People of Today

Debrett's

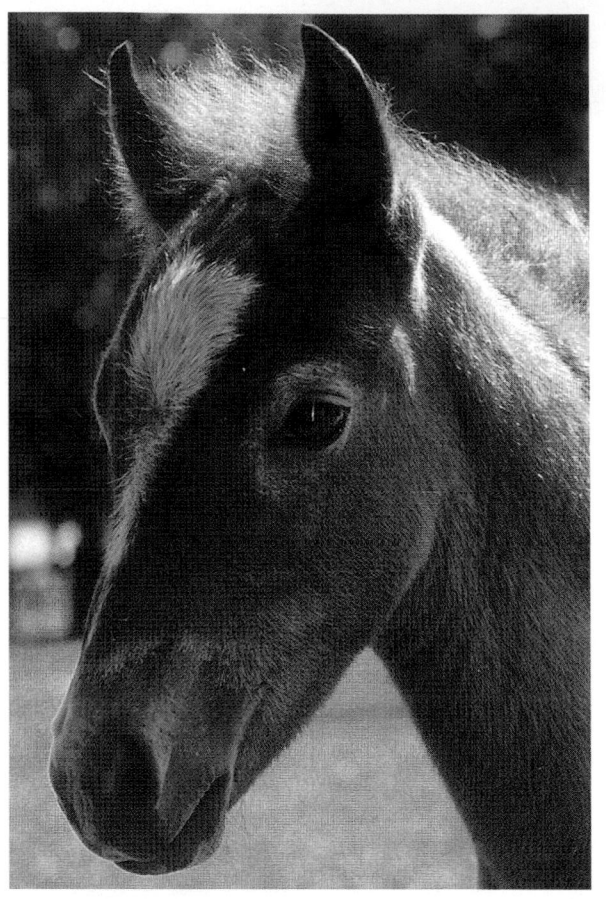

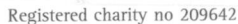

HM THE QUEEN
(Tim Graham, London)

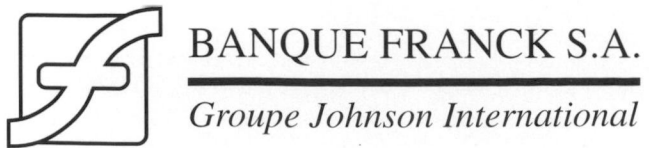

People of Today

Editor
Jonathan Parker

Consulting Editor
David Williamson

Co-Editors
Jessica Hailstone
Lucy Passmore
John Wheatley
Martin Windle

Assistant Editor
Andrew Moulder

Published by

DEBRETT'S PEERAGE LIMITED

73/77 Britannia Road · PO Box 357 · London · SW6 2JY

ISBN 1 870520 34 3

Debrett's People of Today 1997
Published by Debrett's Peerage Limited
73/77 Britannia Road · PO Box 357 · London · SW6 2JY

Printed in England.

Database typesetting by BPC Whitefriars Ltd, Tunbridge Wells.
Printed and bound by BPC Wheatons Ltd, Marsh Barton, Exeter.

CONTENTS

FOREWORD BY DAVID DIMBLEBY P11

INTRODUCTION BY JONATHAN PARKER P13

THE ROYAL NATIONAL THEATRE
BY SIR RICHARD EYRE, CBE P15

CHARITIES AND THE CHARITY COMMISSION TODAY
BY RICHARD FRIES P19

MAN OF INDEPENDENCE
BY BARRY HASSELL P25

BUYING PROPERTY IN TAX HAVENS
BY CHARLES JACOBY P31

ASSOCIATION OF BRITISH TRAVEL AGENTS
BY IAN REYNOLDS P39

Finance and Investment P42-P81

INDUSTRY IN BRITAIN
BY THE RT HON THE LORD HANSON P43

THE FINE ART OF INSURANCE
BY ROBERT HISCOX P49

GUERNSEY
BY WILL OLLARD P53

THE ADVANTAGES OF OFFSHORE BANKING
BY WILL OLLARD P59

PRIVATE BANKING IN SWITZERLAND
BY WILL OLLARD P67

MAKING ADEQUATE PROVISION FOR RETIREMENT
BY JOE PALMER, CBE P73

HONG KONG: 1997 AND BEYOND
BY SIR WILLIAM PURVES P79

THE ROYAL FAMILY P83

THE ORDER OF SUCCESSION P86

THE ROYAL HOUSEHOLDS P87

HER MAJESTY'S OFFICERS OF ARMS P89

GENERAL TABLES OF PRECEDENCE P90

POSITION OF LETTERS AFTER THE NAME P93

FORMS OF ADDRESSING PERSONS OF TITLE P96

CLUBS P101

A READER'S GUIDE P102

ABBREVIATIONS P103

FOREWORD
by DAVID DIMBLEBY

Before you start to browse through this volume spare a thought for its 34,000 authors—the people of today whose names appear here. At first gratified by their inclusion they have grappled with what to reveal about themselves—how to make themselves admirable in your eyes while arousing the envy of their rivals.

How much or how little to include? Too much smacks of insecurity, too little looks like the arrogance of false modesty. What hobbies should they affect (most being too busy to spare time for even a proportion of those they list)? How many spouses should they concede?

Should early achievements be erased in favour of later triumphs? Or are there no recent triumphs, only the nagging fear that they will soon be expunged from the book? Perhaps Debrett should publish a companion volume, a 'People of Yesterday' to accommodate them: a volume to which we will all ultimately be consigned.

In the 1960s, when our social structure was crumbling under the weight of the Beatles, a young deb, keen to put her finger in the dyke of progress, shocked her fiancé by suggesting that The Times should restrict its Forthcoming Marriages column to those whose names were listed in Debrett. She had in mind an earlier publication than this—*Debrett's Peerage, Baronetage, Knightage and Companionage.* The boyfriend, from un-Debrett stock, assumed this was a ploy to break off the engagement until he discovered to his surprise his father's name at the back of the volume, included because he had been awarded the CBE. I was the boyfriend and have had a healthy respect for Debrett publications ever since.

I wonder whether *People of Today* is put to similar use in our meritocratic society. Whatever use you put it to I recommend this book. It serves many purposes and when it is out of date it is still perfect for pressing flowers.

Company Profile

THE BURTON GROUP PLC

With nearly 1,500 outlets in high streets and shopping centres throughout the country, the Burton Group is one of the largest fashion retailers in the UK.

The Burton Group was founded eponymously as 'Montague Burton' in 1900 by a Lithuanian immigrant. When the young Burton found that he couldn't afford to go to university, he borrowed £100 from a relative and set up his own menswear shop in Chesterfield.

Within 10 years, the business had expanded to a chain of 14 shops in Sheffield and Leeds and had introduced the bespoke tailoring operation that was to make Montague Burton a household name in the '20s and '30s.

The outbreak of the First World War brought a temporary halt to the rapid expansion of shops. However, production capacity increased dramatically as Burton had won contracts to supply uniform clothing for nearly a quarter of the armed forces. The end of the War brought an enormous unprecedented demand for men's clothing for which Burton was well placed.

Post War years: growth of production and retail

With the post war years came rapid growth in mass markets—in housing, furniture, consumer goods, entertainment and clothing. It was the era of ribbon development, the Austin Seven, Lyons Corner Houses, Odeon Cinemas, and it was also the era of the Montague Burton suit.

In the mid 1940s demand for tailored menswear remained high and with 600 menswear shops there was hardly a high street in the country without a Burton. Burton was estimated to be clothing about one-fifth of the British male population at that time. When Sir Montague Burton died in 1952, his company was the largest multiples tailor in the world.

In 1946 the company made its first move into the womenswear market with the acquisition of the fashion group Peter Robinson. Expansion continued through the '50s and early '60s and in the mid-sixties Peter Robinson launched 'Top Shop' which to this day has maintained its reputation for putting new ideas on the high street first.

In the 1970s, and as a complement to the suit business which was in decline, the Group started to develop itself significantly in mainstream retail clothing by beginning to target chains to precisely defined markets.

In 1971 the Group acquired Evans—the market leader in large-size fashion for women. In 1979 the Dorothy Perkins chain was acquired, enabling the Group to consolidate its position in the womenswear markets. In 1984 the Group launched a new chain, Principles for Women—for fashion conscious women with a higher disposable income. Principles for Men was launched a year later in 1985.

Also in 1985 the Group acquired Debenhams, the largest department store group in the UK, founded in 1851, and Colliers. The acquisition of Debenhams added another 67 stores, bringing a wide range of goods other than clothing to the Burton Group's portfolio.

By 1991, however, the Group reported a substantial fall in profitability, due to a discount-led pricing strategy and the effect of major diversification into property development. New management was appointed which set about improving the Group's financial position and long term performance.

The Burton Group today

Today, the Group reaches its customers through seven trading divisions, from department stores, to womenswear and menswear fashion chains, and, more recently, through Home Shopping.

Each division targets distinct market segments and most of the Group's divisions operate with leading positions in their respective markets.

The Group's largest division is Debenhams, the UK's leading chain of family department stores. The fashion 'Multiples' store chains Burton Menswear and Dorothy Perkins, both offer affordable, mainstream clothing for men and women respectively. Of the Group's other Multiple chains, Top Shop/Top Man is Britain's biggest provider of young fashion; Evans is the UK's market leader in large-size womenswear, whilst the Principles chain is known for its distinctive clothing for men and women.

The Group has recently created a Home Shopping division following the acquisition of Innovations in August 1996 and Racing Green in October 1996.

Strong own label development is a feature across the Group. In addition, several divisions have teamed up with some of the UK's finest designers to develop fashionable designer ranges at high street prices. Branded storecards have been developed for every division. The Group currently has over 5 million active storecard accounts.

From the original 'Burton' shop which continues to trade in Chesterfield, the Burton Group brands are today available from nearly 1,500 stores in 500 markets throughout the UK. Montague Burton's initial investment of £100 and a handful of staff has been turned into a significant UK group employing 43,000 people and generating sales of over £2 billion.

The Burton Group plc

INTRODUCTION

Many anniversaries and birthdays have come and gone in Debrett's long history, but it is nonetheless pleasing to celebrate the arrival of each new edition of *People of Today.* Indeed, we have even greater cause for celebration in 1997, as our general reference source reaches its tenth year of publication.

In Debrett terms, *People of Today* is still very much in its infancy but we hope it displays a maturity beyond its years. Our aim is, and has always been, to provide information on those who have 'arrived' in their chosen profession, regardless of age or background. Selection (and deselection) policy is driven by the information needs of our users.

In a publication so intrinsically involved with people, it is never an easy task to please all of them. In order to keep *People of Today* up-to-date and relevant, we continually change the cast. I would like to take this opportunity, therefore, to thank all those entrants, past and present, for their assistance in compiling previous editions.

Those entrants who have kindly contributed an article to this edition deserve special mention. They are Sir Richard Eyre, Richard Fries, Lord Hanson, Barry Hassell, Robert Hiscox, Joe Palmer, Sir William Purves and Ian Reynolds. I would also like to thank David Dimbleby for his foreword, including his helpful suggestion for the utilisation of out-of-date editions.

Thanks must also be given to the board of Sterling Publishing Group PLC for their continued support of this project. A final word of acknowledgement goes to Frances Johnston and Charles Kidd for their invaluable assistance on this edition.

JONATHAN PARKER

THE ROYAL NATIONAL THEATRE
by SIR RICHARD EYRE, CBE

I began work as Director of the National Theatre in January 1988. Within the next nine months the theatre had acquired the prefix 'Royal', and I had acquired nightmares about the job that I had taken on. My nightmares reminded me of a Polish film called *The Knights of the Teutonic Order*. The film was set in the early middle ages: a Knight was tortured, his tongue was cut out, and he was imprisoned in an iron box for several years. When he was liberated from his confinement he shambled out, grey-haired, sightless and tongueless, to rediscover a world whose features he could now only guess at. Mercifully, the reality of my life has not mimicked the experiences of the Polish Knight. The Royal National Theatre hasn't proved to be an immutable bureaucracy, nor a cultural colossus riddled with institutional inertia; to state what ought to be obvious, it's demonstrated for me—to parody Gertrude Stein—that a theatre is a theatre is a theatre.

There will be many occasions over the time remaining to me to calibrate my sadness at saying goodbye to the Royal National Theatre against my excitement at the possibilities which seem to present themselves in the future. I won't miss the drizzle of journalistic jeremiads predicting the demise of the art of theatre, the cowpats of columnists plopping into the Sunday papers, cataloguing litanies of complaint about how difficult it is to travel to the theatre, how difficult it is to get a drink at the theatre, how expensive it is, how boring it is, and how much more vital is the medium of film, or fiction, or even football. I will not miss the conditions that conspire to ensure that whenever two or three theatre practitioners are gathered together the talk invariably turns to funding. I will not miss the necessary evangelical exhortations to government and to the opposition to accept that funding the arts is in *all* our interests, and I will not miss the disappointment endemic to an art form in which true success—the achievement of doing something really well in its own terms—is so exasperatingly difficult to achieve.

What I will miss, paradoxically, is what might be regarded as the burden from which one would devoutly wish to be delivered: being responsible for a national institution. The National Theatre was the dream of three men at the start of this century: the playwright Bernard Shaw, the critic William Archer, and the playwright, actor and director Harley Granville-Barker. They dreamt of a building which presented the best of new plays, classical drama and experimental work in three auditoria in repertoire, 52 weeks of the year. 'I would not give a straw,' said Barker, 'for a national theatre which did not set out to be better—just that—than the theatre round the corner.' Their dream has been embodied in the building, opened in 1976, which sits on the South Bank of the Thames.

The Royal National Theatre presents at least six different productions in any week, and seeks to take artistic risks, to sustain the best of tradition, and to develop new talent. We feed the West End and Broadway with productions—*An Inspector Calls, Carousel, Dealer's Choice, Arcadia, Les Parents Terribles, Skylight*, to name a few; we inspire films for the cinema—*Amadeus, Plenty, The Madness of King George*, and many actors, directors, writers and designers progress (or regress if you prefer) from the stages of the National Theatre to stardom on TV or in Hollywood.

We have three auditoria to produce plays, rehearsal rooms to prepare them, and workshops to make the costumes, the sets and the props; we tour our productions nationally and internationally; we have an Education Department that works with thousands of schools and takes small-scale productions to all corners of the country; we present Platform performances of readings by well-known playwrights, novelists and poets; we have music, nightly, in the foyers, and we have bookshops, bars, buffets and restaurants which are open all day—and we do all this at prices which do not exclude all but the very rich.

Theatre companies through the ages of Euripedes, Shakespeare, Calderon, Molière, Chekhov, Ibsen, Shaw and Stoppard have relied on royal, state, civic, corporate and private patrons. They have also relied on the patronage of the public: those who live to please have to please to live. At the RNT we receive a subsidy partly from the government—via the Arts Council, and partly from numerous corporate and private sponsors. When we speak of subsidy we're not asking for the money to hear the sound of our own voices echoing in an empty room: we aim at a target of 75% capacity for every performance—that's over 1,700 seats a night. We depend on box-office income for well over half of our revenue. Unless we earn nearly £18 million a year through our own efforts we are faced, like Mr Micawber, with the result: misery.

We seek to uplift and entertain from the moment the public enters the doors of our building, and these aims are reflected in its architecture. There are many criticisms that can be made and have been made of its design, but it is indisputable that the National Theatre building asserts clarity of vision, boldness, dignity and classical simplicity.

Any theatre which fails to respond to the spirit of the day, both in the demands of its audiences and the aspirations of its management, deserves to wither. We are the National Theatre's tenants; we have a responsibility not only to our current audiences, actors and technicians, but also to their successors. Consequently we are embarking on a programme of work that will guarantee that the interior and exterior of the building is preserved and enhanced, and that the three auditoria will be able to operate to the highest standards for the next twenty-five years. In short, we are seeking to guarantee the physical future of the RNT for the audiences and artists of the future.

We will improve signage, lighting, service access, access to the river, and traffic flow; we will relocate the bookshop and box office, add a lift for the disabled to allow access to the mezzanine level, provide a link between the Olivier and Lyttelton foyers, and a permanent ticket counter in the Cottesloe; create a 'theatre square', making a focal point to the entrance to the building, and harmonising with the plans for the rest of the South Bank. In addition we will improve the long term acoustic defects in the Olivier, replace the carpets throughout, and give the exterior a much-overdue cleaning.

The technical equipment in the three auditoria was 'state of the art' when it was installed in the mid 1970s. Much of it cannot now be repaired or brought up to date. Within a few years it will be literally impossible to continue to operate the entire flying and lighting systems safely and reliably. We are nothing if not pragmatic, but there comes a point at which it is impossible to keep a theatre running with equipment for which parts are no longer manufactured, whose operation depends on constant extemporisation, whose consistency cannot be guaranteed, and whose safety the Local Authority will refuse to endorse.

The total cost of the work is £42 million. We have received £31.5 million from the Lottery, and we have to raise matching funds of £10.5 million from private and corporate sources to draw down the Lottery money. Through the generosity of a number of donors we have already—by December 1996—raised over £6 million by asking the question of prospective patrons: do you believe that it's worth trying to assure the future of the Royal National Theatre?

Theatre depends on the relationship of a performer to a group of spectators, and to the disposition of mankind to tell each other stories. Theatre only ever exists in the present tense. It always prospers under the logic of plot, and it always thrives on metaphor—a room becomes a world, a group of characters becomes a whole society. Above all, the art of theatre depends on the scale of the human figure and the human voice; it is resolutely humane in form and content, and as long as human beings continue to want to talk to each other I, at least, believe that it is an art worth fighting for, and that our National Theatre is worth saving for successive generations of theatre-makers and theatre-goers.

Sir Richard Eyre, CBE

Director, Royal National Theatre

CHARITIES AND THE CHARITY COMMISSION TODAY
by RICHARD FRIES

Charity is an immensely important part of our national life. Every day the media has headlines about charities, what they are doing and what they are saying. Charity has been a cornerstone of our way of life for centuries. The word itself has ancient roots. It is amazing that so ancient a word continues to exercise such a hold over people's imagination despite all the changes in society. That is because, behind the unchanging label, the practice of charity has kept apace with social change.

We must make sure charity continues to be relevant to modern life. We cannot take it for granted. The question of what role charity should play in the modern world must be asked. Behind the vitality of charities there are questions and confusions in the public's mind. The Duke of Devonshire was asked recently what legislative change he would most like to make. Noting that there are 180,000 registered charities—and that is England and Wales only—he said that he would most like to see a moratorium on new charities. I sense that many people agree with that. Proliferation of charities is an anxiety. Another anxiety is that charities are inefficient or wasteful—does the money I give go effectively to the cause I want to support? The opposite question is also asked—aren't charities too much like businesses? Where is the charitable ethos? Or aren't charities too political? And again the opposite question aren't they becoming simply agents of the state?

The fact that there are 180,000 charities on the Commission's register—and quite a lot more which are not required to register—indicates the scale of the charitable sector. Actually the sheer number does not necessarily mean that there are too many. Only a couple of thousand have an annual turnover of more than £1 million, and of these only a couple of hundred are over the £10 million mark. Some of the 180,000 are not really separate charities at all, but subsidiaries of others. Over 100,000 are very small—with a turnover of less than £10,000 a year. They are for example genuinely local charities or special funds of one sort or another. And the range of issues which charity tackles is so broad that the sheer number does not necessarily indicate duplication. But that very fact means that charities must demonstrate to their supporters, and the public at large, that they live up to the values and ethos which charity represents. Otherwise public confidence will be undermined.

I imagine that the ordinary person thinks of charities first as bodies which seek to meet need—poverty, illness and the like. That is indeed a central part of charity now as always. It includes the well-known national, and indeed international, charities—world-renowned names like the Salvation Army. Education in all its forms is a sphere to which charity has long made a vital contribution. It remains a basic element of charity—one of the four 'heads' as defined by the courts. People do not always remember the other issues which charity covers—heritage, the environment, animal welfare, the arts, and so on and on—covering practically everything which serves the public interest. But they instantly acknowledge the names of national institutions, such as the National Trust, RSPCA, RSPB and the like. The very origins of charity are religious, and of course the advancement of religion remains a continuing strand of charity.

It is therefore perhaps not surprising that there is some confusion about what charity actually is. It has surfaced recently for example in the public and media response to the range of 'good causes' to which lottery money goes. I think it is a natural reflection of the range of issues embraced by charity. Part of it also is an uncertainty about what is distinctive about charity and where it stands in the modern world. For some it smacks of an outmoded Victorian attitude—patronising do gooding by the comfortable to the unfortunate. Concern for fellow beings in distress is indeed one of the roots of charity. Generosity of spirit and concern for others remains as worthy and as necessary today as ever. Charity gives public spiritedness a wide scope. It is about the community and its needs. There is nothing new in questioning its role. Questioning and change is a sign of vitality in society. The Victorian age is itself an example. What some see as out of date now was a great reforming zeal in those days. The growth of philanthropy stands as an inspiring example of an age which responded to the novel problems which society faced in those times. Many of our leading charities were founded then. It is an example from which we can retain the spirit even if the letter is sometimes in need of modernisation.

Victorian philanthropy met many of the needs which people experienced in the dislocation of the Industrial Revolution out of which our great cities arose. In the years after the Second World War public statutory authorities took over much which charity had come to provide, but that was a challenge to charity, not a signal for it to contract. Recent decades have been a period of exceptional vitality for charity and indeed have contributed to what the Americans euphemistically call the 'reinventing of Government'. The contraction of the State which that signals is an opportunity—as well as a challenge—to charity.

I have explained the diversity of the charitable sector. There are nevertheless some core characteristics which charities with all their diversity share. Two essential features are independence and commitment to the public good. Charity is a distinctive legal framework. It is a complicated framework based on continuous development over centuries. One of the functions of the Charity Commission is to develop as well as apply to charity law—and by definition, as society changes, charity law *must* develop. But the framework is there to ensure that charities exist for publicly beneficial purposes, that they are in the hands of independent trustees who safeguard those purposes, and that the charity's resources are devoted to those purposes.

One issue is what purposes are publicly beneficial in our changing world. As society changes so its needs change. Our society is itself diverse, comprising many communities. The charitable sector has responded to these changes. Charities have sprung up to help migrants, to encourage good community relations. Education in all its forms is as important in our age as it was in the past. With electronic information it takes new forms. Charities respond to the need for education in new forms. Issues concerning the environment are becoming more critical for the planet itself. Charities play a major part in action to tackle environmental problems. They also play an important role in public debate and education.

The register of charities is the public record of what charities there are and what they do. The Charity Commission, answerable to the courts, determines charitable status; it is not laid down in statute law. This enables the Commission and the courts to keep charitable status up to date by responding to change. Part of the modernisation of the Charity Commission involves developing the register of charities in a full blown computerised form. As part of that process we shall be reviewing the scope of charitable status to make sure that it is up to date within the existing law and identifying issues which may need changing. This is going to be the first thoroughgoing review of charitable status and will be a very exciting and challenging process. Many controversial issues will no doubt arise. It must be a public process and we shall be engaging in a range of consultation activities. I hope that readers of this article will contribute.

It is not just what charities do which is distinctive, it is how they are constituted that makes for the real ethos of charity. Charities are voluntary bodies—part of the voluntary sector. They use volunteers, they get funding from voluntary donations, but above all they are managed by volunteers. It is the trustees of charities who under law have responsibility for their charity, its activities and its resources. They embody the individuality, independence and commitment which is the essence of charity. The fact that we have so many charities is in part a reflection of the fact that individuals see issues which need tackling. The law supports them—as does the tax man with tax relief! Charities owe their existence to the wish of an individual or group of individuals to tackle some public need or public issue. One reason why charities are still being formed at the rate of 3,000–4,000 a year is that personal commitment. It is easy to engage in rhetorical talk of community. Charities are the reality of that rhetoric.

Independence, in particular from the State and its authorities, is the necessary essence of charities. The trustees must be the guardians of that. Much innovation has arisen through individual initiative. The hospice movement is one striking example. If there are too many charities part of the reason is the right to establish a charity. (The Charity Commission registers charities to make them accessible and accountable—not to ration them.) Diversity, idiosyncracy, even inefficiency, are inevitable features of the charitable sector.

But charities are public bodies in the sense that they receive the protection of the law and fiscal benefits—and attract public support—because they serve the public interest. Alongside their independence must lie accountability—accountability of the right sort, to enhance confidence without stultifying independence. The task of the Charity Commission, under the Charities Act 1993 which has given the Charity Commission new powers and responsibilities, is to provide that framework of accountability. Details of charities must be easily available on the register. One reason for computerising it is to make charities open and accessible. The Charity Commission now has its own site on the Internet. Sooner, rather than later, the register will be available on the Internet. Requirements, graduated according to complexity and scale of activities, for reporting and accounting will ensure that charities account for how they are seeking to fulfil their charitable objects and use the resources. All that will be publicly available. The Commission's role is to provide regular support and guidance to charities, and, as from this year annual monitoring of the 40,000 or so with an income of above £10,000 a year. The Commission is both adviser and regulator. Charities need advice and guidance on the law. Public confidence depends on their handling their resources with proper care and managing their affairs well. Where minimum standards are not met, the Commission has the power to intervene. If things have broken down we can even suspend trustees and appoint a receiver and manager to take its administration. But the Commission's powers are 'remedial'—designed to put charities back on course, not to impose sanctions on trustees, who mostly are seeking to fulfil an essential public duty on a voluntary basis as best they can. Our aim is to work with charities, to ensure that their legal and administrative framework suits their purposes and that they operate effectively within it. We rely so far as possible on co-operation and agreement. That fits the ethos of an independent sector.

The task of charities is complex, perhaps for many increasingly so. It must be remembered however that many—like Barnardos to take just one example—have run important services for years. People sometimes criticise charities for being 'no better than big businesses'. This begs the question of whether being businesslike is such a bad thing in any case. But the criticism ignores the fact that many charities are handling hundreds of thousands or even tens of millions of pounds and running sophisticated services. Good management is necessary. So is the charitable ethos. It is a challenge to be both businesslike and charitable. They are not incompatible. Professional staff, well managed, are essential to provide services to a high standard. But charities provide these services to a charitable ethos—for the public benefit not for private profit. The trustees and

Tim, aged 15

Starts skipping class
Falls in with bad crowd
Starts stealing
Stops going to school
Steals cars
Tries drugs
Sells drugs
Gets arrested
Gets jailed
Gets out
Can't get job
Commits robbery
Gets jailed
Gets out
Can't get job
Sells drugs
Takes drugs
Convicted aggravated assault
Suspended sentence
Meets girl
Has baby
Can't get job
Commits armed robbery
Gets caught
Gets jailed

Starts skipping class
Falls in with bad crowd
Starts stealing
Stops going to school
Steals cars
Tries drugs
Sells drugs
Gets arrested
Is referred to The Children's Society Remand Project
Receives counselling
Gets home tuition
Goes back to school
Gets GCSEs
Is helped to get training
Gets job
Meets girl
Settles down
Gets married
Has family

Charity Registration No. 221124

PA9106

volunteers—and the commitment of staff working for their cause rather than create a profit—make charities, however large, distinctively charitable—and different from statutory services or commercial organisations.

And the trustees are the guarantors of the independence of these charities. That may not be easy if too much funding comes from one source, particularly if it is in fulfilment of a public sector contract. But it is the essence of charity. One element in the independence of charities is that they have their own view of their sphere and the problems with which they are dealing. It is important that charities should make their experience available in public debate on crucial issues, even if (as with matters of such importance is often the case) they are the stuff of politics. The law permits charities to engage in political activities and to campaign provided that they do so in pursuit of their properly charitable objects and do so responsibly and knowledgeably. One of the Charity Commission's functions is to safeguard this right while advising and supervising charities on where the line is drawn. The guidelines we published in 1995 are designed to draw the right line between the legitimate public view of charities and illegitimate incursion into party politics. So far they have worked well.

As the charitable sector approaches the Millennium, and as the 1601 framework of charity law completes 400 years, the need for a healthy sector, and the challenge facing it, is great. Public confidence cannot be taken for granted. But public support remains high. With greater openness and with flexibility and imagination, charities, supported by the Charity Commission, can face the next century with confidence.

RICHARD FRIES

Chief Charity Commissioner

MAN OF INDEPENDENCE
by BARRY HASSELL

My experience as the Chief Executive of the first unit to leave the NHS some twelve years ago taught me a great deal about the daily pressures faced by those who have to cope with a caring and rapidly changing environment. Specialising in treating and caring for children with chronic or disabling conditions, the hospital I then managed—Tadworth Court Children's Hospital in Surrey—proved to me beyond doubt the benefits of independence and freedom from a highly politicised and unresponsive centre.

Today in my role as Chief Executive of the Independent Healthcare Association (IHA), I represent the majority of the UK's independent health and social care sector's organisations. IHA's members cover a diverse range of small and large, charitable and for profit entities. They provide acute elective surgery, psychiatric treatment, long term care and many other services. The sector has always prided itself on giving its employees the means by which to deliver the highest standards of quality and care. Committed to the highest standards of professionalism, the sector's providers boast an outstanding record when it comes to investment in both its people and its services.

However, it was not that long ago when most opinion formers seemed to believe that the state could correct all of society's ills and that Government would provide all the resources necessary to cope with the demand for health and social care. Such assumptions were certainly the life blood of the UK's post-war settlement and they were at the heart of a political consensus which dominated public policy for more than forty years.

Unsustainable Utopianism

Fifty years ago, the ideas underpinning the UK's National Health Service (NHS) were busy circling the globe and leading the developed world (particularly Commonwealth countries) into a brave new technocratic age of centrally planned, 'command and control' healthcare.

Significantly, the 1944 White Paper, *A National Health Service*, initially estimated that the state system would cost £132 million per year. However, in its first full year of operation, 1949–1950, the NHS actually ended up costing the tax payer a massive £305 million.

Popularising the view that after an 'initial surge' for spectacles and false teeth, healthcare expenditure might even fall, the utopianism of the early NHS instilled in the population a lasting belief that healthcare could be managed on the basis of the state providing 'unlimited' healthcare 'free' at the point of delivery. To establish the NHS the state took into public ownership some 3,118 independent hospitals and clinics with a total of 388,000 staffed and 57,000 unstaffed beds.

However, in reality it did not take the 1945 Labour administration long to realise that the NHS will always present Government with the same fundamental challenge: that of managing a service which is based on the promise of providing unlimited healthcare which is 'free' at the point of demand. Although this was one of the founding principles of the NHS, it was actually abandoned within five years of the 1944 White Paper.

In 1949, an amending Act was passed to allow the levying of a 1 shilling charge for prescriptions and after the Conservative victory of 1951, further charges were introduced for prescriptions, spectacles and dental treatment. Since then rationing by cash limits, queues and exclusion have all become familiar features of the service.

Mixed Economy Reform

By the mid-1980s it had become obvious that the old, heavy, top down structures of NHS centralisation would no longer suffice. Under a new system introduced in the early 1990s, the NHS was divided between purchasers and providers, and hospitals given a greater degree of freedom from the centre.

Signalling an important departure from the post-war world of largely uncosted, bureaucratic and producer led healthcare, it is interesting to note that politicians are—the world over—embracing a more mixed economy approach in health and social care. Under pressure from the forces of economic globalisation, adverse demographic trends and rising consumer expectations, politicians everywhere are busy exploring new ways in which private finance and expertise can be reintroduced into national healthcare systems.

Today, the UK's independent providers of health and social care are building ever stronger bridges with statutory purchasers and winning business by demonstrating their ability to deliver high quality, value for money services. Policies such as the 'Internal Market', the 'Private Finance Initiative', 'Market Testing' and 'Contracting Out' are all encouraging bridges between, what some increasingly see as, a utopian and unsustainable past and a de-politicised, sustainable future.

Today's Independent Sector

The quiet revolution that has taken place in UK health and social care in recent years means that there are now more beds in the country's independent sector than in the statutory sector. Indeed, the independent sector supplies more health and social care beds (443,000) than the NHS and Local Authorities combined (356,000).

The sector is an important employer. It currently employs 500,000 people, the majority of whom are women. There are also 76,000 independent professionals working under contract to the NHS, including doctors in general practice, dentists, pharmacists and opticians. Additionally, three quarters of all hospital consultants have some form of private practice.

Like any other major industry driven by reputation and quality, the independent sector invests heavily in developing the skills and talent of its workforce. Against the myth that training for health and social care is only undertaken by the NHS, today's independent sector provides a vast and ever expanding range of learning opportunities for its employees.

Deeply rooted in the Libertarian traditions of Mutuality, Co-operation, and non-state collective self-help—as well as for-profit and charity—the independent sector is again a rich tapestry of competing organisational philosophies.

Independent acute hospitals provide at least 20% of elective surgery including, for example, 20% of all coronary heart bypass operations and 30% of all hip replacements. Overall, the operations performed range from the simple to the very complex. In a recent survey of independent hospitals 25% of surgical procedures were identified as being 'major complex' while 48% were classified as 'intermediate'. Only 27% were found to be 'minor'.

The independent sector provides 76% of all long-term nursing and residential care. Here the sector is particularly diverse offering nursing, convalescent, respite and rehabilitation care to a wide range of client groups which include: elderly people, the elderly mentally ill, and those adults and children with physical disabilities and learning difficulties. Offering highly specialised care in such areas as brain injury rehabilitation or challenging behaviour, many homes and hospitals are at the forefront of innovation. The sector also provides and is expanding in other areas of care such as domiciliary, day and respite care, which are often centred around an existing care home.

The proportion of psychiatric services provided by the independent sector has also grown significantly in recent years. There are now 69 independent psychiatric and substance abuse units in the country: which represents a six fold increase since 1980. Twenty-eight per cent of consultant psychiatrists make regular admissions to independent sector facilities and virtually all acute substance abuse and brain injury rehabilitation care is undertaken in the sector. Overall, it now provides 72% of the UK's acute brain injury rehabilitation beds.

Making such a major contribution to care and having seen such spectacular growth in recent years, today's independent sector is far too large for opinion formers to ignore. By the year 2000 it will be virtually left up to the independent sector to provide the estimated additional 72,000 beds required by an ageing population.

10,000,000 People Can't be Wrong!

Medical care in the independent sector, as in the NHS, has to be paid for. It is clear, however, that taking out insurance against medical costs is no longer the exclusive luxury of the rich. Around 6,700,000 people have private medical insurance in the UK. A further 3,000,000 people have health insurance which pays out cash benefits when they are ill and in need of treatment.

Together 9,700,000 have some sort of medical or health insurance: which is more people than belong to trade unions or regularly attend church and there are yet more people who simply pay for care as and when they require it. In terms of total expenditure, independent health and social care is comparable to all consumer spending on DIY or on air travel. Recent projections show that private medical insurance is set to grow a further 27% by the year 2000.

Beyond Naïve Statism

While some people still believe that the NHS had its heyday in the 1950s, 60s and 70s, and that during this period it was a largely unchanging institution, history reveals that the service has always had to adapt and change to circumstance. There has never been a time when it could afford to stand still.

In the 1940s, the Fabian Society was in the vanguard of the country's healthcare reforms. As the devout advocates of public ownership and the nationalisation of provision it was the Fabians who toured the globe championing the rationality of state ownership and central planning.

Yet as the most influential of the centre-left think tanks in the UK, the Fabians are once again mapping out the type of healthcare reform demanded by the age. In a recent paper by Kathy Jones called *Accountability not Ownership* the Society demonstrated its ability to change with the times. The report stated: 'High quality private sector providers, mainly hospices and nursing homes, have long histories of providing care for NHS patients at the expense of the taxpayer. This is neither sinister, nor damaging to the concept of public service. ... Labour should recognise that private provision does not mean the end of free health care at the point of need. Publicly-purchased services can be, and are, delivered by privately owned institutions without users having to pay. There is no reason why health care providers should be publicly owned.'

As politicians the world over begin to face the challenges of the twenty first century it is clear that a new era is dawning in health and social care. Instead of relying upon the somewhat naïve and outdated assumption that the state can do everything, politicians of the left and right are increasingly coalescing around a new agenda which recognises the benefits of a dynamic mixed economy and the services that a powerful non-state sector can provide.

Accountability

Overall, the theory behind the NHS reforms is both understandable and worthy. In attempting to move the system towards a more market based and mixed economy approach the Government has clearly set out to encourage a greater degree of competition, innovation and efficiency; yet preserve its core—public service—ethos and function.

Nevertheless, like many politicians, IHA wholeheartedly supports a concern to see public funds

used properly and believes that an essential part of this stewardship must be the effective use of public resources. In this context the Association believes that the government would do well to question the rationale behind NHS pay-beds for acute surgery. These units are engaged in risky commercial ventures in a highly competitive market and yet are ultimately financed by government funds.

As the Audit Commission has repeatedly made clear, NHS Trusts as they currently stand not only lack the most basic costings systems but in pursuing so called 'private work' leave open the possibility for massive cross subsidisation by the taxpayer and therefore the wholesale undermining of public accountability. Today, serious questions arise over the accountability of NHS Trusts for their private practice:

- The so called 'six principles' that govern NHS private practice still apply—but who is enforcing them?
- How are NHS hospitals proving that private patients are not significantly prejudicing non-paying patients. How is this audited?

The issues of cross subsidisation and public accountability are important because if we are going to make the mixed economy work and thereby enable purchasers to make effective decisions, it is vital that NHS institutions become more transparent in their actions and open to judgement.

While it is right that we pursue a mixed economy which encourages greater efficiency, innovation and higher standards in the delivery of health and social care, it is vital that the Government thinks through reforms more clearly and then sets some basic ground rules so that all the players concerned are ultimately held accountable for their actions.

Opportune Future

As we enter the twenty first century, and the necessary regulatory environment is established, the emerging—mixed economy—market will lead to a new and unrecognisable structure to UK health and social care services.

- The State will fund but not necessarily provide health and social care services.
- More specialised, niche services will be developed providing highly skilled specialised services.
- Independent operators will, in a variety of ways, manage NHS and local authority facilities.
- Less capital funding will be available from the state and more sought from the private sector.
- Joint ventures between public and private sector partners will be the norm and not the exception.

Rising Consumerism

Given the general trend towards consumer choice, higher living standards and the demographic changes facing the UK, there can be little doubt that the independent sector will have a major role to play in the development of high quality services for an ever increasing range of people. Today, the UK's independent health and social care sector already makes a massive contribution to the health and social well-being of the nation and is a substantial sector of the economy in its own right: it is our 10th largest employer.

Just as the UK blazed a trail in the 1940s so the country is once again proving its ability to institute major reforms. As time passes, we can be confident that more and more people will come to accept the view that what really matters in health and social care is not whether a service is delivered in an independently or publicly owned hospital or home, but that the level and quality of the service offered is the best and provides the greatest value for money. After all, surely that is the real challenge for everyone involved in the business of delivering the best in health and social care.

Barry Hassell

Chief Executive, Independent Healthcare Association

BUYING PROPERTY IN TAX HAVENS

Whether it is the warmth of the people and climate of the Channel Islands, the Mediterranean heat of Monaco and its Casino, or the gentle and drizzly way of life in Ireland or the Isle of Man, there is a steady stream of Britons looking to leave Blighty to save on tax. And this year the numbers of people loading removal lorries take on a special significance.

The market for properties abroad booms in the run up to the election. It is the same every time. 'The recurring trend at this time in the political calendar is that we suddenly seem to receive a lot more enquiries for properties in the Channel Islands and other low tax areas, such as Monaco,' says Paddy Dring of estate agent Knight Frank. 'Many people believe that an incoming Labour administration may raise taxes on the wealthy and they want to move before their money is taxed any further.'

John Allen, managing director of Guernsey estate agent Swoffers, reports a dramatic rise in sales. 'For the last 18 months the market has—as one might expect in this stage of the UK political cycle—increased,' he says. 'It's been getting busier and busier. The number of open market sales on the island this year are, at 120, going to be double what they were three years ago. Then it was just 63. It is a tiny market, which is one of the reasons the UK Government has never tried to do anything about it.'

The way Dring and Allen talk, anyone might think Britain was like Casablanca in the days of Rick's Bar, with people nervously waiting to leave for a better life as the invading armies—then the Nazis, now Labour—rumble inexorably towards them. Others do not notice so much election activity. 'For several years in the early 1990s there were very few people leaving the UK for capital gains tax reasons. That picked up two or three years ago,' says David Piesing of tax planner Pannell Kerr Forster (Guernsey), based in St Peter's Port. 'The open market has been very buoyant since then—though whether it's only for capital gains tax reasons or whether it takes account of the possibility of a Labour Government nobody knows.'

David King of Hamptons is a Monaco specialist. He has not been stampeded by anxious Tory buyers either. 'There is a demand,' he says. 'It has been quite slow, but economies have been picking up. There hasn't been a rush from UK buyers worried about the threat of a Labour Government. It's a bit like Hong Hong. There doesn't seem to be the mad panic that everyone thought, but perhaps there will be as the election gets closer.'

Moving to a tax haven is not for everyone. The first costs of going abroad to the sunnier spots like the Channel Islands or Monaco are enormous. A five-bedroomed house in Berkshire with an acre of garden which sells for between £350,000 and £500,000 would cost between £700,000 to £1 million on Guernsey. In nearby Jersey, the Government is not keen to admit you unless you can show assets of between £10 and £12 million. Of the accessible tax havens, only Ireland is substantially cheaper than the UK.

Jersey's exclusivity means it is rare for people to move there. According to Peter De Las Casas, who manages Hamptons' St Helier office, only three families moved to Jersey in 1996. 'In 1995 we saw nine families come,' he says. 'I am anticipating good results in 1997. It's unusual for us to have two bad years in a row. I'm getting a lot of verbal enquiries at the moment and am looking forward to firming them up in the next year.'

This exclusivity comes with a hint of snobbery. 'We like to call ourselves an 'offshore financial centre' rather than a tax haven,' De Las Casas adds, pofaced.

Conrad Coutanche of St Helier-based solicitor Mourant du Feu & Jeune agrees. 'Well, is there anywhere else to live?' he asks. 'Jersey is arguably one of the most civilised places in which one can expect to live. It is clean, the bureaucracy is not overpowering, it is—in my submission—a combination of rural and urban life, and it is very easy to switch from one to the other. It arguably has more first-class restaurants in its square miles than anywhere else in the world. And add to this a tax rate of a maximum of 20% income tax, slightly reduced by allowances which all persons are allowed.'

Coutanche, too, expects a good year in 1997. 'There was a lull in the market between autumn 1995 and autumn 1996,' he says. 'Since then there has been a noticeable increase in numbers of people enquiring about moving to the island. It should not be taken that that is a direct result of people worried about a Labour Government. Enquiries are coming from continental Europe, and even further afield.'

He describes the kind of applicants he is seeing: 'They are, generally speaking, middle-aged entrepreneurs, who have spent 25 years building up a business and have disposed all or part of the business for cash. They want to move here (a) for the tax benefits (b) because of the stability of the island—it is not a changing government because we have no party politics—and (c) because of the quality of life, notably the crime rate. The television series *Bergerac* was jolly good fun, but like all fiction it has to be taken with a pinch of salt.'

John Pickles, a partner with accountants Moore Stephens, observes that Jersey's over-riding drawback is that it is full. But he has to agree with De Las Casas and Coutanche. If Pickles could afford it, he would move to Jersey of all the accessible tax havens. 'I like Jersey as a place, but I couldn't get in there,' he says. 'I'm slightly short on the £12 million. It's the sunshine that attracts me.'

Pickles is less keen on the living conditions in one of the Channel Islands' greatest rivals, Monaco, though he admits it has greater tax advantages. 'If you can put up with living in a very small place, you can effectively be living completely tax free in Monaco—apart from French TVA [like British VAT],' he says. 'The authorities are getting tougher, though. People were getting their carte de sejour and just pretending to live there.'

At that level, why not? The tax-avoiding flotsam of Europe jet and yacht from one haven to another. 'Normally people rent for three years in Monte Carlo to fulfil their tax requirements and then go home,' says King. 'Not many people live there full time. We sell or rent the odd apartment there. Indeed, we have some very luxurious ones for sale, but normally people who go there want two or three-bedroomed pied-à-terres. There is a shortage of the smaller type apartments.'

For the less well-keeled, there are plenty of good tax reasons to move to the rest of mainland Europe. 'People do move to France, Spain or Portugal for tax reasons and keep their money in, for example, the Channel Islands,' says King.

Kevin Brown of property company Swissinvest says: 'Most of the people who buy just want a second home near skiing and the lakes and they happen to like Switzerland. It's not such a good tax haven any more, but people who have retired like it. It's a secure investment. The Swiss franc has traditionally been one of the strongest currency in the world. And property prices have risen very steadily. It's not like the horror stories you hear in France.'

'It depends on what you are advised to do by your tax people,' adds King. 'If you have your money in the Cayman Islands and then move to France, you are only taxed on your assets in France.'

This inevitably brings the roving house-buyers' thoughts back to the unashamedly cheap tax haven Ireland. The market is booming. Actress Patsy Kensit and *Formula 1* racing driver Damon Hill both moved there in recent years. 'People go to Ireland for very specific reasons,' says Pickles. 'They do have a good regime for authors there. You can collect loads of royalties effectively tax free.'

Robert Ganley, who manages estate agent Ganley Walters in Dublin, says that between 40% and 50% of country house sales last year went to overseas buyers. 'We have advantageous tax laws,' he comments. 'A lot of people in the music business live here because of the legislation on artists.'

As for the Isle of Man, it is difficult to find a non-Manxman or trial-biker who really likes the place, despite the vexed question of tax. 'The Isle of Man is very much like the Channel Islands from a tax point of view,' says Pickles. 'But you do suffer from VAT and you do suffer from the weather.'

Dring says all this is worth it. Well he would, wouldn't he? Every area has slightly different financial advantages and each offers a different kind of lifestyle, he observes. 'Some people go into tax exile with long faces thinking they will have to sit out three or four years to avoid capital gains tax,' he says, 'but they often end up enjoying the lifestyle in somewhere like Guernsey so much that they never leave.'

THE BAILIWICK OF GUERNSEY, ALDERNEY AND SARK

Immigration qualifications: British buyers are restricted to buying homes on Guernsey's 'open market' where prices can be double those on the 'local' market from which islanders buy.

Tax advantages: 20% rate on taxable income, no capital gains tax or VAT. No inheritance tax or death duties. Generous personal allowances are given before tax.

Lifestyle: Guernsey is the largest island, 26 square miles with a population of 60,000. More than 20,000 of the homes on the island are restricted to local market. Only 1,700 are on the open market. Alderney is three square miles and Sark one square mile. The people of the Bailiwick have a very British lifestyle and speak English, though they live closer to France. They benefit from a much gentler and sunnier climate than Britain with an average of 1,800–2,000 hours of sunshine per year. The Bailiwick has almost full employment and a very low crime rate. It is governed by a single house of parliament, the States of Deliberation, comprising elected representatives with no political party allegiance.

JERSEY

Immigration qualifications: a desire to prevent overcrowding and protect the beautiful countryside in Jersey has resulted in stiff immigration laws. To be considered for residency and for buying a property in Jersey you have to be a multi-millionaire with minimum assets of £12 million and guaranteed annual income to ensure income tax payable to the States of Jersey of between £150,000 and £200,000. Other routes for consideration are the possibility of bringing substantial local employment to the island, or to be a sportsperson, entertainer, artist or professional bringing unique talents to the island.

Tax advantages: income tax of 20% on worldwide income after personal allowances. No capital gains tax, inheritance tax or VAT.

Lifestyle: Jersey has a population of 82,000 on 45 square miles. It is rare to find a house with more than seven acres of land. Like Guernsey—though the atmosphere is British—Jersey is nearer to France and has a much gentler and sunnier climate. Zero unemployment and a low crime rate add to the feelgood factor for Jersey residents. There are several large yacht marinas and golf courses. Like Guernsey, the island is also governed by a non-political body, the States of Jersey.

IRELAND

Immigration qualifications: a national of the European Community, Austria, Finland, Sweden or Iceland is entitled to apply for residency if they can support themselves without recourse to state assistance. UK nationals are exempt from these controls.

Tax advantages: this is a haven for artists, painters, writers, composers and poets from all over the world who are given a warm welcome in Ireland and allowed to live free of tax on any of their artistic earnings. In 1995, there were some 2,600 'artists' resident in Ireland—a third of whom are non-Irish nationals.

Lifestyle: as well as benefiting from the international centre of Dublin, Ireland boasts a laid back lifestyle, spectacular countryside, and lots and lots of sport. It could see a mini-boom from the hunting/shooting/fishing set if any, or all, of these activities are banned in the UK. Its rich and widespread cultural and sporting roots are annually on show at events like the Wexford Opera Festival, the Royal Dublin Horse Show, the Cork Jazz Festival and the Irish Derby.

ISLE OF MAN

Immigration qualifications: none necessary for British passport holders.

Tax advantages: no death or estate duties. No inheritance, gift or capital gains tax. Income tax is set at 15% on the first £8,750 and 20% on the balance.

Lifestyle: 227 square miles of glens, sandy beaches and mountains. Much bigger and less crowded than all the other havens apart from Ireland. The easiest to get into. Property prices on a par with south-east England. Tucked between the north-west coast of Britain and Ireland, the climate of the Isle of Man is very British.

MONACO

Immigration qualifications: you must be employed in Monaco, or be able to prove you have adequate financial support to live there. There is no restriction on foreigners owning property.

Tax advantages: no tax on private incomes. Limited inheritance tax on Monegasque assets. There are, however, tax considerations if you have a secondary residence in France.

Lifestyle: certainly the most glamorous of all the accessible tax havens. A tiny principality headed by a royal family, this Côte d'Azur state—capital Monte Carlo—is a much-loved resort of the rich and famous. It also has a fantastic supply of banks, accountants and lawyers to cater for 'exiled' residents on its 190 hectares. Monaco is internationally famous for its tennis tournament and for the Monte Carlo Grand Prix. It also boasts glitzy hotels and restaurants including the Hermitage and Café de Paris, as well as the Casino. There is a substantial British expatriate community, who either lease or buy property.

GUIDE TO ACCESSIBLE LOW TAX AREAS
Compiled with the help of Knight Frank

- John Allen, Swoffers (Guernsey) 01481 711766
- Kevin Brown, Swissinvest (UK) 01902 688514
- Conrad Coutanche, Mourant du Feu & Jeune (Jersey) 01534 609000
- Paddy Dring, Knight Frank (UK) 0171 629 8171
- Jonathan Evans, Bishops International Holdings (UK) 01832 274408
- Robert Ganley, Ganley Walters (Ireland) 00 353 1 662 3255
- David King, Hamptons (UK) 0171 824 8822
- Norma Linds, European Estates (Spain) 00 34 28 80 43 42
- Fredi Littlefair-Molin, The Reality Center (USA) 00 1 615 292 3745
- John Pickles, Moore Stephens (UK) 0171 248 4499
- David Piesing, Pannell Kerr Forster (Guernsey) 01481 729930

Charles Jacoby

Bishops International

Bishops International Property Consultants specializes in all aspects of the property market on a global scale. Having dealt mainly in Europe to date, we now have properties and developments as far afield as South Africa and Australia.

The international property market is a buoyant one, with some European countries enjoying 'mini booms', such as that in Italy. Purchasers are far more confident of buying internationally, and coupled with today's technology, including the Internet, this task is now far easier.

The trend for UK buyers is no longer in France but South Africa, where prices are increasing steadily with the end of apartheid and the lifting of international sanctions. Where UK residents were buying in Normandy and the Dordogne, many have found themselves selling to Dutch, Swiss and even German buyers and this has certainly been more common than not with ourselves. As a nation, we are still buying in Italy; this is mainly due to the quick profits being offered by the Italian property market, as previously mentioned. The Dutch, Swiss and Germans are also buying in Spain where we previously would have done.

The international 'exodus' from Hong Kong has now all but dried up, with many choosing to stay with a 'suck it and see' approach, though not knowing what the economy will do after the changeover many have poured their assets into buying in the UK where property prices, despite predictions of increase, remain pretty stagnant overall. Many in Hong Kong are still doing this and it is still a relatively lucrative market for selling country properties.

Bishops International cater for both buyers and sellers alike, dealing in worldwide property sales and rentals, and negotiating on behalf of buyers through our comprehensive search programme.

We have sales representatives in many European countries and will cater for a client's needs on the spot, whether it is searching for a property or selling abroad. Our international advertising is second to none and we will give your property extensive cover through our marketing network.

Property Consultants

For further information on our wide range of services, telephone:- +44 1780 482861, Fax:- +44 1780 482869 or write to:- Bishops International Property Consultants, Star Lane House, Star Lane, Stamford, Lincolnshire, PE9 1PH, UK.

CHATEAU DE LA PERELLE
4,000,000 Francs

La Perelle is an outstanding early 19th Century Napoleon III style Chateau, situated in eight acres of landscaped grounds and parkland, and surrounded by a large forest of 250 acres and some beautiful breathtaking countryside.

The Chateau is approximately 30km (20 miles) from Honfleur and Deauville, 40km (25 miles) from Rouen and Le Havre, 70km (40 miles) from Caen, and 150km (90 miles) from Paris. The new Normandy bridge to Le Havre is some ten miles away.

CHATEAU DE LA PERELLE

The property is situated on a plateau in the Risle Valley and is 3.5km (2 miles) from the picturesque village of Campigny and 5km (3 miles) from Pont Audemer, a gem of Normandy with its wood-panelled houses, many dating back to the 15th century, the canal system of the Venise Normande, and its twice weekly markets.

The ground floor contains a large entrance hall, four reception rooms, two kitchens, a study (used as an artist's studio), two large terraces and two WCs. The entrance hall has a mosaic floor and largely intact original wall paintings. A beautiful oak carved staircase leads to the upstairs rooms. The Napoleon III style dining room is wood-panelled with caisson ceilings and parquet floors, beautiful doors and an oak carved fireplace.

The original billiard room is now used as a living room with a marble fireplace and two large mirrors and parquetry flooring. A second living room has mural walls in the 19th century style (the theme is the five continents) with a period light fitting, marble fireplace and parquetry floors. The other salon was originally the orangerie; it has oil painted wall panels (not original), a marble fireplace and parquet floors, and opens onto the park with a small terrace and steps.

The original kitchen is very large with original earthenware wall tiles and terracotta floors, and opens onto the park. The artist's studio comes off the kitchen and has a large mirror and terracotta floors.

The first floor is on two levels, and contains six bedrooms, two large bathrooms, two WCs and three cabinets de toilette, a small fitted kitchen, two linen rooms, a dining and living room. One of the bedrooms, originally the library, is huge and has magnificent views over the grounds and plateau through two picture windows.

There are six further bedrooms and two cabinets de toilette as well as a WC and a large artist's studio.

There are 12 cellars including a wood and wine cellar, and three underground rainwater reservoirs which can be used for spraying the lawns and gardens. Hot water is supplied by three electric boilers. Heating is by gas and electrical radiators as well as the fireplaces. Both gas and electric cooking are available. The original central heating is still existent, but not in working order. The attic is used for storage.

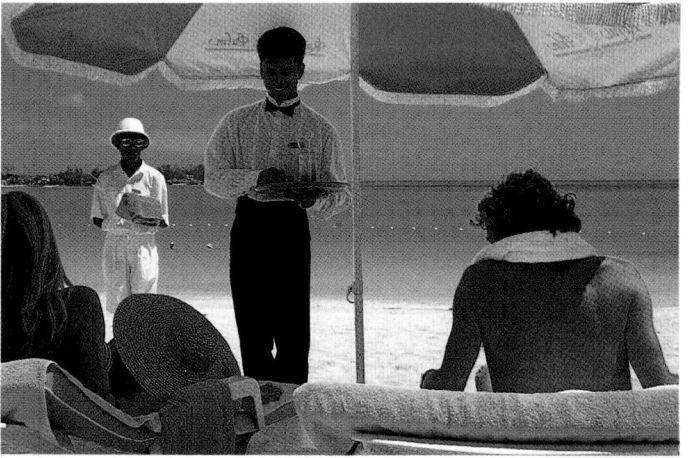

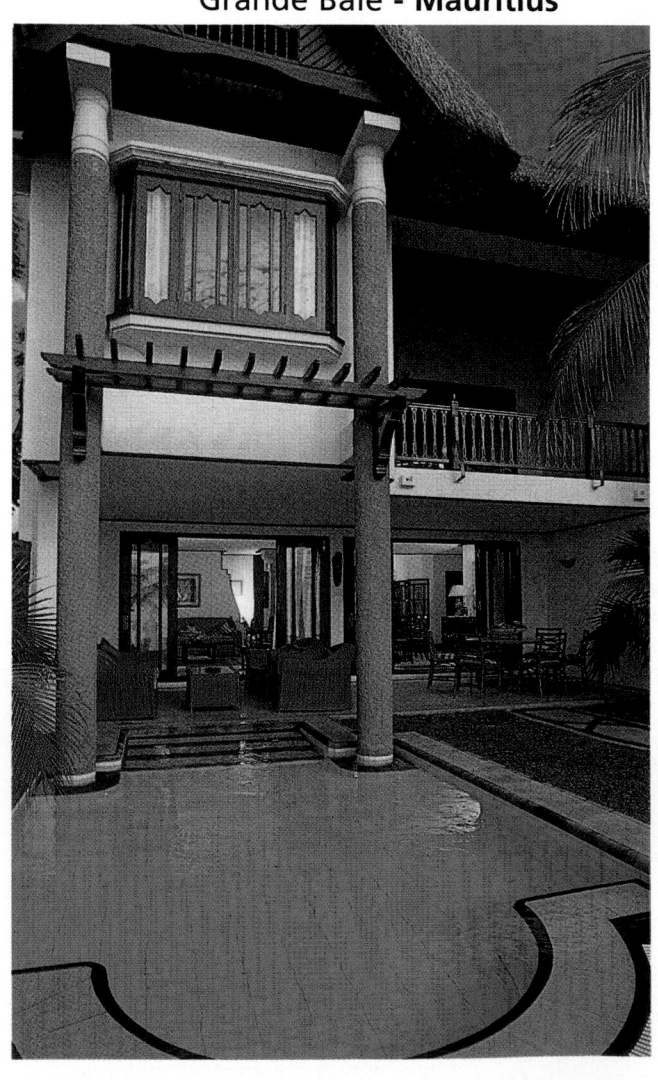

ASSOCIATION OF BRITISH TRAVEL AGENTS
by IAN REYNOLDS

Like most others of my generation, childhood holidays were spent in Britain. The jet engine had not been introduced into civil aircraft and the package holiday had not been invented. A Mediterranean holiday remained a dream.

Although now much more readily available, an overseas holiday remains the fulfilment of a dream for most of us and for many it is the largest single item of annual expenditure. This puts a tremendous responsibility on the travel industry to 'get it right'. It is an exciting and challenging time to be involved in the tourism industry, as customers look for ever more exotic hotels and exciting itineraries. British holidaymakers expect, and receive, some of the most competitive prices in Europe.

ABTA, the Association of British Travel Agents, has been at the forefront of the travel industry since its formation in 1950. It is a self-regulatory body, run by its membership and for over 20 years it has offered the holidaymaker a financial protection scheme. ABTA aims to ensure high standards of service and business throughout its membership and specifies Codes of Conduct with which its members must comply.

The 'Package Holiday' market has developed and widened significantly in recent years. The improving economic circumstances in the United Kingdom in the post-war years, the invention of the jet aircraft engine and the 'entrepreneurial' flair of the British travel industry have brought holidays abroad within the reach of millions of citizens. As a nation we make over 28 million holiday trips a year, with the result that a higher percentage of our population enjoys a holiday abroad than anywhere else in the world.

The industry can be very volatile and, in recent years, we have seen increases in passenger numbers of up to 20 per cent. There is evidence that we may now be reaching a levelling off and tour operators may have to concentrate their efforts on their own market share, rather than increasing the market by any noticeable amount. This has certainly meant a diversification of destinations and experiences.

Tour operators are continuously striving to satisfy the criteria of the most demanding traveller. Quality accommodation, flexible itineraries and a huge variety of destinations are required in order to attract an ever more discerning customer.

In addition to the traditional beach holidays in Europe, tour operators now offer an increasing number of exotic, long haul and luxury holidays in their main programmes. Spain remains the top destination for British travellers but many holidaymakers are looking further afield for their holiday experience. In a recent MORI survey, conducted for ABTA, Australia emerged as the country that British holidaymakers would visit if money were no object. The next destination cited was the United States, already the long haul destination with the highest number of British visitors.

The introduction of charter flights has brought many exciting, long haul destinations within the reach of the average holidaymaker. Florida, as the most popular long haul destination, provides a wonderful introduction to the United States. There is so much to see in the United States that a large number will visit time and again, choosing to see a different area on subsequent visits.

Numbers to the Caribbean are increasing, with islands such as Cuba and the Dominican Republic attracting many tourists for the first time. Recent research for ABTA shows that Mexico, with an astounding 236 per cent growth rate, was the fastest growing destination in 1996. The Far East, a long time favourite of independent travellers, is now appearing as an inclusive tour destination. Thailand is a firm favourite, as are Malaysia and Singapore. India, particularly Goa, is attracting many more visitors seeking winter sunshine.

There are numerous different ways to experience these countries—travelling on carefully planned escort trips or travelling independently—with accommodation to suit every taste, luxurious hotels and resorts, guesthouses or even 'under the stars' in tents. Flexibility is now important, with many operators encouraging clients to construct a tailor-made product from the published programme.

The brochures themselves, which adorn the travel agents' shelves, reflect the move to develop and mature the British package holiday market. Gone are the days of artists' impressions, scantily clad women tempting us to look closer and vague, flowery language. Holidaymakers, and the law, require that tour operators provide accurate, detailed information on the countries, resorts and relevant health and visa requirements. Many current brochures, produced to inform and tempt, are almost coffee table books in their own right.

For those with access to the Internet there are now over 40,000 travel and tourism sites on the world wide web. Many of these provide pictures of the destination, some with full motion video and sound. So it is now possible to experience a 'virtual reality' holiday without even leaving the armchair!

Cruising, long considered the ultimate in luxury holidays, is now the fastest growing sector of the holiday industry. Once considered as the preserve of the old and wealthy, cruising was seen as the ultimate holiday statement, available only to those with sufficient time and money. While cruises are still the epitome of luxury, the expansion of this lucrative sector has resulted in the availability of a wider range of prices and itineraries. Fly cruises are now available at well below £1,000 and this has led to over 400,000 people taking a cruise in 1996.

Working hard to dispel the myth that cruising is purely a luxury product for the elderly, the travel industry has been responsible for re-educating the public to appreciate the value for money represented by a cruise. Last year, over half of those who travelled on a cruise were first-timers and this is an encouraging trend.

Itineraries feature over two hundred destinations and include the Caribbean, Mediterranean, Alaska and round-the-world trips. River cruising, featuring the Nile, Danube, Rhine, Mississippi and the Amazon is also available. Cruise holidays are now as varied as the people who take them. With its emphasis on entertainment and socialising, it is also a popular holiday with the single traveller. With nearly a quarter of the population now living alone, this sector of the market is a huge potential source of customers.

The all-inclusive element found in cruise programmes has also been developed within other holidays. Several years ago this was to be found almost exclusively in the up-market, top of the range product but the concept is now being introduced into the less expensive short haul market. The appeal of one price covering all food, entertainment, activities and even some alcoholic drinks has definite potential.

The British, once called a 'nation of shopkeepers', are now turning to shopping overseas. Several years ago this market was taking cross-channel day-trips to France. Today, as the cross-channel routes offer better value than ever, with healthy competition under, over and on the Channel, business is booming. In addition though, we now see shopping trips to the United States, Canada and the United Arab Emirates.

In recent years, as we work harder and our leisure time becomes more precious, we have seen many people combine their holiday with a leisure interest or pursuit. Holidays are now available for those who want to improve their painting, bowls or archery, those who want to prepare or consume fine foods and wines or those who enjoy visiting battlefields. For the more adventurous there are opportunities for adrenaline-seeking skidoo trips, sensational four-wheel drive safaris, horse trekking, white water rafting or bungee jumping. These so-called 'soft' adventures may form a small part of your holiday or may be the activity around which your holiday is built. Adventure travel has increased by 500 per cent during the past five years.

While the travel industry is encouraged to note the trend towards taking more adventurous holidays, it is important to look at what may be the factors influencing this propensity to book further afield. Initially, most people choose a simple, familiar holiday close to home. Research indicates that as they become more experienced and confident they begin to look at new destinations and experiences.

In recent years we have seen the number and variety of holiday programmes on television and radio increase. Images, on television in particular, can certainly excite the interest of potential visitors. With the continuing success of local radio and the growth in cable television networks, we are confident that there will be a growing opportunity for holiday ideas on the airwaves.

The importance of the media in influencing travel trends was emphasised in an ABTA survey at the end of last year. We found that 34 per cent of customers felt that television and radio programmes offered them useful, unbiased information. We were delighted to note that 50 per cent felt that travel agents would do the same. Clearly, while the ideas may come from various sources, it is still imperative for clients to talk through their requirements with a travel agent.

The reality in our business, as in any other, is that competitive pricing is key to success. While increasing numbers may aspire to travel outside Europe and participate in ever more challenging activities, it is the cost or the value for money that determines whether the aspiration can become the reality.

Development inevitably means change and, in some cases, this brings its own problems. The travel industry seeks to work with national governments to ensure that the very reasons why a destination is so appealing are not demolished with the beginning of mass tourism. As with most things, it is achieving the balance that is so important.

There are a number of destinations that have achieved this balance very successfully. Mauritius, for example, has restricted the height of its buildings to that of the surrounding trees. Thailand and many other Asian countries have worked with groups such as the Coalition on Child Prostitution and Tourism to discourage the wrong type of visitor. Many African destinations have also successfully involved the community in the expansion of their tourism programmes and this has ensured that both local needs and commercial ones are given consideration.

In recent years, nearly one third of the British public have left the purchase of their holiday until the last minute. When one considers how important a holiday is to most of us, it seems strange that we should be prepared to leave this decision so late. Creative marketing by the tour operators and a better balance between supply and demand last year seem to have halted this trend and we are hopeful that it may have been reversed, as the experience of 1996 showed that early bookers fared best for both choice and price. Tour operators will be taking further steps this year to encourage holidaymakers to book early in order to obtain the holiday they want at the right price.

If the travel industry could invite us all to imagine our dream holiday, consider the amount of money we have to spend and then consult with our travel agent, many of us would be surprised at the breadth of choice available and the width of price range that facilitates it. Whether your ideal holiday includes peace and quiet, the adventure of a lifetime, or a little of both, you may be pleased to find spectacular and unforgettable destinations in both familiar and unfamiliar areas of the world.

Ian Reynolds

Chief Executive, Association of British Travel Agents

Kredietbank & Kredietrust Luxembourg

Serving your trust...

Kredietbank Luxembourg (KBL), an internationally active investment and private bank, provides international private investors with a complete range of private banking services and products in the Grand Duchy as well as through its branches and subsidiaries in Geneva, Basle, Lugano, London (see bookmark), Dublin, Jersey and Monaco.

Kredietrust (KTL), a company associated with KBL in Luxembourg and also represented in Geneva, Madeira and Jersey, works closely with the bank to provide more specialised services such as private wealth management and asset structuring, including setting up and managing companies and trusts.

For nearly fifty years Kredietbank Luxembourg and Kredietrust have gained and kept the confidence of thousands of private investors. This confidence explains:

- the steady increase of the assets entrusted to KBL (by this criterion, KBL ranks as one of the most important of the 222 banks established in Luxembourg);
- the leading position held, year after year, by number of incorporations and companies administered, by the Companies and Trusts department at KTL.

There are excellent reasons for this confidence:

- the strength of the principal KBL/KTL shareholder- the Almanij-Kredietbank Group - with more than 16 000 employees in over 100 financial sector companies engaged in worldwide cooperation;
- the exemplary solidity of KBL, a bank with a consolidated solvency ratio of 19.8% (the bank has ranked first in solvency in the Grand Duchy for several years);
- the state-of-the-art IT and communications resources available to KBL and KTL;
- more than 1200 committed employees within KBL and 340 people at Kredietrust;
- the quality of the top-class specialised services provided.

Expert credentials

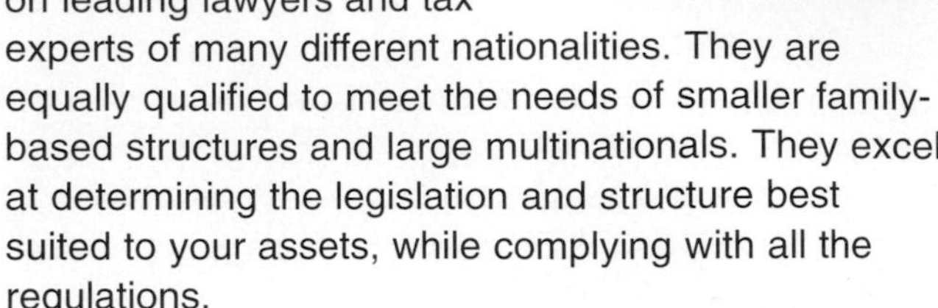

The Companies and Trusts department of Kredietrust relies on leading lawyers and tax experts of many different nationalities. They are equally qualified to meet the needs of smaller family-based structures and large multinationals. They excel at determining the legislation and structure best suited to your assets, while complying with all the regulations.

The ins and outs of holding companies, SOPARFIs, trusts, foundations, fiduciary contracts and similar legal structures are an open book to these experts. Throughout the lifetime of the structure, their services also include ongoing advice, administrative management, help in preparing your tax declarations and, when necessary, the provision of directors, trustees and auditors.

In synergy with this department, KTL Private Asset Management offers a choice of management styles (advisory or discretionary management, according to a diversified, bond-based or personal strategy) in order to optimise the funds held in the structure that our Companies and Trusts specialists establish for you.

"Every day, all over the world, we grow the trust and assets of thousands of private investors."

Contacts:

Kredietbank Luxembourg
43 bd Royal L-2955 Luxembourg
General Inquiries
Tel.: + 352 4797 2021 Fax: +352 4797 2060

Kredietrust Luxembourg
11 rue Aldringen L-2960 Luxembourg
Private Asset Structuring
Carlo Schlesser/Françoise Stamet
Tel. : +352 46 819 2609/2611 Fax: +352 47 11 01

Private Asset Management
Charles Vandevelde
Tel.: +352 46 819 3896 Fax: +352 46 54 93

KBL and KTL are not regulated in the United Kingdom and do not conduct investment business in the UK. The protection afforded to investors under the United Kingdom regulatory system would not apply and compensation under the Investors Compensation Scheme would not be available. This advertisment has been approved by Brown, Shipley & Co. Limited who are regulated by the SFA.

INDUSTRY IN BRITAIN
by THE RT HON THE LORD HANSON

In Britain today industry is presented with a great opportunity which is shown by many key indicators of economic strength. Private consumption in Britain is higher per capita than it is in Germany, Sweden or Australia. Our national income is currently fifth in the world. Median real wages here have increased by 19% in real terms in the last ten years, more than in Japan, France or Canada. Even our lowest paid workers have enjoyed a 10% increase in their real earnings over the period, more than their counterparts in France, Sweden or the USA.

Although the tax burden on the average household has increased over the last fifteen years, average income has *risen* twice as much as taxes. All of which amounts to considerably increased spending power in Britain. The consumer has more to spend and looks to industry to provide the goods and services wanted.

Our increased individual spending power here is mirrored by our having, since 1992, a higher rate of economic growth than the USA, France, Japan or Germany. Over the period since 1979, our growth among G-7 countries has been second only to Japan.

In Britain we currently provide jobs for a higher proportion of our working age population than Germany, France or Italy and we have a lower rate of unemployment than any of those countries. So it is not surprising that the OECD's Economic Survey for 1996 speaks of our maintaining 'an economic environment conducive to job creation' which is paying off in a 'better jobs and unemployment record than in many continental European countries'.

With a rapidly reviving economy under this Government, continuing very low interest rates, realistic rates of exchange and no so-called *'Social Chapter'* to blunt competitiveness, it is also not surprising that the IMF speaks of Britain's 'enviable' economic performance. Nor is it surprising that we lead the inward investment league in Europe, currently attracting 38% of *all* investment into the European Union.

In 1995–96 alone there were 477 projects begun by overseas investors here, including 208 from the USA, 48 from Japan and 12 from Korea. Since then the LG group from Korea has announced the largest ever single inward investment in the UK or Europe, a £1.7 billion manufacturing investment near Newport in South Wales. So enterprises from abroad clearly understand the opportunities for industry in Britain.

A key question for all of us is: Will British industry grasp this great opportunity, rather than leave it to our foreign competitors? Can enterprise here exploit the chance it now has to move onwards and upwards?

Not so long ago it was fashionable to hold that we had lost our traditional industrial strength in manufacturing and that the British economy was set to be a centre of finance and services rather than of invention and making. I have never believed that our future lay in services at the expense of manufacturing. The smokestack industries of the Industrial Revolution have gone, but constructive ideas and people are pouring out of the universities and industry.

For exciting proof of that, you only have to look at the dominance of British designers and engineers in *Formula 1* racing cars. Indeed, amid all the gloom about our supposedly unskilled workforce, it may surprise many to learn that even before our recent expansion of higher education we had the same proportion of young people gaining degrees and higher level vocational qualifications as France and more than Germany.

But we have much ground to make up at the lower levels of skills. Far too many of our young people are appallingly ill-educated. Real as these problems certainly are to those of us in industry, they are not discouraging firms from abroad from choosing to base their manufacturing plant here. Nor do they impugn our skills base at the higher levels essential to a competitive economy today. Could it be they feel they have better managerial skills?

British industry has a great opportunity if only it will grasp it. It can be done, but only if we adopt the right philosophy of management. Intellectually, the philosophy is simplicity itself. Whatever problems it poses lie in the application. For example, the tendency to fudge hard decisions and opt for any easy life. But fudging could be fatal, locally and nationally. If we blur the clean lines of correct managerial strategy, money, time and effort will be diverted from developing the best chances and profiting from them. Individual businesses will suffer and even die. Collectively the country would fluff the opportunity now afforded us as we come out of the struggle and difficulties of the last few years.

What no-one should forget is that while it is those on the ground who actually make things and designers, engineers and inventors who plan what they make, any operation depends on management leadership at every turn. It depends on management to raise the capital needed in the first place; it depends on management to ensure that the process of production goes smoothly and it depends on management to ensure that potential customers know of the product and its benefits and that it is available when and where it is wanted.

In very small enterprises many of these functions will be undertaken by the same individual and individuals, as when an inventor finances, builds and markets his own brainwave out of his own resources. But in the vast majority of cases efficiency and scale demand division of labour. In this division of labour, management must facilitate everything else. Unfortunately, too often, rather than facilitating, management obstructs, stifles initiative and confuses lines of command. Typical of management in state-run enterprises here in the past and abroad even today.

But it is not only public-sector management which is sclerotic. Private corporations and companies also have an in-built tendency to develop a culture in which the primary aim of management appears to be its own well-being and expansion, at the expense of efficiency and profit.

At least, this can happen for a time but it is the virtue of the private sector that, in the end, inefficient, top-heavy and self-serving management will be weaned out by market forces. You live by the market and you can die by the market. The enterprise will fold or be taken over by others more willing and able to understand and grasp its potential. Takeovers occur precisely because people outside a company often know more about what it is worth and what it could do than those currently charged with running it. Such a situation implies that shareholders are in effect being short-changed.

It is indeed from the premise that any private concern has to make a profit to survive and has to produce a return for those who invest in it, that our conception of management follows. Without return on investment, no company will flourish, nor will it attract the further funds to sustain and expand its activity. From this key point the priorities of company management follow.

The over-riding priority must be to shareholders. The shareholders, who have entrusted their money to a company, create both a moral and commercial obligation. The money they invest is money they have earned and on which they paid taxes; for which they have worked, at great personal effort and risk.

It would be wrong, as well as commercial suicide, not to ensure a return on investment, for it is money which has been made freely available and in good faith. This principle would hold good no matter the source of the investment, but the obligation of a company to its shareholders is reinforced when we reflect that the biggest shareholders these days are institutions to whom millions of ordinary people have entrusted their savings and pensions.

There is nothing anti-social or divisive in a company management treating its first duty as being to its shareholders, however much socialist talk about 'stakeholding' and 'the wider community' may muddy the waters. Such talk is intellectually confused and is more the old cry that those who have contributed nothing to a company should be given a free-ride on its benefits and success.

Directly or indirectly we are all shareholders now and we all have an interest in the success of our investments, whether we realise it or not. Shareholders' trust in a company will only be honoured if the company makes a profit. From this follows the second duty of a company management, the satisfaction of its customer. If customers are not satisfied, the company's products will not be bought and there will be nothing for the shareholders. A company has a moral duty to its customers in the same direct way it has to its shareholders and it will not fulfil its duty to them unless it succeeds commercially with its customers.

Immediately following shareholders and customers, management has very serious responsibility to its employees. They invest their efforts and skills in the company and should be treated fairly and reasonably, which first and foremost means good pay and conditions. However, the only sure way of achieving good pay and conditions for employees is success in the market place. So logically there is no contradiction in recognising a responsibility to employees and focusing one's primary gaze and effort on the shareholders and customers. Without that focus, the company will fail, which will be of no benefit to employees. Logically, then, the well-being of a company's employees should be seen as a by-product of success in its other activities.

The success of the 'de-nationalisation' process has illuminated the difference between management in the private sector and what happened in nationalised bureaucracies. Private sector management has to set its face resolutely against treating its own interests as any kind of priority. Bureaucracies tend to promote their own interests before those of their clients or customers. In the public sector this went on for years because of an apparently bottomless public purse and because of a public too easily conned by emotive talk of public services. You've all seen the difference now between the old GPO telephone system or the former British Airways 'service' before and after. Once freed from the bureaucratic yoke, they have been able to lead the world.

In the private sector self-serving activity on the part of management is not unknown, but its undesirability becomes more transparent, leading ultimately to the destruction of any company which puts the interest of those running it, before those of its customers and shareholders. Within the structure implied by its duties to shareholders and customers, management's role is to facilitate and energise the efforts of others.

To do this effectively, managers at every level must be free to exercise their judgement. Only if they are free, will they respond creatively to the demands and opportunities which arise continually in whatever sector of the company for which they have responsibility. In management, difficult as it may be to apply in practice, subsidiarity must mean something. Budgeting and decision-making must always be at the lowest appropriate level. This will motivate the decision-takers while allowing the company to make full use of their experience, knowledge and expertise.

In appointing managers, seek to identify the individuals at the sharp end of things who have enough insight to analyse the information required to make the business succeed and the strength of character to take the necessary decisions. The individuals identified should then be trusted to make the decisions and this trust should be backed up from the centre with finance and support.

If people are not competent to make good decisions, they should not be made managers or should be removed. Having a top-heavy management structure will not

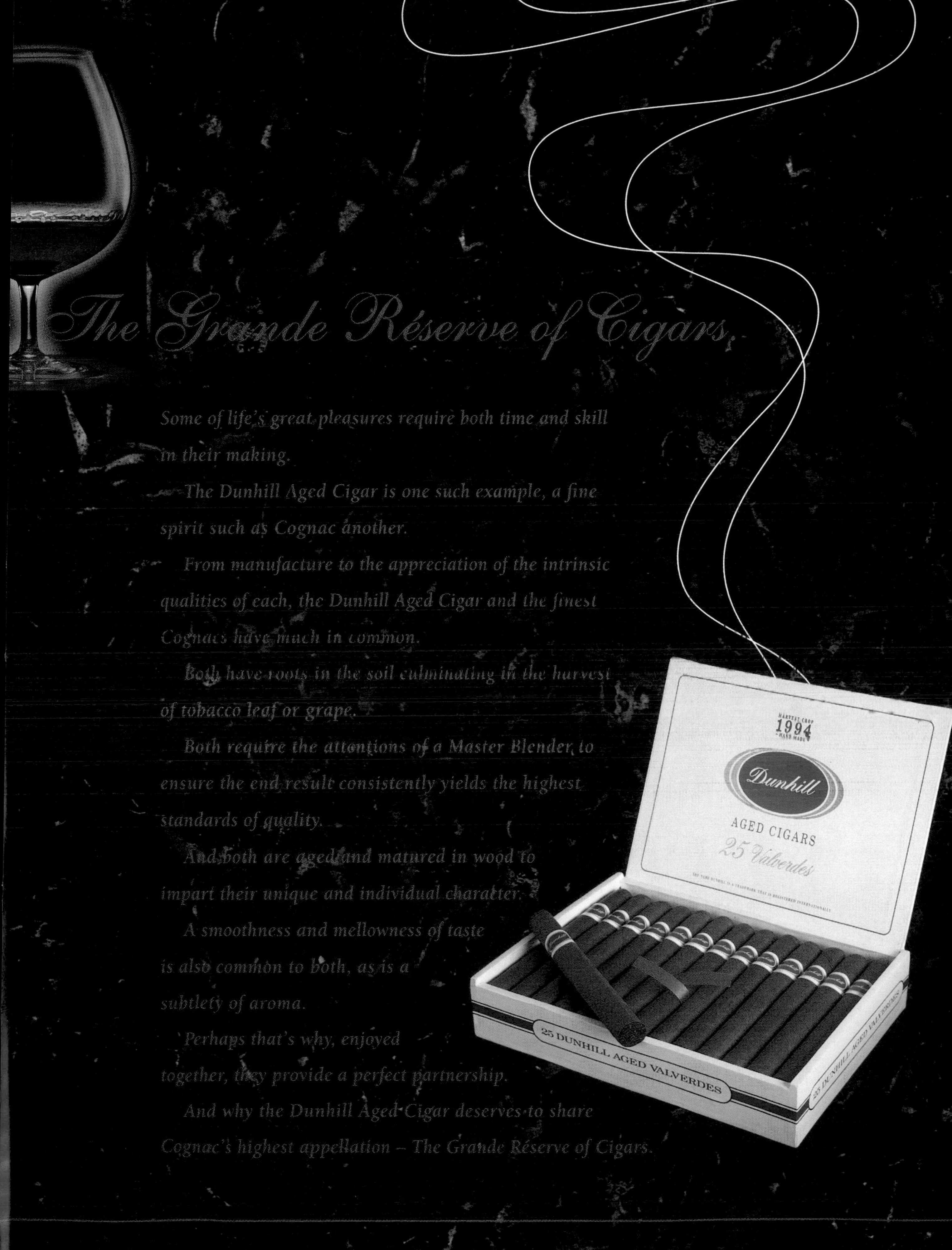
The Grande Réserve of Cigars.
Some of life's great pleasures require both time and skill in their making.
The Dunhill Aged Cigar is one such example, a fine spirit such as Cognac another.
From manufacture to the appreciation of the intrinsic qualities of each, the Dunhill Aged Cigar and the finest Cognacs have much in common.
Both have roots in the soil culminating in the harvest of tobacco leaf or grape.
Both require the attentions of a Master Blender, to ensure the end result consistently yields the highest standards of quality.
And both are aged and matured in wood to impart their unique and individual character.
A smoothness and mellowness of taste is also common to both, as is a subtlety of aroma.
Perhaps that's why, enjoyed together, they provide a perfect partnership.
And why the Dunhill Aged Cigar deserves to share Cognac's highest appellation – The Grande Réserve of Cigars.
HARVEST CROP
1994
HAND MADE
Dunhill
AGED CIGARS
25 Valverdes
25 DUNHILL AGED VALVERDES
25 DUNHILL AGED VALVERDES
CHIEF MEDICAL OFFICERS' WARNING
TOBACCO SERIOUSLY DAMAGES HEALTH

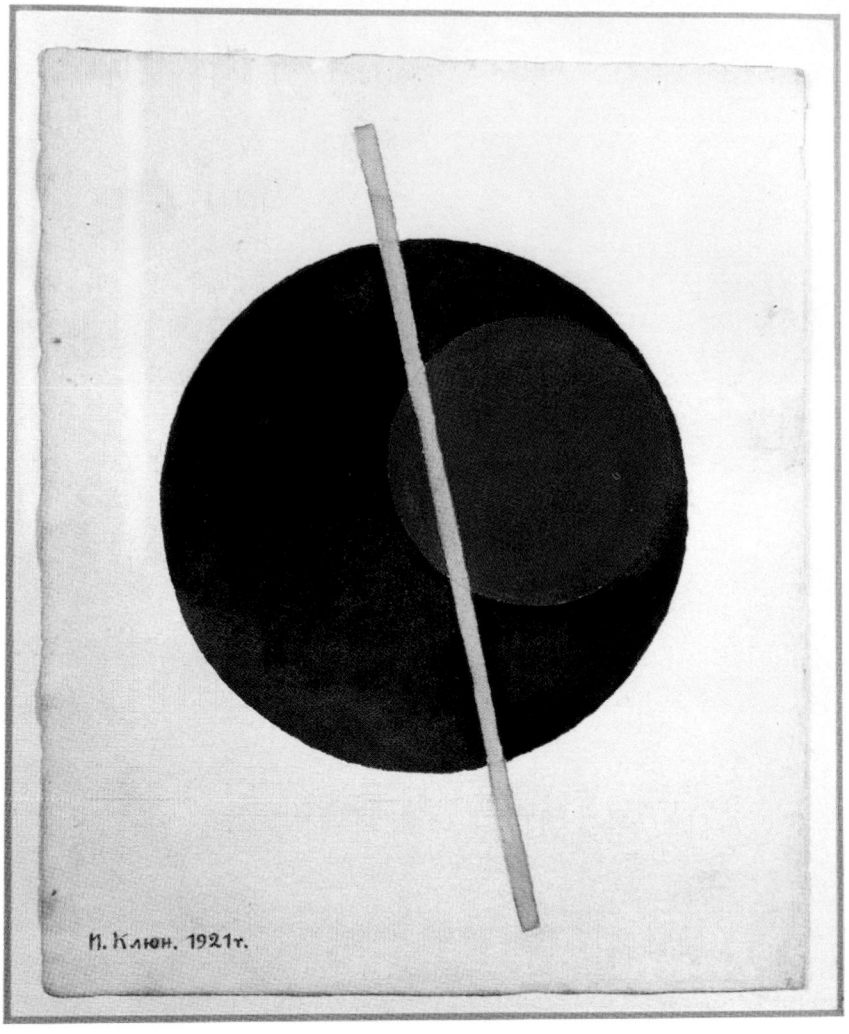

compensate for incompetent managers, for the company will still lack the information the managers are supposed to be supplying. On the other hand, a top-heavy management will undoubtedly curtail the initiative of a good manager, thus depriving the company of the very thing he or she is there to provide.

The general economic situation right now gives British industry a great launch-pad for success in the near future. To take the opportunity, business, like the Scouts, must be prepared. Those running them must be clear about their responsibilities to shareholders and customers. In their own organisations, businesses must have enough faith in their managers to given them their head. For they are the people who are best placed to make vital decisions at whatever level.

A company bold enough to give its key managers their head will not be disappointed. For the managers the challenge will motivate and enthuse; for the company the benefit will be flexibility, creativity, speed of response **and profit**. These are just the things which mark out successful enterprises from their more staid and bureaucratic competitors. A great opportunity awaits British industrial enterprise. Let us not miss this chance to shine.

The Rt Hon The Lord Hanson

Chairman, Hanson PLC

THE FINE ART OF INSURANCE
by ROBERT HISCOX

As a collector of fine art, I am only too aware of the emotional attachment that can apply to collections, let alone the financial asset they represent. In fact, my experience as chairman of a major insurer of art and high value households in the UK, makes me more wary than most of the constant threat of damage, not only from accidents, but also from theft and other acts of deliberate vandalism. Estimates of the value of stolen art vary between $3bn and $5bn per annum, so the risks are real.

Any careful owner will have noted the substantial increase in art theft during the height of the recession in the early 1990s and will have taken physical precautions to protect their assets. Unfortunately, it is probably fair to say that physical deterrents will not prevent a professional thief or gang, particularly if they are stealing to order. Insurance is the last line of asset protection.

Whilst it is the theft of famous paintings and sculpture that makes the headlines, art theft does not just involve art galleries or national exhibitions. On the contrary, the majority of thefts involve art that is not known on a national level and is stolen from country houses and small private collections.

As a company with a long term interest in art (and a considerable corporate collection of its own), Hiscox started specialising in the insurance of fine art, antiques and all collectibles in the 1960s. With the increasing interest in recent years in the value of such items, encouraged by programmes such as the Antiques Roadshow, there has been a growing realisation that collections of art and houses with valuable contents need specialist insurance. Hiscox has led the way in providing that specialist cover.

Many owners of fine art simply have conventional home insurance without recognising the benefits of broader cover, specialist claims service and importantly, financial incentives for, and practical advice about, valuations.

A recent survey published revealed that there are around 800,000 homes in the UK that could be classified as 'high net worth'. Of these homes, 90% had conventional home insurance where specialist insurance would be more appropriate.

There are only a handful of specialist insurers in the world, many of them operating in the London market. These insurers are being approached by more and more discerning owners of art who recognise the importance of insuring with someone who can provide personal, informal service and who is committed to an exceptional claim service based on a detailed knowledge of the art market. I personally want to speak to an insurer or professional intermediary who understands that the difference between a Monet and a Manet is not just a spelling mistake. Art is a volatile market place, and knowledge of its vagaries is an important consideration in the service provided by your insurer.

'Standard' home contents policies pose a particular problem to the owner of fine art, antiques or jewellery—they often will not pay out more than one third of the total cover on 'valuables'. Many also include a single article limit that restricts payment on any one item that is lost or stolen to a small percentage of the total insurance cover (often 5%). If you want more cover for each item in your collection, you will have to pay more and itemise each item—few people remember this requirement. I doubt if few readers have a complete, up to date view on the values at risk in their home(s). We, all of us, take for granted our furnishings and few have the discipline to value their property regularly.

One of the keys to successful relationships between insurers and their clients is the agreement of value. A professional valuation is extremely useful. It has to be said that for many people, it is a genuine shock to find out how much the maiden aunt's inheritance is actually worth. The difference between perception and valuation is often staggering.

Inevitably, a specialist insurer is managed by staff with an absorbing interest in art. Underwriters have close ties with the art world; valuers, framers and auctioneers are able to understand quickly the whimsical nature of pricing—and the possible markets for stolen goods!

Advice on security, including complex alarms, is all part of the service offered by a specialist insurer. This will usually include a visit by a highly trained surveyor to give advice on the particular security needs of the house, including emergency procedures such as how to get paintings or objects out of the house, how to handle them properly and in what order.

Few readers will have missed the much publicised thefts recently of important fine art. Two Turners on loan from the Tate Gallery to a gallery in Germany in 1994, worth £24m and insured by my own underwriters, are still missing—but not forgotten. It is a matter of personal pride that they are tracked down—they are certainly unsaleable in a gallery—and that they are actually returned to their rightful owners. Edward Munch's 'The Scream' was of course recovered after a ransom demand. Unfortunately, the owner of Titian's 'Rest on the Flight into Europe' stolen from Longleat House, has not been so lucky. If paintings of this quality can disappear (hopefully for only a short time), it is little wonder that less well known paintings and objects are still attractive to unscrupulous collectors. All the more reason to protect your property and insure it for its full value with a specialist insurer, whose underwriters believe that risk assessment and pricing is more than the product of a computer programme.

ROBERT HISCOX

Chairman, Hiscox plc

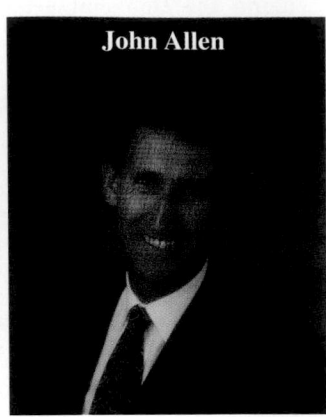

GUERNSEY—A MATURE INTERNATIONAL FINANCE CENTRE

Although a close trading relationship exists with the UK, as it has for centuries, today Guernsey's speciality is attracting funds and assets from around the world.

In 1995 an estimated 57% of the Island's annual export earnings arose from international finance compared with 15% from tourism, 9% from light industry and 4% from horticulture. The other 15% came from 'rentiers'—wealthy Guernsey residents who live off investment income and who comprise both Islanders and settlers mainly from the UK and former Commonwealth countries.

The latter have been attracted for many reasons not the least of which is that for UK and EU citizens the Island's housing legislation, through which immigration is controlled, is fairly straightforward. Of Guernsey's 21,000 or so dwellings nearly 1,800 are classed as Open Market, which means they can be bought and occupied by people without the residential qualifications which are essential for legal occupation of any of the remaining 19,200 homes. In 1995 the estimated average price for an Open Market property was £414,200 although, typically, prices range from £250,000 to around £1 million. Recently the highest asking price for a single, substantial Open Market property was £7 million. Unlike some other offshore centres, where the residence requirements are more complicated, the Guernsey requirement rests simply on the potential newcomer's ability to afford an Open Market home. For 'essential' workers licences are available enabling the occupation of Local Market homes usually on condition that these properties are relatively expensive and that the licence holder will be staying only three or five years.

Quite apart from the relative simplicity of the local housing laws there are many other reasons why newcomers choose to settle in the Island: it offers a pleasant lifestyle with relatively high standards of living for individuals and families, the climate is good and Guernsey is virtually crime and strike-free. There are also excellent educational, medical, recreational and cultural facilities, there is almost no unemployment, taxation and rates are low and there are no party politics.

It is perhaps not without cause that estate agents in Guernsey claim that interest by wealthy UK citizens in the purchase of Open Market homes increases when a Labour government seems imminent or, indeed, comes into power.

However, while some of the above attractions have undoubtedly helped the Island's expansion as a premier international finance centre, there are other additional key factors to take into account.

Guernsey was part of William the Conqueror's Norman possessions when he defeated King Harold at Hastings in 1066 and still remains an 'appanage' of the Crown. It has been self-governing for centuries and even today the UK government is responsible only for defence and foreign affairs. The absence of party politics has produced decades of political and economical stability and regular annual budget surpluses. For nearly forty years income tax for individuals and companies has been at a standard rate of 20% and there are no other forms of direct taxation, in particular inheritance tax and death duties. There is also no VAT and bank interest is paid gross. Such a benign regime was originally introduced to benefit Islanders themselves who, following five devastating years of German occupation, faced severe economic problems after liberation in 1945.

Along with proximity to the City (Guernsey is less than an hour's flying time from London) low taxes were among the reasons why the first British merchant banks established operations in the Island in the 1960s with the intention of offering their international clients secure and tax-efficient services including portfolio management, offshore trusts and corporate administration.

Since then many other changes, beyond the Island's control, have helped generate further growth. The most important include the abolition of exchange controls by the UK government and the negotiation of a special relationship for Guernsey with the EU. The latter is enshrined in Protocol 3 of the Treaty of Accession and places the Island in the EU for trade in physical goods but out for everything else including the need to comply with Financial Directives and any measures to harmonise taxation. The Protocol can only be changed by unanimous vote of all EU members.

During the 1970s and 1980s Guernsey's growth as an international finance centre continued apace and to help accommodate and control this growth, along with enhancing the Island's reputation as a well-regulated centre, a variety of legislation was introduced, the overall effect of which has been to improve investor confidence. In February 1988 the Guernsey Financial Services Commission was established with statutory powers over banking, insurance and investment businesses—mainly collective investments schemes (offshore funds).

It is to the credit of the Commission, which is staffed by professional regulators including three former Bank of England executives and which has always approached its task in a 'firm but flexible' manner, that Guernsey has continued to attract and retain only top quality financial services businesses. BCCI, for example, never gained a foothold in the Island.

For several years in succession Guernsey has been Europe's fastest growing location for the formation of captives, established not only for parent organisations based in the UK, but also for those from many other parts of the world. There are 38 insurance company management companies, between them handling over 300 captive insurance companies. Captive insurance, incidentally, is a form of self-insurance by which medium to large corporations and organisations can cover risks that are expensive or difficult to place in the conventional insurance market, for example professional indemnity, catastrophe, pollution, public liability and product guarantee risks.

As at the end of March 1996, Guernsey had 75 banks including Coutts, Rothschilds, Hambros, Credit Suisse, Royal Bank of Canada, Bank of Bermuda and subsidiaries of several UK building societies. Together they held deposits of nearly £46 billion, three quarters in foreign currency. In addition, Guernsey had over 30 fund management companies providing services to more than 330 Guernsey offshore funds holding assets of almost £14 billion for over 114,000 investors worldwide. There were also six international life and pension companies.

Over the past 30 years the controlled progression towards a mature international finance centre has laid a solid foundation for the future of Guernsey.

Patrick Murrin, FCA

Partner, Saffery Champness
Chairman, Guernsey International Business Association

GUERNSEY

Guernsey likes to portray itself as Europe's offshore centre. It points out that it has most of the benefits of membership of the European Union but few of the hassles. Guernsey lies within the European Community as far as the single market for the free movement of manufactured goods is concerned, yet lies outside the EU for taxation and exchange of information purposes.

This means that a bank or trust company based in Guernsey has no obligation to provide information to regulators other than its own. What is more, since Guernsey has a relationship with the British crown rather than the British parliament, it is not necessarily bound by parliamentary decisions. This means that for all political issues, except defence and foreign policy, the island's own legislature, the States of Deliberation, can make laws to suit Guernsey's own circumstances.

For most British taxpayers, the main advantage of using an offshore centre such as Guernsey is to avoid (not evade, which is a criminal offence) tax. Currency funds are one common way of enjoying the advantages of offshore investment. These funds allow investors to earn interest free of tax by investing in safe bank deposits in sterling and other currencies. Yet unlike a Tessa or an issue of National Savings certificates (which are their tax-free onshore equivalents), investors in offshore funds are not locked into the investment for a set period. Nor does the investor have to declare (for tax purposes) the annual interest payments from the fund, since these can be rolled up and remitted when the onshore investor decides that it now suits him to pay the tax for which he is liable.

This combination of tax efficiency and flexibility has contributed to the strong growth of the fund management industry in the island. Over the past five years, Guernsey's fund management business has doubled: the island now has over £15bn of funds under management. Its banks have deposits of over £45bn. Over the past five years international banks have started to make greater use of the advantages offered by the island. There are two clear signs of this: Swiss banks now account for 40% of the deposits held on the island and, secondly, currencies other than sterling now account for over 70% of the deposits held on the island.

Besides offering investment accounts, most financial companies in Guernsey also specialise in trusts. Here, figures are harder to come by but informed estimates reckon that the total wealth managed from Guernsey is in the order of £80bn (which includes banks deposits and assets under management). Offshore trusts are set up to help people manage their wealth efficiently. Trusts are the most common way of enabling individuals and families to avoid unnecessary taxation on the wealth they have either inherited or created.

Establishing trusts in Guernsey is attractive for several reasons. Some are simple, such as the fact that Guernsey is in the European time-zone and everyone speaks English. There are several more technical attractions. One is that a trust based in Guernsey is not liable for any income tax on the income the trust derives from non-Guernsey assets where the beneficiaries are not residents of Guernsey. Another technical attraction is that the courts in Guernsey will uphold the validity of the trust against any legal challenge from the jurisdiction in which the person setting it up is based. The courts in Guernsey will simply refuse to accept any interference from foreign courts over the legality of the way the assets of the trust are being settled. A third technical attraction that a Guernsey trust possesses is efficient management. Companies offering fiduciary services in the island have a proven management record. They also have a wide experience of the advantages of other jurisdictions and can therefore design and service a trust or private company to suit most requirements.

The benefits enjoyed by offshore investors pale besides the privileges that Guernsey residents possess. Some of Britain's super-rich in fact move to the island to benefit from its maximum income tax rate of 20%. The rate has not varied since it was introduced 40 years ago.

Although Guernsey has a large offshore business aimed at serving individuals it also has made a considerable effort to develop captive insurance. Guernsey ranks as one of the top five locations for captive insurance companies in the world; it is also the most popular location for captives in Europe. It is handling a widening range of business.

The captive insurance business is becoming increasingly important as professionals (such as lawyers, doctors and accountants) find it more difficult to buy some sorts of insurance cover, particularly professional negligence, at reasonable prices from their usual insurance companies. The traditional insurance companies have become alarmed at the settlements courts have started to make in professional negligence actions. As a result they have jacked up everyone's premiums and reduced the scope of their cover.

The professionals' solution to the problem is to set up their own (captive) insurance company to cover at least some of the risks they run. This lowers the premiums they pay to the insurance company, and since, almost by definition, they will not want to claim from their captive insurance company, it enables the captive insurer to build up its reserves. Guernsey's captive insurance industry has been the fastest growing in Europe in the 1990s. Already at least four groups of British solicitors have set up Guernsey captives to insure themselves. This business could increase immensely in Continental Europe if the US habit of litigation takes root. One problem though is that, because of the EU rules on insurance, captive companies on the continent can only handle international business (such as maritime and transport risks) and reinsurance.

The captive insurance market is not limited to professional indemnity. In 1994 four British building societies all set up captive insurance companies in

Guernsey to handle their mortgage guarantee business. There is also growing interest in travel-agent bonding.

Traditionally, Guernsey's captive business has come from the UK. Indeed, 28 of the 35 companies that set up in 1995 were UK based. The island also gets a significant amount of business from Scandinavia. Interestingly, a US/Russian reinsurer has set up a captive in Jersey as did an Italian short-tail reinsurer for excess of loss.

The strength and scope of the financial services industry in Guernsey has helped to draw in other industries. The needs of the financial services industry have created a heavy demand for ancillary services such as accountants, lawyers and technologists. The buoyancy of the financial services industry on the island has created a healthy demand for upmarket property. Indeed, the Guernsey property market is one of the strongest in the English-speaking world: there are tight building restrictions and only a limited amount of land available. This has led to even modest properties fetching well into six figures: Swoffers, one of the island's leading estate agents and property management companies, produces a quarterly market review which illustrates the properties and prices available on the island.

The core of the island's financial services industry remains its banks. Among the international banks with substantial Guernsey operations, is Coutts & Co, the global private banking arm of the NatWest group. Coutts focuses on providing trust and managed company services from Guernsey. Managed companies are essentially holding companies which control an individual's assets: they make the management, and especially the taxation, of these assets more efficient.

Guernsey has 72 commercial banks and has recently pioneered the concept of administered banking facilities. These are banks in which international banks subcontract the back-office operations of their Guernsey businesses to banks already based in the island. This allows the newer banks to concentrate on front-office services and to control their costs.

Guernsey also has its indigenous financial institutions. One such institution is the Bachmann Trust, which although having only 85 staff, all in Guernsey, is as international in its outlook as any of the big banks operating from the island. The company was founded by Peter Bachmann and is once again controlled by him. It started off in, and is still involved with, the business of managing the corporate ownership of large yachts but has also moved into trust and company management (especially involving property in Portugal). It also now has Bachmann Asset Management which manages global investments funds. The heart of the company now is the asset management side, which offers traditional private banking services. The investment philosophy of the company is to preserve the real value of capital: the firm prefers to deal with people who have assets of more than £250,000.

Offshore centres have traditionally tried to undercut each other in taxation and regulation. This trend has now reversed and adequate regulation, especially, has become an important qualification for an offshore centre. Guernsey has always enjoyed what practitioners in all its financial businesses call firm but accessible regulation. The authorities are proud of the fact they refused to give the Bank for Credit & Commerce International a licence to operate from Guernsey. The island also has tight rules to prevent money laundering. This should reassure Britons eyeing the dangers that a change of government might pose to their wealth.

Will Ollard

Offshore Banking with Coutts

One objective Coutts' clients look for in their relationship with us is peace of mind. This is where international private banking and relationship management, delivered by Coutts through our offices in Jersey, Guernsey and the Isle of Man, is a great source of comfort.

Coutts has offered private banking services in the UK for over 300 years. Coutts has numbered amongst its clients some of the wealthiest and most influential men and women of their time.

Today, our clients include entrepreneurs, professionals, captains of industry, civil servants and sports and media personalities. Coutts understands the financial needs of such people and the care and professionalism they expect from their bankers. Our objective is to ensure that their expectations are consistently met.

To meet our clients' ever growing needs, Coutts provides a global perspective and, through its international representation, a fully confidential offshore administration service is offered together with additional international estate and tax planning benefits.

A particular feature of Coutts' service is to work very closely with a client's own professional advisers to design a structure precisely suited to a client's needs and circumstances.

Coutts believes that the essence of private banking lies in the combination of trust, professionalism and personal service. Our aim is to establish close and long-term relationships.

As a client, you will be assigned an experienced and highly skilled client relationship manager who will become your first point of contact. The client relationship manager will take time to understand your present and future needs and be responsible for ensuring that all matters are carried out efficiently, effectively and to your complete satisfaction.

Offshore services comprise, banking including deposit accounts in all major currencies, credit facilities, foreign exchange, currency management and a selection of payment services. More structured arrangements include trusts, offshore company management and international investment management.

Matching dedication to service with an equal commitment to banking innovation has made Coutts today one of the world's leading private banks.

Please see advertisement opposite for important regulatory information.

LIECHTENSTEIN—AN OFFSHORE CENTRE WITH A VARIETY OF SOLUTIONS

For anyone owning substantial assets or active in international business, it can make sense to use the advantages of an offshore centre to secure assets for the future or to have profits accumulate where taxation is low. Thanks to its political and economic stability, its well-developed banking and trustee sector and its advantageous legal and tax environment, the Principality of Liechtenstein offers international investors ideal conditions.

Security and stability

The Principality of Liechtenstein meets all the criteria which should be checked by any investor for whom security is essential. With an area of 160 square km and some 30,000 inhabitants, the country has been a soveriegn state since 1806. Its foreign policy position is secured by its membership of the UN, the Council of Europe, the Organisation for European Security and Co-operation (OESC), the European Economic Area (EEA) and the World Trade Organisation. According to the Constitution of 1921, the system of government in Liechtenstein is a constitutional hereditary monarchy operating on a democratic and parliamentary basis. The Prince, as the Head of State, and the people, as the holders of the democratic right, have a duty to work together and it is this which establishes Liechtenstein's political stability. The State regularly reports fiscal surpluses and there is no national debt. The economy of the country is dynamic and varied, providing employment for 20,000 people. There is a peaceful social climate; there have been no strikes for over 100 years and the unemployment rate is less than 1 per cent. About 50 per cent of the working population are employed in the industrial sector, which is highly specialised and markets its products throughout the world.

The well-developed banking and trust sector, with its modern technical infrastructure, profits from this stability. The legal basis for its success results from the tax law, which has special privileges for domiciliary and holding companies, and the Liechtenstein Persons and Companies Act which dates back to 1926. The aim of the legislation was not only to take account of the needs of the domestic economy but also to attract foreign investors by offering liberal provisions and a variety of forms of enterprise.

Reference should also be made to the Bank Act—amended in 1992—which although based on EU directives, contains very clear provisions on banking secrecy which are comparable to those of Switzerland or Luxembourg, yet formulated in even stricter terms. The said Act applies not only to banks but also to finance companies and imposes on their staff (and to representatives of the authorities) the obligation of secrecy. Such secrecy may only be lifted in the case of criminal proceedings.

Membership of two economic areas

In 1923, Liechtenstein concluded a Customs Treaty with Switzerland and since that date has formed a common economic area with her. A year later, the Swiss franc was introduced in Liechtenstein as the national currency. The stability of the currency and the proximity of Switzerland has helped promote Liechtenstein as an investment centre.

Since May 1st 1995, Liechtenstein has been a member of the EEA which, in addition to the 15 EU states, also includes Norway and Iceland. Although Switzerland belongs neither to the EEA nor the EU, it has maintained its close links with Liechtenstein. Thus, Liechtenstein is a member of two economic areas and profits both from the advantages of the Swiss economic area and from the privileges of the Single European Market.

Since the EEA Agreement excludes taxation—quite in contrast to the legal system within the European Union—Liechtenstein has been able to retain its advantageous conditions for offshore business; no tax harmonisation is planned and there is no provision for official or mutual legal assistance in tax matters. The strict banking secrecy is not affected either and the tax privileges for holding and domiciliary companies remain in place.

Tailor-made solutions for clients

Of course, this favourable environment must be supplemented by competent counselling on the possible ways of utilising offshore structures. Codex Treuhand Aktiengesellschaft, an independent fiduciary company in Liechtenstein, has specialised in such a service for some years. Its partners hold international qualifications, have acquired experience over many years and maintain worldwide links with legal and tax experts. To their largely English-speaking clients, they are able to offer international solutions to the problems of structuring company groups, managing assets or tax planning.

Codex Treuhand Aktiengesellschaft's services include both the analysis of the client's specific problem and the development of appropriate structures, taking account of all the legal possibilities both in Liechtenstein and abroad. It can also handle the formation and administrative support of companies and will accept mandates for company, trust and foundation boards. Although its service package embraces all forms of company structure in Liechtenstein, Codex Treuhand Aktiengesellschaft has specialised in trusts above all. This legal form is highly suitable for succession and tax planning. It enables assets to be withdrawn from the property of the trust and to have them managed and employed via the trust for the client's own needs or those of his family and descendants. Codex Treuhand Aktiengesellschaft has acquired a great deal of expertise in this field and is able to offer its clients the guarantee of a long and successful collaboration, based on mutual trust.

Dr Thomas Wilhelm

Partner, Codex Treuhand Aktiengesellschaft
Austrasse 15, PO Box 1150
FL-9490 Vaduz
Principality of Liechtenstein
tel: 00 41 75 237 67 00
fax: 00 41 75 237 67 01

THE ADVANTAGES OF OFFSHORE BANKING

The prospect of higher rates of tax and fewer loopholes is prompting Britain's rich and successful to look at ways of reducing their tax liabilities. One way of minimising or of avoiding tax altogether is to set up an offshore trust or company. Taxable assets are transferred to the trust and thus out of the reach of the taxman. Trusts have a long history of being adapted to suit particular needs. The essence of a trust is separating the ownership of an asset from the benefits conferred by ownership. The first trusts demonstrated this. They were set up so that Medieval monks could both run vast estates and yet abide by their vow of poverty: the property was owned by a trust whose beneficiaries were the Abbeys where the monks lived and worked.

Offshore companies have a less illustrious pedigree: their growth has accelerated as governments have tried to raise more revenues from taxes on the rich and successful. There are two easy ways for an individual or a company to lower his (or its) tax bills: the first is to move to a tax haven and therefore swap Britain's comparatively high rates of taxation for the zero income tax of the Bahamas or Bermuda. The second is to move the ownership of the assets that produce the taxable revenues offshore.

A recent survey found that European private banks expected their trust and offshore company business to be their fastest growing area over the next five years. Essentially the trust and offshore company business is a facet of the asset management business: trust and offshore companies are often the most effective ways to organise the management of an individual or a company's assets.

Moving the ownership of assets is comparatively simple, but convincing the taxman that ownership of them has changed can be much more complicated. This is where disclosure requirements can be so important. If the taxman cannot provide evidence of his suspicions he cannot bring a case before the courts. One centre which has almost no disclosure requirements is Liechtenstein.

The Principality of Liechtenstein is famous for two things in the business world. The first is that it is Europe's (if not the world's) biggest manufacturer of false teeth. The second and more widely broadcast claim to fame is the deep secrecy it offers investors. The deepest secrecy is reserved for the various sorts of trusts and companies which can be set up in the Principality. It is all but impossible for the curious to find out who are the beneficiaries of a Liechtenstein-registered trust, foundation, establishment or company. What makes Liechtenstein doubly unusual is that it is one of the few civil code jurisdictions (i.e. a jurisdiction that applies Roman rather than Common Law principles) to recognise trusts.

Indeed, even finding out the numbers, let alone the identity, of companies registered in Liechtenstein is difficult. The current official estimate is that there are at least 70,000 entities such as companies, trusts and foundations registered there. Even the number of companies on the company register, however, remains confidential and many of the foundations registered in Liechtenstein are not registered in the public register.

Robert Maxwell, the disgraced financier who stole from the pension funds of his publicly quoted companies to keep his private companies going, eventually abused the secrecy Liechtenstein offered. He had several foundations and establishments based there. He set up the first in the early 1950s and was still using Liechtenstein foundations and trusts at the time of his death in 1991. Foundations and trusts undertake not to pursue trade or commercial activities. If a foundation does want to carry out commercial activities these activities have to be not-for-profit.

In Maxwell's case, his foundation seemed to have large stakes in his publishing and other interests. Under Liechtenstein law, foundations neither have to name their beneficiaries nor, since they do not trade, publish a balance sheet. Indeed, many foundations meet only the minimum requirement of lodging their articles with the Register of Commerce in Vaduz, the Principality's capital. The beneficiaries of a foundation (a Stiftung) are usually charities or the heirs of the foundation's founder. Essentially, a foundation is created to provide support for the beneficiaries or to manage the assets of pension and welfare plans and individuals.

As a foundation's articles are open to public inspection, most do not detail who (or what) are to be the beneficiaries of it. These matters are usually recorded on a separate document which is not available for public inspection. The beneficiaries of a foundation, however, have the right to insist that it takes steps to protect their interests. Furthermore, the beneficiaries' creditors can have no claim on the assets held in a foundation that provides an income to the beneficiaries.

Maxwell also used Liechtenstein establishments (Anstalts). These are even more discreet than foundations, though they have some drawbacks: the chief one being that the founder is the only person who can decide to liquidate the establishment. The rights of a founder to transfer his interest in the establishment are usually contained in a bearer document: unlike registered documents where there has to be a record of transfer of ownership, the holder of a bearer document owns the title to assets referred to in the document. As most establishments are not considered to be commercial operations (invariably they are holding companies for assets) the establishment does not have to submit to an audit or keep records.

These privileges are useful to scrupulous businessmen and investors who want to deter their rivals or the taxman from finding out too much about the organisation of their affairs. These businessmen and investors use the facilities offered by Liechtenstein, which lies along an Alpine valley between Switzerland and Austria, for more honourable reasons. These are chiefly concerned with simplifying the management of their assets.

In sum, a Liechtenstein foundation or establishment is one of the easiest ways for an individual to protect his assets from potential creditors while retaining personal control over his assets. The lack of interest regulators in the Principality have in getting information on the assets controlled by entities registered there means that it is usually impossible for taxmen and others to unravel an ownership web in which the strands pass through a Liechtenstein establishment or foundation.

Setting up a company, trust or foundation in Liechtenstein is not cheap. The minimum capital for a company is 50,000 Swiss francs (£23,000). For an establishment, a trust or a foundation the minimum capital required is 30,000 Swiss francs. In addition it costs about 3,000 Swiss francs in administration charges and fees to set up the company, trust or foundation.

Once the entity is up and running, though, the annnual costs are small. For a company, the annual capital tax is 0.1% of the company's net assets. Foundations face a capital tax of 0.075% if they have net assets of less than 2m Swiss francs and 0.05% if they have more than 10m Swiss francs in net assets. The minimum tax in both cases is 1,000 Swiss francs.

Besides the low running costs and secrecy the Principality also offers investors an attractive tax regime. Liechtenstein does not levy taxes on income, turnover or profit. The only tax that the Principality does levy is a 4% coupon tax on distributions or dividends paid by a company whose capital is divided into shares. This tax is not levied on distributions to the beneficiaries of a Liechtenstein trust, so the beneficiaries are not subject to taxes on the income distributed by the trust or foundation.

Even banking secrecy is tighter in Liechtenstein than it is in Switzerland, whose currency and legal system the Principality uses. Unlike Switzerland, where banks have to know the beneficial owners of all their accounts, in Liechtenstein banks do not need to know about beneficial owners if the business has been referred to them by a registered local lawyer-trustee. This difference is crucial for those people who want to keep their business affairs shrouded in secrecy.

The attractions of the secrecy Liechtenstein offers have enabled it to pull money from Switzerland, where banks face ever-tighter regulatory controls in order to reduce the amount of money being laundered through the country. In recent years, the Liechtenstein banks have seen their asset management businesses boom. The onus will now be on the banks to retain this money by improving the performance of the funds they manage. The country's biggest bank, the Bank in Liechtenstein, which is 99% controlled by the ruling family through the Prince of Liechtenstein Foundation, has built up its fund management business (buying GT Management in Britain in 1989).

Other financial centres, which make it hard for the nosy to get information lie further west. Luxembourg is a popular centre to set up an offshore company to do business in Europe. So too are the Channel Islands and the Isle of Man. Ireland also offers some advantages, especially if the company creates jobs. Gibraltar too has its adherents. Bermuda, the Bahamas, the Turks and Caicos Islands and the Cayman Islands as well as the British Virgin Islands, Belize and Panama are all popular locations for the registration of offshore companies and trusts. In the Pacific, the Cook Islands and Vanuatu have proved to be useful locations: the Cook Islands have long been used by Australian businessmen to run the international parts of their businesses. Labuan, Malaysia's offshore centre, is also gaining adherents and weight.

Bermuda offers several advantages over both its local and international competitors. The first is that it has three international but Bermuda-based banks which have a long experience in setting up and running offshore trusts and companies. The second is that Bermuda has a reputation to maintain: it prides itself on only doing business with top quality clients worldwide and is extremely careful to check on the quality of the client before accepting any business.

Bermuda recently reformed its trust law. This allowed for the setting up of a Special Purpose Trust. This is a trust which has no beneficiaries, only a purpose. The SPT can be combined with a Private Trustee Company. The combination can enable families to act as the trustee for trusts they have set up. Special Purpose Trusts have also been used to own and lease aircraft.

The quality and range of the financial business done in Bermuda means that the island can claim with some justification to have the best legal and accounting services of any offshore centre with the exception of Hong Kong. Bermuda is one of the main re-insurance centres in the world and a growing centre for mutual funds: hedge funds, the aggressive fund managers who take massive punts on the direction of and relationship between different financial markets have also been major users of the facilities offered by the island.

All this means that the financial institutions on the island now have the infrastructure to handle investments in less obvious markets. The stellar performance of the emerging markets of Asia, Eastern Europe and Latin America in recent years has prompted investors to put chunks of their portfolios in these markets. Few offshore centres, however, have the financial plumbing in place (such as custodian banks in the emerging markets which can get and deliver share certificates, collect dividends from companies, and keep track of the value of the portfolio). Bermuda is an exception.

Mauritius has also developed as an important centre for company formation. Its target market is people and companies interested in doing business with India, especially fund management companies. The Indian market is developing fast: India is making it much easier for foreign companies to invest and do business in the

subcontinent. The lure for the foreign companies is that India has a middle class that is 200 million strong.

Mauritius has developed as the main offshore financial centre for fund management companies wanting to invest in India. The island has developed the infrastructure so that all the central administration of an investment fund can be managed from Mauritius. The income of offshore companies in Mauritius is taxed at 0%, but the companies may choose to be taxed at any rate between 0% and 35% in order to take advantage of double taxation treaties. These treaties ensure that international investors are not taxed more than once on the same income: if they pay tax in Mauritius they will not have to pay again when the money is sent on to Britain. The island has double taxation treaties with most of Europe and India.

There is no capital gains tax in Mauritius. This has proved particularly advantageous for investors in India. India taxes capital gains made by overseas investors at rates of between 20% and 55%. The lower rate applies if investors have held their investments for more than two years.

One clear distinction between reputable financial centres such as Liechtenstein, Bermuda and Mauritius and some of the other offshore financial centres is the care the authorities in the three centres take over the names of the companies which they register. All three jurisdictions make it clear that offshore companies cannot use words like 'National' or 'Government' in their names. This is to prevent companies with such names being used by the unscrupulous to try and con money from the gullible. These three centres want to preserve their reputations as places where bona fide investors can manage their affairs more efficiently. Regulators do not want the centres to be used as bases for hard selling, get-rich-quick schemes.

Will Ollard

MAURITIUS: AN INTERNATIONAL FINANCIAL SERVICES CENTRE

The economy of Mauritius had traditionally been based upon the growing and milling of sugar cane. However, as the population grew following the eradication of malaria in the 1950s, it became necessary to diversify the economy. Tourism started to be developed in the late 1950s and the natural beauty of the island and the high level of service has put Mauritius firmly as a world class destination with over 450,000 visitors in 1996.

From the early 1970s legislation was introduced creating the Mauritius Exports Processing Zone. Today over 80,000 are employed in light manufacturing, principally of textiles, with Mauritius being the third largest exporter of woollen knitted goods in the world.

The latest diversification of the economy took place in 1992 with the passing of The Mauritius Offshore Business Activities Act 'MOBAA' which created the regulatory body for an international financial services centre. During the past four years the sector has grown rapidly with 4,500 companies incorporated.

The success of Mauritius as an international financial services centre is due to a number of reasons amongst which are:

- The high quality of service offered by bilingual Mauritian professionals, lawyers and accountants trained in Europe and America.
- An expanding network of double taxation treaties making Mauritius attractive to tax planners.
- A low rate of taxation, no capital gains tax and no inheritance tax.
- Active support by the Government.
- State of the art communications.
- An ideal location which allows Mauritius to communicate with the Far East, Europe and America during working hours of the same day.
- Free repatriation of dividends—exchange control was removed in 1992.
- A stable political climate with a democracy based on the Westminster model.
- A tradition of respect for law with the highest court of appeal being The Privy Council.
- Modern legislation which has created the Limited Life Company, the Investment Company which has the characteristics of an open ended structure and Offshore Trusts.
- A regulator Authority which has upheld the reputation of Mauritius as a professional centre.

International Management (Mauritius) Ltd, 'IMM', was licensed in 1992 by MOBAA to operate as a management company in 'offshore' Mauritius. It is a wholly owned subsidiary of Rogers, a group established in 1876, which has grown into the largest investment and trading house in Mauritius.

IMM is staffed by a majority of professionals who have qualified in Europe.

We offer the following services:

- Legal and tax advice.
- Structuring of corporate entities and trusts.
- Fund administration including NAV calculations.
- Accounting, domiciliation, corporate and secretarial services.
- Provision of professional directors, nominee shareholders and trustees.
- Opening of bank accounts.
- Ship and aircraft registration.

We are one of the few independent management companies in Mauritius not affiliated to an international network and as such we live or die by the quality of our service.

What of the future?

Legislation has also been introduced to create a freeport which will act as a bridge between the Far East, Asia and Africa. Construction of the necessary infrastructure has already started.

Mauritius is known primarily as the route into India with over US$4 billion already invested. Diversification is therefore required and the treaties which are thought to offer the best potential are those with China, Italy, Luxembourg and South Africa. However, treaties have been ratified with six European, five Asian and Far East countries and four African countries with six others waiting ratification or signature.

This makes Mauritius an ideal base for regional funds.

At the same time, Mauritius has learned a great deal in the four years that the centre has been operational. We have learned that there is strong competition and that there is no room for complacency. It is therefore proposed that new legislation be introduced to cover offshore unit trusts, UCITS, an anti money laundering act and most importantly of all, a Financial Services Authority, which will be the ultimate regulatory authority in Mauritius and which we hope will result in Mauritius being granted 'designated status' by authorities in the United Kingdom allowing the wider marketing of funds.

The next development will be the introduction of asset management companies which will considerably broaden the scope of products offered by Mauritius and further increase its attractiveness.

There is plenty of work to be done but Mauritius is determined to make a success of the centre as it has done with tourism and the exports processing zone and IMM intends to play a full part in that success.

Sydney Bathfield

Managing Director, International Management (Mauritius) Ltd

THE BERMUDA NAMES
(or FROM COFFEE SHOPS TO GOLF COURSES)

ACE, Zurich, American, XL, Centre Re, Partner Re, Mid Ocean Re, Johnson & Higgins, International Risk Management, SCUUL, Renaissance Re, are just some of the Bermuda names that attract to Bermuda the formation of an increasing number of insurance and reinsurance companies and captive insurance companies.

When Bermudians in 1995 voted a resounding 'No' to independence for Bermuda, little did the average Bermudian realise the importance and excitement in the forging of new business relationships between Bermuda and London. Key players in this dynamic industry are becoming worldwide organisations with offshoots in other key markets around the world; so, Bermuda based Trident Partnership LP acquired Lloyd's managing agency Venton Underwriting Agencies Ltd; ACE purchased a majority stake in Lloyd's managing agency, Methuen. Terra Nova (Bermuda) Holdings has completed the purchase of Octavian Syndicate Management Ltd, which manages five Lloyd's active syndicates. In this way Terra Nova was provided the opportunity to participate in the world's oldest insurance market in London. In the words of Terra Nova's key executive: 'In softening price markets you're better off growing by purchasing rather than trying to expand your existing business... for the same reason we came to Bermuda, we have chosen to go into the Lloyd's market, underlying our basis philosophy of physically being where the business is offered. ...Indeed, you are seeing other Bermuda-based companies moving to London, and you are seeing London companies coming to Bermuda. ...Bermuda has grown rapidly both in capital and talent, and it will continue to grow.' Terra Nova, through its Bermuda and UK subsidiaries, is an international speciality underwriter of property, marine, and liability insurance and reinsurance. From Octavian's perspective: 'Ready access to secure capital and the growing strength of Terra Nova's balance sheet will enhance our syndicates' ability to provide reliable capacity to meet the needs of brokers and clients.' Chief Executive of Methuen, Leslie Goodman, believes 'the London market is starting to see Bermuda as increasingly a centre for expertise in this industry; there is a substantial and growing pool of talent (in Bermuda), and a lot of surplus capital.' A London presence makes logical sense for Bermuda companies for several reasons, not the least of which are the ability to acquire expertise and the ability to have a larger physical presence than may be possible on this tiny dependent territory.

A recent spate of acquisitions and strategic alliances by Bermuda insurers (for example, Ace Limited's recent acquisition of property catastrophe reinsurer, Tempest Re) strengthens further the image Bermuda has gained as the only business centre of its kind providing ready access to a commercial insurance and reinsurance market. By 1993 Bermuda's relatively young reinsurance industry had already captured more than 9% of the world reinsurance capacity when measured by net premiums written; its market share has grown significantly since that time. In virtually every sector of the Bermuda insurance industry Bermuda is now seen as a global leader. It is the undisputed captive insurance capital of the world; it has the largest concentration of financial reinsurers; its property catastrophe reinsurers have grabbed more than a 20% global market share and the excess liability carriers are now industry giants. A. M. Best, America's oldest insurance rating agency which began rating Bermuda's property catastrophe reinsurers in April 1996, described Bermuda reinsurers as 'well capitalised and well staffed' companies that have 'dramatically improved the level of sophistication and expertise of the catastrophe reinsurance industry'. Bermuda now boasts the largest concentration of capital dedicated to the finite reinsurance sector.

Reinsurance markets have traditionally exchanged high-level information among high-value professionals practising high-level analysis. The only real asset is knowledge. Throughout history, the industry has organised itself to enhance the ability to receive, assess, and transfer information to help people make informed decisions. The first underwriters gathered in coffee shops in the heart of the City of London, for more than 100 years. In 1996, the most sophisticated and innovative brokers in the industry exchange ideas on Bermuda's lush golf courses.

ACE chairman reportedly said the Bermuda market has the most forward-thinking capital in the world. It has the highest concentration of financial and intellectual capital, and it can be utilised to look for opportunities where other markets are caught up in the past.

Bermuda's names have become recognised for coming up with the right product at the right time. Perhaps too late to cover Texaco's recent losses arising out of the class action brought by its black employees following the appalling demonstration of race discrimination, XL Insurance and Marsh & McLennan Global Broking (Bermuda) Ltd have developed the first single, stand-alone insurance programme offering employers up to $100 million in protection against the rising cost of claims resulting from employee lawsuits. In a business environment increasingly marked by restructuring, downsizing and greater awareness of job discrimination and sexual harassment, the Bermuda-based companies expect the surge of interest already demonstrated in this new product to remain extremely high. ACE Insurance and Zurich American are acting as reinsurers of XL.

Convergence and consolidation are the new buzz words in the reinsurance industry. Buyers of reinsurance are becoming more sophisticated and are requiring partners who can offer superior financial strength, creative solutions and global expertise. Reinsurance companies are undergoing a convergence and consolidation resulting in a rationalisation of risk capital allocation which is providing a more diversified range of financial products over a broader spectrum of risk. The role of the reinsurance intermediary is being redefined as investment banks and reinsurance companies develop capital market/insurance solutions which provide lower cost and more efficient tax and accounting treatments of securitisations, swaps, liquidity facilities and credit enhancements. What's next? 'The only thing we know for sure is that the revolution has begun and that in a mature and consolidating financial services industry, business will be won by proactive players with the lowest cost of capital and the most creative and efficient solutions that meet the client's objectives', says David Kaplon, Senior Vice President at Exel. Bermuda is certainly at the forefront of this revolution. And, if the new Bermuda Catastrophe Futures Exchange (CATEX) is any indication, Bermuda will be leading the way well into the next millennium.

The Insurance Amendment Act of 1995 provides a regulatory system which at once protects the policy holders whilst nurturing the growth of this very vital industry with its increasingly significant Bermuda-London connection.

KEREN V P LOMAS, LLB (Hons), FCIArb

Barrister & Attorney
Member of the Executive Committee of the North American Branch of the Chartered Institute of Arbitrators

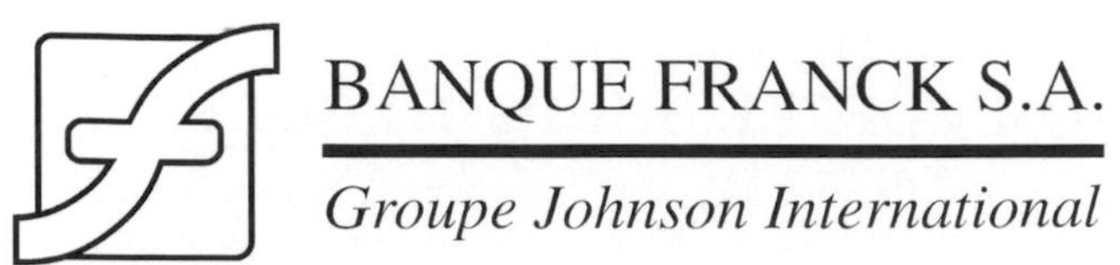

SAFETY

The Bank's location is its advantage. Switzerland is neutral, politically stable and secure. Nestled in the old town of Geneva, the heart of Swiss Private Banking, Banque Franck S.A. reflects the solidity of the fortified city around it. Unlike other Swiss Private Banks, which rely upon the undisclosed goodwill and unlimited liability of their partners, Banque Franck S.A. receives the support of a large and resourceful group with published balance sheets. The Bank boasts an uncommonly high "safety ratio" of capital to assets of over 30%. High risk management priorities forbid it from engaging in commercial lending, merchant banking, or proprietary futures and derivatives trading. Its core business is investment management, with accessory asset protection and trust services provided by a Group subsidiary in Grand Canyon.

DISCRETION

Switzerland affords the strictest confidentiality. The privacy and protection of Bank customers is a legal imperative, required not only of Swiss financial institutions, but also of their staff. Transgressions are punishable by law, with sanctions levied upon individual offenders.

As Banque Franck S.A. is governed by Swiss Law, its first assurance of discretion towards its customers is by virtue of its legal status. Its size, low profile, location and private group backing offer an additional level of discretion, not easily maintained by more visible financial groups.

A FAMILY OF FUNDS

Global Bond ECU
Designed to achieve Central European Bond diversification with an exposure to standard market credit risk in order to outperform index returns.

Capital Protection Fund
Designed to enhance returns from cash without placing normal initial capital risk.

European Equities Portfolio
Designed to achieve European equity diversification with an exposure to standard market risk, in order to obtain index returns.

North American Equity Portfolio
Designed to achieve superior returns from US equities with an exposure to less than standard market risk in order to outperform the S&P 500 Index.

Asian Equities Portfolio
Designed to achieve equity exposure to Japan, Hong Kong and Singapore with standard market risk, in order to obtain index returns.

Special Opportunities Portfolio
Designed to achieve superior returns from international equities and equity linked instruments, in order to outperform the Morgan Stanley Capital International World Equity Index, expressed in Swiss Francs.

Multi Manager Fund
Used to enhance investment performance with acceptable risk, and to reduce standard portfolio risk by diversification into securities non-correlated to standard markets.

TRADITION

S.C. Johnson's family traditions serve as the foundation for Banque Franck's Private Banking. The Group's devotion to integrity, innovation and personalised service, has arisen from the synergy of two corporate cultures with a single purpose: to please their customers.

Founded in 1886 in Bacine, Wisconsin, S.C. Johnson & Son, Inc. is known internationally for its Johnson Wax. Still a family business, the company employs more than 15,000 people in 45 countries on every continent. Corporate growth has been generated by constant innovation and an omnipresent desire to develop increasing consumer loyalty.

The Johnson family believes in people: the people it serves and the people it works with. At Banque Franck, they also believe in people. Their size and attitude allow them to exemplify Geneva's Private Banking tradition of Trust, Absolute Discretion, and Customised Service.

Their business is Asset Management, but their focus is upon enduring and stable relationships. Getting to know their customers is not just a matter of due diligence, it is their driving force and the leitmotif of the S.C. Johnson family business.

PRIVATE BANKING IN SWITZERLAND

The prospect of a victory by the Labour Party in the British General Election is frightening a lot of people who have prospered under eighteen years of Conservative government. Under Conservative governments successful entrepreneurs and even professional people were encouraged to keep their money in the country as income tax rates were lowered and tax incentives to invest in new businesses established. Now Britain's rich (and not so rich) fear that an incoming Labour government will raise tax rates and make private investment less rewarding.

Already there have been reports that up to £2 billion of private wealth could leave Britain in the run up to the election if Labour maintains its strong lead in the opinion polls. A good chunk of this money should find its way to Switzerland, where wealth preservation is probably the country's biggest business.

Figures on how much money is managed from Switzerland are hard to come by. The most reputable estimates speak of US$1.1 trillion (£700 billion) of foreign money being managed from Swiss banks. To put this into context, the most plausible estimate for the total assets owned by the world's high net worth individuals at the end of 1994 was between US$11 trillion and US$12 trillion (quoted in *Private Banking*, Euromoney Books, 1996). Of this US$11 trillion to US$12 trillion, around US$3 trillion is held offshore (i.e., outside the owners' domestic markets). If these figures are right, Swiss banks manage around a third of the assets owned by the world's rich.

Swiss banks used to feel that they could not add much value for private banking customers whose net assets were less than US$1 million (£700,000). This minimum is beginning to become more flexible. Banks now distinguish more sharply between assets and income. Few private banks will accept accounts from people whose annual income is much below £100,000 though some Swiss banks will, if they believe that the client has the potential to earn a substantially higher income in the future. Swiss banks are especially keen to build a long term relationship with their customers; offering them the cachet of a Swiss bank account when, objectively, the client has not earned it is one way of getting a relationship off to a good start.

Swiss banks provide their clients with a product that is a combination of three basic elements: personal service, investment management and security. Security has traditionally been the Swiss banks' greatest advantage over other locations. Switzerland has been a byword for political stability in Europe. It has been ruled by the same coalition of political parties for the past forty years. Its independence has become almost proverbial: for years Switzerland only had observer status at the IMF and the World Bank because the government believed that full membership would compromise the country's independence. Although Switzerland lies, geographically at least, closer to the heart of Europe it has stayed outside the European Union. Switzerland rejected EU membership in a referendum in 1992.

This streak of independence and self-reliance has helped the economy develop, which has reinforced the country's political stability and made the currency one of the strongest in the world. These two qualities, political and economic stability, were bolstered by laws deliberately designed to promote the country as a financial centre. The best known of these laws is banking secrecy, which makes it a serious offence for a bank to reveal any information about a customer unless that customer has committed what the Swiss penal code regards as a criminal offence: tax evasion is not a crime in Switzerland. A second, equally important law is the law guaranteeing Swiss neutrality which specifically stops the authorities from blocking or freezing bank accounts for political reasons.

Swiss banks' investment management skills have improved dramatically since the last Labour government held office in Britain. Then Swiss banks relied on the strength of the Swiss franc and the inflation proofing qualities of gold to provide their British customers with satisfactory returns. Now Swiss investment management is much more sophisticated. The influx of business from the new rich Asia and Eastern Europe has meant that Swiss banks have had to improve the investment management side of their business. Asian private banking customers, in particular, want their private banks to provide them with access to wholesale international financial markets (such as foreign exchange) and to trade these markets actively and successfully on their behalf. The Asian new rich also tend to want their bankers to extend them margin credits to allow them to take gambles in the futures and options markets on the direction of financial and commodity markets. These sorts of services may be a bit too racy for the traditional Geneva private banks which plan on building up relationships with clients that will last for generations rather than making them a quick buck but some of the other banks based in Switzerland are only too keen to provide what the customer wants.

For all but the most exclusive private banking partnerships, investment performance is now becoming the decisive element in the private banking service. The emphasis on investment performance is nothing new for American banks which have seen private banking as a way of selling products to their customers. They are used to demonstrating that their products are better than their rivals'. US banks, especially investment banks, have set up in Switzerland offering all the service advantages of a Swiss private bank plus the performance of a US fund manager.

For Swiss banks, the new emphasis on performance has had some strange consequences. The banks have started to raise their profiles. Several Swiss private banks, which have traditionally relied on personal recommendation for new business, have started to demonstrate their investment management expertise by creating international investment funds which are publicly quoted and sold throughout Europe. Often these funds are targeted at investing in either emerging markets (such as South East Asia) or at specific industries or market segments of mature markets. Their performance is designed to demonstrate their managers' expertise, though sometimes the management of these funds is contracted out to independent money managers. Some private bankers argue that they sit across one of the most important information flows in the world's financial markets: what the elites of countries are doing with their money. This information, they say, can give an edge to their performance.

These international funds, usually listed in Luxembourg, developed from the Swiss banks' success in devising in-house mutual funds for their traditional private banking customers. Often these funds would contain parts of a portfolio and thus enable smaller customers to diversify further than the size of their portfolio would warrant. Often the in-house funds would be targeted at particular industries (bio-technology or high technology) or regions (Latin America or Eastern Europe). From a more or less standing start in 1988, the size of the pooled investment funds managed through Swiss banks reached SwFr 200 billion (US$160 billion) in 1995.

Some Swiss banks have been meeting the performance challenge by subcontracting out some of their investment management activities to independent money managers (or *gerants de fortune*). The Geneva private banks have been especially active in this field. By some reckonings the independent money managers now account for between 10% and 15% of the foreign money managed from Switzerland. Altogether, foreign investment managers are now reckoned to manage around 30% of the international private banking assets managed from Switzerland. The foreign managers range from the *gerants de fortune* to the private banking subsidiaries of the US investment banks. They also include the specialist Swiss private banking operations of the big international commercial banks such as NatWest from Britain, the Hongkong & Shanghai Banking Corporation and the big US financial services companies. By some measures, foreign private banking operations in Switzerland have been growing much faster than the indigenous private banks.

Service is the third quality that a Swiss bank provides. The Swiss banks' pivotal position and long experience in international private banking means that they often have a greater range of expertise: they will know where the best location for a trust with largely British assets and beneficiaries in retirement in Spain would be. They will also know how best to tax plan for assets that straddle several jurisdictions. Just as importantly, the Swiss private banker's long experience of customers and their needs should mean that he is able to anticipate what a customer might want before the customer really understands what he needs.

The essence of private banking is building up a relationship between the bank and the customer. The private banker sees himself as the customer's professional man of affairs, able to advise on the financial structure of his customer's business, the management of his assets and liabilities.

For the traditional private banking customer service, repeated surveys have shown, is the key element in the private banking package. To provide a superior service, the private banker has to know his customer and, just as importantly, his own bank. As customers' needs become more complicated and more demanding some private banks are considering acting more as an adviser than as an actual manager. In this way they can ensure that their customers get the products that are best for them, while the bank itself focuses on delivering a superior service.

Switzerland is still the world's premier private banking centre, but it is the premier centre because it has allowed international financial institutions to exploit the advantages it offers: stability, service, communications and attractive holiday resorts. It would have been relatively easy for the authorities to have restricted privileges such as banking secrecy to Swiss banks. The more open approach is now providing more jobs and the competition and experience provided by the foreigners is helping to enhance the investment performance of the indigenous banks, creating a more vibrant and successful centre.

Although Zurich is now Switzerland's main financial centre, it ranks behind Geneva as a private banking centre. Private banks, originally Protestant, began life as merchant banks first in Geneva and then Basle, Zurich and Berne. Fiscally responsible local governments in Switzerland and booming domestic economies quickly turned these banks into international banks, with a bias to financing ruling families. By the start of the century, the private banks had developed a business that was sharply different from that of their foreign competitors such as Barings or Rothschild. The Swiss private banks were entirely focused on preserving the wealth of their customers while the other banks were equally interested in backing companies and entrepreneurs and forming business relationships with them.

This difference was recognised under the Swiss Banking Act of 1934. The authorities drew a distinction between private banks and other banks. The private banks did not have to publish balance sheets, nor (at that time) meet the capital adequacy or liquidity requirements imposed on commercial banks. In return, private banks could not solicit deposits.

Geneva's private banks still form the largest group accounting for seven of the seventeen private banks. Zurich is home to five private banks and Basle four. Two of the traditional private banking partnerships decided in the mid 1970s that the partnership structure was no longer adequate for the needs of their customers and they became quoted companies. Of the twenty-two private banking partnerships at the beginning of the

Legal & Fiscal Services

We assure you legal advice of the highest standard through knowledge and experience and always with full discretion

- *Enforcement of client's privacy*
- *Set up of international tax planning structures*
- *Drafting of trusts, contracts and other documents*
- *Representation of clients in worldwide operations*

Trust Services

We organize your asset protection structures by offering complete trust services

- *Individually designed asset protection plans*
- *Set up and administration of trusts worldwide*
- *Trustees and protectors provided by our own subsidiaries*

Investment Management Services

We manage your personal or company assets

- *Research and definition of the client's specific targets*
- *Management of assets with top ranked custodian banks*
- *All type of investments through specialized team of professionals*
- *Direct computer links with the custodian banks and international markets*

Corporation Services

We assist you in the incorporation and administration of companies in Switzerland and abroad

- *Constitution of all kinds of companies, foundations in all jurisdictions*
- *Full administration by putting at your disposal directors and board members*
- *Correspondence, invoicing, payments and collection of funds*
- *Loan and documentary credit negotiations on an international level*
- *Bookkeeping and auditing according to all local legislations*

I.C.C. Building, P.O. Box 1918, 20 route de Pré-Bois, CH - 1215 Geneva 15 Airport
Tel. : +41.22.798.51.55 Fax : +41.22.798.54.39 E-Mail : 101643.2031@compuserve.com

1980s, six have either merged or allowed themselves to be bought out by larger, non-partnership competitors.

Geneva is still generally reckoned to be the world's biggest private banking centre. Although all the remaining private banks have become international, they still have their traditional biases. Geneva's private banks traditionally have a pre-eminent position in the French market, where tax avoidance and evasion have been a way of life for over 200 years. Zurich's banks have looked to Germany as their main private banking market. Basle's private banks look down the Rhine valley (and thus to both France and Germany) for business. Lugano developed as a banking centre to serve the Italian market, though it does not have any indigenous private banks.

Swiss private banks tend to benefit when governments try to force the pace of economic growth. They benefited hugely from the expansionist US policies in the early 1960s: the Cuba crisis, the assassination of President Kennedy and the steadily escalating involvement in Vietnam all contributed to a shift of money out of the US and into Switzerland. In Britain, a succession of governments tried to live beyond the country's means by borrowing large amounts before cheating foreign creditors by devaluing and domestic creditors by inflating. It was from this period that George Brown's famous jibe about the 'gnomes of Zurich' (more correctly Geneva) undermining sterling dates. Brown, economics minister, made his comment at the end of 1964, as the new Labour government faced the first of a series of sterling crises that culminated in the humiliating devaluation of 1967 which destroyed sterling's reputation as a reserve currency.

Although the East Asia region has now overtaken Europe in terms of the amount of private wealth it has created, Europeans still account for the biggest slice of the offshore market: around 35% of the money managed by international private bankers comes from Europe. The next biggest slice is US money (20%) followed by 15% each from East Asia, Latin America and the Middle East. For Swiss banks, the business is even more clearly European. Around 60% of the foreign private client assets they manage are owned by Europeans. Britain's share of this pool of money is probably around 20%. It has probably been dwindling for the past 17 years as Britons took advantage of the more attractive domestic economic environment to invest domestically.

Now that they perceive that this wealth might be threatened they are once again looking to stash away some funds in Switzerland. The rich are always cautious about politics: 'the wise man makes his arrangements before he hopes' is their motto.

So far, Labour has not said anything about restoring exchange controls. Ending exchange controls was probably the boldest move by the first Thatcher government which took office in 1979. Mrs Thatcher's first Chancellor of the Exchequer, Geoffrey Howe recalled lying awake at night just before he ended exchange controls wondering whether he was doing the right thing. It was: investment flowed into the country rather than out of it. Restoring exchange controls, which would make it an offence for a person to either move money out of the country or keep money out of the country, could lead to a flood of money into safe havens, such as Swiss banks, as Britons prepared themselves for the worst.

Will Ollard

MAKING ADEQUATE PROVISION FOR RETIREMENT
by JOE PALMER, CBE

Sufficient private provision for retirement is becoming increasingly important: demographic trends are forcing all European governments, including our own, to consider very carefully the extent to which the state will be able to support people in their later years. A combination of improving mortality rates and the post war baby boom means that in the United Kingdom, for example, somewhere between the year 2015 and 2030 less than one third of the population will have to support the other two thirds. Consequently, the level of taxation required to maintain the current standard of benefits may be unacceptable and it does seem likely that future governments of whatever political persuasion will need to target benefits to a greater extent than they do now and provide a lower level of support to the population as a whole. The scale of the challenge faced in the future can perhaps be best illustrated by reference to some statistics: the Rowntree report stated in 1993 that, with sustainable economic growth, the rise in public expenditure to fully meet demographic changes might amount to an extra 5% of GDP, which was equated by some commentators at the time to an immediate increase of 20p in the basic rate of tax, or, put another way, extending VAT from 17.5% to 30%. Furthermore, the need to make private provision can already be seen by the reduction in the value of the UK state pension in comparison with average earnings which has occurred since the government in 1980 decided to peg pension increases to prices rather than earnings. Since then the state pensions' comparative value to average earnings has fallen from 20% in 1977 to around 15% at the current time and by the year 2030, based on projections, it will represent only 8%.

So it is difficult to see circumstances where the state pension will do anything more than help meet people's basic needs and will certainly not allow them to enjoy the retirement they might wish. The questions which then arise are whether individuals are currently making sufficient private provision and, if they are not, what can be done to encourage them to do so? With regard to the former the evidence is clear that many people are not making sufficient provision for their retirement: independent surveys indicate that the majority of people believe that a retirement income of two-thirds of pay, including pensions available from the state, is necessary. In order to provide such a pension someone aged 35 would need to save at least 8.5% of all their earnings and increase contributions as their earnings rise. However, the average annual premium for all personal pension plans sold since 1988 has only been around 2% of earnings. This means that many investors will fail to have their expectations met when they reach retirement.

How then can the need to make greater provision be addressed and in particular what is PIA's role in this? In answering this question I am not going to debate political initiatives that might be undertaken in this area but will restrict myself to what can be done within current arrangements. The key issues, in my opinion, that need to be tackled, and which are intertwined, are consumer confidence and consumer awareness.

There is no doubt that the financial services industry is presently not held in high esteem by the general public. The mis-selling of personal pension plans to investors in the late 1980s and early 1990s has heightened mistrust and left many investors wary of purchasing investment products. Consequently, PIA has sought in three main ways to rebuild an environment where consumers can have confidence in the products they're buying. They are:

- PIA's Admissions Process;
- Training and Competence;
- Disclosure.

PIA's Admissions Process

One very important consideration for investors is that firms are adequately checked before being allowed to conduct investment business with the general public. Consequently, PIA took the decision at the time it was being established in early 1994 that admission into membership of PIA would not be automatic for any firm. All applications for authorisation by PIA are thoroughly vetted to ensure that a firm meets PIA's high standards for membership. To date just under 4,000 firms have been admitted into membership and there is only a small residual number of applications of less than 100 outstanding. The admissions process has been a time consuming exercise but, PIA believes an extremely valuable one: by rejecting or deterring firms from applying because they can not meet PIA's high standards, the admissions process provides consumers with comfort as to the quality of professional service they will receive in the marketplace which is beneficial to both investors and those many ethical firms offering financial services.

Training and Competence

With regard to training and competence it cannot be ignored that one of the main reasons for investors being sold inappropriate products in the past was the fact that some advisers had been inadequately trained to be able to advise their clients. As a result, PIA requires all firms, as a condition of membership, to maintain high quality training programmes, together with arrangements for securing and monitoring the competence of those individuals who provide investment advice. However, PIA feels that additional measures are necessary to provide investors with adequate comfort as to the quality of advice they are likely to receive; consequently, on 1st October 1995, PIA introduced for all the firms it authorises a new training and competence regime which requires all those involved in the financial planning process to:

- take a relevant benchmark examination to demonstrate an adequate level of knowledge. For most advisers this will be the Financial Planning Certificate produced by the Chartered Insurance Institute;
- undertake an appropriate programme of Continuing Professional Development so that they remain up to date with industry developments;
- be the subject of ongoing supervision, with the exception of practitioner principals, from, in most cases, an in-house supervisor.

Every element of PIA's new scheme is to be implemented by 1st July 1997 and it is PIA's belief that these arrangements will contribute to a more professional environment which should significantly enhance investors' confidence.

Disclosure

PIA's view though, is that adequate training and competence requirements are insufficient in themselves to fully revive consumer confidence: investors also need to be furnished with all relevant information necessary to make informed investment decisions and this information should be provided in an intelligible form. Accordingly, PIA has from 1st January 1995 implemented a new product and commission disclosure regime for life and pensions products which provides investors with key information on products in clear terms. It enables the investor to understand the aims of the product on offer; the financial commitment involved; any risk factors associated with the product; the effect which charges have on the investment; and the amount of the commission in cash terms which will be paid to the adviser if he is successful in recommending a product. A similar regime for non-life products, such as unit trusts, is also being introduced. PIA has issued rules and guidance to firms on this subject and the new regime for unit trusts and other collective investments will come into force on 1st May 1997. This again will enable investors to better understand the product they are being offered and to make broad comparisons between different types of products. It is therefore PIA's view that investors are now placed in a far better position than in the past to understand the nature of the product which is being offered to them and this transparency, combined with high standards of advice, should contribute to a marked improvement over time in investor confidence.

PIA's Evolution Project

However, PIA still believes more can be done to encourage investors to save for retirement. Despite the improvements that disclosure has delivered, many investors still find the buying of an investment a daunting prospect: the selling process can be protracted and the amount of paperwork that the investor is supplied with can, in some cases, be off-putting to the extent that they do not buy products that they may need. PIA, having established a framework of greater openness and professionalism, now wants to work towards a streamlining of the sales process and the further demystification of the buying of investments. It is currently addressing these issues through something called the Evolution Project. As the name suggests PIA is looking at ways in which the current regulatory regime can be modified, not revolutionised, so that investors can more easily purchase products without any diminution in investor protection. We have already published a discussion paper to this end which focuses on the way in which investments are sold in practice to the public. The paper contains guidance and proposals which should contribute to a more effective method of delivering products to investors. In particular it addresses the issue of 'information overload' in two main ways: firstly, by considering the amount of information that is necessary for a firm to obtain from an investor before recommending a product; and secondly, by looking at how much information needs to be provided by a firm to the client. With regard to the former, PIA has issued detailed guidance—with immediate effect—as to what information it expects as a minimum an adviser to obtain on a client. This should help firms from misinterpreting PIA's 'know your customer' requirements and avoid the 'belt and braces' approach which can create an unduly long sales process disconcerting some investors from buying products that they need.

In relation to information from firms to investors PIA is looking at ways of making the disclosure regime work even better. We are considering how the paper mountain might be reduced by allowing all essential information about a product to be contained within a single brochure for the investor; and whether added flexibility can be built into the disclosure requirements so that investors can be presented with information in a more timely and efficient manner.

The Evolution Project is not yet complete but PIA believes that through this initiative and the work that has already been done in relation to training and competence and disclosure we are making significant strides toward an environment where investors can have substantially greater confidence in the quality of

information on products that they receive. PIA believes that if investors are presented with information on products that they can more readily understand and advice that they can have confidence in, then the likelihood of greater provision being made for retirement is considerably increased. Greater clarity should also stimulate competition in the marketplace and enable investors a greater choice of investments. I consider that the regulatory regime is playing a key role in helping investors make informed choices for their benefit in the next century.

Joe Palmer, CBE

Chairman, Personal Investment Authority

HONG KONG: 1997 AND BEYOND
by SIR WILLIAM PURVES

China's resumption of sovereignty over Hong Kong takes place at midnight on 30th June 1997. The world is waiting to see how Hong Kong's position as one of its leading financial and trading centres will be affected by the new political arrangements.

This is entirely understandable. Handing back a territory to a motherland with a different social, political and economic evolution is, as far as I know, unique in constitutional history. It was inevitable that the process would be perceived as difficult. However, the number of sceptical views I hear about the future of the territory, particularly from those outside Hong Kong, surprises me.

Headline-grabbing articles say that Hong Kong's demise is close at hand: Betrayal; the Beginning of The End; Flight and Exodus. Some fund managers, on the other hand, predict that the Hang Sang Stock Market Index will hit 30,000 by the end of 1998. On 31st October 1996, it stood at 12,478.

I have no wish to underrate the difficulties that Hong Kong may face, but despite what some may say the vast majority of the territory's business leaders, myself included, believe wholeheartedly in the success of Hong Kong after the change of sovereignty.

Not only because China has an enormous interest in Hong Kong's success. Not only because Hong Kong has an enormous interest in China's success. Not only because Japan, the United States, the United Kingdom, Canada, the European Union and a host of Asian countries have an interest in the success of both. But because Hong Kong people are going to be running Hong Kong, just as they do now, and because their hunger for success and their ability to a challenge have created one of the most competitive economies in the world.

No one has made money betting against Hong Kong, although the predictions of doom that greeted the Joint Declaration in 1984 may have tempted a few to try. How wrong they would have been. In the last 12 years, Hong Kong has seen a 140 per cent growth in export of services, a 200 per cent growth in investment, a 250 per cent growth in per capita GDP, a 600 per cent growth in fiscal reserves, and a 1,000 per cent growth in stock market capitalisation.

Hong Kong in transition

Hong Kong has really been preparing for two transitions. The territory has been putting in place the arrangements that will realise the promises made to Hong Kong by Britain and China in the Joint Declaration of 1984. At the same time, Hong Kong has been laying the foundations for its continued success as one of the world's most important centres for high-quality financial services. Preparations for both these transitions are at an advanced stage.

Hong Kong is the world's third-largest international banking centre, its fifth-largest foreign exchange market and its eighth-largest trading economy. It is among the highest GDP per capita economies in the world, the leading provider of foreign direct investment in ASEAN and APEC countries, and by far the major source of capital for China.

The territory has an increasingly international investor base and stock market and more than 1,000 authorised funds and unit trusts domiciled in more than a dozen jurisdictions. The Hong Kong Investment Funds Association estimates that Hong Kong fund managers manage in excess of US$50 billion of portfolio investments from Hong Kong into the domestic market, the region and the world.

As an international financial centre, Hong Kong has developed a market infrastructure and a regulatory environment that inspires confidence in investors worldwide. It is characterised by user-friendly, regulatory policies that are adaptable, predictable, transparent and written to the highest international standards. The market flourishes under an effective common law system and a philosophy of non-interventionism and equal success for all. Adam Smith would have made Hong Kong the number one example of free trade in *The Wealth of Nations*, as did Milton Friedman some 200 hundred years later when he said: 'If you want to see how capitalism works, go to Hong Kong.'

It is a financial system whose development mirrors the tremendous infrastructure developments that are taking place in Hong Kong as a whole: the expansion of its port; its roads and railways; and the building of its new airport at Chek Lap Kok, currently the largest civil engineering project in the world.

And Hong Kong's financial infrastructure has come even further in the last decade. With its highly-efficient dealing, clearing and settlement and risk management systems, the territory possesses the latest in banking technology and financial management expertise. Indeed, the Hong Kong Monetary Authority is establishing ever-more advanced facilities for the banking sector and for monetary co-operation between Hong Kong and China.

No other market in the world can access information about China and react to it as quickly as Hong Kong can. No pool of retail investors has the same knowledge, and hence appreciation, of Chinese enterprises, the Chinese economy and China risk.

Hong Kong: 1997 and beyond

So what then of 1997? I believe it is against all logic and experience to suggest that the structures of Hong Kong will change significantly when the territory resumes its former position as part of China. Indeed, in all the encounters of Hong Kong's business leaders with Chinese government leaders, there has never been any suggestion that Hong Kong's international nature, free society and free flow of information, capital and people will alter in

1997. Indeed, every Chinese official has stressed—and many international economists agree—that the transition will mean further enhancement of Hong Kong's position, both as a developed market within the emerging and strongly performing economy of China, and as an international financial centre.

The Joint Declaration and the Basic Law guarantee the continuity of Hong Kong's way of life, its financial and monetary autonomy, its law and regulations, and its free flow of capital. In particular, Article 109 of the Basic Law guarantees Hong Kong's status as an international financial centre after 1997, which, as far as I know, is the only such constitutional guarantee in the world.

All of Hong Kong's financial and regulatory institutions, including the Hong Kong Monetary Authority and the Securities and Futures Commission, will remain in place in 1998, in the year 2000 and well into the future. A change in political sovereignty does not mean interference in Hong Kong's financial autonomy.

On the contrary, although Hong Kong has built excellent relationships with the People's Bank of China, the Hong Kong Monetary Authority will continue to regulate Hong Kong's banking system after 1997. And Hong Kong will continue to be a signatory to a wide range of international treaties and a separate member of economic organisations such as APEC.

This autonomy in monetary and financial affairs is a vital guarantor of Hong Kong's future as an international financial centre. As Chen Yuan, the Deputy Governor of the People's Bank of China, has declared, 'after 1st July 1997, Hong Kong will be part of one country, two systems, two currencies and two monetary systems'.

On the basis of such declarations, several credit rating agencies have decided that Hong Kong should receive a separate rating from that of China after China's resumption of sovereignty.

Confidence depends on perception. Although there has been widespread international scepticism about Hong Kong—scepticism fuelled to some extent by the media—there are those who take a more optimistic view, and many are to be found in Hong Kong.

Among them is the HSBC Group. We continue to demonstrate our commitment to Hong Kong by making substantial investments in our branch network, in our personal banking, in our unit trust and credit card products, in our treasury and capital markets businesses, and in major projects like our new dealing room in Hong Kong.

We are also investing strongly in China, where HongkongBank now has 14 offices and where we have developed additional expertise in China-related business through HSBC Investment Bank Asia, HSBC Capital, HSBC Markets, HSBC Corporate Finance, Wayfoong Property, and so on.

Like Hong Kong, we have a tremendous depth of experience in understanding China risk, and in structuring and negotiating China-related projects. And this is of vital importance to a country which, according to World Bank estimates, will need half of Asia's projected spending of US$1.5 trillion on infrastructure in the next 15 years.

The Future

The opportunities for Hong Kong and for those who invest in and through Hong Kong are virtually limitless in the decades ahead. The territory will have a vital role to play within China, both as its international financial centre and as its capital formation base. The major proportion of China's H share trading already takes place in Hong Kong. The development of a debt market and of financial futures for China will be the next stage. The eventual convertibility of the renminbi will present even greater possibilities for the Hong Kong markets. But the opportunity for Hong Kong does not reside exclusively in China.

Hong Kong is one of the leaders in the development of Asian debt markets, which will soon gain a further boost from the projected establishment of a Mandatory Provident Fund System in Hong Kong somewhat similar to that in Singapore. The expected injection of some US$5.5. billion a year into the local fund management industry will mean a rapid accumulation of reserves and fierce competition to handle those reserves. Hong Kong Government reserves at 30th June 1996 stood at US$60 billion.

And let us not forget Hong Kong as the leading catalyst and arranger of deals and loans throughout the region—the number one source of foreign investment for APEC and ASEAN countries.

Of course, there are other regional financial centres in Asia, but such competition is healthy. There is every reason to believe that further integration of markets will work to the overall benefit of Hong Kong, and of Asia as a whole.

As for confidence, let me assure you that there is no net flight of capital or people from Hong Kong. Quite the opposite. There is net inflow and Hong Kong dollar money supply, measured by deposits, grew faster in 1995 than GDP growth. The scale of investment and construction in Hong Kong challenges any other area in the world.

Survey after survey shows that regional headquarters are staying in Hong Kong and local and overseas companies are expanding their investments enormously in Hong Kong and China.

Hong Kong is China's best asset, and China is Hong Kong's biggest asset. I have a feeling that in the years to come we may look back on China's resumption of sovereignty and say that this was the moment when Hong Kong realised its position as a truly world-class financial centre.

Sir William Purves

Chairman, HSBC Holdings plc

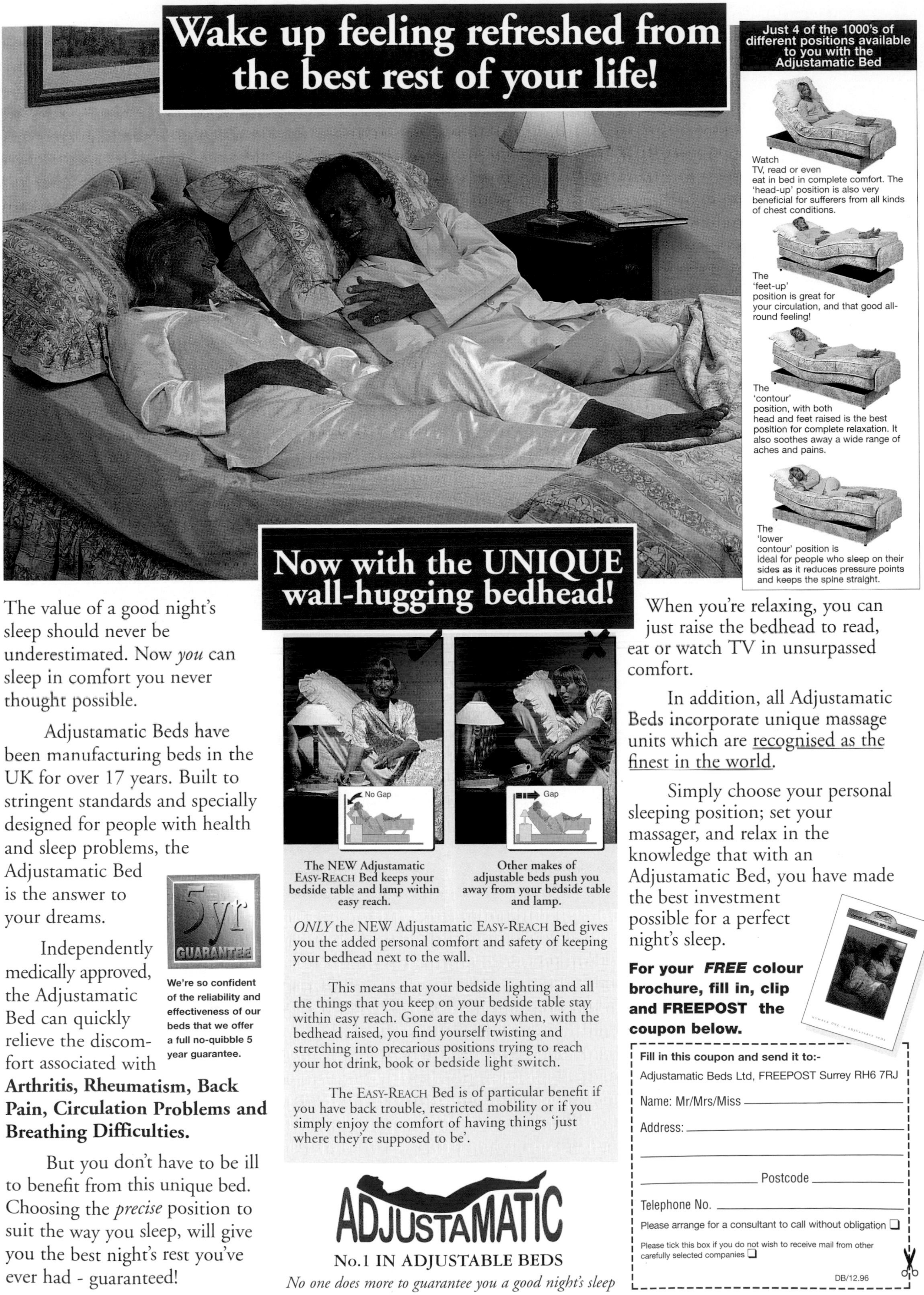

THE ROYAL FAMILY

For full details see *Debrett's Peerage and Baronetage*

HER MAJESTY THE QUEEN, Elizabeth Alexandra Mary; style in the United Kingdom: Elizabeth II, by the Grace of God, of the United Kingdom of Great Britain and Northern Ireland and of Her Other Realms and Territories Queen, Head of the Commonwealth, Defender of the Faith; crowned at Westminster Abbey 2 June 1953; celebrated her Silver Jubilee 1977; er da of His Majesty King George VI (d 6 Feb 1952) and of Lady Elizabeth Angela Marguerite Bowes-Lyon (HM Queen Elizabeth The Queen Mother, *qv*), da of 14 Earl of Strathmore and Kinghorne; *b* 21 April 1926; *m* 20 Nov 1947, HRH The Prince Philip, Duke of Edinburgh, KG, KT, OM, GBE, PC, *qv*; 3 s, 1 da (*see below*); *Heir* s, HRH The Prince of Wales, *qv*; Lord High Adm of the United Kingdom; Col-in-Chief: Life Guards, Blues and Royals (Royal Horse Gds and 1 Dragoons), Royal Scots Dragoon Gds (Carabiniers and Greys), 16/5 Queen's Royal Lancers, Royal Tank Regt, RE, Grenadier Gds, Coldstream Gds, Scots Gds, Irish Gds, Welsh Gds, Royal Welch Fus, Queen's Lancashire Regt, Argyll and Sutherland Highlanders (Princess Louise's), Royal Green Jackets, RAOC, Queen's Own Mercian Yeo, Duke of Lancaster's Own Yeo, Corps of Royal Mil Police, Corps of Royal Canadian Engrs, Canadian Forces Mil Engrs Branch, King's Own Calgary Regt, Royal 22e Regt, Govr-Gen's Foot Gds, Canadian Grenadier Gds, Le Regiment de la Chaudière, Royal New Brunswick Regt, 48 Highlanders of Canada, Argyll and Sutherland Highlanders of Canada (Princess Louise's), Royal Canadian Ordnance Corps, Malawi Rifles; Capt-Gen: RA, HAC, Combined Cadet Force, Royal Canadian Artillery, Royal Malta Artillery; Air Cdre-in-Chief: RAuxAF, RAF Regt, Royal Observer Corps, Royal Canadian Air Force Aux; Hon Air Cdre RAF Marham, Cmdt-in-Chief RAF Coll Cranwell, Hon Cmmr Royal Canadian Mounted Police, Master of the Merchant Navy and Fishing Fleets, Head Civil Defence Corps and Nat Hosp Service Reserve; Sovereign of all British Orders of Knighthood, Order of Merit, Royal Order of Victoria and Albert, Order of Crown of India, Order of Companions of Honour, Distinguished Service Order, Imperial Service Order, Order of Canada; Sovereign Head of Order of Hosp of St John of Jerusalem, Order of Australia, The Queen's Service Order of NZ; patron Royal Coll of Physicians Edinburgh and Victoria League for Cwlth Friendship; FRS 1947; *Residences:* Buckingham Palace, London SW1A 1AA; Windsor Castle, Berkshire; Balmoral Castle, Aberdeenshire; Sandringham House, Norfolk

EDINBURGH, HRH The Duke of; HRH The Prince Philip; KG (1947), KT (1952), OM (1968), GBE (mil 1953), PC (1951, Canada 1957); *cr* Baron Greenwich, of Greenwich, Co London, Earl of Merioneth, and Duke of Edinburgh (UK 1947); naturalized a British subject and adopted surname of Mountbatten 1947; granted title, style and attribute of Royal Highness 1947; granted style and titular dignity of a Prince of UK 1957; only s of HRH Prince Andrew of Greece and Denmark, GCVO (d 1944), and HRH Princess (Victoria) Alice Elizabeth Julia Marie, RRC (d 1969), da of 1 Marquess of Milford Haven; *b* 10 June 1921; *Educ* Cheam Sch, Salem, Baden, Gordonstoun, RNC Dartmouth; *m* 20 Nov 1947, HM Queen Elizabeth II, *qv*; 3 s, 1 da; 1939-45 War, Mediterranean Fleet (Home Waters) and with British Pacific Fleet in SE Asia and Pacific (despatches, Greek War Cross; 1939-45, Atlantic, Africa, Burma (with Pacific rosette), and Italy Stars; War Medal 1939-45 (with oak leaf) and French Croix de Guerre (with Palm); a personal ADC to HM King George VI 1948; Field Marshal; Capt-Gen RM; Col-in-Chief: Queen's Royal Irish Hussars, Duke of Edinburgh's Royal Regt (Berks and Wilts), Queen's Own Highlanders (Seaforth and Camerons), REME, Intelligence Corps, Army Cadet Force, Royal Canadian Regt, Seaforth Highlanders of Canada, Cameron Highlanders of Ottawa, Queen's Own Cameron Highlanders of Canada, Royal Canadian Army Cadets; Col Grenadier Gds; Hon Col: Edinburgh and Heriot-Watt Univs OTC, Trinidad and Tobago Regt; *Navy:* Adm of the Fleet; Sea Cadet Corps, Royal Canadian Sea Cadets; Marshal of the RAF; Air Cdre-in-Chief: ATC, Royal Canadian Air Cadets; Hon Air Cdre RAF Kinloss; Cmdt-in-Ch and Extra Master Merchant Navy; memb cncl Duchy of Cornwall 1952-, Ranger of Windsor Great Park 1952-, Lord High Steward of Plymouth 1960-; chllr of univs: Salford 1967-71, Wales 1948-, Edinburgh 1952-, Cambridge 1977-; master bench Inner Temple 1954-, elder bro Trinity House 1952 (master 1969-; hon bro Hull 1953-); pres: Amateur Athletic Bd 1952-, Cwlth Games Fedn 1955-, Br Sportsman's Club 1958-, Central Cncl of Physical Recreation 1951-, City & Guilds of London Int 1951-, ESU of Cwlth 1952-, Guards' Polo Club 1955-, RAS of Cwlth 1958-, Royal Household Cricket Club 1953-, Royal Merchant Navy Sch 1952-, RSA 1952-, World Wild Life Fund British Nat Appeal 1961-; third pres Inst Wild Life Fund 1981-; Royal pres Soc of Friends of St George's and Descendants of KGs 1948-; patron and trustee Duke of Edinburgh's Award, chm Duke of Edinburgh's Ctee for Queen's Awards to Industry 1965-; patron UK branch Soc d'Entr'aide of Legion of Honour; Adm and Cdre Royal Yacht Sqdn 1961-68; Adm of Yacht Clubs: House of Lords, Royal Motor, Royal Southern, Bar, Dart, Royal Gibraltar, RNSA, Royal Yacht Club of Victoria (Australia) and of Great Navy State of Nebraska USA; King George VI Coronation Medal 1937, Queen Elizabeth II Coronation Medal 1953; Grand Master and First or Princ Kt of Order of British Empire 1953; FRS 1951

HM QUEEN ELIZABETH THE QUEEN MOTHER; Lady Elizabeth Angela Marguerite, *née* Bowes-Lyon; Lady of the Order of the Garter (1936), Lady of the Order of the Thistle (1937), CI (1931), GCVO (1937), GBE (1927); da of 14 Earl of Strathmore and Kinghorne, KG, KT, GCVO, TD, JP, DL (d 1944) and Nina Cecilia, GCVO (d 1938), da of Rev Charles William Frederick Cavendish-Bentinck (gs of 3 Duke of Portland, who was twice Prime Minister during King George III's reign); *b* 4 Aug 1900: *m* 26 April 1923, HM King George VI (d 6 Feb 1952); 2 da (HM The Queen and HRH The Princess Margaret, *qqv*); Col-in-Chief: 1 Queen's Dragoon Gds, The Queen's Own Hussars, 9/12 Royal Lancers (Prince of Wales's), King's Regt, Royal Anglian Regt, Light Inf, The Black Watch (Royal Highland Regt), RAMC, The Black Watch (Royal Highland Regt) of Canada, The Toronto Scottish Regt, Canadian Forces Medical Services; Hon Col: Royal Yeo, London Scottish (Gordon Highlanders) (TA), Univ of London Contingent OTC; Cmdt-in-Chief: WRNS, WRAC, RAF Central Flying Sch, WRAF, Nursing Corps and Divs St John Ambulance Bde; hon member of Lloyd's; pres British Red Cross Soc 1937-52, since when dep pres; pres Royal Highland and Agric Soc 1963-64; Gold Albert Medal of RSA 1952; Grand Master Royal Victorian Order 1937-; pres Univ Coll of Rhodesia and Nyasaland 1957-70, chllr London Univ 1955-81, first chllr Dundee Univ 1967; bencher Middle Temple 1944 (tres 1949); hon fellow London Univ, and of King's Coll London; FRS; appointed Lord Warden and Admiral of the Cinque Ports and Constable of Dover Castle (the first woman to hold this office) 1978; received Royal Victorian Chain 1937; Grand Cross of Legion of Honour; GCStJ; *Residences:* Clarence House, London SW1A 1BA; Royal Lodge, Windsor Great Park, Berks; Birkhall, Ballater, Aberdeenshire; Castle of Mey, Caithness-shire.

WALES, HRH The Prince of; HRH The Prince Charles Philip Arthur George; KG (1958, invested and installed 1968), KT (1977), GCB and Great Master of Order of the Bath (1975), AK, QSO, PC 1977; cr Prince of Wales and Earl of Chester 1958 (invested 1969); also Duke of Cornwall and Rothesay, Earl of Carrick and Baron of Renfrew, Lord of the Isles and Great Steward of Scotland; eldest s and h of HM Queen Elizabeth II, *qv*; *b* 14 Nov 1948; *Educ* Cheam Sch, Gordonstoun, Geelong GS Australia, Trinity Coll Cambridge (MA, Polo Half-Blue), Univ Coll of Wales, Aberystwyth; Bar of Gray's Inn 1974 (hon bencher 1975); *m* 29 July 1981 (*m* dis 1996), Lady Diana Spencer (*see* Wales, Diana, Princess of); 2s (*see below*); *Heir*, HRH Prince William of Wales, *qv*; Col-in-Chief: The Royal Regt of Wales (24/41 Foot) 1960-, The Cheshire Regt 1977-, The Gordon Highlanders 1977-, Lord Strathcona's Horse (Royal Canadian) Regt 1977-, The Parachute Regt 1977-, The Royal Regt of Canada 1977-, 2 King Edward VII Own Goorkhas 1977-, The Royal Winnipeg Rifles 1977-; personal ADC to HM 1973-; Col Welsh Guards 1974-; Cdr RN 1976-, Wing Cdr RAF 1976-; Hon Air Cdre RAF Brawdy 1977-; Col-in-Chief Air Reserves Gp of Air Cmd in Canada 1977-, pres: Soc of Friends of St George's and Descendants of KG's 1975-, United World Colls 1978-, The Prince's Trust 1975-; Cdre Royal Thames Yacht Club 1974-, High Steward Royal Borough of Windsor and Maidenhead 1974-; chm: Queen's Silver Jubilee Trust 1978-, The Prince of Wales' Ctee for Wales 1971-; chllr The Univ of Wales 1976-, memb bd Cwlth Devpt Corpn 1979-; patron: The Press Club, Transglobe Expedition, Welsh National Opera, Royal Sch for the Blind, Mary Rose Trust; author of: The Old Man of Lochnagar, A Vision of Britain; Coronation Medal 1953, Queen's Silver Jubilee Medal 1977; *Residence:* Highgrove House, Doughton, Tetbury, Glos GL8 8TG

WALES, Diana, Princess of; Lady Diana Frances, *née* Spencer; 3 da of 8 Earl Spencer, LVO, DL (*d* 1992) and (first wife) Hon Mrs Shand Kydd; *b* 1 July 1961; *Educ* Riddlesworth Hall, West Heath, Switzerland; *m* 29 July 1981 (*m* dis 1996), HRH The Prince of Wales, *qv*; 2 s (*see below*); former kindergarten teacher; *Residence:* Kensington Palace, London W8 4PU

WALES, HRH Prince William of; Prince William Arthur Philip Louis; s and h of HRH The Prince of Wales, *qv*; *b* 21 June 1982; *Educ* Eton

WALES, HRH Prince Henry (Harry) of; Prince Henry Charles Albert David; yr s of HRH The Prince of Wales, *qv*; *b* 15 Sept 1984

YORK, HRH The Duke of; HRH The Prince Andrew Albert Christian Edward; CVO (1979); *cr* Baron Killyleagh, Earl of Inverness, and Duke of York (UK 1986); 2 s of HM The Queen; *b* 19 Feb 1960; *Educ* Gordonstoun, Lakefield Coll Sch Ontario, RNC Dartmouth; Lieut RN, served S Atlantic Campaign 1982 as helicopter pilot HMS *Invincible*;

personal ADC to HM The Queen 1984; *m* 23 July 1986 (*m* dis 1996), Sarah Margaret, da of Maj Ronald Ivor Ferguson, The Life Guards, and his 1 w, Susan Mary, *née* Wright (later Mrs Hector Barrantes); 2 da (*see below*) *Residence;* Buckingham Palace, London SW1A 1AA

YORK, HRH Princess Beatrice of; Princess Beatrice Elizabeth Mary; er da of HRH The Duke of York; *b* 8 Aug 1988

YORK, HRH Princess Eugenie of; Princess Eugenie Victoria Helena; yr da of HRH The Duke of York; *b* 23 March 1990

HRH The Prince Edward Antony Richard Louis; CVO (1989); 3 and yst s of HM The Queen; *b* 10 March 1964; *Educ* Gordonstoun, Jesus Coll Cambridge; former house tutor and jr master Wanganui Collegiate Sch NZ; 2 Lieut RM 1983; *Residence:* Buckingham Palace, London SW1A 1AA

HRH THE PRINCESS ROYAL; HRH The Princess Anne Elizabeth Alice Louise; LG (1994), GCVO (1974); declared Princess Royal 13 June 1987; o da of HM The Queen; *b* 15 Aug 1950; *Educ* Benenden; *m* 1, 14 Nov 1973 (*m* dis 1992), Capt Mark Anthony Peter Phillips, CVO, ADC(P) (*see main text*); 1 s, 1 da (*see below*); *m* 2, 12 Dec 1992, Cdr Timothy James Hamilton Laurence, MVO, RN (*see main text*); Col-in-Chief: 14/20 King's Hussars, Worcs and Sherwood Foresters Regt (29/45 Foot) and 8 Canadian Hussars (Princess Louise's), Royal Corps of Signals, Canadian Forces Communications and Electronics Branch, Grey and Simcoe Foresters Militia; Ch Cmdt WRNS, Hon Air Cdre RAF Lyneham; pres: Save The Children Fund, British Acad of Film and Television Arts, WRNS Benevolent Trust, Windsor Horse Trials, Royal Sch for Daughters of Offrs of RN and RM (Haslemere); patron: Assoc of WRNS, Communications and Electronics Assoc, Riding for the Disabled Assoc, Jersey Wildlife Trust, R Corps of Signals Assoc, Royal Corps of Signals Instn, Breast Cancer Research Trust, Save the Children Action Group, Army and RA Hunter Trials, Gloucester and N Avon Fedn of Young Farmers' Clubs, Horse of the Year Ball, Benenden Ball; vice-patron British Show Jumping Assoc; Cmdt-in-Ch St John Ambulance and Nursing Cadets; chllr London Univ 1981-; *Residence:* Gatcombe Park, Minchinhampton, Stroud, Glos GL6 9AT

PHILLIPS, Peter Mark Andrew; s of HRH The Princess Royal, *qv*; *b* 15 Nov 1977; *Educ* Gordonstoun

PHILLIPS, Zara Anne Elizabeth; da of HRH The Princess Royal, *qv*; *b* 15 May 1981

SNOWDON, HRH The Princess Margaret, Countess of; HRH The Princess Margaret Rose; CI (1947), GCVO (1953), Royal Victorian Chain (1990); yr da of His late Majesty King George VI and Lady Elizabeth Angela Marguerite Bowes-Lyon (HM Queen Elizabeth The Queen Mother, *qv*); *b* 21 Aug 1930; *m* 6 May 1960 (m dis 1978), 1 Earl of Snowdon, GCVO (*see main text*); 1 s, 1 da (*see below*); Col-in-Chief: Royal Highland Fus (Princess Margaret's Own Glasgow and Ayrshire Regt), 15/19 King's Royal Hussars, Princess Louise Fus, Highland Fus of Canada, QARANC; Dep Col-in-Chief Royal Anglian Regt, Hon Air Cdre RAF Coningsby, chllr Univ of Keele; pres: Barnado's Scottish Children's League, Victoria League, Sunshine Homes and Schs for Blind Children (Royal Nat Inst for the Blind), Royal Ballet, NSPCC (and Royal Scottish Soc), Dockland Settlements, Friends of the Elderly and Gentlefolk's Help, Invalid Children's Aid Assoc (also chm cncl), Sadler's Wells Fndn, English Folk Dance and Song Soc, Horder Centres for Arthritics, Girl Guides Assoc, RASE; patron: Princess Margaret Rose Hosp Edinburgh, Royal Coll of Nursing, Nat Cncl of Nurses of UK, London Festival Ballet, Tenovus (Inst of Cancer Research); bencher Lincoln's Inn and tres 1967; Grand Pres of St John Ambulance Assoc and Bde, hon memb and patron of Grand Antiquity Soc of Glasgow; CStJ; *Residence:* Kensington Palace, London W8 4PU

LINLEY, Viscount; David Albert Charles Armstrong-Jones; s of HRH The Princess Margaret and s and h of 1 Earl of Snowdon (*see main text*); *b* 3 Nov 1961; *Educ* Bedales, John Makepeace Sch of Woodcraft, Beaminster, Dorset; *m* 8 Oct 1993, Hon Serena Alleyne Stanhope, only da of Viscount Petersham (*qv*)

CHATTO, Lady Sarah Frances Elizabeth; *née* Armstrong-Jones; da of HRH The Princess Margaret and 1 Earl of Snowdon; *b* 1 May 1964; *Educ* Bedales; *m* 14 July 1994, Daniel Chatto, yr s of late Thomas Chatto; 1 s (Samuel David Benedict *b* 28 July 1996)

GLOUCESTER, HRH 2 Duke of; HRH Prince Richard Alexander Walter George; GCVO (1974); also Earl of Ulster and Baron Culloden (both UK 1928); 2 but only surv s of HRH the late Prince Henry, 1 Duke of Gloucester (d 1974, 3 s of King George V) and HRH Princess Alice, Duchess of Gloucester, *qv*; *b* 26 Aug 1944; *Educ* Eton, Magdalene Coll Cambridge (MA, Dip Arch); *m* 8 July 1972, Birgitte Eva, GCVO (1989), DStJ (Col-in-Ch Royal Army Educational Corps; pres: London Region WRVS, Royal Alexander and Albert Sch, Cambridge House; patron: Asthma Research Cncl, Bobath Centre), da of Asger Preben Wissing Henriksen, lawyer, of Odense, Denmark, and his 1 w, Vivian, da of late Waldemar Oswald Van Deurs, whose name she assumed; 1 s, 2 da (*see below*); *Heir* s, Earl of Ulster, *qv*; *Career* RIBA, FSA, FRSA; Col-in-Chief: The Gloucestershire Regt 1975-, Royal Pioneer Corps 1977-; Hon Col Royal Monmouthshire RE (Militia) 1977-; pres: Inst of Advanced Motorists 1971-, Cancer Research Campaign 1973-, Nat Assoc of Boys' Clubs 1974-, British Consultants Bureau 1978-, E England Agric Soc 1979-; vice-pres British Leprosy Relief Assoc 1971-; patron: ASH 1974-, Victorian Soc 1976-, Bulldog Manpower Services 1976; ranger of Epping Forest 1975-; Grand Prior Order of St John of Jerusalem 1975-; KStJ; *Residence* Kensington Palace, London W8 4PU

ULSTER, Earl of; Alexander Patrick Gregers Richard; s and h of HRH 2 Duke of Gloucester, GCVO, *qv*; *b* 24 Oct 1974

WINDSOR, Lady Davina Elizabeth Alice Benedikte; er da of HRH 2 Duke of Gloucester, GCVO, *qv*; *b* 19 Nov 1977

WINDSOR, Lady Rose Victoria Birgitte Louise; yr da of HRH 2 Duke of Gloucester, GCVO, *qv*; *b* 1 March 1980

GLOUCESTER, HRH Princess Alice, Duchess of; Lady Alice Christabel, *née* Montagu Douglas Scott; GCB (1975), CI (1937), GCVO (1948), GBE (1937); 3 da of 7 Duke of Buccleuch and Queensberry, KT, GCVO JP (d 1935), and Lady Margaret Alice, *née* Bridgeman (d 1954), 2 da of 4 Earl of Bradford; *b* 25 Dec 1901; *Educ* St James's Sch W Malvern, Paris; *m* 6 Nov 1935, HRH The Prince Henry William Frederick Albert, KG, KT, KP, GCB, GCMG, GCVO, 1 Duke of Gloucester (d 10 June 1974, 3 s of King George V); 1 s (*see above*) and 1 s decd (HRH Prince William, who was killed in an aeroplane accident 28 Aug 1972); Air Chief Marshal WRAF; Col-in-Chief: KOSB, Royal Hussars, RCT; Dep Col-in-Chief Royal Anglian Regt; memb cncl British Red Cross Soc; Dep Cmdt-in-C Nursing Corps and Divs of St John Ambulance Bde 1937-; GCStJ; *Residence* Kensington Palace, London W8 4PU

KENT, Field Marshal HRH 2 Duke of; Prince Edward George Nicholas Paul Patrick; KG (1985), GCMG (1967), GCVO (1960); also Earl of St Andrews and Baron Downpatrick (both UK 1934); er s of HRH 1 Duke of Kent, KG, KT, GCMG, GCVO, PC (killed on active service 25 Aug 1942, 4 s of King George V), and HRH Princess Marina, CI, GCVO, GBE (d 27 Aug 1968), yst da of HRH late Prince Nicholas of Greece and Denmark; *b* 9 Oct 1935; *Educ* Eton, Switzerland, RMA Sandhurst; *m* 8 June 1961, Katharine Lucy Mary, GCVO (1977) (Controller-Cmdt WRAC and Hon Maj-Gen; Col-in-Chief Army Catering Corps, Hon Col Yorks Volunteers TAVR, chllr Leeds Univ), only da of late Sir William Arthington Worsley, 4 Bt; 2 s, 1 da (*see below*); Maj-Gen (ret) Royal Scots Dragoon Gds; Col-in-Chief: Royal Regt of Fusiliers, Devonshire and Dorset Regt; Col Scots Gds, personal ADC to HM 1966-, GSO II E Cmd 1966-68, company instr RMA Sandhurst 1968-70, cmd C Sqdn Royal Scots Greys 1970-71; Grand Master United Grand Lodge Freemasons of England and Grand Master Order of St Michael and St George; pres: Wellington Coll, Cwlth War Graves Cmmn. Scout Assoc, Technician Educn Cncl; vice-chm British Overseas Trade Bd 1976-; chllr Surrey Univ 1977-; dir British Insulated Callender's Cables 1981-; FRS 1990; *Residence* York House, St James's Palace, London SW1A 1BQ

ST ANDREWS, Earl of; George Philip Nicholas Windsor; er s, and h of HRH 2 Duke of Kent, KG, GCMG GCVO, *qv*; *b* 26 June 1962; *Educ* Eton, and Downing Coll Camb; *m* 9 Jan 1988, Sylvana Palma, da of Maximilian Karl Tomaselli; 1 s (Edward Edmund Maximilian George, Lord Downpatrick *b* 2 Dec 1988), 2 da (Lady Marina-Charlotte Alexandra Katharine Helen Windsor *b* 30 Sept 1992, Lady Amelia Sophia Theodora Mary Margaret Windsor *b* 24 Aug 1995)

WINDSOR, Lord Nicholas Charles Edward Jonathan; 2 s of HRH 2 Duke of Kent, KG, GCMG, GCVO, *qv*; *b* 25 July 1970

TAYLOR, Lady Helen Marina Lucy; *née* Windsor; da of HRH 2 Duke of Kent, KG, GCMG, GCVO, *qv*; *b* 28 April 1964; *m* 18 July 1992, Timothy Verner Taylor, eldest s of Cdr Michael Verner Taylor, RN, of Stoke St Gregory, Taunton, and Mrs Colin Walkinshaw; 2 s (Columbus George Donald *b* 6 Aug 1994, Cassius Edward *b* 26 Dec 1996)

KENT, HRH Prince Michael of; HRH Prince Michael George Charles Franklin; KCVO (1992); 2 s of HRH 1 Duke of Kent (killed on active service 1942); *b* 4 July 1942; *Educ* Eton, RMA Sandhurst; *m* 30 June 1978, Baroness Marie Christine Agnes Hedwig Ida, da of late Baron Günther Hubertus von Reibnitz, and formerly wife of Thomas Troubridge, yr bro of Sir Peter Troubridge, 6 Bt; 1 s, 1 da (*see below*); Maj Royal Hussars to 1981; foreign attaché liaison sec MOD 1968-70, UN Force Cyprus 1971,

Defence Intelligence Service 1974-76, Army Recruiting Directorate 1976-78, GSO Defence 1974-76, Army Recruiting Directorate 1976-78, GSO Defence Intelligence Staff 1978-81; pres: British Bobsleigh Assoc 1977-, Soc of Genealogists, Inst of Motor Industry 1978-, Royal Patriotic Fund Corpn 1980-, Soldiers', Sailors' and Airmen's Families Assoc 1982-; Cwlth pres Royal Lifesaving Soc; memb: RAC British Motor Sports Cncl, British Olympic Assoc 1977-, HAC; *Residences* Kensington Palace, London W8 4PU; Nether Lypiatt Manor, Stroud, Glos GL6 7LS

WINDSOR, Lord Frederick Michael George David Louis; o s of HRH Prince Michael of Kent, *qv*; *b* 6 April 1979

WINDSOR, Lady Gabriella (Ella) Marina Alexandra Ophelia; o da of HRH Prince Michael of Kent, *qv*; *b* 23 April 1981

HRH Princess Alexandra, the Hon Lady Ogilvy; HRH Princess Alexandra Helen Elizabeth Olga Christabel; GCVO (1960); da of HRH 1 Duke of Kent (killed on active service 1942); *b* 25 Dec 1936; *Educ* Heathfield, Paris: *m* 24 April 1963, Rt Hon Sir Angus James Bruce Ogilvy, KCVO (*see main text*), 2 s of 12 Earl of Airlie, KT, GCVO, MC; 1 s, 1 da (*see below*); Col-in-Chief: 17/21 Lancers, Queen's Own Rifles of Canada, The King's Own Border Regt, The Canadian Scottish Regt (Princess Mary's); Dep Col-in-Chief LI, Dep Hon Col Royal Yeo TAVR, Air Chief Cmdt Princess Mary's RAF Nursing Service; Hon Cmdt-Gen: Royal Hong Kong Police Force, Royal Hong Kong Aux Police Force; pres: Royal Commonwealth Soc for the Blind, Children's Country Holidays Fund, Queen Alexandra's House Assoc, Star and Garter Home for Disabled Sailors, Soldiers and Airmen, Alexandra Rose Day, British Sch at Rome, Royal Humane Soc; vice-pres British Red Cross Soc; patron Queen Alexandra's Royal Naval Nursing Service: chllr: Lancaster Univ 1964-, Univ of Mauritius 1974-, Hon FRCPS, Hon FRCOG, Hon FFA RCS; *Residences* Thatched House Lodge, Richmond Park, Surrey; 22 Friary Court, St James's Palace, London SW1A 1BQ

OGILVY, James Robert Bruce; o s of HRH Princess Alexandra and Hon Sir Angus Ogilvy, KCVO, *qv*; *b* 29 Feb 1964 (*see main text*)

MOWATT, Mrs Paul; Marina Victoria Alexandra; *née* Ogilvy; o da of HRH Princess Alexandra and Hon Sir Angus Ogilvy, KCVO, *qv*; *b* 31 July 1966; *m* 2 Feb 1990, Paul Julian Mowatt, s of David Mowatt; 1 s (Christian Alexander *b* 4 June 1993), 1 da (Zenouska May *b* 26 May 1990)

For other members of the Royal Family, the Earl of Harewood, KBE, the Hon Gerald Lascelles, the Duke of Fife and Captain Alexander Ramsay of Mar, see their entries in the main body of the work

THE ORDER OF SUCCESSION

The first twenty-five persons in line of succession to the throne

HRH The Prince of Wales
HRH Prince William of Wales
HRH Prince Henry of Wales
HRH The Duke of York
HRH Princess Beatrice of York
HRH Princess Eugenie of York
HRH The Prince Edward
HRH The Princess Royal
Peter Phillips
Zara Phillips
HRH The Princess Margaret, Countess of Snowdon
Viscount Linley
Lady Sarah Chatto
Samuel David Benedict Chatto
HRH The Duke of Gloucester
Earl of Ulster
Lady Davina Windsor
Lady Rose Windsor
HRH The Duke of Kent

(NB Earl of St Andrews would be next in line but for his marriage to a Roman Catholic. His rights are, however, transmitted to his children.)

Lord Downpatrick
Lady Marina-Charlotte Windsor
Lady Amelia Windsor
Lord Nicholas Windsor
Lady Helen Taylor
Columbus Taylor

THE ROYAL HOUSEHOLDS

THE QUEEN'S HOUSEHOLD

Lord Chamberlain, The Earl of Airlie, KT, GCVO, PC
Lord Steward, The Viscount Ridley, KG, GCVO, TD
Master of the Horse, The Lord Somerleyton, KCVO
Mistress of the Robes, The Duchess of Grafton, GCVO
Lords in Waiting, Lt Col the Lord Charteris of Amisfield, GCB, GCVO, QSO, OBE (Permanent); The Lord Moore of Wolvercote, GCB, GCVO, CMG, QSO (Permanent); The Lord Camoys; The Viscount Long, CBE; The Lord Lucas of Crudwell; The Earl of Courtown
Baronesses in Waiting, The Baroness Trumpington; The Baroness Miller of Hendon, MBE
Captain, Gentlemen at Arms, The Lord Strathclyde
Captain, Yeomen of the Guard, The Lord Chesham
Treasurer of the Household, Andrew MacKay, MP
Comptroller of the Household, Timothy Wood, MP
Vice-Chamberlain of the Household, Derek Conway, MP
Ladies of the Bedchamber, The Countess of Airlie, DCVO; The Lady Farnham
Extra Lady of the Bedchamber, The Marchioness of Abergavenny, DCVO
Women of the Bedchamber, The Hon Mary Morrison, DCVO; The Lady Susan Hussey, DCVO; Lady Dugdale, DCVO; The Lady Elton
Extra Women of the Bedchamber, The Hon Mrs van der Woude, CVO; Mrs John Woodroffe, CVO; Mrs Michael Wall, DCVO; Lady Abel Smith, DCVO; Mrs Robert de Pass
Equerries, Lt Col Sir Guy Acland, Bt, MVO; Lt Cdr Toby Williamson, RN
Temporary Equerry, Capt Charles Winter
Private Secretary, The Rt Hon Sir Robert Fellowes, GCVO, KCB
Deputy Private Secretary, Robin Janvrin, CB, CVO
Assistant Private Secretary, Mrs Mary Francis
Special Assistant to Private Secretary, Simon Gimson
Chief Clerk, Mrs Graham Coulson, LVO
Press Secretary, Geoffrey Crawford, LVO
Deputy Press Secretary, Miss Penelope Russell-Smith
Assistant Press Secretary, Vacant
Defence Services Secretary, Air Vice-Marshal Peter Harding, CB, CBE, AFC
Keeper of the Privy Purse and Treasurer to The Queen, Michael Peat, CVO
Deputy Keeper and Deputy Treasurer, John Parsons, LVO
Chief Accountant and Paymaster, Ian McGregor
Personnel Officer, Miss Patricia Lloyd
Director of Property Services, John Tiltman
Director of Finance Property Services and Royal Travel, Stephen Cawley
High Almoner, The Rt Rev John Taylor, MA
Secretary, Royal Almonry, Christopher Williams, RVM
Master of the Household, Maj Gen Sir Simon Cooper, KCVO
Deputy Master of the Household, Lt Col Sir Guy Acland, Bt, MVO
Chief Clerk, Michael Jephson, MVO
Comptroller, Lord Chamberlain's Office, Lt Col Malcolm Ross, CVO, OBE
Secretary, LCO, Jonathan Spencer, MVO
Assistant Secretary, LCO, Miss Ana Krysztofiak
State Invitations Assistant, John Hope
Marshal of the Diplomatic Corps, Vice Admiral Sir James Weatherall, KBE
Vice-Marshal of the Diplomatic Corps, Philip Astley, LVO
First Assistant Marshal of the Diplomatic Corps, Robin Gorham
Assistant Marshal of the Diplomatic Corps, Mrs Lesley Dean
Secretary, Central Chancery of the Orders of Knighthood, and Assistant Comptroller, LCO, Lt Col Anthony Mather, OBE
Assistant Secretary, Miss Rachel Wells, MVO
Crown Equerry, Lt Col Seymour Gilbart-Denham, CVO
Superintendent, Royal Mews, Major Albert Smith, MBE
Master of The Queen's Music, Malcolm Williamson, CBE, AO
Poet Laureate, Edward Hughes, OBE
Gentlemen at Arms: Lieutenant, Colonel Thomas Hall, OBE
Clerk of the Cheque and Adjutant, Lt Col Richard Mayfield, DSO
Yeomen of the Guard: Lieutenant, Colonel Greville Tufnell
Clerk of the Cheque and Adjutant, Colonel Shaun Longsdon
Clerk of the Closet, The Bishop of Derby (The Rt Rev Jonathan Bailey)
Deputy Clerk of the Closet, The Rev William Booth
Dean of the Chapels Royal, The Bishop of London (The Rt Rev and Rt Hon Richard Chartres)
Sub-Dean of the Chapels Royal, The Rev William Booth
Head of the Medical Household and Physician, Dr Richard Thompson, DM, FRCP
Apothecary to The Queen, Dr Nigel Southward, CVO, MB, BChir, MRCP
Serjeant Surgeon, Barry Jackson, MS, FRCS
Windsor Castle: Constable and Superintendent, General Sir Patrick Palmer, KBE: *Superintendent,* Major Barrie Eastwood, LVO, MBE
Director of the Royal Collection and Surveyor of The Queen's Works of Art, Hugh Roberts, LVO, FSA
Surveyor of The Queen's Pictures, Christopher Lloyd, LVO
Librarian, Royal Library, Oliver Everett, CVO
Deputy Surveyor of The Queen's Works of Art, Jonathan Marsden
Director of Media Affairs, Richard Arbiter
Curator of the Print Room, Royal Library, The Hon Mrs Roberts, LVO
Heralds and Persuivants, see HER MAJESTY'S OFFICERS OF ARMS

HOUSEHOLD OF QUEEN ELIZABETH THE QUEEN MOTHER

Apothecary to the Household, Dr Nigel Southward, CVO, MB, BChir, MRCP
Clerk Comptroller to the Household, Malcolm Blanch, CVO
Equerries, Major Sir Ralph Anstruther, Bt, GCVO, MC; Major Raymond Seymour, CVO; Captain Sir Alastair Aird, KCVO
Temporary Equerry, Major Charles MacEwan
Information Officer, Mrs Roy Murphy, LVO
Ladies of the Bedchamber, The Lady Grimthorpe, DCVO; The Countess of Scarbrough
Women of the Bedchamber, Dame Frances Campbell-Preston, DCVO; The Lady Angela Oswald, LVO; The Hon Mrs Rhodes; Mrs Michael Gordon-Lennox
Lord Chamberlain, The Earl of Crawford and Balcarres
Page of Honour, The Hon Thomas Lumley
Private Secretary and Comptroller, Captain Sir Alastair Aird, GCVO
Assistant Private Secretary, Major Raymond Seymour, CVO
Apothecary to the Household at Royal Lodge, Windsor, Dr John Briscoe, MB, BChir, MRCGP, DObst, RCOG
Treasurer, Major Sir Ralph Anstruther, Bt, GCVO, MC

HOUSEHOLD OF THE PRINCE PHILIP, DUKE OF EDINBURGH

Chief Clerk and Accountant to the Household, Graham Partington
Equerry, Lt Col Charles Richards
Temporary Equerries, Capt the Hon James Geddes, Major John Crosby, RM; Capt Richard Goodfellow, REME
Extra Equerry, Sir Brian McGrath, KCVO
Private Secretary, Brigadier Miles Hunt-Davis, CBE

HOUSEHOLD OF THE PRINCE OF WALES

Apothecary to the Household, Dr Peter Wheeler, MB BS, MRCP, MRCGP
Equerry, Lt Cdr John Lavery, RN
Temporary Equerry, Capt Fergus Williams
Private Secretary and Treasurer, Stephen Lamport
Deputy Private Secretary, Vacant
Assistant Private Secretaries, Dr Manon Williams, Jonathan Skan

HOUSEHOLD OF DIANA, PRINCESS OF WALES

Comptroller, Michael Gibbins, Esq
Ladies in Waiting, Miss Anne Beckwith-Smith, LVO; Viscountess Campden, LVO; Mrs Max Price; Mrs Duncan Byatt; Mrs James Lonsdale
Extra Lady in Waiting, The Lady Sarah McCorquodale

HOUSEHOLD OF THE DUKE OF YORK

Equerry, Major Timothy Allan
Private Secretary, Treasurer and Extra Equerry, Capt Neil Blair, LVO, RN
Comptroller and Assistant Private Secretary, Cdr Charlotte Manley, OBE, RN

HOUSEHOLD OF THE PRINCE EDWARD

Private Secretary and Equerry, Lt Col Sean O'Dwyer, LVO
Assistant Private Secretary, Mrs Richard Warburton, MVO

HOUSEHOLD OF THE PRINCESS ROYAL

Ladies in Waiting, Lady Carew Pole, LVO; Mrs Andrew Feilden, LVO; The Hon Mrs Legge-Bourke LVO; Mrs William Nunneley; Mrs Timothy Holderness-Roddam; Mrs Charles Ritchie; Mrs David Bowes-Lyon
Extra Ladies in Waiting, Miss Victoria Legge-Bourke, LVO; Mrs Malcolm Innes, LVO; The Countess of Lichfield, LVO
Private Secretary, Lt Col Peter Gibbs, CVO
Assistant Private Secretary, The Hon Mrs Louloudis

HOUSEHOLD OF THE PRINCESS MARGARET, COUNTESS OF SNOWDON

Apothecary to the Household, Dr Nigel Southward, CVO, MB, BChir, MRCP
Lady in Waiting, The Hon Mrs Whitehead, LVO
Extra Ladies in Waiting, The Lady Elizabeth Cavendish, CVO; Lady Aird, LVO; Mrs Robin Benson, LVO, OBE; The Hon Mrs Wills, LVO; Mrs Jane Stevens, LVO; The Lady Juliet Townsend, LVO; The Lady Glenconner, LVO; The Countess Alexander of Tunis, LVO; Mrs Charles Vyvyan
Private Secretary, Comptroller and Equerry, Major the Lord Napier and Ettrick, KCVO

HOUSEHOLD OF PRINCESS ALICE, DUCHESS OF GLOUCESTER

Apothecary to the Household, Dr Nigel Southward, CVO, MB, BChir, MRCP
Extra Equerry, Lt Col Sir Simon Bland, KCVO
Ladies in Waiting, Dame Jean Maxwell-Scott, DCVO; Mrs Michael Harvey, LVO
Private Secretary, Comptroller and Equerry, Maj Nicholas Barne, LVO

HOUSEHOLD OF THE DUKE AND DUCHESS OF GLOUCESTER

Apothecary to the Household, Dr Nigel Southward, CVO, MB, BChir, MRCP
Extra Equerry, Lt Col Sir Simon Bland, KCVO
Ladies in Waiting, Mrs Michael Wigley, CVO; Mrs Euan McCorquodale, LVO; Mrs Howard Page, LVO
Extra Ladies in Waiting, The Lady Camoys, Miss Jennifer Thomson
Assistant Private Secretary to the Duchess of Gloucester, Miss Suzanne Marland, LVO
Private Secretary, Comptroller and Equerry, Maj Nicholas Barne, LVO

HOUSEHOLD OF THE DUKE AND DUCHESS OF KENT

Apothecary to the Household, Dr Nigel Southward, CVO, MB, BChir, MRCP
Clerk Comptroller, Mrs Paul Christodoulou
Temporary Equerry, Capt Marcus Barnett
Ladies in Waiting, Mrs Colin Marsh, LVO; Mrs Peter Troughton; Mrs Julian Tomkins; Mrs Richard Beckett; Mrs Charles Holbech
Private Secretary, Nicolas Adamson, OBE
Personal Secretary to the Duchess of Kent, Miss Claire Almonds
Extra Equerry, Lt Cdr Sir Richard Buckley, KCVO, RN

HOUSEHOLD OF PRINCE AND PRINCESS MICHAEL OF KENT

Apothecary to the Household, Dr Nigel Southward, CVO, MB, BChir, MRCP
Ladies in Waiting, Mrs Julian Fellowes; Miss Anne Frost; The Hon Mrs Sanders
Personal Secretary to Prince Michael of Kent, Miss Claudia Jenkins
Personal Secretary to Princess Michael of Kent, Miss Claire Butler
Extra Equerry, Lt Col Sir Christopher Thompson, Bt

HOUSEHOLD OF PRINCESS ALEXANDRA, THE HON LADY OGILVY

Comptroller, Cdr Charlotte Manley, OBE, RN
Extra Equerry, Major Sir Peter Clarke, KCVO
Lady in Waiting, The Lady Mary Mumford, DCVO
Extra Ladies in Waiting, Mrs Peter Afia; The Lady Nicholas Gordon Lennox; Dame Mona Mitchell, DCVO; The Lady Mary Colman; The Hon Lady Rawley
Private Secretary, Capt Neil Blair, LVO, RN
Personal Secretary, Mrs Valerie Hampton, MVO

THE QUEEN'S HOUSEHOLD IN SCOTLAND

Hereditary Lord High Constable, The Earl of Erroll
Hereditary Master of the Household, The Duke of Argyll
Hereditary Standard Bearer for Scotland, The Earl of Dundee
Hereditary Bearer of the National Flag of Scotland, The Earl of Lauderdale
Hereditary Carver in Scotland, Major Sir Ralph Anstruther, Bt, GCVO, MC
Hereditary Keepers:-
  Holyrood, The Duke of Hamilton and Brandon
  Falkland, Ninian Crichton-Stuart
  Rothesay, The Marquess of Bute
  Stirling, The Earl of Mar and Kellie
  Dunstaffnage, The Duke of Argyll
  Dunconnel, Sir Charles Maclean of Dunconnel, Bt
Keeper of Dumbarton Castle, Brig Donald Hardie, TD
Governor of Edinburgh Castle, Maj Gen Jonathan Hall, OBE
Dean of the Order of the Thistle, The Very Rev Gilleasbuig Macmillan, MA, BD
Dean of the Chapel Royal, The Very Rev James Harkness, CB, OBE
Physicians in Scotland, Dr Peter Brunt, OBE, MD, FRCP; Dr Anthony Toft, CBE, FRCPE
Surgeons in Scotland, Jetmund Engeset, ChM, FRCS; Sir David Carter, MD, FRCS
Apothecary to the Household at Balmoral, Dr Douglas Glass, MB, ChB
Apothecary to the Household at the Palace of Holyroodhouse, Dr Jack Cormack, MD, FRCPE, FRCGP
Royal Company of Archers:
  Gold Stick for Scotland and Captain General, Major Sir Hew Hamilton-Dalrymple, Bt, KCVO
  Adjutant, Major the Hon Sir Lachlan Maclean of Duart, Bt
Heralds and Pursuivants, see HER MAJESTY'S OFFICERS OF ARMS

HER MAJESTY'S OFFICERS OF ARMS

ENGLAND
College of Arms, Queen Victoria Street, London EC4V 4BT

EARL MARSHAL
His Grace the Duke of Norfolk, KG, GCVO, CB, CBE, MC

KINGS OF ARMS
Garter–Peter Llewellyn Gwynn-Jones, LVO
Clarenceux–John Philip Brooke Brooke-Little, CVO, FSA
Norroy and Ulster (and Registrar)–David Hubert Boothby Chesshyre, LVO, FSA

HERALDS
Somerset–Thomas Woodcock, LVO, FSA
Richmond (and Earl Marshal's Secretary)–Patric Laurence Dickinson
York–Henry Edgar Paston-Bedingfeld
Chester–Timothy Hugh Stewart Duke
Lancaster–Vacant
Windsor–Vacant

PURSUIVANTS
Bluemantle–Robert John Baptist Noel
Portcullis–William George Hunt, TD
Rouge Croix–David Vines White
Rouge Dragon–Vacant

HERALDS EXTRAORDINARY
New Zealand–Phillippe Patrick O'Shea, LVO
Surrey–Sir Walter John George Verco, KCVO
Beaumont–Francis Sedley Andrus, LVO
Maltravers–John Martin Robinson, DPhil, FSA
Norfolk–David Rankin-Hunt, MVO, TD
Wales–Michael Powell Siddons

PURSUIVANT EXTRAORDINARY
Howard–Lt Cdr John Henry Bruce Bedells, JP, RN

SCOTLAND
Court of the Lord Lyon, HM New Register House, Edinburgh EH1 3YT

THE RT HON THE LORD LYON KING OF ARMS
Sir Malcolm Rognvald Innes of Edingight, KCVO, WS

HERALDS
Albany–John Alexander Spens, RD, WS
Rothesay–Sir Crispin Hamlyn Agnew of Lochnaw, Bt, QC
Ross–Charles John Burnett, FSA Scot

PURSUIVANTS
Kintyre–John Charles Grossmith George, FSA Scot
Unicorn–Alastair Lorne Campbell of Airds, FSA Scot
Carrick–Mrs Christopher Roads, MVO, FSA Scot

PURSUIVANTS OF EARLS
(Not forming part of Her Majesty's Household and not under the control of Lord Lyon)
Pursuivants to the Earl of Erroll, the Countess of Mar and the Earl of Crawford
Slains–Peter Drummond-Murray of Mastrick
(Pursuivant to the Earl of Erroll)
Garioch–David Gordon Allen d'Aldecamb Lumsden of Cushnie
(Pursuivant to the Countess of Mar)
Endure–The Hon Alexander Walter Lindsay
(Pursuivant to the Earl of Crawford)

GENERAL TABLE OF PRECEDENCE IN ENGLAND AND WALES

The Queen
The Duke of Edinburgh
The Prince of Wales
The Sovereign's younger sons
The Sovereign's grandsons (according to the seniority of their fathers)
The Sovereign's cousins (according to the seniority of their fathers)
Archbishop of Canterbury
Lord High Chancellor
Archbishop of York
The Prime Minister
Lord High Treasurer (no such office exists at present)
Lord President of the Council
The Speaker of the House of Commons
Lord Privy Seal
Ambassadors and High Commissioners

Above all Peers of their own degree:
- Lord Great Chamberlain
- Lord High Constable (no such office exists at present)
- Earl Marshal
- Lord High Admiral (office held by HM The Queen)
- Lord Steward of the Household
- Lord Chamberlain of the Household

Master of the Horse
Dukes of England
Dukes of Scotland (none created since 1707)
Dukes of Great Britain (1707–1801)
Dukes of Ireland (created before 1801)
Dukes of the United Kingdom (created since 1801)
Eldest sons of Dukes of the Blood Royal (when they are not brothers, grandsons, uncles, or nephews of the reigning sovereign)
Marquesses of England
__________ Scotland (none created after 1707)
__________ Great Britain (1707–1801)
__________ Ireland (created before 1801)
__________ the United Kingdom (created since 1801)
Eldest sons of Dukes
Earls of England (anterior to 1707)
Earls of Scotland (none created after 1707)
Earls of Great Britain (1707–1801)
Earls of Ireland (created before 1801)
Earls of the United Kingdom (created since 1801)
Younger sons of Dukes of the Blood Royal (when they are not brothers, grandsons, uncles or nephews of the reigning sovereign)
Eldest sons of Marquesses
Younger sons of Dukes
Viscounts of England
__________ Scotland (anterior to 1707)
__________ Great Britain (1707–1801)
__________ Ireland (anterior to 1801)
__________ the United Kingdom (created since 1801)
Eldest sons of Earls
Younger sons of Marquesses
Bishop of London
_______ Durham
_______ Winchester
English Diocesan Bishops (according to date of consecration)
Bishops Suffragan (according to date of consecration)
Secretaries of State (if barons)
Barons of England
Barons of Scotland (none created since 1707)
_______ Great Britain (1707–1801)
_______ Ireland (anterior to 1801)
_______ the United Kingdom (created since 1801)
Lords of Appeal in Ordinary
Commissioners of the Great Seal (those persons who execute the office of Lord High Chancellor when it happens to be vacant)
Treasurer of the Household
Comptroller of the Household
Vice-Chamberlain of the Household
Secretaries of State (when not barons)
Eldest sons of Viscounts
Younger sons of Earls
Eldest sons of Barons
Knights of the Garter
Privy Councillors
Chancellor of the Exchequer
____________ Duchy of Lancaster
Lord Chief Justice
Master of the Rolls
President of the Family Division
The Vice-Chancellor of the Chancery Division
Lord Justices of Appeal, ranking according to date of appointment
Judges of the High Court of Justice, ranking according to date of appointment
Vice-Chancellor of the County Palatine of Lancaster
Younger sons of Viscounts
____________ Barons
Younger sons of Life Peers
Baronets
Knights of the Thistle
Knights Grand Cross of the Bath
Knights Grand Commanders of the Star of India
Knights Grand Cross of St Michael and St George
Knights Grand Commanders of the Order of the Indian Empire
Knights Grand Cross of the Royal Victorian Order
Knights Grand Cross of the Order of the British Empire
Knights Commanders of the Bath
Knights Commanders of the Star of India
Knights Commanders of St Michael and St George
Knights Commanders of the Order of the Indian Empire
Knights Commanders of the Royal Victorian Order
Knights Commanders of the Order of the British Empire
Knights Bachelor
Circuit Judges
Masters in Chancery
Master of Court of Protection
Companions of the Bath
Companions of the Star of India
Companions of St Michael and St George
Companions of the Indian Empire
Commanders of the Royal Victorian Order
Commanders of the Order of the British Empire
Companions of the Distinguished Service Order
Lieutenants of the Royal Victorian Order
Officers of the Order of the British Empire
Companions of the Imperial Service Order
Eldest sons of the younger sons of Peers
Eldest sons of Baronets
Eldest sons of Knights of the Garter
Eldest sons of Knights, according to the precedence of their fathers
Members of the Royal Victorian Order
Members of the Order of the British Empire
Younger sons of Baronets
Younger sons of Knights
Esquires
Gentlemen

RELATIVE RANK AND PRECEDENCE IN THE NAVY, ARMY AND AIR FORCE

Navy	Army	Air Force
Admiral of the Fleet	Field Marshal	Marshal of the RAF
Admiral	General	Air Chief Marshal
Vice Admiral	Lieutenant-General	Air Marshal
Rear Admiral	Major-General	Air Vice-Marshal
Commodore	Brigadier	Air Commodore
Captain	Colonel	Group Captain
Commander	Lieutenant-Colonel	Wing Commander
Lieutenant Commander	Major	Squadron Leader
Lieutenant	Captain	Flight Lieutenant
Sub Lieutenant	Lieutenant	Flying Officer
Commissioned Officers from Warrant Rank	Second Lieutenant	Pilot Officer

PRECEDENCE AMONG LADIES

The daughter of a peer does not lose her own rank should she marry a person not a peer, but if she marries a peer her title and precedence are merged in his, *e.g.* if the daughter of a duke marries a baron, she takes the rank of a baroness. The widow of a peer, baronet or knight who re-marries does not retain any title or precedence acquired from her previous husband, but may do so only by courtesy. A dowager peeress or the widow of a baronet, while a widow, takes precedence of the wife of the living holder of the title. The divorced wife of a peer or baronet derives no rank or precedence from her former husband but unless she remarries usually retains the title with her christian or forename prefixed (e.g. Mary, Lady Jones). Official rank and precedence is not communicable to the wife, but the wife of a lord mayor has precedence derived from her husband's office.

The Queen
The Queen Mother
The Princess of Wales
The Duchess of York
The Princess Royal
Sister of the Sovereign
Granddaughters of the Sovereign
Wives of the Sovereign's uncles
Wives of the Sovereign's cousins
Cousin of the Sovereign
The Prime Minister (if female)
Duchesses of England
__________ Scotland
__________ Great Britain
__________ Ireland
__________ the United Kingdom
Wives of the eldest sons of Dukes of the Blood Royal
Marchionesses (in the same order as the Duchesses)
Wives of the eldest sons of Dukes
Daughters of Dukes (while unmarried, or when married to commoners)
Countesses (in the same order as the Duchesses)
Wives of the younger sons of Dukes of the Blood Royal
Wives of the eldest sons of Marquesses
Daughters of Marquesses (while unmarried or when married to commoners)
Wives of the younger sons of Dukes
Viscountesses (in the same order as the Duchesses)
Wives of the elder sons of Earls
Daughters of Earls (while unmarried, or when married to commoners)
Wives of younger sons of Marquesses
Baronesses (in the same order as the Duchesses)
Wives of the eldest sons of Viscounts
Daughters of Viscounts (while unmarried or when married to a commoner)
Wives of the younger sons of Earls
Wives of the eldest sons of Barons
Daughters of Barons (if unmarried, or when married to a commoner)
Wives of Knights of the Garter
Privy Councillors (Women)
Wives of the younger sons of Viscounts
Wives of the younger sons of Barons
Daughters of Lords of Appeal
Wives of the sons of Legal Life Peers
Wives of Baronets (according to the dates of creation of titles held by their husbands)
Wives of Knights of the Thistle
Dames Grand Cross of St Michael and St George
Dames Grand Cross of the Royal Victorian Order
Dames Grand Cross of the Order of the British Empire
Wives of Knights Grand Cross of the Bath
Wives of Knights Grand Commanders of the Star of India
Wives of Knights Grand Cross of St Michael and St George
Wives of Knights Grand Commanders of the Indian Empire
Wives of Knights Grand Cross of the Royal Victorian Order
Wives of Knights Grand Cross of the Order of the British Empire
Dames Commanders of the Bath
Dames Commanders of St Michael and St George
Dames Commanders of the Royal Victorian Order
Dames Commanders of the Order of the British Empire
Wives of Knights Commanders of the Bath
Wives of Knights Commanders of the Star of India
Wives of Knights Commanders of St Michael and St George
Wives of Knights Commanders of the Indian Empire
Wives of Knights Commanders of the Royal Victorian Order
Wives of Knights Commanders of the Order of the British Empire
Wives of Knights Bachelor
Commanders of St Michael and St George
Commanders of the Royal Victorian Order
Commanders of the Order of the British Empire
Wives of Commanders and Companions of the Orders of the Bath, the Star of India, St Michael and St George, Indian Empire, Royal Victorian Order, and the British Empire
Wives of Companions of the Distinguished Service Order
Officers of the Order of the British Empire
Wives of Lieutenants of the Royal Victorian Order
Wives of Officers of the Order of the British Empire Companions of the Imperial Service Order
Wives of Companions of the Imperial Service Order
Wives of the eldest sons of the younger sons of Peers
Daughters of the younger sons of Peers
Wives of the eldest sons of Baronets
Daughters of Baronets
Wives of the eldest sons of Knights of the Garter
Wives of the eldest sons of Knights Bachelor
Daughters of Knights Bachelor
Members of the Royal Victorian Order
Members of the Order of the British Empire
Wives of members of the Royal Victorian Order
Wives of members of the Order of the British Empire
Wives of the younger sons of Baronets
Wives of the younger sons of Knights
Wives of Esquires
Wives of Gentlemen

GENERAL TABLE OF PRECEDENCE IN SCOTLAND

GENTLEMEN

The Duke of Edinburgh*
Lord High Commissioner to the General Assembly of the Church of Scotland (during sitting of General Assembly)
Duke of Rothesay (The Prince of Wales)
Sovereign's younger sons
Sovereign's grandsons
Sovereign's Cousins
Lord-Lieutenants of Counties†
Lord Provosts of Cities being *ex-officio* Lord-Lieutenants of Counties of Cities†
Sheriffs Principal†
Lord Chancellor of Great Britain
Moderator of General Assembly of Church of Scotland (during office)
The Prime Minister (if male)
Keeper of the Great Seal of Scotland (the Secretary for Scotland) (if a Peer)
Keeper of the Privy Seal of Scotland (if a Peer)
Hereditary High Constable of Scotland
Hereditary Master of the Household in Scotland
Dukes (as in English Table)
Eldest sons of Dukes of the Blood Royal
Marquesses (as in English Table)
Eldest sons of Dukes
Earls (as in English Table)
Younger sons of Dukes of the Blood Royal
Eldest sons of Marquesses
Younger sons of Dukes
Keeper of the Great Seal (the Secretary for Scotland) (if not a Peer)
Keeper of the Privy Seal (if not a Peer)
Lord Justice-General
Lord Clerk Register
Lord Advocate
Lord Justice-Clerk
Viscounts (as in English Table)
Eldest sons of Earls
Younger sons of Marquesses
Barons or Lords of Parliament (Scotland) (as in English Table)
Eldest sons of Viscounts
Younger sons of Earls
Eldest sons of Barons or Lords of Parliament
Knights of the Garter
Knights of the Thistle
Privy Counsellors
Senators of the College of Justice (Lords of Session), including Chairman of Scottish Land Court
Younger sons of Viscounts
Younger sons of Barons or Lords of Parliament
Baronets
Knights Grand Cross and Knights Grand Commanders of Orders (as in English Table)
Knights Commanders of Orders (as in English Table)
Solicitor-General for Scotland
Lord Lyon King of Arms
Sheriffs Principal (when not within own county)††
Knights Bachelor
Sheriffs
Companions of the Bath
Thence as in English Table

Lord-Lieutenants of Counties and of Counties of Cities during their term of office and within the limits of their jurisdiction have precedence before the Sheriffs Principal having concurrent jurisdiction.

LADIES

The Queen
The Queen Mother
Duchess of Rothesay (The Princess of Wales)
Duchess of York (Countess of Inverness)
Sovereign's Daughter
Sovereign's Sister
Sovereign's Granddaughters
Wives of Sovereign's Uncles
Wives of Dukes of the Blood Royal
Wives of Princes of the Blood Royal
Sovereign's Cousin
The Prime Minister (if female)
Duchesses (as in English Table)
Wives of the eldest sons of Dukes of the Blood Royal
Marchionesses (as in English Table)
Wives of eldest sons of Dukes
Daughters of Dukes
Wives of younger sons of Dukes of the Blood Royal
Wives of eldest sons of Marquesses
Daughters of Marquesses
Wives of younger sons of Dukes
Countesses (as in English Table)
Viscountesses (as in English Table)
Wives of eldest sons of Earls
Daughters of Earls
Wives of younger sons of Marquesses
Baronesses, or Ladies of Parliament (Scotland) (as in English Table)
Wives of eldest sons of Viscounts
Daughters of Viscounts
Wives of younger sons of Earls
Wives of eldest sons of Barons or Lords of Parliament
Daughters of Barons or Lords of Parliament
Ladies of the Order of the Garter
Wives of Knights of the Garter
Ladies of the Order of the Thistle
Wives of Knights of the Thistle
Privy Counsellors (women)
Wives of younger sons of Viscounts
Wives of younger sons of Barons
Wives of Baronets
Dames Grand Cross of Orders (as in English Table)
Wives of Knights Grand Cross and Knights Grand Commanders of Orders (as in English Table)
Dames Commanders of Orders (as in English Tables)
Wives of Knights Commanders of Orders (as in English Tables)
Wives of Knights Bachelor and Wives of Senators of the College of Justice (Lords of Session) including the wife of the Chairman of the Scottish Land Court**
Companions of the Order of the Bath
Thence as in English Table

* By Royal Warrant dated 18 September 1952, it was declared that HRH the Duke of Edinburgh was henceforth to have Precedence next to HM the Queen, thus having place before the Lord High Commissioner.

** Taking precedence among themselves according to the dates of their husbands' creation as Knights or appointment as Senators of the College of Justice, respectively.

† During term of office, and within their respective Counties, Cities and Sheriffdoms.

†† In Scotland Sheriffs exercise judicial functions.

POSITION OF LETTERS AFTER THE NAME

The abbreviations 'Bt' or 'Bart' (for a Baronet) and 'Esq', if applicable, precede all other letters.

The series of other letters are grouped either by regulations or by custom as follows:

1. Orders and Decorations conferred by the Crown.
2. Appointments in the following order, Privy Counsellor, Aide de Camp to Her Majesty, Honorary Physician to The Queen, Honorary Surgeon to The Queen, Honorary Dental Surgeon to The Queen, Honorary Nursing Sister to The Queen, and Honorary Chaplain to The Queen, viz. PC, ADC, QHP, QHS, QHDS, QHNS and QHC.
3. Queen's Counsel, Justice of the Peace and Deputy Lieutenant, viz. QC, JP and DL.
4. University Degrees.
5. (a) Religious Orders.
   (b) Medical Qualifications.
6. (a) Fellowships of Learned Societies,
   (b) Royal Academicians and Associates,
   (c) Fellowships, Memberships, etc., of Professional Institutions, Associations, etc.,
   (d) Writers to the Signet.
7. Member of Parliament, viz. MP.
8. Membership of one of the Armed Forces, such as RN or RAF.

The following notes are given for guidance.

It is important to keep the group order, even if the individual series of letters in Groups 4, 5 and 6 present difficulties. For further details see the appropriate section.

The nature of the correspondence determines which series of letters should normally be included under Groups 4, 5 and 6. For instance, when writing a professional letter to a doctor of medicine one would normally add more medical qualifications than in a social letter.

On a formal list all the appropriate letters are usually included after each name.

Those who have letters signifying Crown Honours and Awards are usually given only the principal letters in Groups 3, 4 and 5 (e.g. MD, FRCS, FRS).

A peer who is a junior officer in the Armed Forces, is not usually addressed by his Service rank in social correspondence, unless he so wishes, or a letter is forwarded to him at a Service address or club.

1. ORDERS AND DECORATIONS

All the appropriate letters are obligatory in correspondence and lists. The order is laid down for Knights, Dames and others.

They are addressed according to their rank, with the appropriate letters after their name in order of precedence. The use of all these letters is obligatory, e.g John Brown, Esq, CBE, MVO, TD.

The recipient is allowed to use the appropriate letters for the Order from the date of announcement in the 'London Gazette'.

Those promoted within the same Order of Chivalry do not continue to show the letters of the lower class of that Order, e.g. if Brigadier John Smith, OBE, is promoted to CBE he is addressed as Brigadier John Smith, CBE, the OBE being dropped.

Precedence of letters

The full list of honours and awards in order of precedence *of letters* is given below. A baronet has the letters Bt or Bart immediately after the name, and before any letters which signify honours.

It should be noted the VC and GC have precedence of *all* letters signifying Orders (including Knightly grades therein), Decorations and Medals.

The Order of Merit (OM) and Companion of Honour (CH) are important honours which bestow no title on the holder. The letters OM follow GCB, and CH follow GBE.

Some people prefer PC after KG since that is its correct position in order of precedence.

Victoria Cross	VC
George Cross	GC
Knight of the Garter	KG
Knight of the Thistle	KT
Knight/Dame Grand Cross of the Order of the Bath	GCB
Order of Merit	OM
Knight Grand Commander of the Star of India	GCSI
Knight/Dame Grand Cross of the Order of St Michael and St George	GCMG
Knight Grand Commander of the Indian Empire	GCIE
Knight/Dame Grand Cross of the Royal Victorian Order	GCVO
Knight/Dame Grand Cross of the British Empire	GBE
Companion of Honour	CH
Knight Commander of the Bath	KCB
Dame Commander of the Bath	DCB
Knight Commander of the Star of India	KCSI
Knight Commander of St Michael and St George	KCMG
Dame Commander of St Michael and St George	DCMG
Knight Commander of the Indian Empire	KCIE
Dame Commander of the Royal Victorian Order	DCVO
Knight Commander of the British Empire	KBE
Dame Commander of the British Empire	DBE
Companion of the Order of the Bath	CB
Companion of the Order of the Star of India	CSI
Companion of the Order of St Michael and St George	CMG
Companion of the Order of the Indian Empire	CIE
Commander of the Royal Victorian Order	CVO
Commander of the Order of the British Empire	CBE
Distinguished Service Order	DSO
Lieutenant of the Royal Victorian Order	LVO
Officer of the Order of the British Empire	OBE
Imperial Service Order	ISO
Member of the Royal Victorian Order	MVO
Member of the Order of the British Empire	MBE
Indian Order of Merit (Military)	IOM
Royal Red Cross	RRC
Distinguished Service Cross	DSC
Military Cross	MC
Distinguished Flying Cross	DFC
Air Force Cross	AFC
Associate, Royal Red Cross	ARRC
Order of British India	OBI
Distinguished Conduct Medal	DCM
Conspicuous Gallantry Medal	CGM
George Medal	GM
Distinguished Conduct Medal of the Royal West African Frontier Force and the King's African Rifles	DCM
Indian Distinguished Service Medal	IDSM
Distinguished Service Medal	DSM
Military Medal	MM
Distinguished Flying Medal	DFM
Air Force Medal	AFM
Medal for Saving Life at Sea	SGM
Indian Order of Merit (Civil)	IOM
Colonial Police Medal for Gallantry	CPM
Queen's Gallantry Medal	QGM
British Empire Medal	BEM
King's Police Medal	KPM
King's Police and Fire Service Medal	KPFSM
Queen's Police Medal	QPM
Queen's Fire Service Medal	QFSM
Colonial Police Medal for Meritorious Service	CPM
Meritorious Service Medal	MSM
Army Emergency Reserve Decoration	ERD
Volunteer Officer's Decoration	VD
Territorial Decoration	TD
Efficiency Decoration	ED
Decoration for Officers of the Royal Naval Reserve	RD
Decoration for Officers of the Royal Naval Volunteer Reserve	VRD
Air Efficiency Award	AE
Canadian Forces Decoration	CD

ORDER OF CANADA

The formation of the Order of Canada was announced in 1967.

The Order, of which the Queen is Sovereign, is divided into the following grades according to its last revised constitution:

CC Companion of the Order of Canada, with precedence after VC and GC before all other letters.
OC Officer of the Order of Canada, with precedence after CC.
CM Member of the Order of Canada, with precedence after OC.

The Cross of Valour, The Star of Courage and The Medal of Bravery have no letters.

ORDER OF AUSTRALIA

The Order of Australia was established in 1975.

The Order, of which The Queen is Sovereign, consists of a General Division and a Military Division and is divided into the following classes:

AK Knight of the Order of Australia, with precedence after the Order of Merit.

AD Dame of Order of Australia, with the same precedence as Knight of the Order of Australia.

AC Companion of the Order of Australia, with precedence after Knight Grand Cross of the Order of the British Empire.

AO Officer of the Order of Australia, with precedence after the Knight Bachelor.

AM Member of the Order of Australia, with precedence after the Distinguished Service Order.

OAM Medal of the Order of Australia, with precedence after the Royal Red Cross (2nd class).

THE QUEEN'S SERVICE ORDER OF NEW ZEALAND

This order was established in 1975. The Order, of which The Queen is Sovereign, is divided into two parts, for Community Service and for Public Services.

There are two divisions:

QSO Companions of The Queen's Service Order, with precedence after Officer of the Order of the British Empire.

QSM The Queen's Service Medal, with precedence after Queen's Gallantry Medal, and before British Empire Medal.

2. PRIVY COUNSELLORS AND APPOINTMENTS TO THE QUEEN

For peers the letters PC are obligatory. For other Privy Counsellors, 'Rt Hon' before the name is sufficient identification. As the other appointments to the Crown (QHP, QHS, etc.) are held for a limited period only, they are not always used by recipients.

3. UNIVERSITY DEGREES

Doctorates in the faculties of Divinity and Medicine (DD, MD) and Masters degrees in the latter (eg MS) are given in all correspondence. Other divinity degrees (eg BD) are sometimes included.

Other degrees in medicine (e.g. MB BS) are sometimes included, especially in professional correspondence, but if one progresses in the same degree only the higher is given.

Doctorates in other faculties are sometimes given, especially if the correspondence concerns the particular profession or subject (e.g. LLD, DSc). Alternatively, except for surgeons, the envelope may be addressed as 'Doctor' before his name, without giving his (or her) degrees.

Other degrees are seldom, and MA and BA never, used in social correspondence, but they are generally included in a formal list.

4. (a) RELIGIOUS ORDERS

Letters for members of religious communities, when used, should be included, e.g. SJ. Some Members of the Order of St. Benedict do not normally use the letters OSB as the prefix of 'Dom' or 'Dame' is held to be a sufficient identification.

(b) MEDICAL QUALIFICATIONS

Fellowships are given in all correspondence (e.g. FRCP, FRCS)

Other qualifications are sometimes given, especially those which are the highest held. They are usually included when writing professionally.

When all letters signifying qualifications are included, as for example in a nominal list, they should appear in the following order. (*Note:* Fellows and Members of each category precede the next category):

Medicine
Surgery (except MRCS)
Obstetrics, Gynaecology and other specialities
Qualifying diplomas (e.g. MRCS, LRCP)
Other diplomas (e.g. DPH, DObst, RCOG)

In practice, a maximum of three series of letters including MD (see Group 3 above) is usually sufficient in ordinary correspondence (e.g. MD, MS, FRCS).

5. (a) FELLOWSHIPS OF LEARNED SOCIETIES

Fellowships fall into two categories:

(a) honorific, i.e. nomination by election,
(b) nomination by subscription.

Normally only honorific fellowships are used in social correspondence (e.g. FRS, FBA). Fellowships by subscription are generally restricted to correspondence concerning the same field of interest, e.g. a writer to a Fellow of the Zoological Society on the subject of zoology will include FZS after the name.

There is no recognized order for placing these letters. Strictly speaking, they should be arranged according to the date of foundation or incorporation of the societies concerned, but some hold that those with a Royal Charter should precede others.

In practice the following is usually adhered to:

(1) Where one society is indisputably of greater importance than another, the letters may be placed in that order; or alternatively the fellowship of the junior society may be omitted.

(2) If such precedence cannot be determined, the letters may be placed in order of conferment. Where this is not known, they may be placed in alphabetical order.

(3) Where a fellow is pre-eminent in a particular subject, his fellowship of a society connected with this interest may either be placed first, or his other fellowships omitted.

The following are some of the principal learned societies, with their dates of incorporation:

Fellow of The Royal Society	FRS	1662
Fellow of The Society of Antiquaries	FSA	1707
Fellow of The Royal Society of Edinburgh	FRSE	1783
Fellow of The Royal Society of Literature	FRSL	1823
Fellow of The British Academy	FBA	1901
Fellow of the Fellowship of Engineering	FEng	1983

Presidents of some societies have special letters to signify their appointment, e.g. The President of the Royal Society has PRS after his name, but these letters are only used within the particular society.

The Royal Society of Literature bestows an award limited to ten recipients, the Companion of Literature. The letters CLit are placed before the Fellowship.

(b) ROYAL ACADEMY OF ARTS, THE ROYAL SCOTTISH ACADEMY, ETC.

It is not suggested that Royal Academicians yield in precedence to fellows of learned societies. In practice the two lists do not coincide.

The President and Past Presidents are indicated as follows:

President of the Royal Academy	PRA
Past President of the Royal Academy	PPRA
President of the Royal Scottish Academy	PRSA
Past President of the Royal Scottish Academy	PPRSA

Royal Academicians and Associates are included as follows:

Royal Academician	RA
Royal Scottish Academician	RSA
Associate of the Royal Academy	ARA
Associate of the Royal Scottish Academy	ARSA

Similarly with other Academies, e.g. President Royal Hibernian Academy (PRHA) and Academicians (RHA).

Honorary Academicians and Associates do not normally use the relevant letters.

(c) FELLOWSHIPS AND MEMBERSHIPS OF PROFESSIONAL INSTITUTIONS, ASSOCIATIONS, ETC.

These letters are usually restricted to correspondence concerning the particular profession.

It is not suggested that professional societies as such yield precedence to learned societies, but in point of fact the two groups do not coincide to any great extent. Most of the senior learned societies which elect fellows are senior in age and importance to the professional. Those whose fellowships are by subscription are generally only used in the particular field of interest. For example, if Mr. John Smith is a Chartered Engineer and a Fellow of the Royal Historical Society, he would normally be described professionally as John Smith, Esq, CEng, FIMechE. When corresponding on historical subjects he is normally described as John Smith, Esq, FRHistS. If both series of letters are placed after his name, it is usual to place first those which concern the particular function or subject.

As there is no recognized order for placing qualifications awarded by different bodies, a recipient usually places these letters on headed paper, business cards, etc. in order of importance to his particular profession.

The Engineering Council

The Engineering Council was granted a Royal Charter in 1981. The object of the Council is to advance the education and training of engineers and technologists, and to promote the science and practice of engineering for the public benefit. The Engineering Council accredits engineering academic courses and training programmes in the UK and registers qualified engineers.

There are 47 Professional Engineering Institutions which are Nominated bodies of The Engineering Council and which work closely with the Council in the qualification and registration areas. Of these 47 Professional Institutions, 17 are chartered. The Engineering Council, through its Board for Engineers' Registration, determines the standards and criteria for the education, training and levels of experience by which Chartered Engineers, Incorporated Engineers and Engineering Technicians may be registered, enabling them to use the designatory letters CEng, IEng, and EngTech respectively. Chartered Engineers must be in membership of a nominated Chartered Engineering Institution, or an institution affiliated body.

The designatory letters CEng, denoting Chartered Engineer, follow immediately after an individual's name and decorations and are followed in turn by the letters F (Fellow) or M (Member) identifying him with the particular institution(s) to which he belongs. Thus J. Smith, Esq, OBE, CEng, FICE, MIMechE, is a Chartered Engineer who is a Fellow of the Institution of Civil Engineers and a Member of the Institution of Mechanical Engineers.

The nominated Bodies which are also Chartered Engineering Institutions are: Royal Aeronautical Society, Institution of Civil Engineers, Institution of Chemical Engineers, Institution of Electrical Engineers, Institute of Energy, Institution of Gas Engineers, Institute of Marine Engineers, Institution of Mechanical Engineers, Institute of Metals, Institution of Mining Engineers, Institution of Mining and Metallurgy, Royal Institution of Naval Architects, Institution of Production Engineers, Institution of Structural Engineers, Institute of Measurement and Control, Chartered Institution of Building Services Engineers and the British Computer Society.

Chartered Societies of the Land

Three chartered societies of the land, viz.:

The Royal Institution of Chartered Surveyors
The Chartered Land Agents' Society
The Chartered Auctioneers' and Estate Agents' Institute

united in June 1970 to become the Royal Institution of Chartered Surveyors. Fellows and Professional Associates respectively have the letters FRICS and ARICS.

Incorporated Society of Valuers and Auctioneers

The Incorporated Society of Auctioneers and Landed Property Agents united in April 1968 with The Valuers Institution to form The Incorporated Society of Valuers and Auctioneers, with the letters FSVA and ASVA.

(d) WRITERS TO THE SIGNET

It is customary for the letters WS to follow the name after University degrees and those which signify Fellowship or Membership of a Society or Institution, despite the fact that the WS Society (an ancient Society of Solicitors in Scotland) is frequently considerably older than many Institutions. This is a way of indicating the profession. It is not customary for the letters WS to be used socially.

6. APPOINTMENTS

The letters MP are always shown for a Member of Parliament.

The letters QC are always shown for a Queen's Counsel including a County Court Judge, but not a High Court Judge.

The letters JP for a Justice of the Peace and DL for a Deputy Lieutenant may be included *in that order.* In practice they are often omitted for a peer, or for one with several honours and awards.

Note: There is no official abbreviation for a Lord-Lieutenant, HM Lieutenant or a Vice-Lieutenant.

7. MEMBERSHIP OF ONE OF THE ARMED FORCES

Royal Navy.—The letters 'RN' (or 'Royal Navy', which the Service prefers) are placed after the names of serving officers of and below the rank of Captain. They are also placed after the names of retired Captains, Commanders, and Lieutenant-Commanders where they are prefixed by Naval rank. The letters RNR are likewise used by officers of the Royal Naval Reserve.

Army.—The appropriate letters which signify a Regiment or Corps may be placed after the name for officers on the active list of and below the rank of Lieutenant-Colonel, but are often omitted in social correspondence. These letters are not used for retired officers.

Corps have letter abbreviations (e.g. RE, RAMC, RAOC, RAPC). Most regiments are written in full.

Royal Air Force.—The letters RAF are placed after serving and retired officers, except for Marshals of The Royal Air Force. Officers above the rank of Group Captain do not often use these letters. Similarly with RAFVR.

Royal Marines.—The letters 'RM' (or 'Royal Marines' which some officers prefer) are placed after the names of serving and retired officers of and below the rank of Lieutenant-Colonel. Similarly RMR (Royal Marines Reserve).

FORMS OF ADDRESSING PERSONS OF TITLE

Ecclesiastical and Services prefixes of rank are written before other titles. A High Officer of State or an official holding an important office, should be addressed by his official title when the communication refers to official business.

Eldest Sons of Dukes, Marquesses, and Earls bearing courtesy titles should not be styled "The Rt. Hon." or "The" unless they themselves are Peers or Members of the Privy Council.

Formal conclusion to letters to Peers. The style "I am, my Lord, Your obedient servant" may be used (as applicable), but "Yours faithfully" and "Yours truly" are now more customarily adopted, except for letters to Members of the Royal Family. After the Lambeth Conference 1968 under the guidance of the Archbishop of Canterbury, a simplified form of address for the Clergy of the Church of England was announced.

Commanders, Companions, Officers or Members of any Order and recipients of Decorations and Medals are addressed according to their rank and are entitled to place the recognised initials after their names in the following order:—VC, GC, OM, VA, CI, CH, CB, CSI, CMG, CIE, CVO, CBE, DSO, LVO, OBE, QSO, ISO, MVO, MBE, RRC, DSC, MC, DFC, AFC, ARRC, DCM, CGM, GM, DSM, MM, DFM, AFM, SGM, CPM (for Gallantry), QGM, BEM, KPM, KPFSM, QPM, QFSM, CPM (for Meritorious Service), ERD, TD, ED, RD, VRD, AE, CD.

Succession to hereditary titles. By custom those who have succeeded to peerages and baronetcies are not so addressed until after their predecessor's funeral.

New honours. Knights and Dames of Orders of Chivalry may use their style of "Sir" and "Dame" and the appropriate letters after their names, and Knights Bachelor their style of "Sir" immediately their honours have been announced. Other recipients of honours may also use the appropriate letters. Peers may use their titles after the patent of creation has passed the Great Seal, when their respective Peerage titles will be announced. Full details of forms of address are included in DEBRETT'S CORRECT FORM.

Air Efficiency Award.—The Air Efficiency Award, introduced in 1942 to recognize meritorious Service in the Royal Auxiliary Air Force and the RAFVR, since 1975 officers including retired officers who have received the Award may place AE after their names.

Albert Medal.—In Oct. 1971, The Queen approved the exchange by which holders of the Albert Medal (AM) receive the George Cross. *See* George Cross.

Ambassador (British).—LETTERS.—*Superscription.* (When in the country to which he is accredited only). "His Excellency [preceding all other ranks and titles], HM Ambassador to_____." *Commencement,* "Sir" or socially according to rank. *Conclusion,* "I have the honour to be Sir, Your Excellency's obedient servant." PERSONAL ADDRESS, "Your Excellency."

Ambassador's Wife. She is not entitled to the style "Her Excellency" and is referred to and addressed by name or conversationally as the Ambassadress.

Archbishop.—LETTERS.—*Superscription,* "The Most Rev The Lord Archbishop of_____," *Commencement,* "Dear Archbishop." PERSONAL ADDRESS, "Your Grace" or "Archbishop." On retirement from office he reverts to the style of Bishop.

Archbishop's Wife.—As the wife of an Esquire.

Archdeacon.—LETTERS.—*Superscription,* "The Venerable the Archdeacon of [Ely]." *Commencement,* "Dear Archdeacon." The prefix of the Venerable is not retained after retirement unless the title of Archdeacon Emeritus has been conferred.

Baron.—LETTERS.—*Superscription,* "The Right Hon the Lord_____" or socially "The Lord_____." *Commencement,* "My Lord" or socially "Dear Lord_____." PERSONAL ADDRESS, "My Lord."

Baroness.—LETTERS.—*Superscription,* if a Baroness in her own right "The Right Hon the Baroness_____." or socially "The Baroness _____," or "The Right Hon the Lady." or "The Lady_____." If the wife of a Baron "The Right Hon the Lady_____," or socially "The Lady_____." *Commencement,* "Madam" or socially "Dear Lady _____." PERSONAL ADDRESS, "Madam." [See also Baron's Widow.]

***If a Baroness in her own right marry a commoner and has issue, the children have the same rank and are addressed as if their father were a Baron.

Baronet.—LETTERS.—*Superscription,* "Sir [Charles]_____Bt." (The abbreviation "Bart." is also sometimes used). *Commencement,* "Sir." PERSONAL ADDRESS, "Sir" or socially "Dear Sir [Charles]".

Baronet's Widow.—*Same as Baronet's Wife* if present baronet is unmarried. For widows where present incumbent of the title is married ["Dowager"]. As to re-marriage, see "Widows."

Baronet's Wife.—LETTERS.—*Superscription,* if the daughter (i) of a commoner. "Lady_____"; (ii) of a Baron or a Viscount, "The Hon Lady _____"; (iii) of an Earl, a Marquess, or a Duke, "The Lady [Emily] _____." *Commencement,* "Madam.", or socially, "Dear Lady_____." PERSONAL ADDRESS, "Madam."

Baron's Daughter.—LETTERS.—*Superscription,* if married (i) to an esquire, "The Hon Mrs_____"; (ii) to a knight, or a baronet, "The Hon Lady_____"; (iii) to the son of a baron, or Viscount, or to the younger son of an Earl, "The Hon Mrs_____," or if her husband has a married brother. "The Hon Mrs [William]_____"; (iv) to the younger son of a Marquess or a Duke, "The Lady [Henry] _____."If unmarried, The Hon [Mary] _____"; (v) to the eldest son of a Duke, Marquess, or Earl by his courtesy title. [*See* also under "Duke's Daughter."] *Commencement,* "Madam." PERSONAL ADDRESS, "Madam," or socially if married to an esquire, "Dear Mrs _____," or according to her husband's rank if a Peer.

Baron's Son.—LETTERS.—*Superscription,* "The Hon [John]_____." *Commencement,* "Sir." PERSONAL ADDRESS, "Sir." or socially "Dear Mr_____." See also "Master of_____.".

Baron's Son's Widow.—*Same as Baron's Son's Wife* so long as she remains a widow. As to re-marriage, see "Widows."

Baron's Son's Wife.—LETTERS.—*Superscription,* "The Hon Mrs [Edward]_____," but if the daughter (i) of a Viscount or Baron "The Hon Mrs_____," (ii) of an Earl, a Marquess, or a Duke, "The Lady [Ellen]." [*See* also under "Duke's Daughter." *Commencement,* "Madam," or socially, if her father an esquire "Dear Mrs_____" or according to her father's rank, if a Peer. PERSONAL ADDRESS, "Madam."

Baron's Widow.—*Same as Baroness* if present Baron is unmarried. For widows where present incumbent of title is married [see "Dowager"]. As to re-marriage, see "Widows."

Bishop (Diocesan).—LETTERS.—*Superscription,* "The Rt Rev the Lord Bishop of_____," *Commencement,* "Dear Bishop."

Bishop (Commonwealth, Church Overseas, Irish, Scottish Episcopal, Suffragan and Welsh).—LETTERS.—*Superscription,* "The Right Rev the Bishop of_____." Exceptions, The Bishop of Meath (Premier Bishop of Ireland), and the Primus of Scotland, who are styled "Most Rev" *Commencement,* "Dear Bishop."

(Bishop retired).—Letters commence "Dear Bishop," and are addressed "The Right Rev [John Smith], DD."

Bishop's Wife.—As wife of Esquire.

Cabinet Ministers.—Are Invariably Privy Counsellors, which see.

Canon.—LETTERS.—*Superscription,* "The Rev Canon [John Smith]." *Commencement,* "Dear Canon," or "Dear Canon [Smith]." On retirement from office he reverts to the style of other clergy unless he has been appointed a Canon Emeritus.

Chairman of Scottish Land Court, as for Lord of Session.

Circuit Judge.—See "Judge, Circuit."

Clergy.—LETTERS.—*Superscription,* "The Rev John_____." *Commencement,* "Dear Mr (Smith)" or "Dear Father Smith." PERSONAL ADDRESS, "Sir." The Reverend precedes any title: The Rev the Hon. It is *incorrect* to write "The Hon and Rev" or "The Rev *Mr.*" Christian name or initials should always be shown.

Consuls [British].—LETTERS.—*Superscription,* "_____, Esq, HM ['Consul-General,' 'Consul,' or 'Vice-Consul,' as the case may be]_____," In other respects as an Esquire.

Countess.—LETTERS.—*Superscription,* "The Rt Hon the Countess of _____." or socially "The Countess of_____," In other respects, as Baroness. [See also "Earl's Widow."] *Commencement,* formally "Madam," socially "Dear Lady_____." If a Countess in her own right marries a gentleman of lesser degree than herself, and has issue, the children would have same rank and are addressed as if their father were an Earl.

Dames of Orders of Chivalry prefix "Dame" to their Christian names, adding the initials "GCB," "GCMG," "GCVO," "GBE" "DCB," "DCMG," "DCVO," or "DBE," as the case may be, after the surname. *Commencement,* formally "Madam" or socially "Dear Dame Edith_____" or "Dear Dame Edith." PERSONAL ADDRESS, "Dame Edith."

Dean.—LETTERS.—*Superscription,* "The Very Rev the Dean of_____." *Commencement,* "Dear Dean." PERSONAL ADDRESS, "Sir." The prefix of "The Very Rev" is not retained on retirement.

Degrees.—Those with doctorates of any faculty may be addressed by the appropriate abbreviations after their names, following those of orders, decorations and medals conferred by the Crown. DD should always be included. Masters' and bachelors' degrees are not used in social correspondence. The order of letters signifying doctorates and degrees depends on the individual university which confers them.

Deputy Lieutenant.—The letters DL are usually put after name. They follow JP.

Divorced Ladies. When a lady is divorced she loses any precedence which she gained by marriage. With regard to divorced Peeresses, the College of Arms, acting on an opinion of the Lord Chancellor, has long held that such persons cannot claim the privileges or status of Peeresses which they derived from their husbands. Divorced Peeresses are not summoned to a Coronation as Peeresses. The above remarks apply to ladies who have divorced their husbands as well as to those who have been divorced.

The correct style and description of divorced ladies who have not re-married, nor have taken steps to resume their maiden name with the prefix of Mrs, is as follows:

The former wife of a Peer or courtesy Peer,—Mary, Viscountess _____.

The former wife of a Baronet or Knight,—Mary, Lady_____.

The divorced wife of an "Honourable,"—The Hon Mrs John _____, or alternatively she may prefer to be known as Mrs Mary_____.

The divorced wife of a younger son of a Duke or Marquess,—The Lady John_____.

The divorced wife of an untitled gentleman,—Mrs Mary _____initials.

Dowager Lady is addressed according to her rank. Immediately a peer, or a baronet, marries, the widow of the previous incumbment of the title becomes "The Dowager"; but if there is more than one widow living of previous incumbents of a title, use must be made of the Christian name as a distinction, since the style of Dowager belongs to the senior of the widows for her lifetime. This prefix, however, is very much less used than formerly, use of the Christian name generally being preferred. In such cases ladies are addressed as The Right Hon [Mary], Countess of _____"; or socially as "[Mary], Countess of_____," etc., etc., if a peeress; or, as Ellen, Lady_____," if a Baronet's widow.

Duchess.—LETTERS.—*Superscription,* "Her Grace the Duchess of _____," or socially "The Duchess of_____." *Commencement,* formally "Madam," or socially "Dear Duchess of_____" or "Dear Duchess." PERSONAL ADDRESS, "Your Grace." [See also "Duke's Widow," and for "Duchess of the Blood Royal" *see* "Princess."]

Duke.—LETTERS.—*Superscription,* "His Grace the Duke of_____" or socially "The Duke of_____." The very formal style of "The Most Noble" is now rarely used. *Commencement,* "My Lord Duke," "Dear Duke of_____," or [more usual] "Dear Duke." PERSONAL ADDRESS, "Your Grace." [For "Duke of the Blood Royal" *see* "Prince."]

Duke's Daughter.—LETTERS.—*Superscription,* "The Lady [Henrietta]." *Commencement,* "Madam," or socially "Dear Lady Henrietta _____" or "Dear Lady Henrietta." PERSONAL ADDRESS, "Madam."

***If the daughter of a Duke, a Marquess, or an Earl marries a Peer she is addressed according to the rank of her husband. If she marries the eldest son of a Duke, Marquess or Earl she is known by her husband's courtesy title, but if the daughter of a *Duke* or *Marquess* marries the eldest son of an Earl she is sometimes addressed by the courtesy title of her husband, but she may revert to the style of Lady [Mary] Stavordale, i.e. her own title, followed by her husband's courtesy title. His surname must never be used. This form is invariably used by such ladies after divorce.

Duke's Eldest Son, assumes by courtesy a secondary title of his father, and is addressed personally as if he were a Peer without 'The Most Hon' or 'The Rt Hon' *Superscription,* "Marquess of_____" (or as title adopted may be).

Duke's Eldest Son's Daughter is by courtesy addressed as if her father were a Peer.

Duke's Eldest Son's Eldest Son assumes by courtesy the third title of his grandfather, and is addressed personally as if he were a peer provided such courtesy title is the title of a Peerage vested in his grandfather. *Superscription,* "Earl of_____" or "Lord_____" (or as title adopted may be).

Duke's Eldest Son's Younger Son is by courtesy addressed as if his father were a Peer.

Duke's Eldest Son's Widow, *Same as Duke's Eldest Son's Wife* so long as she remains a widow. As to re-marriage, *see* "Widows."

Duke's Eldest Son's Wife is known by his courtesy title, and is addressed personally as a peeress without 'The Most Hon' or 'The Rt Hon'.

Duke's Widow, *same as Duchess* if present Duke is unmarried. For widows where present incumbent of title is married [*see* "Dowager"]. As to remarriage, *see* "Widows."

Duke's Younger Son.—LETTERS.—*Superscription,* "The Lord [Robert] _____." *Commencement,* formally "My Lord," or socially "Dear Lord Robert_____," or "Dear Lord Robert." PERSONAL ADDRESS, "My Lord."

Duke's Younger Son's Widow, *same as Duke's Younger Son's Wife.* As to re-marriage, *see* "Widows."

Duke's Younger Son's Wife.—LETTERS.—*Superscription,* "The Lady [Thomas]_____." *Commencement,* "Madam," or socially "Dear Lady Thomas_____," or "Dear Lady Thomas."

Earl.—LETTERS. —*Superscription,* "The Right Hon the Earl of_____," or socially "The Earl of_____." In other respects as Baron.

Earl's Daughter, *same as Duke's Daughter.*

Earl's Eldest Son bears by courtesy a lesser (usually the second) title of his father, and is addressed as if he were a Peer but without 'The Rt Hon'. *Superscription,* "Viscount_____."

Earl's Eldest Son's Daughter is by courtesy addressed as if her father were a Peer.

Earls Eldest Son's Son is by courtesy addressed as if his father were a Peer. [If a Scottish Earldom, the eldest may be addressed as "The Master of_____." *See* Master.]

Earl's Eldest Son's Widow, *same as eldest son's Wife* so long as she remains a widow. As to re-marriage, *see* "Widows."

Earl's Eldest Son's Wife is usually known by his courtesy title (for exception see under "Duke's Daughter"), and is addressed personally as if a Peeress but without 'The Rt Hon'.

Earl's Widow, *same as Countess* if present Earl is unmarried. For widows where present incumbent of the title is married [*see* "Dowager"].

Earl's Wife.—*See* "Countess."

Earl's Younger Son, *same as Baron's Son.*

Earl's Younger Son's Widow, *same as Baron's Son's Wife.*

Earl's Younger Son's Wife, *same as Baron's Son's Wife.*

Edward Medal.—In Oct. 1971, The Queen approved the exchange by which holders of the Edward Medal (EM) receive the George Cross. (see George Cross).

Esquire.—LETTERS.—*Superscription,* "[Edward]_____, Esq." *Commencement,* "Sir." PERSONAL ADDRESS, "Sir."

Esquire's Widow, *same as Esquire's Wife.* She continues to use her late husband's christian name unless she re-marries, e.g. Mrs John Smith *not* Mrs Mary Smith.

Esquire's Wife.—*Superscription.* "Mrs [Egerton]," or "Mrs [John Egerton]." The former style is applicable if she is the wife of the head of the family, provided that there is no senior widow living, who retains the style for life or until re-marriage.—LETTERS.—*Commencement,* "Madam." PERSONAL ADDRESS, "Madam."

Fire Service Medals.—See Police Medals.

George Cross. The letters GC take precedence after VC, and before all other honours and decorations.

Governor of a Country within the British Commonwealth is styled "His Excellency" [preceding all other ranks and titles] while actually administering a Government and within its boundary (also an officer administering in his absence). If the Governor has not been knighted he is styled "His Excellency Mr John Smith." Esquire should not be used with HE.

Governor-General.—The style of His Excellency precedes all other titles and ranks, and is used while actually administering a Government and within the territory administered.—LETTERS.—*Superscription,* "His Excellency [Sir John]_____, Governor-General of_____" (also an officer administering in his absence). In other respects as for Governor.

Governor-General's Wife.—The style of "Her Excellency" has, since 1924, been confined to the wives of the Govs-Gen of Countries of the Commonwealth within the country administered by her husband.

Governor's Wife.—She is not accorded the style of "Her Excellency."

Grandchildren of Peers.—If the eldest son of a peer predeceases his father and the grandson succeeds to the peerage held by his grandfather, a Royal Warrant is necessary (when such succession has eventuated) to grant to his younger brothers and his sisters, the "rank, title, place, pre-eminence, and precedence" which would have been due to them if their father had survived to inherit the Peerage.

High Commissioner.—*Superscription,* His Excellency [preceding all other ranks, and titles] the High Commissioner for_____." Otherwise as for an Ambassador.

"Honourable" in Commonwealth Countries. The title of "Honourable" is borne *for life* by all Members of the Queen's Privy Council in Canada, Members of the Canadian Senate and Premiers and Lieutenant-Governors of Canadian Provinces, and of the Executive Councils of the Commonwealth of Australia and of the States of Victoria and Tasmania. In Canada the title of "Honourable" is borne *during office* by the following categories of Judges in Canada—Judges of Supreme and Exchequer Courts of Canada the Chief Justices and Judges of the Supreme Courts of Ontario, Nova Scotia, New Brunswick, Alberta and Newfoundland, the Court of Queen's Bench and the Superior Court of Quebec, the Court of Appeal and the Court of Queen's Bench of Manitoba and Saskatchewan, the Court of Appeal and the Supreme Court of British Columbia, the Supreme Court of Judicature of Prince Edward Island, and the Territorial Courts of NW Territories and Yukon Territory. They are eligible to be personally recommended by the Governor-General for Her Majesty's permission to retain the title on retirement. Also in Commonwealth countries all Members of Executive Councils, all Members of Legislative Councils (other than Legislative Councils of Provinces of Canada), and by the Speaker of the Lower House of the Legislatures. It is also used locally by Members of the Executive and Legislative Councils of territories not possessing Responsible Government. The following in Commonwealth Countries are eligible to be recommended to retain the title of "Honourable" on retirement. Executive Councillors who have served for at least three years as Ministers or one year as Prime Minister; Presidents of Senates and Legislative Councils and Speakers of Legislative Assemblies on quitting office after having served three years in their respective offices: Senators and Members of the Legislative Councils on retirement or resignation after a continuous service of not less than ten years. [*See* also Judges in Commonwealth and Overseas Territories]

Invitations. When sent jointly to married couples at their home address, the envelope should always be addressed to the wife.

Judge of City of London Court, as for Circuit Judge.

Judge in Commonwealth and Overseas Territories. —The title of "The Right Honourable" is borne for life by the Chief Justice of Canada. The title of "Honourable" during tenure of office is borne by Chief Justices and Judges of the High Court of Australia, and the Supreme Courts of New South Wales, Vic, Queensland, S Aust, W Aust, Tasmania, NZ, and the Judges of the Supreme and Exchequer Courts, and the Chief Justices and Judges of certain other Courts in the provinces of Canada; also such Chief Justices and Judges of those Courts as may be specially permitted to bear it after retirement. *Superscription,* "The Hon the Chief Justice," or "The Hon Mr Justice_____." Judges of the Supreme Courts in Commonwealth Countries are styled "The Honourable."

Judge, Circuit.—For the various appointments see Table of General Precedence.—LETTERS.—*Superscription,* "His Honour Judge _____." PERSONAL ADDRESS—"Sir", but when on the Bench, "Your Honour." The prefix of "His Honour," but not "Judge," is retained after retirement from office, but personal address as "Judge" or "Judge Brown" may be continued unofficially in retirement.

Judge, District.—LETTERS.—*Superscription,* "District Judge_____." *Commencement,* "Dear Judge."

Judge of High Court. —LETTERS.—*Superscription,* (official) "The Hon Mr Justice_____." (private) "Sir John_____." *Commencement,* "Sir." PERSONAL ADDRESS, "Sir," but when on the Bench, "My Lord," or, "Your Lordship." *See also* "Lord Chief Justice of England," "Master of the Rolls," "Lord Justice of Appeal," and "Lord of Appeal in Ordinary."

Judges of High Court, Ladies.—LETTERS.—*Superscription,* (official) "The Hon Mrs Justice_____" (private) "Dame Mary Smith_____." *Commencement,* "Madam." PERSONAL ADDRESS, "Madam," but when on the Bench "My Lady" or "Your Ladyship."

Justice of the Peace.—PERSONAL ADDRESS.—When on the Bench, "Your Worship," and in other respects as an Esquire. The letters JP are usually put after name.

Knight Bachelor. —LETTERS.—*Superscription,* "Sir [George]_____." In other respects same as Baronet. The letters KB should *not* be used.

Knight's Wife, *same as Baronet's Wife.* The wife of a clergyman of the Church of England who receives a Knighthood of an Order of Chivalry but consequently not the accolade, retains the style of "Mrs_____."

Knight of an Order of Chivalry, *same as Knight Bachelor,* but adding to the superscription the recognised letters of the Order, such as "GCB." or "KCB". Clergymen of the Church of England and Honorary Knights do not receive the accolade, and consequently are addressed by the letters of the Orders but not the prefix "Sir."

Knight's Widow, *same as Knight's Wife* so long as she remains a widow. As to re-marriage, *see* "Widows."

Lady (untitled). *See* Esquire's wife and widow. Of unmarried daughters, the eldest of the senior generation is styled "Miss [Egerton]." A younger daughter is addressed as "Miss [Helen Egerton]."

Lady Mayoress. *See* "Lord Mayor's Wife."

Lieutenant-Governor.—Isle of Man, Jersey and Guernsey, as for Governor. The style of a Lt-Gov of a Canadian Province is "*The Hon*" (borne for life).

Life Peer.—He is addressed as for an hereditary peer.—*See* "Baron."

Life Peer's Son.—*See* "Baron's son."

Life Peer's Daughter.—*See* "Baron's daughter."

Life Peeress. *See* "Baroness."

Life Peeress in her own right. She is addressed as for an hereditary peeress. *See* "Baroness."

Lord, in Peerage of Scotland.—*See* "Baron."

Lord Advocate.—LETTERS.—*Superscription,* "The Rt Hon the Lord Advocate," or, "The Rt Hon [George]_____." In other respects as an esquire. [The prefix of Rt Hon is not retained after retirement from office, unless a Member of the Privy Council.]

Lord Chancellor.—LETTERS.—*Superscription,* "The Rt Hon the Lord High Chancellor." In other respects as a peer according to his rank.

Lord Chief Justice.—LETTERS.—*Superscription,* "The Lord Chief Justice of England," or "To the Right Hon Lord_____, Lord Chief Justice of England." In other respects as a Judge, except when of noble rank, when he is addressed according to his degree.

Lord High Commissioner to General Assembly of Church of Scotland.—LETTERS.—*Superscription,* "To His Grace the Lord High Commissioner." *Commencement,* "Your Grace." PERSONAL ADDRESS. "Your Grace."

Lord Justice-Clerk.—LETTERS.—*Superscription,* "The Rt Hon the Lord Justice-Clerk" (if a Privy Counsellor), otherwise "The Hon the Lord Justice-Clerk". *Commencement,* "Dear Lord Justice-Clerk." PERSONAL ADDRESS, Addressed for all purposes by their appointments and not by the Judicial Titles with which they take their seats on the bench.

Lord Justice-General.—LETTERS.—*Superscription,* "The Rt Hon the Lord Justice-General". *Commencement,* "Dear Lord Justice-General." PERSONAL ADDRESS, *See* Lord Justice-Clerk.

Lord Justice of Appeal.—LETTERS.—*Superscription,* "The Right Hon Lord Justice," or "To the Right Hon Sir [Robert]_____." In other respects as a Judge of High Court.

Lord Mayor.—LETTERS.—The Lord Mayors of London, York, Belfast, and Cardiff have the privilege of being styled "The Rt Hon"; and permission to use this style has also been granted to the Lord Mayors of Sydney (NSW), Melbourne (Vic), Adelaide (S Aust), Perth (W Aust.). Brisbane (Queensland), and Hobart (Tasmania). *Superscription,* "The Rt Hon the Lord Mayor of_____." or "[Henry_____,] The Rt Hon Lord Mayor of_____," [The prefix of Right Hon is not retained after retirement from office. [*See also* "Lord Provost."]. *Commencement,* "My Lord," or less formally, "Dear Lord Mayor." *Superscription* for other Lord Mayors "The Right Worshipful the Lord Mayor of_____."

Lord Mayor's Wife or Lady Mayoress.—LETTERS.—*Superscription,* "The Lady Mayoress." In other respects as Knight's or Esquire's wife.

Lord of Appeal-in-Ordinary.—*See Baron.*

Lord of Session, Scottish.—LETTERS.—*Superscription,* "The Hon Lord_____." In other respects as a Baron, but children have no courtesy styles. *See* also Lord Justice Clerk and Lord Justice General.

Lord of Session's Wife or Widow.—LETTERS.—*Superscription,* "Lady." In other respects as Baron's wife.

Lord Provost.—LETTERS.—*Superscription,* The Lord Provosts of Edinburgh and Glasgow are addressed as "The Rt Hon the Lord Provost," while in office. The prefix may be placed before the name of the holder in the case of the Lord Provost of Edinburgh. In other respects as a Baron. The Lord Provost of Perth, Dundee and Aberdeen are styled "The Lord Provosts of_____."

Lord Provost's Wife. Same as the wife of an Esquire. The style of Lady Provost is incorrect.

Marchioness.—LETTERS.—*Superscription,* "The Most Hon the Marchioness of_____," or socially, "The Marchioness of_____." In other respects as Baroness. [*See also* "Marquess's Widow."]

Marquess.—LETTERS.—*Superscription,* "The Most Hon the Marquess of_____," or less formally, "The Marquess of_____." In other respects as Baron.

Marquess's Daughter, *same as Duke's Daughter.*

Marquess's Eldest Son, *same as Duke's Eldest Son. Superscription,* "Earl of_____" (or as title adopted may be).

Marquess's Eldest Son's Daughter is by courtesy addressed as if her father were a peer.

Marquess's Eldest Son's Eldest Son, *same as Duke's Eldest Son. Superscription,* "Viscount_____" (or as title adopted may be).

Marquess's Eldest Son's Younger Son is by courtesy addressed as if his father were a Peer, viz. "The Hon_____."

Marquess's Eldest Son's Widow, *same as Duke's Eldest Son's Widow.*

Marquess's Eldest Son's Wife is known by his courtesy title, and is addressed personally as a peeress without 'The Rt Hon'.

Marquess's Widow, *same as Marchioness,* if present Marquess is unmarried. For widows where present incumbent of title is married [see "Dowager"]. As to re-marriage see "Widows."

Marquess's Younger Son, *same as Duke's Younger Son.*

Marquess's Younger Son's Widow, *same as Duke's Younger Son's Wife,* As to re-marriage, see "Widows."

Marquess's Younger Son's Wife, *same as Duke's Younger Son's Wife.*

Master.—This title is borne in the *Peerage of Scotland* by the heir apparent or presumptive of a Peer. It is also used *by courtesy* by the eldest son of a Peer by courtesy. In the case of the heir apparent, "Master" is normally used by the eldest son of a Viscount and Lord, as the heirs of the senior grades of the Peerage normally use a courtesy title. He is styled "The Master of_____" (the appropriate title will be found under the Peerage article). If the heir be a woman, she is officially designated "The Mistress of_____" but this title is seldom used. A Master's wife is styled "The Hon Mrs [Donald Campbell"] or according to her husband's rank.

Master of the Rolls.—LETTERS.—*Superscription,* "The Right Hon the Master of the Rolls," or "The Right Hon_____," according to *Commencement,* as "Judge." PERSONAL ADDRESS, "Sir," but when on the Bench, "My Lord," or "Your Lordship."

Mayor (whether man or woman).—LETTERS.—*Superscription,* (if Mayor of a City), "The Right Worshipful the Mayor of_____", (if a Mayor of a Borough or Town Mayor), "The Worshipful the Mayor of _____." *Commencement,* "Sir (or Madam)." In other respects as an Esquire or an Esquire's wife. The form "Dear Mr Mayor" may be used for a man or woman.

Members of the Executive and Legislative Councils.—See Honourable in Commonwealth Countries.

Members of Parliament.—According to rank, but adding the initials "MP" after title or name and honours.

Military Officers.—See "Naval, Military, and Air Force Officers."

Minister of the Crown.—If a Privy Counsellor, see that section, otherwise see Member of Parliament or Grade of Peerage. The social form of "Dear Secretary of State," or "Dear Minister" may be used if the matter concerns the Department.

Moderator of the General Assembly of Church of Scotland. By Order in Council the Moderator has precedence in Scotland and at Court functions immediately after Bishops of the Church of England, and while in office is addressed as "Rt Rev" Former Moderators, "Very Rev."

Naval, Military, and Air Force Officers.—Professional rank should always precede any titles, *e.g.,* "Adm (the Right Hon) the Earl of _____," "Gen the (Right Hon) Lord_____," "Air-Marshal Sir," but Lieutenants in the Army, Flying Officers and Pilot Officers in the Air Force are addressed by their social and not their professional rank, *e.g.,* "The Hon Benjamin_____, Irish Guards," "George_____, Esq., 11th Hussars," or "William_____, Esq., RAF."

Peers and Peeresses by courtesy.—As commoners they are not addressed as "Rt Hon" or "The" but "Viscount [Brown]" or appropriate title.

Police and Fire Service Medals. The letters KPM, KPFSM, QPM, QFSM and CPM are now placed after the name. If the Colonial Police Medal were awarded for gallantry the letters CPM are placed before BEM, and if for meritorious service after QFSM (see paragraph 4 at beginning of section).

Prebendary.—As for Canon, but substituting the word Prebendary for Canon.

Prime Minister, The.—See Privy Counsellors. The social form of "Dear (Mr.) Prime Minister" may be used if the matter concerns his office.

Prince.—LETTERS.—*Superscription,* (i) the son of a Sovereign "His Royal Highness The Prince [Edward]"; (ii) other Princes "His Royal Highness Prince [Michael of Kent]"; (iii) Duke "His Royal Highness The Duke of [Gloucester]." *Commencement,* "Sir," *Conclusion,* "I have the honour to be, Sir. Your Royal Highness's most humble and obedient servant." PERSONAL ADDRESS, "Your Royal Highness," and thenceforward as "Sir." [*See also* Royal Family.]

Princess.—LETTERS.—*Superscription,* (i) the daughter of a Sovereign "Her Royal Highness The Princess [Royal]"; (ii) other Princesses "Her Royal Highness Princess [Alexandra], the Hon Lady Ogilvy"; (iii) Duchess "Her Royal Highness The Duchess of [Kent]." *Commencement,* "Madam." *Conclusion,* "I have the honour to be, Madam, Your Royal Highness's most humble and obedient servant." PERSONAL ADDRESS, "Your Royal Highness," and thenceforward as "Ma'am." [*See also* Royal Family.]

Privy Counsellors, also spelt PRIVY COUNCILLORS.—Letters.—*Superscription,* "The Right Hon_____," but if a peer than as such, followed by the letters "PC," *after* all Orders and Decorations. *Commencement, &c.,* according to the rank of the individual. Privy Counsellors of Northern Ireland, which are no longer created, are entitled to the prefix of Right Hon and are included in this section. Members of the Privy Council of Canada are entitled to the style of "Hon" for life. *Commencement,* as for Esquire or appropriate rank.

Privy Counsellors, Wives of.—They enjoy no special style or precedence as such.

Provost.—As for Dean, but substituting the word Provost for Dean.

Provost (Scotland)—LETTERS.—*Superscription,* "The Provost of _____." *Commencement,* "Dear Provost." PERSONAL ADDRESS, "Provost."

Queen Mother.—LETTERS.—*Superscription,* for formal and state documents, "Her Gracious Majesty Queen Elizabeth The Queen Mother," otherwise "Her Majesty Queen Elizabeth The Queen Mother." *Commencement,* as for the Queen Regnant. *Conclusion,* "I have the honour to remain, Madam, Your Majesty's most humble and obedient servant." PERSONAL ADDRESS, as for the Queen Regnant.

Queen Regnant.—LETTERS.—*Superscription,* for formal and state documents. "The Queen's Most Excellent Majesty." otherwise "Her Majesty The Queen," *Commencement,* "Madam," or "May it please your Majesty." *Conclusion,* "I have the honour to remain Madam, Your Majesty's most humble and obedient servant." PERSONAL ADDRESS, "Your Majesty," and thenceforward as "Ma'am."

Queen's Counsel.—LETTERS.—*Superscription,* "_____Esq, QC." In other respects as an Esquire. The letters are used after the name by Circuit Judges, but not by High Court Judges.

Rt Honourable.—This prefix is borne by Privy Counsellors of Great Britain and Northern Ireland, the Governor General of Canada, and Prime Minister and Chief Justice of Canada *for life*; by Earls, Viscounts and Barons: (except peers by courtesy) their wives and widows; and certain Lord Mayors (see Lord Mayors), and Provosts of Edinburgh and Glasgow (see Lord Provosts).

Royal Dukes.—See "Prince."

Royal Family.—On 11 Dec 1917, it was ordained that "The children of any Sovereign of the United Kingdom and the children of the sons of any such Sovereign and the eldest living son of the eldest son of the Prince of Wales, shall have and at all times hold and enjoy the style, title, or attribute of Royal Highness with their titular dignity of Prince or Princess prefixed to their respective Christian names, or with their other titles of honour; and that the grandchildren of the sons of any such Sovereign in the direct male line (save only the eldest living son of the eldest son of the Prince of Wales) shall have the style and title enjoyed by the children of Dukes." [*See* also "Queen Regnant," "Queen Mother." "Prince," and "Princess."]

Rural Deans. No special form of address.

Secretary of State. See "Minister of the Crown" and "Privy Counsellors."

Sheriff.—LETTERS.—*Superscription,* "Sheriff." PERSONAL ADDRESS, Addressed on the bench as "My Lord" or "My Lady" and formally and socially as "Sheriff_____."

Sheriff Principal.—LETTERS.—*Superscription,* "Sheriff Principal _____." *Commencement,* "Sheriff Principal." PERSONAL ADDRESS, Addressed on the bench as "My Lord" or "My Lady", and formally and socially as "Sheriff_____."

Sovereign, The. —See "Queen Regnant."

Titles just announced.—See paragraph at commencement of this section.

Trinity House, Elder Brethren of are entitled to be called "Captain," with precedence after Naval Captains.

Victoria Cross.—The letters VC take precedence of all other honours and decorations.

Viscount,—LETTERS.—*Superscription,* "The Right Hon the Viscount _____," or socially "The Viscount_____." In other respects as Baron.

Viscountess.—LETTERS.—*Superscription,* "The Right Hon the Viscountess_____." or socially, "The Viscountess." In other respects as Baroness and Baron's widow. [See also "Viscount's Widow"].

Viscount's Son, and his Wife or Widow *same as Baron's.*

Viscount's Daughter, *same as Baron's.*

Viscount's Widow, *same as Viscountess* if present Viscount is unmarried. For widows where present incumbent of title is married [*see* "Dowager"]. As to re-marriage, see "Widows."

Wales, Prince of. See "Prince" and "Royal Family."

Widows.—A Widow who re-marries *loses* any title or precedence she gained by her previous marriage, and is not recognised as having any claim to bear the title of her deceased husband, *e.g.:* at a coronation or other State ceremonial, the widow of a peer would not be summoned as a peeress if she had subsequently married a commoner; and, if having espoused a peer of lesser degree than her former husband, she would only be recognised by the rank acquired by her last marriage. [*See also* Esquire's Widow.]

LONDON CLUBS

Army and Navy	36 Pall Mall, SW1	0171-930 9721
Anglo-Belgian	60 Knightsbridge, SW1	0171-235 2121
Arts	40 Dover Street, W1	0171-499 8581
Athenaeum	107 Pall Mall, SW1	0171-930 4843
Beefsteak	9 Irving Street, WC2	0171-930 5722
Boodle's	28 St James's Street, SW1	0171-930 7166
Brooks's	St James's Street, SW1	0171-493 4411
Buck's	18 Clifford Street, W1	0171-734 6896
Caledonian	9 Halkin Street, SW1	0171-235 5162
Canning	94 Piccadilly, W1	0171-499 5163
Carlton	69 St James's Street, SW1	0171-493 1164
Cavalry and Guards'	127 Piccadilly, W1	0171-499 1261
Chelsea Arts	143 Old Church Street, SW3	0171-376 3311
City Livery	Sion College, Victoria Embankment, EC4	0171-353 2431
City of London	19 Old Broad Street, EC2	0171-588 7991
East India, Devonshire, Sports and Public Schools	16 St James's Square, SW1	0171-930 1000
Farmers'	3 Whitehall Court, SW1	0171-930 3557
Flyfishers'	24a Old Burlington Street, W1	0171-734 9229
Garrick	15 Garrick Street, WC2	0171-836 1737
Groucho	45 Dean Street, W1	0171-439 4685
Hurlingham	Ranelagh Gardens, SW6	0171-736 8411
Lansdowne	9 Fitmaurice Place, Berkeley Square, W1	0171-629 7200
MCC (Marylebone Cricket Club)	Lord's Cricket Ground, NW8	0171-289 1611
National Liberal	Whitehall Place, SW1	0171-930 9871
Naval	38 Hill Street, W1	0171-493 7672
Naval and Military	94 Piccadilly, W1	0171-499 5163
New Cavendish	44 Great Cumberland Place, W1	0171-723 0391
Oriental	Stratford House, Stratford Place, W1	0171-629 5126
Portland	42 Half Moon Street, W1	0171-499 1523
Pratt's	14 Park Place, St James's Street, SW1	0171-493 0397
Queen's	Palliser Road, W14	0171-385 3421
Reform	104 Pall Mall, SW1	0171-930 9374
Royal Air Force	128 Piccadilly, W1	0171-499 3456
Royal Automobile	89-91 Pall Mall, SW1	0171-930 2345
Royal Ocean Racing	20 St James's Place, SW1	0171-493 2248
Royal Over-Seas League	Over-Seas House, St James's Street, SW1	0171-408 0214
Royal Thames Yacht	60 Knightsbridge, SW1	0171-235 2121
St Stephen's Constitutional	34 Queen Anne's Gate, SW1	0171-222 1382
Savage	1 Whitehall Place, SW1	0171-930 8118
Savile	69 Brook Street, W1	0171-629 5462
Ski Club of Great Britain	118 Eaton Square, SW1	0171-245 1033
Travellers'	106 Pall Mall, SW1	0171-930 8688
Turf	5 Carlton House Terrace, SW1	0171-930 8555
United Oxford & Cambridge University	71 Pall Mall, SW1	0171-930 5151
University Women's	2 Audley Square, South Audley Street, W1	0171-499 6478
White's	37 St James's Street, SW1	0171-493 6671

CLUBS OUTSIDE LONDON

Bath and County	Queen's Parade, Bath BA1 2NJ	01225 423732
Caledonian	32 Abercromby Place, Edinburgh EH3 6QE	0131 557 2675
Jockey	101 The High Street, Newmarket CB8 8JL	01638 663101
Kildare St and University	17 St Stephen's Green, Dublin 2	00 353 1 676 2975
Leander	Henley-on-Thames RG9 2LP	01491 575782
New	86 Prince's Street, Edinburgh EH2 2BB	0131 226 4881
Northern Counties	Hood Street, Newcastle-upon-Tyne NE1 6LH	0191 232 2744
Royal and Ancient	St Andrews, Fife KY16 9JD	01334 472112
Royal Irish Automobile	34 Dawson Street, Dublin 2	00 353 1 677 0668
Royal Scottish Automobile	11 Blythswood Square, Glasgow G2 4AG	0141 221 3850
Royal Yacht Squadron	The Castle, Cowes, Isle of Wight PO31 7QT	01983 292743
Scottish Arts	24 Rutland Square, Edinburgh EH1 2BW	0131 229 1076
Ulster Reform	4 Royal Avenue, Belfast BT1 1DA	01232 323411
Western	32 Royal Exchange Square, Glasgow G1 3AB	0141 221 2016

A Reader's Guide

The following notes should be borne in mind when reading an entry in *People of Today.*

Brackets around entrants' first forenames indicate names not used, while brackets around later forenames denote nicknames by which they are generally known. If clarification is needed, see the Style section towards the end of each entry.

It is standard genealogical practice to list sons first, followed by daughters. In recent times the editors have felt it appropriate to relax this rule, and newer entries will generally list daughters first if the entrant's first-born child was female.

Careers generally begin by detailing the entrant's main professional career, including military service where applicable, in chronological order. This will typically be followed by involvements with other career-related organisations, then any charitable, public or other appointments. Honours, distinctions and awards are listed next, with the section concluding with memberships or fellowships of professional bodies. Because of the wide range of entrants' activities in *People of Today,* however, there is necessarily considerable variation in the way career information is presented.

Clubs are generally in London unless stated otherwise. The word 'Club' is normally omitted from their names.

The entrant's style is the preferred way to address him or her in correspondence, in line with commonly accepted correct form and as agreed by the entrant. The styles given in *People of Today* do not include professional qualifications or academic distinctions after an entrant's name, though it may be appropriate to do so in correspondence pertaining to the entrant's particular profession (see the foregoing section on Position of Letters after the Name for further information).

Addresses and telephone numbers are given as required for writing or dialling from within the UK.

DISCLAIMER

Debrett's make every effort to check and update the extensive information contained in this publication.

Any errors or omissions which remain are unintentional, and no liability of any kind is accepted by the publisher or distributor in respect of them.

Such errors or omissions should be drawn to Debrett's attention for correction in future editions.

ABBREVIATIONS

A

AA	Automobile Association; Architectural Association; Anti-Aircraft
AAA	Amateur Athletic Association (now BAF)
AAAS	American Association for the Advancement of Science
AAC	Army Air Corps
AACCA	Associate of the Association of Certified and Corporate Accountants
AACI	Accredited Appraiser, Canadian Institute
AADipl	Diploma of the Architectural Association
A&AEE	Aeroplane and Armament Experimental Establishment
AAF	Auxiliary Air Force
AAFCE	Allied Air Forces Central Europe
AAG	Assistant Adjutant-General
AAGBI	Associate, Anaesthetists of Great Britain and Ireland
AAI	Associate of the Chartered Auctioneers' and Estate Agents' Institute
AALPA	Association of Incorporated Auctioneers and Landed Property Agents
AAM	Association of Assistant Mistresses in Secondary Schools
AAMC	Australian Army Medical Corps
AAPG	American Association of Petroleum Geologists
AA&QMG	Assistant Adjutant & Quarter Master General
AASA	Associate of the Australian Society of Accountants
AASC	Australian Army Service Corps
AASF	Advanced Air Striking Force
AAT	Association of Accounting Technicians
AB	Bachelor of Arts (USA); Able-bodied Seaman
ABA	Associate of the British Archaeological Association; Antiquarian Booksellers' Association; Amateur Boxing Association
ABCC	Association of British Chambers of Commerce
ABI	Association of British Insurers
ABIA	Associate, Bankers' Institute of Australia
ABIBA	Associate of the British Institute of Brokers Association
ABIM	Associate of the British Institute of Management (now AIMgt)
ABOD	Advance Base Ordnance Depot
ABP	Associated British Ports (formerly BTDB)
ABPS	Associate of the British Psychological Society
ABRC	Advisory Board for the Research Councils
ABSA	Association for Business Sponsorship of the Arts
ABTA	Association of British Travel Agents
AC	Companion of the Order of Australia
ACA	Associate of the Institute of Chartered Accountants
Acad	Academy
ACARD	Advisory Council for Applied Research and Development
ACAS	Advisory, Conciliation and Arbitration Service
ACBSI	Associate, Chartered Building Societies Institute
ACC	Association of County Councils
ACCA	Associate of the Chartered Association of Certified Accountants
ACCM	Advisory Council for the Church's Ministry
ACCS	Associate of the Corporation of Secretaries
AcDipEd	Academic Diploma in Education
ACDS	Assistant Chief of Defence Staff
ACE	Association of Consulting Engineers
ACENVO	Association of Chief Executives of National Voluntary Organisations
ACF	Army Cadet Force
ACFA	Army Cadet Forces Association
ACG	Assistant Chaplain General
ACGI	Associate of the City & Guilds of London Institute
ACGS	Assistant Chief of General Staff
ACIArb	Associate, Chartered Institute of Arbitrators
ACIB	Associate, Chartered Institute of Bankers
ACII	Associate of the Chartered Insurance Institute
ACInstT	Associate, Chartered Institute of Taxation (formerly AInstT)
ACIS	Associate of the Institute of Chartered Secretaries (now ICSA)
ACMA	Associate, Institute of Cost and Management Accountants
ACNS	Assistant Chief of Naval Staff
ACommA	Associate, Society of Commercial Accountants
ACORD	Advisory Committee on Research and Development
ACOS	Assistant Chief of Staff
ACOST	Advisory Council on Science and Technology
ACP	Association of Clinical Pathologists; Associate, College of Preceptors
ACPO	Association of Chief Police Officers
ACRE	Action with Rural Communities in England
ACS	American Chemical Society
ACSEA	Allied Command SE Asia
ACT	Australian Capital Territory; Australian College of Theology; Association of Corporate Treasurers
Actg	Acting
ACTT	Association of Cinematograph, Television and Allied Technicians
ACVO	Assistant Chief Veterinary Officer
ACWA	Associate, Institute of Cost and Works Accountants
ADAS	Agricultural Development and Advisory Service (MAFF)
ADB	Associate of the Drama Board
ADC	Aide-de-Camp
AD Corps	Army Dental Corps
ADC(P)	Personal Aide-de-Camp to HM The Queen
ADGB	Air Defence of Great Britain
ADGMS	Assistant Director-General of Medical Services
Adj	Adjutant
Adj-Gen	Adjutant-General
Adm	Admiral
Admin	Administration; Administrative; Administrator
ADMS	Assistant Director of Medical Services
Admty	Admiralty
ADNI	Assistant Director of Naval Intelligence
ADOS	Assistant Director of Ordnance Service
ADP	Automatic Data Processing
ADPR	Assistant Director Public Relations
ADS&T	Assistant Director of Supplies and Transport
Adv-Gen	Advocate-General
ADVS	Assistant Director of Veterinary Services
Advsr	Advisor
Advsy	Advisory
Advtg	Advertising
A/E	Accident and Emergency
AE	Air Efficiency Award (see AEA)
AEA	Air Efficiency Award; Atomic Energy Authority
AEAF	Allied Expeditionary Air Force
AEC	Army Educational Corps (now RAEC); Agricultural Executive Committee
AED	Air Efficiency Decoration
AEF	Amalgamated Union of Engineering and Foundry Workers
AEM	Air Efficiency Medal
AER	Air Emergency Reserve
AERE	Atomic Energy Research Establishment
AEU	Amalgamated Engineering Union
AF	Air Force
AFAEP	Association of Fashion Advertising and Editorial Photographers (now Association of Photographers)
AFAIM	Associate Fellow of the Australian Institute of Management
AFB	Air Force Base (US)
AFBPsS	Associate Fellow, British Psychological Society
AFC	Air Force Cross; Association Football Club
AFCENT	Allied Forces Central Europe
Affrs	Affairs
AFHQ	Allied Forces Headquarters
AFI	Associate of the Faculty of Insurance; American Film Institute
AFIMA	Associate Fellow, Institute of Mathematics and its applications
AFM	Air Force Medal
AFOM	Associate, Faculty of Occupational Medicine
AFRAeS	Associate Fellow of the Royal Aeronautical Society
AFRC	Agricultural and Food Research Council (now BBSRC)
AFS	Auxiliary Fire Service
AFV	Armoured Fighting Vehicles
AFVPA	Advertising, Film and Video Producers' Association
AG	Attorney-General
Agent-Gen	Agent-General
AGI	Alliance Graphique Internationale
AGRA	Association of Genealogists and Record Agents
Agric	Agriculture, Agricultural
AGSM	Associate, Guildhall School of Music and Drama
AHA	Area Health Authority
AHA(T)	Area Health Authority (Teaching)
AHQ	Army Headquarters
AHSM	Associate, Institute of Health Services Management
AIA	American Institute of Architects; Associate, Institute of Actuaries; Association of International Artists
AIAA	Associate of the Institute of Administrative Accountants
AIAC	Associate of the Institute of Company Accountants
AIAS	Associate Surveyor Member, Incorporated Association of Architects and Surveyors
AIB	Associate of the Institute of Banking
AIBD	Associate, Institute of British Decorators
AICA	Associate Member Commonwealth Institute of Accountants
AICE	Associate, Institute of Civil Engineers
AIChor	Associate of the Institute of Choreography
AICS	Associate of the Institute of Chartered Shipbuilders
AICTA	Associate, Imperial College of Tropical Medicine
AIEE	Associate of the Institution of Electrical Engineers
AIF	Australian Imperial Forces
AIG	Adjutant-Inspector-General
AIIA	Associate of the Institute of Industrial Administration
AIIMR	Associate of the Institute of Investment Management and Research
AIL	Associate, Institute of Linguists
AIM	Associate of the Institution of Metallurgists
AIMarE	Associate of the Institute of Marine Engineers
AIMSW	Associate, Institute of Medical Social Workers
AINA	Associate of the Institute of Naval Architects
AInstBRM	Associate, Institute of Baths and Recreation Management
AInstM	Associate Member of the Institute of Marketing
AInstP	Associate of the Institute of Physics
AInstT	Associate, Institute of Taxation (now ACInstT)
AInstTport	Associate, Institute of Transport
AIP	Association of Independent Producers
AIPM	Associate of the Institute of Personnel Management
AIRC	Association of Independent Radio Contractors

Air Cdre Air Commodore
AIRMIC Associate, Insurance & Risk Managers in Industry and Commerce
AISVA Associate, Incorporated Society of Valuers and Auctioneers
AIYL Association of International Young Lawyers
AK Knight of the Order of Australia
aka Also known as
AKC Associate, King's College London
ALA Associate, Library Association
ALAM Associate, London Academy of Music and Dramatic Art
ALAS Associate Member of Chartered Land Agents' Society
ALCD Associate, London College of Divinity
ALCM Associate, London College of Music
ALFSEA Allied Land Forces South East Asia
ALI Argyll Light Infantry; Associate, Landscape Institute
ALIA Associate, Life Insurance Association
ALL Association of Language Learning
ALLC Association for Literary and Linguistic Computing
Alta Alberta (Canada)
AM Member of the Order of Australia; Albert Medal; Master of the Arts (USA); Alpes Maritimes
AMA Associate, Museum Association; Association of Metropolitan Authorities
Ambass Ambassador
AMBIM Associate, Member of the British Institute of Management
AMCT Associate, Manchester College of Technology
AMDEA Associate of Manufacturers of Domestic and Electrical Appliances
AMEC Association of Management Education for Clinicians
AMEME Association of Mining, Electrical and Mechanical Engineers
AMF Australian Military Forces
AMGOT Allied Military Government Occupied Territory
AMI Association of Media Independents
AMIBE Associate Member of the Institution of British Engineers
AMICE Associate Member of the Institution of Civil Engineers
AMIChemE Associate Member of the Institution of Chemical Engineers
AMIED Associate Member of the Institution of Engineering Designers
AMIEE Associate Member of the Institution of Electrical Engineers
AMIEEIE Associate Member, Institute of Electronic and Electrical Incorporated Engineers
AMIMechE Associate Member of the Institution of Mechanical Engineers
AMIMinE Associate Member of the Institution of Mining Engineers
AMInstNA Associate Member of the Institution of Naval Architects
AMIPE Associate Member of the Institution of Production Engineers
AMIStructE Associate Member, Institute of Structural Engineers
AMP Air Ministry Personnel; Advanced Management Programme
AMPC Auxiliary Military Pioneer Corps
AMRAes Associate Member, Royal Aeronautical Society
AMRINA Associate Member, Royal Institution of Naval Architects
AMS Army Medical Service; Assistant Military Secretary
AMSI Associate Member of the Securities Institute
AMSO Air Member for Supply and Organisation
AMTPI Association of the Town Planning Institution
AnalaR Analytical Reagents
ANU Australian National University
AO Air Officer; Officer of the Order of Australia
AOA Air Officer in Charge of Administration
AOC Air Officer Commanding
AOC-in-C Air Officer Commanding-in-Chief
AOD Army Ordnance Department
AOEng Air Officer Engineering
AOER Army Officer's Emergency Reserve
AOM Air Officer Maintenance
APA American Psychiatric Association
APEX Association of Professional, Executive, Clerical and Computer Staffs
APM Assistant Provost Marshal
APP Associate of Psychoanalytic Psychotherapy
Appt Appointment
APR Accredited Public Relations Practitioner
APRA Association of Political Risks Analysts
APS American Physical Society
AQ Administration and Quartering
AQH Association of Quality Assurance in Healthcare
AQMG Assistant Quarter-Master General
ARA Associate of the Royal Academy
ARAD Associate, Royal Academy of Dancing
ARAeS Associate of the Royal Aeronautical Society
ARAM Associate of the Royal Academy of Music
ARB Architects' Registration Board (formerly ARCUK); Airworthiness Requirements Board
ARBA Associate of the Royal Society of British Artists
ARBS Associate of the Royal Society of British Sculptors
ARC Agricultural Research Council
ARCA Associate of Royal College of Art
ARCM Associate of the Royal College of Music
ARCO Associate of the Royal College of Organists
ARCS Associate, Royal College of Science
ARCST Associate, Royal College of Science and Technology
ARCUK Architects' Registration Council of the UK (now ARB)
ARCVS Associate of the Royal College of Veterinary Surgeons
ARE Associate, Royal Society of Painter-Etchers and Engravers
ARELS Association of Recognised English Language Schools
ARIAS Associate, Royal Incorporation of Architects in Scotland
ARIBA Associate of the Royal Institute of British Architects
ARIC Associate of the Royal Institute of Chemistry
ARICS Associate of the Royal Institution of Chartered Surveyors
ARINA Associate of the Royal Institution of Naval Architects
ARMCM Associate, Royal Manchester College of Music
Armd Armoured
ARP Air Raid Precautions
ARPS Associate of the Royal Photographic Society
ARRC Associate of the Royal Red Cross
ARSA Associate of the Royal Scottish Academy
ARSM Associate of the Royal School of Mines
ARTC Associate of the Royal Technical College
ARWS Associate of the Royal Society of Painters in Water Colours
ASA Associate Member of the Society of Actuaries; Australian Society of Accountants; Army Sailing Association
ASAA Associate of the Society of Incorporated Accountants and Auditors
ASC Army Service Corps
ASCAP American Society of Composers, Authors and Publishers
ASD Armament Supply Department
ASEAN Association of South East Asian Nations
ASF Associate of the Institute of Shipping and Forwarding Agents
A&SH Argyll and Sutherland Highlanders
ASIAD Associate, Society of Industrial Artists and Designers
ASLIB Association of Special Libraries and Information Bureaux
ASM Association of Senior Members
ASME American Society of Mechanical Engineers; Association for the Study of Medical Education
ASO Air Staff Officer
assas assassinated
ASSC Accounting Standards Steering Committee
Assoc Association; Associate; Associated
Asst Assistant
Assur Assurance
ASTD Associate Member, Society of Typographic Designers
ASTMS Association of Scientific, Technical and Managerial Staff (now MSF)
ASVO Association of State Veterinary Officers
ASWE Admiralty Surface Weapons Establishment
ATA Air Transport Auxiliary
ATAF Allied Tactical Air Force
ATC Air Training Corps; Art Teachers' Certificate
ATCL Associate, Trinity College of Music, London
ATD Art Teachers' Diploma
ATI Associate, Textile Institute
ATII Associate Member, Institute of Taxation
ATO Ammunitions Technical Officer
ATS Auxiliary Territorial Service
AUEW Amalgamated Union of Engineering Workers
Aust Australian, Australia
AUT Association of University Teachers
Authy Authority
Aux Auxiliary
Ave Avenue
AVMA Action for the Victims of Medical Accidents
AVR Army Volunteer Reserve
AWeldI Associate of the Welding Institute
AWPR Association of Women in Public Relations
AWRE Atomic Weapons Research Establishment
AWS Graduate of Air Warfare Course

B

b born
BA Bachelor of Arts; British Airways
BAAB British Amateur Athletics Board
BAAL British Association for Applied Linguistics
BAAS British Association for the Advancement of Science
BAc Bachelor in Acupuncture
BAC Battersea Arts Centre; British Aircraft Corporation
BACB British Association of Communicators in Business
Bacc Baccalauréat
BADA British Antique Dealers' Association
BAEM British Association for Accident and Emergency Medicine
BAF British Athletic Federation (formerly AAA)
BAFO British Air Forces Occupation
BAFSEA British Air Forces South East Asia
BAFTA British Academy of Film and Television Arts
BAgric Bachelor of Agriculture
BAI Baccalarius in Arte Ingeniaria
BAIE British Association of Industrial Editors (now BACB)
BALPA British Airline Pilots' Association
BAO Bachelor of Obstetrics
BAOL British Association of Otolaryngologists
BAOMS British Association of Oral and Maxillo-Facial Surgeons
BAOR British Army of the Rhine
BARB Broadcasters' Audience Research Board
BARC British Automobile Racing Club
BArch Bachelor of Architecture
BARR British Association of Rheumatology Rehabilitation (now BSR)
Barr Barrister
Bart's St Bartholomew's Hospital
BAS Bachelor in Agricultural Science

BASc Bachelor of Applied Science
BASC British Association of Shooting and Conservation
BASCA British Academy of Songwriters, Composers and Authors
Batty Battery
BAUA Business Aviation Users' Association
BBA British Bankers' Association; Bachelor of Business Administration
BBC British Broadcasting Corporation
BBS Bachelor of Business Studies
BBSRC Biotechnology and Biological Sciences Research Council (formerly AFRC)
BC British Columbia; Borough Council
BCE Bachelor of Civil Engineering
BCh Bachelor of Surgery
BChir Bachelor of Surgery
BCL Bachelor in Civil Law
BCOF British Commonwealth Occupation Force in Japan
BCom Bachelor of Commerce
BCS British Computer Society; Bengal Civil Service
BCU British Canoeing Union
BD Bachelor in Divinity
Bd Board
BDA British Dental Association; Broadcasting Design Association
Bdcast Broadcast
Bde Brigade
BDF Barking Dog of Fulham (now decd)
BDMA British Direct Marketing Association (now DMA)
BDS Bachelor of Dental Surgery
BE Bachelor of Engineering
BEA British European Airways
BEAMA Federation of British Electrotechnical and Allied Manufacturers Association
BEC Business Education Council (now see BTEC)
BEcon Bachelor of Economics
BECTU Broadcast Entertainment Cinematograph and Theatre Union
BEd Bachelor of Education
BEE Bachelor of Electrical Engineering
BEF British Expeditionary Force
BEM British Empire Medal
BEng Bachelor of Engineering
BERA British Educational Research Association
BESO British Executive Services Overseas
BETRO British Export Trade Organisation
BFBS British Forces Broadcasting Service
BFI British Film Institute
BFME British Forces Middle East
BFPO British Forces Post Office
BFSS British Field Sports Society
BGGS Brigadier-General, General Staff
BGS Brigadier, General Staff
BHA British Hoteliers' Association (formerly BHRCA)
BHRA British Hydromechanics Research Association
BHRCA British Hotel, Restaurant and Catering Association (now BHA)
BHS British Horse Society
BHy Bachelor of Hygiene
BIBA British Insurance Brokers' Association
BICC British Insulated Callender's Cables
BIEE British Institute of Energy Economics
BIFU Banking, Insurance and Finance Union
BIIBA British Insurance and Investment Brokers' Association
BIID British Institute of Interior Design
BIM British Institute of Management
BINDT British Institute of Non-destructive Testing
BIPP British Institute of Professional Photographers
BIR British Institute of Radiology
BISPA British Independent Steel Producers' Association
BJSM British Joint Service Mission
BJur Bachelor in Jurisprudence
BL Bachelor of Law; British Leyland
BLA British Army of Liberation
Bldgs Buildings
BLESMA British Limbless Ex-servicemen's Association
BLitt Bachelor of Letters
BM Bachelor of Medicine (Oxford); Brigade Major
BMA British Medical Association
BMedSci Bachelor of Medical Science
BMet Bachelor of Metallurgy
BMH British Military Hospital
BMJ British Medical Journal
BMM British Military Mission
BMus Bachelor of Music
Bn Battalion
BNAF British North Africa Force
BNC Brasenose College (Oxford)
BNES British Nuclear Energy Society
BNF British Nuclear Fuels
BNFL British Nuclear Fuels Ltd
BNMS British Nuclear Medicine Society
BNSC British National Space Centre
BNurs Bachelor of Nursing
BOA British Olympic Association
BOAC British Overseas Airways Corporation
BOT Board of Trade
BOTB British Overseas Trade Board
BP British Petroleum
BPA British Paediatric Association
BPG Broadcasting Press Guild
BPharm Bachelor of Pharmacy
BPhil Bachelor of Philosophy
BPI British Phonographic Industry
BPIF British Printing Industries' Federation
BPMF British Postgraduate Medical Federation
BPNA British Paediatric Neurology Association
Br British
BR British Railways
BRA British Rheumatism and Arthritis Association
BRCS British Red Cross Society
BRDC British Racing Drivers' Club
Brig Brigadier
BRNC Britannia Royal Naval College
bro brother
BS Bachelor of Surgery; Bachelor of Science (US)
BSA Building Societies' Association
BSAC British Sub Aqua Club
BSACI British Society for Allergy and Clinical Immunology
BSc Bachelor of Science
BSC British Steel Corporation; British Society of Cinematographers
BSCC British-Soviet Chamber of Commerce
BSDA British Soft Drinks Association
BSI British Standards Institution; British Society for Immunology
BSIRA British Scientific Instrument Research Association
BSR British Society of Rheumatology
BSS Bachelor of Social Sciences (USA)
Bt Baronet
BT British Telecom
BTA British Troops in Austria; British Tourist Authority; British Theatre Association
Bt-Col Brevet-Colonel
Btcy Baronetcy
BTDB British Transport Docks Board (now ABP)
BTEC Business and Technicians Education Council
BTh Bachelor of Theology
Btss Baronetess
BUPA British United Provident Association
BV Besloten Vennootschap (Netherlands, Ltd)
BVA British Veterinary Association
BVetMed Bachelor of Veterinary Medicine
BVMS Bachelor of Veterinary Medicine and Surgery
BVSc Bachelor of Veterinary Science
BWI British West Indies
BWM British War Medal
BWS Member of the British Watercolour Society

C

c children
C Conservative
ca circa
CA Chartered Accountant; County Alderman
CAA Civil Aviation Authority
CAABU Council for the Advancement of Arab and British Understanding
CAB Citizens' Advice Bureau
CACA Chartered Association of Certified Accountants
CACTM Central Advisory Council of Training for the Ministry
Calif California
CAM Communications, Advertising and Marketing
CAMC Canadian Army Medical Corps
CAMRA Campaign for Real Ale
Cantab Of Cambridge University
Capt Captain
CARE Cottage and Rural Enterprises
CAS Chief of Air Staff
CB Companion of the Order of the Bath
CBA Council for British Archaeology
CBC County Borough Council
CBE Commander of the Order of the British Empire
CBI Confederation of British Industry
CBIM Companion, British Institute of Management (now CIMgt)
CBiol Chartered Biologist
CBIREE Companion, British Institute of Radio and Electronic Engineers
CBSO City of Birmingham Symphony Orchestra
CC County Council; Companion of the Order of Canada; Cricket Club
CCA County Councils' Association
CCAB Consultative Committee of Accounting Bodies
CCBE Consultative Council of European Bars and Law Societies (Commission Consultative des Barreaux de la Communant Europèene)
CCBI Council of Churches for Britain and Ireland
CCC Corpus Christi College; County Cricket Club
CCF Combined Cadet Force
CCG(BE) Control Commission, Germany (British Element)
CChem Chartered Chemist
CCHMS Central Committee for Hospital and Medical Services
CCIBS Companion, Chartered Institute of Building Services
CCncllr County Councillor
CCO Conservative Central Office

CCPR Central Council of Physical Recreation
CCRA Commander Corps, Royal Artillery
CCRE Commander Corps of Royal Engineers
CCRSigs Commander Corps of Royal Signals
CCS Casualty Clearing Station
CCSC Central Consultants and Specialists' Committee
CD Canadian Forces Decorations; Compact Disc
CDipAF Certified Diploma in Accounting and Finance
Cdr Commander
Cdre Commodore
CD-ROM Compact Disc read-only memory
CDS Chief of Defence Staff
CE Chief Engineer; Church of England
CEDEP Centre Européen d'Education Permanente
CEDR Centre for Dispute Resolution
CEFIC Conseil Européen des Federations de l'Industrie Chimique
CEGB Central Electricity Generating Board
CEI Council of Engineering Institutions
CEng Chartered Engineer
CERI Centre d'Etudes et de Recherches Internationales (Paris)
CERN Conseil (now Organisation) Européenne pour la Recherche Nucléaire
CertEd Certificate of Education
CertTheol Certificate of Theology
CEST Council for the Exploitation of Science and Technology
CF Chaplain to the Forces
CFBOA Companion Fellow, British Orthopaedic Association
CFM Canadian Forces Medal
CFR Commander, Order of the Federal Republic of Nigeria
CFS Central Flying School
CFTC Commonwealth Fund for Technical Cooperation
C&G City and Guilds of London Institute (formerly CGLI)
CGA Country Gentlemen's Association
CGeol Chartered Geologist
CGIA City and Guilds of London Insignia Award
CGLI City and Guilds of London Institute (now C&G)
CGS Chief of the General Staff
CH Companion of Honour
ChB Bachelor of Surgery
CHB Companion of Honour Barbados
CHC Community Health Council
ChCh Christ Church (Oxford)
Chem Chemical
Chev Chevalier
Chllr Chancellor
Chm Chairman
ChM Mastery of Surgery
ChStJ Chaplain of the Order of St John of Jerusalem
CI Order of the Crown of India; Channel Islands
CIAgrE Companion, Institute of Agricultural Engineers
CIArb Chartered Institute of Arbitrators
CIBS Chartered Institute of Building Services
CIBSE Chartered Institution of Building Services Engineers
CIC Construction Industry Council
CICeram Companion, Institute of Ceramics
CICHE Committee for International Co-operation in Higher Education
CID Criminal Investigation Department
CIE Companion of the Order of the Indian Empire
CIEE Companion, Institution of Electrical Engineers
CIGE Companion, Institute of Gas Engineers
CIGRE Conference Internationale des Grands Résaux Electriques
CIGS Chief of the Imperial General Staff
CII Chartered Insurance Institute
CIM Chartered Institute of Marketing
CIMA Chartered Institute of Management Accountants
CIMarE Companion of the Institute of Marine Engineers
CIMechE Companion of the Institution of Mechanical Engineers
CIMgt Companion, Institute of Management
C-in-C Commander-in-Chief
CInstE Companion of the Institute of Energy
CInstSMM Companion, Institute of Sales and Marketing Management
CIOB Chartered Institute of Building
CIPD Companion, Institute of Personnel and Development (formerly CIPM)
CIPFA Chartered Institute of Public Finance and Accountancy
CIPM Companion, Institute of Personnel Management (now CIPD)
CIRIA Construction Industry Research and Information Association
CIT Chartered Institute of Transport
CLA Country Landowners' Association
CLit Companion of the Royal Society of Literature
CLP Constituency Labour Party
CM Member of the Order of Canada; Master of Surgery
CMA Cost and Management Accountant (NZ)
CMath Chartered Mathematician
Cmd Commanded, command
Cmdg Commanding
Cmdt Commandant
CMF Commonwealth Military Forces; Central Mediterranean Force
CMG Companion of the Order of St Michael and St George
Cmmn Commission
cmmnd commissioned
Cmmr Commissioner
CMO Chief Medical Officer
CMP Corps of Military Police
CMS Church Missionary Society
CNAA Council for National Academic Awards
Cncl Council
Cncllr Councillor
CND Campaign for Nuclear Disarmament
CNRS Centre Nationale du Recherche Scientifique
Cnsllr Counsellor
CO Commanding Officer
Co Company; County
COD Communications and Operations Department (FO)
C of C Chamber of Commerce
C of E Church of England
COGS Chief of General Staff
COHSE Confederation of Health Service Employees
COI Central Office of Information
Co L Coalition Liberal
Col Colonel
Coll College
COMMET Council of Mechanical and Metal Trade Associations
Comp Comprehensive
Conf Conference
Confedn Confederation
Conn Connecticut
Cons Conservative
Conslt Consultant
consltg consulting
contrib contributor, contributed, contribution
Co-op Co-operative
Corp Corporation, corporate
Corpl Corporal
Corr Correspondent
COS Chief of Staff
COSIRA Council for Smaller Industries in Rural Areas
cous cousin
CP Captain of a Parish (IOM)
CPA Commonwealth Parliamentary Association; Chartered Patent Agent
CPC Conservative Political Centre
CPE Common Professional Examination (of the Law Society)
CPhys Chartered Physicist
CPL Chief, Personnel & Logistics
CPM Colonial Police Medal
CPRE Council for the Protection of Rural England
CPRS Central Policy Review Staff
CPS Crown Prosecution Service; Canadian Pacific Steamships
CPSA Civil and Public Services Association
CPsychol Chartered Psychologist
CPU Commonwealth Press Union
CQSW Certificate of Qualification in Social Work
cr created
CRA Commander Royal Artillery
CRAC Careers Research and Advisory Council
CRAeS Companion, Royal Aeronautical Society
CRASC Commander, Royal Army Service Corps
CRC Community Relations Commission
CRD Conservative Research Department
CRE Commanding Royal Engineers
CRMP Corps of Royal Military Police
CRO Commonwealth Relations Office
CS Clerk to the Signet
CSA Commonwealth Society of Artists; Chair Schools Association
CSCE Conference on Security and Co-operation in Europe
CSD Chartered Society of Designers
CSERB Computer Systems and Electronics Requirements Board
CSI Companion of the Order of the Star of India; Council for the Securities Industries
CSIR Council for Scientific and Industrial Research
CSIRO Commonwealth Scientific and Industrial Research Organisation
CSO Chief Signal Officer; Chief Staff Officer; Chief Scientific Officer; Central Statistical Office
CSS Council for Science and Society
CStat Chartered Statistician
CSTI Council of Science and Technology Institutes
CStJ Commander of the Order of St John of Jerusalem
CSV Community Service Volunteers
Ct Court
CTC City Technology College
Ctee Committee
CText Chartered Textile Technologist
CUF Common University Fund
CUP Cambridge University Press
CVCP Committee of Vice-Chancellors and Principals of the UK
CVL Central Veterinary Laboratory
CVO Commander of the Royal Victorian Order
CWA Crime Writers' Association
Cwlth Commonwealth
CzMC Czechoslovakian Military Cross

D

d died; death

da daughter
DA Diploma in Anaesthetics; Diploma in Art
DAAG Deputy-Assistant-Adjutant-General
DAA & QMG Deputy Assistant-Adjutant and Quartermaster-General
DACG Deputy Assistant Chaplain General
D & AD Designers & Art Directors' Association
DAD Deputy-Assistant Director
DADGMS Deputy Assistant Director General of Medical Services
DADMS Deputy Assistant Director Medical Services
DADOS Deputy Assistant Director of Ordnance Services
DADR Deputy Assistant Director of Remounts
DADST Deputy Assistant Director of Supplies and Transport
DAG Deputy-Adjutant-General
DAMS Deputy-Assistant Military Secretary
DAPM Deputy Assistant Provost Marshal
DAPS Director of Army Postal Services
DA & QMG Deputy-Adjutant and Quartermaster-General
DAQMG Deputy-Assistant-Quartermaster-General
DBA Doctor of Business Administration; Design Business Association
DBE Dame Commander of the Order of the British Empire
DBO Diploma of British Orthoptics
DC District Council; Doctor in Chiropractic
DCAe Diploma of the College of Aeronautics
DCAS Deputy Chief of Air Staff
DCB Dame Commander of the Order of the Bath
DCGS Deputy Chief of General Staff
DCH Diploma in Child Health
DCL Doctor of Civil Law
DCLI Duke of Cornwall's Light Infantry
DCM Distinguished Conduct Medal
DCMG Dame Commander Order of St Michael and St George
DCMS Deputy Commissioner Medical Services
DCSO Deputy Chief Scientific Officer
DCVO Dame Commander Royal Victorian Order
DD Doctor in Divinity
DDDS Deputy Director of Dental Services
DDes Doctor of Design
DDME Deputy Director of Mechanical Engineering
DDMS Deputy Director of Medical Services
DDO Diploma in Dental Orthopaedics
DDOS Deputy Director of Ordnance Services
DDPS Deputy Director of Personal Services
DDR Deputy Director of Remounts
DDS Doctor of Dental Surgery; Director of Dental Services
DDSD Deputy Director of Staff Duties
DDS & T Deputy Director Supplies and Transport
DDVS Deputy Director of Veterinary Services
DDWE & M Deputy Director of Works, Electrical and Mechanical
DE Doctor of Engineering (US)
DEA Department of Economic Affairs
decd deceased
DEd Doctor of Education
Def Defence
Del Delegate
Delgn Delegation
Dem Democrat
DEM Diploma in Education Management
DEME Director of Electrical and Mechanical Engineering
DEng Doctor of Engineering
Dep Deputy
Dept Department
DES Department of Education and Science (now DfEE)
DèsL Docteur ès Lettres
DesRCA Designer of the Royal College of Art
Devpt Development
DFA Doctor of Fine Arts
DFC Distinguished Flying Cross
DFE Department for Education
DfEE Department for Education and Employment
DFFP Diploma, Faculty of Family Planning and Reproductive Health
DFH Diploma of the Faraday House
DFM Distinguished Flying Medal; Diploma in Forensic Medicine
DG Director General
DGAMS Director-General of Army Medical Services
DGCStJ Dame Grand Cross of the Order of St John of Jerusalem
DGDP Diploma in General Dental Practice
DGMS Director-General of Medical Services
DGS Diploma in Graduate Studies
DGStJ Dame of Grace of the Order of St John of Jerusalem
DH Doctor of Humanities
DHA District Health Authority
DHL Doctor of Humane Letters; Doctor of Hebrew Literature
DHMSA Diploma in the History of Medicine (Society of Apothecaries)
DHQ District Headquarters
DHSS Department of Health and Social Security
DHy Doctor of Hygiene
DIC Diploma of the Imperial College
DIH Diploma in Industrial Health
Dio Diocese
Dip Diploma; Diplomatic
DipAD Diploma in Arts and Design
DipAg Diploma in Agriculture
DipArch Diploma in Architecture
DipAvMed Diploma in Aviation Medicine
DipBA Diploma in Business Administration
DipCAM Diploma in Communications, Advertising and Marketing of the CAM Foundation
DipCD Diploma in Civic Design
DipEd Diploma in Education
DipESL Diploma in English as a second Language
DipHA Diploma in Hospital Administration
DipHSM Diploma in Health Services Management
DipLA Diploma in Landscape Architecture
DipLD Diploma in Landscape Design
DipLOR Diploma in Operations Research
DipM Diploma in Marketing
DipMRS Diploma of the Market Research Society
DipN Diploma in Nursing
DipOrthMed Diploma in Orthopaedic Medicine
DipTh Diploma in Theology
DipTP Diploma in Town Planning
Dir Director
dis dissolved (marriage)
Dist District
Div Division
Divnl Divisional
DJAG Deputy Judge Advocate General
DJStJ Dame of Justice of the Order of St John of Jerusalem
DK Most Esteemed Family Order of Brunei
DL Deputy-Lieutenant for the County of
DLC Diploma Loughborough College
DLI Durham Light Infantry
DLit Doctor of Literature
DLitt Doctor of Letters
DLO Diploma in Laryngology and Otology/Otorhinolaryngology
DM Doctor of Medicine
DMA Direct Marketing Association; Diploma in Municipal Administration
DMD Doctor in Dental Medicine
DME Director of Mechanical Engineering
DMGO Division Machine Gun Officer
DMI Director Military Intelligence
DMJ Diploma in Medical Jurisprudence
DMO & I Director Military Operations and Intelligence
DMRD Diploma in Medical Radiological Diagnosis
DMRE Diploma in Medical Radiology and Electrology
DMRT Diploma in Medical Radiotherapy
DMS Director of Medical Services; Diploma in Management Studies
DMSI Director of Management and Support Intelligence
DMT Director of Military Training
DMus Doctor of Music
DNI Director of Naval Intelligence
DNO Director of Naval Ordnance
DO Diploma in Ophthalmology; Divisional Officer; Diploma in Osteopathy
DOAE Defence Operational Analysis Establishment
DObstRCOG Diploma Royal College of Obstetricians and Gynaecologists
DOC District Officer Commanding
DOE Department of Environment
DOI Department of Industry
DOMS Diploma in Ophthalmic Medicine
DOR Director of Operational Requirements
DOrthRCS Diploma in Orthodontics Royal College of Surgeons
DOS Director of Ordnance Services
DPA Diploma in Public Administration
DPCP Department of Prices and Consumer Protection
DPH Diploma in Public Health
DPhil Doctor of Philosophy
DPL Director of Pioneers and Labour
DPM Diploma in Psychological Medicine
DPMO Deputy Principal Medical Officer
DPP Director of Public Prosecutions
DPR Director of Public Relations
DPS Director of Personal Services
DQMG Deputy Quartermaster-General
Dr Doctor
DRC Diploma of the Royal College of Science and Technology, Glasgow
DRCOG Doctor of the Royal College of Obstetricians and Gynaecologists
DRD Diploma in Restorative Dentistry
Dr jur Doctor of Laws
DrPA Doctor of Public Administration (USA)
DRSAMD Diploma of the Royal Scottish Academy of Music and Drama
DRVO Deputy Regional Veterinary Officer
DS Directing Staff
DSA Diploma in Social Administration
DSAC Defence Scientist Advisory Committee
DSAO Diplomatic Service Administration Office
DSC Distinguished Service Cross
DSc Doctor of Science
DSCHE Diploma of the Scottish Council for Health Education
DSD Director of Staff Duties
DSIR Department of Scientific and Industrial Research
DSLitt Doctor of Sacred Letters
DSM Distinguished Service Medal (USA)
DSO Companion of the Distinguished Service Order
DSocSc Doctor of Social Sciences (see also DSSc)
dsp decessit sine prole (died without issue)
DSP Docteur en Sciences Politiques (Montreal)

DSS Department of Social Security
DSSc Doctor of Social Sciences (see also DSocSc)
DSSS Doctor of Science in Social Sciences
DS & T Director of Supplies and Transport
DStJ Dame of Grace of the Order of St John of Jerusalem
DTech Doctor of Technology
DTh Doctor of Theology
DTI Department of Trade and Industry
DTM Diploma in Tropical Medicine
DTM&H Diploma in Tropical Medicine and Hygiene
DUniv Doctor of the University
DVFS Director, Veterinary Field Services
DVM Doctor of Veterinary Medicine
DVO Divisional Veterinary Officer
DVS Director of Veterinary Services
DVSM Diploma of Veterinary State Medicine
DX Document Exchange

E

E East; Earl; England
EASA Ecclesiastical Architects and Surveyors' Association
EBRD European Bank for Reconstruction & Development
EBU European Broadcasting Union
EC European Commission
ECGD Export Credit Guarantee Department
Econ Economic
Ed Editor; edited
ED Efficiency Decoration; European Democratic (Group)
EDC Economic Development Committee
EDG European Democratic Group (UK Conservative Group, European Parliament)
edn edition
Educn Education
educnl educational
EEA European Economic Area
EEF Engineering Employers' Federation
EETPU Electrical, Electronic, Telecommunications and Plumbing Union
EFTA European Free Trade Association
EIU Economist Intelligence Unit
eld eldest
EMBL European Molecular Biology Laboratory
EMBO European Molecular Biology Organisation
EMS Emergency Medical Service
Eng English; England
Engr Engineer
Engrg Engineering
ENO English National Opera
ENSA Entertainments National Services Association
ENT Ear, Nose and Throat
EPLP European Parliamentary Labour Party
EPP European People's Party
EPSRC Engineering and Physical Sciences Research Council (formerly SERC)
er elder
ERA Electrical Research Association
ERD Emergency Reserve Decoration
ESN Educationally Sub Normal
Esq Esquire
ESRC Economic and Social Research Council
ESRO European Space Research Organisation
Estab Established; Establishment
EU European Union (formerly European Community)
Eur Ing European Engineer
Euro European
Exec Executive
Exhbn Exhibition
Expdn Expedition
Ext Extinct; Extension

F

f father
FA Football Association
FAA Fellow of the Australian Academy of Science
FAAAS Fellow, American Academy of Arts & Sciences
FAAP Fellow, American Academy of Paediatrics
FAAV Fellow, Central Association of Agricultural Valuers
FACC Fellow, American College of Cardiology
FACCA Fellow of the Association of Certified and Corporate Accountants
FACD Fellow, American College of Dentistry
FACE Fellow, Australian College of Education
FACOG Fellow, American College of Obstetricians and Gynaecologists
FACP Fellow, American College of Physicians
FACS Fellow, American College of Surgeons
FACT Fellow, Association of Corporate Treasurers
FACVT Fellow, American College of Veterinary Toxicology
FAE Fellow of the Academy of Experts (formerly FBAE)
FAES Fellow of the Audio Engineering Society
FAI Fellow of the Chartered Auctioneers and Estate Agents' Institute; Fellow, Financial Accountants' Institute
FAIA Fellow, American Institute of Architects
FAIE Fellow, British Association of Industrial Editors (now FCB)
FAIM Fellow of the Australian Institute of Management
FAIP Fellow of the Australian Institute of Physics
FAIRE Fellow of the Australian Institute of Radio Engineers
FALPA Fellow of the Incorporated Auctioneers and Land Property Agents
FAMEME Fellow, Association of Mining, Electrical and Mechanical Engineers
FAMI Fellow of the Australian Marketing Institute
FAMS Fellow of the Ancient Monuments Society
FANY First Aid Nursing Yeomanry
FANZCA Fellow of the Australian and New Zealand College of Anaesthetists
FAO Food and Agricultural Organisation
FAPA Fellow, American Psychiatric Association
FAPM Fellow of the Association of Project Managers
FAQMC Fellow, Association of Quality Management Consultants
FARELF Far East Land Forces
FAS Fellow, Antiquarian Society
FASA Fellow of the Australian Society of Accountants
FASCE Fellow of the American Society of Civil Engineers
FASI Fellow of the Architects and Surveyors' Institute
FASME Fellow of the American Society of Mechanical Engineers
FBA Fellow of the British Academy
FBAA Fellow, British Acupuncture Association; Fellow, British Archaeological Association
FBAE Fellow of the British Academy of Experts (now FAE)
FBAM Fellow, British Academy of Management
FBCO Fellow of British College of Opticians
FBCS Fellow, British Computer Society
FBEC(S) Fellow, Business Education Council (Scotland)
FBEng Fellow of the Association of Building Engineers
FBHI Fellow of the British Horological Institute
FBI Federation of British Industries
FBIAC Fellow, British Institute of Agricultural Consultants
FBIBA Fellow of the British Insurance Brokers' Association
FBICSc Fellow, British Institute of Cleaning Science
FBID Fellow, British Institute of Interior Design
FBIEE Fellow of the British Institute of Energy Economists
FBIM Fellow of the British Institute of Management (now FIMgt)
FBIPP Fellow of the British Institute of Professional Photographers
FBIS Fellow of the British Interplanetary Society
FBKSTS Fellow, British Kinematograph, Sound and Television Society
FBOA Fellow of the British Optical Association; Fellow, British Orthopaedic Association
FBPsS Fellow, British Psychological Society
FBSI Fellow of the Boot and Shoe Industry
FC Football Club
FCA Fellow of the Institute of Chartered Accountants
FCAI Fellow of the Canadian Aeronautical Institute
FCAM Fellow, Communications Advertising & Marketing Educational Foundation
FCAnaes Fellow, College of Anaesthetists
FCB Fellow, British Association of Communicators in Business (formerly FAIE)
FCBSI Fellow of the Chartered Building Societies Institute
FCCA Fellow of the Chartered Association of Certified Accountants
FCCS Fellow of the Corporation of Certified Secretaries
FCDA Fellow of the Company Directors' Association of Australia
FCEC Federation of Civil Engineering Contractors
FCFA Fellow of the Cookery and Food Association
FCFI Fellow, Clothing and Footwear Institute
FCGI Fellow, City and Guilds of London Institute
FCIA Fellow, Corporation of Insurance Agents
FCIArb Fellow, Chartered Institute of Arbitrators
FCIB Fellow of the Corporation of Insurance Brokers; Fellow, Chartered Institute of Bankers
FCIBS Fellow, Chartered Institution of Building Services; Fellow, Chartered Institute of Bankers of Scotland
FCIBSE Fellow, Chartered Institution of Building Service Engineers
FCII Fellow of the Chartered Insurance Institute
FCIM Fellow, Chartered Institute of Marketing (formerly FInstM)
FCInstT Fellow, Chartered Institute of Taxation (formerly FInstT)
FCIOB Fellow, Chartered Institute of Building
FCIPA Fellow, Chartered Institute of Patent Agents (now CPA)
FCIPS Fellow, Chartered Institute of Purchasing and Supply (received Royal Charter 1992)
FCIS Fellow of the Institute of Chartered Secretaries and Administrators (formerly Chartered Institute of Secretaries)
FCIT Fellow of the Chartered Institute of Transport
FCIWEM Fellow, Chartered Institution of Water and Environmental Management (formerly FIWEM)
FCMA Fellow, Institute of Cost and Management Accountants
FCO Foreign and Commonwealth Office
FCOG Fellow of the College of Obstetrics and Gynaecology
FCollP Ordinary Fellow, College of Preceptors
FCommA Fellow of the Society of Commercial Accountants
FCOphth Fellow of the College of Ophthalmology (now FRCOphth)

FCP	Academic Fellow, College of Preceptors
FCPA	Fellow, Australian Society of Certified Practising Accountants
FCPS	Fellow of the College of Physicians and Surgeons
FCS	Fellow of the Chemical Society; Federation of Conservative Students (now Conservative Collegiate Forum)
FCSD	Fellow, Chartered Society of Designers
FCT	Fellow of the Institute of Corporate Treasurers
FCWA	Fellow of the Institute of Cost and Works Accountants
FDI	Fédération Dentaire Internationale
FDR	Federalische Deutsche Republik
FDS	Fellow in Dental Surgery
FDSRCS	Fellow in Dental Surgery Royal College of Surgeons of England
FE	Further Education
FEAF	Far East Air Force
FEBU	Fellowship of European Boards of Urology
Fed	Federal
Fedn	Federation
FEIS	Fellow of the Educational Institute of Scotland
Fell	Fellow
FEng	Fellow, Royal Academy of Engineering
FES	Fellow of the Entomological Society
FESC	Fellow, European Society of Cardiology
FESH	Federation of Ethical Stage Hypnotists
FFA	Fellow of the Faculty of Actuaries (Scotland); Fellow of the Institute of Financial Accountants
FFAEM	Fellow, Faculty of Accident & Emergency Medicine
FFARACS	Fellow, Faculty of Anaesthetists Royal Australasian College of Surgeons
FFARCS	Fellow, Faculty of Anaesthetists, Royal College of Surgeons (now FRCA)
FFARCSI	Fellow, Faculty of Anaesthetists Royal College of Surgeons of Ireland
FFAS	Fellow of the Faculty of Architects and Surveyors
FFB	Fellow of the Faculty of Building
FFCM	Fellow, Faculty of Community Medicine (now FFPHM)
FFDRCSI	Fellow, Faculty of Dentistry, Royal College of Surgeons in Ireland
FFHom	Fellow, Faculty of Homeopathy
FFOM	Fellow, Faculty of Occupational Medicine
FFPHM	Fellow, Faculty of Public Health Medicine (formerly FFCM)
FFPM	Fellow, Faculty of Pharmaceutical Medicine
FFR	Fellow of the Faculty of Radiologists
FFY	Fife and Forfar Yeomanry
FGA	Fellow of the Gemmological Association
FGIS	Fellow, Guild of Incorporated Surveyors
FGS	Fellow of the Geographical Society
FGSM	Fellow, Guildhall School of Music
FHA	Fellow, Institute of Health Service Administrators
FHCIMA	Fellow of the Hotel Catering and Institutional Management Association
FHG	Fellow in Heraldry and Genealogy
FHKIE	Fellow, Hong Kong Institute of Engineers
FHSM	Fellow, Institute of Health Services Management
FIA	Fellow, Institute of Actuaries; Fédération Internationale de L'Automobile
FIAAS	Fellow Architect Member of the Incorporated Association of Architects and Surveyors
FIAC	Fellow, Institute of Company Accountants
FIAeS	Fellow of the Institute of Aeronautical Sciences
FIAgrE	Fellow, Institution of Agricultural Engineers
FIAL	Fellow, International Institute of Arts and Letters
FIAM	Fellow, International Academy of Management
FIArb	Fellow of the Institute of Arbitration
FIAS	Fellow, Institute of Aeronautical Sciences (US); Fellow of the Incorporated Society of Architects
FIB	Fellow of the Institute of Bankers (now FCIB)
FIBC	Fellow, Institute of Business Counsellors
FIBF	Fellow, Institute of British Foundrymen
FIBiol	Fellow, Institute of Biology
FIBM	Fellow, Institute of Builders' Merchants
FIBrew	Fellow of the Institute of Brewing
FIBScot	Fellow of the Institute of Bankers in Scotland
FICA	Fellow of the Institute of Chartered Accountants in England and Wales (now FCA); Fellow of the Independent Consultants' Association
FICAS	Fellow, Institute of Chartered Accountants in Scotland
FICD	Fellow of the Institute of Civil Defence
FICE	Fellow of the Institution of Civil Engineers
FICeram	Fellow, Institute of Ceramics
FICFor	Fellow, Institute of Chartered Foresters
FIChemE	Fellow of the Institution of Chemical Engineers
FICM	Fellow, Institute of Credit Management
FICMA	Fellow, Institute of Cost and Management Accountants
FICS	Fellow of the Institute of Chartered Shipbrokers; Fellow of the International College of Surgeons
FICSA	Fellow of the Institute of Chartered Secretaries and Administrators
FIDM	Fellow, Institute of Direct Marketing
FIDPM	Fellow, Institute of Data Processing Management
FIE(Aust)	Fellow, Institution of Engineers (Australia)
FIED	Fellow, Institution of Engineering Design
FIEE	Fellow of the Institution of Electrical Engineers
FIEEE	Fellow, Institution of Electrical and Electronics Engineers (New York)
FIElecIE	Fellow, Institution of Electronic Incorporated Engineers
FIERE	Fellow of the Institution of Electronics and Radio Engineers
FIEx	Fellow, Institute of Export
FIFF	Fellow, Institute of Freight Forwarders
FIFireE	Fellow, Institute of Fire Engineers
FIFM	Fellow, Institute of Fisheries Management
FIFor	Fellow, Institute of Forestry
FIFST	Fellow of Food Science and Technology
FIGasE	Fellow of the Institute of Gas Engineers
FIGD	Fellow, Institute of Grocery Distribution
FIGE	Fellow, Institute of Gas Engineers
FIGeol	Fellow, Institute of Geology
FIHE	Fellow, Institute of Health Education
FIHort	Fellow of the Institute of Horticulture
FIHospE	Fellow, Institute of Hospital Engineering
FIHSM	Fellow, Institute of Health Service Managers
FIHT	Fellow, Institute of Highways and Transportation
FIHVE	Fellow, Institution of Heating and Ventilating Engineers
FIIA	Fellow, Institute of Internal Auditors
FIIM	Fellow, Institute of Industrial Managers
FIInfSc	Fellow, Institute of Information Scientists
FIInst	Fellow of the Imperial Institute
FIL	Fellow of the Institute of Linguists
FILA	Fellow of the Institute of Landscape Architects
FILDM	Fellow, Institute of Logistics and Distribution Management
FilDr	Doctor of Philosophy
FILog	Fellow, Institute of Logistics
FIM	Fellow, Institute of Materials (formerly Institute of Metals)
FIMA	Fellow of the Institute of Mathematics and its Applications
FIMarE	Fellow, Institute of Marine Engineers
FIMBRA	Financial Intermediaries, Managers and Brokers' Regulatory Association
FIMC	Fellow, Institute of Management Consultants
FIMechE	Fellow of the Institution of Mechanical Engineers
FIMF	Fellow, Institute of Metal Finishing
FIMfgE	Fellow, Institution of Manufacturing Engineers (merged with Institution of Electrical Engineers, 1991)
FIMFT	Fellow, Institute of Maxillo-Facial Technology
FIMgt	Fellow, Institute of Management (following merger of British Institute of Management and Institution of Industrial Managers in 1992)
FIMH	Fellow, Institute of Material Handling; Fellow, Institute of Military History
FIMI	Fellow, Institute of Motor Industry
FIMinE	Fellow, Institute of Mining Engineers
FIMIT	Fellow, Institute of Musical Instrument Technology
FIMLS	Fellow, Institute of Medical and Laboratory Sciences
FIMM	Fellow, Institution of Mining and Metallurgy
FIMT	Fellow of the Institute of the Motor Trade
FIMTA	Fellow of the Institute of Municipal Treasurers & Accountants
Fin	Finance; Financial
FInstAA	Fellow of the Institute of Administrative Accountants
FInstAM	Fellow, Institute of Administrative Management
FInstCES	Fellow of the Institution of Civil Engineering Surveyors
FInstCS	Fellow, Institute of Chartered Secretaries
FInstD	Fellow, Institute of Directors
FInstE	Fellow of the Institute of Energy
FInstF	Fellow of Institute of Fuel
FInstFF	Fellow, Institute of Freight Forwarders
FInst GasE	Fellow, Institution of Gas Engineers
FInstGeol	Fellow, Institute of Geologists
FInstHE	Fellow, Institution of Highway Engineers
FInstLEx	Fellow, Institute of Legal Executives
FInstM	Fellow, Institute of Marketing (now FCIM)
FInstMC	Fellow, Institute of Measurement and Control
FInstMSM	Fellow of the Institute of Marketing and Sales Management
FInstNDT	Fellow, Institute of Non-Destructive Testing
FInstP	Fellow of the Institute of Physics
FInstPet	Fellow of the Institute of Petroleum
FInstPI	Fellow, Institute Patentees (Incorporated)
FInstPS	Fellow, Institute of Purchasing and Supply (now FCIPS)
FInstSMM	Fellow, Institute of Sales and Marketing Management
FInstT	Fellow, Institute of Taxation (now FCInstT)
FInstTT	Fellow, Institute of Travel and Tourism
FINucE	Fellow of the Institute of Nuclear Engineers
FIOA	Fellow, Institute of Acoustics
FIOB	Fellow, Institute of Building
FIOP	Fellow of the Institute of Printing
FIOSc	Fellow of the Institute of Optical Science
FIP	Fellow, Institute of Packaging; Fellow Australian Institute of Petroleum
FIPA	Fellow of the Institute of Public Administration; Fellow of the Institute of Practitioners in Advertising; Fellow, Insolvency Practitioners' Association
FIPD	Fellow, Institute of Personnel and Development (following merger of FIPM and FITD)
FIPHE	Fellow of the Institution of Public Health Engineers
FIPI	Fellow, Institute of Professional Investigators
FIPlantE	Fellow, Institute of Plant Engineers
FIPM	Fellow, Institute of Personnel Management (now FIPD)
FIPR	Fellow of the Institute of Public Relations
FIProdE	Fellow of the Institute of Production Engineers (now FIEE)
FIPS	Fellow, Institute of Purchasing and Supply
FIPSM	Fellow, Institute of Physical Sciences in Medicine
FIQ	Fellow, Institute of Quarrying

FIQA Fellow, Institute of Quality Assurance
FIRE Fellow of the Institution of Radio Engineers
FIRI Fellow of the Institution of the Rubber Industry
FIRM Fellow, Institute of Risk Management
FIRSE Fellow, Institute of Railway Signalling Engineers
FIS Fellow, Institute of Stationers
FISA Fédération Internationale Societé d'Aviron
FISE Fellow of the Institute of Sanitary Engineers
FISP Fellow, Institute of Sales Promotion
FISTC Fellow, Institute of Scientific and Technical Communicators
FISTD Fellow, Imperial Society of Teachers of Dancing
FIStructE Fellow, Institution of Structural Engineers
FISVA Fellow, Incorporated Society of Valuers and Auctioneers
FITA Fellow, International Archery Federation
FITD Fellow, Institute of Training and Development (now FIPD)
FIWEM Fellow, Institution of Water and Environmental Management (now FCIWEM)
FIWES Fellow, Insititute of Water Engineers and Scientists
FIWSc Fellow, Institute of Wood Science
FJI Fellow, Institute of Journalists
FKC Fellow, King's College London
FLA Fellow, Library Association
FLAS Fellow, Land Agents Society
FLCM Fellow, London College of Music
FLCOM.ND Fellow, London College of Osteopathic Medicine with a Diploma in Naturopathy
FLI Fellow, Landscape Institute
FLIA Fellow, Life Assurance Association
FLS Fellow, Linnean Society
Flt Flight
Flt Lt Flight Lieutenant
FMA Fellow of the Museums Association
FMPA Fellow, Master Photographers' Association
FMS Fellow, Institute of Management Services; Fellow of the Medical Society; Fellow, Manorial Society
FNAEA Fellow, National Association of Estate Agents
Fndn Foundation
Fndr Founder
FNI Fellow, Nautical Institute
FNIAB Fellow, National Institute of Agricultural Botany
FO Foreign Office
FODA Fellow, Overseas Doctors' Association
FOR Fellowship of Operational Research
FPA Family Practitioners' Association
FPC Family Practitioner Committee
FPCA Fellow of Practising and Commercial Accountants
FPCS Fellow, Property Consultants' Society
FPEA Fellow, Physical Education Association
FPhS(Eng) Fellow, Philosophical Society of England
FPMI Fellow, Pensions Management Institute
FPMS Institution of Professionals, Managers and Specialists (formerly IPCS)
FPRI Fellow, Plastics and Rubber Institute
FPS Fellow of Philological Society of Great Britain
FRACDS Fellow, Royal Australian College of Dental Surgeons
FRACI Fellow, Royal Australian Chemical Institute
FRACP Fellow of the Royal Australasian College of Physicians
FRACR Fellow, Royal Australian College of Radiologists
FRACS Fellow of the Royal Australasian College of Surgeons
FRAeS Fellow, Royal Aeronautical Society
FRAgS Fellow, Royal Agricultural Societies
FRAI Fellow of the Royal Anthropological Institute
FRAIC Fellow, Royal Architectural Institute of Canada
FRAM Fellow of the Royal Academy of Music
FRAS Fellow of the Royal Astronomical Society; Fellow, Royal Asiatic Society
FRBS Fellow of the Royal Botanic Society; Fellow of the Royal British Society of Sculptors
FRCA Fellow, Royal College of Art; Fellow, Royal College of Anaesthetists (formerly FFARCS)
FRCAA Fellow of the Royal Cambrian Academy of Art
FRCGP Fellow, Royal College of General Practitioners
FRCM Fellow of the Royal College of Music
FRCN Fellow, Royal College of Nursing
FRCO Fellow of the Royal College of Organists
FRCO(CHM) Fellow of the Royal College of Organists with Diploma in Choir Training
FRCOG Fellow of the Royal College of Obstetricians and Gynaecologists
FRCOphth Fellow, Royal College of Ophthalmologists (formerly FCOphth)
FRCP Fellow of the Royal College of Physicians
FRCPA Fellow, Royal College of Pathologists of Australia
FRCPath Fellow, Royal College of Pathologists
FRCPE Fellow of the Royal College of Physicians of Edinburgh
FRCPEd Fellow of the Royal College of Physicians of Edinburgh
FRCPGlas Fellow, Royal College of Surgeons and Physicians, Glasgow
FRCPI Fellow, Royal College of Physicians in Ireland
FRCPS Fellow of the Royal College of Physicians and Surgeons (Glasgow)
FRCPsych Fellow, Royal College of Psychiatrists
FRCR Fellow, Royal College of Radiologists
FRCS Fellow of the Royal College of Surgeons; Fellow of the Royal Commonwealth Society (formerly Royal Empire Society)
FRCSEd Fellow, Royal College of Surgeons Edinburgh
FRCSGlas Fellow, Royal College of Surgeons and Physicians, Glasgow
FRCSI Fellow, Royal College of Surgeons in Ireland
FRCVS Fellow, Royal College of Veterinary Surgeons
FREconS Fellow of the Royal Economic Society
FRES Fellow, Royal Entomological Society
FRG Federal Republic of Germany
FRGS Fellow of the Royal Geographical Society
FRHistS Fellow of the Royal Historical Society
FRHS Fellow of the Royal Horticultural Society
FRIA Fellow, Royal Institute of Arbitrators
FRIAS Fellow of the Royal Incorporation of Architects in Scotland
FRIBA Fellow of the Royal Institute of British Architects
FRIC Fellow of the Royal Institute of Chemistry
FRICS Fellow of the Royal Institute of Chartered Surveyors
FRIN Fellow of the Royal Institute of Navigation
FRINA Fellow of the Royal Institution of Naval Architects
FRIPHH Fellow, Royal Institute of Public Health and Hygiene
FRMetS Fellow of the Royal Meteorological Society
FRMIA Fellow of the Royal Management Institute of Australia
FRMS Fellow of the Royal Microscopical Society
FRNCM Fellow, Royal Northern College of Music
FRNS Fellow of the Royal Numismatic Society
FRPharmS Fellow, Royal Pharmaceutical Society
FRPI Fellow, Institute of Rubber and Plastics Industry
FRPS Fellow of the Royal Photographic Society
FRPSL Fellow of the Royal Philatelic Society, London
FRS Fellow of the Royal Society
FRSA Fellow of the Royal Society of Arts
FRSAIre Fellow of the Royal Society of Antiquaries of Ireland
FRSAMD Fellow, Royal Scottish Academy of Music and Drama
FRSBS Fellow, Royal Society of British Sculptors
FRSC Fellow of the Royal Society of Canada; Fellow, Royal Society of Chemistry
FRSCM Fellow, Royal School of Church Music
FRSE Fellow of the Royal Society of Edinburgh
FRSGS Fellow of the Royal Scottish Geographical Society
FRSH Fellow of the Royal Society of Health
FRSL Fellow of the Royal Society of Literature
FRSM Fellow of the Royal Society of Medicine
FRSNZ Fellow, Royal Society of New Zealand
FRSocMed Fellow of the Royal Society of Medicine
FRSS Fellow, Royal Statistical Society
FRSTM & H Fellow, Royal Society of Tropical Medicine and Health
FRTPI Fellow, Royal Town Planning Institute
FRTS Fellow, Royal Television Society
FRVA Fellow of the Rating and Valuation Association
FRZS Scot Fellow of the Royal Zoological Society of Scotland
FSA Fellow of the Society of Antiquaries
FSAA Fellow of the Society of Incorporated Accountants and Auditors
FSAE Fellow, Society of Arts Education
FSAI Fellow, Society of Architectural Illustrators
FSAS Fellow, Society of Antiquaries of Scotland
FSCA Fellow, Society of Company and Commercial Accountants
FScotvec Fellow, Scottish Vocational Educational Council
FSDC Fellow, Society of Dyers and Colourists
FSE Fellow of Society of Engineers
FSF Fellow of the Institute of Shipping and Forwarding Agents
FSG Fellow of the Society of Genealogists
FSI Fellow, Royal Institution of Chartered Surveyors (see also FRICS)
FSIA Fellow of the Society of Industrial Artists
FSIAD Fellow, Society of Industrial Artists and Designers (now FCSD)
FSLAET Fellow, Society of Licensed Aircraft Engineers and Technologists
FSLGD Fellow, Society for Landscape and Garden Designs
FSMC Freeman, Spectacle Makers Company
FSMPTE Fellow of the Society of Motion Pictures and Television Engineers (USA)
FSS Fellow of the Royal Statistical Society (now CStat)
FSScA Fellow of the Royal Society of Science and Art, of London
FSTD Fellow, Society of Typographical Designers
FSUT Fellow, Society for Underwater Technology
FSVA Fellow, Incorporated Society of Valuers and Auctioneers
FTC Flying Training Command
FTCL Fellow of Trinity College of Music, London
FTI Fellow of the Textile Institute
FTII Fellow, Institute of Taxation
FTMA Fellow of the Telecommunications Managers' Association
FTS Fellow of the Tourism Society
Fus Fusiliers
FVI Fellow, Valuers' Institution
FWA Fellow, World Academy of Arts and Sciences
FWeldI Fellow, Welding Institute
FZS Fellow of the Zoological Institute

G

g great
Ga Georgia (USA)
GA Geologists' Association
GAA Gaelic Athletic Association
Gall Gallery
GAMTA General Aviation Manufacturers' Association
GATT General Agreement on Tariffs and Trade
GB Great Britain

GBA Governing Bodies Association
GBE Knight of the Grand Cross of the Order of the British Empire
GBSM Graduate, Birmingham and Midland Institute School of Music
GC George Cross; Grand Cross
GCB Knight Grand Cross of the Order of the Bath
GCBS General Council of British Shipping
GCGI Graduate, City and Guilds of London Institute
GCH Knight Grand Cross of Hanover
GCHQ Government Communications Headquarters
GCIE Knight/Dame Grand Commander of the Indian Empire
GCMG Knight/Dame Grand Cross of the Order of St Michael and St George
GCON Grand Cross, Order of the Niger
GCSE General Certificate in Secondary Education
GCSI Knight Grand Commander of the Star of India
GCStJ Bailiff or Dame Grand Cross of the Order of St John of Jerusalem
GCVO Knight or Dame of the Grand Cross of the Royal Victorian Order
gda granddaughter
GDBA Guide Dogs for the Blind Association
gdns gardens
GDR German Democratic Republic
Gds Guards
Gen General
Ger Germany
gf grandfather
ggda great granddaughter (and so forth)
ggs great grandson (and so forth)
GHQ General Headquarters
GIFireE Graduate, Institute of Fire Engineers
GIMechE Graduate Institution of Mechanical Engineers
GLC Greater London Council
GLR Greater London Radio
GM George Medal
gm grandmother
GMB Great Master of the Bath; (Union for) General, Municipal, Boilermakers
GMBATU General Municipal Boilermakers and Allied Trade Unions (now see GMB)
GMC General Medical Council
GME General Ministerial Examination
GMIE Grand Master of the Indian Empire
GMMG Grand Master of St Michael and St George
GMSI Grand Master of the Star of India
G&MWU General & Municipal Workers' Union
GMWU General and Municipal Workers' Union (later GMBATU, now see GMB)
gn great nephew; great niece
GO Grand Officier (de la Légion d'Honneur)
GOC General Officer Commanding
GOC-in-C General Officer Commanding-in-Chief
Govr Governor
Govt Government
GP General Practitioner; General Practice
Gp Group
Gp Capt Group Captain
GPDST Girls' Public Day School Trust
GPO General Post Office
grad graduate; graduated
GRCM Graduate of the Royal College of Music
GRSM Graduate of the Royal Schools of Music
GS General Staff; Grammar School
gs grandson
GSA Girls' School Association
GSM General Service Medal; Guildhall School of Music and Drama
GSO General Staff Officer
Gt Great
GTCL Graduate, Trinity College of Music, London
Gtr Greater
Guy's Guy's Hospital
GWR Great Western Railway

H

h heir
ha heir apparent
HA Health Authority; Historical Association
HAA Heavy Anti-Aircraft
HAC Honourable Artillery Company
HBM His/Her Britannic Majesty
hc honoris causa
HCF Hon Chaplain of the Forces
HCIMA Hotel, Catering and Institutional Management Association
HCITB Hotel and Catering Industry Training Board
HDipEd Higher Diploma in Education
HDip in Ed Honorary Diploma in Education
HE His/Her Excellency; Higher Education
HEFCE Higher Education Funding Council of England
HEQC Higher Education Quality Council
HESIN Higher Education Support for Industry in the North
HG Home Guard
HH His/Her Highness
HHA Historic Houses Association
HHD Doctor of Humanities (US)
High Cmmr High Commissioner
HIH His/Her Imperial Highness
HIllH His/Her Illustrious Highness
HIM His/Her Imperial Majesty
Hist Historical
HKIA Member, Hong Kong Institute of Architects
Hldgs Holdings
HLI Highland Light Infantry
HM His/Her Majesty('s)
HMC Headmasters' Conference; Hospital Management Committee
HMEH His Most Eminent Highness
HMHS Her Majesty's Hospital Ship
HMI Her Majesty's Inspectorate
HMOCS Her Majesty's Overseas Civil Service
HMS Her Majesty's Ship
HMSO Her Majesty's Stationery Office
HNC Higher National Certificate
HND Higher National Diploma
Hon Honourable; Honour (Judges); Honorary
Hons Honours
Hort Horticulture; Horticultural
Hosp Hospital
hp heir presumptive
HQ Headquarters
HRE Holy Roman Empire
HRH His/Her Royal Highness
HRHA Honorary Member, Royal Hibernian Academy
HRI Hon Member of the Royal Institute of Painters in Water Colours
HRSA Hon Member Royal Scottish Academy
HS High School
HSE Health and Safety Executive
HSH His/Her Serene Highness
husb husband
HVCert Health Visitors' Certificate

I

I Ireland
IA Indian Army
IAAF International Amateur Athletics Federation
IAB Brazilian Institute of Architects
IACP International Association of Chiefs of Police (USA)
IADR International Association for Dental Research
IAEA International Atomic Energy Agency
IAF Indian Air Force; Indian Auxiliary Force
IAMC Indian Army Medical Corps
IAOC Indian Army Ordnance Corps
IAOMS International Association of Oral and Maxillo-Facial Surgeons
IAP Institute of Analysts and Programmers
IAPS Incorporated Association of Preparatory Schools
IAPSO International Association for Physical Sciences of the Ocean
IARO Indian Army Reserve of Officers
IAS Indian Administrative Service
IASC Indian Army Service Corps
IATA International Air Transport Association
IATEFL International Association of Teachers of English as a Foreign Language
IBA Independent Broadcasting Authority
IBF International Boxing Federation
IBP Institute of British Photographers
IBPA International Bridge Players' Association
IBRC Insurance Brokers' Registration Council
IBRD International Bank for Reconstruction and Development (World Bank)
IBRO International Brain Research Organisation
i/c in charge of
ICA Institute of Contemporary Arts; Institute of Chartered Accountants
ICAEW Institute of Chartered Accountants of England and Wales
ICAS Institute of Chartered Accountants in Scotland
ICE Institution of Civil Engineers; In Car Entertainment
ICEF International Federation of Chemical, Energy and General Workers' Unions
ICF International Canoe Federation
ICFC Industrial and Commercial Finance Corporation
ICI Imperial Chemical Industries
ICL International Computers Ltd
ICOM International Council of Museums
ICRA International Centre for Research in Accounting
ICS Indian Civil Service
ICSA Institute of Chartered Secretaries and Administrators
ICSID International Council of Societies of Industrial Design
idc has completed a course at, or served for a year on the staff of, The Imperial Defence College
IDC Imperial Defence College
IDS Institute of Development Studies
IEA Institute of Economic Affairs
IEE Institution of Electrical Engineers
IEEE Institute of Electrical and Electronic Engineers (NY)

IEF Indian Expeditionary Force
IEng Incorporated Engineer
IERE Institute of Electronic and Radio Engineers (now part of IEE)
IFAD International Fund for Agricultural Development (UN)
IFC International Finance Corporation
IFLA International Federation of Library Associations
IFPA Industrial Fire Protection Association
IG Instructor in Gunnery
IGasE Institute of Gas Engineers
IHSM Institute of Health Services Management
IIEP International Institute for Educational Planning
IIM Institution of Industrial Managers
IIP Institute of Incorporated Photographers
IISS International Institute of Strategic Studies
ILAM Institution of Landscape & Amenity Management
ILEA Inner London Education Authority
Ill Illinois (USA)
ILO International Labour Office
ILP Independent Labour Party
IMA International Music Association; Institute of Mathematics and its Applications
IMCB International Management Centre Buckingham
IMechE Institution of Mechanical Engineers
IMEDE Institut pour l'Etude des Méthodes de Direction de l'Enterprise
IMER Institute of Marine Environmental Research
IMF International Monetary Fund
Imp Imperial
IMRO Investment Management Regulatory Organisation
IMS Indian Medical Service, International Military Services
Inc Incorporated
incl include; including
Ind Independent
Indust Industry
Industl Industrial
Industs Industries
Inf Infantry
Info Information
INSEAD Institut Européen d'Administration des Affaires
Inspr Inspector
Inst Institute
Instn Institution
Instr Instructor
Insur Insurance
Int International
Investmt Investment
IOC International Olympic Committee
IOD Institute of Directors
IOM Isle of Man
IOW Isle of Wight
IPA Institute of Practitioners in Advertising; Insolvency Practitioners' Association
IPCS Institution of Professional Civil Servants (now IPMS)
IPFA Member or Associate, Chartered Institute of Public Finance and Accountancy
IPHE Institution of Public Health Engineers
IPI Institute of Patentees and Inventors
IPM Institute of Personnel Management
IPMS Institute of Professionals, Managers and Specialists
IPPA Independent Programme Producers' Association
IPR Institute of Public Relations
IProdE Institute of Production Engineers
IPS Indian Political Service
IQA Institute of Quality Assurance
Ir Irish
IRA Irish Republican Army
IRC Industrial Re-organisation Corporation
IRE Indian Corps of Royal Engineers
IRN Independent Radio News
IRRV Institute of Revenues, Rating and Valuation
Is Island(s)
ISBA Incorporated Society of British Advertisers
ISC Indian Staff Corps; Imperial Service College
ISCO Independent Schools' Careers Organisation
ISE Indian Service of Engineers
ISI International Statistical Institute
ISID International Society of Interior Design
ISIS Independent Schools' Information Service
ISJC Independent Schools' Joint Council
ISM Imperial Service Medal; Incorporated Society of Musicians (member/associate)
ISO Imperial Service Order; International Organisation for Standardisation
ISOCARP International Society of City and Regional Planning
ISPP International Society of Political Psychology
IStructE Institution of Structural Engineers
ISVA Incorporated Society of Valuers and Auctioneers
IT Information Technology
ITA Independent Television Authority
ITC Independent Television Commission
ITCA Independent Television Companies Association
ITN Independent TV News
ITU International Telecommunications Union
ITV Independent Television
ITVA Independent Television Association
IUCN International Union for the Conservation of Nature and Natural Resources
IUPAC International Union of Pure and Applied Chemistry
IUPAP International Union of Pure and Applied Physics
IUTAM International Union of Theoretical and Applied Mechanics
IWEM Institution of Water and Environmental Management
IY Imperial Yeomanry

J

JAG Judge Advocate General
JCD Doctor of Canon Law (Juris Canonici Doctor)
Jcl Licentiate of Canon Law
JD Doctor of Jurisprudence
JDipMA Joint Diploma in Management Accounting Services
Jl Journal
jl/s journal/s
JMN Johan Mangku Negara (Malaysia)
JP Justice of the Peace
jr junior
JSDC Joint Services Defence College
jsdc Qualified at Joint Service Defence College
JSM Johan Seita Mahkota (Malaysia)
JSSC Joint Services Staff College
jssc Qualified at Joint Services Staff College
jt joint
jtly jointly

K

k killed
ka killed in action
KAR King's African Rifles
KASG Knightly Association of St George the Martyr
KBE Knight Commander of the Order of the British Empire
KC King's Counsel
KCB Knight Commander of the Order of the Bath
KCH King's College Hospital
KCIE Knight Commander of the Order of the Indian Empire
KCL King's College London
KCMG Knight Commander of the Order of St Michael and St George
KCS King's College School
KCSG Knight Commander of St Gregory
KCSI Knight Commander of the Star of India
KCVO Knight Commander of the Royal Victorian Order
KDG King's Dragoon Guards
KEH King Edward's Horse Regiment
KEO King Edward's Own
KG Knight of the Order of the Garter
KGStJ Knight of Grace, Order of St John of Jerusalem
KGVO King George V's Own
KHC Honorary Chaplain to the King
KHDS Honorary Dental Surgeon to the King
KHP Honorary Physician to the King
KHS Honorary Surgeon to the King; Knight of the Holy Sepulchre
K-i-H Kaisar-i-Hind
KJStJ Knight of Justice, Order of St John of Jerusalem
KM Knight of Malta
KMN Kesatria Mangku Negara (Malaysian Decoration)
KORR King's Own Royal Regiment
KOSB King's Own Scottish Borderers
KOYLI King's Own Yorkshire Light Infantry
KP Knight of the Order of St Patrick
KPFSM King's Police and Fire Service Medal
KPM King's Police Medal
KRI King's Royal Irish
KRRC King's Royal Rifle Corps
KSG Knight of the Order of St Gregory the Great
KSLI King's Shropshire Light Infantry
KStJ Knight of the Order of St John of Jerusalem
KT Knight of the Order of the Thistle
kt knighted (Knight Bachelor)

L

L Labour
LA Los Angeles
La Louisiana
LAA Light Anti-Aircraft
Lab Labour; Laboratory
LAC Leading Aircraftsman
LACOTS Local Authorities' Co-ordination of Trading Standards Committee

LACSAB Local Authorities' Conditions of Service Advisory Board
LAH Licentiate of Apothecaries Hall, Dublin
LAMDA London Academy of Music and Dramatic Art
LBC London Broadcasting Company
LCC London County Council
LCDS London Contemporary Dance Studio
LCDT London Contemporary Dance Theatre
LCGI Licentiate, City and Guilds of London Institute
LCh Licentiate in Surgery
LCJ Lord Chief Justice
LCP Licentiate of the College of Preceptors
Ldr Leader
LDS Licentiate in Dental Surgery
LDV Local Defence Volunteers
LEA Local Education Authority
LEB London Electricity Board
lectr lecturer
LEPRA British Leprosy Relief Association
LesL Licenciees Lettres
LF Land Forces
LFAA Look first, ask afterwards
LG Life Guards; Lady Companion, Order of the Garter
LGSM Licentiate, Guildhall School of Music and Drama
LH Light Horse
LHD Literarum Humaniorum Doctor
LHSM Licentiate, Institute of Health Service Management
LI Light Infantry
Lib Liberal
LIBC Lloyd's Insurance Brokers' Committee
Lib Dem Liberal Democrat
Lieut Lieutenant
LIFFE London International Financial Futures Exchange
LIOB Licentiate, Institute of Building
Lit Literature
LittD Doctor of Letters (Cambridge & Dublin)
LLA Lady Literate in Arts
LLB Bachelor of Laws
LLCM Licentiate, London College of Music
LLD Doctor of Laws
LLM Master of Laws
LM Licentiate in Midwifery
LMA League Managers' Association
LMBC Lady Margaret Boat Club
LMCC Licentiate of Medical Council of Canada
LMH Lady Margaret Hall (Oxford)
LMRTPI Legal Member of the Royal Town Planning Institute
LMSSA Licentiate in Medicine and Surgery, Society of Apothecaries
LNER London and North East Railway
LPh Licentiate in Philosophy
LPO London Philharmonic Orchestra
LPTB London Passenger Transport Board
LRAM Licentiate of the Royal Academy of Music
LRCP Licentiate of the Royal College of Physicians
LRCPE Licentiate, Royal College of Physicians Edinburgh
LRCSE Licentiate, Royal College of Surgeons Edinburgh
LRFPS Licentiate of the Royal Faculty of Physicians and Surgeons (Glasgow)
LRIBA Licentiate of the Royal Institute of British Architects
LRPS Licentiate, Royal Photographic Society
LSA Licentiate of the Society of Apothecaries
LSCA London Society of Chartered Accountants
LSE London School of Economics
LSHTM London School of Hygiene and Tropical Medicine
LSO London Symphony Orchestra
Lt Lieutenant
LTA Lawn Tennis Association
LTCL Licentiate, Trinity College of Music, London
Lt-Col Lieutenant-Colonel
Ltcy Lieutenancy
Ltd Limited (company)
Lt-Gen Lieutenant-General
LTh Licentiate in Theology
LU Liberal Unionist
LVO Lieutenant of the Royal Victorian Order
LWT London Weekend Television

M

m married, marriage
M & A Mergers & Acquisitions
MA Master of Arts; Military Assistant
MAAEM Member, American Association of Electrodiagnostic Medicine
MAAF Mediterranean Allied Air Forces
MAAT Member, Association of Accounting Technicians
MACC Member, American College of Cardiology
MACE Member, Association of Conference Executives; Member, Association of Consulting Engineers
MACM Member, Association of Computing Machines
MACP Member, Association of Child Psychotherapists
MAE Member of the Academy of Experts (formerly MBAE)
MAFF Ministry of Agriculture, Fisheries and Food
MAI Master of Engineering
MAIAA Member, American Institute of Aeronautics and Astronautics
MAIE Member, British Association of Industrial Editors (now MCB)
Maj Major
Maj-Gen Major-General
mangr manager
Mans Mansions
MAOT Member of the Association of Occupational Therapists
MAP Ministry of Aircraft Production
MArch Master of Architecture
Marq Marquess
MASAE Member, American Society of Agricultural Engineers
MASCE Member, American Society of Civil Engineers
MASME Member, American Society of Mechanical Engineers
Mass Massachusetts (US)
MB Bachelor of Medicine
MBA Master of Business Administration
MBAE Member, British Academy of Experts (now MAE)
MBC Metropolitan/Municipal Borough Council
MBCS Member, British Computer Society
MBE Member of the Order of the British Empire
MBEDA Member, Bureau of European Design
MBHI Member of the British Horological Institute
MBII Member of the British Institute of Innkeeping
MBIM Member of the British Institute of Management (now MIMgt)
MBISC Member, British Institute of Sports Coaches
MBKS Member, British Kinematograph Society
MBO Management Buy Out
MBOU Member, British Ornithologists' Union
MBSG Member, British Society of Gastroenterology
MC Military Cross
MCAM Member, Institute of Communications, Advertising and Marketing
MCB Master of Clinical Biochemistry; Member, British Association of Communicators in Business (formerly MAIE)
MCC Marylebone Cricket Club; Metropolitan County Council
MCD Master of Civic Design
MCFA Member of the Cookery and Food Association
MCGI Member, City and Guilds of London Institute
MChir Master in Surgery
MChOrth Master of Orthopaedic Surgery
MCIA Member, Chartered Institute of Arbitrators
MCIB Member, Chartered Institute of Banking
MCIBSE Member, Chartered Institution of Building Services Engineers
MCIH Member of the Chartered Institute of Housing
MCII Member, Chartered Insurance Institute
MCIM Member, Chartered Institute of Marketing
MCIOB Member, Chartered Institute of Building
MCIPS Member, Chartered Institute of Purchasing and Supply
MCIT Member of the Chartered Institute of Transport
MCIWEM Member, Chartered Institution of Water and Environmental Management (formerly MIWEM)
MCom Master of Commerce
MConsE Member, Association of Consulting Engineers
MCOphth Member, College of Ophthalmologists (formerly Faculty of Ophthalmologists, FacOph, and Ophthalmic Society of UK, OSUK)
MCP Member of Colonial Parliament; Member, College of Preceptors
MCPath Member of the College of Pathologists
MCPCH Member, College of Paediatrics and Child Health
MCPS Member, College of Physicians and Surgeons
MCSD Member, Chartered Society of Designers
MCSP Member of the Chartered Society of Physiotherapy
MCT Member, Association of Corporate Treasurers
MD Doctor of Medicine
md managing director
MDC Metropolitan District Council
MDes Master of Design
m dis marriage dissolved
MDiv Master of Divinity
MDS Master of Dental Surgery
ME Middle East
MEAF Middle East Air Force
MEC Member, Executive Council
MECAS Middle East Centre for Arab Studies
MECI Member, Institute of Employment Consultants
MEd Master of Education
Med Medical; medicine; Mediterranean
MEF Mediterranean Expeditionary Force
MEIC Member of the Engineering Institute of Canada
MELF Middle East Land Forces
memb member
Meml Memorial
MENCAP Royal Society for Mentally Handicapped Children and Adults
MEP Member of the European Parliament
MESC Member, European Society of Cardiology
Met Metropolitan
MFA Master of Fine Arts (USA)
MFARCS Member of the Faculty of Anaesthetists, Royal College of Surgeons
MFB Member, Faculty of Building
MFC Mastership in Food Control
MFCM Member, Faculty of Community Medicine (now MFPHM)
MFH Master of Fox Hounds
MFHom Member, Faculty of Homeopathy
MFOM Member, Faculty of Occupational Medicine

MFPHM Member, Faculty of Public Health Medicine
mfr manufacturer
mfrg manufacturing
MGC Machine Gun Corps
MGDS RCS Member in General Dental Surgery, Royal College of Surgeons
MGGS Major-General General Staff
Mgmnt Management
MGO Master General of the Ordnance
Mgr Monsignor
MGRA Major-General Royal Artillery
MH Military Hospital
MHCIMA Member, Hotel Catering and Institutional Management Association
MHK Member of the House of Keys (IOM)
MHR Member of the House of Representatives
MHRA Modern Humanities Research Association
MHSM Member, Institute of Health Services Management
MI Military Intelligence
MIAA Member of the International Advertising Association
MIAeE Member, Institute of Aeronautical Engineers
MIAM Member Institute of Administrative Management
MIBE Member of the Institution of British Engineers
MIBG Member, Institute of British Geographers
MIBiol Member, Institute of Biology
MICAS Member of the Institute of Chartered Accountants of Scotland
MICE Member, Institution of Civil Engineers
MICEI Member, Institution of Civil Engineers of Ireland
MICFM Member of the Institute of Charity Fund-Raising Managers
MIChemE Member of the Institution of Chemical Engineers
MICM Member, Institute of Credit Management
MIConsE Member, Institute of Consulting Engineers
MIDM Member, Institute of Direct Marketing
MIDPM Member, Institute of Data Processing Management
MIEA Member of the Institution of Engineers, Australia
MIED Member, Institution of Engineering Design
MIEE Member of the Institution of Electrical Engineers
MIEEE Member, Institute of Electrical and Electronics Engineers (NY)
MIEI Member of the Institute of Engineering Inspection
MIEIE Member, Institute of Electronic Incorporated Engineers
MIERE Member of the Institution of Electronic and Radio Engineers
MIES Member of the Institution of Engineers and Shipbuilders in Scotland
MIEx Member of the Institute of Export
MIFA Member, Institute of Field Archaeologists
MIH Member of the Institute of Housing (now the Chartered Institute of Housing)
MIHE Member, Institute of Health Education
MIHort Member, Institute of Horticulture
MIHT Member, Institute of Highways and Transportation
MIIA Member, Institute of Internal Auditors
MIIExE Member, Institute of Incorporated Executive Engineers
MIIM Member, Institute of Industrial Managers
MIInfSc Member, Institute of Information Sciences
MIL Member, Institute of Linguists
Mil Military
MILDM Member, Institute of Logistics and Distribution Management
MILE Member of the Institution of Locomotive Engineers
MILog Member of the Institute of Logistics
MIM Member, Institute of Materials (formerly Institute of Metals)
MIMarE Member of the Institute of Marine Engineers
MIMC Member of the Institute of Management Consultants; Corporate Member of the Institute of Measurement and Control
MIMCE Member of the Institute of Municipal and County Engineers
MIME Member of the Institution of Mining Engineers
MIMechE Member of the Institution of Mechanical Engineers
MIMfgE Member, Institution of Manufacturing Engineers (merged with Institution of Electrical Engineers, 1991)
MIMgt Member, Institute of Management
MIMI Member of the Institute of the Motor Industry
MIMM Member of the Institution of Mining and Metallurgy
Min Minister
MIngF Member, Danish Engineers' Association
MInstB Member, Institute of Bankers
MInstD Member of the Institute of Directors
MInstE Member, Institute of Energy
MInstEnvSci Member, Institute of Environmental Sciences
MInstGasE Member of the Institution of Gas Engineers
MInstHE Member of the Institution of Highway Engineers
MInstM Member, Institute of Marketing
MInstMC Member, Institute of Measurement and Control
MInstME Member of the Institution of Mining Engineers
MInstMet Member of the Institute of Metals
MInstP Member of the Institute of Physics
MInst Pet Member of the Institute of Petroleum
MInstPS Member, Institute of Purchasing and Supply (now MCIPS)
MInstR Member, Institute of Refrigeration
MInstTT Member of the Institute of Travel and Tourism
MInstW Member of the Institution of Welding
MINucE Member of the Institution of Nuclear Engineers
Miny Ministry
MIOB Member of the Institute of Building
MIOSH Member, Institution of Occupational Safety & Health
MIPA Member of the Institution of Practitioners in Advertising; Member, Insolvency Practitioners' Association
MIPD Member of the Institute of Personnel and Development
MIPharmM Member, Institute of Pharmacy Management
MIPHE Member of the Institute of Public Health Engineers
MIPlantE Member, Institute of Plant Engineers
MIPM Member of the Institute of Personnel Management
MIPR Member of the Institute of Public Relations
MIProdE Member of the Institute of Production Engineers (now MIMfgE)
MIQ Member, Institute of Quarrying
MIRA Motor Industry Research Association
MIRE Member of the Institution of Royal Engineers
MIRS Member, Investor Relations Society
MIS Member of the Institute of Statisticians
MISA Member, Institute of South African Architects
Misc Miscellaneous
MISI Member of the Iron and Steel Institute
Miss Mississippi (USA)
MIStructE Member of the Institution of Structural Engineers
MIT Massachusetts Institute of Technology (USA)
MITD Member, Institute of Training and Development (now MIPD)
MITI Member, Institute of Translation and Interpreting
MIWEM Member of the Institution of Water and Environmental Management (now MCIWEM)
MJI Member of the Institute of Journalists
MJInstE Member of the Junior Engineers' Institute
Mktg Marketing
MLA Member, Legislative Assembly; Modern Language Association; Master in Landscape Architecture
MLC Member of the Legislative Council
MLIA Member, Life Insurance Association
MLitt Master of Literature
MLO Military Liaison Officer
MM Military Medal
MMC Monopolies and Mergers Commission
MMechE Master of Mechanical Engineering
MMet Master of Metallurgy
MMIM Member, Malaysian Institute of Management
MMin Master of Ministry
MMRS Member, Market Research Society
MMS Masters in Management Services; Member, Institute of Management Services
MMSA Master of Midwifery, Society of Apothecaries
MMus Master of Music
MN Merchant Navy
MNECInst Member, North East Coast Institution of Engineers and Shipbuilders
MNI Member, Nautical Institute
MNYAS Member, New York Academy of Sciences
MNZIE Member of the New Zealand Institution of Engineers
Mo Missouri (USA)
MO Medical Officer
MOD Ministry of Defence
MOH Medical Officer of Health
MOI Ministry of Information
MOP Ministry of Power
MOS Ministry of Supply
MP Member of Parliament
MPA Master of Public Administration
MPBW Ministry of Public Building Works
MPH Master of Public Health
MPhil Master of Philosophy
MPO Management and Personnel Office
MPRISA Member of the Public Relations Institute of South Africa
MPS Member of the Pharmaceutical Society of Great Britain
MR Master of the Rolls
MRAC Member of the Royal Agricultural College
MRAD Member of the Royal Academy of Dancing
MRAeS Member, Royal Aeronautical Society
MRAS Member of the Royal Asiatic Society
MRC Medical Research Council
MRCGP Member, Royal College of General Practitioners
MRCOG Member of the Royal College of Obstetricians and Gynaecologists
MRCP Member of the Royal College of Physicians
MRCPath Member, Royal College of Pathologists
MRCPGlas Member, Royal College of Physicians and Surgeons of Glasgow
MRCPI Member, Royal College of Physicians in Ireland
MRCPsych Member, Royal College of Psychiatrists
MRCR Member, Royal College of Radiologists
MRCS Member of the Royal College of Surgeons
MRCVS Member of the Royal College of Veterinary Surgeons
MRI Member, Royal Institution
MRIA Member of the Royal Irish Academy
MRIAI Member, Royal Institute of the Architects of Ireland
MRIC Member, Royal Institute of Chemistry
MRICS Member of the Royal Institution of Chartered Surveyors
MRIN Member of the Royal Institute of Navigation
MRINA Member of the Royal Institution of Naval Architects
MRIPHH Member, Royal Institute of Public Health and Hygiene
MRN Member, Register of Naturopaths
MRO Member of the Register of Osteopaths
MRPharmS Member, Royal Pharmaceutical Society
MRS Market Research Society; Medical Research Society
MRSC Member, Royal Society of Chemistry
MRSH Member of the Royal Society of Health
MRST Member of the Royal Society of Teachers

MRTPI Member of the Royal Town Planning Institute
MRUSI Member of the Royal United Service Institution
MRVA Member, Rating and Valuation Association
MS Master of Surgery; Manuscript; Master of Science (US)
MSAE Member, Society of Automotive Engineers (US)
MSC Manpower Services Commission
MSc Master of Science
MScD Master of Dental Science
MSCI Member, Society of Chemical Industry
MScL Member, Society of Construction Law
MSE Member of the Society of Engineers; Master of Science in Engineering (US)
MSEE Member, Society of Environmental Engineers
MSF Manufacturing, Science and Finance Union (formerly ASTMS)
MSI Member of the Securities Institute (formerly member of the Stock Exchange)
MSIA Member of the Society of Industrial Artists
MSIAD Member of the Society of Industrial Artists and Designers
MSM Meritorious Service Medal
MSocSci Master of Social Sciences
MSPI Member, Society of Practitioners of Insolvency
MSR Member, Society of Radiographers
MSSCC Member, Scottish Society of Contamination Control
MSST Member of the Society of Surveying Technicians
MSt Master of Studies (Oxford)
MSTD Member, Society of Typographic Designers
MTAI Member, Institute of Travel Agents
MTB Motor Torpedo Boat
MTG Member of the Translators' Guild
MTh Master of Theology
MTPI Member, Town Planning Institute
MTTA Machine Tool Trades' Association
MUniv Master of the University
MusB Bachelor of Music
MusD Doctor of Music (Cambridge)
MusM Master of Music
MV Motor Vessel
MVO Member, Royal Victorian Order
MVSc Master of Veterinary Science
MW Master of Wine
MWB Metropolitan Water Board
MWeldI Member, Welding Institute
MY Motor Yacht

N

N North; Nationalist
n nephew
NAAFI Navy, Army and Air Force Institutes
NABC National Association of Boys' Clubs
NAC National Agriculture Centre
NACF National Art Collectors' Fund
NACRO National Association for the Care and Resettlement of Offenders
NADFAS National Association of Decorative and Fine Arts Societies
NAEB National Association of Educational Broadcasters
NAG Northern Army Group
NAHAT National Association of Health Authorities and Trusts
NAHT National Association of Head Teachers
NALGO National and Local Government Officers' Association
NAMH National Association for Mental Health
NAO National Audit Office
NAPE National Association of Primary Education
NAPM National Association of Paper Merchants
NAQA National Association of Quality Assurance in Healthcare (now AQM)
NASDAQ National Association of Securities Dealers Automated Quotations (USA)
Nat National
NATCS National Air Traffic Control Services
NATFHE National Association of Teachers in Further and Higher Education
Nat Lib National Liberal
NATO North Atlantic Treaty Organisation
NBL National Book League
NBPI National Board for Prices and Incomes
NC Nautical College
NCA National Cricket Association; National Certificate of Agriculture
NCB National Coal Board
NCCI National Committee for Commonwealth Immigrants
NCCL National Council for Civil Liberties
NCLC National Council of Labour Colleges
NCO Non-commissioned officer
NCTJ National Council for the Training of Journalists
NCVCCO National Council for Voluntary Child Care Organisations
NCVO National Council for Voluntary Organisations
NCVQ National Council for Vocational Qualifications
ND Diploma in Naturopathy
NDA National Diploma in Agriculture
NDC National Defence College
NDD National Diploma in Dairying; National Diploma in Design
NEAC New English Art Club
NEAF Near East Air Force
NEC National Executive Committee
NEDC National Economic Development Council
NEDO National Economic Development Office
NERC Natural Environment Research Council
NFER National Foundation for Educational Research
NFL National Football League
NFS National Fire Service
NFU National Farmers' Union
NFWI National Federation of Women's Institutes
NGO Non-governmental Organisation
NGW Nice Glass of Water
NHS National Health Service
NI Northern Ireland
NICS Northern Ireland Civil Service
NID Naval Intelligence Department
NIESR National Institute of Economic and Social Research
NIH National Institute of Health (US)
NILP Northern Ireland Labour Party
NJ New Jersey (USA)
NLF National Liberal Federation
NMCU National Meteorological Co-ordinating Unit Committee
NP Notary Public
NRA National Rifle Association
NRDC National Research Development Corporation
NRPB National Radiological Protection Board
ns Graduate of the Royal Naval Staff College, Greenwich
NS Nova Scotia
NsgMD Nursing Management Diploma
NSocIs Member Societé des Ingenieurs et Scientifiques de France
NSPCC National Society for the Prevention of Cruelty to Children
NSW New South Wales
NT National Theatre
NTDA National Trade Development Association
NUBE National Union of Bank Employees (now BIFU)
NUGMW National Union of General and Municipal Workers
NUI National University of Ireland
NUJ National Union of Journalists
NUM National Union of Mineworkers
NUMAST National Union of Marine, Aviation and Shipping Transport Officers
NUPE National Union of Public Employees
NUR National Union of Railwaymen
NUS National Union of Students
NUT National Union of Teachers
NV Naamlose Vennootschap (Netherlands, plc)
NVQ National Vocational Qualification
NWFP North West Frontier Province
NY New York
NYBG New York Botanical Garden
NYC New York City
NYSE New York Stock Exchange
NZ New Zealand
NZEF New Zealand Expeditionary Force

O

o only
OA Officier d'Académie
OAS Organisation of American States
OB Order of Barbados
OBE Officer of the Order of the British Empire
OC Officer Commanding; Officer of the Order of Canada
OCF Officiating Chaplain to the Forces
OCS Officer Cadet School
OCTU Officer Cadet Training Unit
ODA Overseas Development Administration
ODI Overseas Development Institute
ODM Ministry of Overseas Development
OE Order of Excellence (Guyana)
OECD Organisation for Economics Co-operation and Development
OEEC Organisation for European Economic Co-operation
OER Officers' Emergency Reserve
Offr Officer
OFMCap Order of Friars Minor Capuchin (Franciscans)
OFMConv Order of Friars Minor Conventual (Franciscans)
OFS Orange Free State
OFT Office of Fair Trading
OGS Order of the Good Shepherd
OIC Officer in Charge
OJ Order of Jamaica
OM Order of Merit
O & M Organisation and Method
OMC Oxford Military College
ON Order of the Nation (Jamaica)
OND Ordinary National Diploma
ONZ Order of New Zealand
O & O Oriental and Occidental Steamship Co
OP Observation Post
OPB Occupational Pensions Board
Oppn Opposition

Ops Operations
OR Order of Roraima (Guyana)
Orch Orchestra
Orgn Organisation
ORS Operational Research Society
ORT Organisation for Rehabilitation by Training
OSB Order of St Benedict
OSC Graduate of Overseas Staff College
OSNC Orient Steam Navigation Company
OSRD Office of Scientific Research and Development
OStJ Officer of the Order of St John of Jerusalem
OTC Officers' Training Corps
OUAC Oxford University Athletics Club
OUBC Oxford University Boat Club
OUDS Oxford University Dramatic Society
OUP Oxford University Press

P

pa per annum
Pa Pennsylvania (USA)
PA Personal Assistant
pac Passed final exam of advanced class Military College of Science
PACT Producers' Alliance for Cinema and Television
Paiforce Palestine and Iraq Force
PAO Prince Albert's Own
Parl Parliament
Parly Parliamentary
PBWS President, British Watercolour Society
PC Privy Councillor; Peace Commissioner (Ireland); Parish Council
PCC Parochial Church Council; Press Complaints Commission
PCFC Polytechnics and Colleges Funding Council
PCL Polytechnic of Central London
PDSA People's Dispensary for Sick Animals
PDTC Professional Dancers' Training Course Diploma
PE Procurement Executive; Physical Education
PEI Prince Edward Island
PEN Poets, Playwrights, Editors, Essayists, Novelists' Club
PEng Registered Professional Engineer (Canada); Member, Society of Professional Engineers
PEP Political and Economic Planning
Perm Permanent
PFA Professional Footballers' Association
PGA Professional Golfers' Association
PGCE Post Graduate Certificate of Education
PHAB Physically Handicapped and Able Bodied
PhC Pharmaceutical Chemist
PhD Doctor of Philosophy
PhL Licentiate of Philosophy
PIA Personal Investment Authority
PID Political Intelligence Department
PIRA Paper Industries Research Association
PLA Port of London Authority
plc Public Limited Company
Plen Plenipotentiary
PLP Parliamentary Labour Party
PM Prime Minister
PMG Postmaster-General
PMN Pangilma Mangku Negara (Malaysia)
PMO Principal Medical Officer
Pmr Paymaster
PMRAFNS Princess Mary's Royal Air Force Nursing Service
PNEU Parents' National Educational Union
PNG Papua New Guinea
PO Pilot Officer; Post Office
POD Personnel Operations Department
POEU Post Office Engineering Union
Poly Polytechnic
P & OSNCo Peninsular and Oriental Steam Navigation Company
post grad post graduate
POUNC Post Office Users' National Council
POW Prisoner of War
PPA Periodical Publishers' Association
PPARC Particle Physics and Astronomy Research Council (formerly SERC)
PPE Philosophy, Politics and Economics (Oxford University)
PPL Private pilot's licence
PPRA Past President of the Royal Academy
PPS Parliamentary Private Secretary
PR Public Relations
PRA President of the Royal Academy
PRCA Public Relations Consultants Association
PRCS President, Royal College of Surgeons
PRE President of the Royal Society of Painters, Etchers and Engravers
Preb Prebendary
Prep Preparatory
Pres President
Prev Previously
PRI President, Royal Institute of Painters in Water Colours; Plastics and Rubber Institute (now part of Inst of Materials)
Princ Principal
PRO Public Relations Officer; Public Records Office
Prodn Production
Prodr Producer
Prods Products
Prof Professor
prog/s programme/s
prop proprietor
Prov Provost; Provincial
PRS President of Royal Society
PRWS President, Royal Society of Painters in Water Colours
PS Pastel Society
psa Graduate of RAF Staff College
PSA President of the Society of Antiquaries; Property Services Agency
psc Staff College Graduate
PSD Petty Session Division
PSI Policy Studies Institute
psm Certificate of the Military School of Music
PSM President of the Society of Miniaturists
PSNC Pacific Steam Navigation Society
PSO Principal Staff Officer
PSPA Professional Sports Photographers' Association
pt part
PT Physical Training
PTA Parent-Teacher Association
PTE Passenger Transport Executive
ptnr partner
ptsc passed Technical Staff College
pt/t part time
Pty Proprietary; Party
Pub Public
Pubns Publications
PWD Public Works Department
PWO Prince of Wales' Own
PWR Pressurised Water Reactor
PYBT Prince's Youth Business Trust

Q

QAIMNS Queen Alexandra's Imperial Nursing Service
QALAS Qualified Associate of Land Agents' Society
QARANC Queen Alexandra's Royal Army Nursing Corps
QARNNS Queen Alexandra's Royal Naval Nursing Service
QC Queen's Counsel
QCVSA Queen's Commendation for Valuable Service in the Air
QDR Qualified Dispute Resolver
QFSM Queen's Fire Service Medal for Distinguished Service
QGM Queen's Gallantry Medal
QHC Honorary Chaplain to The Queen
QHDS Honorary Dental Surgeon to The Queen
QHNS Honorary Nursing Sister to The Queen
QHP Honorary Physician to The Queen
QHS Honorary Surgeon to The Queen
Qld Queensland
QMAAC Queen Mary's Army Auxiliary Corps
QMC Queen Mary College, London
QMG Quartermaster-General
QO Qualified Officer
QOH Queen's Own Hussars
QPM Queen's Police Medal
qqv Qua Vide (which see, plural)
QRIH Queen's Royal Irish Hussars
QS Quarter Sessions
QSM Queen's Service Medal (NZ)
QSO Queen's Service Order (NZ)
qv Quod Vide (which see)

R

(R) Reserve
R & A Royal and Ancient (St Andrews) Club
RA Royal Artillery; Royal Academician
RAAF Royal Australian Air Force
RAAMC Royal Australian Army Medical Corps
RAC Royal Armoured Corps; Royal Automobile Club; Royal Agricultural College
RACGP Royal Australian College of General Practitioners
RAChD Royal Army Chaplains' Department
RACP Royal Australasian College of Physicians
RACS Royal Australasian College of Surgeons
RADA Royal Academy of Dramatic Art
RADC Royal Army Dental Corps
RAE Royal Australian Engineers; Royal Aircraft Establishment
RAEC Royal Army Educational Corps
RAeS Royal Aeronautical Society
RAF Royal Air Force
RAFA Royal Air Force Association

RAFO Reserve of Air Force Officers
RAFRO Royal Air Force Reserve of Officers
RAFVR Royal Air Force Volunteer Reserve
RAI Royal Anthropological Institute
RAIA Royal Australian Institute of Architects
RAIC Royal Architectural Institute of Canada
RAM (member of) Royal Academy of Music
RAMC Royal Army Medical Corps
RAN Royal Australian Navy
RANR Royal Australian Naval Reserve
RANVR Royal Australian Naval Volunteer Reserve
RAOC Royal Army Ordnance Corps
RAPC Royal Army Pay Corps
RARDE Royal Armament Research and Development Establishment
RARO Regular Army Reserve of Officers
RAS Royal Agricultural Society; Royal Astronomical Society; Royal Asiatic Society
RASC Royal Army Service Corps (now RCT)
RASE Royal Agricultural Society of England
RAuxAF Royal Auxiliary Air Force
RAVC Royal Army Veterinary Corps
RB Rifle Brigade
RBA (Member of) Royal Society of British Artists
RBC Royal British Colonial Society of Artists
RBK & C Royal Borough of Kensington and Chelsea
RBS Royal Society of British Sculptors
RC Roman Catholic
RCA Royal College of Art
RCAC Royal Canadian Armoured Corps
RCAF Royal Canadian Air Force
RCAMC Royal Canadian Army Medical Corps
RCDS Royal College of Defence Studies
RCGP Royal College of General Practitioners
RCHA Royal Canadian Horse Artillery
RCM (member of) Royal College of Music
RCN Royal College of Nursing; Royal Canadian Navy
RCNC Royal Corps of Naval Constructors
RCNR Royal Canadian Naval Reserve
RCNVR Royal Canadian Naval Volunteer Reserve
RCO Royal College of Organists
RCOG Royal College of Obstetricians and Gynaecologists
RCP Royal College of Physicians, London
RCPath Royal College of Pathologists
RCPE(d) Royal College of Physicians, Edinburgh
RCPI Royal College of Physicians in Ireland
RCPSGlas Royal College of Physicians and Surgeons, Glasgow
RCPsych Royal College of Psychiatrists
RCR Royal College of Radiologists
RCS Royal College of Surgeons of England; Royal Corps of Signals; Royal College of Science
RCS(Ed) Royal College of Surgeons of Edinburgh
RCSI Royal College of Surgeons Ireland
RCST Royal College of Science and Technology
RCT Royal Corps of Transport
RCVS Royal College of Veterinary Surgeons
Rd Road
RD Royal Naval Reserve Officers' Decoration
R & D Research and Development
RDA Royal Defence Academy
RDC Rural District Council
RDF Royal Dublin Fusiliers
RDI Royal Designer for Industry (RSA)
RDS Royal Dublin Society
RE Royal Engineers; Fellow, Royal Society of Painter-Etchers and Engravers
Rear-Adm Rear-Admiral
Rec Recorder
Reg Regular
Regnl Regional
Regt Regiment
Regtl Regimental
Rels Relations
REME Royal Electrical and Mechanical Engineers
REngDes Registered Engineering Designer
Rep Representative; Repertory (theatre)
Repub Republic(an)
RERO Royal Engineers Reserve of Officers
Res Reserve; Research; Resident
RES Royal Empire Society (now Royal Commonwealth Society)
ret retired
Rev Reverend
RFA Royal Field Artillery
RFC Royal Flying Corps; Rugby Football Club
RFU Rugby Football Union
RGA Royal Garrison Artillery
RGI Royal Glasgow Institute of Fine Arts
RGN Registered General Nurse
RGS Royal Geographical Society
RHA Royal Horse Artillery; Royal Hibernian Academy; Regional Health Authority
RHB Regional Hospital Board
RHF Royal Highland Fusiliers
RHG Royal Horse Guards
RHR Royal Highland Regiment
RHS Royal Horticultural Society
RI Member, Royal Institute of Painters in Water Colours; Rhode Island
RIAI Royal Institute of Architects of Ireland
RIAS Royal Incorporation of Architects in Scotland
RIASC Royal Indian Army Service Corps
RIBA (Member of) Royal Institute of British Architects
RIC Royal Irish Constabulary
RICS Royal Institution of Chartered Surveyors
RIF Royal Irish Fusiliers
RIIA Royal Institute of International Affairs
RIM Royal Indian Marine
RIN Royal Indian Navy
RINA Royal Institute of Naval Architects
RINVR Royal Indian Navy Volunteer Reserve
RIOP Royal Institute of Oil Painters
RIPA Royal Institute of Public Administration
RIPHH Royal Institute of Public Health and Hygiene
RIrR Royal Irish Rifles
RL Retired List
RLFC Rugby League Football Club
RLSS Royal Life Saving Society
RM Royal Marines
RMA Royal Military Academy; Royal Marine Artillery; Royal Musical Association
RMC Royal Military College, Sandhurst (now Royal Military Academy)
RMCS Royal Military College of Science
RMFVR Royal Marine Forces Volunteer Reserve
RMLI Royal Marine Light Infantry
RMN Registered Mental Nurse
RMO Resident Medical Officer
RMP Royal Military Police
RMPA Royal Medico-Psychological Association
RMR Royal Marine Reserve
RMS Royal Meteorological Society
RN Royal Navy
RNAS Royal Naval Air Service
RNC Royal Nautical College; Royal Naval College
RNCM (Member of) Royal Northern College of Music
RND Royal Naval Division
RNEC Royal Naval Engineering College
RNIB Royal National Institute for the Blind
RNID Royal National Institute for Deaf People
RNLI Royal National Lifeboat Institution
RNR Royal Naval Reserve
RNSA Royal Naval Sailing Association
RNSD Royal Naval Store Department
RNT Royal National Theatre
RNVR Royal Naval Volunteer Reserve
RNVSR Royal Naval Volunteer Supplementary Reserve
RNZADC Royal New Zealand Army Dental Corps
RNZAF Royal New Zealand Air Force
RNZN Royal New Zealand Navy
RNZNVR Royal New Zealand Naval Volunteer Reserve
ROC Royal Observer Corps
R of O Reserve of Officers
ROI Member, Royal Institute of Painters in Oils
RORC Royal Ocean Racing Club
ROSPA Royal Society for the Prevention of Accidents
RP Member of the Royal Society of Portrait Painters
RPC Royal Pioneer Corps
RPMS Royal Postgraduate Medical School
RPO Royal Philharmonic Orchestra
RPS Royal Photographic Society
RR Royal Regiment
RRAF Royal Rhodesian Air Force
RRC Royal Red Cross
RRF Royal Regiment of Fusiliers
RSA Royal Scottish Academician; Royal Society of Arts
RSAA Royal Society for Asian Affairs
RSAC Royal Scottish Automobile Club
RSAMD Royal Scottish Academy of Music and Drama (Diploma of)
RSBA Royal Society of British Artists
RSBS Royal Society of British Sculptors
RSC Royal Shakespeare Co; Royal Society of Canada; Royal Society of Chemistry
RSCN Registered Sick Children's Nurse
RSE Royal Society of Edinburgh
RSF Royal Scots Fusiliers
RSL Royal Society of Literature; Returned Services League of Australia
RSM Royal Society of Medicine; Royal Society of Music; Regimental Sergeant Major
RSMA Royal Society of Marine Artists
RSME Royal School of Military Engineers
RSNC Royal Society for Nature Conservation
RSPB Royal Society for the Protection of Birds
RSPCA Royal Society for the Prevention of Cruelty to Animals
RSPP Royal Society of Portrait Painters
RSRE Royal Signals and Radar Establishment
RSS Royal Statistical Society
RSSPCC Royal Scottish Society for the Prevention of Cruelty to Children
RSW Member, Royal Scottish Society of Painters in Water Colours
Rt Right

RTC Royal Tank Corps
RTE Radio Telefis Eireann
Rt Hon Right Honourable
RTO Railway Transport Officer
RTPI Royal Town Planning Institute
RTR Royal Tank Regiment
Rt Rev Right Reverend
RTS Royal TV Society
RUA Royal Ulster Academy
RUC Royal Ulster Constabulary
RUFC Rugby Union Football Club
RUI Royal University of Ireland
RUKBA Royal United Kingdom Beneficent Association
RUR Royal Ulster Regiment
RUSI Royal United Services Institute for Defence Studies (formerly Royal United Services Institution)
RVC Royal Veterinary College
RVO Regional Veterinary Officer
RWA Member, Royal West of England Academy
RWAFF Royal West African Frontier Force
RWAR Royal West African Regiment
RWF Royal Welch Fusiliers
RWS Member, Royal Society of Painters in Water Colours
RYA Royal Yachting Association
RYS Royal Yacht Squadron
RZS Royal Zoological Society

S

s son
S South; Scotland/Scottish (Peerages)
SA South Africa; South Australia; Societé Anonyme; Sociedad anónima
SAAF South African Air Force
sac Qualified at Small Arms Technical Long Course
SAC Senior Aircraftsman; Scientific Advisory Committee
SACEUR Supreme Allied Commander Europe
SACLANT Supreme Allied Commander Atlantic
SACRO Scottish Association for the Care and Resettlement of Offenders
SACSEA Supreme Allied Commander, S E Asia
SADG Societé des Architectes Diplomés par le Gouvernement
Salop (now) Shropshire
SAS Special Air Service
Sask Saskatchewan
SASO Senior Air Staff Officer
SAT Senior Member Association of Accounting Technicians
SATRO Science & Technology Regional Organisation
SBAC Society of British Aircraft Constructors (now Society of British Aerospace Companies)
SBNO Senior British Naval Officer
SBStJ Serving Brother of the Order of St John of Jerusalem
S4C Sianel Pedwar Cymru (Channel 4 Wales)
sc Student at the Staff College
SC Senior Counsel (Eire, Guyana, South Africa)
SCAR Scientific Commission for Antarctic Research
SCB Sausage, chips and beans
ScD Doctor of Science (Cambridge and Dublin)
SCF Senior Chaplain to the Forces
SCGB Ski Club of Great Britain
Sch School
Sci Science
SCI Society of Chemical Industry
SCL Student in Civil Law
SCM State Certified Midwife
SCONUL Standing Conference of National and University Libraries
Scot Scottish; Scotland
SCUA Scottish Conservative Unionist Association
SDA Scottish Diploma in Agriculture
SDLP Social Democratic and Labour Party
SDP Social Democratic Party
SEAC South East Asia Command
SEATAG South East Asia Trade Advisory Group
Sec Secretary
Secdy Secondary
Sec-Gen Secretary-General
Sen Senator
SEN State Enrolled Nurse
sep separated
SERC Science and Engineering Research Council (now EPSRC and PPARC)
SERT Society of Electronic and Radio Technicians
Serv Service
SFA Securities and Futures Authority
SFInstE Senior Fellow Institute of Energy
SFTA Society of Film and Television Arts
SG Solicitor-General
SGM Sea Gallantry Medal
Sgt Sergeant
SHA Secondary Heads Association
SHAEF Supreme Headquarters, Allied Expeditionary Force
SHAPE Supreme Headquarters, Allied Powers Europe
SHHD Scottish Home and Health Department
SHMIS The Society of Headmasters and Headmistresses of Independent Schools
SHO Senior House Officer
SIAD Society of Industrial Artists and Designers
SIB Securities and Investments Board
SICOT Societé Internationale de Chirurgie Orthopédique et de Traumatologie
sis sister
SJ Society of Jesus (Jesuits)
SJD Doctor of Juristic Science
SLAET Society of Licensed Aircraft Engineers and Technologists
SLD Social and Liberal Democrats
SLDP Social, Liberal and Democratic Party
slr solicitor
SM Service Medal of the Order of Canada; Master of Science (USA); Member, Society of Miniaturists
SME School of Military Engineering
SMIEEE Senior Member, Institute of Electrical and Electronic Engineers (NY)
SMMT Society of Motor Manufacturers and Traders
SMN Seri Maharaja Mangku Negara (Malaysia)
SMO Senior Medical Officer; Sovereign Military Order
SMOM Sovereign Military Order of Malta
SNO Senior Naval Officer
SNP Scottish Nationalist Party
SNTS Society for New Testament Studies
SO Scottish Office; Staff Officer
SOAS School of Oriental and African Studies
Soc Society
SOE Special Operations Executive
SOGAT Society of Graphical and Allied Trades
SOLACE Society of Local Authority Chief Executives
SOLT Society of London Theatres (formerly SWET)
Som Somerset
SOTS Society for Old Testament Studies
Sov Sovereign
sp sine prole (without issue)
SPCK Society for Promoting Christian Knowledge
SPG Society for the Propagation of the Gospel
SPNM Society for the Promotion of New Music
SPSO Senior Personnel Staff Officer
SPTL Society of Public Teaching of Law
SPUC Society for the Protection of the Unborn Child
Sq Square
Sqdn Squadron
Sqdn Ldr Squadron Leader
sr senior
SR Special Reserve; Southern Railway; Southern Region
SRC Science Research Council
SRDE Signals Research and Development Establishment
SRHE Society for Research in Higher Education
SRN State Registered Nurse
SRO Supplementary Reserve of Officers
SRP State Registered Physiotherapist
SRR State Registered Radiographer
SSA Society of Scottish Artists
SSAFA Soldiers', Sailors', and Airmen's Families Association
SSC Solicitor, Supreme Court (Scotland); Short Service Commission
SSEES School of Slavonic and East European Studies
SSMLL Society for the Study of Modern Languages and Literature
SSO Senior Supply Officer
SSRC Social Science Research Council
SSStJ Serving Sister of the Order of St John of Jerusalem
STA Society of Technical Analysts
STC Senior Training Corps
STD Doctor of Sacred Theology
STh Scholar in Theology
STL Licentiate of Sacred Theology
STM Master of Sacred Theology
STSO Senior Technical Staff Officer
Subalt Subaltern
Subs Submarines (RN)
subseq subsequent(ly)
Subsid Subsidiary
Subst Substitute
suc succeeded
Sup Supérieure
Supp Supplementary
Supt Superintendent
Surgn Surgeon
Survg Surviving
SWA Sports Writers' Association
SWB South Wales Borderers
SWEB South Western Electricity Board
SWET Society of West End Theatres (now SOLT)

T

t/a trading as
TA Territorial Army

TAA	Territorial Army Association; Tropical Agriculture Association
TAF	Tactical Air Force
T & AFA	Territorial and Auxiliary Forces' Association
TANS	Territorial Army Nursing Service
TARO	Territorial Army Reserve of Officers
TAS	Torpedo and Anti-Submarine Course
Tas	Tasmania
T & AVR	Territorial & Army Volunteer Reserve
TAVRA	Territorial Auxiliary and Volunteer Reserve Association
Tbnl	Tribunal
TC	Order of Trinity Cross (Trinidad and Tobago)
TCCB	Test and County Cricket Board
TCD	Trinity College Dublin
TD	Territorial Officers' Decoration; Teachta Ðala (member of the Dail, Parliament of Eire)
TEC	Training & Enterprise Council
Tech	Technical
Technol	Technology; Technological
TEFL	Teaching English as a Foreign Language
TEM	Territorial Efficiency Medal
Temp	Temporary
TEP	Member, Society of Trust and Estate Practitioners
TES	Times Educational Supplement
TF	Territorial Force
TGWU	Transport and General Workers' Union
Theol	Theological
ThM	Master of Theology
TLS	Times Literary Supplement
TMA	Theatre Managers' Association
Tport	Transport
Trans	Translation; translated; translator
TRE	Telecommunications Research Establishment
Treas	Treasurer
Treasy	Treasury
Trg	Training
TRH	Their Royal Highnesses
TRIC	Television and Radio Industries' Club
Tst	Trust
Tstee	Trustee
TUC	Trades Union Congress
TV	Television
TVEI	Technical and Vocational Educational Initiative

U

U	Unionist
UAE	United Arab Emirates
UAR	United Arab Republic
UAU	Universities' Athletic Union
UC	University College
UCAS	Universities and Colleges Admissions Service
UCCA	Universities' Central Council on Admissions
UCH	University College Hospital (now UCHL)
UCHL	University College Hospital, London
UCL	University College London
UCLA	University of California at Los Angeles
UCNS	Universities' Council for Non-Academic Staff
UCNW	University College of North Wales
UCS	University College School
UCW	University College of Wales
UDC	Urban District Council
UDF	Union Defence Force; Ulster Defence Force
UDR	Ulster Defence Regiment
UDS	United Drapery Stores
UDUP	Ulster Democratic Unionist Party
UEA	University of East Anglia
UFAW	Universities' Federation of Animal Welfare
UFC	Universities' Funding Council
UFO	Unidentified Flying Object
UGC	University Grants Committee
UHS	University High School
UK	United Kingdom
UKAEA	United Kingdom Atomic Energy Authority
UKLF	United Kingdom Land Forces
UKMIS	UK Mission
UMDS	United Medical and Dental Schools
UMIST	University of Manchester Institute of Science and Technology
UN	United Nations
UNA	United Nations' Association
unc	uncle
UNCTAD	United Nation's Commission for Trade and Development
UNDP	United Nation's Development Programme
UNESCO	United Nation's Educational, Scientific and Cultural Organisation
UNFAO	United Nation's Food and Agricultural Organisation
UNHCR	United Nation's High Commissioner for Refugees
UNICE	Union des Industries de la Communauté Européenne
UNICEF	United Nation's International Children's Emergency Fund
UNIDO	United Nation's Industrial Development Organisation
UNIDROIT	Institut International pour l'Unification du Droit Privé
UNIPEDE	Union Internationale des Producteurs et Distributeurs d'Energie Electrique
Univ	University
UNO	United Nation's Organisation
UNRRA	United Nation's Relief and Rehabilitation Administration
UP	Uttar Pradesh; United Provinces; United Presbyterian
UPNI	Unionist Party of Northern Ireland
URCC	United Kingdom Central Council for Nurses, Midwives and Health Visitors
URSI	Union Radio-Scientifique Internationale
US	United States
USA	United States of America
USAF	United States Air Force
USDAW	Union of Shop, Distributive and Allied Workers
USM	Unlisted Securities Market
USMC	United States Military College
USN	United States Navy
USNR	United States Naval Reserve
USPG	United Society for the Propagation of the Gospel
USSR	Union of Soviet Socialist Republics
UTC	University Training Corps
UU	Ulster Unionist
UWIST	University of Wales Institute of Science and Technology

V

v	versus (against)
V & A	Victoria and Albert (Museum)
VA	Lady of the Order of Victoria and Albert
Va	Virginia
VAD	Voluntary Aid Detachment
VAT	Value Added Tax
VBF	Veterinary Benevolent Fund
VC	Victoria Cross
VCAS	Vice-Chief of the Air Staff
VCC	Vintage Car Club
VD	Volunteer Officers' Decoration (now VRD); Venereal Disease
VDC	Volunteer Defence Corps
Ven	Venerable
Very Rev	Very Reverend
Vet	Veterinary
VHF	Very High Frequency
Visc	Viscount
VM	Victory Medal
VMH	Victoria Medal of Honour (Royal Horticultural Society)
VO	Veterinary Officer
Vol	Volunteer
VPRWS	Vice President, Royal Society of Painters in Water Colours
VRD	Volunteer Reserve Officers Decoration
VSCC	Vintage Sports Car Club
VSO	Voluntary Service Overseas

W

w	wife
W	West
WA	Western Australia
WAAA	Women's Amateur Athletics Association
WAAF	Women's Auxiliary Air Force (later WRAF)
WBA	World Boxing Association
WBC	World Boxing Council
WBO	World Boxing Organisation
WEA	Worker's Educational Association
WEU	Western European Union
WFN	World Fund for Nature
WFTU	World Federation of Trade Unions
WHO	World Health Organisation
WI	West Indies; Women's Institute
wid	widow
WIPO	World Intellectual Property Organisation
Wm	William
WNO	Welsh National Opera
WNSM	Welsh National School of Medicine
WO	War Office
WRAC	Women's Royal Army Corps
WRAF	Women's Royal Air Force
WRNR	Women's Royal Naval Reserve
WRNS	Women's Royal Naval Service
WRVS	Women's Royal Voluntary Service (formerly WVS)
w/s	War Substantive
WS	Writer to the Signet
WVS	Women's Voluntary Service
WWF	World Wide Fund for Nature (formerly World Wildlife Fund)
WWI	First World War
WWII	Second World War

Y

YCs Young Conservatives
Yeo Yeomanry
YHA Youth Hostels' Association
YMCA Young Men's Christian Association
yr younger
yst youngest
YWCA Young Women's Christian Association

à BRASSARD, Nigel Courtenay; s of Maj Herbert Forbes à Brassard, of Oxfordshire, and Elisabeth Kane, *née* McCue; *b* 7 June 1955; *Educ* Cheltenham Coll, King's Coll London (BA); *m* 16 March 1996, Adele, da of Dr Herman Dexter Webster, of New Orleans, Louisiana, USA; 1 s (Louis Forbes b 20 Dec 1996); *Career* joined Samuel Montagu Co Ltd London 1977, seconded to Dominguez Barry Samuel Montagu Ltd Sydney Australia 1984–85; dir of int corporate fin Kleinwort Benson Ltd 1986–, dir Kleinwort Benson Iberfomento SA; *Recreations* polo, cricket, opera, ballet and wine; *Clubs* Buck's, Cirencester Park Polo; *Style—* Nigel à Brassard, Esq; ✉ Kleinwort Benson Ltd, 20 Fenchurch St, London EC3P 3DB (☎ 0171 623 8000, fax 0171 929 7945, telex 888531)

AARONS, John Julius Emile; s of Jacob Henry Aarons (d 1945), of Hampstead, and Esther, *née* Cohen (d 1975); *b* 12 Aug 1936; *Educ* Kent Coll Canterbury, St John's Coll Cambridge (BA, MA), Sch of Mil Survey Newbury; *m* 14 Jan 1962, Maureen (Mo) Finley; 1 s (Matthew David Edward b 3 Aug 1969), 3 da (Emma Julia b 25 June 1963, (Sarah) Annabel (Mrs McMahon) b 6 Jan 1965, Olivia Rachel b 20 Sept 1967); *Career* surveyor Directorate of Overseas Surveys 1959–63, systems analyst London Boroughs Orgn and Methods Ctee 1963–65, conslt CEIR 1965–67, data processing mangr Wates Ltd 1967–71; The Stock Exchange: systems analyst 1971, asst dir Policy and Planning 1983–87, dir Inter Market Projects 1987, head Quality of Markets Unit and ed Stock Exchange Quarterly 1990–93; head of supervision Stock Exchange and Service Cos Securities and Investments Bd 1993–96, ret; parent govr Montpelier Middle Sch 1975–80; MSI 1993; *Books* The Useless Land (with Claudio Vita-Finzi); *Recreations* squash, sculling, etymology; *Style—* John Aarons, Esq; ✉ 8 Winscombe Crescent, London W5 1AZ (☎ 0181 997 7961)

AARONSON, Edward John (Jack); s of Samuel Wolf Aaronson (d 1943), and Sara Jochebed Chalkin (d 1989); *b* 16 Aug 1918; *Educ* C F S London; *m* 7 Sept 1946, Marian, da of Lodwick Davies (d 1984); 2 s (Michael John Aaronson, *qv* b 1947, Robin Hugh Aaronson, *qv* b 1951); *Career* RA, Palestine to Tunisia 1940–44, India 1945–46, W/S Capt; articled Jackson Pixley & Co 1946–49, fndr gen sec The Anglo Israel C of C London 1950–53, econ advsr (export) GEC 1954–61 (gen mangr overseas operations 1961–63), Celmac Ltd 1964–65, dep chm and pt/t chief exec The Steel Barrel Scammells & Associated Engrs Ltd (later Anthony Carrimore Ltd) 1965–68, industl advsr (later dir) Armitage Industrial Holdings Ltd 1965–68, dir (later chm) George Turton Platt 1966–68, dir E R & F Turner Ltd 1967–68, chm Br Northrop Ltd 1968–73, chm and chief exec (also scheme mangr and Creditors Ctee chm) The G R A Property Tst Ltd 1975–83, non-exec chm Wand F C Bonham and Sons Ltd 1981–88, non-exec dir Camlab Ltd 1982–89, non-exec chm The Reject Shop plc 1985–90; memb: FBI Standing Ctees on overseas credit and overseas investmt from inception 1958–63, Cncl The Export Gp for the Construction Industs 1960–63, Br Greyhound Racing Bd 1975–83, Gen Ctee The Reform Club 1976–79 and 1980–83; chm NGRC Race Course Promoters Assoc 1978–83; FCA 1960, FInstD 1980; *Recreations* family, music, reading, swimming, current affairs; *Clubs* Reform; *Style—* Jack Aaronson, Esq; ✉ Bushey House, Upper Wanborough, nr Swindon, Wilts SN4 0BZ (☎ 01793 790642)

AARONSON, Graham Raphael; QC (1982); s of Jack Aaronson (d 1973), of London, and Dora, *née* Franks; *b* 31 Dec 1944; *Educ* City of London Sch, Trinity Hall Cambridge (MA); *m* 12 Sept 1967 (m dis 1992), Linda Esther, da of Maj William Smith, of Oxford; 2 s (Oran b 1968, Avi b 1974), 1 da (Orit b 1970); m 2, 12 May 1993, Pearl Isobel, da of Harold Rose; *Career* called to the Bar Middle Temple 1966, md Worldwide Plastics Development Ltd 1973–77, fndr Standford Grange Rehabilitation Centre for Ex-Offenders, advsr on taxation Treasy Israel 1986–92, chm Tax Law Review Ctee 1994–; chm Dietary Res Fndn 1989–91; bencher Middle Temple 1991; *Recreations* photography; *Style—* Graham Aaronson, Esq, QC; ✉ 1 Essex Court, Temple, London EC4Y 9AR (☎ 0171 583 2000, fax 0171 583 0118)

AARONSON, Michael John (Mike); s of Edward John (Jack) Aaronson, *qv*, of Wanborough, Wilts, and Marian, *née* Davies; *b* 8 Sept 1947; *Educ* Merchant Taylors' Sch Northwood, St John's Coll Oxford (Sir Thomas White scholar, Trevelyan scholar, MA); *m* 27 Aug 1988, Andrene Margaret Dundas, da of late John Sutherland; 1 da (Katherine Sara Dundas b 22 Feb 1989), 2 s (Benedict Lodwick MacGregor b 24 Aug 1991, Nathanael Aeron Sutherland b 10 Feb 1994); *Career* field co-ordinator Nigeria Save the Children Fund 1969–71; HM Dip Serv 1972–88: third rising to first sec HM Embassy Paris 1973–77, Br High Cmmn Lagos 1981–83, HM Embassy Rangoon 1987–88; dir gen Save the Children Fund 1995– (overseas dir 1988–95); Freeman: City of London, Worshipful Co of Merchant Taylors; *Recreations* sports, the performing arts; *Clubs* MCC; *Style—* Mike Aaronson, Esq; ✉ Dingley Dell, Glaziers Lane, Normandy, Guildford, Surrey GU3 2EB (☎ 01483 811655); Save the Children Fund, Mary Datchelor House, 17 Grove Lane, London SE5 8RD (☎ 0171 703 5400, fax 0171 703 2278, telex 892809 SCFLON G)

AARONSON, Robin Hugh; s of Edward John (Jack) Aaronson, *qv*, of Wanborough, Wilts, and Marian, *née* Davies; *b* 7 July 1951; *Educ* Merchant Taylors' Sch, Balliol Coll Oxford (MA, OU Prize for Comparative Philology, pres Dramatic Soc), LSE (MSc, Eli Devons Prize for Economics); *m* 19 June 1976 (sep), Janet Charmian Christabel, da of Joseph Evans; *Career* admin trainee MOD 1974–80 (on secondment to LSE 1978–80), economic advsr HM Treasy 1980–86 (speechwriter to Chancellor of the Exchequer, advsr on economic effects of tax changes in 3 successive budgets), sr economic advsr Monopolies and Mergers Cmmn 1986–89 (advsr on numerous investigations); Coopers and Lybrand: joined as mangr 1989, ptnr responsible for competition policy advice servs 1993–, chm Regulatory Servs Gp; visiting lectr on Euro competition policy Centre des Études Européennes Strasbourg, specialist advsr House of Commons Trade and Indust Ctee 1991; *Recreations* mountains, running, photography, gardening; *Style—* Robin Aaronson, Esq; ✉ Cob Cottage, Lower Assendon, Henley-on-Thames, Oxon RG9 6AH; Coopers & Lybrand, 1 Embankment Place, London WC2N 6NN (☎ 0171 213 1595, fax 0171 213 1893)

ABBADO, Claudio; *b* 26 June 1933, Milan; *Educ* Conservatorio Giuseppe Verdi Milan, Hochschule für Musik Vienna; *Career* conductor; music dir: La Scala Milan 1968–86, LSO 1979–88, Vienna State Opera 1986–91, European Community Youth Orchestra (fndr) 1978–; artistic dir: Gustav Mahler Jugendorchester (fndr) 1988–, contemporary art festival Wien Modern (fndr) 1988–, Berlin Philharmonic 1989–, Vienna International Competition for Composers 1991, chamber music festival Encounters in Berlin 1992, Salzburg Easter Festival 1994–; Generalmusikdirektor City of Vienna 1987–; artistic advsr Chamber Orchestra of Europe; hon doctorates: Univ of Aberdeen 1986, Univ of Ferrara 1990, Univ of Cambridge 1994; Sergei Koussewitzky Prize Tanglewood 1958, Mozart-Medaille Vienna 1973, Goldmedaille International Gustav Mahler Gesellschaft Vienna 1985, numerous major international awards for recordings; Gran Croce della Repubblica Italiana 1984, Croix de Legion d'Honneur 1986, Bundesverdienstkreuz Republic of Germany 1992, Ehrenring City of Vienna 1994; *Style—* Claudio Abbado, Esq; ✉ Berliner Philharmonisches Orchester, Matthaikirchstrasse 1, D-10785 Berlin, Germany

ABBOT, Russ; *Career* comedian and actor; turned professional 1965, fndr leader The Black Abbots (cabaret act) 1965–80, solo career launched 1980; early TV guest appearances incl: London Night Out, What's on Next, Who Do You Do, The Comedians, Bruce Forsyth's Big Night; solo TV work: Russ Abbot's Madhouse (ITV) 1981–85, TV specials for ITV, The Russ Abbot Show (BBC) 1986–91, Russ Abbot's Christmas Show, The Russ Abbot Show (WGBO TV Chicago, screened throughout US) 1991, September Song (2 series, ITV) 1993–94, The Russ Abbot Show (ITV) 1994, Married for Life 1996; TV guest star appearances incl: Des O'Connor Tonight, Live from Her Majesty's, Tarby And Friends, Wogan, The Bob Monkhouse Show, Live from the Palladium; pantomime seasons incl: New Theatre Oxford 1980–81, Davenport Theatre Stockport 1981–82, Alhambra Theatre Bradford 1982–83, Palace Theatre Manchester 1986–87, Hippodrome Theatre Birmingham 1988–89, Mayflower Theatre Southampton 1989–90; star own theatre show: Torquay 1981, Great Yarmouth 1982 and 1987, Blackpool 1983, 1986 (biggest ever money making show of seaside theatre), 1988 and 1992, Southampton 1983–84, Cardiff 1985–86, Bournemouth 1985 and 1991, Edinburgh 1986; star of Madhouse show theatre tours 1982–85, 1990 and 1991, Russ Abbot and Friends 1989; West End stage work: Little Me (Prince of Wales Theatre) 1984, One for the Road (Lyric Theatre) 1987, Russ Abbot's Palladium Madhouse (London Palladium) 1990, Oliver (London Palladium) 1996; other work: Ted in September Song (2 series, ITV) 1993–94; comic creations incl: Cooperman, See You Jimmy, Vince Prince, Boggles, Fritz Crackers, Basildon Bond, Wilf, Honest Sid, Barrett Holmes, Val Hooligan, Julio Doubleglazias, Miss Marbles, Dr Profile, Hans Van Rental, Fat Man; chart hits: Atmosphere, All Night Holiday, Lets Go to the Disco (all taken from album I Love a Party); *Awards* five times winner Funniest Man on Television TV Times, Funniest Man on Television in Europe (Euro TV Magazine Assoc) 1983, Best Actor in a TV Commercial (Golden Break Awards) 1990, Top Variety Act (British Comedy Awards) 1990, voted Comedian of the Decade by TV viewers; *Style—* Russ Abbot, Esq; ✉ c/o Mike Hughes, Prince of Wales Theatre, Coventry Street, London W1V 8AS

ABBOTT, Diane Julie; MP (Lab) Hackney North and Stoke Newington (majority 10,727); *b* 27 Sept 1953; *Educ* Harrow County Girls' GS, Newnham Coll Cambridge; *children* 1 s (James Alexander Abbott-Thompson b 21 Oct 1991); *Career* successively: admin trainee Home Office, race relations offr NCCL, researcher Thames TV, reporter TV-am, equality offr ACTT, press and PR offr GLC, princ press offr Lambeth Borough Cncl; joined Lab Pty 1971, memb Westminster City Cncl 1982–86, MP (Lab) Hackney North and Stoke Newington 1987–; currently memb Treasy Select Ctee and also memb Lab Pty Nat Exec; sec Campaign Gp of Lab MPs 1992–; *Style—* Ms Diane Abbott, MP; ✉ House of Commons, London SW1A 0AA (☎ 0171 219 4426, fax 0171 219 4964)

ABBOTT, Adm Sir Peter Charles; KCB (1994); *b* 12 Feb 1942; *Educ* St Edward's Sch Oxford, Queens' Coll Cambridge (MA), RCDS; *m* 1965, Susan, *née* Grey; 3 da; *Career* articled clerk Blackburn Robson Coates and 2 Lt RMFVR 1963, resigned and joined RN as Sub Lt 1964; CO HMS Chawton 1972, on staff of Sr Naval Offr W Indies and promoted Cdr 1975, CO HMS Ambuscade 1976, 2 i/c HMS Bulwark and promoted Capt 1980, Chief of Defence Staff briefer during Falklands War 1982, CO HMS Ajax and First Frigate Sqdn 1983, RCDS 1985, Dir of Navy Plans 1985–89, promoted Rear Adm 1989, Flag Offr Second Flotilla 1989–91 in HM Ships Ark Royal, Cumberland, London, Argonaut and Cardiff, Asst Chief of Naval Staff 1991–93, promoted Vice Adm 1993, Dep Supreme Allied Cdr Atlantic 1993–95, promoted Adm 1995, C-in-C Fleet 1995–; *Style—* Adm Sir Peter Abbott, KCB; ✉ CINCFLEET, Northwood HQ, Eastbury Park, Northwood, Middx HA6 3HB (☎ 01923 837265, fax 01923 837597)

ABBOTT, Roderick Evelyn; s of Stuart Evelyn Abbott, OBE (d 1992), of Cambridge, and Jocelyn, *née* Niemeyer; *b* 16 April 1938; *Educ* Rugby, Merton Coll Oxford (BA); *m* 22 June 1963, Elizabeth McLean, da of Dr Neil McLean; 3 da (Nicola b 1964, Mary b 1966, Melissa b 1972); *Career* Nat Serv RCS 1956–58; Bd of Trade 1962–71; sec SE Econ Planning Cncl 1966–68, FCO 1971–73; Cmmn of the EU: DG external rels 1973–75 and 1979–82, dep head of mission Geneva 1975–79, dir Directorate Gen of External Economic Rels 1982–96, ambass to the UN and Int Orgns Geneva 1996–; *Style—* Roderick Abbott, Esq; ✉ EC Delegation, 37 Rue de Vermont, 1202 Geneva, Switzerland (☎ 00 41 22 734 2236)

ABBOTT, Ronald William; CVO (1989), CBE (1979); s of Edgar Abbott (d 1956); *b* 18 Jan 1917; *Educ* St Olave's GS; *m* 1, 1948, Hilda Mary (d 1972), da of William George Clarke (d 1918); 2 da (Mary Elaine b 1949, Christine Margaret b 1956); m 2, 1973, Barbara Constance, da of Gilbert Hugh Clough (d 1961); *Career* consltg actuary; Bacon & Woodrow: sr actuary 1946, ptnr 1948, sr ptnr 1972–81, conslt ptnr 1982–94, memb Departmental Ctee on Property Bonds and Equity Linked Life Assurance 1971–73; memb Cncl: Inst of Actuaries 1966–74 (treas 1971–73), Indust Soc 1964–84 (life memb 1984), Pensions Mgmnt Inst 1977–81 (vice pres 1978–80); chm Occupational Pensions Bd 1982–87 (dep chm 1973–82); contrib Jl of Inst of Actuaries; memb Court Worshipful Co of Ironmongers (Master 1986–87); Finlaison medallist Inst of Actuaries 1988; FIA, ASA, FPMI, FRSA; *Books* A Short History of the Association of Consulting Actuaries (1991); *Recreations* music, theatre; *Clubs* Royal Automobile; *Style—* Ronald W Abbott, Esq, CVO, CBE; ✉ 43 Rottingdean Place, Falmer Rd, Rottingdean, E Sussex (☎ 01273 303302, fax 01273 309949)

ABBOTT, Stephen (Steve); s of Wilfrid Lockley Abbott, of Bradford, W Yorks, and Lily Templeton, *née* Limbert; *b* 28 July 1954; *Educ* Bradford GS, CCC Cambridge (MA); *m* (sep 1993), Karen Lesley Lewis; 1 s (James Alexander b 1989), 1 da (Francesca b 1986); *Career* producer; Price Waterhouse London 1976–79, Hand Made Films London 1979–81, Mayday Management Ltd 1981–, chm Prominent Features Ltd 1989– (md

1986–89); exec prodr: A Fish Called Wanda 1988, Fierce Creatures 1995 (released 1997); prodr: American Friends 1990, Blame It On the Bellboy 1991, Brassed Off 1996; FCA 1990 (ACA 1979); *Style*— Steve Abbott, Esq; ✉ Prominent Features Ltd, 68A Delancey St, London NW1 7RY (☎ 0171 284 0242, fax 0171 284 1004)

ABBS, Dr Peter Francis; s of Eric Charles Abbs (d 1987), and Mary Bertha, *née* Bullock (d 1994); *b* 22 Feb 1942; *Educ* Norwich Tech Coll, Univ of Bristol (BA), Univ of Sussex (PhD); *m* Barbara Ann, da of Jack Beazeley; 2 da (Annabel b 20 Oct 1964, Miranda b 22 July 1966), 1 s (Theodore b 29 March 1973); *Career* English teacher Bristol 1966–70, res asst Univ of Wales 1970–76, reader in educn Univ of Sussex 1976–; has lectured widely in USA, Aust, Denmark, Ireland, Belgium and elsewhere; memb: Soc of Authors, Assoc of Univ Teachers; *Poetry* For Man and Islands, Songs of a New Taliesin, Icons of Time, Personae, Angelic Imagination; *Non-Fiction* English For Diversity, Root and Blossom - The Philosophy, Practice and Politics of English Teaching, English Within the Arts, The Forms of Poetry, The Forms of Narrative, Autobiography in Education, Proposal for a New College (with Graham Carey), Reclamations - Essays on Culture, Mass-Culture and the Curriculum, A is for Aesthetic - Essays on Creative and Aesthetic Education, The Educational Imperative, The Polemics of Imagination - Selected Essays on Art, Culture and Society; ed: The Black Rainbow - Essays on the Present Breakdown of Culture, Living Powers - The Arts in Education, The Symbolic Order - A Contemporary Reader on the Arts Debate; *Recreations* swimming, walking; *Style*— Dr Peter Abbs; ✉ The Gryphon Press, 38 Prince Edwards Road, Lewes, East Sussex BN7 1BE (☎ 01273 472410); The Institute of Education, University of Sussex, Falmer, Brighton BN1 9RG (☎ 01273 678447, fax 01273 678568)

ABDELA, Lesley Julia; MBE (1990); da of Frederick Abdela (d 1985), and Henrietta, *née* Hardy (d 1959); *b* 17 Nov 1945; *Educ* Glendower London, Queen Anne's Caversham, Châtelard Sch Les Avants Switzerland, Queen's Coll Harley St, Hammersmith Coll of Art, London Sch of Printing; *m* 1972 (m dis); 1 s (Nicholas b 1973); *Career* feature writer, author, TV and radio bdcaster on politics and travel, after dinner speaker specialising in women in the 1990s; formerly advtg exec Royds London, researcher House of Commons and House of Lords 1976–77, Parly candidate (Lib) Herts E 1979, fndr All-Party 300 Gp for Women in Politics 1980, USA Leader Grant visiting Washington DC, LA and Seattle 1983, studied Third World by residence in the Gambia 1984–86; currently sr ptnr Eyecatcher Associates (journalism, copywriting, research, conference speakers); conslt on women and politics in East and Central Europe Project Liberty Kennedy Sch of Government Harvard Univ 1992–, political ed Cosmopolitan 1993–, accredited journalist UN 4th World Conf on Women Beijing 1995, chief exec Project Parity 1996–; memb: Bd International Inst for Environment and Devpt 1992–, Bd of Govrs Westminster Fndn for Democracy 1996–; a govr Nottingham Trent Univ 1997–; winner EC's UK Woman of Europe Award (for servs to EU) 1995; FRGS, FRSA 1991; *Books* Women with X Appeal (1989), Breaking Through The Glass Ceilings (Met Authys Recruitment Agency guide, 1991), What Women Want, 1993–2000 (ed, 1993), DO IT! - Walk the Talk (1994); travel books incl: Driving in the USA, Stay Healthy When You Travel (To the Tropics); *Recreations* travel, painting, desert agriculture; *Style*— Ms Lesley Abdela, MBE; ✉ Eyecatcher Associates, The Lodge, Conock Manor, Wilts SN10 3QQ (☎ 01380 840594, fax 01380 840028); 46 Portland Place, London W1N 3DG (☎ 0171 631 1545, fax 0171 631 1544); La Boursaie, 14140 Tortisambert, France

ABDY, Sir Valentine Robert Duff; 6 Bt (UK 1850), of Albyns, Essex; s of Sir Robert Abdy, 5 Bt (d 1976), and Lady Diana, *née* Bridgeman (d 1967), da of 5 Earl of Bradford; *b* 11 Sept 1937; *Educ* Eton; *m* 1971 (m dis 1982), Mathilde, da of Etienne Coche de la Ferté; 1 s (Robert); *Heir* s, Robert Etienne Eric Abdy b 22 Feb 1978; *Career* set up (with Peter Wilson) Sotheby's first office abroad in Paris and Munich; special advsr Int Fund for Promotion of Culture UNESCO, first rep Smithsonian Inst (Washington DC) in Europe 1983–95; currently: memb Nat Bd Smithsonian Inst Washington DC, conseil d'administration Union National des Arts Décoratifs Paris, memb Comité Scientifique Conservatoire National des Arts et Métiers Paris; Chev des Arts et des Lettres (France) 1995; *Clubs* Jockey (Paris), The Travellers (Paris); *Style*— Sir Valentine Abdy, Bt; ✉ 13 Villa Molitor, 75016 Paris, France; 19 Belgrave Place, London SW1; Hadsley House, Lefebore Street, St Peter Port, Guernsey

ABEL, Prof Edward William; s of Sydney John Abel (d 1952), of Kenfighill, and Donna Maria, *née* Grabham (d 1981); *b* 3 Dec 1931; *Educ* Bridgend GS Glamorgan, Univ Coll Cardiff (BSc), Northern Poly London (PhD); *m* 6 Aug 1960, Margaret Rosina, da of Glyndwr Vivian Edwards (d 1974), of Porthcawl; 1 s (Christopher b 23 Oct 1963), 1 da (Julia b 4 April 1967); *Career* Nat Serv 1953–55; res fell Imperial Coll London 1957–59, lectr and reader Univ of Bristol 1959–71, prof of inorganic chemistry Univ of Exeter 1972–95 (head of dept 1977–88, dep vice chllr 1991–94); visiting prof: Univ of Br Columbia 1970, Japan 1971, Tech Univ of Braunschweig 1973, Australian Nat Univ Canberra 1990; int sec Int Confs on Organometallic Chemistry 1972–88; Royal Soc of Chemistry: memb Cncl 1978–82, 1983–89 and 1990–, pres 1996–98, chm Local Affairs Bd 1983–87, chm Divnl Affairs Bd 1990–92, chm Scientific Affairs Bd 1992–95, memb Dalton Divnl Cncl 1977–83 and 1987–91 (sec and treas 1977–82, vice pres 1989–91, pres 1987–89); Univ Grants Ctee: memb 1986–89, chm Physical Sci Sub Ctee 1986–89; Cncl for Nat Academic Awards: chm Physical Sci Ctee 1987–91, memb Academic Affairs Ctee 1987–91, memb Cncl 1991–93; nat advsr for chemistry to Exec Univ Funding Cncl 1989–93, assessor to Res Ctee Poly and Coll Funding Cncl 1988–90; Royal Soc of Chemistry: Main Gp Chemistry award 1976, Tilden medal and lectr 1981; FRSC; *Books* Royal Soc Chemistry Specialist Periodical Reports on Organometallic Chemistry (Vols 1–25, jt ed, 1970–), Comprehensive Organometallic Chemistry (9 Vols, exec ed, 1984), Comprehensive Organometallic Chemistry II (14 Vols, ed 1995); *Recreations* gardening; *Style*— Prof Edward Abel; ✉ 1A Rosebarn Avenue, Exeter, Devon EX4 6DY (☎ 01392 270272); Department of Chemistry, University of Exeter, Exeter EX4 4QD (☎ 01392 263489, fax 01392 263434)

ABEL, Kenneth Arthur; CBE (1984), DL (Dorset 1976); s of Arthur Abel, CBE (d 1988), of Yorks, and Francis Ethel, *née* Roome (d 1973); *b* 4 April 1926; *Educ* Durham Sch, Univ of Glasgow, Univ of Durham; *m* 22 Sept 1955, Sarah Matilda, da of Capt Maurice Pugh Poynor, TD (d 1950), of Leics; 3 s (David Arthur b 4 Oct 1957, Paul Anthony b 28 Feb 1959, Godfrey Andrew b 2 July 1960); *Career* RA 1944–48; admitted slr 1952; asst slr: Warwickshire CC 1952–53, Leicestershire CC 1954–59; sr asst slr Northamptonshire CC 1959–63, dep clerk of the peace and of North Riding CC 1963–67, chief exec Dorset CC 1967–91 (clerk of the peace 1967–73), clerk to the Ltcy Dorset 1967–91; memb Assoc of County Chief Execs (past chm), memb Int City Management Assoc, memb Dorset Co Golf Union (past pres); *Recreations* golf, gardening; *Clubs* Sherborne Golf (vice pres); *Style*— Kenneth Abel, Esq, CBE, DL; ✉ Herne's Oak, Bradford Rd, Sherborne, Dorset DT9 6BP (☎ 01935 813200)

ABEL SMITH, Caroline Bridget; OBE (1994); da of late Capt Howard Bennett Bartlam (d 1970), of Carnforth, Lancs, and Mary Isobel Bartlam; *b* 26 Sept 1945; *Educ* Casterton Sch Cumbria; *m* 1970, John Lawrence Abel Smith, s of late Maj Desmond Abel Smith; 2 s (Alexander Howard Lawrence b 19 March 1971, Oliver Desmond b 13 June 1974), 1 da (Helen Isobel Katherine b 18 Aug 1976); *Career* trained as med lab technician Lancaster and Guy's Hosps, subsequently personal asst in PR The Times and The Sunday Times, lay memb GDC 1989– (memb Professional Conduct Ctee), non-exec dir S Bucks NHS Tst 1992–; Cons Women's Nat Ctee: memb 1988–, dep chm 1994–95, chm 1996–; memb Cons Pty Nat Union Exec Ctee 1991–; parish cncllr, church warden and memb Deanery Synod; *Recreations* gardening, fishing, tennis, tapestry work; *Style*— Mrs Caroline Abel Smith, OBE; ✉ The Old Rectory, Great Hampden, Great Missenden, Bucks HP16 9RL (☎ 01494 488556)

ABEL SMITH, David Francis; s of Sir Alexander Abel Smith, KCVO, TD, JP (d 1980), of Quenington Old Rectory, Cirencester, Glos, and Elizabeth, *née* Morgan (d 1948); *b* 3 Feb 1940; *Educ* Gordonstoun, Stockton and Billingham Tech Coll; *m* 18 Nov 1982, Lucy Marie, da of Col Sir Bryce Muir Knox, KCVO, MC, TD (former Lord Lt of Ayr and Arran); 1 da (Eliza Violet Daria b 15 March 1991); *Career* exec dir The Delta Group plc 1974–82 (joined 1961), md Benjamin Priest Group plc 1983–91, chief exec Marling Industries plc 1992–; memb Quenington Parish Cncl 1987–93; Freeman City of London, memb Worshipful Co of Fishmongers; *Recreations* foxhunting; *Clubs* Pratt's; *Style*— David Abel Smith, Esq; ✉ Quenington Old Rectory, Cirencester, Glos GL7 5BN (☎ 01285 750358, fax 01285 750540); Marling Industries plc, 17 Aylmer Parade, London N2 0PF (☎ 0181 340 4046, fax 0181 348 5878)

ABEL SMITH, Lady; Henriette Alice; DCVO (1977, CVO 1964); o da of Cdr Francis Charles Cadogan, RN (d 1970), and Ruth Evelyn, *née* Howard (d 1962); *b* 6 June 1914; *m* 1, 4 Sept 1939, Sir Anthony Frederick Mark Palmer, 4 Bt (ka 1941); 1 s (Sir Mark Palmer, 5 Bt, *qv*), 1 da; m 2, 17 Feb 1953, Sir Alexander Abel Smith, KCVO, TD, JP (d 1980); 1 s, 1 da; *Career* an Extra Lady-in-Waiting to HM The Queen 1987– (a Lady-in-Waiting 1949–87); JP: Tunbridge Wells 1955, Glos 1971; *Style*— Lady Abel Smith, DCVO; ✉ The Garden House, Quenington, Cirencester, Glos (☎ 01285 750231)

ABEL SMITH, Ralph Mansel; o s of Thomas Abel Smith, JP (d 1983), of Woodhall Park, Watton at Stone, Hertford, and Alma Mary Agatha, *née* de Falbe; *b* 11 Dec 1946; *Educ* Eton; *m* 18 July 1985, Alexandra Clare Ragnhild, da of Maj Ian Stuart Rae Bruce, MC (d 1967), of Highfield, Bells Yew Green, Sussex; 2 s (Thomas Ralph Bruce Abel b 1989, Edward Mansel Ian Abel b 1991); *Career* landowner and farmer; chm: Herts/Middx Branch CLA 1981–86, Herts Co Award Liaison Panel of Duke of Edinburgh's Award Scheme 1976–81; patron of livings of: Watton-at-Stone, Sacombe, Bramfield with Stapleford, Bengeo; High Sheriff Herts 1984–85; memb: E Herts DC 1976–83, Herts CC 1985–89; life govr Haileybury and Imperial Serv Coll 1985; *Recreations* shooting, fishing, music, classical architecture; *Clubs* Buck's, Pratt's, Turf; *Style*— Ralph Abel Smith, Esq; ✉ Woodhall Park, Watton-at-Stone, Hertford SG14 3NF; Cambusmore Lodge, Dornoch, Sutherland IV25 3JF

ABEL SMITH, Col Richard Francis; DL; s of Col Sir Henry Abel Smith, KCMG, KCVO, DSO, DL (d 1993), and Lady May Helen Emma, *née* Cambridge (d 1994), da of 1 Earl of Athlone, KG, GCB, GCMG, GCVO, DSO, PC (d 1957), and HRH Princess Alice of Albany, VA, GCVO, GBE (d 1981); *b* 11 Oct 1933; *Educ* Eton, Sandhurst, RAC Cirencester; *m* 1960, Marcia, DL Notts 1993, da of Maj-Gen Sir Douglas Kendrew, KCMG, CB, CBE, DSO (d 1989); 1 da (Katherine Emma); *Career* RHG (Blues): Escort Cdr and ADC to Govrs of Cyprus 1957–60, Instr RMA Sandhurst 1960–63, ret; co cmmr for Scouts (Notts) 1966–75, cmd Sherwood Rangers Sqdn, Royal Yeo Regt 1967–69 (Hon Col 1979–89); High Sheriff Notts 1978; Vice Lord-Lt of Notts 1991; chm Sports Aid Fndn East Midlands 1979–89, sr fell Midland Div Woodard Fndn; Liveryman Worshipful Co of Vintners; farmer; *Recreations* shooting, fishing, riding; *Clubs* White's, Farmers', Army and Navy; *Style*— Col Richard Abel Smith, DL; ✉ Blidworth Dale, Ravenshead, Nottingham NG15 9AL (☎ 01623 792241)

ABELL, (John) David; s of Leonard Abell, and Irene Craig, *née* Anderson; *b* 15 Dec 1942; *Educ* Univ of Leeds (BA), LSE (Dip Business Admin); *m* 1, 1967 (m dis 1977), Anne Janette, *née* Priestley; 3 s; m 2, 1981 (m dis), Sandra Dawn, *née* Atkinson; 1 s, 1 da; m 3, 1988, Juliana, da of late Prof John Lister Illingworth Fennell, of Canterbury Rd, Oxford; *Career* Ford Motor Co 1962–65, AEI 1965–67, various appts British Leyland 1968–72 and 1974–81, First National Finance Corp 1972–73, chm and chief exec Suter plc 1981–96; CIMgt; *Style*— J David Abell, Esq; ✉ The Old Rectory, Branston-by-Belvoir, Grantham, Lincs NG32 1RU

ABELL, Prof Peter Malcolm; s of John Raymond Abell (d 1987), and Constance, *née* Moore; *b* 18 Aug 1939; *Educ* Wakefield GS, Univ of Leeds (BSc, PhD); *m* (m dis); 3 s (Paul b 1963, Simon b 1968, Johnathon b 1988); *Career* dir of research Industrial Sociology Unit Imperial Coll London 1970–75; prof of sociology: Dept of Sociology Univ of Birmingham 1976–79, Univ of Surrey 1979–91; dir The Interdisciplinary Inst of Mgmnt London Sch of Economics and Political Science 1991–; *Books* Model Building in Sociology (1972), Socio-Economic Potential of Producer Co-ops in Developing Countries (1987), The Syntax of Social Life (1988), Support Systems for Co-ops in Developing Countries (1988), Rational Choice (1991); *Recreations* walking, music; *Style*— Prof Peter Abell; ✉ 37 The Ridgeway, Radlett, Herts; London School of Economics, Houghton Street, London WC2A 2AE

ABELL, Timothy George (Tim); s of Sir George Edmond Brackenbury Abell, KCIE (d 1989), and Susan, *née* Norman Butler; *b* 29 April 1930; *Educ* Marlborough, CCC Oxford (MA); *m* 8 April 1961, Philippa Joan, da of Sir Charles Percival Law Whishaw; 3 s (James b 11 Feb 1962, Mark b 13 Aug 1963, Richard b 30 June 1966); *Career* dir Baring Brothers & Co Ltd 1969–86 (joined 1953), dep chm Baring Investment Management Ltd 1986–89 (ret); non-exec chm: F & C Eurotrust plc 1989–, CCLA Investment Management Ltd; non-exec vice pres Equitable Life Assurance Soc (ret 1995); also non-exec dir: Baring Tribune Investment Trust plc, Greig Fester Group Ltd, Herald Investment Trust plc; chm Assoc of Investmt Tst Cos 1985–87 (dep chm 1983–85); *Clubs* MCC, Flyfishers'; *Style*— Tim Abell, Esq; ✉ Eastrop Farm House, Up Nately, Hook, Hants RG27 9PS (☎ 01256 762695)

ABER, Prof Geoffrey Michael; s of David Aber (d 1988), of Leeds, and Hilda, *née* Madeloff (d 1982); *b* 19 Feb 1928; *Educ* Leeds GS, Univ of Leeds (MB ChB, MD), Univ of Birmingham (PhD); *m* 27 June 1964, Eleanor Maureen, da of Gerald Christopher Harcourt; 1 da (Alison Jane b 1965), 1 s (Mark Barrington b 1967); *Career* Lt and Capt RAMC 1954–56; house physician Brompton Hosp 1957–58, res fell McGill Univ Montreal 1959–60, sr registrar Queen Elizabeth Hosp Birmingham 1960–64, Wellcome sr res fell in clinical sci and hon sr lectr Univ of Birmingham 1964–65, conslt physician N Staffs Hosp Centre 1965–93; Univ of Keele: prof and advsr in clinical res Dept of Postgrad Med 1979–82, prof of renal med 1982–93, head Dept of Postgrad Med 1982–89, dean of postgrad med 1989–91; memb Cncl RCP 1984–87; FRCP 1973; *Publications* Recent Advances in Renal Medicine (contrib, 1983), Postgraduate Nephrology (contrib, 1985), Textbook of Genitourinary Surgery (contrib, 1985); author of scientific papers in learned jls; *Recreations* music, sport, motor cars; *Style*— Prof Geoffrey Aber; ✉ Greenleaves, Seabridge Lane, Westlands, Newcastle-under-Lyme, Staffs ST5 3LS (☎ 01782 613692, fax 01782 625104)

ABERCONWAY, 3 Baron (1911 UK); Sir Charles Melville McLaren; 3 Bt (UK 1902); eld s of 2 Baron Aberconway, CBE (d 1953), and Christabel (d 1974), da of Sir Melville Macnaghten, CB; bro of Hon Christopher Melville McLaren, *qv*; *b* 16 April 1913; *Educ* Eton, New Coll Oxford (BA); *m* 1, 1941 (m dis 1949), Deirdre, da of John Knewstub; 1 s, 2 da; m 2, 1949, Ann, o da of Mrs Alexander Lindsay Aymer, of New York, and formerly w of Maj Robert Lee Bullard III; 1 s; *Heir* s, Hon (Henry) Charles McLaren, *qv*; *Career* 2 Lt RA 1939–45; called to the Bar Middle Temple 1937; dir National Westminster Bank (formerly National Provincial Bank) 1953–83; chm: John Brown & Co Ltd 1953–78 (pres 1978–85), Sheepbridge Engineering 1961–79, English China Clays 1963–84 (pres 1984–); dep chm: Sun Alliance & London Insurance Co Ltd 1976–85, Westland plc 1979–85; pres RHS 1961–84 (pres emeritus 1984–); cmmr-gen Int

Garden Festival of Liverpool 1984, dir Nat Garden Festival Stoke-on-Trent 1986; pres of judging: Glasgow Garden Festival 1988, Gateshead Garden Festival 1990, Ebbw Vale Garden Festival 1992; JP Denbighshire 1946, High Sheriff Denbighshire 1950; Liveryman Worshipful Co of Fishmongers; Hon FIHort 1985; *Recreations* gardening, travel; *Style*— The Rt Hon Lord Aberconway, JP; ✉ 25 Egerton Terrace, London SW3 (☎ 0171 589 4369); Bodnant, Tal-y-Cafn, N Wales (☎ 01492 650 200)

ABERCORN, 5 Duke of (I 1868); Sir James Hamilton; 15 Bt (I 1660); also Lord Paisley (S 1578), Lord Abercorn (S 1603), Earl of Abercorn and Lord Paisley, Hamilton, Mountcastell, and Kilpatrick (S 1606), Baron of Strabane (I 1617), Baron Mountcastle and Viscount Strabane (I 1701), Viscount Hamilton (GB 1785), Marquess of Abercorn (GB 1790 - title in House of Lords), and Marquess of Hamilton (I 1868); s of 4 Duke of Abercorn (d 1979), and Lady Kathleen Mary, GCVO, *née* Crichton (d 1990), sis of 5 Earl of Erne; *b* 4 July 1934; *Educ* Eton, RAC Cirencester; *m* 1966, Alexandra Anastasia, da of Lt-Col Harold Pedro Phillips (d 1980), of Checkendon Court, nr Reading, also sis of Duchess of Westminster and gda through her m, Georgina, of late Sir Harold Wernher, 3 Bt, GCVO, TD, DL, by his w, late Lady Zia, CBE, *née* Countess Anastasia Mikhailovna (er da of HIH Grand Duke Mikhail Mikhailovitch of Russia, himself gs of Tsar Nicholas I); 2 s (Marquess of Hamilton, Lord Nicholas b 1979), 1 da (Lady Sophie b 1973); *Heir* s, Marquess of Hamilton, *qv*; *Career* 2 Lt Grenadier Gds; MP (UU) Fermanagh and S Tyrone 1964–70; dir Local Enterprise Devpt Unit 1971–77; memb Cncl of Europe 1968–70; memb Econ and Social Ctee EEC 1973–78; pres RUKBA 1979–; dir: NI Indust Devpt Bd 1982–87, Northern Bank Ltd 1970–; chm Laganside Devpt Corp 1989–96; High Sheriff Co Tyrone 1970, Lord-Lt Co Tyrone 1987–; pres: Building Socs Assoc 1986–92, NI Concrete Soc 1991–, NI Business in the Community 1992–; patron Royal Ulster Agric Soc 1990–95; *Recreations* shooting; *Clubs* Brooks's; *Style*— His Grace the Duke of Abercorn; ✉ Barons Ct, Omagh, Co Tyrone, N Ireland BT78 4EZ (☎ 0166 26 61470); Baronscourt Estate Office, Omagh, Co Tyrone (☎ 016626 61683, fax 01662 662059)

ABERCROMBIE, (George) Forbes; s of George Francis Abercrombie, VRD, RNVR (d 1978), and Marie, *née* Underhill; *b* 28 March 1935; *Educ* Charterhouse, Gonville and Caius Coll Cambridge, St Bartholomew's Hosp Med Coll (MA, MD); *m* 15 August 1959, Jennifer Elizabeth Dormer, da of Richard Valentine Dormer Kirby (d 1957); 2 s (John Forbes b 1961, Colin Francis b 1963); *Career* conslt urological surgn St Mary's Hosp Portsmouth 1971–95; cncl memb Br Assoc of Urological Surgns 1984–87, memb Int Urological Soc; Liveryman Worshipful Soc of Apothecaries 1964 (former memb Livery Ctee); FRCS; *Recreations* golf, salmon fishing, chess; *Style*— Forbes Abercrombie, Esq; ✉ Church House, Catherington Lane, Catherington, Hants PO8 0TE (☎ 01705 597 676)

ABERCROMBIE, Ian Ralph; QC (Scot 1994); s of Ralph Abercrombie, of Edinburgh, and Jean Hamilton Brown Lithgow (d 1992); *b* 7 July 1955; *Educ* Milton HS Bulawayo, Univ of Edinburgh (LLB (Hons)); *Career* admitted to Faculty of Advocates 1981; *Style*— Ian Abercrombie, Esq, QC; ✉ 7 Lauder Road, Edinburgh EH9 2EW (☎ 0131 668 2489); c/o Advocates' Library, Parliament House, Edinburgh EH1 1RF (☎ 0131 226 5071)

ABERCROMBIE, Prof Nicholas; s of Michael Abercrombie (d 1978), and Jane Abercrombie (d 1984); *b* 13 April 1944; *Educ* University Coll Sch, The Queen's Coll Oxford (BA), LSE (MSc), Univ of Lancaster (PhD); *m* 1969, Brenda, da of Harry Patterson; 2 s (Robert b 1971, Joseph b 1974); *Career* hon research asst UCL 1968–70; Univ of Lancaster: lectr in sociology 1970–83, sr lectr 1983–88, reader 1988–90, prof of sociology 1990–, dean of undergraduate studies 1992–95, pro-vice-chllr 1995–; memb British Sociological Soc 1968; *Books* The Dominant Ideology Thesis (with S Hill and B Turner, 1980), The Penguin Dictionary of Sociology (with S Hill and B Turner, 1984), Sovereign Individuals of Capitalism (with S Hill and B Turner, 1986), Contemporary British Society (jtly, 1988), Television and Society (1996); also author of numerous articles in learned jls; *Recreations* gardening; *Style*— Prof Nicholas Abercrombie; ✉ University of Lancaster, Lancaster LA1 4YL (☎ 01524 65201, fax 015424 36841, e-mail n.abercrombie@lancaster.ac.uk)

ABERCROMBY, Sir Ian George; 10 Bt (NS 1636), of Birkenbog, Banffshire; s of Robert Ogilvie Abercromby, gs of 5 Bt; suc kinsman 1972; *b* 30 June 1925; *Educ* Lancing, Bloxham Sch Banbury; *m* 1, 1950 (m dis 1957), Joyce Beryl, da of Leonard Griffiths; m 2, 1959, Fanny Mary Udale (Molly), da of Dr Graham Udale-Smith, of Sitio Litre, Puerto de la Cruz, Tenerife; 1 da; m 3, 1976, Diana Marjorie, da of Horace Geoffrey Cockell, and wid of Capt Ian Charles Palliser Galloway; *Heir* none; *Style*— Sir Ian Abercromby, Bt

ABERDARE, 4 Baron (UK 1873); Morys George Lyndhurst Bruce; KBE (1984), PC (1974), DL (Dyfed 1985); s of 3 Baron Aberdare, GBE (d 1957); *b* 16 June 1919; *Educ* Winchester, New Coll Oxford; *m* 1946, (Maud Helen) Sarah, da of Sir John Dashwood, 10 Bt, CVO (d 1966); 4 s; *Heir* s, Hon Alastair Bruce; *Career* Welsh Guards 1939–46; J Arthur Rank Orgn 1947–49, BBC 1949–56; min of state DHSS 1970–74, min without portfolio 1974, chm Ctees House of Lords 1976–92; chm: Albany Life Assurance 1975–92, Metlife (UK) Ltd 1986–92; chm The Football Tst 1979–; pres: YMCA of Wales, Tennis and Rackets Assoc, Kidney Research Unit for Wales Fndn; Hon LLD Wales 1985; GCStJ; *Books* The Story of Tennis, Willis Faber Book of Tennis and Rackets; *Recreations* real tennis, rackets; *Clubs* Lansdowne, MCC, All England Lawn Tennis, Queen's (pres); *Style*— The Rt Hon Lord Aberdare, KBE, PC, DL; ✉ 32 Elthiron Rd, London SW6 4BW (☎ 0171 736 0825)

ABERDEEN, Bishop of (RC) 1977–; Rt Rev Mario Joseph Conti; s of Louis Conti, and Josephine Panicali; *b* 1934; *Educ* St Marie's Convent Sch Springfield Elgin, Blairs Coll Aberdeen, Pontifical Gregorian Univ Rome (STL, PhL); *Career* ordained Rome 1958, curate St Mary's Cathedral Aberdeen 1959–62, jt parish priest St Joachim's Wick and St Anne's Thurso 1962–77; pres/treas Scottish Catholic Int Aid Fund 1978–85, Scottish memb Episcopal Bd Int Cmmn for English in the Liturgy 1978–87; chm: Cmmn for the Pastoral Care of Migrant Workers 1978–85, Scottish Catholic Heritage Cmmn 1980–; pres: Nat Liturgy Cmmn 1981–85, Nat Cmmn for Christian Doctrine and Unity 1985–; memb: Bishops' Jt Ctee for Bio-ethical Issues 1982–, Cncl for Promotion of Christian Unity (Rome) 1984–; convener Action of Churches Together in Scotland 1990–93, princ chaplain Br Assoc of the Order of Malta 1995, co-moderator Jt Working Gp (RC Church and WCC) 1995; Commendatore Dell'Ordine Al Merito Della Repubblica Italiana 1981, Kt Cdr of the Holy Sepulchre 1989, Conventual Chaplain Ad Honorem Sovereign Military Order of St John of Jerusalem 1991; Hon DD Aberdeen 1989; FRSE 1995; *Style*— The Rt Rev the Bishop of Aberdeen; ✉ Bishop's House, 3 Queen's Cross, Aberdeen AB15 4XU (☎ 01224 319154)

ABERDEEN AND ORKNEY, Bishop of 1992–; Rt Rev (Andrew) Bruce Cameron; s of Andrew Cameron (d 1975), of Dunoon, Argyll, and Helen, *née* Adam McKechnie (d 1989); *b* 2 May 1941; *Educ* Eastwood Secdy Sch, Edinburgh Theol Coll (Luscombe scholar), New Coll Univ of Edinburgh (Cert in Pastoral Studies), Urban Theol Unit Sheffield (Dip in Theol and Mission); *m* 1974, Elaine; 2 s (Ewan b 1979, Dermot b 1981); *Career* ordained: deacon 1964, priest 1965; curate: St Michael and All Angels Helensburgh 1964–67, Holy Cross Church Edinburgh 1967–70; chaplain St Mary's Cathedral Edinburgh and diocesan and provincial youth chaplain 1970–75, rector St Mary's Church Dalmahoy and Anglican chaplain Heriot Watt Univ 1975–82, team priest and churches devpt offr Livingston Ecumenical Parish Livingston New Town 1982–88, rector St John's Church Perth 1988–92; convenor Scottish Episcopal Church's Mission Bd 1988–92; *Recreations* sport (golf and swimming), music, theatre, reading; *Clubs* Rotary; *Style*— The Rt Rev the Bishop of Aberdeen and Orkney; ✉ Bishop's House, Ashley House, Ashley Gardens, Aberdeen AB10 6RQ (☎ and fax 01224 208142); Diocesan Centre, 39 Kings Crescent, Aberdeen AB24 3HP (☎ 01224 636653, fax 01224 636186)

ABERDEEN AND ORKNEY, Dean of; *see:* Stranraer-Mull, Very Rev Gerald

ABERDEEN AND TEMAIR, 6 Marquess of (UK 1916); Sir Alastair Ninian John Gordon; 14 Bt (NS 1642); also 12 Earl of Aberdeen (S 1682), Lord Haddo, Methlic, Tarves, and Kellie (S 1682), Viscount Formartine (S 1782), Viscount Gordon (UK 1814), and Earl of Haddo (UK 1916); s of 3 Marquess of Aberdeen and Temair, DSO (d 1972), by his 1 w, Cecile, da of George Drummond (ggggs of Andrew Drummond, yr bro of 4 Viscount Strathallan and fndr of Messrs Drummond, the bankers) by Elizabeth (da of Rev Frederick Norman and Lady Adeliza Manners, da of 5 Duke of Rutland); suc er bro 5 Marquess of Aberdeen and Temair 1984; *b* 20 July 1920; *Educ* Harrow; *m* 1950, Anne, da of Lt-Col Gerald Barry, MC; 1 s, 2 da; *Heir* s, Earl of Haddo, *qv*; *Career* served WWII Capt Scots Gds; painter; one man exhibitions in London, New York, Chicago, Baltimore and Sydney; memb Int Assoc of Art Critics, chm Arts Club 1966–76; memb Bach Choir 1939–82; *Recreations* music, people; *Clubs* Arts, MCC, Puffins; *Style*— The Most Hon the Marquess of Aberdeen and Temair; ✉ Quicks Green, Ashampstead, Berks RG8 8SN (☎ 01491 671331)

ABERDEEN AND TEMAIR, June, Marchioness of; (Beatrice Mary) June Gordon; CBE (1989, MBE 1971), DL (Aberdeenshire 1971); da of late Arthur Paul Boissier (d 1953); *b* 29 Dec 1913; *Educ* Southlands Sch Harrow, RCM; *m* 29 April 1939, 4 Marquess of Aberdeen and Temair, CBE, TD, KStJ (d 1974); 2 adopted s, 2 adopted da; *Career* music teacher Bromley HS for Girls 1936–39, musical dir and conductor Haddo House Choral and Operatic Soc 1945–, tstee Haddo House Hall Arts Tst; chm: Scottish Children's League 1969–94, NE Scotland Music Sch 1975–, Advsy Cncl Scottish Opera 1979–92, local advsy ctee Aberdeen Int Festival of Music and the Performing Arts 1980–93 (patron 1993–); govr: Gordonstoun Sch 1971–86, Royal Scottish Acad of Music and Drama 1979–82; Hon LLD Aberdeen 1968, Hon DMus Robert Gordon's Univ 1992; GCStJ 1996; FRCM 1967, FRSE 1983, FRSAMD 1985; *Style*— The Most Hon June, Marchioness of Aberdeen and Temair, CBE, DL, FRSE; ✉ Haddo House, Aberdeen AB41 0ER (☎ 01651 851216)

ABERDOUR, Lord; (John) Stewart Sholto Douglas; s and h of 21 Earl of Morton, *qv*; *b* 17 Jan 1952; *Educ* Dunrobin Castle Sch, Aberdeen Univ; *m* 20 July 1985, Amanda Kirsten, yr da of David John Macfarlane Mitchell, of Castle St, Kirkcudbright; 1 s (Hon John David Sholto, Master of Aberdour b 28 May 1986), 2 da (Hon Katherine Florence b 3 Aug 1989, Hon Jennifer Mary b 29 March 1991); *Career* ptnr Dalmahoy Farms; *Style*— Lord Aberdour; ✉ Haggs Farm, Kirknewton, Midlothian EH27 8EE

ABERGAVENNY, 5 Marquess of (UK 1876); John Henry Guy Nevill; KG (1974), OBE (1945), JP (Sussex 1948); also Baron Abergavenny (E 1450 as Baron Bergavenny; 14 Baron, who held the title 1724–45, was the first to be styled Lord Abergavenny), Viscount Nevill, Earl of Abergavenny (both GB 1784), and Earl of Lewes (UK 1876); s of 4 Marquess of Abergavenny (d 1954); *b* 8 Nov 1914; *Educ* Eton, Trinity Coll Cambridge; *m* 1938, Patricia (*see* Abergavenny, Marchioness of); 3 da (and 1 s and 1 da decd); *Heir* nephew, Christopher George Charles Nevill b 1955; *Career* 2 Lt LG 1935, Maj 1942, served NW Europe (despatches), Temp Lt-Col 1945, ret 1946; Hon Col Kent and Co of London Yeo 1948–62, Alderman E Sussex CC 1954–62, tstee Ascot Authy 1952–82, HM Representative at Ascot 1972–82, pres Royal Agric Soc of England 1967 (dep pres 1968 and 1972); former pres: Royal Assoc of Br Dairy Farmers, Assoc of Agric; pres Br Horse Soc 1970–71, memb Nat Hunt Ctee (former Sr Steward), former vice chm Turf Bd; Lord-Lt of E Sussex 1974–89 (DL 1955, Vice-Lt 1970–74), Chllr of Order of the Garter 1977–, pres Cncl of Order of St John Sussex 1975– (KStJ 1976); former chm: Lloyds Bank Property Co Ltd, Lloyds Bank SE Regional Bd; former dir: Lloyds Bank plc, Lloyds Bank UK Management, Massey-Ferguson Holdings Ltd (ret 1985), Whitbread Investment Co Ltd, Br Equestrian Promotions Ltd; *Clubs* White's; *Style*— The Most Hon the Marquess of Abergavenny, KG, OBE, JP; ✉ Eridge Park, Tunbridge Wells, Kent TN3 9JT (☎ 01892 527378); Flat 2, 46 Pont St, London SW1 (☎ 0171 581 3967)

ABERGAVENNY, Marchioness of; (Mary) Patricia; DCVO (1981, CVO 1970); da of late Lt-Col John Fenwick Harrison, RHG, and Hon Margery, da of 3 Baron Burnham, DSO; *b* 1915; *m* 1938, 5 Marquess of Abergavenny, *qv*; 3 da (and 1 s and 1 da decd); *Career* Lady of the Bedchamber to HM The Queen 1966– (an Extra Lady of the Bedchamber 1960–66); *Style*— The Most Hon The Marchioness of Abergavenny, DCVO; ✉ Eridge Park, Tunbridge Wells, Kent TN3 9JT (☎ 01892 527378); Flat 2, 46 Pont St, London SW1 (☎ 0171 581 3967)

ABERNETHY, Hon Lord; (John) Alastair Cameron; s of William Philip Legerwood Cameron (d 1977), of Edinburgh, and Kathleen Milthorpe, *née* Parker (d 1966); *b* 1 Feb 1938; *Educ* St Mary's Sch Melrose, Glenalmond Coll Perth, Pembroke Coll Oxford (MA); *m* 1968, Elspeth Mary Dunlop, da of James Bowie Miller (d 1994), of E Lothian; 3 s (Hamish b 1970, Neil b 1972, Iain b 1975); *Career* Nat Serv 2 Lt RASC Aldershot & Malta 1956–58; called to the Bar Inner Temple 1963, advocate 1966, advocate depute 1972–75, vice dean Faculty of Advocates 1983–92; standing jr counsel to: Dept of Energy 1976–79, Scot Devpt Dept 1978–79; QC Scotland 1979; pres Pensions Appeal Tbnls for Scotland 1985–92 (legal chm 1979–85), chm Faculty Services Ltd 1983–89 (dir 1979–89); Lord of Session (Senator of the College of Justice) 1992–; chm Judges' Forum Int Bar Assoc 1994– (vice chm 1993–94); memb Exec Ctee Soc for the Welfare and Teaching of the Blind (Edinburgh and SE Scotland) 1979–92; hon fell Pembroke Coll Oxford 1993–; *Publications* Medical Negligence: An Introduction (1983), contrib to Reproductive Medicine and the Law (ed A A Templeton and D J Cusine, 1990); *Recreations* sport, travel, Africana, nature conservation; *Style*— The Hon Lord Abernethy; ✉ Court of Session, Parliament House, Edinburgh EH1 1RQ (☎ 0131 225 2595, fax 0131 225 8213)

ABINGDON, Earl of *see:* Lindsey and Abingdon, Earl of

ABINGER, 8 Baron (UK 1835); James Richard Scarlett; s of 7 Baron Abinger, DSO (d 1943); *b* 28 Sept 1914; *Educ* Eton, Magdalene Coll Cambridge; *m* 1957, Isla Carolyn, niece of Sir Henry Rivett-Carnac, 7 Bt, and da of late Vice Adm J W Rivett-Carnac, CB, CBE, DSC; 2 s; *Heir* s, Hon James Harry Scarlett, *qv*; *Career* served Royal Artillery 1936–47, Capt (Hon Lt-Col); sits as Cons in House of Lords; retired co dir and farmer; memb Ct Univ of Essex, fndr memb Euro-Atlantic Gp, a vice pres Byron Soc; formerly chm: Keats-Shelley Meml Soc, Mid Anglia Centre Nat Tst; former govr ESU, memb Chapter-Gen OstJ; served Halstead and Braintree DCs and on Cncl CPRE; DL Essex 1968–89; KStJ; *Recreations* field sports; *Clubs* Carlton, RAC; *Style*— The Rt Hon the Lord Abinger; ✉ Sheepcote House, 23 Queen Street, Castle Hedingham, Halstead, Essex CO9 3HA (☎ 01787 460388); 7 Cumberland Street, London SW1V 4LS (☎ 0171 828 4708)

ABLE, Graham George; s of George Jasper Able, and Irene Helen, *née* Gaff; *b* 28 July 1947; *Educ* Worksop Coll Notts, Trinity Coll Cambridge (MA, PGCE), Univ of Durham (MA); *m* Mary Susan, da of John Sidney Thomas Munro; 1 s (Richard Graham Munro b 10 May 1973), 1 da (Lisa Maria b 17 June 1976); *Career* Sutton Valence Sch: teacher of chemistry 1969–83, cricket master 1971–76 and 1980–83, hockey master 1972–83, boarding housemaster 1976–83; second master Barnard Castle Sch 1983–88, headmaster Hampton Sch 1988–96, master Dulwich Coll 1997–; fndr memb Kent Schs Sports Cncl 1976–83; chm of Conf Ctee BSA Housemasters' and Headmistresses' Conf 1980 and

1981; memb: Sports Sub Ctee HMC 1989–91, Assisted Places Working Party HMC 1991–96, Academic Policy Sub Ctee HMC 1995–; memb Assisted Places Ctee ISJC 1991–96; memb: HMC 1988– (chm London Div 1993–94), Assoc for Science Educn 1968–88, SHA 1988–, IOD; FRSA 1994; *Recreations* cricket and hockey, fell-walking, contract bridge, the theatre; *Clubs* East India & Public Schools (hon memb), MCC; *Style*— Graham Able, Esq; ✉ Elm Lawn, Dulwich Common, London SE21 7EW (☎ 0181 693 0546); Dulwich College, London SE21 7LD (☎ 0181 693 3601, fax 0181 693 6319)

ABLEMAN, Sheila; da of Dennis Hutton-Fox, of Hove, Sussex, and late Rosamund Alice Evelyn, *née* Tapsell; *b* 3 Feb 1949; *Educ* Cheam Co Sch for Girls, Epsom Art Sch, Cambridge Art Sch, Queen Mary Coll Univ of London (BA); *m* 1978, Paul Victor Ableman, novelist and playwright; 1 s (Thomas Mark b 7 July 1981); *Career* designer's asst Weidenfeld & Nicolson Ltd 1970, editorial asst Victor Gollancz 1976–78; BBC Books: editorial asst 1978–82, dep books ed 1982–87, sr commissioning ed 1987–90, jt head of editorial 1990–94, editorial dir 1994–; *Clubs* Academy; *Style*— Mrs Sheila Ableman; ✉ BBC Books, BBC Worldwide, Woodlands, 80 Wood Lane, London W12 0TT (☎ 0181 576 2630)

ABRAHAM, Ann; *b* 25 Aug 1952; *Educ* Bedford Coll London (BA), City of London Poly (postgrad DMS); *Career* graduate trainee (latterly estate mangr) London Borough of Tower Hamlets 1975–79, estate action mangr London Borough of Islington 1979–80; The Housing Corp: joined 1980, regnl dir 1986–89, ops dir 1989–90; chief exec Nat Assoc of Citizens Advice Bureaux 1991–; MCIH; *Recreations* family, friends, football and walking; *Style*— Ms Ann Abraham; ✉ National Association of Citizens Advice Bureaux, Myddelton House, 115–123 Pentonville Road, London N1 9LZ (☎ 0171 833 2181, fax 0171 833 4371)

ABRAHAM, Sir Edward Penley; kt (1980), CBE (1973); s of Albert Penley Abraham, and Mary, *née* Hearn; *b* 10 June 1913; *Educ* King Edward VI Sch Southampton, Queen's Coll Oxford (MA, DPhil); *m* 1939, Asbjörg Harung, of Bergen, Norway; 1 s; *Career* fell Lincoln Coll Oxford 1948–80 (hon fell 1980–), prof of chemical pathology Oxford 1964–80 (now emeritus prof); hon fell: Queen's Coll Oxford 1973, Linacre Coll Oxford 1976, Lady Margaret Hall Oxford 1978, Wolfson Coll Oxford 1982, St Peter's Coll Oxford 1983; Chemical Soc Award in Medicinal Chemistry 1975, Royal Soc Mullard Medal and Prize 1980 (Royal medal 1973), Int Soc of Chemotherapy Award 1983; author of med and scientific papers on penicillins, cephalosporins and other substances with biological activity 1941–93; fndr and tstee two charitable tst funds for the support of research or educn in med, biological and chemical sciences 1967–; foreign hon memb American Acad of Arts and Sciences 1983; Hon DSc: Univ of Exeter 1980, Univ of Oxford 1984, Univ of Strathclyde 1989; FRS 1958; *Publications* Biochemistry of Some Peptide and Steroid Antibiotics (1957), Biosynthesis and Enzymic Hydrolysis of Penicillins and Cephalosporins (1974); *Clubs* Athenaeum; *Style*— Sir Edward Abraham, CBE, FRS; ✉ Badger's Wood, Bedwells Heath, Boars Hill, Oxford (☎ 01865 735395); Sir William Dunn School of Pathology, Oxford (☎ 01865 275500, fax 01865 275501)

ABRAHAM, Maj-Gen (Sutton) Martin O'Heguerty; CB (1973), MC (1942, and Bar 1943); s of Capt Edgar Gaston Furtado Abraham, CB, late ICS (d 1955), and Ruth Eostre, da of Rev Gerald S Davies, master of the Charterhouse, London; *b* 26 Jan 1919; *Educ* Eton, Trinity Coll Cambridge (BA); *m* 1950, Iona Margaret, da of Sir John Stirling, KT, MBE; 2 s, 1 da; *Career* dir of Combat Devpt MOD 1968–71, chief of Jt Servs Liaison Orgn BAOR 1971–73, FO Balanced Force Reductions in Europe 1973–76; sec Bedford Coll Univ of London 1976–82 (govr 1983–85); Col 9/12 Royal Lancers 1978–82; *Style*— Maj-Gen Martin Abraham, CB, MC; ✉ c/o Hoare & Co, 37 Fleet St, London EC4P 4DQ

ABRAHAM, Neville Victor; s of Solomon Abraham (d 1991), and Sarah Raphael; *b* 22 Jan 1937, Calcutta; *Educ* Brighton Coll, Univ of London, LSE (BSc); *Career* sr princ Board of Trade and private sec to Minister of State 1963–71; corporate policy advsr Whitehead Consulting Group 1971–76; fndr chm and md Amis du Vin Gp and Les Amis du Vin Ltd 1974–86; visiting lectr at leading Business Schs 1974–83; gp exec dir Kennedy Brookes plc 1984–86; dir Creative Business Communications plc 1986–91; chm and chief exec: Groupe Chez Gérard Restaurants Ltd 1986–, Groupe Chez Gérard plc 1994–; jt exec chm BOC Covent Garden Festival 1991–, vice chm Restaurateurs Assoc of GB 1994–; *Books* Big Business and Government: The New Disorder (1974); *Recreations* music (especially opera), walking, eating out, reading menus and wine lists; *Clubs* RAC, MCC; *Style*— Neville Abraham, Esq; ✉ 82 Addison Road, London W14 8ED; Groupe Chez Gérard Restaurants Ltd, 8 Upper St Martin's Lane, London WC2H 9EN (☎ 0171 240 9240)

ABRAHAM, Prof Raymond John; s of Judah H Abraham (d 1989), and Elizabeth, *née* Harrop; *b* 26 Nov 1933; *Educ* Magnus GS Newark, Univ of Birmingham (BSc, PhD, DSc); *m* 1, 16 Aug 1958 (m dis 1986), June Roslyn; 2 s (David Joseph b 3 Sept 1962, Simon Douglas b 27 Oct 1969), 1 da (Susan Elizabeth b 8 Sept 1959); m 2, 17 Sept 1988, Barbara Ann, da of Henry Broadbent (d 1982); *Career* postdoctoral fell NRC Canada 1957–59, sr fell Nat Physical Lab 1959–61, Univ of Liverpool 1961– (lectr, sr lectr, reader, prof); visiting prof: Carnegie-Mellon Univ Pittsburgh 1966–67, Univ of California 1981–89; Ciba-Geigy fell Univ of Trondheim 1979; memb American Chemical Soc 1981–; *Books* The Analysis of NMR Spectra (1971), Proton and Carbon 13 NMR Spectroscopy (with P Loftus, 1978), Introduction to NMR Spectroscopy (with J Fisher and P Loftus, 1988); *Recreations* squash, gardening, theatre; *Clubs* Birkenhead Constitutional; *Style*— Prof Raymond Abraham; ✉ 11 Lawns Ave, Raby Mere, Wirral L63 0NF; The Robert Robinson Labs, The Chemistry Department, The University of Liverpool, PO Box 147, Liverpool L69 3BX (☎ 0151 794 3511, fax 0151 794 3588, telex 627095 UNILPLG)

ABRAHAMS, Lt-Col (Sidney) Anthony George; TD; s of Anthony Claude Walter Abrahams, of Goldsmith Building, Temple, London, and Laila, *née* Myking; *b* 30 Oct 1951; *Educ* Bedford Sch; *m* 6 Oct 1979, Kathryn Helen Anne, da of Humphrey John Patrick Chetwynd-Talbot, of South Warnborough, Basingstoke, Hants; 1 s (Thomas b 1985), 2 da (Annika b 1983, Harriett b 1988); *Career* cmmnd 1976, Lt-Col 1994, Royal Green Jackets (V); admitted slr 1978; Wade-Gery and Brackenbury 1980–84, Alexander Farr and Son 1984–88, Pictons (formerly Wade Gery Farr) 1988–, dep district judge Co Ct 1989; Freeman City of London 1985; memb: Worshipful Co of Glazier's 1985, Law Soc; *Recreations* TA, squash, food and drink; *Clubs* Army & Navy; *Style*— Lt-Col Anthony Abrahams, TD; ✉ Woodfield, Honeydon Rd, Colmworth, Beds MK44 2LZ (☎ 01234 378996); Pictons, 30–32 Bromham Rd, Bedford MK40 2QD (☎ 01234 273273, fax 01234 353110)

ABRAHAMS, Gerald Milton; CBE (1967); s of Isidor Abrahams (d 1943); *b* 20 June 1917; *Educ* Westminster; *m* 1, 1946, Doris, da of late Mark Cole, of Brookline, Mass, USA; 2 da; m 2, 1972, Mrs Marianne Wilson, da of late David Kay, of London; *Career* Maj Br Army WWII, HAC, RHA, served Greece, W Desert and Ceylon; chm and md Aquascutum Group plc and associated cos 1947–91, former pres Aquascutum Group plc; memb: Br Menswear Guild (chm 1959–61 and 1964–66), Cncl CBI 1965–87, Br Nat Export Cncl Ctee for Exports to Canada 1965–70, Consumer Goods Ctee Export Cncl for Europe, Clothing Export Cncl (chm 1966–70, vice pres 1970–87), Economic Devpt Ctee for Clothing Indust 1966–69, Clothing Manufacturers' Fedn of GB 1960–82 (chm Exec Cncl 1965–66), North American Advsy Gp BOTB 1978–86 (vice chm 1983–86), Br Clothing Indust Assoc 1982–87; FRSA 1972, CIMgt 1979; *Recreations* swimming, golf; *Clubs* Buck's; *Style*— Gerald Abrahams, Esq, CBE

ABRAHAMS, Ivor; s of Harry Abrahams (d 1984), of Southport, and Rachel, *née* Kalisky (d 1983); *b* 10 Jan 1935; *Educ* Wigan GS, Southport Sch of Arts and Crafts, St Martin's Sch of Art, Camberwell Sch of Art (NDD); *m* 1, Victoria, da of Henry James Taylor; 1 s (Saul Benjamin b 27 March 1966 (decd)); m 2, Evelyne, da of Andre Horvais; 1 s (Etienne b 17 April 1973); *Career* artist, sculptor, photographer; solo exhibitions incl: Arnolfini Gallery Bristol 1971, Mappin Art Gallery Sheffield and Aberdeen Art Gallery 1972, Lijnbaan Centrum Rotterdam 1973, Kölnischer Kunstverien Cologne 1973, Ferens Art Gallery Kingston upon Hull 1979, Portsmouth City Art Gallery 1979, Middlesbrough Art Gallery 1979, Stoke on Trent City Museum 1979, St Enoch's Gallery Glasgow 1980, Warwick Arts Tst London 1982, Bolton Museum and Art Gallery 1984, Yorkshire Sculpture Park Wakefield 1984; gp exhibitions incl: 26 Young Sculptors (Inst of Contemporary Arts London) 1961, Br Art Today (Palazzo Realle Milan) 1976, Silver Jubilee Exhibition (contemporary sculpture, Battersea Park) 1977, New Orleans Museum of Art 1978, Br Art Show 1980, Landscape Prints (Tate Gallery) 1981, Br Sculpture in the 20th Century 1951–80 (Whitechapel Art Gallery) 1982; public collections incl: Aberdeen Art Gallery and Museum, Arts Cncl of GB, Bibliotheque Nationale Paris, Br Cncl London, Metropolitan Museum New York, Museum of Modern Art New York, Nat Gallery of Australia Canberra, Tate Gallery London, V & A Museum London, Buymans Museum Rotterdam, Denver Museum Colorado, Minneapolis Art Inst, Strasbourg Museum, Walker Art Gallery Liverpool, Wedgwood Museum Stoke on Trent, Wilhem Lembruke Museum Duisburg, Williams Coll Museum of Art Williamstown; work incls: book illustrations and photographs, short films and videos; visiting lectr: Birmingham Coll of Art and Crafts 1960–63, Coventry Coll of Art and Crafts 1964–66, Goldsmiths' Coll of Art 1968–69, Royal Coll of Art 1980–81, Slade Sch UCL 1982, Winston Churchill fell 1990; RA 1991 (ARA 1989); *Recreations* golf, photography, reading, collecting; *Clubs* Chelsea Arts, Colony Room; *Style*— Ivor Abrahams, Esq, RA; ✉ c/o The Royal Academy, Burlington House, Piccadilly, London W1V 0DS

ABRAHAMS, Michael David; CBE 1994 (MBE 1988), DL (N Yorks 1994); s of Alexander Abrahams, and Anne, *née* Sokoloff; *b* 23 Nov 1937; *Educ* Shrewsbury, Worcester Coll Oxford; *m* 1967, Amanda, *née* Atha; 2 da (Emily, Victoria), 1 s (Rupert); *Career* cmmnd Royal Marines; md A W (Securities) Ltd 1968; dir: John Waddington plc 1984–, Drummond Group plc 1989–; dep chm: York Trust plc 1985–88, John Crowther plc 1985–88, Prudential Corporation plc 1991– (dir 1984–); chm Cavaghan and Gray Group plc (formerly Dalepak Foods plc) 1992– (dir 1987–); dir The Rank Fndn 1992–; pres British Carpet Manufacturers' Assoc 1979–80; chm: Ripon Improvement Tst 1994–, The London Clinic 1996– (govr 1990–); dep chm Cncl Prince of Wales's Inst of Architecture 1991–; High Sheriff for Co of N Yorks 1993–94; breeder of pedigree beef shorthorns; jt master and huntsman West of Yore Hunt 1970–81, jt master Bedale Hunt 1971–79; Master Worshipful Co of Woolmen 1996; *Recreations* architecture, literature, shooting, sailing; *Clubs* Garrick, Pratt's; *Style*— Michael Abrahams, Esq, CBE, DL; ✉ Newfield, Mickley, Ripon, N Yorks HG4 3JH (☎ 01765 635426, fax 01765 635461)

ABRAHAMS, Paul Richard; s of Anthony Claud Walter Abrahams, of London, and Laila, *née* Myking; *b* 20 April 1962; *Educ* Radley, Downing Coll Cambridge (BA, MA), Darwin Coll Cambridge (PhD, Fencing half blue); *Career* Financial Times: technol corr 1988–89, dep defence and aerospace corr 1989–91, chemicals and pharmaceuticals corr 1991–94, Lex columnist 1994–95, int cos ed 1995–; *Recreations* skiing; *Clubs* Ski Club of GB; *Style*— Paul Abrahams, Esq; ✉ Financial Times, 1 Southwark Bridge, London SE1 9HL (☎ 0171 873 3650, fax 0171 873 4344)

ABRAMOVICH, Solomon; s of Dr Jacob Abramovich, MD (d 1977), and Bronia Maisel (d 1980); *b* 12 Dec 1946; *Educ* Sch of Music, Kaunas Med Sch (MSc, MB BS); *children* 1 s (Alexander b 5 Jan 1991), 1 da (Natalia b 6 Jan 1996); *Career* The Radcliffe Infirmary Oxford 1974–75, The Hammersmith Hospital London 1975, UCH 1976–78, King's Coll Hosp 1979, clinical fell Univ of Toronto 1982, chief asst and sr registrar St Bartholomew's and Nat Hosp for Neurology and Neurosurgery London 1982, conslt ENT surgn St Mary's Hosp London and Central Middlesex Hosp 1988; hon clinical sr lectr The Imperial Coll of Science, Technol and Med London 1989; hon conslt to Gibraltar; memb: Int Barany Soc, Int Maniere's Soc, Cochlear Implant Study Gp; FRCS (MRCS), LRCP, MRSM; *Books* Electric Response Audiometry in Clinical Practice (1990); *Recreations* tennis, skiing, playing the violin; *Clubs* Athenaeum; *Style*— Solomon Abramovich, Esq; ✉ 24 Downshire Hill, London NW3 1NT (☎ 0171 435 8342); 152 Harley St, London W1N 1HH (☎ 0171 935 3834, fax 0171 224 2574)

ABRAMS, Anita Rosalie; da of Mark Berlyne (d 1981), and Cissie, *née* Spurgin (d 1981); *b* 22 Dec 1928; *Educ* Manchester HS for Girls, Newnham Coll Cambridge (MA); *m* 22 Aug 1954, (Joseph) David Abrams, s of Julius Maurice Abrams (d 1974), of Leeds; 5 da (Susan b 1955, Janet b 1959, Hester b 1963, Wendy b 1966, Rachel b 1973); *Career* asst lectr Dept of Psychiatry Univ of Leeds 1951–53; educnl psychologist: Child Guidance Clinic Sheffield 1953–55, London Borough of Enfield 1965–73; chartered psychologist (educn and clinical) in private practice 1973–; hon sec Assoc of Chartered Clinical Psychologists in Private Practice 1985–90 (fndr memb 1982); AFBPsS 1952, affiliate memb Assoc of Educn Psychologists; *Recreations* craft fairs and quirky humour; *Style*— Mrs Anita R Abrams; ✉ 11 Mercers Place, Brook Green, London W6 7BZ; Hospital of St John and St Elizabeth, London NW8 9NH (☎ 0171 266 1797, fax 0171 603 8807)

ABRAMS, Charles; s of Mozus Mischa Abrams (d 1987), of London, and Evelyn Joyce, *née* Spitzel; *b* 2 Nov 1952; *Educ* St Paul's, Trinity Coll Cambridge (BA); *m* 30 Aug 1987, Georgia Gitelle Devora, da of James Leo Rosengarten, of Hampstead, and Naomi Rosengarten, *née* Alexander; 1 s (Boris Yoshua Avitzur b 27 July 1992), 1 da (Alexandra Berina Amelia b 29 May 1990); *Career* slr Linklaters & Paines 1976–85 (articled 1974), ptnr S J Berwin & Co 1986– (slr 1985–86); various pubns in jls and speaker at seminars on securities law; arbitrator Securities and Futures Authy Consumer Arbitration Scheme; memb: City Regulatory Panel CBI, Law Soc; ACIArb; *Books* Guide to the Financial Services Act 1986 (jtly, 2 edn 1989); contrib to: CCH Financial Services Reporter, Pension Fund Investment (1987), Bond Market Compliance (1992), Futures Trading Law and Regulation (1993); *Recreations* looking after babies, theatre; *Style*— Charles Abrams, Esq; ✉ S J Berwin & Co, 222 Gray's Inn Rd, London WC1X 8HB (☎ 0171 533 2222)

ABRAMS, Dr Michael Ellis; CB (1992); s of Sam Philip Abrams, OBE (d 1964), and Ruhamah Emmie, *née* Glieberman (d 1989); *b* 17 Sept 1932; *Educ* King Edward's Sch Birmingham, Univ of Birmingham (MB ChB, BSc); *m* 1962, Rosalind June, da of Nathan Beckman (d 1970); 4 c (Rebecca, Jonathan, Jeremy, Nathan); *Career* dep chief med offr Dept of Health 1985–92; non-exec vice chm Haringey Healthcare NHS Tst 1993–; Liveryman Worshipful Soc of Apothecaries; FRCP, FFPHM; *Recreations* beachcombing; *Style*— Dr Michael Abrams, CB; ✉ 97 Wood Vale, London N10 3DL

ABRAMSKY, Jennifer (Jenny); da of Chimen Abramsky, and Miriam, *née* Nirenstein; *b* 7 Oct 1946; *Educ* Holland Park Sch, UEA (BA); *m* Alasdair D MacDuff Liddell, *qv*; 1 s, 1 da; *Career* BBC: joined 1969 as progs ops asst, prodr The World At One 1973 (ed 1981), jt prodr special prog on Nixon 1974, ed PM 1978, prodr Radio 4's Budget progs 1979–86, ed Today Prog 1986–87, ed News and Current Affrs Radio 1987–93 (set up Radio 4 Gulf FM for duration of Gulf War), controller Radio 5 Live and head of Ceefax 1994–96, head Continuous News 1996–; special award for Radio 5 Live Sony Radio Awards 1995, UK Station of the Year Sony Radio Awards 1996; Woman of Distinction award (Jewish Care) 1990; appointed to ESRC 1992–96; hon prof Thames Valley Univ

1994; *Recreations* theatre, music; *Style—* Ms Jenny Abramsky; ✉ Room 4084, BBC Broadcasting House, Portland Place, London W1A 1AA (☎ 0171 580 4468)

ABSE, Dr Dannie; s of Rudolf Abse (d 1964), of Cardiff, and Kate, *née* Shepherd (d 1981); bro of Leo Abse, *qv*; *b* 22 Sept 1923; *Educ* St Illtyd's Coll Cardiff, Univ of Wales Cardiff, King's Coll London, Westminster Hosp London (MRCS, LRCP); *m* 4 Aug 1951, Joan, da of John Mercer, of St Helens, Lancs; 1 s (Jesse David b 1958), 2 da (Keren Danielle b 1953, Susanna Ruth b 1957); *Career* RAF 1951–54 Sqdn Ldr i/c Chest Clinic Central Med Estab London 1954–82; poet, playwright and novelist; sr fell of humanities Princeton Univ 1973–74; pres: Poetry Soc 1979–92, Welsh Acad of Letters 1995–; Hon DLitt Wales 1989; FRSL 1983, fell The Welsh Acad 1991; *Poetry* After Every Thing Green (1948), Walking Under Water (1952), Tenants of the House (1957), Poems Golders Green (1962), A Small Desperation (1968), Funland and Other Poems (1973), Collected Poems (1977), Way Out in the Centre (1981), Ask the Bloody Horse (1986), White Coat, Purple Coat (1989), Remembrance of Crimes Past (1990), On The Evening Road (1994); *Prose* A Strong Dose of Myself (1983), Journals from the Ant-Heap (1986), Intermittent Journals (1994); *Novels* Ash on a Young Man's Sleeve (1954), Some Corner of an English Field (1957), O Jones, O Jones (1970), There Was a Young Man from Cardiff (1991); *Autobiography* A Poet in the Family (1974); *Plays* House of Cowards (1960), The Dogs of Pavlov (1969), Pythagoras (1976), Gone in January (1978); *Anthologies* ed: Mavericks (with Howard Sergeant, 1957), Modern European Verse (1964), Voices in the Gallery (with Joan Abse, 1986), The Music Lover's Literary Companion (with Joan Abse, 1988), The Hutchinson Book of Post-War British Poets (1989); *Style—* Dr Dannie Abse; ✉ Green Hollows, Craig-yr-Eos Rd, Ogmore-by-Sea, Glamorgan, S Wales

ABSE, Leo; s of Rudolph Abse (d 1964), of Cardiff, and Kate, *née* Shepherd (d 1981); bro of Dr Dannie Abse, *qv*; *b* 22 April 1917; *Educ* Howard Gardens HS, LSE; *m* 1955, Marjorie Davies (d 1996); 1 s (Tobias), 1 da (Bathsheba); *Career* WWII serv RAF 1941–46 (arrested for political activities in ME 1944, precipitated Parly debate); slr, sr ptnr in Cardiff law firm, first slr granted right of audience in the High Ct 1986; chm Cardiff City Lab Pty 1951–53, memb Cardiff CC 1953–58, Parly candidate (Lab) Cardiff N 1955; MP (Lab): Pontypool 1958–83, Torfaen 1983–87; chm Welsh Parly Pty 1976–87; memb Home Office Advsy Ctees on: the Penal System 1968, Adoption 1972; first chm Select Ctee on Welsh Affairs 1980, memb Select Ctee on Abortion 1975–76, sec Br-Taiwan Parly Gp 1983–87; sponsor or co sponsor of Private Memb's Acts relating to: divorce, homosexuality, family planning, legitimacy, widow's damages, industrial injuries, congenital disabilities and relief from forfeiture; sponsor: Children's Bill 1973 (later became Children's Act 1975), Divorce Bill 1983 (later became Matrimonial and Family Proceedings Act 1985); initiated first Commons debates on: genetic engrg, Windscale, in vitro pregnancies; led Lab anti-devolution campaign Wales 1979; vice pres Inst for Study and Treatment of Delinquency 1994– (memb Cncl 1964–94), tstee Winnicott Clinic of Psychotherapy 1980–, pres Nat Cncl for the Divorced and Separated 1974–92, vice pres Br Assoc for Counselling 1985–90, chm Parly Friends of WNO 1985–87; memb Ct: Univ of Wales 1981–87, UWIST; Regents lectr Univ of Calif 1981; *Awards* Best Dressed Man Award Clothing Fedn 1962, Order of Brilliant Star (China) 1988, Wingate Fndn Jewish Quarterly Literary Award for Non-Fiction 1994; *Books* Private Member: a psychoanalytically orientated study of contemporary politics (1973), In Vitro Fertilisation: past, present and future (contrib 1986), Margaret, daughter of Beatrice: a psychobiography of Margaret Thatcher (1989), Wotan my enemy; can Britain live with the Germans in the European Union? (1994), The Man Behind the Smile (1996); *Recreations* Italian wines, psychobiography; *Style—* Leo Abse, Esq; ✉ 54 Strand on the Green, London W4 3PD (☎ 0181 994 1166); Via Poggio di Mezzo, Nugola Vecchia, Livorno, Italy (☎ 00 39 586 977022)

ACHER, Gerald (Gerry); s of David Acher (d 1979), and Andrée Diana, *née* Laredo; *b* 30 April 1945; *Educ* King's Coll Sch Wimbledon; *m* 18 July 1970, Joyce Kathleen, *née* White; 2 s (James David b 4 July 1973, Mark Gerald b 3 Jan 1976); *Career* articled clerk Bird Potter & Co 1961–66; KPMG (and predecessor firms): asst mangr 1967–73, mangr 1973–75, sr mangr 1975–80, ptnr 1980–, memb UK Bd 1987–, head Corp Fin 1990–93, UK head Audit and Accounting 1993 , chm World-Wide Audit and Accountancy Ctee 1995–; memb Cncl and chm Audit Faculty ICAEW 1995–; govr and vice chm Motability, tstee Motability 10th Anniversary Tst, chm of Govrs Milbourne Lodge Jr Sch; William Quilter Prize, Plender Prize for Auditing ICA 1966; Liveryman Worshipful Co of Chartered Accountants; FCA 1977 (ACA 1967), fell Securities Industries Assoc; *Recreations* mountain walking, classic and vintage cars, opera and music, gardening, watching rugby; *Clubs* Travellers'; *Style—* Gerry Acher, Esq; ✉ Orchard Close, 1 Oxshott Way, Cobham, Surrey KT11 2RU (☎ 01932 865224); KPMG, 8 Salisbury Square, London EC4Y 8BB (☎ 0171 311 8640, fax 0171 311 8718)

ACHESON, Prof Sir (Ernest) Donald; KBE (1986); s of Malcolm King Acheson, MC, and Dorothy Josephine, *née* Rennoldson; *b* 17 Sept 1926; *m* Barbara Mary, *née* Castle; 1 s, 5 da; *Career* Flt Lt actg Sqdn Ldr RAF Med Branch 1953–55, med practitioner 1951, various clinical posts Middx Hosp, Radcliffe travelling fell UC Oxford 1957–59, med tutor Nuffield Dept of Med Radcliffe Infirmary Oxford 1960, dir Oxford Record Linkage Study and Unit of Clinical Epidemiology 1962, May reader in med 1965, fell BNC Oxford 1968 (hon fell 1991), prof of clinical epidemiology Univ of Southampton and hon conslt physician Royal S Hants Hosp 1963–83, fndn dean Faculty of Med Southampton Univ 1968–78, dir MRC Unit in Environmental Epidemiology 1979–83, chief med offr Depts of Health and Social Security, DES and Home Office 1984–91; visiting prof of international health London Sch of Hygiene and Tropical Med 1991–96 (hon fell), chm Int Centre for Health and Soc UCL 1996–; chm Health Advsy Ctee for the Prison Service 1992–, memb World Bank Close the Gap Ctee 1993–; Hon DM Univ of Southampton 1984; Hon DSc: Univ of Newcastle 1984, Univ of Salford 1991; Hon MD: Queen's Univ Belfast 1987, Univ of Nottingham 1989, Univ of Birmingham 1991; Hon LLD Univ of Aberdeen 1988; memb Assoc of Physicians of GB and I 1965 (pres 1979), pres BMA 1996–97; FRCP, FRCS, FRCOG, FFPHM, FFOM; *Books* Medical Record Linkage (1967), Multiple Sclerosis, a reappraisal (1966), Medicine, an outline for the intending student (1970); scientific papers on epidemiology of cancer and chronic desease, med educn and orgn of med care; *Style—* Prof Sir Donald Acheson, KBE; ✉ International Centre for Health & Society, University College London, 1–19 Torrington Place, London WC1E 6BT

ACHESON, Dr (Enid) Joan; da of Ernest Barnett (d 1980), and Eva, *née* Hodgkinson (d 1955); *b* 14 Oct 1926; *Educ* Orme Girls' Sch Newcastle-under-Lyme, Univ of Birmingham (MB ChB, MD, FRCP); *m* Harold William Kennedy (Bill) Acheson, OBE, s of Samuel Acheson (d 1957); 1 s (David b 1955); *Career* Dept of Neurology N Staffs Royal Infirmary: res asst 1960–64, clinical res fell Br Heart Fndn 1964–70; clinical res fell Dept of Med Manchester Royal Infirmary 1970–77 (memb Married Women's Re-Trg Scheme 1977–86), clinical res fell and hon conslt Dept of Med Univ of Manchester Med Sch 1986–89, conslt advsr in clinical computing Central Manchester Healthcare Trust 1989–96; memb Sch Cncl Newcastle-under-Lyme Endowed Schs 1981– (govr 1958–81, vice chm Bd of Govrs 1959–76, pres of Old Girls' Soc 1963–66, chm Bd of Govrs 1976–79); memb: BMA 1951, Manchester Med Soc 1971; *Books* Strokes - Natural History, Pathology and Surgical Treatment (1975); *Recreations* music, embroidery; *Style—* Dr Joan Acheson; ✉ Braegarth, Elterwater, Ambleside, Cumbria LA22 9JB (☎ and fax 01539 437355); 6 Appleby Lodge, Wilmslow Rd, Manchester M14 6HZ (☎ 0161 224 9469)

ACHESON, Hon Patrick Bernard Victor Montagu; s of 5 Earl of Gosford, MC (d 1954), and Caroline Mildred Carter, Countess of Gosford (d 1965); unc and hp of 7 Earl of Gosford; *b* 4 Feb 1915; *Educ* Harrow, Trinity Coll Cambridge (BA), Harvard Univ (MBA); *m* 1946, Judith, da of Frederick B Bate (d 1970), of Waterford, Virginia, USA; 3 s, 2 da; *Career* with International Bank for Reconstruction and Development 1947–65, pres Culligan Water Conditioning Corporation of N Virginia 1966–80; *Recreations* golf, gardening; *Clubs* Loudoun Golf; *Style—* The Hon Patrick Acheson; ✉ 207 Cornwall St, NW Leesburg, VA 20176, USA (☎ 00 1 703 777 8381)

ACHESON, Prof Roy Malcolm; s of Malcolm King Acheson, MC, MD (d 1962), of Castlecaufield, Co Tyrone, and Dorothy Josephine, *née* Rennoldson (d 1976); *b* 18 Aug 1921; *Educ* Merchiston Castle Sch Edinburgh, Trinity Coll Dublin (BA, MA, ScD), Brasenose Coll Oxford (BA, MA), Radcliffe Infirmary Oxford (BM BCh, DM); *m* 16 March 1950 (m dis 1990), Fiona Marigo, da of Wing-Cdr Vincent O'Brien (d 1950), of Altrincham, Cheshire; 2 s (Malcolm O'Brien b 1950, Vincent Rennoldson b 1960), 1 da (Marigo Fiona b 1963); *Career* enlisted WWII RAC (N Irish Horse) 1942, active serv Algeria and Tunisia, cmmnd RMC Sandhurst 1944, rejoined N Irish Horse, active serv Italy, discharged Lt 1946; clinical and res posts Radcliffe Infirmary and Univ of Oxford, Rockefeller travelling fell Western Reserve and Harvard Univs 1955–56, Radcliffe travelling fell Univ of Oxford 1955–57, lectr in social med Univ of Dublin 1955–59, fell Trinity Coll Dublin 1957–59, sr lectr then reader in social and preventive med Guy's Hosp Med Sch and London Sch of Hygiene and Tropical Med 1959–62, prof of epidemiology Yale Univ 1964–72 (assoc prof 1962), fell Jonathan Edwards Coll 1966–75; London Sch of Hygiene and Tropical Medicine: Cwlth Fund sr travelling fell in med 1968–69, dir Centre for Extension Trg in Community Med 1972–76; prof of health serv studies Univ of London 1974–76, prof of community med Univ of Cambridge 1976–88 (emeritus prof 1988–); fell Churchill Coll Cambridge 1977–; author and ed of several texts and scientific papers; memb: GMC 1978–88, GDC 1983–88, Cambridge Health Authy 1986–88; Hon MA Yale Univ 1964; hon fell: Acad of Med in Buenos Aires (elected 1974), Acad of Med in Singapore (elected 1987); FRCP, FFOM 1984, FFCM (vice pres 1986–89); *Books* Health, Society and Medicine: An Introduction to Community Medicine (with S Hagard, 1985), Costs and Benefits of the Heart Transplant Programmes at Harefield and Papworth Hospitals (with M Buxton, N Caine, S Gibson and B O'Brien, 1985), A History of Education in Public Health (1991); *Recreations* choral singing, occasional bird watching, golf; *Clubs* Utd Oxford and Cambridge Univ, Gog Magog Golf; *Style—* Prof Roy Acheson; ✉ 21 The Cliff, Roedean, Brighton, E Sussex BN2 5RF (☎ 01273 698518)

ACKERS, Sir James George; kt (1987); s of James Ackers, and Vera Harriet, *née* Edwards; *b* 20 Oct 1935; *Educ* Oundle, LSE; *Career* chm Fedn of Univ Cons Assocs 1958, contested (C) Walsall N 1959, vice chm Bow Group 1962–63; Ackers Jarrett Ltd: md 1963–74, chm 1974–91; chm Ackers Jarrett Leasing Ltd 1982–91; memb: Ctee of Inquiry into Civil Serv Pay 1981, Monopolies and Mergers Cmmn 1981–90, Nat Trg Task Force 1989–91, NEDC 1989–92; chm West Midlands RHA 1982–93; pres Walsall Chamber of Indust and Commerce 1978; Assoc of Br Chambers of Commerce 1982–91: dep chm 1982–84, chm 1984–86, pres 1986–90; pres Jerome K Jerome Soc 1985–93; Liveryman Worshipful Co of Loriners; *Style—* Sir James Ackers

ACKERY, Graham Bernard; s of Bert George Ackery (d 1974), and Elsie Violet Ackery (d 1987); *b* 25 April 1932; *Educ* Chiswick Poly Coll; *m* 21 Dec 1957, Gillian Margaret, da of Leslie Charles Abraham (d 1985); 2 s (Mark Richard b 16 May 1966, Peter Michael b 31 Oct 1967); *Career* joined Hodgson Harris (now Kidsons Impey) 1949; Nat Serv 1950–52; Hodgson Harris: rejoined as articled clerk, qualified 1964, ptnr 1966–; FCA, ATII; *Recreations* music (playing electronic organ), golf, gardening, woodwork, DIY; *Clubs* Chartered Accountants Dining, Flackwell Heath Golf, Hole In One, Uxbridge Supper; *Style—* Graham B Ackery, Esq; ✉ Little Glebe, Manor Lane, Gerrards Cross, Bucks SL9 7NH; Kidsons Impey, Spectrum House, 20–26 Cursitor Street, London EC4A 1HY (☎ 0171 405 2088, fax 0171 831 2206, car 0836 610777)

ACKFORD, Paul John; *b* 26 Feb 1958; *m* Suzie Mumme; *Career* former rugby union player (lock); clubs: Plymouth Albion, Rosslyn Park, Metropolitan Police, Harlequins; England: B debut 1979, full debut v Aust 1988, Five Nations debut v Scotland 1989, memb Grand Slam winning team 1991, memb World Cup runners-up team 1991, 22 caps; 3 test appearances Br Lions 1989; memb: Rugby Football Union Ctee 1992–94, Surrey RFU Ctee 1992–94; former police offr; currently rugby correspondent The Sunday Telegraph and occasional TV pundit; *Recreations* cooking, entertaining, golf; *Style—* Paul Ackford, Esq; ✉ c/o The Sunday Telegraph, 1 Canada Square, Canary Wharf, London E14 5AR (☎ 0171 538 5000)

ACKLAND, Joss (Sidney Edmond Jocelyn); s of Maj Sidney Norman Ackland (d 1981), and Ruth, *née* Izod (d 1957); *b* 29 Feb 1928; *Educ* Dame Alice Owens Sch, Central Sch of Speech Training and Dramatic Art; *m* 18 Aug 1951, Rosemary Jean, da of Capt Robert Hunter Kirkcaldy (d 1954); 2 s (Toby b 1966, Paul b 1953, d 1982), 5 da (Melanie b 1952, Antonia b 1956, Penelope b 1958, Samantha b 1962, Kirsty b 1963); *Career* actor; worked in theatre since 1945, tea planter Central Africa 1954–55, disc jockey in Cape Town 1955–57; memb: Drug Helpline, Amnesty International, Covent Garden Community Assoc; *Theatre* rep work incl: Stratford-on-Avon, Arts Theatre, Buxton, Croydon, The Embassy Coventry, Oxford, Pitlochry; Old Vic Theatre Co 1958–61, roles incl: Toby Belch, Caliban, Pistol, Lord Froth in The Double Dealer, Aegisthus in The Oresteia and Falstaff in Henry IV part 1, The Merry Wives of Windsor; artistic dir Mermaid Theatre 1961–63; roles incl: Galileo, Long John Silver, Bluntschli in Arms and the Man, Scrofulovsky in The Bedbug, Kirilov in the Possessed; dir Plough and the Stars; *West End* roles incl: Professor in The Professor, Gus in Hotel in Amsterdam, Come As You Are, Sam in The Collaborators, Mitch in A Streetcar Named Desire, Brassbound in Captain Brassbound's Conversion, Stewart in A Pack of Lies; *Other* roles incl: Gaev in The Cherry Orchard (Chichester), Petruchio in The Taming of the Shrew, Sir in The Dresser (both nat tours), Eustace Perrin State in The Madras House, Romain Gary in Jean Seburg (both NT); Opening of the Barbican Theatre: Falstaff in Henry IV Parts 1 and 2, Captain Hook and Mr Darling in Peter Pan; most recently Alfred Ill in The Visit (Chichester) 1995; *West End Musicals* incl: Squeezum in Lock Up Your Daughters, title role in Jorrocks, Fredrik in A Little Night Music, Peron in Evita, Captain Hook and Mr Darling in Peter Pan - The Musical; *Television* numerous appearances incl: Kipling, D'Artagnan in Twenty Years After, Barrett in The Barretts of Wimpole Street, C S Lewis in Shadowlands, Clarence Darrow in Never the Sinner, Terence Fielding in A Murder of Quality, Archie in Voices in the Garden, Alan Holly in First and Last; most recently Bondarchuk in Citizen X 1995; mini-series incl: Herman Goering in The Man Who Lived at The Ritz, Sir Burton in Queenie, Onassis in A Woman Named Jackie; *Films* incl: Seven Days to Noon, Forbush and the Penguins, The House that Dripped Blood, Villain, Crescendo, The Happiness Cage, England Made Me, Hitler - The Last Ten Days, The Black Windmill, The Little Princess, S-P-Y-S, Royal Flash, One of our Dinosaurs is Missing, Operation Daybreak, Silver Bears, Watership Down, Who is Killing the Great Chefs of Europe?, Saint Jack, The Apple, Rough Cut, Lady Jane, A Zed and Two Noughts, It Couldn't Happen Here, Don Masino in The Sicilian, The Colonel in To Kill a Priest, Sir Jock Delves Broughton in White Mischief, Arjen Rudd in Lethal Weapon 2, Russian Ambassador in The Hunt for Red October, The Man of Power in The Palermo Connection, Tre Colonne in Cronaca, The Object of Beauty, The Sheltering Desert, The Bridge, Georgino, Brando in Occhio Pinocchio, Hale in Nowhere to Run, The Bible, Miracle on 34th Street, Stringer in Mad Dogs and Englishmen, Gerald Carmody in Daisies in December, King Francis in Till the End of Time, King Arthur in A Kid at the Court of King Arthur, Mighty Ducks 1 & 3, Matisse in Surviving Picasso, The Captain in Deadly Voyage, Lord Claire in Firelight, Swaffer in Amy Foster; *Books* I Must Be in There Somewhere (autobiography, 1989); *Recreations* writing, painting, reading, 23 grandchildren; *Clubs* Garrick; *Style—* Joss Ackland, Esq; ✉ c/o Garrick Club, Garrick St, London WC2

ACKLAND-SNOW, Brian Percy; s of Frank Whittlesey Ackland-Snow (d 1974), and Ivy Jesse Byway; *b* 31 March 1940; *Educ* Harrow Sch of Art; *m* 24 Sept 1960, Carol Avis, da of James Dunsby (d 1963); 1 s (Andrew b 1961), 1 da (Amanda b 1963); *Career* prodn designer and art director; films incl: Death on the Nile, McVicar, Superman III, Room with a View (BAFTA Award for Production Design, Academy Award for Art Direction), Maurice, Man in the Brown Suit, Without a Clue, The Secret Garden, Scarlett (Emmy Award for Art Direction); memb: BAFTA, AMPAS, ATAS; *Recreations* historical architecture, archaeology; *Style—* Brian Ackland-Snow, Esq; ✉ Quarry Edge, Cookham Dean, Berks (☎ 01628 483387)

ACKNER, Baron (Life Peer UK 1986), of Sutton, Co of W Sussex; Desmond James Conrad Ackner; PC (1980); s of Dr Conrad Ackner, of Yew Tree House, Jordans, Beaconsfield, Bucks, and Rhoda Ackner; *b* 18 Sept 1920; *Educ* Highgate, Clare Coll Cambridge; *m* 1946, Joan Ackner, JP, da of late John Evans, JP, and wid of K B Spence; 1 s, 1 da, 1 adopted (step) da; *Career* served WWII RA and Admiralty Naval Law Branch; called to the Bar Middle Temple 1945, QC 1961, rec of Swindon 1962–71, judge High Court Queen's Bench 1971–80, judge Jersey and Guernsey Courts of Appeal 1967–71, presiding judge W Circuit 1976–79, Lord Justice of Appeal 1980–86, Lord of Appeal in Ordinary 1986–92; Gen Cncl of the Bar: memb 1957–70, hon treas 1964–66, vice chm 1966–68, chm 1968–70; pres: Senate of Inns of Court and Bar 1980–82, Soc of Sussex Downsmen 1993–96 (vice pres 1996–); chm Law Advsy Ctee Br Cncl 1981–90; treas Middle Temple 1984 (dep treas 1983), memb Br Cncl 1991; pres Arbitration Appeal Panel Securities and Futures Authy 1993, appeal cmmr Personal Investment Authy 1994; dir City Disputes Panel; hon memb Canadian Bar Assoc 1973, hon fell Clare Coll Cambridge 1983; *Recreations* swimming, gardening, theatre; *Style—* The Rt Hon Lord Ackner, PC; ✉ House of Lords, London SW1A 0PW (☎ 0171 219 3295, fax 0171 219 2082); Browns House, Sutton, Petworth, W Sussex (☎ 017988 69206, fax 017988 69407)

ACKROYD, Christopher Edward; s of Anthony Ackroyd (d 1988), of Rustington, Sussex, and May Patricia Jean, *née* Dixon; *b* 21 Aug 1942; *Educ* Hurstpierpont Coll, Gonville and Caius Coll Cambridge (MA), Middx Hosp Med Sch (MB BChir); *m* 1, 21 Sept 1968 (m dis 1992); 1 s (Oliver Edward b 21 April 1977), 2 da (Emily Kate b 21 Jan 1974, Jessica Louise b 30 Oct 1975); m 2, 18 June 1994, Alexandra, da of Joseph Stanley Jephcott, of Clevedon, Avon; *Career* sr registrar Robert Jones & Agnes Hunt Orthopaedic Hosp Oswestry 1973, lectr Dept of Orthopaedic Surgery Nuffield Orthopaedic Centre Oxford 1974–76 (reader Dept of Orthopaedic Surgery 1976–79), conslt orthopaedic surgn Southmead Gen Hosp and Avon Orthopaedic Centre 1979–, hon clinical sr lectr Univ of Bristol 1979–; memb: Bd of Injury 1982–85, Bd of Jl of Bone and Joint Surgery 1983–86; sec Br Orthopaedic Assoc 1987–88 (memb 1973, hon sec 1988–89); memb: Br Orthopaedic Res Soc 1976, Girdlestones Soc 1976; FRCS; *Books* The Severely Injured Limb (1983); *Recreations* sailing, gardening, photography, music; *Style—* Christopher Ackroyd, Esq; ✉ 2 Clifton Park, Clifton, Bristol BS8 3BS (☎ 0117 973 0958, fax 0117 973 0887)

ACKROYD, David Edward; s of John Edward Ackroyd (d 1976), and Betty, *née* Mitchell; *b* 9 Aug 1955; *Educ* Chesterfield Sch, Univ of Durham (BSc); *m* 7 July 1984, Sandra Joan; 3 s (Mark Edward b 10 April 1985, Simon William b 24 Sept 1986, Jonathan Paul b 30 July 1988); *Career* actuarial trainee Phoenix Assurance 1976–78; Williams De Broë: joined 1978, head of Gilt Edged Dept 1982, dir 1987–95; FIA 1982; *Recreations* squash, golf; *Style—* David Ackroyd, Esq

ACKROYD, Jane Victoria Macleod; da of late Sir John Robert Whyte Ackroyd, 2 Bt, and Jennifer Eileen Macleod, *née* Bishop; *b* 25 Feb 1957; *Educ* Godolphin and Latymer Sch Hammersmith, St Martin's Sch of Art (BA), Royal College of Art (MA); *m* David Robert Ewart Annesley; 1 s (William Harry Macleod b 31 August 1992); *Career* artist; exhibitions incl: The Albert Exhibition 1983, Anti-thesis (Angela Flowers Gallery) 1986, Anderson O'Day summer exhibition 1987 and 1988; solo exhibitions: Kingsgate Workshops Gallery 1984, 1985, 1986 and 1987, Anderson O'Day Gallery 1988 and 1991, The Royal Academy Summer Exhibition 1988 and 1989; work in public and private collections incl: The Arts Cncl of GB, The Contemporary Arts Soc, The Harlow Arts Tst; cmmn: Moonlight Ramble (Haymarket) 1992, Limehouse Narrow Street (Herring Gull) 1994; Pollock/Krasner Fndn Award USA 1995; Freeman: Worshipful Co of Carpenters, City of London 1980; *Recreations* walking, music; *Style—* Miss Jane Ackroyd; ✉ Kingsgate Workshops, 116 Kingsgate Rd, London NW6 (☎ 0171 328 7878); Anderson O'Day Fine Art, 5 Quintin Avenue, London W10 6NX (☎ 0181 969 8085)

ACKROYD, Keith; CBE (1994); *Career* The Boots Company plc: joined 1952, dir 1979–94, md Boots The Chemists 1983–84, md Retail Div 1984–94; chm: Trent RHA 1994–, Silentnight Holdings plc 1995– (non-exec dir 1993–), British Retail Consortium; non-exec dir: T Cowie Group plc, Takare plc, Nottingham Group Holdings plc; memb: Passport Agency Advsy Bd, Nat Bd for Crime Prevention 1992–95; Liveryman Worshipful Soc of Apothecaries; FRPharmS; *Style—* Keith Ackroyd, Esq, CBE; ✉ Trent Regional Health Authority, Loughborough Hospital, Epinal Way, Loughborough, Leics LE11 0JY (☎ 01509 213858, fax 01509 268536); Silentnight Holdings plc, Silentnight House, Salterforth, Colne, Lancs BB8 5UE (☎ 01282 815888, fax 01282 816840)

ACKROYD, Norman; s of Albert Ackroyd (d 1976), of Leeds, and Clara Briggs (d 1979); *b* 26 March 1938; *Educ* Cockburn HS Leeds, Leeds Coll of Art, RCA; *m* 1, 1963 (m dis 1975), Sylvia, *née* Buckland; 2 da (Felicity b 1964, Justine b 1966); m 2, 1978, Penelope, da of Blair Hughes-Stanton; 1 s (Simeon b 1983), 1 da (Poppy b 1981); *Career* artist (painter and etcher); tutor in etching Central Sch of Arts London 1965–93; one-man exhibitions incl: Anderson O'Day Gallery London 1980 and 1988, Associated American Artists Philadelphia 1981 and 1983, Mickelson Gallery Washington DC 1982, Yehudi Menuhin Sch Surrey 1983, Jersey Arts Centre Channel Islands 1984, Dolan/Maxwell Gallery Philadelphia 1985, 1987 and 1989, Dena Clough Gallery Halifax 1986, Nat Museum of Art Santiago Chile 1987, Royal Soc of Painter-Etchers and Engravers London 1988, Compass Gallery Glasgow 1990; public collections incl: The Br Museum, Tate Gallery, Albertina Museum Vienna, Arts Cncl GB, Boston Museum of Fine Arts, Br Cncl, Chicago Art Inst, Musée D'Art Historie Geneva, Museum of Modern Art NY, National Galleries of Norway, Canada, Scotland and SA, Queensland Art Gallery Aust, Rijksmuseum, V & A; cmmnd murals for: Albany Hotel Glasgow 1974, Albany Hotel Birmingham 1977, Haringey Cncl 1982–83, Lloyds Bank 1990, British Airways 1991; TV appearances: Artists in Print (BBC 2) 1981, Paul Sandby (Central) 1987, Prospects of Rivers (Channel 4) 1988; awards: SE States Open exhibition 1969, Bradford International Biennale 1972 and 1982, Royal Soc of Painter-Etchers and Engravers 1984 and 1985, Frechen Triennale Germany 1986; RE 1985, RA 1991 (ARA 1988); *Recreations* cricket; *Clubs* Chelsea Arts, Arts; *Style—* Norman Ackroyd, Esq, RA

ACKROYD, Peter; s of Graham Ackroyd, and Audrey, *née* Whiteside; *b* 5 Oct 1949; *Educ* Clare Coll Cambridge, Yale Univ; *Career* writer; The Spectator: lit ed 1971–77, managing ed 1977–81; chief book reviewer The Times 1986–; Somerset Maugham Prize 1984, The Guardian Fiction Award 1985, Whitbread Prize for Best Biography 1984/85; Hon DLitt Exeter 1992; FRSL; *Poetry* London Lickpenny (1973), Country Life (1978), The Diversions of Purley (1987); *Non-Fiction* Notes for a New Culture (1976), Ezra Pound and His World (1980), T S Eliot (1984), Dickens (1990), Introduction to Dickens (1991), Blake (1995), Milton in America (1996); *Novels* The Great Fire of London (1982), The Last Testament of Oscar Wilde (1983), Hawksmoor (1985), Chatterton (1987), First Light (1989), English Music (1992), The House of Doctor Dee (1993), Dan Leno and the Limehouse Golem (1994), Milton in America (1996); *Style—* Peter Ackroyd, Esq, FRSL; ✉ c/o Sheil Land Associates, 43 Doughty Street, London WC1N 2LF (☎ 0171 405 9351)

ACKROYD, Rev Prof Peter Runham; s of Rev Jabez Robert Ackroyd (d 1978), and Winifred, *née* Brown (d 1971); *b* 15 Sept 1917; *Educ* Harrow County Sch, Downing and Trinity Colls Cambridge (MA, PhD), Univ of London (BD, MTh, DD); *m* 1, 1940, Evelyn Alice (d 1990), da of William Young Nutt (d 1926); 2 s (William, Simon), 3 da (Jane, Jenny, Sarah); m 2, 1991, Ann, da of Arthur James Golden (d 1984); *Career* clerk in Holy Orders 1957; univ lectr: Leeds 1948–52, Cambridge 1952–61; Samuel Davidson prof of Old Testament studies King's Coll London 1961–82 (emeritus 1982–); visiting prof: Lutheran Sch of Theology Chicago 1967 and 1976, Univ of Toronto 1972, Univ of Notre Dame Indiana 1982, Emory Univ Atlanta 1984; special lectures: Selwyn Lectures New Zealand 1970, Haskell Lectures Oberlin Ohio 1984; lecture tour Japanese univs 1984; pres Soc for Old Testament Study 1972 (foreign sec 1987–90); chm: Cncl Br Sch of Archaeology in Jerusalem 1980–84, Palestine Exploration Fund 1986–90 (hon sec 1962–70); Hon DD Univ of St Andrews 1970; hon memb Soc of Biblical Literature 1982; *Books include* Exile and Restoration (1968), Israel under Babylon and Persia (1970), I and II Samuel (1971, 1977), I, II Chronicles, Ezra, Nehemiah (1973), Doors of Perception (1978), Studies in the Religious Tradition of the Old Testament (1987), The Chronicler in His Age (1990); ed: Bible Key Words 1961–64, Soc for Old Testament Study Book List 1967–73, Palestine Exploration Quarterly 1971–86; *Recreations* music, reading; *Style—* The Rev Prof Peter R Ackroyd; ✉ 155 Northumberland Road, North Harrow, Middx HA2 7RB (☎ 0181 429 0396)

ACKROYD, Sir Timothy Robert Whyte; 3 Bt (UK 1956), of Dewsbury, W Riding of Yorks; s of Sir John Robert Whyte Ackroyd, 2 Bt (d 1995), and Jennifer Eileen MacLeod, *née* Bishop; *b* 7 Oct 1958; *Educ* Bradfield, LAMDA; *Heir* bro, Andrew John Armitage Ackroyd b 17 Sept 1961; *Career* actor; dir Martingale Productions 1985–, fndr Archview Film Prodns, dir LISA 1991–; hon memb Theatre of Comedy 1984, fndr tstee and patron of charity Tusk 1989, tstee: Marjorie & Dorothy Whyte Memorial Fund 1992, The Ackroyd Tst 1994, Ackroyd/Pullan Prodns 1994; Freeman City of London, Liveryman Worshipful Co of Carpenters 1982; *Theatre* incl: Agamemnon (West End Theatre Critics' Award nomination Most Promising Newcomer) 1976, On Approval 1979, Much Ado About Nothing 1980, A Month in the Country 1981, Man and Superman 1982, A Sleep of Prisoners 1983, Pygmalion 1984, Another Country 1986, No Sex Please - We're British 1987, Black Coffee 1988, The Reluctant Debutante 1989, Jeffrey Bernard is Unwell 1989–91, Journey's End 1993, The Bad Soldier Smith 1995; *Films and Television* incl: Jack Be Nimble 1979, Martin Luther - Heretic 1983, Creator 1984 (Hollywood), Man and Superman 1985, That Has Such People In It 1987, Pied Piper 1989, Bullseye 1989, The Wildlands (Kenya) 1992, A Royal Scandal 1996; *Recreations* rugby, literature, history, sumo wrestling; *Clubs* MCC, Garrick; *Style—* Sir Timothy Ackroyd, Bt; ✉ c/o Tim Scott, The South Bank Commercial Centre, 140 Battersea Park Road, London SW11 4NB (☎ 0171 978 1352)

ACLAND, Sir Antony Arthur; GCMG (1986, KCMG 1982, CMG 1976), GCVO (1991, KCVO 1976); s of Brig Peter Bevil Edward Acland, OBE, MC, TD (d 1993), and Bridget Susan, *née* Barnett (d 1996); bro of Maj-Gen Sir John Hugh Bevil Acland, KCB, CBE, DL, *qv*; *b* 12 March 1930; *Educ* Eton, ChCh Oxford (MA 1956); *m* 1, 6 Nov 1956, (Clare) Anne (d 1984), da of Francis Reynolds Verdon (d 1960), of Liverpool and Sidbury, Devon; 2 s (Simon b 27 March 1958, Nicholas b 6 Feb 1960), 1 da (Katharine (Mrs George Weston) b 30 June 1965); m 2, 28 July 1987, Mrs Jennifer Joyce McGougan, da of Col R Dyke, OBE (d 1976), of Bicton, Devon, and former w of John McGougan; *Career* HM Dip Serv: joined 1953, ME Centre for Arab Studies 1954, Dubai 1955, Kuwait 1956, FO 1958–62, asst private sec to Sec of State 1959–62, UK Mission to UN 1962–66, head of Chancery UK Mission Geneva 1966–68, head Arabian Dept 1970–72, PPS to Foreign Sec 1972–75; ambass: Luxembourg 1975–77, Spain 1977–79; dep under-sec FCO 1980–82, head HM Dip Serv and perm under-sec FCO 1982–86, ambass Washington USA 1986–91; provost of Eton 1991–; non-exec dir: Shell Transport and Trading 1991–, Booker plc 1992–; chm: Cncl of the Ditchley Fndn 1991–96, Tidy Britain Gp 1991–96; a tstee: National Portrait Gallery 1991–, Esmée Fairbairn Charitable Tst 1991–; chllr Order of St Michael and St George 1994–; Hon DCL Exeter 1988, Hon LLD College of William and Mary Virginia USA 1991, Hon DCL Reading 1992; 1 class Order of Orange-Nassau (Luxembourg), 1 class Order of Isabel the Catholic (Spain); *Recreations* riding, gardening, country pursuits; *Clubs* Brooks's; *Style—* Sir Antony Acland, GCMG, GCVO; ✉ The Provost's Lodge, Eton College, Windsor, Berks SL4 6DH

ACLAND, David Alfred; DL (Glos); s of Lt-Col Arthur William Acland, OBE, MC, TD (d 1992), and Violet Gwendolen, *née* Grimston (d 1984); *b* 21 Oct 1929; *Educ* Eton, ChCh Oxford (MA); *m* 19 Oct 1960, Serena Elizabeth, da of late Cyril Hugh Kleinwort; 1 s (Harry Alexander b 1963), 1 da (Lucy Henrietta b 1962); *Career* 2 Lt XI Hussars (PAO) 1947–49; dir Barclays Bank Private Bank Ltd; chm: Electric & General Investment Co plc, Fleming Natural Resources Investment Trust plc, Kleinwort Overseas Investment Trust plc; dir BZW Convertible Investment Trust; chm RNLI; *Recreations* sailing, hunting, tennis; *Clubs* Royal Yacht Squadron, Cavalry & Guards; *Style—* David Acland, Esq, DL; ✉ 24 Caroline Place, London W2 4AN (☎ 0171 229 4189)

ACLAND, Lt-Col Sir (Christopher) Guy Dyke; 6 Bt (UK 1890), of St Mary Magdalen, Oxford; MVO (1990); s of Sir Antony Acland, 5 Bt (d 1983), and Margaret, Lady Acland; *b* 24 March 1946; *Educ* Allhallows Sch, RMA Sandhurst; *m* 1971, Christine Mary Carden, da of late John William Brodie Waring; 2 s (Alexander b 1973, Hugh b 1976); *Heir* s, Alexander John Dyke Acland b 29 May 1973; *Career* cmmnd RA 1966, served UK, Germany and Hong Kong, 2 i/c 1 RHA 1985–88, equerry to HRH The Duke of Edinburgh 1988–90, Lt-Col 1990, SO1 Mgmnt Servs (Org 3) MOD 1990–92, cmd Southampton UOTC 1992–94, ret; dep master HM Household and equerry to HM The Queen 1994–; FRSA 1990; *Recreations* sailing, gardening, shooting; *Clubs* Royal Yacht Sqdn, Royal Artillery Yacht; *Style—* Lt-Col Sir Guy Acland, Bt, MVO

ACLAND, Sir John Dyke; 16 Bt (E 1678, with precedence from 1644), of Columb-John, Devon; eldest s of Sir Richard Thomas Dyke Acland, 15 Bt (d 1990), and Anne Stella, *née* Alford (d 1992); *b* 13 May 1939; *Educ* Clifton, Magdalene Coll Cambridge (MA), Univ of West Indies (MSc); *m* 9 Sept 1961, Virginia, yr da of Roland Forge, of The Grange, Barnoldby-le-Beck, Lincs; 2 s (Dominic Dyke b 1962, Piers Dyke b 1965), 1 da (Holly b 1972); *Heir* s, Dominic Dyke Acland b 19 Nov 1962; *Style—* Sir John Acland, Bt; ✉ Sprydon, Broadclyst, Exeter, Devon EX5 3JN

ACLAND, Maj-Gen Sir John Hugh Bevil; KCB (1980), CBE (1978), DL (Devon 1983); s of Brig Peter Bevil Edward Acland, OBE, MC, TD (d 1993), and Bridget Susan, *née* Barnett (d 1996); bro of Sir Antony Arthur Acland, GCMG, GCVO, *qv*; *b* 26 Nov 1928; *Educ* Eton; *m* 1953, Myrtle, da of Brig Alastair Crawford (d 1978), and Helena Beatrice, *née* Dundas (d 1976), of Auchentroig, Stirlingshire; 1 s (Peter b 1954), 1 da (Victoria (Mrs Thomas Goddard) b 1958); *Career* enlisted Scots Gds 1946 (cmmnd 1948), served with 1 or 2 Bn in Malaya, Cyprus, Egypt, Germany, Kenya, Zanzibar and NI 1949–70, equerry to HRH the Duke of Gloucester 1957–59, Staff Coll 1959, Bde Maj 4 Gds Armd

Bde 1964–66, CO 2 Bn Scots Gds 1968–71, Col and BGS MOD 1972–75, Cdr Land Forces Cyprus 1976–78, GOC SW Dist 1978–81, Cdr Commonwealth Monitoring Force S Rhodesia/Zimbabwe and mil advsr to Govr 1979–80, ret 1981; Hon Col: Univ of Exeter OTC 1980–90, Royal Devon Yeo 1983–92, Royal Wessex Yeo 1989–92; farmer; pres Devon RBL 1982–89; dir of liaison research Allied Vintners 1982–93; govr: Allhallows Sch 1982–95, Kings Sch Ottery St Mary 1994–; memb: Dartmoor Nat Park Authy 1986, Steering Ctee for Schs Health Educn Unit Univ of Exeter 1987–93; chm: Gallant Ordnance 1986–93, SW Regnl Working Party on Alcohol 1987–93; tstee Exeter Cathedral Preservation Tst 1994; Vice Lord-Lt Devon 1995; *Recreations* fly-fishing, arboriculture, destroying vermin; *Clubs* Army and Navy, MCC, Blue Seal; *Style*— Maj-Gen Sir John Acland, KCB, CBE, DL; ✉ Feniton Court, Honiton, Devon EX14 0BE

ACLAND, Martin Edward; JP (Herts 1964), DL (Herts 1996); s of Lt-Col Arthur Acland, OBE, MC, TD (d 1992); *b* 31 July 1932; *Educ* Eton; *m* 1956, (Anne) Maureen Acland, *qv*, da of late Stanley Ryder Runton, of Ilkley, Yorks; 3 s; *Career* formerly 2 Lt 11 Hussars; dir: Mercantile Credit 1970–85, Alexander Holdings plc 1985–87, Redfearn National Glass 1985–88, Cambridge Corporate Consultants Ltd 1985–87; UK dir of Christian Children's Fund 1985–94; memb: Legal Aid Bd 1988–94, Herts Family Health Servs Authy 1990–95, Herts Police Authy 1993–; High Sheriff Herts 1978–79; *Recreations* shooting, gun dog training, sailing; *Clubs* Royal Yacht Sqdn, Seaview Yacht; *Style*— Martin Acland, Esq, JP, DL; ✉ Standon Green End, Ware, Herts (☎ 01920 438233)

ACLAND, (Anne) Maureen; *née* Runton; OBE (1988); da of Stanley Ryder Runton (d 1983), of Ilkley, W Yorkshire, and Kathleen Ryder Runton, CBE, *née* Carter (d 1974); *b* 3 Oct 1934; *Educ* privately in England and Paris; *m* 1956, Martin Edward Acland, *qv*; 3 s (Michael Christopher Dyke b 1958, Richard Arthur Dyke b 1962, Peter Edward Dyke b 1964); *Career* FO 1954–56; memb Cncl: St John Herts 1970, London Choral Soc 1973–78 (memb 1970–78); Nat Gardens Scheme: co-organiser 1971–87, memb Nat Cncl 1978–, tstee 1989–; pres and tstee Herts Nursing Tst 1975–, chm Queen's Nursing Inst 1978–, vice pres and exec Ctee Dist Nursing Assoc UK 1979–95, memb Cncl and Grants Ctee Nation's Fund for Nurses 1980, Cdr St John Ambulance Herts 1987 (dep co cmmr 1982–87), chm Florence Nightingale Fndn, assoc tstee Florence Nightingale Museum Tst 1988; Order of St John: Dame of Justice, Chapter Gen 1987–, memb Cncl 1993; FRSM 1990 (memb Cncl Open Section 1985–, treas 1990–93, vice pres 1993), LRAM, FRSA, FRSH; *Recreations* life (country, family, wild), music, and the arts (creative, performing and spectator), gardening, tennis, designing and making; *Clubs* Seaview Yacht, RSM; *Style*— Mrs Maureen Acland, OBE; ✉ Standon Green End, Ware, Hertfordshire SG11 1BN (☎ 01920 438233, fax 01920 438527)

ACLAND HOOD GASS, *see:* Gass

ACLOQUE, Hon Mrs (Camilla Anne Bronwen); *née* Scott-Ellis; da of 9 Baron Howard de Walden and 5 Baron Seaford, and his 1 w, Countess Irene Harrach (d 1975); *b* 1 April 1947; *Educ* Convent of the Sacred Heart Woldingham Surrey; *m* 1971, Guy, s of John Acloque (d 1971), of Reigate, Surrey; 1 s, 2 da (twin); *Career* co-heiress to Barony of Howard de Walden; *Style*— The Hon Mrs Acloque; ✉ Alderley Grange, Wotton-under-Edge, Glos (☎ 01453 842161)

ACRES, Dr Douglas Ian; CBE (1987, OBE 1981), JP (Essex 1958), DL (Essex 1978); s of Sydney Herbert Acres, MBE (d 1952), of Benfleet, Essex, and Hilda Emily, *née* Chatton (d 1979); *b* 21 Nov 1924; *Educ* Westcliff HS, Borland's Victoria, London Hosp Med Coll (MRCS, LRCP, DMJ (clinical), MRCGP); *m* 17 Sept 1949, Joan Marjorie, da of Charles William Bloxham (d 1966), of Benfleet, Essex; 3 da (Mary b 1952, Jane b 1955, Elizabeth b 1957); *Career* RAF Med Branch 1951–53 (Acting Sqdn Ldr, vice pres Med Bd, Air Crew Selection Centre, Hornchurch); house surgeon and casualty registrar King George Hosp Ilford 1949–51, GP 1953–84; md Remploy Ltd 1962–, med corr SE Essex Evening Echo 1967–95, med advsr Congregational Fedn 1985–; author of articles and chapters on medico-legal matters 1968–; memb: Benfleet UDC 1960–65 (chm Public Health Ctee), Ctee on Mentally Abnormal Offenders 1972–75, Lord Chancellor's Essex Advsy Ctee 1973–84, Int Dept Ctee on Alcoholism 1975–78, Parole Bd 1984–87; chm: Governing Body King John Sch Thundersley 1971–89, Rochford Bench 1974–84 (memb 1958–91), Essex Cncl on Alcoholism 1981–86, Cncl Magistrates' Assoc 1984–87; pres Essex Branch Nat Assoc of Probation Offrs 1983–89; memb Governing Body SE Essex Sixth Form Coll 1982–86; lay pastor: Battlesbridge Free Church 1984–, Woodham Ferrers Congregational Church 1984–92; AOC's commendation and vote of thanks Order of St John east coast flood disaster 1953; Freeman City of London, Liveryman Worshipful Soc of Apothecaries 1968; CStJ; *Clubs* RSM; *Style*— Dr Douglas Acres, CBE, JP, DL; ✉ Thundersley Lodge, Runnymede Chase, Thundersley, Benfleet, Essex SS7 3DB (☎ 01268 793241)

ACTON, Prof the Hon Edward David Joseph LYON-DALBERG-; 4 s of 3 Baron Acton, CMG, MBE, TD (d 1989); *b* 4 Feb 1949; *Educ* Univ of York (BA), Univ of Cambridge (PhD); *m* 1972, Stella Marie, da of Henry Conroy (d 1990), of Bolton; 2 da; *Career* sr lectr in history Univ of Manchester 1988–91, prof of modern Euro history UEA 1991–; *Books* Alexander Herzen and the Role of the Intellectual Revolutionary (1979); Russia: the present and the past (1986), Rethinking the Russian Revolution (1990), Russia: the Tsarist and Soviet Legacy (1995); *Recreations* tennis, bridge, racing; *Style*— Prof the Hon Edward Acton; ✉ 365 Unthank Road, Norwich NR4 7QG (☎ 01603 505673); School of History, Universtiy of East Anglia, Norwich NR4 7TJ (☎ 01603 56161)

ACTON, Hon John Charles Ferdinand Harold LYON-DALBERG-; o s and h of 4 Baron Acton, *qv*; *b* 19 Aug 1966; *Educ* Winchester, Balliol Coll Oxford; *Career* freelance journalist (obituaries, book reviews); bd memb The James J Norris Fndn for Migrants and Refugees; *Style*— The Hon John Lyon-Dalberg-Acton; ✉ Flat A, 199 Portobello Road, London W11 1LV (☎ 0171 221 9369)

ACTON, 4 Baron Acton (UK 1869); Sir Richard Gerald Lyon-Dalberg-Acton; 11 Bt (E 1644); also a Patrician of Naples; patron of one living (but being a Roman Catholic cannot present); eldest s of 3 Baron Acton, CMG, MBE, TD (d 1989), and Hon Daphne, *née* Strutt, da of 4 Baron Rayleigh; *b* 30 July 1941; *Educ* St George's Coll Salisbury Rhodesia, Trinity Coll Oxford (BA, MA); *m* 1, 28 Aug 1965, Hilary Juliet Sarah (d 1973), 2 da of Dr Osmond Laurence Charles Cookson, of Perth, WA; 1 s (Hon John Charles Ferdinand Harold); m 2, 1974 (m dis 1987), Judith Garfield, da of the Hon Garfield Todd, of Hokonu Ranch, P O Dadaya, Rhodesia (formerly PM of S Rhodesia); m 3, 19 March 1988, Patricia, o da of late M Morey Nassif, of 115 34th Street, South East, Cedar Rapids, Iowa 53403, USA; *Heir* s, Hon John Charles Ferdinand Harold Lyon-Dalberg-Acton b 19 Aug 1966; *Career* barr Inner Temple 1976; dir Coutts & Co 1971–74; sr law offr Zimbabwe Miny of Justice Legal and Parly Affairs 1981–85; vice patron Apex Tst 1995–; patron Mind's Jubilee Appeal 1996; writer in anthologies, academic journals and magazines; *Books* (with Patricia Nassif Acton) To Go Free: A Treasury of Iowa's Legal Heritage (Benjamin F Suam Baugh Award 1996); State Historical Society of Iowa's Throne (Aldrich Award best article 1995); *Style*— The Rt Hon the Lord Acton; ✉ House of Lords, London SW1; 100 Red Oak Lane SE, Cedar Rapids, Iowa 52403, USA; 152 Whitehall Court, London SW1A 2EL

ACTON DAVIS, Jonathan James; QC (1996); s of Michael James Acton Davis (d 1994), of London, and Elizabeth Margaret, *née* Sim; *b* 15 Jan 1953; *Educ* Harrow, PCL (LLB); *m* 1987, Lindsay Alice Boswell; 1 s (Matthew James); *Career* called to the Bar Inner Temple 1977 (bencher 1995); memb Gen Cncl of the Bar 1993–; *Recreations* cricket, walking, South West France; *Clubs* MCC, Garrick; *Style*— Jonathan Acton Davis, Esq, QC; ✉ 4 Pump Court, Temple, London EC4Y 7AN (☎ 0171 353 2656, fax 0171 583 2036)

ACTON-STOW, Derek; OBE (1979); s of Ivor Acton-Stow (d 1972), of E Dean, E Sussex, and Ada Beatrice, *née* Smith; *b* 20 Sept 1929; *Educ* Epsom GS, Kingston College of Art; *m* 1955 (m dis 1959), Julia Weightman; m 2, 25 May 1959, Gwyneth, da of David John Pugh (d 1965), of London; 3 da (Anna b 1959, Katherine b 1962, Harriet b 1968); *Career* architect; Powell and Moya 1953–62; sr ptnr: Derek Stow & Ptnrs 1962–, Halpin Stow Ptnrship 1992–; awards incl: Civic Tst 1970, 1973, 1978 and 1986, Concrete Soc 1973, Euro Prize for Architecture 1974, RIBA 1978, Structural Steel 1978 and 1980; memb Cncl Cities of London and Westminster Soc Architects, assoc Soc of Artist Architects; Freeman City of London 1984, Liveryman Worshipful Co of Chartered Architects 1989; FRIBA 1951; *Recreations* visual arts, music, literature; *Clubs* Arts; *Style*— Derek Acton-Stow, Esq, OBE; ✉ 57 Sutherland St, Pimlico, London SW1V 4JY (☎ 0171 834 2599); 29 Tufton St, Westminster, London SW1P 3QL (☎ 0171 222 9237, fax 0171 222 8773)

ACWORTH, Ven Richard Foote; s of Oswald Roney Acworth, of Zeals, Warminster, Wilts, and Jean Margaret, *née* Coupland; *b* 19 Oct 1936; *Educ* St John's Sch Leatherhead, Sidney Sussex Coll Cambridge (MA), Cuddesdon Theol Coll; *m* 22 Oct 1966, Margaret Caroline Marie, da of Edward Knight Jennings; 1 da (Rachel Margaret b 15 Aug 1967), 2 s (Thomas Richard b 28 Sept 1968, Edward Roney b 20 July 1971); *Career* Nat Serv RNVR 1956–58, Univ of Cambridge 1958–61, Cuddesdon Theol Coll 1961–63; ordained: deacon (St Paul's Cathedral) 1963, priest (Manchester Cathedral) 1964; asst curate: St Etheldreda's Fulham 1963, All Saints and Martyrs Langley Manchester 1964–66, St Mary's Bridgwater 1966–69; vicar of St Mary the Virgin Yatton 1969–81, priest-in-charge St John's and St Mary's Taunton 1981–84, vicar of St Mary Magdalene Taunton 1984–93, archdeacon of Wells 1993–; memb Gen Synod C of E 1980–95; *Recreations* walking, gardening, ornithology, DIY; *Style*— The Ven the Archdeacon of Wells; ✉ The Rectory, Croscombe, Wells, Somerset BA5 3QN (☎ 01749 342242, fax 01749 330060)

ACWORTH, Brig Robert William; CBE (1986); s of Oswald Roney Acworth, of Zeals, Wiltshire, and Jean Margaret Acworth; *b* 11 Dec 1938; *Educ* St John's Sch Leatherhead Surrey, RMA Sandhurst; *m* 8 July 1967, Elizabeth Mary, da of J N S Ridgers; 1 da (Victoria Mary b 4 April 1969), 2 s (Richard John Ridgers b 20 June 1971, Nicholas Robert Julian b 24 May 1973); *Career* cmmnd Queen's Royal Regt 1958, served Germany, UK, Norway, Holland, Gibraltar, Aden, Hong Kong, Oman and NI, Staff Coll 1970, CO 10 UDR 1981–83, Asst COS HQ NI 1983–85, Coll Cdr RMA Sandhurst 1985–87, Asst COS (Intelligence) HQ AFCENT 1987–90, Dep Cdr and COS HQ SE Dist 1990–91, ret; Dep Col: The Queen's Regt 1986–92, The Princess of Wales's Royal Regt 1992–94; pres The Queen's Royal Surrey Regt Assoc 1995–; registrar St Paul's Cathedral 1991–; *Recreations* shooting, fishing, gardening, tennis; *Clubs* Army and Navy; *Style*— Brig Robert Acworth, CBE; ✉ St Paul's Cathedral, London EC4M 8AD (☎ 0171 246 8311, fax 0171 248 3104)

ADAIR, Gilbert; *b* 1944; *Career* writer and journalist; contrib to: The Sunday Times, Esquire, The Guardian, The Independent, The Independent on Sunday, The Connoisseur, Tatler, Harpers & Queen, The Evening Standard, The Sunday Correspondent, Sight and Sound, The Listener, Mirabella, TLS, The New Statesman and Society, Marxism Today, The Spectator, The Washington Post, The Boston Globe, Punch, The Illustrated London News, Time Out, The Movie, The Sunday Telegraph, The European, Al Majalla, Radio Times; *TV appearances* Saturday Review, Comment, The Late Show, Film Club, Film 1990; *Radio* Critics' Forum, Kaleidoscope, New Premises, Meridian, Le Journal des Arts, Midi Magazine, Third Opinion, Night Waves; *Books* fiction: Alice Through the Needle's Eye (1984), Peter Pan and the Only Children (1987), The Holy Innocents (1988), Love and Death on Long Island (1990), The Death of the Author (1992); The Rape of the Cock (poetry, 1992); non-fiction: Hollywood's Vietnam (1981), Myths & Memories (1986), The Postmodernist Always Rings Twice (1992), Flickers (1995); translations: Orson Welles (André Bazin, 1974), Kubrick (Michel Ciment, 1983), John Boorman (Michel Ciment, 1986), Letters (François Truffaut, 1990), Wonder Tales (ed Marina Warner, 1994), A Void (Georges Perec, 1994); contribs: Anatomy of the Movies (1981), What's What in the 1980s (1982), Rediscovering French Film (1983), La Petite Voleuse (1989), The Time Out Film Guide (1989), Ariel at Bay (1990), New Writing (1992); *Style*— Gilbert Adair, Esq

ADAM, *see:* Forbes Adam

ADAM, Beverley Ann; da of Clement Alfred Adam, and Nora Margaret, *née* Willis; *b* 11 Feb 1953; *Educ* King George V Sch Hong Kong, Univ of Warwick (LLB); *m* 16 April 1977, Graham Robert Starling, s of Arthur Ewart Starling, MBE; 2 s (Gareth b 20 April 1982, Sean b 12 Dec 1985), 1 da (Natasha 12 Nov 1990); *Career* slr and ptnr Linklaters & Paines; memb Worshipful Co of City of London Slrs; memb: Law Soc, UKELA, Financial Sector Working Gp of Advsy Ctee on Business in the Environment, LSLA; *Style*— Miss Beverley Adam; ✉ Linklaters & Paines, Barrington House, 59–67 Gresham St, London EC2V 7JA (☎ 0171 606 7080, fax 0171 606 5113, telex 884349)

ADAM, Dr Gordon Johnston; MEP (Lab) Northumbria (majority 66,158); s of John Craig Adam (d 1969), of Carlisle, and Deborah Armstrong, *née* Johnston (d 1978); *b* 28 March 1934; *Educ* Carlisle GS, Univ of Leeds (BSc, PhD); *m* 22 Dec 1973, Sarah Jane, da of John Lockhart Seely (d 1990), of Stakeford, Northumberland; 1 s ((John) Duncan b 11 May 1979); *Career* mining engr NCB 1959–79; cncllr Whitley Bay BC 1971–74; North Tyneside Met BC: cncllr 1973–80, chm 1973–74, mayor 1974–75, dep ldr 1975–80; memb Northern Econ Planning Cncl 1974–79; Parly candidate (Lab) Tynemouth 1966, Berwick-upon-Tweed Nov 1973 (by-election), Feb 1974 and 1992; MEP (Lab) Northumbria 1979–, vice chm Euro Parliament's Energy Res and Technol Ctee 1984–; memb: Northern Arts Gen Cncl 1975–77, Northern Sinfonia Mgmnt Ctee 1978–80, Whitley Bay Playhouse Theatre Tst 1975– (chm 1975–80); chm Newcastle Free Festival 1992– (Bd memb 1989–); Bd memb Northern Stage Co 1989–; chm: Northumbira Energy Advice Centre 1993–, Northern Energy Initiative 1995–; MInstME 1953, CEng; *Style*— Dr Gordon Adam, MEP; ✉ East House Farm, Killingworth Village, Newcastle upon Tyne NE12 0BQ (☎ 0191 216 0154); office: 10 Coach Rd, Wallsend, Tyne and Wear NE28 6JA (☎ 0191 287 5410, fax 0191 287 5411)

ADAM, Ian Clark; s of George Adam (d 1976), of Dundee, and Natalie Jane Gibson, *née* Clark; *b* 2 Sept 1943; *Educ* Harris Academy; *m* 25 Sept 1967, Betty Anne, da of Norman James McKie Crosbie; 1 da (Allison Jane b 26 July 1968), 1 s (Garry Clark b 19 Dec 1970); *Career* trainee accountant Henderson & Logie 1962–67; Price Waterhouse: audit sr and asst mangr (Rio de Janeiro) 1967–70, mangr Bristol 1970–76, ptnr Edinburgh 1976–86, sr ptnr Scotland 1986–95; fin dir Christian Salvesen PLC 1995–; govr: Queen Margaret Coll Edinburgh 1993, Daniel Stewart's and Mary Erskine Schs; memb Co of Merchants of the City of Edinburgh 1987; MICAS 1967, MAE 1990; *Recreations* reading, golf, shooting and travel; *Clubs* New (Edinburgh), Royal Burgess Golfing Soc of Edinburgh, Royal & Ancient Golf (St Andrews), Rotary (Murrayfield Cramond); *Style*— Ian C Adam, Esq; ✉ Christian Salvesen PLC, 50 East Fettes Avenue, Edinburgh EH4 1EQ (☎ 0131 559 3600, fax 0131 552 5809)

ADAMISHIN, HE Anatoly Leonidovich; s of Leonid Adamishin (d 1943), of Kiev, and Vera Vladimirovna, *née* Gusovskaya (d 1984); *b* 11 Oct 1934; *Educ* Lomonosov Moscow State Univ (PhD); *m* 1979, Olga Nikolaevna; 1 da (Vera b 1960), 1 s (Alexander b 1962); *Career* Russian diplomat; Miny of Foreign Affrs: First Euro Dept 1957–59,

Embassy of the USSR Rome 1959–65, First Euro Dept 1965–71, Foreign Policy Planning Dept 1971–73, head Gen Inter Issues Dept 1973–78, head First Euro Dept and memb Miny of Foreign Affairs Collegium 1978–86, dep foreign min 1986–90, concurrently head USSR Cmmn for UNESCO Affrs 1987–90, ambass to Italy 1990–92, first dep foreign min of Russia 1992–94, ambass to the Ct of St James's 1994–; memb: Foreign Policy Cncl of Russia 1993, Foreign Investments Cncl of Russia 1995; *Books* Tramonto e Rinascita di una Grande Potenza (1995); *Recreations* lawn tennis; *Clubs* RAC, Athenaeum, Travellers, Queens, Army and Navy; *Style*— HE Mr Anatoly Adamishin; ✉ Embassy of the Russian Federation, 13 Kensington Palace Gardens, London W8 4QX (☎ 0171 229 3620, fax 0171 229 5804)

ADAMS, Dr Aileen Kirkpatrick; CBE (1988); da of Dr Joseph Adams, MC (d 1985), of Sheffield, and Agnes, *née* Munro (d 1983); *b* 5 Sept 1923; *Educ* Farringtons Sch Chislehurst Kent, Univ of Sheffield (MB ChB); *Career* hosp posts in Cambridge, London, Bristol and clinical fell Massachusetts Gen Hosp Boston USA 1955–57, first asst Nuffield Dept of Anaesthetics Oxford 1957–59, conslt anaesthetist Addenbrooke's Hosp Cambridge 1960–84, sr lectr Lagos Univ Med Sch Nigeria 1963–64, assoc lectr Univ of Cambridge 1977–84, dean Faculty of Anaesthetists RCSEng 1985–88; Hunterian prof RCSEng 1993, Hunterian tstee RCS 1995–; examiner: Final MB Clinical Pharmacology Univ of Cambridge 1977–80, Final FFARCS 1979–82; memb Trinity Hall Cambridge; hon memb Assoc of Anaesthetists of GB and Ireland 1989 (hon sec 1970, vice pres 1976–78), memb Editorial Bd Anaesthesia 1972–85; pres: Soc of Anaesthetists of SW Region 1981, East Anglian Assoc of Anaesthetists 1983–85, History of Anaesthesia Soc 1990–92; memb Cncl RCS 1982–84 and 1985–88, hon archivist Royal Coll of Anaesthetists; author of papers on topics related to anaesthesia and history of med; Royal Soc of Med: pres Anaesthetics Section 1985–86, pres History of Med Section 1994–95, hon treas 1995–; FRSM, FFARCS 1954, FFA(SA) 1987, FRCS(Eng) 1988, FDSRCS 1989, FFA(SA); *Recreations* choral singing, hill walking, history of medicine; *Style*— Dr Aileen Adams, CBE; ✉ 12 Redwood Lodge, Grange Road, Cambridge CB3 9AR (☎ and fax 01223 356460)

ADAMS, Prof Anthony Peter; s of Sqdn Ldr Henry William John Adams (d 1986), and Winifred Louise, *née* Brazenor (d 1989); *b* 17 Oct 1936; *Educ* Epsom Coll, Univ of London (MB BS, PhD); *m* 1, 30 Sept 1961 (m dis 1972), Martha Jill Vearncombe, da of Herbert William Davis (d 1985), of Yeovil, Somerset; 2 s (Christopher b 1963, Paul b 1965); m 2, 12 May 1973, Veronica Rosemary, da of Raymond Ashley John, of Maidenhead, Berks; 1 s (Adrian b 1979), 1 da (Jenny b 1975); *Career* conslt anaesthetist and clinical lectr Nuffield Dept of Anaesthetics Oxford 1969–79, prof of anaesthetics Univ of London at United Med and Dental Schs of Guy's and St Thomas's Hosps 1979–, chm Div of Anaesthetics United Med and Dental Schs 1984–89 and 1995– (vice chm 1989–95); hon conslt anaesthetist: Guy's Hosp 1979–, St Thomas' Hosp 1990–, The Maudsley Hosp 1992–95, King's Coll Hosp 1995–; examiner: FFARCS 1974–86, RCVS 1986–93, Univ of the W Indies 1986–88 and 1995, Univ of Wales 1988–93, Univ of Singapore 1988, Chinese Univ Hong Kong 1990; regnl advsr in anaesthetics SE Thames 1980–88, conslt SE Asia WHO 1982; Royal Coll of Anaesthetists: memb Cncl 1989–, chm Educn Ctee 1990–93, chm Info Technol Ctee 1996–, chm Standing Ctee on Dental Anaesthesia 1996–, memb Examinations Ctee; memb: Exec Ctee Anaesthetic Res Soc 1983 (chm 1990–94), Safety Ctee Assoc of Anaesthetists GB and Ireland 1987–; sr Euro Acad of Anaesthesiology 1985–95 (academician 1981–); visiting professorships incl: Univ of Texas 1983, Johns Hopkins Hosp Baltimore 1983, Univ of Yale 1984, Univ of Zimbabwe 1985, Univ of W Ontario 1985; assoc ed: Survey of Anesthesiology 1984–, Euro Jl of Anaesthesiology 1987–94; memb: Editorial Bd Br Jl of Anaesthesia 1984–, Jl of Anaesthesia (Japan) 1995–; memb: Shabbington Parish Cncl 1977–79, Bd of Govrs Sutton HS 1988–96; FRCA, FFARCS, FANZCA, FFARACS; *Books* Principles and Practice of Blood - Gas Analysis (jtly, 2 edn 1982), Intensive Care (jtly, 1984), Emergency Anaesthesia (jtly, 1986), Recent Advances in Anaesthesia (jtly, 18 edn 1993, 19 edn 1995), Anaesthesia, Analgesia and Intensive Care (jtly, 1991), Principles and Practice Series (jt series ed, BMJ Publications, 1994–); *Recreations* cinema, croquet, tennis, badger watching; *Clubs* Royal Soc of Med; *Style*— Prof Anthony Adams; ✉ Department of Anaesthetics, NGH-2, Guy's Hospital, London SE1 9RT (☎ 0171 955 4047)

ADAMS, Barbara Georgina; *née* Bishop; da of Charles Bishop (d 1980), and Ellaline, *née* Cowdrey (d 1972); *b* 19 Feb 1945; *Educ* Godolphin & Latymer GS, Univ of London (Dip in Archaeology, Cert in Geology); *m* 27 Sept 1967, Robert Frederick Adams, s of Frederick Adams (ka 1943); *Career* sci asst Entomology and Sub-Dept of Anthropology Br Museum of Nat History 1962–65, curator Petrie Museum of Egyptian Archaeology 1984– (asst 1965–75, asst curator 1975–84); memb: London Fedn of Museums and Art Galleries, London Museum Consultative Ctee, Egypt Exploration Soc, Int Assoc of Egyptologists, Geologists' Assoc, Palaeopathology Assoc; active memb Lib Pty, candidate for GLC 1982; *Books* Ancient Hierakonpolis (1974), The Koptos Lions (1984), The Fort Cemetery at Hierakonpolis (1987), Predynastic Egypt (1988), The Followers of Horus (jt ed with Renée Friedman, 1992), Ancient Nekhen (1995); ed Shire Egyptology series; *Recreations* geology, cinema, countryside, museums and galleries; *Style*— Mrs Barbara Adams; ✉ Petrie Museum of Egyptian Archaeology, University College London, Gower St, London WC1E 6BT (☎ 071 387 7050, ext 2882)

ADAMS, Bernard Charles; s of Charles Willoughby Adams (d 1963), of Ryde, IOW, and Emily Alice, *née* Ambrose (d 1950); *b* 29 Oct 1915; *Educ* King James I Sch IOW; *m* 1, 1942, Marjorie Barrett (d 1986), da of William Henry Frederick Weller (d 1918), of Barnoldswick, Yorks; 3 da (Jane, Gillian d 1983, Catherine d 1973); m 2, 1989, Betty Isabel Tucker, *née* Feist (d 1992); m 3, 1995, Ruth Atkinson, *née* Johnson; *Career* TA 1938–39, War Serv WWII 219 Battery, 43 Wessex Heavy Anti-Aircraft Regt RA, Battle of Britain def of Portsmouth and Southampton, 107 HAA Regt (Mobile) RA in UK, France (Normandy), Belgium, Holland, Germany, Capt RA (despatches); architect; sr architect Derbyshire CC 1951–54, asst co architect Kent CC 1954–59, dep co architect Herts CC 1959–60, co architect Somerset CC 1960–80, vice pres RIBA 1970–72 (memb Cncl 1963–69 and 1970–76); chm: SW Regnl Cncl RIBA 1972–74, Structure of the Profession Study RIBA 1976–79; pres: Co Architects' Soc 1973–74 (vice pres 1971–73), Soc of Chief Architects of Local Authorities (SCALA) 1975–76 (vice pres 1974–75, hon memb 1983–); memb: Nat Consultative Cncl for the Bldg and Civil Engrg Industs 1974–80, Bd of Architectural Studies Univ of Bristol 1964–74; architect advsr to Assoc of CC's 1971–80, fndr chm Architects' Ctee Consortium for Method Bldg 1961–6; Taunton Theatre Tst (became Brewhouse Theatre & Arts Centre April 1989): fndr memb 1972, chm 1986–Nov 1989, memb Cncl of Mgmnt; RIBA Architecture Award 1970, Commendation 1974, Heritage Year Award (Euro Architectural Heritage Year) 1975, Civic Tst Awards 1962, 1968, 1971 and Commendation 1965; ARIBA, FRIBA, FRSA; *Publications* contrib to jl of the RIBA and other professional jls; *Recreations* arts, theatre, languages; *Style*— Bernard Adams, Esq; ✉ Meadowside, Wild Oak Lane, Trull, Taunton, Somerset TA3 7JT (☎ 01823 272485)

ADAMS, Dr Bernard George; s of Arthur Adams (d 1975), and Sarah, *née* Morris (d 1971); *b* 9 Aug 1931; *Educ* Univ of London, London Hosp (MSc, MB BS, DPM Acad); *m* 21 Sept 1958, Caryle Ann, da of Robert Julius Steen (d 1968); 2 s (Peter Neil b 1963, James Robert b 1968), 1 da (Madeleine Clare b 1965); *Career* sr registrar: Bethlem Royal and Maudsley Hosps 1965–67, Royal Hammersmith Postgraduate Hosp 1965–67; conslt and hon sr lectr UCH London 1968; conrib to literature on psychopharmacology and liaison psychiatry; FRCP 1973, FRCPsych 1974, FRSM; *Recreations* music, theatre; *Style*— Dr Bernard Adams; ✉ Coutancie, Nanteuil Auriac de Bourzac, France; 7 Wimpole St, London W1 (☎ 0171 436 6346, fax 0181 340 1122)

ADAMS, Air Commodore Colin Ronald; CBE (1995), AFC (1973); s of Maj Ronald Adams, RAC and Chindits (ka Burma 1944), of Wimbledon, Surrey, and Margaret Amelia, *née* Carne (d 1987); *b* 1 April 1940; *Educ* Christ's Hosp, RAF Coll Cranwell; *m* Josephine (Jo) Mary Adams, da of Herbert Colton; 2 da (Sophie b 1 Nov 1965, Philippa (Pip) b 23 April 1967), 1 s (Nicholas b 23 May 1969); *Career* cmmnd RAF 1961; successively served in reconnaissance flying appts: UK, ME, Far East, Malta and Cyprus; flying instr; RN Staff Coll 1974, memb Tornado Aircraft Project Team Munich 1977–81, dep dir RAF Personnel Mgmnt 1983–86, CO RAF Akrotiri Cyprus 1986–88, project dir RAF Estate Rationalisation 1989–90, defence attaché Br Embassy Paris 1990–95, ret RAF 1995; dir British Consultants Bureau 1995–; Hon Cdr Ordre National du Merité (France) 1992, Humanitarian Gold Medal (France) 1993; FIPD 1989; *Recreations* offshore sailing, golf, skiing, fly fishing, visual arts; *Clubs* Royal Thames Yacht, RAF; *Style*— Colin Adams, CBE, AFC; ✉ British Consultants Bureau, 1 Westminster Palace Gardens, 1–7 Artillery Row, London SW1P 1RJ (☎ 0171 222 3651); West House, Maltravers Street, Arundel, West Sussex BN18 9BQ

ADAMS, David Howard; s of Capt Bernard Adams, RA (d 1982), of Newcastle, and Eve, *née* Glass (d 1987); *b* 15 Nov 1943; *Educ* Manchester GS; *m* 22 June 1969, Zoe, da of Victor Joseph Dwek (d 1989), of Manchester; 2 da (Gisele b 1970, Zanine b 1975); *Career* chief exec Henry Cooke Lumsden plc (dir 1975–94), exec dir Private Client Gp Capel-Cure Myers Capital Management Ltd 1994–96, managing conslt to Professional Practice 1996–; past chm: Manchester Stock Exchange, Inst for Fiscal Studies NW, Gtr Manchester Arts Centre Ltd (Cornerhouse); memb Royal Ct Theatre Devpt Bd; memb Worshipful Co of CAs 1978; past memb MENSA, FCA 1967, FRSA 1988, MSI (Dip) 1992; *Recreations* cycling, computers, reading; *Style*— David H Adams, Esq; ✉ David H Adams Ltd, Hamilton House, No 1 Temple Avenue, London EC4Y 0HA (☎ 0171 353 4212, fax 0171 353 3325, e-mail david@dhadams.demon.co.uk, pager 0941 176553)

ADAMS, Prof David Keith; s of Sidney Adams (d 1976), of Bredon, Worcestershire, and Dagmar Ruth Cawnpore, *née* Judge (d 1985); *b* 11 Aug 1931; *Educ* Abbey House and William Ferrer's GS Tewkesbury, Univ of Rennes, Clare Coll Cambridge (BA, MA), Yale Univ (AM), Oriel and Nuffield Coll Oxford (MA, DPhil); *m* 1, 23 March 1961 (m dis 1981), Virginia Mary Hope, da of Walton White (d 1976), of Edinburgh; 3 s (Giles b 4 March 1963, Roderick b 25 Nov 1965, Thomas b 9 June 1967); m 2, 5 Sept 1992, Sarah Louise, da of Peter and Jennifer Shuttleworth, of Bishop's Sutton, Hampshire; *Career* Henry fellowship Yale 1954–55, tutor in modern history Univ of Oxford 1955–59, visiting lectr in American studies Univ of Manchester 1959–60, lectr in American studies UCNS 1961 (asst lectr in history 1957–60), ACLS fellowship George Washington Univ 1965–66; Univ of Keele: sr lectr in American studies 1965–72, dir David Bruce Centre for American Studies 1969–96, head Dept of American Studies 1965–93, prof 1972–97; visiting sr scholar Clare Coll Cambridge 1970, visiting prof Univ of Tulsa 1981, visiting scholar Western Carolina Univ 1987; chm: Br-American-Canadian Assocs London, Canada-UK Colloquia 1990–93; memb Advsy Ctee Roosevelt Study Centre Middelburg The Netherlands; memb: BAAS, EAAS, OAH, SHAFR; *Books* America in the Twentieth Century (1967), An Atlas of North American Affairs (1969 and 1979), Franklin D Roosevelt and the New Deal (1979), British Documents on Foreign Affairs - North America 1919–1939 (ed 25 vols, 1986–95), American Literary Landscapes - The Fiction and the Fact (ed, 1988), Studies in US Politics (ed, 1989), Britain and Canada in the 1990s (ed, 1992), Environmental Issues (ed, 1993), Facing the Energy Challenge (ed, 1993), Reflections on American Exceptionalism (ed, 1994); *Recreations* books, gardening; *Style*— Prof David Adams; ✉ 17 Springpool, Keele, Newcastle-under-Lyme, Staffs ST5 5BN (☎ 01782 627392); David Bruce Centre for American Studies, University of Keele, Keele, Staffs ST5 5BG (☎ 01782 583010, fax 01782 583460)

ADAMS, Douglas Noël; s of Christopher Douglas Adams, and Janet, *née* Donovan (now Mrs Thrift); *b* 11 March 1952; *Educ* Brentwood Sch Essex, St John's Coll Cambridge (BA, MA); *m* 1991, Jane Belson; 1 da (Polly Jane Rocket b 22 June 1994); *Career* radio and TV writer 1974–78, BBC Radio producer 1978, BBC TV script ed 1978–80, novelist 1979–; dir The Digital Village; *Books* The Hitch Hiker's Guide to The Galaxy (1979), The Restaurant at the End of the Universe (1980), Life, The Universe and Everything (1982), So Long, and Thanks for all the Fish (1984), The Meaning of Liff (with John Lloyd, 1984), The Original Hitch Hiker Radio Scripts (1985), Dirk Gently's Holistic Detective Agency (1987), The Long Dark Tea-Time of the Soul (1988), Last Chance to See (with Mark Cawardine, 1990), The Deeper Meaning of Liff (with John Lloyd, 1990), Mostly Harmless (1992), The Illustrated Hitch Hiker's Guide to The Galaxy (1994); *Recreations* acoustic guitar playing, scuba diving, fiddling with computers; *Clubs* Groucho; *Style*— Douglas Adams; ✉ e-mail dna@tdv.com; c/o Ed Victor Ltd, 6 Bayley Street, Bedford Square, London WC1B 3HB (☎ 0171 304 4100, fax 0171 304 4111)

ADAMS, Douglas William; s of William Adams, of Perth, and Elizabeth, *née* Black; *b* 17 May 1953; *Educ* Perth Acad, Univ of Glasgow (MA, univ golf champion), Univ of Strathclyde (MBA); *m* 28 June 1975, Jacqueline Mary, da of Alfred John Ferguson; 1 s (Euan b 6 Sept 1980), 1 da (Keren Mhairi b 10 Dec 1982); *Career* sr economic asst Scottish Office Edinburgh 1975–78, admin Euro Cmmn Brussels 1978–82; economist: Scottish Devpt Agency Glasgow 1982–86, Scottish Provident Edinburgh 1968–88; mktg dir Templeton Investment Management Ltd Edinburgh 1988–94, currently head of regnl servs Oxford Economic Forecasting Ltd; *Recreations* golf, running; *Clubs* Dunbar Golf, Luffness Golf, Islay Golf; *Style*— Douglas Adams, Esq; ✉ Oxford Economic Forecasting Ltd, Abbey House, 121 St Adgates, Oxford OX1 1HB (☎ 01865 202828)

ADAMS, Gerald Edward; *b* 8 March 1930; *Educ* Royal Tech Coll Salford (BSc London), Univ of Manchester (PhD, DSc); *m* 1955, Margaret, *née* Ray; 3 s; *Career* post-doctoral fell Chemical Div Argonne Nat Laboratory Argonne Illinois 1958–60, visiting scientist Centre d'Etude Nucléaire Saclay France 1960–61, Res Unit in Radiobiology (later Gray Laboratory) Cancer Res Campaign 1962–76 (dep dir 1969–76), prof of physics as applied to med Univ of London Inst of Cancer Res London and Sutton 1976, dir MRC Radiobiology Unit Chilton Oxon 1982–95; chm Gray Laboratory Cancer Research Tst 1995–; numerous honorary appts various nat and int med orgns incl: memb Cncl Imperial Cancer Res Fund, memb Dirs' Sub-ctee UK Co-ordinating Ctee on Cancer Res, pres British Inst of Radiology 1995–96 (vice pres 1992–93); assoc ed various periodicals incl: Radiation Res, Int Jl of Radiation, Biology, Physics and Chemistry, Int and Euro Jls of Radiation Oncology; specialist ed Encylopaedia of Pharmacology and Therapeutics; ed-in-chief British Jl of Cancer 1994–; external examiner Univs of Cambridge, London, Edinburgh, Manchester, Leicester, Newcastle, Liverpool, Nottingham, Salford, Brunel, Stockholm, Oslo, Toronto, Delhi and Cape Town; author of over 250 res pubns incl book chapters and patents; Radiation Res Award Radiation Res Soc USA 1969, David-Anderson-Berry Prize RSE 1969, Sylvanus Thomson Medal British Inst of Radiology 1979, Milford Schulz Lectureship and Award Harvard Med Sch 1979, Maurice Lenz Lectureship and Award Columbia Univ 1981, hon doctorate in chem and technological pharmaceutics Univ of Bologna 1982, Röntgen Medal Soc of the Friends and Supporters of the German Röntgen Museum 1989, Failla Gold Medal Radiation Soc USA 1990, Weiss Medal Assoc of Radiation Research 1994, Kaplan Award Int Assoc of Radiation Research 1995, The Klaas Breur Medal Euro Soc for Therapeutic Radiology and Oncology 1996; fell American Coll of Radiology 1981, memb

Academia Scienze di Bologna 1983; *Style*— Gerald Adams, Esq; ✉ c/o Medical Research Council, Harwell, Didcot, Oxon OX11 0RD (☎ 01235 832139)

ADAMS, Gerard (Gerry); s of Gerard Adams; *b* 6 Oct 1948; *Educ* St Mary's GS Belfast; *m* 1971, Colette McArdle; 1 s; *Career* fndr memb Northern Ireland Civil Rights Assoc; interned by British Govt 1971, released for talks with Govt 1972, re-interned 1973; sentenced to 18 months imprisonment for attempted escape; released 1977; charged with IRA membership 1978, but charges unproven and released after seven months; elected to Northern Ireland Assembly 1982, MP (Sinn Fein) Belfast West 1983–92; pres Sinn Fein 1983– (vice pres 1978–83); *Books* Peace In Ireland, Politics of Irish Freedom, Pathway to Peace, Falls Memories, Cage 11, The Street & Other Stories, Free Ireland: Towards A Lasting Peace; *Style*— Gerry Adams, Esq; ✉ 51–53 Bothar na bhFal, Beal Feirste BT12 4PD

ADAMS, Prof (James) Hume; s of John Boyd Adams (d 1979), of Paisley, and Elizabeth Scott, *née* Neill (d 1975); *b* 31 Dec 1929; *Educ* Paisley GS, Univ of Glasgow (MB ChB, MD), Univ of London (PhD, DSc); *m* 9 Sept 1954, Eileen Rachel, da of James Lawson (d 1967), of Glasgow; 3 s (Nigel b 21 Jan 1956, Peter b 8 June 1959, Robin b 5 Feb 1961); *Career* Nat Serv RAMC 1955–57; specialist in pathology RAMC 1955–57, MRC res fell London 1957–59; Univ of Glasgow: successively lectr, sr lectr, reader 1959–71, prof of neuropathology 1971–92, hon sr res fell 1992–; pres Br Neuropathological Soc 1981–83 (sec 1968–76), pres Int Soc of Neuropathology 1990–94 (sec gen 1978–86); FRCPath 1973 (MRCPath 1963), FRCPGlas 1977 (MRCPGlas 1973), FRSE 1988; *Books* Brain Biopsy (1982), Atlas of Post-Mortem Techniques in Neuropathology (1982), An Introduction to Neuropathology (1988); *Recreations* golf, bridge; *Style*— Prof J Hume Adams, FRSE; ✉ 31 Burnhead Rd, Newlands, Glasgow G43 2SU (☎ 0141 637 1481); Institute of Neurological Sciences, Southern General Hospital, Glasgow G51 4TF (☎ 0141 201 2046)

ADAMS, Sir (William) James; KCMG (1991, CMG 1976); s of late William Adams, and late Norah, *née* Walker; *b* 30 April 1932; *Educ* Wolverhampton GS, Shrewsbury Sch, Queen's Coll Oxford; *m* 1961, Donatella, da of late Andrea Pais-Tarsilia; 2 s (Andrew, Charles), 1 da (Julia); *Career* Nat Serv RA 1950–51, ME Land Forces; Foreign Office 1954–92: MECAS 1955, third sec Bahrain 1956, asst political agent Trucial States 1957, London 1958, second sec 1959, Manila 1960, first sec and private sec to Min of State FO 1963, first sec (info) Paris 1965–69, FCO 1969, counsellor 1971, head of Euro Integration Dept (2) FCO 1971–72, seconded to Econ Cmmn for Africa Addis Ababa 1972–73, cnsllr (developing countries) UK Perm Rep to EC 1973–77, head of Chancery and econ cnsllr Rome 1977–80, asst under sec of state FCO 1980–84; ambassador: Tunisia 1984–87, Egypt 1987–92; conslt Control Risks Group 1992–, chm Egyptian-Br C of C 1992–, memb Roman Catholic Ctee for Other Faiths 1995–; Order of the Star of Honour (hon) Ethiopia 1965, Order of the Two Niles (hon) Sudan 1965; *Clubs* Reform; *Style*— Sir James Adams, KCMG; ✉ 13 Kensington Court Place, London W8 5BJ

ADAMS, James Macgregor David; s of Ronald Shaw Adams (d 1974), and Elizabeth Frances Mary, *née* Hunter; *b* 22 April 1951; *Educ* Harrow, Neuchatel Univ Switzerland; *m* 1 July 1990, René Riley-Adams, da of Robert Sanford Riley III; 2 da (Ella Riley-Adams b 12 July 1991, Grace Katherine Riley-Adams b 13 May 1993); *Career* Evening Chronicle Newcastle 1972–75, freelance Africa and USA 1975–78, 8 Days Magazine 1978–81 (reporter, chief reporter, news ed); The Sunday Times: foreign mangr 1981–82, special asst to Ed 1982–84, defence corr 1984–91 (managing ed and defence corr 1989–91), Washington Bureau chief 1991–; regular writer for Washington Post and Los Angeles Times; broadcaster for BBC, Nightline and Today Show (US); lectr: US Army War Coll, Defence Intelligence Coll, Brookings, British Special Branch; *Books* The Artist in the Marketplace (with Patricia Frischer, 1980), The Unnatural Alliance (1984), The Financing of Terror (1986), Secret Armies (1988), Ambush - The War Between the SAS and the IRA (1988), Engines of War (1990), The Final Terror (1991), Bull's Eye (1992), Taking the Tunnel (1993), New Spies (1993), Sellout (1995), Hard Target (1995); *CD-ROMs* Spycraft (1995), SSN (1996); *Recreations* fly fishing, scuba diving; *Clubs* Piscatorial Soc; *Style*— James Adams, Esq; ✉ c/o The Sunday Times, 1 Pennington Street, London E1 9XW (☎ 0171 782 5700, fax 0171 782 5050)

ADAMS, Prof James Noel; *b* 24 Sept 1943; *Educ* North Sydney Boys' HS, Univ of Sydney (BA, Univ medal), Brasenose Coll Oxford (DPhil); *m* 22 March 1971 (sep 1992), Geneviève Lucienne, *née* Baudon; 1 s (Nicholas James b 20 July 1976); *Career* teaching fell Dept of Latin Univ of Sydney 1965–67, Rouse res fell in classics Christ's Coll Cambridge (MA on election) 1970–72; Univ of Manchester: lectr 1972–78, sr lectr 1978–82, reader 1982–93, prof of Latin 1993–95; prof of Latin Univ of Reading 1995–; visiting sr res fell St John's Coll Oxford 1994–95; memb Philological Soc 1972; FBA 1992; *Books* The Text and Language of a Vulgar Latin Chronicle (1976), The Vulgar Latin of the Letters of Claudius Terentianus (1977), The Latin Sexual Vocabulary (1982), Wackernagel's Law and the Placement of the Copula esse in Classical Latin (1994), Pelagonius and Latin Veterinary Terminology in the Roman Empire (1995); *Recreations* cricket; *Style*— Prof J N Adams, FBA; ✉ Department of Classics, University of Reading, Whiteknights, PO Box 218, Reading RG6 2AA (☎ 0118 931 8420, fax 0118 931 6661)

ADAMS, Jennifer; *née* Crisp; LVO (1993); da of Arthur Roy Thomas Crisp, and Joyce Muriel, *née* Davey; *b* 1 Feb 1948; *Educ* City of London Sch IPRA Staff Coll; *m* 21 Sept 1968, Terence William Adams; *Career* mangr Central Royal Parks 1983– (actg bailiff 1990–92); pres Inst of Horticulture 1996–98 (pres-elect 1994–96); Liveryman Worshipful Co of Gardners; FILAM, Dip PRA, FIHort; *Style*— Mrs Jennifer Adams, LVO; ✉ Central Royal Parks, Ranger's Lodge, Hyde Park, London W2 2UH (☎ 0171 298 2102)

ADAMS, John Crawford; OBE (1977); s of Dr Archibald Crawford Adams (d 1943), of W Hallam, Derbyshire, and Ethel, *née* Parkin (d 1943); *b* 25 Sept 1913; *Educ* Oakham Sch, Univ of London (MD, MS), FRCS (Eng); *m* 1, 10 Oct 1940, Joan (d 1981), da of W Spencer Elphinstone, MBE (d 1969); m 2, 23 Feb 1990, Marguerite, da of Norman H Cross (d 1968); *Career* MO RAF 1939–45; conslt orthopaedic surgn: Brighton Gen Hosp 1948–58, St Mary's Hosp London 1948–80 (hon conslt surgn 1980–), St Vincent's Orthopaedic Hosp Eastcote Pinner 1948–68; hon civil conslt in orthopaedic surgery RAF, orthopaedic specialist RAFVR; memb Cncl Jl of Bone and Joint Surgery 1984–88 (prodn ed 1954–84); fell Br Orthopaedic Assoc (hon sec 1959–62, vice pres 1974–75); hon fell American Acad of Orthopaedic Surgns 1973; FRSM; *Books* Outline of Orthopaedics (1956, 12 edn 1995), Outline of Fractures (1957, 10 edn 1992), Ischio-Femoral Arthrodesis (1966), Arthritis and Back Pain (1972), Standard Orthopaedic Operations (1976, 4 edn 1992), Shakespeare's Physic, Lore and Love (1989), Francis, Forgiven Fraud (1992); *Recreations* silversmithing, music; *Style*— John Crawford Adams, Esq, OBE; ✉ 126 Harley St, London W1 (☎ 0171 935 2030); 33 Denman's Lane, Lindfield, W Sussex RH16 2JN

ADAMS, John Douglas Richard; s of Gordon Arthur Richard Adams (d in enemy hands 1944), and Marjorie Ethel, *née* Ongley (d 1983); *b* 19 March 1940; *Educ* Watford GS, Univ of Durham (LLB); *m* 12 April 1966, Anne Easton, da of Robert Easton Todd (d 1967); 2 da (Katharine b 1975, Caroline b 1978); *Career* called to the Bar Lincoln's Inn 1968; lectr in law: Univ of Newcastle upon Tyne 1963–71, UCL 1971–78; also practised at the Revenue Bar until 1978; special cmmr of Income Tax 1978–82, Registrar of Civil Appeals 1982–, recorder of the Crown Court 1992–; hon lectr St Edmund Hall Oxford 1975–, visiting lectr Univ of Oxford 1995–; *Books* International Taxation of Multinational Enterprises (with J Whalley, 1977), Supreme Court Practice (ed, 1991), Atkin's Court Forms (ed, 1991), Chitty & Jacob's Queen's Bench Forms (ed, 1987); *Recreations* music, walking, dining; *Style*— John Adams, Esq; ✉ Royal Courts of Justice, Strand, London WC2A 2LL (☎ 0171 936 6017)

ADAMS, Rear Adm John Harold; CB (1967), LVO (1957); s of H V Adams (d 1938), of Alnmouth, Northumberland; *b* 19 Dec 1918; *Educ* Glenalmond; *m* 1, 1943 (m dis 1961), Mary, da of Arthur Parker, of London; 1 s (decd); m 2, 1961, Ione, MVO, JP, da of late Col James Alister Eadie, DSO, TD; 2 s, 2 da; *Career* joined RN 1936, served WWII (despatches), Lt 1941, Lt Cdr 1949, Cdr 1951, Capt 1957, Rear Adm 1966, ACNS (policy) 1966–68, ret; dir Paper Indust Trg Bd and Employers' Fedn of Papermakers 1968–74, dir gen Br Paper and Bd Indust Fedn 1974–83; md DUO (UK) Ltd (Interview Guidance) 1983–93, sr ptnr John Adams Interviews 1994–, chm BFR Ltd; chm Bd of Govrs Cheam Sch 1975–87; FIPM 1975–93; *Recreations* photography, fishing; *Clubs* Army and Navy; *Style*— Rear Adm John Adams, CB, LVO; ✉ The Oxdrove House, Burghclere, Newbury, Berks RG20 9HJ (☎ 01635 278385)

ADAMS, Prof John Norman; s of Vincent Smith Adams, of Lintz Green Cottage, Lintz Green, Tyne & Wear, and Elsie, *née* Davison (d 1964); *b* 24 Dec 1939; *Educ* Newcastle upon Tyne Royal GS, Univ of Durham; *Career* slr in private practice 1965–71, lectr in law Univ of Sheffield 1971–79, called to the Bar Inner Temple 1984, prof of commercial law Univ of Kent 1987–94 (sr lectr in law 1979–87), prof of intellectual property Univ of Sheffield 1994–; visiting prof: Univ of Maryland 1974–75, Nat Law Centre Washington DC 1981, Notre Dame Law Sch Concannon Centre 1986–87, Université Paris X 1989–91; dir Intellectual Property Inst; *Books* incl: A Bibliography of Eighteenth Century Legal Literature (1982), Franchising (3 edn, 1990), Merchandising Intellectual Property (1987, 2 edn 1996), Understanding Contract Law (1987, 2 edn 1994), Commercial Hiring and Leasing (1989), Understanding Law (1992), A Bibliography of Nineteenth Century Legal Literature (Vol 1 1992, Vol 2 1994, Vol 3 1996), Key Issues in Contract (1995); *Recreations* music, walking; *Clubs* Savage, Lansdowne; *Style*— Prof John N Adams; ✉ 26 Priory Terrace, London NW6 4DH (☎ 0171 328 8676); 49 Endcliffe Hall Avenue, Sheffield S10 3EL (☎ and fax 0114 268 7311); One Raymond Buildings, Gray's Inn, London WC1R 5BZ (☎ 0171 430 1234, fax 0171 430 1004); 17 Russell Square, London WC1B 5DR (☎ 0171 637 1721, fax 0171 580 4273)

ADAMS, John Trevor; s of Claude Walter Adams (d 1985) of Wembley, Middx, and Ann Fletcher Gordon, *née* Taylor; *b* 2 April 1936; *Educ* UCS; *m* 6 July 1963, Elizabeth Mary, da of Montague William Lacey (d 1981), of Lytham, Lancs; 1 s (David John b 1968), 1 da (Caroline Mary b 1965); *Career* Nat Serv RASC 1954–56; articled to Temple Gothard 1957–63, audit sr Shipley Blackburn Sutton & Co 1963–68, tax sr Arthur Andersen 1966–68, tax sr and tax ptnr Josolyne Miles and Cassleton Elliot 1968–71, ptnr Clark Whitehill 1972–96; FCA 1964; *Recreations* rugby, cricket, badminton, tennis, music, fine art; *Style*— John Adams, Esq; ✉ 4 Grove Rd, Northwood, Middx HA6 2AP (☎ 01923 824933)

ADAMS, Prof Judith Elizabeth; da of late Percy Charles Lockyer, of Hale, Cheshire, and Barbara, *née* Bailey; *b* 16 May 1945; *Educ* Roedean, UCH London (MB BS, MRCP); *m* 16 Sept 1972, Prof Peter Harold Adams, s of late Alfred Adams, of Penarth, Wales; 2 s (Charles Edward b 25 Dec 1978, James Lindsay b 26 Jan 1983); *Career* prof of diagnostic radiology Univ of Manchester 1993– (lectr 1976–79, sr lectr 1979–), hon conslt radiologist Royal Infirmary Manchester 1978–, dean Faculty of Clinical Radiology RCR 1993–; vice pres RCR 1994–95; author of scientific pubns on: quantitative computed tomography for bone mass measurement, imaging in metabolic bone disorders and endocrine diseases, effective use of radiological resources; chm Examining Bd pt 1 FRCR 1984–89 (examiner 1980–84); memb: Editorial Bd British Journal of Radiology 1984–89, Editorial Bd Skeletal Radiology 1987–95, Int Skeletal Soc 1987–; non-exec memb Manchester Health Authy 1995–, chm Congress Ctee Radiology 1997; hon sec Br Assoc Clinical Anatomists 1990–93; FRCR 1975, FRCP 1988; *Recreations* embroidery, flower arranging, sewing, swimming; *Style*— Prof Judith Adams; ✉ Fairholm, Hawley Lane, Hale Barns, Altrincham, Cheshire WA15 0DR; Department of Diagnostic Radiology, University of Manchester, Stopford Building, Oxford Road, Manchester M13 9PJ (☎ 0161 275 5114, fax 0161 275 5594)

ADAMS, Maj Kenneth Galt; CVO (1979), CBE (1989); s of William Adams, OBE (d 1949), of Retford, Notts, and Christina Elisabeth, *née* Hall (d 1948); *b* 6 Jan 1920; *Educ* Doncaster GS, Staff Coll Camberley (psc); *m* 23 Dec 1988, Sally, da of late Col John Middleton, of Fleet, Hants, and wid of Douglas Long; *Career* RASC 1940–59; cmmnd Cairo 1941, WWII served ME and N Africa, DADST WO 1946–48, CO Cdr Kenya 1949–51, DAA & QMG Aldershot 1952, Staff Coll Camberley 1953, DAA & QMG HQ Northern Cmd 1954–56, sr instr RASC 1956–59; dir and conslt COS 1962–85, dir Proprietors of Hays Wharf Ltd 1966–70 (joined 1960); St George's House Windsor Castle: dir of studies 1969–76, fell 1976–82, hon fell 1990; Comino fell RSA 1979–89; vice chm Archbishops' Cncl on Evangelism 1965–77; chm: Industl Christian Fellowship 1977–86, Southwark Cathedral Cncl 1967–70, Tstees Fndn for Manufacturing and Indust 1993–94; indust fell Comino Fndn 1987–; memb: Advsy Ctee Christian Assoc of Business Execs 1975–, Advsy Ctee Inst of Business Ethics 1986–; tstee Industl Trg Fndn 1980–91; Liveryman Worshipful Co of Pattenmakers; MA (Lambeth) 1979, Hon DPhil Int Mgmnt Coll 1991; CIMgt 1975, FRSA 1979, FCIT 1980; *Recreations* reading 19th century novels, border terriers; *Clubs* Army and Navy; *Style*— Maj Kenneth Adams, CVO, CBE; ✉ 8 Datchet Rd, Windsor, Berks SL4 1QE (☎ 01753 869 708)

ADAMS, Michael; s of William John Walter (Bill) Adams, and Margaret Anne Jane, *née* Uglow; *b* 17 Nov 1971; *Educ* King Charles Sch, Truro Sch; *Career* chess player; titles incl: Br Championship 1989, Brussels Rapidplay 1992, Tilbury 1992; as England rep: third World Team Championships Lucerne 1989, second Visa Match Reykjavik 1990, third Olympiad Novi Sad 1990, third Euro Team Championship Debrecen 1992, first Groningen International 1993, winner PCA quarter final match NY 1994, winner Intel Grand Prix London 1995; *Books* Development of a Grandmaster (with Bill Adams, 1991); *Style*— Michael Adams, Esq

ADAMS, (Adrian) Neil; MBE (1983); s of Alfred Cyril Adams, of Seaton, Devon, and Jean, *née* Wrighley; *b* 27 Sept 1958; *m* 27 Aug 1984, Alison Louise, da of Alan Charles Walker; 1 s (Ashley Neil James); *Career* 8 times Br Open Judo Champion, European Title holder 1979, 1980, 1983, 1984 and 1985, 2 Olympic Silver medals, World Champion 1981; nat coach to GB Team; *Books* A Life in Judo (1985), Olympic Judo (Tachiwaza) Standing, Olympic Judo (Newaza) Groundwork, The Neil Adams Guide to Better Judo, Olympic Judo Preparation Training, Judo - Children's Judo, Armlocks, Gripps; *Style*— Neil Adams, Esq, MBE; ✉ The Neil Adams Club, Kenpas Highway, Coventry, Warwicks, (☎ 01203 418282)

ADAMS, Prof Norman Edward Albert; s of Albert Henry Adams, and Elizabeth Winifred Rose, *née* Humphreys; *b* 9 Feb 1927; *Educ* Harrow Art Sch, RCA (ARCA); *m* 1947, Anna Theresa, da of George Baseden Butt (d 1963), and Dorothy, *née* Till (d 1969), of London; 2 s (Jacob b 17 March 1956, Benjamin b 28 Jan 1958); *Career* artist (painter); head Dept of Painting Manchester Poly 1962–70, prof of fine art Univ of Newcastle upon Tyne 1981–86, prof of painting Royal Acad of Arts London 1986– (keeper 1986–95); works incl: murals St Anselm's Church Kennington London 1970, Stations of the Cross Our Lady of Lourdes Milton Keynes 1975, decor for ballets Covent Garden and Sadler's Wells in 1950s, Stations of the Cross St Mary's Manchester 1995; paintings in many public collections incl Tate Gallery and Fitzwilliam Coll Cambridge; Hon MA Newcastle; RWS 1988, RA 1972 (ARA 1967); *Publications* Alibis and Convictions (with Glyn Hughes, 1978), A Decade of Painting 1971–81 (1981), Angels of

Soho (with A Adams, 1988), Islands Chapters (with A Adams), Life on Limestone (with A Adams, 1994); *Recreations* all the arts; *Clubs* Arts; *Style*— Prof Norman Adams, RA; ✉ Butts, Horton-in-Ribblesdale, Settle, N Yorks BD24 0HD (☎ 01729 860284); 6 Gainsborough Road, London W4 1NJ

ADAMS, Sir Philip George Doyne; KCMG (1969, CMG 1959); s of Dr George Basil Doyne Adams (d 1957), and Arline Maud, *née* Dodgson (d 1986); *b* 17 Dec 1915; *Educ* Lancing, ChCh Oxford (MA); *m* 1954, Hon (Mary) Elizabeth Lawrence; 2 da (Lucy b 1955, Harriet b 1959), 2 s (Geoffrey b 1957, Justin b 1961); *Career* HM Consular and Dip Serv 1939–75; ambass to Jordan 1966–70, dep sec Cabinet Office 1971–72, ambass to Egypt 1973–75; dir Ditchley Fndn 1977–82; *Clubs* Brooks's; *Style*— Sir Philip Adams, KCMG; ✉ 54 Sussex Square, London W2 2SR (☎ 0171 262 1547)

ADAMS, Ralph Gange; s of Ralph Noel Adams (d 1988), and Catherine Anne, *née* Reid (d 1988); *b* 30 Oct 1955; *Educ* Trinity Coll Glenalmond, Univ of Dundee (LLB); *m* 3 Aug 1989, Kirstine Mary Park, da of Rev Keith Campbell (d 1994); 1 da (Catherine Christine Campbell b 27 May 1992), 2 s (Angus Keith Gange b 5 May 1994, Gavin Graham McFarlane b 11 March 1996); *Career* Deloitte & Touche (formerly Touche Ross): specialist in corp fin, indentured student 1976–79, CA 1979, seconded to Melbourne office 1980, seconded to Bank of Scotland Glasgow and Edinburgh 1984–85, ptnr 1986–, ptnr i/c Edinburgh office 1989–93, ptnr i/c Scottish offices 1993–, memb Bd of Ptnrs 1993–; MICAS 1979; *Recreations* Golf; *Clubs* Prestwick Golf; *Style*— Ralph Adams, Esq; ✉ Westering, 2 Inverleith Grove, Edinburgh, Scotland EH3 5PB; Deloitte & Touche, 39 George Street, Edinburgh, Scotland EH2 2HZ (☎ 0131 225 6834, fax 0131 225 4049)

ADAMS, Richard Borlase; CBE (1982); s of James Elwin Cokayne Adams (d 1961), and Susan Mercer, *née* Porter (d 1985); *b* 9 Sept 1921; *Educ* Winchester, Trinity Coll Oxford; *m* 1951, Susan Elizabeth, da of Col Ronald Streeter Lambert, MC (d 1976); 2 s (Christopher, Jeremy), 1 da (Jill); *Career* served WWII with Rifle Bde ME and Italy; chm Islay Kerr & Co Ltd Singapore 1963–66; British India Steam Navigation Co Ltd: dir 1966–69, md 1969–70, chm 1970–84; P & O: dir 1970–74, dep md 1974–79, md 1979–84, chief exec 1981–84; dir Clerical Medical and General Life Assurance Soc 1975–88; chm Kent Assoc for the Disabled 1986–91; *Recreations* gardening, tennis, golf; *Clubs* Oriental; *Style*— Richard Adams, Esq, CBE; ✉ 6 Leicester Close, Henley-on-Thames, Oxon RG9 2LD (☎ 01491 574184)

ADAMS, Richard George; s of Evelyn George Beadon Adams, and Lilian Rosa, *née* Button; *b* 9 May 1920; *Educ* Bradfield, Worcester Coll Oxford (MA); *m* 1949, (Barbara) Elizabeth Acland; 2 da (Juliet, Rosamond); *Career* author; Army Serv 1940–46; entered Civil Serv 1948, ret as asst sec DOE 1974; writer in residence: Univ of Florida 1975, Hollins Coll Virginia 1976; pres RSPCA 1980–82; Carnegie Medal 1972; FRSL 1975; *Books* Watership Down (1972, filmed 1978), Shardik (1974), Nature Through the Seasons (with Max Hooper, 1975), The Tyger Voyage (narrative poem, 1976), The Ship's Cat (narrative poem, 1977), The Plague Dogs (1977, filmed 1982), Nature Day and Night (with Max Hooper, 1978), The Iron Wolf (short stories, 1980), The Girl in a Swing (1980, filmed 1988), Voyage Through The Antarctic (travel book, 1982), Maia (1984), The Bureaucats (1985), Nature Diary (1985), Traveller (1988), The Day Gone By (autobiography, 1990), Tales from Watership Down (1996); contrib to and ed: Occasional Poets anthology (1986), The Legend of Te Tuna (narrative poem, 1986); *Style*— Richard Adams, Esq, FRSL; ✉ 26 Church St, Whitchurch, Hants, RG28 7AR

ADAMS, Robert; *Career* planning and devpt dir RTZ Corporation plc 1991–, dir CRA Ltd 1995–; *Style*— Robert Adams, Esq; ✉ The RTZ Corporation plc, 6 St James's Square, London SW1Y 4LD (☎ 0171 930 2399)

ADAMS, Prof Robert David; s of William Peter Adams (d 1973), and Marion, *née* Lawton; *b* 13 April 1940; *Educ* Hanley HS, Imperial Coll London (BSc, ACGI, DSc), St John's Coll Cambridge (PhD); *m* 28 Sept 1963, Susan, da of John Felix Waite, GM, of Aston, Market Drayton; 1 s (Joss b 26 Sept 1970), 1 da (Rosie b 11 April 1968); *Career* Dept of Mech Engrg Univ of Bristol: successively lectr, reader and prof 1967–, head of dept 1994–; memb Adhesives Gp Inst of Materials; FIMechE, FInstP, FPRI; *Books* Structural Adhesive Joints in Engineering (with William C Wake, 1984), over 150 papers in scientific and tech jls; *Recreations* rowing, gardening, wine; *Clubs* Rotary Club of Clifton; *Style*— Prof Robert Adams; ✉ 17 Cotham Lawn Road, Bristol BS6 6DU (☎ 0117 924 7977); Department of Mechanical Engineering, University of Bristol, University Walk, Bristol BS8 1TR (☎ 0117 928 7743, fax 0117 929 4423)

ADAMS, Robin William; s of William Edward Leo Adams, of Edmonton, London, and Jennie Alfreda Adams; *b* 17 Oct 1944; *Educ* Huxley Sch Enfield, Enfield Tech Coll; *m* 1967, Pauline; 1 da (Julia b 1968), 1 s (John b 1972); *Career* dep press offr The Rank Organisation 1962–65, press offr Rank Audio Visual Ltd 1965–67, central press offr The Rank Organisation 1967–70, press and publicity mangr Guild Holdings Ltd 1970–72; dir: McLeish Associates Ltd 1972–79, GEA Public Relations Ltd 1979–; memb Professional Practices Ctee and former memb Cncl IPR; hon press offr Film '69, '71 and '73 (int conf and exhbn for film and TV industs); corp memb Br Kinematograph Sound and TV Soc, memb Int Bldg Press; FIPR 1995 (MIPR 1974); *Books* The After-Dinner Speaker's Handbook (ed, 1990–91); ed Architectural Ironmongery Jl; *Recreations* reading and writing; *Style*— Robin Adams, Esq; ✉ GEA Public Relations Ltd, 89 Great Eastern Street, London EC2A 3HY (☎ 0171 729 0586, fax 0171 729 7765)

ADAMS, His Hon Judge (John) Roderick Seton; s of George G Adams (d 1980), of Edinburgh, and M Winifred, *née* Wilson (d 1990); *b* 29 Feb 1936; *Educ* Whitgift Sch, Trinity Coll Cambridge (MA); *m* 19 April 1965, (Pamela) Bridget, da of Rev David Edmund Rice, MC (d 1978), of Hexham; 3 s (Robert b 5 Jan 1966, James b 14 Aug 1967, John b 9 Oct 1973); *Career* 2 Lt Seaforth Highlanders 1955–56, Capt Parachute Regt 1960–65; called to the Bar Inner Temple 1962, in practice 1968–90, recorder Crown Ct 1980–90; circuit judge: SE Circuit 1990–96, NE Circuit 1996–; *Recreations* music, fishing; *Style*— His Hon Judge Roderick Adams; ✉ 6 Pump Court, Temple, London EC4 (☎ 0171 583 6013, fax 0171 353 0464); Melness House, Sutherland (☎ 01847 601255)

ADAMS, Tate; *b* 26 Jan 1922; *Educ* Central Sch of Art London, Royal Melbourne Inst of Technol; *Career* studied wood engraving with Gertrude Hermes; sr lectr in printmaking Art Sch Royal Melbourne Institute of Technology 1960–82; fndr: Crossley Gallery Melbourne 1966, Crossley Print Workshop 1970, Lyre Bird Press 1977 (merged with James Cook Univ of N Queensland 1990); currently prodr artists' books; RE 1992 (ARE 1985); *Books* The Soul Cages (1958), Diary of a Vintage (1982), Port of Pearls (1989); *Recreations* study of Australian wines; *Style*— Tate Adams, Esq; ✉ 20 Ethel Street, Hyde Park, Townsville, Queensland, Australia (☎ 00 61 77 215712)

ADAMS, Tony; *b* 10 Oct 1966; *Career* professional footballer (defender); with Arsenal FC 1983– (currently capt); honours with Arsenal: League Championship 1989 and 1991, League Cup 1993, FA Cup 1993, Euro Cup Winners' Cup 1994; England: played for youth, under-21 and B teams, 46 full caps and 4 goals (as at Jan 1997), capt 1994, 1995 and Euro 96; PFA Young Player of the Year 1987; *Style*— Tony Adams; ✉ c/o Jerome Anderson Management, 248 Station Road, Edgware, Middx HA8 7AU (☎ 0181 958 7799)

ADAMS, William Horace; s of David Horace Adams (d 1965), and Patience, *née* Dixon (d 1963); *b* 15 Aug 1925; *Educ* Stamford Sch, Oakham Sch; *m* 1947, Joan, da of James Pugh (d 1960); 2 s, 2 da; *Career* chartered surveyor; chm: RICS Continental Euro Branch 1981, Waterglade International Holdings plc 1987–92; pres: Br Chapter Int Real Est Fndn (FIABCI) 1982–83, Arbitration and Conciliation Cncl FIABCI 1982–90; dir Property Intelligence Ltd 1984–94; conslt: Security Pacific National Bank 1984–90, Privatbanken (now Unibank) 1985–91, Bankers' Trust Co 1990–91; Freeman City of London, Liveryman Worshipful Co of Gardeners; *Clubs* RAC; *Style*— William H Adams, Esq; ✉ 7 Doran Court, Pembury Road, Tunbridge Wells, Kent TN2 3RH

ADAMSON, Sir (William Owen) Campbell; kt (1976); o s of late John Adamson, of Kinross; *b* 26 June 1922; *Educ* Rugby, Corpus Christi Coll Cambridge; *m* 1, 1945 (m dis 1984), Gilvray, da of Dr William Allan, of Baildon, Yorks; 2 s, 2 da; m 2, 1984, Mrs J (Mimi) Lloyd-Chandler; *Career* with Richard Thomas & Baldwins and Steel Co of Wales 1947–69; former memb: BBC Advsy Ctee, NEDC, SSRC, Design Cncl, Industl Soc Cncl; formerly vice chm Nat Savings Ctee for England and Wales; dir gen CBI 1969–76; chm: Abbey National Building Society (now Abbey National plc) 1978–91, Revertex Chemicals 1978–81, Renold Ltd 1982–86 (dir 1976–, dep chm 1981–82); dir: Imperial Group 1976–86, Yule Catto until 1982, Lazard Brothers 1976–87, Doulton & Co 1977–83, Tarmac plc 1980–90; author of various tech pubns; vice pres Inst of Manpower Studies 1982–; special tstee Charing Cross Hosp 1983–, chm Re-Action Tst 1991–, pres NCVO 1992–; govr Rugby Sch 1979–93; Hon DSocSci Univ of Birmingham 1993, hon fell Corpus Christi Coll Cambridge 1996; *Recreations* walking, music; *Clubs* Naval and Military; *Style*— Sir Campbell Adamson; ✉ c/o Abbey National plc, 32 Grosvenor Square, London W1X 9LL (☎ 0171 491 4616)

ADAMSON, (Ronald) Crawfurd; s of Ronald Adamson, of Edinburgh, and Janette Elizabeth Minna, *née* Bauermeister, of Edinburgh; *b* 24 March 1953; *Educ* Duncan of Jordanstone Coll of Art Dundee (Scottish Educn Dept travelling scholar, post-grad commendation), Elizabeth Greenshields Fndn Canada; *m* 1974, Mary Ann Elizabeth, da of Andrew Alexander Hansen Phimister; 1 s (Matthew Andrew b 1978), 1 da (Cassie Francesca b 1981); *Career* artist; gave up teaching to paint full time 1983; *Solo Exhibitions* incl: Cylinder Gallery London 1984 and 1985, Trinity Arts Centre Kent 1985, Scottish Gallery Edinburgh 1987, 1988 and 1989, Thumb Gallery London 1988, Scottish Gallery London 1989, Parnham House Dorset 1991, Jill George Gallery London 1991, 1993 and 1995, Château de la Muette Paris 1993; *Gp Exhibitions* incl: Soc of Scottish Artists 1978 and 1979, Royal Scottish Acad 1979, Prix International d'Art Contemporain de Monte-Carlo 1984 and 1993, Contemporary Scottish Art (touring Japan, 1990), Scottish Art in the 20th Century (Royal W of England Acad Bristol) 1991, invited artist Salon d'Automne Paris 1993; works in numerous collections incl The Met Museum of Art NYC; *Recreations* woodworking, music; *Style*— Crawfurd Adamson, Esq; ✉ Jill George Gallery, 38 Lexington Street, London W1R 3HR (☎ 0171 439 7343/7319, fax 0171 287 0478)

ADAMSON, Dr Donald; JP (Cornwall 1993); s of Donald Adamson (d 1982), of Lymm, Cheshire, and Hannah Mary, *née* Booth (d 1994); *b* 30 March 1939; *Educ* Manchester GS, Magdalen Coll Oxford, Univ of Paris (MA, MLitt, DPhil); *m* 24 Sept 1966, Helen Freda, da of Frederick Percival Griffiths, TD (d 1970), of Mossley Hill, Liverpool; 2 s (Richard Henry Egerton b 17 Jan 1970, John Daniel b 21 April 1971); *Career* author and historian; visiting fell Wolfson Coll Cambridge 1989–90; judge Museum of the Year Awards 1979–83, memb Exec Ctee Nat Heritage 1980–92; Liveryman: Worshipful Co of Haberdashers 1976, Worshipful Co of Curriers 1991; JP City of London 1983–92; Lord of the Manor of Dodmore; Chevalier Ordre des Palmes Académiques France 1986; Order of St John: OStJ 1985, CStJ 1992, dir of ceremonies Essex 1992, asst dir of ceremonies Order of St John 1995; FSA 1979, FRSL 1983, FIL 1989; *Books* The Genesis of Le Cousin Pons (1966), Dusty Heritage (1971), The House of Nell Gwyn (jtly, 1974), A Rescue Policy for Museums (1980), Balzac: Illusions Perdues (1981), Les Romantiques Français devant la Peinture espagnole (1989), Blaise Pascal: Mathematician, Physicist, and Thinker about God (1995), Rides Round Britain, the travel journals of John Byng, 5th Viscount Torrington (ed, 1996); translations of works by Balzac (1970, 1976) and Maupassant (1993), contrib to various reviews; *Recreations* collecting, gastronomy, water sports; *Clubs* Reform, Beefsteak, City Livery; *Style*— Dr Donald Adamson, JP; ✉ Topple Cottage, Polperro, Cornwall PL13 2RS (☎ 01523 107182, car 0468 281277); Dodmore House, The Street, Meopham, Kent DA13 OAJ

ADAMSON, Hamish Christopher; OBE (1996); s of John Adamson (d 1985), of Perth, Scotland, and Denise, *née* Colman-Sadd; *b* 17 Sept 1935; *Educ* Stonyhurst, Lincoln Coll Oxford (MA); *Career* admitted slr 1961; The Law Soc: asst sec 1966–81, sec Law Reform and Int Rels 1981–87, dir Int Div 1987–95; sec UK Delgn Cncl of Bars and Law Soc's of Euro Community 1981–95, exec sec Cwlth Lawyers Assoc 1983–95, dir Franco-Br Lawyers Soc 1991–, chm Tstee Ctee Commonwealth Human Rights Initiative 1993–95; memb Law Soc; *Books* The Solicitors Act 1974 (1975), Butterworth's Free Movement of Lawyers (1992); *Recreations* plants, books, travel; *Style*— Hamish Adamson, Esq, OBE; ✉ 133 Hartington Rd, London SW8 2EY (☎ 0171 720 4406, fax 0171 720 4406)

ADAMSON, Norman Joseph; CB (1981), QC (Scot 1979); s of Joseph Adamson, and Lily, *née* Thorrat, of Glasgow; *b* 29 Sept 1930; *Educ* Hillhead HS, Univ of Glasgow (MA, LLB); *m* 1961, Patricia Mary, er da of Walter Scott Murray Guthrie, of Edinburgh; 4 da; *Career* advocate (Scot) 1957, called to the Bar Gray's Inn 1959; Army Legal Aid (Civil) (UK) 1956–57, in practice Scottish Bar 1957–65; standing jr counsel: Bible Bd 1962, MOD (Army) 1963–65; Parly draftsman and legal sec Lord Advocate's Dept London 1965–89, legal sec to Lord Advocate and first Parly draftsman for Scot 1979–89, asst counsel to Lord Chm of Ctees House of Lords 1989–95, ret; elder of Church of Scotland; *Style*— Norman J Adamson, Esq, CB, QC; ✉ Prospect House, 53 Lodge Hill Road, Lower Bourne, Farnham, Surrey GU10 3RD (☎ 01252 721988)

ADAMSON, Stephen James Lister; s of James Lister Adamson (d 1985), and Helen Galloway Begg Adamson (d 1980); *b* 10 July 1942; *Educ* John Lyon Sch, Harrow; *m* 20 May 1972, Elizabeth Margaret, da of John Leslie Tunley (d 1965), of Heswall, Cheshire; 3 s (Neil b 15 Feb 1974, Stuart b 25 Jan 1977, Ross b 19 March 1981); *Career* CA 1966; ptnr: Arthur Young 1978, Ernst & Young 1989–; pres: Insolvency Practitioners' Assoc 1989–90 (memb 1978–), INSOL Int 1993–95; memb Faringdon Ward Club 1988; FIPA 1978; *Recreations* fishing, golf, theatre; *Clubs* IOD, Oriental; *Style*— Stephen Adamson, Esq; ✉ Englewood, Ridgemead Rd, Englefield Green, Surrey; Ernst & Young, Becket House, 1 Lambeth Palace Rd, London SE1 7EU (☎ 0171 928 2000, fax 0171 931 4184)

ADAMSON, Stewart Marr; s of Stewart Marr Adamson (d 1996), of Newcastle upon Tyne, and Josephine, *née* Mooney; *Educ* ONC and HNC in Mechanical Engrg, Univ of Durham (BSc Marine Engrg); *m* 29 Aug 1964, Margaret, da of Alan Kennedy (d 1957), of Newcastle upon Tyne; 1 da (Debra Jane b 20 Nov 1969), 1 s (Stewart Marr b 17 Feb 1972); *Career* indentured engrg apprentice and jig and tool designer Hawthorn Leslie (Engineers) Ltd 1954–61, Univ of Durham 1961–64, head Main Propulsion Research Gp Br Ship Research Assoc (BSRA) 1964–68, chief engrg designer and tech servs mangr Vosper Thornycroft Ltd 1968–74, tech mangr/project mangr David Brown Vosper (Offshore) Ltd 1974–78, euro mangr Lockheed Petroleum Services (UK) Ltd (later CanOcean Resources (UK) Ltd) 1978–81, md Kongsberg Engineering Ltd 1981–85, md Fuel Subsea Engineering Smit International Group (formerly part of Costain Group plc) 1985–; Offshore Technology Conference (OTC, USA): memb Program Ctee 1978–94 (vice-chm 1994), program chm 1995 (first non-American), memb Bd and dir Offshore Technology Conferences Inc 1995– (first non-American); FEng 1996, FIMechE, FIMarE, memb American Inst of Chemical Engrs; *Publications include* The Type 21 Frigate (RN Jl, 1970), Offshore LNG Terminal Review: Small Scale Gas Recovery Systems for Hostile Environments (OTC, 1978), Garoupa Subsea Production System (Offshore Europe Conf, 1979), Impact of Subsea Maintenance Activities on Floating Production Facilities in Deep Water (OTC, 1984), The Development of Diverless Subsea Production Systems (Brazil

Oil and Gas Seminar, 1987), Application of Subsea Production Systems Offshore USSR (Neftegas Conf, 1987), The Development of Diverless Subsea Production Systems (Inst of Marine Engrs, 1988), Application of Diverless Subsea Production Systems to Gulf of Mexico (Houston, 1990); *Recreations* making classical guitars and occasionally lutes and balalaikas, attending concerts (especially for classical guitar and lute), photography; *Style—* Stewart M Adamson, Esq, FEng; ✉ Managing Director, Fuel Subsea Engineering, Smit International, Chobham House, Christchurch Way, Woking, Surrey GU21 1JG (☎ 01483 777301, fax 01483 777315, e-mail stewartadamson@fuelsubsea.sprint.com)

ADCOCK, Fleur; OBE (1996); da of Cyril John Adcock, and Irene, *née* Robinson; *b* 10 Feb 1934; *Educ* Wellington Girls' Coll NZ, Victoria Univ of Wellington (MA); *m* 1, 1952 (m dis 1958), Alistair Teariki Campbell; 2 s (Gregory Stuart b 1954, Andrew Robert Teariki b 1957); m 2, 1962 (m dis 1966), Barry Crump; *Career* poet; asst librarian: Univ of Otago 1959–61 (asst lectr 1958), Alexander Turnbull Library 1962, FCO 1963–79; freelance writer 1979–; Northern Arts Fellowship in Literature Univs of Newcastle upon Tyne and Durham 1979–81, Eastern Arts Fellowship Univ of East Anglia 1984, writer in res Univ of Adelaide 1986; FRSL 1984; *Awards* Buckland Award 1967 and 1979, Jessie MacKay Award 1968 and 1972, Cholmondeley Award 1976, NZ Book Award 1984, Arts Cncl Bursaries 1982 and 1988; *Books* The Eye of the Hurricane (1964), Tigers (1967), High Tide in the Garden (1971), The Scenic Route (1974), The Inner Harbour (1979), Below Loughrigg (1979), The Oxford Book of Contemporary NZ Poetry (1982), Selected Poems (1983), The Virgin and the Nightingale: medieval Latin poems (1983), Hotspur: a ballad for music (1986), The Incident Book (1986), The Faber Book of 20th Century Woman's Poetry (1987), Orient Express: poems by Grete Tartler (trans, 1989), Time Zones (1991), Letters from Darkness: poems by Daniela Crasnaru (trans, 1991), Hugh Primas and the Archpoet (ed and trans, 1994), The Oxford Book of Creatures (ed with Jacqueline Simms, 1995); *Style—* Ms Fleur Adcock, OBE, FRSL; ✉ 14 Lincoln Road, London N2 9DL

ADCOCK, Robert Wadsworth; CBE (1992), DL (Essex 1978); s of Sir Robert Adcock, CBE, DL (d 1990), of Torquay, and Mary Hannah, *née* Wadsworth; *b* 29 Dec 1932; *Educ* Rugby; *m* 26 Oct 1957, Valerie Colston, da of Col Stanley Robins, MBE (Indian Army, d 1974), of Hereford; 1 s (Robert Charles b 1961), 1 da (Olivia Charlotte b 1961); *Career* asst slr Lancs CC 1955–56, asst slr Manchester CC 1956–59, sr slr Berks CC 1959–63, asst clerk (later dep clerk) Northumberland CC 1963–70, dep chief exec Essex CC 1970–76, chief exec Essex CC 1976–95, clerk of Essex Lieutenancy 1976–95; Assoc of County Cncls: advsr Police Ctee 1976–83, advsr Policy Ctee 1983–, chm Officers' Advsy Gp 1987– (memb 1983–); Assoc of County Chief Execs: hon sec 1983–90, chm 1991–92; chm Officers' Advsy Panel SE Region Planning Conf 1984–88; *Recreations* gardening, ornithology; *Style—* Robert Adcock, Esq, CBE, DL; ✉ The Christmas Cottage, Great Sampford, Saffron Walden, Essex CB10 2RQ (☎ 01779 586363); Essex County Council, County Hall, Chelmsford, Essex (☎ 01245 492211 ext 20011, fax 01245 352710, telex 995910)

ADDINGTON, 6 Baron (UK 1887); Dominic Bryce Hubbard; s of 5 Baron Addington (d 1982), and Alexandra Patricia, *née* Millar; *b* 24 Aug 1963; *Educ* Hewett Sch, Norwich City Coll, Univ of Aberdeen (MA); *Heir* bro, Hon Michael Hubbard, *qv*; *Recreations* rugby football; *Clubs* National Liberal; *Style—* The Rt Hon the Lord Addington; ✉ 9/11 Chalk Hill Rd, Norwich NR1 1SC

ADDINGTON, Hon Jeremy Francis; s and h of 7 Viscount Sidmouth; *b* 29 July 1947; *Educ* Ampleforth; *m* 1, 1970, Grete, *née* Henningsen, of Randers, Denmark; 1 s (Steffan b 1966), 1 da (Laura Grete b 1975); m 2, 1986, Una, eldest da of James Coogan, of Calne, Wilts; 1 s (John b 29 Nov 1990), 1 da (Anna Frances b 1988); *Style—* The Hon Jeremy Addington; ✉ Highway Manor, nr Calne, Wilts SN11 8SR

ADDIS, Dr Bruce John; s of John Henry Addis (d 1942), and Muriel Florence, *née* Cattell; *b* 11 Oct 1942; *Educ* King Edward's Five Ways Sch Birmingham, St Bartholomew's Hosp Med Coll (MB BS); *m* 6 Aug 1966, Rosemary, da of Charles Eltham Kidner, of Bovey Tracey, Devon; 1 s (Mark b 1970), 1 da (Chania b 1968); *Career* Surgn Cdr RN 1968–84, conslt pathologist Royal Naval Hosp Haslar 1978–83; conslt histopathologist: Brompton Hosp 1984–87, Salisbury Dist Hosp 1987–94; chm of pathology HCI International Medical Centre 1994–; sr lectr Nat Heart and Lung Inst 1984–87, ed Jl of Pathology 1987–94; memb Cncl Assoc of Clinical Pathologists 1992–95; author of papers on histopathology; FRCPath 1989 (MRCPath 1977); *Books* Lung Tumours (ed, 1988), Textbook of Uncommon Cancer (contrib, 1988); *Recreations* music, painting; *Style—* Dr Bruce Addis; ✉ Auchengare, Station Road, Rhu, Helensburgh, Argyll and Bute G81 8LW (☎ 01436 820536); Department of Pathology, HCI International Medical Centre, Clydebank, Scotland G81 4DY (☎ 0141 951 5904)

ADDISON, Edward Norman; OBE (1987); *b* 28 May 1918; *Educ* Realgymnasium Vienna; *m* 1 May 1945, Patricia, *née* Saint; 2 da (Vivien b 1946, Jacqueline b 1949); *Career* WWII Army 1940–46; fndr and chm The Addison Tool Co Ltd 1956–; pres MTTA 1985–86 and 1990–91, chm COMMET 1986–87, pres Comité Européen de Liaison des Importateurs de Machines-Outils 1977–80, vice pres Comité Européen de Co-opération des Industries de la Machine-Outil (CECIMO) 1990–; FRSA 1988; *Recreations* racehorse owner; *Style—* Edward Addison, Esq, OBE; ✉ The Addison Tool Co Ltd, Elliott House, Victoria Road, London NW10 6NY (☎ 0181 965 6600, fax 0181 993 8767)

ADDISON, Mark Eric; *b* 22 Jan 1951; *Educ* Marlborough, St John's Coll Cambridge (BA), City Univ (MSC), Imperial Coll London (PhD); *Career* Dept of Employment: admin trainee 1978, private sec to the PM 1985–88, regnl dir for London Trg Agency 1988–91, dir of Fin and Resource Mgmnt 1991–94; dir of Safety Policy HSE 1994–; *Recreations* British motor cycles, Dorset, windsurfing and the opus of Robert Zimmerman and James Hendrix; *Style—* Mark Addison, Esq; ✉ Health and Safety Executive, Rose Court, 2 Southwark Bridge, London SE1 9HS (☎ 0171 717 6000, fax 0171 717 6717)

ADDISON, Terry Robert; s of Keith Roy Addison (d 1982), and Dorothy Phyllis, *née* Hind (d 1969); *b* 27 Dec 1932; *Educ* Hinckley GS Leics, Leicester Coll of Art, RCA London (Royal scholar, Des RCA); *m* 4 Oct 1958, Anne Jennifer (d 1982), da of Percival White (d 1947); 2 s (Scott b 1961, Ben b 1961), 1 da (Elizabeth b 1970); *Career* Nat Serv 1 RHA, BAOR; interior design conslt; ptnr YRM Architects 1960–78; own practice: Addison Marc 1978– (associate offices in Singapore, Kuala Lumpur, Riyadh, Boston, Miami and Chicago); dir: Devpt & Investmt Co, Adsul Ltd 1986–; fell Soc of Artists and Designers; *Recreations* piano; *Clubs* IOD; *Style—* Terry R Addison, Esq; ✉ Addison Marc, 5 Portpool Lane, London EC1N 7UU (☎ 0171 831 2800, fax 0171 831 0274)

ADDISON, 4 Viscount (UK 1945); William Matthew Wand Addison; also 4 Baron Addison (UK 1937); s of 3 Viscount Addison (d 1992), and Kathleen, da of Rt Rev and Rt Hon John William Charles Wand, KCVO, DD, 110 Bishop of London; *b* 13 June 1945; *Educ* King's Sch Bruton, Essex Inst of Agric; *m* 1, 1970 (m dis), Joanna Mary, eldest da of late John Ivor Charles Dickinson, of Blyborough Grange, Gainsborough, Lincs; 1 s (Hon Paul Wand b 1973), 2 da (Hon Sarah Louise b 1971, Hon Caroline Amy b 1979); m 2, 1991, Lesley Ann, da of George Colin Mawer, of Sudbeck Lane, Welton, Lincs; *Heir* s, Hon Paul Wand Addison b 1973; *Career* vice pres The Cncl for Nat Parks 1995–; *Style—* The Rt Hon the Viscount Addison; ✉ Church Barn, Oundle, Peterborough PE8 4AX

ADDYMAN, Peter Vincent; s of Erik Thomas Waterhouse Addyman (d 1963), of Harrogate, and Evelyn Mary, *née* Fisher (d 1961); *b* 12 July 1939; *Educ* Sedbergh Sch Cumbria, Peterhouse Cambridge (open exhibitioner, MA); *m* 1965, Shelton Oliver Addyman, da of Stanley Matthews Oliver; 1 s (Thomas Oliver b 28 May 1967), 1 da (Susannah Mary b 1 June 1969); *Career* lectr in archaeology: Queen's Univ of Belfast 1964–67 (asst lectr 1962–64), Univ of Southampton 1967–72; dir York Archaeological Tst 1972–; pres Cncl for Br Archaeology 1992–95 (vice pres 1981–85), vice pres Royal Archaeological Inst 1979–83; chm Standing Conf of Archaeological Unit Mangrs 1975–78; Bd dir Heritage Projects Ltd; hon fell Univ of York 1972– (Hon DUniv 1985), hon reader Univ of Bradford 1974–81 (Hon DSc 1984): MIFA 1982 (chm 1983–85), FSA 1967; *Books* The Archaeology of York Vols 1–20 (gen ed 1976–93), Archaeological Papers from York (with V E Black, 1984); *Recreations* gardening, watercolours, travel; *Clubs* Athenaeum; *Style—* Peter Addyman, Esq, FSA; ✉ 50 Bootham, York YO3 7BZ (☎ 01904 624311); York Archaeological Trust, Cromwell House, 11 Ogleforth, York YO1 2JG (☎ 01904 663003)

ADEBOWALE, Victor; s of E O Adebowale, and Grace Adebowale; *b* 21 July 1962; *Educ* Thornes House Wakefield; *m* (sep); 1 s (Adam); *Career* London Borough of Newham: private sector repairs admin 1983, estate offr 1983–84, sr estate mangr 1984–86; permanent property mangr Patchwork Community Housing Assoc 1986–88, regnl dir Ujima Housing Assoc 1988–90, dir Centrepoint Soho (alcohol recovery project) 1990–; chm Special Info Trg Resource Agency (SITRA); memb: Nat Cncl Nat Fedn of Housing Assocs, Bd ACENVO; *Publications* Alcohol Problems in the Community: Drinking Problems Among Black Communities (Routledge, 1996); *Recreations* kite flying, reading, writing poetry, music; *Style—* Victor Adebowale, Esq; ✉ Centrepoint Soho, Bewlay House, 2 Swallow Place, London W1V 7AA (☎ 0171 629 2229, fax 0171 409 2027, mobile 0802 449107)

ADENEY, David William; s of Rev Dr Harold Walter Adeney, of Reepham, Norwich, and Dr Isobel McDonald, *née* Anderson; *b* 22 Oct 1940; *Educ* Monkton Combe Sch, Queens' Coll Cambridge (BA); *m* 11 Jan 1964, Ann; 1 s (Mark Howard b 16 Nov 1964), 2 da (Suzan Elizabeth, Alison Clare (twins) b 15 Feb 1967); *Career* Reckitt & Colman plc 1963–86: export mgmnt 1964–67, product mangr India 1967–69, md Sri Lanka 1970–71, Asia Div mangr 1971–73, md Pakistan 1973–78, export dir Household Div 1978–84, md Nigeria 1984–86; exec dir Tear Fund 1988–95 (joined as operational dir 1986); diocesan sec Norwich Dio; *Recreations* international affairs; *Style—* David Adeney, Esq

ADENEY, (Howard) Martin; s of Rev Arthur Webster Adeney, and Edith Marjorie, *née* Blagden (d 1987); *b* 7 Sept 1942; *Educ* Monkton Combe Sch, Queens' Coll Cambridge (BA); *m* 18 Dec 1971, Ann Valerie, *née* Corcoran; 2 s (William Edward b 3 Sept 1973, Thomas Henry b 7 June 1976), 1 step s (Samuel John Stanton Moore b 29 April 1963); *Career* reporter Guardian 1965–77 (labour corr 1972–77), feature writer Colombo Pubn Bureau 1968–69, industl corr Sunday Telegraph 1977–78, industl ed BBC TV 1982–89 (labour corr 1978–82); gp PR mangr ICI plc 1993– (head int media rels 1989–93); memb Westminster City Cncl 1971–74; *Books* The Miners Strike: Loss Without Limit (with John Lloyd, 1986), The Motormakers: The Turbulent History of Britain's Car Industry (1988), Nuffield: a biography (1993); *Recreations* walking, garden labouring; *Style—* Martin Adeney, Esq; ✉ ICI plc, 9 Millbank, London SW1P 3JF

ADÈS, Thomas Joseph Edmund; s of Timothy Raymond Ades, of London, and Prof Dawn Ades, *née* Tylden-Pattenson; *b* 1 March 1971; *Educ* Univ Coll Sch, Guildhall Sch of Music, King's Coll Cambridge, St John's Coll Cambridge; *Career* pianist, conductor, composer; awarded Lutine Prize 1985; composer- in-association Hallé Orch 1993–95, fell commoner in creative arts Trinity Coll Cambridge 1995–97; *Performances* as pianist: Park Lane Group (Purcell Room) 1993, Composers Ensemble (Almeida Theatre 1994 and 1995, Cheltenham Festival 1994, Tirane Festival Albania 1995), Thomas Adès and Friends (Almeida Festival 1994, Cheltenham Festival 1995 and 1996, Aldeburgh Festival 1995), Endellion Quartet (Spitalfields Festival) 1995, London Sinfonietta Soloists (Cheltenham Festival 1995, London South Bank 1996), Berkeley Symphony Orch (and as composer) 1995, Hallé Orch 1996, Lindsay Quartet 1996; conducted orchs and ensembles incl: Birmingham Contemporary Music Gp 1994, Hallé Orch 1994, Nash Ensemble 1996; *Compositions* Five Eliot Landscapes 1989 (broadcast by BBC 1993), Chamber Symphony 1990, ... but all shall be well 1993, Living Toys 1993 (winner Paris Int Rostrum of Composers for composers under 30 1994), Arcadiana String Quartet 1994, Powder Her Face (cmmnd by Almeida Opera) 1995; *Recreations* dining out; *Clubs* Black's; *Style—* Thomas Adès, Esq; ✉ c/o Faber Music, 3 Queen Square, London WC1N 3AU (☎ 0171 278 7436, fax 0171 278 3817)

ADEY, John Fuller; s of Frank Douglas Adey (d 1978), and Doreen Adey; *b* 12 May 1941; *Educ* Glyn Sch Epsom, St Edmund Hall Oxford (MA), Harvard Business Sch (MBA); *m* 25 Sept 1965, Marianne, da of George Hugh Banning; 2 da (Helen Doreen b 1 July 1971, Francesca Ruth b 26 May 1977), 2 s (Matthew Frank George b 19 May 1975, Michael Douglas John b 31 Dec 1984); *Career* manufacturing mangr then int mktg dir Raychem Ltd 1973–83, md Courtaulds Chemicals and Plastics 1983–86, md Baxter Healthcare 1986–93, chief exec National Blood Authority 1993–; CEng 1970, MIMechE 1970, MIEE 1976, FInstD 1994; *Recreations* tennis, cycling; *Style—* John Adey, Esq; ✉ National Blood Authority, Oak House, Reeds Crescent, Watford, Herts WD1 1QH (☎ 01923 212121, fax 01923 211031)

ADGEY, Prof (Agnes Anne) Jennifer; da of Robert Henry Adgey (d 1973), of Newtownards, Co Down, and Sarah Jane, *née* Menown (d 1990); *b* 2 Oct 1941; *Educ* Regent House Sch Newtownards Co Down, Queen's Univ Belfast (MB, MD); *Career* res fell in cardiology Presbyterian Med Centre San Francisco 1967–68; Royal Victoria Hosp Belfast: jr house offr 1964–65, sr house offr and registrar 1965–67, sr registrar in cardiology 1968–71, conslt cardiologist 1971–, prof of cardiology 1991–; examiner RCP London, expert Advsy Panel on Cardiovascular Diseases WHO, examiner RCP Ireland 1988; memb: Cncl Br Cardiac Soc 1995–, Cncl Med Defence Union 1995–; memb: Br Cardiac Soc 1973, Assoc of Physicians of GB and Ireland 1980, NY Acad of Sci 1983, Resuscitation Cncl UK 1987; fell American Coll of Cardiology 1975; MRCP 1967, FRCP 1978; *Books* The Acute Coronary Attack (with J F Pantridge, J S Geddes and S W Webb, 1975), Developments in Cardiovascular Medicine (1982), Acute Phase of Ischemic Heart Disease and Myocardial Infarction (ed), numerous papers on cardiology; *Recreations* piano and classical music; *Style—* Prof Jennifer Adgey; ✉ Mossvale House, 71 Ballyskeagh Road, Lisburn, Co Antrim BT27 5TE (☎ 01232 629773); Regional Medical Cardiology Centre, Royal Victoria Hospital, Belfast BT12 6BA (☎ 01232 894975, fax 01232 312907)

ADIE, Kathryn (Kate); OBE; adopted da of John Wilfrid Adie (d 1993), and Maud, *née* Fambely (d 1990); *b* 19 Sept 1945; *Educ* Sunderland Church HS, Univ of Newcastle upon Tyne (BA Hons); *Career* technician and prodr BBC local radio 1969–76, reporter BBC TV South 1977–78; BBC TV News: reporter 1979–81, corr 1982, chief news corr 1989–; Hon MA: Univ of Bath 1987, Univ of Newcastle upon Tyne 1990; Hon DLitt: City Univ 1989, Univ of Sunderland 1991, Univ of Loughborough 1991; RTS: News Award 1981 and 1987, Judges' Award 1989; Monte Carlo Int TV News Award 1981 and 1990, BAFTA Richard Dimbleby Award 1989; Freedom of City of Sunderland; *Style—* Ms Kate Adie, OBE; ✉ c/o BBC TV, Wood Lane, London W12

ADIE, Rt Rev Michael Edgar; CBE (1994); s of Walter Granville Adie and Kate Emily, *née* Parish; *b* 22 Nov 1929; *Educ* Westminster, St John's Coll Oxford (MA); *m* 1957, Anne Devonald Roynon; 1 s, 3 da; *Career* former res chaplain to Archbishop of Canterbury, vicar St Mark Sheffield 1960–69, rural dean of Hallam 1966–69, rector of Louth 1969–76, vicar of Morton with Hacconby 1976–83, archdeacon of Lincoln 1977–83, bishop of Guildford 1983–94; chm Gen Synod Bd of Educn and Nat Soc for Promoting Religious Educn 1989–94; Provost (Southern Div) Woodard Corporation (largest gp of independent church schs in England including Lancing Coll, Hurstpierpoint Coll, Ardingly Coll and Bloxham Sch) 1996–; Hon DUniv Surrey 1995; *Style*— The Rt Rev Michael Adie, CBE; ✉ Greenslade, Froxfield, Petersfield, Hants GU32 1EB (01730 827266)

ADKINS, Richard David; QC (1995); s of Walter David Adkins, and Patricia, *née* Chimes; *b* 21 Oct 1954; *Educ* Leamington Coll for Boys, Hertford Coll Oxford (MA); *m* 1977, Jane Margaret, da of Derek and Ella Sparrow; 2 s, 1 da; *Career* Lovell White & King: articled clerk 1976–78, admitted slr 1978, slr 1978–79; slr Freshfields 1979–82; called to the Bar Middle Temple 1982; memb Ctee Chancery Bar Assoc 1991–93; *Publications* Encyclopaedia of Forms and Precedents (Vol 3, 1985), Company Receivers: A New Status? (1988), Gore-Browne on Companies (contrib 44 edn, 1992–); *Recreations* opera, tennis; *Clubs* Bromley Cricket; *Style*— Richard Adkins, Esq, QC; ✉ 3–4 South Square, Gray's Inn, London WC1R 5HP (☎ 0171 696 9900)

ADKINS, Roy Ewart; OBE (1992); s of Samuel William Ewart Adkins (d 1980), and Elsie, *née* Spooner; *b* 21 June 1931; *Educ* Handsworth GS; *m* 14 May 1960, Barbara May, da of Horace Benjamin Loach; 2 s (John Ewart b 3 Jan 1963, Timothy Benjamin b 3 Feb 1966), 1 da (Louise Elizabeth b 26 May 1961); *Career* Nat Serv 1953–54; ptnr: Ault & Co 1966–71 (qualified chartered accountant 1963), Thornton Baker (following merger) 1971; Grant Thornton (formerly Thornton Baker): ptnr 1971–91, chm Insolvency Panel 1973–87, memb and former chm Policy Bd 1978–83, non-exec chm Thornton Baker Associates Limited (Mgmnt Conslts) 1976–80, chm Ptnrs Nat Annual Conf 1988–90, chm Nat Equity Ptnrs Meetings 1986–91; Insolvency Practitioners Assoc: memb 1971–, memb Law Reform Ctee 1972–78, chm Tech Ctee 1982–84 (memb 1978–84), memb Ethics Ctee 1986–88, chm Regnl Meetings Ctee 1985–88, pres Cncl 1984–85 (memb 1980–86); Soc of Practitioners of Insolvency: fndr memb 1990–, memb Cncl 1990–92, chm Ethics Ctee 1990–92; memb: Insolvency Practitioners Ctee ICAEW 1986–89, Ethics Ctee ICAEW 1986–88; chm Insolvency Practioners Jt Liaison Ctee 1984–89; memb: Insolvency Serv Steering Bd DTI 1989–96, Inst of Credit Mgmnt 1980–91; FCA (ACA 1963); *Recreations* theatre, golf; *Style*— Roy Adkins, Esq, OBE; ✉ 36 Wyvern Road, Sutton Coldfield, West Midlands B74 2PT (☎ 0121 240 0443)

ADLAM, Lance Edward Stott; s of Edward Douglas Stott Adlam (d 1991), of Cotleigh, nr Honiton, Devon, and Margaret Elsie, *née* May-Arrindell (d 1996); *b* 3 April 1944; *Educ* Acton Central Sch, The Elms Secdy Sch Acton, Chiswick Poly, Thames Poly (formerly Hammersmith Coll of Art & Building), Poly of Central London; *m* 1 July 1967, Angela Marie, da of Vivian Egerton Saunders; 2 s (Mark Edward Vivian b 1970, Paul Andrew John b 1972); *Career* architect; Fitzroy Robinson & Partners 1960–71, Bucks Co Architects Dept 1971–78, section ldr Architects' Dept Ind Coope Ltd 1978–80, sr architect Fitzroy Robinson Partnership 1980–83; T P Bennett Partnership (formerly T P Bennett & Son) assoc 1983–89, ptnr 1989–93, conslt 1993–; princ Lance Adlam Architects 1993–; vice-chm Princes Risborough Chamber of Trade 1995–; memb: Great Western Soc, N Gauge Soc, Buckinghamshire Family History Soc, Bucks Genealogical Soc; memb ARCUK 1974, RIBA 1974; *Recreations* badminton, tennis, railway modelling, railway history, philately, genealogy, music, reading; *Clubs* Thame Badminton (chm 1988–96); *Style*— Lance Adlam, Esq; ✉ Chartered Architect, 6 Salisbury Close, Princes Risborough, Bucks HP27 0JF (☎ and fax 01844 345423)

ADLAM, Nicholas Rolfe; s of Bernard Stephen Adlam (d 1976), of The Walnuts, Hail Weston, nr St Neots, Cambs, and (Avis) Marjorie Adlam, OBE (d 1995); *b* 1 Oct 1945; *Educ* Kimbolton Sch; *m* 1, 10 April 1971 (m dis 1993), Heather Miranda, da of George May (d 1974), of Wyboston, Beds; m 2, 6 Sept 1995, Sarah Ann, da of John Fentiman (d 1980), of Kearnsey, Kent, and Theadora, *née* Instone (d 1976); *Career* chm: Gordon Watts & Co Ltd 1981–89, B S Adlam & Co Ltd 1977; md: Cavingston Properties Ltd 1974–, Cavingston Ltd, Wincomblee Estates Ltd 1985–; non-exec dir Omnibus Workspace Ltd 1977–; jt md: Fennstone Investments Ltd 1990–, Fennstone Properties Ltd 1990–; Freeman City of London 1967, Liveryman Worshipful Co of Spectacle Makers 1971 (Freeman 1966); memb Guild of Freemen of City of London 1969; *Recreations* horse-racing, travelling, reading balance sheets, cutting grass; *Clubs* East India, RAC; *Style*— Nicholas R Adlam, Esq; ✉ c/o East India Club, 16 St James's Square, London SW1Y 4LH (☎ 0171 930 1000, fax 0171 321 0217, telex 938 041)

ADLARD, David Boyd; s of Clifford Boyd Adlard (d 1985), of Norwich, and Elsie Lawrence, *née* Fielder (d 1990); *b* 13 June 1944; *Educ* Gresham's, Univ of Sussex (BSc), Middlesex Poly (Dip Mgmnt Studies), Kilburn Poly (Catering Studies); *m* Aug 1984, Mary Ellen, da of Edward Patrick Healy, of North Worcester, Mass; 1 da (Lucy Elizabeth b Nov 1987), 1 s (Matthew John Boyd b Aug 1991); *Career* work study engr then prodn mangr Alcan Industries Ltd 1966–73, prodn mangr Cape Universal Building Products 1973–74; chef: various hotels and restaurants 1975–77, Connaught Hotel Mayfair 1978–81; chef tournant Le Talbooth Restaurant Dedham Colchester Essex 1981–82, pastry chef and asst to Maître D'Hotel Castle Restaurant Leicester Mass USA 1982, restaurant mangr The Terrace Restaurant Dedham Vale Hotel Dedham Colchester Essex 1982, opened Adlard's Restaurant Wymondham Norfolk 1983 (moved restaurant to 79 Upper St Giles St Norwich 1989); memb Académie Culinaire de France (filiale Grande Bretagne) 1988–; *Awards* (for Adlard's restaurant) Michelin one rosette 1987–92 and 1995–96, AA (three Rosettes), Egon Ronay rosette, Good Food Guide 4/5 rating 1990–96 and Exceptional Wine Cellar ranking 1990–95, Decanter Badoit Restaurant of The Month 1990, regnl winner Decanter/Sandeman Wine List Competition 1995; *Recreations* wine, computing, reading cookery books, searching for wild mushrooms and dining out; *Style*— David Adlard, Esq; ✉ 79a Upper St Giles Street, Norwich, Norfolk NR2 1AB (☎ 01603 661988, fax 01603 617733); Adlards Restaurant, 79 Upper St Giles Street, Norwich, Norfolk NR2 1AB (☎ 01603 633522)

ADLER, David Harold; *b* 14 Oct 1941; *Educ* Felsted; *Career* articled clerk Edward Moore & Sons 1961–66, qualified chartered accountant 1966, Roth Manby & Co 1966–68; KPMG: joined 1968, ptnr 1972–95, senior ptnr Norwich office 1991–95; pres E Anglian Soc of CAs 1987, chm E Anglian Dist Training Bd 1990–94; memb Broads Authy (and memb Navigation Ctee) 1995–, chm Cox Boatyard Ltd 1995–, dir Thetford Moulded Products Ltd, dir Whitlingham Charitable Tst 1995–; FCA (ACA 1966); *Recreations* sailing, squash, skiing, bridge; *Style*— David Adler, Esq; ✉ 1 Eaton Road, Norwich, Norfolk NR4 6PY (☎ 01603 458556)

ADLER, Eur Ing George Fritz Werner; OBE (1982); s of Fritz Jacob Sigismund Adler (d 1949), of Cardiff, and Hildegard Julie Lippmann (d 1982); *b* 12 Jan 1926; *Educ* Co GS Penarth, Univ of London (BSc), Univ of Cardiff (Jt Dip in Mechanical Engrg), Imperial Coll London (DIC); *m* 11 June 1949, June Moonaheim Margaret, da of William Charles Nash; 3 da (Helen Margaret Suzanne b 26 April 1951, Fiona Ruth b 22 April 1955, Caroline Francesca Mathilde b 15 Dec 1965); *Career* mangr Water Turbine Valve & Hydraulic Products Divs English Electric Co 1966–71 (graduate apprentice 1945–47, chief devpt engr Rugby 1956–58), mangr Mechanical Products Div Marconi 1962–66 (chief mechanical engr 1958–62), dir of res British Hydromechanics Research Association 1971–86, sec Assoc of Independent Res and Technol Orgns 1986–89; contrib to Kempe's Engineers Yearbook 1956–; memb: Governing Body Imperial Coll 1985–, Engrg Cncl 1986–89; chm Br Nat Ctee for Int Engrg Affairs 1986–89, vice pres Euro Fedn of Nat Engrg Assocs 1987–89; Freeman City of London 1984, Liveryman Worshipful Co of Engrs 1984; Fell Univ of Wales Coll of Cardiff, FIMechE (pres 1983–84), FICE 1980, FEng 1981 (treas and memb Cncl 1988–91), FIMgt, FInstD; *Recreations* crafts, gardening, music, golf; *Clubs* Carlton; *Style*— Eur Ing George Adler, OBE, FEng; ✉ The Haining, Orchard Close, Longburton, Sherborne, Dorset DT9 5PP (☎ 01963 210641)

ADLER, John James; JP (Chelmsford 1987); s of Cdr Alan Adler, RNVR (d 1966); *b* 16 Sept 1935; *Educ* Felsted; *m* 1962, Hilary Anne, da of Reginald Drew, of Essex; 2 s (Michael b 1962, Harry b 1970), 2 da (Fiona b 1964, Julia b 1967); *Career* chm: Cadogan Investments 1970–95 (md 1966), Tobacco Trade Benevolent Assoc 1977–82, A Oppenheimer & Co Ltd 1979–95 (remaining dir); dir Thetford Moulded Products; chm Mid Essex Hosp Servs NHS Tst 1991–94; chm: Eastern Cos Rugby Referees 1987–92, Bd of Visitors HM Prison Chelmsford 1985–87 (now ordinary memb); Master Worshipful Co of Tobacco Makers and Tobacco Blenders City of London 1982; *Recreations* squash, sailing (Albacore 'Phee Anna'), rugby refereeing; *Clubs* City Livery, Thorpe Bay Yacht; *Style*— John Adler, Esq, JP; ✉ A Oppenheimer & Co, 20 Vanguard Way, Shoeburyness, Southend-on-Sea, Essex SS3 9RA (☎ 01702 297 785, fax 01702 294 225)

ADLER, Lawrence Cecil (Larry); s of Louis Adler, and Sadie Hack; *b* 10 Feb 1914; *Educ* Baltimore City Coll; *m* 1, 1938 (m dis 1961), Eileen Walser; 1 s, 2 da; m 2, 1969 (m dis 1977), Sally Cline; 1 da; *Career* mouth organist, journalist and critic; winner Maryland Harmonica Championship 1927, first British stage appearance in CB Cochran's Streamline revue 1934, debut as soloist with Symphony Orchestra Sydney Aust 1939; jt recital tours with dancer Paul Draper US 1941–49; soloist with NY Philharmonic and other maj orchs in US, Eng, Japan and Europe; war tours: for Allied Troops 1943, 1944 and 1945, Germany 1947 and 1949, Korea 1951, Israel 1967 (Six Day War) and 1973 (Yom Kippur War); contrib articles and book reviews: Sunday Times, New Statesman, Spectator, New Society, Observer, Punch; restaurant critic: Harpers and Queen, London Portrait, Boardroom, Chamber Life; columnist: What's On in London, Jazz Express, Jewish Gazette; film scores composed: Genevieve, King and Country, High Wind in Jamaica, The Great Chase; Hon Dip: Peabody Conservatory of Music Baltimore 1986, City Coll Baltimore 1986; Duke Ellington fell Yale Univ 1988; *Books* How I Play (1937), Larry Adler's Own Arrangements (1960), Jokes and How to Tell Them (1963), It Ain't Necessarily So (autobiography, 1985); *Recreations* tennis, journalism, conversation; *Clubs* Groucho, Paddington Tennis; *Style*— Larry Adler, Esq; ✉ c/o MBA Literary Agents Ltd, 45 Fitzroy Street, London W1P 5HR (☎ 0171 387 2076)

ADLER, Prof Michael William; s of late Gerhard Adler, and Hella, *née* Hildergard; *b* 12 June 1939; *Educ* Middlesex Hosp Med Sch (MB BS, MD); *m* 1 (m dis 1978), Susan Jean Burnett; m 2, 23 June 1979 (m dis 1994), Karen Hope Dunnell, da of Richard Henry Williamson (d 1984); 2 da (Zoe b 1980, Emma b 1982); m 3, 26 March 1994, Baroness Jay of Paddington, *qv*; *Career* house offr and registrar in med (Middx Hosp, Central Middx Hosp, Whittington Hosp) 1965–69, lectr St Thomas' Hosp Med Sch 1970–75, sr lectr Middx Hosp Med Sch 1975–79, prof of genito urinary med Univ Coll London Med Sch (formerly Middx Hosp Med Sch) 1979–; non-exec dir Camden and Islington Community Health Servs NHS Tst 1993; MRC memb: Res Advsy Gp on epidemiological studies of sexually transmitted dieases 1975–80, Working Pty to coordinate lab studies on the gonococcus 1979–83, Working Pty on AIDS 1981–87 (Sub Ctee therapeutic studies 1985–87), Ctee epidemiological studies on AIDS 1985–94, Ctee on clinical studies of prototype vaccines against AIDS 1987; Jt Ctee of Higher Med Trg: memb Advsy Ctee on genito urinary med 1981–86, sec 1982–83, chm 1984–86; memb EC Working Gp on AIDS 1985–, chm RCP Ctee on Genito Urinary Med 1987–91 (memb 1981–91), advsr Parly All Pty Ctee on AIDS 1987–, chm and tstee Nat AIDS Tst 1987–, dir AIDS Policy Unit 1988–89, memb Cncl Med Soc for Study of Venereal Diseases; DOH: memb Expert Advsy Gp AIDS 1984–92, memb Gp on health care workers 1987–91; memb: Exec Ctee Int Union against Venereal Diseases 1986–, BMA AIDS Working Pty 1986–, RCS Ctee on HIV Infection/AIDS 1991–; advsr in venereology WHO 1983–, memb Med Advsy Ctee Brook Advsy Centres 1984–94, memb Cncl Royal Inst of Public Health and Hygiene 1993–94, memb Advsy Bd Int AIDS Soc 1993–; dir Terence Higgins Tst 1982–88; fndr ed AIDS (monthly jl) 1986–94; memb Editorial Panel: Genitourinary Medicine, Current Opinion on Infectious Diseases; Evian Health Award 1990; FFPHM, FRCP; *Books* ABC of Sexually Transmitted Diseases (1984, 3 edn 1995), ABC of AIDS (1987, 3 edn 1993), Diseases in the Homosexual Male (ed, 1988); also articles on sexually transmitted diseases and AIDS in medical jls; *Recreations* yoga, jogging; *Style*— Prof Michael Adler; ✉ Academic Department of Genito-Urinary Medicine, The Mortimer Market Centre, Mortimer Market, off Capper Street, London WC1E 6AU (☎ 0171 380 9660, fax 0171 380 9669)

ADLINGTON, Jonathan Peter Nathaniel; s of Sidney Roy Adlington, JP (d 1982), of Mylor, Cornwall, and Patricia, *née* Moxon; *b* 26 April 1949; *Educ* Downside, Univ of Liverpool (LLB); *m* 2 June 1973, Carolyn Patricia Lilian Marie, da of Brian BW Bromley, of Crowborough, E Sussex; 1 s (Edward b 25 Dec 1983), 2 da (Emily b 3 May 1975, Tamsin b 19 Sept 1976); *Career* admitted slr 1973; ptnr Trowers and Hamlins 1976– (articled clerk 1971–73); memb Law Soc; *Recreations* sailing; *Clubs* RAC; *Style*— Jonathan Adlington, Esq; ✉ Trowers & Hamlins, 6 New Square, Lincoln's Inn, London WC2A 3RP (☎ 0171 831 6292, telex 21422, fax 0171 831 8700)

ADMANI, Dr (Abdul) Karim; OBE (1987), JP (City of Sheffield 1974); s of Haji Razzak Admani (d 1954), of Palitana, India, and Hajiani Rahima Admani; *b* 19 Sept 1937; *Educ* Gujarat Univ (BSc), Karachi Univ (MB BS), Univ of London; *m* Seema, da of Charles Robson (d 1947), of South Shields; 1 s (Nadim b 1969), 1 da (Nilofer b 1971); *Career* conslt physician with special interest in strokes and the elderly; teacher Health Authority 1970–, clinical lectr Sheffield Medical Sch 1972–; dir: Ranmoor Grange Nursing Home Ltd 1975–80, Overseas Doctors' Assoc in the UK Ltd 1976– (chm 1981–87, pres 1987–94); chm Sunningdale Yorks Ltd 1983–, chm PAK-Br Med Fndn in UK 1995–; county pres S Yorks BRCS 1982– (also patron); memb: Exec Ctee for Racial Equality in Sheffield 1972– (chm 1978–), Exec Ctee BMA Sheffield 1974–, Gen Medical Cncl in UK 1979–, Central Ctee of Consultant and Specialists in UK 1979–93, Exec Ctee Age Concern Sheffield 1982–90, Sheffield Health Authy; memb Editorial Bd: Pakistan Medical Bulletin 1974–94, Medi-Scene 1981–, ODA News Review 1985–; chm: Educn and Graduate Trg Ctee ODA 1978, ODTS of ODA 1982–, Trent Regnl Geriatric Soc 1989–93, Region III BRCS 1991–94, Inst of Transcultural Health 1991–, GlenEagle Nursing Home Ltd 1993–, Pakistan Enterprise Cncl Ltd 1993–; cncl memb: Br Geriatric Soc in UK 1989–93, BRCS 1991–94; memb Editorial Bd Ethnicity and Health 1996–; pres: Muslim Cncl of Sheffield Rotherham and Dists 1978–, Union of Pakistani Orgns in UK and Europe 1979–93; fell: Overseas Doctors' Assoc, BMA, Coll of Physicians and Surgns Bangladesh (FCP&S); DTM&H (Eng) 1963, FRCP, FRCPE 1979, FRCPGlas 1988, FRSM 1988, FRIPH; *Publications* Guidance for Overseas Doctors in National Health Service in UK (ed, 1982 and 1991); *Recreations* tennis, table tennis, snooker, chess; *Clubs* Abbeydale Rotary, Conservative, Medico-Chirurgical Soc; *Style*— Dr Karim Admani, OBE, JP; ✉ 1 Derriman Glen, Silverdale Rd, Sheffield S11 9LQ (☎ 0114 236 0465)

ADRIAN (aka WARNE), John Adrian Marie Edward Warne; s of Col John Edward Marie William Warne, REME (d 1971), and Agnes Amelia Diana, *née* Mills; *b* 29 Jan 1938; *Educ* Dulwich Coll London, Salesian Coll Burwash Sussex; *Career* served RAF Cyprus 1955–58; singer and dancer 1959–72; performed at: London Palladium, Moulin Rouge Paris, Carre Theatre Amsterdam; theatre mangr 1972–86: Nat Youth Theatre, Stoll Moss Theatres London, St George's Shakespeare Theatre, Garrick Theatre London, Royal Cultural Theatre Amman Jordan, Theatre Royal Windsor; admin and sec Grand Order of Water Rats 1986–; Freeman City of London, memb Co of

Firefighters; memb: Br Actors' Equity, Soc for Theatre Res; *Recreations* historical research, swimming and cycling; *Clubs* East India & Public Schools, Green Room; *Style*— John Adrian, Esq; ✉ Grand Order of Water Rats, 328 Gray's Inn Rd, London WC1X 8BZ (☎ 0171 278 3248, fax 0171 278 1765)

ADRIANO, Dino B; *Educ* Highgate Coll, Strand GS; *Career* J Sainsbury plc: joined as accountant 1964, gen mangr Homebase 1981–86, area dir 1986–89, md Homebase 1989–93 (chm 1991–Sept 1996), main bd dir 1990–, dep chm Shaw's Supermarkets Inc 1993–96, dir Giant Food Inc 1994–96, asst md 1995–96, chief exec supermarket business April 1997– (dep chief exec 1996–April 1997); non-exec dir Laura Ashley Holdings plc 1996–; FCCA; *Style*— Dino Adriano, Esq; ✉ J Sainsbury plc, Stamford House, Stamford Street, London SE1 9LL (☎ 0171 921 6000)

ADRIEN, *see:* Latour-Adrien

ADSETTS, (William) Norman; OBE (1988); s of Ernest Norman Adsetts (d 1992), and Hilda Rachael, *née* Wheeler (d 1986); *b* 6 April 1931; *Educ* King Edward VII Sch, The Queen's Coll Oxford (MA); *m* 20 Oct 1956, Eve, da of Eric Stefanuti (d 1985); 1 s (Philip Norman b 1959), 1 da (Helen Eve b 1957); *Career* appts in sales and mktg and research and devpt Fibreglass Ltd (joined as graduate trainee 1955); chm: Sheffield Insulating Company Ltd 1985–89 (dir 1966, md 1970), Sheffield Insulations Group plc 1989–96, Sheffield Partnerships Ltd 1988–93, South Yorkshire Supertram Trust Ltd 1993–; non-exec dir Sheffield Theatres Ltd 1988–94, deputy chm Sheffield Development Corporation 1991– (bd memb 1988–91), chm Kelham Island Museum Ltd 1994–, chm Sheffield Theatres Tst 1996–; chm Association for the Conservation of Energy Ltd 1985–90 and 1993–95 (vice pres 1990–93); pres Sheffield C of C 1988–89, chm CBI Yorkshire and Humberside 1989–91, chm Bd of Govrs Sheffield Hallam Univ 1993–, tstee Hillsborough Disaster Appeal 1989–95; memb: Advsy Ctee on Business and the Environment 1991–93, Yorkshire and Humberside Arts Bd 1991–94, Bd Opera North Ltd 1991–94; MInstM 1959, FRSA 1989; *Recreations* reading, local history, grandchildren; *Clubs* United Oxford and Cambridge, Sheffield; *Style*— Norman Adsetts, Esq, OBE; ✉ 28 Endcliffe Hall Avenue, Sheffield, South Yorkshire S10 3EL (☎ 0114 268 3881, fax 0114 266 6093)

ADSHEAD, John E; CBE (1997); *Career* gp personnel dir J Sainsbury plc 1989– (also i/c Gp Sec's Dept); *Style*— John Adshead, Esq, CBE; ✉ J Sainsbury plc, Stamford House, Stamford Street, London SE1 9LL (☎ 0171 921 6000)

AEBERHARD, John Peter; s of Armin Aeberhard (d 1988), of Switzerland, and Winifred Florence, *née* Ryland (d 1992); *b* 6 March 1937; *Educ* Bromley Co GS, CCC Oxford (MA); *m* 1964, Penelope Jane, da of Eric John Rankin, MC; 3 s (Matthew John b 25 May 1966, Daniel Edwin b 28 Oct 1969, Peter Joseph b 24 Sept 1971); *Career* press offr: Michelin Tyre Co Ltd 1962–66, English Electric Computers 1966–69; Honeywell: PRO N Europe 1969–75, dir Public Relations UK Ops 1975–78, dir Public Relations and Advertising Honeywell Information Systems Inc Boston Mass 1978–80; chm and chief exec A Plus Group Ltd 1981–96; *Recreations* running, walking, jazz; *Style*— John Aeberhard, Esq; ✉ Millstones, Egypt Lane, Farnham Common, Buckinghamshire SL2 3LF (☎ 01753 642739)

AFSHAR, Farhad; s of Aziz Afshar Yazdi, and Btoul, *née* Ameli; *b* 4 Dec 1941; *Educ* Lord Wandsworth Coll Hants, London Hosp Med Coll Univ of London (BSc, MB BS, MD); *m* 1, 23 Aug 1968 (m dis 1983), Lucille Anne, da of William E Goodfellow (d 1985); 3 s (Iain b 1970, Daniel b 1973, Brett b 1974), 1 da (Nina b 1977); *Career* fell in neurosurgery Ohio State Univ USA 1974–75, conslt neurosurgeon and sr lectr in neurosurgery London Hosp 1975–85, sr registrar in neurosurgery London and St Bartholomew's Hosp 1977, conslt neurosurgeon St Bartholomew's Hosp 1985–, also currently sr conslt neurosurgeon Royal London Hosp; author of numerous chapters and scientific papers on neurosurgery, examiner in surgery Univ of London; FRSM, MRCS, LRCP, FRCS; memb: Soc of Br Neurosurgeons, Congress of American Neurosurgeons, Euro and World Sterotaxic Surgns, World Pituitary Surgns; *Books* Stereotaxic Atlas of Human Brain Stem and Cerebellar Nuclei (1978); *Recreations* photography, natural history, walking; *Style*— Farhad Afshar, Esq; ✉ 149 Harley St, London W1 (☎ 0171 935 7505); Department of Neurosurgery, St Bartholomew's Hosp, London EC1 (☎ 0171 601 8888); Senior Consultant Neurosurgeon, Royal London Hospital, London E1 (☎ 0171 377 7000)

AGA KHAN, Prince Sadruddin; s of Mohamed Shah Aga Khan III, and Andrée Joséphine, *née* Carron; *Educ* Harvard Univ (BA, Phi Beta Kappa), Centre for Middle Eastern Studies Harvard Univ; *m* Catherine Aleya, *née* Sursock; *Career* special conslt UNESCO 1958, head of mission and advsr to UN High Cmmr for Refugees 1959–60, special advsr to DG of UNESCO for orgn of Campaign for the Preservation of Nubia (responsible for int archeological excavations) 1961, UN dep high cmmr for refugees 1962–65, UN high cmmr for refugees 1965–77 (UN coordinator Special Operations for Displaced Persons: Bangladesh 1972, Uganda 1972, Sudan 1973, Chile 1973, Cyprus 1974), special conslt and chargé de mission to the Sec-Gen of the UN 1978–; special rapporteur of UN Human Rights Cmmn 1981, convenor and co-chm Independent Cmmn on Int Humanitarian Issues 1983–87, convenor and co-chm of independent working gp on UN financial emergency Crisis and Opportunity 1986, memb int panel of UN Assoc (USA) Decision-Making Project on the Future of the UN 1987, coordinator for UN Humanitarian and Economic Assistance Progs relating to the people of Afghanistan 1988–90, personal rep of the Sec-Gen of the UN for a UN Inter-Agency Humanitarian Prog for Iraq, Kuwait and Iraq/Turkey and Iraq/Iran border areas 1991; fndr and pres Bellerive Fndn and Gp de Bellerive Geneva, chm Alp Action, fndr memb Geneva Int Peace Res Inst (GIPRI), tstee World Wide Fund for Nature Int, fndr and sec Harvard Islamic Assoc, former pres and fndr Cncl on Islamic Affairs NYC; memb: Ct Univ of Leeds, Int Bd United World Colls, Bd of Dirs TV Tst for the Environment (UK), Better World Soc (USA), Bd Beijer Inst Stockholm, Bd Int Acad of the Environment Geneva; Doctorate Honoris Causa: Fletcher Sch of Law and Diplomacy Tufts Univ Boston, Univ of Nice, Univ of Leeds; Commandeur de la Légion d'Honneur (France), Order of the Star of the Nile (Sudan), Cdr's Cross with Star of the Order of Merit (Poland), Cdr of the Golden Ark (Netherlands), Bourgeois d'Honneur de Genève (Switzerland); UN Human Rights Award (NY), Dag Hammarskjöld Hon Medal (FDR), Onassis Fndn Olympia Prize (Greece), Int Rescue Ctee's Freedom Award (USA), Man for Peace Award 1989 Together for Peace Fndn, Hilal-e-Pakistan Award 1991 (Pakistan); FAAAS; *Publications* The Paris Review (ed), Nuclear War, Nuclear Proliferation and their Consequences (ed, 1986), International Protection of Refugees (ed, Hague Acad of Int Law); author of many articles on humanitarian, disarmament and environmental subjects in jls and newspapers; *Recreations* Islamic art, sailing, skiing, hiking, kite flying; *Style*— Prince Sadruddin Aga Khan; ✉ Secretariat de Bellerive, 4 rue Munier-Romilly, 1206 Geneva, Switzerland (☎ 00 41 22 346 88 66)

AGA KHAN (IV), HH The; Prince Karim; s of late Prince Aly Khan, and Hon Joan, *née* Yarde-Buller (now Viscountess Camrose), da of 3 Baron Churston, MVO, OBE; gs of HH Rt Hon the Aga Khan (III), GCSI, GCIE, GCVO (d 1957); *b* 13 Dec 1936; *Educ* Le Rosey, Harvard; *m* 1969 (m dis 1995), Sarah Frances (Sally), o da of Lt-Col Arthur Edward Croker Poole, and former w of Lord James Charles Crichton-Stuart (d 1982), s of 5 Marquess of Bute; 2 s (Prince Rahim b 1971, Prince Hussain b 1974), 1 da (Princess Zahra b 1970); *Career* Spiritual Leader and Imam of Ismaili Muslims, granted title HH by HM The Queen 1957, and HRH by late Shah of Iran 1959; leading owner and breeder of race horses in France and Ireland; winner Derby: 1981 (Shergar), 1986 (Shahrastani), 1988 (Kahyasi); winner Prix de L'Arc de Triomphe 1982 (Akiyda); winner Prix de Jockey Club: Top Ville 1979, Charlottesville 1980, Darshaan 1984, Mouktar 1985, Natroun 1987; pres: Aga Khan Fndn Geneva 1967 (other branches in Bangladesh, Canada, India, Kenya, Pakistan, Portugal, Tanzania, Uganda, UK and USA), Aga Khan Award for Architecture 1977–, Inst of Ismaili Studies 1977–, Aga Khan Tst for Culture Geneva 1988; fndr and chllr Aga Khan Univ Pakistan 1983; Dr of Laws (hc): Peshawar Univ Pakistan 1967, Sind Univ Pakistan 1970, McGill Univ Canada 1983, McMaster Univ Canada 1987, Univ of Wales Cardiff 1993; Hon DLitt Univ of London 1989; Thomas Jefferson Meml Fndn Medal in Architecture 1984, American Inst of Architects Honor 1984, Medalla de Oro Consejo Superior de Colegios de Arquitectos Spain 1987, Huesped de Honor de Granada Spain 1991, hon fell RIBA, Medaille d'Argent Académie d'Architecture Paris 1991; Commandeur Ordre du Mérite Mauritanien 1960; Grand Croix: Order of Prince Henry the Navigator Portugal 1960, l'Ordre National de la Côte d'Ivoire 1965, l'Ordre National de la Haute-Volta 1965, l'Ordre Malgache 1966, l'Ordre du Croissant Vert des Comores 1966; Grand Cordon Order of the Raj Iran 1967, Nishan-i-Imtiaz Pakistan 1970, Cavaliere di Gran Croce della Repubblica Italiana 1977, Grand Officier l'Ordre National du Lion Sénégal 1982, Nishan-e-Pakistan 1983, Grand Cordon Ouissam-al Arch Morocco 1986, Cavaliere del Lavoro Italy 1988, Cdr de la Légion d'Honneur France 1990, Gran Cruz de la Orden del Merito Civil Spain 1991; *Recreations* yachting, skiing; *Clubs* Royal Yacht Squadron, Yacht Club Costa Smeralda (Sardinia, fndr pres); *Style*— His Highness the Aga Khan; ✉ Aiglemont, 60270 Gouvieux, France

AGAR, Hon Mark Sidney Andrew; s of 5 Earl of Normanton (d 1967), and Lady Fiona (d 1985), da of 4 Marquess Camden; *b* 2 Sept 1948; *Educ* Gordonstoun; *m* 1, 1973 (m dis 1979), Rosemary, da of Maj Philip Marnham; m 2, 8 Feb 1985, Arabella Clare, da of John Gilbert Gilbey (d 1982), and formerly w of Thomas Charles Blackwell; 2 s (Max John Andrew b 6 April 1986, Charles Christopher Edward b 29 July 1989); *Career* Lt Blues and Royals; farmer and landowner (1200 acres); *Style*— The Hon Mark Agar; ✉ Inholmes, Woodlands St Mary, Hungerford, Berks RG17 7SY

AGGETT, Valerie; da of James William Cocksey (d 1986); *b* 15 Dec 1950; *Educ* Bury GS, Univ of Durham (BA), Coll of Law Guildford; *m* 1 (m dis), Gareth Aggett; m 2 (m dis), John Allan Grenier, *qv*; *Career* former slr; princ and md The HLT Group Ltd 1976–95 (Queen's Award for Export 1982); int mktg advsr Liverpool Inst for Performing Arts; finalist Times Businesswoman of the Year 1981; fell Univ of Wolverhampton; memb Law Soc; *Recreations* theatre, tennis, interior design, fashion; *Clubs* Reform; *Style*— Ms Valerie Aggett; ✉ c/o Reform Club, 104 Pall Mall, London SW1Y 5EW

AGGISS, Liz; da of James Henry Aggiss, of Terling, Essex, and Marie Elizabeth, *née* Chamberlain (d 1975); *b* 28 May 1953; *Educ* Hornchurch GS, Madeley Coll, Nikolais/Louis Dance Theatre NY; *Career* choreographer, dancer, performer and artistic dir (in collaboration with Billy Cowie); memb The Wild Wigglers (formed 1982, touring worldwide); work with Divas Dance Co (formed 1985, touring worldwide) incl: Torei en Veran Veta Arnold! 1986–87, Eleven Executions 1988, Dorothy and Klaus 1989–91, Die Orchidee im Plastik Karton 1989–91, Drool and Drivel They Care 1990–91, La Petite Soupe 1990–91, La Chanson Bien Douce 1991; solo performances incl: Grotesque Dancer 1986–89, Stations of the Angry 1989, Tell Tale Heart 1989, El Puñal Entra En El Corazón 1991, Vier Tänze (reconstructions from the 1920s and '30s by Hilde Holger) 1992, Falling Apart at the Seams (So it Seems) 1993, No Man's Land 1993, Absurditties 1994, Hi Jinx 1995, The Fetching Bride 1995; cmmns incl: Dead Steps/Die Totenschritte (for Extemporary Dance Theatre) 1988–89, Banda Banda and La Soupe (for Carousel) 1989–90, Bird in A Ribcage (for Transitions Dance Co) 1994; awards: Colorado Coll scholarship to study with Hanya Holm 1980, Brighton Festival Special award 1989, Brighton Festival Zap award for Dance 1989, Brighton Festival BBC Radio award 1990, Alliance and Leicester award 1990 and 1992, Time Out/Dance Umbrella award 1990, Arts Cncl and BBC2 Dance for Camera award 1992 Beethoven in Love, Bonnie Bird choreography award 1994; contrib dance entries Fontana Dictionary of Modern Thought (1988); *Recreations* music, cinema; *Style*— Ms Liz Aggiss; ✉ 20 Montpelier Street, Brighton, East Sussex BN1 3DJ (☎ 01273 327894)

AGIS, Gaby; *b* 1960; *Career* independent choreographer 1983–; choreographer in residence Riverside Studios 1984–86, launched own co 1985; progs incl: Close Streams 1983, Crossing Under Upwards 1983, Surfacing 1984, Borders 1984, Shouting Out Loud 1984, Between Public Places 1985, Undine and the Still 1985, This Is, What, Where 1985, In Anticipation of Surrender 1986, Fow Fold 1986, Lying On the Warm Concrete 1986, Trail 1986, Kin 1987, Freefall 1988, Don't Trash My Altar/Don't Alter My Trash 1988, Mlada (London Symphony Orchestra) 1989, Hess Is Dead (Royal Shakespeare Co) 1989, Dark Hours And Finer Moments 1989, Pale Shelter 1990, Cold Dark Matter 1991, The Family 1994; performance art venues incl: Tate Gallery Liverpool, Chisenhale Gallery, Whitechapel Art Gallery, Riverside Studios Gallery, The Museum of Modern Art Oxford and Cornerhouse Gallery Manchester; TV and film appearances incl: Hail the New Puritan 1985, Imaginary Women 1986, Freefall 1988, Dark Hours and Finer Moments 1994; awards incl Distinguished Visitors award of US Govt 1986; *Style*— Ms Gaby Agis; ✉ c/o Bolton & Quinn, 8 Pottery Lane, London W11 4LZ (☎ 0171 221 5000, fax 0171 221 8100)

AGIUS, Marcus Ambrose Paul; s of Lt-Col Alfred Victor Louis Benedict Agius, MC, TD (d 1969), and Ena Eleanora, *née* Hueffer; *b* 22 July 1946; *Educ* St George's Coll Weybridge, Trinity Hall Cambridge (MA), Harvard Business Sch (MBA); *m* 1971, Kate Juliette, da of Maj Edmund Leopold de Rothschild, TD, of Hants; 2 da (Marie-Louise Eleanor b 1977, Lara Sophie Elizabeth b 1980); *Career* Lazard Bros & Co Ltd: dir 1981–85, md 1985–90, vice chm 1990–; md Lazard Frères & Co LLC 1995–; non exec dir: Exbury Gardens Ltd 1977–, BAA plc 1995–, Credit Agricole Lazard Financial Products Ltd; *Recreations* gardening, tennis, shooting, skiing, sailing; *Clubs* White's, Swinley Forest; *Style*— Marcus A P Agius, Esq; ✉ Lazard Bros & Co Ltd, 21 Moorfields, London EC2P 2HT (☎ 0171 588 2721, telex 886438, fax 0171 638 1051)

AGLIONBY, His Hon Judge; Francis John; s of Francis Basil Aglionby, and Marjorie Wycliffe Aglionby; *b* 17 May 1932; *Educ* Charterhouse, CCC Oxford; *m* 1967, Susan Victoria Mary, *née* Vaughan; 1 s, 1 da; *Career* called to the Bar Inner Temple 1956 (bencher 1976); recorder of the Crown Court 1975–80, circuit judge (SE Circuit) 1980–; chllr: Birmingham Diocese 1971–, Portsmouth Diocese 1978–, Carlisle Diocese 1991–; *Clubs* Brooks's; *Style*— His Hon Judge Aglionby; ✉ The Croft, Houghton, Carlisle, Cumbria CA3 OLD; Knightsbridge Crown Court, 1 Pocock Street, London SE1 0BT

AGNEW, (Alexander James) Blair; s of James Percival Agnew, DL, and Jessie Blair, *née* Anderson (d 1978), of Racecourse Rd, Ayr; *b* 6 Oct 1935; *Educ* Rugby; *m* 1958, Gillian Margaret, da of Maj W D Gray-Newton, of Little Court, Warboys, Cambs; 2 s (Blair, Angus), 1 da (Caroline); *Career* regular offr Royal Scots Fus then Royal Highland Fus 1954–65 (Capt); Hon Col 3 (V) Bn Royal Highland Fus; memb Royal Co of Archers (Queen's Body Guard for Scotland); stockbroker; dir Greig Middleton & Co Ltd, memb Cncl Stock Exchange 1979–85, memb Bd Securities and Futures Authority Ltd 1989–95; CIMgt; *Recreations* gardening, walking; *Clubs* Army and Navy, Western (Glasgow); *Style*— Blair Agnew, Esq; ✉ Drumbarr, Ayr KA6 6BN (☎ 01292 441312); Greig Middleton & Co Ltd, 155 St Vincent Street, Glasgow G2 5NN (☎ 0141 204 1886)

AGNEW, Sir John Keith; 6 Bt (UK 1895), of Great Stanhope Street, St George, Hanover Square, Co London; s of Sir (George) Keith Agnew, 5 Bt, TD (d 1994), and his w, *née* Baroness Anne Merete Louise Schaffalitzky de Muckadell; *b* 19 Dec 1950; *Heir* bro,

George Anthony Agnew b 1953; *Style*— Sir John Agnew, Bt; ✉ The Estate Office, Rougham, Bury St Edmunds, Suffolk IP30 9LZ

AGNEW, Jonathan Geoffrey William; s of late Sir Geoffrey Agnew, and late Hon Doreen, da of 1 Baron Jessel, CB, CMG; *b* 30 July 1941; *Educ* Eton, Trinity Coll Cambridge (MA); *m* 1966 (m dis 1986), Hon Agneta Joanna Middleton, yr da of Baron Campbell of Eskan (life peer, d 1994); 1 s (Caspar Jonathan William b 1967), 2 da (Lara Joanna b 1969, Katherine Agneta b 1971); m 2, 1990, Marie-Claire, da of Bernard Dreesmann; 1 da (Clarissa Virginia b 1992); *Career* The Economist 1964–65, World Bank 1965–67, Hill Samuel & Co 1967–73 (dir 1971), Morgan Stanley & Co 1973–82 (md 1977), fin conslt 1983–86, chief exec ISRO 1986, gp chief exec Kleinwort Benson Group plc 1989–93 (joined 1987); chm: J G W Agnew & Co Ltd, HTR Income and Growth Split Trust plc, London Insurance Market Investment Trust plc; dir: Thos Agnew and Sons Ltd, Greenfriar Investment Company Ltd, Apollo Fund plc; *Clubs* White's, Automobile (Paris); *Style*— Jonathan Agnew, Esq; ✉ 51E Eaton Sq, London SW1W 9BE (☎ 0171 235 7589)

AGNEW, Jonathan Philip; s of Philip Agnew, of Ketton, Lincs, and Margaret, *née* McConnell; *b* 4 April 1960; *Educ* Uppingham; *m* 1, 8 Oct 1983 (m dis 1994), Beverley Measures; 2 da (Jennifer Ann b 31 Oct 1985, Rebecca Louise b 18 Sept 1988); m 2, 4 May 1996, Emma Norris; *Career* former cricketer (bowler); joined Leics CCC 1978, took 101 wickets 1987 season, ret 1990; played for Eng 1984 and 1985 (3 tests, 3 one day ints); cricket corr Today 1990–91, BBC cricket corr 1991–; Radio Acad Best Sports Reporter Sony Radio Awards 1993; *Books* 8 Days a Week (1988); *Recreations* golf, gardening; *Style*— Jonathan Agnew, Esq; ✉ Cricket Correspondent, BBC Radio 5, Broadcasting House, London W1A 1AA (☎ 0171 927 5050)

AGNEW, (Morland Herbert) Julian; yr s of Sir Geoffrey William Gerald Agnew (d 1986), and Hon Doreen Maud Jessel, da of 1 Baron Jessel, CB, CMG; *b* 1943; *Educ* Eton, Trinity Coll Cambridge (scholar and sr scholar, MA); *m* 1, 1973 (m dis), Elizabeth Margaret, yst da of William B Mitchell, of Gateside, Blanefield, Stirlingshire; 1 s (Thomas Julian Noel b 1975), 2 da (Amelia Elizabeth b 1979, Georgina Helen b 1982); m 2, 4 Sept 1993, Victoria, 2 da of Maj (Henry) Ronald Burn Callander, MC, and Penelope, Countess of Lindsay; 1 s (Benjamin Geoffrey David Callander b 6 Oct 1996); *Career* Agnew's: joined 1965, dir 1968, md 1987, chm 1992–; pres BADA 1979–81, chm Soc of London Art Dealers 1986–90, treas Friends of the Courtauld Inst, chm Evelyn Hosp Cambridge; FRSA; *Recreations* grand opera, music, books, tennis, golf; *Style*— Julian Agnew, Esq; ✉ Thos Agnew & Sons Ltd, 43 Old Bond St, London W1X 4BA (☎ 0171 629 6176, fax 0171 629 4359)

AGNEW OF LOCHNAW, Sir Crispin Hamlyn; 11 Bt (NS 1629), of Lochnaw, Wigtownshire; QC (Scot 1995); Chief of the Name of Agnew; s of Sir Fulque Melville Gerald Noel Agnew of Lochnaw, 10 Bt (d 1975), and Swanzie, da of Maj Esme Nourse Erskine, CMG, MC (descended from the Earls of Buchan), late Consular Serv; *b* 13 May 1944; *Educ* Uppingham, RMA Sandhurst; *m* 27 Sept 1980, Susan Rachel Strang, da of late Jock Wykeham Strang Steel, of Logie (2 s of Sir Samuel Strang Steel of Philiphaugh, 1 Bt, TD, DL, and Vere Mabel, 2 da of 1 Baron Cornwallis) and Lesley (da of Lt-Col Sir John Graham of Larbert, 3 Bt, VC, OBE, and Rachel, 5 da of Col Sir Alexander Sprot of Stravithie, 1 Bt, CMG); 1 s (Mark Douglas Noel younger of Lochnaw b 1991), 3 da (Isabel Sevilla Wilhelmina b 1984, Emma Rachel Elizabeth b 1986, Roseanna Celia Nancy b 1989); *Heir* s, Mark Douglas Noel Agnew of Lochnaw, yr b 24 April 1991; *Career* Maj RHF (ret 1981); admitted Faculty of Advocates 1982; Slains Pursuivant of Arms to the Lord High Constable of Scotland (The Earl of Erroll) 1978–81, Unicorn Pursuivant of Arms 1981–86, Rothesay Herald of Arms 1986–; ldr of expeditions to: Greenland 1968, Patagonia 1972, Api Himal 1980; memb of expeditions to: Greenland 1966, Elephant Island, Antarctica 1970, Nuptse Himal 1975, Everest 1976; tstee John Muir Tst; *Books* The Licensing (Scotland) Act 1976 (co-author with Heather Baillie, 4 edn, 1996), Connell on the Agricultural Holdings (Scotland) Act (co-author with Donald Rennie, OBE, 7 edn, 1996), Agricultural Law in Scotland (1996); *Recreations* mountaineering, yachting (yacht 'Pippa's Song'), heraldry, genealogy; *Clubs* Army and Navy; *Style*— Sir Crispin Agnew of Lochnaw, Bt, QC; ✉ 6 Palmerston Rd, Edinburgh EH9 1TN (☎ 0131 668 3792, fax 0131 668 4357, e-mail sir_crispin_agnew@link.org)

AGNEW-SOMERVILLE, Sir Quentin Charles Somerville; 2 Bt (UK 1957), of Clendry, Co Wigtown; s of Sir Peter Agnew, 1 Bt (d 1990), and his 1 w, Enid Frances (d 1982), da of Henry Boan, of Perth, W Australia; assumed by Royal Licence 1950 additional surname of Somerville after that of Agnew, and the arms of Somerville quarterly with those of Agnew, on succeeding to the Somerville estate of his maternal unc by m, 2 and last Baron Athlumney, who d 1929, leaving a widow, Margery, da of Henry Boan and sis of Enid, Sir Quentin's mother; *b* 8 March 1929; *Educ* RNC Dartmouth; *m* 1963, Hon (Margaret Irene) April Drummond, da of 15 Baron Strange (d 1982); 1 s, 2 da (Amelia Rachel b 1965, Geraldine Margaret b 1967); *Heir* s, James Lockett Charles Agnew-Somerville b 26 May 1970; *Career* Sub Lt RN to 1950, when invalided from serv; co dir; *Clubs* Brooks's, Kildare Street and University; *Style*— Sir Quentin Agnew-Somerville, Bt; ✉ Mount Auldyn House, Jurby Rd, Ramsey, Isle of Man (☎ 01624 813724, fax 01624 816498)

AGRAN, Linda; *Career* television prodr; head of devpt and exec prodr Euston Films Ltd (subsid of Thames Television) 1976–86, dep controller drama and arts London Weekend Television 1986–89, md Paravision UK (independent film and TV prodn co) 1989, currently jt chief exec AB TV; presenter/viewers' ombudsman Right to Reply (Channel Four) 1990–92; *Programmes* drama films/series for Euston Films incl: Out, Danger UXB, Fox, Quatermas, Charlie Muffin, Leon Griffiths' Minder 1980, Lynda La Plante's Widows 1982, Jack Rosenthal's The Knowledge, John Mortimer's Paradise Postponed 1984; for LWT incl: Jack Rosenthal's London's Burning (film, later several series), Piece of Cake, Agatha Christie's Hercule Poirot; for Paravision incl: Jack Rosenthal's Bye Bye Baby (for Channel Four, winner Prix Europa, Writers' Guild of GB Best Screenplay 1993), John Byrne's Boswell and Johnson's Tour of the Western Isles 1993, Jack Rosenthal's Moving Story 1994, Nigel Williams' The Wimbledon Poisoner 1994; *Style*— Ms Linda Agran; ✉ AB TV, 114 The Chambers, Chelsea Harbour, London SW10 0XF (☎ 0171 351 7070)

AGUTTER, Jennifer Ann (Jenny); da of Derek Brodie Agutter, OBE, of London, and Catherine (Kit), *née* Lynam; *b* 20 Dec 1952; *Educ* Elmhurst Ballet Sch Camberley Surrey; *m* 4 Aug 1990, Johan Carl Sebastian Tham; *Career* actress; *Theatre* incl: School for Scandal 1972, Rooted 1973, The Ride Across Lake Constance, Arms and the Man 1973, The Tempest (NT) 1974, Spring Awakening (NT) 1974, The Unified Field LA 1987, Breaking the Code (Neil Simon Theatre, NY) 1987; RSC 1982–83 and 1985 and 1995: Fontanelle in Lear, Regan in King Lear, Alice Arden in Arden of Faversham, Grace in the Body, Breaking the Silence 1985, Love's Labour's Lost 1995, English Places English Faces 1996, Mothers and Daughters 1996; *Television* incl: Long After Summer 1967, The Wild Duck 1971, The Snow Goose 1971, A Legacy 1971, A War of Children 1972, Amy 1980, Love's Labours Lost 1984, Silas Marner 1985, Murder She Wrote 1986, The Equaliser 1988, Not a Penny More Not a Penny Less 1989, TECX 1990, Boon 1991, The Good Guys 1991, Love Hurts 1994, Heartbeat (ITV) 1994, The Buccaneers (BBC) 1995, September 1995, Alexis Sayle Show 1995, Connie in And The Beat Goes On (Channel 4) 1996, Heartbeat 1996; *Radio* Jamaica Inn (BBC Radio 2) 1996; *Films* incl: East of Sudan (debut) 1964, Ballerina 1964, Gates of Paradise 1967, Star! 1968, I Start Counting, Walkabout 1969, The Railway Children 1970, Logan's Run 1975, The Eagle Has Landed 1976, The Man in the Iron Mask 1976, Equus 1976, Dominique 1977, China 9 Liberty 37 1978, Riddle of the Sands, Sweet William, The Survivor 1980, An American Werewolf in London 1981, Secret Places 1983, Dark Tower 1987, King of the Wind 1989, Child's Play II 1989, The Dark Man 1990, Freddie as Fro7 1992, Blue Juice 1995; *Awards* incl: Royal Variety Club Most Promising Artist 1971, Emmy Award Best Supporting Actress (for The Snow Goose) 1971, BAFTA Award Best Supporting Actress (for Equus) 1976; *Books* Snap (1984); *Style*— Miss Jenny Agutter; ✉ c/o Yvonne de Valera, JY Publicity, 54a Ebury Street, London SW1W 9QD (☎ 0171 730 2112)

AGUTTER, Richard Devenish; JP; s of Anthony Tom Devenish Agutter (d 1960), and Joan Hildegarde Sabina, *née* Machen (now Mrs Fleming); *b* 17 Sept 1941; *Educ* Marlborough; *m* 29 June 1968, Lesley Anne, da of Kenneth Alfred Ballard, MC, of Giles Barn Cottage, Horsted Keynes, Sussex; 3 s (Rupert William Devenish b 3 Nov 1972, Tom Alexander Devenish b 17 July 1975, Giles Edward Devenish b 6 April 1979); *Career* CA 1964, articled W T Walton & Sons 1960; KPMG (formerly KPMG Peat Marwick Mitchell): joined 1964, ptnr 1977–, chm KPMG Int Corp Fin Network 1990–96; treas Wine Guild of UK; Liveryman: Worshipful Co of Goldsmiths, Worshipful Co of Chartered Accountants; Alderman City of London (Castle Baynard Ward) 1995–; FCA (ACA 1964), MSI, FRSA; *Recreations* sailing, gardening, wine; *Clubs* City Livery; *Style*— Richard Agutter, Esq, JP; ✉ Great Frenches Park, Snow Hill, Crawley Down, West Sussex RH10 3EE (☎ 01342 716 816); Flat 3, President's Quay House, 72 St Katharines Way, London E1 (☎ 0171 702 9113); KPMG Corporate Finance, 8 Salisbury Square, Blackfriars, London EC4Y 8BB (☎ 0171 311 8700, fax 0171 311 8276, car 0802 617184)

AGYEPONG, Jacqueline Akosua (Jacqui); da of Joseph Kwabena Agyepong, and Victoria Adwoa, *née* Senyah; *b* 5 Jan 1969; *Career* athlete; Br rep: Euro Juniors 1987, World Juniors 1988; achievements at 100m hurdles: quarter-finalist Olympic Games Barcelona 1992, semi-finalist World Championships Stuttgart 1993, finalist Euro Championships Helsinki 1994, Silver medal Commonwealth Games 1994, Gold medal Europa Cup 1994, Bronze medal World Cup 1994, finalist World Championships Gothenburg 1995; *Recreations* reading, listening to music; *Style*— Ms Jacqui Agyepong

AHEARNE, Stephen James; s of James Joseph Ahearne (d 1972), and Phyllis Eva, *née* Grigsby; *b* 7 Sept 1939; *Educ* St Ignatius Coll London; *m* 24 April 1965, Janet Elizabeth, da of Jack Ronald Edwards; 2 s (Jeremy b 1966, Thomas b 1968); *Career* British Petroleum Co plc 1964–96: joined 1964, various accounting and planning posts in UK, W Africa and Middle E 1964–78, md BP Denmark 1978–81, dir BP Chemicals International 1981–86, gp controller British Petroleum Co plc 1986–90, gen mangr corporate planning 1988–90, chief fin offr 1990–96, md 1992–96; chm: BP Nutrition 1992–95, BP Finance 1993–96; also dir: BP Exploration 1986–92 and 1995–96, BP Oil 1986–96, BP International 1986–96, BP Pension Services 1992–96, BP Chemicals 1995–96; ret; memb Restrictive Practices Court; govr Felsted Sch 1996–; *Recreations* tennis, gardening; *Style*— Stephen J Ahearne, Esq

AHLÅS, (Lars) Peter Richard; *b* 22 Sept 1948; *Educ* Högre Allmana Lanoverket å Kungsholmen Stockholm, Royal Swedish Naval Aacd, London Sch of Foreign Trade (Dip Shipping & Marine Insur); *m* 1973, Sian Fiona, *née* Holford-Walker; 2 da; *Career* Lt Cdr Royal Swedish Navy 1969–71, Res 1971–; marine insurance broker; W K Webster 1971–73, gen mangr Liberian Insurance Agency 1973–74, broker Bland Payne 1974–78; dir: Jardine Glanvill Marine 1978–86, Gibbs Insurance Holdings Ltd 1986–; chief exec Marine and Aviation Divs Gibbs Hartley Cooper Ltd 1986–; memb IBRC; *Recreations* shooting, tennis, riding; *Clubs* Lansdowne; *Style*— Peter Ahlås, Esq; ✉ Gibbs Hartley Cooper Ltd, Bishops Court, 27–33 Artillery Lane, London E1 7LP (☎ 0171 247 5433, fax 0171 377 2139, telex 8950791)

AHM, Povl Borge; CBE (1993); *b* 26 Sept 1926; *Educ* Technical Univ of Denmark (MSc); *Career* Nat Serv 2 Lt Army 1951; engr Ramboell & Hannemann Consulting Engrs 1951–53; Ove Arup & Partners: joined 1953, assoc ptnr 1956–, engr 1953–65, sr ptnr 1965, fndr Civil Engrg Div UK (1965) and Hong Kong (1975), chm Ove Arup & Partners 1984–89 (dep chm 1977–84), chm Ove Arup Partnership 1989–92, dir of Hong Kong Co and Arup Atkins Int 1984–92, tstee and conslt 1993–; memb Cncl: Prestressed Concrete Devpt Gp 1963–66, Concrete Soc 1966–71 (vice pres 1969–71); memb Govt Advsy Ctee on Falsework 1973, memb Bd BR Design Panel 1982–; chm: Relationship Ctee FIDIC 1981–86, Assoc of Consulting Engrs 1992–93 (memb Cncl 1987–90 and 1991–94, vice chm 1991–92); vice pres Registered Engrs for Disaster Relief 1989–; awarded Gold Medal ICE 1993; Hon DSc Univ of Warwick 1994; FICE (memb Cncl 1972–75 and 1983–86), FEng 1981, FIStructE, FIHT, FASCE, Kt of the Order of Dannebrog (Denmark) 1980 (1st Class 1994); *Style*— Povl Ahm, Esq, CBE, FEng; ✉ Ove Arup Partnership, 13 Fitzroy Street, London W1P 6BQ (☎ 0171 465 3362, fax 0171 465 3107)

AHMED, Prof Haroon; s of Mohammad Nizam Ahmed (d 1980), and Bilquis Jehan, *née* Abbasi (d 1988); *b* 2 March 1936; *Educ* St Patrick's Sch Karachi, Imperial Coll London (BSc), King's Coll Cambridge (PhD), ScD 1996; *m* 4 July 1969, Evelyn Anne Travers, da of Alec Thorpe Goodrich; 1 s (Imran Saleem b 28 Nov 1982), 2 da (Ayesha Fehmina b 12 March 1971, Rehana Sara b 17 Aug 1972); *Career* GEC and Hirst Research Centre 1958–59; Univ of Cambridge: res studentship King's Coll 1959–62, Turner and Newall res fell 1962–63, univ demonstrator Dept of Engrg 1963–66, fell Corpus Christi Coll 1967–, lectr in engrg 1966–84, reader in microelectronics Cavendish Laboratory 1984–92 (prof of microelectronics 1992–); FEng 1990, FIEE, FInstP; *Books* Introduction to Physical Electronics (with A H Beck, 1968), Electronics for Engineers (with P J Spreadbury, 1973, 2 edn 1984); *Recreations* golf, tennis, skiing; *Style*— Prof Haroon Ahmed, FEng; ✉ Microelectronics Research Centre, Cavendish Laboratory, Madingley Rd, Cambridge CB3 OHE (☎ 01223 337557, fax 01223 337706)

AHRENDS, Peter; s of Steffen Bruno Ahrends, and Margarete Maria Sophie Ahrends; *b* 30 April 1933; *Educ* Architectural Assoc Sch of Architecture (AADipl); *m* 1954, Elizabeth Robertson; 2 da; *Career* architect: Steffen Ahrends & Ptnrs Johannesburg 1957–58, Dennys Lasdun & Ptnrs and Julian Keable & Ptnrs 1959–60; fndr ptnr and dir Ahrends Burton & Koralek 1961–; princ works incl: Berkeley Library Trinity Coll Dublin 1972, Arts Faculty Bldg 1979, residential bldg Keble Coll Oxford 1976 (RIBA Architecture Award 1978), Templeton Coll Oxford 1969–88, Nebenzahl House Jerusalem 1972, warehouse and showroom for Habitat Wallingford 1974 (Structural Steel Design Award, FT Industl Architecture Award 1976), Whitmore Court Housing 1975 (RIBA Good Design in Housing Award 1977), factory for Cummins Engines Shotts 1975–83 (Structural Steel Design Award 1980), J Sainsbury Supermarket Canterbury 1984 (Structural Steel Design Award 1985), retail HQ WH Smith Swindon 1985, John Lewis Dept Store Kingston 1990, St Mary's Hosp Newport IOW 1990, Heritage Centre Dover, stations for extensions Docklands Railway, Poplar Bridge (Structural Design Award Commendation 1993), Br Embassy Moscow, campus devpt plan Univ of Grenoble France, Whitworth Art Gallery, Loughborough Univ Departmental Bldgs, Chiswick Park Buildings J & K, Techniquest Science Centre Cardiff Bay, Dublin Dental Hosp, St Leonard's Healthcare Centre; memb: Cncl AA 1965–67, Design Cncl 1988–93; chm UK Architects Against Apartheid 1988–93; prof of architecture Bartlett Sch of Architecture and Planning UCL 1986–89; pt/t teaching posts and workshops: AA Sch of Architecture, Canterbury Sch of Art, Univ of Edinburgh, Winter Sch Edinburgh, Plymouth Poly, Plymouth Sch of Art, Kingston Poly; visiting critic and/or external examiner: Kumasi Univ, AA Sch of Architecture, Nova Scotia Tech Univ, Kingston Poly, Strathclyde Univ; chm Camden Design Advsy Gp 1995–; exhibitions of drawings and works incl: RIBA Heinz Gallery 1980, Douglas Hyde Gallery Dublin 1981, Alvar Aalto Museum Finland

1982, AA HQ Oslo 1983; RIBA 1959; *Books* Monograph on Ahrends Burton & Koralek (Academy Editions, 1991); *Style—* Peter Ahrends, Esq; ✉ Ahrends Burton & Koralek, 7 Chalcot Road, London NW1 8LH (☎ 0171 586 3311, fax 0171 722 5445)

AICHROTH, Paul Michael; s of Gerald Paul Aichroth, of Vancouver, Canada, and Elsie, *née* Webb; *b* 30 April 1936; *Educ* Alleyn's Sch, King's Coll London, Westminster Med Sch (MB BS, MS); *m* 17 June 1961, Angela, da of Frederick George Joslin, of Bournemouth, Dorset; 1 s (Mark Jonathan Paul); *Career* conslt orthopaedic surgn 1971– (Chelsea and Westminster Hosp, Wellington Hosp); author of various papers and theses on knee disorders; Hunterian prof RCS 1973, Robert Jones Gold medallist 1973, annual orator London Med Soc 1991–; pres Br Assoc for Surgery of the Knee 1992; memb: Br Orthopaedic Assoc, RSM, BMA 1963; FRCS 1965; *Books* Harris's Orthopaedics (contrib, 1975 and 1995), Operative Surgery (contrib, 1990), Insall Knee Surgery (contrib, 1992), Knee Surgery: Current Practice (1992); *Recreations* boats, countryside, Mozart, claret; *Clubs* Athenaeum; *Style—* Paul Aichroth, Esq; ✉ Flat 7, 43 Wimpole St, London W1M 7AF (☎ Rooms - 0171 935 2349, Res - 0171 935 7034); Hydon Wood, Feathercombe Lane, Hambledon, Surrey GU8 4DP (☎ 01483 860 377); Wellington Hospital, London NW8 9LE (fax 0171 483 0297)

AIKEN, Joan Delano; da of Conrad Potter Aiken, and Jessie McDonald Aiken; *b* 4 Sept 1924; *Educ* privately, Wychwood Sch Oxford; *m* 1, 7 July 1945, Ronald George Brown (d 1955), s of Albert Brown (d 1953); 1 s (John b 1949), 1 da (Elizabeth b 1951); m 2, 2 Sept 1976, Julius Goldstein; *Career* author of novels, plays and poetry; BBC 1942–43, librarian Information Ctee UN 1943–49, sub ed and features ed Argosy magazine 1955–60, copywriter J Walter Thompson London 1960–61; Guardian Award for Children's Literature 1969, Mystery Writers of America Edgar Allan Poe Award 1972, Lewis Carroll Shelf Award 1962; memb: Soc of Authors, Writers' Guild, Mystery Writers of America, PEN; *Books* children's books: All You've Ever Wanted (1953), The Kingdom and the Cave (1960), Black Hearts in Battersea (1964), The Whispering Mountain Cape (1968), Armitage, Armitage, Fly Away Home (1970), Smoke From Cromwell's Time (1970), The Kingdom Under the Sea (1971), A Harp of Fishbones (1972), Winterthing (play, 1972), The Mooncusser's Daughter (1973), The Escaped Black Mamba (1973), Tales of Arabel's Raven (1974), Tale of a One-Way Street (1978), The Skin Spinners (poems, 1976), A Bundle of Nerves (1976), The Faithless Lollybird (1977), Mice and Mendelson (1978), Street (1979), Mortimer's Portrait on Glass (1982), Bridle the Wind Cape (1983), Mortimer's Cross (1983), Up the Chimney Down (stories, 1984), The Last Slice of Rainbow (stories, 1985), Dido and Pa Cape (1986), The Teeth of the Gale Cape (1988), The Erl King's Daughter (1988), Voices Hippo (1988); adult pubns: The Silence of Herondale (1964), The Fortune Hunters (1965), Hate Begins at Home (1967), The Embroidered Sunset (1970), Died on a Rainy Sunday (1972), Castle Barebane (1976), The Smile of the Stranger (1978), The Weeping Ash (1980), A Whisper in the Night (1982), The Way to Write for Children (1982), Foul Matter (1983), Mansfield Revisited (1985), Voices (1988), Blackground (1989), Jane Fairfax (1990), A Fit of Shivers (1990), The Haunting of Lamb House (1991), Morningquest (1992), Is (1992), Mortimer and Arabel (1992), The Midnight Moropus (1993), Hatching Trouble (1993), Eliza's Daughter (1994), The Winter Sleepwalker (1994), Cold Shoulder Road (1995), A Handful of Gold (1995), The Cockatrice Boys (1996), Emma Watson (1996), The Jewel Seed (1997); *Recreations* walking, gardening, listening to music, looking at art, travel; *Style—* Ms Joan Aiken; ✉ c/o A M Heath and Co Ltd, 79 St Martin's Lane, London WC2N 4AA

AIKEN, Air Chief Marshal Sir John Alexander Carlisle; KCB (1973, CB 1967); s of Thomas Leonard and Margaret Aiken; *b* 22 Dec 1921; *Educ* Birkenhead Sch; *m* 1948, Pamela Jane, da of late H F W Bartlett, of Brook Lodge, Stock, Essex; 1 s, 1 da; *Career* joined RAF 1941, Fighter Sqdns Europe and Far East 1942–45, Fighter Cmd 1946–47, CFS 1948, Staff of RAF Coll Cranwell 1948–50, OC Univ of Birmingham Air Sqdn 1950–52, Staff Coll 1953, HQ Fighter Cmd 1954–55, OC 29 Fighter Sqdn 1956–57, jssc 1958, HQ AF North 1958–60, Air Miny 1960–63, Station Cdr RAF Finningley 1963–64, Air Cdre Intelligence MOD 1965–67, idc 1968, Dep Cdr RAF Germany 1969–71, DG Trg RAF 1971–72, Head of Economy Project Team RAF 1972–73, AOC-in-C NEAF 1973–76, Air Memb for Personnel 1976–78, DG Intelligence MOD 1978–81; pres: RAFA 1984–85 and 1987–88 (chm Central Cncl 1981–84), Cncl Chatham House 1984–90; *Recreations* skiing, walking; *Clubs* RAF; *Style—* Air Chief Marshal Sir John Aiken, KCB; ✉ c/o The RAF Club, 128 Piccadilly, London W1V 0PY

AIKENS, Richard John Pearson; QC (1986); s of Maj Basil Aikens (d 1983), and Jean Eleanor, *née* Pearson; *b* 28 Aug 1948; *Educ* Norwich Sch, St John's Coll Cambridge (MA); *m* 3 March 1979, Penelope Anne Hartley, da of Hartley Baker (d 1961); 2 s (Christopher b 1979, Nicholas b 1981), 2 step da (Jessica b 1964, Anna b 1966); *Career* called to the Bar Middle Temple 1973, in practice 1974–, a jr counsel to the Crown common law 1981–86, recorder of the Crown Court 1993–, bencher Middle Temple 1994–; memb Supreme Court Rules Ctee 1984–88; dir Bar Mutual Indemnity Fund Ltd 1988–, dir ENO 1995–; govr Sedbergh Sch 1988–; *Books* Bullen and Leake on Pleadings and Practice (contributing ed, 13 edn 1991); *Recreations* music, the country; *Clubs* Leander, Groucho's; *Style—* Richard Aikens, QC; ✉ Brick Court Chambers, 15–19 Devereux Court, London WC2R 3JJ (☎ 0171 583 0777)

AIKIN, Olga Lindholm (Mrs J M Driver); CBE (1997); da of late Sidney Richard Daly, of Buckley, Clwyd, and Lilian May, *née* Lindholm (d 1966); *b* 10 Sept 1934; *Educ* Ilford Co HS for Girls, LSE (LLB), King's Coll London, London Business Sch; *m* 1, 1959 (m dis 1979), Ronald Sidney Aikin; 1 da (Gillian); m 2, 1982, John Michael Driver; 1 step da (Katie); *Career* called to the Bar Gray's Inn 1956; lectr: King's Coll London 1956–59, LSE 1959–70, London Business Sch 1971–90; dir gen Law Div Lion Int 1985–90, ptnr Aikin Driver Partnership 1988–; ed Law & Employment series Inst of Personnel Mgmnt; chm Bd of Mgmnt Nat Conciliation Service Qualitas Furnishing Standards Ltd 1992–94, memb Cncl ACAS 1982–; *Books* Employment, Welfare and Safety at Work (1971), Legal Problems of Employment (1990), Contracts (1992); *Recreations* collecting cookery books and glass; *Style—* Mrs Olga Aikin, CBE; ✉ Aikin Driver Partnership, 22 St Lukes Rd, London W11 1DP (☎ 0171 727 9791)

AILESBURY, 8 Marquess of (UK 1821); Sir Michael Sydney Cedric Brudenell-Bruce; 14 Bt (E 1611); also Baron Brudenell (E 1628), Earl of Cardigan (E 1661), Baron Bruce (GB 1746), Earl of Ailesbury (GB 1776), and Earl Bruce and Viscount Savernake (both UK 1821); 30 Hereditary Warden of Savernake Forest (until 1987, when he was succeeded by his son); s of 7 Marquess of Ailesbury (d 1974); *b* 31 March 1926; *Educ* Eton; *m* 1, 1952 (m dis 1961), Edwina, da of late Lt-Col Sir Edward Wills, 4 Bt; 1 s, 2 da; m 2, 1963 (m dis 1974), Juliet, da of late Hilary Kingsford; 2 da; m 3, 1974 (m dis 1992), Caroline, da of late Cdr Owen Wethered, JP, DL, RN; *Heir* s, Earl of Cardigan; *Career* late Lt RHG (reserve); memb London Stock Exchange 1954–; *Style—* The Most Hon the Marquess of Ailesbury; ✉ Luton Lye, Savernake Forest, Marlborough, Wilts

AILSA, 8 Marquess of (UK 1831); Archibald Angus Charles Kennedy; also Lord Kennedy (S 1452), Earl of Cassillis (S 1509), and Baron Ailsa (UK 1806); s of 7 Marquess of Ailsa, OBE, DL (d 1994), and Mary, *née* Burn; *b* 13 Sept 1956; *m* 1979 (m dis 1989), Dawn Leslie Anne, o da of David A Keen, of Paris; 2 da (Lady Rosemary Margaret b 1980, Lady Alicia-Jane Lesley b 1981); *Heir* bro, Lord David Thomas Kennedy, *qv*; *Recreations* shooting, skiing, youth work; *Clubs* New (Edinburgh); *Style—* The Most Hon the Marquess of Ailsa; ✉ Cassillis House, Maybole, Ayrshire (☎ 01292 56310)

AINGER, David William Dawson; TD (1969); s
Lt Cdr RN), of Weston Super Mare, and Fried
Educ Marlborough, Univ of Oxford (MA), Cor
da of Albert William Lewis (d 1991), of I
Ruairidh b 1980), 2 da (Katharine b 1966
1953–55, AER and TA&VR RE and RCT 19
conveyancing counsel of the Supreme Ct 1991–
lectr in law Univ of Southampton 1961–71; *Style*
Northampton Park, London N1 2PJ (☎ 0171 226 1401
London WC2A 3SU (☎ 0171 242 5002, fax 0171 831 9188)

AINGER, Nicholas (Nick); MP (Lab) Pembroke (majority
Netherthorpe GS Staveley Derbys; *m* Sally; 1 da; *Career* rigger Ma
Ltd Pembroke Dock, sr TGWU shop steward and branch sec 1
Pembroke 1992–; Dyfed CC: cncllr 1981–93, served on various ctees; m
International, Dyfed Wildlife Tst, RSPB; *Style—* Nick Ainger, Esq, MP; ✉
Commons, London SW1A 0AA

AINSCOW, Robert Morrison; CB (1989); s of Robert Ainscow, of Salford, Lancs
1974), and Hilda, *née* Cleminson; *b* 3 June 1936; *Educ* Salford GS, Univ of Liverpool (BA); *m* 1965, Faye Bider; 1 da (b Dec 1972), 1 s (b May 1977); *Career* Govt of the Fedn of Rhodesia and Nyasaland 1957–61, UN Secretariat New York 1961–65, Dept of Econ Affairs London 1965–66, UN Secretariat New York 1966–68; ODA: econ advsr 1968–70, sr econ advsr 1971–76, head of S Asia Dept 1976–79, under sec (Educn and Tech Cooperation Div) 1979–80, princ fin offr and under sec (Fin and Aid Policy Div) 1980–86, dep sec 1986–96; chm OECD/DAC Working Pty on Fin Aspects of Devpt Assistance 1982–86, memb IBRD/IMF Devpt Ctee Task Force on: Concessional Flows 1983–85, Future of Multilateral Devpt Banks 1994–96; *Style—* Robert Ainscow, Esq, CB; (☎ and fax 0171 435 2218)

AINSLEY, David Edwin; s of Edwin Ainsley, of Bebington, Wirral, Merseyside, and Gertrude Mary, *née* Fletcher (d 1978); *b* 13 Sept 1944; *Educ* Portsmouth GS, Sch of Architecture Univ of Liverpool (BArch); *m* 1, 28 Feb 1970 (m dis 1984), Pauline Elisabeth, da of Aubrey Highton; 2 s (Sam b 21 Sept 1975, Christian b 24 May 1978); m 2, Beatrix Hinchliffe Parry, da of William Ellis, of Tettenhall; 2 step s (Nathan b 22 Dec 1971, Benjamin b 7 Feb 1976); *Career* ptnr in firm of architects and landscape architects Ainsley Gommon Wood; winner of thirteen national and international design awards incl: Royal Town Planning Inst commendation, Housing Centre Tst Award, Liverpool Int Garden Festival Best Home Garden, twice winner of RIBA Community Enterprise Scheme Award, RIBA Housing Design Award, Civic Tst commendations, Welsh Nat Eisteddfod Architecture Prize; pres Liverpool Architectural Soc 1993–94, memb Cncl Liverpool Chamber of Commerce and Indust 1993–95, bd memb Liverpool Architecture and Design Tst 1994–, tstee Artsworks Wirral Arts Devpt Agency 1994–; fndr memb and former chm Oxton Soc; govr Christchurch CE Primary Sch Birkenhead 1992–; RIBA 1972, FASI 1986; *Recreations* music (keyboard and saxaphone in Low Flier), sailing; *Style—* David Ainsley, Esq; ✉ 10 South Bank, Arno Road, Oxton, Birkenhead L43 5UP (☎ 0151 652 4064); Tynyllwyn, Llanrhaeadr YM, Shropshire SY10 0DA; Ainsley Gommon Wood, Architects and Landscape Architects, 1 Price St, Hamilton Square, Birkenhead, Merseyside L41 6JN (☎ 0151 647 5511, fax 0151 666 2195)

AINSLEY, John Mark; s of John Alwyn Ainsley, of Maidenhead, and (Dorothy) Sylvia *née* Anderson; *b* 9 July 1963; *Educ* Nunnery Wood Secdy Modern Worcester, Worcester Royal GS, Magdalen Coll Oxford; *Career* tenor; currently studies with Diane Forlano, professional debut singing Stravinsky's Mass (Royal Festival Hall under Simon Rattle) 1984, operatic debut in Scarlatti's Gli Equivoci nel Sembiante (Innsbruck Festival) 1988; former memb Deller Consort, former memb Gothic Voices, has sung with all major Baroque ensembles, also soloist in later repertoire; performed with numerous orchs incl: London Philharmonic, Royal Liverpool Philharmonic, BBC Symphony, City of Birmingham Symphony, English Chamber, Scottish Chamber, Bournemouth Symphony, London Classical Players, Berlin Philharmonic, Montreal Symphony; appeared at numerous international venues incl: Konzerthaus Vienna, Musikverein Vienna, Philarmonic Berlin, Gewandhaus Leipzig, Stuttgart Festival, Göttingen Festival, others in New York, Boston, France, Holland and Switzerland; lay clerk Christ Church Oxford 1982–84; *Performances* operatic roles incl: Return of Ulysses (ENO) 1989, Fenton in Falstaff (Scottish Opera), Idamantes in Idomemeo (WNO under Sir Charles Mackerras and Munich), Don Ottavio in Don Giovanni (Lyon Opera and Aix en Provence Festival, Glyndebourne Festival and San Francisco), Ferrando in Cosi fan Tutte (Glyndebourne Festival, La Monnaie Brussels) 1992; concert performances incl world première of Tavener's We Shall See Him as He Is (Chester Festival, later BBC Proms) 1992; *Recordings* incl: Handel's Nisi Dominus (with Choir of Westminster Abbey under Simon Preston, Deutsche Grammophon), Purcell's Odes (with English Concert under Trevor Pinnock, Deutsche Grammophon), Mozart's C Minor Mass and Handel's Acis and Galatea (with Acad of Ancient Music under Christopher Hogwood, Decca), Handel's Saul (under John Eliot Gardiner, Philips), Handel's Acis and Galatea and Joshua (under King, Hyperion), title role in Monteverdi's Orfeo (Decca), Mozart's Requiem (under Roger Norrington, EMI), Charlie in Brigadoon (EMI), Ottavio in Mozart's Don Giovanni (under Roger Norrington, EMI) Frederic in Gilbert and Sullivan's Pirates of Penzance (Mackerras/Telare), Mendelssohn's Elijah (under Herrewege, Harmonia Mundi), Berlioz's Les Troyens (under Dutoit, Decca), various works by Britten for EMI, Decca and Philips, Haydn's Die Schpfung (under Bruggen, Philips), Purcell's Odes (under Trevor Pinnock, DG Archiv), Quilter Songs (with Malcolm Martineau on piano, Hyperion), Complete Schubert Edition (with Graham Johnson on piano, Hyperion), Stravinsky's Oedipus Rex (under Welser-Möst, EMI), Stravinsky's Pulcinella (under Bernard Haitink, Philips), Finzi's Dies Natalis/Intimations of Immortality (under Best, Hyperion), Vaughan Williams's Serenade to Music (under Roger Norrington, Decca); *Recreations* chocolate, early Flemish painting; *Style—* John Mark Ainsley, Esq; ✉ c/o Robert Rattray, Lies Askonas Ltd, 6 Henrietta Street, London WC2E 8LA (☎ 0171 379 7700)

AINSLIE, David Galbraith; s of Patrick David Lafone Ainslie, of Aynhoe Pk, Aynho, nr Banbury, Oxon, and Agnes Ursula, *née* Galbraith; *b* 13 Oct 1947; *Educ* Wellington Coll, Pembroke Coll Cambridge (MA); *m* 16 July 1993, Catherine Mary Ruth, *née* Green; 1 s (Jonathan David Alexander b 6 April 1996); *Career* admitted slr 1973; joined Dawson & Co 1969; ptnr: Lovell White & King 1981–83 (joined 1976), Towry Law Financial Planning Ltd (ind fin advsrs) 1983–; dir: Towry Law Trustee Co Ltd 1984–, Castle School Fees Ltd 1985–, Towry Law Financial Planning Ltd 1987–, Towry Law Pension Services Ltd 1994–; memb: UK Falkland Islands Ctee 1973–, Exec Ctee Falkland Islands Assoc 1977–; tstee UK Falkland Islands Tst 1981–; memb Law Soc 1971; Freeman City of London, Liveryman Worshipful Co of Haberdashers 1971; *Books* Practical Tax Planning with Precedents (contrib, 1987–); *Recreations* fishing, shooting; *Style—* David Ainslie, Esq; ✉ The Old Bakehouse, Hampstead Norreys, nr Newbury, Berks RG18 0TE (☎ 01635 201 355); Towry Law Group, Baylis House, Stoke Poges Lane, Slough, Berks SL1 3PB (☎ 01753 554400, fax 01753 558220)

AINSWORTH, Anthony Thomas Hugh; s and h of Sir (Thomas) David Ainsworth, 4 Bt, *qv*; *b* 30 March 1962; *Educ* Harrow; *Career* Lt Royal Hussars (PWO) 1982–85; *Style—* Anthony Ainsworth, Esq; ✉ 10 Paultons House, Paultons Square, London SW3 5DU

RTH, Sir (Thomas) David; 4 Bt (UK 1916), of Ardanaiseig, Co Argyll; s of mas Ainsworth, 2 Bt, by his 2 w, Marie, da of Compton Domvile; suc half-bro, n Ainsworth, 3 Bt, 1981; *b* 22 Aug 1926; *Educ* Eton; *m* 6 May 1957, Sarah Mary, Lt-Col Hugh Carr Walford, 17/21 Lancers (ka 1941); 2 s (Anthony, Charles David Aug 1966), 2 da (Serena Mary (Mrs Peratinos) b 13 March 1958, Tessa Jane (Mrs rtescue) b 6 Aug 1959); *Heir* s, Anthony Thomas Hugh Ainsworth, *qv*; *Recreations* hooting, fishing; *Style*— Sir David Ainsworth, Bt; ✉ 80 Elm Park Gardens, London SW10; Ashley House, Wootton, nr Woodstock, Oxon OX20 1DX (☎ 01993 811650)

AINSWORTH, (Mervyn) John; s of Gordon John Ainsworth (d 1974), and Eileen, *née* MacDonald; *b* 28 Jan 1947; *Educ* Stanfield HS Stoke-on-Trent, Goldsmiths' Coll Univ of London (CertEd, Dip in Educn); *m* Marta Christina, o da of Piotr Marmolak (d 1973); 2 s (Andrew Edward John b 5 Dec 1975, Peter Gordon John b 10 July 1983), 1 da (Stephanie Mary b 28 Sept 1978); *Career* asst clerk to the Governors and Bursar Dulwich Coll 1969–74, princ asst CEGB 1974–77, secretarial asst and mangr Secretariat Servs BTDB (now ABP) 1977–78; BPIF: sec 1978–84, fin dir 1983–84; sec gen Inst of Admin Mgmnt 1984–90, chief exec and sec Inst of Chartered Secretaries and Administrators 1990–; Freeman City of London, Liveryman Worshipful Co of Secs and Admins; FIMgt 1978, FCIS 1980, FInstAM 1983, hon fell Canadian Inst of Certified Admin Mangrs 1987; *Recreations* golf, gardening, travel, family life; *Style*— John Ainsworth, Esq; ✉ Institute of Chartered Secretaries and Administrators, 16 Park Crescent, London W1N 4AH (☎ 0171 580 4741, fax 0171 323 1132)

AINSWORTH, District Judge John David; s of George Irving Ainsworth (d 1989), of Bournemouth, and Moyra Rosetta Ainsworth (d 1994); *b* 27 July 1943; *Educ* Emanuel Sch London, Univ of Southampton (LLB); *m* 1, 4 June 1966, Sally Georgina (d 1990), da of George Goater (d 1990), of Christchurch, Dorset; 2 s (Nicholas Robert b 13 Jan 1969, Jeremy John b 18 July 1971); m 2, 8 April 1994, Ann, da of Frederick Pledge, of Thorpe Bay, Essex; *Career* admitted slr 1968; asst slr: White Brooks & Gilman Winchester 1968–71 (articled clerk 1966–68), Harry Ellis & Co Bournemouth 1971–72; ptnr Lester & Russell Bournemouth 1975–88 (asst slr 1972–75), ptnr and head of litigation Lester Aldridge Bournemouth 1988–92, pt/t dep High Ct and Co Ct district judge 1988–92, full time dist judge of the High Ct Southampton District Registry and Southampton County Ct 1992–; former sec Bournemouth RFC, former chm Dorset Schs Badminton Assoc, former chm No 3 Area Legal Aid Bd; memb: Law Soc, Bournmouth District Law Soc, Western Circuit; FCIArb 1991; *Recreations* golf, tennis, swimming; *Clubs* Ferndown Golf, David Lloyd, Hazards Golf Soc, Penpushers Golf Soc, Old Emanuel Assoc, Mansion House (Poole); *Style*— District Judge J D Ainsworth; ✉ 23 Meyrick Park Crescent, Bournemouth, Dorset BH3 7AG (☎ 01202 553839); Southampton Combined Court Centre, Southampton (☎ 01703 228586, e-mail jainsworth@lix.comulink.co.uk)

AINSWORTH, Mavis; OBE (1997); da of Reginald Frederick Davenport (d 1967), of Totley, Sheffield, and Wilhelmina, *née* Mynette; *b* 6 Sept 1931; *Educ* Univ of London (BA, PGCE), Univ of Illinois (MA); *m* 8 Aug 1953, Stanley Ainsworth, step s of late Andrew Rutherford, of Heaton Chapel, Stockport; 2 s (Jonathan Grieve b 1960, Quentin Paul b 1961); *Career* head of English Dept Totley Thornbridge Coll of Educn Sheffield 1969–76; Sheffield Hallam Univ: head of English Dept 1976–87, dean Faculty of Cultural Studies (with overall responsibility for initial and inservice teacher trg) 1987–89, dir Sch of Cultural Studies 1989–96; FRSA 1994; *Recreations* theatre, travel, visiting London; *Style*— Mrs Mavis Ainsworth, OBE; ✉ c/o School of Cultural Studies, Sheffield Hallam University, Psalter Lane, Sheffield S11 8UZ (☎ 0114 253 2601, fax 0114 253 2603, telex 54680 SHPOLY6)

AINSWORTH, Peter; MP (C) Surrey East (majority 17,656); s of Lt Cdr Michael Lionel Yeoward Ainsworth (d 1978), and Patricia Mary, *née* Bedford; *b* 16 Nov 1956; *Educ* Ludgrove Sch, Bradfield Coll, Lincoln Coll Oxford; *m* 1981, Claire, *née* Burnett; 1 s, 2 da; *Career* res asst to Sir John Stewart-Clark MEP 1979–81, investmt analyst Laing & Cruickshank 1981–85, dir S G Warburg Securities 1989–92 (joined as investmt analyst 1985); MP (C) Surrey E 1992–; PPS: to Jonathan Aitken as Chief Sec to the Treasy 1994–95, to Virginia Bottomley as Sec of State for Nat Heritage 1995–96; asst govt whip 1996–; memb Environment Select Ctee 1993–94; cncllr London Borough of Wandsworth 1986–92 (sometime chm Cons Gp); memb Bow Gp 1983– (memb Cncl 1984–86); *Recreations* family, music, gardening; *Clubs* MCC; *Style*— Peter Ainsworth, Esq, MP; ✉ House of Commons, London SW1A 0AA

AINSWORTH, (Edward) Peter Richard; s of Edward Ainsworth (d 1955), of Sale, Cheshire, and Sara Katharina, *née* Healy (d 1962); *b* 31 July 1932; *Educ* Sale HS, Manchester GS; *m* 12 August 1959, Moira Josephine Gabrielle, da of Albert Grant; 4 s (Michael Edward b 12 Sept 1960, Timothy Grant b 2 July 1962, John Benedict b 28 July 1964, Mark Justin b 26 Nov 1967); *Career* articled to Edward Ainsworth; ptnr: Edward Ainsworth & Son 1954–58, Booth Ainsworth (sr ptnr) 1959–; pres Manchester Soc of Chartered Accountants 1983–84, memb Cncl ICAEW 1985–; FCA 1959 (ACA 1954); *Recreations* sailing, skiing; *Clubs* Royal Mersey Yacht, Budworth Sailing, Trearddur Bay Sailing; *Style*— Peter Ainsworth, Esq; ✉ Booth Ainsworth, Ashfield House, Ashfield Road, Cheadle, Cheshire SK8 1BE (☎ 0161 491 0200, fax 0161 491 0660)

AINSWORTH, Robert (Bob); MP (Lab) Coventry North East (majority 11,676); s of late Stanley Ainsworth, and Pearl Ainsworth; *b* 19 June 1952; *Educ* Foxford Comp Sch Coventry; *m* 22 June 1974, Gloria, *née* Sandall; 2 da; *Career* sheet metal worker Jaguar Cars Ltd Coventry 1971–91, MP (Lab) Coventry NE 1992–; oppn whip 1995–; TGWU (now MSF): shop steward 1974–80, sr steward 1980–91, sec jt shop stewards 1980–91, branch pres 1983–87; Coventry City Cncl: cncllr 1984–92, dep ldr 1988–91, chm Fin Ctee 1989–92; *Recreations* walking, chess, reading; *Style*— Bob Ainsworth, Esq, MP; ✉ House of Commons, London SW1A 0AA (☎ 0171 219 4047, fax 0171 219 2889, constituency ☎ 01203 226707, fax 01203 226707)

AINSWORTH, William Robert; s of William Murray Ainsworth (d 1964), of Stockton-on-Tees, Co Durham, and Emma Laura Mary, *née* Easley (d 1981); *b* 24 June 1935; *Educ* Holy Trinity Sch Stockton-on-Tees, Stockton GS, Sch of Architecture Univ of Durham (BArch); *m* 7 Nov 1959, Sylvia Vivian, da of Norman Brown, of Buenos Aires, Argentina, S America; 3 da (Graciela Glenn b 1960, Anita Susan b 1964, Lucia Emma b 1977); *Career* chartered architect, designer and urban planner, fndr ptnr Ainsworth Spark Assocs 1963– (completed over 3,000 projects throughout UK and Europe for local, nat and int companies); working tours of: S America, USA, and Europe; visiting studio tutor Sch of Architecture Newcastle upon Tyne 1961–63; external examiner: Sch of Architecture, Coll of Arts and Technol Newcastle; memb Bd and govr Newcastle Coll 1991–; RIBA: chm Northern Region 1972–73, fndr chm Nat Ctee for Environmental Educn 1977, dir Bd of Servs Ltd London, memb and vice pres Nat Cncl 1980–82; vice pres and hon librarian Br Architectural Library 1987–90; bd govr Coll of Arts and Technol 1984–86, vice chm Bd of Govrs Newcastle Coll 1996–; initiator of World Day of Architecture in UK 1989; chm Sculpture Tst Northern Arts (fndr) 1981–, memb Bd Arts Resources 1995–; fndr chm Northumberland and Durham Lord's Taverners; memb Union of Int Architects (UIA); FRIBA 1967, MCSD 1977, IOB 1980, FRSA 1985; *Recreations* cricket, golf, gardening, reading, painting (watercolours); *Clubs* Arts (London), Northumberland Golf; *Style*— William Ainsworth, Esq; ✉ 1 Edgewood, Darras Hall, Ponteland, Newcastle upon Tyne; Ainsworth Spark Associates, Summerhill House, 9 Summerhill Terrace, Newcastle upon Tyne NE4 6EB (☎ 0191 232 3434, fax 0191 261 0628)

AIRD, Capt Sir Alastair Sturgis; GCVO (1997, KCVO 1984, CVO 1977, LVO 1969); s of Col Malcolm Aird (d 1965); *b* 14 Jan 1931; *Educ* Eton, RMA Sandhurst; *m* 1963, Fiona Violet, LVO (1980), da of Lt-Col Ririd Myddelton (d 1988); 2 da (Caroline (Mrs Allfrey) b 1964, Henrietta (Mrs Seidler) b 1966); *Career* cmmnd 9 Queen's Royal Lancers 1951, Adjutant 1956–59, ret 1964; equerry to HM Queen Elizabeth The Queen Mother 1960–63, asst private sec 1964–74, comptroller to HM Queen Elizabeth The Queen Mother 1974–93 (private sec 1993–); memb Cncl Feathers Assoc of Youth Clubs 1973–93, tstee RSAS Devpt Tst 1986–; Hon Master of the Bench Middle Temple 1991; *Recreations* shooting, fishing, golf, tennis; *Clubs* Cavalry and Guards; *Style*— Capt Sir Alastair Aird, GCVO; ✉ 31B St James's Palace, London SW1 (☎ 0171 839 6700)

AIRD, Catherine; *see:* McIntosh, Kinn Hamilton

AIRD, Sir (George) John; 4 Bt (UK 1901), of Hyde Park Terrace, Paddington, Co London; s of Col Sir John Renton Aird, 3 Bt, MVO, MC, JP, DL (d 1973), sometime Extra Equerry to King George VI and to HM The Queen, of Forest Lodge, Windsor Great Park, and Lady Priscilla, *née* Heathcote-Drummond-Willoughby, yr da of 2 Earl of Ancaster; *b* 30 Jan 1940; *Educ* Eton, ChCh Oxford (MA), Harvard (MBA); *m* 31 Aug 1968, Margaret Elizabeth, yr da of Sir John Harling Muir, 3 Bt, TD, DL; 1 s, 2 da (Rebecca b 1970, Belinda Elizabeth b 1972); *Heir* s, James John Aird b 12 June 1978; *Career* page of honour to HM 1955–57; engineer Sir Alexander Gibb & Partners 1961–65, mangr John Laing & Co 1967–69, chm and md Sir John Aird & Co 1969–; chm: Matcon Group plc 1981–, Healthcare Development Services 1995–, Advanced Fluid Systems Ltd 1996–; Liveryman Worshipful Company of Drapers; MICE 1965; *Recreations* skiing, hunting; *Clubs* White's; *Style*— Sir John Aird, Bt; ✉ Grange Farm, Evenlode, Moreton-in-Marsh, Glos GL56 0NT (☎ 01608 650607, fax 01608 652442, e-mail john_aird@matcon.compulink.co.uk)

AIREY, Clifford; s of Maj William Airey (d 1986), of Preston, Lancashire, and Ellen, *née* Hogg (d 1974); *b* 16 Jan 1939; *Educ* Br Army Schs Overseas, Univ of Liverpool, Univ of Manchester; *m* 1, 23 Jan 1960 (m dis 1980), Maureen, *née* Fowler; 1 s (Shawn James b 1965), 2 da (Dawn Elizabeth Airey, *qv*, b 1960, Rachel Louise b 1967); m 2, 1982, Gina Margarita, *née* Kingdon, 2 s (Sebastian Jon b 1983, Clifford Lloyd b 1985), 1 da (Dominique Ellen 1984); *Career* res ptnr Jubb & Partners consulting engrs 1964–73, sr ptnr Airey and Coles consulting engrs 1973–; sr lectr Plymouth Poly 1967–70; past chm Inst of Structural Engrs, memb Plymouth Philatelic Soc; CEng, FIStructE, MConsE, FFB; *Recreations* fly-fishing, sailing, shooting, stamp and coin collecting; *Style*—Clifford Airey, Esq; ✉ 8 Whiteford Rd, Mannamead, Plymouth PL3 5LX (☎ 01752 266 456); Airey and Coles Consulting Engineers, Kirkby Lodge, Portland Square Lane North, Plymouth, Devon (☎ 01752 229119/227983, fax 01752 222115)

AIREY, Dawn Elizabeth; da of Clifford Airey, *qv*, and Maureen Airey; *b* 1960; *Career* controller then dir of prog planning Central Independent Television until 1992 (joined as mgmnt trainee 1985), controller of daytime and children's progs ITV Network Centre 1993–94, controller of arts and entertainment Channel Four Television 1994–96, dir of progs Channel 5 Broadcasting 1996–; *Style*— Ms Dawn Airey; ✉ Channel 5 Broadcasting Ltd, 22 Long Acre, London WC2E 9LY (☎ 0171 911 0055)

AIRLIE, 13 Earl of (S 1639) David George Coke Patrick Ogilvy; KT (1985), GCVO (1984), PC (1984), JP (Angus 1989); also Lord Ogilvy of Airlie (S 1491) and Lord Ogilvy of Alyth and Lintrathen (S 1639); s of 12 Earl of Airlie, KT, GCVO, MC (d 1968), and Lady Alexandra Coke (d 1984), da of 3 Earl of Leicester; *b* 17 May 1926; *Educ* Eton; *m* 1952, Virginia Fortune, DCVO (1995; vice-pres Women of the Year, tstee Tate Gallery 1980–94 and Nat Gallery of Scotland, Lady in Waiting to HM The Queen 1973–), da of John Barry Ryan (d 1966), of Newport, RI, USA, and Margaret Dorothy (Nin) (d 1995), da of Otto Kahn, of New York; 3 s (David (Lord Ogilvy), Bruce b 1959, Patrick b 1971), 3 da (Doune b 1953, Jane b 1955, Elizabeth b 1965); *Heir* s, Lord Ogilvy, *qv*; *Career* Lt Scots Gds 1944; Capt ADC to High Cmmr and C-in-C Austria 1947–48, Malaya 1948–49, resigned cmmn 1950; chief cmmr for Scotland Scout Assoc 1960–61 (treas 1962–86, hon pres 1988); Capt Royal Co of Archers (Queen's Body Guard for Scotland) 1996– (Ensign 1975–85, Lt 1985–96); chm: Schroders plc 1977–84, Ashdown Investment Trust Ltd 1968–82, Westpool Investment Trust until 1982 (also resigned directorships), General Accident Fire & Life Assurance Corporation 1987– (dir 1962, dep chm 1975–87); dir: J Henry Schroder Wagg & Co 1961–84 (chm 1973–77), Scottish & Newcastle Breweries 1969–83, Royal Bank of Scotland Group plc 1983–93, Royal Bank of Scotland 1991–93, Baring Stratton Investment Trust plc (formerly Stratton Investment Trust) 1986–; Lord Chamberlain of the Queen's Household 1984–, Chllr Royal Victorian Order 1984–; govr Nuffield Hosps 1984–89, hon pres Scout Assoc in Scotland 1988–, dep chm of tstees Royal Collection Tst 1993–, first chllr Univ of Abertay Dundee 1994–; Lord-Lt Tayside Region District of Angus 1989 (DL Angus 1964); KStJ 1995; Hon LLD Dundee 1990; CStJ 1981; *Clubs* White's; *Style*— The Rt Hon the Earl of Airlie, KT, GCVO, PC, JP; ✉ Cortachy Castle, Kirriemuir, Angus; 5 Swan Walk, London SW3 4JJ; Lord Chamberlain's Office, Buckingham Palace, London SW1

AIRS, Graham John; s of George William Laurence Airs, of Saltash, and Marjorie, *née* Lewis (d 1967); *b* 8 Aug 1953; *Educ* Newport GS Essex, Emmanuel Coll Cambridge (MA, LLB); *m* 4 April 1981, Stephanie Annette, da of William Henry Marshall; *Career* admitted slr 1978; Slaughter and May 1976–80; ptnr: Airs Dickinson 1980–84, Slaughter and May 1987– (rejoined as asst slr 1984–87); memb Law Soc; *Books* Tolley's Tax Planning (contrib); *Style*— Graham Airs, Esq; ✉ Slaughter and May, 35 Basinghall St, London EC2V 5DB (☎ 0171 600 1200, fax 0171 726 0038, 0171 600 0289, telex 883486, 888926)

AITCHISON, Sir Charles Walter de Lancey; 4 Bt (UK 1938), of Lemmington, Co Northumberland; s of Sir Stephen Charles de Lancey Aitchison, 3 Bt (d 1958), and Elizabeth Anne Milburn, *née* Reed (now Mrs Roland Antony Cookson); *b* 27 May 1951; *Educ* Gordonstoun; *m* 1984, Susan, yr da of late Edward Ellis, of Hest Bank, Lancs; 1 s (Rory), 1 da (Tessa Charlotte b 1982); *Heir* s, Rory Edward de Lancey Aitchison b 7 March 1986; *Career* late Lt 15/19 KRH, RARO 1974–78; dir Leamington Hall Properties Ltd; ARICS 1984; *Recreations* fishing; *Style*— Sir Charles Aitchison, Bt; ✉ Park House, Barbon, Kirkby Lonsdale, Cumbria LA6 2LG

AITCHISON, Craigie Ronald John; yr s of Rt Hon Lord Aitchison, PC, KC, LLD (Scottish Lord of Session, Lord Justice-Clerk and Lord Advocate Scotland under Ramsay MacDonald; noted for never losing a case involving an indictment on a capital charge when defending); yr bro of Raymund Craigie Aitchison, the writer; *b* 13 Jan 1926; *Educ* Edinburgh Univ, Middle Temple London, Slade Sch of Fine Art; *Career* painter; *Solo Exhibitions* Beaux Arts Gallery London 1959, 1960 and 1964, Marlborough Fine Arts (London) Ltd 1968, Compass Gallery Glasgow 1970, Basil Jacobs Gallery London 1971, Rutland Gallery London 1975, Scottish Arts Cncl 1975, M Knoedler & Co Ltd London 1977, Kettles Yard Gallery Cambridge 1979, Arts Cncl Retrospective Exhibition Serpentine Gallery London 1981, David Grob Fine Art London 1981, Artis Monte Carlo Monaco 1985, Albemarle Gallery London 1987, 1989, Thomas Gibson Fine Art 1993, Harewood House Leeds (retrospective 1954–94) 1994, Gallery of Modern Art Glasgow (retrospective) 1996; has participated in many mixed exhibitions; *Work in Collections* Aberdeen Art Gallery and Museum, Arts Cncl of GB, Glasgow Art Gallery and Museum, Grundy Art Gallery Blackpool, Newcastle Region Art Gallery NSW Australia, Perth City Art Gallery and Museum, Rugby Borough Cncl Collection, Scottish Arts Cncl Edinburgh, Scottish Nat Gallery of Modern Art Edinburgh, Tate Gallery, Walker Art Gallery Liverpool; *Awards* British Cncl Italian Govt Scholarship 1955, Arts Cncl

Purchase Award 1965, Edwin Austin Abbey Premier Scholarship 1970, Prizewinner John Moores Liverpool Exhibition 1974, Lorne Scholarship 1974–75, Arts Cncl Bursary 1976, First Johnson Wax Prize RA 1984, Korn Ferry Int Award RA 1989 and 1991, First Jerwood Fndn Painting Prize 1994; RA 1988 (ARA 1978); *Style*— Craigie Aitchison, Esq, RA; ✉ c/o Royal Academy of Arts, Burlington House, London W1

AITCHISON, Prof Jean Margaret; da of John Frederick Aitchison, of Debden Green, Essex, and Joan Eileen, *née* Chivers (d 1994); *b* 3 July 1938; *Educ* Wimbledon HS GPDST, Girton Coll Cambridge (MA), Radcliffe Coll Harvard (AM); *partner* John Robert Ayto; *Career* asst lectr in Greek Bedford Coll Univ of London 1961–65; LSE 1965–92: lectr, sr lectr, reader in linguistics; Rupert Murdoch prof of language and communication Univ of Oxford 1993–, professorial fell Worcester Coll Oxford 1993–; BBC Reith lectr 1997; *Books* The articulate mammal: An introduction to psycholinguistics (3 edn, 1989), Language change: Progress or decay? (2 edn, 1991), Introducing Language and mind (1992), Linguistics (4 edn, 1992), Words in the mind: An introduction to the mental lexicon (2 edn, 1994), Language Joyriding (1994), The seeds of speech: Language origin and evolution (1996), The Language web: The power and problems of words (1996); *Recreations* windsurfing; *Style*— Prof Jean Aitchison; ✉ Worcester College, Oxford OX1 2HB (☎ 01865 278392, fax 01865 278387, e-mail jean.aitchison@worcester.oxford.ac.uk)

AITKEN, Alexander William; s of Alexander John Aitken (d 1979), and Freda, *née* Trueman, of Rownhams, nr Southampton; *b* 9 May 1958; *Educ* RAF Changi GS Singapore, Leamington Coll for Boys, The Mountbatten Sch Romsey Hants (played rugby and basketball to County Level); *m* 9 May 1977, Caroline, da of Herbert Douglas Abbott; 2 s (Justin Richard b 1 April 1980, Alexander Joseph b 28 June 1983); *Career* deck hand Scot fishing trawler 1975, waiter Whitbread Wessex Potters Heron Motel Ampfield 1976, asst head waiter The Slipway Restaurant Lymington 1976, head waiter Grosvenor Hotel Stockbridge 1976, catering mangr Silhouette Casino 1976–77, restaurant mangr Le Chanteclere Restaurant Cadham Hants 1977–82, The Elizabethan Restaurant Winchester 1982–83, opened Le Poussin Restaurant 1983; featured in The Best of Europe series Discovery Channel TV; memb: Master Chefs of GB 1986, Br Culinary Inst 1989; *Awards* three rosettes AA Restaurant Guide, one star Egon Ronay Guide, one star Michelin Guide, 4/5 Good Food Guide, Good Food Guide Hampshire Restaurant of the Year 1987 and 1992, Clover Award Ackerman Guide, Out of Town Restaurant of the Year The Times 1990–91; *Recreations* sailing, dressage, scuba diving, mushroom hunting; *Style*— Alexander Aitken, Esq; ✉ Le Poussin Restaurant, The Courtyard, Brookley Rd, Brockenhurst, Hampshire S042 7RB (☎ 01590 623063, fax 01590 622912)

AITKEN, Rt Hon Jonathan William Patrick; PC (1994), MP (C) Thanet South (majority 11,513); s of Sir William Aitken, KBE, MP (d 1964), and Hon Lady Aitken, MBE, JP, *qv*; is gn of 1 Baron Beaverbrook and gs of 1 Baron Rugby; bro of Maria Aitken, *qv*, the actress; *b* 30 Aug 1942; *Educ* Eton, ChCh Oxford; *m* 1979, Lolicia Olivera (economist), da of O A Azucki, of Zürich; 1 s (William b 7 Sept 1982), twin da (Victoria, Alexandra b 14 June 1980); *Career* private sec to Selwyn Lloyd 1964–66, foreign corr Evening Standard 1966–71, md Slater Walker (ME) 1973–75, fndr and chm Aitken Hume International 1979–90, temp chief exec TV-am March-April 1983; MP (C): Thanet E 1974–1983, Thanet S 1983–; min of state Miny of Defence 1992–94, chief sec to the Treasy 1994–95; *Books* A Short Walk on the Campus (1966), The Young Meteors (1967), Land of Fortune: A Study of the New Australia (1971), Officially Secret (1971), Nixon: A Life (1993); *Clubs* Beefsteak, Turf, Pratt's; *Style*— Rt Hon Jonathan Aitken, MP; ✉ House of Commons, London SW1A 0AA

AITKEN, Maria Penelope Katharine; da of Sir William Aitken, KBE, MP Bury St Edmunds 1950–64 (d 1964, s of Joseph Aitken, 2 s of Rev William Aitken and eld bro of 1 Baron Beaverbrook; Sir William's yr sis Margaret Annie was a Canadian MP in the early 1970s), and Hon Lady Aitken, *qv*; sis of Jonathan Aitken, MP, *qv*; *b* 12 Sept 1945; *Educ* privately, Riddlesworth Hall Norfolk, Sherborne Girls' Sch, St Anne's Coll Oxford; *m* 1, 1968 (m dis), Mark Durden-Smith, yst s of A J Durden-Smith, FRCS, of Kensington; m 2, 1972 (m dis 1980), Nigel Davenport, the actor, *qv*; 1 s (Jack); m 3, 28 Dec 1991, Patrick J McGrath, the novelist, eldest s of Dr Patrick Gerard McGrath, CB, CBE; *Career* actress; visiting assoc prof of drama Yale Univ 1991; *Theatre* for NT incl: Bedroom Farce, Blithe Spirit; for RSC incl: Travesties, The Happiest Days of Your Life 1984, Waste 1985; numerous roles incl: Amanda in London prodn of Noel Coward's Private Lives 1979–80, Gilda in Coward's Design for Living 1982–83, Sister Mary Ignatius (Ambassadors) 1983, Florence Lancaster in Coward's The Vortex (Garrick) 1989, Hay Fever (Albery) 1992, Kate in Sylvia (Apollo) 1996; also dir: Happy Family by Giles Cooper (Duke of York's) 1983, Private Lives by Noel Coward (Oxford Playhouse) 1984, After the Ball by William Douglas Home (Old Vic) 1985, The Rivals by Sheridan (Court Theatre Chicago) 1985, Irma Vep (Ambassadors) 1989, Lady Bracknell's Confinement (Vineyard Theatre NY) 1991, As You Like It (Regents Park) 1992, School for Scandal (Theatr Clwyd) 1992; *Television* own chat show (Private Lives) on BBC2; own prodn co Dramatis Personae produced: Happy Family 1983, Sister Mary Ignatius 1983, Acting (series) for BBC2 1988–90; part-time journalist, documentary (made Going up the Amazon) for the BBC 1985; *Films* incl: A Fish Called Wanda (with John Cleese, *qv*) 1988, The Grotesque 1996, Fierce Creatures 1996; *Books* A Girdle Round the Earth (1986, paperback 1988), Style: Acting in High Comedy (1996); *Style*— Miss Maria Aitken; ✉ c/o Michael Whitehall Ltd, 125 Gloucester Road, London SW7 4TE (☎ 0171 244 8466, fax 0171 244 9060)

AITKEN, Matthew James (Matt); s of John Aitken (d 1965), and Joan, *née* Stockdale-Edge; *b* 25 Aug 1956; *Educ* Leigh Boys' GS, Manchester Poly; *m* Katherine, *née* Williams; 2 da (Isabelle Keeble b 8 March 1990, Romy Marianne b 31 Aug 1992); *Career* professional freelance musician and musical dir 1980–, audio engr and record prodr 1982–, formerly in prodn team Stock Aitken Waterman; artists incl: Princess, Hazell Dean, Dead or Alive, Bananarama, Mel and Kim, Sinitta, Rick Astley, Kylie Minogue, Brother Beyond, Jason Donovan, Donna Summer, Sonia, Big Fun, Cliff Richard, Sybil and SLAMM; currently working with Mike Stock writing and/or producing artists incl: Jocelyn Brown, Kym Mazelle and Darren Day; charity records incl: Let it Be (Ferry Aid), Help (Comic Relief), Let's All Chant (Help a London Child), Ferry Cross the Mersey (Mersey Aid), Do They Know It's Christmas? (Ethiopia Famine Appeal), You've Got A Friend (Childline); *Awards* BPI Best British Producers 1988; Music Week Top Producers for: Singles (1st) and Albums (3rd) 1987, Singles (1st) and Albums (1st) 1988 and 1989; Ivor Novello Awards (UK): Songwriters of the Year 1987, 1988 and 1989, Writers of Most Performed Works 1987, 1988 and 1989; BMI Awards (USA) Writers of Most Performed Works 1987, 1988 and 1989; Jasrac Awards (Japan) and Cash Awards (Hong Kong) Writers of Most Performed Foreign Works 1989; *Recreations* motor racing, gourmet, computers; *Style*— Matt Aitken, Esq; ✉ c/o Love This Records, 100 House, 100 Union Street, London SE1 0NL (☎ 0171 928 4444)

AITKEN, Michael William (Mike); s of Matthew Alastair Aitken, and Joan Elizabeth, *née* Graham; *b* 9 July 1952; *Educ* Royal HS Edinburgh, Macalester Coll St Paul Minnesota, Univ of Stirling (MA); *m* 27 March 1978, (Mary) Elaine, da of late Henry Rutherford; 1 s (Nicholas Henry b 6 Oct 1983); *Career* The Scotsman: joined as grad trainee 1974, NCTJ cert, football corr 1976–90 (covered World Cup finals in Argentina 1978, Spain 1982, Mexico 1986, Italy 1990 and Euro Cup and championships), chief sports writer 1990– (covered Olympics, Wimbledon, Ryder Cup, Five Nations etc), specialising in golf 1994–; Regnl Sports Writer of the Yr Br Sports Journalism Awards 1992 and 1995, commended Scottish Press Awards 1996; memb: Scottish Football Writers' Assoc, Sports Writers' Assoc of GB; *Books* When Will We See Your Like Again (1977), Glorious Hearts (1986), The Sandy Jardine Story (1987), Heart to Heart (1988); *Recreations* golf, swimming, tennis, reading, home computing, listening to the music of Brian Wilson; *Clubs* Ratho Park Golf; *Style*— Mike Aitken, Esq; ✉ The Scotsman, 20 North Bridge, Edinburgh EH1 1YT

AITKEN, Hon Lady (Penelope); *née* Maffey; MBE (1955), JP, WRVS Long Service Medal; da of 1 Baron Rugby, GCMG, KCB, KCVO, CSI, CIE (d 1969); *b* 2 Dec 1910; *m* 1939, Sir William Aitken, KBE, MP (d 1964), s of Joseph Aitken, bro to first Lord Beaverbrook; 1 s (Jonathan Aitken, MP, *qv*), 1 da (Maria Aitken, actress, *qv*); *Style*— The Hon Lady Aitken, MBE, JP; ✉ 2 North Court, Gt Peter Street, London SW1P 3LL (☎ 0171 222 44166)

AITMAN, David Charles; s of Gabriel Aitman, and Irene Bertha, *née* Polack; *b* 11 April 1956; *Educ* Clifton, Univ of Sheffield (BA); *m* 26 March 1983, Marianne Lucille, da of Edward Atherton; 1 s (Marcus), 2 da (Lauren, Polly); *Career* admitted slr 1982; ptnr Denton Hall (formerly Denton Hall Burgin & Warrens) 1988–, dir Bertelsmann UK Ltd; memb Law Soc; LRAM; *Books* Butterworth's Encyclopaedia of Competition Law (chapter on intellectual property licensing, 1991), Practical Intellectual Property (chapter on competition law), Yearbook of Media Law (chapter on competition law); *Recreations* tennis, wind surfing, music (performing and concert going); *Style*— David Aitman, Esq; ✉ Denton Hall, 5 Chancery Lane, Clifford's Inn, London EC4A 1BU (☎ 0171 320 6332)

AITON, Keith Martyn Hamilton; s of Alexander Hamilton Aiton, and Margaret Helen Elizabeth, *née* Martyn; *b* 14 Sept 1958; *Educ* Nottingham HS, Sidney Sussex Coll Cambridge; *children* 1 da (Laura Margaret b 17 Jan 1995), 1 s (Alexander Cameron Hamilton b 18 April 1996); *Career* croquet player 1980–; played for Cambridge in Varsity Match 1980, 1981 and 1982 (capt); team player Nottingham Croquet Club 1983– (joined 1981); played Scotland Home Internationals 1983–85 and 1987–90 (capt 1990); championships incl: British Men's (winner 1987 and 1989), British Open (second 1983, third 1988), President's Cup (third 1984 and 1986), Chairman's Salver (winner 1983); coach: of GB Under 21 Squad 1988–92, of winning GB Team for matches v Aust and NZ 1990 and v Aust, NZ and USA 1993 and 1996; qualified as slr 1989, tax conslt Price Waterhouse Nottingham 1990–96, tax mangr Pannell Kerr Forster 1996–; memb Inst of Taxation 1992; *Recreations* chess, golf, Greek mathematics; *Style*— Keith Aiton, Esq; ✉ The Coach House, Church Hill, Old Bilsthorpe, Newark, Notts NG22 8RU

AKABUSI, Kriss Kezie Uche-Chukwu Duru; MBE (1991); s of Daniel Kambi Duru Akabusi, and Clara, *née* Adams; *b* 28 Nov 1958; *Educ* Edmonton Co Comp; *m* 2 April 1982, Monika, da of Heinrich Bernard Udhöfer; 2 da (Ashanti b 19 June 1984, Shakira b 20 Oct 1987); *Career* Army: jr signalman 1975, signalman 1976 (data telegraphist), Lance Corpl (AIPT) 1978, Corpl (AITP) 1980, Sgt SI APTC 1981, Staff Sgt SSI APTC 1985, WOII (QMSI) APTC 1988; athlete: Bronze medal 4 x 400m relay World Championships 1983, Silver medal 4 x 400m relay Olympic Games 1984, UK 400m champion 1984, capt Eng Athletics Team v USA 1985, Gold medal 4 x 400m relay Euro Championships and Cwlth Games 1986, finalist 400m hurdles and Silver medal 4 x 400m relay World Championships 1987, UK 400m hurdles champion 1987 and 1992, finalist 400m hurdles Olympic Games 1988, AAA champion 400m 1988, Gold medal 400m hurdles Euro Championships and Cwlth Games 1990, Gold medal 4 x 400m relay Euro Championships 1990, Gold medal 4 x 400m relay and Bronze medal 400m hurdles World Championships Tokyo 1991, Bronze medals 400m hurdles and 4 x 400m relay Olympic Games 1992, Gold medal 4 x 400m relay Euro Cup 1993; Br record holder 400m hurdles 1990; involved with: Cwlth Games Appeal 1985–86, Olympic Games Appeal 1986–88; British Athletics Writers' Athlete of the Year 1991; *Clubs* Team Solent Athletics; *Style*— Kriss Akabusi, Esq, MBE

AKEHURST, Gen Sir John Bryan; KCB (1984), CBE (1976); s of Geoffrey Akehurst, and Doris Akehurst; *b* 12 Feb 1930; *Educ* Cranbrook Sch, RMA Sandhurst; *m* 1955, Shirley Ann, er da of Maj W G Webb, MBE; 1 s, 1 da (both decd); *Career* formerly with Northamptonshire Regt and Malay Regt, cmd 2 Royal Anglian Regt 1968–70, DS IDC 1970–72, Cdr Dhofar Bde Sultan of Oman's Armed Forces 1974–76, Dep Mil Sec (A) MOD 1976–79, GOC Armd Div BAOR 1979–82, Cmdt Staff Coll Camberley 1982–83 (instr 1966–68 and 1972–74), cmd UK Field Army and inspr gen TA 1984–87, Dep Supreme Allied Cdr Europe 1987–90, Col The Royal Anglian Regt 1986–91, chm Cncl TA&VRA 1990–95; govr Harrow Sch 1982– (chm of Govrs 1991–); cmmr Cwlth War Graves Cmmn 1993–; Order of Oman (Third Class Mil) 1976; *Books* We Won a War (1982); *Recreations* golf, fly fishing; *Clubs* Army and Navy, Lord's Taverners; *Style*— Gen Sir John Akehurst, KCB, CBE; ✉ 46 Vicarage Street, Warminster, Wiltshire BA12 8JF

AKENHEAD, Robert; QC (1989); s of Lt-Col Edmund Akenhead, TD (d 1990), and Angela Miriam, *née* Cullen; *b* 15 Sept 1949; *Educ* Rugby, Univ of Exeter (LLB); *m* 9 Dec 1972, Elizabeth Anne, da of Capt Frederick Hume Jackson, CMG, OBE, of Tonbridge, Kent; 1 s (Edmund b 1983), 3 da (Eleanor b 1978, Isobel b 1980, Rosalind b 1985); *Career* called to the Bar Inner Temple 1972, recorder of the Crown Court 1994– (asst recorder 1991); examiner Diocese of Canterbury 1991; *Books* Site Investigation and the Law (with J Cottington, 1984); *Recreations* cricket, skiing, theatre; *Style*— Robert Akenhead, Esq, QC; ✉ 1 Atkin Building, Gray's Inn, London WC1R 5BQ (☎ 0171 404 0102, fax 0171 405 7456, telex 298623 HUDSON)

AKERS, Colin Arthur; s of Lt Arthur William Akers, JP, RNVR (d 1985), of the Bryn, Yewlands, Hoddesdon, Herts, and Nora Edith, *née* Archer (d 1983); *b* 29 Sept 1931; *Educ* Canford, University Coll Oxford; *m* 8 April 1978, Jean, da of Albert Mills (d 1983), of Cheshire; *Career* Nat Serv 1950–52, Gunner tech asst RA Korean War 1951–52; md: EJ Woollard Ltd (horticultural suppliers) 1968–81 (joined 1953), Selfridges Ltd (sr wine conslt) 1984–; dir Cheshunt Building Soc 1975–91; local dir Bristol & West Building Soc 1992–93; former chm Cheshunt & Waltham Cross C of C; vice pres: Herts LTA, Herts CHA; hon life memb Broxbourne Sports Club (formerly chm), memb Herts CCC, 105 Caps Herts Co Hockey XI (capt 1958–61); chm Herts Fine Wine Soc 1991–93 and 1995–; *Recreations* hockey, wine-tasting, classical music; *Clubs* Les Compagnons du Beaujolais, Wine and Spirit Trade; *Style*— Colin Akers, Esq; ✉ The Fernery, 110 Bengeo Street, Bengeo, Hertford, Herts SG14 3EX (☎ 01992 587300); Selfridges Ltd, 400 Oxford Street, London W1 (direct ☎ 0171 318 3730, fax 0171 491 1880)

AKERS-DOUGLAS, Francis Alexander Moreton (Frank); s of Anthony George Akers-Douglas (d 1991), and Dorothy Louise, *née* Gage; *b* 23 Sept 1948; *Educ* Eton, Brown Univ; *m* 1974, Hon Julian Mary, eld da of 2 Baron Bruntisfield, *qv*; 2 s (Joseph Michael Aretas b 1979, James George b 1989); *Career* Binder Hamlyn: articled clerk 1967, ptnr 1978–, head Private Client Servs 1980–; memb: Tax Faculty ICAEW, Soc of Trust and Estate Practitioners 1993; FCA 1971; *Books* Butterworths: Self Assessment and Simplification (1994); *Recreations* tennis, cricket, woodlands management; *Style*— Frank Akers-Douglas, Esq; ✉ Binder Hamlyn, 17 Lansdowne Road, Croydon CR9 2PL (☎ 0181 666 9723, fax 0181 666 9090, car 0850 968703)

AKERS-JONES, Sir David; KBE (1985), CMG (1978); s of Walter George Jones, and late Dorothy, *née* Akers; *b* 14 April 1927; *Educ* Worthing HS, Brasenose Coll Oxford (MA); *m* 8 Sept 1951, Jane, da of Capt Sir Frank Todd Spickernell, KBE, CB, CVO, DSO (d 1959), and Amice Ivy Delves Broughton (d 1974); 1 s (decd), 1 da; *Career* with Br India Steam Navigation Co 1945–49, Malayan Civil Serv 1954–57; Hong Kong Civil Serv: sec for New Territories 1973–81, sec for City and New Territories Admin 1981–83, sec for dist admin 1983–85, chief sec 1985–86, actg govr 1986–87, advsr to Govr 1987,

Hong Kong affrs advsr to China 1993–; chm: Hong Kong Housing Authy 1988–93, National Mutual Insurance Asia Ltd, Global Asset Management Hong Kong, WWF Hong Kong 1986–94, Cncl Australian Nat Gallery; dir: Sime Darby Hong Kong, Hysan Development Co Ltd, The China Investment Co; vice chm CNT Group Hong Kong; pres Outward Bound Tst Hong Kong 1986–96, hon pres Hong Kong Mountaineering Union; hon vice pres: Hong Kong Girl Guide Assoc, Scout Assoc of Hong Kong; vice patron Hong Kong Football Assoc; Hon DCL Univ of Kent 1987, Hon LLD Chinese Univ of Hong Kong 1988, Hon DSSc City Univ of Hong Kong 1993; *Recreations* painting, gardening, walking, music; *Clubs* Athenaeum, Royal Over-Seas League, Hong Kong, Kowloon, Dynasty, The China; *Style—* Sir David Akers-Jones, KBE, CMG; ✉ Dragon View, Tsing Lung Tau, New Territories, Hong Kong (☎ 00 852 2491 9319, fax 00 852 2491 1300)

AKHTAR, Prof Muhammad; s of Muhammad Azeem Chaudhry; *b* 23 Feb 1933; *Educ* Punjab Univ Pakistan (MSc), Imp Coll Univ of London (PhD, DIC); *m* 3 Aug 1963, Monika E, *née* Schurmann; 2 s (Marcus, Daniel); *Career* res scientist Res Inst for Med and Chemistry Cambridge USA 1959–63; Univ of Southampton: lectr 1963–, reader then sr lectr, chm Sch of Biochemical and Physiological Sciences 1983–87, prof of biochemistry 1978–, head Dept of Biochemistry 1978–93, chm Inst of Biomolecular Sciences 1989–91; dir SERC Centre for Molecular Recognition 1990–94; author of articles in learned jls; founding fell Third World Acad of Sci 1984 (treas 1993–); FRS (memb Cncl 1983–85); memb: Royal Soc of Chemistry, American Chem Soc, Biochemical Soc; award of Sitara-I-Imtiaz by Govt of Pakistan 1981, Flintoff medal 1993; *Style—* Prof Muhammad Akhtar, FRS; ✉ Department of Biochemistry, The University of Southampton, Bassett Crescent East, Southampton SO16 7PX (☎ 01703 594323/594338)

AKHURST, Julie; da of Philip Akhurst (d 1979), and Valerie, *née* Pearcey; *b* 19 Dec 1963; *Educ* Univ of Oxford (Abbots scholar, Coll scholar, MA); *Career* assoc ed Reader's Digest Magazine 1988–90, features ed Take A Break 1990–92, launch ed That's Life! Magazine (Sydney, Australia) 1993–95, ed Best 1995–; *Recreations* writing horror fiction, collecting children's books; *Style—* Ms Julie Akhurst; ✉ Best Magazine, Gruner & Jahr of the UK, Portland House, Stag Place, London SW1E 5AU (☎ 0171 245 8870, fax 0171 245 8825)

AKISTER, (Roy) Edward; s of Aaron Akister (d 1975), of Lindale in Furness, Cumbria, and Jennie, *née* Shaw (d 1974); *b* 22 Oct 1933; *Educ* The Friends' Sch Lancaster, Pinewood Students Unit Berks, Owens Coll Univ of Manchester; *children* 1 s (Simeon James b 15 April 1964), 2 da (Louise b 7 Feb 1962, Victoria b 26 Aug 1972); *Career* aviation mangr Marchwiel Plant and Engrg 1970–79, site mangr McAlpine (civil engrg) 1979–85, sr ptnr Easthope Trading Co Ltd (design and devpt) 1985–90, ptnr Abc Partnership (design and build) 1990–; former ed of 244 magazine; chm: Shropshire and Dist Br Inst of Mgmnt 1978–79, Shropshire Lib Party 1981–84; MBIM, MIIM; *Recreations* bee-keeping, painting, shooting, Guild of One Name Studies, walking; *Clubs* Horsfall Museum (Manchester); *Style—* Edward Akister, Esq; ✉ Easthope Coppice, Bridge Bank, Iron-Bridge, Shropshire; Abc Partnership, Bridge Road, Iron-Bridge, Shropshire (☎ 01952 432101)

AKKER, John Richard; s of Alec Akker (d 1964), and Ruby, *née* Bryant (d 1973); *b* 6 May 1943; *Educ* S W Essex Tech Coll, Ruskin Coll Oxford (L C White scholar, DipEcon), Univ of York (BA), Cranfield Mgmnt Sch (various mgmnt courses); *m* Gillian Kulwicki; 1 s (Michael b 27 Nov 1979), 2 da (Caroline b 12 Oct 1973, Harriet b 7 Feb 1975); *Career* dep local govt offr NALGO 1971–73 (asst nat offr 1969–71), dep gen sec AUT 1977–94 (asst gen sec 1973–77), gen sec NATFHE (univ and coll lectrs union) 1994–; Churchill fell 1976; *Recreations* sailing, motor sport, growing vegetables; *Clubs* National Liberal; *Style—* John Akker, Esq; ✉ Flat 5, 64–68 Princelet Street, London E1 5LP (☎ and fax 0171 247 5595); National Association of Teachers in Further and Higher Education, 27 Britannia Street, London WC1X 9JP (☎ 0171 837 3636, fax 0171 278 3177)

AL-AMRI, HE Dr Hussein Abdullah; yst s of 'Abd Allah ben Al-'Al-Hussein Al-'Amri, judge and scholar; *b* 28 April 1944, Sana'a; *Educ* Faculty of Arts Univ of Damascus, Univ of Cambridge, Univ of Durham (PhD); *Career* Yemeni diplomat; Miny of Foreign Affrs: joined 1964, dep min 1975–79, min for foreign affrs 1979–83; dir PM's Office 1983–84, min of educn 1984–86, min of agriculture and fisheries 1986–93, MP and chm Culture and Educn Ctee of Parl (Majilis al-niyab) 1988–93, ambass to the Ct of St James's 1995–; prof of modern Yemen and Arab history Univ of Sana'a 1994– (joined Dept 1983); *Books* Yemen and the Western World (Arabic trans of Eric Macro's work, 2 edn 1978), The Yemeni Manuscripts of the Sources of Yemen Culture at the British Library (1980), Hundred Years of Yemen History (2nd edn 1988); various studies and annotations; *Style—* HE Dr Hussein Abdullah Al-Amri; ✉ Embassy of the Republic of Yemen, 57 Cromwell Road, London SW7 2ED (☎ 0171 584 6607, fax 0171 589 3350)

AL AZMEH, Prof Aziz; s of Ahmad Malak Azmeh, of Damascus, Syria, and Salma Naboulsi; *b* 23 July 1947; *Educ* Brummana HS Lebanon, Tübingen (MA), Univ of Oxford (DPhil); *m* 31 Aug 1979, Dr Kasturi Sen, da of Keshab Chandra Sen; 1 s (Omar b 27 Dec 1986); *Career* prof of Islamic studies Univ of Exeter 1985–96, author of numerous articles on Islam; radio and TV broadcaster on Islamic and Arabic affrs and conslt to various bodies; chm UK Section Arab Human Rights Orgn 1987; memb: Arab Club of GB, Br Soc Middle Eastern Studies, Medieval Soc of America, Nat Conf of Univ Profs, Arab Philosophical Assoc, Arab Writers' Union, Lesh Beirut; fell: Nuffield Fndn 1993–94, Inst for Advanced Studies Berlin 1994–95 and 1996–; awarded Republican Order of Merit (Tunisia) 1993; *Books* Ibn Khaldun in Modern Scholarship (1981), Ibn Khaldun (1982), Historical Writing and Historical Knowledge (Arabic, 1983), Arabic Thought and Islamic Societies (1986), The Politics and History of Heritage (Arabic, 1987), Arabs and Barbarians (Arabic, 1990), Secularism in Modern Arab Life and Thought (Arabic, 1991), Islams and Mordernities (1993), Muslim Kingship (1996), Religion and Society in Modern Arab History (Arabic, 1996); *Style—* Prof Aziz Al Azmeh; ✉ Wissenschaftskolleg zu Berlin, Wallotstrasse 19, D-14193 Berlin, Germany (☎ 00 49 30 89001 264, fax 00 49 30 89001 300)

AL-DUWAISAN, HE Khaled; Hon GCVO; *b* 15 Aug 1946; *Educ* Cairo Univ (BA), Univ of Kuwait (business admin dipl); *m*; 2 c; *Career* Kuwaiti diplomat; researcher Miny of Foreign Affairs 1970–71, diplomatic attaché 1971–72, third sec 1972–74, second sec 1974–76, joined Embassy of Kuwait in Washington DC 1975, first sec 1976–80, counseller 1980–84, ambass extraordinary and plenipotentiary to the Netherlands 1984–90, appointed non-resident ambass to Romania 1988, ambass to the Ct of St James's 1993–; non-resident ambass: Denmark, Norway and Sweden 1994–95, Republic of Ireland 1995–; coordinator with UN during creation of the demilitarised zone and with UN ctee for return of missing and stolen property 1992; memb: IOD, RIIA; *Clubs* Queen's Tennis; *Style—* HE Mr Khaled Al-Duwaisan, GCVO; ✉ Embassy of the State of Kuwait, 2 Albert Gate, London SW1X 7JU (☎ 0171 590 3400)

AL-KHALIFA, HE Sheikh Abdulaziz bin Mubarak; *b* 10 Oct 1962; *Educ* Wellington, Newbury Coll Berks (HND), American Univ Sch of Int Serv Washington DC (BA Int Affrs), Harvard Univ Cambridge Massachusetts; *m*; *Career* Bahrainian diplomat; HH The PM's Court Bahrain: researcher for political and economic affrs Directorate of Info and Follow Up 1987–90, asst dir of info and follow up 1990–94, actg dir of admin and PR 1994–96; ambass of the State of Bahrain to the Ct of St James's (concurrently non-resident ambass to the Kingdom of Denmark and to Ireland) 1996–; *Style—* HE Sheikh Abdulaziz bin Mubarak Al-Khalifa; ✉ Embassy of the State of Bahrain, 98 Gloucester Road, London SW7 4AU (☎ 0171 370 5132/3, fax 0171 370 7773)

ALAGIAH, George Maxwell; *b* 22 Nov 1955, Sri Lanka; *Educ* St John's Coll Southsea, Univ of Durham; *m*; 2 s; *Career* BBC: joined 1989, foreign affrs corr 1989–94, Southern Africa corr 1995–; BBC assignments incl news reports/documentaries on: trade in human organs India, street children Brazil, civil war in Liberia, Earth Summit Rio, famine and civil war in Somalia, persecution of Kurds in Iraq, effects on developing countries of GATT Agreement, ethnic conflict in Burundi, civil war in Afghanistan, genocide in Rwanda, human rights violations in Ethiopia, war in Liberia; *Awards* Monte Carlo TV Festival and RTS awards for Somalia reports 1993, BAFTA commendation for Newsnight Kurdistan reports 1994, Amnesty International Press Awards Journalist of the Year 1994, Bdcasting Press Guild Journalist of the Year 1994, Bayeux War Reporting Award 1994, 1995 and 1996, James Cameron Memorial Tst Award 1995, One World Bdcasting Tst TV News Premier Award 1995, Asian Film and TV Acad Best TV Journalist 1995; *Style—* George Alagiah, Esq; ✉ BBC, 1 Park Road, Richmond 2092, Johannesburg, South Africa (☎ 00 27 11 482 2305, fax 00 27 11 482 3400); c/o Foreign Desk, BBC TV News, BBC Television Centre, Wood Lane, London W12 7RJ

ALANBROOKE, 3 Viscount (UK 1946); Alan Victor Harold Brooke; s of 1 Viscount Alanbrooke, KG, GCB, OM, GCVO, DSO (d 1963), and his 2 w, Benita Blanche (d 1968), da of Sir Harold Pelly, 4 Bt, JP, and wid of Sir Thomas Lees, 2 Bt; suc half-bro, 2 Viscount, 1972; *b* 24 Nov 1932; *Educ* Harrow, Bristol Univ (BEd); *Heir* None; *Career* served Army 1952–72, Germany, Korea, Malaya, UK, Capt RA ret; qualified teacher 1975; lectr for MOD Princess Marina Coll Arborfield 1978–; hon pres Salisbury and Dist Branch The 1940 Dunkirk Veterans 1970; The UK Veterans of King Leopold III: patron 1977–87, hon pres 1987–; *Recreations* private flying, radio control model aircraft, fencing, walking round the edge of Cornwall, restoring property ravaged by tenants; *Style—* The Rt Hon the Viscount Alanbrooke

ALBARN, Damon; *b* 23 March 1968; *Career* singer; memb Blur 1990–; 8 top twenty singles: There's No Other Way, Girls & Boys, To The End, Parklife, End Of A Century, Country House, The Universal, Stereotypes; albums: Leisure (UK no 7, Gold), Modern Life Is Rubbish (UK no 15, Gold), Parklife (UK no 1, 4 x Platinum) 1994, The Great Escape (UK no 1, Triple Platinum) 1995; videos: Starshaped, Showtime (1995); awards: Best Band, Best Album, Best Video and Best Single (all for Parklife) BRIT Awards 1995, jt winner Songwriter of the Year Ivor Novello Awards 1996; *Style—* Damon Albarn; ✉ c/o Kate Hanson, CMO Management International Ltd, Unit 32, Ransomes Dock, 35–37 Parkgate Road, London SW11 4NP (☎ 0171 228 4000)

ALBEMARLE, Countess of; Dame Diana Cicely; DBE (1956); da of Maj John Grove; *b* 6 Aug 1909; *Educ* Sherborne Sch for Girls; *m* 1931, as his 2 w, 9 Earl of Albemarle, MC (d 1979); 1 da (Lady Anne-Louise Hamilton-Dalrymple); *Career* cnclir Wayland Rural DC Norfolk 1935–46, Norfolk Co organiser WVS 1939–44; chm: Exec Ctee Nat Fedn of Women's Insts 1946–51, Devpt Cmmn 1948–74, Departmental Ctee on Youth Serv 1958–60, Nat Youth Employment Cncl 1962–68, The Drama Bd 1964–78; vice chm Br Cncl 1959–74; memb: Arts Cncl 1951, Royal Cmmn on Civil Serv 1954, UGC 1956–70, Standing Cmmn on Museums and Galleries 1958–71, Youth Devpt Cncl 1960–68, Harkness Fellowship Ctee of Award 1963–69, Cncl Univ of E Anglia 1964–72, English Local Govt Boundary Cmmn 1971–77; life tstee Carnegie UK Tst (chm 1977–82); tstee: The Observer until 1977, Glyndebourne Arts Tst 1968–80; Hon DLitt Reading 1959, Hon DCL Oxon 1960, Hon LLD London 1960; *Style—* The Rt Hon the Countess of Albemarle, DBE; ✉ Seymours, Melton, Woodbridge, Suffolk (☎ 01394 382151)

ALBEMARLE, 10 Earl of (E 1696); Rufus Arnold Alexis Keppel; also Baron Ashford and Viscount Bury (both E 1696); s of Viscount Bury (d 1968, eld s of 9 E of Albemarle, MC) and his 2 w, Marina, da of late Lt Cdr Count Serge Orloff-Davidoff, RNVR, and late Hon Elisabeth, *née* Scott-Ellis, 2 da of 8 Baron Howard de Walden; *b* 16 July 1965; *Heir* cousin Crispian Walter John Keppel; *Style—* The Rt Hon the Earl of Albemarle; ✉ Piazza di Bellosguardo 10, Florence 50124, Italy; 20A Pembroke Sq, London W8 6PA

ALBERGE, Dalya; da of Maurice Ernest, and Ella, Alberge; *b* 29 Aug 1959; *Educ* S Hampstead HS, Trinity Coll of Music London (GTCL), Univ of Keele (MA); *Career* asst ed Brevet Publishing magazines 1981–83, freelance journalist 1983, asst ed Classical Music Magazine 1984–86, art market corr and arts writer The Independent 1986–94, arts corr The Times 1994–; memb Educn Advsy Bd Dulwich Picture Gallery 1991–, Arts Cncl adjudicator British Gas Working for Cities public art award 1992–93; *Recreations* the arts; *Style—* Miss Dalya Alberge; ✉ The Times, 1 Pennington Street, London E1 9XN (☎ 0171 782 5950, fax 0171 782 5959)

ALBERY, Ian Bronson; s of Sir Donald Arthur Rolleston Albery (d 1988), and Ruby Gilchrist, *née* Macgilchrist (d 1956); Ian Albery is the fifth generation in the theatre and both f (Sir Donald Albery) and gf (Sir Bronson Albery) as well as step ggf (Sir Charles Wyndham) were all knighted for servs to the theatre; *b* 21 Sept 1936; *Educ* Stowe, Lycée de Briançon France; *m* 1, 1966 (m dis 1985), Barbara Yuling, *née* Lee; 2 s (Wyndham b 1968, Bronson b 1971); 1 da (Caitlin b 1985), by Jenny Beavan; *Career* Soc of W End Theatres (SWET): exec 1965–89, pres 1977–79, vice pres 1979–82; tstee Theatres Tst 1977–96; memb: Drama Panel Arts Cncl of GB 1974–76, Drama and Dance Panel Br Cncl 1978–88; dep chm London Festival Ballet Ltd/English National Ballet 1984–90, dir Ticketmaster Ltd 1985–92, chm and md Donmar Ltd 1986–, md The Wyndham Theatres Ltd and associated companies 1978–87, chief exec Sadler's Wells Tst Ltd 1994–; prodr or co-prodr of over 50 West End prodns; prodr and md: Theatre of Comedy Co Ltd 1987–90, Wyndham Ltd 1987–; *Clubs* Garrick; *Style—* Ian B Albery, Esq; ✉ 12 Granville Mansions, Shepherds Bush Green, London W12 8QA; Wyndham Ltd, 54 Cavell St, Whitechapel, London E1 2HP (☎ 0171 790 2007, fax 0171 790 6634)

ALBU, Sir George; 3 Bt (UK 1912), of Grosvenor Place, City of Westminster, and Richmond, Province of Natal, Repub of S Africa; s of Sir George Werner Albu, 2 Bt (d 1963); *b* 5 June 1944; *Educ* Michaelhouse S Africa, Cedara Agric Coll; *m* 23 April 1969, Joan Valerie, da of late Malcolm Millar, of Weybridge, Surrey; 2 da (Camilla Jane b 22 Aug 1972, Victoria Mary b 14 Jan 1976); *Heir* none; *Career* trooper Imperial Light Horse Regt 1963, rifleman Commandos 1989; gen investor; *Recreations* horse racing (flat), motor racing; *Clubs* Victoria (Pietermaritzburg, Natal, SA), Richmond Country (SA), Natal; *Style—* Sir George Albu, Bt; ✉ Glen Hamish, PO Box 62, Richmond 3780, Natal, S Africa (☎ 00 27 3322 2587)

ALBUM, Edward Jonathan Corcos; s of Harry Album (d 1988), of London N3, and Matilda, *née* Corcos; *b* 8 Sept 1936; *Educ* Emanuel Sch, ChCh Oxford (MA); *m* 14 July 1970, Elizabeth Ann, da of Lancelot Ezra, of Belsize Rd, London NW6; 1 s (Richard b 1974), 1 da (Victoria b 1977); *Career* Capt Res TA 1962–70; slr; dir: Macsteel International UK Ltd, Leopold Lazarus Ltd, The London Metal & Ore Co Ltd, LMO Investments Ltd; chm Sanderling Ltd; tstee Settle & Carlisle Railway Tst; Liveryman Worshipful Co of Basketmakers; *Recreations* military history, ornithology, railway preservation; *Clubs* Sir Walter Scott (Edinburgh), Army & Navy, AC Owners'; *Style—* Edward Album, Esq; ✉ Sanderling House, High St, Cley, Norfolk (☎ 01263 740810); 47 Lyndale Ave, London NW2 2QB (☎ 0171 431 2942)

ALBURY, Simon Albert; s of Cyril Lyon Albury (d 1971), and Eileen Palmer, *née* Lloyd-Jones (d 1986); *b* 9 Feb 1944; *Educ* West House Sch Birmingham, Clifton Coll, Univ of Nottingham (BA), Brandeis Univ, Univ of Sussex (MA); *m* 14 Jan 1989, Phillida Bartels-Ellis; 1 s (David Kwamena Bartels b 25 March 1989); *Career* info offr Government Social Survey 1967, res assoc American Psychological Assoc project on Scientific Info Exchange in Psychology 1968, reporter World in Action Granada

Television 1969, with BBC Current Affrs Gp 1969–73, BBC Open Univ 1973–74, sr prodr Granada Television (progs incl World in Action, What the Papers Say, End of Empire, The Outrageous Millie Jackson) 1974–89, dir Campaign for Quality Television 1989–90; dir of public affrs: MAI Broadcasting 1994–95 (dir of strategy 1990), Meridian Broadcasting 1991– (dir of strategy 1991), MAI Media 1995–96, United Broadcasting and Entertainment 1996–; tstee Meridian Broadcasting Charitable Tst 1993–; presenter (as Sam Scott) gospel music show Hallelujah (Capital Radio) 1973–75; *Recreations* opera, gospel music and jazz; *Style*— Simon Albury, Esq; ✉ United Broadcasting and Entertainment, Ludgate House, 245 Blackfriars Road, London SE1 9UY (☎ 0171 579 4412, fax 0171 579 4435)

ALCOCK, Prof Leslie; OBE (1991); s of Philip John Alcock, and Mary Ethel, *née* Bagley; *b* 24 April 1925; *Educ* Manchester GS, Brasenose Coll Oxford (BA, MA); *m* 29 July 1950, Elizabeth Annie, da of Robert Blair; 1 s (John b 1960), 1 da (Penelope b 1957); *Career* WWII Gurkha Rifles 1943–47; supt of exploration and excavation Dept of Archaeology Govt of Pakistan 1950–52, curator Leeds City Museums 1952–53; prof of archaeology: Univ Coll Cardiff (also lectr and reader) 1953–73, Univ of Glasgow 1973–90 (hon professorial res fell 1990–); pres: Cambrian Archaeological Assoc 1982, Soc of Antiquaries of Scotland 1984–87; tstee Nat Museum of Antiquities of Scotland 1973–85, memb Ancient Monuments Bd Scotland 1974–90; cmmr RC Ancient Monuments: Scotland 1977–92, Wales 1986–90; FSA 1957, FRHistS 1969, FRSE 1976–87, Hon FSAScot 1994; *Books* Dinas Powys (1963), Arthur's Britain (1971), By South Cadbury is that Camelot (1972), Economy Society and Warfare (1987), Cadbury Castle, Somerset; the early medieval archaeology (1994); *Recreations* music, landscape; *Style*— Prof Leslie Alcock, OBE; ✉ 29 Hamilton Drive, Glasgow G12 8DN (☎ 0141 339 7123)

ALCOCK, Air Chief Marshal Sir Michael; GCB (1996, CB 1989), KBE (1992); *b* 11 July 1936; *Educ* Cathedral HS Bombay, Copthorne Sch Sussex, Victoria Coll Jersey; *m* 1965, Pauline; 2 da; *Career* student apprentice RAE Farnborough, joined RAF as graduate engr Bomber Cmd Devpt Unit 1958, Tech Coll Henlow, various engrg appts on V-bombers RAF Wyton, Goose Bay, Wittering and Finningley until 1967, i/c engrg aspects of Vulcan aircraft HQ Bomber Cmd 1967–69, Sqn Ldr 1970, RAF Staff Coll 1970, personal staff offr to DG Engrg (RAF) 1971–73, Wing Cdr 1973, OC Engrg Wing RAF Coningsby (Phantoms) 1973–75, Air Warfare Course RAF Coll Cranwell 1975, Gp Capt 1975, OC No 23 Maintenance Unit RAF Aldergrove N Ireland 1975–77, Gp Capt Plans HQ Support Cmd Andover then Brampton 1977–79, Air Cdre 1979, Dir of Trg (Ground) 1979–81, Dep Cmdt RAF Staff Coll Bracknell 1981–84, RCDS 1984, Air Vice-Marshal 1984, DG Communications/Info Systems and Orgn 1985–88, Air Offr Engrg and Supply HQ Strike Cmd 1988–91, Air Marshal 1991, Chief of Logistic Support and Chief Engr (RAF) 1991–93, Air Chief Marshal and memb Air Force Bd 1993 (first Ground Branch offr to reach 4-star rank), Air Memb for Supply and Orgn 1993–94, AOC-in-C, Air Memb for Logistics and Chief Engr 1994–96, ret; dir Cygnae Ltd; pres: RAF Golfing Assoc, Assoc of Air Warfare and Flying Colls, RAF Model Aircraft Assoc; Hon DSc Cranfield 1994; FEng 1995, FIMechE, FRAeS; *Recreations* golf; *Style*— Air Chief Marshal Sir Michael Alcock, GCB, KBE, FEng; ✉ c/o National Westminster Bank, PO Box 61, 2 Alexandra Road, Farnborough, Hants GU14 6YR

ALDCROFT, Prof Derek Howard; s of Leslie Howard Aldcroft, and Freda, *née* Wallen; *b* 25 Oct 1936; *Educ* Univ of Manchester (BA (Econ), PhD); *Career* lectr in economic history Univ of Leicester and Univ of Glasgow 1960–71; prof of economic history: Univ of Sidney 1973–76, Univ of Leicester 1976–94 (reader 1971–73); research prof in economic history Manchester Metropolitan Univ 1994–; visiting prof Anglia Poly Univ 1993–; memb Economic History Soc; *Books include* From Versailles to Wall Street (1977), The European Economy 1914–90 (1993), Full Employment: The Elusive Goal (1984), The British Economy 1920–51 (1986), Economic Change in Eastern Europe since 1918 (with Steven Morewood, 1995); *Recreations* tennis, swimming, the Stock Exchange and gardening; *Style*— Prof Derek Aldcroft; ✉ Department of Economics and Economic History, Manchester Metropolitan University, Manchester M13 9PL (☎ 0161 247 6494)

ALDENHAM (AND HUNSDON OF HUNSDON), 6 (and 4) Baron (UK 1896 and 1923 respectively); Vicary Tyser Gibbs; s of 5 Baron Aldenham and 3 Baron Hunsdon of Hunsdon (d 1986); *b* 9 June 1948; *Educ* Eton, Oriel Coll Oxford, RAC Cirencester; *m* 16 May 1980, Josephine Nicola, er da of John Richmond Fell, of Lower Bourne, Farnham, Surrey; 2 s (Hon Humphrey William Fell b 31 Jan 1989, Hon Thomas Antony John b 13 Oct 1992), 1 da (Hon Jessica Juliet Mary b 1984); *Heir* s, Hon Humphrey William Fell Gibbs b 31 Jan 1989; *Career* dir: Hundred Oaks Co 1978–, Montclare Shipping Co 1986–; chm Herts & Middx CLA 1995–; Liveryman, Merchant Taylors' Co 1979; *Style*— The Rt Hon Lord Aldenham; ✉ c/o House of Lords, London SW1A 0PW

ALDER, Samuel George (Sam); s of George Parker Alder (d 1981), of Douglas, IOM, and Brenda Margaret, *née* Moore (d 1980); *b* 28 Jan 1944; *Educ* King Williams Coll IOM, Grey Coll Univ of Durham (BA); *m* 6 Sept 1983, Helen Mary, da of Dr Algernon Ivor Boyd, OBE, of St Johns, Antigua; 1 s (Samuel Moore Boyd b 6 Oct 1991), 1 da (Alison Margaret b 16 Feb 1989); *Career* Whinney Murray & Co (CAs) 1966–71, fin dir EG Management Ltd 1971–77, md EG Music Ltd 1977–88; mangr: Roxy Music 1972–83, King Crimson 1972–85; chm: EG Group Ltd 1980–, Villiers Group plc 1985–, Yeoman Security Group plc 1986–91; sr ptnr Alder Dodsworth & Co (CAs) 1985–, dir Douglas Gas plc 1990–96; hon treas: Music Therapy Charity Fund Raising Ctee 1975–81, Duke of Edinburgh's Award Int Project 1987, Duke of Edinburgh's Award Special Projects Gp 1988–92 (dep chm 1992–), Museum of Garden History Appeal Ctee 1989–; tstee: Bishop Barrow's Charity 1985–, British Record Industry Tst 1994–; sec, treas and govr Nordoff-Robins Music Therapy Centre 1981–, chm Int Tst for Nordoff-Robins Music Therapy 1996–; govr King William's Coll IOM; ACA 1971, FCA 1977; *Recreations* music, farming, history; *Clubs* RAC; *Style*— S G Alder, Esq; ✉ The Grange, Clypse Moar, Onchan, Isle of Man IM4 5BG; EG Group Ltd, 63A Kings Rd, London SW3 4NT (☎ 0171 730 2162, fax 0171 730 1330)

ALDERDICE, Baron (Life Peer UK 1996), of Knock in the City of Belfast; John Thomas Alderdice; s of Rev David Alderdice, of Glenariff, Ballymena, NI, and (Annie Margaret) Helena, *née* Shields; *b* 28 March 1955; *Educ* Ballymena Acad, Queen's Univ Belfast (MB BCh, BAO); *m* 30 July 1977, Dr Joan Margaret Hill, da of late James Hill, of Ballymena, NI; 2 s (Hon Stephen b 1980, Hon Peter b 1983), 1 da (Hon Anna b 1988); *Career* conslt psychotherapist E Health and Social Servs Bd 1988, hon lectr in psychotherapy Queen's Univ Belfast 1990–, exec med dir South and East Belfast Health & Social Servs Tst 1994–; Alliance Pty of NI: memb Exec Ctee 1984, vice chm 1987, leader 1987–; Parly candidate 1987 and 1992, Euro Parly candidate June 1989; cnclr (Victoria Area) Belfast City Cncl 1989–; leader Alliance Delgns: to Inter-Party and Intergovernmental talks on the future of NI 1991–, to Forum for Peace and Reconciliation Dublin Castle 1994–; vice pres Liberal International 1992–, treas Euro Liberal Democrat and Reform Party 1995–, elected to NI Forum May 1996–; dir NI Inst of Human Rels 1990–95; MRCPsych 1983; *Recreations* reading, music, gastronomy; *Clubs* Ulster Reform (Belfast), National Liberal; *Style*— The Rt Hon Lord Alderdice; ✉ House of Lords, London SW1A 0PW; Alliance Party Headquarters, 88 University St, Belfast BT7 1HE (☎ 01232 324274, fax 01232 796689)

ALDERMAN, Prof Geoffrey; s of Samuel Alderman (d 1987), of London, and Lily, *née* Landau; *b* 10 Feb 1944; *Educ* Grocers' Company's Sch Hackney London, Lincoln Coll Oxford (open exhibitioner, MA, DPhil); *m* 9 Sept 1973, Marion Joan, yr da of Eliezer and Stella Freed; 1 da (Naomi Alicia b 1974), 1 s (Eliot Daniel b 1978); *Career* res asst Dept of History UCL 1968–69, temp lectr Dept of Political Theory and Govt Univ Coll of Swansea 1969–70, postdoctoral res fell Univ of Reading 1970–72; Royal Holloway Coll Univ of London: lectr in politics 1972–84, reader in politics 1984–88, prof of politics and contemporary history 1988–94; Univ of London: chm Academic Cncl 1989–94, pro-vice chllr for academic standards 1992–93, dean of arts 1992–94; head of Academic Devpt and Quality Assurance Unit Middlesex Univ 1994–; visiting prof: Univ of Northumbria at Newcastle 1993–96, Sheffield Hallam Univ 1994–97; sr assoc Oxford Centre for Hebrew and Jewish Studies 1996–99, professorial research assoc Sch of Oriental and African Studies 1996–98; Loewenstein-Wiener fell American Jewish Archives Cincinnati Ohio; FRHistS 1971, FRSA 1991, FIQA 1995; *Books* incl: The Railway Interest (1973), The Jewish Community in British Politics (1983), Pressure Groups and Government in Great Britain (1984), Modern Britain (1986), London Jewry and London Politics (1989), Modern British Jewry (1992); *Recreations* music, reading; *Clubs* Athenaeum; *Style*— Prof Geoffrey Alderman; ✉ Middlesex University, Trent Park, Bramley Road, London N14 4YZ (☎ 0181 362 5963, fax 0181 362 6499)

ALDERMAN, John; s of Edward George Alderman (d 1978), and Eunice, *née* Childs (d 1987); *b* 24 Feb 1936; *Educ* Rotherham GS, Battersea Coll of Tech (Dip Tech in Hotel Mgmnt); *m* 1965, Jean Gwendolen, da of John Raymond Blake; 1 s (Maxwell John b 8 April 1966), 2 da (Jennifer Jean b 29 Nov 1967, Alison Jane b 10 Sept 1969); *Career* hotel mgmnt Jamaica 1961–64, gen mangr 1964–71 (Hertford Hotel, Gifford Hotel, Both Worlds), area mangr CCH 1971–73, md Lithgow Hotels 1973–83, conslt Hall & Woodhouse 1983–88, proprietor Streamside Restaurant and Hotel 1988–; chm Master Innholders 1980–81, nat pres HCIMA 1984–85; Freeman City of London 1978; FHCIMA 1976, Master Innholder 1978, FTS 1980; *Recreations* golf, crossword puzzles; *Clubs* Broadstone Golf; *Style*— John Alderman, Esq; ✉ Streamside Hotel & Restaurant, 29 Preston Rd, Weymouth, Dorset DT3 6PX (☎ 01305 833121)

ALDERSLADE, Prof Richard; s of Herbert Raymond Alderslade, and Edna F Alderslade; *b* 11 Aug 1947; *Educ* Chichester HS for Boys, ChCh Oxford (BA, BM BCh, MA), St George's Hosp Med Sch London; *m* 1974, Elizabeth Rose; 2 s, 1 da; *Career* house physician Dorset Co Hosp Dorchester 1972–73, casualty offr St George's Hosp London 1974 (house surgn 1973–74), GP Kirklees and asst police surgn W Yorks 1974–76, clinical asst A/E Dewsbury Gen Hosp 1975–76, registrar in community med NW Thames RHA 1976–78 (hon sr registrar 1978–79), lectr in community med Middx Hosp Med Sch 1978–79; DHSS: MO 1979–82, SMO 1982–83, private sec to Chief Med Offr 1984–85 (also med staff offr 1984); specialist in community med Hull Health Authy 1985–88 (community unit gen mangr 1986–88), hon res fell Dept of Social Policy and Professional Studies Univ of Hull 1985–88, regnl dir of public health and regnl med offr Trent RHA 1988–94 (exec memb 1990–94), prof of community care Univ of Sheffield 1994–96; regnl advsr co-ordination and humanitarian assistance WHO Regnl Office for Europe 1995–; pt/t sec MRC Health Servs Res Ctee 1986–88; memb: Central Ctee for Community Med BMA 1977–79, BMA/DHSS Working Pty on Future of Community Health Doctors 1978–79, Microbiological Sub-Gp Nat Water Cncl 1980–81, MRC Standing Ctee on use of Med Info for Res 1981–82, Educn Ctee of Faculty of Public Health Med 1989–95, Standing Med Advsy Ctee 1989–92; FFPHM 1987 (MFCM 1982), FRCP 1993; *Publications* various articles on public health; *Recreations* railway history, music, theatre; *Style*— Prof Richard Alderslade; ✉ 85 Market Place, South Cave, Brough, N Humberside HU15 2AS (☎ 01430 421362); Strandagervej 9, 2900, Hellerup, Denmark (☎ 00 45 39 62 07 41)

ALDERSON, Derek; s of Frederick Alan Alderson, of Birtley, Co Durham, and Mary Annie, *née* Brown; *b* 18 Jan 1953; *Educ* Chester-le-Street GS, Univ of Newcastle upon Tyne (MB BS, MD); *m* 19 Oct 1975, Lyn Margaret, da of Anthony Smith, of Pelton, Co Durham; 1 s (Kevin b 1979), 1 da (Helen b 1981); *Career* house offr Royal Victoria Infirmary Newcastle upon Tyne 1976–77, surgical registrar Newcastle AHA 1979–81, Wellcome surgical training fell 1981–83, sr registrar in surgery Northern RHA 1983–88, res fell Washington Univ St Louis USA 1985–86; Univ of Bristol: conslt sr lectr in surgery 1988–96, conslt surgn 1997–; memb: Surgical Res Soc, Assoc of Surgns of GB and I, Br Assoc of Surgical Oncology, Br Soc of Gastroenterology, Ctee Pancreatic Soc of GB and I; FRCS 1980; *Recreations* jogging; *Style*— Derek Alderson, Esq; ✉ Bristol Royal Infirmary, University Department of Surgery, Marlborough Street, Bristol BS2 8HW (☎ 0117 923 0000)

ALDERSON, John Cottingham; CBE (1981), QPM (1974); s of late Ernest Cottingham Alderson, and Elsie Lavinia Rose; *b* 28 May 1922; *Educ* Barnsley; *m* 1948, Irene Macmillan Stirling; 1 s; *Career* served WWII Warrant Offr Army Physical Training Corps N Africa and Italy; called to the Bar Middle Temple; Police Coll 1954, inspr 1955, dep chief constable Dorset 1964–66, dep asst cmmr (Training) 1968, Cmdt Police Coll 1970, asst cmmr (Personnel and Trg Div) 1973, chief constable Devon and Cornwall 1973–82; visiting prof Centre for Police Studies Univ of Strathclyde 1983–89; conslt on human rights to Cncl of Europe 1981–, dir of Human Rights Strasbourg; fell commoner CCC Cambridge 1982, fell Inst of Criminology Cambridge 1982, Gwilym Gibbon res fell Nuffield Coll Oxford 1982–83, Aust Cwlth fell Aust Govt 1987, hon research fell Centre for Police Studies Univ of Exeter 1987–93, research fell Inst for Police and Criminal Studies Univ of Portsmouth 1995–; Parly candidate (Lib) Teignbridge Devon 1983; Hon LLD Exeter 1979, Hon DLitt Bradford 1981; *Books* Encyclopaedia of Crime and Criminals (contrib, 1960), The Police We Deserve (with P J Stead, 1973), Policing Freedom (1979), Law and Disorder (1984), Human Rights and Police (1984); *Clubs* Royal Over-Seas League; *Style*— John Alderson, Esq, CBE, QPM; ✉ Gorselands, Hawkins Lane, West Hill, Ottery St Mary, Devon EX11 1XG

ALDERSON, Matti; *b* 20 Dec 1951; *Educ* Bearsden Acad Scotland, Open Univ (BA Hons); *Career* legal exec 1970–72, Advtg Agency Poster Bureau 1972–74, Royd's Advertising 1974–75, currently DG Advertising Standards Authority (joined 1975); memb Editorial Bd Jl of Regulatory Law and Practice, fndr vice chm Euro Advtg Standards Alliance Brussels; FRSA 1993, FCAM 1993; *Recreations* architecture and design, reading, studying, driving; *Clubs* Arts; *Style*— Mrs Matti Alderson; ✉ Director General, The Advertising Standards Authority, 2 Torrington Place, London WC1E 7HW (☎ 0171 580 5555, fax 0171 631 3051)

ALDERTON, John; *b* 27 Nov 1940; *m* 1 (m dis); m 2, Pauline Collins; 2 s, 1 da; *Career* actor; debut in Emergency Ward 10 (York Repertory Co) 1961, West End debut Spring and Port Wine (Apollo); *Theatre* incl: Dutch Uncle (Aldwych) 1969, The Night I chased the Woman with an Eel (Comedy) 1969, Judies, The Birthday Party, Confusions, Rattle of a Simple Man (Savoy) 1980, Casebook (Young Vic), Haven't We Met Before? (The Mill at Sonning), Special Occasions (Theatre of Comedy (fndr memb and dir)), Humphrey in See How They Run (with Maureen Lipman), dir Reluctant Heroes (Churchill Theatre Bromley) 1985, lead in The Maintenance Man (Thorndike Theatre Leatherhead and Comedy Theatre) 1986, Estragon in Waiting for Godot (NT) 1987, Dr Prentice in What the Butler Saw (RNT) 1995; *Television* incl: The Rivals, Macbeth and Trelawney of the Wells (plays), Please Sir (also a feature film), My Wife Next Door (with Hannah Gordon), Upstairs Downstairs, No Honestly, Wodehouse Playhouse, Upchat Line, Father's Day (Channel 4), Forever Green (3 series, with Pauline Collins) 1988–91, Keeping Tom Nice (play, with Gwen Taylor, BBC) 1990, Still Life, The Astonished Heart and Family Album (3 plays, BBC's Tonight At Eight-Thirty series, with Pauline Collins) 1991; *Films* incl: Duffy (with James Mason), Zardo, It Shouldn't Happen to a Vet, Clockwork Mice 1995;

Style— John Alderton, Esq; ✉ c/o ICM Ltd, Oxford House, 76 Oxford Street, London W1N 0AX (☎ 0171 636 6565, fax 0171 323 0101)

ALDINGTON, 1 Baron (UK 1962); Toby Austin Richard William Low; KCMG (1957), CBE (1945, MBE 1944), DSO (1941), TD and Clasp (1950), PC (1954), DL (Kent 1973); s of Col Stuart Low, DSO (d on active serv 1942; s of Sir Austin Low, CIE, JP), and Hon Gwen Atkin, da of Baron Atkin, PC (Life Peer, d 1944); *b* 25 May 1914; *Educ* Winchester, New Coll Oxford (BA, MA); *m* 10 April 1947, (Felicité Ann) Araminta, er da of Sir Harold Alfred MacMichael, GCMG, DSO (d 1969), and former w of Capt Paul Humphrey Armytage Bowman; 1 s (Charles b 1948), 2 da (Jane (see Hon Mrs Roberts, LVO) b 1949, *qv*, Ann (Hon Mrs Laing) b 1956); *Heir* s, Hon Charles Low, *qv*; *Career* served WWII KRRC 1939–45, Brig BGS5 Corps 1944–45; called to the Bar Middle Temple 1939; MP (C) Blackpool N 1945–62, Parly sec MOS 1951–54, min of state BOT 1954–57, dep chm Cons Pty Orgn 1959–63; chm: House of Lords Select Ctee on Overseas Trade 1984–85, Sub-Ctee A House of Lords Euro Communities Ctee 1989–93, Ctee of Mgmnt Inst of Neurology 1961–78, Grindlays Bank 1964–76, Port of London Authy 1971–77, BBC Gen Advsy Cncl 1971–79, Sun Alliance & London Insurance 1971–85, National Nuclear Corp 1973–80, Westland plc 1978–85, Leeds Castle Fndn 1984–94; dep chm GEC 1968–84 (chm 1964–68); dir: Lloyds Bank 1967–85, Citicorp (USA) 1969–83; pres Ashford Div Cons Assoc 1965–95, pres Brain Res Tst 1985– (chm 1973–85), warden Winchester Coll 1979–87, hon fell New Coll Oxford 1976; *Recreations* gardening, golf; *Clubs* Carlton, Royal St George's Golf, Rye Golf, Royal and Ancient Golf; *Style*— The Rt Hon the Lord Aldington, KCMG, CBE, DSO, TD, PC, DL; ✉ Knoll Farm, Aldington, Ashford, Kent TN25 7BY (☎ 01233 720292)

ALDISS, Brian Wilson; s of Stanley Aldiss, and May, *née* Wilson; *b* 18 Aug 1925; *Educ* Framlingham Coll, West Buckland Sch; *m* 1, 1949 (m dis 1965); 1 s (Clive b 1955), 1 da (Wendy b 1959); m 2, 11 Dec 1965, Margaret Christie, da of John Manson; 1 s (Tim b 1967), 1 da (Charlotte b 1969); *Career* author and critic; served RCS 1943–47, India, Assam, Burma, Sumatra, Singapore, Hong Kong; bookseller Oxford 1948–56, lit ed Oxford Mail 1948–56; pres Br Science Fiction Assoc 1960–64, ed SF Horizons 1964–70, chm Oxford Branch Conservation Soc 1968–69, vice pres The Stapledon Soc 1975–, jt pres Euro SF Ctees 1976–79, pres World SF 1982–84 (fndr memb); Soc of Authors: memb Ctee of Mgmnt 1976–78, chm 1978, chm Cultural Exchanges Ctee 1979–; memb: Arts Cncl (Lit Panel) 1978–80, Cncl Cncl for Posterity 1990–; prolific lectr, contrib articles to newspapers and jls; Observer Book Award for Science Fiction 1956, Ditmar Award for Best Contemporary Writer of Science Fiction 1969, James Blish Award for SF Criticism (only recipient) 1977, Pilgrim Award 1978, Award for Distinguished Scholarship Int Assoc for the Fantastic in the Arts (first recipient) 1986; FRSL 1990; *Books* novels incl: The Brightfount Diaries (1955), Non-Stop (1958), Greybeard (1964), Barefoot in the Head (1969), The Hand-Reared-Boy (1970), Soldier Erect (1971), Frankenstein Unbound (1973), The Malacia Tapestry (1976), A Rude Awakening (1978), Life in the West (1980), The Helliconia Trilogy (1982–85), Forgotten Life (1988), Dracula Unbound (1990), Remembrance Day (1993), Somewhere East of Life (1994); short stories collections incl: Space, Time and Nathaniel (1957), The Canopy of Time (1959), The Saliva Tree (1966), Intangibles Inc (1969), The Moment of Eclipse (1970), Last Orders (1977), Seasons in Flight (1984), Best Science Fiction Stories of Brian W Aldiss (1988), A Romance of the Equator (1989), A Tupolev Too Far (1993), The Secret of This Book (1995); non-fiction incl: Cities and Stones (travel, 1966), The Shape of Further Things (1970), Billion Year Spree (1973), Trillion Year Spree (update, 1986), Bury My Heart at W H Smiths (1990), The Detached Retina (1995); poetry incl: At the Caligula Hotel (1995), The Poems of Makhtumkuli (1996); *Recreations* amateur theatricals; *Style*— Brian Aldiss, Esq, FRSL; ✉ Hambleden, 39 St Andrews Road, Old Headington, Oxford OX3 9DL (☎ 01865 62464, fax 01865 744435)

ALDOUS, Bernard Russell; s of Bertie William Aldous, of Haughley, Stowmarket, Suffolk, and Evelyn Rose, *née* Dorling; *b* 5 July 1944; *Educ* Stowmarket County GS; *m* 3 Aug 1968, Patricia Ann, da of Alfred Charles William Greengrass, of Stowmarket; 2 s (Timothy James b 12 Feb 1974, David William b 3 Oct 1981), 2 da (Claire Louise b 16 April 1971, Anna Victoria b 14 May 1978); *Career* qualified mangr Whiting & Partners (chartered accountants) 1967–73 (articled clerk 1962–67), audit mangr Coopers & Lybrand Bristol 1974–76, regnl int mgmnt auditor for SW England and Wales Vestric Ltd (subsid of Glaxo) 1976–78, in practice Bristol 1978–80; ptnr Andrew Moore & Co 1984–93 (qualified mangr 1980–84), princ Aldous & Co 1993–; memb for E Anglia Gen Practitioner Bd ICAEW 1989–95, past pres Ipswich & Colchester Soc of CAs; FCA 1979 (ACA 1968); *Recreations* photography, ornithology, fly-fishing, caravanning; *Clubs* Sudbury Institute; *Style*— Bernard Aldous, Esq; ✉ 29 Lambert Drive, Acton, Sudbury, Suffolk CO10 6EB (☎ 01787 371507)

ALDOUS, Charles; QC (1985); s of Guy Travers Aldous (d 1981), of Suffolk, and Elizabeth Angela, *née* Paul; *b* 3 June 1943; *Educ* Harrow, Univ Coll London (LLB); *m* 17 May 1969, Hermione Sara, da of Montague George de Courcy-Ireland (d 1987), of Abington Pigotts Hall, Royston, Herts; 1 s (Alastair b 1979), 3 da (Hermione b 1971 (d 1972), Charlotte b 1973, Antonia b 1975); *Career* called to the Bar Inner Temple 1967, bencher Lincoln's Inn 1993, head of chambers; *Style*— Charles Aldous, Esq, QC; ✉ 7 Stone Buildings, Lincoln's Inn, London WC2 (☎ 0171 405 3886)

ALDOUS, Chief Constable Dirk Wayne; QPM (1995); s of Donald William Aldous (d 1990), of Plymouth, and Margaret, *née* Boothroyd; *b* 13 May 1944; *Educ* Torquay Boys' GS, St John's Coll Oxford (MA); *m* 1, 1965 (m dis 1988), Elaine Mary Burstow; 2 da (Karen Alayne b 27 Feb 1967, Kelly Jayne b 2 Dec 1970); m 2, 1990, Susan Mary Ware; *Career* police cadet Bristol 1960; Bristol Constabulary (now part of Avon and Somerset Constabulary): joined 1963, inspr 1975–77, chief inspr 1977–82, supt 1982–87 (Police Staff Coll Bramshill 1984 and 1986), dep head Avon and Somerset CID 1987–88, chief supt 1988–89; asst chief constable Hampshire Police 1989 then dep chief constable Wiltshire Constabulary, chief constable Dorset Police 1994–; memb ACPO 1989; *Recreations* motor boating, badminton, shooting; *Clubs* Royal Motor Yacht; *Style*— Chief Constable Dirk Aldous, QPM; ✉ Dorset Police, Dorset Police HQ, Winfrith, Dorchester, Dorset DT2 8DZ (☎ 01202 223727)

ALDOUS, Hugh Graham Cazalet; s of Maj Hugh Francis Travers Aldous (d 1979), and Emily, *née* Watkinson; *b* 1 June 1944; *Educ* Cheam Sch, Scarborough HS, Univ of Leeds (BCom); *m* 25 Aug 1967, Christabel, da of Alan Marshall (d 1974); *Career* accountant; Robson Rhodes: ptnr 1976, head corp fin consultancy 1983–85, dep managing ptnr 1985–87, managing ptnr 1987–, currently sr ptnr; seconded to Dept of Tport 1976–79; dir: Freightliner Ltd 1979–84, Sealink UK Ltd 1981–84; memb Br Waterways Bd 1983–86, DTI inspr into affairs of House of Fraser Holdings plc 1987–88, chm Cilntec 1994– (dir 1991–); memb Tech Directorate ICAEW 1995–; FCA 1979 (ACA 1970); *Recreations* walking, tennis, music; *Clubs* RAC; *Style*— Hugh Aldous, Esq; ✉ Robson Rhodes, 186 City Road, London EC1V 2NU (☎ 0171 251 1644, fax 0171 250 0801, telex 885734)

ALDOUS, Lucette (Mrs Alan Alder); da of Charles Fellows Aldous (d 1983), of Sydney, Aust, and Marie, *née* Rutherford; *b* 26 Sept 1938; *Educ* Dux Randwick HS for Girls; *m* 17 June 1972, Alan Richard Alder, s of Richard Alder; 1 da (Floeur Lucette b 2 July 1977); *Career* ballet dancer; prima ballerina Ballet Rambert London England 1957–62; ballerina: London Festival Ballet 1962–66, Royal Ballet Covent Garden 1966–71; prima ballerina Australian Ballet 1972–76; sr adjudicator Nat Eisteddfods 1979–, head of classical dance Dance Dept WA Acad, guest teacher Australian Ballet, Royal New Zealand Ballet and W Australian Ballet Co 1988–; memb: Dance Panel for Performing Arts Bd of Australian Cncl 1986–88, Advsy Cncl Care Australia, Exec Ctee WA Ballet Co, Australia Cncl for the Arts 1996–; hon memb Imperial Soc of Teachers of Dancing, London patron Cecchetti Soc of Australia Inc; American Biographical Inst Woman of the Year 1996; *Style*— Ms Lucette Aldous; ✉ c/o Dance Department, Western Australian Academy of Performing Arts, 2 Bradford St, Mount Lawley, Perth, WA 6050, Aust (☎ 00 619 370 6442, fax 00 619 370 2910)

ALDOUS, Rt Hon Lord Mr Justice; Rt Hon Sir William; kt (1988), PC (1995); s of Guy Travers Aldous, QC (d 1981), and Elizabeth Angela, *née* Paul; *b* 17 March 1936; *Educ* Harrow, Trinity Coll Cambridge (MA); *m* 1960, Gillian Frances, da of John Gordon Henson, CBE; 1 s, 2 da; *Career* called to the Bar Inner Temple 1960, memb jr counsel DTI 1972–76; QC 1976; chm Performing Right Tbnl 1987–88; judge of the High Ct of Justice (Chancery Div) 1988–95, a Lord Justice of Appeal 1995–; *Recreations* horses; *Style*— The Rt Hon Lord Justice Aldous; ✉ Royal Courts of Justice, Strand, London WC2A 2LL

ALDRIDGE, (Harold Edward) James; s of William Thomas Aldridge, and Edith, *née* Quayle; *b* 10 July 1918; *Educ* Swan Hill HS Aust, Bradshaw Coll; *m* 16 Oct 1942, Dina, *née* Shenoudah; 2 s (William Daoud, Thomas Hilal); *Career* author; reporter: Herald and Sun Melbourne 1937–38, Daily Sketch and Sunday Dispatch London 1939; Euro and ME war corr Aust Newspaper Serv and N American Newspaper Alliance 1939–44, Teheran corr Time and Life 1944; recipient: Rys Meml Prize 1945, World Peace Cncl Gold Medal, Int Orgn of Journalists Prize 1967, Lenin Meml Peace Prize 1972, Aust Children's Book Cncl Book of Year Award 1985; *Novels* Signed With their Honours (1942), Of Many Men (1946), Heroes of the Empty View (1954), I Wish He Would Not Die (1958), The Hunter (1961), The Statesmen's Game (1966), A Sporting Proposition (1973), Mockery In Arms (1974), The Untouchable Juli (1976), Goodbye Un-America (1979); *Short stories* Gold and Sand (1960); *Plays* The 49th State (produced 1947), One Last Glimpse (produced 1981); *Children's books* The Flying 19 (1966), The Marvellous Mongolian (1974), The Broken Saddle (1983), The True Story of Lilli Stubek (1984), The True Story of Spit MacPhee (1986, Guardian Children's Fiction Prize); *Plays* 49th State (New Lindsay Theatre London) 1947, One Last Glimpse (Vinohrady Theatre Prague) 1981; TV scripts for Robin Hood; *Recreations* trout and salmon fishing; *Style*— James Aldridge, Esq; ✉ c/o Curtis Brown Group Ltd, 28–29 Haymarket, London SW1Y 4SP (☎ 0171 396 6600, fax 0171 396 0110)

ALDRIDGE, (Michael) John; s of John Edward Aldridge (d 1991), of Derbyshire, and Margery, *née* Taft (d 1969); *b* 1 Dec 1942; *Educ* Beckett Sch Nottingham, Univ of Birmingham Med Sch (BSc, MB ChB); *m* 4 April 1970, Eva Robin, da of James Nicholson, of Harare, Zimbabwe; 4 s (James Hugh b 1971, Gregory b 1972, Stephen b 1974, Nicholas b 1978); *Career* RAMC Lt Col 202 Midland Gen Hosp (cmmnd Capt 1973), ret 1993; house offr Queen Elizabeth Hosp Birmingham 1968–69, then trained in gen and orthopaedic surgery, conslt orthopaedic surgn Coventry and Warwickshire Hosp Coventry 1977–, orthopaedic advsr to Br Amateur Gymnastics Assoc 1979–; team doctor: World Gymnastics Championship 1981, 1983, 1985, 1987 and 1989, Men's Euro Championship Gymnastics 1981, 1983, 1985, 1987, 1989 and 1990, Women's Euro Championship Gymnastics 1989, 1990 and 1992, Jr Euro Championships 1982, 1984, 1986, 1988 and 1991, Seoul Olympics 1988; HQ doctor: Cwlth Games Auckland 1990, Barcelona Olympics 1992, Atlanta Olympics 1996; memb Med Cmmn of Int Gymnastics Fedn 1990–; course writer for Nat Coaching Fndn, presented papers at int meetings on sports injuries; memb BMS, fell Br Orthopaedic Assoc; FRCSE 1973; *Publications* Stress Injuries to Adolescent Gymnasts' Wrists (1988); contrib to orthopaedic jls on gymnastic injuries; *Style*— John Aldridge, Esq; ✉ South Lodge, 29 Westfield Rd, Rugby, Warwickshire CV22 6AS (☎ 01788 576583); Coventry and Warwickshire Hospital, Stoney Stanton Rd, Coventry CV1 4FH (☎ 01203 224055); 15 Palmerston Rd, Coventry (☎ 01203 678472)

ALDRIDGE, Simon Anthony; s of Maj Anthony Harvey Aldridge, TD (d 1994), of The Gables, Elstead, Surrey, and Betty Angela, *née* Harbord; *b* 12 April 1942; *Educ* Marlborough, Grenoble Univ France; *m* 23 Feb 1968, Jennifer Roberta Anne, da of Maj Denzil Robert Noble Clarke (d 1986), of Puffins, South Drive, Wokingham; 1 da (Victoria Helmore Elizabeth b 1 May 1969); *Career* md Savory Milln 1986–89 (ptnr 1969–86), co chm SBC Stockbroking 1988–89; dir: Baring Securities Ltd 1989–93, Baring Securities (Europe) Ltd 1991–93, Baring Securities Bourse SA 1992–93; md BZW Securities Ltd 1993–; dir: Northgate Pacific Fund Jersey 1982–, French Prestige Fund Paris 1985–, Croissance Immobilier Paris 1987–; dep chm Croissance Britannia Paris 1987–; Ordre Nationale du Merité (France) 1989; *Recreations* art, golf, shooting, tennis; *Clubs* Cercle de L'Union Interalliée (Paris), City of London; *Style*— Simon Aldridge, Esq; ✉ 31 Cadogan St, London SW3 2PP (☎ 0171 589 3895); Barclays de Zoete Wedd Securities Ltd, Ebbgate House, 2 Swan Lane, London EC4R 3TS (☎ 0171 956 4520, fax 0171 956 3181, telex 8812124)

ALDRIDGE, Trevor Martin; Hon QC (1992); s of Dr Sidney Aldridge (d 1972), and Isabel Rebecca, *née* Seelig (d 1960); *b* 22 Dec 1933; *Educ* Frensham Heights Sch, Sorbonne, St John's Coll Cambridge (MA); *m* 1966, Joanna van Dedem, da of Cyril van Dedem Edwards (d 1992), of Isle of Man; 1 s (Neil b 1969), 1 da (Deborah b 1968); *Career* admitted slr 1960; ptnr Bower Cotton & Bower 1962–84; law cmmr 1984–93; pres Special Educational Needs Tbnl 1994–; gen ed Property Law Bulletin 1980–84; pres Bd of Govrs Frensham Heights Sch 1996– (chm 1976–95); hon visiting prof City Univ 1994–95; hon life memb Law Soc 1995; *Books* Boundaries, Walls and Fences (1962, 7 edn 1992), Finding Your Facts (1963), Directory of Registers and Records (1963, consltg ed 5 edn 1993), Service Agreements (1964, 4 edn 1982), Aldridge's Residential Lettings (1965, 10 edn 1993), Betterment Levy (1967), Letting Business Premises (1971, 7 edn 1996), Your Home and the Law (1975, 2 edn 1979), Managing Business Property (jtly, 1978), Criminal Law Act 1977 (1978), Guide to Enquiries of Local Authorities (1978, 2 edn 1982), Guide to Enquiries Before Contract (1978), Guide to National Conditions of Sale (1979, 2 edn 1981), Leasehold Law (1980), Housing Act 1980, and as amended 1984 (2 edn 1984), Powers of Attorney (ed, 5 edn 1986 to 8 edn 1991), Guide to Law Society's Conditions of Sale (1981, 2 edn 1984), Questions of Law: Homes (1982), Law of Flats (1982, 3 edn 1994), Practical Conveyancing Precedents (1984), Practical Lease Precedents (1987), Companion to Standard Conditions of Sale (1990, 2 edn 1992), Companion to Property Information Forms (1990), First Registration (1991); *Clubs* United Oxford and Cambridge Univ; *Style*— Trevor M Aldridge, Esq, QC

ALEKSANDER, Prof Igor; s of Branimir Aleksander (d 1972), and Maja, *née* Unger (d 1990); *b* 26 Jan 1937; *Educ* Marist Bros Coll Johannesburg SA, Univ of Witwatersrand (BSc), Univ of London (PhD); *m* 23 March 1963 (m dis 1977), Myra Jeanette, *née* Kurland; *Career* section head Standard Telephone & Cable Co 1958–61, reader Univ of Kent 1968–74; prof and head: Electrical Engrg Dept Brunel Univ 1974–84, Kobler Unit Mgmnt IT Imperial Coll 1984–88; head Electrical Engrg Dept Imperial Coll London 1988–; FRSA 1983, FIEE 1988, FEng 1989; *Books* Introduction To Logic Circuit Theory (1971), Microcircuit Learning Computers (1971), Automata Theory: An Engineering Approach (with FK Hanna 1978), The Human Machine (1978), Reinventing Man (with Piers Burnett 1984), Designing Intelligent Systems (1985), Decision And Intelligence (with Forraney and Ghalab 1986), Thinking Machines (with Piers Burnett 1987), An Introduction To Neural Computing (with H Morton 1989), Neurons and Symbols: The Stuff That Mind Is Made Of (with H Morton 1993), Impossible Minds, My Neurons My

Consciousness; *Style*— Prof Igor Aleksander, FEng; ✉ Department of Electrical & Electronic Engineering, Imperial College of Science, Technolology and Medicine, Exhibition Road, London SW7 2BT (☎ 0171 594 6188, fax 0171 823 8125, e-mail i.aleksander@ic.ac.uk)

ALESBURY, Alun; s of George Alesbury, and Eveline, *née* Richards, of Weybridge, Surrey; *b* 14 May 1949; *Educ* Cambridge and Seville Univs; *m* 26 June 1976, Julia Rosemary, 6 da of Herbert Archibald Graham Butt (d 1971), of Sibford Gower, Oxon; 1 s (Rupert b 1980), 2 da (Lucy b 1982, Katie b 1990); *Career* called to the Bar Inner Temple 1974, legal corr The Architect 1976–80, memb Panel of Jr Treasy Counsel (Lands Tbnl) 1978–, memb Supplementary Panel Common Law (Planning) 1991–; memb Parly Bar Mess; fndr memb Planning and Environment Bar Assoc 1986 (hon sec 1986–88), appointed to hold inquiry into Palmeira Avenue fire Hove 1992 and Lake Windermere speed limit inquiry 1994–95; *Publications* incl: Highways (contrib 4 edn Halsburys Laws of England), articles on planning law; *Recreations* walking, travel, old buildings, skiing, sailing; *Style*— Alun Alesbury, Esq; ✉ 2 Mitre Court Buildings, Temple, London EC4Y 7BX (☎ 0171 583 1380, fax 0171 353 7772); West Marden, West Sussex

ALEXANDER, *see:* Hagart-Alexander

ALEXANDER, Prof Alan; *b* 13 Dec 1943; *Educ* Univ of Glasgow (MA); *Career* res and educn offr General and Municipal Workers' Union 1965, asst prof Dept of Political Science Lakehead Univ 1969–71 (lectr 1966–69), lectr in politics Univ of Reading 1971–87; Strathclyde Business Sch Univ of Strathclyde: dir Scottish Local Authys Mgmnt Centre and prof of mgmnt in local govt 1987–93, prof of local and public mgmnt 1993–, head Dept of Resource Mgmnt 1993–96; scholar Rockefeller Fndn 1984, Fulbright visiting prof of politics Randolph-Macon Woman's Coll 1986; Parly candidate (Lab) Henley general election 1974; memb: Reading Co Borough Cncl 1972–74, Berks CC 1973–77, Bd Housing Corp 1977–80, Working Gp on internal mgmnt of local authys Scottish Office 1992–93; memb Editorial Bd: Scottish Affairs 1991–, Strategic Government 1992–; *Books* Local Government in Britain since Reorganisation (1982), The Politics of Local Government in the United Kingdom (1982), L'amministrazione locale in Gran Bretagna (1984), Borough Government and Politics: Reading 1835–1985 (1985), Managing the Fragmented Authority (1994); author of numerous articles in jls and contribs to books; *Style*— Prof Alan Alexander; ✉ Scottish Local Authorities Management Centre, The Graham Hills Building, 50 Richmond Street, Glasgow G1 1XT (☎ 0141 553 4167, fax 0141 552 6587)

ALEXANDER, Andrew Clive; s of Ronald Fergus Alexander (d 1972), and Doreen, *née* Davies (d 1956); *b* 12 May 1935; *Educ* Lancing; *Career* leader writer Yorkshire Post 1960–65, Parly sketch-writer Daily Telegraph 1966–72, city ed Daily Mail 1984– (Parly sketch-writer and political columnist 1972–84); dir Associated Newspapers; Parly candidate (C) Colne Valley 1963 and 1964; *Books* The Making of the Prime Minister (with Alan Watkins, 1970); *Recreations* landscape gardening, music, weight training; *Clubs* Reform; *Style*— Andrew Alexander, Esq; ✉ Daily Mail, 141–143 Drury Lane, Covent Garden, London WC2B 5TS (☎ 0171 938 6000)

ALEXANDER, Anthony Ernest; s of Henry Gustav Alexander (d 1986), and Alice, *née* Polackova; *b* 7 Oct 1945; *Educ* St Paul's, Downing Coll Cambridge (MA); *m* 1, 6 July 1969, Ilana, da of Maurice Raphael Setton, of Jerusalem, Israel; 1 s (Daniel b 17 Sept 1974), 1 da (Sharon b 10 May 1973); m 2, 14 July 1996, Louise, da of Bernard Tupling Hart and Doris Hart, of Brisbane, Aust; *Career* ptnr: Herbert Oppenheimer, Nathan & Vandyk 1973–88 (sr ptnr 1988), Denton Hall 1988–; ctee memb Slrs' Euro Gp, sec Br Czech and Slovak Law Assoc; Freeman Worshipful Co of Slrs 1988; memb: Law Soc 1971, The Pilgrims, RIIA; *Books* England-Legal Aspects of Alien Acquisition of Real Property (contrib); *Recreations* music and classical studies; *Style*— Anthony Alexander, Esq; ✉ 14 Mecklenburgh Square, London WC1N 2AD (☎ 0171 278 1662, fax 0171 278 3755); Denton Hall, Five Chancery Lane, Clifford's Inn, London EC4A 1BU (☎ 0171 242 1212, fax 0171 404 0087, car tel 0802 260129)

ALEXANDER, Anthony George Laurence; s of G W Alexander, of Beaconsfield; *b* 4 April 1938; *Educ* St Edward's Sch Oxford; *m* Frances, *née* Burdett; 1 s, 2 da; *Career* dir Hanson plc 1976–96 (UK chief operating offr 1986–96), dep chm Imperial Tobacco Group plc; non-exec dir: Shanks & McEwan Group plc, Inchcape plc, Misys plc; FCA; *Recreations* tennis, golf; *Style*— Anthony Alexander, Esq; ✉ Crafnant, Gregories Farm Lane, Beaconsfield, Bucks; office: 1 Grosvenor Place, London SW1X 7JH (☎ 0171 245 1245, fax 0171 235 3455)

ALEXANDER, Anthony Victor; CBE (1987); s of Aaron Alexander (d 1945); *b* 17 Sept 1928; *Educ* Dragon Sch Oxford, Harrow, St John's Coll Cambridge (MA, LLB); *m* 1958, Hélène Esther, da of late Victor Adda; 1 da (Susannah); *Career* insur broker; md Sedgwick Collins (non marine div) 1968–73, chm Sedgwick Forbes UK and dir Sedgwick Forbes Holdings 1973–78, dir Securicor Group and Securicor Services 1977–, dep chm Sedgwick Forbes Ltd 1978–79, dir Sedgwick Group 1980–89; chm: Sedgwick Group Special Services 1980–83, Sedgwick Group Underwriting Services 1982–85, Br Insur Brokers Assoc (BIBA) 1982–87 (dep chm to 1982); dir ARV Aviation Ltd 1985–88; chm: Fan Museum Tst 1984–, Victor Adda Fndn 1984–; memb: Mktg of Investmts Bd Organising Ctee 1984–85, Securities and Investmts Bd 1985–88; Liveryman Worshipful Co of Insurers; FCIB, FINucE; *Recreations* home and garden, sailing, fishing, antique collecting, woodlands; *Style*— Anthony Alexander, Esq, CBE; ✉ 1 St Germans Place, Blackheath, London SE3 0NH (☎ 0181 858 5509); c/o The Fan Museum Trust, 12 Crooms Hill, Greenwich SE10 8ER (☎ 0181 853 3849)

ALEXANDER, Hon Brian James; s of 1 Earl Alexander of Tunis, KG, GCB, OM, GCMG, CSI, DSO, MC, PC (d 1969 - 3 s of 4 Earl of Caledon); hp of bro, 2 Earl; *b* 31 July 1939; *Educ* Harrow; *Career* Lt Irish Gds (Res); Liveryman Worshipful Co of Mercers; *Clubs* White's; *Style*— The Hon Brian Alexander; ✉ 11 The Little Boltons, London SW10 9LJ (☎ 0171 370 4158)

ALEXANDER, Capt Byron John; s of Capt Dimitrius Alexander (d 1975), of Athens, and June Doreen, *née* Eddy; *b* 18 May 1942; *Educ* Monkton House Sch; *m* 4 June 1969, Eileen May, da of Eric Leslie Page, of Eastcote, Middx; 2 s (Marc Byron b 4 Oct 1972, James Philip b 25 Dec 1976), 1 da (Nicola Jane b 10 March 1970); *Career* MN 1959–69; md: Alexander Advertising International Ltd 1969–, Illustra Graphics Ltd 1984–; memb HM Coastguard (Auxiliary Afloat Section) 1973–; memb Guild of Masters, Mates and Engineers; Capt (merchant marine), Master Mariner, River Master; MIPR 1973, MIMgt 1975, MRIN; *Books* Buying a Boat (1972); *Recreations* motor yachting, computers; *Clubs* Leander, Royal Temple Yacht; *Style*— Capt Byron Alexander; ✉ Alexander Advertising International, Alexander House, Wallingford, Oxon OX10 0XF (☎ 01491 834966, fax 01491 833475, car 0860 877766)

ALEXANDER, Sir Charles Gundry; 2 Bt (UK 1945), of Sundridge Park, Co Kent; s of Sir Frank Alexander, 1 Bt, JP (d 1959), and Elsa, da of Sir Charles Collett, 1 Bt; *b* 5 May 1923; *Educ* Bishop's Stortford Coll, St John's Coll Cambridge (BA 1943, MA 1947); *m* 1, 1944, Mary Neale, o da of late Stanley Robert Richardson, of Maple Lawn, Lyndhurst, Hants; 1 s (Richard b 1947), 1 da (Jennifer b 1949); m 2, 1979, Eileen Ann, da of Gordon Stewart, of Inveresk, Finchampstead; *Heir* s, Richard Alexander, *qv*; *Career* served WWII Lt RN N Atlantic and Far East; chm Alexander Shipping Co 1959–87; chm Bd of Govrs Care Ltd 1975–86; memb Ct of Assts Worshipful Co of Merchant Taylors (Master 1981–82), Prime Warden Worshipful Co of Shipwrights 1983–84; AIMarE; *Clubs* RAC; *Style*— Sir Charles Alexander, Bt; ✉ Hollytree Farmhouse, North Cadbury, Yeovil, Somerset BA22 7DD (☎ 01963 440159)

ALEXANDER, Maj-Gen David Crichton; CB (1976); s of James Alexander (d 1978), and Margaret, *née* Craig; *b* 28 Nov 1926; *Educ* Edinburgh Acad, Staff Coll Camberley, RCDS; *m* 1, 1957, Diana Joyce (Jane) (d 1995), da of Sydney Fisher, CVO (d 1980); 1 s, 2 da, 1 step s; m 2, 1996, Elizabeth Patricia, da of Hugh Geoffrey Herrington, CBE (d 1980); *Career* served RM 1944–77, equerry and acting treas to Duke of Edinburgh 1957–60, staff of CDS 1966–69, Col GS to CGRM 1970–73, ADC to HM The Queen 1973–75, MGRM Trg 1975–77; dir gen ESU 1977–79, cmdt Scottish Police Coll 1979–87; memb Tport Users' Consultative Ctee for Scot 1989–93, pres SSAFA Fife 1990–94, pres Corps of Commissionaires 1994–; Freeman City of London, Liveryman Worshipful Co of Painter-Stainers; *Recreations* gardening, fishing, golf; *Clubs* Army and Navy, Golf House (Elie); *Style*— Maj-Gen David Alexander, CB

ALEXANDER, Sir Douglas; 3 Bt (UK 1921), of Edgehill, Stamford, Connecticut, USA; s of Lt-Cdr Archibald Gillespie Alexander, US Coast Guard (d 1978), and Margery Isabel, *née* Griffith; n of Sir Douglas Hamilton Alexander, 2 Bt (d 1983); *b* 9 Sept 1936; *Educ* Rice Univ Houston Texas (MA 1961), Univ of N Carolina (PhD 1967); *m* 1958, Marylon, da of Leonidas Collins Scatterday, of Worthington, Ohio, USA; 2 s (Douglas Gillespie *qv*, Andrew Llewellyn b 14 Jan 1967); *Heir* s, Douglas Gillespie Alexander b 24 July 1962; *Career* pres Edgehill Investment Co; *Style*— Sir Douglas Alexander II, Bt; ✉ 2499 Windsor Way Court, Wellington, Florida 33414, USA

ALEXANDER, Douglas Gillespie; s and h of Sir Douglas Alexander II, 3 Bt, *qv*; *b* 24 July 1962; *Educ* Reed Coll Portland Oregon (BA); *Style*— Douglas G Alexander, Esq

ALEXANDER, Prof (Albert) Geoffrey; s of William Francis Alexander (d 1969), of Kingston upon Hull, and Muriel Katherine, *née* Boreham (d 1989); *b* 22 Sept 1932; *Educ* Bridlington Sch, UCH Dental Sch Univ of London (BDS, MDS, LDSRCS, FDSRCS); *m* 2 June 1956, (Dorothy) Constance, da of Harry Johnson (d 1980), of Orpington; 1 da (Susan Elizabeth b 1959); *Career* Nat Serv Capt RADC 1956–58; dental house surgn UCH 1955–56, lectr in conservative dentistry UCH Med Sch 1960–62, sr lectr conservation and periodontics UCL Dental Sch, prof of conservative dentistry Univ of London 1972–92 (reader 1969), appointed to chair of conservative dentistry UCL Sch of Med 1976, dean UCL Sch of Dentistry 1977–92 (vice dean 1974–77), chair of conservative dentistry and assoc dean Faculty of Dentistry Univ of Hong Kong 1992–94; fell: Int Coll of Dentists 1975, UCL 1986, Hong Kong Acad of Med 1993; memb: Gen Dental Cncl 1986–92 (treas 1989–92), BDA; *Books* The Prevention of Periodontal Disease (1971), Self Assessment Manual No 3 - Clinical Dentistry (1978), A Companion to Dental Studies (volumes 2 and 3, 1988); *Recreations* photography; *Style*— Prof Geoffrey Alexander

ALEXANDER, Helen Anne; da of Bernard Gustav Alexander (d 1990), of Great Haseley, Oxon and London SW7, and Tania von Benckendorff; *b* 10 Feb 1957; *Educ* St Paul's Girls' Sch (head girl), Hertford Coll Oxford (2 half blues), INSEAD (MBA); *m* Feb 1985, Timothy John Suter, s of Martin Edward Hayles Suter; 1 da (Nina Joscelin b 6 May 1990), 2 s (Gregory Constantine b 1 Feb 1992, Leo Martin Bernard b 26 Sept 1993); *Career* Duckworth & Co 1978–79, Faber & Faber 1979–83, The Economist Newspaper Ltd 1985–93: dir of circulation and distbn The Economist 1987–89, int circulation and mktg dir 1989–93; md The Economist Intelligence Unit 1993–97, chief executive The Economist Group plc London 1997–; memb Advsy Cncl DEMOS (all-party think tank) 1996–; non-exec dir Northern Foods plc; former bd memb: Dept of the Environment Exec Agency, QEII Conf Centre; interviewer Civil Serv Fast Stream prog; FRGS; *Clubs* Reform; *Style*— Ms Helen Alexander; ✉ The Economist Intelligence Unit, 15 Regent Street, London SW1Y 4LR (☎ 0171 830 1070, fax 0171 839 1466)

ALEXANDER, Ian Douglas Gavin; QC (1989); s of Dr Archibald Douglas Park Alexander (d 1968), of Lancing, Sussex, and Dilys, *née* Edwards; *b* 10 April 1941; *Educ* Tonbridge, UCL (LLB); *m* 13 Dec 1969, Rosemary Kirkbridge, da of Kenneth Richards; 1 s (Justin b 6 June 1978), 1 da (Victoria b 26 Jan 1980); *Career* called to the Bar Lincoln's Inn 1964, recorder Midland and Oxford Circuit 1982–; *Recreations* field sports, skiing, sailing, gardening; *Clubs* Naval and Military; *Style*— Ian Alexander, Esq, QC; ✉ 11 Bolt Court, Fleet Street, London EC4A 3DQ (☎ 0171 353 2300, fax 0171 353 1878, DX 01022 LDE)

ALEXANDER, John Bernard Alexei; s of B G Alexander, of Great Haseley, Oxford, and T Alexander, *née* Benckendorf; *b* 23 Aug 1941; *Educ* Westminster, Balliol Coll Oxford; *m* 1 July 1969, Jacquelyn, da of John Bray, of Sydney, Aust; 2 s (Nicolas b 1971, Christopher b 1974); m 2, 14 April 1981, Judy, da of Maj Patrick Chilton, of West Ashling, Sussex; 1 da (Tania b 1982); *Career* merchant banker; dir Hill Samuel & Co Ltd 1973–83, md LCF Edmond de Rothschild Securities 1984–; dir: Banque Privée Edmond de Rothschild Geneva 1994–, Port of Bristol 1991–, Sterling Insurance Group Ltd 1995–; *Recreations* skiing, tennis, gardening; *Clubs* Brooks's; *Style*— John B A Alexander, Esq; ✉ The Old Rectory, Great Haseley, Oxford; LCF Edmond de Rothschild Ltd, 5 Upper St Martin's Lane, London WC2H 9EA (☎ 0171 240 1870)

ALEXANDER, Dr John Huston (Ian); s of John Alexander, of Bath, and Agnes Margaret Crawford, *née* Huston; *b* 5 April 1941; *Educ* Campbell Coll Belfast, St Edmund Hall Oxford (BLitt, MA, DPhil); *m* 1970, Flora Munro, da of late Angus Ross, of Invergordon; 2 da (Ruth b 1971, Jane b 1974), 2 s (Mark b 1976, Patrick John b 1977); *Career* sessional lectr in English Univ of Saskatchewan Saskatoon Canada 1966–67, reader in English Univ of Aberdeen 1996– (lectr in English 1968–84, sr lectr 1984–96); ed: The Scott Newsletter 1982–, Scottish Literary Journal 1991–; gen ed Edinburgh Edn Waverley Novels 1984–; *Books* Two Studies in Romantic Reviewing (1976), The Lay of the Last Minstrel: Three Essays (1978), The Reception of Scott's Poetry by his Correspondents (1979), Marmion: Studies in Interpretation and Composition (1981), Scott and His Influence (ed with David Hewitt, 1983), Reading Wordsworth (1987), The Tavern Sages: Selections from the Noctes Ambrosianae (ed, 1992), Scott in Carnival (ed with David Hewitt, 1993), Walter Scott: Kenilworth - A Romance (ed, 1993), Walter Scott: The Bride of Lammermoor and A Legend of the Wars of Montrose (ed, 1995), Walter Scott: Tales of a Grandfather: The History of France (second series, ed with William Baker, 1996); *Recreations* music, walking; *Style*— Dr J H Alexander; ✉ 45A Queen's Road, Aberdeen AB1 6YN (☎ 01224 317424); Department of English, University of Aberdeen, Aberdeen AB9 2UB (☎ 01224 272626, fax 01224 272624, e-mail j.h.alexander@abdn.ac.uk)

ALEXANDER, Dr John Innis; s of William Bahudur Alexander (d 1984), of Surbiton, Surrey, and Winifred Edith, *née* Cottle; *b* 17 April 1942; *Educ* King's Coll Sch Wimbledon, Univ Coll and Med Sch London (MB BS, MRCS, LRCP); *m* 22 April 1978, Susan Diane, da of Philip Lionel Taylor, of Newport, Gwent; 1 s (Christopher b 1982), 1 da (Phyllida b 1980); *Career* sr house offr in anaesthesia Norfolk and Norwich Hosp 1967–68, registrar in anaesthesia Royal Free Hosp London 1968–69, res fell in anaesthesia Scottish Home and Health Dept 1970–72, conslt in anaesthesia and pain mgmnt United Bristol Hosps 1974– (sr registrar in anaesthesia 1969–74); memb Editorial Bd Frontiers of Pain 1990–92, examiner in pharmacology Royal Coll of Anaesthetists 1990–; FRCA 1969; chm Bristol and District Research Ethics Ctee 1993–; memb: Anaesthetic Res Soc 1970–, Int Assoc for the Study of Pain 1975–; *Books* Postoperative Pain Control (1987); *Recreations* woodwork, swimming; *Style*— Dr John Alexander; ✉ Sir Humphry Davy Department of Anaesthesia, Bristol Royal Infirmary, Bristol BS2 8HW (☎ 0117 928 2163)

ALEXANDER, Kenneth Alston; s of Brig-Gen Sir William Alexander, KBE, CB, CMG, DSO, MP (d 1954), and his 1 wife Beatrice Evelyn, *née* Ritchie (d 1928); *b* 21 Nov 1928; *Educ* Winchester, Trinity Coll Cambridge (BA); *m* 1957, Linda Mary, da of Edward

Lefevre, of Cochin and Gargrave, Yorks; 1 s, 3 da; *Career* Royal Tank Regt; chem merchant and manufacturer; chm and chief exec Tennants Consolidated Ltd 1972– (previously holding various directorships within the Tennant Group); *Recreations* shooting, music; *Clubs* RAC; *Style*— Kenneth Alexander, Esq; ✉ Tennants Consolidated Ltd, 69 Grosvenor Street, London W1X 0BP (☎ 0171 493 5451)

ALEXANDER, Prof Sir Kenneth John Wilson; kt (1978); only s of late William Wilson Alexander; *b* 14 March 1922; *Educ* George Heriot's Sch Edinburgh, Dundee Sch of Econs; *m* 1949, Angela-May, da of late Capt G H Lane, RN; 1 s, 4 da; *Career* prof of economics Univ of Strathclyde 1963–80 (on leave 1976–80), dean Scottish Business Sch 1973–75, princ and vice chllr Univ of Stirling 1981–86, chllr Univ of Aberdeen 1987–; chm Highlands and Islands Devpt Bd 1976–80; dir: Fairfields (Glasgow) Ltd 1966–68, Upper Clyde Shipbuilders Ltd 1968–71, Scottish Television 1982–92, Stakis plc 1987–93, Aberdeen Univ Press 1989–92 (chm 1990), Scottish Daily Record and Sunday Mail (1986) Ltd 1990–93; chm: Govan Shipbuilders 1974–76, Michael Kelly Associates 1986–94, Scottish Industrial Exhibitions Ltd 1991–; dir Glasgow C of C 1969–73, econ conslt to Sec of State for Scotland 1968–90, chm Ctee on Adult Educn in Scotland 1970–73, dep chm Scottish Cncl (Devpt and Indust) 1982–92 (memb Exec Ctee 1962–92); memb: Scottish Tport Gp 1969–76 (pt/t), SSRC 1975–76, Scottish Devpt Agency 1975–86, Bd UK Centre for Econ and Environmental Devpt 1985–; govr: Tech Change Centre 1981–87, Newbattle Abbey Coll 1967–73; pres: Section F Br Assoc 1974, Saltire Soc 1975–81, Scottish Section Town and Country Planning 1982–; hon pres The Highland Fund 1983–, pres Scottish Nat Dictionary Assoc 1984–; chm: John Muir Tst 1985–88, Edinburgh Book Festival 1987–91, Paxton Tst 1989–93; tstee Nat Museums of Scotland 1985–87; Hon LLD: CNAA 1976, Univ of Aberdeen, Univ of Dundee 1985, Univ of Strathclyde 1986; Hon DUniv Stirling 1977, Hon DUniv Open Univ 1985, Hon DLitt Univ of Aberdeen 1987, Hon DUniv Heriot-Watt 1995; FRSE 1978 (vice pres 1994–96); CIMgt 1980, FEIS 1983, FBEC(S) 1984, FRIAS 1988, FRSA 1992; *Books* The Economist in Business (1967), Productivity Bargaining and the Reform of Industrial Relations (1969), Fairfields, a study of industrial change (with C L Jenkins, 1971), The Political Economy of Change (ed, 1976); *Recreations* sea fishing; *Clubs* Caledonian, Scottish Arts; *Style*— Prof Sir Kenneth Alexander, FRSE; ✉ 9 West Shore, Pittenweem, Fife KY10 2NV

ALEXANDER, Sir (John) Lindsay; kt (1975); s of Ernest Daniel Alexander, MC (d 1975), and Florence Mary, *née* Mainsmith; *b* 12 Sept 1920; *Educ* Alleyn's Sch, BNC Oxford (MA); *m* 1944, Maud Lilian, 2 da of Oliver Ernest Collard; 2 s, 1 da; *Career* chm: Ocean Transport & Trading 1971–80, Overseas Container Holdings 1976–82, Lloyds Bank International 1980–85; dep chm Lloyds Bank 1980–88 (dir 1970–91); dir: BP 1975–91, Jebsens Drilling 1980–86, Hawker Siddeley 1981–91, Wellington Underwriting Holdings 1986–, Lloyds Abbey Life 1988–91, Britoil 1988–90; chm Ctee of Euro Shipowners' Assoc 1972–73; pres Chamber of Shipping 1974–75; hon memb Worshipful Co of Master Mariners 1974, hon fell BNC Oxford 1977; JP Cheshire 1965–75; Cdr Royal Order of St Olav (Norway) 1980; FCIT, CIMgt 1980 (FIMgt 1972); *Recreations* gardening, music, photography; *Style*— Sir Lindsay Alexander; ✉ c/o Lloyds Bank plc, 71 Lombard St, London EC3P 3BS (☎ 0171 626 1500)

ALEXANDER, Prof (Robert) McNeill; s of Robert Priestley Alexander (d 1973), of Lisburn, Co Antrim, and Janet, *née* McNeill; *b* 7 July 1934; *Educ* Tonbridge Sch, Trinity Hall Cambridge (MA, PhD); *m* 29 July 1961, Ann Elizabeth, da of Gordon Francis Coulton (d 1947), of Pentney, Norfolk; 1 s (Gordon b 1964), 1 da (Jane b 1962); *Career* sr lectr in zoology Univ Coll of N Wales 1968–69 (asst lectr 1958–61, lectr 1961–68), prof of zoology Univ of Leeds 1969– (head Dept of Pure and Applied Zoology 1969–78 and 1983–87); visiting prof: Harvard 1973, Duke 1975, Nairobi 1976, 1977 and 1978, Basle 1986, St Francis Xavier 1990, California (Davis) 1992; memb Biological Scis Ctee SRC 1974–77, sec Zoological Soc of London 1992– (vice pres 1990–91, memb Cncl 1988–91), pres Soc for Experimental Biology 1995–97 (vice pres 1993–95); hon memb American Soc of Zoologists 1986; Scientific Medal Zoological Soc 1969, Linnean Medal Linnean Soc 1979, Muybridge Medal Int Soc for Biomechanics 1991; DSc (Wales) 1969; FRS 1987, FIBiol, memb Academia Europaea 1996; *Books* Functional Design in Fishes (1967), Animal Mechanics (1968), Size and Shape (1971), The Chordates (1975), The Invertebrates (1979), Optima for Animals (1982), Elastic Mechanisms in Animal Movement (1988), Dynamics of Dinosaurs and other Extinct Giants (1989), Animals (1990), The Human Machine (1992), Exploring Biomechanics (1992), Bones (1994), and other books and papers; *Recreations* local history, history of natural history; *Style*— Prof McNeill Alexander, FRS; ✉ 14 Moor Park Mount, Leeds LS6 4BU (☎ 0113 275 9218); Department of Biology, University of Leeds, Leeds LS2 9JT (☎ 0113 233 2911, fax 0113 233 2835, telex 556473 UNILDS G)

ALEXANDER, Rt Rev Mervyn Alban Newman; *see:* Clifton, Bishop of (RC)

ALEXANDER, Michael Charles; s of Rear Adm Charles Otway Alexander (d 1970), and Antonia, *née* Geermans; *b* 20 Nov 1920; *Educ* Stowe, RMC Sandhurst; *m* 5 July 1961 (m dis), Sarah, da of Lt-Col Frederick Wignall; 1 da; *Career* WWII DCLI; 5 (Ski) Bn Scots Gds, 8 Commando (Layforce), HQ 13 Corps GSO3, SBS (POW Colditz 1942–44), 2 SAS Regt; WO (civil affrs) Intergovernmental Ctee on Refugees 1946, editorial dir Common Ground Ltd 1946–50; located Firuzkoh Central Afghanistan 1952, Himalayan Hovercraft Expedition 1972, Yucatan Straits Hovercraft Expedition 1975, Upper Ganges Hovercraft Expedition 1980, dir Adastra Productions Ltd 1980–; fndr: Woburn Safari Serv 1977, Chelsea Wharf Restaurant 1983; co-publisher Wildlife Magazine; hon pres Br Inflatable Boat Owners' Assoc (BIBOA) 1994; FZS, FRGS, fell Royal Soc for Asian Affrs; *Books* The Privileged Nightmare (with Giles Romilly 1952, republished as Hostages at Colditz 1975), Offbeat in Asia (1953), The Reluctant Legionnaire (1955), The True Blue (1957), Mrs Fraser on the Fatal Shore (1972), Discovering the New World (1976), Omai: Noble Savage (1977), Queen Victoria's Maharajah (1980), Delhi-Agra: A Traveller's Companion (1987); *Clubs* Beefsteak, Chelsea Arts; *Style*— Michael Alexander, Esq; ✉ 48 Eaton Place, London SW1 (☎ 0171 235 2724)

ALEXANDER, Prof Michael Joseph; s of Joseph Brian Alexander, MBE, JP (d 1984), and Winefred, *née* Gaul (d 1985); *b* 21 May 1941; *Educ* Downside, Trinity Coll Oxford (MA); *m* 1, 1 Sept 1973, Eileen Mary (d 1986), da of Anthony Hamilton McCall; 1 s (Patrick b 1980), 2 da (Lucy b 1977, Flora b 1982); m 2, 11 July 1987, Mary Cecilia Sheahan; *Career* ed William Collins 1963, fell Princeton Graduate Sch 1965, lectr Univ of Calif 1966, ed André Deutsch 1967, lectr UEA 1968, reader Univ of Stirling 1985 (lectr 1969), Berry prof of Eng lit Univ of St Andrews 1985–; *Books* translations incl: The Earliest English Poems (1966), Beowulf (1973); other publications: Twelve Poems (1977), The Poetic Achievement of Ezra Pound (1979), MacMillan Anthology of English Literature (jt ed, 1989), Beowulf (ed, 1995), Sons of Ezra (jt ed, 1995), The Canterbury Tales: The First Fragment (ed, 1996); *Style*— Prof Michael Alexander; ✉ 62 Hepburn Gardens, St Andrews KY16 9DG; School of English, The University, St Andrews KY16 9AL

ALEXANDER, Sir Michael O'Donel Bjarne; GCMG (1992, KCMG 1988, CMG 1982); s of late Conel Hugh O'Donel Alexander, CMG, CBE, and Enid Constance Crichton Neate; *b* 19 June 1936; *Educ* Foyle Coll Londonderry, St Paul's, King's Coll Cambridge, Yale and Berkeley Univs USA (Harkness fell); *m* 1960, Traute Krohn; 2 s, 1 da; *Career* served RN 1955–57; joined FO 1962, asst private sec to Sir Alec Douglas-Home then James Callaghan as successive Foreign Secs 1972–74, cnsllr (Conference on Security and Co-operation in Europe) and subsequently head Chancery UK Mission to the UN Geneva 1974–77, head POD FCO 1978–79 (dep head 1977–78), private sec (Overseas Affairs) to PM Margaret Thatcher 1979–81, UK ambass to Vienna 1982–86, UK permanent rep on N Atlantic Cncl Brussels 1986–92; chm Royal United Servs Inst 1993–, dep chm Wasserstein Perella Eastern Europe 1992–; *Style*— Sir Michael Alexander, GCMG; ✉ 3 Burlington Gardens, London W1X 1LE

ALEXANDER, Sir Norman Stanley; kt (1966), CBE (1959); s of Charles Monrath Alexander (d 1941), of NZ, and Flora Elizabeth, *née* Reid (d 1944); *b* 25 Oct 1906; *Educ* Hamilton HS NZ, Univ Coll Auckland (MSc), Trinity Coll Cambridge (PhD); *m* 1, 1935, Frances Elizabeth Somerville, da of Kenneth Caldwell (d 1950); 1 s, 2 da; m 2, 1959, Constance Lilian Helen (d 1990), da of Henry Geary (d 1950); m 3, Evelyn, da of Herbert Henry Hyde (d 1917); *Career* prof of physics: Univ of Malaya 1936–52, Univ Coll Ibadan Nigeria 1952–59; vice chllr Ahmadu Bello Univ of Nigeria 1961–66; advsr on Higher Educn Miny Overseas Devpt; hon memb Order of the Niger (Nigeria) 1966; *Recreations* gardening; *Style*— Sir Norman Alexander, CBE; ✉ Burrowland, Crediton, Devon (☎ 01363 773200)

ALEXANDER, Richard; s and h of Sir Charles Alexander, 2 Bt, *qv*, and his 1 w, Mary, da of Stanley Richardson; *b* 1 Sept 1947; *Educ* Bishop's Stortford Coll; *m* 1971, Lesley Jane, da of Frederick William Jordan, of Orpington; 2 s (Edward Samuel b 1974, James Gundry b 1977); *Career* PR conslt Alexander Jordan Associates, archivist and historian Furness Withy Group; chm Mid-Kent Gp Br Cardiac Patients Assoc; Freeman City of London, Liveryman Worshipful Co of Merchant Taylors; MIPR; *Recreations* motoring, barebow archery; *Clubs* Bentley Drivers'; *Style*— Richard Alexander, Esq; ✉ Wealden Hall, Pilgrims Way, Detling, nr Maidstone, Kent ME14 3JY; Alexander Jordan Associates (☎ 01622 739134, fax 01622 734611)

ALEXANDER, Richard Thain; MP (C) Newark (majority 8,229); s of Richard Rennie Alexander, of Cockerham, Lancaster, and Gladys Alexander; *b* 29 June 1934; *Educ* Dewsbury GS, UCL, Inst of Advanced Legal Studies London; *m* 1, 1966 (m dis 1984), Valerie Ann, da of Harold Winn (d 1959); 1 s (Nicholas), 1 da (Emma); m 2, 1987, Patricia Diane Hanson; *Career* slr and cmmr for oaths; former chm Doncaster Nat Insur Appeal Tbnl, sr ptnr Jones Alexander & Co Retford 1964–85 (conslt 1985–90); MP (C) Newark 1979–; *Recreations* theatre, opera, reading, a little golf; *Clubs* Newark Cons; *Style*— Richard Alexander, Esq, MP; ✉ 409 Howard House, Dolphin Square, London SW1V 3PF; House of Commons, London SW1A 0AA

ALEXANDER, Roger Michael; s of Hyman Isador Alexander, of London, and Anna, *née* Blumberg; *b* 29 June 1942; *Educ* Dulwich, Law Soc Coll of Law; *m* 26 June 1966, Monica Anne, da of Freddie Freedman; 2 da (Jessica Louise b 6 June 1969, Lucy Katharine b 27 Feb 1971); *Career* admitted slr 1965; Lewis Silkin: ptnr 1965, lead ptnr 1989–, head of Mktg Servs Law Gp 1990–92; non-exec dir EDS Financial Services Div 1995–96; hon slr London Marriage Guidance Cncl 1988 (memb Exec Cncl 1986–90); memb Law Soc 1965; *Recreations* books, photography, gardening, travel; *Style*— Roger Alexander, Esq; ✉ Lewis Silkin, 1 Butler Place, Buckingham Gate, London SW1H 0PT (☎ 0171 222 8191, fax 0171 222 4633)

ALEXANDER, Stephen H; s of Sir Alex Alexander (d 1994), and Marga, *née* Vogel; *b* 12 Dec 1955; *Educ* Winchester, Emmanuel Coll Cambridge (MA Law); *m* 1980, Amanda, *née* Fletcher-Brewer; 3 s (Robert b 26 Sept 1981, Benjamin b 31 July 1985, Michael b 30 June 1987), 1 da (Kate (twin) b 26 Sept 1981); *Career* Imperial Foods Ltd 1978–82, int dir Lyons Tetley Ltd 1982–86, md Lyons Maid Ltd 1986–88, dir J Lyons & Co Ltd 1988–92 (chm Beverages Div 1989–92), md J Lyons & Co Ltd 1992–95, dir Allied Domecq plc and chief exec Allied Domecq Retailing 1995–; non-exec dir Devro plc 1993–; *Recreations* shooting, tennis, theatre, music; *Style*— Stephen Alexander, Esq; ✉ Allied Domecq plc, 24 Portland Place, London W1N 4BB (☎ 0171 323 9000, fax 0171 462 4017, mobile 0836 387815)

ALEXANDER, Terence Joseph; s of Joseph Edward William Alexander (d 1951), of Knaresborough, Yorks, and Patricia, *née* O'Flynn (d 1960); *b* 11 March 1923; *Educ* Ratcliffe Coll Leicester, Norwood Coll Harrogate; *m* 1, 14 Jan 1949 (m dis 1973), Juno St John Stevas; 2 s (Nicholas Edward St John b 18 May 1955, Spiro Marcus St John b 12 May 1958); m 2, 2 June 1976, Jane Downs; *Career* actor; *Theatre* incl: Macbeth, Mrs Willie, Ring for Catty, In at the Death, Move Over Mrs Markham, Two and Two Make Sex, There Goes the Bride, Fringe Benefits, Bit Between the Teeth, The Pleasure of His Company, Poor Bitos, Joie de Vivre, Party Manners; *Television* incl: Hancock's Half Hour, The Man in the Suitcase, The Champions, The Baron, The Avengers, Comedy Playhouse, Nicholas Nickleby, The Forsyth Saga, Dr Finlay's Casebook, Please Sir, Father Dear Father, Unpleasantness at the Belladona Club, The Solarium, Flea in her Ear, The Pallisers, Moody and Peg, The Good Old Days, Les Dawson Show, Churchill and the Generals, Terry and June, Suntrap, Jim Davidson Show, Unity, Just Liz, 7 Dials Mystery, Strangers and Brothers, The New Statesman, Charlie Hungerford in Bergerac 1981–91; *Films* incl: The League of Gentlemen, All the Way Up, Waterloo, The Boy Who Never Was, The Internecine Project, Only When I Larf, Bulldog Breed, The Magic Christian, The Day of the Jackal, Ike - the War Years, The Vault of Horror, Run a Crooked Mile, The Intelligence Men, Danger Within; *Recreations* walking, reading, buying wine at keen prices; *Style*— Terence Alexander, Esq; ✉ c/o Brunskill Management Ltd, Suite 8a, 169 Queen's Gate, London SW7 5EH (☎ 0171 584 8060, fax 0171 589 9460)

ALEXANDER, William (Bill) (*né* Paterson); s of William Paterson, of Warton, Lancs, and Rosemary, *née* McCormack; *b* 23 Feb 1948; *Educ* St Lawrence Coll Ramsgate, Univ of Keele (BA); *m* 1 June 1977, Juliet Linda, da of Michael Hedley Harmer, of Petworth, W Sussex; 2 da (Jessie b 1974, Lola b 1979); *Career* director; seasons with The Other Company, Bristol Old Vic and Royal Court 1972–78, hon assoc dir RSC 1991– (assoc dir RSC 1978–91), artistic dir Birmingham Rep Theatre 1992–; *Theatre* Bristol Old Vic incl: The Ride Across Lake Constance, Twelfth Night, Old Times, Butley, How the Other Half Loves; Royal Court incl: Sex and Kinship in a Savage Society 1976, Amy and the Price of Cotton 1977, Class Enemy 1978, Sugar and Spice 1979; RSC incl: Factory Birds 1977, Shout Across the River, The Hang of the Gaol, Captain Swing 1978, Men's Beano 1979, Bastard Angel, Henry IV (tour) 1980, Accrington Pals 1981, Volpone 1983, Richard III 1984, The Merry Wives of Windsor 1985, A Midsummer Night's Dream 1986, Twelfth Night, The Merchant of Venice, Cymbeline 1987, Duchess of Malfi 1989, The Taming of the Shrew 1990, Much Ado About Nothing 1991, Taming of the Shrew 1992, The School of Night 1992; Troilus and Cressida (Shakespeare Theatre Washington) 1992; Birmingham Rep incl: Othello 1993, Volpone 1993, Old Times 1993, The Snowman 1993, Awake and Sing 1994, The Tempest 1994, The Servant 1995, Macbeth 1995, Way of the World 1995, Divine Right 1996, Dr Jekyll and Mr Hyde 1996, The Alchemist 1996; *Style*— Bill Alexander, Esq; ✉ Rose Cottage, Tunley, nr Cirencester, Glos; Birmingham Repertory Theatre, Broad Street, Birmingham (☎ 0121 236 4532)

ALEXANDER, Dr William David; s of Rev Hugh Crighton Alexander, of Oakington, Cambridge, and Monica, *née* Hill; *b* 9 June 1945; *Educ* Clifton, St Thomas' Hosp Med Sch London (MB BS), MRCP; *m* 12 June 1968, Prof Dorothy Hanson Crawford, da of late Sir Theo Crawford, of Langton Green, Tunbridge Wells, Kent; 2 s (Danny b 1970, Theo b 1973); *Career* conslt physician and dir Diabetes Unit Queen Mary's Hosp Sidcup and Bexley Health Authy 1978–; author of various reports and papers on diabetes related topics; chm: Queen Mary's Hosp Med Staff and Exec Ctees 1983–85, SE Thames Diabetes Physicians Gp 1984–88; govr Chislehurst and Sidcup GS 1984–86; Br Diabetic Assoc: hon sec Med Advsy Ctee and med advsr 1984–89, conslt memb Dist Mgmnt Bd

1988–, memb Exec Cncl, chm Diabetes Servs Advsy Ctee; FRCP 1989, FRSPB; memb: BMA, BDA, EASD; *Recreations* taxidermy, Bexley borough choir, beekeeping; *Clubs* Chislehurst Golf; *Style*— Dr William Alexander; ✉ Yeomans Hall, 27 Halfway St, Sidcup, Kent DA15 8LQ (☎ 0181 302 2678); Diabetes Unit, Queen Mary's Hospital, Sidcup, Kent (☎ 0181 302 2678)

ALEXANDER, William J (Bill); *b* 15 Feb 1947, Corbridge, Northumberland; *m* Dorothy; 1 s, 1 da; *Career* British Coal Corp (formerly NCB): joined as graduate trainee 1970, area mech engr Scotland 1982–83, chief engr Scottish Region 1983–86, chief mech engr HQ 1986–87, head of engrg 1987–89; Thames Water Utilities Ltd: engrg dir 1989–91, tech dir 1991–92, md 1992–, exec main bd dir Thames Water plc (incl responsibility for construction of Thames Water London Ring Main) 1994–; former pres Inst of Mining Electrical and Mining Mechanical Engrs (IMEMME); CEng, FIMechE, FIMinE, Hon FIMEMME, FInstD, FEng 1996; *Style*— Bill Alexander, Esq, FEng; ✉ Thames Water plc, 14 Cavendish Place, London W1M 0NU (☎ 0171 636 8686, fax 0171 833 6135)

ALEXANDER OF TUNIS, Countess; Hon Davina Mary; *née* Woodhouse; LVO (1991); da of 4 Baron Terrington; *b* 12 April 1955; *m* 1981, as his 2 w, 2 Earl Alexander of Tunis; 2 da (Lady Rose b 1982, Lady Lucy b 1984); *Career* lady in waiting to HRH The Princess Margaret, Countess of Snowdon 1975–79; extra lady in waiting 1979–; special events conslt and co-ordinator; pres: SOS (stars orgn supporting action for people with cerebral palsy) 1992–95, Society of Stars (celebrity support for children and adults with cerebral palsy) 1996–; memb Governing Cncl Friends of The Elderly and Gentlefolk's Help; *Style*— The Rt Hon the Countess Alexander of Tunis, LVO; ✉ 59 Wandsworth Common West Side, London SW18 2ED

ALEXANDER OF TUNIS, 2 Earl (UK 1952); Shane William Desmond Alexander; also Viscount Alexander of Tunis (UK 1946) and Baron Rideau (UK 1952); s of Field Marshal 1 Earl Alexander of Tunis, KG, GCB, OM, GCMG, CSI, DSO, MC, PC (3 s of 4 Earl of Caledon), and Lady Margaret Bingham, GBE, JP (d 1977), da of 5 Earl of Lucan (gs of the Crimean War commander); *b* 30 June 1935; *Educ* Harrow, Ashbury Coll Ottawa; *m* 1, 1971 (m dis 1976), Hilary, da of John van Geest, of Lincs; m 2, 1981, Hon Davina Woodhouse, Extra Lady-in-Waiting to HRH The Princess Margaret, da of 4 Baron Terrington; 2 da (Lady Rose Margaret b 23 April 1982, Lady Lucy Caroline b 20 Sept 1984); *Heir* bro, Hon Brian Alexander, *qv*; *Career* sits as Cons peer in House of Lords; Lt Irish Gds (res); Lord in Waiting to HM The Queen 1974; patron Br-Tunisian Soc 1975–, dir: International Healthcare Pharmaceuticals Hotels Group 1981–, Kyrgoil Corp (Canada) 1995–, Marketform Ltd 1996–; pres Br-American Canadian Assocs 1988–94, chm and tstee Canada Meml Fndn 1990–; Liveryman Worshipful Co of Mercers 1965; Order of Republic of Tunisia 1996; *Clubs* MCC; *Style*— The Rt Hon Earl Alexander of Tunis; ✉ 59 Wandsworth Common West Side, London SW18 2ED (☎ 0181 874 4831, fax 0181 877 9487)

ALEXANDER OF WEEDON, Baron (Life Peer UK 1988); Robert Scott Alexander; QC (1973); s of late Samuel James Alexander, and Hannah May Alexander; *b* 5 Sept 1936; *Educ* Brighton Coll, King's Coll Cambridge (MA); *m* 3, 1985, Marie Sugrue; 2 s and 1 da (by first m); *Career* called to the Bar Middle Temple 1961, bencher 1979; judge of the Cts of Appeal of Jersey and Guernsey 1985–88; chm Bar Cncl 1985–86 (vice chm 1984–85), chm Panel of Takeovers and Mergers 1987–89; chm National Westminster Bank plc 1989–; non-exec dir: RTZ Corporation plc 1991–96 (non-exec dir CRA Ltd Dec 1995–96), Int Stock Exchange of the UK and Republic of Ireland 1991–93; dep chm SIB 1994–; memb Govt's Panel on Sustainable Devpt 1994–; chm: Cncl Justice 1990–, Tstees Crisis 1990–96; govr and chm Fndn Bd Royal Shakespeare Co 1994–, pres Parkinson's Disease Soc 1990–93; tstee National Gallery 1987–93, pres King's Coll Assoc 1980–81, memb Cncl of Govrs Wycombe Abbey Sch 1986–92; Hon LLD: Sheffield 1991, Buckingham 1992, Keele 1993, Exeter 1995; presentation fell King's Coll London 1995; FRSA 1991; *Recreations* theatre, literature, tennis; *Clubs* Garrick; *Style*— The Lord Alexander of Weedon, QC; ✉ c/o National Westminster Bank plc, 41 Lothbury, London EC2P 2BP (☎ 0171 726 1000)

ALEXANDER-SINCLAIR OF FRESWICK, Maj-Gen David Boyd; CB (1980); s of Cdr Mervyn Boyd Alexander-Sinclair of Freswick, RN (d 1979), and Avril Nora, *née* Fergusson-Buchanan (d 1980); *b* 2 May 1927; *Educ* Eton; *m* 1958, Ann Ruth, da of late Lt-Col Graeme Daglish; 2 s, 1 da; *Career* cmdg 3 Bn Royal Green Jackets 1967–69, Cdr 6 Armd Bde 1971–73, GOC 1 Div 1975–77, Chief of Staff UKLF 1978–79, Cmdt Staff Coll 1980–82, ret; *Style*— Maj-Gen David Alexander-Sinclair, CB

ALFÖLDY, HE Tádé; s of László Alföldy (d 1977), of Budapest, and Erzsébet, *née* Újvári (d 1980); *b* 6 Aug 1946; *Educ* Kölcsey Ferenc GS, Karl Marx Univ Budapest; *m* 26 Oct 1968, Orsolya, da of József Baraczka; 2 da (Orsolya b 22 April 1971, Virág b 30 Aug 1974); *Career* Hungarian diplomat; sales exec Hungarian Shipping Agency 1968–70, teacher Hungarian Youth Union 1970–74, sec gen Int Ctee of Children's and Adolescents' Movements (CIMEA) 1974–79; Arab desk offr Miny of Foreign Affrs 1979–80, second then first sec Kuwait 1980–85; Miny of Foreign Affrs: Br desk offr 1985–89, dir N Atlantic Dept 1989–90, dep sec of state 1990–91; ambass: to Greece 1991–94, to Ct of St James's 1994–; *Recreations* family, gardening, tennis; *Clubs* Athenaeum, Army and Navy, Queen's, Foreign Policy Assoc (Budapest); *Style*— HE Mr Tádé Alföldy; ✉ Embassy of the Republic of Hungary, 35 Eaton Place, London SW1X 8BY (☎ 0171 235 0214, fax 0171 823 1348)

ALFORD, Prof Bernard William Ernest; s of Ernest Edward Alford (d 1970), of Uffculme, Devon, and Winifred Daisy Alford (d 1966); *b* 17 Oct 1937; *Educ* Tiverton GS, LSE (BSc (Econ), PhD); *m* 18 Aug 1962, Valerie Sandra, da of Albert Thomas North (d 1963), of Cullompton, Devon; 1 da (Naomi Elizabeth b 1968), 2 s (Jonathan Edward b 1970, Dominic James Henry b 1973); *Career* asst lectr in econ history LSE 1961–62; Univ of Bristol: lectr then reader in econ and social history 1962–82, prof of econ and social history 1982–, head Dept of Historical Studies; numerous contribs to books and learned jls; treas Economic History Soc 1988–96 (memb Cncl 1979, chm Pubns Ctee 1983–88); memb: Lord Chllr's Advsy Ctee on The Public Records 1988–94, Advsy Cncl Inst of Contemporary Br History 1989–, Research Grants Bd ESRC 1989–93; *Books* A History of the Carpenters' Company (with T C Barker, 1968), Depression and Recovery? British Economic Growth, 1918–1939 (1972), W D and H O Wills and the Development of the UK Tobacco Industry 1783–1965 (1973), British Economic Performance, 1945–1975 (1988), Economic Planning in Britain 1943–1951 (with R Lowe and N Rollings, 1992), Britain and the World Economy since 1880 (1995); *Recreations* family life; *Style*— Prof Bernard Alford; ✉ The Bank House, High St, Marshfield, Chippenham, Wilts SN14 8LT (☎ 01225 891660); Department of Historical Studies, University of Bristol, 13–15 Woodland Rd, Bristol BS8 1TB (☎ 0117 9287937, fax 0117 928 8276, telex 445938 BSUNIV G)

ALFORD, George Francis Onslow; s of Cdr Ian Francis Onslow Alford, RN (ret), of London, and Jacqueline Louise, *née* Herbert; *b* 10 Oct 1948; *Educ* Winchester, UCL (BScEcon); *m* 12 Jan 1974, Adronie Elizabeth, da of late Douglas Crisp Gall, of Chantersell, Nutley, Sussex; *Career* Kleinwort Benson Group 1970–: rep Tokyo Office 1976–80, mangr Middle East Dept 1980–83, gp personnel dir 1987–91, head of Private Banking 1991–; md Fendrake Ltd 1982–87; dir London Human Resource Gp 1994 (chm 1991–93), dep chm City and Inner London North Trg and Enterprise Cncl, chm Int Private Banking Advsy Gp Br Bankers' Assoc 1995–, memb London Stock Exchange Working Pty on Private Share Ownership 1995–; memb: Langbourne Ward Club, United Ward Club; memb Cncl Br Export Houses Assoc 1984–87; Freeman City of London, Asst Worshipful Co of Basketmakers; FCIS, FIPM; *Recreations* sailing, skiing, riding; *Clubs* Royal Solent Yacht, City Livery; *Style*— George Alford, Esq; ✉ 28 Eagle Wharf Court, Lafone Street, Southwark SE1 (☎ 0171 407 6125); Kleinwort Benson Group, 20 Fenchurch Street, London EC3P 3DB (☎ 0171 623 8000, telex 888531)

ALFORD, Richard Harding; OBE (1988); s of Jack Harding Alford, of London (d 1984), and Gertrude Sylvia, *née* Buckland (d 1990); *b* 28 Dec 1943; *Educ* Dulwich, Keble Coll Oxford (Open Grove exhbn in modern history, BA, Dip in History and Philosophy of Science); *m* Penelope Jane, da of James Wort; 2 da (Harriet Jane b 18 April 1971, Jessica Louise b 21 March 1973), 1 s (Joseph William b 1 June 1973); *Career* vol VSO Aitchison Coll Lahore 1966–67; British Cncl: asst cultural attaché British Embassy Prague 1969–72, various posts (Middle East Dept, Policy Res Dept and Educn Contracts Dept) 1972–77; Project Planning Centre Univ of Bradford and Inst of Educn Univ of London 1977–78; British Cncl: asst rep New Delhi 1978–81, dir E Europe and N Asia Dept 1982–85, rep Poland 1985–89, dir Personnel 1989–93, regnl dir Central Europe 1993–96, dir Italy 1996–; govr Centre for Int Briefing Farnham Castle 1992–96; *Recreations* squash, tennis, theatre; *Clubs* Friends of Dulwich Coll; *Style*— Richard Alford, Esq, OBE; ✉ British Council, 10 Spring Gardens, London SW1A 2BN (☎ 0171 389 4792)

ALFREDS, Michael Guy Alexander (Mike); s of John Mark Alfreds (d 1978), and Hylda, *née* Metz; *b* 5 June 1934; *Educ* Bradfield, American Theater Wing NY, Carnegie-Mellon Inst Pittsburgh Pa USA (BFA); *Career* director; dir of prodns Summer Stock Kennebunkport Maine 1958–59; freelance dir 1963–70 (Israeli theatre and TV 1970–75), and 1983–; assoc dir NT 1985 and 1987–88; appts as artistic dir incl: Theatre West Tucson Arizona 1960, Cincinnati Playhouse-in-the-Park 1961–62, Khan Theatre Jerusalem 1972–75, Shared Experience 1975–87 (fndr), Cambridge Theatre Co 1991–95, Method & Madness 1995–; teacher of acting and directing at various instns incl: LAMDA, Beijing Central Acad of Drama, Univ of Tel Aviv, Arts Cncl Wellington NZ, Royal Shakespeare Co; author of several articles in professional jls and co-adaptor of Eugene Sue's The Wandering Jew (1987); memb: Arts Cncl Drama Panel 1981–85, Arts Cncl Drama Projects Sub Ctee 1982–85, Mgmnt Ctee The Actor's Centre 1988, Working Pty of Gulbenkian Fndn Enquiry Into Dir Trg (report A Better Direction) 1987–89; Bd dir: Almeida Theatre 1982–89, Shared Experience 1975–, David Glass Ensemble 1990–94; *Theatre* prodns at Shared Experience incl: Arabian Nights Trilogy 1975–77, Bleak House 1977–78, Science Fictions 1978–79, Cymbeline 1979–80, The Merchant of Venice 1981, The Seagull 1981, La Ronde 1982, A Handful of Dust 1982, The Comedy Without A Title 1983, Successful Strategies 1983, False Confidences 1983, Marriage 1984, The Three Sisters, Too True To Be Good 1986; Cambridge Theatre Co incl: Lady Windermere's Fan, The Country Wife 1991, The Revenger's Tragedy, The Game of Love and Change (and NT) 1992, The Hypochondriac 1993, The Dearly Beloved 1993, Les Enfants du Paradis 1993, A Handful of Dust 1994, Uncle Silas 1994, Emma 1994, What I Did in the Holidays 1995; prodns for Method & Madness incl: Jude the Obscure 1995, Private Lives, Flesh and Blood, Ghosts 1996, The Winter's Tale 1997; other prodns incl: Suitcase Packers (Cameri Theatre Tel Aviv 1983, Le Theatre des Nations 1984, Edinburgh Festival 1985), 1001 Nights (Theater der Stadt Heidelberg) 1984, The Cherry Orchard (NT) 1985, The Wandering Jew (NT) 1987, Countrymania (NT) 1987, Blood Wedding (Tarragon Theatre Toronto and Banff Centre) 1988, A Streetcar Named Desire (Tianjin People's Art Theatre China) 1988, Ghosts (Beersheba Municipal Theatre Israel) 1989, The Miser (Oxford Stage Co) 1990, Trouble in Paradise (Talking Pictures) 1990, The Seagull (Oxford Stage Co) 1991, A Flea in her Ear (Theatr Clwyd and W Yorks Playhouse); *Awards* Best Revival BTA Drama Awards for The Seagull 1982, Best Dir BTA Drama and Plays and Players Awards for The Cherry Orchard 1986, Israel Kinoor David Award for Best Dir and Best Prodn for Mandragola (Haifa Theatre) 1971 and Suitcase Packers (Cameri Theatre) 1984); *Style*— Mike Alfreds, Esq; ✉ Method & Madness, 25 Short Street, London SE1 8LJ (☎ 0171 401 9797, fax 0171 401 9777)

ALGOSAIBI, HE Dr Ghazi Abdulrahman; *b* 1940; *Educ* Univ of Cairo (LLB), Univ of Southern Calif (MA), Univ of London (PhD); *m* 1968; 1 da, 3 s; *Career* Saudi Arabian diplomat; King Saud Univ Riyadh 1965–74: asst prof, prof, head Political Science Dept, dean Faculty of Commerce, also advsr to numerous govt depts (incl Miny of Def and Civil Aviation, Miny of Finance and Nat Economy and Inst of Public Admin Miny of Foreign Affairs); dir Saudi Railways 1974–75, min of industry and electricity 1975–82, min of health 1982–84, ambass to Bahrain 1984–92, ambass to the Ct of St James's 1992–; involved in numerous charitable orgns (incl receiving first Human Serv Award from Soc of Handicapped Children Riyadh 1992 for role as fndr and first chm); decorations from Saudi Arabia, Kuwait, Qatar, Spain, Germany, France, Sweden, Finland, Venezuela, Indonesia, Taiwan and Zaire; *Poetry* Poems from the Pearl Islands, Drops of Thirst, Battle without Flag, Love Verses, You Are Riyadh, Fever, Return to Old Places, Flowers in Sana's Braids, Obituary of a Former Knight, Necklace of Stones, Dusting the Colour from Roses (1994); *Prose* From Here and There, In My Humble Opinion, More of My Humble Opinion, Face to Face with Development, Poems I Liked, A Life in Poetry, A Hundred Rose Petals, The Cultural Invasion, The Gulf Crisis: An Attempt to Understand (1993), The Dilemma of Development (1994), An Apartment Called Freedom (1996); *Recreations* swimming, fishing and ping-pong; *Style*— HE Dr Ghazi Algosaibi; ✉ Royal Embassy of Saudi Arabia, 30 Charles Street, London W1X 7PM

ALI, Dr (Mohammad) Shaukat; s of Shahamat Ali (d 1973), and Hashena Begum (d 1992); *b* 1 June 1939; *Educ* Kasba High English Sch, Dhaka Govt Coll, Univ Med Coll Dhaka (MB BS), Univ of Liverpool (DTM & H); *m* 30 Sept 1962, Hasina, da of Yakub Ali Bhuiyan, of Chittagong, Bangladesh; 2 s (Sanwar b 1965, Shahrar b 1969), 2 da (Sherlia b 1967, Shabrina b 1977); *Career* registrar in gen med Professorial Unit Chittagong Med Coll Hosp 1964–65, sr registrar in geriatric and gen med KCH 1971–74, conslt physician in geriatric and gen med Greenwich Dist Hosp 1974–; author of various articles; actively involved with: BMA, Overseas Doctors' Assoc UK, Bangladesh Med Assoc UK (past pres); chm Dist Div of Med 1989–91; memb: NHS Health Advsy Service 1994–, GMC 1994–; BMA: memb 1966–, memb Regnl Conslts and Specialists Ctee 1988–91, currently chm Greenwich and Bexley Div; FRCP (London) 1994 (MRCP 1973), FRCPI 1984 (MRCPI 1971), FRCP (Glas) 1984, FRCPE 1984; *Books* British Medical Journal (contrib, 1978); *Recreations* photography, gardening, cooking and entertaining; *Clubs* West Kent Medico-Chirurgical Soc; *Style*— Dr Shaukat Ali; ✉ Greenwich District Hospital, Vanbrugh Hill, London SE10 9HE (☎ 0181 858 8141)

ALISON, Fiona; da of Harry Widdup (d 1976), of Weymouth, Dorset, and Nell Roberts (d 1968); *b* 7 March 1939; *Educ* Weymouth GS, Weymouth Coll, Univ of London (CertEd); *m* 30 June 1962, Peter Alison (d 1995), s of Youssof Alison; 1 s (Julian Piers b 16 June 1969), 1 da (Elizabeth Charlotte b 10 Jan 1973); *Career* int child photographer 1980–; works incl: children's portraiture 1980–84, children's fashion and advertising photography GB 1984–87, photographic assignments and lectures worldwide 1988– (BIPP nat conf speaker 1990, Enfield Arts Cncl photographic convention speaker 1990, Les Journées Mondiales de L'Image Congres Corsica speaker 1990), exhibition of work at Glaziers' Hall London 1983, numerous appearances on radio and tv, first woman judge BP Chemicals World Photographic Competition 1990, tutor Fuji Film UK Sch of Photography Cyprus and GB 1991; speaker: 13th Congreso Internacional de Foto/Ventas Madrid 1994, MPA/Kodak Delphi UK Tour 1996; FBIPP 1988 (LBIPP 1981, ABIPP 1982), FRSA 1982, FRPS 1992 (Fellowship and Associateship Appied Distinctions Panel,

1993), FMPA 1995; *Awards* Kodak Nat Portrait Award winner (first woman to win) 1980, 3M Nat Portfolio Award winner (first woman to win) 1983, BIPP Peter Grugeon Award (first woman to win) 1988; *Recreations* reading, theatre, croquet; *Clubs* London Portrait Gp; *Style—* Mrs Fiona Alison; ✉ Fiona Alison Studio, 89 Broughton Avenue, Aylesbury, Bucks HP20 1QB (☎ 01296 23670)

ALISON, Rt Hon Michael James Hugh; PC (1981), MP (C) Selby (majority 9,508); s of J S I Alison, of London and Sydney, Australia; *b* 27 June 1926; *Educ* Eton, Wadham Coll Oxford, Ridley Hall Cambridge; *m* 1958, Sylvia Mary, da of Anthony Haigh, CMG; 2 s, 1 da; *Career* served Lt Coldstream Gds 1944–48; clerk Lazard Bros merchant bankers 1951–53, res offr London Municipal Soc 1954–58, memb Kensington Cncl 1956–59, Cons Research Dept 1958–64; MP (C): Barkston Ash 1964–83, Selby 1983–; jt Parly under sec DHSS 1970–74; min of state: NI Office 1979–81, Dept of Employment 1981–83; PPS to the Prime Minister 1983–87; second church estates cmmr 1987; *Books* Christianity and Conservatism (ed jtly, 1990); *Style—* The Rt Hon Michael Alison, MP; ✉ House of Commons, London SW1A 0AA (☎ 0171 219 3000)

ALKER, Doug; *b* 23 Nov 1940; *Educ* Royal Cross Sch for Deaf Children Preston, Mary Hare GS Berks, Univ of London (BSc Maths (external)), Univ of Birmingham (MBA (Public Sector)); *Career* analytical chemist Pilkington Brothers 1959–64, experimental offr Plastics Div ICI 1964–85, researcher BBC 1985–87; RNID: dir of community servs 1987–90, dir of quality and res 1990–94, chief exec 1994–; patron Cncl for the Advancement of Communication with Deaf People (CACDP); hon fell Univ of Central Lancs 1995; memb: ACENVO, Inst of Dirs; *Recreations* football, rugby, chess, magic; *Style—* Doug Alker, Esq; ✉ Royal National Institute for Deaf People, 19–23 Featherstone Street, London EC1Y 8SL (☎ 0171 296 8000, fax 0171 296 8199)

ALLAIRE, Paul Arthur; s of Arthur E Allaire (d 1960), of Worcester, Mass, USA, and Mrs G P Murphy; *b* 21 July 1938; *Educ* Worcester Polytechnic Inst (BS), Carnegie Mellon Univ (MS); *m* 1963, Kathleen, da of Thomas Buckley (d 1959), of New York; 1 s (Brian b 1964), 1 da (Christiana b 1967); *Career* engr Univac 1960–62, project mangr General Electric 1962–64, mangr of fin planning and pricing Xerox Corp 1966–70, fin conroller Rank Xerox Ltd 1970–73; Xerox Corp: dir of int fin 1973–74, dir of int ops 1974–75; Rank Xerox Ltd: chief staff offr 1975–79, dep md 1979–80, md 1980–83, memb Bd of Dirs; Xerox Corp: sr vice pres 1983–86, pres 1986–, chief exec offr 1990–, chm Bd 1991–, dir Fuji Xerox Co; non-exec dir: SmithKline Beecham plc 1993–, Sara Lee Corp, NY City Ballet, NY Stock Exchange; memb: Business Cncl, Bd Catalyst, Bd Cncl on Foreign Rels; tstee: Carnegie Mellon Univ (memb Business Advsy Cncl Grad Sch of Industl Admin), Worcester Poly Inst Mass; *Recreations* skiing, riding, tennis; *Style—* Paul Allaire; ✉ Xerox Corporation, PO Box 1600, Stamford, CT 06904, USA

ALLAM, Roger William; s of The Rev William Sydney Allam (d 1977), of London, and Kathleen, *née* Service; *b* 26 Oct 1953; *Educ* Christ's Hosp Horsham Sussex, Univ of Manchester (BA); *Career* actor; fndr memb Monstrous Regiment Theatre Co; repertory work in Manchester, Birmingham and Glasgow; author of contribs on Mercutio and Duke Vincentio in Players of Shakespeare II and III; *Theatre* roles incl: Angelo in Measure for Measure, title role in Macbeth, Macheath in Threepenny Opera, Dr Rock in The Doctor and The Devils; RSC (joined RSC 1981 (assoc artist 1990)) roles incl: Richmore in Twin Rivals, Conrad in Our Friends in The North, Theseus and Oberon in A Midsummer Night's Dream, Mercutio in Romeo and Juliet, Victor in Today, Ford in The Party, The Officer in The Dream Play, Javert in Les Miserables, Adrian in The Archbishop's Ceiling, Clarence in Richard III, Pimm in Heresies, Brutus in Julius Caesar, Sir Toby Belch in Twelfth Night, Duke Vincentio in Measure for Measure, Benedick in Much Ado About Nothing, Trigorin in The Seagull, Dr Jekyll in The Strange Case of Dr Jekyll and Mr Hyde, Macbeth, Trissotin in The Learned Ladie; other roles incl: Oberon in The Fairy Queen (Aix-en-Provence Festival) 1989, Angelo in Una Pooka (London) 1992, Philip Madras in The Madras House (London) 1992, Stone in City of Angels (London) 1993, Bernard Nightingale in Arcadia (London) 1994, John Watling in The Importance of Being Earnest (Birmingham Rep and Old Vic) 1995, Mirabell in The Way of the World (RNT) 1995; *Television* incl: Who Bombed Birmingham?, Summerchild in A Landing on the Sun (BBC) 1994, Between the Lines, Richard II in Henry IV; *Radio* incl: Valmont in Les Liaisons Dangereuse and title role in Peter Grimes; *Films* incl: Wilt, 5000 Francs; *Recreations* playing and listening to music, cooking, drinking red wine; *Clubs* Peg's; *Style—* Roger Allam, Esq; ✉ Meg Poole, c/o The Richard Stone Partnership, 25 Whitehall, London SW1A 2BS (☎ 0171 839 6421, fax 839 5002)

ALLAN, *see:* Havelock-Allan

ALLAN, Alexander Claud Stuart; s of Lord Allan of Kilmahew, DSO, OBE (Life Peer, d 1979), and Maureen Catherine Flower, *née* Stuart Clark; *b* 9 Feb 1951; *Educ* Harrow, Clare Coll Cambridge (MA), UCL (MSc); *m* 1978, Katie Christine, da of Keith Clemson (d 1988); *Career* HM Customs and Excise 1973–76; HM Treasury: joined 1976, princ private sec to Chllr of the Exchequer 1986–89, under sec for international finance 1989–90, under sec for general expenditure policy 1990–92, princ private sec to Prime Minister 1992–; *Recreations* Grateful Dead music, sailing, computers; *Clubs* Royal Ocean Racing; *Style—* A C S Allan, Esq; ✉ 10 Downing Street, London SW1A 2AA

ALLAN, Andrew Norman (Andy); *b* 26 Sept 1943; *Career* early career as presenter, prodr and editor with ABC and ITN, various positions rising to head of news Thames Television 1969–78, prog controller rising to md Tyne Tees Television 1978–84; Central Independent Television: dir of progs 1984–93, also md Central Broadcasting 1990–93, md Central Independent Television plc 1993–94; Carlton UK Television (following takeover of Central by Carlton Communications plc): chief exec 1994–95, dir of progs 1996–; memb ITV Cncl 1993–96; *Style—* Andy Allan, Esq; ✉ Carlton UK Television Ltd, 35–38 Portman Square, London W1H 0NU (☎ 0171 486 6688, fax 0171 612 7447)

ALLAN, (Gordon) David; s of Joseph Allan (d 1981), of Banbury, Oxon, and Isobel Joyce, *née* Williams (d 1982); *b* 7 Aug 1940; *Educ* Bury GS Lancs; *m* 1972, Margaret Elizabeth, da of John Beresford Humphries; 2 s (Simon b 24 Oct 1978, Robin b 2 June 1981); *Career* country music disc jockey; gen factotum then asst stage mangr Manchester Library Theatre 1957–59, backstage jobs in various rep theatres incl Theatre Royal Windsor 1959–64, stage mgmnt in West End incl asst stage mangr for Barbra Streisand's Funny Girl 1964–67, disc jockey Radio 390 (pirate station) 1967–68, announcer/newsreader Anglia TV 1968–69; BBC TV and Radio: continuity announcer BBC2 1969–94, freelance country music bdcaster Radio 2 1969–, presenter/co-prodr TV coverage of annual Wembley Country Music Festival 1969–89, presenter Sunday Early Show (Radio 2) 1988–92, currently presenter: in-flight country prog for British Airways, Country Club (BBC Radio 2), Melody Radio London; hon citizen Nashville Tennessee 1978; memb Country Music Assoc of America 1970; *Awards* Disc Jockey of the Year Br Country Music Assoc 1977, 1978 and 1979, Most Popular Euro Country Music Disc Jockey (poll taken in 5 countries by Br Jl Country Music Roundup) 1990; *Recreations* photography, swimming, lying in the (preferably Spanish) sun; *Style—* David Allan, Esq; ✉ Redmayne, Bull Lane, Gerrards Cross, Bucks SL9 8RF (☎ 01753 882541)

ALLAN, David Ian; s of Ian Allan, OBE, and Mollie Eileen, *née* Franklin; *b* 7 July 1954; *Educ* Seaford Coll; *m* 30 Sept 1978, Gillian Susan, da of Canon Dennis Walter Hedges; 2 s (Marc Ian b 21 June 1982, Nicholas David b 29 Sept 1984), 1 da (Victoria Jane b 15 June 1986); *Career* WH Smith & Son 1974–78; Ian Allan Ltd: gen trg 1978–83, sales dir 1983–85, md 1985–89, chm 1986–, chm Ian Allan Regalia Ltd 1986–, chm Ian Allan Printing Ltd 1989–, chm Chase Organics 1992–, jt md Ian Allan Group (Graphics) 1990–; govr Halstead Prep Sch Woking 1993–; Freedom City of London 1987; Liveryman Worshipful Co of Stationers and Newspaper Makers 1988; MIDM 1994, FInstD 1995; *Recreations* soccer, hockey, skiing, golf, tennis, cricket; *Clubs* Staines Hockey (vice pres), Exeter Cavaliers CC (vice pres); *Style—* David Allan, Esq; ✉ Terminal House, Shepperton TW17 8AS (☎ 01932 255500)

ALLAN, Prof Dennis Joseph; s of Joseph Sharp Allan (d 1963), and Annie Irene, *née* Parker (1975); *b* 10 May 1933; *Educ* Lawrence Sheriff Sch Rugby, Rugby Coll of Engrg (BSc(Eng) external); *m* Glenis Carole Elizabeth, *née* Lake; 2 da (Karen Grace b 1957, Melanie Jane b 1962); *Career* student/graduate apprentice BTH Co Ltd Rugby 1951–56, Nat Serv Tech Servs REME 1957–58, asst chief engr AEI Transformers Ltd Wythenshaw 1964–68 (devpt section ldr Rugby 1959–64); GEC Transformers Ltd Stafford: chief devpt engr 1968–78, quality mangr 1978–80, engrg mangr 1980–83; dir and tech mangr GEC Alsthom T & D Transformers Ltd Stafford 1983–; Royal Acad of Engrg chair in principles of engrg design UMIST 1991–; chm: Study Ctee 12 (Transformers) CIGRE 1986–94 (chm BNC 1994–), TC14 (Transformers) IEC 1993–, Power Div IEE 1990–91; FIEE 1971, FIMechE 1971, FIEEE 1992, FEng 1993; *Recreations* industrial archaeology, mediaeval architecture; *Style—* Prof Dennis Allan, FEng; ✉ Crosswinds, Battle Ridge, Hopton, Stafford ST18 0BG (☎ 01785 42773); Director and Technical Manager, GEC Alsthom T & D Transformers Ltd, PO Box 26, Lichfield Road, Stafford ST17 4LN (☎ 01785 274380, fax 01785 274407)

ALLAN, Geoffrey Robert John; s of Dr Robert Leitch Allan (d 1976), and Elsie Kathleen, *née* Stewart; *b* 25 March 1941; *Educ* Strathallan Sch Forgandenny Perthshire, Univ of Glasgow (BDS Glas, FDS RCPS Glas, MRD RCPS Glas, Rugby blue), Univ of London (MSc); *m* 1, 1969; 2 s (Christopher Geoffrey b 4 Nov 1973, Nicholas Cochrane Robert b 4 Jan 1975), 1 da (Kimberley Kathleen b 12 Nov 1977); m 2, Dec 1984, Rosalind Mary, da of David Smith; 1 step s (Gavin David b 10 April 1973), 1 step da (Suzanne Mary b 27 Feb 1975); *Career* trainee rising to shift supt Clyde Paper Co 1960–64; house offr, sr house offr, registrar and sr registrar Glasgow Dental Hosp Canniesburn and Stobhill 1969–77, Eastman Dental Hosp London 1975, conslt in restorative dentistry Guy's Hosp 1977–79, joined Glynn Setchell (now called Glynn, Setchell and Allan) 1979; examiner RCPS Glasgow 1985–; memb: BDA, Int Coll of Dentists; *Books* BDA Booklet on Treatment of the Cleft Palate Patient; *Recreations* family, golf, skiing; *Clubs* Wilderness; *Style—* Geoffrey Allan, Esq; ✉ Glynn, Setchell & Allan, 35 Devonshire Place, London W1N 1PE (☎ 0171 935 3342)

ALLAN, George Alexander; s of William Allan (d 1976), of Edinburgh, and Janet Peters, *née* Watt (d 1976); *b* 3 Feb 1936; *Educ* Daniel Stewart's Coll Edinburgh, Univ of Edinburgh (MA); *m* 1 Sept 1962, Anne Violet, da of Vibert Ambrose George Veevers, of Kelso; 2 s (Victor Julian Douglas b 1964, Timothy Edward Douglas b 1966); *Career* Edinburgh Univ Air Sqdn 1953–56, CCF RAFVR 1958–66; classics master Glasgow Acad 1958–60; Daniel Stewart's Coll Edinburgh: classics master 1960–63, head of classics 1963–73, housemaster 1966–73; Robert Gordon's Coll Aberdeen: dep headmaster 1973–77, headmaster 1978–96; schoolmaster fell commoner Corpus Christi Coll Cambridge 1972–; played rugby for Edinburgh XV 1960–62, Scottish trial 1963; Scottish Div HMC: sec 1980–87, rep on Nat Ctee 1982–83, chm 1988–89; memb Ctee Scottish Cncl of Ind Schs 1988–96; govr Welbeck Coll 1980–89, burgess of guild City of Aberdeen 1981–; memb HMC 1978–96; dir Edinburgh Acad 1996–, memb Scottish Advsy Ctee Imperial Cancer Research Fund 1996; *Recreations* golf, gardening, music, travel; *Clubs* East India and Public Schools, Royal Northern and Univ (Aberdeen); *Style—* George Allan, Esq; ✉ Maxwiel, 5 Abbey View, Kelso TD5 8HX (☎ 01573 225128)

ALLAN, James Nicholas; CMG (1989), CBE (1976); s of late Morris Edward Allan, and Joan Bach; *b* 22 May 1932; *Educ* Gresham's, LSE; *m* 1961, Helena Susara Crouse; 1 s, 1 da; *Career* HM Forces 1950–53, asst princ CRO 1956–58, 3 later 2 sec Cape Town/Pretoria 1958–59, private sec to Parly Under Sec 1959–61; 1 sec: Freetown 1961–64, Nicosia 1964; CRO later FCO 1964–68, head of chancery Peking 1969–71, Luxembourg 1971–73, cnsllr seconded to NI Office Belfast 1973–75, cnsllr FCO 1976, head of Overseas Info Dept FCO 1978–81, high cmmr Mauritius 1981–85, concurrently ambass (non-resident) to the Comoros 1984–85, ambass to Mozambique 1986–89, sr directing staff RCDS 1989–92; *Style—* James Allan, Esq, CMG, CBE; ✉ c/o Foreign and Commonwealth Office, King Charles St, London SW1A 2AH

ALLAN, Prof James Wilson; *b* 5 May 1945; *Educ* Marlborough, St Edmund Hall Oxford (MA, DPhil); *m* 1970, Jennifer Robin, *née* Hawksworth; 2 s, 2 da; *Career* Dept of Eastern Art Ashmolean Museum: asst keeper 1966–88, sr asst keeper 1988–91, keeper 1991–, prof of eastern art 1996–; memb Cncl: Br Inst of Persian Studies, Br Sch of Archaeology Jerusalem; fell St Cross Coll 1990–; *Publications* Medieval Middle Eastern Pottery (1971), Persian Metal Technology 700–1300 AD (1978), Islamic Metalwork (Nuhad Es-Said Collection, 1982), Nishapur: Metalwork of the Early Islamic Period (1982), Metalwork of the Islamic World: the Aron Collection (1986), A Short Account of Early Muslim Architecture (1989); *Recreations* music, ornithology, walking, travel; *Style—* Prof James Allan; ✉ Ashmolean Museum, Oxford OX1 2PH (☎ 01865 278067, fax 01865 278078)

ALLAN, John; *b* 20 Aug 1948; *Educ* Univ of Edinburgh (BSc); *Career* mktg trainee then brand mangr Lever Bros 1970–74, mktg appts Consumer Products Div Bristol-Myers 1974–77, various appts rising to mktg and buying dir Fine Fare 1977–85, main bd dir i/c business servs Europe and gp mktg dir BET plc 1985–94, chief exec Ocean Group plc 1994–; non-exec dir Hamleys plc 1996–; memb Cncl IOD; *Style—* John Allan, Esq; ✉ Ocean Group plc, Ocean House, The Ring, Bracknell, Berkshire RG12 1AN (☎ 01344 302000, fax 01344 710031)

ALLAN, Sheriff John Douglas; s of Robert Taylor Allan, of Edinburgh, and Christina Helen Blythe Allan (d 1970); *b* 2 Oct 1941; *Educ* George Watson's Coll Edinburgh, Univ of Edinburgh (LLB, Dip Mgmnt Studies); *m* 1966, Helen Elizabeth Jean, da of William Aiton (d 1959); 1 s (Graeme b 1967), 1 da (Anne b 1970); *Career* slr and Notary Public; slr 1963–67, dep procurator fiscal 1967–71, sr legal asst Crown Office 1971–76, asst procurator fiscal Glasgow 1976–77, sr asst procurator fiscal Glasgow 1978–79, asst slr Crown Office 1979–83, regnl procurator fiscal for Lothians & Borders 1983–88; Sheriff of S Strathclyde, Dumfries and Galloway at Lanark 1988–; sec Sheriffs' Assoc 1991–; FIMgt; *Recreations* youth work, church work, walking; *Style—* Sheriff J Douglas Allan; ✉ Minard, 80 Greenbank Crescent, Edinburgh EH10 5SW (☎ 0131 447 2593); Sheriff Court, Hope St, Lanark ML11 7NQ (☎ 01555 661531)

ALLAN, Richard Bellerby; *b* 2 Aug 1940; *Educ* Marlborough, Merton Coll Oxford (BA); *m* 17 Sept 1966, Diana Rosemary Cotton, QC, *qv*; 2 s (Jonathan Bellerby b 28 June 1972, Jeremy Richard b 7 Aug 1974), 1 da (Joanna Frances b 10 March 1977); *Career* KPMG Peat Marwick: articled clerk 1962–65, qualified sr 1965–69, mangr 1969–77, ptnr 1977–; *Style—* Richard Allan, Esq; ✉ KPMG, 8 Salisbury Square, London EC4Y 8BB (☎ 0171 311 1000)

ALLAN, Dr Robert Norman; s of Dr Malcolm Allan (d 1994), and Kathleen Mary, *née* Tuck (d 1972); *b* 26 July 1941; *Educ* Ashby-de-la-Zouch Boys' GS, Univ of Birmingham (MB ChB, MD, PhD, FRCP 1980); *m* 8 July 1978, Ann-Marie Teresa, da of Bernard Sommereux; 2 da (Charlotte Louise b 16 May 1981, Sophie Marie b 25 March 1989); *Career* house physician: Queen Elizabeth Hosp Birmingham 1965 (house surgn Dept of Neuro-Surgery 1964), Children's Hosp Birmingham 1965; sr house offr Warick Hosp 1966–67, Sheldon clinical res fell Dept of Pathology Warick Hosp and Dept of Biochemistry Queen Elizabeth Hosp 1967–68, house physician Dept of Neurology

Hammersmith Sch London 1968, asst lectr Dept of Med Royal Post Grad Med Sch London 1968–69, med registrar The Gen Hosp Birmingham 1970–71, sr med registrar Nutritional and Intestinal Unit Utd Birmingham Hosps 1972–74, US post-doctoral res fell Gastroenterology Unit Mayo Grad Sch of Med Rochester Minnesota 1974–75, asst tutor Univ of Birmingham 1975–76, conslt physician (with an interest in gastroenterology) to S Birmingham Health Dist and clinical sr lectr Univ of Birmingham 1977–; Br Soc of Gastronenterology: memb Cncl 1984–, ed GUT 1988–95, memb Educn and Sci Ctee 1980–86 and 1990–95, memb Clinical Servs Ctee 1993–; chm: Ctee on Gastroenterology and regnl Royal Coll advsr RCP 1993–, Endowment Res Fund S Birmingham Health Dist 1993–; memb British Soc of Gastroenterology 1974; *Books* Inflammatory Bowel Diseases (1983, 2 edn 1990, 3 edn 1996), Gastroenterology Textbook of Clinical Science and Practice (1984, 2 edn 1993), author of numerous other pubns on the epidemiology, incidence, prognosis and cancer risk in inflammatory bowel disease; *Recreations* opera, political biography, gardening; *Style—* Dr Robert Allan; ✉ 5 Carpenter Road, Edgbaston, Birmingham B15 2JT (☎ 0121 454 1943); Queen Elizabeth Hospital, Edgbaston, Birmingham B15 2TH (☎ 0121 472 1311 ext 3377, fax 0121 472 8135)

ALLAN, Robert William; s of William Bennett Allan (d 1986), of NY, USA, and Mona Theresa, Bradley, *née* Langford; *b* 4 May 1945; *Educ* Xaverian Coll Brighton; *m* 15 July 1979, Elizabeth, da of John Jackson, of Newcastle; 2 da (Charlotte b 1979, Kirsty b 1982); *Career* admitted slr 1967; ptnr: Roney & Co 1971–73, Simons Muirhead & Allan 1973–86, Denton Hall 1986–; memb Law Soc; *Recreations* skiing, clay pigeon shooting, travel; *Clubs* Groucho's; *Style—* Robert W Allan, Esq; ✉ Denton Hall, 5 Chancery Lane, Clifford's Inn, London EC4A 1BU (☎ 0171 242 1212, fax 0171 404 0087)

ALLAN, Stephen David; s of Gerry Allan, of London, and Sonja, *née* Geiringer; *b* 26 June 1963; *Educ* City of London Sch; *m* 21 March 1991, Hayley Sara, da of Jeffrey Frankel; *Career* mangr Fotofast 1981, trainee media exec Yershon Media 1981; The Media Business Group plc (floated 1995): media exec 1982, assoc dir 1986, bd dir holding co 1987, equity shareholder 1988, first dir of new business 1989–93, md 1993–; MIPA 1988; *Recreations* golf, shooting, travel; *Clubs* Coombe Hill Golf; *Style—* Stephen Allan, Esq; ✉ The Media Business Group plc, 70 North Row, London W1R 1DE (☎ 0171 408 4400)

ALLAN, Dr William Craig; s of William Allan (d 1962), of Tunbridge Wells, and Doris Craig Bowman (d 1993); *b* 8 Nov 1942; *Educ* Aberdeen GS, Univ of Aberdeen (BSc), Univ of Edinburgh (PhD); *m* 2 April 1966, Ann Marjorie, da of Sqdn Ldr Robert Alfred Miller, RAF; 3 da (Victoria b 13 July 1967, Susan b 12 July 1968, Kirsty 5 Jan 1974); *Career* res asst in mineralogy Hunterian Museum Univ of Glasgow 1968–72, county museum curator Warwickshire Museum Warwickshire CC 1978– (dep curator and keeper of geology 1972–77); pres Midlands Fedn of Museums and Galls 1983–85, memb Bd of Mgmnt W Midlands Area Mus Serv 1980–; FMA 1983 (AMA 1976); *Style—* Dr William C Allan; ✉ Warwickshire Museum, Market Hall, Warwick CV34 4SA (☎ 01926 412500, fax 01926 412471)

ALLANBRIDGE, Hon Lord; William Ian Stewart; s of John Stewart, FRIBA (d 1954), and Mrs Maysie Shepherd Service or Stewart (d 1968), of Drimfearn, Bridge of Allan; *b* 8 Nov 1925; *Educ* Loretto, Univ of Edinburgh, Univ of Glasgow (MA, LLB); *m* 1955, Naomi Joan, da of Sir James Boyd Douglas, CBE (d 1964), of Barstibly, Castle Douglas; 1 s (John), 1 da (Angela); *Career* served WWII Sub-Lt RNVR, escort gp Western Approaches; advocate 1951, advocate depute 1959–64, QC (Scot) 1965, memb Criminal Injuries Compensation Bd 1969–70, home advocate depute 1970–72, slr gen for Scotland 1972–74, temp sheriff princ of Dumfries and Galloway 1974, senator Coll of Justice in Scotland (Scottish Lord of Session) 1977–95; *Recreations* hill walking; *Clubs* New (Edinburgh); *Style—* The Hon Lord Allanbridge; ✉ 60 Northumberland St, Edinburgh EH3 6JE (☎ 0131 556 2823)

ALLARDICE, His Hon Judge; William Arthur Llewellyn Allardice; DL (Staffs 1980); s of late W C Allardice, MD, FRCSEd, JP, and late Constance Winifred Allardice; *b* 18 Dec 1924; *Educ* Stonyhurst, Univ Coll Oxford (MA); *m* 1956, Jennifer Ann, da of late G H Jackson; 1 s, 1 da; *Career* joined Rifle Bde 1943, cmmnd 1944, served 52 LI Europe and Palestine 1945; called to the Bar Lincoln's Inn 1950; practised Oxford Circuit 1950–71, judge Midland and Oxford circuit 1972–; chm William Salt Library 1991–96; *Recreations* local history, matters equestrian; *Style—* His Hon Judge Allardice, DL; ✉ c/o Courts Administrator, Stafford (☎ 01785 55219)

ALLARDYCE, Fiona M; *b* 18 Aug 1954; *Educ* Cheltenham Ladies' Coll, Univ of Edinburgh (MA), Instituto Centrale del Restauro Rome (dip), Courtauld Inst (MA); *m* Stephen Garratt; 2 c (b 1990 and 1992); *Career* art conservator, non stipendiary publisher; sr asst wall paintings workshop Canterbury Cathedral 1980–84, pt/t asst to the Surveyor of Conservation for the Nat Tst 1984–86, freelance conservator 1986– (pt/t 1984–86), freelance advsr on wall paintings NT 1988–; freelance mural/panel conslt projects incl: Durham Deanery, Rievaulx Ionic Temple (NT) 1986, Packington Hall 1989, Temple Island Henley 1989–90, Mortimer House 1991, St John's Lodge Regent's Park 1991; conslt Cliveden Conservation Workshop 1992–; publisher Allardyce, Barnett, Publishers 1992–; *Style—* Ms Fiona Allardyce

ALLASON, Julian Edward Thomas; s of Lt-Col James Harry Allason, OBE, FRSA; *Educ* Downside, Univs of Sussex, Aix-en-Provence and Nottingham; *m* 1976 (m dis 1991), Jessica Marland, da of Richard Thomas Wingert, of Westport, Connecticut, USA; 2 s (James b 1980, Benjamin b 1984), 1 da (Chloe b 1982); *Career* dir: Apricot Computers plc 1979–86, Sharp Technology Fund plc 1984–; md The Blackthorn Gp 1989–; author; publisher Microcomputer Printout Magazine 1979–83; columnist: The Observer 1981–83, Daily Telegraph 1983–86; JP Inner London 1973–78; memb Information Technol NEDC 1984–86; Kt Sov Mil Order of Malta 1985 (Cdr of Merit 1989), Kt Constantinian Order of St George 1986 (Cdr of Grace 1994), Kt Order of St Maurice & St Lazarus 1995; *Books* The Pet Companion (1981), English Legal Heritage (co-ed 1979), Prayers of the Order of Malta (1990); *Recreations* photography, messing about in boats; *Clubs* White's, Jet, Bembridge Sailing; *Style—* Julian Allason, Esq; ✉ PO Box 41, Wallingford, Oxon OX10 6TD (☎ 01491 641044, fax 01491 641017)

ALLASON, Rupert William Simon; MP (C) Torbay (majority 5,787); s of Lt-Col James Harry Allason, OBE, FRSA; *b* 8 Nov 1951; *Educ* Downside, Univ Hall Buckland, Univ of Lille, Univ of Grenoble; *m* 1979, Nicole Jane, da of M L Van Moppes (d 1963), of Bermuda; 1 s (Thomas b 1980), 1 da (Alexandra b 1987); *Career* author (pen name Nigel West); special constable 1975–82, BBC TV 1978–82, Euro ed Intelligence Quarterly 1985–; Parly candidate (C): Kettering 1979, Battersea 1983; MP (C) Torbay 1987–; *Books* The Branch - A History of the Metropolitan Police Special Branch 1883–1983 (1983); as Nigel West: SPY! (with Richard Deacon, 1980), MI5 (1981), A Matter of Trust (1982), MI6 (1983), The Branch (1983), Unreliable Witness (1984), GARBO (with Juan Pujol, 1985), GCHQ (1986), Molehunt (1987), The Friends (1988), Games of Intelligence (1989), The Blue List (1989), Cuban Bluff (1990), Seven Spies (1991), Secret War (1992), The Faber Book of Espionage (ed, 1993), The Illegals (1993), The Faber Book of Treachery (1995); *Recreations* skiing, sailing; *Clubs* White's, Special Forces, Royal Yacht Sqdn, Royal Torbay Yacht; *Style—* Rupert Allason, Esq, MP; ✉ 96 Eaton Terrace, London SW1W 8UG (☎ 0171 352 1110); House of Commons, London SW1A 0AA (☎ 0171 219 4142)

ALLCOCK, Anthony (Tony); MBE; s of Ernest Stacey Allcock, and Joan Winifred Allcock (d 1986); *b* 11 June 1955; *Educ* Norwich City Coll; *Career* bowls player; world outdoor champion 1980, 1984 and 1988, world outdoor singles champion 1992 and 1996, world indoor singles champion 1986 and 1987, world indoor pairs champion (with David Bryant, CBE, *qv*) 1986, 1987, 1989, 1990, 1991 and 1992; pres Western Div MENCAP, patron English Nat Assoc of Visually Handicapped Bowlers; *Books* Improve your Bowls (1988), Step by Step Guide to Bowls (1988), End to End - a year in bowls (1989), Bowl to Win (1994); *Recreations* countryside, opera, horses, antiques; *Clubs* Cheltenham Bowling, Cotswold and Bentham Country; *Style—* Tony Allcock, Esq, MBE; ✉ Rose Cottage, Little Shurdington, Cheltenham, Gloucestershire GL51 5TX

ALLCOCK, James; s of James Allcock (d 1950), and Margery, *née* Higginbotham (d 1980); *b* 2 June 1926; *Educ* Audenshaw GS, Univ of Liverpool (BVSc, MRCVS); *m* 1950, Pamela, da of E C Bovett (d 1955); 2 s (Stephen James b 1952, Christopher Charles b 1961), 2 da (Sarah Louise (Mrs Hodnett) b 1954, Victoria Jane (Mrs Thomas) b 1963); *Career* in gen vet practice Bristol 1948–83; vet advsr: Bristol Corporation 1958–90, Woodspring District Cncl 1974–90; advsr to various industl companies on environmental pollution, frequent radio and TV progs and interviews on animal topics; memb Avon CC 1983–88; memb Cncl: BVA 1968–83 (hon sec 1979–83), RCVS 1983–96; *Books* A Dog of Your Own (1978), A Cat of Your Own (1980), Pet Bird of Your Own (1981), Small Pet of Your Own (1983, trans German and Norwegian), Pets in Particular (1986); *Recreations* orchid growing, sheep farming, watching cricket and rugby; *Style—* James Allcock, Esq; ✉ Shepherd's Hey, Ham Green, Pill, Bristol BS20 0HF (☎ 01275 372327)

ALLCOCK, John Paul Major; s of John Gladding Major Allcock, CB (d 1986), and Eileen Winifred Arnold, *née* Baiss; *b* 8 July 1941; *Educ* St Edward's Sch Oxford, King's Coll London (BSc), Faculté Polytechnique de Mons Belgium (Maitrise en Science Appliquée); *m* 7 Nov 1981 (m dis 1992), Caroline Anne, da of Arthur Frederick Lyle Rocke, of Olney, Maryland, USA; 1 s (Oliver John Llewelyn b 1 March 1985), 2 da (Arabella Louise b 27 April 1983, Lucinda Anne b 20 Feb 1990); *Career* chartered patent agent 1968, admitted slr 1977, ptnr specialising in intellectual property Bristows Cooke & Carpmael 1981–; memb Law Soc; fell Chartered Inst of Patent Agents 1968, MIEE 1971, CEng 1971; *Recreations* sailing and walking; *Style—* John Allcock, Esq; ✉ Bristows Cooke & Carpmael, 10 Lincoln's Inn Fields, London WC2A 3BP (☎ 0171 400 8000, fax 0171 400 8050, telex 27487)

ALLDAY, Coningsby; CBE (1971); s of late Esca Allday, and Margaret Allday, of Birmingham; *b* 21 Nov 1920; *Educ* Solihull Sch, Univ of London (BSc); *m* 1, 1945, Iris Helena (d 1990); 1 s, 1 da; m 2, 1993, Rosalind Myra Roberts; *Career* UK Atomic Energy Authority 1959–71 (chief chemist, tech dir, commercial dir, dep md), memb UKAEA 1976–85, md British Nuclear Fuels plc 1971–86 (chief exec 1975–86, chm 1983–86), chm Allday Nuclear Conslts Ltd 1986–, non-exec dir National Westminster Bank Northern Region 1985–92, chm Nimtech NW 1986–90; CEng, FIChemE, FRSA; Hon DSc Univ of Salford 1985; Chevalier de la Legion d'Honneur 1983; *Recreations* gardening, music, bridge; *Style—* Coningsby Allday, Esq, CBE; ✉ Bredon, 54 Goughs Lane, Knutsford, Cheshire WA16 8QN

ALLDAY, John Philip; s of Philip Frederick Allday (d 1994), of Northwood, Middx, and Kathleen Mary Clifford Green; *b* 8 Sept 1939; *Educ* Bradfield; *m* 22 Aug 1992, Leonie Ann, da of (Leonard) Keith Robinson, CBE, DL, *qv*; 1 s (Andrew Charles Philip b 8 Oct 1971), 1 da (Susannah Mayne b 2 Sept 1969), 1 step s (Christopher Michael b 10 July 1975), 1 step da (Catherine Clara b 12 Nov 1977); *Career* Turquands Barton Mayhew & Co (formerly Barton Mayhew & Co): articled clerk 1958–63, accountant 1963–75, ptnr 1975–79; ptnr Ernst & Young (formerly Ernst & Whinney) 1979– (nat dir of valuation 1989–); memb Worshipful Co of: Needlemakers, Chartered Accountants; FCA; *Recreations* golf, cricket, gardening, music; *Clubs* MCC, City Livery, Burnham & Berrow Golf; *Style—* John Allday, Esq; ✉ The Old Farmhouse, Bullocks Lane, Kingston Seymour, North Somerset BS21 6XA (☎ 01934 876528); Ernst & Young, Becket House, 1 Lambeth Palace Road, London SE1 7EU (☎ 0171 931 4711, fax 0171 261 1073)

ALLDIS, Air Cdre Cecil Anderson; CBE (1962), DFC (1941), AFC (1953); 2 s of John Henry Alldis (d 1943), of Birkenhead, Cheshire, and Margaret Wright Alldis (d 1953); *b* 28 Sept 1918; *Educ* Birkenhead Inst, Emmanuel Coll Cambridge (MA); *m* 1942, Jeanette Claire, da of Albert Edward Collingwood Tarrant (d 1924), of Johannesburg, SA; *Career* served WWII (despatches), Pilot RAF, Asst Air Attaché Moscow 1947–49, Air Attaché Bonn 1963–66, ret 1966; entered Home Civil Serv 1966, MOD 1966–69, seconded to HM Dip Serv 1969, cnsllr (def supply) Bonn 1969–80, ret 1980; sec gen The Air League 1982–90, ret 1990; *Recreations* golf, fishing; *Clubs* Naval & Military; *Style—* Air Cdre Cecil Alldis, CBE, DFC, AFC; ✉ Tudor Cottage, 31 Oxshott Way, Cobham, Surrey KT11 2RU (☎ 01932 866092)

ALLDIS, Christopher John; s of John Henry Alldis (d 1981), and Isabel Marjorie, *née* Carter; *b* 16 May 1947; *Educ* Birkenhead Sch, Emmanuel Coll Cambridge (MA, LLB); *m* 14 Sept 1985, Marcia Elizabeth, *née* Kidman; 2 da (Amy Elizabeth b 1987, Rebecca Isabel Amelia b 1989); *Career* called to the Bar Gray's Inn 1970, practising Northern Circuit, recorder of the Crown Court 1994–; *Recreations* gliding, light aviation, skiing, fishing; *Clubs* Naval & Military; *Style—* Christopher Alldis, Esq; ✉ Romsdal, 3 Prenton Lane, Birkenhead, Merseyside (☎ 0151 608 1828); Peel House, Harrington St, Liverpool (☎ 0151 236 4321, fax 0151 236 3332)

ALLDIS, John; s of William Alldis, and Nell, *née* Bennet; *b* 10 Aug 1929; *Educ* Felsted, Univ of Cambridge (MA); *m* 23 July 1960, Ursula, da of William Mason; 2 s (Dominic b 1962, Robert b 1964); *Career* Nat Serv Essex Regt 1947–49; formed John Alldis Choir 1962, choral prof Guildhall Sch of Music and Drama 1964–77, fndr and conductor London Symphony Chorus 1966–69, conductor London Philharmonic Choir 1969–82, jt chief conductor Radio Denmark 1971–77, Artistic Dir Groupe Vocal de France 1979–83; guest conductor Hallé Choir 1992–93; memb Vaughan Williams Trust 1976–; fell Westminster Choir Coll Princeton USA; ARCO 1956, FGSM 1976, Chev des Arts et des Lettres (France) 1984; FRSA 1990; *Style—* John Alldis, Esq; ✉ 3 Wool Rd, Wimbledon, London SW20 0HN (☎ 0181 946 4168)

ALLEN, Prof Adrian; s of Philip John Frances Allen (d 1979), of Bognor Regis, and Mary Isobel, *née* Parry (d 1985); *b* 27 Jan 1938; *Educ* Ch Ch Oxford (MA, DPhil); *m* 22 July 1960, Pauline Elizabeth; 1 s (Adam b 1969), 3 da (Susan b 1961, Deborah b 1965, Katherine b 1967); *Career* Univ of Newcastle upon Tyne: lectr 1967, reader 1976, prof of physiological biochemistry 1980–; *Recreations* ornithology, hill walking; *Style—* Prof Adrian Allen; ✉ Department of Physiological Sciences, Medical Sch, Framlington Place, Newcastle upon Tyne NE2 4HH (☎ 0191 222 6991)

ALLEN, Anthony John; CBE (1994); s of William Raymond Houghton Allen (d 1987), and Elsie Zillah Primrose, *née* Russ (d 1986); *b* 7 Oct 1939; *Educ* Battersea GS, Univ of Exeter (LLB); *m* 1, 1964 (m dis 1984), Suzanne Davies; 2 s (Richard b 1966, Phillip b 1967); m 2, 27 May 1987, Helen Leah Graney; 2 s (Tristan John b 4 May 1993, Rhodric George b 2 February 1995); *Career* admitted slr of the Supreme Ct 1964; asst slr: London Borough of Barnet 1964–65, Borough of Watford 1965–67; asst chief exec: Coventry City 1968–71, London Borough of Lewisham 1971–72; dep town clerk and slr to the Cncl London Borough of Southwark 1972–76, chief exec London Borough of Hammersmith and Fulham 1976–86, chief exec and clerk to the Lieutenancy Royal Co of Berkshire 1986–93; chief exec National House Building Council Ltd 1994–96; non-exec dir: London Youth Games Ltd 1986–, BSI 1991–; memb Soc of Local Authy Chief Execs 1976, CIMgt 1992; *Recreations* golf, travel; *Style—* Anthony Allen, Esq, CBE; ✉ The Fifteenth, 7 Broadlands Close, Calcot Park, Reading, Berks RG3 5RP (☎ 0118 942 7310)

ALLEN, Carol; da of William Joseph Allen (d 1949), of Greenford, Middx, and Winifred Rose, *née* Bicknell (d 1973); *Educ* Notting Hill and Ealing HS, Central School of Speech and Drama (Univ of London Dip in Drama, Teaching Dip); *m* 15 June 1973 (m dis 1978), James Dyer, s of Sidney Dyer; *Career* prodn asst BBC TV, prodr COI, freelance broadcaster, LBC Radio 1980–87 (prog presenter, newsreader and cinema specialist), freelance writer, reviewer and broadcaster specialising in the Arts 1987–; dir Cat's Whiskers Productions; memb: London Screenwriters' Workshop, Critics' Circle, NUJ, Assoc of Ind Radio Prodrs; *Books* The Virgin Encyclopaedia of the Movies (part author, 1995); *Recreations* the company of friends, books, films, theatre, television; *Style*— Miss Carol Allen; ✉ c/o Cat's Whiskers Productions, 132 Dawes Road, London SW6 7EF

ALLEN, Charles Lamb; *Career* with British Steel 1974–79, TM Group div of Galaghers plc 1979–82; Grand Metropolitan plc: dir GrandMet International Services Ltd 1982–85, gp md Compass Vending and Grand Metropolitan Innovations Ltd 1986–87, md GIS Middle East Ltd 1987–88; md Compass Group plc (following buyout from GrandMet) 1988–91; Granada Group plc: chief exec Granada Television Ltd and gp main bd dir 1992–, chm Granada Leisure and Services to Business Div 1994–, chief exec London Weekend Television (following takeover) 1994–96 (chm 1996–), gp chief exec Granada Group plc 1996–, chm Forte plc (following takeover) 1996–; chm GMTV 1996– (dep chm 1994–96); *Style*— Charles Allen, Esq; ✉ Granada Group plc, Stornoway House, 13 Cleveland Row, London SW1A 1GG (☎ 0171 451 3000)

ALLEN, (Michael) Christopher Kinkead; s of Col Robert Langley Kinkead Allen, OBE (d 1976), and Phyllis Mary, *née* Serjeant; *b* 7 Jan 1940; *Educ* Haileybury, Jesus Coll Oxford (MA); *m* 10 April 1976, Jennifer Anne, da of Sir John Rogers Ellis, MBE, of Woodford Green, Essex; 1 s (Robert b 1978), 1 da (Kate b 1980); *Career* ptnr: Penningtons slrs 1966–90, Mishcon de Reya slrs 1990–; *Recreations* squash, tennis, sailing, gardening; *Clubs* Lansdowne; *Style*— Christopher Allen, Esq; ✉ Nowhurst Farmhouse, Nowhurst Lane, Broadbridge Heath, N Horsham, W Sussex RH12 3PJ (☎ 01403 69512); Mischon de Reya, 21 Southampton Row, London WC1B 5HS (☎ 0171 405 3711)

ALLEN, Dr Christopher Michael Colquhoun; s of Christopher Oswald Colquhoun Allen, of Kingsbridge, S Devon, and Barbara Louise, *née* Archer; *b* 1 Dec 1948; *Educ* Eastbourne Coll, Christ's Coll Cambridge (MA, MD, FRCP), Guy's Hosp Med Sch; *m* 28 July 1973, Susan Valerie, da of Alan Douglas Belcher (d 1971), of Sheffield; 1 s (Samuel b 1982), 2 da (Kate b 1978, Joanna b Dec 1979); *Career* sr house offr: renal medicine St Thomas's Hosp 1976–77, Nat Hosp for Nervous Diseases 1977; hon sr registrar Dept of Neurology Guy's Hosp 1979–82 (house offr Med Professorial Unit 1973–74, med registrar 1977–79), neurology registrar Middx Hosp 1982–84, sr registrar in neurology Charing Cross Hosp 1984–86, conslt neurologist Addenbrooke's Hosp Cambridge 1986–, dean Sch of Clinical Med Univ of Cambridge 1996–; FRCP; *Books* The Management of Acute Stroke (1988); *Recreations* listening to Mozart, writing book reviews, windsurfing; *Style*— Dr Christopher Allen; ✉ 232 Hills Rd, Cambridge CB2 2QE (☎ 01223 247694, fax 01223 414904); Department of Neurology, Addenbrooke's Hospital, Cambridge CB2 2QQ (☎ 01223 216759)

ALLEN, Colin Mervyn Gordon; CBE (1978); s of Cecil Gordon Allen (d 1980), of Saltford, Bristol, and Gwendoline Louise Allen, *née* Hutchinson (d 1974); *b* 17 April 1929; *Educ* King Edward's Sch Bath, Open Univ (BA), Univ of London (MA); *m* 1953, Patricia Mary, da of William Thomas Seddon (d 1943); 2 s (Timothy, Mark), 1 da (Claire); *Career* Naval Store Dept Admty 1948–56; NCB: London HQ 1956–59, area stores offr NE Div 1959–64; Covent Garden Market Authy: planning offr 1964–66, asst gen mangr 1967, gen mangr 1967–89; pt/t consultancy work on horticulture marketing and wholesale markets mainly in E Europe 1992–; pres: Assoc of Wholesale Markets within Int Union of Local Authys 1972–78, Inst of Purchasing and Supply 1982–83; chm Vauxhall Cross Amenity Tst 1982–83; author of various papers on horticultural mktg and allied topics, and on supply and logistics matters; *Recreations* archaeology; *Style*— Colin Allen, Esq, CBE; ✉ 33 Butts Road, Horspath, Oxford OX33 1RJ

ALLEN, (Francis John) David; s of Stanley Roy Allen (d 1942), of Harrow, and Eve Maude, *née* Poulton; *b* 9 Jan 1939; *Educ* Harrow Weald GS, Balliol Coll Oxford (BA); *m* 12 Aug 1965, Gillian Lilias, da of Jack Johnstone, of West Kirby, Wirral; 1 s (Hugo Richard b 12 Oct 1972), 1 da (Charlotte Luise b 2 Jan 1976); *Career* sr prodr BBC TV, ed BBC Computer Literacy Project 1981–86, prodr and ed Micro Live series BBC TV, currently exec prodr BBC Interactive Trg and Info Unit; recipient US Govt Int Visitors Prog 1978, award winner NY Film Festival 1981, Judges Award RTS 1982, Times Technol Prog of the Year 1985–86, Sony Innovation award 1989 and 1990; *Books* Early Years at School, Measurement in Education, That's the Way the Money Goes, The Computer Book (ed); *Recreations* windsurfing, singing, BBC Symphony Chorus (chm); *Style*— David Allen, Esq; ✉ BBC Interactive Training and Information Unit, BBC Elstree Centre, Borehamwood, Herts (☎ 0181 953 6100)

ALLEN, Donald George; CMG (1981); s of Sydney George Allen (d 1971), and Doris Elsie, *née* Abercrombie (d 1969); *b* 26 June 1930; *Educ* Southall GS; *m* 1955, Sheila Isobel, da of Wilfred Bebbington (d 1976); 3 s (Stephen, d 1991, David, Mark); *Career* HM Forces 1949–51; FO 1951–54, The Hague 1954–57, second sec (Commercial) La Paz 1957–60, FO 1961–65, first sec 1962, asst private sec to Lord Privy Seal 1961–63 and to Min without Portfolio 1963–64, first sec head of Chancery, consul Panama 1966–69, FCO 1969–72, cnsllr on secondment to NI Office Belfast 1972–74, cnsllr and head of Chancery UK Perm Delgn to OECD Paris 1974–78, inspr 1978–80, dir Office of Parly Cmmr 1980–82, dep Parly cmmr for admin (ombudsman) 1982–90; memb Broadcasting Complaints Cmmn 1990–97; *Recreations* squash, golf, tennis; *Clubs* RAC, Princes Squash; *Style*— Donald Allen, Esq, CMG; ✉ 99 Parkland Grove, Ashford, Middx TW15 2JF (☎ 01784 255617)

ALLEN, Eric; s of Rose Allen; *b* 10 March 1938; *Educ* Harthill Secdy Sch, Glasgow Coll of Commerce; *m* 13 May 1961, Elizabeth Ann, da of Ephraim Belcher; 1 s (Graeme Robert b 29 Nov 1966); *Career* hotelier; apprentice surveyor NCB 1954–59, Regular Sgt Scots Gds 1959–62, prodn controller Telegraph Condenser Co 1962–64, med rep Pfizer 1964–66, regnl mangr Squibb 1970–72 (med rep 1966–70); hotelier 1972– (Glen Eldon Hotel Largs 1972–78, Airds Hotel Port Appin 1978–); Chevalier du Tastevin St Hubert Chapter 1990; *Recreations* study of wine, history of Scotland; *Clubs* Caledonian; *Style*— Eric Allen, Esq; ✉ The Airds Hotel, Port Appin, Appin, Argyll PA38 4DF (☎ 0163 173 236, fax 0163 173 535)

ALLEN, Fergus Hamilton; CB (1969); s of Charles Winckworth Allen (d 1971), of Dublin, and Marjorie Helen, *née* Budge (d 1986); *b* 3 Sept 1921; *Educ* Newtown Sch Waterford, Trinity Coll Dublin (MA, MAI, ScD); *m* 1947, Margaret Joan, da of Prof Michael J Gorman (d 1982), of Dublin; 2 da (Mary (m Robin George Woodhead, *qv*, Elizabeth); *Career* asst engr Sir Cyril Kirkpatrick and Partners 1943–48, Port of London Authy 1949–52, dir Hydraulics Res Station Dept of Scientific and Industl Res (now SERC) 1958–65 (asst dir 1952–58), chief scientific offr Cabinet Office 1965–69, civil serv cmmr 1969–74, first civil serv cmmr Civil Serv Dept 1974–81; sr consit Boyden Int 1982–86; ICE: memb 1947–57, fell 1957–86, Telford Gold Medal 1958, memb Cncl 1962–67 and 1968–71; *Books* The Brown Parrots of Providencia (1993), Who Goes There (1996); *Recreations* reading, gardening; *Clubs* Athenaeum; *Style*— Fergus Allen, Esq, CB; ✉ Dundrum, Wantage Rd, Streatley, Berks RG8 9LB (☎ 01491 873234)

ALLEN, His Hon Judge Francis Andrew; s of Andrew Eric Allen and Joan Elizabeth Allen; *b* 7 Dec 1933; *Educ* Solihull Sch, Merton Coll Oxford (MA); *m* 1, 1961, Marjorie Pearce; 1 s, 3 da; m 2, 1994, Sheila Baggaley; *Career* called to the Bar Gray's Inn 1958; recorder of the Crown Ct 1978–79, circuit judge (Midland & Oxford Circuit) 1979–; memb Judicial Studies Bd 1990–95 (chm Magisterial Ctee), chm Area Criminal Justice Liaison Ctee (Northants and Leicester) 1993–; *Recreations* walking; *Clubs* Mountain Bothies Assoc (Scottish Highlands); *Style*— His Hon Judge Francis Allen; ✉ The Crown Court, Lady's Lane, Northampton NN1 3HQ (☎ 01604 250131)

ALLEN, Gary James; CBE (1991), DL (1993); s of late Alfred Allen, of Sutton Coldfield, W Midlands, and Alice Jane Allen; *b* 30 Sept 1944; *Educ* King Edward VI GS Birmingham, Univ of Liverpool (BCom); *m* 10 Sept 1966, Judith Anne, da of William Nattrass (d 1961); 3 s (Andrew b 1969, Anthony b 1971, James b 1979); *Career* md IMI Range Ltd 1973–77; IMI plc: dir 1978–, asst md 1985–86, md and chief exec 1986–; chm Eley Ltd 1981–85; non-exec dir: NV Bekaert SA Belgium 1987–, Marley plc 1989– (dep chm 1993–), Birmingham European Airways 1989–91, London Stock Exchange 1994–; memb Cncl: CBI 1986 (W Midlands Regnl Cncl 1983–89), Birmingham Chamber of Indust and Commerce 1983 (pres 1991–92, memb Bd 1994–96), Univ of Birmingham 1985–90 (hon life memb Ct 1984); The Lord's Taverners: memb Cncl 1995–, pres W Midlands Region 1994– (chm 1987–93, memb Cncl 1985–); memb Bd Birmingham Royal Ballet 1993–; pres Midlands Club Cricket Conf 1995–; Freeman Worshipful Co of Gunmakers; FCMA 1985, CIMgt 1986, FRSA 1988; *Recreations* sport, reading; *Style*— Gary J Allen, Esq, CBE, DL; ✉ IMI plc, PO Box 216, Birmingham B6 7BA (☎ 0121 356 4848, telex 336771 IMI KYN G)

ALLEN, Prof Sir Geoffrey; kt (1979); s of John James Allen and Marjorie Allen, of Wingerworth, Derbyshire; *b* 29 Oct 1928; *Educ* Clay Cross Tupton Hall GS, Leeds Univ (BSc, PhD); *m* 1973, Valerie Frances, da of Arthur Duckworth (d 1979); 1 da (Naomi); *Career* scientist; prof of chemical physics Univ of Manchester 1965–75, prof of chemical technol Imperial Coll 1976–81; chm Sci Res Cncl 1977–81 (memb 1976); pres: SCI 1990–, Plastics and Rubber Inst 1990–; visiting fell Robinson Coll Cambridge 1980–; head res engrg Unilever 1981–90, dir Unilever Plc and Unilever NV 1982–90, exec advsr Kobe Steel Ltd 1990–; dir: Courtaulds Plc (non-exec) 1987–93, Cambridge Quantum Fund 1990–; chllr UEA 1994–; Hon MSc Univ of Manchester; Hon DUniv: Open Univ 1981, UEA, Bath, Bradford and Loughborough 1985, Essex, Keele and Leeds 1986, Cranfield 1988, Surrey 1989, Sheffield 1993; Hon DSc Univ of Durham 1984; hon fell UMIST; Hon FIChemE 1989, Hon FCGI 1990, FIC, CEng 1986, FInstP, FRICS, FPRI, FRS 1976, FEng 1993; *Recreations* opera, walking, talking; *Style*— Prof Sir Geoffrey Allen, FRS, FEng; ✉ Kobe Steel Ltd, Alton House, 174–177 High Holborn, London WC1V 7AA (☎ 0171 836 1225, fax 0171 240 7460, telex 25309 KOBE G)

ALLEN, Graham William; MP (Lab) Nottingham N (majority 10,743); s of William Allen, and Edna, *née* Holt; *b* 11 Jan 1953; *Educ* Robert Shaw Primary, Forest Fields GS; *Career* warehouseman Nottingham 1971–72, Lab Pty res offr 1978–83, Local Govt offr GLC 1983–84, Trades Union nat co-ordinator Political Fund Ballots Campaign 1984–86, regnl res and educn offr GMBATU 1986–87, MP (Lab) Nottingham N 1987–; memb: Public Accounts Ctee 1988–90, Procedure Ctee, 1990 Fin Bill Ctee; chm PLP Treasy Ctee 1990–92; oppn frontbench spokesman on social security 1991–92, shadow min (democracy and the constitution) Home Office 1992–94, shadow min (media) Dept of Nat Heritage 1994–95, shadow min (buses, air and sea) Dept of Tport 1995–96, shadow min (health and safety) Dept of Environment 1996–; *Recreations* cricket, walking, democratising the UK; *Clubs* Strelley Social, Dunkirk Cricket, Beechdale Community Assoc, Lords and Commons Cricket; *Style*— Graham W Allen, Esq, MP; ✉ House of Commons SW1A 0AA (☎ 0171 219 4343)

ALLEN, Prof Howard Godfrey; s of Thomas Charles Allen (d 1971), and Elsie, *née* Fell (d 1979); *b* 17 Oct 1931; *Educ* Haverfordwest GS, Univ of Liverpool (BEng, PhD); *m* 27 July 1957, Margaret, da of late William Edward Bourner, of Middlesbrough; 1 s (Martin b 1963), 1 da (Elizabeth b 1961); *Career* stressman AV Roe Manchester 1955–57, engr Sir William Halcrow and Ptnrs London 1958–60; Univ of Southampton: lectr Dept Civil Engrg 1960, sr lectr 1967, reader 1971, prof of structural engrg 1984–96, emeritus 1996–; FIStructE, MICE; *Books* Analysis and Design of Structural Sandwich Panels (1969), Background to Buckling (with P Bulson, 1980); *Recreations* walking, cycling, folk dancing, reading; *Style*— Prof Howard Allen; ✉ Department of Civil and Environmental Engineering, Southampton University, Southampton SO17 1BJ (☎ 01703 592870, fax 01703 594986)

ALLEN, Hugh Edward Keith; *b* 22 April 1934; *Educ* Oundle, Univ of Cambridge (MA), Royal Sch of Mines Imperial Coll London (BScEng); *m* 8 Aug 1959, Ann, *née* Barling; 5 c; *Career* Anglo/De Beers Gp: engr 1959–78, mangr Orapa Diamond Mine Botswana 1973–76; reader Imperial Coll Univ of London 1978–87, mining advsr RTZ Corporation plc 1987–90, dir RTZ Technical Services Ltd 1990–96, ptnr Allen Associates 1996–; ARSM, FIMM (pres 1991–92), FEng 1993; *Style*— Hugh Allen, Esq, FEng; ✉ 12 Roxborough Park, Harrow on the Hill, Middlesex HA1 3BE (☎ 0181 422 0300, fax 0181 426 4544)

ALLEN, Prof Ingrid Victoria (Mrs Barnes Thompson); CBE (1993), DL (1989); da of Rev Dr Robert Allen (d 1968), of Belfast, and Doris Victoria, *née* Shaw (d 1990); *b* 30 July 1932; *Educ* Ashleigh House Belfast, Cheltenham Ladies' Coll, Queen's Univ Belfast (MB BCh, BAO, MD, DSc); *m* 1, 30 May 1972, Alan Watson Barnes (d 1987), s of Sidney W Barnes (d 1992), of Martin Cross, nr Fordingbridge, Salisbury; m 2, 6 Sept 1996, Prof John Thompson; *Career* house offr Royal Victoria Hosp Belfast 1957–58; Queen's Univ Belfast: Musgrave res fell 1958–59, tutor in pathology 1959–61, Calvert res fell in multiple sclerosis 1961–64; sr registrar Pathology Dept Royal Victoria Hosp 1964–65; Queen's Univ Belfast and Royal Victoria Hosp: sr lectr and consIt in neuropathology 1966–78, reader and consIt in neuropathology 1978–79, prof of neuropathology, consIt and head Dept of Neuropathology 1979–; memb: MRC, Multiple Sclerosis Soc, Univ Funding Cncl, Br Malaysian Soc; FRCPath 1975, FRCPI 1985, FRCPGlas 1987 (MRCPGlas 1985), MRIA 1993, FRCPE 1995; *Books* Demyelinating Diseases in Greenfield's Neuropathology (5 edn), Pathology of Multiple Sclerosis in McAlpine's Multiple Sclerosis (2 edn, 1980); *Recreations* sailing, tennis, reading, Irish history, fashion, architecture; *Clubs* Royal Soc of Med, Royal Ulster Yacht; *Style*— Prof Ingrid V Allen, CBE, DL; ✉ Department of Neuropathology, Institute of Pathology, Queen's University of Belfast, Grosvenor Rd, Belfast BT12 6BA (☎ 01232 894742, fax 01232 438024, car 0836 361920)

ALLEN, Janet Rosemary; da of John Algernon Allen (d 1972), of Leicester, and Edna Mary, *née* Orton (d 1991); *b* 11 April 1936; *Educ* Cheltenham Ladies' Coll, Univ Coll Leicester (BA (London)), Hughes Hall Cambridge (CertEd); *Career* Howell's Sch Denbigh: schoolmistress 1959–75, head of History Dept 1961–75, head of Sixth Form 1965–75, housemistress 1968–75; headmistress Benenden Sch 1976–85; memb: Boarding Schs Assoc Ctee 1980–83, GSA Educnl Sub-Ctee 1983–85, Cncl of Friends of Gloucester Cathedral, Cncl Gloucester Diocesan Bd of Educn 1992–; vice pres Women's Careers Fndn 1982–, sch govr St Catherine's Bramley Sch 1986–; govr: Winchcombe C of E Infants' Sch 1991–, King's Sch Worcester 1996–; *Recreations* music, drama, walking, swimming, history, archaeology; *Clubs* Royal Over-Seas League; *Style*— Miss Janet Allen; ✉ Bourne Rise, Queen's Square, Winchcombe, Cheltenham, Glos GL54 5LR

ALLEN, Prof John Anthony; s of George Leonard John Allen (d 1968), and Dorothy Mary, *née* Willoughby (d 1964); *b* 27 May 1926; *Educ* High Pavement Sch Nottingham, Univ of London (BSc, PhD, DSc); *m* 1, 1952 (m dis 1983), Marion Ferguson, da of late Dr John Crow, of Largs; 1 s (Hamish John Allen b 1955), 1 da (Elspeth Ferguson Allen b 1959); m 2, 1983, Margaret Porteous, da of James Aitken, of Motherwell; 1 adopted step s (Andrew Alexander Murdoch b 1972); *Career* Sherwood Foresters 1945–46, RAMC 1946–48; asst lectr Univ of Glasgow 1951–54, John Murray student Royal Soc 1952–54, lectr, sr lectr and reader in zoology and marine biology Univ of Newcastle upon Tyne 1954–76, prof of marine biology Univ of London 1976–91, dir Univ Marine Biology Station 1976–91, emeritus prof and hon res fell 1991–; visiting prof: Univ of Washington 1968/70/71, Univ of W Indies 1976; post doctoral fell and guest investigator Woods Hole Oceanographic Inst 1965–; author numerous pubns and articles on deep sea organisms and shellfish, etc; memb: Natural Environment Res Cncl 1977–83 (chm Univ Affrs Ctee 1978–83), Nature Conservancy Cncl 1982–90 (chm Advsy Ctee on Sci 1984–90), Cncl Scottish Marine Biol Assoc 1977–83, Cncl Marine Biol Assoc UK 1981–83 and 1989–93, Life Scis Bd CNAA 1981–84, Br Nat Ctee for Oceanic Res 1988–90; pres Malacological Soc of London 1982–84; FRSE 1968, FIBiol 1969; *Recreations* travel, admiring gardens, pub lunching, wild flower photography; *Style*— Prof John A Allen, FRSE; ✉ Drialstone, Isle of Cumbrae, Scotland KA28 0EP (☎ 01475 530 479); University Marine Biological Station, Millport, Isle of Cumbrae, Scotland KA28 0EG (☎ 01475 530 581, fax 01475 530601)

ALLEN, Sir John Derek; kt (1995), CBE (1987); s of William Henry Allen (d 1956), of Cardiff, and Lalla Dorothy, *née* Bowen (d 1987); *b* 6 Nov 1928; *Educ* Cardiff HS, Cardiff Coll of Tech (HND in Bldg, BA 1990); *m* 14 July 1951, Thelma Jean, da of John Henry Hooper (d 1971), of Cardiff; 1 s (Nicholas John b 1961); *Career* civil engr then chm and md John Morgan Group of Cardiff 1947–79, memb Land Authy for Wales 1976– (dep chm 1988–), dep chm then chm Cwmbran Devpt Corp 1979–88, chm Housing for Wales 1988–; treas Nat Fedn of Bldg Trade Employers 1980–83 (pres 1979); Freeman City of London 1980; FCIOB 1980, FIMgt 1980; *Recreations* fly fishing and golf; *Clubs* Cardiff and County, Cardiff Golf; *Style*— Sir John Allen, CBE; ✉ 6 Egremont Rd, Penylan, Cardiff CF2 5LN (☎ 01222 499461); Housing for Wales, 25–30 Lambourne Crescent, Llanishen, Cardiff CF4 5ZJ (☎ 01222 747979)

ALLEN, Very Rev John Edward; s of Rev Canon Ronald Edward Taylor Allen, MC (d 1984), and Isabel Edith, *née* Otter-Barry; *b* 9 June 1932; *Educ* Rugby, Univ Coll Oxford (MA), Fitzwilliam Coll Cambridge (MA), Westcott House Cambridge; *m* 1957, Eleanor, *née* Prynne; 1 s (Christopher), 3 da (Rebecca, Madeleine, Isabel); *Career* chaplain Univ of Bristol 1971–79, vicar Chippenham 1979–82, provost Wakefield West Yorks 1982–; memb: Gen Synod C of E 1985–, Bd of Social Responsibility C of E 1985–90, Bd of Mission 1991–96; vice chm Partnership for World Mission 1987–96, chm Wakefield Med Research Ethics Ctee 1991–, chm of govrs Cathedral HS 1992–, religious advsr Yorkshire Television 1994–; vice chm Wakefield HA 1991–, govr Queen Elizabeth GS Wakefield 1982–; *Recreations* walking, fishing, people; *Style*— The Very Rev John Allen; ✉ 1 Cathedral Close, Margaret St, Wakefield, W Yorks WF1 2DQ (☎ 01924 210005, fax 01924 210009); The Glebe Barn, Sawdon, nr Scarborough, N Yorks YO13 9DY (☎ 01723 859854)

ALLEN, Maj-Gen John Geoffrey Robyn; CB (1976); s of R A Allen, of Leatherhead, Surrey, and Mrs R A Allen, *née* Youngman; *b* 19 Aug 1923; *Educ* Haileybury; *m* 1959, Ann Monica, da of Kenneth Morford, CBE; 1 s (Christopher b 1962), 1 da (Julia b 1965); *Career* cmmnd KRRC 1942, transfd RTR 1947, dir gen Fighting Vehicles and Engr Equipment MOD 1973–74, dir RAC 1974–76, Sr Army Directing Staff RCDS 1976–78, ret 1979; Col Cmdt RTR 1976–80 (Rep 1978–80); lay observer attached to Lord Chllr's Dept 1979–85; memb: Lord Chllr's Advsy Ctee on Legal Aid 1979–85, Booth Ctee on Matrimonial Procedure 1982–85; Hon Col Royal Yeo (TA) and Hon Col HQ (Westminster Dragons) Sqdn 1982–87; *Recreations* dinghy sailing, gardening; *Clubs* Army and Navy; *Style*— Maj-Gen John Allen, CB; ✉ Meadowleys, Charlton, Chichester, West Sussex PO18 0HU (☎ 01243 811638)

ALLEN, John Piers; OBE (1979); s of Percy Allen, and Marjorie Isabel Agnes Nash; ggs on the paternal side of Fanny Stirling (1815–1895), the 19th century actress; *b* 30 March 1912; *Educ* Aldenham, St John's Coll Cambridge; *m* 1, 1937 (m dis 1944), Modwena Sedgwick; 2 s (Jemmy, Toby); m 2, 1945, Anne Preston (d 1968); 2 s (Simon, Benjamin), 2 da (Charlotte, Harriet); m 3, 1981, Margaret Wootton; *Career* memb Old Vic Co 1933–35, Victor Gollancz Ltd 1936–37, drama organizer Left Book Club Theatre Guild 1937, London Theatre Studio 1938–39; RNVR 1940–45; prodr and admin Glyndebourne Children's Theatre 1945–51, script-writer and prodr BBC Sch Bdcasting Dept 1951–61, adjudicator Dominion Drama Festival Canada 1956, UNESCO drama specialist Aust 1959 and 1961, HM inspr of schs with nat responsibility for drama 1961–72, princ Central Sch of Speech and Drama 1972–78, visiting prof of drama Westfield Coll Univ of London 1979–82, visiting lectr Centre for Arts City Univ 1979–83, currently visiting lectr UC Scarborough; vice chm Br Theatre Assoc 1978–83; chm: Accreditation Bd Nat Cncl of Drama Trg 1979–83, Dance Educn and Trg 1982–95 (chm Accreditation Bd 1979–82); memb CNNA Dance and Drama Panels 1979–82; vice pres Br Centre Int Amateur Theatre Assoc 1982–86, chm Old Meeting House Tst Helmsley 1993–96; FRSAMD, FGSM, FRSA; *Books* Producing Plays for Children (1950), Going to the Theatre (1951), Great Moments in the Theatre (ed 1953), Masters of British Drama (1957), Masters of European Drama (1962), An Elizabethan Actor (1966), Three Medieval Plays (1953), Education Survey No2 - Drama (1968), Drama in Schools: theory and practice (1979), Theatre in Europe (a study of the European Theatre cmmnd by Cncl of Europe, 1981), A History of the Theatre in Europe (1983); *Style*— John Allen, Esq, OBE; ✉ The Old Orchard, Lastingham, York YO6 6TQ (☎ 01751 417334)

ALLEN, Prof John Walter; s of Walter Allen (d 1992), and B M Allen; *b* 7 March 1928; *Educ* King Edward's HS Birmingham, Sidney Sussex Coll Cambridge (open major scholar, MA); *m* 1, Mavis Joan, *née* Williamson (d 1972); 1 s (Matthew John b 1962); m 2, 1981, Hania Renata, *née* Szawelska; *Career* Nat Serv RAF Educn Branch 1949–51; staff scientist Ericsson Telephones Beeston Nottingham (now part of GEC) 1951–56; research scientist Royal Naval Scientific Serv Electronics Research Lab 1956–64; visiting assoc prof Stanford Univ California 1964–66; Univ of St Andrews: Tullis Russell fell Dept of Physics 1968–72, reader in physics 1972–80, personal chair in solid state physics 1980–; memb American Physical Soc; fell former Physical Soc, FSA(Scot), FRSE 1985; *Recreations* traditional dance, archaeology; *Style*— Prof John W Allen, FRSE; ✉ 2 Dempster Terrace, St Andrews, Fife KY16 9QQ (☎ 01334 474163); Department of Physics and Astronomy, University of St Andrews, North Haugh, St Andrews, Fife KY16 9SS (☎ 01334 463331, fax 01334 463104)

ALLEN, Dr Justin Norman Bertram; *b* 7 Dec 1945; *Educ* Northgate GS for Boys Ipswich, Guy's Hosp Med Sch (MB BS, LRCP MRCS, DObstRCOG, FRCGP 1986); *m* Sue; 3 c; *Career* pre-registration appts Guy's and Lewisham Hosps 1969–70, internship Pittsfield Massachusetts 1970–71, Ipswich Vocational Trg Scheme 1971–73, in gen practice 1973– (sr ptnr 1980–); regional assoc advsr Trent Region 1993–; RCGP: coll rep Euro Acad of Teachers in Gen Practice 1991–, co-opted memb Cncl 1993–, memb Int Ctee 1993–, jt sec Jt Ctee on Postgraduate Educn for Gen Practice 1993–; author of various pubns in academic jls; *Style*— Dr Justin Allen; ✉ Countesthorpe Health Centre, Central Street, Counteshorpe, Leicester LE8 5QJ (☎ 0116 277 6336, fax 0116 278 0851)

ALLEN, Keith Howell Charles; s of Edward Allen, and Mary Elizabeth, *née* John; *b* 2 Sept 1953; *Educ* Sir Anthony Browns Brentwood Essex, Brune Park Comp Gosport Hants; 1 s (Alfie b 11 Sept 1986), 2 da (Sarah b 12 Dec 1979, Lily Rose b 2 May 1985); *Career* actor and writer; writer England World Cup Song (World in Motion) 1990 and Euro Cup Song (Englands Irie, with Black Grape) 1996; *Theatre* roles incl: Street Trash (NT Studio), DC Barry Hooper in Murmuring Judges (RNT) 1993; as writer and performer: The Yob, The Bullshitters, Detectives on The Verge of a Nervous Breakdown, Whatever You Want; *Television* roles incl: Comic Strip Presents..., Born to Run, Martin Chuzzlewit, Sharman, Dangerfield, A Very British Coup; *Films* incl: Shallowgrave, Trainspotting, Second Best, Lochness, Blue Juice, Scandal, Chicagoe Joe and the Showgirl, Kafka, Beyond Bedlam; *Clubs* The Colony Room, Groucho; *Style*— Keith Allen, Esq; ✉ c/o Lou Coulson, 37 Berwick Street, London W1V 3RF (☎ 0171 734 9633)

ALLEN, Sir (William) Kenneth Gwynne; kt (1961); er s of Harold Gwynne Allen (d 1960), of Bedford, and Hilda Margaret, *née* Langley (d 1969); *b* 23 May 1907; *Educ* Westminster, Neuchâtel Univ of Switzerland; *m* 1931, Eleanor Mary (d 1990), o da of late Henry Eeles, of Newcastle-upon-Tyne; 1 s (Charles), 1 da (Caroline); *Career* chm: W H Allen Sons & Co 1955–70 (dir 1937–70, md 1946–70), Amalgamated Power Engineering 1968–70; dir: Whessoe Ltd 1954–65, Electrolux 1970–78; chm: Br Internal Combustion Engine Mfrs' Assoc 1955–57, BEAMA 1959–61; pres: Br Engrs' Assoc 1957–59, Engrg Employers' Fedn 1962–64; memb Cncl CBI 1965–67; Freeman City of London, Liveryman Worshipful Co of Shipwrights; High Sheriff Beds 1958–59, DL Beds 1978–92; CEng, FIMarE, MRINA; *Style*— Sir Kenneth Allen; ✉ 12 The Mews, Amesbury Abbey, Amesbury, Wilts SP4 7EX (☎ 01980 624048)

ALLEN, Prof Kevin John; s of John Allen, of Warrington, and Ellen, *née* Wilcock; *b* 25 Nov 1941; *Educ* Boteler GS, Univ of Nottingham (BA), Univ of Newcastle; *m* 1969, Kirsten Margaret, da of James Paton; 1 s (James Keir b 1973), 1 da (Kirsty Anne b 1971); *Career* lectr in applied economics Dept of Social and Economic Research Univ of Glasgow 1966–75 (asst lectr 1964–66), research fell Int Inst of Management Berlin 1975–77 (gp leader int team studying Euro regnl incentives); Centre for the Study of Public Policy Univ of Stathclyde: co-dir 1977–82, prof and co-dir 1983–87; Euro Policies Research Centre Univ of Strathclyde: prof and dir 1987–95; assoc dean (research) Strathclyde Business Sch Univ of Strathclyde 1991–93; econ conslt to Sec of State for Scotland 1989–; *Books* Nationalised Industries (1970), Regional Problems and Policies in Italy and France (1971), An Introduction to the Italian Economy (1974), Small Area Employment Forecasting: Data and Problems (1978), Regional Incentives in the European Community: A Comparative Study (1979), European Regional Incentives (1980–), Industrial Aids in Britain: A Businessman's Guide (1981, 4 edn 1985), Regional Incentives and the Investment Decision of the Firm (1986), Government Support for British Business (1986–); *Recreations* wood turning; *Style*— Prof Kevin Allen; ✉ 38 Mitre Road, Glasgow G14 9LE (☎ 0141 959 1692); European Policies Research Centre, University of Strathclyde, 141 St James' Road, Glasgow G4 0LT (☎ 0141 552 4400, fax 0141 552 1757)

ALLEN, Leonard; s of Joseph Allen (d 1956), of Bournemouth, and Henrietta Emily, *née* Fowle; *b* 30 Nov 1930; *m* 1, 1955 (m dis 1969), Diana, *née* Love; m 2, 27 April 1970, Theodora Jane, da of John Russell (d 1984), of Caversham, Reading; 1 da (Henrietta Sophie b 1972); *Career* Nat Serv RTR 1949–50; Cons Central Office: agent Reading 1959–64, political educn offr Eastern Area 1964–67 (dep area agent 1967–74), dep dir and head Local Govt Dept Cons Central Office 1974–77; chief exec Fedn of Recruitment and Employment Servs 1977–93, dep chm Machinery Users' Assoc 1995–, dep chm MUA Management Services Ltd 1995–; sec gen Int Confedn of Temp Work Businesses 1990–93 (currently advsr); conslt T L Dallas (City) Ltd 1995–, corp affairs dir Stirling Recruitment Group Ltd 1996–; vice chm Southern Region UNs Assoc 1955–57, chm Recruitment Soc 1982–84, memb Governing Body SPCK 1977–80, vice chm Bow Gp 1959–64, memb DOE Advsy Ctee on Women's Employment 1980–92; govr Battle Abbey Sch; Freeman: City of London 1978, Worshipful Co of Woolmen; memb NUJ, FRSA; *Recreations* conversation, music, reading, art galleries, dining out and in; *Clubs* Athenaeum, Arts; *Style*— Leonard Allen, Esq; ✉ 8 Carmel Court, Highfield, Marlow, Bucks SL7 2LQ (☎ 01628 472325, fax 01628 476484); MUA, Roman House, Wood Street, London EC2Y 5BA (☎ 0171 638 4383); Stirling Recruitment Group Ltd, 49 Old Steine, Brighton BN1 1NH (☎ 01273 702555)

ALLEN, Mary; *b* 22 Aug 1951; *Educ* Sch of St Helen and St Katherine, New Hall Cambridge (BA); *Career* actress BBC, West End and repertory 1973–76, agent London Management 1977–78, arts sponsorship mangr Mobil Oil Company Ltd 1978–81, asst dir Assoc for Business Sponsorship of The Arts 1982–83, training conslt 1986–90, arts mgmnt conslt 1983–90, dir Watermans Arts Centre 1990–92, sec-gen Arts Cncl of England 1994– (dep sec-gen 1992–94); Arts Cncl 1986–90: memb Art Panel, memb Ethnic Minority Arts Ctee, advsr to Percent for Art Steering Gp; chm Public Art Devpt Tst 1983–92, memb Bd Cheek by Jowl 1989–92; lectr in arts mgmnt for: Br Cncl, City Univ, Leics Poly; *Books* Sponsoring The Arts: New Business Strategies for the 1990s; *Style*— Ms Mary Allen; ✉ Arts Council of England, 14 Great Peter Street, London SW1P 3NQ (☎ 0171 333 0100)

ALLEN, Michael John; s of Edward Thomas Allen, of Bedford, and Dorothy May, *née* Leigh; *b* 11 July 1941; *Educ* Bedford Sch, St Catharine's Coll Cambridge (MA); *m* 22 Oct 1977, Marjolein Christina, da of Hendrik Casper Wytzes, of Bloemendaal, Netherlands; 2 da (Elizabeth b 1981, Caroline b 1983); *Career* Univ of Cambridge: dir of extramural studies 1980–90, bursar Churchill Coll 1990– (fell 1985–), dir of studies in English 1991–; *Recreations* natural history, gardening, squash; *Clubs* Royal Soc of Arts; *Style*— Michael Allen, Esq; ✉ Churchill College, Cambridge CB3 0DS (☎ 01223 336112)

ALLEN, Peter Dobson; CBE (1988), DL (1989); s of Frederick Allen (d 1957), of Dewsbury, and Ethel, *née* Dobson (d 1990); *b* 4 Jan 1931; *Educ* Wheelwright GS Dewsbury, Univ of Birmingham (BSc); *m* 15 Sept 1956, Janet, da of Cyril Thurman (d 1983), of Dewsbury; 3 s (Timothy b 1958, Christopher b 1959, Nicholas b 1963); *Career* Lt RA 1957; British Steel Corporation 1972–90: dir Port Talbot Works 1972–76, md Welsh Div 1976–80, md ops Strip Products Gp 1980–89, md British Steel Strip Products 1989–90, ret 1990; dir: Benzole Producers Ltd 1982–89, Benzene Marketing Co Ltd 1982–89, ASW Holdings plc 1987–89; High Sheriff Mid Glamorgan 1987–88; chm: W Wales Trg and Enterprise Cncl 1989–90, Morriston Hosp NHS Tst Swansea 1994–; memb: Bd West Glamorgan Health Authy 1990–94 (chm 1991–94), Cncl and Jt Planning and Resources Ctee Univ of Wales 1990–, Bd BR 1991–; CEng, FIM; *Recreations* rugby football, cricket, the turf, music; *Style*— Peter D Allen, Esq, CBE, DL; ✉ Furzebrook, Merthyr Mawr Road, Bridgend, Mid Glam CF31 3NS (☎ 01656 655803, fax 01656 655147)

ALLEN, Peter John; s of William George Allen (d 1974), and Florence Rose, *née* Betambeau; *b* 3 July 1949; *Educ* Wallington; *m* 23 June 1973, Jennifer, da of Cyril Robert Groves, of East Sussex; *Career* Kenneth Anderson and Co 1967–68, Centre File 1968–69, Rowe Swann and Co 1969–75, Sheppards and Chase Discretionary Fund Mgmnt 1975–77; Kleinwort Benson Investment Management: joined 1977, asst dir 1985–87, dir 1987–, dir Kleinwort Emerging Markets Trust plc 1993–; MInstD, MSI, MIMgt; *Recreations* riding, ballet; *Clubs* RAF; *Style*— Peter Allen, Esq; ✉ Hestia, Woodland Way, Kingswood, Surrey KT20 6PA; 1 Churchill Villas, Churchill Rd, The Bourne, Brimscombe, Glos GL5 2UB; Kleinwort Benson Investment Management Ltd, 10 Fenchurch St, London EC3M 3LB (☎ 0171 623 8000, telex 9413545)

ALLEN, Peter William; s of Alfred William Allen (d 1987), of Sittingbourne, Kent, and Myra Nora, *née* Rogers (d 1982); *b* 22 July 1938; *Educ* Borden GS, Sidney Sussex Coll Cambridge (MA); *m* 1965, Patricia Mary, da of Joseph Frederick Dunk, of Sheffield; 3 da (Samantha, Joanna, Annabel); *Career* RAF 1957–59; Coopers & Lybrand: joined 1963, qualified CA 1966, ptnr 1973, chm Int Personnel Ctee 1975–78, ptnr i/c London Office

1983, managing ptnr 1984–90, memb UK Mgmnt Ctee 1984–90, memb Int Exec Ctee 1988–90 and 1992–94, dep chm Coopers & Lybrand 1990–94 (memb Bd 1990–94), chm Mgmnt Consulting Servs UK 1990–94; non-exec dir: Charter plc 1994–, Schroder Ventures Group 1994–, The Post Office May 1995–, Samantha Allen Interior Design Ltd; Freeman City of London 1988, Liveryman Worshipful Co of Glaziers and Painters of Glass 1989; FCA 1969, CIMgt 1993; *Recreations* golf, painting; *Clubs* Reform; *Style*— Peter W Allen, Esq; ✉ John O'Gaddesden's House, Little Gaddesden, Berkhamsted, Herts HP4 1PF (☎ 01442 842148)

ALLEN, Prof Raymond William Kenneth (Ray); s of Raymond Kenneth Allen, of Bishopstoke, and Dee, *née* Powell; *b* 14 Feb 1948; *Educ* Portsmouth GS, UMIST (MSc), McGill Univ Montreal (PhD); *m* April 1978, Rosemarie; 3 da (Aemelia Catherine Payard b 1979, Hermione Sarah Payard b 1990, Beatrice Eleanor Payard b 1994), 1 s (Sebastian Alexander Payard b 1983); *Career* Harwell Res Laboratory: indust res fell 1975–77, sr scientific offr 1977–82, princ scientific offr 1982–88, head Environmental and Process Engrg Dept 1988–93, head Tech Area for Chemical and Process Engrg 1990–, business devpt dir 1993–95; prof of chemical engrg Univ of Sheffield 1995– (head Dept of Chemical and Process Engrg 1996–), seconded DTI Innovation Unit 1995–; visiting prof Dept of Chem Engrg Univ of Newcastle 1989–93; tech ed Filtration and Separation Jl 1983–88; memb: Editorial Bd Journal of Separation Technol 1979–89, Tech Ctee NSCA 1986–91, Academic Advsy Panel Hughenden Fndn 1986–89, Process Engrg Ctee SERC 1989–92, Mgmnt Ctee SERC Clean Technologies Unit 1989–93, DOE Advsy Gp on Air Pollution Abatement Technol 1990–94, Mgmnt Ctee DTI Carrier Technol Prog 1992–; memb Cncl: Filtration Soc 1985–86 (chm 1985–86), Nat Soc for Clean Air 1986–91; FIChemE 1986 (memb Cncl 1990–92), FEng 1993; *Recreations* practical politics, almost any activity with my family; *Style*— Prof Ray Allen, FEng; ✉ Department of Chemical and Process Engineering, University of Sheffield, Mappin Street, Sheffield S1 3DJ (☎ 0114 222 7600, fax 0114 276 2154)

ALLEN, (Phillip) Richard Hernaman; s of Philip Hernaman Allen (d 1972), and Dorothy, *née* Modral; *b* 26 Jan 1949; *Educ* Loughborough GS, Merton Coll Oxford (BA); *m* 11 July 1970, Vanessa, da of Laurence Alfred Lampard; 2 da (Joanna Kirstie Hernaman b 6 April 1978, Katharine Rhiannon Lampard b 1 Aug 1981); *Career* asst private sec to: Paymaster Gen (Treasy) 1973–74, Chancellor of the Duchy of Lancaster (Cabinet Office) 1974–75; HM Customs & Excise: asst princ 1970–73, high exec offr (admin) 1973, princ 1975–84, asst sec 1984–90, cmmr and dir of internal taxes 1990–91, cmmr and dir of organisation 1991–94; policy dir Dept of Social Security 1994–; *Recreations* music, badminton, gardening, keeping fit; *Style*— Richard Allen, Esq; ✉ Department of Social Security, Adelphi, 1–11 John Adam Street, London WC2N 6HT (☎ 0171 962 8010)

ALLEN, Richard Ian Gordon; s of Reginald Arthur Hill Allen, and Edith Alice, *née* Manger; *b* 13 Dec 1944; *Educ* Edinburgh Acad, Univ of Edinburgh (MA), Univ of York (BPhil); *m* 20 May 1988, Lynn Conroy; *Career* conslt UN Econ Cmmn for Euro 1970, res offr NIESR 1971–75, econ advsr Dept of Energy 1975–78, econ advsr HM Treasy 1978–81, sr econ advsr, later asst sec HM Treasy 1981–85, cnsllr econ Br Embassy Washington 1985–87, press sec to Chllr of the Exchequer 1987–88, under sec Int Fin HM Treasy 1988–90; dir European Investment Bank 1988–90; HM Treasy: under sec Local Govt Fin 1990–93, under sec Mgmnt Policy 1993–95; with Miny of Fin and Nat Economy Bahrein 1995–; *Recreations* arts, golf; *Clubs* Royal Wimbledon Golf; *Style*— Richard Allen, Esq; ✉ c/o Office of the Financial Adviser, Ministry of Finance and National, Economy, PO Box 333, Manama, Bahrein

ALLEN, Richard Robert Edward; s of Robert Edward Allen (d 1976), of Worcester, and Agnes Mary, *née* Clarke (d 1950); *b* 8 Feb 1933; *Educ* Worcester Sch of Art, Bath Acad of Art, Dept of Educn Univ of Bristol, Italian Govt scholar in Fine Art, Cwlth scholar in Fine Art (India), Univ of Sussex (Fellowship in Fine Art); *m* 13 April 1961, Evelyn Beatrice, da of Phillip Raymond Laurens; 2 da (Rebecca Emily Laurens-Allen b 16 June 1966, Alice Mary b 27 Oct 1971); *Career* artist and exhibition/art conslt; lectr in art in colls of art and univ art depts throughout UK (visiting lectr Dept of Fine Art Univ of Wales 1993–), participation in numerous exhibitions, contrib public and private art collections, organiser numerous art photography and other exhibitions in UK, Germany and Belgium; dir: Festival France Jersey, Exart Ltd, Exhibition Art and Design Conslts; memb: working party for trg exhibition organisers Arts Cncl, Art Info Registry London, Industl Sponsors Ctee London, Barreau Art Fndn Jersey, Arts Advsy Panel Jersey Heritage Tst; Br Forces Korea Medal 1950–53, UN Serv Medal; FCSD, FRSA; *Recreations* walking, travelling; *Style*— Richard Allen, Esq; ✉ Knapp Cottage, Brilley, Whitney-on-Wye, Herefordshire HR3 6JD (☎ and fax 01497 831405)

ALLEN, Rick; *b* 1 Nov 1963; *Career* drummer; joined Def Leppard 1978; Def Leppard tours: Pyromania 1983, Hysteria 1987, Adrenalize 1992; 1 UK top ten single (Animal 1987), 3 US top ten singles (Hysteria 1988, Pour Some Sugar On Me 1988, Armageddon 1989); albums with Def Leppard: On Through The Night (1980, UK no 15), High 'N' Dry (1981, UK no 26), Pyromania (1983, UK no 18, US no 2), Hysteria (1987, UK and US no 1), Adrenalize (1992), Retro-Active (1993), Slang (1996); awards incl: Favourite Heavy Metal Artist, Favourite Heavy Metal Album (for Hysteria) American Music Awards 1989; *Style*— Rick Allen, Esq; ✉ c/o Bludgeon Riffola, Mercury, Chancellors House, 72 Chancellors Road, London W6 9QB (☎ 0181 910 5678, fax 0181 910 5896)

ALLEN, Robert Edward; s of Edward Allen (d 1964), of Liverpool, and Elsie Allen; *b* 2 Sept 1946; *Educ* Liverpool Collegiate Sch; *m* 1972, Ann-Marie; 1 da (Sophie Elizabeth b 1978), 1 s (Oliver Edward b 1982); *Career* NHS mgmnt trainee Liverpool 1965–69, asst hosp sec Winchester 1969–71, dep hosp sec Wolverhampton 1971–74, sector administrator Hull 1974–76, dist support servs mangr SE Kent Health Authy 1976–79, asst dist administrator S Nottingham Dist Health Authy 1979–82, dep dist administrator Nottingham Dist Health Authy 1982–85, gen mangr Seacroft and Killingbeck Hosps Leeds 1985–90, dist gen mangr Airedale Health Authy 1990–92, chief exec Airedale NHS Tst 1992–; MHSM (memb Nat Cncl, former chm Yorks Branch); *Recreations* family, squash, golf, swimming, cycling; *Clubs* Collingham and Linton Sports Association; *Style*— Robert E Allen, Esq; ✉ Airedale NHS Trust Headquarters, Airedale General Hospital, Skipton Road, Skeeton, Keighley, W Yorks BD20 6TD (☎ 01535 652511, fax 01535 676366)

ALLEN, Robert Geoffrey Bruère (Robin); QC (1995); s of Rev Canon Ronald Edward Taylor Allen (d 1984), of Ludlow, and Isabel Edith, *née* Otter-Barry (d 1994); *b* 13 Feb 1951; *Educ* Rugby, Univ Coll Oxford (BA (PPE)); *m* 3 Sept 1977, (Elizabeth) Gay, da of Dr Anthony James Moon, of Rickmansworth; 2 s (Christopher Francis (Kit) b 19 Feb 1983, Luke Anthony b 10 June 1986); *Career* co-organiser Free Representation Unit 1973; called to the Bar Middle Temple 1974; in practice 1976–, employment law advsr to Legal Action Gp 1978–80, legal advsr to Local Govt Gp Inst of PR 1988–90; expert advsr to EC on UK law affecting the most disadvantaged 1993; sec Lambeth Central Constituency Lab Party 1977; chm: London Youth Advsy Centre 1984–90, Bd of Govrs Eleanor Palmer Sch 1988–91, Brandon Centre 1991–93; Employment Law Bar Assoc: fndr ctee memb 1994–, vice chm 1996–; vice chm Bar Pro Bono Unit 1996–; *Television* The Great Ape Trial (Channel 4) Dec 1995; *Books* How to Prepare a Case for an Industrial Tribunal (1987), Employment Law Manual (contrib, 1988), Civil Liberty (contrib, 1989); *Recreations* family life, fishing; *Style*— Robin Allen, Esq, QC; ✉ Cloisters, 1 Pump Court, Temple, London EC4Y 7AA (☎ 0171 583 0303, fax 0171 583 2254)

ALLEN, Susan Jennifer (Susie); da of Henry Francis Metcalfe (d 1991), of Scotland, and Yolande, *née* Senior-Ellis; *b* 12 May 1949; *Educ* Kingston Poly (BA), RCA (MA), Cite Int des Arts Paris (RCA travelling scholarship); *m* 1, 1969 (m dis 1985); m 2, 1990, Paul Huxley; *Career* artist and curator RCA Collection 1989– (Fine Art Devpt Office RCA 1994); pt/t and visiting lectr 1981–: RCA, Wimbledon Sch of Art, Kingston Poly, Ruskin Sch of Drawing Univ of Oxford, Chelsea Coll of Art, Central/St Martin's Coll of Art, Edinburgh Coll of Art; selected exhibitions: New Contemporaries ICA 1978–79, Demarco Gallery Edinburgh 1979, Edinburgh City Art Gall 1980, Mulhouse Print Biennale France 1981, 35 printmakers RCA touring exhbn UK and France 1983–86, Works on Paper Raab Gallery 1987, Artist's Choice V & A 1987, RCA Anniversary exhbn Barbican Art Gall 1987, Homage to the Square Flaxman Gallery 1988, Galerie zur Alten Deutschen Schule Switzerland 1989, 1990, 1992 and 1993, Cabinet Paintings Gillian Jason Gallery London and touring 1991–92, Artistic Assocs Gillian Jason Gallery 1992, Gallery 7 Hong Kong 1995, Thinking Eye Gallery 7 Hong Kong 1996; cmmnd to design sets and costumes IBIS Dance Co Theatre Royal Stratford East 1982; work in public collections: Scottish Arts Cncl, British Cncl, V & A; curator: British Art Britain in Vienna Festival Contemporary Art Soc Vienna 1986, Exhbn Road Painters at the RCA 1988, 3 Ways British Cncl touring exhbn E Europe and Africa 1989–96, An American Passion Contemporary Br Painting The Kaser/Summer Collection 1994–95, Decorative Forms Over the World - Edward Allington London and NY (Virgin Atlantic) 1996; contemporary art conslt: NACF, CAS, Wedgwood, TI Group, Visa Int, Virgin Atlantic Airways, Absolut Vodka, Start Int; NACF Award for outstanding services to the arts 1988–89; FRCA 1990; *Style*— Ms Susie Allen; ✉ 2 Dalling Road, Hammersmith, London W6 0JB (☎ 0181 563 9495); Royal College of Art, Kensington Gore, London SW7 2EU

ALLEN, Thomas Boaz; CBE (1989); s of Thomas Boaz Allen (d 1987), of Seaham, Co Durham, and Florence, *née* Hemmings (d 1990); *b* 10 Sept 1944; *Educ* Robert Richardson GS Ryhope Co Durham, RCM London (ARCM); *m* 1, 30 March 1968 (m dis 1986), Margaret, da of George Holley (d 1980), of Seaham, Co Durham; 1 s (Stephen Boaz b 31 Jan 1970); m 2, 12 March 1988, Jeannie Gordon Lascelles, da of Norman Gordon Farquharson, of Southbroom, Natal, SA; *Career* opera singer; princ baritone: Welsh Nat Opera 1969–72, Royal Opera House Covent Garden 1972–77; guest appearances: Metropolitan Opera NY (debut) 1981, Bayerische Staatsoper München 1985, Wiener Staatsoper, Paris Opera, La Scala Milan (opened 1987/88 season as Don Giovanni), ENO, San Francisco Opera, Chicago Lyric Opera, Los Angeles, Glyndebourne, Aldeburgh and Salzburg Festivals, Count in Le Nozze di Figaro (Covent Garden) 1995; memb The Arts for the Earth, bd memb London Opera Festival; Prince Consort prof RCM; Hon MA Newcastle 1984, Hon DMus Durham 1988, Hon RAM 1988; FRCM 1988; *Books* Foreign Parts: A Singer's Journal; *Recreations* golf, drawing and painting, ornithology; *Clubs* Garrick; *Style*— Thomas Allen, Esq, CBE; ✉ c/o Lies Askonas Ltd, 6 Henrietta Street, London WC2E 8LA

ALLEN, Dr William Alexander; CBE (1980); s of Frank Allen (d 1965), of Winnipeg, Canada, and Sarah Estelle, *née* Harper (d 1915); *b* 29 June 1914; *Educ* Univ of Manitoba (BArch); *m* 10 Sept 1938, Beatrice Mary Theresa (Tessa), da of Clarence Henry Pearson (d 1930), of Cheriton Fitzpaine, Devon, and Dr Beatrice Mary Pearson, *née* Knowles; 2 s (Christopher b 1942, Nicholas b 1944), 1 da (Deborah b 1948); *Career* chief architect Building Research Establishment 1953–61 (joined 1938), princ Architectural Assoc Sch of Architecture 1961–66, jt fndr ptnr Bickerdike Allen Partners 1962–89 (conslt 1989–); memb Cncl RIBA 1954–72 and 1982–89; pres: Inst of Acoustics 1975–76, Ecclesiastic Architects & Surveyors Assoc 1980–81; former vice chm Govrs Sir Frederic Osborn Sch; advsr for bldg research to US Nat Bureau of Standards 1966–92, hon scientific advsr Nat Gallery 1970–; Hon LLD Univ of Manitoba 1977; Cdr Ordem do Merito (Portugal) 1972; fndr memb Acoustics Soc (later Inst) 1946, hon assoc memb NZ Inst Arch 1965, memb Ecclesiastic Architects & Surveyors 1975; hon fell: American Inst of Architects 1983, Acad of Experts (former vice pres); FRIBA 1965 (ARIBA 1937); *Publications* incl: Sound Transmission in Buildings (with R Fitzmaurice, 1940), Professionalism and Architecture (paper in Encyclopedia of Architecture, 1989), other papers on bldg tech sci and arch; *Recreations* walking, gardening, drawing, writing; *Clubs* Athenaeum; *Style*— Dr William Allen, CBE; ✉ 4 Ashley Close, Welwyn Garden City, Herts AL8 7LH (☎ 01707 324178, fax 01707 391992); Bickerdike Allen Partners, 121 Salusbury Rd, London NW6 6RG (☎ 0171 625 4411, fax 0171 625 0250, telex 263889)

ALLEN, William Anthony; s of Derek William Allen, and Margaret Winifred, *née* Jones; *b* 13 May 1949; *Educ* King's Coll Sch Wimbledon, Balliol Coll Oxford (BA), LSE (MScEcon); *m* 29 July 1972, Rosemary Margaret, da of Richard Kelland Eminson; 1 s (Edmund James b 1979), 2 da (Rosalind Jane b 1976, Lucy Ruth b 1983); *Career* Bank of England: Econ Intelligence Dept 1972–77, Cashiers Dept 1977–78, secondment Bank for International Settlements Basle Switzerland 1978–80, Economics Div 1980–82, Gilt-Edged Div 1982–86, head of Money Market Ops Div 1986–90, head of Foreign Exchange Div 1990–94, dep dir (monetary analysis) 1994– (concurrently pt/t advsr to National Bank of Poland); *Recreations* gardening, jazz; *Style*— William Allen, Esq; ✉ Deputy Director, Monetary Analysis, Bank of England, Threadneedle St, London EC2R 8AH (☎ 0171 601 4444, fax 0171 601 4404)

ALLEN, Maj-Gen William Maurice; CB (1983); s of William James Allen, and Elizabeth Jane Henrietta Allen; *b* 29 May 1931; *m* 1956, Patricia Mary Fletcher; 1 da (decd); *Career* cmmnd RASC 1950, RCT 1965, regtl and staff appts Korea, Cyprus, Germany and UK, Staff Coll Camberley 1961, Instr Staff Coll Camberley and RMCS Shrivenham 1968–70, RCDS 1976, Asst Cmdt RMA Sandhurst 1979–81, Dir-Gen Tport and Movements (Army) 1981–83, ret; dir of trg and educn Burroughs Machines Ltd 1983–85; dir European Management Information 1988–89; conslt: Mondial Defence Systems 1989–, Fortis Aviation Group; md: Fortis International Ltd 1990–93, Pulsar Aviation Ltd, Aviation Services Inc; memb Cncl: IAM 1982–85, NDTA 1983–; chm Milton Keynes IT Trg Centre 1983–85, assoc St George's House; Freeman City of London 1981, Hon Liveryman Worshipful Co of Carmen 1981; FCIT, FIMI, FIFDM, FIMgt, MInstPet; *Recreations* vigneron du Languedoc, economics, gardening, ocean cruising, squash, keeping fit; *Clubs* Overseas, Bristol Channel Yacht; *Style*— Maj-Gen William Allen, CB; ✉ c/o Royal Bank of Scotland plc, Holts Farnborough Branch, Lawrie House, 31–37 Victoria Rd, Farnborough, Hants GU14 7NR

ALLEN-JONES, Charles Martin; s of Air Vice-Marshal John Ernest Allen-Jones, CBE, of Dunmow, Essex, and Margaret Ena, *née* Rix (d 1974); *b* 7 Aug 1939; *Educ* Clifton Coll Bristol; *m* 25 June 1966, Caroline, da of Keith Beale, OBE (d 1979), of Woodchurch, Kent; 1 s (Christof b 1968), 2 da (Nicola b 1970, Anna b 1972); *Career* articled to Clerk of the Justices Uxbridge Magistrates Ct 1958–60, articled to Vizard Oldham Crowder and Cash 1960–63; admitted slr 1963; Linklaters and Paines: joined 1964, ptnr 1968–, Hong Kong Office 1976–81, head Corporate Dept 1985–91, sr ptnr 1996–; memb Hong Kong Banking Advsy Ctee 1978–80, memb City Taxation Ctee 1973–75; *Recreations* gardening, tennis, travel, reading; *Style*— Charles Allen-Jones, Esq; ✉ Linklaters and Paines, Barrington House, 59–67 Gresham St, London EC2V 7JA (☎ 0171 606 7080, fax 0171 606 5113, telex 884349)

ALLEN OF ABBEYDALE, Baron (Life Peer UK 1976); Philip; GCB (1970, KCB 1964, CB 1954); yr s of Arthur Allen (d 1962), of Sheffield, and Louie, *née* Tipper; *b* 8 July 1912; *Educ* King Edward VII Sch Sheffield, Queens' Coll Cambridge (MA); *m* 1938, Marjorie Brenda, da of Thomas John Colton Coe (d 1944); *Career* sits as Independent in House of Lords; entered Home Office 1934, Offices of War Cabinet 1943–44, Cwlth fellowship in USA 1948–49, dep chm of Prison Cmmn for England and Wales 1950–52, asst under sec of state Home Office 1952–55, dep sec Miny of Housing and Local Govt 1955–60, dep under sec of state Home Office 1960–62, second sec Treasy 1963–66, perm under sec of state Home Office 1966–72; memb Security Cmmn 1973–91, chm Gaming Bd for GB 1977–85, chm Mencap 1982–88; memb Tbnl of Inquiry into Crown Agents 1978–82; chief counting offr EEC Referendum 1975; hon fell Queens' Coll Cambridge and Royal Holloway Univ of London; *Style*— The Rt Hon the Lord Allen of Abbeydale, GCB; ✉ Holly Lodge, Englefield Green, Surrey TW20 0JP (☎ 01784 432291)

ALLENBY, 3 Viscount (UK 1919); Michael Jaffray Hynman Allenby; s of 2 Viscount Allenby (d 1984), s of Capt Frederick Allenby, CBE, JP, RN; n of 1 Viscount Allenby, GCB, GCMG, GCVO, and his 1 w (Gertrude) Mary Lethbridge, *née* Champneys (d 1988); *b* 20 April 1931; *Educ* Eton; *m* 29 July 1965, Sara Margaret, o da of Lt-Col Peter Milner Wiggin; 1 s; *Heir* s, Hon Henry Jaffray Hynman Allenby b 29 July 1968; *Career* cmmnd 2 Lt 11 Hussars (PAO) 1951, served Malaya 1953–56, ADC to Govr Cyprus 1957–58, Bde Maj 51 Bde Hong Kong 1967–70, Lt-Col Royal Hussars, CO Royal Yeo 1974–77, GS01 Instr Nigerian Staff Coll Kaduna 1977–79; chm Quickrest Ltd 1987–91, dep chm The International League for the Protection of Horses 1992–; dep speaker House of Lords 1993–; *Clubs* Cavalry and Guards'; *Style*— The Rt Hon the Viscount Allenby; ✉ The House of Lords, Westminster, London SW1A 0PW

ALLENDALE, 3 Viscount (UK 1911); Wentworth Hubert Charles Beaumont; DL (Northumberland 1961); also Baron Allendale (UK 1906); s of 2 Viscount Allendale, KG, CB, CBE, MC (d 1956), and Violet (d 1979), da of Sir Charles Seely, 2 Bt; *b* 12 Sept 1922; *Educ* Eton; *m* 1948 (m dis), Hon Sarah Ismay, da of Gen 1 Baron Ismay, KG, GCB, CH, DSO, PC; 3 s; *Heir* s, Hon Wentworth Beaumont, *qv*; *Career* served WWII Flt Lt RAFVR (POW); ADC to Viceroy of India 1946–47; Hon Air Cdre 3508 Northumberland; pres Northumberland & Durham Assoc Bldg Socs; OStJ; steward Jockey Club 1963–65; *Style*— The Rt Hon the Viscount Allendale, DL; ✉ Allenheads Hall, Allenheads, Hexham, Northumberland; Bywell Hall, Stocksfield-on-Tyne, Northumberland

ALLERTON, Air Vice-Marshal Richard Christopher; CB (1988), DL (Cornwall 1995); er s of Air Cdre Ord Denny Allerton, CB, CBE (d 1977), and Kathleen Mary, *née* Tucker (d 1993); *b* 7 Dec 1935; *Educ* Stone House Broadstairs, Stowe; *m* 14 March 1964, Marie Isobel Campbell, er da of Capt Sir Roderick Edward François McQuhae Mackenzie (11 Bt, cr 1703), CBE, DSC, RN (d 1986), and Marie Evelyn Campbell, *née* Parkinson (d 1993); 2 s (James Roderick Ord b 1967, Christopher Edward Ord b 1970); *Career* Mil Serv RAF, cmmnd 1954; served 1955–78: RAF Hullavington, Oakington, Feltwell, Kinloss, HQ Coastal Cmd, RAF MB SAFI (Malta), HQ Maintenance Cmd, No 3 Sch TT Hereford, RAF Central Flying Sch Little Rissington, RAF Coll Cranwell, student RAF Staff Coll Bracknell, staff HQ RAF Germany, chief instructor S&S WG RAF Coll Cranwell, student Nat Def Coll Latimer, MOD Harrogate; dep dir RAF supply policy MOD 1978–80, station cdr RAF Stafford 1980–82, ADC to HM The Queen 1980–82, student RCDS 1983, air cdre supply and movements HQ Strike Cmd 1983–86, dir gen of supply RAF 1987–90, ret; chm Sharpe's of Aberdeen 1995; memb Cncl Order of St John for Cornwall; *Recreations* shooting, fishing, cricket (pres RAF Cricket Assoc 1987–89); *Style*— Air Vice-Marshal Richard Allerton, CB, DL; ✉ c/o Lloyds Bank, 13 Broad St, Launceston, Cornwall PL15 8AG

ALLEYNE, Rev Sir John Olpherts Campbell; 5 Bt (GB 1769), of Four Hills, Barbados; s of Capt Sir John Alleyne, 4 Bt, DSO, DSC, RN (d 1983), and Alice Violet Emily, *née* Campbell (d 1984); *b* 18 Jan 1928; *Educ* Eton, Jesus Coll Cambridge (BA, MA); *m* 28 Sept 1968, Honor Emily Margaret, da of late William Albert Irwin, of Linkview Park, Upper Malone, Belfast; 1 s, 1 da (Clare Emma Gila b 1969); *Heir* s, Richard Meynell Alleyne b 23 June 1972; *Career* deacon 1955, priest 1956; curate Southampton 1955–58; chaplain: Coventry Cathedral 1958–62, Clare Coll Cambridge 1962–66, to Bishop of Bristol 1966–68; Toc H area sec SW England 1968–71, vicar of Speke 1971–73, rector 1973–75, rector of St Matthew's Weeke Dio of Winchester 1975–93; *Recreations* supporting asylum seekers, sailing, mountain walking, astronomy; *Style*— The Rev Sir John Alleyne, Bt; ✉ 2 Ash Grove, Guildford, Surrey GU2 5UT (☎ 01483 573824)

ALLFREY, Maj (Henry) John; OBE (1990); s of Maj Henry Sydney Allfrey, JP, DL (d 1975), of The Grange, How Caple, Hereford, and Vera, *née* Hazlehurst (d 1965); *b* 30 Dec 1924; *Educ* Winchester; *m* 1, 18 May 1957 (m dis 1980), Jocelyne, da of Cdr The Hon Maurice FitzRoy-Newdegate (d 1976), of Arbury Hall, Nuneaton, Warwicks; 2 s (David, Charles), 1 da (Lucia); m 2, 18 Oct 1980, Sonia Elisabeth, da of Col Juan Beresford Hobbs (d 1978), of Easthorpe Hall, Kelvedon, Colchester, Essex; *Career* cmmnd RHA 1944, WWII 1945–46 India Malaya and Java, Staff Capt SE Asia Land Forces HQ 1946–48; regtl serv: airborne RHA, Jr Ldrs Regt and Berks Yeo 1948–59, staff coll 1956, GSO II HQ 4 Infantry Div 1957–59, GSO II Brig Author MOD 1959–61; dir: Harp Lager (Southern) 1965–70, Courage (Central) 1967–69, Courage (Eastern) 1969–70, Courage (Brewing) 1973–80; md Courage (Central) 1971–79; memb Cncl Southern Region CBI 1972–78; dir Research into Ageing (registered charity) 1980–89, appeal dir Brentwood Sch 1990–91, sec Hedingham & Halstead Div SSAFA 1991–, chm Friends of Elderly Accomodation Counsel (registered charity) 1989–, vice chm and chm Wokingham Cons Assoc 1966–72, govr Elstree Sch 1975–88, fndr and patron Berks Retirement Assoc 1976–89; memb Braintree DC 1994–; memb Exec Cncl: Assoc of Med Res Charities, Br Soc for Res into Ageing; Lord of the Manor of Robertsbridge in Kent; FInstD, memb Inst of Mktg, memb Inst of Fund Raising Mangrs; *Books* from 1959–61: The Nuclear Land Battle, Keeping The Peace, Training For War; *Recreations* fishing, shooting, gardening; *Clubs* MCC; *Style*— Maj John Allfrey, OBE; ✉ The Dower House, Castle Hedingham, nr Halstead, Essex CO9 3DG (☎ 01787 61108)

ALLFREY, Peter Charles Scudamore; s of Lt-Gen Sir Charles Walter Allfrey, KBE, CB, DSO, MC, JP, DL (d 1964), and Geraldine Clara, *née* Lucas Scudamore (d 1982); *b* 13 Jan 1942; *Educ* Eton, Univ of Grenoble; *m* 19 Sept 1991, Delia Rose Anne, da of Lt-Col Hugh G E Dunsterville; 2 step s (William Robert Templer b 1964, Tristram James Templer b 1969), 1 step da (Sophie Anne Templer b 1966); *Career* Whitbread & Co plc: joined 1967, dir Whitbread (London) Ltd 1972–73, overseas investmt mangr Stowells of Chelsea 1973–75, Thresher & Co Ltd 1976–79, left Whitbread group 1982; with Grant Thornton Charterd Accountants 1983–90, own mgmnt consultancy firm 1991–; dir: Malcolm Innes Gallery Ltd 1973–, Mark Wilkinson Furniture Ltd 1985–, Royal Nat Hosp for Rheumatic Diseases 1990–; also involved with The Continence Fndn; FCA 1965; *Recreations* country sports, pictures, music, food and drink; *Style*— Peter C S Allfrey, Esq; ✉ 13 Lansdown Crescent, Bath BA1 5EX (☎ 01225 316698); office: 7 Old King Street, Bath BA1 2JW (☎ 01225 336575, fax 01225 444560)

ALLGOOD, Joseph William Edwin; s of Joseph Philip Allgood (d 1938), and Blanche, *née* Strutt (d 1966); *b* 6 Jan 1922; *Educ* Spring Grove GS; *m* 24 Sept 1949, Ann Elizabeth, da of Richard Halsey (d 1955), of Richmond, Surrey; 1 da (Suzanne b 1964), 1 step s (Geoffrey b 1943); *Career* WWII RA 1943–47; served in: N Africa, Italy, Greece, Trieste, Germany (despatches); jeweller; joined Cartier 1938, md Cartier Ltd 1976–83 (vice chm UK 1983–93); former holder Royal Warrant for HM Queen Elizabeth the Queen Mother (former holder for HM The Queen) on behalf of Cartier; chm Bond St Assoc 1981–83; FGA; *Recreations* golf; *Style*— Joseph W E Allgood, Esq

ALLINGTON, Edward Thomas; s of Ralph Allington, of Troutbeck Bridge, Cumbria, and Evelyn Hewartson (d 1988); *b* 24 June 1951; *Educ* Lancaster Sch of Art, Central Sch of Art (DipAD), RCA (Herbert Read meml prize); *m* 1974 (sep 1981), Susan Jean Bradley (d 1984); partner, 1983, Julia Wood; 1 s (Harry Roland Allington Wood b 1991), 1 da (Thalia Evelyn Allington Wood b 1988); *Career* sculptor; *Solo Exhibitions* incl: 1B Kensington Church Walk London 1977, Spacex Gallery Exeter 1981, Exe Gallery Exeter 1982, Spectro Gallery Newcastle upon Tyne 1983, ICA London 1983–84, Lisson Gallery London 1984, Midland Gp Arts Centre Nottingham 1984, Gallery Schmela Düsseldorf 1984, Riverside Studios London 1985, Lisson Gallery 1985, Northern Centre for Contemporary Art Sunderland 1985–86, Abbot Hall Art Gallery Kendal 1986, Diane Brown Gallery NY 1986, Galerie 565 Aalst Belgium 1986, Galerie Adrien Maeght Paris 1986, Galerie Montenay-Delsol Paris 1986, Marlene Eleini Gallery London 1987, Diane Brown Gallery NY 1987, Fuji TV Gallery Tokyo 1988, Gallery Face Tokyo 1988, Lisson Gallery 1990, Galerie Faust Geneva 1990, Vaughan and Vaughan Minneapolis, Kohji Ogura Gallery Nagoya; *Group Exhibitions* incl: Summer Show (Serpentine Gallery London) 1976, Objects and Sculpture (Arnolfini Gallery Bristol) 1981, London/NY 1982, Lisson Gallery 1982, Teme Celeste (Museo Civico D'Arte Contemporanea Gibellina Sicily) 1983, Beelden/sculpture 1983 (Rotterdam Arts Cncl) 1983, The Sculpture Show (Hayward and Serpentine Galleries London) 1983, Metaphor and/or Symbol (Nat Museum of Modern Art Tokyo and Nat Museum of Osaka) 1984–85, Space Invaders (Mackenzie Art Gall Regina and tour Canada) 1985, Time after Time (Diane Brown Gallery NY) 1986, Britain in Vienna 1986, British Art (Kunstlerhaus Vienna) 1986, 3eme Ateliers Internationaux FRAC Pays de la Loire 1986, Prospect 86 (Kunstverein Frankfurt) 1986, Vessel (Serpentine Gallery) 1987, Inside/Outside (Museum van Hedendaagse Kunst Antwerp) 1987, Die Grosse Oper (Bonner Kunstverein Bonn and tour) 1987–88, Britannia 30 Ans de Sculpture (Musée des Beaux Arts Brussels) 1988, British Now Sculpture et Autre Dessins (Musée D'Art Contemporain de Montreal) 1988–89, 2000 Jahre Die Geganwart der Vergangenheit (Bonner Kunstverein Bonn) 1989; *Major works* His Favourite Was David Smith But She Preferred Dame Barbara Hepworth 1975, Ideal Standard Forms 1980, The Fruit of Oblivion 1982, We Are Time 1985, Building With Missing Columns 1986, Seated in Darkness 1987, Victory Boxed 1987, Light Temple PAS Heizcraftwerk Saarbrucken 1989, Inverted Architrave 1990, set for prodn of Apollon La Nuit 1990; *Awards* prizewinner John Moores 16 Liverpool Exhbn 1989, Gregory fell in Sculpture Univ of Leeds; *Style*— Edward Allington, Esq; ✉ Lisson Gallery, 67 Lisson St, London NW1 5DA (☎ 0171 724 2739, fax 0171 724 7124)

ALLINSON, Sir (Walter) Leonard; KCVO (1979, MVO 1961), CMG (1976); s of Walter Allinson (d 1965), and Alice Frances, *née* Cassidy; *b* 1 May 1926; *Educ* Friern Barnet GS, Merton Coll Oxford (MA), RCDS; *m* 1951, Margaret Patricia, *née* Watts; 3 da (incl twins); *Career* dep high cmmr Kenya 1972–73, RCDS 1974, dep high cmmr and min New Delhi 1975–78, high cmmr Lusaka 1978–80, asst under sec (Africa) FCO 1980–82, Br high cmmr Kenya 1982–86 (ret); non-serv memb Home Office Assessment Consultancy Unit 1986–96; vice pres Royal African Soc 1982–, memb Cncl Br Inst for E Africa 1988–92, hon vice chm Kenya Soc 1990–; treas Wendron Parochial Church Cncl 1988–96, fndn govr Wendron Sch 1989–, chm Fin Ctee Enwall Red Cross 1996–; *Recreations* reading, collecting driftwood, rough gardening; *Clubs* Oriental; *Style*— Sir Leonard Allinson, KCVO, CMG; ✉ Tregarthen, Wendron, Helston, Cornwall TR13 0NA

ALLIOTT, Hon Mr Justice; Hon Sir John Downes Alliott; kt (1986); s of Alexander Clifford Alliott (d 1967), and Ena Kathleen, *née* Downes, later Mrs Richard Ellson (d 1994); *b* 9 Jan 1932; *Educ* Charterhouse, Peterhouse Cambridge (scholar, BA); *m* 1957, Patsy Jennifer, da of late Gordon Beckles-Willson; 2 s (George Alliott b 1958, Julian b 1968), 1 da (Katharine b 1967); *Career* cmmnd Coldstream Gds 1950–51; called to the Bar Inner Temple 1955, dep chm E Sussex QS 1970–71, recorder of the Crown Court 1972–86, QC 1973, bencher Inner Temple 1980, ldr SE Circuit 1983–86, memb Home Office Advsy Bd on Restricted Patients 1983–86, judge of the High Court of Justice (Queen's Bench Div) 1986–, presiding judge SE Circuit 1989–92; vice chm Parole Bd 1996– (memb 1994–); *Recreations* rural pursuits, France, Italy, military history; *Style*— The Hon Mr Justice Alliott; ✉ Royal Courts of Justice, Strand, London WC2A 2LL

ALLISON, (Samuel) Austin; s of Dr Samuel Allison, of Stedham, W Sussex, and Helen Burns Brighton, *née* Wilson; *b* 30 June 1947; *Educ* Liverpool Coll, Wadham Coll Oxford (BA, BCL); *m* 5 June 1971, June, da of late Henry Edward Brassington, of Crofton, Kent; 2 s (Giles b 1973, Jonathan b 1975); *Career* called to the Bar Middle Temple 1969; private practice at the Bar 1970–87, head of gp compliance Standard Chartered Bank 1987–95, dir West Merchant Bank 1996–; memb: Panel of Arbitrators The Securities and Futures Authy, Panel of Arbitrators City Disputes Panel, Commercial Ct Ctee, Gen Cncl of the Bar, Bar Assoc of Commerce Fin and Indust Ctee (chm 1995); FCIArb, fell Indian Cncl of Arbitration, fell Indian Soc of Arbitrators; *Publications* Banking and the Financial Services Act (jtly, 1993); *Recreations* the turf; *Style*— Austin Allison, Esq; ✉ 156 Kingston Lane, Teddington, Middlesex TW11 9HD; West Merchant Bank, 33/36 Gracechurch Street, London EC3V 0AX (☎ 0171 623 8711)

ALLISON, Prof David John; s of Denis Allison (d 1982), of Leeds, and Eileen, *née* O'Connell (d 1986); *b* 21 March 1941; *Educ* Prince Rupert Sch Germany, Wimbledon Coll, KCH London (BSc, MB BS, MD, DMRD, MRCS, FRCP, FFR, FRCR); *m* 16 April 1966, Deirdre Mary, da of Patrick Flynn (d 1975), of New Malden, Surrey; 1 s (Richard b 1970), 2 da (Catherine b 1967, Helen b 1969); *Career* conslt and sr lectr Royal Post Grad Med Sch Univ of London 1975–83, dir of radiology Hammersmith Hosp and Royal Post Grad Med School Univ of London 1983–, author of several publications on cardiovascular and interventional radiology and physiology; memb Fleischner Soc 1979–; memb Cncl: Br Inst of Radiology 1985–88, RCR 1987–; Cardiovascular and Interventional Soc of Europe: memb Exec Ctee 1986–, pres 1990–95; memb: RCR 1973, Br Inst of Radiology 1973, BSG 1978, CIRSE 1980; *Books* Diagnostic Radiology: An Anglo-American Textbook of Imaging Volumes 1, 2 and 3 (with R G Grainger, 1985, 2 edn 1991); *Recreations* gardening, food and wine (at others' expense); *Style*— Prof David Allison; ✉ Department of Imaging, Royal Postgraduate Medical School, Hammersmith Hospital, Du Cane Rd, London W12 0HS (☎ 0181 383 3123, fax 0181 743 5409)

ALLISON, Air Vice-Marshal Dennis; CB (1987); s of George Richardson Allison (d 1951), and Joan Anne Sarah, *née* Little (d 1949); *b* 15 Oct 1932; *Educ* RAF Halton, RAF Coll Cranwell; *m* 16 June 1964, Rachel Anne, da of Air Vice-Marshal John Gerald Franks, CB, CBE; 1 s (Peter b 1970), 4 da (Jennifer b 1965, Susan b 1965, Rosemary b 1967, Rachel b 1970); *Career* No 87 Sqdn RAF 1955–58, flying instr and Coll Adj Cranwell 1959–61, Sqdn Ldr 1961, OC RAF Sharjah 1961–62, OC Standards Sqdn RAF Strubby 1962–64, Indian Def Servs Staff Coll 1964–65, staff HQ 224 Gp Singapore 1965–68, Wing Cdr 1967, MOD Central Staffs 1968–70, OC Flying Wing RAF Bruggen 1970–72, Nat Def Coll 1972–73, MOD Central Staffs 1973–74, Gp Capt 1974, OC RAF Coningsby 1974–76, Canadian Nat Def Coll 1976–77, MOD Central Staffs 1977–79, Air Cdre 1979, cmdt Central Flying Sch 1979–83, dir flying trg MOD 1983–85, Air Vice-Marshal 1985, dir of Mgmnt and Support of Intelligence 1985–86; chief exec N Western RHA 1990–94 (regnl gen mangr 1985–90); memb: NHS Trg Authy 1987–90, Standing Ctee on Postgrad Educn 1988–93, Steering Ctee on Pharmacist Postgrad Educn 1991–94, NHS Estates Advsy Bd 1991–95, Nat Blood Authy 1993– (vice chm 1994–); govr Salford Coll of Technol 1987–89; QCVSA 1959; Hon MA Univ of Manchester 1994; *Recreations* golf, bridge, keeping bantams; *Clubs* RAF; *Style*— Air Vice-Marshal Dennis Allison, CB; ✉ The Old Forge, Castle Bytham, Grantham, Lincs NG33 4RU (☎ 01780 410372)

ALLISON, John; CBE (1975), JP (Swansea 1966), DL (W Glam 1975); s of Thomas William Allison (d 1954), and Margaret, *née* Grey (d 1958); *b* 4 Oct 1919; *Educ* Glanmor Secdy Sch, Swansea Tech Coll; *m* 12 April 1948, Elvira Gwendoline (d 1992), da of William Evan Lewis (d 1945); 1 s (Richard Thomas William b 12 Aug 1956), 2 da (Susan Margaret b 12 May 1949, Jillian b 15 May 1955); *Career* dir: Picton Music Ltd 1969–87, Swansea Sound 1974–95, Municipal and Mutual Insurance Ltd 1982–91; memb Swansea Co Borough Cncl 1957–73, ldr City Authy 1967–73, dep mayor 1966–67 and 1972–73; memb: W Glamorgan CC 1973–89 (chm 1975–76, ldr 1979–89), Assoc of CCs 1973–89 (chm 1986–88); chm S Wales Police Authy 1987–89; Parly candidate (Lab) Barry 1970; *Recreations* gardening, fishing, golf; *Clubs* Morriston Golf; *Style—* John Allison, Esq, CBE, JP, DL; ✉ 155 Vicarage Rd, Morriston, Swansea SA6 6DT (☎ 01792 771331)

ALLISON, Air Chief Marshal Sir John Shakespeare; KCB (1995), CBE (1986); s of Walter Allison (d 1971), and Mollie Emmie, *née* Poole; *b* 24 March 1943; *Educ* Hillside Sch Haslemere, Royal Grammar Sch Guildford; *m* 5 Aug 1966, Gillian Patricia, da of Kenneth Douglas Middleton; 3 da (Katherine Louise b 1967, Elizabeth Jane b 1970, Anne Rosemary b 1974), 2 s (James Shakespeare b 1968, David Walter Kenneth b 1974); *Career* RAF Coll Cranwell 1961–64, advanced flying trg/operational conversion 1964–65, sqn pilot No 5 Sqn (Lightnings) 1966–68, weapons instr No 226 OCU (Lightnings) 1968–70, USAF exchange Luke AFB Arizona (Phantoms) 1970–72, Sqn Cdr No 228 OCU (Phantoms) 1972–74, staff duties HQ 11 Gp 1974–76, attended RAF Staff Coll Bracknell 1977, OC No 228 OCU (Phantoms) 1977–79, Air Plans Dept MOD 1979–82, OC RAF Wildenrath 1982–85, Sec Chiefs of Staff Ctee 1985–87, Dir of Air Force Plans and Progs 1987–89, RCDS 1989, ACDS Operational Requirements (Air Systems) 1990–92, AOC No 11 Gp 1992–94, Dep C-in-C and COS Strike Cmd 1994–96, Air Member for Logistics and AOC-in-C Logistics Cmd 1996–; *Recreations* air display flying and testing of old aircraft, gliding, restoration and preservation of old aircraft, gliders and cars; *Clubs* RAF; *Style—* Air Chief Marshal Sir John Allison, KCB, CBE; ✉ HQ Logistics Command, RAF Brampton, Huntingdon, Cambridgeshire PE18 8QL (☎ 01480 434177)

ALLISON, Julia; da of Alfred Arthur Richley, of Nottingham, and Amelia, *née* Douglas (d 1992); *b* 26 Sept 1939; *Educ* Lilley & Stone Newark HS, Wolverhampton Poly (CertEd), Univ of Nottingham (MA); *m* 1960, Barrie Allison, s of Harry Allison; 1 da, 1 s; *Career* trainee midwife 1970–72, community midwife 1972–76, hosp midwife 1976–77, community midwife 1979–86, midwife teacher 1986–89, sr midwife advsr and assoc res Univ of Nottingham 1989–91, head Faculty of Midwifery Norfolk 1991–94, gen sec Royal Coll of Midwives 1994– (former chm and pres); memb: Royal Coll of Midwives, RSM; *Recreations* labradors, watercolour painting, collecting antiquarian books; *Style—* Mrs Julia Allison; ✉ Trevans, Hospital Road, Wicklewood, Wymondham, Norfolk NR18 9PR (☎ 01953 600087); Royal College of Midwives, 15 Mansfield Street, London WC1M 0BE (☎ 0171 872 5100, fax 0171 872 5101)

ALLISON, Roderick Stuart; CB (1996); s of Stuart Frew Allison (d 1960), and Poppy, *née* Hodges (d 1974); *b* 28 Nov 1936; *Educ* Dumfries Acad, Manchester GS, Balliol Coll Oxford (MA); *m* 1968, Anne Allison; 1 s (Edward b 16 Nov 1972), 1 da (Carrie b 5 May 1974); *Career* Ministry of Labour: asst princ 1959–63, private sec to Perm Sec 1963–64, princ 1964–69, seconded to Civil Serv Dept 1969–71, grade 5 1971, grade 3 1977; Health and Safety Executive: dir Special Hazards 1989–92, dir Safety Policy and memb Channel Tunnel Safety Authy 1992–94, chief exec Offshore Safety Div 1994–; *Recreations* sailing, music, languages, reading; *Style—* Roderick Allison, Esq, CB; ✉ Health and Safety Executive, Rose Court, 2 Southwark Bridge Road, London SE1 9HS (☎ 0171 717 6701, fax 0171 717 6907)

ALLISON, Ronald William Paul; CVO (1978); s of Percy Allison, and Dorothy, *née* Doyle; *b* 26 Jan 1932; *Educ* Weymouth GS, Taunton's Sch Southampton; *m* 1, 1956, Maureen Angela Macdonald (d 1992); 2 da; m 2, 1993, Jennifer Loy Weider; 1 s (David William Helton b 28 Feb 1996); *Career* reporter and corr BBC 1957–73, press sec to HM The Queen 1973–78, md Ronald Allison & Assocs 1978–80; Thames TV: presenter 1978–, controller of sport and outside bdcasts 1980–85, dir corp affrs 1986–89; conslt freelance writer and broadcaster 1989–; chm: TV Barter International 1990–, Grand Slam Sports Ltd 1992–96 (md 1993); dir of corp affrs: BAFTA 1993–, The Sponsorship Group 1996–; *Books* Look Back in Wonder (1968), The Queen (1973), Charles, Prince of our Time (1978), Britain in the Seventies (1980), The Royal Encyclopedia (ed, with Sarah Riddell, 1993); *Clubs* RAC; *Style—* Ronald Allison, Esq, CVO

ALLISON, Shaun Michael; s of Lt Cdr Jorgen Leslie William Michael Allison (d 1983), of White Cottage, Beenham, Berks, and Honoria Brenda, *née* Magill; *b* 12 Jan 1944; *Educ* Rugby; *m* 14 Sept 1968, Lucy Howard Douglas, da of Lt-Col Charles Robert Douglas Gray, of Chilcombe, Greywell, Basingstoke, Hants; 2 s (Piers Michael Douglas b 1971, Charles Howard b 1977), 1 da (Sophie Louise b 1974); *Career* stockbroker 1965; ptnr Hoare Govett Ltd 1978–85, dir Hoare Govett Securities Ltd 1986–92, corp fin dir Panmure Gordon 1992–; *Recreations* skiing, shooting, sailing; *Clubs* City of London; *Style—* Shaun M Allison, Esq; ✉ Panmure Gordon, New Broad Street House, 35 New Broad Street, London EC2M 1NH (☎ 0171 638 4010)

ALLISON, Prof Wade William Magill; s of Lt Cdr (Jorgen Leslie William) Michael Allison, RN (d 1983), and Honoria Brenda, *née* Magill; *b* 23 April 1941; *Educ* Rugby, Trinity Coll Cambridge (MA), ChCh Oxford (MA, DPhil); *m* 1, 9 Sept 1967 (m dis 1988); 1 s (Thomas b 1977), 3 da (Emma b and d 1968, Harriet (Mrs James Cridland) b 1972, Rachel b 1974); m 2, 6 Dec 1988, Marilyn Frances (Kate), *née* Easterbrook; 2 step da (Helen Mary Foss b 1973, Frances Margaret Foss b 1974); *Career* Univ of Oxford: res offr Nuclear Physics Laboratory 1970–75, lectr Christ Church 1973–75 (res lectr 1966–71), univ lectr 1976–96, sr tutor Keble Coll 1985–89 (tutorial fell 1976–), assoc chm of physics 1990–92, prof of physics 1996–; author of numerous papers and articles on elementary particle physics and experimental methods; fell Royal Cmmn for the Exhibition of 1851 1966–68; MRIN; *Recreations* sailing, motoring, navigation; *Clubs* Cruising Association; *Style—* Prof Wade Allison; ✉ Southfields, Ludgershall, Aylesbury, Bucks HP18 9PB (☎ 01844 237602, e-mail southfields@dial.pipex.com); Keble Coll, Oxford; Nuclear Physics Laboratory, Oxford (☎ 01865 272734, fax 01865 273418, e-mail w.allison@physics.oxford.ac.uk)

ALLISS, Peter; s of Percy Alliss (d 1975), of Sheffield, and Dorothy, *née* Rust (d 1973); *b* 28 Feb 1931; *Educ* Queen Elizabeth GS Wimborne Dorset, Crosby House Sch Winton Bournemouth; *m* 1, 1953 (m dis 1968), Joan; 1 s (Gary b 1954), 1 da (Carol b 1960); m 2, 1969, Jaqueline Anne, da of Col Geoffrey Bridgeman Grey, CB, CBE, TD, DL, of Birmingham; 2 s (Simon b 1975, Henry b 1983), 1 da (Sara b 1972); *Career* Nat Serv RAF Regt 1949–51; professional golfer 1946; played in 8 Ryder Cup matches and 10 Canada Cup (now World Cup) matches, winner of 21 maj events incl open championships of Spain, Portugal, Italy and Brazil; golf commentator and broadcaster following retirement, also golf course designer; former pres: Br Greenkeepers' Assoc 1977–86, Ladies Professional Golfers' Assoc 1980–86; twice capt PGA 1962–87, pres Nat Assoc of Public Golf Courses; *Books* Easier Golf (with Paul Trevillion, 1969), Bedside Golf (1980), Shell Book of Golf (1982), The Duke (1983), Play Golf with Peter Alliss (1983), The Who's Who of Golf (1983), The Open (with Michael Hobbs, 1984), Golfer's Logbook (1984), Lasting the Course (1984), More Bedside Golf (1984), Peter Alliss' Most Memorable Golf (1986), Yet More Bedside Golf (1986), Play Better Golf with Peter Alliss (1989), Peter Alliss' Best 100 Golfers (1989), The Best of Golf (with Bob Ferrier, 1989); autobiographies: Alliss in Wonderland (1964), Peter Alliss: An Autobiography (1981); *Recreations* conversation (with wine!); *Clubs* Lansdowne, Motcombs, Ritz, Crockfords; *Style—* Peter Alliss, Esq; ✉ Peter Alliss Golf Designs, 10 St George's Yard, Farnham, Surrey GU9 7LW (☎ 01252 717711, fax 01252 717722)

ALLOTT, Air Cdre Molly Greenwood; CB (1975); da of late Gerald William Allott; *b* 28 Dec 1918; *Educ* Sheffield HS for Girls; *Career* joined WAAF 1941, serv WWII Fighter and Coastal Cmds, Supply Branch 1944; appts: Egypt 1945–47, Singapore 1948–50; staff of: AOC in C RAF Germany 1960–63, AOC Fighter Cmd 1963–66, Trg Cmd 1971–73; dir WRAF 1973–76, ADC to HM The Queen 1973–76; nat chm Girls Venture Corps 1977–83; cncl memb: Union Jack Club 1976–91, Main Grants Ctee and Educn Ctee RAF Benevolent Fund 1976–84; FIMgt; *Recreations* foreign travel, decorative and fine arts; *Clubs* RAF, Royal Lymington Yacht; *Style—* Air Cdre Molly Allott, CB; ✉ 15 Camden Hurst, Milford-on-Sea, Lymington, Hants SO41 0WL

ALLOTT, Paul John Walter; s of John Norman Allott, and Lillian Patricia, *née* Walker; *b* 14 Sept 1956; *Educ* Altrincham GS, Bede Coll Durham; *m* 1, 27 Oct 1979 (m dis 1991), Helen Crago; 1 s (Ben b 20 July 1984), 1 da (Susie b 4 Aug 1986); m 2, 24 Oct 1992, Pamela Allott; *Career* professional cricketer; Lancashire CCC: debut 1978, awarded county cap 1981, benefit 1990, 200 first class appearances, 500 first class wickets; England: schools rep 1973–75, young cricketers tour W Indies 1976, 13 test matches 1981–85, 13 one day ints 1982–85, tour India/Sri Lanka 1981 and India/Aust 1984–85; currently mktg conslt and freelance journalist, broadcaster and commentator with Sky Sports and BBC Test Match Special, sports travel conslt with ITC Sports Chester; dir Cricketer International Magazine; *Recreations* golf, travel; *Style—* Paul Allott, Esq; ✉ Lancashire CCC, Old Trafford, Manchester M16 0PX (☎ 0161 282 4000, fax 01625 828263)

ALLPORT, Denis Ivor; s of late A R Allport, and E M, *née* Mashman; *b* 20 Nov 1922; *Educ* Highgate Sch; *m* 1949, Diana, *née* Marler; 2 s, 1 da; *Career* served WWII Indian Army; Metal Box plc: dir 1973, md 1977–79, chief exec 1977–85, dep chm 1979, chm 1979–85; memb Nat Enterprise Bd 1980–83; dir: Beecham Gp 1981–88, Marley plc 1986–91; chm Castle Underwriting Agents Ltd 1989–94; govr Highgate Sch 1981–94, memb Neill Cmmn of Enquiry into Lloyd's 1986; CIMgt, FRSA; *Style—* Denis Allport, Esq; ✉ The Barn, Highmoor, Henley on Thames, Oxon RG9 5DH (☎ 01491 641283)

ALLRED, Prof Henry; s of William Allred (d 1970), of Leigh, Lancashire, and Beatrice Ellen Cooke (d 1960); *b* 4 July 1929; *Educ* Leigh GS Lancashire, Univ of Manchester (DDS, MDS, BDS, LDS); *m* 9 June 1954, Brenda, da of Willam Hoyle (d 1985); 1 da (Josephine Elizabeth b 1960); *Career* house surgn Manchester Dental Hosp 1954, dental practice Walkden Manchester 1954–56, lectr Univ of Manchester 1956–60, conslt in cons dentistry London Hosp 1966–94, dean of dental studies London Hosp Med Coll Univ of London 1979–85 (sr lectr in cons dentistry 1961–66, reader 1966–69, prof 1969–94, govr 1977–94), ret; pres Assoc for Dental Educn in Europe; memb: UGC 1984–89, WHO; govr St Dunston's Coll Catford London; tstee Wakefield and Tetley Tsts; Freeman City of London, Liveryman Worshipful Society of Apothecaries; memb: BDA, BSDR, BSRD; FRSM 1961; *Books* Assessment of the Quality of Dental Care (1977), Public Health in Europe No 7 - The Training and Use of Dental Auxiliary Personnel (1977); *Recreations* reading, travel, music; *Clubs* Royal Society of Medicine; *Style—* Prof Henry Allred; ✉ 50 Tower Bridge Wharf, St Katharine's Way, London E1 9LB (☎ 0171 265 0643); 2 Magistrates Court, Church Lane, Ledbury, Herefordshire

ALLSOP, Peter Henry Bruce; CBE (1984); s of late Herbert Henry Allsop, and Elsie Hilpern, *née* Whittaker; *b* 22 Aug 1924; *Educ* Haileybury, Gonville and Caius Coll Cambridge (MA); *m* 1950, Patricia Elizabeth Kingwell Bown; 2 s, 1 da; *Career* called to the Bar Lincoln's Inn 1948, bencher 1989; chm Sweet & Maxwell 1974–80 (ed 1950–59, dir 1960–64, md 1965–73), chm Associated Book Publishers 1976–87 (dir 1963, asst md 1965–67, md 1968–76, chief exec to 1982), chm Teleordering Ltd 1978–91, dir J Whitaker & Son Ltd 1987–, publishing conslt PUMA 1983–, tstee Yale Univ Press 1981– (vice chm 1984–), dir Lloyd's of London Press Ltd 1991–95; memb Cncl Publishers' Assoc (treas 1973–75 and 1979–81, pres 1975–77, vice pres 1977–78); dir Woodard Schs (Western Div) Ltd 1985–95; chm: Book Trade Benevolent Soc 1986–92 (tstee 1976–85 and 1994–), King's Coll and King's Hall Taunton 1986–94; FRSA, FIMgt; *Style—* Peter Allsop, Esq, CBE; ✉ Manor Farm, Charlton Mackrell, Somerton, Somerset TA11 7BQ

ALLSOP, Prof Richard Edward; OBE (1997); s of Edward James Allsop, of Mackworth, Derby, and Grace Ada, *née* Tacey (d 1984); *b* 2 May 1940; *Educ* Bemrose Sch Derby, Queens' Coll Cambridge (MA), UCL (PhD, DSc); *m* 23 June 1990, Frances Elizabeth, da of Henry James Killick (d 1978); *Career* sci offr Road Res Laboratory 1964–66, res fell UCL 1967–69, lectr in tport studies UCL 1970–72, dir Tport Ops Res Gp Univ of Newcastle upon Tyne 1973–76, prof of tport studies UCL 1976–, visitor to Traffic Gp Tport and Road Res Laboratory 1987–92, ext res advsr Dept of Tport 1993–; dir Parly Advsy Cncl for Tport Safety, chm Road Infrastructure Working Pty Euro Tport Safety Cncl; memb: Road Traffic Law Review 1985–88, War on Want, Chiltern Soc; FCIT 1981, FIHT 1983, CEng, FICE 1990, FEng 1996; *Recreations* photography, theatre, walking; *Style—* Prof Richard Allsop, OBE, FEng; ✉ Centre for Transport Studies, University College London, Gower St, London WC1E 6BT (☎ 0171 391 1555, fax 0171 391 1567)

ALLSOPP, (Harold) Bruce; s of Henry Allsopp (d 1953), of Worthing, Sussex, and Elizabeth May, *née* Robertson (d 1956); *b* 4 July 1912; *Educ* Manchester GS, Univ of Liverpool Sch of Architecture (BArch); *m* 29 Dec 1936, (Florence) Cyrilla (d 1991), da of John Victor Hearn Woodroffe, MD (d 1938), of Dorking, Surrey; 2 s (Roger Henry b 1941, Christopher John b (twin) 1941); *Career* served WWII RE N Africa and Italy Capt RE; author, artist, historian; chm: Oriel Press Ltd 1962–87, Ind Publishers' Guild 1971–72; dir Routledge & Kegan Paul Books 1974–86; fndr memb and chm Soc of Architectural Historians of Great Britain 1959–65, pres Fedn of Northern Arts Socs 1980–83; sr lectr in architecture Univ of Durham 1955 (lectr 1946); Univ of Newcastle: dir of architectural studies 1965–69, sr lectr in history of architecture 1969–73, reader 1973–77; occasional TV presenter; Master Art Workers' Guild 1970; ARIBA 1935, FRIBA 1955, AMTPI (now MRTPI) 1936, FSA 1968; *Books* incl: Decoration and Furniture (Vol 1 1952, Vol 2 1953), Art and the Nature of Architecture (1952), A General History of Architecture (1955), The Future of the Arts (1959), A History of Renaissance Architecture (1959), Possess (ed, 1959), The Naked Flame (1962), A History of Classical Architecture (1965), To Kill a King (1965), Civilization, the Next Stage (1969), Modern Architecture of Northern England (1970), Romanesque Architecture (1971), Ecological Morality (1972), Towards a Humane Architecture (1974), Return of the Pagan (1974), A Modern Theory of Architecture (1977), Appeal to the Gods (1980), The Country Life Companion to British and European Architecture (1985), Social Responsibility and the Responsible Society (1985), Guide de l'Architecture (1985), Larousse Guide to European Architecture (1985), Spirit of Europe - a Subliminal History (1997); with Ursula Clark: Architecture of France (1963), Architecture of Italy (1964), Architecture of England (1964), Historic Architecture of Northumberland (1969), Historic Architecture of Northumberland and Newcastle (1977), English Architecture (1979); with U Clark and H W Booton: The Great Tradition of Western Architecture (1966); articles in various publications incl Encyclopedia Americana, Encyclopaedia Britannica and Routledge Companion to Contemporary Architectural Thought (1993); *Recreations* music, gardening; *Clubs* Athenaeum; *Style—* Bruce Allsopp, Esq, FSA; ✉ Ferndale, Mount View, Stocksfield, Northumberland NE43 7HL (☎ 01661 842323)

ALLSOPP, Michael Edward Ranulph; s of Samuel Ranulph Allsopp, CBE (d 1975), of Stansted, Essex, and Hon Norah Hyacinthe, *née* Littleton; *b* 9 Oct 1930; *Educ* Eton;

m 1953, Patricia Ann, da of Geoffrey H Berners (d 1972), of Faringdon, Oxon; 4 da (Frances Jane Berners (Mrs David Woodd) b 1956, Carolyn Ann Berners b 1957, Davina Hyacinth Berners (m 1987, Sir Nicholas Powell, 4 Bt, *qv*) b 1960, Jessica Elizabeth Berners (twin) (Mrs Edward Leigh Pemberton) b 1960); *Career* Subaltern 7 QOH, Capt Royal Wilts Yeo (TA); chm: Allen Harvey & Ross Ltd 1968–79, London Discount Market Assoc 1974–76, Allied Dunbar & Co Ltd 1979–86, Granville Holdings plc 1987–, Granville & Co Ltd 1987–, Granville Bank, St David's Investment Trust plc, Berners Allsopp Estate Management Co; *Recreations* foxhunting (Master of Old Berks Hounds 1960–81); *Clubs* White's, Pratt's; *Style*— Michael Allsopp, Esq; ✉ Little Coxwell Grove, Faringdon, Oxon SN7 7LW (☎ 01367 240580, office 01367 240138); Granville Holdings plc, Mint House, 77 Mansell Street, London E1 8AF (☎ 0171 488 1212, fax 0171 481 3911)

ALLTHORPE-GUYTON, Marjorie; da of Maurice Jack Allthorpe-Guyton, of Norwich, and Edith Florence, *née* Clark (d 1972); *b* 29 July 1948; *Educ* Blyth GS Norwich, UEA (BA), Leverhulme scholarship, Courtauld Inst London; *m* 27 Oct 1989, John Mullis; 1 da (Elise Charlotte Allthorpe-Mullis b 30 Sept 1984), 1 s (Theodore Edmund Allthorpe-Mullis b 14 Feb 1991); *Career* asst keeper Norwich Castle Museum Norfolk 1969–79, researcher Norwich Sch of Art 1980–82, lectr Open Univ 1983, lectr London program Univ of Connecticut 1982–88, visiting lectr in theoretical studies Norwich Sch of Art 1985–88; co-selector Art Cncl British Art Show 1982–84; external assessor: BA and MA Fine Art Goldsmith's Coll London 1988–, BA Fine Art Plymouth Univ (formerly Poly SW) and Exeter Coll of Art 1989–93; UK contrib ed Flash Art 1987–89, ed Artscribe 1991–92 (assoc ed 1989–91), conslt VIART 1993, dir of visual arts Arts Cncl of GB 1993–; author of several oeuvre catalogues, numerous articles for art jls and press, contrib to various exhbn catalogues; assoc: Museums Assoc 1975, Art Historians' Assoc 1979; memb exec Ctee Int Assoc of Art Critics 1996; FRSA 1993; *Recreations* family, art, food, film (especially European); *Clubs* Chelsea Arts, Blacks; *Style*— Miss Marjorie Allthorpe-Guyton; ✉ Director of Visual Arts, The Arts Council of England, 14 Great Peter Street, London SW1P 3NQ (☎ 0171 973 6470, fax 0171 973 6590)

ALLUM, William Herbert; s of Herbert Edward Allum (d 1987), of Oxford, and Gladys Marion, *née* Bolton; *b* 9 Feb 1953; *Educ* St Edward's Sch Oxford, Univ of Birmingham (BSc, MB ChB, MD); *m* 23 April 1983, (Pamela) Anne, da of Joseph Anthony Collier (d 1995), of Stratford-upon-Avon; 3 s (Charles b 1985, Henry b 1987, James b 1990); *Career* house offr posts 1977–78, demonstrator in anatomy Univ of Southampton 1978–79, sr house offr in surgery Reading Hosps 1979–80; registrar in surgery: Central Birmingham 1980–82, Hereford Hosps 1982–83; lectr in surgery Univ of Birmingham 1985–88 (hon res fell 1983–85), sr lectr Univ of Leicester and hon conslt surgn Leicester Hosps 1988–90; conslt surgn: Bart's London 1991–93, Epsom Dist Gen Hosp 1993–; memb Physiotherapists' Bd Cncl of Professions Supplimentary to Med; hon sec Br Stomach Cancer Gp; memb Ct of Examiners RCS; memb: Surgical Res Soc, Br Assoc of Surgical Oncology (nat ctee memb); FRCS 1982; *Books* Cancer of the Stomach - Clinical Cancer Monographs 1989 (co-author); *Recreations* golf, cricket; *Clubs* Marylebone Cricket; *Style*— William Allum, Esq; ✉ The Chestnuts, 21 Greville Park Road, Ashtead, Surrey KT21 2QU (☎ 01372 813318); Epsom District General Hospital (☎ 01372 735114)

ALLVEY, David Philip; s of Edgar Frederick Allvey, and Kathleen Beatrice, *née* Lamb; *b* 13 March 1945; *Educ* Lewes County GS; *m* 26 April 1969, Brenda Cunningham; 2 s (Mark James b 11 Dec 1979, Philip Duncan b 4 May 1982); *Career* various mgmnt positions in construction industry until 1972, articled clerk with accountancy firm, mangr International Tax Dept Price Waterhouse London until 1980; BAT Industries plc: joined as gp dep tax mangr 1980, fin dir gp cosmetic interests and fin advsr and taxation mangr British-American Tobacco Co Ltd 1984–86, head of Finance Dept BAT Industries 1986, gp fin dir 1989–, dir various gp subsids incl Eagle Star and Allied Dunbar, memb Chief Exec's Ctee (formerly Chm's Policy Ctee) 1992–; non-exec dir McKechnie plc 1993–; memb UK Accounting Standards Bd, chm Fiscal Ctee Hundred Gp of Financial Dirs 1994–; FCA, ATII; *Recreations* golf; *Style*— David Allvey, Esq; ✉ BAT Industries plc, Windsor House, 50 Victoria Street, London SW1H 0NL (☎ 0171 222 7979, fax 0171 222 4094)

ALLWEIS, His Hon Judge; Martin Peter; s of Jack Allweis (d 1993), and Iris, *née* Mosco; *b* 22 Dec 1947; *Educ* Manchester GS, Sidney Sussex Coll Cambridge (BA); *m* 1 April 1984, Tracy Ruth, da of Bernice and late Hyam Barr; 2 c (Sophie May b 21 June 1990, Steven Charles b 8 Aug 1992); *Career* called to the Bar Inner Temple 1970, in practice 1970–94, recorder 1990–94, circuit judge (Northern Circuit) 1994–, designated family judge for Gtr Manchester 1996–; *Recreations* family, football (Manchester City FC), squash; *Style*— His Hon Judge Allweis; ✉ c/o Manchester County Court, Courts of Justice, Crown Square, Manchester M60 9DJ

ALMENT, Sir (Edward) Anthony John; kt (1980); s of Edward Alment, and Alice Alment; *b* 3 Feb 1922; *Educ* Marlborough, Bart's; *m* 1946, Elizabeth Innes Bacon; *Career* conslt obstetrician and gynaecologist Northampton 1960–85; prev: Bart's, Norfolk and Norwich Hosp, Queen Charlotte's and Chelsea Hosp for Women, London Hosps; author of various articles on med and wine subjects; former memb Oxford Regnl Hosp Bd and chm Med Advsy Ctee; memb: Oxford RHA 1973–75, UK Central Cncl for Nursing Midwifery and Health Visiting 1980–83; Hon DSc Leicester 1982; MRCS, LRCP, FRCOG (MRCOG 1951, memb Cncl RCOG 1961–67, hon sec 1968–73, pres 1978–81); hon fell American Assoc of Obstetricians and Gynaecologists 1973 (Joseph Price Oration 1972), Hon FRCPI 1979, Hon FRCPEd 1981, Hon FRCGP 1982, Hon FRACOG 1985; *Books* Competence to Practise (jtly, 1976); *Recreations* engineering, fishing, wine; *Style*— Sir Anthony Alment

ALMOND, (Thomas) Clive; OBE (1989); s of Thomas Almond (d 1976), and Eveline, *née* Moss (d 1986); *b* 30 Nov 1939; *Educ* Bristol GS; *m* 4 Sept 1965, Auriol Gala Elizabeth Annette, da of Dr H C Hendry; *Career* joined Dip Serv 1967, FO 1967–68 and 1975–78, High Cmmn Accra 1968–71, Paris Embassy 1971–75, Brussels Embassy 1978–80, Jakarta Embassy 1980–83, HM ambass Brazzaville Embassy 1987–88 (chargé d'affaires 1983–87), asst marshal of the Dip Corps and asst head of Protocol Dept FO 1988–92, HM consul-gen Bordeaux 1992–; *Recreations* travel, golf; *Style*— Clive Almond, Esq, OBE; ✉ c/o FCO (Bordeaux), King Charles St, London SW1A 2AH

ALMOND, David William; s of George Sydney Almond, of Lymington, Hants, and Madge Lilian, *née* Skegg; *b* 24 Oct 1945; *Educ* Purley GS Surrey; *m* 6 June 1970, Elizabeth (Liz), da of Percy Thomas Bisby (d 1978), of Aldwick, Sussex; 2 da (Amanda Jane b 25 Feb 1974, Juliette b 10 March 1977); *Career* CA; articles City of London 1962–67, ptnr Alliotts (formerly Evans Peirson) 1969–; chm Alliott Peirson Associates 1974–86; Alliott Peirson International Ltd: chm 1979–89, md and sec 1989–; dir Accounting Firms Associates Inc 1982–92; chm: Croydon Soc of CAs 1979–80 (sec 1975–79), Storrington Rural Preservation Soc 1995–; Freeman City of London 1976, memb Ct of Assts Worshipful Co of Coachmakers and Coach Harness Makers 1977, Liveryman Worshipful Co of CAs 1980; FCA 1967, ATII 1967, FIMgt 1978; *Recreations* sailing, gardening; *Clubs* East India; *Style*— David Almond, Esq; ✉ Fryern Place, Storrington, West Sussex RH20 4HG (☎ 01903 743030); Alliotts, 96 High St, Guildford, Surrey GU1 3DL (☎ 01483 33119, fax 01483 37339)

ALMOND, Prof Jeffrey William; s of Stanley Peter Almond, of Lyndale, Sutton under Whitestone Cliffe, N Yorks, and late Joyce Mary, *née* Fountain; *b* 28 June 1951; *Educ* Thirsk Grammar and Mod Sch, Univ of Leeds (BSc), Univ of Cambridge (PhD); *m* 6 Aug 1976, Karen Elizabeth, da of late Joseph Batley, of 10 Northolme Circle, Hessle, Humberside; 2 s (Maximilian b 13 Sept 1979, Adam b 8 Nov 1989), 1 da (Gemma b 16 Oct 1981); *Career* scientist Sandoz Forschungsinstitut Vienna 1977–79, lectr Univ of Leicester 1979–85, res fell Lister Inst of Preventative Med 1985, memb Lister Inst 1994–, prof of microbiology Univ of Reading 1985–; memb Cncl Soc for Gen Microbiology 1993–; memb Steering Ctee of MRC's AIDS directed programme 1990–94, co-ordinator and chm of Biotech and Biol Sci Res Cncl's res programme on Biology of the Spongiform Encephalopathies 1991–, chm Virology Div Int Union of Microbiological Societies 1996–99, memb Govt's Spongiform Encephalopathies Advsy Ctee (SEAC); *Style*— Prof Jeffrey Almond; ✉ School of Animal and Microbial Sciences, University of Reading, Whiteknights, PO Box 228, Reading RG6 2AJ (☎ 0118 931 8901, fax 0118 931 6537, e-mail J.W.Almond@reading.ac.uk)

ALMOND, Martin John; s of Stanley Wilton Almond, and Helen Prescott, *née* Baron (d 1979); *b* 8 May 1946; *Educ* Brooksby, Univ of Stirling (MSc); *m* 12 Dec 1970, Elizabeth; 2 da (Jennifer b 1977, Susan b 1979); *Career* CA 1967; articled City of London; ptnr: H R Davison & Co 1978–, Robert Parkinson & Co 1981–, Abbey Nursing Homes 1986–; Abbey Care Group 1993–; md Comparative Business Information Ltd 1983–; dir Queenscrest Ltd 1991–; FTC 1967, FCA 1973; Dip M 1993, MCIM 1993; *Recreations* climbing, history, research, reading, family; *Clubs* Royal Over-Seas League; *Style*— M J Almond, Esq; ✉ Kingswood House, Buckfastleigh, Devon TQ11 0BL; 100 Queen St, Newton Abbot, Devon TQ12 2E9 (☎ 01626 53392); Hawkhurst Castle, Hawkhurst, Kent TN18 5EG

ALMOND, Peter John; s of Herbert John Almond (d 1991), and Winifred Mary, *née* Munds; *b* 18 Jan 1946; *Educ* Woolverstone Hall Sch Ipswich Suffolk; *m* 27 Dec 1969, Anna, da of R Collinson, of Skirlaugh, Hull; 2 s (Nicholas b 28 Feb 1979, Jeffrey b 28 Dec 1981); *Career* trainee reporter Northern Echo Darlington 1964, apprentice journalist Yorkshire Evening Press York 1965–68 (NCTJ cert), info offr Br Army W Germany 1969; Cleveland Press Ohio USA: police reporter 1970–71, suburban reporter 1971–73, educn reporter 1973–78, labour reporter 1978–79, environment reporter 1979–80, Nieman fell in journalism Harvard Univ 1980–81, investigative reporter 1981–82; Washington Times Washington DC: State Dept corr 1982–83, Br, Euro and ME corr 1983–87, defence corr Washington 1987–90; defence corr Daily Telegraph 1990–95; currently freelance defence writer; pres Defence Correspondents' Assoc; *Recreations* jogging, movies, reading, walking; *Style*— Peter Almond, Esq; ✉ The Daily Telegraph, 1 Canada Square, Canary Wharf, London E14 5DT (☎ 0171 538 5000)

ALPORT, Baron (Life Peer UK 1961), of Colchester, Co Essex; Cuthbert James McCall Alport; TD (1949), PC (1960), DL (Essex 1974); s of Prof Arthur Cecil Alport, FRCP (d 1958), of Cairo, and Janet, *née* McCall; *b* 22 March 1912; *Educ* Haileybury, Pembroke Coll Cambridge (BA, MA); *m* 26 Oct 1945, Rachel Cecilia (d 1983), da of Lt-Col Ralph Charles Bingham, CVO, DSO (s of Maj-Gen Sir Cecil Bingham GCVO, KCMG, 2 s of 4 Earl of Lucan, KP, JP); 1 s (Hon Arthur Edward b 22 May 1954), 2 da (Hon Cecilia Alexandra Rose (Hon Mrs Lang) b 3 Sept 1946, d 1995, Hon Lavender Lilias Carole (Hon Mrs Taylor) b 13 Dec 1950); *Career* served WWII Lt-Col (GSO 1 E Africa 1944–45); barr Middle Temple; dir Cons Political Centre 1945–50, MP (C) Colchester Div Essex 1950–61; chm Jt E and Central African Bd 1953–55, govr Charing Cross Hosp 1954–55, asst postmaster-gen 1955–57, min of state CRO 1959–61 (Parly under sec of state 1957–59), Br high cmmr Fedn of Rhodesia and Nyasaland 1961–63, memb Cncl of Europe 1964–65, Br Govt rep to Rhodesia June-July 1967; sits as Ind Cons House of Lords, a dep speaker 1971–82 and 1983–96, advsr to Home Sec 1974–82; chm New Theatre Tst 1970–83, pres Minories Art Gallery Colchester 1978–88; pro-chllr City Univ 1972–79, chm Academic Advsy Ctee Gresham Coll 1984–86, life govr Haileybury Coll; High Steward of Colchester 1967– (Hon Freeman 1992); Liveryman Worshipful Co of Skinners (Master 1969–70 and 1982–83; Hon DCL City Univ 1979; *Books* Kingdoms in Partnership (1937), Hope in Africa (1952), The Sudden Assignment (1965); *Clubs* Farmers'; *Style*— The Rt Hon the Lord Alport, PC, TD, DL; ✉ The Cross House, Layer de la Haye, Colchester, Essex (☎ 01206 634217)

ALSOP, Prof William Allen; s of Francis John Alsop (d 1964), and Brenda Ethelwyn, *née* Hight; *b* 12 Dec 1947; *Educ* Eaglehurst Coll Northampton, AA London, Br Sch in Rome (Bernard Webb scholar); *m* 1972, Sheila Elizabeth, da of George Bean; 2 s (Oliver b 1977, Piers b 1984), 1 da (Nancy b 1980); *Career* architect; with: Maxwell Fry 1971, Cedric Price 1973–77, Roderick Ham 1977–79; currently sole princ Alsop and Störmer; visiting prof Faculty of the Built Environment Univ of Central England (formerly Birmingham Poly) 1992–93, hon prof Bremen Acad for Art and Music, prof Vienna Tech Univ 1995; Société Architectes Diplômes par le Gouvernement, awarded William Van Allen Medal for Architects; memb: AA 1968, Soc of Architects 1973, RIBA 1977; FRSA 1983; *Recreations* architecture, fishing; *Clubs* Reform; *Style*— Prof William Alsop; ✉ Alsop & Störmer, Bishops Wharf, 39–49 Parkgate Road, London SW11 4NP (☎ 0171 978 7878, fax 0171 978 7879)

ALSTEAD, Brig (Francis) Allan Littlejohns; CBE (1984), DL (City of Edinburgh 1996); s of Prof Stanley Alstead, CBE (d 1992), of Dunblane, Perthshire, and his 1 w, Nora, *née* Sowden (d 1980); *b* 19 June 1935; *Educ* Glasgow Acad, RMA Sandhurst, Univ Coll Wales Aberystwyth (MPhil), Univ of Edinburgh (NATO research fell); *m* 4 April 1964, Joy Veronica, da of George Alexander Edwards (d 1991), of Carlisle, Cumbria; 2 s (Robert b 24 Dec 1965, Jonathan b 13 Nov 1968); *Career* cmmnd KOSB 1955, RN Staff Coll 1966, Jt Servs Staff Coll 1971, cmd 1 Bn KOSB 1974–76 (despatches 1976), MA to QMG 1976–79, ACOS Log Plans BAOR 1981–84, cmd 51 Highland Bde 1984–87; NATO reinforcement co-ordinator 1987–90; chief exec Scottish Sports Cncl 1990–; memb Royal Co of Archers (Queen's Body Guard for Scotland), regimental tstee KOSB, Dep Hon Col City of Edinburgh Univs OTC 1990–; govr Moray House Coll Edinburgh 1991–, pres Edinburgh and Midlothian SSAFA 1991–; memb: Exec Scottish Cncl for Devpt and Indust 1995–, Lowland Territorial and Volunteer Assoc 1995–; tstee Seagull Tst 1995–, govr Glasgow Acad 1995–; FIMgt 1984, FIPD 1986, FCIT 1989, FInstAM 1990, FRSA 1991, FInstD 1993; *Recreations* skiing, running, tennis, classical music; *Style*— Brig Allan Alstead, CBE, DL; ✉ Scottish Sports Council, Caledonia House, South Gyle, Edinburgh EH12 9DQ (☎ 0131 317 7200)

ALSTON, James Douglas; CBE (1967), JP (1960), DL (Norfolk 1981); s of James Alston (d 1958), of Uphall, Norfolk; *b* 6 May 1913; *Educ* Thetford GS, Midland Agric Coll; *m* 1943, Gale Violet May, da of Edward Tyrrell Lewis (d 1934), of Manitoba, Canada; 2 s, 2 da; *Career* served WWII RAF; farmer, chm Eastern Counties Farmers Ltd 1954–68 (pres 1973–83); memb Agric Res Cncl 1957–67, vice chm Royal Norfolk Agric Assoc 1963–83 (pres 1981), chm Plant Breeding Inst Cambridge 1971–83, vice chm Norfolk Agric Station 1973–84, pres Br Friesian Cattle Soc 1983; tstee TSB of Eastern England 1960–80 (vice chm 1979–80); memb Norfolk CC 1969–73; memb Ct and Cncl UEA; *Recreations* shooting; *Clubs* Farmers', Norfolk; *Style*— James D Alston, Esq, CBE, JP, DL; ✉ South Lopham Hall, Diss, Norfolk IP22 2LW (☎ 01379 687286)

ALSTON, John Alistair; CBE (1988), DL (Norfolk 1991); s of David Alston (d 1989), of Lavenham, Suffolk, and Bathia Mary Davidson (d 1987); *b* 24 May 1937; *Educ* Orwell Park, Sherborne, RAC Cirencester; *Career* farmer; elected Norfolk CC 1973 (ldr 1981–87 and 1989–93, chm 1988); chm: Norwich Health Authy 1994–96, East Norfolk Health Cmmn 1994–96, Norfolk Health Authy 1996–, Broads Bill Steering Ctee; memb: Cncl UEA, Broads Authy 1988–, Regnl Ctee Nat Tst 1994–; tstee Norwich City FC 1992–; *Recreations* shooting, gardening, fishing; *Style*— J A Alston, Esq, CBE, DL; ✉ Besthorpe Hall, Norfolk NR17 2LJ (☎ 01953 452138, fax 01953 453054)

ALSTON, HE Robert John; CMG (1987); s of Arthur William Alston (d 1993), and late Rita Alston; *b* 10 Feb 1938; *Educ* Ardingly Coll, New Coll Oxford (BA); *m* 1969, Patricia Claire, *née* Essex; 1 s (Jeremy b 1972), 1 da (Nadine b 1970); *Career* Dip Serv: third sec Kabul 1963, Eastern Dept FO 1986, head Computer Study Team FCO 1969, first sec (Econ) Paris 1971, first sec and head of Chancery Tehran 1974, Energy Sci and Space Dept FCO 1977, head Jt Nuclear Unit FCO 1978, political cnsllr UK Delgn to NATO 1981, head Def Dept FCO 1984, ambass Oman 1986–90, seconded Home Civil Serv 1990–92, asst under sec (Public Depts) FCO 1992–94, high cmmr Wellington NZ and concurrently non-resident high cmmr to Independent State of Western Samoa and non-resident govr Pitcairn, Henderson, Ducie and Oeno Islands 1994–; *Recreations* gardening, travel, music; *Style—* HE Mr Robert J Alston, CMG; ✉ c/o Foreign and Commonwealth Office (Wellington), King Charles St, London SW1A 2AH

ALSTON, Robin Carfrae; OBE; s of Wilfred Louis Alston (d 1993), and Margaret Louise, *née* Mackenzie (d 1975); *b* 29 Jan 1933; *Educ* Queen's Royal Coll Trinidad, Lodge Sch Barbados, Rugby, Univ of Br Columbia (BA), Univ of Oxford (MA), Univ of Toronto (MA), Univ of London (PhD); *m* m 2, 1996, Janet Pedley, da of Ronald A King; *Career* bibliographer; teaching fell Univ Coll Toronto 1956–58, lectr Univ of New Brunswick 1958–60, lectr in Eng lit Univ of Leeds 1964–76, hon res fell UCL 1987–, prof of library studies Univ of London 1990–, dir Sch of Library, Archive and Info Studies UCL 1990–; David Murray lectr Univ of Glasgow 1983, Cecil Oldman lectr Univ of Leeds 1988–89, Klein visiting prof Univ of Texas 1990; fndr chm and ed Scolar Press 1965–73 (md 1984–), fndr and md Janus Press 1973–80; conslt bibliographer to Br Library 1977– (memb Advsy Ctee 1975–77), ed-in-chief Eighteenth Century Short Title Catalogue 1978–90, editorial dir The Nineteenth Century 1985–; Bibliographical Soc: pres 1986–88, memb Cncl 1968–86, memb Pubns Ctee 1970–92, ed Occasional Papers 1984–92; memb: Organising Ctee 18th Century Short Title Catalogue 1976–80, Advsy Ctee MLA of America for the Wing Project 1978–, Advsy Panel Aust Res Grants Ctee 1983–, Ctee Br Book Trade Index 1984–92; external examiner Inst of Bibliography Univ of Leeds 1983–91; fndr memb Cncl Ilkley Literature Festival 1973–, co-fndr Sir Frederic Madden Soc 1990 (ed Soc's occasional pubns); Samuel Pepys Gold Medal Ephemera Soc 1984, Smithsonian Instn Award 1985, Gold Medal Bibliographical Soc of London 1996; Hon FLA 1986, FSA 1988; *Publications* incl: Anglo-Saxon Composition for Beginners (1959), Materials for a History of the English Language (2 vols, 1960), An Introduction to Old English (1961, 1962), A Concise Introduction to Old English (1966), Alexander Gil's Logonomia Anglica 1619 (ed with B Danielsson, 1979), Cataloguing Rules for the Eighteenth Century Short Title Catalogue (1977), Bibliography, Machine Readable Cataloguing and the ESTC (with M J Jannetta, 1978), Eighteenth Century Subscription Lists (with F J G Robinson and C Wadham, 1983), The Eighteenth Century Short Title Catalogue: the British Library Collection (ed, 1983), The Nineteenth Century Subject Scope & Principles of Selection (1986), The Nineteenth Century - Cataloguing Rules (1986), Bibliography of the English Language 1500–1800 (22 vols, 1–12 published to date), The British Library: Past Present Future (1989), A Checklist of Women Writers 1801–1900 (1990), Handlist of Unpublished Finding Aids to the London Collections of the British Library (1991), The Journal of Sir Frederic Madden: abstract (1991), Books with Manuscript (1994); *Style—* Robin Alston, Esq, OBE, FSA; ✉ 16 Medburn St, London; The British Library, Great Russell St, London WC1B 3DG (☎ 0171 323 7609)

ALSTON-ROBERTS-WEST, Lt-Col George Arthur; CVO (1988), DL (Warwickshire 1988); yr s of Maj William Reginald James Alston-Roberts-West (ka 1940; the Major's gf James added Alston to his patronymic of Roberts-West 1918. James's ggf, another James, added the name Roberts to his patronymic of West 1808. This second James had as mother one Sarah, da of Christopher Wren, of Wroxall Abbey, Staffs, and a descendant of Sir Christopher Wren the architect), and Constance Isolde (d 1987), er da of Lord Arthur Grosvenor, JP, DL, 2 s of 1 Duke of Westminster; *b* 23 Nov 1937; *Educ* Eton, RMA Sandhurst; *m* 20 May 1970, Hazel Elizabeth Margaret, yst da of Lt-Col Sir Thomas Russell Albert Mason Cook, JP (d 1970, ggs of Thomas Cook, fndr of the eponymous tourist agency, and Lady Cook); extra lady-in-waiting to HRH The Princess of Wales 1981–91; *Career* served Grenadier Gds 1957–80; comptroller Lord Chamberlain's Office 1987–90 (asst comptroller 1981–87), extra equerry to HM The Queen 1982–; dir of fundraising and PR CARE (for people with a mental handicap) 1991–95; Freeman City of London 1991; *Style—* Lt-Col George Alston-Roberts-West, CVO, DL; ✉ Atherstone Hill Farmhouse, Stratford-on-Avon, Warwickshire CV37 8NF

ALT, Anthony; *b* 23 March 1946; *Educ* Westminster City Sch, Univ of Hull; *m* Catherine Lurie; 1 s (Nicholas), 1 da (Alexandra); *Career* md N M Rothschild & Sons Ltd; *Recreations* sports, reading, music and family; *Clubs* MCC, Hurlingham, Wentworth; *Style—* Anthony Alt, Esq; ✉ N M Rothschild & Sons Limited, New Court, St Swithin's Lane, London EC4P 4DU (☎ 0171 280 5000)

ALTHAUS, Sir Nigel Frederick; kt (1989); s of Frederick Rudolph Althaus, CBE (d 1975), and Margaret Frances, *née* Twist (d 1990); *b* 28 Sept 1929; *m* 1958, Anne, da of P G Cardew; 3 s, 1 da; *Career* memb Stock Exchange 1955–89; sr ptnr: Pember & Boyle (stockbrokers) 1975–82, Mullens & Co (stockbrokers to the Government and the Bank of England) 1982–86; sr Govt broker (formally known as sr broker to the National Debt Commissioners) 1982–89; treas Imperial Cancer Research Fund; memb Ct of Assts Worshipful Co of Skinners; *Style—* Sir Nigel Althaus; ✉ c/o Bank of England, Threadneedle St, London EC2R 8AH

ALTMAN, His Hon Judge; John; s of Lionel Altman (d 1987), of Leeds, and Vita, *née* Levi (d 1969); *b* 21 June 1944; *Educ* Moorlands Sch Leeds, Bootham Sch York, Univ of Bristol (LLB); *m* 25 Feb 1968, Elizabeth, da of Ralph and Helen Brown; 2 da (Claire Rose b 11 Aug 1973, Vivien Simone b 10 April 1976); *Career* called to the Bar Middle Temple 1967, practised at the Bar in London and N Eastern Circuit, chm Industrial Tbnls 1986–91 (pt/t chm 1983–86), recorder 1989–91 (asst recorder 1985–89), circuit judge (NE Circuit) 1991–; memb Hon Soc of Middle Temple; *Recreations* reading, music, theatre, photography, gardening; *Style—* His Hon Judge Altman

ALTMAN, John; *b* 2 March 1952; *Educ* Sir William Nottidge Sch Kent, High Wycombe Sch of Art, York Acad of Speech and Drama; *m*, Brigitte; 1 da (Rosanna); *Career* actor; *Theatre* incl: nat tours incl: Whodunnit, Up in the Gallery, Dangerous Obsession; other credits incl: Dream of a Ridiculous Man (Pip Simmons Theatre), Dracula (Citizens, Glasgow), Masque of the Red Death (Mickery, Amsterdam), Woyzeck (Cardiff Chapter), Rent (Finborough Theatre), Down by the Greenwood Side (Bath Festival), Little Tramp (Horseshoe Theatre, Basingstoke), The Adventures of Robinson Crusoe (Hazlitt Theatre, Maidstone), Oliver (De Montfort Hall, Leicester), Deadfall (Thorndike Theatre Leatherhead and Theatre Royal Windsor); *Television* incl: Minder, Bouncing Back, the Scarlet Pimpernel, Lucky Jim, Remembrance, Life After Death, Take Two, Going to Work, EastEnders, Gentlemen and Players, The Paradise Club, Up Yer News, Scrag Tag and Toddles, Jack and the Beanstalk, The Ghosts of Oxford Street, TV Squash, The Famous Five, Black Hearts in Battersea, Cold Lazarus, Ant and Dec; *Films* incl: The First Great Train Robbery, Quadrophenia, The Birth of the Beatles, An American Werewolf in London, The Revenge of the Jedi, Memoirs of a Survivor, Remembrance, Seekers, The Higher Mortals, To Die For; *Recreations* writing, swimming, photography, playing the drums and the guitar; *Style—* John Altman, Esq; ✉ c/o George Heathcote Management, Suite 4, Neals Yard, London WC2H 9DP (☎ 0171 379 1081, fax 0171 379 6625)

ALTMAN, Lionel Phillips; CBE (1979); s of late Arnold Altman, and late Catherine, *née* Phillips; *m* 1989, Diana; 1 s and 2 da by previous marriages; *Career* dir: Carmo Holdings 1947–63, Sears Holdings Motor Group 1963–73, C & W Holdings 1974–77, chm Westminster Consultancy 1992–; chm and chief exec Pre-Divisional Investments 1972–94; dir: H P Information plc 1985–91, Equity & General plc Group of Companies (chm 1978–91); chm: United Technologists 1981–93, European Cleaning Services Group 1991–94, Hydro-Lock Europe Ltd 1992–96; dep chm Technology Transfers 1984–90, advsr to public bodies, charities and private sector 1990–; pres Motor Agents Assoc 1975–77 (memb Nat Cncl 1965–), vice pres and memb Cncl Inst of Motor Industry 1970–78; chm: Industry Taxation Panel 1975–82, Publicity Club of London 1961–63, Automotive VIP Club 1988–91, Retail Motor Indust Working Pty on SE Market 1988–93, Barbican Assoc 1995–; memb: Cncl CBI 1977–89, CBI Industl Policy Ctee 1979–86, Dun & Bradstreet Industry Panel 1982–86; life vice pres Devon Agricultural Assoc; Liveryman and former hon treas Worshipful Co of Coachmakers and Coach Harness Makers' Co, Burgess Guild Bro Worshipful Co of Cordwainers; Freeman: City of London 1973, City of Glasgow 1974; FIMI, FCIM, fndr MIPR (1948), FInstD; *Style—* Lionel P Altman, Esq, CBE; ✉ 405 Gilbert House, Barbican, London EC2Y 8BD (☎ and fax 0171 638 3023)

ALTON, David Patrick; MP (Lib Dem) Liverpool Mossley Hill (majority 2,606); s of late Frederick Alton, and Bridget, *née* Mulroe; *b* 15 March 1951; *Educ* Campion Sch, Christ Coll Liverpool; *m* 23 July 1988, Elizabeth, *née* Bell; 1 da (Marianne b 1989), 2 s (Padraig b 1990, Philip b 1992); *Career* teacher of children with special needs 1972–79; cncllr Liverpool City Cncl 1972–80 (dep ldr Cncl 1978–79, chm Housing Ctee 1978–79), nat pres Nat League of Young Liberals 1979; MP (Lib): Liverpool Edge Hill March 1979–83, Liverpool Mossley Hill 1983–; chm Lib Pty Standing Ctee (Policy) 1980–81, memb Select Ctee on the Environment 1981–85, Lib chief whip 1985–87, Lib and Alliance spokesman on NI 1986–87; memb House of Commons Privileges Ctee 1994–96, chm All-Pty Mersey Barrage Group 1990–; vice chm: All-Pty Drug Abuse Group 1992–96, All-Pty Mental Health Gp; fndr Movement for Christian Democracy 1990; nat vice pres Life, pres Liverpool Old People's Hostels Assoc, vice pres Liverpool YMCA, dir Florence Inst Liverpool, vice pres Assoc of Cncllrs; tstee: Crisis, Liverpool Hostels for Victims of Violent Crime, Western Care Assoc; pres Liverpool Branch NSPCC; patron: Jubilee Campaign for the release of prisoners of conscience 1986–, Belfast Tst for Integrated Educn; chm Forget-me-Not Appeal, memb Exec Ctee Andrew Lloyd Webber's Open Churches Tst; columnist: Catholic Pictorial 1982–95, The Universe 1989–; memb Inst of Journalists, FRSA 1994–95; *Books* What Kind of Country (1987), Whose Choice Anyway? (1988), Faith in Britain (1991), Signs of Contradiction (1996); *Style—* David Alton, Esq, MP; ✉ 25 North Mossley Hill Road, Liverpool L18 (☎ 0151 724 6106); House of Commons, London SW1A 0AA (☎ 0171 219 3000)

ALTRINCHAM, Barony of *see:* Grigg, John Edward Poynder

ALTY, Prof James Lenton; s of William Graham Alty (d 1959), of Haslingden, Lancs, and Annie Alty (d 1989); *b* 21 Aug 1939; *Educ* King Edward VII Sch Lytham, Univ of Liverpool (BSc, PhD); *m* 16 Jan 1965, Mary Eleanor, da of Thomas Roberts (d 1986), of Llanerchymedd, Anglesey; 2 s (Gareth Thomas b 1965, Graham James b 1971), 2 da (Carys Ann b 1967, Sian Cathryn b 1968); *Career* account exec IBM (UK) Ltd 1971–72 (sr systems engr 1968–71), dir Computer Laboratory Univ of Liverpool 1972–82 (Oliver Lodge res fell 1962–64, Leverhulme res fell 1966–68), exec dir Turing Inst 1984–90, BT prof of computer sci Univ of Strathclyde 1989–90 (prof of computer sci 1982–89, dir Scot HCI Centre 1984–90), prof of computer sci Univ of Loughborough 1990–, head Computer Studies Dept 1991–; over seventy pubns in academic jls and conf proceedings; memb: Computer Bd for Univs and Res Cncls 1975–81, Cncl Br Computer Soc 1981–84 (fell 1982); FIEE 1993; *Books* Computing Skills and the User Interface (with M J Coombs, 1982), Human Computer Interaction (with G R S Weir, 1990), Industrial Applications of Artificial Intelligence (with Mikulich, 1991), People and Computer VIII (with Diaper and Guest, 1993), Expert Systems: Concepts and Examples (with M J Coombs, 1984); *Recreations* skiing, musical composition; *Clubs* National Liberal; *Style—* Prof James Alty; ✉ 168 Station Rd, Cropston, Leicestershire; Loughborough University of Technology, Loughborough, Leicestershire LE11 3TU (☎ 01509 222648, fax 01509 211586)

ALUN-JONES, Sir (John) Derek; kt (1987); s of Thomas Alun-Jones (d 1951), and Madge Beatrice, *née* Edwards (d 1968); *b* 6 June 1933; *Educ* Lancing, St Edmund Hall Oxford (MA); *m* 1960, Gillian, da of Ian Palmer; 2 s (Jeremy b 1961, Nicholas (triplet) b 1968), 3 da (Carella (Mrs James McGrigor) b 1963, Sophie and Emma (Mrs Oliver Hassall) (triplets) b 1968); *Career* dir: Burmah Oil Trading Co 1970–74, Reed International 1984–90, GKN 1986–88; non-exec dir Royal Insurance Holdings plc 1981–96; dir Spectrum Energy and Information Technology Ltd 1990–; chm: Straker Holdings Ltd 1991–, Boulton & Paul Holdings Ltd 1993–, Astro Technology Systems Ltd 1996–; chm and md Ferranti 1975–90; CIMgt; *Recreations* shooting, fishing, golf; *Style—* Sir Derek Alun-Jones; ✉ The Willows, Effingham Common, Surrey KT24 5JE (☎ 01372 458158, fax 01372 459151)

ALVAREZ, Alfred; s of Bertie Alvarez (d 1965), of London, and Katie, *née* Levy (d 1982); *b* 5 Aug 1929; *Educ* Oundle, CCC Oxford (BA, MA); *m* 1, 1956 (m dis 1961), Ursula Barr; 1 s (Adam); m 2, 1966, Anne, da of Jack Gilmore Adams, of Toronto, Canada; 1 s (Luke b 1968), 1 da (Kate b 1971); *Career* poet and author; sr scholar CCC Oxford 1952–55 and Goldsmiths' Co 1952–55; Procter visiting fellowship Princeton 1953–54, visiting fell Rockefeller Fndn USA 1955–56 and 1958, lectr in creative writing and Gauss Seminarian Princeton 1957–58, D H Lawrence fellowship Univ of New Mexico 1958; visiting prof: Brandeis Univ 1960, New York State Univ Buffalo 1966; poetry critic The Observer 1956–66; Vachel Lindsay Prize for Poetry 1961; *Books* The Shaping Spirit (1958), The School of Donne (1961), The New Poetry (ed and introduction, 1962), Under Pressure (1965), Beyond All This Fiddle (1968), Lost (poems, 1968), Penguin Modern Poets No18 (1970), Apparition (poems, 1971), The Savage God (1971), Beckett (1973), Hers (1974), Hunt (1978), Autumn to Autumn and Selected Poems (1978), Life After Marriage (1982), The Biggest Game in Town (1983), Offshore (1986), Feeding the Rat (1988), Rainforest (1988), Day of Atonement (1991), The Faber Book of Modern European Poetry (ed and introduction, 1992), Night (1995); *Recreations* poker, music; *Clubs* Climbers', Alpine, Beefsteak; *Style—* A Alvarez, Esq; ✉ c/o Aitken & Stone, 29 Fernshaw Rd, London SW10 OTG

ALVEY, John; CB (1980); s of George Clarence Vincent Alvey (d 1929), and Hilda Eveline, *née* Pellat (d 1955); *b* 19 June 1925; *Educ* Reeds Sch, Univ of London (BSc); *m* 1955, Celia Edmed, da of Dr Cecil Brittain Marson (d 1932); 3 s (David, Peter, Stephen); *Career* London Stock Exchange until 1943, RN 1943–46, RN Scientific Serv 1950, head of weapons projects Admty Surface Weapons Estab 1968–72, DG Electronics Radar PE MOD 1972–73, DG Airborne Electronic Systems PE MOD 1974–75, dir Admty Surface Weapons Estab 1976–77, dep controller R & D Estabs and Res C and chief scientist (RAF) MOD 1977–80, md Devpt and Procurement and engr-in-chief British Telecom 1983–86 (sr dir Technol 1980–83), LSI Logic Ltd 1986–91; chm SIRA Ltd 1987–94; memb Cncl: Fellowship of Engrg 1985–92 (vice pres 1989–92), Fndn for Sci and Technol 1986–90, City Univ 1985–93; Hon DSc City Univ 1984, Hon DTech CNAA 1991; fell Queen Mary and Westfield Coll London 1988; FIEE, FRSA, FEng 1984; *Recreations* skiing, walking, reading, travel; *Style—* John Alvey, Esq, CB, FEng; ✉ 9 Western Parade, Emsworth, Hants PO10 7HS

ALVINGHAM, 2 Baron (UK 1929); Robert Guy Eardley; CBE (1977, OBE 1972); s of 1 Baron Alvingham (d 1955), and Dorothea Gertrude Yerburgh (d 1927); *b* 16 Dec 1926; *Educ* Eton; *m* 1952, Beryl Elliot, da of William D Williams, of Hindhead; 1 s (Robert), 1 da (Susannah); *Heir* s, Capt Hon Robert Yerburgh; *Career* formerly Coldstream Gds (joined 1945, cmmnd 1946), served Palestine, Tripoli, FARELF, S America; Head Staff CDS 1972–74, RCDS 1975, dep dir Army Staff Duties 1975–78, Maj-Gen 1978, dir Army Quartering MOD 1978–81; patron Oxfordshire County of The Royal British Legion; *Style*— Maj-Gen The Rt Hon Lord Alvingham, CBE; ✉ c/o House of Lords, Westminster, London SW1

AMANN, Prof Ronald; s of George James Amann, of Newcastle upon Tyne, and Elizabeth Clementson, *née* Towell (d 1983); *b* 21 Aug 1943; *Educ* Heaton GS Newcastle upon Tyne, Univ of Birmingham (MSocSci, PhD); *m* 28 Aug 1965, Susan Frances, da of Leslie Peters, of S Porcupine, Ontario, Canada; 2 s (Edmund b 1968, Timothy Francis b 1970), 1 da (Jessica Louise b 1974); *Career* conslt OECD 1965–68; Univ of Birmingham: sr lectr (formerly asst lectr and lectr) 1968–83, dir Centre for Russian and E Euro Studies 1983–89, prof of comparative politics 1985–, dean Faculty of Commerce and Social Sci 1989–91, pro vice-chllr 1991–94; chief exec and dep chm ESRC 1994–; former memb Cncl Sch of Slavonic and E Euro Studies Univ of London, specialist advsr and witness Foreign Affrs Ctee and Ctee on Sci and Technol House of Commons; memb ESRC Res Centres Bd Res Resources Bd, chm Steering Ctee ESRC E-W Res Initiative; currently non-exec dir City Hosp NHS Tst Birmingham, memb nat Technol Foresight Steering Gp, memb Ctee on the Public Understanding of Science (COPUS); *Books* Science Policy in the USSR (with Berry and Davies, 1968), The Technological Level of Soviet Industry (with Cooper and Davies), Industrial Innovation in the Soviet Union (with Cooper, 1982), Technical Progress and Soviet Economic Development (with Cooper); *Recreations* walking, modern jazz, cricket; *Clubs* Athenaeum; *Style*— Prof Ronald Amann; ✉ Chief Executive, Economic and Social Research Council, Polaris House, North Star Avenue, Swindon SN2 1UJ (☎ 01793 413000)

AMBLER, Eric; OBE (1981); s of Alfred Percy Ambler (d 1929), and Amy Madeleine Ambler; *b* 28 June 1909; *Educ* Colfe's GS, Univ of London; *m* 1, 1939, Louise Crombie; m 2, 1958, Joan Mary Harrison (d 1994); *Career* novelist and screenwriter; apprenticeship in engrg 1927–28, advtg copywriter 1929–35, professional writer 1936–; served WWII Lt-Col RA Europe, asst dir of army kinematography War Office 1944–46, Bronze Star (USA) 1946; screenplays incl: The Way Ahead (1944), The October Man (1947), The Passionate Friends (1948), Highly Dangerous (1950), The Magic Box (1951), Gigolo and Gigolette in Encore (1952), The Card (1952), Rough Shoot (1953), The Cruel Sea (1953), Lease of Life (1954), The Purple Plain (1954), Yangtse Incident (1957), A Night to Remember (1958), Wreck of the Mary Deare (1959), Love Hate Love (1970); *Books* incl: The Dark Frontier (1936), Uncommon Danger (1937), Epitaph for a Spy (1938), Cause for Alarm (1938), The Mask of Dimitrios (1939), Journey into Fear (1940), Judgement on Deltchev (1951), The Schirmer Inheritance (1953), The Night-Comers (1956), Passage of Arms (1959), The Light of Day (1962), The Ability to Kill (essays, 1963), To Catch a Spy (ed and intro, 1964), A Kind of Anger (Edgar Allen Poe award, 1964), Dirty Story (1967), The Intercom Conspiracy (1969), The Levanter (1972, Golden Dagger award, 1973), Dr Frigo (1974, MWA Grand Master award 1975), Send No More Roses (1977), The Care of Time (1981), Here Lies (autobiog, 1985, Diamond Dagger Award CWA, 1986), The Story So Far (1993); Hon DLitt City Univ; *Clubs* Garrick; *Style*— Eric Ambler, Esq, OBE; ✉ 14 Bryanston Square, London W1H 7FF

AMBLER, Prof Richard Penry; s of Henry Reason Ambler, OBE (d 1970), and Anne Sarah Ellen, *née* Evans (d 1993); *b* 26 May 1933; *Educ* Haileybury Coll, Pembroke Coll Cambridge (minor scholar, MA, PhD); *m* 1, 1957 (m dis), Ann Patricia, da of Leonard Waddington (d 1991); 2 da (Anne b 9 April 1962, Jane b 14 Sept 1964); m 2, 1994, Susan, da of Stanley Hewlett; *Career* 2 Lt Royal Signals 1953–55; Univ of Cambridge: res fell Pembroke Coll 1959–62, res MRC Laboratory of Molecular Biology 1962–65; Univ of Edinburgh: lectr 1965–73, sr lectr 1973–75, reader 1975–87, head Dept of Molecular Biology 1984–90, prof of protein chemistry 1987–, head Inst of Cell and Molecular Biology 1990–93; memb: Biochemical Soc 1958, Euro Molecular Biology Orgn 1985, Soc of Antiquaries of Scotland 1985; tstee Darwin Tst of Edinburgh 1984–94; *Recreations* railways and ancient history; *Style*— Prof Richard Ambler; ✉ Institute of Cell and Molecular Biology, University of Edinburgh, Mayfield Road, Edinburgh EH9 3JR (☎ 0131 650 5394)

AMBRASEYS, Prof Nicholas; s of Neocles Amvrasis, of Athens, and Cleopatra, *née* Yambani (d 1986); *b* 19 Jan 1929; *Educ* Nat Tech Univ of Athens, Imperial Coll London (DIC), Univ of London (PhD, DSc); *m* 25 Aug 1955, Xeni, da of Alexander Stavrou; *Career* lectr in civil engrg Imperial Coll London 1958–62, assoc prof of civil engrg Univ of Illinois 1963, prof of hydrodynamics Nat Tech Univ Athens 1964; Imperial Coll London: lectr in engrg seismology 1965–68, univ reader 1969–72, prof 1973–94, head of Engrg Seismology Section 1969–94, sr res fell Imperial Coll 1994–; chm Br Nat Ctee for Earthquake Engrg 1961–71, dir Int Assoc for Earthquake Engrg 1961–77, vice pres Euro Assoc for Earthquake Engrg 1964–75, vice chm UNESCO Int Advsy Ctee on Earthquake Risk 1979–81 (memb 1969–81); ldr UN/UNESCO earthquake reconnaissance missions to Pakistan, Iran, Turkey, Romania, Yugoslavia, Italy, Greece, Algeria, Nicaragua, E and Central Africa; chm Int Cmmn for Earthquake Protection of Historical Monuments 1977–81, hon memb Int Assoc Earthquake Engrg 1993–; Dr (hc) Univ of Athens 1993; Decennial Award Euro Assoc for Earthquake Engrg 1975, Busk Medal RGS 1975; FEng 1985, FICE, FGS, FRGS; *Books* The Seismicity of Egypt, Arabia and the Red Sea - A History of Persian Earthquakes (with C Melville, 1982 and 1994), The Seismicity of Turkey (with C Finkel, 1995); *Recreations* historical geography, archaeology; *Style*— Prof Nicholas Ambraseys, FEng; ✉ 19 Bede House, Manor Fields, London SW15 3LT (☎ 0181 788 4219); Department of Civil Engineering, Imperial College of Science & Technology, London SW7 2BU (☎ 0171 594 6059, fax 0171 225 2716)

AMBROSE, Prof (Edmund) Jack; s of Harry Edmund Ambrose (d 1940), of Cambridgeshire, and Kate, *née* Stanley (d 1926); *b* 2 March 1914; *Educ* Perse Sch Cambridge, Emmanuel Coll Cambridge (BA, MA), Univ of London (DSc); *m* 31 July 1943, Andrée, da of Alphonse Huck, of Seine, France; 1 s (Edmund David b 1945), 1 da (Philippa Jane b 1948); *Career* WWII secret res Admty 1940–45; res offr (protein structure) Courtauld Basic Res Inst Maidenhead 1945–53, res on cell surfaces in normal and cancer cells Chester Beatty Res Inst 1953–73, prof and head of Dept of Cell Biology Univ of London 1966–75 (now emeritus); chm Sci Advsy Ctee and advsr in cancer to Govt of India Tata Meml Hosp Res Inst Bombay 1965–73, advsr Regnl Cancer Centre Kerala India 1978–, co fndr and advsr Fndn for Med Res (leprosy) Bombay 1975–; recorder Zoology Section Br Assoc for Advancement of Sci 1968–73, fndr and convener Br Soc of Cell Biology, emeritus memb Int Soc of Biological Differentiation; diocesan reader in Westfield Church Chichester Diocese 1981–; Queen Elizabeth of Hungary medal Ordre de St Jean de Malte Paris 1981 (for leprosy work in India); *Books* Cell Electrophoresis (1962), The Cancer Cell in Vitro (jtly, 1968), Biology of Cancer (ed, 1968, 2 edn 1975), Cell Biology (jtly, 1970, 2 edn 1975), Nature and Origin of the Biological World (1981), The Mirror of Creation (1990); *Recreations* sailing, pastel sketching; *Clubs* Chelsea Arts, Royal Bombay Yacht; *Style*— Prof Jack Ambrose

AMBROSE, (Neil) Simon; s of Neil Trevor Ambrose (d 1952), and Margaret, *née* Donaldson; *b* 17 May 1950; *Educ* Campbell Coll Belfast, King's Coll Hosp Med Sch (MB BS, MS); *m* 11 Sept 1976, (Elizabeth) Jane, da of William John Arthur Cowley; 2 s (Benjamin Neil b 1981, Jeremy William b 1983), 1 da (Felicity Jane b 1986); *Career* lectr in surgery Univ of Birmingham 1983–88, conslt surgn and sr clinical lectr Univ of Leeds 1988–, surgical tutor Leeds Eastern Health Authy 1989–94, chm Leeds Eastern Dist Audit Ctee 1990–91; sec Assoc of Surgns in Trg 1985–87; chm: St James's Univ Hosp Tst Audit Ctee 1991–, Yorks Gastrointestinalo Tumour Gp 1989–93; memb: Yorks Regnl Audit Ctee 1991–, Yorks Regnl Cancer Orgn Policy Ctee 1993–, Regnl Higher Surgical Trg Ctee 1994–; FRCS 1979; *Recreations* travel, reading, swimming, golf, gardening, DIY; *Style*— Simon Ambrose, Esq; ✉ St James's University Hospital, Beckett St, Leeds LS9 7TF (☎ 0113 243 3144)

AMBROSE, Timothy Michael; s of Henry Ambrose, and Janet, *née* Millard; *b* 8 Dec 1949; *Educ* Dauntseys Sch Wilts, Univ of Southampton (BA, CertEd); *m* 21 Sept 1974, Hon Angela Francesca Hayward Blanch, 3 da of Rt Rev Baron Blanch, PC, DD (Life Peer, d 1994); 2 da (Bethany Beatrice Hayward b 24 July 1978, Emily Kate b 15 May 1981); *Career* res asst Univ of Oxford Inst of Archaeology and archivist Ashmolean Museum Library 1972–74, pubns asst DOE 1974–75, res asst in Euro archaeology Univ of Oxford 1975–77, asst keeper of archaeology Lincolnshire Museums 1977–82; Scottish Museums Cncl: dep dir 1982–86, acting dir 1986–89, dir 1989–94; sr res fell City Univ Dept of Arts Policy and Mgmnt 1994–96, head of practice Museum Resource Management (UK and int museum advsrs) 1994–; chm Exec Bd ICOM UK, dir and tstee Sussex Archaeological Soc; author of numerous reports, reviews and papers; FMA 1990 (AMA 1980), FSA 1993; *Books* New Museums - A Start-Up Guide (1987), Education in Museums, Museums in Education (1987), Working with Museums (1988), Presenting Scotland's Story (1989), Money, Money, Money and Museums (1991), Forward Planning - a Handbook (1991), Museum Basics (1993), Managing New Museums (1993); *Recreations* gardening; *Style*— Timothy M Ambrose, Esq, FSA; ✉ Museum Resource Management, Holdings Old Farmhouse, The Street, Kingston, Lewes, E Sussex BN7 3NT (☎ 01273 478423)

AMES, Dr Anthony Cyril; s of Cyril Frederick Ames (d 1991), and Amy Edith, *née* Casey; *b* 7 April 1934; *Educ* Mercers' Sch, St Mary's Hosp Med Sch Univ of London (BSc, MB BS); *m* 20 May 1961, Gillian Rosemary Tyson, da of Lt-Col J P Walters (d 1952); 1 s (Anthony b 1968), 2 da (Sally b 1963, Samantha b 1965); *Career* conslt chemical pathologist 1969–96 (ret), postgraduate clinical tutor 1971–96; memb: Nat Quality Assur Advsy Panel for Chemical Pathology 1987–90, Royal Coll of Pathologists Standing Advsy Ctee for Chemical Pathology 1988–90; hon treas Assoc of Clinical Pathologists 1990–95, Welsh Cncl for Postgraduate Medical and Dental Education 1988–94; memb: Welsh Lawn Tennis Coaches' Assoc, Assoc of Clinic Pathologists; author of numerous papers on biochemistry and clinical pathology; LRCP, MRCS, FRCPath; *Recreations* marathon running, mountaineering, fly fishing, tennis; *Clubs* Old Mercers, Neath Harriers Athletic; *Style*— Dr Anthony Ames; ✉ Tyn-Y-Cwm, Rhos, Pontardawe, W Glamorgan SA8 3EY (☎ 01792 862513)

AMES, Ethan Ojai; s of Richard McCurdy Ames, of Santa Barbara, and Ann, *née* Jones (d 1992); *b* 16 June 1949; *Educ* Summerhill Sch, East Ham Tech Coll (LSIAD); *m* 11 Aug 1973 (m dis 1985), Julia Rosemary, *née* Stone; 1 da (Tacita Amelia Charlotte Inez Tora b 1 March 1974); *partner*, Robert William Thomas Chapman; *Career* graphic designer; sr lectr/course tutor East Ham Coll of Technol 1973–78, sr graphic designer Thames TV 1978–82, head of design and graphics TV-am 1982–88, prodn graphic designer Thames TV 1988–92, head of graphic design BBC TV 1994– (graphic design mangr News and Current Affairs 1992–94); work published in D&AD, Modern Publicity, Print Magazine, Graphics World, Monotype Recorder, Changing Image, Television Graphics - From Pencil to Pixel; memb: D&AD 1978, RTS 1982, BDA 1993; FRSA; *Style*— Ethan Ames, Esq; ✉ Graphic Design Department, BBC, Television Centre, Wood Lane, London W12 7RJ (☎ 0181 576 1628, fax 0181 576 4889)

AMES, Gerald George Singleton; s of George Singleton Ames (d 1956), and Florence Christian, *née* Hart (d 1982); *b* 15 April 1927; *Educ* Wade Deacon GS, Manchester Sch of Architecture (DipArch); *m* 4 Feb 1950, Margaret, da of Frederick Atherton (d 1983), of Hillcrest, Cheshire; 2 s (Stephen b 1956, Mark b 1960); *Career* dir John Finlan Ltd 1956–70, md and deputy chm Finlan Group plc 1970–85, dir Finlan Group plc (company concerned in property design and development, export of building services and components, materials handling and merchanting) 1985–87, chm and md Sefton Group Ltd (property devpt, mgmnt and investmt); dir: Sefton Land Ltd, Sefton Securities Ltd, Sefton Plard Ltd; ARIBA; *Recreations* sailing, music; *Clubs* Liverpool Artists'; *Style*— Gerald Ames, Esq; ✉ Tyn-Yr-Ynn Farm, Llanferres, Mold, Clwyd; Sefton Group Ltd, Queen Insurance Buildings, 16 Queen Avenue, Liverpool L2 4TX (☎ 0151 227 1553, fax 0151 236 1046)

AMESS, David Anthony Andrew; MP (C) Basildon (majority 1,480); s of James Henry Valentine Amess (d 1986), and Maud Ethel, *née* Martin; *b* 26 March 1952; *Educ* St Bonaventures GS, Bournemouth Coll of Technol (BSc); *m* 1983, Julia Margaret Monica, da of Graham Harry Arnold, of Southend-on-Sea; 1 s (David James b 1984), 4 da (Katherine Louise b 1985, Sarah Elizabeth b 1988, Alexandra Charlotte Clementine b 1990, Florence Rebecca b 26 Sept 1991); *Career* teacher 1970–71, insurance underwriter Leslie & Godwin Agency 1974–76, sr conslt Accountancy Personnel 1976–80, ptnr Accountancy Aims Employment Agency 1981–87; chm: Accountancy Solutions 1987, Accountancy Aims Group 1990–96; memb Cons Pty 1968–, Parly candidate (C) Forest Gate 1974 and 1978, GLC candidate Newham NW 1977, Parly candidate (C) Newham NW 1979, MP (C) Basildon 1983–; Redbridge Cncl: elected 1981, vice chm Housing Ctee 1981–85, vice chm until 1985; PPS at DHSS 1987 to: Edwina Currie, Michael Portillo, Lord Skelmersdale; PPS to Michael Portillo: as Min of State Dept of Transport 1988–90, at DOE 1990–92, as Chief Sec to the Treasury 1992–94, as Sec of State for Employment 1994–95, as Sec of State for Def 1995–; *Recreations* reading, writing, sport, theatre, gardening, popular music; *Clubs* Carlton, Kingswood Squash and Racketball (Basildon); *Style*— David Amess, Esq, MP; ✉ House of Commons, London SW1A 0AA (☎ 0171 219 6387, fax 0171 219 2245)

AMEY, Julian Nigel Robert; s of Robert Amey, of Fieldways, Barton Seagrave, Kettering, Northants, and Diana, *née* Coles; *b* 19 June 1949; *Educ* Wellingborough Sch, Magdalene Coll Cambridge (MA); *m* 16 Dec 1972, Ann Victoria, da of Thomas Frank Brenchley, CMG, of London SW1, and Edith, *née* Helfand; 3 da (Joanna b 9 Sept 1981, Frances b 12 Oct 1984, Charlotte b 7 Jan 1990); *Career* dir of int sales and marketing Longman Group Ltd 1985–89, exec dir BBC English World Service 1989–94, seconded to DTI 1994–96, DG Canning House (Hispanic and Luso Brazilian Cncl) 1996–; tstee International House, govr Bath Coll of Higher Educn; *Books* Spanish Business Dictionary (1979), Portuguese Business Dictionary (1981); *Recreations* cricket, travel; *Clubs* Hawks', Travellers', ESU; *Style*— Julian Amey, Esq; ✉ Canning House, 2 Belgrave Square, London SW1X 8PJ (☎ 0171 235 2303, fax 0171 235 3587)

AMHERST OF HACKNEY, 4 Baron (UK 1892); (William) Hugh Amherst Cecil; s of 3 Baron Amherst of Hackney, CBE (d 1980), and Margaret, Baroness Amherst of Hackney; *b* 28 Dec 1940; *Educ* Eton; *m* 1965, Elisabeth, da of Hugh Humphery Merriman, DSO, MC, TD, DL (d 1983); 1 s (Hon (Hugh) William Amherst), 1 da (Hon Aurelia Margaret Amherst b 1966); *Heir* s, Hon (Hugh) William Amherst Cecil b 17 July 1968; *Career* dir E A Gibson Shipbrokers Ltd; *Recreations* sailing (yacht "Hal"); *Clubs* Royal Yacht Sqdn, Royal Ocean Racing; *Style*— The Rt Hon the Lord Amherst of Hackney

AMIEL, Jonathan Michael (Jon); s of Barry Conrad Amiel (d 1978), of London, and Anita, *née* Barron; *b* 20 May 1948; *Educ* William Ellis Sch London, Univ of Cambridge (MA); *m* Quinny, da of Leslie Sacks; 2 s (Leo Barry, Jack Barry); *Career* freelance director; admin Oxford & Cambridge Shakespeare Co 1970–73, literary mangr then assoc dir Hampstead Theatre Club 1973–76, asst then assoc dir Royal Shakespeare Co 1976–78, story ed BBC TV 1978–79; directed numerous prodns for BBC Play for Today 1980–85, incl: Preview, Lunch, A Sudden Wrench, Busted, Gates of Gold, Nobody's Property; other credits as dir incl: Tandoori Nights (series, Channel 4) 1985, Silent Twins (film) 1986, The Singing Detective (BBC) 1986, Queen of Hearts (feature film) 1988, Aunt Julia & The Scriptwriter (US title Tune In Tomorrow) 1990, Sommersby (US feature film, with Richard Gere and Jodie Foster) 1993, Copycat (US feature film, with Sigourney Weaver and Holly Hunter) 1995; winner numerous awards for The Singing Detective, several festival awards for Queen of Hearts and Tune In Tomorrow; *Style*— Jon Amiel, Esq; ✉ Angel Films, c/o Judy Daish Associates, 2 St Charles Place, London W10 6EG (☎ 0181 964 8811, fax 0181 964 8966)

AMIES, Sir (Edwin) Hardy; KCVO (1989, CVO 1977); s of late Herbert William Amies; *b* 17 July 1909; *Career* dressmaker by appointment to HM The Queen 1955–; previously: trainee W & T Avery Ltd Birmingham 1930–34, managing designer Lachasse Farm Street London W1 1934–39; joined Intelligence Corps 1939, served WWII becoming Lt-Col and head Special Forces Mission to Belgium 1944; fndr dir own dressmaking business Hardy Amies Ltd 1946–; design conslt to mfrs in UK, EEC, USA, Canada, Aust, NZ, Japan and Korea; chm Incorporated Soc of London Fashion Designers 1959–60 (vice chm 1954–56); awards: Harper's Bazaar 1962, Caswell-Massey 1962, 1964 and 1968, Ambassador Magazine 1964, Sunday Times (Special Award) 1965, Personnalité de l'Année (Haute Couture) Paris 1986, Br Fashion Cncl (Hall of Fame Award) 1989; Officier de l'Ordre de la Couronne (Belgium) 1946; RDI 1964, FRSA 1965; *Books* Just So Far (1954), ABC of Men's Fashion (1964), Still Here (1984), The Englishman's Suit (1994); *Recreations* lawn tennis, gardening, opera; *Clubs* Queen's, Buck's; *Style*— Sir Hardy Amies, KCVO; ✉ 29 Cornwall Gardens, London SW7; Hardy Amies Ltd, 14 Savile Row, London W1 (☎ 0171 734 2436)

AMIES, Timothy John (Tim); s of Maj George Amies (d 1977), of Drumdevan House, Inverness, and Elizabeth Mary, *née* MacDonald (who m 2, Reginald Phillips (d 1992) and d 1993); *b* 1 July 1938; *Educ* Oundle; *m* 6 Nov 1969, Clare Rosemary, da of John Robert Payne Crawfurd, of Surrey; 3 s (Tom b 1971, Edward b 1973, Harry b 1979), 2 da (Sarah b 1974, Alice b 1985); *Career* 2 Lt Queen's Own Cameron Highlanders 1956–58; CA Casselton Elliott and Co 1959–64, merchant banker Morgan Grenfell and Co 1964–68, stockbroker and ptnr Laurie Milbank & Co 1968–86, Chase Manhattan Bank London 1986–90, Amies Mergers 1991–; dir: Chase Investment Bank Ltd 1987–90, Mercury Grosvenor Trust plc (formerly Grosvenor Development Capital plc) 1991–, ApT Design and Development Ltd 1992–, World Vision (UK); FCA, MSI; *Recreations* children, reading, walking, gardening, golf; *Clubs* City of London, Inst of Directors, Woburn Country; *Style*— Tim Amies, Esq; ✉ The Old Farm, Great Brickhill, Milton Keynes, Buckinghamshire MK17 9AH (☎ 01525 261243, fax 01525 261005); Ballachar, Loch Ruthven, Farr, Inverness (☎ 01808 521258)

AMIS, Martin Louis; s of Sir Kingsley William Amis, CBE (d 1995), and his 1 w, Hilary Ann, *née* Bardwell; *b* 25 Aug 1949; *Educ* Exeter Coll Oxford (BA); *m* (m dis 1996), Antonia; *Career* writer; literary ed New Statesman 1977–79, special writer The Observer 1980–; tennis corr The New Yorker 1992–; *Books* The Rachel Papers (1973, Somerset Maugham Award 1974), Dead Babies (1975), Success (1978), Other People: A Mystery Story (1981), Money (1984), The Moronic Inferno and Other Visits to America (1986), Einstein's Monsters (1987), London Fields (1989), Time's Arrow (1991), The Information (1995); *Style*— Martin Amis, Esq; ✉ Wylie Agency, 36 Parkside, 52 Knightsbridge, London SW1X 7JP (☎ 0171 235 6394)

AMIS, Richard Henry Allen; CBE (1983); s of Maj Ivan Roll Amis (d 1970), of Ripley, Surrey, and Sylvia Emily, *née* Booth (d 1968); *b* 4 May 1932; *Educ* Eton; *Career* Capt (TA) 1955; chm Alfred Booth & Co plc 1974–86, dir Michelin Tyre Co 1982–, chm CBI Health & Safety Ctee 1978–83; JP 1984–87; cncllr Guildford Borough Cncl 1972–83; *Recreations* gardening, walking, historical reading; *Clubs* Carlton; *Style*— Richard H Amis, Esq, CBE; ✉ The Georgian House, Ripley, Woking, Surrey GU23 6AF (☎ 01483 224353)

AMLOT, Roy Douglas; QC (1989); s of Air Cdre Douglas Lloyd Amlot, CBE, DFC, AFC (d 1979), of Casa Jacaranda, Praia da Luz, Algarve, Portugal, and Ruby Luise, *née* Lawrence; *b* 22 Sept 1942; *Educ* Dulwich; *m* 26 July 1969, Susan Margaret, da of Sir Henry McLorinan McDowell, KBE, *qv*, of Dulwich; 2 s (Thomas b 1971, Richard b 1978); *Career* called to the Bar Lincoln's Inn 1963, bencher 1987, second prosecuting counsel to Inland Revenue (Central Criminal Ct and London Crown Ct) 1974, first prosecuting counsel to the Crown (Inner London Ct) 1975, jr prosecuting counsel to the Crown (Central Criminal Ct) 1977, sr prosecuting counsel to the Crown (Central Criminal Ct) 1981, first sr prosecuting counsel to the Crown 1987; *Publications* Phipson on Evidence (ed 11 edn); *Recreations* skiing, windsurfing, music, squash; *Clubs* St James's; *Style*— Roy Amlot, Esq, QC; ✉ 6 King's Bench Walk, Temple, London EC4

AMOORE, Alan David John; s of John Bradly Rendell Amoore, of Aberdeen, and Marie Gladys, *née* Rennie; *b* 16 March 1944; *Educ* Robert Gordon's Coll Aberdeen; *m* 1 Oct 1975, Catherine Moir, da of Robert Glentworth; 2 da (Catherine Marie b 10 Nov 1977, Lesley Helen b 3 Feb 1980); *Career* articled clerk Bower & Smith CA's, chartered accountant G & J McBain; KPMG: ptnr 1976–, managing ptnr Aberdeen office 1994–; burgess City of Aberdeen; MICAS (area sec (Grampian) 1984–), MIPA, MSPI; *Recreations* charity work especially Save the Children, golf, gardening; *Clubs* Royal Northern and University; *Style*— Alan Amoore, Esq; ✉ KPMG, 37 Albyn Place, Aberdeen AB10 1JB (☎ 01224 591000, fax 01224 590009)

AMORY, *see:* Heathcoat-Amory

AMOS, Francis John Clarke; CBE (1973); s of Frank Amos (d 1970), and Alice Mary, *née* Clarke (d 1974); *b* 10 Sept 1924; *Educ* Dulwich, Univ of London (BSc), London Poly (DipArch), Sch of Planning London (Dip in Planning); *m* Geraldine Mercy Amos, MBE, JP, da of Capt Egbert Spear Sutton (d 1977); 1 s (Gideon), 2 da (Zephyr, Felicity); *Career* served Royal Corps of Signals 1942–44, RIASC 1944–47, Capt; Harlow Devpt Corp 1951, LCC Planning Div 1953–58, Miny of Housing and Local Govt 1958–59 and 1962–63, advsr to Imperial Ethiopian Govt 1959–62, Liverpool Corp City Planning Dept 1962–73 (chief planning offr 1966–73), chief exec Birmingham CC 1973–77; asst cmmr Local Boundary Cmmn 1986–, conslt Halcrow Fox Assocs 1986–, freelance int conslt 1991–; sr fell Univ of Birmingham 1977–, special prof of planning and mgmnt Univ of Nottingham 1980– (memb Ct 1975–), visiting prof Queen's Univ Belfast 1991–; chm Sir Herbert Manzoni Scholarship Tst 1975–95; sometime lectr: Workers' Educnl Assoc, Univ Extension Serv, various locations incl USA, India, Utrecht, Belgrade and Barcelona; various seminars organised by: UN, OECD, Int Fedn of Housing & Planning, Int Soc of City & Regnl Planners; advsr UN Centre of Human Settlements 1974–; advsr various govt aid progs in countries incl: Venezuela (1978), Tanzania (1978–80 and 1991–92), India (1979–), Turkey (1979–80), Kenya (1981–), Germany (1981–), Pakistan (1981–93), Zimbabwe (1981–83), Bangladesh (1983–), Hong Kong (1983), Hungary (1984), Ghana (1985), Iraq (1985–87), Uganda (1987–), Zambia (1987–94), Lesotho (1987), Trinidad and Tobago (1988 and 1992), Ethiopia (1958–61 and 1988–89), Br Virgin Islands (1989), Indonesia (1989), Laos (1990), Malta (1990), Poland (1991–), China (1991), Belize (1993 and 1996), Romania (1993), Latvia (1994 and 1996), Jordan (1994), Dubai (1994 and 1996), Hungary (1994 and 1995); dir Foreign Office Local Govt Asst Prog in Poland 1992–; tstee Community Project Fndn 1977–88, tstee dir Action Resource Centre 1976–87; memb: Community Work and Area Research Centres Gp 1970–86, Int Soc of City and Regnl Planners 1973–, Exec Ctee Public Serv Announcements 1978–86, Arts Cncl Regnl Ctee 1979–, Nat Exec Ctee and Cncl Nat Assoc of CAB 1982–86, St George's House Windsor 1981–, Jt Land Requirements Ctee 1982–89; hon sec Royal Town Planning Inst 1979– (pres 1971–72); Freeman City of London 1968; ARIBA 1954, FRTPI 1967 (AMTPI 1955), FRSA 1977; *Books* Education for Planning and Urban Governance (1973), City Centre Redevelopment (1973), Planning and the Future (1977), Low Income Housing in the Developing World (1984), and various articles, conference papers and government papers; *Recreations* voluntary social work; *Style*— Francis Amos, Esq, CBE; ✉ Grindstones, 20 Westfield Rd, Edgbaston, Birmingham B15 3QG (☎ 0121 454 5661, fax 0121 454 8331); Coach House, Ashton Gifford, Codford St Peter, Warminster, Wilts (☎ and fax 01985 50610); School of Public Policy, University of Birmingham, PO Box 363, Birmingham B15 2TT (☎ 0121 414 5004)

AMOS, Roy; s of Leonard Alfred Amos, of Birmingham; *b* 8 Sept 1934; *Educ* King Edward's Sch Aston Birmingham, Birmingham Coll of Commerce; *m* 1956, Marjorie Ann, da of Arnold Hall, of Birmingham; *Career* chm and md Lightning International Ltd 1969–74, exec gp dir IMI plc 1974–96; non-exec chm Manders plc 1987–; FCMA; *Recreations* tennis, golf; *Clubs* Four Oaks, Sutton Coldfield Golf; *Style*— Roy Amos, Esq; ✉ The Lodge, Roman Rd, Little Aston Park, Sutton Coldfield, W Midlands B74 3AA (☎ and fax 0121 353 5373)

AMOS, Valerie; *b* 13 March 1954; *Educ* Univ of Warwick (BA), Univ of Birmingham (MA), UEA; *Career* Lambeth Borough Cncl 1981–82, women's advsr London Borough of Camden 1983–85, freelance organisational and mgmnt devpt conslt 1984–89, head of mgmnt servs London Borough of Hackney 1987–89 (head of trg and devpt 1985–87); chief exec Equal Opportunities Cmmn 1989–94, md Quality and Equality 1994–95, dir Amos Fraser Bernard 1995–; non-exec dir UCLH; author and presenter numerous papers at nat and int confs; external examiner Univ of Liverpool, hon prof Thames Valley Univ; memb: Cncl Inst of Employment Studies, Cncl King's Fund; dep chair Runnymede Tst; chair: Bd of Govrs RCN, Advsy Bd Windsor Leadership Tst, AFIYA Tst; dir Hampstead Theatre, tstee Inst of Public Policy Research; FRSA; *Style*— Ms Valerie Amos; ✉ Amos Fraser Bernard Consultancy and Training Partnership, 4 Avenue Mansions, St Paul's Avenue, London NW2 2UG (☎ and fax 0181 830 4379)

AMPHLETT, Philip Nicholas; s of Colin Bernard Amphlett, of Wootton Village, Oxford, and Hilda, *née* Price (d 1972); *b* 20 Oct 1948; *Educ* Winchester, Balliol Coll Oxford (BA); *m* 4 Aug 1969, Marjolein Erantha, da of Jan Cornelius de Vries (d 1952), of Eindhoven, Holland; 1 s (Jan b 17 Aug 1972), 2 da (Jessica b 9 Jan 1970, Catherine b 14 Nov 1974); *Career* trainee mangr W H Brandts Sons and Co Ltd 1971–73, dir Henry Ansbacher and Co Ltd 1981–85 (joined 1973), sr vice pres Bank Julius Baer and Co Ltd 1985–; *Recreations* sailing, swimming, tennis; *Style*— Philip Amphlett, Esq; ✉ Howletts, Gt Hallingbury, Bishops Stortford, Herts (☎ 01279 54563); Ballaminers Cottage, Little Petherick, nr Wadebridge, N Cornwall; Bank Julius Baer and Co Ltd, Bevis Marks House, Bevis Marks, London EC3A 7NE (☎ 0171 623 4211, fax 0171 283 6146, telex 887272)

AMPTHILL, 4 Baron (UK 1881); Geoffrey Denis Erskine Russell; CBE (1986), PC (1995); s of late 3 Baron Ampthill, CBE, by his 1 w, Christabel, da of Lt-Col John Hart, by his w, Blanche, 4 da of Capt David Erskine (2 s of Sir David Erskine, 1 Bt); suc 1973; *b* 15 Oct 1921; *Educ* Stowe; *m* 1, 1946 (m dis 1971), Susan Mary Sheila, da of Hon Charles Winn (2 s of 2 Baron St Oswald, JP, DL) by his 1 w, Hon Olive Paget (da of 1 and last Baron Queenborough, GBE, JP); 2 s (and 1 s decd), 1 da; m 2, 1972 (m dis 1987), Elisabeth Anne-Marie, da of late Claude Mallon, of Paris, and of Mme Chavane; *Heir* s, Hon David Russell; *Career* WWII Capt Irish Gds; gen mangr Fortnum & Mason 1947–51, chm New Providence Hotel Co Ltd 1952–58, md various theatre owning and producing cos 1953–81; dir: Dualvest 1980–87, United News & Media plc (formerly United Newspapers) 1981–96 (dep chm 1991–96), Express Newspapers plc 1985– (dep chm 1989–); dep chm of Ctees House of Lords 1981–92 (chm 1992–94), dep speaker 1983–; chm Select Ctee on: Channel Tunnel Bill 1987, Channel Tunnel Rail Link Bill 1996; dir Leeds Castle Fndn 1980–82; *Style*— The Rt Hon the Lord Ampthill, CBE, PC; ✉ 6 North Court, Great Peter Street, London SW1P 3LL

AMWELL, 3 Baron (UK 1947), of Islington, Co London; Keith Norman Montague; s of 2 Baron Amwell (d 1990), and Kathleen Elizabeth, *née* Fountain; *b* 1 April 1943; *Educ* Ealing GS, Nottingham Univ (BSc); *m* 1970, Mary, o da of Frank Palfreyman, of Potters Bar, Herts; 2 s (Hon Ian b 1973, Hon Christopher b 1977); *Heir* s, Hon Ian Montague b 1973; *Career* consulting civil engr Brian Colquhoun and Partners 1965–94; dir Thorburn Colquhoun Ltd 1994–96; CEng, CGeol, FICE, FGS, MIHT, MIQA; *Recreations* walking, gardening, photography, badminton; *Style*— The Rt Hon Lord Amwell

AMY, Dennis Oldrieve; CMG (1992), OBE (1984); s of George Arthur Amy (d 1969), and Isabella Thompson, *née* Crosby (d 1973); *b* 21 Oct 1932; *Educ* Southall GS Middx; *m* 31 March 1956, Helen Rosamunde, da of Wilfred Leslie Clemens (d 1991); 1 s (Robin Clemens b 1957), 1 da (Bryony Crosby (Mrs Bryony Matthews) b 1960); *Career* Nat Serv RM 1951–53; HM Dip Serv: FO 1949–51 and 1953–58, Athens 1958–61, second sec Moscow 1961–63, FO and DSAO 1963–66, second sec Canberra 1966–70, first sec Ibadan 1971–74, FCO 1974–78 (seconded to Dept of Trade 1974–76), first sec Santiago 1978–83 (chargé d'affaires 1979), first sec FCO 1983–85, cnsllr and head of dept FCO 1985–86, consul gen Bordeaux 1986–89, ambass Republic of Madagascar 1990–92, non-resident ambass to Federal Islamic Republic of the Comoros 1991–92; *Recreations* golf, Scottish dancing, church; *Style*— Dennis Amy, Esq, CMG, OBE; ✉ Timbers, Hambledon Road, Godalming, Surrey GU7 1PJ

AMYES, Prof Sebastian Giles Becket; s of Julian Charles Becket Amyes (d 1992), of London, and Katherine Anne Smith, *née* Allan; *b* 6 May 1949; *Educ* Cranleigh Sch, UCL (BSc), Univ of Reading (MSc), Univ of London (PhD, DSc); *m* 17 April 1976, Dorothy Mary, da of William Thomas Gregory; 1 s (Rupert William Becket b 26 May 1978), 1 da (Alexandra Katherine Becket b 15 Nov 1979); *Career* teaching fell Sch of Pharmacy Univ of London 1974–77, prof of microbial chemotherapy Univ of Edinburgh 1992– (lectr 1977–88, reader 1988–92); Annual Science award Royal Pharmaceutical Soc 1984, C L Oakley lectureship Pathological Soc 1987; author of 250 pubns; FRCPath 1995 (MRCPath 1985), FIBiol 1988; *Recreations* fishing, foreign exploration, golf, opera; *Style*— Prof Sebastian Amyes; ✉ Department of Medical Microbiology, The Medical School, University of Edinburgh, Teviot Place, Edinburgh EH8 9AG (☎ 0131 650 3163, fax 0131 650 6882)

ANAND, Valerie May Florence; da of John McCormick Stubington (d 1967), of Mitcham, and Florence Louise, *née* Sayers; *b* 1937; *Educ* Mitcham Co Sch for Girls; *m* 26 March 1970, Dalip Singh Anand, s of Sunder Singh Anand; *Career* novelist; typist Sudanese Embassy 1956, shorthand typist then sec Odhams Press 1956–59, sec then editorial asst Quarry Managers' Journal 1959–60, asst PR offr Institute of Launderers, editorial asst Accountancy 1963–66, journalist Index to Office Equipment & Supplies 1966–69, PR offr E J Poole Associates 1969–71, asst ed then ed house magazine of Heals 1971–75, ed Matthew Hall News 1975–88, full time novelist 1988–; memb: Richard III Soc 1981–, Exmoor Soc 1985– (memb Ctee London Area Branch 1994–), Soc of Authors 1989–, Tolkein Soc 1992–; *Novels* Gildenford (1978), The Norman Pretender (1979), The

Disputed Crown (1981), To A Native Shore (1984), King of the Wood (1988), Crown of Roses (1989), The Proud Villeins (1990), The Ruthless Yeomen (1991), West of Sunset (1992), Women of Ashdon (1992), The Faithful Lovers (1993), The Cherished Wives (1994), The Dowerless Sisters (1995), The Robsart Mystery (as Fiona Buckley, 1997); *Recreations* reading, conversation and argument, good food and wine, used to ride horses; *Style*— Mrs Valerie Anand; ✉ c/o Mr David Grossman, David Grossman Literary Agency, 118b Holland Park Avenue, London W11 4VA (☎ 0171 221 2770)

ANASTASI, George; s of Michael Anastasi, and Paraskevou, *née* Mattheou; *b* 20 Oct 1941; *Educ* The Quintin Sch London, Goldsmiths' Coll London; *m* 19 Dec 1964, Maureen Gillian Gloria, da of Alfred Charles Adams (d 1959); 1 s (Robert Matthew b 23 Nov 1979); *Career* asst vice pres Deltec Trading Co Ltd London 1969–73; mangr: First Boston Corp London 1973–74, Williams & Glyn's Bank Ltd London 1974–78; dir Donaldson Lufkin & Jenrette London 1978–80, exec mangr Arab International Finance Ltd London 1980–83, Svenska International plc London 1983–91, Svenska Handelsbanken 1983–; *Clubs* National Liberal; *Style*— George Anastasi, Esq; ✉ 7 Clarendon Way, Chislehurst, Kent BR7 6RE (☎ 01689 820112); Svenska Handelsbanken, Svenska House, 3–5 Newgate St, London EC1A 7DA (☎ 0171 329 4467, fax 0171 329 0036/7, telex 89471)

ANCASTER, Earl of *see:* Willoughby de Eresby, Baroness

ANCRAM, Rt Hon Earl of; Michael Andrew Foster Jude Kerr; PC (1996), QC (1996), DL (Roxburgh, Ettrick and Lauderdale, 1990), MP (C) Devizes (maj 19,712); s and h of 12 Marquess of Lothian; *b* 7 July 1945; *Educ* Ampleforth, ChCh Oxford (MA), Edinburgh Univ (LLB); *m* 1975, Lady Jane Fitzalan-Howard, da of 16 Duke of Norfolk, KG, GCVO, GBE, TD, PC (d 1975), and Lavinia, Duchess of Norfolk, LG, CBE (d 1995); 2 da (Lady Clare b 1979, Lady Mary b 1981); *Heir* bro, Lord Ralph Kerr; *Career* advocate (Scot) 1970; MP (C): Berwickshire and E Lothian Feb-Sept 1974, Edinburgh S 1979–87 (also contested 1987), Devizes 1992–; memb Public Accounts Ctee 1992–93; Parly under sec NI Office 1993–94; min of state NI Office 1994–; chm Cons Party in Scotland 1980–83 (vice chm 1975–80), memb Select Ctee on Energy 1979–83, Parly under-sec Scottish Office (Home Affairs and Environment) 1983–87; chm Northern Corporate Communications Ltd 1989–91, memb Bd Scottish Homes 1988–90; chm Scottish Cncl of Ind Schs 1988–90; govr Napier Poly of Edinburgh 1989–90, pres Environmental Medicine Fndn 1988–92, chm Waverley Housing Tst 1988–90; *Recreations* photography, folksinging; *Clubs* New (Edinburgh), Pratt's, Beefsteak; *Style*— The Rt Hon Earl of Ancram, DL, QC, MP; ✉ c/o House of Commons, London SW1A 0AA

ANDERSON, Alastair William; TD (1966); s of Cecil Brown Anderson, of 5 Dorchester Court, Glasgow (d 1965), and Janet Davidson, *née* Bell (d 1966); *b* 9 Aug 1931; *Educ* The High Sch of Glasgow, Univ of Glasgow (BSc); *m* 6 Sept 1957, Jennifer Mary, da of Maj Charles W Markham (d 1942), of Clarkston, Glasgow; 1 s (Keith Charles b 30 July 1962); *Career* Nat Serv cmmnd 2 Lt RE 1954, served Britcom Engr Regt Br Cwlth Forces Korea 1954–56, TA 1956–67, Maj RE; Crouch and Hogg Consultant Engineers: joined 1956, assoc 1966–, ptnr 1971, sr ptnr 1981–90; chm Crouch Hogg Waterman Consulting Engineers 1990–92 (conslt 1992–); memb Court Univ of Glasgow 1996–; CEng, MConsE, FICE, FIHT, FRSA; *Recreations* golf, gardening, reading, walking; *Clubs* Royal Scottish Automobile; *Style*— Alastair Anderson, Esq, TD; ✉ Storrs, 7 Greenbank Ave, Whitecraigs, Giffnock, Glasgow G46 6SG (☎ 0141 639 2343); Crouch Hogg Waterman Consulting Civil and Structural Engineers, The Octagon, 35 Baird St, Glasgow G4 0EE (☎ 0141 552 2000, fax 0141 552 2525, telex 779860)

ANDERSON, Dr Alun Mark; s of Peter Marchmont Anderson, of Clwyd, North Wales, and Jane Watkin James; *b* 27 May 1948; *Educ* Rhyl GS, Univ of Sussex (BSc), Univ of Edinburgh (PhD), Univ of Oxford (IBM res fell), Univ of Kyoto Japan (Royal Soc fell); *Career* Nature (Int Jl of Sci): news and views ed 1980–83, Tokyo bureau chief 1983–86, Washington bureau chief 1986–90; int ed Science 1991–92, ed New Scientist 1992–; *Books* Science Technology In Japan (1984, 2 edn 1990); *Recreations* mountain walking, photography; *Style*— Dr Alun Anderson; ✉ Editor, New Scientist, King's Reach Tower, Stamford Street, London SE1 9LS (direct ☎ 0171 261 7301, fax 0171 261 6464)

ANDERSON, Anthony John; QC (1982); s of A Fraser Anderson (d 1982), and Margaret Gray, *née* Spence (d 1986); *b* 12 Sept 1938; *Educ* Harrow, Magdalen Coll Oxford (MA); *m* 1970, Fenja Ragnhild, da of Havard Gunn, OBE; *Career* 2 Lt Gordon Highlanders 1957–59; called to the Bar Inner Temple 1964, bencher 1992, recorder of the Crown Court 1995–; chm of tbnls Securities and Futures Authy (formerly The Securities Assoc) 1988–; *Recreations* golf, fishing; *Clubs* Garrick, MCC; *Style*— Anthony Anderson, Esq, QC; ✉ 2 Mitre Court Buildings, Temple, London EC4 (☎ 0171 583 1380)

ANDERSON, Brett; *Career* singer; fndr memb Suede 1989–; 3 top twenty singles (Metal Mickey 1992, We Are the Pigs 1994, The Wild Ones 1994), 3 top ten singles (Animal Nitrate 1993, Stay Together 1994, Trash 1996); albums: Suede (1993, UK no 1), Dog Man Star (1994), Coming Up (1996, UK no 1); Mercury Music Award 1993; *Style*— Brett Anderson, Esq; ✉ c/o Interceptor Enterprises, 98 White Lion Street, London N1 9PF (☎ 0171 278 8001, fax 0171 713 6298)

ANDERSON, Clive Stuart; *Educ* Selwyn Coll Cambridge (MA, pres Cambridge Footlights); *Career* television presenter and barrister; called to the Bar Middle Temple 1976; host The Cabaret Upstairs (BBC Radio 4) 1986–88, chairman Whose Line Is It Anyway? (Radio 4 1988, Channel Four Television 1988–), host Clive Anderson Talks Back (Channel Four) 1989–, presenter Notes and Queries (BBC2) 1991–93, presenter Great Railway Journeys of the World: Hong Kong to Outer Mongolia (BBC2) 1994, documentary series Our Man In... (BBC2) 1995– (author of book to accompany the series entitled Our Man In...), presenter Our Man In Heaven & Hell 1996, presenter Clive Anderson All Talk (BBC 1) 1996–, occasional presenter/guest numerous other progs; formerly scriptwriter: Weekending (BBC Radio 4), The Frankie Howerd Variety Show (Radio 4), Not the Nine O'Clock News (BBC2), Alas Smith & Jones (notably head-to-head dialogues, BBC2), Around Midnight (LWT), The World According to Smith & Jones (LWT); memb revue group An Evening Without (toured England, Scotland and Australia) 1979, numerous stand-up comedy appearances Comedy Store and other venues in early 1980s; author of various articles in The Times, The Observer and The Guardian, former regular columnist Sunday Correspondent; *Awards* Comedy Presenter of the Year RTS Awards 1991, Top Channel 4 Presenter British Comedy Awards 1992; for Whose Line Is It Anyway?: Best Light Entertainment Prog RTS Awards 1990, Best International Comedy Series ACE Awards 1991, Best Light Entertainment Prog Br Academy Awards 1991 (also nominated 1990 and 1992), also nominated for Top Entertainment Series Br Comedy Awards 1991 and Best Popular Arts Prog International Emmy Awards 1991, TRIC Best ITV/Channel 4 TV Personality Award 1995; *Style*— Clive Anderson, Esq; ✉ c/o London Management & Representation Ltd, 2 Noel Street, London W1V 3RB (☎ 0171 287 9000)

ANDERSON, (Richard James) Colin; s of Richard Henry Anderson (d 1979), and Roseina, *née* Blaney; *b* 11 May 1954; *Educ* Regent House GS, Univ of Ulster; *m* 18 May 1978, Hilary Ann, da of Wilson Somerville Smyth; 2 s (Kyle, Jeffrey), 1 da (Kelly); *Career* trainee Thomson Newspapers Orgn, fndr md and princ shareholder Anderson Advertising Ltd, chm Anderson Group of Companies; visiting prof Dept of Communication Faculty of Social and Health Scis Univ of Ulster; pres NI C of C and Indust; dir NI Quality Centre 1993–96; memb NI Tourist Bd (Govt appt) 1988–94, former cncl memb NI Branch Inst of Mktg; rugby rep for: Ulster, Ards Rugby Club, CIYMS Rugby Club; Duke of Edinburgh's Gold Award (ctee memb NI 1989–92); MInstD, MCIM; *Recreations* yachting, skiing, golf, rugby; *Clubs* Royal Ulster Yacht; *Style*— Colin Anderson, Esq; ✉ Anderson Group Holdings (NI) Ltd, Anderson House, Holywood Rd, Belfast BT4 2GU (☎ 01232 768714, fax 01232 760991)

ANDERSON, Colin William; s of Laurence Robert Dacre Anderson (d 1971), of Reading, Berks, and Margaret Alice, *née* Wynn-Evans (d 1991); *b* 15 Jan 1930; *Educ* Rugby; *m* 1, 1957 (m dis 1985), Elizabeth Davinia, *née* Leyshon; 1 da (Rachel b 5 Aug 1959), 3 s (Charles b 10 Dec 1960, Guy b 26 Jan 1963, Harry b 18 Oct 1964); m 2, 1986, Felicity Anne Leader, da of Lt Harold Chapman, RN (ka 1939); *Career* Geo Peters & Co wine merchants Portsmouth 1950–60: joined as office boy to Gen Mangr, Vintners scholarship 1953, MW 1957; buyer Friary Meux Guildford 1960–64; Grants of St James's (Allied Lyons) 1964–86: quality control mangr 1965–69, buyer 1969–72, buying dir 1972–86; wine devpt dir European Cellars Ltd 1986, int wine conslt 1987– (currently wine conslt to BA); Inst of Masters of Wine: vice chm 1988–89, chm 1989–90, chm Cert of Excellence Ctee 1992–; Ordre du Merite Agricole France 1974; *Recreations* fishing, ornithology, food and wine; *Style*— C W Anderson, Esq; ✉ Coralclass Ltd, The Toll House, Frensham, Farnham, Surrey GU10 3DZ (☎ 01252 792622, fax 01252 795342)

ANDERSON, Rear Adm (Charles) Courtney; CB (1971); s of Lt-Col Charles Anderson (d 1919), Australian Light Horse, and Constance Powell-Anderson, OBE, JP; *b* 8 Nov 1916; *Educ* RNC Dartmouth; *m* 1940, Pamela Ruth, da of Lt-Col William Miles, RM (d 1947); 3 s; *Career* RN 1930, served WWII in cmd of Motor Torpedo Boats, Destroyers and Frigates, Naval Intelligence 1946–49 and 1955–57, cmd HMS Contest 1949–51, Cdr 1952, BJSM Washington 1953–55, Capt 1959, naval attaché Bonn 1962–64, dir Naval Recruiting 1965–68, ADC to HM The Queen 1968, Rear-Adm 1969, flag offr Admty Interview Bd 1969–71, ret; ed The Board Bulletin 1971–78; *Books* The Drum Beats Still (1951), Bats in my Belfry (1997); numerous articles and short stories; *Recreations* gardening, Sea Cadets; *Style*— Rear Adm Courtney Anderson, CB; ✉ Bybrook Cottage, Bustlers Hill, Sherston, Malmesbury, Wilts SN16 0ND (☎ 01666 840323)

ANDERSON, David Colville; VRD (1947, clasp 1958), QC (Scot 1957); s of John Lindsay Anderson, of Pittormie, Fife (d 1943), and Etta Colville (d 1949); *b* 8 Sept 1916; *Educ* Trinity Coll Glenalmond (Ashburton Shield winner 1933), Pembroke Coll Oxford (BA), Univ of Edinburgh (Thow scholar, LLB, Maclagan prize in forensic med); *m* 1948, Juliet, yr da of Hon Lord Hill Watson, MC, of Barlanark, Edinburgh (d 1957); 2 s (Laurence and Gavin), 1 da (Lorraine); *Career* WWII Lt RNVR N Sea destroyers and in Norway (despatches); Admty Egerton Prize for 1943 in Naval Gunnery; advocate 1946, lectr in Scots law Univ of Edinburgh 1948–60, standing jr counsel War Office 1955–57; Parly candidate (C): Coatbridge 1955, East Dunbartonshire 1959; MP (C) Dumfries Dec 1963–Sept 1964; slr-gen Scotland 1960–64; chief reporter for public inquiries Scottish Office 1972–74, under-sec Civil Serv 1972–74; cmmr Northern Lighthouses 1960–64 (vice chm 1964); Hon Sheriff Lothians 1965–74; chm Industl Appeal Tbnls (Scot) 1970–72; King Haakon VII Freedom Medal (Norway) 1945; subject of the play The Case of David Anderson, QC by John Hale (Manchester 1980, Edinburgh 1980, Lyric Hammersmith 1981); *Clubs* New (Edinburgh), Scottish Ornithologists (fndr memb 1936); *Style*— David Anderson, Esq, VRD, QC; ✉ Barlanark, 8 Arboretum Rd, Edinburgh EH3 5PD, Scotland (☎ 0131 552 3003)

ANDERSON, HE Judge David Heywood; CMG (1982); *b* 14 Sept 1937; *Educ* Univ of Leeds (LLB), LSE (LLM); *Career* called to the bar Gray's Inn 1963; FCO: asst legal advsr 1960–69, legal advsr British Embassy Bonn 1969–72, legal cnsllr 1972–79, legal advsr UK Mission to the UN New York 1979–82, legal cnsllr 1982–87, dep legal advsr 1987–89, second legal advsr 1989–96; judge Int Tbnl for the Law of the Sea 1996–; memb: Study Gp of the British Inst of Int and Comparative Law on Jt Devpt of Offshore Oil and Gas 1989, British Branch Int Law Assoc, Ctee on Public Int Law British Inst of Int and Comparative Law 1992–; memb UK Delgn to: Vienna Conf on the Law of Treaties 1968, UN Ctee on Peaceful Uses of the Seabed 1973, Third UN Conf on the Law of the Sea 1973–77, S Atlantic Fisheries Cmmn (Argentina and UK) 1991–96; ldr UK Delgn for: Preparatory Cmmn for the Int Sea Bed Authy and the Int Tribunal for the Law of the Sea 1990–94, Maritime Boundary Negotiations 1986–, UN Conf on Straddling Fish Stocks and Highly Migratory Fish Stocks 1993–95; *Style*— HE Judge David Anderson, CMG; ✉ International Tribunal for the Law of the Sea, Wexstrasse 4, 20354 Hamburg, Germany (☎ 00 49 40 3589 683, fax 00 49 40 3589 686)

ANDERSON, David Munro; s of Alexander Anderson, of St Clements, Jersey, CI, and Jessica Hope, *née* Vincent-Innes; *b* 15 Dec 1937; *Educ* Strathallan Sch Perth; *m* 1, 3 April 1965, Veronica Jane, da of Reginald Eric Stevens; 2 s (Angus b 1 Oct 1967, Duncan b 10 Nov 1968), 1 da (Lucy b 29 Sept 1973); m 2, Ruth, da of Lt-Col E Lewis-Bowen (late RAVC); *Career* cmmnd The Black Watch 1956–59; The London Scottish 1963–68; chm Allingham Anderson Roll Ross Ltd 1990–; churchwarden Holy Innocents Lamarsh, memb Lamarsh PCC; tstee The Wilderness Tst; MSI; *Recreations* shooting, skiing, gundog training, the arts; *Clubs* Caledonian; *Style*— David Anderson, Esq; ✉ Clees Hall, Bures, Suffolk CO8 5DZ; Allingham Anderson Roll Ross Ltd, 23 Camomile St, London EC3A 7PP

ANDERSON, Donald; MP (Lab) Swansea E (majority 23,482); s of David Robert Anderson (d 1954), of Swansea, and Eva, *née* Mathias (d 1994); *b* 17 June 1939; *Educ* Swansea GS, Univ Coll Swansea (BA); *m* 28 Sept 1963, Dorothy Mary, da of Rev Frank L Trotman (d 1969), of Bolivia; 3 s (Robert b 24 Dec 1964, Hugh b 17 Nov 1967, Geraint b 20 Sept 1972); *Career* called to the Bar Inner Temple 1969; HM Foreign Serv 1960–64 (third sec Br Embassy Budapest 1963–64); lectr in politics Univ Coll Swansea 1964–66; MP (Lab): Monmouth 1966–70, Swansea E 1974–; PPS to: Min of Defence 1969–70, Attorney Gen 1974–79; chm Select Ctee on Welsh Affairs 1981–83, oppn spokesman: foreign affairs 1983–92, defence 1993–94; memb Chairmen's Panel 1995–; chm: Welsh Lab Gp 1977–78, Br Zimbabwe Gp, Parly Christian Fellowship 1990–93, chm Br German Parly Gp 1994–; vice chm: Br French Parly Gp, Br Norwegian Gp; vice chm and treas IPU 1986–90 (treas 1990–91 and 1993–95); cncllr Royal Borough of Kensington and Chelsea 1971–75; chm Nat Prayer Breakfast 1989, bd memb World Vision of Britain 1991–94, pres The Boys' Brigade in Wales 1991–; hon fell Univ Coll Swansea; Cdr's Cross Order of FRG for contrib to Br German Relations 1986; *Style*— Donald Anderson, Esq, MP; ✉ c/o House of Commons, London SW1A 0AA (☎ 0171 219 3425/6562)

ANDERSON, Douglas Hardinge; s of James Alasdair Anderson (d 1982), of Tullichewan, and Lady Flavia Joan Lucy Anderson, *née* Giffard; *b* 8 Aug 1934; *Educ* Eton; *m* 1, 1962 (m dis), Mary Jenkins; 1 da (Lucy Elizabeth b 1962), 1 s (James Henry Wallace b 1964); m 2, 1974, Veronica, da of John Markes; 1 da (Sophie Esme b 1977); *Career* portrait painter and wildlife artist; trained with Pietro Annigoni in Florence; exhbns in Florence, Munich, RA London, Royal Hibernian Acad Ireland, Gothenberg, Stockholm, New York and others; paintings in private collections in Europe, USA, etc; cmmnd for portraits of HM The Queen, HM Queen Elizabeth, The Queen Mother and HRH The Princess of Wales (for The Royal Marsden Hospital); memb RSPP 1957; *Recreations* painting, fishing, shooting, gardening, orchids and cooking; *Clubs* Turf; *Style*— Douglas Anderson, Esq; ✉ 56036 Palaia (Pisa), Italy (☎ and fax 00 39 587 622382)

ANDERSON, Douglas Kinloch; OBE (1983); s of William James Kinloch Anderson, of Edinburgh, and Margaret, *née* Gowenlock Harper; *b* 19 Feb 1939; *Educ* George Watson's Coll Edinburgh, Univ of St Andrews (MA), Univ of Edinburgh; *m* 16 June 1962, Deirdre Anne Kinloch, da of Leonard Walter Loryman (d 1985); 2 s (Peter Douglas b 1968, John William b 1972), 1 da (Claire Deirdre b 1964); *Career* Kinloch Anderson Ltd: dir 1962–72, md 1972–, chm 1980– (Queen's Award for Export Achievement 1979), chm Kinloch Anderson (Holdings) Ltd; dir: Carnegie Robertson & Black Ltd, Scottish Eastern Investment Trust plc, Fidelity Special Values plc; pres: Edinburgh Assoc of Royal Tradesmen 1986–88, Edinburgh C of C 1988–90, Royal Warrant Holders Assoc 1994–95; memb: Bd Scottish Tourist Bd 1986–92, Edinburgh Festival Cncl 1988–90, Scottish Ctee IOD; hon memb St Andrews Soc Washington DC 1985; Edinburgh Merchant Company: asst 1976–79, treas 1988–90, Master 1990–92; *Recreations* fishing, golf, travel, reading; *Clubs* New (Edinburgh), The Honourable Co of Edinburgh Golfers, Bruntsfield Golfing Soc, Caledonian; *Style*— Douglas Kinloch Anderson, Esq, OBE; ✉ Brockham Green, 36A Kings Road, Longniddry, E Lothian EH32 0NN (☎ 01875 52302); Kinloch Anderson Ltd, Commercial Street/Dock Street, Leith, Edinburgh EH6 6EY (☎ 0131 555 1355, fax 0131 555 1392)

ANDERSON, Eric George; s of Charles G Anderson (d 1984), of Alyth, Perthshire, and Margery Drysdale, *née* Taylor (d 1992); *b* 7 June 1940; *Educ* Dundee HS, Univ of St Andrews (MB ChB), Univ of Salford (MSc); *m* 26 March 1966, Elizabeth Clare (Liz), da of Donald George Cracknell (d 1995), of Appin, Argyll; 1 s (Colin b 1967), 2 da (Fiona b 1969, Heather b 1973); *Career* sr registrar Robert Jones and Agnes Hunt Orthopaedic Hosp Oswestry and Birmingham Accident Hosp 1973–78, conslt orthopaedic surgn Western Infirmary and Gartnavel Gen Hosp Glasgow 1978–, hon clinical sr lectr Univ of Glasgow 1978–, clinical assoc Univ of Strathclyde 1979–, visiting lectr in surgery Glasgow Caledonian Univ 1994–; memb Surgical Faculty Coll of Podiatrists, hon med advsr Scot Amateur Swimming Assoc, past pres Br Orthopaedic Foot Surgery Soc, sec gen Int Fedn of Foot and Ankle Socs, memb Cncl Euro Fedn of Foot and Ankle Socs; dep ed Injury; memb Editorial Bd: Foot, Foot Diseases, Foot and Ankle Surgery; memb Int Soc Prosthetics and Orthotics 1976, fell Br Orthopaedic Assoc 1978, memb Br Orthopaedic Foot Surgery Soc 1981, corresponding memb American Orthopaedic Foot and Ankle Soc 1996; FRCS (Edinburgh 1971, Glasgow 1981), FRSM 1973, Hon FChS; *Books* contrib: Common Foot Disorders (1989), The Foot and its Disorders (1991), Airds Companion to Surgical Studies (1997); *Recreations* philately, modelling buses and tramways, music; *Style*— Eric Anderson, Esq; ✉ 102 Prestonfield, Milngavie, Glasgow G62 7PZ (☎ 0141 956 3594, fax 0141 955 0324); Department of Orthopaedic Surgery, Western Infirmary, Glasgow G11 6NT (☎ 0141 211 1853, fax 0141 339 0462); Glasgow Nuffield Hospital, Beaconsfield Rd, Glasgow G12 0PJ (☎ 0141 334 9441)

ANDERSON, Dr (William) Eric Kinloch; s of William James Kinloch Anderson, of Edinburgh; *b* 27 May 1936; *Educ* George Watson's Coll, Univ of St Andrews (MA), Balliol Coll Oxford (MLitt); *m* 1960, Anne Elizabeth (Poppy), da of William Mattock Mason (d 1988), of Yorks; 1 s (David b 1961), 1 da (Catherine b 1963); *Career* asst master: Fettes 1960–64 and 1966–70, Gordonstoun 1964–66; headmaster: Abingdon Sch 1970–75, Shrewsbury Sch 1975–80, Eton Coll 1980–94; rector Lincoln Coll Oxford 1994–; tstee Nat Heritage Meml Fund 1996–; hon fell Balliol Coll Oxford 1989; Hon DLitt: Univ of St Andrews 1981, Univ of Hull 1994; Liveryman Worshipful Company of Drapers; FRSE 1985; *Books* Journal of Sir Walter Scott (ed, 1972), The Percy Letters Vol IX (ed, 1989); *Recreations* golf, fishing; *Style*— Dr Eric Anderson, FRSE; ✉ Lincoln College, University of Oxford, Oxford OX1 3DR (☎ 01865 279800)

ANDERSON, Prof Sir (William) Ferguson; kt (1974), OBE (1961); s of Capt James Kirkwood Anderson, 7 Scottish Rifles (ka Gaza 1917), and late Sarah Barr Anderson; *b* 8 April 1914; *Educ* Merchiston, Glasgow Acad, Univ of Glasgow (MB ChB, MD); *m* 1940, Margaret Gebbie; 1 s, 2 da; *Career* physician in geriatric med Stobhill Gen Hosp and advsr in diseases of old age and chronic sickness; W Region Hosp Bd Scotland 1952–74, David Cargill prof of geriatric med Univ of Glasgow 1965–79; hon pres Crossroads (Scot) Care Attendant Scheme; awarded Brookdale Prize from The Gerontological Soc of America 1984; FRCPGlas, FRCPEd, FRCP, FRCP (C), FRCPI, FACP, KStJ 1974; *Books* Practical Management of the Elderly (jtly, 1989); *Recreations* golf; *Clubs* Royal Scottish Automobile; *Style*— Prof Sir Ferguson Anderson, OBE; ✉ Rodel, Moor Rd, Strathblane, Glasgow G63 9EX (☎ 01360 770862)

ANDERSON, Gordon Alexander; s of Cecil Brown Anderson (d 1965), of Glasgow, and Janet Davidson, *née* Bell (d 1966); *b* 9 Aug 1931; *Educ* The High Sch of Glasgow; *m* 12 March 1958, Eirené Cochrane Howie, da of Richmond Douglas (d 1980), of Troon; 2 s (David b 1958, Colin b 1961), 1 da (Carolyn b 1967); *Career* Nat Serv RN (Sub Lt RNVR) 1955–57; CA 1955; Moores Carson & Watson Glasgow (which became McClelland Moores 1958, Arthur Young McClelland Moores 1968, Arthur Young 1985, Ernst & Young 1989): trainee 1949–55, sr asst 1957–58, ptnr 1958–90, memb Exec Ctee 1972–84, office managing ptnr Glasgow 1976–79, chm 1987–89, dep sr ptnr 1989–90; memb Cncl on Tribunals and its Scottish Ctee 1990–96; chm Bitmac Ltd 1990–96 (dir 1985–96), dir Douglas Firebrick Co Ltd 1960–70, chm TSB Bank Scotland plc 1994– (dir 1991–), dir TSB Group plc (now Lloyds TSB Group) 1993–; dir HS of Glasgow Ltd 1975–81 and 1990– (chm Govrs 1992–), dir Merchants House of Glasgow 1996, pres Glasgow HS Club 1978–79, memb Scot Milk Mktg Bd 1979–85; Inst of Chartered Accountants of Scot: memb Cncl 1980–84, vice pres 1984–86, pres 1986–87; FCMA 1984; *Recreations* golf, gardening, opera; *Clubs* Caledonian, Western (Glasgow), Glasgow Golf, Buchanan Castle Golf; *Style*— Gordon A Anderson, Esq; ✉ Ardwell, 41 Manse Road, Bearsden, Glasgow G61 3PN (☎ and fax 0141 942 2803); TSB Bank Scotland plc, Henry Duncan House, 120 George Street, Edinburgh EH2 4TS (☎ 0131 225 4555, fax 0131 220 0240)

ANDERSON, Hamish; s of Dr James Anderson, of Plymouth, and Joan, *née* Caughey; *b* 12 July 1948; *Educ* Clifton Coll, Kingston Poly (LLB), UCL (LLM); *m* 19 Aug 1972, Linda Stuart, da of Dr Norman Rutherford Carlson; 1 s (James b 1975), 1 da (Bryony b 1977); *Career* admitted slr 1973; pt/t lectr in law and res asst Kingston Poly 1969–71, licensed insolvency practitioner 1987–; ptnr: Bond Pearce 1977–96 (joined 1971), Norton Rose 1996–; memb: Consumer and Commercial Law Ctee Law Soc (memb Insolvency Sub-ctee), Cncl (and past pres) Insolvency Lawyers' Assoc, Cncl Soc of Practitioners of Insolvency, Law Soc, Plymouth Law Soc; ed Insolvency Practitioner, memb Editorial Bd Insolvency Law & Practice; *Books* Administrators - Part II of the Insolvency Act 1986, Anderson's Notes on Insolvency Conveyancing, Agricultural Charges and Receivership, Commercial Aspects of Trusts and Fiduciary Obligations (contrib), Current Issues in Insolvency Law (contrib), Lightman and Moss: The Law of Receivers of Companies (contrib); *Recreations* shooting, cycling, photography; *Style*— Hamish Anderson, Esq; ✉ Maristow Cottage, Maristow, Roborough, Devon PL6 7BZ (☎ 01752 730186); Norton Rose, Kempson House, PO Box 570, Camomile Street, London EC3A 7AN (☎ 0171 283 6000, fax 0171 283 6500)

ANDERSON, Janet; MP (Lab) Rossendale and Darwen (majority 120); da of late Tom Anderson, and late Ethel, *née* Pearson; *b* 6 Dec 1949; *Educ* Kingsfeld Comp Sch Bristol, Poly of Central London (Dip in Bilingual Business Studies), Univ of Nantes; *m* 2 Oct 1972, Vincent Humphreys, s of late William Humphreys; 2 s (James, David), 1 da (Katie); *Career* sec The Scotsman and Sunday Times 1971–74; PA to: Rt Hon Barbara Castle MP (later MEP) 1974–81, Jack Straw 1981–87; PLP campaign offr 1987–89, co-ordinator Lab Pty's Industry 2000 Campaign for Gordon Brown 1989–90, northern regnl organiser Shopping Hours Reform Cncl 1990–92, MP (Lab) Rossendale and Darwen 1992– (also contested 1987), PPS to Margaret Beckett MP (Dep Ldr of the Lab Pty) 1992–93, memb Select Ctee on Home Affrs 1994–95, oppn whip for Home & Legal Affrs 1995–96, shadow min for women 1996–; PLP rep House of Commons Cmmn 1993–94, co-ordinator Home Affrs Campaigns 1994–95, sec Tribune Gp of Labour MPs 1994–96, memb Lab Pty Nat Policy Forum 1995–; chair All Pty Footwear Gp 1992–, vice chair All Pty Exports Gp, treas All Pty Opera Gp; memb Steering Ctee Lab Women's Network, vice pres Assoc of Dist Cncls, memb Parly Panel RCN, vice chair Lab Campaign for Electoral Reform, hon advsr Emily's List UK; memb: GMB Union, Blackburn & Darwen CND, Blackburn & Darwen Anti-Apartheid, Rossendale & Dist Amnesty Int, League Against Cruel Sports; visiting fell St Antony's Coll Oxford; FRSA; *Recreations* playing the piano, opera, my family; *Style*— Ms Janet Anderson, MP; ✉ Constituency Office: 23 Bolton Road, Darwen, Lancashire BB3 1DF; House of Commons, London SW1A 0AA (☎ 0171 219 3000)

ANDERSON, Prof John; s of John Anderson (d 1963), of Newcastle upon Tyne, and Norah, *née* French (d 1992); *Educ* Royal GS Newcastle upon Tyne, The Med Sch Kings Coll Univ of Durham (Philipson scholar, MB BS), FRCP 1973 (MRCP 1961); *m* 12 May 1959, Mary, o da of Percival Bynon; 1 s (David Guy b 14 Aug 1960), 1 da (Deborah Jane b 13 Sept 1963); *Career* med registrar Royal Victoria Infirmary Newcastle upon Tyne 1962–64, research fell Univ of Virginia Charlottesville 1965–66; Univ of Newcastle: first asst in med 1967–68, sr lectr in med 1968–85, academic sub-dean Med Sch 1975–85, postgrad dean and dir Postgrad Inst for Med and Dentistry and prof of med educn 1985–; hon conslt physician Royal Victoria Infirmary 1968–; memb GMC 1980–; memb: Assoc for the Study of Med Educn (vice pres), BMA; FRCOG (ad eundem) 1983, FRCPGlas 1992; *Books* The Multiple Choice Question in Medicine (1976, 2 edn 1982); numerous chapters in books and papers in scientific jls on med, diabetes and med educn; *Recreations* listening to music, watching cricket, reading (anything), walking; *Clubs* Yorkshire CCC; *Style*— Prof John Anderson; ✉ 6 Wilson Gardens, Newcastle upon Tyne NE3 4JA; Postgraduate Institute for Medicine and Dentistry, 10–12 Framlington Place, Newcastle upon Tyne NE2 4AB (☎ 0191 222 6772, fax 0191 221 1049)

ANDERSON, Prof John Allan Dalrymple; TD (1967), DL (Richmond 1987–90, Greater London 1990–); s of Lt-Col John Allan Anderson, RAMC (d 1942), and Mary Winifred, *née* Lawson (d 1973); *b* 16 June 1926; *Educ* Loretto, Univ of Oxford (BA, MA), Univ of Edinburgh (MB ChB, MD), Univ of London (DPH); *m* 3 April 1965, Mairead Mary, da of Dr P D Maclaren (d 1967), of Edinburgh; 3 da (Sheena b 1966, Mary b 1968, Anne b 1972); *Career* Nat Serv Capt RAMC 1950–52, Maj RMO 7/9 Royal Scots (TA) 1953–63, Maj 51 Highland Vols OC G Co 1967–70, Lt-Col CO 221 Field Ambulance RAMC (TA), Col London Dist TA 1981–83, Regtl and Dep Hon Col 51 Highland Vols 1983–89, hon civilian conslt to Army (public health med); lectr Dept of Gen Practice Univ of Edinburgh 1954–59, physician and res fell Industrial Survey Unit Dept of Rheumatology Univ of Edinburgh 1960–63, sr lectr in preventive med London Sch of Hygiene and Tropical Med 1963–69, dir Dept of Community Med Guy's Hosp Med Sch (subsequently merged with St Thomas's to form Utd Med and Dental Schs) 1969–90, hon conslt Guy's Hosp 1969–90, med dir Occupational Health Serv Lewisham and N Southwark Health Dist 1984–90, academic registrar Faculty of Community Med 1983–89, prof and chm Dept of Public Health and Occupational Med Univ of UAE 1990–94; hon physician Royal Scottish Corp 1972–95, emeritus prof Univ of London and emeritus conslt Guy's Hosp 1990; Freeman City of London, Liveryman Worshipful Soc of Apothecaries; elder St Columbas Church of Scotland; FRCP 1987, FFCM 1974, FRCGP 1985, FFOM 1990; *Books* A New Look at Community Medicine (1966), Self-Medication (1970), Bibliography of Back Pain (1978), Epidemiological, Sociological and Environmental Aspects of Rheumatic Diseases (1987); *Recreations* hill walking, golf, bridge; *Clubs* New (Edinburgh); *Style*— Prof John Anderson, TD, DL; ✉ The Lanterns, 11 D Ettrick Road, Edinburgh EH10 5BJ (☎ 0131 229 0433)

ANDERSON, Maj-Gen Sir John Evelyn; KBE (1971, CBE 1963); s of Lt-Col John Gibson Anderson, of Christchurch, NZ, and Margaret, *née* Scott; *b* 28 June 1916; *Educ* King's Sch Rochester, RMA Woolwich; *m* 1944, Jean Isobel, 2 da of Charles Tait, of Tarves, Aberdeenshire; 1 s, 1 da; *Career* cmmnd Royal Signals 1936, Lt-Col 1956, Col 1960, Brig 1964, Maj-Gen 1967, Signal Offr in Chief (Army) MOD 1967–69, ACDS (Signals) 1969–72; Hon Col: 71 (Yeo) Signal Regt TAVR 1969–76, Women's Tport Corps (FANY) 1970–76 (vice pres 1994–); dir-gen NATO Integrated Communication System Mgmnt Agency 1977–81, conslt electronics and communications 1981–93, exec dir AFCEA Europe Gp 1981–88, dir Space & Maritime Applications Inc 1988–92; *Recreations* fishing, gardening; *Clubs* Army & Navy, Flyfishers'; *Style*— Maj-Gen Sir John Anderson, KBE; ✉ The Beeches, Amport, nr Andover, Hants SP11 8BW

ANDERSON, John Heugh; s of Samuel Caldwell Anderson (d 1974), and Jemima Fraser, *née* Cameron (d 1980); *Educ* Queens Park Sr Secdy Sch Glasgow, Jordanhill Coll of Educn, Univ of Strathclyde, Open Univ; *m* 19 Nov 1988, Dorothy Margaret, da of James Holton Beresford; *Career* Nat Serv 1953–55; athletics coach and leisure conslt; teacher Glasgow 1955–64, nat coach AAA 1964–65, Scot nat coach 1965–70, dir of physical recreation Heriot-Watt 1970–74, chief leisure and recreation offr Nuneaton and Bedworth Borough Cncl 1974–84, dir of leisure and recreation London Borough of Southwark 1984–89 (leisure conslt 1989–), external examiner BSc (Hons) sport course Univ of Nottingham 1987–91, dir of trg and referee Gladiators TV prog (ITV) 1992–; athletics coordinator Br Paralympic Assoc 1991–92, chief coach special needs Br Athletics 1992–94, race dir The Standard Life Prince's Street Mile 1992; GB team coach track and field for all major championships 1981–90 incl: Olympic Games 1984 and 1988, Cwlth Games 1982 and 1986, World Championships 1983 and 1987, Euro Championships 1982, 1986, 1990, Euro Cup 1981, 1985 and 1989; team mangr Scotland for Cwlth Games Kuala Lumpur 1998; over 100 GB athletes coached incl: David Moorcroft, David Bedford, David Jenkins, Linsey Macdonald, Liz McColgan, Judy Simpson, Eugene Gilkes, Lynne McDougall (formerly McIntyre); only person to have coached athletes to GB standard in every event, first person to pass all sr AAA coaching awards in all events 1964, first Scotsman to pass full FA Badge 1961, fndr original Passport to Leisure Scheme Nuneaton and Bedworth; first chm Nat Assoc of Sports Coaches 1993–95; sporting achievements: Scot Schs football 1950, footballer Scot Amateur League, finalist LTA W of Scot Doubles Shield; Churchill fell 1971; Olympic coach of the year 1988; *Recreations* coaching the disabled in athletics, reading, walking the dog in the country, jogging, cycling, tennis, golf, computer use; *Style*— John H Anderson, Esq; ✉ 3 The Heathery, Masterton Road, Dunfermline, Fife KY11 5TS (☎ 01383 723555, fax 01383 732321)

ANDERSON, John Stewart; TD (and Bar); s of Percy Stewart Anderson (d 1960), and Mabel France, *née* Jones (d 1962); *b* 3 Aug 1935; *Educ* Shrewsbury, Univ of Manchester (BA), Univ of Salford (MSc); *m* 28 Sept 1963, Alice Beatrice, da of Arthur Shelmerdine (d 1996), of Holmes Chapel, Cheshire; 1 s (Guy Stewart b 1964); *Career* 2 Lt RE 1954, Lt Suez Reserve 1956, Maj RE TA and RCT 1956–76; architect and planner in private and public offices 1962–74, dir of planning and architecture Lincoln City Cncl 1974–85, conslt architect and town planner (ptnr John Anderson Planning) specialising in urban design and conservation (UK and overseas) 1985–; memb Cncl RTPI 1977–91 and 1993–95 (pres 1984), sr vice pres Euro Cncl of Town Planners 1988–90, memb Leicester Diocesan Panel of Architects 1990–; Freeman: City of London 1988, Worshipful Co of Watermen and Lightermen 1989; ARIBA, FRTPI, FRSA; *Style*— John S Anderson, Esq, TD; ✉ The Old Stables, Harston, Grantham, Lincs NG32 1PP (☎ 01476 870424, fax 01476 870816)

ANDERSON, John Victor Ronald; OBE (1997); s of Ronald Anderson (d 1971), of Caer Rhun Hall, Conwy, and Muriel Dorothy, *née* Hilton (d 1985); *b* 10 April 1937; *Educ* Sidney Sussex Coll Cambridge (MA); *m* 1986, Rosemary, *née* Ditchburn; *Career* ptnr V

R Anderson & Son (chartered accountants) 1962–90, ptnr Accountancy Tuition Centre 1983–90, dir Accountancy Tuition Centre Ltd 1985–; memb Cncl ICAEW 1995–, pres Liverpool Soc of Chartered Accountants 1989–90; ACA 1962; *Style*— John Anderson, Esq, OBE; ✉ Accountancy Tuition Centre Ltd, Caer Rhun Hall, Conwy, Gwynedd LL32 8HX (☎ 01492 650012, fax 01492 650639)

ANDERSON, Julian Anthony; s of Sir Kenneth Anderson (d 1992), and Helen Veronica, *née* Grose (d 1986); *b* 12 June 1938; *Educ* King Alfred Sch, Wadham Coll Oxford (MA); *Career* entered civil serv as asst princ MAFF 1961, asst private sec to Min 1964–66, princ 1966; seconded FCO as memb UK EEC Accession Negotiation Team 1970–73, asst sec 1973; seconded to FCO as min (Food and Agric), UK perm rep to EEC 1982–85, under sec Lands and Environmental Affrs 1985–90, resigned Civil Service 1990; dir gen Country Landowners' Assoc 1990–; *Recreations* music, sport, travel, photography, gardening, DIY; *Clubs* United Oxford & Cambridge Univ, Civil Service; *Style*— Julian A Anderson, Esq; ✉ Country Landowners' Association, 16 Belgrave Square, London SW1X 8PQ

ANDERSON, Keith David; s of Dr Redvers Edward Anderson (d 1947), of Luton, Bedfordshire, and Norah Mary Agnes, *née* Payne (d 1972); *b* 3 June 1939; *Educ* Alton Castle Sch Alton Staffordshire, St Bernardine's Coll Buckingham; *m* 1, 27 July 1963 (m dis 1974), Sarah Jane, *née* Beddow; 1 s (Timothy Stuart b 26 Sept 1967), 1 da (Jane Ann b 24 May 1964); m 2, 21 March 1975, Susan Lesley, da of late Gordon Rodney Kent; 1 s (Stuart David b 20 July 1978); *Career* Nat Serv 1959–61, RAPC attached to RNF in 1 Gurkha Inf Bde; local govt offr Aylesbury 1954–64; BBC TV: mangr Alexandra Palace 1965–69, organiser Arts Dept 1970–74, prog planning mangr 1974–78, head prog planning resources 1978–82, gen mangr prog planning 1982–89, controller planning and prog servs 1989–92; md: Keith Anderson Associates 1992–, Production Finance and Management Ltd (PFM) 1995–; chm Independent Wildlife Ltd 1996–; FRTS 1991; *Recreations* golf, squash; *Clubs* Groucho, Ellesborough Golf, Holmer Green Squash, Wendover Squash, The Cricketers (London), The Rugby (London); *Style*— Keith Anderson, Esq

ANDERSON, Leslie William; s of Robert Anderson (d 1966), of Edinburgh, and Janetta Urquart, *née* Wishart; *b* 3 Aug 1940; *Educ* Daniel Stewart's College Edinburgh; *m* 8 Jan 1964, Alexandra Angus, da of Bruce Rennie, of Alexandria, Dunbartonshire; 2 da (Emma b 23 Nov 1972, Sacha b 9 May 1975); *Career* news reporter Scot Daily Mail Glasgow 1963–66; Scot Daily Express: news reporter 1966–67, dep industl corr 1967–70, industl corr 1970–78; BBC Scot: industl corr 1979–84, parliamentary corr 1984–89, home affairs corr 1989–; *Recreations* watching rugby; *Clubs* Caledonian, London; *Style*— Leslie Anderson, Esq; ✉ BBC Scotland, Broadcasting House, Queen Margaret Drive, Glasgow (☎ 0141 338 2793, fax 0141 338 2955)

ANDERSON, Prof Malcolm; s of James Armstrong Anderson (d 1959), and Helen, *née* Potts (d 1985); *b* 13 May 1934; *Educ* Altrincham GS for Boys, University Coll Oxford; *m* 1, 1957 (m dis), Eileen Mary, *née* Callan; 2 s (Denis Ian Gervaise b 7 June 1958, Keith James b 18 Feb 1961), 1 da (Helen Catherine b 17 Oct 1963); m 2, 1991, Marie Jacqueline Larrieu; *Career* lectr in govt Univ of Manchester 1960–64, Rockefeller research fell Fondation Nationale des Sciences Politiques Paris 1964–65, prof of politics Univ of Warwick 1973–79 (sr lectr 1965–73); Univ of Edinburgh: prof of politics 1979–, dean of Faculty and provost of Faculty Gp of Law and Social Scis 1989–93, dir Int Social Scis Inst 1994–; temp teaching posts in Canada USA and France; fell ESRC 1976–77, Nuffield fell 1986–87; pres Euro Community Studies Assoc; FRSE 1995, FRSA 1995; *Books* Government in France (1970), Conservative Politics in France (1974), Frontiers Regions in Western Europe (ed, 1983), Policing the World (1989), Policing the European Union (1995), Frontiers (1996); *Recreations* reading, walking; *Style*— Prof Malcolm Anderson, FRSE; ✉ 72 Dundas Street, Edinburgh EH3 6QZ (☎ 0131 556 9300); Department of Politics, University of Edinburgh, 31 Buccleuch Place, Edinburgh EH8 9JT (☎ 0131 650 4254/3, fax 0131 650 6546, e-mail malcolm.anderson@ed.ac.uk)

ANDERSON, Brig Hon Dame Mary McKenzie; *see:* Pihl, Brig Hon Dame M M

ANDERSON, Mary Margaret; CBE (1996); *Educ* Forres Acad, Univ of Edinburgh (MB ChB); *Career* jr posts Scotland and England (incl Hammersmith and St Mary's Hosps), sr registrar St Mary's Hosp London until 1967, conslt obstetrician and gynaecologist Lewisham Hosp London 1967–; chm: Div of Obstetrics and Gynaecology Lewisham Hosp, SE Thames Specialist Sub Ctee (Obstetrics and Gynaecology), Hosp Recognition Ctee RCOG; memb: Scientific Ctee Nat Birthday Tst, Cncl Med Def Union; jr vice pres RCOG 1989–92; FRCOG 1974 (MRCOG 1962); *Books* Anatomy and Physiology of Obstetrics (1979), Handbook of Obstetrics and Gynaecology for House Officers (1981), The Menopause (1983), Pregnancy After Thirty (1984), The A-Z of Gynaecology (1986), Infertility (1987); *Style*— Miss Mary Anderson, CBE; ✉ 96 Harley St, London W1N 1AF (☎ 0171 487 4146)

ANDERSON, Prof Michael; *b* 21 Feb 1942; *Educ* Queens' Coll Cambridge (MA, PhD); *Career* Univ of Edinburgh: reader Dept of Sociology 1975–79 (asst lectr 1967–68, lectr 1969–75), prof of economic history Dept of Economic and Social History 1979– (head of Dept 1979–85 and 1988–), dean Faculty of Social Sciences 1985–89, vice-princ (responsible for Information Infrastructure) 1989–93; chm Res Resources Bd ESRC 1992–94 (memb ESRC 1990–94); memb: Scottish Records Advsy Cncl 1984–93, History of Medicine Ctee Wellcome Tst 1988–93, Soc and Politics Res Devpt Gp ESRC (vice-chm 1991–92); FBA 1989, FRSE 1990; *Publications include* Family Structure in Nineteenth Century Lancashire (1971), Sociology of the Family: Readings (ed with introductions, 2nd edn 1979), Approaches to the History of the Western Family 1500–1914 (1981), Population Change in North-Western Europe 1750–1850 (1988); *Style*— Prof Michael Anderson, FBA, FRSE; ✉ Department of Economic History, University of Edinburgh, Edinburgh EH8 9JY (☎ 0131 650 1000)

ANDERSON, Michael Arthur; JP (Chester 1979); s of Alexander William Anderson (d 1971), and Winifred Ann, *née* Pusill (d 1978); matriculation of Arms granted in 1980 by Lord Lyon, King of Arms, based on Arms granted in 1780 but in use prior to 1665; *b* 23 March 1928; *Educ* LSE (BSc); *m* 1954, Anne, da of Joseph Beynon (d 1965); 2 s (Michael (d 1992), Richard), 2 da (Sarah, Deborah); *Career* fin dir Caribbean Printers Ltd Trinidad 1960–61, sr fin appts Ford Motor Co and Ford of Europe 1962–67, fin dir Manchester Guardian and Evening News Ltd 1968–69, gp fin dir Tillotson & Son Ltd 1970–71, sr fin appts BL 1972–75, fin dir Mersey Docks & Harbour Co 1975–84; dir: Liverpool Grain Storage & Transit Co Ltd 1979–89, Anderson & Co (CAs) 1984–96, Small Firms Business Advisors Ltd 1989–96; business cnsllr to Govt Small Firms Serv 1985–91, business cnsllr 1994–; chm The Anderson Association 1993–; FCA, FCMA, FIBC; *Books* Anderson Families (1984); *Recreations* genealogy, walking, opera, classical music; *Style*— Michael A Anderson, Esq, JP; ✉ Business Counsellor, Kintrave, Wood Lane, Burton, Cheshire, S Wirral L64 5TB (☎ 0151 336 4349)

ANDERSON, Prof Michael John; s of Ronald Arthur Anderson (d 1981), of Llantwit Major, and Dorothy Alma Anderson; *b* 4 June 1937; *Educ* Taunton Sch, Univ of Bristol (BA); *m* 29 Dec 1973, Alessandra Pierangela Lucia, da of dott Girolamo di Gregorio (d 1983), of Bisceglie, Italy; 2 da (Silvia b 1977, Marina b 1980); *Career* The Welch Regt 1956–58; mangr New Theatre Cardiff 1963–64, lectr in drama Univ of Bristol 1964–78; prof of drama: Univ Coll of North Wales Bangor 1978–90 (chm Standing Ctee of Univ Drama Depts 1979–82), Univ of Kent 1990–; memb Welsh Arts Cncl 1985–90 (chm Drama Ctee), joint sec gen Int Fndn for Theatre Res 1989–; FRSA; *Books* Classical Drama and its Influence (ed, 1965), Anger and Detachment: A Study of Osborne Arden and Pinter (1976); *Recreations* travel, films; *Clubs* Royal Commonwealth Soc, Circolo Unione Bisceglie (Italy); *Style*— Prof Michael Anderson; ✉ 28 Nunnery Fields, Canterbury, Kent (☎ 01227 464578); Eliot College, The University, Canterbury, Kent (☎ 01227 764000, fax 01227 827464)

ANDERSON, Prof Olive Ruth; da of Donald Henry Frere Gee (d 1964), and Ruth Winifred, *née* Clackson (d 1950); *b* 27 March 1926; *Educ* King Edward VI GS Louth, St Hugh's Coll Oxford (BA, BLitt, MA); *m* 10 July 1954, Matthew Smith, s of Matthew Smith Anderson (d 1960), of Perth; 2 da (Rachel b 1955, Harriet b 1957); *Career* Dept of History Westfield Coll London: asst lectr 1949–56, lectr 1958–69, reader 1969–86, prof and head of dept 1986–89; Queen Mary and Westfield Coll: prof and dep head of dept 1989–91, emeritus prof and hon res fell 1991–, fell 1995–; James Ford special lectr Univ of Oxford 1992; Royal Hist Soc: assoc 1953, fell 1968, cncllr 1986–90, vice pres 1991–95; memb Academic Cncl Univ of London 1989–91 (memb Exec Ctee 1990–91), tstee Theodora Bosanquet Tst 1995–, memb Fin Ctee Br Fedn of Women Graduates Charitable Fndn 1996–; *Books* A Liberal State at War (1967), Suicide in Victorian and Edwardian England (1987); *Style*— Prof Olive Anderson; ✉ 45 Cholmeley Crescent, Highgate, London N6 5EX (☎ 0181 340 0272); Queen Mary and Westfield College, London E1 4NS (☎ 0171 975 5555, fax 0171 975 5500)

ANDERSON, Robert Charles (Bob); s of Harry Charles Anderson (d 1980), and Hazel Irene, *née* Grant; *b* 7 Nov 1947; *Educ* Headlands GS; *m* 26 Sept 1970, Florence Mary, da of Cyril Roy Benstead (d 1976); 1 s (David b 1977), 1 da (Jennie b 1975); *Career* darts player; Gold Cup Winner 1983 and 1986, British Open Champion 1987, World Matchplay Champion 1987, World Masters Winner 1986, 1987 and 1988, World Champion 1988, Pacific Masters Winner 1987, 1988 and 1989; former Eng Int capt; *Recreations* golf, snooker, bowls; *Clubs* Marlborough Golf; *Style*— Bob Anderson, Esq; ✉ 45 Queensfield, Upper Stratton, Swindon, Wiltshire SN2 6SS (☎ 01793 722026)

ANDERSON, Dr Robert David; s of Robert David Anderson (d 1956), of London, and Gladys, *née* Clayton (d 1973); *b* 20 Aug 1927; *Educ* Harrow, Gonville and Caius Coll Cambridge (MA); *Career* dir of music Gordonstoun Sch 1958–62, extra mural lectr in Egyptology Univ of London 1966–77, assoc ed The Musical Times 1967–85, conductor Bart's Hosp Choral Soc 1965–90, visiting fell in music City Univ 1983–90; hon sec Egypt Exploration Soc 1971–82 (admin dir EES dig at Qasr Ibrim 1976–79); music critic for The Times, radio and TV for BBC, co-ordinating ed Elgar Complete Edition 1984–93; Freeman: City of London 1977, Worshipful Co of Musicians 1977; Hon DMus City Univ 1985; FSA 1983; *Books* Catalogue of Egyptian Antiquities in the British Museum III, Musical Instruments (1976), Wagner (1980), Egypt in 1800 (jt ed, 1988), Elgar in Manuscript (1990), Elgar (1993); *Recreations* modulating from music to Egyptology; *Style*— Dr Robert Anderson, FSA; ✉ 54 Hornton St, London W8 4NT (☎ 0171 937 5146)

ANDERSON, Dr Robert Geoffrey William; er s of Herbert Patrick Anderson, and Kathleen Diana, *née* Burns; *b* 2 May 1944; *Educ* Oxford (BSc, MA, DPhil); *m* 1973, Margaret Elizabeth Callis, da of John Austin Lea; 2 s (William b 1979, Edward b 1984); *Career* keeper of chemistry Science Museum 1980–84; dir: Royal Scottish Museum 1984–85 (formerly curator scientific instruments), Nat Museums of Scotland 1985–92, British Museum 1992–; memb Cncl: Soc for the History of Alchemy and Chemistry 1978–, Gp for Scientific Technological and Medical Collections 1979–83, Br Soc for the History of Sci 1981–84 (pres 1988–90), Scottish Museums 1984–91, Museums Assoc 1988–92; memb Editorial Bd: Annals of Sci 1981–, Annali di Storia della Scienza 1986–; pres Scientific Instrument Cmmn Int Union of the History and Philosophy of Sci 1982–, memb Br Nat Ctee for the Hist of Sci 1985–89; tstee Boerhaave Museum Leiden 1994–; Dexter Prize American Chemical Soc 1986; Hon DSc Edinburgh 1995; FRSC 1984, FSA 1986, FRSE 1990; *Books* The Mariner's Astrolabe (1972), Edinburgh and Medicine (1976), The Early Years of the Edinburgh Medical School (1976), The Playfair Collection and the Teaching of Chemistry at the University of Edinburgh (1978), The History of Technology Vol VI (contrib, 1978), Science in India (1982), Science, Medicine and Dissent - Joseph Priestley 1733–1804 (ed, 1987), Joseph Black: A Bibliography (1992), Making Instruments Count (jt ed, 1993); *Clubs* Athenaeum; *Style*— Dr R G W Anderson, FRSE, FSA; ✉ The British Museum, Great Russell St, London WC1B 3DG (☎ 0171 636 1555)

ANDERSON, Prof Robert Henry; s of Henry Anderson (d 1981), and Doris Amy, *née* Callear (d 1977); *b* 4 April 1942; *Educ* Wellington GS, Univ of Manchester (BSc, MB ChB, MD); *m* 9 July 1966, Christine, da of Keith Ibbotson, of Grantham, Lincs; 1 s (John b 1972), 1 da (Elizabeth b 1970); *Career* travelling fell MRC Univ of Amsterdam 1973, sr res fell Br Heart Fndn Brompton Hosp 1974, Joseph Levy prof of paediatric cardiac morphology Nat Heart and Lung Inst (formerly Cardiothoracic Inst) Imperial Coll Sch of Med Univ of London 1979– (reader 1977); visiting prof Univ of Pittsburgh 1984–, hon prof Univ of North Carolina 1984–, visiting prof Univ of Liverpool 1988–; Excerpta Medica Travel Award 1977, Br Heart Fndn Prize for Cardiovasular Res 1984; FRCPath 1986; *Publications* 435 articles, 225 chapters in books; 33 books incl: Cardiac Anatomy (1978), Cardiac Pathology (1983), Surgical Anatomy of the Heart (1985), Paediatric Cardiology (2 volumes, 1987); *Recreations* music, golf, wine; *Clubs* Roehampton, Saintsbury; *Style*— Prof Robert Anderson; ✉ Department of Paediatrics, National Heart & Lung Institute, Imperial College of Medicine, Dovehouse Street, London SW3 6LY (☎ 0171 351 8751, fax 0171 351 8230)

ANDERSON, Prof Roy Malcolm; s of James Anderson, and Elizabeth, *née* Watson-Weatherburn; *b* 12 April 1947; *Educ* Duncombe Sch, Richard Hale Sch, Imperial Coll Univ of London (BSc, PhD, DIC); *m* 1, 16 Aug 1974 (m dis 1989), Mary Joan, da of Peter Mitchell; m 2, 21 July 1990, Claire, da of Rev Peter Baron; *Career* IBM res fell Oxford Univ 1971–73; lectr Dept of Zoology King's Coll London 1973–77; Dept of Biology Imperial Coll London: lectr 1977–80, reader 1980–82, prof 1982–93, head of dept 1984–93; Linacre prof of zoology and head of Zoology Dept Univ of Oxford 1993–, dir Wellcome Trust Centre for the Epidemiology of Infectious Disease 1994–, fell Merton Coll Univ of Oxford 1993, hon fell Linacre Coll Univ of Oxford 1993; dir Wellcome Centre for Parasite Infections 1989–93; visiting prof Imperial Coll Univ of London 1993, Genentech distinguished prof Dept of Biostatistics Univ of Washington USA 1996–97; author of over 300 scientific jls and books; awarded: Huxley Meml medal 1982, Zoological Scientific medal 1982, CA Wright Meml medal 1986, David Starr Jordan prize 1986, Chalmers medal 1988, Weldon prize 1989, John Grundy Lecture medal 1990, Frink medal for Br Zoologists 1993; Storer lectr Univ of California Davis 1994, Croonian lectr Royal Soc 1994, Joseph Smadel lectr Univ of N Carolina 1994, P H Thiel lectr Boerhaave Course on Travel Med Leiden 1995, Thomas Francis Meml Lectr Univ of Michigan 1995; memb: Natural Environment Res Cncl 1988–91, Cncl Zoological Soc 1988–90, Advsy Cncl On Science and Technol 1989–91, Cncl Royal Soc 1989–91, Cncl London Sch of Hygiene and Tropical Medicine 1993–, Cncl RPMS Hammersmith 1993–; tstee and then govr The Wellcome Tst 1991–; Hon MRCP 1991, FRS 1986, FIBiol, FRSS, ARCS; *Books* Population Dynamics of Infectious Diseases (1982), Infectious Diseases of Humans: Dynamics and Control (jtly, 1990); *Recreations* croquet, hill walking, music, natural history; *Clubs* Athenaeum; *Style*— Prof Roy Anderson, FRS; ✉ Department of Zoology, University of Oxford, South Parks Road, Oxford OX1 3PS (☎ 01865 281239, fax 01865 281241)

ANDERSON, Sarah Pia; da of Stewart Angus Anderson, and Eldina Pia Anderson; *b* 19 July 1952; *Educ* The Cedars Sch, Univ of Swansea (BA); *Career* theatre and television director; prof in Dramatic Art Univ of California at Davis; memb: Dirs' Guild of GB, Dirs' Guild of America, Women in Film (UK), Soc of Stage Dir and Choreographers USA, BAFTA LA; *Theatre* trained at the Crucible Theatre Sheffield prodns incl: Hello and Goodbye, What The Butler Saw, Ashes, The Caucasian Chalk Circle; prodns for the Bush Theatre incl: Blisters, Gin Trap, First Blush Last Resort, The Estuary, These Men, The Nest; prodns for RSC incl: Indigo, Old Year's Eve, Across Oka, Mary and Lizzie; other prodns incl: Rosmersholm (NT, La Mama Theatre NY), Carthagians (Abbey & Hampstead), Mary Stuart and St Joan (Shakespeare Theatre Washington DC), The Winters Tale (Univ of Santa Cruz Shakespeare Festival), Hedda Gabler (Roundabout Theatre NY); *Television* incl: Blisters, Stepping Out, Shaping Up, Pity in History, A Silly Little Habit, A Woman Calling (Samuel Beckett Award), Summers Awakening, The Raving Beauties Make It Work, In My Experience, This Is History Gran, The Bill (15 episodes), The Alleyn Mysteries, Dr Finlay, Prime Suspect, The Profiler (for NBC); *Recreations* photography, tennis, swimming; *Style—* Ms Sarah Pia Anderson

ANDERSON, Prof Thomas; s of Frederick Anderson (d 1992), and May, *née* Barrett (d 1987); *b* 24 July 1947; *Educ* Blaydon GS, Univ of Newcastle upon Tyne (BSc, PhD); *m* 3 Aug 1968, Patricia, da of Robert Ormston; 1 s (Iain b 1972), 1 da (Claire b 1975); *Career* Univ of Newcastle upon Tyne: dir Centre for Software Reliability 1982–, prof 1986–, head Computing Sci Dept 1992–; MIEEE, FBCS; *Books* Fault Tolerance - Principles and Practice (with P A Lee, 2 edn 1990), also ed 11 other volumes 1979–97; *Recreations* fell walking, singing; *Style—* Thomas Anderson, Esq; ✉ Centre for Software Reliability, University of Newcastle, Newcastle upon Tyne NE1 7RU (☎ 0191 212 2222, fax 0191 222 7995, e-mail Tom.Anderson@newcastle.ac.uk)

ANDERTON, Darren Robert; s of Norman Anderton, of Bitterne Park, Southampton, and Jane, *née* Smith, of West End, Southampton; *b* 3 March 1972; *Educ* Bitterne Park Sch; *partner* Kate Randall; *Career* professional footballer; Portsmouth FC: joined as apprentice, turned professional 1990, full debut v Cardiff City 1990, 54 appearances, FA Cup semi-finalists 1992; transferred to Tottenham Hotspur FC 1992–; England: under 19 and under 21 int, 16 full caps (first v Denmark 1994), memb squad Euro 96; Barclays Young Eagle of the Month (regnl winner twice, nat winner March 1993); *Style—* Darren Anderton, Esq; ✉ Tottenham Hotspur FC, 748 High Rd, Tottenham, London N17 0AP (☎ 0171 808 6666)

ANDERTON, Sir (Cyril) James; kt (1990), CBE (1982), QPM, DL (Greater Manchester); s of late James Anderton, and Lucy, *née* Occleshaw; *b* 24 May 1932; *Educ* Wigan GS, Univ of Manchester; *m* 1955, Joan; 1 da; *Career* Royal Mil Police 1950–53, Constable rising to Chief Inspr Manchester City Police Force 1953–67, Chief Supt Cheshire Constabulary 1967–68, Asst Chief Constable Leicester & Rutland Constabulary 1968–72, asst to HM Chief Inspr of Constabulary for England and Wales Home Office London 1972–75, Dep Chief Constable Leicestershire Constabulary 1975, Chief Constable Gtr Manchester Police 1976–91 (Dep Chief Constable 1975–76); pres ACPO 1986–87; Cdr St John Ambulance Gtr Manchester 1989–96 (county dir 1976–89), chm Manchester Salvation Army Advsy Bd; pres: Christian Police Assoc 1979–81, Manchester Branch BIM 1984–93, Wythenshawe Hosp League of Friends, Bolton Outward Bound Assoc, Altrincham Town Centre Partnership, Gtr Manchester Youth Field Gun Assoc, Disable Living Manchester; hon nat vice pres The Boy's Brigade; vice pres: Univ of Birmingham Visual Impairment Appeal, Manchester YMCA, Adelphi Lads' Club Salford, Sharp St Ragged Sch Manchester, Gtr Manchester W Scout Cncl, Gtr Manchester Fedn Boys Clubs, Manchester Salford and Dist Branch NSPCC, Wigan Hospice, Manchester & Dist Branch of the Royal Life Saving Soc; patron: Gtr Manchester LUPUS Gp, Br Coll of Accordionists, The Br Tst, N Manchester Hosp Broadcasting Serv, NW Campaign for Kidney Donors, Henshaws Soc for the Blind, Stockport Canal Tst, Hindley Community Assoc Wigan, North Cheshire (Trafford) Branch Multiple Sclerosis Soc, Mottram & Hattersley Amateur Boxing Club, Stockport Branch ACROSS; memb Manchester Olympic Bid Ctee 1985–93; memb: The Chief Constables' Club, The Christian Police Assoc, Royal Mil Police Assoc, The Catholic Union of GB, Assoc for the Propagation of the Faith, Royal Sch of Church Music, The Royal Soc of St George, Friends of Israel Assoc, Cncl of Christians and Jews, Broughton Catholic Charitable Soc, Manchester Portico Library, Manchester Literary and Philosophical Soc, The Nat Tst, RSPB, RSPCA (pres Manchester and Dist, patron Wigan and Dist), Wigan Little Theatre, RLSS; Mancunian of the Yr 1980; hon fell British Coll of Accordionists 1976, hon memb RNCM 1984; Freeman City of London; KStJ; Cross Pro Ecclesia et Pontifice 1982, Chevalier de la Confrerie des Chevaliers du Tastevin 1985; *Recreations* home, family; *Clubs* St John House; *Style—* Sir James Anderton, CBE, QPM, DL; ✉ 9 The Avenue, Sale, Trafford, Greater Manchester M33 4PB

ANDERTON, Kenneth John; s of Leslie George Anderton (d 1968), of 10 Windsor Terrace, Penarth, S Glam, and Nina Mary, *née* Harwood; *b* 22 July 1940; *Educ* Penarth GS, Welsh Nat Sch of Med Cardiff; *m* 1, 6 June 1962 (m dis), Elizabeth Sarah, da of Gwillym Jones, of Dinas Powis, Cardiff; 1 s (Nicholas Simon b 31 Aug 1974), 2 da (Helen Claire b 19 Feb 1970, Susan Jane b 28 Sept 1972); m 2, 21 Feb 1978, Norah; *Career* house offr: Llandough Hosp Cardiff 1963–64, St Woolos Hosp Newport 1964, Glossop Terrace Hosp Cardiff 1965; sr house offr, then registrar Royal Victoria Hosp Newcastle upon Tyne 1965–68, registrar Ashington Hosp Northumbria 1968–72, lectr Univ Dept Jessop Hosp for Women Sheffield 1972–76, conslt obstetrician and gynaecologist Rotherham Gen Hosp 1976–, clinical dir Dept of Obstetrics and Gynaecology Rotherham Gen Hosp; author of papers in relevant med jls; chm: Rotherham Branch Relate 1985–86, Rotherham Div BMA 1986–87; FRCOG 1982; *Books* Hormone Replacement Therapy of the Menopause (1976), Psychosexual Problems in Gynaecology (1978); *Style—* Kenneth Anderton, Esq; ✉ Department of Obstetrics and Gynaecology, Rotherham District General Hospital, Moorgate Rd, Rotherham, South Yorks S60 2AU (☎ 01709 820000)

ANDOVER, Viscount; Alexander Charles Michael Winston Robsahm Howard; s and h of 21 Earl of Suffolk and Berkshire; *b* 17 Sept 1974; *Style—* Viscount Andover

ANDRAE, Michael Anton; s of Emile Anton Andrae (d 1974), of London, and Minnie Jenette Isobel, *née* Nisbett (d 1984); *b* 20 Sept 1932; *Educ* Hornsey County GS, Enfield Tech Coll; *m* 12 March 1955, Laura, da of Alfred George Smith; 2 da (Vivienne Jane b 11 June 1960, Gillian Louise b 16 Oct 1963); *Career* Nat Serv RAF 1951–53; mgmnt apprentice British Oxygen 1950–51, sales rep A Ling & Co 1953–56, PA to md Medico-Therapeutics Ltd 1956–58, PA to md rising to sales mangr then sales and mktg dir Heinke Ltd 1959–65, dir Heinke-Trelleborg Ltd 1959–65, mktg dir Gemma Group 1965–75, dir Mecco Marine Ltd (UK mktg and distribution co for Pirelli Milan inflatable craft) 1965–75, md and chief exec Hunt Instrumentation Ltd 1972–77; dir: Midar Systems Ltd 1975–87, Bond Instrumentation Gibraltar Ltd 1975–87, Bond Instrumentation (Singapore) PTE Ltd 1975–87 (and alternating chm); commercial dir and co sec Bond Instrumentation and Process Control Ltd 1975–87, mktg and business conslt and various non-exec directorships 1987–, memb Bd of Mgmnt Services Sound and Vision Corporation 1991–; Chartered Inst of Mktg: nat treas 1987–88, nat chm 1989–90, President's Award 1988; Freeman City of London 1989, Liveryman Worshipful Co of Marketors 1989; MCIM 1964, Hon FCIM 1990, fell Mktg Inst of Singapore 1988, FInstD 1985, FRSA 1990; *Recreations* fine art, shooting, fishing; *Style—* Michael Andrae, Esq; ✉ Andrae Ryder Associates, Business & Marketing Consultants, Carpenders, Eastwell Towers, Kennington, Ashford, Kent TN25 4PQ (☎ 01233 626868, fax 01233 638528)

ANDRÉ, Martin; *b* 10 Dec 1960; *Educ* Univ of Cambridge; *m* m Karin; 1 da (Sophie), 1 s (Ben); *Career* conductor; sometime resident conductor Welsh Nat Opera, freelance conductor, music dir English Touring Opera 1993–96; performances with Welsh Nat Opera incl: chamber version of Aida (professional debut), Falstaff, Jenufa, Ernani, Rigoletto, Madama Butterfly, Un Ballo in Maschera, Eugene Onegin, Il Barbiere de Siviglia; freelance productions incl: The Merry Widow and La Clemenza di Tito (Scottish Opera), The Love for Three Oranges and John Buller Bakxai (world première, ENO), Madama Butterfly (Opera North), Le Nozze di Figaro, Mozart Die Entführung aus dem Serail (Opera 80), Janacek From the House of the Dead (N American première for Vancouver Opera), Ariadne (Vancouver Opera), La Traviata (Opera Zuid Maastricht and Vancouver Opera), L'amour des Trois Oranges (Lisbon and New Israeli Opera), Carmen (US debut, Seattle Opera), Un Ballo in Maschera (Royal Opera House debut), Christoph Rilke's Song of Love and Death (UK première, Glyndebourne Touring Opera), Don Pasquale (New Israeli Opera), world premières by James MacMillan and Craig Armstrong Edinburgh Int Festival, Cosi fan Tutte, Orpheus and Euridice, La Bohème, Werther, Rigoletto (all for English Touring Opera); also performances with English Chamber Orch, Scottish Chamber Orch, Northern Sinfonia, Jerusalem Symphony Orch; 1996–97 season performances incl: Cunning Little Vixen (Scottish Opera), La Traviata (Opera Northern Ireland), Cav and Pag (Staastheater Stuttgart), Makropolus Case (Glyndebourne Touring Opera); *Recreations* has season ticket for Arsenal FC; *Style—* Martin André, Esq; ✉ c/o Ingpen & Williams Ltd, 14 Kensington Court, London W8 5DN (☎ 0171 937 5158, fax 0171 938 4175)

ANDRESKI, Prof Stanislav Leonard; s of Teofil Andrzejewski (d 1967), and Zofia, *née* Karaszewicz-Tokarzewska (d 1939); *b* 8 May 1919; *Educ* Secdy Sch in Poznan, Univ of Poznan, LSE (BSc, MSc, PhD); *m* 1974, Ruth, da of Maurice Ash (d 1976); 2 s (Adam, Lucas), 2 da (Wanda, Sophia); *Career* Mil Serv Polish Army 1937–47, cmmnd 1944; lectr in sociology Rhodes USA 1947–53, sr res fell in anthropology Univ of Manchester 1954–56; lectr in: econs Acton Tech Coll London 1956–57, mgmnt studies Brunel Coll of Technol London 1957–60; prof of sociology Sch of Social Sciences Santiago Chile 1960–61, sr res fell Nigerian Inst of Social and Econ Res Ibadan Nigeria 1962–64, prof and head of Dept of Sociology Univ of Reading 1964–84 (prof emeritus 1984), prof Polish Univ of London 1978–92 (prof emeritus 1993); visiting prof: Dept of Sociology and Anthropology City Coll, City Univ of NY 1968–69, Dept of Sociology Simon Fraser Univ Canada 1976–77, pt/t prof INTEGER Centre of Business Studies Monterey Mexico 1985–; memb IPI; *Books* Elements of Comparative Sociology (1964), The African Predicament - a Study in Pathology of Modernisation (1968), The Uses of Comparative Sociology (1969, Spanish ed 1972), Parasitism and Subversion - The Case of Latin America (1970, Spanish ed 1968), Military Organization and Society (1970), Social Sciences as Sorcery (1972; ed: Spanish 1973, German 1974, French 1975, Italian 1977, Japanese 1981), The Prospects of a Revolution in the USA (1973), Max Weber's Insights and Errors (1984, Polish ed 1991), Syphilis, Puritanism and Witch hunts - Historical Explanations in the Light of Medicine and Psychoanalysis with a Forecast about Aids (1989), Wars, Revolutions, Dictatorships - Studies of Historical and Contemporary Problems from a Comparative Viewpoint (1992); *Recreations* sailing (yacht Metamorfoza); *Clubs* Cruising Assoc; *Style—* Prof Stanislav Andreski

ANDREW, Elizabeth Honora; *née* Thomas; da of Dilwyn Thomas, of Pontypridd, S Wales, and Morfydd, *née* Horton (d 1979); *b* 6 March 1946; *Educ* Pontypridd Girls' GS, Univ of London (LLB); *m* 21 July 1967, Kenneth Andrew, s of Arthur James Andrew, of Benfleet, Essex; 2 s; *Career* trainee retail and personnel mgmnt Marks & Spencer 1963–65, res asst Welsh Hosp Bd 1965–66, fashion buyer 1966–68, mangr wholesale and retail fashion trade 1968–70; called to the Bar Middle Temple 1974; practitioner in employment and professional negligence law and local govt law; asst recorder; former parish cncllr Three Rivers Parish Cncl; memb: Commercial Bar Assoc, Admin Law Bar Assoc, Employment Lawyers Assoc, Employment Law Bar Assoc; FRSA; *Recreations* writing, travel, antiques; *Style—* Mrs Elizabeth Andrew; ✉ Devereux Chambers, Devereux Court, London WC2R 3JJ (☎ 0171 353 7534, fax 0171 353 1724)

ANDREW, Dr Kenneth; s of Arthur James Andrew, of Benfleet, Essex, and Emily Sarah, *née* Elderkin; *b* 21 Dec 1944; *Educ* Enfield Coll of Technol (ONC), Imperial Coll London (MSc, DIC), Univ of Wales (BEng), Int Mgmnt Centre (DPhil); *m* 21 July 1967, Elizabeth Honora, da of Dilwyn Thomas, of Pontypridd, S Wales; 2 s; *Career* apprentice draughtsman 1961–64; NatWest Bank plc 1969–84: various posts including head of operational res, branch mgmnt City and West End London, head of mktg; gp markets dir Good Relations Group plc 1984–85, dir consumer mktg Europe The Chase Manhattan Bank NA 1985–87, gp dir strategy and mktg National & Provincial Building Society 1987–90, independent business conslt 1990–91; dir: DBS Management plc 1993–, Manitous 1991–, St James International 1995–, Mount Vernon Watford Hosp NHS Tst 1994–; chm St James Business Group Ltd 1995–; sr vice pres, chm and md Aetna UK 1991–93, industl prof of fin servs mgmnt IMC; Hon MPhil IMCB 1984; MIMgt, AIB, MBBA, MInstScB, FInstD, FRSA; *Books* The Bank Marketing Handbook (1986), The Financial Public Relations Handbook (1990), Bank Marketing in a Changing World (1991); *Recreations* swimming, reading, writing, travel; *Clubs* MCC, Carlton, Athaeneum; *Style—* Dr Kenneth Andrew; (☎ 0171 706 3672)

ANDREW, Prof Malcolm Ross; s of John Malcolm Young Andrew, of Latchley, nr Gunnislake, Cornwall, and Mary Lilian, *née* Faulkner; *b* 27 Jan 1945; *Educ* The Perse Sch Cambridge, St Catharine's Coll Cambridge (BA, MA), Simon Fraser Univ BC Canada (MA), Univ of York (DPhil); *m* 17 Aug 1968, Lena Margareta, da of Gustaf Bernström, of Göteborg, Sweden; 1 s (Christopher b 1980), 1 da (Elizabeth b 1982); *Career* asst English master Haileybury Coll 1973–74, lectr then sr lectr Sch of English and American Studies Univ of East Anglia 1974–85; The Queen's Univ Belfast: prof of English 1985–, head of dept then dir Sch of English 1986–92, dean Faculty of Arts 1992–96, provost of humanities 1993–; memb: Steering Ctee Cncl for Univ English 1989–92, English Panel Humanities Research Bd British Acad 1995–; DLit Queen's Univ Belfast 1995; *Books* On the Properties of Things, Book VII (1975), Poems of the Pearl Manuscript (with R Waldron, 1978), The Gawain-Poet: An Annotated Bibliography (1979), Two Early Renaissance Bird Poems (1984), Critical Essays on Chaucer's Canterbury Tales (1991), Variorum Chaucer: General Prologue to the Canterbury Tales (1993), Geoffrey Chaucer, The Canterbury Tales (ed with A C Cawley, 1996); *Recreations* literature, art, architecture, music; *Style—* Prof Malcolm Andrew; ✉ 39 Cranmore Gardens, Belfast BT9 6JL (☎ 01232 667869); School of English, The Queen's University of Belfast, Belfast BT7 1NN (☎ 01232 245133 ext 3317, fax 01232 249864)

ANDREW, Nicholas Anthony Samuel; s of Samuel Ogden Lees Andrew (d 1966), of Winchester, and Rosalind Molly Carlyon, *née* Evans (d 1984); *b* 20 Dec 1946; *Educ* Winchester, Queens' Coll Cambridge (MA); *m* 28 Nov 1981, Jeryl Christine, da of Col John George Harrison, OBE, TD, DL, of Devon; 2 da (Venetia b 1989, Olivia Rose b 1992); *Career* CA; ptnr: Robson Rhodes 1986–90, Rawlinson & Hunter 1990–92; md: Robson Rhodes Financial Services Ltd 1986–90, Nicholas Andrew Financial Planning Ltd 1992–; FIMBRA Membership Ctee 1986–90; FCA, FCCA; *Books* Yuppies and their Money (1987), Robson Rhodes Personal Financial Planning Manual (jtly, 2–6 edns), How to Make Yourself Wealthy in the 1990's; *Recreations* golf, music, travel; *Clubs* MCC, RAC; *Style—* Nicholas A S Andrew, Esq; ✉ Nicholas Andrew Financial Planning Ltd, 10 Orange Street, Haymarket, London WC2H 7DQ (☎ 0171 312 6515, fax 0171 312 0022)

ANDREW, (John) Patrick Ramsay; s of John Ramsay Andrew, of St Saviours, Guernsey, and Betty, *née* Arnold (now Mrs Reginald MacLeod); *b* 25 June 1937; *m* 1, 11 Sept 1976, Philippa Rachel (d 1988), da of Cdr Felix Johnstone (d 1964) (*see* Debrett's

Peerage and Baronetage, B Derwent); 2 da (Edwina Elizabeth b 1981, Emily Katharine b 1983); m 2, 17 Nov 1995, Peta-Carolyn Pope, *née* Stocker, wid of Lt Col Julian Pope, MBE (d 1988); *Career* co dir and int conslt; formerly with Courtaulds, EMI, Rank Xerox, Guinness; currently chm: Strategy Resources Group 1983–, Parks and Reserves Company (Parc) 1993–; *Recreations* the Arts (fndr Connaught Gallery 1972), building restoration, sailing, fly fishing, sculpture, international affairs (memb RIIA); *Style—* Patrick Ramsay Andrew, Esq; ✉ Upton Grove, Tetbury, Gloucestershire GL8 8LP

ANDREW, Richard Arnold; s of John Ramsay Andrew, of St Saviours, Guernsey, and Beatrice Marjorie Kathleen Betty, *née* Arnold; *b* 4 July 1944; *Educ* Cheltenham; *m* 1, 19 Sept 1965 (m dis 1972), Gillian Kathrine, da of Prof Frank Elliott, of Philadelphia; 2 s (James Richard Elliott b 20 July 1966, Edward Alexander b 7 May 1968); m 2, 27 April 1978 (m dis 1989), Lady Serena Mary Bridgeman, da of 6 Earl of Bradford; *Career* Gallaher Ltd 1964–66, Kleinwort Benson Ltd 1966–72, md Service Holdings Ltd 1972–74, Scandinavian Bank Group plc 1974–91 (gp dir 1981–91); chm: Private Capital Group 1986–91, Mortgage Trust Ltd 1986–91; dir: Brewin Dolphin Ltd 1987–91, Adams & Nevile Asset Management Ltd 1991–92, George Wimpey plc 1992–95 (chm and chief exec Homes Div); non-exec dir: Wates Building Group Ltd 1995–, Wellman plc 1995–; FInstD; *Recreations* golf; *Clubs* Brook's; *Style—* Richard Andrew, Esq; ✉ 13 Redcliffe St, London SW10 9DR (☎ 0171 373 2706); Cornwell Hill Farm, Chipping Norton, Oxon OX7 5YG (☎ 01608 641206)

ANDREW, (Christopher) Robert (Rob); MBE (1995); *b* 18 Feb 1963; *Educ* Barnard Castle, Univ of Cambridge (BA, Rugby blue, Cricket blue); *m* 18 Aug 1989, Sara; 2 da (Emily b 5 July 1990, Beth b 29 March 1995); *Career* rugby union fly-half; clubs: Middlesbrough RUFC, Cambridge Univ 1981–84, Nottingham RFC 1984–87, Gordon RFC (Aust), Wasps FC 1987–91 and 1992–96, Toulouse 1991–92, Barbarians RFC, Newcastle RFC Jan 1996– (devpt dir Sept 1995–); rep: North 1985 and 1987, London 1989, Eng B (debut 1988), Home Unions 1989 (capt v France); England: debut v Romania 1985, Five Nations debut v France 1985, memb World Cup squad (2 appearances) 1987, tour Aust & Fiji 1988 (3 test appearances), tour Romania 1989, memb Grand Slam winning team 1991, 1992 and 1995, memb runners-up team World Cup 1991, memb team semi-finalists World Cup 1995, tour to S Africa 1994, over 50 caps, ret; kicked 6 penalties and scored 21 points v Wales 1986, record holder for drop goals in internationals, highest individual scoring mark (30 points v Canada, equalling world record) 1994; memb Br Lions tour Aust (2 tests) 1989; cricket: first class Yorkshire CCC 2nd XI, Cambridge Univ CC (capt 1985); chartered surveyor until Sept 1995; *Style—* Rob Andrew, Esq, MBE; ✉ c/o Newcastle RFC, Newcastle Upon Tyne NE3 2DT (☎ 0191 214 0422)

ANDREW, Sir Robert John; KCB (1986, CB 1979); s of Robert Young Andrew (d 1980), of Walton-on-the-Hill, Surrey; *b* 25 Oct 1928; *Educ* King's Coll Sch Wimbledon, Merton Coll Oxford (MA); *m* 1963, Elizabeth, da of Walter de Courcy Bayley (d 1951), of Barbados; 2 s (Christopher b 1967, John b 1968); *Career* serv Intelligence Corps 1947–49; joined Civil Serv 1952, serv in MOD, Dip Serv and Civil Serv Dept, dep under sec of state Home Office 1976–83, perm under sec of state NI Office 1984–88; dir Esmée Fairbairn Charitable Tst 1989–94; conservator of Wimbledon and Putney Commons 1973–, govr King's Coll Sch Wimbledon 1976– (chm 1990–), memb Cncl Royal Holloway and Bedford New Coll 1989– (chm 1992–); tstee BBC Children in Need 1994–; non-exec dir of several cos; FRSA; *Recreations* carpentry, walking, canal boats; *Clubs* Utd Oxford and Cambridge Univ; *Style—* Sir Robert Andrew, KCB

ANDREWS, Anthony; *b* 12 Jan 1948; *Educ* Royal Masonic Sch; *Career* actor; *Theatre* incl: 40 Years On (Apollo), One of Us (Greenwich) 1986, Coming Into Land (NT) 1986, Dragon Variation (Chichester Festival Theatre), Tima and the Conways (The New Shakespeare Co); *Television* incl: Brideshead Revisited, Danger UXB, Much Ado About Nothing, Romeo and Juliet, Jewels, Bluegrass, The Law Lord, Columbo Goes To The Guillotine, A Ware of Children, The Fortunes of Nigel, The Beast with Two Backs, Suspicion, Z For Zachariah, Burning Bridges, A Superstition, The Woman He Loved, Dixon of Dock Green, The Judge's Wife, Alma Mater, AD, Sparkling Cyanide, The Scarlet Pimpernel, Ivanhoe, La Ronde, Upstairs Downstairs, David Copperfield, The Pallisers, Follyfoot, A Day Out, French Without Tears, The Country Wife, London Assurance, QBVII, As the Actress Said to the Bishop, Woodstock, Doomwatch, The Duchess of Duke Street, Hands of a Murderer (USA), The Strange Case of Dr Jekyll and Mr Hyde (USA), Ruth Rendell's Heartstones; *Film* incl: The Scarlet Pimpernel, Under the Volcano, The Holcroft Covenant, Second Victory, The Light Horseman, Hannah's War, Percy's Progress, Take Me High, Operation Daybreak, Mistress of Paradise, Lost in Siberia (also prodr), Haunted (also prodr); *Style—* Anthony Andrews, Esq; ✉ c/o Peters Fraser & Dunlop Ltd, 503 The Chambers, Chelsea Harbour, London SW10 0XF (☎ 0171 376 7676, fax 0171 352 7356)

ANDREWS, Anthony Peter Hamilton; s of Col Peter Edward Clinton Andrews, of Hants, and Margaret Jean Hamilton, *née* Cooke; *b* 23 Dec 1946; *Educ* King's Sch Worcester, Univ of St Andrews (Kitchener scholar, MA, PGCE); *m* 8 Sept 1973, Alison Margaret Dudley, da of (David) Dudley Morgan, of Essex; 2 da (Jocelyn Amanda Hamilton b 30 July 1977, Gail Louise Hamilton b 15 June 1980), 1 s (David Dudley Hamilton b 1 March 1983); *Career* Offr Royal Marines 1964–71 (scholar 1962); trainee land agent J T Sutherland & Co 1975–76; British Council: VSO support offr Nigeria 1976–78, Br Information Centre Belgrade 1979–82, asst dir Oman 1982–85, dir NE Brazil 1985–89, dir Scotland 1990–96 (Glasgow 1989–90), dir Br Cncl Russia and cultural cnsllr Br Embassy Moscow April 1996–; *Recreations* river management, fly fishing, sailing, painting, music, Scotland's history and culture; *Clubs* New (Edinburgh), Scottish Arts; *Style—* Anthony Andrews, Esq; ✉ Milton of Finavon House, By Forfar, Angus DD8 3PY (☎ and fax 01307 850275); c/o The British Council, 10 Spring Gardens, London SW1A 2BN; Moscow (☎ 00 7 095 234 0201, fax 007 095 975 2561)

ANDREWS, Dr Christopher John Horner; s of Prof William Henry Horner Andrews (d 1978), and Dr Jean Romer, *née* Young; *b* 31 Dec 1946; *Educ* High Wycombe Royal GS, St George's Coll Jamaica, Univ of London (MB BS, PhD); *m* 21 Oct 1972, Victoria Catherine, da of Charles Samuel Weston (d 1987); 2 s (Jeremy Charles Horner b 1977, William Jonathan Horner b 1979); *Career* MO Br Antarctic Survey 1972–76, sr house offr in anaesthetics The London Hosp 1976–77, registrar Royal Devon and Exeter Hosp 1977–80, sr registrar Bristol Royal Infirmary 1980–84, conslt Plymouth Health Authy 1984–, med dir Plymouth Hosps NHS Tst 1996– (clinical dir (anaesthetics) 1992–95); memb: BMA 1972, Assoc of Anaesthetists 1977; FFARCS 1980; *Recreations* fell walking; *Style—* Dr Christopher Andrews; ✉ 21 Seymour Park, Mannamead, Plymouth PL3 5BQ (☎ 01752 664830); Derriford Hospital, Department of Anaesthetics, Derriford Rd, Plymouth PL6 8DH (☎ 01752 792691)

ANDREWS, David Roger Griffith; CBE (1980); s of C H R Andrews, and G M Andrews; *b* 27 March 1933; *Educ* Abingdon Sch, Pembroke Coll Oxford (MA); *m* 1963, (Dorothy) Ann, da of B A Campbell, CBE (d 1962); 2 s, 1 da; *Career* exec vice chm BL 1977–81, chief exec Land Rover-Leyland Group 1982–86 (chm 1981–86), chm Gwion Ltd 1986–95; dir: Clarges Pharmaceutical Trustees Ltd 1983–91, Glaxo Trustees Ltd 1983–91, Ex-Cell-O Ltd 1987–88, Fndn for Sci and Technol 1990–95 (Fndn Medal 1996); memb: Cncl CBI 1981–86, Exec Ctee SMMT 1981–86; FCMA, FRSA, CIMgt; *Recreations* sailing, photography; *Style—* David Andrews, Esq, CBE; ✉ Gainford, Mill Lane, Gerrards Cross, Bucks

ANDREWS, (William) Denys Cathcart; CBE (1980); s of Eugene Andrews (d 1947), of Girvan, and Agnes, *née* Armstrong (d 1964); *b* 3 June 1931; *Educ* Girvan HS, Worksop Coll Notts, Univ of Edinburgh (BL); *m* 11 Nov 1955, May, da of Thomas O'Beirne (d 1985), of Ayr; 2 s (Patrick b 1962, Martin b 1964), 2 da (Caroline (Mrs Harris) b 1960, Alison (Mrs Cosslett) b 1967); *Career* slr; ptnr Shepherd & Wedderburn 1962–91, ret; pres Law Soc of Scotland 1978–79 (cncl memb 1972–81, vice pres 1977–78), pt/t memb Lands Tbnl for Scotland 1980–91; memb Soc of Writers to HM Signet (fiscal 1987–91); *Recreations* gardening; *Style—* Denys Andrews, Esq, CBE; ✉ Auchairne, Ballantrae, South Ayrshire (☎ 01465 831344)

ANDREWS, Sir Derek Henry; KCB (1991, CB 1984), CBE (1970); s of late Henry Andrews, and late Emma Jane Andrews; *b* 17 Feb 1933; *Educ* LSE (BA); *m* 1, 1956, Catharine May, *née* Childe (d 1982); 2 s, 1 da; m 2, 29 Nov 1991, Mrs Alison M Blackburn, *née* Nield; *Career* MAFF: asst princ 1957, asst private sec to Min of Agric, Fisheries & Food 1960–61, princ 1961, private sec to PM 1966–70, asst sec 1968, under sec 1973, dep sec 1981–87, perm sec 1987–93; chm Residuary Milk Mktg Bd 1994; Harvard Univ USA 1970–71; *Style—* Sir Derek Andrews, KCB, CBE; ✉ c/o The Reform Club, 104 Pall Mall, London SW1V 5EW

ANDREWS, Prof Edgar Harold; s of Richard Thomas Andrews (d 1968); *b* 16 Dec 1932; *Educ* Dartford GS, Univ of London (BSc, PhD, DSc); *m* 1961, Thelma Doris, da of Selby John Walker, of Watford; 1 s (Martyn b 1964), 1 da (Rachel b 1962); *Career* dean Faculty of Engrg QMC (now Queen Mary and Westfield Coll) 1971–74 (prof of materials 1968–); dir: QMC Industrial Research Ltd 1970–88, Denbyware Ltd 1971–81, Materials Technol Consultants Ltd 1974–, Evangelical Press 1975–, Fire and Materials Ltd 1985–88, Metal Technology Inc; recipient A A Griffith Silver Medal 1977; FIP, FIM, CEng, CPhys; *Books* Fracture in Polymers (1968), From Nothing to Nature (1978), God, Science and Evolution (1980), The Promise of the Spirit (1982), Christ and the Cosmos (1986), Free in Christ (1996); *Recreations* writing, music, church work; *Style—* Prof Edgar Andrews; ✉ Redcroft, 87 Harmer Green Lane, Welwyn, Herts (☎ 01438 798376); Queen Mary and Westfield College, Mile End Rd, London E1 4NS (☎ 0171 975 5152)

ANDREWS, Ernest Somers; s of Charles Andrews (d 1961), of Manchester, and Dorothy, *née* Tonks (d 1989); *b* 10 June 1928; *Educ* Chorlton GS Manchester, Wigan Mining Coll, Salford Tech Coll, UMIST; *m* 22 Sept 1973, Norma, da of William Wilkinson (d 1974), of Manchester; 3 da (Elizabeth Sarah b 1974, Alexandra Dorothy b 1976, Victoria Mary Jane b 1983); *Career* WWII REME 1946–49; princ Charles Andrews & Sons Consltg Engrs 1956–; former pres: Manchester Assoc of Engrs, Rotary Club of Manchester South; former chm Manchester Branch Inst Plant Engrs; CEng, FIMechE, FIPlantE, FFB, MConsE; *Recreations* military history, industrial archaeology, gardening; *Style—* Ernest Andrews, Esq; ✉ Charles Andrews & Sons, Charter Buildings, Ashton Lane, Sale, Manchester M33 IWT (☎ 0161 973 6782, fax 0161 962 0617)

ANDREWS, Graham Eric; s of Leonard Christopher Andrews (d 1980), and Gladys, *née* Blackburn (d 1989); *b* 9 May 1932; *Educ* Preston GS, Plympton GS; *m* 1, 11 Dec 1955, Muriel Dorothy (d 1984), da of Alfred Thomas Adams (d 1975); 2 da (Sheila (Mrs Thomas) b 1958, Linda (Mrs Stone) b 1961); m 2, 21 Dec 1985, Mrs Margaret Eileen Alker, da of Frederick Gardner Suckling (d 1963); *Career* retail mgmnt 1948–83, conslt retail mangr 1983–91; memb: Combe Martin Parish Cncl 1967– (del to Nat Assoc of Local Cncls 1970–), Barnstaple Rural Dist Cncl 1970–74, Devon Co FA 1970–85 and 1996–, SW Sports Cncl 1972–91, N Devon Dist Cncl 1973–76 and 1979–91, Assoc of Dist Cncls 1974–76, N Devon Community Health Cncl 1974–80, Devon Family Practitioner Ctee 1981–90, Exmoor Nat Park Authy 1985–89, Devon CC 1985–89, N Devon Health Authy 1986–89, Devon Sea Fisheries Authy 1986–89, Berrynarbor Parish Cncl 1987–, Cncl of Assoc of CCs 1988–89, Ofwat SW Customer Serv Ctee 1989–93, Gas Consumer Cncl 1991–; non-exec dir Northern Devon Healthcare NHS Tst 1990–94; chm: N Devon Community Health Cncl 1976–79, Conf of SW Sports Orgns 1976–85, Devon Assoc of Parish Cncls 1978–, SW Advsy Ctee Sports Aid Fndn 1980–85, SW Water Consultative 1983–89, N Devon Dist Cncl 1984–86, N Devon Cons Assoc 1993–96; pres Plymouth Argyle Vice-Presidents Club 1995–96; MRSH 1976; Maistre De Ordre International De Anysetiers (France) 1987; *Books* The Councillor's Role (1974); *Recreations* sport spectator; *Clubs* Clubmans, Barnstaple Cons; *Style—* Graham Andrews, Esq; ✉ Treetops, 1 Old Coast Rd, Berrynarbor, Ilfracombe, North Devon EX34 9RZ (☎ 01271 883385, fax 01271 883375)

ANDREWS, Prof John A; JP (1975, supplemental list 1992); s of Arthur George Andrews (d 1980), of Newport, Gwent, and Hilda May Andrews (d 1989); *b* 29 Jan 1935; *Educ* Newport HS, Wadham Coll Oxford (MA, BCL); *m* 2 April 1960, Elizabeth Ann Mary, da of Frederick Edward Wilkes (d 1939), of King's Heath, Birmingham; 2 da (Carolyn Elizabeth b 1963, Susan Rebecca b 1966); *Career* called to the Bar Gray's Inn 1960, bencher 1991; asst lectr Univ of Manchester 1957–58, lectr Univ of Birmingham 1958–67; Univ of Wales Aberystwyth: head Dept of Law 1970–92, prof of law 1967–92, vice princ 1985–88, hon prof of law 1992–; chief exec Further and Higher Educn Funding Cncls for Wales 1992–; visiting prof Univs of: Thessaloniki 1974 and 1990, Cracow 1978, Maryland 1983; ed Legal Studies 1981–; chm: Cncl of Validating Univs 1987–90, Police Promotions Examinations Bd 1987–; pres SPTL 1988–89, memb Police Trg Cncl 1987–, memb Lord Chllr's Advsy Ctee on Legal Educn 1987–90, chm Wales Advsy Body for Local Authy Higher Educn Standing Working Gp 1990–92, memb Welsh Economic Cncl 1994, tstee Hamlyn Tst 1969–; *Books* Welsh Studies in Public Law (ed, 1970), Human Rights in Criminal Procedure (ed, 1982), The Welsh Language in the Courts (jtly, 1984), The International Protection of Human Rights (jtly, 1987), Criminal Evidence (jtly, 1987, 2nd edn 1992), Criminal Evidence - Cases and Materials (1990); *Recreations* walking, theatre, food; *Clubs* Brynamlwg; *Style—* Prof John Andrews, JP; ✉ 7 Maeshendre, Aberystwyth, Dyfed SY23 3PR (☎ 01970 623921); Welsh Funding Councils, Lambourne House, Cardiff Business Park, Llanishen, Cardiff CF4 5GL (☎ 01222 761861, fax 01222 763163); Department of Law, University College of Wales, Aberystwyth, Dyfed SY23 3DY (☎ 01970 622712, fax 01970 622729)

ANDREWS, John Malcolm; s of Leslie Andrews (d 1980), and Gwen, *née* Eite; *b* 11 June 1942; *Educ* Bromley GS; *m* Elizabeth Faith, da of Harry Crispin Smith; 2 s (Thomas Crispin b 2 Feb 1970, James Henry b 7 July 1972); *Career* Inland Revenue 1962–65; Coopers & Lybrand: joined 1965, head of tax 1986–93, sr tax ptnr 1994–; memb Cncl Chartered Inst of Taxation 1992– (dep pres 1996–97); FTII 1967, FCA 1974; *Books* Taxation of Directors and Employees (4 edn, 1995); *Recreations* all sport; *Style—* John Andrews, Esq; ✉ Coopers & Lybrand, 1 Embankment Place, London WC2N 6NN (☎ 0171 212 4504)

ANDREWS, Mark Björnsen; s of Harry Field Andrews, of Reading, and Ruth Margaret, *née* Legge; *b* 12 July 1952; *Educ* Reading GS, Hertford Coll Oxford (BA); *Career* admitted slr 1976; Wilde Sapte: ptnr 1979–, head of Insolvency Gp 1990–, sr ptnr 1996–; tstee Pimlico Opera; memb: Law Soc 1974, Soc of Practitioners of Insolvency 1991, City of London Slrs' Co 1994, IOD 1994, Int Bar Assoc 1994; *Recreations* music, history, outdoor activities, ornithology; *Style—* Mark Andrews, Esq; ✉ Wilde Sapte, Number 1 Fleet Place, London EC4M 7WS (☎ 0171 246 7000, fax 0171 246 7777)

ANDREWS, Mark Canter; s of Peter J Andrews (d 1993), of Bristol, and Joyce, *née* Abbey; *b* 9 Nov 1954; *Educ* Bristol Cathedral Sch; *Career* trainee architect Moxley Jenner & Partners 1973–74; graphic designer: BBC Bristol 1974–76, ITV (ATV, HTV, Westward TV) 1976–78; prodr Freeman Mathews & Milne advtg agency 1978–80; Collett Dickenson Pearce & Partners: prodr 1980–86, bd dir/head of TV 1986–89, fndr chm Independent Image (subsid) 1989–92; fndr md Propaganda Films Europe (subsid of Polygram Plc) 1992–95, md Rogue Films (subsid of Carlton Plc) 1995–96; numerous awards for TV campaigns incl: 7 Gold, 14 Silver and 23 Bronze Lions Int Advtg Festival Cannes, 39 Clio awards; chm Pliatsky II Ctee 1994–95; former memb: ACTT, IPA; memb AFVPA 1992; *Recreations* skiing, wine, fly fishing, lunch and big hi-fi; *Clubs* The Lunch, Soho House; *Style*— Mark Andrews, Esq; ✉ 25 Battersea Church Road, London SW11 3LY (☎ 0171 801 0025)

ANDREWS, (J) Michael G; s of Air Vice-Marshal J O Andrews, CB, DSO, MC (d 1989), and Bertha Winifred, *née* Bisdee (d 1992); *b* 6 Nov 1926; *Educ* Shrewsbury, Magdalen Coll Oxford (MA), Harvard Business Sch (MBA); *m* Oct 1988, Sylvia, da of Dr Charles Rothschild (d 1988); 2 da (Carolyn b 1955, Victoria b 1959); *Career* dir: Hill Samuel & Co 1963–68, Samuel Montagu & Co 1968–72; chief exec Brandts 1972–75; non-exec directorships incl: Bankside Underwriting Agencies Ltd, Bluebird Toys plc, Hambro Countrywide plc, National Mortgage Bank plc, Angerstein Underwriting Trust plc, Credit Lyonnais Capital Markets Plc, Laing & Cruickshank Investment Management, Michael Page Group Plc; former non-exec dir: Royal Worcester, Teachers (Distillers); external memb Cncl Lloyd's of London 1985–87, former memb Chemical Indust EDC; FCA; *Recreations* fishing; *Clubs* Leander; *Style*— Michael Andrews, Esq; ✉ Credit Lyonnais Capital Markets Plc, 5 Appold St, London EC2A 2DA (☎ 0171 229 5954)

ANDREWS, Peter John; QC (1991); s of Reginald Percy Andrews, of Sutton Coldfield, and Dora, *née* Carter; *b* 14 Nov 1946; *Educ* Bishop Veseys GS, Univ of Bristol (undergraduate scholar), Christ's Coll Cambridge; *m* 10 Sept 1976, (Hilary) Ann, da of Graham Chavasse (d 1978); 2 da (Emily Alice b 19 May 1979, Fleur Victoria b 17 May 1981); *Career* called to the Bar Lincoln's Inn 1970 (Hardwicke scholar), jr Midland and Oxford Circuit 1973–74, dir Birmingham Legal Advice Centre 1974–75, recorder of the Crown Court 1990– (asst recorder 1986–90), chm Fountain Court Chambers Ltd 1994–; *Books* Catastrophic Injuries: A Guide to Compensation (1997); *Style*— Peter Andrews, Esq, QC; ✉ 199 Strand, London WC2R 1DR (☎ 0171 379 9779, fax 0171 379 9481)

ANDREWS, Raymond Denzil Anthony; MBE (1953), VRD (1960); s of Michael Joseph Andrews (d 1975), of Herts, and Phyllis Marie, *née* Crowley (d 1972); *b* 5 June 1925; *Educ* Highgate Sch, Christ's Coll Cambridge, Univ of London, Univ of Michigan; *m* 28 Sept 1958, (Anne) Gillian Whitlaw, da of David Small (d 1933); 1 s (Michael James b 1964), 1 da (Emily Justine b 1968); *Career* Lt RM 1946, Maj RMR 1968; sr ptnr Andrews Downie & Ptnrs Architects 1960–; first prize Royal Mint Square Housing Competition 1974; pres Architectural Assoc 1977–78, RIBA (vice pres 1984); Order of Al Rafidan of Iraq 1956; *Recreations* sailing (sloop 'Blaise'); *Style*— Raymond Andrews, Esq, MBE; ✉ 34 Clarendon Rd, Holland Park, London W11 3AD (☎ 0171 727 4129); Andrews Downie & Partners, 6 Addison Ave, London W11 4QR (☎ 0171 602 7701, fax 0171 602 8480)

ANDREWS, Richard Edward; s of William Reginald Andrews (d 1983), and Agnes Ruby Whiffen (d 1994); *b* 15 Aug 1936; *Educ* Cambridge HS, St Catharine's Coll Cambridge (MA); *m* 20 Aug 1982, Stephanie Elizabeth, da of Percy Craig, of Motueka, NZ; 1 s, 1 da; *Career* Fly Offr RAF Fighter Cmd 1955–57; sr conslt PA 1965–72, personnel mangr BLMC 1972–74, personnel dir Franklin Mint USA 1974–78, business mangr Cassells 1979, gp personnel dir Dixons Group plc 1980–95; dir Dixons Bradford CTC Trust 1988–, memb Industl Tbnls 1995–; FIPD, FRSA; *Recreations* golf, watching cricket, rugby, sketching; *Clubs* Savile, Achilles, Elstree Golf; *Style*— Richard Andrews, Esq; ✉ 14 Grange Gardens, Pinner, Middlesex HA5 5QE (☎ and fax 0181 429 2305)

ANDREWS, Stuart Morrison; s of William Hannaford Andrews (d 1975), and Eileen Elizabeth, *née* Morrison (d 1987); *b* 23 June 1932; *Educ* Newton Abbot GS, St Dunstan's Coll, Sidney Sussex Coll Cambridge (MA); *m* 1962, Marie Elizabeth, da of Jacobus Petrus van Wyk, of SA; 2 s (Jeremy b 1963, Christopher b 1966); *Career* headmaster: Norwich Sch 1967–75, Clifton 1975–90; ed Conference 1971–82; dep chm Assisted Places Ctee 1981–91, nat rep HMC Ctee 1986–87; HMC lead inspr of schs 1994–; FRSA; *Books* Eighteenth Century Europe (1965), Enlightened Despotism (1967), Methodism and Society (1970); *Recreations* walking, writing; *Style*— Stuart Andrews, Esq; ✉ 34 St Thomas St, Wells, Somerset BA5 2UX (☎ 01749 674123)

ANDRUS, (Francis) Sedley; LVO (1982); s of late Brig-Gen Thomas Alchin Andrus, CMG, JP (d 1959), and Alice Loveday, *née* Parr (d 1984); b on first anniversary of d of gf Adm Alfred Arthur Chase Parr, FRGS, sometime a Naval ADC to Queen Victoria; *b* 26 Feb 1915; *Educ* Wellington, St Peter's Coll Oxford (MA); *Career* Bluemantle Pursuivant of Arms 1970–72, Lancaster Herald of Arms 1972–82, Beaumont Herald of Arms Extraordinary 1982–; landowner; Freeman City of London 1988; *Books* Written for Fun (1996), Written to Order: A Book Within a Book (1996); *Style*— Sedley Andrus, Esq, LVO; ✉ College of Arms, Queen Victoria St, London EC4V 4BT (☎ 0171 248 2762); 8 Oakwood Rise, Longfield, Kent DA3 7PA (☎ 01474 705424)

ANG, Dr Swee Chai; da of P L Ang, of Singapore, and L H Ang, *née* Lee; *b* 26 Oct 1948; *Educ* Raffles GS, Univ of Singapore (MB BS, MSc); *m* 29 Jan 1977, Francis Khoo, s of Anthony T E Khoo (d 1972), of Singapore; *Career* orthopaedic surgn HS of Beirut 1976–, surgn UN Gaza Strip 1988–89, conslt surgn WHO Gaza and W Bank 1989, sr conslt orthopaedic surgn Newham Gen Hosp London, conslt orthopaedic surgn Royal London Hosp; fndr memb Br Charity Medical Aid for Palestinians; memb BMA, FBOA, FRCS; *Books* From Beirut to Jerusalem (1989), Manual of War Surgery (1994); *Recreations* music, poetry; *Style*— Dr Swee Ang; ✉ Medical Aid for Palestinians, 33A Islington Park Street, London N1 1QB (☎ 0171 226 4114, fax 0171 226 0880)

ANGADI, Patricia Clare; da of Robert Fell-Clark (d 1948), of London, and Clare, *née* Williams (d 1966); *b* 23 Sept 1914; *Educ* Frognal Sch Hampstead, Prior's Field Sch Godalming, Heatherly's Sch of Art, Paris; *m* 1 May 1943, Ayana Deva Angadi (d 1993); 3 s (Daniel Shankara b 1944, Dominic Ashoka b 1946, Darien Kabir b 1949), 1 da (Chandrika Clare Eulalie b 1953); *Career* writer and painter; co-fndr (with husband) Asian Music Circle to promote Asian music and dance 1946–60s; chm Hampstead Artists' Cncl 1950s-60s; portraits incl: James Maxton (Glasgow People's Art Gall), Baron Reuter (Reuter's Press Assoc Library Archive Aachen), Ali Akbar Khan, Vilayat Khan, Ravi Shankar, George and Patti Harrison; exhibited at: RSPP, Soc of Women's Artists, Women's Int Art Club and others; *Books* The Governess (1985, runner up Best First Work Yorkshire Post, finalist First Work David Higham Award), The Done Thing (1986), The Highly Flavoured Ladies (1987), Sins of the Mothers (1989), Playing for Real (1990), Turning the Turtle (1991), My Mother Said (1994); numerous contribs to magazines and jls; *Recreations* gardening; *Style*— Mrs Patricia Angadi; ✉ c/o Jane Conway Gordon, 1 Old Compton Street, London W1V 5PH (☎ 0171 494 0148)

ANGEL, Anthony Lionel; s of William Angel, of London N3, and Frances Beatrice, *née* Berman; *b* 3 Dec 1952; *Educ* Haberdashers' Aske's, Queens' Coll Cambridge (MA); *m* 2 Nov 1975, Ruth Frances Barbara, da of Ivan Frank Hartog, of Northwood, Middx; 2 s (Benjamin b 3 Dec 1978, Jonathan b 18 Sept 1982); *Career* admitted slr 1978; ptnr Linklaters & Paines 1984– (joined 1976, head of tax 1994–); memb: Worshipful Co of Slrs, Law Soc; *Recreations* tennis, swimming, skiing; *Style*— Anthony Angel, Esq; ✉ Linklaters & Paines, Barrington House, 59–67 Gresham St, London EC2V 7JA (☎ 0171 606 7080, fax 0171 606 5113, e-mail tangel@linklaters.com)

ANGEL, Donald; CBE; s of Bertram Angel (d 1951), and Alice Amelia, *née* Peterson (d 1993); *b* 20 Oct 1926; *Educ* East Ham GS, LSE (BSc Econ); *m* 1, 1948 (m dis), Anne Helene Jenny Schwarze; 1 s, 1 da; m 2, 1983, Elisabeth Joanna Young; *Career* chm: Lipton Ltd 1972–74, Wall's Meat Co Ltd 1974–78, Birds Eye Foods Ltd 1979–81, Birds Eye Wall's Ltd 1981–88; dir: Trebor Ltd 1987–89, Associated Fresh Foods Ltd 1988–91, Travellers Fare Ltd 1989–92; pres UK Assoc of Frozen Food Producers 1984–86, exec memb Cncl Food and Drink Fedn 1986–88; govr Francis Holland Schs 1975–, memb Cncl GPDST 1988–; CIMgt; *Recreations* opera, antique furniture, gardening; *Style*— Donald Angel, Esq, CBE; ✉ 41 Canonbury Square, London N1 2AW (☎ 0171 359 4645)

ANGEL, District Judge; Gerald Bernard Nathaniel Aylmer; s of Bernard Francis Angel (d 1963), and Ethel Angel (d 1988); *b* 4 Nov 1937; *Educ* St Mary's Sch Nairobi Kenya; *m* 1968, Lesley Susan, da of Rev Preb Cyril Kenneth Alfred Kemp (d 1987); 4 s (Matthew b 1971, Thomas b 1975, Benedict b and d 1978, Christopher b 1979), 1 da (Katharine b 1969); *Career* served Kenya Regt 1956–57; called to the Bar Inner Temple 1959, advocate Kenya 1960–62, practised at Bar 1962–80, registrar Family Div High Ct 1980–90; memb: Civil and Family Sub-Ctee Judicial Studies Bd 1985–90, Judicial Studies Bd 1989–90; dist judge 1990, sr dist judge of the Family Div 1991–; memb: Supreme Court Procedure Ctee 1990–, Matrimonial Causes Rule Ctee 1991, Family Proceedings Rule Ctee 1991–; ed Industrial Tribunal Reports 1966–78, advsy ed and contributor Atkin's Court Forms 1988–; *Style*— District Judge Angel; ✉ 9 Lancaster Avenue, London SE27 9EL; Principal Registry of the Family Division, Somerset House, Strand, London WC2

ANGEL, Dr Heather; da of Stanley Paul Le Rougel, and Hazel Marie, *née* Sherwood; *b* 21 July 1941; *Educ* 14 schs in England and NZ, Univ of Bristol (BSc, MSc); *m* 3 Oct 1964, Martin Vivian Angel, s of Thomas Huber Angel; 1 s (Giles Philip b 25 May 1977); *Career* marine biologist, professional wildlife photographer, author and lectr; special prof Dept of Life Science Univ of Nottingham 1994–; columnist Amateur Photographer 1990–; solo exhibitions: Kodak Exhibition The Natural History of Britain and Ireland (Science Museum) 1981, Nature in Focus (Nat Hist Museum) 1987, The Art of Wildlife Photography (Nature in Art, Gloucester) 1989; television appearances (demonstrating photographic techniques): Me and My Camera 1981 and 1983, Gardeners' World 1983 and 1991, Nature 1984, Nocon on Photography 1988; pres Royal Photographic Soc 1984–86; RPS Hood medal 1975, Medaille de Salverte (Société Française de Photographie) 1984; Hon DSc Univ of Bath 1986; Hon FRPS 1986 (FRPS 1972), FBIPP 1972; *Books incl* Nature Photography: Its Art and Techniques (1972), Photographing Nature (5 vols, 1975), A Life in The Oceans (1977), The Book of Nature Photography (1983), Camera in the Garden (1984), The Book of Close-up Photography (1986), A View from a Window (1988), Nature in Focus (1988), Landscape Photography (1989), Animal Photography (1991), Kew: A World of Plants (1993), Photographing the Natural World (1994); *Recreations* travelling to remote parts of the world to photograph wilderness areas and unusual aspects of animal behaviour; *Style*— Dr Heather Angel; ✉ Highways, 6 Vicarage Hill, Farnham, Surrey GU9 8HJ (☎ 01252 716700, fax 01252 727464)

ANGEL, Marie Louise; da of Francis John Angel (d 1968), of Australia, and Thelma Lilie, *née* Sandow (d 1974); *b* 30 July 1953; *Educ* Methodist Ladies' Coll Adelaide; *m* 1985, David Charles Freeman, s of Howard Freeman; 1 da (Catherine Elinor b 13 May 1989), 1 s (Lachlan John b 28 Feb 1993); *Career* soprano; with Opera Factory London 1982–; winner Gulbenkian prize 1977, Countess of Munster prize 1977; *Performances* with Opera Factory incl: Pretty Polly 1983, Donna Anna in Don Giovanni 1990 and 1992, Countess Almaviva in Don Giovanni 1992 (later filmed for Channel 4), Fiordiligi in Cosi fan Tutte 1986 (later filmed for Channel 4), Hannah in Yan Tan Thethera 1992, title role in L'Incoronazione di Poppea 1992, Sarajevo 1994 (several roles incl Cassandra in Trojan Women), Dido in Dido & Aeneas London and Zurich 1995; others incl: Oracle of the Dead in The Mask of Orpheus (ENO) 1986, Donna Anna (Melbourne State Opera) 1990, cr role Morgan le Fay in Gawain (Royal Opera House Covent Garden) 1991, cr role Esmerelda in Rosa (Peter Greenaway and Louis Andriessen, Netherlands Opera) 1994, cr role Ingrid in Lovendier Esmée Holland Festival 1995, Countess in Soldaten (ENO) 1996; also appeared in Peter Greenaway's film Prospero's Books 1991; *Recreations* gardening; *Style*— Ms Marie Angel; ✉ c/o Allied Artists' Agency, 42 Montpelier Square, London SW7 1JZ

ANGELL, Prof Ian Oakley; s of Roy Oakley Angell, of Bargoed, Mid Glamorgan, and Eluned (d 1972); *b* 8 July 1947; *Educ* Lewis Sch Pengam Mid Glamorgan, Univ of Wales (BSc), Univ of London (PhD); *m* 30 July 1971, Florence Mary, da of John Graham Davies, of Bargoed, Mid Glamorgan; *Career* Univ of London: lectr Royal Holloway Coll 1971–84, sr lectr UCL 1984–86, prof of info systems LSE 1986–; ed MacMillan Info Systems Series; fndr memb Euro Orgn for East-West Cooperation, memb Steering Ctee of UNESCO Regnl Office for Sci and Tech for Europe (Venice), conslt strategic information systems and int and organisational information tech policies; *Books* incl: A Practical Introduction To Computer Graphics (1981), High Resolution Computer Graphics Using C (1990), Information Systems Management (1991), Advanced Graphics on VGA and XGA cards with Borland C++ (1992); *Recreations* opera, ballet, cats, computing; *Style*— Prof Ian Angell; ✉ London School of Economics and Political Science, Department of Information Systems, Houghton Street, London WC2A 2AE (☎ 0171 405 7686, fax 0171 242 0392, telex 24655 BLPES G)

ANGERS, Brian Mason; s of Ernest Angers (d 1953), and Eunice Mason (d 1990); *b* 18 Nov 1936; *Educ* Lancaster Royal GS, Univ of Oxford (Cert in Mgmnt Studies); *m* 2 May 1992, Sarah Prendergast; 2 s (Harry b 19 April 1993, John b 18 June 1995); *Career* formerly dir: The Cunard Steamship Co plc, Cunard Line Ltd, Ritz Hotel (London) Ltd, Cunard Ellerman Ltd, Dartford River Crossing Company Ltd, HeavyLift Cargo Airlines Ltd, Midland Expressway Ltd (Birmingham Northern Relief toll rd, also gen mangr), currently dir: Kvaerner Corporate Development Ltd, Cunard Sea Goddess Ltd; exec dir Eurorail CTRL Ltd; FCA; *Recreations* tennis, golf; *Clubs* Wentworth; *Style*— Brian M Angers, Esq; ✉ Ku-Ring-Gai, Broomfield Park, Sunningdale, Ascot, Berkshire SL5 0JT (☎ 01344 20296); Kvaerner Corporate Development Ltd, 20 Eastbourne Terrace, London W2 6LE (☎ 0171 262 8080)

ANGLESEY, 7 Marquess of (UK 1815); Sir George Charles Henry Victor Paget; 10 Bt (I 1730); also Lord Paget of Beaudesert (E 1552) and Earl of Uxbridge (GB 1784); s of 6 Marquess of Anglesey (d 1947), and Lady Marjorie Manners, da of 8 Duke of Rutland; *b* 8 Oct 1922; *Educ* Eton; *m* 16 Oct 1948, Elizabeth Shirley Vaughan, DBE, LVO, da of Charles Langbridge Morgan, the writer (*see* Anglesey, Marchioness of); 2 s, 3 da; *Heir* s, Earl of Uxbridge; *Career* Maj RHG 1946; JP 1959–68 and 1983–89; dir Wales Nationwide Building Society 1973–89; pres Anglesey Cons Assoc 1949–83, chm Historic Bldgs Cncl for Wales 1977–92, tstee National Portrait Gallery 1979–90; memb: National Heritage Memorial Fund 1980–92, Royal Cmmn on Historical Manuscripts 1984–91; DL Anglesey 1960, Vice Lord-Lt of Anglesey 1960–83, Lord-Lt for Gwynedd 1983–89; Hon DLitt Univ of Wales 1984, hon prof UCW (Bangor) 1986; FSA, FRHistS, FRSL, Hon FRIBA; *Books* The Capel Letters (1955), One-Leg (1961), Sergeant Pearman's Memoirs (1968), Little Hodge (1971), A History of the British Cavalry 1816–1919 (Vol I 1973, Vol II 1975, Vol III 1982, Vol IV 1986, Vol V 1994, Vol VI 1995, Vol VII 1996); *Recreations* music, gardening; *Style*— The Most Hon the Marquess of Anglesey, FSA; ✉ Plâs Newydd, Llanfairpwll, Anglesey, Gwynedd (☎ 01248 714330)

ANGLESEY, Marchioness of; (Elizabeth) Shirley Vaughan Paget; DBE (1982, CBE 1977), LVO (1993); da of late Charles Morgan (novelist), and Hilda Vaughan (novelist); *b* 4 Dec 1924; *Educ* Francis Holland Sch, St James' Sch W Malvern, Kent Place Sch USA; *m* 1948, 7 Marquess of Anglesey; 2 s, 3 da; *Career* chm Nat Fedn of Women's Insts 1966–69, vice chm Govt Working Pty on Methods of Sewage Disposal 1969–70, dep chm Prince of Wales Ctee 1970–80, chm Welsh Arts Cncl 1975–81, memb IBA 1976–81, chm Br Cncl Drama and Dance Advsy Ctee 1981–91, chm Broadcasting Complaints Cmmn 1987–91, vice chm Museums and Galleries Cmmn 1981–96; tstee: Pilgrim Tst 1982–, Theatres Tst 1992–95; hon fell UCNW Bangor 1990; Hon LLD Univ of Wales 1977; *Style*— The Most Hon the Marchioness of Anglesey, DBE, LVO; ✉ Plâs Newydd, Llanfairpwll, Gwynedd (☎ 01248 714330)

ANGUS, Rev (James Alexander) Keith; LVO (1990), TD; s of Rev Walter Chalmers Smith Angus (d 1956), and Isabella Margaret Stephen (d 1979); *b* 16 April 1929; *Educ* HS of Dundee, Univ of St Andrews (MA); *m* 1956, Alison Jane, da of Donald Cargill Daly (d 1951), of Kirkcubrightshire; 1 s (Hugh), 1 da (Alison); *Career* Nat Serv Army TA, RA Capt, TA Royal Chaplains Dept; min: Hoddam Parish Church 1956–67, Gourock Old Parish Church 1967–79, Braemar and Crathie Parish Churches 1979–95, ret; domestic chaplain to HM The Queen 1979–96 (extra chaplain 1996–); *Recreations* fishing, hillwalking, golf; *Clubs* New (Edinburgh); *Style*— The Rev Keith Angus, LVO, TD; ✉ Darroch Den, Hawthorn Place, Ballater, Aberdeenshire (☎ 013397 56260)

ANGUS, Sir Michael Richardson; kt (1990); s of William Richardson Angus, and Doris Margaret Breach; *b* 5 May 1930; *Educ* Marling Sch Stroud Glos, Univ of Bristol (BSc); *m* Eileen Isabel May; 2 s, 1 da; *Career* served RAF 1951–54; Unilever: joined 1954, mktg dir Thibaud Gibbs Paris 1962–65, md Res Bureau 1965–67, sales dir Lever Brothers UK 1967–70, dir Unilever PLC 1970–92, toilet preparations co-ordinator 1970–76, chemicals co-ordinator 1976–80, regnl dir N America 1979–84, chm and chief exec offr Unilever United States Inc NY 1980–84, chm and chief exec offr Lever Brothers Co NY 1980–84, vice chm Unilever NV 1986–92, chm Unilever PLC 1986–92 (vice chm 1984–86); Whitbread PLC: non-exec dir 1986–, dep chm Jan 1992, chm May 1992–; chm The Boots Company plc 1994–, non-exec dep chm British Airways Plc 1989– (dir 1988–), non-exec dir National Westminster Bank PLC 1991– (dep chm 1991–94), non-exec dir Thorn EMI plc 1988–93; pres CBI 1992–94 (dep pres 1991–92 and 1994–95); memb Greenbury Ctee on executive pay 1995; chm of govrs: Ashridge Management Coll, RAC Cirencester; tstee Leverhulme Tst, dir The Ditchley Fndn, int cnsllr emeritus Conference Bd (NY); Holland Trade Award 1990; Hon DSc: Univ of Bristol 1990, Univ of Buckingham 1994; Hon LLD Univ of Nottingham 1996; CIMgt; hon memb RICS; Cdr Order of Oranje Nassau (Netherlands) 1992; *Recreations* countryside, wine, mathematical puzzles; *Clubs* Athenaeum, Univ (NY), Knickerbocker (NY); *Style*— Sir Michael Angus; ✉ Whitbread PLC, Chiswell St, London EC1Y 4SD (☎ 0171 606 4455, fax 0171 615 1012)

ANGUS, Robin John; s of Ian Gordon Angus, of Forres, Moray, Scotland (d 1991), and Morag Ann (Sally), *née* Macdonald; *b* 15 Sept 1952; *Educ* Forres Acad, Univ of St Andrews (MA), Peterhouse Cambridge; *m* 20 Aug 1977, Lorna Christine, da of James Smith Campbell (d 1986), of Drumlemble, Argyll, Scotland; *Career* investment mangr Baillie Gifford & Co 1977–81, investment tst analyst Wood Mackenzie & Co 1981–85, dir Personal Assets Trust plc 1984–, asst dir Wood Mackenzie & Co Ltd 1985–88; dir: Hill Samuel Securities Ltd 1985–88, NatWest Securities Ltd (incorporating Wood Mackenzie & Co Ltd) 1988–91 (dir equities 1991–), Charlotte Marketing Services Ltd 1991–94, The Edinburgh Agency Ltd 1991–, The Edinburgh Dealing Co Ltd 1993–95, Ivory & Sime Trustlink Ltd 1994–, Personal Assets Investments Ltd 1995–; memb Advsy Cncl Inst of Investmt Mgmnt 1990–, tstee and memb Ctee Scottish Centre for Economic and Social Research, ambass Highlands & Islands Enterprise 1993–, advsr Centre for Fin Markets Res Univ of Edinburgh 1995–; Gen Synod Scottish Episcopal Church 1987–91: memb, memb Faith and Order Bd, convenor Orgn Review Ctee; memb Working Pty on Fin and Ethics Centre for Theology and Public Issues Univ of Edinburgh, auditor and fin advsr Diocese of Moray Ross and Caithness Scottish Episcopal Church, dir Scottish Episcopal Church Clergy Widows and Orphans' Fund 1986–89; MSI 1993; *Books* Independence - The Option for Growth (1989), Haec Olim - Exploring the World of Investment Trusts 1981–1991 (1991), Capital - A Moral Instrument? (contrib, 1992), Dictionary of Scottish Church History and Theology (contrib, 1993); *Recreations* church work, politics (Scottish Nationalist), history, music, reading, writing verse; *Clubs* New (Edinburgh), Scottish Arts (Edinburgh), Royal Scottish Automobile (Glasgow), McSkate's (St Andrews); *Style*— Robin Angus, Esq; ✉ Director, Equities, NatWest Securities Ltd Incorporating Wood Mackenzie & Co Ltd, Kintore House, 74–77 Queen St, Edinburgh EH2 4NS (☎ 0131 225 8525, fax 0131 243 4269, telex 72555)

ANKARCRONA, Jan Gustaf Theodor Stensson; s of Sten Stensson Ankarcrona, RVO (d 1981), of Stockholm, Sweden, and Ebba, *née* Countess Mörner; *b* 18 April 1940; *Educ* Östra Real Stockholm, Stockholm Sch of Econ (MBA), Univ of California Berkeley (MBA); *m* 1, 16 June 1968 (m dis 1978), E Margaretha Antonie, da of Erik von Eckermann, of Ripsa, Sweden; 2 s (Johan b 1969, Edward b 1972); *m* 2, 6 March 1981, Sandra, da of E B Coxe, of New York, USA; 2 da (Aurore b 1983, Ariane b 1988); *Career* Royal Swedish Navy 1958–61, Lt-Cdr Royal Swedish Navy Reserve 1974; Stockholms Enskilda Bank Stockholm 1964–65, Gränges AB Stockholm 1966–69, American Express Securities SA Paris 1969–70, dep md Nordic Bank Ltd London 1971–83, md and chief exec Fennoscandia Bank Ltd London 1983–91, md Lexa UK Ltd London 1992–, non-exec dir Lindab AB Sweden 1994–; OStJ Sweden; *Recreations* shooting, sailing, tennis, music, history; *Clubs* Brooks's, Hurlingham, Nya Sällskapet Stockholm; *Style*— Jan Ankarcrona, Esq; ✉ 29 Argyll Rd, London W8 7DA (☎ 0171 937 9438); Lexa UK Ltd, 14 Queen Anne's Gate, London SW1H 9AA (☎ 0171 222 0400, fax 0171 222 0125)

ANNALY, 6 Baron (UK 1863); Luke Richard White; o s of 5 Baron Annaly (d 1990), and his 1 w, Lady Marye Isabel Pepys (d 1958), da of 7 Earl of Cottenham; *b* 29 June 1954; *Educ* Eton, RMA Sandhurst, RAC Cirencester; *m* 1983, Caroline Nina, yr da of Col Robert Hugh Garnett, MBE, of Hope Bowdler Court, nr Church Stretton, Shropshire; 1 s (Hon Luke Henry b 1990), 2 da (Hon Lavinia Marye b 1987, Hon Iona Elizabeth b 1989); *Heir* s, Hon Luke Henry White b 20 Sept 1990; *Career* Lt Royal Hussars 1974–78, RAC Reserve 1978–86; govt whip and Lord-in-Waiting 1994–; jt master The Bicester Hunt 1985–88; *Recreations* cricket, tennis, fox hunting, country pursuits; *Style*— The Rt Hon Lord Annaly; ✉ House of Lords, London SW1A 0PW

ANNAN, Baron (Life Peer UK 1965), of Royal Burgh of Annan, Co Dumfries; Noel Gilroy Annan; OBE (1946); s of James Gilroy Annan (d 1965), and Fannie Mildred, *née* Quinn (d 1970); *b* 25 Dec 1916; *Educ* Stowe, King's Coll Cambridge (BA, MA); *m* 30 June 1950, Gabriele, da of Louis Ferdinand Ullstein, of Berlin; 2 da (Hon (Amanda) Lucy (Hon Mrs de Grey) b 13 June 1952, Hon Juliet Louise (Hon Mrs Le Fanu) b 7 Jan 1955); *Career* served WO, War Cabinet Offices and Military Intelligence 1940–44, France and Germany 1944–46, GSO1 Political Div Br Control Cmmn 1945–46; Univ of Cambridge: fell King's Coll 1944–56 and 1966, asst tutor 1947, lectr in politics 1948–66, provost King's Coll 1956–66; sr fell Eton Coll 1956–66, provost UCL 1966–78, vice chllr Univ of London 1978–81; chm: Departmental Ctee on the Teaching of Russian in Schs 1960, Academic Planning Bd Univ of Essex 1965–70, Enquiry into the Disturbances at the Univ of Essex 1974, Ctee on Future of Broadcasting 1974–77, Bd of Tstees Nat Gallery 1980–85 (tstee 1978–85); memb: Academic Advsy Ctee Brunel Coll 1966–73, Academic Planning Bd UEA 1964–71, Public Schs Cmmn 1966–70; govr: Stowe Sch 1945–66, QMC London 1956–60; tstee: Churchill Coll Cambridge 1958–76, Br Museum 1963–78; Gulbenkian Fndn: memb Arts Ctee 1957–64, chm Educn Ctee 1971–76; dir Royal Opera House Covent Garden 1967–78, pres London Library 1980–96; FRHistS; *Clubs* Brooks's; *Style*— The Rt Hon the Lord Annan, OBE; ✉ 45 Ranelagh Grove, London SW1W 8PB (☎ 0171 730 4930)

ANNAND, Richard Wallace; VC (1940), DL (Co Durham 1956); s of Lt Cdr Wallace Moir Annand, Adj Collingwood Bn Royal Navy Div (ka Gallipoli 1915), and late Dora Elizabeth Chapman, of South Shields; *b* 5 Nov 1914; *Educ* Pocklington Sch E Yorks; *m* 1940, Shirley Osborne, JP, MBE; *Career* staff National Provincial Bank 1933–37; cmmnd RNVR (Tyne and London Divs) midshipman 1933, Sub-Lt 1936, transfd Durham LI 1938, served France and Belgium 1939–40, wounded, VC (first Army VC WWII), invalided (severe deafness) as Capt RARO 1948; personnel offr Finchale Trg Coll for the Disabled 1948–79, ret; Hon Freeman Co Borough of South Shields 1940; Col-in-Chief Euro Legion of Frontiersmen; pres: Royal British Legion Durham and Cleveland Counties Branch, Durham Co Assoc for the Disabled, North Eastern League of the Hard of Hearing, Durham City Branch DLI Assoc, South Shields Branch Normandy Veterans; past pres Newcastle and Gateshead Branch Dunkirk Veterans' Assoc, fndr memb British Assoc of the Hard of Hearing 1946; *Recreations* golf; *Clubs* Royal Over-Seas, Durham County; *Style*— Richard Annand, Esq, VC, DL

ANNANDALE AND HARTFELL, 11 Earl of (S, by Charter, 1662); Patrick Andrew Wentworth Hope Johnstone of Annandale and of that Ilk; DL (Dumfrieshire 1987); also Lord of Johnstone (S 1662), Hereditary Steward of Stewartry of Annandale, Hereditary Keeper of Castle of Lochmaben, and Chief of Clan Johnstone; s of Maj Percy Wentworth Hope Johnstone, TD, JP, RA (TA), *de jure* 10 Earl (d 1983), by his 2 w, Margaret Jane Hunter-Arundell (Dowager Countess of Annandale and Hartfell); claim to Earldom (which had been dormant since 1792) admitted by Ctee for Privileges of House of Lords, and a writ issued summoning him to Parl in the Upper House 1986; *b* 19 April 1941; *Educ* Stowe, RAC Cirencester; *m* 1969, Susan, o da of Col Walter John Macdonald Ross, CB, OBE, TD, JP, Lord Lt of the Stewartry, of Netherhall, Castle Douglas, Kirkcudbrightshire; 1 s (Hon David Patrick Wentworth, Hope Johnstone, Lord Johnstone and Master of Annandale & Hartfell b 13 Oct 1971), 1 da (Lady Julia Clare b 1974); *Heir* s, Lord Johnstone; *Career* underwriting memb Lloyd's 1976–; memb: Solway River Purification Bd 1970–86, Scottish Valuation Advsy Cncl to Sec of State for Scotland 1984–86, Annan Fishery Bd 1983–, Standing Cncl of Scottish Chiefs, various ctees Dumfries CC 1970–75, Dumfries & Galloway Regnl Cncl 1974–86; chm Royal Jubilee and Prince's Tst for Dumfries and Galloway 1984–88, Royal Scottish Forestry Soc 1981–84; dir: Bowerings Members Agency 1985–88, Murray Lawrence Members Agency 1988–92; Vice Lord Lt Dumfriesshire 1992; *Recreations* golf; *Clubs* Puffin's (Edinburgh), Brooks's; *Style*— The Rt Hon the Earl of Annandale and Hartfell, DL; ✉ c/o House of Lords, London SW1

ANNESLEY, Hon Francis William Dighton; s and h of 15 Viscount Valentia, *qv*; *b* 29 Dec 1959; *Educ* Falcons Bulawayo; *m* 1982, Shaneen Hobbs; 2 da (Kirsten b 1986, Sarah Ashleigh b 1989); *Style*— The Hon Francis Annesley

ANNESLEY, Sir Hugh Norman; QPM; *Career* chief constable RUC until 1996; *Style*— Sir Hugh Annesley, QPM; ✉ c/o RUC, Brooklyn, Knock Road, Belfast, Northern Ireland BT5 6LE (☎ 01232 650222)

ANNESLEY, (Arthur) Noël Grove; s of Edmund Patrick Grove Annesley, OBE (d 1975), of Castletownroche, Co Cork, and Ruth, *née* Rushforth; *b* 28 Dec 1941; *Educ* Harrow, Worcester Coll Oxford (open scholarship, MA); *m* 7 Sept 1968, Caroline Susan, da of Thomas Henry Waldore Lumley; 2 s (Marcus Robert Grove b 27 March 1972, James Alexander Grove b 22 May 1974); *Career* Christie, Manson & Woods Ltd: joined 1964, fndr Dept of Prints, Drawings and Watercolours, dep chm 1985–91 (dir 1969–91), dep chm Christie's International plc 1992– (dir 1989–); *Recreations* music (esp chamber), gardening, watching cricket, marine life, Ireland; *Clubs* Brooks's; *Style*— Noël Annesley, Esq; ✉ Christie's International plc, 8 King Street, St James's, London SW1Y 6QT (☎ 0171 389 2241, fax 0171 389 2530)

ANNESLEY, 10 Earl (I 1789); Patrick Annesley; also Baron Annesley (I 1758) and Viscount Glerawly (I 1766); s of 9 Earl Annesley (d 1979), and Nora, *née* Harrison (d 1992); *b* 12 Aug 1924; *m* 1947, Catherine, da of John Forrest Burgess; 4 da; *Heir* bro, Hon Philip Annesley, *qv*; *Style*— The Rt Hon The Earl Annesley

ANNESLEY, Hon Philip Harrison; s of 9 Earl Annesley (d 1979), and hp of bro, 10 Earl, *qv*; *b* 29 March 1927; *Educ* Strode's GS Egham, Army Tech Sch; *m* 1951, Florence Eileen (d 1995), da of late John Arthur Johnston, of Gillingham, Kent; *Career* REME: leading artisan 1948, armament artificer 1951; test and calibration engr Rediffusion Simulation Ltd 1957, system designer 1963, systems trg mangr Hughes Rediffusion Simulation Ltd 1989–91; *Style*— The Hon Philip Annesley; ✉ 17 Folly Mill Gardens, Bridport, Dorset DT6 3RN

ANNETT, Prof John; s of Frederick Annett, and Irene Laura Annett; *b* 11 July 1930; *Educ* Sir Joseph Williamson's Mathematical Sch Rochester, St Peter's Coll Oxford (MA, DPhil); *m* 9 April 1955, Marian Elsie, da of Harold Drabble; 1 s (James Frederick b 1961), 1 da (Lucy Elizabeth b 1958); *Career* Nat Serv RN 1948–50; asst psychologist Burden Mental Res Dept Univ of Bristol 1953–55, res worker Inst of Experimental Psychology Oxford 1955–60, sr res worker Univ of Sheffield 1960–63, lectr Univ of Aberdeen 1963–65, reader Univ of Hull 1968–72 (sr lectr 1965–68); prof of psychology: Open Univ 1972–74, Univ of Warwick 1974–94 (prof emeritus 1994–); FBPsS 1980, fell Ergonomics Soc 1985, CPsychol 1987; *Books* Feedback and Human Behaviour (1969), Introduction to Psychology (1974); *Recreations* music, watercolouring, gardening; *Style*— Prof John Annett; ✉ Department of Psychology, University of Warwick, Coventry CV4 7AL (☎ 01203 523165)

ANNING, Raymon Harry; CBE (1982), QPM (1975); *b* 22 July 1930; *m* 1949, Beryl Joan; 1 s (Nicholas b 17 April 1959), 1 da (Julie b 22 July 1955); *Career* E Surrey Regt and Royal Military Police 1948–50; Met Police 1952–79, HM Inspr of Constabulary for England and Wales 1979–83, cmmr of Police Royal Hong Kong Police Force 1985–90 (dep cmmr 1983–85); chm Securicor Consultancy Ltd 1991–96 (joined Securicor Group 1990); CIMgt 1980; *Style*— Raymon Anning, Esq, CBE, QPM

ANNIS, Philip Geoffrey Walter; s of Walter Annis, of Windermere, Cumbria, and Lilian Alice, *née* Norris; *b* 7 Feb 1936; *Educ* Sale Co GS, Kelsick GS Ambleside Westmorland, Univ of Manchester (BA); *m* 15 July 1967, Olive Winifred, da of Edward Walter Scarlett, OBE, of Ilford, Essex; 1 s (Edward Philip b 30 April 1970); *Career* Nat Serv 2 Lt RA 1957–59, actg Flt Lt RAFVR (T) 1960–62, Lt RA (TA) 1961–67; inspr Grade 3 Bd of Inland Revenue 1959–62; Nat Maritime Museum: joined 1962, co-ordinator of museum servs 1971–79, dep dir 1979–86; mangr of regtl history project RA Inst 1986–; FSA 1973, FRHistS 1975; Cdr of the Order of the Lion of Finland 1987; *Books* Naval Swords (1970), Swords for Sea Service (with Cdr W E May, 1970); *Recreations* gardening, reading; *Style*— Philip Annis, Esq, FSA; ✉ Royal Artillery Institution, Old Royal Military Academy, Woolwich, London SE18 4DN (☎ 0181 781 5613)

ANSARI, Dr Joseph Mohammad Ayub; s of Hakim Mohammad Yusuf Ansari (d 1971), and Hasina Khatoan, *née* Kidwai (d 1971); *b* 25 June 1938; *Educ* Shia Degree Coll Lucknow India (BSc), King Edward VII Med Coll Lahore Pakistan (MB BS); *m* 26 May 1972, Ruth, da of William Haughton Hill (d 1975), of Merseyside; 1 s (Arif b 20 Oct 1974), 1 da (Sarah b 16 Jan 1977); *Career* Dept of Psychiatry Univ of Liverpool: lectr 1971–75, sr lectr 1975–76, clinical lectr 1976–; conslt in psychological med 1976, med dir Regnl Alcohol Univ of Liverpool 1976–, surpervisor for Sr Registrar Training in Psychiatry Merseyside 1986–89; sec and treas NW Div RCPsych, treas Liverpool Psychiatric Soc (former pres); memb: Nat Cncl of Alcohol 1980–, World Psychiatric

Assoc 1985–, BMA 1988–; DPM 1970, MPsyMed 1975, FRCPsych 1985; *Publications* several contribs on psycho-sexual problems and mental illness in leading medical jls; *Recreations* photography, painting and reading; *Style*— Dr Joseph Ansari; ✉ 31 Rodney St, Liverpool L1 9EH (☎ 0151 709 8522)

ANSBRO, David Anthony; s of David Thomas Ansbro (d 1963), and Kathleen Mary, *née* Mallett; *b* 3 April 1945; *Educ* Xaverian Coll Manchester, Univ of Leeds (LLB), Coll of Law, Univ of Birmingham (Advanced Mgmnt Course); *m* 1967, Veronica Mary, *née* Ashton; 2 da (Lucy b 10 Aug 1965, Kate b 10 Sept 1970); *Career* admitted slr 1969, dep dir of admin W Yorks CC 1977–81 (asst dir of admin 1973–77), town clerk & chief exec York City Cncl 1981–85; chief exec: Kirklees Cncl 1985–87, Leeds City Cncl 1988–91; Eversheds: ptnr Leeds 1991, managing ptnr Leeds 1994–95, managing ptnr Leeds & Manchester 1995–; memb Local Govt Cmmn for England 1992–95, dir Leeds TEC 1990–, memb Cncl Leeds C of C; awarded Papal Medal 1982; memb: Law Soc 1969, SOLACE 1981; *Recreations* golf, wine, sport of any kind (except synchronised swimming!), passionate supporter of Manchester City FC; *Clubs* Honley Cricket, Upper Wharfedale RUFC; *Style*— David Ansbro, Esq; ✉ The Green, Airton, Skipton, North Yorkshire BD23 4AH (☎ 01729 830451); Eversheds, Cloth Hall Court, Infirmary Street, Leeds LS1 2JB (☎ 0113 200 4400, fax 0113 245 6188, mobile 0421 868684, e-mail pilot.ansbrod@eversheds.com)

ANSELL, His Hon Judge; Anthony Ronald Louis; s of Samuel Ansell (d 1974), of London, and Joan Teresa, *née* Berman; *b* 9 Sept 1946; *Educ* Dulwich Coll, UCL (LLB); *m* 28 June 1970, Karen Judith (Kaye); 1 s (Simon b 1 Jan 1978), 1 da (Naomi b 4 May 1979); *Career* called to the Bar Gray's Inn 1968, in practice until 1979, slr 1980–95, circuit judge (SE Circuit) 1995–; vice pres United Synagogue 1992–, memb Lawyers' Gp Jewish Cncl; *Books* Kalms Review - A Time for Change (co-author, 1992); *Recreations* opera, music, theatre, walking, swimming, gardening; *Style*— His Hon Judge Ansell; ✉ Barnet County Court, St Mary's Close, Regent's Park Road, London N3 1BQ (☎ 0181 343 4272, fax 0181 343 1324)

ANSELL, Mark John; s of John Frederick Ansell, of Birmingham, and Irene Francis, *née* Spiers (d 1982); *b* 2 Jan 1952; *Educ* Waverley GS Birmingham; *m* 2 March 1974, Sheila Mary, da of Victor William Marston, of Sutton Coldfield; *Career* CA 1973; ptnr Joslyne Layton Bennett & Co Birmingham 1977 (later merging with Binder Hamlyn), managing ptnr BDO Binder Hamlyn 1988–94 (Birmingham office taken over by Touche Ross 1994), head of corp fin Touche Ross (now Deloitte & Touche) 1994–; non-exec dir Good Hope Hosp NHS Tst, sr vice pres Aston Villa Football Club plc; formerly: chm City of Birmingham Round Table, treas Birmingham Rotary Club; FCA 1977 (ACA 1973), BMA 1987; *Recreations* golf, football (watching Aston Villa FC); *Clubs* Walmley Golf, Variety Club; *Style*— Mark Ansell, Esq; ✉ Deloitte & Touche, Colmore Gate, 2 Colmore Row, Birmingham B3 2BN (☎ 0121 200 2211)

ANSELL, Maj-Gen Nicholas George Picton; CB (1992), OBE (1980), JP (Bideford and Gt Torrington 1994), DL (Devon 1996); s of Col Sir Michael Picton Ansell, CBE, DSO, DL (d 1994), Bideford, Devon, and his 1 w, Victoria Jacintha Fleetwood, *née* Fuller (d 1969); *b* 17 Aug 1937; *Educ* Wellington, Magdalene Coll Cambridge (MA); *m* 17 June 1961, Vivien, da of Col Anthony Donnithorne Taylor, DSO, MC (d 1986), of N Aston, Oxon; 2 s (Mark b 1963, Julian b 1964), 1 da (Clare b 1968); *Career* cmmnd 5 Royal Inniskilling Dragoon Guards 1956 (served BAOR, Libya, Cyprus), Staff Coll Camberley 1970, Bde Maj RAC HQ 1 (BR) Corps 1971–72, instr Staff Coll Camberley 1976–77, CO 5 Royal Inniskilling Dragoon Guards 1977–80, Col GS Staff Coll Camberley 1980–81, OC 20 Armd Bde 1982–83, RCDS 1984, dep chief of staff HQ BAOR 1985–86, dir RAC 1987–89; Sr Directing Staff (Army) RCDS 1990–92; clerk of the course Exeter Racecourse 1995–; *Recreations* country pursuits; *Style*— Maj-Gen Nicholas Ansell, CB, OBE, JP, DL; ✉ Exeter Racecourse, Kennford, Exeter EX6 7XS

ANSELM, Marilyn; da of Henry Charlton (d 1961), and Mabel, *née* Draisey (d 1966); *b* 30 Dec 1944; *Educ* Homelands GS Derby, Derby Sch of Art, Central Sch of Art (DipAD); *m* 1968, Yoram Anselm, s of Isaac Anselm; 2 da (Aimie b 1969, Kate b 1972); *Career* fndr own retail business 1970, co-fndr/designer Bertie Shoes 1977, fndr/designer Hobbs clothing and shoe retailers 1980– (currently international with 35 UK outlets); *Recreations* opera, theatre, literature, equestrian pursuits, gardening; *Style*— Marilyn Anselm; ✉ Hobbs Ltd, 122 Gloucester Avenue, London NW1 8HX (☎ 0171 722 1576, fax 0171 586 3687)

ANSON, Cdr (Norman) Alastair Bourne; OBE (1983); s of Sir (George) Wilfrid Anson, MBE, MC (d 1974), of Bristol, and Dinah Maud Lilian, *née* Bourne; *b* 14 Oct 1929; *Educ* Winchester; *m* 23 Feb 1952 (m dis 1965), Collette Lavinia, da of Lt-Col Richard Eldred Hindson (d 1964), of Liss, Hants; 1 s (Richard b 11 Nov 1952), 1 da (Crispin b 4 Sept 1955); m 2, 27 Nov 1968, Lavinia Maude, da of Rear Adm Ion Tower, DSC (d 1941); *Career* RN 1947–82; CO HMS Carhampton Med 1956–58, Lt Cdr 2 i/c HMS Loch Lomond Persian Gulf 1959–61, Naval rep RMA Sandhurst 1961–63, CO HMS Keppel Arctic Fishery Sqdn 1963–65, CO HMS Londonderry Far E 1965–66, asst sec Chiefs of Staff Ctee 1967–69, 2 i/c HMS Fearless 1969–71, Cabinet Office 1972–75, NATO HQ Naples 1975–78, trg dir Sea Cadet Corps 1979–82, ret 1982; memb Panel Lord Chllr's Ind Inquiry Insprs responsible for inquiries on maj trunk road and motorway schemes; churchwarden St Martin-in-the-Fields, dir St Martin-in-the-Fields Enterprise Ltd; Freeman City of London 1982, Liveryman Worshipful Co of Tin Plate Workers 1982; FIL 1959, FRGS 1983; *Recreations* music (organist), tennis, skiing, photography; *Clubs* City Livery, The Queen's, Hurlingham; *Style*— Cdr Alastair Anson, OBE; ✉ 38 Catherine Place, London SW1E 6HL (☎ 0171 834 5991)

ANSON, Charles Vernon; CVO (1996, LVO 1983); s of Philip Vernon Anson, of E Sussex, and Stella, *née* Parish; *b* 11 March 1944; *Educ* Lancing, Jesus Coll Cambridge (BA), Johns Hopkins Univ; *m* 1976, Clarissa Rosamund, da of Christopher John Denton, of Lavant, W Sussex; 1 s (Louis b 1979), 1 da (Gemma b 1977); *Career* HM Dip Serv 1966–87, third then second sec (commercial) Br Embassy Washington 1968–71, FCO 1971–74, asst private sec to Min of State 1974–76, second sec (commercial) Tehran 1976–79, seconded to Press Office 10 Downing Street 1979–81, first sec (info) Br Embassy Washington 1981–85, FO 1985–87; dir of PR Kleinwort Benson Ltd 1987–90, press sec to HM The Queen 1990–97, gp corp rels dir Grand Metropolitan plc Feb 1997–; *Clubs* Hurlingham; *Style*— Charles Anson, Esq, CVO; ✉ Grand Metropolitan plc, 8 Henrietta Place, London W1M 9AG (☎ 0171 518 5200, fax 0171 518 4641)

ANSON, Colin Shane; s of Anthony John Anson (d 1981), of Highdown, Horam, Sussex, and Rosalind Désirée, *née* Arbuthnot (d 1985); *b* 29 July 1931; *Educ* Dragon Sch, Stowe, Slade Sch of Fine Art (Dip Fine Art); *Career* Art Dept Arts Cncl of GB 1956–66, Picture Dept Christie's 1967–70, Artemis Group 1971–96; dir: David Carritt Ltd (art dealers) 1981–96 (res asst 1971–81), Artemis Fine Arts Ltd 1981–96; ret; chm Villiers David Fndn 1991–; *Clubs* Brooks's; *Style*— Colin Anson, Esq; ✉ 18 Ripplevale Grove, London N1 1HU (☎ 0171 607 2995)

ANSON, Vice Adm Sir Edward Rosebery; KCB (1984); s of Ross Rosebery Anson (d 1959), and Ethel Jane, *née* Green; *b* 11 May 1929; *Educ* Prince of Wales Sch Nairobi, RNC Dartmouth; *m* 1960, Rosemary Anne, *née* Radcliffe; 1 s (Jonathan b 1965), 1 da (Mea); *Career* served Naval Air Sqdns 1952–64, graduated Empire Test Pilots Sch 1957, RN Test Pilot on Buccaneer Blackburn Aircraft Ltd 1959–61, CO 801 Sqdn 1962–64, CO HMS Eskimo 1964–66, Cdr (Air) RNAS Lossiemouth 1967–68, Cdr (Air) HMS Eagle 1969–70, CO InterService Hovercraft Unit 1971 (Capt 1971), Naval and Air Attaché Tokyo and Seoul 1972–74; cmd: HMS Juno and Capt 4 Frigate Sqdn 1974–76 (Capt 1971), HMS Ark Royal 1976–78 (last CO of the last traditional Br aircraft carrier); Flag Offr Naval Air Cmd 1979–82, Rear Adm 1980, Vice Adm 1982, COS to C-in-C Fleet 1982–84; Naval Weapons Div Br Aerospace 1984–86, pres and chief exec offr Br Aerospace Inc Washington DC USA 1986–89, sr naval advsr Br Aerospace plc 1989–91, aerospace conslt IAD Aerospace Ltd Worthing 1991–93; FRAeS 1982; *Recreations* golf, photography, walking; *Style*— Vice Adm Sir Edward Anson, KCB; ✉ c/o Lloyds Bank, 9 High St, Yeovil, Somerset BA20 1RN

ANSON, Lady Elizabeth; *see:* Shakerley, Lady Elizabeth Georgiana

ANSON, Sir John; KCB (1990, CB 1980); s of Sir Edward Anson, 6 Bt (d 1951), and Alison, da of Hugh Pollock (gs of Sir George Pollock, 1 Bt, GCB, GCSI); bro of Rear Adm Sir Peter Anson, 7 Bt, *qv*; *b* 3 Aug 1930; *Educ* Winchester, Magdalene Coll Cambridge (MA); *m* 1957, Myrica, da of Dr Harold Fergie-Woods (d 1961); 2 s, 2 da; *Career* HM Treas 1954–68, fin cnsllr Br Embassy Paris 1968–70, Cabinet Office 1971–74, under-sec HM Treas 1974–77, dep sec HM Treas 1977–87, econ min Br Embassy Washington and UK exec dir IMF and World Bank 1980–83, second perm sec HM Treas 1987–90; chm Public Finance Fndn 1991–94, chm Retirement Income Inquiry 1994–96; *Style*— Sir John Anson, KCB; ✉ 18 Church Rd, Barnes, London SW13 9HN (☎ 0181 748 6557)

ANSON, Rear Adm Sir Peter; 7 Bt (1831), of Birch Hall, Lancashire; CB (1974), DL (Surrey 1993); s of Sir Edward Reynell Anson, 6 Bt (d 1951), and Alison, da of Hugh Pollock (gs of Sir George Pollock, 1 Bt, GCB, GCSI); bro of Sir John Anson, KCB, *qv*; *b* 31 July 1924; *Educ* RNC Dartmouth; *m* 16 April 1955, Dame Elizabeth Audrey Anson, DBE, JP, DL, da of Rear Adm Sir (Charles) Philip Clarke, KBE, CB, DSO (d 1966); 2 s (Philip Roland b 1957, Hugo William b 1962), 2 da (Louisa Frances b 1956, Sarah Elizabeth b 1966); *Heir* s, Philip Anson, *qv*; *Career* RN: Cdr Naval Forces, Gulf 1970–71 (Cdre), asst chief of Def Staff (Signals) 1972–74 (Rear Adm), ret 1975; divnl mangr satellites Marconi Space and Defence Systems Ltd 1977 (asst mktg dir 1975), chm Matra Marconi Space UK Ltd 1985–91 (md 1984–85); chm IGG Component Technology Ltd 1992–; High Sheriff Surrey 1993–94; CEng, FIEE; *Recreations* gardening, golf; *Style*— Rear Adm Sir Peter Anson, Bt, CB, DL; ✉ Rosefield, 81 Boundstone Rd, Rowledge, Farnham, Surrey GU10 4AT (☎ and fax 01252 792724)

ANSON, Philip Roland; s and h of Rear Adm Sir Peter Anson, 7 Bt, CB, *qv*; *b* 4 Oct 1957; *Educ* Charterhouse, Chelsea Coll London (BPharm); *Career* pharmacist; Boots 1979–84, Waremoss Chemists Ltd 1984–; MRPharmS 1980, MIPharmM 1980; *Style*— Philip Anson, Esq; ✉ 34 Martello Rd, Eastbourne, East Sussex BN22 7SS (☎ and fax 01323 411906); Guy's Pharmacy, 26 Eastbourne Rd, Pevensey Bay, East Sussex BN24 6ET (☎ and fax 01323 761321)

ANSON, Viscount; Thomas William Robert Hugh Anson; s and h of 5 Earl of Lichfield, *qv*; *b* 19 July 1978; *Style*— Viscount Anson; ✉ c/o The Rt Hon The Earl of Lichfield, Shugborough Hall, Stafford

ANSORGE, Peter James; s of Kurt Ansorge (d 1967), of London, and Anneliese, *née* Töpfer; *b* 5 Nov 1944; *Educ* Kilburn GS, King's Coll Cambridge (scholarship, MA); *m* 1970 (m dis 1984), Jocelyne Claude, *née* Douvre; 1 s (Paul Francis b 13 April 1977); *Career* freelance journalist and pt/t teacher 1967–69, teacher of English and Drama Sir William Collins Comp Sch London 1970–72, ed Plays and Players 1972–75 (asst ed 1972–75), script ed and prodr BBC Eng Regions Drama Dept Birmingham 1975–83, ind writer and prodr 1983–85, fndr ptnr Angel Films 1985–86, dep head Drama Series and Serials Channel 4 1990– (commissioning ed 1987–90); worked on progs and films incl: Gangsters (script ed), Licking Hitler (script ed, BAFTA Best Single Drama Award 1978), Empire Road (prodr), Moon Over Soho (writer) 1984, Tandoori Nights (developer and prodr); also cmmnd: The Real Eddy English, A Very British Coup (Int Emmy 1988, BAFTA and Golden Fleece Awards, Bdcasting Press Guild Best Drama Series Award), Behaving Badly (Golden Gate Best Drama Award), Traffik (Int Emmy 1989, Cannes TV Festival Best Drama Award, BAFTA Best Drama Series Award 1990, various other awards), GBH, Lipstick on your Collar, The Camomile Lawn, Tales of the City (RTS Award for Best Drama Series, Peabody Award), Hearts and Minds, The Politician's Wife, Jake's Progress, Cold Lazarus, Karaoke, The Fragile Heart, Family Money; memb BAFTA 1987–; *Books* Disrupting the Spectacle - Five Years of Fringe Theatre (1974); *Style*— Peter Ansorge, Esq; ✉ Channel Four Television Corporation, 124 Horseferry Road, London SW1P 2TX (☎ 0171 396 4444)

ANSTEE, Prof John Howard; s of Stanley George Anstee (d 1978), of Milford Haven, and Anne May, *née* Griffiths (d 1992); *b* 25 April 1943; *Educ* Milford Haven GS, Univ of Nottingham (BSc, PhD); *m* 18 July 1966, Angela June, da of Emlyn Havard Young, JP; 1 s (Quentin Mark b 7 Feb 1973); *Career* Univ of Durham: sr demonstrator in zoology 1968–71, lectr 1971–81, sr lectr 1981–96, dean Faculty of Science 1994– (dep dean 1991–94), prof of insect physiology 1996–; hon sec Soc for Experimental Biology 1990–94 (memb 1972); author of numerous articles on insect physiology and biochemistry; FRES (memb Cncl 1991–94), FZS 1967; *Recreations* cricket, dinghy sailing and rugby; *Style*— Prof John H Anstee; ✉ Faculty of Science Science Laboratories, University of Durham, South Road, Durham DH1 3LE (☎ 0191 374 7029/3336, fax 0191 374 7479)

ANSTEE, Dame Margaret Joan; DCMG (1994); da of Edward Curtis Anstee (d 1971), and Anne Adaliza, *née* Mills (d 1972); *b* 25 June 1926; *Educ* Chelmsford Co HS for Girls, Newnham Coll Cambridge (MA), Univ of London (BSc); *Career* lectr in Spanish Queen's Univ Belfast 1947–48, 3 sec FO 1948–52, admin offr UN Tech Assistance Bd Manila Philippines 1952–54, Spanish supervisor Univ of Cambridge 1955–56; UN Tech Assistance Bd: offr i/c Bogota Colombia 1956–57, resident rep Uruguay 1957–59, dir Special Fund progs and UN Info Centre La Paz Bolivia 1960–65, resident rep UNDP Ethiopia 1965–67, liaison offr with UN Econ Cmmn for Africa 1965–67, sr econ advsr PM's UK 1967–68, sr asst to cmmr i/c of Study of Capacity of UN Devpt System 1968–69; resident rep UNDP: Morocco 1969–72, Chile and liaison offr with UN Econ Cmmn for Latin America 1972–74; dep to UN Under Sec Gen i/c of UN relief operation to Bangladesh and dep coordinator of UN emergency assistance to Zambia 1973; UNDP NY: dep asst admin and dep regnl dir for Latin America 1974–76, dir Admins Unit for Special Assignments 1976, asst dep admin 1976, asst admin and dir Bureau for Prog Policy and Evaluation 1977–78, asst Sec Gen UN Dept of Tech Cooperation for Devpt 1978–87, special rep of Sec Gen for coordination of int assistance following Mexico earthquake 1985–87, chm Advsy Gp on review of UN World Food Cncl 1985–86, special coordinator of UN Sec Gen to ensure implementation of Gen Assembly resolution on fin and admin reform of the UN 1986–87; special rep of UN Sec Gen for Bolivia 1982–92, rep UN Sec Gen at Conf for the Adoption of a Convention Against Illicit Traffic in Narcotic Drugs and Psychotropic Substances 1988, sec gen Eighth UN Congress on the Prevention of Crime and the Treatment of Offenders Havana 1990, special rep of the UN Sec Gen for Peru 1990–92, Sec Gen's co-ordinator for addressing the effects of the Chernobyl disaster 1991–92, Sec Gen's personal rep to co-ordinate UN efforts to counter impact of burning oilfields in Kuwait and region 1991–92; dir gen UN office Vienna, under sec gen UN, head of centre for Social Devpt and Humanitarian Affrs 1987–92, co-ordinator of all UN drug control related activities 1987–91, under sec-gen and special rep of UN Sec-Gen for Angola and head UN Angolan Verification Mission (UNAVEM II) 1992–93, ind conslt and advsr to Pres and Govt of Bolivia 1993–; hon fell Newnham Coll Cambridge; Hon DSc: Univ of Essex 1994, Univ of Westminster 1996; foreign honours: Commandeur Ouissam Alaouite (Morocco) 1972, Dama Gran Cruz Condor of the Andes (Bolivia) 1986, Das Grosse Goldene Ehrenzeichen am Bande (Austria) 1993,

Reves Peace Prize William & Mary Coll USA 1993; *Books* The Administration of International Development Aid (USA 1969), Gate of the Sun: a Prospect of Bolivia (1970, USA 1971), Africa and the World (ed with R K A Gardiner and C Patterson, 1970), Orphan of the Cold War: The Inside Story of the Collapse of the Angolan Peace Process 1992–93 (1996, UK, US and Portugal); *Style*— Dame Margaret J Anstee, DCMG; ✉ c/o PNUD, Casilla 9072, La Paz, Bolivia

ANSTIS, Toby; s of Ray Anstis, of Bray-on-Thames, Berks, and Janet, *née* Fisk; *b* 14 Dec 1969; *Educ* Royal Ballet Sch, Desborough Boys Comp Sch, Univ of Surrey (Froebel Coll, BSc Hons); *Career* television presenter; credits incl: Children's BBC 1992–95, The Ozone (voted Top Music Prog in Smash Hits), Fan TC (two series with Danni Minogue) 1994–95, The Fast Forward Summer Parties (tours) 1992 and 1993, host The Smash Hits Arena Tour 1993 and 1994, co-host Prince's Tst Concert (BBC) 1994, Childline Extravaganza at Wembley Arena, Smash Hits Shows on the Road, The 11th Hour (two series) 1995–; National Lottery Live (presenting weekly films) 1995–96, hosted Children's Comic Relief Live (BBC) 1995, Bright Sparks 1996, Grandstand (film contrib) 1996–, Live and Kicking 1996–, hosting Children in Need (BBC) 1996; starred in Cinderella (Derngate Theatre Northampton) 1995, starring as Dick in Dick Whittington (Orchard Theatre Dartford) 1996; ambass Prince's Youth Tst, involved with Childline and NCH Action for Children; *Recreations* tennis, skiing, sailing; *Clubs* Holmes Place Health, Chelsea Rocks Lane Tennis; *Style*— Toby Anstis, Esq; ✉ c/o James Grant Media Group Ltd, Syon Lodge, London Road, Syon Park, Middlesex TW7 5BH (☎ 0181 232 4100, fax 0181 232 4101)

ANSTRUTHER, Harriet Joan Campbell; da of Ian Fife Campbell Anstruther, of Barlavington, Petworth, W Sussex, and Susan Margaret, *née* Paten; *b* 24 March 1967; *Educ* Queen's Coll London, City & Guilds Sch of Art, Byam-Shaw Sch of Fine Art; *m* 19 July 1991 (m dis), Hamish Howard Anthony Summers, s of Anthony Gilbert Summers; 1 da (Celestia Nell Campbell b 23 Aug 1993); *Career* textile designer; fndr Hufitts (T-shirt design/wholesale business) 1991–92, fndr Harriet Anstruther (accessories, men's and women's ready to wear and furnishing fabrics) 1991–, jt fndr Selina Blow, Harriet Anstruther, Lulu Guiness (shop in Elizabeth St SW1) 1995–, fndr Harriet Anstruther Design Studio (incorporating all areas of design and styling incl china, fashion, textile, furnishing fabric, wallpaper, costume, set and interior design and illustrations) 1996–; over 340 stockists worldwide (Australia, Japan, Europe and America); design projects/cmmns incl: exclusive print design for Perry Ellis USA 1991, commemorative scarf for Hokusai exhbn (RA) 1991, exclusive fabric print for Xavier Foley 1993, printed silk scarf for Past Times 1993, printed scarf and tie for Daphne's Restaurant 1994 and for Covent Garden Hotel 1994, Vogue illustration Dec 1995, consultancy for Margaret Howell Ltd 1996, illustration for The Pelham Hotel 1996, commemorative scarf for Catherine Cookson (private cmmn) 1996, interior design for Covent Garden Hotel 1996, set and costume design for BBC2's An Audience with Charles Dickens 1996; currently writing book on design and its many aspects; included in The Best of British Women (specialist designers section) 1993; *Recreations* tapestry, reading, painting, music, collecting pictures and prints; *Clubs* Kartouche, Soho House; *Style*— Harriet Anstruther; ✉ Harriet Anstruther Design Studio, 15a Cromwell Mews, South Kensington, London SW7 2LA (☎ 0171 584 7312, fax 0171 584 8285)

ANSTRUTHER, Ian Fife Campbell; s of Douglas Tollemache Anstruther (d 1956, gs of Sir Robert Anstruther, 5 Bt), and his 1 w Enid (d 1964), 2 da of Lord George Granville Campbell; *b* 11 May 1922; *Educ* Eton, New Coll Oxford; *m* 1, 1951 (m dis 1963), (Geraldine) Honor, elder da of late Capt Gerald Stuart Blake, MC; 1 da; m 2, 1963, Susan Margaret Walker, da of Henry St John Paten; 2 s, 3 da; *Career* Capt Royal Corps of Signals, former attaché Br Embassy Washington; author; memb Royal Co of Archers (Queen's Body Guard for Scotland); Lord of the Manor of Barlavington; FSA; *Books* I Presume, The Knight and the Umbrella, The Scandal of the Andover Workhouse, Oscar Browning, Coventry Patmore's Angel; *Clubs* Brooks's; *Style*— Ian Anstruther, Esq, FSA; ✉ Estate Office, Barlavington, Petworth, Sussex GU28 0LG (☎ 01798 869260, fax 01798 869401)

ANSTRUTHER-GOUGH-CALTHORPE, Sir Euan Hamilton; 3 Bt (UK 1929), of Elvetham Hall, Elvetham, Co Southampton; s of Niall Hamilton Anstruther-Gough-Calthorpe (d 1970), and Martha (who m 2, 1975, Charles Nicholson), da of Stuart Warren Don; suc gf, Brig Sir Richard Anstruther-Gough-Calthorpe, 2 Bt, CBE (d 1985); *b* 22 June 1966; *Educ* Harrow, Royal Agric Coll Cirencester; *Style*— Sir Euan Anstruther-Gough-Calthorpe, Bt; ✉ Elvetham, Hartley Wintney, Hants RG27 8BE

ANSTRUTHER OF THAT ILK, Sir Ralph Hugo; 7 Bt (NS 1694) and 12 Bt (NS 1700), GCVO (1992, KCVO 1976, CVO 1967), MC (1943), DL (Fife 1960, Caithness 1965); s of late Capt Robert Anstruther, MC, and Marguerite (d 1992), da of Hugo de Burgh, 3 s of Thomas de Burgh, of Oldtown, Co Kildare; suc gf Sir Ralph Anstruther, 6 Bt, JP, Lord-Lt of Fife, 1934 and cous Sir Windham Carmichael-Anstruther 11 Bt 1980; *b* 13 June 1921; *Educ* Eton, Magdalene Coll Cambridge (BA); *Heir* cous, Ian Anstruther, *qv*; *Career* Maj (ret) Coldstream Gds; equerry to HM Queen Elizabeth The Queen Mother 1959– (treas 1961–, asst private sec 1959–64); memb Royal Co of Archers (Queen's Body Guard for Scotland); hereditary carver to HM The Queen; *Style*— Major Sir Ralph Anstruther, Bt, GCVO, MC, DL; ✉ Balcaskie, Pittenweem, Fife; Watten Mains, Caithness

ANTEBI, Raymond Nathan; s of Moise Antebi (d 1970), and Miriam, *née* Farhi; *b* 4 March 1930; *Educ* Lycée Français Alexandria Egypt, Univ of Bologna (MD), Apothecaries' Hall Dublin (LAH), Univ of London (DPM); *m* 1956, Anna, da of Philip Van der Velde; 2 s (Daniel Leo b 2 April 1957, David Joel b 25 Feb 1960), 2 da (Laura Jane b 7 April 1963, Helen Clare b 10 Nov 1966); *Career* rotating internship United Hosp NY State USA 1954–55, sr house offr Gen Hosp Durham Co 1955–56, registrar Wordsley Hosp Stourbridge 1956–57, pre-registration medicine Darlington Meml Hosp Co Durham 1957–58, pre-registration obstetrics and gynaecology Greenbank Maternity Hosp Co Durham 1958, GP asst Newcastle upon Tyne 1958–59, jr hosp med offr (psychiatry) Moorhaven Hosp S Devon 1959–62, sr registrar and clinical tutor North Regnl Bd Univ of Aberdeen 1962–64, conslt psychiatrist All Saints Hosp Birmingham, Duke St Hosp and Glasgow Royal Infirmary 1966–80, acting head of Dept of Psychiatry Duke St Hosp 1980–87, physician supt and clinical services mangr Eastern Psychiatric Services Glasgow 1987–92; clinical teacher Univ of Glasgow, former psychiatric advsr Student Health Serv Univ of Strathclyde, conslt psychiatrist Glasgow Univ Student Health Serv; hon memb Scottish Branch Med and Dental Hypnotic Soc 1982; MRCPSGlas, FRCPS, FRCP, FRCPsych; *Publications:* Seven Principles to Overcome Resistance in Hypno-Analysis, Effect of Serum of Schizophrenics on Evoked Cortical Potentials in the Rat, The Need for Elementary Knowledge of Psychology in Dentistry, State Benefits as a Cause of Unwillingness to Work, Accident Neurosis - Entity or Non-Entity, Sexual Dysfunction, Value of Forensic Psychiatry in a Court of Law, Homicide On-lookers, Medical Role of Drug Abuse, Psychological Characteristics of Offenders and Violent Offenders in the West of Scotland; *Style*— Raymond Antebi, Esq

ANTHONY, Barbara (pen name Antonia Barber); da of Derek Wilson, and (Edith Jessie) Julie, *née* Jeal; *Educ* Rye GS, UCL (BA); *m* 1956, Kenneth Charles Anthony (k 1981), s of the late Charles Arthur Anthony; 2 s (Jonathan Charles b 1968, Nicholas James b 1972), 1 da (Gemma Thi-Phi-Yen b 1974); *Career* writer of children's books 1966–; supporter of: Friends of the Earth, Greenpeace, Amnesty International, Ramblers ASP, Woodland Tst, Nat Tst; memb Soc of Authors; *Books* incl: The Ghosts (1969, filmed as The Amazing Mr Blunden 1971), The Ring in the Rough Stuff (1983), The Enchanter's Daughter (1987), The Mousehole Cat (1990), Catkin (1994), The Monkey and the Panda (1995), Tales from the Ballet (1996); *Recreations* walking, sailing, reading, theatre, TV; *Style*— Mrs Barbara Anthony; ✉ Hornes Place Oast, Appledore, Ashford, Kent TN26 2BS; c/o David Higham Associates, 5–8 Lower John Street, Golden Square, London W1R 4HA (☎ 0171 437 7888, fax 0171 437 1072)

ANTHONY, David Gwilym; s of Ernest Anthony (d 1990), and Megan Euron, *née* Davies; *b* 10 Feb 1947; *Educ* Hull GS, St Catherine's Coll Oxford (MA); *m* 8 Oct 1974, (Ellen) Brigid, da of Air Vice-Marshal W J Crisham (d 1987); 1 s (Peter b 1979), 1 da (Jane b 1980); *Career* Barton Mayhew (now Ernst & Young) 1969–73, Dymo Business Systems Ltd 1973–75, Slater Walker Finance Ltd 1975–77, Forward Trust (Ireland) Ltd 1977–82, dir and gen mangr Hitachi Credit (UK) PLC 1982–, dir Fleetlease (UK) Ltd 1991–; FCA 1973; *Recreations* walking, table tennis; *Style*— David G Anthony, Esq; ✉ Retreat, Church Lane, Stoke Poges, Bucks SL2 4NZ (☎ 01753 530895); Hitachi Credit (UK) PLC, Wallbrook Business Centre, Green Lane, Hounslow, Middx TW4 6NW (☎ 0181 572 7554, fax 0181 577 9939)

ANTHONY, Dr Donald William James (Don); s of George Anthony, of Sidcup, Kent, and Annie Eva Starkey (d 1962); *b* 6 Nov 1928; *Educ* Loughborough Univ of Sci and Technol (Dip Physical Educn), Univ of London (Dip Health Educn), Univ of Leicester (MEd, PhD); *m* 6 June 1958, Jadwiga, da of Wladeslaw Rzeszowski (d 1942); 1 s (Anthony Marek Louis b 14 July 1964); *Career* asst lectr in physical educn Univ of Manchester 1954–56, lectr Loughborough Univ of Technol 1956–59, princ lectr Avery Hill Coll 1959–85; author of several books, journalist, broadcaster; holder of English hammer throwing record and AAA champion 1953, memb Br Olympic Hammer Throwing Team 1956; memb Br Olympic Ctee (chm BOA Educn Tst), fndr and hon pres English Volleyball Assoc; advsr: IOC Olympic Solidarity, IOC; sports admin, conslt to govt and commercial cos; memb: Sports Writers' Assoc, Devpt Studies Assoc, World Future Soc, NATFHE, Int Fund for Animal Welfare; awarded IOC Centennial Trophy 1994; *Books* Know the Game Volleyball (1948), Keeping Fit for All Ages (1962), Success in Volleyball (1962), The PE Teacher's A-Z (1970), How to Keep Fit (1972), A Strategy for British Sport (1980), Field Athletics (1982), Olympic English (1986), Britain and the Olympic Games (1986), Man of Sport - Man of Peace (1991); *Recreations* tennis, reading, walking; *Style*— Dr Don Anthony

ANTHONY, Evelyn Bridgett Patricia; DL (Essex 1995); da of Lt Cdr Henry Christian Stephens, RNVR (d 1953), of Cholderton, Wilts, and Elizabeth, *née* Sharkey (d 1968), of Lower Leeson St, Dublin; father invented Dome anti-aircraft trainer 1939–45, ggf Henry Stephens invented Stephens writing ink; *b* 3 July 1928; *Educ* Convent of Sacred Heart Roehampton; *m* 1955, Michael Ward-Thomas, s of Richard Ward-Thomas (d 1954), of Hunsdonbury, Hunsdon, Herts; 4 s (Anthony, Ewan, Christian, Luke), 2 da (Susan, Katharine (decd)); *Career* author; has produced 32 novels which have been translated into 19 languages and have sold over 14 million copies; Freeman City of London 1987, Liveryman Needlemakers' Co 1987; High Sheriff Co of Essex 1994–95; *Books* 12 historical novels incl Anne Boleyn (1956, US Literary Guild Award); thrillers incl: The Rendezvous (1967), Anne of Austria (1968), The Legend (1969), The Assassin (1970), The Tamarind Seed (1971, filmed 1973), The Poellenberg Inheritance (1972), The Occupying Power (1973, Yorkshire Post Fiction Prize), The Malaspiga Exit (1974), The Persian Ransom (1975), The Silver Falcon (1977), The Return (1978), The Grave of Truth (1979), The Defector (1980), The Avenue of the Dead (1981), Albatross (1982), The Company of Saints (1983), Voices on the Wind (1985), No Enemy but Time (1987), The House of Vandekar (1988), The Scarlet Thread (1989), The Relic (1991), The Doll's House (1992), Exposure (1993), Bloodstones (1994), The Legacy (1997); *Recreations* National Hunt racing, music, gardening, salerooms; *Style*— Miss Evelyn Anthony, DL; ✉ Horham Hall, Thaxted, Essex

ANTHONY, Lysette; *b* 26 Sept 1963; *Educ* Stoodley Knowle Convent Torquay, Nat Youth Theatre; *m* Luc Leestemaker; *Career* actress; *Theatre* Reproductions (Bridge Lane Theatre), Ghosts (Shaw Theatre), Lady's Not For Burning (Northcott Theatre, Exeter), Toys in the Attic (Watford Palace), Balmoral (Bristol Old Vic); *Television* Frost in May (BBC), Dombey and Son (BBC), Beauty and the Beast (Thames), Jemima Shore (Thames), Night Train to Murder (Thames), Auf Wiedersehn Pet (Central), The Gentle Touch (LWT), The House on Kirov Street (BBC), Three Up, Two Down (3 series, BBC), Oliver Twist (BBC), Lovejoy (BBC), 1936 Truth! (BBC), The Bretts (Central), Home to Roost (Yorkshire), Campion (BBC), Cleudo (Granada), Dark Shadows (NBC); *Films* Oliver Twist, Krull, Ivanhoe, Princess Daisy, Tug of Love, A Drop in the Ocean, Looking for Eileen, The Emperor's New Clothes, Without A Clue, Jack The Ripper, The Lady and The Highwayman, Ghost of Monte Carlo, Switch, The Pleasure Principle, Husbands and Wives (dir Woody Allen); *Style*— Ms Lysette Anthony; ✉ c/o William Morris Agency (UK) Ltd, 31/32 Soho Square, London W1V 6DG (☎ 0171 434 2191, fax 0171 437 0238)

ANTHONY, Prof Peter Paul; s of Dr Miklos Anthony (d 1989), and Maria, *née* Sedon (d 1966); *b* 22 June 1933; *Educ* Gymnasia of Eger and Jaszapati, Univ of Budapest Hungary, St Bartholomew's Hosp Med Coll Univ of London; *m* 27 May 1961, Mary, da of Norman Capstick (d 1983); 1 s (Stephen), 1 da (Nicola); *Career* sr lectr in pathology and conslt: Univ of East Africa 1969–71, Middx Hosp Med Sch Univ of London 1971–77; Exeter and Royal Devon and Exeter Hosps: sr lectr 1977, later reader, currently prof of clinical histopathology and conslt; author of over 100 articles, reviews and chapters in books; memb Cncl: Int Acad of Pathology 1988–91 (also 1978–81), Assoc of Clinical Pathologists 1988–91 (also 1981–84), RCPath 1993–96 (also 1983–87 and 1989–92); memb ctees: WHO, BMA, SW RHA; pres Assoc of Clinical Pathologists 1992–93; FRCPath 1982 (MRCPath 1968); *Books* Recent Advances in Histopathology vols 10–16 (jtly, 1978–1994), Pathology of the Liver (jt ed, 1 edn 1978, 2 edn 1987, 3 edn 1994); *Recreations* sailing, walking, photography; *Clubs* Starcross Yacht, Exe Yacht; *Style*— Prof Peter Anthony; ✉ 2 St Leonards Place, Exeter EX2 4LZ; Royal Devon & Exeter Hospital (Wonford), Pathology Laboratory, Barrack Road, Exeter, Devon EX2 5DW; Postgraduate Medical School, University of Exeter, Barrack Rd, Exeter (☎ 01392 403006)

ANTHONY, Ronald Desmond; s of William Arthur Anthony (d 1987), and Olive Francis, *née* Buck (d 1986); *b* 21 Nov 1925; *Educ* Sidcup and Chistlehurst GS, Imperial Coll of Sci and Technol (BSc, ACGI); *m* Betty Margaret, da of Walter Frederick Newton Croft (d 1971); 4 da (Frances b 1951, Jennifer b 1953, Rebecca b 1957, Sarah b 1958); *Career* served RCS 1943–48; Vickers Armstrongs (Supermarine) 1950–57, Nuclear Power Plant Co 1957–60; HSE (and predecessor orgns): inspr of nuclear installations 1960, head Safety Policy Div 1977–80, bd memb 1977–85, chief inspr of nuclear installations 1980–85; engrg conslt 1985–; pres BNES 1987–89, FIMechE, FINucE, MRAeS; *Recreations* golf; *Style*— Ronald Anthony, Esq; ✉ 2 Perry House, Chislehurst Road, Sidcup, Kent DA14 6BE

ANTHONY, Vivian Stanley; s of Capt Arthur Stanley Anthony (d 1983), of Llandaff, Cardiff, and Ceinwen, *née* Thomas (d 1965); *b* 5 May 1938; *Educ* Cardiff HS, Univ of London, LSE (BSc Econ), Fitzwilliam Coll Cambridge (DipEd); *m* 1969, Rosamund Anne, da of Col Frank McDermot Byrn, of Co Wicklow, Eire; 1 s (Thomas b 1971), 1 da (Jennifer b 1970); *Career* asst master Leeds GS 1960–64, asst master and housemaster Tonbridge 1964–69; sch master fellowship Merton Coll Oxford 1969; lectr in educn Univ of Leeds 1969–71, dep headmaster The King's Sch Macclesfield 1971–76, headmaster Colfe's Sch 1976–90, sec HMC 1990–; external examiner: Univ of Manchester PGCE

1972–75, Univ of Birmingham Cert of Educn at Dudley Coll 1975–78, Univ of Lancaster 1977–79; chief examiner in A and S level economics for Oxford and Cambridge Bd 1975–92 (examiner 1970–75); chm Economics Assoc 1974–77; memb: Ctee of Chief Examiners to examine common core in A level economics 1980–81, HMC Academic Policy Ctee 1985–90 (chm 1989–90), Professional Devpt Ctee 1983–88, Teacher Shortage Working Pty 1987–88, CBI/Schools Panel; chm Area 1 SHA 1988–89 (memb Educn Ctee 1989–); SHA rep on London Univ Examination Bd 1984–87, SEAC 1980–88, scrutineer Oxford and Welsh Bds; memb: Admty Interview Bd 1985–, HMC Inspection Working Pty 1993–; tstee E Euro Scholarship Scheme 1993–; govr: Stamford Endowed Schs 1993–, King's Sch Macclesfield 1994–96, Bromsgrove Sch 1995–, Uppingham Sch 1996–; Hon Freeman Worshipful Co of Leathersellers 1990; Hon FCP 1991; *Books include* Monopoly (1968), Overseas Trade (4 edn, 1981), Banks and Markets, Objective Test in A Level Economics (1973), Tour of American Independent Schools (1984), History of Cricket at Colfe's (1986); articles incl: The Economics Association and the Training of Teachers (Economics 1972), The Report of the Working Party on Economics and Economic History (Economics 1973), The Impact of ERA: Standards (1992), Head to Head (1992), A Coherent and Unified System for 16–19 Education (1992), The HMC and the National Curriculum KS3 (1993), Manual of Guidance (HMC, 1994), Access and Affordability (NAIS, 1994); *Recreations* music (choral singing), rugby football, squash, tennis; *Clubs* E India, Old Colfeians; *Style*— Vivian Anthony, Esq; ✉ Headmasters' Conference, 130 Regent Rd, Leicester LE1 7PG (☎ 0116 285 4810, fax 0116 247 1167)

ANTICO, Sir Tristan; AC (1983), kt (1973); s of Terrible Giovanni Antico (d 1965), and Erminia Bertin (d 1979); *b* 25 March 1923, Pioveite, Italy; *Educ* Sydney HS; *m* 1950, Dorothy Bridget, da of William Shields; 3 s (William, Damien, Stephen), 4 da (Virginia, Helen, Elizabeth, Veronica); *Career* fndr chm and md Pioneer International Ltd (formerly A&C Concrete) 1952–94 (now life pres), chm Tregoyd Holdings Pty Ltd, chm Ampol/Ampol-Ex Ltd 1982–92; former dir: Société Générale, Arena Management Pty Ltd, Convex (Qld) Pty Ltd, Qantas Airways Ltd; memb Business Cncl of Australia, former chm St Vincent's Hosp Bd, former tstee Art Gallery of New South Wales Fndn; Commendatore dell'Ordine della Stella Solidarieta Italiana 1967; *Recreations* horseracing and breeding, swimming, cruising, tennis; *Clubs* Royal Sydney Yacht Squadron, Manly Golf, Tattersall's Australian Jockey, Sydney Turf, American National, Balmoral Beach; *Style*— Sir Tristan Antico, AC; ✉ 161 Raglan Street, Mosman, NSW 2088, Australia

ANTON, David; s of James Martin Anton (d 1966), and Sarah Anton (d 1968); *b* 14 April 1936; *Educ* Harrow Co GS; *m* Cynthia Maureen; 1 s (Richard Phillip b 1964), 1 da (Sara Jane b 1969); *Career* CA; articled clerk J & J Sawyer & Co 1952–57, sr chartered accountant Deloitte & Co 1958–66; ptnr: Harmood Banner & Co 1969–70 (mangr 1966–69), Coopers & Lybrand (formerly Deloitte Haskins & Sells) 1974–94 (ptnr i/c litigation support incl forensic accounting), conslt 1994– (expert witness incl forensic accounting); FCA 1958, MAE 1989; *Recreations* sailing, skiing, bridge; *Style*— David Anton, Esq; ✉ 50 Florin Court, Charterhouse Square, London EC1M 6EU (☎ and fax 0171 608 2053)

ANTONELLI, Count Pietro Hector Paolo Maria; s of Count Giacomo Antonelli (d 1963; Cavalry Gen Italian Army), and Countess Luisa Antonelli, *née* Piva (d 1954); of the same family as Cardinal Giacomo Antonelli, sec of State to Pope Pius IX, and of Count Pietro Antonelli, African explorer and diplomat; *b* 14 March 1924; *Educ* Univ of Rome (Degree in Philosophy); *m* (m dis 1976), Countess Maria Benedetta Bossi Pucci; 3 da (Sibilla b 27 April 1947, Santa b 12 Nov 1950, Serena b 18 Jan 1953); *Career* official Banca Commerciale 1948–62; md: Caboto Spa 1962–72, Banca Provinciale di Depositi e Sconti 1971; mangr and subsequently dir Hambros Bank Ltd 1972–; chm Piaggio & Co SpA 1994–; Grande Ufficiale Ordine al Merito della Repubblica Italiana 1991 (Commendatore 1983); *Recreations* yachting; *Clubs* Circolo della Caccia (Rome); *Style*— Count Pietro Antonelli; ✉ Hambros Bank Ltd, 41 Tower Hill, London EC3N 4HA (☎ 0171 480 5000, fax 0171 702 9262, telex 883851)

ANTONIOU, James Demetrios (Jim); s of Platon Antoniou (d 1982), and Sotiria, *née* Demetriou (d 1958); *b* 11 Nov 1937; *Educ* Sir Walter St John's GS London, The Poly Coll of Architecture and Advanced Bldg Technol London (DipArch, post dip in town planning); *m* 18 Sept 1964, Carole Olivia, da of Frederick Prior; 1 s (Platon James b 20 April 1968), 1 da (Zoe Olivia b 29 Sept 1970); *Career* architect Lyons Israel & Ellis 1961–65, first planning asst working on urban design and urban planning schemes Corp of London 1966–69, PA to C A Doxiadis Athens working on res and devpt of int projects 1970–72, int conslt working in various countries 1972–88, md ESP Planning Ltd 1988–90 (fndr memb 1988), currently int conslt involved with numerous int projects dealing with construction indust, educn bldgs, urban design, conservation and planning, housing for the poor and rural devpt; projects incl: the conservation of the Old City of Cairo Egypt 1980, rehabilitation of squatter areas in Khartoum for World Bank, urban design proposals for a waterside devpt in the ME five times the size of Venice 1990, design of Oasis at Um Al Osh in Al Ain region 1993, contrib and illustrator European Urban Charter for the Cncl of Europe 1993, participated Petra Master Plan for UNESCO 1994, advsr to UNESCO on Giza Pyramid Project Egypt 1994–, urban design conslt Chambacu Devpt Project Cartagena Columbia for Bank of Columbia 1995–; agencies worked with incl: ODA, UNDP, UNESCO, UNHCR, OECD, World Bank, OPEC Fund, EC, Cncl of Europe and numerous private orgns; visiting lectr numerous instns in UK and USA; memb Editorial Advsy Panel Official Architecture and Planning Jl 1969, urban devpt corr Middle East Construction Jl 1980, monthly column in Building Design Magazine 1986–, series of articles (Designs on London) in Evening Standard 1993, Traveller's Notebook in Business Life magazine 1994–; nominator Aga Khan Award for Architecture 1980, chm Assoc of Conslt Planners UK 1992–94, memb Case Ctee and memb Cncl Architects' Benevolent Soc UK 1989–; Freeman and memb Guild of Freemen City of London 1968; memb Worshipful Co of Constructors 1977; RIBA 1966, MRTPI, FFB 1974, FRSA 1992; *Books* incl: Environmental Management - Planning for Traffic (1971), Plaka - The Historic District of Athens (1972), Greece - The Land and its People (1974), Construction in the Middle East (1978), Islamic Cities and Conservation (1981), Urban Transportation Perspectives and Prospects (contrib, 1982), The Arab City - Its Character and Islamic Cultural Heritage (contrib, 1982), Building Roads by Hand (jtly, 1990), Cities: Then and Now (1994), UK Aid for Human Settlements (1996); *Recreations* sketching, writing, photography, walking, reading; *Clubs* Reform; *Style*— Jim Antoniou, Esq; ✉ Jim Antoniou and Associates, 86 Priory Road, London N8 7EY (☎ 0181 340 5367, fax 0181 348 1411)

ANTRIM, 9 Earl of (I 1785); Alexander Randal Mark McDonnell; also Viscount Dunluce; s of 8 Earl of Antrim, KBE (d 1977), and Angela Christina, da of Col Sir Mark Sykes; *b* 3 Feb 1935; *Educ* Downside, ChCh Oxford, Ruskin Sch of Art; *m* 1, 1963 (m dis 1974), Sara Elizabeth Anne, 2 da of St John Bernard Vyvyan Harmsworth (d 1995); 1 s, 2 da (Lady Flora Mary b 1963, Lady Alice Angela Jane (Lady Alice Gwinn) b 1964); *m* 2, 1977, Elizabeth, da of Michael Moses Sacher; 1 da (Lady Rachel Frances b 1978); *Heir* s, Viscount Dunluce, *qv*; *Career* Tate Gallery: restorer 1965–75, keeper of conservation 1975–90, head of collection servs 1990–93, dir of collection servs 1994–95; chm Rathlin Island Tst 1990–93; memb: Exec Ctee City and Guilds of London Art Sch, Art Advsry Ctee Nat Museums and Galleries of Wales 1995–; dir: Ulster TV, Northern Salmon Co, Antrim Estates Co; Prime Warden Hon Co of Fishmongers 1995–96; FRSA; *Style*— The Rt Hon the Earl of Antrim; ✉ Deer Park Cottage, Glenarm, Co Antrim BT44 0BQ

ANTROBUS, Sir Edward Philip; 8 Bt (UK 1815), of Antrobus, Cheshire; s of Sir Philip Coutts Antrobus, 7 Bt (d 1995), and Dorothy Margaret Mary, *née* Davis (d 1973); *b* 28 Sept 1938; *Educ* Witwatersrand Univ (BSc), Magdalene Coll Cambridge (MA); *m* 7 Oct 1966, Janet Sarah Elizabeth (d 1990), da of Philip Walter Sceales, of Johannesburg; 1 s (Francis Edward Sceales b 24 Oct 1972), 2 da (Barbara Joanna b 27 Jan 1968, Sarah Diana b 9 April 1970); *Heir* s, Francis Edward Sceales Antrobus b 24 Oct 1972; *Career* mangr Marley Johannesburg, landowner; *Recreations* golf, tennis; *Clubs* Johannesburg Country, Royal Johannesburg Golf; *Style*— Sir Edward Antrobus, Bt; ✉ PO Box 695, Rivonia 2128, South Africa

ANWAR, Tariq Rafiq; s of Rafiq Anwar (d 1976), of Chiswick, and Edith Fordham, *née* Reich (d 1994); *b* 21 Sept 1945; *Educ* Walpole GS, Sir John Cass Coll London; *m* 29 Sept 1966, Shirley Natalie, da of John Richard Hills (d 1990), of Hainault, Essex; 1 s (Dominic b 1967), 1 da (Gabrielle b 1970); *Career* film ed with BBC; films incl: Under Suspicion, The Madness of George III, The Crucible, Wings of the Dove; best ed BAFTA Awards: Caught on a Train, Oppenheimer; BAFTA nominations: Monocled Mutineer, Fortunes of War, Summer's Lease, The Madness of George III; ACE nomination for Tender is the Night; memb ACTT; *Recreations* music, tennis; *Style*— Tariq Anwar, Esq; ✉ c/o Peters Fraser and Dunlop, Chelsea Harbour, London SW10 0XF (☎ 0171 376 7676)

ANWYL, Her Hon Judge; Shirley Anne; QC (1979); da of James Ritchie (d 1991), of Johannesburg, and Helen Sutherland, *née* Peters; *b* 10 Dec 1940; *Educ* St Mary's Diocesan Sch for Girls Pretoria, Rhodes Univ S Africa (BA, LLB); *m* 23 May 1969, Robin Hamilton Corson, s of Douglas Fraser Corson (d 1978); 2 s (Jonathan Hamilton Corson Anwyl b 7 Oct 1973, James Douglas Corson Anwyl b 8 June 1975); *Career* called to the South African Bar 1963, called to the English Bar Inner Temple 1966 (bencher 1985), recorder of the Crown Court 1981–95, circuit judge (SE Circuit) 1995–; memb: Senate of the Inns of Court and Bar 1978–81, Criminal Injuries Compensation Bd 1981–95, Mental Health Review Tbnl 1983–, Gen Cncl of the Bar 1987; chair Barristers' Benevolent Assoc 1989–95; Freedom City of London 1994, memb Worshipful Co of Fruiterers 1996; *Recreations* theatre, music, sailing; *Clubs* Royal Soc of Arts; *Style*— Her Hon Judge Anwyl, QC; ✉ c/o Woolwich Crown Court, 2 Belmarsh Road, London SE28 0EY

ap ROBERT, His Hon Hywel Wyn Jones; s of Rev Robert John Jones (d 1973), and Mrs Jones, *née* Evans (d 1986); *b* 19 Nov 1923; *Educ* Cardiff HS, CCC Oxford (MA); *m* 1956, Elizabeth, da of J Gareth Davies, of Penarth; 2 da; *Career* WWII FO and Intelligence Corps; called to the Bar Middle Temple 1950, contested Cardiganshire (Plaid Cymru) 1970, chm Industl Tbnls 1970–72, recorder of the Crown Ct 1972–75, stipendiary magistrate Cardiff (now S Glamorgan) 1972–75, circuit judge 1975–94; hon memb of the Gorsedd of Bards 1972; co ct judge: in Mid and W Glamorgan 1985–93, Cardiff 1993–94; *Recreations* Welsh and classical literature, modern languages; *Clubs* Cardiff & County; *Style*— His Hon Hywel ap Robert; ✉ Cefn Bryn, 56 Heol Plymouth, Penarth, De Morgannwg CF6 2DJ

APPIO, Isabel Anne; da of Chief Gabriel Fenton Appio (d 1992), of Lagos, Nigeria, and Marguerite, *née* Lancaster-Cooper; *b* 30 June 1959; *Educ* Blackheath HS London, Central London Poly (BA); *Career* asst ed Caribbean Times newspaper 1981–83, asst music ed Time Out 1986–91, ed The Weekly Journal 1992–, chief editorial dir Voice Communications Group 1994–95, editorial dir Wishes Services (Big Properties in the Tropics) 1996–; *Style*— Ms Isabel Appio; ✉ Positive Time and Space Ltd, 36 Skylines, London E14 9TS (☎ and fax 0171 537 3222)

APPLEBY, His Hon Judge; Brian John; QC (1971); s of Ernest Joel Appleby; *b* 25 Feb 1930; *Educ* Uppingham, St John's Coll Cambridge; *m* 1958, Rosa Helena, *née* Flitterman; 1 s, 1 da; *Career* called to the Bar Middle Temple 1953, recorder of the Crown Ct 1972–88, circuit judge (Midland & Oxford Circuit) 1988–; dep chm Notts QS 1970–71, bencher Middle Temple 1980; dist referee Notts Wages Conciliation Bd NCB 1980–88; memb Notts City Cncl 1955–58 and 1960–63; *Style*— His Hon Judge Appleby, QC; ✉ The Poplars, Edwalton Village, Edwalton, Notts NG12 4AB (☎ 0115 922 3814)

APPLEBY, (Lesley) Elizabeth (Mrs Michael Collins); QC (1979); o da of Arthur Leslie Appleby, and Dorothy Evelyn, *née* Edwards; *b* 12 Aug 1942; *Educ* Dominican Convent Brewood Staffs, Wolverhampton Girls' HS, Univ of Manchester (LLB); *m* 6 Jan 1978, Michael Kenneth Collins, OBE; 1 s (Andrew b 23 Jan 1980), 1 da (Emma b 13 Feb 1984); *Career* called to the Bar Gray's Inn 1965, ad eundem Lincoln's Inn 1975; in practice Chancery Bar 1966–; memb of Senate of Inns of Court and Bar 1977–80 and 1981–82; bencher Lincoln's Inn 1986, recorder of the Crown Court 1989–, jt head of chambers; *Recreations* gardening, swimming, golf; *Style*— Miss Elizabeth Appleby, QC; ✉ The Glebe House, West Grinstead, Horsham, W Sussex RH13 8LR (☎ 01403 711228); 4/5 Gray's Inn Square, Gray's Inn, London WC1R 5AY (☎ 0171 404 5252, fax 0171 242 7803)

APPLEBY, John Montague; s of Montague Eric Appleby (d 1983), and Carmen Irene Appleby (d 1993); *b* 8 Nov 1945; *Educ* Dauntsey's, Univ of Nottingham (LLB, pres Univ Law Students' Soc, capt Univ and UAU hockey); *m* 30 May 1970, Barbara Joan, da of Arthur Plumb; 1 s (Luke Justin b 17 July 1976); *Career* admitted slr 1970, asst slr Leicester 1970–72; Truman Close Kendall & Appleby (formerly Truman & Appleby): joined 1972, ptnr 1974–88, managing ptnr (following merger of Truman & Appleby and Close Kendall & Co) 1988–; asst recorder 1993–; sec Notts Young Slrs Gp 1973 (Nat Ctee rep 1976–82), chm Nat Ctee Young Slrs Gp 1980–81; vice pres Notts Law Soc 1996; Law Soc: memb 1970–, memb Regnl Cncl (for Lincs and Notts) 1984, memb Cncl 1984–, chm Family Law Ctee 1987–90, chm Cts and Legal Servs Ctee 1990–93, memb Remuneration & Practice Devpt Ctee 1986–89, dir Slrs Indemnity Fund 1987–90, memb Practice Devpt Ctee 1993–96, memb Civil Litigation Ctee 1993–, memb Trg Ctee 1996–; *Books* Professional Management of a Solicitors Practice (contrib); *Recreations* hockey, golf, jogging, travel, wine, theatre; *Clubs* Notts Hockey Assoc (pres 1994–96), Nottingham Hockey (vice-pres), Notts Forest CCC (vice-pres), Bacchanalians Hockey, Wollaton Park Golf; *Style*— John Appleby, Esq; ✉ Trumans, 22 Park Row, Nottingham NG1 6GX (☎ 0115 941 7275, fax 0115 948 4272)

APPLEBY, Keith David; s of Cornelius Appleby, of Amersham, Bucks, and Doreen Mary, *née* Briscoe; *b* 14 May 1953; *Educ* Bucks Coll of Higher Educn (BA), RCA (MA); *m* 1987, Margaret Ann, da of Anthony Lepps; 1 s (Frederick William b 25 March 1990); *Career* designer Habitat Designs Ltd 1978–81, sr designer Habitat-Mothercare plc 1981–84, assoc dir Storehouse plc 1984–88, mktg dir RSCG Conran Design 1993–96 (design dir 1988–93), design dir Home Furnishings Division Coats Viyella plc 1996–; *Style*— Keith Appleby, Esq; ✉ Home Furnishings Division, Coates Viyella plc, PO Box 7, Newtown Mill, Lees Street, Manchester M27 6DB (☎ 0161 794 4781)

APPLEBY, Malcolm Arthur; s of James William Appleby (d 1976), of West Wickham, Kent, and Marjory, *née* Stokes (d 1991); *b* 6 Jan 1946; *Educ* Hawesdown Co Secdy Mod Sch for Boys, Beckenham Sch of Art, Ravensbourn Coll of Art and Design, Central Sch of Art and Design, Sir John Cass Sch of Art, Royal Coll of Art; *Career* started career as engraver 1968, currently designer for silver and specialist gun engraver (developed gold fusing onto steel and created new silver engraving techniques); research into platinum engraving techniques for Ayrton Metals 1992 (resulting in a platinum and gold collection); fndr chm Br Art Postage Stamp Soc, former memb Crathes Drumoak and Durris Community Cncl (chm 1992); memb: Br Art Medal Soc, Soc for the Protection of Ancient Bldgs, Butterfly Conservation Soc, Berwick upon Tweed Swan Tst, Silver Soc; Liveryman Worshipful Co of Goldsmiths London 1991; *Work* incl: engraving orb on Prince of Wales's Coronet, King George VI Diamond Stakes trophy 1978, 500th anniversary silver cup for London Assay Office, V & A seal, condiment set destined for 10 Downing St, major silver cmmn (cup and cover) for Royal Museum of Scotland 1990, designer to Holland & Holland Gunmaker; *Collections* work in collections incl: Aberdeen Art Gallery Nat Museum of Scotland, Aland's Bay Maritime Museum, Nat Museum of Finland, South Aust Maritime Museum, Royal Armouries, V & A, Crafts Cncl, BR Museum, Contemporary Arts Soc, Goldsmiths' Co; *Exhibitions* Br Cncl Crafts Exhibition to Japan, Sotheby's Contemporary Arts Exhibition to Japan, Chicago New Art Forms Exhibition (with the Scottish Gallery), one-man show Pier Arts Centre Stromness Orkney (prints and silver); *Recreations* work, standing in the garden, cups of herbal tea with friends and neighbours, stilton cheese, still darning my very old but colourful pullover; *Style*— Malcolm Appleby, Esq; ✉ Aultbeay, Grand Tully, Perthshire PH15 2QU (☎ 01887 840484)

APPLETON, Lt-Col George Fortnam; OBE (1946), TD (1947), JP (1954), DL (Lancs 1971); s of James Arthur Appleton, JP (d 1961), of Ainsdale, Lancs and Wetwood, Staffs, and Ethel Maude, *née* Fortnam; *b* 23 July 1913; *Educ* Warwick Sch; *m* 1940, Patricia Margaret (d 1990), da of Henry J L Dunlop (memb Shackleton Antarctic Expedition 1907–09, d 1931), of Lancs; 1 da (Jayne (Mrs Anthony Cant)), 1 s (His Hon Judge Appleton, *qv*); *Career* 2 Lt 5 (Rifle) Bn The King's Regt 1933, Staff Capt 165 Inf Bde 1938, served WWII, Staff Coll 1940, Gen Staff A & Q Branch appts HQ II Corps and HQ Eastern Cmd, Beach Co Cmd D Day Invasion 1944 (despatches twice, OBE for servs in NW Europe), DAQMG HQ 12 Corps, 2 Army and Port of Antwerp, AA & QMG HQ 20 L of C Sub Area BAOR; ret co dir and farmer; cmdt Special Constabulary 1950–54; chm: Southport and N Sefton PSD's 1971–83, Southport Juvenile Court Panel 1954; former chm N Lancs and Merseyside Branches Magistrates' Assoc; Co Borough Cncllr 1949–61; High Sheriff of Merseyside 1977–78, hon co dir W Lancs BRCS 1964–74, pres Merseyside Co BRCS 1974–79; fndr chm Merseycare Charitable Tst, former Lancs pres Forces Help Soc and Lord Roberts' Workshops; patron: Southport and W Lancs Branch Normandy Veterans' Assoc, Southport and Dist Branch Burma Star Assoc, Dunkirk Veterans' Assoc; pres: Southport Branch Royal Br Legion, Southport and Dist Youth Band; former govr School for Hearing Impaired Children Birkdale; OStJ 1974; *Style*— Lt-Col George Appleton, OBE, TD, JP, DL; ✉ Shore House, Shore Rd, Ainsdale, Southport, Lancs PR8 2PU (☎ 01704 578211)

APPLETON, His Hon Judge; John Fortnam; s of Lt-Col George Fortnam Appleton, OBE, TD, JP, DL, *qv*, of Southport, and Patricia Margaret, *née* Dunlop (d 1990); *b* 8 April 1946; *Educ* Harrow, Univ of Bristol (LLB); *m* 1 July 1983, Maureen, da of Frederick Williams; 1 s (George Frederick Fortnam b 12 April 1984); *Career* Northern Circuit: barr, circuit jr 1970, recorder 1985–92, circuit judge 1992–; *Recreations* salmon fishing, shooting, gardening, stalking; *Style*— His Hon Judge Appleton; ✉ The Old Vicarage, Abbeystead, Lancaster LA2 9BG (☎ 01524 791727); c/o Northern Circuit Office, 15 Quay Street, Manchester M60 9FD

APPLEYARD, Bryan Edward; s of Cyril John Snowdon Appleyard (d 1965), and Freda Bendelsen (d 1971); *b* 24 Aug 1951; *Educ* Bolton Sch, King's Coll Cambridge; *m* Christena Marie-Thérèse; 1 da (Charlotte Mary Freda b 26 June 1982); *Career* journalist; South London News Group 1972–75, United Newspapers City Office 1975–76, journalist The Times 1976– (financial news ed and dep arts ed 1981–84), freelance journalist and author 1985–; columnist: The Independent (The Bryan Appleyard Interview 1990–), The Times; weekly columnist The Sunday Times (Bryan Appleyard's Forum), also writer The Sunday Times Magazine; also contrib to: Vogue, Spectator, London Review of Books; TV critic The Tablet; British Press Awards: General Feature Writer of the Year 1986, commended Feature Writer of the Year 1992, Feature Writer of the Year 1996; *Books* The Culture Club (1984), Richard Rogers - A Biography (1986), The Pleasures of Peace (1989), Understanding the Present - Science and the Soul of Modern Man (1992), The First Church of the New Millennium (1994); *Recreations* writing; *Clubs* Groucho's, The Academy; *Style*— Bryan Appleyard, Esq

APPLEYARD, Dr (William) James; s of Edward Rollo Appleyard (d 1937), and Maud Oliver, *née* Marshall (d 1979); *b* 25 Oct 1935; *Educ* Canford Sch Wimborne Dorset, Exeter Coll Oxford, Guy's Hosp London, Univ of Louisville Sch of Med Kentucky USA (Alumnus award); *m* 1964, Elizabeth Anne, *née* Ward; 1 s (Richard James b 1966), 2 da (Lisa Jane b 1968, Suzanne Mary b 1970); *Career* SHO Hosp for Sick Children Gt Ormond St London 1967, Dyers' Co research registrar St Thomas' Hosp London 1968, sr paediatric registrar Guy's Hosp London 1969–71, conslt paediatrician Kent and Canterbury Hosp 1971–; dean of clinical studies (UK) St George's Univ Sch of Med Grenada WI 1995– (prof of paediatrics 1983–95); memb: Kent AHA 1974–79, Supra Regnl Servs Advsy Ctee Dept of Health 1990–95; treas: Br Paediatric Assoc 1983–88, BMA 1996– (chm Representative Body 1993–95); memb: GMC 1984–, Cncl World Med Assoc 1994– (chm Ethical Ctee 1996–); patron Dyspraxia Tst; Liveryman Worshipful Soc of Apothecaries London; FRCP 1978; *Publications* articles in refereed based med jls on the new born, disabled children and medical manpower; *Recreations* lawn tennis, photography; *Clubs* Athenaeum, RSM, Penn; *Style*— Dr James Appleyard; ✉ Kent and Canterbury Hospital, Canterbury, Kent CT1 3NG (☎ 01227 766877, fax 01227 783185)

APPLEYARD, Joan Ena; da of William Jefferson, and Ruth Ena, *née* Leake; *b* 15 Aug 1946; *Educ* Univ of Newcastle (BA), Westminster Coll Oxford (DipEd); *m* 27 Aug 1994, Sir Leonard Appleyard, KCMG, *qv*; *Career* head of history Scarborough Girls' HS 1970–73 (asst mistress 1968–70), head of humanities Graham Sch Scarborough 1973–75; headmistress: Hunmanby Hall Sch Filey 1979–86 (dep headmistress 1975–79), St Swithun's Sch Winchester 1986–94; dep chm Common Entrance Bd until 1994; memb: Cncl GSA (pres 1992–93), Bloxham Project Steering Ctee; FRSA; *Recreations* drama, theatre, reading, cooking; *Style*— Lady Appleyard; ✉ Outward Bag Room (Peking), FCO, King Charles Street, London SW1A 2AH

APPLEYARD, Sir Leonard Vincent; KCMG (1994, CMG 1986); s of Thomas William Appleyard (d 1979), of Cawood, W Yorks, and Beatrix, *née* Golton (d 1982); *b* 2 Sept 1938; *Educ* Read Sch Drax W Yorks, Queens' Coll Cambridge (MA); *m* 1, 3 May 1964 (m dis), Elizabeth Margaret, da of John Lees West, of Grasmere, Cumbria; 2 da (Caroline b 1965, Rebecca b 1967); m 2, 27 Aug 1994, Joan Jefferson (Lady Appleyard, *qv*); *Career* FO 1962, third sec Hong Kong 1964, second sec Peking 1966, second (later first) sec FO 1969; first sec: Delhi 1971, Moscow 1975, HM Treasy 1978; fin cnsllr Paris 1979–82, head of Econ Rels Dept FCO 1982–84, princ private sec 1984–86, ambass to Hungary 1986–89, dep sec Cabinet Office 1989–91, political dir FCO 1991–94, ambass to China 1994–; *Recreations* music, reading, tennis; *Clubs* Brooks's; *Style*— Sir Leonard Appleyard, KCMG; ✉ c/o Foreign and Commonwealth Office (Peking), King Charles St, London SW1

APPLEYARD, (Walter) Philip; OBE (1987); s of Walter Appleyard (d 1970), and Hilda, *née* Teanby (d 1974); *b* 22 July 1923; *Educ* Humberston Fndn Sch Cleethorpes; *m* Jill, da of Arthur Brook Mellor (d 1974); 1 da (Lynne b 20 March 1950); *Career* Midland Bank 1939–42; Lincolnshire Regt and King's African Rifles 1942–47; Walter Appleyard Ltd 1947–51; Ross Group Ltd 1951–68: jt md Ross Fish Merchants 1951–57, jt md Ross Foods 1957–62, md Ross International 1962–68; Food and Agric Orgn of UN 1968–79: project dir (fisheries) Korea 1968–69, project dir (fisheries) Peru 1970–73, dir Industs Div HQ Rome 1974–79; gen mangr Oman Fishing Co 1980, chm MacAlister Elliott & Partners and subsid cos 1980–, fisheries conslt to int agencies 1980–; memb Inst of Fisheries Economics and Technol 1982–; author of over 200 books, documents and articles relevant to int fisheries, issues and devpt; pres The Hockey Assoc 1985–95, chm GB Men's Hockey Bd 1989–95, treas Int Hockey Fedn 1992– (memb Cncl 1992–); *Recreations* administering and watching hockey, theatre, cricket, watching TV, sport; *Clubs* Army & Navy; *Style*— Philip Appleyard, Esq, OBE; ✉ 1 Ashfield House, Martock, Somerset TA12 6EE (☎ 01935 826336, fax 01935 826503); MacAlister Elliott & Partners Ltd, 56 High Street, Lymington, Hampshire SO41 9AH (☎ 01590 679016, fax 01590 671573)

APSLEY, Lord; Allen Christopher Bertram Bathurst; s and h of 8 Earl Bathurst; *b* 11 March 1961; *m* 1, 31 May 1986 (m dis 1995), Hilary Jane, da of John F George, of Weston Lodge, Albury Surrey; 1 s (Hon Benjamin George Henry b 6 March 1990), 1 da (Hon Rosie Meriel Lilias b 20 April 1992); m 2, 5 June 1996, Sara Lucille, da of Christopher Chapman, of Ilminster, Somerset; *Style*— Lord Apsley; ✉ Cirencester Park, Cirencester, Glos GL7 2BT (☎ 01285 656037)

APTED, Michael D; *b* 10 Feb 1941; *Educ* Univ of Cambridge (BA); *Career* film director; began as researcher Granada TV; credits as TV dir incl: Coronation Street, The Lovers (Best Comedy Series BAFTA), Folly Foot (Best Children's Series BAFTA), Another Sunday & Sweet FA and Kisses at Fifty (Best Dramatic Dir BAFTA); film dir: Triple Echo 1972, Stardust 1975, The Squeeze 1977, Agatha 1979, Coal Miner's Daughter 1980 (nominated Directors' Guild of America award), Continental Divide 1981, Gorky Park 1983, Kipperbang 1983 (BAFTA nomination), First Born 1984, Bring on the Night 1985 (Grammy award), Critical Condition 1987, Gorillas in the Mist 1988, The Long Way Home 1989, Class Action 1990, Incident at Oglala 1992, Thunderheart 1992, Blink 1993, Moving the Mountain 1993, Nell 1994, Extreme Measures 1996; exec prodr: Bram Stoker's Dracula, Strapped, Criminal Justice; dir on-going documentary series revisiting gp of 14 people every 7 years (began with 7 Up 1963), 28 Up won BAFTA, Int Emmy and Int Documentary awards, 35 Up won BAFTA; *Style*— Michael Apted, Esq; ✉ Michael Apted Film Co, 1901 Avenue of the Stars, Suite 1245, Los Angeles, CA 90067–6013, USA

AQUILECCHIA, Prof Giovanni; s of Gen Vincenzo Aquilecchia (d 1959), and Maria Letizia, *née* Filibeck; *b* 28 Nov 1923; *Educ* Liceo T Tasso Rome, Univ of Rome, Univ of Paris, Univ of London; *m* 1, 7 May 1951 (m dis 1973), Costantina Maria, da of Adolfo Bacchetta (d 1940); 2 s (Adolfo b 1952, Vincent b 1956), 1 da (Maria Letizia b 1960); m 2, 24 April 1992, Catherine Mary, da of John Albert Posford (d 1996); *Career* libero docente di letteratura Italiana Univ of Rome 1958–, reader in Italian UCL 1959–61 (lectr 1955–59); prof of Italian: Univ of Manchester 1961–70, Univ of London 1970–89 (now emeritus), hon research fell UCL 1984–; visiting prof: Univ of Melbourne 1983, Univ of Naples 1990; chm Manchester Dante Soc 1961–70, memb Byron Soc 1979–; memb: AUT 1953–89, Soc of Italian Studies 1954, Soc of Renaissance Studies 1981, Associazione per gli Studi di Lingua e Letteratura Italiana; fell Arcadia Accademia Letteraria Italiana 1961; Hon MA Univ of Manchester 1965, Serena Medal British Acad 1996; *Books* Collected Essays on Italian Language and Literature (1971), numerous academic pubns in Italian and French; *Recreations* walking, swimming; *Style*— Prof Giovanni Aquilecchia; ✉ 49 Hanover Gate Mansions, Park Road, London NW1 (☎ 0171 723 8337); Department of Italian, University College, Gower Street, London WC1E 6BT (☎ 0171 387 7050 ext 3023)

ARBON, Paul; s of Paul Arbon (d 1929), of London, and Elizabeth, *née* Ashe (d 1977); *Educ* Taft Sch, Fountain Valley Sch; *m* 18 May 1946, Joan, da of James Ward Alker (d 1931), of NY City; 4 da (Carol b 1948, Joyce b 1950, Robin b 1952, April b 1958); *Career* banker; WWII Maj US Air Force 1941–45 (served 8 and 20 Air Force, DFC); chm of Bd Roosevelt & Sons; *Recreations* hunting, fishing; *Clubs* Union Club (Seawanhaka Corinthian Yacht), Soc of the Cincinnati, Pilgrims; *Style*— Paul Arbon, Esq; ✉ 46 Limerston St, London SW10 0HH (☎ 0171 351 9558); 128 East 95, New York 10028, USA

ARBUTHNOT, David William Patrick; s of Sir Hugh Fitzgerald Arbuthnot, 7 Bt (d 1983), and his 1 w, Elizabeth Kathleen (d 1972); hp of bro, Sir Keith Arbuthnot, 8 Bt; *b* 7 March 1953; *Educ* Wellington; *m* 12 March 1988, Diane, o da of John Yeomans, of Baughurst, Hants; 2 da (Phoebe Elizabeth b 18 Nov 1988, Rosanna Mary b 28 Nov 1989); *Career* racehorse trainer; *Recreations* rugby, shooting; *Clubs* Turf; *Style*— David Arbuthnot, Esq; ✉ Yew Tree Stables, Compton, nr Newbury, Berks RG16 0QT (☎ fax 01635 578427)

ARBUTHNOT, James Norwich; MP (C) Wanstead and Woodford (majority 16,885); yr s of Sir John Sinclair-Wemyss Arbuthnot, 1 Bt, MBE, TD (d 1992), and (Margaret) Jean, *née* Duff; hp of brother, Sir William Reierson Arbuthnot, 2 Bt, *qv*; *b* 4 Aug 1952; *Educ* Eton, Trinity Coll Cambridge (MA); *m* 6 Sept 1984, Emma Louise, da of (John) Michael Broadbent, of Avon; 1 s (Alexander Broadbent b 1986), 2 da (Katherine Rose Joste b 1989, Eleanor Sophie Duff b 1992); *Career* called to the Bar Inner Temple 1975; practising barr 1977–92; cncllr Royal Borough of Kensington and Chelsea 1978–87; Parly candidate (C) Cynon Valley 1983 and May 1984, MP (C) Wanstead and Woodford 1987–; PPS to: Min of State for Armed Forces 1988–90, Sec of State DTI 1990–92; asst whip 1992–94, Parly under sec of state DSS 1994–95, min of state (Def Procurement) MOD 1995–; pres Cynon Valley Cons Assoc 1983–92; *Recreations* skiing, computers, guitar, theatre; *Clubs* West Essex Cons; *Style*— James Arbuthnot, Esq, MP; ✉ House of Commons SW1A 0AA (☎ 0171 219 3000)

ARBUTHNOT, Sir Keith Robert Charles; 8 Bt (UK 1823), of Edinburgh; s of Sir Hugh Arbuthnot, 7 Bt (d 1983), and his 1 w, Elizabeth Kathleen (d 1972), da of Sqdn Ldr George Algernon Williams; *b* 23 Sept 1951; *Educ* Wellington, Univ of Edinburgh (BSc); *m* 22 May 1982, Anne, yr da of Brig Peter Moore (d 1992), of Hastings Hill House, Churchill, Oxon; 2 s (Robert Hugh Peter, Patrick William Martin b 13 July 1987), 1 da (Alice Elizabeth Mary b 22 March 1990); *Heir* s, Robert Hugh Peter Arbuthnot, b 2 March 1986; *Style*— Sir Keith Arbuthnot, Bt; ✉ Whitebridge, Peebles, Peebleshire, Scotland

ARBUTHNOT, Sir William Reierson; 2 Bt (UK 1964), of Kittybrewster, Aberdeen; s of Sir John Sinclair-Wemyss Arbuthnot, 1 Bt, MBE, TD (d 1992), and (Margaret) Jean, *née* Duff; *b* 2 Sept 1950; *Educ* Eton; *Heir* bro, James Norwich Arbuthnot, MP, *qv*; *Career* Scottish American Investment Co 1969–70, Arbuthnot Latham Holdings Ltd 1970–76, Joynson-Hicks & Co (slrs) 1978–81; memb Lloyd's; Liveryman Worshipful Co of Grocers; *Recreations* Lloyd's, genealogy, computers; *Style*— Sir William Arbuthnot, Bt; ✉ 14 Ashburn Gardens, London SW7 4DG (☎ and fax 0171 370 4907); 37 Cathcart Road, London SW10 9JG (☎ 0171 823 3344)

ARBUTHNOTT, Hugh James; CMG (1984); 2 s of Cdr James Gordon Arbuthnott, RN (d 1985; ggs of 8 Viscount of Arbuthnott), and Margaret Georgiana, *née* Hyde (d 1993); *b* 27 Dec 1936; *Educ* Ampleforth, New Coll Oxford; *m* 1964, Vanessa Rose, o da of Edward Dyer, of Tunbridge Wells; 3 s (Dominic b 1965, Justin b 1967 d 1989, Giles b 1970); *Career* Nat Serv 2 Lt Black Watch 1955–57; joined FO (subsequently FCO) 1960, third sec Tehran 1961–64, FO 1964–68 (private sec to Min of State 1966–68), first sec and head Chancery Tehran 1971–74, asst then head of Euro Integration Dept (External) FCO 1974–77, cnsllr (Agric and Econ) Paris 1978–80, head of Chancery Paris 1980–83, under sec Int Div ODA 1983–85, ambass to Romania 1986–89, ambass to Portugal 1989–93, ambass to Denmark 1993–96, ret; *Books* The Common Man's Guide to the Common Market (with Geoffrey Edwards, 2 edn 1989); *Style*— Hugh Arbuthnott, Esq, CMG; ✉ 65 Winchendon Road, London SW6 5DH (☎ 0171 736 2783)

ARBUTHNOTT, 16 Viscount of (S 1641); John Campbell Arbuthnott; KT (1996), CBE (1986), DSC (1945); also Lord Inverbervie (S 1641); s of 15 Viscount of Arbuthnott (d 1966), and Ursula, *née* Collingwood (d 1989); Lord Arbuthnott is the thirty third Laird of Arbuthnott and the twenty seventh in descent from Hugh de Swinton, who acquired the estate of Aberbothenoth, of which he is recorded as having been styled *thanus* and *dominus*, towards the end of the twelfth century, and who was ggggggggggs of Edulf Edulfing, 1 Lord of Bamburgh (d 912); *b* 26 Oct 1924; *Educ* Fettes, Gonville and Caius Coll Cambridge; *m* 1949, Mary Elizabeth Darley, er da of Cdr Christopher Oxley, DSC, RN (himself 2 s of Adm Charles Oxley, JP, and whose yst sis m 14 Viscount of Arbuthnott); 1 s, 1 da (*see* Hon Mrs Smith); *Heir* s, Master of Arbuthnott, *qv*; *Career* served RNVR Fleet Air Arm Far E & Pacific 1942–46; chartered surveyor and land agent; Agricultural Land Serv 1949–55, land agent Scottish Nature Conservancy 1955–67; dir: Aberdeen & Northern Marts 1973–91 (chm 1986–91), Scottish Widows' Fund and Life Assurance Soc 1978– (chm 1984–87), Scottish North Investment Trust 1979–85, Clydesdale Bank 1985–92, Britoil plc 1988–90, BR Scottish Advsy Bd 1990–; Lord-Lt Grampian Region (Kincardineshire) 1977–; pres: Br Assoc for Shooting and Conservation (formerly Wildfowlers Assoc of GB and Ireland) 1973–92, RZS Scotland 1976–, Royal Scottish Geographical Soc 1982–87; dep chm Nature Conservancy Cncl 1980–85 (chm Scottish Advsy Ctee); memb: Aberdeen Univ Court 1978–84, Royal Cmmn on Historical Manuscripts 1987–94; Liveryman Worshipful Co of Farmers; HM Lord High Cmmr to Gen Assembly of Church of Scotland 1986 and 1987; Bailiff Grand Cross and Prior of the Order of St John of Jerusalem in Scotland 1983–95; Hon LLD Aberdeen 1995; FRSE 1984, FRSA, FRICS; GCStJ; *Recreations* countryside activities, historical research; *Clubs* Army and Navy, New (Edinburgh); *Style*— The Rt Hon the Viscount of Arbuthnott, KT, CBE, DSC, FRSE; ✉ Arbuthnott House, by Laurencekirk, Kincardineshire AB30 1PA (☎ home 01561 361226, office fax 01561 320476)

ARBUTHNOTT, Master of; Hon John Keith Oxley; s and h of 16 Viscount of Arbuthnott, CBE, DSC, *qv*; *b* 18 July 1950; *Educ* Fettes, N Scotland Coll of Agric Aberdeen (HND, Dip in Farm Business, Orgn and Mgmnt), Robert Gordons Inst of Technol Aberdeen (Dip in Mgmnt Studies); *m* 1974, Jill Mary, eld da of Capt Colin Farquharson, of Whitehouse, Alford, Aberdeenshire; 1 s (Christopher Keith b 20 July 1977), 2 da (Clare Anne b 1974, Rachel Sarah b 1979); *Career* owner/mangr Arbuthnott Estate; memb Grampian Health Bd 1993–; *Style*— The Master of Arbuthnott; ✉ Kilternan, Arbuthnott, Laurencekirk, Kincardineshire AB30 1NA

ARBUTHNOTT, Prof John Peebles; s of James Anderson Arbuthnott (d 1961), and Jean, *née* Kelly (d 1982); *b* 8 April 1939; *Educ* Hyndland Sr Secdy Sch, Univ of Glasgow (BSc, PhD), Trinity Coll Dublin (MA, ScD); *m* 2 July 1962, Elinor Rutherford, da of John Smillie (d 1986); 1 s (Andrew b 10 Feb 1969), 2 da (Anne b 6 March 1966, Alison b 11 Nov 1974); *Career* res fell Royal Soc 1968–72, sr lectr Dept of Bacteriology Univ of Glasgow 1972–75 (asst lectr 1960–63, lectr 1963–67), bursar Trinity Coll Dublin 1983–86 (prof of microbiology 1976–88), prof of microbiology Univ of Nottingham 1988–91, princ and vice chllr Univ of Strathclyde 1991–; chm Joint Information Systems Ctee 1993–, convener Ctee of Scottish Higher Educn Princs until 1996; author of many papers on microbial pathogenicity; memb Cncl Soc of Gen Microbiology 1981–86 (sr ed 1980–84, treas 1987–92), meetings sec Fedn of Euro Microbiology Socs 1986–90; memb: Microbiological Safety of Food Ctee 1989–90, AFRC Animal Res Bd 1989–92, Public Health Laboratory Service Bd 1991–, DTI Multimedia Indust Advsy Gp 1994–, Educn Counselling Serv Bd British Cncl 1995–96, Nat Ctee of Enquiry into Higher Educn 1996–; memb: Soc of Gen Microbiology, Pathological Soc; hon fell Trinity Coll Dublin 1992; MRIA 1985, FIBiol 1988, FRSA 1989, FRSE 1993, FIIB 1993, FRCPath 1995; *Books* Isoelectric Focussing (jt ed, 1974), Determinants of Microbial Pathogenicity (jt ed, 1983), Foodborne Illness: a Lancet review (jtly, 1991); *Recreations* watching football, Scottish country dancing; *Style*— Prof John Arbuthnott, FRSE; ✉ University of Strathclyde, 16 Richmond St, Glasgow G1 1XQ (☎ 0141 552 4400, fax 0141 553 1521)

ARBUTHNOTT, Robert; CBE (1991); s of Archibald Arbuthnott, MBE, ED (d 1977), and Barbara Joan, *née* Worters (d 1988); *b* 28 Sept 1936; *Educ* Sedbergh, Emmanuel Coll Cambridge (BA, MA); *m* 19 May 1962, (Sophie) Robina, da of Robin Alan and Sophie Maud Axford; 1 s (Robert Keith b 1968), 2 da (Alison b 1963, Catherine b 1965); *Career* Nat Serv 2 Lt The Black Watch (RHR) 1955–57; British Council: Karachi 1960–62, Lahore 1962–64, London 1964–67, rep Nepal 1967–72, rep Malaysia 1973–76, dir Educational Contracts Dept 1976–77, controller Personnel and Staff Recruitment Div 1978–81, rep Germany 1981–85, RCDS 1986, controller America Pacific and S Asia Div 1987, minister (cultural affairs) New Delhi 1988–93; memb: Mgmnt Ctee St Anthony's Cheshire Home Wolverhampton, Organising Ctee English Haydn Festival Bridgnorth; fell and memb Cncl Royal Asiatic Soc; memb: Royal Soc for Asian Affrs, Royal Horticultural Soc, Nat Tst; *Recreations* making music, gardening, sport, historic places; *Clubs* United Oxford and Cambridge University; *Style*— Robert Arbuthnott, Esq, CBE; ✉ Glazeley Old Rectory, nr Bridgnorth, Shropshire WV16 6AB

ARCHDALE, Sir Edward Folmer; 3 Bt (UK 1928), of Riversdale, Co Fermanagh; DSC (1943); s of Vice Adm Sir Edward Archdale, 2 Bt, CBE (d 1955), and Gerda, da of Frederik Sievers, of Copenhagen; *b* 8 Sept 1921; *Educ* Copthorne Sch, RNC Dartmouth; *m* 24 July 1954 (m dis 1978), Elizabeth Ann Stewart, da of Maj-Gen Wilfrid Boyd Fellowes Lukis, CBE, RM (d 1969); 1 s (Nicholas Edward), 2 da (Annabel Frances b 1956, d 1996, Lucinda Grace b 1958); *Heir* s, Nicholas Edward Archdale b 2 Dec 1965; *Career* RN: joined 1935, serv WWII (despatches), Capt (ret); def conslt, political economist; NI rep The Henry George Fndn; *Recreations* civilisation; *Style*— Sir Edward Archdale, Bt, DSC; ✉ 46 Coleshill Park, Enniskillen, Co Fermanagh BT74 7LD, Northern Ireland (☎ 01365 320349)

ARCHDEACON, Antony; s of Maurice Ignatius Archdeacon (d 1973), of Ruislip, Middx, and Nora Margery May, *née* Ball; *b* 25 Jan 1925; *Educ* Oxford House Sch, Buckingham Univ (LLB); *m* 1, 3 Dec 1956 (m dis 1965), Elizabeth, da of Samuel Percy Ball, of The Cottage, Great Horwood, Bucks; 1 s (Timothy b 1957); m 2, 24 Aug 1992, Ursula, da of Fritz Mentze, of Iserlohn, Germany; *Career* admitted slr 1950; dir: Skim Milk Supplies Ltd 1967–, Business Mortgages Trust plc 1969–86; chm Forum of St Albans plc 1985–; pres: Rotary Club Buckingham 1968, Northampton Anglo-German Club 1988–; town clerk Buckingham 1951–71; Freeman: City of London 1972, Worshipful Co of Feltmakers 1972; *Recreations* walking, languages; *Clubs* St Stephen's Constitutional, City Livery; *Style*— Antony Archdeacon, Esq; ✉ Trolly Hall, Buckingham MK18 1PT (☎ 01280 812126, fax 01280 822105)

ARCHER, Prof Brian Harrison; s of Arthur Cecil Arthur (d 1969), and Elizabeth, *née* Summerscales; *b* 31 July 1934; *Educ* Liverpool Coll, Fitzwilliam House Cambridge (MA), Univ of London (BSc), Univ of Wales (PhD); *Career* cmmnd King's Regt Liverpool 1955, Maj TAVR 1955–65; schoolmaster Monmouth 1958–69, Inst of Economic Res Univ Coll of N Wales 1969–77 (sr res offr, lectr, sr lectr, dir); Univ of Surrey: prof and head Dept of Mgmnt Studies 1978–91, pro vice chllr 1987–94, prof 1994–; conslt to: Cwlth Secretariat, UNDP, World Bank, WTO; author of numerous pubns in jls; ind memb devpt and mktg ctees Br Tourist Authy 1984–94, govr Charterhouse Sch 1991–95; *Books* The Impact of Domestic Tourism (1973), Demand Forecasting in Tourism (1976), Tourism Multipliers: The State of the Art (1977); *Recreations* travel, watching cricket and rugby; *Style*— Prof Brian Archer; ✉ 3 The Cedars, Milford, Godalming, Surrey GU8 5DH; Department of Management Studies, University of Surrey, Stag Hill, Guildford, Surrey GU2 5XH (☎ 01483 259184, fax 01483 509387, telex 859331)

ARCHER, Bryan Russell; s of Donald Charles Archer (d 1990), and Lillian May, *née* Smith; *b* 18 April 1928; *Educ* Watford GS, Architectural Assoc Sch of Architecture (DipArch); *m* 31 March 1955, Nancy Sheila, da of Stanley James Dean (d 1995), of Welwyn Garden City, Herts; 2 s (Richard b 1959, Andrew b 1960), 1 da (Susan b 1963); *Career* registered architect 1956; fndr ptnr Archer Boxer Partners 1963; dir: Archer Boxer Group Ltd 1978–96, Archer Boxer Partners (International) Ltd 1993–95, Savoy Homes Ltd 1996; pres Hatfield C of C 1969–71, dir Herts C of C 1972–80; govr Sherrardswood Sch 1974–96, dist govr Rotary Int (dist 1260) 1985–86; memb The Lord's Taverners 1992–; Freeman Worshipful Co of Constructors 1978–; FRIBA 1968, FFB 1970; *Recreations* boating, travelling; *Clubs* IOD; *Style*— Bryan Archer, Esq; ✉ Pennyfathers, Pennyfathers Lane, Harmer Green, Welwyn, Herts AL6 0EL (☎ 01438 714627)

ARCHER, Colin Robert Hill; s of Robin Hamlyn Hill Archer, of Richmond, and Cherrie Mary, *née* Gourlay; *b* 13 Aug 1949; *Educ* Stowe, Univ of Essex (BA); *m* 27 March 1976, (Mary) Jane, da of John Rutherford Blaikie; 1 s (Charles b 18 Aug 1983), 1 da (Sarah b 11 March 1981); *Career* articled clerk then asst mangr Thomson McLintock 1971–77, mangr corp fin Kleinwort Benson 1977–85, divnl dir corp fin BHS plc 1985–86, gp fin controller Storehouse plc 1988–89 (gp co sec 1986–88), gp fin dir Higgs and Hill plc 1989–; FCA; *Recreations* tennis, golf, skiing, reading; *Clubs* Hurlingham, Berkshire Golf; *Style*— Colin Archer, Esq; ✉ Higgs and Hill plc, Crown House, Kingston Rd, New Malden, Surrey KT3 3ST (☎ 0181 942 8921)

ARCHER, Geoffrey Wilson; s of Thomas Wilson Archer, of Salisbury, and Dorothy Maude, *née* Monahan; *b* 21 May 1944; *Educ* Highgate; *m* 17 Aug 1974, Eva Jenny Lucia, da of Gustaf Janson; 1 s (James Alexander b 22 Dec 1977), 1 da (Alison Susanne b 24 July 1975); *Career* author; trainee Southern Television 1964, reporter/prodr Anglia Television 1965–69, reporter/presenter Tyne-Tees Television 1969; ITN: news reporter 1969–79, defence/science corr 1979–83, defence/dip corr 1983–95; *Books* Sky Dancer (1987), Shadow Hunter (1989), Eagle Trap (1993), Scorpion Trail (1995), Java Spider (1997); *Recreations* walking, gardening, sailing; *Style*— Geoffrey Archer, Esq; ✉ c/o Century/Arrow Books, 20 Vauxhall Bridge Road, London SW1V 2SA

ARCHER, Dr Gordon James; s of Sqdn Ldr Percival John Archer, of 53 Birch Ave, Cleveleys, Lancs, and Doris Elizabeth Archer; *b* 21 Aug 1942; *Educ* Kirkham GS, Univ of Manchester (MB ChB); *m* 21 Sept 1968, Barbara, da of Alwyn Johns, of Penllergaer, W Glamorgan; 1 s (Gareth b 9 Oct 1974), 1 da (Joanne b 3 Sept 1976); *Career* med registrar Cardiff Royal Infirmary 1969–71, thoracic med registrar London Chest Hosp 1971–73, sr med registrar Leeds Gen Infirmary 1973–74, conslt physician with special interest chest diseases Stockport AHA 1974–, clinical teacher Univ of Manchester 1983–; memb: Regnl Med Ctee Br Thoracic Soc, NW Regnl Assoc Physicians; med dir Stockport Health Authy, chm Stockport Asthma Care Fund; pres Macclesfield Castle Rotary Club 1994–95; MRCP 1969, FRCP 1990; *Books* numerous pubns in jls incl: Treatment of Pneumothorax by Simple Aspiration (1983), Results of Pneumothorax Aspiration (1985); *Recreations* golf; *Clubs* Tytherington Golf and Country; *Style*— Dr Gordon Archer; ✉ Ryley Mount Consulting Rooms, 432 Buxton Rd, Gt Moor, Stockport, Cheshire SK2 (☎ 0161 483 9333)

ARCHER, HE Graham Robertson; *b* 4 July 1939; *m* 1963, Pauline, *née* Cowan; 2 da (b 1965 and 1968); *Career* HM Dip Serv: entered 1962, Cwlth Rels Office FCO 1962–64, private sec to High Cmmr New Delhi 1964–66, vice consul Kuwait 1966–67, FCO 1967–70, second sec Washington 1970–72, FCO 1972–75, head of Chancery Wellington 1975–79, FCO 1979–81, scrutiny exercise 1981–82, head of chancery Pretoria 1982–86, dep head of mission The Hague 1986–90, FCO 1990–95, high cmmr to Republic of Malta 1995–; *Style*— HE Mr Graham Archer; ✉ c/o Foreign & Commonwealth Office (Valletta), King Charles Street, London SW1H 2AH

ARCHER, Jasper Rodney; s of Lt-Col Rodney Archer, MC (d 1974); *b* 14 Aug 1941; *Educ* Cheltenham, RMA Sandhurst; *m* 10 Feb 1967, Victoria, da of Eric Leigh (d 1981); 1 s (Nicholas b 1971), 1 da (Sophie b 1973); *Career* 4/7 Royal Dragoon Gds 1962–70 (Capt 1965); dir Cardew & Co; *Recreations* skiing; *Clubs* Cavalry and Guards; *Style*— Jasper Archer, Esq; ✉ The Malt House, Stapleford, Wiltshire; Cardew & Co, 12 Suffolk Street, London SW1Y 4HG (☎ 0171 930 0777)

ARCHER, Gen Sir (Arthur) John; KCB (1976), OBE (1964, MBE 1960); s of Alfred Arthur Archer, of Fakenham, Norfolk, and Mildred Archer; *b* 12 Feb 1924; *Educ* King's Sch Peterborough, St Catharine's Coll Cambridge; *m* 1950, (Cynthia) Marie, da of Col Alexander Allan, DSO, MC (d 1967), of Swallowcliffe, Wilts; 2 s; *Career* entered Army 1943, cmmnd 1944, reg cmmn Dorset Regt 1946, psc 1956, jssc 1959, GSO1 3 Div 1963–65, CO 1 Devon and Dorset Regt 1965–67, Cdr Land Forces Gulf 1968–69, idc 1970, dir of PR (Army) 1970–72, Cdr 2 Div 1972–74, dir Army Staff Duties 1974–76, Cdr Br Forces Hong Kong 1976–78, Lt Gen Bde of Gurkhas 1977–78, C-in-C UKLF 1978–79; Col Devonshire & Dorset Regt 1977–79; chief exec Royal Hong Kong Jockey Club 1980–86; dir The Hongkong & Shanghai Banking Corpn 1982–86; pres Officers Pensions Soc 1994– (memb Cncl 1989–94); CIMgt; *Recreations* light aviation, gliding, sailing; *Clubs* Army and Navy, Hong Kong, Royal Hong Kong Jockey, Royal Motor Yacht; *Style*— Gen Sir John Archer, KCB, OBE; ✉ c/o Lloyds Bank, Blue Boar Row, Salisbury, Wilts

ARCHER, John Francis Ashweek; QC (1975); s of late George Eric Archer, and Frances, *née* Ashweek; *b* 9 July 1925; *Educ* Winchester, New Coll Oxford (BA); *m* 1, 1960, Doris Mary, *née* Hennessey (d 1988); m 2, 1995, Vivienne Frances Weatherhead, *née* Ecclestone; *Career* served WWII, Lt RA 1948; called to the Bar Inner Temple 1950, bencher 1984; recorder of the Crown Court 1974–; memb Criminal Injuries Compensation Bd 1987–; *Recreations* bridge, motoring; *Style*— John Archer, Esq, QC; ✉ 3 Hare Court, London EC4; 2 Crown Office Row, Temple, London EC4Y 7HT (☎ 0171 797 8100)

ARCHER, Prof John Stuart; s of Stuart Leonard Gordon Archer, of Hounslow, Middx, and Joan, *née* Watkinson; *b* 15 June 1943; *Educ* GS for Boys Chiswick, City Univ London (BSc), Imperial Coll London (PhD, DIC); *m* 30 Sept 1967, Lesley, da of Leslie Arthur Oaksford, of Yeovil, Somerset; 1 s (Adam John b 21 Feb 1975), 1 da (Louise b 19 Jan 1973); *Career* student trainee Imperial Chemical Industs 1961–64, res reservoir engr ESSO Resources Canada 1969–73, petroleum reservoir engr British Gas Corp 1973–74, mangr reservoir studies D&S Petroleum Conslts 1974–77, conslt ERC (Energy Resource Conslts) 1977–84 (fndr and dir Reservoir Studies 1977–80); Imperial Coll London: joined 1980, prof of petroleum engrg (former reader), head Dept of Mineral Resources Engrg 1986–94, dean Royal Sch of Mines 1989–91, pro rector 1991–94, dep rector 1994–96; princ and vice-chllr Heriot-Watt Univ 1997–; princ Prof J S Archer and Associates conslts; dir: Impel, MTD Ltd, Clyde Petroleum plc; memb Soc of Petroleum Engrg 1973, CEng 1974, FEng 1992, FInstPet 1977, FCGI 1996, FInstE, FIMM, FRSA; *Books* Petroleum Engineering - Principles and Practice (1986); *Recreations* golf, skiing, walking, gardening, theatre; *Clubs* Athenaeum; *Style*— Prof John Archer, FEng; ✉ Heriot-Watt University, Edinburgh EH14 4AS (☎ 0131 451 3360, fax 0131 449 3330)

ARCHER, Prof Margaret Scotford; da of Ronald Archer (d 1964), and Elise, *née* Scotford; *b* 20 Jan 1943; *Educ* Sheffield HS for Girls, LSE (BSc, PhD), Ecole Pratique des Hautes Etudes Paris; *m* 1 May 1973, (Gilbert) Andrew Jones, s of Kingsley Boardman (d 1975); 2 s (Kingsley b 1975, Marcus b 1979); *Career* lectr Univ of Reading 1966–73, prof Univ of Warwick 1979– (reader 1973–79); memb Br Sociological Assoc, pres Int Sociological Assoc; counsellor Pontifical Acad of Social Scis; *Books* Social Conflict and Educational Change in England and France 1789–1848 (with M Vaughan, 1971),

Contemporary Europe, Class, Status and Power (ed with S Giner, 1971), Students, University and Society (ed, 1972), Contemporary Europe, Social Structures and Cultural Patterns (ed with S Giner, 1978), Social Origins of Educational Systems (1979), The Sociology of Educational Expansion (ed, 1982), Culture and Agency (1988), Realist Social Theory: the Morphogenetic Approach (1995); *Recreations* equestrian; *Style—* Prof Margaret Archer; ✉ Department of Sociology, University of Warwick, Coventry, Warwickshire CV4 7AL (☎ 01203 523499, fax 01869 37146)

ARCHER, Neill John; s of Peter Archer, of Leicester, and Margaret Anne, *née* Munns; *b* 31 Aug 1961; *Educ* Wyggeston Boys' GS Leicester, UEA Norwich, Brevard Music Centre North Carolina USA; *m* 30 Aug 1986, Marilyn, da of late Oscar Dale; 3 da (Sally Anne b 9 Jan 1990, Rosemary Jane b 29 Oct 1992, Grace Elizabeth b 25 Oct 1995); *Career* tenor; *Performances* operatic roles incl: Tamino in The Magic Flute (Kent Opera) 1987, title role in Don Chisciotti in Conti's Sierra Morena (Buxton Festival) 1987, Don Ottavio in Don Giovanni (WNO) 1988, Edoardo IV in Testi's Riccardo III (Teatro Regio Torino) 1988, Ubaldo in Haydn's Armide (Buxton Festival) 1988, Ferrando in Cosi fan Tutte (Opera Factory, QEH) 1988, young man and naked youth in Schonberg Moses and Aaron (BBC Symphony Orchestra and BBC Radio 3) 1988, Ferrando in Cosi fan Tutte (Scottish Opera 1988, Channel Four 1989), Clem in Britten's The Little Sweep by Britten (Thames) 1989, Andres in Wozzeck (Teatro Regio Parma) 1989, Paradies und Peri (Paris Opera) 1989, Count Almaviva in The Barber of Seville (Norske Oper Oslo and Opera North) 1989, Cassio in Otello (WNO 1990, Tamino in The Magic Flute (ENO) 1990, Jacquino in Fidelio (Covent Garden and BBC Radio) 1990, Pylades in Gluck's Iphegenia auf Taurus (Basel Opera House) 1991, Ferrando (Glyndebourne Festival and Touring Opera) 1991, Achilles in King Priam (Opera North) 1991, Pelleas in Pelleas et Melisande (WNO 1992), Der Steuermann in Der Fliegender Holländer (Covent Garden) 1992, Ferrando in Cosi fan Tutte (Sydney Aust) 1994, Tamino in The Magic Flute (ENO) 1994; concert and recital performances incl: Handel's Messiah (QEH 1988, St Davids Hall with WNO 1989), Orff's Carmina Burana (Edinburgh Festival and BBC TV) 1988, arias from St Matthew Passion (Stavanger Symphony Orchestra) 1989; *Style—* Neill Archer, Esq; ✉ c/o IMG Artists Europe, Media House, 3 Burlington Lane, London W4 2TH (☎ 0181 233 5800, fax 0181 233 5801)

ARCHER-JONES, Patricia Ann; da of Herbert Taylor (d 1986), and Dorothy, *née* Beardall, of Lancs; *b* 12 July 1948; *Educ* Accrington HS, Univ of Warwick (BA), Manchester Poly (Postgrad Dip in Personnel Mgmnt and Industl Trg); *Career* Cheshire CC: grad trainee 1969–71, trg offr 1971–74, personnel mangr 1974–82, asst co sec 1982–87; borough manpower servs offr Sefton MBC 1987–90, dir of personnel and mgmnt servs Liverpool City Cncl 1990–91, exec dir of strategic planning and performance review W Glamorgan Health Authy 1991–94, chief exec Powys Health Authy 1994–96, dir of contractor servs Dyfed Powys Health Authy 1996–; FIPM 1989; *Style—* Mrs Patricia Archer-Jones; ✉ Dyfed Powys Health Authority, PO Box 13, Carmarthen SA31 2AB (☎ 01267 232691, fax 01267 234251, mobile 0585 378677)

ARCHER OF SANDWELL, Baron (Life Peer UK 1992), of Sandwell in the County of West Midlands; Peter Kingsley Archer; PC (1977), QC (1971); s of Cyril Kinglsey Archer, MM (d 1974), and May, *née* Baker (d 1976); *b* 20 Nov 1926; *Educ* Wednesbury Boys' HS, Univ of London (external LLB), LSE (LLM), UCL (BA); *m* 7 Aug 1954, Margaret Irene, da of Sydney John Smith (d 1936), of London, Ontario, Canada; 1 s (Hon John Kingsley b 1962); *Career* called to the Bar Gray's Inn 1952, bencher 1974; commenced practice 1953, recorder of the Crown Court 1982–; MP (Lab): Rowley Regis and Tipton 1966–74, Warley W 1974–92; PPS to Attorney Gen 1967–70, Slr Gen 1974–79; oppn front bench spokesman on: legal affrs 1979–82, trade 1982–83; shadow NI sec 1983–87; front bench spokesman on foreign affairs House of Lords 1992–; chm: Parly Gp for World Govt 1970–74, Br section Amnesty Int 1971–74, Cncl on Tribunals 1992–; vice chm Anti-Slavery Soc 1970–74; pres: Fabian Soc 1993– (chm Exec Ctee 1980–81, memb 1974–86), Methodist Homes for the Aged 1993–, Soc of Labour Lawyers 1993– (chm 1971–74 and 1980–93), World Disarmament Campaign 1994–; ombudsman Mirror Group Newspapers 1989–; fell UCL 1978; *Books* The Queen's Courts (1956), Social Welfare and the Citizen (ed, 1957), Communism and the Law (1963), Freedom at Stake (with Lord Reay, 1966), Human Rights (1969), Purpose in Socialism (jtly, 1973), The Role of the Law Officers (1978), More Law Reform Now (co-ed, 1984); *Recreations* music, writing, talking; *Style—* The Rt Hon Lord Archer of Sandwell, PC, QC; ✉ 7 Old School Court, Wraysbury, Staines, Middx (☎ 01784 483136)

ARCHER OF WESTON-SUPER-MARE, Baron (Life Peer UK 1992), of Mark in the County of Somerset; Jeffrey Howard Archer; s of William Archer (d 1956), and Lola, *née* Cook; *b* 15 April 1940; *Educ* Wellington Sch Somerset, BNC Oxford (Athletics blues 1963–65, Gymnastics blue 1965, Oxford 100 yds record 1966); *m* 11 July 1966, Dr Mary Doreen Archer, *qv*, da of Harold Weeden (d 1971); 2 s (Hon William Harold b 1972, Hon James Howard b 1974); *Career* politician and author; memb GLC Havering 1966–70, MP (C) Louth 1969–74; dep chm Cons Pty 1985–86; tstee RWS 1989–; pres: Somerset AAA 1973, Somerset Wyverns 1983; hon pres Glasgow Univ Dialectic Soc 1984–; FRSA 1973; *Books* Not a Penny More, Not a Penny Less (1975, televised 1990), Shall We Tell The President? (1977), Kane and Abel (1979, televised 1986), A Quiver Full of Arrows (1980), The Prodigal Daughter (1982), First Among Equals (1984, televised 1986), A Matter of Honour (1986), Beyond Reasonable Doubt (play, 1987), A Twist in The Tale (short stories, 1989), Exclusive (play, 1989), As the Crow Flies (1991), Honour Among Thieves (1993), Twelve Red Herrings (1994); *Recreations* theatre, cinema, watching Somerset play cricket; *Clubs* MCC, Louth Working Men's; *Style—* The Rt Hon Lord Archer of Weston-super-Mare; ✉ Alembic House, 93 Albert Embankment, London SE1 7TY (☎ 0171 735 0077)

ARCHER OF WESTON-SUPER-MARE, Baroness; Dr Mary Doreen Archer; da of Harold Norman Weeden (d 1971), and Doreen, *née* Cox; *b* 22 Dec 1944; *Educ* Cheltenham Ladies' Coll, St Anne's Coll Oxford (BA, MA), Imperial Coll London (PhD); *m* 11 July 1966, Baron Archer of Weston-super-Mare (Life Peer), *qv*; 2 s; *Career* jr res fell St Hilda's Coll Oxford 1968–71, temp lectr in chemistry Somerville Coll Oxford 1971–72, res fell Royal Inst of Great Britain 1972–76, fell and lectr Newnham Coll Cambridge and lectr in chemistry Trinity Coll Cambridge 1976–86, bye-fell Newnham Coll Cambridge 1987–; non-exec dir: Anglia Television Group 1987–95, Mid Anglia Radio plc 1988–, Cambridge and Newmarket FM Radio Ltd 1988–; dir Fitzwilliam Museum Tst 1984–91, chm Nat Energy Fndn 1989–, memb Cncl Lloyd's 1988–92, tstee Science Museum 1990–; memb Cncl Cheltenham Ladies' Coll 1991–; visiting prof Dept of Biochemistry Imperial Coll London; memb Addenbrooke's Hosp NHS Tst; visitor Univ of Hertfordshire; FRSC, FRSA; *Books* Rupert Brooke and the Old Vicarage, Grantchester (1989); various contribs to chem jls; *Recreations* singing, theatre, cats, squash; *Style—* The Rt Hon Lady Archer of Weston-super-Mare; ✉ The Old Vicarage, Grantchester, Cambridge CB3 9ND (☎ 01223 840213, fax 01223 842882); Alembic House, 93 Albert Embankment, London SE1 7TX (☎ 0171 735 0077, fax 0171 582 2406)

ARCHIBALD, Liliana; da of Dr Noah Barou (d 1955), and Sophie Barou (d 1956); sis of Eur Ing Prof Alexander Kennaway, *qv*; *b* 25 May 1928; *Educ* Kingsley Sch, Geneva Univ; *m* 1951 (m dis 1965), Prof George Christopher Archibald (d 1996); *Career* lectr Otago Univ 1952–55; dir: Const & Co Ltd 1955–73 and 1977–94, Credit Consultants Ltd 1957–73 and 1977–85, Adam Bros Contingency Ltd 1970–85 (chm 1991–92), Fenchurch Group International Ltd 1985–87, Holman Wade Ltd insur brokers 1989–92; head of Credit Insur and Export Credit Div EEC 1973–77, EEC advsr Lloyd's 1978–85, conslt Belmont Euro Community Law Office Brussels 1985–88, conslt Coopers & Lybrand 1989–, dir CLM Insurance Fund plc 1993–; memb Lord Chllr's Advsy Ctee on Legal Educn and Conduct 1991–94; memb Lloyd's 1973–94; Liveryman Worshipful Co of Insurers; *Books* trans and ed: Peter the Great (1958), Rise of the Romanovs (1970); *Recreations* driving fast cars, skiing, gardening; *Style—* Mrs Liliana Archibald; ✉ 21 Langland Gardens, London NW3 6QE

ARCHIBALD, Prof (Andrew) Ronald; *b* 12 May 1934; *Educ* Univ of Edinburgh (BSc, PhD); *m* Angela Carr; 3 da (Sarah b 1968, Rachael b 1970, Charlotte b 1972); *Career* Univ of Newcastle upon Tyne: prof of microbiological chemistry 1979, head Dept of Microbiology 1989–93, pro-vice-chllr 1993–; special res in bacterial cell walls; author of various pubns in scientific lit; *Style—* Professor Ronald Archibald; ✉ 19 Linden Rd, Gosforth, Newcastle upon Tyne (☎ 0191 285 7920); Pro-Vice-Chancellor's Office, University of Newcastle upon Tyne, 6 Kensington Terrace, Newcastle upon Tyne NE7 7RH (☎ 0191 222 5058, fax 0191 222 6229, e-mail A.R.Archibald@newcastle.ac.uk)

ARCHIBALD, Wilfred William; s of Cyril Nadalie Archibald (d 1966), of London, and Ethele, *née* Polonski (d 1990); *Educ* Victoria Coll Alexandria Egypt; *m* 28 June 1947, Jean Pauline Scott, da of Alexander William Gibson (d 1961), of Ferring, W Sussex; 1 s (Duncan Archibald b 1948), 2 da (Juliet (Mrs Billingham) b 1949, Christine (Mrs Brewster) b 1959); *Career* WWII Navigator RAF 1940–44; inspr for Middle East Guardian Royal Exchange Assurance Co 1947–56 (mangr Singapore, Malaysia, Thailand and Borneo 1957–67), seconded to Union Insurance Society of Canton as md 1968–69, overseas mangr GRE Gp Head Office London 1970–77, asst gen mangr (overseas) 1977–86, ret 1986; govr: City of London Freeman's Sch Ashstead, Mitchell City of London Charity and Educnl Fndn (dep chm), Lady Eleanor Holles Sch (Cripplegate Schs Fndn), Christ's Hosp Sch Horsham, City Literary Inst London, St Andrew Holborn City Fndn; memb London Court Int Arbitration Consultative Ctee; memb: St Michael's Cornhill PCC, Ct of Common Cncl City of London, Cncl St Lawrence Jewry Guild Church dep for Ward of Cornhill; memb: Cripplegate Ward Club, Lime St Ward Club, Utd Ward Club, Broad Street Ward Club; Freeman City of London 1980, Liveryman Worshipful Co of Insurers 1980; *Recreations* farming; *Style—* Wilfred Archibald, Esq; ✉ Deakes Manor, Deakes Lane, Cuckfield, West Sussex RH17 5JA (☎ 01444 454151); 184 Andrewes House, Barbican, London EC2

ARCULUS, (Thomas) David Guy; s of Thomas Guy Arculus, and Mary, *née* Barton (d 1971); *b* 2 June 1946; *Educ* Bromsgrove Sch, Oriel Coll Oxford (MA), London Business Sch (MSc); *m* 11 Aug 1974, Anne Murdoch, da of Howard Leslie Sleeman; 1 da (Suzanne b 1 April 1976), 2 s (Thomas b 30 Jan 1978, Nicholas b 13 Nov 1979); *Career* VSO 1964–65, prodr BBC 1968–70; EMAP plc: joined 1972, gen mangr mags 1974–81, md business mags and exhbns 1981–84, gp dep md 1984–89, gp md 1989–; non-exec dir: Norcros plc 1993–, Severn Trent plc 1996–; chm PPA 1990, treas Fedn of Int Periodical Press 1992–, memb Nat Consumer Cncl 1993–96; Freeman City of London 1990, Liveryman Worshipful Co of Stationers and Newspaper Makers 1992; memb Assoc of MBAs 1972, MInstD 1993, fell Indust and Parl Tst; *Recreations* cricket, golf; *Clubs* United Oxford & Cambridge Univ, MCC, Groucho; *Style—* David Arculus, Esq; ✉ EMAP plc, Lincoln Court, 1 Lincoln Road, Peterborough PE1 2RF (☎ 01733 68900, fax 01733 62636)

ARCULUS, Sir Ronald; KCMG (1979, CMG 1968), KCVO (1980); s of Cecil Arculus, MC (d 1968), and Ethel L Arculus (d 1982); *b* 11 Feb 1923; *Educ* Solihull Sch, Exeter Coll Oxford (MA), Imperial Defence Coll; *m* 1953, Sheila Mary, da of Arthur Faux (d 1982); 1 s (Gerald), 1 da (Juliet); *Career* Capt 4 Queen's Own Hussars 1942–45; HM Dip Serv: FO 1947, San Francisco 1948, La Paz 1950, FO 1951, Ankara 1953, FO 1957, Washington 1961, cnsllr NY 1965–68, IDC 1969, head Sci and Technol Dept FCO 1970–72, min (econ) Paris 1973–77, ambass and perm ldr UK Delgn UN Law of the Sea Conf 1977–79, ambass to Italy 1979–83, ret; dir Glaxo Holdings 1983–92 (conslt 1992–95); conslt: Trusthouse Forte 1983–86, London and Continental Bankers 1984–88; govr Br Inst of Florence 1984–93; dir King's Med Res Tst 1984–88; special advsr to Min of T'port on Channel Tunnel Trains 1987–88; Freeman City of London 1981; hon fell Exeter Coll Oxford 1989; Grand Cross Italian Order of Merit 1980; *Recreations* travel, opera, ballet, fine arts; *Clubs* Army and Navy, Hurlingham, Cowdray Park; *Style—* Sir Ronald Arculus, KCMG, KCVO; ✉ 20 Kensington Court Gardens, London W8 5QF

ARDEE, Lord; John Anthony Brabazon; s and h of 14 Earl of Meath; *b* 11 May 1941; *Educ* Harrow; *m* 1973, Xenia Goudime; 1 s, 2 da (Hon Corinna Lettice b 9 Nov 1974, Hon Serena Alexandra b 23 Feb 1979); *Heir* s, Hon Anthony Jaques Brabazon b 30 Jan 1977; *Career* page of hon to HM The Queen 1956–57, served Grenadier Gds 1960–63; *Style—* Lord Ardee; ✉ Ballinacor, Rathdrum, Co Wicklow, Ireland

ARDEN, Andrew Paul Russel; QC (1991); s of Sidney Russel Arden, of Cannes, France, and Helen Anne, *née* Prevezer (d 1991); *b* 20 April 1948; *Educ* Stowe, Univ Coll Sch, UCL (LLB); *m* 19 Sept 1991, Joanne, da of Joseph Leahy, of Cramlington, Northumberland; 1 da (Emma b 1992); *Career* called to the Bar Gray's Inn 1974; dir Small Heath Community Law Centre Birmingham 1976–78; *Legal Publications* Manual of Housing Law (1978, 6 edn with C Hunter 1997), Housing Act 1980 (1980), Homeless Persons: Part III, Housing Act 1985 (1982, 5 edn with C Hunter 1997), Private Tenants Handbook (1985, 2 edn 1989), Public Tenants Handbook (1985, 2 edn 1989), Homeless Persons Handbook (1986, 2 edn 1988), Housing Act 1985 (1986), Quiet Enjoyment (with Prof M Partington 1980, 2 edn 1985), Housing Law (with Prof M Partington 1983, 2 edn with Prof M Partington and C Hunter 1994), Rent Acts & Regulations, Amended and Annotated (with Prof J T Farrand, 1981), Housing & Building Control Act 1984 (with C Cross, 1984), Landlord & Tenant Act 1985 (with S McGrath, 1986), Housing Associations Act 1985 (with J Ramage, 1986), Housing Act 1988 (with C Hunter, 1989), Local Government & Housing Act 1989 (with C Hunter, 1990), Assured Tenancies (Vol 3 'The Rent Acts', with Sir Robert Megarry, 1989), Local Government Finance Law and Practice (with C Hunter, 1994), Housing Act 1996 (with C Hunter, 1996), Housing Grants, Construction and Regeneration Act 1996 (with C Hunter, 1996); gen ed: Encyclopaedia of Housing Law (1978–), Housing Law Reports (1981–); *Fiction* The Motive Not The Deed (1985), No Certain Roof (1975), The Object Man (1986); also author series of 4 thrillers (written under pseudonym); *Recreations* Southern Comfort, Camels, Hill St Blues; *Clubs* Manzis Luncheon; *Style—* Andrew Arden, Esq, QC; ✉ Arden Chambers, 59 Fleet Street, London EC4Y 1JV (☎ 0171 353 3132, fax 0171 353 2774)

ARDEN, Rt Rev Donald Seymour; CBE (1981); s of Stanley Arden, FLS (d 1942), of Sitiawan (Lower Perak) and Worthing, and Winifred, *née* Morland (d 1968); family a collateral branch of Arden of Harden Hall, Stockport who descend from Eustace de Arden, of Watford, Northants; *b* 12 April 1916; *Educ* St Peter's Coll Adelaide S Aust, Univ of Leeds (BA), Coll of the Resurrection Mirfield; *m* 1962, Jane Grace, da of Gerald Riddle (d 1967), of East Ogwell, Devon; 2 s (Bazil, Christopher); *Career* ordained: deacon 1939, priest 1940; curate: St Catherine's Hatcham 1939–40, Nettleden with Potten End 1941–43; asst priest Pretoria African Mission 1944–51; dir Usuthu Swaziland 1951–61 (canon of Zululand and Swaziland); bishop of: Nyasaland 1961–64, Malawi 1964–71, Southern Malawi 1971–81; archbishop of Central Africa 1971–80; commissary to bishops of: Malawi 1981–, Niassa Mozambique 1988–; priest i/c St Margaret Uxbridge 1981–86, asst bishop London 1981–, vol asst priest St Alban's N Harrow 1986–; *Books* Youth's Job in the Parish (1938), Out of Africa Something New (1976); *Recreations* photography; *Style—* Bishop Donald Arden, CBE; ✉ 6 Frobisher Close, Pinner, Middx HA5 1NN (☎ and fax 0181 866 6009)

ARDEN, John; s of C A Arden, and A E Layland; *b* 26 Oct 1930; *Educ* Sedbergh, King's Coll Cambridge, Edinburgh Coll of Art; *m* 1957, Margaretta Ruth D'Arcy; 4 s (and 1 decd); *Career* playwright and novelist; *Plays* incl: All Fall Down (for radio, 1955), The Life of Man (1956), The Waters of Babylon (1957), Live Like Pigs (1958), Sergeant Musgrave's Dance (1959), Soldier Soldier (for TV, 1960), Wet Fish (for TV, 1962), The Workhouse Donkey (1963), Ironhand (1963), Armstrong's Last Goodnight (1964), Left-Handed Liberty (1965), The True History of Squire Jonathan and his Unfortunate Treasure (1968), The Bagman (for radio, 1970), Pearl (for radio, 1978), To Put It Frankly (for radio, 1979), Don Quixote (for radio, 1980), Garland for a Hoar Head (for radio, 1982), The Old Man Sleeps Alone (for radio, 1982); *with Margaretta D'Arcy* The Business of Good Government (1960), The Happy Haven (1960), Ars Longa Vita Brevis (1964), Friday's Hiding (1966), The Royal Pardon (1966), The Hero Rises Up (1968), Muggins is a Martyr (1968), Island of the Mighty (1972), The Ballygombeen Bequest (1972), The Non-Stop Connolly Cycle (1975), Vandaleur's Folly (1978), The Little Gray Home in the West (1978), The Manchester Enthusiasts (for radio, 1984), Whose is the Kingdom? (radio, 1988), A Suburban Suicide (for radio, 1994); *Publications* To Present The Pretence (essays on theatre, 1978), Silence Among The Weapons (novel, 1982), Books of Bale (novel, 1988), Awkward Corners (essays, etc with Margaretta D'Arcy, 1988), Cogs Tyrannic (novel, 1991), Jack Juggler and the Emperor's Whore (novel, 1995); *Recreations* antiquarianism, mythology; *Style—* John Arden, Esq; ✉ c/o Casarotto Ramsay Ltd, National House, 4th Floor, 60–66 Wardour Street, Londo W1V 3HP (☎ 0171 287 4450, fax 0171 287 9128)

ARDEN, Hon Mrs Justice; Hon Dame Mary Howarth; DBE (1993); da of Lt-Col Eric Cuthbert Arden (d 1973); *m* 26 May 1973, Sir Jonathan Hugh Mance (Hon Mr Justice Mance, *qv*); 2 da (Abigail b 1976, Jessica b 1978), 1 s (Henry b 1982); *Career* called to the Bar 1971, QC 1986, asst recorder of Crown and Co Courts 1990–93, dep High Court judge 1990–93, attorney-gen Duchy of Lancaster 1991–93, judge of the High Court of Justice (Chancery Div) 1993–; chm Appeal Ctee Royal Courts of Justice 1994–; inspector Rotaprint Plc under sections 432 and 444 of the Companies Act 1985 1988–91; elector Herchel Smith professorship in intellectual property law Univ of Cambridge 1993–94; memb: Law Soc's Company Law Ctee 1976– (ldr Insolvency Working Pty), Insolvency Sub-Ctee Consumer and Commercial Law Ctee of Law Soc (previously Jt Working Pty of the Bar and the Law Soc on Insolvency) 1978–, Financial Law Panel 1993–; hon memb Soc of Public Teachers of Law 1993–; *Style—* The Hon Mrs Justice Arden, DBE; ✉ c/o Royal Courts of Justice, Strand, London WC2A 2LL

ARDILES, Osvaldo (Ossie); s of Arturo Ardiles, of Cordoba, Argentina, and Blanca, *née* Vignoli; *b* 3 Aug 1952; *Educ* Montserrat Sch, Univ of Cordoba and Buenos Aires (studied law); *m* 29 Dec 1973, Silvia Navarro; 2 s (Pablo b 1 Feb 1975, Federico b 23 Sept 1978); *Career* former professional football player and manager; player: apprentice Instituto Cordoba 1964 (first team debut 1970), Huracan Buenos Aires 1975–78, Tottenham Hotspur 1978–88, on loan Paris St Germain France 1982, Queens Park Rangers 1988–89, Fort Lauderdale USA 1989, 42 full caps Argentina (debut 1975); manager: Swindon Town 1989–91, Newcastle Utd 1991–92, West Bromwich Albion 1992–93, Tottenham Hotspur 1993–Nov 1994, Guadalajara Mexico (for ten matches) until Nov 1995; honours in Argentina: Cordoba League Championship 1972, runners up Argentinian League 1976, World Cup winners 1978; honours with Tottenham Hotspur: FA Cup 1981 and 1982 (runners up 1987), runners up Littlewoods Cup 1982, UEFA Cup 1984; promotion to Div 1 Swindon Town 1990 (later cancelled), promotion Div 1 West Brom 1993; film actor Escape to Victory 1981; conslt Barnett Alexander Chart (lawyers) 1995–; *Recreations* golf, chess, cinema, theatre, reading; *Style—* Ossie Ardiles, Esq; ✉ c/o Barnett Alexander Chart, 60 Gray's Inn Road, London WC1X 8LT (☎ 0171 242 4422)

ARDRON, Peter Stuart; s of Wilfred Ardron, MBE (d 1982), of Annfield Plain, Co Durham, and Lucy Muriel, *née* Hawkins (d 1988); *b* 11 June 1927; *Educ* Stanley GS Stanley Co Durham, INSEAD Fontainebleau, Oxford Centre for Mgmnt Studies; *m* 1956, Marion McWilliams, da of William Ross (d 1972), of Dunoon; 1 s (David), 2 da (Carol, Lesley); *Career* Barclays Bank International Ltd: gen mangr 1977–83, sr gen mangr 1983–84, dir 1983–87, vice chm 1986–87; dir Barclays International Holdings 1985–87, dir and sr gen mangr Barclays Bank plc 1985–87, vice chm BAII Ltd 1987–90, chm Anglo-Romanian Bank Ltd 1987–, dep chm Italian International Bank plc 1987–, exec vice chm Sabanci Bank Ltd 1987–; dir: Banque de la Société Financière Européenne Paris 1980–87, Société Financière Européenne Luxembourg 1980–87, Euro-Latinamerican Bank Ltd London 1983–87; FCIB, FInstD, FRSA; *Recreations* cricket, tennis, gardening; *Clubs* Bankers', MCC; *Style—* P S Ardron, Esq; ✉ Oriel Cottage, Rookery Close, Fetcham, Leatherhead, Surrey KT22 9BG (☎ 01372 372958)

ARGENT, Denis John; s of Robert Argent (d 1983), and Ellen, *née* Newman (d 1992); *b* 28 Aug 1943; *Educ* Cardinal Vaughan Sch; *m* 30 July 1966, Marie Rose, da of John Barnard (d 1980); 3 s (Nicholas b 1968, Phillip b 1970, Christopher b 1973), 1 da (Marianne b 1981); *Career* mgmnt conslt Coopers & Lybrand 1972–79, chief accountant Cancer Res Fund 1979–87, fin dir Royal Pharmaceutical Soc of GB 1987–; FCCA; *Recreations* rugby, squash, golf; *Clubs* MCC, East India; *Style—* Denis Argent, Esq; ✉ 112 Waxwell Lane, Pinner, Middx (☎ 0171 866 1526); 1 Lambeth High St, London SE1 7JN (☎ 0171 735 9141)

ARGENT, Douglas; *Career* BBC floor mangr, prodn mangr then dir and prodr; TV series incl: Till Death Us Do Part, Taxi, Feydeau Farces, The Liver Birds, Steptoe and Son, Fawlty Towers (BAFTA award 1979), Crimewriters; freelance 1980; TV series incl: The Cuckoo Waltz, The Schoolmistress, Astronauts, That Beryl Marsden, Union Castle, The Lady is a Tramp, It Takes a Worried Man, Lonelyhearts Kids, Flying Lady, Never the Twain, Anybody for Murder, Edge of Fear, EastEnders; dir corporate video ideas for: Shell Chemicals (UK) Ltd, Lloyds Bank Ltd, Mobil Oil, British Airways, Crown Paints, Guardian Royal Exchange, Trustee Savings Bank; memb: Dirs' Guild of GB, BAFTA (memb Cncl 1978–82, 1984–86 and 1990–91); *Style—* Douglas Argent, Esq; ✉ 55 Kenton Ave, Sunbury on Thames, Middlesex TW16 5AS (☎ 01932 785892); Michael Ladkin Personal Management (☎ 0171 436 4626, fax 0171 436 4627)

ARGENT, (Bernard) Godfrey; s of Godfrey Stanley Albert Argent (d 1972), and Helena, *née* Smith; *b* 6 Feb 1937; *Educ* Bexhill GS for Boys Sussex; *m* 1, 1956, Janet Rosemary, *née* Boniface (d 1970); 3 da (Lisa b 1957, Gina b 1958, Susan b 1960); m 2 (m dis 1973), Anne Yvonne, *née* Coxon; m 3, 1975 (m dis 1990), Sally Dorothy, *née* McAlpine; 1 da (Jenna b 1980); *Career* Household Cavalry (The Life Gds) 1954–63; freelance photographer 1963, chm Godfrey Argent Ltd 1964–; owner mangr: Walter Bird Photographic Studios (London) 1968, Baron Studios (London) 1974; one man shows incl: Nat Portrait Gallery (London) 1971, Johannesburg, Cape Town and Durban SA 1975–76, Los Angeles 1978, Camera Club (London) 1988; photographer Royal Family 1964–; official photographer: Nat Portrait Gallery (London) 1967–71, Royal Soc of GB 1967–; *Books* The Royal Mews (1965), The Household Brigade (1966), The Queen's Guards (1966), The Queen Rides (1966), Horses in the Sun (1966), Charles 21st Prince of Wales (1969), World of Horses (1969), Royalty on Horseback (1974); *Recreations* running, cooking for friends; *Clubs* Inanda (SA); *Style—* Godfrey Argent, Esq; ✉ 8 Ladbroke Walk, London W11 3PW (☎ 0171 229 4440); 12 Holland St, London W8 4LT (☎ 0171 937 4008/0441)

ARGENT, Malcolm; CBE (1985); s of Leonard James Argent (d 1989), and Winifred Hilda Argent (d 1980); *b* 14 Aug 1935; *Educ* Palmer's Sch Grays Essex; *m* 1, 4 March 1961, Mary Patricia Addis, da of Geoffrey Vivian Stimson (d 1989); m 2, 5 Dec 1986, Thelma Hazel, da of Leonard Eddleston, of Eastry, Kent; 1 s, 1 da; *Career* GPO London Telecom Region: exec offr 1953–62, higher exec offr 1962–66, princ PO HQ 1966–70, private sec to md Telecom 1970–74, personnel controller External Telecom Exec 1974–75; dir: Chm's Office PO Central HQ 1975–77, Eastern Telecom Region 1977; sec: The PO 1978–81, BT Corp 1981–94; BT plc: sec 1984–94, gp dir 1989–94, non-exec dir 1994–; dep chm Civil Aviation Authy 1995–, chm National Air Traffic Services Ltd 1996–; dir: McCaw Cellular Communications Inc 1989–94, Westminster Health Care plc 1992–, Clerical Medical & General Assurance Society 1994–; tstee: BT Staff Superannuation Fund 1981–94, BT New Pension Scheme 1986–89; Freeman City of London 1987; CIMgt 1991 (FIMgt 1980); *Recreations* tennis; *Style—* Malcolm Argent, Esq, CBE; ✉ Chestnuts, Fryerning Lane, Fryerning, Ingatestone, Essex CM4 0DF; Civil Aviation Authority, CAA House, 45–59 Kingsway, London WC2B 6TE (☎ 0171 832 5199, fax 0171 832 6368)

ARGENTI, (Ambrose) John Alexander; s of Nicholas A Argenti (d 1961), of London, and Elfrida Mary, *née* Ionides (d 1988); *b* 10 Feb 1926; *Educ* Charterhouse, Trinity Coll Oxford (MA); *m* 29 Dec 1948, Mildred Elfrida (d 1995), da of Alan George Marshal (d 1973), of Taunton; 1 s (Matthew b 1953), 1 da (Hilary b 1949); *Career* aircraftman (pilot under trg) RAF 1944–45; mgmnt positions Fisons Fertilizers Ltd 1954–68, chm Argenti Systems Ltd 1980–; fndr and first treas: Strategic Planning Soc London, Civic Tst Widnes; MIMgt 1966; *Books* Corporate Planning - A Practical Guide (1968), Management Techniques (1970, Matra prize Best Mgmnt Book 1970), A Management System for The Seventies (1971), Systematic Corporate Planning (1974), Corporate Collapse (1976), Practical Corporate Planning (1980 and 1989), Your Organization: What is it for? (1993); *Style—* John Argenti, Esq; ✉ Pettistree Lodge, Woodbridge, Suffolk IP13 0HX; Argenti Systems Ltd, 12 Lower Brook St, Ipswich IP4 1AT (☎/fax 01728 746466)

ARGYLE, His Hon Michael Victor; MC (1945), QC (1961); s of Harold Victor Argyle (d 1965), of Highways, Repton, Derby, and Elsie Marion, *née* Richards; *b* 31 Aug 1915; *Educ* Westminster, Trinity Coll Cambridge (MA); *m* 1951, Ann Norah (d 1994), da of late C A Newton, of Derby; 3 da; *Career* served WWII 7 QOH, Maj; called to the Bar Lincoln's Inn 1938, bencher 1967, treas 1984–85; recorder: Northampton 1962–65, Birmingham 1965–70; dep chm Holland QS 1965–71, lay judge Ct of Arches Canterbury 1968–92, circuit judge 1970–88 (formerly additional judge of the Central Criminal Ct); contested (C): Belper 1950, Loughborough 1955; pres: Nat Campaign for Restoration of Capital Punishment 1988–92, Midland Counties Canine Soc 1988–92; memb Victim Support Notts 1990–; Master Worshipful Co of Playing Cards Makers 1984–85 (Jr Warden 1982–83, Sr Warden 1983–84); *Books* Phipson on Evidence (10th edition); *Recreations* chess, boxing; *Style—* His Hon Michael Argyle, MC, QC; ✉ The Red House, Fiskerton, nr Southwell, Notts NG25 0UL (☎ 01636 830530)

ARGYLL, 12 Duke of (S 1701 and UK 1892); Sir Ian Campbell; 14 Bt (NS 1627), JP (1996); also Lord Campbell (S 1445), Earl of Argyll (S 1457), Lord Lorne (S 1470), Marquess of Kintyre and Lorne, Earl of Campbell and Cowal, Viscount Lochow and Glenila, and Lord Inveraray, Mull, Morvern and Tiry (all S 1701), Baron Sundridge (GB 1766), Baron Hamilton (GB 1776), Hereditary Master of HM's Household in Scotland, keeper of the Great Seal of Scotland, keeper of Dunoon, Carrick, Dunstaffnage and Tarbert Castles, Admiral of the Western Coasts and Isles, hereditary sheriff of Argyll, 26 Chief of Clan Campbell; s of 11 Duke of Argyll (d 1973), and his 2 w Louise, da of Henry Clews; *b* 28 Aug 1937; *Educ* Le Rosey, Trinity Coll Glenalmond, McGill Univ of Canada; *m* 1964, Iona, da of Capt Sir Ivar Iain Colquhoun of Luss, 8 Bt, JP, DL; 1 s, 1 da (Lady Louise Iona b 26 Oct 1972); *Heir* s, Marquess of Lorne, *qv*; *Career* late Capt Argyll & Sutherland Highlanders; stockbroker Decoppet & Doremus New York USA 1958–59; First Nat City Bank London 1962–63; export sales executive Rank Xerox USSR, Poland, Romania, DDR 1964–67; chm Beinn Bhuidhe Holdings 1969–; dir: Campbell Distillers, Muir Mackenzie & Co, White Heather Distillers, Aberlour Glenlivet Distillery Co and Associated Cos 1983–, Cetec Int, Visual Sound Programmes Glasgow 1974–90; pres: Royal Highland Soc of London 1987–88, Argyll Scouts Assoc, Argyll & Bute Conservative Assoc 1973–96; dir then pres Royal Caledonian Schs 1972–96; govr Dollar Acad 1985–90; Lord-Lt Argyll and Bute 1996– (Vice Lord-Lt 1994–95, DL 1987); ret memb Royal Co of Archers (Queen's Body Guard for Scotland), Hon Col Argyll & Sutherland Highlanders, ACF Bn 1982–92; KStJ 1975; *Clubs* White's, New (Edinburgh); *Style—* His Grace the Duke of Argyll, JP; ✉ Inveraray Castle, Inveraray, Argyll PA32 8XF (☎ 01499 302275, fax 01499 302421)

ARGYLL AND THE ISLES, Dean of; *see:* Macleay, Very Rev John Henry James (Ian)

ARGYLL AND THE ISLES, Bishop of 1992–; Rt Rev Douglas MacLean Cameron; s of Andrew Cameron (d 1975), of Dunoon, Argyll, and Helen, *née* Adam (d 1988); *b* 23 March 1935; *Educ* Eastwood GS Glasgow, Edinburgh Theol Coll, Univ of The South Sewanee Tennessee USA; *m* Feb 1969, (Anne) Patricia, da of Dr Richard H Purnell (d 1994); 2 da (Josephine Helen b 28 April 1972, Anne Patricia b 17 June 1974); *Career* ordained: deacon 1962, priest 1963; curate Christ Church Falkirk 1962–65, mission priest Eiwo Papua New Guinea 1966–67, priest-in-charge Movi Papua New Guinea 1967–72, rector St Francis Church Goroka Papua New Guinea 1972–74, archdeacon of New Guinea Mainland 1972–74; rector: St Fillan's Edinburgh 1978–88 (priest-in-charge 1974), St Hilda's Edinburgh 1977–88, St Mary's Dalkeith and St Leonard's Lasswade 1988–92; canon of St Mary's Cathedral and Synod clerk Edinburgh 1990–92, dean of Edinburgh 1991–92; *Recreations* walking, cooking, reading, music; *Style—* The Rt Rev the Bishop of Argyll and The Isles; ✉ The Pines, Ardconnel Road, Oban PA34 5DR (☎ 01631 566912)

ARGYRIS, Prof John; *b* 19 Aug 1916; *Educ* Classical HS Athens, Tech Univ of Athens, Tech Univ of Munich (DiplIng), Univ of Berlin, Univ of Zurich (DSc(Eng)); *m*; 1 s; *Career* sr scientific asst Dept of Structures Tech Univ of Munich 1936–37, projects engr/head Project Office J Gollnow and Sohn (Stettin) 1937–39, tech offr Engrg Dept RAeS London 1942–49 (head Structures Gp 1948–49), lectr American univs and research insts (incl NASA) summer 1949; Imperial Coll of Sci and Technol London: sr lectr 1949–50, reader 1950–55, prof of aeronautical structures 1955–75, visiting prof 1975–80, emeritus prof 1975; visiting research scientist Nat Research Cncl Ottawa summer 1952; Univ of Stuttgart: univ prof and dir Institut für Statik and Dynamik der Luft-und Raumfahrtkonstruktionen and Aeronautical Computing Centre 1959–84, dir Inst for Computer Applications 1984–; visiting prof Univ of Calif Los Angeles and MIT Boston Massachusetts 1967, 12th Lanchester Meml lectr RAeS London May 1969, princ ed Computer Methods in Applied Mechanics and Engineering jl 1972–, organiser first Int Conf on Finite Element Methods in Nonlinear Mechanics Stuttgart Aug 1978; memb: Managing Bd and Scientific Prog Ctee Euro Research Community on Flow Turbulence and Combustion (ERCOFTAC) 1985–, High Performance Computing Advsy Ctee of the EC CERN Geneva 1990–, Scientific Ctee Centre for Advanced Studies, Research and Devpt Cagliari Sardinia 1990–, Bd of Advsrs Poly Univ of Madrid 1991–; George Taylor Prize and Silver Medal RAeS 1971, Copernicus Medal Polish Acad of Scis Warsaw 1979, Gold Medal Land Baden-Württemberg FRG 1980, Timoshenko Medal American Soc of Mechanical Engrs 1981, I B Laskowitz Award with Gold Medal NY Acad of Scis 1982, von Kármán Medal American Soc of Civil Engrs 1985, Grand Cross of Merit (FRG) 1985, Royal Medal (awarded by HM the Queen and the Royal Soc London) 1985, Deadalus Medal in Gold Sir George Cayley Inst for Computational and Information Mechanics London 1988, Grand Cross of Merit with Star (FRG) 1990, Gold Medal

Bulgarian Acad of Scis 1991, Euro Henri Coenda Medal in Gold Poly Inst of Iasi Romania 1992; hon prof Northwest Poly Univ Xian China 1980, hon prof Tech Univ of Beijing 1983, hon prof Chinghua Univ of Peking Beijing 1984; Hon DrIng Tech Univ of Hanover 1983, Hon DTech Univ of Linköping Sweden 1986; Hon DSc (Maths) Univ of Athens 1989, Hon DSc (Mechs) Univ of Vilnius 1991; Hon DSc (Computer Mechs and Informatics): Poly Inst of Iasi Romania 1992, Tech Univ Tallinn Estonia 1993, Tech Univ St Petersburg 1993; Hon DSc (Computer Mechs) Tech Univ Timisoara Romania 1995; Hon DSc(Eng) (Computer Mechs): Tech Univ of Athens 1995, Univ of Ioannina Greece 1995; hon memb and medallist Greek Assoc of Computational Mechanics 1994; hon fell Groupe pour l'Avancement des Methodes Numeriques de l'Ingenieur (GAMNI) Paris 1974, Hon FCGI 1976 (Hon ACGI 1962), FIC hon fell Imperial Coll of Sci and Technol London 1985, hon fell Aeronautical Soc of India 1985, hon fell Inst of Engrs India 1985, Hon FRAeS 1986 (FRAeS 1955), hon fell Romanian Acad 1992; corresponding memb Acad of Scis Athens 1973, life memb American Soc of Mechanical Engrs 1981, memb NY Acad of Scis 1981, fell American Inst of Aeronautic and Astronautics 1983, fell American Soc for the Advancement of Sci Washington DC 1985, FRS 1986, foreign assoc US Nat Acad of Engrg 1986, FEng 1990, fell American Soc of Civil Engrs 1991 (memb 1979); *Books* Structural Analysis - Part II of Handbook of Aeronautics (with P C Dunne, Vol 1 1952), Stressing of Conical Tubes (with P C Dunne, Vol 2 1949–50), Energy Theorems and Structural Analysis (1960, 3 edn 1967), Modern Fuselage Analysis and the Elastic Aircraft (with S Kelsey, 1963), Recent Advances in Matrix Methods of Structural Analysis (Vol 4 1964), Die Methode der Finiten Elemente in der Elementaren Strukturmechanik (with H-P Mlejnek, Vols 1–III 1986–88), Dynamics of Structures (with H-P Mlejnek, Vol 5 1991), Die Erforschung des Chaos (with G Faust and M Haase, 1993), An Exploration of Chaos (with G Faust and M Haase, Vol VII 1994); *Style*— Prof John Argyris, FRS, FEng; ✉ Institute for Computer Applications, University of Stuttgart, Pfaffenwaldring 27, D-70569 Stuttgart, Germany (☎ 00 49 711 685 35 94, fax 00 49 711 685 36 69)

ARIE, Prof Thomas Harry David; CBE (1995); s of Dr O M Arie (d 1983), of Reading, and Hedy, *née* Glaser (d 1994); *b* 9 Aug 1933; *Educ* Reading Sch, Balliol Coll Oxford (MA, BM BCh); *m* 5 July 1963, Dr Eleanor Arie, FRCP, da of Sir Robert Aitken, of Birmingham; 1 s (Samuel b 1974), 2 da (Laura b 1968, Sophie b 1971); *Career* sr lectr in social med London Hosp 1967–77, conslt psychiatrist Goodmayes Hosp 1969–77, fndn prof of health care of the elderly Univ of Nottingham 1977–95 (now emeritus), hon conslt psychiatrist Nottingham Hosps 1977–95; Fotheringham lectr Univ of Toronto 1979, visiting prof NZ Geriatrics Soc 1980, Dozor visiting prof Univ of the Negev 1988, Frölich visiting prof RSM Fndn Univ of California Los Angeles 1991; memb: Central Cncl for Educn and Trg in Social Work 1975–81, Standing Med Advsy Ctee DHSS 1980–84, Ctee on Review Medicines 1981–91, Res Ctee Nat Inst Social Work 1983–90, Cncl Royal Surgical Aid Soc 1995–; chm Geriatric Psychiatry Section World Psychiatric Assoc 1989–93, govr Centre for Policy on Ageing 1991–; Royal Coll of Psychiatrists: chm Specialist Section on Old Age 1981–86, vice pres 1983–85, memb Ct of Electors 1985–91, memb Cncl 1991–; a patron Abbeyfield Soc 1996–; Dhole-Eddleston Meml Prize Br Geriatrics Soc 1996; FRCPsych, FRCP, FFPHM; *Books* Health Care of the Elderly (ed, 1981), Recent Advances in Psychogeriatrics (ed, 1985, 2 edn 1992); *Style*— Prof T H D Arie, CBE; ✉ Department of Health Care of the Elderly, Medical School, Queen's Medical Centre, Nottingham NG7 2UH (☎ 0115 970 9408, 0115 978 0608, fax 0115 942 3618)

ARIF, Saleem; s of Dr S A Quadri, and Sayeed Unisa Quadri; *b* 28 May 1949; *Educ* Birmingham Coll of Art, RCA (MA); *Career* artist; selected solo exhibitions: Art Heritage Gallery New Delhi 1984, Ipswich Museum 1986, Winchester Art Gallery 1987, Anderson O'Day Gallery London 1988, Laing Art Gallery Newcastle upon Tyne 1991, Birds of Breath (Midland Art Centre Birmingham) 1993, The Downstairs Art Gallery Burnley 1994; selected gp exhibitions: Serpentine Gallery Summer Show London 1981, Hayward Annual London and Edinburgh 1982, From Two Worlds (Whitechapel Gallery London and Fruitmarket Gallery Edinburgh) 1986, Graven Images (Harris Museum Preston) 1988, The Other Story (Hayward Gallery ondon and tours Wolverhampton Art Gallery and Cornerhouse Manchester) 1989–90, The Third World and Beyond (Art Int Confrontation of Contemporary Galleria Civica D'Arte Contemporanea Marsala Sicily) 1991, Cagnes-sur-Mer Int Exhibition (British Cncl) France; most important works: Itinerary 1972, Dante's Inferno (set of forty) 1980–81, Birds of Aspirations 1989, Birds of Breath 1991–93; selected collections: Govt collection London, Ipswich Museum, Arts Cncl of GB, David Villiers Fndn Geneva, Birmingham Museum and City Art Gallery, Manchester City Art Gallery; selected awards: prize winner Young Sculptor of the Year Sunday Telegraph Competition 1971, Italian Govt Bursary Florence 1982, Villers David Fndn travel award 1989; tstee and memb Exhibitions Ctee Camden Art Centre 1989–, memb Advsy Arts Panel Eastern Arts Bd 1989–; *Recreations* collecting Indian contemporary folk art, photography, travelling; *Style*— Saleem Arif, Esq; ✉ 1 Boadicea Street, Islington, London N1 0UA

ARIS, Brian; *Career* portrait and feature photographer; cmmns int magazines incl: Life, Paris Match, Stern, Gente, Sunday Times, Newsweek; charity work incl: Save the Children Fund, Prince's Trust, Band Aid, Nordoff Robbins Music Therapy; estab stock library (actors, musicians, pop stars and industrialists); *Recreations* golf, tennis; *Style*— Brian Aris, Esq; ✉ Brian Aris Associates, 22–24 Link House, New Covent Garden, London SW8 5PA (☎ 0171 627 2523, fax 0171 627 2524)

ARIS, John Bernard Benedict; TD (1967); s of John Woodbridge Aris (d 1977), of Sedlescombe, Sussex, and Joyce Mary, *née* Williams (d 1986); *b* 6 June 1934; *Educ* Eton, Magdalen Coll Oxford (BA, MA); *Career* Nat Serv 2 Lt RA Korea, Hong Kong 1952–54, Territorial Serv RA RHA serv in 44 Para Bde (Maj) 1954–72; LEO Computers Ltd 1958–63, English Electric Computers Ltd 1963–69, ICL 1969–75 (directeur technique Europe de l'Ouest 1972–75), Imperial Group plc 1975–85 (mangr Gp Mgmnt Serv 1982–85), chief exec Nat Computer Centre Ltd 1985–90 (non-exec dir 1981–85), dir IMPACT Programme KPMG 1990–95; chm FOCUS Private Sector Users' Ctee 1984–85, Alvey User Panel 1985–88, DTI User Requirements Working Pty 1990; Freeman City of London 1988, Liveryman Worshipful Co of Info Technologists 1992 (fndr Freeman 1987); FBCS, FInstD, FRSA; *Books* User Driven Innovation (jtly, 1996); *Recreations* travel, music, art, scuba diving, gastronomy; *Style*— John Aris, Esq, TD; ✉ c/o IMPACT Programme, KPMG, 8 Salisbury Square, London EC4Y 8BB (☎ 0171 311 1000, fax 0171 311 3311)

ARKELL, Lt Col James Rixon; TD, DL (Wiltshire 1996); s of Peter Arkell, and Anne, *née* Falcon; *b* 28 May 1951; *Educ* Milton Abbey; *m* 7 Sept 1974, Carolyn Jane, da of Charles Ralph Woosnam; 3 s (George b 9 Dec 1978, John b 17 April 1983, Alexander b 15 Aug 1985), 1 da (Emma 6 Feb 1976); *Career* Royal Wiltshire (Yeo) TA 1974, Sqdn-Ldr 1983, 2 i/c 1989, CO Royal Yeo Regt 1993–95; md Arkells Brewery Ltd Swindon; *Recreations* shooting, fishing, hunting, skiing; *Clubs* Cavalry; *Style*— Lt-Col James Arkell, TD, DL; ✉ Arkells Brewery Ltd, Kingsdown Brewery, Stratton St Margaret, Swindon, Wilts SN2 6RU (☎ 01793 823026)

ARKELL, John Hardy; *b* 10 July 1939; *Educ* Stowe, Selwyn Coll Cambridge (MA, pres JCR); *m* Jean, *née* Harding; 2 s (Peter, James), 1 da (Nicola); *Career* Sub Lt HM's Submarines RN 1958–60; teacher Abingdon Sch 1963–64, head of VI form English and house tutor Framlington Coll 1964–70; Fettes Coll 1970–83: head English Dept 1971–73 and 1976–78, fndr headmaster Fettes Jr Sch 1973–79, housemaster Glencorse House 1979–83; headmaster: Wrekin Coll 1983–91 (co-educational since 1983), Gresham's Sch Holt 1991–; govr Old Hall Prep Sch Wellington, chm Central Region ISIS; memb: Gen Teaching Cncl Scotland, HMC (sec Midland Div); *Recreations* literature, drama, music, playing tennis, golf and cricket, rowing occasionally, sailing, elderly motor cars; *Style*— John Arkell, Esq; ✉ Gresham's School, Holt, Norfolk NR25 6EA (☎ 01263 713271)

ARKELL, John Heward; CBE (1961), TD; s of Rev H H Arkell, Vicar of Chipping Norton, Oxon, and Gertrude Mary, *née* Heward; *b* 20 May 1909; *Educ* Radley, ChCh Oxford (MA); *m* 1, 1940, Helen Birgit, da of HE Emil Huitfeldt, sometime Norwegian ambass to Denmark; 2 s, 1 da; *m* 2, 1956 (m dis), Meta, da of Otto Bäche Grundtvig, of Trondheim, Norway; 1 s; *Career* cmmnd 1 Bn Queen's Westminsters KRRC 1939 (TA), Chief Instr Inf Wing Sch of Signals, served BLA 1944, demobbed 1945, Maj; sec Sir Max Michaelis Investment Trust 1931–37, asst sec Cncl for Protection of Rural Eng 1937–39 (vice pres 1984), personnel mangr J Lyons & Co 1945–49; BBC: controller of staff 1949–58, dir of staff 1958–60, dir of admin 1960–70; chm Air Tport and Travel Indust Trg Bd 1970–80; dir: The Boots Co 1970–79, The Coates Group of Cos 1970–76, UK Provident Inst 1971–80; sr assoc Leo Kramer International Ltd 1980–86; lay memb Nat Indust Rels Ct 1972–74, memb Cncl Nat Tst 1971–84 (chm Advsy Ctee on Communications 1983), visiting fell Henley Mgmnt Coll 1971–90; memb: Cncl CBI 1973–75, Final Selection Bd Civil Serv Cmmn 1978–82; Inst of Mgmnt (formerly Br Inst of Mgmnt): chm Cncl 1972–74, vice pres 1974–, dir BIM Fndn 1976–81; govr Radley Coll 1965–70, chm Radley Coll War Meml Ctee 1963–88; gen hon sec and fndr ChCh Oxford Utd Clubs SE London 1932 (later chm, jt pres 1986–); inherited Lordship of the Manor and Patron of the Living of Fawley 1992; composer of light music; CIMgt, FRSA, FIPM; *Recreations* music, walking, swimming; *Clubs* Savile, Leander, Lansdowne; *Style*— John Arkell, Esq, CBE, TD; ✉ Fawley Manor, Pinnocks, Fawley, nr Henley-on-Thames, Oxon RG9 6JH (☎ 01491 573017); Glen Cottage, Ringstead Bay, nr Dorchester, Dorset DT2 8NG (☎ 01305 852686)

ARKELL, Julian; OBE (1992); 2 s of William Joscelyn Arkell (d 1958), and Ruby Lilian, *née* Percival (d 1983); *b* 22 Oct 1934; *Educ* Bryanston, King's Coll Cambridge (MA); *m* 1, 5 Sept 1964 (m dis 1976); 2 da (Claire b 25 Aug 1966, Katie b 8 July 1968); m 2, 29 April 1983, Elaine; *Career* Shell-Mex and BP Ltd 1956–62, ptnr Robert Matthew Johnson-Marshall & Partners 1972–86 (partnership sec 1962–72), co sec RMJM Ltd 1986–91; in practice as conslt t/a International Trade and Services Policy (clients have incl British Invisibles, RMJM Group, EC, ICC, OECD, UNCTAD, UNICE, US Dept of Commerce, UPS), dir Applied Service Economics Centre Geneva 1991–; memb: Fees Ctee RIBA 1974–92, Lotis Ctee BI 1981–, Exec Ctee British Conslts Bureau 1992, Export Fin Panel LCCI 1983–91, Bd Services World Forum Geneva 1992–, Global Services Leadership Cncl San Francisco 1993–; services rapporteur GATT Working Gp UNICE Brussels 1990–94; chm: Euro Community Servs Gp Working Pty Brussels 1986–93, Servs Gp WTO Ctee UNICE 1994–95; Hon ARICS 1991; *Style*— Julian Arkell, Esq, OBE; ✉ International Trade and Services Policy, Box 41, Mussupta 2, 07712 San Clemente, Menorca, Spain (☎ and fax 00 34 71 35 08 45, e-mail arkell@infotelecom.es)

ARKELL, Peter; s of Sir Noel Arkell, DL (d 1981), and Olive Arscott, *née* Quick (d 1988); *b* 24 Jan 1923; *m* 12 Aug 1949, Anne, da of Michael Falcon (d 1976), of Burlingham House, Norwich, Norfolk; 1 s (James b 1951), 3 da (Jane b 1950, Alison b 1952, Rosalind b 1954); *Career* Mil Serv RAFVR 1941–45, Flt Lt 26 Sqdn Mustangs 161 Sqdn (Special Duty) Lysander, Tempsford 357 Sqdn (Special Duty) Lysanders BURMA; chm Arkell's Brewery Ltd; Liveryman Worshipful Co of Brewers; *Recreations* fishing, shooting, gardening; *Clubs* Special Forces, RAF, Leander; *Style*— Peter Arkell, Esq; ✉ Whelford Mill, Fairford, Gloucestershire; Arkell's Brewery Ltd, Kingsdown, Swindon SN2 6RU

ARKWRIGHT, Thomas James; s of Thomas Joseph Arkwright (d 1963), of Wigan, Lancs, and Mary Edna, *née* Ashurst (d 1995); *b* 22 March 1932; *Educ* Mount St Mary's Coll Sheffield, Univ of Liverpool (LLB); *m* 27 Aug 1958, (Margaret) Muriel, da of Wilfred Hague (d 1973), of Wigan, Lancs; 5 da (Louise b 1960, Julie b 1963, Clare b 1966, Lucy b 1968, Helen b 1971), 1 s (Paul b 1962); *Career* admitted slr 1955; articled to Sir John B McKaig Liverpool 1950–55; winner: Sheffield Prize for highest Slr's finals results, John Mackrell Prize, Daniel Reardon Prize, Enoch Harvey Prize, Timpron Martin Gold Medal Prize, Rupert Bremner Gold Medal Prize, Vice-Chllr of the Duchy of Lancaster Prize; ptnr Cyril Morris & Co (Cyril Morris Arkwright & Co from 1965) 1957–71, sr ptnr Cyril Morris Arkwright Bolton 1971–92, practising as Tom Arkwright & Co 1992–96, Notary Public; pres: Bolton Catholic Musical and Choral Soc 1968–, Bolton C of C and Indust 1971–73, Bolton Law Soc 1972, Bolton West Cons Assoc 1973–76 and 1989–93 (sec 1961–66, tstee 1965–96, chm 1966–71, treas 1981–84, hon life vice pres); memb Jt Standing Ctee Law Soc and HM Land Registry 1972–91; dep pres Bolton Coronary Care 1970–, dep treas NW Cons Pty 1972–73, chm NW C of C and Indust 1973, treas and mangr N W Catholic History Soc 1987–90 (hon life memb 1990), memb Ctee Friends of Lancashire Archives 1992– (hon sec 1992–95), govr Mount St Mary's Coll Sheffield 1992–96; pres The Mount Assoc 1994–95, memb Ctee Chorley Civic Soc 1995– (treas 1996–); memb: Law Soc 1955, Notaries Soc 1960; *Recreations* historical studies, genealogy, industrial archaeology, canal walking, gardening and garden design; *Clubs* Bolton; *Style*— Thomas Arkwright, Esq; ✉ Ivy Cottage, Limbrick, Chorley, Lancashire PR6 9EE (business ☎ and fax 01257 230055)

ARMAGH, Archbishop of (RC) and Primate of All Ireland 1990–; His Eminence Cardinal Cahal Brendan Daly; s of Charles Daly (d 1939), of Loughguile, Co Antrim, and Susan Daly (d 1974); *b* 1 Oct 1917; *Educ* St Malachy's Coll Belfast, Queen's Univ Belfast (MA), St Patrick's Coll Maynooth (DD), Institut Catholique Paris (LPh); *Career* ordained 1941, classics master St Malachy's Coll Belfast 1945–46, reader in scholastic philosophy Queen's Univ Belfast 1963–67 (lectr 1946–63); consecrated bishop 1967; bishop of: Ardagh and Clonmacnois 1967–82, Down and Connor 1982–90; created Cardinal 1991; *Books* Morals, Law and Life (1962), Natural Law Morality Today (1965), Violence in Ireland and Christian Conscience (1973), Peace, the Work of Justice (1979), The Price of Peace (1991), Morals and Law (1993), Tertullian The Puritan (1993), Northern Ireland - Peace - Now is the Time (1993), Moral Philosophy in Britain from Bradley to Wittgenstein (1996); *Recreations* reading, writing; *Style*— His Eminence The Cardinal Archbishop of Armagh; ✉ Ara Coeli, Armagh, N Ireland BT61 7QY

ARMAGH, Dean of; *see:* Cassidy, Very Rev Herbert

ARMAGH, Archbishop of and Primate of All Ireland 1986–; Baron Eames (Life Peer UK 1995), of Armagh, in the County of Armagh; Most Rev the Rt Hon Robert Henry Alexander Eames; s of William Edward Eames, of Belfast, and Mary Eleanor Thompson, *née* Alexander; *b* 27 April 1937; *Educ* Belfast Royal Acad, Methodist Coll Belfast, Queen's Univ Belfast (LLB, PhD), Trinity Coll Dublin (LLD); *m* 1966, (Ann) Christine, da of Capt William Adrian Reynolds Daly (d 1943), of London; 2 s (Hon Niall b 1967, Hon Michael b 1969); *Career* curate of Bangor Co Down 1963–66; incumbent of: Gilnahirk Down 1966–74, Dundela Down 1974–75; bishop of: Derry and Raphoe 1975–80, Down and Dromore 1980–86; chm Archbishop of Canterbury's Int Cmmn on Communion and Women in the Episcopate 1988, govr Church Army 1985–; Hon LLD Queen's Univ Belfast 1989, Hon DLitt Greenwich Univ 1993; Hon DD Camb 1994; *Books* A Form of Worship for Teenagers (1965), The Quiet Revolution: Irish Disestablishment (1970), Through Suffering (1973), Thinking Through Lent (1978), Through Lent (1984), Chains to be Broken (1992); *Recreations* sailing, reading; *Clubs* Strangford Yacht, Ringhaddy Yacht, Kildare St and Univ Club (Dublin); *Style*— The Most Rev the Rt Hon Lord Eames, Archbishop of Armagh; ✉ The See House, Cathedral

Close, Armagh BT61 7EE (☎ 01861 527144, fax 01861 527823); House of Lords, London SW1A 0PW

ARMAND SMITH, Dr Nicholas Godfrey; s of Rev Lt Cdr Francis Armand Smith (ret), and Monica Ella Mary, *née* Harden (d 1975); *b* 16 Feb 1943; *Educ* Bryanston, St Mary's Hosp Med Sch Univ of London (MB BS); *m* 13 Sept 1973, Margaret Winifred, da of Francis John Hebbert, ERD, of Wilton, Salisbury, Wilts; 1 s (Henry b 1977), 2 da (Josephine b 1979, Celia b 1985); *Career* conslt epidemiologist WHO 1974–75, specialist in community med Lothian Health Bd 1977–82, dir of public health Salisbury Health Authy 1982–94, currently conslt public health physician Wilts HA; pres Assoc of Dirs of Public Health 1992–94, chm Salisbury branch Alzheimer's Disease Soc; FFPHM; *Recreations* cycling, old cars; *Style—* Dr Nicholas Armand Smith; ✉ Health Commission for Wiltshire and Bath, Southgate House, Pans Lane, Devizes, Wilts (☎ 01380 728899)

ARMATRADING, Joan Anita Barbara; da of Amos Ezekiel Armatrading, and Beryl Madge, *née* Benjamin; *b* 9 Dec 1950; *Educ* Secdy Sch Birmingham; *Career* singer and songwriter; first album Whatever's For Us 1972 (with Pam Nestor), stage debut Fairfield Hall Croydon 1972, first non-jazz act downstairs at Ronnie Scott's 1973, first major hit Love and Affection 1976, first Gold album Joan Armatrading 1976, recent album What's Inside 1995; numerous silver, gold and platinum discs; concerts: Blackbush with Bob Dylan (before 100,000 plus audience) 1978, Prince's Tst 1982 and 1986, Amnesty Int (Giant Stadium) 1986, Amnesty Int (Secret Policeman's Ball) 1987, Nelson Mandela's 70th Birthday 1988, First King's Tst Swaziland 1989 and 1990; nominated: Grammy Best Female Vocal 1980 and 1983, Best Female Vocal UK 1976 and 1983; Key to Sydney 1983, guest of honour St Kitt's Independence Celebration 1983; *Recreations* reading British comics, owner of two vintage cars; *Style—* Miss Joan Armatrading

ARME, Prof Christopher; s of Cyril Boddington Arme, of Smalley, Derbyshire, and Monica Henriette, *née* Hawkins; *b* 10 Aug 1939; *Educ* Heanor GS, Univ of Leeds (BSc, PhD), Keele Univ (DSc); *m* 1962, Mary Arme; 3 s (Patrick b 16 May 1965, Mark b 19 April 1967, Peter b 12 Aug 1969); *Career* SRC/NATO res fell Univ of Leeds 1964–66, RES fell Rice Univ Houston 1966–68, lectr/reader in zoology Queen's Univ Belfast 1968–76, princ lectr in biology and head of biology N Staffs Poly 1976–79, prof of zoology Keele Univ 1979–, secondment as dir of terrestrial and freshwater sciences NERC 1993–95; Br Soc of Parasitology: memb, Silver Jubilee lectr 1987, pres 1990–92, hon memb 1992; memb: American Soc of Parasitology, Royal Soc of Tropical Med and Hygiene, Zoological Soc London, Linnean Soc, Inst of Biology (hon treas 1986–93), Soc of Experimental Biology; hon memb All Russia Soc of Helminthologists 1992, hon treas Euro Fedn of Parasitologists 1992, hon memb Czechoslovak Parasitological Soc 1990; K I Skryabin Medal 1995, Charter Award Inst of Biology 1995; Hon DSc Slovak Acad of Sciences 1995; *Publications* author of several books and over 100 scientific pubns incl Parasitology (ed with F E G Cox); *Style—* Prof Christopher Arme; ✉ Department of Biological Sciences, Keele University, Keele, Staffs ST5 5BG (☎ 01782 583025, fax 01782 630007, e-mail c.arme@keele.ac.uk)

ARMES, Timothy Joseph Patrick; s of Harry Armes (d 1986), and Teresa, *née* O'Mahony; *b* 1 Oct 1953; *Educ* St Richard of Chichester Sch, Westminster Tech Coll (ONC), The City Univ; *m* 14 July 1989, Susan McKenzie, da of John Self, of Oxted, Surrey; 1 da (Olivia Charlotte McKenzie b 31 March 1990), 1 s (Henry Timothy Alexander b 30 Nov 1991); *Career* advertising exec; J Walter Thompson 1976–78 (trainee buyer rising to media buyer), media gp head MWK & P 1978–83, media gp dir Young & Rubicam 1983–89, devpt dir The Media Shop 1990–92; DMB&B The Media Centre: media gp dir 1992–94, dir of press buying 1994–, concurrently bd dir; memb Exec Ctee The Media Circle; *Recreations* cricket, horse racing, wine, collecting antiques, being a father, opera, theatre, cinema, restaurants, travel; *Clubs* RAC, Middlesex CCC; *Style—* Timothy Armes, Esq; ✉ The Media Centre, 123 Buckingham Palace Road, London SW1W 9DZ (☎ 0171 233 5678, fax 0171 592 1038)

ARMFIELD, Diana Maxwell; da of (Joseph) Harold Armfield (d 1981), of Ty Newydd, Parc, Bala, Gwynedd, and Gertrude Mary, *née* Uttley (d 1984); *b* 11 June 1920; *Educ* Bedales, Slade Sch, Central Sch of Arts and Crafts; *m* 12 Feb 1949, (Andrew Harold) Bernard Dunstan, RA, *qv*, s of Dr Albert Ernest Dunstan (d 1960), of Cambridge; 3 s (Andrew Joseph b 1950, David James b 1952, Robert Maxwell b 1955); *Career* painter; cultural activities organiser Miny of Supply 1942–46; tutor: Textile Dept Central Sch Art 1949–50, Byam Shaw Art Sch 1959–90; visiting tutor various art schs 1959–91, reg exhibitor Royal Acad 1966–; memb Cncl Royal Acad 1991–92; exhibitor: Festival of Britain 1951, Tonic for the Nation (V&A), Diana Armfield's Choice (Albany Gallery Cardiff) 1991, Albany Gallery Cardiff 1995, Glyn-Y-Weddw Llandrog Llanbedrog N Wales 1995; artist in residence: Perth W Aust 1985, Jackson Wyoming USA 1989; NEAC Centenary Sothebys' 1986; one man show Browse & Darby London 1979, 1981, 1984, 1987, 1990 and 1993, gp show Hollis Taggart Gall Washington DC 1993; perm collections: V&A (textiles), cmmns Reuters 1986–87, Contemporary Art Soc Wales 1987, Nat Tst 1988–89, HRH Prince of Wales 1989, Farringdon Tst, Yale Centre Br Art, Govt Picture Collection, Br Museum, Royal Watercolour Soc, Lancaster Co Museum, Royal W England Acad, Royal Acad Diploma Collection; retrospective exhbn RA 1995; group exhibitions: Hollis Taggart Gallery Washington DC 1993, Barneys Greenwich Connecticut USA 1993 and 1995; buyer for Contemporary Art Soc Wales 1990–91; memb: Cncl of the Protection of Rural Wales, Friends of the Earth; subject of book 'The Art of Diana Armfield' by Julian Halsby 1994; MCSD 1951, memb Royal Cambrian Acad, memb NEAC 1970, RWA 1975, RWS 1980, RA 1992 (ARA 1989); *Books* Painting In Oils (1982); *Recreations* musical appreciation, singing, gardening; *Clubs* Arts; *Style—* Miss Diana Armfield, RA; ✉ 10 High Park Rd, Kew, Richmond, Surrey TW9 4BH (☎ 0181 876 6633); Llwynhir, Parc, Bala, Gwynedd (☎ 01678 540289)

ARMIGER, Paul Gower; s of Wing Cdr Brian Armiger, OBE, of Edinburgh, and Peggy Joyce, *née* Oldfield; *b* 25 Aug 1942; *Educ* Karachi GS India, Cranbrook Sydney Aust, Haileybury and ISC Windsor, Bloxham Sch Banbury Oxon; *m* 28 June 1964, Patricia Gillian, da of Sqdn Ldr Charles Clinch; 2 s (Andrew Gower b 9 April 1968, Steven Paul b 21 Feb 1971); *Career* photographer; staff photographer Montgomery Advertiser and Alabama Journal USA 1960–61, freelance photographer Washington DC (work for Time, Life, Newsweek, Washington Post, Nat Geographic) 1961–64, freelance photographer The Daily Telegraph London 1965, staff photographer The Daily Telegraph 1967– (covered NI 1969–74, Darien Gap Expedition 1971); hon memb Naval Air Cmd Sub Aqua Club, fndr memb Br Soc of Underwater Photographers 1969, memb Underwater Archaeological Expeditions Assoc Hollandia Colossus 1967–72; second class diver BSAC 1970, holder commercial diver's licence (Part IV Diver at work) 1980; *Recreations* scuba diving, photography, golf, model shipwright (18th century ship models); *Clubs* Press Club (Washington and London), Royal Over-Seas League; *Style—* Paul Armiger, Esq; ✉ The Daily Telegraph, 1 Canada Square, Canary Wharf, London E14 5DT (☎ 0171 538 6399, car 0836 256671)

ARMITAGE, Edward Phillip (Phil); s of Leslie Armitage, of Barnsley, and Alice Emily, *née* Dufton; *b* 20 Jan 1947; *Educ* Barnsley Holgate GS, Univ of Sussex (BSc, MSc, MA); *m* 24 Aug 1974, Elizabeth, da of Joseph Blackburn Sweeney; 1 s (Richard John b 27 Dec 1978), 1 da (Jennifer Elizabeth b 16 Oct 1980); *Career* sr lectr in statistics Coventry Poly 1968–78, res fell and lectr in student assessment Open Univ 1978–85, dir educn and training ICAEW 1990– (examinations offr 1985–90); *Recreations* music, squash, fell walking; *Style—* Phil Armitage, Esq; ✉ Institute of Chartered Accountants, Chartered Accountants Hall, Moorgate Place, London EC2P 2BJ (☎ 0171 920 8511, fax 0171 920 0547)

ARMITAGE, Jeremy John; s of Maj Edward John Armitage (d 1992), of London, and Marthe Ada, *née* Cleyndert; *b* 10 June 1954; *Educ* St Paul's, Edinburgh Coll of Art (BArch, Dip Arch); *m* 4 Jan 1978, Rowena Kathleen, da of Alexander Johnston, JP (d 1988); 2 s (John Joseph b 1981, James William b 1987), 1 da (Hannah Mary b 1979); *Career* architectural asst Western Isles Cncl 1979–80; Campbell and Arnott: joined 1980, opened new Glasgow office and became assoc 1985, ptnr 1987, dir 1989–94; in practice Armitage Associates 1994–; RIBA 1980, ARIAS 1985; *Recreations* sailing, hill walking; *Clubs* Clyde Canoe; *Style—* Jeremy Armitage, Esq; ✉ 7 Kirklee Road, Glasgow G12 0RH (☎ 0141 334 8522); Armitage Associates, Fleming House (13th Floor), 134 Renfrew Street, Glasgow G3 6ST (☎ 0141 332 8011, fax 0141 332 8374)

ARMITAGE, John Patrick; s of Rev Cyril Moxon Armitage, MVO (d 1966), of St Bride's Rectory, Fleet St, London, and Eva, *née* Brinsmead; *b* 17 March 1935; *Educ* Marlborough; *m* 1, 28 Aug 1965 (m dis 1973), Marah Helen, *née* Douglas; 1 s (Edward b 8 Dec 1967); m 2, 14 Oct 1984, Nicola Caroline, da of Larry Gaines, of Crosstrees, Saltwood, Kent; *Career* Nat Serv cmmnd 2 Lt E Yorks Regt UK, Malaya, Germany 1954–56; sales exec Noel Gay Music Co Ltd 1956–59, dir Ogilvy & Mather Ltd 1971–85 (account exec 1959–71); chm: Primary Contact Ltd 1985–, Ogilvy & Mather Focus Ltd 1988–90; memb Mark Soc; *Recreations* golf; *Clubs* Littlestone Rye, Royal & Ancient; *Style—* John Armitage, Esq; ✉ Primary Contact Ltd, Knightway House, Soho Square, London W1V 6AU (☎ 0171 437 4947)

ARMITAGE, (William) Kenneth; CBE (1969); *b* 18 July 1916; *Educ* Slade Sch; *Career* sculptor; served Army 1939–46; teacher of sculpture Bath Acad of Art 1946–56; work in private and public collections worldwide; Hon Dr RCA 1969 (hon fell 1965), RA 1994; *Solo Exhbns* Gimpel Fils London 1952, 1957 and 1980, Bertha Schaefer NY 1956, Paul Rosenberg NY 1958–62, Br Cncl exhbns Venice Biennale, then touring museums Paris, Cologne, Brussels, Zürich, Rotterdam, Whitechapel Art Gall 1959, Br Cncl world touring exhbn 1959–76, Kestner Gesselschaft Hanover and Japan 1960–61, Marlborough Gall London 1962 and 1965, Art Cncl exhbn touring 10 Eng cities 1972–73, Fuji TV Gall Tokyo then Galerie Humanite Nagoya and Gallery Kasahara 1978, Sala Mendoza Caracas Venezuela 1982, Artcurial Paris (retrospective) 1985, 80th Birthday Survey Yorks Sculpture Park 1996, Works on Paper Royal Acad 1996; *Group Exhbns* incl: The New Decade Mus of Modern Art NY 1955, Guggenheim Int Exhbn NY 1967, Br Sculpture of 20 Century Whitechapel Gall 1982, Br Art of the 20th Century RA 1987 then Staatsgalerie Stuttgart, EXPO 88 Brisbane, Olympiad of Art Seoul Olympics 1988, Chelsea Harbour Sculpture 1993; *Style—* Kenneth Armitage, Esq, CBE, RA; ✉ 22A Avonmore Rd, London W14 8RR

ARMITAGE, Air Chief Marshal Sir Michael John; KCB (1983), CBE (1975); *b* 25 Aug 1930; *Educ* Newport GS IOW, RAF Coll Cranwell; *m* 1, 1955 (m dis 1969); 3 s; m 2, 1970, Gretl Renate Steinig; *Career* Halton apprentice 1947–50, RAF Coll Cranwell 1950–53, cmmnd 1953, various flying, staff, cmd and academic appts, OC 17 Sqdn 1967–69, OC RAF Luqa Malta 1972–74, RAF Dir of Forward Policy 1976–78, Dep Cdr RAF Germany 1978–80, Sr RAF Dir Staff RCDS 1980–82, Dir of Service Intelligence 1982–83, Dep Chief Def Staff (Intelligence) 1983, Chief of Def Intelligence MOD 1984–85, Air Memb for Supply and Orgn, Air Force Bd 1985–87, Cmdt RCDS 1988–89, ret 1990; memb: IISS, RUSI; *Books* Air Power in the Nuclear Age (jtly 2 edn 1985), Unmanned Aircraft (1988), History of the Royal Air Force (1993); author of numerous articles in professional journals and newspapers; lectures on air power and mil history; *Recreations* field shooting, military history, writing, lecturing; *Clubs* RAF; *Style—* Air Chief Marshal Sir Michael Armitage, KCB, CBE; ✉ c/o Lloyds Bank, 7 Pall Mall, London SW1

ARMITAGE, Peter Lockhart; s of Dennis Lockhart Armitage, of Rushton Temple Lane, East Meon, Hants, and Dorothy Margaret, *née* Lamb; *b* 13 Jan 1949; *Educ* Malvern, Univ of Manchester (BA); *m* 7 Aug 1976, Fiona Christine Lilli, da of John Kingsley Hill, of Hen Ysgol, Llanfaethly, Holyhead, Anglesey; 2 s (Michael b 1980, Jonathan b 1985), 1 da (Melanie b 1982); *Career* CA; co sec and fin dir: OCS Group Ltd 1987, Smarts Group Ltd 1981, Collie Carpets Ltd 1980; jt md: Smarts Group Ltd 1985–87 (all cos owned by OCS Gp), J Mason & Son Leek Ltd 1977–78; *Recreations* tennis, sailing, gardening; *Style—* Peter Armitage, Esq; ✉ OCS Group Ltd, 79 Limpsfield Road, Sanderstead, Surrey CR2 9LB (☎ 0181 651 3211, fax 0181 651 4832)

ARMITAGE, Roger Stuart; s of Eric Armitage (d 1970), and Elsie, *née* Hollingworth; *b* 17 April 1943; *Educ* Elland GS; *m* 3 Sept 1966, Wendy, da of Frank Lockwood; 1 s (Martin James b 26 Dec 1970); *Career* CA 1965; Revell Ward (formerly Hirst & Elmslie): articled clerk 1959–64, ptnr 1969, sr ptnr 1990–; former pres Huddersfield CAs Students Soc, pres Huddersfield Soc of CAs 1993–94; ACA 1965, ATII 1965; *Recreations* golf, walking, theatre; *Clubs* Woodsome Hall Golf, Colne Valley Soc (treas); *Style—* Roger S Armitage, Esq; ✉ Messrs Revell Ward, Chartered Accountants, Norwich Union House, High St, Huddersfield HD1 2LN (☎ 01484 538351, fax 01484 513522)

ARMITAGE, (Henry) St John Basil; CBE (1978, OBE 1968); s of (Henry) John Armitage (d 1978), of Co Tipperary and Lincoln, and Amelia Eleanor, *née* Hall (d 1967); *b* 5 May 1924; *Educ* Lincoln Christ's Hosp, Trinity Coll Cambridge; *m* 1956, Jennifer Gerda, da of Prof Walter Horace Bruford; 1 s (Richard), 1 da (Elizabeth); *Career* served Army 1943–45, Arab Legion 1946, Br Mil Mission to Saudi Arabia 1946–49, mil advsr to Saudi Arabian MOD 1946–51, Desert Locust Control Kenya and Aden Protectorates 1952, mil serv Sultan of Muscat and Oman 1952–59; resident mangr Gen Geophysical Co (Houston) Libya 1959–60, oil conslt Astor Assocs Libya 1960–61, business conslt ME 1962; HM Dip Serv: entered 1962; first sec (commercial): Baghdad 1963–67, Beirut 1967–68, Jedda 1968–74; chargé d'affaires Jedda 1968, 1969 and 1973, HM cnsllr and consul gen Dubai 1974–78, chargé d'affaires Abu Dhabi 1975, 1976 and 1977, ret 1978; hon sec All Party British Saudi Arabian Parly Gp; conslt on ME affrs; *Recreations* cricket, reading, travel; *Clubs* Travellers'; *Style—* St John Armitage, Esq, CBE; ✉ The Old Vicarage, East Horrington, Wells, Somerset

ARMITAGE, Simon Robert; s of Peter Armitage, and Audrey May Armitage, of Huddersfield; *b* 26 May 1963; *Educ* Colne Valley HS, Portsmouth Poly (BA), Univ of Manchester (CQSW, MA); *m* 21 Sept 1991, Alison Claire, *née* Tootell; *Career* probation offr Greater Manchester Probation Serv 1988–, ed Poetry Chatto and Windus; Eric Gregory Award, Forward Poetry Prize 1992, Sunday Times Young Writer of the Year 1993; *Poetry Collections* Zoom! (1989, Poetry Book Soc Choice), Xanadu (1992), Kid (1992), Book of Matches (1993), The Dead Sea Poems (1995); *Recreations* as expected; *Style—* Simon Armitage, Esq; ✉ c/o Faber & Faber Ltd, 3 Queen Square, London WC1N 3AU (☎ 0171 465 0045, fax 0171 465 0034)

ARMITAGE, Dr (John) Vernon; s of Horace Armitage, and Evelyn, *née* Hauton; through his mother, Dr Armitage is 2 cous of Baron Richardson of Duntisbourne, *qv*; *b* 21 May 1932; *Educ* Rothwell GS, UCL (BSc, PhD), Cuddesdon Coll Oxford; *m* 1963, Sarah Catherine Clay; 2 s; *Career* asst master: Pontefract HS 1956–58, Shrewsbury Sch 1958–59; lectr in maths Univ of Durham 1959–67, sr lectr in maths King's Coll London 1967–70, prof of mathematical educn Univ of Nottingham 1970–75 (special prof 1976–79); Univ of Durham: princ Coll of St Hild and St Bede 1975–, dean of colleges 1988–93; chm Mathematical Instruction Sub-Ctee of Br Nat Ctee for Maths Royal Soc 1975–78; *Books* A Companion to Advanced Mathematics (with H B Griffiths, 1969); papers on theory of numbers in professional jls; *Recreations* railways, cricket and most games; *Clubs* Athenaeum; *Style*— Dr Vernon Armitage; ✉ The Principal's House, Pelaw Leazes Lane, Durham DH1 1TB (☎ 0191 374 3050, fax 0191 374 4740)

ARMITSTEAD, Claire Louise; da of Charles Henry Wilfrid Armitstead (d 1996), of Haywards Heath, W Sussex, and Gillian Louise, *née* Bartley (d 1987); *b* 2 Dec 1958; *Educ* Bedales Sch Hants, St Hilda's Coll Oxford (BA); *m* 17 Sept 1983, John Christopher Yandell, s of Canon Owen James Yandell; 1 s (Arthur James Armitstead b 7 Sept 1990); *Career* journalist; sub-ed and theatre critic: South Wales Argus Newport 1983–84 (trainee reporter The News 1980–83), Hampstead & Highgate Express 1984–89; theatre critic: The Financial Times 1986–92, The Guardian 1992–96; arts ed The Guardian 1996–; memb: NUJ 1980, Critics' Circle 1990, Int Assoc of Theatre Critics 1988; *Recreations* finding time to read novels and keep fit; *Style*— Ms Claire Armitstead; ✉ The Guardian, 119 Farringdon Road, London EC1R 3ER (☎ 0171 278 2332)

ARMOUR, Prof Sir James; kt (1995), CBE (1989); s of James Angus Armour (d 1948), and Margaret Brown, *née* Roy (d 1959); *b* 17 Sept 1929; *Educ* Marr Coll Troon, Univ of Glasgow (Golf blue, MRCVS, PhD); *m* 1, 1953, Irene (d 1988), da of Arthur Brunton Morris (d 1971); 2 s (Donald George b 10 Dec 1955, Malcolm Craig 30 Sept 1961), 2 da (Linda Margaret 17 June 1954, Fiona Marion 22 Sept 1957); m 2, 1992, Christine McTavish Strickland; *Career* research offr Colonial Vet Serv Nigeria 1953–60, vet researcher Cooper McDougall & Robertson 1960–63; Univ of Glasgow: research fell 1963–67, lectr in vet parasitology 1967–71, sr lectr 1971–73, reader 1973–76, prof 1976–95, vice-princ 1990–95; chm: Vet Products Ctee 1987–95, Governing Body Inst for Animal Health 1990–95, Glasgow Dental Hosp and Sch NHS Tst 1995–99; RCVS: memb 1952, fell 1995, John Henry Steel Medal; BVA: memb 1952, Wooldridge Medal; Bledisloe award RASE, Pfizer award for research World Assoc for Vet Parasitology; Dr (hc) Univ of Utrecht 1981, DVMS Univ of Edinburgh 1995; FRSE 1990; *Books* Veterinary Parasitology (1 edn 1988, 2 edn 1995); *Recreations* golf, watching football and rugby; *Clubs* Royal Troon, Turnberry Golf; *Style*— Prof Sir James Armour, CBE, FRSE; ✉ Mokoia, 11 Crosbie Road, Troon, Scotland KA10 6HE (☎ 01292 314068)

ARMSON, (Frederick) Simon Arden; s of Frank Gerald Arden Armson (d 1982), and Margaret Fenella, *née* Newton; *b* 11 Sept 1948; *Educ* Denstone Coll, Univ of London (MSc 1997); *m* 8 Feb 1975, Marion Albinia, da of David Hamilton-Russell (d 1988), and Pauline, *née* Slade; 3 c (Meriel Albinia b 1979, Patrick David Arden b 1982, Katharine Geraldine b 1984); *Career* early trg in health serv mgmnt, various managerial and admin posts NHS 1970–84; pt/t lectr in NHS industl rels Oxford Poly 1977–82; The Samaritans: asst gen sec 1984–89, gen sec 1989–90, chief exec 1990–; chm Telephone Helpline Gp 1992–96, memb Exec Ctee Assoc of Chief Execs of Nat Vol Orgns (ACENVO) 1992–94, chm BBC Radio Helpline Advsy Cncl 1995–, dir Samaritan Enterprises Ltd 1996–, UK nat rep Int Assoc for Suicide Prevention (IASP) 1996–; chm Panel of Judges Guardian Jerwood Award 1995–; FRSA 1993, CIMgt 1995; *Recreations* sailing, walking, music, cycling (cross country); *Style*— Simon Armson, Esq; ✉ Broad Oak, Hurley, Maidenhead, Berks SL6 5LW (☎ 01628 824322, fax 01628 826867); Chief Executive, The Samaritans, 10 The Grove, Slough SL1 1QP (☎ 01753 532713, fax 01753 819004)

ARMSTRONG, Andrew Charles; s of Terence George Armstrong, of Linton, Cambs, and Marion, *née* Rigg; *b* 15 March 1959; *Educ* Newport GS Essex; *m* 4 July 1981, Jacqueline Mary, da of Anthony Rokeby Roberts, of Stansted, nr Bishop's Stortford, Herts; 2 s (Robert Charles b 1985, David Alexander b 1989); *Career* dir Robert Fleming & Co Ltd 1986–; *Recreations* flying, golf; *Style*— A C Armstrong, Esq; ✉ Robert Fleming & Co Ltd, 25 Copthall Ave, London EC2R 7DR (☎ 0171 638 5858, fax 0171 256 5036)

ARMSTRONG, Sir Andrew Clarence Francis; 6 Bt (UK 1841), of Gallen Priory, King's Co; CMG (1959); er s of Edmund Clarence Richard Armstrong, FSA (d 1923), Bluemantle Pursuivant of Arms, and Mary Frances, *née* Cruise, 2 da of Sir Francis Cruise (d 1953); suc his cousin Sir Andrew St Clare Armstrong, 5 Bt (d 1987); *b* 1 May 1907; *Educ* St Edmund's Coll Ware, Christ's Coll Cambridge (BA 1928); *m* 1, 8 Jan 1930, Phyllis Marguerite (d 18 Jan 1930), da of Lt-Col Roland Henry Waithman, DSO; m 2, 17 June 1932, Laurel May (d 1988), er da of late Alfred Wellington Stuart, of New Zealand; 1 s (1 s decd); *Heir* s, Lt-Col Christopher John Edmund Stuart Armstrong, MBE, *qv*; *Career* Colonial Admin Serv: W Pacific 1929, Nigeria 1941, perm sec Fed Miny of Mines and Power Nigeria; ret 1961; *Recreations* croquet; *Clubs* Phyllis Court; *Style*— Sir Andrew Armstrong, Bt, CMG; ✉ 5 Isis, Thamesfield Court, Wargrave Road, Henley-on-Thames, Oxon RG9 2LX (☎ 01491 577635)

ARMSTRONG, Anne; *Career* US ambass to UK 1976–77; dir: Glaxo Wellcome plc (formerly Glaxo Holdings plc) 1991–, American Express Inc, Boise Cascade Inc, General Motors Corp, Halliburton; chm Bd of Tstee Center for Strategic and Int Studies Washington DC; *Style*— Hon Anne Armstrong; ✉ Glaxo Wellcome plc, Lansdowne House, Berkeley Square, London W1X 6BQ (☎ 0171 493 4060, fax 0171 408 0228)

ARMSTRONG, Lt-Col Christopher John Edmund Stuart; MBE (1979); s and h of Sir Andrew Clarence Francis Armstrong, 6 Bt, CMG, *qv*; *b* 15 Jan 1940; *Educ* Ampleforth, RMA; *m* 1972, Georgina Elizabeth Carey, 2 da of late Lt-Col W G Lewis, of Hayling Island; 3 s (Charles Andrew b 1973, James Hugo b 1974, Sam Edward b 1986), 1 da (Victoria Jane b 1980); *Career* Lt-Col RLC; *Style*— Lt-Col Christopher Armstrong, MBE

ARMSTRONG, Colin Robert; s of Arthur Armstrong (d 1957), and Sylvia Ann, *née* Williamson (d 1945); *b* 4 July 1934; *Educ* Haileybury; *m* 10 Oct 1959, Stella Margaret, da of Harold Bracht (d 1985), of Bogota, Colombia; 1 s (Arthur Guthrie b 9 April 1962), 1 da (Annabel Clare b 16 Sept 1966); *Career* Nat Serv 1952–54: cmmnd Middx Regt 1953, seconded to KAR (active serv E Africa and Malaya); 7 Middx Regt TA 1955–57; dir Tracey & Co (subsidiary of Bank of London and S America) 1963–71, mangr head office Bank of London and S America 1971–74, regnl mangr Lloyds Bank Int 1974–77, gen mangr Banco Anglo Colombiano 1977–81, dir and chief exec (Latin America & Caribbean) Inchcape Overseas Ltd 1981–86, exec dir Inchcape plc 1986–91, currently dir Inchcape Family Investments; chm: Latin American Trade Advsy Gp 1984–86, British Chilean C of C, Gray Dawes Travel; memb: Exec Ctee Canning House 1986–, Lloyd's 1983–88; *Recreations* fly fishing, cricket, ornithology; *Clubs* MCC, East India; *Style*— Colin Armstrong, Esq; ✉ The Old House, The Folly, Lightwater, Surrey (☎ 01276 473258, fax 01276 451049)

ARMSTRONG, Prof David Gilford; s of Arthur Armstrong (d 1930), of Whitley Bay, Tyne and Wear, and Beatrice Mary, *née* Walton (d 1972); *b* 9 July 1926; *Educ* Whitley Bay GS, Univ of Durham (BSc, MSc, PhD), Univ of Newcastle (DSc); *m* 31 Aug 1963, Susan, da of James Edward Hannah (d 1971), of Ayr, Scotland; 1 s (Neil b 1965), 1 da (Helen b 1967); *Career* lectr in agricultural chemistry Univ of Durham 1951–54 (demonstrator 1946–51), study year Univ of Illinois USA 1952–53, staff appt Nutrition Dept Hannah Res Inst Ayr 1954–62; Univ of Newcastle: reader and head of dept 1963–68, prof of agriculture biochemistry and nutrition Univ of Newcastle 1968–91, head Dept of Biological and Nutritional Sciences 1991, emeritus prof 1991–; visiting prof Univ of New England Aust 1971; memb Governing Body: Hill Farming Res Orgn 1970–85, Grassland Res Inst 1974–85, Macauley Land Use Res Inst 1985–88; memb: Ind Merit Review Ctee 1985–89, Meat and Livestock Res Ctee 1986–, AFRC Animals Ctee 1987–89, Inst of Animal Health 1988–90, Scientific Ctee on Animal Nutrition EEC 1972–87; pres Nutrition Soc 1986–89, pres Northumberland Branch Holstein-Friesian Club 1989–, hon res assoc Inst of Grassland and Animal Prodn 1987, hon res fell Hannah Res Inst 1989; hon life memb: British Soc Animal Prodn 1992, Nutrition Soc 1993; Hon DSc Univ of Louvain la Neuve 1988; FRSE 1969, FRIC, FIBiol; Ordre du Merite Agricole France 1981; *Recreations* fishing, shooting, golf; *Style*— Prof David Armstrong, FRSE; ✉ Woodcote, 44 North Rd, Ponteland, Northumberland NE20 9UR (☎ 01661 822316, fax 01661 860440); University of Newcastle, Dept of Biological and Nutritional Sciences, Newcastle upon Tyne NE1 7RU (☎ 0191 222 6000, ext 6907, fax 0191 222 1182, telex 53654)

ARMSTRONG, Prof David Millar; s of James Armstrong, of Workington, Cumbria, and Jean Alexandra, *née* Millar; *b* 25 May 1941; *Educ* Workington GS, Univ of Oxford (BA, BSc), Australian Nat Univ (PhD); *m* 12 Aug 1964, Lucinda Russell, da of George Graham Kennedy (d 1955); 1 s (James Graham b 1966), 1 da (Katherine Anne b 1965); *Career* Univ of Bristol: lectr 1968–78, reader 1978–84, prof of physiology 1984–, head of dept 1990–95; memb: Neurosciences and Mental Health Bd of MRC 1987–91, Trg Awards Ctee MRC 1989–93; memb: Marine Biological Assoc 1965, Physiological Soc 1968; *Recreations* walking, reading, social and medical historical research; *Clubs* Bristol Scientific; *Style*— Prof David Armstrong; ✉ Department of Physiology, School of Medical Sciences, University of Bristol, University Walk, Bristol BS8 1TD (☎ 0117 928 9101, fax 0117 928 8923 attn D M Armstrong)

ARMSTRONG, Dr Ernest McAlpine; s of Ernest Armstrong (d 1988), and Mary Brownlie McLean, *née* McAlpine (d 1980); *b* 3 June 1945; *Educ* Hamilton Acad, Univ of Glasgow (BSc, MB, ChB); *m* 15 July 1970, Dr Katherine Mary Dickson, da of Dr William C Young; 2 s (Euan McAlpine b 1 March 1972, Neil William b 4 Feb 1976); *Career* jr house offr Glasgow 1970–71, lectr in pathology Univ of Glasgow 1971–74, clinical asst (anaesthetics) West Highland Hosp 1975–81, trainer in general practice 1980–90, princ in general practice Connel 1975–93 (trainee asst 1974–75), sec BMA 1993–; chm: Scottish General Medical Servs Ctee 1989–92, Scottish Cncl BMA 1992–92; dep chm General Medical Servs Ctee 1992–93, memb numerous BMA and NHS Ctees; FRCP (Glas), FRCGP; *Recreations* music, travelling, sailing; *Clubs* Caledonian; *Style*— Dr Ernest Armstrong; ✉ 526 Willoughby House, Barbican, London EC2Y 8BN; Craiglora, Connel, Argyll PA37 1PH; British Medical Association, BMA House, Tavistock Square, London WC1H 9JP (☎ 0171 387 4499, fax 0171 383 6400)

ARMSTRONG, Fiona Kathryne; da of Robert Armstrong, of Lancs, and Pauline, *née* Moreland; *b* 28 Nov 1956; *Educ* A R Tuson Coll Preston, Univ of London (BA); *m* 12 Sept 1987, Rodney Thomas Potts, s of Thomas Potts, of Canonbie, Dumfriesshire; *Career* reporter Radio 210 Reading 1980–82, regnl journalist BBC TV Manchester 1982–85, reporter Border TV Cumbria 1985–87, newscaster ITN 1987–92, presenter Jan-March GMTV 1993, currently freelance working with BBC TV, BBC Radio 2 and 4 and NBC Superchannel; *Books* 'F' is for Flyfishing, The Commuter's Cookbook; *Recreations* fishing, cooking; *Clubs* Reform; *Style*— Ms Fiona Armstrong

ARMSTRONG, Frank William; s of Frank Armstrong (d 1965), and Millicent Armstrong (d 1989); *b* 26 March 1931; *Educ* Stretford GS, Royal Tech Coll Salford, Queen Mary Coll London (MSc); *m* 1957, Diane Tranter, da of Stanley and Doreen Varley; 3 da (Catherine Mary b 6 Nov 1961, Jennifer Clare b 10 June 1963, Rachel Jane b 23 April 1967); *Career* engrg trg Massey-Harris Ltd Manchester 1947–51, Queen Mary Coll London 1951–56, tech asst De Havilland Engine Co Edgware 1956–58, Admty Engrg Lab West Drayton 1958–59; Nat Gas Turbine Estab Pyestock: joined 1959, head of Noise Research 1971–75, head of Performance and Design Research 1975–78; Engine Div MOD (PE) London 1978–81, dep dir R & D Nat Gas Turbine Establishment 1981–83; Royal Aircraft Establishment Farnborough (later Royal Aerospace): head of Propulsion Dept 1983–87, dep dir (Aircraft) 1987–89, dir (Aerospace Vehicles) 1989–91; ind tech conslt 1991–; specialist areas incl: gas turbines for aircraft and non-aeronautical applications, heat engines and energy conversion systems, aerospace technol and design, mgmnt and orgn of research (incl int collaboration); contrib to learned society jls on aeronautical research, gas turbines and aircraft propulsion; winner Akroyd Stuart Prize Royal Aeronautical Soc 1975; FRAeS 1981, FIMechE 1981, FEng 1991; *Recreations* walking and mountaineering, aviation history, music; *Style*— Frank W Armstrong, Esq, FEng; ✉ 6 Corringway, Church Crookham, Fleet, Hampshire GU13 0AN (☎ and fax 01252 616526)

ARMSTRONG, Gary; s of Lawrance Albert Armstrong, of Jedburgh, and Margret, *née* Paxton; *b* 30 Sept 1966; *Educ* Berwickshire HS, Dumfermline Agric Coll; *m* 1989, Shona, da of William Ramsay; 1 s (Darren James b 24 Oct 1990); *Career* professional rugby union scrum-half; clubs: Jed Thistle under 18's 1981–84, Jed-Forest RFC 1984–95, Newcastle RFC 1995–; rep: Scot Midlands under 15's, Scot South under 18's, Scot South; Scotland: under 18 and under 21 rep, full debut v Aust 1988, Five Nations debut v Wales 1989, memb Grand Slam winning team 1990, memb World Cup team (fourth place) 1991, over 30 caps; memb British Lions' team touring NZ 1993; *Recreations* golf; *Style*— Gary Armstrong, Esq; ✉ c/o Newcastle RFC, New Ground, Great North Road, Gosforth, Newcastle Upon Tyne NE3 2DT (☎ 0191 214 0422)

ARMSTRONG, Hilary Jane; MP (Lab) Durham NW (majority 13,987); da of Rt Hon Ernest Armstrong (d 1996), and Hannah, *née* Lamb; *b* 30 Nov 1945; *Educ* Monkwearmouth Comp Sch Sunderland, West Ham Coll of Technol (BSc), Univ of Birmingham (Dip in Social Work); *Career* VSO teacher Murray Girls' HS Kenya 1967–69, social worker Newcastle City Social Servs Dept 1970–73, community worker Southwick Neighbourhood Action Project Sunderland 1973–75, lectr in community and youth work Sunderland Poly 1975–86, sec/researcher to father Ernest Armstrong MP 1986–87, MP (Lab) Durham NW 1987–; oppn spokesman on educn 1988–93, PPS to John Smith, Leader of the Oppn 1992–94, Treasy Team 1994–95, shadow min for local govt 1995–; memb Educn Select Ctee 1988, chm PLP Educn Ctee; memb Durham CC 1985–87; *Recreations* theatre, reading; *Style*— Ms Hilary Armstrong, MP; ✉ House of Commons, London SW1A 0AA

ARMSTRONG, Prof Isobel Mair; da of Richard Aneurin Jones (d 1953), and Marjorie, *née* Jackson; *b* 25 March 1937; *Educ* Friends Sch Saffron Walden Essex, Univ of Leicester (BA, PhD); *m* 9 Aug 1961, (John) Michael Armstrong, s of Rev Charles Armstrong (d 1947); 2 s (Thomas b 5 Oct 1968, Stephen b 24 April 1975), 1 da (Ursula b 16 Aug 1971); *Career* post doctoral fell in English Westfield Coll London 1962–63, asst lectr then lectr in English UCL 1963–70, lectr then sr lectr in English Univ of Leicester 1970–79; prof of English: Univ of Southampton 1979–89, Birkbeck Coll London 1989–; visiting prof: Dept of English Princeton Univ, Breadloaf Sch of English MA Prog Middlebury Coll Vermont, English Dept Harvard Univ; fndr ctee memb Ctee for Univ English, co-ed Women - A Cultural Review 1988; FRSA 1991; *Books* incl: Every Man Will Shout (with R Mansfield, 1964), The Major Victorian Poets - Reconsiderations (1969), A Sudden Line (1976), Language as Living Form in Nineteenth Century Poetry (1982), Jane Austen - Mansfield Park (1988), Victorian Poetry: Poetry, Poetics and Politics (1993), Jane Austen - Sense and Sensibility (1994), Nineteenth Century Women Poets: An Oxford Anthology (co-ed, 1996); contrib to various other books incl: Victorian Poetry (1968), Critical Essays on George Eliot (1970), Augustan Worlds (1978), The Oxford Literary Review (1981), Women Reading Women's Writing (1987), Dickens and Other Victorians (1988), Textuality and Sexuality (1993); contrib reviews to various jls incl: Women's Review 1986, Times Literary Supplements 1986–94; *Recreations* travel, drawing, writing; *Style*— Prof Isobel Armstrong; ✉ 15 Furzedown Rd, Highfield, Southampton SO2 1PN; 36 Jenner House, Hunter Street, London WC1; Department of English, Birkbeck College, Malet St, London WC1E 7HX (☎ 0171 631 6070, fax 0171 631 6072)

ARMSTRONG, Dr James Hodgson; OBE (1996); s of John James Armstrong (d 1958), of Carlisle, Cumbria, and Margaret Eleanor, *née* Hodgson (d 1959); *b* 11 May 1926; *Educ* Carlisle GS, Univ of Glasgow (BSc); *m* 18 March 1950, Marjorie, da of Allan Victor Cartner (d 1960); 1 s (Hugh b 1954 d 1994), 1 da (Jane b 1951); *Career* engr; Duff and Geddes consulting engrs Edinburgh 1946–49, Rendel Palmer and Tritton 1949–54 (Scotland, Tyneside and London), specialist geotechnical engr Soil Mechanics Ltd London 1954–60, Harris and Sutherland conslts 1960–63, ptnr Building Design Partnership London 1966–89 (joined 1963); visiting prof: Cooper Union Coll NY 1978–82, Kingston Univ (formerly Kingston Poly) 1983–, Queen's Univ Belfast 1988, Univ of Leeds 1987–93; external examiner: Univ of Herts 1985–88, Univ of Strathclyde 1989–94; past pres: IStructE 1990, Br Masonry Soc 1991; chm Bd of Tstees Euro Christian Industl Movement 1978–, chm of tstees and chm Devpt Ctee Higher Educn Fndn 1990–, govr St James's Schools Kensington; dep chm Tstees Partnership Awards 1990–, tstee Varanasi Educnl Tst 1989–, chm Tstees Maryport Heritage Tst 1990–; chm Design Matters Gp Royal Acad of Engrg; memb several professional/educnl ctees; Hon DEng Kingston Univ 1993; FEng 1990, FICE 1951, FIStructE 1951, MConsE, FASCE, FGS, FID, FRSA; *Recreations* philosophy, reading, walking, photography; *Clubs* Reform; *Style—* Dr James Armstrong, OBE, FEng; ✉ 32 Langford Green, London SE5 8BX (☎ 0171 733 6808, fax 0171 326 5149)

ARMSTRONG, Rear Adm John Herbert Arthur James (Louis); s of John William Armstrong, of Frome, Somerset, and Marie Helen, *née* Clarke (d 1979); *b* 4 Sept 1946; *Educ* King's Sch Canterbury, BRNC Dartmouth, Magdalen Coll Oxford (MA Law); *m* 7 April 1973 (sep), Marjorie Anne (Darjie), *née* Corbett; 1 s (Mark b 21 Feb 1976), 1 da (Mandy b 10 June 1978); *Career* served Royal Navy 1964–; serv at sea in HM Ships Fife, Intrepid, Zulu, Illustrious and HM Yacht Britannia (also various staff, legal and admin posts ashore) 1970–87, called to the Bar Middle Temple 1976, seconded to Cabinet Office (Oversea and Def Secretariat) 1987–89, dep dir Naval Operational Requirements MOD 1989–91, RCDS 1992, dir Naval Manpower Planning 1993, dir Corp Programming Naval Personnel 1994, cmdt RN Staff Coll Greenwich 1994–95, Sr Naval Directing Staff RCDS 1996–; *Recreations* music (choral singing), the arts, tennis, skiing, parties; *Style—* Rear Adm Louis Armstrong; ✉ Royal College of Defence Studies, Seaford House, 37 Belgrave Square, London SW1X 8NS (☎ 0171 915 4834, fax 0171 915 4999)

ARMSTRONG, Karen Andersen; da of John Oliver Seymour Armstrong (d 1975), and Eileen Hastings, *née* McHale; *b* 14 Nov 1944; *Educ* Convent of the Holy Child Jesus Edgbaston Birmingham, St Anne's Coll Oxford (MA, MLitt, Violet Vaughan Morgan prize); *Career* writer and broadcaster; Soc of the Holy Child Jesus (RC teaching order of nuns) 1962–69, tutorial res fell Bedford Coll London 1973–76, head of English James Allen's Girls' Sch Dulwich 1976–82, freelance writer and bdcaster 1982–; winner Calamus Fndn Annual Award 1991; *TV* work incl: The First Christian (six part documentary on St Paul) 1984, Varieties of Religious Experience (interview series) 1984, Tongues of Fire (interview series) 1985; *Books* Through the Narrow Gate (1981), Beginning the World (1983), The First Christian (1983), Tongues of Fire (1985), The Gospel According to Woman (1986), Holy War - The Crusades and their Impact on Today's World (1988), Muhammed - A Western Attempt to Understand Islam (1991), A History of God (1993), The End of Silence - Women and Priesthood (1993), A History of Jerusalem: One City, Three Faiths (1996), In the Beginning - A New Interpretation of Genesis (1996); *Recreations* music, theatre, fiction, travel; *Style—* Ms Karen Armstrong; ✉ c/o Felicity Bryan, 2A North Parade, Banbury Road, Oxford OX2 6PE (☎ 01865 513816, fax 01865 310055)

ARMSTRONG, Prof Peter; s of Alexander Armstrong, of London, and Ada, *née* Lapidas (d 1963); *b* 31 Aug 1940; *Educ* Marylebone GS, Middx Hosp Med Sch (MB BS); *m* Carole Jennifer Armstrong; 1 da (Natasha Janine b 23 Nov 1972), 2 s (Damon Oliver b 17 Oct 1971 d 1972, Jethro Karl b 22 Feb 1974); *Career* house physician Middx Hosp 1963, house surgn Kettering General Hosp 1964; sr registrar in radiology: Middx Hosp 1965–68 (registrar 1964–65), Guy's Hosp 1968–70; conslt in radiology KCH 1970–77, prof and vice chm Univ of Virginia Hosp 1981–89 (assoc prof 1977–81), prof of radiology and Mercer chair of diagnostic radiology Bart's 1989–; RCR: warden clinical radiology 1994–, George Simon lectr 1993; ed Clinical Radiology 1990–94; Robley Dunglison Prize Univ of Virginia Med Sch 1983 and 1984; memb: Br Inst of Radiology 1966, RSM 1984; FRCR 1968; *Books* Diagnostic Imaging, Critical Problems in Diagnostic Radiology, Imaging of Diseases of the Chest, Diagnostic Radiology in Surgical Practise; *Recreations* reading, theatre, chess, collecting art; *Clubs* Shadow's Radiology; *Style—* Prof Peter Armstrong; ✉ Academic Department of Radiology, St Bartholomew's Hospital, London EC1A 7BE (☎ 0171 601 8864, fax 0171 601 8868)

ARMSTRONG, Robert Walter; s of Frederick Lakin Armstrong (d 1981), of Newmarket, and Maureen, *née* Greenwood (d 1979); *b* 15 Jan 1944; *Educ* Kings Mead, Seaford, Uppingham; *m* 1, 5 Nov 1968 (m dis), Elizabeth, da of Marcus Marsh; m 2, 21 April 1979, Mary Anne (d 1989), da of Maj David Charles Innes-Kerr (d 1957); m 3, 18 Nov 1989, Jane Robinson, da of John Roberts; *Career* racehorse trainer; best horses trained: Maroof, Moorestyle, Never So Bold, Shady Heights, Mujtahid, Be My Native; big races won: Prix du Moulin (Longchamp), July Cup (twice, Newmarket), Prix de la Forêt (twice, Longchamp), Coronation Cup (Epsom), Prix de l'Abbaye (Longchamp), Premio Roma (Rome), Vernons Sprint (Haydock), Lockinge (Newbury), Ribbesdale (Royal Ascot), Great Voltigeur Stakes (York), Gimcrack (York), July Stakes (Goodwood), International Stakes (York), Jersey Stakes (Royal Ascot), Diadem Stakes (Ascot), St Simon Stakes (Newbury), Yorkshire Cup (York), Prix Maurice de Gheest (Deauville), Queen Elizabeth II Stakes (Ascot); *Recreations* tennis, travel, music, arts, flying, motor racing; *Style—* Robert Armstrong, Esq; ✉ St Gatien, Newmarket, Suffolk CB8 8HJ (☎ 01638 663333)

ARMSTRONG, William O'Malley; s of Brig Alfred Elliott Armstrong, OBE, MC (d 1956), and Maeve Josephine Armstrong (d 1987); *b* 9 Nov 1938; *Educ* Worth Priory, Downside, Merton Coll Oxford (sr exhibitioner, MA); *m* 22 May 1965, Clare Theresa, da of Bernard Collins, CBE (d 1989), of Tonbridge, Kent; 1 s (Rowland Constantine O'Malley b 1966), 1 da (Florian Cloud de Bouneviale b 1971); *Career* ed: Knowledge 1963–65, Purnell's History of the Twentieth Century 1966–68; md: Sidgwick & Jackson 1971–96, Trusthouse Forte Publishing 1982–86; dir Pan Macmillan 1989–96; Macmillan General Books: non-fiction publisher 1994–96, assoc publisher 1996–; vice chair Islington MIND; *Recreations* tennis; *Clubs* Garrick; *Style—* William Armstrong, Esq; ✉ Macmillan General Books, 25 Eccleston Place, London SW1W 9NF (☎ 0171 373 6070, fax 0171 370 0746, telex 917466)

ARMSTRONG OF ILMINSTER, Baron (Life Peer UK 1988), of Ashill, Co Somerset; Sir Robert Temple Armstrong; GCB (1983, KCB 1978, CB 1974), CVO (1975); s of Sir Thomas (Henry Wait) Armstrong (d 1994), and Hester Muriel, *née* Draper (d 1982); *b* 30 March 1927; *Educ* Eton, Ch Ch Oxford; *m* 1953 (m dis 1985), Serena Mary Benedicta (d 1994), er da of Sir Roger James Ferguson Chance, 3 Bt, MC; 2 da (Hon Jane Orlanda b 1954, Hon Teresa Brigid b 1957); m 2, 1985, (Mary) Patricia, o da of Charles Cyril Carlow (d 1957); *Career* asst sec: Cabinet Office 1964–66, Treasury 1967–68; under sec Treasury 1968–70, princ private sec to PM 1970–75, dep under sec Home Office 1975–77, perm under sec 1977–79, sec of the Cabinet 1979–87, head Home Civil Service 1981–87; chm Bd of Tstees V & A 1988–, memb Bd of Dirs Royal Opera House Covent Garden 1988–93 (sec 1968–87); chm: Biotechnology Investments Ltd 1989–, Bristol and West Building Society 1993– (non-exec dir 1988–); non-exec dir: BAT Industries plc 1988–, NM Rothschild and Sons Ltd 1988–, RTZ Corporation plc 1988– (non-exec dir CRA Ltd Dec 1995–), Shell Transport and Trading plc 1988–, Inchcape plc 1988–95, Lucas Industries plc 1989–92, Carlton Television Ltd 1991–95; chllr Univ of Hull 1994–; Liveryman Salters' Co 1983 (hon memb 1996); fell Eton Coll 1979–94; hon student Ch Ch Oxford 1985, Rhodes tstee 1975, hon fell Royal Acad of Music 1985; hon bencher Inner Temple 1986; Hon LLD Univ of Hull 1994; *Recreations* music; *Clubs* Athenaeum, Brooks's; *Style—* The Rt Hon the Lord Armstrong of Ilminster, GCB, CVO; ✉ House of Lords, Westminster, London SW1A 0PW

ARMYTAGE, Capt David George; CBE (1981); s of Rear Adm Reginald William Armytage, GC, CBE (d 1984), and Sylvia Beatrice, *née* Staveley (d 1996); cous and hp of Sir Martin Armytage, 9 Bt, *qv*; *b* 4 Sept 1929; *Educ* RNC Dartmouth; *m* 3 April 1954, Countess Antonia Cosima, er da of Count Cosimo Diodono de Bosdari, and his w Enid, o da of Lt-Col Sir Peter Carlaw Walker, 2 Bt; 2 s (Hugh b 1955, Charles b 1962), 1 da (Davina b 1956); *Career* RN: cmmnd Motor Torpedo Boats 1952–53, cmdg HMS Minerva 1968–70, Def Policy Staff 1970–72, Naval Asst to 1 Sea Lord 1972–74, Int Mil Staff Brussels 1975–76, cmd HMS Scylla 1976 and HMS Jupiter 1977, Capt 7 Frigate Sqdn 1976–77, dep dir Naval Warfare 1977–79, Cdre cmdg Standing Naval Force Atlantic 1980–81; ADC to HM The Queen 1981, sec gen Br Diabetic Assoc 1981–91, vice pres SSAFA Wilts; *Recreations* sailing, shooting; *Clubs* Oriental, Royal Naval Sailing Association, Royal Channel Island Yacht; *Style—* Capt David Armytage, CBE, RN; ✉ Sharcott Manor, Pewsey, Wilts SN9 5PA

ARMYTAGE, Sir (John) Martin; 9 Bt (GB 1738), of Kirklees, Yorkshire; s of Capt Sir John Lionel Armytage, 8 Bt (d 1983), and Evelyn Mary Jessamine, *née* Fox; *b* 26 Feb 1933; *Educ* Eton, Worcester Coll Oxford; *Heir* cousin, Capt David George Armytage, CBE, RN, *qv*; *Clubs* Naval and Military; *Style—* Sir Martin Armytage, Bt; ✉ Kirklees Park, Brighouse, Yorkshire; Halewell, Withington, Cheltenham, Glos GL54 4BN

ARNANDER, Christopher James Folke; s of Per Erik Folke Arnander (d 1933), and Cynthia Anne, *née* Lindsay; *b* 22 Dec 1932; *Educ* Harrow Sch, Oriel Coll Oxford (MA); *m* 7 April 1961, Pamela Primrose, da of David McKenna, CBE; 3 s (Conrad b 1963, Michael b 1964, Magnus b 1970), 1 da (Katharine b 1967); *Career* lectr Univ of Minnesota (USA) 1956–57, Hill Samuel Merchant Bankers 1958–65, Williams & Glyn's Bank 1965–73 (dir 1970), financial exec in Kuwait 1973–79, chief advsr Riyad Bank Saudi Arabia 1979–85, dir Barclays de Zoete Wedd 1985–90, advsr Barclays Bank 1991–92; dir: Record Treasury Management 1993–, Capital Trust 1991–96, Shirescot 1992–; memb: Glyndebourne Arts Tst 1964–73 (memb Cncl 1973–), cncllr Royal Coll of Music 1986–96 (FRCM 1990), treas Nat Assoc for Care & Resettlement of Offenders (NACRO) 1967–73; *Recreations* music, sports, reading, travel; *Style—* Christopher Arnander, Esq; ✉ 6 Prince Edward Mansions, Hereford Road, London W2 4WB (☎ 0171 229 3993, fax 0171 221 7520)

ARNELL, Richard Anthony Sayer; s of Richard Sayer Arnell (d 1952), and Hélène Marie Ray Scherf (d 1942); *b* 15 Sept 1917; *Educ* The Hall Hampstead, Univ Coll Sch, RCM; *m* 1992, Joan Cynthia Nita Heycock; 3 da from prev m (Jessie, Claudine, Jennifer); *Career* composer, conductor and impresario; princ lectr Trinity Coll of Music 1981–87 (teacher of composition 1949–81), music conslt BBC N American Serv 1943–46, lectr Roy Ballet Sch 1958–59, ed The Composer 1961–64; vice pres Composers' Guild of GB 1991 (chm 1965 and 1974–75); chm: Young Musicians' Symphony Orch Soc 1973–75, Tadcaster Civic Soc - Music and Arts 1988–91, Saxmundham Music and Arts 1992– (pres 1995–); visiting lectr (Fullbright Exchange) Bowdoin Coll Maine 1967–68, visiting prof Hofstra Univ NY 1968–70, music dir and bd memb London Int Film Sch 1971–80, music dir Ram Filming Ltd 1980–91, dir Organic Sounds Ltd 1982–84, Composer of the Year 1966 (Music Teachers' Assoc award), Tadcaster Town Cncl Merit Award 1991; compositions include: 6 symphonies, 2 concertos for violin, concerto for harpsichord, 2 concertos for piano, 6 string quartets, 2 quintets, piano trio, piano works, songs, cantatas, organ works, music for string orchestra, wind ensembles, brass ensembles, song cycles, electronic music, music theatre; opera: Love in Transit, Moonflowers; puppet operetta: Petrified Princess; ballet scores: Punch and the Child for Ballet Soc NY 1947, Harlequin in April Sadler's Wells Theatre Ballet 1951, The Great Detective for Sadler's Wells Theatre Ballet 1953, The Angels for Royal Sadler's Wells Theatre Ballet 1957, Giselle (Adam) reorchestrated for Ballet Rambert 1965; film scores: The Land 1941, The Third Secret 1963, The Visit 1964, The Man Outside 1966, Topsail Schooner 1966, Bequest for a Village 1969, Second Best 1972, Stained Glass 1973, Wires over the Border 1974, Black Panther 1977, Antagonist 1980, Dilemma 1981, Toulouse Lautrec 1984, Light of the World 1990; other works: Symphonic Portrait Lord Byron for Sir Thomas Beecham 1953, Landscapes and Figures for Sir Thomas Beecham 1956, Robert Flaherty Impression for Radio Eireann 1960, Musica Pacifica for Edward Benjamin 1963, Festival Flourish for Salvation Army 1965, 2nd piano concerto for RPO 1967, Overture Food of Love for Portland Symphony Orch 1968, My Lady Green Sleeves for Hofstra Univ 1968, Nocturne Prague 1968, I Think of All Soft Limbs for Canadian Broadcasting Corp 1971, Astronaut One 1973, Life Boat Voluntary for RNLI 1974, Call for LPO 1982, Ode to Beecham for RPO 1986, Xanadu for Harlow Choral Society 1992–93, Fanfare for a Lifeboat for RNLI 1994; Hon FTCL; *Clubs* Savage; *Style—* Richard Arnell, Esq; ✉ Benhall Lodge, Benhall, Suffolk IP17 1JD

ARNISON, Val (Mrs Arthur Brittenden); da of Thomas Arnison, of Wargrave, Berks, and Vera Arnison, *née* Christian, of Woodstock, Oxon; *b* 30 Aug 1940; *Educ* Lowther Coll Abergele N Wales; *m* 24 Oct 1975, (Charles) Arthur Brittenden, *qv*, s of Tom Edwin Brittenden (d 1926); *Career* press and PR offr ICI Ltd 1970–79, asst vice pres and dir PR AMI Health Care Ltd 1982–87, assoc dir Countrywide Communications 1988–91, independent PR conslt 1991–; pres Assoc of Women in PR 1978–79 (memb 1975–), exec chm Women of the Year Luncheon 1987–92 (vice pres 1992–); non-exec dir: NHS Trust Devpt Bd The Horton Gen Hosp Banbury Oxon 1991–92, The Horton Gen Hosp NHS Tst 1992–; MIPR; *Recreations* gardening, reading, music, needlepoint; *Clubs* New Cavendish, RSM; *Style—* Miss Val Arnison; ✉ 22 Park St, Woodstock, Oxfordshire OX20 1SP (☎ 01993 813545, fax 01993 813556)

ARNOLD, Bruce; *b* 1936; *Educ* Kingham Hill Sch, Trinity Coll Dublin (BA); *m*; 3 c; *Career* journalist 1960s: The Irish Times, The Irish Press, The Sunday Independent, Hibernia National Review; corr The Guardian 1962–68; Irish Independent: political commentator and parly corr 1972–86, London ed 1986–87, literary ed and art critic 1987–; FRSL 1994; *Novels* A Singer at the Wedding, The Song of the Nightingale, The Muted Swan, Running to Paradise; *Non-Fiction* A Concise History of Irish Art, Orpen: Mirror to an Age, What Kind of Country, Margaret Thatcher: A Study in Power, An Art Atlas of Britain and Ireland (1991), William Orpen (1991), The Scandal of Ulysses (1991), Mainie Jellett and the Modern Movement in Ireland (1991), Haughey: His Life and Unlucky Deeds (1993); *Style—* Bruce Arnold, Esq, FRSL; ✉ c/o Giles Gordon, Curtis Brown Group Ltd, 28–29 Haymarket, London SW1Y 4SP (☎ 0171 396 6600, fax 0171 396 0110)

ARNOLD, Dr David; s of Ernest Edward, (d 1984), and Teresa Eliza Mary, *née* Grimsdell; *b* 18 June 1943; *Educ* St Ignatius Coll, Wandsworth Tech Coll (HNC), South Bank Poly, Univ of Bristol (MSc), Cranfield Inst (PhD); *m* 28 Sept 1963, Jean Selina, da of Charles Owen George Brodie; 2 da (Melanie b 8 March 1967, Louise b 14 Oct 1979), 1 s (Mark b 19 April 1969); *Career* trainee engr 1962, trainee Edward A Pearce and Partners Consulting Engrs 1962–66; Troup Bywaters and Anders Consulting Engrs: intermediate engr 1962–73, sr ptnr 1991– (ptnr 1973); co-fndr CIBSE Thermal Storage

Gp (formerly chm); chm: Strategy 2000 Ctee, CLIMA 2000 Exec Ctee 1989–93, NES 1993– (pres 1994–95); memb ASHRAE (Ed Bd ASHRAE Jl, Publishing Cncl 1993–); Liveryman Worshipful Co of Fanmakers; CEng, FCIBSE (memb 1969–, chm Meetings Ctee 1980–85, memb Cncl 1984–87), MIMechE 1970, FEng 1993; author of numerous tech papers; *Recreations* photography, jogging, cycling; *Clubs* Royal Photographic Soc, Sonning Working Men's; *Style—* Dr David Arnold, FEng; ✉ Troup, Bywaters and Anders, 51 Praed Street, Paddington, London W2 1NR (☎ 0171 262 1041, fax 0171 262 1041)

ARNOLD, David Philip James; s of Philip Arthur Arnold (d 1988), and Christine May, *née* Rowe; *b* 13 Aug 1955; *Educ* Merchant Taylors', Univ of Exeter; *m* 19 Aug 1978, Carol Alice, da of Arthur George Edward Williams (d 1973); 2 da (Kirsten b 7 Feb 1986, Lucy b 4 May 1993), 1 s (James b 7 July 1995); *Career* CA; ptnr Ernst & Young 1988–; Freeman City of London 1976, Liveryman Worshipful Co of Fishmongers 1982; FCA 1979; *Recreations* golf, squash; *Clubs* Royal Automobile; *Style—* David Arnold, Esq; ✉ Ernst & Young, Rolls House, 7 Rolls Buildings, Fetter Lane, London EC4A 1NH (☎ 0171 931 1913, fax 0171 931 2214)

ARNOLD, Graham; s of Charles Arnold (d 1971), of Brighton, E Sussex, and Mildred, *née* King (d 1963); *b* 24 May 1932; *Educ* Beckenham Sch of Art, RCA; *m* 1961, Ann, da of Prof Edmund Telfer; *Career* painter in residence Digswell House Herts 1960–63, sr lectr in fine art Kingston Poly 1963–72; visiting tutor in fine art: Westminster Sch 1961–65, The Royal Acad Schs 1966–71; fndr memb The Brotherhood of Ruralists (with Ann Arnold, David Inshaw, Peter Blake, Jann Howarth, Graham Ovenden, and Annie Ovenden) 1975; work in public collections incl: Royal Acad of Arts, Bristol City Art Gallery, Contemporary Arts Soc, Univ of Liverpool Gallery, Nat Gallery of NZ, The Br Museum, Southport Museum and Art Gallery; RCA travelling scholarship to Italy 1958–60, Univ of London scholarship for painting 1973, Chichester Nat Art Exhibition prize for painting 1975; illustrations for numerous books incl: Round about a Great Estate, The Epic of Gilgamesh; *Exhibitions* Royal Acad Summer Exhibition 1950, 1959 and 1976, Festival Gallery Bath 1977, The Fine Arts Soc Edinburgh 1977, Doncaster Museum and Art Gallery 1977, Southampton Univ Art Gallery 1977, Bodmin Fine Arts Cornwall 1978, Southampton City Art Gallery 1978, Upottery Arts Festival Devon 1978, Gainsborough's House Museum Sudbury 1979, Charleston Manor Festival Sussex 1979, Wren Library Trinity Coll Cambridge 1980, Bristol City Art Gallery 1980, Brotherhood of Ruralists touring exhibition supported by the Arts Cncl and the Eng Tourist Bd (Arnolfini Gallery Bristol, Birmingham City Art Gallery, Third Eye Centre Glasgow and Camden Arts Centre London) 1981, The Definitive Nude (Ruralist project shown at Tate Gallery as part of Peter Blake exhibition) 1983, Salute to Elgar (The David Paul Gallery Chichester) 1984, The Continuing Tradition (touring David Paul Gallery Chichester, Tunbridge Wells Art Gallery, Devizes Museum and Art Gallery, The Fine Art Soc Glasgow and Piccadilly Gallery London) 1985–86, The Secret Garden (touring) 1989, Alice (touring Bearnes Rainbow Torquay, Machynlleth Wales, Plymouth Art Gallery, Christchurch Gallery Oxford and Piccadilly Gallery London) 1990, The Power of the Image (Berlin) 1996; solo incl: Brighton Art Gallery (with Ann Arnold) 1971, Festival Gallery Bath 1976, George Gallery Bristol 1978, Brillig Art Centre Bath 1979, Festival Gallery Bath 1980, Bodmin Gallery 1981, David Paul Gallery Chichester 1982, Piccadilly Gallery London 1983, 1986, 1988 (with Ann Arnold), 1991, 1993 and 1995, major retrospective Museum of Modern Art Wales Machynlleth 1992; *Recreations* beekeeping, music, poetry and writing, astronomy, being in deep countryside, gardening; *Style—* Graham Arnold, Esq; ✉ The Piccadilly Gallery, 16 Cork St, London W1 (☎ 0171 629 2875)

ARNOLD, Jacques Arnold; MP (C) Gravesham (majority 5,493); s of Samuel Arnold (d 1985), and Eugenie, *née* Patentine; *b* 27 Aug 1947; *Educ* sch in Brazil, LSE (BSc Econ); *m* 22 May 1976, Patricia Anne, da of Dennis Maunder, of Windsor, Berks; 1 s (David Samuel b 1984), 2 da (Hazel Jane b 1979, Philippa Rachel b 1981); *Career* asst gp rep Midland Bank Brazil 1976–78, regnl dir Thomas Cook Gp 1978–84, asst trade fin dir Midland Bank 1984–85, dir American Express Europe Ltd 1985–87; Parly candidate (C) Coventry SE 1983, MP (C) Gravesham 1987–; memb Educn, Sci and Arts Select Ctee 1989–92; sec: Cons Backbench Foreign and Cwlth Affrs Ctee 1990–92 and 1996–, Br-Latin American Parly Gp 1987–; chm: Br-Brazil Parly Gp 1992–, Br-Portuguese Parly Gp 1994–; vice chm Cons Backbench: Constitutional Affrs Ctee 1996–, Pty Orgn Ctee 1996–; PPS to David Maclean Min of State for the Environment & Countryside 1992–93, Min of State Home Office 1993–95; tstee Environment Fndn 1989–; Grand Official Order of the Southern Cross (Brazil) 1993; co cncllr Oundle 1981–85; *Recreations* family life, gardening, philately; *Clubs* Carlton; *Style—* Jacques A Arnold, Esq, MP; ✉ Fairlawn, 243 London Rd, West Malling, Kent ME19 5AD (☎ 01732 848573); House of Commons, London SW1A 0AA (☎ 0171 219 4150, fax 0171 219 2942)

ARNOLD, Prof John André; s of Capt André Eugene Arnold (d 1974), and May, *née* Vickers (d 1977); *b* 30 April 1944; *Educ* Haberdashers' Aske's, LSE (MSc); *children* 2 da (Kate Lynne b 1976, Mandy Louise b 1978); *Career* teaching fell Mgmnt Studies LSE 1967–69, lectr in accounting Univ of Kent 1969–71; Univ of Manchester: lectr in accounting 1971–75, sr lectr 1975–77, prof of accounting 1977–86, KPMG Peat Marwick prof of accounting 1986–94, dean Faculty of Econ and Social Studies 1987–89, pro-vice chllr 1990–94, dir Manchester Business Sch and KPMG prof of accounting and fin mgmnt 1994–; visiting prof Univ of Washington USA 1981–82; dir of research ICAEW 1987–94; pres Manchester Soc of CAs 1991–92 (vice pres 1989–90, dep pres 1990–91); Hon MA (Econ) Univ of Manchester; FCA 1967; *Books* Pricing and Output Decisions (1973), Topics in Management Accounting (1980), Accounting for Management Decisions (1983, 3 edn 1996), Management Accounting Research and Practice (1983), Financial Accounting (1985, 2 edn 1994), Management Accounting: British Case Studies (1987), Management Accounting: Expanding the Horizons (1987), Financial Reporting: The Way Forward (1990), The Future Shape of Financial Reports (1991); *Recreations* squash, opera; *Clubs* Marple Cricket & Squash; *Style—* Prof John Arnold; ✉ Manchester Business School, Booth Street West, Manchester M15 6PB (☎ 0161 275 6413, fax 0161 275 6585)

ARNOLD, Rt Hon Sir John Lewis; kt (1972), PC (1979); s of Alfred Lewis Arnold (d 1917), of London, and E K Arnold; *b* 6 May 1915; *Educ* Wellington; *m* 1, 1940 (m dis 1963), Alice Margaret Dorothea, da of George Cookson (d 1949), of Thursley, Surrey; 1 s, 1 da; m 2, 1963, Florence Elizabeth, da of late H M Hague, of Montreal; 1 s, 2 da; *Career* served WWII Army (despatches 1945); called to the Bar Middle Temple 1937, QC 1958, chm Bar Cncl 1970–72, High Court judge (Family Div) 1972–88, pres Family Div 1979–88, treas Middle Temple 1982; Hon DLitt Univ of Reading 1982; *Recreations* cricket, travel; *Style—* The Rt Hon Sir John Arnold; ✉ Villa La Pergola, Via B Bonci 14, Vagliagli 53010, Siena, Italy (☎ 00 39 577 322728)

ARNOLD, Very Rev John Robert; s of John Stanley Arnold (d 1977), of Rowan Cottage, Laleham, Middx, and Ivy, *née* Ireland (d 1981); *b* 1 Nov 1933; *Educ* Christ's Hosp, Sidney Sussex Coll Cambridge (MA), Westcott House Theol Coll; *m* 29 Sept 1963, Livia Anneliese, da of Capt Ernst Konrad Franke (d 1944), of Eisleben, Sachsen-Anhalt, Germany; 1 s (Matthew b 1965), 2 da (Frances b 1964, Miriam b 1972); *Career* Nat Serv Intelligence 1952–54, 2 Lt Civil Serv Cmmn Serv Interpreter Cert 1954; ordained: deacon 1960, priest 1961; curate Holy Trinity Millhouses Sheffield 1960–63, Sir Henry Stephenson fell Univ of Sheffield 1962–63, chaplain and lectr Univ of Southampton 1963–72, sec Bd for Mission and Unity 1972–78; dean of: Rochester 1978–89, Durham 1989–; memb Central Ctee Conf of Euro Churches 1986–, dir First Conference Estate plc 1978–; chm of Govrs Durham Bow and Chorister Schs 1989–, memb Cncl Univ of Durham 1989–, pres Conf of Euro Churches 1993; Order of St Vladimir (Russian Orthodox Church) 1974, Offr's Cross OM (FRG) 1991; *Books* The Eucharistic Liturgy of Taizé (trans, 1962), Strategist for the Spirit (contrib, 1985), Rochester Cathedral (1987); *Recreations* music, literature; *Clubs* Cwlth Tst, Christ's Hosp; *Style—* The Very Rev John Arnold; ✉ The Deanery, Durham DH1 3EQ (☎ 0191 384 7500, fax 0191 386 4267)

ARNOLD, Malcolm; s of Colin William Arnold (d 1988), of Northwich, Cheshire, and Jane, *née* Powell; *b* 4 April 1940; *Educ* Verdin GS Winsford Cheshire, Loughborough Univ; *m* Madelyn, *née* Morrissey; 1 s (Andrew b 20 Jan 1966), 1 da (Helen b 26 Sept 1964); *Career* athletics coach; dir of coaching Uganda 1968–72, nat athletics coach Wales 1974–94, hd of coaching and devpt British Athletic Federation 1994–; coach to Olympic teams: Uganda 1968 and 1972, GB and NI 1980, 1984, 1988 and 1992; head coach GB and NI Olympic Team 1996; coach to: John Akii-Bua (Olympic 400m hurdles champion 1972, world record holder 1972–76), Colin Jackson (world record holder 110m hurdles), Kay Morley (Cwlth 100m hurdles champion 1990), Mark McKoy (Olympic 110m hurdles Gold medal 1992), numerous Br int athletes; *Books* author of six athletics books; *Recreations* rally driver of enthusiasm but no distinction; *Style—* Malcolm Arnold, Esq; ✉ 22 Sundbury Rise, Northfield, Birmingham B31 2EZ; c/o British Athletic Federation, 225a Bristol Road, Edgbaston, Birmingham B5 7UB (☎ 0121 440 5000)

ARNOLD, Sir Malcolm Henry; kt (1993), CBE (1970); s of William and Annie Arnold, of Northampton; *b* 21 Oct 1921; *Educ* RCM; *m* 1, 1942, Sheila, da of Herbert Nicholson; 1 s, 1 da; m 2, 1963, Isobel Katherine (d 1992), da of David Inglis Wood Gray; 1 s; *Career* composer; princ trumpet London Philharmonic Orchestra 1942–44 and 1946–48, served Army 1944–45; Ivor Novello Award for music for Inn of Sixth Happiness 1952, awarded Oscar for music for film Bridge on the River Kwai 1957, bard of the Cornish Gorsedd 1969, Ivor Novello Award for outstanding servs to Br music 1986, Wavendon All Music Composer of the Year 1987; Hon Freeman Borough of Northampton 1989; Hon DMus: Univ of Exeter 1969, Univ of Durham 1982, Univ of Leicester 1984; Hon Dr Arts and Humane Letters Miami Univ Ohio 1990; Hon RAM; Liveryman Worshipful Co of Musicians; FRCM 1983; *Works* symphonies: No 1 1949, No 2 1953, No 3 1957, No 4 1960, No 5 1961, No 6 1967, No 7 1973, No 8 1978, No 9 1986, Symphony for Brass Instruments 1979; overtures: Beckus the Dandipratt 1943, Tam O'Shanter 1955, Peterloo 1967; other compositions: eighteen concertos, five ballets, two one-act operas, two string quartets, two brass quintets, vocal, choral and chamber music; Hon DMus Trinity Coll London 1991; *Recreations* reading, foreign travel; *Clubs* Savile; *Style—* Sir Malcolm Arnold, CBE; ✉ 26 Springfields, Attleborough, Norfolk NR17 2PA (☎/fax 01953 455420)

ARNOLD, Michael; s of Dr Alan George Arnold (d 1990), and Kathleen, *née* McGuirk (d 1947); *b* 16 Sept 1947; *Educ* Royal Wolverhampton Sch, Univ of Reading (BSc); *m* 8 April 1972, Pauline Ann, da of Berwyn Elvet Pritchard; 2 s (David Paul b 4 July 1975, Stuart Michael b 12 May 1978); *Career* actuarial trainee Prudential Assurance Co Ltd 1969–71; Hymans Robertson: joined as actuarial trainee 1971, ptnr 1974, currently sr ptnr; memb Cncl Inst of Actuaries; memb Worshipful Co of Actuaries 1985; FIA 1973; *Recreations* golf, travel; *Clubs* City Livery, Kingswood Golf, Walton Heath Golf, RAC; *Style—* Michael Arnold, Esq; ✉ Hymans Robertson, 190 Fleet St, London EC4A 2AH (☎ 0171 831 9561, fax 0171 831 6800)

ARNOLD, Michael John; s of Thomas Henry Arnold (d 1991), and Cecily May Arnold; *b* 1 April 1935; *m* 21 Jan 1989, Jane, *née* Benson; *Career* Nat Serv Lt RA 1958–59; Hilton Sharpe & Clark 1951–57, qualified CA 1967, ptnr Arthur Young 1966–89 (joined 1960), chm AY Management Consultants 1973–83, nat dir Corporate Recovery and Insolvency 1975–89, sole practitioner (corp restructuring and recoveries) 1989–; dir Roux Restaurants 1987–; chm: Prelude Technology Holdings 1991–96, Luminar plc 1994–; court appointed receiver NUM 1984–86; hon treas Racehorse Owners' Assoc, memb Fin Ctee Br Horseracing Bd; FCA, FIMC, FIPA; *Recreations* horse racing, hunting, country; *Clubs* Turf; *Style—* Michael Arnold, Esq; ✉ Brockhill, Naunton, Cheltenham, Glos GL54 3AF (☎ 01451 850191, fax 01451 850199)

ARNOLD, Sheila May; da of John Millar Arnold (d 1949), and Mabel, *née* Walker (d 1951); *b* 24 May 1930; *Educ* RCSI (LPCP, LPCS); *m* 4 April 1955, Thomas Matthew Maguire, s of Philip Francis Maguire (d 1932); 2 da (Ailsa Catherine b 1965, Kim Caroline b 1970); *Career* house surgn and physician Richmond Hosp Dublin 1954–55; sr house surgn: Kent and Sussex Hosp 1956, Derbys Royal Infirmary 1957, Newcastle Royal Infirmary 1959; personal physician and surgn to Pres Kwame Nkruma Ghana Med Serv investigating deafness in village children 1959–62, St Mary Abotts Hosp London 1963, sr registrar Guy's and Lewisham Hosps 1970–73, sr conslt ENT surgn Frimley Park Hosp Surrey 1973–; memb: Royal Soc of Med, Regnl Med Advsy Ctee Br Soc of Otolaryngologists; LRCP, LRCS 1954, DLO 1961, FRCS 1973; *Publications* The Vulnerability of the Chorda Tympani Nerve & Middle Ear Disease (paper, 1973); *Recreations* badminton, skiing, swimming, foreign travel, squash; *Style—* Miss Sheila Arnold; ✉ Robin Hill, 18 Murdoch Rd, Wokingham, Berks RG11 2DE (☎ 0118 978 7027); Frimley Park Hospital, Portsmouth Rd, Frimley, Surrey GU16 5UJ (☎ 01276 692777)

ARNOLD, Simon Rory; s of Rory Watkin Williams Arnold (d 1950), and Rosemary Arnold (d 1948); *b* 10 Sept 1933; *Educ* Diocesan Coll S Africa; *m* 1960, Janet Linda, da of Peter J May (d 1980); 1 s (Guy Rory b 1964), 1 da (Clare Louise b 1963); *Career* Lt Duke of Wellington's Regt 1957–59; various directorships with Minet Holdings 1952–84 (dep chm and gp md 1982); Bain Clarkson Ltd (Bain Dawes plc until 1987): chief exec 1984–, chm 1986–94; dep chm Bain Hogg Group plc 1994–, dir Inchcape plc 1988–94; chm: Lloyd's Brokers Ctee 1986–92 (memb 1979–), British Insurance and Investment Brokers' Assoc 1994–; memb Cncl Lloyd's 1991–; memb Ct of Assts Worshipful Co of Insurers; *Recreations* tennis, golf, walking; *Clubs* Royal Ashdown Golf; *Style—* Simon R Arnold, Esq; ✉ Meadows, Ditchling Common, Ditchling, nr Hassocks, W Sussex BN6 8TN (☎ 01273 844246); Bain Hogg Group plc, Lloyds Chambers, 1 Portsoken Street, London E1 8DF (☎ 0171 680 4000, fax 0171 480 4007, telex 884633)

ARNOLD, Susan Hillary (Sue); da of Morny McHarg, and Marjorie James; *Educ* Elmhurst Ballet Sch Camberley, Trinity Coll Dublin (MA); *m* twice; 6 c; *Career* journalist: Lancashire Evening Telegraph Blackburn 1967–68, Evening Standard 1968–69, Tehran Jl 1969–70, The Observer 1970–; *Awards* commended Magazine Writer Br Press awards 1982, Magazine Writer of the Year 1983; *Books* Little Princes (1981), Curiouser & Curiouser (1984); *Recreations* Housewifery; *Clubs* Chelsea Arts; *Style—* Ms Sue Arnold; ✉ c/o The Observer, 119 Farringdon Road, London EC1R 3ER

ARNOLD, Sir Thomas Richard; kt (1990), MP (C) Hazel Grove (majority 929); s of Thomas Charles Arnold, OBE (d 1969), of London, and Helen, *née* Breen (later Mrs Cyril Daniels; d 1994); *b* 25 Jan 1947; *Educ* Bedales, Le Rosey, Pembroke Coll Oxford (MA); *m* 4 July 1984 (m dis 1993), Elizabeth Jane Mary, da of Capt Sir Henry Nicholas Nevile, KCVO, of Aubourn Hall, Lincoln, and wid of Robin Irwin Smithers; 1 da (Emily Minna Mary b 29 Dec 1986); *Career* theatre prodr and publisher; Parly candidate (C): Manchester Cheetham 1970, Hazel Grove Feb 1974; MP (C) Hazel Grove Oct 1974–; PPS to: Sec of State for NI 1979–81, Lord Privy Seal/FCO 1981–82; chm Treasy and Civil Serv Select Ctee 1994– (memb 1992–94); a vice chm Cons Pty 1983–92; Freeman City of London, Liveryman of Worshipful Co of Bakers; *Clubs* Carlton, RAC; *Style—* Sir Thomas Arnold, MP; ✉ House of Commons, London SW1A 0AA (☎ 0171 219 4096)

ARNOLD, Wallace; *see:* Brown, Craig Edward Moncrieff

ARNOLD-BAKER, Prof Charles; OBE (1966); s of Baron Albrecht von Blumenthal, and Alice Wilhelmine, *née* Hainsworth; *b* 25 June 1918; *Educ* Winchester, Magdalen Coll Oxford; *m* 1943, Edith, *née* Woods; 1 s, 1 da; *Career* served WWII Army Inf and War Office 1940–46; called to the Bar Inner Temple 1948; Admty Bar 1948–52, sec Nat Assoc of Local Cncls 1953–78, memb Royal Cmmn on Common Lands 1955–58; dep chm: Eastern Traffic Cmmrs 1978–90, E Midlands Traffic Cmmrs 1981–86; visiting prof City Univ 1983–93 (conslt lectr 1978–83); ed Road Law 1991–96; author and occasional broadcaster; King Haakon VII Freedom medal (Norway) 1946; *Books* Everyman's Dictionary of Dates (1954), Parish Administration (1958), New Law and Practice of Parish Administration (1966), The Five Thousand and the Power Tangle (1967), The Local Government Act 1972 (1973), The Local Government, Planning and Land Act 1980 (1981), Practical Law for Arts Administrators (1983, 2 edn 1992), The Five Thousand and the Living Constitution (1986), Local Council Administration (4 edn, 1995), Companion to British History (1996); *Recreations* travel; *Clubs* Oxford Union; *Style*— Prof Charles Arnold-Baker, OBE; ✉ Top Floor, 2 Paper Buildings, Inner Temple, London EC4Y 7ET (☎ 0171 353 3490)

ARNOTT, Sir Alexander John Maxwell; 6 Bt (UK) 1896, of Woodlands, St Anne, Shandon, Co Cork; s of Sir John Robert Alexander Arnott, 5 Bt (d 1981), and Ann Margaret, *née* Farrelly; *b* 18 Sept 1975; *Heir* bro, Andrew John Eric Arnott b 20 June 1978; *Style*— Sir Alexander Arnott, Bt

ARNOTT, Eric John; s of Capt Sir Robert Arnott, 4 Bt (d 1967), of Ounavarra, Lucan, Co Dublin, Ireland, and Cynthia Anita Amelia, *née* James (d 1948); *b* 12 June 1929; *Educ* Harrow, Trinity Coll Dublin (BA, MB BCh, BAO), Univ of London (DO); *m* 19 Nov 1960, Veronica Mary, da of Capt Arvid Langué Querfeld von der Seedeck (d 1986), of Hazel Bank, Sandy Lane, Hartley, Wintney, Hants; 2 s (Stephen John b 1962, Robert Lauriston John b 1971), 1 da (Tatiana Amelia b 1963); *Career* house offr Adelaide Hosp Dublin 1954–55, registrar Royal Victoria Eye and Ear Hosp Dublin 1956–57, resident offr (later sr resident offr) Moorfields Eye Hosp London 1959–61, sr registrar UCH 1962–65; conslt ophthalmologist: Royal Eye Hosp 1966–72, Charing Cross Hosp and Charing Cross Gp of Hosps 1967–94; hon conslt ophthalmologist Royal Masonic Hosp 1970–, reader Univ of London 1972–; pres and fndr Euro Soc for Phaco and Laser Surgery, pres Int Assoc of Ocular Surgeons 1994, former examiner Br Orthoptic Cncl; pioneer of phacoemulsification in Europe 1968–75, designer intraocular lens implants 1976–, pioneer of excimer laser for correction of refractive disorders of the eye 1991–; fndr and chm Arnott Tst and Gtr London Treasure Hunt; FRCS 1963; Hon FCOphth 1988; *Books* Emergency Surgery (jtly, 1977), Cataract Extraction and Lens Implantation (jtly, 1983), Phacoemulsification (contrib, 1988); *Recreations* swimming, golf, sailing; *Clubs* Kildare St (Dublin), Garrick; *Style*— Eric Arnott, Esq; ✉ Trottsford Farm, Headley, nr Bordon, Hampshire GU35 8TF (☎ 01420 472136, fax 01420 473477); 22a Harley Street, London W1N 2BP (☎ 0171 580 1074, fax 0171 255 1524)

ARNOTT, Prof (William) Geoffrey; s of Bertie Arnott (d 1975), of Bury, Lancs, and Edith May, *née* Smith (d 1982); *b* 17 Sept 1930; *Educ* Bury GS, Pembroke Coll Cambridge (MA, PhD); *m* 20 Aug 1955, Vera, da of Wilfrid Hodson (d 1934), of Greenmount, nr Bury, Lancashire; 3 da (Rosemary, Alison, Hilary); *Career* asst master Bristol GS 1952, asst lectr in Greek Bedford Coll Univ of London 1955–59, asst dir of examinations Civil Serv Cmmn 1959–60, asst lectr in classics Univ of Hull 1960–61; lectr in classics: Univ of Durham 1961–63, Univ of Newcastle upon Tyne 1963–66; sr lectr in classics Univ of Newcastle upon Tyne 1966–67, prof of Greek Univ of Leeds 1968–91 (now emeritus); memb Inst for Advanced Studies Princeton USA 1973, visiting foreign scholar Univ of British Columbia Vancouver 1982; visiting prof: Univ of Wellington NZ 1982, Univ of Alexandria Egypt 1983, Univ of Queensland 1987; visiting fell Gonville and Caius Coll Cambridge 1987–88; memb Classical Jls Bd 1970–92, govr St Peter's Sch York 1971–83, lectr for NADFAS 1979–, memb Editorial Bd of Texts and Commentaries Univs of London and Urbino 1980–, pres Leeds Birdwatchers' Club 1981–84; fell Italian Soc for Study of Classical Antiquity 1981; *Books* Menander's Dyskolos (translated, 1960), Menander Plautus Terence (1975), Menander vol I (1979), Alexis: A Commentary (1996), Menander vol II (1996); *Recreations* birdwatching, 19th century bird-painting, crosswords, photography; *Style*— Prof Geoffrey Arnott; ✉ 35 Arncliffe Road, Leeds LS16 9JT (☎ 0113 275 2751, fax 0113 233 6017, telex 556473 UNILDS G)

ARNOTT, Ian Emslie; s of Henry Arnott (d 1967), of Galashiels, and Margaret Hume Paton Emslie (d 1961); *b* 7 May 1929; *Educ* Galashiels Acad, Edinburgh Coll of Art (DA (Edin), Dip TP (Edin)); *m* 17 Sept 1955, Mildred Stella; 1 da (Gillian Elisabeth b 1958); *Career* Flying Offr RAF 1955–57; architect; chm Campbell & Arnott Architects 1963–94 (conslt 1994–); awards: Gold Medal for Architecture Royal Scot Acad, Civic Tst (5), Edinburgh Architectural Assoc (2); recent projects: Scot Fin Centre Castle Terrace Edinburgh, Maybury Business Technol Park Edinburgh, AEU HQ London; OStJ; ARSA, RIBA, ARIAS; *Recreations* walking, travel, music, reading, photography; *Clubs* New (Edinburgh); *Style*— Ian Arnott, Esq; ✉ The Rink, Gifford, East Lothian (☎ 01620 810278); Campbell & Arnott, Albany Lane, Edinburgh EH1 3QP (☎ 0131 557 1725, fax 0131 556 1199)

ARNOTT, John Michael Stewart; s of George Arnott (d 1970), of Kirriemuir, and Winifred Douglas, *née* Livingston; *b* 12 June 1933; *Educ* King Edward's Sch Birmingham, Peterhouse Cambridge (BA); *m* 2 Jan 1965, (Hazel) Lynne, da of Rev W E Gladstone-Millar, MC (d 1982), of Arbroath; 1 s (Martin b 1967), 1 da (Hilary b 1970); *Career* Pilot RAF 1952–54; BBC: studio mangr 1960, announcer 1961–67, producer 1967–85 (Sony Award 1985), ed and mangr Edinburgh 1985–90; vice chm Countryside Cmmn Scotland 1986–92 (memb 1982–92); chm: Isle of May Bird Observatory 1980–85, Fair Isle Bird Observatory Tst 1983–84; pres: Scottish Ornithologists' Club 1984–87, Scottish Arctic Club 1995–; memb: Ctee for Scot Nature Conservancy Cncl 1986–91, Nat Parks Review Panel Eng and Wales 1990–91, SE Regnl Bd Nature Conservancy Cncl for Scot 1991–92, SE Regnl Bd Scottish Natural Heritage 1992–95; *Recreations* ornithology, hill walking, arctic travel; *Style*— John Arnott, Esq; ✉ East Redford House, Redford Rd, Edinburgh EH13 0AS (☎ 0131 441 3567)

ARNOTT, Sir (William) Melville; kt (1971), TD (and Clasps 1944); s of Rev Henry Arnott (d 1952), of Edinburgh, and Jeanette Main Arnott; *b* 14 Jan 1909; *Educ* George Watson's Coll Edinburgh, Univ of Edinburgh (MB ChB, BSc, MD), MD (Birmingham) 1947; *m* 1938, Dorothy Eleanor, er da of George Frederick Seymour Hill, of Edinburgh; 1 s; *Career* 2 Lt RA 1929, TA 1929–39, served WWII as specialist physician (siege of Tobruk, despatches 1945), Lt-Col 1942; physician Utd Birmingham Hosps 1946–74, hon conslt physician Queen Elizabeth Hosp Birmingham 1974–; Univ of Birmingham: William Withering prof of med 1946–71, Br Heart Fndn prof of cardiology 1971–74, emeritus prof of med 1974–; Sims travelling prof 1957; sr vice pres and sr censor Royal Coll of Physicians London 1973–74, pres Br Lung Fndn 1984–87 (fndr memb); Hon Lt-Col RAMC; Hon DSc: Univ of Edinburgh 1975, Chinese Univ of Hong Kong 1983; Hon LLD: Rhodesia 1976, Univ of Dundee 1976; FRCP, FRCPEd, Hon FRCP(C), FRCPath, Hon FACP, FRSE 1971; *Recreations* travel; *Clubs* Naval and Military; *Style*— Sir Melville Arnott, TD, FRSE; ✉ Bushwood Court Flats, 32 St James's Road, Edgbaston, Birmingham B15 2NX (☎ 0121 440 2195)

ARNOTT, Prof Struther; CBE (1996); s of Charles McCann, and Christina Struthers; *b* 25 Sept 1934; *Educ* Hamilton Acad Lanarkshire, Univ of Glasgow (BSc, PhD); *m* 11 June 1970, Greta Maureen, da of James Reginald Edwards, of Dudley; 2 s; *Career* King's Coll London: res sci MRC Biophysics Unit, physics demonstrator 1960–67, dir postgrad studies in biophysics 1967–70; Purdue Univ Indiana USA: prof of biology 1970–86, head of bio scis 1980–86, vice pres for res and dean of Graduate Sch 1980–86; Univ of Oxford: sr visiting fell Jesus Coll 1980–81, Nuffield res fell Green Coll 1985–86; princ and vice-chllr Univ of St Andrews 1986–; Guggenheim Memorial fell 1985; govr Sedbergh Sch; Hon ScD St Andrews Laurenburg 1994; FRS 1985, FRSE 1988; *Recreations* birdwatching, botanizing; *Clubs* Athenaeum, Caledonian, Royal and Ancient (St Andrews); *Style*— Prof Struther Arnott, CBE, FRS, FRSE; ✉ 9 The Scores, St Andrews KY16 9AR (☎ 01334 472492); University of St Andrews, College Gate, North Street, St Andrews KY16 9AJ (☎ 01334 462551, fax 01334 462543)

ARONSTAM, Dr Anthony; s of Alfred Aronstam (d 1975), and Golda, *née* Kagan; *b* 27 May 1934; *Educ* S African Coll Sch, Univ of Cape Town (MB ChB), Univ of Southampton (DM); *m* 28 Feb 1967, Gillian Lesley, da of Leslie Ludlow Hawdon; 2 s (Jeremy b 1968, Benjamin b 1972), 1 da (Suzanne b 1969); *Career* lectr St George's Hosp Med Sch 1969–70, conslt haematologist Basingstoke 1970–, res fell Univ of Western Ontario 1976–77; memb: Paediatric Advsy Gp World Fedn of Haemophilia, Wessex Region AIDS Expert Advsy Ctee, N Hampshire Drug Abuse Liaison Ctee; chm: N Hampshire AIDS Working Pty, N Hampshire Pathology Care Gp; FRCPath 1981 (MRCPath 1969); *Books* Haemophilic Bleeding (1985); contrib: Br Journal of Haematology (1976 and 1981), Journal of Clinical Pathology (1977, 1978 and 1979), Practitioner (1977), Thrombosis and Haemostasis (1977 and 1978), British Medical Journal (1975, 1979 and 1990), Lancet (1981), Journal of Pediatrics (1982), Clinical and Laboratory Haematology (1981, 1982, 1983 and 1984), Journal of Bone and Joint Surgery (1985 and 1987), Thrombosis Research (1985), Nouvelle Revue Francais d'Hematologie (1982 and 1986), Med Laboratory Science (1988), Folia Haematologica (1990), Archives of Diseases of Childhood (1993); *Recreations* thinking, sun bathing; *Style*— Dr Anthony Aronstam; ✉ The North Hampshire Hospital, Basingstoke, Hants (☎ 01256 473202, fax 01420 84472)

ARRAN, 9 Earl of (I 1762); Sir Arthur Desmond Colquhoun Gore; 11 Bt (I 1662); also Viscount Sudley, Baron Saunders (both I 1758), and Baron Sudley (UK 1884); s of 8 Earl of Arran (d 1983), and Fiona, Countess of Arran; *b* 14 July 1938; *Educ* Eton, Balliol Coll Oxford; *m* 1974, Eleanor, er da of Bernard van Cutsem and Lady Margaret Fortescue, da of 5 Earl Fortescue; 2 da (Lady Laura Melissa b 1975, Lady Lucy Katherine b 1976); *Heir* kinsman, Paul Annesley Gore, CMG, CVO, JP, *qv*; *Career* Nat Serv cmmnd Grenadier Gds; asst mangr Daily Mail 1972–73, md Clark Nelson 1973–74, asst gen mangr Daily and Sunday Express 1974; dir Waterstone & Co Ltd 1984–87; a lord-in-waiting (Govt whip) 1987–89 and July 1994–Jan 1995; spokesman for: Home Office, DES and DHSS 1987–89, Dept of the Environment 1988–89; Parly under sec of state: for the Armed Forces MOD 1989–92, Northern Ireland Office 1992–94, Dept of the Environment 1994–94; dep chief whip (House of Lords) 1994–95; co-chm Children's Country Holidays Fund; non-exec dir HMV (Thorn/EMI) 1995–; *Recreations* tennis, golf, gardening; *Clubs* Turf, Beefsteak, Pratt's, White's; *Style*— The Rt Hon the Earl of Arran; ✉ House of Lords, London SW1A 0PW

ARRAND, Ven Geoffrey William; s of Thomas Staniforth Arrand (d 1992), and Alica Ada, *née* Costello (d 1995); *b* 24 July 1944; *Educ* Scunthorpe GS, KCL (BD, AKC), St Boniface Coll Warminster; *m* (m dis 1986), Mary Marshall; 2 da (Bridget Mary b 1972, Rebekah Kate b 1974), 1 s (Thomas William b 1976); *Career* curate: Washington Dio of Durham 1967–70, South Ormsby Gp Dio of Lincoln 1970–73; team vicar Great Grimsby Dio of Lincoln 1973–79, team rector Halesworth Dio of St Edmundsbury and Ipswich 1979–85, rector of Hadleigh, Layham and Shelley 1985–94, dean of Bocking 1985–94, rural dean of Hadleigh 1986–94, canon of St Edmundsbury 1992–, archdeacon of Suffolk 1994–; OStJ 1994; *Recreations* golf; *Style*— The Ven the Archdeacon of Suffolk; ✉ 38 Saxmundham Road, Aldeburgh, Suffolk IP15 5JE (☎ 01728 454034, fax 01728 452794); Diocese of St Edmundsbury & Ipswich, Diocesan House, 13/15 Tower Street, Ipswich, Suffolk IP1 3BG (☎ 01473 211028, fax 01473 232407)

ARRINDELL, HE Sir Clement Athelston; GCMG (1984), GCVO (1985), kt (1982), QC (1984); s of George Ernest Arrindell, and Hilda Iona Arrindell (d 1975); *b* 16 April 1931; *Educ* Bradley Private Sch, Basseterre Boys' Elementary, St Kitts-Nevis GS (Island scholar); *m* 1967, Evelyn Eugenia, da of Michael Cornelius O'Loughlin (d 1934), of Basseterre, St Kitts, and his w Dulcie (d 1972); *Career* treasy clerk Treasy Dept St Kitts 1951–54; called to the Bar Lincoln's Inn 1958, in practice 1958–66, dist magistrate 1966–72, chief magistrate 1972–78, judge W Indies Assoc States Supreme Ct 1978–81; govr gen St Kitts-Nevis 1983– (govr 1981–83); *Recreations* gardening, piano playing, classical music; *Style*— Sir Clement Arrindell, GCMG, GCVO, QC

ARROWSMITH, Anthony; s of Arthur Arrowsmith and Winifred, *née* McDonough; *b* 11 May 1945; *Educ* St Chad's Coll Wolverhampton (DipCAM); *m* 4 May 1968, Yvonne Mary da of George Brannon; 1 s (Aidan b 1970), 2 da (Alexa b 1973, Sian b 1982); *Career* chm and chief exec Barkers Birmingham 1976, chm Barkers Scotland 1986, chm and chief exec Barkers Regional Communications Ltd 1989; dir: BNB Resources Group 1984, BNB Resources plc 1987; chm Bd of Govrs St Christopher's Sch Codsall; FIPA; *Style*— Anthony Arrowsmith, Esq; ✉ The Hollies, Histons Hill, Codsall, Staffs WV8 2ER (☎ 01902 843987); Barkers Birmingham, Kennedy Tower, Snow Hill, Queensway, Birmingham B4 (☎ 0121 236 9501)

ARROWSMITH, Pat; da of George Ernest Arrowsmith (d 1976), and Margaret Vera, *née* Kingham (d 1976); *b* 2 March 1930; *Educ* Stover Sch, Cheltenham Ladies' Coll, Newnham Coll Cambridge (BA), Univ of Ohio, Univ of Liverpool; *lesbian partner*, 1962–76, Wendy Butlin; m, 11 Aug 1979 (for one day, m dis), Donald Gardner; *Career* pacifist and socialist; many short term jobs incl: community organizer Chicago 1952–53, cinema usher 1953–54, social caseworker Family Service Unit Liverpool 1954, childcare offr 1955 and 1964, nursing asst Deva Psychiatric Hosp 1956–57, reporter Peace News 1965, gardener Camden BC 1966–68, researcher Soc of Friends Race Relations Ctee 1969–71, case worker NCCL 1971, also worked on farms and in cafes, factories and offices; asst ed Amnesty International 1971–94; organizer: Direct Action Ctee Against Nuclear War, Ctee of 100, CND 1958–68; Parly candidate: (Radical Alliance) Fulham 1966, (Stop the SE Asia War Ctee) Hammersmith 1970, (Independent Socialist) Cardiff SE 1979, gaoled 11 times as political prisoner 1958–85, twice adopted as Prisoner of Conscience by Amnesty International; awarded Holloway Prison Green Arm band 1964, peace prize of US gp ARISE; memb: Ver Poets, CND; *Books* Jericho (novel, 1965), Somewhere Like This (novel, 1970), To Asia in Peace (1972), The Colour of Six Schools (1972), Breakout (poems and drawings, 1975), On the Brink (poems with pictures, 1981), The Prisoner (novel, 1982), Thin Ice (poems, 1984), Nine Lives (poems and pictures, 1990), I Should Have Been a Hornby Train (fiction-cum-memoirs, 1995); *Recreations* painting, writing poetry, swimming; *Style*— Ms Pat Arrowsmith; ✉ 132c Middle Lane, London N8 7JP (☎ 0181 340 2661)

ARROWSMITH, Sue; *b* 1950; *Educ* Nottingham Fine Art, The Slade Sch of Art London; *Career* artist; *Solo Exhibitions* incl: Beside Myself (Matt's Gallery London) 1982, Ancient Mirrors: Fragile Traces (Serpentine Gallery London) 1985, Egg of Night (Ikon Gallery Birmingham) 1986, Anthony Reynolds Galley 1987, Qualities of Silence (Kettle's Yard Cambridge) 1987, Works on Paper (Lime Kiln Gallery London) 1996; *Group Exhibitions* incl: Young Contemporaries (RA) 1970, The Lisson Wall Show (Lisson Gallery) 1970, The British Avant-Garde (NY Cultural Centre) 1971, Art Systems (Museum of Modern Art Buenos Aires) 1971, Experiment 4 (Midland Gp Nottingham) 1975, British Polaroid Exhibition (Spectro-Arts Newcastle and touring) 1982, Home and Abroad (Serpentine

Gallery and touring) 1984, Between Identity/Politics (Gimpel Fils London and NYC) 1986, John Moores Exhbns 15 and 16 (Walker Art Gallery Liverpool) 1987 and 1989–90, Athena Art Awards (Barbican London) 1987, On a Plate (Serpentine Gallery) 1987, Artists in Dialogue (Kettle's Yard) 1987, Public Workshop (Riverside Studios London) 1987, Excavations (Galerie Hubert Winter Vienna and John Hansard Gallery Southampton) 1988, Polaroid work with Jan Hnizdo (V&A) 1989, Shocks to the System (Arts Cncl touring exhbn) 1991, Art for Amnesty (Bonham's London) 1991, invited artist RA Summer Show 1993 and numerous exhbns at Anthony Reynolds Gallery, Faith, Hope, Love and Death (Kunsthalle Vienna) 1995–96; *Curator of Exhibitions* Photo(graphic) Vision (Winchester Gallery) 1983, Incidentally... (Winchester Gallery and Goldsmiths' Gallery London) 1986, Artists in Dialogue (Kettle's Yard) 1987; *Public Collections* incl: Arts Cncl of GB, V&A, Wolfson Coll Cambridge (artist/fell); *Awards* Arts Cncl of GB major award 1987, prizewinner John Moores Liverpool Exhbn 16 1990; *Style—* Ms Sue Arrowsmith; ✉ 117 Devons Road, Bow, London E3 3QX

ARTAZA, HE Mario; *b* 2 Sept 1937; *Educ* Law Sch Univ of Chile, Univ of Virginia (MA Foreign Affrs), American Univ Sch of Int Serv (PhD programme); *m* Anita Valsasnini; *Career* Chilean diplomat; Miny of Foreign Affrs: Legal Advsy Dept 1958–59, Political Dept 1963, third then second sec Chilean Embassy Washington 1964–67, second then first sec Chilean Delgn to OAS 1968–69, on sabbitical as dir and prof of int politics and int orgns Inst of Political Scis Catholic Univ of Chile 1969, head UN Dept Miny of Foreign Affrs 1970, cnsllr Chilean Embassy Peru 1971–73, chargé d'affaires Chilean Embassy Washington Sept 1973, visiting prof Univ of the Pacific Calif Jan-June 1974, Overseas Devpt Cncl visiting fell Washington DC June-Sept 1974; World Bank Washington DC: i/c ops with Pakistan 1974–80, i/c ops with Argentina and Paraguay 1980–87; sr offr infrastructure ops South Zone LATAM 1987–90, Chilean ambass Geneva 1990–92; Miny of Foreign Rels: head Dept of Multilateral Policy 1992–94, head Planning Dept 1994; Foreign Min's rep before Bd of Dirs of Int Agency for Co-operation and Devpt 1994–95, Chilean ambass to the Ct of St James's 1996–; *Books* Overall Development of Chile (jtly, 1967), América 70 (jtly, 1970); *Style—* HE Señor Mario Artaza; ✉ Embassy of Chile, 12 Devonshire Street, London W1N 2DS (☎ 0171 580 6392, fax 0171 436 5204)

ARTHUR, Alan David; s of David Edward John Arthur, of Bedwas, Gwent, and Elizabeth Ann, *née* Howell; *b* 3 July 1949; *Educ* Bedwellty GS, Univ Coll of Wales Aberystwyth (BSc); *Career* chartered accountant; ptnr int practice Deloitte Haskins & Sells 1983–84 (previous posts in S Wales, W Yorks and Zambia), fndr and first md Bradford Enterprise Agency 1984–86, ptnr Booth & Co CAs 1986–89, currently dir of corp fin Ernst & Young; FCA 1974, FCIArb 1987; *Recreations* work; *Clubs* Bradford; *Style—* Alan Arthur, Esq; ✉ 76 Hallowes Park Rd, Cullingworth BD13 5AR (☎ 01535 273074); Ernst & Young, Cloth Hall Court, 14 King Street, Leeds LS1 2JN (☎ 0113 285 5153, fax 0113 243 4195)

ARTHUR, Christine; da of W J Arthur, of Hemel Hempstead, Herts, and R Arthur, *née* Campion; *b* 14 July 1966; *Educ* Parmiters Sch Watford Herts, Univ of Birmingham (BA); *m* 1990, N J S Davies, s of Brian Davies; *Career* Rote PR 1988–92, assoc dir Haslimann Taylor Birmingham 1992–93, md and main bd dir Key Communications Birmingham 1993–; memb: Arts, Sports and Leisure Ctee Young City 2000 1993–, City 2000 1993– (memb Mktg Ctee 1994–); author of various feature articles for nat, local and trade press; memb PRCA; *Recreations* tennis, foreign travel, piano, antiques; *Clubs* Swallow Hotel Health, Birmingham Aerobics; *Style—* Ms Christine Arthur; ✉ Key Communications Ltd, 9 The Apex, 6 Embassy Drive, Edgbaston, Birmingham B15 1TP (☎ 0121 456 3199, fax 0121 456 3192)

ARTHUR, Gavyn Farr; s of Maj the Hon (George) Leonard Arthur, of Bath and London SW3, and (Gladys) Raina Arthur; *b* 13 Sept 1951; *Educ* Harrow, Ch Ch Oxford (MA); *Career* called to the Bar 1975; memb W Circuit Ctee 1988–; chm Res Ctee on Child Care Proceedings 1987, memb Soc of Conservative Lawyers; treas Coningsby Club 1987, memb Ct of Common Cncl Ward of Farringdon Without 1988–91; govr: St Bride's Inst Fndn 1989, City of London Sch for Girls 1991–, Christ's Hosp, Bridewell Royal Hosp, Cripplegate Fndn, City of London Freemen's Sch 1996–; Alderman Ward of Cripplegate 1991; tstee Sir John Soane Museum; Freeman City of London 1979, pres Cripplegate Ward Club, vice pres Br Red Cross; memb Worshipful Co of Gardeners; *Recreations* travel, writing, British India, the South Tyrol question; *Clubs* Carlton, Coningsby, City Livery; *Style—* Gavyn Arthur, Esq; ✉ 2 Harcourt Buildings, Temple, London EC4Y 9DB (☎ 0171 353 6961, fax 0171 353 6968)

ARTHUR, Prof Geoffrey Herbert; s of William Gwyn Arthur (d 1945), of Llangibby, Gwent, and Ethel Jessie Parry (d 1967); *b* 6 March 1916; *Educ* Abersychan Secdy Sch, Univ of Liverpool (BVSc, MVSc), Univ of London (FRCVS); *m* 22 Feb 1948, Lorna Isabel, da of Isaac Alec Simpson (d 1969), of Ranworth, Heswall, Cheshire; 4 s (Richard b 1950, Hugh b 1954, Charles b 1960, James b 1963), 1 da (Angela (Mrs Sheard) b 1948); *Career* lectr in vet med Univ of Liverpool 1945–49, prof of vet obstetrics Univ of London 1964–73, head of Dept of Surgery RVC 1972–73, prof of vet surgery Univ of Bristol 1974–79 (emeritus 1980), clinical vet prof King Faisal Saudi Arabia 1980–83; regnl postgrad vet dean RCVS 1985–95, memb Cncl RCVS 1989–97; former chm Soc for the Protection of Animals Abroad (SPANA); former pres: Br Cattle Vet Assoc, Soc for the Study of Animal Breeding; former memb Cncl Br Vet Assoc; *Books* Veterinary Reproduction and Obstetrics (7 edn 1989); *Recreations* observing natural phenomena and experimenting, North African travel; *Style—* Prof Geoffrey Arthur; ✉ Fallodene, Stone Allerton, Axbridge, Somerset BS26 2NH (☎ 01934 712 077)

ARTHUR, Lt-Col John Reginald; OBE (1985); s of Col Lionel Francis Arthur, DSO, OBE (d 1952), of Camberley, Surrey, and Muriel Irene, *née* Tilley (d 1995); *b* 25 June 1935; *Educ* Winchester; *m* 21 Dec 1965, Princess Valerie Isolde Mary de Mahe, da of Prince John Bryant Digby de Mahe, MBE; 2 s (Malcolm Ian Charles b 5 Sept 1969, John Benjamin George b 25 Nov 1971), 1 da (Anneliese Mary b 8 March 1967); *Career* RMA Sandhurst 1954–55, cmmnd Scots Gds 1955, Staff Coll Camberley 1966, Lt-Col 1976, ret 1984; co sec: Laurence Prust & Co Ltd 1986–89, Credit Commercial de France (UK) Ltd 1989–90, md The Wisley Golf Club plc 1991–; *Recreations* golf, gardening, music; *Clubs* MCC, I Zingari, Free Foresters, Berkshire Golf, Royal St George's Golf, Hon Co of Edinburgh Golfers; *Style—* Lt-Col John Arthur, OBE; ✉ Garden Lodge, Whitmore Lane, Sunningdale, Berkshire SL5 0PX

ARTHUR, His Hon John Rhys; DFC (1944), JP (Lancs 1970); s of John Morgan Arthur (d 1973), and Eleanor Arthur (d 1965); *b* 29 April 1923; *Educ* Mill Hill Sch, Christ's Coll Cambridge (MA); *m* 1951, Joan Tremearne (d 1995), da of Richard Pickering (d 1961), and Dorothy Pickering (d 1991); 2 s, 1 da; *Career* cmmnd RAF 1943, demobbed 1946; called to the Bar Inner Temple 1949; asst recorder Blackburn 1970, dep chm Lancs County QS 1970–71, recorder 1972–75, circuit judge 1975–93; *Clubs* MCC, Old Millhillians, Athenaeum (Liverpool), Cardiff Athletic; *Style—* His Hon John Arthur, DFC, JP; ✉ Orovales, Caldy Road, Caldy, Wirral, Merseyside L48 1LP (☎ 0151 625 8624)

ARTHUR, Michael Anthony; CMG (1992); s of John Richard Arthur (d 1982), and Mary Deirdre, *née* Chaundy; *b* 28 Aug 1950; *Educ* Rugby, Balliol Coll Oxford (Nettleship music scholar, BA); *m* 1974, Plaxy Gillian Beatrice, *née* Corke; 2 da (Zoe Mary b 1978, Olivia Anne b 1980), 2 s (Julian J B b 1982, Guy Tristram b 1985); *Career* HM Dip Serv: joined FCO 1972, third sec UK Mission to UN NY 1972–73, UN Dept FCO 1973–74, second sec UK Perm Rep to EEC Brussels 1974–76, second sec Kinshasa Zaire 1976–78, FCO 1978–80, private sec to Lord Privy Seal (successively Sir Ian Gilmour, Humphrey Atkins, Lord Belstead, Lady Young) 1980–83, first sec Bonn 1983–88, head EC Dept (internal) FCO 1988–93, sr assoc memb St Antony's Coll Oxford spring/summer 1993, cnsllr and head of Chancery Paris 1993–; Freeman City of Oxford 1971; *Recreations* music, travel, books; *Clubs* Cercle Interallie (Paris); *Style—* Michael Arthur, Esq, CMG; ✉ c/o FCO (Paris), King Charles Street, London SW1A 2AH

ARTHUR, Lt-Gen Sir (John) Norman Stewart; KCB (1985), JP; s of Col Evelyn Stewart Arthur (d 1963), of Montgomerie, Mauchline, Ayrshire, and Elizabeth, *née* Burnett-Stuart (d 1976); *b* 6 March 1931; *Educ* Eton, RMA Sandhurst; *m* 1960, Theresa Mary, da of Francis Hopkinson and Ursula Hopkinson, of Dundas Farm, Elmsted, Kent; 1 s (Simon b 1967), 1 da (Camilla b 1962), 1 s decd; *Career* cmmnd Royal Scots Greys 1951; CO Royal Scots Dragoon Gds 1972–74 (despatches 1974), 7 Armd Bde 1976–77, GOC 3 Armd Division 1980–82, Dir Personal Servs (Army) MOD 1983–85, Col Cmdt Mil Provost Staff Corps 1983–88, GOC Scotland Govr Edinburgh Castle 1985–88, Col The Royal Scots Dragoon Gds (Carabiniers and Greys) 1985–92, Col 205 (Scot) Gen Hosp RAMC (V) 1988–93, Col Scottish Yeomanry 1992–; offr Royal Co of Archers (Queen's Body Guard for Scot); memb Br Olympic Team (equestrian three-day event) 1960; vice-pres Riding for the Disabled Edinburgh and Borders 1988–94; chm: Army Benevolent Fund Scotland 1988–, Carnsalloch Cheshire Home Dumfries 1994–; pres Scottish Conservation Projects Tst 1989–94; memb: Ctee AA 1990–, Bd of Dirs Edinburgh Military Tattoo Co 1988–91; HM Lord Lt Kirkcudbright 1996– (DL 1989); *Recreations* country pursuits, reading, field sports; *Clubs* Cavalry and Guards', Caledonian Hunt; *Style—* Sir Norman Arthur, KCB, JP; ✉ Newbarns, Colvend, by Dalbeattie, Kirkcudbrightshire DG5 4PY (☎ 01556 630227)

ARTHUR, Peter Alistair Kennedy; s of Jack Kennedy Arthur (d 1993), of Troon, Ayrshire, and Margaret Kerr, *née* Morisson; *b* 16 June 1956; *Educ* Loretto, Univ of Edinburgh (LLB); *m* 5 June 1982, Dorothy, da of William Erskine; 3 s (Michael Kennedy b 22 Aug 1984, Graeme Erskine b 4 March 1987, Duncan Robert b 26 Oct 1989); *Career* trainee then asst slr Murray Beith & Murray 1977–80; co sec: Noble & Co 1980–83, ESCO Oil Management Ltd 1983–87; Edinburgh Fund Managers plc: asst co sec and compliance offr 1987–89, co sec 1989–90, admin dir 1990–95, jt md 1995–; pres Edinburgh Branch Br Red Cross Soc; FCIS; *Recreations* golf, skiing, family; *Clubs* HCEG, Murrayfield Golf, Royal Troon, Royal Portrush; *Style—* Peter Arthur, Esq; ✉ Edinburgh Fund Managers plc, Donaldson House, 97 Haymarket Terrace, Edinburgh EH12 5HD (☎ 0131 313 1000, fax 0131 313 6300, telex 72453)

ARTHUR, Sir Stephen John; 6 Bt (UK 1841), of Upper Canada; s of Hon Sir Basil Malcolm Arthur, 5 Bt, MP (d 1985), and Elizabeth Rita, da of late Alan Mervyn Wells; *b* 1 July 1953; *Educ* Timaru Boys' HS; *m* 1978 (m dis), Carolyn Margaret, da of Burnie Lawrence Diamond, of Cairns, Qld, Australia; 1 s, 2 da (Amanda b 1975, Melanie b 1976); *Heir* s, Benjamin Nathan Arthur b 27 March 1979; *Style—* Sir Stephen Arthur, Bt

ARTHUR, Terence Gordon (Terry); s of William Gordon Arthur (d 1971), of West Hartlepool, and Dorothy, *née* Baker; *b* 5 Sept 1940; *Educ* West Hartlepool GS, Univ of Manchester (BSc), Univ of Cambridge (Dip Statistics, rugby blue); *m* 1, 15 May 1965 (m dis 1983), Valerie Ann Marie, da of Stephen Daniels, of Suffolk; 1 s (Richard b 1970), 2 da (Louise b 1966, Frances b 1968); m 2, 25 Nov 1983, Mary Clare, *née* Austick; *Career* asst sec Equity & Law Life Assur Soc 1967 (joined 1963), ptnr Duncan C Fraser & Co Actuaries 1969–76 (joined 1967), T G Arthur Hargrave Actuaries 1976–91 (fndr 1976) (merged with Bacon and Woodrow 1989); professional non-exec 1991–; memb: Cncl Inst of Actuaries 1977–94 (treas 1985–86), Co of Actuaries; 2 caps England rugby football 1966; Freeman City of London; FIA 1966, FIS 1975, fell Inst of Pensions Mgmnt 1977; *Books* 95 per cent is Crap - A Plain Man's Guide to British Politics (1975); *Clubs* Birmingham Area Sports Internationalists, Oriental, Hawks (Cambridge); *Style—* Terry Arthur, Esq; ✉ 23 St Mary's Street, Stamford, Lincs PE9 2DG (☎ 01780 53525, fax 01780 65610)

ARTHURS, Prof Arnold Magowan; s of James Arthurs (d 1969), of Islandmagee, Antrim, and Mary, *née* Scott (d 1992); *b* 2 Sept 1934; *Educ* Royal Belfast Academical Instn, Queen's Univ Belfast (BSc), Jesus Coll Oxford (MA, DSc); *m* 6 July 1963, Elspeth Marie, da of Arthur John Lonsdale (d 1977), of Hornsea, E Yorks; 3 s (William b 1965, Henry b 1967, Jack b 1971); *Career* praelector in mathematics and fell Queen's Coll Oxford 1962; Univ of York: reader 1964, prof of mathematics 1976–; memb York Blood Donor Ctee 1983–; FIMA 1970; *Books* Probability Theory (1965), Complementary Variational Principles (1970), Calculus of Variations (1975); *Recreations* music, visual and decorative arts; *Style—* Prof Arnold Arthurs; ✉ Department of Mathematics, University of York, Heslington, York YO1 5DD (☎ 01904 433075)

ARTUS, Ronald Edward; CBE (1991); s of Ernest Edward Artus (d 1980), and Doris Isobel, *née* Goddard (d 1994); *b* 8 Oct 1931; *Educ* Sir Thomas Rich's Sch Gloucester, Magdalen Coll Oxford (MA); *m* 1, 1956 (m dis 1987), Brenda Margaret, *née* Touche; 3 s (Colin, Alan, Philip), 1 da (Lucy); m 2, Dr Joan Mullaney; *Career* Prudential Corporation plc: joined 1954, head of econ intelligence 1958–71, sr asst mangr 1973–75, jt sec and chief investmt mangr 1975–82, gp chief investmnt mangr 1982–90, exec dir 1984–90, non-exec dir 1990–93; non-exec dir: GEC plc 1990–, Electro-components plc 1990–, The Solicitors' Indemnity Fund Ltd 1990–, The Securities and Futures Authy Ltd 1990–, Imperial Cancer Research Technology Ltd 1988–, Celltech Ltd 1980–91, CLM Insurance Fund plc 1993–; hon fell Inst of Investment Management & Res (formerly Soc of Investment Analysts) 1980; memb: Accounting Standards Ctee 1982–86, City Capital Markets Ctee 1982–90 (chm 1988–90), Cncl for Inst of Fiscal Studies 1988–94, CBI City Indust Task Force 1987, Lloyd's Task Force 1991, Fin Law Panel 1993–; *Recreations* music, learning about art (especially British School and English watercolours); *Clubs* MCC; *Style—* Ronald Artus, Esq, CBE; ✉ General Electric Company plc, 1 Stanhope Gate, London W1A 1EH (☎ 0171 493 8484, fax 0171 493 1974)

ARULAMPALAM, Thankarajah; s of Richard Kunaratnam Arulampalam (d 1969), of Jaffna, Sri Lanka, and Anna Annammah, *née* Amerasingham (d 1990); *b* 28 Dec 1933; *Educ* Jaffna Central Coll Jaffna, St Thomas Coll Mt Lavinia Sri Lanka, Univ of Ceylon Sri Lanka (MB BS); *m* 18 Dec 1967, (Jannette) Lokeswarie, da of Dr John Rasiah Wilson, MBE (d 1984); 1 s (Thanjakumar Hermon Arichandran b 20 Dec 1968), 1 da (Lohini Hemangini b 3 June 1973); *Career* sr house offr in ophthalmology St Paul's Eye Hosp Liverpool 1968–69, registrar in ophthalmology Royal Hallamshire Hosp Sheffield 1970–72, sr registrar in ophthalmology Guy's Hosp and St George's Hosp London 1973–77, conslt ophthalmologist North Notts Health Authy King's Mill Hosp Notts 1978–; North Notts Health Authy rep: Med Advsy Sub Ctee in Ophthalmology, Regnl Med Manpower Ctee; memb: GMC, Med Def Union; DO, FRCS, FRCOphth, fell Int Assocs of Ocular Surgns; *Recreations* cricket, soccer, hockey, athletics; *Style—* Thankarajah Arulampalam, Esq; ✉ 22 Black Scotch Lane, Berry Hill, Mansfield, Nottinghamshire NG18 4JX (☎ 01623 25500); Department of Ophthalmology, Kings Mill Centre for Health Care Services, Mansfield Rd, Sutton in Ashfield, Nottinghamshire (☎ 01623 22515 ext 3366)

ARUNDEL AND BRIGHTON, Bishop (RC) of 1977–; Rt Rev Cormac Murphy-O'Connor; s of Dr George Patrick Murphy-O'Connor (d 1960), of Reading, Berks, and Ellen Theresa, *née* Cuddigan (d 1971); *b* 24 Aug 1932; *Educ* Prior Park Coll Bath, The Ven English Coll Rome, Gregorian Univ Rome (PhL, STL); *Career* ordained to RC Priesthood 1956; parish priest Portswood Southampton 1970–71, rector Venerable Eng Coll Rome 1971–77; first chm Bishops' Ctee for Europe 1979–82, RC co chm of

Anglo-Roman Catholic Int Cmmn (ARCIC-II) 1983–; *Recreations* walking, music, reading; *Style—* The Rt Rev the Bishop of Arundel and Brighton; ✉ St Joseph's Hall, Storrington, Pulborough, W Sussex RH20 4HE (☎ 01903 742172, fax 01903 746336)

ARUNDEL AND SURREY, Earl of; Edward William Fitzalan-Howard; s and h of 17 Duke of Norfolk, KG, CB, CBE, MC, DL; *b* 2 Dec 1956; *Educ* Ampleforth, Lincoln Coll Oxford; *m* 27 June 1987, Georgina Susan, yr da of John Temple Gore; 3 s (Henry Miles, Lord Maltravers b 3 Dec 1987, Hon Thomas Jack b 14 March 1992, Hon Philip b 14 July 1996), 2 da (Lady Rachel Rose b 10 June 1989, Lady Isabel Serena b 7 Feb 1994); *Heir* s, Lord Maltravers; *Career* chm: Sigas Ltd 1979–88, Parkwood Group Ltd 1989–; Liveryman Worshipful Co of Fishmongers; *Recreations* motor racing, skiing, shooting; *Clubs* British Racing Drivers (Silverstone); *Style—* Earl of Arundel and Surrey; ✉ Arundel Castle, Arundel, W Sussex (☎ 01903 883979)

ARUNDELL, Hon Richard John Tennant; JP (1991); s and h of 10 Baron Talbot of Malahide, *qv*; *b* 28 March 1957; *Educ* Stonyhurst, RAC Cirencester; *m* 1984, Jane Catherine, da of Timothy Heathcote Unwin, MFH; 4 da (Isabel Mary b 1986, Emily Rose b 1988, Frances Laura b 1990, Lucinda Jane b 1991); *Career* farmer; *Style—* The Hon Richard Arundell, JP; ✉ Hook Manor, Donhead, Shaftesbury, Dorset SP7 9ET (☎ 01747 828423)

ASBURY, Dr (Adrian) John; *b* 16 April 1948; *Educ* Sandbach GS Cheshire, Univ of Birmingham (MB ChB, FRCA), Univ of Sheffield (PhD, MD); *m*; 2 c; *Career* SHO E Birmingham Hosp 1972–73 (house appts 1971–72), registrar E Birmingham Hosp, E Birmingham Chest Branch Marston Green Maternity Hosp and Hollymoor Psychiatric Hosp 1973, lectr in anaesthesia Huggins Sch of Med Salisbury Rhodesia 1974–75, registrar Dudley Road Hosp Birmingham, Birmingham and E Midlands Eye Hosp and Ear Nose and Throat Hosp 1975–76; sr registar (Midland rotation): Queen Elizabeth Hosp, Birmingham Maternity Hosp, Gen Hosp, Birmingham Dental Hosp and Smethwick Centre for Neurology and Neurosurgery 1976–77, Stoke City Gen Hosp and N Staffs Royal Infirmary 1977, Dudley Rd Hosp Clinical Investigation Unit, Birmingham and E Midlands Eye Hosp and Ear Nose and Throat Hosp 1977–78; lectr in anaesthesia Dept of Anaesthetics Univ of Sheffield 1978–84, reader in anaesthesia Univ of Glasgow 1995– (sr lectr 1984–95); hon conslt anaesthetist 1984–: Gtr Glasgow Health Bd, Western Infirmary Glagow (head Dept of Anaesthetics 1994–96); Hartree Premium IEE jtly 1986 and 1993, Cybernetics Soc Prize Edinburgh jtly 1991; memb: BMA, Assoc of Anaesthetists, Anaesthetic Research Soc, Intensive Care Soc, IEE (assoc), Scottish Soc of Anaesthetists, Euro Acad of Anaesthesiology, Glasgow and W Soc of Anaesthetists, Northern Br Pain Assoc; *Books* ABC of Computers (BMA, 1989), A Career and Study Guide to Anaesthesia (Glasgow Univ Press, 1989); contrib various book chapters and author of numerous articles in learned jls; *Recreations* local church and its activities, industrial history and its ramifications, recreational mathematics and the history of mathematics, fell walking; *Style—* Dr A J Asbury; ✉ 24 Kilmardinny Avenue, Bearsden, Glasgow G61 3NS (☎ 0141 942 4784); University Department of Anaesthesia, Western Infirmary, Glasgow G11 6NT (☎ 0141 211 2698, fax 0141 211 1807)

ASCOTT, Robert Henry Charles; s of James Robert Ascott, of London, and Joan Daisy, *née* Le Feuvre; *b* 7 March 1943; *Educ* St Paul's, Trinity Coll Cambridge (MA), Admin Staff Coll Henley; *Career* pres EMI-Capitol de Mexico SA de CV 1975–79, md Emidata 1979–82, gp sr exec Intermed 1982–84, bursar Univ of Reading 1984–, dir Kleinwort High Income Trust plc 1991–; *Recreations* coaching rowing, choral conducting, singing, organ playing, foreign languages; *Clubs* Leander; *Style—* Robert Ascott, Esq; ✉ 114 High St, Burbage, Marlborough, Wilts; Univ of Reading, Whiteknights, Reading, Berks

ASFOURY, Dr Zakara Mohamed; s of Prof Mohamed El Asfoury (d 1983), of Port Said, Egypt; *b* 5 Aug 1921; *Educ* Port Said Secdy Sch, Cairo Univ, Liverpool Univ, London Univ (BSc, MSc, PhD, MB BCh, MRCS, LRCP), assoc res MD (Univ of Cambridge); *m* 1983, Prof Fadia Hassan, da of late Mohammed Katamesh; *Career* medical practitioner 1947–; res fell, hon demonstator, registrar, sr registrar, conslt physician working at various hosps incl: St Thomas', The London, The N Middx, St Mary's, The High-Land, Red Hill, Liverpool, Cairo; med specialisations incl gen, rheumatic, tropical and geriatric med; res work incl: first organ transplant RCS 1950, first time discovery of the collagenase enzyme and anticollegenese in man and animals 1965, first time breaking of kidney stones by VHF currents 1958, treatment of Biharziasis and other tropical infections by diathermy 1965, first time treatment of heart ischemic diseases by VHF currents 1965, treatment of Psoriasis 1992; memb: The Renal Assoc, The Anatomical Soc, Geriatric Soc, Hunterian Soc; FRSM; *Publications* numerous articles in learned jls, Pregnancy Nephropathy (contrib, 1971), Sympathectomy and the Innervation of the Kidney (1971); *Style—* Dr Z Asfoury; ✉ office: 27 Devonshire Place, London W1N 1PD (☎ 0171 486 4342)

ASH, Charles John; s of Leonard John Ash (d 1965), of Cirencester, Glos, and Mary Elizabeth, *née* Watson; *b* 26 Nov 1945; *Educ* Cirencester GS, Hatfield Poly (BSc); *m* 1976, Pamela Monica, da of late Cecil Jenkins; 1 da (Emily Clare b 1978); *Career* Hawker Siddeley Dynamics: jr design engr 1964, design engr 1966, sr design engr 1968–72; design engr Broomwade 1967, project leader Instron 1978–82, mangr mechanical engrg and head of ops IDEO Product Development (formerly Moggridge Associates) 1982–; Br Design Award for cordless telephone 1990; Eur Ing 1996, MIMechE; *Style—* Eur Ing Charles Ash; ✉ IDEO Product Development, 7–8 Jeffrey's Place, Jeffrey's St, London NW1 9PP (☎ 0171 485 1170, fax 0171 482 3970)

ASH, Douglas Terence (Doug); s of Sydney Alexander Ash (d 1994), and Doreen Victoria, *née* Gornall; *b* 19 Dec 1947; *Educ* Wallington GS, Univ of Nottingham (BA), Harvard Business Sch (MBA); *m* 19 Aug 1972, Rhona Helen, da of Harold James Bennett (d 1978), former vice-pres Rotary Int; 1 s (Laurence b 1981), 3 da (Belinda 1975, Isobel b 1976, Amelia b 1981); *Career* exec dir Ocean Group PLC, chief exec MSAS Cargo International, dir various MSAS subsids throughout the world; non-exec dir Direct Wines (Windsor) Ltd; *Recreations* rugby football; *Style—* Doug Ash, Esq; ✉ Cherry Croft, Kingwood Common, Henley on Thames, Oxon R69 5NA (☎ 01491 628234); MSAS Cargo International, Ocean House, Bracknell, Berks RG12 1AW (☎ 01344 52222)

ASH, Prof Sir Eric Albert; kt (1990), CBE (1982); s of Walter J Ash (d 1970), and Dorothea Cecily, *née* Schwarz (d 1974); *b* 31 Jan 1928; *Educ* Univ Coll Sch, Imperial Coll of Science & Technol (BSc, DIC, PhD, DSc); *m* 30 May 1954, Clare Mosher, *née* Babb; 5 da (Gillian Carol (Mrs Barr) b 1958, Carolyn Dian b 1960, Lucy Amanda b 1962, Emily Jane b 1966, Jennifer Dian (twin) b 1966); *Career* res fell Stanford Univ California 1952–54, res engr Standard Telecom Labs 1954–63; Dept of Electronic and Electrical Engrg UCL: sr lectr 1963–65, reader 1965–67, prof 1967–85, Pender prof and head of dept 1980–85; rector Imperial Coll London 1985–93, prof Dept of Physics UCL 1993–; non-exec dir: BT plc 1987–93, SLC 1994–; chm: Cncl Royal Inst 1995– (sec 1984–88), Sci Advsy Ctee BBC 1987–94; tstee: Sci Museum 1988–94, Wolfson Fndn 1988–; memb: Exec Bd Fellowship of Engrg (now Royal Acad of Engrg) 1981–84, ABRC 1989–93, Academia Europaea 1989–; Faraday Medal IEE 1980, Royal Medal Royal Soc 1986; hon doctorates: Aston Univ 1987, Univ of Leicester 1988, Univ of Edinburgh 1988, Institut National Polytechnique de Grenoble 1987, Poly Univ NY 1988, Univ of Surrey 1993, Univ of Glasgow 1994, Chinese Univ of Hong Kong 1994; hon fell: UCL 1985, Imperial Coll 1995; FEng 1978, FRS 1977, FCGI, FIEE, FIEEE, FInstP, MInstD; *Recreations* reading, music, swimming, skiing; *Style—* Prof Sir Eric Ash, CBE, FRS, FEng; ✉ 11 Ripplevale Grove, London N1 1HS (☎ 0171 607 4989, fax 0171 700 7446)

ASH, Ian William; s of Sidney Ewart Ash (d 1987), and Joan Mary, *née* Boultwood; *b* 18 Sept 1941; *Educ* St Alban's GS, Queen Mary Coll London (BSc); *m* 17 Oct 1964, Jacqueline Maureen, da of James Lawrence Hardy; 3 s (Michael Richard b 10 Aug 1965, Duncan Ian b 7 July 1967, Christopher James b 22 June 1976), 1 da (Clare Jacqueline b 23 Nov 1969); *Career* IBM: scientific support 1963–65, sales 1965–70, asst to Pres Europe (Paris) 1971–72, sales and mktg mgmnt (UK) 1973–77, serv mktg worldwide (USA) 1978–80, UK region mangr 1981–83; divnl dir of technol and mktg Coopers & Lybrand 1983–85, pres Valid International (San José California) 1985–90; BT: dir of mktg (Personal Customers) 1990–94, dir of corp relations 1994–; *Recreations* rugby, sailing, walking; *Style—* Ian Ash, Esq; ✉ British Telecommunications plc, BT Centre, 81 Newgate Street, London EC1A 7AJ (☎ 0171 356 5350, fax 0171 356 6577)

ASH, Rear Adm Walter William Hector; CB (1962); s of Hector Sidney Ash (d 1953), of Portsmouth, Hants, and Mabel Jessy Ash; *b* 2 May 1906; *Educ* City and Guilds Engrg Coll Kensington, RNC Greenwich (Whitworth scholar, John Samuel scholar); *m* 1932, Louisa Adelaide, da of late William Salt, of Jarrow-upon-Tyne; 3 da; *Career* chartered electrical engr; electrical engr Admty 1937–39 (asst 1932–37), fleet electrical engr Staff C-in-C Med 1939–40; supt electrical engr: Admty 1940–45, HM Dockyard Hong Kong 1945–48; Cdr RN HMS Montclare 1950–51, Capt RN Admty 1951–54, electrical engrg mangr HM Dockyard Devonport 1954–58, chm IEE SW Sub-Centre 1958–59, Rear Adm 1960, ship design directorate Admty 1959–63, ret 1963; ADC to HM The Queen 1958–60; CEng, FIEE; *Recreations* music (piano and organ); *Style—* Rear Adm Walter Ash, CB; ✉ 4 Vavasour Hse, North Embankment, Dartmouth, Devon TQ6 9PW (☎ 01803 834630)

ASHBEE, Dr Paul; s of Lewis Ashbee, and Hannah Mary Elizabeth, *née* Brett; *b* 23 June 1918; *Educ* Maidstone Sch, Univ of Leicester (MA, DLitt), Univ of London (Postgrad Dip in Archaeology); *m* 4 Sept 1952, Richmal Crompton Lamburn, da of Thomas Frederick Rhodes Disher (d 1963), of Dulwich; 1 s (Edward b 1953), 1 da (Catherine b 1956); *Career* WWII Royal W Kent and REME 1939–46, control cmmn for Germany Aachen and Dusseldorf HQs 1946–49; excavations carried out for Miny of Works (now English Heritage) 1949–76, co dir Br Museum excavations at Sutton Hoo 1964–71, archaeologist UEA 1968–83; author of numerous papers, articles and reviews for archaeological jls; memb: Royal Archaeological Inst, Wilts Archaeological Soc, Cornwall Archaeological Soc (pres 1976–80, vice pres 1980–84), Kent Archaeological Soc, Prehistoric Soc (memb Cncl and meetings sec 1960–74), Sutton Hoo Research Ctee 1982–; sec Sub Ctee Br Assoc for Archaeological Field Experiments 1961–, former sec Neolithic and Bronze Age Ctee Br Archaeology Cncl, Royal Cmmr on Historical Monuments of England 1975–85, memb Area Archaeological Advsy Ctee for Norfolk and Suffolk 1975–79, chm Scole Ctee for E Anglian Archaeology 1979–84; FSA 1958, FRSAIre 1987; *Books* The Bronze Age Round Barrow in Britain (1960), The Earthen Long Barrow in Britain (1970, 2 edn 1984), Ancient Scilly (1974), The Ancient British (1978), Sutton Hoo (contrib, 1976), Wilsford Shaft (1989); *Recreations* bibliophilia, historical architecture, East Anglia; *Clubs* The Norfolk (Norwich); *Style—* Dr Paul Ashbee, FSA; ✉ The Old Rectory, Chedgrave, Norwich NR14 6ND (☎ 01508 520595)

ASHBOURNE, 4 Baron (UK 1885); (Edward) Barry Greynville Gibson; s of Vice Adm 3 Baron Ashbourne, CB, DSO, JP (d 1983), and Reta Frances Manning, *née* Hazeland (d 1996); *b* 28 Jan 1933; *Educ* Rugby; *m* 25 March 1967, Yvonne Georgina, da of late Mrs Flora Ham; 3 s (Hon Charles b 1967, Hon Rodney b 1970, Hon Patrick b 1977); *Heir* s, Hon Edward Charles d'Olier Gibson b 31 Dec 1967; *Career* RN 1951–72: Lt Cdr, cmd HMS Crofton 1963–64; RN Staff Coll 1965; stockbroker 1972–79; investmt mktg 1979–88; pres Petersfield Branch E Hampshire Cons Assoc; vice pres Hampshire Autistic Soc; chm Joshua Christian Tst, sec and treas Lords' and Commons' Family and Child Protection Gp; chm All Party Royal Yacht Parly Gp; *Recreations* golf, sailing, gardening; *Style—* The Rt Hon the Lord Ashbourne; ✉ 107 Sussex Rd, Petersfield, Hants GU31 4LB (☎ 01730 264636)

ASHBROOK, Kate Jessie; da of John Benjamin Ashbrook, of Denham Village, Bucks, and Margaret, *née* Balfour; *b* 1 Feb 1955; *Educ* High March Sch, Benenden Sch, Univ of Exeter (BSc); *Career* sec Dartmoor Preservation Assoc 1981–84 (pres 1995–), gen sec Open Spaces Soc 1984– (memb Exec Ctee 1978–), ed Open Space 1984–; Ramblers' Assoc: memb Nat Exec Ctee 1982–, vice chm 1993–95, chm 1995–, footpath sec and press offr Bucks and W Middx area 1986–; chm Central Rights of Way Ctee 1991–, sec Countryside Link Gp 1989–92; memb: Gen Cncl CPRE 1984–95, Exec Ctee Cncl for Nat Parks 1983–; chm Turville Sch Tst 1994–95; *Books* Severnside - A Guide to Family Walks (contrib The Southern Quantocks, 1977), The Walks of SE England (contrib A Walk Round Denham, 1975), Common Place No More, Common Land in the 1980s (1983), Make for the Hills (1983), Our Common Right (1987); *Recreations* walking, campaigning for access to countryside, music; *Style—* Miss Kate Ashbrook; ✉ Telfer's Cottage, Turville, Henley-on-Thames RG9 6QL (☎ 01491 638396); Open Spaces Society, 25A Bell St, Henley-on-Thames RG9 2BA (☎ 01491 573535)

ASHBROOK, 11 Viscount (I 1751); Michael Llowarch Warburton Flower; JP (Cheshire 1983), DL (Cheshire 1982); s of 10 Viscount Ashbrook, KCVO, MBE (d 1995), and Elizabeth, *née* Egerton-Warburton; *b* 9 Dec 1935; *Educ* Eton, Worcester Coll Oxford (MA); *m* 8 May 1971, Zoë Mary, da of Francis Henry Arnold Engleheart, of The Priory, Stoke-by-Nayland, Suffolk (d 1963); 2 s (Hon Rowland Francis Warburton b 1975, Hon Harry William Warburton b 1977), 1 da (Hon Eleanor Filumena b 1973); *Heir* s, Hon Rowland Francis Warburton Flower b 1975; *Career* 2 Lt Gren Gds 1955; landowner; admitted slr 1963; ptnr: Farrer & Co 1966–76, March Pearson & Skelton 1986–91, Pannone March Pearson 1991–92, conslt Pannone & Partners 1992–96; chm Taxation Sub Ctee CLA 1984–86, pres Cheshire Branch CLA 1990–; Vice Lord Lt for Cheshire 1990–; *Recreations* gardening, shooting, the countryside; *Clubs* Brooks's; *Style—* The Rt Hon the Viscount Ashbrook, JP, DL; ✉ The Old Parsonage, Arley Green, Northwich, Cheshire CW9 6LZ (☎ 01565 777277)

ASHBURNHAM, Capt Sir Denny Reginald; 12 Bt (E 1661), of Broomham, Sussex; s of Sir Fleetwood Ashburnham, 11 Bt (d 1953); co-heir to Barony of Grandison (abeyant since 1328); *b* 24 March 1916; *m* 22 June 1946, Mary Frances, da of Maj Robert Pascoe Mair, of Wick, Udimore, Sussex; 1 s (decd), 2 da (Frances (Mrs Robert C Taylor) b 1947, Honor Rosemary (Mrs Frank Cooke) b 1949); *Heir* gs, James Fleetwood Ashburnham b 17 Dec 1979 (s of John Anchitel Fleetwood Ashburnham (b 1951 d 1981) by his w Corinne, da of D W J O'Brien, of The Grey House, Hooe Common, E Sussex); *Career* Capt S Staffs Regt; *Style—* Capt Sir Denny Ashburnham, Bt; ✉ Little Broomham, Guestling, E Sussex TN35 4HS

ASHBURTON, 7 Baron (UK 1835) John Francis Harcourt Baring; KG (1994), KCVO (1990, CVO 1980), kt (1983), DL (1994); s of 6 Baron Ashburton, KG, KCVO, JP, DL (d 1991), and Hon Doris Mary Thérèse (d 1981), da of 1 Viscount Harcourt; *b* 2 Nov 1928; *Educ* Eton (fell 1982), Trinity Coll Oxford (MA); *m* 1, 1955 (m dis 1984), Hon Susan Mary Renwick, da of 1 Baron Renwick, KBE; 2 s (Hon Mark Francis Robert b 1958, Hon Alexander Nicholas John b 1964), 2 da (Hon Lucinda Mary Louise (Hon Mrs Michael Vaughan) b 1956, Hon Rose Theresa b 1961); m 2, 27 Oct 1987, Mrs Sarah Crewe, da of John George Spencer Churchill, and Mrs Angela Culme Seymour; *Career* chm: British Petroleum plc 1992–95 (non-exec dir 1982–95), Baring Bros & Co Ltd 1974–89 (md 1955–74), Barings plc 1985–89 (non-exec dir 1985–94), Baring Stratton Investment Trust plc 1986–, Baring Fndn; dir: Bank of England 1983–91, Jaguar plc 1989–91, Outwich Investment Tst 1965–86, Royal Insurance Co 1964–82 (dep chm 1975–82), Dunlop

Holdings 1981–84; memb: Br Tport Docks Bd 1966–71, President's Ctee of CBI 1976–79; chm: Ctee on Fin for Industry (NEDC) 1980–86, Accepting Houses Ctee 1977–81; receiver-gen Duchy of Cornwall 1974–90, Lord Warden of the Stannaries and Keeper of the Privy Seal of the Duke of Cornwall 1990–94; pres Overseas Bankers' Club 1977–78, vice pres Br Bankers' Assoc 1977–81, memb Exec Ctee NACF 1989–, Rhodes tstee 1970– (chm 1987–); tstee: Royal Jubilee Tsts 1979–95, Nat Gallery 1981–87, Univ of Southampton Devpt Tst 1986–96, Winchester Cathedral Tst 1989– (chm 1993–), The Police Fndn (hon treas) 1989–; hon fell: Hertford Coll Oxford 1976, Trinity Coll Oxford 1989; High Steward of Winchester Cathedral 1991–; *Clubs* Pratt's, Flyfishers'; *Style*— The Rt Hon Lord Ashburton, KG, KCVO, DL; ✉ Lake House, Northington, Alresford, Hants SO24 9TG (☎ 01962 734293)

ASHBY, Brian Sterry; s of Roland Sterry Ashby (d 1978), of Manor House, Moulton, Northants, and Marion Elizabeth, *née* Phillips (d 1976); *b* 28 Aug 1930; *Educ* Bloxham Sch, Trinity Coll Cambridge (MA), Westminster Med Sch (MB MChir); *m* 1, 5 Dec 1953 (m dis 1960), Avis Jean, da of Daniel Howell Harding Thomas (d 1948); 1 s (Phillip Sterry b 31 Jan 1955); m 2, 14 Aug 1961 (m dis 1992), Gillian Mary Elizabeth, da of William Victor Dawson (d 1946), of Canterbury, Kent; m 3, 19 Oct 1996, Greta Geraldine, da of Arthur Chester Smith (d 1996), of Westcliff, Essex; *Career* surgical registrar St James Hosp Balham 1961–63, sr surgical registrar Westminster Hosp 1964–69, res fell Univ of California San Francisco 1966–67, conslt surgn Southend Gen Hosp 1970–91; Cutlers' Surgical award Worshipful Co of Cutlers 1983, Hunterian prof RCS 1984; memb: Br Soc of Gastroenterology, RSM; FRCS; *Books* Renal Preservation (1969), contrib to books on surgery of gallstones and choledochoscopy; *Recreations* gardening, walking, flying, collecting contemporary paintings; *Style*— Brian Ashby, Esq; ✉ Keigwin, Mousehole, Penzance, Cornwall TR19 6RR (☎ 01736 731688)

ASHBY, David Glynn; MP (C) Leicestershire NW (majority 979); s of Robert M Ashby and Isobel A Davidson; *b* 14 May 1940; *Educ* Royal GS High Wycombe, Bristol Univ (LLB); *m* 1965, Silvana Morena; 1 da (Alexandra); *Career* called to the Bar Gray's Inn 1963, in practice on SE Circuit; memb: Hammersmith Borough Cncl 1968–71, GLC for W Woolwich 1977–81, ILEA 1977–81; MP (C) Leicestershire NW 1983–; *Recreations* gardening, skiing, music; *Style*— David Ashby, Esq, MP; ✉ c/o House of Commons, London SW1A 0AA

ASHBY, Prof the Hon Michael Farries; er s of Baron Ashby, FRS (Life Peer; d 1992), and Elizabeth Helen Margaret, *née* Farries; *b* 20 Nov 1935; *Educ* Campbell Coll Belfast, Queens' Coll Cambridge (MA, PhD); *m* 1962, Maureen, da of James Stewart, of White House, Montgomery, Powys; 2 s, 1 da; *Career* asst Univ of Göttingen 1962–65, asst prof Harvard Univ 1965–69, prof of metallurgy Harvard Univ 1969–73, prof of engineering materials Univ of Cambridge 1973–89, Royal Society research prof Dept of Engineering Univ of Cambridge 1989–; ed Acta Metallurgica 1974–; memb Akademie der Wissenschaften zu Göttingen 1980–; Hon MA Harvard 1969; FRS 1979, FEng 1993; *Books* Engineering Materials (parts 1 and 2), Deformation-Mechanism Maps, The Structure and Properties of Cellular Solids, Materials Selection in Mechanical Design; *Recreations* music, design; *Style*— Prof the Hon Michael Ashby, FRS, FEng; ✉ 51 Maids Causeway, Cambridge CB5 8DE

ASHCOMBE, 4 Baron (UK 1892); Henry Edward Cubitt; s of 3 Baron Ashcombe (d 1962) by his 1 w, Sonia, da of Lt-Col Hon George Keppel, MVO, (3 s of 7 Earl of Albemarle); *b* 31 March 1924; *Educ* Eton; *m* 1, 12 Sept 1955 (m dis 1968), Ghislaine, o da of Cornelius Willem Dresselhuys, of Long Island and formerly w of late Maj Denis James Alexander (later 6 Earl of Caledon); m 2, 1973 (m dis 1979), Hon Virginia Carington, yr da of 6 Baron Carrington; m 3, 1979, Elizabeth, da of Dr Henry Davis Chipps, of Lexington, Kentucky, and widow of Geoffrey Mark Dent-Brocklehurst, of Sudeley Castle, Glos; *Heir* kinsman, Mark Cubitt b 1964; *Career* served WWII RAF; consul-gen for Monaco in London 1961–68, chm Cubitt Estates Ltd; *Clubs* White's; *Style*— The Rt Hon the Lord Ashcombe; ✉ Sudeley Castle, Winchcombe, Cheltenham, Glos GL54 5JD; Flat H, 14 Holland Park Road, London W14 8LZ

ASHCROFT, Kenneth; s of James Martland Ashcroft (d 1969), of Preston, and Mary Winifred, *née* Walker; *b* 22 March 1935; *Educ* Preston GS; *m* 1957, Patricia Maria, da of Henry Hothersall (d 1946), of Preston; 2 da (Jill (Mrs Campion) b 1961, Jayne (Mrs Bowtell) b 1963); *Career* formerly with Philips Holland and Ford of Europe; dir: Ideal Standard 1970–73, Comet 1973–75, Hepworth-Next 1975–82, Dixons Ltd 1983–85, Amstrad plc 1985–92; chm Betacom Plc 1992–94; non-exec dir Trinity House (and chm Audit Ctee); memb Advsy Gp to Employment Serv Bd; treas Br Deaf Assoc; FCA, FCMA; *Recreations* music, gardening; *Style*— Kenneth Ashcroft, Esq; ✉ Fendley Corner, Sauncey Wood, Harpenden, Herts AL5 5DW (☎ 01582 715549, fax 01582 712838)

ASHCROFT, Philip Giles; s of Edmund Samuel Ashcroft (d 1957), of Newcastle upon Tyne, and Constance Ruth, *née* Giles (d 1960); *b* 15 Nov 1926; *Educ* Newcastle Royal GS, Univ of Durham (LLB); *m* 1, 27 April 1968 (m dis 1983), Kathleen Margaret, *née* Senior; 1 s (Richard b 1969); m 2, 14 Sept 1985, Valerie May, da of Edgar Thomas George Smith (d 1966), of London; *Career* Royal Signals 1944–48; admitted slr 1951; Treasy Slrs Dept 1955–67, asst legal advsr Land Cmmn 1967–71, asst treasy slr 1971–73, under sec legal DTI 1973, legal advsr Dept of Energy 1974–80, dep slr Post Office 1980–81, slr BT 1981–87, ret; legal conslt Building Societies Cmmn 1988–96; memb Law Soc 1951; *Recreations* walking, music; *Style*— Philip Ashcroft, Esq; ✉ 24A Rudds Lane, Haddenham, Aylesbury, Bucks HP17 8JP (☎ 01844 291921)

ASHDOWN, David William (Dave); s of William Curtis Thomas, and Jean Vida Ashdown; *b* 11 Dec 1950; *Educ* Wandsworth Comp; *m* 12 Aug 1978, Carol, da of Andrew Allan Smith (d 1963); 2 s (Michael b 1974, Peter b 1979); 1 da (Elizabeth Rose b 22 Aug 1991); *Career* photographer: Keystone Press 1968–78, Daily Star 1978–86; chief sports photographer The Independent 1986–; FRPS; *Awards* Ilford Press Photographer of the Year 1974, runner-up Br Press Picture Awards 1979, Ilford Sports Picture of the Year 1985 and 1991, Nikon Press Sports Photographer of the Year 1987, Adidas Euro Sports Picture of the Year 1987, Sports Photographer of the Year 1987 and 1990, winner Euro Sports Photographer of the Year 1993; *Recreations* golf, old motorbikes; *Style*— Dave Ashdown, Esq; ✉ The Independent, 1 Canada Square, Canary Wharf, London E14 5DL (☎ 0171 293 2000, fax 0171 293 2435, car 0836 236340)

ASHDOWN, Rt Hon Jeremy John Durham (Paddy); PC (1989), MP (Lib Dem) Yeovil (majority 8,833); s of John W R D Ashdown, and Lois A Ashdown; *b* 27 Feb 1941; *Educ* Bedford Sch, Language Sch Hong Kong (qualified first class Chinese interpreter); *m* 1961, Jane Courtenay; 1 s (Simon), 1 da (Kate); *Career* RM 1959–72, served Borneo, Persian Gulf and Belfast, cmd Special Boat Section (SBS) in the Far East; first sec (Foreign Office) Br Mission to UN Geneva 1971–76, with Westland Helicopters 1976–78, sr mangr Morlands Ltd 1978–81, youth offr Dorset CC 1981–83; Parly candidate (Lib) 1976, MP (Lib until 1988, Lib Dem 1988–) Yeovil 1983–, leader Liberal Democrats 1988–; Lib/Alliance/Lib Dem spokesman: on trade and indust 1983–86, on educn and science 1987–88, on Northern Ireland 1989–90; *Clubs* National Liberal; *Style*— The Rt Hon Paddy Ashdown, MP; ✉ House of Commons, London SW1A 0AA

ASHDOWN, Baroness; Lillian Nell; *née* King; CBE (1971); da of Ralph King (d 1966), of Rhodesia (now Zimbabwe) and London, and Mabel Kathleen King (d 1969); *b* 19 May 1915; *Educ* St Margaret's Harrow, Paris, King's Coll London; *m* 1937, Arnold Silverstone, kt 1964, cr Baron Ashdown (Life Peer) 1974 and d 1977; *Career* served WWII with Mechanised Tport Corps; Westminster City cncllr 1955–65; memb Nat Union Cons Pty 1963–79, vice chm NWAC 1967, chm SE Area Cons Pty 1971–75 (previously chm of women), serv Cons Pty Policy Ctee 1973–79; fndr memb Women's Nat Cancer Campaign 1964– (vice chm 1967–70); govr St George's Hosp 1971–75, pres E Sussex DGAA 1974–78, chm Friends of Moorfield Hosp 1979 and govr Moorfields Special Health Authy; conservator Ashdown Forest 1973–78; pres Westminster SSAFA 1988– (hon sec 1982–88); *Recreations* politics, reading; *Clubs* Carlton; *Style*— The Rt Hon the Lady Ashdown, CBE; ✉ c/o Barclays Bank, 8 West Halkin St, London SW1X 8JE

ASHE, Sir Derick Rosslyn; KCMG (1978, CMG 1966); s of Frederick Charles Allen Angelo Patrick Donnelly Ashe (d 1930), and Rosalind, *née* Mitchell; *b* 20 Jan 1919; *Educ* Bradfield, Trinity Coll Oxford (MA); *m* 1957, Mrs Rissa Guinness, da of late Capt Hon Trevor Tempest Parker, DSC, RN (s of Baron Parker of Waddington of the first creation); 1 s (Dominick), 1 da (Victoria); *Career* served WWII Capt (despatches); entered HM Dip Serv 1947; cnsllr: Addis Ababa 1962–64, Havana 1964–66; head Security Dept FO 1966–69, min Br Embassy Toyko 1969–71; HM ambass: Romania 1972–75, Argentina 1975–77; ambass and perm del: First UN Special Session on Disarmament NY 1977–78, Disarmament Conf Geneva 1977–79; ret 1979; Knight of the Order of Orange Nassau with Swords (Netherlands) 1945; *Recreations* gardening, fine arts; *Clubs* Travellers', Beefsteak; *Style*— Sir Derick Ashe, KCMG; ✉ Dalton House, Hurstbourne Tarrant, Andover, Hants (☎ 01264 736276)

ASHE, (Thomas) Michael; QC (1994); s of John Ashe (d 1977), and Nancy, *née* O'Connor (d 1992); *b* 10 March 1949; *Educ* Finchley Catholic GS, Inns of Court Sch of Law; *m* 23 April 1977, Helen Morag, da of Lt Col Kenneth Wheeler Nicholson (d 1963); *Career* Estate Duty Office Inland Revenue 1967–70; called to the Bar: Middle Temple 1971, Ireland 1975, Northern Ireland 1993; with Schroders and Arbuthnot Latham (merchant banks) 1971–76; in practice at Bar 1978–; *Books* Money (4 edn, Halsbury's Laws of England, 1980), Injunctions (4 edn (reprint), Halsbury's Laws of England, 1991), Insider Trading (2 edn, 1993), Insider Crime (1993); *Recreations* walking, railways, music; *Style*— Michael Ashe, Esq, QC; ✉ First Floor, 11 Stone Buildings, Lincoln's Inn, London WC2A 3TG (☎ 0171 404 5055, chambers fax 0171 405 1551, private fax 0171 430 2631)

ASHE, Rosemary Elizabeth; da of Philip Stephen Ashe, of Wakefield, W Yorks, and Dorothy May, *née* Watts; *b* 28 March 1953; *Educ* Lowestoft GS, RAM, London Opera Centre; *Career* soprano; operatic roles incl: The Queen of Night in The Magic Flute (Opera North), Marionette in The Cunning Widow (Wexford Festival), Fiakermilli in Arabella, Esmeralda in The Bartered Bride, Papagena in The Magic Flute, Venus in Orpheus in the Underworld (ENO), Lucy Lockitt in The Beggar's Opera and Despina in Cosi fan Tutte (directed by Jonathan Miller for BBC TV), Musetta in La Bohème (Opera Northern Ireland), Frasquita in Carmen (Earls Court prodn repeated in Japan), Violetta in La Traviata (Holland Park); roles in musicals incl: Janet in The Rocky Horror Show, Maria in West Side Story, Hortense in The Boy Friend, Yum Yum in The Mikado, created the role of Carlotta in The Phantom of the Opera, Manon and Sari in Bitter Sweet (Sadler's Wells Opera), title role in La Belle Hélène (New Sadler's Wells Opera), Cunegonde in Candide (Old Vic Theatre), Josephine in HMS Pinafore (City Center Opera NY), Julie in Showboat (RSC/Opera North), The Witch in Into the Woods (Wolsey Theatre Ipswich), Madame Thénardier in Les Misérables (Palace), Widow Corney in Oliver (Palladium), Dinah in Trouble in Tahiti (Music Theatre Transparant Belgium); other performances incl: Masterpiece Theatre Anniversary Celebrations (New York Forbidden Broadway Company Los Angeles and Washington), Think Pink (one-woman show), Annie in Annie Get Your Gun (Wolsey Theatre Ipswich), Hermia in A Midsummer Night's Dream (Barbados Festival), Lottie Grady in When We Are Married and Orinthia in The Applecart (both Wolsey Theatre Ipswich), Asphynxia in Salad Days (nat tour), Zou Zou in La Belle Vivette (ENO), Mrs Darling in Peter Pan (Theatre Royal Nottingham); regular broadcaster on Friday Night is Music Night and Songs From The Shows (Radio 2); TV incl: The Music Game (Channel 4), Whale On (Channel 4), House of Eliot (BBC); recordings incl: The Phantom of the Opera, The Boyfriend, Bitter Sweet, Kismet, The Student Prince, The Song of Norway, Oliver; *Style*— Ms Rosemary Ashe; ✉ c/o Hilary Fagan, Caprice House, 3 New Burlington Street, London W1X 1FE (☎ 0171 439 1371, fax 0171 439 4108)

ASHER, Bernard Harry; *Career* dir HongKong Bank 1989–92 (joined 1980), exec dir investmt banking HSBC Holdings plc 1992–, chm HSBC Investment Banking plc (subsid); *Style*— Bernard Asher, Esq; ✉ HSBC Investment Bank plc, Thames Exchange, 10 Queen Street Place, London EC3R 6AE (☎ 0171 621 0011)

ASHER, Jane; da of Richard Alan John Asher (d 1969), and Margaret, *née* Eliot; *b* 5 April 1946; *Educ* North Bridge House, Miss Lambert's PNEU; *m* Gerald Anthony Scarfe, *qv*, s of Reginald Thomas Scarfe (d 1972); 2 s (Alexander b 1981, Rory b 1983), 1 da (Katie b 1974); *Career* actress; proprietor Jane Asher's Party Cakes Shop and Tea Room Chelsea, cake designer Sainsbury's, conslt/spokeman McVities; contrib: TV and radio current affairs progs, newspaper and magazine articles; reg columns Daily Telegraph and The Independent; memb BBC Gen Advsy Cncl, involved with Dept of Tport's promotion of use of child car restraints, patron numerous charities, govr Molecule Theatre; tstee: WWF, BBC Children In Need, Ford Martin Fund for Children with Cancer, Child Accident Prevention Tst; memb BAFTA, assoc RADA; FRSA; *Theatre* incl: Housemaster 1957, Muriel Webster in Will You Walk A Little Faster (Duke of York's) 1960, Wendy in Peter Pan (Scala) 1961, Eliza Doolittle in Pygmalion (Watford), Juliet in Romeo and Juliet, Julietta in Measure for Measure (both City Centre NY) 1967, Celia in The Philanthropist (Mayfair and Broadway) 1970, Sally in Old Flames (Bristol Old Vic) 1974, Ann in Treats (Royal Court and Mayfair) 1975, Charlotte in Strawberry Fields, To Those Born Later (NT) 1976, Dr Scott in Whose Life Is It Anyway? (Mermaid and Savoy), Peter in Peter Pan 1979, Before The Party (also prodn, Queens Theatre) 1981, Ruth in Blithe Spirit (Vaudeville) 1986, Robot/Wife in Hence forward.... (Vaudeville) 1989, Lady Sneerwell in The School for Scandal (RNT) 1990, Diana in Making It Better (Hampstead & Criterion) 1992/93; Bristol Old Vic 1965–72: Cleo, Great Expectations, The Happiest Days of Your Life, Sixty Thousand Nights, Romeo and Juliet, Measure For Measure; *Television* incl: The Mill on The Floss, The Recruiting Officer, Hedda Gabler, Brideshead Revisited 1981, Love is Old Love is New, Voyage Round My Father, East Lynne, Bright Smiler, The Mistress 1986, Wish Me Luck 1987–89, Eats for Treats 1990, Closing Numbers 1993, The Choir 1995; *Radio* incl: Crown House; *Films* incl: Mandy 1951, Greengage Summer 1961, Alfie 1966, Deep End 1970, Henry VIII and His Six Wives 1970, Runners 1984, Dream Child 1985, Paris By Night 1988; *Books* Jane Asher's Party Cakes (1982), Jane Asher's Quick Party Cakes (1983), Jane Asher's Fancy Dress (1983), Silent Nights for You and Your Baby (1984), Easy Entertaining (1987), Moppy Is Happy (with G Scarfe, 1987), Moppy Is Angry (with G Scarfe, 1987), Keep Your Baby Safe (1988), Jane Asher's Children's Parties (1988), Calendar of Cakes (1989), Eats for Treats (1990), Jane Asher's Complete Book of Cake Decorating Ideas (1993), Time to Play (1995), The Longing (1996), 101 Things I wish I'd Known (1996); *Recreations* times crossword, reading, music; *Style*— Jane Asher; ✉ c/o ICM Ltd, Oxford House, 76 Oxford Street, London W1N 0AX (☎ 0171 636 6565, fax 0171 323 0101)

ASHER, Prof Ronald E; s of Ernest Asher, and Doris, *née* Hurst; *b* 23 July 1926; *Educ* King Edward VI GS Retford Notts, UCL (BA, PhD), Univ of Edinburgh (DLitt 1992); *m* 1960, Chin; 2 s (David b 1966, Michael b 1968); *Career* asst Dept of French UCL 1951–53, lectr in linguistics and Tamil SOAS Univ of London 1953–65; Univ of Edinburgh: sr lectr Dept of Linguistics 1965–70, reader 1970–77, prof of linguistics 1977–93, dean of Faculty of Arts 1986–89, memb of Univ Ct 1989–92, vice-princ 1990–93, curator of patronage 1991–93; visiting prof: of Tamil Univ of Chicago 1961–62, of linguistics Univ of Illinois 1967, of Tamil and Malayalam Michigan State Univ 1968, of linguistics Univ of Minnesota 1969, Collège de France Paris 1970, of linguistics and int communication Int Christian Univ Tokyo 1994–95, of 20th century Malayalam lit Mahatma Gandhi Univ Kottayam S India 1995–96; fell of the Kerala Sahitya Akademi (Kerala Academy of Letters) India 1983, Gold medal of the Akademi for distinguished servs to Malayalam language and lit; FRAS 1964, FRSE 1991; *Books* A Tamil Prose Reader (1971), Aspects de la Littérature en Prose dans le Sud de l'Inde (1972), Some Landmarks in the History of Tamil Prose (1973), Scavenger's Son (translation from Malayalam, 1975), Me Grandad 'ad an Elephant (translation from Malayalam, 1980), Towards a History of Phonetics (ed with E J A Henderson, 1981), Tamil (1982), Malayala Bhasha-Sahitya Pathanangal (Malayalam - Studies on Malayalam Language and Literature) (1989), National Myths in Renaissance France (1993), Atlas of the World's Languages (jt ed, 1994), The Encyclopedia of Language and Linguistics (ed in chief, 1994), Concise History of the Language Sciences from the Sumerians to the Cognitivists (jt ed, 1995), Malayalam (1996); *Style*— Prof R E Asher, FRSE; ✉ Department of Linguistics, University of Edinburgh, Adam Ferguson Building, Edinburgh EH8 9LL (☎ 0131 650 3484, fax 0131 650 3962, telex 727442 UNIVED G, e-mail rea@ed.ac.uk)

ASHFORD, Prof Norman Joseph; s of Robert Edward Ashford (d 1979), of London, and Gladys Kathleen, *née* Norman (d 1975); *b* 21 Aug 1935; *Educ* Gunnersbury Sch, UCL (BSc), Georgia Inst of Technol (MSCE, PhD); *m* 13 June 1957, Joan Allison, da of Maurice Hornsby (d 1959), of Sutton in Ashfield; 1 s (Robert Simon b 12 Sept 1962), 1 da (Elizabeth b 18 Nov 1966); *Career* Royal Canadian Engr (Militia) 2 Lt 1961–63, Lt 1963–66; conslt engr Canada 1957–63, asst and assoc prof Florida State Univ 1967–72, prof of tport planning Loughborough Univ of Technol 1972–; dir Norman Ashford (Consulting Engineers) Ltd; author of numerous articles in jls; FICE 1971, FCIT 1972, MASCE 1967; *Books* Transportation Engineering (1972, 3 edn 1989), Airport Engineering (1979, 3 edn 1992), Airport Operations (1984, 2 edn 1991), Airport Finance (1992); *Recreations* photography; *Clubs* Royal Cwlth Soc; *Style*— Prof Norman Ashford; ✉ 15 The Drive, Woodhouse Eaves, Leicestershire LE12 8RE (☎ 01509 890260); Department of Transport Technology, Loughborough University of Technology, Loughborough, Leicestershire LE11 3TU (☎ 01509 223400, fax 01509 223946, telex 34319)

ASHFORD, Peter Desmond; s of Walter George Ashford (d 1985), and Beatrice Narcissa, *née* Davis (d 1985); *b* 31 July 1934; *Educ* Rutlish Sch; *m* 19 Dec 1969, Jennifer Anne, da of Robert James Patrick; 2 da (Elizabeth Anne b 13 July 1971, Catherine Anne b 16 Oct 1974); *Career* articled clerk then accountant Lever Honeyman & Co Chartered Accountants 1951–63; Annan & Dexter & Co: joined 1963, seconded to Deloitte Plender Griffiths Annan & Co Ndola Zambia 1965–66, ptnr 1968–71; ptnr: Dearden Lord Annan Morrish 1971–73, Dearden & Co (name change) 1973–76, Dearden Farrow (following merger) 1976–87, Binder Hamlyn (following merger) 1987–89, BDO Binder Hamlyn (name change) 1989–94, Binder Hamlyn (name change following merger with Arthur Andersen Worldwide Organisation) 1994–95, ret; FCA (ACA 1961); *Recreations* travel, photography; *Clubs* City of London; *Style*— Peter Ashford, Esq; ✉ 3 Rozeldene, Hindhead, Surrey GU26 6TW (☎ 01428 605064)

ASHFORD, Ronald; CBE (1992); s of Russell Sutcliffe Ashford (d 1960), of Alton, Hants, and Dorothy, *née* Shorland (d 1963); *b* 24 Aug 1932; *Educ* St Edward's Sch Oxford, De Havilland Aeronautical Tech Sch; *m* 18 June 1955, Francoise Louisa Gabrielle, da of Camille Genestal Du Chaumeil (d 1978), of Le Havre, France; 2 s (Mark b 1959, Peter b 1961); *Career* Nat Serv PO RAF 1956–58; flt test engr De Havilland Aircraft Co 1953–56, flt test engr and sr aerodynamicist De Havilland Aircraft Co and Hawker Siddeley Aviation 1958–68, design surveyor Air Registration Bd 1968–72; CAA: design surveyor 1972–82, head Flt Dept 1982–83, dir gen airworthiness 1983–87, head of operational safety 1987–88, gp dir safety 1988–92, bd memb 1988–92; sec gen Euro Jt Aviation Authorities 1992–94; aviation and safety conslt 1992–; vice chm Aerospace Industs Bd IMechE 1991–96, memb Cncl IMechE 1992–95; Liveryman Guild of Air Pilots and Air Navigators 1991; CEng 1970, FRAeS 1983, FIMechE 1986; *Recreations* walking, gardening, light aircraft flying; *Style*— Ronald Ashford, Esq, CBE; ✉ Chartcote, Goodley Stock Rd, Crockham Hill, Edenbridge, Kent TN8 6TA (☎ 01732 866252, fax 01732 867928)

ASHKEN, Kenneth Richard; CB (1996); s of Karol Maksymilian Ashken, and Dulcinea, *née* Cook; *b* 13 June 1945; *Educ* Whitgift Sch, Univ of London (LLB), Cambridge Inst of Criminology (DipCrim); *m* 1, Linda Salemink; 2 s (Toby b 1977, Sam b 1978), 1 da (Lucy b 1981); m 2, Patricia Almond; 1 da (Claudia b 1991); *Career* slr; Office of Dir of Public Prosecutions: joined 1972, asst dir 1984–86; Crown Prosecution Serv: joined as head of Policy and Info Div 1986, dir Policy Gp 1990–96; FRSA; *Clubs* RAC; *Style*— Kenneth Ashken, Esq, CB

ASHKENAZY, Vladimir; s of David Ashkenazy, of Moscow, and Evstolia Plotnova (d 1979); *b* 6 July 1937; *Educ* Moscow Central Sch of Music, Moscow Conservatory (second prize Chopin int piano competition 1955, first prize Brussels int piano competition 1956, first prize Tchaikovsky int piano competition 1962); *m* 25 Feb 1961, Thorunn Sofia, da of Johann Tryggvason, of Iceland; 2 s (Vladimir Stefan b 1961, Dimitri Thor b 1969), 3 da (Nadia Liza b 1963, Sonia Edda b 1974, Alexandra Inga b 1979); *Career* concert pianist and conductor; studied under Lev Oborin class Moscow Conservatory 1955, debut with London Symphony Orch 1962, debut solo recital London (Festival Hall) 1963, music dir Royal Philharmonic Orch London 1987–95, music dir Radio Symphony Orch (now Deutsches Sinfonie-Orchester) Berlin 1989–; Hon RAM 1972, Order of Falcon Iceland 1988; *Books* Beyond Frontiers (with Jasper Parrott, 1985); *Style*— Vladimir Ashkenazy, Esq

ASHLEY, Lord; Anthony Nils Christian Ashley-Cooper; s and h of 10 Earl of Shaftesbury; *b* 24 June 1977; *Style*— Lord Ashley

ASHLEY, Bernard John; s of Alfred Walter Ashley (d 1967), and Vera, *née* Powell (d 1978); *b* 2 April 1935; *Educ* Sir Joseph Williamson's Mathematical Sch Rochester, Trent Park Coll of Educn Herts, Cambridge Inst of Educn (Advanced DipEd); *m* 1957, Iris Frances, da of Harold Edward Holbrook; 3 s (Christopher b 1 Jan 1961, David b 1 June 1963, Jonathan b 17 April 1965); *Career* writer; teacher in Kent until 1965; head teacher: Hertford Heath CP Sch 1965–71, Hartley Jr Sch Newham 1971–77, Charlton Manor Jr Sch London 1977–95; memb Writers' Guild of GB; *Novels* The Trouble with Donovan Croft (1974, The Other Award 1975), Terry on the Fence (1975), All My Men (1977), A Kind of Wild Justice (1979), Break in the Sun (1981), Dodgem (1983), High Pavement Blues (1984), Janey (1985), Running Scared (1986), Bad Blood (1988), Johnnie's Blitz (1995); *Short Story Collections* Clipper Street (1988), Seeing Off Uncle Jack (1991), Dockside School (1992), The Puffin Book of School Stories (1993); *Picture Books* Cleversticks (with Derek Brazell, 1992), I Forgot, said Troy (with Derek Brazell, 1996), A Present for Paul (with David Mitchell, 1996); *Television* BBC TV serials: Break In the Sun (1981), Running Scared (1986), The Country Boy (1989), Dodgem (1991, winner Best Children's Entertainment Prog, RTS 1992); Three Seven Eleven (Granada TV series), Justin and the Demon Drop Kick (Carlton for EBU); *Plays* The Old Woman who lived in a Cola Can (tour, 1988/89), The Secret of Theodore Brown (Unicorn Theatre London, 1990); *Recreations* travel, watching football at Tottenham, theatre, concerts; *Style*— Bernard Ashley, Esq; ✉ 128 Heathwood Gardens, London SE7 8ER (☎ 0181 854 5785, fax 0181 244 0131)

ASHLEY, Cedric; CBE (1984); s of Ronald Bednall Ashley (d 1980), and Gladys Vera, *née* Fincher; *b* 11 Nov 1936; *Educ* King Edward's Sch Birmingham, Univ of Birmingham (BSc, PhD); *m* 1, 1960, Pamela Jane (decd), da of William Turner; 1 s (Paul); m 2, 1965 (m dis 1989), (Marjorie) Vivien, da of Arnold Joseph Gooch (d 1960); 1 s (William b 1971), 1 da (Juliet b 1967); m 3, 1991, Auriol Mary Keogh, da of John Kelly; *Career* with Rolls-Royce Ltd Derby 1955–60; lectr Univ of Birmingham 1965–73 (ICI research fell 1963), int tech dir Bostrom Div UOP Ltd 1973–77, dir Motor Indust Res Assoc 1977–87, md Lotus Engineering Ltd 1987–88, chm Cedric Ashley and Associates 1988–, chief exec British Internal Combustion Engine Research Inst 1989–91, md Steyr Power Technology Ltd 1992–; dir: Euromoter 1992–, Joalto Design Inc USA; chm: SEE 1970–72, RAC Tech Ctee 1980–87; memb: SMMT Tech Bds 1977–87, Bd Assoc of Independent Contract Research Orgns 1977–86 (pres 1982–84), Coventry and District Engrg Employers' Assoc 1978–85, Court Cranfield Inst of Technol 1977–87, Engine and Vehicles Ctee DTI 1980–88, Three Dimensional Design Bd CNAA 1981–87; Liveryman Worshipful Co of Carmen; FIMechE 1978 (chm Automobile Div 1990–91), FRSA 1983; *Awards* Cementation Muffelite Award SEE 1968, Design Cncl Award 1974; *Recreations* walking, motoring; *Clubs* RAC; *Style*— Cedric Ashley, Esq, CBE; ✉ 29 High Street, Burnham, Bucks SL1 7JD (☎ and fax 01628 662399)

ASHLEY, Jackie; da of Lord Ashley of Stoke, *qv*, and Pauline Kay, *née* Crispin; *b* 10 Sept 1954; *Educ* Rosebery GS Epsom Surrey, St Anne's Coll Univ of Oxford (BA); *m* Aug 1987, Andrew Marr, *qv*, *s of Donald Marr; 1 s (Harry Cameron b 5 July 1989), 2 da (Isabel Claire b 4 Oct 1991, Emily Catherine b 3 Nov 1994); Career* news trainee BBC 1978–80, prodr Newsnight 1980–82, politics prodr C4 News 1982–86, presenter Their Lordships House and The Parliament Programme 1986–88, political corr ITN 1988–; *Recreations* my children, walking, reading; *Style*— Ms Jackie Ashley; ✉ ITN Ltd, 200 Gray's Inn Road, London WC1X 8XZ (☎ 0171 833 3000)

ASHLEY-MILLER, Dr Michael; CBE (1995); s of Cyril Ashley-Miller (d 1963), and Marjorie, *née* George (d 1975); *b* 1 Dec 1930; *Educ* Charterhouse, Hertford Coll Oxford (BA, BM BCh, MA), KCH, London Sch of Hygiene (DPH); *m* 31 May 1958, Yvonne Marcell, da of Cyril Marcell Townend; 3 da (Amanda b 1959, Tessa b 1961, Penny b 1964); *Career* house surgn and physician KCH 1956, SMO Dulwich Hosp 1957; Nat Serv Flt Lt RAF: MO Oakington 1958–60, SMO Colerne 1960; SMO IOW CC 1961–64, MO and SMO MRC HQ 1964–74, sr princ MO Scottish Home and Health Dept 1983–86; sec Nuffield Provincial Hosps Tst 1986–95 (conslt 1996–), visiting research fell Brookes Univ 1996–; Hon FRCGP 1995; FRCP, FRCPEd, FFPHM, FRSM; *Books* Screening for Risk of Coronary Heart Disease (jtly, 1986); *Recreations* walking, reading, visiting cathedrals; *Clubs* RSM; *Style*— Dr Michael Ashley-Miller, CBE; ✉ 28 Fitzwarren Gardens, London N19 3TP (☎ 0171 272 7017)

ASHLEY MILLER, Lt Cdr Peter; s of Cyril Ashley Miller (d 1963), of Seafield, Overstrand, Norfolk, and Marjorie, *née* George (d 1975); *b* 26 Dec 1925; *Educ* RNC Dartmouth; *m* 11 Feb 1956, Catherine Jill, da of Maj John MacNaughton, MC (d 1959), of Upavon, Wilts, and Hon Mrs Doris MacNaughton (d 1976); 2 da (Bridget b 1957, Catherine b 1959), 1 s (Mark b 1962); *Career* RN 1939–59 in Home, Med and Far East Fleets and Admty; dir: Ionian Bank Ltd 1972–77, Arbuthnot Latham Bank Ltd 1978–90, Arbuthnot Fund Managers Ltd 1990–; md Archimedes Investment Trust plc 1973–; chm: Norland Nursery Trg Coll 1983–88, Burlingham House Home for Mentally Handicapped 1984–95; FCA, AIIMR; *Recreations* sailing; *Clubs* Bankers', Norfolk (Norwich); *Style*— Lt Cdr Peter Ashley Miller; ✉ 7 Ballygate, Beccles, Suffolk NR34 9NA

ASHLEY OF STOKE, Baron (Life Peer UK 1992), of Widnes in the County of Cheshire; Jack Ashley; CH (1975), PC (1979); s of John Ashley (d 1927), and Isabella, *née* Bridge; *b* 6 Dec 1922; *Educ* Ruskin Coll Oxford (scholarship 1946–48), Gonville and Caius Coll Cambridge (scholarship 1948–51, chm Cambridge Lab Club 1950, pres Cambridge Union 1951); *m* 1951, Pauline Kay, da of Clarence Adley Crispin, of Liverpool; 3 da (Hon Jacqueline (Hon Mrs Marr) b 1954, Hon Jane Elizabeth (Hon Mrs Rosenbaum) b 1958, Hon Caroline (Hon Mrs Dewdney) b 1966); *Career* labourer and cranedriver 1936–46, cncllr Borough of Widnes 1945, shop steward convenor and memb Nat Exec Chem Workers' Union 1946; student 1946–51; BBC: radio prodr 1951–57, sr television prodr 1957–66, memb Gen Advsy Cncl 1967–69 and 1970–74; MP (Lab) Stoke-on-Trent S 1966–92; PPS to Sec of State for: Econ Affairs 1966–67, Health and Social Security 1974–76; memb Nat Exec Ctee of Lab Pty 1976–78; chllr Univ of Staffordshire 1993–; pres: Hearing and Speech Tst 1985–, Royal Nat Inst for the Deaf; *Books* Journey into Silence (1973), Acts of Defiance (1992); *Style*— The Rt Hon Lord Ashley of Stoke, PC, CH; ✉ c/o House of Lords, London SW1A OPW

ASHLEY-SMITH, Dr Jonathan; s of Ewart Trist Ashley-Smith (d 1972), of Sutton Valence, Kent, and Marian Tanfield, *née* Smith; *b* 25 Aug 1946; *Educ* Sutton Valence, Univ of Bristol (BSc, PhD), Univ of Cambridge; *m* 19 Aug 1967, Diane Louise, *née* Wagland; 1 s (Joseph Daniel b 1975), 1 da (Zoë Elizabeth b 1985); *Career* V & A: scientific offr 1973–77, head of Conservation Dept 1977–; memb: Conservation Ctee Cncl for Care of Churches 1978–85, Crafts Cncl 1980–83 (memb Conservation Ctee 1978–83), Bd of Govrs London Coll of Furniture 1983–85; UK Inst for Conservation: memb 1974–, memb Exec Ctee 1978–84, vice chm 1980–83, chm 1983–84; hon fell RCA 1992, Leverhulme fell 1994–95; FIIC 1985, FRSC 1987, CChem 1987, FMA 1988; *Books* Science for Conservators (scientific ed, Vols 1–3, 1984); author of articles in learned jls; *Recreations* legal combinations of driving fast, getting drunk, and heavy rock music; *Clubs* Anglesea; *Style*— Dr Jonathan Ashley-Smith; ✉ Conservation Department, Victoria and Albert Museum, London SW7 2RL (☎ 0171 938 8568, fax 0171 938 8477)

ASHMALL, Harry A; *b* 22 Feb 1939; *Educ* Kilsyth Acad, Univ of Glasgow (MA, MLitt), Jordanhill Coll of Educn; *m*; 2 da; *Career* asst The High Sch of Glasgow 1961–66 (princ teacher of history 1968–71); rector: Forfar Acad 1971–79, Morrison's Acad 1979–; lectr and religious presenter; series incl: In Opposite Corners, The Church and...., The Apostles' Creed, Sunday Worship; individual presentations incl: Crossfire, Does God Exist After 1984?, Thought for the Day, A Personal View, Voyager, Sixth Sense; lectr Malaysian Inst of Mgmnt; chm Scottish Educnl Research Assoc 1980–83, chm Educnl Broadcasting Cncl for Scotland 1991–94; vice chm: UNICEF Exec Bd (UK), UNICEF Mgmnt Ctee, SCIS Governing Bd, Mgmnt Ctee of Scot Cncl for Ind Schs; chm ISIS (Scotland); FIMgt, MMIM; *Books* The High School of Glasgow - A History (1976); also various pamphlets and articles; *Recreations* reading, writing, scuba diving; *Clubs* New (Edinburgh), East India; *Style*— Harry Ashmall, Esq

ASHMORE, Adm of the Fleet Sir Edward Beckwith; GCB (1974, KCB 1971, CB 1966), DSC (1942); s of Vice Adm Leslie Haliburton Ashmore, CB, DSO (d 1974), and late Tamara Vasilievna, *née* Schutt, and bro of Vice Adm Sir Peter William Beckwith Ashmore, KCB, KCVO, DSC, *qv*; *b* 11 Dec 1919; *Educ* RNC Dartmouth; *m* 1942, Elizabeth, da of late Rear Adm Sir Lionel Sturdee, 2 Bt, CBE; 1 s, 1 da (and 1 da decd); *Career* joined RN 1933; served 1938–42 HMS: Birmingham, Jupiter, Middleton; qualified in Signals 1943, staff of C-in-C Home Fleet Flag Lt 4 Cruiser Sqdn 1944–45, qualified interpreter in Russian 1946, asst naval attaché Moscow 1946–47, Sqdn Communications Offr 3 Aircraft Carrier Sqdn 1950, Cdr 1950, cmd HMS Alert 1952–53, Capt 1955, Capt (F) 6 Frigate Sqdn and CO HMS Blackpool 1958, dir of plans Admty and MOD 1960–62, Cdr Br Forces Caribbean Area 1963–64, Rear Adm 1965, Asst Chief of the Defence Staff Signals 1965–67, Flag Offr second in cmd Far East Fleet 1967–68, Vice Adm 1968, Vice-Chief Naval Staff 1969–71, Adm 1970, C-in-C Western Fleet 1971, C-in-C Fleet

1971–74, First and Princ Naval ADC to HM The Queen 1974–77, Chief of Naval Staff and First Sea Lord 1974–77, Chief of Defence Staff 1977; non-exec dir Racal Electronics plc 1978–; govr Sutton's Hosp 1976–; *Clubs* Naval and Military; *Style*— Adm of the Fleet Sir Edward Ashmore, GCB, DSC; ✉ c/o Naval Secretary, Victory Building, HM Naval Base, Portsmouth, Hampshire

ASHMORE, Fionna Margaret; da of John Michael Campbell Stewart, and Ann Margaret, *née* Symington; *b* 21 May 1950; *Educ* Oporto British Sch, Convent of the Sacred Heart Tunbridge Wells, Univ of Wales Cardiff (BA), Univ of Glasgow; *m* 22 April 1972, Peter John Ashmore, s of Prof P Ashmore; 2 s (Alexander b 2 Aug 1974, James b 12 Nov 1976), 1 da (Jessica b 19 July 1981); *Career* res into Portugese Iron Age 1971–73, archaeological indexing, excavation and res 1973–; dir Soc of Antiquaries of Scotland 1992–; memb Cncl Cockburn Assoc 1992– (asst sec 1990–92); FSA Scot 1974, FSA 1996; *Recreations* reading, walking, visiting archaeological sites, countryside recreations, visiting art galleries and museums; *Style*— Mrs Fionna Ashmore, FSA; ✉ Society of Antiquaries of Scotland, Royal Museum of Scotland, Chambers Street, Edinburgh EH1 1JF (☎ 0131 225 7534)

ASHMORE, Gillian Margaret; da of John Roger Oxenham, of Heytesbury, Wilts, and Joan, *née* Palmer; *b* 14 Oct 1949; *Educ* Walthamstow Hall Sch Sevenoaks, Winchester Co HS for Girls, Newnham Coll Cambridge (BA); *m* 1971, Frederick Scott Ashmore, s of Prof Philip George Ashmore; 2 da (Beatrice b 1980, Olivia (Polly) b 1989), 2 s (Edward (Ned) b 1982, John b 1986); *Career* civil servant; various housing and tport positions DOE 1971–78 (Housing Corp 1974), various positions (incl fin, vehicle safety, bus deregulation and privatisation) Dept of Tport 1979–85, dep dir Enterprise & Deregulation Unit Dept of Employment (became unit of DTI 1987) 1986–89, head Central Fin Div Dept of Tport 1990–92, dir Privatisation and Internal Communication BR 1992–94, regnl dir Govt Office for the SE 1994–; tstee Kingston Friends Workshop Gp; FRSA; *Recreations* walking, swimming, novels, tennis, dancing, socialising, children; *Style*— Ms Gillian Ashmore; ✉ Government Office for the, South East, Bridge House, Walnut Tree Close, Guildford, Surrey GU1 4GA (☎ 01483 882260, fax 01483 882269)

ASHMORE, Prof Jonathan Felix; s of Eric Peter Ashore, of Fermoy, Co Cork, Eire, and Rosalie Sylvia, *née* Crutchley; *b* 16 April 1948; *Educ* Westminster (Queen's scholar), Univ of Sussex (BSc), Imperial Coll London (PhD), Univ Coll London (MSc); *m* 1974, Sonia Elizabeth Newby, da of George Eric Newby, CBE, MC, *qv*; 1 s (Joseph Prospero b 14 Nov 1974), 1 da (Lucia b 30 May 1979); *Career* visiting scientist ICTP Trieste Italy 1971–72, Nuffield biological scholar 1972–74, research asst Dept of Biophysics UCL 1974–77, visiting research physiologist Dept of Ophthalmology Univ Coll San Francisco USA 1977–80; Univ of Sussex: temp lectr 1980–82, MRC research assoc 1982–88; Univ of Bristol: lectr 1983–88, reader in physiology 1988–93, prof of biophysics 1993–96; Bernard Katz prof of biophysics UCL 1996–; Fulbright scholar 1977–80, G L Brown prize lectr Physiological Soc 1992–93; author of various research reports in learned jls; memb Physiological Soc 1980; FRS 1996; *Recreations* reading, travel (virtual and actual); *Style*— Prof Jonathan Ashmore, FRS; ✉ Department of Physiology, University College London, Gower Street, London WC1E 6BT (☎ 0171 380 7133, e-mail j.ashmore@ucl.ac.uk)

ASHMORE, Vice Adm Sir Peter William Beckwith; KCB (1972, CB 1968), KCVO (1980, MVO (4 Class) 1948), DSC (1942); s of late Vice Adm Leslie Haliburton Ashmore, CB, DSO (d 1974), and late Tamara Vasilievna, *née* Schutt, of St Petersburg; yr bro of Adm of the Fleet Sir Edward Ashmore, GCB, DSC, *qv*; *b* 4 Feb 1921; *Educ* Yardley Court, RNC Dartmouth; *m* 1952, Patricia Moray, da of late Adm Sir Henry Tritton Buller, GCVO, CB (d 1960), and Lady Hermione, *née* Stuart, da of 17 Earl of Moray (d 1989); 1 s, 3 da; *Career* midshipman RN 1939, served WWII (despatches), Lt 1941; Equerry (temp) to HM The King 1946–48; Extra Equerry to: HM The King 1948–52, HM The Queen 1952–; Cdr 1951, Capt 1957, Dep Dir RN Staff Coll Greenwich 1957, Capt (F) Dartmouth Training Sqdn 1960–61, Imperial Defence Coll 1962, Plans Div Admty 1963, Rear Adm 1966, Flag Offr Admty Interview Bd 1966–67, Chief of Staff to C-in-C Western Fleet and NATO C-in-C E Atlantic 1967–69, Vice Adm 1969, Chief of Allied Staff NATO Naval HQ S Europe 1970–72, ret; Master of HM's Household 1973–86; *Recreations* golf, tennis, fishing; *Style*— Vice Adm Sir Peter Ashmore, KCB, KCVO, DSC

ASHTON, Andrew Keith Maxwell; s of Sqdn Ldr Hugh Alan Ashton, DFC (d 1989), and Joan Maxwell, *née* Mann; *b* 18 Sept 1950; *Educ* Framlingham Coll, Wells Cathedral Sch, Trent Poly, Univ of London (LLB); *m* 20 April 1985, Dr Patricia Mary White, da of Norman Ernest White (d 1981); 1 s (Richard), 1 da (Catherine); *Career* admitted slr 1974; ptnr Herbert Mallam Gowers 1976–; memb: Wallingford Rowing Club, Warborough and Shillingford Soc, Friends of Oratory Sch; memb Law Soc; *Recreations* bringing up children, bar mgmnt, taming the garden; *Clubs* Law Soc; *Style*— Andrew Ashton, Esq; ✉ Little Cranford, Moulsford, Oxon OX10 9HU (☎ 01491 651305); Herbert Mallam Gowers, West Way House, Elms Parade, Oxford OX2 9LL (☎ 01865 244661, fax 01865 241842)

ASHTON, David Julian; *b* 23 Oct 1948; *Educ* LSE (BSc); *m* April 1976, Marilyn Joy Ashton; 2 s (Richard b July 1977, Michael b March 1981); *Career* ptnr Arthur Andersen 1982– (joined 1970); memb Exec Ctee Centre for Alternative Dispute Resolution, sec Shipping Discussion Gp; MInstPet, FCA; fell: Inst of Arbitrators, Acad of Experts; *Recreations* skiing, walking; *Clubs* Carlton; *Style*— David Ashton, Esq; ✉ Arthur Andersen, 1 Surrey Street, London WC2R 2PS (☎ 0171 438 3352, fax 0171 438 5582)

ASHTON, George Arthur; s of Lewis Arthur Ashton (d 1952), and Mary Annie Ashton (d 1964); *b* 27 Nov 1921; *Educ* Llanidloes GS, Birmingham Coll of Technol; *m* 1, 1948, Joan Rutter (decd); 1 s (Stephen); m 2, 1978, Pauline Jennifer, *née* Margett; *Career* HM Forces 1943–47, Maj Far East; works dir Tubes Ltd, dep md TI Steel Tube Div 1966 (tech dir 1962); dir: TI Group plc 1969–84 (md Machine Div 1974, tech dir and business area chm 1978–84), Arthur Lee & Sons plc 1981–91; chm Seamless Tubes Ltd 1983–86; engrg and mgmnt conslt, ret; dep chm Steering Ctee WINTECH Welsh Devpt Agency 1984–87; pres BISPA 1973–74, vice pres Advanced Mfrg Technol Research Inst (AMTRI) 1986– (chm Cncl 1982–86); hon memb American Iron & Steel Inst 1974–94, assoc memb Parly & Scientific Ctee 1978–84; CEng, FIMechE, CIMgt, FRSA 1981; *Recreations* walking, cycling, gardening; *Clubs* Naval and Military; *Style*— George Ashton, Esq; ✉ Barn Cottage, Longford, Ashbourne, Derbyshire DE6 3DT (☎ 01335 330561)

ASHTON, Hon (Thomas) Henry; s and h of 3 Baron Ashton of Hyde; *b* 18 July 1958; *Educ* Eton, Trinity Coll Oxford; *m* 31 October 1987, Emma Louise, da of Colin Allinson, of Bath; 3 da (Harriet Emily b 11 July 1990, Isabel Louise b 22 Sept 1992, Flora Juliet b 17 April 1995); *Career* C T Bowring Ltd; Guy Carpenter & Co Inc NY; D P Mann Underwriting Agency Ltd; *Clubs* Boodle's; *Style*— The Hon Henry Ashton; ✉ Broadwell Hill, Moreton-in-Marsh, Glos GL56 0UD (☎ 01451 830626)

ASHTON, Hubert Gaitskell (Hugh); DL (Essex 1983); s of Sir Hubert Ashton, KBE, MC (d 1979), of Brentwood, and Dorothy Margaret, *née* Gaitskell (d 1983); *b* 27 Jan 1930; *Educ* Winchester, Trinity Coll Cambridge (MA); *m* 1956, Anna-Brita, da of Gustav Bertil Rylander, of Sweden (d 1976); 3 s (Hubert, Peter, Charles), 1 da (Katherine); *Career* 2 Lt Irish Gds 1948–50; Peat Marwick Mitchell 1953–61, J Henry Schroder Wagg & Co (merchant bankers) 1961–85; dir: The Housing Corp 1979–85, Brixton Estate plc 1983–85, Hanson plc 1985–89, BAA plc 1986–93, Wheway plc 1989–93, Rosehaugh plc 1991–92, Albert Fisher Group plc 1991–; chm Close Brothers Group plc 1989–95; High Sheriff Essex 1983–84; pres: Essex Co Football Assoc 1984–, Essex Friends of YMCA 1985–95; chm Govrs Brentwood Sch 1989–; memb Ct of Assts Worshipful of Skinners (Master 1986–87); FCA; *Recreations* shooting, eating, drinking, swimming; *Clubs* MCC, City of London; *Style*— H G Ashton, Esq, DL; ✉ Wealdside, South Weald, Brentwood, Essex (☎ 01277 373406, fax 01277 374936); 32 Garrick House, Carrington St, London W1 (☎ 0171 499 3989)

ASHTON, Prof John Richard; *b* 27 May 1947, Liverpool; *Educ* Univ of Newcastle upon Tyne (Nuffield Fndn scholar in tropical med Fiji Islands, Charlton scholar in med, MB BS, MRCPsych), London Sch of Hygiene and Tropical Med London (MSc, Sir Allen Daley meml prize in social med); *m*; 3 c; *Career* house physician and house surgn Newcastle upon Tyne Univ Hosp Gp 1970–71, gen practice locum July-Oct 1971, SHO in gen med and geriatrics Newcastle Univ Hosp Gp Oct 1971–72, SHO and registrar Dept of Psychological Med Univ of Newcastle upon Tyne Rotational Trg Scheme 1972–74, princ in gen practice Newcastle and Northumberland Family Practitioner Ctees Newcastle Univ Student Health Serv 1974–75, lectr in primary med care (mental health) Univ of Southampton and princ in gen practice Hants Family Practitioner Ctee 1975–76, postgraduate student in social med London Sch of Hygiene and Tropical Med 1976–78, sr registrar in community med Hants AHA and lectr in community med Univ of Southampton 1978–79, sr lectr Dept of Community Med London Sch of Hygiene and Tropical Med 1980–82, sr lectr Dept of Public Health Univ of Liverpool 1983–93 (personal chair in public health policy and strategy 1993); regional dir of public health and regional med offr: Mersey RHA 1993–94 (hon specialist in public health med 1983–93, dir Liverpool Public Health Observatory 1990–93, head Dept of Public Health and dir Public Health Team 1991–93), North West RHA 1994–; visiting prof Valencian Inst for Public Health Studies Spain 1988, professorial fell Liverpool Sch of Tropical Med 1994; inaugural coordinator Euro WHO Healthy Cities Project 1986–88; formerly occasional advsr to WHO on the devpt of educn progs, currently advsr to WHO on the devpt of city-based public health strategies; gen rapporteur 44th World Health Assembly Tech Discussions on urban health Geneva 1991; memb: Int Scientific Advsy Gp Inst of Public Health Valencia 1995, Bd Faculty of Public Health Med and Exec Royal Coll of Physicians of England, Chief Med Offr's Academic Forum; FFPHM 1986, FRCPsych; *Books* Everyday Psychiatry (1980), Esmedune 2000 (A Healthy Liverpool) - Vision or Dream? (1986), The New Public Health - The Liverpool Experience (with H Seymour, 1988, Spanish edn 1990), Healthy Cities (ed, 1991), The Urban Health Crisis - Strategies for All in the Face of Rapid Urbanisation (ed, 1991); also author of numerous book chapters, papers and editorials in learned jls; *Style*— Prof John Ashton; ✉ North West Regional Health Authority, 930 Birchwood Boulevard, Millenium Park, Birchwood, Warrington WA3 7QN (☎ 01925 704233, fax 01925 704241)

ASHTON, Joseph William (Joe); MP (Lab) Bassetlaw (majority 9,997); s of Arthur and Nellie Ashton, of Sheffield; *b* 9 Oct 1933; *Educ* High Storrs GS, Rotherham Tech Coll; *m* 1957, Margaret Patricia, da of George Lee, of Andover St, Sheffield; 1 da; *Career* engrg apprentice 1949–54; Nat Serv RAF 1954–56; design engr 1956–68; cncllr Sheffield City Cncl 1962–69, MP (Lab) Bassetlaw 1968–; journalist; columnist: Sheffield Star 1970–75 and 1979–80, Labour Weekly 1971–82, Daily Star 1979–88, Sunday People 1988–89, Plus magazine 1988–89; PPS to Sec of State for Energy 1974–76, asst govt whip 1976–77, front bench spokesman on Energy 1979–81; memb Select Ctee on: Trade and Indust 1987–89, Home Affairs 1989–92, Nat Heritage 1992–; winner What the Papers Say (Granada TV) award for Columnist of the Year 1984; dir Sheffield Wednesday FC 1990–; chm House of Commons Football Ctee 1992–; *Books* Grassroots (Novel, 1977), A Majority of One (Play, 1981); *Clubs* Foundry Working Men's (Sheffield), Doncaster Road Working Men's (Langold); *Style*— Joe Ashton, Esq, MP; ✉ 16 Ranmoor Park Rd, Sheffield (☎ 0114 230 1763); House of Commons, London SW1A 0AA (☎ 0171 219 3000)

ASHTON, Rt Rev Leonard James; CB (1970); s of late Henry Ashton, of Chesham, Bucks, and late Sarah, *née* Ing; *b* 27 June 1915; *Educ* Tyndale Hall Trinity Coll Bristol; *Career* ordained 1942, curate Cheadle 1942–45, chaplain RAF 1945–74; served: Far E (incl Br Cwlth Occupation Forces in Japan) 1945–48, Middle E 1954–55 and 1960–61; RAF Coll Cranwell 1956–60, Br Forces Arabian Peninsular and ME Cmd 1960–61, asst chaplain-in-chief Training Cmds 1962–65, res chaplain St Clement Danes 1965–69, chaplain-in-chief and archdeacon RAF (rank of Air Vice-Marshal) 1969–73; hon canon and preb of Lincoln Cathedral 1969–73 (canon emeritus 1973–), asst bishop in Jerusalem 1974–76, episcopal canon St George's Cathedral Jerusalem 1976–83, bishop in Cyprus and the Gulf 1976–83, hon asst bishop of Oxford 1983–, commissary for bishops in Jerusalem and Iran 1983–, episcopal canon St Paul's Cath Nicosia Cyprus 1989–; hon chaplain to HM The Queen 1967–73; ChStJ 1976; *Books* Winged Words (1990); *Recreations* photography, gardening; *Clubs* RAF; *Style*— The Rt Rev Leonard Ashton, CB; ✉ 60 Lowndes Avenue, Chesham, Bucks HP5 2HJ (☎ 01494 782952)

ASHTON, Prof Norman Henry; CBE (1976); 2 s of late Henry James Ashton, of Herts, and late Margaret Ann, *née* Tuck; *b* 11 Sept 1913; *Educ* West Kensington Sch, King's Coll London and Westminster Hosp Med Sch Univ of London, DSc (London) 1961, FRCP, FRCS, FRCPath, FRCOphth; *Career* Lt-Col RAMC, asst dir of pathology and offr i/c Central Pathological Laboratory Middle East 1946; dir of pathology Kent and Canterbury Hosp 1941, blood transfusion offr East Kent 1941, pathologist Gordon Hosp 1947; Inst of Ophthalmology Univ of London: dir Dept of Pathology 1948–78, reader in pathology 1953, prof of pathology 1957–78, fell and emeritus prof 1978–; conslt pathologist Moorfields Eye Hosp 1948–78; fell in residence Johns Hopkins Hosp Baltimore 1953 (visiting prof 1959), emeritus fell Leverhulme Tst, visiting research fell Merton Coll Oxford 1980; memb: Cncl RCPath 1963–66 and 1976–78 (fndr fell), Governing Body Br Postgrad Med Fedn 1967–82 (chm Central Acad Cncl 1967–70), Cncl RSM 1971–79 (memb Exec Ctee 1976–8), Br Nat Ctee for Prevention of Blindness 1973–78, Royal Postgrad Med Sch Cncl 1977–80, Pathological Soc of GB and Ireland, Euro Assoc for Study of Diabetes, Medical Art Soc; memb Ctee of Mgmnt: Inst of Ophthalmology 1953–78 and 1984–92, Inst of Child Health 1960–65, Cardio-Thoracic Inst 1972–78, Inst of Rheumatology 1973–77; memb Bd of Govrs: Moorfields Eye Hosp 1963–66 and 1975–78, Hosp for Sick Children Gt Ormond St 1977–80, Royal Nat Coll for the Blind 1977–, Brendoncare Fndn 1984–; pres: Br Div Int Acad of Pathology 1962, Ophth Section RSM 1972–74, Assoc of Clinical Pathologists 1978–79, Ophth Soc of UK 1979–81, European Ophthalmic Pathology Soc (life pres); tstee Fight for Sight Appeal 1965–91 (chm 1980–91); Freeman City of London, Master Worshipful Soc of Apothecaries of London 1984–85 (currently asst emeritus); Hon DSc Chicago, fell Coll of Physicians Philadelphia USA; KStJ 1971; FRS 1971; *Awards* Edward Nettleship Prize for Research in Ophthalmology 1953, BMA Middlemore Prize 1955, Proctor Medal for Research in Ophthalmology USA 1957, Doyne Medal Oxford 1960, William Julius Mickle Fellow Univ of London 1961, Bowman Medal 1965, Donder's Medal 1967, Wm Mackenzie Memorial Medal 1967, Gonin Medal 1978, first Jules Stein Award USA 1981, Francis Richardson Cross Medal 1982, Lord Crook Gold Medal Spectacle Makers' Co 1989, International Pizart Vision Award USA 1991, Buchanan Medal Royal Soc 1996; *Recreations* painting, gardening; *Clubs* Athenaeum, Garrick; *Style*— Prof Norman Ashton, CBE, FRS; ✉ 4 Blomfield Rd, Little Venice, London W9 1AH (☎ 0171 286 5536)

ASHTON, Prof Robert; s of Joseph Ashton (d 1979), of Chester, and Edith Frances, *née* Davies (d 1954); *b* 21 July 1924; *Educ* Magdalen Coll Sch Oxford, Univ Coll Southampton, LSE (BA, PhD); *m* 30 Aug 1946, Margaret Alice, da of T W Sedgwick (d

1948), of Dover; 2 da (Rosalind Helen b 1954, Celia Elizabeth b 1960); *Career* WWII served RAF 1943–46; sr lectr in econ history Univ of Nottingham 1961–63 (asst lectr 1952–54, lectr 1954–61), visiting assoc prof of history Univ of Calif Berkeley 1962–63, emeritus prof UEA 1989 (prof of Eng history 1963–89, dean Sch of Eng Studies 1964–67), Leverhulme emeritus fell 1989–91; visiting fell All Souls Coll Oxford 1973–74 and 1987, James Ford special lectr in History Oxford 1982; FRHistS 1961 (vice pres 1983–86); *Books* The Crown and The Money Market 1603–1640 (1960), James I By His Contemporaries (1969), The English Civil War: Conservatism and Revolution 1603–1649 (1978, 2 edn 1989), The City and the Court 1603–1643 (1979), Reformation and Revolution 1558–1660 (1984), Counter-Revolution: the Second Civil War and Its Origins 1646–48 (1994); *Recreations* wine, food, music, old buildings; *Style*— Prof Robert Ashton; ✉ The Manor House, Brundall, Norwich NR13 5JY (☎ 01603 713368)

ASHTON, Prof Rosemary; *b* 11 April 1947; *Educ* Univ of Aberdeen (MA, Seafield medal, Senatus prize), Newnham Coll Cambridge (Lucy fell, PhD); *m*; 3 c; *Career* temp lectr in English Univ of Birmingham 1973–74; Univ Coll London: lectr in English 1974–86, reader in English 1986–91, prof of English 1991–; Deutscher Akademischer Austauschdienst (DAAD) Stipendium Univ of Heidelberg 1966–67, Literary Review Award for The German Idea 1980, DAAD Travel Scholarship 1983, British Acad Thank-Offering to Britain fell 1984–85, British Acad Res Readership 1988–90, visiting fell Beinecke Library Yale Univ 1989, Leverhulme Res Fellowship 1995; memb: Int Assoc of Univ Profs of English, Humanities Research Bd Br Acad; *Books* The German Idea: Four English Writers and the Reception of German Thought 1800–1860 (1980), George Eliot (1983), Little Germany: Exile and Asylum in Victorian England (1986), The Mill on the Floss: A Natural History (1990), G H Lewes: A Life (1991), The Life of Samuel Taylor Coleridge: A Critical Biography (1996), George Eliot: A Life (1996); author of numerous edition introductions and articles and reviews in jls; *Style*— Prof Rosemary Ashton; ✉ University College London, Gower Street, London WC1E 6BT (☎ 0171 419 3143, fax 0171 916 2054)

ASHTON, Ruth Mary (Mrs E F Henschel); OBE (1991); da of Leigh Perry Ashton, and Marion Lucy, *née* Tryon; *b* 27 March 1939; *Educ* Kenya HS for Girls, Clarendon Sch (lately Abergele), The London Hosp, Queen Mother's Hosp and High Coombe Midwife Teachers' Trg Coll (RN 1965, RM 1967, MTD 1970); *m* 7 April 1984, E Fred Henschel; *Career* staff midwife and midwifery sister Queen Mother's Hosp Glasgow 1967–69, nursing offr and midwifery tutor King's Coll Hosp London 1971–75; Royal Coll of Midwives: tutor 1975–79, professional offr 1979, gen sec 1980–94; non-exec dir Optimum NHS Tst 1995–; temp prof March of Dimes LA 1982; offr sister OStJ 1988; memb and vice pres Royal Coll of Midwives, ACIArb 1995; *Books* Your First Baby (ed and author, 1980), Report on Activities, Responsibilities and Independence of Midwives in the European Union (1996); *Recreations* gardening, sailing, travel; *Clubs* Queenborough Yacht; *Style*— Miss Ruth Ashton, OBE; (☎ and fax 0181 851 7403)

ASHTON, William Michael Allingham; MBE (1978); s of Eric Sandiford Ashton (d 1983), of Lytham St Annes, and Zilla Dorothea, *née* Miles (d 1944); *b* 6 Dec 1936; *Educ* Rossall Sch, St Peter's Coll Oxford (BA, DipEd); *m* 22 Oct 1966, Kay Carol, da of John Stallard Watkins, of New Quay, Dyfed; 2 s (Grant b 1967, Miles b 1968), 1 da (Helen b 1983); *Career* Nat Serv RAF 1955–57; fndr and musical dir Nat Youth Jazz Orchestra (NYJO) 1965–; numerous appearances before royalty incl Royal Variety Performance 1978, toured many countries on behalf of Br Cncl (USA, USSR, Aust, Turkey); chm NYJO Ltd 1972–; memb: Musicians' Union, Br Assoc of Jazz Musicians; owner Stanza Music; fell Leeds Coll of Music 1995; *Awards* for NYJO: Best Br Big Band Br Jazz Awards 1993 and 1995, Critics' Choice 1992 and 1995, winner BBC Radio 2 Award for Servs to Jazz 1995, Silver Jazz Medal Worshipful Co of Musicians 1996; *Recreations* reading, song writing, snorkelling; *Style*— William Ashton, Esq, MBE; ✉ 11 Victor Rd, Harrow, Middx HA2 6PT (☎ 0181 863 2717, fax 0181 863 8685)

ASHTON-BOSTOCK, David Ashton; s of Cdr John Bostock, DSC, RN; additional surname and arms assumed by Royal Licence 1953, at the wish of his great-uncle Samuel Ashton-Yates; *b* 17 Feb 1930; *Educ* Wellington, Maidstone Coll of Art, Byam Shaw Art Sch; *m* 1965 (m dis 1983), Victoria Rosamond, da of Capt Richard White, DSO, RN; 1 s (decd), 1 da; *Career* interior designer; vice pres Alexandra Rose Day; memb Lloyd's; fell Interior Decorators and Designers' Assoc; FIAL; *Recreations* painting, gardening, genealogy; *Style*— David Ashton-Bostock, Esq; ✉ Danes Bottom Place, Wormshill, Sittingbourne, Kent (☎ 01622 884476); 28 Sutherland St, London SW1 4LA (☎ 0171 834 1696)

ASHTON-JONES, Christopher James; *b* 18 March 1948; *Educ* Nailsea GS; *m* 1972, Carmen Mary, *née* Don-Fox; 1 s (George John b 1978), 2 da (Joanna Mary b 1973, Amelia Jane b 1975); *Career* trainee N M Rothschild and Sons 1966–69, institutional sales Hoare Govett 1969–71, investmt analyst and mangr Eastminster Group 1971–73, fin PR exec Leo Burnett 1973–76, exec Dewe Rogerson 1976–79 (dir 1979–83), PR mangr The BOC Group 1983–85, investor relations dir Dewe Rogerson 1985–88, dir Brunswick Public Relations Ltd 1988–93, dir Ludgate Communications Ltd 1994–95, ind conslt 1996–; memb Cncl Inst of PR 1985–86 (chm City and Fin Gp 1983–84); memb Communications Advsy Ctee World Wide Fund for Nature (WWF) 1992–95; FIPR 1992 (MIPR 1978); *Books* This Public Relations Consultancy Business (contrib, 1984); *Recreations* motorboating, gardening, classic cars; *Clubs* City of London, Chichester Yacht; *Style*— Christopher Ashton-Jones, Esq; ✉ Minster Oak, 8 Quartermile Road, Godalming, Surrey GU7 1TG (☎ and fax 01483 428234)

ASHTON OF HYDE, 3 Baron (UK 1911); Thomas John Ashton; TD; s of 2 Baron Ashton of Hyde, JP, DL (d 1983), and Marjorie Nell, *née* Brooks (d 1993); *b* 19 Nov 1926; *Educ* Eton, New Coll Oxford (MA); *m* 18 May 1957, Pauline Trewlove, er da of Lt-Col Robert Henry Langton Brackenbury, OBE, of Yerdley House, Long Compton, Shipston on Stour; 2 s, 2 da; *Heir* s, Hon Thomas Henry Ashton b 18 July 1958; *Career* formerly Lt 11 Hussars, Maj Royal Glos Hussars (TA); sr exec local dir Barclays Bank Manchester 1968–81, dir Barclays Bank plc and subsidiary cos 1969–87; Liveryman Worshipful Co of Goldsmiths; JP Oxon 1965–68; *Clubs* Boodle's; *Style*— The Rt Hon the Lord Ashton of Hyde, TD, JP; ✉ Fir Farm, Upper Slaughter, Bourton on the Water, Glos GL54 2JR (☎ 01451 830652)

ASHTOWN, 7 Baron (I 1800); Sir Nigel Clive Cosby Trench; KCMG (1976, CMG 1966); s of Clive Newcome Trench (d 1964, s of Hon Cosby Godolphin Trench, 2 s of 2 Baron Ashtown), and Kathleen, da of Maj Ivar MacIvor, CIE; suc kinsman, 6 Baron Ashtown (d 1990); *b* 27 Oct 1916; *Educ* Eton, CCC Cambridge; *m* 1 Dec 1939, Marcelle Catherine (d 1994), da of Johan Jacob Clotterbooke Patyn van Kloetinge, of Zeist, Holland; 1 s; *Heir* s, Hon Roderick Nigel Godolphin Trench b 1944; *Career* serv KRRC WWII (UK and NW Europe, despatches); Foreign Serv 1946, first sec 1948, first sec (commercial) Lima 1952, cnsllr Tokyo 1961, cnsllr Washington 1963, Cabinet Office 1967, ambass to Korea 1969–71, memb Civil Serv Selection Bd 1971–73, ambass to Portugal 1974–76, memb Police Fire and Prison Serv Selection Bds 1977–86; Order of Dip Serv Merit (Rep of Korea) 1984; *Recreations* golf, looking at other people's gardens; *Clubs* Naval and Military; *Style*— The Rt Hon Lord Ashtown, KCMG; ✉ 4 Kensington Court Gardens, Kensington Court Place, London W8 5QE

ASHURST, Prof John; *b* 14 March 1937; *Career* architect; asst architect in private practice with Scott Brownrigg and Turner and J Brian Cooper 1961–69, architect Directorate of Ancient Monuments and Historic Buildings DOE 1969–75, princ architect DAMHB (later English Heritage) 1975–90, heritage restoration conslt in private practice 1990–91; prof of heritage conservation Dept of Conservation Sciences Univ of Bournemouth 1991– (also dir Historic Building and Site Servs); sometime lectr: Inst of Advanced Architectural Studies Univ of York, Int Centre for the Study of the Preservation and the Restoration of Cultural Property (Rome), Architectural Assoc Sch of Architecture, Soc for the Protection of Ancient Buildings, Standing Joint Ctee on Natural Stones, Directorate of Ancient Monuments and Historic Buildings, Heriot Watt Sch of Architecture, Univ of Edinburgh, Oxford Brookes Univ, Inst of Archaeology; research projects: Surface Treatments for Stone 1970–72, Desalination of Masonry Walls 1970–74, Biocide Performance 1970–75, Stone Consolidant Development 1972–81, Limestone Consolidation 1975–84, Plaster Consolidation 1984–87, Conservation of Clunch 1985–87, Smoke Deposited Insecticides 1970–90, Mortar Performance 1989–; *Books Specification* - Stone Masonry (with Francis Dimes, 1975), *Stone in Building* - Its Use and Potential Today (with Francis Dimes, 1977), Mortars, Plasters and Renders in Conservation (1983 and 1996), Practical Building Conservation (5 vols, with Nicola Ashurst, 1988), The Conservation of Building and Decorative Stone (2 vols, with Francis Dimes, 1990), Stone Cutter, Restoration Mason (with Keith Blades, 1991); also author of various tech papers; *Style*— Prof John Ashurst; ✉ Resurgam Conservation Consultancy, Netley House, Gomshall, Guildford, Surrey GU5 9QA (☎ 01483 203221, fax 01483 202911)

ASHURST, (Kenneth William) Stewart; s of Kenneth Latham Ashurst, OBE, and Helen Ferguson, *née* Rae; *b* 19 May 1945; *Educ* Royal GS Newcastle upon Tyne, King Edward VI GS Lichfield, Exeter Coll Oxford (MA Jurisprudence), Coll of Law Guildford, Univ of Birmingham (MSocSc Corp Mgmnt); *m* 1984, Catherine Mary, da of George Sample; 1 da (Olivia b 6 Jan 1985), 2 s (William b 5 June 1987, Edward b 19 June 1989); *Career* articled clerk Leicester County BC 1967–68, articled clerk then asst slr Newcastle upon Tyne County BC 1968–71, SSRC post graduate Univ of Birmingham 1971–72, asst slr Cumberland CC 1972–73, asst county clerk Cumbria CC 1973–79, county slr and dep county clerk Suffolk CC 1981–85 (dep county sec 1979–81), chief exec Essex CC 1994– (dep chief exec and clerk 1985–94); dir: Essex TEC, Year of Opera and Music Theatre; memb Senate Univ of Essex; other positions incl: clerk to Essex Police Authy, clerk to Essex Lieutenancy, local govt memb Cncl Law Soc of England and Wales, memb Local Govt Gp Law Soc (former chm), sec Lord Chllr's Advsy Ctee, clerk to River Crouch Harbour Authy, sec Stansted Airport Consultative Ctee; former chm: Planning and Environmental Law Ctee Law Soc, Para Legal Trg Gp Law Soc, Post Qualification Casework Ctee Law Soc, Slrs' Mgmnt Devpt Gp; memb Law Soc 1971; *Recreations* family, wine tasting, daydreaming; *Style*— Stewart Ashurst, Esq; ✉ Essex County Council, County Hall, Duke Street, Chelmsford, Essex CM1 1LX (☎ 01245 430015, fax 01245 256731)

ASHWORTH, Prof Andrew John; s of Clifford Ashworth (d 1993), and Amy, *née* Ogden; *b* 11 Oct 1947; *Educ* Rishworth Sch, LSE (LLB), New Coll Oxford (DCL), Univ of Manchester (PhD); *m* 1971 (sep), Gillian, *née* Frisby; 2 da (Susannah b 1974, Alison b 1976); *Career* lectr then sr lectr in law Univ of Manchester 1970–78, fell and tutor in law Worcester Coll Oxford 1978–88, Edmund-Davies prof of criminal law and criminal justice KCL 1988–; ed Criminal Law Review 1975–; FBA 1993; *Books* Principles of Criminal Law (1991, 2 edn 1995), Sentencing and Criminal Justice (1992, 2 edn 1995), The Criminal Process (1994); *Recreations* travel, bridge, golf; *Style*— Prof Andrew Ashworth, FBA; ✉ School of Law, King's College, Strand, London WC2R 2LS (☎ 0171 836 5454)

ASHWORTH, Anne Mary Catherine; s of Peter Ashworth, of Wimbledon, and Joan, *née* Kay (d 1975); *b* 13 June 1954; *Educ* Ursuline Convent Wimbledon, King's Coll London (BA); *m* 1985, Tom Maddocks; 1 s (George b 1990); *Career* journalist; Accountancy magazine 1980–82, Sunday Express 1982–86, Today 1986, Daily Mail 1986–87, personal fin ed and assoc city ed Mail on Sunday 1987–94, personal fin ed The Times 1994–; *Style*— Ms Anne Ashworth; ✉ The Times, 1 Pennington Street, London E1 9XN (☎ 0171 782 5000)

ASHWORTH, David Anthony; s of Dr Harold Kenneth Ashworth (d 1978), and Maimie Margery, *née* Baldwin; *b* 18 July 1944; *Educ* Uppingham, St Edmund Hall Oxford (MA, rep univ at rugby and cricket); *children*; 1 s (Nicholas David b 17 March 1980), 2 da (Tamsin Lucy b 9 March 1974, Katherine Emma b 20 Oct 1975); *Career* Norton Rose: articled clerk 1967–69, admitted slr 1970, ptnr 1977–, departmental managing ptnr Commercial Property & Planning Dept 1987–94; Freeman Worshipful Co of Slrs of the City of London 1977, Freeman City of London 1992; memb Law Soc; *Recreations* golf, cricket, avoiding gardening, being educated by my children; *Clubs* City of London, Vincent's, British Sportsman's, MCC, Harlequins CC, Free Foresters CC, I Zingari CC; *Style*— David Ashworth, Esq; ✉ Norton Rose, Kempson House, Camomile Street, London EC3A 7AN (☎ 0171 283 6000, fax 0171 283 6500); Richmond, Surrey

ASHWORTH, Prof Graham William; CBE (1980), DL (Lancs 1991); s of Frederick William Ashworth (d 1978), and Ivy Alice, *née* Courtiour (d 1982); *b* 14 July 1935; *Educ* Devonport HS, Univ of Liverpool (BArch); *m* 2 April 1960, Gwyneth Mai, da of John Morgan Jones (d 1959); 3 da (Clare, Alyson, Kate); *Career* architect and planner: London CC 1959–62, Graeme Shankland Associates 1962–64; architect Civic Tst 1964–65, dir Northwest Civic Tst 1965–73 (chm Exec Ctee 1973–87); Univ of Salford: prof of urban environmental studies 1973–87, dir Environmental Inst 1978–87, dir Campaign to Promote Univ of Salford (CAMPUS) 1981–87, res prof of urban environmental studies 1987–; dir gen Tidy Britain Group 1987–; chm Ravenhead Renaissance Ltd 1988–, chm Going for Green 1994–; dir: Merseyside Devpt Corpn 1981–92, Norweb 1985–88; memb: NW Economic Planning Cncl 1968–79 (chm of sub-gp), Skeffington Ctee on Public Participation in Planning 1969, NW Advsy Cncl of BBC 1970–75, Countryside Cmmn 1974–77; pres RTPI 1973–74, chm Inst of Environmental Sciences 1980–82; memb: Baptist Union Cncl 1975–, Cncl St George's House Windsor 1982–88; tstee Manchester Museum of Science and Industry 1988–91; assoc pastor Carey Baptist Church Preston 1977–86; RIBA 1962, FRSA 1968, FRTPI 1969, FIMgt 1986; *Books* An Encyclopaedia of Planning (1973), International Journal of Environmental Education and Information (ed 1981–), Britain in Bloom (1991), The Role of Local Government in Environmental Protection (1992); *Clubs* Nat Lib, Athenaeum; *Style*— Prof Graham Ashworth, CBE, DL; ✉ Manor Court Farm, Preston New Road, Samlesbury, Preston, Lancs PR5 0UP (☎ 01254 812011); Tidy Britain Group, The Pier, Wigan WN3 4EX (☎ 01942 824620); Going for Green, 56 Oxford Street, Manchester M60 7HJ (☎ 0161 237 4158)

ASHWORTH, Sir Herbert; kt (1972); s of Joseph Hartley Ashworth (d 1954), of Burnley, Lancs; *b* 30 Jan 1910; *Educ* Burnley GS, Univ of London (BSc, LLB); *m* 1936, Barbara Helen Mary, da of Douglas D Henderson (d 1932), of London; 2 s, 1 da; *Career* gen mangr: Portman Building Soc 1938–50, Co-operative Permanent Building Soc 1950–61; dir and gen mangr Hallmark Securities Ltd 1961–66; chm: Housing Corporation 1968–73 (dep chm 1964–68), Nationwide Building Society 1970–82 (dep chm 1968–70); dir The Builder Ltd 1975–80; chm: Surrey and W Sussex Agric Wages Ctee 1974–88, Nationwide Housing Tst 1983–87; vice pres Building Socs Assoc; *Publications* Housing in Great Britain (1951), Building Society Work Explained (1977), The Building Society Story (1980); *Style*— Sir Herbert Ashworth; ✉ 8 Tracery, Park Road, Banstead, Surrey SM7 3DD (☎ 01737 352608)

ASHWORTH, Dr John Michael; s of Jack Ashworth (d 1975), and Mary Constance, *née* Ousman (d 1971); *b* 27 Nov 1938; *Educ* West Buckland Sch, Exeter Coll Oxford (BA, BSc, MA), Univ of Leicester (PhD), Univ of Oxford (DSc); *m* 1, 13 July 1963, Ann (d

1985), da of Peter Knight (d 1977); 1 s (Matthew b 24 Sept 1971), 3 da (Harriet b 23 Oct 1964, Sophia b 2 Dec 1968, Emily b 3 Aug 1970); m 2, 23 July 1988, Auriol Hazel Dawn Stevens, *qv*; *Career* Dept of Biochemistry Univ of Leicester: research demonstrator 1961–63, lectr 1963–71, reader 1971–73; prof of biology Univ of Essex 1974–79, seconded to central policy review staff 1976–79, under sec Cabinet Office 1979–81, chief scientist CPRS 1979–81, vice chllr Univ of Salford 1981–90, dir LSE 1990–96, chm Bd British Library 1996–; chm: Salford University Business Services Ltd and Business Enterprises Ltd 1981–90, Bd National Computer Centre Ltd 1983–92; dir: BR (London Mainland) 1987–92, Granada TV 1986–89, Granada Group plc 1990–, J Sainsbury plc 1993–; memb: Library and Info Servs Cncl 1980–84, Electronics Indust EDC (NEDO) 1983–86, Info Technol Econ Devpt Cncl 1983–86, Nat Accreditation Cncl for Cert Bodies BSI 1984–88; pres Res and Devpt Soc 1988; Colworth Medal Biochemical Soc 1972; FIBiol 1973, CIMgt 1984; *Books* The Slime Moulds (with J Dee, 1970), Cell Differentiation (1972); *Recreations* fell walking; *Style*— Dr John Ashworth; ✉ The British Library, 96 Euston Road, London NW1 2DB (☎ 0171 412 7264, fax 0171 412 7268)

ASHWORTH, Piers; QC (1973); s of Tom and Mollie Ashworth; *b* 27 May 1931; *Educ* Christ's Hosp Sch, Pembroke Coll Cambridge (scholar, MA), Harmsworth Law scholar 1956; *m* 1, 1959 (m dis 1978), Jennifer, da of W G Foxley; 3 s, 1 da; m 2, 1980, Elizabeth, da of A J S Aston; *Career* cmmnd Royal Signals 1951; called to the Bar Middle Temple 1956, bencher 1984, recorder of the Crown Court 1974–, in practice Midland and Oxford Circuit; chm of the Bar Mutual Indemnity Fund Ltd; govr and almoner Christ's Hospital Sch 1986–; *Recreations* sailing, squash, tennis, bridge; *Style*— Piers Ashworth, Esq, QC; ✉ 2 Harcourt Buildings, Temple, London EC4Y 9DB (☎ 0171 583 9020)

ASKE, Rev Sir Conan; 2 Bt (UK 1922), of Aughton, East Riding of Yorkshire; s of Sir Robert William Aske, 1 Bt, TD, QC, JP (d 1954), by his 2 w Edith; *b* 22 April 1912; *Educ* Rugby, Balliol Coll Oxford (MA); *m* 1, 13 Dec 1948, Vera (d 1960), yr da of late George Rowbotham, of Iffley, Oxford, and former w of Roland Faulkner; m 2, 23 Aug 1965, Rebecca (d 1996), yr da of Hugh Fraser Grant (d 1967), of Wick, Caithness; *Heir* bro, Robert Edward Aske, *qv*; *Career* served WWII Dunkirk 1940, Maj E Yorks Regt, ME 1941–51, Sudan Defence Force, Maj Civil Affairs Offr Reserved Area of Ethiopia and The Ogaden 1949–51; schoolmaster Hillstone Malvern 1952–69; asst curate: Hagley 1970–72, St John's Worcester 1972–80; chaplain to Mayor of Worcester 1979–80; hon padre 1940 Dunkirk Veterans' Assoc Worcs Branch 1988–; *Style*— The Rev Sir Conan Aske, Bt; ✉ 167 Malvern Road, Worcester WR2 4NN (☎ 01905 422817)

ASKE, Robert Edward; 2 s of Sir Robert Aske, 1 Bt, TD, QC, JP, LLD, sometime MP Newcastle E; hp to bro, Rev Sir Conan Aske, 2 Bt, *qv*; *b* 21 March 1915; *m* 1940, Joan Bingham, o da of Capt Bingham Ackerley, of White Lodge, Cobham; 1 s (Robert John Bingham b 1941); *Style*— Robert Aske, Esq; ✉ 45 Holland Rd, London W14 (☎ 0171 602 9714)

ASKEW, Sir Bryan; kt (1989); s of John Pinkney Askew (d 1940), and Matilda Brown; *b* 18 Aug 1930; *Educ* Wellfield GS Wingate Co Durham, Fitzwilliam Coll Cambridge (MA); *m* 10 Aug 1955, Millicent Rose, da of Thomas Henry Holder (d 1966); 2 da (Penelope Jane b 1957, Melissa Clare b 1966); *Career* ICI Ltd 1952–59, Consett Iron Co Ltd (later part of Br Steel Corp) 1959–71, own consultancy 1971–74; Samuel Smith Old Brewery Tadcaster: joined 1974, personnel dir 1982–95; chm Yorks RHA 1983–94; cncllr Consett UDC 1967–71; Parly candidate gen election (C): Penistone 1964 and 1966, York 1970; memb: Duke of Edinburgh's Third Cwlth Study Conf Australia 1968, Ct Univ of Leeds 1985– (memb Cncl 1988–), Working Gp on Young People and Alcohol Home Office Standing Conf on Crime Prevention 1987; Hon LLD Univ of Hull 1992; FRSA 1986, FRSM 1988; *Style*— Sir Bryan Askew; ✉ 27 Golf Links Avenue, Tadcaster, N Yorks LS24 9HF (☎ 01937 833216)

ASKEW, Henry John; s of John Marjoribanks Askew, CBE (d 1996), of Ladykirk, Berwick-upon-Tweed, and Lady Susan Alice, *née* Egerton; *b* 5 April 1940; *Educ* Eton; *m* 27 Jan 1978, Rosemary Eileen, da of Dr Charles Edmunds Darby Taylor, of Alnwick House, Little Shelford, Cambridge; 3 s (Jack b 1984, George b 1986, William b 1992); *Career* cmmnd Grenadier Guards 1959–62; dir then md Gerrard & Nat Hldgs plc (formerly Gerrard & Nat Ltd) 1967–94; *Recreations* reading, music, opera, ballet; *Clubs* Pratt's; *Style*— Henry Askew, Esq; ✉ Ladykirk House, Berwick-upon-Tweed TD15 1SU (☎ 01289 382309); 77 Chester Row, London SW1W 8JL (☎ 0171 730 6151)

ASKEW, Rev Canon Reginald James Albert; s of Paul Askew (d 1953, pioneer of Br Broadcasting), and Amy, *née* Wainwright (d 1976); *b* 16 May 1928; *Educ* Harrow, CCC Cambridge (BA, MA), Lincoln Theol Coll; *m* 1953, Kate, yr da of Rev Henry Townsend Wigley (d 1970, gen sec Free Church Federal Cncl); 1 s (Paul), 2 da (Catherine, Rachel); *Career* curate Highgate 1957–61, lectr and vice princ Wells Theological Coll 1961–69, priest vicar Wells Cathedral 1961–69, vicar of Christ Church Lancaster Gate London 1969–73, princ Salisbury and Wells Theol Coll 1973–87, chm The Southern Dioceses' Ministerial Training Scheme 1973–87, canon of Salisbury Cathedral and prebendary of Grantham Borealis 1975–87, canon emeritus Salisbury Cathedral 1988–, dean King's Coll London 1988–93; chair of contemporary theology at Lafayette Orinda California 1992; proctor Univ of London, memb Gen Synod of the C of E 1990–93, chaplain Worshipful Co of Merchant Taylors 1996–97; memb The Corrymeela Community; *Books* The Tree of Noah (1971), Muskets and Altars, Jeremy Taylor and the last of the Anglicans (1997); *Recreations* music, gardening, making lino-cuts, cricket; *Clubs* Athenaeum; *Style*— The Rev Canon Reginald Askew; ✉ Carters Cottage, North Wootton, Somerset BA4 4AF (☎ 01749 890728)

ASKHAM, (Francis) Guy Lewis; s of Francis Joe Askham, of Braishfield, Hants, and Beatrice Marjorie, *née* Lewis; *b* 10 April 1931; *Educ* Hurstpierpoint; *m* 12 Sept 1957, Marlene Joan, da of Leonard Peacock; 2 da (Hilary Jane b 5 Jan 1960, Mary Frances b 31 March 1965); *Career* Nat Serv cmmnd offr RAPC 1955–57; ptnr Burnett Swayne 1962–82 (articled 1949), business conslt and co dir 1982–; currently chm: Southampton Football Club Ltd, Wilshaw plc; also dir: Baldwin plc, M & W plc, International Energy Group Ltd; tstee Nuffield Theatre Southampton; FCA (ACA 1955), FInstD, FRSA; *Recreations* professional sport, golf, theatre; *Clubs* Hampshire CCC (vice pres), Royal Southampton Yacht, Romsey Golf; *Style*— Guy Askham, Esq; ✉ Charter Court, Third Ave, Southampton, Hants SO9 1QS (☎ 01703 702345, fax 01703 702570); Southampton Football Club, The Dell, Milton Road, Southampton SO9 4XX (☎ 01703 220505, fax 01703 330360)

ASLET, Clive William; s of Kenneth Charles Aslet, and Monica, *née* Humphreys; *b* 15 Feb 1955; *Educ* King's Coll Sch Wimbledon, Peterhouse Cambridge (MA); *m* 27 Sept 1980, Naomi Selma, da of Prof Sir Martin Roth; 1 s (William Kenneth Samuel b 26 May 1995); *Career* Country Life: architectural writer 1977–84, architectural ed 1984–88, dep ed 1988–92, ed 1993–; founding hon sec The Thirties Soc 1979–87; FRSA; *Books* The Last Country Houses (with Alan Powers, 1982), The National Trust Book of the English House (1985), Quinlan Terry, The Revival of Architecture (1986), The American Country House (1990), Countryblast (1991); *Recreations* reading, riding, roaming; *Clubs* Garrick; *Style*— Clive Aslet, Esq; ✉ c/o Country Life, King's Reach Tower, Stamford St, London SE1 9LS (☎ 0171 261 6969, fax 0171 261 5139)

ASLETT, Judy Jane; da of Michael Eric Aslett, and Gillian, *née* Kenyon; *b* 1 Oct 1962; *Educ* Culford Sch, Univ of St Andrews, Central London Poly (BA); *m* 1991, John Stephen, s of Stephen Parkin; 1 da (Emily Claire b 16 June 1992); *Career* editorial trainee ITN 1986–87, prodr Independent TV News 1987–90, corr S Africa Channel 4 News 1991–95 (Sky News 1990–91), foreign ed Channel 4 News 1995–; *Style*— Ms Judy Aslett; ✉ ITN, 200 Gray's Inn Road, London WC1X 8XZ (☎ 0171 833 3000)

ASPEL, Michael Terence; OBE (1993); s of Edward Aspel, and Violet Aspel; *b* 12 Jan 1933; *Educ* Emanuel Sch; *m* 1, 1957 (m dis), Dian; 2 s (Gregory (decd), Richard); m 2, 1962 (m dis), Ann; 1 s (Edward), 1 da (Jane (twin)); m 3, 1977, Elizabeth Power; 2 s (Patrick, Daniel); *Career* writer and broadcaster; Nat Serv KRRC and Para Regt TA 1951–53; radio actor 1954–57, BBC TV news reader 1960–68 (announcer 1957–60), freelance 1968–; daily show Capital Radio 1974–84; presenter: Aspel & Company (LWT) 1984–93, This Is Your Life (LWT until 1994 whereafter BBC1) 1988–, ITV Telethon 1988, 1990 and 1992, BAFTA Awards, Strange... But True? (LWT); Independent Radio Personality Variety Club Award 1983, ITV Personality Variety Club Award 1988; pres Stackpole Tst 1985–, vice pres Baby Life Support Systems (BLISS) 1981–, hon vice pres Assoc for Spina Bifida and Hydrocephalus (ASBAH) 1985–, patron Plan International 1986–; *Books* Polly Wants a Zebra (autobiog, 1974), Hang On! (for children, 1982), Child's Play (with Richard Hearsey, 1985); *Recreations* theatre, cinema, eating, travel, water sports; *Clubs* Lord's Taverners, RYA; *Style*— Michael Aspel, Esq, OBE; ✉ c/o API Personality Management Ltd, 141–143 Drury Lane, London WC2B 5TB (☎ 0171 379 4625, fax 0171 836 1735)

ASPIN, William George; s of George Francis Aspin, of The Elms, Willow Ave, Constable Lee, Rawtenstall, Rossendale, Lancs, and Margaret, *née* Joyce; *b* 16 Aug 1954; *Educ* Cardinal Langley GS; *m* 18 June 1994, Lynne Elizabeth Pfau; *Career* CA; formed W G Aspin & Co 1980, ptnr Dymond Ashworth & Co Accountants 1981–90, fndr W Aspin & Co Chartered Accountants 1990–; memb Rossendale Round Table; FICA (1983); *Recreations* reading, wine tasting; *Style*— William George Aspin, Esq; ✉ 95 Goodshaw Avenue North, Loveclough, Rossendale, Lancs (☎ 01706 217401); W Aspin & Co, Chartered Accountants, Sutherland House, 89 Albert Road, Colne, Lancs (☎ 01282 871871)

ASPINALL, Prof David; s of William Aspinall (d 1966), of Blackpool, and Hilda, *née* Whittle (d 1975); *b* 11 Aug 1933; *Educ* King Edward VII Lytham, Univ of Manchester (MSc, PhD); *m* 29 March 1958, Ina Paterson, da of William Kennedy Sillars, of Lytham St Annes; 2 s (Robert b 1962, Edward b 1965), 1 da (Mary b 1960); *Career* visiting assoc prof Univ of Illinois 1966, sr lectr of computer sci Univ of Manchester 1967–70 (lectr in electrical engrg 1960, lectr in computer sci 1964), prof of electrical engrg Univ Coll Swansea 1970, IEE Silvanus P Thompson lectr 1977–79, prof of computation UMIST 1978–93 (vice princ 1984–86), emeritus prof Univ of Manchester 1993–; FBCS 1968, FIEE 1977, CEng 1977; *Books* Introduction To Microprocessors (with E L Dagles, 1976), The Microprocessor & Its Application (1978), Introduction to Microcomputers (with E L Dagles, 1982); *Recreations* gardening, fell walking; *Style*— Prof David Aspinall; ✉ 16A Darley Ave, West Didsbury, Manchester M20 2XF (☎ 0161 445 6622); Department of Computation, UMIST, PO Box 88, Manchester M60 1QD (☎ 0161 200 3300, fax 0161 228 7040, telex 666 094)

ASPINALL, Robin Michael; *b* 3 Aug 1949; *Educ* Cathedral Sch Bristol, Univ of Lancaster (BA (Econ)), Univ of Manchester (MA (Econ)); *m*; 2 s; *Career* Barclays Bank plc 1966–69, university 1969–73, mangr of forecasting Economic Models Ltd 1973–76, head of economics Imperial Group plc 1976–86, chief economist Schroder Securities Ltd 1986–89, dir of currency economics Security Pacific/Hoare Govett 1989–90, chief economist Schroders 1991–92, chief economist/strategist Panmure Gordon & Co 1992–96, chief economist Financial Mkts Europe National Australia Bank 1996–; *Style*— Robin Aspinall, Esq; ✉ National Australia Bank, Ground Floor, 6–8 Tokenhouse Yard, London EC2R 7AJ (☎ 0171 710 2188)

ASPINALL, Wilfred; *b* 14 Sept 1942; *Educ* Poynton Secdy Modern Sch, Stockport Coll for Further Educn; *m* 1973, Judith Mary; 1 da (Isabel b 1980); *Career* memb Econ and Social Consultative Assembly Brussels (MESC) 1986–, princ Aspinall & Assocs Eurolink Professionals in Europe 1990–; with National Provincial Bank Ltd 1960–69, asst gen sec Nat Westminster Staff Assoc 1969–75, memb Banking Staff Cncl 1970–77, gen sec Confedn of Bank Staff Assoc 1975–79, treas and conslt Managerial Professional and Staff Liaison Gp 1978–79; exec dir and conslt Fedn of Managerial Professional and General Assocs (MPG) 1979–94, vice pres Confédération Européen des Cadres 1979–94; memb: Hammersmith Special Health Authy 1982–90, North Herts District Health Authy 1982–86, North West Thames RHA 1986–88; *Style*— Wilfred Aspinall, Esq; ✉ The Croft, 19 Shillington Rd, Pirton, Hitchin, Herts (☎ 01462 712316, fax 01462 712293); Brussels Bureau, Rue de la Tourelle 23, Brussels 1040, Belgium (☎ 00 32 2 230 8510, fax 00 32 2 230 7818)

ASPINWALL, Jack Heywood; MP (C) Wansdyke (majority 13,341); *b* 1933; *Educ* Prescot GS Lancs, Marconi Coll Chelmsford; *m* Brenda Jean Aspinwall; *Career* RAF 1949–56; Parly candidate: (Lib) Kingswood Feb and Oct 1974, (C) Kingswood 1979–83; MP (C) Wansdyke 1987–; co dir; *Books* Kindly Sit Down, Tell Me Another, Hit Me Again, After Dinner Stories; *Style*— Jack Aspinwall, Esq, MP; ✉ House of Commons, London SW1A 0AA

ASQUITH, Viscount; Raymond Benedict Bartholomew Michael Asquith; OBE; s and h of 2 Earl of Oxford and Asquith, KCMG; *b* 24 Aug 1952; *Educ* Ampleforth, Balliol Oxford; *m* 1978, Clare, da of Francis Pollen (d 1987), and Thérèse, da of His Hon Sir Joseph Sheridan, and gda of late Arthur Pollen (gn of Sir Richard Pollen, 3 Bt) by his w Hon Daphne Baring, da of 3 Baron Revelstoke; 1 s (Hon Mark Julian b 13 May 1979), 4 da (Hon Magdalen Katharine b 1981, Hon Frances Sophia b 1984, Hon Celia Rose b 1989, Hon Isabel Anne b 1991); *Heir* s Hon Mark Julian Asquith b 13 May 1979; *Career* HM Dip Serv; FCO 1980–83, first sec (Chancery) Moscow 1983–85, FCO 1985, on loan to Cabinet Office 1985–92, cnsllr (Political) Kiev 1992–; *Style*— Viscount Asquith, OBE; ✉ The Manor House, Mells, Frome, Somerset BA11 3PN

ASSCHER, Prof Sir (Adolf) William; kt (1992); s of William Benjamin Asscher (d 1982), and Roosje, *née* van der Molen (d 1993); *b* 20 March 1931; *Educ* Maerlant Lyceum The Hague Netherlands, London Hosp Med Coll (BSc, MB BS, MD); *m* 1, 1960, Corrie, *née* van Welt (d 1961); m 2, 3 Nov 1962, Jennifer, da of Wynne Lloyd, CB (d 1973), of Cardiff; 2 da (Jane (Mrs Stephen Barrett) b 1963, Sophie (Mrs Philip Hughes) b 1965); *Career* Nat Serv 1949–51, cmmnd Lt RE; jr med appts London Hosp 1957–59, lectr in medicine London Hosp Med Coll 1959–64; WNSM Cardiff (later Univ of Wales Coll of Med): conslt physician and sr lectr in med 1964–70, reader in med 1970–76, prof of med 1976–80, prof and head Dept of Renal Med 1980–87; princ St George's Hosp Med Sch London Univ 1988–96, hon conslt physician St George's Hosp 1988–96, chm Morriston Hosp NHS Tst 1996–; RCP: regnl advsr 1973–77, cncllr 1977–80, pres Faculty of Pharmaceutical Med 1995–; memb Medicines Cmmn DHSS 1981–84, chm Ctee on Review of Medicines DHSS 1984–87, memb Welsh Arts Cncl 1985–88; chm: Ctee on Safety of Medicines Dept of Health 1987–93 (memb 1984–87), Med Benefit Risk Fndn 1993–96, UKCCCR 1997–; memb SW Thames RHA 1988–90; non-exec dir: Wandsworth DHA 1988–93, St George's Healthcare Tst 1993–; Liveryman Worshipful Soc of Apothecaries 1960; memb: Renal Assoc 1962 (sec 1972–77, pres 1986–89), Assoc of Physicians 1970, Med Res Soc 1957 (memb Cncl 1966); FRCP 1970 (MRCP 1959), FFPM 1993, FRSA 1995; *Books* Urinary Tract Infection (1973), The Challenge of Urinary Tract Infections (1981), Nephrology Illustrated (with D B Moffat and E Sanders, 1982), Nephro-Urology (with D B Moffat, 1983), Microbial Diseases in Nephrology (with W Brumfitt, 1986), Medicines and Risk-Benefit Decisions (with S R Walker, 1986), Clinical Atlas of the Kidney (with J D Williams, 1990); *Recreations* visual arts, golf; *Clubs*

Reform, Cardiff and County, Radyr Golf, Radyr Lawn Tennis (chm 1972–78); *Style*— Prof Sir William Asscher; ✉ The Old Rectory, Llangan, nr Bridgend, Vale of Glamorgan CF35 5DW (☎ and fax 01656 646351); Morriston Hospital, Morriston, Swansea SA6 6NL (☎ 01792 702222, fax 01792 703632)

ASSENTI, David James Alexander; *b* 11 Dec 1947; *Educ* Blairgowrie HS; *m* Ailsa; 2 da (Sinead b 18 Aug 1971, Imogen b 4 Sept 1976); *Career* hotelier; mangr and ptnr Berkeley Hotel Southampton 1975–77 (trainee/asst 1969–72), fndr mangr Seafield Arms Cullen Banffshire 1972–77 (first hotel in Scotland to gain 3 AA red stars), md The Stewart Hotel Duror 1979–85, gen mangr Ballathie House Hotel by Stanley Perthshire 1985–93 (raised from basic 3 star fish hotel to 3 AA red stars), proprietor Cromlix House 1993–; dir Scotlands Heritage Hotels 1991–; Which? Good Hotel Guide Regional Hotel of the Year 1996; *Recreations* country leisure, reading; *Style*— David Assenti, Esq; ✉ Cromlix House, Kinbuck, by Dunblane, Perthshire FK15 9JT (☎ 01786 822125, fax 01786 825450)

ASSHETON, Hon Nicholas; s of 1 Baron Clitheroe, KCVO, PC (d 1984), and Sylvia, Lady Clitheroe (d 1991), da of 6 Baron Hotham; *b* 23 May 1934; *Educ* Eton, ChCh Oxford (MA); *m* 29 Feb 1960, Jacqueline Jill, da of Marshal of the RAF Sir Arthur Harris, 1 Bt, GCB, OBE, AFC (d 1984), of Goring-on-Thames, by his 2 w; 1 s (Thomas b 1963), 2 da (Caroline b 1961, Mary Thérèse b 1967); *Career* formerly 2 Lt Life Gds, Lt Inns of Court Regt; memb The Stock Exchange (memb Cncl 1969); sr ptnr Montagu Loebl Stanley & Co 1978 (ptnr 1960); dep chm Coutts & Co; Liveryman Worshipful Co of Vintners; Lord of the Manor and Liberty of Slaidburn, Grindleton and Bradford; FSA; *Clubs* Pratt's, White's; *Style*— The Hon Nicholas Assheton, FSA; ✉ 15 Hammersmith Terrace, London W6 9TS; Coutts & Co, 440 Strand, London WC2R 0QS (☎ 0171 753 1000)

ASSHETON, Hon Ralph Christopher; Lord of the Manors of Downham and Cuerdale; Lord of the Honor of Clitheroe and Hundred of Blackburn; s and h of 2 Baron Clitheroe, *qv*; *b* 19 March 1962; *Educ* Eton; *m* 19 Oct 1996, Olivia S, o da of Anthony Warrington, of Low Burton Hall, Masham, N Yorkshire; *Career* ARICS; *Clubs* Cavalry and Guards'; *Style*— The Hon Ralph C Assheton; ✉ The Lidgett, Downham, Clitheroe, Lancs BB7 4BL (☎ 01200 440173)

ASTAIRE, Edgar; s of Max Astaire; *b* 23 Jan 1930; *Educ* Harrow; *m* 1958 (m dis 1975); 3 s (Mark b 1959, Simon b 1961, Peter b 1963); *Career* stockbroker; chm Jewish Meml Cncl; dir Angela Flowers plc; Master Worshipful Co of Pattenmakers 1982; *Clubs* MCC, Queen's, Chelsea Arts; *Style*— Edgar Astaire, Esq; ✉ 11 Lowndes Close, Lowndes Place, London SW1X 8BZ (☎ 0171 235 5757); Cold Comfort Farm, Wendover, Bucks (☎ 01296 623172); Edgar Astaire & Co Ltd, 14 Ryder Street, St James's, London SW1Y 6QB (☎ 0171 925 2555, fax 0171 925 2625)

ASTILL, His Hon Judge Michael John; s of late Cyril Norman Astill, of Thurnby, Leics, and late Winifred, *née* Tuckley; *b* 31 Jan 1938; *Educ* Blackfriars Sch Laxton Northants; *m* 1 June 1968, Jean Elizabeth, da of late Dr John Chisholm Hamilton Mackenzie; 3 s (Matthew b 28 Dec 1972, James (twin) b 28 Dec 1972, Mark b 11 Nov 1975), 1 da (Katherine b 11 July 1971); *Career* admitted slr 1962, called to the Bar Middle Temple 1972, recorder 1980–84, circuit judge Midland and Oxford Circuit 1984–; pres Mental Health Tribunals 1986–; *Recreations* reading, music, gardening, sport; *Style*— His Honour Judge Michael Astill; ✉ c/o Midland and Oxford Circuit Office, The Priory Courts, 33 Bull Street, Birmingham B4 6DW

ASTLEY, Hon Delaval Thomas Harold; s and h of 22 Baron Hastings, *qv*; *b* 25 April 1960; *Educ* Radley, Hatfield Coll Durham; *m* 26 July 1987, Veronica M, er da of Richard A Smart, of Chester; 1 s (Jacob Addison b 5 Sept 1991), 2 da (Molly b 20 Oct 1993, another b 21 June 1996); *Style*— The Hon Delaval Astley; ✉ 39 Colville Gardens, London W11

ASTLEY, Dr Neil Philip; s of Philip Thomas Astley, of Adelaide, Aust, and Margaret Ivy Astley (d 1976); *b* 12 May 1953; *Educ* Price's Sch Fareham Hants, Univ of Newcastle upon Tyne (BA); *m* 1, 4 Sept 1976 (m dis 1983), Julie Marie Callan; m 2, 8 Oct 1988 (sep 1993), Katharine Keens-Soper, da of Henry John Stuffins, of Harrogate; *Career* md and ed Bloodaxe Books Ltd (fndr 1978); *Awards* Eric Gregory Award 1982, Poetry Book Soc Recommendation 1988, Dorothy Tutin Award for Servs to Poetry 1989, Hon DLitt Univ of Newcastle 1996; *Books* Ten North-East Poets (ed, 1980), The Speechless Act (1984), Bossy Parrot (ed, 1987), Darwin Survivor (1988), Poetry with an Edge (ed, 1988 and 1993), Dear Next Prime Minister (ed, 1990), Tony Harrison (ed, 1991), Wordworks (ed, 1992), Biting My Tongue (1995); *Recreations* reading books and enjoying countryside; *Style*— Dr Neil Astley; ✉ Bloodaxe Books Ltd, PO Box 1SN, Newcastle upon Tyne NE99 1SN (☎ 0191 232 5988, fax 0191 222 0020)

ASTLEY-COOPER, Alexander Paston; s and h of Sir Patrick Graham Astley-Cooper, 6 Bt; *b* 1 Feb 1943; *Educ* Kelly Coll Tavistock; *m* 1974, Minnie Margeret, da of Charles Harrison (d 1959); *Career* sales office mangr Carton Industry; *Recreations* cricket, badminton, rugby union, theatre, travel; *Style*— Alexander Astley-Cooper, Esq; ✉ Gadebridge, 8 Berkshire Close, Leigh-on-Sea, Essex (☎ 01702 421920)

ASTLEY-COOPER, Sir Patrick Graham; 6 Bt (UK 1821) of Gadebridge, Herts; s of late Col Clifton Graham Astley Cooper, DSO, RA (gs of 2 Bt); suc kinsman Sir Henry Lovick Cooper, 5 Bt (d 1959); *b* 4 Aug 1918; *Educ* Marlborough; *m* 7 April 1942, Audrey Ann Jervoise, yr da of late Major Douglas Philip Jervoise Collas, Military Knight of Windsor; 1 s, 2 da; *Heir* s, Alexander Paston Astley-Cooper; *Career* former sr asst land cmmr MAFF, dir Crendon Concrete Ltd Long Crendon 1973–; *Style*— Sir Patrick Astley-Cooper, Bt; ✉ The White Cottage, 3 Townside, Haddenham, Aylesbury, Bucks HP17 8BG

ASTON, Archdeacon of; *see:* Barton, Ven (Charles) John Greenwood

ASTON, John Russell; s of Mona Aston; *b* 16 Feb 1937; *Educ* Coalbrookdale Co HS Shropshire, Burslem Coll of Art Stoke-on-Trent, Shrewsbury Sch of Art & Design (NDD); *m* 20 Oct 1962, Martina Jane, da of Col John Elcho Hamilton-Selway; 2 da (Sophie Jane b 23 June 1970, Gemma Rose b 5 June 1973); *Career* art ed: Condé Nast Publishing Group London 1961–62, Fountain Press London 1962–63; designer BBC Publications London 1963–65, graphic designer BBC TV London 1965–69, sr graphic designer and gp ldr BBC Open University Productions 1969–74, mangr of prodn servs BBC TV Network Production Centre Manchester 1974–75, chief asst to Head of Graphic Design BBC TV London 1975–82, mangr and dep head of graphic design BBC TV London 1982–91, princ Berkshire Coll of Art & Design 1992–97; external examiner: CSD CNAA 1977–92, Bristol Poly BA (Hons) Graphic Design 1988–91, The London Inst 1994–96; memb: Graphic Design Bd CNAA 1977–86, Educn and Trg Bd CSD 1978–93, Editorial Bd Designer magazine 1980–86, Euro Ctee Institut National de l'Audiovisuel 1986–88, Industl Liaison Ctee Middlesex Poly 1990–92, Indust Lead Body for Design Bedford Square London 1991–, Educn and Trg Advsy Gp Design Cncl 1995–97; chm Information Bd SIAD 1982–86; govr: W Surrey Coll of Art & Design 1978–89, Falmouth Sch of Art & Design 1987–92; advsr/conslt Design Faculty Cornwall Coll of HE 1985–87, specialist advsr CNAA 1986–91; FCSD, FRSA; *Publications* author of numerous articles for jls incl: Le Mond, Television (RTS jl), Designer Magazine, Graphic Design - World Views (UK, USA and Japan); *Recreations* sailing, walking, conversing, travelling; *Style*— John Aston, Esq; ✉ Berkshire College of Art & Design, Raymond Rd, Maidenhead, Berks SL6 6DF (☎ 01628 24302, fax 01628 23797)

ASTON, Prof Peter George; s of Dr George William Aston (d 1980), and Dr Elizabeth Oliver Aston, *née* Smith (d 1979); *b* 5 Oct 1938; *Educ* Tettenhall Coll, Birmingham Sch of Music (GBSM), Univ of York (DPhil); *m* 13 Aug 1960, Elaine Veronica, da of Harold Neale (d 1942); 1 s (David b 1963); *Career* sr lectr in music Univ of York 1972–74 (lectr 1964–72), dean Sch of Fine Arts and Music UEA 1981–84 (prof and head of music 1974–); music dir: Tudor Consort 1959–65, Eng Baroque Ensemble 1967–70; conductor Aldeburgh Festival Singers 1975–88; princ guest conductor: Zephyr Point Church Music Festival Nevada 1991, 1993 and 1995, Sacramento Bach Festival Calif 1993–97; gen ed UEA Recordings 1979–, jt fndr and artistic dir Norwich Festival of Contemporary Church Music 1981–; published compositions incl chamber music, church music, opera, choral and orch works; ed complete works of George Jeffreys and music by various Baroque composers; numerous recordings and contribs to int jls; hon patron: Gt Yarmouth Musical Soc, Lowestoft Choral Soc 1986–; chm: Eastern Arts Assoc Music Panel 1975–81, Norfolk Assoc for the Advancement of Music 1990–93, Acad Bd Guild of Church Musicians 1996–; pres Norfolk Assoc for the Advancement of Music 1993–; chorus master Norfolk & Norwich Triennial Festival 1982–85, hon pres Trianon Music Gp 1984–96; hon fell Curwen Inst 1987; FTCL, FCI, ARCM, FRSA 1980, Hon RCM 1991 Hon FGCM 1995; *Books* George Jeffreys and the English Baroque (1970), Sound and Silence (jtly 1970, German edn 1972, Italian edn 1980, Japanese edn 1981), The Music of York Minster (1972), The Collected Works of George Jeffreys (3 vols, 1977), Music Theory in Practice (jtly, 3 vols 1992–93); *Recreations* travel, bridge, chess, cricket; *Clubs* Athenaeum, Norfolk (Norwich); *Style*— Prof Peter Aston; ✉ University of East Anglia, Music Centre, School of Music, Norwich NR4 7TJ (☎ 01603 56161, fax 01603 250454, telex 975197)

ASTOR, Viscountess; (Janet) Bronwen Alun; yst da of His Hon Judge Sir (John) Alun Pugh (d 1971), and Kathleen Mary, *née* Goodyear (d 1970); *b* 6 June 1930; *Educ* Dr William's Sch Dolgellau, Central Sch of Speech and Drama (Dip); *m* 1960, as his 3 w, 3 Viscount Astor (d 1966); 2 da (Hon Janet Elizabeth (Countess of March and Kinrara) b 1961, Hon Pauline Marian (Hon Mrs Case) b 1964); *Career* teacher, TV announcer, model girl, psychotherapist; currently runs a Christian retreat house; *Recreations* fishing, tennis, windsurfing; *Style*— Bronwen, Viscountess Astor; ✉ Tuesley Manor, Tuesley, Godalming, Surrey GU7 1UD (☎ 01483 417281, fax 01483 420415)

ASTOR, (Hon) (Francis) David Langhorne; CH (1994); s of 2 Viscount Astor (d 1952), and Nancy, Viscountess Astor, CH, MP (d 1964); *b* 5 March 1912; *Educ* Eton, Balliol Oxford; *m* 1, 1945, Melanie Hauser; 1 da; m 2, 1952, Bridget Aphra Wreford; 2 s, 3 da; *Career* served WWII with RM 1940–45 (Croix de Guerre 1944); The Observer: foreign ed 1946–48, ed 1948–75, dir 1976–81; *Books* Peace in the Middle East: Super Powers and Security Guarantees (with V Yorke, 1978); *Clubs* Reform, Athenaeum; *Style*— David Astor, CH; ✉ 24 St Ann's Terrace, London NW8 6PJ (☎ 0171 586 8689); Manor House, Sutton Courtenay, Oxon

ASTOR, David Waldorf; CBE (1994); s of Hon Michael Langhorne Astor (MP for Surrey East 1945–51, d 1980, 3 s of 2 Viscount Astor), and his 1 w, Barbara Mary (d 1980), da of Capt Ronald McNeil; n of Hon Sir John Astor, *qv*; *b* 9 Aug 1943; *Educ* Eton, Harvard Univ; *m* 19 Sept 1968, Clare Pamela, er da of Cdr Michael Beauchamp St John, DSC, RN; 2 s (Henry b 17 April 1969, Tom b 24 July 1972), 2 da (Joanna b 23 June 1970, Rose b 9 June 1979); *Career* short service cmmn in Royal Scots Greys 1962–65; farmer 1973–; dir: Jupiter Tarbutt Merlin 1985–91, Priory Investments Holdings 1990–; chm Classic FM 1989–91; chm Cncl for the Protection of Rural England 1983–93; Parly candidate (SDP) Plymouth Drake 1987; tstee Glyndebourne Arts Tst 1995–; FRSA 1988; *Recreations* books, sport; *Clubs* Brooks's, MCC; *Style*— David Astor, Esq, CBE; ✉ Bruern Grange, Milton-under-Wychwood, Chipping Norton, Oxfordshire OX7 6HA (☎ 01993 830413)

ASTOR, Hon Hugh Waldorf; JP (Berks 1953); s of 1 Baron Astor of Hever (d 1971), and Violet Mary Elliot, da of Earl of Minto; *b* 20 Nov 1920; *Educ* Eton, New Coll Oxford; *m* 1950, Emily Lucy, da of Sir Alexander Kinloch, 12 Bt; 2 s (Robert, James), 3 da (Virginia, Rachel, Jean); *Career* WWII Lt-Col Intelligence Corps Europe and SE Asia; dep chm The Times 1959–67; dir: Hambros plc 1960–91, Winterbottom Energy Trust plc 1961–86, Phoenix Assurance plc 1962–85; memb Cncl Trusthouse Forte 1962– (chm 1971–), exec vice chm Olympia Ltd 1971–73; dep chm Middlesex Hosp 1965–74; chm: Times Trust 1967–82, Peabody Donation Fund 1981–92 (dep chm 1979), Mgmnt Ctee King Edward's Hosp Fund for London 1983–88 (chm 1981); hon treas: Marine Biology Assoc, Franco-British Soc 1969–76; memb Ct of Assts Fishmongers' Co (Prime Warden 1976–77); High Sheriff Berks 1963; *Recreations* shooting, sailing, flying; *Clubs* Brooks's, Buck's, Pratt's, Royal Yacht Sqdn, Royal Ocean Racing; *Style*— The Hon Hugh Astor, JP; ✉ Folly Farm, Sulhamstead, Berks RG7 4DF (☎ 0118 930 2326); 79 Ashley Gardens, Thirleby Road, London SW1P 1HG (☎ 0171 976 6818)

ASTOR, Hon Sir John Jacob; kt (1978), MBE (1945), ERD (1989), DL (Cambs 1962); s of 2 Viscount Astor; unc of David W Astor, *qv*; *b* 29 Aug 1918; *Educ* Eton, New Coll Oxford; *m* 1, 1944 (m dis 1972), Ana Inez (d 1992), da of Señor Dr Don Miguel Angel Carcano, (Hon) KCMG, (Hon) KBE, sometime Argentine Ambass to UK; 1 s (Michael Ramon Langhorne m 1979 Daphne Warburg), 1 da (Stella); m 2, 1976 (m dis 1985), Mrs Susan Sheppard, da of late Maj Michael Eveleigh; m 3, 1988, Mrs Marcia de Savary; *Career* served WWII as Maj (French Croix de Guerre and Legion d'Honneur 1945); MP (C) Plymouth Sutton 1951–59, PPS to Fin Sec of Treasy 1951–52; chm: Governing Body of Nat Inst of Agric Engrg 1963–68, Agric Res Cncl 1968–78, NEDC for Agric Indust 1978–83; steward Jockey Club 1968–71 and 1983–85; memb: Horserace Totalisator Bd 1962–68, Horserace Betting Levy Bd 1976–80; JP Cambs 1960–74, High Sheriff Cambs and Isle of Ely 1967; *Clubs* White's; *Style*— The Hon Sir John Astor, MBE, ERD, DL; ✉ The Dower House, Hatley Park, Hatley St George, Sandy, Beds SG19 3HL (☎ 01767 650266)

ASTOR, 4 Viscount (UK 1917); William Waldorf Astor; also Baron Astor (UK 1916); only child of 3 Viscount Astor (d 1966), by his 1 w, Hon Sarah, *née* Norton, da of 6 Baron Grantley; the recurrent forename Waldorf commemorates a village near Heidelberg from which John Jacob Astor (ggf of 1 Viscount) emigrated to the New World in the end of the eighteenth century and later bought lands in the area now covered by New York; *b* 27 Dec 1951; *Educ* Eton; *m* 1976, Annabel Lucy Veronica, da of Timothy Jones (himself s of Sir Roderick Jones, KBE, sometime chm of Reuters, and his w, better known as the writer Enid Bagnold). Annabel's mother was Pandora, *née* Clifford (niece of 11 and 12 Barons Clifford of Chudleigh and sis of Lady Norwich - *see* 2 Viscount Norwich); 2 s (Hon William Waldorf b 18 Jan 1979, Hon James Jacob b 4 March 1981), 1 da (Hon Flora Katherine b 7 June 1976); *Heir* s, Hon William Waldorf Astor; *Career* a Lord in Waiting (Govt whip) 1990–93; Govt House of Lords spokesman: for DOE 1990–91, on home affrs 1991–92, on national heritage 1992–; Parly under-sec of state: Dept of Social Security 1993–94, Dept of Nat Heritage 1994–95; dir: Trocadero plc, Cliveden plc, various property cos in UK and USA; *Recreations* field sports; *Clubs* White's, Turf; *Style*— The Rt Hon The Viscount Astor; ✉ Ginge Manor, Wantage, Oxon OX12 8QT (☎ 01235 833228)

ASTOR OF HEVER, Irene, Lady; Lady Irene Violet Freesia Janet Augusta; da of Field Marshal 1 Earl Haig, KT, GCB, DM, GCVO, KCIE (d 1928); *b* 7 Oct 1919; *m* 4 Oct 1945, 2 Baron Astor of Hever (d 1984); 2 s, 3 da; *Career* hon life memb BRCS (holder of Queen's Badge of Honour, chm and pres Kent Branch 1976–82), patron Kent Co Royal Br Legion Women's Section, pres Kent Agric Soc 1981 and 1982, vice pres RNIB, nat vice pres Women's Section (SE region) Royal British Legion; CStJ; *Style*— The Rt Hon Irene, Lady Astor of Hever; ✉ Holly Tree House, French St, Westerham, Kent TN16 1PW (☎ 01959 562141); 11 Lyall St, Eaton Sq, London SW1X 8DH (☎ 0171 235 4755)

ASTOR OF HEVER, 3 Baron (UK 1956); John Jacob Astor; 3 Baron (UK 1956); s of 2 Baron Astor of Hever (d 1984), by his w, Lady Irene Violet Freesia Janet Augusta Haig, da of FM 1 Earl Haig, KT, GCB, OM, GCVO, KCIE; *b* 16 June 1946; *Educ* Eton; *m* 1, 1970 (m dis 1990), Fiona Diana Lennox, da of Capt Roger Harvey, JP, DL, Scots Gds, and Diana (da of Sir Harry Mainwaring, 5 and last Bt, by his w Generis, eld da of Sir Richard Williams-Bulkeley, 12 Bt, KCB, VD, JP, and Lady Magdalen Yorke, da of 5 Earl of Hardwicke); 3 da (Hon Camilla Fiona b 1974, Hon Tania Jentie b 1978, Hon Violet Magdalene b 1980); m 2, 5 May 1990, Hon Elizabeth Constance, da of 2 Viscount Mackintosh of Halifax, OBE, BEM (d 1980), 1 s (Hon Charles Gavin John b 10 Nov 1990), 1 da (Hon Olivia Alexandra Elizabeth b 21 Aug 1992); *Heir* s, Hon Charles Gavin John Astor b 10 Nov 1990; *Career* Lt LG 1966–70, served Malaysia, Hong Kong, NI; md: Terres Blanches Services SARL 1975–77, Valberg Plaza SARL 1977–82, Honon et Cie 1982–; pres: Astor Enterprises Inc 1983–, Astor France SARL 1990–; dir Cobham Hall Enterprises Ltd 1995–96; pres: Sevenoaks Westminster Patrons Club 1991–, Earl Haig Branch Royal British Legion 1994–, Kent Federation of Amenity Socs 1995–, Motorsport Industry Assoc 1995–; dep-pres ROSPA 1995–; chm Cncl of St John Kent 1987–, sec Anglo-Swiss Parly Assoc 1992–; treas Brit-S Africa Parly Gp; Liveryman Worshipful Co of Goldsmiths; patron: Edenbridge Music and Arts Tst 1989–, Bridge Tst 1993–, Kent Assoc of Youth Clubs 1994–; govr Cobham Hall Sch 1992–; tstee: Rochester Cathedral Tst 1988–, Canterbury Cathedral Appeal Fund 1992–, Astor of Hever Tst 1986–, Astor Fndn 1988–; *Clubs* White's, Riviera Golf; *Style*— The Rt Hon the Lord Astor of Hever; ✉ Frenchstreet House, Westerham, Kent TN16 1PW (☎ 01959 562051, fax 01959 561286)

ASTWOOD, Hon Sir James Rufus; KBE (1994), kt (1982), JP; s of late James Rufus Astwood, and Mabel Winifred Astwood; *b* 4 Oct 1923; *Educ* Berkeley Inst Bermuda, Univ of Toronto; *m* 1952, Gloria Preston Norton; 1 s, 2 da; *Career* called to the Bar Gray's Inn 1956; started practice at Jamaican Bar 1956; Jamaican Legal Serv 1957–74: dep clerk of courts Jamaica 1957–58, stipendiary magistrate and judge of Grand Court Cayman Islands 1958–59, clerk of courts Jamaica 1958–63, resident magistrate Jamaica 1963–74, puisne judge Jamaica 1971–73; sr magistrate Bermuda 1974–76, slr gen Bermuda 1976–77, acting attorney gen Bermuda 1976 and 1977, temp acting dep govr Bermuda during 1977, chief justice Bermuda 1977–93, justice of appeal Bermuda 1994–95, pres Ct of Appeal Bermuda 1995–; Hon MA Gray's Inn 1985; *Style*— The Hon Sir James Astwood, KBE, JP; ✉ The Pebble, 7 Astwood Walk, Warwick WK08, Bermuda (☎ 00 809 236 1097, fax 00 809 236 8816); Appeal Court, Hamilton HM12, Bermuda (☎ 00 809 292 1350)

ASTWOOD, Lt-Col Sir Jeffrey Carlton; kt (1972), CBE (1966, OBE (mil) 1946), ED (1942); s of late Jeffrey Burgess Astwood, of Neston, Bermuda, and Lilian Maude, *née* Searles; *b* 5 Oct 1907; *Educ* Saltus GS Bermuda; *m* 1928, Hilda Elizabeth Kay, da of Henry George Longhurst Onions, of Aberfeldy, Somerset, Bermuda; 1 s, 1 da; *Career* joined local TF 1924, cmmnd 2 Lt 1926, Capt 1928, Maj 1930, Lt-Col CO Local Forces 1943, organised amalgamation of 2 local forces to form Bermuda Regt 1957; House of Assembly Bermuda: memb 1948–72, memb Exec Cncl and dep speaker 1957–68, speaker 1968–72; min: Agric, Immigration and Lab, Health; chm Vestry St James Church Parish 1950–60; pres: Exec Ctee Sandys GS 1950–57 (chm of tstees 1950–74), Bermuda Sea Cadet Assoc 1974–78; *Recreations* horticulture, theatre; *Clubs* Royal Bermudan Yacht, Directors', RHS Vincent Square; *Style*— Lt-Col Sir Jeffrey Astwood, CBE, ED; ✉ Greenfield, Somerset MA03, Bermuda (☎ 234 1729)

ATCHERLEY, Sir Harold Winter; kt (1977); s of L W Atcherley, and Maude Lester, *née* Nash; *b* 30 Aug 1918; *Educ* Gresham's, Univ of Heidelberg, Univ of Geneva; *m* 1, 1946 (m dis), Anita Helen, *née* Leslie; 1 s, 2 da; m 2, 25 June 1990, Mrs Elke Jessett, er da of late Dr Carl Langbehn and Mrs Irmgard Langbehn, of Long Melford, Suffolk; *Career* served WWII, Queen's Westminster Rifles 1939, cmmnd Intelligence Corps 1940, 18 Inf Div Singapore (POW) 1942–45; with Royal Dutch Shell Group 1937–39 and 1946–70 (personnel coordinator 1964–70); 1 recruitment advsr to MOD 1970–71; chm: Armed Forces Pay Review Body 1971–82, Police Negotiating Bd 1983–86 (dep chm 1982–83); memb: Top Salaries Review Body 1971–87, Nat Staff Ctee for Nurses and Midwives 1973–77, Halsbury Ctee of Enquiry into Pay and Conditions of Nurses and Midwives 1974, Ctee of Inquiry into Remuneration of Membs of Local Authorities 1977; dir British Home Stores Ltd 1973–87; chm: Tyzack & Ptnrs 1979–85, Toynbee Hall 1985–90 (memb Mgmnt Ctee 1979–85), Aldeburgh Fndn 1989–94 (dep chm 1988–89); vice chm Suffolk Tst for Nature Conservation 1987–90, chm Suffolk and N Essex Branch European Movement 1996–; Empress Leopoldina Medal Brazil 1958; *Style*— Sir Harold Atcherley; ✉ Conduit House, The Green, Long Melford, Suffolk (☎ 01787 310897)

ATHA, Bernard Peter; OBE (1991); s of Horace Michael Atha, of Leeds (d 1984), and Mary, *née* Quinlan (d 1951); *b* 27 Aug 1928; *Educ* Leeds Modern GS, Univ of Leeds (LLB), RAF Sch of Educn (DipEd); *Career* Nat Serv FO RAF 1950–52; called to the Bar Gray's Inn 1950; actor and variety artist; films and TV incl: Kes, Coronation Street; princ lectr in business studies Huddersfield Tech Coll 1973–90; elected Leeds City Cncl 1957, chm Leeds Leisure Services Ctee 1988–90; vice chm: West Leeds HA 1988–90, St James Hosp 1993–; contested (Lab): Penrith and Border 1959, Pudsey 1964; vice chm Sports Cncl 1976–80, memb Arts Cncl 1979–82; chm: Nat Watersports Centre 1978–84, Educn Social Servs and Watch Ctees; currently chm: Northern Ballet Theatre, Cultural Servs Ctee, Leeds Co-op Soc, Grand Theatre, City of Varieties, Red Ladder Theatre Co, Yorkshire Dance Centre Tst, Leeds Playhouse, UK Sports Assoc for People with Mental Handicap, Br Paralympics Assoc, Int Sports Assoc for People with Mental Handicap; dir Opera North; memb: Sports Aid Fndn, Sports Aid Tst; UK rep EU Ctee on Sport for the Disabled; FRSA; *Recreations* the arts, sport, politics; *Style*— Bernard Atha, Esq, OBE; ✉ 25 Moseley Wood Croft, Leeds LS16 7JJ (☎ 0113 267 2485, 0113 247 8328)

ATHANASOU, Dr Nicholas Anthony; s of Anthony James Athanasou (d 1964), and Angela, *née* Pappas (d 1974); *b* 26 April 1953; *Educ* Sydney Boy's High Sch, Univ of Sydney (MB BS), Univ of London (PhD); *m* 27 April 1985, Linda Joan, da of Anthony Hulls, of Chislehurst; *Career* conslt pathologist Nuffield Orthopaedic Centre (hon clinical lectr Univ of Oxford) 1991–; memb Wolfson College Oxford; MRCP 1981, MRCPath 1986; *Recreations* cricket, reading, writing; *Style*— Dr Nicholas Athanasou; ✉ Pathology Department, Nuffield Orthopaedic Centre, Headington, Oxford OX3 7LD (☎ 01865 227619)

ATHERTON, David; s of Robert Atherton, and Lavinia, *née* Burton; *b* 3 Jan 1944; *Educ* Univ of Cambridge (MA); *m* 5 Sept 1970, Ann Gianetta, da of Cdr J F Drake (d 1978), of Ware, Herts; 1 s (John b 14 May 1979), 2 da (Elizabeth b 13 Feb 1974, Susan b 10 June 1977); *Career* conductor and musical dir London Sinfonietta 1967–73 (fndr 1967); Royal Opera House: repetiteur 1967–68, resident conductor 1968–79; Royal Liverpool Philharmonic Orch: princ conductor and artistic advsr 1980–83, princ guest conductor 1983–86; musical dir and princ conductor San Diego Symphony Orch 1980–87, princ guest conductor BBC Symphony Orch 1985–89, musical dir and princ conductor Hong Kong Philharmonic Orch 1989–; artistic dir and conductor: London Stravinsky Festival 1979–82, Ravel/Varèse Festival 1983–84; artistic dir and fndr Californian Mainly Mozart Festival 1989–, princ guest conductor BBC Nat Orch of Wales 1994–; youngest conductor Henry Wood Promenade Concerts Royal Albert Hall and Royal Opera House 1968; Royal Festival Hall debut 1969; performances abroad incl: Europe, M East, Far East, Australasia, N America; major works conducted incl: Billy Budd (San Francisco Opera 1978, Met Opera NY 1985, ENO 1988 and 1991), Peter Grimes (Dallas Opera 1980, Met Opera 1985, ENO 1991 and 1994), Stravinsky Le Rossignol and Ravel L'Enfant et les Sortileges (Royal Opera House 1987 and 1989), Berlioz Romeo and Juliet (Philharmonia Orch) 1989, The Love for Three Oranges (ENO) 1989, Wozzeck (Canadian Opera) 1990, Les Huguenots (Royal Opera House) 1991, Death in Venice (Metropolitan Opera) 1994, The Barber of Seville (Met Opera) 1995, Turandot (ENO) 1995; awards incl: Composers' Guild of GB Conductor of the Year 1971, Edison Award 1973, Grand Prix du Disque 1977, Koussevitzky Award 1981, Int Record Critics' Award 1982, Prix Caecilia 1982; adapted and arranged Pandora by Robert Gerhard for Royal Ballet 1975; FRSM 1976; *Books* The Complete Instrumental and Chamber Music of Arnold Schoenberg and Roberto Gerhard (ed, 1973), Pandora and Don Quixote Suites by Roberto Gerhard (ed, 1973), The Musical Companion (contrib, 1978), The New Grove Dictionary (1981); *Recreations* travel, squash, theatre; *Style*— David Atherton, Esq; ✉ c/o Harold Holt Ltd, 31 Sinclair Rd, London W14 0NS (☎ 0171 603 4600, fax 0171 603 0019)

ATHERTON, Dr David John; s of Dr Desmond Joseph Atherton, of Coventry, and Hildegard, *née* Rowe, MBE; *b* 24 April 1949; *Educ* Ampleforth, Pembroke Coll Cambridge (MA, MB BChir); *m* 11 Sept 1971, (Hazel) Anne, da of Dr Rex Malcolm Chaplin Dawson, FRS, of Langham, Norfolk; 2 s (James b 1976, Joseph b 1984); *Career* conslt in paediatric dermatology 1982–: Gt Ormond St Hosp for Children, St John's Inst of Dermatology; sr lectr in paediatric dermatology Inst of Child Health 1986–; FRCP; *Books* Eczema in Childhood (1994); *Recreations* tennis, gardening; *Style*— Dr David Atherton; ✉ Great Ormond Street Hospital for Children, London WC1N 3JH (☎ 0171 405 9200, fax 0171 829 8643)

ATHERTON, Howard William; s of William Atherton (d 1989), of Sudbury, Suffolk, and Rose Charlotte Atherton (d 1984); *b* 12 Aug 1947; *Educ* Sudbury GS, London Film Sch; *m* 12 Aug 1972, Janet Ruth, da of Ronald William Simpson, of Lavenham, Suffolk; 1 s (Oliver Luke b 1979), 2 da (Rebecca Louise b 1977, Charlotte Letitia Rose b 1985); *Career* director of photography; memb Br Soc of Cinematography; *Films* incl: Helen, Runners, Keep Off the Grass, Fatal Attraction 1986, The Boost 1987, Mermaids 1989, Indecent Proposal 1992, Bad Boys 1994, Gullivers Travels 1995, Lolita 1995, Deep Rising 1996; *Style*— Howard Atherton, Esq; ✉ St Ann's Lodge, St Ann's Hill, Chertsey, Surrey KT16 9NH

ATHERTON, Kevin; s of William Edward Atherton, of Douglas, Isle of Man, and Elizabeth, *née* Clague; *b* 25 Nov 1950; *Educ* Douglas HS for Boys IOM, IOM Coll of Art, Leeds Poly (BA); *m* 1977, Victoria, da of Francis Sidney Thomas Robinson; *Career* sculptor, artist and lectr in art; pt/t teacher 1978–86: Slade Sch of Fine Art, RCA, Norwich Sch of Art, Winchester Sch of Art, Maidstone Coll of Art, Chelsea Sch of Art, Fine Art Dept Middx Poly, Fine Art Dept South Glamorgan Inst of Higher Educn Cardiff; artist in residence London Borough of Richmond upon Thames 1989; Kingston Poly: Picker lectr in public art Fine Art Dept 1989, Stanley Picker lectr in video performance and public art 1990; lecture tour of Australia 1990; princ lectr in combined media Fine Art Dept Chelsea Sch of Art 1990– (project ldr research project into Virtual Reality as a Fine Art Medium); organiser and speaker Virtual Reality and the Gallery conf (Tate Gallery) 1995; external examiner Fine Art Dept Kingston Univ 1993–; specialist advsr CNAA 1985–; judge Arts Cncl Br Gas Awards 1990–91; awards incl ABSA Award for Best Cmmn in Any Media 1986; numerous exhbns in England and Europe incl one-man exhbn Perth Inst of Contemporary Art 1990; *Work in Public Collections* Sheffield City Poly, Merseyside CC, Graves Art Gallery Sheffield; *Commissions* incl: A Body of Work (Tower Hamlets) 1982, Upon Reflection (Islington) 1985, Platforms Piece (BR Brixton) 1986, Cathedral (Forest of Dean, Glos) 1986, Iron Horses (BR) 1986–87, The Architect (Harlow New Town) 1990, Conversation Piece (Leicester CC) 1990, Art Within Reach (Hampshire Sculpture Tst) 1991, To The Top (New Civic Offices Twickenham) 1990, The Complete Angler (Prudential Assurance Bldg Reading Berks) 1992, A Different Ball Game (Kingshill W Malling Kent) 1993, A Private View (Taff Viaduct Cardiff Bay) 1995; *Recreations* the turf; *Style*— Kevin Atherton, Esq; ✉ 77 Kenworthy Rd, London E9 5RB (☎ 0181 533 1173)

ATHERTON, Brig Maurice Alan; CBE (1981), DL (Kent 1984); s of Rev Harold Atherton (d 1975), of Sheffield, and Beatrice, *née* Shaw (d 1958); *b* 9 Oct 1926; *Educ* St John's Sch Leatherhead, Staff Coll Camberley; *m* 28 Aug 1954, Guendolene Mary (Wendi), da of Col James Bryan Upton, MBE, TD, JP, DL (d 1976), of Hotham, York; 1 s (James Patrick b 7 Sept 1966), 1 da (Christine Wendy b 6 March 1965); *Career* cmmnd E Yorks Regt 1946 (serv in Egypt, Sudan, Malaysia, Austria, Germany, UK), MA to CBF Hong Kong 1959–62, coll chief instr RMA Sandhurst 1964–67, CO 1 Green Howards 1967–69, GSO 1 NI 1969–70, def advsr Ghana 1971–73; cdr Dover Shorncliffe Garrison and Dep Constable Dover Castle 1976–81; magistrate Dover Bench Kent 1982–91; High Sheriff of Kent 1983–84; county pres: Royal Br Legion 1982–91, Men of the Trees 1985–95; chm Kent Ctee Army Benevolent Fund 1984–, chm Christ Church Coll Canterbury 1993–; *Recreations* shooting, gardening, skiing; *Clubs* Army and Navy, Lansdowne; *Style*— Brig M A Atherton, CBE, JP, DL; ✉ Digges Place, Barham, Canterbury, Kent CT4 6PJ (☎ 01227 831420, fax 01227 832311)

ATHERTON, Michael Andrew (Mike); s of Alan Atherton, and Wendy, *née* Fletcher; *b* 23 March 1968; *Educ* Manchester GS, Downing Coll Cambridge (MA, Cricket blue and capt); *Career* professional cricketer; first class debut Cambridge Univ v Essex April 1987; Lancashire CCC: debut v Warwickshire July 1987, awarded county cap 1989, vice capt 1992–; England: former English School's rep, capt Young England to Sri Lanka 1987 and Australia 1988, first team debut v Australia Aug 1989, first full tour Aust and NZ 1990/91, memb team touring India and Sri Lanka 1992/93, capt England July 1993–, capt team touring West Indies 1993–94, Australia 1994/95 and S Africa 1995–96, Zimbabwe and New Zealand 1996–97; highest test score 185 v S Africa 1995; Professional Cricketers' Assoc Young Cricketer of Year 1990, Cricket Writers' Young Cricketer of Year 1990, Cornhill Player of the Year 1994; *Recreations* reading, golf, squash, rugby, football (Manchester United supporter), good food; *Style*— Mike Atherton, Esq; ✉ c/o Lancashire CCC, Old Trafford, Manchester M16 0PX (☎ 0161 848 7021)

ATHERTON, Peter; s of Joseph Ignatius Atherton (d 1984), of Wrightington, and Winifred, *née* Marsh; *b* 8 Nov 1952; *Educ* Mount St Mary's Coll Derby, Univ of Birmingham (LLB), Coll of Law; *m* 17 Oct 1981, Jennifer Marie, da of Charles Birch, of Ontario, Canada; 1 s (Timothy Peter b 4 Sept 1985), 1 da (Hilary Anne b 4 Jan 1984); *Career* called to the Bar Gray's Inn 1975; jr Northern Circuit 1978–79, asst recorder of the Crown Court 1994–; chm Young Barrs Ctee Senate of Inns of Ct and Bar Cncl for England and Wales 1982–83; *Recreations* tennis, golf, theatre; *Style*— Peter Atherton, Esq; ✉ Deans Court Chambers, Crown Square, Manchester (☎ 0161 834 4097)

ATIYAH, Sir Michael Francis; OM (1992), kt (1983); s of Edward Selim Atiyah (d 1964), and Jean, *née* Levens (d 1964); bro of Prof Patrick Atiyah, QC, FBA, *qv*; *b* 22 April 1929; *Educ* Victoria Coll Egypt, Manchester GS, Univ of Cambridge (MA, PhD); *m* 1955, Lily Jane Myles, da of John Cameron Brown (d 1970); 3 children; *Career* fell Trinity Coll Cambridge 1954–58, Savilian prof of geometry Univ of Oxford 1963–69, prof of mathematics Inst for Advanced Study Princeton USA 1969–72, Royal Soc res prof Mathematical Inst Univ of Oxford 1973–90, pres Royal Soc 1990–95, Master Trinity Coll Cambridge 1990–, dir Isaac Newton Inst for Mathematical Scis Cambridge 1990–96; Hon ScD Univ of Cambridge; FRS 1962, Hon FEng 1993; *Recreations* gardening; *Style*—

Sir Michael Atiyah, OM, FRS; ✉ The Master's Lodge, Trinity College, Cambridge CB2 1TQ (☎ 01223 338412, fax 01223 338500)

ATIYAH, Prof Patrick Selim; QC (1989); s of Edward Selim Atiyah (d 1964), and Jean, *née* Levens (d 1964); bro of Sir Michael Atiyah, OM, FRS, *qv*; *b* 5 March 1931; *Educ* Woking County GS for Boys, Magdalen Coll Oxford (BA, BCL, MA, DCL); *m* 1951, Christine Ann, da of Reginald William Best (d 1978); 4 s (Julian, Andrew, Simon, Jeremy); *Career* asst lectr LSE 1954–55, lectr Univ of Khartoum 1955–59, called to the Bar Inner Temple 1956, crown counsel Ghana 1959–61, legal asst Bd of Trade 1961–64, fell New Coll Oxford 1964–70; prof of law: Aust Nat Univ 1970–73, Univ of Warwick 1973–77; prof of English law and fell of St John's Coll Univ of Oxford 1977–88 (hon fell 1988), ret 1988; Hon LLD Warwick 1989; FBA 1978; *Publications* The Sale of Goods (1957, 8 edn 1990), Introduction to the Law of Contract (1961, 5 edn 1995), Vicarious Liability (1967), Accidents, Compensation and the Law (1970, 5 edn (ed Peter Cane) 1994), The Rise and Fall of Freedom of Contract (1979), Promises, Morals and Law (1981, Swiney Prize RSA/RSP 1984), Oxford Journal of Legal Studies (gen ed, 1981–86), Law and Modern Society (1983, 2 edn 1995), Essays on Contract (1987), Pragmatism and Theory in English Law (1987), Form and Substance in Anglo-American Law (with R S Summers, 1987); articles in legal jls; *Style*— Prof Patrick Atiyah, QC, FBA; ✉ 75 Main Rd, Long Hanborough, Witney, Oxon OX8 8JX (☎ 01993 882938)

ATKIN, Alec Field; CBE (1978); s of Alec and Grace Atkin; *b* 26 April 1925; *Educ* Riley HS, Hull Tech Coll, Univ of Hull (BSc, Dip Aero); *m* 1, 1948 (m dis 1982), Nora Helen Darby; 2 s (and 1 adopted s), 1 da; m 2, 1982, Wendy Atkin; *Career* asst md BAC (Military Aircraft Div) 1976–77, md (Military) Aircraft Gp British Aerospace 1978–81, chm Warton Kingston-Brough and Manchester Div 1978–81, md (Marketing) Aircraft Gp British Aerospace 1981–82; aviation conslt 1982–; FEng 1979, FIMechE, FRAeS, FRSA; *Style*— Alec Atkin, Esq, CBE, FEng; ✉ Les Fougeres d'Icart, Icart Rd, St Martin, Guernsey, Channel Islands GY4 6JG (☎ 01481 37628, fax 01481 37709)

ATKIN, Peter Richard (Pete); s of Cyril William Atkin, of Cambridge, and Elsie Rose Cowell (d 1980); *b* 22 Aug 1945; *Educ* Perse Sch Cambridge, St John's Coll Cambridge (BA); *m* 24 Nov 1973, Mary Louise, da of Lewis Lynch Lowance, of Manassas, Virginia, USA; *Career* radio producer; scriptwriter, critic, songwriter (with Clive James) and recording artist of 6 albums 1970–75 (collection reissued 1991); former furniture maker and woodwork corr Vole magazine 1976–77; chief prodr BBC Radio Light Entertainment 1986–89 (producer 1981, script ed 1983), head of network radio BBC South Bristol 1989–93, ind prodn coordinator BBC Radio 4 1993; ind radio prodr and conslt 1994–, script ed Hat Trick Productions 1994–; prodr This Sceptred Isle (BBC Radio 4 History of Britain) 1995–96; winner Best Non-Fiction Talkie of the Year Talkie Awards 1996; tstee St George's Music Tst Bristol, memb Mgmnt Ctee Cheltenham Festival of Literature; *Recreations* words, music, wood; *Clubs* Meccano, Eddie Grundy Fan; *Style*— Pete Atkin, Esq; ✉ 19 Archfield Rd, Bristol BS6 6BG (☎ 0117 942 1582, fax 0117 924 0138); Hat Trick Productions, 10 Livonia Street, London W1V 3PH

ATKIN, Ron; s of Oscar Ridgeway, of Barrow-on-Soar, Leics, and Agatha Victoria, *née* Hull; *b* 3 Feb 1938; *Educ* Loughborough Coll of Art, Royal Acad Schs (Cert); *m* 23 July 1960, Ann, da of Capt Arthur Charles Fawssett, DSO, RN (d 1961); 2 s (Francis Charles Edward b 1961, Richard Bernard b 1963); *Career* artist; exhibited at Royal Soc of Br Artists 1959, Southampton Museum and Art Gallery 1959, RA summer exhibition 1960, 1970 and 1975, Royal Watercolour Soc Galleries Bond Street 1961, mixed exhibition Roland Browse and Delbanco Cork Street London and SA 1961 and 1964, Paintings and Sculpture from some Oxford Jr Common Rooms Leics Museum and Art Gallery 1962; one-man shows: Plymouth City Museum and Art Gallery 1976, Chenil Art Gallery King's Road London 1982; paintings in private collections: GB, Aust, USA, Canada, Germany, Zurich, Lucerne; paintings in public collections incl: Dartington Tst Devon, Devon CC Schs Museum Serv, Lincoln Coll Oxford, Plymouth City Museum and Art Gallery; shortlisted for a Gulbenkian Printmakers' award 1984; featured in Dictionary of British Art Vol VI, 20th Century Painters; *Recreations* walking; *Style*— Ron Atkin; ✉ Studio 7, Abbots Bickington, Devon EX22 7LQ

ATKINS, Prof Anthony George; s of Walter George Atkins (d 1975), and Emily Irene, *née* Aldridge; *b* 10 Oct 1939; *Educ* Canton HS Cardiff, Univ Coll Cardiff (BSc), Trinity Coll Cambridge (PhD, ScD), Exeter Coll Oxford (MA); *m* 4 March 1971, Margaret Ann, da of Lt-Col Richard Risely Proud, CVO, OBE (d 1976); 2 s (Philip George b 1973, Richard James b 1976), 1 da (Margaret Ruth b 1980); *Career* US Steel Corpn 1965–67, BSC fell Univ of Oxford 1967–70, assoc prof in mechanical engrg Univ of Michigan 1970–75, res mangr Delta Metal 1975–81, prof of mechanical engrg Univ of Reading 1981–; memb CPRE; FIM 1986, FIMechE 1987, CEng; *Books* Strength and Fracture of Engineering Solids (jtly, 1984, 2 ed 1996), A History of GWR Goods Wagons (jtly, 2 edn, 1986), Manufacturing Engineering (jtly, 1987), Elastic and Plastic Fracture (jtly, 2 edn, 1988); *Recreations* music, skiing, woodwork; *Style*— Prof Anthony Atkins; ✉ White House, Heads Lane, Inkpen Common, Hungerford, Berks RG17 9QS (☎ 01488 668253); Department of Engineering, Box 225, University of Reading, Whiteknights, Reading RG6 6AY (☎ 0118 931 8562, telex 847813, fax 0118 931 3327)

ATKINS, Eileen June; CBE (1990); da of late Arthur Thomas Atkins, and Annie Ellen, *née* Elkins (d 1984); *b* 16 June 1934; *Educ* Latymer GS, Guildhall Sch of Music and Drama (AGSM); *m* 1, 1957 (m dis 1966), Julian Glover, *qv*; m 2, Feb 1978, William B Shepherd; *Career* actress; hon memb GSM; *Theatre* incl: Twelfth Night, Richard III, The Tempest (Old Vic) 1962, The Killing of Sister George (Bristol Old Vic transfd Duke of York, Best Actress Standard Award) 1963, The Cocktail Party (Wyndham's transfd Haymarket) 1968, Vivat! Vivat! Regina! (Piccadilly, Variety Award) 1970, Suzanne Andler (Aldwych) 1973, As You Like It (Stratford) 1973, St Joan (Old Vic) 1977, Passion Play (Aldwych) 1981, Medea (Young Vic) 1986, Winter's Tale, Cymbeline (Olivier Award), Mountain Language (NT) 1988, A Room of One's Own (Hampstead, NY Critics' Special citation) 1989, Exclusive (Strand) 1989, Prin (NY) 1990, Hannah Jelkes in The Night of the Iguana (Critics' Circle Award) 1992; *Television* incl: The Duchess of Malfi, Sons and Lovers, Smiley's People, Nelly's Version, The Burston Rebellion, Breaking Up, The Vision, Mrs Pankhurst in In My Defence (series) 1990, A Room of One's Own 1990, Lost Language of Cranes 1992, The Maitlands 1993; *Film* incl: Equus 1974, The Dresser 1984, Let Him Have It 1990, Wolf 1993, Jack and Sarah 1995; *Style*— Miss Eileen Atkins, CBE; ✉ c/o Jonathan Altaras Associates Ltd, 27 Floral Street, London WC2E 9DP (☎ 0171 836 8722, fax 0171 836 6066)

ATKINS, Frances Elizabeth (Mrs Gerald Atkins); da of Thomas Colyer Venning, MBE, of Ilkley, Yorks, and Hilary Susan, *née* Harris; *b* 8 Sept 1950; *m* 1, 1976 (m dis 1984), George Alfred Carman, QC, *qv*; m 2, 1984, Gerald Atkins; *Career* restaurateur; Atkins Restaurant: Great Missenden 1984–86, The Old Plow Inn Speen 1986–88, Farleyer House Aberfeldy 1988–92; chef proprietor Shaw's Restaurant 1994–; Masterchef 1993, memb Bd of Scottish Chefs 1992; *Recreations* work, art appreciation, collecting furniture; *Style*— Mrs Gerald Atkins; ✉ Farleyer Field House, Aberfeldy, Perthshire PH15 2JE (☎ 01887 829553); Shaw's Restaurant, 119 Old Brompton Road, London SW7

ATKINS, Prof Peter William; s of William Henry Atkins (d 1988), and Ellen Louise, *née* Edwards (d 1978); *b* 10 Aug 1940; *Educ* Dr Challoner's Amersham, Univ of Leicester (BSc, PhD), Univ of Oxford (MA), UCLA; *m* 1, 20 Aug 1964 (m dis 1983), Judith Ann Kearton; 1 da (Juliet b 1970); m 2, 30 March 1991, Susan Adele Greenfield; *Career* Harkness fell 1964–65; Univ of Oxford: univ lectr in physical chemistry 1965–96, prof of chemistry 1996–, fell and tutor Lincoln Coll 1965–; visiting prof: China, France, Israel, Japan, New Zealand; Dreyfus lectr California 1980, Firth visiting prof Univ of Sheffield 1984; Meldola Medal 1969; Hon DSc Univ of Utrecht 1992; *Books* The Structure of Inorganic Radicals (1967), Molecular Quantum Mechanics (1970, 3 edn 1996), Quanta: A Handbook of Concepts (1974, 2 edn 1991), Physical Chemistry (1978, 5 edn 1994), Solutions Manual for Physical Chemistry (1978, 5 edn 1994), The Creation (1981), Principles of Physical Chemistry (1982), Solutions Manual for MQM (1983, 2 edn 1997), The Second Law (1984), Molecules (1987), Chemistry: Principles and Applications (1988), General Chemistry (1989, 2 edn 1992), Inorganic Chemistry (1990, 2 edn 1994), Atoms, Electrons and Change (1991), Elements of Physical Chemistry (1992, 2 edn 1996), Creation Revisited (1992), The Periodic Kingdom (1995), Concepts of Physical Chemistry (1995), Chemistry: Molecules, Matter and Change (1997); *Recreations* art; *Style*— Prof Peter Atkins; ✉ Lincoln Coll, Oxford OX1 3DR (☎ 01865 279797, fax 01865 279802)

ATKINS, Rt Hon Robert James; PC (1995), MP (C) South Ribble (majority 5,973); s of late Reginald Alfred Atkins, of Gt Missenden, and Winifred Margaret Atkins; *b* 5 Feb 1946; *Educ* Highgate; *m* 1969, Dulcie Mary, da of Frederick Moon Chaplin, of Bexley; 1 s (James b 1979), 1 da (Victoria b 1976); *Career* MP (C): Preston N 1979–1983, South Ribble 1983–; former jt sec Cons Parly Def and vice chm Aviation Ctees, nat pres Cons Trade Unionists 1984–87; PPS to: Norman Lamont as Min of State for Indust 1982–84, Lord Young of Graffham as Min Without Portfolio and Sec of State for Employment 1984–87; Parly under-sec of State DTI 1987–89, min for roads and traffic Dept of Tport 1989–90, Parly under sec of state Dept of the Environment and min for sport July-Nov 1990, Parly under sec of state Dept of Educn and Science and min for sport 1990–92, min of state Northern Ireland Office 1992–94, min of state Dept of Environment 1994–95; *Recreations* cricket, Holmesiana, ecclesiology, wine; *Style*— The Rt Hon Robert Atkins, MP; ✉ House of Commons, London SW1 0AA (☎ 0171 219 5080)

ATKINSON, Prof Anthony Barnes (Tony); s of Norman Joseph Atkinson (d 1988), and Esther Muriel, *née* Stonehouse; *b* 4 Sept 1944; *Educ* Cranbrook, Churchill Coll Cambridge (MA); *m* 11 Dec 1965, Judith Mary, da of Alexander Mandeville, of Swansea; 2 s (Richard b 1972, Charles b 1976), 1 da (Sarah b 1974); *Career* fell St John's Coll Cambridge 1967–71, prof of economics Univ of Essex 1971–76, prof Univ of London 1976–92 (Thomas Tooke prof of econ sci and statistics 1987–92), fell Churchill Coll and prof of political economy Univ of Cambridge 1992–94, warden Nuffield Coll Oxford 1994–; ed Journal of Public Economics 1971–; pres: Econometric Soc 1988, Euro Econ Assoc 1989, Int Econ Assoc 1989–92, Royal Econ Soc 1995–; memb: Royal Cmmn on Distribution of Income and Wealth 1978–79, Retail Prices Advsy Ctee 1984–90; vice pres Br Acad 1988–90; Freeman City of London 1983, memb Worshipful Co of Barbers (Liveryman 1985); UAP Sci prize 1986; Hon Dr Rer Pol Univ of Frankfurt 1987; Hon DSc Econ Univ of Lausanne 1988; Hon DUniv: Liège 1989, Athens 1991, Stirling 1992, Edinburgh 1994, École Normale Supérieur Paris 1995, Essex 1995; hon memb American Econ Assoc 1985; FBA 1984; *Books* Poverty in Britain and the Reform of Social Security (1969), Unequal Shares (1972), The Tax Credit Scheme (1973), Economics of Inequality (1975), Distribution of Personal Wealth in Britain (with A J Harrison, 1978), Lectures on Public Economics (with J E Stiglitz, 1980), Social Justice and Public Policy (1982), Parents and Children (jtly, 1983), Unemployment Benefits and Unemployment Duration (with J Micklewright, 1986), Poverty and Social Security (1989), Economic Transformation in Eastern Europe and the Distribution of Income (with J Micklewright, 1992), Public Economics in Action (1995), Incomes and the Welfare State (1996); *Recreations* sailing; *Style*— Prof Tony Atkinson; ✉ 39 Park Town, Oxford OX2 6SL (☎ 01865 556064)

ATKINSON, Prof Anthony Curtis; s of Harold Atkinson (d 1944), of Sidcup, Kent, and Iris Madge, *née* Ellison (d 1990); *b* 22 June 1937; *Educ* Christ's Hosp, Univ of Cambridge (MA), Imperial Coll London (PhD); *m* 13 June 1972, Ruth Mary, da of Robert Mantle Rattenbury (d 1970), of Cambridge; 2 da (Alison b 1972, Rachel b 1975); *Career* Shell Chemical Co 1960–64, American Cyanamid NJ USA 1965–67, prof of statistics Imperial Coll 1983–89 (lectr 1969–78, reader 1978–83), prof of statistics LSE 1989–; MISI, FSS; *Books* A Celebration of Statistics (with S Fienberg, 1985), Plots, Transformations and Regression (1985), Optimum Experimental Designs (with A N Donev, 1992); *Recreations* music, architecture; *Style*— Prof Anthony Atkinson; ✉ 2 Eton Villas, London NW3 4SX (☎ 0171 722 7021); Department of Statistics, London School of Economics, Houghton Street, London WC2A 2AE (☎ 0171 955 7622, fax 0171 955 7416, e-mail a.c.atkinson @ lse.ac.uk)

ATKINSON, David Anthony; MP (C) Bournemouth E (majority 14,823); s of late Arthur Joseph Atkinson, and Joan Margaret, *née* Zink, of Southbourne, Bournemouth; *b* 24 March 1940; *Educ* St George's Coll Weybridge, Coll of Automobile and Aeronautical Engrg Chelsea; *m* 1968, Susan Nicola, da of Dr Roy Pilsworth, of Benfleet, Essex; 1 s (Anthony b 1977), 1 da (Katherine b 1973); *Career* dir Chalkwell Motor Co Westcliff on Sea 1963–72, md David Graham Ltd 1972–78; memb: Southend County BC 1969–72, Essex CC 1973–78; nat chm Young Conservative Orgn 1970–71; MP (C) Bournemouth E 1979–; PPS to Rt Hon Paul Channon MP as: Min for Civil Service 1979–81, Min for Arts 1981–83, Min for Trade 1983–86, Sec of State for Trade & Indust 1986–87; author of Licensing (Occasional Permissions) Act 1983 Private Membs Bill; UK rep on Cncl of Europe and Western European Union 1979– (chm Ctee for Non-Memb Countries 1991–95), UK pres Christian Solidarity Int 1983– (chm 1979–83); *Recreations* mountaineering, art, architecture; *Style*— David Atkinson, Esq, MP; ✉ House of Commons, London SW1A 0AA

ATKINSON, Ven Dr David John; s of Thomas John Collins Atkinson (d 1986), and Adèle Mary, *née* Cox; *b* 5 Sept 1996; *Educ* Maidstone GS, KCL (BSc, PhD, AKC), Univ of Bristol (MLitt), Univ of Oxford (MA), London Cert in Student Counselling; *m* 1969, Suzan; 1 s (Jonathan b 1972), 1 da (Rachel b 1974); *Career* sci teacher Maidstone HS 1968–69; ordained deacon 1972, priest 1973; curate St Peter Halliwell Bolton 1972–74, sr curate St John Harborne 1974–77, librarian Latimer House Oxford 1977–80; Corpus Christi Coll Oxford: chaplain 1980–93, fell and lectr 1984–93; residentiary canon Southwark Cathedral 1993–96, archdeacon of Lewisham 1996–; co-fndr Oxford Christian Inst for Counselling, dir Mildmay Mission Hosp, formerly theol conslt Care and Counsel; memb Soc of Ordained Scientists (SOSc); *Books* To Have and to Hold (1979), Homosexuals in the Christian Fellowship (1979), Peace in Our Time? (1985); Bible Speaks Today: Ruth (1984), Genesis 1–11 (1990), Job (1992), Proverbs (1996); Life and Death (1986), Pastoral Ethics (1989, 2 edn 1994); *Recreations* music, painting, walking; *Style*— The Ven the Archdeacon of Lewisham; ✉ 3a Court Farm Road, Mottingham, London SE9 4JH (☎ 0181 857 7982, fax 0181 249 0350); Trinity House, 4 Chapel Court, Borough High Street, London SE1 1HW (☎ 0171 403 8686, fax 0171 403 4770, e-mail trinity@ dswark.org.uk)

ATKINSON, Air Marshal Sir David William; KBE (1982); s of late David William Atkinson, and late Margaret Atkinson; *b* 29 Sept 1924; *Educ* Univ of Edinburgh (MB ChB, DPH, DIH); *m* 1948, Mary Sowerby; 1 s; *Career* joined RAF as med offr 1949 (appts UK Jordan and Egypt 1949–52), student RAF Staff Coll 1963–64, SMO RAF Brüggen Germany 1964–67, dep PMO HQ Air Support Command 1967–70, PMO HQ British Forces Gulf Bahrain 1970–71, OC RAF Hosp Wegberg Germany 1971–73, dir Health and Research RAF 1974–78, PMO RAF Strike Command 1978–81, QHP 1978–84, dir gen RAF Med Servs 1981–84; dir gen The Stroke Assoc 1985–93; Freeman City of London 1984, Liveryman Worshipful Soc of Apothecaries; CStJ 1981; FFPHM, MFOM 1978, FFOM 1983, FRCPE 1983; *Books* Double Crew Continuous Flying Operations: a study of aircrew sleep patterns (jtly, 1970); *Clubs* RAF; *Style*— Air Marshal Sir David

Atkinson, KBE; ✉ Rosedene, Woodside Lane, Lymington, Hampshire SO41 8FJ (☎ 01590 670438)

ATKINSON, Sir Frederick John (Fred); KCB (1979, CB 1971); s of George Edward Atkinson, and Elizabeth Sabina Cooper; *b* 7 Dec 1919; *Educ* Dulwich, Jesus Coll Oxford; *m* 1947, Margaret Grace, da of Sidney Jeffrey Gibson; 2 da; *Career* lectr Jesus and Trinity Colls Oxford 1947–49, Economic Section Cabinet Office 1949–51, Br Embassy Washington 1952–54, HM Treasy 1955–62, economic advsr Foreign Office 1962–63, HM Treasy 1963–69 (dep dir Economic Section 1965–69), controller economics and statistics Min of Technology 1970, chief econ advsr Dept of Trade and Indust 1970–73, an asst sec gen OECD Paris 1973–75, dep sec and chief econ advsr Dept of Energy 1975–77, chief econ advsr to Treasy 1977–79, head Govt Economic Serv 1977–79; hon fell Jesus Coll Oxford 1979–; *Books* Oil and the British Economy (with S Hall, 1983); *Style—* Sir Fred Atkinson, KCB; ✉ 26 Lee Terrace, Blackheath, London SE3 (☎ 0181 852 1040); Tickner Cottage, Aldington, Kent (☎ 01233 720514)

ATKINSON, Brig Geoffrey Arthur; s of Arthur Vivian Atkinson (d 1983), and Flora Muriel, *née* Lucas (d 1984); *b* 17 March 1931; *Educ* Berkhamsted Sch, Royal Mil Coll of Sci (BSc, ptsc), Manchester Business Sch; *m* 20 Dec 1952, Joyce Eileen, *née* Pavey; 1 s (Nicholas James Vivian b 1962), 1 da (Sally Elizabeth b 1957); *Career* Nat Serv 2 Lt 1949–52; Army Serv 1952–84, Lt 1952–57, Capt 17 Gurkha Div Malaya and Inf Bde Workshop Malaya 1957–60, Regtl electrical and mechanical engr The Queen's Own Hussars 1960–62, instr RMA Sandhurst 1962–63, Staff Course 1963–65, Maj 20 Armd Bde Germany 1965–67, tech staff offr Trials Section Mechanical Tport Wing Army Sch of Tport 1967–69, Mgmnt Course 1969, Lt-Col CO 7 Armd Workshop REME 1970–72, staff offr to DG Fighting Vehicles & Engr Equipment MOD (Procurement Exec) 1972–75, offr and soldier recruitment for Dir of Electrical & Mechanical Engrg 1975–76, Mil Dir of Studies Weapons & Vehicles RMCS Shrivenham 1976–78, Brig REME 1 Br Corps Germany 1979–81, Dir of Equipment Engrg MOD Logistic Exec Andover 1981–83, Cdr HQ REME TA 1983–84, ret; Hon Col REME Specialist Units TA 1986–89; The Fellowship of Engineering: dep sec 1984–88, head of Secretariat 1988–90, exec sec 1990–92; exec sec The Royal Acad of Engineering 1992–93; memb: Cncl Parly and Scientific Ctee 1991–93, Ctee Parly Gp for Engrg Devpt 1990–93; Freeman: Worshipful Co of Engrs 1990 (Liveryman 1991), City of London 1990; CEng 1962, FIMgt 1981, FIMechE 1982; *Style—* Brig Geoffrey Atkinson

ATKINSON, Dr Harry Hindmarsh; s of Harry Temple Atkinson (late Cmmr of Patents NZ, d 1961), and Constance Hindmarsh, *née* Shields (d 1973); gf, Sir Harry Atkinson (Prime Min of NZ five times between 1873 and 1890, d 1892); *b* 5 Aug 1929; *Educ* Nelson Coll Nelson NZ, Canterbury Univ Coll NZ (BSc, MSc), Cornell Univ, Corpus Christi Coll & Cavendish Lab Cambridge (PhD); *m* 25 March 1958, Anne Judith, da of Thomas Kenneth Barrett (d 1964); 2 s ((Harry) David b 1960, (John) Benedict b 1966), 1 da (Katherine Hindmarsh b 1959); *Career* asst lectr in physics Canterbury Univ Coll NZ 1952–53, res asst Cornell Univ USA 1954–55, sr res fell AERE Harwell UK 1958–61, head Gen Physics Gp Rutherford Lab UK 1961–69, staff chief sci advsr to UK Govt Cabinet Office UK 1969–72; UK Sci Res Cncl: head Astronomy Space & Radio Div 1972–78, under sec dir of astronomy space & nuclear physics 1979–83; under sec dir of sci UK Sci & Engrg Res Cncl (incl responsibility for int affrs) 1983–88, under sec (special responsibilities) 1988–92; research conslt 1992–; assessor Univ Grants Ctee 1986–89, UK memb EISCAT Cncl 1976–86, chm of Cncl Euro Space Agency 1984–87 (vice chm 1981–84); UK memb: S African Astronomical Observatory Ctee 1979–85, Anglo-Aust Telescope Bd 1979–88; chm Anglo-Dutch Astron Ctee 1981–88, UK delegate Summit Gp on High Energy Physics 1982–88; chm and memb steering ctee of Inst Laue Langevin (ILL) Grenoble France 1984–88; UK delegate to Cncl Synchrotron Radiation Facility 1986–88, memb NI Ctee Univ Funding Cncl 1989–93, coordinator UK Aust NZ Science Collaboration 1989–94, pt/t chief scientist Loss Prevention Cncl 1990–; FRAS; *Recreations* cars, travelling; *Clubs* Athenaeum; *Style—* Dr Harry Atkinson; ✉ Atkinson Associates, Ampney Lodge, Bampton, Oxford OX18 2JN (☎ 01993 850120)

ATKINSON, Prof the Rev Canon James; s of Nicholas Ridley Atkinson (d 1944), and Margaret Patience Bradford, *née* Hindhaugh (d 1970); *b* 27 April 1914; *Educ* Tynemouth HS, Univ of Durham (MA, MLitt), Univ of Muenster (DTh); *m* 1 Aug 1939, Laura Jean, da of George Nutley (d 1967); 1 s (Nicholas b 1949), 1 da (Mary b 1945); *Career* curate Newcastle upon Tyne 1937–41, precentor of Sheffield Cathedral 1941–44, vicar St James and Christopher Sheffield 1944–51, res fell Univ of Sheffield 1951–54, canon theologian Leicester Cathedral 1954–56, reader in theology Univ of Hull 1956–66, visiting prof Chicago 1966–67, prof of biblical studies Univ of Sheffield 1967–79, univ memb of Gen Synod 1975–80, fndr and hon dir Centre for Reformation Studies Univ of Sheffield 1979–, special prof of reformation theology Univ of Nottingham 1993–, examining chaplain to several dioceses; memb: Prep Cmmn on Anglican/Roman Catholic Relations, several ctees on Lutheran/Anglican relations, L'Academie Internationale des Sciences Religieuses Brussels; pres Soc for the Study of Theology; *Books* Library of Christian Classics Vol XVI (1962), Luther's Early Theological Works (1962), Rome and Reformation (1966), Luther's Works Vol 44 (1967), Luther and the Birth of Protestantism (1968, 1982), The Reformation, Paternoster Church History Vol 4 (1968), The Trial of Luther (1971), Martin Luther - Prophet to the Church Catholic (1983), The Darkness of Faith (1987); *Recreations* music, gardening; *Style—* Prof the Rev Canon James Atkinson; ✉ Leach House, Hathersage, Via Sheffield S30 1BA (☎ 01433 650570)

ATKINSON, Jane Elizabeth; da of William Gledhill (d 1969), and Ethel, *née* Stopps (d 1978); *b* 20 July 1947; *Educ* Kesteven and Seaford HS for Girls; *m* 1, 1967 (m dis 1973), David Hayward; 1 s (Anthony b 1967); m 2, 1975, George Ronald Atkinson; 1 s (Nicholas b 1980), 1 da (Caroline b 1984); *Career* sec until 1975, asst account exec Planned Public Relations International 1975–76, account exec Welbeck PR 1976–78, sr client conslt Bell Capper PR 1978–80, bd dir Eurocom PR 1980, jt md Granard Communications (after merger with Eurocom PR 1982) 1988, dep chm The Rowland Company (result of Granard merger with Kingsway PR) 1990–94, jt md Affinity Consulting Ltd (Countrywide Group) 1992–95, ptnr Atkinson Courage Communications 1995–97, with Lowe Bell Consultants 1997–; media advsr to HRH The Princess of Wales Jan-July 1996 (resigned); ptnr Best Bib and Tucker Catering; Prince's Youth Business Tst: small business advsr, vice chm E London Bd; past pres Assoc of Women in Public Relations; MIPR; *Recreations* cooking, reading, walking; *Style—* Mrs Jane Atkinson; ✉ Best Bib and Tucker Catering, 77 Sutton Court Rd, London W4 3EG (☎ 0181 546 0553); Lowe Bell Consultants, 7 Hertford Street, London W1Y 8LP (☎ 0171 495 4044)

ATKINSON, Prof John; s of John Jennings Atkinson (d 1974), and Cecil Priscilla, *née* Sully; *b* 10 March 1942; *Educ* Norwich Sch, Imperial Coll London; *m* 17 July 1978, Josephine, da of John Thomas Kirby, of Brentford, Middx; 2 s (Robert b 1978, Nicholas b 1981); *Career* engr; Coffey & Ptnrs Brisbane 1967–69, Imperial Coll London 1969–73, Univ of Cambridge 1973–76, Univ Coll Cardiff 1976–80, City Univ 1980–; CEng, CGeol, FICE, FGS; *Books* The Mechanics of Soils (1978), Foundations and Slopes (1981), The Mechanics of Soils and Foundations (1993); *Recreations* sailing, surfing, the countryside; *Clubs* Norfolk Punt; *Style—* Prof John Atkinson; ✉ Geotechnical Engineering Research Centre, The City University, Northampton Square, London EC1V 0HB (☎ 0171 477 8000)

ATKINSON, Sir John Alexander (Alec); KCB (1978, CB 1976), DFC (1943); yr s of Rev Robert F Atkinson (d 1943), and Harriet Harrold, *née* Lowdon; *b* 9 June 1919; *Educ* Kingswood Sch Bath, Queen's Coll Oxford (MA); *m* 1945, Marguerite Louise, da of George Pearson (d 1974); 1 da (Charlotte); *Career* served WWII Flt Lt; entered Civil Serv 1946, princ Ministry of Nat Insurance 1949–50 (asst princ 1946–49), Cabinet Office 1950–52, PPS to Min of Pensions and Nat Insurance 1957–58 (asst sec 1958), under sec Miny of Social Security 1966–73, dep sec DHSS 1973–76, second perm sec DHSS 1977–79; memb: Panel of Chairmen Civil Serv Selection Bd 1979–88, Occupational Pensions Bd 1981–88; specialist advsr to House of Lords Ctee on the Euro Communities Sub Ctee C on Draft Directives on Equal Treatment for Men and Women in Pensions (1988–89) and on Pension Funds (1992); pres Kingswood Assoc 1983, chm ind Working Gp on Pensions and Divorce (appointed by The Pensions Mgmnt Inst in agreement with The Law Soc) 1992–93; *Recreations* walking, reading, theatre; *Clubs* United Oxford and Cambridge Univ; *Style—* Sir Alec Atkinson, KCB, DFC; ✉ Bleak House, The Drive, Belmont, Sutton, Surrey SM2 7DH (☎ 0181 642 6479)

ATKINSON, (Charles) Keith; s of Joseph Atkinson (d 1974), of Atherton, Lancs, and Elizabeth, *née* Glover; *b* 18 Dec 1937; *Educ* Nottingham Bluecoat, St John's Coll Durham (BA, dip in educn); *m* Sept 1962, Celia, da of James Kelly; 2 da (Clare Jane b 24 Nov 1963, Juliet Rachel b 4 Nov 1970); *Career* gen subjects teacher Bingham Toot Hill 1961–64, head Humanities Faculty Wilsthorpe Sch Long Eaton 1964–74, dep head South Wolds Sch Keyworth Notts 1974–78, headteacher Tuxford Sch Tuxford Notts 1978–96; JP Shire Hall Nottingham 1980–90; umpire FISA (int rowing) 1980–94; *Recreations* rowing, running, walking, stage productions; *Clubs* Nottingham Boat (pres 1976–), Nottinghamshire County Rowing Association; *Style—* Keith Atkinson, Esq; ✉ 67 Newark Road, Southwell, Notts NG25 0ES (☎ 01636 814526)

ATKINSON, Kenneth Neil; s of William Atkinson (d 1972), and Alice, *née* Reid (d 1990); *b* 4 April 1931; *Educ* Kingussie HS; *Career* various appts Miny of Labour and Dept of Employment 1948–67, dep chief conciliation offr Dept of Employment 1968–72, dir youth trg MSC Trg Agency 1983–89 (dir indust trg bd relations 1975–78, dir Scotland 1979–82), md The Travel Training Co (Nat Trg Bd ABTA until 1994, of which dir) 1989–95; chm Prince's Tst Community Venture 1989–92; memb Cncl: CGLI 1991–, Prince's Tst Volunteers 1993–94; ARCM 1961, FIPD 1986; *Recreations* tennis, choral singing, conducting; *Clubs* Royal Scottish Automobile; *Style—* Kenneth N Atkinson, Esq; ✉ 3 St Catherines Road, Ruislip, Middlesex HA4 7RX

ATKINSON, Peter; MP (C) Hexham (majority 13,438); s of Maj Douglas Atkinson (ka 1945), and Amy Atkinson; *b* 19 Jan 1943; *Educ* Cheltenham Coll; *m* 7 April 1976, Brione, da of Cdr A T Darley; 2 da; *Career* Evening Standard: journalist 1961–73, various posts rising to news ed 1973–81; chm Southern Free Press Gp 1981–87, public affrs conslt 1983–92, MP (C) Hexham 1992–; PPS to: Armed Forces Min 1994, Rt Hon Jeremy Hanley as min without portfolio and chm of Cons Pty 1994–95, Sir Nicholas Bonsor and Rt Jeremy Hanley as Mins of State for Foreign and Cwlth Affrs 1995–96 (resigned); memb: Scottish Affrs Select Ctee 1992–, Euro Legislation Ctee 1992–; sec Cons Agriculture Backbench Ctee 1992–94; cncllr: London Borough of Wandsworth 1978–82, Suffolk CC 1989–92; memb Wandsworth Health Authy 1982–89, dir of public affrs Br Field Sports Soc 1983–92; *Recreations* shooting, gardening, racing; *Clubs* Albert Edward (Hexham), Turf, Northern Counties; *Style—* Peter Atkinson, Esq, MP; ✉ House of Commons, London SW1A 0AA

ATKINSON, Rev Canon Peter Gordon; s of Thomas John Collins Atkinson (d 1986), of Maidstone, and Adèle Mary, *née* Cox; *b* 26 Aug 1952; *Educ* Maidstone GS, St John's Coll Oxford (scholar, sr scholar, Denyer and Johnson student, Liddon student, MA), Westcott House Cambridge; *m* 1983, Lynne, da of Brian Wilcock; 2 s (James David b 1985, Leo Francis b 1992), 1 da (Elizabeth Grace b 1987); *Career* ordained: deacon 1979, priest 1980; asst curate Clapham Old Town Team Miny 1979–83, priest-in-charge St Mary's Tatsfield 1983–90, rector of Holy Trinity Bath 1990–91, princ Chichester Theol Coll 1991–94, Bursalis preb and residentiary canon Chichester Cathedral 1991–, rector of Lavant 1994–; *Style—* The Rev Canon Peter Atkinson; ✉ The Rectory, Pook Lane, East Lavant, Chichester, W Sussex (☎ 01243 527313)

ATKINSON, Sir Robert; kt (1982), DSC (1941, 2 Bars 1943 and 1944), RD (1947); s of Nicholas Atkinson (d 1944), and Margaret Patience Bradford; *b* 7 March 1916; *Educ* Univ of London (BSc), McGill Univ Canada; *m* 1, 1941, Joyce, *née* Forster (d 1973); 1 s (Robert), 1 da (Gillian); m 2, 1977, Margaret Hazel Walker; *Career* served WWII 1939–45 (despatches 1943); md: Wm Doxford 1957–61, Tube Investments (Eng) 1961–67, Unicorn Industries 1967–72; chm: Aurora Holdings Sheffield 1972–84, British Shipbuilders 1980–84; non-exec dir Stag Furniture Holdings 1971–90; CEng 1960, FIMechE 1962 (James Clayton Medal 1960), FEng 1983; *Publications* The Design and Operating Experience of an Ore Carrier Built Abroad (1957), The Manufacture of Steel Crankshafts (1960), Some Crankshaft Failures - Investigation into Causes and Remedies (1960), British Shipbuilders Offshore Division (paper, 1982); *Recreations* salmon fishing, gardening, walking; *Clubs* Royal Thames Yacht; *Style—* Sir Robert Atkinson, DSC, RD, FEng; ✉ Southwood House, Itchen Abbas, Winchester, Hants SO21 1AT (☎ 01962 779610)

ATKINSON, Dr Ronald James; s of Robert William Atkinson (d 1974), and Ellen, *née* Whiteside (d 1991); *b* 8 Sept 1945; *Educ* Bangor GS, Queen's Univ Belfast (MD); *m* 25 Oct 1974, (Sarah) Pamela, da of Robert Samuel Gawley (d 1990); 2 da (Claire b 1977, Sarah b 1981); *Career* fell Cancer Res Campaign 1976–78, sr lectr Queen's Univ Belfast 1980– (acting head Oncology Dept 1993–96), conslt Belfast City Hosp 1980–; numerous contribs to med jls; sec British Gynaecological Cancer Soc; FRCS, FRCOG; *Recreations* wind surfing, gardening; *Style—* Dr Ronald J Atkinson; ✉ 29A Carnreagh, Hillsborough, Co Down, N Ireland BT26 6LJ; Oncology Department, University Floor, Belfast City Hospital Tower, Lisburn Road, Belfast BT9 7AB (☎ 01232 329241 ext 2229/2264, 01232 314055)

ATKINSON, Rowan Sebastian; s of Eric Atkinson (d 1984), and Ella May Atkinson; *b* 6 Jan 1955; *Educ* Durham Cathedral Choristers' Sch, St Bees' Cumbria, Univ of Newcastle (BSc), Queen's Coll Oxford (MSc); *m* 1990, Sunetra Sastry; *Career* actor and writer; *Theatre* West End performances incl: One Man Show 1981 and 1986 (SWET Award for Comedy Performance of the Year), The Nerd 1984, Chekhov's The Sneeze 1988; one man show tours to Aust, Canada, USA, and Far East; *Television* for BBC incl: Not The Nine O'Clock News 1979–82, The Black Adder 1983, Blackadder II 1985, Blackadder the Third 1987, Blackadder Goes Forth 1989; other credits incl: Mr Bean (Tiger Aspect for ITV) 1990–95, The Thin Blue Line (Tiger Aspect for BBC) 1995 and 1996; *Films* The Tall Guy 1989, The Appointments of Dennis Jennings 1989, The Witches 1990, Hot Shots - Part Deux 1993, Four Weddings and a Funeral 1994, The Lion King (voiceover) 1994; *Awards* BBC TV Personality of the Year 1980 and 1989, Br Acad Award 1980 and 1989; *Recreations* motor cars (regular columnist Car magazine 1992–94), motor sport; *Style—* Rowan Atkinson, Esq; ✉ c/o PBJ Management Ltd, 5 Soho Square, London W1V 5DE (☎ 0171 287 1112, fax 0171 287 1448)

ATKINSON, Dr Sue; *b* 10 Aug 1946; *Educ* Merchant Taylors' Sch for Girls, UCNW Bangor (BSc), Univ of Cambridge (MA), Middx Hosp Med Sch London (MB BChir, LRCP, MRCS, FFPHM 1990 (MFPHM 1985)); *Career* SHO Addenbrooke's Hosp Cambridge 1975–76, registrar (paediatrics) Southmead Hosp Bristol 1976, gen paediatrics and paediatric oncology Royal Hosp for Sick Children Bristol 1977, DCH 1977, res assoc Dept of Child Health Univ of Bristol/Avon Area Health Authy 1977–79, registrar then sr registrar in community med Avon Area Health Authy 1980, res fell Nat Health and MRC Unit of Epidemiology and Preventative Med Univ of Western Australia 1980–81, GP 1981–82, specialist in public health med Bristol and Western Health Authy 1985–87 (sr registrar 1982–85), sr lectr UMDS and conslt in public health

Lewisham and N Southwark Health Authy 1987, dir of public health and serv devpt Lewisham and N Southwark Health Authy and sr lectr UMDS 1988–91, dir of public health SE London Health Authy 1991–93 (actg chief exec 1993), dir of health strategy/regnl dir of public health Wessex RHA 1993–94, dir of public health/med dir S Thames RHA/RO 1994–; special advsr to House of Commons Select Ctee in its examination of NHS Reforms and NHS Tsts 1991–92; Faculty of Public Health Med: bd memb 1990–93, exec ctee memb 1990–93, examiner and visitor for jr doctor posts; memb: Soc for Social Med 1983, 24 Gp (Community Med) 1984, Bristol Chirological Soc 1986; *Publications* author of numerous papers in professional jls; *Style*— Dr Sue Atkinson; ✉ South Thames Regional Office, NHS Executive, 40 Eastbourne Terrace, London W2 3QR (☎ 0171 725 2500)

ATKINSON, Terry; s of Reginald Atkinson (d 1951), of Thurnscoe, Rotherham, Yorkshire, and Lily, *née* Hampshire; *b* 16 July 1939; *Educ* Wath-upon-Dearne GS South Yorkshire, Barnsley Sch of Art, Slade Sch of Fine Art Univ of London; *m*; 2 c; *Career* artist; fndr memb Art & Language 1966–74, currently reader in rhetorics and practices of fine art Univ of Leeds (lectr in fine art 1977); Turner prize nominee 1985; author of numerous articles and essays; *Art & Language Group Exhibitions* incl: The British Avant-Garde (NY Cultural Centre) 1971, Dokumenta 5 (Museum Friedericianum Kassel) 1972, The New Art (Hayward Gallery) 1972; *Other group exhibitions* incl: Art for Society (Whitechapel Gallery) 1979, 5th Sydney Biennale 1984, Aperto Venice Biennale 1984, Turner Prize Nominee's Exhbn (Tate Gallery) 1985, State of the Art Exhbn (ICA) 1987, Innocence and Childhood (Manchester City Art Galleries) 1992, Mind the Gap (Gimpel Fils Gallery) 1992; *Solo exhibitions* incl: Work 1977–83 (Whitechapel Art Gallery) 1983, Art for the Bunker (Gimpel Fils London) 1985, Mute 1 (Galleri Prag Copenhagen) 1988, Work (Stampa Basel) 1989, Greasers & Mutes (Galerie Sophia Ungers Cologne) 1990, Mute 3 - Work 1988–91 (Kuntsmuseum Sorø Denmark) 1992, Irish Mus of Modern Art Dublin 1992, Cornerhouse Manchester 1992, Ruses Mutes Monochromes & Bombers (Galerie Patricia Asback Copenhagen) 1992, Bunker Entrance outside site specific project Furka Pass Switzerland 1992, Fragments of a Career (Kunstwerk Berlin) 1994–95, Work 1974: in leaving Art & Language (Archivio Di Nuovo Scrittura Milan) 1995, Enola Gay Works (Galleria Inga-Pin Milan) 1995; *Sculpture* with Sue Atkinson for: Mute 2 Exhbn (Orchard Gall Derry) 1988, A New Necessity (Gateshead Garden Festival) 1991; *Style*— Terry Atkinson, Esq; ✉ 12 Milverton Crescent, Leamington Spa, Warwickshire CV32 5NG (☎ 01926 311894); Department of Fine Art, University of Leeds, Leeds LS2 9JT (☎ 0113 533 5271, fax 0113 545 1977)

ATKINSON, Dr Thomas; s of Thomas Bell Atkinson (d 1968), of Sacriston, Durham, and Elizabeth Dawson (d 1967); descendant of J J Atkinson, the pioneer of the science of mine ventilation; *b* 23 Jan 1924; *Educ* Sacriston Sch, Royal Sch of Mines London (PhD, DIC, DEng, DSc); *m* 1948, Dorothy, da of Harold Price (d 1967), of Tyne and Wear; 1 da (Dorothy b 1951); *Career* Charlaw and Sacriston Collieries Ltd Durham 1938–42; served RN 1942–46, W/O N Atlantic & SEAC; NCB 1946–49, Andrew Yule India 1949–53, KWPR Australia 1953–56, mining engr Powell Duffryn Technical Services Ltd 1956–68, sr lectr Imperial Coll 1968–73, dir British Mining Consultants Ltd 1969–88, head Coal Mining Div Shell International Petroleum Maatschappij BV Holland 1973–77, prof and head Dept of Mining Engrg Univ of Nottingham 1977–88 (emeritus prof 1988), chm Consolidated Coalfields Ltd 1986–92; chm Nat Awards Tbnl British Coal (formerly NCB) 1984–; various contribs to technical jls; FIMM, FIMinE, FIEE, FIMechE, FRSA, FEng 1987; *Recreations* oil painting; *Clubs* Chaps, Snobs; *Style*— Prof Thomas Atkinson, FEng; ✉ Suite 209, 4875 Valley Drive, Vancouver BC, V6J 4B8, Canada

ATKINSON, William Silver; s of Arthur George Atkinson (d 1971), and Kathleen Evelyn May, *née* Fitzgerald (d 1986); *b* 14 Sept 1937; *m* 1963 (m dis 1974), Mary, da of Mark Breadmore, of Bracknell, Berks; *Career* oil company exec; dir: Continental Oil Co Ltd 1979–82, Conoco (UK) Ltd 1982–93, Conoco Ltd 1982–93, The Arts Club (London) Ltd 1984–95, Du Pont Treasury Ltd 1990–93; writer and speaker on taxation; sec UK Oil Indust Taxation Ctee 1976–85, hon treas The Arts Club 1985–88 (tstee 1987–95); FCA, FTII; *Recreations* opera, walking, wine; *Clubs* Arts, Oriental; *Style*— William Atkinson, Esq; ✉ 1 Eton College Road, London NW3 2BS

ATLAY, Robert David; s of Robert Henry Atlay, of Freshfield, nr Southport, Lancs, and Sarah, *née* Griffiths; *b* 26 June 1936; *Educ* Wirral GS, Univ of Liverpool (MB ChB, FRCOG); *m* 11 Feb 1967, Jean, da of William Alfred Stephen Cole, of Prenton, Wirral, Merseyside; 2 da (Josephine b 8 May 1969, Victoria b 3 April 1973); *Career* conslt obstetrician and gynaecologist; formerly at: Mill Road Maternity Hosp 1970, Royal Liverpool Hosp 1978; clinical lectr in obstetrics and gynaecology and chm Faculty of Med Univ of Liverpool, med dir Liverpool Women's Hosp Obstetrics and Gynaecology NHS Tst; chm Euro Ctee RCOG; examiner: RCOG, Royal Aust Coll of Obstetrics and Gynaecology, Univs of Liverpool, Cambridge, Manchester, Birmingham, Glasgow, London and the W Indies; hosp visitor Royal Women's Hosp Brisbane Aust 1981, papers in specialist jls, contrib RCOG Yearbooks, clinics in obstetrics and gynaecology 1989–; past pres Union Professionelle Internationale Obstetrics and Gynaecology; Sec of State appointee memb: Maternity Servs Advsy Ctee, Nat Transplant Panel, English Nat Bd Nursing Midwifery and Health Visiting; hon sec RCOG 1980–87 (memb Cncl 1973–95), govr Wirral GS, past pres Waterloo Rugby Union FC; *Recreations* rugby union football, golf, skiing, traditional jazz; *Clubs* Waterloo Football, Formby Golf, Liverpool Artists, Gynaecological Travellers; *Style*— Robert Atlay, Esq; ✉ 27 Merrilocks Rd, Blundellsands, Merseyside L23 6UL (☎ 0151 924 1160); 35 Rodney St, Liverpool, Merseyside L1 9EN (☎ 0151 708 9528); Liverpool Women's Hospital, Crown Street, Liverpool L8 7SS (☎ 0151 708 9988)

ATTA, Hatem Riad; s of Riad Gorgi Atta (d 1995), of Egypt, and Jozephine Matta, *née* Abrahim (d 1989); *b* 12 Aug 1951; *Educ* Private Mission Sch Egypt, DO London (MB BCh); *m* 26 June 1982, Janet Ann, da of Samuel John Saunders (d 1988); *Career* sr registrar in ophthalmology West Midlands RHA 1983–88, fell in ophthalmic ultrasonography Miami Sch of Med 1986–87, conslt ophthalmic surgn Aberdeen Royal Infirmary 1988–; hon sr lectr Univ of Aberdeen 1988; author of papers in scientific jls; memb: Oxford Congress, Int Soc of Ophthalmic Ultrasound; FRCSEd 1980, FRCOphth 1988; *Books* Techniques and Application of Diagnostic Ultrasound (1990), Ophthalmic Ultrasound - a practical guide (1996); *Recreations* racquet sports, golf, scuba diving; *Clubs* Aberdeen Petroleum, British Subaqua, Aberdeen Medical Golf Society; *Style*— Hatem Atta, Esq; ✉ Eye Department, Aberdeen Royal Infirmary, Foresterhill, Aberdeen (☎ 01224 681818)

ATTALLAH, Naim Ibrahim; s of Ibrahim and Genevieve Attallah; *b* 1 May 1931; *Educ* Battersea Poly; *m* 1957, Maria, da of Joseph Nykolyn; 1 s; *Career* foreign exchange dealer 1957, fin conslt 1966, dir of companies 1969–; book publisher and proprietor: Quartet Books 1976–, The Women's Press 1977–, Robin Clark 1980–; magazine proprietor: The Literary Review 1981–, The Wire 1984–, The Oldie 1991–94; Asprey plc: fin dir and jt md 1979–92, chief exec 1992–; md Mappin & Webb 1990–, md Watches of Switzerland 1992–, exec dir Garrard 1990–; proprietor The Academy Club 1989–; parfumier: launched Parfums Namara 1985 with Avant l'Amour and Aprés l'Amour, Naïdor in 1986, l'Amour de Namara 1990; theatrical prodr: Happy End (co-presenter, Lyric) 1975, The Beastly Beatitudes of Balthazar B (presenter and prodr, Duke of York's) 1981, Trafford Tanzi (co-prodr, Mermaid) 1982; film prodr: The Slipper and the Rose (co-prodr with David Frost) 1974–75, Brimstone and Treacle (exec prodr) 1982; also produced and presented of TV documentaries; *Books* Women (1987), Singular Encounters (1990), Of a Certain Age (1992), More of a Certain Age (1993), Speaking for the Oldie (1994), A Timeless Passion (1995); articles in The Literary Review, princ interviewer Oldie magazine; *Recreations* classical music, opera, theatre, cinema, photography; *Clubs* Arts, Beefsteak; *Style*— Naim Attallah, Esq; ✉ 106 Regent Street, London W1R 3JH (☎ 0171 734 5842)

ATTENBOROUGH, Sir David Frederick; CH (1996), kt (1985), CVO (1991), CBE (1974); s of Frederick Levi Attenborough (d 1973), and Mary, *née* Clegg (d 1961); bro of Lord Attenborough, *qv*; *b* 8 May 1926; *Educ* Wyggeston GS for Boys Leicester, Clare Coll Cambridge (hon fell 1980); *m* 1950, Jane Elizabeth Ebsworth Oriel; 1 s, 1 da; *Career* naturalist, traveller, broadcaster and writer; served RN 1947–49; editorial asst in an educational publishing house 1949–52, prodr talks and documentary progs BBC 1952, controller TV BBC2 1965–68, dir of Programmes TV and memb Bd of Management BBC 1969–72; zoological and ethnographic filming expeditions to: Sierra Leone 1954, Br Guiana 1955, Indonesia 1956, New Guinea 1957, Paraguay and Argentina 1958, South West Pacific 1959, Madagascar 1960, Northern Territory Australia 1962, Zambesi 1964, Bali 1969, Central New Guinea 1971, Celebes 1973, Borneo 1973, Peru 1973, Columbia 1973, Mali 1974, Br Columbia 1974, Iran 1974, Solomon Islands 1974, Nigeria 1975; writer and presenter BBC series: Zoo Quest 1954–64, Tribal Eye 1976, Life on Earth 1979, The Living Planet 1984, The First Eden 1987, Lost Worlds Vanished Lives 1989, The Trials of Life 1990, The Private Life of Plants 1995; tstee: World Wildlife Fund UK 1965–69, 1972–82 and 1984–90, World Wildlife Fund Int 1979–86, Br Museum 1980–, Science Museum 1984–87, Royal Botanic Gardens Kew 1986–92, Learning Through Landscapes 1990–; memb Nature Conservancy Cncl 1973–82, corresponding memb American Museum of Natural History 1985, Huw Wheldon Meml Lecture RTS 1987; fell BAFTA 1980; awards: Special Award SFTA 1961, Silver Medal Zoological Soc of London 1966, Silver Medal RTS 1966, Desmond Davis Award SFTA 1970, Cherry Keaton Medal RGS 1972, Kalinga Prize UNESCO 1981, Washburn Award Boston Museum of Science 1983, Hopper Day Medal Acad of Natural Sciences Philadelphia 1983, Founder's Gold Medal RGS 1985, Int Emmy Award 1985, Encyclopaedia Britannica Award 1987, Livingstone Medal RSGS 1990; Hon Freeman City of Leicester 1990; hon fell: Manchester Poly 1976, UMIST 1980; Hon DLitt: Univ of Leicester 1970, City Univ 1972, Univ of London 1980, Univ of Birmingham 1982; Hon LLD: Univ of Bristol 1977, Univ of Glasgow 1980; Hon DSc: Univ of Liverpool 1974, Heriot-Watt Univ 1978, Univ of Sussex 1979, Univ of Bath 1981, Ulster Univ 1982, Univ of Durham 1982, Keele Univ 1986, Univ of Oxford 1988; Hon DUniv: Open Univ 1980, Univ of Essex 1987; Hon ScD Univ of Cambridge 1984; Cdr of the Golden Ark (Netherlands) 1983; Hon FRCP 1991, FRS 1983; *Books* Zoo Quest to Guiana (1956), Zoo Quest for a Dragon (1957), Zoo Quest in Paraguay (1959), Quest in Paradise (1960), Zoo Quest to Madagascar (1961), Quest under Capricorn (1963), The Tribal Eye (1976), Life on Earth (1979), The Living Planet (1984), The First Eden (1987), The Trials of Life (1990), The Private Life of Plants (1995); *Recreations* tribal art, natural history; *Style*— Sir David Attenborough, CH, CVO, CBE, FRS; ✉ 5 Park Road, Richmond, Surrey TW10 6NS

ATTENBOROUGH, Hon Michael John; s of Baron Attenborough, CBE (Life Peer), *qv*, and Sheila Beryl Grant, *née* Sim; *b* 13 Feb 1950; *Educ* Westminster, Univ of Sussex (BA, pres Univ Drama Soc); *m* 1, 10 July 1971 (m dis 1976), Jane Seymour, *qv*; *m* 2, 14 April 1984, Karen Esther, yr da of Sydney Victor Lewis (d 1990), of London; 2 s (Thomas Frederick Richard b 13 Oct 1986, William Grant Oliver b 26 June 1991); *Career* freelance theatre director; asst dir Gardner Centre Theatre 1972; assoc dir: Mercury Theatre Colchester 1972–74, Leeds Playhouse 1974–79, Young Vic Theatre 1979–80; artistic dir: Palace Theatre Watford 1980–84, Hampstead Theatre 1984–89, Turnstyle Group 1989–90; principal assoc dir RSC 1990–; freelance work as dir incl prodns for: Open Space Theatre, Red Ladder, Newcastle Playhouse, Citadel Theatre Edmonton, Abbey Theatre Dublin, Tricycle Theatre, Royal Court Theatre London and Nat Theatre; dir of over 70 plays to date; former memb: Drama Panel Arts Cncl, Greater London Arts, Bd Bubble Theatre, Cncl Directors' Guild; currently dir Susan Smith Blackburn Prize, memb Cncl RADA; Time Out Theatre Award for Observe The Sons of Ulster Marching Towards The Somme 1986, nominated for Best Dir London Theatre Critics Awards 1985, nominated for Outstanding Achievement Award (as dir Hampstead Theatre) Olivier Awards 1986; *Recreations* being with my family, football, music, theatre; *Style*— The Hon Michael Attenborough; ✉ Royal Shakespeare Company, Barbican, London EC2Y 8BQ (☎ 0171 628 3351, fax 0171 638 2812)

ATTENBOROUGH, Neil Richard; RD (1980, and Bar 1989); s of John William Attenborough, and Eileen, *née* Ward; *b* 4 May 1940; *m* 1, 10 Sept 1968 (m dis 1980), Josephine; 2 s (Paul Alexander b 1971, Tristan Alistair b 1973); m 2, 10 June 1982, Jennifer Mary; 1 s (Thomas William b 1983); *Career* conslt oral and maxillo-facial surgn SW Surrey and NE Hants Dist Authys, dir Guildford Dental Trg and Treatment Centre; inventor and prodr Attenborough Sea Drogue; CO London Sailing Project, memb: RNSA, BDA, RSM; FDSRCS, FDSRCSEd; *Recreations* sailing, squash, cricket; *Style*— Neil Attenborough, Esq, RD; ✉ Mount Alvernia, Harvey Rd, Guildford, Surrey (☎ 01483 38066 and 01483 455307)

ATTENBOROUGH, Peter John; s of John Frederick Attenborough (d 1967), and Eileen Mabel, *née* Reavell; *b* 4 April 1938; *Educ* Christ's Hosp, Peterhouse Cambridge; *m* 1967, Alexandra Deidre, da of Alexander Henderson Campbell (d 1982), of Derby; 1 s (James b 1969), 1 da (Charlotte b 1971); *Career* £sst master Uppingham Sch 1960–75 (head of Classics Dept and housemaster, housemaster Starehe Boys Centre Nairobi 1966–67; headmaster: Sedbergh Sch 1975–81, Charterhouse 1982–93; dir of Educational and Community Care Projects Rank Foundation 1994–; chm: Ind Schs Central Subject Panel for Classics 1976–80, Ind Sch Cmmn Entrance Ctee 1983–88, Schs Arabic Project 1986–87; memb: Ind Schs Curriculum Ctee 1980–83, HMC Academic Policy Ctee 1982–83, HMC Ctee 1986–87 and 1989–90; Almoner Christ's Hosp 1987–; govr: Ashdown House 1983–93, Haslemere Prep Sch 1986–93, St Edmund's Sch 1986–94, Brambletye Sch 1989–, Caldicott Sch 1990–92, Haberdashers' Monmouth Schs 1995–; tstee: Uppingham Sch 1993–, Starehe Endowment Fund (UK) 1995–; Freeman City of London 1965; Liveryman Worshipful Co of Skinners 1978; *Clubs* East India; *Style*— Peter Attenborough, Esq; ✉ Rawmarsh Cottage, Linton, nr Ross on Wye, Herefordshire HR9 7RX (☎ 01989 720746, fax and answerphone 01989 720530)

ATTENBOROUGH, Philip John; CBE (1994); s of (Ralph) John Attenborough, CBE (d 1994), and Barbara, *née* Sandle (d 1988); *b* 3 June 1936; *Educ* Rugby, Trinity Coll Oxford; *m* 1963, Rosemary, da of Dr (William) Brian Littler, CB; 1 s, 1 da; *Career* publisher; Nat Serv Sgt 68 Regt RA Oswestry 1954–56; Hodder & Stoughton: joined 1957, export mangr 1960, dir 1963, sales dir 1969, chm Hodder & Stoughton Ltd 1975–93, chm Hodder & Stoughton Holdings 1975–93; dep chm Hodder Headline plc 1993–96; chm Lancet Ltd 1977–92, dir Book Tokens Ltd 1985–; Publishers' Assoc: memb Cncl 1976–92, treas 1981–82, vice pres 1982–83 and 1985–86, pres 1983–85; chm: Book Devpt Cncl 1977–79, Br Cncl Publishers' Advsy Ctee 1989–93 (memb 1977–93); vice pres Int Publishers' Assoc 1992–96 (memb Exec Ctee 1988–96); memb Br Library Advsy Cncl 1986–89, chm PA Freedom to Publish Ctee 1987–91; govr Judd Sch Tonbridge 1987–; Liveryman Skinners' Co 1970 (memb Ct 1995, Warden 1996); rep Fédération des Editeurs Européens 1986–93; *Publications* The Rebirth of European Publishing: An Anglo-European Perspective of '1992' (1991); *Clubs* Garrick, MCC, Kent Cricket, Rye Golf, Senior Golfers' Soc, Piscatorial Soc; *Style*— Philip Attenborough, Esq, CBE; ✉ Coldhanger, Seal Chart, Sevenoaks, Kent TN15 0EJ (☎ 01732 761516)

ATTENBOROUGH, Baron (Life Peer 1993), of Richmond upon Thames in the London Borough of Richmond upon Thames; Sir Richard Samuel Attenborough; kt (1976), CBE (1967); s of Frederick Levi Attenborough (d 1973), and Mary, *née* Clegg (d 1961); bro of Sir David Attenborough, *qv*; *b* 29 Aug 1923; *Educ* Wyggeston GS for Boys Leicester, RADA (Leverhulme scholar, Bancroft Medal); *m* 22 January 1945, Sheila Beryl Grant, *née* Sim, JP (actress), da of Stuart Grant Sim (d 1975), of Hove, Sussex; 1 s (Hon Michael John, *qv*, b 13 February 1950), 2 da (Hon Jane (Hon Mrs Holland) b 30 September 1955, Hon Charlotte (Hon Mrs Sinclair) b 29 June 1959); *Career* actor, film producer and director; joined RAF 1943, flt sgt airgunner/cameraman, seconded RAF Film Unit 1944 (for Journey Together, 1944), demobbed 1946; formed: Beaver Films (with Bryan Forbes) 1959, Allied Film Makers 1960; memb: Cncl Br Actors' Equity Assoc 1949–73, Cinematograph Films Cncl 1967–73, Arts Cncl of GB 1970–73; chm: BAFTA 1969–70 (vice pres 1971–94), RADA 1970– (memb Cncl 1963–), Capital Radio 1972–92 (life pres 1992), Help a London Child 1975–, UK Tstees Waterford-Kamhlaba Sch Swaziland 1976– (govr 1987–), Duke of York's Theatre 1979–92, BFI 1981–92, Goldcrest Films & TV 1982–87, Ctee of Inquiry into the Arts and Disabled People 1983–85, Channel 4 TV 1987–92 (dep chm 1980–86), Br Screen Advsy Cncl 1987–, Euro Script Fund 1988–; pres: Muscular Dystrophy Gp of GB 1971– (vice pres 1962–71), The Gandhi Fndn 1983–, Brighton Festival 1984–, Br Film Year 1984–86, The Actors' Charitable Tst 1988– (chm 1956–88), Combined Theatrical Appeals Cncl 1988– (chm 1964–88), Arts for Health 1989–, Gardner Centre for the Arts Univ of Sussex 1990– (patron 1969–90); tstee: Tate Gallery 1976–82 and 1994–, Tate Fndn 1986–, Fndn for Sport and the Arts 1991–; dir: Chelsea FC 1969–82, Young Vic 1974–84; govr Nat Film Sch 1970–81, pro-chllr Univ of Sussex 1970–, govr Motability 1977–; patron: Kingsley Hall Community Centre 1982–, RA Centre for Disability and the Arts Leicester 1990–; goodwill ambassador for UNICEF 1987–; Evening Standard Film Award for 40 Years Service to Br Cinema 1983, Award of Merit for Humanitarianism in Film Making Euro Film Awards 1988, Academy Award Sony Radio Awards 1992, Shakespeare Prize for Outstanding Contrib to Euro Culture 1992; Fleming Meml Lecture RTS 1989; Freeman City of Leicester 1990; Hon DLitt: Leicester 1970, Kent 1981, Sussex 1987; Hon DCL Newcastle 1974, Hon LLD Dickinson Pa 1983; fell: BAFTA 1983, BFI 1992; fell King's Coll London 1993; Martin Luther King Jr Peace Prize 1983, Padma Bhushan India 1983, Commandeur Ordre des Arts et des Lettres France 1985, Chevalier Ordre de la Légion d'Honneur France 1988; *Theatre* debut as Richard Miller in Ah Wilderness (Intimate Theatre Palmers Green) 1941, West End debut as Ralph Berger in Awake and Sing (Arts Theatre) 1942, The Little Foxes (Piccadilly) 1942, Brighton Rock (Garrick) 1943, The Way Back (Home of the Brave (Westminster)) 1949, To Dorothy a Son (Savoy 1950, Garrick 1951), Sweet Madness (Vaudeville) 1952, The Mousetrap (Ambassadors) 1952–54, Double Image (Savoy 1956–57, St James's 1957), The Rape of the Belt (Piccadilly) 1957–58; *Film* appearances incl: debut in In Which We Serve 1942, School for Secrets, The Man Within, Dancing with Crime, Brighton Rock 1947, London Belongs to Me, The Guinea Pig 1948, The Lost People, Boys in Brown, Morning Departure 1950, Hell is Sold Out, The Magic Box, Gift Horse, Father's Doing Fine, Eight O'Clock Walk, The Ship that Died of Shame, Private's Progress 1956, The Baby and the Battleship, Brothers in Law, The Scamp, Dunkirk 1958, The Man Upstairs, Sea of Sand, Danger Within, I'm All Right Jack 1959, Jet Storm, SOS Pacific, The Angry Silence (also co-prodr) 1960, The League of Gentlemen 1960, Only Two Can Play, All Night Long 1961, The Dock Brief, The Great Escape 1963, Séance On A Wet Afternoon (prodr, Best Actor San Sebastian Film Festival and Br Film Acad) 1964, The Third Secret, Guns At Batasi (Best Actor Br Film Acad) 1964, The Flight of The Phoenix 1966, The Sand Pebbles (Hollywood Golden Globe) 1967, Dr Dolittle (Hollywood Golden Globe) 1967, The Bliss of Mrs Blossom 1967, Only When I Larf 1968, The Last Grenade, A Severed Head, David Copperfield, Loot 1969, 10 Rillington Place 1970, And Then There Were None, Rosebud, Brannigan, Conduct Unbecoming 1974, The Chess Players 1977, The Human Factor 1979, Jurassic Park 1993, Miracle on 34th Street 1994; prodr: Whistle Down The Wind 1961, The L-Shaped Room 1962; prodr and dir: Oh! What A Lovely War (16 Int Awards incl Hollywood Golden Globe and BAFTA UN Award) 1969; dir: Young Winston (Hollywood Golden Globe) 1972, A Bridge Too Far (Evening News Best Drama Award) 1977, Magic 1978; prodr and dir: Gandhi (8 Oscars, 5 BAFTA Awards, 5 Hollywood Golden Globes, Dirs' Guild of America Award for Outstanding Directorial Achievement) 1980–81, A Chorus Line 1985, Cry Freedom (Berlinale Kamera and BFI Tech Achievement Award) 1987, Chaplin 1992, In Love and War, Shadowlands 1993 (BAFTA Alexander Korda Award for Outstanding Br Film of the Year); *Books* In Search of Gandhi (1982), Richard Attenborough's Chorus Line (with Diana Carter, 1986), Cry Freedom A Pictorial Record (1987); *Recreations* collecting paintings and sculpture, listening to music, watching football; *Clubs* Garrick, Beefsteak; *Style*— The Rt Hon Lord Attenborough, CBE; ✉ Old Friars, Richmond, Surrey TW9 1NQ

ATTER, John Perkins; *b* 27 July 1938; *Educ* Worksop Coll; *m*; 2 da (1 decd); *Career* Lieut Robin Hood Foresters TA; articled clerk Mellors Basdon & Mellors Nottingham 1956–61, audit clerk Peat Marwick Mitchell London 1962–63; fin dir and co sec: J Clarke & Co (Arnold) Ltd 1963–64, Venus Packaging Ltd Ilkeston 1964–70; Shield Packaging Ltd Washington Tyne & Wear: fndr, co sec 1970–75, fin dir 1970–85, commercial dir 1977–79, md 1979–85; sr business advsr English Estates North 1985–86, business support mangr English Estates 1988–93 (business devpt offr 1986–88), fndr own consultancy business 1993, md Drillturn Engineering Ltd 1995–; non-exec dir Mazel (1980) Ltd, co sec Newcastle Playhouse Trust Ltd 1992–; chm Industl & Commercial Membs' Ctee A ICAEW (memb 1985–88), fndr memb Bd of Chartered Accountants in Business 1990–91 (chm Membs' Communication Gp 1990–91), chm Dina Atter/Shield Cancer Res Fund 1982–; FCA (ACA 1962); *Recreations* rugby, charity work, wood carving, gardening; *Style*— John Atter, Esq; ✉ 4 Lumley Thicks, Chester-Le-Street, Co Durham DH3 4HF (☎ 0191 385 7189)

ATTERTON, Dr David Valentine; CBE (1981); s of Maj Frank Arthur Shepherd Atterton, MBE (d 1950), and Ella Constance, *née* Collins (d 1940); *b* 13 Feb 1927; *Educ* King's Sch Rochester Kent, Bishop Wordsworth's Sch Salisbury, Peterhouse Cambridge (MA, PhD); *m* 1948, Sheila Ann, da of John McMahon (d 1960); 2 s (Charles, Edward), 1 da (Victoria); *Career* post doctorate research Cambridge 1950–52, Foundry Services Ltd 1952; md: Foseco Ltd 1966, Foseco Minsep Ltd 1969 (chm 1979–87); chm Guinness Mahon Holdings plc 1993–; dir: Associated Engineering plc 1972–86 (dep chm 1979–86), 3i Group plc (formerly ICFC then Investors in Industry) 1974–92, IMI plc 1976–89, Barclays Bank plc 1982–92, Bank of England 1984–92, British Coal (pt/t) 1986–95, CIN Management Ltd 1986–, Marks & Spencer plc 1987–92, The Rank Organisation plc 1987–; memb Bd of Govrs United World Coll of the Atlantic 1968–85 (chm 1973–79), chm NEDO Iron and Steel Sector Working Pty 1977–82, memb Advsy Cncl for Applied Research and Devpt 1982–85; pres: Birmingham Chamber of Commerce and Industry 1974–75, Inst of Metals 1987–88; Asst Worshipful Co of Founders (Master 1994–95); FEng 1982, FRSA, FIM; *Recreations* cartography, notaphilia, Japanese language; *Style*— Dr David Atterton, CBE, FEng; ✉ Cathedral Green House, Wells, Somerset BA5 2UB (☎ 01749 674907, fax 01749 670495); 14 Chesterfield House, South Audley St, London W1Y 5TB (☎ 0171 499 8191)

ATTEWELL, Brian; s of William Joan Geldard Attewell (d 1987), and Marie Evelyn, *née* Little (d 1991); *b* 29 May 1937; *Educ* Dulwich, LSE (BScEcon); *m* 14 Dec 1963, Mary Gillian Tandy, da of Mrs Hilda Austin; 2 s (Alexander Mark b 1964, Guy Nicholas Anthony b 1969), 1 da (Zoë Jane b 1966); *Career* Bd of Trade 1956–58 and 1961–66, private sec to Parly sec 1964–66; HM Dip Serv: joined 1966, Washington 1967–70, Buenos Aires 1970–73, FCO 1974–78, Canberra 1978–80, asst head of W Indian and Atlantic Dept FCO 1980–83, Dubai 1984–87, cnsllr (commercial) Brussels 1988–92, high cmmr Nassau 1992–96, ret; *Recreations* golf, listening to music (classical and jazz), reading; *Clubs* Wimbledon Park Golf; *Style*— Brian Attewell, Esq; ✉ c/o Foreign and Commonwealth Office, King Charles Street, London SW1A 2AH

ATTEWELL, Prof Peter Brian; s of Ernest Attewell (d 1966), of Ilkeston, Derbys, and Ida Caroline, *née* Bexon (d 1961); *b* 20 Oct 1931; *Educ* Univ of Birmingham (BSc), Univ of Sheffield (PhD, DEng); *m* 21 Dec 1957, Doreen Mary, da of Flt Lt Granville Atack (d 1969), of Heysham, Lancs; 2 da (Jane Elizabeth b 12 Sept 1961, Linda Christine (twin)); *Career* mangr and civil engrg contractor NCB 1950–53 and 1956–59; res asst then res fell Univ of Sheffield 1959–65, reader then prof Univ of Durham 1965–94, emeritus prof and civil engrg consIt 1994–; FICE; *Books* Principles of Engineering Geology (1976), Soil Movements Induced by Tunnelling and their Effects on Pipelines and Structures (1986), Ground Pollution (1993), Tunnelling contracts and site investigation (1995); *Recreations* walking; *Style*— Prof Peter Attewell; ✉ 50 Archery Rise, Durham DH1 4LA (☎ 0191 386 7298)

ATTLEE, Air Vice-Marshal Donald Laurence; CB (1977), LVO (1964), DL (Devon 1991); s of Maj Laurence Gillespie Attlee (d 1968; bro of 1 Earl Attlee, PM of GB 1945–51), of Groombridge, Sussex, and Letitia, *née* Rotton (d 1973); *b* 2 Sept 1922; *Educ* Haileybury; *m* 2 Feb 1952, Jane Hamilton, da of Capt Robert Murray Hamilton Young, RFC (d 1974), of Tichborne Grange, Hants; 1 s (Charles b 1955), 2 da (Carolyn (Mrs Kevin Moloney) b 1957, Jenny (Mrs Luke Ellis) b 1963); *Career* joined RAF 1942, Flying Instructor 1944–48, Staff Training Cmd 1949–52, 12 Sqdn 1952–54, Air Staff Air Miny 1954–55, RAF Staff Coll 1956, 59 Sqdn 1957–59, CO The Queen's Flight (Wing Cdr) 1960–63, HQ RAF Germany 1964–67, CO RAF Brize Norton 1968–70, IDC 1970, Policy Staff MOD 1971–72, dir of RAF Recruiting 1973–74, Air Cdre Intelligence 1974–75, Air Vice-Marshal 1975, AOA Trg Cmd Brampton 1975–77 (ret 1977); fruit farmer 1977–; memb Mid Devon DC 1982– (vice chm 1987–89, chm 1989–91), chm Mid Devon Business Club 1985–87, dir Mid Devon Enterprise Agency 1983–93; *Recreations* genealogy; *Clubs* RAF; *Style*— Air Vice-Marshal Donald Attlee, CB, LVO, DL; ✉ Jerwoods, Culmstock, Cullompton, Devon (☎ 01823 680317)

ATTLEE, 3 Earl (UK 1955); John Richard Attlee; also Viscount Prestwood (UK 1955); o s of 2 Earl Attlee (d 1991), and his 1 w, Anne Barbara, eldest da of James Henderson, CBE, of Bath; gs of 1 Earl Attlee, KG, OM, CH, PC (d 1967, Lab PM 1945–51); *b* 3 Oct 1956; *Educ* Stowe; *m* 31 July 1993, Celia Jane, yst da of Dexter Plummer, of Bishop's Stortford, Herts; *Career* pres Heavy Haulage Assoc 1994–, International Aid; *Style*— The Earl Attlee; ✉ c/o House of Lords, London SW1 0PW

ATTOUNGBRE, HE Gervais Yao; *b* 19 June 1936; *Educ* L'Institut des Hautes Etudes d'Outmer Iheom (licencie en droit, diplome), Section Diplomatique Paris; *Career* diplomat of the Côte d'Ivoire; first cnsllr Rome 1962–66, dir of political affairs Miny of Foreign Affairs 1966–70, ambass in E Africa with residence in Ethiopia 1970–71, ambass to Italy 1971–81, dir of political affairs Miny of Foreign Affairs 1982–89, ambass to the Ct of St James's 1989–; memb Côte d'Ivoire delegation to UN Int Confs 1966–87; *Style*— HE Monsieur Gervais Attoungbre; ✉ Embassy of the Republic of Côte d'Ivoire, 2 Upper Belgrave Street, London SW1X 8BJ (☎ 0171 235 6991)

ATTRIDGE, Elizabeth Ann Johnston; da of Rev John Worthington Johnston (d 1952), and Mary Isobel Giraud, *née* McFadden (d 1957); *b* 26 Jan 1934; *Educ* Richmond Lodge Sch Belfast, Univ of St Andrew (MA); *m* 1 Sept 1956, John Attridge, s of William Christopher Attridge (d 1958), of Worthing; 1 s (John Worthington b 1959); *Career* civil servant; asst princ Miny of Educn NI 1955–56; MAFF 1956–94: asst princ Land Div, princ Plant Health 1963–66, princ Finance 1966–69, princ External Relations (GATT) 1969–72, asst sec Animal Heatlh 1972–75, asst sec Marketing Policy and Potatoes 1975–78, asst sec Tropical Products (chm Int Coffee Orgn) 1978–83, under sec EC Gp 1983–85, under sec Emergencies Food Quality Pesticide Safety Gp 1985–89, under sec Animal Health Gp 1989–91, under sec Horticulture Plant Protection and Agricultural Resources Gp (re-organised as Agricultural Input, Plant Protection and Emergencies) 1991–94, ret; sr clerk/advsr European Legislation Ctee House of Commons 1994–; *Clubs* Royal Over-Seas League; *Style*— Mrs John Attridge; ✉ Croxley East, The Heath, Weybridge, Surrey KT13 0UA

ATTWELL, Michael Nielen; s of John Knowles Attwell (d 1969), and Veronique Wobecke Kellner, *née* Marais (d 1969); *b* 23 July 1949; *Educ* General Smuts HS South Africa, St Catherine's Coll Oxford (MA); *Career* journalist Western Mail Cardiff 1974–76; London Weekend Television: researcher Weekend World 1976–78, prodr Babylon 1979, prodr Gay Life 1980–81, prodr Six O'Clock Show and Weekend World 1981–85; independent prodr for LWT and Channel 4 1987–88, commissioning ed science, business and features Channel 4 1988–93, independents' commissioning exec factual progs BBC TV 1994–96, controller of features and arts Channel 5 Broadcasting 1996–; *Books* South Africa - Background to the Crisis (1986); *Style*— Michael Attwell, Esq; ✉ Channel 5 Broadcasting Ltd, 22 Long Acre, London WC2E 9LY (☎ 0171 421 7113)

ATTWOOD, Frank Albert; s of Eric George Attwood, of Broadstairs, Kent, and Dorothy May, *née* Gifford; *b* 19 Jan 1943; *Educ* Simon Langton GS Canterbury, Leighton Park Sch Reading, Univ of Hull (BSc); *m* 10 July 1965, Pamela Ann Paget, da of late Samuel Kennedy Pickavor Hunter; 1 da (Rebecca b 1980); *Career* articled Sir Lawrence Robson 1965–68, CA 1968, chartered sec 1969, ptnr Robson Rhodes 1974–, chief exec offr RSM International 1990–95; memb CAs Jt Int Cmmn, former memb Auditing Practices Ctee; ICAEW: former memb Insur Sub Ctee and Res Bd, jt auditor 1988–95; chm APC Lloyd's Working Pty, hon treas and dep chm Schoolmistresses and Governesses' Benevolent Inst, memb Bretton Woods Ctee; Freeman City of London 1989, Liveryman Worshipful Co of Scriveners 1989; FCA, ACIS; *Books* De Paula's Auditing (jtly 1976, 1982, 1986), Auditing Standards From Discussion Drafts to Practice (jtly 1978); *Recreations* rambling, gardening, travel, modern novels, weight training, watching cricket; *Style*— Frank Attwood, Esq; ✉ RSM Robson Rhodes, 186 City Rd, London EC1 (☎ 0171 251 1644/071 865 2385, fax 0171 250 0801, telex 885 734)

ATTWOOD, Thomas Jaymril (Tom); s of Cdr George Frederick Attwood (d 1969), and Avril Sandys, *née* Cargill (d 1963), of NZ, who was ggda of Capt William Cargill (b 1784) who founded Otago province in NZ; *b* 30 March 1931; *Educ* Haileybury, Sandhurst, Harvard Business Sch, INSEAD; *m* 1963, Lynette, da of late C Lewis; 1 s (Alistair b 1964), 1 da (Caroline b 1966); *Career* mgmnt conslt; chm Cargill Attwood & Thomas (Mgmnt Consultancy Gp) 1965–; conductor of seminars: UN Secretariat, EC, World Cncl of Churches, Cncl of Europe and Euro Space Agency 1979–; pres Int Consits Fndn 1978–81, memb Exec Ctee Br Mgmnt Trg Export Cncl 1978–85, pt/t chm POUNC 1982–83; former GLC borough cncllr, memb Richmond upon Thames BC 1969–71; memb Ct Worshipful Co of Marketors 1985–93 (Liveryman 1980–); FCIM, FIMC, FIMgt, FInstD; *Recreations* cricket, chess, travel, music; *Clubs* City Livery, MCC, Lord's Taverners; *Style*— Tom Attwood, Esq; ✉ 8 Teddington Park, Teddington, Middx TW11 8DA (☎ 0181 977 8091, fax 0181 943 1393)

ATTWOOLL, David; *b* 22 April 1949; *Educ* Lancing, Pembroke Coll Cambridge (open exhibitioner, MA); *m*; 3 c; *Career* publisher; Oxford University Press: trainee ed London 1970–71, ed Ibadan Nigeria 1971–73, Nigerian branch ed London 1973–74, ed Paperbacks Dept London 1974–76, editorial dir Paperbacks Dept Oxford 1976–80, editorial dir i/c gen books (trade hardbacks and paperbacks) Academic & Gen Div Oxford 1980–83, exec ed i/c reference books NY 1983–85, editorial dir Reference & Gen Dept Arts & Reference Div Oxford 1985–89; Random Century: md Paperback Div 1989–90, md Reference Div 1990–92; md Helicon Publishing Ltd 1992–; hon fell Oxford Business Sch Oxford Poly (memb Advsy Bd); *Style*— David Attwooll, Esq; ✉ Helicon, 42 Hythe Bridge Street, Oxford OX1 2EP (☎ 01865 204204)

ATWELL, Very Rev James Edgar; s of Joseph Norman Edgar Atwell (d 1965), of Rough Leaze Farm, Calne, Wilts, and Sybil Marion, *née* Burnett (d 1978); *b* 3 June 1946; *Educ* Dauntsey's Sch West Lavington Wilts, Exeter Coll Oxford (MA), The Divinity Sch Harvard Univ (ThM), Cuddesdon Theol Coll, Univ of Oxford (BD); *m* 1976, Lorna, da of Prof Geoffrey Goodwin (d 1995); 1 s (Luke Alexander Goodwin b 16 July 1978), 2 da (Elizabeth Anne Burnett b 8 Aug 1980, Mary Ellen Frances b 5 Nov 1982); *Career* ordained (Southwark Cathedral): deacon 1970, priest 1971; curate: of St John the Evangelist E Dulwich 1970–74, of Great St Mary's The Univ Church Cambridge 1974–77; chaplain of Jesus Coll Cambridge 1977–81, vicar of Towcester 1981–95 (rural dean 1983–91), provost of St Edmundsbury 1995–; *Recreations* driving a Land Rover, walking, the countryside, travelling, fairground organs; *Style*— Provost of St Edmundsbury; ✉ The Provost's House, Bury St Edmunds, Suffolk IP33 1RS (☎ 01284 754852); The Cathedral Office, Abbey House, Angel Hill, Bury St Edmunds, Suffolk IP33 1LS (☎ 01284 754933, fax 01284 768655)

ATWELL, John David; s of Percival John Cyril Atwell, MBE (d 1990), of Hamble, Hants, and Doris May, *née* Gardiner (d 1995); *b* 17 May 1929; *Educ* Peter Symonds Sch Winchester, Univ of Leeds (MB ChB); *m* 30 April 1960, (Penelope) Susan, da of Lt-Col Roland Douglas Nightingale, MC (d 1962), of Gloucestershire; 2 s (Christopher John b 1961, Michael James b 1965), 1 da (Caroline Susan b 1962); *Career* Nat Serv 2 Lt Royal Corps Signals 1947–49; sr lectr in paediatric surgery Gt Ormond St Hosp 1963–66, conslt neonatal surgn to St Thomas' Hosp and conslt paediatric surgn to the Westminster Hosp London 1966–69, conslt paediatric surgn to Wessex RHA 1969–94, civilian conslt in paediatric surgery to RN 1986–94, ret; chm Ct of Examiners RCS 1989 (memb 1983–89), pres Br Assoc of Paediatric Surgns 1989–90; external examiner: Univ of London, Univ of Glasgow, RCS Ireland; invited cncl memb RCS; FRCS 1955, FRSM; *Books* contrib: Current Surgical Practice (1981), Operative Surgery (1983), Management of Vesicoureteric Reflux (1984), Pathology in Surgical Practice (1985), Operative Surgery and Management (1987), Surgery for Anaesthetists (1988); *Recreations* sailing, old English glass; *Clubs* Army and Navy; *Style*— John Atwell, Esq; ✉ Church Cottage, Common Road, Whiteparish, Salisbury, Wilts SP5 2SU (☎ 01794 884152)

AUBER, Thomas Frederick; s of Eric Auber, of Ilford, and Margaret, *née* Wolf (d 1984); *b* 11 Aug 1939; *Educ* Bancroft's Sch Woodford Green Essex, Univ of Oxford (MA); *m* 1965, Jennifer Jane, da of John Berry (d 1942); 2 s (Daniel b 1968, Toby b 1971); *Career* admitted slr 1965; ptnr Gouldens 1971–94, ret; past pres Old Bancroftians Assoc; memb Law Soc 1965; *Recreations* sailing, skiing; *Style*— Thomas Auber, Esq; ✉ 23 Church Street, Woodbridge, Suffolk IP12 1DS (☎ and fax 01394 384419)

AUBREY, Juliet Emma; da of Roland Aubrey, of Llanelli, Dyfed, and Sylvia, of Datchet, Berks, *née* Sturgess; *b* 17 Dec 1966; *Educ* Farnborough Hill Convent, Queen Anne's Caversham, King's Coll London (BA Classics & Classical Archaelology), Central Sch of Speech and Drama; *Career* actress; *Theatre* incl: Branwell in The Long Mirror (Theatr Clwyd), Miranda in The Tempest (Oxford Stage Co), Pegeen in Playboy of the Western World (King's Theatre Co), Irena in Three Sisters, Olivia in Twelfth Night (both Cry Havoc); *Television* incl: Isabella in Measure for Measure (BBC), Dorothea in Middlemarch (BBC), Susan in Big Battalions (Carnival Films/Channel 4), Miss Forsythe in Death of a Salesman (BBC); *Radio* incl: Eleanor in Chronicles of Barchester, Poria in Merchant of Venice; *Films* incl: Karen in Go Now (Revolution Films), Hannah in Jonah Who Lived in the Whale (Jean Vigo Prodns), Eva in Take Pity (JSP Ltd/British Screen); *Awards* Efebo D'oro and David Di Donatello Awards (both for Jonah Who Lived in the Whale 1993), Broadcasting Press Guild Best Actress Award 1994, BAFTA Best Actress Award 1994 (both for Middlemarch); *Style*— Miss Juliet Aubrey; ✉ c/o Michael Foster, ICM Ltd, Oxford House, 76 Oxford Street, London W1N 0AX (☎ 0171 636 6565, fax 0171 323 0101)

AUBREY-FLETCHER, Sir Henry Egerton; 8 Bt (GB 1782), of Clea Hall, Cumberland; o s of Sir John Henry Lancelot Aubrey-Fletcher, 7 Bt (d 1992), and Diana Mary Fynvola, *née* Egerton (d 1996); *b* 27 Nov 1945; *Educ* Eton; *m* 1976, (Sara) Roberta, da of late Maj Robert Buchanan, of Blackpark Cottage, Evanton, Ross-shire; 3 s (John Robert b 1977, Thomas Egerton b 1980, Harry Buchanan b 1982); *Heir* s, John Robert Aubrey-Fletcher b 20 June 1977; *Career* co dir; High Sheriff for Co of Bucks 1995; *Style*— Sir Henry Aubrey-Fletcher, Bt; ✉ Estate Office, Chilton, Aylesbury, Bucks HP18 9LR (☎ 01844 265201, fax 01844 265203)

AUCKLAND, Archdeacon of; *see:* Gibson, Ven (George) Granville

AUCKLAND, 9 Baron (I 1789 & GB 1793); Ian George Eden; s of 8 Baron Auckland, MC (d 1957), and Evelyn, 3 da of Col Arthur Hay-Drummond, of Cromlix (nephew of 12 Earl of Kinnoull), the latter's mother Arabella being maternal gda of the 1 Duke of Cleveland. The Duke's paternal gm Grace was gda of Barbara, cr Duchess of Cleveland, by whom Lord Auckland is ninth in descent from Charles II; *b* 23 June 1926; *Educ* Blundell's; *m* 1954, Dorothy Eden, JP (Surrey), da of Henry Joseph Manser, of Eastbourne; 1 s, 2 da; *Heir* s, Hon Robert Eden, *qv*; *Career* served: Royal Signals 1945–48, London Yeo Sharpshooters TA 1948–53; non-exec dir: George S Hall & Co, C J Sims & Co, BAA Housing; Lloyd's underwriter 1948–64 (working memb 1956–64); pres Inst of Insur Consltss 1977–89, memb Cncl Royal Soc for Prevention of Accidents; takes Conservative Whip in House of Lords, memb Anglo-Finnish, Danish, Swedish and Czech Parly Gps; chm All Party Anglo-South Pacific Gp CPA; county pres Surrey Royal Br Legion, memb New Zealand Soc; Master Broderers' Co 1967–68, hon memb Ct of Assts Blacksmiths' Co; Knight First Class Order of White Rose (Finland) 1984; *Recreations* music, theatre, tennis, walking; *Clubs* City Livery; *Style*— The Rt Hon the Lord Auckland; ✉ Tudor Rose House, 30 Links Rd, Ashtead, Surrey KT21 2HF (☎ 01372 274393)

AUCOTT, John Adrian James; s of Arthur Aucott (d 1955), of Kingsbury, Staffs, and Beryl Joan, *née* Simmonds (d 1984); *b* 20 Jan 1946; *Educ* Coleshill GS; *m* 16 Sept 1969, Angela, da of Alan Baillie, of Rock, Cornwall; 2 da (Katherine Joanne (Kate) b 16 July 1971, Lucy Elizabeth (Lucie) b 6 March 1973); *Career* articled clerk Birmingham, admitted slr 1969; Edge & Ellison: ptnr 1974–, sr ptnr 1990–95; chm Young Slrs Gp 1979–80 (memb 1975–80), pres Birmingham Law Soc 1992–93 (memb 1969–, memb Cncl 1978–); Law Society Services Ltd; dep registrar High Ct and Co Ct 1983–87; memb Law Soc 1969 (memb Cncl 1984–); *Books* contrib to various law pubns and to The Law of Meetings (1987); *Recreations* country sports, wine and gastronomy, family and friends; *Clubs* Carlton, Little Aston Golf, Wig and Pen; *Style*— John Aucott; ✉ Edge & Ellison Solicitors, Rutland House, 148 Edmund St, Birmingham B3 2JR (☎ 0121 200 2001, fax 0121 200 1991)

AUDI, Pierre; *b* 9 Nov 1957, Beirut; *Educ* Exeter Coll Oxford (BA); *Career* opera and stage director; fndr the Almeida Theatre Islington 1979; dir numerous operas and plays by living composers and playwrights incl David Rudkin, Botho Strauss, Bernard-Marie Koltès, Wolfgang Rihm, Claude Vivier, Michael Finnissy, John Casken, Sylvano Bussotti and Luis de Pablo; artistic dir De Nederlandse Opera Amsterdam 1988–; Leslie Boosey Award 1990; *Productions* dir for De Nederlandse Opera: Monteverdi Il Ritorno d'Ulisse in Patria 1990–91 and revival 1992–93, double bill of Schönberg Die Glückliche Hand and Morton Feldman Neither 1990–91, double bill of Theo Loevendie Gassir (world premiere) and Monteverdi Il Combattimento di Tancredi e Clorinda 1990–91 and revival 1992–93, Mozart Mitridate Re di Ponto 1991–92, double bill Param Vir Snatched by the Gods/Broken Strings winner BMW Musiktheaterpreis Munich Biennale 1992), La Bohème 1992–93, Birtwistle Punch and Judy 1992–93, L'Incoronazione di Poppea 1993–94, Mozart Il Re Pastore 1993–94, Guus Janssen Noach 1993–94, Schönberg Erwartung/Die Glückliche Hand/Von heute auf morgen 1995, Monteverdi L'Orfeo 1995, Die Zauberflöte 1996, Wagner Ring Cycle projected for 1997–99; dir for Toneelgroep Amsterdam: Timon of Athens (Transformatorhuis Amsterdam) 1995; dir for others incl: Verdi Jérusalem (Br premiere for Opera North) 1990, Henze Venus and Adonis (world premiere at Bayerische Staatsoper) 1996; *Style*— Pierre Audi, Esq; ✉ De Nederlandse Opera, Waterlooplein 22, 1011 PG Amsterdam, The Netherlands (☎ 00 31 20 551 8922, fax 00 31 20 551 8311)

AUDLAND, Sir Christopher John; KCMG (1987, CMG 1973), DL; s of Brig Edward Gordon Audland, CB, CBE, MC (d 1976), and Violet Mary, *née* Shepherd-Cross (d 1981); *b* 7 July 1926; *Educ* Winchester; *m* 1955, Maura Daphne, da of Gp Capt John Sullivan, CBE (d 1953); 2 s (Rupert b 1960, William b 1966), 1 da (Claire b 1963); *Career* served Br Army 1944–48; RA Temp Capt; entered HM Dip Serv 1948; served in FO: Bonn, Strasbourg, Washington, Brussels; memb UK delgn to the negotiations with memb states of the EEC 1961–63, head of chancery Buenos Aires 1963–67, ldr UK delgn to UN Ctee on the Seabed and Ocean Floor at Rio de Janeiro 1968, head Sci and Technol Dept FO 1968–70, cnsllr and head of Chancery Bonn 1970–73, also dep ldr of the UK delgn to the Four Power negotiations on Berlin, dep sec-gen Cmmn of the Euro Communities 1973–81, dir-gen for energy CEC 1981–86, ret 1986; hon fell Faculty of Law and visiting lectr on Euro insts Univ of Edinburgh 1986–, pro chancellor Univ of Lancaster 1990– (memb Cncl 1988–); memb: Euro Strategy Bd ICL 1988–96, Lake District Special Planning Bd 1989–95, NW Regnl Ctee Nat Tst 1987–95; vice pres Europa Nostra 1989–91, pres Int Castles Inst 1990–91 (vice pres 1988–90), exec pres Europa Nostra united with the Int Castles Inst 1992 (vice pres 1991–92 and 1993–96), tstee Ruskin Fndn 1993–; *Recreations* gliding, skiing, gardening, walking; *Clubs* United Oxford and Cambridge; *Style*— Sir Christopher Audland, KCMG, DL; ✉ The Old House, Ackenthwaite, Milnthorpe, Cumbria LA7 7DH (☎ 015395 62202, fax 015395 64041)

AUDLEY, Sir (George) Bernard; kt (1985); s of Charles Bernard Audley (d 1958), of Stoke-on-Trent, and Millicent Claudia, *née* Collier (d 1989); *b* 24 April 1924; *Educ* Wolstanton GS, Corpus Christi Coll Oxford (MA); *m* 17 June 1950, Barbara, da of Richard Arthur Heath (d 1964); 2 s (Maxwell Charles b 1954, Robert James b 1956), 1 da (Sally Anne b 1959); *Career* Lt Kings Dragoon Gds 1943–46; asst gen mangr Hulton Press Ltd 1949–57, md TAM Ltd 1957–61, fndr and chm AGB Research plc 1962–89; chm: Pergamon AGB plc 1989–90, Caverswall Holdings 1990–, Arts Access 1986–, Netherhall Tst 1962–; memb: Indust and Commerce Advsy Ctee William & Mary Tercentenary Tst 1985–89, St Brides Appeal for Restoration and Devpt 1987–; vice pres Periodical Publishers Assoc 1989– (pres 1985–89), visiting prof in business and mgmnt Middlesex Univ 1989–, govr Hong Kong Coll 1984–; Liveryman Worshipful Co of Gold and Silver Wyre Drawers 1975, Freeman City of London 1978; FSS 1960, FMRS 1986, FRSA 1986; *Recreations* golf, reading, travel; *Clubs* Cavalry & Guards', MCC, Rye Golf, Hadley Wood Golf; *Style*— Sir Bernard Audley; ✉ 56 River Court, Upper Ground, London SE1 9PE (☎ 0171 928 6576)

AUDLEY, 25 Baron (E 1312–13); Richard Michael Thomas Souter; s of Sir Charles Alexander Souter, KCIE, CSI, and Charlotte Dorothy Jesson (sis of Thomas Tuchet-Jesson, f of 23 Baron and the 23 Baron's sis who as Baroness Audley was 24 holder of that title; Charlotte and Thomas were children of Charlotte, da of John Thicknesse-Tuchet, bro of 21 Baron Audley, by her husb Thomas Jesson); suc cous 1973; *b* 31 May 1914; *Educ* Uppingham; *m* 1941, Lily Pauline, da of Dallas Louis Eskell; 3 da (Hon Patricia Ann (Hon Mrs Mackinnon) b 10 Aug 1946, Hon Jennifer Michelle (Hon Mrs Carrington) b 23 May 1948, Hon Amanda Elizabeth b 5 May 1958); *Heir* all 3 da as coheiresses presumptive: Hon Mrs Carey Mackinnon, Hon Mrs Michael Carrington, *qv*, Hon Amanda Souter, *qv*; *Career* WWII Capt RA, Control Cmmn Germany 1946–50; insur broker until 1955, loss adjuster 1955–84; dir Graham Miller & Co, ret 1982; fell Chartered Inst of Loss Adjusters; *Recreations* shooting, gardening; *Style*— The Rt Hon The Lord Audley; ✉ Friendly Green, Cowden, nr Edenbridge, Kent (☎ 01342 850682)

AUDLEY, Prof Robert John; s of Walter Audley (late Warrant Offr RE, d 1981), and Agnes Lilian, *née* Baker; *b* 15 Dec 1928; *Educ* Battersea GS, UCL (State scholar, BSc, PhD); *m* 1, 1952 (m dis 1977), Patricia Mary, *née* Bannister; 2 s (Matthew John b 1961, Thomas Giles b 1963); m 2, 24 April 1990, (Vera) Elyashiv, da of Guttmann (d 1942); *Career* Nat Serv Sgt RE (mainly BAOR) 1947–49; Fulbright scholar and res asst Washington State Univ USA 1952–53; UCL: res scientist MRC Gp for the Experimental Investigation of Behaviour 1955–57, lectr in psychology 1957–64, reader in psychology 1964, prof of psychology 1965–, head Dept of Psychology 1979–93, dean Faculty of Sci 1985–88, vice provost 1988–, fell 1989; memb Bd of Tstees Academia Istropolitana Czechoslovakia 1991–; visiting prof Columbia Univ NY USA 1962, visiting fell Inst for Advanced Study Princeton USA 1970, Miller visiting prof Univ of California Berkeley USA 1971; pres: Br Psychological Soc 1969 (hon librarian 1962–65), Experimental Psychology Soc 1975–76 (hon sec 1962–65); ed Br Jl of Mathematical and Statistical Psychology 1963–69, assoc ed Jl of Mathematical Psychology 1979–81; memb: MRC/RAF Flying Personnel Ctee 1965–75, Equipment Sub-Ctee UGC 1982–88, Computer Bd Universities and Res Cncl 1986–90; chm Psychology Sub-Ctee MRC/RN Personnel Res Ctee 1984–; FBPsS 1972; *Recreations* crosswords, cooking; *Style*— Prof Robert Audley; ✉ 22 Keats Grove, London NW3 2RS (☎ 0171 435 6655); Department of Psychology, University College London, Gower Street, London WC1E 6BT (☎ 0171 391 1297)

AUEL, Jean Marie; da of late Neil Solomon Untinen, and late Martha Amelia, *née* Wirtanen; *b* 18 Feb 1936; *Educ* Univ of Portland (MBA); *m* 19 March 1954, Ray Bernard Auel; 2 s (Kendall Poul b 1959, Marshall Philip b 1961), 3 da (RaeAnn Marie b 1954, Karen Jean b 1956, Lenore Jerica b 1958); *Career* writer; Tektronix Inc 1964–76: credit mangr, mgmnt training, tech writer, circuit bd designer; Golden Plate Award American Academy of Achievement 1986, Silver Trowel Award Sacramento Archeological Soc 1990, National Zoo Award Centennial Medal Smithsonian Institution 1990, Award for Contributions to Cultural Resources Mgmnt Dept of the Interior and Soc for American Archeology 1990; Oregon Cncl for the Humanities Campaign Chair 1991; formerly memb Bd Int Women's Forum; memb: Advsy Bd of Dirs Oregon Writers Colo, Bd of Dirs Oregon Museum of Sci and Indust 1993; advsr Oregon Center for the Book; hon vice pres Int MENSA 1991; Hon Dr of Letters: Univ of Portland 1984, Pacific Univ 1995; Hon Dr of Humanities Univ of Maine 1986, Hon Dr of Humane Letters Mt Vernon Coll 1986; memb: Authors Guild, PEN American Center NW Branch, Int MENSA, Acad of American Poets, Willamette Writers, Oregon Writers Colony, Soc for American Archeologists, Pacific NW Archeological Soc, Oregon High Desert Mus, Oregon Historical Soc; *Books* The Clan of the Cave Bear (1980, Friends of Literature Vicki Penziner Matson Memorial Award 1980, Pacific NW Booksellers' Award for Excellence in Writing 1980, nominee American Book Award (Nat Book Awards) Best First Novel

1981), The Valley of Horses (1982), The Mammoth Hunters (1985), The Plains of Passage (1990, Persie Award 1990, Waldo Award Waldenbooks Books Bestselling Book of 1990, Publieksprijs voor het Nederlandse Boek Holland Most Popular Foreign Language Novel 1990); *Recreations* travel, research; *Style—* Ms Jean M Auel

AUERBACH, Frank Helmuth; s of Max Auerbach (d 1942), of Berlin, and Charlotte Norah, *née* Borchardt (d 1942); *b* 29 April 1931; *Educ* Bunce Ct Sch Kent, Borough Poly Sch of Art, St Martin's Sch of Art, RCA; *m* 10 March 1958, Julia, da of James Wolstenholme (d 1981); 1 s (Jake b 1958); *Career* painter; public collections incl: Tate Gallery, Arts Cncl, Br Cncl, Museum of Modern Art NY, Metropolitan Museum NY, Nat Gallery of Australia; one-man exhibitions incl: Beaux Arts Gallery 1956, 1959, 1961, 1962 and 1963, Marlborough Fine Art 1965, 1967, 1971, 1974, 1983, 1987, 1990 and 1997, Marlborough-Gerson NY 1969, Villiers Sydney Aust 1972, Bergamini Milan 1973, Univ of Essex 1973, Municipal Gallery of Modern Art Dublin 1975, Marlborough Zurich 1976, Arts Cncl Retrospective (Hayward Gallery) 1978, Jacobson NY 1979, Marlborough NY 1982 and 1994, Anne Berthoud London 1983, Venice Biennale 1986 (Golden Lion Prize), Kunstverein Hamburg 1986, Museum Folkwang Essen 1986, Centro de Arte Reina Sofia Madrid 1987, Rijksmuseum Vincent van Gogh Amsterdam 1989, Yale Center for British Art 1991, National Gallery London 1995; numerous mixed exhibitions; ARCA 1955; *Style—* Frank Auerbach, Esq; ✉ c/o Marlborough Fine Art (London) Ltd, 6 Albemarle St, London W1X 4BY (☎ 0171 629 5161)

AUGER, George Albert; s of Thomas Albert Auger (d 1977), and Lilian Daisy, *née* McDermott (d 1991); *b* 21 Feb 1938; *Educ* Finchley Co GS; *m* 8 Sept 1962, Pauline June; 2 da (Jacqueline Susan (Mrs Bull) b 1965, Deborah Anne (Mrs Auld) b 1969); *Career* Nat Serv RAF 1957–59; sr insolvency ptnr BDO Stoy Hayward 1978–95 (currently conslt); memb Cncl Chartered Assoc Certified Accountants 1980–86 and 1994–, pres Insolvency Practitioners' Assoc 1981–82; chm govrs Channing Sch London; FCCA 1962, MIPA 1967 (sr moderator Jt Insolvency Exam Bd 1994–); *Books* Hooper's Voluntary Liquidation (1978); *Recreations* cricket, tennis, opera, porcelain; *Style—* George Auger, Esq; ✉ BDO Stoy Hayward, 8 Baker St, London W1M 1DA (☎ 0171 486 5888, fax 0171 935 3944, telex 367716 H)

AUKIN, David; s of Charles Aukin (d 1981), and Regina, *née* Unger; *b* 12 Feb 1942; *Educ* St Paul's, St Edmund Hall Oxford (BA); *m* 20 June 1969, Nancy Jane, da of Herman Meckler, of London and New York; 2 s (Daniel b 1970, Jethro b 1976); *Career* admitted slr 1965; literary advsr Traverse Theatre Club 1970–73, admin Oxford Playhouse Co 1974–75; dir: Hampstead Theatre 1978–83 (admin 1975–78), Leicester Haymarket Theatre 1983–86; exec dir Royal Nat Theatre 1986–90, head of drama Channel 4 TV 1990–; FRSA 1989; *Recreations* golf; *Clubs* Groucho, RAC; *Style—* David Aukin, Esq; ✉ 27 Manor House Court, Warrington Gardens, London W9 2PZ; Channel 4 Television, 124 Horseferry Road, London SW1P 2TX (☎ 0171 396 4444)

AULD, Prof (Alan) Graeme; s of Alan Talbert Auld, and Alice Jolly, *née* Coull; *b* 14 Aug 1941; *Educ* Robert Gordon's Coll Aberdeen (Classical Dux, Mackenzie Shield), Univ of Aberdeen (MA, DLitt 1994), Univ of Edinburgh (BD, PhD); *m* 23 Sept 1967, Dr Sylvia Joyce Auld, da of Maj Gen Stephen Lamplugh; 2 s (Alan Hamish b 20 Sept 1970, Fergus Stephen b 17 Feb 1973), 1 da (Caroline Mary b 28 April 1975); *Career* asst dir Br Sch of Archaeology Jerusalem 1969–72; Univ of Edinburgh: lectr 1972–85, sr lectr 1985–95, prof of Hebrew Bible 1995–; foreign sec Soc for Old Testament Study 1997–; tstee Br Sch of Archaeology in Jerusalem 1996–; FSAS; *Books* Joshua, Moses and the Land (1980), Amos (1986), Kings without Privilege (1994), Jerusalem I: From the Bronze Age to the Maccabees (with Margreet Steiner, 1996); *Recreations* music, travel, walking; *Style—* Prof Graeme Auld; ✉ University of Edinburgh, New College, Mound Place, Edinburgh EH1 2LX (☎ 0131 650 8975, fax 0131 650 6579, e-mail a.g.auld@ed.ac.uk)

AULD, Margaret Gibson; da of Alexander John Sutton Auld (d 1988), of Cardiff, and Eleanor Margaret, *née* Ingram (d 1980); *b* 11 July 1932; *Educ* Cardiff HS for Girls, Univ of Edinburgh (Cert in Nursing Admin, MPhil); *Career* departmental sister Cardiff Maternity Hosp 1957–59 and 1961–66, ward sister Queen Mary Hosp Dunedin NZ 1960, matron Simpson Meml Maternity Pavilion Edinburgh 1968–73 (asst matron 1967), actg chief regnl nursing offr SE Region Scot 1973, chief area nursing offr Borders Health Bd 1973–77, chief nursing offr Scot Home and Health Dept 1977–88; memb: Ctee on Nursing 1970–72, Gen Nursing Cncl Scot 1973–76, Central Midwives Bd Scot 1972–76, Scot Bd BIM 1983–90, Human Fertilization and Embryo Authy 1990–92; conslt WHO, fndr memb Nuffield Cncl on Bioethics; chair Scottish Mgmnt Exec Gp/Clinical Resource Advsy Gp on Maternity Servs in Scot 1992–95, memb Ctee on the Ethics of Gene Therapy 1991–93; vice pres Royal Coll of Midwives 1988; vice-chair Bd of Govrs Queen Margaret Coll Edinburgh 1995– (govr 1989–); Hon DSc Queen Margaret Coll Edinburgh 1987; FRCN 1980, CIMgt 1981; *Books* How Many Nurses? (1977); *Recreations* reading, music, entertaining; *Style—* Miss Margaret Auld; ✉ Staddlestones, Neidpath Rd, Peebles, Scotland EH45 8NN (☎ 01721 729594)

AULD, Rt Hon Lord Justice; Rt Hon Sir Robin Ernest; kt (1988), PC (1995); s of late Ernest Auld; *b* 19 July 1937; *Educ* Brooklands Coll, King's Coll London (LLB, PhD, FKC); *m* 1963, Catherine Eleanor Mary, elder da of late David Henry Pritchard; 1 s, 1 da; *Career* called to the Bar Gray's Inn 1959, QC 1975, Dept of Trade inspr Ashbourne Investments Ltd 1975–79, recorder of the Crown Court 1977–87, bencher 1984, judge of the High Court of Justice (Queen's Bench Div) 1987–95, memb Judicial Studies Bd 1989–91 (chm Criminal Ctee 1989–91), presiding judge Western Circuit 1991–94, a Lord Justice of Appeal 1995–, sr presiding judge Eng and Wales 1995–; admitted New York State Bar 1984; memb Cmmn of Inquiry into Casino Gambling in the Bahamas 1967, chm William Tyndall Schs' Inquiry 1975–76, legal assessor to Gen Med and Dental Cncls 1982–87, chm Home Office Ctee of Inquiry into Sunday Trading 1983–84; Master Worshipful Co of Woolmen 1984–85; *Clubs* Athenaeum; *Style—* The Rt Hon Lord Justice Auld; ✉ Royal Courts of Justice, Strand, London WC2A 2LL

AUMONIER, John Martin; s of Lt Cdr Timothy Peppercorn Aumonier (d 1983), of Billingshurst, W Sussex, and Maureen, *née* Leonard (d 1985); *b* 5 Jan 1952; *Educ* John Fisher Sch Purley Surrey, Ledsham Ct Hastings, St Mary's Coll Guildford; *m* 17 Feb 1979, Sally Wallace, da of Maj John Wallace Goodwyn Kay (d 1972), of Cranleigh, Surrey; 2 da (Jessica b 1985, Lucy b 1987); *Career* Advtg Dept London Evening News 1969–70, advtg exec Vogue 1970–72, media gp head Stewart & Jefferies Advertising 1972, sr exec Associated Independent Radio Services Ltd 1972–76, sales mangr Broadcast Marketing Services Ltd 1976–80; md: The Radio Business Ltd 1980–82, Radio Mercury plc 1982–92, Virgin Radio Ltd 1992–93, Talk Radio UK (third national independent station) 1993–95; dir Phoenix Radio 1995–; visiting examiner Crawley Coll of Technol; Ordre des Chevaliers du Bellay; *Recreations* radio, wine, food, travel; *Style—* John Aumonier, Esq

AUSTEN, David Lee; s of David Robert Austen, of Cambridge, and Joan Ellen, *née* Waters; *b* 11 April 1960; *Educ* Maidstone Coll of Art, RCA; *partner* Mary Doyle; 1 s (Sam Joseph David b 21 Sept 1986), 1 da (Mia India b 19 Aug 1982); *Career* artist; solo exhibitions: Anthony Reynolds Gallery London 1986, 1988, 1991, 1992, 1994, 1995 and 1997, Serpentine Gallery 1987, Arnolfini Bristol 1988, Castle Museum and Art Gallery Nottingham 1989, Cirrus Los Angeles 1989, 1991, 1993 and 1994, Frith Street Gallery London 1990, Cornerhouse Manchester 1993, Barbican London and tour 1997; gp exhibitions incl: Between Identity & Politics (Gimpel Fils London/NY) 1986, Works on Paper (Anthony Reynolds Gallery London) 1986, Object and Image: Aspects of British Art in the 1980s (City Museum and Art Gallery Stoke-on-Trent) 1988, Poiesis (Graeme Murray Gallery Edinburgh 1990 and Fruitmarket Gallery Edinburgh 1992), New Voices (Centre de Conférences Albert Borshette Brussels) 1992, Twelve Stars (Belfast, Edinburgh and London) 1992–93, MOMA Oxford 1996, Whitechapel London 1997; *Style—* David Austen, Esq; ✉ 12 Prospect Cottages, Point Pleasant, London SW18 1NW (0181 877 1525); c/o Anthony Reynolds Gallery, 5 Dering Street, London W1R 9AB (☎ 0171 491 0621)

AUSTEN, Mark Edward; s of Capt George Ernest Austen (d 1987), of Ashtead, Surrey, and Eileen Gladys, *née* Thirkettle; *b* 25 Aug 1949; *Educ* City of London Freemen's Sch; *m* 28 May 1977, Priscilla, da of Reginald Cyril Hart (d 1984), of Chiddingfold, Surrey; 1 s (Timothy b 1980), 1 da (Rachel b 1982); *Career* corp accounts trainee Reed International 1967–72, asst fin controller Henry Ansbacher 1972–75; Price Waterhouse Management Consultants: conslt 1975–82, ptnr 1982–, ptnr in charge fin servs consltg UK 1985–90, Europe 1990–96 and worldwide 1996–, memb Global Consltg Mgmnt Bd 1996–; Freeman City of London; FCMA 1976; *Recreations* music, squash, food; *Clubs* Carlton, Colets; *Style—* Mark Austen, Esq; ✉ 18 Imber Park Rd, Esher, Surrey KT10 8JB (☎ 0181 398 3144); Price Waterhouse Management Consultants, Southwark Towers, 32 London Bridge Street, London SE1 9SY (☎ 0171 939 3000, fax 0171 378 0647)

AUSTEN-SMITH, Air Marshal Sir Roy David; KBE (1979), CB (1975), CVO (1994), DFC (1953); s of D Austen Smith, of Kingsdown, Kent; *b* 28 June 1924; *Educ* Hurstpierpoint; *m* 1951, Patricia Ann, *née* Alderson; 2 s; *Career* RAF; served WWII, Cdr Br Forces Cyprus, AOC Air HQ Cyprus and Admin Sovereign Base Areas Cyprus 1976–78; head Br Def Staff Washington and Def Attaché 1978–81, ret; Gentleman Usher to HM the Queen 1982–94, Extra Gentleman Usher 1994–; *Recreations* golf; *Clubs* RAF; *Style—* Air Marshal Sir Roy Austen-Smith, KBE, CB, CVO, DFC; ✉ c/o Nat West Bank, Swanley, Kent

AUSTICK, David; s of Bertie Lister Austick (d 1938), and Hilda, *née* Spink (d 1968); *b* 8 March 1920; *Educ* City of Leeds Sch; *m* 1944, Florence Elizabeth Lomath; *Career* currently master bookseller Austicks Bookshops; memb: Leeds City Cncl 1969–74, Leeds MDC 1974–75, W Yorks CC 1974–79; MP (Lib) Ripon July 1973 - Feb 1974; contested (Lib): Ripon 1974, Cheadle 1979, Leeds Euro Parl 1979; vice pres Electoral Reform Soc Ltd 1993– (exec chm 1984–86, treas and co sec 1987–91), fin sec Electoral Reform (Ballot Services) Ltd 1989–90; *Recreations* antiquarian books, illustrated books, limited editions, sailing (yacht 'Frontispiece'), nat 12 foot class; *Clubs* Nat Liberal, Fellowship of Reconciliation; *Style—* David Austick, Esq

AUSTIN, Sir Anthony Leonard; 6 Bt (UK 1894), of Red Hill, Castleford, West Riding of York; s of Sir William Ronald Austin, 4 Bt (d 1989), and his 1 w, Dorothy Mary, *née* Bidwell (d 1957); suc bro, Sir Michael Trescawen Austin, 5 Bt (d 1995); *b* 30 Sept 1930; *Educ* Downside; *m* 1, 1956 (m dis 1966), Mary Annette, da of Richard Kelly, of Greenogue, Kilsallaghan, Co Dublin; 2 s (Peter John b 1958, Nicholas Michael James b 1960), 1 da (Caroline Dorothy b 1957); m 2, 1967, Aileen Morrison Hall, da of William Hall Stewart; 1 da (Rebecca Dorothy Mary b 1968); *Heir* s, Peter John Austin b 29 July 1958; *Style—* Sir Anthony Austin, Bt; ✉ Stanbury Manor, Morwenstow, Bude, Cornwall EX23 9JQ

AUSTIN, Prof Brian; *b* 5 Aug 1951; *Educ* Mount Grace Comp Sch, Univ of Newcastle (BSc, PhD), Heriot-Watt Univ (DSc); *m* Dawn Amy, *née* Allen; 1 da (Aurelia Jean b 30 Sept 1987); *Career* res assoc Dept of Microbiology Univ of Maryland 1977–78 (post doctoral fell 1975–77), sr scientific offr Fish Diseases Laboratory MAFF 1978–84; Dept of Biological Sciences Heriot-Watt Univ: lectr in aquatic microbiology 1984–89, reader 1989–92, head Div of Aquaculture 1990–93, prof 1992–, head of dept 1993–; visiting prof: Central Univ of Venezuela 1985, 1992 and 1995, Univ of Kebangsaam 1989, Universidad del Zulia 1991; visiting scientist Ocean Univ of Shandong 1990 and 1995; external examiner: Univ of Stirling 1982–83, Univ of Bombay 1984, Univ of Wales 1994, Univ of Rouen 1996; non-exec dir Aquaculture Vaccines Ltd 1990–; memb: American Soc of Microbiology, Euro Assoc of Fish Pathologists, Soc of Applied Bacteriology, Soc for General Microbiology, UK Fedn of Culture Collections; author of numerous pubns and papers in learned jls; FRSA 1996; *Books* Modern Bacterial Taxonomy (with F G Priest, 1986), Bacterial Fish Pathogens: disease in farmed and wild fish (with D A Austin, 1987, 2 edn 1993), Marine Microbiology (1988), Methods in Aquatic Bacteriology (ed, 1988), Methods for the Microbiological Examination of Fish and Shellfish (ed, 1989), Pathogens in the Environment (ed, 1991), Modern Bacterial Taxonomy (with F G Priest, 2 edn 1993), The Genus *Aeromonas* (ed, 1996); *Recreations* gardening, literature, hiking, music, photography, theatre, travel, writing; *Style—* Prof Brian Austin; ✉ Department of Biological Sciences, Heriot-Watt University, Riccarton, Edinburgh EH14 4AS (☎ 0131 451 3452)

AUSTIN, Dr Colin François Lloyd; s of Prof Lloyd James Austin (d 1994), of Cambridge, and Jeanne Françoise, *née* Guérin; *b* 26 July 1941; *Educ* Lycée Lakanal Paris, Manchester GS, Jesus Coll Cambridge (MA), Ch Ch Oxford (DPhil), Freie Univ W Berlin; *m* 28 June 1967, Mishtu, da of Sreepada Mojumder (d 1963), of Calcutta; 1 s (Topun b 1 Aug 1971), 1 da (Teesta b 21 Oct 1968); *Career* Univ of Cambridge: dir of studies in classics and fell Trinity Hall 1965–, asst lectr 1969–72, lectr 1973–88, reader in Greek language and literature 1988–; treas: Cambridge Philological Soc 1971–, Jt Ctee Greek and Roman Socs 1983–; FBA 1983; *Books* Nova Fragmenta Euripidea (1968), Menandri Aspis et Samia (1969–70), Comicorum Graecorum Fragmenta in Papyris Reperta (1973), Poetae Comici Graeci 6 vols (1983–); *Recreations* cycling, philately, wine tasting; *Style—* Dr Colin Austin, FBA; ✉ 7 Park Terrace, Cambridge CB1 1JH (☎ 01223 362732); Trinity Hall, Cambridge CB2 1TJ (☎ 01223 332520)

AUSTIN, David Charles Henshaw; s of Charles Frederick Austin (d 1980), of Broad Oak, Shrewsbury, and Lilian, *née* Kidson (d 1981); *b* 16 Feb 1926; *Educ* Shrewsbury; *m* 24 March 1956, Patricia Josephine, da of Leonard Dudley Braithwaite (d 1970); 2 s (David Julian Charles b 1958, James b 1959), 1 da (Claire Rose 1957); *Career* farmer 1943–70; professional rose breeder 1970– (non-professional 1946–70), fndr David Austin Roses 1970 (introduced 97 new English roses, distributed worldwide); memb Br Assoc of Rose Breeders; *Books* The Heritage of the Rose (1988), Old Roses and English Roses (1992), Shrub Roses and Climbing Roses (1993), David Austin's English Roses (1993); *Recreations* reading and writing poetry, current affairs, swimming, looking at gardens and countryside, farming and walking with my Staffordshire Bull Terrier; *Style—* David Austin, Esq; ✉ David Austin Roses, Bowling Green Lane, Albrighton, Wolverhampton, West Midlands WV7 3HB (☎ 01902 373931, fax 01902 372142)

AUSTIN, Ven George Bernard; s of Oswald Hulton Austin (d 1975), of Bury, Lancs, and Evelyn, *née* Twigg (d 1955); *b* 16 June 1931; *Educ* Bury HS, St David's Coll Lampeter (BA), Chichester Theol Coll; *m* 21 July 1962, Roberta (Bobbie) Anise, da of George Edward Thompson (d 1988), of Luton, Beds; 1 s (Jeremy Paul b 1969); *Career* ordained: deacon 1955, priest 1956; asst chaplain Univ of London 1960; vicar: St Mary's Eaton Bray 1964–70, St Peter's Bushey Heath 1970–88; archdeacon of York 1988–; proctor in convocation 1970–95, church cmmr 1978–95, memb Crown Appointments Cmmn 1992–95; broadcaster on radio and TV 1959–; contributor to newspapers (feature articles) 1958–; *Books* Life of Our Lord (1960), When Will Ye Be Wise? (contrib, 1983), Building In Love (contrib, 1990), Journey to Faith (1992), Affairs of State (1995), Quo Vaditis (contrib, 1996), But This I Know (1996); *Recreations* cooking, theatre, photography; *Style—* The Ven the Archdeacon of York; ✉ North Back House, Main Street, Wheldrake, York YO4 6AG (☎ 01904 448509)

AUSTIN, Ian; s of Jack Austin, and Ursula, *née* Ingham; *b* 30 May 1966; *Educ* Haslingden HS; *Career* professional cricketer; Lancashire CCC: joined 1986, first class debut 1987, awarded county cap 1990; memb England under 19 tour Bermuda 1985; amateur Lancs League record for highest individual score (149 not out), scored fastest first class century (64 balls) 1991; *Recreations* golf; *Style*— Ian Austin, Esq; ✉ Lancashire CCC, Old Trafford, Manchester M16 OPX (☎ 0161 848 7021)

AUSTIN, James Lucien Ashurst; s of Prof Lloyd James Austin, of Cambridge, and Jeanne, *née* Guérin; *b* 4 June 1940; *Educ* Lycée Lakanal Paris, Manchester GS, Jesus Coll Cambridge (MA), Courtauld Inst of Art London (post grad degree); *m* 30 July 1969, Pauline Jeannette, da of Paul Aten; 2 s (Thomas b 18 Oct 1974, Benjamin b 7 June 1977), 1 da (Lucie b 27 May 1980); *Career* photographer; Courtauld Inst: asst Photographic Dept 1962–63, photographer to the Conway Library 1973–85; freelance photographer 1965–73 and 1985–; major cmmns incl: Emile Male: Religious Art in France (3 volumes published), The Buildings of England by Nicholas Pevsner (over 15 volumes published), photography of Sainsbury Collection Univ of E Anglia, photographer to artist Ben Nicholson (4 exhibition catalogues published), inventory photography for Nat Trust and English Heritage, catalogue photography for Tate Gallery; photographs for facsimile edns of: Lambeth Palace Apocalypse, Bank of Eng Royal Charter, Commission and Subscriptions Book, Turner water colours for book on Turner at Petworth; FBIPP 1977 (assoc 1970), memb Assoc of History and Fine Art Photographers 1986; *Style*— James Austin, Esq; ✉ 24 George Street, Cambridge CB4 1AJ (☎ 01223 365776); Fine Art Photography, 24 George St, Cambridge CB4 1AJ (☎ 01223 359763, fax 01223 314271)

AUSTIN, John; TD (1961); s of John Austin (d 1972), of Chesterfield; *b* 13 April 1927; *Educ* St George's Sch Harpenden, Univ of Glasgow; *m* 1959, Shirley Frances Bonner, da of Maj G Proctor (d 1979), of Tullydoey, Co Tyrone; 1 s (James b 1960), 1 da (Frances b 1964); *Career* former Capt RASC; former dir and chief exec: J Mann & Son Ltd, Claas (UK) Ltd; former dir: Howard Machinery plc, Ransomes & Rapier Ltd, Ruston-Bucyrus Ltd; former memb Eastern Electricity Bd, former chm Eastern Electricity Consumers' Ctee; current vice chm Ipswich Port Authy; CEng, MIProdE; *Recreations* walking, gardening; *Clubs* RAC; *Style*— John Austin, Esq, TD; ✉ The White Cottage, Woodbridge, Suffolk IP12 4BT (☎ and fax 01394 383044)

AUSTIN, Dr Michael; s of Henry George Austin, and Phyllis Minnie, *née* Huntley; *b* 23 Dec 1938; *Educ* City of London Sch, Magdalen Coll Oxford (BA), Poly of Central London (PhD); *m* 14 Sept 1963, Penelope Jane Ingrid, da of George Raymond Faulks; 2 s (James Huntley b 4 April 1966, Peter Michael b 6 Nov 1968); *Career* photographer/holographer; res chemist Ilford Ltd 1962–65, devpt offr International Publishing Corp 1965–71, princ lectr in photographic scis Poly of Central London 1971–89, ptnr Hickmott & Austin holograms 1979–87, ed Jl of Photographic Sci 1986–; FRPS 1989 (pres 1990–92), Hon FRPS 1992; *Recreations* mountaineering, natural history, photography, travel, gardening; *Style*— Dr Michael Austin; ✉ Royal Photographic Society, The Octagon, Milsom St, Bath BA1 1DN (☎ 01225 462841, fax 01225 448688)

AUSTIN, Vice Adm Sir Peter Murray; KCB (1976); s of Vice Adm Sir Francis Murray Austin, KBE, CB (d 1953), and Marjorie Jane, *née* Barker (d 1968); *b* 16 April 1921; *Educ* RNC Dartmouth; *m* 1959, Josephine Rhoda Ann Shutte-Smith; 3 s, 1 da; *Career* Naval Cadet 1935, serv WWII at sea, qualified as pilot Fleet Air Arm 1946, Capt 1961, Rear Adm 1971, Flag Offr Naval Air Cmd 1973–76, Vice Adm 1974, ret 1976; ops dir Mersey Docks and Harbour Co 1976–80, dir Avanova International Consultants 1980–89, chm Special Trg Servs 1984–89, dir Mastiff Electronic Systems 1987–; Liveryman Guild of Air Pilots and Air Navigators 1987; CIMgt; *Recreations* skiing, sailing, bicycling, golf; *Clubs* Army and Navy, Royal Yacht Sqdn; *Style*— Vice Adm Sir Peter Austin, KCB

AUSTIN, Air Marshal Sir Roger Mark; KCB (1992), AFC (1973); s of Mark Austin (d 1982), and Sylvia Joan, *née* Reed; *b* 9 March 1940; *Educ* King's Alfred GS Wantage; *m* 1, 1963 (m dis 1981), Carolyn de Recourt, *née* Martyn; 2 s (Stuart b 1965, Patrick b 1971), 1 da (Rachel b 1964); m 2, 26 July 1986, Glenys Amy Beckley, da of Hugh Glyn Roberts, of Holyhead; 2 step da (Sarah b 1969, Emma b 1972); *Career* RAF: cmmnd 1957, Flying Instr 1960; flying appts: 20 Sqdn 1964, 54 Sqdn 1966, cmd 54 Sqdn 1969, 4 Sqdn 1970; Staff Coll Camberley 1973, cmd 233 OCU 1974, PSO to AOC in C Strike Cmd 1977, cmd RAF Chivenor, ADC to HM the Queen 1980, Staff HQ Strike Cmd 1982, DOR 2 MOD 1984, RCDS 1986, AOIC Central Tactics and Trials Orgn 1987, Dir Gen Aircraft 1 MOD (Procurement Exec) 1987, AOC and Cmdt RAF Coll Cranwell 1989–92, DCDS (Systems) MOD 1992–94, DCDP (Ops) and Controller Aircraft 1994–96; FRAeS 1991; *Recreations* walking, transport systems; *Clubs* RAF; *Style*— Air Marshal Sir Roger Austin, KCB, AFC

AUSTIN, Wendy Elizabeth; da of Cecil William Stead Austin, of Londonderry and Belfast, and Irene Elizabeth Simpson, *née* Wilson; *b* 19 Nov 1951; *Educ* Victoria Coll Belfast, Queen's Univ; *m* 1982 (m dis 1995), Peter Hutchinson; 1 s (Niall b 27 Sept 1983), 2 da (Kerry b 10 June 1985, Clare b 8 April 1988); *Career* freelance broadcaster/presenter: Children in Need (BBC TV) 1980–, Inside Ulster (BBC NI TV) 1980–85, Woman's Hour (from NI and London, BBC Radio) 1981–, Breakfast Time (BBC NI TV) 1982–87, Morning Extra (Radio Ulster) 1982–89, PM (Radio 4) 1990–, Open House (BBC NI TV) 1990–, Good Arts Guide (BBC NI Radio) 1991, Breakfast Show (BBC Radio 5 Live), Good Morning Ulster/PM Ulster (BBC Radio Ulster) 1992–; patron: NI Pre-School Playgroups Assoc, Enniskillen Integrated Primary Sch, Women on the Move Against Cancer; chm Spirit of Enniskillen Bursaries; *Recreations* motor racing (as a spectator), lunch, reading diet books; *Clubs* Belfast Boat; *Style*— Ms Wendy Austin; ✉ BBC, Broadcasting House, Belfast BT2 8HQ (☎ 01232 660358)

AUSTIN-COOPER, Richard Arthur; o s of late Capt Adolphus Richard Cooper, Croix de Guerre, of Ditton, Kent, and Doris Rosina, *née* Wallen; see Burke's Irish Family Records under Cooper (of Killenure Castle, Co Tipperary, and Abbeyville House, Co Dublin); assumed additional surname of Austin by Deed Poll 1963; *b* 21 Feb 1932; *Educ* Wellingborough GS, Tottenham GS; *m* 1, 28 March 1953 (m dis 1963), Sylvia Anne Shirley Berringer; m 2, 28 Sept 1963 (m dis 1974), Valerie Georgina, da of Henry Drage, of Tottenham, London; 1 s (Matthew b 1969), 1 da (Samantha b 1967); m 3, 1979 (m dis 1981), Mariola Danuta Sikorska; m 4, 19 June 1986, Rosemary Swaisland, *née* Gillespie; 1 step s (Richard Swaisland), 1 step da (Lucy Swaisland); *Career* served RA 1950–52 and TAVR in the RA, Intelligence Corps, 21 SAS Regt (Artists' Rifles), Essex ACF 1952–69 and the Hon Artillery Co 1978–79 (cmmnd 2 Lt TAVR 1968), OC ACF Canvey Island; head cashier Bank of Baroda 1960–63, and Lloyd's Bank 1963–69, dep head Stocks & Shares Dept Banque de Paris et des Pays Bas 1969–74, mangr Banking Div Brook St Bureau of Mayfair Ltd 1974–75, chief custodian and London registrar of Canadian Imperial Bank of Commerce and registrar in London for Angostura Bitters Ltd 1975–78, personnel offr Deutsche Bank AG London Branch 1978–85, sr mangr and head of personnel Deutsche Bank Capital Markets Ltd 1985–90, ret; fndr fell Inst of Heraldic and Genealogical Studies; memb Ct of Common Cncl City of London for Cripplegate Ward 1978–81; memb Bd of Mgmnt: Barbican YMCA, City of London Central Markets (Leadenhall Market, Billingsgate Market); memb: City of London TAVR Assoc, Coal Corn and Rates Ctee, Mgmnt Ctee Barbican Sch of Music and Drama (and mature student (tenor)), Irish Peers Assoc 1964–; govr: City of London Sch for Girls 1979–80, City of London Freemen's Sch 1980–81, Lansbury Adult Educn Inst 1979–82; life govr Sheriffs' and Recorders' Fund at the Old Bailey 1979–; represented the City of London Corp on the Gtr London Arts Cncl 1979–80, Freeman City of London 1964, final tstee City of London Imperial Vols 1980–81; parish cncllr Wansford Cambs 1989–90, PCC memb Thurlby Lincs 1991–93; vice pres Bourne Lincs Family History Soc 1993–; chm Stamford Lincs Arthritis Care 1994–95; prizes for athletics (including winning Barclays Bank Cross-Country Championships), operatic singing (tenor), painting; FHG 1965, FRSA 1974, FRSAI 1980, FCIB 1987; *Books* Butterhill and Beyond (1991), The Beavers of Barnack (1995); *Recreations* genealogical research, tenor concerts, gardening, painting, sketching, judging art; *Clubs* Special Forces, SAS Old Comrades Assoc, Intelligence Corps Old Comrades, Artists' Rifles Assoc, Wellingborough GS Old Boys, Probus (Bourne, Lincs); *Style*— Richard Austin-Cooper, Esq; ✉ Butterhill House, 6 Woodside East, Northorpe, Nr Bourne, Lincolnshire PE10 0HT (☎ 01778 424398, fax 01778 422172)

AUSTIN-WALKER, John Eric; MP (Lab) Woolwich (majority 2,225); s of late Stanley Austin, and late Ellen Austin; *b* 21 Aug 1944; *Educ* Glyn GS Epsom, Goldsmiths' Coll London, Univ of Bristol; *m* 1965 (sep 1988), Linda, *née* Walker; 2 s, 1 da; *Career* medical lab technician 1961–63; organiser and agent: Swindon CLP 1965–66, Greenwich CLP 1966–70; social worker London Borough of Bexley 1972–74, dir Bexley Cncl for Racial Equality 1974–92, MP (Lab) Woolwich 1992– (also contested 1987); memb House of Commons Health Select Ctee 1994–, chair Socialist Campaign Gp of Lab MPs 1995–; London Borough of Greenwich: cncllr 1970–92, chm Social Services Ctee 1974–78, dep ldr 1981–82, ldr 1982–87, mayor 1987–89; chm: Greenwich MIND 1978–82, Assoc of Community Health Cncls for England and Wales 1981–83, London Boroughs Emergency Planning Info Ctee 1990–92, London Ecology Unit 1990–92; vice chm: Assoc of London Authorities 1983–87 (environment spokesman 1989–92), London Strategic Policy Unit 1986–88, London Gp of Labour MPs; tstee: London Marathon Charitable Tst Ltd, Adolescent & Children's Tst; memb MSF; *Recreations* cooking, gardening, marathon running; *Style*— John Austin-Walker, Esq, MP; ✉ House of Commons, London SW1A 0AA (☎ 0171 219 5195, fax 0171 219 2706)

AUSTWICK, Prof Kenneth; JP (Bath 1970); s of Harry Austwick (d 1984), of Morecambe, Lancs, and Beatrice, *née* Lee (d 1954); *b* 26 May 1927; *Educ* Morecambe GS, Univ of Sheffield (BSc, DipEd, MSc, PhD); *m* 18 Aug 1956, Gillian, da of Frank Griffin (d 1983), of Bromsgrove, Worcs; 1 s (Malcolm b 1959), 1 da (Dawn b 1960); *Career* schoolmaster 1950–59, lectr then sr lectr Univ of Sheffield 1959–65, dep dir Inst of Educn Univ of Reading 1965–66; Univ of Bath: prof of educn 1966–91, pro-vice chllr 1972–75, emeritus prof 1991–; advsr Home Office 1967–81, chm Nat Savings SW Regnl Educn 1975–78; conslt: OECD, UTA, Br Rail; govr Bath Coll; FSS 1962, FSA 1970; *Books* Teaching Machines (1962), Aspects of Educational Technology Vol Six (1972), Trigonometry (1967), Maths at Work (1985), Mathematics Connection (1985), National Curriculum Mathematics Skills Level 4 (1990), Work Related Assignments (ed, 1991–93), National Curriculum Mathematics Assessments Level 8 (1992); *Recreations* gardening, wine-making; *Clubs* Royal Cwlth, Bath and County; *Style*— Prof Kenneth Austwick, JP; ✉ Brook House, Combe Hay, Bath BA2 7EG (☎ 01225 832541)

AUTY, Helen Rees; da of Norman Auty (d 1980), of Little Common, E Sussex, and Eirwen Auty (d 1990); *b* 31 Dec 1939; *Educ* St Catherine's Sch Bramley Surrey, Univ of London (Dip in History of Art); *Career* sec: The Distillers' Co 1958–60, RSA 1960–64, W D Scott & Co NZ 1964–65, The Northern Employers' Group Australia 1965; RSA: PA to Chief Exec 1966–70, head of design 1970– (i/c RSA annual Student Design Awards, RSA Art for Architecture and Young Designers into Industry scheme); memb Design Cncl 1990–, dir Design for Transformation 1993–; govr: Falmouth Coll of the Arts 1989–, Berkshire Coll of Art and Design 1990–; Conf for Higher Educn in Art and Design (CHEAD) Medal for servs to art and design educn 1989, hon fell RCA 1993, RSA Bicentenary Medal 1994, Hon Doctor of Design De Montfort Univ 1996; *Recreations* country walks, gardening, art exhibitions, theatre, travelling, photography, second hand book shops, pottering; *Clubs* Chelsea Arts; *Style*— Ms Helen Auty; ✉ RSA, 8 John Adam Street, London WC2N 6EZ (☎ 0171 930 5115, fax 0171 839 5805)

AUTY, Capt Richard Ian; s of Keith Ian Auty, of Nyali, Huntersfield Close, Reigate, Surrey, and Marjorie, *née* Gwinnell; *b* 9 April 1946; *Educ* Trinity Sch of John Whitgift, RAF Coll Cranwell, Coll of Air Trg Hamble; *m* 4 June 1971 (m dis 1984), Carole Marie Brenda Hazel, da of Albert Bacuez (d 1951); 1 s (Charles b 1974), 1 da (Natalie b 1976); *Career* joined BEA 1967, overseas div 1976, sr capt BA; memb: BALPA, RHS; *Recreations* reading, water sports, tennis, golf, theatre; *Clubs* Naval; *Style*— Capt R I Auty; ✉ 24 Beechcrest View, Hook, Hampshire

AVEBURY, 4 Baron (UK 1900); Sir Eric Reginald Lubbock; 7 Bt (UK 1806); s of Hon Maurice Fox Pitt Lubbock (yst s of 1 Baron Avebury) and Hon Mary Stanley (eldest da of 5 Baron Stanley of Alderley and sis of the actress Pamela Stanley); suc cousin, 3 Baron 1971; *b* 29 Sept 1928; *Educ* Upper Canada Coll, Harrow, Balliol Coll Oxford (BA, boxing blue); *m* 1, 1953 (m dis 1983), Kina Maria, da of Count Joseph O'Kelly de Gallagh (a yr s of the family whose head is a Count of the Holy Roman Empire by Imperial Letters Patent of 1767); 2 s (Hon Lyulph Ambrose Jonathan, Hon Maurice Patrick Guy), 1 da (Hon Mrs Binney); m 2, 1985, Lindsay Jean, da of Gordon Neil Stewart, and of late Pamela Hansford Johnson (Lady Snow), writer; 1 s (Hon John William Stewart b 8 Aug 1985); *Heir* s, Hon Lyulph Ambrose Jonathan Lubbock, *qv*; *Career* Lt Welsh Gds 1949–51; engr with Rolls Royce 1951–56; mgmnt conslt: Production Engineering Ltd 1953–60, Charterhouse Group 1960; sits as Liberal in House of Lords; MP (Lib) Orpington 1962–70, Lib chief whip 1963–70, chm Br Parly Human Rights Gp 1976–; conslt Morgan-Grampian Ltd 1970–; dir C L Projects Ltd 1966–; pres: Data Processing Mgmnt Assoc 1972–75, Fluoridation Soc 1972–85, Conservation Soc 1973–82, London Bach Soc and Steinitz Bach Players 1984–; memb: Cncl Inst of Race Relations 1972–74, Royal Cmmn on Standards of Conduct in Public Life 1974–76; Liveryman Worshipful Co of Fishmongers; MIMechE, MBCS; *Recreations* listening to music, reading; *Style*— The Rt Hon the Lord Avebury; ✉ 26 Flodden Rd, London SE5 9LH

AVERY, Dr Brice Johnson; s of William Johnson Avery, of Haultwick, Herts, and Margaret Norma, *née* Booth; *b* 31 Dec 1959; *Educ* Bishop's Stortford Coll, Univ of Reading (BSc), Univ of Southampton (BMBS), Univ of Edinburgh; *m* 10 Sept 1993, Tina Louise, da of Barry Stott; *Career* trained in psychology, med, psychiatry and psychoanalytic psychotherapy; child and family psychiatrist, adult psychotherapist, business conslt and writer; regular appearer on radio and TV in religious, psychological and science programmes; princ PsychoDynamics Business Consultants; PPL 1989 MRCPsych 1991, memb Soc of Authors 1994; *Books* Churches and How to Survive Them (1994), The Pastoral Encounter - hidden depths in human contact (1996), Principles of Psychotherapy (1996); *Style*— Dr Brice Avery; ✉ 4 Millerfield Place, Edinburgh EH9 1LW (☎ 0131 662 0687, fax 0131 667 0252)

AVERY, Dr Charles Henry Francis; s of Richard Francis Avery, of Richmond, Surrey, and Dorothea Cecilia, *née* Wharton; *b* 26 Dec 1940; *Educ* KCS Wimbledon, St John's Coll Cambridge (MA, PhD), Courtauld Inst of Art London (Academic Dip); *m* 11 June 1966, (Kathleen) Mary, da of Charles Gwynne Jones (d 1969); 3 da (Charlotte Frances b 24 Feb 1970, Susanna Mary (triplet), Victoria Jane (triplet); *Career* dep keeper of sculpture V & A 1965–79, dir Sculpture Dept Christie's 1979–90, currently ind fine art conslt; FSA 1985; Cavaliere Dell'ordine Al Merito della Repubblica Italiana 1979, medal of Ministry of Culture Poland; *Books* Florentine Renaissance Sculpture (1970), Studies in European Sculpture (1981, 1987), Giambologna the Complete Sculpture (1987), Renaissance and Baroque Bronzes in the Frick Art Museum (1993), Donatello: An

Introduction (1994), David Le Marchand (1674–1726), An Ingenious Man for Carving in Ivory (1996); *Recreations* writing, reading, tennis; *Clubs* United Oxford and Cambridge Univ, Beckenham Tennis; *Style*— Dr Charles Avery, FSA; ✉ Holly Tree House, 20 Southend Road, Beckenham, Kent BR3 1SD (☎ 0181 650 9933, fax 0181 650 9950)

AVERY, Gillian Elise (Mrs A O J Cockshut); da of Maj Norman Bates Avery, MC (d 1957), of Redhill, Surrey, and Grace Avery (d 1989); *b* 30 Sept 1926; *Educ* Dunottar Sch Reigate; *m* 1952, Anthony Oliver John Cockshut, s of Dr Rowland William Cockshut (d 1977), of Hendon; 1 da; *Career* writer; chm Children's Books History Soc 1987–90, memb American Antiquarian Soc 1988; ed Gollancz revivals of early children's books 1967–70; *Books* children's fiction: The Warden's Niece (1957), Trespassers at Charlcote (1958), James Without Thomas (1959), The Elephant War (1960), To Tame a Sister (1961), The Greatest Gresham (1962), The Peacock House (1963), The Italian Spring (1964), The Call of the Valley (1966), A Likely Lad (1971, Guardian award 1972), Huck and Her Time Machine (1977); adult fiction: The Lost Railway (1980), Onlookers (1983); non-fiction: Nineteenth Century Children: Heroes and Heroines in English Children's Stories (with Angela Bull, 1965), Victorian People in Life and Literature (1970), The Echoing Green: Memories of Regency and Victorian Youth (1974), Childhood's Pattern (1975), Children and Their Books: a Celebration of the Work of Iona and Peter Opie (ed with Julia Briggs, 1989), The Best Type of Girl: a History of Girls' Independent Schools (1991), Behold the Child: American Children and Their Books 1621–1922 (1994); *Recreations* walking, music; *Style*— Miss Gillian Avery; ✉ 32 Charlbury Rd, Oxford (☎ 01865 56291)

AVERY, Graham John Lloyd; s of The Rev Edward Avery (d 1979), and Alice, *née* Lloyd; *b* 29 Oct 1943; *Educ* Kingswood Sch Bath, Balliol Coll Oxford (MA); *m* 1967, Susan (sep 1982); 2 s (Matthew b 1974, John b 1976); partner 1989, Annalisa Cecchi; 1 s (Nicholas b 1993); *Career* MAFF: entered 1965, princ responsible for negotiations for entry to EC 1969–72, princ private sec to Fred Peart then John Silkin 1976; European Commission Brussels 1973–; memb cabinets of: Christopher Soames (vice pres external rels) 1973–76, Roy Jenkins (pres) 1977–80, Finn Gundelach (cmmr for agric) 1981, Poul Dalsager (cmmr for agric) 1981, Frans Andriessen (vice pres for agric) 1985–86; served in Directorate Gen for Agric 1981–84 and 1987–90, Directorate Gen for External Rels 1990–93, Task Force for Enlargement 1993–94, head of foreign policy planning 1995, chief advsr Enlargement 1996–; author of articles in various econ and political jls; Freeman City of Indianapolis, fell Center for Int Affairs Harvard; *Style*— Graham Avery, Esq; ✉ European Commission, 1049 Brussels, Belgium (☎ 00 32 2 299 2202)

AVERY JONES, John Francis; CBE (1987); s of Sir Francis Avery Jones, CBE, of Chichester, W Sussex, and Dorothea Bessie, *née* Pfirter (d 1983); *b* 5 April 1940; *Educ* Rugby, Trinity Coll Cambridge (MA, PhD, LLM); *Career* admitted slr 1966, ptnr Bircham & Co 1970–85, sr ptnr Speechly Bircham 1985–; jt ed British Tax Review 1974–, memb Editorial Bd Simon's Taxes 1977–, visiting prof of taxation LSE 1986–; pres Inst of Taxation 1980–82, dep special cmmr of income tax 1991–, pt/t chm of VAT Tbnls 1991–; memb: Keith Ctee 1980–84, Cncl Law Soc 1986–90, Cncl Inst of Fiscal Studies 1988–, Exec Ctee Int Fiscal Assoc 1988–94 (chm Br Branch 1989–91), Bd of Tstees Int Bureau of Fiscal Documentation 1989– (chm 1991–), Bd of Govrs Voluntary Hosp of St Bartholomew 1984–, Court of Govrs LSE 1995–; Sr Warden and memb Ct of Assts Worshipful Co of Barbers (Master 1985–86), City of London Solicitors Co (former Steward); memb Law Soc; *Books* Encyclopedia of VAT (1972), Tax Havens and Measures Against Tax Avoidance and Evasion in the EEC (1974); *Recreations* music (particularly opera); *Clubs* Athenaeum; *Style*— John Avery Jones, Esq, CBE; ✉ 65 Castlebar Rd, Ealing, London W5 2DA (☎ 0181 998 2143, fax 0181 997 9736); Speechly Bircham, Bouverie House, 154 Fleet St, London EC4A 2HX (☎ 0171 353 3290, fax 0171 353 4825)

AVIS, Helen-Lela Kyriacopoulou (Lela); da of Dionysius Kyriacopoulos (d 1978), and Cleoniki, *née* Panagiotourou (d 1989); *b* 22 Sept 1928; *Educ* privately in Greece and Switzerland, Athens Univ (BA, PhD); *m* 9 Jan 1958, Anthony Charles Avis, s of Charles and Alice Mary Avis, of Gaywood, Norfolk; 1 s (Charles Dionysius b 7 Nov 1959), 1 da (Alice Mary Cleoniki b 31 May 1962); *Career* lectr in classical history and archaeology Athens Univ 1956–58, concurrently offical guide to guests of the Greek royal family and the Greek govt (helped re-start classical tourism during 1950s), teacher of French, classics and philosophy at local grammar schs Yorkshire 1958–74, subsequently hotelier and night club owner (later sold for devpt), currently proprietor The Box Tree Restaurant Ilkley; *Publications* a standard textbook on Daphni Monastery (with Argyris Petronotes, 1956); *Recreations* the live theatre in particular, the arts in general, collecting fine wines, combating male prejudice; *Style*— Mme Lela Avis; ✉ Crescent Estates (Ilkley) Ltd, Crescent Hotel, Brook Street, Ilkley, W Yorks LS29 8DG (☎ 01943 600062, fax 01943 607186); The Box Tree Restaurant, Church Street, Ilkley, W Yorks

AVON, Countess of; Clarissa; only da of late Maj John Strange Spencer-Churchill, DSO (himself bro of Rt Hon Sir Winston Churchill, KG, OM, CH, TD, PC); *b* 28 June 1920; *m* 1952, as his 2 w, Anthony Eden, 1 Earl of Avon, KG, MC, PC (d 1977); *Style*— The Rt Hon the Countess of Avon; ✉ 32 Bryanston Square, London W1H 7LS

AWDRY, William Richard (Will); s of Richard Charles Visger Awdry, of Penn, Bucks, and Jocelyn Genesta St George, *née* Poole (d 1990); *b* 11 Feb 1961; *Educ* Marlborough, BNC Oxford (BA); *m* 5 Dec 1992, Claire Julia, *née* Marshall; *Career* advtg exec; account mgmnt trainee rising to exec McCormick Intermarco Farmer 1983–85; Bartle Bogle Hegarty 1986–94: copywriter 1986–94, bd dir 1992–94, gp creative head 1993–94; copywriter, head of copy and bd dir The Leagas Delaney Partnership 1994–96, rejoined Bartle Bogle Hegarty 1996–; *Recreations* music (percussion drummer on various infrequent occasions), practical as opposed to theoretical oenology; *Style*— Will Awdry, Esq; ✉ Bartle Bogle Hegarty, 60 Kingly Street, London W1R 6DS (☎ 0171 734 1677, fax 0171 437 3666)

AWFORD, Ian Charles; s of Joseph Arthur Awford, of Lyme Regis, Dorset, and Eva Rhoda, *née* McPherson; *b* 15 April 1941; *Educ* Wellingborough Sch, Univ of Sheffield (LLB); *m* 1, 24 July 1965 (m dis 1983), Claire Sylvia, da of late Ralph Linklater, of Bexleyheath, Kent; 3 s (James b 16 Nov 1967, Giles b 13 Jan 1969, Guy b 27 Sept 1970); m 2, 2 Sept 1989, Leonora Maureen, da of late Robert James Wilson, of Sydney; 2 s (Alexander b 18 July 1991, Thomas b 26 April 1993), 1 da (Katherine Louise b 11 Dec 1995); *Career* admitted slr 1967; ptnr with Barlow Lyde & Gilbert 1973– (currently head Aviation & Space); admitted slr Hong Kong 1988; dir Int Court of Aviation and Space Arbitration; chm: Outer Space Ctee of the Int Bar Assoc 1985–90, Aerospace Law Ctee of the Asia Pacific Lawyers' Assoc 1987–90, Aerospace Law Ctee of the Inter Pacific Bar Assoc 1990–94; memb: Int Inst of Space Law of the Int Aeronautics Fedn, Int Soc of Air Safety Investigators, Shipping and Aviation Sub Ctee of the City of London Law Soc, Air Law Gp of the Royal Aeronautical Soc, Air Law Working Gp Int C of C, American Bar Assoc, Int Assoc of Defence Counsel, Product Liability Advsy Cncl, Euro Centre for Space Law, Euro Soc for Air Safety Investigators, Fedn of Insur and Corp Counsel, Int Forum of Travel and Tourism Advocates; FRAeS 1987; *Books* Developments in Aviation Products Liability (1985), author of various pubns on outer space and aviation legal issues; *Recreations* golf, skiing, art, music, theatre; *Style*— Ian Awford, Esq; ✉ 28 Belitha Villas, Islington, London N1 1PD (☎ 0171 700 6341, fax 0171 700 0981); Barlow, Lyde & Gilbert, Beaufort House, 15 St Botolph St, London EC3A 7NJ (☎ 0171 782 8454, fax 0171 782 8505, telex 913281)

AXE, Royden (Roy); s of Bernard Axe (d 1969), of Scarbrough, Yorkshire, and Ruth Ann, *née* Fillingham (d 1992); *b* 17 June 1937; *Educ* Scarborough HS, Coventry Tech Coll; *m* 1961, Brenda Patricia, da of Charles Edgar Tomes; 1 da (Victoria Jane b 25 Dec 1961), 1 s (Christopher Royden b 13 March 1964); *Career* designer; Rootes Motors: joined as body engr/stylist, chief stylist until 1969; design dir Chrysler Europe (following t/o of Rootes) 1969–75, design dir Chrysler Corp USA 1975–82, design dir Austin Rover then Rover Group 1982–92, md Design Research Associates Ltd 1992–; Hon DUniv Univ of Central England; fell Univ of Coventry; Liveryman Worshipful Co of Coach Makers and Coach Harness Makers; FCSD, FRSA, IBCAM; *Designs* for Rootes/Chrysler incl: Sunbeam Rapier, Hillman/Chrysler Avenger, Simca 1301, Chrysler 180, Chrysler/Talbot Sunbeam and Alpine, Chrysler Voyager (USA); for Rover incl: 200/400, 800, MG EX-E and Rover CCV concept cars; various others incl Bentley Java 1994, numerous VIP aircraft interiors; *Recreations* travel, design, reading, writing, family, all things related to classic cars; *Style*— Roy Axe, Esq; ✉ Design Research Associates Ltd, Tachbrook Park Drive, Warwick CV34 6RH (☎ 01926 313325, fax 01926 313327)

AXFORD, Dr David Norman; s of Norman Axford (d 1961), and Joy Alicia (d 1970); *b* 14 June 1934; *Educ* Merchant Taylors', Plymouth Coll, St John's Coll Cambridge (BA, MA, PhD), Univ of Southampton (MSc); *m* 1, 26 May 1962 (m dis 1979), Elizabeth Anne Moynihan, da of Ralph J Stiles (d 1973); 1 s (John b 1968), 2 da (Katy b 1964, Sophie b 1966); m 2, 8 March 1980, Diana Rosemary Joan, da of Leslie George Bufton (d 1970); 3 step s (Simon b 1959, Timothy b 1961, Jeremy b 1963), 1 step da (Nicola b 1968); *Career* Nat Serv RAF 1958–60, PO 1958, Flying Offr 1959; Meteorological Office: Forecasting and Res 1960–68, Meteorological Res Flight and Radiosondes 1968–76, asst dir Operational Instrumentation 1976–80, asst dir Telecommunications 1980–82, dep dir Observational Servs (grade 5) 1982–84, dir of Servs and dep to DG of Meteorological Office (under sec grade 3) 1984–89; dep sec gen World Meteorological Orgn 1989–95, ret; independent conslt in int meteorology 1995–; conslt to EarthWach Europe 1996–; pres N Atlantic Observing Stations Bd 1983–86, chm Ctee of Operational Systems Evaluation 1986–89, vice pres RMS 1989–91 (memb Cncl and hon gen sec 1983–88), tstee Thames Valley Hospice Windsor 1996–, memb Exec Ctee Br Assoc of Former UN Civil Servants (BAFUNCS) 1996–; L G Groves Memorial prize for Meteorology 1970; CEng 1975, FIEE 1982, CMet 1994; *Recreations* swimming, reading, good food and wine, garden, music; *Clubs* Phyllis Court (Henley-on-Thames); *Style*— Dr David Axford; ✉ Rudgewick Cottage, Binfield Heath, Henley-on-Thames, Oxon RG9 4JY (☎ 01491 574423)

AXTON, Henry Stuart (Harry); s of Wilfrid George Axton, and Mary Louise Laver; *b* 6 May 1923; *Educ* Rock Ferry, RMC Sandhurst; *m* 1947, Constance Mary (d 1996), da of Lycurgus Godefroy; 1 da (Louise); *Career* served WWII N Africa (RTR) and NW Europe, Fife and Forfar Yeo, wounded 3 times, invalided out 1945; CA 1948; treas United Sheffield Hosps and other hosp appointments 1948–55, co sec Midland Assurance 1955–61; Brixton Estate plc: joined 1961, md 1964–83, dep chm 1971–83, chm 1983–93; chm investmt cos in Australia and Switzerland; British Property Fedn: memb Gen Cncl 1974–93, vice pres 1983–84, pres 1984–86; dep chm Audit Cmmn 1987–91 (memb 1986–91); chm: BUPA Med Centre 1973–82 (govr 1970–82), Nuffield Hosps 1976–93 (govr 1968–93, dep chm 1975–76), St George's Hosp Med Sch 1977–92 (memb 1969–92, dep chm 1974–77); govr: BUPA 1969–80, St George's Hosp 1970–74 (special tstee 1974–77); memb: Chichester Health Authy 1985–87, The Archbishop of Canterbury's Cncl for the Church Urban Fund 1990–94; dir Cathedral Works Organisation (Chichester) Ltd 1985–91, chm Chichester Festivities 1989–, tstee Chichester Festival Theatre 1995–; first hon fell St George's Hosp Med Sch 1992–; Freeman City of London; Lord of the Manor of Aldingbourne; *Recreations* sailing (yacht 'Alpha IV'), music; *Clubs* Royal Thames Yacht, Royal Ocean Racing; *Style*— Harry Axton, Esq; ✉ Hook Place, Hook Lane, Aldingbourne, nr Chichester, W Sussex PO20 6TS (☎ 01243 542291)

AYCKBOURN, Sir Alan; kt (1997), CBE (1987); s of Horace Ayckbourn, and Irene Maude, *née* Worley; *b* 12 April 1939; *Educ* Haileybury; *m* 1959, Christine Helen, *née* Roland; 2 s (Steven, Philip); *Career* playwright and theatre director; worked in rep as stage mangr/actor Edinburgh, Worthing, Leatherhead, Oxford and with late Stephen Joseph's Theatre-in-the-Round Scarborough (currently artistic dir Stephen Joseph Theatre), fndr memb Victoria Theatre Stoke-on-Trent 1962, BBC Radio drama prodr Leeds 1964–70, co dir NT 1986–87, Cameron Mackintosh visiting prof of contemporary theatre and fell St Catherine's Coll Oxford 1991–92; Hon DLitt: Hull 1981, Keele 1987, Leeds 1987, Bradford 1994, Cardiff 1995; Hon DUniv York 1992; *London Prodns* Mr Whatnot (Arts) 1964, Relatively Speaking 1967 (Duke of York's (Greenwich 1986, televised 1969 and 1989)), How the Other Half Lives 1970 (Lyric, Duke of York's 1988), Time and Time Again 1972 (Comedy, televised 1976), Absurd Person Singular 1973 (Criterion (Evening Standard Drama Award Best Comedy 1975, televised 1985)), The Norman Conquests 1974 (trilogy, Globe (Evening Standard Drama Award Best Play, Variety Club of GB Award, Plays and Players Award, televised 1977)), Jeeves (musical with Andrew Lloyd Webber, Her Majesty's) 1975, Absent Friends 1975 (Garrick, televised 1985), Confusions (Apollo) 1976, Bedroom Farce 1977 (NT, televised 1980), Just Between Ourselves 1977 (Queen's, (Evening Standard Drama Award Best Play, televised 1978)), Ten Times Table (Globe) 1978, Joking Apart (Globe, Plays and Players Award) 1979, Sisterly Feelings (NT) 1980, Taking Steps (Lyric) 1980, Suburban Strains (musical with Paul Todd, Round House) 1981, Season's Greetings (Apollo) 1982, Way Upstream (NT, televised 1988) 1982, Making Tracks (musical with Paul Todd, Greenwich) 1983, Intimate Exchanges (Ambassadors) 1984, A Chorus of Disapproval 1985 (also dir, Evening Standard Drama Award Best Comedy, Olivier Award Best Comedy, Drama Award Best Comedy 1985, transferred Lyric 1986, film 1989), Woman in Mind (also dir, Vaudeville) 1986, A Small Family Business 1987 (NT, Evening Standard Drama Award Best Play), Henceforward... (also dir, Vaudeville (Evening Standard Drama Award Best Comedy 1989)) 1988, Man of the Moment 1990 (also dir, Globe (Evening Standard Drama Award Best Comedy 1990)), Invisible Friends (also dir, NT) 1991, The Revengers' Comedies (also dir, Strand) 1991, Mr A's Amazing Maze Plays (also dir, NT) 1993, Time of my Life (also dir, Vaudeville) 1993, Wildest Dreams (also dir, Barbican) 1993, Communicating Doors (also dir, Gielgud (Olivier Award nomination for Best Comedy 1996)) 1995; *Scarborough Prodns* Body Language 1990, This Is Where We Came In (for children) 1990, Callisto 5 (for children) 1990, Wildest Dreams 1991, My Very Own Story (for children) 1991, Time of my Life 1992, Dreams From A Summer House (a comedy with music by John Pattison) 1992, Haunting Julia 1994, The Musical Jigsaw Play (with music by John Pattison) 1994, By Jeeves 1996 (transfered to Duke of York's, Lyric Theatres (Brit Regional Theatre Awards 1996 Best Musical), The Champion of Paribanou 1996; *Plays Directed for NT* Tons of Money 1986, A View from the Bridge 1987, A Small Family Business 1987, 'Tis Pity She's a Whore 1988; *Books* The Norman Conquests (1975), Three Plays (Absurd Person Singular, Absent Friends, Bedroom Farce, 1977), Joking Apart and Other Plays (Just Between Ourselves, Ten Times Table, 1979), Sisterly Feelings and Taking Steps (1981), A Chorus of Disapproval (1986), Woman in Mind (1986), A Small Family Business (1987), Henceforward.... (1988), Mr A's Amazing Maze Plays (1989), Man of the Moment (1990), Invisible Friends (1991), The Revengers' Comedies (1991), Time of My Life (1993), Wildest Dreams (1993), Communicating Doors (1995); *Clubs* Garrick; *Style*— Sir Alan Ayckbourn, CBE; ✉ c/o Casarotto Ramsay Ltd, National House, 4th Floor, 60–66 Wardour Street, London W1V 4ND (☎ 0171 287 4450, fax 0171 287 9128)

AYERST, Rev Edward Richard; s of Edward Vigne Ayerst (d 1963), and Winifred, *née* Tucker (d 1977); *b* 21 Oct 1925; *Educ* Coopers' Co's Sch, Univ of Leeds, Coll of the Resurrection Mirfield; *m* 1960, Pauline, *née* Clarke; 1 s (Stephen b 23 July 1963), 2 da (Rachel b 9 June 1965, Elizabeth b 4 July 1968); *Career* vicar St John Edmonton London 1960–66, rector Whippingham with E Cowes IOW 1966–77, vicar Bridgwater 1977–90, ret 1990; chaplain to HM the Queen 1987; memb Philosophical Soc 1983; *Style—* The Rev Edward Ayerst; ✉ 56 Maple Drive, Burnham-on-Sea, Somerset TA8 1DH (☎ 01278 780701)

AYKROYD, Sir James Alexander Frederic; 3 Bt (UK 1929), of Birstwith Hall, Harrogate, Co York; s of Bertram Aykroyd (d 1983), and his 1 w, Margot, *née* Graham-Brown (now Dame Margot Smith, DBE, *qv*); suc his uncle Sir Cecil William Aykroyd, 2 Bt (d 1993); *b* 6 Sept 1943; *Educ* Eton, Univ of Aix-en-Provence, Univ of Madrid; *m* 1973, Jennifer, da of late Frederick William Marshall, of Porthcawl, Glam; 2 da (Gemma Jane b 1976, Victoria Louise b 1977); *Heir* half-bro, Toby Nigel Bertram Aykroyd b 13 Nov 1955; *Style—* Sir James Aykroyd, Bt; ✉ Birstwith Hall, nr Harrogate, North Yorkshire HG3 2JW

AYKROYD, Michael David; s of late George Hammond Aykroyd, TD (s of late Sir William Henry Aykroyd, 1 Bt); hp of cous, Sir William Aykroyd, 3 Bt, MC, *qv*; *b* 14 June 1928; *m* 1952, Oenone Gillian Diana, da of Donald George Cowling, MBE, of Leeds; 1 s, 3 da; *Style—* Michael Aykroyd, Esq; ✉ The Homestead, Killinghall, Harrogate, Yorks

AYKROYD, Sir William Miles; 3 Bt (UK 1920), of Lightcliffe, W Riding, Co of York, MC (1944); s of Sir Alfred Hammond Aykroyd, 2 Bt (d 1965), and Sylvia, *née* Walker (d 1992); *b* 24 Aug 1923; *Educ* Charterhouse; *Heir* cous, Michael David Aykroyd, *qv*; *Career* Lt 5 Royal Inniskilling Dragoon Gds 1943–47; dir Hardy Amies 1950–69; *Clubs* Boodle's; *Style—* Sir William Aykroyd, Bt, MC; ✉ Buckland Newton Place, Dorchester, Dorset (☎ 01300 345259)

AYLEN, Leo William; s of The Rt Rev Bishop Charles Arthur William Aylen (d 1972), and Elisabeth Margaret Anna, *née* Hills (d 1975); bro of Walter Aylen, QC, *qv*; *Educ* New Coll Oxford (MA), Univ of Bristol (PhD); *m* Annette Elizabeth, da of Jack Scott Battams (d 1982); *Career* writer, actor, director; poetry incl: Discontinued Design (1969), I, Odysseus (1971), Sunflower (1976), Return to Zululand (1980), Red Alert: this is a god warning (1981), Jumping-Shoes (1983); for children: The Apples of Youth (opera 1980), Rhymoceros (poems 1989), Dancing the Impossible: New and Selected Poems (1996); contrib to anthologies incl: The Sun Dancing, What Makes Your Toenails Twinkle, Toughie Toffee, The Songmakers, Never Say Boo to a Ghost, Spaceways, Open the Door; other pubns incl: Greek Tragedy and the Modern World (1964), Greece for Everyone (1976), The Greek Theater (1985); writer/director films for TV incl: 1065 and All that, Dynamo: a life of Michael Faraday, Who'll Buy a Bubble, Celluloid Love, 'Steel be my Sister', Six Bites of the Cherry (series), The Drinking Party (nominated for BAFTA award), The Death of Socrates, Soul of a Nation (documentary); radio plays and features incl: The Birds, An Unconquered God, Le Far West, Woman's Brief Season, Zulu Dreamtime, Dancing Bach, Poetry in Action (3 series); theatre works incl: Down the Arches (lyrics), No Trams to Lime Street (adaption of Alun Owen's play), Antigone (dir of own trans); subject of 3 CBS programmes devoted to his work as poet/actor; formerly: Hooker Distinguished visiting prof McMaster Univ Ontario, poet in residence Fairleigh Dickinson Univ New Jersey; awarded C Day Lewis Fellowship, prizewinner Arvon Int Poetry Competition 1992; memb: Poetry Soc of America, Poetry Soc of GB, Writers' Guild of GB, Writers' Guild of America, ACTT, Br Actors' Equity, BAFTA, Int PEN; *Recreations* church organ playing, distance running, mountains; *Clubs* BAFTA; *Style—* Leo Aylen; ✉ 13 St Saviour's Road, London SW2 5HP (☎ 0181 674 5949)

AYLEN, Walter Stafford; QC (1983); s of The Rt Rev Bishop Charles Arthur William Aylen (d 1972), and Elisabeth Margaret Anna, *née* Hills (d 1975); bro of Leo Aylen, *qv*; *b* 21 May 1937; *Educ* Winchester, New Coll Oxford (scholar, sr scholar, MA, BCL); *m* 1967, Peggy Elizabeth Lainé Woodford, *qv*, da of Ronald Curtis Woodford; 3 da (Alison b 1968, Frances b 1970, Imogen b 1974); *Career* Nat Serv cmmnd 2 Lt 1 Bn KRRC 1956–57; called to the Bar Middle Temple 1962 (Harmsworth entrance exhibitioner and scholar); recorder of the Crown Court 1985– (asst recorder 1982), bencher Middle Temple 1991, head of chambers 1991; memb Gen Cncl of the Bar 1994–96, chm BSITC 1994 (vice chm Fin Ctee 1995–96); FRSA 1989, ACIArb 1996; *Recreations* music (especially lieder and opera), theatre, literature; *Style—* Walter Aylen, Esq, QC; ✉ 27 Gauden Road, London SW4 6LR (☎ 0171 622 7871); Hardwicke Building, New Square, Lincoln's Inn, London WC2A 3SB (☎ 0171 242 2523, fax 0171 831 6968)

AYLESFORD, 11 Earl of (GB 1714); Charles Ian Finch-Knightley; JP (Warwicks 1948); also Baron Guernsey (GB 1702); s of 10 Earl of Aylesford (d 1958); *b* 2 Nov 1918; *Educ* Oundle; *m* 1946, Margaret Rosemary (d 1989), da of Maj Austin Tyer, MVO, TD; 1 s, 2 da; *Heir* s, Lord Guernsey; *Career* served WWII Capt Black Watch; Vice-Lt Warwicks 1964–74, Lord-Lt W Midlands 1974–94; former regnl dir Lloyds Bank Birmingham & W Midlands Bd (resigned 1989); memb Water Space Amenity Cmmn 1973–83; patron Warwicks Boy Scouts Assoc 1974– (co cmmr 1949–74); pres: Warwicks CCC 1980–, TAVRA 1982; Hon LLD Birmingham 1989; KStJ 1974; *Recreations* shooting, fishing, archery, nature conservation, preservation of wildlife; *Clubs* Flyfishers'; *Style—* The Rt Hon the Earl of Aylesford, JP; ✉ Packington Old Hall, Coventry, W Midlands CV7 7HG (☎ 01676 523273, office 01676 522020)

AYLIFFE, Prof Graham Arthur John; s of Arthur Ayliffe (d 1930), of Hambrook, Glos and Winifred Lily, *née* Hart (d 1984); *b* 2 March 1926; *Educ* Queen Elizabeth Hosp Sch Bristol, Univ of Bristol (BSc, MB ChB, MD); *m* 14 Sept 1963, Janet Esther, da of Edwin Alfred Lloyd (d 1977), of Clophill, Beds; 1 s (Richard b 1966), 1 da (Margaret b 1968); *Career* memb scientific staff MRC Industl Injuries and Burns Unit 1964–81, pres Infection Control Nurses Assoc 1976–79, chm Hosp Infection Soc 1979–84, hon dir Hosp Infection Res Laboratory Birmingham 1980–91 (hon conslt 1964–81 and 1991–), prof of med microbiology Univ of Birmingham 1981–89, dir WHO Collaborating Centre In Hosp Infection 1981–93, WHO conslt in bacterial diseases, member EC Ctee On Intensive Care Infection 1986–, chm DHSS Microbiology Advsy Ctee 1986–89; pres: Sterile Servs Mgmnt Inst 1988–94, Hosp Infection Soc 1988–94; chm Int Fedn Infection Control 1990–94; FRCPath; *Books* Principles and Practice of Disinfection, Preservation and Sterilisation (co-ed, 1991), Drug Resistance in Antimicrobial Therapy (jtly, 1975), Control of Hospital Infection, A Practical Handbook (co-ed, 1992), Hospital Acquired Infection, Principles and Practice (jtly, 1990), Chemical Disinfection in Hospital (jtly, 1984); *Recreations* fencing, fly fishing; *Style—* Prof Graham Ayliffe; ✉ 50 Halesowen Rd, Halesowen, West Midlands B62 9BA (☎ 0121 422 4233); Hospital Infection Research Laboratory, City Hospital NHS Trust, Dudley Rd, Birmingham B18 7QH (☎ 0121 554 3801 ext 4822, fax 0121 551 7763)

AYLMER, Dr Gerald Edward; s of late Capt E A Aylmer, RN, and Mrs G P Aylmer, *née* Evans; *b* 30 April 1926; *Educ* Winchester, Balliol Coll Oxford (MA, DPhil); *m* 1955, Ursula Nixon; 1 s, 1 da; *Career* historian; served RN 1944–47; Jane Eliza Proctor visiting fell Princeton Univ NJ USA 1950–51, jr res fell Balliol Coll Oxford 1951–54, lectr in history Univ of Manchester 1957–62 (asst lectr 1954–57), prof of history and head of dept Univ of York 1963–78, memb Univ of Oxford History Faculty 1978–, master St Peter's Coll Oxford 1978–91 (hon fell 1991); hon vice pres: Royal Hist Soc 1988– (pres 1984–88), Historical Assoc 1992–; chm: Royal Cmmn on Hist Manuscripts 1989–94 (memb 1978–), Editorial Bd History of Parl Tst 1989– (memb 1969–); Hon DLitt: Univ of Manchester 1991, Univ of Exeter 1991; FBA 1976; *Books* The King's Servants (1961, 2 edn 1974), The Diary of William Lawrence (ed, 1962), The Struggle for the Constitution (1963, 5 edn 1975), The Interregnum (ed 1972, 2 edn 1974), The State's Servants (1973), The Levellers in the English Revolution (ed, 1975), A History of York Minster (ed with Reginald Cant, 1978), Rebellion or Revolution? England 1640–1660 (1986); articles and reviews in learned jls; *Style—* Dr G E Aylmer, FBA; ✉ 18 Albert St, Jericho, Oxford OX2 6AZ (☎ 01865 512383); The Old Captain's, Hereford Rd, Ledbury, Herefordshire HR8 2PX (☎ 01531 670817)

AYLMER, Hon (Anthony) Julian; only s and h of 13 Baron Aylmer; *b* 10 Dec 1951; *Educ* Westminster, Trinity Hall Cambridge; *m* 5 May 1990, Belinda Rosemary, o da of Maj Peter Parker (gs of 6 Earl of Macclesfield), of The Hays, Ramsden, Oxford; 1 s (Michael Henry b 21 March 1991), 1 da (Rosemary Sofia b 11 Dec 1993); *Career* admitted slr 1976, ptnr Reynolds Porter Chamberlain 1982–; *Style—* The Hon Julian Aylmer; ✉ 16 Edgarley Terrace, London SW6 6QF; Reynolds Porter Chamberlain, Chichester House, 278–282 High Holborn, London WC1V 7HA (☎ 0171 242 2877, fax 0171 242 1431)

AYLMER, 13 Baron (I 1718); Sir Michael Anthony Aylmer; 16 Bt (I 1662); s of Christopher Aylmer (d 1955), and his 1 w, Marjorie Marianne Ellison, *née* Barber; suc 2 cous, 12 Baron Aylmer, 1982; *b* 27 March 1923; *Educ* privately, Trinity Hall Cambridge (MA, LLM); *m* 1950, Contessa Maddalena Sofia Maria Gabriella Cecilia Stefania Francesca, da of Count Arbeno Maria Attems di Santa Croce (d 1968), of Aiello del Friuli, and Sofie, eldest da of Prince Maximilian Karl Friedrich zu Löwenstein-Wertheim-Freudenberg; 1 s, 1 da; *Heir* s, Hon Julian Aylmer; *Career* admitted slr 1948; Legal Dept Equity & Law Life Assurance Society 1951–83; Liveryman City of London Solicitors' Co; *Recreations* reading, music; *Style—* The Rt Hon The Lord Aylmer; ✉ 42 Brampton Grove, London NW4 4AQ (☎ 0181 202 8300)

AYLMER, Sir Richard John; 16 Bt (I 1622), of Donadea, Co Kildare; s of Sir Fenton Gerald Aylmer, 15 Bt (d 1987), and Rosalind Boultbee, *née* Bell (d 1991); *b* 23 April 1937; *m* 16 June 1962, Lise, da of Paul Emile Demers, of Montreal, Canada; 1 s (Fenton Paul), 1 da (Geneviève b 16 March 1963); *Heir* s, Fenton Paul Aylmer b 31 Oct 1965; *Career* writer; *Style—* Sir Richard Aylmer, Bt; ✉ 3573 Lorne Ave, Montreal, Quebec H2X 2A4, Canada

AYLOTT, Robert Alexander William; s of Rueben David Aylott (d 1978), of Hampshire, and Colleen Joy, *née* Horne; *b* 21 Dec 1948; *Educ* Charterhouse, Harrison Road Hampshire; *m* 24 Oct 1970, Heather Jean, da of Philip Foot; 1 s (James Alexander Robert b 17 Dec 1973), 1 da (Michelle Heather b 28 Oct 1976); *Career* photo-journalist; darkroom asst: Sport & General Photo Agency Fleet Street 1964–65, Fox Photos London 1966–67; press photographer: Keystone Press Agency Fleet Street 1967–69, Daily Sketch 1969–70, Daily Mail 1970–75; photographer National Enquirer USA 1975–78; proprietor Front Page Press (Newspaper and Publishers) Hampshire 1978–87, photographer Express Newspapers 1987–95; winner various awards incl: News Photographer of the Year 1968, Colour Sequence of the Year 1971, Nikon Picture of the Year 1972, World Press Photos Portrait Section 1977; work exhibited at: World Press Photographers of the Year 1969, ICA Gallery 1972, first Press Exhibition (Photographers' Gallery London) 1972; contrib various books incl: Photography Year Books 1973–89, Eye Witness and Headline Photography (by Harold Evans), Chronicles of the 20th Century, Slip-Up, Naked Eye Astronomy (by Patrick Moore); fell Inst of Inc Photographers 1973, FRPS 1973; *Publications* Cry for Tomorrow (novel, 1973); Local History Publications: Fareham Two Views (1981), Unofficial Guide to Fareham (1982), Isle of Wight - Two Views (1982), Gosport - Two Views (1982), The Story of Porchester Castle (1983); *Recreations* painting, writing, travel, gardening, art collecting, photographic history; *Clubs* Press; *Style—* Robert Aylott, Esq; ✉ Earls Charity, Titchfield, Hampshire PO14 4PD (☎ 01329 842301)

AYLWIN, John Morris; s of Walter Edgar Aylwin (d 1978), of Worcs, and Rosamund, *née* Byng-Morris (d 1978); *b* 23 July 1942; *Educ* Uppingham, Emmanuel Coll Cambridge (MA), Guildford Coll of Law; *m* 4 July 1970, Angela, da of Conningsby Deryck Phillips (d 1995); 2 s (Michael Deryck Morris b 22 April 1972, Christopher John b 16 May 1974); *Career* Richards Butler solicitors: articled clerk 1965–67, asst slr 1967–72, ptnr 1972–, exec ptnr 1984–91, head of Environmental Law Gp 1991–; Freeman City of London Slrs Co 1988; memb: Law Soc 1965, City of London Law Soc 1988; *Recreations* tennis, golf, rugby, gardening, theatre; *Clubs* Richmond FC, Dorking RFC, Cottesmore Country Club; *Style—* J M Aylwin, Esq; ✉ Richards Butler, Beaufort House, 15 St Botolph St, London EC3A 7EE (☎ 0171 247 6555, fax 0171 247 5091)

AYOUB, HE Fouad; *b* 1944, Amman; *Educ* Calif State Univ San Francisco (BA, MA); *m* 1974, Marie, *née* Vernazza; 2 s (Hussein, Rakan), 1 da (Lana); *Career* Jordanian Dip Serv; press sec to HM King Hussein 1977, fell Harvard Univ Center for Int Affrs 1983–84, memb Jordanian Delgn to Madrid Peace Conf 1991, ambass to Ct of St James 1991–, non-resident ambass to Iceland and Ireland 1992–; decorations incl awards from Jordan, Germany, France, Greece, Italy, Spain, Indonesia, Finland, Austria and Sweden; *Recreations* reading; *Style—* HE Mr Fouad Ayoub; ✉ Embassy of The Hashemite Kingdom of Jordan, 6 Upper Phillimore Gardens, London W8 7HB

AYRE, John Victor; s of Gp Capt John Macdonald Ayre, CBE (d 1980), and Mary Annie, *née* Hibberd; *b* 11 May 1942; *Educ* King Edward VII Sch King's Lynn; *m* 18 June 1966, Jean Eva, da of Sqdn Ldr Arthur Frederick Plant, DFM; 1 s (Christopher John William b 12 Dec 1970), 1 da (Caroline Jean b 17 Jan 1968); *Career* CA; articled Allen Baldry Holman & Best London 1959–64, Finnie Ross Welch & Co 1965–72, Buckley Hall Devin & Co Hull 1972–73; ptnr: Whinney Murray & Co 1973–89, Ernst & Young 1989–; pres: Humberside & Dist Soc of CAs 1990–91, Hull Literary & Philosophical Soc 1995–96; FCA 1965; *Clubs* Hull Golf; *Style—* John Ayre, Esq; ✉ 4 The Paddock, Swanland, East Yorkshire HU14 3QW; Ernst & Young, Cloth Hall Court, 14 King Street, Leeds LS1 2JN

AYRE, Richard; *b* 1949; *Educ* Univ of Durham; *Career* BBC 1972–: news trainee working on Today prog Radio 4, Radio Solent and Belfast 1972–74, regnl journalist Belfast 1974, reporter Belfast 1975–76, dep news ed NI 1976–79, dep news ed Intake TV News rising to home news ed TV News 1979–82, six month fellowship in bdcast journalism Univ of Chicago 1984–85, ed Special Projects TV News 1985–87, chief asst to Dep Dir News and Current Affrs then to Dir News and Current Affrs 1987–88, head of editorial devpt News and Current Affrs 1988–89, head of BBC Westminster 1990–93, controller Editorial Policy 1993–96, dep chief exec BBC News 1996–; *Style—* Richard Ayre, Esq; ✉ Controller, Editorial Policy, BBC, Broadcasting House, Portland Place, London W1A 1AA (☎ 0171 580 4468)

AYRES, Gillian; OBE (1986); da of Stephen Ayres (d 1969), of Barnes, London, and Florence Olive, *née* Beresford Brown (d 1968); *b* 3 Feb 1930; *Educ* St Paul's Girls' Sch, Camberwell Sch of Art; *m* (m dis); 2 s (James, Sam); *Career* artist; teacher 1959–81 (Corham 1959–65, St Martin's 1966–78, head BA Painting Dept Winchester Sch of Art 1978–81); one-woman exhibitions 1956–: Knoedler Gallery London 1966–88, retrospective Serpentine Gallery 1983, Knoedler Gallery NY 1985, Fischer Fine Art 1990; sole Br rep in Indian Triennale Delhi 1991; works in public collections incl: Tate Gallery, Museum of Modern Art NY, V & A; maj Arts Cncl bursary 1979; Br Cncl prizewinner Tokyo Biennale 1963, John Moores 2nd prize 1982, Charles Woolaston Award RA 1989, Critics' Prize RA 1990, Indian Triennale Gold Medal 1991; Hon DLit London 1994; sr fell RCA 1996; RA 1991 (ARA 1982); *Recreations* gardening; *Style—* Miss Gillian Ayres,

OBE, RA; ✉ c/o Gimpel Fils Gallery, 30 Davies Street, London W1Y 1LG (☎ 0171 493 2488)

AYRES, Prof Jonathan Geoffrey (Jon); s of Geoffrey Walter Ayres, and Brenda Ruby, *née* Turpin; *b* 14 Feb 1950; *Educ* Woodhouse GS Finchley, Guy's Hosp (BSc, MB BS, MD); *m* Susan Marian Ayres; 1 s (Peter b 1981), 1 da (Katherine b 1982); *Career* Guy's Hosp: house offr 1974–75, sr house offr 1976–78, res registrar 1979–81, registrar 1978–79 and 1981–82; sr house offr Brompton Hosp 1977–78, sr registrar E Birmingham Hosp 1982–84, conslt physician in respiratory and gen med Birmingham Heartlands Hosp and hon sr lectr Univ of Birmingham 1984–, prof of respiratory med Univ of Warwick 1996–; author of numerous scientific pubns; memb: Br Thoracic Soc (sec Epidemiology Section), Midland Thoracic Soc and W Midlands Physicians' Assoc, American Thoracic Soc 1986, Int Epidemiology Assoc 1986, Euro Respiratory Soc 1988; FRCP 1989; *Recreations* sketching in pencil and watercolours, singing; *Style—* Prof Jon Ayres; ✉ Department of Respiratory Medicine, Birmingham Heartlands Hospital, Birmingham B9 5SS (☎ 0121 766 6611 ext 4475)

AYRES, Pam (Mrs Dudley Russell); da of Stanley William Ayres (d 1981), of Stanford-in-the-Vale, Oxon, and Phyllis Evelyn, *née* Loder; *b* 14 March 1947; *Educ* Faringdon Secdy Modern Sch; *m* 1982, Dudley Russell, s of late Joe Russell; 2 s (William Stanley b 12 Dec 1982, James Joseph b 20 July 1984); *Career* writer and entertainer 1974–; presenter The Pam Ayres Radio Show (BBC Radio 2) 1996–; *Style—* Ms Pam Ayres; ✉ PO Box 64, Cirencester, Glos GL7 5YD (☎ 01285 644622, fax 01285 642291)

AYRES, Rosalind Mary (Mrs Martin Jarvis); da of Sam Johnson (d 1986), of Westbury, Wilts, and Daisy, *née* Hydon (d 1987); *b* 7 Dec 1946; *Educ* George Dixon GS for Girls Birmingham, Loughborough Coll of Educn (Dip Educn); *m* 23 Nov 1974, Martin Jarvis, *qv*, s of Denys Jarvis, of Sanderstead, Surrey; *Career* actress; memb: RSC, Stars Organisation for Spastics; *Theatre* incl: Hamlet, The Three Sisters, Uncle Vanya, The Perfect Party (Greenwich), Dracula (Shaftesbury), I Claudius (Queens's), A Dolls House (Thorndike), Exchange (Vaudeville), Just Between Ourselves (Greenwich), Now You Know (Hampstead); for LA Theatre Works: Make and Break, Exchange, Private Lives, The Third Man, Table Manners; *Radio* A Room With A View, The Circle, Alphabetical Order; *Television* incl: The Mill, The House of Bernarda Alba, Juliet Bravo, The Bounder (series), Father's Day (series), Hindle Wakes, The Good Guys, Casualty, The Cinder Path (mini-series), A Face to Die For (mini-series, US); *Films* incl: The Lovers, Tales from Beyond the Grave, Mr Smith, Cry Wolf, That'll be the Day, Stardust, The Slipper and the Rose, Emily's Ghost, Black Beauty, Titanic; *Recreations* interior design, illustration; *Style—* Ms Rosalind Ayres; ✉ c/o Lou Coulson, 37 Berwick Street, London W1V 3RF (☎ 0171 734 9633, fax 0171 439 7569); c/o Badgley Connor, 9229 Sunset Blvd, Suite 311, Los Angeles, California, 90069 USA (☎ 00 1 310 278 9313)

AYRTON, Norman Walter; *b* 25 Sept 1924; *Career* WWII service with RNVR; int theatre and opera dir; trained as actor Old Vic Sch 1947–48, joined Old Vic Co 1949, rep work Farnham and Oxford 1949–50, on staff Old Vic Sch 1949–51, rejoined Old Vic Co 1951 Festival Season, opened own teaching sch 1952, began dramatic coaching for Royal Opera House Covent Garden 1953, princ LAMDA 1966–72 (asst princ 1954–66); guest dir: Aust Cncl for the Arts Sydney and Brisbane 1973–74, Loeb Drama Center Harvard 1974, 1976 and 1978, Faculty Juillard Sch NY 1974–85, Melbourne Theatre Co 1974–75, Nat Inst of Dramatic Art Sydney 1973–76, Vancouver Opera Assoc 1975–83, Sydney Opera House 1976–81 and 1983, Williamstown Festival USA 1977, Hartford Stage Co and American Stage Festival 1978 , Missouri Rep Theatre 1980–81, Nat Opera Studio London 1980–81, Oberlin Coll USA 1982, Spoleto Festival USA 1984; resident stage dir: American Opera Center NY 1981–85, Vassar Coll NY 1990–96, Sarah Lawrence Coll NY 1993–, Utah Shakespeare Festival 1994, Cornell Univ NY 1995; dir of opera: Royal Acad of Music 1986–90, Great Elm Music Festival 1988–; dean: British American Drama Acad 1986–96, Florida State Univ 1996–; Hon RAM 1989; *Recreations* music, travel, gardens; *Style—* Norman Ayrton, Esq; ✉ 40A Birchington Rd, W Hampstead, London NW6 4LJ (☎ 0171 328 6056)

AYRTON-GRIME, Philip; CVO (1979); s of Philip Grime (d 1982), of Bushells House, Goosnargh, Lancs, and May, *née* Chadwick (d 1968); *b* 20 Nov 1926; *Educ* Preston GS, Univ of Liverpool (MRCVS); *m* 1958, Anne, da of Douglas Arthur Dadley; 3 da (Charlotte b 1959, Deborah b 1962, Olivia b 1965), 1 s (Gerard b 1961); *Career* in gen vet practice Windsor 1950–92 (retired as sr ptnr), conslt vet surgn to HM The Queen 1992–; vet surgn to: Royal Windsor Horse Show 1951– (memb Ctee 1979–), Royal Windsor Racecourse 1951–92, Ascot Racecourse 1963–; dir: Ascot Finance (UK) Ltd 1986–, Ayrton Construction Ltd 1986–; memb Lloyds 1978–; memb Nat Panel Int Equestrian Fedn 1980–, vice pres Royal South Bucks Agricultural Assoc 1982–; hon memb: Br Vet Hosps Assoc 1985 (fndr memb 1968, pres 1979–80), Br Vet Zoological Assoc 1995 (fndr memb 1963); *Recreations* horse racing, tennis, gardening; *Clubs* Royal Society of Medicine; *Style—* Philip Ayrton-Grime, Esq, CVO; ✉ Woodland Manor, St Leonard's Hill, Windsor, Berks SL4 4AT

AZA, HE Alberto; *b* 23 May 1937; *m*; 6 c; *Career* Spanish diplomat; joined diplomatic serv 1965, second sec Spanish Embassy Libreville 1965–67, second sec Spanish Embassy Algiers 1967–72, first sec Spanish Embassy Rome 1972–75, dir of Near and Middle East Africa Dept Miny of Foreign Affairs Madrid 1975; Diplomatic Information Bureau Miny of Foreign Affairs Madrid: dir of int information 1975, dir of media relations 1976, dep DG 1977; dir of the Cabinet of the Pres of the Govt Madrid 1977–83, chief dir of Orgn of American States Latin-American Dept Miny of Foreign Affairs Madrid 1983, min cnsllr Spanish Embassy Lisbon 1983–85, ambass to the Orgn of American States Washington DC 1985–89, ambass to Belize with residence in Washington DC 1989–90, ambass to Mexico 1990–92, ambass to the Ct of St James's 1992–; Gran Cruz del Mérito Civil (Spain) 1979; *Style—* HE Señor Alberto Aza; ✉ Spanish Embassy, 24 Belgrave Square, London SW1X 8QA

AZIS, Jonathan Giles Ashley; s of Osman Azis, and Irene Elizabeth Winifred May, *née* Dean; *b* 14 April 1957; *Educ* Millfield, Pembroke Coll Oxford (MA); *m* 18 Aug 1984, Emily Susanna, da of Michael Fenwick Briggs, of Bath, and Isabel Colegate, *qv*; 1 s (Arthur Jonathan Osman b 25 March 1993), 2 da (Matilda Winifred Katherine b 18 Dec 1986, Constance Irene Isabel b 28 Nov 1988); *Career* Barretts (slrs) 1979–82 and 1984–87, Walker Martineau (slrs) 1982–84, Nabarro Nathanson 1987, Kingston Smith (CAs) 1987–90, Beazer plc 1990–92, co sec Hanson PLC 1995– (joined 1992); memb Law Soc; *Recreations* books, music, ironing; *Clubs* Brooks's, Lansdowne; *Style—* Jonathan Azis, Esq; ✉ Westwood Manor, Bradford on Avon, Wiltshire BA15 2AF (☎ 01225 863374); Hanson PLC, 1 Grosvenor Place, London SW1X 7JH (☎ 0171 245 1245, fax 0171 235 3455)

AZIZ, Khalid; s of Ahmad Aziz (d 1978), of London, and Sheila Frances, *née* Light; *b* 9 Aug 1953; *Educ* Westminster City Sch, Aitcheson Coll Lahore; *m* 1, 27 March 1974 (m dis), Barbara Elizabeth, da of Harry Etchells, of Sherburn-in-Elmet, Yorks; 2 da (Nadira b 1977, Fleur b 1981); m 2, 16 June 1994, Kim Kemp, da of Muriel Haslam, of Bassett, Southampton; *Career* broadcaster, journalist and dir; prodr/presenter: BBC Radio and TV 1970–81, TVS 1981–91; presenter: On Course (C4) 1988–89, The Small Business Programme (BBC2/C4) 1990, Starnet Business Programme 1990; TV Journalist of the Year 1987–88; chm The Aziz Corporation (specialists in spoken communication) 1991–; sr visiting fell Sch of Mgmnt Univ of Southampton 1991–; chm: The Wessex Children's Hospice Tst, Communication Ctee RAC Cirencester 1991–94; memb Advsy Ctee Office for Nat Statistics; tstee Winchester Med Tst; chm: Prince's Tst Hants, S Counties Bd Prince's Youth Business Tst; vice pres Pestalozzi Int Children's Village; author of 9 books (principally on Indian cooking); *Books* The Barclays Guide to Small Business Computing (1990); *Recreations* aviation, fishing, shooting, computers; *Clubs* Naval and Military; *Style—* Khalid Aziz, Esq; ✉ West Stratton, Winchester, Hants (☎ 01962 774766)

AZIZ, Suhail Ibne; s of Azizur Rahnan (d 1971), of Bangladesh, and Lutfunnessa Khatoon; *b* 3 Oct 1937; *Educ* RNC Dartmouth, Univ of London (MSc Econ); *m* 1960, Elizabeth Ann, da of Alfred Pyne, of Dartmouth; 2 da (Lisa, Rebecca); *Career* served Pakistan Navy 1954–61, served as RAF Offr 1966–70; personnel mangr Lever Bros Pakistan Ltd 1963–66, industl rels offr London 1970–73, labour rels exec Ford Motor Co UK 1973–74, personnel offr Pedigree Petfoods 1974–78, dir Gen Servs Divs Cmmn for Racial Equality 1978–81, PA Int Mgmnt Conslts 1981–83, head Econ and Employment Div and dep dir London Borough of Lewisham 1984–89, mgmnt conslt Fullemploy Consultancy 1989–90, chm and md The Brettonwood Partnership Ltd 1990–; exec memb Nottingham Community Relations Cncl 1975–78; memb: Race Relations Bd Conciliation Ctee 1971–74, Gulbenkian Fndn 1976–82, Home Sec's Standing Advsy Cncl 1977–78, Dept of Employment Min's Employment Advsy Gp 1977–78, Advsy Ctee BBC 1977–82, Employers Panel Industl Tbnls 1978–, Bd of Tstees Brixton Neighbourhood Community Assoc 1979–82, Cncl Inst of Mgmnt Conslts 1988–91, Exec Ctee Common Purpose 1991–, Isle of Dogs Community Tst 1991–, Res Advsy Ctee Queen Mary and Westfield Coll London Univ; chm: Third World Specialist Gp Inst of Mgmnt Conslts 1984–91, Developing Countries Gp Queen Mary and Westfield Coll 1991–; fndr chm E London Bangladeshi Enterprise Agency 1985, advsr Minority Business Devpt Unit City of London Poly 1986, tstee and dir East End Tourism Tst 1991–, govr Tower Hamlets Coll 1991–; CRE bursary to USA to study minority econ devpt initiatives 1986, led preparation of Bangladeshi community response to House of Commons Select Ctee report "Bangladeshis in Britain" and assisted organisations in the preparation of implementation plans 1986; FIMgt, FIMC (MIMC 1986); *Recreations* travel, reading political economy; *Clubs* Sudan (Khartoum), RAF; *Style—* Suhail Aziz, Esq; ✉ The Brettonwood Partnership, 126 St Julian's Farm Road, West Norwood, London SE27 0RR (☎ 0181 766 6118, fax 0181 766 0212)

B

BAART, Leonard William; s of Lein Wilhelmus Baart (d 1973), of S Africa, and Florence Emily, *née* Gilchrist (d 1967); *b* 5 April 1927; *Educ* Kimberley Boys' HS, Witwatersrand Univ (BArch); *m* 21 March 1953, Diana Ingrid, da of Richard John Southwell Crowe (d 1980), of Avon; 1 s (John b 1960), 3 da (Veronica b 1954, Fiona b 1956, Angela b 1958); *Career* chartered architect in private practice, cmmnd architect to English Heritage 1986–89, conslt architect to English Heritage for Re-Survey of Listed Buildings 1984–87; Fellow Worshipful Co of Arbitrators 1985, Freeman City of London 1984; FRIBA, FCIArb; *Recreations* painting (water-colour), golf, tennis, choir singing; *Clubs* Bulawayo (Zimbabwe); *Style—* Leonard W Baart, Esq; ✉ Cobden House, Hanwood, nr Shrewsbury SY5 8LT (☎ 01743 860322); Wilderhope House, Bellevue, Shrewsbury (☎ 01743 361261/2)

BABB, Phil; *b* 30 Nov 1970; *Career* professional footballer; Millwall 1988–90, 80 appearances (14 goals) Bradford City 1990–92, Coventry City 1992–94; Liverpool: transferred for fee of £3.6m 1994–, winners Coca-Cola Cup 1995; Ireland: over 10 full caps, memb World Cup team 1994; *Style—* Phil Babb, Esq; ✉ c/o Liverpool FC, Anfield Road, Anfield, Liverpool L4 0TH (☎ 0151 263 2361)

BABBIDGE, Adrian Vaughan; JP (1983); s of William Henry Vaughan Babbidge, of Cwmbran, Gwent, and Violet, *née* Jenkins (d 1990); *b* 10 July 1949; *Educ* Jones' West Monmouth Sch Pontypool, Univ Coll Cardiff (BA), Univ of Leicester (post grad mus studies cert, MA); *Career* asst curator Thurrock Local History Mus Grays Essex 1971–74, mus curator Borough of Torfaen Pontypool 1974–78, dir and sec Torfaen Mus Trust Pontypool 1978–89, dir and sec E Midlands Mus Serv Nottingham 1992– (dir 1989–); dir: Gwent Area Broadcasting Ltd 1981–89 (company sec 1981–85), Cardiff Broadcasting Co plc 1985–89, Midlands Arts Marketing Ltd 1992–95 (vice chair), Museum Enterprises Ltd 1991–, E Midlands Regnl Recognition Panel, Investors in People 1995–; external examiner (heritage management) Nottingham Trent Univ 1995–; memb: Exec Ctee E Midlands Tourist Bd 1989–92, Inst of Leisure and Amenity Mgmnt; tstee Glamorgan-Gwent Archaeological Trust 1985–89; FMA 1982 (hon treas 1988–91), FRSA; *Recreations* cinema, discovering Britain, learning about the law; *Clubs* Royal Over-Seas League; *Style—* Adrian Babbidge, Esq, JP; ✉ Director, East Midlands Museums Service, Courtyard Buildings, Wollaton Park, Nottingham NG8 2AE (☎ 0115 985 4534, fax 0115 928 0038)

BABINGTON, His Hon Anthony Patrick; s of Oscar John Gilmore Babington (d 1930), of Monkstown, Co Cork; *b* 4 April 1920; *Educ* Reading Sch; *Career* serv WWII Royal Ulster Rifles and Dorset Regt (twice wounded), Maj; called to the Bar Middle Temple 1948, bencher 1977, autumn reader 1994; SE Circuit: prosecuting counsel to PO 1959–64, metropolitan stipendiary magistrate 1964–72, circuit judge 1972–87; memb: Home Office Working Pty on Bail 1971–73, NEC Int PEN English Centre 1979–82; hon bencher Kings Inns Dublin 1995; Croix de Guerre with Gold Star (France) 1944; *Books* No Memorial (1954), The Power To Silence (1968), A House In Bow Street (1969), The English Bastille (1971), The Rule of Law In Britain (1978), For The Sake of Example (1983), Military Intervention in Britain (1990), The Devil to Pay (1991), Shell-Shock (1997); *Recreations* music, theatre, reading; *Clubs* Garrick, Special Forces; *Style—* His Hon Anthony Babington; ✉ 3 Gledhow Gardens, Kensington, London SW5 0BL (☎ 0171 373 4014); Thydon Cottage, Chilham, nr Canterbury, Kent CT4 8BX (☎ 01227 730300)

BABINGTON, His Hon Robert John; DSC (1942), QC (NI 1965); s of Maj David Louis James Babington (d 1973), and Alice Marie, *née* McClintock (d 1978); *b* 9 April 1920; *Educ* St Columba's Coll Dublin, Trinity Coll Dublin (BA); *m* 2 Jan 1954, (Elizabeth) Bryanna Marguerite, da of Dr Ernest Henry Alton, MC, provost Trinity Coll Dublin (d 1952); 2 s (Philip b 30 Oct 1954, David b 2 Feb 1961), 1 da (Jane b 22 Sept 1956); *Career* Fleet Air Arm 1940–45; called to the Bar Inns of Court NI 1947; county court judge: Fermanagh and Tyrone 1978–90, Co Down 1990–94; MP N Down Stormont 1968–72; *Recreations* golf, birdwatching; *Clubs* Tyrone County (Omagh), Special Forces, Fermanagh County (Enniskillen), Royal Belfast Golf, RUYC; *Style—* His Hon Robert Babington, DSC, QC; ✉ c/o Royal Courts of Justice, Chichester Street, Belfast BT1 3JF

BACH, John Theodore; s of late Dr Francis Bach, and Matine, *née* Thompson; *b* 18 Feb 1936; *Educ* Rugby, New Coll Oxford (MA); *m* 15 April 1967, Hilary Rose, da of late Gp Capt T E H Birley, OBE; 1 s (Alexander b 1969), 2 da (Emily b 1968, Susannah b 1973); *Career* slr; ptnr Stephenson Harwood 1966–; dir Moorfields Eye Hosp NHS Tst; memb Ct of Assts Worshipful Co of Barbers; *Clubs* City Univ; *Style—* John Bach, Esq; ✉ Stephenson Harwood, St Paul's Churchyard, London EC4M 8SH (☎ 0171 329 4422, fax 0171 606 0822)

BACHE, HE Andrew Philip Foley; CMG (1992); s of Robert Philip Sydney Bache, OBE (d 1984), and late Jessie, *née* Pearman-Smith; *b* 29 Dec 1939; *Educ* Shrewsbury, Emmanuel Coll Cambridge (MA); *m* 20 July 1963, Shân, da of late Rev L V Headley, OBE, of E Tisted, Hants; 2 s (Richard b 1964, Alexander b 1966), 1 da (Xenia b 1974); *Career* HM Dip Serv: entered 1963, FCO 1963–64, 1968–71 and 1974–78, third sec Nicosia 1964–66, second sec Sofia 1966–68, first sec Lagos 1971–74, first sec (commercial) Vienna 1978–81, cnsllr and head of chancery Tokyo 1981–85, cnsllr Ankara 1985–87, head of Personnel Servs Dept FCO 1988–90, chm Civil Serv Selection Bd (on secondment) 1990–91; ambass: to Romania 1992–96, to Denmark 1996–; *Recreations* sport, skiing, fine arts, travel, ornithology; *Clubs* Jesters, MCC, Combined Oxford and Cambridge Univ; *Style—* HE Mr Andrew Bache, CMG; ✉ c/o Foreign & Commonwealth Office (Copenhagen), King Charles Street, London SW1A 2AH

BACHMANN, Lawrence Paul; s of Jacob G Bachmann (d 1950), of Los Angeles, California, and Beatrice, *née* Lashins; *b* 12 Dec 1911; *Educ* Univ of Southern California (BA), Univ of Oxford (MA); *m* 1 (m dis 1966), Jean, *née* Campbell; m 2, 8 May 1967, Bettina, da of Alfred Hart (d 1936), of Rochester, NY; *Career* USAAF: main overseas corr Air Force official jl 1942–45, served S Pacific 1943, Europe 1944, Europe and Pacific 1944–45, China, Burma and India 1945, Lt-Col USAFR; asst to Head: RKO Studios Hollywood 1933–35, MGM Studios Culver City Ca 1936–42; co-author of many Dr Kildare films and others 1936–42, screen writer and novelist 1945–48, in Berlin for US War Dept OMGUS 1948–50, in Berlin for US State Dept 1950–52, novelist 1952–56, chm and md Paramount Br Prodns London 1956–58, head MGM Br Studios 1959–66; prodr MGM films: Village of the Damned (Agatha Christie Miss Marple series), Zero One (39 part TV series for MGM/BBC), Whose Life is it Anyway 1982; fell Green Coll Oxford 1983– (memb Vice Chllr's Appeals & Income Generating Ctee); Domus fell St Catherine's Coll Oxford 1990; memb: Writers' Guild of America 1935, Acad Motion Picture Arts & Scis 1960; fell Royal Soc of Med 1986; *Books* Death in the Dolls House (1943), The Kiss of Death (1946), The Phoenix (1955), The Valley of the Kings (1956), The Lorelei (1957), The Bitter Lake (1969), The Legend of Joseph Nokato (1971), The Ultimate Act (1972); *Recreations* lawn tennis; *Clubs* All England Lawn Tennis & Croquet, Garrick, RAF, Beverly Hills Tennis; *Style—* Lawrence Bachmann, Esq; ✉ The Manor House, Great Haseley, Oxford OX44 7JY (☎ 01844 279317)

BACK, Patrick; QC (1970); s of late Ivor Back, and Barbara, *née* Nash; *b* 23 Aug 1917; *Educ* Marlborough, Trinity Hall Cambridge; *m* 1971, Rosina Selina Alice Hare, QC, *qv*; *Career* Capt 14 Punjab Regt 1941–46; called to the Bar 1940, bencher Gray's Inn 1978, commenced practice Western Circuit 1948 (leader 1984–89), dep chm Devon QS 1968; recorder of the Crown Court 1972–; *Recreations* fly-fishing; *Style—* Patrick Back, Esq, QC; ✉ 3 Temple Gardens, Temple, London EC4Y 9AU (☎ 0171 353 3102, fax 0171 353 0960); 9–11 Broad Street, All Saints Chambers, Bristol BS1 2HP (☎ 0117 921 1966, fax 0117 927 6493)

BACK, Prof Paul Adrian Auchmuty; CBE (1994); s of Arthur William Back, QC (d 1960), of Grahamstown, S Africa, and Mary Helen Margaret, *née* Carter; *b* 30 May 1930; *Educ* St Andrew's Coll Grahamstown S Africa, Rhodes Univ S Africa (BSc), Univ of Cape Town (BSc), Trinity Coll Oxford (Rhodes scholar, PhD, Desborough Medal for servs to rowing, Hack Trophy for flying Univ Air Squadron); *m* 1965, Jacqueline Sarah, da of Walter Hide; 3 s (Jonathan Paul b 1966, Rupert James b 1968, Nicholas Hugo b 1976); *Career* Sir Alexander Gibb & Partners: joined 1955, assoc 1967–70, ptnr 1970–89, co dir and chief tech dir 1989–95; prof of design Univ of Oxford 1992–; worked on Kariba Hydro-Electric Power Station and Dam 1955–60, worked on several hydro-electric projects incl Samanalawewa and Victoria Dam and Hydro-Electric Projects in Sri Lanka and Kariba North Hydro-Electric Power Station Zambia 1970–, advsr to World Bank on Tarbela Dam 1976–, memb Bd of Advsrs Nat Irrigation Admin of the Philippines Magat Dam 1977–, chm Advsy Panel Shaqikou Hydro-Electric Project China 1984–, chm Panel of Enquiry Kantalai Tank failure Sri Lanka 1986, chm Lesotho Highlands Consltss Review Panel for the Katse Dam 1987–, project dir for design and supervision of construction Cardiff Bay Barrage Wales 1989–; Construction News Award of the Year for the Victoria Dam Project Sri Lanka (ptnr i/c) 1985; chief guest speaker Sri Lanka Assoc for the Advancement of Sci 1989, lectr (Dams in Difficulties) Br Assoc for Advancement of Science 1995; memb Cncl ICE 1989; memb Assoc of Consulting Engrs 1971, FICE 1971 (MICE 1961), FEng 1981; *Books* Seismic Design Study of a Double Curvative Arch Dam (jt author, 1969), P K Le Roux Dam - Spillway Design and Energy Dissipators (jt author, 1973), Hydro-Electric Power Generation and Pumped Storage Schemes Utilising the Sea (1978), Aseismic Design of Arch Dams (jt author, 1980), The Influence of Geology on the Design of Victoria Dam Sri Lanka (jt author, 1982), Automatic Flood Routing at Victoria Dam Sri Lanka; *Recreations* sailing, skiing; *Clubs* RAF London; *Style—* Prof Paul Back, CBE, FEng; ✉ Parsonage Farm, How Lane, White Waltham, Berks SL6 3JP (☎ 0118 934 3973)

BACKHOUSE, David John; s of Joseph Helme Backhouse (d 1989), and Jessie, *née* Chivers, of Devizes, Wilts; *b* 5 May 1941; *Educ* Lord Weymouth Sch Warminster, W of England Coll of Art; *m* 19 July 1975, Sarah Patricia, da of Philip Gerald Barber, CBE (d 1988); 1 s (Theodore b 1980), 2 da (Katharine b 1977, Rosalind b 1984); *Career* sculptor; many public sculptures in UK; cmmns incl: Aspiration for James Capel House City of London, Dance of the Centaurs for Whiteleys of Bayswater, The Young Mozart for the City of Bath; recent portraits incl: José Carreras for The Royal Opera House Covent Garden, The Marquess of Bath for Longleat House; portrait heads and bronzes in collections worldwide; one man exhibitions in: London, NY, Washington DC; RWA, FRBS, FRSA; *Recreations* landscape gardening, walking, cycling; *Style—* David Backhouse, Esq; ✉ Lullington Studio, Lullington, Frome, nr Bath, Somerset BA11 2PW (☎ 01373 831318, fax 01373 830319); La Chapelle Pommier, 24340 Mareuil, Dordogne, France

BACKHOUSE, David Miles; s of Jonathan Backhouse (d 1993), and Alice Joan (d 1984), *née* Woodroffe; *b* 30 Jan 1939; *Educ* Eton; *m* 1969, Sophia Ann, da of Col Clarence Henry Southgate Townsend (d 1953); 2 children; *Career* investmt banker; dir: Bassett Trust Ltd 1985–, Bradstock Group plc 1990–, Clayhithe plc 1994–, Johnson Fry Holdings plc 1995–; govr RAC Cirencester 1987–; *Recreations* tennis, riding; *Clubs* Boodle's, Vanderbilt Racquet; *Style—* David Backhouse, Esq; ✉ c/o Bradstock Group plc, 18 London Street, London EC3R 7JP

BACKHOUSE, Oliver Richard; s of Maj Sir John Edmund Backhouse, 3 Bt, MC (d 1944), and Jean Marie Frances, *née* Hume-Gore; hp of bro, Sir Jonathan Roger Backhouse, 4 Bt; *b* 18 July 1941; *Educ* Ampleforth, RMA Sandhurst; *m* 1970, Gillian Irene, o da of L W Lincoln, of Northwood, Middx; 1 adopted s, 1 adopted da; *Career* memb Securities Institute; FCA; *Style—* Oliver Backhouse, Esq; ✉ Highcroft, 141 Quickley Lane, Chorleywood, Rickmansworth, Herts WD3 5PD

BACKHOUSE, William; s of Jonathan Backhouse (d 1993), of Essex, and Alice Joan, *née* Woodroffe (d 1984); *b* 29 May 1942; *Educ* Eton; *m* 1971, Deborah Jane, da of Hon David Edward Hely-Hutchinson (d 1984), of Wilts; 1 s (Timothy b 1981), 2 da (Harriet b 1975, Tessa b 1977); *Career* Baring Brothers & Co Ltd 1970–84, Baring Asset Management Ltd 1985–93; non-exec dir Essex Rivers Healthcare Tst 1994–; memb Cncl King Edward's Hosp Fund for London 1991– (treas 1993–); Liveryman Worshipful Co of Gunmakers; FCA; *Recreations* travel, photography; *Style—* William Backhouse, Esq; ✉ Layer Marney Wick, Colchester, Essex CO5 9UT (☎ 01206 330267, fax 01206 330647)

BACKLEY, Steven James; MBE (1995); s of John Backley, and Pauline, *née* Hogg; *b* 12 Feb 1969; *Educ* Bexley and Erith Tech HS, Loughborough Univ of Technol; *Career* javelin thrower; holder of world jr record in 1988, finished third in overall athletics Grand Prix to Said Aouita and Roger Kingdom 1989, UK record holder 85.90m set in Barcelona 1989, England rep Cwlth Games Auckland NZ 1990 (Gold medal), Euro champion 1990 and 1994, world record holder 91.46m Auckland 1992, Bronze medal Olympic Games Barcelona 1992, Gold medal World Cup 1994, Silver medal World Championships Gothenburg 1995, Silver medal Olympic Games Atlanta 1996; *Recreations* athletics; *Clubs* Cambridge Harriers (Bexley); *Style—* Steven Backley, Esq,

MBE; ✉ c/o Mr E C Nash, Cambridge Harriers, 12 Margaret Road, Bexley, Kent DA5 1DU

BACON, Anthony Gordon (Tony); TD (1973); s of Frederick Gordon Bacon (d 1990), of Ingatestone, Essex, and Dorothy Winifred, *née* Ramsay; *b* 12 May 1938; *Educ* Highgate Sch, Hertford Coll Oxford (BA, MA); *m* 1, 18 Aug 1962, (Margaret) Jocelyn (d 1992), da of George Ronald Percival Ross, of Blackmore End, Herts; 3 s (Richard b 1965, Michael b 1967, d 1995, Timothy b 1970); m 2, 18 Feb 1994, Robina (d 1995), da of Col C J Y Dallmeyer, DSO and bar, of East Lothian; *Career* Nat Serv RA UK and Hong Kong 1956–58; TA Essex Yeo RHA 1959–74 (EY Signal Sqdn, 71 Signal Regt (V)); banker Barclays Bank Gp 1961–92 (UK, Australia, Cote d'Ivoire, Hong Kong); exec sec Anglo Ghanaian Business Assoc 1992–, funding offr Utd Soc for the Propagation of the Gospel 1992–; advsr to the Church of the Province of the Indian Ocean 1993–; ACIB 1966, FCIS 1985; *Recreations* real tennis, golf, music, country pursuits; *Clubs* Australian, Naval & Military (Melbourne Australia), The Bankers'; *Style*— Tony Bacon, Esq, TD; ✉ USPG, Partnership House, 157 Waterloo Road, London SE1 8XA (☎ 0171 928 8681)

BACON, Jennifer Helen (Jenny); CB (1995); da of Dr Lionel James Bacon, of Winchester, Hants, and Joyce, *née* Chapman; *b* 16 April 1945; *Educ* Bedales Sch Petersfield, New Hall Cambridge (BA); *Career* Civil Serv: entered as asst princ Miny of Labour 1967, private sec to Min of State for Employment 1971–72, princ Health and Safety at Work Act 1972–74, industl rels legislation 1974–76, princ private sec to Sec of State for Employment 1977–78, asst sec Head of Skillcentres in Manpower Servs Cmmn 1978–80, sabbatical travelling in Latin America 1980–81, head Machinery of Govt Div Cabinet Office 1981–82, dir of Adult Trg Manpower Servs Cmmn 1982–86, head Schs Branch 3 Nat Curriculum and Assessment Dept of Educn and Sci 1986–89, princ fin offr Dept of Employment 1989–91, dir of resources and strategy Dept of Employment 1991–92, dir gen Health and Safety Executive 1995– (dep dir gen 1992–95); visiting fell Nuffield Coll Oxford 1989–; memb Sheffield Development Corporation 1992–95 (resigned); *Recreations* travel, walking, classical music and opera; *Style*— Miss Jenny Bacon, CB; ✉ Health and Safety Executive, Rose Court, 2 Southwark Bridge, London SE1 9HS (☎ 0171 717 6633, fax 0171 928 6639)

BACON, John Maxwell; s of John Anthony Bacon (d 1985), of Beckenham, Kent, and Irene, *née* Roberts; *b* 6 Jan 1949; *Educ* Hawesdown Co Secdy Modern Sch Kent; *m* 3 July 1976, Rita, da of Patrick Dempsey; *Career* jr copywriter Young & Rubicam advtg 1969–71, copywriter Collett Dickinson Pearce 1971–73, sr copywriter BMP 1973–78, gp head and creative dir Saatchi & Saatchi 1978–88; exec creative dir: Ogilvy & Mather 1988–94, Foote Cone & Belding 1994–; winner various advtg awards incl: 3 D&AD Silver, 3 Gold and 5 Silver Campaign Press Awards, 3 Cannes Silver Lions, 5 Clios; memb D&AD; *Recreations* shooting, fencing, collecting vintage wristwatches, wine; *Style*— John Bacon, Esq; ✉ Foote Cone and Belding, 110 St Martin's Lane, London WC2N 4DY (☎ 0171 240 7100, fax 0171 240 5500)

BACON, Sir Nicholas Hickman Ponsonby; 14 and 15 Bt (E 1611 and 1627), of Redgrave, Suffolk, and of Mildenhall, Suffolk, respectively; Premier Baronet of England; s of Sir Edmund Bacon, 13 and 14 Bt, KG, KBE, TD, JP, by his w Priscilla, da of Col Sir Charles Ponsonby, 1 Bt, TD, and Hon Winifred Gibbs (da of 1 Baron Hunsdon), Sir Nicholas is 12 in descent from Rt Hon Sir Nicholas Bacon, Lord Keeper of the Great Seal under Elizabeth I 1558–78 (in which latter year he d), His eld s was cr a Bt 1611 and this eld son's 3 s cr a Bt in 1627, Lord Keeper Bacon's 5 s by a second m (but yr s by this w, Anne, da of Sir Anthony Cooke, sometime tutor to Edward VI) was Lord High Chllr & was cr Baron Verulam 1618 and Viscount St Albans 1621 both ext 1626; *b* 17 May 1953; *Educ* Eton, Univ of Dundee (MA); *m* 1981, Susan Henrietta, da of Raymond Dinnis, of Delaware Farm, Edenbridge; 4 s (Henry Hickman b 1984, Edmund b 1986, Nathaniel b 1989, Thomas Castell b 1992); *Heir* s, Henry Hickman Bacon b 23 April 1984; *Career* called to the Bar Gray's Inn 1978; page of honour to HM The Queen 1966–69; Liveryman Worshipful Co of Grocers; *Clubs* Pratt's; *Style*— Sir Nicholas Bacon, Bt; ✉ Raveningham Hall, Norwich NR14 6NS (☎ 01508 548206)

BACON, Priscilla, Lady; Priscilla Dora; *née* Ponsonby; DL (Norfolk); eld da of Sir Charles Edward Ponsonby, 1 Bt, TD, DL (d 1976), sometime MP for Sevenoaks (gs of 1 Baron De Mauley), and Hon Winifred Gibbs, JP, eld da of 1 Baron Hunsdon; *b* 3 June 1913; *m* 15 Jan 1936, Sir Edmund Castell Bacon, 13 and 14 Bt, KG, KBE, TD, JP (Lord Lieut of Norfolk 1949–78, d 1982); 1 s (Nicholas Hickman Ponsonby, 14 and 15 Bt), 4 da (Mrs John Bruce (d 1994), Mrs Stephen Gibbs, Mrs Ronald Hoare, Lady Nicholson); *Career* Queen Elizabeth II Coronation Medal; *Publications* contributed article on Raveningham Hall gardens to New Englishwoman Gardener (1987); *Style*— Priscilla, Lady Bacon, DL; ✉ Orchards Raveningham, Norfolk NR14 6NS (☎ 01508 548322)

BACON, Sir Sidney Charles; kt (1977), CB (1971); s of Charles Bacon; *b* 11 Feb 1919; *Educ* Woolwich Poly, Univ of London (BSc Eng); *Career* Mil Serv 1943–48, Capt REME, Royal Arsenal Woolwich 1933–58, regnl supt of inspection N Midlands 1958–60; Royal Ordnance Factories: asst dir Nottingham 1960–61, dir Leeds 1961–62, dir Woolwich 1962–63, idc 1964, dir Birtley 1965, dir Weapons and Fighting Vehicles 1965–66, dep controller 1966–69, controller 1969–72, md 1972–79, dep chm Bd 1972–79; dir Short Brothers Ltd 1980–89; memb Cncl City and Guilds of London Inst 1983–91, pres IProdE 1979; FEng 1979, FIMechE, FIEE; Hon FCGI; *Style*— Sir Sidney Bacon, CB, FEng; ✉ 228 Erith Rd, Bexleyheath, Kent DA7 6HP

BACON, Timothy Roger; s of Christopher Henry Bacon (d 1956), and Diana Sybil, *née* Richmond Brown (d 1995); *b* 4 Dec 1947; *Educ* Eton, Univ of Bristol (BSc); *m* 14 Sept 1985, Marylyn Rowan Ogilvie, da of William Arthur Grant; 2 da (Rosalind Sarah b 12 Jan 1987, Laura Charlotte b 11 July 1988); *Career* Brown Shipley & Co Ltd 1970–92 (dir 1988–92), dir Colville Estate Ltd 1976–, conslt Columbus Asset Management Ltd 1992–; memb Inst of Bankers; *Recreations* opera, theatre, travel; *Clubs* City University, Pratt's; *Style*— Timothy Bacon, Esq; ✉ 67 Britannia Rd, London SW6 2JR (☎ 0171 731 0408)

BACQUIER, Gabriel; *Educ* Paris Conservatoire (first prize for singing 1950); *Career* baritone; international debut as Figaro in The Barber of Seville at Théâtre Royal de la Monnaie Brussels 1953, joined Vienna Staatsoper 1960; has appeared at numerous international venues incl: Royal Opera House Covent Garden, La Scala Milan, Paris Opera, Met Opera NY, Lyric Opera Chicago, Geneva Opera; *Roles* incl: Scarpia in Tosca 1960, title role in Don Giovanni (Aix-en-Provence Festival) 1960, I Puritani (Royal Opera House Covent Garden debut) 1964, The King in The Love for Three Oranges (Aix-en-Provence Festival) 1989, title role in Don Pasquale (Aix-en-Provence Festival) 1990, Dr Bartolo in The Barber of Seville (Royal Opera House Covent Garden) 1993, title role in Falstaff, Iago in Otello, Don Alfonso in Cosi fan Tutte, Doctor Bartolo in The Marriage of Figaro, title role in Boris Godunov; *Recordings* numerous incl: Don Giovanni, Le Nozze di Figaro, Guillaume Tell, Les Contes d'Hoffman; *Style*— Gabriel Bacquier, Esq; ✉ c/o Marks Management Ltd, 14 New Burlington Street, London W1X 1FF (☎ 0171 494 2404, fax 0171 494 1380)

BADAWI, Zeinab Mohammed-Khair; da of Mohammed-Khair El Badawi, of Southgate, London N14, and Asia Mohammed, *née* Malik; *b* 3 Oct 1959; *Educ* Hornsey Sch for Girls, St Hilda's College Oxford (BA), Univ of London (MA); *partner* David Crook; 1 s (Joseph Badawi-Crook b 1994), 1 da (Sophia Badawi-Crook b 1996); *Career* presenter and journalist in current affairs and documentaries Yorkshire TV 1982–86, current affairs reporter BBC TV 1987–88, newscaster and journalist ITN (Channel Four News) 1988–; memb NUJ; *Recreations* languages, piano, cinema, music, reading; *Style*— Miss Zeinab Badawi; ✉ ITN, 200 Gray's Inn Road, London WC1X 8XZ (☎ 0171 833 3000)

BADCOCK, Maj-Gen John Michael Watson; CB (1976), MBE (1969), DL (Kent 1980); s of late R D Badcock, MC, JP; *b* 10 Nov 1922; *Educ* Sherborne, Worcester Coll Oxford; *m* 1948, Gillian Pauline, *née* Attfield; 1 s, 2 da; *Career* enlisted in ranks (Army) 1941, cmmnd RCS 1942, served UK, BAOR and Ceylon 1945–47, served UK, Persian Gulf, BAOR and Cyprus 1947–68, cdr 2 Inf Bde and dep constable Dover Castle 1968–71, dep mil sec 1971–72, manning dir (Army) 1972–74, defence advsr and head Br Defence Liaison Staff Canberra 1974–77, ret; Col Cmdt RCS 1974–80 and 1982–90, Master of Signals 1982–90, Hon Col 31 (London) Signal Regt (Vol) 1978–83, chm SE TA & VRA 1979–85; chief appeals offr Cancer Res Campaign 1978–82, chm S W Mount & Sons 1982–86; *Recreations* shooting, fishing, watching rugby, football, cricket and hockey; *Style*— Maj-Gen John Badcock, CB, MBE, DL; ✉ c/o RHQ Royal Signals, Blandford Camp, Dorset DT11 8RH

BADDELEY, Prof Alan David; *b* 23 March 1934; *Educ* Cockburn HS Leeds, UCL (BA), Princeton Univ (MA), Univ of Cambridge (PhD); *m* 1964, Hilary Ann White; 3 s; *Career* memb scientific staff MRC Applied Psychology Unit Cambridge 1958–67, lectr then reader Univ of Sussex 1967–72, prof of psychology Univ of Stirling 1972–74, dir MRC Applied Psychology Unit Cambridge 1974–96, sr res fell Churchill Coll Cambridge 1987–95; prof of psychology Univ of Bristol 1995–; hon prof of cognitive psychology Univ of Cambridge 1991–95; memb: Advsy Ctee Age and Cognitive Performance Res Centre, Advsy Ctee to the MRC Nat Survey of Health and Devpt, Scientific Ctee Amnesia Assoc, ESRC Psychology Ctee 1979–81, Advsy Cncl Int Assoc for the Study of Attention and Performance; chm MRC Neurosciences Bd 1987–89 (memb 1981–85); memb Editorial Bds: Applied Cognitive Psychology (special editorial advsr), Cognition and Emotion, Consciousness and Cognition, Essays in Cognitive Psychology, European Jl of Cognitive Psychology, Learning and Individual Differences, Learning and Memory, Neuropsychological Rehabilitation; President's Award British Psychological Soc 1982 (Myers lectr 1980); pres: Experimental Psychology Soc 1984–86 (Bartlett lectr 1988), Euro Soc for Cognitive Psychology 1986–90; hon foreign memb American Acad of Arts and Scis 1996; Hon DPhil Umeå Univ Sweden 1991, Hon DUniv Stirling 1996; Hon FBPsS 1995, FRS 1993; *Books* The Psychology of Memory (1976), Your Memory: A User's Guide (1982, 2 edn 1993), Working Memory (1986), Human Memory: Theory and Practice (1990), Working Memory and Language (with S Gathercole, 1993); jt ed: Attention and Performance IX (1981), Research Directions in Cognitive Science: A European Perspective - Vol 1: Cognitive Psychology (1989), Human Factors in Hazardous Situations (1990), Attention: Selection, Awareness and Control - A Tribute to Donald Broadbent (1993), Handbook of Mermory Disorders (1995); *Style*— Professor Alan Baddeley, FRS; ✉ Department of Psychology, University of Bristol, 8 Woodland Road, Bristol BS8 1TN (☎ 0117 928 8541, fax 0117 928 8562)

BADDELEY, Sir John Wolsey Beresford; 4 Bt (UK 1922), of Lakefield, Parish of St Mary Stoke Newington, Co London; s of Sir John Beresford Baddeley, 3 Bt (d 1979), and Nancy Winifred, *née* Wolsey; *b* 27 Jan 1938; *Educ* Bradfield Coll Berks; *m* 1962 (m dis 1992), Sara Rosalind, da of late Colin Crofts, of Scarborough; 3 da (Sara Alexandra (Mrs Andrew Turner) b 1964, Anna Victoria (Mrs Brian A Chambers) b 1965, Emma Elisabeth b 1972); *Heir* kinsman, Mark David Baddeley b 12 May 1921; *Career* FCA (ACA 1961); *Recreations* inland waterways, destructive gardening; *Style*— Sir John Baddeley, Bt; ✉ Springwood, Sandgate Lane, Storrington, Sussex (☎ 01903 743054)

BADDELEY, Mark David; s of late Mark Baddeley (d 1930), gs of Sir John Baddeley, 1 Bt, and hp of kinsman Sir John Wolsey Baddeley, 4 Bt; *b* 12 May 1921; *Educ* Cliftonville Coll; *Style*— Mark Baddeley, Esq; ✉ 22 Woodberry, George V Avenue, Margate, Kent CT9 5PX

BADDELEY, Ven Martin James; *b* 10 Nov 1936; *Educ* Keble Coll Oxford (MA), Lincoln Theol Coll; *m* 10 July 1963, Judith Clare, da of Rev R J W Hill; 2 s (Andrew b 23 May 1964, David b 30 Aug 1966), 1 da (Margaret b 28 Jan 1971); *Career* asst curate St Matthew Stretford 1962–65, staff memb Lincoln Theol Coll 1965–69, chaplain Fitzwilliam Coll and New Hall Cambridge 1969–74 (fell Fitzwilliam Coll 1972–74), residentiary canon Rochester Cathedral 1974–80, princ Southwark Ordination Course 1980–94, jt princ SE Inst for Theol Educn 1994–96, archdeacon of Reigate 1996–; *Style*— The Ven the Archdeacon of Reigate; ✉ St Matthew's House, 100 George Street, Croydon CR0 1PE (☎ 0181 681 5496)

BADDELEY, Brig Robert John; s of Lt-Col Robert John Halkett Baddeley, MC (d 1954), and Hilda Maitland Dougall, *née* Wardle (d 1989); *b* 2 July 1934; *Educ* Wellington, RMA Sandhurst; *m* Susan Marian, da of Edwin Colin Neale Edwards, of Eton Coll, Windsor; 2 da (Charlotte b 1965, Emma b 1968); *Career* cmmnd 4/7 Royal Dragoon Gds, ADC Chief of Defence Staff Ghana UN Congo 1960, HQ Malta and Libya 1966, CO 4/7 Royal Dragoon Gds, directing staff Staff Coll Camberley 1976, Def Attaché Tehran 1978, dep dir Army Recruiting 1980, Cdr Br Military Advsy Team Bangladesh 1983, dir of Army Trg 1987, ADC to HM the Queen 1988–89, Col 4/7 Royal Dragoon Gds 1988–92; cncllr Wilts CC 1989– (chm Planning & Environment 1992–94); chm Wilts BFSS; memb Royal Soc of Asian Affrs; Freeman City of London, Liveryman Worshipful Co of Coachmakers and Coach Harness Makers; FRGS; *Clubs* Cavalry and Guards'; *Style*— Brig R J Baddeley; ✉ Hazeldon House, Tisbury, Wilts SP3 6RD (☎ and fax 01747 870867)

BADDELEY, Stephen John; s of William Baddeley, and Barbara Isabel; *b* 28 March 1961; *Educ* Chelsea Coll Univ of London (BSc); *m* 16 June 1984, Deirdre Ilene, *née* Sharman; 1 s (James Scott William b 25 Jan 1991), 1 da (Selene Sharman b 16 April 1993); *Career* former badminton player; Eng nat singles champion 1981, 1985 and 1987, Eng nat men's doubles champion 1985, 1987 and 1989; Euro singles champion 1990; Cwlth Games: Gold medal team event 1982, 1986 and 1990, Gold medal singles 1986; winner men's singles: Indian Open 1985, Scottish Open 1986; represented Europe v Asia 1983, 1984 and 1986; 143 caps for Eng; hon memb Badminton Writers' Assoc, memb and chair Eng Badminton Players' Assoc 1989–90, chm World Badminton Players' Fedn 1989–90, ret as player 1990; dir of coaching and devpt Scottish Badminton Union 1990–92, mangr Br Olympic Badminton Team 1990–92, coach Nat Centre de Badminton Lausanne (asst nat Swiss coach) 1992–96, dir of tournament World Badminton Championships Lausanne 1995, dir Elite Play and Nat Coaching Policy Badminton Assoc of England Ltd 1996–; *Books* Badminton In Action (1988), Go and Play Badminton (1992); *Recreations* golf, sailing; *Style*— Stephen Baddeley, Esq; ✉ National Badminton Centre, Bradwell Road, Loughton Lodge, Milton Keynes MK8 9LA (☎ 01908 568822, fax 01908 566922)

BADDILEY, Prof Sir James; kt (1977); s of late James Baddiley, and Ivy Logan Cato; *b* 15 May 1918; *Educ* Manchester GS, Univ of Manchester (BSc, PhD, DSc), Univ of Cambridge (ScD); *m* 1944, Hazel, yr da of Wesley Wilfrid Townsend; 1 s; *Career* ICI fell Univ of Cambridge 1945–49, Swedish MRC fell Wenner-Grens Inst for Cell Biology Stockholm 1947–49, memb of staff Dept of Biochemistry Lister Inst of Preventive Med London 1949–54, Rockefeller fellowship Harvard Med Sch (Mass Gen Hosp) 1954, prof of organic chemistry King's Coll Univ of Durham 1954–77 (later Univ of Newcastle upon Tyne), Karl Folkers visiting prof of biochemistry Univ of Illinois 1962, head Sch of Chemistry Univ of Newcastle upon Tyne 1968–78, prof of chemical microbiology and dir Microbiological Chemistry Res Laboratory 1977–83 (now emeritus prof), SERC sr fell Dept of Biochemistry Univ of Cambridge 1981–83, fell Pembroke Coll Cambridge

1981 (now emeritus); vice pres Alzheimer's Res Tst; memb Advsy Ctee CIBA (later CIBA-Geigy) Fellowships 1966–88, tstee EPA Cephalosporin Fund 1979–; memb Cncl: Royal Soc 1977–79, SERC 1979–81; hon memb American Soc of Biochemistry and Molecular Biology; Meldola medal Royal Inst of Chemistry 1947, Corday-Morgan medal Chem Soc 1952 (Tilden lectr 1959, Pedler lectr 1980); Hon DSc: Heriot-Watt Univ 1979, Univ of Bath 1986; FRS 1961 (Leeuwenhoek lectr 1967, Davy medal 1974), FRSE 1962; *Publications* numerous pubns on coenzymes, structure of COA, bacterial cell walls and membranes and dicovery of teichoic acids in jls incl: Journal of the Chemical Society, Nature, Biochemical Journal; articles in various microbiological and biochemical reviews; *Recreations* swimming, mountaineering, photography, music, fine arts; *Style*— Prof Sir James Baddiley, FRSE, FRS; ✉ Hill Top Cottage, Hildersham, Cambridge CB1 6DA (☎ 01223 893055); Dept of Biochemistry, Univ of Cambridge, Tennis Court Rd, Cambridge CB2 1QW (☎ 01223 333600)

BADEL, Sarah; da of Alan Badel (d 1982), of Chichester, West Sussex, and Yvonne, *née* Owen (d 1990); *b* 30 March 1943; *Educ* Poles Convent Sch Herts, Royal Acad of Dramatic Art; *Career* actress; *Theatre* incl: Ellie Dunn in Heartbreak House, Raina in Arms and the Man, Solveig in Peer Gynt, Varya in The Cherry Orchard, Mrs Crawford in The Right Honourable Gentleman, Vivie Warren in Mrs Warren's Profession (NT), (created role of) Rachel in The Black Prince (Aldwych Theatre) 1989, Mme Arbeziat in Tovarich 1991; *Television* incl: Flora Poste in Cold Comfort Farm, Katharine in The Taming of the Shrew, Goneril in King Lear, Lizzy Eustace in The Pallisers, Alice in Dear Brutus, Olwen in Dangerous Corner, Joy/Hilary in Small World, Babs in The Irish RM, The Baroness Weber in A Perfect Spy, Angela in The Cloning of Joanna May, Lady Julia Fish in Heavy Weather, Rachel in The Tenant of Wildfell Hall; TV appearances: Casualty, Cadfael, Poirot; *Films* incl: The Shooting Party, Not Without My Daughter, Sally Seton in Mrs Dalloway; *Radio* incl: Anna Karenina, Becky Sharp in Vanity Fair, Sister Jeanne in The Devils, Caesar and Cleopatra, Vinnie in Mourning Becomes Electra; *Awards* Best Actress for Josie in A Moon for the Misbegotten 1978; *Recreations* cooking; *Style*— Miss Sarah Badel; ✉ c/o Peters Fraser & Dunlop Ltd, 503 The Chambers, Chelsea Harbour, Lots Road, London SW10 0XF (☎ 0171 344 1010, fax 0171 352 7356)

BADEN, (Edwin) John; s of Percy Baden (d 1972), of Parkstone, Dorset, and Jacoba Geertruij, *née* de Blank; *b* 18 Aug 1928; *Educ* Winchester, Corpus Christi Coll Cambridge (MA); *m* 6 Sept 1952, Christine Irene, da of Edward Miall Grose (d 1973), of Farm View, Laughton, Sussex; 2 s (Peter b 1954, David b 1959), 3 da (Ann b 1956, Susan b 1958, Zoë b 1962); *Career* RA and RHA 1947–48, cmmnd 2 Lt, served Eng, Palestine and Tripolitania; audit clerk Deloitte Haskins & Sells London 1951–54, sec and dir H Parrot & Co Ltd London 1954–61, fin advsr C & A Modes Ltd London 1961–63, dir Samuel Montagu & Co Ltd London 1963–78, chm Midland Montagu Industrial Finance 1975–78, md and chief exec Italian International Bank plc 1978–89; Girobank plc: dir 1987–, dep chm 1989–90 and 1996–, chief exec 1989–91, md 1990–91, chm 1995–96; sec gen Eurogiro (formerly Post/Giro Directors' Gp) 1993– (chm 1990–92); non-exec dir Alliance & Leicester Building Society (following purchase of Girobank) 1991– (exec dir 1990–91); memb Mgmnt Ctee (from inception) Pan European Property Unit Tst London 1973–, chm N American Property Unit Tst London 1980–93 (memb Mgmnt Ctee from inception 1975); tstee Int Centre for Res in Accounting Univ of Lancaster 1975–95; ICAS: memb Res Ctee 1966–74, 1985–88 and 1991–95, memb Cncl 1984–90, memb Fin Reporting Review Panel 1990–95; memb Payment Systems Tech Devpt Gp EU 1993–; chm Drascombe Assoc 1987–94; Freeman City of London 1987, Liveryman Worshipful Co of Information Technologists 1992; MICAS 1954, memb Inst of Taxation 1954; FRSA, CIMgt, FCIB; Cavaliere Ufficiale (Order of Merit of the Italian Republic) 1986; *Publications* Making Corporate Reports Valuable (jtly, 1988), Post Giro Banking in Europe (jtly, 1993), Auditing into the 21st Century (jtly, 1993), Internal Control and Financial Reporting (jtly, 1994); and numerous articles in professional magazines; *Recreations* sailing, shooting, reading; *Style*— John Baden, Esq; ✉ Lanaways Barn, Two Mile Ash, Horsham, West Sussex RH13 7LA (☎ 01403 733834, fax 01403 732860); Alliance & Leicester Building Society/Girobank plc, 49 Park Lane, London W1Y 4EQ (☎ 0171 629 5552, fax 0171 396 6466)

BADEN HELLARD, Ronald; s of Ernest Baden Hellard (d 1975), of Longfield, Kent, and Alice May, *née* Banks (d 1980); *b* 30 Jan 1927; *Educ* Liskeard GS, The Poly Sch of Architecture (Univ of Westminster) (DipArch), Loughborough Tech Coll (now Loughborough Univ of Technol); *m* 16 Dec 1950, Kay Peggy, *née* Fiddes; 2 da (Sally b 1953, Diana Jacqueline b 1956); *Career* WWII Duke of Cornwall's LI 1945–48, Capt GHQ MELF 1947–48; fndr ptnr: Polycon Group 1952–, Polycon Building Industrial Consultants 1955–; chm Polycon AIMS Ltd 1984–, chief exec TQM/Polycon 1988–; architect of various industl and commerical bldgs incl Oxford Air Trg Sch at Kidlington; first chm Mgmnt Ctee RIBA 1956–64, developed a number of mgmnt techniques which are now standard mgmnt practice in construction indust; pres S London Soc of Architects 1967–69; Br Inst of Mgmnt: chm SE London Branch 1969–72, chm SE Region 1972–76, memb Nat Cncl 1971–77; cncl memb CIArb 1970–84 (actg sec 1973); Freeman City of London 1981, Liveryman Worshipful Co of Arbitrators 1981; FCIArb 1952, FRIBA 1955, FIMgt 1966, FAQMC 1992; *Books* Management in Architectural Practice (1964), Metric Management Action Plan (1971), Training for Change (1972), Construction Quality Coordinators Guide (1987), Managing Construction Conflict (1988), Management Auditing in Construction (1990), Total Quality in Construction Projects (1993), Project Partnering: Principle and Practice (1995); *Recreations* tennis, travel; *Style*— Ronald Baden Hellard, Esq; ✉ 97 Vanbrugh Park, Blackheath, London SE3 (☎ 0181 853 2006); Polycon Group, 70 Greenwich High Rd, London SE10 (☎ 0181 691 7425, fax 0181 692 9453)

BADEN-POWELL, Hon (David) Michael; s of 2 Baron Baden-Powell (d 1962); hp of bro, 3 Baron Baden-Powell, *qv*; *b* 11 Dec 1940; *Educ* Pierrepont House; *m* 1966, Joan, da of late Horace Berryman, of Melbourne; 3 s; *Career* insurance consultant, agent with Australian Mutual Provident Soc 1972–; Freeman City of London, memb Worshipful Co of Mercers; *Style*— The Hon Michael Baden-Powell; ✉ 18 Kalang Rd, Camberwell, Vic 3124, Australia (☎ 00 61 39 889 5009, fax 00 61 39 889 1818)

BADEN-POWELL, Baroness; Patience Hélène Mary; CBE (1986); da of Maj Douglas Batty (d 1982), of Zimbabwe; *b* 27 Oct 1936; *Educ* St Peter's Diocesan Sch Bulawayo; *m* 1963, 3 Baron Baden-Powell, *qv*; *Career* Girl Guides Assoc: cmmr 1970–79, chief cmmr 1980–85, vice pres 1990–; pres: Cwlth Youth Exchange Cncl 1982–85, National Playbus Assoc, Surrey Cncl for Voluntary Youth Servs 1986–; patron: Surrey Antiques Fair, Woodlarks Campsite Tst for the Disabled; tstee Painshill Park Tst; dir: Laurentian Financial Group plc 1984–94, Fieldguard Ltd; *Style*— The Rt Hon the Lady Baden-Powell, CBE; ✉ Clandon Manor Farm, Back Lane, East Clandon, Guildford, Surrey GU4 7SA (☎ 01483 224262)

BADEN-POWELL, 3 Baron (UK 1929); Sir Robert Crause Baden-Powell; 3 Bt (UK 1922); s of 2 Baron Baden-Powell (d 1962); *b* 15 Oct 1936; *Educ* Bryanston; *m* 1963, Patience (*see* Baden-Powell, Baroness); *Heir* bro, Hon (David) Michael Baden-Powell, *qv*; *Career* vice pres: Scout Assoc 1982– (chief scouts cmmr 1965–82), World Scout Fndn 1978–88; memb Cncl Scout Assoc 1965– (memb Ctee 1972–78), pres W Yorks Scout Cncl 1972–88; dir Boulton Building Soc 1972–88; chm: Quarter Horse Racing UK 1985–88, Br Quarter Horse Assoc 1989–90 (memb Cncl 1984–90); pres The Camping and Caravan Club 1992–; Liveryman Worshipful Co of Mercers; *Recreations* breeding racing Quarter Horses; *Style*— The Rt Hon the Lord Baden-Powell; ✉ Clandon Manor Farm, East Clandon, Guildford, Surrey GU4 7SA

BADENOCH, (Ian) James Forster; QC (1989); s of Sir John Badenoch (d 1996), and Anne Newnham, *née* Forster; *b* 24 July 1945; *Educ* Dragon Sch Oxford, Rugby, Magdalen Coll Oxford (MA); *m* Marie-Thérèse Victoria, da of Martin Hammond Cabourn Smith; 2 s (William James Cabourn b 30 Jan 1982, Rory Martin Cabourn b 3 Nov 1984), 1 da (Isabel Grace b 1 Jan 1980); *Career* called to the Bar Lincoln's Inn 1968, memb Inner Temple, recorder of the Crown Court 1987–; memb: The Harveian Soc of London, The Medico-Legal Soc; *Books* Medical Negligence (contrib, Butterworths 1990, 2 edn 1994); *Recreations* family, tennis, travel; *Style*— James Badenoch, Esq, QC; ✉ 1 Crown Office Row, Temple, London EC4Y 7HH (☎ 0171 797 7500, fax 0171 797 7550)

BADERMAN, Dr Howard; OBE (1996), JP (London, 1981); s of Maxwell Baderman (d 1988), and Esther, *née* Collier (d 1990); *b* 12 Nov 1934; *Educ* Ealing Co GS London, UCL (BSc), UCH Med Sch (MB BS); *m* 4 Sept 1970, Susan, da of Wallace Patten (d 1945); 2 s (Rupert b 1974, James b 1977), 1 da (Sophie b 1972); *Career* conslt physician accident and emergency med UCH London 1970–, hon sr clinical lectr Dept of Med Univ of London 1971–, sec and chm Specialist Advsy Ctee Accident and Emergency Med RCPS 1975–84, examiner RCS(Ed) 1982–, conslt memb Bloomsbury DHA 1985–89, conslt advsr accident and emergency med to CMO Dept of Health 1989–, advsr accident and emergency servs WHO, civilian conslt to Army in A&E med 1994–; coordinator accident servs: UK Egypt Health Agreement 1983–, UK USSR Health Agreement 1986–; memb: Bd Visitors HM Prisons Wandsworth and Holloway 1982–89, Ind Ctee supervision Telephone Info Servs 1986–94, Working Pty Child Sex Abuse Standing Med Advsy Ctee 1987–88, mission on Turkish-Bulgarian migration WHO 1989, Standing Ctee Br Paediatric Assoc on Child Abuse; sec Working Pty Prison Med Servs 1988–89; dep chm Inner London Family Proceedings Courts 1991–96; Wilfred Trotter medal surgery 1957, Fellowes Gold medal and Sir William Gower prize medal 1958, Sir Ernest Finch visiting prof Sch Med Univ of Sheffield 1981; Freeman City Corpus Christi Texas USA 1963; memb BAEM, fell UCL 1988, sci fell Zoological Soc of London; MRCS(Eng) 1959, FRCP(London) 1974 (LRCP 1959, MRCP 1967), FFAEM 1994; *Books* Admission of Patients to Hospital (1973), Management of Medical Emergencies (ed, 1978); *Recreations* European history, fell walking; *Style*— Dr Howard Baderman, OBE, JP; ✉ 21 Churchill Rd, London NW5 1AN (☎ 0171 267 4281); Banty Ghyll, Howgill, Cumbria LA10 5HZ; Accident Department, University College Hospital, London WC1E 6AU (☎ 0171 387 9300, fax 0171 380 9977)

BADGER, Prof Anthony John; s of Kenneth Badger (d 1979), of Bristol, and Iris Gwendoline, *née* Summerill; *b* 6 March 1947; *Educ* Cotham GS, Sidney Sussex Coll Cambridge (MA), Univ of Hull (PhD); *m* 28 June 1979, Ruth Catherine, da of Ronald Davis; 2 s (Nicholas b 22 Aug 1981, Christopher (twin)); *Career* Dept of History Univ of Newcastle: lectr 1971–81, sr lectr 1981–91, head of dept 1988–91, prof 1991; Paul Mellon prof of American history Univ of Cambridge 1992–; fell Sidney Sussex Coll Cambridge; *Books* Prosperity Road: The New Deal, North Carolina and Tobacco (1980), North Carolina and The New Deal (1981), The New Deal: The Depression Years 1933–1940 (1989); *Recreations* walking, supporting Bristol Rovers FC; *Style*— Prof Anthony J Badger; ✉ 15 Cabbage Moor, Great Shelford, Cambridge CB2 5NB (☎ 01223 844698); Sidney Sussex College, Cambridge CB2 3HU (☎ 01223 338876, fax 01223 338884)

BADHAM, Douglas George; CBE (1975), JP (Glamorgan 1962); s of late David Badham, JP; *b* 1 Dec 1914; *Educ* Leys Sch Cambridge; *m* 1939, Doreen Spencer Phillips; 2 da; *Career* CA 1937; exec dir: Powell Duffryn Group 1938–69, Pascoe Holdings 1983–88; chm: Powell Duffryn Wagon Co 1965–86, Hamell (West) Ltd 1968–, Economic Forestry Gp 1981–88 (dir 1978–88), T T Pascoe 1983–89, Minton Treharne and Davies 1960–84, Worldwide Travel (Wales) until 1985; dir: Align-rite Ltd 1985–88, T H Couch 1985–88, World Trade Centre Wales Ltd 1985–; High Sheriff of Mid Glamorgan 1976, HM Lt for Mid Glamorgan 1982–85, HM Lord Lt for Mid Glamorgan 1985–89 (DL 1975–82); memb: Welsh Cncl 1971–80, Wales and the Marches Telecommunications Bd 1973–80, Br Gas Corp 1974–84 (pt/t), Cncl UWIST 1975–80, BR (Western) Bd 1977–82, Welsh Devpt Agency 1978–84 (dep chm 1980–84); chm: Devpt Corp for Wales 1971–80 (memb 1965–83), Nat Health Serv Staff Cmmn 1972–75; KStJ 1991; *Recreations* forestry, trout breeding; *Clubs* Cardiff and County; *Style*— Douglas Badham, Esq, CBE, JP; ✉ Swyn-y-Coed, Watford Rd, Caerphilly, Mid Glamorgan CF8 1NE (☎ 01222 882094)

BADHAM, John; s of John William Badham, of Rotherham, Yorks (d 1978), and Wilhemina Frances, *née* Ratcliffe (d 1969); *b* 9 Dec 1934; *Educ* Mexborough GS, Univ of Sheffield (Dip Arch, ARIBA, Dip TP); *m* 11 Sept 1958, Penelope, da of Francis Henry Stokes, of Potters Bar, Herts; 2 da (Francesca b 1964, Imogen b 1964); *Career* architect; dir: Fitzroy Robinson Ltd 1972–, Edwards Stepan Assocs 1964–72, Sir John Burnet Tait & Ptnrs 1961–64, T P Bennett & Son 1959–61; Liveryman Worshipful Co of Chartered Architects; *Recreations* music, piano playing, skiing; *Clubs* Ski (GB); *Style*— John Badham, Esq; ✉ 23 Onslow Gardens, London N10 3JT (☎ 0181 883 2500); Fitzroy Robinson Ltd, 77 Portland Place, London W1 (☎ 0171 636 8033)

BADRAWY, Dr Galal Akasha; s of Akasha Badrawy (d 1985), of Cairo, and Sanya Ahmed; *b* 4 June 1946; *m* 1974, Sylvia Anne, da of Edward Hatcher; 1 s (Adam b 1977), 1 da (Sarah b 1980); *Career* house surgn Mansoura Univ Hosp Egypt 1970–71, house physician Dar El Saha Hosp Beirut Lebanon 1971; sr house offr: Accident Emergency & Orthopaedics Princess Margaret Hosp Swindon 1972, Geriatric Med Stratton St Margaret's Hosp Swindon 1972–73, Orthopaedic Surgery Co Hosp York 1973–74; registrar: Naburn & Bootham Park Hosps York 1974–78 (sr house offr 1974), Child and Adolescent Psychiatry Southfield & Fairfield Units York 1978–79, York & Community Psychiatry St Andrew Day Hosp 1979–80; conslt psychiatrist and head Psychiatry Dept Abdulla Fouad Hosp Dammam Saudi Arabia, clinical asst Maudsley & The Bethlem Royal Hosp/Inst of Psychiatry 1982, registrar in psychiatry Horsham and Crawley Gen Hosp 1982–83; locum conslt psychiatrist: Yorkshire RHA (with duties at St Mary's Hosp, Scarborough and Clifton Hosp, Scarborough Dist Hosp) 1983, Trent RHA (with duties at Rauceby Hosp Lincolnshire, Boston Gen Hosp, Skegness Gen Hosp) 1982–85, Ashford Gen Hosp Middx 1985–86; locum conslt: St Thomas' Hosp (based at Tooting, duties at Bec Hosp and Day Hosp Putney) 1986–87, Psychiatric Unit Basingstoke Hosp 1987, Abraham Cowley Unit St Peter's Hosp Chertsey 1987–88; locum conslt psychiatrist Wexham Park Hosp Slough 1988–90; in private practice Harley St 1983–, conslt psychiatrist Charter Nightingale Hosp Lisson Grove 1989– (med dir Arab Unit 1987–89); subject of interviews by Harpers and Queen, several Arabic newspapers and by BBC Arabic stations; hon memb American Psychiatric Assoc; memb: RCP, BMA; FRSM; *Recreations* golf; *Clubs* Wentworth, Les Ambassadeurs; *Style*— Dr Galal Badrawy; ✉ High Hedges, 31 London Rd, Camberley, Surrey GU15 3UQ (☎ 01276 22219); 121 Harley St, London W1N 1DH (☎ 0171 935 6875, fax 0171 224 0651)

BAELZ, Rev Peter Richard; s of Eberhard Baelz (d 1986), and Dora, *née* Focke (d 1970); *b* 27 July 1923; *Educ* Dulwich Coll, Christ's Coll Cambridge (MA, BD), Westcott House Cambridge, Univ of Oxford (DD); *m* 15 July 1950, Anne Thelma, da of Edward Cleall-Harding (d 1942); 3 s (Simon b 1951, Nicholas b 1955, Timothy b 1956); *Career* asst curate: Bournville Birmingham 1947–50, Sherborne Dorset 1950–52; asst chaplain Ripon Hall Oxford 1952–53, rector Wishaw Birmingham 1953–56, vicar Bournville Birmingham 1956–60, fell and dean Jesus Coll Cambridge 1960–72, univ lectr in divinity Univ of Cambridge 1966–72, canon of Christ Church and regius prof of moral and pastoral theology Univ of Oxford 1972–79, dean of Durham 1980–88 (dean emeritus 1988–); cncllr Llandrindod Wells Town Cncl 1995–; Hon DD Univ of Durham 1993, hon prof Univ of Wales Lampeter 1993–; OStJ; *Books* Prayer and Providence (1966), The Forgotten Dream (1974); *Recreations* walking and cycling; *Style*— The Rev Peter Baelz; ✉ 36 Brynteg, Llandrindod Wells, Powys LD1 5HB (☎ 01597 825404)

BAER, Sir Jack Mervyn Frank; kt (1997); yr s of late Frank Baer, and Alix Baer; *b* 29 Aug 1924; *Educ* Bryanston, Slade Sch of Fine Art, UCL; *m* 1, 1952 (m dis 1969), Jean (d 1973), only child of late L F St Clair; 1 da; m 2, 1970, Diana Downes Baillieu, da of Aubrey Clare Robinson; 2 step da; *Career* served RAF (Combined Ops) 1942–46; Hazlitt Gallery: joined as ptnr 1948, md 1957, chm 1960–82; md Hazlitt Gooden & Fox 1973–93; pres Fine Art Provident Inst 1972–75; chm: Fine Arts and Antiques Export Advsy Ctee to Dept of Trade 1971–73 (vice chm 1969–71), Soc of London Art Dealers 1977–80 (vice chm 1974–77); tstee Burlington Magazine 1991–; memb: Reviewing Ctee on the Export of Works of Art 1992–, Museums and Galleries Cmmn 1993–; *Publications* numerous exhibition catalogues and articles in various jls; *Recreations* drawing; *Clubs* Brooks's, Beefsteak; *Style*— Sir Jack Baer; ✉ 9 Phillimore Terrace, London W8 (☎ 0171 937 6899)

BAGGALEY, David Anthony; s of Geoffrey (d 1944), and Joan, *née* Shackleton (d 1969); *b* 9 Jan 1943; *Educ* Merchant Taylors', Portsmouth Poly (Dip Business Admin); *m* 1965, Betty; 1 s (Jason b 1969), 1 da (Sasha b 1970); *Career* dir fin and investment Girobank plc 1979–85, fin dir Abbey Life Group plc 1985–88, dep md Lloyds Bowmaker Finance Ltd 1989–; FCMA, FCT; *Recreations* sailing, mountaineering; *Clubs* Fell and Rock Climbing, David LLoyd; *Style*— David Baggaley, Esq; ✉ Broadwater, 37 Alyth Rd, Talbot Woods, Bournemouth, Dorset BH3 7DG; Lloyds Bowmaker Finance Ltd, Finance House, 51 Holdenhurst Road, Bournemouth BH8 8EP (☎ 01202 299777)

BAGGE, (Alfred) James Stephen; 2 s of Sir John Alfred Picton Bagge, 6 Bt, ED, DL (d 1990); *b* 7 Dec 1952; *Educ* Eton; *m* 10 Oct 1981, Victoria I, er da of Michael A Lyndon Skeggs, of Oakhall, Cornhill-on-Tweed, Northumberland; 1 da (Edwina Rose b 1985); *Career* Capt Blues and Royals, ADC to Govr S Australia 1975–77; barr 1979–93; ptnr Norton Rose Slrs; memb Hon Soc of Lincoln's Inn 1975–93, memb Law Soc; *Clubs* Boodle's; *Style*— James Bagge, Esq; ✉ 8 Egliston Mews, London SW15; Norton Rose, Kempson House, Camomile Street, London EC3A 7AN (☎ 0171 283 6000, fax 0171 283 6500)

BAGGE, Sir (John) Jeremy Picton; 7 Bt (UK 1867), of Stradsett Hall, Norfolk; DL (Norfolk 1996); s of Sir John Alfred Picton Bagge, 6 Bt, ED, DL (d 1990), and Elizabeth Helena (Lena), *née* Davies (d 1996); *b* 21 June 1945; *Educ* Eton; *m* 1979, Sarah Margaret Phipps, da of late Maj James Shelley Phipps Armstrong, Agent-Gen for Ontario; 2 s (Alfred James John b 1 July 1980, Albert Daniel Bracewell b 1 April 1985), 1 da (Alexandra Mary Pleasance b 26 Dec 1982); *Heir* s, Alfred James John Bagge b 1 July 1980; *Career* farmer; FCA; fin advsr to HIH The Crown Prince of Ethiopia 1969–70; chm: West Norfolk Enterprise Agency 1985–94, Norfolk RDC 1989–; Cncllr King's Lynn and West Norfolk Borough 1981–95 (chm Planning 1991–94); memb: Norfolk Ctee CLA 1986–, Ely Diocesan Synod 1994–; Freeman Worshipful Co of Haberdashers; Freeman City of London; FCA 1968; *Recreations* shooting, stalking, skiing, water skiing; *Clubs* Boodle's, Air Squadron, Allsorts; *Style*— Sir Jeremy Bagge, Bt, DL; ✉ Stradsett Hall, Stradsett, King's Lynn, Norfolk PE33 9HA (☎ 01366 347562); Stradsett Estate Office, Stradsett, King's Lynn PE33 9HA (☎ 01366 347642, fax 01366 347846)

BAGGE, Richard Anthony; s of Gordon Roy Bagge (d 1980), and Barbara Joan, *née* Sympson; *b* 5 Aug 1949; *Educ* Broad Green GS, Croydon Tech Coll, London Poly; *m* 1, 15 June 1974; 2 s (Jonathan Richard, Jeremy Edward); m 2, 31 August 1991, Kirsty Jane, da of Ian Somerled Macdonald, of The Coach House, Netherexe, Devon; 1 s (Rupert Richard Somerled), 1 da (Phoebe Elizabeth); *Career* Barclays Bank 1966–70, Northcote & Co 1970–75, dir INVESCO MIM 1975–92, dir White Square Communications 1993, assoc dir Newton Investment Management 1994–; FInstSMM; *Recreations* sailing, gardening, antiques, music, theatre; *Style*— Richard Bagge, Esq; ✉ Bridgeham Lodge, Smallfield, Surrey; Newton Investment Management Ltd, 71 Queen Victoria Street, London (☎ 0171 332 9000)

BAGGE, Thomas Philip (Tom); 3 s of Sir John Alfred Picton Bagge, 6 Bt, ED (d 1990); *b* 4 May 1955; *Educ* Eton, RMAS and RAC Cirencester; *Career* Capt Blues and Royals, ADC to Gen Cmdg 4 Armed Div 1977–78; land agent; ptnr Strutt & Parker; FRICS; *Style*— Tom Bagge, Esq; ✉ Hall Farm, Irnham, Grantham, Lincolnshire NG33 4JD (office ☎ 01476 565886, fax 01476 567291)

BAGNALL, Air Marshal Anthony John Crowther (Tony); CB (1994), OBE; *Educ* Stretford Grammar Sch, RAF Coll Cranwell; *m* Pamela; 3 c; *Career* cmmnd RAF 1967, sqdn pilot then weapons instr (Lightnings) 1967–75, promoted Sqdn Ldr 1975, flt cdr 1975–78, attended RAF Staff Coll 1978, staff duties MOD 1978–80, promoted Wing Cdr 1980, Wing Cdr Air Defence HQ Strike Cmd 1980–83, CO No 43 Sqdn then CO No 23 Sqdn (Phantoms) Falkland Is 1983–85, promoted Gp Capt 1985, Dir of Air Staff Briefing and Co-ordination 1985–87, CO RAF Leuchars 1987–91, promoted Air Cdre 1990, RCDS 1990, Dir of Air Force Staff Duties MOD 1990–92, promoted Air Vice-Marshal 1992, Asst Chief of Air Staff 1992–94, AOC No 11 Gp 1994–96, promoted Air Marshal 1996, Dep C-in-C Allied Forces Central Europe 1996–; *Recreations* fell walking, golf, bridge; *Style*— Air Marshal A J C Bagnall, CB, OBE; ✉ Deputy Commander-in-Chief, Headquarters Allied Forces Central Europe, BFPO 28, The Netherlands (☎ 00 31 45 5262610)

BAGNALL, John Keith; s of Alfred Studley Bagnall (d 1992), of Otley, West Yorks, and Margaret, *née* Kirkham (d 1983); *b* 30 Dec 1941; *Educ* Oundle; *m* 10 Oct 1964, Valerie, da of Leslie Moxon (d 1985); 1 s (Stephen b 1968), 1 da (Caroline b 1966); *Career* Alfred Bagnall & Sons Ltd: dir 1962, gp md 1972–; treas Keighley and Dist Trg Assoc 1966–70; memb Standing Ctee: Safety Health and Welfare 1976–79, Fin 1976–, Econ and Public Affrs Gp 1983–93; pres: Nat Fedn Painting and Decorating Contractors 1979–80, Fedn of Bldg Specialist Contractors 1983–84; chm Bldg Employers' Confedn 1992–93 (memb Nat Cncl 1978–85, vice pres 1986–90, dep chm 1991–92); FCA 1965, FIMgt 1972; *Recreations* tennis, chess; *Style*— John Bagnall, Esq; ✉ Dale Lodge, Gilstead Lane, Bingley, West Yorkshire BD16 3LN (☎ 01274 563867); Alfred Bagnall & Sons Ltd, 6 Manor Lane, Shipley, West Yorks BD18 3RD (☎ 01274 587227, fax 01274 530171)

BAGNALL, Kenneth Reginald; QC (England and Wales 1973, Hong Kong 1983); s of Reginald Bagnall, and Elizabeth Bagnall; *b* 26 Nov 1927; *Educ* King Edward VI Sch Birmingham, Univ of Birmingham (LLB, Yardley scholar); *m* 1, Margaret Edith Wall; 1 s, 1 da; m 2, Rosemary Hearn; 1 s, 1 da; *Career* served RAF, Pilot Offr 1947, Flt Lt 1948; called to the Bar Gray's Inn 1950, dep judge Crown Court 1975–83; chm The Hurstwood Timber Co 1972–79; Anglo-American Real Property Inst: co-fndr 1980, chm 1980–82, life govr 1983; memb Crafts Cncl 1982–84; co-fndr: Bagnall Gallery (operated by the Crafts Cncl) 1982, The New Law Publishing Co plc (chm 1991–); ed-in-chief New Property Cases 1986–; Freeman City of London 1972, Liveryman Barber Surgeons' Co 1972; MInstD; *Books* Guide to Business Tenancies (1956), Development Land Tax (with K Lewison, 1978), Judicial Review (1985); *Recreations* motoring, travel, yachting; *Clubs* Carlton, 1900; *Style*— Kenneth Bagnall, Esq, QC; ✉ Brookfield House, Pornall Rise, Wentworth, Surrey GU25 4JZ (☎ 01344 843696)

BAGNALL, Field Marshal Sir Nigel Thomas; GCB (1985, KCB 1980), CVO (1978), MC (1950, and Bar 1953); s of Lt-Col Harry Stephen Bagnall, and Marjory May Bagnall; *b* 10 Feb 1927; *Educ* Wellington; *m* 1959, Anna Caroline Church; 2 da (Emma, Sarah); *Career* joined Army 1945, cmmnd Green Howards 1946, 6 Airborne Div Palestine 1946–48, Malaya 1949–52, GSO1 (Intelligence) Borneo 1966–67, Cmd 4/7 Royal Dragoon Gds BAOR and NI 1967–69, Cmd RAC BAOR 1970–72, defence fell Balliol Coll Oxford 1972–73, sec COS Ctee MOD 1973–75, GOC 4 Div BAOR 1975–77, ACDS (Policy) MOD 1978–80, Cmd 1 (Br) Corps BAOR 1980–83, C-in-C BAOR and Cmd N Army Gp BAOR 1983–85, Chief of Gen Staff 1985–88, Col Cmdt RAC 1985–88, Col Cmdt Army Physical Trg Corps 1981–88, ADC Gen to HM The Queen 1985–88; co-pres Anglo-German Officers' Assoc 1991–; Commander's Cross of the Federal Republic of Germany 1994; hon fell Balliol Coll Oxford 1986; *Books* The Punic Wars (1991); *Recreations* reading, writing, walking, gardening, breeding ornamental ducks; *Clubs* Cavalry and Guards'; *Style*— Field Marshal Sir Nigel Bagnall, GCB, CVO, MC

BAGNALL, Peter Hill; DL (Oxon 1996); s of Reginald Stuart Bagnall (d 1974), and Mary Adelaide, *née* Hill (d 1993); *b* 8 Oct 1931; *Educ* Newcastle-under-Lyme Sch, St Catharine's Coll Cambridge (MA); *m* 1, 1955 (m dis 1979), Edith Ann, *née* Wood; 1 s (Miles), 1 da (Sarah) and 1 s decd; m 2, 1979, Diana Elizabeth, *née* Rayner; *Career* Nat Serv and TA cmmns N Staffs Regt; dir WH Smith & Sons Ltd 1968–88, dir and md WH Smith plc 1974–88, dep chm WH Smith Pension Trustees Ltd 1979–; chm Book Club Associates 1972–88; dir: Book Tokens 1975–, TSB/Trustcard 1986–89, Longman/Ladybird 1987–90, Blackwell Ltd 1988–95, British Museum Company 1988–; The Book Tst: dir 1986–93, chm 1989–91; dir Oxfordshire HA 1990–93; chm: Oxford Radcliffe NHS Tst 1993–, Oxford Brookes Univ 1993–; memb: Bd of Visitors HM Prison Oxford 1987–92, Visiting Ctee Open Univ 1988–92; *Recreations* fell walking, book collecting, travel, theatre; *Clubs* Garrick, Sloane; *Style*— Peter Bagnall, Esq, DL; ✉ Oxford Radcliffe Hospital NHS Trust, The John Radcliffe, Headley Way, Headington, Oxford OX3 9DU (☎ 01865 741741)

BAGOT, 9 Baron (GB 1780); Sir Heneage Charles Bagot; 14 Bt (E 1627); s of late Charles Frederick Heneage Bagot, ggs of 1 Baron; suc half-bro 1979; *b* 11 June 1914; *Educ* Harrow; *m* 1939, Muriel Patricia, da of late Maxwell James Moore Boyle; 1 s, 1 da; *Heir* s, Hon Shaun Bagot; *Career* late Maj 6th Queen Elizabeths' Own Gurkha Rifles; plantation interests in Sri Lanka; *Recreations* sailing, shooting, skiing; *Clubs* Alpine Ski, Himalayan; *Style*— The Rt Hon The Lord Bagot; ✉ 16 Barclay Road, London SW6; Tyn-y-Mynydd, nr Llithfaen, Gwynedd

BAGOT, Hon (Charles Hugh) Shaun; s and h of 9 Baron Bagot, *qv*; *b* 23 Feb 1944; *Educ* Abbotsholme; *m* 16 July 1986, Mrs Sally A Stone, da of D G Blunden, of Farnham, Surrey; 1 da (Grace Lorina Kitty b 17 Aug 1993); *Style*— The Hon Shaun Bagot; ✉ 16 Barclay Road, London SW6

BAGSHAWE, Prof Kenneth Dawson; CBE (1990); s of Capt Harry Bagshawe (d 1959), of Cliff House, Beesands, Devon, and Gladys, *née* Dawson (d 1983); *b* 17 Aug 1925; *Educ* Harrow County Sch, LSE, St Mary's Hosp Med Sch (MB BS, MD); *m* 1, 12 Dec 1946 (m dis 1976), Alice, da of Thomas Kelly (d 1924); 1 s (James b 26 April 1959), 1 da (Janita b 2 Mar 1956); m 2, 29 Jan 1977, Sylvia Dorothy Lawler (d 1996), da of Capt Fred Corben, MC (d 1969); *Career* Sub Lt RNVR 1943–46; jr med appts St Mary's Hosp London 1952–60, res fell Johns Hopkins Hosp Baltimore 1955–56, conslt physician Charing Cross Hosp 1963–75 (sr lectr in med 1961–63), prof of med oncology Charing Cross Hosp Med Sch 1975–90 (prof emeritus 1990); author of 300 papers on various aspects of cancer incl reverse role chemotherapy and generating cytotoxic agents at cancer sites; Cancer Research Campaign: chm Scientific Ctee 1983–88, chm Exec Ctee 1988–90, vice chm Bd 1988–; Hon DSc Univ of Bradford 1990; FRCOG 1979, FRCR 1984, FRCP 1969, FRS 1989; *Books* Choriocarcinoma (1969), Medical Oncology (1975); *Recreations* walking, photography, invention; *Clubs* Athenaeum; *Style*— Prof Kenneth Bagshawe, CBE, FRS; ✉ 115 George St, London W1H 5TA (☎ 0171 262 6033)

BAGULEY, Maurice Grant; s of Capt William Albert Baguley (d 1947), of Hounslow, Middx, and Phyllis Amy, *née* Laverne (d 1987); *b* 2 May 1926; *Educ* Spring Grove GS, Acton Tech Coll, Brighton Poly, City Univ (MSc); *m* 1, 20 Nov 1948, Ivy Ethel (d 1983), da of Reginald Arthur Coomber (d 1952), of Ashford, Middx; 1 da (Claire Susan b 1953); m 2, 19 Nov 1983, Julie Elizabeth, *née* Barker, wid of Alec John Shickle; *Career* structural draughtsman The Square Grip Co Ltd 1945–46, jr engr J H Coombs and Partners 1946–47, design engr Peter Lind & Co Ltd 1947–48, sr design engr Woodall Duckham 1948–53, ptnr Malcolm Glover and Partners 1953–62, fndr Maurice Baguley and Partners 1962, ret 1973, currently practising as Maurice Baguley Consultants; structural and civil engrg bldg control conslt: City of Westminster, Royal Borough of Kensington and Chelsea, London Borough of Hackney, Wandsworth Corp, Heathrow Airport; IStructE awards: Wallace Premium 1950, Husband Prize 1953, Andrews Prize 1953; FICE 1973, FIStructE 1953, FFB 1982; MAmerSCE 1974, MConsE 1960, FRSA 1994; *Recreations* sailing, cruising, pianoforte; *Clubs* RYA, Naval; *Style*— Maurice Baguley, Esq; ✉ The Barn, Ivy Mill Lane, Godstone, Surrey RH9 8NF (☎ 01883 724500, fax 01883 744719)

BAHCHELI, Tylan; s of Salih Bahcheli (d 1986), and Zehra, *née* Mustafa (d 1989); *b* 20 Aug 1943; *Educ* The English Sch Nicosia Cyprus, Westminster; *m* 18 March 1965, Marylin Ann, da of Eric Dudley Jenkins, of Downend, Bristol; 1 s (Simon George b 24 Dec 1966), 1 da (Tezel Jane b 19 Sept 1965); *Career* mktg exec T Bath and Co Ltd 1964–70; chm: Dudley Jenkins Associates Ltd 1984–88 (proprietor 1971–84), Dudley Jenkins Group plc 1988–; *Recreations* gardening, shooting, reading; *Clubs* Wig and Pen; *Style*— Tylan Bahcheli, Esq; ✉ 9 Rostrevor Rd, London SW6 (☎ 0171 731 2358); Telford House, Coaley, Nr Dursley, Glos (☎ 01453 860230); Dudley Jenkins Group plc, 2A Southwark Bridge Office Village, Thrale Street, London SE1 9JG (☎ 0171 407 4753, fax 0171 407 6294)

BAHL, Kamlesh; da of Swinder Nath Bahl (d 1978), and Leela Wati, *née* Madan; *b* 28 May 1956; *Educ* Minchenden Sch Southgate, Univ of Birmingham (LLB); *m* 1986, Dr Nitin Nanji Lakhani; *Career* slr: GLC 1978–81, BSC 1981–84, Texaco Ltd 1984–87; Data Logic Ltd: legal and commercial mangr 1987–89, co sec and mangr Legal Servs 1989–93, legal conslt 1993–; chairwoman Equal Opportunities Cmmn 1993–; chm Commerce and Indust Gp Law Soc 1988–89; non exec memb: Barnet Health Authy 1989–90, Parkside Health Authy 1990–93; memb: Ethnic Minorities Advsy Ctee 1991–94, Judicial Studies Bd 1991–93, Justice Sub-ctee on Judiciary 1991–92, Cncl of Justice 1993–95, Cncl of Nat Assoc of Health Authys and Tsts 1993–94, Cncl Law Soc 1990–, EC Advsry Ctee on Equal Opportunities for Women and Men 1993–, Cncl of Justice 1993–95; independent memb No 1 Diplomatic Service Appeal Bd of Foreign and Cwlth Office 1993–; EC Rep EC Consultative Cmmn on Racism & Xenophobia 1994–; patron UN Year for Tolerance 1995; memb Cncl Scouts Assoc 1996–; FRSA 1993; *Books* Managing Legal Practice in Business (ed, 1989); *Recreations* swimming, dancing, travelling, theatre; *Style*— Kamlesh Bahl; ✉ Equal Opportunities Commission, Overseas House, Quay Street, Manchester M3 3HN (☎ 0161 838 8231, fax 0161 832 8816)

BAHRANI, Prof Aladdin Saleem; s of Saleem Bahrani (d 1986), and Bahija, *née* Shamma (d 1991); *b* 10 March 1930; *Educ* Baghdad Coll Iraq, Queen's Univ Belfast (BSc, MSc, PhD); *m* 1952, Margaret, *née* Sawrey; 1 s (David b 1964), 1 da (Linda b 1955); *Career* apprentice: Ruston and Hornsby Lincoln 1955–56, Metropolitan Vickers Manchester 1956–57; chief marine and mechanical engr Iraq Ports Admins Basrah 1959–63, sr pipeline engr Iraq Petroleum Company Kirkuk 1967–69, chief engr Iraq National Oil Company 1969–70; Queen's Univ of Belfast: lectr 1970–72, sr lectr 1972–77, reader 1977–83, prof of manufacturing engrg 1983–92, prof emeritus 1992; MIM 1967,

FWeldI 1976, FIMechE 1980, FEng 1989; *Recreations* gardening, listening to music, country walking; *Style*— Prof Aladdin Bahrani, FEng; ✉ 30 Circular Road, Belfast, Northern Ireland BT4 2GA (☎ 01232 768112)

BAIER, Frederick John Watt; s of Francis Clair Wolfgang Baier, of Birkenhead, and Violet, *née* Wood; *b* 15 April 1949; *Educ* Bootham Sch York, Hull GS Kingston upon Hull, Canterbury Coll of Art, Birmingham Coll of Art (DipAD Furniture), RCA (MA, fell); *m* 1988, Lucy Elizabeth Strachan, the sculptor, da of David Rankin Strachan (d 1979); 2 da (Billie Anna b 26 Jan 1989, Rebecca b 4 Feb 1990); *Career* furniture designer; in partnership with Barry Joseph Leister and Keith Clarke in Empire Workshops (architectural reclamation, interior schemes and prototype furniture) 1977–79; teaching: pt/t at Brighton Poly 1979–82, Wendell Castle Sch USA 1986–88, pt/t at RCA and Wiltshire Studio 1989–; consultancy work incl: Design Cncl, Crafts Cncl, A B K Architects, Terry Farrell, *qv*, David Davies; exhibitions incl: Furniture Designer Craftsman (RCA) 1977, New Faces (Br Crafts Centre London) 1978, Furniture into Sculpture (Ikon Gallery Birmingham) 1979, The Maker's Eye (Crafts Cncl London) 1982, The Furniture Fellow (solo, Northern Arts touring) 1983, Going for Baroque (Midland Gp Nottingham) 1985, British Design (COI/Kunstlerhaus Vienna) 1986, Keeping up with the Jones (Art and Architecture Gallery USA) 1987, 2D/3D, Art and Craft Made and Designed for the Twentieth Century (Laing Art Gallery Newcastle upon Tyne and Northern Centre for Contemporary Art Sunderland) 1987, New Traditions in British Design (Boymans Museum Rotterdam) 1989, Three Ways of Seeing (Crafts Cncl London and touring) 1990, Design '91 (Ishikawa Japan) 1991, 50 Years of Craft (Festival Hall) 1992, Visions of Craft (Crafts Cncl) 1993, British Studio Furniture (The Gallery Cork Street) 1994, Furniture Today (Craft Cncl touring) 1995; collections and cmmns incl: V & A Museum, Birmingham Museum and Art Gallery, Southern Arts, Crafts Cncl Gallery, Shipley Art Gallery, Templeton Coll Oxford, City of Leeds Museums, Carnegie Museum of Art Pittsburg Pa; awards: Royal Soc of Arts Bursary 1971, Major award Craft Advsy Ctee 1976, Minor award Midlands Arts 1978, Br Crafts award Telegraph Sunday Magazine 1978, Northern Arts Fellowship 1982–83, Craft Cncl Research award 1990; *Style*— Frederick Baier, Esq; ✉ 45 High St, Pewsey, Wiltshire SN9 5AF (☎ 01672 562974, fax 01672 563043)

BAILES, Alyson Judith Kirtley; da of John-Lloyd Bailes, and Barbara, *née* Martin; *b* 6 April 1949; *Educ* The Belvedere Sch GPDST Liverpool, Somerville Coll Oxford (MA); *Career* HM Dip Serv: FCO 1969–70, Budapest 1970–74, UK delgn to NATO 1974–76, MOD and FCO 1976–80, Bonn 1981–84, FCO 1984–87, cnsllr Peking 1987–89, on attachment to RIIA 1990, consul-gen and dep head of mission Oslo 1990–93, head Security Policy Dept FCO 1994–; *Recreations* travel, music, nature; *Style*— Miss Alyson Bailes; ✉ c/o Foreign & Commonwealth Office, King Charles St, London SW1A 2AH (☎ 0171 270 3000)

BAILEY, (Thomas) Alan; s of Thomas Dobson Bailey (d 1983), of Ryde, IOW, and Violet Vera, *née* Walker (d 1983); *b* 28 Oct 1928; *Educ* Maidstone; *m* 7 Aug 1950, Mary (d 1995), da of Maj Percy Baldock, IA (d 1973); 1 s (Kimball b 1957); *Career* Nat Serv 1946–49, TA 1949–64 (Capt Intelligence Corps); various local govt appts (incl asst clerk Brentwood DC) 1950–62, under sec RICS 1962–69, chief exec World of Property Housing Trust (now Sanctuary Housing Group) 1969–79, chm Focus Group of Cos 1969–79, md Andrews Group of Cos 1979–84, chm (and formerly md) ABS Group of Cos 1979–; chm Placemakers 1971–, non-exec dir Asset Corporation Ltd 1989–, chm Merchant International Group 1995–; former tstee Voluntary and Christian Serv and Phyllis Tst (later dir Help The Aged, Action Aid and other charities), dir Int Shakespeare Globe Centre 1981–90, tstee Cyril Wood Meml Tst 1980–91; visiting lectr Coll of Estate Mgmnt Univ of Reading; MCAM, MIPR, MCIM, MCIJ; *Books* How To Be A Property Developer (1988, 2 edn 1991), How to be an Estate Agent (1992), All Write (1993); *Recreations* drawing, painting, writing, walking; *Clubs* Special Forces, Wig & Pen; *Style*— Alan Bailey, Esq; ✉ The Bridge House, Sible Hedingham, Essex; 7 Bradbrook House, Studio Place, London SW1 (☎ 0171 235 3397); ABS Group of Companies, 14 Kinnerton Place South, Kinnerton St, London SW1X 8EL (☎ 0171 245 6262, fax 0171 235 3916)

BAILEY, Sir Brian Harry; kt (1983), OBE (1976), JP (Somerset 1964), DL (Somerset 1988); s of Harry Bailey, and Lilian, *née* Pulfer; *b* 25 March 1923; *Educ* Lowestoft GS; *m* 1948, Nina Olive Sylvia Saunders; 2 da; *Career* served RAF 1941–45; orgn offr SW District NALGO 1951–82, SW regnl sec TUC 1968–81; chm Television South West 1980–93; dir: Oracle Teletext Ltd 1983–94, Channel Four Television 1985–91 (dep chm 1989–91); memb: Somerset CC 1966–84, SW Econ Planning Cncl 1969–79, BBC West Regnl Advsy Cncl 1973–78, Advsy Ctee Severn DOE 1978–81, MRC 1978–86, Business Educn Cncl 1980–84, NHS Mgmnt Inquiry Team 1983–85; vice chm BBC Radio Br Advsy Cncl 1971–78; chm: SW RHA 1975–82, Health Educn Cncl 1983–87, ITVA Cncl 1991; pres Assoc of Commercial Television (Europe) 1991–92; dir Bournemouth Orchestras 1982–, tstee Euro Community Chamber Orchestra 1987–; SW regnl pres MENCAP 1984–90, chm Dartington Coll 1993–; *Recreations* watching sport, music, golf; *Clubs* Enmore Park Golf; *Style*— Sir Brian Bailey, OBE, JP, DL; ✉ 32 Stonegallows, Taunton, Somerset (☎ 01823 461265)

BAILEY, Christopher Bruce (Chris); s of Robert Malcolm Bailey, and Pamela Marion Bailey; *b* 29 April 1968; *Educ* Taverham HS, Norwich City Coll; *Career* former professional tennis player; Br under 12 champion 1980, formerly ranked Norfolk number 1 at under 12, under 14, under 16 and under 18, ranked Norfolk sr number 1 1980, 1982, 1984 and 1986, formerly ranked East Region number 1 at under 12, under 16 and under 18, ranked East Region sr number 1 1980, 1984 and 1986; memb and player Br Davis Cup Team 1987–89 and 1992–93; winner Central African Satellite, quarter-finalist Stella Artois Championships Queen's Club London, semi-finalist Livingstone NJ Grand Prix USA, winner French Satellite 1992, winner Bristol Challenger 1993 (semi-finalist 1991), ret due to injury 1994; currently tennis commentator BBC and commentator/presenter Sky TV; conslt Reebok UK; *Style*— Chris Bailey, Esq; ✉ 17A St Ann's Road, London SW13 9LH

BAILEY, Hon Christopher Russell; TD; only s and h of 4 Baron Glanusk; *b* 18 March 1942; *Educ* Eton, Clare Coll Cambridge (BA); *m* 1974, Frances Elizabeth, da of Air Chief Marshal Sir Douglas Charles Lowe, GCB, DFC, AFC, *qv*; 1 s (Charles Henry b 1976), 1 da (Rosemary Elizabeth b 1979); *Career* computer systems engr: English Electric 1964–66, Ferranti 1966–78; product mktg mangr Bestobell Mobrey Ltd 1978–83, sales engr (Defence Systems) STC Telecommunications Ltd 1984–86, gen mangr Lumenition 1986–; memb Chobham Parish Cncl 1987–; TA: Lt 7 Bn Cheshire Regt 1964–67, Capt 94 (Berks Yeo) Signals Sqdn 1967–78, Capt 80 (Cheshire Yeo) Signals Sqdn 1978–80, Maj (HQ11) Signals Bde 1980–83; *Style*— The Hon Christopher Bailey, TD; ✉ 51 Chertsey Rd, Chobham, Surrey GU24 8PD (☎ 01276 85 6380)

BAILEY, Chief Constable Colin Frederick; QPM (1993); s of Fred Bailey (d 1994), of Tattershall, Lincs, and Mary Meletha, *née* Sivill; *b* 17 Oct 1943; *Educ* Queen Elizabeth GS Horncastle Lincs, Univ of Sheffield (LLB); *m* 17 Sept 1966, Christine, da of late Thomas Lound; 1 s (Nicholas b 9 Sept 1967), 1 da Louise (b 21 Dec 1969); *Career* Lincolnshire Constabulary: joined 1962, sgt 1967–71, inspr 1971–77, chief inspr 1977–81, detective supt and dep head Lincs CID 1981–83, chief supt and head Lincs CID 1983–86; asst chief constable Crime Operations W Yorks Police 1986–90, chief constable Nottinghamshire Constabulary 1995– (dep chief constable 1990–95); *Recreations* antiques (particularly porcelain, crested china, commemoratives), reading, gardening, walking, wildlife; *Style*— Chief Constable Colin Bailey, QPM; ✉ Nottinghamshire Constabulary HQ, Sherwood Lodge, Arnold, Nottingham NG5 8PP (☎ 0115 967 2005, fax 0115 967 2009)

BAILEY, David; s of William Bailey, and Agnes, *née* Green; *b* 2 Jan 1938; *m* 1, 1960, Rosemary Bramble; m 2, 1967 (m dis), Catherine Deneuve, the film actress; m 3, 1975 (m dis 1985), Marie Helvin, *qv*; m 4, 1986, Catherine Dyer; 1 s, 1 da; *Career* photographer; photographer for Vogue (British, American, Italian and French) 1959–, dir of commercials (over 500) 1966–, dir and prodr of TV documentaries 1968–71 (subjects include Beaton, Warhol and Visconti); memb Arts Cncl 1983–; FRPS, FSIAD, FRSA, FCSD; *Exhibitions* Nat Portrait Gallery 1971, V & A Museum (one man retrospective) 1983, Int Centre of Photography NY 1984, Photographs from the Sudan for Live Aid (ICA and tour) 1985, Bailey Now! (Royal Photographic Soc, Bath) 1989, Hamiltons Gallery London 1989 and 1992–, Fahey Klein Gallery LA 1990; *Awards* for commercials incl: The Golden Lion (Cannes), The Cleo (USA), American TV Award, D&AD Gold (London), EMMY Award (USA); *Books* Box of Pin-Ups (1964), Goodbye Baby and Amen (1969), Warhol (1974), Beady Mincers (1974), Papua New Guinea (1975), Mixed Moments (1976), Trouble and Strife (1980), David Bailey's London NW1 (1982), Black and White Memories (1983), Nudes 1981–84 (1984), Imagine (1985), If We Shadows (1991), The Lady is a Tramp (1995); *Recreations* photography, aviculture, travel, painting; *Style*— David Bailey, Esq; ✉ c/o RSA Films Ltd, 42–44 Beak Street, London W1R 3DA (☎ 0171 437 7426, fax 0171 734 4978)

BAILEY, Dennis; s of Leonard Charles Bailey, and Ethel Louise, *née* Funnell; *b* 20 Jan 1931; *Educ* West Tarring Secdy Mod Sch Worthing, W Sussex Sch of Art Worthing, RCA (ARCA, RCA travelling scholar); *m* 20 July 1985, Nicola Anne, da of John Roberts; 1 da (Catherine Anne b 6 May 1984), 1 s (Peter John Leonard b 23 Dec 1990); *Career* graphic designer and illustrator; asst ed Graphics Zürich 1956; art ed: Olympus Press Paris 1962–63, Town magazine London 1964–66; ptnr Bailey and Kenny 1988–; lectr in graphic design Chelsea Sch of Art London 1970–81; *Catalogues and Graphics for Exhibitions* incl: Pompeii AD 79 (Royal Acad) 1977, Dada and Surrealism Reviewed 1978, Picasso's Picassos 1981, Le Corbusier 1987 (Arts Cncl of GB, Hayward Gallery); other work incl: House Styles, Royal Soc of Arts, design of business print for NM Rothschilds, design of British Med Jl 1996, New Statesman 1996; RDI 1980; *Style*— Dennis Bailey, Esq; ✉ Bailey and Kenny, 102 Coppergate House, 16 Brune Street, London E1 7NS (☎ 0171 721 7705, fax 0171 721 7763)

BAILEY, Sir Derrick Thomas Louis; 3 Bt (UK 1919), of Cradock, Province of Cape of Good Hope, Union of South Africa; DFC; s of late Sir Abe Bailey, 1 Bt, KCMG; suc half-bro, Sir John Milner Bailey, 2 Bt (d 1946); *b* 15 Aug 1918; *Educ* Winchester, Ch Ch Oxford; *m* 1, 1946 (m dis), Katharine Nancy, da of Robin Stormonth Darling (d 1956), of Kelso, Scotland; 4 s (John Richard b 1947, Thomas Noel b 1948, William Abe b 1950, Patrick James b 1959), 1 da (Patricia Rosemary (Mrs Collins) b 1951); m 2, 1980 (m dis 1990), Mrs Jean Roscoe; *Heir* s, John Richard Bailey b 11 June 1947; *Career* Capt S African Air Force, formerly 2 Lt S African Irish; farmer; *Recreations* sports, games; *Clubs* Rand (Johannesburg); *Style*— Sir Derrick Bailey, Bt, DFC; ✉ Bluestones, Alderney, CI

BAILEY, Diane Jane; MBE (1988); da of William Howard Robb (d 1988), and Doris Elizabeth Robb; *b* 31 Aug 1943; *Educ* Bilston Girls HS; *m* 1, 13 Jan 1962, Alastair Frearson (d 1968), s of Raymond Frearson, of Skegness, Lincolnshire; 1 s (Karl b 1964), 1 da (Caroline b 1963); m 2, John Michael Bailey; 1 da (Abigail b 1975); *Career* golf player; Br Girl int 1957–61, Sr Girls' Open Stroke Play champion 1959 and 1961, Staffordshire champion 1961, Br Girls' champion 1961, finalist Br Ladies Championship 1961, Br int 1961, 1962, 1968 and 1972, Eng int 1961 and 1971, Midland champion 1966, Lincolnshire champion 1966 and 1967, memb World Cup Team 1968, Avia Foursomes Championship 1972; capt: Cwlth Team 1983, Br Team Vagliano 1983 and 1985, Curtis Cup Team 1984, 1986 and 1988 (memb 1962 and 1972), English Ladies Team Euro Team Championships 1991 and 1993; currently account mangr; *Recreations* motor cruising, fishing; *Clubs* Sussex Motor Yacht, Enville Golf, Reigate Heath Golf, Walton Heath Golf; *Style*— Mrs Diane Bailey, MBE; ✉ Clubhouse Developments Ltd, Hatchways House, Gomshall, Surrey GU5 9QF (☎ 01483 202001, fax 01483 202847)

BAILEY, Air Vice-Marshal Dudley Graham (Bill); CB (1979), CBE (1970); s of P J Bailey, and D M Bailey, *née* Taylor; *b* 12 Sept 1924; *m* 15 May 1948, Dorothy Barbara, *née* Lovelace-Hunt; 2 da (Deborah b 1956, Caroline b 1957); *Career* served RAF 1943–80; trained as pilot in Canada 1943–45, intelligence duties in Middle East 1946–48, Berlin Airlift No 47 Sqdn 1949, Adjutant 50 Sqdn and Flt Cdr 61 Sqdn (Lincolns) 1950–52, exchange duties with USAF 1952–54 (B36 Aircraft), Flt Cdr 58 Sqdn and OC 82 Sqdn (Canberras) 1955–56, Dept of Operational Requirements Air Miny 1957–58, Army Staff Coll Camberley 1959, OC 57 (Victors) Sqdn 1960–62, Wing Cdr Ops HQ Middle East Aden 1963–65, Staff of Chief of Def Staff 1965–66, dep dir Air Plans MOD 1966–68, OC RAF Wildenrath 1968–70, sr personnel staff offr HQ Strike Cmd 1970–71, RCDS 1972, dir of personnel (RAF) 1973–74, Sr Air Staff Offr RAF Germany 1974–75, Dep Cdr RAF Germany 1975–76, DG of Personal Services (RAF) MOD 1976–80, ret; dep md and co sec Services Sound and Vision Corp 1980–93; chm RAFA 1991–, vice chm of govrs Piper's Corner Sch 1991–; *Clubs* RAF; *Style*— Air Vice-Marshal Bill Bailey, CB, CBE; ✉ Firs Corner, Abbotswood, Speen, Princes Risborough, Bucks HP27 0SR (☎ 01494 488462)

BAILEY, George Henry Selborne; s of Dr Alison George Selborne Bailey, of High Wycombe, Bucks, and Christine, *née* Delfosse (d 1982); *b* 13 Aug 1953; *Educ* Radley, Downing Coll Cambridge (BA); *m* 8 Nov 1986, Allison Gail; 2 s (Henry George Selborne b 15 Jan 1989, Matthew John Selborne b 15 March 1991); *Career* md Sotheby's (dir 1979–); ARICS 1978; *Clubs* Leander; *Style*— George Bailey, Esq; ✉ Sotheby's, 34 New Bond St, London W1 (☎ 0171 493 8080)

BAILEY, Glenda Adrianne; da of John Ernest Bailey, and Constance, *née* Groome; *b* 16 Nov 1958; *Educ* Noel Baker Sch Derby, Kingston Poly (BA), Hon Dr 1995; *Career* fashion forecasting Design Direction 1983–84, prodr dummy magazine for IPC 1985; ed: Honey magazine 1986, Folio magazine 1987, marie claire magazine (UK) 1988–96, marie claire magazine (US) 1996–; Women's Magazine Ed of the Year award Br Soc of Magazine Eds 1989, Best Magazine award Periodical Publishers' Assoc 1991, Consumer Magazine of the Year Media Week Press Awards and Periodical Publishers Assoc 1991, Magazine of the Year award Media Week Awards 1992, Editor's Editor of the Year and Women's Magazine Editor of the Year British Soc of Magazine Editors 1992, Consumer Magazine of the Year Periodical Publishers Assoc 1993, Consumer Magazine of the Year IPC Annual Editorial Awards 1993, Best International Magazine and Best International Consumer Magazine IDP International Press Awards 1994; *Style*— Miss Glenda Bailey; ✉ c/o Marie Claire, 250W 55 Street, New York, NY 10019, USA

BAILEY, Ian Campbell; s of James Rowland Bailey (d 1979), and Hilda Maud, *née* Campbell (d 1958); *b* 5 Oct 1929; *Educ* St Andrew's Coll Dublin, Trinity Coll Dublin (BA, MB BCh, BAO, LM); *m* 18 June 1955, Ruth Kathleen, *née* Johnson; 2 s (Christopher b 1957, Michael b 1961), 1 da (Caroline b 1966); *Career* conslt neurological surgn and sr lectr Univ of E Africa Uganda, sr conslt neurological surgn Royal Victoria Hosp Belfast; FRCS, FRCSI; *Recreations* athletics, tennis, sailing; *Style*— Ian Bailey, Esq; ✉ The Blackstone House, Magheragall, Lisburn, Northern Ireland (☎ 01846 621 333); The Royal Victoria Hospital, Belfast (☎ 01232 240503)

BAILEY, Jack Arthur; s of Horace Arthur Bailey, and Elsie Winifred Bailey; *b* 22 June 1930; *Educ* Christ's Hosp, Univ Coll Oxford (BA); *m* 1, 1957, Julianne Mary Squier; 1 s,

2 da; m 2, 1991, Vivian Mary Robins; *Career* asst master Bedford Sch 1958–60, Reed Paper Group 1960–67; rugby football corr Sunday Telegraph 1962–74; sec: MCC 1974–87 (asst sec 1967–74), Int Cricket Conf 1974–87; reg contrib to The Times 1987–; *Publications* Conflicts in Cricket (1989), Trevor Bailey, a life in cricket (1993); *Recreations* cricket (played for Essex and Univ of Oxford), golf; *Clubs* Wig & Pen, MCC (hon life memb), Vincent's (Oxford); *Style—* Jack Bailey, Esq; ✉ Sports Desk, The Times, 1 Pennington Street, London E1 9XN (☎ 0171 782 5000, fax 0171 488 3242)

BAILEY, Rt Rev Jonathan Sansbury; *see:* Derby, Bishop of

BAILEY, Kim Charles; s of K Bailey, of Brackley, Northants, and Bridgett Anne, *née* Courage (d 1987); *b* 25 May 1953; *Educ* Radley; *m* 31 Oct 1983, Tracey Louise, da of Julian Sutton; *Career* racehorse trainer 1979–; major races won: Seagram Grand National (Mr Frisk), Whitbread Gold Cup (twice, Mr Frisk and Docklands Express 1991), SGB Chase (Man O Magic), Bollinger Chase (twice, Man O Magic and Kings Fountain), Golden Spurs Chase (Man O Magic), H & T Walker Chase (twice, Man O Magic and Kings Fountain), Scottish Champion Hurdle (Positive), BIC Razor Hurdle (Carnival Air), Anthony Mildway & Peter Cazalet Meml Handicap Chase (twice, Mr Frisk and Shifting Gold), Crown Paints Hurdle (Positive), Cheltenham Tote Gold Cup (Master Oats) 1995, Cheltenham Champion Hurdle (Alderbrook) 1995; *Recreations* shooting, cricket, tennis; *Style—* Kim Bailey, Esq

BAILEY, (Robert) Malcolm; s of Brian Bailey, of Holmfirth, Yorks, and Annie, *née* Hinchliffe; *b* 19 Dec 1950; *Educ* Holme Valley GS, Imperial Coll London (BSc); *m* 26 Aug 1972, Anne Elizabeth, da of late Thomas Edward Dawson; 2 da (Hannah Victoria b 19 Dec 1977, Ruth Mary b 18 Oct 1979), 1 s (Thomas Matthew b 20 June 1981); *Career* Price Waterhouse: joined 1972, qualified CA 1975, ptnr 1984–, nat dir of human resources Nat Exec 1993–, sr client ptnr, vice chm World Petroleum Industry Gp 1995–; ARCS, FCA 1980; *Style—* Malcolm Bailey, Esq; ✉ Price Waterhouse, Southwark Towers, 32 London Bridge Street, London SE1 9SY (☎ 0171 939 5757, fax 0171 939 4400)

BAILEY, (Christian) Martin; s of Dr Leslie Bailey, of Harpenden, Hertfordshire, and Marie Elisabeth, *née* Phillips; *b* 4 Aug 1949; *Educ* Aldwickbury Sch Harpenden Hertfordshire, St Albans Sch Hertfordshire, The Royal Free Hosp Sch of Med (BSc, MB BS, FRCS); *m* 24 April 1971, Dr Jane Nicola Rotha Bailey, da of John Stewart Barnfield; 1 s (Simon John Martin b 7 Aug 1975), 1 da (Laura Jane Susanna b 7 June 1978); *Career* past appts: The Royal Free Hosp London (house surgn, house physician, sr house offr), sr house offr in otolaryngology Royal Nat Throat Nose & Ear Hosp London, sr house offr in gen surgery The Royal Northern Hosp London, registrar then sr registrar in otolaryngology Royal Nat Throat Nose & Ear Hosp, sr registrar in otolaryngology Sussex Throat & Ear Hosp Brighton; TWJ Fndn clinical & research fell in otology & neuro-otology Univ of Michigan USA; conslt otolaryngologist Great Ormond Street Hospital for Children London and The Royal Nat Throat Nose & Ear Hosp London 1982–, hon conslt otolaryngologist St Luke's Hosp for the Clergy London 1984–; hon sr lectr: Inst of Laryngology & Otology London 1982–, Inst of Child Health 1985–; memb: BMA 1973, RSM 1976, Br Assoc of Otolaryngologists 1982; *Books* Ear Nose & Throat Nursing (jtly, 1986) Scott-Brown's Otolaryngology (contrib, 1987), Recent Advances in Otolaryngology (contrib, 1995), author of papers on various aspects of Paediatric Otolaryngology; *Recreations* fell walking, computers, cars; *Style—* Martin Bailey, Esq; ✉ 7 Heathgate, Hampstead Garden Suburb, London NW11 7AR (☎ 0181 455 8628, fax 0181 381 4292); 55 Harley St, London W1N 1DD (☎ 0171 580 2426, fax 0171 436 1645)

BAILEY, Norman Stanley; CBE (1977); s of Stanley Bailey (d 1986), and Agnes, *née* Gale; *b* 23 March 1933; *Educ* East Barnet GS Herts, Rhodes Univ SA (BMus), Vienna State Acad (Dip in Opera, Lieder, Oratorio); *m* 1, 21 Dec 1957 (m dis 1983), Doreen, da of late Leonard Simpson, of Kenya; 2 s (Brian Emeric b 1960, Richard Alan b 1967), 1 da (Catherine Noorah (Mrs Osbourne) b 1961); m 2, 25 July 1985, Kristine Ciesinski, *qv*, da of Roman Anthony Ciesinski, of Delaware, USA; *Career* operatic and concert baritone; princ baritone Sadler's Wells Opera 1967–71; prof of music RCM 1990–; regular engagements at world major opera houses and festivals incl: La Scala Milan, Royal Opera House Covent Garden, Bayreuth Wagner Festival, Vienna State Opera, Met Opera NY, Paris Opera, Edinburgh Festival, Hamburg State Opera, English Nat Opera; Schigolch in Berg's Lulu (BBC Proms) 1996; BBC TV performances: Falstaff, La Traviata, The Flying Dutchman, Macbeth; recordings incl: The Ring (Goodall), Meistersinger and Der Fliegende Holländer (Solti), Walküre (Klemperer); Hon DMus Rhodes Univ S Africa 1986; Hon RAM 1981; *Recreations* memb Baha'i world community, chess, notaphily, golf, microcomputing; *Style—* Norman Bailey, Esq, CBE; ✉ c/o Robert Gilder and Co, Enterprise House, 59–65 Upper Ground, London SE1 9PQ (☎ 0171 928 9008)

BAILEY, Paul; s of Arthur Oswald Bailey (d 1948), and Helen Maud, *née* Burgess (d 1984); *b* 16 Feb 1937; *Educ* Sir Walter St John's Sch London, Central Sch of Speech and Drama London; *Career* freelance writer and radio broadcaster; actor 1956–64, writer in residence Univ of Newcastle and Univ of Durham 1972–73, visiting lectr in Eng lit North Dakota State Univ 1976–79; frequent radio bdcaster (mainly Radio 3), writer and presenter progs on Karen Blixen, Henry Green, I B Singer and Primo Levi; winner: Somerset Maugham award 1968, E M Forster award 1973, George Orwell Memorial prize 1977; FRSL 1982–84; *Books* At The Jerusalem (1967), Trespasses (1970), A Distant Likeness (1973), Peter Smart's Confessions (1977), Old Soldiers (1980), An English Madam (1982), Gabriel's Lament (1986), An Immaculate Mistake (autobiog, 1990), Sugar Cane (1993), Oxford Book of London (ed, 1995); *Recreations* visiting churches, opera, watching tennis; *Style—* Paul Bailey, Esq; ✉ 79 Davisville Road, London W12 9SH (☎ 0181 749 2279, ☎ and fax 0181 248 2127)

BAILEY, Sir Richard John; kt (1984), CBE (1977); s of Philip Bailey, and Doris Margaret, *née* Freebody; *b* 8 July 1923; *Educ* Newcastle and Shrewsbury; *m* Marcia Rachel Cureton Webb; 1 s, 3 da; *Career* served RN 1942–46, Lt (Destroyers); Doulton Fine China: joined 1950, tech dir 1955–63, md 1963–72; chm: Royal Doulton Ltd 1980–87 (md 1972–80), Royal Crown Derby Porcelain Co Ltd 1983–87, British Ceramic Research Ltd 1982–83 and 1987–90; dir Central Independent Television plc 1986–94; chm North Staffs Business Initiative 1981–91, dir West Midlands Industrial Development Assoc 1983–87; memb: Ceramics Indust Nat Jt Cncl 1961–84 (jt chm 1969–84), Ceramics Indust Trg Bd 1967–70, Cncl Keele Univ; pres: N Staffs Med Inst, Stoke-on-Trent Repertory Theatre, Br Ceramic Manufacturers Fedn 1973–74, Br Ceramic Soc 1980–81; Hon Freeman City of Stoke-on-Trent 1987; Hon MUniv Keele 1983, Hon Fell Staffordshire Poly 1988; FICeram 1955 (fndr fell), FRSA 1977; *Recreations* golf, walking, gardening; *Style—* Sir Richard Bailey, CBE

BAILEY, Prof Richard Nigel; s of William Bailey, of Spilsby, Lincs, and Hilda Bailey (d 1959); *b* 21 May 1936; *Educ* Spilsby GS, Univ of Durham (MA, PhD); *m* 3 Sept 1960, Mary Isabel, da of Norman Carmichael (d 1984), of Morpeth, Northumberland; 1 s (Nigel), 1 da (Alison); *Career* lectr in English UCNW 1960–66; Univ of Newcastle: lectr in English 1966–74, sr lectr 1974–80, prof of Anglo Saxon civilisation 1980–, dean Faculty of Arts 1985–88, pro vice chllr 1988–93 and 1995–; FSA 1975; *Books* Viking-Age Sculpture (1980), Corpus of Anglo-Saxon Sculpture: Cumbria (1988), Dowsing and Church Archaeology (1988), England's Earliest Sculptors (1995); *Recreations* visiting churches and country houses; *Style—* Prof Richard Bailey, FSA; ✉ 22 Ridgely Drive, Ponteland, Newcastle upon Tyne NE20 9BL (☎ 01661 823128); University of Newcastle, Newcastle upon Tyne NE1 7RU (☎ 0191 222 6000)

BAILEY, Robin; s of George Henry Bailey (d 1925), of Hucknall, Nottingham, and Thirza Ann Mettam (d 1979); *b* 5 Oct 1919; *Educ* Henry Mellish Sch Nottingham; *m* 6 Sept 1941, Patricia Mary (d 1993), da of William Oliver Weekes; 3 s (Nicolas, Simon, Justin); *Career* actor; Lt RASC 1940–44; *Theatre* London appearances incl: Othello 1947, The Rivals 1948, Love in Albania 1949, The Cocktail Party 1950, Pygmalion 1951, Duel of Angels 1958, A Severed Head 1964, Quartermaine's Terms 1981, Camelot 1982, Beethoven's Tenth 1983, Look Look 1990; RNT 1978–93: Volpone, The Country Wife, The Cherry Orchard, Macbeth, For Services Rendered, When We Are Married, Rough Crossing, Mrs Warren's Profession, Six Characters in Search of an Author, Fathers and Sons, Black Snow, The Night of the Iguana, Pygmalion, Trelawny of the "Wells", Macbeth, Absence of War; *Television* incl: Bleak House, Potter, Rumpole of the Bailey, I Didn't Know You Cared, Tales From A Long Room, Charters and Caldicott, The Good Guys, Tales from Hollywood, Bed, Dalziel and Pascoe; *Clubs* Garrick, MCC; *Style—* Robin Bailey, Esq; ✉ 130 Merton Road, London SW18 5SP (☎ 0181 874 8571)

BAILEY, Ronald William; CMG (1961); s of William Staveley Bailey (d 1956), of Southampton, and May Eveline Bailey, *née* Cudlipp; *b* 14 June 1917; *Educ* King Edward VI Sch Southampton, Trinity Hall Cambridge (Wootton Isaacson scholar); *m* 1946, Joan Hassall, da of A E Gray, JP (d 1959), of Stoke-on-Trent; 1 s, 1 da; *Career* HM Dip Serv: Beirut 1939–41, Alexandria 1941–45, Cairo 1945–48, FO 1948–49, first sec Beirut 1949–52, cnsllr Washington 1955–57 (first sec 1952–55), Khartoum 1957–60, chargé d'affaires Taiz 1960–62, consul gen Gothenburg 1963–65, min Baghdad 1965–67, ambass Bolivia 1967–71 and Morocco 1971–75, ret; memb Cncl Anglo-Arab Assoc 1978–85, hon life vice pres Soc for the Protection of Animals Abroad 1989 (vice pres 1975–87, pres 1987–89), hon life pres Br-Moroccan Soc 1987, chm Black Down Ctee Nat Trust 1982–87 (memb 1977–87), town cncllr Haslemere 1976–79; *Books* Records of Oman 1867–1960 (12 vols, 1988–92); *Recreations* gardening, walking, photography; *Clubs* Oriental; *Style—* Ronald Bailey, Esq, CMG; ✉ Redwood, Tennyson's Lane, Haslemere, Surrey GU27 3AF (☎ 01428 642800)

BAILEY, Dr (Theodore Robert) Simon; s of Herbert Wheatcroft Bailey (d 1989), of Shepshed, Leics, and Norah Violet, *née* Roberts; *b* 20 Dec 1943; *Educ* King Edward VII GS Coalville Leics, UCL (BSc), UCH Med Sch (MB BS, FRCGP, DRCOG); *m* 26 July 1975, Elizabeth Frances, da of John Harper, OBE, of Oakfield, Salwick, Preston, Lancs; 2 s (Jonathan b 1978, Timothy b 1981); *Career* GP 1973–, sr MO Newmarket Races, clinical teacher Faculty of Med Univ of Cambridge, assoc advsr in general practice Anglia and Oxford Regnl Health Authy; *Recreations* music, classic cars, fine art; *Style—* Dr Simon Bailey; ✉ Lincoln Lodge, Newmarket, Suffolk CB8 7AB (☎ 01638 663 792); Orchard Surgery, Newmarket, Suffolk CB8 8NU (☎ 01638 663 322, fax 01638 561921)

BAILEY, Sir Stanley Ernest; kt (1986), CBE (1980), QPM (1975), DL (Tyne & Wear 1986); s of John William Bailey (d 1962), of London, and Florence Mary, *née* Hibberd (d 1945); *b* 30 Sept 1926; *Educ* Lyulph Stanley Sch Camden Town London; *m* 27 March 1954, Marguerita Dorothea (Rita), da of George Whitbread (d 1963), of London; *Career* Met Police to supt 1947–66, asst chief constable Staffs Police 1966–70, dir Police Res Home Office 1970–72, dep chief constable Staffs 1973–75, chief constable Northumbria Police 1975–91, police cdr designate No 2 Home Def Region until 1991; memb Assoc of Chief Police Offrs (ACPO) England Wales and N Ireland (vice pres 1984–85, pres 1985–86), chm Ctee first Int Police Exhibition and Conf (IPEC) London 1987, dir and vice chm Crime Concern 1988–94, dir Northumbria Coalition Against Crime 1988–91; police advsr Assoc of Metropolitan Authorities and memb Chernobyl Task Force Ctee 1987–91; chm (until 1991): ACPO Standing Ctee on Intruder Alarms, ACPO Sub Ctee on Crime Prevention, chm BSI Tech Ctee on Security Systems; former memb: CBI Business and Crime Prevention Working Gp and Business Crime Prevention Sub-Gp, Br Vehicle Retailers Leasing Assoc Steering Gp on Crime Prevention, Nat Approval Cncl for Security Systems; vice pres Police Mutual Assur Soc 1986–94, active memb Int Assoc of Police Chiefs (memb Exec Ctee 1986), chm Advsy Ctee on Int Policy IACP 1985–89 (dir European World Regnl Office, observer on Private Security Ctee and memb Membership Ctee IAPC); graduate of Nat Exec Inst FBI Acad Washington; ACPO rep at INTERPOL 1986–88, govr Int Inst of Security, observer Eighth UN Conf on Crime Prevention Havana Cuba 1990, fndr and chm First Conf Sr Police at UN Conf 1990; conslt on policing, crime prevention and security 1991–; dir: Industrial Communication and Security Services Ltd, Security Auditors Ltd 1993–; vice pres Ex-Police in Commerce and Industry (EPIC) 1992–, pres Security Services Assoc (SSA) now Security Systems and Alarms Inspection Bd (SSAIB) 1992–, tstee Suzy Lamplugh Tst 1991–93; fndr and jt chm Newcastle Univ/Northumbria Police Centre for Res into Crime, Community and Policing 1989–91; memb Editorial Bd Professional Security; ABIS Ken Bolton award for outstanding contribution to security and crime prevention 1990; lectr on crime prevention, policing and security: USA, Pacific, Far East and Europe; Freeman City of London 1988; CIMgt 1987, OStJ 1981; *Publications* Community Policing and Crime Prevention in America and England (with Robert C Wadman, 1993); author of articles in various police journals on specialist subjects incl management and research; *Recreations* gardening, travel; *Style—* Sir Stanley Bailey, CBE, QPM, DL; ✉ 2 Hadrian Court, Darras Hall, Newcastle upon Tyne NE20 9JU (☎ 01661 825529)

BAILEY, Terence Michael; s of Thomas Sturman Bailey, and Margaret Hilda, *née* Wright; *b* 22 Oct 1946; *Educ* Kettering GS, Lanchester Poly Coventry (BA); *m* 1, 21 Oct 1972 (m dis), Penelope Ann, da of Geoffrey Lever Butler; 1 s (Tobin b 1976); m 2, 20 July 1985, Susan Jane, da of Frederick Peter Runacres; 3 s (Tim b 1986, Christopher b 1987, David b 1990); *Career* slr to Corby Devpt Corp 1972–73, ptnr Toller Hales & Collcutt (Northants) 1973–; chm Corby Industrial Group (for promotion of industry in Corby area) 1991–94; *Recreations* skiing, motor-cycling, gardening, keep-fit, reading; *Clubs* Northants Law Soc, Kettering Golf, RHS; *Style—* Terence M Bailey, Esq; ✉ Yew Tree Farm House, Little Oakley, Corby, Northants NN18 8HA (☎ 01536 742233); Toller Hales & Collcutt, 53–57 High St, Corby, Northants NN17 1UY (☎ 01536 276727, fax 01563 276700)

BAILHACHE, Sir Philip Martin; kt (1996); s of Sqdn Ldr Lester Vivian Bailhache, RAF, and Nanette Ross, *née* Ferguson; *b* 28 Feb 1946; *Educ* Charterhouse, Pembroke Coll Oxford (MA); *m* 1, 1967 (m dis 1982); 2 s (Robert b 1968, John b 1974), 2 da (Rebecca b 1969, Catherine b 1972); m 2, 2 June 1984, Linda, da of Martin Geoffrey Le Vavasseur dit Durell; 1 s (Edward b 1990), 1 da (Alice b 1988); *Career* called to the Bar Middle Temple 1968, called to the Jersey Bar 1969, advocate Jersey 1969–74 (dep for Grouville 1972–74), slr gen Jersey 1975–86, attorney gen Jersey 1986–93, QC 1989, bailiff of Jersey 1995– (dep bailiff 1994–95), pres Jersey Court of Appeal 1995–; chm Jersey Arts Cncl 1987–89; hon fell Pembroke Coll Oxford 1995; *Recreations* music, the arts, gardening, wine; *Clubs* Reform, United (Jersey); *Style—* Sir Philip Bailhache; ✉ L'Anquetinerie, Grouville, Jersey, Channel Islands (☎ 01534 852533); Bailiff's Chambers, Royal Court House, St Helier, Jersey (☎ 01534 502100, fax 01534 502199)

BAILIE, Rt Hon Robin John; PC (NI 1971); *b* 6 March 1937; *Educ* Queen's Univ Belfast (LLB); *m* 1961, Margaret Frances, da of Charles Boggs; 1 s, 3 da; *Career* slr Supreme Ct of Judicature NI 1961–, MP (NI) Newtownabbey 1969–72, Min of Commerce NI 1971–72; dir: Goodyear Tyre & Rubber Co (GB), Jones Engineering Services Ltd; *Recreations* wine drinking, skiing, squash, golf, tennis; *Style—* The Rt Hon Robin Bailie; ✉ Adaragh House, Camber, Co Down (☎ 01247 870490)

BAILLIE, Andrew Bruce; s of Edward Oswald Baillie (d 1974), and (Molly Eva Lavers) Renée, *née* Andrews (d 1985); *b* 17 May 1948; *Educ* King's Coll Sch Wimbledon,

Université De Besancon, Univ of Kent (BA); *m* 11 Sept 1976, Mary Lou Meech (d 1988), da of Stanley Harold Palmer (d 1988), of Portsmouth, Hants; 1 s (Oliver b 1984), 2 da (Emma b 1979, Victoria b 1981); *Career* called to the Bar Inner Temple 1970, recorder of the Crown Court 1989–; *Recreations* golf; *Clubs* Caledonian; *Style*— Andrew Baillie, Esq; ✉ 9 Gough Square, London EC4 (☎ 0171 353 5371)

BAILLIE, Hon Evan Michael Ronald; s and h of 3 Baron Burton, *qv*, by his 1 w Elizabeth Ursula Forster, *née* Wise (d 1993); *b* 19 March 1949; *Educ* Harrow; *m* 1970 (m dis 1984), Lucinda Anne, da of Robin Law, of Haverhill; 2 s, 1 da; *Clubs* Brooks's; *Style*— The Hon Evan Baillie

BAILLIE, Sir Gawaine George Hope; 7 Bt (UK 1823), of Polkemmet, Linlithgowshire; s of Sir Adrian Baillie, 6 Bt (d 1947), and Hon Olive, *née* Paget, da of 1 and last Baron Queenborough, GBE, JP (gs of 1 Marq of Anglesey); *b* 8 March 1934; *Educ* Eton, Univ of Cambridge; *m* 1966, Mrs Lucile Margot Gardner, da of Hon Sen Louis P Beaubien, of Ottawa, Canada; 1 s (Adrian Louis b 1973), 1 da (Liza Katharine b 1969); *Heir* s, Adrian Louis Baillie b 26 March 1973; *Career* co dir; *Recreations* golf, tennis, skiing; *Clubs* St George's Golf, Berkshire Golf; *Style*— Sir Gawaine Baillie, Bt; ✉ Freechase, Warninglid, West Sussex RH17 5SZ (☎ 01444 461296)

BAILLIE, Iain Cameron; s of David Brown Baillie (d 1976), and Agnes Wiseman, *née* Thomson (d 1992); *b* 14 July 1931; *Educ* Glasgow HS, Univ of Glasgow (BSc), Fordham Law Sch NY (JD); *m* 1959, Joan Mary Christine, da of Dr Allan Miller (d 1967), and Dr Margaret Miller (d 1971), of Rickmansworth, Herts; 1 s (Gordon); *Career* int lawyer; sr Euro ptnr Ladas & Parry (of NY, Chicago, Los Angeles, London, and Munich); admitted NY Bar and Fed Cts incl Supreme Ct (USA); chartered patent attorney, registered UK trade mark agent, Euro patent attorney; dir MRC Collaborative Centre 1993–; author of numerous articles and frequent lectr on business law; fell: Inst of Int Licensing Practitioners, Inst of Trade Marks; *Books* Practical Management of Intellectual Property (1986), Licensing - A Practical Guide for the Businessman (1987); *Recreations* law, walking, model making; *Clubs* Caledonian; *Style*— Iain Baillie, Esq; ✉ 20 Chester St, London SW1X 7BL (☎ 0171 235 1975, fax 0171 235 4784); Ladas and Parry, 52 High Holborn, London WC1V 6RR (☎ 0171 242 5566, fax 0171 405 1908)

BAILLIE, Prof John; s of Arthur Baillie (d 1979), of Glasgow, and Agnes Baillie (d 1981); *b* 7 Oct 1944; *Educ* Whitehill Sr Secdy Sch; *m* 3 June 1973, Annette, da of James Alexander; 1 s (Kenneth b 22 Feb 1979), 1 da (Nicola b 13 Oct 1975); *Career* CA 1967; ptnr: KPMG Peat Marwick (formerly Thomson McLintock) 1978–93, Scott-Moncrieff 1993–; author of various tech and professional papers to professional jls; ICAS: memb various ctees 1978–, convenor Research Ctee 1996–; Johnstone Smith chair of accountancy Univ of Glasgow 1983–88, visiting prof of accountancy Heriot-Watt Univ 1988–; Hon MA Univ of Glasgow 1983; *Books* Systems of Profit Measurement (1985), Consolidated Accounts and The Seventh Directive (1985); *Recreations* keeping fit, reading, golf, music, hill walking; *Clubs* Western (Glasgow); *Style*— Prof John Baillie; ✉ The Glen, Glencairn Rd, Kilmacolm, Renfrewshire PA13 4PJ (☎ 01505 873254)

BAILLIE, Robin Alexander MacDonald; *b* 20 Aug 1933; *Educ* Larkhall Acad Scotland; *m* 7 Feb 1959, Dr Elizabeth Susan Baillie, da of John Ordish; 1 s (Jonathan Michael b 20 Oct 1962), 1 da (Caroline Elizabeth b 2 March 1971); *Career* Nat Serv Sub Lt RNVR 1952–54; divnl dir Grindlays Bank plc 1973 (bank offr in Kenya, Uganda and India 1955–66), chief exec Exporters Refinance Corporation Ltd 1972 (joined 1966), md Wallace Brothers Group 1976–77 (joined 1973); Standard Chartered Group: md Standard Chartered Merchant Bank 1977–85, md MAIBL PLC 1983, exec dir 1983–87, non-exec dir 1987–94; chm Burson-Marsteller Ltd 1987–92; chm: Finsbury Underwriting Investment Trust PLC, INVESCO Asia Trust plc, Henderson TR India Fund Sicav; non-exec dir: Boustead PLC, City Merchants High Yield Trust plc, Capital & Counties plc, Henderson plc, Gartmore Smaller Companies Trust plc, NatWest Irish Smaller Companies Investment Trust plc, Standard Chartered PLC until 1994, The Emerging Markets Country Investment Trust PLC, Liberty International Holdings PLC, Control Risks Group; FCIBS, FRSA, FInstD; *Recreations* the opera, victorian watercolours, Indian art; *Style*— Robin Baillie, Esq; ✉ Henderson plc, 3 Finsbury Avenue, London EC2H 2PA (☎ 0171 410 4100)

BAILLIEU, Christopher Latham; MBE (1977); s of Hon Edward Latham Baillieu, and Betty Anne Jardine, *née* Taylor; *b* 12 Dec 1949; *Educ* Radley, Jesus Coll Cambridge (Rowing blue); *m* 8 Sept 1984, Jane Elizabeth, da of Robert Price Bowie; 2 s (Charles Latham b 31 May 1985, Edward Latham b 22 July 1990), 1 da (Olivia Clare b 3 Oct 1987); *Career* oarsman; rowed for: Radley Coll 1967–68 (competed Jr Int 1967), Univ of Cambridge 1970–73, Leander Club 1973–84, GB 1973–83; Bronze medal double sculls Euro Championships 1973; World Championships: Bronze medal double sculls 1974 and 1975, Gold medal double sculls 1977, Silver medal double sculls 1978 (fourth place 1979), fourth place single sculls 1981 (sixth place 1982); Silver medal double sculls Olympic Games 1976 (fourth place double sculls 1980); Henley Royal Regatta: winner double sculls 1973, 1975, 1977, 1978, 1979 and 1983, winner diamond sculls 1981, 1982 and 1984; called to the Bar Lincoln's Inn (Walter Wrigglesworth scholarship 1975), co dir, TV rowing commentator; Sir Winston Churchill travelling fellowship 1976, steward Henley Royal Regatta 1984; govr Sports Aid Fndn 1992; *Recreations* old buildings, most art, modern history; *Clubs* Hawks' (Cambridge), Leander (Henley); *Style*— Christopher Baillieu, Esq, MBE; ✉ 11 Woodthorpe Rd, London SW15 6UQ

BAILLIEU, 3 Baron (UK 1953); James William Latham Baillieu; er s of 2 Baron Baillieu (d 1973), and his 1 w, Anne Bayliss, *née* Page; *b* 16 Nov 1950; *Educ* Radley, Monash Univ Melbourne (BEc); *m* 1, 1974 (m dis 1985), Cornelia, da of late William Ladd; 1 s; m 2, 1987, Clare, da of Peter Stephenson; *Heir* s, Hon Robert Latham Baillieu, b 2 Feb 1979; *Career* 2 Lt Coldstream Gds 1970–73; Banque Nationale de Paris (Melbourne) 1978–80, Rothschild Australia Ltd 1980–88 (assoc dir 1985–88), gen mangr capital markets Manufacturers Hanover Australia Ltd 1988–90, dir Standard Chartered Asia Ltd 1990–; *Clubs* Boodle's, Australian (Melbourne); *Style*— The Rt Hon the Lord Baillieu; ✉ c/o Mutual Trust Pty Ltd, 360 Collins Street, Melbourne, Vic 3000, Australia

BAIN, Angus Hugh Uniacke; s of Dr George Alexander Bain (d 1981), of Sheffield, and Sheila Beatrice, *née* Uniacke (d 1988); *b* 31 July 1940; *Educ* Uppingham; *m* 1, 24 March 1965 (m dis 1972); m 2, 3 May 1973, Jane Verel, da of Wing Cdr Coleman, AFC, of Malta; 1 s (Hugo Alastair Uniacke b 28 April 1974); *Career* memb Stock Exchange 1962, dir SGST Investment Advisers 1989–; *Recreations* golf, tennis, racing, cricket, football; *Clubs* City of London, Royal Wimbledon Golf; *Style*— Angus Bain, Esq; ✉ 27 Titchwell Rd, London SW18 8LW (☎ 0181 874 9461); SGST Investment Advisers, 36–44 Moorgate, London EC2R 6EL (☎ 0171 638 5699, fax 0171 628 2711)

BAIN, Prof George Sayers; s of George Alexander Bain, of Winnipeg, Canada, and Margaret Ioleen, *née* Bamford (d 1988); *b* 24 Feb 1939; *Educ* Winnipeg State Sch System, Univ of Manitoba (BA, MA), Univ of Oxford (DPhil); *m* 1, 24 Aug 1962 (m dis 1987), Carol Lynne Ogden, da of Herbert Fyffe White (d 1986); 1 s (David Thomas b 1969), 1 da (Katharine Anne b 1967); m 2, 28 Dec 1988, (Frances) Gwynneth Rigby, *née* Vickers; *Career* Royal Canadian Navy Reserve, Midshipman 1957–60, Sub Lt 1960, Lt 1963, ret 1963; lectr in economics Univ of Manitoba 1962–63, res fell in industl rels Nuffield Coll Oxford 1966–69, Frank Thomas prof of industl rels UMIST 1969–70; Industl Rels Res Unit of SSRC Univ of Warwick: dep dir 1970–74, acting dir 1974, dir 1975–81; Univ of Warwick: titular prof 1974–79, Pressed Steel Fisher prof of industl rels 1979–89, chm Sch of Industl and Business Studies 1983–89; princ London Business Sch 1989–; Distinguished visiting prof Univ of Manitoba 1985, Cecil H and Ida Green visiting prof Univ of British Columbia 1987; memb res staff Royal Cmmn on Trade Unions and Employers' Assoc (The Donovan Cmmn) 1966–67, conslt to Nat Bd for Prices and Incomes 1967–69; memb: Mechanical Engrg Econ Devpt Ctee NEDO 1974–76 (conslt to NEDO 1982–85), Ctee of Inquiry on Industl Democracy 1975–76, Cncl ESRC 1986–91, Nat Forum for Mgmnt Educn and Devpt 1988–90, Exec British Univs Industl Rels Assoc 1971–80 (sec 1971–74), Cncl Nat Forum for Mgmnt Educn and Devpt 1987–90, American Assembly of Collegiate Schs of Business 1992–94, Bd of Tstees Euro Fndn for Mgmnt Devpt 1990–96 (memb Exec Ctee 1991–96, exec vice pres 1991–95), Cncl Fndn for Mgmnt Educn 1991–, Int Cncl American Mgmnt Assoc 1993–96, Bd Fndn for Canadian Studies in the UK 1993–, Sr Salaries Review Body 1993–96, Cncl BESO 1995–; chm: Cncl Univ Mgmnt Schs 1987–90 (exec memb 1984–90), Food Sector Working Gp NEDO 1991–92, Cmmn on Public Policy and Br Business Inst Public Policy Research 1995–; dir: Blackwell Publishers Ltd 1990–, Rover Learning Business 1991–, The Economist Group 1993–, Canada Life Assurance Company of Great Britain Ltd 1994–, Canada Life Assurance Company 1995–; frequent arbitrator/mediator for ACAS; Hon DBA De Montfort Univ 1995; FRSA 1987, CIMgt 1991; *Books* Trade Union Growth and Recognition (1967), The Growth of White-Collar Unionism (1970), The Reform of Collective Bargaining at Plant and Company Levels (1971), Social Stratification and Trade Unionism (1973), Union Growth and the Business Cycle (1976), A Bibliography of British Industrial Relations (1979 and 1985), Profiles of Union Growth (1980), Industrial Relations in Britain (ed 1983); *Recreations* genealogy, family history, Western riding; *Clubs* Reform; *Style*— Prof George Bain; ✉ London Business School, Sussex Place, Regent's Park, London NW1 4SA (☎ 0171 262 5050, fax 0171 724 3881)

BAIN, Iain Stuart; s of James Bain, MC (d 1971), of Cromarty and Kirkcudbright, and Frances Mary Hamilton, *née* Shaw (d 1984); *b* 16 Feb 1934; *Educ* Fettes, St Edmund Hall Oxford; *m* 14 June 1958, Susan, da of Kenneth Herbert Forbes (d 1981), of Englefield Green; 2 da (Kirsty b 1961, Catriona b 1964); *Career* Nat Serv cmmnd 2 Lt 1 Bn Seaforth Highlanders 1953–55; Scottish Champion Hammer Thrower 1956–57 and 1959, Scotland and GB rep 1959; prodn mangr The Bodley Head 1966–72, publisher The Tate Gallery 1972–94; chm Printing Hist Soc 1984–89, tstee Thomas Bewick Birthplace Tst 1985–90, pres Private Libraries Assoc 1992–95, tstee Wordsworth Tst 1993–, memb Cncl Bibliographical Soc 1993–; Liveryman Worshipful Co of Stationers and Newspaper Makers 1990; FSA 1988, FSTD 1992, FRSA 1993; *Books* A Memoir of Thomas Bewick (1975, 1979), Thomas Bewick: Vignettes (1979), The Watercolours & Drawings of Thomas Bewick & His Workshop Apprentices (1981), The Workshop of Thomas Bewick: A Pictorial Survey (1989); *Recreations* printing and publishing history, printing and typography at the hand-press, folk music and pipe music of Scotland and Northumberland; *Clubs* Athenaeum, Double Crown; *Style*— Iain Bain, Esq, FSA

BAIN, Dr Neville Clifford; s of Charles Alexander Bain (d 1990), of St Kilda, Dunedin, NZ, and, Gertrude Mae, *née* Howe (d 1986); *b* 14 July 1940; *Educ* King's HS Dunedin NZ, Otago Univ Dunedin NZ (MCom, LLD); *m* 18 Sept 1987, Anne Patricia; from previous m, 1 s (Peter John b 1965), 1 da (Susan Mary b 1963), 1 step da (Kristina Knights b 1979); *Career* trainee inspr Inland Revenue NZ 1957–59, mangr Anderson & Co CA's NZ 1960–62, various mgmnt posts Cadbury Schweppes plc 1963–90 (latterly gp fin dir and dep chief exec), gp chief exec Coats Viyella plc 1990–; non-exec dir: Gartmore Scotland Investment Trust plc, Safeway plc (formerly Argyll Group plc); formerly dir: Cadbury Schweppes Overseas Ltd, Cadbury Schweppes Australia, Cadbury Schweppes SA, Cadbury India Ltd, Amalgamated Beverages GB, Reading Scientific Services Ltd, Itnet Ltd; CMA, FCIS 1962, CIMgt 1988, FCA 1989 (ACA 1959), FRSA; *Books* Successful Management (1995), Winning Ways through Corporate Governance (with Professor David Band, 1996); *Recreations* music, sport, photography; *Style*— Dr Neville C Bain; ✉ High Trees, Cavendish Road, Weybridge, Surrey KT13 0JX; Coats Viyella plc, 28 Savile Row, London W1X 2DD (☎ 0171 292 9200, car 0860 860135)

BAINBRIDGE, Beryl; da of Richard Bainbridge, and Winifred Baines; *b* 21 Nov 1934; *Educ* Merchant Taylors' Sch Liverpool, Arts Educnl Schs Tring; *m* 1954 (m dis), Austin Davies; 1 s, 2 da; *Career* actress and writer; columnist Evening Standard 1987–; Hon LittD Univ of Liverpool 1986; FRSL 1978; *Books* A Weekend with Claud (1967, revised edn 1981), Another Part of the Wood (1968, revised edn 1979), Harriet Said.... (1972), The Dressmaker (1973, film 1989), The Bottle Factory Outing (1974, Guardian Fiction Award), Sweet William (1975, film 1980), A Quiet Life (1976), Injury Time (1977, Whitbread Award), Young Adolf (1978), Winter Garden (1980), English Journey (1984, TV series), Watson's Apology (1984), Mum and Mr Armitage (1985), Forever England (1986, TV series 1986), Filthy Lucre (1986), An Awfully Big Adventure (1989, theatre adaptation Liverpool Playhouse 1992, film 1995), The Birthday Boys (1991), Something Happened Yesterday (1993, articles from Evening Standard), Collected Stories (1994), Every Man For Himself (1996); *Plays* Tiptoe Through the Tulips (1976), The Warrior's Return (1977), It's a Lovely Day Tomorrow (1977), Journal of Bridget Hitler (1981), Somewhere More Central (TV 1981), Evensong (TV 1986); *Recreations* painting, sleeping; *Style*— Miss Beryl Bainbridge, FRSL; ✉ 42 Albert St, London NW1 (☎ 0171 387 3113)

BAINBRIDGE, Cyril; s of Arthur Herman Bainbridge (d 1966), and Edith, *née* Whitaker (d 1988); *b* 15 Nov 1928; *Educ* Negus Coll Bradford; *m* 20 Jan 1953, Barbara Hannah, da of Sydney Crook (d 1991); 1 s (Christopher b 1958), 2 da (Susan b 1954, Amanda b 1958); *Career* Nat Serv Army 1947–49; author and journalist; reporter: provincial newspapers 1944–54, Press Association 1954–63; The Times: joined 1963, dep news ed 1967–69, regnl news ed 1969–77, managing news ed 1977–82, asst managing ed 1982–86, editorial data mangr 1986–88; pres Inst of Journalists 1978–79 (vice pres 1977–78, fell 1986); memb: Press Cncl 1980–90, Nat Cncl for Trg of Journalists 1983–87; *Books* Taught With Care: a Century of Church Schooling (1974), The Brontës and Their Country (1978, revised edns 1990 and 1993), Brass Triumphant (1980), North Yorkshire and North Humberside (1984, revised edn 1989), One Hundred Years of Journalism (ed, 1984), Pavilions on the Sea (1986), The News of the World Story (1993); *Recreations* reading, walking, collecting old bookmarks; *Style*— Cyril Bainbridge, Esq; ✉ 6 Lea Road, Hemingford Grey, Huntingdon, Cambs PE18 9ED (☎ 01480 468973)

BAINBRIDGE, John Philip; s of Philip James Bainbridge, of Mottingham, London, and Joan Winifred, *née* Walker; *b* 28 Aug 1946; *Educ* Chislehurst and Sidcup GS; *m* 2 May 1970, Marilynne Ailsa, da of Stanley Joseph Kesler (d 1985), of Cranleigh, Surrey; 2 s (Daniel John b 1979, James Ashley b 1981); *Career* dir Schroder Unit Trusts Ltd 1988– (joined Schroder Group 1973); FCA; *Recreations* reading, cricket; *Style*— John Bainbridge, Esq; ✉ Baltic House, The Common, Cranleigh, Surrey GU6 8SL (☎ 01483 275949); Schroder Unit Trusts Ltd, 85 Queen Victoria Street, London EC4V 4EJ (☎ 0171 382 6742, fax 0171 382 3538, telex 885029)

BAINES, Alan Leonard; s of Leonard Baines (d 1989), of Edwalton, Nottingham, and Edna, *née* Hackston (d 1985); *b* 7 May 1948; *Educ* Chadderton GS Lancashire; *m* 1982, Carole, da of Colin Johnson; *Career* articled clerk Joseph Crossley & Sons Manchester; accountant Price Waterhouse 1970–74; Stoy Hayward (now BDO Stoy Hayward): joined 1975, ptnr 1976–, specialist advsr on problems of corp strategies and family owned businesses; FCA, FIMgt, FInstD; *Recreations* the British coast and countryside, music, theatre; *Style*— Alan Baines, Esq; ✉ BDO Stoy Hayward, Foxhall Lodge, Gregory Boulevard, Nottingham NG7 6LH (☎ 0115 962 6578, fax 0115 969 1043)

BAINES, Garron John; s of Roy Hubert Baines, of Tadgells, Housham Tye, Harlow, Essex, and Jillian Ann, *née* Wheeley; *b* 25 Aug 1952; *Educ* Oundle; *m* 6 July 1974, Irene Joyce, da of Richard Rennie Williams, of 19 Broadstone Ave, Port Glasgow,

Renfrewshire, Scotland; 2 da (Laura Lockhart b 1 Nov 1978, Fiona Suzanne b 8 June 1982); *Career* former newspaper journalist E Midland Allied Press; ITN: joined as writer 1977, head Channel Four News until 1995 (news ed from launch 1982, dep ed 1989), ed international news progs 1995–; *Recreations* talking, walking, television; *Style—* Garron Baines, Esq; ✉ ITN, 200 Gray's Inn Road, London WC1X 8HB (☎ 0171 833 3000)

BAINES, Peter; s of Jonathan Baines (d 1979), of Warrington, Cheshire, and Florrie, *née* Bent (d 1981); *b* 26 May 1942; *Educ* Newton-Le-Willows GS; *m* 29 May 1967, Eleanor May Baines; 1 s (Simon Alexander b 24 March 1970), 1 da (Eleanor Anne b 25 Feb 1972); *Career* CA; trainee, sr then mangr D J Dunn & Co 1958–63, sr mangr Tunstall & Co 1964–66, self employed CA 1966–67, jt sr ptnr Haslams 1967–88, chm M6 Cash & Carry PLC 1986–90, gp fin dir Ashall Group Ltd Property Devpt and Construction 1987–, self employed corp finance conslt 1988–; chm Skyway Group plc 1990–, non-exec dir Sonomatic Ltd 1990–93, fin dir Venezia Trustees Ltd (Ferranti family tst co) 1990–; dir Arderne plc 1993–; fndr and treas Ash Investment Gp 1970–90, fndr memb and nat treas The Urostomy Assoc Charity 1972–, treas CPRE Warrington Branch 1980–93; chm: Warrington Gp of Chartered Accountants 1984–86, Warrington and Dist Business Club 1985–87; ICAEW: memb Working Party Devpt of Taxation Databases 1984–86, fndr memb Faculty of Taxation and chm Dist Socs Liaison Ctee 1988–; FInstD, FCA 1976 (ACA 1966); *Style—* Peter Baines, Esq; ✉ Oak Tree Farm, Lord Street, Croft, Warrington WA3 7DB (☎ 01925 766209, fax 01925 766205, car 0421 641117)

BAINES, Stephen Philip; s of Charles Philip Baines (d 1986), and Edna, *née* Millard; *b* 16 Jan 1947; *Educ* Neath GS, Avery Hill Coll of Educn London (CertEd), Univ of Oregon USA (BSc, MSc); *m* 14 Sept 1985, (Emilie) Micheline; 1 s (David Alexander b 3 Oct 1988), 1 da (Katherine Sian b 27 April 1986); *Career* physical educn teacher: Wandsworth Comp Sch 1969–71, Pendle Hill HS Sydney Aust (also sportsmaster) 1971–73; exec dir Canadian Rugby Union Ottawa 1975–81, md Pro-Motion International Toronto 1981–83, dir of mktg Nat Assoc of Boys' Clubs London 1983–86, chief exec The Hockey Assoc 1986–; sec The Hockey Assoc Youth Tst, sec and memb Cncl Nat Hockey Fndn; spoken at numerous conferences worldwide, author of various articles for magazines; memb: Henley Royal Regatta Stewards Enclosure; vice chm Br Inst of Sports Administration; MIMgt, FCIM; *Recreations* international sport, rugby, photography, travel, golf; *Clubs* London Welsh RFC, Neath RFC, British Sportsman's; *Style—* Stephen Baines, Esq; ✉ The Hockey Association, The Stadium, Silbury Boulevard, Milton Keynes MK9 1HA (☎ 01908 241100, fax 01908 241106)

BAINS, Lawrence Arthur; CBE (1983), DL (Gtr London 1978); s of late Arthur Bains, and Mabel, *née* Payn; *b* 11 May 1920; *Educ* Stationers' Co's Sch; *m* 1954, Margaret, da of Sir William J Grimshaw (d 1958); 2 s, 1 da; *Career* served WWII Middx Yeo, N Africa 1940, POW 1942 (escaped 1943); Hornsey BC: memb 1949–65, dep leader 1958–64, mayor 1964–65; cncllr London Borough of Haringey 1964–74 (chm fin 1968–71); GLC: memb for Hornsey/Haringey 1967–81, chm 1977–78, chm S Area Planning Bd 1971–73, dep leader Housing Policy Ctee 1979–81, chm GLC/Tower Hamlets Jt Mgmnt Ctee 1979–81, memb Lee Valley Regnl Park Authy 1968–81 (chm 1980–81); chm Haringey Health Authy 1981–93; dir: Bains Brothers Ltd, Crowland Leasing Ltd, Bains Finance Management Ltd; chm N London Coll of Health Studies 1991–95; memb Lloyd's; Liveryman Worshipful Co of Basketmakers; *Clubs* City Livery; *Style—* Lawrence Bains, Esq, CBE, DL; ✉ Crowland Lodge, 100 Galley Lane, Arkley, Barnet, Herts EN5 4AL (☎ 0181 440 3499)

BAIRD, (James) Andrew Gardiner; s and h of Sir James Baird, 10 Bt, MC, *qv*, and Mabel Ann (Gay) Tempest, *née* Gill; *b* 2 May 1946; *Educ* Eton; *m* 1984 (m dis), Jean Margaret, da of Brig Sir Ian Liddell Jardine, 4 Bt, OBE, MC (d 1982), of Coombe Place, Meonstoke, Southampton; 1 s (Alexander b 28 May 1986); *Recreations* shooting, fishing, photography; *Clubs* Boodle's; *Style—* Andrew Baird, Esq; ✉ 68 Lessar Avenue, Clapham Common, London SW4 9HQ (☎ 0171 673 2035)

BAIRD, (Eric) Anthony Bamber; s of Oswald Baird, and Marion, *née* Bamber; *b* 11 Dec 1920; *Educ* LSE (BSc Econ); *m* 10 Oct 1959 (m dis 1977), Inger Bohman; 2 da (Karoline Ann Sofi b 1961, Madeleine Susan Sofi b 1964); *Career* served RA 1941–46; Swedish Broadcasting Corp 1950–65, Public Relations Ltd 1965–72, Civil Serv 1972–78, dir Institute for Complementary Medicine 1980– (joined 1979); FRSA; *Books* Notes on Canada (1955), The Charm of Sweden (co-author, 1958); *Recreations* writing children's stories, gardening; *Style—* Anthony Baird, Esq; ✉ Institute for Complementary Medicine, PO Box 194, London SE16 1QZ (☎ 0171 237 5165)

BAIRD, Sir David Charles; 5 Bt (UK 1809), of Newbyth, Haddingtonshire; s of William Arthur Baird, JP, DL (himself 2 s of Sir David Baird, 3 Bt, JP, DL, by his w Hon Ellen Stuart, 2 da and co-heir of 12 Lord Blantyre); the present Bt's mother was Lady Hersey Conyngham, 3 da of 4 Marquess Conyngham; suc unc, Sir David Baird, 4 Bt, MVO, JP, DL, 1941 (Sir David's ggg uncle, the Rt Hon Sir David Baird, 1 Bt, KCB, PC, was a distinguished soldier and himself gn of Sir James Baird, 2 Bt, of Saughton); *b* 6 July 1912; *Educ* Eton, Univ of Cambridge; *Heir* nephew, Charles William Stuart Baird b 8 June 1939; *Style—* Sir David Baird, Bt; ✉ Byrlaw, 38 Dalbeattie Road, Dumfries DG2 7PL

BAIRD, Prof David Tennent; s of Sir Dugald Baird (d 1986), and Mathilda Deans, *née* Tennent, CBE (d 1983); *b* 13 March 1935; *Educ* Aberdeen GS, Univ of Aberdeen, Trinity Coll Cambridge (BA), Univ of Edinburgh (MB ChB, DSc); *m* 29 Jan 1964 (m dis), Frances Diana, da of Francis Lichtveld, of Amsterdam, Holland; 2 s (Dugald Francis b 1967, Gavin Tennent b 1969); *Career* jr med posts Royal Infirmary Edinburgh 1960–65, MRC travelling res fell Worcester Fndn of Experimental Biology USA 1965–68, lectr then sr lectr Dept of Obstetrics Univ of Edinburgh 1968–72, conslt gynaecologist Royal Infirmary Edinburgh 1970–, dep dir MRC Unit of Reproductive Biology Edinburgh 1972–77, prof of obsterics and gynaecology Univ of Edinburgh 1977–85, MRC clinical res prof of reproductive endocrinology Univ of Edinburgh 1985–; FRCPE 1971, FRCOG 1972, FRSE 1990, FRCP 1996; *Books* Mechanism of Menstruation (1983); *Recreations* ski-mountaineering, golf; *Clubs* RSM; *Style—* Prof David Baird, FRSE; ✉ Department of Obstetrics and Gynaecology, University of Edinburgh, 37 Chalmers St, Edinburgh (☎ 0131 229 2575)

BAIRD, James Hewson; s of James Baird, MBE, of Carlisle, and Ann Sarah, *née* Hewson (d 1988); *b* 28 March 1944; *Educ* Austin Friars, Creighton Sch Carlisle, Univ of Newcastle (BSc); *m* 7 March 1969, Clare Rosalind, da of Frederick Sidney Langstaff, of Colchester; 3 da (Emma Jane b 6 April 1973, Deirdre Helen b 13 Feb 1975, Katherine Sally b 26 July 1978); *Career* hydrologist and agriculturalist Essex River Authy 1968–74, princ engr Anglian Water Authy 1974–75, policy offr Nat Water Cncl 1975–80, dir of admin Inst of Civil Engrs 1982–85 (asst dir 1980–82), dir Assoc of Municipal Engrs 1985–86, dir of external affrs Fedn of Civil Engrg Contractors 1986–87, chief exec and co sec British Veterinary Assoc 1987–; MIWES 1970–87; *Recreations* rugby, gardening, farming, countryside; *Clubs* Farmers', London Rugby; *Style—* James Baird, Esq; ✉ British Veterinary Association, 7 Mansfield St, London (☎ 0171 636 6541, fax 0171 436 2970)

BAIRD, Lt-Gen Sir James Parlane; KBE (1973); s of Rev David Baird, of Lochgoilhead, Argyllshire, and Sara Kathleen Black; *b* 12 May 1915; *Educ* Bathgate Acad, Univ of Edinburgh (MD); *m* 1948, Anne Patricia, da of David Patrick Anderson, of Houghton, Arundel, Sussex; 1 s, 1 da; *Career* cmmnd RAMC 1939, Lt-Col 1956, prof of mil med Royal Army Med Coll 1965, conslt physician BAOR 1967, dir of med and consltg physician to the Army 1969–71, Cmdt and dir of studies Royal Army Med Coll 1971–73, Dir-Gen AMS 1973–77; med advsr Nat Advice Centre for Postgrad Educn 1977–84; QHP 1969; awarded Hilal-i-Quaid-i-Azam (Pakistan); FRCP 1959, FRCPE 1952; *Publications* Tropical Diseases Supplement to Principles and Practice of Medicine (1968), The Oxford Companion to Medicine (contrib, 1986); *Recreations* golf; *Clubs* West Sussex Golf; *Style—* Lt-Gen Sir James Baird, KBE

BAIRD, Sir James Richard Gardiner; 10 Bt (NS 1695), of Saughton Hall, Edinburghshire, MC; s of Capt William Frank Gardiner Baird (ka 1914), 2 s of 8 Bt; suc unc, Maj Sir James Hozier Gardiner Baird, 9 Bt, MC, 1966; *b* 12 July 1913; *Educ* Eton, Univ Coll Oxford; *m* 1941, Mabel Ann (Gay) Tempest, da of Algernon Gill; 2 s ((James) Andrew Gardiner b 1946, William Julian Gardiner b 1947), 1 da (Lavinia Mary Arabella b 1951); *Heir* s, (James) Andrew Gardiner Baird, *qv*; *Career* Lt RA 1940, Capt Kent Yeo 1944; hon treas The Ada Cole Meml Stables Ltd; *Recreations* shooting; *Clubs* Naval and Military; *Style—* Sir James Baird, Bt, MC; ✉ Church Farm House, Guist, Norfolk NR20 5AJ (☎ 01362 683808)

BAIRD, Dr John Alexander; s of John Wilson Baird (d 1963), of Edinburgh, and Agnes Fairrie, *née* Newlands (d 1990); *b* 28 Aug 1947; *Educ* Daniel Stewart's Coll, Univ of Edinburgh (BSc, MB ChB, MD); *m* 6 Oct 1972, Ann, da of Robert Easson (d 1988), of Edinburgh; 3 s (Colin b 1974, Douglas b 1977, Andrew b 1979); *Career* physician supt State Hosp Carstairs 1985–92 (conslt forensic psychiatrist 1981–85), conslt forensic psychiatrist Douglas Inch Clinic Glasgow 1993–; chm Standing Ctee on Difficult Prisoners 1988–91 (memb 1985–); memb: Parole Bd for Scotland 1992–94, Advsy Ctee on Prisoner Mgmnt 1993–; FRCPsych 1978; *Recreations* hill walking, wine; *Clubs* Medico Legal Soc; *Style—* Dr John Baird

BAIRD, Kenneth William; s of William Stewart Baird, of Northampton, and Christine Bowie, *née* Salton; *b* 14 July 1950; *Educ* Uppingham (music scholar), Univ of St Andrews (MA), RCM (LRAM, ARCM); *Career* with ENO 1974–82, gen mangr Aldeburgh Fndn 1982–88, music dir Arts Cncl 1988–94; chm Snape Historical Tst 1986–; *Clubs* Chelsea Arts; *Style—* Kenneth Baird, Esq

BAIRD, Roger Neale; s of late John Allan Baird, of Edinburgh, and Margaret Edith, *née* Shand (d 1994); *b* 24 Dec 1941; *Educ* Daniel Stewarts Coll Edinburgh, Univ of Edinburgh (BSc, MB ChB, ChM); *m* 12 Oct 1968, Affra Mary, da of Douglas Varcoe-Cocks (d 1964); 1 s (Richard b 1972), 1 da (Susan b 1970); *Career* sr house offr and registrar Royal Infirmary Edinburgh 1969–73 (house surgn 1966–67), res scholar in clinical surgery 1967–69, lectr and sr lectr Univ of Bristol 1973–81, Fulbright scholar Harvard Med Sch Mass 1975–76, conslt surgn Royal Infirmary Bristol 1981–; dir and tstee Euro Soc for Vascular Surgery; pres British Medico-Chirurgical Soc 1994–95; memb: Cncl Bristol Clifton and W of Eng Zoological Soc, Vascular Surgical Soc of GB and Ireland (fomer memb Cncl), American Soc for Vascular Surgery (corresponding) 1993; FRCS, FRCSEd; *Books* Diagnosis and Monitoring in Arterial Surgery (1980), Human Disease for Dental Students (1981); *Recreations* golf, skiing, travel; *Clubs* Army and Navy; *Style—* Roger Baird, Esq; ✉ 23 Old Sneed Park, Stoke Bishop, Bristol BS9 1RG (☎ 0117 968 5523); Consultant Surgeon, Royal Infirmary, Bristol BS2 8HW (☎ 0117 928 2737, fax 0117 928 2000)

BAIRD, Ronald (Ron); s of Richard Baird (d 1975), and Emma, *née* Martin (d 1986); *b* 9 Dec 1930; *Educ* GS Blyth Northumberland, Kings Coll Durham; *m* 4 March 1957, Helen Lilian, da of His Hon Judge John Charlesworth; *Career* Nat Serv 13/18 Royal Hussars (QMO); Saward Baker & Co Ltd 1954–63, chief exec offr Stuart Advertising Ltd 1963–66, mktg dir Queen Street Warehouse Ltd 1966–68, md Holmwood Advertising Ltd 1968–74, dir Notley Advertising Ltd 1970–74, vice chm Saatchi & Saatchi Advertising 1974–95; bd dir NT 1984–91 (vice chm Devpt Bd 1985–95), vice pres Royal Life Saving Soc; *Style—* Ron Baird, Esq; ✉ c/o Saatchi & Saatchi Advertising Ltd, 80–84 Charlotte Street, London W1A 1AQ (☎ 0171 636 5060, fax 0171 637 8489)

BAIRD, (John) Stewart; s of John Baird (d 1971), and Louisa Jane Wright, *née* Stewart (d 1993); *b* 8 June 1943; *Educ* Allan Glens Sch Glasgow, Univ of Glasgow; *m* 22 March 1985, Lorna Jane, da of Andrew Bayne, of Stanley, Perthshire; 1 s (Andrew b 14 Aug 1977), 3 da (Karen b 12 May 1969, Emma b 12 Nov 1972, Amanda b 1 Jan 1977); *Career* Pannell Kerr Forster: apprentice Glasgow 1962–67, audit sr Liberia 1967–68, ptnr Gambia 1968–72, ptnr Sierra Leone 1972–85, ptnr London 1985–87, managing ptnr London 1987–, ptnr in charge Corporate Recovery 1992–94, managing ptnr Edinburgh 1994–96; osp conslt Kidsons Impey 1996–; Freeman City of London 1987, Liveryman Worshipful Co of Loriners 1987; memb: Inst CAs of Scotland 1967–, Inst of CAs of Ghana 1977–, Inst of CAs of Sierra Leone 1988–, Insolvency Practioners Assoc 1989–; MInstD; Royal Order of the Polar Star (Sweden) 1985; *Recreations* golf, reading; *Clubs* Caledonian, Walton Health Golf, Kingswood Golf; *Style—* Stewart Baird, Esq; ✉ Glenshee, 10 Warren Lodge Drive, Kingswood, Surrey, KT20 6QN (☎ 01737 832010, fax 01737 830126); Kidsons Impey, Spectrum House, 20–26 Cursitor Street, Cursitor Street, London EC4A 1HY

BAIRD, Vice Adm Sir Thomas Henry Eustace; KCB (1980), DL (Ayrshire and Arran 1982); s of Geoffrey Henry Baird, and Helen Jane Baird; *b* 17 May 1924; *Educ* RNC Dartmouth; *m* 1953, Angela Florence Ann Paul, of Symington, Ayrshire; 1 s, 1 da; *Career* joined RN 1941, Capt of the Fleet 1973, Rear Adm 1976, COS to C-in-C Naval Home Cmd 1976–77, dir gen Naval Personal Servs 1978–79, Vice Adm 1979, Flag Offr Scotland & NI and Cdr N Sub Area E Atlantic and N Sub Area Channel 1979–82, ret 1982; chm Exec Ctee Erskine Hosp 1986–95; *Recreations* shooting, fishing, golf, DIY; *Clubs* Prestwick Golf; *Style—* Vice Adm Sir Thomas Baird, KCB, DL

BAIRD-SMITH, Robin Jameson; s of John Helenus Baird-Smith (d 1977), and Jean Marjorie Guthrie, *née* Priestman, OBE (d 1993); *b* 21 July 1946; *Educ* Winchester, Royal Acad of Music, Trinity Coll Cambridge (BA); *m* 17 Jan 1976, Sarah Mary-Ann (d 1994), da of Charles Stevens Hedley, MC (d 1976); 2 s (Max John b 1978, Archibald Victor b 1979, d 1994), 1 da (Leonora Frances b 1981); *Career* publisher; Darton Longman and Todd Ltd: ed 1968–71, editorial dir 1971–78; Collins Publishers: ed 1978–81, editorial dir 1981–85; Constable Publishers: editorial dir 1985–95, publishing dir 1992–95, jt md 1992–95; publisher and md Gerald Duckworth and Company Ltd 1995–; opera critic Mail on Sunday Newspaper 1989–90; chm Guild of Catholic Writers 1984–85, memb Analytical Psychology Club 1985–; *Books* Living Water (1988), Winter's Tales Vols 2 - 11 (1986–95), God of the Impossible (1989); *Recreations* music, travel, gardening, reading; *Clubs* Travellers'; *Style—* Robin Baird-Smith, Esq; ✉ 8 Lawn Road, London NW3 2XS (☎ 0171 722 0716); Gerald Duckworth and Company Ltd, The Old Piano Factory, 48 Hoxton Square, London N1 6PB (☎ 0171 729 5986, fax 0171 729 0015)

BAIRSTO, Air Marshal Sir Peter Edward; KBE (1981, CBE 1973), CB (1980), AFC (1957), DL (Fife 1992); s of late Arthur Bairsto, and Beatrice, *née* Lewis; *b* 3 Aug 1926; *Educ* Rhyl GS; *m* 1947, Kathleen, *née* Clarbour; 2 s, 1 da; *Career* RN 1944–46, RAF 1946–84, ret as Air Marshal; mil aviation advsr Ferranti Scottish Group 1984–93, vice chm (Air) Highland TAVRA 1984–90, HM cmmr Queen Victoria Sch Dunblane 1984–93; memb: Scottish Sports Cncl 1985–90, Cncl RAF Benevolent Fund 1985–94, Scottish Air Cadet Cncl 1988–92, St Andrews Links Tst 1989–95 (chm 1992–95); Hon Col RE Field Sqdns Northern Gp ADR(V) 1989–92; CIMgt; *Recreations* gardening, shooting, fishing, golf; *Clubs* RAF, Royal and Ancient Golf (St Andrews); *Style—* Air Marshal Sir Peter Bairsto, KBE, CB, AFC, DL; ✉ Bearwood, 124 Hepburn Gardens, St Andrews, Fife KY16 9LT (☎ and fax 01334 475505)

BAKER, *see also:* Arnold-Baker, Sherston-Baker

BAKER, Prof Alan; s of late Barnet, and Bessie, Baker; *b* 19 Aug 1939; *Educ* Stratford GS, UCL (BSc), Trinity Coll Cambridge (MA, PhD); *Career* Trinity Coll Cambridge: fell 1964–, res fell 1964–68, dir of studies in Mathematics 1968–74; prof of Pure Mathematics Univ of Cambridge 1974–; visiting prof Stanford Univ 1974 and other US univs, Royal Soc Kan Tong Po prof Univ of Hong Kong 1988, guest prof ETH Zürich 1989; MSRI Univ of Calif Berkeley 1993; Fields medal Int Congress of Mathematicians Nice 1970, Adams prize Univ of Cambridge 1972; hon fell Indian Nat Science Acad 1980; fell UCL 1979; FRS 1973; *Publications* Transcendental Number Theory (1975), A Concise Introduction to the Theory of Numbers (1984), New Advances in Transcendence Theory (ed, 1988); numerous papers in scientific jls; *Style*— Professor Alan Baker, FRS; ✉ Department of Pure Mathematics and Mathematical Statistics, 16 Mill Lane, Cambridge CB2 1SB (☎ 01223 337999); Trinity College, Cambridge CB2 1TQ (☎ 01223 338400)

BAKER, Anthony Frank (Tony); s of Frank Cyril Baker, of Southampton, and Gwendoline Maggie, *née* Bushell; *b* 29 March 1940; *Educ* Taunton's Sch Southampton; *m* 19 Sept 1964, Sally, *née* Slinn, step da of Dudley Fitzroy Harding; 2 s (Paul Michael b 4 April 1968, Jonathan Alan b 30 April 1971); *Career* cricket administrator; chief exec Hampshire CCC 1986– (hon treas 1978–86), pres (former chm) Southern Cricket League; tax offr Inland Revenue 1958–60, trainee CA 1961–66, mangr chartered accountants Winchester 1966–68, ptnr Brooking Knowles and Lawrence 1968–86; ACA 1966; former cricket player: Old Tauntonians CC, Southampton Touring CC, Club Cricket Conference, Hampshire CCC second eleven; represented Southampton and Southern Area basketball; *Recreations* playing golf, watching football and cricket, travel, collecting cigarette cards; *Style*— Tony Baker, Esq; ✉ Hampshire CCC, Northlands Rd, Southampton, Hants SO15 2UE (☎ 01703 333788, fax 01703 330121)

BAKER, Anthony James Morton; s of Harris James Morton Baker (d 1960), of N Barningham, Norfolk, and Cicely Margaret, *née* Howgate (d 1986); *b* 30 Jan 1932; *Educ* Gresham's, Emmanuel Coll Cambridge (MA, LLM); *m* 19 July 1958, Vivienne Marguerite, da of Alexander Barclay Loggie, MBE (d 1967); 1 s (Malcolm b 1961), 1 da (Katherine (Mrs McGoldrick) b 1963); *Career* Nat Serv 2 Lt RA 1951–52; TA: Lt RA 1952–54, Lt Norfolk Yeo 1954–55, Lt RA 1955–58, Capt RA 1958–60; admitted slr 1958; ptnr: Walters and Hart 1960–72, Walters Vandercom and Hart 1972–78, Walters Fladgate 1978–87, Fladgate Fielder 1988–96 (sr ptnr 1988–91); dir: CT Baker Ltd, Larner Brothers Ltd; pres: Old Greshamian Club 1985–87, Bucks Co Hockey Assoc 1981–84; memb Cncl Hockey Assoc 1986–87; memb Law Soc; *Recreations* men's hockey, golf, reading; *Clubs* The Norfolk, Sheringham Golf, Royal Norwich Golf; *Style*— Anthony Baker, Esq; ✉ The Old Farm, West Runton, Cromer, Norfolk NR27 9QJ (☎ 01263 837268)

BAKER, His Honour (John) Burkett; QC (1975); s of Philip and Grace Baker, of Finchley; *b* 17 Sept 1931; *Educ* Finchley Catholic GS, Univ Coll Exeter (LLB London); *m* Margaret Mary Smeaton, of East Ham; 3 s (1 decd), 7 da; *Career* RAF 1955–58; called to the Bar Gray's Inn 1957, prosecuting counsel to DHSS 1969–75, dep chm Shropshire QS 1970–71, recorder of the Crown Ct 1972–78, circuit judge (SE Circuit) 1978–96, ret; marriage cnsllr Catholic Marriage Advsy Cncl 1970–87 (chm 1981–83), pres Barnet, Haringey and Hertsmere Marriage Guidance Cncl 1982–92; govr: Bedford Coll London 1983–85, Holy Family Covent Enfield 1984–89; memb Ctee Cncl of Circuit Judges 1991–95; Papal Cross Pro Ecclesia et Pontifice 1986; *Recreations* theatre; *Style*— His Hon J Burkett Baker, QC; ✉ 43 The Ridgeway, Enfield, Middx EN2 8PD

BAKER, Caroline Christian; da of Maj Hugh Armitage Baker, MC (d 1972), of Argentina, and Nettie Christian, *née* Cook; *b* 8 Jan 1943; *Educ* Northlands Buenos Aires; *children* 1 da (Elodene Baker Murphy b 1984); *Career* asst to Shirley Conran at the Observer 1966–68, fashion ed Nova Magazine 1968–76, freelance fashion contributor Vogue Magazine 1976, fashion ed Cosmopolitan 1980–83; fashion ed: Sunday Times 1987–90, Mirabella 1990–91, Good Housekeeping 1991–; *Recreations* living in the imagination and dreaming impossible romances; *Style*— Ms Caroline Baker; ✉ Good Housekeeping Magazine, National Magazine House, 72 Broadwick St, London W1

BAKER, Christopher James; s of James Alfred Baker, and Alice Marjorie Baker, *née* Yeomans (d 1991); *b* 5 Nov 1951; *Educ* Dulwich, Christ's Coll Cambridge (MA); *m* 27 March 1978, Anne Elizabeth Sylvia, da of Francis George James Morris, of Stockton-on-Tees; 2 s (James b 1981, Francis b 1985), 2 da (Amy b 1983, Hannah b 1988); *Career* principal HM Treasy 1973–80, banker Morgan Grenfell & Co Ltd 1981–83, dir Hill Samuel Bank Ltd 1987–89 (joined 1983), corp fin ptnr Coopers & Lybrand 1990–93, corp strategy dir The Littlewoods Organisation plc 1993–; *Recreations* walking, motoring, photography; *Style*— Christopher J Baker, Esq; ✉ Woodlands, 18 Carrwood Road, Wilmslow, Cheshire SK9 5DL (☎ 01625 529663, fax 01625 528349); The Littlewoods Organisation plc, 100 Old Hall Street, Liverpool L70 1AB (☎ 0151 235 3428, fax 0151 235 3351)

BAKER, Christopher Paul; s of Roland Midelton Baker (d 1949), and Hilda May, *née* Paul (d 1968), of Clifton; *b* 31 Oct 1925; *Educ* Marlborough; *m* 1956, Jane, da of Maj-Gen Sir Charles Dunphie, CB, CBE, DSO, *qv*, of Wincanton; 2 s, 1 da; *Career* Army 1944, served Egypt and Palestine 1945–47 (Capt); insur broker (Lloyd's), ret; former dir Glanvill Enthoven & Co Ltd and subsidiary cos; former dep chm: Mid Southern Water Co and Cncl of Water Cos (Pension Fund) Tstee Co; chm Byways Tst 1993–; *Recreations* gardening, steam trains, preservation of the Book of Common Prayer, field sports; *Style*— Christopher Baker, Esq; ✉ Broad Oak House, Odiham, Hants RG29 1AH (☎ 01256 702482)

BAKER, Colin Charles; s of Charles Ernest Baker (d 1971), and Lily Catherine Baker; *b* 8 June 1943; *Educ* St Bede's Coll Manchester, Coll of Law, LAMDA; *m* 1, 1976 (m dis 1979), Liza Goddard, the actress; m 2, 20 Sept 1982, Marion Elizabeth, da of Kenneth Wyatt; 1 s (Jack b and d 1983), 4 da (Lucy b 1985, Belinda b 1988, Lalage b 1990, Rosie b 1992); *Career* actor; major roles incl: Prince Anatol in War and Peace (BBC) 1971, Paul Merroney in The Brothers (BBC) 1973–76, The Doctor in Dr Who (BBC) 1983–86; dir Equity Tst Fund 1992–; memb: Cncl of Mgmnt and Appeals Ctee Fndn for the Study of Infant Deaths 1984– (chm 1996–), memb Equity 1969 (Cncl 1990–94, Equity Exec 1992–94); memb and vice pres Wildlife Hosp Tst, govr Frieth CEC Sch Bucks 1993–; *Style*— Colin Baker, Esq; ✉ c/o Evans and Reiss, 100 Fawe Park Road, Putney, London SW15 2EA (☎ 0181 877 3755, fax 0181 877 0307)

BAKER, David Kenneth; s of Kenneth William Baker (d 1991), of Lincoln, and Mary Evelyn, *née* Billingham; *b* 21 Oct 1937; *Educ* Ardingly; *m* 3 June 1967, Susan Patricia, da of Edward Thornton Denton, MBE, FCA, JP; 3 s (William David b 20 Feb 1969, Charles Nicholas b 10 Aug 1970, Edward Kenneth b 17 April 1973); *Career* trainee rising to sales dir C S Dickinson Ltd Lincoln (flour millers) until 1971, md A W Tindall Ltd Holbeach until 1993 (joined to become sales dir 1972); owner Narborough Trout Farm Ltd 1993–; High Sheriff of Lincolnshire 1995–96, vice pres Lincs Agric Soc; chm: Complaints Review Panel Social Servs Lincs CC, Spalding Area Lincoln Cathedral Preservation Cncl; memb: Cncl East of England Agric Soc, Exec Ctee Lincs Cathedral Preservation Cncl, Holbeach Hurn PCC, Upper River Nar Drainage Board, Social Servs Secure Accommodation Panel Lincs CC, Ctee Holbeach and District Civic Soc, Nat Assoc of Br and Irish Millers 1955–89; *Recreations* shooting, fishing, golf, sailing, DIY, gardening; *Style*— David K Baker, Esq; ✉ Narborough Trout Farm Ltd, Narborough, Kings Lynn, Norfolk PE32 1TE (☎ 01760 338005)

BAKER, David Leon; s of late Jack Charles Baker, of Baker St, London, and Joan, *née* Grannard; *b* 14 May 1950; *Educ* St Marylebone GS London, Eaton & Wallis Coll London; *m* 23 June 1974, Helen Amanda (Mandy), da of Gerald and Joyce Stone, of Regents Park, London; *Career* Erdman Lewis International Ltd Int (now Colliers Erdman Lewis) Property Conslts: asst negotiator 1968, assoc dir 1973, dir 1978, sr office dir 1987 (network mangr for USA, Canada and Europe 1987–90), dir corp business 1989–93, exec dir UK Offices and Business Space 1994–95, dir business devpt 1995–; dep res Brokerage Ctee Int Real Estate Fedn, fndr memb Steering Ctee Office Agents Soc, memb Ctee of Mgmnt Br Cncl for Offices; hon surveyor Thames Valley Univ 1992; Freeman City of London 1990; memb Land Inst, fell Property Conslts Soc, FPCS, FFB; *Recreations* rugby, football, cricket, athletics, tennis, local government, historic London, architecture, theatre; *Style*— David Baker, Esq; ✉ Colliers Erdman Lewis Ltd, 9 Marylebone Lane, London (☎ 0171 629 8191, fax 0171 409 3124, telex 28169, car 0468 500148)

BAKER, Duncan; s of Frank Baker, and Janet, *née* Craddock; *Educ* Huntingdon GS Cambs, Open Univ (BA); *m* 27 July 1974, Bridget; 1 s (Brendan b 13 Sept 1988); *Career* journalist: Eastern Counties Newspapers 1971–75, Birmingham Post and Mail 1975–79; press offr W Midlands RHA 1979–81, PR exec European Ferries 1981–85, PR mangr Port of Felixstowe (P&O Group) 1986–89, head of PR Cable & Wireless Business Networks 1989–92, mangr of PR Cable & Wireless plc 1992–95, sr mangr of corp rels HSBC Holdings plc March-Sept 1995, dir of public affrs Midland Bank plc Sept 1995–96, gp brand mangr Cable & Wireless plc Oct 1996–; *Recreations* skiing, mountain biking, travel, reading, family; *Style*— Duncan Baker, Esq; ✉ Cable & Wireless plc, 124 Theobalds Road, London WC1X 8RX (☎ 0171 315 4000, fax 0171 315 5000)

BAKER, His Hon Judge (Michael) Findlay; QC (1990); s of Rt Hon Sir George Baker, PC (d 1984), of Rickmansworth, Herts and Portpatrick, Wigtownshire, and Jessie Raphael, *née* Findlay; *b* 26 May 1943; *Educ* Haileybury and ISC, BNC Oxford (BA); *m* 1973, Sarah Hartley Overton; 2 da (Helen Mary Hartley b 1976, Hannah Elizabeth Findlay b 1979); *Career* called to the Bar Inner Temple 1966, recorder of the Crown Court 1991–95, circuit judge (SE Circuit) 1995–; sec Nat Reference Tribunals for the Coal-Mining Indust 1973–95; *Recreations* mountaineering, cross country running; *Clubs* Alpine, Climbers'; *Style*— His Hon Judge Findlay Baker, QC; ✉ Oakford, Standon, Ware, Herts SG11 1LT (☎ 01920 822144); St Albans Crown Court, 4 Bricket Road, St Albans, Herts AL1 3HY

BAKER, His Hon Geoffrey; QC (1970); er s of Sidney Baker (d 1963), of Bradford, and Cecilia Baker; *b* 5 April 1925; *Educ* Bradford GS, Univ of Leeds (LLB); *m* 1948, Sheila, da of M Hill, of Leeds; 2 s, 1 da; *Career* called to the Bar Inner Temple 1947; recorder: Pontefract 1967–71, Sunderland 1971–72, Crown Ct 1972–78; circuit judge (NE Circuit) 1978–95 (dep circuit judge 1995–); pres: Leeds Univ Law Graduates' Assoc 1981–, Leeds and W Riding Medico-Legal Soc 1984–85 (memb Ctee 1980–); memb: Standing Cncl Convocation of Leeds Univ 1980– (chm 1986–90), Advsy Ctee on Law Univ of Leeds 1983–, Ct Univ of Leeds 1984–; *Recreations* gardening, painting, photography; *Style*— His Hon Geoffrey Baker, QC; ✉ c/o Courts Administrator, Symons House, Belgrave Street, Leeds LS2 8DD

BAKER, Prof Geoffrey Howard; s of Albert Baker (d 1976), of Marton, Blackpool, and Dorothy, *née* Howard; *b* 27 Dec 1931; *Educ* Arnold Sch Blackpool, Sch of Architecture Univ of Manchester (DipArch), Univ of Newcastle upon Tyne (PhD); *m* 1, 11 Jan 1966 (m dis 1988), Margaret Anne, *née* Gilmour; 1 s (Kieran Roderick Michael b 14 April 1968); m 2, Carolynn, da of Carl E Gillum, of Chanute, Kansas, USA; *Career* architect; Grenfell Baines and Hargreaves Preston 1957–59, S W Cooke and Ptnrs Birmingham 1959–60, Norman and Dawbarn London 1960–62; lectr: Plymouth Sch of Architecture 1962–64, Univ of Newcastle upon Tyne Sch of Architecture 1964–76; reader Sch of Architecture and Interior Design Brighton Poly 1976–87, currently prof of architecture Tulane Univ New Orleans USA; visiting lectr and critic: Univ of Plymouth (formerly Plymouth Poly), Univ of Sheffield; visiting prof: Queen's Univ Belfast 1981, Univ of Arkansas (also programme dir); distinguished visiting prof Univ of N Carolina 1993; Open Univ: co-organiser course A305 1973–74, writer and presenter of course materials and TV programmes, dir of summer sch at Univ of Sussex 1975, external examiner course A305 1975–81, external examiner Huddersfield Poly 1981–85; ARIBA 1959; *Books* Le Corbusier: An Analysis of Form (1984, 3 edn 1996), Le Corbusier: Early Works by Charles-Edouard Jeanneret-Gris (1987), Design Strategies in Architecture: An Approach to the Analysis of Form (1989), Le Corbusier: The Creative Search (1996); *Recreations* swimming, travel, soccer, opera; *Style*— Prof Geoffrey Baker; ✉ School of Architecture, Tulane University, New Orleans, Louisana 70118 USA (☎ 00 1 504 891 3451)

BAKER, HE Gordon Meldrum; s of Ralph Gordon Walter John Baker, of Burnham-on-Sea, Somerset, and Kathleen Margaret Henrietta Dawe, *née* Meldrum; *b* 4 July 1941; *Educ* St Andrew's Sch Bridgwater, Univ of Bradford (MSc); *m* 8 April 1978, Sheila Mary, da of Edward Megson (d 1977); *Career* Lord Chllr's Dept 1959–66; HM Dip Serv: Cwlth Office 1966–68, FCO (formerly FO) 1968–69, Br High Commision Lagos 1969–72, first sec W Africa Dept FCO 1973–75, res clerk FCO 1974–75 and 1976–78, sabbatical at Bradford Univ 1975–76, FCO 1976–78 (Sci and Technol (later Maritime, Aviation and Environment) Dept), first sec, head of Chancery and HM consul Brasilia 1978–81, asst head Mexico and Central America Dept FCO 1982–84, cnsllr FCO 1984, seconded to British Aerospace plc 1984–86, cnsllr, head of Chancery then dep hd of Mission and HM Consul-Gen Santiago 1986–90, RCDS 1990–91, head of W Indian and Atlantic Dept FCO 1991–95, high cmmr Belize 1995–; *Recreations* reading, walking, watching birds, amateur dramatics; *Style*— HE Mr G M Baker; ✉ c/o FCO (Belmopan), King Charles St, London SW1A 2AH

BAKER, Guy Christopher Scott; s of George Henry Baker (d 1980), of Rothley, Leics, and Phyllis Harriett Scott (d 1985); *b* 18 March 1945; *Educ* Loughborough GS; *m* 3 Nov 1979, Caroline Anne, da of Thomas Matthew Lockton; 1 da (Josephine Elizabeth b 10 Dec 1981); *Career* articled clerk A C Palmer & Co 1962, CA 1968, ptnr Ernst & Young 1989– (ptnr with previous merged firms 1974–); memb: Insolvency Practitioners Assoc, Soc of Practitioners of Insolvency 1990; *Recreations* golf; *Clubs* Rothley Park Golf, The Farmers; *Style*— Guy Baker, Esq; ✉ 90 Swithland Lane, Rothley, Leicestershire LE7 7SE (☎ 0116 230 3004); Ernst & Young, Provincial House, 37 New Walk, Leicester LE1 6TU (☎ 0116 254 9818, fax 0116 255 1357)

BAKER, Dr (John) Harry Edmund; s of late Joseph Elmer Grieff Baker, and Mary Irene Elizabeth, *née* Bolton; *b* 8 Jan 1949; *Educ* Epsom Coll, The Middx Hosp Med Sch Univ of London (BSc, MB BS, MRCP); *Career* Maj RAMC TA, specialist pool HQ AMS, Br Army Trauma Life Support Team, chief med advsr ACFA/CCFA, lately DADMS (TA) HQ W Mid Dist; lectr Univ of Nottingham Med Sch 1976–77, registrar Nat Hosp for Nervous Diseases 1977–80, sr registrar Nat Spinal Injuries Centre Stoke Mandeville 1980–83, Midland Spinal Injury Centre Oswestry 1983–85, conslt in spinal injuries and rehabilitation med S Glamorgan Health and Welsh Health Common Servs Authy 1985–, conslt advsr in rehabilitation Dept of Social Security War Pensions Office; author of pubns in med jls on immediate care & emergency handling of spinal cord injury, mgmnt of spinal injuries at accident sites, accident and disaster med; former dep chm Med Exec St John Ambulance Bde, past chm Professional Panel St John Aero Med Servs, vice chm Wales and memb Exec Bd (UK) Br Assoc of Socs of Immediate Care, memb Med Bd of St John Ambulance (Priory for Wales), med advsr Nat Rescue Trg Cncl; memb Cncl: Int Soc of Aeromedical Servs, Int Med Soc of Paraplegia, World Assoc of Emergency and Disaster Med; conslt advsr to Conjoint Ctee of the Voluntary Aid Socs; advsr and lectr in mgmnt of spinal cord injury to: Fire Servs, NHS Trg Directorate,

Ambulance Serv, Med Equestrian Assoc, various equestrian bodies, RAC, MSA, various other motor sports orgns, Mountain Rescue Team, RLSS; CStJ 1988; Fell NY Acad of Sci (USA) 1988; *Books* Management of Mass Casualties (jtly, 1980), ABC of Major Trauma (1994); *Style—* Dr Harry Baker; ✉ 56 Bridge St, Llandaff, Cardiff CF5 2EN (☎ 01222 578091); 5 Bridge Rd, Llandaff, Cardiff CF5 2PT (☎ 01222 569900); Rookwood Hospital, Fairwater Rd, Llandaff, Cardiff CF5 2YN (☎ 01222 566281, 01222 555677, fax 01222 555156, answering service 01426 910256, e-mail 73064.2232@compuserve.com)

BAKER, Dr Harvey; s of Isaac Baker (d 1971), and Rose, *née* Rifkin (d 1982); *b* 19 Aug 1930; *Educ* Univ of Leeds (MB ChB, MD); *m* 6 June 1960, Adrienne Dawn, da of Leonard Lever, of London; 1 s (Laurence b 1961), 2 da (Caroline b 1962, Marion b 1967); *Career* Capt RAMC served KAR Kenya 1955–57; conslt dermatologist 1968–, conslt physician The London Hosp 1968–90; pres St John's Hosp Dermatological Soc 1973, pres Br Assoc of Dermatologists 1990–91; FRCP (London); *Books* Concise Text Book of Dermatology (1979), Clinical Dermatology (1989); *Recreations* music, literature; *Style—* Dr Harvey Baker; ✉ 16 Sheldon Ave, Highgate, London N6 4JT (☎ 0181 340 5970); 152 Harley St, London W1 (☎ 0171 935 8868, fax 0171 224 2574)

BAKER, Maj-Gen Ian Helstrip; CBE (1977, MBE 1965); s of Henry Hubert Baker, and Mary Clare, *née* Coles; *b* 26 Nov 1927; *Educ* St Peter's Sch York, St Edmund Hall Oxford, Open Univ (BA 1994); *m* 1956, Susan Anne, da of Maj Henry Osmond Lock, of York House, Dorchester, Dorset; 2 s, 1 s decd, 1 da; *Career* cmmnd 2 Lt RA 1948, transferred to RTR 1955, Staff Coll Camberley 1959, Maj 1960, DAAG HQ17 Gurkha Div Malaya and Singapore 1960–62, OC Parachute Sqdn RAC 1963–65, Instr Staff Coll and Brevet Lt-Col 1965, GSO1 Chiefs of Staff Ctee MOD 1966–67, Lt-Col 1966, CO 1 RTR UK and BAOR 1967–69, Col 1970, Col RTR 1970–71, Brig 1972, Cdr 7 Armd Bde BAOR 1972–74, RCDS 1974, BGS HQ UKLF 1975–77, Maj Gen 1978, Asst Chief of Gen Staff MOD 1978–80, GOC NE Dist 1980–82, Col Cmdt RTR 1981–86, ret Army 1982; Univ Coll London: sec 1982–91, hon pres Med Students' Soc 1983–88, hon pres UCL Boat Club 1986–93, pres The Crabtree Fndn UCL 1995; memb Int Ctee of Univ Administrators 1984–91; govr Welbeck Coll 1980–82; fell St Catharine's Coll Cambridge 1977; various contribs to service and univ papers and jls; *Recreations* sailing, outdoor pursuits, reading, modern history; *Style—* Maj-Gen Ian Baker, CBE; ✉ c/o Barclays Bank, Dorchester, Dorset DT1 1BT

BAKER, Dame Janet Abbott; CH (1994), DBE (1976, CBE 1970); da of Robert Abbott Baker and May, *née* Pollard; *b* 21 Aug 1933; *Educ* The Coll for Girls York; *m* 1957, James Keith Shelley; *Career* singer; memb Munster Tst, tstee Fndn for Sport and the Arts 1991–, Opera Bd Royal Opera House 1994–; chllr Univ of York 1991–; Hon DMus: Univ of Birmingham 1968, Univ of Leicester 1974, Univ of London 1974, Univ of Hull 1975, Univ of Oxford 1975, Univ of Leeds 1980, Univ of Lancaster 1983, Univ of York 1984; Hon MusD Univ of Cambridge 1984, Hon DLitt Univ of Bradford 1983, Hon LLD Univ of Aberdeen 1980; hon fell: St Anne's Coll Oxford 1975, Downing Coll Cambridge 1985; Daily Mail Kathleen Ferrier Award 1956, Queen's Prize RCM 1959, Hamburg Shakespeare Prize 1971, Copenhagen Sonning Prize 1979, Gold Medal Royal Philharmonic Soc 1990; Commandeur Ordre des Arts et des Lettres (France); FRSA 1979; *Books* Full Circle (autobiog, 1982); *Recreations* reading, walking; *Style—* Dame Janet Baker, CH, DBE

BAKER, Jeffrey; s of Peter Baker, of Norton-on-Tees, Cleveland, and Barbara Baker; *b* 22 Oct 1967; *Educ* Blakeston Comp Stockton-on-Tees; *Partner* Daphne Latimer; 1 s (Jack Bosco b 12 Oct 1994), 1 da (Jasmine b 31 Aug 1996); *Career* chef; commis chef de partie Greenhouse Mayfair, chef de partie Rue St Jacques London, chef de partie Waltons London, estagé Restaurant Riesbachli Zurich, estagé Chateau Montreuil France, sous chef Bishopstrow House Relais & Chateau Wilts, sous chef Sud Ouest Knightsbridge, sous chef Stephen Bull Restaurant London, head chef Brasserie Fourty Four Ltd Leeds 1992–, head chef Pool Court at 42 1994– (Michelin Star 1996); *Recreations* eating out, following Middlesbrough FC; *Style—* Jeffrey Baker, Esq; ✉ Brasserie 44 & Pool Court at 42, 42/44 The Calls, Leeds LS2 7EW (☎ 0113 244 4242, fax 0113 234 3332)

BAKER, His Honour Judge John Arnold; DL (Surrey 1986); s of late William Sydney Baker, MC, and late Hilda Dora, *née* Swiss; *b* 5 Nov 1925, Calcutta; *Educ* Plymouth Coll, Wellington Sch Somerset, Wadham Coll Oxford (MA, BCL); *m* 1954, (Edith Muriel) Joy, *née* Heward; 2 da; *Career* admitted slr 1951, called to the Bar Gray's Inn 1960, recorder 1972–73, circuit judge (SE Circuit) 1973–; contested (Lib): Richmond 1959 and 1964, Dorking 1970; chm: Nat League of Young Libs 1952–53, Lib Party Exec 1969–70; vice pres Lib Pty 1968–69; pres Medico-Legal Soc 1986–88, lay fell RSM 1989; *Recreations* music; *Style—* His Honour Judge Baker, DL; ✉ c/o The Crown Court, Canbury Park Rd, Kingston upon Thames, Surrey (☎ 0181 549 5241)

BAKER, Rt Rev Dr John Austin; s of George Austin Baker and Grace Edna; *b* 11 Jan 1928; *Educ* Marlborough, Oriel Coll Oxford (DD); *m* 1974, Gillian Leach; *Career* ordained priest 1955, official fellow, chaplain and lectr in Divinity Corpus Christi Coll Oxford 1959–73, also lectr in theology Brasenose Coll Oxford and Lincoln Coll Oxford 1959–73, canon Westminster 1973–82, sub-dean and Lector Theologiae 1978–82, rector St Margaret's Westminster and Speaker's chaplain 1978–82, bishop of Salisbury 1982–93; memb C of E Doctrine Cmmn 1967–87; *Books* The Foolishness of God (1970), Travels in Oudamovia (1976), The Whole Family of God (1981), The Faith of a Christian (1996); *Clubs* Royal Over-Seas League; *Style—* The Rt Rev Dr John Baker; ✉ 4 Mede Villas, Kingsgate Road, Winchester, Hants SO23 9QQ (☎ 01962 861388)

BAKER, Prof John Hamilton; Hon QC (1996); s of Kenneth Lee Vincent Baker, QPM, of Hintlesham, Suffolk, and Marjorie, *née* Bagshaw; *b* 10 April 1944; *Educ* King Edward VI GS Chelmsford, Univ Coll London (LLB, PhD), Univ of Cambridge (MA, LLD); *m* 20 April 1968, Veronica Margaret, da of Rev William Stephen Lloyd, TD (d 1971), Vicar of Southsea and Berse Drelincourt, Denbighshire; 2 da (Alys b 1973, Anstice b 1978); *Career* called to the Bar Inner Temple 1966 (hon bencher 1988); lectr in law UCL 1967–71 (asst lectr 1965–67, fell 1990); Univ of Cambridge: fell St Catharine's Coll 1971–, librarian Squire Law Library 1971–73, lectr in law 1973–83, jr proctor 1980–81, reader in English legal history 1983–88, prof of English legal history 1988–, chm Faculty of Law 1990–92; lectr in legal history Inns of Ct Sch of Law 1973–78; visiting prof: Euro Univ Inst Florence 1979, Harvard Law Sch 1982, Yale Law Sch 1987, NY Univ Sch of Law 1988–; literary dir Selden Soc 1992– (jt literary dir 1981–91); Ames prize Harvard 1985; Hon LLD Univ of Chicago 1992; FRHistS 1980, FBA 1984; *Books* Introduction to English Legal History (1971, 3 edn 1990), English Legal Manuscripts (1975, 1978), The Reports of Sir John Spelman (1977–78), Manual of Law French (1979, 2 edn 1990), The Order of Serjeants at Law (1984), English Legal Manuscripts in the USA (1985, 1990), The Legal Profession and the Common Law (1986), Sources of English Legal History: Private Law to 1750 (with S F C Milsom, 1986), The Notebook of Sir John Port (1986), Readings and Moots in the Inns of Court, Part II: Moots (with S E Thorne, 1990), Reports from the Lost Notebooks of Sir James Dyer (1994); *Style—* Prof J H Baker, QC, FBA; ✉ St Catharine's College, Cambridge CB2 1RL (☎ 01223 338317, fax 01223 338340)

BAKER, John W; *Educ* Univ of Oxford (BA); *Career* various appts in transport policy & finance then urban regeneration & housing rising to dep chief exec The Housing Corporation until 1979; Central Electricity Generating Bd: joined as co sec 1979, bd memb 1980, corp md (incl responsibility for privatisation) until 1990; National Power plc (following privatisation): chief exec 1990–95, non-exec chm 1995–; non-exec dir Royal & Sun Alliance Insurance Group plc 1995–, non-exec chm Medeva plc April 1996–, memb Business Cncl A P Moller Group; chm World Energy Cncl, memb Euro Advsy Cncl Air Products & Chemicals Inc and Bankers Tst, chm English Nat Opera, govr London Business Sch; *Style—* John Baker, Esq; ✉ National Power plc, Senator House, 85 Queen Victoria Street, London EC4V 4DP (☎ 0171 615 3400)

BAKER, (Norman) Keith; s of Norman Baker (d 1985), of Bedford, and Lilian Hopper, *née* Robson (d 1994); *b* 25 April 1945; *Educ* Doncaster GS, Bedford Modern Sch; *m* 1973, Elizabeth Rhoda, da of John Avery Stonehouse; 2 da (Amelia Elizabeth b 1978, Alice Harriet Clarissa b 1981); *Career* Coopers & Lybrand: Bedford 1964–70, London 1970–73, mangr 1972, expert witness 1973, audit gp mangr Hong Kong 1973–75, sr mangr Audit & Investigations Bedford 1976–87; Neville Russell Chartered Accountants: joined 1987, ptnr 1988–, tech ptnr for Chilterns region, in charge of Litigation Support Servs; FCA 1975 (ACA 1970); *Recreations* golf, crosswords, furniture renovation, squash; *Clubs* Mowsbury Golf; *Style—* Keith Baker, Esq; ✉ Neville Russell Chartered Accountants, Sovereign Court, 202 Upper Fifth St, Silbury Boulevard, Central Milton Keynes MK9 2JB (☎ 01908 664466, fax 01908 690567, car 0831 388272)

BAKER, Rt Hon Kenneth Wilfred; CH (1992), PC (1984), MP (C) Mole Valley (majority 15,950); s of late Wilfred M Baker, OBE, of Twickenham, Middx, and Mrs Baker, *née* Harries; *b* 3 Nov 1934; *Educ* St Paul's, Magdalen Coll Oxford; *m* 1963, Mary Elizabeth Baker, *qv*, da of William Gray Muir, of Edinburgh; 1 s, 2 da; *Career* Nat Serv Lt Gunners N Africa 1953–55, artillery instr to Libyan Army; industl conslt; memb Twickenham BC 1960–62; contested (C): Poplar 1964, Acton 1966; MP (C): Acton 1968–70, St Marylebone 1970–83, Mole Valley 1983–; Parly sec CSD 1972–74, PPS to Ldr of Oppn 1974–75, min of state for indust (special responsibility for info technol) 1981–84, min for local govt DOE 1984–85, sec of state for the environment 1985–86, sec of state for educn and sci 1986–89, chm of the Cons Party and Chllr of the Duchy of Lancaster 1989–90, home sec 1990–92; memb: Public Accounts Ctee 1969–70, Exec 1922 Ctee 1975–81; chm Hansard Soc 1978–81, sec gen UN Conf of Parliamentarians on World Population and Devpt 1978; dir: Hanson plc 1992–, Videotron Corporation Ltd 1992–, Wavetek Corporation 1992–, Bell Cablemedia plc 1994–; chm MTT plc 1996–; *Books* I Have No Gun But I Can Spit (ed, 1980), London Lines (ed, 1982), The Faber Book of English History in Verse (ed, 1988), Unauthorised Versions: Poems and Their Parodies (ed, 1990), The Faber Anthology of Conservatism (ed, 1993), The Turbulent Years: my life in politics (1993), The Prime Ministers - An Irreverent Political History in Cartoons (1995), Kings and Queens - An Irreverent History of the British Monarchy (1996); *Recreations* collecting books; *Clubs* Athenaeum, Carlton, Garrick; *Style—* The Rt Hon Kenneth Baker, CH, MP; ✉ House of Commons, London SW1A 0AA

BAKER, Mark Alexander Wyndham; s of Lt Cdr Alexander Arthur Wyndham Baker (d 1969), and Renée Gavrelle Stenson, *née* Macnaghten; *b* 19 June 1940; *Educ* Prince Edward Sch Salisbury Rhodesia, Univ Coll Of Rhodesia and Nyasaland (BA), Christ Church Oxford (BA, MA); *m* 30 July 1964, Meriel, da of Capt Edward Hugh Frederick Chetwynd-Talbot, MBE, of Milton Lilbourne, Pewsey, Wilts; 1 s (Alexander b 1968), 1 da (Miranda b 1970); *Career* UKAEA: various admin appts 1964–76, sec AERE Harwell 1976–78 (gen sec 1978–81), dir of personnel and admin Northern Div 1981–84, authy personnel offr 1984–86, authy sec 1986–89; exec dir of corp affairs and personnel Nuclear Electric plc 1989–95, chm Magnox Electric plc 1996–; FRSA 1992; *Recreations* golf, bridge, walking, gardening, words; *Clubs* Reform, United Oxford and Cambridge Univ, Antrobus Dining (Cheshire); *Style—* Mark Baker, Esq; ✉ Magnox Electric plc, Berkeley Centre, Berkeley, Glos GL13 9PB (☎ 01453 813370)

BAKER, Mary Elizabeth; da of William Gray Muir, WS (d 1959), of Edinburgh, and Betty, *née* Montgomery (d 1976); *b* 5 Feb 1937; *Educ* Rothesay House Edinburgh, St Mary's Wantage, Univ of St Andrews (MA); *m* 1963, Rt Hon Kenneth Baker, CH, MP, *qv*; 2 da, 1 s; *Career* teacher 1959–67, non-exec dir Thames TV 1975–90, govr Bedford Coll 1980–85, chm London Tourist Bd 1980–83; non-exec dir: Avon Cosmetics Ltd 1981–, Barclays Bank UK Ltd 1983–88, Barclays Bank plc 1989–, Prudential Corp plc 1988–94, MFI Furniture Group plc 1992–, Camelot Group plc 1994–; memb Women's National Cmmn 1973–78; chm: Holiday Care Serv 1986–92, Thames/LWT Telethon Tst 1987–89; govr Westminster Sch 1982–88, tstee Ind Bdcasting Telethon Tst 1989–93, chm Tourism for All campaign 1988–; pres Women in Mgmnt 1990–95; vice pres: Opportunities for People with Disabilities 1990–, Women in Banking & Finance 1996–; fndr memb FORUM UK; hon fell Nene Coll; Freeman City of London; CIMgt; *Books* Days of Decision-Women (part author, 1987); *Style—* Mrs Mary Baker; ✉ c/o The Secretary, Fifth Floor, 54 Lombard Street, London EC3P 3AH

BAKER, Mary Geraldine; MBE (1995); *Educ* Univ of Leeds (BA), Inst of Almoners (post grad dip); *m*, 3 s; *Career* almoner St Thomas's Hosp 1959, marriage guidance cnsllr, lectr in sociology Open Univ, med social worker 1975–83, princ med social worker 1983–84, dir of welfare Parkinson's Disease Soc 1984–; pres European Parkinson's Disease Assoc 1992– (re-elected 1994), nat and int devpt conslt 1995–; exec memb Neurological Alliance; lay memb London Implementation Gp for Neurosciences 1993–; memb: Dept of Health Advsy Gp on Rehabilitation 1992–, Working Pty on Neurological Services in District General Hosps RCP, Working Pty and Patients' Liaison Ctee RCP 1993–, Movement Disorders Cochrane Review Gp (rep patients') 1995; govr Nat Hosp for Neurology & Neurosurgery 1994–96; memb Cncl: Chartered Soc of Physiotherapists 1994, Queens Nursing Inst 1994; hon fell Coll of Speech & Language Therapists 1992; AIMSW; *Style—* Mrs Mary Baker, MBE; ✉ Parkinson's Disease Society of the UK, 22 Upper Woburn Place, London WC1H 0RA (☎ 0171 383 3513, fax 0171 383 5754)

BAKER, Prof Michael John; TD (1971); s of John Overend Baker (d 1960), of York, and Constance Dorothy, *née* Smith (d 1979); *b* 5 Nov 1935; *Educ* Worksop Coll, Gosforth & Harvey GS, Univ of Durham (BA), Univ of London (BSc), Harvard (Cert ITP, DBA); *m* 1959, Sheila, da of Miles Bell (d 1964), of Carlisle; 1 s (John), 2 da (Fiona, Anne); *Career* served in TA 1953–55, 2 Lt RA 1956–57, Lt 624 LAA Regt RA (TA) 1958–61, Capt City of London RF 1961–64, Capt PWO 1965–67; salesman Richard Thomas & Baldwins (Sales) Ltd 1958–64, asst lectr Medway Coll of Technol 1964–66, lectr Hull Coll of Technol 1966–68, Fndn for Mgmnt Educn fell Harvard Business Sch 1968–71 (res assoc 1969–71); Univ of Strathclyde: prof of mktg 1971–, dean Strathclyde Business Sch 1978–84, dep princ Strathclyde Univ 1984–91; chm: Westburn Publishers Ltd 1982–, Scottish Mktg Projects Ltd 1986–, Inst of Mktg 1987, SGBS Ltd 1990–; dir: Stoddard Sekers Int plc 1983–, Scottish Tport Gp 1987–90, ARIS PLC 1989–94; Secretary of State for Scotland's Nominee Scottish Hosps Endowment Res Tst 1984–96; memb: Chief Scientist's Ctee SHHD 1985–96, SCOTBEC 1973–85 (chm 1983–85), UGC Business & Mgmnt Sub-Ctee 1985–89; dean Coll of Mktg 1994–, pres Acad of Mktg 1986–; fndr ed Jl of Marketing Management 1985; FRSE, FCIM, FCAM, FRSA, FScotVec; *Books* Marketing New Industrial Products (1975), Innovation - Technology, Policy & Diffusion (1979), Marketing - Theory & Practice (3 edn, 1995), Market Development (1983), Marketing Management and Strategy (1985, 2 edn 1992), Organisational Buying Behaviour (1986), The Role of Design in International Competitiveness (1989), Marketing and Competitive Success (1989), Macmillan Dictionary of Marketing and Advertising (2 edn, 1990), Marketing - An Introductory Text (6 edn, 1996), The Marketing Book (3 edn, 1994), Research for Marketing (1991), Companion Encyclopedia of Marketing (1995); *Recreations* travel, gardening, walking, sailing ('Ornsay', 'Mary Rose of Morar'); *Clubs* Royal Over-Seas League; *Style—* Prof Michael Baker, TD, FRSE; ✉ Westburn, Helensburgh, Strathclyde G84 8NH (☎ 01436 674686); University of Strathclyde, Glasgow G4 0RQ (☎ 0141 552 4400)

BAKER, His Hon Judge Michael John David; s of Ernest Bowden Baker (d 1979), and Dulcie, *née* Davies; *b* 17 April 1934; *Educ* Trinity Sch of John Whitgift, Univ of Bristol (LLB); *m* 4 April 1958, Edna Harriet, da of John Herbert Lane (d 1950); 1 s (Matthew b 1963), 1 da (Amanda b 1961); *Career* Flying Offr RAF 1957–60; admitted slr 1957, ptnr Glanvilles 1962–88 (joined 1960), coroner S Hants 1973–88 (dep coroner 1972), recorder Crown Ct 1980–88, circuit judge (SE Circuit) 1988–; memb Cncl Coroners Soc of Eng and Wales 1979–88 (jr vice pres 1987–88), pres Southern Coroners Soc 1975–76; *Recreations* walking, swimming, tennis, theatre, photography; *Clubs* The Law Soc, RAF, Emsworth Sailing; *Style*— His Hon Judge Michael Baker; ✉ Chichester Combined Court Centre, The Court House, Southgate, Chichester, West Sussex PO19 1SX

BAKER, Michael Verdun; s of Albert Ernest Thomas Baker, of Frinton-on-Sea, Essex, and Eva Louisa Florence, *née* Phillips; *b* 30 July 1942; *Educ* Caterham Sch; *m* 21 Sept 1963, Rita Ann, da of Walter James Marks, of Ilford, Essex; 2 da (Carolyn b 1967, Louise b 1970); *Career* insur official Alliance Assurance Co Ltd 1959–63, O & M systems analyst Plessey Co 1963–66, sr consIt Coopers & Lybrand 1967–72; The Stock Exchange: talisman project dir 1972–78, settlement dir 1978–82, admin dir 1982–84, divnl dir settlement servs 1984–87, exec dir mkts 1987–90, chief exec Assoc of Private Client Investmt Mangrs and Stockbrokers 1990–94, chm Consort Securities Systems Ltd 1994–96; memb Advsy Bd International Securities Consultancy 1993–; author of various booklets and brochures on O & M, clerical work mgmnt and Stock Exchange settlement; *Recreations* running, photography, travel, golf, record collecting; *Clubs* Bigbury Golf; *Style*— Michael Baker, Esq; ✉ 10 Maclarens, Wickham Bishops, Witham, Essex CM8 3XE (☎ 01621 892158)

BAKER, Sir Nicholas Brian; kt (1997), MP (C) Dorset N (majority 10,080); s of late Col Harold Stanley Baker, OBE; *b* 23 Nov 1938; *Educ* Clifton, Exeter Coll Oxford (MA); *m* 1970, (Penelope) Carol, da of Maj Edward Nassau Nicolai d'Abo, KOYLI (RARO); 1 s, 1 da; *Career* ptnr Frere Cholmeley slrs 1973–94, conslt Frere Cholmeley Bischoff 1994; MP (C) Dorset N 1979–; PPS to: Min of State for the Armed Forces 1981–83, Min of State for Def Procurement 1983–84, Michael Heseltine as Sec of State for Def 1984–86, Lord Young of Graffham as Sec of State for Trade and Indust 1987–88; a Lord Cmmr of the Treasy (govt whip) 1990–94 (asst govt whip 1989–90), pairing whip 1993–94, Parly under sec of state for home affairs 1994–95; *Recreations* exercise, music, English countryside; *Clubs* Blandford Constitutional, Wimborne Cons; *Style*— Sir Nicholas Baker, MP; ✉ House of Commons, London SW1A 0AA

BAKER, (William) Nigel Whiston; s of Francis Cecil Whiston Baker (d 1952), and Gladys, *née* Davies; *b* 4 Jan 1934; *Educ* St Edward's Sch Oxford, Univ of London Middx Hosp Med Sch (MB, MS); *m* 29 Nov 1962, Daphne Cicely Kempe, da of John Kempe Clarke (d 1977); 2 da (Helen b 1964, Charlotte b 1966); *Career* Capt RAMC 1960–62; res fell St Mark's Hosp 1967–69 (former resident surgical offr), sr registrar Westminster Gp of Hosps 1970–77, conslt gen surgn Ashford Hosp 1977–; memb RSM, Br Soc of Gastroenterology; *Style*— Nigel Baker, Esq; ✉ Ashford Hospital, Ashford, Middx TW15 3AA (☎ 01784 251188, fax 01784 255696)

BAKER, Nik; s of Herbie Baker, of Shoreham, W Sussex, and Maria Baker; *b* 11 May 1971; *Educ* Steyning GS; *Career* professional windsurfer; *Achievements* winner Robbie Naish Trophy 1986, Indoor World champion 1993, 1994 and 1995; memb Professional Windsurfers' Assoc world tour; placed 4th overall in PWA world rankings 1995; *Recreations* snowboarding, surfing, mountain biking; *Style*— Nik Baker, Esq; ✉ c/o SSM Ltd, 21 Chelsea Wharf, 15 Lots Road, Chelsea, London SW10 0QJ (☎ 0171 376 7446, fax 0171 376 7786)

BAKER, His Hon Paul Vivian; QC (1972); s of Vivian Cyril Baker (d 1976), and Maud Lydia, *née* Jiggins (d 1979); *b* 27 March 1923; *Educ* City of London Sch, Univ Coll Oxford (BA, BCL, MA); *m* 2 Jan 1957, Stella Paterson, da of William Eadie (d 1942); 1 s (Ian David b 1958), 1 da (Alison Joyce b 1960); *Career* Flt Lt RAF 1941–46; called to the Bar Lincoln's Inn 1950, practised at Chancery Bar 1951–83, bencher Lincoln's Inn 1979, circuit judge (SE Circuit) 1983–96; chm Incorporated Cncl of Law Reporting 1992–; ed Law Quarterly Review 1971–87 (asst ed 1960–70); Freeman City of London 1946; *Books* Snell's Principles of Equity (jt ed 24–29 edn, 1954–90); *Recreations* music, walking, reading; *Clubs* Athenaeum, Authors; *Style*— His Hon Paul Baker, QC; ✉ 9 Old Square, Lincoln's Inn, London WC2A 3SR (☎ 0171 242 2633)

BAKER, Peter Alan; s of Alan Baker, of Wolverhampton, and Joan, *née* Price; *b* 7 Oct 1967; *Educ* Codsall HS; *m* 6 Oct 1990, Helen; 2 da (Georgina b 14 Oct 1992, Grace b 7 June 1994); *Career* professional golfer 1986–; winner: Benson & Hedges Int Open Championship 1988, UAP Under 25's Championship 1990, Dunhill British Masters 1993, Scandinavian Masters 1993, Perrier Paris European 4–Ball 1994; memb team: Ryder Cup 1993–, Dunhill Cup 1993–; Rookie of the Year 1987; *Recreations* music, cars, sports, Wolves FC; *Style*— Peter Baker, Esq; ✉ c/o IMG, Pier House, Strand on the Green, Chiswick, London W4 3NN (☎ 0181 233 5000, fax 0181 233 5001)

BAKER, His Hon Judge Peter Maxwell; QC (1974); s of Harold Baker (d 1971), and Rose Baker (d 1994); *b* 26 March 1930; *Educ* King Edward VII Sch Sheffield, Exeter Coll Oxford (MA); *m* 1, 1954, Jacqueline Mary, *née* Marshall (d 1986); 3 da; *m* 2, 1988, Sandra Elizabeth Hughes; *Career* called to the Bar Gray's Inn 1956, jr NE Circuit 1960, recorder Crown Court 1972–83, circuit judge (NE Circuit) 1983–, resident judge Doncaster 1991–; *Recreations* music, watching other gardens, yachting, fishing, shooting; *Style*— His Hon Judge Peter Baker, QC; ✉ c/o Circuit Administrator, 17th Floor, West Riding House, Albion Street, Leeds LS1 5AA

BAKER, Peter Portway; AFC (1957); s of Wing Cdr Alfred Guy Baker (d 1955), of Beaconsfield, Bucks, and Luciana Maria Lorenza, *née* Castelli; *b* 2 Sept 1925; *Educ* Merchant Taylors', St John's Coll Oxford; *Career* RAF: U/T Aircrew 1944, GD Offr (Pilot Offr) 1945, memb 201, 209 and 230 Sqdns as pilot 1946–49, Central Flying Sch 1949, flying instr (Flt Lt) 1949–52, Empire Test Pilots Sch 1953, test pilot A and AEE Boscombe Down 1954–56, tutor (Sqdn-Ldr) Empire Test Pilots Sch 1957–59, voluntarily resigned 1959, test pilot Handley Page Ltd 1959 (test flying Dart Herald and Victor aircraft); BAC Weybridge: joined 1962, test pilot for VC10 BAC 1–11 and Concorde aircraft, asst chief test pilot Concorde 1969, dep chief test pilot BAe Filton Div 1980 (ret 1982); memb CAA Airworthiness Div 1982 (chief test pilot 1986–87, ret 1987), self employed aviation conslt; QCVSA, RP Alston Meml Medal 1978; Liveryman Guild of Air Pilots and Air Navigators 1971 (Upper Freeman 1961–); memb: Bd Air Requirements until 1996, Royal Aeronautical Soc 1964, Soc of Experimental Test Pilots 1965; *Recreations* walking, reading, aviation; *Clubs* RAF, MCC; *Style*— Peter Baker, Esq, AFC; ✉ Flat 2, 44 Elsworthy Rd, London NW3 3BU (☎ 0171 722 4759)

BAKER, Raymond Edwin (Ray); OBE; *Educ* Lanchester Coll, Dunchurch Coll; *Career* served HM Forces; early business career with Courtaulds, Armstrong Siddeley Motors and the Post Office, subsequently various positions within GEC rising to regnl mangr Scotland GEC Telecomms, currently dir GEC Scotland Ltd; currently chm: Fife Enterprise, Fife Health Board, Fife Coll, Assoc of Scottish Colls, Fife Indust Cncl, Fife Euro Vocational Trg Partnership, Fife Area Bd Young Enterprise, Youth Clubs Fife; currently vice chm Fife Economic Forum; FRSA, FIMgt, MInstD; *Recreations* music, reading, gardening, walking; *Style*— Ray Baker, Esq, OBE; ✉ Chairman, Fife Health Board, Springfield House, Cupar, Fife KY15 5UP (☎ 01334 656200, fax 01334 652606)

BAKER, Richard Douglas James; OBE (1976), RD (1979); s of Albert Baker (d 1974), of Kilburn, London, and Jane Isobel, *née* Baxter; *b* 15 June 1925; *Educ* Kilburn GS, Peterhouse Cambridge (MA); *m* 1961, Margaret Celia, da of Thomas Herbert Martin; 2 s (Andrew b 1962, James b 1964); *Career* served WWII RN 1943–46; broadcaster and author; actor 1948–49, teacher 1949–50; BBC 1950–95; announcer BBC Third Programme 1950–53, newsreader BBC TV 1954–82; TV commentaries on state and musical events incl Last Night of the Proms, New Year Concert from Vienna 1960–95 and Festival of Remembrance 1990–; presenter: Omnibus (BBC 1) 1983, Start the Week (Radio 4) 1970–87; record programmes with BBC incl: These You Have Loved (Radio 4) 1972–77, Baker's Dozen 1977–87, Music in Mind (Radio 4) 1987–88, Melodies For You (Radio 2) 1988–95, Richard Baker Compares Notes (Radio 4) 1988–95, Mainly for Pleasure and In Tune (Radio 3) 1988–95, Music for Awhile (BBC World Service) 1990–91, Classic Countdown (Classic FM) 1995–; one man theatre show Music In My Life; other theatre incl: Grand Tour to Melody, The Best of British (narrator), Mr Gilbert and Mr Sullivan (scriptwriter and Sullivan), Viva Verdi! (scriptwriter and narrator); memb Broadcasting Standards Cncl 1989–94, dir Youth and Music, govr Nat Youth Orch of GB 1985–, tstee D'Oyly Carte Opera Co 1985–; TV Newscaster of the Year (Radio Industries Club) 1972, 1974 and 1979, BBC Radio Personality of the Year (Variety Club of GB) 1984, Man of the Year 1990, Gold Award Sony Radio Awards 1996; Freeman City of London, memb Worshipful Co of Plaisterers; Hon LLD: Univ of Strathclyde 1979, Univ of Aberdeen 1982; Hon FLCM 1974, Hon RAM 1988; *Books* incl: Here is the News (1964), The Terror of Tobermory (1972), The Magic of Music (1975), Dry Ginger (1977), Richard Baker's Music Guide (1979), Mozart (1982, 2 edn 1991), Richard Baker's London (1990), Mozart (1991), Richard Baker's Companion to Music (1993); *Recreations* gardening, the gramophone; *Clubs* Garrick; *Style*— Richard Baker, Esq, OBE, RD; ✉ c/o Bagenal Harvey Organisation, 141–143 Drury Lane, London WC2B 5TB (☎ 0171 379 4625, fax 0171 836 1735)

BAKER, Richard William Shelmerdine; s of Lt-Col Charles Bradbeer Baker (d 1979), and Vera Margaret, *née* Shelmerdine (d 1994); *b* 17 Dec 1933; *Educ* Buxton Coll; *m* 1 (m dis 1975), Teresa Mary Elizabeth, *née* Smith; 1 s (David b 22 Feb 1960), 1 da (Lisa b 31 July 1962); m 2, 30 May 1975, Vanda, da of Percy William Macey (d 1989); *Career* Nat Serv 1951–53, cmmnd 2 Lt, transfd AER 1953, Lt 1954, Actg Capt 1960; mgmnt post Marks and Spencer 1954–60, sales dir and gp md Barbour Index Ltd 1972–79; sr vice pres and gen mangr Sun Life Assurance Co of Canada (rep 1960–72, memb Sr Advsy Cncl for Int Ops), md Sun Life of Canada (UK) Ltd; chm: Sun Life of Canada Unit Managers Ltd, Sun Life of Canada Home Loans Ltd; dir Life Assurance and Unit Trust Regulatory Orgn (LAUTRO); pres GB Wheelchair Basketball Assoc; MInstD; *Recreations* racing, golf, tennis; *Clubs* Canada, East India, MCC, Turf; *Style*— Richard Baker, Esq; ✉ Wissenden House Oast, Bethersden, Kent TN26 3EL (☎ 0123 382 0352); Fisher House, Hillside Park, Sunningdale, Berks SL5 9RP (☎ 01344 22664); Sun Life of Canada, Basing View, Basingstoke, Hants RG21 2DZ (☎ 01256 849210, fax 01256 811129, telex 858654)

BAKER, Dr Robert George; s of Reginald Henry Baker (d 1981), of Dinton, Wilts, and Ellen Louise (d 1984); *b* 6 Dec 1930; *Educ* Bishop Wordsworth's Sch Salisbury, Fitzwilliam House Cambridge (MA, PhD); *m* 30 July 1955, Anne, da of Norman Watts Ramsden (d 1965), of Boughton, Northants; 1 s (Stephen John b 1957, d 1975), 2 da (Caroline Jane b 1958, Katharine Elizabeth b 1962); *Career* head of metallurgical res Welding Inst 1959, asst res mangr British Steel 1970, supt Materials Applications Div Nat Physical Laboratory 1973, dir of res Glacier Metal Co 1977, conslt materials engr 1982–, industl fell Wolfson Coll Oxford 1983–85, assoc prof Brunel Univ 1984–95; FIM 1969, FWeldI 1968, CEng 1978; *Books* The Microstructure of Metals (with Prof J Nutting, 1965); *Recreations* painting, walking, reading, photography; *Style*— Dr Robert Baker; ✉ Wayland Farm, Ashford Road, Bethersden, Kent TN26 3AP (☎ 01233 820094)

BAKER, Robert James; s of John Edward Baker (d 1990), and Margaret Elsie Mary, *née* Palmer; *b* 9 Dec 1947; *Educ* Univ of East Anglia (BA); *m* 15 June 1973, Beverley Joan, da of Paul Archdale Langford (d 1976); 2 da (Hannah Alice b 1979, Amy Margaret b 1981); *Career* dep md Hobsons Publishing plc 1992– (formerly dir), dir Harmsworth Publishing 1994–; md: Hobsons Academic Relations 1996–, Communication Resources Ltd 1996–; dir Harmsworth Information Publishing 1996–; *Recreations* art, antique collecting, racing; *Clubs* Reform; *Style*— Robert Baker, Esq; ✉ Porters Farm, Over, Cambridge CB4 5NS (☎ 01954 230761); Hobsons Publishing plc, Bateman St, Cambridge (☎ 01223 354551)

BAKER, Prof Robin Richard; s of Walter Richard Baker (d 1975), and Victoria Rebecca, *née* Martin (d 1988); *b* 31 Dec 1942; *Educ* RCA (maj travelling scholar, Fulbright scholar, MA), Univ of California, Thames Poly; *m* 1, 1966 (m dis 1970), Teresa Osborne-Saul; m 2, 1971 (m dis 1975), Tamar Avital; m 3, 1981 (m dis 1990), Angela Mary Piers Dumas; m 4, 1991, Katherine Knowles; *Career* designer; designer with: Joseph Ezcherick Associates San Francisco 1964–65, Russell Hodgeson & Leigh (architects) 1965–66; fndr own design practice (maj exhibitions cmmns from Arts Cncl of GB, Br Airports Authy and Nat Tst) 1966–79, princ lectr (with responsibility for computer studies) Chelsea Sch of Art 1982–83, computer advsr Art & Design Inspectorate ILEA 1984–86, specialist advsr in computing Ctee for Arts & Design CNAA 1985–88, visitor in computing Art & Design Inspectorate and Poly of Hong Kong 1985, prof and dir of computing RCA 1987–94, dir Ravensbourne Coll of Design and Communication 1994–; design computing conslt to: Conran Fndn's Museum of Design 1987–, Comshare Ltd 1987–88, Arthur Young 1988–89, Burtons Ltd 1988–89, Design Cncl 1990–, Marks & Spencer 1990–; author of numerous articles in design technology jls; *Style*— Prof Robin Baker; ✉ Ravensbourne College of Design and Communication, Walden Road, Chislehurst, Kent BR7 5SN (☎ 0181 468 7071)

BAKER, Dr Robin William; s of William John David Baker (d 1971), and Brenda Olive, *née* Hodges (d 1978); *b* 4 Oct 1953; *Educ* Bishop Wordsworth Sch, SSEES (BA), Univ of E Anglia (scholar, PhD); *m* 1974, Miriam Joy, da of Bernard Frederick Turpin (d 1968); 2 s (Simeon Scott b 12 Nov 1979, Joel William b 3 Feb 1983); *Career* exec offr MOD 1976–80, doctoral res Univ of E Anglia 1981–84; British Council: trainee 1984–85, asst rep S Africa 1985–89, head of recruitment London 1989–90, asst dir Hungary 1990–93, dir Thessaloniki 1994–; memb Société Finno-Ougrienne 1982; *Books* The Development of the Komi Case System (1985); *Recreations* opera, walking, languages; *Style*— Dr Robin Baker; ✉ The British Council, 10 Spring Gardens, London SW1A 2BN (☎ 0171 930 8466)

BAKER, Roy Horace Ward; s of Horace John Baker (d 1964), of London, and Florence Amelia, *née* Ward (d 1971); *b* 19 Dec 1916; *Educ* Lycée Corneille Rouen, City of London Sch; *m* 1, 1940 (m dis 1944), Muriel Constance, da of late Evelyn Edward Bradford; m 2, 1948 (m dis 1987), Joan Sylvia Davies, da of Alfred William Robert Dixon; 1 s (Nicholas Roy b 18 Aug 1950); *Career* director; army serv 1940–46 (cmmnd Bedfordshire and Hertfordshire Regt 1941, Army Kinematograph serv 1943); prodn runner to Asst Dir Gainsborough Studios Islington 1934–40; *Television* over 100 series incl: The Avengers, Danger UXB, Minder, Irish RM, Flame Trees of Thika, The Good Guys; *Films* over 30 feature films incl: The October Man 1946, Morning Departure 1949, Don't Bother to Knock (in Hollywood, 1952–53), Night Without Sleep (in Hollywood), Inferno (in Hollywood), Tiger in the Smoke 1956, The One That Got Away 1957, A Night to Remember 1958, The Singer Not the Song 1960, Two Left Feet 1962, Quatermass and the Pit 1967, The Anniversary 1967, Asylum 1972; *Awards* incl: NY Critics Circle Best Ten 1959, Golden Globe 1959 (for A Night to Remember), Christopher (for direction), Paris Convention du Cinema Fantastique Grand Prix (for Asylum) 1972; *Recreations* woodwork; *Clubs* Athenaeum; *Style*— Roy Baker, Esq; ✉ 2 St Albans Grove, London W8 5PN (☎ 0171 937 3964)

BAKER, Hon Mr Justice; Hon Sir (Thomas) Scott Gillespie; kt (1988); s of Rt Hon Sir George Gillespie Baker, OBE (d 1984), and Jessie McCall, *née* Findlay (d 1983); *b* 10 Dec 1937; *Educ* Haileybury, Brasenose Coll Oxford; *m* 1973, Margaret Joy Strange; 2 s, 1 da; *Career* called to the Bar Middle Temple 1961, bencher 1985; recorder of the Crown Court 1976–88, QC 1978, judge of the High Court of Justice (Queen's Bench Div) 1993– (Family Div 1988–92), Family Div liaison judge (Wales and Chester Circuit) 1990–92, presiding judge Wales and Chester Circuit 1991–95; memb: Senate Inns of Ct 1977–84, Bar Cncl 1988, Govt Ctee of Inquiry into Human Fertilisation (Warnock Ctee) 1982–84, Chorleywood UDC 1965–68; dep chm Appeals Ctee Cricket Cncl 1986–88, govr Caldicott Sch 1991–; *Recreations* golf, fishing; *Clubs* MCC, Denham Golf; *Style*— The Hon Mr Justice Scott Baker; ✉ Royal Courts of Justice, Strand, London WC2A 2LL

BAKER, Susan Mary; da of Lt Leo Kingsley Baker, DFC, RFC (d 1986), and Eileen Frida, *née* Brooks (d 1982); *b* 22 July 1930; *Educ* Stroud HS, Francis Holland Sch, RCM; *m* 12 July 1958, William Bealby-Wright, s of George Edward Wright (d 1931) (stage name George Bealby); 1 s (Edmund b 1962), 1 da (Sarah b 1960); *Career* violinist mangr Barrow Poets 1960–; princ performances incl: UK festivals 1960s and 1970s, 4 tours in America 1969–71; one woman show Violins Fiddles and Follies 1976–; princ performances incl: Edinburgh Int Festival, Brighton Festival, Belfast Festival; solo album Fiddles and Follies; promoter of classical concerts in Somerset; memb Musicians Union; ARCM; *Recreations* cooking, swimming; *Style*— Miss Susan Baker; ✉ Beckington Abbey, Beckington, nr Bath BA3 6TD (☎ and fax 01373 830695)

BAKER, Prof Terry George; s of George William John (d 1987), of Lymington, Hants, and Eugenia, *née* Bristow; *b* 27 May 1936; *Educ* Coventry Tech Secdy Sch, UCNW Bangor (BSc), Univ of Birmingham (PhD), Univ of Edinburgh (DSc); *m* 23 Aug 1958, Pauline, da of Alfred Archer (d 1970), of Coventry; 3 s (Paul Stephen b 7 Jan 1960, Noel Terence b 4 Dec 1961, Martin Christopher b 20 June 1966); *Career* science master Woodlands Boys Sch Coventry 1959–61; Univ of Birmingham: res student 1961–64, MRC res fell 1964–67, lectr in anatomy 1967–68; sr lectr in obstetrics and gynaecology Univ of Edinburgh 1975–79 (lectr 1968–75), pro vice chllr Univ of Bradford 1986–89 (prof of biomedical sciences 1980–); author of numerous pubns in learned jls; memb Bradford Health Authy 1982–86, memb Sub-Ctee on Educn Inst of Med Laboratory Sci 1985–88, pres Bradford Medico-Chirurgical Soc 1990–91, vice chm Res Ctee Yorks RHA 1992–94; govr Huddersfield Poly 1986–89; FRCPath 1991, FIBiol, FIMLS, FRSA, FRSE 1980; *Books* incl: Radiation Biology of the Fetal and Juvenile Mammal (contrib, 1969), Human Reproduction: Conception and Contraception (contrib, 1973), Ovarian Follicular Development and Function (contrib, 1978), Functional Morphology of the Human Ovary (contrib, 1981), Comparative Primate Biology (contrib, 1986), Visual Problems in Childhood (contrib, 1993); *Recreations* music, wood carving, photography; *Style*— Prof Terry Baker, FRSE; ✉ Hollybrook, 30 Queen's Rd, Ilkley, W Yorkshire LS29 9QJ (☎ 01943 430080); Department of Biomedical Sciences, University of Bradford, Richmond Rd, Bradford BD7 1DP (☎ 01274 383563, fax 01274 309742, telex 51309 UNIBFD)

BAKER-BATES, Merrick Stuart; CMG (1996); s of Eric Tom Baker-Bates (d 1986), and Norah Stuart, *née* Kirkham (d 1981); *b* 22 July 1939; *Educ* Shrewsbury, Hertford Coll Oxford (MA), Coll of Europe Bruges; *m* 6 April 1963, Chrystal Jacqueline, da of John Hugh Mackenzie Goodacre; 1 s (Jonathan b 1966), 1 da (Harriet b 1969); *Career* journalist Brussels 1962–63; HM Dip Serv: third later second sec Tokyo 1963–68, first sec FCO 1968–73, first sec (info) Washington 1973–76, first sec (commercial) Tokyo 1976–79, cnsllr (commercial) Tokyo 1979–82; dir Cornes & Co Ltd and rep dir Gestetner (Japan) Ltd Tokyo 1982–85; HM Dip Serv: re-joined 1985, dep high cmmr and cnsllr (commercial and economic) Kuala Lumpur 1986–89, head South America Dept FCO 1989–90, head S Atlantic and Antarctic Dept FCO and cmmr Br Antarctic Territory 1990–92, consul-gen Los Angeles 1992–; *Recreations* photography, golf, things Japanese; *Clubs* Brooks's, Tokyo; *Style*— Merrick Baker-Bates, Esq, CMG; ✉ c/o FCO (Los Angeles), London SW1A 2AH

BAKER-CARR, Air Marshal Sir John Darcy; KBE (1962, CBE 1951), CB (1957), AFC (1944); s of Brig-Gen Christopher Teesdale Baker-Carr, CMG, DSO (d 1949), and Sarah de Witt, *née* Quinan; *b* 13 Jan 1906; *Educ* Harrow, Phillips Acad USA, MIT; *m* 30 June 1934, Margery Alexandra Grant, da of Maj-Gen Alister Grant Dallas, CB, CMG (d 1931); *Career* joined RAF 1929, No 32 Fighter Sqdn UK 1930–31, flying boats RAF Calshot and Iraq 1931–34, special armament course 1934–35, Western Area Andover 1935–37, No 3 Bomber Gp Mildenhall 1937–38, R & D air testing of aircraft rocket 1938–45, Br Air Cmmn Washington 1945–46, Central Fighter Estab 1947–48, dir Dept of Personnel 1948–49, dir of armament R & D Miny of Supply 1949–51, Imperial Def Coll 1951–52, Cmdt RAF St Athan 1953–56, HQ Fighter Cmd 1956–59, AOC No 41 Gp Andover 1959–61, Air Marshal controller Engrg and Equipment 1962–64; ret 1964; *Recreations* carpentry, sailing; *Clubs* RAF Yacht (Hamble, Hants); *Style*— Air Marshal Sir John Baker-Carr, KBE, CB, AFC; ✉ Thatchwell Cottage, King's Somborne, Hants

BAKER WILBRAHAM, Randle; s & h of Sir Richard Baker Wilbraham, 8 Bt, DL, *qv*; *b* 28 May 1963; *Educ* Harrow; *Career* London Fire Bde 1983–89; Fine Art Course The Study Centre 1989–90, London-Cape Town Motorcycle Expedition 1990–91, Trans America Combi Expedition 1992, Leith's Cookery Sch 1992, London Coll of Printing 1994–95; *Recreations* astronomy, bookbinding; *Style*— Randle Baker Wilbraham, Esq; ✉ Rode Hall, Scholar Green, Cheshire ST7 3QP (☎ 01270 873237)

BAKER WILBRAHAM, Sir Richard; 8 Bt (GB 1776); DL; s of Sir Randle John Baker Wilbraham, 7 Bt, JP, DL (d 1980); *b* 5 Feb 1934; *Educ* Harrow; *m* 2 March 1962, Anne Christine Peto, da of late Charles Peto Bennett, OBE, of Jersey; 1 s, 3 da; *Heir* s, Randle Baker Wilbraham, *qv*; *Career* Lt Welsh Gds 1952–54; dir: J Henry Schroder Wagg & Co 1969–89 (joined 1954), Westpool Investment Trust plc 1974–92, Brixton Estate plc 1985– (dep chm), Charles Barker plc 1986–89, Really Useful Group plc 1985–90, Severn Trent plc 1989–94, Bibby Line Group Ltd 1989– (chm 1992–), Majedie Investments plc 1989–, Grosvenor Estate Holdings 1989– (dep chm); non-exec dir Christie Hosp NHS Tst 1990–96; tstee Grosvenor Estate 1981–; govr: Harrow Sch 1982–92, King's Sch Macclesfield 1986–, Nuffield Hosps 1990–; church cmmr 1994; High Sheriff of Cheshire 1991–92; Upper Bailiff Worshipful Co of Weavers 1994–95; *Recreations* field sports; *Clubs* Brooks's; *Style*— Sir Richard Baker Wilbraham, Bt, DL; ✉ Rode Hall, Scholar Green, Cheshire ST7 3QP (☎ 01270 882961)

BAKEWELL, Joan Dawson; da of John Rowlands, and Rose, *née* Bland; *b* 16 April 1933; *Educ* Stockport HS for Girls, Newnham Coll Cambridge (BA); *m* 1, 1955 (m dis 1972), Michael Bakewell, 1 s, 1 da; m 2, 1975, Jack Emery (theatre and TV prodr); *Career* broadcaster and writer 1964–; TV critic The Times 1978–81, arts corr BBC 1981–87, columnist Sunday Times 1987–91; govr BFI 1994–; memb Cncl Aldeburgh Fndn; pres Soc of Arts Publicists 1988–92, fell Royal Coll of Art, memb Cncl Friends of the Tate Gallery; *BBC TV* incl: Meeting Point 1964, The Second Sex 1964, Late Night Line Up 1965–72, The Youthful Eye 1968, Moviemakers at the National Film Theatre 1971, Film '72 and Film '73, For the Sake of Appearance 1973, Where is Your God? 1973, Who Cares? 1973, The Affirmative Way (series) 1973, What's it all About? (2 series) 1974, Time Running Out (series) 1974, The Brontë Business 1974, The Shakespeare Business 1976, Generation to Generation (series) 1976, My Day with the Children 1977, The Moving Line 1979, Arts UK: OK? 1980, The Heart of the Matter 1988–; *ITV* incl: Sunday Break 1962, Home at 4.30 1964, Thank You Ron (writer and prodr) 1974, Fairest Fortune 1974, Edinburgh Festival Report 1974, Reports Action (4 series) 1976–78; also Memento (Channel 4) 1993; *Radio* Away from it All 1978–79, PM 1979–81, There and Back (play), Parish Magazine (play, 3 episodes); *Books* The New Priesthood: British Television Today (with Nicholas Garnham, 1970), A Fine and Private Place (with John Drummond, 1977), The Complete Traveller (1977), The Heart of Heart of the Matter (1996); *Recreations* theatre, travel, talk; *Style*— Ms Joan Bakewell; ✉ Knight Ayton Management, 10 Argyll St, London W1V 1AB (☎ 0171 287 4405)

BALAGUER-MORRIS, José; s of Vicente Balaguer Martin (d 1975), of Barcelona, Spain, and Emma Morris Irrisarry; *b* 6 Oct 1933; *Educ* Jesuit Sch Barcelona, Barcelona Univ Med Sch, King's Coll Dental Sch London (BDS, Sr Conservation prize), Karolinska Institutet Stockholm (Leg Tand); *m* 8 Sept 1962, Ann-Britt, da of late Vidar Sahlin; 1 da (Anna Cristina b 28 May 1967); *Career* dental technician Barcelona and London, house surgeon King's Coll London 1970, lectr Karolinska Institutet Tandlakare Hogskolan Stockholm 1970–71, private dental surgeon and pt/t clinical lectr KCH and UCH Dental Schs 1971–72, clinical lectr UCH 1971–72, sr clinical lectr UCH Dental Sch 1975–82 (pt/t clinical lectr 1972–75); in private practice London and Oxford 1972–; UK corr Revista Europea de Estomatologia, advsr in Spanish language to FDI Lexicon; memb: BDA 1970, Swedish Dental Assoc 1971, Euro Prosthodontic Assoc (fndr) 1979, Int Coll of Dentists 1985, Int Prosthodontic Assoc 1986, Br Soc of Endodontics (memb Cncl 1987), Br Soc of Periodontology, Br Soc of Cons Dentistry, Int Dental Fedn (FDI); memb Delta Sigma Delta fraternity; *Recreations* tennis, mountain walking, collecting wine, Latin and Punic wars, historical literature, travel to historical places; *Clubs* Maidenhead Tennis; *Style*— José Balaguer-Morris, Esq; ✉ 90 Harley St, London W1N 1AF (☎ 0171 935 2240, fax 0171 224 4158); 4 Moreton Rd, Oxford OX2 7AX (☎ 01865 557808)

BALCHIN, Sir Robert George Alexander; kt (1993); s of Leonard George Balchin (d 1968), and Elizabeth, *née* Skelton; the Balchin family settled in Surrey c 1190, Sir Roger de Balchen owning lands in both Normandy and Surrey, Adm Sir John Balchin (1669–1744) was Adm of the White and Governor of Greenwich RN Hosp; *b* 31 July 1942; *Educ* Bec Sch, Univ of London, Univ of Hull (MEd, Advanced DipEd); *m* 1970, Jennifer, da of Bernard Kevin Kinlay (d 1975), of Cape Town; 2 s (Alexander b 1975, Thomas (twin) b 1975); *Career* asst master Chinthurst Sch 1964–68, head of English Dept Ewell Sch 1968–69, res Inst of Educn Univ of Hull 1969–71, headmaster Hill Sch Westerham 1972–80 (chm 1980–); chm: Grant-Maintained Schs Fndn (formerly Tst) 1989–, Pardoe-Blacker Publishing Ltd 1989–, Choice in Educn 1989–94, Grant-Maintained Schools Mutual Insurance Co 1992–95; St John Ambulance: nat schs advsr 1978–82, asst DG 1982–84, DG 1984–90; fndr chm: Campaign for a Gen Teaching Cncl 1981–84, Balchin Family Soc 1993–; chm St John Nat Schools Project 1990–95; memb: Standing Conf on Sch Sci and Technol 1976–79, Surrey CC 1981–85 (memb Educn and Social Servs Ctees), Editorial Bd Education Today 1981–87, Centre for Policy Studies 1982–, Funding Agency for Schs 1994–, Ct Univ of Leeds 1995–, Cncl Imperial Soc of Knights Bachelor 1995–; dep area treas Cons Pty 1983–86, chm Cons Pty SE England 1993–96 (vice chm 1986–90), Cons treas for SE England 1990–93; conslt dir: Cons Central Office 1988–93, Cons Bd of Fin 1990–93; treas Catch 'em Young Project Tst 1984–; Hon DPhil Northland Open Univ Canada 1985; Liveryman Worshipful Co of Goldsmiths 1987 (Freeman 1981); Hon FCP 1987 (FCP 1971), Hon FHS 1987, hon memb CGLI 1983; KStJ 1984, Commander's Cross (Pro Merito Melitensi SMOM) 1987, Commander (first class) Order of Polonia Restituta 1990; *Books* Emergency Aid in Schools (1984), New Money (1985, 2 edn 1989), Choosing a State School (jtly, 1989), Emergency Aid at Work (jtly, 1990); *Recreations* restoration of elderly house; *Clubs* Athenaeum; *Style*— Sir Robert Balchin; ✉ New Place, Lingfield, Surrey RH7 6EF (☎ 01342 834543); 88 Marsham Court, Westminster, London SW1P 4LA; 36 Great Smith St, London SW1P 3BU (☎ 0171 233 4666, fax 0171 233 2795)

BALCHIN, Prof William George Victor; s of Victor Balchin (d 1944), of Aldershot, Hants, and Ellen Winifred Gertrude, *née* Chapple (d 1988); *b* 20 June 1916; *Educ* Aldershot HS, St Catharine's Coll Cambridge (BA, MA), King's Coll London (PhD); *m* 10 Dec 1939, Lily, da of Henry Gordon Kettlewood (d 1965), of Otley, Yorks; 1 s (Peter Malcolm b 6 Sept 1940), 2 da (Anne Catharine b 10 Oct 1948, Joan Margaret b 10 May 1942 d 1985); *Career* WWII hydrographic offr Hydrographic Dept Admiralty 1939–45; jr demonstrator in geography Univ of Cambridge 1937–39 (geomorphologist Cambridge Spitsbergen Expedition 1938), lectr Univ of Bristol Regnl Ctee on Educn and WEA tutor 1939–45, lectr King's Coll London 1945–54 (geomorphologist on US Sonora-Mohave Desert Expedition 1952); Univ of Wales Swansea: prof and head Dept of Geography 1954–78 (emeritus prof 1978, Leverhulme emeritus fell 1982), dean of science 1959–61, vice-princ 1964–66 and 1970–73; RGS: Open Essay Prize 1936–37, Gill Memorial Award 1954, memb Cncl 1962–65 and 1975–88, chm Educn Ctee 1975–88, vice pres 1978–82, chm Ordnance Survey Ctee 1983–91; Geographical Assoc: conference organiser 1950–54, memb Cncl 1950–81, tstee 1954–77, pres 1971, hon memb 1980; BAAS: pres (Section E Geography) 1972, treas 2 Land Utilisation Survey of Britain 1961–, chm Land Decade Educnl Cncl 1978–83; memb: Meteorological Ctee MOD 1963–69, Br Nat Ctee for Geography 1964–70, 1976–78 and Cartography 1961–71, Nature Conservancy Ctee for Wales 1959–68, Hydrology Ctee ICE 1962–76, Ct of Govrs Nat Museum of Wales 1966–74, Ct of St David's Coll Lampeter 1968–80, Ct of Univ Coll Swansea 1980–, Univ of Bradford Disaster Prevention Unit 1989–; vice pres Glamorgan Co Naturalist Tst 1961–80, pres Balchin Family Soc 1993–; Hon FKC 1984; FRGS 1937, FRMetS 1945, FRCSoc 1978, fell British Cartographic Soc (FBCartS) 1996; *Books* Geography and Man (3 vols, ed 1947), Climatic and Weather Exercises (with A W Richards 1949), Practical and Experimental Geography (with A W Richards 1952), Cornwall - The Making of the English Landscape (1954), Geography for the Intending Student (ed 1970), Swansea and its Region (ed, 1971), Living History of Britain (ed, 1981), Concern for Geography (1981), The Cornish Landscape (1983), The Geographical Association - The First Hundred Years 1893–1993 (1993); *Recreations* travel, writing; *Clubs* Royal Cwlth Soc, Geographical; *Style*— Prof William Balchin; ✉ 10 Low Wood Rise, Ben Rhydding, Ilkley, W Yorks LS29 8AZ (☎ 01943 600 768)

BALCOMBE, Rt Hon Sir (Alfred) John; kt (1977), PC (1985); er s of Edwin Kesteven Balcombe (d 1986), of London, and Jane Phyllis, *née* Abrahams (d 1982); *b* 29 Sept 1925; *Educ* Winchester, New Coll Oxford (BA, MA); *m* 24 May 1950, Jacqueline Rosemary, yr da of Julian Cowan (d 1957), of Harrow, Middx: 2 s (Peter b 1955, David b 1958), 1 da (Jennifer (Mrs Suthers) b 1952); *Career* cmmnd Royal Signals 1945, served 1943–47; called to the Bar Lincoln's Inn 1950, QC 1969, bencher 1977; practised at Chancery Bar 1951–77, judge of the High Court of Justice (Family Div) 1977–85, judge of Employment Appeal Tbnl 1983–85, a Lord Justice of Appeal 1985–95, ret; memb Gen Cncl of the Bar 1967–71, chm London Marriage Guidance Cncl 1982–88, pres SW London Branch Magistrates' Assoc 1993–; Liveryman Worshipful Co of Tin Plate Workers (Master 1971–72, memb Ct of Assts); hon fell Hebrew Univ of Jerusalem 1996; *Books* Exempt Private Companies (1953); *Clubs* Garrick; *Style*— The Rt Hon Sir John Balcombe; ✉ Alban Place, 1A Lingfield Road, London SW19 4QA (fax 0181 944 0527)

BALCON, Raphael; *b* 26 Aug 1936; *Educ* King's Coll Med Sch (MB BS, LRCP, MRCP, MD); *Career* resident house physician King's Coll Hosp London 1960, resident house surgn Dulwich Hosp London 1961, resident house physician London Chest Hosp 1961, sr house physician St Stephen's Hosp London 1962–63, US public health fell Dept of

Med Wayne State Univ Coll of Med Detroit USA 1963–64, fell and hon registrar King's Coll Hosp London 1965, med registrar King's Coll Hosp London 1966, sr registrar Nat Heart Hosp London 1967–70 (registrar 1966–67); conslt cardiologist, hon sr lectr Nat Heart and Lung Inst; dean Cardiothoracic Inst 1976–80, memb DHSS Pacemaker Advsy Ctee 1979–84, hon treas Br Cardiac Soc 1981–86; memb: Cardiology Ctee RCP (chm) 1992–95, Fin Ctee RCP 1986–92, Cncl Br Coronary Intervention Soc 1990–94; pres Br Cardiac Soc 1995–; memb Br Cardiac Soc 1969, FACC 1970, FRCP 1977, fndr fell Euro Soc of Cardiology 1986; author of numerous pubns in learned jls; *Recreations* skiing, tennis, mountain walking; *Style—* Raphael Balcon, Esq; ✉ 13 Park Village West, London NW1 4AE

BALDING, Gerald Barnard (Toby); s of Capt Gerald Matthews Balding (d 1957), of Weyhill, nr Andover, Hants, and Eleanor, *née* Hoagland (d 1987); bro of Ian Balding, LVO, *qv*; *b* 23 Sept 1936; *Educ* Marlborough; *m* 21 Jan 1960, Carolyn Anne, da of Anthony Lister Barclay; 1 s (Gerald Barclay b 9 Jan 1961), 2 da (Serena Anne (Mrs J A Geake) b 1 Aug 1962, Camilla (Mrs T G Bridgewater) b 17 Oct 1963); *Career* Nat Serv HM Lifeguards 1955–57; point-to-point jockey 1954–57, racehorse trainer 1957–; trained ca 2000 winners on flat and over jumps incl: Grand National twice, Topham Trophy, Eider Chase four times, Portland Handicap, Coronation Hurdle, Whitbread Trial Chase, Mildmay of Flete Chase twice, Irish Sweeps Hurdle, John Porter Stakes, Stewards Cup, Cheltenham Gold Cup, Ayr Gold Cup, Tote Gold Trophy, Glen Int Gold Cup, Waterford Crystal Champion Hurdle twice, Martell Aintree Hurdle five, Nat Hunt Chase twice, Prix d'Arenberg France, Breeders Cup Chase USA twice; horses trained incl: Highland Wedding, Little Polveir, Grandpa's Legacy, Caduval, Dozo, New World, Official, Tudor Legend, Belgrano, Reality, Bybrook, Decent Fellow, Green Ruby, Via Delta, Lucky Vane, Lonach, Sheer Gold, Far Bridge, So True, Neblin, Kildimo, Beech Road, Boraceva, Morley Street, Forest Sun, Palace Street, Regal Scintilla, Cool Ground; world record for Nat Hunt prize money won on one day Aintree 8 April 1989, Morley Street voted Nat Hunt Horse of the Year UK and USA 1990 (first horse to win both awards); former jr rugby rep Dorset and Wilts; *Recreations* tennis, reading, eating, pretty girls (not necessarily in that order!); *Style—* Toby Balding, Esq; ✉ Fyfield Stables, Fyfield, Nr Andover, Hampshire SP11 8EW (☎ 01264 772278, fax 01264 771221)

BALDING, Ian Anthony; LVO (1992); s of Capt Gerald Matthews Balding (d 1957), of Weyhill, nr Andover, Hants, and Eleanor, *née* Hoagland (d 1987); bro of Toby Balding, *qv*; *b* 7 Nov 1938; *Educ* Marlborough, Millfield, Christ's Coll Cambridge (Rugby blue); *m* 25 Aug 1969, Emma Alice Mary, da of late Peter Hastings-Bass; 1 s (Andrew Matthews b 29 Dec 1972), 1 da (Clare Victoria b 29 Jan 1971); *Career* racehorse trainer 1964–; notable horses trained incl: Glint of Gold, Mrs Penny, Mill Reef, Forest Flower, Diamond Shoal, Selkirk, Crystal Spirit, Lochsong; trained for: HM Queen Elizabeth The Queen Mother (won Imperial Cup with Insular), HM The Queen 1964–, Paul Mellon KBE 1964–; maj races won in UK and Ireland incl: Derby, King George VI & Queen Elizabeth Stakes, Eclipse Stakes, Dewhurst Stakes (4 times), Imperial Cup (nat hunt), 1000 Guineas (Ireland), Nat Stakes (Ireland, twice), Queen Elizabeth II Stakes (1991); races won abroad incl: Italian Derby, Prix de l'Arc de Triomphe, Prix Ganay, Prix de Diane, Prix Vermaille, Prix de l'Abbaye de Long Champ (3 times), Grosser Preis von Baden (twice), Preis von Europa (3 times); second leading flat trainer in first full year 1965, leading trainer 1971, leading int trainer 3 times; amateur nat hunt jockey winning over 70 races 1954–64 (incl Nat Hunt Chase Cheltenham), winning jockey various hunter chase and point to point races 1964–92; rugby: Bath 1956–66, Dorset & Wiltshire 1956–66, Cambridge Univ 1959–62, various appearances Southern Cos, Newbury FRC 1966–80; boxing Cambridge Univ, cricket Crusaders; *Recreations* jt master Berks & Bucks Drag Hunt, skiing, squash, tennis, golf, cricket; *Style—* Ian Balding, Esq, LVO; ✉ Park House, Kingsclere, Newbury, Berks RG15 8PZ (☎ 01635 298274/298210, fax 01635 298305)

BALDOCK, Brian Ford; s of Ernest John Baldock, of Teddington, Middx, and Florence, *née* Ford (d 1983); *b* 10 June 1934; *Educ* Clapham Coll London; *m* 1 (m dis 1966), Mary Lillian, *née* Bartolo; 2 s (Simon b 1958, Nicholas b 1961); m 2, 30 Nov 1968, Carole Anthea, da of F R Mason (d 1978); 1 s (Alexander b 1970); *Career* Lt Royal W Kent Regt 1952–53, Corps of Royal Mil Police 1953–55; mgmnt trainee Procter & Gamble Ltd 1956–61, assoc dir Ted Bates Inc 1961–63, mktg mangr Rank Organisation 1963–66, dir Smith & Nephew 1966–75, vice pres Revlon Inc (Europe, ME and Africa) 1975–78, md Imperial Leisure & Retail 1978–86; Guinness plc: dir 1986–, gp md 1989–, dep chm 1992–; non-exec dir Dalgety plc 1992–; Freeman: Worshipful Co of Brewers 1988, City of London 1988; Liveryman Worshipful Co of Marketors; FInstM 1976, fell Mktg Soc 1988, FRSA 1987, CIMgt 1992; *Recreations* theatre, music, travel; *Clubs* Lord's Taverners' (cncl memb, chm 1992–95), Mark's; *Style—* Brian Baldock, Esq; ✉ Guinness plc, 39 Portman Square, London W1H 0EE (☎ 0171 486 0288, fax 0171 935 2884, telex 23368)

BALDOCK, (Richard) Stephen; s of John Allan Baldock (d 1989), and Marjorie Procter, *née* Taylor; *b* 19 Nov 1944; *Educ* St Paul's, King's Coll Cambridge (MA, John Stewart of Rannoch scholarship), King's Coll London; *m* 5 July 1969, Dr Janet Elizabeth Cottrell, MA, MB, BChir, MRCGP; 3 da (Sarah Ruth b 5 April 1975, Emma Stephanie b 6 Aug 1978, Rachel Elizabeth b 17 June 1980), 1 s (Andrew James b 23 July 1976); *Career* St Paul's Sch: asst master 1970–77, housemaster 1977–84, surmaster 1984–92, high master 1992–; Cncl memb and educnl advsr Overseas Missionary Fellowship 1989–; govr: Durston House Prep Sch 1992–, The Hall Sch Hampstead 1993–, Orley Farm Sch 1996–; memb: Soc for the Promotion of Hellenic Studies, Tyndale Fellowship for Biblical Res, Jt Assoc of Classical Teachers, HMC; *Recreations* sport, travel, computers, music; *Clubs* MCC, East India; *Style—* Stephen Baldock, Esq; ✉ St Paul's School, Lonsdale Road, London SW13 9JT (☎ 0181 748 9162, fax 0181 748 9557)

BALDRY, Antony Brian (Tony); MP (C) Banbury (majority 16,720); eldest s of Peter Edward Baldry, and Oina, *née* Paterson; *b* 10 July 1950; *Educ* Leighton Park, Univ of Sussex (BA, LLB); *m* 1979 (m dis 1996), Catherine Elizabeth, 2 da of Capt James Weir, RN (ret), of Chagford, Devon; 1 s, 1 da; *Career* barr and publisher; called to the Bar Lincoln's Inn 1975; dir: New Opportunity Press 1975–90, Newpoint Publishing Group 1983–90; PA to Mrs Thatcher in Oct 1974 election, in ldr of oppn's office Mar-Oct 1975, memb Carlton Club Political Ctee, Parly candidate (C) Thurrock 1979, MP (C) Banbury 1983–; memb Parly Select Ctee on Employment 1983–85; PPS to: Min of State for Foreign and Cwlth Affrs 1985–87, Lord Privy Seal and Leader of the House 1987–89, Sec of State for Energy 1989–90; Parly under sec of state: Dept of Energy 1990, DOE 1990–94, FCO 1994–95; min of state MAFF 1995–; Robert Schuman Silver medal (Stiftung FVS Hamburg) for contribs to Euro politics 1978; Liveryman: Worshipful Co of Merchant Taylors, Worshipful Co of Stationers & Newspaper Makers; *Recreations* walking, beagling; *Clubs* Carlton, Brass Monkey, Banbury Cons; *Style—* Tony Baldry, Esq, MP; ✉ House of Commons, London SW1A 0AA

BALDWIN, Barry Anthony; s of Joseph Patrick Baldwin (d 1977), and Nina, *née* Brazier; *b* 7 Jan 1935; *Educ* King's Coll Sch Wimbledon; *m* 1, 1958 (m dis 1973); m 2, 1976, Liz, da of John McKeown; 3 s (Christopher Richard b 15 July 1959, Mark Jonathan b 31 Aug 1961, Paul Stephen b 27 March 1964); *Career* articled clerk Russell and Mason 1953–58; Price Waterhouse: joined 1958, mangr 1963–69, ptnr Bristol 1969–75, ptnr i/c Ind Business Gp London 1975–83, seconded to CRD 1980–82, ptnr i/c Windsor office 1983–85, nat dir Ind Business Servs 1985–88, dir Ind Business Servs Europe 1988–91, chm Emerging Business World Executive 1991, left PW 1991; chm Union of Ind Cos 1986–87, head of research Small Business Bureau, hon special advsr to Small Firms Min 1991–92, econ advsr to the Union of Ind Cos 1977–93, rapporteurs expert Econ and Social Ctee of EC 1983, 1985 and 1986; chm XEBEC Multimedia Solutions Ltd; dir: A T Poeton & Son Ltd, Shield Guarding Company Ltd; gen mangr Interactive Productions Ltd; chm 3i Communication Club 1993; memb: Lambeth Lewisham and Southwark AHA 1980–82, Lewisham and N Southwark DHA 1982–83; co-opted special tstee Guy's Hosp 1976–93, hon dir Theatre Royal Windsor, memb Fin Ct and Cncl Cranfield Univ; FCA (ACA 1958); *Books* Management Training for Owners of SMEs (with Sue Palmer, 1983), A UK Loan Guarantee Scheme (with Bill Poeton, 1981); *Recreations* golf, theatre, rugby football; *Style—* Barry Baldwin, Esq; ✉ Zahra, Lakeside Drive, Stoke Poges, Bucks SL2 4LX

BALDWIN, Clarissa Mary; da of Rev Basil Alderson Watson, OBE, RN, of Greenwich, and Janet Isabel, *née* Roderick; *b* 9 Feb 1949; *Educ* St Agnes & St Michael's Sch, Dartmouth Coll; *m* 18 March 1977, Roger Douglas Baldwin, s of Douglas Baldwin; 1 s (James Douglas Alderson b 18 Dec 1980); *Career* fashion model 1968–70, positions with Cambridge Evening News and Evening Standard, chief exec National Canine Defence League 1986– (author slogan: A dog is for life.... not just for Christmas); chm Welfare Ctee Pet Plan Charitable Tst, tstee Hearing Dogs for the Deaf, memb Bd Pet Advsy Ctee, advsy dir World Soc for the Protection of Animals; FRSA 1985; *Recreations* tennis, theatre, ballet; *Clubs* Lansdowne; *Style—* Mrs Clarissa Baldwin; ✉ Chief Executive, National Canine Defence League, 17 Wakley Street, London EC1V 7LT (☎ 0171 837 0006, fax 0171 833 2701, mobile 0831 135849)

BALDWIN, Dr David Arthur; CBE (1990); s of Isaac Arthur Baldwin (d 1983), of Twickenham, and Edith Mary, *née* Collins; *b* 1 Sept 1936; *Educ* Twickenham Tech Coll, Wimbledon Tech Coll; *m* 1961, (Jacqueline) Anne, da of Frederick Edward Westcott (d 1947), of Twickenham; 1 s (Richard David b 1975), 1 da (Sarah b 1967); *Career* radio engr EMI Ltd 1954–63, sales engr Solartron Ltd 1963–65, sales engr and mangr Hewlett Packard Ltd 1965–73, Euro mktg mangr Hewlett Packard SA 1973–78; Hewlett Packard Ltd: md 1978–88, chm 1988–96, dir emeritus 1996–; exec dir Hewlett Packard Switzerland; memb: Electronics Indust Sector Gp NEDO, ITSA and Butcher IT Skills Shortage Ctee, Cncl Econ and Fin Planning Ctee CBI, Ct of Brunel Univ, Ct of Cranfield Inst of Technol, Cncl for Indust and Higher Educn, PITCOM, Berks Assoc of Boys' Clubs; chm Euro Trade Ctee and memb Bd of Trade, chm Thames Action Res Gp for Educn and Trg, memb Cncl RSA; Freeman City of London, Liveryman Guild of Info Technologists; Hon Dr Strathclyde Univ 1990; FIEE, FInstD, FInstM, CIMgt; *Recreations* golf, skiing, photography, painting; *Clubs* RAC; *Style—* Dr David Baldwin, CBE; ✉ Hewlett Packard Ltd, Cain Road, Bracknell, Berks RG12 1HN (☎ 01344 360000, fax 01344 362224)

BALDWIN, Gordon Nelson; OBE (1992); s of Lewis Nelson Baldwin (d 1982), of Lincoln, and Elsie, *née* Hilton (d 1982); *b* 10 July 1932; *Educ* Lincoln Sch, Lincoln Sch of Art, Central Sch of Art & Design; *m* Nancy Dorothy, da of Thomas Hayden Chandler (d 1989), and Dorothy Frances, *née* Ward (d 1969); 1 s (Raef Ashcroft b 9 Sept 1959), 2 da (Amanda Louise 30 Oct 1962, Flavia Sophia b 16 April 1967); *Career* potter; resident teacher Eton Coll 1957–; visiting lectr: Goldsmiths' Coll 1954–63, Central Sch of Art & Design 1957–86; one time assoc lectr Camberwell Sch of Art & Craft; *Exhibitions* incl: Clay and Walls (Whitechapel Gallery London) 1969, International Ceramics (V&A) 1972, The Craftman's Art (V&A) 1973, Ceramic Forms I (Crafts Advsy Ctee and Br Cncl Euro touring exhbn) 1974, Kettles Yard Univ of Cambridge 1975, British Ceramics (Penn State Univ) 1976, British Potters (Graham Gallery NYC) 1978, Br Cncl touring exhbn Aust 1980, British Ceramics (Knokke-Heiste Belgium 1981, restrospective touring UK 1983, Univ of Wales Ceramic Series 1984, Schneider Gallery W Germany 1984, British and German Ceramics (Fitzwilliam Museum Cambridge) 1985, Soloman Gallery London 1986, International Ceramics (Chatearoux France) 1987, New Art Objects (London and Amsterdam) 1988, Retrospective (Boymans Museum Rotterdam) 1989, solo show (Hetjens Museum Dusseldorf) 1990, solo show (Galerie Bowig Hanover) 1990, International Ceramics (Korea) 1991, Configura 1 (Erfurt Germany) 1991, The Abstract Vessel (Welsh Arts Cncl Cardiff) 1991, International Ceramics (Fulda Germany) 1992, Raw & the Cooked (Barbican Gallery, touring UK, Japan and France) 1993, Pandora's Box (Crafts Cncl London, Garth Clark Gallery NY) 1995, Gordon Baldwin (V&A) 1995; *Public Collections* incl: V&A, Crafts Cncl London, Southampton City Art Gallery, Portsmouth Art Gallery, Usher Gallery Lincoln, Ulster Museum Belfast, Boymans Van Beuningen Rotterdam, Bellrive Museum Zurich, Penn State Univ, Museum of Art Melbourne, Museum of Art Perth Aust, Glasgow Museum and Art Gallery, Keramion Centre Germany, Knokke-Heiste Belgium, Octagon Center Iowa, Kettles Yard Cambridge, Württembregisches Landesmuseum Stuttgart, Univ of Wales Collection, Museum für zietgenössische Keramik Deidesheim, Los Angeles Co Museum USA; *Recreations* reading, walking, other arts; *Style—* Gordon Baldwin, Esq, OBE; ✉ Contemporary Applied Arts, 43 Earlham Street, Covent Garden, London WC2H 9LD (☎ 0171 836 6993)

BALDWIN, Jan; da of late Joseph John Baldwin, and Catherine Agnes, *née* Freeman; *b* 12 Dec 1946; *Educ* Chipping Norton GS, Bicester GS, Royal Coll of Art (MA); *m* 10 Dec 1988, Prof Henry Philip Wynn, s of Arthur Wynn; 2 step s (Hamish, Robin); *Career* therapy radiographer NY 1967–74, freelance photographer 1981–; memb AFAEP; *Recreations* film, theatre, travelling; *Style—* Ms Jan Baldwin; ✉ 11 Gibraltar Walk, London E2 7LH (☎ 0171 729 2664)

BALDWIN, Prof John Evan; s of Evan Baldwin (d 1976), and Mary, *née* Wild (d 1983); *b* 6 Dec 1931; *Educ* Merchant Taylors' Crosby, Queens' Coll Cambridge (Clerk Maxwell scholar, BA, MA, PhD); *m* 20 Sept 1969, Joyce, da of Alexander Thomas Cox (d 1979); *Career* Univ of Cambridge: res fell later fell Queens' Coll Cambridge 1956–74 and 1989–, demonstrator in physics 1957–62, asst dir of res 1962–81, reader 1981–89, dir Mullard Radio Astronomy Observatory 1987–, prof of radioastronomy 1989–; memb SERC Ctees and Bds 1971–, memb Int Astronomical Union 1961–; FRAS 1957, FRS 1991; *Recreations* mountain walking, gardening; *Style—* Prof John Baldwin, FRS; ✉ Cavendish Laboratory, Madingley Rd, Cambridge CB3 0HE (☎ 01223 337299, fax 01223 354599)

BALDWIN, Dr John Paul; QC (1991); s of Frank Baldwin, of Grange-over-Sands, Cumbria, and Marjorie Baldwin (d 1966); *b* 15 Aug 1947; *Educ* Nelson GS, Univ of Leeds (BSc), St John's Coll Oxford (DPhil); *m* 19 Sept 1981, Julie, da of Merle Gowan, of N Adelaide, Aust; 2 da (Melissa Jay b 20 Sept 1982, Sarah Elizabeth b 21 March 1985); *Career* res fell Univ of Oxford 1972–75, called to the Bar Gray's Inn 1977; *Books* Patent Law of Europe and UK (ed jtly, 1983); *Recreations* tennis, gardening; *Clubs* Portcullis, Harbour, Campden Hill Lawn Tennis; *Style—* Dr John Baldwin, QC; ✉ 8 New Square, Lincoln's Inn, London WC2A 3QP (☎ 0171 405 4321, fax 0171 405 9955, pager 0459 115439)

BALDWIN, Mark Phillip; s of Ronald William Baldwin, of Australia, and Rose Thersa Evans (d 1969); *b* 16 Jan 1954; *Educ* St Kentigerns Coll NZ, Pakuranga Coll NZ, Suva GS Fiji, Elam Sch of Fine Arts, Univ of Auckland NZ (BA); *Career* choreographer; dancer with: Limbs Dance Co NZ, NZ Ballet, Australian Dance Theatre, Rambert Dance Co 1982–92; major roles incl: Glen Etley's Pierot Lunaire, Richard Alston's Sonda Lake; fndr The Mark Baldwin Dance Co 1992 (over 17 works in rep to date); choreographer Rambert Dance Co 1992–94, choreographer in res Sadlers Wells 1994–95, res artist The Place 1995–96, choreographer in res Scottish Ballet 1996–; works for Rambert Dance Co: Island to Island 1991, Gone 1992, Spirit 1994, Banter Banter 1994; Scottish Ballet:

Hyden Pieces 1995, Ae Fond Kiss 1996, More Poulenc 1996; choreographed Hans Werner Henze's Laberinth for Statsopera Berlin 1997; *Awards* Time Out Dance Award 1996, Special Judges' Prize for dance film video Danse 8 Grand Prix Int 1996; *Recreations* all forms of music, serious painting, tennis, modern technological culture, ethnic issues; *Style—* Mark Baldwin, Esq; ✉ Mark Baldwin Dance Company, 20 Chancellors Street, London W6 9RN (☎ 0181 746 3600, fax 0181 741 7902)

BALDWIN, Air Vice-Marshal Nigel Bruce; CBE (1992); *b* 20 Sept 1941; *Educ* Peter Symond's Sch Winchester, RAF Coll Cranwell; *m* Jenny; 1 da (Kate) and 1 da decd; *Career* cmmnd RAF 1962; co-pilot No 9 Sqn (Vulcans) RAF Coningsby 1963–64, capt No 35 Sqn (Vulcans) RAF Cottesmore 1964–67 (incl active serv in Far E), ADC to AOC No 11 Gp RAF Bentley Priory, Sqn Ldr/Flt Cdr No 35 Sqn RAF Akrotiri, attended RAF Staff Coll 1974, Staff Offr to Sr Air Staff Offr HQ Strike Cmd, Wing Cdr OC No 50 Sqn (Vulcans) RAF Waddington, attended Air War Coll Maxwell AFB Alabama 1980, instr USAF Air Cmd and Staff Coll Maxwell AFB 1981–83, Gp Capt and Stn Cdr RAF Wyton (Canberras and Nimrods) 1983–85, int fell Nat Defense Univ Washington DC 1985–86, Asst Dir of Defence Policy MOD 1986–88, Air Cdre Plans HQ Strike Cmd and Dep ACOS HQ UK Air Forces 1988–91, ACOS Plans JHQ High Wycombe during Operation GRANBY, Asst Chief of the Defence Staff (Overseas) MOD 1993–; *Style—* Air Vice-Marshal N B Baldwin, CBE; ✉ Assistant Chief of the Defence Staff (Overseas), Ministry of Defence, Main Building, Whitehall, London SW1A 2HB

BALDWIN, Maj-Gen Peter Alan Charles; CBE (1994); s of Alec Baldwin, and Anne, *née* Dance; *b* 19 Feb 1927; *Educ* King Edward VI GS Chelmsford; *m* 1, 1953, Judith Elizabeth Mace; m 2, 1982, Gail J Roberts; *Career* enlisted 1942, cmmnd Royal Signals 1947, served WWII, Korean War and Borneo Ops (despatches 1967), Cdr 13 Signal Regt BAOR 1969–71, sec for studies NATO Def Coll 1971–74, Cdr 2 Signal Gp 1974–76, ACOS Jt Exercises Div AFCENT 1976–77, Maj-Gen CSO HQ BAOR 1977–79; dir of radio IBA 1987–90 (dep dir 1979–87), chief exec Radio Authy 1991–95, ret; conslt Thomson Fndn 1995–; fell Radio Acad 1992; FRSA 1993; *Recreations* cricket, theatre, music; *Clubs* Army and Navy, MCC; *Style—* Maj-Gen Peter Baldwin, CBE; ✉ c/o Lloyds Bank plc, 7 Pall Mall, London SW1Y 5NA

BALDWIN, Sir Peter Robert; KCB (1977, CB 1973); s of Charles Baldwin (d 1962) and Katie Isobel, *née* Field (d 1957); *b* 10 Nov 1922; *Educ* City of London Sch, CCC Oxford (hon fell); *m* 1951, Margaret Helen Moar; 2 s; *Career* served FO 1942–45, Gen Register Office 1948–54, Treasy 1954–62, Cabinet Office 1962–64; Treasy: re-entered 1964, princ private sec to Chllr of Exchequer 1966–68, under sec 1968–72, dep sec 1972–76; second perm sec DOE 1976, perm sec Dept of Tport 1976–82, ret; chm: SE Thames RHA 1983–91, Disabled Persons Transport Advsy Ctee 1986–93, Tripscope 1987–93, RSA 1985–87, PHAB 1982–87, RADAR 1993–, Civil Serv Sports Cncl 1978–82; vice chm Automobile Assoc Ctee 1990–93; memb: Public Fin Fndn 1984–, Charities Aid Fndn 1990– (currently chm); former memb City Literary Inst; vice pres: RSA 1987–, RNID 1983–90; vice chm AA 1990–; FKC, FCIT, Hon FIHT, CIMgt; *Recreations* painting, watching cricket; *Clubs* Reform; *Style—* Sir Peter Baldwin, KCB; ✉ 123 Alderney St, London SW1V 4HE (☎ and fax 0171 821 7157)

BALDWIN, Prof Robert William; s of William Baldwin, and Doris, *née* Mellor; *b* 12 March 1927; *Educ* Univ of Birmingham (BSc, PhD); *m* 19 July 1952, Lilian Baldwin; 1 s (Robert Neil b 1957); *Career* dir Cancer Res Campaign Laboratories 1960–, prof of tumour biology Univ of Nottingham 1971–92 (prof emeritus 1992–); vice pres of res Allergene (California), GIBB Fell Cancer Res Campaign 1971–92; FRCPath 1973, FIBiol 1979; *Books* Monoclonal Antibodies for Cancer Detection and Therapy (1985), Immunology of Malignant Diseases (1987), Cancer Medicine (1993), Biological Approaches to Cancer Treatment (1993); ed Cancer Immunotherapy and Immunotherapy 1976–; *Recreations* gardening; *Style—* Prof R W Baldwin; ✉ Department of Surgery, Floor E - West Block, University Hospital, Queen's Medical Centre, Nottingham NG7 2UH (☎ 0115 942 0807, fax 0115 942 0653)

BALDWIN, Simon John; s of William John Baldwin, of Leigh, Lancs, and Patricia Ann, *née* Downs; *b* 31 March 1975; *Educ* St Mary's RC HS Astley, Wigan Coll of Technol; *partner* Angela Louise Walford; *Career* Rugby League second row forward; rep sch/town team and Lancs: Leigh Rangers 1982–86, Leigh East ARLFC 1986–91; Warrington Academy 1991–92; professional clubs: Leigh RLFC 1992–94 (approx 50 appearances with first team), Halifax RLFC 1994– (approx 20 appearances, debut v Featherstone 1994); Academy level: 3 caps against France 1993 and 1994, 1 cap against NZ 1993, 2 caps against Aust 1994; U21: 1 cap against France 1995; England: 1 cap against France 1995, 1 cap against Wales 1995; non-sporting career: plumber; *Recreations* golf, cycling; *Style—* Simon Baldwin, Esq; ✉ Halifax RLFC, Thrum Hall, Gibbet Street, Halifax HX1 4TL (☎ 01422 361026, fax 01422 349019)

BALDWIN OF BEWDLEY, 4 Earl (UK 1937); Edward Alfred Alexander Baldwin; also Viscount Corvedale (UK 1937); s of 3 Earl (d 1976, 2 s of 1 Earl, otherwise Stanley Baldwin, thrice PM and 1 cous of Rudyard Kipling); *b* 3 Jan 1938; *Educ* Eton, Trinity Coll Cambridge (MA, PGCE); *m* 1970, Sarah MacMurray, da of Evan James, of Upwood Park, Abingdon, Oxon (and sis of Countess of Selborne); 3 s (Viscount Corvedale, Hon James Conrad b 1976, Hon Mark Thomas Maitland b 1980); *Heir* s, Viscount Corvedale, *qv*; *Career* school teacher 1970–77, LEA educn offr 1978–87; former memb Research Cncl for Complementary Medicine, chm Br Acupuncture Accreditation Bd 1990–, jt chm Parly Gp for Alternative and Complementary Medicine 1992–; *Recreations* mountains, tennis; *Clubs* MCC; *Style—* The Rt Hon The Earl Baldwin of Bewdley; ✉ Manor Farm House, Godstow Rd, Upper Wolvercote, Oxon OX2 8AJ (☎ and fax 01865 552683)

BALE, Stephen William; s of Dennis Alfred Amer Bale (d 1981), of Cardiff, and Ida, *née* George (d 1994); *b* 3 May 1952; *Educ* Univ Coll Cardiff (BA); *m* 14 July 1974, Fleur Elizabeth, da of late Richard John Gregory; 1 s (Owen John b 29 June 1980), 1 da (Lara Claire b 25 March 1985); *Career* Neath Guardian 1973–78 (NCTJ Proficiency Cert 1975), South Wales Evening Post Swansea 1978–80, South Wales Argus Newport 1980–83, Western Mail Cardiff 1983–86, Rugby Union corr The Independent 1988–96 (joined 1986), rugby ed Sunday Express 1996–; memb: Welsh Rugby Writers' Assoc (chm 1996–97), Sports Writers' Assoc of GB, Rugby Union Writers' Club (vice chm 1996–98); *Style—* Stephen Bale, Esq; ✉ Orchard Barns, Broughton Lane, Shoreditch, Taunton, Somerset TA3 7BH (☎ and fax 01823 325567); Sunday Express, Ludgate House, 245 Blackfriars Road, London SE1 9UX (mobile 0468 446160)

BALEN, Malcolm; s of Henry Balen, and Elswyth Honor Balen; *b* 9 Feb 1956; *Educ* Peterhouse Cambridge (BA); *Career* news trainee BBC 1978, regnl journalist Manchester 1980–82, sr prog ed Channel Four News ITN 1989–94 (joined ITN 1982), ed BBC Nine O'Clock News 1994–; BAFTA award 1991 (for Channel 4 coverage of resignation of Margaret Thatcher 1990); *Books* Kenneth Clarke (1994); *Style—* Malcolm Balen, Esq; ✉ BBC News and Current Affairs, Television Centre, Wood Lane, London W12 7RJ (☎ 0181 576 7779, fax 0181 749 7534)

BALES, Kenneth Frederick; CBE (1990); s of Frederick Charles Bales (d 1981), of Ilford, Essex, and Deborah Alice (d 1983); *b* 2 March 1931; *Educ* Buckhurst Hill GS, LSE (BSc), Univ of Manchester (DSA); *m* 16 Aug 1958, (Margaret) Hazel, da of John Austin (d 1946), of Dumfries, Scotland; 2 s (Stewart Mark b 22 Oct 1959, Craig Austin b 2 Sept 1961), 1 da (Shona Kay b 9 April 1963); *Career* hosp sec Southport Hosp Mgmnt Ctee 1958–62, regnl staff offr Birmingham Regnl Hosp Bd 1965–68 (regnl trg offr 1962–65), sec W Birmingham Hosp Mgmnt Ctee 1968–73; W Midlands Regnl Health Authy: regnl admin 1973–84, regnl gen mangr 1984–90, regnl md 1990–92; assoc Inst of Health Serv Mgmnt; *Recreations* swimming, sports viewing and painting; *Style—* Kenneth Bales, Esq, CBE; ✉ Stronefield, 4 St Catherine's Close, Blackwell, nr Bromsgrove, Worcs B60 1BG (☎ 0121 445 1424)

BALFE, Richard Andrew; MEP (Lab) London S Inner (majority 59,220); s of Dr Richard Joseph Balfe (d 1985), of Yorks, and Dorothy Lillias, *née* De Cann (d 1970); *b* 14 May 1944; *Educ* Brook Secdy Modern Sch Sheffield, LSE (BSc); *m* 1, 1978 (m dis 1984), Vivienne Patricia, *née* Job; 1 s (Richard Geoffrey Clement b 10 April 1980); m 2, 22 March 1986, Susan Jane, da of John Honeyford, of Cambridge; 1 da (Alexandra Mary Jane b 9 March 1988), 1 s (James Patrick John b 1 Sept 1991); *Career* 1 Bn London Irish Rifles TA 1961–67; HM Dip Serv 1965–70, res offr Finer Ctee on One Parent Families 1970–72, political sec Royal Arsenal Co-operative Soc 1973–79, dir CWS Ltd 1979–80; Parly candidate (Lab): Paddington S 1970, Southwark and Bermondsey 1992; MEP (Lab) London South Inner 1979–; Euro Parl: quaestor, Lab spokesman on defence and Turkey and N Cyprus, rapporteur on Turkey, Bangladesh and Rumania; memb Southwark/Dulwich GLC 1973–77; chm: Thamesmead New Town Ctee 1973–75, GLC Housing Ctee 1975–77; memb: Exec Ctee Fabian Soc 1981–82, London Lab Pty Exec 1973–95 (chm Policy Ctee 1983–85), Ct of Govrs LSE 1973–91; *Books* Housing in London (1977), Human Rights in Turkey (1985); *Recreations* reading, walking; *Clubs* Reform, Lewisham Labour; *Style—* Richard Balfe, Esq, MEP; ✉ 132 Powis St, London SE18 6NL (☎ 0181 855 2128, fax 0181 316 1936); 97–113 rue Belliard, 1040 Bruxelles, Belgium (☎ 00 322 284 5406, fax 00 322 284 9406)

BALFOUR, Charles George Yule; s of Eustace Arthur Goschen Balfour, *qv*, and (Dorothy Melicent) Anne, *née* Yule; *b* 23 April 1951; *Educ* Eton; *m* 1, 18 Sept 1978 (m dis 1985), Audrey Margaret, da of H P Hoare (d 1983), of Stourhead, Wilts; m 2, 1987, Svea Maria, da of Ernst-Friedrich Reichsgraf von Goess, of Carinthia, Austria; 1 da (Eleanor Cecilly Isabelle b 4 April 1989), 1 s (George Eustace Charles b 8 Dec 1990); *Career* Hoare Govett 1971–73, Hill Samuel 1973–76, Dillon Read 1976–79, exec dir Banque Paribas London 1979–91, dir Cragnotti and Partners Capital Investment (UK) Ltd 1991–92, md Nasdaq Int 1993–; sr vice pres The Nasdaq Stock Market Inc, memb Queen's Body Guard for Scotland (The Royal Co of Archers); *Recreations* gardening, shooting, fishing; *Clubs* White's, Puffins; *Style—* Charles Balfour, Esq; ✉ 15 Oakley St, London SW3 (fax 0171 352 2764); Nasdaq Stock Market, Durrant House, 8–13 Chiswell Street, London EC1Y 4XY (☎ 0171 825 5501, fax 0171 374 4488)

BALFOUR, Christopher Roxburgh; s of Archibald Roxburgh Balfour (d 1958), and Lilian, *née* Cooper (d 1989); strong links with S America 1850–1960 via Balfour Williamson & Co; *b* 24 Aug 1941; *Educ* Ampleforth, Queen's Coll Oxford (BA); *Career* merchant banker Hambros Bank Ltd 1968–95; dir: Hambros Bank Ltd 1984–, Dunhill Holdings plc (non-exec) 1991–93, Vendôme plc and Vendôme SA (non-exec) 1993–; exec dir Christies International plc 1995– (chm Christies Europe); *Recreations* horses, tennis, shooting, bridge, skiing; *Clubs* Pratt's, Brookes's; *Style—* Christopher R Balfour, Esq; ✉ 35 Kelso Place, London W8 (☎ 0171 937 7178); Christies International plc, 8 King Street, St James's, London SW1 (☎ 0171 839 9060)

BALFOUR, Cdr Colin James; DL (Hants 1973); s of Maj Melville Balfour, MC (d 1962), of Wintershill Hall, Durley, Hants, and Margaret (Daisy) Mary, *née* Lascelles (d 1972); *b* 12 June 1924; *Educ* Eton; *m* 27 Aug 1949, Prudence Elisabeth, JP, da of Adm Sir Ragnar Colvin, KBE, CB (d 1954), of Curdridge House, Curdridge, Hants; 1 s (James b 1951), 1 da (Belinda (Mrs Hextall) b 1953); *Career* RN 1942, serv HMS Nelson Med 1943, D Day and N Russian Convoys 1944–45, HMS Cossack Korean War 1950–52, RN Staff Coll 1955, 1 Lt HM Yacht Britannia 1956–57, Cdr 1957, Cmd HMS Finisterre 1960–62, resigned 1965; CLA: chm Hants Branch 1980–81 (pres 1987–94), chm Legal and Parly Sub Ctee and memb Nat Exec Ctee 1982–87; pres Hants Fedn of Young Farmers' Clubs 1982; liaison offr Hampshire Duke of Edinburgh's Award Scheme 1966–76, memb Hampshire Local Valuation Panel 1971–81 (chm 1977–), govr and vice chm Lankhills Special Sch Winchester 1975–80, chm of govrs Durley C of E Primary Sch 1980–95; High Sheriff of Hampshire 1972; Vice Lord-Lieut of Hampshire 1996–; Freeman City of London, Liveryman Worshipful Co of Farmers 1983; *Recreations* shooting, small woodland mgmnt; *Clubs* Brook's, Pratt's; *Style—* Cdr Colin Balfour, DL, RN; ✉ Wintershill Farmhouse, Durley, Hants SO32 2AH; Flat 4, Cygnet House, 188 Kings Rd, London SW3

BALFOUR, Doug John; s of Gwyn Balfour, of Bury St Edmunds, and Joy Balfour, of London; *b* 12 June 1958; *Educ* Univ of Southampton (MSc Geology), Cranfield Sch of Mgmnt (MBA); *m* 1984, Anne Mary, da of Robin Watson; 1 da (Alexandra b 1988), 2 s (Jonathan b 1990, Ryan b 1993); *Career* sr exploration geologist De Beers (Kalahari desert) 1980–83, Lucas Industries (sr mgmnt conslt, materials mangr, sales and mktg mangr) 1984–89, support mangr Youth With A Mission Amsterdam 1989–92, relief dir MEDAIR Relief Agency (following Liberian Civil War) 1991–92, commercial mangr Lucas Engineering & Systems Ltd (internal mgmnt consultancy Lucas Gp) 1992–95, gen dir Tear Fund (charity) 1995–; memb ACENVO 1996; *Recreations* travelling, history, gym; *Style—* Doug Balfour; ✉ Tear Fund, 100 Church Road, Teddington, Middlesex TW11 8QE (☎ 0181 977 9144, fax 0181 943 3594)

BALFOUR, Eustace Arthur Goschen; s of late Lt-Col Francis Cecil Campbell Balfour, CIE, CVO, CBE, MC, and gn of 1 E of Balfour, KG, OM, PC (d 1930), and Hon Phyllis Evelyn Goschen (d 1976), da of 2 Viscount Goschen; h to Earldom of Balfour; *b* 26 May 1921; *Educ* Eton; *m* 1, 1946 (m dis 1971), Anne, da of late Maj Victor Yule; 2 s (Roderick Francis Arthur Balfour, *qv*, Charles George Yule Balfour, *qv*); m 2, 1971, Mrs Paula Susan Cuene-Grandidier, da of late John Maurice Davis, MBE; *Career* served N Africa, Italy and Greece 1939–46, Capt Scot Guards, wounded Anzio beach head; *Clubs* Naval and Military; *Style—* Eustace Balfour, Esq; ✉ Le Pavillon, Ancenis-les-Bois, 44440 Riaillé, France (☎ 00 33 2 40 97 83 63, fax 00 33 2 40 97 83 64)

BALFOUR, 4 Earl of (UK 1922); Gerald Arthur James Balfour; JP (E Lothian 1970); also Viscount Traprain (UK 1922); s of 3 Earl (d 1968, nephew of 1 Earl, otherwise Arthur Balfour, PM (C) 1902–05) and Jean Lily (d 1981), da of late Rev John James Cooke-Yarborough (fourth in descent from George, 2 s of Sir George Cooke, 3 Bt); *b* 23 Dec 1925; *Educ* Eton, HMS Conway; *m* 14 Dec 1956, Mrs Natasha Georgina Lousada (d 1994), da of late Capt George Anton, of Archangel, Russia; *Heir* kinsman, Eustace Balfour; *Career* master mariner, served MN WWII; cncllr E Lothian 1960–75; currently farmer; Liveryman Worshipful Co of Clothworkers; *Clubs* Association of International Cape Horners, English Speaking Union; *Style—* The Rt Hon the Earl of Balfour, JP; ✉ Whittingehame Tower, Haddington, E Lothian EH41 4QA (☎ 01368 850208)

BALFOUR, Rear Adm (George) Ian Mackintosh; CB (1962), DSC (1943); s of Tom Stevenson Balfour (d 1912), and Ina Mary, *née* Tabuteau (d 1953); *b* 14 Jan 1912; *Educ* RNC Dartmouth; *m* 8 Aug 1939, (Gertrude) Pamela Carlyle, da of late Maj Hugh Carlyle Forrester, DL, of Tullibody House, Cambus; 2 s (David b 1944 ka HMS Sheffield Falklands 1983, Patrick b 1950), 1 da (Jane b 1953); *Career* HMS Emperor of India 1929–30, HMS Cornwall and HMS Kent (China) 1930–32, Sub Lt's courses 1932–33, HMS Viceroy 1933–34, HMS Carlisle (SA), and on loan as ADC to Govr Gen, Flag Lt to C in C 1935–37, HMS Caledonia 1937–39, 1 Lt HMS Kelvin 1939–42 (despatches 1941); i/c: HMS Foxhound 1942, HMS Decoy 1942–43, HMS Tuscan 1943, HMS Scourge 1943–45, HMS Solebay 1945–46, HMS Onslow 1946; jt planning staff Cabinet Offices 1946–48, American jt staff course 1948, exec offr HMS Triumph 1948–50, jt servs staff course 1950, asst dir of Plans Admty 1951, Capt Plans Washington 1952–54, i/c HMS

Osprey 1954–56, i/c and Capt D2 HMS Daring 1956–58, dir of offrs appointments Admty 1958–60, sr directing staff (Navy) IDC 1960–63, ret 1963; chief appeals offr and dep sec Cancer Res Campaign 1963–78 (memb Cncl 1978–86), vice pres RN Sch Haslemere (formerly govr); *Recreations* fishing; *Style*— Rear Adm Ian Balfour, CB, DSC; ✉ Westover, Farnham Lane, Haslemere, Surrey GU27 1HD (☎ 01428 643876)

BALFOUR, Dr (Elizabeth) Jean; CBE (1981), JP (Fife 1963); da of late Maj-Gen Sir James Syme Drew, KBE, CB, DSO, MC (d 1955), and late Victoria Maxwell of Munches; *b* 4 Nov 1927; *Educ* Univ of Edinburgh (Hons BSc); *m* 1950, John Charles Balfour, OBE, MC, JP, DL, *qv*; 3 s; *Career* dir A J Bowen & Co Ltd, ptnr Balbirnie Home Farms and Balbirnie Dairy Farm; dir: Chieftain Industries 1983–85, Scot Dairy Trade Fedn 1983–86; pres Royal Scot Forestry Soc 1969–71, chm Countryside Cmmn for Scot 1972–83, A New Look at the Northern Ireland Countryside (report to govt) 1984, hon vice pres Scot YHA 1983–, vice pres E Scot Coll of Agric 1982–88 (govr 1958–88), dir Scot Agric Colls 1987–89; memb: Fife CC 1958–70, Nature Conservancy Cncl 1973–80, Scot Economic Cncl 1978–83, Ct Univ of St Andrews 1983–87; vice chm Scottish Wildlife Tst 1969–72 (hon vice pres 1983–), memb Cncl Inst of Chartered Foresters 1984–87, chm Regnl Advsy Ctee (Mid Scotland) Forestry Cmmn 1987–, memb Ctee of Enquiry on Handling of Geographical Info 1987–89; dep chm: Seafish Indust Authy 1987–90, Women's Sci Ctee Office of Sci and Technol (Cabinet Office) 1993–; memb Forth River Purification Bd 1992, govr Duncan of Jordanston Coll of Art 1992–94, tstee Royal Botanic Garden Edinburgh 1992, memb Cncl Scottish Landowners' Fedn 1992; Hon DSc Univ of St Andrews 1977, Hon DUniv Stirling 1991; FRSA 1981, FRSE 1980, FICFor, FIBiol 1988, FRZS Scot 1983; *Recreations* hill walking, fishing, painting, exploring arctic vegetation, shooting; *Clubs* Farmers', New (Edinburgh, assoc); *Style*— Dr Jean Balfour, CBE, JP, FRSE; ✉ Kirkforthar House, Markinch, Glenrothes, Fife (☎ 01592 752233, fax 01592 610314); Scourie, by Lairg, Sutherland

BALFOUR, John Charles; OBE (1978), MC (1943), JP (Fife 1957), DL (Fife 1958); s of late Brig Edward Balfour, CVO, DSO, OBE, MC, and Lady Ruth, CBE, *née* Balfour (d 1967), da of 2 Earl of Balfour (d 1945), and Lady Elizabeth Bulwer-Lytton, da of 1 Earl of Lytton; bro of Peter Edward Gerald Balfour, CBE, *qv*; *b* 28 July 1919; *Educ* Eton, Trinity Coll Cambridge; *m* 1950, Dr (Elizabeth) Jean Balfour, CBE, JP, FRSE, *qv*, *née* Drew; 3 s; *Career* served RA (Maj) N Africa and Europe 1939–45; memb: Inter-Deptl Ctee on Children and Young Persons (Scotland) 1961–64, Scottish Cncl on Crime 1972–75; chm: Children's Panel Fife Co 1970–75 and Fife Region 1975–77, Scottish Assoc of Youth Clubs 1968–79, Fife Area Health Bd 1983–87 (memb 1981–87); memb Royal Co of Archers (Queen's Body Guard for Scotland) 1949–; tstee Nat AIDS Tst 1987–96; Vice Lord-Lt Fife 1988–96; *Recreations* fishing, shooting; *Clubs* New (Edinburgh); *Style*— John Balfour, Esq, OBE, MC, JP, DL; ✉ Kirkforthar House, Markinch, Glenrothes, Fife KY7 6LS (☎ 01592 752233, fax 01592 610314)

BALFOUR, John Manning; s of James Richard Balfour, and Eunice Barbara, *née* Manning; *b* 2 Oct 1952; *Educ* Fettes, Worcester Coll Oxford (MA); *Career* ptnr Frere Cholmeley Bischoff 1986– (slr 1979); *Books* Air Law (contrib ed, 1988–96), European Community Air Law (1995); *Recreations* swimming, reading; *Clubs* Lansdowne; *Style*— John Balfour, Esq; ✉ 1 Launceston Place, London W8 5RL (☎ 0171 937 9006); Frere Cholmeley Bischoff, 4 John Carpenter Street, London EC4Y 0NH (☎ 0171 615 8000)

BALFOUR, Michael John; JP (Roxburgh 1988); s of Duncan Balfour (d 1952), of Englefield Green, Surrey, and Jeanne Germaine, *née* Picot (d 1974); *b* 17 Oct 1925; *Educ* Eton, Christ Church Oxford (MA); *m* 15 Sep 1951, Mary Campbell, da of Maj-Gen Sir William Ronald Campbell Penney, KBE, CB, DSO, MC (d 1964), of Stanford Dingley, Berks; 3 s (James b 1952 d 1974, William b 1955, Andrew b 1963), 1 da (Emma b 1953); *Career* WWII RAF 1944–47; Bank of England: joined 1950, sr advsr Euro affrs 1973, chief advsr 1976, asst dir overseas affrs 1980–85, alternate dir Bank for International Settlements 1972–85; chm: Balgonie Estates 1975– (dir 1955–), IMI Capital Markets (UK) Ltd 1987–92, IMI Securities Ltd 1988–94; non-exec dir SIGECO (UK) Ltd (formerly IMI Capital Markets (UK) Ltd) 1992–95, dir IMI Bank (International) 1987–; memb EEC Monetary Ctee 1974–85; *Recreations* fishing, boating, music; *Style*— M J Balfour, Esq, JP; ✉ Harrietfield, Kelso, Roxburghshire TD5 7SY (☎ 01573 224825); 17 Shrewsbury Mews, London W2 5PN

BALFOUR, Nancy; OBE (1965); da of Alexander Balfour, and Ruth Macfarland Balfour; *b* 1911; *Educ* Wycombe Abbey Sch, Lady Margaret Hall Oxford (MA); *Career* Res Dept FO 1941–45, BBC N American Serv 1945–48, The Economist 1948–72 (asst ed 1954–72); Contemporary Art Soc: hon treas 1971–76, chm 1976–82, pres 1984–; vice chm Crafts Cncl 1983–85 (memb 1980–85); chm: Art Servs Grants 1983–89, Southern Arts Craft Panel 1986–90, Arts Research Ltd 1990–; memb: Cncl RIIA 1963–84, Bd Br-American Arts Assoc 1980–; tstee Public Art Devpt Tst 1983–91; FRSA 1985; *Recreations* sightseeing, viewing work by living artists; *Clubs* Arts; *Style*— Miss Nancy Balfour, OBE; ✉ 36E Eaton Square, London SW1W 9DH (☎ 0171 235 7874)

BALFOUR, Neil Roxburgh; s of Archibald Roxburgh Balfour, and Lilian Helen, *née* Cooper (d 1989); *b* 12 Aug 1944; *Educ* Ampleforth, Univ Coll Oxford (BA); *m* 1, 23 Sept 1969 (m dis 1978), HRH Princess Elizabeth of Yugoslavia; 1 s (Nicholas b 6 June 1970); m 2, 4 Nov 1978, Serena Mary Churchill, da of Edwin F Russell, and Lady Sarah Churchill; 1 s (Alastair b 20 Aug 1981), 1 da (Lily b 29 Nov 1979), 2 step da (Morgan b 19 June 1973, Lucinda b 14 Aug 1975); *Career* called to the Bar Middle Temple 1968; Baring Bros & Co 1968–74, European Banking Co Ltd 1974–83 (exec dir 1980–83); chm: York Trust Ltd 1983–, York Trust Group plc 1986–91, York Mount Group plc 1986–89, Yorkshire General Unit Trust 1985–88; non-exec dir: Oceonics Group plc 1988–90, Carter Plc 1989–; non-exec chm Acsis Group plc 1991–93 (formerly non-exec dir); MEP (C) Yorks N 1979–84; *Books* Official Biography of Prince Paul of Yugoslavia (1980); *Recreations* bridge, golf, tennis, fishing and shooting; *Clubs* Pratt's, Turf, White's, Royal St George's (Sandwich); *Style*— Neil Balfour, Esq; ✉ 55 Warwick Sq, London SW1V 2AJ (☎ 0171 834 6974); York Trust Ltd 12th Floor, Moor House, 119 London Wall, London EC2Y 5ET (☎ 0171 374 2344)

BALFOUR, (George) Patrick; s of David Mathers Balfour, CBE, of Little Garnstone Manor, Seal, Sevenoaks, Kent, and Mary Elisabeth, *née* Beddall (d 1988); gs of George Balfour, MP; *b* 17 Sept 1941; *Educ* Shrewsbury Sch, Pembroke Coll Cambridge (MA); *m* 18 March 1978, Lesley Ann, da of John Denis Johnston, of Glenfuir, Fidra Rd, N Berwick, Scotland; 3 s (James David Johnston b 1980, Matthew Alexander Patrick b 1982, Hugo Charles Beddall b 1989); *Career* slr; ptnr Slaughter & May 1973–; dir Slrs Benevolent Assoc; memb Law Soc; *Recreations* theatre, opera, golf, country pursuits; *Style*— Patrick Balfour, Esq; ✉ Slaughter & May, 35 Basinghall St, London EC2V 5DB (☎ 0171 600 1200, fax 0171 726 0038, telex 883486)

BALFOUR, Peter Edward Gerald; CBE (1984); s of Brig Edward William Sturgis Balfour, CVO, DSO, OBE, MC (d 1955), and Lady Ruth, CBE (d 1967), *née* Balfour, da of 2 Earl of Balfour (d 1945); bro of John Charles Balfour, OBE, MC, JP, DL, *qv*; *b* 9 July 1921; *Educ* Eton; *m* 1, 1948 (m dis 1967), Lady Grizelda, *née* Ogilvy, da of 7 (12 but for attainder) Earl of Airlie, KT, GCVO, MC (d 1968); 2 s, 1 da; m 2, 1968, Diana Wainman; 1 s, 1 da; *Career* served Scots Guards 1940–54; joined William McEwan & Co Ltd 1954, chm and chief exec Scottish and Newcastle Breweries 1970–83; chm: Selective Assets Trust 1978–92, Charterhouse plc 1985–90, First Charlotte Assets Trust 1981–92; dir: Royal Bank of Scotland 1971–90 (vice chm 1985–90), Royal Bank of Scotland Group 1978–91, British Assets Trust plc 1962–92; memb Hansard Soc Cmmn on Electoral Reform 1975–76, pres Scottish Cncl for Devpt and Indust 1986–91 (chm Exec Ctee 1978–85); *Clubs* Cavalry and Guards', New (Edinburgh); *Style*— Peter Balfour, Esq, CBE; ✉ Scadlaw House, Humbie, E Lothian (☎ 01875 33252)

BALFOUR, Robert Roxburgh; s of Alastair Norman Balfour (d 1996), and Elizabeth Eugenie, *née* Cowell; *b* 29 June 1947; *Educ* Tabley House, Grenoble Univ (Dip), Madrid Univ (Dip); *m* 31 Jan 1973, (Camilla) Rose, da of Michael George Thomas Webster, of Hants; 1 s (Rupert Alastair b 23 April 1976), 2 da (Camilla Louise b 11 May 1979, Lara Selina b 1 June 1983); *Career* md Bell Lawrie White Financial Services Ltd 1984–93, dir Bell Lawrie White & Co 1987–; chm Personal Equity Plan Mangrs Assoc 1995–; memb: Red Deer Cmmn 1984–92, Firearms Consultative Ctee 1989–90; IBRC 1980; *Recreations* shooting, photography; *Style*— Robert Balfour, Esq; ✉ Wester Dawyck, Stobo, Peeblesshire EH45 9JU (☎ 01721 760226); 10 Murrayfield Avenue, Edinburgh EH12 6AX (☎ 0131 337 6403); Bell Lawrie White & Co, 7 Drumsheugh Gardens, Edinburgh EH3 7QH (☎ 0131 225 2566, fax 0131 225 3134, telex 72260)

BALFOUR, Roderick Francis Arthur; s of Eustace Arthur Goschen Balfour, *qv*, and Anne, *née* Yule; *b* 9 Dec 1948; *Educ* Eton, London Business Sch (Sr Exec Program); *m* 14 July 1971, Lady Tessa Balfour, da of 17 Duke of Norfolk, *qv*; 4 da (Willa b 1973, Kinvara b 1975, Maria b 1977, Candida b 1984); *Career* ptnr Grieveson Grant and Co Stockbrokers 1972–81, investmt dir Jessel Toynbee and Co 1981–83, International and UK investmt dir Union Discount Co of London plc 1983–90, dir Rothschild Trust Corporation 1990–; Freeman City of London 1977, Liveryman Worshipful Co of Clothworkers 1986; *Recreations* music, painting, tennis, cricket, skiing, water skiing; *Clubs* White's, City of London, Hurlingham, Eton Ramblers; *Style*— Roderick Balfour, Esq; ✉ NM Rothschild & Sons Ltd, New Court, St Swithin's Lane, London EC4P 4DU (☎ 0171 280 5000, fax 0171 929 5239)

BALFOUR, William Harold St Clair; s of Francis Edmund Balfour (d 1974), of Edinburgh, and Isobel MacIntosh Shaw, *née* Ingram (d 1980); *b* 29 Aug 1934; *Educ* Hillfield Sch Ontario Canada, Edinburgh Acad, Univ of Edinburgh; *m* 1, 10 June 1961 (m dis 1983), (Janette) Patricia, da of late Donald Mowbray Waite; 1 s (Michael St Clair b 1966), 2 da (Sonia Jane b 1962, Jillian Clare b 1964); m 2, 1989, Mrs (Alice) Ingsay Macfarlane; 2 step da (Catherine b 1974, Emma b 1972); *Career* TA 1953–60; slr; ptnr Balfour & Manson 1962–; clerk to Admission of Notaries Public in Scotland 1973–92; pt/t tutor Univ of Edinburgh 1981–86, memb Scottish Home and Health Dept Prison Visiting Ctee 1965–70; chm: Basic Space Dance Theatre 1980–86, Friends of Talbot Rice Art Centre 1985–, Garvald Tst 1987–, Wellspring 1985–96; sec Scottish Photography Gallery 1975–96, Fruit Market Gallery Edinburgh 1986–96, tstee Edinburgh Rudolf Steiner Sch 1982–94; memb: Law Soc of Scotland 1960, City of Edinburgh Business Club 1962; MInstD 1980–88; *Recreations* sailing, walking, wine, travel; *Clubs* New (Edinburgh); *Style*— William Balfour, Esq; ✉ Balfour & Manson, 58 Frederick St, Edinburgh EH2 1LS (☎ 0131 200 1200, fax 0131 200 1377); 11 Nelson St, Edinburgh EH3 6JF (☎ 0131 556 7298)

BALFOUR-LYNN, Dr Lionel Peter; *b* 4 May 1928; *Educ* Hurstpierpoint Coll, Christ's Coll Cambridge, Guy's Hosp London (MD, MA, MB BCh, MRCS, LRCP, DCH); *m* 1952, June Anne, *née* Herbert; 1 da (Alison b 1955), 2 s (Simon b 1957, John b 1961); *Career* Flt Lt RAF 1954–56; paediatric registrar Hillingdon Hosp 1956–58; American Hosp Ruislip: sr paediatric specialist 1958–68, conslt paediatrician 1968–70; hon lectr Dept of Paediatrics: Brompton Hosp London 1970–74, Royal Postgraduate Med Sch Hammersmith Hosp London 1974–; hon conslt paediatrician Hammersmith Hosp London 1984–; vice pres Br Fellowship of the Israel Med Assoc 1995– (chm 1985–94); memb: Hampstead Med Soc, Windsor Med Soc, Hosp Conslts and Specialists Assoc, British Paediatric Assoc; FRSM; *Publications* author of papers on the relationship of childhood asthma with puberty, growth and exercise, Encyclopedia of Adolescence (contrib, 1991), Childhood Asthma and Other Wheezing Disorders (contrib, 1995); *Recreations* golf, tennis, cricket, skiing; *Clubs* RSM, Wentworth Golf, Relics CC; *Style*— Dr Lionel Balfour-Lynn; ✉ 120 Harley St, London W1N 1AG (☎ 0171 935 2220); 7 Kidderpore Gardens, London NW3 7SS (☎ 0171 435 5400)

BALFOUR OF BURLEIGH, Lady; (Dr Janet Morgan); da of Frank Morgan, and Sheila, *née* Sadler; *b* 5 Dec 1945; *Educ* Newbury Co Girls GS, St Hugh's Coll Oxford (MA), Nuffield Coll Oxford (DPhil), Univ of Sussex (MA), Kennedy Meml Scholar Harvard Univ; *m* 1993, 8 Lord Balfour of Burleigh, *qv*; *Career* res fell Wolfson Coll Oxford and res offr Univ of Essex 1971–72, res fell Nuffield Coll Oxford 1972–74, lectr in politics Exeter Coll Oxford 1974–76, dir of studies St Hugh's Coll Oxford 1975–76 and lectr in politics 1976–78, visiting fell All Souls Coll Oxford 1983; memb Central Policy Review Staff Cabinet Office 1978–81, dir Satellite Television plc 1981–83, special advsr to Dir-Gen BBC 1983–86, advsr to Bd Granada Group plc 1986–89, vice pres Videotext Indust Assoc 1985–91; dir Hulton Deutsch Collection 1988–89; non-exec dir: Cable & Wireless plc 1988–, WH Smith Group plc 1989–95, Midlands Electricity plc 1990–96, Pitney Bowes plc 1991–92, Scottish American Investment Tst plc 1991–, Scottish Oriental Smaller Companies Tst plc 1995–, Scottish Life plc 1995–, Nuclear Generation Decommissioning Fund Ltd 1996–; chm: Dorothy Burns Charity, Readiscovery (Scotland's Nat Book Campaign) 1994–96, Scottish Cultural Resources Access Network, Cable & Wireless Flexible Resource Ltd; tstee: American Sch in London 1985–88, Fairground Heritage Tst 1987–91, Cyclotron Tst 1988–89, Carnegie Endowment for the Univs of Scotland 1994–; memb: Lord Chllr's Advsy Cncl on Public Records 1982–86, Editorial Bd Political Quarterly, Bd Br Cncl 1989–, Ancient Monuments Bd for Scotland 1990–, Scottish Hosp Endowments Research Tst 1992–; FSA(Scot); *Books* The House of Lords and the Labour Government 1964–70 (1975), Reinforcing Parliament (1976), The Diaries of a Cabinet Minister 1964–70 by Richard Crossman 3 Vols (ed, 1975, 1976, 1977), Backbench Diaries 1951–63 by Richard Crossman (ed, 1980), The Future of Broadcasting (ed with Richard Hoggart, 1982), Agatha Christie: A Biography (1984), Edwina Mountbatten: A Life of her Own (1991); *Recreations* music of Handel, sea-bathing, ice skating out of doors, gardens; *Style*— Lady Balfour of Burleigh, professionally known as Dr Janet Morgan; ✉ Cable & Wireless plc, Mercury House, Theobalds Rd, London WC1X 8RX (☎ 0171 315 4000, fax 0171 315 5000, telex 920000)

BALFOUR OF BURLEIGH, Jennifer, Lady; Jennifer Ellis; da of E S Manasseh (d 1962), of London, and Phyllis Annette, *née* Barnard (d 1970); *b* 27 Oct 1930; *Educ* St Paul's Girls' Sch, Lady Margaret Hall Oxford; *m* 1, 12 Dec 1951 (m dis 1968), John Edward Jocelyn Brittain-Catlin (d 1987), s of Sir George Edward Gordon Catlin (d 1979), and his 1 w, Vera Brittain; 3 s (Daniel b 1953, Timothy b 1961, William b 1966); m 2, 30 Oct 1971 (m dis 1993), 8 Lord Balfour of Burleigh, *qv*; 2 da (Hon Victoria b 1973, Hon Ishbel b 1976); *Career* public relations executive: Butter Information Cncl 1953–55, Patrick Dolan & Assoc 1955–56; sr public relations executive Erwin Wasey Ruthrauff & Ryan 1956–61; conslt PR advsr to various companies incl Acrilan, Hoover, Vono, Carnation Milk, Littlewoods Stores, Scottish Crafts Centre 1961–71; dir Jamaica Street Ltd property developers 1980–, mangr London & Scottish Property Services 1985–; dir: Scottish Opera 1990–, ECAT Ltd (Edinburgh Contemporary Arts Tst) 1989–, Boxcar Films plc (non-exec) 1994–; memb Bd Link Housing Assoc 1974– (former chm Central Region Ctee), life pres Ochil View Housing Assoc (chm 1988–93); memb: Visiting Ctee HM Instn Glenochil 1980–85, CAB Alloa 1988–92, Exec Ctee Clackmannan Social & Liberal Democrats until 1993, Cncl National Tst for Scotland 1991–96, Bd The Grassmarket Project 1994–, Bd Children's Music Fndn Scotland 1994–; writer of numerous booklets, pamphlets, newspaper and magazine articles; *Recreations* music, theatre; *Style*— Jennifer, Lady Balfour of Burleigh; ✉ 5A Belford Park, Edinburgh EH4 3DP (☎ 0131 332 9348)

BALFOUR OF BURLEIGH, 8 (*de facto* and 12 but for the Attainder) Lord (S 1607); Robert Bruce; er s of 7 Lord Balfour of Burleigh (11 but for the Attainder, d 1967); *b* 6 Jan 1927; *Educ* Westminster; *m* 1, 30 Oct 1971 (m dis 1993), Jennifer, Lady Balfour of Burleigh, *qv*, da of E S Manasseh (d 1962), and former w of John Edward Jocelyn Brittain-Catlin; 2 da (Hon Victoria b 7 May 1973, Hon Ishbel b 28 Sept 1976); m 2, 29 Aug 1993, Dr Janet P Morgan, *qv*, da of Frank Morgan; *Heir* (hp) da, Hon Victoria Bruce b 7 May 1973; *Career* served RN 1945–48; foreman and supt English Electric Co Ltd Stafford & Liverpool 1952–57; gen mangr: English Electric Co India Ltd 1957–64, English Electric Netherton Works 1964–66, D Napier & Son Ltd 1966–68; dir: Bank of Scotland 1968–91 (dep govr 1977–91), Scottish Investment Trust plc 1971–, Tarmac plc 1981–90, William Lawson Distillers Ltd 1984–, UAPT Infolink plc 1991–94; chm: Scottish Arts Cncl 1971–80, Viking Oil Ltd 1971–80, Fedn of Scottish Bank Employers 1977–86, Nat Book League Scotland 1981–86, Edinburgh Book Festival 1982–87 (dir 1982–), United Artists (Communications) Scotland Ltd (formerly Cablevision (Scotland) plc) 1983–, The Turing Inst 1983–92, Canongate Press plc 1991–93; memb: BR (Scottish) Bd 1982–93, Forestry Cmmn 1971–74, Cncl ABSA 1976–94 (chm Scot Ctee 1990–94); treas: Royal Soc of Edinburgh 1989–94, Royal Scottish Corp 1967–; chllr Univ of Stirling 1988–; Hon DUniv Stirling 1988, Hon DLitt Robert Gordon Univ of Aberdeen 1995; CEng, FIEE, Hon FRIAS 1982, FRSE 1986; *Recreations* music, climbing, woodwork; *Style*— The Rt Hon the Lord Balfour of Burleigh, FRSE; ✉ Brucefield, Clackmannan FK10 3QF (☎ 01259 730228)

BALFOUR OF INCHRYE, 2 Baron (UK 1945); Ian Balfour; s of 1 Baron Balfour of Inchrye, MC, PC (d 1988), and his 1 w Diana Blanche (d 1982), da of Sir Robert Grenville Harvey, 2 Bt; *b* 21 Dec 1924; *Educ* Eton, Magdalen Coll Oxford (MA); *m* 28 Nov 1953, Josephine Maria Jane, o da of Morogh Wyndham Percy Bernard; 1 da (Roxane (Hon Mrs Laird Craig)); *Heir* none; *Career* business conslt, composer and gem historian; compositions include 6 operas, 5 symphonies, concertos for viola (2), violoncello, violin and violoncello, orchestral, vocal and instrumental works; performances: Two Pieces for Strings - Haifa 1976; In Memoriam II for Oboe, Strings, Harp and Percussion - Dublin 1982; Suite No 1 for Cello Solo - Edinburgh and London 1986; Oxford Memories for small orchestra - Oxford 1996; *Books* Famous Diamonds (1987, 2nd edn 1992); *Recreations* reading, walking, watching cricket and association football; *Style*— The Rt Hon Lord Balfour of Inchrye; ✉ 10 Limerston Street, London SW10 0HH

BALGONIE, Lord; David Alexander Leslie Melville; s and h of 14 Earl of Leven and (13 of) Melville, DL; *b* 26 Jan 1954; *Educ* Eton; *m* 1981, Julia Clare, yr da of Col I R Critchley, of Lindores, Muthill, Perths; 1 s (Hon Alexander b 1984), 1 da (Hon Louisa Clare b 1987); *Heir* s Hon Alexander Leslie Melville; *Career* Lt (acting Capt) Queen's Own Highlanders, RARO 1979–81; dir: Wood Conversion Ltd Basingstoke 1984–, Treske Shop Ltd London 1988–; *Style*— Lord Balgonie; ✉ The Old Farmhouse, West Street, Burghclere, Newbury, Berks RG15 9LB (☎ 01635 278241)

BALKWILL, Bryan Havell; *b* 2 July 1922; *Educ* Merchant Taylors', RAM; *m* Susan Elizabeth, *née* Roberts; 1 s (Chris Russell), 1 da (Maryan); *Career* served Intelligence Corps 1943–46; asst conductor New London Opera Co 1947–49, assoc conductor Int Ballet Co 1948–50, musical dir and princ conductor London Festival Ballet 1950–52, assoc conductor Glyndebourne Opera 1950–64, princ conductor Wexford Festival 1953–58, conductor Royal Opera House Covent Garden 1959–66, musical dir WNO 1963–67, musical dir Wells Co Sadler's Wells Opera 1966–69, prof of conducting Indiana Univ Sch of Music Bloomington 1977–92; numerous freelance concert and operatic engagements worldwide 1970–; life memb Royal Philharmonic Soc; FRAM; *Recreations* open air; *Style*— Bryan Balkwill, Esq; ✉ 8 The Green, Wimbledon Common, London SW19 5AZ (☎ 0181 947 4250)

BALKWILL, Richard Stephen; s of Michael Y Basanta Balkwill (d 1985), of Semley, Shaftesbury, Dorset, and Bridget Home de Selincourt (d 1970); *b* 12 June 1946; *Educ* Charterhouse, ChCh Oxford (MA); *m* 5 July 1975, Elisabeth Ruth, da of Air Marshal Sir Thomas Warne-Browne, KBE, CB, DSC (d 1963), of Chilbolton, Stockbridge, Hants; 1 da (Emily Victoria b 14 April 1976); *Career* Ginn & Co 1968–72, primary schs ed Thos Nelson & Sons 1972–77; Macmillan Education: sr primary ed 1977–78, dir primary sch publishing 1979–83, dir schs publishing 1983–84, publishing dir 1984–88, dir of operations and servs 1989; md Heinemann Children's Reference 1990–92, currently writer and publishing conslt in trg and copyright; *Books* Trafalgar: Great Battles and Sieges (1993), Guinness Book of Rail Facts and Feats (jtly with John Marshall, 6 edn 1993), Food and Feasts in Ancient Egypt/Tudor Times (1994), Multi-Lingual Dictionary of Copyright, Rights and Contracts (1994), Milton's Mystery (1996); *Recreations* music, choral singing, writing, canal cruising, steam railways; *Clubs* Savile; *Style*— Richard Balkwill, Esq; ✉ Pitts, Great Milton, Oxfordshire OX44 7NF (☎ 01844 279506)

BALL, Air Marshal Sir Alfred Henry Wynne; KCB (1976, CB 1967), DSO (1943), DFC (1942); s of Capt J A E Ball, MC (d 1957), and Josephine Hilda Wynne, *née* Rowland-Thomas, of Rostrevor, Co Down and BNR India; *b* 18 Jan 1921, Rawalpindi, Br India; *Educ* Campbell Coll Belfast, RAF Coll Cranwell, RAF Staff Coll, JSSC, IDC; *m* 1942, Nan, da of late A G McDonald, of Tipperary; 3 s, 1 da; *Career* cmmnd 1939, served WWII RAF Lysander Spitfire and Mosquito Sqdn (despatches twice), cmd 682, 542 and 540 and 13 Sqdns, Air Medal (USA) 1943, Wing Cdr 1944, Gp Capt 1959, BJSM Washington DC 1959–62, cmd Honington V Bomber Base 1963–64, Air Cdre AOA Aden 1964–66, Air Vice Marshal 1968, asst COS SHAPE, NATO 1968–71, DG of RAF Orgn 1971–75, UK mil rep CENTO Ankara 1975–77, Dep C-in-C RAF Strike Cmd 1977–78, ret 1979; mil advsr ICL 1979–83; vice chm (Air) TAVRA Cncl 1979–84, Hon Air Cdre RAuxAF Regt Sqdn 1984–90; Hon FBCS 1984; *Recreations* golf, bridge; *Clubs* RAF, Phyllis Court, Huntercombe; *Style*— Air Marshal Sir Alfred Ball, KCB, DSO, DFC

BALL, Anthony George (Tony); MBE (1986); s of Harry Clifford Ball, of Bridgwater, Somerset, and Mary Irene Ball; *b* 14 Nov 1934; *Educ* Bridgwater GS, Bromsgrove Coll of FE; *m* 27 July 1957, Ruth, da of Ivor Parry Davies (d 1976), of Mountain Ash, S Wales; 2 s (Kevin, Michael), 1 da (Katherine); *Career* indentured engrg apprentice Austin Motor Co 1951, responsible for launch of Mini 1959, UK sales mangr Austin Motor Co 1962–66, sales and mktg exec BMC 1966–67, chm Barlow Rand UK Motor Group 1967–78 (md Barlow Rand Ford S Africa 1971–73 and Barlow Rand Euro Ops 1973–78); dir: BL Cars, BL International, Rover Gp, Austin Morris, Jaguar Cars, Jaguar Rover Triumph Inc (USA) and BL overseas subsids; chm Nuffield Press 1978–80, chm and md BL Europe and Overseas 1979–82, world sales chief BL Cars 1979–82 (responsible for BL's Buy British campaign and launch of Austin Metro 1980); chief exec Henlys plc 1982–84; chm: Tony Ball Associates plc (mktg, product launch and sales promotion agency) 1983–; dep chm: Lumley Insurance Consultants Ltd 1985–95, Lumley Warranty Services Ltd 1985–95; dir: Customer Concern Ltd 1986–92, Jetmaster Int 1989–, Billy Marsh Associates Ltd (theatre agency) 1992–; mktg advsr to: Sec of State for Agric 1982, Sec of State for Energy 1983–87, Sec of State for Wales 1987–91; responsible for UK dealer launch of Vauxhall Astra for General Motors 1984; launches for: Rover, Mercedes-Benz, Fiat, Bedford, Proton, Lada, Leyland DAF, Daihatsu, Optare Buses, GM Europe; organiser Rugby World Cup Launch and opening ceremony 1991; responsible for prodn and promotion of SMMT Br International Motor Show; mktg advsr to relaunch of London Zoo 1993–; creator and producer Lloyds Private Banking Playwright of the Year Award 1995–; producer Euro 96 opening and closing ceremonies at Wembley Stadium of 1996 European Football Championships; responsible for launch production of British Motor Industry Centenary Year 1996 for SMMT; broadcaster, writer, lectr and after-dinner speaker, Mason Meml Lecture Univ of Birmingham 1982, various TV and radio documentaries, prodr ITV documentary The Birth of Rugby 1991, panellist BBC Any Questions; Benedictine Awards Business After Dinner Speaker of the Year 1992–93; Freeman City of London 1980; Liveryman: Worshipful Co of Coach Makers and Coach Harness Makers 1980, Worshipful Co of Carmen 1983; hon memb City & Guilds of London, Prince Philip Medal for Mktg Achievement and Servs to Br Motor Indust 1984; FCIM 1981, FIMI, ACIArb; *Books* Metro - The Book of the Car (contrib), A Marketing Study of the Welsh Craft Industry (Govt report, 1988), Tales Out of School - Early Misdeeds of the Famous (contrib), Successful Business Presentations (contrib); *Recreations* military history, theatre, after-dinner speaking, sharing good humour; *Clubs* Oriental, RAC; *Style*— Tony Ball, Esq, MBE; ✉ 249 Grove End Gardens, Grove End Rd, St John's Wood, London NW8 (☎ 0171 286 0899); Tony Ball Associates plc, 174/178 North Gower St, London NW1 2NB (☎ 0171 380 0953)

BALL, Sir Charles Irwin; 4 Bt (UK 1911), of Merrion Square, City of Dublin, and Killybegs, Co Donegal; s of Sir Nigel Gresley Ball, 3 Bt (d 1978), and Florine Isabel, *née* Irwin; *b* 12 Jan 1924; *Educ* Sherborne; *m* 1, 2 Sept 1950 (m dis 1983), Alison Mary, o da of Lt-Col Percy Holman Bentley, MBE, MC, of Farnham, Surrey; 1 s, 1 da (Diana Margaret b 1955); m 2, 1994, Christine Trilby Knowles; *Heir* s, Richard Bentley Ball, *qv*; *Career* served RA 1942–47 (Capt 1946); chartered accountant Peat Marwick Mitchell & Co 1950–54, joined Robert Benson Lonsdale & Co Ltd (now Kleinwort Benson Ltd) 1954; dir: Kleinwort Benson Ltd 1964–76 (vice chm 1974–76), Kleinwort Benson Lonsdale Ltd 1974–76, Cadbury Schweppes Ltd 1971–76, Chubb & Son Ltd 1971–76, Sun Alliance and London Insurance Ltd 1971–83, Telephone Rentals plc 1971–89 (vice chm 1978–81, chm 1981–89), Tunnel Holdings Ltd 1976–82, Barclays Bank Ltd 1976–77, Rockware Group plc 1978–84, Peachey Property Corporation plc 1978–88 (chm 1981–88), British Transport Docks Bd 1971–82; chm: Barclays Merchant Bank Ltd 1976–77, Silkolene plc 1989–94; dep chm: Associated British Ports Holdings plc 1982–, Century Oils Group plc 1991–94; Liveryman Worshipful Co of Clockmakers 1960 (Master 1985); FCA 1960; *Style*— Sir Charles Ball, Bt; ✉ Killybegs, Eddystone Road, Thurlestone, Kingsbridge, Devon TQ7 3NU

BALL, Christopher Charles; s of Reginald Charles Ball, of Essex, and Amelia Ellen, *née* Garner; *b* 25 Dec 1945; *Educ* Harold Hill GS; *m* 17 July 1971, Frances Jean, da of Philip Elliott, of Barry Island, Wales; 1 s (Ian b 1987); *Career* dir: Capel-Cure Myers 1986, Linton Nominees Ltd 1986, Richardson Glover and Case Nominees Ltd 1986, Capel-Cure Myers Unit Trust Management Ltd 1990, National Investment Group 1990; chm Ridgefield Unit Trust Administration Ltd; MSI; *Recreations* golf, reading, shooting; *Style*— Christopher Ball, Esq; ✉ 147 Western Rd, Leigh-on-Sea, Essex (☎ 01702 711032); The Registry, Royal Mint Court, London EC3N 4EY (☎ 0171 488 4000, fax 0171 481 3798, telex 9419251)

BALL, Sir Christopher John Elinger; kt (1988); er s of late Laurence Elinger Ball, OBE, and Christine Florence Mary, *née* Howe; *b* 22 April 1935; *Educ* St George's Sch Harpenden, Merton Coll Oxford (MA); *m* 1958, Wendy Ruth, da of Cecil Frederick Colyer; 3 s (David, Peter, Richard), 3 da (Helen, Diana, Yasmin); *Career* 2 Lt Para Regt 1955–56; lectr in English language Merton Coll Oxford 1960–61, lectr in comparative linguistics SOAS Univ of London 1961–64; Lincoln Coll Oxford: fell and tutor of English language 1964–79, sr tutor for admissions 1971–72, bursar 1972–79, hon fell 1981; Keble Coll Oxford: warden 1980–88, hon fell 1989; hon fell Merton Coll Oxford 1987; chm Bd of Nat Advsy Body for Public Sector Higher Educn in England 1982–88, sec Linguistics Assoc of GB 1964–67, pres Oxford Assoc of Univ Teachers 1968–71, publications sec Philological Soc 1969–75, chm Univ of Oxford English Bd 1977–79, founding fell Kellogg Forum for Continuing Educn Univ of Oxford 1988–89, chm Educn-Indust (Indust Matters) RSA 1988–90, RSA fell in continuing educn 1989–92, RSA dir of learning 1992–; memb: Jt Standing Ctee for Linguistics 1979–82, Conf of Colls Fees Ctee 1979–85, Gen Bd of the Faculties 1979–82, Hebdomadal Cncl 1985–89, CNAA 1982–88 (chm English Studies Bd 1973–80, chm Linguistics Bd 1977–82), BTEC 1984–90, IT Skills Shortages Ctee (Butcher Ctee) 1984–85, CBI IT Skills Agency 1985–88, CBI Trg Task Force 1988–89, CBI Educn and Trg Affrs Ctee 1989–; chm: Strategic Educn Fora for Kent, Oxfordshire and Greater Peterborough 1992–, Educn Policy Ctee RSA Exams Bd 1993–; memb Cncl and Exec Templeton Coll Oxford 1981–92; govr: St George's Sch Harpenden 1985–89, Centre for Medieval and Renaissance Studies Oxford 1987–90; chm: Brathay Hall Tst 1990–91, Manchester Poly 1989–91 (hon fell 1988); chm High Educn Info Servs Tst 1987–90, visiting prof of higher educn Leeds Poly 1989–92, chm Nat Inst for Careers Educn and Counselling 1989–92, chm Pegasus 1989–92, pres Assoc of Colls for Further and Higher Educn 1987–90; educnl conslt to Price Waterhouse 1989–92; founding chm: Nat Advsy Cncl for Careers and Educnl Guidance (NACCEG) 1994–96, Nat Campaign for Learning 1995–; Chllr of Univ of Derby 1995–; jt founding ed (with late Angus Cameron) Toronto Dictionary of Old English 1970, memb Editorial Bd Oxford Review of Education 1984–; hon fell Poly of Central London 1990, NT hon fell North East Wales Inst 1996; Hon DLitt CNAA 1989; FRSA 1987; *Publications* Fitness for Purpose (1985), Aim Higher (1989), Higher Education into the 1990s (jt ed with Heather Eggins, 1989), More Means Different (1990), Learning Pays (1991), Sharks and Splashes!: The Future of Education and Employment (1991), Profitable Learning (1992), Start Right (1993); various contribs to philological, linguistic and educnl jls; *Style*— Sir Christopher Ball; ✉ 45 Richmond Rd, Oxford OX1 2JJ (☎ and fax 01865 310800)

BALL, David Martin James; s of Rev Thomas William Ball, of Perth, W Aust, and late Anne, *née* Rice; *b* 29 Sept 1943; *Educ* Annadale GS, Lisburn Tech Coll, Belfast Coll of Arts and Tech (Dip Civil Engrg); *m* 1, 1969 (m dis 1985); 2 da (Heidi b 5 Oct 1974, Joanna b 14 Aug 1977); m 2, 31 May 1986, Jacqueline Bernadette Margaret Mary, da of Maj Fredrick Jocelyn Clarke, of Weybridge, Surrey; 1 da (Victoria b 20 Nov 1989); *Career* civil engr Middle Level Cmmrs March Cambridge 1965–66, gen mangr A L Curtis (ONX) Ltd Chatteris Cambridge 1966–70, chm and md David Ball Group Cambridge 1970–; chm: Cambridge Energy Management Group 1982, Cambridge Philharmonic Soc 1986, Q 103 FM (local commercial radio) 1988; regnl chm East Anglia Energy Managers Gps 1990; dir Business Link Central and South Cambs; memb Cncl Midland Examining Group, vice chm and co fndr Cambridge Enterprise Agency; chm: Cambridge Work Relations Gp, Parochial Church Cncl; memb Synod; tstee Pye Fndn; memb Concrete Soc (MCS); FIMgt 1981, Fell Inst of Refractory Engrs 1981, FRSA 1985; *Recreations* gardening, tennis, walking; *Style*— David Ball, Esq; ✉ Freckenham House, Freckenham, Suffolk IP28 8HX (☎ 01638 720975); David Ball Group plc, Huntingdon Rd, Bar Hill, Cambridge CB3 8HN (☎ 01954 780687, fax 01954 782912, telex 817213 BALL CO G, car 0831 878600)

BALL, Denis William; MBE (1971); s of William Charles Thomas Ball, of Eastbourne, Sussex, and late Dora Adelaide, *née* Smith; *b* 20 Oct 1928; *Educ* Tonbridge, BNC Oxford (MA); *m* 5 Aug 1972, Marja Tellervo (d 1987), da of Osmo Lumijarvi, of Sontula 42, Toijala, Finland; 2 s (Christian b 1975, Robin b 1976), 1 da (Sasha b 1981); *Career* served RN 1947–49, RNR 1953–85 (Lt Cdr 1958); housemaster The King's Sch Canterbury 1954–72 (asst master 1953–72); headmaster: Kelly Coll Tavistock 1972–85, St Michael's Sch Tawstock 1986; dir: Western Bloodstock Ltd 1986–92, James Wilkes plc 1987–88, Perkins Foods plc 1987–96, Redbridge Properties Ltd 1990–96; conslt Throgmorton Investment Management Ltd 1987–88; squash rackets for Oxford Univ and Kent, real tennis for MCC and Jesters; memb: HMC 1972–85, HMA 1972–85; tstee Tavistock Coll 1972–85, hon govr St Michael's Sch Tawstock 1993– (vice chm 1974–93); memb: Ickham PCC 1986– (treas 1990–), Johnson Club 1987–; *Recreations* Elizabethan history, cryptography, literary and mathematical puzzles, cricket, real tennis, golf; *Clubs* East India, Devonshire, Sports and Public Schools, MCC; *Style*— Denis Ball, Esq, MBE; ✉ Ickham Hall, Ickham, nr Canterbury, Kent CT3 1QT

BALL, Geoffrey Arthur (Geoff); s of Henry Arthur Ball, of Bristol, and Phyllis Edna, *née* Webber; *b* 4 Aug 1943; *Educ* Cotham GS Bristol; *m* 1968, Mary Elizabeth, da of late S George Richards, of Bristol; 3 s (Nicholas b 1971, Nathan b 1972, Thomas b 1975), 1 da (Esther b 1977); *Career* chm and chief exec CALA plc; dir: The Scottish Mortgage & Tst plc, The Standard Life Assurance Co; Clydesdale Bank Young Business Personality of the Year 1983; FCA; *Recreations* golf, music; *Clubs* New (Edinburgh), MCC; *Style*— Geoff Ball, Esq; ✉ 26 Hermitage Drive, Edinburgh EH10 6BY (☎ 0131 447 7909); CALA plc, 42 Colinton Rd, Edinburgh EH10 5BT (☎ 0131 346 0194, fax 0131 346 4190)

BALL, Prof Sir (Robert) James; kt (1984); s of Arnold James Hector Ball; *b* 15 July 1933; *Educ* St Marylebone GS, Queen's Coll Oxford (BA, MA), Univ of Pennsylvania (PhD); *m* 1, 1954 (m dis 1970), Patricia Mary Hart Davies; 1 s (Charles), 3 da (Stephanie, Deborah, Joanne) and 1 da decd; m 2, 1970, Mrs Lindsay Jackson, *née* Wonnacott; 1 step s (Nigel); *Career* Flying Offr Navigator RAF 1952–54; res offr Oxford Univ Inst of Statistics 1957–58, IBM fell Univ of Pennsylvania 1958–60, lectr (subsequently sr lectr) Univ of Manchester 1960–65; London Business Sch: prof of economics 1965–, govr 1968–84, dep princ 1971–72, princ 1972–84; chm Legal & General Group plc 1980–94; dir: Ogilvy & Mather Ltd 1969–71, Economic Models Ltd 1971–72, Barclays Bank Trust Co 1973–86, Tube Investments 1974–84, LASMO plc 1988–94, IBM UK Ltd 1979–94, dir IBM UK Ltd Pensions Trust Ltd 1994–, Royal Bank of Canada 1990–, chm Royal Bank of Canada Holdings (UK) Ltd 1995–; econ advsr Touche Ross & Co 1984–94; tstee: Foulkes Fndn 1984–, Civic Tst 1986–91, Economist Newspaper 1987–; memb: Page Ctee to review Nat Savings 1971–73, British-North American Ctee 1985–; Marshall Aid Commemoration cmmr 1987–94; vice pres CIM 1991–94, fell Econometric Soc 1973, CIMgt 1974, FIAM 1985; Freeman City of London 1987; Hon DSc Aston Univ 1987, Hon DSocSci Univ of Manchester 1988; *Books* An Econometric Model of the United Kingdom (1961), Inflation and the Theory of Money (1964); ed: Inflation (1969), The International Linkage of National Economic Models (1973); Money and Employment (1982), Toward European Economic Recovery in the 1980s (with M Albert, 1984), The Economics of Wealth Creation (ed, 1992), The World Economy: Trends and Prospects for the Next Decade (1994); numerous articles in professional jls; *Recreations* gardening, chess, fishing; *Clubs* RAC; *Style*— Prof Sir James Ball; ✉ London Business School, Sussex Place, Regent's Park, London NW1 4SA (☎ 0171 262 5050, fax 0171 724 7875, telex 27461)

BALL, Prof John Macleod; *b* 19 May 1948; *Educ* Mill Hill Sch, St John's Coll Cambridge (open exhibitioner, BA), Univ of Sussex (DPhil); *Career* SRC postdoctoral res fell Brown Univ USA 1972–74; Heriot-Watt Univ: joined Dept of Mathematics 1972, lectr in mathematics 1974–78, reader in mathematics 1978–82, prof of applied analysis 1982–96; Sedleian prof of natural philosophy Mathematical Inst Univ of Oxford 1996–; visiting prof Dept of Mathematics UC Berkeley USA 1979–80, sr fell SERC 1980–85, visiting prof Laboratoire d'Analyse Numérique Université Pierre et Marie Curie Paris 1987–88 and 1994, Ordway visiting prof Univ of Minnesota 1990, visiting prof Inst for Advanced Study Princeton Univ 1993–94; pres London Mathematical Soc 1996–97; memb Engrg and Physical Sciences Research Cncl 1994–; memb editorial bds various mathematical and scientific jls and book series, author of numerous mathematical and scientific pubns; Whittaker Prize Edinburgh Mathematical Soc 1981, jr Whitehead Prize London Mathematical Soc 1982, Keith Prize RSE 1990, Naylor Prize London Mathematical Soc 1995; FRSE 1980, FRS 1989; *Recreations* chess, music, travel; *Style*— Prof John Ball, FRS, FRSE

BALL, Johnny; *b* 23 May 1938; *Educ* Bolton County GS; *m* 1; 1 da (Zoë Louise b 23 Nov 1970); m 2, 14 June 1975, Dianne Cheryl; 2 s (Nicholas Alexander b 19 Aug 1976, Daniel James b 8 Dec 1977); *Career* television writer and presenter; early career in accountancy with DeHavilland Aircraft Co, Nat Serv RAF; Butlin's redcoat and drummer Liverpool then stand-up comedian, compered first Rolling Stones UK tour and tours of Dusty Springfield, Engelbert Humperdinck and others; TV career 1966–; dir The Living History of Science (agency supplying historical characters as an educnl resource), advsr Techniquest museum project Cardiff; numerous lectures and presentations incl: Royal Society Lecture 1979, Humphrey Davy Lecture 1982, British Telecom Christmas Lectures 1984 and 1988, British Gas Lectures 1984–85, Br Assoc of Young Scientists, numerous colls and univs; also writer/presenter numerous educnl and corporate video prodns; Lord Rector Univ of Glasgow 1993–, pres Nat Assoc for Gifted Children, patron CREST Creativity in Science and Technol Awards, memb Research & Devpt Soc; *Programmes* early progs incl: Late Date with Johnny Ball (Tyne Tees) 1966, host ITV Christmas Night Spectacular 1967, Val Doonican and Harry Secombe Shows; writer/presenter children's and educnl progs incl: presenter Play School (BBC) for 16 years, comedy writer Playaway (BBC), Cabbages and Kings (2 series, BBC), writer and regular guest Star Turn (5 series, BBC), writer Crackerjack (BBC), Think of a Number (6 series, BBC), Think Again (5 series, BBC), Think It - Do It (2 series, BBC), Think Backwards (BBC), Think This Way (BBC), Playdays (BBC), Philomena (BBC), Knowhow (BBC), Help your Child with Maths (BBC), Away with Numbers (BBC), Johnny Ball's Maths Games (BBC Radio), Sixth Sense (2 series, Anglia TV), Johnny Ball Reveals All (5 series, Central TV) 1990–; presenter other series incl: The Great Egg Race, Snooker Taylor Made, Secrets Out (2 series), Fun and Games (Yorkshire TV); writer other shows/series incl: Don't Ask Me (3 series, BBC), Battle of the Sexes, The Hot Shoe Show (BBC); *Awards* incl: BAFTA Harlequin Award for Best Children's Prog (for Think of a Number) 1979, Asian Bdcasting Union Best Children's Prog Award (for Think Again: Chairs) 1982, Prix Jeunesse Munich Best Information Prog Award (for Think Again: Flight) 1982, Int Emmy nomination (for Think Again: Doors) 1983, Boston Radio Award (for Johnny Ball's Maths Games) 1984, ITVA Merit Award and BISFA Medical Cncl Bronze Award for You Are What You Eat (video for Flour Advsy Bureau) 1985, ITVA Craft Award for Best Presenter (for What's Wessex Up To?) 1986, NY Film & TV Awards Silver Medal (for Johnny Ball Reveals All: Blood) 1993; *Books* Think of a Number (1980), Johnny Ball's Think Box (1982), Plays for Laughs (1983), Second Thinks (1987), Games from Around the World (1990); *Recreations* recreational maths, the history of maths and science, chess, cricket, golf, charity work; *Clubs* Lord's Taverners', Variety Club of GB, Farnham Common CC; *Style*— Johnny Ball, Esq; ✉ Ball Games Ltd, Highfield, Beaconsfield Road, Farnham Common, Bucks SL2 3JD (☎ 01753 643621, fax 01753 646880, car 0860 639132)

BALL, Jonathan Macartney; MBE (1992); s of Christopher Edward Ball (d 1978), and Dorothy Ethel, *née* Macartney; *b* 4 June 1947; *Educ* Truro Sch, The Architectural Assoc (AADipl); *m* 29 June 1974, Victoria Mary Ogilvie, da of Dr Anthony Blood, of Bude; 2 da (Jemima Veryan b 1976, Morwenna Victoria b 1979); *Career* chartered architect; princ The Jonathan Ball Practice 1974–; dep chm Land Architects Ltd London, chm The Eden Project; Concrete Soc Award (mention) 1981 and 1986, RIBA Award (commendation) 1983, CPRE/CLA Henley Award 1981; occasional lectr, conference speaker, assessor for architecture awards; RIBA: memb Cncl 1981–, chm Parly Liaison Ctee 1981–87, vice pres 1983–85, hon sec 1988–91, vice pres 1991–93, hon sec 1993–95; former RNLI sr helmsman Bude Lifeboat; pres Cornwall region Surf Life Saving Assoc of GB; memb Ct of Assistants Worshipful Co of Chartered Architects 1986, Freeman City of London 1987; ACIArb 1978, FRSA 1985; *Recreations* enjoying Cornwall and the Isles of Scilly; *Clubs* Athenaeum; *Style*— Jonathan Ball, Esq, MBE; ✉ Tregarthens, Diddies Rd, Stratton, Bude, Cornwall EX23 9DW (☎ 01288 352198); The Jonathan Ball Practice, Chartered Architects, 5 Belle Vue, Bude, Cornwall EX23 8JJ (☎ 01288 355557, fax 01288 355826)

BALL, Michael Ashley; s of Anthony George (Tony) Ball, MBE, *qv*, of Bidford-on-Avon, Warwicks, and Ruth Parry Davies; *b* 27 June 1962; *Educ* Plymouth Coll, Farnham Sixth Form Coll, Guildford Sch of Acting; *Career* actor and singer; *Theatre* Surrey Youth Theatre 1980–81: The Boyfriend (1980), Under Milk Wood (1981); drama sch 1981–84, first professional role Judas/John the Baptist in Godspell 1984, first starring role Frederick in The Pirates of Penzance (Manchester Opera House) 1985, West End debut cr role of Marius in original prodn of Les Miserables (Barbican and Palace) 1985; other major roles incl: Raoul in Phantom of the Opera (Her Majesty's) 1987, cr role of Alex in Aspects of Love (Prince of Wales 1989, Broadway debut 1990), Giorgio in Passion (Queen's) 1996; *Television* incl: Coronation Street, Late Expectations, Save the Children Christmas Spectacular, Top of the Pops, Royal Variety Performance, GB rep Eurovision Song Contest 1992, two series of Michael Ball 1993 and 1994; *Recordings* incl: Les Miserables (original London cast album 1986, int cast album 1987), Rage of the Heart 1987, London cast album Aspects of Love 1989, Michael Ball 1992, West Side Story 1993, Always 1993, One Careful Owner 1994, The Best of Michael Ball 1994; *Awards* Most Promising Artiste Award Variety Club of GB 1989; *Recreations* music, theatre, keeping fit, contemplating country life; *Style*— Michael Ball, Esq; ✉ management: James Sharkey Associates, 21 Golden Square, London W1R 3PA (☎ 0171 434 3801, fax 0171 494 1547); press and PR agent: Alex Ritchie, Dennis Davidson Associates, Royalty House, 72–74 Dean Street, London W1V 5HB (☎ 0171 439 6391, fax 0171 437 6358)

BALL, Michael George; JP (1968), DL (Isle of Wight 1984); s of Stanley George Ball (d 1969), of Yarmouth, Isle of Wight, and (Winifred Maud) Nesta, *née* Pilling (d 1988); *b* 22 Aug 1937; *Educ* Charterhouse, Highbury Tech Coll; *m* 10 Sept 1966, Jane Rosemary, da of Lt Col David Everard Baird; 1 da (Nicola Jane b 1 July 1967), 1 s (Charles Baird Cecil b 14 April 1969); *Career* served 13/18 Royal Hussars 1957–60; shipbroker 1961–66, farmer and mangr family business 1967–; fndr memb Isle of Wight Grain Cooperative 1978; chm: Isle of Wight Magistrates Courts Ctee 1981–88, Isle of Wight Magistrates 1988–93, Isle of Wight branch NFU 1982; High Sheriff of Isle of Wight 1994–95; assoc memb Inst of Br Engrs 1965; *Clubs* Royal Yacht Squadron, Island Sailing, Old Carthusian Yacht; *Style*— Michael Ball, Esq, JP, DL; ✉ Ashengrove, Calbourne, Isle of Wight PO30 4HU (☎ 01983 531209)

BALL, Rt Rev Michael Thomas; patron of 2 archdeaconries, 24 canonries, 64 livings, one alternately with the Crown, one other alternately and three jointly; The See of Cornwall existed independently 865–1050, whereafter merged with Diocese of Exeter until 1876, when the See was refounded; it comprises the old archdeaconry of Cornwall within the Diocese of Exeter; s of Thomas James Ball (d 1966), of Eastbourne, and Kathleen Obena Bradley, *née* Morris (d 1980); *b* 14 Feb 1932; *Educ* Lancing, Queens' Coll Cambridge (BA, MA); *Career* schoolmaster 1955–75; prior of Stroud Glos 1963–75, chaplain for higher educn in Brighton Area 1975–80, curate Whiteshill Stroud 1971–75, parish priest Stanmer and Falmer 1975–80, bishop of Jarrow 1980–90, bishop of Truro 1990–97, ret; co fndr Community of the Glorious Ascension 1960; involved in: governing body various ind schools, drug rehabilitation unit, school for violent or difficult children; pres various institutions and concerns; *Recreations* sport, music, housework; *Style*— The Rt Rev Michael Ball

BALL, Rev Canon Peter William; s of Leonard Wevell Ball (d 1976), of St Albans, and Dorothy Mary, *née* Burrows; *b* 17 Jan 1930; *Educ* Aldenham Sch, Worcester Coll Oxford (MA), Cuddesdon Coll Oxford; *m* 11 Sept 1956, Angela Jane, *née* Dunlop; 1 s (Michael b 1961), 2 da (Lucy b 1957, Katharine b 1959); *Career* 2 Lt RA 1948; curate All Saints Poplar 1955–61, vicar The Ascension Wembley 1961–68, rector St Nicholas Shepperton 1968–84, area dean Spelthorne 1972–84, prebendary St Paul's Cathedral 1976–84, canon residentiary and chllr St Paul's Cathedral 1984–90 (canon emeritus 1990–), chapter treas 1985–89, dir Post Ordination Trg and Continuing Ministerial Educn Kensington Area 1984–87; chaplain: Associated Rediffusion TV 1961–68, Thames Television 1970–92; fndr and chm Catechumenate Network 1984–, dir Samaritans Brent and NW Surrey 1965–75; Freeman City of London 1986; *Books* Journey into Faith (1984), Adult Believing (1988), Adult Way to Faith (1992), Journey into Truth (1995); *Recreations* gardening, walking, music; *Style*— The Rev Canon Peter Ball; ✉ Whittonedge, Whittonditch Road, Ramsbury, Wilts SN8 2PX (☎ 01672 520259)

BALL, Richard Bentley; s and h of Sir Charles Irwin Ball, 4 Bt, *qv*; *b* 29 Jan 1953; *Educ* Dragon Sch Oxford, Sherborne, Univ of Leicester; *m* 31 Aug 1991, Beverley Ann, da of late Bertram Joffre Wright; 1 da (Anna Frances b 20 Feb 1996); *Career* CA; Peat Marwick Mitchell 1975–82, International Computers Ltd 1982–, currently dir of finance Africa Region and International Distributors; Liveryman Worshipful Co of Clockmakers; ACA; *Recreations* tennis, hockey; *Clubs* Hampstead and Westminster Hockey; *Style*— Richard Ball, Esq; ✉ Evenshade, Sandown Road, Esher, Surrey KT10 9TT (☎ 01372 464293)

BALLANTINE, (David) Grant; s of James Williamson Ballantine (d 1990), and Robertha, *née* Fairley; *b* 24 March 1941; *Educ* Daniel Stewart's Coll Edinburgh, Univ of Edinburgh (BSc); *m* 30 Oct 1969, Marjorie Campbell, *née* Brown; 1 da (Jane Helena b 30 Nov 1972), 1 s (Keith Campbell b 2 March 1977); *Career* actuarial trainee Scottish Widows Fund Edinburgh 1963–68, asst vice pres (Employee Benefits) American Insurance Gp 1968–73; Govt Actuary's Dept: joined 1973, chief actuary (Pensions) 1983–91, directing actuary (Pensions) 1991–; FFA 1968 (memb Cncl 1991–94); *Recreations* hill walking, politics; *Style*— Grant Ballantine, Esq; ✉ Government Actuary's Department, 22 Kingsway, London WC2B 6LE (☎ 0171 211 2623, fax 0171 211 2630)

BALLANTYNE, Prof Colin Kerr; s of Robert Morrison Ballantyne (d 1991), and Isabella Sturrock, *née* Kerr (d 1970); *b* 7 June 1951; *Educ* Hutchesons' GS Glasgow, Univ of Glasgow (MA), McMaster Univ (MSc), Univ of Edinburgh (PhD); *m* 1996, Rebecca Josephine, da of Graeme Trengove; *Career* teaching asst McMaster Univ 1973–75, demonstrator Univ of Edinburgh 1977–79; Univ of St Andrews: lectr in geography 1980–89, sr lectr 1989–94, prof of physical geography 1994–; Gordon Warwick Award Br Geomorphological Research Gp 1987, President's Medal Royal Scottish Geographical Soc 1991, Newbigin Prize Royal Scottish Geographical Soc 1992, Scottish Science Award Saltire Soc 1996; FRSE 1996, FRSA 1996; *Books* The Quaternary of the Isle of Skye (1991), The Periglaciation of Great Britain (1994); *Recreations* mountaineering, skiing, music, modern history, travel; *Style*— Prof Colin Ballantyne, FRSE; ✉ Birchwood, Blebo Craigs, Fife KY15 5UF; Department of Geography, University of St Andrews, St Andrews, Fife KY16 9ST (☎ 01334 463907, fax 01334 463940)

BALLARD, Maj Anthony William; s of Maj John Francis Ballard, of Over Worton Heath Farm, Chipping Norton, Oxon, and Jean Carolina, *née* Rawle; *b* 27 May 1957; *Educ* Eton, RMA Sandhurst; *m* 25 Oct 1986, Petronella Johanna Antonia Maria, da of Sjoerd Wiegersma, of Amsterdam; 1 s (Sebastian Hendrik Aloysius b 23 Jan 1993), 1 da

(Charlotte Antonia Carolina b 25 Oct 1989); *Career* Sandhurst 1976, cmmnd 1 Bn Welsh Gds 1977, Gds Depot 1979, Capt 1 Bn Welsh Gds 1980 (Falklands 1982), SO3 G2/G3 HQ Logistic Support Gp 1987, SO3 G3 (Log/Trg) HQ UK Mobile Force 1988, Maj 1 Bn Welsh Gds 1988–91, SO2 G1 HQ London Dist 1991–93; hon sec and treas Combined Services Polo Assoc 1990–93; conslt project mangr Fired Earth plc 1994–96, partnership sec Woolf Simmonds Slrs 1996–; *Recreations* polo, hunting; *Clubs* Cavalry and Guards', Mounted Infantry, Guards' Polo; *Style*— Maj A W Ballard; ✉ Over Worton Cottage, Chipping Norton, Oxon OX7 7EP (☎ and fax 01608 683419)

BALLARD, Beatrice Rosalind; da of James Graham Ballard, of Shepperton, Middx, and Mary, *née* Matthews (d 1964); *b* 29 May 1959; *Educ* St David's Sch Ashford Middx, UEA (BA), City Univ of London (Journalism Dip); *Career* reporter New Statesman 1981, writer and researcher Radio Times 1981–82, asst prodr and dir John Craven's Newsround BBC TV 1983–85, prodr special progs LWT 1986–88; series prodr: Saturday Night Clive, Fame in the Twentieth Century, Clive James Postcards From Miami, New York and Paris, Clive James Meets Ronald Reagan BBC TV 1988; exec prodr Entertainment Gp BBC TV 1994–; exec prodr incl: BBC TV 60th Anniversary, Br Academy Awards, Carrie Fisher on Hollywood, Aunties All Time Greats, Ruby Wax Meets Madonna; memb: ACTT, NUJ; *Recreations* reading, cinema, travel, eating out; *Style*— Ms Beatrice Ballard; ✉ 225 Westbourne Grove, London W11 2SE; BBC Television, Room 4146, Television Centre, Wood Lane, London W12 7RJ (☎ 0181 576 9633, fax 0181 576 1168)

BALLARD, (Richard) Graham John; s of Alfred John Ballard (d 1979), of Worcs, and Ada Mary Ballard (d 1981); *b* 17 Jan 1927; *Educ* Prince Henry's GS Evesham, Wadham Coll Oxford (MA), Univ of Cambridge (MA); *m* 10 July 1954, Domini Gabrielle, da of Dr Alfred Johannes Wright (d 1942), of Bucks; 2 s (Sebastian John b 1961, Toby Graham Dominic b 1963); *Career* chm and md Liebigs Rhodesia Ltd 1973–78, md Brooke Bond Kenya 1978–83, dir Tea Board of Kenya 1978–83, chm British Business Assoc Kenya 1982–83; fell commoner Christ's Coll Cambridge 1994– (bursar and fell 1983–94); administrator American Friends of Cambridge University 1996–; fndr memb Glyndebourne Festival Soc; *Recreations* opera, chamber music, reading, travel, bridge, holidays in France; *Style*— Graham Ballard, Esq; ✉ 23 Bentley Rd, Cambridge CB2 2AW (☎ 01223 323547)

BALLARD, Dr Howard Frederick; *b* 19 Jan 1937; *Educ* Glasgow HS, Univ of Glasgow (BDS, DGDP(UK)); *Career* princ in mixed dental practice Ballard Associates; dental practice advsr Gtr Glasgow Health Bd; memb GDC (memb Servs Ctee) until 1996; *Clubs* motorcycling, golf, opera, cats; *Style*— Dr Howard Ballard; ✉ Sundrum Castle, by Ayr KA6 5JY; Ballard Associates, 1806 Paisley Road West, Glasgow G52 3TP (☎ 0141 883 0056)

BALLARD, John Frederick; s of Frederick Ballard, and Margaret Ballard; *b* 8 Aug 1943; *Educ* Roundhay GS Leeds, Ifield GS W Sussex, Univ of Southampton (BA), Univ of Exeter (CertEd); *m* 1976 (sep 1986); 1 s, 2 da; *Career* Academic Registar's Dept Univ of Surrey 1965–69, asst princ Miny of Tport 1969–72; princ: DOE 1972–76, HM Treasy 1976–78; sec Top Salaries Review Body and Police Negotiating Bd DOE 1979–83 (sec 1978–79), princ private sec to Sec of State for the Environment 1983–85, under sec DOE 1986–92, dir Maxwell Pension Unit DHSS 1992–93, dir of planning DOE 1993–; assoc special tstee Gt Ormond St Hosp for Sick Children 1992–, tstee Maxwell Pensions Tst 1993–; *Recreations* squash, singing, reading; *Style*— J F Ballard, Esq; ✉ Department of the Environment, Eland House, Bressenden Place, Victoria, London SW1E 5DU (☎ 0171 890 3900, fax 0171 890 3979)

BALLARD, Richard Michael; s of Michael Agar Ballard, and Junella, *née* Ashton (d 1960); *b* 3 Aug 1953; *Educ* St Edmund's Coll Ware, Queens' Coll Cambridge (MA); *m* 28 Feb 1981, Penelope Ann, da of Dilwyn John Davies, DFC (d 1988), of Glamorgan; 3 s (Hayden b 1984, Thomas b 1985, James b 1992), 1 da (Sophie b 1987); *Career* admitted slr 1978; ptnr Freshfields 1984–; memb Law Soc; *Recreations* country pursuits; *Clubs* Oriental; *Style*— Richard Ballard, Esq; ✉ Freshfields, 65 Fleet Street, London EC4Y 1HS (☎ 0171 936 4000, fax 0171 832 7001)

BALLESTEROS, Severiano (Seve); s of Baldomero Ballesteros, of Spain, and Carmen, *née* Sota; *b* 9 April 1957; *m* 1988, Carmen, *née* Botin; 2 s (Baldomero Javier b 20 Aug 1990, Gonzalo Miguel b 3 Sept 1992), 1 da (Carmen b 23 Aug 1994); *Career* professional golfer 1974–; tournament victories: Dutch Open 1976, 1980 and 1986, Lancome Trophy 1976, 1983, 1986 (tied) and 1988, French Open 1977, 1982, 1985 and 1986, Uniroyal Int 1977, Swiss Open 1977, 1978 and 1989, Japanese Open 1977 and 1978, Dunlop Phoenix Japan 1977 and 1981, Otago Classic NZ 1977, Martini Int 1978 and 1980, German Open 1978 and 1988, Scandinavian Open 1978, 1981 and 1988, Kenya Open 1978, Greater Greensboro Open USA 1978, English Golf Classic 1979, Open Championship 1979, 1984 and 1988, Madrid Open 1980, 1982 and 1989, US Masters 1980 and 1983, Spanish Open 1981 and 1985, World Match-Play Championship 1981, 1982, 1984, 1985 and 1991, Australian PGA Championship 1981, English PGA Championship 1983, Irish Open 1983, 1985 and 1986, Westchester Classic USA 1983 and 1988, Sanyo Open 1985, USF & G Classic USA 1985, Br Masters 1986 and 1991, Monte Carlo Open 1986, Suze Open 1987, Mallorca Open de Baleares 1988, 1990 and 1992, Taiheiyo Masters Japan 1988, Epson Grand Prix 1989, Euro PGA Championship (formerly English PGA) 1991, Chunichi Crowns 1991, Dubai Open 1992, Benson and Hedges Int Open 1994; team events: Double Diamond Euro Team 1975, 1976 and 1977, Hennessey Cup 1976, 1978 and 1980, Ryder Cup 1979, 1983, 1985 (winners), 1987 (winners), 1989 (winners), 1991 and 1995 (winners), World Cup 1975, 1976 (winner with Manuel Pinero), 1977 (winner with Antonio Garrido) and 1991, Dunhill Cup 1985, 1986 and 1988; awards: Vardon Trophy 1976, 1977, 1978, 1986, 1988 and 1991, Ritz Club Golfer of the Year 1986 and 1991, Best Current Golfer Golf Digest 1986, Alerta de Plata Spain 1988, Sports Personality of the Year France 1988, Premio Principe de Asturias de los Deportes Spain 1989, Golden Tee USA 1989, No 1 Euro Order of Merit 1976, 1977, 1978, 1986, 1988 and 1991, Golfer of the Year Assoc of Golf Writers 1979, 1984, 1991; *Recreations* cycling, fishing; *Style*— Seve Ballesteros, Esq; ✉ c/o Roddy J Carr, Fairway SA, Pasaje de Peña 2, Cuarta Planta, 39008 Santander, Spain (☎ 00 34 42 314512, fax 00 34 42 314559)

BALLIN, Robert Andrew; s of Harold Ballin (d 1976), of East Dean, E Sussex, and Mollie Ballin, *née* Dunn (d 1989); *b* 8 July 1943; *Educ* Highgate Sch, City of London Coll; *m* 27 Nov 1975, Serena Mary Ann, da of Richard Goode, OBE (d 1966), of Chelsea, London SW3; 1 s (Edward b 1980), 2 da (Annabel b 1981, Chloe b 1985); *Career* Shell-Mex and BP 1962–67, SH Benson 1967–69, Gallagher-Smail/Doyle Dane Bernbach 1969–73; Foote Cone & Belding 1973–: int account dir and dep to md Impact-FCB Belgium 1975–77, dir 1977, dep chm 1988–; memb Epsom Race Ctee 1994–; MCIM, MIPA; *Recreations* music, theatre, sport; *Clubs* White's, RAC, MCC; *Style*— Robert Ballin, Esq; ✉ The Old Vicarage, Froxfield, Marlborough, Wilts SN8 3JY (☎ 01488 682736); Foote Cone & Belding, 110 St Martin's Lane, London WC2N 4DY (☎ 0171 240 7100)

BALLS, Alastair Gordon; CB (1995); s of Rev Ernest George Balls, of Stevenson, Ayrshire, Scotland, and Elspeth Russell, *née* McMillan; *b* 18 March 1944; *Educ* Hamilton Acad Lanarkshire, Univ of St Andrews (MA), Univ of Manchester (MA); *m* 26 Nov 1977, Beryl May, da of John Nichol, of Harlow, Essex; 1 s (Thomas b 1979), 1 da (Helen b 1982); *Career* asst sec Treasy Govt of Tanzania 1966–68, economist Dept of Tport UK Govt 1969–73, sec Cairncross Ctee on Channel Tunnel 1974–75, sr econ advsr HM Treasy 1976–79, under sec DOE 1983–87 (asst sec 1979–83), chief exec Tyne & Wear Urban Devpt Corp 1987–; CIMgt 1988; *Recreations* fishing, sailing, camping; *Clubs* Royal Northumberland Yacht, Wylam Angling; *Style*— Alastair Balls, Esq, CB; ✉ Tyne and Wear Development Corporation, Scotswood House, Newcastle Business Park, Newcastle upon Tyne NE4 7YL (☎ 0191 226 1234, fax 0191 226 0905)

BALLS, Geoffrey Robert; s of Victor Leslie Balls, of Carshalton, Surrey, and Ellen, *née* MacNaboe; *Educ* Trent Poly (BA), Garnett Coll (CertEd), Univ of Warwick (MSc); *m* 31 Aug, Eileen Mary, da of Patrick O'Regan, of Baltimore, Co Cork; 1 s (Matthew), 3 da (Jessica, Stephanie, Catherine); *Career* Plessey Radar Ltd 1979–82, Cray Research (UK) Ltd 1982–87, head of Info Systems Channel Four TV Ltd 1987–; *Style*— Geoffrey Balls, Esq; ✉ Channel Four Television Corporation, 124 Horseferry Road, London SW1P 2TX (☎ 0171 306 8646, fax 0171 306 8370)

BALMER, Colin Victor; s of Peter Lionel Balmer (d 1982), and Adelaide Currie, *née* Hamilton; *b* 22 Aug 1946; *Educ* Liverpool Inst HS; *m* 20 May 1978, Frances Mary, da of John Montrésor; 2 s (Thomas Montrésor b 29 June 1979, William John b 24 April 1987), 1 da (Lucy Caroline b 27 March 1981); *Career* clerical offr War Office 1963–68; MOD: exec offr 1968–70, asst princ 1970–72, asst private sec to Min of State 1972–73, private sec to Under Sec of State (RAF) 1973, princ civil advsr GOC NI 1973–77; Cabinet Office 1977–80, private sec to Min of State (Def Procurement) 1980–82, first sec UK Delgn NATO 1982–84, asst sec 1984–90, Min (Defence Materiél) Br Embassy Washington 1990–92, asst under sec of state (Mgmnt Strategy) 1992–94, asst under sec of state (Fin Mgmnt) 1994–96, dep under sec of state (Resources, Progs and Fin) 1996–; *Recreations* golf, tennis, gardening, bridge, rock and roll music, playing guitar (badly); *Style*— Colin Balmer, Esq; ✉ 36 Pensford Avenue, Richmond, Surrey TW9 4HP (☎ 0181 878 2224); Deputy Under Secretary of State (Resources, Programmes and Finance), Ministry of Defence, Main Building, Whitehall, London SW1A 2HB (☎ 0171 218 2616, fax 0171 218 7718)

BALMFORD, Prof David Ernest Hall; OBE (1993); s of Edgar Balmford (d 1986), of Stockton, Cleveland, and Edna Hinchliffe (d 1974); *b* 3 April 1932; *Educ* Huddersfield Coll, Univ of Durham (BSc); *m* 22 Feb 1958, Irene Mary, da of Joseph Reece Williams; 1 da (Julia Dawn b 13 July 1967), 1 s (Richard Anthony Hall b 30 Dec 1968); *Career* chief dynamicist Fairey Aviation 1959–64 (stressman 1953–59); Westland Helicopters Ltd: chief dynamicist 1964–69, head Tech Dept 1971–77 (dep head 1969–71), dep chief engr (research) 1977–80, head of advanced engrg 1980–89, chief scientist 1989–94 (ret); conslt 1994–; visiting industl prof Univ of Bristol 1991–; chm Res Ctee Soc of British Aerospace Companies 1989–93, dep chm Cncl Aircraft Research Assoc 1993–95; *Awards* (with Westland Helicopters Ltd) MacRobert Award (jtly) for innovative technical design of Lynx helicopter 1975, Design Cncl Award (jtly) for design of Westland 30 helicopter 1983; FRAeS 1993, FEng 1994; *Recreations* recreational flying (PPL), fell walking; *Style*— Prof David Balmford, OBE, FEng; ✉ 4 Springfield Crescent, Sherborne, Dorset DT9 6DN (☎ and fax 01935 813462)

BALNIEL, Lord; Anthony Robert Lindsay; s and h of 29 Earl of Crawford and (12 of) Balcarres, PC, *qv*; *b* 24 Nov 1958; *Educ* Eton, Univ of Edinburgh; *m* 12 Aug 1989, Nicola A, yst da of Antony Bicket, of Derwas, Dolwen, N Wales; 2 s (Master of Lindsay b 1991, Hon James Antony b 10 Nov 1992), 1 da (Hon Katherine Ruth Vere b 4 Sept 1996); *Heir* s, Alexander Thomas, Master of Lindsay b 5 Aug 1991; *Career* dir J O Hambro Investment Management Ltd 1987–; *Clubs* New (Edinburgh); *Style*— Lord Balniel; ✉ Balcarres, Colinsburgh, Fife; 6 Pembridge Place, London W2 4XB

BALOGH, Baroness; Catherine; da of Arthur Cole (d 1968), of London, and Margaret Henrietta, *née* Gaselee (d 1971); *Educ* St Paul's Girls' Sch, Newnham Coll Cambridge, W London Hosp (MRCS, LRCP); *m* 1, 1942 (m dis 1970), Dr Anthony Storr, s of Vernon Faithfull Storr; 3 da (Sophia Jane b 1946, Polly Cecilia b 1946, Emma Faithfull b 1953); m 2, 1970, as his 2 w, Baron Balogh (d 1985; Life Peer UK 1968), of Hampstead; *Career* psychotherapist: West London Hosp 1948–50, Middlesex Hosp 1950–63; writer (over 30 children's books and 6 adult novels); FRSM; *Books* under the name Catherine Storr incl: Clever Polly & the Stupid Wolf (Faber, 1952), Polly & the Wolf Again (Faber, 1954), Marianne Dreams (Faber, 1958), Robin (1962), The Catchpole Story (1965), The Chinese Egg (1967), The World of Freud (contrib, 1972), Discipline in Schools (contrib, 1973), Growing Up (1975), The Boy & the Swan (1987, Friends of the Earth prize 1988); *Recreations* opera, cooking, walking, swimming; *Style*— The Rt Hon the Lady Balogh; ✉ c/o Peters, Fraser & Dunlop, 5th Floor, The Chambers, Chelsea Harbour, Lots Rd, London SW10 0XF (☎ 0171 376 7676)

BALSTON, His Hon Judge Antony Francis; s of Cdr Edward Francis Balston, DSO, RN, of Merlins, Ewhurst Lane, Northam, E Sussex, and Diana Beatrice Louise, *née* Ferrers (d 1993); *b* 18 Jan 1939; *Educ* Downside, Christ's Coll Cambridge (MA); *m* 1966, Anne Marie Judith, da of Gerald Ball (d 1971); 2 s (James b 1967, Andrew b 1969), 1 da (Alexandra b 1972); *Career* RN 1957–59; admitted slr 1966, ptnr Herington Willings & Penry Davey (Hastings) 1966–85; recorder Crown Ct 1980–85, hon recorder Hastings 1984–, circuit judge (SE Circuit) 1985–; *Recreations* gardening; *Clubs* Farmers'; *Style*— His Hon Judge Antony Balston; ✉ Elmside, Northiam, Rye, E Sussex (☎ 01797 252270); The Law Courts, Barker Road, Maidstone ME16 8EQ

BAMBER, David James; s of late Ernest Bamber, of Walkden, Salford, and late Hilda, *née* Wolfendale; *b* 19 Sept 1954; *Educ* Walkden Co Secdy Modern Sch, Farnworth GS, Univ of Bristol, RADA; *m* July 1982, Julia Swift (the actress), da of David Swift; 1 s (Theo Elia b 27 Dec 1991); *Career* actor; RADA William Peel Prize, Carol Brahams Musical Comedy Prize, Bancroft Gold Medal; *Theatre* for NT incl: Oresteia 1981, Charlie in The Strangeness of Others 1988, John Littlewit in Bartholomew Fair 1988, Horatio in Hamlet 1989, Streaky Bacon in Racing Demon 1990–91, Mole in Wind in the Willows 1990–91; others incl: Joseph and His Amazing Technicolor Dreamcoat (Palace Theatre Westcliff) 1979, Outskirts (RSC Warehouse) 1981, Masterclass (Leicester Haymarket, Old Vic, Wyndhams) 1983–84, Kissing God (Hampstead) 1984, Amadeus 1986, Three Birds Alighting on a Field (Royal Court) 1991, Hikatier in Schippel (Greenwich Theatre & Edinburgh Festival), Martin Mirkheim in Search and Destroy (Theatre Upstairs), Guy in My Night with Reg (Theatre Upstairs and Criterion (winner Olivier Award for Best Actor 1995)) 1994; *Television* incl: Call Me Mister (BBC) 1986, Cockles (BBC) 1983, Buddha of Suburbia (BBC) 1993, Stalag Luft (YTV) 1993, Wycliffe, Pride and Prejudice; *Films* incl: Privates on Parade 1982, High Hopes 1988; *Recreations* listening to music, playing the piano, trying to keep fit usually at a gym, being married to Julia, son, Theo born 1991; *Style*— David Bamber, Esq; ✉ c/o Jonathan Altaras Associates Ltd, 27 Floral Street, London WC2E 9DP (☎ 0171 836 8722, fax 0171 836 6066)

BAMBER, Roger; s of Frederick William Bamber (d 1987), of Leicester, and Vera Lilian, *née* Stephenson; *b* 31 Aug 1944; *Educ* Beaumont Leys Secdy Modern Leicester, Leicester Coll of Art; *m* 1970 (m dis 1973), Joan Bergquist; *partner* 1983, Shân Lancaster; *Career* news photographer; Fleetway Publications 1963–64, Leicester Coll of Art 1964–65, Daily Mail 1965–69, The Sun 1969–88, The Observer 1988–89, The Guardian 1989–; *Exhibitions* Royal Photographic Soc 1992, Brighton Museum and Art Gallery 1993, Tom Blau Gallery London 1994, Month of the Image Dieppe 1995, Worthing Museum and Art Gallery 1996; *Awards* Br News Photographer of the Year 1973, Photographer of the Year and News Photographer of the Year (Br Press Awards) 1983, Nikon Features Photographer of the Year 1991, Kodak Features Photographer of the Year 1991, Ilford Press Photographer of the Year 1992 (runner up 1991), UK Picture Editors' Guild Award for features photography 1996; FRPS; *Style*— Roger Bamber, Esq; ✉ c/o The Guardian,

119 Farringdon Road, London EC1R 3ER (☎ 0171 278 2332 and 01273 723689, mobile 0860 381255)

BAMBERG, Harold Rolf; CBE (1966); s of Ernest Bamberg; *b* 17 Nov 1923; *Educ* Fleet Sch, William Ellis Sch Hampstead; *m* 1957, June Winifred, da of John Clarke; 1 s, 2 da (and 1 s, 1 da of a former m); *Career* fndr chm: British Eagle International Airways Ltd, Lunn Poly, Eagle Aircraft Ltd, Glos Air Ltd, Via Nova Properties Ltd and subsids; various business interests and chairmanships of trade assocs; Cavaliere al Merito della Republic Italiana 1960; FRAeS; *Recreations* equestrian, tennis, swimming; *Clubs* Guards' Polo, Wentworth Golf; *Style*— Harold Bamberg Esq, CBE; ✉ Park House, Pinecote Drive, Sunningdale, Berkshire SL5 9PS

BAMBOROUGH, John Bernard; s of John George Bamborough (d 1931), and Elsie Louise, *née* Brogden; *b* 3 Jan 1921; *Educ* Haberdashers' Aske's, Hampstead Sch, New Coll Oxford; *m* 1947, Anne, da of Olav Indrehus (d 1984), of Indrehus, Norway; 1 s (Paul), 1 da (Karin Cecilia); *Career* RN 1941–46, Lt Instr Europe; fell and tutor Wadham Coll Oxford 1947–62 (lectr in English 1951–62), princ Linacre Coll Oxford 1962–88, pro vice chllr Univ of Oxford 1966–88; *Style*— John Bamborough, Esq; ✉ 18 Winchester Rd, Oxford OX2 6NA (☎ 01865 559886)

BAMBRIDGE, Anthony Martin; s of Sidney Ernest Bambridge, and Millicent Rose, *née* Reekie (d 1990); *b* 27 Aug 1935; *Educ* Buckhurst Hill County HS, LSE; *m* 1960, Judith Pauline, *née* Swingland; 2 s (Daniel b 1967, Jacob b 1969), 1 da (Emma b 1965); *Career* reporter The Economist 1960–64, business and news ed The Observer 1964–76, PR dir Unilever 1976–77, The Sunday Times 1977– (business ed, managing ed news, managing ed features, exec ed, currently managing ed); dir Times Newspapers Holdings Ltd; *Books* Ambush (with Robin Morgan and James Adams, 1989); *Style*— Anthony Bambridge, Esq; ✉ The Sunday Times, 1 Pennington St, London E1 9XW (☎ 0171 782 5000)

BAMBRIDGE, Ron; *b* 6 Nov 1953; *m* 15 Feb 1986, Rose Angela, *née* Nielsen; 1 da (Daisy b 10 Nov 1988); *Career* photographer; asst to Nigel Hartnup (fashion photographer) 1972–73, asst photographer Photographic Dept Foote Cone & Belding (advtg agency) 1973–77, freelance photographer 1977–; specialist in still life photography until 1985, landscape, people and special panoramic photography since 1985; work for various clients incl: BA, ICI, London Transport, Rothschilds, British Gas, National Power, British Airports Authy, Welsh Devpt Agency, Seacontainers, Peugeot; work included in English Landscape in Danger (exhbn and auction cmmnd by CPRE) 1987; cmmn Royal Mail London Landmark stamps 1996; memb AFAEP; *Awards* incl: highly commended Advtg People Category Ilford Awards 1984, AFAEP Gold Award (for landscape series) 1986, AFAEP Merit Award (for people series) 1988, Best Photography Award (Nat Business Calendar Awards) 1988, AFAEP Merit Award (for landscape) 1993, Bronze Award (Best of Book in Contact Photographers) 1993; *Style*— Ron Bambridge, Esq; ✉ Jolly Robin Forge, Hawkley, Hampshire GU33 6NQ (☎ 01730 827460); c/o Jenny Ungless (☎ 0181 870 7916)

BAMFORD, Alan George; CBE (1985); s of James Ross Bamford (d 1976), of Liverpool, and Margaret Emily, *née* Ramsay (d 1994); *b* 12 July 1930; *Educ* Prescot GS, Borough Road Coll (CertEd), Univ of Liverpool (DipEd, MEd), Univ of Cambridge (MA); *m* 7 Aug 1954, Joan Margaret, da of Arthur William Vint (d 1985), of Hastings; 4 s (Stephen Mark b 1955, Timothy David b 1959, Simon John b 1960, Peter Andrew b 1967); *Career* Corpl RAF 1948–50; teacher then dep headmaster Lancs Primary Schs 1952–62, lectr in educn Univ of Liverpool 1962–63, sr lectr Chester Coll 1963–66, princ lectr and head of dept S Katharine's Coll Liverpool 1966–71; princ: Westhill Coll Birmingham 1971–85, Homerton Coll Cambridge 1985–91; chm Birmingham Assoc of Youth Clubs 1972–85 (vice pres 1985–), memb Cncl Nat Youth Bureau 1974–80, govr London Bible Coll 1981–89; memb: Advsy Ctee on Religious Broadcasts BBC Radio Birmingham 1972–80, Cncl Br and Foreign Sch Soc 1972–85; vice pres Colls of Educn Christian Union 1965–86 (pres 1966–67 and 1972–73); memb: Br Cncl of Churches Standing Ctee on Theological Educn 1979–82, Cncl of Mgmnt Central Register and Clearing House 1982–92, Exec Ctee Assoc of Voluntary Colls 1979–86, Voluntary Sector Consultative Cncl 1987–88, Exec Ctee Standing Conf on Studies in Educn 1978–87 (sec 1982–84), Educn Ctee Free Church Fed Cncl 1978–90, Ctee Standing Conf of Principals of Colls and Insts of Higher Educn 1986–91, Standing Ctee of Educn and Trg of Teachers (vice chm 1988, chm 1989), Cambridge Health Health Authy (and tstee) 1987–90; JP Birmingham 1977–85; Hon MA Univ of Birmingham 1981; FRSA 1975; *Recreations* travel, photography; *Clubs* Royal Cwlth Soc; *Style*— Alan G Bamford, Esq, CBE; ✉ 2 Bayham Road, Tunbridge Wells, Kent TN2 5HP (☎ 01892 530942)

BAMFORD, Sir Anthony Paul; kt (1990), DL (Staffs 1989); s of Joseph Cyril Bamford, CBE, *qv*; *b* 23 Oct 1945; *Educ* Ampleforth Coll, Grenoble Univ; *m* 1974, Carole Gray Whitt; 2 s, 1 da; *Career* joined JCB 1962, chm and md J C Bamford Group 1975–; dir Tarmac plc 1987–95; memb: President's Ctee CBI 1986–88, Design Cncl 1987–89; pres: Staffs Agric Soc 1987–88, Burton on Trent Cons Assoc 1987–90; High Sheriff of Staffs 1985–86; Hon MEng Birmingham 1987, Hon DUniv Keele 1988, Hon DSc Cranfield 1994; Young Exporter of the Year 1972, Young Businessman of the Year 1979, Top Exporter of the Year 1995; Chevalier de l'Ordre National du Mérite (France) 1989, Commendatore al merito della Repubblica Italianna 1995; *Recreations* farming and gardening; *Clubs* Pratt's, White's, British Racing Drivers'; *Style*— Sir Anthony Bamford, DL; ✉ c/o J C Bamford Excavators Ltd, Rocester, Uttoxeter, Staffs ST14 5JP

BAMFORD, Colin; s of Firth Bamford (d 1986), of Blackburn, Lancs, and Edna, *née* Cockshutt; *b* 28 Aug 1950; *Educ* Queen Elizabeth's GS Blackburn, Trinity Hall Cambridge (scholar, MA); *m* 31 Jan 1975, Nirmala Rajah Bamford, da of Hon Mr Justice AP Rajah, of Singapore; 2 s (Rowan Firth Rajah b 13 March 1980, Daniel Chelva Rajah b 26 July 1986), 1 da (Roxanne Vijaya Rajah b 6 May 1990); *Career* Herbert Oppenheimer Nathan and Vandyk: articled clerk 1972–74, asst slr 1974–77, ptnr 1977–88; ptnr Richards Butler 1988–, chief exec Financial Law Panel 1993–; *Style*— Colin Bamford, Esq; ✉ Financial Law Panel, 125 Wood Street, London EC2V 7AQ (☎ 0171 606 2566, fax 0171 606 0040)

BAMFORD, David John; s of Samuel John Bamford, of Wellingborough, Northants, and Joan Sullivan, *née* Greenwood; *b* 28 June 1955; *Educ* Wellingborough GS, Univ of Aberdeen (MA); *m* 19 July 1979, Meyni Maria, da of Cornelis Timmer, of Oosterend, Texel, Netherlands; 2 s (Thomas Rosh b 1981, Oliver Samuel b 1993); *Career* BBC: political researcher Monitoring Serv 1980–83, journalist World Serv News 1983–86, Ankara corr 1986–87, N Africa corr 1988–89, Nigeria corr 1991–93, W Africa corr 1994–; contrib 1986–: The Guardian, Middle East Int, Middle East Economic Digest, Daily Telegraph, Economist; *Style*— David Bamford, Esq; ✉ 1 The Crofts, Little Paxton, Huntingdon, Cambs (☎ 01480 212581); BBC World Service News, PO Box 76, Bush House, Strand, London (☎ 0171 257 2684)

BAMFORD, Joseph Cyril; CBE (1969); Cyril Joseph Bamford (d 1953), of the Parks, Uttoxeter, Staffs; *b* 21 June 1916; *Educ* St John's Alton Staffs, Stonyhurst; *m* 1941, Marjorie, da of William Griffin, of Uttoxeter, Staffs; 2 s (Sir Anthony Paul Bamford, DL, *qv*, Mark Joseph); *Career* fndr chm and md J C Bamford Excavators Ltd 1945–76; inventor and engr designer of world famous JCB machines; Hon DTech Loughborough Univ 1983, Hon DEng Univ of Sheffield 1992; *Style*— Joseph Bamford, Esq, CBE; ✉ PO Box 496, Rue du Maupas 49, Ch-1000 Lausanne 9, Switzerland

BAMJI, Dr Andrew Nariman; s of Dr Nariman Sorabji Bamji (d 1978), of Highgate, London, and Dr Joan Elizabeth Bamji, *née* Jermyn; *b* 14 Aug 1950; *Educ* Highgate Sch, The Middlesex Hosp Med Sch Univ of London (MB BS); *m* 10 June 1978, Elizabeth Mary, da of Raymond William Millard, of Wembdon, Bridgwater, Somerset; 1 s (Nicholas b 1985), 1 da (Alexandra b 1981); *Career* conslt in rheumatology and rehabilitation: SE Thames RHA Brook Gen Hosp 1983–89, Queen Mary's Hosp Sidcup 1983– (dir Elmstead Younger Disabled Unit 1985–, clinical tutor and dir of med educn 1990–95), Chelsfield Park Hosp Kent 1987–; chm: Jt Care Planning Gp for the Younger Disabled Bexley Health Authy 1990–92, SE Thames Region Specialty Sub-Ctee in Rheumatology 1992–; memb: BMA, London Topographical Soc; FRCP 1989; *Books* Atlas of Clinical Rheumatology (jt ed, 1986), Queen Mary's Hospital: A Commemoration 1974–94 (1994); *Recreations* antiques, gardening, pianola; *Style*— Dr Andrew Bamji; ✉ Queen Mary's Hospital, Frognal Ave, Sidcup, Kent DA14 6LT (☎ 0181 302 2678, fax 0181 308 3058); Chelsfield Park Hospital, Bucks Cross Road, Chelsfield, Kent BR6 7RG (☎ 01689 877855, fax 01689 837439, e-mail 100741.1557@compuserve.com, homepage http://ourworld.compuserve.com/homepages/Andrew_Bamji)

BAMPTON, Deborah Ellen; da of Albert Richard Bampton, of 68 Castlefields, Istead Rise, Meopham, Kent, and Ann Ceila, *née* Johnson; *b* 7 Oct 1961; *Career* footballer; clubs: former player manager Millwall Lionesses, Trani WFC Italy, Arsenal Ladies' FC 1992–93, currently player manager Croydon WFC; honours with Arsenal LFC: The Treble, WFA Cup, League Cup, The Nat League 1992/93; sometime capt England Women's Football Team (82 caps), quarter-finalists World Cup Sweden 1995; *Style*— Miss Deborah Bampton; ✉ 1 The Spires, Wilmington, Kent

BANATVALA, Prof Jangu Edal; s of Dr Edal Banatvala (d 1981), and Ratti, *née* Shroff; *b* 7 Jan 1934; *Educ* Forest Sch London, Gonville & Caius Coll Cambridge (MA), London Hosp Med Coll (MD, DCH, DPH, Sir Lionel Whitby Medal), FRCP, FRCPath; *m* 15 Aug 1959, Roshan, da of Jamshed Mugaseth (d 1950); 3 s (Nicholas b 1961, Jonathan b 1963, Christopher b 1967), 1 da (Emma-Jane b 1968); *Career* res fell Univ of Cambridge 1961–64, post doctoral fell Yale Sch of Med 1964–65; St Thomas' Hosp Med Sch (later Utd Med and Dental Sch): sr lectr 1965–71, reader in clinical virology 1971–75, prof 1975–; chm W Lambeth Dist Mgmnt Team and Med Advsy Ctee St Thomas' Hosp 1983–84; vice pres: RCPath 1987–90 (registrar 1985–87, memb Cncl 1993–96), Cncl Med Def Union 1987–; pres Euro Assoc Against Virus Disease 1981–83; chm: Sub Ctee on Measles Mumps and Rubella (CDVIP) Med Res Cncl 1985–95, Dept of Health Advsy Gp on Hepatitis 1990–; memb Jt Ctee on Vaccination and Immunisation 1986–95; examiner in pathology for MB Univs of: London, Cambridge, W Indies, Riyadh; examiner in virology RCPath; elected memb Univ of London Senate 1987; hon conslt microbiologist to the Army 1992–; govr Forest Sch Snaresbrook Essex; Freeman City of London 1987, Liveryman Worshipful Soc of Apothecaries; memb: Soc of Gen Microbiology 1970, BMA 1970, Royal Soc of Tropical Med and Hygiene 1983; *Books* Current Problems in Clinical Virology (1971), Principles and Practice of Clinical Virology (jtly, 1987, 3 edn 1994), Viral Infections of the Heart (1993); *Recreations* watching sports in which one no longer performs (rowing, cricket), playing tennis, exercising retrievers (infrequently), music; *Clubs* Athenaeum, Leander, MCC, Hawk's (hon); *Style*— Prof Jangu Banatvala; ✉ Little Acre, Church End, Henham, nr Bishop's Stortford, Herts CM22 6AN; Department of Virology, United Medical and Dental School of Guy's and St Thomas' Hospitals, St Thomas' Campus, Lambeth Palace Rd, London SE1 7EH (☎ 0171 928 9292 ext 2405, fax 0171 922 8387)

BANBURY, (Frederick Harold) Frith; s of Rear Adm Frederick Arthur Frith Banbury, RN (d 1951), of Buddington, Midhurst, Sussex, and Winifred, *née* Fink (d 1960); *b* 4 May 1912; *Educ* Stowe Sch, Hertford Coll Oxford, RADA; *Career* theatrical director, producer and actor; stage debut If I Were You (Shaftesbury) 1933; made numerous TV and film appearances and worked with most of the leading actors and actresses of the past 40 years; memb: Equity, SWET; *Theatre* roles incl: Hamlet (New) 1934, Goodness How Sad (Vaudeville) 1938, New Faces (Comedy) 1939, Uncle Vanya (Westminster) 1943, Jacobowsky and the Colonel (Piccadilly) 1945, Caste (Duke of York's) 1947; as prodr and dir of plays incl: Dark Summer (Lyric Hammersmith, St Martin's) 1947, The Holly and the Ivy (Duchess) 1950, Waters of the Moon (Haymarket) 1951, The Deep Blue Sea (Duchess, Morosco New York) 1951 and 1952, A Question of Fact (Piccadilly) 1953, Love's Labour's Lost (Old Vic) 1954, Marching Song (St Martin's) 1954, The Diary of Anne Frank (Phoenix) 1956, Flowering Cherry (Haymarket, Lyceum New York) 1957 and 1959, A Dead Secret (Piccadilly) 1957, A Touch of the Sun (Saville) 1958, The Ring of Truth (Savoy) 1959, The Tiger and the Horse (Queen's) 1960, The Wings of the Dove (Lyric) 1963, The Right Honourable Gentleman (Billy Rose New York) 1965, Howards End (New) 1967, Dear Octopus (Haymarket) 1967, Le Valet (Théâtre de la Renaissance Paris) 1968, Enter A Free Man (St Martin's) 1968, A Day In the Death of Joe Egg (Cameri Tel Aviv) 1968, On the Rocks (Dublin Theatre Festival) 1969, The Winslow Boy (New) 1970, My Darling Daisy (Lyric) 1970, Captain Brassbound's Conversion (Cambridge) 1971, Reunion in Vienna (Chichester Festival, Piccadilly) 1971 and 1972, The Day After the Fair (Lyric) 1972, Shubert Los Angeles 1973, Glasstown (Westminster) 1973, Ardèle (Queen's) 1975, On Approval (Canada, SA, Vaudeville) 1976 and 1977, Motherdear (Ambassadors) 1980, Dear Liar (Mermaid) 1982, The Aspern Papers (Haymarket) 1984, The Corn is Green (Old Vic) 1985, The Admirable Crichton (Haymarket) 1988, Screamers (Arts) 1989; *Recreations* piano playing; *Style*— Frith Banbury, Esq

BANBURY, Martin John; s of Raymond Francis Banbury, of Fareham, and Molly Louise Banbury; *b* 30 March 1957; *Educ* Chelsea Coll London (BSc); *m* 1 (m dis 1992), Sarah, da of Peter Andrew Campbell; 2 da (Amber Sarah Edna b 1 Dec 1986, Emma Lucie b 24 June 1988); m 2, Carol, da of Colin White; 1 da (Jasmine b 5 April 1993), 1 s (Daniel Ray); *Career* mktg exec; Mktg Dept of Procter & Gamble 1979–82, Cussons 1982–84, Britvic 1984–85; jt chm Connect One plc 1985–; memb: Inst of Sales Promotion, Sales Promotion Conslts Assoc; FInstD; *Recreations* flying, sailing; *Style*— Martin Banbury, Esq; ✉ 48 Kelvedon Road, Coggeshall, Essex CO6 1RQ; Connect One plc, 2–4 Boundary Street, London E2 7JE (☎ 0171 739 6633, fax 0171 739 6565)

BANBURY, (Nigel Graham Cedric) Peregrine; s of Ralph Cecil Banbury (d 1951), of Ebury St, London, and Florence Leslie St Clair Keith; *b* 23 May 1948; *Educ* Gordonstoun; *m* 1, 17 Nov 1973, Rosemary Henrietta Dorothy, da of Capt Anthony Henry Heber Villiers, of Woodchester, Glos; m 2, 28 Sept 1978, Susan Margaret, da of Lt-Col Joseph Patrick Feeny, of Estoril, Portugal (d 1970); 2 s (Alexander b 1981, Ralph b 1987); m 3, 7 July 1992, Mrs Carol A Whistler, da of John Groves, CB, and former wife of Laurence Whistler, CBE; *Career* Coutts & Co 1967–70, stockbroker 1971–81, Robert Fleming 1981–86, dir EBC Amro Asset Management Ltd 1986–87; Coutts & Co: head Asset Mgmnt 1987–, ptnr Private Banking 1996–; dir: Exeter Preferred Capital Investment Trust 1992–, Schroder Income Growth Trust 1995–, Securities Inst 1995–; Freeman City of London; MSI (Dip); *Recreations* shooting, skiing, gardening, golf; *Style*— Peregrine Banbury, Esq; ✉ Coutts & Co, 440 Strand, London WC2R 0QS (☎ 0171 753 1000, fax 0171 753 1054)

BANBURY OF SOUTHAM, 3 Baron (UK 1924); Sir Charles William Banbury; 3 Bt (UK 1902); s of 2 Baron Banbury, DL (d 1981), and Hilda, *née* Carr (m dis 1958; she m 2, Maj Robert O G Gardner, MC (d 1987), and 3, Richard Frederick Norman); *b* 29 July 1953; *Educ* Eton; *m* 1, 1984 (m dis 1986), Lucinda, er da of John Frederick Trehearne; m 2, 1989, Inger Marianne Norton, *née* Wiegert; 2 da (Hon Charlotte Rosa b 15 April 1990, Hon Poppy Isobel b 13 Nov 1991); *Style*— The Rt Hon the Lord Banbury of Southam; ✉ The Mill, Fossebridge, nr Cheltenham, Glos

BANCE, Prof Alan Frederick; s of Frederick Bance, and Agnes Mary, *née* Wilson; *b* 7 March 1939; *Educ* Hackney Downs Sch (aka Grocers' Co Sch), UCL (BA), Univ of Cambridge (PhD); *m* 30 Aug 1964, Sandra, da of John Davis, of Hove, W Sussex; 2 da (Georgia b 1972, Miriam b 1976); *Career* lectr Univ of Strathclyde 1965–67, sr lectr Univ of St Andrews 1981 (lectr 1967–81); prof of German: Univ of Keele 1981–84, Univ of Southampton 1984–; pres Conf of Univ Teachers of German in GB and Ireland 1994–96 (vice pres 1993–94); memb: Res Selectivity Exercise UFC/HEFCE Res Assessment Panel for German Studies 1992 and 1996, Ctee Univ Cncl for Modern Languages 1994–; ed Germanic Section Modern Language Review 1988–94; hon life memb Modern Humanities Res Assoc 1995; *Books* The German Novel 1945–60 (1980), Theodor Fontane: The Major Novels (1982), Weimar Germany: Writers and Politics (ed, 1982), Ödön von Horváth 50 Years On (ed with I Huish, 1988), Theodor Fontane: The London Symposium (ed with H Chambers and C Jolles, 1995); *Recreations* walking, gardening, foreign travel, theatre; *Style*— Prof Alan Bance; ✉ German Studies, School of Modern Languages, University of Southampton, Highfield, Southampton SO17 1BJ (☎ 01703 592210, fax 01703 672693, tlx 47661)

BANCEWICZ, John; s of Dr Anthony Bancewicz, of Airdrie, Lanarkshire, and Helen, *née* Ulinskas (d 1950); *b* 26 March 1945; *Educ* St Aloysius Coll Glasgow, Univ of Glasgow (BSc, MB ChB), Univ of Manchester (ChM); *m* 5 Jan 1972, Margaret Kathleen, da of Dr Charles Douglas Anderson, MC; 1 s (Peter b 1973), 1 da (Ruth b 1976); *Career* res fell Harvard Med Sch 1974–75, lectr in surgery Univ of Glasgow 1976–79, reader in surgery and conslt surgn Univ of Manchester 1988– (sr lectr 1979–88); Salford Royal Hosps NHS Tst: clinical dir in general surgery 1994–96, med dir for surgical specialities 1996–; dir Hope Hosp Total Quality Mgmnt Prog 1989–92, chm Salford Dist Med Audit Ctee 1990–93, memb Cncl Int Soc for Diseases of the Esophagus 1989–, memb Cncl Br Soc of Gastroenterology 1991–94; examiner in surgery RCPSGlas 1988–; memb: MRC Working Party on Oesophageal Cancer 1991–, MRC Working Party on Gastric Cancer 1993–, Surgical Gastroenterology Gp Assoc of Surgns of GB and Ireland 1993–, Cncl Assoc of Upper Gastrointestinal Surgns of GB and Ireland 1996– (chm Educn and Research Ctee); chm: Upper Gastrointestinal Specialty Working Gp NHS Clinical Terms Project 1992–95, Surgical Section Br Soc of Gastroenterology 1994–, NW Deanery Surgical Trg Ctee 1996– (vice chm 1993–96); hon memb Romanian Soc of Surgery 1993; FRCSGlas 1973; *Recreations* sailing, hill walking; *Style*— John Bancewicz, Esq; ✉ 10 Syddal Rd, Bramhall, Cheshire SK7 1AD (☎ 0161 439 2508); University of Manchester, Dept of Surgery, Hope Hospital, Salford M6 8HD (☎ 0161 789 5128, fax 0161 787 5992)

BAND, His Hon (Robert) Murray Niven; MC (1944), QC (1974); s of Robert Niven, and Agnes Jane Band; *b* 23 Nov 1919; *Educ* Trinity Coll Glenalmond, Hertford Coll Oxford (MA); *m* 1948, Nancy Margery Redhead; 2 da; *Career* served RA 1940–46; called to the Bar Inner Temple 1947, jr Treasy counsel in probate matters 1972–74, chm Family Law Bar Assoc 1972–74, recorder Crown Ct 1977–78, circuit judge 1978–91; chm St Teresa's Hosp Wimbledon 1969–83; Liveryman Worshipful Co of Fanmakers; *Recreations* countryside, gardens, old buildings; *Style*— His Hon Murray Band, MC, QC

BAND, Thomas Mollison (Tom); s of late Robert Boyce Band, and Elizabeth, *née* Mollison; *b* 28 March 1934; *Educ* Perth Acad; *m* 9 May 1959, Jean McKenzie, da of Robert Brien, JP; 1 s (Ewan b 1960), 2 da (Susan b 1962, Margaret b 1966); *Career* Nat Serv RAF 1952–54; joined Civil Serv 1954, princ BOT 1966–73, dir Location of Indust DOI Scotland 1973–76, asst sec Scot Office 1976–84, dir Historic Buildings & Monuments 1984–87, chief exec Scottish Tourist Bd 1987–94; chm: Made in Scotland Ltd 1994–95, Edinburgh Europa Ltd 1994–, Anderson Enterprises 1994–, Perth Rep Theatre 1996; dir Perth Housing Assoc 1993–; govr Queen Margaret Coll 1995–; FSA (Scot) 1984, FTS 1988, FRSA 1993; *Recreations* skiing, gardening, beating; *Style*— Tom Band, Esq; ✉ Heathfield, Pitcairngreen, Perth (☎ 01738 583403, fax 01738 583063)

BANERJEE, Dr Arup Kumar; OBE (1996), JP; s of Ansumali Banerjee (d 1984), and Maya, *née* Chatterjee; *b* 28 Nov 1935; *Educ* Univ of Calcutta Med Coll (MB BS); *m* 23 March 1959, Dr Aleya Banerjee, da of late Nakuleswar Banerjee; 3 s (Arpan b 14 Feb 1960, Anjan b 12 Sept 1962, Avijit b 2 Dec 1969); *Career* various jr hosp appts in India and UK 1958–67, sr registrar in med Southend Gen Hosp 1967–68, lectr in med Univ of Malaya Med Sch Kuala Lumpur 1968–71, sr registrar in elderly med Portsmouth and Southampton Univ Hosps 1971–73, conslt physician in elderly med Bolton Gen Hosp 1973– (med dir Bolton Hosp Tst), hon clinical lectr in geriatric med Univ of Manchester 1975–; conslt to Nat Health Advsy Serv; memb NW RHA 1987–94 (vice chm 1992–94); pres Br Geriatrics Soc 1996–98; memb: Geriatrics Ctee RCP London, Panel of Experts for Nat Registered Homes Tbnl; author of various pubns on med topics; memb: Br Geriatrics Soc, BMA (memb Med Specialities Ctee 1986–94, memb CCSC 1986–94); FRCPGlas 1979 (MRCPGlas 1965), FRCPEd 1980 (MRCPEd 1967), FRCP 1982 (MRCP 1967); *Books* Haematological Aspects of Systematic Disease (contrib 1976), The Principles and Practice of Geriatric Medicine (contrib 1985 and 1991), A Guide to the Care of the Elderly (1995); *Recreations* travel, music, literature; *Style*— Dr Arup Banerjee, OBE, JP; ✉ 2 Pilling Field, Egerton, Bolton BL7 9UG (☎ 01204 305482); Department of Medicine for the Elderly, Bolton General Hospital, Minerva Rd, Farnworth, Bolton BL4 0JR (☎ 01204 390685/6, 01204 390390)

BANERJI, Sara Ann; da of Sir Basil Mostyn, Bt, and Anita Mostyn; *b* 6 June 1932; *Educ* various schs and convents in GB and S Rhodesia; *m* Ranjit Banerji; 3 c (Bijoya b 13 Dec 1957, Sabita b 26 Jan 1961, Juthika b 18 Nov 1963); *Career* writer; memb Soc of Authors; *Novels* Cobwebwalking, The Wedding of Jayanthi Mandel, The Teaplanter's Daughter, Shining Agnes, Absolute Hush, Writing On Skin; *Recreations* transcendental meditation, painting, gardening, cooking, interior decor, company (especially of husband, daughters, sons-in-law and grandchildren); *Style*— Mrs Sara Banerji; ✉ c/o Merrick Davidson, Literary Agent, 12 Priors Heath, Goudhurst, Cranbrook, Kent TN17 2RE

BANFIELD, Ven David John; s of Norman Charles Banfield (d 1980), and Muriel Gladys Honor, *née* Pippard (d 1986); *b* 25 June 1933; *Educ* Yeovil Sch, Univ of London, London Coll of Divinity (ALCD); *m* 1967, Rita, da of William Everson Woolhouse; 3 da (Mary Christine b 19 June 1968, Helen Margaret b 20 June 1970, Rachel Ann b 20 Aug 1971); *Career* Nat Serv RAF 1951–53; curate Middleton Manchester 1957–62, chaplain/asst warden Scargill Community 1962–67; vicar: Addiscombe Croydon 1967–80, Luton Bedfordshire 1980–90; archdeacon of Bristol 1990–; *Recreations* walking, travel, music, gardening; *Style*— The Ven the Archdeacon of Bristol; ✉ 10 Great Brockeridge, Westbury-on-Trym, Bristol BS9 3TY (☎ 0117 962 2438); Diocese of Bristol, Church House, 23 Great George Street, Bristol BS1 5QZ (☎ 0117 921 4411)

BANG, Christian Francis Lanyon; s of Christian Lucien Bang, of White House, Old Bosham, nr Chichester, W Sussex, and Agnes Elizabeth Lanyon, *née* Penno; *b* 12 Aug 1948; *Educ* Forres and Crookham Court; *m* 3 Sept 1994, Kirsten Frances, da of Mogens Christian Christoff Vind, of Brundeanlaws House, Jedburgh; *Career* HAC 1967–75; CA Blease Lloyd & Co 1967–72, Thomson McLintock & Co 1973–76, Robson Rhodes 1977–78, Norton Warburg Ltd 1979–80, sr ptnr Christian Bang and Co 1981–; dir several cos; memb Bow Gp 1975–84; FCA; *Recreations* riding, sailing; *Clubs* HAC, Itchenor Sailing; *Style*— Christian Bang, Esq; ✉ 15 Bowfell Road, London W6 9HE; 4 and 5 Domingo Street, London EC1Y 0TA (☎ 0171 608 3707, fax 0171 608 3714)

BANGOR, Bishop of 1993–; Rt Rev Dr Barry Cennydd Morgan; s of Rhys Haydn Morgan (d 1983), and Mary Gwyneth, *née* Davies (d 1988); *b* 31 Jan 1947; *Educ* UCL (BA), Selwyn Coll Cambridge (MA), Westcott House Cambridge (Powis exhibitioner), Univ of Wales (PhD); *m* Aug 1969, Hilary Patricia, da of Ieuan Lewis; 1 s (Jonathan Rhodri b 19 July 1975), 1 da (Lucy Rachel Angharad b 4 Feb 1977); *Career* ordained (Llandaff): deacon 1972, priest 1973; curate St Andrew's Major Dinas Powis 1972–75, chaplain Bryn-y-Don Community Sch 1972–75, chaplain and lectr St Michael's Coll Llandaff 1975–77, lectr UC Cardiff 1975–77, warden Church Hostel Bangor, Anglican chaplain and lectr in theol UCNW 1977–84, ed Welsh Churchman 1975–82; examining chaplain: to Archbishop of Wales 1978–82, to Bishop of Bangor 1983; in-serv trg offr 1979–84, warden of ordinands Dio of Bangor 1982–84, canon of Bangor Cathedral 1983–84, rector Rectorial Parish of Wrexham 1984–86, archdeacon of Merioneth and rector of Criccieth 1986–93; chm: Div of Stewardship Provincial Bd of Mission 1988–94, Archbishop's Doctrinal Cmmn 1983–93 (memb 1982); hon fell UCW Bangor; *Publications* O Ddydd i Ddydd, Pwyllgor Darlleniadau Beiblaidd Cyngor Eglwysi Cymru (1980), History of the Church Hostel and Anglican Chaplaincy at University College of North Wales Bangor (1986), Concepts of Mission and Ministry in Anglican University Chaplaincy Work (1988); *Recreations* golf; *Style*— The Rt Rev the Bishop of Bangor; ✉ Ty'r Esgob, Bangor, Gwynedd LL57 2SS (☎ 01248 362895, fax 01248 354866)

BANGOR, Dean of; *see:* Edwards, Very Rev (Thomas) Edward Pryse

BANGOR, Rt Hon Viscountess; *see:* Bradford, Sarah Mary Malet

BANGOR, 8 Viscount (I 1781); William Maxwell David Ward; also Baron Bangor (I 1770); s of 7 Viscount Bangor (d 1993), and his 3 w, Leila Mary, *née* Heaton (d 1959); *b* 9 Aug 1948; *Educ* Univ Coll London; *m* 1976, Sarah Bradford, *qv*, da of Brig Hilary Anthony Hayes, DSO, OBE, and formerly wife of Anthony Bradford; *Heir* half-bro, Hon (Edward) Nicholas Ward, *qv*; *Career* antiquarian bookseller; patron Bangor FC; *Recreations* Bolton Wanderers; *Style*— The Rt Hon the Viscount Bangor; ✉ 31 Britannia Road, London SW6 2HJ

BANHAM, Belinda Joan; CBE (1977), JP; da of Col Charles Henry Unwin (d 1939), of Chelsea, and Winifred Unwin, *née* Woodman Wilson (d 1922); *Educ* privately, West Bank Sch Brussels, Univ of London (BSc, RGN, Dip in Social Studies); *m* 1939, Terence Middlecott Banham (d 1995), s of Rev Vivian Greaves Banham, MC (d 1973); 2 s (Sir John Banham, *qv*, Simon), 2 da (Susan, Joanna); *Career* work in health servs 1937–; chm: Cornwall & Isles of Scilly HMC 1967–74 (memb 1964–77), Cornwall & Isles of Scilly AHA 1974–77, Kensington Chelsea & Westminster FPC 1979–85 (memb 1977–79), Paddington & N Kensington DHA 1981–86; memb: SW Regnl Hosp Bd 1965–74, MRC 1979–87, Lambeth Southwark & Lewisham FPC 1987–90; Lambeth Southwark and Lewisham Family Health Authy: non-exec dir 1990–, vice chm 1990–93, chm 1993–; vice chm Lambeth Southwark and Lewisham Health Cmmn 1993–; memb MRC 1979–87; pt/t conslt Health Div Business Sciences Ltd 1986–; marriage guidance cnsllr 1960–72; vice chm: Disabled Living Fndn 1983–90, Wytham Hall 1990–93 (tstee 1985–); vice pres AFASIC 1989–, pres Friends of St Mary's Hosp 1993–; *Publications* Partnership in Action (jtly, 1990), Snapshots in time: Some experiences in health care 1936–1991 (1991), General Practice in the NHS or football round The Mulberry Bush 1918–1995 (1995); *Recreations* gardening, plant biology, theatre; *Clubs* Sloane; *Style*— Mrs Belinda Banham, CBE, JP; ✉ Ponsmaen, St Feock, Truro, Cornwall TR3 6QG (☎ 01872 862275); 27 Vandon Court, Petty France, London SW1H 9HG (☎ 0171 222 3676)

BANHAM, Sir John Michael Middlecott; kt (1992); s of Terence Middlecott Banham (d 1995), and Belinda Joan Banham, CBE, JP, *qv*; *b* 22 Aug 1940; *Educ* Charterhouse, Queens' Coll Cambridge (MA); *m* 30 Oct 1965, Frances Barbara Molyneux, da of Cdr Richard Molyneux Favell, DSC, RN (d 1995), of St Buryan, Cornwall; 1 s (Mark Richard Middlecott b 1968), 2 da (Serena Frances Tamsin b 1970, Morwenna Bridget Favell b 1972); *Career* temp asst princ HM Dip Serv 1962–64, mktg exec J Walter Thompson 1964–65, mktg dir Wallcoverings Div Reed International 1965–69; McKinsey & Co Inc: assoc 1969–75, princ 1975–80, dir 1980–83; first controller Audit Cmmn for Local Authorities 1983–87; dir gen CBI 1987–92; chm: Local Govt Cmmn for England 1992–95, Westcountry Television 1991–, Labatt Breweries of Europe 1992–95, ECI Ventures (venture capital mangrs) 1992–, Tarmac Plc 1994–, Kingfisher plc 1996– (non-exec dir 1995–); dir: National Westminster Bank plc 1992–, National Power plc 1992–, Merchants Trust plc 1992–; managing tstee Nuffield Fndn 1988–, hon treas Cancer Research Campaign 1991–; hon fell Queens' Coll Cambridge 1989; Hon LLD Univ of Bath 1987, Hon DSc Loughborough Univ 1989 and Univ of Exeter 1993, Hon LLD Univ of Strathclyde 1995; *Books* Anatomy of Change (1994); author of numerous reports on mgmnt, health and local authy servs; *Recreations* gardening, cliff walking, sailing, ground clearing; *Clubs* Travellers', Oriental; *Style*— Sir John Banham; ✉ Westcountry Management, 64A Neal Street, Covent Garden, London WC2H 9PA (☎ 0171 379 1697)

BANKHEAD, Jack William; s of Frank James Bankhead, and Rita, *née* Jones; *b* 29 Dec 1942; *Educ* Wandsworth Comp; *m* 30 Sept 1967, Ann Christina, da of Frank Trottier; 2 s (William Johnnie b 17 May 1972, Barney Jack b 28 May 1974), 1 da (Corina Ann b 13 Jan 1979); *Career* advertising photographer; art studio mangr 1972, estab own studio 1979; notable campaigns incl series for John Player Special; *Recreations* tennis, skiing, swimming; *Style*— Jack Bankhead, Esq; ✉ 31B Harbour Yard, Chelsea Harbour, SW10

BANKS, Brian; s of Albert Edward Banks (d 1981), of London, and Evelyn Lilian, *née* Bilyard (d 1981); *b* 2 July 1938; *Educ* Henry Thornton GS; *m* 6 Oct 1962, Barbara Eileen, da of Edward Townsend (d 1973), of London; 2 s (Andrew Nicholas b 1964, Alexander James b 1973), 1 da (Joanne b 1967); *Career* res analyst L Messel & Co 1964–66, investmt mangr Nat Provident Inst 1966–68, md Britannia Arrow Holdings 1975–78 (investmt dir 1968–78), dir Dunbar Group and md Dunbar Fund Managers 1978–83, chm Guildhall Investment Management 1983–86, md Asset Trust plc 1986–89, chm Guildhall Investment Management Ltd 1989–; Freeman City of London; memb Worshipful Co of Carmen; *Recreations* golf; *Clubs* RAC, MCC; *Style*— Brian Banks, Esq; ✉ Guildhall Investment Management Ltd, 5–7 Southwark St, London SE1 1RQ (☎ 0171 403 7572, fax 0171 403 7147)

BANKS, Colin; s of William Banks (d 1985), and Ida Jenny, *née* Hood (d 1976); *b* 16 Jan 1932; *Educ* Mid Kent Coll of Printing; *m* 1961, Dr Caroline Grigson, *qv*; 1 s, 1 da (decd); *Career* fndr ptnr Banks & Miles (graphic designers): London 1958–, Amsterdam 1975–82, Hamburg 1990–92, Brussels 1991–94; design conslt: Zoological Soc 1962–82, Br Cncl 1968–83, E Midlands Arts Assoc 1974–77; art ed Which? and other Consumers' Assoc magazines 1964–93; design advsr: NERC, London Tport, BT, PSA, IMechE, SERC, Fndn Roi Baudouin, Mott MacDonald Consltg Engrs, Portsmouth Univ, UN Univ Tokyo and Helsinki, Univ of S W Bristol, UNHCR major publication; curator True To Type (touring exhbn) 1994–96; conslt designer Oxford University Press 1996–; mangr Blackheath Sch of Art 1981–90; pres Soc of Typographic Designers 1988–93; IBA medal 1971, Gold medal Brno Biennale 1986, Green Award for redesign of phonebook RSA, Silver medal Leipzig Book Fair, Best German Printed Book Frankfurt 1989, BBC Environmental prize 1990, Paris Cité Concours for Technical Innovation, 2nd Felici Feliciano triannale 1991; treas Mala Project for Children's Educn and Welfare India 1989–92, hon memb City and Guilds, memb Association Typographique Internationale; FRSA, FCSD; *Books* Social Communication, 26 Letters, London's Handwriting; *Recreations* Indian life; *Clubs* Arts, Wynkyn de Worde (past chm), Double Crown (past pres); *Style*— Colin Banks, Esq; ✉ Banks & Miles, 29 Langton Way, Blackheath, London SE3 7TJ (☎ 0171 318 1131)

BANKS, (Arthur) David; s of Arthur Banks (d 1988), of Warrington, Cheshire, and Helen, *née* Renton; *b* 13 Feb 1948; *Educ* Boteler GS Warrington; *m* Gemma, da of Francis Xavier Newton; 1 da (Natasha Kate b 12 Dec 1978), 1 s (Timothy James b 28 Sept 1982); *Career* jr reporter Warrington Guardian 1965–68, reporter/subed Newcastle Journal

1968–71, sub ed Daily Express 1971–72, asst night ed Daily Mirror 1972–79, asst managing ed New York Post 1979–81, night ed/asst ed The Sun 1981–86, dep managing ed New York Daily News 1986–87, dep ed The Australian 1987–89, ed Daily Telegraph Mirror Sydney 1989–92, ed Daily Mirror 1992–94; Mirror Group Newspapers Ltd: editorial dir 1994–96, new media advsr 1996–; broadcaster LBC, BBC Radio, presenter Live TV, Channel 4; *Recreations* dining, dieting; *Style—* David Banks, Esq; ✉ Mirror Group Newspapers Ltd, One Canada Square, Canary Wharf, London E14 5AP (☎ 0171 293 3691, fax 0171 293 3594, e-mail dbanks@media.co.uk)

BANKS, Dr David Charles; JP (1993); s of Charles William John Banks (d 1961), of Brighton, and Jenny Frances Kathleen, *née* Puttick (d 1981); *b* 11 Dec 1938; *Educ* Varndean GS Brighton, The London Hosp Univ of London (MB BS, MD); *m* 3 Aug 1963, Judith Elizabeth, da of Horace Kingsley Evershed; 2 s (Peter b 1964, Philip b 1971), 2 da (Elizabeth b 1966, Gill b 1969); *Career* house offr London Hosp and sr house offr assoc hosps 1962–67, med registrar KCH 1967–69, MRC res fell Med Unit Univ of Nottingham 1969–72, Anglo American res fell Br Heart Fndn and American Heart Assoc 1972–73, assoc in med Harvard Univ 1972; City Hosp Nottingham: conslt physician and pt/t sr lectr in therapeutics 1973–82, conslt physician 1982–, unit gen mangr 1984–86; dist gen mangr Nottingham Health Authy 1986–93; memb: Exec Ctee Univ Hosp Assoc, Ethical Ctee SmithKline Beecham Pharmaceuticals 1987–92, Liver Club 1975, European Cardiac Soc, Cardiac Soc 1979, Assoc of Physicians 1982; hon memb Ceylon Coll of Physicians 1996; fell Univ of Nottingham 1992; FRCP 1979 (MRCP 1966); *Books* ABC of Medical Treatment (1979); *Recreations* walking, golf, photography; *Style—* Dr David Banks, JP; ✉ The Mill House, Caythorpe, Nottingham NG14 7ED (☎ 0115 966 3092); City Hospital, Hucknall Rd, Nottingham NG5 1PB (☎ 0115 969 1169)

BANKS, Derek John; s of John Gerard (d 1983), of Bellshill, Lanarkshire, and Jane, *née* Rowan; *b* 25 Sept 1947; *Educ* St Joseph's Coll Dumfries, Univ of Glasgow (MA), Simon Fraser Univ Canada (MA); *m* 10 April 1976, Moira, *née* Bridges; 1 da (Catriona Frances b 25 Sept 1980), 2 s (Gregory James b 21 May 1983, Nicholas Charles b 26 May 1987); *Career* civil servant 1973–86, dir of planning and information Crewe Health Authy 1986–88, exec dir of planning and information N Lincs Health Authy 1988–92, gen mangr Dumfries and Galloway Health Bd 1993–; MHSM; *Recreations* chess, travel, hill walking; *Style—* Derek Banks, Esq; ✉ Dumfries and Galloway Health Board, Nithbank, Dumfries DG1 2SD (☎ 01387 41800)

BANKS, Baron (Life Peer UK 1974); Desmond Anderson Harvie Banks; CBE (1972); s of James Banks, OBE; *b* 23 Oct 1918; *Educ* UCS Hampstead; *m* 1948, Barbara, da of Richard Taylor Wells; 2 s; *Career* served WWII Middle East & Italy, KRRC & RA as Maj (Chief PRO to Allied Mil Govt Trieste 1946); subsequently joined Canada Life Assurance Co; life assurance broker 1959–; dir: Tweddle French & Co (Life & Pensions) Ltd 1973–, Lincoln Consultants Ltd 1982–89; Lib Pty: chm Exec 1961–63 and 1969–70, pres 1968–69, dir of policy promotion 1972–74; pres: Nat Liberal Club 1981–93, Lib Euro Action Gp 1971–87; memb Foreign Affrs and Social Securities Panels 1961–88; Parly candidate (Lib): Harrow E 1950, St Ives 1955, SW Herts 1959; sits as Lib Dem Peer in House of Lords; vice chm Lib Pty Standing Ctee 1973–79, dep Lib whip House of Lords 1977–83; Lib spokesman on: social security 1975–89, social servs 1977–83; vice chm: Euro Atlantic Gp 1979–85 (vice pres 1985–), Br Cncl Euro Movement 1979–86 (pres 1986–94); elder United Reformed Church; *Recreations* Gilbert and Sullivan operas, Clyde river steamers, reading; *Clubs* Nat Lib; *Style—* The Rt Hon Lord Banks, CBE; ✉ Lincoln House, The Lincolns, Little Kingshill, Great Missenden, Bucks HP16 0EH

BANKS, James Alastair Crawford (Jamie); s of Maj Alastair Arthur Banks, MC, of Thursley, Surrey, and Ann Paton, *née* Crichton; *b* 11 March 1947; *Educ* Dover Coll, Greenwich HS USA, Grenoble Univ France; *m* 15 May 1976, Sally Christable, da of late Richard Geoffrey Hugh Coles, of Fordingbridge, Hants; 2 s (Alastair b 1979, Stuart b 1981); *Career* works mangr H Taylor (Drums) Ltd 1972–78, dir and gen mangr Victor Blagden Ltd 1978–88, gp business devpt exec Blagden Industs plc 1988–94, independent business advsr 1994–, dir Anglia Business Resources 1995–; chm E London Area Ctee CBI 1987 (memb London Regnl Cncl 1987), pres Barking & Dagenham C of C 1987–89, chm Barking & Dagenham Trg Initiative Ltd 1987–89, govr Meadgate Primary Sch Gt Baddow 1988–92 (chm Fin Ctee 1990–92); *Recreations* sailing, squash, bridge, skiing, badminton, theatre; *Style—* Jamie Banks, Esq; ✉ Brickwalls, 36 High St, Great Baddow, Essex CM2 7HQ (☎ and fax 01245 472053); business fax 01279 813362, mobile 0860 481535

BANKS, (Ernest) John; s of Ernest Frederick Banks (d 1995), and Marian Blanche, *née* Nuttall (d 1991); *b* 2 July 1945; 1 da (Charlotte Frederique Marianne b 3 May 1983); *Career* former gp chm and chief exec offr Young and Rubicam Gp Advertising Agency; currently chm/managing ptnr Banks Hoggins O'Shea (formerly The Banks Partnership); memb Market Res Soc of GB, FIPA; *Clubs* Buck's, Carlton, Turf, MCC; *Style—* John Banks, Esq; ✉ Banks Hoggins O'Shea Ltd, 54 Baker Street, London W1M 1DJ (☎ 0171 314 0000, fax 0171 314 0004)

BANKS, (William) Lawrence; s of Richard Alford Banks, CBE, of Herefords, and Lilian Jean, *née* Walker (d 1973); *b* 7 June 1938; *Educ* Rugby, ChCh Oxford (MA); *m* 1963, Elizabeth Christina, da of Capt Leslie Swain Saunders, DSO, RN (d 1988), of Northants; 2 s (Richard b 1965, Edward b 1967); *Career* merchant banker; dep chm Robert Fleming & Co Ltd; chm Cncl (former treas) Royal Postgrad Med Sch Hammersmith 1990–; chm: Caledonian Publishing 1993–96, Kington Connected Community Co Ltd 1993–; non-exec dir Nat Blood Authy; a cmmr of the 1851 Exhbn, memb Devpt Cncl Nat Art Collections Fund; hon treas RHS 1981–92; awarded Victoria Medal of Honour (RHS); tstee: Chevening Estate, Chelsea Physic Garden, Hergest Tst, Hereford Mappa Mundi Tst; *Recreations* gardening, fishing, shooting, theatre; *Clubs* MCC, Pratt's; *Style—* Lawrence Banks, Esq; ✉ 13 Abercorn Place, London NW8 9EA (☎ 0171 624 5740); Ridgebourne, Kington, Herefordshire (☎ 01544 230218); Robert Fleming & Co Ltd, 25 Copthall Ave, London EC2R 7DR (☎ 0171 638 5858, fax 0171 588 7219)

BANKS, Lynne Reid; da of Dr James Reid-Banks (d 1953), and Muriel Alexandra Marsh (d 1981, actress, stage name Muriel Alexander); *b* 31 July 1929; *Educ* various schs in England and Canada, Italia Conti Stage Sch, RADA; *m* Chaim Stephenson, sculptor; 3 s (Adiel b 1965, Gillon b 1967, Omri b 1968); *Career* actress 1949–54, reporter ITN 1955–62, teacher of English in Israel 1963–71; full time writer and lectr 1971–; visiting teacher to international schs: Tanzania 1988, Israel (Arab Sector) 1989, Nepal 1990, US (Navajo Reservation) 1991, India 1992 and 1996; author of several plays for stage, TV and radio, numerous articles in The Observer, The Guardian, TES, The Times, The Independent and various magazines; memb: Soc of Authors, Equity, PEN; *Plays* It Never Rains (1954), All in a Row (1956), The Killer Dies Twice (1956), Already It's Tomorrow (1962), The Eye of the Beholder (1975), A Question of Principle (1987), Travels of Yoshi and the Tea-Kettle (for children, Polka Theatre 1991–92, Fringe Award); *Fiction* The L-Shaped Room (1960, film 1962), An End to Running (1962), Children at the Gate (1968), The Backward Shadow (1970), Two is Lonely (1974), Defy the Wilderness (1981), The Warning Bell (1984), Casualties (1987); *Biographical novels* Dark Quartet - the story of the Brontës (1976, Yorks Arts Literary Award), Path to the Silent Country (sequel, 1977); *For young adults* One More River (1973, rewritten and reissued 1992), Sarah and After (1975), My Darling Villain (1977), The Writing on the Wall (1981), Melusine - a Mystery (1988), Broken Bridge (sequel to One More River, 1994); *Children's* The Adventures of King Midas (1977, rewritten and reissued 1993), The Farthest-Away Mountain (1977), I, Houdini (1978), The Indian in the Cupboard (1980, also film, Pacific NW Choice Award 1984, Calif Young Readers' Medal 1985, Virginia Children's Choice 1988, Massachusetts Children's Choice 1988, Rebecca Caudill Award 1988, Arizona Children's Choice 1989 and others), Maura's Angel (1984), The Fairy Rebel (1985), Return of the Indian (1986, Indian Paintbrush Award Wyoming 1989), Secret of the Indian (1989, Great Stone Face Children's Book Award Vermont 1991), The Magic Hare (1991), The Mystery of the Cupboard (1993, West Virginia Children's Book Award, 1995), Harry the Poisonous Centipede (1996), Angela and Diabola (1997); *History* Letters to My Israeli Sons (1979), Torn Country: An Oral History of Israel's War of Independence (1982); *Recreations* theatre, travel, gardening, talking; *Style—* Ms Lynne Reid Banks; ✉ c/o Sheila Watson, Watson Little Ltd, Capo di Monte, Windmill Hill, Hampstead, London NW3 6RJ (☎ 0171 431 0770, fax 0171 431 0770)

BANKS, Matthew R W; MP (C) Southport (majority 3,063); s of Harry Banks, and Audrey Banks; *b* 21 June 1961; *Educ* Calday Grange Sch Wirral, Sheffield City Poly, RMA Sandhurst; *m* 5 Dec 1992, Jane, da of Michael Miller, of London; *Career* cmmnd 1 Bn Gordon Highlanders 1981, served until 1984; with Barclays Bank plc NW Region 1983–87, private sec House of Commons 1987–89, dir LBJ Ltd 1989–; Parly candidate (C) Manchester Central 1987, MP (C) Southport 1992–, PPS to Mins of State Dept of Environment 1996–; memb Select Ctee on Tport 1992–, vice chm Cons Tport Ctee 1994– (sec 1992), served on Crossrail Bill 1993–94; sec: Anglo-Venezuelan Gp, Anglo-Moroccan Gp; treas Anglo-Manx Parly Gp; cncllr Wirral BC 1984–90; *Recreations* reading, travel, golf, flying; *Clubs* Heswall Golf, West Lancashire Yacht, Caledonian, Montes; *Style—* Matthew Banks, Esq, MP; ✉ House of Commons, London SW1A 0AA (☎ 0171 219 3000)

BANKS, Robert George; MP (C) Harrogate (majority 12,589); s of late George Walmsley Banks, MBE, and Olive Beryl, *née* Tyler; *b* 18 Jan 1937; *Educ* Haileybury; *m* 1967, Diana Margaret Payne Crawfurd; 4 s, 1 da; *Career* Lt Cdr RNR; memb Paddington Borough Cncl 1959–65, jt fndr dir Antocks Lairn Ltd 1963–67; MP (C) Harrogate Feb 1974–; jt sec Cons Parly Def Ctee 1976–79; PPS to: Min of State FCO 1979–81, Min of State for Overseas Devpt FCO 1981–82; memb Select Ctee on: Foreign Affrs 1982, Trade and Industry 1994–; memb: Cncl of Europe 1977–81, WEU 1977–81, N Atlantic Assembly 1981–, Alcohol Educn & Res Cncl 1982–87; chm All-Pty: Anglo-Sudan Gp 1983– (sec 1978–83), Tourism Ctee 1992–; vice-chm Br-Ecuador Parly Gp, vice-chm Arts and Heritage Ctee, jt vice-chm Yorkshire Members Gp; dir: BDO Hospitality Consulting, Credit Management Resources Ltd; fell Industry and Parly Tst; FRSA; *Publications* The Technology of Military Space Systems, Britain's Home Defence Gamble (jtly, 1979), Nuclear, Biological and Chemical Protection (1980), New jobs from Pleasure 1985, Tories for Tourism (1995); *Recreations* travel, sport, contemporary art, architecture; *Style—* Robert Banks, Esq, MP; ✉ House of Commons, London SW1

BANKS, Robert James; s of Maj Kenneth Banks (d 1986), and Nona Banks; *b* 26 Feb 1951; *Educ* Dover Coll, Univ of Wales (BSc); *Career* called to the Bar Inner Temple 1978; *Style—* Robert Banks; ✉ 132 Great Portland Street, London W1N 5PH

BANKS, Roderick Charles I'Anson; s of Charles I'Anson Banks (d 1991), and Suzanne Mary Gwendoline, *née* Hall; *b* 5 Dec 1951; *Educ* Westminster, UCL (LLB); *m* 11 Aug 1979, Susan Elizabeth Lavington, da of His Hon Albert William Clark, *qv*, of Worthing, Sussex; 2 s (Oliver b 1982, Frederick b 1986); *Career* called to the Bar Lincoln's Inn 1974, head of chambers 48 Bedford Row; legal author; accredited CEDR mediator; fndr memb Centre for Dispute Resolution; memb Country Landowners' Assoc; hon assoc Br Veterinary Assoc; *Books* Lindley on Partnership (co-ed, 14 edn 1979, 15 edn 1984), Lindley & Banks on Partnership (ed, 16 edn 1990, 17 edn 1995), Encyclopedia of Professional Partnerships (ed, 1987), Halsbury's Laws of England: Partnership Vol (conslt ed, 4 edn reissue 1994); *Recreations* reluctant gardener, TV/video addict, collecting autographs and Art Deco; *Style—* R C I'Anson Banks, Esq; ✉ 48 Bedford Row, London WC1R 4LR (☎ 0171 430 2005, fax 0171 831 1510)

BANKS, Tony; MP (Lab) Newham North West (majority 9,171); s of Albert Banks; *b* 8 April 1943; *Educ* Archbishop Tenison's GS Kennington, Univ of York (BA), LSE; *Career* head of res AUEW 1968–75, asst gen sec Assoc of Bdcasting and Allied Staffs 1976–83, political advsr to Min for Overseas Devpt (Dame Judith Hart) 1975; memb Lab Pty 1964–; memb GLC for Hammersmith 1970–77 and Tooting 1981–86 (chm 1985–86); Parly Candidate (Lab): East Grinstead 1970, Newcastle N Oct 1974, Watford 1979; MP (Lab) Newham NW 1983–; memb Select Ctee on: Treasy 1986–87, Procedure 1989–; oppn frontbench spokesman on: Tport 1992–93, Environment 1992–93; London whip 1988–; memb: Jt Lords/Commons Ctee on Private Bill Procedure 1987–88, Cncl of Europe and WEU 1989–91; chm: London Gp Lab MPs 1987–, Br-Nicaragua Inter Parly Union Gp 1987–; memb Bd: Nat Theatre 1981–85, ENO 1981–83, London Festival Ballet 1981–83; *Recreations* soccer, trade union history; *Style—* Tony Banks, Esq, MP; ✉ House of Commons, London SW1

BANKS, Tony; *b* 27 March 1951; *Educ* Charterhouse, Univ of Sussex; *Career* musician (keyboard player); co fndr Genesis 1966 (with Mike Rutherford, *qv*, and Peter Gabriel, *qv*); albums with Genesis: From Genesis to Revelation (1969), Trespass (1970), Nursery Cryme (1971), Foxtrot (1972), Genesis Live (1973), Selling England by the Pound (1973), The Lamb Lies Down On Broadway (1974), A Trick of the Tail (1976), Wind and Wuthering (1977), Seconds Out (live, 1978), And Then There Were Three (1978), Duke (1980, UK no 1), Abacab (1981, UK no 1), Three Sides Live (live and studio, 1982), Genesis (1983, UK no 1), Invisible Touch (1986, UK no 1), We Can't Dance (1992), Genesis Live - The Way We Walk (Vol 1, The Shorts 1992, Vol 2, The Longs 1992); solo albums: A Curious Feeling (1979), The Wicked Lady (soundtrack, 1983), The Fugitive (1983), Soundtracks (1986), Bankstatement (1989), Still (1991); *Style—* Tony Banks, Esq; ✉ c/o Hit & Run Music Ltd, 30 Ives St, London SW3 2ND (☎ 0171 581 0261, fax 0171 584 5774)

BANNEN, Ian; s of John James Bannen (d 1958), of Coatbridge, Scotland, and Agnes Clare, *née* Galloway (d 1976); *b* 29 June 1928; *Educ* St Aloysius Jesuit Sch Glasgow, Grace Dieu Prep Sch Leics, Ratcliffe Coll Leics; *m* 16 Nov 1978, Marilyn, da of John Salisbury (d 1984), of Wrexham; *Career* actor; Nat Serv RE; vice pres Catholic Stage Guild; memb: St Vincent de Paul Soc, American Acad (AMPAS) 1966–, BAFTA; awarded BAFTA: Scotland's Life Time Achievement Award presented by Mel Gibson in Los Angeles 1995; *Theatre* RSC 1951–54, Marco in A View from the Bridge (first West End role, Comedy Theatre) 1956–57, title role in Sergeant Musgrave's Dance (Royal Court) 1958, Jamie in Long Day's Journey into Night (Globe) 1958–59, Julian in Toys in the Attic (Piccadilly) 1960; RSC 1961–62: title role in Hamlet, Orlando (to Vanessa Redgrave's Rosalind) in As You Like It, Mercutio in Romeo and Juliet, Iago to Sir John Gielgud's Othello; Yvonne Arnaud Theatre: Dick Dudgeon in The Devils Disciple 1965, The Brass Hat 1972; Hickey in The Iceman Cometh (Royal Lyceum Edinburgh 1974, London Arts and Wintergarten Theatres 1958), Judge Brack to Janet Suzmann's Hedda Gabler (Duke of York's and Edinburgh Festival) 1977, Hugh in Translations (Hampstead Theatre and NT, winner Critics' Award Actor of the Year) 1981–82, Tyrone in Moon for the Misbegotten (Riverside, Mermaid, American Repertory Harvard and Broadway) 1983–84, All My Sons (Young Vic) 1992; *Films and Television* incl: Hope and Glory (Best Supporting Actor nomination BAFTA), Flight of the Phoenix (Oscar nomination), Gandhi, Gorky Park, Eye of the Needle, Defence of the Realm, Tinker Tailor Soldier Spy, George's Island, Ghost Dad, The Big Man, Uncle Vanya, The Common Pursuit, Murder in Eden, Ashenden, Arise and Go Now, The Treaty, The Sound and The Silence, Damage, Doctor Finlay's Casebook (TV film), Doctor Finlay (third series), A Pin for the Butterfly, Measure for Measure (TV film), The Politician's Wife (Channel 4 mini series), Braveheart (with Mel Gibson), Dr Finlay (special), Dead-Sea Reels, Original Sin (3 part mini-series); *Recreations* walking, swimming, reading, photography; *Style*— Ian Bannen, Esq; ✉ c/o London Management, 2–4 Noel Street, London W1V 3RB (☎ 0171 287 9000, fax 0171 287 3036)

BANNENBERG, Jon; *b* 8 July 1929; *Educ* Canterbury HS Sydney NSW, Sydney Conservatorium of Music; *m* 1960, Beaupré Bannenberg; 2 s (Benedict, Cam); *Career* yacht designer; produced around 200 designs for motor and sail yachts and four interiors for aircraft; RDI 1978, AMRINA; *Exhibitions* Siecle d'Elegance Exhibition Louvre Paris 1959, CIONA Exhibition V&A London 1960, Eye for Industry Exhibition V&A London 1986; *Motor and Sail Boat Designs* incl: QEII (1967), Carinthia V and VI, Persephone, Sandpiper, Mediterranean Sky, Mediterranean Sea, Odyssey, Southern Breeze, Solitaire of the Isles, Nabila, Gee Dee, Lady Ghislaine, Parts VI, Silver Leopard, CRN 35, 45 and 50, 140 Royal Yacht, Althani Hydrojet, State of Kuwait 72, Highlander, Southern Cross III, Never Say Never, Antipodean, Sun Paradise, Stefaren, Mystique, Oceana, Siran, Kremlin Princess, Coral Island, Limitless, Talitha G; *Recreations* running, swimming, sailing, music, Polynesian and Pacific history; *Style*— Jon Bannenberg, Esq; ✉ Jon Bannenberg Ltd, 6 Burnsall St, London SW3 3ST (☎ 0171 352 4851, fax 0171 352 8444)

BANNER, Norman Leslie; s of Frank Leslie Banner (d 1986), of Warrington, and Clarice, *née* Rutter (d 1986); *b* 6 Nov 1947; *Educ* Lymm GS, Manchester Poly (BA); *m* 1, 1972 (m dis 1981), Andrea, *née* Atkinson; m 2, 1995, Louise, *née* Astley; *Career* Robert Davies & Co slrs Warrington: articled clerk 1971, admitted slr 1973, ptnr 1978–95; ptnr Ridgway Greenall Warrington 1995–; chm: Warrington Ctee for the Disabled 1978–91, Warrington Crossroads Care Attendant Scheme 1980–, Birchwood Project (Warrington) Ltd 1984–, Warrington Hosp NHS Tst 1993–; non-exec dir Mersey RHA 1991–93; pres Assoc of Crossroads Care Attendant Schemes 1992– (chm 1983–92); dir Warrington Festival Tst 1982–93; memb Law Soc 1973, Rotary of Warrington 1984– (past pres); *Clubs* Warrington; *Style*— Norman Banner, Esq; ✉ 12 Melton Ave, Walton, Warrington, Cheshire (☎ 01925 268186); Warrington Hospital NHS Trust, Lovely Lane, Warrington WA5 1QG (☎ 01925 662299)

BANNERMAN, Celia Elizabeth; da of Hugh Bannerman, and Hilda, *née* Diamond; *b* 3 June 1944; *Educ* Drama Centre London; *m* Edward Klein; *Career* director and actress; memb Dirs' Guild of GB; staff dir NT 1978–80 (Lies In Plastic Smiles, Making Love, The Passion, Lark Rise, Strife, Fruits of Enlightenment), assoc dir Bristol Old Vic 1982–83 (Quartermaine's Terms, Translations, The White Devil, Good Fun, Enemy of The People, The Price), assoc dir Theatre Royal Stratford (Sleeping Beauty, Magni, The Proposal); directed: Hank Wangford Band (Edinburgh Festival), La Ronde (Bristol Old Vic), Jack And The Beanstalk (Shaw Theatre London); worked on setting up and prodn of Little Dorrit with Derek Jacobi for Sands Films 1985–86; dir: Beached (Croydon Warehouse) 1987, Bet Noir (Young Vic Studio) 1987, Sinners and Saints (Croydon Warehouse) 1988, Brookside (Mersey TV) 1990; assoc prodr: The Fool 1989, A Dangerous Man 1991, As You Like It 1992; *Theatre* roles incl: Dolly in you Never Can Tell (Haymarket London), Lucy in The Rivals (Haymarket), Miranda in The Tempest (Glasgow Citizens), Cecily in The Importance of Being Earnest (Haymarket), Cynthia in The Double Dealer (Royal Ct), Come As You Are (New Theatre London), Viola in Twelfth Night (Regents Park), Katherine in Perkin Warbeck (Other Place RSC), Lady Anne in Richard III (Other Place RSC), Mrs Galy Gay in Man is Man (Other Place RSC), Rosalind in As You Like It (Acter USA), Mrs Weston in Emma (Cambridge Theatre Co) 1994, Ruth in Blythe Spirit (world tour); *Television* roles incl: Elizabeth Bennett in Pride and Prejudice, Cecily in The Importance of Being Earnest, Lady Diana Newbury in Upstairs Downstairs; *Film* incl: Rachel in The Tamarind Seed, title role in Biddy 1983, Milliner in Little Dorrit 1987, Celia in As You Like It 1992; *Style*— Ms Celia Bannerman; ✉ Harriet Cruickshank, 97 Old South Lambeth Rd, London SW8 1XU (☎ 0171 735 2933, fax 0171 735 1081)

BANNERMAN, Prof (James Charles) Christopher; s of Prof Lloyd Charles Bannerman, of Ontario, Canada, and Ethel Leah, *née* Dakin; *b* 23 Feb 1949; *Educ* Univ of Kent at Canterbury (BA); *m* 2 Sept 1988, Sara Elizabeth, da of Thomas Haig; *Career* dancer Nat Ballet of Canada 1968–72, dancer and choreographer London Contemporary Dance Theatre 1975–90; works choreographed incl: Treading, The Singing, Sandsteps, Shadows in the Sun, Unfolding Field, Ascending the Climbing Frame, Colls of Silence; head Sch of Dance Middx Univ; chm: Dance UK, Nat Dance Co-ordinating Ctee Arts Cncl; memb Dance Panel Arts Cncl; fndr artistic dir Lilian Baylis Youth Dance Co Sadlers Wells; *Recreations* gardening, travel, wilderness canoe trips in Canada; *Style*— Prof Christopher Bannerman; ✉ 136 Dukes Ave, Muswell Hill, London N10 2QB (☎ 0181 883 1314); c/o Middlesex University, Trent Park, Bramley Road, London N14 4XS (☎ 0181 362 5610)

BANNERMAN, Sir David Gordon; 15 Bt (NS 1682), of Elsick, Kincardineshire; OBE (1976); yr s of Sir Donald Arthur Gordon Bannerman, 13 Bt (d 16 Sept 1989), and Barbara Charlotte, *née* Cameron; suc bro Sir Alexander Patrick Bannerman, 14 Bt (d 21 Nov 1989); *b* 18 Aug 1935; *Educ* Gordonstoun, New Coll Oxford (MA); *m* 25 June 1960, Mary Prudence, er da of Rev Philip Frank Ardagh-Walter, Vicar of Woolton Hill, Hants; 4 da (Clare Naomi (Mrs Michael O'Neill) b 1961, Margot Charlotte b 1962, Arabella Rose b 1965, Clodagh Isobel Rose b 1975); *Career* 2 Lt Queen's Own Cameron Highlanders 1954–56, HOMCS (Tanganyka) 1960–63, MOD 1963–; *Recreations* painting, ornithology, architecture; *Style*— Sir David Bannerman, Bt, OBE; ✉ Drummond's, 49 Charing Cross, London SW1A 2DX

BANNERMAN, (George) Gordon; s of George Bannerman (d 1964), of Glasgow; *b* 25 Feb 1932; *Educ* Glasgow HS, Glasgow Acad, Sidney Sussex Coll Cambridge (MA); *m* 1959, Ann, da of James Gemmell (d 1977), of Milngavie; 1 s, 1 da; *Career* actuary; dir and actuary C T Bowring & Layborn Ltd 1972–87, dir and chief actuary Fenchurch Fin Servs Ltd 1987–91, currently in own practice; Liveryman Worshipful Co of Actuaries; ACII, AIA, ASA, FPMI, FFA; *Style*— Gordon Bannerman, Esq; ✉ 37 Westbury Rd, London N12 7PB (☎ 0181 445 1795)

BANNISTER, Brian; s of Norman Bannister, and Sarah Ann, *née* Jolly; *b* 31 Dec 1933; *Educ* King Edward VII Sch Lytham St Annes, Birmingham Sch of Architecture (DipArch); *m* 1, 5 April 1961 (m dis 1973), Pauline Mary, da of Jack Miller (d 1987), of Preston, Lancs; 1 s (Dominic b 3 Feb 1964, d 1981), 1 da (Karen b 23 July 1962); m 2, 25 May 1973, Avril, da of James Wigley Allen (d 1987); 1 s (Richard Allen b 8 July 1975), 1 da (Katie Louise b 10 Feb 1979); *Career* Nat Serv 1958–59; architect Lancs CC 1956–58 and 1960; John H D Madin and Ptnrs: sr architect 1960–64, assoc 1964–68; assoc i/c Watkins Grey Woodgate International (Birmingham Office) 1968–70; ptnr: Burman Goodhall and Ptnrs 1970–72, Brian Bannister and Assocs 1972–85, Brian Bannister Partnership 1985–93; dir Co-ordinated Project Management Ltd 1971–92, dir and co sec BMW Properties Ltd 1986–93; dir: Tweedale Planning and Design Group Ltd (trading as Bloomer Tweedale) 1993–94, Bloomer Tweedale Ltd (trading as Alex Gordon Tweedale) 1994–96, Brian Bannister Projects 1996–; sub ed Architecture West Midlands 1970–75, memb Ctee Birmingham Architectural Assoc 1972–84 (vice pres 1980–82, pres 1982–84), memb Ctee W Midlands Div Faculty of Building 1991–; ARIBA 1958, FIMgt 1980; *Recreations* golf, squash, sailing; *Clubs* Edgbaston Golf, Edgbaston Priory Squash; *Style*— Brian Bannister, Esq; ✉ 10 Strutt Close, Edgbaston, Birmingham B15 3PW (☎ 0121 455 7431); Brian Bannister Projects, 202 Hagley Road, Edgbaston, Birmingham B16 9PQ (☎ 0121 454 7373, fax 0121 454 3675)

BANNISTER, (Richard) Matthew; s of Richard Neville Bannister, of Sheffield, and Olga Margaret, *née* Bennett; *b* 16 March 1957; *Educ* King Edward VII Sch Sheffield, Univ of Nottingham (LLB); *m* 1, 23 June 1984, Amanda Gerrard, da of Dr (Alexander) Percy Walker, of Bentfield, Prestwick, Ayrshire; 1 da (Jessica b 3 Dec 1984); m 2, 14 Jan 1989, Shelagh Margaret, *née* MacLeod; 1 s (Joseph b 1 May 1990); *Career* presenter and reporter BBC Radio Nottingham 1978–81, presenter and prodr Capital Radio 1981–83, presenter Radio One Newsbeat 1983–85, head of news Capital Radio 1987–88 (asst head of news 1985–87); BBC: rejoined as managing ed Greater London Radio 1988–91, chief asst to BBC's Dir of Corporate Affrs 1991–92, project co-ordinator BBC Charter Renewal 1992–93, controller Radio One 1993–97, dir BBC Radio 1997–; memb: Radio Acad, Nat Tst; *Recreations* opera, theatre, rock music, collecting P G Wodehouse first editions; *Clubs* Reform; *Style*— Matthew Bannister, Esq; ✉ BBC Radio, Broadcasting House, London W1A 1AA (☎ 0171 580 4468)

BANNISTER, (Arthur) Neil; s of Arthur Bannister (d 1974), of Lytham, Lancashire, and Ida, *née* Powner; *b* 27 Aug 1936; *Educ* Manchester GS, Blackpool Catering Coll; *Career* Nat Serv personal cook GOC-C London dist 1955–57, stagiaire La Tour d'Argent Paris 1957–59, various asst mgmnt posts George Hotel Edinburgh 1960–68, co-proprietor Tullich Lodge 1968–; travelling scholarship HCI, Master Innholder 1981; Freeman City of London 1981; FCMA 1976 (MHCIMA 1955); *Clubs* Travellers'; *Style*— Neil Bannister, Esq; ✉ Tullich Lodge, By Ballater, Aberdeenshire, Scotland AB35 5SB (☎ 013397 55406, fax 013397 55397)

BANNISTER, Sir Roger Gilbert; kt (1975), CBE (1955); s of late Ralph Bannister and Alice Bannister, of Harrow; *b* 23 March 1929; *Educ* Univ Coll Sch London, Exeter and Merton Colls Oxford (MA, MSc, BM BCh, DM, MRCS, LRCP, MRCP), St Mary's Hosp Med Sch London; *m* 1955, Moyra, da of Per Jacobsson (chm IMF), of Sweden; 2 s, 2 da; *Career* athletics: winner Oxford v Cambridge Mile 1947–50, pres OUAC 1948, capt Oxford and Cambridge Combined American Team 1949, finalist Olympic Games Helsinki 1952, Br mile champion 1951, 1953 and 1954, first man to run 4 minute mile 1954, Br Empire Mile title and record 1954, Euro 1500m title and record 1954; jr med specialist RAMC 1958, Radcliffe travelling fell from Oxford Univ at Harvard 1962–63, conslt neurologist Western Ophthalmic Hosp 1963–85; hon conslt physician Nat Hosp for Nervous Diseases London (formerly conslt physician); hon conslt neurologist: St Mary's Hosp London (formerly conslt neurologist), Oxford Regnl and Dist Health Authy 1985–93; master Pembroke Coll Oxford 1985–93; chm Govt Working Gp on Sport in Univs 1995–96; memb: Cncl King George's Jubilee Tst 1961–67, Miny of Health Advsy Ctee on Drug Dependence 1967–70; chm: Sports Cncl 1971–74, Med Ctee St Mary's Hosp 1983–85; pres: Nat Fitness Panel NABC 1956–59, Sussex Assoc of Youth Clubs 1972–79, Int Cncl for Sport and Physical Recreation 1976–83, Alzheimer's Disease Soc 1982–84; govr: Atlantic Coll 1985–92, Sherborne Sch 1989–93; Liveryman Worshipful Soc of Apothecaries; hon fell: UMIST 1974, Exeter Coll Oxford 1979, Merton Coll Oxford 1986; Hon LLD Univ of Liverpool 1972, Hon DLitt Univ of Sheffield 1978; Hon Doctorate: Jyvaskyla Univ Finland 1983, Univ of Bath 1984, Imperial Coll London 1984, Srinnell USA 1984, Univ of Rochester NY USA 1985, Univ of Pavia Italy 1986, Williams Coll USA 1987, Univ of Wales Cardiff 1995, Univ of Loughborough 1996; FRCP; *Books* Brain's Clinical Neurology (ed, 3–7 edn 1966–92), Autonomic Failure (1 and 2 edn 1983 and 1988, 3 edn (with C J Mathias) 1992); author of numerous papers on neurology and disorders of the autonomic nervous system; *Clubs* Athenaeum, United Oxford & Cambridge Univ, Vincent's (Oxford); *Style*— Sir Roger Bannister, CBE; ✉ 21 Bardwell Road, Oxford OX2 6SU (☎ 01865 511413)

BANNOCK, Graham Bertram; s of Eric Burton Bannock (d 1977), and Winifred, *née* Sargent (d 1972); *b* 10 July 1932; *Educ* Crewkerne Sch, LSE (Bsc); *m* 26 Feb 1971, Françoise Marcelle, *née* Vranckx; 1 s (Laurent Graham b 1972); *Career* Sgt RASC 1950–52; market analyst Ford Motor Co 1955–56; asst mangr; market res Richard Thomas & Baldwins Ltd 1957–58, Rover Co 1958–60; sr admin OECD Paris 1960–62; chief of econ and market res Rover Co 1962–67; mangr Advanced Progs Ford of Europe Inc 1968–69, dir Res Ctee of Inquiry on Small Firms 1970–71; md: Econ Advsy Gp Ltd 1971–81, Economist Intelligence Unit Ltd 1981–84; chm: Graham Bannock & Ptnrs Ltd 1985–, Nutrafit Ltd 1996–; exec dir Central Banking Publications Ltd 1990–, dir Dai (USA) 1996–; *Books* Business Economics and Statistics (with A J Merrett, 1962), The Juggernauts (1971), The Penguin Dictionary of Economics (with R E Baxter and Evan Davis, 1972), How to Survive the Slump (1975), Smaller Business in Britain and Germany (1976), The Economics of Small Firms (1981), Going Public (1987), The Economist International Dictionary of Finance (1989, revised 1995), Governments and Small Business (with Sir Alan Peacock, 1989), Taxation in the European Community (1990), Small Business Policy in Europe (with Horst Albach, 1991), Corporate Takeovers and the Public Interest (with Sir Alan Peacock, 1991), Small Business Statistics (with Michael Daly, 1994); *Recreations* karate, the arts; *Clubs* Royal Automobile; *Style*— Graham Bannock, Esq; ✉ Graham Bannock & Partners Ltd, 53 Clarewood Court, Crawford St, London W1H 5DF (☎ 0171 723 1845)

BANSKI, Norman Alexander Fyfe Ritchie; s of Richard Carol Stanislaw Bański, Lt 9 Polish Lancers, of Kincardineshire (d 1970), and Marion Alexandra Watt Fyfe (now Mrs George A Ritchie); *b* 3 Aug 1955; *Educ* Laurencekirk Secdy Sch, Mackie Acad Stonehaven, Univ of Aberdeen (LLB); *Career* slr and NP; ptnr W J C Reed & Sons, registrar births deaths and marriages, cemetery clerk, census offr (S Kincardine) 1981 and 1991; sec and dir Milltown Community (adults with special needs); tstee various local charitable tsts, dir Howe O'The Mearns Developments Ltd; sec Villages in Control, memb Laurencekirk and Dist Business Club; hon vice pres: Laurencekirk and Dist Angling Assoc, PM Lodge St Laurence 136; past princ: Chapter Haran 8; memb: Law Soc of Scotland, Scottish Law Agents Soc, Assoc of Registrars for Scotland, WWF, Esk Dist Fishery Bd, Laurencekirk Business Club; *Recreations* golf, angling, clay pigeon shooting, sailing, philately, rugby, gliding; *Clubs* Laurencekirk and Dist Angling Assoc, Laurencekirk and District Business, F P Rugby, Lodge St Laurence 136, Chapter Haran 8, Auchenblae Golf; *Style*— Norman Bański, Esq; ✉ W J C Reed & Sons, Royal Banks Buildings, Laurencekirk

BANSZKY VON AMBROZ, Baroness Caroline Janet; da of Harold Arthur Armstrong While (d 1982), of East Molesey, Surrey, and Janet Bell Symington, *née* Clark; *b* 24 July 1953; *Educ* Wycombe Abbey Sch, Univ of Exeter (BA); *m* 31 March 1984 (m dis 1995), Baron Nicholas Laszlo Banszky von Ambroz, *qv*, s of Baron Dr Laszlo Banszky von Ambroz; 2 da (Genevra b 15 April 1985, Antonella b 1 Aug 1987); *Career* formerly articled clerk rising to audit asst mangr KPMG Peat Marwick McLintock; N M Rothschild & Sons Ltd: Corp Fin Div 1981–84, Fin Div 1984–, chief fin offr 1988–89, exec dir 1989–, fin dir 1995–; Liveryman Worshipful Co of Farriers 1978–; FCA 1991 (ACA 1978); *Recreations* children, riding, skiing; *Style*— Baroness Nicholas Banszky von Ambroz; ✉ N M Rothschild & Sons Ltd, New Court, St Swithins Lane, London EC4P 4DU (☎ 0171 280 5000, fax 0171 283 4278)

BANSZKY VON AMBROZ, Baron (Hungary) Nicholas Laszlo; s of Baron Dr Laszlo Banszky von Ambroz (d 1965), of London, and Veronica, *née* Racz (now Lady Wyatt of Weeford); *b* 18 July 1952; *Educ* Westminster, Worcester Coll Oxford (MA); *m* 31 March 1984 (m dis 1995), Caroline Janet, *qv*, da of Harold Arthur Armstrong While, of East Molesey, Surrey; 2 da (Genevra b 15 April 1985, Antonella b 1 Aug 1987);

Career merchant banker; N M Rothschild & Sons Ltd 1974–84, Charterhouse J Rothschild Gp 1984–86, Smith New Court plc 1986–95 (dir 1988–95), dir Smith Borkum Hare (Pty) Ltd SA 1996– (joined 1995, currently head of corp fin); *Recreations* riding, skiing, cooking; *Style—* Baron Nicholas Banszky von Ambroz; ✉ Smith Borkum Hare (Pty) Ltd, 27 Diagonal Street, Johannesburg 2001, Republic of South Africa (☎ 00 27 11 498 6195, fax 00 27 11 836 9540, telex 4-87002)

BANTING, Ven (Kenneth) Mervyn Lancelot Hadfield; s of Rev Canon H M Bantang (d 1985), and P M Bantang, *née* Hadfield (d 1993); *b* 8 Sept 1937; *Educ* Tonbridge, Pembroke Coll Cambridge (MA), Cuddesdon Coll Oxford; *m* 1970, Linda, da of Rear Adm P D Gick; 4 da (Jessica b 1972, Frances Mary b 1974, Alice Elizabeth Ingrid 1977, Ruth Eleanor b 1979); *Career* Nat Serv RN 1956–58; asst chaplain Winchester 1965–70 (asst master 1961–64), asst curate St Francis' Leigh Park Dio of Portsmouth 1970–73, team vicar St Paul's Highfield Hemel Hempstead Dio of St Albans 1973–79, vicar St Mary the Virgin Goldington Dio of St Albans 1979–88, rural dean of Bedford Dio of St Albans 1984–87, vicar St Cuthbert's Portsea Dio of Portsmouth, rural dean of Portsmouth 1994–96, hon canon Portsmouth Cathedral 1995–96, archdeacon of the Isle of Wight 1996–; *Recreations* sailing, electrical vehicles, horology; *Style—* The Ven the Archdeacon of the Isle of Wight; ✉ 3 Beech Grove, Ryde, Isle of Wight PO33 3AH (☎ 01983 565522, fax 01983 565522, mobile 0385 588906)

BANTON, Prof Michael Parker; JP (Bristol 1966); s of Francis Clive Banton (d 1985), of Maids Morton, Buckingham, and Kathleen Blanche, *née* Parkes (d 1945); *b* 8 Sept 1926; *Educ* King Edward's Sch Birmingham, LSE (BScEcon), Univ of Edinburgh (PhD, DSc); *m* 23 July 1952, (Rut) Marianne, da of Lars Robert Jacobson (d 1954), of Lulea, Sweden; 2 s (Sven Christopher b 1953, Nicholas b 1956 d 1994), 2 da (Ragnhild b 1955, Dagmar b 1959); *Career* Sub-Lt RNVR 1946–47; reader in social anthropology Univ of Edinburgh 1962–65 (lectr 1955–62); Univ of Bristol: prof of sociology 1965–92, emeritus prof 1992–, pro-vice chllr 1985–88; visiting prof: MIT 1962–63, Wayne State Univ Detroit 1971, Univ of Delaware 1976, ANU 1981, Duke Univ 1982; ed Sociology 1966–69; memb Royal Cmmn on: Criminal Procedure 1978–81, Civil Disorders in Bermuda 1978; memb: UK Nat Cmmn for UNESCO 1963–66 and 1980–85, UN Ctee for Elimination of Racial Discrimination 1986– (chm 1996–98); pres Royal Anthropological Inst 1987–89; FRSA 1981; *Books* The Coloured Quarter (1955), West African City (1957), White and Coloured (1959), The Policeman in the Community (1964), Roles (1965), Race Relations (1967), Racial Minorities (1972), Police-Community Relations (1973), The Idea of Race (1977), Racial and Ethnic Competition (1983), Promoting Racial Harmony (1985), Investigating Robbery (1985), Racial Theories (1987), Racial Consciousness (1988), Discrimination (1994), International Action Against Racial Discrimination (1996), Ethnic and Racial Consciousness (1996); *Style—* Prof Michael Banton, JP; ✉ The Court House, Llanvair Discoed, Gwent NP6 6LX (☎ and fax 01633 400208)

BANVILLE, John; *Educ* Christian Brothers' Schs, St Peter's Coll Wexford; *m* Janet Dunham; 2 s (Colm, Douglas); *Career* novelist and journalist 1969–; currently lit ed The Irish Times; *Awards* incl: Allied Irish Banks Fiction Prize, American-Irish Fndn Award, James Tait Black Meml Prize, Guardian Prize for fiction, Guinness Peat Aviation Award, Premio Ennio Flaiano 1991; *Books* Long Lankin (short stories, 1970), Nightspawn (1971), Birchwood, Doctor Copernicus, Kepler, The Newton Letter, Mefisto, The Book of Evidence (shortlisted Booker Prize 1989), Ghosts (1993), Athena (1995); *Style—* John Banville, Esq; ✉ c/o Sheil Land Associates, 43 Doughty Street, London WC1N 2LF (☎ 0171 405 9351, fax 0171 831 2127)

BARBARITO, HE the Most Rev Luigi; Hon GCVO (1996); s of Vincenzo Barbarito (d 1923), and Alfonsina Armerini (d 1986); *b* 19 April 1922, Atripalda, Italy; *Educ* Pontifical Seminary Benevento Italy, Gregorian Univ Rome (JCD), Papal Diplomatic Acad (Dip); *Career* ordained priest 1944, served Dio of Avellino 1944–52; Dip Serv of Holy See: sec Apostolic Delgn in Aust 1953–59, Secretariat of State of Vatican (Cncl of Public Affrs for the Church) 1959–67, cnsllr Apostolic Nunciature Paris 1967–69, titular archbishop of Fiorentino 1969, papal nuncio to Haiti and del to Antilles 1969–75, pro-nuncio to Senegal, Bourkina Fasso, Niger, Mauritania, Cape Verde Is and Guinea Bissau 1975–78, apostolic pro-nuncio to Aust 1978–86, apostolic nuncio 1993– to Ct of St James's (apostolic pro-nuncio 1986–93); memb Papal Missions of Pope Paul VI to India 1964 and Portugal 1967, head Special Mission of Holy See for inauguration of new Philippines repub 1981; dean of Dip Corps: Canberra 1985–86, Ct of St James's 1993–; memb Mexican Acad of Int Law; Grand Cross: Nat Order of Haiti 1975, Order of the Lion (Senegal) 1978; Knight Cdr Order of Merit: Italy 1966, Portugal 1967; *Recreations* music, walking; *Style—* HE The Most Rev Luigi Barbarito, GCVO; ✉ Apostolic Nunciature, 54 Parkside, Wimbledon, London SW19 5NE (☎ 0181 946 1410, fax 0181 947 2494)

BARBENEL, Prof Joseph Cyril; s of Tobias and Sarah Barbenel; *b* 2 Jan 1937; *Educ* Hackney Down GS (Grocers' Co), Univ of London (BDS, prize in anatomy and dental anatomy), Univ of St Andrews (Nuffield fell, BSc, physics medal), Univ of Strathclyde (MSc, PhD, MRC Award for the further education in medical sciences); *m* 6 Aug 1964, Lesley Mary Hyde, *née* Jowett BDS LDS RCS(Eng); 1 da (Rachel b 14 July 1966), 2 s (David b 31 March 1968, Daniel b 2 Feb 1970); *Career* house surgn London Hosp 1960; Nat Serv Lt RADC Malaya 1960–61(Capt 1961–62); gen dental practice NHS London 1962–63; student Univ of St Andrews 1963–66; student Bioengineering Unit Univ of Strathclyde 1966–67; lectr Dept of Dental Prosthetics Dental Sch and Hosp Univ of Dundee 1967–69; Bioengineering Unit Univ of Strathclyde: sr lectr 1970–73, head of Tissue Mechanics Div 1973–82, reader 1982–85, personal prof 1985–89, prof 1989–, head of dept 1992–; visiting prof: Chongqing Univ China 1986–, Univ of Technology Vienna 1987–; pres: Biological Engrg Soc 1988–90, Tissue Viability Soc 1989–92; President's Medal Soc of Cosmetic Scientists 1994; FRSE 1986, FIBiol 1987, FInstP 1988, fell Inst of Physical Sciences in Medicine 1988, FRSM 1989, fell Biological Engrg Soc 1993; *Books* Progress in Bioengineering (co-ed, 1989), Blood Flow in the Brain (co-ed, 1989), Blood Flow in Artificial Organs and Cardiovascular Prostheses (co-ed, 1989); *Recreations* work, music, theatre, cinema, reading, travel; *Style—* Prof Joseph Barbenel, FRSE; ✉ 151 Maxwell Drive, Glasgow G41 5AE (☎ 0141 427 0765); University of Strathclyde, Bioengineering Unit, Wolfson Centre, 106 Rottenrow, Glasgow G4 0NW (☎ 0141 552 4400 ext 3221, fax 0141 552 6098, telex 77472 UNSLIB G)

BARBER, Prof Anthony Douglas; s of Douglas Robert Barber, of Southwold, Suffolk, and Jean, *née* Arnold; *b* 9 Oct 1946; *Educ* Ashlyns Sch Berkhamsted, Univ of Nottingham (BSc, PhD); *m* 4 July 1970, Margaret Rose, da of Evalds Liepnieks; 1 s (Jeremy Janis b 19 Aug 1973), 1 da (Julia Zahra b 13 Oct 1976); *Career* research fell Swiss Federal Inst of Technol (ETH) Zurich 1972–74, various positions as separations specialist Shell Research and Development 1974–84, research advsr Shell UK Exploration & Production 1982–84, head offshore research Koninklijke/Shell Exploratie en Produktie Laboratorium Rijswijk 1984–88, mangr equipment engrg Koninklijke/Shell Laboratorium Amsterdam 1988–96, dir engrg Institution of Chemical Engineers 1997–; special prof in chemical engrg Univ of Nottingham 1992–; memb: Syndicate Dept of Chemical Engrg Univ of Cambridge, Advsy Cncl Stevin Centre Tech Univ of Eindhoven; winner Moulton Medal (Instn of Chemical Engrs) 1974; CEng 1979, FIChemE 1986, MIMgt 1986, FEng 1996; *Publications* author of various papers on educn, foaming and offshore equipment incl: A Model for a Cellular Foam (1974), Foaming in Crude Distillation Units (1979), Some New Offshore Techniques (1988); *Recreations* genealogy, motor cruising, gardening; *Style—* Prof Anthony Barber, FEng; ✉ Longridge House, Church Lane, Church Brampton, Northampton NN6 8AT (☎ 01604 846593, fax 01604 846593); The Institution of Chemical Engineers, 165–189 Railway Terrace, Rugby, Warwicks CV21 3HQ (☎ 01788 578214, fax 01788 560833, e-mail adbarber@icheme.org.uk)

BARBER, Baron (Life Peer UK 1974), of Wentbridge, W Yorks; Anthony Perrinott Lysberg Barber; PC (1963), TD, DL; s of late John Barber, CBE, of Doncaster, and Musse, *née* Lysberg; *b* 4 July 1920; *Educ* Retford GS, Oriel Coll Oxford (MA); *m* 1, 1950, Jean Patricia (d 1983), da of Milton Asquith, of Wentbridge; 2 da (Hon Louise Patricia Lysberg b 1951, Hon Josephine Julia Asquith (Hon Mrs Bradby) b 1952); m 2, 8 Sept 1989, Mrs Rosemary Youens, da of Canon Youens of Brodsworth; *Career* cmmnd Army 1939, seconded pilot RAF 1940–45 (despatches, POW); called to the Bar Inner Temple 1948; MP (C): Doncaster 1951–64, Altrincham and Sale Feb 1965–Sept 1974; PPS to Under Sec of State for Air 1952–55, asst whip 1955–57, Lord Cmmr of the Treasy 1957–58, PPS to the PM 1958–59, econ sec to the Treasy 1959–62, fin sec to the Treasy 1962–63, min of health and memb Cabinet 1963–64, Chllr of the Duchy of Lancaster June-July 1970, Chllr of the Exchequer 1970–74; chm Cons Pty Orgn 1967–70; chm Standard Chartered Bank plc 1974–87 and dir of other banks, dir BP 1979–88; memb: Franks Ctee on The Falklands 1982, Cwlth Eminent Persons Gp on SA 1985–86; chm: Cncl Westminster Med Sch 1975–84, RAF Benevolent Fund 1991–; hon fell Oriel Coll Oxford 1971; *Clubs* Carlton, RAF; *Style—* The Rt Hon The Lord Barber, PC, TD, DL; ✉ House of Lords, London SW1

BARBER, Antonia; *see:* Anthony, Barbara

BARBER, Daniel Mark; s of David and Gillian Barber; *b* 21 Sept 1964; *Educ* JFS Comp Sch, St Martin's Sch of Art (BA Graphic Design); *m* 6 June 1992, Sandra, da of Léo Rogg; *Career* designer/dir Lambie Nairn & Co 1988–93; creator of title sequence for BBC Nine O'Clock News and station identities for BBC1, BBC2, Carlton TV and various Euro TV stations; Rose Hackney Barber Productions (formerly Rose Hackney): commercials dir 1993–, ptnr 1995–; creator of TV and cinema commercials for clients incl BMW, Sony, Orange and Ford; recipient of numerous awards/honours from indust bodies incl BAFTA, D&AD, BTA, RTS, Clio and Creative Circle; subject of profile articles in many indust magazines in Europe and America, work published in major design and advtg pubns; memb D&AD; *Recreations* cinema, tennis, shopping, dieting, travel; *Style—* Daniel Barber; ✉ Rose Hackney Barber Productions, 6–8 Kingly Court, London W1R 5LE (☎ 0171 439 6697)

BARBER, Sir (Thomas) David; 3 Bt (UK 1960), of Greasley, Co Nottingham; s of Sir William Francis Barber, 2 Bt, TD (d 1995), and his 1 w, Diana Constance, *née* Lloyd (d 1984); *b* 18 Nov 1937; *Educ* Eton, Trinity Coll Cambridge (MA); *m* 1, 1972 (m dis 1975), Amanda Mary, da of Frank Rabone, and wid of Maj Michael Healing, Gren Guards; 1 s (Thomas Edward b 14 March 1973); m 2, 1978, Jeannine Mary, former w of John Richard Boyle (gs of Col Lionel Boyle, CMG, MVO, himself gs of 7 Earl of Cork and Orrery), by whom she had 3 s, and da of Capt Timothy John Gurney by his w Bridget, half sister of Sir Christopher de Bathe, 6 and last Bt; 1 s (William Samuel Timothy b 23 Sept 1982), 1 da (Sarah Emily b 19 June 1981); *Heir* s, Thomas Edward Barber b 14 March 1973; *Career* 2 Lt RA 1957–58; *Style—* Sir David Barber, Bt; ✉ Windrush House, Inkpen, nr Hungerford, Berks RG17 9QY (☎ 01488 668 419)

BARBER, Prof David John; s of George William Barber (d 1981), and Amelia Sarah, *née* Harris (d 1973); *b* 14 Feb 1935; *Educ* Wanstead HS London, Univ of Bristol (BSc, PhD); *m* 1, 26 July 1958 (m dis 1974), Vivien Joan, da of Leslie George Hayward (d 1969); 2 s (Douglas b 1961, Peter b 1961, d 1979), 2 da (Rosalind b 1964, Alison b 1966); m 2, 17 Oct 1975, Jill Elizabeth Edith, da of Frank Joseph Sanderson, of Great Holland, Essex; 1 s (Alastair b 1978); *Career* investigator Alcan International 1959–62, gp leader Nat Bureau of Standards USA 1963–65 (scientist 1962–63); Univ of Essex: lectr 1965–74, sr lectr 1974–78, prof of physics 1979–96, pro vice chllr 1981–85; prof Dept of Physics Univ of Sci and Technol Hong Kong 1989–96; visiting prof: Dept of Physics Univ of Essex 1996–, Sch of Industl and Mfrg Sci Cranfield Univ 1996–; visiting scholar: Univ of California 1970–71, 1980, 1989, 1991 and 1995, Pennsylvania State Univ 1979–80, State Univ of NY 1989; vice pres Mineralogical Soc (GB) 1987–88 (memb Cncl 1985–88); memb: Mineralogical Soc GB, Mineralogical Soc USA; CPhys, FInstP, CEng, FIM; *Books* Introduction to the Properties of Condensed Matter (with R Loudon, 1989), Deformation Processes in Minerals, Ceramics and Rocks (ed with P G Meredith, 1990); *Recreations* sailing, gardening, carpentry; *Clubs* Royal Harwich Yacht; *Style—* Prof David Barber; ✉ Department of Physics, University of Essex, Colchester, Essex (☎ 01206 872850, fax 01206 873598); School of Industrial and Manufacturing Science, Cranfield University, Cranfield, Bedfordshire MK43 0AL

BARBER, David Stewart; s of Jack Barber (d 1961), of Manchester, and Margaret, *née* Hall (d 1960); *b* 21 Sept 1931; *Educ* Rossendale GS; *m* 25 Jan 1965, Hazel Valerie, da of Francis Smith (d 1968), of Whitstable, Kent; 1 s (Nicholas b 1968), 1 da (Suzanna b 1971); *Career* 2 Lt Lancs Fus 1950–52; trainee and subsequently mangr Imperial Tobacco Co (John Player & Sons) 1952–57, PA Mgmnt Conslts (various appts) 1958–69, divnl chief exec Bovis Ltd 1969–71, chm and chief exec Halma plc 1972–95 (chm 1995–); *Recreations* tennis, golf; *Style—* David Barber, Esq; ✉ Halma plc, Misbourne Court, Rectory Way, Amersham, Bucks HP7 0DE (☎ 01494 721111, fax 01494 728032)

BARBER, Donald Christopher (Chris); OBE; s of Donald Barber, CBE (d 1957), of West Byfleet, Surrey, and Henrietta Mary Evelyn Barber, JP, *née* Dunne; *b* 17 April 1930; *Educ* King Alfred Sch, St Paul's, Guildhall Sch of Music; *m* 1, 1954 (m dis 1959), Naida Lane, of London; m 2, 1959 (m dis 1983), Ottilie Patterson, of Comber, Co Down; m 3, 1984 (m dis 1992), Renate Barber-Hilbich, of Germany; 1 da (Caroline Mary b 1980), 1 s (Christopher Julian b 1985); *Career* jazz musician; instruments played: trombone, trumpet, baritone horn, double bass; formed amateur 1949 band then played in cooperative band with Ken Colyer 1953–54; fndr and ldr Chris Barber's Jazz and Blues Band 1954–: over 150 LPs, CDs, etc, extensive tours to USA, Japan, Aust, Middle East and E and W Europe, playing approx 250 engagements each year; hon citizen New Orleans USA; *Recreations* motor racing, snooker, collecting Jazz and Blues records and antiques; *Style—* Chris Barber, Esq, OBE; ✉ Cromwell Management, 4/5 High St, Huntingdon, Cambridgeshire PE18 6TE (☎ 01480 435600 fax 01480 435155)

BARBER, Edmund Patrick Harty; s of Maj Leslie Bernard Michael Barber (d 1983), of Marley House, Marley Commom, Haselmere, and Ellen, *née* Harty; *b* 25 Aug 1946; *Educ* Glenstal Abbey Sch Co Limerick, Univ Coll Dublin; *m* 20 Dec 1969, Elizabeth Marguerite, da of Eric Fowler Sherriff, of Tewin, Welwyn, Herts; 1 s (Samuel), 2 da (Catherine, Lucy); *Career* CA 1973– (specialising in int tax work and acquisition and disposal); dir: Rigidized Metals Ltd, Courtyard Leisure plc; Freeman City of London, memb Worshipful Co of Chartered Accountants; FCA 1973; *Recreations* squash, golf; *Clubs* Naval and Military, Leander, Reform, MCC; *Style—* Edmund Barber, Esq; ✉ 1 Harmer Green Lane, Digswell, Welwyn, Herts (☎ 01438 716088, fax 01438 840841); Flat 2, 25 Maiden Lane, Covent Garden, London WC2E 7NA (☎ 0171 379 0422, fax 0171 379 6141); 17–18 Henrietta St, Covent Garden, London WC2E 8QH (☎ 0171 379 7711, fax 0171 240 2618)

BARBER, Frances Jennifer; da of S W Brookes, of Wolverhampton, and Gladys, *née* Simpson (d 1991); *b* 13 May 1958; *Educ* Municipal GS Wolverhampton, Univ of Bangor, Univ of Cardiff; *Career* actress; memb: Dr Barnados, Terence Higgins Tst, Cancer Research, The Labour Party; prodn bd memb BFI 1995–; *Theatre* incl: Ooh La La for Hull Truck (Plays and Players Award Most Promising Newcomer nomination 1980), Riff Raff Rules, Space Ache (Tricycle Theatre), La Guerra, Desperado Corner, Madam

Louise (Glasgow Citizen's and Venice Festival), The Treat (ICA), The Mission (Soho Poly), Hard Feelings (Oxford Playhouse and Bush Theatre), Summer and Smoke (Leicester Haymarket), Viola in Twelfth Night, Lady Macbeth in Macbeth (Exchange Manchester), Eliza Doolittle in Pygmalion, Maxine Faulk in The Night of the Iguana (RNT), My Heart's A Suitcase (Royal Court), Over a Barrel (Palace Theatre Watford), Imagine Drowning (Hampstead), Insignificance (Donmar); for RSC credits incl: Camille (Olivier Award for Most Promising Newcomer 1985), Ophelia in Hamlet, Jacquetta in Love's Labour's Lost, Dolores in The Dead Donkey; *Television* incl: Home Sweet Home, A Flame to the Phoenix, Those Glory Days, Reilly Ace of Spies, Hard Feelings, Clem, Twelfth Night, Duck, Annie Besant, Behaving Badly, The Grasscutter, The Nightmare Years, The Storey Teller - The Greek Myths, Do Not Disturb, The Orchid House, Hancock, Inspector Morse, The Leaving of Liverpool, A Statement of Affairs, Inspector Alleyn, Spitting Image - Thatcherworld, Return to Blood River, In the Cold Light of Day, Dirty Old Town, Circle of Deceit, Rules of Engagement, Space Precinct, Rhodes, It Might be You, Royal Scandal; *Films* incl: Rosie in Sammy and Rosie Get Laid, Megan in We Think the World of You, Leonie Orton in Prick up your Ears, A Zed and Two Noughts, Castaway, The Missionary, Acceptable Levels, White City, The Soul of the Machine, Young Soul Rebels, Secret Friends, The Lake, Soft Top, Hard Shoulder, The Fish Tale, Scarborough Ahoy! (Best Foreign Student American Academy Award), Three Steps to Heaven; also three french speaking films: Chambre a Part, Giorgino, Germaine et Benjamin; *Recreations* swimming, reading, walking the dog, poetry; *Style*— Ms Frances Barber

BARBER, Frank; s of Sidney Barber, and Florence, *née* Seath; *b* 5 July 1923; *Educ* W Norwood Central Sch; *m* 1, Dec 1945, Gertrude Kathleen, *née* Carson (d 1994); 2 s (John b 1951, Alan b 1947 decd), 1 da (Ann b 1948); m 2, Elizabeth Joan Charvet; *Career* WWII Flt Lt RAFVR 1942–46; Lloyd's 1939–, underwriter Frank Barber & others 1962–81; ptnr: Morgan Fentiman & Barber 1968– (sr ptnr 1994), GS Christensen and Partners 1986–; chm Alan Grant (Underwriting Agencies) Ltd 1991–; Lloyd's of London: memb Ctee 1977–80, 1981–85 and 1987, memb Cncl 1983–85 and 1987, dep chm 1983–84; chm Lloyd's Underwriters Non Marine Assoc 1972 (dep chm 1971); dep chm Br Insurers' Euro Ctee 1983; *Recreations* music, walking, sailing; *Style*— Frank Barber, Esq; ✉ Doiley Hill House, Hurstbourne Tarrant, Andover, Hants SP11 0ER (☎ 01264 736595, fax 01264 736229)

BARBER, Giles Gaudard; s of Eric Arthur Barber (d 1965), and Alice Madeleine, *née* Gaudard (d 1968); *b* 15 Aug 1930; *Educ* Dragon Sch Oxford, Leighton Park Sch Reading, St John's Coll Oxford (MA, BLitt, Gordon Duff prize); *m* 1, 3 Sept 1958, Monique (d 1969), da of H Fluchère, of Sainte Tulle, France; 1 da (Isabelle b 1962); m 2, 19 July 1970 (m dis 1997), Gemma, da of G Miani, of Venice, Italy; 2 s (Simon b 1973, Mark b 1977), 1 da (Francesca b 1974); *Career* Univ of Oxford: asst Bodleian Library 1954–70, fell Linacre Coll 1963–96, emeritus fell 1996–, lectr in continental bibliography 1969–96, librarian Taylor Instn 1970–96, vice princ Linacre Coll 1989–91; Graham Pollard meml lectr 1984, Moses Tyson lectr Univ of Manchester 1985, Panizzi lectr Br Library 1988, Homee Randeria lectr 1994; memb: Cncl Int Soc for Eighteenth Century Studies 1979–83, Univ of Oxford Libraries Bd, Cncl The Bibliographical Soc London (vice pres 1983–92); dir Voltaire Fndn Oxford (chm 1987–89); pres Oxford Bibliographical Soc 1992–96; officer Ordre des Arts et des Lettres (France) 1992; author of numerous articles in learned jls; *Books* Fine Bindings in Oxford Libraries 1500–1700 (co-author, 1968), A Checklist of French Printing Manuals (1969), Textile and Embroidered Bindings (1971), Book Making in Diderot's Encyclopédie (1973), N Contat - Anecdotes Typographiques (ed, 1980), Buch und Buchhandlung in Europa im Achtzehnten Jahrhundert (co-ed, 1981), Enlightenment Essays in Memory of Robert Shackleton (co-ed, 1988), Daphnis and Chloe (1989), Studies in the Booktrade of the European Enlightenment (1994), Arks for Learning (1995); *Recreations* book collecting, gardening, looking at Oxford; *Style*— Giles Barber, Esq; ✉ 66 Woodstock Close, Oxford OX2 8DD (☎ 01865 556807); Linacre College, Oxford OX1 3JA (fax 01865 271668)

BARBER, Glynis; da of Frederick Werndly Barry van der Riet, of Durban, SA, and Heather Maureen, *née* Robb (d 1973); *Educ* Mountview Theatre Sch; *m* 1989, Michael Brandon, *qv*; *Career* actress; *Television* incl: Blake's 7 1981, Jane 1982, Harriet Makepeace in Dempsey and Makepeace 1984–86, Visitors 1980, Miss Marple, The Mirror Cracked 1992; *Films* incl: The Wicked Lady 1982, Jekyll and Hyde - The Edge of Sanity 1988, Tangier, The Hound of the Baskervilles; *Recreations* tennis, yoga; *Style*— Miss Glynis Barber; ✉ c/o Susan Shaper Management, 174–178 North Gower Street, London NW1 2NB (☎ 0171 388 6996, fax 0171 388 6848)

BARBER, Prof James; *b* 16 July 1940; *Educ* Univ Coll of Swansea (tech state scholar, BSc), UEA (Nuffield biological fell, MSc, PhD); *m* 1 s (b 1971), 1 da (b 1972); *Career* Unilever Biochemical Soc European fell Biophysics Dept Univ of Leiden 1967; Imperial Coll London: lectr Dept of Botany 1968–74, reader in plant physiology 1974–79, prof of plant physiology 1979–90, dean Royal Coll of Science 1989–91, head Dept of Biochemistry 1989–, dir Centre for Photomolecular Science 1990–, Ernst Chain prof of biochemistry 1990–; Miller visiting prof Univ of Calif Berkeley 1989; memb Exec Ctee Weizmann Inst Fndn London 1991–; memb editorial bds of numerous scientific jls; memb Academiae Europaeae 1989; Hon Dr Univ of Stockholm 1992; CChem, FRSC; *Books* Topics in Photosynthesis Vol 1–12 (series ed, 1976–92), Techniques and New Developments in Photosynthesis Research (ed with R Malkin), Trends in Photosynthesis Research (ed with H Medrano & M G Guerrero), Advances in Molecular Biology Vol 11 (ed), Frontiers in Molecular Biology (ed with B Andersson); published over 400 papers; *Recreations* sailing, gardening, carpentry; *Style*— Prof James Barber; ✉ Department of Biochemistry, Wolfson Laboratories, Imperial College of Science, Technology and Medicine, Exhibition Road, London SW7 2AY (☎ 0171 581 1316, fax 0171 581 1317)

BARBER, Prof James Peden; s of John Barber (d 1973), and Carrie Barber (d 1967); *b* 6 Nov 1931; *Educ* Liverpool Inst HS, Pembroke Coll Cambridge, Queen's Coll Oxford (MA, PhD); *m* 3 Sept 1955, (Margaret) June Barber, da of Henry James McCormac, of Beetham, Cumbria; 3 s (Michael James b 1958, Andrew John b 1959, Mark Henry b 1965), 1 da (Anne Elizabeth b 1965); *Career* Nat Serv PO RAF 1950–52; Colonial Serv Uganda: dist offr 1956–61, asst sec to PM and clerk to cabinet 1961–63; lectr Univ of NSW Aust 1963–65, lectr in govt Univ of Exeter 1965–69 (seconded to Univ Coll Rhodesia 1965–67), prof of political sci Open Univ 1969–80; Univ of Durham: master Hatfield Coll 1980–96, pro vice chllr 1987–92, sub warden 1990–92, prof of politics 1992–96; advsr to House of Commons Select Ctee on Foreign Affrs 1990–91; JP Bedford 1977–80; memb RIIA 1968; pres: Durham Univ Soc of Fellows 1988, Durham Univ Hockey Club 1981–96, Bd Cambridge Centre of Int Studies 1996–; Uganda Independence Medal; *Books* Rhodesia: The Road to Rebellion (1967), Imperial Frontier (1968), South Africa's Foreign Policy (1973), European Community: Vision and Reality (1974), The Nature of Foreign Policy (1975), Who Makes British Foreign Policy? (1977), The West and South Africa (1982), The Uneasy Relationship: Britain and South Africa (1983), South Africa: The Search for Status and Security (1990), The Prime Minister since 1945 (1991), The New South Africa (1994); *Recreations* hockey, walking, choral singing; *Clubs* Royal Cwlth Soc; *Style*— Prof James Barber; ✉ 14 North Terrace, Midsummer Common, Cambridge CB5 8DJ (☎ 01223 313453)

BARBER, John Norman Romney; s of George Ernest Barber, and Gladys Eleanor Barber; *b* 22 April 1919; *Educ* Westcliff HS; *m* 1941, Babette, da of Louis Chalu (d 1975); 1 s; *Career* co dir and business conslt; served Army 1939–46 (Capt); Miny of Supply 1946–55; fin dir: Ford Motor Co Ltd 1962–65 (joined 1955), AEI 1965–67; chm Telephone Cables Ltd 1967; British Leyland Motor Corporation Ltd: dir of fin and planning 1968–71, dep md 1971–73, dep chm 1973–75, md 1974–75; chm: Pullmaflex International Ltd 1976–79, Aberhurst Ltd 1976–89, A C Edwards Engineering Ltd 1977–81, Cox & Kings Financial Services Ltd 1980–85, C & K Consulting Group Ltd 1982–88; dir: Acrow plc 1977–84, Good Relations Group plc 1979–84, Amalgamated Metal Corporated Ltd 1980–81, Spear and Jackson International plc 1980–85, Economists Advisory Group Ltd 1981–, UK Investments Ltd 1985–, The Communications Group Holdings plc 1990–; dep chm: John E Wiltshier Group plc 1980–88 (dir 1979–88), Cox & Kings Ltd 1980–81; chm Advsy Ctee on Investmt Grants BOT 1967–68; memb: Royal Cmmn on Med Educn 1965–68, Cncl BIM 1967–71, Advsy Cncl for Energy Conservation 1974–75; vice pres SMMT 1974–76; CIMgt; *Clubs* British Automobile Racing; *Style*— John Barber, Esq; ✉ Balcary, Earleswood, Cobham, Surrey KT11 2BZ; Economists Advisory Group Ltd, 38 Spring St, London W2 1JA (☎ 0171 224 9100, fax 0171 224 9061)

BARBER, Lynn; da of Richard Barber, of Ebbesborne Wake, Wilts, and Beryl Barber; *b* 22 May 1944; *Educ* The Lady Eleanor Holles Sch for Girls, St Anne's Coll Oxford (BA); *m* 1 Sept 1971, David Maurice Cloudesley Cardiff, s of Maj Maurice Cardiff, CBE, of Little Haseley, Oxford; 2 da (Rose b 1975, Theodora b 1978); *Career* asst ed Penthouse magazine 1967–72, staff writer Sunday Express Magazine 1984–89, feature writer Independent on Sunday 1990–93, contributing ed Vanity Fair 1992; columnist Sunday Times 1993, currently feature writer The Observer; Br Press Awards: Magazine Writer of the Year 1986 and 1987 (commended 1992), Feature Writer of the Year 1990; What the Papers Say Award Feature Writer of the Year 1990; *Books* How to Improve Your Man in Bed (1973), The Single Woman's Sex Book (1975), The Heyday of Natural History (1980), Mostly Men (1991); *Recreations* gossip; *Style*— Ms Lynn Barber; ✉ The Observer, 119 Farringdon Road, London EC1R 3ER (☎ 0171 278 2332, fax 0171 263 2991)

BARBER, Nicholas Charles Faithorn; s of Bertram Harold Barber (d 1982), and Nancy Lorraine, *née* Belsham (d 1984); *b* 7 Sept 1940; *Educ* Ludgrove, Shrewsbury, Wadham Coll Oxford (MA), Univ of Columbia NY (MBA); *m* 8 Jan 1966, Sheena Macrae, da of Donald Graham (d 1984); 2 s (James Henry b 1969, George Belsham b 1974), 1 da (Fenella Macrae b 1972); *Career* lectr Marlboro Coll Vermont 1963–64; Ocean Group plc (formerly Ocean Steam Ship Ltd) 1964–94: dir 1980–94, gp md 1986–87, gp chief exec 1987–94; dir: Costain Group plc 1990–93, Royal Insurance Holdings plc 1991–96 (dep chm 1994–96), Royal & Sun Alliance Insurance Group plc 1996–, Barings plc 1994–95, Bristol & West Building Society 1994–, Albright & Wilson plc 1995–; chm: Innovative Electronics Co 1996–, Agepower PLC 1996–; tstee: Nat Museums and Galleries Merseyside 1986–94, British Museum 1993– (chm British Museum Soc 1992–, chm British Museum Co 1996–); govr: Shrewsbury Sch 1983–, NIESR 1991–, London Business Sch 1993–; dir Liverpool Playhouse 1982–87, vice pres Liverpool Sch of Tropical Med 1988–; memb: Cncl Univ of Liverpool 1985–88, Advsy Ctee Tate Gall Liverpool 1988–92, Cncl Industrial Soc 1993–; *Recreations* cricket, mountain walking, destructive gardening; *Clubs* Oxford and Cambridge, MCC; *Style*— Nicholas Barber, Esq; ✉ Flat 6, Lytton Court, 14 Barter Street, London WC1A 2AH (☎ 0171 831 3393)

BARBER, Rt Rev Paul Everard; *see:* Brixworth, Bishop of

BARBER, Ralph Gordon; s of John Leslie Barber, and Margaretta Primrose, *née* Sanders; *b* 2 Jan 1951; *m* Elizabeth Anne Barber; *Career* co sec: The Hongkong and Shanghai Banking Corporation 1986–92, HSBC Holdings plc 1990–, Midland Bank 1994–96; FCIS, FRSA; *Clubs* The Royal Hong Kong Golf, The Bankers; *Style*— Ralph Barber, Esq; ✉ HSBC Holdings plc, 10 Lower Thames Street, London EC3R 6AE (☎ 0171 260 6688, fax 0171 260 8249)

BARBER, Dr Richard William; s of Dr Geoffrey Osborn Barber (d 1988), of Dunmow, Essex, and Daphne, *née* Drew (d 1982); *b* 20 Oct 1941; *Educ* Felsted Sch, Marlborough (sr scholarship), Corpus Christi Coll Cambridge (MA, PhD, Trevelyan scholarship); *m* 1970, Helen Rosemary, *née* Tolson; 1 s (Humphrey Thomas b 1974), 1 da (Elaine Mary b 1976); *Career* publisher and author; fndr md Boydell Press (now Boydell & Brewer Ltd) 1969–; founding dir Univ of Rochester Press NY 1989; FRSL 1970, FRHistS 1976, FSA 1978; *Books* Arthur of Albion (1961), Henry Plantagenet (1963), The Knight and Chivalry (1970, Somerset Maugham Award, new edn 1995), The Figure of Arthur (1974), Edward Prince of Wales and Aquitaine (1976), Companion Guide to Southwest France (1977, new edn 1991, TES Info Book Award 1978), A Companion to World Mythology (1979), The Arthurian Legends (1979), King Arthur (1986), Tournaments (with Juliet Barker, 1989), Pilgrimages (1991); ed for Folio Soc: Aubrey's Brief Lives (1975), Life and Campaigns of the Black Prince (1979), The Pastons (1981), Fuller's Worthies (1987), The Worlds of John Aubrey (1988), Bestiary (1992); *Recreations* sailing, gardening, travel, music; *Style*— Dr Richard Barber, FSA, FRSL; ✉ Boydell & Brewer Ltd, PO Box 9, Suffolk IP12 3DF

BARBER, Stephen David; s of Dr Frederick Barber, and Edith Renate Wolfenstein (d 1987); *b* 15 March 1952; *Educ* Univ Coll Sch, LSE (BScEcon); *m* 1 April 1978, Suzanne Jane, da of Graham Hugh Presland (d 1986); 1 s (Andrew Charles b 1985), 1 da (Claire Louise b 1982); *Career* ptnr Price Waterhouse 1985– (joined 1973); FCA; *Recreations* family, skiing, running, tennis, films; *Style*— Steve Barber, Esq; ✉ Price Waterhouse, 1 London Bridge Street, London SE1 9QL (☎ 0171 939 3000, fax 0171 403 5265, telex 884 657)

BARBER OF TEWKESBURY, Baron (Life Peer UK 1992), of Gotherington in the County of Gloucestershire; Sir Derek Coates Barber; kt (1984); s of Thomas Smith-Barber (d 1967), of Suffolk, and Elsie Agnes, *née* Coates (d 1967); descendant of John Coats whose three sons due to a disagreement swore not to bear his name 1870, instead they adopted Coates, Cotts and Coutts; *b* 17 June 1918; *Educ* RAC Cirencester; *m* 1 (m dis 1981); m 2, 1983, Rosemary Jennifer Brougham, da of Lt Cdr Randolph Brougham Pearson, RN (ka 1946); *Career* farmer and land conslt; fndr memb Farming & Wildlife Advsy Gp 1969–, environment conslt Humberts Chartered Surveyors 1972–93, ed chm BBC's Central Agric Advsy Ctee 1974–80, conslt Humberts Landplan 1974–89, chm Countryside Cmmn 1981–91, chm Booker plc Countryside Advsy Bd 1990–96; pres: Glos Naturalists Soc 1982–, RSPB 1990–91 (chm 1976–81, vice pres 1982–); patron Lancs Heritage Tst 1990, bd memb Centre for Econ and Environmental Devpt 1983–, tstee Farming and Wildlife Tst 1984–91, memb Advsy Ctee Centre for Agric Strategy 1985–88, dep chm The Groundwork Fndn 1985–91, vice pres Ornithology Soc of Middle East 1987–; memb Cncl: Rare Breeds Survival Tst 1987– (pres 1991–95), Br Tst for Ornithology 1987–89; pres: Royal Agric Soc of England 1991–92, The Hawk and Owl Tst 1992–96, Br Pig Assoc 1995–96; chm New Nat Forest Advsy Bd 1991–95; *Awards* John Haygarth Gold Medal in Agric 1939, Bledisloe Gold Medal for Distinguished Servs to UK Agric 1969, RSPB Gold Medal for Servs to Wildlife Conservation 1983, Massey-Ferguson Agric Award 1989, Royal Agric Soc of England Gold Medal for Distinguished Service to Agric 1991; Hon FRASE 1986, Hon DSc Univ of Bradford 1986; Queen's Silver Jubilee Medal 1977; *Books* Farming for Profits (with Keith Dexter, 1961), Farming in Britain Today (with Frances and J G S Donaldson, 1969), Farming and Wildlife: a Study in Compromise (1971), A History of Humberts (1980); *Recreations* birds, farming; *Clubs* Farmers'; *Style*— The Rt Hon Lord Barber of Tewkesbury; ✉ Chough House, Gotherington, Glos GL52 4QU (☎ 01242 673908)

BARBIERI, Margaret Elizabeth; da of Ettore Barbieri, and Lea Barbieri; *b* 2 March 1947; *Educ* Durban, Royal Ballet Sr Sch; *m* 1982, Iain Webb, soloist with the Royal Ballet; 1 s (Jason Alexander b July 1987); *Career* Sadler's Wells Royal Ballet: joined 1965, princ 1970, sr princ 1974–90; guest artist with Birmingham Royal Ballet 1990 and 1991; prodr, freelance teacher and coach 1990–, dir Classical Graduates Course London Studio Centre, artistic dir Images of Dance Co 1990–, govr Royal Ballet 1992–; since 1990 has staged: Ashton's Facade, De Valois' Rake's Progress, Cranko's Pineapple Doll, Markova's Les Sylphides, Petipa's Raymonda Act III and Kingdom of the Shades Act from La Bayadere, Swan Lake Act II, Paquita Act II; appeared with Royal Ballet throughout Europe and in Canada, USA, S America, Australia, New Zealand, China, Japan, Yugoslavia, India, Egypt, Israel and elsewhere; made guest appearances in USA, Germany, S Africa, France, Norway and Czechoslovakia; *Performances* with Royal Ballet incl: Giselle (first performance in the role at Covent Garden 1968), Sleeping Beauty (first performance Leeds 1969), Swan Lake (first performance Frankfurt 1977), Romeo and Juliet (first performance Covent Garden 1979), Papillon, The Taming of the Shrew, Coppélia, Les Sylphides, Raymonda Act III, Le Spectre de la Rose, La Vivandière, Petrushka, Ashton's La Fille Mal Gardée, Two Pigeons, The Dream, Façade, Wedding Bouquet and Rendezvous, Cranko's Lady and the Fool, Card Game and Pineapple Poll, MacMillan's The Invitation and Solitaire, Elite Syncopation, Summer in The Four Seasons, de Valois' Checkmate and The Rake's Progress, van Manen's Grosse Fugue and Tilt, Tudor's The Lilac Garden, Howard's Fête Etrange, Layton's Grand Tour, Hynd's Summer Garden, both Killar's and Rodrigues' Cinderella; created roles in ballets incl: Tudor's Knight Errant, Drew's From Waking Sleep, Sacred Circles and The Sword, Cauley's Ante-Room, Layton's Oscar Wilde, Thorpe's Game Piano, Killar's The Entertainers, Hynd's Charlotte Brontë, Wright's Summertide, Bintley's Metamorphosis and Flowers of the Forest, Corder's The Wand of Youth; *Recreations* classical music, theatre, gardening; *Style*— Miss Margaret Barbieri; ✉ Chiswick, London W4; The Royal Ballet Company, Covent Garden, London WC2

BARBOSA, HE Rubens Antonio; LVO; s of José Orlando Barbosa, and Lice Farina Barbosa; *b* 13 June 1938, São Paulo, Brazil; *Educ* Univ of Brazil (law degree), Instituto Rio Branco (grad), LSE (MA); *m* Maria Ignez Correa, da of Sergio Afonso Correa da Costa; 1 s (João Bernardo), 1 da (Mariana Correa da Costa); *Career* Brazilian diplomat; exec sec Brazilian Trade Cmmn with the Socialist countries of Eastern Europe 1976–84, head of staff of Min of External Rels 1985–86, under sec-gen for multilateral and special political affrs 1986–87, sec for int affrs Miny of Economy 1987–88, ambass/Brazilian perm rep to Latin-American Integration Assoc (ALADI) 1988–91, pres Ctee of Reps ALADI 1991–92, under sec-gen for regnl integration, economic affrs and foreign trade Miny of External Rels 1991–93, co-ordinator Brazilian section Mercosul - Southern Cone Common Market 1991–93, vice pres Perm Ctee on Foreign Trade Miny of External Rels 1992–93, Brazilian ambass to Ct of St James's 1994–; pres Assoc of Coffee Producing Countries 1994–; Grand Cross: Order of Rio Branco (Brazil), Order of the Liberator San Martin (Argentina), Order of the Aztec Eagle (Mexico); Cdr Legion d'Honneur, Kt Cdr Order of Merit (Italy); *Books* América Latina em Perspectiva: a Integração Regional da Retórica à Realidade (1991); articles in Brazilian newspapers and magazines; *Style*— HE Mr Rubens Barbosa, LVO; ✉ Brazilian Embassy, 32 Green Street, Mayfair, London W1Y 4AT (☎ 0171 499 0877, fax 0171 493 5105)

BARBOUR, Anthony George; adopted s of George Richard Barbour (d 1989), of Bolesworth Castle, Tattenhall, Chester, and s of Eva Elizabeth, *née* Houry (d 1983); *b* 19 Oct 1938; *Educ* Stowe, New Coll Oxford; *m* 12 Nov 1976, Diana Caroline, da of David Blackwell, of Combe, Oxford; 2 da (Nina Caroline b 1980, Cleo Diana b 1986); *Career* dir Bolesworth Estate Co Ltd 1960–, chm Cheshire CLA 1986–87, Parly candidate (Cons) Crewe 1964 and 1966; High Sheriff of Cheshire 1987–88; chm: Lady Verdin Tst, Tstees British Sporting Art Tst; memb Agric Land Tbnl 1976–89; *Recreations* collector of 20th century art, gardening, tennis; *Clubs* Brooks's, Mill Reef; *Style*— Anthony Barbour, Esq; ✉ Bolesworth Castle, Tattenhall, Chester CH3 9HQ (☎ 01829 782369, fax 01829 782294)

BARBOUR, James; OBE (1992); s of Thomas Jack Barbour (d 1985), and Flora Jean Barbour; *b* 16 Jan 1953; *Educ* Madras Coll, St Andrews Univ (BA Politics and Sociology); *partner* Rosalind Marjorie Doig; 1 s, 2 da; *Career* grad mgmnt trainee NHS Scotland 1977–79, admin Gtr Glasgow Health Bd 1979–83, unit admin Gt Ormond St Hosps 1983–86, gen mangr Royal Manchester Children's Hosp 1986–87, gen mangr Acute Servs Grampian Health Bd 1987–92; chief exec: Aberdeen Royal Hosps NHS Tst 1992–94, Central Manchester Healthcare NHS Tst 1994–; burgess City of Aberdeen, memb Ct and hon sr fell Univ of Manchester; EEC exchange scholarship W Germany 1981, alumnus London Business Sch 1989; memb RSA; *Recreations* sport, keeping fit, family; *Clubs* Royal Northern (Aberdeen); *Style*— James Barbour, Esq, OBE; ✉ Central Manchester Healthcare NHS Trust, Manchester Royal Infirmary, Oxford Road, Manchester M13 9WL (☎ 0161 276 1234, fax 0161 273 6211)

BARBOUR OF BONSKEID, Very Rev Prof Robert Alexander Stewart (Robin); KCVO (1991), MC (1945); s of Dr George Freeland Barbour of Bonskeid and Fincastle (d 1946), of Pitlochry, and Hon Helen Victoria, *née* Hepburne-Scott (d 1982), eldest da of 9 Lord Polwarth, CBE, DL; *b* 11 May 1921; *Educ* Rugby, Balliol Coll Oxford (MA), St Mary's Coll St Andrews (BD), Yale Univ (STM); *m* 18 March 1950, Margaret Isobel, da of Lt-Col Harold Pigot (d 1982), of Beccles; 3 s (Freeland b 1951, David b 1954, Andrew b 1959), 1 da (Alison b 1956); *Career* late Maj Scot Horse; lectr then sr lectr in New Testament language, literature and theology Univ of Edinburgh 1955–71, prof of New Testament exegesis Univ of Aberdeen 1971–85; dean Chapel Royal Scot 1981–91, Chaplain in Ordinary to HM The Queen in Scot 1976–91, prelate Priory of Scot of Order of St John 1977–93; master Christ's Coll Aberdeen 1977–82; chm Bd of Govrs Rannoch Sch 1971–77, chm Scot Churches' Cncl 1982–86; Hon DD St Andrews 1979; *Books* The Scottish Horse 1939–45 (1950), Traditio-Historical Criticism of the Gospels (1972), What is the Church for? (1973); *Recreations* music, rural pursuits; *Clubs* New (Edinburgh); *Style*— The Very Rev Prof Robert Barbour of Bonskeid, KCVO, MC; ✉ Old Fincastle, Pitlochry, Perthshire PH16 5RJ (☎ 01796 473209)

BARCLAY, Christopher Francis Robert; CMG (1967); s of Capt Robert Barclay (d 1941), of Toddington, Beds, and Annie Douglas Dowdeswell, *née* Davidson (d 1958); *b* 8 June 1919; *Educ* Summer Fields, Eton, Magdalen Coll Oxford (MA); *m* 1, 29 Sept 1950 (m dis 1962), Clare Justice, da of Sir John Monro Troutbeck, GBE, KCMG (d 1970), of Horsham; 2 s (Christopher b 1951, John b 1954), 1 da (Jane b 1955); m 2, 14 June 1962, Diana Elizabeth, da of Cdr (John) Michael Goodman (ka 1940); 1 s (Charles b 1963), 1 da (Henrietta b 1966); *Career* Army Offr Cadet 1939; RB: 2 Lt 1940, Capt 1942, Maj 1943; served ME (Egypt, Palestine, Iraq), demobbed 1946; HM Dip Serv: FO 1946, second sec Cairo 1947, first sec FO 1950, Bonn 1953, FO 1956, regnl info offr Beirut 1959, FO 1960, cnsllr and head Info Res Dept 1962, head Personnel Dept (trg and gen) FCO 1967, asst sec Civil Serv Dept 1969, DOE 1973, sec Govt Hospitality Fund 1976–80; memb Cncl City Univ 1976–84, chm Jt Nat Horse Educn and Trg Cncl 1988–90; Freeman City of London 1942, memb Ct of Assts Worshipful Co of Saddlers (Master 1983–84, Liveryman 1942); FRSA 1984; Cdr of the Order of the Infante DOM Henrique (Portugal) 1979; *Recreations* fishing, gardening; *Clubs* Army and Navy; *Style*— Christopher Barclay, Esq, CMG; ✉ Croft Edge, Hollyhock Lane, Painswick, Glos GL6 6XH (☎ 01452 812332)

BARCLAY, Sir Colville Herbert Sanford; 14 Bt (NS 1668), of Pierston, Ayrshire; s of late Rt Hon Sir Colville Adrian de Rune Barclay, KCMG, 3 s of 11 Bt; suc unc, Sir Robert Cecil de Belzim Barclay, 13 Bt, 1930; *b* 7 May 1913; *Educ* Eton, Trinity Coll Oxford (BA, MA); *m* 1949, Rosamond Grant Renton, da of late Dr Walter Armstrong Elliott, of Chandlers Ford, Hants; 3 s (Robert Colraine b 1950, Alistair James Elliott b 1952, Colville Edwin Ward b 1956); *Heir* s, Robert Colraine Barclay, *qv*, b 12 Feb 1950); *Career* third sec HM Dip Serv 1937–41; enlisted Navy 1941, Sub-Lt RNVR 1942, Lt 1943, Lt Cdr 1945, demobbed 1946; painter; exhibitor: Royal Acad, RBA, London Gp, Bradford City Gallery, Brighton Gallery; chm Royal London Homoeopathic Hosp 1970–74 (vice chm 1961–65); plant-hunting expeditions to Crete, Turkey, Cyprus, Réunion, Mauritius and Nepal 1966–81; *Books* Crete: Checklist of Vascular Plants (1986); *Recreations* gardening; *Clubs* Naval; *Style*— Sir Colville Barclay, Bt; ✉ Pitshill, Petworth, W Sussex GU28 9AZ (☎ 01798 861341)

BARCLAY, Hugh Maben; CB (1992); s of William Barclay (d 1972), and Mary Frances, *née* Laird (d 1983); *b* 20 Feb 1927; *Educ* Fettes, Gonville and Caius Coll Cambridge (MA); *m* 8 Sept 1956, Margaret Hilda Hope, da of George Gilbert Hope Johnston (d 1973), of Beith, Ayrshire and latterly of Sevenoaks, Kent, and Margaret Elizabeth Hope, *née* Johnstone (d 1986); 2 c (Alison b 1957, David b 1961); *Career* served RA Egypt 1948–50; Dept of the Clerk of the House of Commons: asst clerk 1950, sr clerk 1955, dep princ clerk 1967, princ clerk 1976, clerk of Standing Ctees 1976, clerk of Private Bills 1982, clerk of Public Bills 1988–91; *Style*— Hugh Barclay, Esq, CB; ✉ 37 Stockwell Green, London SW9 9HZ (☎ 0171 274 7375)

BARCLAY, James Christopher; s of Theodore David Barclay (d 1981), and Anne Millard, *née* Bennett (d 1996); *b* 7 July 1945; *Educ* Harrow; *m* 1975, Rolleen Anne, da of Lt-Col Walter Arthur Hastings Forbes (d 1987); 2 c; *Career* served 15/19 King's Royal Hussars 1964–67; bill broker; chm and jt md Cater Allen Ltd (bankers) 1981–, chm Cater Allen Holdings plc 1985– (dep chm 1981–85); chm London Discount Market Assoc 1988–90; *Recreations* fishing, shooting; *Clubs* Pratt's, Boodle's; *Style*— James Barclay, Esq; ✉ Cater Allen Holdings plc, 20 Birchin Lane, London EC3V 9DJ (☎ 0171 623 2070, fax 0171 283 0604)

BARCLAY, Dr John Martyn Gurney; s of Dr Oliver Rainsford Barclay, of Leicester, and Dorothy, *née* Knott (d 1963); *b* 31 July 1958; *Educ* Univ Coll Sch London, Queens' Coll Cambridge (scholar, MA, PhD); *m* 22 Aug 1981, Diana Jane, da of Hon Mr Justice Knox, *qv*; 2 s (Robert James b 14 July 1986, David Timothy b 3 Sept 1988), 1 da (Frances Elizabeth b 14 May 1991); *Career* res student Univ of Cambridge 1981–84, sr lectr Dept of Theology and Religious Studies Univ of Glasgow 1996– (lectr 1984–96); memb: Studiorum Novi Testamenti Societas 1990, Soc of Biblical Literature 1993; *Books* Obeying the Truth (1988), Jews in the Mediterranean Diaspora (1996); *Recreations* music, cycling, walking; *Style*— Dr John Barclay; ✉ Department of Theology and Religious Studies, University of Glasgow, Glasgow G12 8QQ (☎ 0141 330 4603, fax 0141 330 4943)

BARCLAY, Joseph Gurney; s of Sir Roderick Edward Barclay, GCVO, KCMG (d 1996); *b* 17 Jan 1946; *Educ* Harrow, St Edmund Hall Oxford, INSEAD; *m* 1978, Joanna, da of late Brig Anthony Douglas Brindley, CBE; 1 s, 2 da; *Career* Barclays Bank PLC: joined 1969, mangr Mayfair 1976–78, local dir Birmingham 1978–85, res dir (then dep chm) Barclays Bank SA Paris 1986–91, city dir 54 Lombard Street 1992–, dir London C of C and Industry 1992–94; *Recreations* shooting, wine, travel; *Clubs* Brooks's; *Style*— Joseph Barclay, Esq; ✉ c/o Barclays Bank, 54 Lombard Street, London EC3V 9EX

BARCLAY, Brig Neil; DL (Shropshire 1986); s of Eric Lionel Barclay (d 1974), of Chelmsford, Essex, and Muriel Clare, *née* Copeland (d 1975); *b* 18 April 1917; *Educ* private; *m* 27 Sept 1941, Mary Emma (Mollie), da of David Scott-Shurmer (d 1964), of Bicknacre, Essex; 1 s (John Allardice b 7 Aug 1944), 3 da (Jane Allardice b 13 Jan 1947, Mary Allardice b 23 Sept 1954 (d 19 March 1991), Emma Allardice b 4 Nov 1957); *Career* RHA TA 1933–38, RA and Airborne RA 1939–51; served: Gibraltar, Malta, Cyprus, Egypt, Palestine, at sea with the RN, W Africa, NW Europe (Airborne Forces), India; transferred RAOC 1951; served: Libya, Persia, Egypt, Germany, E Africa, S Arabia and Persian Gulf; Lt-Col 1958, Col 1964, Brig 1968; writer and journalist 1933–39; sr princ planning inspr DOE 1972–89; vice pres St John Cncl Shropshire; memb: Co Ctee SSAFA, jt TA/Cadet Ctee; vice chm ABF Shropshire; pres: ACF League Branch, RA Assoc Branch; FASMC 1962, FIMgt 1968, FCIArb 1973; KStJ 1987; *Recreations* travelling, good companions, gardening; *Clubs* Army & Navy, Muthaiga (Nairobi); *Style*— Brig Neil Barclay, DL; ✉ Strinebrook House, The Hincks, Lilleshall, Newport, Shropshire (☎ 01952 604204)

BARCLAY, Norman Veitch Lothian; s of James Barclay, JP (d 1963), and Florence, *née* Lothian (d 1976); *Educ* Trinity Coll Glenalmond, St John's Coll Cambridge (MA); *m* 1, 20 Jan 1954, Joan, da of George Ogg; 3 s (James b 1955, Rupert b 1957, Jeremy b 1958); m 2, 20 Sept 1969, Thérèse Ann, da of Lt Cdr O M De Las Casas, LVO, OBE, RN; 2 s (Maxwell b 1970, Alexander b 1974); *Career* dir (former chief exec) MacFarlane Group plc (formerly Aberdeen Combworks Ltd) until 1995; GB bobsleigh champion 1958–60, Gold medallist 4 man bob Cwlth Winter Games 1958, GB luge champion 1960–63, memb luge team 1964–68, winner of many class 1 and 2 powerboat races, first powerboat round Britain 1969, first Trans-Irish waterskier, first winter Trans-Alpine balloon crossing 1972; *Recreations* all winter sports, speedsports, golf, diving, ballooning; *Clubs* Turf, Lyford Cay, RSAC, St Moritz Sporting, St Moritz Tobogganing (Cresta), UKOBA Dracula and others; *Style*— Norman Barclay, Esq; ✉ Eyreton House, Quarterbridge, Douglas, Isle of Man

BARCLAY, Patrick; s of Guy Deghy (d 1992), and Patricia Barclay (d 1978); *b* 15 Aug 1947; *Educ* Dundee HS; *children* 1 da (Jennifer b 29 Nov 1968), 1 s (Duncan b 9 Nov 1972); *Career* journalist; trainee Evening Telegraph Dundee 1963–64; sub-ed: Evening Express Aberdeen 1965, Scottish Daily Mail 1966, The Sun 1966–67; football reporter and columnist The Guardian 1976–86 (sub-ed 1967–76); football corr: Today 1986, The Independent 1986–90, The Observer 1990–96; football columnist The Sunday Telegraph 1996–; Sports Journalist of the Year British Sports Journalism Awards 1993; *Style*— Patrick Barclay, Esq; ✉ Sunday Telegraph, 1 Canada Square, London E14 5AR (☎ 0171 538 7380)

BARCLAY, Sir Peter Maurice; kt (1992), CBE (1984); s of George Ronald Barclay, OBE (d 1975), and Josephine Stephanie, *née* Lambert (d 1968); *b* 6 March 1926; *Educ* Bryanston, Magdalene Coll Cambridge (MA); *m* 1953, Elizabeth Mary, da of Herbert H S Wright, of Wellington Coll; 1 s (Simon), 2 da (Alison, Nicola); *Career* RNVR 1944–46, Sub Lt; admitted slr 1952; sr ptnr Beachcroft & Co 1964–74, ptnr Beachcrofts 1974–88; govr Bryanston Sch 1972–88, chm Joseph Rowntree Fndn 1996– (tstee 1974–, vice chm 1994–96); chm: Ctee on Role and Tasks of Social Workers 1981–82, Social Security Advsy Ctee 1985–93, Nat Family Mediation 1994–96, tstees Home-Start UK 1994–; non-exec memb Departmental Bd Dept of Social Security 1994–; vice pres St Pancras Housing Assoc 1994– (chm 1983–91); pres Nat Inst for Social Work 1988 (chm 1973–85), cncl memb Policy Studies Inst 1989–96; Hon DUniv: Stirling 1994, York 1996; *Recreations* gardening, walking, painting; *Clubs* United Oxford & Cambridge Univs; *Style*— Sir Peter Barclay, CBE; ✉ Ferry Hill, E Portlemouth, nr Kingsbridge, Devon TQ8 8PU (☎ 01548 843443); Flat 4, 43 Ladbroke Grove, London W11 3AR (☎ 0171 727 4613, fax 0171 243 8969)

BARCLAY, Robert Colraine; s and h of Sir Colville Herbert Sanford Barclay, 14 Bt, *qv*; *b* 12 Feb 1950; *Educ* Eton, Univ of East Anglia; *m* 1980, Lucilia Saboia, da of Carlos Saboia de Albuquerque, of Ipanema, Rio de Janeiro; 1 s, 1 da; *Career* country mangr Baring Securities Brazil 1992–95, dir Banco Bozano Simonsen Rio Brazil 1995–; FCA;

Style— Robert Barclay, Esq; ✉ Av Lineu de P Machado 1005/COB, Jardim Botanico, 22470-040 Rio de Janeiro, Brazil (☎ 00 55 21 512 6048, fax 00 55 21 271 8199)

BARCLAY, Stephen Robert; s of James Barclay, and Edna, *née* Brown; *b* 8 Nov 1961; *Educ* Ardrossan Acad, Glasgow Sch of Art (BA); 1 da (Gwen Johannsen b 17 April 1990); *Career* artist 1985–; with Paton Gallery London 1985–88, joined Raab Gallery London 1988; *Solo Exhibitions* incl: Paton Gallery London 1987, Raab Gallerie Berlin 1989, Raab Gallery London 1989 and 1992, Visions of Albion (Collyer Bristow Gallery London), Figurative to a Degree (Paton Gallery London), Northlands Festival 1994, St Fergus Gallery 1994; *Group Exhibitions* incl: Royal Glasgow Inst of Fine Arts Annual Exhibition 1984, Christmas Show (Compass Gallery Glasgow) 1984–85, Smith Biennial (Third Eye Centre Glasgow) 1985, Ayr Midland Gp Nottingham 1985, Contemporary Art on the Theme of Gardens (Stoke-on-Trent City Museum and Art Gallery) 1985, New Art New World (Jack Barclay's Ltd London) 1985, Autumn Show (Paton Gallery London) 1986 and 1987, British Art in Malaysia 1987, New British Painting - Object and Image Aspects of British Art in the 1980's (touring USA) 1988, Metropolis (Raab Gallery London) 1988, Opening Exhibition (Raab Gallery Millbank London) 1989, Turning the Century: The New Scottish Painting (Raab Gallery Millbank London) 1990, Gallerie Gian Ferrari Milan 1980, Three Generations of Scottish Painters (Beaux Arts Gallery Bath) 1990, Modern Painters, a memorial exhibition for Peter Fuller 1990, Galerie Bureaux et Magasins Ostend 1991, Visions of Albion (Collyer Bristow Gallery) 1992, Figurative to a Degree (Paton Gallery) 1993, Art 94 (Islington Business and Design Centre) 1994, New Work (with Sally Heywood and Alexander Guy, Paton Gallery) 1994, Autumn Exhibition (Paton Gallery) 1995; *Work in Public Collections* incl: Aust Nat Gallery, Contemporary Arts Soc London, Cleveland Gallery, Tyne and Wear Museum Newcastle, Metropolitan Museum of Modern Art NY, Texaco, Deutsche Bank, Laing Art Gallery, Robert Fleming and Co; work in private collections in UK and abroad; *Awards* Hospitalfield Summer Scholarship 1983, Adam Bruce Thomson award 1984; *Recreations* gliding, sailing; *Clubs* Angus Gliding; *Style—* Stephen Barclay, Esq; ✉ The Guynd, Carmyllie, Arbroath, Angus, Scotland DD11 2QR (☎ 01241 860296)

BARCLAY, Timothy Humphrey; s of Rev Humphrey Gordon Barclay, CVO, MC (d 1955), of Thurgarton Lodge, Norwich, and Evermar Beatrice, *née* Bond Cabbell (d 1975); *b* 18 June 1923; *Educ* Stowe; *m* 23 June 1947, June, da of Thomas Ramsden (d 1960), of Middleton Tower, King's Lynn; 1 s (Thomas Julian b 12 June 1950); *Career* RN 1941–46; Rootes Group 1946–50, farmer and agent 1950–, rep Bonhams Auctioneers E Anglia 1965–85, dealer fine arts 1960–; High Sheriff of Norfolk 1983–84; master and huntsman: W Norfolk Foxhounds 1958–68 (sec 1953–58), Sennow Park Harriers 1970–75; pres N W Norfolk Cons Assoc 1984, steward and dir Fakenham Race Course 1955; Liveryman Worshipful Co of Farriers 1976, hon life memb BHS; *Recreations* hunting, fishing, shooting, coursing; *Clubs* MCC, Norfolk, Allsorts; *Style—* Timothy Barclay, Esq; ✉ Middleton Tower, King's Lynn, Norfolk PE32 1EE (☎ 01553 840203)

BARCLAY-WHITE, Dr Barclay Egon Oram; s of Jack Barclay-White (d 1981), of Weybridge, Surrey, and Phyllis Blanche, *née* Showler; *b* 27 June 1927; *Educ* King's Coll Sch Wimbledon, Univ of London (LDS RCS), Univ of California USA (DDS); *m* 1, 1952 (m dis 1979), Sheila Meredith Bailey; 2 s (Adam Meredith Barclay b 1966, Jason Meredith Barclay b 1969), 2 da (Belinda Meredith Barclay b 1951, Amanda Meredith Barclay b 1953); m 2, 16 Sept 1979, Cathy Mary Bernadette, da of John Gregson (d 1975), of Weybridge and Shepperton; 1 s (Barclay John Gregson b 1987), 1 da (Genevieve Gregson b 1983); *Career* dentist in Weybridge until 1978, dir Dominfast Investments Ltd 1970–91, fndr and non-exec dir Capital Radio plc 1973–; *Recreations* worrying (so I'm told); *Clubs* Naval & Military; *Style—* Dr Barclay Barclay-White; ✉ Balla Awin, Davis Road, Brooklands, Weybridge, Surrey KT13 0XH (☎ 01932 827161, fax 01932 827162, mobile 0976 244107)

BARDA, Robin John Blackmore; s of Gaston Barda (d 1978), of Lausanne, Switzerland, and Cecilia Marjorie, *née* Blackmore; *b* 19 Oct 1947; *Educ* Bryanston, Magdalen Coll Oxford (BA); *m* 6 Sept 1980, Louisa Anne Maxwell, da of Lawrence Thorne Stevenson (d 1985); 3 da (Tabitha b 1983, Arabella b 1986, Persephone b 1988); *Career* freelance singer and musician 1970–75, called to the Bar Gray's Inn 1975; dir and chm The Sixteen Ltd, dir Singcircle Ltd; memb Family Law Bar assoc; *Recreations* singing, music, squash; *Clubs* Savage; *Style—* Robin Barda, Esq; ✉ 4 Paper Buildings, Temple, London EC4Y 7EX (☎ 0171 583 0816, fax 0171 353 4979)

BARDEN, Prof Laing; CBE; *b* 29 Aug 1931; *Educ* Washington GS Durham, Kings Coll Durham (BSc, MSc), Univ of Liverpool (PhD), Univ of Manchester (DSc); *Career* engr R T James Consulting Engineers 1955–59, lectr in civil engrg Univ of Liverpool 1959–62, lectr, sr lectr then reader in engrg Univ of Manchester 1962–69; Univ of Strathclyde: prof of civil engrg 1969–74, chm of Dept of Civil Engrg 1969–71, year secondment to Mowlem Ltd London 1973; Newcastle upon Tyne Poly: dep dir 1974–77, acting dir 1977, dir 1978–92; vice chllr Univ of Northumbria at Newcastle 1992–96, prof emeritus 1996–; dir: MARI (Microelectronic Applications Res Inst) 1980–90, NRMC (Northern Regnl Mgmnt Centre) 1980–, ENTRUST (Tyne & Wear Enterprise Trust) 1982–90, NTC (Newcaste Technology Centre) 1985–89; memb: SRC/SSRC Jt Ctee 1974–77, S Tyneside Educn Ctee 1974–77, CIHE (Cncl for Industry and Higher Educn) 1987–96, Bd of Govrs TNI (The Newcastle Initiative) 1988–, CICHE Br Cncl 1989–92; *Style—* Professor Laing Barden, CBE; ✉ 7 West Farm Road, Cleadon, Tyne and Wear SR6 7UG

BARDEN-STYLIANOU, Stephen; s of Eugene Stylianou (d 1983), and Constantia Stylianou, of East London, SA; *b* 26 June 1950; *Educ* Paul Roos Gymnasium Stellenbosch SA, Centre for Applied Social Science Univ of Natal SA (postgrad dip), Harvard Business Sch (PMD); *m* 1, Aug 1970; 1 c (Sascha b 27 July 1972); m 2, 9 Feb 1979, Foszia Bebe Turner-Stylianou, da of Essop Valodia; 2 c (Rishad b 1 Sept 1980, Nuria b 11 Feb 1983); *Career* South African Broadcasting Corp Durban 1970–76, radio and TV writer/prodr 1977–81, dir of info Inst of Industrial Relations Johannesburg 1981, prodr London Broadcasting Co 1981–82; TV-AM: labour reporter 1982–84, news ed 1984–85, foreign ed 1986–87, managing ed 1988–92, exec dir news 1988–92; gen mangr BSkyB 1992, md and chief exec offr News Datacom Ltd and News Digital Systems Ltd 1992–95; dir 1995–: Worldpipe Ltd, Millennium New Media Ltd, Sigma Squared Ltd; Dir of the Year Natal Critics' Circle 1976; memb RTS; *Clubs* Harvard Club of London; *Style—* Stephen Barden, Esq; ✉ 21 Seymour Road, East Molesey, Surrey KT8 0PB (☎ 0181 941 6208, fax 0181 979 6175)

BARDER, Sir Brian Leon; KCMG (1992); s of late Harry Barder, and late Vivien Barder; *b* 20 June 1934; *Educ* Sherborne, St Catharine's Coll Cambridge (BA); *m* 1958, Jane Maureen; 3 c (Virginia b 1961, Louise b 1962, Owen b 1967); *Career* 2 Lt 7 RTR 1952–54; Colonial Office: entered 1957, private sec to Perm Under Sec 1960–61; HM Dip Serv: entered 1965, first sec UK mission to UN 1964–68, FCO 1968–70, first sec and press attaché Moscow 1971–73, cnsllr and head of Chancery Br High Cmmn Canberra 1973–77, Canadian Nat Def Coll Kingston Ontario 1977–78, head Central and Southern (later Southern) African Dept FCO 1978–82, ambass Ethiopia 1982–86, ambass Poland 1986–88, high cmmr Nigeria and ambass (non resident) Benin 1988–91, high cmmr Australia 1991–94, ret; Hon Cdr of the Order of the Niger (Nigeria) 1989; *Clubs* Utd Oxford & Cambridge Univ; *Style—* Sir Brian Barder, KCMG; ✉ 10 Melrose Road, Southfields, London SW18 1NE (e-mail 100345.3126@compuserve.com.)

BARDHAN, Dr (Pokalath) Gouri; da of Maj-Gen Pokalath Ram Kumar, of Bangalore, India, and Rohini, *née* Ezhuthachan; *b* 6 March 1943; *Educ* Univ of Madras (MB BS, DCH); *m* 15 Dec 1972, Karna Dev Bardhan, *qv*, s of Maj-Gen Pramathanath Bardhan (d 1966); 1 s (Satyajeet b 11 Nov 1977), 1 da (Suchitra Kaveri b 30 Sept 1980); *Career* conslt haematologist Doncaster Royal Infirmary 1984–; former memb Doncaster DHA; regnl rep Br Soc of Haematology; practitioner acupuncture and homeopathy; FRCP, FRCPath; *Recreations* reading, music, crafts; *Style—* Dr Gouri Bardhan; ✉ Haematology Department, Doncaster Royal Infirmary, Armthorpe Rd, Doncaster DN2 5LT (☎ 01302 366666)

BARDHAN, Dr Karna Dev; s of Maj-Gen Pramatha Nath Bardhan (d 1966), of Pune, India, and Anima, *née* Chaudhuri; *b* 16 Aug 1940; *Educ* Christian Med Coll of Vellore Univ of Madras (MB BS), Univ of Oxford (Rhodes scholar, DPhil); *m* 15 Dec 1972, Dr Gouri Bardhan *qv*, da of Maj-Gen P Ram Kumar, of Bangalore, India; 1 s (Satyajeet b 11 Nov 1977), 1 da (Suchitra Kaveri b 30 Sept 1980); *Career* house physician Oxford and Hammersmith Hosp London 1968–69, registrar Royal Hosp Sheffield 1969–70, conslt physician Dist Gen Hosp Rotherham 1973–, hon lectr in gastroenterology Sheffield Univ 1973– (lectr in med 1970–72); memb: Br Soc of Gastroenterology, Assoc of Physicians of GB and Ireland, American Gastroenterological Assoc, American Coll of Gastroenterology, American Coll of Physicians; FRCP, FACP; *Books* Perspectives in Duodenal Ulcer (1980), Topics in Peptic Ulcer Disease (ed, 1987), Non-Responders in Gastroenterology (ed 1991); *Recreations* photography; *Style—* Dr K D Bardhan; ✉ 26 Melrose Grove, Rotherham S60 3NA (☎ 01709 372288); District General Hospital, Moorgate Road, Rotherham S60 2UD (☎ 01709 820000, fax 01709 824168)

BARDSLEY, Andrew Tromlow; s of Andrew Bardsley (d 1950), of Ashton-under-Lyne, Lancs, and Gladys Ada, *née* Tromlow; *b* 7 Dec 1927; *Educ* Ashton-under-Lyne GS, Manchester Regnl Coll of Art, UMIST; *m* 27 Nov 1954, (June) Patricia, da of Patrick Ford (d 1968), of Ashton-under-Lyne; 1 s (Dr Philip Andrew b 6 April 1958), 1 da (Catherine Patricia b 17 March 1962); *Career* served RN communications branch 1946–49; borough engr and surveyor Worksop Borough Cncl 1963–69; dir of tech servs; Corby New Town 1969–71, Luton Co Borough Cncl 1971–73; gen mangr and chief exec Harlow Development Corp 1973–80, princ Westgate Development Consultancy 1981–95; gen cmmr of Taxes for England and Wales 1987–92; JP Essex 1975–92; CEng, FICE; *Recreations* golf, music appreciation, most spectator sports; *Clubs* Ferndown Golf (Dorset); *Style—* Andrew Bardsley, Esq; ✉ 25 Charlotte Close, Talbot Village, Poole, Dorset (☎ 01202 537954)

BAREFOOT, Peter Thomas; s of Herbert John Leslie Barefoot, GC (d 1958), and Amy Gladys, *née* Goddard (d 1991); *b* 20 Jan 1924; *Educ* Ipswich Sch, Architectural Assoc Sch of Architecture (AADipl); *m* 3 July 1948, Patience Heaslop (d 1996), da of John Francis Cunningham, OBE (d 1932), of London; 1 s (Guy b 1957), 3 da (Ann b 1949, Julia b 1951, Sara b 1953); *Career* WWII RN 1943–46, Petty Offr Med Combined Ops; chartered architect in private practice 1954–, chartered designer 1976–; architect: Stevenage Devpt Corp 1949–50, County Hall LCC 1951–54; work incl: Suffolk Hosp Buildings (Bronze Medal RIBA), Elizabeth Court sheltered housing for old people at Aldeburgh (Miny of Housing and Civic Tst Awards) 1962–63, Club House for Royal Harwich Yacht Club 1966–68, housing for WVRS Housing Assoc (DOE Award) 1969–70, Peter Runge House conf centre in Westminster for Industl Soc (The Times/RICS Conservation Award) 1970–71, Children's Cancer Ward and Lab St Bart's Hosp London 1989, East Bergholt Sports Pavilion 1993; drawings and models exhibited at: Royal Acad Summer Exhibition, RIBA, AA, Le Grand Palais Paris; memb: Hellenic Soc, Br Inst of Archaeology Ankara; FRIBA, FRSA; *Recreations* sailing, travel; *Clubs* Waldringfield Sailing; *Style—* Peter Barefoot; ✉ 1 Gaston Street, East Bergholt, Colchester CO7 6SD (☎ and fax 01206 298422)

BARENBOIM, Daniel; s of Enrique Barenboim, and Aida, *née* Schuster; *b* 15 Nov 1942, Buenos Aires; *Educ* Santa Cecilia Acad Rome, coached by Edwin Fischer, Nadia Boulanger and Igor Markevitch; *m* 1, 1967, Jacqueline du Pré, OBE (d 1987), the violoncellist, da of Derek du Pré (d 1990); m 2, Nov 1988, Elena Bashkirova; *Career* pianist and conductor; debut as pianist with: Israel Philharmonic Orch 1953, RPO 1956, Berlin Philharmonic Orch 1963, NY Philharmonic Orch 1964; musical dir: Orchestre de Paris 1975–89, Chicago Symphony Orch 1991–; artistic dir Staatsoper Berlin 1992–; regular tours to Aust, N and S America, Far East; regular appearances at Bayreuth, Edinburgh, Lucerne, Prague and Salzburg Festivals; appeared with Chicago Symphony Orch BBC Proms 1996; Beethoven Medal 1958, Paderewski Medal 1963; Legion of Honour (France) 1987; *Books* A Life in Music (1992); *Style—* Daniel Barenboim, Esq; ✉ c/o Celia Willis, Harold Holt Ltd, 31 Sinclair Road, London W14 0NS (☎ 0171 603 4600, fax 0171 603 0019); c/o Daniel Barenboim Secretariat, 5 Place de la Fusterie, 1204 Geneve, Switzerland

BARFIELD, Brian Michael; s of Isom Bennett Barfield, and Georgina Margaret, *née* Aiken (d 1983); *b* 21 Jan 1945; *Educ* Friends Sch Lisburn, Trinity Coll Dublin (BA); *Career* BBC: announcer and presenter BBC N Ireland 1968–72, sr prodr arts progs BBC N Ireland 1972–77, sr prodr talks and documentaries BBC Radio 1977–79, dep ed Kaleidoscope Radio 4 1979–85, planning ed Radio 3 1985–88, head of planning and business mgmnt Radio 3 1988–94, managing ed Radio 3 1994–; *Recreations* walking and visiting country graveyards; *Style—* Brian Barfield, Esq; ✉ BBC Radio 3, Broadcasting House, London W1A 1AA (☎ 0171 580 4468)

BARFORD, Clive Julian Stanley; s of Maj Edward James Barford, MC (d 1979), late Royal Horse Guards (Special Reserve), and Hon Grace Lowrey Stanley (later Hon Mrs Buckmaster), da of 1 and last Baron Ashfield; *b* 11 May 1933; *Educ* Eton; *m* 1961, Helen Gay Woodroffe, da of Hon Mr Justice (Sir Peter Harry Batson Woodroffe) Foster, MBE, TD; 1 s (James Edward Clive b 1972), 3 da (Emma Jane b 1962, Amanda Helen b 1964, Charlotte Gay b 1967); *Career* chm and md Aldworth Investments Ltd and Abex Ltd, memb Lloyd's; *Recreations* shooting, golf, gardening; *Clubs* Buck's; *Style—* Clive Barford, Esq; ✉ Pibworth House, Aldworth, Berks (☎ 01635 578495)

BARGH, Elizabeth (Liz); *Educ* Univ of Essex (BA); *children*; 1 da; *Career* formerly: staff mangr Marks & Spencer Ltd, personnel mangr NHS, head Pepperell Unit Industl Soc 1988 (joined 1986), dir Domino Consultancy Ltd (involved with equal opportunities and women's devpt and training); dir Opportunity 2000 Business in the Community 1991–; FRSA; *Recreations* tennis, sailing, swimming, skiing, theatre, music, reading; *Style—* Ms Liz Bargh; ✉ Opportunity 2000, Business in the Community, 44 Baker Street, London W1M 4DH (☎ 0171 224 1600, fax 0171 486 1700)

BARHAM, Edmund Justin; s of Donald Arthur Barham (d 1980), of Beckenham, Kent, and Margaret Justine, *née* Prichard; *b* 22 March 1954; *Educ* Christ's Hosp Horsham, Trinity Coll of Music, London Opera Centre; *m* 1980 (m dis 1994); m 2, 1994, Christine Ferraro; 1 s (Donald Sebastian b 1994); *Career* tenor; continental debut Theatre de la Monnaie Brussels 1977, ENO debut 1985, Opera North 1987 and Welsh Nat Opera 1994; princ tenor Gartnerplatz Theater Munich 1984–86; performed at venues incl: Royal Festival Hall, Royal Albert Hall, New Concert Hall Birmingham, Glasgow, Edinburgh, Concertgebau Amsterdam, Bolshoi and Kirov Operas (ENO tour 1990), Sydney Opera House 1993, Teatro Municipale Sao Paolo, Teatro Municipale Rio de Janeiro 1994, Lyric Opera of Queensland 1995, Minneapolis Opera 1995, Seattle Opera 1996, Victoria State Opera Melbourne; performed with orchs incl: Royal Philharmonic, Hallé Orch, City of Birmingham Symphony Orch, Ulster Orch, Orchestre de Paris, Greek Nat Orch, Prague Radio Orch; Ricordi Opera Prize 1974, Green Room Award (Melbourne, Australia) 1994; *Recreations* record collecting, cricket; *Style—* Edmund Barham, Esq; ✉ c/o Stafford Law Associates, 6 Barham Close, Weybridge, Surrey KT13 9PR (☎ 01932 854489)

BARHAM, His Hon Judge; (Geoffrey) Simon; s of Denis Patrick Barham (d 1978), of Cavendish, Suffolk, and Pleasance, *née* Brooke; *b* 23 Dec 1945; *Educ* Malvern, Christ's Coll Cambridge (BA, MA); *m* 18 Sept 1976, Sarah, da of Rev Godfrey Seebold; 1 s (Thomas b 1980), 1 da (Lucy b 1979); *Career* called to the Bar Lincoln's Inn 1968, recorder of the Crown Ct 1987–93, circuit judge (SE Circuit) 1993–; *Clubs* Norfolk; *Style—* His Hon Judge Barham; ✉ Norwich Combined Court Centre, Bishopgate, Norwich NR3 1UR

BARING, Sir John Francis; 3 Bt (UK 1911), of Nubia House, Northwood, Isle of Wight; s of Capt Raymond Alexander Baring (d 1967), and Margaret Fleetwood, OBE, JP, DL, *née* Cambell-Preston (who m 2, 6 Earl of Malmesbury and d 1994); suc unc Sir Charles Christian Baring, 2 Bt (d 1990); *b* 21 May 1947; *m* 1971, Elizabeth Anne, yr da of late Robert David Henle Pillitz, of Buenos Aires, Argentina; 2 s (Julian Alexander David b 1975, James Francis b 1984), 1 da (Andrea Hermione b 1977); *Heir* s, Julian Alexander David Baring b 10 Feb 1975; *Career* Citibank NA 1971–72, Chemical Bank 1972–84, Kidder Peabody & Co 1984–89, GPA Group Ltd 1989, Hackman Baring & Co 1991–, HB Communications Acquisition Corp (now Source Media Inc) 1993–95; *Recreations* gardening; *Clubs* Union (NY); *Style—* Sir John Baring, Bt; ✉ 89 June Road, North Salem, NY 10560–0322, USA

BARING, Louise Olivia; da of Aubrey George Adeane Baring (d 1987), and Marina, *née* Bessel; *b* 28 July 1957; *Educ* Queen's Gate Sch; *Career* journalist; letters arts and home affrs writer Britain section The Economist 1983–89, commissioning ed You magazine The Mail on Sunday 1989–90, asst features ed The Independent on Sunday 1990–93, feature writer Condé Nast Publications 1994–; *Style—* Ms Louise Baring; ✉ Flat 7, 39–40 Queens Gate, London SW7 5HR (☎ 0171 581 8641)

BARING, Nicholas Hugo; s of Francis Anthony Baring (ka 1940), and Lady Rose Gwendolen Louisa McDonnell DCVO (d 1993); *Educ* Eton, Magdalene Coll Cambridge; *Career* late Lt Coldstream Gds; Commercial Union plc: dir Northern & Employers Assurance Co 1966, dir Commercial Union (following merger) 1968–, chm 1990–; non-exec dir Unilever Pension Investments Ltd; chm Bd of Tstees National Gallery 1992–96, memb Cncl National Trust, memb Cncl The Baring Fndn; *Style—* N H Baring, Esq; ✉ Commercial Union plc, St Helen's, 1 Undershaft, London EC3P 3DQ (☎ 0171 283 7500)

BARING, Peter; *Career* chm Barings plc 1989–95; non-exec dir Inchcape plc 1978–96, dep chm Provident Mutual Life Assurance Assoc 1989–94; chm London Investmt Banking Assoc (formerly British Merchant Banking and Securities Houses Assoc) 1991–94; govr London Business Sch 1991–, chm Glyndebourne Arts Tst 1994–; *Style—* Peter Baring, Esq; ✉ office: 60 London Wall, London EC2M 5TQ (☎ 0171 767 1000)

BARING, Hon Mrs (Susan Mary); *née* Renwick; OBE (1984), JP (Hants 1965); da of 1 Baron Renwick, KBE (d 1973); *b* 5 June 1930; *m* 1955 (m dis 1984), Hon John Francis Harcourt Baring, now 7 Baron Ashburton; 2 s, 2 da; *Career* chm Hampshire Probation Ctee 1978–82; vice chm Central Cncl of Probation Ctees 1979–82; memb Parole Bd for England and Wales 1971–74 and 1979–83; pres Hampshire Assoc of Youth Clubs 1977–79; devpt offr Richmond Fellowship 1984–86; prospective Parly candidate: (Alliance) Reading East 1987, (Lib Dem) E Hampshire 1992; memb Cncl King's Coll London 1979–94; vice chm Delegacy King's Coll Med Sch 1989–95; chm: Br Inst of Human Rights 1989–, Nat Birthday Tst 1989–93, Inner London Probation Ctee 1996– (vice chm 1993–96), New Lease Tst (formerly NW London Housing Assoc); memb: London Action Tst 1992–, Bd Almeida Theatre 1993–, Wellbeing Cncl 1993–95; *Recreations* walking, reading, music, family; *Style—* The Hon Mrs Baring, OBE, JP; ✉ 13 Alexander St, London W2 5NY (☎ 0171 727 2438, fax 0171 243 8412)

BARING, Hon Vivian John Rowland; 2 s of 3 Earl of Cromer, KG, GCMG, MBE, PC (d 1991); *b* 12 June 1950; *Educ* Royal Farms Windsor, RAC Cirencester; *m* 1974, his 2 cous, Lavinia Gweneth, eldest da of Maj Sir Mark Baring, KCVO (d 1988); 2 s (Rowley Mark Thomas b 1977 (page of honour to HM The Queen 1989–92), Thomas Patrick Vivian b 1979), 1 da (Camilla Rose b 1985); *Career* dir: Northcliffe Newspapers Group Ltd, Northern Star Insurance Co Ltd; OStJ; *Recreations* sailing (yacht Milanto), skiing; *Clubs* White's, Royal Yacht Sqdn; *Style—* The Hon Vivian Baring; ✉ The Stone House, Lower Swell, Stow on the Wold, Glos GL54 1LQ

BARKER, Hon Adam Campbell; s of Baroness Trumpington (Life Baroness), *qv*, and William Alan Barker, of Sandwich, Kent (d 1988); *b* 31 Aug 1955; *Educ* King's Sch Canterbury, Queens' Coll Cambridge (MA); *m* 1985, Elizabeth Mary, da of Eric Marsden, OBE; 1 s (Christopher Adam b 1989), 1 da (Virginia Giverny b 1987); *Career* solicitor and attorney; barr 12 King's Bench Walk 1978–80; assoc Webster & Sheffield NY 1980–90, ptnr Sedgwick Detert Moran & Arnold (NY and London) 1990–; *Recreations* golf, tennis, horse racing (steward Lingfield Park Racecourse 1992–), bridge; *Clubs* Oxford and Cambridge, Royal St George's (Sandwich), Hever Golf, Hurlingham, Pilgrims; *Style—* The Hon Adam Barker; ✉ October Cottage, Town Croft, Hartfield, East Sussex TN7 4AD (☎ 01892 770014); Sedgwick Detert Moran & Arnold, 6 Lloyds Ave, Lloyds Avenue House, London EC3N 3AX (☎ 0171 929 1829)

BARKER, Sir Alwyn Bowman; kt (1969), CMG (1962); s of late Alfred James Barker, of Mt Barker, S Australia; *b* 5 Aug 1900; *Educ* St Peter's Coll Adelaide, Geelong CE GS, Adelaide Univ (BE, BSc); *m* 1926, Isabel Barron, da of Sir Edward Lucas (d 1950); 1 s (Donald, decd), 1 da (Shirley); *Career* British Thomson Houston Co Rugby 1923–24, Hudson Motor Car Co Detroit 1924–25, prodn mangr Holden's Motor Body Builders Ltd Adelaide 1925–31, works mangr Kelvinator Australia Ltd Adelaide 1931–40, gen mangr Chrysler Australia Ltd Adelaide 1940–52; chm: Kelvinator Australia Ltd 1967–80 (md 1952–67), Municipal Tramways Trust SA 1953–68; chm: Adelaide Electrolysis Ctee 1935–78, Industl Devpt Advsy Cncl 1968–70; dep chm Aust Mineral Fndn 1969–83; pres: Australian Inst of Mgmnt Adelaide Div 1952–54 (federal pres 1952–53 and 1959–61), Instn of Prodn Engrs (Aust Cncl) 1970–72; memb: Faculty of Engrg Univ of Adelaide 1937–66 (lectr in industl engrg 1929–54), Mfrg Industs Advsy Cncl 1958–72, R & D Advsy Ctee 1967–72; John Storey Meml Medal 1965, Jack Finlay Nat Award 1965; grazier (7000 acres); Hon FAIM, CEng, FIEE, FIAM, FIEAust; *Publications* Three Presidential Addresses (1954), William Queale Memorial Lecture (1965); *Recreations* pastoral; *Clubs* Adelaide; *Style—* Sir Alwyn Barker, CMG; ✉ 51 Hackney Rd, Hackney, 5069, South Australia (☎ 00 618 362 2838)

BARKER, Anthony; QC (1985); s of Robert Herbert Barker, of Barlaston, Stoke-on-Trent, Staffs, and Ellen Doreen, *née* Maskery; *b* 10 Jan 1944; *Educ* Newcastle-under-Lyme HS, Clare Coll Cambridge (BA); *m* 1, 1969 (m dis 1980); m 2, 12 Feb 1983, Valerie Anne, da of late Dr William Chatterley Baird, of Caterham, Surrey; 2 da (Sarah Louise b 1971, Vanessa Ann b 1973), 1 step s (Scott William Kenneth Ellis b 1975); *Career* called to the Bar Middle Temple 1966; asst recorder 1981, recorder of the Crown Court 1985–, head of chambers; *Recreations* gardening, music, walking; *Style—* Anthony Barker, Esq, QC; ✉ Hilderstone House, Hilderstone, nr Stone, Staffs ST15 8SQ (☎ 01889 505331); 5 Fountain Court, Steelhouse Lane, Birmingham B4 (☎ 0121 606 0500)

BARKER, (Brian) Ashley; OBE (1975); s of George Henry Barker (d 1980), of Aley Green, Beds, and Evelyn Dorothy, *née* Chandler (d 1994); *b* 26 May 1927; *Educ* Luton GS, AA London (AADipl); *m* 1, 27 Feb 1960 (m dis 1973); 2 s (James b 1961, David b 1964), 2 da (Rhiannon b 1963, Charlotte b 1967); m 2, 29 May 1973, (Sheila) Ann Margaret, da of Lt-Col George Broadhurst (d 1954), of Cheltenham; *Career* architect and conslt on historic bldgs; Surveyor of Historic Bldgs GLC (head of div) 1970–86, head of London Div Historic Bldgs and Monuments Cmmn for England 1986–88; chm: Assoc for Studies in the Conservation of Historic Bldgs 1970–89, Culverin Holdings Ltd 1988–91; chm Canterbury Cathedral Fabric Ctee 1992– (memb 1987–); memb: London Diocesan Advsy Ctee for the Care of Churches 1978–95, Faculty Jurisdiction Cmmn 1980–84, Cathedrals Advsy Cmmn for England 1986–91, St Paul's Cathedral Fabric Ctee 1990–, Bd Heritage of London Trust Ltd 1988–, Bd Taylor Warren Developments Ltd 1994–; tstee: Civic Tst 1989–, Florence Tst 1988–93; pres Surveyors' Club 1984–85; Freeman City of London 1972, Liveryman Worshipful Co of Chartered Architects 1988 (Master 1993–94); Queen's Silver Jubilee Medal 1977; FSA 1966, FRIBA 1967 (assoc 1949); *Recreations* music, visual arts; *Clubs* Athenaeum; *Style—* Ashley Barker, Esq, OBE, FSA; ✉ 25 Brandon Mews, Barbican, London EC2Y 8BE (☎ 0171 638 9096)

BARKER, Audrey Lilian; da of Harry Barker (d 1963), and Elsie Annie Dutton (d 1976); *b* 13 April 1918; *Educ* secdy schs in Kent and Surrey; *Career* writer; Editorial Office Amalgamated Press 1936, publisher's reader Cresset Press 1947, BBC 1949–78; memb Exec Ctee Eng Centre Int PEN 1981–85; memb Panel of Judges for: Katherine Mansfield Prize 1984, Macmillan Silver Pen Award for Fiction 1986, Short Stories 1989, Arts Cncl Writers' Bursaries 1989, Arts Cncl Library Fund 1993–; FRSL 1970; *Awards* Atlantic Award in Lit 1946, Somerset Maugham Award 1947, Cheltenham Festival of Lit Award 1963, Arts Cncl Award 1970, SE Arts Creative Book Award 1981, Macmillan Silver Pen Award 1987, Soc of Authors Travelling Scholarship 1988; *Books* Innocents (1947), Apology for a Hero (1950), Novelette (1951), The Joy Ride (1963), Lost Upon the Roundabouts (1964), A Case Examined (1965), The Middling (1967), John Brown's Body (1969), Femina Real (1971), A Source of Embarrassment (1974), A Heavy Feather (1979), Life Stories (1981), Relative Successes (1984), No Word of Love (1985), The Gooseboy (1987), The Woman Who Talked to Herself (1989), Any Excuse for a Party (1991), Zeph (1992), The A L Barker Omnibus (1992), Element of Doubt (1992); *Style—* A L Barker, FRSL; ✉ Carshalton, Surrey

BARKER, Bridget Caroline; da of Michael John Barker, of Wilmslow Park, Wilmslow, Cheshire, and Brenda, *née* Sawdon (d 1987); *b* 7 March 1958; *Educ* Haberdashers' Monmouth Sch for Girls, Univ of Southampton (LLB); *m* 10 Sept 1994, W Iain Cullen; *Career* admitted slr 1983; Macfarlanes: joined 1981, ptnr 1988, currently head fin services; Skadden Arps Slate Meagher & Flom NY 1986–87; memb: Law Soc, Int Bar Soc, Assoc of Women Slrs, City of London Slrs Co; *Recreations* tennis, travel, gardening; *Style—* Ms Bridget Barker; ✉ Macfarlanes, 10 Norwich Street, London EC4A 1BD (☎ 0171 831 9222, fax 0171 831 9607)

BARKER, Christopher Shelley; DL (S Yorks 1984); s of Ernest Anthony Barker, CBE (d 1979), of Lindrick, nr Worksop, and Barbara Mary, *née* Bishop; *b* 13 Nov 1932; *Educ* Rugby, New College Oxford (BA); *m* 11 June 1960, Jennifer Mary, da of Harold Sydney Biggs (d 1981), of Hornsea; 3 da (Caroline, Victoria, Belinda); *Career* Nat Serv RE 1950–52 (cmmnd 1951), TA RE 1952–62; admitted slr 1959; ptnr: H Shelley Barker & Son 1960–68, Neals & Shelley Barkers 1969–77, Broomheads 1978–87 (sr ptnr from 1981); sr ptnr Dibb Lupton Broomhead 1988–93; tstee Sheffield Town Tst 1984–, Talbot Tsts 1962–; gen cmmr of taxes 1967–72, memb Cncl Univ of Sheffield 1964– (treas 1971–79, pro chllr 1979–87, chm 1981–87); High Sheriff S Yorkshire 1993–94; Freeman Co of Cutlers in Hallamshire; Hon LLD Univ of Sheffield 1988; memb Law Soc; *Recreations* golf; *Style—* Christopher Barker, Esq, DL; ✉ Roy's Barn, Market Place, Burnham Market, Norfolk PE31 8HA (☎ 01328 730443)

BARKER, Rt Rev Clifford Conder; TD (1971); s of Rev Sidney Barker (d 1979), and Kathleen Alice, *née* Conder (d 1973); *b* 22 April 1926; *Educ* Middlesbrough HS, Oriel Coll Oxford (BA, MA), St Chad's Coll Durham (Dip Theol); *m* 1, 14 Aug 1952, Marie (d 1982), da of Richard Edwards (d 1958); 1 s (Richard b 1960), 2 da (Helena b 1954, Catherine b 1962); m 2, 23 July 1983, Audrey Vera Gregson, da of Charles Ernest Fisher (d 1961); 2 step s (Timothy b 1954, Simon b 1955), 1 step da (Louise b 1959); *Career* Green Howards 1944–48 (cmmnd 1946), Chaplain TA 1958–74; ordained: deacon 1952, priest 1953; curate: All Saints Scarborough 1952–55, Redcar 1955–57; vicar: Sculcoates Hull 1957–63, Rudby in Cleveland with Middleton 1963–70, St Olave York 1970–76; rural dean: Stokesley 1965–70, City of York 1971–76; canon and prebendary York Minster 1973–76, consecrated bishop 1976, bishop of Whitby 1976–83, bishop of Selby 1983–91; *Recreations* most sports, gardening, music, travel, crosswords, natural history; *Style—* The Rt Rev C C Barker, TD; ✉ 15 Oak Tree Close, Strensall, York YO3 5TE (☎ 01904 490406)

BARKER, Clive; s of Leonard Barker, of Liverpool, and Joan Ruby Revill; *b* 5 Oct 1952; *Educ* Quarry Bank GS Liverpool, Univ of Liverpool (BA); *Career* playwright, screenwriter, painter, producer and film director; *Theatre* plays incl: Dog, Subtle Bodies, Paradise Street, Crazyface, Secret Life of Cartoons, Incarnations: Three Plays 1995; *Films* incl: Hellraiser (dir/writer) 1987, Hellraiser II: Hellbound (exec prodr/story) 1988, Nightbreed (dir/writer) 1990, Hellraiser III: Hell on Earth (exec prodr/story) 1992, Candyman (exec prodr/story) 1992, Candyman: Farewell to the Flesh (exec prodr/story) 1995, Lord of Illusions (dir/writer/co-prodr) 1995, Hellraiser IV: Bloodline (exec prodr/story) 1996, The Thief of Always (animated, writer/exec prodr) 1996; *Exhibitions and Art Publications* incl: Clive Barker Illustrator, vol I (text by Fred Burke, 1990), Frontier Tales (LACE LA, 1990), Los Angeles Art Fare (1993), Clive Barker Illustrator vol II (text by Fred Burke, 1993), One Person Show (Bess Cutler Gallery NY, 1993–94), One Person Show (Laguna Art Museum/Gallery, 1995); *Books* Books of Blood Vols I-III (1984), Vols IV-VI (1985), The Damnation Game (1986), The Inhuman Condition (short stories, 1986), In the Flesh (short stories, 1986), The Hellbound Heart (1986), Weaveworld (1987), Cabal (short stories, 1989), The Great and Secret Show (1989), Imajica (1991), The Thief of Always (1992), Everville (1994), Sacrament (1996); biographies incl: Pandemonium (ed Michael Brown, 1991), Shadows in Eden (ed Steven Jones, 1992),; *Style—* Clive Barker, Esq; ✉ c/o HarperCollins, 77–85 Fulham Palace Road, London W6 8JB

BARKER, Clive; s of Samuel Lawrence Barker (d 1987), of Middlesbrough, Yorkshire, and Lily, *née* Dawson (d 1970); *b* 29 June 1931; *Educ* Acklam Hall GS Middlesbrough, Bristol Old Vic Theatre Sch, Univ of Birmingham (BA); *m* 1, 21 March 1964, Josephine Benson, *née* Smith (decd); 2 s (John Jesse b 30 Dec 1960, Brendan Samuel b 5 March 1965); m 2, 15 Aug 1983, Susan Edna, da of Raymond George Bassnett; 1 s (Luke Alexander Bassnett Barker b 31 July 1989), 2 da (Vanessa Jane Bassnett Barker b 11 Aug 1977, Rosanna Bassnett Barker b 7 Feb 1985), 1 step da (Lucy Mercedes Bassnett-McGuire b 30 Sept 1972); *Career* freelance actor, dir, writer and other theatrical employment 1955–66; festivals organiser Centre 42 1961–63, lectr in theatre practice Dept of Drama and Theatre Arts Univ of Birmingham, assoc dir Northcott Theatre Exeter 1974–75, lectr Jt Sch of Theatre Studies Univ of Warwick 1975–96 (ret); memb Theatre Workshop Co 1955–; performing first prodns incl: The Hostage 1958, Fings Ain't Wot They Used T'be, The Good Soldier Schweik 1956, The Merry Roosters Pantomime 1963, Twang!!! 1965, Oh! What A Lovely War 1964; worked repertory theatres: Carlisle 1956, Canterbury and Exeter 1960–63, Royal Ct Theatre 1960; dir first Br prodns incl: The Lion in Love 1960, Enter Solly Gold 1962, The Dice 1963, The Police 1963, Vassa Zhelessnova 1972; work abroad: acting coach Bühne der Stadt Köln 1974, dir Dr Faustus (Deutsches Nationaltheater Weimar) 1983, assoc dir Teatro Libre de Bogota 1985, dir Oroonoko (Teatro Colon Bogota) 1986; teaching posts incl: dir of courses Nat Youth Theatre 1964–70, Br Cncl exchange fell Humboldt Univ of Berlin 1981, Landsdown visitor Univ of Victoria BC Canada 1986; memb Bd of Dirs: Centre 42 1961–71, 7:84 Theatre Co 1980–, Albatross Arts Project and Geese Theatre 1987–

(chm 1989–), Int Workshop Festival 1990– (chm 1995–); memb: Int Symposium on the Trg of Theatre Dirs Warsaw 1980, Int Sch of Theatre Anthropology Bologna 1990–; pres Br Pirandello Soc 1983–88, assoc dir Almost Free Theatre 1974–82, chm of the Tstees Inst of Drama Therapy 1989–94, chm Int Festival for Theatre Research 1995–; tstee Interaction 1967–92; assoc ed Theatre Quarterly 1978–81; jt ed: New Theatre Quarterly 1984–, (with Simon Trussler); various radio documentaries, author of plays for TV, theatre and radio; *Books* Theatre Games, A New Approach to Theatre Training (1977), Brecht: The Days of the Commune (translation with Arno Reinfrank, 1978), Woche Für Woche (1971); *Recreations* cricket; *Style—* Clive Barker, Esq; ✉ Woodstock House, The Square, Wolvey, Hinckley, Leics LE10 3LJ

BARKER, Sir Colin; kt (1991); *b* 20 Oct 1926; *Educ* Hull GS, London and Edinburgh Univs; *m* 15 Sept 1951, Beryl; 3 s (Keith, Roger, Paul), 1 da (Heather); *Career* fin dir: Ford UK 1967 (joined 1960), Blue Circle 1968–70, STC 1970–80, British Steel Corp 1980–83; chm: British Technology Group 1983–93 (chief exec 1983–85), British Investment Trust plc 1985–93, CIN Management Limited 1985–93, MCD Group Limited 1990–95, Torotrack (Holdings) Limited 1989–93, Anglia Group plc 1991–96; dir: Reed International plc 1983–92, British Coal Corp 1984–91, Edinburgh Fund Managers 1988–93 FRSA; *Style—* Sir Colin Barker

BARKER, David; QC (1976); s of Frederick Barker (d 1987), of The Old Cottage, Woodhouse, Leics, and Amy Evelyn, *née* Lundie; *b* 13 April 1932; *Educ* Sir John Deane's GS Northwich, Univ Coll London (LLB), Univ of Michigan (LLM); *m* 1957, Diana Mary Vinson, da of Alan Duckworth (d 1981), of Hill House, Rochdale, Lancs; 1 s (Jonathan), 3 da (Jane, Rachel, Caroline); *Career* RAF Flt Lt 1956–58; called to the Bar Inner Temple 1954, bencher 1985; practised Midland and Oxford Circuit, recorder of the Crown Court 1974–; memb: Senate of Inns of Ct and the Bar 1981–84, Criminal Injuries Compensation Bd 1990–; contested (Lab) Runcorn 1955; *Recreations* gardening, sailing, walking; *Clubs* Western (Glasgow); *Style—* David Barker, Esq, QC; ✉ Nanhill, Woodhouse Eaves, Leics (☎ 01509 890 224); 7 King's Bench Walk, EC4; Francis Taylor Building, Temple, London EC4 (☎ 0171 353 7768)

BARKER, David Edward; s of Edward Reginald Barker, of Radlett, Herts, and Frances Barker, *née* Solly; *b* 28 May 1946; *Educ* Bushey Sch, Watford Art Coll; *m* 9 Oct 1971, Jennifer Ann, da of Ernest Farnham (d 1960), of Morden, Surrey; 1 s (Leo Farnham b 1979), 1 da (Cassia Eve b 1978); *Career* art dir Leo Burnett London 1966–68, creative gp head J Walter Thompson London and New York 1970–75 (art dir 1968–70); creative dir: Rupert Chetwynd 1975–79, Benton & Bowles London 1979–80, Geers Gross 1980–84; fndr and creative dir Humphreys Bull & Barker 1984–86, fndr and exec creative dir KHBB 1986–90, dir The Reject Shop plc 1990–94, fndr chm and creative dir Barker and Ralston 1991–; *Recreations* motor racing, photography, music; *Clubs* BARC, BRSCC; *Style—* David Barker, Esq; ✉ Barker and Ralston, 2 Marshall Street, London W1V 1LQ (☎ 0171 437 4371, fax 0171 437 2727)

BARKER, Prof David Faubert; s of Faubert Barker (d 1980), and Doreen Maude, *née* Hitchcock (d 1955); *b* 18 Feb 1922; *Educ* Bryanston, Magdalen Coll Oxford (BA, DPhil, MA, DSc); *m* 1, 16 June 1945 (m dis 1977), Kathleen Mary Frances, da of William Pocock (d 1951); 3 s (Ian b 1947, Jolyon b 1952, Guy b 1954), 2 da (Susan b 1948, Jillian b 1955); m 2, 29 Jan 1978, Patricia Margaret, *née* Drake; 1 s (John b 1970), 1 da (Annabel b 1974); *Career* demonstrator Dept of Zoology Univ of Oxford 1947–50, prof of zoology Univ of Hong Kong 1950–62 (dean Faculty of Sci 1959–60), prof of zoology Univ of Durham 1962–87, Sir Derman Christopherson fell Univ of Durham Res Fndn 1985–86 (emeritus prof 1987–); emeritus fell Leverhulme Tst 1989–91; memb Physiological Soc, sr memb Anatomical Soc; *Recreations* gardening; *Style—* Prof David Barker; ✉ Department of Biological Sciences, University of Durham, South Road, Durham DH1 3LE (☎ 0191 374 3341)

BARKER, David Frank; *b* 7 June 1941; *Educ* Gresham's Sch Holt; *m*; 2 c, 2 step c; *Career* Norwich Union Life Insurance Society (NULIS): joined 1959, actuarial student 1960–66, actuarial asst 1966–71, seconded to Scottish Union and National Insurance Co Edinburgh 1967–68, seconded to Pakistan Branch (Karachi) April - Oct 1969, actuary NZ Head Office Wellington 1971–76 (dep mangr 1973–76), asst investmt mangr Head Office Norwich 1976–78, investmt mangr 1978–84, chief investmt mangr 1984–86; md: Hill Samuel Investment Management Ltd 1986–90, Royal Insurance Asset Management Ltd 1990–96; gp dir of Worldwide Life Ops and memb Mgmnt Bd Royal & Sun Alliance Insurance Group plc 1996–, gp dir Life and Investmt Royal Insurance Holdings Ltd 1996– (dir 1991–96); also currently dir: Royal Insurance plc, Royal Insurance UK Ltd, Royal Life Holdings Ltd (dep chm), Royal Life Canada (chm), Royal Financial Services Inc USA (chm), Royal Life Insurance International Ltd, Royal Insurance Property Services, Royal Life España (chm); *Style—* David Barker, Esq; ✉ Royal & Sun Alliance Insurance Group plc, 1 Cornhill, London EC3V 3QR (☎ 0171 283 4300, fax 0171 283 4841)

BARKER, Dennis Malcolm; s of George Walter Barker (d 1970), of Oulton Broad, and Gertrude Edith, *née* Seeley (d 1979); *b* 21 June 1929; *Educ* Royal GS High Wycombe, Lowestoft GS; *m* Sarah Katherine, *née* Alwyn; 1 da (Eleanor Lucy); *Career* journalist and author; Suffolk Chronicle and Mercury 1947–48, E Anglian Daily Times 1948–58, Express and Star Wolverhampton 1958–63 (property ed, theatre and radio critic, columnist), The Guardian 1963– (Midlands corr, then in London, feature writer, general columnist, media corr, People profile columnist, obituarist); regular bdcaster BBC Radio Stop The Week programme 1974–76; chm: Suffolk branch NUJ 1958 (sec 1953–58), Home Counties Dist Cncl 1956–57; memb: Writers' Guild of GB, Soc of Authors, Broadcasting Press Guild; life memb NUJ; *Books* non-fiction: The People of the Forces Trilogy (Soldiering On 1981, Ruling The Waves 1986, Guarding The Skies 1989), One Man's Estate (1983), Parian Ware (1985), Fresh Start (1990); novels: Candidate of Promise (1969), The Scandalisers (1974), Winston Three Three Three (1987); *Recreations* painting, sailing, music, cinema; *Style—* Dennis Barker, Esq; ✉ 67 Speldhurst Road, London W4 1BY (☎ 0181 994 5380); The Guardian, 119 Farringdon Road, London EC1R 3ER (☎ 0171 278 2332)

BARKER, Elspeth; da of Robert Scott Langlands, of Cairnmount House, Kelso, and Elizabeth Cameron, *née* Brash; *b* 16 Nov 1940; *Educ* Drumtochty Castle Sch Scotland, St Leonard's Sch Scotland, Somerville Coll Oxford; *m* 29 July 1989, George Granville Barker; 2 da (Raffaella b 1964, Lily b 1974), 3 s (Alexander 1966, Roderick b 1967, Samuel b 1971); *Career* writer, reviewer and journalist; head of classics Runton Hill Sch 1982–93; *Awards* David Higham Prize 1991, Angel Fiction Prize 1992, Scottish Spring Book Award 1992, RSL Winifred Holtby Prize 1992, shortlisted Whitbread First Novel Prize 1991; memb PEN 1992; *Books* O Caledonia (1991), The War Graves (1995); *Recreations* reading, drinking, talking; *Style—* Mrs Elspeth Barker; ✉ c/o Toby Eady Associates Ltd, 3rd Floor, 9 Orme Court, London W2 4RL (☎ 0171 792 0092, fax 0171 792 0879)

BARKER, Prof Geoffrey Ronald; s of Ronald James Barker (d 1982), and Edith Gertrude, *née* Fisher (d 1985); *b* 4 April 1943; *Educ* Univ of London Guy's Medical Dental Sch (BSc, MB BS, BDS), Univ of Manchester (MSc); *m* 14 Nov 1977, Jane McEwen, da of Daniel Trushell, of Kilbarchan; 2 s (Simon b 26 July 1979, Matthew 15 June 1981); *Career* conslt oral and maxillofacial surgn RAMC (V) 372 MFST, Maj 1985–; med practitioner Alderney and Guernsey 1974–78; Univ of Birmingham Med and Dental Schs 1978–81: hon registrar, hon sr registrar, lectr in oral surgery and oral med; sr lectr and hon conslt in oral and maxillofacial surgery and oral med Manchester Med and Dental Schs 1981–87, prof, conslt and head of dept Dept of Oral Surgery Medicine and Pathology Univ of Wales Coll of Med Cardiff 1987–91, currently med dir Astra Pharmaceuticals Ltd; memb: Br Dental Assoc, BMA, Br Thoracic Soc, Br Soc of Gastroenterology, American Thoracic Soc, American Gastroenterological Assoc, Med Ctee Assoc of Br Pharmaceutical Industries; former memb: Dental Ctee Med Defence Union, local dental ctees for S Wales; former surgn St John Ambulance; FRCS 1985, MRCS, LRCP, LDSRCS, FDSRCS 1979, MFPM 1995; *Recreations* photography, walking, golf; *Clubs* Royal Army Medical; *Style—* Prof Geoffrey Barker; ✉ Astra Pharmaceuticals Ltd, Home Park, Kings Langley, Herts WD4 8DH

BARKER, Godfrey Raymond; s of Harold Lindsey Barker (d 1973), and Alys, *née* Singleton (d 1988); *b* 14 April 1945; *Educ* Dulwich, Cambridge, Oxford and Cornell Univs (MA, DPhil); *m* 1974, Ann, da of Frederick Botsford Callender, of Pasadena, California; 1 s (Frederick George Lindsey b 28 Oct 1983); *Career* Cons Res Dept 1966–67, second sec UN Dept FO 1972; The Daily Telegraph: joined 1972, parly sketchwriter and leader writer 1981–89, arts ed 1986, arts and political columnist 1989–; *Books* Visions of Europe (with Margaret Thatcher and others, 1993), Sovereign Britain (with Norman Lamont, 1995); *Recreations* campaigning for the National Heritage, opera, lieder, cricket; *Clubs* Beefsteak; *Style—* Godfrey Barker, Esq; ✉ 26 Charles St, Berkeley Square, London W1 (☎ 0171 499 8516); The Daily Telegraph, 1 Canada Square, Canary Wharf London E14 5DT (☎ 0171 538 5000)

BARKER, Prof Graeme William Walter; s of Reginald Walter Barker (d 1987), and Kathleen, *née* Walton (d 1981); *b* 23 Oct 1946; *Educ* Alleyn's Sch London, St John's Coll Cambridge (Henry Arthur Thomas open scholar, BA, MA, PhD), Br Sch at Rome (Rome scholar in classical studies); *m* 3 Jan 1976 (m dis 1991), Sarah Miranda Buchanan; 1 s (Lewis William b 26 May 1983), 1 da (Rachel Jessica b 14 Feb 1980); *Career* sr lectr in prehistoric archaeology Univ of Sheffield 1981–84 (lectr 1972–81), dir British Sch in Rome 1984–88, prof and head of Sch of Archaeological Studies Univ of Leicester 1988–; chm Soc for Libyan Studies 1988–94; memb: Mgmnt Ctee Br Sch at Athens 1993–95, Editorial Bd CUP and Journal of Mediterranean Archaeology; co-dir: UNESCO Libyan Valleys Survey 1979–89, Tuscania Project 1986–; FSA 1979; *Books* Landscape and Society: Prehistoric Central Italy (1981), Archaeology and Italian Society (co-ed with R Hodges), Prehistoric Farming in Europe (1985), Beyond Domestication in Prehistoric Europe (co-ed with C Gamble, 1985), Cyrenaica in Antiquity (co-ed with J Lloyd and J Reynolds, 1985), Roman Landscapes (co-ed with J Lloyd, 1991), A Mediterranean Valley: Landscape Archaeology and Annales History in the Biferno Valley (1995), The Biferno Valley Survey: the Archaeological and Geomorphological Record (1995), Farming the Desert: the UNESCO Libyan Valleys Archaeological Survey (with D Gilbertson, B Jones and D Mattingly, 1996); *Recreations* walking, swimming, sailing; *Style—* Prof Graeme Barker, FSA; ✉ 55 Knighton Drive, Leicester LE2 3HD (☎ 0116 270 8132); School of Archaeological Studies, University of Leicester, University Rd, Leicester LE1 7RH (☎ 0116 252 2612, fax 0116 252 5005)

BARKER, Graham Harold; TD (1985); s of Harold George Barker (d 1962), of Cambridge, and Dorothy, *née* Speechley (d 1986); *b* 11 Jan 1949; *Educ* Cambridge GS, King's Coll London, St George's Hosp Med Sch London (MB BS, AKC); *m* 23 Sept 1978, Esther Louise, da of John Owen Farrow, of Norwich; 1 s (Douglas Graham b 23 June 1982), 1 da (Louise Elizabeth b 9 Jan 1987); *Career* Surgn 217 (L) Gen Hosp RAMC (V) 1973–91, Capt 1974, Maj 1980; lectr Inst of Cancer Res London 1977–79, registrar Queen Charlotte's and Chelsea Hosps London 1980, sr registrar in gynaecology and obstetrics Middx Hosp and UCH 1981–87, currently gynaecologist St George's Hosp London and Portland Hosp for Women London; memb: Br Soc for Colposcopy and Cervical Pathology, Br Gynaecological Cancer Soc, Gynaecological Res Soc, Chelsea Clinical Soc; Astor fell Harvard Univ Hosps 1984; Freeman City of London, Liveryman Worshipful Co of Apothecaries 1980; FRCSEd 1979, FRCOG 1993 (MRCOG 1978), MD 1991; *Books* Family Health And Medicine Guide (1979), Your Search For Fertility (1981), Chemotherapy of Gynaecological Malignancies (1983), The New Fertility (1986), Your Smear Test - A Guide To Screening, Colposcopy And The Prevention Of Cervical Cancer (1987), Overcoming Infertility (1990); founding ed Obstetrics and Gynaecology Today; *Recreations* writing, the organ, trumpet, piano; *Style—* Graham Barker, Esq, TD; ✉ 12 Wolsey Close, Kingston Upon Thames, Surrey KT2 7ER (☎ 0181 942 2614); The Chimes, 11 The Suttons, Cambersands, Rye, East Sussex (☎ 01797 226876); St George's Hosp, Blackshaw Rd, London SW17 (☎ 0181 672 1255)

BARKER, John Alfred; s of Alfred Barker (d 1990), of Holborn, London, and Miriam Alice, *née* Kerley (d 1993); *b* 2 Dec 1929; *Educ* Neale's Mathematical Sch, City of London Coll; *m* 22 Sept 1962, Margaret Coutts, da of Thomas Coutts Smith (d 1948), of Stonehouse, Lanark; *Career* Intelligence Corps TA & AVR 1959–69; Stock Exchange 1950–64, Inner London Probation Serv 1965–90, memb Local Review Ctee HM Prison Wandsworth 1986–90; Corp of London common councilman Cripplegate Without 1981– (deputy 1993–); memb: Inner London and City Probation Ctee 1994–, Bd of Mgmnt Barbican YMCA 1986– (chm 1990–), City Parochial Fndn Central Governing Body 1989–, London Boroughs Assoc Environment Ctee (dep) 1991–, City and Hackney Jt Consultative Ctee NHS 1993–; Past Master Cripplegate Ward Club; govr: Bridewell Royal Hosp 1982–, City of London Sch for Girls 1982–, King Edward's Sch Witley Surrey 1989–, Christ's Hosp 1991–; tstee: Soc for Relief of Homeless Poor 1982–, Neale's Educnl Fndn 1983–, Charity of John Land 1983–, Mitchell City of London Charity and Educnl Fndn 1991–, St Luke's Parochial Tst 1995–; Freeman: City of London 1970, Worshipful Co of Basketmakers 1973; FRGS 1979, FZS 1980, FInstD 1984, MIMgt 1985; FRSA 1992; *Recreations* travel, hill and mountain walking, club man; *Clubs* Reform, Guildhall, City Livery, Royal Over-Seas League, Rotary Club of London; *Style—* John Barker, Esq; ✉ 319 Willoughby House, Barbican, London EC2Y 8BL (☎ 0171 628 5381)

BARKER, John Edgar; s of Edgar Barker (d 1975), and Hilda, *née* Hitchinson (d 1992); *b* 23 Sept 1931; *Educ* Christ's Hosp Sch Horsham, RCM London, Salzburg Mozarteum (Lovro von Matačič); *Career* conductor; has worked with Br opera cos incl: Glyndebourne Festival (memb music staff), Sadler's Wells (chorus master, conductor), ENO (head of Music Staff, conductor), The Royal Opera (former head Music Staff and head Music Dept); at Covent Garden has conducted: Le Nozze di Figaro, Don Giovanni, Troilus and Cressida, Peter Grimes, Madam Butterfly, Tosca, Turandot, Lucia di Lammermoor, Il Trovatore, La Bohème, La Cenerentola; conductor Royal Ballet 1988–89: Sleeping Beauty, Romeo and Juliet; repertoire at Sadler's Wells and ENO incl: Mozart, Rossini, Saint-Saëns, Verdi, Offenbach, Johann Strauss, Humperdinck, Stravinsky, Wagner (incl the Ring Cycle), Williamson's The Violins of St Jacques and Lucky Peter's Journey (world premiere); conducted: Carmen in Seoul, concert with Baltsa and Carreras in Tokyo on 1986 Far East Tour, two concerts with Domingo Royal Opera House 1988; conducted orchs incl: London Philharmonia, Boston Symphony, Radio Eireann Symphony, Bournemouth Symphony, Orquestra Sinfonica Mexico City, Iceland Symphony Orch 1992; ARCM, GRSM; *Style—* John Barker, Esq

BARKER, Air Vice-Marshal John Lindsay; CB (1963), CBE (1946), DFC (1945); s of Dr Abraham Cockroft Barker (d 1971), and Lilian Alice, *née* Woods (d 1969); *b* 12 Nov 1910; *Educ* Trent Coll, BNC Oxford (BA); *m* 1948, Eleanor Margaret Hannah, da of E B Williams, of Co Cork; 1 s; *Career* RAFO 1930, RAF 1933, served France 1939–40, N Africa 1942–43, War Cabinet Plans 1943–44, Bomber Cmd 1944–45, Far East 1945–46, Palestine 1946–48, Egypt 1950–53, air attaché Rome 1955–58, Cdr Royal Ceylon Air Force 1958–63, ret Air Vice-Marshal; called to the Bar Middle Temple 1947; Order of

Merit (Italy) 1958; *Recreations* sailing, golf, photography; *Clubs* RAF; *Style*— Air Vice-Marshal John L Barker, CB, CBE, DFC; ✉ The Old Cider Press, Mill Court, Frogmore, Kingsbridge, South Devon TQ7 2PB (☎ 01548 531746)

BARKER, Rear Adm John Perronet; CB (1985); s of Gilbert Barker (d 1969; gs of Thomas Perronet Barker, constructional engr, who built all the waterless gasholders in Britain in the 1930s), and Dorothy Gwendoline, *née* Moore (d 1972), of Edgbaston, Birmingham; *b* 24 June 1930; *Educ* Nautical Coll Pangbourne; *m* 1955, (Evelyn) Priscilla Summerson, da of Sir William Christie, KCIE, CSI, MC (d 1983), of Gerrards Cross, Bucks; 2 s (b 1957 and 1959); *Career* joined RN 1948, Capt's sec HMS CERES 1955–57, supply offr HMS Lagos 1957–58, BRNC Dartmouth 1958–61, sec to Br Naval Attaché Washington 1961–64, sec to ACNS (Warfare) 1964–67, supply offr HMS Hampshire 1967–68, sec to Flag Offr Second in Cmd Far East Fleet 1968–69, sec to Controller of the Navy 1972–76, Royal Coll of Defence Studies 1977, dir Fleet Supply Duties MOD 1978–80, Cdre HMS Centurion 1980–83, Rear Adm 1983, COS to C-in-C Naval Home Cmd 1983–85, ret RN 1986; admin sec Mission to Seamen 1987–93, chm ISAF Youth Sailing Ctee 1986–; memb Cncl: Sea Cadet Assoc 1986–94, Shaftesbury Homes and ARETHUSA 1988–; chm: Assoc of RN Offrs 1987–, TS Royalist Mgmnt Ctee 1986–94; memb Mgmnt Ctee YMCA Nat Centre Fairthorne Manor (nr Southampton) 1994–; Freeman Worshipful Company of Shipwrights 1983; *Recreations* yacht racing and administration, gardening, DIY; *Clubs* RN Sailing, Midland Sailing, Royal Yacht Sqdn; *Style*— Rear Adm John Barker, CB; ✉ c/o Lloyds Bank plc, Colmore Row, Birmingham B3 3AD

BARKER, Prof John Reginald; s of Thomas Reginald Barker (d 1965), of Bamford, Derbys, and Marjorie, *née* Cutler (d 1979); *b* 11 Nov 1942; *Educ* New Mills GS, Univ of Edinburgh (BSc), Univ of Durham (MSc), Univ of Warwick (PhD); *m* 11 Aug 1966, Elizabeth Carol, da of George Patrick Maguire; 1 da (Emma Jane b 26 Aug 1970), 2 s (Tom Alexander Patrick b 31 July 1972, John Luke Patrick b 17 March 1974); *Career* SRC res student Dept of Applied Physics Univ of Durham 1966–67, jr res assoc Dept of Physics Univ of Warwick 1967–69, pt/t physics teacher Henry VIII GS Coventry 1968, pt/t lectr Canley Coll of FE; Univ of Warwick: SRC post doctoral res fell Dept of Physics 1969–70, lectr 1970–84, sr lectr 1984–85; prof of electronics Dept of Electronics and Electrical Engrg Univ of Glasgow 1985–; co-dir: NATO Advanced Study Inst 1979 and 1990, NATO Advanced Res Inst 1982; distinguished science lectr Yale Univ 1992; visiting prof: N Texas State Univ 1978, Colorado State Univ 1978–79 (affiliate prof 1979–83); visiting scientist: IBM T J Watson Res Centre NY 1978, NORDITA Neils Bohr Inst Copenhagen 1980, Bell Telephone Laboratories 1980–81, Electronics and Devices Laboratory US Army 1981; former memb of numerous SERC Ctees, presenter Venture series (Central) 1982, various appearances on Tomorrow's World and other science progs; FRSE 1990, fell Br Interplanetary Soc 1992; *Books* Physics of Non-Linear Transport in Semiconductors (1979), Physics of Granular Electronic Systems (1991); *Recreations* hill walking, reading, cooking, astronomy, Volvo driving; *Style*— Prof John Barker, FRSE; ✉ 45 Hugheaden Gardens, Glasgow G12 9YH (☎ 0141 338 6026); Nanoelectronics Research Centre, Department of Electronics and Electrical Engineering, University of Glasgow, Glasgow G12 8QQ (☎ 0141 330 5221, fax 0141 330 4907)

BARKER, Jonathan David; s of Thomas William Barker, and Dorothy Joan Barker; *b* 17 July 1949; *Educ* Victoria Boys' Sch Watford, Cassio Coll of Futher Educn Watford, Birkbeck Coll London (BA, Frank Newton prize for English), Poly of N London (Postgrad Dip in Librarianship & Info Sci); *m* 23 July 1983, Deirdre Mary, da of Cornelius Joseph Shanahan; *Career* arboriculturalist Whippendell Woods Watford 1969–70, library asst Kensington Central Reference Library 1970–72, poetry librarian Arts Cncl Poetry Library 1973–88, asst sec Poetry Book Soc Ltd 1973–83, literature offr Literature Dept The Br Cncl 1988–; adjudicator numerous poetry competitions (incl Arts Cncl Raymond Williams Prize for Publishing 1992 and 1993); ALA 1985, memb Library Assoc; *Publications* Arts Council Poetry Library Short-Title Catalogue (6 edn 1981), Selected Poems of W H Davies (ed, 1985, new edn 1992), Poetry Book Society Authology (ed, 1986), The Art of Edward Thomas (ed, 1987), Thirty Years of The Poetry Book Society - 1956–1986 (ed, 1988), Norman Cameron Collected Poems and Selected Translations (jt ed, 1990), A Select Bibliography of Poetry in Britain and Ireland (1995); contrib various critical articles to reference books; *Recreations* music, gardening, travelling, book collecting; *Clubs* Centre for English Studies Univ of London; *Style*— Jonathan Barker, Esq; ✉ Literature Department, The British Council, 11 Portland Place, London W1N 4EJ (☎ 0171 389 3175)

BARKER, Katharine Mary (Kate); *b* 29 Nov 1957; *Educ* Stoke-on-Trent Sixth Form Coll, St Hilda's Coll Oxford (PPE); *m* 1982, Peter Donovan; 2 s (b 1988, 1990); *Career* investment analyst Post Office Pension Fund 1979–81, res offr NIESR 1981–85, chief Euro economist Ford of Europe 1985–94, chief econ advsr CBI 1994–; memb HM Treasy independent panel of economic forecasting advsrs 1996–; memb Cncl Royal Econ Soc 1994–; *Recreations* bell ringing; *Style*— Ms Kate Barker; ✉ Confederation of British Industry, Centre Point, 103 New Oxford Street, London WC1A 1DU (☎ 0171 379 7400)

BARKER, Kenneth; s of Raymond Charles Barker, of Leics, and Ivy, *née* Blackburn; *b* 15 Aug 1947; *Educ* Gateway Sch Leics; *m* 1, 30 Oct 1970 (m dis 1983), (Elizabeth) Peris, da of Thomas Stephens (d 1985); 1 s (Michael b 1974); m 2, 8 July 1987, Julie, da of Joseph Casling (d 1984); 1 s (Edward b 1984); *Career* CA; F W Clarke & Co (later Touche Ross & Co) 1964–78, Barker & Co 1978–; treas and memb: Leicester CC 1962–82, Old Lancastrians Football Club 1963–85; treas Leics Badminton Assoc 1981–84; FCA 1979; *Recreations* golf, badminton; *Clubs* Glen Gorse Golf, Coalville Badminton; *Style*— Kenneth Barker, Esq; ✉ The Old Coach House, Church Lane, Dunton Bassett, Lutterworth, Leics (☎ 01455 202140); Barker & Co, Lonsdale House, High St, Lutterworth, Leics (☎ 01455 550440, fax 01455 554144)

BARKER, Prof Kenneth; CBE (1994); s of Thomas William Barker, and Lillian Barker; *b* 26 June 1934; *Educ* Royal Coll of Music (GRSM, ARCM, FTCL, FLCM), King's Coll London (BMus), Univ of Sussex (MA); *m* 1958, Jean Ivy Pearl; 1 s, 1 da; *Career* sch master 1958–62, lectr and univ teacher 1962–75, princ Gipsy Hill Coll 1975, pro-dir Kingston Poly 1975–86, dir Leicester Poly 1987–92 (dep dir 1986–87), chief exec and vice-chllr De Montfort Univ 1992–; chm: Phoenix Arts, Bd De Montfort Enterprise Ltd; Liveryman Worshipful Co of Framework Knitters; Hon DSc; FRSA, CIMgt; *Recreations* music, theatre, watching rugby; *Clubs* Atheneum, Reform, IOD; *Style*— Prof Kenneth Barker, CBE; ✉ Bramshott, Church Road, Long Ditton, Surbiton KT6 5HH (☎ 0181 398 4700); De Montfort University, The Gateway, Leicester LE1 9BH (☎ 0116 257 7007)

BARKER, Capt Nicholas John; CBE (Falklands List, 1982); s of Lt Cdr John Frederick Barker, DSC, RN (ka i/c HMS Ardent, 1940), and Jillian, *née* Paget (d 1943); *b* 19 May 1933; *Educ* Canford, Naval Colls and Staff Coll, Churchill Coll Cambridge (Defence fell); *m* 1, 10 Aug 1957 (m dis 1989), Elizabeth Venetia, *née* Redman; 2 s (Henry b 1959, Benjamin b 1964), 2 da (Louise (Mrs Townsend) b 1961, Emma (Mrs Payne) b 1962); m 2, 4 March 1989, Jennifer Jane, da of Cdr Richard Douglas Cayley, DSO and two bars, RN (ka i/c HM Submarine P311, 1943); 2 step da (Antonia b 1958, Jessica (Mrs Cushnir) b 1963); *Career* RN; eight seagoing cmds incl: HMS Arrow 1975–77, HMS Endurance (Falklands) 1980–82, Fishery Protection Sqdn 1984–86, HMS Sheffield 1987–88; MOD Naval Sec Dept 1977–79; dep chm North European Marine Services Ltd; dir Marr Technical Services; ptnr Nicholas Barker Properties and Consultancy; nat chm Royal Nat Mission to Deep Sea Fishermen, memb Nat Cncl Br Maritime Fndn; memb SW Atlantic Gp; chm/pres local ctees: Sea Cadets, British Legion, Royal Naval Assoc; Younger Bro Trinity House London 1967; Hon Col Royal Marines RMR Tyne, vice chm N of Eng TAVRA; Freeman City of London, Liveryman Worshipful Co of Fishmongers 1986; MNI 1979, FRGS 1982; Royal Order of Merit Class IV Norway 1988; *Books* The Falklands, a Common Denominator (1984), Beyond Endurance (1996); novels incl: Red Ice (1987, voted one of best novels NY Times 1987), Rig (1990); *Recreations* shooting, fishing, golf, spectating almost any sport, championing lost causes; *Clubs* Naval, Northern Counties; *Style*— Capt Nicholas Barker, CBE, RN; ✉ Low Farnham Farmhouse, Sharperton, Rothbury, Morpeth, Northumberland NE65 7AQ (☎ 01669 640275); North European Marine Services Ltd, South Dock, Sunderland SR1 2BU (☎ 0191 514 5037, fax 0191 510 8108)

BARKER, Nicola Jane; da of Derek Royston Barker, of Denver, Colorado, and Rayne, *née* Norma Johnson; *b* 30 March 1966; *Educ* Enfield Chase Girls Comp, King's Coll Cambridge (BA); *Career* writer and freelance journalist; *Awards* David Higham Prize for Fiction 1993, Silver Pen Award (jt winner) 1993, Arts Cncl Literature Bursary 1995; *Books* Love Your Enemies (short stories, 1993), Reversed Forecast (1994), Small Holdings (1995), Heading Inland (short stories, 1996); *Style*— Ms Nicola Barker; ✉ c/o David Miller, Rogers, Coleridge & White, 20 Powis Mews, London, W11 1JN (☎ 0171 221 3717)

BARKER, Nicolas John; s of Sir Ernest Barker (d 1960), and Olivia Stuart, *née* Horner (d 1976); *b* 6 Dec 1932; *Educ* Westminster, New Coll Oxford (MA); *m* 11 Aug 1962, Joanna Mary Nyda Sophia, da of Col Henry Edward Mariano Cotton, OBE (d 1988); 2 s (Christian b 1964, Cosmo b 1973), 3 da (Emma b 1963, Olivia b 1963, Cecilia b 1969); *Career* with Bailliere Tindall & Cox and Rupert Hart-Davis 1959, asst keeper Nat Portrait Gallery 1964, with Macmillan & Co Ltd 1965, with OUP 1971, dep keeper British Library 1976–92, libraries advsr to Nat Tst 1992–; William Andrews Clark visiting prof UCLA 1986–87; pres: Amici Thomae Mori 1978–89, Double Crown Club 1980–81, Bibliographical Soc 1981–85; memb: Publication Bd of Dirs RNIB 1969–92, London Library Ctee 1971–, Appeals Advsy Ctee BBC and ITV 1977–86, Arts Panel Nat Tst 1979–92; tstee The Pilgrim Tst 1977–, chm Laurence Sterne Tst 1984–, London Library 1994–; ed The Book Collector 1965–; Hon DUniv York 1994; *Books* The Publications of the Roxburghe Club (1962), The Printer and the Poet (1970), Stanley Morison (1972), Essays and Papers of ANL Munby (ed, 1977), The Early Life of James McBey - An Autobiography 1883–1911 (ed, 1977), Bibliotheca Lindesiana (1977), The Oxford University Press and the Spread of Learning 1478–1978 (1978), A Sequel to an Enquiry (with John Collins, 1983), Aldus Manutius and the Development of Greek Script and Type (1985), The Butterfly Books (1987), Two East Anglian Picture Books (1988), Treasures of the British Library (compiler, 1989), S Morison: Early Italian Writing-Books (ed, 1990), Medieval Pageant (with A Wagner and A Payne, 1993); *Clubs* Garrick, Beefsteak; *Style*— Nicolas Barker, Esq; ✉ 22 Clarendon Rd, London W11 3AB (☎ 0171 727 4340)

BARKER, Patricia Margaret (Pat); da of Moira Drake; *b* 8 May 1943; *Educ* Grangefield GS, LSE (BSc); *m* 29 Jan 1978, David Faubert Barker, s of Faubert Barker (d 1980); 1 s (John b 1970), 1 da (Annabel b 1974); *Career* novelist; jt winner Fawcett Prize 1983, elected one of twenty Best of British Young Novelists 1983, Guardian Fiction Prize 1993, Special Award Northern Electric Arts Awards 1993, Booksellers' Association Author of the Year Award 1996; Hon MLitt Teesside 1993, Hon DLitt Napier 1996; memb: Soc of Authors 1983, PEN 1989; FRSA 1995; *Books* Union Street (1982, filmed as Stanley and Iris 1990 starring Robert de Niro and Jane Fonda), Blow Your House Down (1984), The Century's Daughter (1986), The Man Who Wasn't There (1989), Regeneration (1991), The Eye in the Door (1993), The Ghost Road (1995, winner Booker Prize 1995); *Recreations* swimming, walking, reading; *Style*— Mrs Patricia Barker, FRSL; ✉ c/o Gillon Aitken, Aitken, Stone & Wylie, 59 Fernshaw Road, London SW10 0TG (☎ 0171 351 7561)

BARKER, Paul; s of Donald Barker (d 1981), and Marion, *née* Ashworth (d 1989); *b* 24 Aug 1935; *Educ* Hebden Bridge GS, Calder HS, BNC Oxford (MA); *m* 1960, Sally, da of James Huddleston (d 1965); 3 s (Nicholas b 1961, Tom b 1966, Daniel b 1973), 1 da (Kate b 1963); *Career* writer and broadcaster; Nat Serv cmmnd Intelligence Corps 1953–55; lectr Ecole Normale Supérieure Paris 1958–59; editorial staff: The Times 1959–63, Economist 1964–65; ed New Society 1968–86 (staff writer 1964, asst ed 1965–68), social policy ed Sunday Telegraph 1986–88, assoc ed The Independent Magazine 1988–90, social and political columnist The Sunday Times 1990–91, planning corr London Evening Standard 1992– (townscape and arts columnist 1987–92); visiting fell Centre for the Analysis of Social Policy Univ of Bath 1986–, Leverhulme res fell 1993–95; BPG Award (jtly) for Outstanding Radio Programme (My Country, Right or Wrong) 1988; dir: The Fiction Magazine 1982–87, Pennine Heritage 1978–86; Inst of Community Studies: tstee 1991–, fell 1992–95, sr fell 1995–; FRSA 1990; *Books* A Sociological Portrait (ed, 1972), One for Sorrow, Two for Joy (ed and contrib, 1972), The Social Sciences Today (ed, 1975), Arts in Society (ed and contrib, 1977), The Other Britain (ed and contrib, 1982), Founders of the Welfare State (ed, 1985), Britain in the Eighties (contrib, 1989), Towards A New Landscape (contrib, 1993), Young at Eighty (contrib, 1995), Gulliver and Beyond (ed and contrib, 1996), Living as Equals (ed and contrib, 1996); *Recreations* architecture; *Style*— Paul Barker, Esq; ✉ 15 Dartmouth Park Ave, London NW5 1JL (☎ 0171 485 8861)

BARKER, Peter William; CBE (1988), DL (1990); s of William Henry George Barker, and Mabel Irene Barker; *b* 24 Aug 1928; *Educ* Royal Liberty Sch Romford, Dorking Co HS, South London Poly; *m* 1961, Mary Rose Hainsworth, JP; 1 s, 1 da; *Career* J H Fenner & Co 1953–67, jt md Fenner International 1967–71, chief exec J H Fenner (Holdings) 1971–82, chm Fenner plc 1982–93; pro-chllr Univ of Hull 1993–; non-exec dir Neepsend plc 1984–93, chm System Freestyle Ltd 1994–; memb: Yorks and Humberside Regnl Cncl CBI 1981–94 (chm 1991–93), Nat Cncl CBI 1985–94, Yorks and Humberside Regnl Industl Devpt Bd 1981– (chm 1992); High Sheriff Humberside 1993–94; Hon DSc (Econ) Univ of Hull 1992; CIMgt, FInstD, FCIM, FRSA; *Recreations* sailing, skiing, tennis, music; *Clubs* Royal Thames Yacht, Royal Yorks Yacht; *Style*— Peter W Barker, Esq, CBE, DL; ✉ Swanland Rise, West Ella, Hull, East Yorkshire HU10 7SF

BARKER, (Colin) Rex; s of Rex Patrick Barker, of Fareham, Hants, and Vera Ivy, *née* Corsham; *b* 16 Feb 1946; *Educ* St Olave's GS, Royal Naval Sch of Physiotherapy (MCSP, Elspeth Curpney Kingdom Prize, RN Student of the Year), Ashridge Mgmnt Coll/City Univ (MBA); *m* 27 Dec 1967, Therese, da of Nikolaus Opers; 2 s (Richard Bernd b 11 Oct 1968, James Rex b 18 Jan 1971); *Career* Royal Navy/Royal Marines: joined RN as sick berth attendant 1963, commando trg 1964, served with 40 Commando RM in Malaya and Borneo 1964, physiotherapy trg 1967–70, cmmnd Sub-Lt 1973, PSO/AO RNH Haslar 1973–76, med admin offr Clyde Submarine Base 1976–78, MA 2 Flag Offr Submarines/SM1 1978–80, MAO HQ Commando Forces RM 1980–82, 3 Commando Bde RM 1982, OC Medical Sqdn Commando Logistic Regt RM 1982–85; unit gen mangr New Forest Hosps and Community Unit Southampton Health Authy 1985–90, MBA 1991, independent mgmnt conslt Morgan Harris Burrows 1992, chief exec NW London Mental Health NHS Trust 1992–95; dir SATORI; memb Ashridge Mgmnt Coll Assoc, dir British Deming Assoc, dir Evidence Based Mgmnt; MHSM; *Recreations* sailing, skiing, music, reading, Oriental philosophy; *Style*— Rex Barker, Esq; ✉ 12 Monks Way, Hill Head, Fareham, Hants PO14 3LU (☎ and fax 01329 668845)

BARKER, Richard Philip; s of Philip Watson Barker (d 1971), and Helen May, *née* Latham (d 1957); *b* 17 July 1939; *Educ* Repton, Trinity Coll Cambridge (MA), Univ of Bristol (CertEd); *m* 30 July 1966, Imogen Margaret, da of Sir Ronald Montague Joseph

Harris, KCVO, CB (d 1995), of Stoke D'Abernon, Surrey; 2 s (Jolyon b 1967, Thorold b 1971), 1 da (Rosalind b 1969); *Career* asst master: Bedales Sch 1963–65, Marlborough Coll 1967–81; dir A-Level Business Studies Project 1966–75, lectr Inst of Educn London 1974–75, headmaster Sevenoaks Sch 1981–96; res govr Br Sch Sri Lanka 1996–97; memb various ctees HMC, memb Employment Ctee IOD 1996–; *Books* Understanding Business (series ed, 1976–); *Recreations* walking, fishing, sailing, beekeeping, educational matters; *Clubs* RSA; *Style*— Richard Barker, Esq; ✉ Slyfield Farmhouse, Stoke D'Abernon, Cobham, Surrey KT11 3QE (☎ 01932 862634, fax 01932 860137)

BARKER, Ronald William George (Ronnie); OBE (1978); s of Leonard Barker, and Edith Barker; *b* 25 Sept 1929; *Educ* Oxford HS; *m* 1957, Joy Tubb; 2 s, 1 da; *Career* actor; began career with Aylesbury Repertory Co 1948; ret from showbusiness 1987, now proprietor of shop in Cotswolds; *Theatre* West End: Mourning Becomes Electra 1955, Summertime 1955, Listen to the Wind 1955, Double Image 1956, Camino Real 1957, Lysistrata 1958, Irma la Douce 1958, Platanov 1960, On the Brighter Side 1961, Midsummer Night's Dream 1962, Real Inspector Hound 1968, The Two Ronnies (Palladium) 1978; *TV series* Seven Faces of Jim 1965, The Frost Report 1966–67, Hark at Barker 1968–69, Six Dates with Barker 1970, The Two Ronnies (10 series) 1971–86, Twenty Years of the Two Ronnies 1986, Porridge 1974–77, Open All Hours 1976 and 1981–82, Going Straight 1978, Clarence 1987; *Films* Robin and Marian 1975, Picnic 1975, Porridge 1979; *Awards* Variety Club of GB 1969, 1974 and 1980, SFTA 1971, Radio Industs Club 1973, 1974, 1977 and 1981, Water Rats 1975, British Acad 1975, 1977 and 1978, RTS award for outstanding creative achievement 1975; *Books* Book of Bathing Beauties (1974), Book of Boudoir Beauties (1975), It's Goodnight From Him (1976), Sauce (1977), Gentlemen's Relish (1979), Sugar and Spice (1981), Ooh-la-la! (1983), Pebbles on the Beach (1985), A Pennyworth of Art (1986); *Recreations* collecting postcards, writing song lyrics; *Style*— Ronnie Barker, Esq, OBE

BARKER, Prof Theodore Cardwell; s of Norman Humphrey Barker (d 1974), and Louie Nettleton, *née* Cardwell (d 1970); *b* 19 July 1923; *Educ* Cowley Sch St Helens, Jesus Coll Oxford (MA), Univ of Manchester (PhD); *m* 2 Aug 1955, Joy Marie (Judith), da of Ernest Pierce (d 1976); *Career* econ history staff LSE 1953–64, first prof of economic and social history Univ of Kent at Canterbury 1964–76, prof of economic history Univ of London 1976–83 (now emeritus, still actively writing); memb Cncl Royal Hist Soc 1967–70 and 1974–77; chm: Oral History Soc 1973–76, Mgmnt Ctee Inst of Hist Res Univ of London 1977–88, History Bd CNAA 1977–81, Mgmnt Ctee Business History Unit Univ of London 1979–86, Debrett's Business History Research Ltd 1984–89, Athlone Press 1988–; memb Exec Int History Congress 1995– (vice pres 1986–90, pres 1990–95); pres: Economic History Soc 1986–89 (hon sec 1960–86), Railway and Canal History Soc 1986–88; FRHistS 1963; *Books* A Merseyside Town in the Industrial Revolution (with J R Harris, 1954, reprint 1994), A History of the Girdlers' Company (1957), Pilkington Brothers and the Glass Industry (1960), Business History (jtly, 1960, 1970 and 1984), A History of London Transport (with R M Robbins, 1963, Vol II 1974), Our Changing Fare - Two Hundred Years of British Food Habits (ed jtly, 1966), A History of the Worshipful Company of Carpenters (with B W E Alford, 1968), The Long March of Everyman (ed, 1974), A History of British Pewter (with M J Hatcher, 1974), An Economic History of Transport (with C I Savage, 1975), The Glassmakers (1977), The Transport Contractors of Rye (1982), The Population Factor (ed with Michael Drake, 1982), The Economic and Social Effects of the Spread of Motor Vehicles (1987), Moving Millions - A Pictorial History of London Transport (1990), Megalopolis: The Giant City in History (ed with A R Sutcliffe, 1993), The Rise and Rise of Road Transport (with Dorian Gerhred, 1993, reprint 1995), A Vision of Glass: An Illustrated Updated History (1994); *Recreations* walking, driving; *Clubs* Reform; *Style*— Prof Theodore Barker; ✉ Minsen Dane, Brogdale Rd, Faversham, Kent ME13 8YA (☎ 01795 533523); Economic History Department, London School of Economics, Houghton St, London WC2A 2AE (☎ 0171 755 7047, fax 0171 955 7750, telex 24655 LSELON G)

BARKER, Thomas Christopher; s of Col Rowland Barker, OBE, MC (d 1965), of Brighton, and Kathleen Maude, *née* Welch (d 1956); *b* 28 June 1928; *Educ* Uppingham, New Coll Oxford (MA); *m* 3 Sept 1960, Griselda Helen, da of Robert Cormack (d 1982), of Ayr; 2 s (Christopher b 1964, Robert b 1966), 1 da (Rosanna b 1961); *Career* 2 Lt 1 Bn Worcs Regt 1947–48; HM Dip Serv: third sec Paris 1953–55, second sec Baghdad 1955–58, first sec Mexico City 1962–67 (also head of Chancery and consul), cnsllr and head of Chancery Caracas 1969–71, FCO 1971–75, seconded as under sec NI Office Belfast 1975–76; curator Scottish Nat War Meml 1978–88 (sec to tstees 1988–93); FSA (Scot) 1988; *Style*— Thomas Barker, Esq

BARKER, Timothy Gwynne; s of Lt-Col (Frank Richard) Peter Barker (d 1974), of Nawton, York, and Hon Olwen Gwynne, *née* Philipps; *b* 8 April 1940; *Educ* Eton, Jesus Coll Cambridge (MA), McGill Univ Montreal; *m* 14 July 1964, Philippa Rachel Mary, da of Brig Mervyn Christopher Thursby-Pelham, OBE, of Finchampstead, Berks; 1 s (Christopher b 1970), 1 da (Camilla b 1968); *Career* vice chm Kleinwort Benson Group plc 1993– (dir 1988–); DG: City Panel on Takeovers and Mergers 1984–85, Cncl for the Securities Indust 1984–85; Liveryman Worshipful Co of Grocers; *Style*— Timothy Barker, Esq; ✉ Kleinwort Benson Ltd, PO Box 560, 20 Fenchurch St, London EC3P 3DB (☎ 0171 623 8000)

BARKER, Trevor; s of Samuel Lawrence Barker (d 1987), of Middlesbrough, and Lilian, *née* Dawson (d 1970); *b* 24 March 1935; *Educ* Acklam Hall GS; *m* 7 Sept 1957, Joan Elizabeth, da of Frederick Cross (d 1972), of Stockton-on-Tees; 1 s (Roy b 21 Feb 1961), 1 da (Karen (Mrs Dent) b 17 July 1958); *Career* articled to Leonard C Bye, FCA (Middlesbrough), Price Waterhouse & Co 1957–58, Cooper Brothers 1958–62, in practice Leyburn Yorks 1962–70, chm and chief exec Gold Case Travel Ltd 1964–77, dir Ellerman Wilson Lines Ltd 1977–80; chm and chief exec: John Crowther Group plc 1981–88, William Morris Fine Arts plc 1982–88, Alpha Consolidated Holdings Ltd 1988–96; dep chm and chief exec Blanchards plc 1988–95, chm Micklegate Group plc 1989–94; memb Bd Peterlee and Aycliffe Development Corp 1986–88; dir: Drew Scientific Group plc 1991–95, Darlington Building Society 1994–; chm Croft Classic and Historic Motorsport Ltd 1995–; Freeman City of London, Liveryman Worshipful Co of Woolmen; FCA 1957, FRSA 1989; *Recreations* racing thoroughbreds, golf, opera, books; *Style*— Trevor Barker, Esq; ✉ Windways, 323 Coniscliffe Rd, Darlington, Co Durham DL3 8AH (☎ 01325 350436, fax 01325 489677, mobile 0860 517839)

BARKSHIRE, Robert Renny St John (John); CBE (1990), TD (1970), JP (Lewes 1980), DL (E Sussex 1986); s of Robert Hugh Barkshire, CBE; *b* 31 Aug 1935; *Educ* Bedford Sch; *m* 1, 1960 (m dis 1990), Margaret Robinson; 2 s (Charles b 1963, William b 1965), 1 da (Sarah b 1969); m 2, 1990, Audrey Witham; *Career* Nat Serv 2 Lt Duke of Wellington's Regt 1953–55, TA HAC 1955–74 (CO 1970–72–, Regt Col 1972–74); banker; Cater Ryder & Co 1955–72 (jt md 1963–72); chm: Mercantile House Holdings plc 1972–87, Alexanders Laing & Cruickshank Holdings Ltd 1984–88, Int Commodities Clearing House 1986–90, Household Mortgage Group 1994 (non-exec dir 1985–94), Chaco Investments Ltd 1994–; non-exec dir: Extel Group 1979–87 (dep chm 1986–87), Savills plc 1988–95, Ctee on Market in Single Properties 1985–, Sun Life and Provincial Holding plc 1988–, TR Property Investment Trust plc 1993–; memb Advsy Bd: IMM Div of Chicago Mercantile Exchange 1981–84, Bank Julius Baer & Co Ltd London 1988–91; dir LIFFE 1982–91 (chm 1982–85); chm: FFWP 1980, LIFFE Steering Ctee 1981; gen cmmr for Income Tax City of London 1981–; memb Cncl Regular Forces Employment Assoc 1985–95; govr: Eastbourne Coll 1980–85 (dep chm 1983–92), Roedean 1984–89; chm Bedford Sch 1984–89, cmmr Duke of York's Royal Mil Sch Dover 1986–95; chm: Reserve Forces Assoc 1983–87, Sussex TA Ctee 1983–85, SE TAVR Assoc 1985–91, City of London TAVRA 1989–91, E Sussex Branch Magistrates Assoc 1986–91, E Sussex Magistrates Courts Ctee 1993–; Hon Col 6/7 Queen's Regt 1986–91, vice chm TA Sport Bd 1983–95 (memb 1979–95), vice pres St James's Branch Royal Br Legion 1992– (chm Chiddingly and Dist 1982–87); fin advsr: Royal Br Legion, Royal Signals, Royal Engrs Funds, Army Sport Control Bd, Army Central Fund TA Sport Bd, Victory Servs Club 1981–95; dir Offrs' Pensions Society Investment Co 1982–95, tstee Duke of Wellingtons Regt; Freeman City of London 1973, Liveryman Worshipful Co of Farmers 1981; ACIB; *Recreations* sailing, shooting; *Clubs* City of London, Cavalry and Guards', MCC, Royal Fowey Yacht; *Style*— John Barkshire, Esq, CBE, TD, JP, DL; ✉ Denes House, High Street, Burwash, East Sussex TN19 7EH (☎ 01435 882646)

BARKWORTH, Paul Raymond Braithwaite; JP; s of Frederic Basil Stileman Barkworth, of Eastbourne, E Sussex, and Beryl Nellie, *née* Wright; *b* 26 Jan 1947; *Educ* Monkton Combe Sch; *m* 18 June 1970, Janet Elizabeth, da of Charles Arthur Crees, of Plymouth; *Career* CA; public practice (ptnr with Solomon Hare), dir Baptist Insurance Co plc 1985–; dep chm English Churches Housing Group 1990; memb: Cncl Baptist Union of GB, Bristol C of C and Indust; Freeman City of London, Freeman Worshipful Co of Patternmakers; MInstD, FCA; *Recreations* motor cycling, music, travel, photography; *Clubs* Lansdowne, Bristol Commercial Rooms; *Style*— P R B Barkworth, Esq, JP; ✉ Tranby House, Norton Lane, Whitchurch, nr Bristol BS14 0BT (☎ 01275 837101); Oakfield House, Oakfield Grove, Clifton, Bristol BS8 2BN (☎ 0117 923 7000, fax 0117 973 2741)

BARKWORTH, Peter Wynn; s of Walter Wynn Barkworth (d 1974), of Bramhall, Cheshire, and Irene May, *née* Brown (d 1972); *b* 14 Jan 1929; *Educ* Stockport Sch, RADA; *Career* actor and director; prodr and dir independent prodn co Astramead Ltd; memb: BAFTA *Theatre* incl: Folkestone and Sheffield Repertory Cos 1948–51, A Woman of No Importance (Savoy) 1953, Roar Like a Dove (Phoenix) 1957–60, The School for Scandal (Haymarket) 1962, Crown Matrimonial (Haymarket, BAFTA Best Actor award 1974) 1972, Donkeys' Years (Globe) 1976, Can You Hear Me At The Back? (Piccadilly) 1979, A Coat of Varnish (Haymarket) 1982, Siegfried Sassoon (Apollo) 1986, Hidden Laughter (Vaudeville) 1990, Shadowlands 1991, Quartermaine's Terms 1993, The Winslow Boy (Globe) 1994; as dir: Night and Day (Leatherhead) 1980, Sisterly Feelings (tour) 1982, The Eight O'Clock Muse (Riverside Studios) 1989; *Television* incl: The Power Game 1966, Manhunt 1969, Professional Foul (BAFTA Best Actor and RTS/BPG Awards 1977), Telford's Change 1979, Winston Churchill: the Wilderness Years 1981, The Price 1985, Late Starter 1985, The Gospel According to St Matthew 1986; *Film* Champions 1984; *Books* About Acting (1980), First Houses (1983), More About Acting (1984), The Complete About Acting (1991); *Recreations* walking, looking at paintings, gardening; *Style*— P Barkworth, Esq; ✉ 47 Flask Walk, London NW3 1HH (☎ 0171 836 8722)

BARLEY, Dr Victor Laurence; s of George Alec Barley (d 1995), of Harrogate, Yorks, and Evelyn Mary Barley (d 1971); *b* 16 June 1941; *Educ* Stamford Sch Lincolnshire, Univ of Cambridge (MA, MB BChir), Univ of Oxford (MA, DPhil); *m* 25 Jan 1969, Janet, da of Dr Stanley Devidson Purcell, of Clevedon, Avon; 1 s (Peter b 3 Dec 1969), 3 da (Elizabeth b 6 Jan 1972, Madeline (twin) b 6 Jan 1972, Christine b 16 July 1981); *Career* conslt clinical oncologist Bristol 1978–, clinical dir Bristol Oncology Centre 1988–96; memb Br Inst of Radiology; FRCSEd, FRCR; *Recreations* music; *Style*— Dr Victor Barley; ✉ 11 Barrow Court Mews, Barrow Court Lane, Barrow Gurney, Bristol BS19 3RW (☎ 01275 463006); Bristol Oncology Centre, Horfield Rd, Bristol BS2 8ED (☎ 0117 928 2415)

BARLING, Gerald Edward; QC (1991); *b* 18 Sept 1949; *Educ* New Coll Oxford (Peel fndn scholar, Thwaites travelling scholar (USA), Burnett open exhibitioner, MA), Inns of Court Sch of Law (Harmsworth entrance exhibitioner, Astbury law scholar); *m* Myriam Frances, née Ponsford; *Career* called to the Bar Middle Temple 1972; in practice: Manchester 1973–81, London and Brussels 1981–; recorder of the Crown Court 1993– (asst recorder 1989–93); memb: Bar Cncl Working Pty on Restrictive Practices 1988–90, Ctee Bar Euro Gp 1988–; chm: Western Euro Sub-Ctee Bar Cncl 1991–92, Bar Euro Gp 1994–96; lectr in law New Coll Oxford 1972–77, tutor in law UC London 1972–73; *Publications* Butterworths European Court Practice (contrib, 1991), Butterworths European Law Service (conslt ed); author of numerous professional papers on aspects of EC law; *Style*— Gerald Barling, Esq, QC; ✉ Brick Court Chambers, 15–19 Devereux Court, London WC2R 3JJ (☎ 0171 583 0777, fax 0171 583 9401); 8 avenue de la Joyeuse Entree, B - 1040 Brussels (☎ 00 322 2303161)

BARLOW, Sir Christopher Hilaro; 7 Bt (UK 1803), of Fort William, Bengal; s of Sir Richard Barlow, 6 Bt, AFC (d 1946), and Rosamund Sylvia, *née* Anderton; *b* 1 Dec 1929; *Educ* Eton, McGill Univ Montreal (BArch); *m* 1952, Jacqueline Claire de Marigny, da of John Edmund Audley (d 1980), of Chester; 1 s (and 1 s decd), 2 da (Persephone Claire (Mrs Robert E Booth) b 1953, Caroline Claire (Mrs James C Jordan) b 1960); *Heir* s, Crispian John Edmund Audley Barlow b 20 April 1958; *Career* architect; former pres Newfoundland Architects' Assoc; *Clubs* Royal Cwlth Soc, The Crow's Nest; *Style*— Sir Christopher Barlow, Bt; ✉ 18 Winter Ave, St John's, Newfoundland A1A 1T3, Canada (☎ 709 726 5913)

BARLOW, Crispian John Edmund Audley; s and h of Sir Christopher Hilaro Barlow, 7 Bt, *qv*; *b* 20 April 1958; *Educ* Marine Electronics, Coll of Fisheries St John's Newfoundland, Technikon SA (Dip in Nature Conservation); *m* 1981, Anne Waiching Siu; 1 da (Jennifer Claire Audley b 1990); *Career* sr inspr of police Royal Hong Kong Police Force 1978–90, chief of Patrol Marina da Gama SA 1992–93, ops exec Sabre Security SA 1991–92, chief ranger Zabalaza Conservation Gp 1993–94, nature conservator Ibhubesi Wildlife Service 1994–; memb: Int Assoc of Bomb Technicians and Investigators, Int Police Assoc, Endangered Wildlife Tst, Wildlife Soc of SA; assoc Inst of Explosive Engrs; *Recreations* shooting, sailing; *Clubs* OCH, 100 Club; *Style*— Crispian Barlow, Esq

BARLOW, Prof David Hearnshaw; s of Archibald Edward Barlow, of Clydebank, and Annie Wilson, *née* Hamilton; *b* 26 Dec 1949; *Educ* Clydebank HS, Univ of Glasgow (BSc, MB ChB, MD), Univ of Oxford (MA); *m* Norma Christie, da of John Campbell Woodrow; 1 s (Neil John b 13 Oct 1975), 1 da (Catriona Charlotte Anne b 11 Feb 1986); *Career* various med trg positions Glasgow 1975–77, MRC trg fell 1977–78, Hall tutorial fell Univ of Glasgow 1979–81, sr registrar Queen Mother's Hosp 1981–84; Univ of Oxford: clinical reader in obstetrics and gynaecology 1984–90, fell Green Coll 1985–90 (hon sr assoc memb 1990–), Nuffield prof of obstetrics and gynaecology 1990–, fell Oriel Coll 1990–; med advsr Endometriosis Soc; memb Cncl: Nat Osteoporosis Soc, RCOG 1996–; treas Br Menopause Soc 1995–; FRCOG 1993 (MRCOG 1980); *Recreations* music (listening and playing the viola), painting; *Style*— Prof David Barlow; ✉ Nuffield Department of Obstetrics and Gynaecology, John Radcliffe Maternity Hospital, Headington, Oxford OX3 9DU (☎ 01865 221008, fax 01865 69141)

BARLOW, David John; s of F Ralph Barlow, of Birmingham, and Joan, *née* Barber; *b* 20 Oct 1937; *Educ* Leighton Park Sch, Queen's Coll Oxford (MA, DipEd), Univ of Leeds (DipESL); *m* 1; 3 s (John, Andrew, Simon); m 2, 1981, Sanchia Beatrice, da of Marcel Oppenheimer; 2 s (Luke, Nathan), 1 da (Imogen); *Career* British Cncl 1962–63; BBC: joined 1963, prog organiser Hindi, Tamil, Nepali and Bengali Serv 1967–70, Further Educn Radio 1970–71; UNESCO: Br Cncl consultancies 1970–73, head of liaison int rels 1974–76, chief asst regions 1977–79; gen sec ITCA 1980–81, sec BBC 1981–83; BBC controller: public affrs and int rels 1983–85, public affrs 1985–87, regnl bdcasting 1987–90; seconded to EBU in Geneva as co-ordinator Audio Visual Eureka Project 1990–91; controller int rels and info servs BBC 1991–92, advsr int rels BBC 1992–; *Recreations* birdwatching, book collecting, photography, mountain walking; *Clubs* English Speaking Union, Royal TV Soc; *Style—* David Barlow, Esq; ✉ 7 Priory Close, Harrold, Beds MK43 7DL; c/o BBC Broadcasting House, 104 HWH, London W1A 1AA

BARLOW, Gary; *b* 20 Jan 1971; *Career* singer and songwriter; memb Take That 1990–96; solo 1996–; 11 top ten singles incl 7 no 1's (Pray 1993, Relight My Fire 1993, Babe 1993, Everything Changes 1994, Sure 1994, Back For Good 1995, How Deep Is Your Love 1996); albums with Take That: Take That and Party (1992, UK no 2), Everything Changes (1993, UK no 1), Nobody Else (1995), Greatest Hits (1996); awards incl: Best British Single (for Could It Be Magic) BRIT Awards 1993, Nordoff Robbins Silver Clef Levis Original Talent Award 1993, Best British Single and Best British Video (for Pray) BRIT Awards 1994, Best Contemporary Song (for Pray) and Songwriter of the Year Ivor Novello Awards 1994, Best Group MTV Euro Pop Awards 1994, Best British Single (for Back For Good) BRIT Awards 1996, Most Performed Work and Best Selling Song Ivor Novello Awards 1966; videos: Take That and Party (1992, UK no 1), Take That - The Party Live At Wembley (1993, UK no 1), Everything Changes (1994, UK no 1), Take That - Berlin (1994, UK no 1); first solo single Forever Love (1996, UK no 1); first solo album Open Road (1996); *Recreations* good food, cinema, hunting for antiques, his two spaniel dogs and alsatian; *Style—* Gary Barlow, Esq; ✉ c/o Nigel Martin-Smith, 41 South King Street, Manchester M2 6DE (☎ 0161 832 8080, fax 0161 832 1613)

BARLOW, George Francis; s of late George Barlow, of Worcester Park, Surrey, and late Agnes Barlow; *b* 26 May 1939; *Educ* Wimbledon Coll, Hammersmith Sch of Art & Building, Poly of Central London; *m* 1969, Judith Alice, da of Alice and the late Alan (Tony) Newton; 2 da (Rachel b 1970, Jacqueline b 1974), 1 s (Daniel b 1972); *Career* chartered surveyor Building Design Partnership 1962–67, devpt surveyor GLC 1967–70, the housing devpt offr London Borough of Camden 1970–76, dir/sec Metropolitan Housing Tst 1976–87, chief exec Peabody Tst 1987–; chm: London Housing Assoc Cncl 1978–82, Prince's Tst/BITC Homelessness Gp 1994–, RICS Housing Policy Panel 1996–; memb: Cncl Nat Fedn of Housing Assocs 1985–89, Housing Ctee RICS 1986–91, Cncl Business in the Community 1989–, Ctee Community Self Build Agency 1989–93, Ctee Broomleigh Health Authy 1989–95, Bd E London Partnership 1994–; govr Univ of East London 1996–; FRICS 1987 (ARICS 1968); *Recreations* theatre, swimming, travelling, Crystal Palace FC; *Clubs* IOD; *Style—* George Barlow, Esq; ✉ Peabody Trust, 45 Westminster Bridge Road, London SE1 7JB (☎ 0171 928 7811)

BARLOW, Gillian Claire Bernadette Judson (Dilly); da of Leonard Alfred Barlow, of Horley, Surrey, and Sarah Elizabeth, *née* Judson (d 1979); *b* 6 May 1952; *Educ* St Anne's Coll Sanderstead Surrey, Univ of Manchester (BA); *Career* TV/radio presenter; newsreader and presentation announcer BBC Radio 4 1978–84; former reporter on progs incl: Today, Breakaway; TV presenter Granada: The Green Life Guide, Hard Cash, House Style, Quest; radio presenter: Enquire Within, Woman's Hour, Cut the Mustard; other work incls freelance conf, voice over and commentary work; *Recreations* looking after Dr John the famous cat, boating; *Clubs* The Academy; *Style—* Ms Dilly Barlow; ✉ 11 Gateley Rd, Brixton, London SW9 9TA (☎ 0171 733 8253)

BARLOW, James Alan; s and h of Sir Thomas Barlow, 3 Bt, DSC, DL, *qv*; *b* 10 July 1956; *Educ* Highgate, Univ of Manchester (BSc); *Career* metallurgist; res engr The Welding Institute Cambridge 1978–82; mangr Harland & Wolff Belfast 1982–84; ptnr Glassdrumman House Annalong 1984–93; Maître d'Hotel Galgorm Manor Ballymena 1993–95; technical conslt Blue Star Ventures Fort St John BC Canada 1996–; pt/t lecturer Covenant Life Coll Fort St John 1996–; *Recreations* walking, ornithology, reading, oenology, the countryside; *Style—* James Barlow, Esq; ✉ c/o Sir Thomas Barlow, Bt, DSC, DL, 45 Shepherds Hill, Highgate, London N6 5QJ (☎ 0171 340 9653)

BARLOW, James Mellodew; s of Capt Cecil Barlow (d 1988), of Oldham, and Florence Patricia, *née* Mellodew; *b* 23 Dec 1943; *Educ* Mill Hill Sch, Univ of Nottingham (LLB); *Career* admitted slr 1967; ptnr Clifford Chance (formerly Coward Chance) 1980–; hon sec Cumberland LTC 1976–82; memb Worshipful Co of Slrs 1980; memb Law Soc 1967, ATII 1968; *Recreations* squash, tennis, skiing, fell walking, bridge; *Clubs* Old Mill Hillians; *Style—* James Barlow, Esq; ✉ 11 Edmunds Walk, London N2 0NH (☎ 0181 883 6972); Clifford Chance, 200 Aldersgate Street, London EC1A 4JJ (☎ 0171 600 1000, fax 0171 600 5555, telex 887847)

BARLOW, Sir John Kemp; 3 Bt (UK 1907), of Bradwall Hall, Sandbach, Co Chester; s of Sir John Denman Barlow, 2 Bt (d 1986), and Hon Diana Helen Kemp, yr da of 1 Baron Rochdale; *b* 22 April 1934; *Educ* Winchester, Trinity Coll Cambridge (MA); *m* 1962, Susan, da of Col Sir Andrew Horsbrugh-Porter, 3 Bt, DSO; 4 s ((John) William Marshal b 1964, Thomas David Bradwall b (Jan) 1966, Andrew Michael Kemp b (Dec) 1966, Charles James Bulkeley b 1970); *Heir* s, (John) William Marshal Barlow b 12 March 1964; *Career* merchant banker and farmer; chm: Thomas Barlow and Bro Ltd, Barlow Services Ltd, Majedie Investments plc; chm Rubber Growers' Assoc 1974–75, steward Jockey Club 1988–90; High Sheriff Cheshire 1979; *Recreations* hunting, shooting, steeplechasing; *Clubs* Brooks's, Jockey, City of London; *Style—* Sir John K Barlow, Bt; ✉ Brindley, Nantwich, Cheshire CW5 8HX

BARLOW, (David) Michael Rigby; CB (1996); s of late Samuel Gordon Barlow, and late Eunice Hodson Barlow; *b* 8 June 1936; *Educ* Shrewsbury, ChCh Oxford (MA); *m* 1 (m dis); 1 da; m 2, 1973, Valeree Elizabeth Rush-Smith; 1 s; *Career* Nat Serv Midshipman RNVR (Submarine Branch RN) 1954–56, Sub-Lt then Lt perm RNR 1956–61; admitted slr England and Wales 1965, admitted slr NI 1991; various appts as lawyer in public serv 1965–73, under sec Govt Legal Serv 1989–96 (asst sec 1973–89), ret 1996; *Recreations* Spanish language and culture, horse riding, cinema; *Style—* Michael Barlow, Esq, CB

BARLOW, Paul Rupert; s of David Barlow, of Jersey, and Belinda, *née* Kidd; *b* 17 Nov 1963; *Educ* Bryanston, St Martin's Sch of Art, Bristol Poly (BA); *Career* creative dir Sampson Tyrrell Enterprise 1994–96 (joined 1988, design dir 1990–94), design dir Ansbach Grossman Enterprise NYC 1996–; cmmns incl: WPP Group annual report 1990, Vernons Pools corp identity 1990, Dun and Bradstreet Euro identitiy and literature system 1991–92, Coates corp identitiy worldwide 1991, Interbank (Turkey) annual report 1992, Univ of Westminster identity 1992, MoDo Merchants corp identity and new Swatch system incl advtg campaign 1993, EMI Classics brand guidelines and complete CD range re-design 1994, Sisu (Finland) corp identity 1994; work published in Design Week, Creative Review, Graphis, Design Magazine and Graphics International; *Recreations* sport and general fitness; *Style—* Paul Barlow, Esq; ✉ Ansbach Grossman Enterprise, 711 Third Avenue, New York, NY 10017, USA (☎ 00 1 212 692 9000)

BARLOW, Roy Oxspring; s of George Barlow, and Clarice Barlow; *b* 13 Feb 1927; *Educ* King Edward VII Sch Sheffield, Queen's Coll Oxford, Univ of Sheffield (LLB); *m* 1957, Kathleen Mary Roberts; 2 s, 1 da; *Career* slr; local govt 1952–62, slr in private practice 1962–91, recorder of Crown Court 1975–95; asst cmmr Parly Boundary Cmmn 1992–95; *Recreations* farming, reading, walking; *Style—* Roy Barlow, Esq; ✉ The Cottage, Oxton Rakes, Barlow, Sheffield S18 5TH (☎ 0114 289 0652)

BARLOW, Sir Thomas Erasmus; 3 Bt (UK 1902), of Wimpole Street, St Marylebone, Co London; DSC (1945), DL (Bucks 1976); s of Sir (James) Alan (Noel) Barlow, 2 Bt, GCB, KBE (d 1968); *b* 23 Jan 1914; *Educ* Winchester; *m* 1955, Isabel, da of late Thomas Munn Body, of Middlesbrough; 2 s (James Alan b 1956, Philip Thomas b 1960), 2 da (Monica Ann b 1958, Teresa Mary b 1963); *Heir* s, James Alan Barlow b 10 July 1956; *Career* RN: entered as cadet 1932, qualified Submarines 1937, served WWII submarines in Atlantic, Med, Indian Ocean and Far East, Cdr 1950, Capt 1954, CSO to Flag Offr Submarines 1960–62, Cdre HMS Drake Devenport 1962–64, ret 1964; memb: Royal Soc for Nature Conservation, Berks Bucks and Oxfordshire Naturalists' Tst, Charles Darwin Fndn for Galapogos Islands; *Recreations* birdwatching, wildlife conservation; *Clubs* Athenaeum, Savile; *Style—* Sir Thomas Barlow, Bt, DSC, DL; ✉ 45 Shepherds Hill, Highgate, London N6 5QJ (☎ 0181 340 9653)

BARLOW, Sir (George) William; kt (1977); s of Albert Edward Barlow, and Annice Barlow; *b* 8 June 1924; *Educ* Manchester GS, Univ of Manchester (BSc); *m* 1948, Elaine Mary Atherton, da of William Adamson; 1 s, 1 da; *Career* served RNVR 1944–47; various appts English Electric Co Ltd (Spain 1952–55, Canada 1958–62); md: English Electric Domestic Appliance Co Ltd 1965–67, English Electric Computers Ltd 1967–68; chm: Ransome Hoffman Pollard 1971–77 (gp chief exec 1969–77), PO 1977–80 (organised separation of PO and British Telecom 1980), BICC plc 1984–91 (dir 1980–); dir: Thorn EMI plc 1980, Vodafone plc 1988–, Waste Management International plc 1992–, Chemring Group plc 1994–; chm Ericsson Ltd 1981–94; chm: Design Cncl 1980–86, Nationalised Industs Chairmen's Gp 1980–, Engrg Cncl 1988–91; pres: BEAMA 1986–87, ORGALIME 1990–92, Royal Acad of Engrg 1991–96, Assoc of Lancastrians in London 1992; Liveryman Worshipful Co of Glaziers, Master Worshipful Co of Engrs 1986–87; hon fell UMIST 1978; Hon DSc: Cranfield Inst of Technol 1979, Univ of Bath 1986, Aston Univ 1988, City Univ 1990; Hon DTech: Liverpool Poly (now Liverpool John Moores Univ) 1988, Univ of Loughborough 1993; Hon DEng UMIST 1996; Hon FICE 1991, Hon FIMechE 1993, CEng, FEng 1979, FIMechE, FIEE, CIMgt 1971; *Recreations* golf; *Clubs* Brooks, Army & Navy, Huntercombe, Royal Birkdale Golf; *Style—* Sir William Barlow, FEng; ✉ 4 Parkside, Henley-on-Thames, Oxon RG9 1TX (☎ 01491 411101, fax 01491 410013)

BARLOW, (John) William Marshall; s and h of Sir John Kemp Barlow, 3 Bt; *b* 12 March 1964; *m* 17 Oct 1991, Sarah Hilary, da of John Nobes, of Windsor, Berks; 2 s (John William Oakley b 4 April 1993, Henry James Marshall b 23 July 1995); *Style—* William Barlow, Esq; ✉ 4 Wharfedale Street, London SW10 9AL

BARLTROP, Prof Donald; s of Albert Edward Barltrop (d 1976), and Mabel, *née* Redding (d 1984); *b* 26 June 1933; *Educ* Southall GS, Univ of London (BSc, MB BS, MD); *m* 1 Aug 1959, Mair Angharad, da of Rev Richard Evan Edwards (d 1971), of Swansea; 2 s (Andrew b 1965, Richard b 1968), 1 da (Elen b 1970); *Career* Capt RAMC 1959–61; Fulbright scholar Harvard Univ 1963–64, Wellcome sr res fell in clinical sci 1968–74; reader in paediatrics: St Mary's Hosp 1975–78, Westminster Hosp 1978–82; prof of child health: Westminster Hosps Univ of London 1982–93, West London Hosp 1984–93, Univ of London 1984–, Charing Cross Hosp 1984–, Chelsea and Westminster Hosp 1993–; adjunct prof of community health Tufts Univ Boston Mass 1984–; examiner: RCP, Univs of London, Leicester, Capetown, Hong Kong, Al-Fateh Tripoli; memb: Lead and Health Ctee DHSS, Working Pty on Composition of Infant Foods Ctee DHSS, Steering Ctee on Chemical Aspects of Food Surveillance MAFF; chm Westminster Children Res Tst; medical advsr: Bliss, Buttle Tst, Inst of Sports Med; Freeman City of London 1977, Master Worshipful Co of Barbers 1995 (Liveryman 1978), memb Lord Mayor and Sheriffs' Ctee 1995; FRCP; *Books* Mineral Metabolism in Paediatrics (jtly, 1969), Children in Health and Disease (jtly, 1977), Paediatric Therapeutics (jtly, 1991); *Recreations* offshore sailing; *Clubs* Naval, RNVR Yacht; *Style—* Prof Donald Barltrop; ✉ 7 Grove Rd, Northwood, Middx HA6 2AP (☎ 01923 826461); Chelsea and Westminster Hospital, Fulham Road, London SW10 9NH (☎ 0181 746 8627, fax 0181 746 8770)

BARLTROP, Roger Arnold Rowlandson; CMG (1987), CVO (1982); s of Ernest William Barltrop, CMG, CBE, DSO (d 1957), and Ethel Alice Lucy, *née* Baker (d 1966); the Barltrop family origins lie in Essex, and those of the Bakers in London and (earlier) Yorkshire; *b* 19 Jan 1930; *Educ* Solihull Sch, Leeds GS, Exeter Coll Oxford (MA); *m* 1962 (sep 1992), Penelope Pierrepont, da of Denys Neale Dalton (d 1986); 2 s (Paul, Richard), 2 da (Fiona, Mary); *Career* RN 1949–50, RNVR and RNR 1950–64 (Lt Cdr); HM Dip Serv: served India, Nigeria, Rhodesia, Turkey, Eastern Caribbean and Ethiopia, ambass (formerly high cmmr) to Fiji and concurrently high cmmr to Nauru and Tuvalu 1982–89, ret 1990; memb Cwlth Observer Gps for elections in: Bangladesh 1991, St Kitts 1995; memb OSCE observer mission for elections in Bosnia 1996; foreign affairs advsr Solomon Islands 1994; chm Pacific Islands Soc of the UK and Ireland 1992–, memb Bd of Govrs Cwlth Tst 1995–; *Recreations* sailing, opera, genealogy; *Clubs* Royal Cwlth Soc, Royal Over-Seas League, Royal Suva Yacht (Fiji); *Style—* R A R Barltrop, Esq, CMG, CVO; ✉ 35 Highfield Drive, Hurstpierpoint, W Sussex BN6 9AU

BARNABY, David Anthony Nathan; s of Michael Nathan Barnaby, of Havering, Hants, and Emily Lucille, *née* Broughton (d 1983); *b* 11 Jan 1955; *Educ* St John's HS, Univ of California Berkeley; *m* 1986, Corinne Elise, *née* Hampton; 1 da (Charlotte Madeleine b 1988), 2 s (Mark Nathan, Dominic Anthony (twins) b 1991); *Career* jr then sr designer (car interiors) General Motors Detroit 1976–79, sr ergonomist Chrysler Corp 1979–81, ptnr Design Ergonomics Ltd UK 1981–85, design dir Consumer Products Div Dae Kim Electronics Corp 1985–88, freelance industl designer and ergonomist 1988–; memb Inst of Ergonomics; *Recreations* travel, food and wine, tennis; *Style—* David A Barnaby, Esq; ✉ Flat 4, 28 D'Arbly Street, London W1V 3FH

BARNABY, Dr (Charles) Frank; s of Charles Hector Barnaby (d 1932), and Lilian, *née* Sainsbury; *b* 27 Sept 1927; *Educ* Andover GS, Univ of London (BSc, MSc, PhD); *m* 19 Dec 1972, Wendy Elizabeth, da of Francis Arthur Field, of Adelaide, Aust; 1 s (Benjamin b 1976), 1 da (Sophie b 1975); *Career* physicist: AWRE Aldermaston 1951–57, UCL 1957–67; exec sec Pugwash Conf on Sci and World Affrs 1967–71, dir Stockholm Int Peace Res Inst 1971–81, guest prof Free Univ of Amsterdam 1981–85, author 1985–; Hon Doctorate: Free Univ of Amsterdam, Univ of Southampton; *Books* Man and the Atom (1972), Nuclear Energy (1975), Prospects for Peace (1975), Verification Technologies (1986), Future Warfare (1986), Star Wars (1987), The Automated Battlefield (1987), The Gaia Peace Atlas (1989), The Invisible Bomb (1989), The Role and Control of Force in the 1990's (1992), How Nuclear Weapons Spread (1993); *Recreations* astronomy, bird watching; *Style—* Dr Frank Barnaby; ✉ Brandreth, Station Rd, Chilbolton, Stockbridge, Hants SO20 6AW (☎ 01264 860423, fax 01264 860868)

BARNARD, 11 Baron (E 1698); Harry John Neville Vane; TD (1960), JP (Durham 1961); patron of ten livings; s of 10 Baron Barnard, CMG, OBE, MC, TD, JP (d 1964), and Sylvia Mary, *née* Straker (d 1993); *b* 21 Sept 1923; *Educ* Eton, Univ of Durham Business Sch (MSc); *m* 8 Oct 1952 (m dis 1992), Lady Davina Mary Cecil, DStJ, (*see* Davina, Lady Barnard), da of 6 Marquess of Exeter (d 1981); 1 s, 4 da; *Heir* s, Hon Henry Vane; *Career* Flying Offr RAFVR 1942–46, Northumberland Hussars 1948–66, Lt-Col Cmdg 1964–66, Hon Col 7 (Durham) Bn LI 1979–89, pres N of England TAVRA 1974–77 (vice pres 1970 and 1977–88); landowner, farmer; cncllr Durham 1952–61, memb Durham Co Agric Exec Ctee 1953–72 (chm 1970–72), pres Durham Co Branch CLA 1965–89 (memb CLA Cncl 1950–80), memb N Regnl Panel MAFF 1972–76; vice chm Cncl BRCS 1987–93 (memb Cncl 1982–85), patron Durham Co Branch BRCS 1993– (pres 1969–87); pres: Farmway Ltd 1965–, Teesdale & Weardale Search & Rescue 1969–, Durham Co St John Cncl 1971–88, Durham Co Scout Assoc 1972–88, Durham and Cleveland Co Branch Royal Br Legion 1973–92, Durham Wildlife Tst 1984–95; Lord Lt and Custos Rotulorum Co Durham 1970–88 (Vice Lt 1969–70, DL 1956); Sr Grand Warden Utd Grand Lodge of England 1970–71 (Provincial Grand Master for Durham 1969–); KStJ 1971; *Clubs* Brooks's, Durham County, Northern Counties (Newcastle); *Style*— The Rt Hon the Lord Barnard, TD, JP; ✉ Raby Castle, P O Box 50, Staindrop, Darlington, Co Durham DL2 3AY (☎ 01833 660751)

BARNARD, Prof John Michael; s of John Claude Southard Barnard (d 1976), and Dora Grace, *née* Epps; *b* 13 Feb 1936; *Educ* King Alfred's GS Wantage Berks, Wadham Coll Oxford (BA, BLitt, MA); *m* 1 (m dis); 1 s (Jason b 1966), 2 da (Josie b 1963, Clio b 1965); m 2, 1991, Hermione Lee; *Career* Nat Serv sr radar technician RAF 1954–56; res asst Dept of English Yale Univ USA 1961–64, visiting lectr English Dept Univ of Calif at Santa Barbara USA 1964–65; Sch of English Univ of Leeds: lectr then sr lectr 1965–78, prof 1978–; foreign expert Miny of Educn and Science Netherlands 1992–93; gen ed Longmans Annotated Poets 1977–, Br Acad Warton lectr 1989; memb Mid Wharfedale Parish Cncl 1974–84; memb Cncl Bibliographical Soc 1990–94; *Books* Congreve's The Way of the World (ed, 1972), Pope: The Critical Heritage (ed, 1973, reprinted 1995), John Keats: The Complete Poems (1973, 3 edn 1988), Etherege's The Man of Mode (ed 1979 (reprinted in Five Restoration Comedies, 1984), John Keats (1987), John Keats: Selected Poems (ed, 1988), The Early Seventeenth-Century Book Trade and John Foster's Inventory of 1616 (with Maureen Bell, 1994); *Recreations* travel; *Clubs* Johnson; *Style*— Prof John Barnard; ✉ School of English, University of Leeds, Leeds LS2 9JT (☎ 0113 233 4730, fax 0113 233 4774, telex 556473 UNILDS G)

BARNARD, Sir Joseph Brian; kt (1986), JP (1973), DL (N Yorks 1988); s of Joseph Ernest Barnard (d 1942), and Elizabeth Loudon Barnard (d 1980); *b* 22 Jan 1928; *Educ* Sedbergh; *m* 21 Jan 1959, Suzanne Hamilton, da of Clifford Bray, of Ilkley, W Yorks; 3 s (Nicholas b 1960, Simon (twin) b 1960, Marcus b 1966); *Career* cmmnd KRRC 1946–48; dir: Joseph Constantine Steamship Line Ltd 1952–66, Teesside Warehousing Co Ltd 1966–, NE Electricity Bd 1987–90; chm: E Harsley Parish Cncl 1973–, Northallerton Petty Sessional Div 1981–93, Govrs Ingleby Arncliffe C of E Primary Sch 1981–91, NE Electricity Consultative Cncl 1987–90, Indeck Energy Services (UK) Ltd 1991–, Worldwide Cargo Control Studies Ltd 1992–93, International Business Group 1993–; pres: Yorks area Cons Trade Unionists, Yorks Magistrates Ct Ctee 1981–93; patron St Oswald's E Harsley; chm: Yorks Area Cons 1983–88, Nat Union of Cons and Unionist Assocs 1990–91 (vice chm 1988–90); *Recreations* walking, shooting, gardening; *Clubs* Carlton; *Style*— Sir Joseph Barnard, JP, DL; ✉ Harsley Hall, Northallerton, N Yorks DL6 2BL (☎ 01609 882203)

BARNARD, Hon Lance Herbert; AO (1979); s of Hon H C Barnard; *b* 1 May 1919; *Educ* Launceston Tech Coll; *m* 1; 1 da; m 2, 1962, Jill, da of Senator H Cant; 1 s, 2 da (and 1 da decd); *Career* elected to Aust House of Reps as memb for Bass 1954, 1955, 1958, 1961, 1963, 1966, 1969, 1972 and 1974, dep ldr Fed PLP 1967–72, min for defence 1972–75, dep PM 1972–74, Australian ambass to Sweden, Norway and Finland 1975–78; state pres Tasmanian Branch Aust Lab Pty, dir Office of Aust War Graves Dept of Veterans' Affrs 1981–83; *Recreations* gardening; *Style*— Hon Lance Barnard, AO; ✉ 6 Bertland Court, Launceston, Tasmania 7250, Australia

BARNARD, Michael John; s of Cecil William Barnard, and Gladys Irene Mary, *née* Hedges; *b* 4 May 1944; *Educ* Licensed Victuallers Sch Slough; *m* 1, 12 March 1965 (m dis 1979), Jennifer, da of Charles Tyrrill; 1 s (Matthew b 15 Sept 1971); m 2, Charlotte Susan, da of Sir Kenneth Berrill; m 3, 1 March 1996, Jayne Ann, da of Brian Jenkinson; *Career* journalist: Kent Web Offset Group 1962–66, Westminster Press 1966–67 and 1968–71; managing ed First Features Ltd 1967–68, prodn dir Macmillan Magazines 1971–79, chm and md Macmillan Production Ltd 1979–; dir: Macmillan Publishers Ltd 1982–, Macmillan Ltd 1985–, Macmillan Publishers Group Administration Ltd 1988–; chm: Macmillan Distribution Ltd 1988–95, Macmillan Information Systems Ltd 1988–95; non-exec dir: Periodical Publishers' Association Ltd 1988–91, Gill & Macmillan Ltd 1990–94; chm New Media Investments Ltd 1994–; chm Printing Industries' Research Assoc 1995–; Liveryman Worshipful Co of Stationers and Newspapermakers 1995 (Freeman 1993); MCB 1988, FRSA 1991, MILog 1993; *Books* Magazine and Journal Production (1986), Introduction to Print Buying (1987), Inside Magazines (1989), Introduction to Printing Processes (1990); *Recreations* swimming, gardening, reading; *Style*— Michael Barnard, Esq; ✉ Macmillan Ltd, Houndmills, Basingstoke, Hants RG21 2XS (☎ 01256 29242, fax 01256 331248, telex 858493)

BARNARD, Surgn Rear Adm (Ernest Edward) Peter; s of Lionel Edward Barnard (d 1964), of Milford on Sea, and Ernestine, *née* Lethbridge (d 1986); *b* 22 Feb 1927; *Educ* schs in UK and S Aust, St John's Coll Oxford (DPhil); *m* 1955, Joan Marion, da of Arthur William Gunn (d 1984), of Grays, Essex; 1 s (Christopher), 1 da (Penelope); *Career* Dep Med Dir Gen (Naval) 1980–82, Surgn Rear Adm (Operational Med Support) 1982–84; publications on underwater medicine and physiology 1962–85; FFCM; *Recreations* gardening, photography; *Style*— Surgn Rear Adm Peter Barnard; ✉ Chesilcote, Chapel Rd, Swanmore, Southampton SO32 2QA (☎ 01489 892373)

BARNARD, Robert; s of Leslie Barnard (d 1969), and Vera Doris, *née* Nethercoat; *b* 23 Nov 1936; *Educ* Colchester Royal GS, Balliol Coll Oxford, Univ of Bergen Norway (DPhil); *m* 1963, Mary Louise Tabor, da of Geoffrey Tabor, of Armidale, Aust; *Career* author; lectr in English lit Univ of New England Armidale NSW 1961–66, lectr and sr lectr Univ of Bergen Norway 1966–76, prof of English lit Univ of Tromsø Norway 1976–83; memb: Soc of Authors, Crime Writers' Assoc (memb Ctee 1988–91); chm Brontë Soc 1996– (memb Cncl and vice chm 1991–95); *Books* incl: Death of An Old Goat (1974), Unruly Son (1978), Mother's Boys (1981), Sheer Torture (1981), A Corpse in a Gilded Cage (1984), A Short History of English Literature (1984), Out of the Blackout (1985), The Skeleton in the Grass (1987), City of Strangers (1990), Dead, Mr Mozart (as Bernard Bastable, 1995); *Recreations* walking, opera, Edwin Drood; *Style*— Robert Barnard, Esq; ✉ Hazeldene, Houghley Lane, Leeds LS13 2DT (☎ 0113 263 8955); agents: Gregory & Radice, 3 Barb Mews, London W6 7PA (☎ 0171 610 4676, fax 0171 610 4686)

BARNARD, Stephen Geoffrey; s of Geoffrey Thomas Barnard, and Diana Pixie, *née* Rivron; *b* 4 May 1950; *Educ* Gresham's Sch, Univ of Southampton (LLB); *m* 4 Oct 1980, Jane Elizabeth Lisa, da of Dr Oliver Vivian Maxim, of Gretton, Northants; *Career* admitted slr 1974; traveller 1974–75; Herbert Smith: joined 1976, NY 1980–82, ptnr 1983–; *Recreations* golf, bridge, walking, birds, skiing, reading, trying to paint, music, talking, wine; *Style*— Stephen Barnard, Esq; ✉ Herbert Smith, Exchange House, Primrose St, London EC2A 2HS (☎ 0171 374 8000, fax 0171 496 1143, telex 886633)

BARNE, Maj Nicholas Michael Lancelot; LVO (1996); *b* 25 Nov 1943; *Educ* Eton; *m* 1974, The Hon Janet Elizabeth Maclean, da of Baron Maclean, KT, GCVO, KBE, PC (Life Peer); 2 s (Alasdair Michael Fitzroy b 1979, Hamish Nicholas Charles b 1981); *Career* Regular Offr Scots Gds 1965–79, fruit farmer 1979–84, Hon Col Norfolk Army Cadet Force 1989– (Co Cmdt 1985–89); Private Sec, Comptroller and Equerry to HRH Princess Alice, Duchess of Gloucester and to TRH The Duke and Duchess of Gloucester 1989–; *Recreations* golf, shooting, skiing; *Style*— Maj Nicholas Barne, LVO; ✉ Blofield House, Blofield, Norwich NR13 4RW; Tower Flat, Kensington Palace, London W8 4PU

BARNES, Adrian Francis Patrick; CVO (1996); s of Francis Walter Ibbetson Barnes, and Heather Katherine, *née* Tamplin; *b* 25 Jan 1943; *Educ* St Paul's, City of London Poly (MA); *m* 31 May 1980, Sally Eve, da of Dr James Lawson Whatley (d 1986); 1 s (William b 1982), 1 da (Sophie b 1983); *Career* called to the Bar Gray's Inn 1973; Slr's Dept DTI 1975–82, dep remembrancer Corp of London 1982, City remembrancer 1986–; doyen Gray's Inn Seniors in Hall 1992–, govr Music Therapy Charity 1995–; Freeman City of London 1982, Liveryman Merchant Taylors' Co 1989; *Recreations* music, cricket, biography, circuit training, chess, City lore; *Clubs* Brooks's, Guildhall, Cannons Sports (City); *Style*— Adrian Barnes, Esq, CVO; ✉ PO Box 270, Guildhall, London EC2P 2EJ (☎ 0171 332 1200, fax 0171 332 1895, telex 265608)

BARNES, Anthony David; s of Cecil James (d 1975), of Hove, and Mary Grace, *née* Pardey; *b* 19 June 1934; *Educ* Brighton Hove and Sussex GS, Univ of Birmingham (BSc, MB ChM); *m* 11 July 1959, Patricia Mary, da of John Frederick Pyatt (d 1977), of Stone; 1 s (Simon David b 1961), 2 da (Sarah Anne Louise b 1963, Joanna Mary b 1966); *Career* Univ of Birmingham: lectr in anatomy 1959–60, Leverhulme res fell 1960–62; United Birmingham Hosp: surgical trainee 1962–69, conslt surgn 1969–; RCS: Arris & Gayle lectr, Hunterian prof, regnl advsr 1984–90; chm UK Transplant 1972–82, pres W Midlands Surgical Soc 1995–96; memb: BMA, Br Transplant Soc, Br Assoc of Endocrine Surgns (pres 1995–97), Assoc of Surgns; FRCS; *Recreations* fishing, farming; *Style*— Anthony Barnes, Esq; ✉ 25 Metchley Park Rd, Edgbaston, Birmingham B15 2PQ (☎ 0121 454 2607); Queen Elizabeth Hospital, Queen Elizabeth Medical Centre, Edgbaston, Birmingham B15 2TH (☎ 0121 627 2523)

BARNES, Carol Lesley; da of Lesley Harry Barnes, of London SW16, and Alexandra Barnes; *b* 13 Sept 1944; *Educ* St Martin in the Fields HS, Univ of Sheffield (BA), Univ of Birmingham (Cert Ed); *m* 30 July 1981, Nigel Thomson, s of Hugh Thomson, of Brighton; 1 s (James b 25 May 1982), 1 da (Clare b 14 July 1979); *Career* presenter LBC Radio 1973–74, reporter World at One BBC Radio 4 1974–75, reporter and newscaster ITN 1974–; TV and Radio Industries Newscaster of the Year 1994; *Recreations* exercise, golf, good food and wine, diving, skiing; *Style*— Ms Carol Barnes; ✉ ITN, 200 Gray's Inn Road, London WC1X 8XZ (☎ 0171 833 3000)

BARNES, Christian William; s of Oswald Edward Barnes, of Gt Houghton Hall, Northants, and Gillian, *née* Ralph; *b* 20 June 1959; *Educ* Uppingham, Univ of Durham (BA); *m* 1987, Melanie Joy, da of Kenneth Roy Eades (d 1996); 3 s (Elliot James Royston b 6 Feb 1991, Hamish William b 25 June 1993, Lewis Gabriel b 1 Jan 1996); *Career* advertisement sales mangr Dominion Press Ltd 1981–82, asst account mangr then account dir Leo Burnett Ltd 1982–87, fndr ptnr and co dir Barnes Vereker Ltd 1987–; *Recreations* music, theatre, travel; *Style*— Christian Barnes, Esq; ✉ Barnes Vereker Ltd, 3 Lloyds Wharf, Mill St, London SE1 2BA (☎ 0171 231 3100, fax 0171 231 6868)

BARNES, Christopher John Andrew (Chris); CB; s of Eric Vernon Barnes (d 1988), and Joan Mary, *née* Benge; *b* 11 Oct 1944; *Educ* City of London Sch, LSE (BSc Econ); *m* 1, 1978 (m dis 1990), Carolyn Elizabeth Douglas Johnston; 2 s (Andrew Peter b 13 July 1978, Timothy Richard b 13 Nov 1980); m 2, 1990, Susan Elizabeth Bridle; 2 s (Nicholas James b 6 Jan 1991, Edward Christopher b 19 Nov 1993); *Career* civil servant; MAFF: exec offr 1962–67, asst princ 1967–69, private sec to Parly Sec 1969–71, princ 1971–80, asst sec 1980, chief regnl offr 1980–83, head Personnel Div 1983–88, head Res Policy Div 1988–90, Near Market R & D Review 1988–89, under sec Arable Crops, Horticulture and Alcoholic Drinks 1990–95, dir of Establishments 1995–96, ret; dir Bucks Health Authy 1996–, dir Drew Associates Ltd 1996–; chair Civil Service Selection Bd 1995–; sr conslt Andersons 1996–; non-exec dir Booker Food Services 1987–90; memb Mgmnt Ctee Civil Serv Healthcare 1992–; *Recreations* off-road vehicles, country living, France; *Style*— Chris Barnes, Esq, CB; ✉ via MAFF, PMDD, Noble House, Smith Square, London SW1P 3JR

BARNES, Colin Angus; s of Maurice Angus Barnes (d 1991), of Stratford-upon-Avon, and Dorothy Edith, *née* Hubbard (1981); *b* 6 July 1933; *Educ* Bradfield Coll; *m* 20 Oct 1962, Brenda Agnes, da of Robert Burnett Loughborough; 1 s (David Angus b 15 Aug 1963), 2 da (Nicola Elizabeth b 11 June 1965, Susannah Dorothy b 17 Dec 1971); *Career* Nat Serv RAF 1952–54, Pilot Offr 1954; BOAC: cadet pilot and trainee navigator 1955–56, flight navigator and second offr 1956, flight navigator Argonauts and Yorks 1956–57, co-pilot and navigator Britannia 102s 1957, first offr 1958, co-pilot and navigator Boeing 707s 1962–71, sr first offr 1963, check first offr (navigation) Boeing 707 and Bd of Trade authorised examiner (Flight Navigator's Licence) 1968, captain 1971, flight superintendent (technical) Boeing 707 1973; British Airways (following merger of BOAC and BEA): flight superintendent (technical) DC10 1974, dep flight mangr (technical) DC10 1977, asst chief pilot 747/Concorde/DC10 1978, chief pilot 1981, dir of flight crew 1986–91, chm subsid British Caledonian Flight Training Ltd 1989–90 (non-exec dir 1988–91), ret 1991; non-exec dir British Airways plc 1991–, chm BA Air Safety Review Ctee 1991–; govr and memb Exec Ctee Flight Safety Fndn 1991–; The Air League: memb Cncl 1993–, memb Exec Ctee 1994–; *Recreations* gardening, tennis; *Clubs* RAF; *Style*— Colin Barnes, Esq; ✉ British Airways plc, c/o X416 Speedbird House (S226), PO Box 10, London Airport Heathrow, Hounslow, Middx TW6 2JA (☎ 0181 562 5394, fax 0181 562 3323)

BARNES, Dr Colin Greenhill; s of Harold Albert Barnes (d 1975), of Pinner, Middx, and Marjorie Mary, *née* Pottle; *b* 4 July 1936; *Educ* Mill Hill Sch, The London Hosp Med Coll Univ of London (BSc, MB BS); *m* 22 Sept 1962, Marian Nora, da of William Goss Sampson (d 1984), of Exeter; 2 s (Graham b 1964, Peter b 1966); *Career* conslt rheumatologist; conslt physician and clinical dir in rheumatology The Royal London Hosp 1968–96, rheumatologist London Independent Hosp 1986–, hon conslt rheumatologist St Luke's Hosp for the Clergy 1987–, hon sr lectr The London Hosp Med Coll Univ of London 1994–96 (teacher 1974–94); chm: Exec Fin Ctee Arthritis and Rheumatism Cncl for Res 1977–93, Mgmnt Ctee Kennedy Inst of Rheumatology 1977–93, Standing Ctee on Devpt of Academic Rheumatology Arthritis and Rheumatism Cncl 1993–; pres: Br League Against Rheumatism 1982–85, Euro League Against Rheumatism 1989–91; assoc ed Annals of the Rheumatic Diseases 1982–88, memb Editorial Bd The Foot 1990–, ed Eular Bulletin/Rheumatology in Europe 1993–; FRCP (London) 1978, fell Royal Soc of Med; memb: BMA, British Soc for Rheumatology; hon memb: French Soc of Rheumatology, Swiss Soc of Rheumatology, Euro League Against Rheumatism (vice pres 1987–89, pres 1989–91), Aust Rheumatology Assoc, Italian Soc of Rheumatology; life govr Mill Hill Sch; *Books* Behçets Syndrome (jt ed, 1979), Behçets Disease (jt ed, 1986); contrib: Clinical Rheumatology, Copeman's Textbook of Rheumatology, The Foot; *Recreations* gardening, music (classical), opera, skiing, travel; *Clubs* Reform, RSM; *Style*— Dr Colin Barnes; ✉ 96 Harley St, London W1N 1AF (☎ 0171 486 0967, fax 0171 935 1107); Newlands, Forest Close, Woodford Green, Essex IG8 0QD (☎ 0181 505 1300)

BARNES, David; s of Tom Barnes, of Fleet, Hants, and Phyllis, *née* Green; *b* 6 Feb 1949; *Educ* Bedford Sch, Univ of Leeds (BA), LSE (MSc), Warwick Univ Business Sch (MSc); *m* 28 July 1972, Lynn Maria Sarah, da of Joseph Johnston; *Career* purchasing offr Philips Industries 1972–73, systems analyst and cost accountant Lucas CAV Ltd 1974–77, asst to fin dir Lucas Girling Koblenz Germany 1977–81, planning mangr then international treasy mangr Cummins Engine Co Ltd 1981–85, asst treas Abbey National Building Society 1985–88; Cheltenham & Gloucester Building Society: gen mangr (fin) 1988–89, fin dir 1989–95; fin dir Britannic Assurance PLC 1995–; ACMA; *Recreations* riding, golf; *Style*— David Barnes, Esq; ✉ Britannic Assurance PLC, Moor Green, Moseley, Birmingham B13 8QF (☎ 0121 449 4444, fax 0121 449 0456)

BARNES, Sir (James) David Francis; kt (1996), CBE (1987); s of Eric Cecil Barnes, CMG (d 1987), and Jean Margaret Procter, *née* Dickens (d 1996); *b* 4 March 1936; *Educ* Shrewsbury, Univ of Liverpool; *m* 1 May 1963, (Wendy) Fiona Mary, da of John Leighton Riddell (d 1994), of Limetree House, Gawsworth, Macclesfield, Cheshire; 1 s (Jonathan Mark b 8 July 1967), 1 da (Alison Jane b 9 Nov 1964); *Career* Nat Serv 1958–60, cmmnd N Battery (The Eagle Troop) 2 Regt RA; ICI Pharmaceuticals Div: Euro mangr 1968, overseas dir 1971–77, dep chm 1977–83; chm ICI Paints Div 1983–86, exec dir ICI plc 1986–93, chief exec offr Zeneca Group plc (following demerger from ICI) 1993–; non-exec dir: Thorn EMI plc 1987–94, Redland plc 1994–; dep chm Business in the Community 1996–; Thames Valley Hospice: chm of Capital Appeal 1984–88, vice pres 1987; NEDO: chm Pharmaceuticals EDC 1983–92, chm Biotechnology Industs Working Party 1989–92; memb Bd Govrs Ashridge (Bonar Law Meml) Tst 1993–; Wooldridge Meml Medal BVA 1995; Hon LLD Univ of Liverpool 1996; FInstD 1983, CIMgt 1987, FRSA 1988, hon assoc memb BVA 1995; *Recreations* fishing, shooting, walking; *Style*— Sir David Barnes, CBE; ✉ Zeneca Group plc, 15 Stanhope Gate, London W1Y 6LN (☎ 0171 304 5000, fax 0171 304 5129, telex 94014000 ZENE G)

BARNES, David Stewart; s of Herbert Stewart Barnes (d 1978), of Salford Lancs, and Kate Myfanwy, *née* Jones; *b* 6 Sept 1938; *Educ* Salford GS, King's Coll Univ of Durham, Univ of Manchester (DipArch, second and third year design prizes, Soccer colours, Univ Athletic Union Soccer colours), RIBA; *m* June 1967, Gwendoline Edith Irene, da of Thomas Foster (d 1986); 1 da (Sarah Kate b 11 May 1972); *Career* asst architect: Cruickshank & Seward Manchester 1964–68, Building Design Partnership Manchester 1968–69; princ ptnr Barnes Heap & Assoc Glossop Derbyshire 1969–74, architect ptnr Building Design Partnership 1979– (project architect 1974–79); *Awards* RIBA Award for Chloride Technical Ltd Swinton Manchester 1978, Structural Steel Design Award 1979; Civic Trust Awards for: Gtr Manchester County Fire Serv HQ 1981, Museum of Sci and Indust Manchester 1989; Class 3 Office of the Year Award for Building Design Partnership Office Sheffield 1983, Office of the Year for Br Cncl Northern Headquarters Manchester 1993; RIBA Regnl Awards for: Museum of Sci and Indust Manchester 1989, Eureka The Children's Museum Halifax 1993; RICS/Times Conservation commendation 1989, Europa Nostra Dip for Christie Building Univ of Manchester 1994, Leeds Award for Architecture for Granary Warehouse 1995; *Recreations* soccer, golf; *Clubs* Manchester Univ Soccer (past pres), Manchester Univ XXI, Mottram Hall Golf; *Style*— David Barnes, Esq; ✉ Building Design Partnership, Sunlight House, PO Box 85, Quay St, Manchester M60 3JA (☎ 0161 834 8441, fax 0161 832 4280)

BARNES, Edward Campbell; s of Hubert Turnbull Barnes, and Annie Mabel, *née* Latham; *b* 8 Oct 1928; *Educ* Wigan Coll; *m* 1950, Dorothy, *née* Smith (d 1992); 1 s, 2 da; *Career* British Forces Network Vienna 1946–49, stage mgmnt provincial and West End theatre 1949–55; BBC TV: studio mgmnt 1955–62, prodr Blue Peter 1962–70, dep head of children's progs 1970–78, head of children's progs 1978–86; ind TV prodr/dir and TV conslt 1986–; prodr/dir: Treasure Houses 1986, All Our Children 1987–90, You Can Do It 1990–91, Boxpops 1991–92, One of Us 1992, The Lowdown: Child to Child 1992, Parallel 9 (exec prodr) 1992; memb: Bd Children's Film and Television Foundation Ltd 1983–, RTS (memb Awards Ctee 1989–91); dir Christian Children's Fund (GB) 1995–; Specialist Prog BAFTA Craft Awards 1969, Silver Medal RTS 1986, Pye Award for services on children's TV 1986; *Books* 25 Blue Peter Books and 8 Blue Peter Mini Books (from 1964), 6 Blue Peter Special Assignment Books (1973–75), Blue Peter Royal Safari (1971), Petra - A Dog for Everyone (1977), Blue Peter - The Inside Story (1989); *Recreations* cricket, Bali, opera, birding; *Clubs* Tewin Irregulars CC; *Style*— Edward Barnes, Esq

BARNES, Edwin; *see:* Richborough, Bishop of

BARNES, Gerald William (Gerry); s of George William Barnes (d 1977), and Violet, *née* Stevens (d 1975); *b* 4 Sept 1928; *Educ* Southend HS, Brentwood Sch; *m* 4 Dec 1954, Jean Dorothy, da of James Robert Hills; 1 s (Robin Richard b 1963); *Career* Nat Serv 13/18 Royal Hussars; CA 1956, budget offr International Computers Ltd 1957–59; fin dir: Pembroke Carton and Printing Co Ltd 1959–64, W S Cowell Ltd and Cowells plc 1964–87; corp conslt 1988–92; chm Allington NHS Tst 1991–; various past offices held in Br Printing Indust Fedn incl: pres E Anglia Alliance, memb Fin Ctee, memb Educn Ctee, memb Eastern Regnl Bd, chm Book Prod Section; FCA 1956; *Recreations* cricket, theatre, travel; *Clubs* Ipswich and Suffolk; *Style*— Gerry Barnes Esq; ✉ Sweynes, 1 Church Crescent, Sproughton, Ipswich, Suffolk IP8 3BJ (☎ and fax 01473 742760)

BARNES, Harold (Harry); MP (Lab) Derbyshire NE (majority 6,270); s of late Joseph Barnes, of Easington Colliery, Co Durham, and Betsy, *née* Gray; *b* 22 July 1936; *Educ* Ruskin Coll Oxford, Univ of Hull (BA); *m* 14 Sept 1963, Elizabeth Ann, da of Richard Stephenson (d 1983); 1 s (Stephen b 1968), 1 da (Joanne b 1972); *Career* Nat Serv RAF 1954–56; railway clerk 1952–54 and 1956–62; lectr Univ of Sheffield 1966–87 (dir mature matriculation courses 1984–87); variety of positions NE Derbys Constituency Lab Pty 1970–87, MP (Lab) Derbyshire NE 1987–; memb Cncl of Nat Admin Cncl of Independent Lab Pubns 1977–80 and 1982–85; memb ctee stage: Local Govt Fin Act 1988, Employment Act 1989, Football Spectator Act 1989, Educn (Student Loans) Act 1990, NI (Emergency Provisions) Bill 1990–91, Tport and Works 1992, Further and Higher Educn 1992, Civil Rights (Disabled Reform) Bill 1995; memb: Select Ctees Euro Legislation 1989–, Members Interests 1990–92, Standing Ctee (A) on Euro Legislation 1991–; assoc memb Br-Irish Inter-Parly Body 1992–; vice chm: Lab Back-Bench Ctee on NI 1989–93, E Midlands Gp Labour MPs 1990–; chm: Lab Back-Bench Ctee on Environmental Protection 1993–, All-Pty UK-Malta Gp 1993–; jt pres New Dialogue 1993–; *Clubs* Dronfield Contact (Sheffield), Chesterfield Labour; *Style*— H Barnes, Esq, MP; ✉ House of Commons, London SW1A 0AA (☎ 0171 219 4521 and 01246 412588)

BARNES, Jack Henry; s of James Barnes (d 1944), and Joan Ivy, *née* Sears; *b* 11 Dec 1943; *Educ* Hatfield Sch Herts, Univ of Sussex (BA), LSE (MSc); *m* 1966, Nicola, *née* Pearse; 2 da (Sarah b 1969, Rachel b 1970); *Career* univ and private sector res conslt 1968–78; Dept of Health 1978–: Chief Scientist's Office 1978–83, Social Servs Inspectorate 1983–88, Res Mgmnt Div 1988–91, Primary Care Div NHS Exec 1991–95, currently with Int and Indust Div; *Style*— Jack Barnes, Esq; ✉ International and Industry Division, Room 505, Richmond House, Whitehall, London SW1A 2NS (☎ 0171 210 5881, fax 0171 710 5660)

BARNES, James Frederick; CB (1982); s of Wilfred Barnes (d 1984), and Doris Martha, *née* Deighton (d 1985); *b* 8 March 1932; *Educ* Taunton's Sch Southampton, The Queen's Coll Oxford (BA, MA); *m* 1957, Dorothy Jean, da of William Jeffrey Drew (d 1980); 1 s (Richard), 2 da (Amanda, Elizabeth); *Career* Engine Div Bristol Aeroplane Co 1953, Nat Gas Turbine Estab Miny of Supply: sci offr 1955, sr sci offr 1957, princ sci offr 1962, sr princ sci offr 1965; asst dir Engine R&D Miny of Aviation 1970, seconded HM Dip Serv as cnsllr (sci and technol) Washington 1972; MOD: under sec 1974, DG Res (C) Procurement Exec 1974–77, dep dir (weapons) RAE 1978–79, dep chief scientific advsr (projects) 1979–82, dep controller (estabs resources and personnel) 1982–84, dep controller (estabs and res) 1984–86, dep chief scientific advsr and head of profession Sci Gp 1987–89, chm MOD Individual Merit Promotion Panel 1990–; chm of govrs Yateley Manor Prep Sch 1981–88, churchwarden All Saint's Farringdon 1984–89, lay memb Winchester Diocesan Synod 1985–89, stewardship advsr Dio of Monmouth 1989–96, chm Churches' Stewardship Network CCBI 1994–96 (treas 1993–94), sec Monmouth Diocesan Advsy Ctee for the Care of Churches 1994–96, memb Church in Wales Working Gps on the Charities Act and on Ecclesiastical Exemption 1996–; tstee Roger Williams and Queen Victoria Almshouses Newport 1990–; memb Ctee: Monmouth and Llandoff Housing Assoc 1991–93, Gwerin (Cymru) Housing Assoc 1993–94; James Clayton Fund prize IMechE 1964; CEng, FRAeS; *Recreations* garden, local history; *Style*— James Barnes, Esq, CB; ✉ Richmond House, 1 Tintern Heights, Catbrook, Chepstow, Monmouthshire NP6 6NH

BARNES, Jeremy; s of John Woodley Barnes, of Cornwall, and Elizabeth Ann, *née* Polkinghorne; *b* 11 Feb 1961; *Educ* Truro Sch, KCL (BA); *m* 8 August 1987, Susan Elizabeth, da of William Alexander Peet; 2 s (Matthew Robert b 1 March 1990, Henry Alexander b 6 Sept 1992); *Career* trainee accountant Saffery Champness 1982–86, fin accountant S G Warburg 1986–87, ptnr Saffery Champness 1990– (rejoined 1987); ACA 1986; *Recreations* rugby, shooting and fishing; *Clubs* RAC; *Style*— Jeremy Barnes, Esq; ✉ Saffery Champness, Fairfax House, Fulwood Place, Gray's Inn, London WC1V 6UB (☎ 0171 405 2828, fax 0171 405 7887, car 0831 308143)

BARNES, John Alfred; CBE (1993); s of John Joseph Barnes (d 1953), of Sunderland, and Margaret Carr, *née* Walker (d 1984); *b* 29 April 1930; *Educ* Bede Boys' GS Sunderland, Univ of Durham (BSc, MA, MEd); *m* 7 Aug 1954, Ivy May, da of Robert Rowntree Walker (d 1981), of Sunderland; 2 da (Shirley May b 30 Oct 1957, Jennifer Anne b 16 June 1960); *Career* Nat Serv RAF 1948–49; teacher Grangefield GS Stockton-on-Tees 1953–57, asst educn offr Barnsley Co Borough 1957–61, dir of educn City of Wakefield 1963–68 (dep dir 1961–63), chief educn offr City of Salford 1968–84, dir-gen City & Guilds of London Inst 1984–93; chm: Assoc Lancs Sch Examining Bd 1972–84, Northern Examining Assoc 1979–82, Assoc Colls of Further Educn 1980–81, Sir Isaac Pitman Ltd 1990– (sec UK Skills 1990–); memb: various industl trg bds 1969–78, MSC Ctees 1978–84, Assoc Examining Bd 1985–93, Nat Examinations Bd for Supervisory Mgmnt 1985–93, Review of Vocational Qualifications Working Gp 1985–86, Exec Standing Conf on Schs Sci and Technol 1985–89 (chm Exec Ctee 1988–89), Further Educn Unit Mgmnt Bd 1986–89, YTS Certification Bd 1986–89, Task Gp of Assessment and Testing 1987–88, Cncl City Technol Colleges Tst 1990–93, Buckinghamshire CC 1993–; hon sec Assoc Educn Offrs 1977–84, treas Nat Fndn for Educnl Res 1979–84, pres Educn Devpt Assoc 1980–85; govr: Imperial Coll London 1987–93, Aylesbury Coll 1996–; tstee City Parochial Fndn and Tst for London 1993–; Freeman City of London 1989; FRSA 1973, FITD 1986, Hon FCP 1991, Hon FCGI 1992, Hon CIPD 1994; *Recreations* cultural activities, foreign travel; *Clubs* Athenaeum; *Style*— John Barnes, Esq, CBE; ✉ Two Oaks, 37 Woodfield Park, Amersham, Bucks HP6 5QH (☎ and fax 01494 726120)

BARNES, Prof Jonathan; s of Albert Leonard Barnes (d 1992), and Kathleen Mabel, *née* Scoltock; *b* 26 Dec 1942; *Educ* City of London Sch, Balliol Coll Oxford; *m* Jennifer Mary, da of Ormond Postgate; 2 da (Catherine, Camilla); *Career* Univ of Oxford: fell Oriel Coll 1968–78, lectr in philosophy 1968, fell Balliol Coll 1978–94, prof of ancient philosophy 1989–94; prof of ancient philosophy Univ of Geneva 1994–; visiting appointments at: Univ of Chicago, Inst for Advanced Study Princeton, Univ of Massachusetts Amherst, Univ of Texas Austin, Wissenschaftskolleg Zu Berlin, Univ of Edmonton, Univ of Zurich, Istituto Italiano per gli Studi Filosofici Naples; FBA 1987; *Books* The Ontological Argument (1972), Aristotle's Posterior Analytics (1975), The Presocratic Philosophers (1979), Aristotle (1982), Early Greek Philosophy (1987), The Toils of Scepticism (1990); *Style*— Prof Jonathan Barnes, FBA; ✉ Département de Philosophie, Université de Genève, 1211 Geneva 4, Switzerland

BARNES, Dame (Alice) Josephine Mary Taylor; DBE (1974); da of late Rev Walter W Barnes (d 1959), and Alice Mary, *née* Ibbetson; *b* 18 Aug 1912; *Educ* Oxford HS, Lady Margaret Hall Oxford (MA, BM BCh, DM), Univ Coll Hosp Med Sch; *m* 1942 (m dis 1964), (Harold) Brian Seymour (later Sir Brian) Warren (d 1996); 1 s (Antony), 2 da (Penelope, Amanda); *Career* dep academic head Obstetric Unit UCH 1947–52, surgn Marie Curie Hosp 1947–67, consulting obstetrician and gynaecologist Charing Cross Hosp and Elizabeth Garrett Anderson Hosp; pres: Med Women's Fedn 1966–67, Women's Nat Cancer Control Campaign 1974– (chm 1969–72, vice pres 1972–74), Nat Assoc of Family Planning Doctors 1976–93, BMA 1979–80, Nat Assoc of Family Planning Nurses 1980–, Royal Med Benevolent Fund 1982–97; memb Cncl: Med Def Union 1961–82 (vice pres 1982–87), RCOG 1965–71 (sr vice pres 1974–75), Advertising Standards Authy 1980–93; hon fell: Lady Margaret Hall Oxford 1980, Chartered Soc of Physiotherapy 1991; Hon MD: Univ of Liverpool 1979, Univ of Southampton 1981; Hon DSc: Univ of Leicester 1980, Univ of Oxford 1990; hon bencher Gray's Inn 1993; Hon FRCOG 1994, FRCP, FRCS, FRCPI, FKC; *Books* Lecture Notes on Gynaecology (6 edn 1988), Scientific Foundations of Obstetrics and Gynaecology (ed 3 edn 1986); *Recreations* music, gastronomy, motoring, foreign travel; *Style*— Dame Josephine Barnes, DBE; ✉ 1 Chartwell House, 12 Ladbroke Terrace, London W11 3PG (☎ 0171 727 9832)

BARNES, Sir Kenneth; KCB (1977, CB 1970); s of Arthur Barnes and Doris Barnes, of Accrington, Lancs; *b* 26 Aug 1922; *Educ* Accrington GS, Balliol Coll Oxford; *m* 1948, Barbara Ainsworth; 1 s, 2 da; *Career* entered Miny of Labour 1948, under sec Cabinet Office 1966–68, perm sec Dept of Employment 1976–82 (dep sec 1968–75); *Style*— Sir Kenneth Barnes, KCB; ✉ South Sandhills, Sandy Lane, Betchworth, Surrey RH3 7AA (☎ 01737 842445)

BARNES, Dr (Nicholas) Martin Limer; s of Geoffrey Lambe Barnes (d 1984), of Craven Arms, Shropshire and Birmingham, and Emily *née* Dicken (d 1976); *b* 18 Jan 1939; *Educ* King Edward's Sch Birmingham, Imperial Coll London (BScEng), Univ of Manchester Inst of Sci and Technol (PhD); *m* 23 Feb 1963, Diana Marion, da of Barrie Campbell (d 1968); 1 s (Matthew b 1966), 1 da (Kate b 1964); *Career* res fell Univ of Manchester 1968–71, ptnr Martin Barnes and Partners 1971–85, ptnr Coopers and Lybrand Associates mgmnt conslt 1985–96; chm International Project Mgmnt Assoc 1991–94; Churchill Fellowship 1971, FEng 1987, FICE, FCIOB, CIMgt, FAPM (chm 1986–91, vice pres 1991–), FInstCES (pres 1978–86, vice pres 1986–), FRSA, MBCS, ACIArb, ACGI; *Books* Measurement in Contract Control (1977), The CESMM2 Handbook (1986), Engineering Management: Financial Control (ed, 1990), The CESMM3 Handbook (1992); *Recreations* railway and canal history, victorian paintings; *Style*— Dr Martin Barnes, FEng; ✉ Cornbrash House, Kirtlington, Oxfordshire OX5 3HF (☎ 01869 350828)

BARNES, Melvyn Peter Keith; OBE (1990); s of Harry Barnes (ka N Africa 1942), and Doris, *née* Milton; *b* 26 Sept 1942; *Educ* Chatham House Sch Ramsgate, NW London Poly (Library Assoc Dip), private study (Dip in Municipal Admin); *m* 18 Sept 1965, Judith Anne, *née* Leicester; 2 s (Jeremy b 1970, Timothy b 1972); *Career* public library posts in Kent, Herts and Manchester 1958–68, dep Borough librarian Newcastle-under-Lyme 1968–72, chief librarian Ipswich 1972–74, Borough librarian and arts offr Royal Borough of Kensington & Chelsea 1974–80, city librarian Westminster 1980–84, Guildhall librarian and dir of libraries and art galleries Corp of London 1984–; Library Assoc: assoc 1965, memb Cncl 1974–, pres 1995 (vice-pres 1991–93); memb Library and Information Servs Cncl (England) 1984–89, pres Int Assoc of Met City Libraries 1989–92; Freeman City of London 1984, Liveryman Clockmakers' Co 1990 (hon librarian), Hon Freeman Worshipful Co of Gardeners 1995; FIMgt 1980, FRSA 1983; *Books* Youth Library Work (1968 and 1976), Best Detective Fiction (1975), Murder in Print (1986), Dick Francis (1986), Root and Branch: A History of the Worshipful Co of Gardeners (1994); *Recreations* reading, writing, theatre, history of the movies and stage musicals, amateur operatics; *Style*— Melvyn Barnes, Esq, OBE; ✉ Guildhall Library, Aldermanbury, London EC2P 2EJ (☎ 0171 332 1850, fax 0171 600 3384)

BARNES, Mervyn; s of late William Eric Barnes, and Marjorie Clark, *née* Walker; *b* 14 Dec 1939; *Educ* Liverpool Collegiate Sch, Liverpool Coll of Building; *m* 1 (m dis); 1 s (Tony John b 26 June 1967), 1 da (Lisa Jane b 10 Sept 1970); m 2, 24 Dec 1980, Jean, da of John James Vose; *Career* formerly surveyor various private practices and orgns, md Specialist Surveying Services PSA (most sr quantity surveyor in govt) until 1992 (joined 1972), md TBV Surveying (following privatisation of PSA) 1992–; memb Divnl Cncl RICS; specialist advsr to NACCB; author and presenter numerous papers on surveying matters; FRICS 1978 (ARICS 1965); *Recreations* walking, music, conservation, animal welfare; *Style—* Mervyn Barnes, Esq; ✉ TBV Surveying, The Lansdowne Building, Lansdown Road, Croydon CR0 2BX (☎ 0181 256 4000)

BARNES, Michael Cecil John; s of Maj Cecil Horace Reginald Barnes, OBE (d 1969), and Katherine Louise, *née* Kennedy (d 1988); *b* 22 Sept 1932; *Educ* Malvern, CCC Oxford (MA); *m* 21 April 1962, Anne, da of Basil Mason (d 1974), of London; 1 s (Hugh b 1963), 1 da (Katy b 1966); *Career* Nat Serv 2 Lt The Wilts Regt, served Hong Kong 1952–53; contested (Lab) Wycombe 1964, MP (Lab) Brentford and Chiswick 1966–Feb 1974, oppn spokesman on food and food prices 1970–71, memb Lab Pty 1957–79 and 1983–, helped form SDP 1981; chm Electricity Consumers Cncl 1977–83, dir UK Immigrants' Advsy Serv 1984–90; Legal Services Ombudsman for England and Wales 1991–, chm Br and Irish Ombudsman Assoc 1995–; chm: Hounslow Arts Tst 1974–82, Notting Hill Social Cncl 1976–79, Housing Action Centre N Kensington 1980–87; memb: Nat Consumer Cncl 1975–80, Advertising Standards Authy 1979–85; Burgess City of Bristol 1953; *Recreations* walking, swimming, dogs; *Style—* Michael Barnes, Esq; ✉ 45 Ladbroke Grove, London W11 3AR (☎ 0171 727 2533); Office of the Legal Services Ombudsman, 22 Oxford Court, Manchester M2 3WQ (☎ 0161 236 9532)

BARNES, Prof Michael Patrick; s of Capt William Edward Clement Barnes, of Broadwey, Weymouth, Dorset, and Gladys Constance, *née* Hooper; *b* 28 June 1940; *Educ* High Canons Sch Herts and Glos, Wynstones Sch Glos, Freie Waldorfschule Stuttgart, UCL (BA, MA, Rosa Morrison prize), Nansenskolen Lillehammer Norway, Univ of Oslo; *m* 8 Aug 1970, Kirsten Heiberg, da of Trygve Ole Mathias Røer (d 1980); 1 s (William Michael b 1978), 3 da (Catherine b 1971, Anne Helen b 1973, Kirsten Emily b 1980); *Career* Dept of Scandinavian Studies UCL: asst lectr 1964–67, lect 1967–75, reader 1975–83, prof of Scandinavian philology 1983–94, prof of Scandinavian studies 1994–; Viking Soc for Northern Res: memb 1963–, ed Saga Book 1970–83, jt hon sec 1983–; memb: AUT 1964–, Royal Gustavus Adolphus Acad Uppsala 1984– (corresponding memb 1977–84); Knight Icelandic Order of the Falcon 1992; *Books* Old Scandinavian Texts (1968), Draumkvæde: an edition and study (1974), The Runic Inscriptions of Maeshowe, Orkney (1993); *Recreations* badminton, drinking real ale, walking disused railways; *Style—* Prof Michael Barnes; ✉ 93 Longland Drive, Totteridge, London N20 8HN (☎ 0181 445 4697); Department of Scandinavian Studies, University College London, Gower St, London WC1E 6BT (☎ 0171 380 7176/7, fax 0171 380 7750)

BARNES, (David) Michael William; QC (1981); s of David Charles Barnes (d 1954), and Florence Maud, *née* Matthews (d 1967); *b* 16 July 1943; *Educ* Monmouth Sch, Wadham Coll Oxford (BA); *m* 5 Sept 1970, Susan Dorothy, da of William Turner; 3 s (Andrew b 1972, Edmund b 1974, Peter b 1979); *Career* called to the Bar Middle Temple 1965, bencher 1989; recorder of the Crown Court 1984–; hon res fell Lady Margaret Hall Oxford 1979; chm Hinckley Point 'C' Public Inquiry 1988; *Publications* Leasehold Reform Act 1967 (1967), Hill and Redman's Law of Landlord and Tenant (ed 15–18 edns, 1970–88); *Recreations* crime fiction, walking; *Clubs* Beefsteak; *Style—* Michael Barnes, Esq, QC; ✉ 4 Breams Buildings, London EC4A 1AQ (☎ 0171 353 5835, fax 0171 430 1677)

BARNES, Neil Richard; s of Maj Harold William Barnes (d 1981), of W Wickham, Kent, and Mary Mabel, *née* Butchart (d 1980); *b* 14 Jan 1947; *Educ* Sutton Valence Sch, Univ of Reading (BSc); *m* 18 Sept 1971, Susan Jane, da of Douglas Norman Smith, of Beckenham, Kent; 1 s (Stephen b 24 May 1979), 1 da (Nicola b 20 Nov 1975); *Career* md IDC Property Investmts 1979–91, md Regent Square Estates Ltd 1991–; pres Round Table W Wickham 1990–91 (chm 1986–87); Freeman City of London, Liveryman Worshipful Co of Masons; FRICS 1983; *Recreations* golf, badminton; *Style—* Neil Barnes, Esq; ✉ Regent Square Estates Ltd, 25 Buckingham Gate, London SW1E 6LD (☎ 0171 834 9377)

BARNES, Peter; s of Frederick Barnes (d 1955), and Martha Barnes (d 1981); *b* 10 Jan 1931; *Educ* Stroud GS; *m* 1, 18 Oct 1961, Charlotte Beck; m 2, 4 March 1995, Christie Horne; *Career* playwright and director; FRSL 1984; plays incl: The Ruling Class (1968), Leonardo's Last Supper (1969), Noonday Demons (1969), Lulu (1970), The Devil is an Ass (1973), The Bewitched (1974), The Frontiers of Farce (1976), Laughter! (1978), Antonio (1979), Red Noses (1985), Sunsets and Glories (1990), Tango at the End of Winter (1991), Lunar Park Eclipsis (1995), Corpsing (1996); directed: Lulu (1970), Bartholomew Fair (1977), Frontiers of Farce (1976), Antonio (1979), The Devil Himself (1980), Somersaults (1981), Bartholomew Fair (1987); radio plays incl: Barnes' People I, II, III (1981–86), More Barnes' People (1989); films incl: Leonardo's Last Supper (1971), The Ruling Class (1972), Enchanted April (1992); written and directed for TV: The Spirit of Man (1989), Nobody Here But Us Chickens (1989), Bye Bye Columbus (1992), Hard Times (1994); *Awards* John Whiting Award 1969, Evening Standard Award 1969, Best Radio Play Award 1981, Olivier Award 1985, RTS Drama Award 1989, New York Festival TV Award 1992, Christopher Award 1992, nominee Academy Award 1993; *Style—* Peter Barnes, Esq, FRSL; ✉ 7 Archery Close, Connaught Street, London W2 2BE; c/o Casarotto Ramsay Ltd, National House, 4th Floor, 60–66 Wardour Street, London W1V 3HP (☎ 0171 287 4450, fax 0171 287 9128)

BARNES, Prof Peter John; s of John Barnes (d 1989), and Eileen, *née* Thurman; *b* 29 Oct 1946; *Educ* Leamington Coll, St Catharine's Coll Cambridge (scholar, MA, numerous prizes), Worcester Coll Oxford (BM, BCh, DM, DSc); *m* 1976, Olivia Mary, *née* Harvard-Watts; 3 s (Adam b 2 Jan 1978, Toby b 20 Feb 1981, Julian b 14 Nov 1988); *Career* med registrar UCH London 1975–78, MRC res fell Royal Postgrad Med Sch 1978–81, MRC travelling fell Cardiovascular Res Inst San Francisco 1981–82, sr registrar Hammersmith Hosp 1979–82, sr lectr/conslt physician Royal Postgrad Med Sch and Hammersmith Hosp London 1982–85, prof of clinical pharmacology Cardiothoracic Inst London 1985–87; currently: prof of thoracic med, dir Dept of Thoracic Med and chm Academic Bd Nat Heart and Lung Inst Univ of London, hon conslt physician Royal Brompton Nat Heart and Lung Hosp London; author of numerous invited review papers and chapters, ed over 15 books on asthma, lung pharmacology and related topics; ed Pulmonary Pharmacology; assoc ed: Euro Respiratory Jl, Br Jl of Clinical Pharmacology, Jl of Applied Physiology; memberships incl: Physiological Soc, Br Pharmacology Soc, Br Thoracic Soc (memb Cncl), MRS; FRCP 1988; *Recreations* travel, gardening; *Style—* Prof Peter Barnes; ✉ Department of Thoracic Medicine, National Heart and Lung Institute, Dovehouse Street, London SW3 6LY (☎ 0171 351 8174, fax 0171 376 3442)

BARNES, Dr Robert Sandford; s of William Edward Barnes (d 1981), of Maghull, Lancs, and Ada Elsie, *née* Sutherst (d 1983); *b* 8 July 1924; *Educ* Ormskirk GS, Univ of Manchester (BSc, MSc, DSc); *m* 16 Aug 1952, Julia Frances Marriott, da of Roger Douglas Marriott Grant (d 1978), of IOW; 1 s (Richard b 1964), 3 da (Philippa b 1956, Alison b 1958, Penelope b 1959); *Career* radar res Admty Res Estab Witley 1944–47; head Irradiation Branch AERE Harwell 1962–65 (res scientist 1948–62), visiting scientist N American Aviation California 1965, head Metallurgy Div Harwell 1966–68, dir BISRA 1969–70 (dep dir 1968), chief scientist Br Steel Corp 1975–78 (dir R & D 1970–75), chm Ruthner Continuous Crop Ltd 1976–78, chm Robert S Barnes Consultants 1978–; tech advsr to the Bd: BOC Ltd 1978–79, BOC International 1979–81; princ Queen Elizabeth Coll Univ of London 1978–85 (fell 1985), fell King's Coll London 1985; Hatfield meml lecture 1972, John Player lecture 1976; memb: Cncl Backpain Assoc 1979–, Fndn for Science and Technology 1980–; pres Inst of Metallurgists 1983–85; Rosenhain medal 1964; Freeman City of London 1984, Liveryman Worshipful Co of Engrs 1984; FInstP 1961, FIM 1965, FRSA 1976, CEng 1977; *Recreations* Mediterranean cruising (yacht Bombero of Southampton); *Clubs* Athenaeum, Cruising Assoc; *Style—* Dr Robert S Barnes; ✉ Pigeon Forge, Daneshill, The Hockering, Woking, Surrey GU22 7HQ (☎ 01483 761529)

BARNES, Hon Ronald Alexander Henry; yr s of 3 Baron Gorell, CBE, MC (d 1963); hp of 4 Baron; *b* 28 June 1931; *Educ* Harrow, New Coll Oxford; *m* 1957, Gillian Picton, yst da of late Picton Hughes-Jones, of Henstridge, Somerset; 1 s, 1 da; *Career* late Lt Royal Fusiliers, seconded KAR, Capt Royal Northumberland Fusiliers (TA); formerly public relations offr P&O-Orient Lines; sr ptnr Stockton & Barnes (estate agents); Liveryman Worshipful Co of Weavers; *Style—* The Hon Ronald Barnes; ✉ Fernbank, Mingoose, Mount Hawke, Truro, Cornwall (☎ 01209 890310)

BARNES, Rosemary Susan (Rosie); da of Alan Allen, of Nottingham, and Kathleen, *née* Brown; *b* 16 May 1946; *Educ* Bilborough GS, Univ of Birmingham (BSocSci); *m* 1967, Graham Barnes; 2 s (Danny b 1973, Joseph b 1985), 1 da (Daisy b 1975); *Career* mgmnt trainee Unilever Research Bureau Ltd 1967–69, mktg exec Yardley of London Ltd 1969–72, primary teacher 1972, freelance researcher 1973–87, MP (SDP 1987–90, Social Democrat 1990–92) Greenwich 1987–92; dir Birthright (now WellBeing) 1992–96; *Style—* Mrs Rosie Barnes

BARNES, Simon Seton; s of Edward Walter Taylor Barnes, of Chelsea, and Joan Constance Barnes (d 1985); *b* 26 Jan 1958; *Educ* Dragon Sch Oxford, Shiplake Coll Oxon, INSEAD (Advanced Mgmnt Prog 1993); *m* 19 Aug 1983, Wendy Clare; 2 s (Oliver b 13 June 1986, Edward b 19 Jan 1988), 1 da (Phoebe b 9 July 1990); *Career* Alexander Howden Reinsurance Brokers Ltd: joined as trainee 1976, dir 1983, md 1986–90, chief exec 1990–95; md and chief operating offr Alexander Howden Non-Marine 1995–; *Recreations* golf, rugby, tennis; *Style—* Simon Barnes, Esq; ✉ Alexander Howden Non-Marine, 8 Devonshire Square, London EC2M 4PL (☎ 0171 623 5500, fax 0171 972 9878)

BARNES, Timothy Paul; QC (1986); s of the late Arthur Morley Barnes, of The Homestead, Seal, Nr Sevenoaks, Kent, and Valerie Enid Mary, *née* Wilks; *b* 23 April 1944; *Educ* Bradfield, Christ's Coll Cambridge (MA); *m* Aug 1969, Patricia Margaret, da of Leslie Ralph Gale (d 1974); 1 s (Christopher b 1973), 3 da (Olivia b 1975, Jessica b 1978, Natasha b 1986); *Career* called to the Bar Gray's Inn 1968; asst recorder 1983–87, recorder of the Crown Court 1987–, memb Midland and Oxford Circuit; *Recreations* hockey, gardening, music; *Clubs* MCC; *Style—* Timothy P Barnes, Esq, QC; ✉ 9 Bedford Row, London WC1R 4AX (☎ 0171 242 3555)

BARNETSON, Hon (William) Denholm; s of Baron Barnetson (Life Peer, d 1981), and Joan Fairley, *née* Davidson; *b* 30 May 1955; *Educ* Cranleigh Sch, Sorbonne; *Career* journalist and foreign corr United Press International Washington DC: Paris 1980–81, NY 1981–83, Washington 1983–85, Hong Kong, New Delhi India 1985–88, Islamabad Pakistan 1988–92, Bangkok Thailand 1992–94, Paris 1994; *Style—* The Hon W Denholm Barnetson; ✉ c/o Broom, Chillies Lane, Crowborough, E Sussex TN6 3TB

BARNETT, Col Anthony Francis (Tony); OBE (1982); s of Walter Francis Barnett (d 1967), of Hockley, Essex, and May Lillian, *née* White (d 1984); *b* 19 May 1933; *Educ* Brentwood Sch Essex; *m* 31 July 1957, Sheila Rose (d 1980), da of Charles Douglas Tomkinson, of Bradford on Avon, Wilts; 1 s (Martin b 1962), 1 da (Caroline 1960); *Career* cmmnd Army 1952, Staff offr RMA Sandhurst 1962–64, 99 Gurkha Inf Bde Sarawak 1965–66, CO Army Catering Corps Army Apprentice Coll 1977–79, HQ Dir Army Catering Corps 1979–81, Cdr Catering Gp 1983–85, Col and dep dir HQ Dir Army Catering Corps 1985–88; Col Cmdt: ACC 1992–93, Royal Logistic Corps 1993–; memb Fencing Ctee Asian Games Singapore 1965; FHCIMA 1984, FIMgt 1989; *Recreations* writing plays and short stories, cricket, eating out, theatre; *Clubs* Army and Navy; *Style—* Col Tony Barnett, OBE; ✉ Little Foxes, 21 Huntsmead, Ashdell Park, Alton, Hants GU34 2SF (☎ 01420 85287); c/o Regimental Headquarters The RLC, The Princess Royal Barracks Blackdown, Deepcut, Camberley, Surrey GU16 6RW

BARNETT, Prof Anthony Howard (Tony); s of Geoffrey Barnett, and Beulah, *née* Statman; *b* 29 May 1951; *Educ* Roundhay GS Leeds, Univ of London King's Coll Hosp (BSc, MB BS, MD); *m* 11 Nov 1975, Catherine Elizabeth Mary, da of John O'Donnell (d 1977); 3 s (James John, Jonathan Andrew, Robert David), 3 da (Clare Joanne, Sarah Suzanne, Anna Lucy); *Career* sr fell MRC 1979–81, sr registrar in med diabetes and endocrinology Christchurch NZ and Southampton 1981–83; Univ of Birmingham: sr lectr and conslt physician 1983, reader in med 1989, prof of med 1992– memb: Assoc of Physicians of GB and Ireland, Br Diabetic Assoc, Euro Assoc for the Study of Diabetes; former sec NZ Diabetes Assoc 1981–82; FRCP 1989 (MRCP 1978); *Books* Immunogenetics of Insulin Dependent Diabetes (1987), Hypertension and Diabetes (1990), Lipids, Diabetes and Vascular Disease (1992); *Recreations* reading, sport and family; *Style—* Prof Tony Barnett; ✉ Birmingham Heartlands Hosp, Undergraduate Centre, Birmingham B9 5ST (☎ 0121 766 6611 ext 4006, fax 0121 753 0214)

BARNETT, Anthony P J; *b* 10 Sept 1941; *Educ* Univ of Essex (MA), Univ of Sussex; *Career* writer and publisher; editorial dir Allardyce Barnett Publishers 1981–, ed Fable Bulletin - Violin Improvisation Studies 1993–; *Poetry*: Poem About Music (1974), Blood Flow (1975), Fear and Misadventure/Mud Settles (1977), A White Mess (1981), North North, I Said, No, Wait a Minute, South, Oh, I Don't Know (148 Political Poems) (1985), The Resting Bell (collected, 1987), Little Stars and Straw Breasts (1993), The Poetry of Anthony Barnett - Essays, Interview and Letters (1993), Carp and Rubato (1995), and others; collaborations with artists: Forest Poems Forest Drawings (with David Nash, 1987), Would You Tread on a Quadruped? An Animal Alphabet of Questionable Rhymes (with Natalie Cohen, 1992); anthologies covered in incl: A Various Art (1987 and 1990), Poets On Writing - Britain, 1970–1991 (1992), The Other: British and Irish Poetry since 1970 (1997); translations from Italian, French and Norwegian; *Music books* Desert Sands: The Recordings and Performers of Stuff Smith, An Annotated Discography and Biographical Source Book (1995); *Recreations* music; *Style—* Mr Anthony Barnett; ✉ Allardyce, Barnett, Publishers, 14 Mount Street, Lewes, E Sussex BN7 1HL

BARNETT, Bernard; s of Samuel Hyman Barnett (d 1978), and Anne, *née* Silver (d 1964); *b* 24 April 1942; *Educ* Torquay GS; *m* (m dis); 2 s (Danny b 10 June 1963, Guy b 3 April 1967), 1 da (Claire b 9 Aug 1965); *Career* reporter: Mid-Devon Advertiser 1960–63, Evening Tribune Nuneaton 1964; ed Mid-Devon Advertiser 1964–68, prodn ed rising to dep ed Campaign magazine 1968–72, exec ed Design magazine 1972; ed: Adweek 1973–75, Parents 1975–78; managing ed Psychology Today 1975–78; ed: Campaign 1978–84, Autocar 1984; ed/publisher Review 1985–86, ed Creative Review 1986, gp communications dir Abbott Mead Vickers advtg 1987–89, gp communications dir Ogilvy & Mather advtg 1989–91, editorial dir Campaign 1991–94, exec vice pres and dir of corp affrs Young & Rubicam Europe 1994–; *Recreations* music, books, cars, cricket; *Style—* Bernard Barnett, Esq; ✉ Young & Rubicam Ltd, Greater London House, Hampstead Road, London NW1 7QP (☎ 0171 387 9366)

BARNETT, His Hon Judge; Christopher John Anthony; QC (1983); s of Richard Adrian Barnett (d 1991), of Battle, Sussex, and Phyllis, *née* Cartwright (d 1947); *b* 18 May 1936; *Educ* Repton, Coll of Law London; *m* 31 Oct 1959, Sylvia Marieliese (Marlies), da of George Lyn Ashby Pritt (d 1983), and Sylvia Marguerite, *née* Castleden (d 1993); 2 s (Peter b 1962, Marcus b 1970), 1 da (Susannah b 1965); *Career* Nat Serv with Kenya Regt and Kenya Govt, Dist Offr (Kikuyu Gd) 1954–56; Kenya Govt Serv 1956–60; dist offr HM Overseas Civil Serv in Kenya 1960–62; called to the Bar Gray's Inn 1965, recorder of the Crown Court 1982–88, circuit judge (SE Circuit) 1988–; chm SE Circuit Area Liaison Ctee 1985–88; memb: Ct Univ of Essex 1983–, Wine Ctee SE Circuit 1984–88; *Recreations* cricket, tennis, walking; *Clubs* Kenya Kongonis Cricket; *Style*— His Hon Judge Barnett, QC; ✉ 9–12 Bell Yard, London WC2A 2LF

BARNETT, Dr Correlli Douglas; s of D A Barnett; *b* 28 June 1927; *Educ* Trinity Sch Croydon, Exeter Coll Oxford (MA); *m* 1950, Ruth Murby; 2 da; *Career* writer and historian; Intelligence Corps 1945–48; N Thames Gas Bd 1952–57, public rels 1957–63; Churchill Coll Cambridge: fell 1977–, keeper of the Churchill Archives Centre 1977–95; lectr in def studies Univ of Cambridge 1980–83; memb: Cncl Royal Utd Servs Inst for Def Studies 1973–85, Ctee London Library 1977–79 and 1982–84; chm Lit Panel and memb Exec Ctee E Arts Assoc 1972–78, pres E Anglian Writers 1969–88; historical conslt/writer to BBC TV series: The Great War 1963–64 (Screenwriters' Guild Award 1964), The Lost Peace 1965–66, The Commanders 1972–73; mil history reviewer The Sunday Telegraph; Chesney Gold medal RUSI 1991; Hon DSc Cranfield Univ 1993; FRHistS, FRSL, FRSA; *Books* The Hump Organisation (1957), The Channel Tunnel (with Humphrey Slater, 1958), The Desert Generals (1960, 2 edn 1983), The Swordbearers (1963), Britain and Her Army (1970, RSL award 1971), The Collapse of British Power (1972), Marlborough (1974), Bonaparte (1978), The Great War (1979), The Audit of War (1986), Hitler's Generals (ed, 1989), Engage the Enemy More Closely: The Royal Navy in the Second World War (1991, Yorkshire Post Book of the Year 1991), The Lost Victory: British Dreams, British Realities 1945–1950 (1996); contrib to: The Promise of Greatness (1968), Governing Elites (1969), Decisive Battles of the Twentieth Century (1976), The War Lords (1976), The Economic System in the UK (1985), Education for Capability (1986); *Style*— Dr Correlli Barnett, FRSL; ✉ Catbridge House, E Carleton, Norwich NR14 8JX

BARNETT, (Ulric) David; s of Peter Cedric Barnett (d 1980), and Sylvia Irina, *née* Kenny; *b* 29 Sept 1942; *Educ* Eton, Magdalen Coll Oxford; *m* 4 Jan 1969, Marie-Jane Hélène, da of Capitaine de Fregate Jean Levasseur (d 1947); 2 s (Rory b 1971, Oliver b 1979), 1 da (Natalie b 1974); *Career* joined Cazenove & Co Stockbrokers 1965 (ptnr since 1972); Liveryman Worshipful Co of Goldsmiths; *Clubs* MCC, City Univ; *Style*— David Barnett, Esq; ✉ Cazenove & Co, 12 Tokenhouse Yard, London EC2R 7AN (☎ 0171 588 2828)

BARNETT, Eric Oliver; s of Eric Everard Barnett (d 1989), of Johannesburg, S Africa, and Maud Emily Louise, *née* Oliver (d 1948); *b* 13 Feb 1929; *Educ* St John's Coll Johannesburg, Witwatersrand Coll of Art, Univ of Cape Town, Univ of S Africa, Univ of Natal, UCL; *m* 1, 13 Feb 1950, Louise Francesca (d 1984), da of Nicholas Peter Lindenberg (d 1978), of Durban; m 2, 13 March 1986, Vivienne, da of Samuel Arthur Goodwin (d 1994), of Northwood, London; *Career* lectr in psychology Univ of Natal 1957; Arthur Barnett Fndn: res dir 1963–71, vice chm 1969–71, chm 1971–; chm Rural Ecology and Resources Ctee Southern Africa 1978–; *Recreations* music, painting, history of science, salmon fishing, shooting; *Style*— Eric Barnett, Esq; ✉ Kirkhill Castle, Colmonell, Ayrshire KA26 0SB

BARNETT, Col Gordon; MBE (1976); s of Ernest Barnett (d 1980), of Stoke on Trent, and Eva Hodgkinson (d 1955); *b* 26 May 1936; *Educ* Newcastle under Lyme HS, RMA Sandhurst; *m* 4 June 1960, Carole Phyllis, da of George Brian Townsend (d 1982), of Weybridge, Surrey; 2 s (Simon b 1963, Jonathan b 1965); *Career* Nat Serv N Staffordshire Regt 1955, Offr Cadet RMA Sandhurst 1956–58, cmmnd RCS 1958, cdr signals Qatar Defence Force (Lt-Col) 1979–81, controller UK Army Telecoms (Col) 1982–86, cdr Sultan of Oman's Armed Forces Signals (Col) 1986–89; mktg mangr Racal Communications Ltd 1989–92, chef du site Racal Datacom Ltd (Channel Tunnel Project) France 1992–; MISM 1966, MIMgt 1978; hon cmd Indian Army Signal Corps (rank Maj) 1976; *Recreations* photography, walking; *Style*— Col Gordon Barnett, MBE; ✉ Hill Cottage, Thames St, Sonning-on-Thames, Berkshire (☎ 0118 969 6693); Racal Datacom Ltd, Eurotunnel Maintenance, Box Postale 18, 62185 Fréthun, France (☎ 00 33 21 00 4575)

BARNETT, Jeremy John; OBE (1982); s of Lt-Cdr Charles Richard Barnett (d 1941), and Audrey, *née* Edmondson (d 1987); *b* 26 Jan 1941; *Educ* St Edwards Sch Oxford, Univ of St Andrews (MA), Univ of London (MA), Univ of Leeds (TEFL Dip); *m* 1968, Maureen Janet, da of Percy Cullum; 1 s (Murray John b 16 Oct 1970), 1 da (Catherine Louise b 30 Sept 1972); *Career* English teacher Garian Sch Libya 1961–62; British Council: joined 1964, seconded as English teacher El-Nasr Coll Cairo 1965–67, seconded as teacher trainer Teacher Trg Coll Istanbul 1967–69, student MECAS Lebanon 1969–70, dir of studies Ankara Turco-British Assoc 1970–72, rep to Saudi Arabia 1972–75, dir of Middle East Dept London 1975–78, cultural affrs cnsllr British Embassy Ankara 1978–82, rep to Poland 1982–85, dir of E Europe and N Asia Dept London 1985–88, controller South and West Asia Div London 1988–89, rep to Egypt and cultural cnsllr British Embassy Cairo 1989–93; Westminster Classic Tours 1994–; *Recreations* long distance walking; *Style*— Jeremy Barnett, OBE; ✉ Oakdene, Station Road, Groombridge, Tunbridge Wells, Kent TN3 9NB (☎ 01892 864626)

BARNETT, Baron (Life Peer UK 1983), of Heywood and Royton, in Greater Manchester; Joel Barnett; PC (1975), JP (Lancs 1960); s of Louis Barnett (d 1964), of Manchester, and Ettie Barnett (d 1956); *b* 14 Oct 1923; *Educ* Derby Street Jewish Sch, Manchester Central HS; *m* 11 Sept 1949, Lilian Stella, da of Abraham Goldstone (d 1965); 1 da (Hon Erica Hazel b 7 Aug 1951); *Career* served WWII RASC and Br Mil Govt Germany; sr ptnr J C Allen & Co Manchester 1954–74; Parly candidate (Lab) Runcorn 1959, MP (Lab) Lancs Heywood and Royton 1964–83; chm Lab Party Econ and Financial Gp 1967–70; memb: Public Accounts Ctee 1966–71, Public Expenditure Ctee 1971–74, Select Ctee on Civil List 1972, Select Ctee on Tax Credits 1973; chief sec Treasury 1974–79 (oppn spokesman Treasury 1970–74), Cabinet memb 1977–79, chm Commons Select Ctee Public Accounts 1979–83; oppn spokesman (Lords) Treasury 1983–86; memb Hallé Soc of Manchester 1982–; hon visiting fell Strathclyde Univ 1980–, tstee V & A 1983–, vice pres Assoc of Metropolitan Authorities 1983–86; vice chm BBC 1986–93; chm Hansard Soc for Parly Govt 1984–90; chm Birkbeck Coll Appeal 1993–96; tstee Open Univ Foundation 1995–; Hon LLD Univ of Strathclyde 1983; fell Birkbeck Coll Univ of London; dir various public and private cos; FCCA; *Books* Inside the Treasury (1982); *Recreations* hiking, reading, music, theatre; *Style*— The Rt Hon the Lord Barnett, PC, JP; ✉ 7 Hillingdon Rd, Whitefield, Manchester M25 7QQ (☎ 0161 257 2345, fax 0161 257 2353); 92 Millbank Court, 24 John Islip St, London SW1 (☎ 0171 927 4620)

BARNETT, Joseph Anthony; CBE (1983, OBE 1975); s of Joseph Edward Barnett (d 1962), and Helen Yanocatis (d 1976); *b* 19 Dec 1931; *Educ* St Albans Sch, Pembroke Coll Cambridge (MA); *m* 1960, Carolina Johnson, da of Baldwin Rice (d 1974), of USA; 1 s (Lindsay b 1965), 1 da (Sujata b 1970); *Career* served Army (2 Lt) 1950–51; teacher Aylesford House St Albans 1954–55, Unilever Ltd 1955–58; British Council: educn offr Dacca 1961 (asst 1958), dir of studies Regnl Inst of Eng Bangalore 1968, rep Ethiopia 1971–75, controller Eng Language Teaching Div 1975–78, rep Brazil 1978–83, dir Japan 1983–91, ret; *Books* Getting on in English (jtly, 1960), Success with English, Books 1–3 (1966–69); *Recreations* cricket, riding, tennis; *Clubs* Athenaeum; *Style*— Joseph Barnett, Esq, CBE; ✉ The Thatch, Stebbing Green, Gt Dummow, Essex CM6 3TE (☎ 01371 856014)

BARNETT, Kenneth Thomas; CB (1979); yr s of Frederick Charles Barnett (d 1975), and Ethel, *née* Powell (d 1965); *b* 12 Jan 1921; *Educ* Howard Gardens HS Cardiff; *m* 1943, Emily May, da of Edward Lovering (d 1962); 1 da; *Career* served RAF 1941–46, radar mechanic (NCO); Miny of Tport: entered 1937, exec offr Sea Tport 1946–51, accountant offr and sec to Divnl Sea Tport Offr ME Port Said 1951–54, higher exec and sr exec posts Roads Divs 1954–61, princ Fin Div 1961–65, asst sec then under sec Ports 1965–71; under sec Cabinet Office (on secondment) 1971–73, dep sec (Housing) Dept of Environment 1976–80 (under sec 1973–76), ret; dir Abbey Data Systems Ltd 1984–; *Recreations* gardening, watching rugby; *Style*— Kenneth Barnett, Esq, CB; ✉ 5 Redan Close, Highcliffe-on-Sea, Christchurch, Dorset BH23 5DJ (☎ 01425 276945)

BARNETT, His Hon Judge Kevin Edward; s of Arthur Barnett (d 1987), of Solihull, W Mids, and Winifred, *née* Jones; *b* 2 Jan 1948; *Educ* Wellesbourne Sch, Tudor Grange GS, City of Birmingham Coll (LLB)(London); *m* 6 May 1972, Patricia Margaret, da of Dr Charles Hanby Smith; 1 da (Elizabeth Clare b 6 Aug 1981); *Career* called to the Bar Gray's Inn 1971, in practice Wales & Chester Circuit, recorder 1994–96 (asst recorder 1991), head of chambers 1995–96, circuit judge (Wales & Chester Circuit) 1996–; *Recreations* photography, painting, cooking; *Clubs* Lansdowne; *Style*— His Hon Judge Kevin Barnett; ✉ c/o Wales and Chester Circuit Office, Churchill House, Churchill Way, Cardiff CF1 4HH

BARNETT, Robert William; OBE (1993); s of Harry Frederick Barnett, of Wells-next-the-Sea, Norfolk, and Dorothy Anne, *née* Williamson; *b* 25 May 1954; *Educ* Wymondham Coll Norfolk, St Catharine's Coll Cambridge (MA); *m* 1979, Caroline Sara, da of Ambrose William Groves Weale; 2 s (Adam Edward b 7 Jan 1982, Oliver James b 17 Dec 1984); *Career* HM Dip Serv; entered FCO 1977, Japanese language trg 1979–80, third sec Tokyo 1980–83, memb Policy Planning Staff FCO 1984, asst private sec to Min of State (Baroness Young) 1984–86, first sec Western Euro Dept FCO 1986–88, first sec Bonn 1988–92, seconded to Saxony State Govt as inward investmt advsr 1992–93, asst head Eastern Adriatic Unit FCO 1993–94, HM ambass to Bosnia-Hercegovina 1994–95, cnsllr Sci and Technol Bonn 1995–; *Recreations* walking, photography, gardening; *Style*— Robert Barnett, Esq, OBE; ✉ c/o Foreign & Commonwealth Office (Bonn), King Charles Street, London SW1A 2AH

BARNETT, His Hon Judge William Evans; QC (1984); s of Alec Barnett (d 1981), of Penarth, S Glam, and Esmé Georgiana, *née* Leon (d 1989); *b* 10 March 1937; *Educ* Repton, Keble Coll Oxford (MA); *m* 24 July 1976, Lucinda Jane Gilbert, JP, da of Richard William Gilbert (d 1980), of Addington, Surrey; 2 s (Nicholas b 1978, James b 1980); *Career* Nat Serv RCS 1956–58; called to the Bar Inner Temple 1962, joined Midland and Oxford Circuit 1963, recorder Crown Ct 1981–94, circuit judge (SE Circuit) 1994–; memb: Personal Injuries Litigation Procedure Working Pty 1976–78, Panel of Arbitrators Motor Insurers' Bureau 1987–94; judicial memb Mental Health Review Tbnl 1993–; *Recreations* golf, photography, gardening, DIY; *Clubs* RAC, Croydon Medico-Legal Soc; *Style*— His Hon Judge William Barnett, QC; ✉ Carleon, 6 Castlemaine Avenue, S Croydon, Surrey CR2 7HQ (☎ 0181 688 9559); Knightsbridge Crown Court, 1 Pocock Street, London SE1 0BT

BARNEWALL, Peter Joseph (Joe); s and h of Sir Reginald Robert Barnewall, 13 Bt, *qv*; *b* 26 Oct 1963; *Educ* St Joseph's Coll Nudgee, Univ of Queensland (BAgrSc (Econ)); *m* 1988, Kathryn Jane, da of Patrick Carroll, of Brisbane, Queensland; 1 s (Christopher Patrick b 3 June 1995), 1 da (Jessica Rose b 10 Nov 1992); *Career* Lt served with Australian Army Reserve, Queensland Univ Regt 1981–86, 2/14 Light Horse (Queensland Mounted Inf) 1987–89; Queensland Dept of Primary Industries 1985–89, GRM International Pty Ltd 1989–94, conslt agric economist; memb: Aust Inst of Agric Sci, Aust Inst of Mgmnt, Aust Agric Economics Soc; CSR Sword of Honour 1986; *Recreations* game shooting, running, photography, tennis; *Clubs* United Service; *Style*— Joe Barnewall, Esq; ✉ 26 Tirrabella Street, Carina Heights, Queensland 4152, Australia (☎ 00 61 7 3395 3478, fax 00 61 7 3397 0376)

BARNEWALL, Sir Reginald Robert; 13 Bt (I 1623), of Crickstown Castle, Meath; s of Sir Reginald John Barnewall, 12 Bt (d 1961); *b* 1 Oct 1924; *Educ* Xavier Coll Melbourne; *m* 1, 1946, Elsie Muriel (d 1962), da of Thomas Matthews Frederick, of Brisbane, Queensland; 3 da; m 2, 1962, Maureen Ellen, da of William Daly, of S Caulfield, Victoria; 1 s; *Heir* s, Peter Joseph Barnewall b 26 Oct 1963; *Career* wool grower, cattle breeder, orchardist; served Royal Australian Engineers Aust Imp Force WWII, cmd B Sqn Victorian Mounted Rifles Royal Australian Armoured Corps 1952–56; md Southern Airlines Ltd of Melbourne 1953–58, fndr and ops mangr Polynesian Airlines W Samoa 1958–62, md Orchid Beach (Fraser Island) Pty Ltd 1962–71, dir and vice chm J Roy Stevens Pty Ltd (printers and publishers) 1962–75, dir Island Airways Pty Ltd Qld 1964–68, operator and owner Coastal-Air Co Qld 1971–76; *Clubs* United Service (Brisbane), Royal Automobile Club of Queensland, Returned Services League of Australia (Surfers' Paradise); *Style*— Sir Reginald Barnewall, Bt; ✉ Innisfree House, Normandie Court, Mount Tamborine, Queensland 4272, Australia

BARNEY, Charlotte Mary Elizabeth; da of Ashley R G Raeburn, *qv*, of Dulwich, London, and Esther, *née* Johns; *b* 29 June 1954; *Educ* James Allen's Girls' Sch Dulwich, Somerville Coll Oxford (MA); *m* 21 Oct 1989, William David Iain Barney, s of (William) Guy Barney; 1 da (b 3 Oct 1992); *Career* analyst/graduate trainee Overseas Dept Bank of England 1975–78, exec Corp Fin Dept Hill Samuel 1980–81 (exec Project Fin Dept 1978–80), journalist Investors Chronicle 1981–85, account dir Good Relations City 1985–86; dir: Streets Financial Strategy 1987 (asst dir 1986–87), Citigate Communications Ltd 1987–; *Recreations* music, skiing, family, Dorset countryside; *Style*— Mrs Charlotte Barney; ✉ Citigate Communications Ltd, 26 Finsbury Square, London EC2A 1DS (☎ 0171 282 8000, fax 0171 282 8010)

BARNSLEY, Prof (David) Graham; s of David Barnsley (d 1982), and Mabel Grace, *née* Beech; *b* 16 Jan 1936; *Educ* Stand GS Whitefield Manchester, Univ of Manchester (LLB, LLM); *m* 1, 21 May 1960, Blanche, *née* Thompson (d 1990); 2 da (Helen Ruth b 1962, Gail Elisabeth b 1964); m 2, 14 Oct 1995, Anne Nest Williams, da of Rev Morris Roberts (d 1953), of Mallwyd, Powys; *Career* admitted slr 1960, lectr Univ of Manchester 1960–66; Univ of Leicester: sr lectr 1966–73, prof of law 1973–, dean Faculty of Law 1976–82; memb: Soc of Public Teachers of Law, Law Soc; *Books* Conveyancing Law and Practice (3 edn, 1988), Land Options (1978); *Recreations* cycling, walking, gardening, philately; *Style*— Prof Graham Barnsley; ✉ Faculty of Law, University of Leicester, Univ Rd, Leics LE1 7RH (☎ 0116 252 2345, fax 0116 252 5023, telex 347250 LEICUN G)

BARNSLEY, Victoria (The Hon Mrs Nicholas Howard); da of late T E Barnsley, OBE, and Margeret Gwyneth, *née* Llewellin; *b* 4 March 1954; *Educ* UCL (BA), Univ of York (MA); *m* Feb 1992, Hon Nicholas Paul Geoffrey Howard, 2 s of Baron Howard of Henderskelfe (d 1984); 1 da (Blanche Mary b 5 Oct 1994); *Career* fndr and publisher Fourth Estate Publishers 1984–, dir Western and Oriental Travel 1994–; *Clubs* Groucho; *Style*— Ms Victoria Barnsley; ✉ 20 St Petersburg Place, London W2; Fourth Estate, 6 Salem Road, London W2 (☎ 0171 727 8993, fax 0171 792 3176)

BARNSTAPLE, Archdeacon of; *see:* Lloyd, Ven (Bertram) Trevor

BARON, Prof Denis Neville; s of Dr Edward Baron (d 1964), of London, and Lilian Dolly, *née* Silman (d 1984); *b* 3 Oct 1924; *Educ* Univ Coll Sch London, Middx Hosp Med Sch Univ of London (MB BS, MD, DSc, MA); *m* 6 Dec 1951, Yvonne Else, da of Hugo Stern (d 1963), of Dresden and London; 1 s (Justin b 1963), 3 da (Leonora b 1954, Jessica b 1956, Olivia b 1958); *Career* Flt Lt RAF (Med Branch) 1946–49; Courtauld Inst of Biochemistry Middx Hosp Med Sch 1949–54; Royal Free Hosp and Sch of Med London: conslt chemical pathologist, reader in chemical pathology 1954–63, prof of chemical pathology 1963–88, vice dean 1977–79; Rockefeller fell Univ of Chicago 1960–61; visiting prof various overseas univs; senator Univ of London 1985–88; tutor in medical ethics St Mary's Hosp Med Sch 1989–; ed in chief Clinical Science 1966–68, chm Assoc of Profs of Clinical Biochemistry 1980–81; memb: Medicines Cmmn 1982–89, Standing Med Advsy Ctee DHSS 1966–74, Med Ctee Chem Def Advsy Bd 1969–76 (conslt 1976–91), Camden & Islington AHA 1978–81, Barnet Health Authy 1982–85 and 1989–90, Assoc 1990–92, Mental Health Appeals Mangr 1994–; govr Henrietta Barnett Sch London 1987–; Liveryman Worshipful Soc of Apothecaries 1951; memb BMA 1945; FRSA 1952, FRCPath 1963 (vice pres 1972–75), FRCP 1971; *Books* New Short Textbook of Chemical Pathology (5 edn, jtly, 1989), Units, Symbols, and Abbreviations (ed, 5 edn, 1994); *Recreations* opera, gardening, bridge, sight-seeing; *Clubs* RSM; *Style*— Prof D N Baron; ✉ 47 Holne Chase, London N2 0QG (☎ 0181 458 2340)

BARON, Francis; *Career* md Guthrie International Ltd until 1983; W H Smith Television Ltd: md until 1993, also md subsid subscription TV channel ScreenSport Gp; chief exec First Choice Holidays PLC (formerly Owners Abroad PLC) 1993–96 (resigned); non-exec dir Yorkshire Television plc until 1991; *Style*— Francis Baron, Esq

BARON, Frank; *b* 15 May 1947; *Educ* Tulse Hill Sch; *m* 1983, Lorna Margaret, da of Brian Dearnaley; 2 s (Christopher b 1983, Alexander b 1987); *Career* asst photographer Keystone Press Agency 1963–67, photographer Daily Sketch 1967–72, fndr and photographer Sporting Pictures 1972–85, sports photographer The Guardian 1985–; winner Sports Picture of the Year 1974; fndr memb Professional Sports Photographers' Assoc, fndr Int Tennis Photographers' Assoc; *Recreations* tennis; *Clubs* Telford Lawn Tennis; *Style*— Frank Baron, Esq; ✉ 12 Ederline Avenue, Norbury, London SW16 (☎ 0181 679 3056); The Guardian, 119 Farringdon Rd, London EC1 (☎ 0171 278 2332)

BARON, Dr (Jeremy) Hugh; s of Dr Edward Baron (d 1964), and Lilian Hannah (Dolly) Baron (d 1984); *b* 25 April 1931; *Educ* Univ Coll Sch Hampstead, Queen's Coll Oxford (MA, DM), Middx Hosp Med Sch London; *m* 1, 8 Sept 1960, Wendy, da of Dr Samuel Barnet Dimson; 1 s (Richard b 1964), 1 da (Susannah b 1968); m 2, 31 Dec 1990, Carla Lord; *Career* Capt RAMC Royal Herbert Hosp Woolwich, BMH Singapore and Malaya, jr specialist med and offr i/c Med Div BMH Kuala Lumpur Malaya 1956–58; house physician, registrar, lectr, sr registrar Middx Hosp and Med Sch London 1954–67, MRC Eli Lilly travelling fell and fell in gastroenterology Mount Sinai Hosp NYC 1961–62, conslt physician Prince of Wales and St Ann's Hosps Tottenham 1968–71, sr lectr and hon conslt Depts of Surgery and Med Royal Postgrad Med Sch and Hammersmith Hosp London 1968–96, conslt physician and gastroenterologist St Charles Hosp London 1971–94, conslt physician and gastroenterologist St Mary's Hosp and hon clinical sr lectr St Mary's Hosp Med Sch Imperial Coll of Sci Technol and Med London 1988–96, co-dir Parkside Helicobacter Study Gp 1988–96; Hunterian prof RCS 1993–94, Goodall lectr RCPSGlas 1994, Fitzpatrick lectr RCP 1994, Burki lectr CPSP 1995, Sydenham lectr Soc of Apothecaries 1996; RSM: pres Clinical Section 1980–81, sr hon ed 1984–90, chm European Ctee 1991–93, vice pres 1991–93; memb: Cncl RCP 1993–96, Governing Body Br Postgrad Med Fedn 1993–96; archivist Br Soc of Gastroenterology 1981–, chm St Charles Hosp Beautification Ctee 1983–93, chm Med Writers' Gp The Soc of Authors 1985–87, chm Hammersmith Hosp Arts Ctee 1996 (vice chm 1988–96), pres Br Soc of Gastroenterology 1988–89, chm Mgmnt Ctee Br Health Care Arts Centre 1989–93; Gold Medal Sociedad Argentina de Gastroenterologia 1973, Koster Prize Danish Gastroenterologists 1981, Siurala Prize Finnish Gastroenterological Assoc 1988; Liveryman Worshipful Soc of Apothecaries 1972; memb BMA; FRCP, FRCS; *Books* Carbenoxolone Sodium (1970), Clinical Tests of Gastric Secretion (1978), Foregut (1981), Cimetidine in the 80s (1981), Vagotomy in Modern Surgical Practice (1982), St Charles Hospital Works of Art (1984, 2 edn 1993), History of The British Society of Gastroenterology, 1937–1987 (1987), Theoretical Surgery (co-ed, 1986–94), Art at the Hammersmith Hospitals and Medical Schools (1996); *Recreations* looking, beautifying hospitals; *Clubs* Royal Society of Medicine; *Style*— Dr J H Baron; ✉ Gastroenterology Unit, St Mary's Hospital, London W2 1NY (☎ 0171 725 1208, fax 0171 725 1138)

BARON, Dr (Ora) Wendy; OBE (1992); da of Dr Samuel Barnet Dimson, of London, and Gladys Felicia, *née* Sieve; *b* 20 March 1937; *Educ* St Paul's Girls', Courtauld Inst of Art (postgrad studentship, BA, PhD); *m* 1, 1960, Dr Jeremy Hugh Baron, s of Edward Baron; 1 s (Archie b 1964), 1 da (Susannah Eve b 1968); m 2, 1990, David Joseph Wyatt, s of Frederick Wyatt; *Career* Leverhulme Tst Fund fellowship 1972–74; dir Govt Art Collection 1978– June 1997; tstee Public Art Cmmns Agency 1990–; *Books* Sickert (1973), Miss Ethel Sands and Her Circle (1977), The Camden Town Group (1979), Sickert Paintings (jt ed, 1992); *Clubs* Chelsea Arts; *Style*— Dr Wendy Baron, OBE

BARR, Prof Allan David Stephen; s of Rev Prof Allan Barr (d 1988), of Edinburgh, and Agnes Christina, *née* Dryburgh (d 1978); *b* 11 Sept 1930; *Educ* Daniel Stewart's Coll Edinburgh, Univ of Edinburgh (BSc, PhD); *m* 16 Dec 1954, Eileen Patricia, da of Patrick Redmond (d 1971), of Frinton-on-Sea; 2 s (David b 28 Jan 1957, Richard b 22 Sept 1960), 1 da (Christina b 7 May 1967); *Career* student apprentice Bristol Aeroplane Co Filton Bristol 1947–49, Fulbright scholar and visiting prof Cornell Univ Ithaca NY USA 1964–65, reader Dept of Mech Engrg Univ of Edinburgh 1965–72 (former asst, lectr, sr lectr 1952–72), prof and head of Dept of Mech Engrg Univ of Dundee 1972–85; Univ of Aberdeen: Jackson prof of engrg 1985–95, dean Faculty of Engrg and Mathematical and Physical Sciences 1991–95 (ret); CEng, FIMechE, FRSE 1983; *Recreations* fly fishing, oil painting; *Clubs* Royal Northern and University (Aberdeen); *Style*— Prof Allan D S Barr, FRSE; ✉ The Orchard, Auchattie, Banchory, Kincardineshire AB31 3PT (☎ 01330 825244)

BARR, David; s of Walter Barr (d 1981), latterly of Glasgow, and Betty, *née* Shulman (d 1990); *b* 15 Oct 1925; *Educ* Largs Higher Grade, Haberdashers' Aske's, Brookline HS Boston USA, Univ of Edinburgh, UCL (LLB); *m* 8 June 1960, Ruth, da of David Weitzman, QC, MP (d 1987); 1 s (Andrew b 9 April 1961), 1 da (Frances b 14 March 1964); *Career* RN 1943–47; admitted slr 1953, met stipendiary magistrate 1976–96; JP Inner London Area 1963–76, dep chm N Westminster PSD 1968–76, chm Inner London Juvenile Panel 1969–92; Finnant House Sch: mangr 1955–73, chm and tstee 1973–; Freeman City of London 1959, Liveryman City of London Solicitors' Co; *Recreations* book collecting, bridge; *Clubs* Garrick, MCC; *Style*— David Barr, Esq; ✉ 19 St Mark's Cresent, London NW1 7TU

BARR, Derek Julian; s of Peter Joachim Barr (d 1993), of London, and Ingrid Gerda, *née* Dannenbaum; *b* 16 Sept 1945; *Educ* St Paul's, Imperial Coll London (BSc, ACGI); *m* 1, 19 Dec 1970 (m dis 1993), Zoe Maxine, da of Wing Cdr Jack Leon Elson-Rees (d 1962); 2 s (James b 1976, Nicholas b 1981), 2 da (Katrina b 1972, Annabelle b 1974); m 2, 10 May 1996, Susan Rose, da of Dr Denis Woodeson (d 1981), and Phyllis Woodeson; *Career* chemical engr (expert in industl drying and process technol), md Barr & Murphy 1974– (founded firm with father 1962); awarded Queen's Award for Export Achievement 1976; FIChemE 1987; *Recreations* skiing, sailing, tennis, music; *Clubs* IOD, Roehampton; *Style*— Derek Barr, Esq; ✉ 43 Corfton Road, London W5 2HR (☎ 0181 998 9531); Barr & Murphy, B & M House, 48 Bell St, Maidenhead, Berks SL6 1BR (☎ 01628 776177, fax 01628 776118)

BARR, Prof James; *b* 20 March 1924; *Educ* Daniel Stewart's Coll Edinburgh, Univ of Edinburgh (MA, BD), Univ of Oxford (DD); *Career* served WWII pilot RN Fleet Air Arm; ordained min Church of Scotland 1951, min Church of Scotland Tiberias Israel 1951–53; prof of New Testament Presbyterian Coll Montreal Canada 1953–55; prof of Old Testament lit and theology: Univ of Edinburgh 1955–61, Princeton Theological Seminary 1961–65; prof of Semitic languages and literatures Univ of Manchester 1965–76; Univ of Oxford: Oriel prof of the interpretation of holy scripture 1976–78, regius prof of Hebrew Oxford 1978–89, emeritus regius prof 1989–; Vanderbilt Univ Nashville Tennessee: prof of Hebrew bible 1989–, distinguished prof 1994–; ed: Jl of Semitic Studies 1965–76, Oxford Hebrew Dictionary 1974–80; del OUP 1979–89, Crown appointee Governing Body SOAS London 1980–85; pres: Soc for Old Testament Study 1973, Br Assoc for Jewish Studies 1978; memb Inst for Advanced Study Princeton 1985; visiting prof: Ormond Coll Melbourne Aust 1968 and 1982, Hebrew Univ Jerusalem 1973, Univ of Chicago 1975 and 1981, Univ of Strasbourg 1975–76, Brown Univ Providence RI 1985, Univ of Otago NZ 1986, Univ of SA Pretoria 1986, Vanderbilt Univ 1987 and 1988, Heidelberg Univ Germany 1993, Brown Univ Providence RI 1994; Burkitt medal for Biblical Studies (Br Acad) 1988; Hon: DD Knox Coll Toronto 1964, MA Univ of Manchester 1969, DD Dubuque Univ Iowa 1974, DD St Andrews 1974, DD Edinburgh 1983, DTheol Univ of SA 1986, doctorate Faculté de Théologie Protestante Paris 1988, DD Victoria Univ Toronto 1988, DTheol Univ of Oslo 1991; Guggenheim Res fellowship 1965, hon fell SOAS 1975, corresponding memb Göttingen Acad of Scis 1976, memb Norwegian Acad of Scis and Letters 1977, hon fell Oriel Coll Oxford 1980, hon memb Soc of Biblical Lit (USA) 1983; memb: Swedish Royal Soc of Scis Uppsala Sweden 1991, American Philosophical Soc 1993; FBA 1969, FRAS 1969, FAAAS 1993; *Books* The Semantics of Biblical Language (1961), Biblical Words for Time (1962), Old and New in Interpretation (1966), Comparative Philology and the Text of the Old Testament (1968), The Bible and the Modern World (1973), Fundamentalism (1977), Holy Scripture: Canon, Authority, Criticism (1983), Escaping from Fundamentalism (1984), The Variable Spellings of the Hebrew Bible (1989), The Garden of Eden and the Hope of Immortality (1992), Biblical Faith and Natural Theology (1993); *Recreations* bird watching; *Style*— Prof James Barr, FBA; ✉ 1432 Sitka Court, Claremont, CA 91711, USA (☎ 00 1 909 621 4189); 6 Fitzherbert Close, Iffley, Oxford OX4 4EN (☎ 01865 772741)

BARR, Sheriff Kenneth Glen; o s of late Rev Gavin Barr, and Catherine McLellan, *née* McGhie; *b* 20 Jan 1941; *Educ* Ardrossan Acad, Royal HS, Univ of Edinburgh (MA, LLB); *m* 1970, Susanne Crichton Keir (d 1996); *Career* admitted Faculty of Advocates 1964, sheriff of S Strathclyde Dumfries and Galloway 1976–; *Style*— Sheriff Kenneth Barr; ✉ Sheriff Court House, Dumfries DG1 2AN

BARR, Lloyd; s of Hyman Barr (d 1963), and Polly Barr; *b* 19 July 1942; *Educ* Copland Sch, Harrow Coll of Further Educn; *m* Helen Marion; 1 s (Philip Adam b 27 March 1969), 1 da (Hayley Jacqueline b 19 Feb 1973); *Career* articled clerk Stoy Hayward; qualified chartered accountant; ptnr Elliotts; chief barker Variety Club of GB 1996 (former treas); Freeman City of London 1996; FCA; *Recreations* golf, collecting 19th century animalier bronzes and showbusiness memorabilia; *Clubs* Potters Bar Golf; *Style*— Lloyd Barr, Esq; ✉ Elliotts, Centre Heights, 137 Finchley Road, London NW3 6JF (☎ 0171 722 7520, fax 0171 586 2528, mobile 0973 799225); Variety Club Children's Charity, 326 High Holborn, London WC1V 7AW

BARR, (John) Malcolm; CBE (1982); s of Robert Barr (d 1961), and Edith, *née* Midgley (d 1963); *b* 23 Dec 1926; *Educ* Shrewsbury, Clare Coll Cambridge (MA, LLM); *m* 27 Aug 1955, Elaine Mary (d 1995), da of Harold Rhodes (d 1956); 2 da ((Margaret) Clare (Mrs Whitaker) b 1956, Janine Ruth (Mrs Oddy) b 1959); *Career* Sub Lt RNVR 1944–48; Barr & Wallace Arnold Trust plc 1952–: chm and gp md 1962–88, gp exec chm 1988–; chm Leeds Permanent Building Society 1989–95 (non-exec dir 1970–95), non-exec dir Hickson International plc 1971–95; treas Br Show Jumping Assoc; High Sheriff W Yorks 1978; FRSA; *Recreations* drama, literature, music, show jumping, sailing; *Clubs* Royal Ocean Racing, Royal Yorkshire Yacht, Royal Thames Yacht, Climbers'; *Style*— Malcolm Barr, Esq, CBE; ✉ Kirkby House, Kirkby Overblow, Harrogate, North Yorkshire HG3 1HJ (☎ 01423 879901, fax 01423 879851)

BARRACLOUGH, Air Chief Marshal Sir John; KCB (1970, CB 1969), CBE (1961), DFC (1942), AFC (1941); s of late Horatio Leonard Barraclough, of London, and Marguerite Maude Barraclough; great nephew of Sir Alfred Gilbert, RA, the sculptor; *b* 2 May 1918; *Educ* Cranbrook Sch; *m* 1946, Maureen, da of Dr William John McCormack, of Wicklow, and niece of George Noble, Count Plunkett; 1 da (Moyra (Mrs David Scott)); *Career* Volunteer Service Artists' Rifles 1935–38; cmmnd RAF 1938, Air Vice-Marshal 1964, Air Chief Marshal 1973, ret 1976; served Coastal, Fighter, Bomber, Strike, Training, Near, Middle and Far East Cmds, flying operations Atlantic, North Sea, Indian Ocean and Madagascar 1939–45 (despatches twice), on staffs of Empire Central and Central Flying Schs (Examining Wing) 1948–51 (made first single-engined jet flight to South Africa 1951), Imperial Def Coll (staff) 1952–54, station cdr RAF Biggin Hill 1954–56 and Middleton St George 1956–58, dir Public Rels Air Miny 1961–64, AOC 19 Gp and NATO Air Cdr Eastern Atlantic 1964–67, Harvard Business Sch 1967 (AMP), AOA Bomber Cmd 1967–68, AOA Strike Cmd 1968–70, Vice-Chief Def Staff 1970–72, Air Sec 1972–74, cmdt Royal Coll of Def Studies 1974–76; co dir and chm The Troika Consortium Ltd; dir Data-Track Fuel Systems Ltd; memb RAF Training and Educn Bd 1976–79, vice chm Air League Cncl 1977–81, vice patron RUSI 1993– (chm Cncl 1977–80, vice pres 1980–88), pres: Air Public Rels Assoc 1976–, West Devon St John Ambulance 1977–85, Coastal Command and Maritime Air Association 1995–; former pres: RAF Modern Pentathlon Assoc, Combined Servs Equitation Assoc; pres Bath Royal Crescent Soc; gentleman usher to the Sword of State 1981–88, hon inspr gen RAuxAF 1984–89 (Hon Air Cdre 1979–89); vice chm: Cwlth War Graves Cmmn 1981–86 (cmmr 1974–86), Ed Bd NATO's Sixteen Nations 1981–86 (ed dir 1978–81), British Export Fin Advsy Cncl 1982–89; OStJ 1985; FRAeS, FRSA, FIPM, FIMgt, MIPR; *Publications* The Third World War (jtly, 1978), Air-Warfare Aspects of The Third World War - The Untold Story; contribs to professional journals; *Recreations* country pursuits, sailing (Irish Admirals' Cup Team 1973); *Clubs* Boodle's, RAF, Royal Anglo-Belgian, Royal Western Yacht; *Style*— Air Chief Marshal Sir John Barraclough, KCB, CBE, DFC, AFC; ✉ 28 The Royal Crescent, Bath, Somerset BA1 2LT

BARRACLOUGH, Robert James; s of Charles Brayshaw Barraclough, of Woosehill, Wokingham, Berks, and Winifred Elizabeth Gibson, *née* Moulton; *b* 17 April 1942; *Educ* Bootham Sch York; *m* 8 Sept 1973, Jillian Mary, da of Frederick George Fennell, RN; 4 s (Paul Anthony b 9 March 1974, Nicholas Charles b 5 Aug 1975, Timothy Nigel b 31 May 1977, Tristan Toby William b 15 Aug 1978); *Career* ptnr Robson Rhodes Chartered Accountants Bradford 1971–90 (gen client serv ptnr, ptnr in charge of audit practice W Yorks); estab Litigation Support Unit in N England Haines Watts Bradford 1990–; memb Yorks Numismatic Soc (pres 1975), hon treas Bradford C of C 1988–95, memb Br Acad of Experts 1989 (memb Cncl 1993–); FCA 1965; *Recreations* badminton, theatre, fell walking, numismatics, scouting; *Clubs* Bradford; *Style*— Robert Barraclough, Esq; ✉ Haines Watts, Sterling House, 133 Barkerend Road, Bradford BD3 9AU (☎ 01274 393666, fax 01274 307364)

BARRAN, Sir John Napoleon Ruthven; 4 Bt (UK 1895), of Chapel Allerton Hall, Chapel Allerton, West Riding of Co York, and of Queen's Gate, St Mary Abbots, Kensington, Co London; s of Sir John Leighton Barran, 3 Bt (d 1974), and Hon Alison (d 1973), da of 9 Lord Ruthven of Freeland, CB, CMG, DSO; n of Sir David Barran, former chm of the Midland Bank and former chm Shell; *b* 14 Feb 1934; *Educ* Winchester, UCL (BA 1994); *m* 1965, Jane Margaret, da of Sir Stanley George Hooker, CBE (d 1984), and his 1 w Hon Margaret Bradbury, da of 1 Baron Bradbury; 1 s, 1 da (Susannah Margaret b 1981); *Heir* s, John Ruthven Barran b 10 Nov 1971; *Career* Lt 5 Royal Inniskillen Dragoon Gds 1952–54; asst account exec: Dorland Advertising Ltd 1956–58, Masius & Fergusson Advertising Ltd 1958–61; account exec Ogilvy Benson & Mather

(NY) Inc 1961–63, Overseas TV News Serv COI 1964, first sec (info) Br High Cmmn Ottawa 1964–67; COI: Home Documentary Film Section 1967–72, Overseas TV and Film News Servs 1972–75, TV Commercials and Fillers Unit 1975–78, head Viewdata Unit 1978–85, head Info Technol Unit 1985–87; memb Cncl Assoc of Lloyd's Members 1990–93; *Recreations* shooting, fishing, cricket (pres East Bergholt Cricket Club), gardening, entertaining; *Style—* Sir John Barran, Bt; ✉ 17 St Leonard's Terrace, London SW3 4QG (☎ 0171 730 2801); The Hermitage, East Bergholt, Suffolk (☎ 01206 298236); Middle Rigg Farm, Sawley, Yorkshire (☎ 01766 20207)

BARRASFORD, Tig; s of Capt Thomas George Barrasford (d 1981), of Wokingham, and Florence Cavell, *née* Mayo; *b* 20 July 1947; *Educ* The John Bright GS Llandudno, Llandrillo Tech Coll Colwyn Bay (Nat Dip in Hotel Keeping and Catering); *m* 5 Oct 1968, Sheelagh Mary, da of Owen O'Hagan; 2 s (Simon b 22 Oct 1971, Paul b 18 March 1974), 1 da (Zoë b 25 March 1978); *Career* trainee mangr Grand Metropolitan Hotels 1968–70; Trust House Forte Hotels: asst mangr Both Worlds Gibraltar 1970–71, dep mangr Eastgate Hotel Lincoln 1972, food and beverage mangr Appollonia Beach Hotel Cyprus 1973, gen mangr Parkview Hotel Durban SA 1974–75, gen mangr Excelsior Hotel Glasgow 1975–77, ops control mangr UK Hotels 1977–78, area dir Scotland UK Hotels 1979–80, ops exec Exclusive Hotels 1981, ops dir International Hotels 1981–82; proprietor Bryn Cregin Garden Hotel Deganwy 1983–86 (responsible for BTA Commendation, Michelin Guide, Relais Routiers, Ashley Courtenay); Aga Khan Fund for Econ Devpt: chief exec Serena Lodges and Hotels Kenya 1986–90, md Serena Tourism Promotion Servs SA 1991–, md Ciga Hotels Italy 1992–93; fndr memb Welsh Rarebits (mktg consortium of ind Welsh hotels), winner Master Innholders Award; Freeman City of London, memb Worshipful Co of Innholders 1985; FHCIMA 1990 (MHCIMA 1977); *Recreations* golf, windsurfing, scuba diving, sailing; *Clubs* North Wales Golf (Llandudno); *Style—* Tig Barrasford, Esq; ✉ Secretariat of His Highness The Aga Khan, Aiglemont, Gouvieux, France (☎ 00 334 458 4000, fax 00 334 458 2000)

BARRASS, Christopher Patrick; s of Maj Patrick Rae Barrass, of Chobham, Surrey, and Ann Delory, *née* Bertram; *b* 12 Nov 1953; *Educ* Dauntsey's Sch Wiltshire; *Career* chief reporter: Westminster Press Surrey Herald 1976–78, Sutton Seibert Publishing 1980–82; md Sovereign Servs 1979–82, conslt Granard Communications 1982–85, dir Edelman Public Relations 1987–89 (assoc dir 1985–87), chief exec Integrated Marketing and Communications 1989–92, sr ptnr Corporate Communications 1989–; memb Exec Ctee: Clandon Soc, Clandon Horticultural Soc, Surrey Downs Gp, Porsche Racing Drivers' Assoc; dir Porsche Drivers' Club; *Recreations* classic cars, literature, arts, water and snow skiing; *Style—* Christopher Barrass, Esq; ✉ Corporate Communications, Brackendene House, Oak Grange Road, Guildford, Surrey

BARRASS, Gordon Stephen; CMG (1992); s of James Stephen Barrass (d 1984), and Mary, *née* Quinn (d 1971); *b* 5 Aug 1940; *Educ* Hertford GS, LSE (BSc Econ), SOAS; *m* 1, 1965, Alice Cecile Oberg (d 1984); m 2, 1992, Kristen Clarke Lippincott; *Career* HM Dip Serv: FCO 1965–67, Peking 1970–72, Cultural Exchange Dept FCO 1972–74, UK Mission Geneva 1974–78, memb Planning Staff FCO 1979–82, cnsllr 1983, RCDS 1983; seconded to: MOD 1984–86, Cabinet Office 1986–93 (under sec 1991–93); int advsr Coopers & Lybrand 1993–; *Recreations* Chinese and Western art, classical archaeology, opera, travel, books; *Style—* Gordon S Barrass, Esq, CMG; ✉ Coopers & Lybrand, 1 Embankment Place, London WC2N 6NN (☎ 0171 213 5543)

BARRATT, Eric George; s of Frank Barratt, of Stokenchurch, Bucks; *b* 15 April 1938; *Educ* Oriel Coll Oxford (MA); *Career* sr ptnr MacIntyre & Co; dir: Esthwaite Estate Ltd, Ely Place Investments Ltd, Land Estates & Property Ltd, World Tour Holland BV, SC Brannan & Sons Ltd, Avonmore Stud Ltd; treas: St Augustine's Fndn, Oriel Coll (and fell); FCA; *Clubs* Athenaeum, Carlton, City of London; *Style—* Eric Barratt, Esq; ✉ Stockfield, Stokenchurch, Bucks (☎ 01494 482284); MacIntyre & Co, 28 Ely Place, London EC1N 6LR (☎ 0171 242 0242)

BARRATT, Jeffery Vernon Courtney Lewis; s of Arnold Douglas Courtney Lewis, and Edith Joyce, *née* Terry; *b* 31 Oct 1950; *Educ* Scots Coll Wellington NZ, Univ of Adelaide (LLB), Univ of Sydney (LLB, LLM); *Career* articled clerk Giovanell and Burges 1971–73, slr Stephen Jaques and Stephen 1973–75; Norton Rose: ptnr 1979– (estab Bahrain Office 1979–82, trg ptnr 1987–91), head SE Asian Project Fin Gp Hong Kong 1993–95, head of Project Finance worldwide 1995–; memb: Editorial Bd Butterworths Jl of Int Banking and Fin Law, Banking Law Sub-Ctee Law Soc 1991–93; author of numerous articles on selling loan assets, sterling commercial paper,securitisation and project fin in learned jls; memb: London Legal Educn Ctee 1987–91, Law Soc, IBA, QMC (Summer Sch Faculty); *Recreations* cricket, squash, skiing, tennis, opera; *Clubs* Hampstead Cricket (capt 1987), RAC, MCC; *Style—* Jeffery Barratt, Esq; ✉ Norton Rose, Kempson House, Camomile Street, London EC3A 7AN (☎ 0171 283 6000, fax 0171 283 6500, telex 883652)

BARRATT, Sir Lawrence Arthur (Lawrie); kt (1982); *b* 14 Nov 1927; *m* 1, 1951 (m dis 1984); 2 s; m 2, 1984, Mary Sheila Brierley; *Career* Barratt Developments PLC: fndr 1958, gp chm until 1988, life pres 1989–91, re-appointed chm 1991; FCIS; *Recreations* golf, shooting, sailing; *Style—* Sir Lawrie Barratt; ✉ Barratt Developments PLC, Wingrove House, Ponteland Rd, Newcastle upon Tyne NE5 3DP (☎ 0191 286 6811)

BARRATT, Michael Fieldhouse; s of Wallace Milner Barratt (d 1980), and Doris, *née* Fieldhouse (d 1934); *b* 3 Jan 1928; *Educ* Rossall and Paisley GS; *m* 1, 1952 (m dis), Joan Francesca Warner; 3 s (Mark, Andrew, Paul), 3 da (Eve, Jane, Rachel); m 2, 1977, Dilys Jane, da of David Morgan (d 1985); 2 s (Oliver, Barnaby), 1 da (Jessica); *Career* communications conslt, broadcaster on radio and TV; entered journalism Kemsley Newspapers 1945, ed Nigerian Citizen 1956, reporter Panorama 1963; BBC TV presenter: 24 Hours 1965–69, Nationwide 1969–77, Songs of Praise 1977–82, Reporting London 1983–88; question master Gardeners' Question Time BBC Radio 4 1973–79; chm: Michael Barratt Ltd 1977–, Commercial Video Ltd 1981–; dir: Travel and Leisure Communications Ltd 1982–, Valley Communications plc; rector Univ of Aberdeen 1973; Hon LLD Univ of Aberdeen 1975; FInstD; *Books* Michael Barratt (1973), Down to Earth Gardening Book (1974), Michael Barratt's Complete Gardening Guide (1977), Golf with Tony Jacklin (1978), Making the Most of the Media (1996); *Recreations* cricket, golf, listening; *Clubs* Lord's Taverners'; *Style—* Michael Barratt, Esq; ✉ Pear Tree Cottage, Ascot Rd, Touchen End, Berks SL6 3LD (☎ 01628 20403, fax 01628 27737)

BARRATT, Oliver William; MBE (1993); s of Lt-Col Roger Barratt, MBE, of Cowmire Hall, Kendal, and Diana Norah, *née* While (d 1992); *b* 7 July 1941; *Educ* Radley, Edinburgh and East of Scotland Coll of Agric (SDA); *Career* sec: The Cockburn Assoc (The Edinburgh Civic Tst) 1971–92, The Cockburn Conservation Tst 1978–92; independent environmental conslt 1992–; vice chm Scottish Assoc for Public Tport; memb Cncl Nat Tst for Scotland 1995–; tstee: Scottish Historic Bldgs Tst, Lothian Bldg Preservation Tst, Cockburn Conservation Tst; Hon FRIAS 1992; *Recreations* the hills, travel, most of the arts; *Style—* Oliver Barratt, Esq, MBE; ✉ Cowmire Hall, Crosthwaite, Kendal, Cumbria LA8 8JJ (☎ and fax 01539 568200); 1 London St, Edinburgh EH3 6LZ (☎ 0131 556 5107)

BARRATT, Peter William; s of Robert Leslie Barratt (d 1974), of Jersey, CI, and Winifrid Irene, *née* Kirton; *b* 7 May 1934; *Educ* De La Salle Coll Salford, Prior Park Coll Bath; *m* 1, 22 June 1960 (m dis 1983), Shirley, da of Charles Littler (d 1955), of Swinton, Lancs; 1 s (Nigel b 1962), 2 da (Elizabeth b 1964, Jacqueline b 1966); m 2, 1990, Pamela Rose, da of Jonah Shapiro; *Career* articled clerk EA Radford Edwards Manchester 1952–59, Ashworth Sons Barratt (stockbrokers) 1959–89: ptnr 1961, sr ptnr 1968–88, dir FPG Securities Ltd (acquired Ashworth Sons & Barratt 1988) 1988; dir: Allied Provincial Securities Ltd 1989–95, Greig Middleton 1995–; memb: Broughton Park RFC 1952–72 (IXV), Lancs RFC 1966–70 (Eng trial 1969); MSI (memb Stock Exchange 1961), FCA; *Recreations* theatre, antiques, reading, history; *Clubs* Broughton Park RFC, Lancs RFC, Sale RFC, Henty Soc; *Style—* Peter Barratt, Esq; ✉ The Corner House, Brook Lane, Alderley Edge, Cheshire SK9 7QQ

BARRATT, Sir Richard Stanley; kt (1988), CBE (1981), QPM (1974); s of Richard Barratt (d 1951), and Mona, *née* Barnes (d 1956); *b* 11 Aug 1928; *Educ* Saltley GS Birmingham; *m* 1 March 1952, Sarah Elizabeth, da of John George Hale (d 1951); 1 s (Richard David b 1953), 2 da (Jennifer Elizabeth b 1956, Penelope Jane b 1965); *Career* Dep Chief Constable Manchester and Salford 1972–74, Dep Chief Constable Greater Manchester 1974–75, Chief Constable S Yorks 1975–78, HM Inspr of Constabulary SE Region 1978–87, HM Chief Inspr of Constabulary for Eng and Wales 1987–90; advsr Police Ctee MOD 1990–95, assessor Guildford and Woolwich Inquiry 1990–94, memb Gaming Bd for GB 1991–95; CStJ 1996; CIMgt 1980; *Recreations* gardening, reading, golf, travel; *Style—* Sir Richard Barratt, CBE, QPM

BARRATT, Robin Alexander; QC (1989); s of Harold Robert Mathew Barratt (d 1974), of Godalming, and Phylis Lily Barratt (d 1968); *b* 24 April 1945; *Educ* Charterhouse, Worcester Coll Oxford (MA); *m* 1 April 1972, Gillian Anne, da of Peter Ellis; 1 s (Richard), 3 da (Sarah, Caroline, Joanna); *Career* called to the Bar Middle Temple 1970; Western Circuit 1971, recorder of the Crown Court 1993–; lectr in law Kingston Poly 1968–71; cncllr London Borough of Merton 1978–86; *Recreations* music, fell walking, reading; *Style—* Robin Barratt, Esq, QC; ✉ 415 Gray's Inn Square, Gray's Inn, London WC1R 5AY (☎ 0171 404 5252)

BARRATT, (Francis) Russell; CB (1975); s of Frederick Russell Barratt (d 1957); *b* 16 Nov 1924; *Educ* Durban HS, Clifton, Univ Coll Oxford; *m* 1, 1949 (m dis 1978), Janet Mary, *née* Sherborne; 3 s; m 2, 1979, Josephine Norah Harrison, da of Brig D McCririck (d 1947); *Career* Intelligence Corps 1943–46 (Capt 1946); HM Treasy: asst princ 1949, princ 1953, first sec UK High Cmmn Karachi 1956–58, asst sec 1962, under sec 1968, dep sec 1973–82; dir Amdahl (UK) 1983–93; memb Review Bd for Govt Contracts 1984–93; *Recreations* reading, music, swimming; *Clubs* Athenaeum; *Style—* Russell Barratt, Esq, CB; ✉ Little Paddocks, Smallhythe Rd, Tenterden, Kent TN30 7LY (☎ 01580 763734)

BARRELL, Alan Walter; s of Leslie Walter Barrell, of Waltham Forest, Essex, and Margaret Louise Emily Barrell; *b* 21 July 1940; *Educ* Willesden GS, Cambridge Coll of Arts and Technol (DipM); *m* 3 March 1963, Pamela Mollie, da of Marcel Herbert Whitley, of Leeds, Yorkshire; 2 s (James, Julian), 2 da (Helene, Louise); *Career* chm and chief exec Domino Printing Sciences plc 1984–90, chm Transatlantic Expansion Ltd 1990–92, dep chm and md Willett International Ltd 1992–, chm Willett Systems Ltd (dir various overseas subsids); dir Centre for Tomorrows Company; FCIM, FInstD, FIMgt, MRSH, FRSA (memb Cncl 1996–); *Books* Exploring New Markets, Building A Global Business, Profit from Innovation, Executive Networking; *Style—* Alan Barrell, Esq; ✉ 6 Hills Ave, Cambridge CB1 4XA (☎ 01223 249597); Willett International Ltd, 3 Cronin Road, Corby, Northants NN18 8AQ (☎ 01536 400777, fax 01536 400888)

BARRELL, Dr Anthony Charles; CB (1994); s of William Frederick Barrell (d 1973), and Ruth Eleanor, *née* Painter (d 1992); *b* 4 June 1933; *Educ* Friars Sch Bangor, Kingston GS, Univ of Birmingham, Imperial Coll London (BSc); *m* 26 Jan 1963, Jean, da of Francis Henry Hawkes, and Clarice Jean Silke, of Budleigh Salterton, Devon; 1 s (Andrew Mark b 1966), 1 da (Samantha Ruth b 1968); *Career* chemist Miny of Supply (later War Dept) 1959–64, commissioning engr African Explosives and Chem Industs 1964–65, shift mangr MOD 1965–66; HM Factory Inspectorate 1966–78 (chem inspr, supt specialist inspr), head Major Hazards Assessment Unit 1978–85, dir of technol Health and Safety Exec 1985–90, dir Hazardous Installations Policy 1990, chief exec North Sea Safety Dept of Energy 1990–91, chief exec North Sea Safety Health and Safety Executive 1991–94, dir BAA plc 1994–; memb Cncl: IChemE 1989–94 (pres 1993–94), Royal Acad of Engrg 1994–; Hon DEng Univ of Birmingham 1995; FIChemE 1984, Eur Ing 1988, FEng 1990 (CEng 1974); *Recreations* offshore sailing, golf, reading; *Clubs* Royal Dart Yacht, Churston Golf; *Style—* Dr Anthony Barrell, CB, FEng; ✉ Sanderling, Ridley Hill, Kingswear, Devon TQ6 0BY (☎ 01803 752266); BAA plc, 130 Wilton Road, London SW1V 1LQ (☎ 0171 932 6645, telex 919268 BAAPLC G)

BARRELL, Joan; *Career* former magazine publisher, currently conslt and freelance journalist; IPC Magazines 1959–71: first female advertisement rep, fndr and advertisement mangr Honey magazine 1965, fndr Fashion magazine 1967, only female advertisement sales co-ordinator (Honey, Fashion and Petticoat magazines) 1969, merchandise mangr all IPC Women's magazines 1970–71; National Magazine Company 1971–95: joined 1971, assoc publisher Vanity Fair magazine 1971, fndr and assoc publisher Cosmopolitan magazine 1972, fndr and publisher Company magazine 1978, only female dir National Magazine Co 1981, dir COMAG distributors 1984, publishing dir Country Living magazine 1986–90, publishing dir Good Housekeeping Magazine and Institute 1990–93, dir of circulation sales 1993–95; ptnr Barrell & Barrell (conslts) Ivy Hatch Kent 1995–; pres Women's Advtg Club of London 1975–, chm Publicity Club of London 1989–90; Greatest Female Contribution Towards Advertising award 1977–78 (Adwoman Awards) 1978, Marcus Morris award for exceptional career and long-standing contrib to the UK magazine indust (PPA) 1995; hon memb WACL; *Books* The Business of Women's Magazines (jtly, 1979, 2 edn 1988); *Style—* Ms Joan Barrell

BARRETT, *see:* Scott-Barrett

BARRETT, Prof Ann; da of R D Brown, of Suffolk; *b* 27 Feb 1943; *Educ* Queen Elizabeth's Girls' GS Barnet, Bart's Hosp Med Sch (LRCP, MRCS, MB BS, MD); *m*; 3 c; *Career* sr house offr in general med Whipps Cross Hosp 1969–70 (house surgn and physician 1968–69), sr house offr in radiotherapy Bart's 1969–70, registrar in radiotherapy UCH and Middx Hosp 1971–72, sr registrar Dept of Radiotherapy Middx Hosp and Mount Vernon Hosp 1972–74, seconded to Fndn Curie and Institut Gustav-Roussy 1974, locum conslt radiotherapist Westminster Hosp 1975–76 (lectr in oncology 1974–75), chef de clinique Hôpital Tenon and Institut Gustav-Roussy 1976–77; Royal Marsden Hosp: sr lectr and hon conslt Inst of Cancer Res 1977–83, conslt in radiotherapy and oncology 1983–86; dir Beatson Oncology Centre Western Infirmary Glasgow 1986–91, prof of radiation oncology Univ of Glasgow 1986–; pres: Scottish Radiological Soc 1995–97, Euro Soc for Therapeutic Radiotherapy and Oncology 1997–99; FRCR 1974, FRCPGlas 1989, FRCP 1990; author of over 100 medical pubns; *Style—* Prof Ann Barrett; ✉ Department of Radiation Oncology, Beatson Oncology Centre, Western Infirmary, Glasgow G11 6NT (☎ 0141 211 2123, fax 0141 337 1712)

BARRETT, Air Cdre (Frederick Onslow) Barrington Oliver (Barry); CBE (1968), DFC (1945); s of Edwin Victor George Oliver Barrett (d 1930), of London, and Edith, *née* Haines (d 1971); *b* 2 Dec 1918; *Educ* City of London Sch; *m* 11 June 1976, Penelope Gay Rowland, da of Ralph Rowland and Elizabeth Absalom, of Brechfa, Carmarthen, Wales; *Career* RAF 1938–72: operational serv Europe and Africa 1939–45, SASO HQ No 38 Gp 1968–71, dir Flight Safety RAF and Army Air Corps 1972–73, graduate RAF Staff Coll, Jt Servs Staff Coll, RAF Flying Coll; md: Air Gregory Ltd, Surrey and Kent Flying Sch; exec Air Birmingham; dir Air Gregory Petroleum Servs 1973–75, conslt GKN 1982–84 (gen mangr Aviation Dept 1976–81), aviation conslt and aircraft broker 1982–; dir Fortis Aviation Group 1990–92; vice pres SSAFA for Warwicks; Freeman City of London 1984, Liveryman Guild of Air Pilots and Air

Navigators 1984 (memb Ct of Assts 1989–92); *Recreations* golf, fishing; *Clubs* RAF; *Style*— Air Cdre Barry Barrett, CBE, DFC; ✉ Court Farm House, Lower Fulbrook, Warwick CV35 8AS (☎ and fax 01926 624379)

BARRETT, Edwin Radford (Ted); s of William Barrett (d 1963), and Florence Adeline, *née* Kohlar (d 1991); *b* 26 March 1929; *Educ* Itchen Sch Southampton, Burnley GS Lancs, Univ of London (BSc); *m* 26 Sept 1957, Patricia, da of Egbert Shuttleworth (d 1991); 1 s (Nicholas Radford b 1960), 1 da (Juliet Jane b 1964); *Career* reporter and sub ed Evening Telegraph Blackburn 1952–56, sub ed Press Assoc London 1956–59; Daily Telegraph: joined 1959, seconded to Sports Room 1959, dep sports ed 1962, sports ed 1979–88, sports managing ed 1988–90; sports broadcaster and freelance writer: Sports Report, Overseas Serv BBC 1960–80s; *Books* Oxford Companion to Sports and Games (contrib, 1975), English Rugby: A Celebration (ed, 1991), The Daily Telegraph Golf Chronicle (1994), The Ultimate Encyclopaedia of Golf (1995); *Recreations* golf; *Clubs* Press Golfing Soc, Upminster Golf; *Style*— Ted Barrett, Esq; ✉ 12 Oak Ave, Upminster, Essex (☎ 01708 224709, fax 01708 223908)

BARRETT, Frank Michael; s of Ernest Edward Barrett (d 1976), of Dagenham, Essex, and Dorothy Sophia, *née* Bentley Allen (d 1988); *b* 17 July 1944; *Educ* Goresbrook Secdy Modern; *m* 16 March 1968, Elaine Joan, da of John Henry Alfred Humby (d 1974); 2 s (Michael Frank b 24 April 1971, Christian David b 15 May 1973); *Career* Keystone Press Agency: messenger 1959, developing boy in glazing room then darkroom, printer, finally full photographer until 1977 (covered Royal Tours and Montreal Olympic Games); freelance photographer 1978; Daily Star: joined 1978, Royal photographer 1988–90, chief photographer 1990; stories covered incl: official birthday pictures of HRH Prince Charles 1977, kidney transplant pictures 1980, Argentina during Falklands War 1982, Boy George pop concerts in Japan, Wham pop tour of China, Bob Geldof in Ethiopia and Live Aid concert at Wembley, Ireland - USA World Championship fights with Barry McGuigan, USSR hero of Chernobyl, drug running in Thailand, Princess Diana in Australia and Middle East, The Romanian Revolution, murder squads in Brazil 1990, the Gulf Conflict, two election tours with Margaret Thatcher, Olympic Games Barcelona 1992, Princess Diana in Pakistan and Nepal, Portuguese Slave Boys 1994, Thailand Slave Workers 1995; Best Agency Photographer 1977, British press photographer of the Year 1977, News Photographer of the Year 1980, British Press Photographer of the Year 1990, highly commended Royals Section Picture Editor's Awards 1994, highly commended Royal Section Martini Awards 1995 (for picture of Duchess of Kent at Children of Courage Awards); memb NUJ; *Recreations* supporting Arsenal Football Club, tennis; *Style*— Frank Barrett, Esq; ✉ Daily Star-Express Newspapers, Ludgate House, 245 Blackfriars Rd, London EC1 (☎ 0171 922 7353, car 0831 345224)

BARRETT, Guy Crossland; OBE (1986); s of John Catton Barrett (d 1982), and Marian Braithwaite (d 1980); *b* 17 March 1925; *Educ* Giggleswick Sch, Bradford Tech Coll; *m* 1950, Mavis, da of Nathaniel James Yeadon (d 1968), of Leeds; 2 s (James b 1955, Richard b 1957), 1 da (Elizabeth b 1951); *Career* RAF 1944–47; structural engr; chm Henry Barrett Group plc 1987–92 (md 1965–87); pres: Royal Pigeon Racing Assoc 1976–79, Bradford C of C 1977–79, Br Constructional Steel Work Assoc 1983–86, La Fédération Colombophile Internationale 1983–87; Euro Convention for Constructional Steelwork 1988–89; vice chm Bd of Govrs Airedale and Wharfedale Coll of FE 1992–95; dir Bradford City Challenge Ltd 1992–; CEng, FIStructE; *Recreations* shooting, pigeon racing; *Clubs* Bradford; *Style*— Guy Barrett, Esq, OBE; ✉ Fence End, Calverley Lane, Horsforth, Leeds LS18 4ED (☎ 0113 258 2655)

BARRETT, John; s of Reginald Frank Barrett (d 1973), of Crewkerne, Somerset, and Doris Elsie, *née* Cummings (d 1992); *b* 7 Jan 1933; *Educ* Crewkerne GS; *m* 29 March 1958, Phyllis Margaret, da of Ernest George Edward Prentice (d 1975), of Croydon, Surrey; 1 s (Andrew John b 1964), 1 da (Helen Margaret b 1967); *Career* RAF 1951–54; Price Waterhouse: joined 1963, sr mangr 1967, ed PW Reporter 1983–92, archivist 1983–, tstee PW Staff Pension Fund 1983–, ed PW Euro News 1988–92; conslt to Drinking Fountain Assoc 1991–; official guide: City of London 1985–, London Borough of Islington 1986–; tutor Merton Adult Educn Authy 1993–; dep chm and sec London Appreciation Soc 1996–, sec Bridge Ward Club 1994–; chm Merton Historical Soc 1977–79, fndr chm Wimbledon Nat Tst Assoc 1981–84, sec Albert Reckitt Charitable Tst 1969–, sec Borough High St Amenity Fndn 1989–; Freeman City of London, memb Guild of Freemen; FCA (ACA 1962); *Recreations* London history, genealogy; *Style*— Mr John Barrett; ✉ 28 Melbury Gardens, London SW20 0DJ (☎ 0181 946 3865)

BARRETT, John Barbenson; s of George William Barrett, of Jersey, and Vera, *née* Simon; *b* 19 July 1950; *Educ* De La Salle Coll Jersey; *m* 1 June 1974, Joan Madelene, da of Francis John Le Corre; 1 s (Simon), 2 da (Caroline, Louise); *Career* CA; ptnr BDO Binder, sr ptnr BDO Carnaby Barrett; FCA 1975; *Recreations* flying, reading; *Style*— John Barrett, Esq; ✉ La Platiere, Le Hocq, St Clement, Jersey; BDO Carnaby Barrett, Seaton House, Seaton Place, St Helier, Jersey (☎ 01534 21565, fax 01534 21987, telex 4912337)

BARRETT, Rev John Charles Allanson; s of Leonard Wilfred Allanson Barrett, of King's Lynn, Norfolk, and Marjorie Joyce, *née* Hares; *b* 8 June 1943; *Educ* Culford Sch, Univ of Newcastle upon Tyne (BA), Fitzwilliam Coll and Wesley House Cambridge (MA); *m* 1967, Sally Elisabeth, da of William Mason Hatley; 1 s (James William Allanson b 16 March 1970), 1 da (Rachel Claire b 24 May 1972); *Career* chaplain and lectr in divinity Westminster Coll Oxford 1968–69, asst tutor Wesley Coll Bristol 1969–71, ordained Methodist min 1970, min Werrington Methodist Church Stoke on Trent and actg head of religious studies Birches HS Hanley 1971–73, chaplain and head of religious studies Kingswood Sch Bath 1973–83; headmaster: Kent Coll Pembury 1983–90, The Leys Sch Cambridge 1990–; World Methodist Cncl: memb Exec Ctee 1981–, sec Br Ctee 1986–, chm Educn Ctee 1991–, chm Prog Ctee 1991–96, memb Presidium 1996–; memb Steering Ctee Bloxham Project 1986–93; Hon DD Florida Southern Coll; FRSA; *Books* What is a Christian School? (1981), Family Worship in Theory and Practice (1982), A New Collection of Prayers (1983), Methodist Education in Britain (1989); sections on Methodism in Encyclopaedia Britannica Year Books 1988–91; *Clubs* East India, Rotary; *Style*— The Rev John Barrett; ✉ Headmaster's House, The Leys School, Cambridge CB2 2AD (☎ 01223 508903)

BARRETT, John Edward; s of Alfred Edward Barrett, and Margaret Helen, *née* Walker; *b* 17 April 1931; *Educ* Univ Coll Sch Hampstead, St John's Coll Cambridge (MA); *m* 1967, (Florence) Angela Margaret, *née* Mortimer; 1 s, 1 da; *Career* former tennis player, tennis promoter, sports conslt; journalist, broadcaster and author; Nat Serv RAF 1950–52; Dunlop Slazenger International Ltd (formerly Slazengers Ltd): mgmnt trainee 1957–59, asst home sales mangr 1959–65, asst mangr Tournament Dept 1965–74, mangr Tournament Dept 1974–75, tournament dir 1975, dir 1978–81, conslt 1981–94; tennis player: Middx jr doubles champion 1947 and 1948, nat schs singles and doubles champion 1949, rep Cambridge Univ v Oxford Univ 1952–54 (capt 1954), rep Oxford and Cambridge Univs v Harvard and Yale (Prentice Cup) 1952 and 1954, RAF champion 1950 and 1951, nat indoor doubles champion (with D Black) 1953, competed at Wimbledon 1950–70, GB rep Davis Cup 1956–57 (non-playing capt 1959–62), ranked nationally 1952–70 (highest position 5); tennis admin: dir LTA Training Squad (Barrett Boys) 1965–68, qualified LTA coach 1969 (memb Trg Ctee), fndr and dir BP Int Tennis Fellowship 1968–80, fndr BP Cup (int under 21 team event) 1973–80, fndr and organiser Pepsi-Cola Jr Int Series 1975–79, memb All England Lawn Tennis Club 1955– (memb Ctee 1989–), fndr bd memb Assoc of Tennis Professionals 1972–73, dep pres Int Lawn Tennis Club of GB 1994– (memb 1953–, memb Ctee 1957–, chm 1983–94); tennis commentator: BBC TV 1971–, Channel 9 Aust 1981–86, Channel 10 Aust 1987, Channel 7 Aust 1988–, various cable networks USA 1977–, Hong Kong Championships for ATV and TVB 1981–, Canadian Open for CTV 1989–; lawn tennis corr Financial Times 1963– (crossword contrib 1986–), editorial conslt and contrib LTA's magazine Serve and Volley (renamed ACE 1996) 1988–; *Books* World of Tennis (fndr ed and contrib, annually 1969–), Tennis and Racket Games (1975), Play Tennis With Rosewall (1975), 100 Wimbledon Championships: a celebration (1986), From Where I Sit (with Dan Maskell, 1988), Oh, I Say! (with Dan Maskell, 1989); *Recreations* music, theatre, reading; *Clubs* United Oxford and Cambridge Univ, All England Lawn Tennis, International Lawn Tennis Club of GB; *Style*— John Barrett, Esq; ✉ All England Lawn Tennis Club, Church Rd, Wimbledon, London SW19 5AE

BARRETT, Rev Prof (Charles) Kingsley; s of Rev Fred Barrett (d 1957), and Clara, *née* Seed (d 1941); *b* 4 May 1917; *Educ* Shebbear, Pembroke Coll Cambridge (BA, MA, BD, DD); *m* 1944, Margaret, da of Percy Leathley Heap (d 1952), of Calverley, Yorkshire; 1 s (Martin), 1 da (Penelope); *Career* asst tutor Wesley Coll Headingley 1942, Methodist min Darlington 1943, prof of divinity Univ of Durham 1958–82 (lectr in theology 1945–58), visiting lectureships and professorships in Europe, Aust, NZ and USA; contrib to learned jls and symposia; pres Studiorum Novi Testamenti Societas 1973–74, vice pres Br and Foreign Bible Soc; hon memb Soc of Biblical Literature USA, memb Royal Norwegian Soc of Scis and Letters 1991; Hon DD: Hull 1970, Aberdeen 1972; Hon DrTheol Hamburg 1981; Burkitt Medal for Biblical Studies 1966, Forschungspreis of the Von Humboldt-Stiftung 1988; hon fell Pembroke Coll Cambridge 1995; FBA 1961; *Books* incl: The Holy Spirit and The Gospel Tradition (1947), Gospel According to St John (1955, 2 edn 1978), The Gospel of John and Judaism (1975), Essays on Paul (1982), Essays on John (1982), Freedom and Obligation (1985), Church, Ministry and Sacraments in the New Testament (1985), Paul (Outstanding Christian Thinkers series, 1994), The Acts of the Apostles (Vol 1, The International Critical Commentary series, 1994), Jesus and the Word, And Other Essays (1996); *Style*— The Rev Prof C K Barrett, FBA; ✉ 22 Rosemount, Plawsworth Rd, Pity Me, Durham DH1 5GA (☎ 0191 386 1340)

BARRETT, Michael Joseph; s of Michael Joseph Barrett, MBE (d 1983), of Middlesbrough, Cleveland, and Hilda Patricia, *née* Davey (d 1991); *b* 15 Oct 1943; *Educ* Ratcliffe Coll Leics, Advanced Mgmnt Programme Harvard Business Sch, ACII; *m* 7 Sept 1967, Sheila Katherine, da of Arnold Willis Little, of Billingham, Cleveland; 1 s (Peter b 1982), 1 da (Louise b 1973); *Career* underwriter and insurance broker; chief exec offr Int Retail Minet Ltd; Liveryman Worshipful Co of Insurers; *Recreations* fishing, shooting; *Clubs* Annabel's; *Style*— Michael Barrett, Esq; ✉ Grey Poplars, Danesbury Park, Bengeo, Herts SG14 3HX (☎ 01992 553485); Minet Ltd, 66 Prescot Street, London E1 8BU (☎ 0171 481 0707, fax 0171 488 9786, telex 8813901)

BARRETT, Michael Paul; OBE (1987); s of William James Barrett, of Nottingham, and Irene Ada, *née* Beynon (d 1979); *b* 30 July 1941; *Educ* Westminster City Sch, Grey Coll Durham (BA); *m* 14 July 1966, Marie-Thérèse Juliette Françoise, da of Joseph Lombard; 2 s (Stephen Michael Lombard b 12 Oct 1967, Matthieu David Fabian Beynon b 26 May 1970); *Career* British Council: trg Madrid 1963–64, asst tutor to overseas students Univ of Birmingham 1964, asst dir Port Harcourt Nigeria 1964–65, asst rep Ethiopia 1966–69, Centre for Educnl Television Overseas London 1969–70, writer/presenter English prog NHK Japan 1970–72, dir Films Dept London 1972–75, educnl technol specialist Media Dept London 1975–77, non-formal educnl specialist Kenya 1977–80, dep rep Japan 1980–84, cultural attaché Washington DC 1984–87, dir Press and Information Dept London 1987–89; managing conslt Goddard, Kay, Rogers & Associates Ltd 1989–93, dir Japan British Council 1993–; chm Bd of Tstees Br Sch in Tokyo 1992–, vice pres Br C of C in Japan 1992–; memb RGS; *Recreations* fishing, music, art, forestry; *Clubs* Travellers'; *Style*— Michael Barrett, Esq, OBE; ✉ 25 Offerton Road, London SW4 0DJ (☎ 0171 720 6598); Rosalbert, Roulens, 11290 France; Sadohara Toyoda House, 2-41-5 Ichigaya Tamachi, Shinjuku-Ku, Tikyo 162, Japan; The British Council, 1-2 Kagurazaka, Shinjuku-Ku, Tokyo 162, Japan

BARRETT, (Alan) Roger; s of Lester Barrett (d 1970), of Leeds, and Nancy Cowling, *née* Clarke (d 1993); *b* 2 Dec 1941; *Educ* St Peter's Sch York; *m* 1977, Diana Kathryn, da of Ernest North (d 1985); 1 da (Jane Elizabeth b 1982); *Career* articled clerk Coulson & Co Scarborough 1958–64, qualified chartered accountant 1963, ptnr's PA Norman Hurtley & Co Leeds 1964–72; ptnr: Spicer & Pegler (now Deloitte & Touche) 1972–91, Barrowcliffs (Leeds) 1991–; chm Leeds Branch Inst of Taxation 1981–83, sec Yorks and Midland Regns Glass & Glazing Fedn 1972–; ACA 1963, ATII 1964, memb Soc of Assoc Execs 1986; *Recreations* theatre, opera, gardening, walking; *Style*— Roger Barrett, Esq; ✉ 2 Oakwood Park, Leeds LS8 2PJ (☎ 0113 240 3420); Barrowcliffs, 46 Park Place, Leeds LS1 2SY (☎ 0113 245 1652, fax 0113 234 1478)

BARRETT, Sir Stephen Jeremy; KCMG (1991, CMG 1982); s of Wilfred Phillips Barrett (d 1978), of Keene Valley, NY, and Dorothy, *née* Sommers (d 1987); *b* 4 Dec 1931; *Educ* Westminster, Ch Ch Oxford (BA, MA); *m* 1958, Alison Mary, da of Col Leonard George Irvine (d 1972); 3 s (Timothy b 1959, Nicholas b 1960, Matthew b 1962); *Career* HM Dip Serv: entered 1955, head of Chancery Helsinki Embassy 1965–68, cnsllr and head of Chancery Prague Embassy 1972–74, head of SW Euro Dept FCO 1974, princ private sec to Foreign and Cwlth Sec 1975, head of Sci and Technol Dept FCO 1976–77, fell Centre for Int Affrs Harvard Univ 1977–78, cnsllr Ankara 1978–81, head Br Interests Section Tehran 1981, dir of communications and tech servs FCO 1981–84; ambass: Prague 1985–88, Warsaw 1988–91; ret; *Recreations* climbing small mountains, reading; *Clubs* Ausable (NY); *Style*— Sir Stephen Barrett, KCMG; ✉ c/o Barclays Bank plc, PO Box 333, 92–93 High St, Oxford OX1 3HS

BARRETT, (Nicholas) Vincent John; s of Sidney Gordon Barrett, of East Hyde, Harpenden, Herts, and Francine Constance Alice, *née* Collins; *b* 9 June 1956; *Educ* Haileybury & ISC, Guy's Hosp (BDS), Univ of Texas San Antonio (MS), M D Anderson Cancer Hosp (Cert in Maxillofacial Prosthodontics); *m* 12 Sept 1991, Gaynor Susan, da of Gerald Duffett, of Tenby, Dyfed; 2 s (James Frederick b 12 Nov 1993, Daniel John b 26 July 1995); *Career* Guy's Hosp: house surgn Dept of Oral and Maxillofacial Surgery Feb-July 1980, house offr Dept of Prosthetic Dentistry 1980–81; assoc in gen dental practice Feb-June 1981, dental practice London 1985–; appts also held: Westminster Hosp 1985–90, King's Coll Dental Sch 1986–87, Guy's Hosp Dental Sch 1986–; Newland Pedley travelling scholar 1981, American Dental Soc award 1981; memb: American Coll of Prosthodontics, M D Anderson Cancer Hosp Assocs, American Dental Soc of London, Int Coll of Prosthodontics, American Dental Soc of Europe, Int Soc for Dental Ceramics; *Books* Colour Atlas of Occlusion and Malocclusion (jtly, 1991); *Recreations* tennis; *Style*— Vincent Barrett, Esq; ✉ 38 Devonshire St, London W1N 1LD (☎ 0171 935 8621)

BARRETT-LENNARD, Rev Sir Hugh Dacre; 6 Bt (UK 1801), of Belhus, Essex; s of Sir Fiennes Cecil Arthur Barrett-Lennard (d 1963), gggs of 1 Bt; suc kinsman, Sir (Thomas) Richard Fiennes Barrett-Lennard, 5 Bt, OBE, 1977; *b* 27 June 1917; *Educ* Radley, Pontifical Beda Coll Rome; *Heir* cous, Richard Fynes Barrett-Lennard b 6 April 1941; *Career* served WWII NW Europe (despatches), enlisted London Scottish 1940, cmmnd 2 Lt 1940, Capt Essex Regt 1945; entered Congregation of the Oratory 1946, ordained priest Rome 1950; *Style*— The Rev Sir Hugh Barrett-Lennard, Bt; ✉ The Oratory, South Kensington, London SW7 (☎ 0171 589 4811)

BARRETT-LENNARD, Richard Fynes; s of Roy Barrett-Lennard (d 1979); hp of kinsman, Rev Sir Hugh Barrett-Lennard, 6 Bt; *b* 6 April 1941; *Style*— Richard Barrett-Lennard, Esq

BARRETTO, Dr John Harold; s of Harold James Barretto (d 1974), and Winifred Annie Alexander (d 1990); *b* 6 Nov 1941; *Educ* Newells Sch Horsham Surrey, King's Coll Sch Wimbledon, St Bartholomew's Hosp Univ of London (MB BS, MRCS, LRCP); *m* 31 July 1964, Jeanette, da of Reginald Owens, of Phoenix, Arizona; 2 s (Mark b 15 July 1965, Dominic b 6 June 1975), 1 da (Roxane b 10 June 1968); *Career* house surgn and house physician Canadian Red Cross Meml Hosp Taplow Bucks 1965; sr house offr: gynaecology St Bartholomew's Hosp 1966, accident and neuro-surgery Radcliffe Infirmary Oxford 1967; in general private practice 1968–; FRSM; *Recreations* shooting, tennis, squash, skiing; *Clubs* Hurlingham; *Style*— Dr John Barretto; ✉ 134 Harley St, London W1 (☎ 0171 580 1101)

BARRIE, Carol Hazel; da of Harry Batson, of Rowley Regis, Warley, W Midlands, and Prudence, *née* Crompton; *b* 23 Dec 1945; *Educ* Rowley Regis GS; *m* 30 Sept 1967, Robert Barrie, s of Robert Barrie; *Career* CA; with Charlton & Co (now part of BDO Binder) Birmingham 1964–72 (articled clerk 1964–70); Peat Marwick Mitchell & Co (now KPMG): joined 1972, tax ptnr 1979–, head of tax Midlands Region 1995–, chm Nat Tax Gp for Partnerships 1988–95; lectr for a variety of Professional Bodies, memb Inst of Bankers' Approved Panel of Speakers, regular radio bdcasts for local radio, contrib to newspapers and technical journals; non-exec memb North Birmingham Health Authy 1988–96; FCA 1971; *Recreations* reading, embroidery, theatre, classical music; *Style*— Mrs Carol Barrie; ✉ KPMG, 2 Cornwall Street, Birmingham B3 2DL (☎ 0121 232 3000, fax 0121 233 3500, car 0836 761455)

BARRIE, Christopher (Chris); s of Alexander Barrie, and Anne, *née* Pitt; *b* 7 Nov 1958; *Educ* St Dunstan's Coll Catford, Univ of Exeter (BA); *m* 7 April 1990, Elspeth Jane, da of Dr Craig Sinclair; 3 s (Thomas Alexander Sinclair b 9 Nov 1993, Gabriel Henry Sinclair b 3 May 1996, William Felix Sinclair (twin) b 3 May 1996); *Career* editorial asst Municipal Group London 1983–85, asst ed Autotrade (Morgan-Grampian publishers) 1985–86; The Engineer: asst ed 1986–89, news ed 1989–91, ed 1991–94; freelance journalist with The Guardian, Evening Standard and BBC 1994–95, fin writer The Guardian 1995–, columnist Evening Standard 1995–; Industrial Magazine Journalist of the Year 1990 (Industrial Journalism Awards); *Recreations* hill walking, reading; *Style*— Chris Barrie, Esq; ✉ c/o The Guardian, 119 Farringdon Road, London EC1R 3ER (☎ 0171 278 2332)

BARRIE, Christopher Jonathan (Chris); *b* 28 March 1960; *Career* actor; worked at The Comedy Store then as voice over for Spitting Image 1984–91; *Television* BBC: Black Adder, The Lenny Henry Show, The Young Ones, Filthy, Rich and Catflap, Red Dwarf, Brittas Empire; contrib to Noel's House Party and Blue Peter, presenter Jackanory; appearances incl: The David Essex Showcase 1982, Jasper Carrott's Election Special 1983, Carrott's Lib 1983; Channel 4: Pushing Up Daisies 1984, Coming Next 1985, Handel - Honour, Profit and Pleasure (film), Zastrozzi (film), Testimony (film); character voices for The Legends of Treasure Island (Central), voice overs for various commercials; *Radio* Son of Cliche (2 series, BBC), Uncyclopaedia of Rock (Capital); *Recreations* classic cars and bikes, photography; *Style*— Chris Barrie, Esq; ✉ Noel Gay Artists, 6th Floor, 76 Oxford Street, London W1N 0AT (☎ 0171 836 3941)

BARRIE, (Charles) David Ogilvy; s of Alexander Ogilvy Barrie (d 1969), and Patricia Mary, *née* Tucker; *b* 9 Nov 1953; *Educ* Bryanston, Brasenose Coll Oxford (MA); *m* 1978, Mary Emily, da of The Rt Hon Sir Ralph Gibson, PC, Lord Justice of Appeal; 2 da (Eleanor Ann Ogilvy b 11 Feb 1983, Miranda Jane Ogilvy b 30 June 1985); *Career* HM Diplomatic Serv: FCO 1975–76, Dublin 1976–80, seconded to Cabinet Office 1980–81, first sec and later asst head of dept FCO 1981–87; transferred to Home Civil Serv Cabinet Office 1988, exec dir Japan Festival 1989–92, dir Nat Art Collections Fund 1992–; dir Guild of St George 1992– (companion 1991); *Books* Modern Painters (ed, by John Ruskin, 1987); *Recreations* sailing, drawing; *Clubs* Royal Cruising, Arts, Emsworth Sailing; *Style*— David Barrie, Esq; ✉ National Art Collections Fund, Millais House, 7 Cromwell Place, South Kensington, London SW7 2JN (☎ 0171 225 4800, fax 0171 225 4848)

BARRIE, Dr Dinah; da of Maj Claude Montague Castle, MC (d 1940), of London, and Mary Alice Patricia, *née* Armstrong; *b* 23 May 1936; *Educ* St James's Convent Sch, St Thomas's Hosp Med Sch (MB BS); *m* Aug 1963, Dr Herbert Barrie, *qv*; 1 da (Caroline Dinah b 1965), 1 s (Michael Robert b 1968); *Career* med registrar: Worthing Gen Hosp 1960–61, Edgware Gen Hosp 1961–63; asst lectr then lectr St Thomas's Hosp 1963–67; currently conslt microbiologist: Charing Cross Hosp (sr registrar 1970–72), Parkside Hosp Wimbledon, New Victoria Hosp Kingston; author of articles on microbiology in med jls; memb: Hosp Infection Soc, Br Soc of Antimicrobial Chemotherapy; FRCPath 1984 (MRCPath 1972); *Recreations* reading and gardening; *Style*— Dr Dinah Barrie; ✉ 3 Burghley Ave, Coombe Hill, Surrey KT3 4SW (☎ 0181 942 2836)

BARRIE, Dr Herbert; *b* 9 Oct 1927; *Educ* Wallington County GS, UCL and Med Sch London (MB BS, MD); *m* 1963, Dr Dinah Barrie, *qv*; *1 s (Michael), 1 da (Caroline)*; *Career* registrar Hosp for Sick Children Gt Ormond St 1955–57, res fell Harvard Univ Children's Med Center 1957, sr registrar and sr lectr Dept of Paediatrics St Thomas' Hosp 1959–65; conslt paediatrician: Moor House Sch for Speech Disorders 1968–74, Ashtead Hosp Surrey 1986–, New Victoria Hosp Kingston 1992–; conslt paediatrician Charing Cross Hosp (paediatrician 1966–84, physician in charge 1984–86); examiner Univ of London and RCP; memb Vaccine Damage Tbnl; FRCP 1972; *Recreations* tennis, writing; *Style*— Dr Herbert Barrie; ✉ 3 Burghley Ave, Coombe Hill, New Malden, Surrey KT3 4SW (☎ 0181 942 2836)

BARRIE, Jane Elizabeth; da of William Pearson, of Somerset, and Bessie, *née* Knowles; *b* 11 Sept 1946; *Educ* Bishop Fox GS for Girls, Imperial Coll of Sci & Technol (BSc); *m* 12 Dec 1970, Dr William Robert Ian Barrie, s of Dr Robert Barrie, of Somerset; *Career* stockbroker; regnl dir NatWest Stockbrokers 1990–93; chm: Avon & Somerset Constabulary Taunton Deane, West Somerset Div Crime Prevention Panel 1987–91; dir Somerset Trg and Enterprise Cncl 1991–93 and 1995–, non-exec dir Taunton and Somerset NHS Tst 1991–94, chm Somerset Health Authority 1994–, pres Soroptimist Int of GB and I 1990–91, chm of govrs Bishop Fox's Sch Taunton 1984–, memb Cncl Taunton Sch; MSI (memb Stock Exchange 1973), ARCS; *Recreations* sailing, bridge; *Clubs* Royal Dart Yacht; *Style*— Mrs Jane E Barrie; ✉ Hollydene, Kingston St Mary, Taunton, Somerset TA2 8HW (☎ and fax 01823 451388)

BARRIE, Lesley; *b* 20 Sept 1944, Glasgow; *Educ* Glasgow HS for Girls, Univ of Glasgow (DPA); *Career* NHS admin trainee 1963–66, hosp mgmnt 1966–77; dist gen mangr: Inverclyde Dist 1977–81, Glasgow SE 1981–83; dir of admin servs Glasgow Royal Infirmary Glasgow, Royal Maternity Hosp and Glasgow Dental Hosp 1983–87, unit gen mangr Stirling Royal Infirmary 1987–91; gen mangr: Forth Valley Health Bd 1991–93, Tayside Health Bd 1993–; chm Social Security Appeal Tbnls 1978–90; Indust Tbnl memb 1992–; table tennis internationalist for Scotland 1963–70, formerly nat and int sec Scottish Table Tennis Assoc; MHSM (DipHSM), MIMgt; *Recreations* table tennis, badminton, reading; *Style*— Miss Lesley Barrie; ✉ Tayside Health Board, PO Box 75, Vernonholme, Riverside Drive, Dundee DD1 9NL (☎ 01382 645151, fax 01382 640166)

BARRINGTON, Douglas John; OBE; s of John Frederick Barrington (d 1964), of Mount Lawley, W Australia, and Ethel Hannah Douglas (d 1981); *b* 9 Oct 1920; *Educ* Modern Sch Perth W Aust; *m* Clare Rachel Mary (d 1989), da of C Cuthbert Brown, of Malaya; 1 da (Prudence Rachel b 1954); *Career* serv WWII Lieut RANVR, Gunnery Offr destroyer flotilla Med (despatches 1945); Lygon Arms Broadway Worcs: mangr 1945, dir 1946, md 1956, owner and chm 1970–86, dir 1986–90; a fndr chm Prestige Hotels 1966; dir: Gordon Russell plc (chm 1980–82), Gleneagles Hotels plc 1980–82, Savoy Hotel Management plc 1986–90, Profile Management & Specialist Recruitment Ltd, Brasseries in the City Plc, Hotel! Hotel! Limited; memb: Main Bd BTA 1973–74, Cncl World Travel Market 1987–93, AA Liaison Ctee Br Hotels Restaurants and Caterers Assoc 1972– (chm Nat Cncl 1980–82, memb Bd of Mgmnt and Hotel Advsy Panel 1972–86); Int Hotel Assoc: chm Fin Ctee 1979–83, pres 1982–84, memb Exec Ctee and Fin Ctee, memb Cncl; pres: Br Assoc of Hotel Accountants 1984–87, The Hotel and Catering Benevolent Assoc 1990–91; Queen's award (first country inn to receive this honour) 1971 and 1985, Catey award for Tourism 1988, Catey award for Lifetime Achievement 1989; cncllr Wychavon DC 1970–76, former chm Broadway Parish Cncl, memb Broadway Cons Assoc, chm Hotel Sector Br Wildlife Year 1986–87; Master Innholder 1978, Freeman City of London 1980, memb Worshipful Co of Innholders 1985; FHCIMA, ACIS; *Recreations* travel, eating and drinking well, reading, tennis and golf (rather badly); *Style*— Douglas Barrington, Esq, OBE

BARRINGTON, Sir Nicholas John; KCMG (1990, CMG 1982), CVO (1975); s of Eric Alan Barrington (d 1974), of Trumpington, Cambridge, and (Agnes) Mildred, *née* Bill (d 1994); *b* 23 July 1934; *Educ* Repton, Clare Coll Cambridge (MA); *Career* 2 Lt RA 1952–54; FO (Persian language trg) 1957–58, language student Tehran 1958–59, oriental sec Kabul 1959–61, FO 1961–63, UK Delgn to Euro Communities 1963–65, first sec Pakistan 1965–67, Euro Econ Dept FCO and private sec Perm Under Sec CRO 1967–68, asst private sec FO 1968–72, head of Chancery and cnsllr Japan 1972–75, FO 1975–78, cnsllr Cairo 1978–81, head of Br Interests Section Tehran 1981–83, UK Mission to UN (NYC) 1983, econ summit coordinator 1984, asst under sec of state (Public Depts) 1984–87, ambass (1987–89) then high cmmr Pakistan 1989–94, concurrently non-resident ambass to Afghanistan 1994; tstee Ancient India and Iran Tst 1993; memb: Cncl Royal Soc of Asian Affairs, Exec Ctee Asia House, Exec Ctee Pakistan Soc; chm Mgmnt Ctee Southwold Summer Theatre; memb: Support Ctee Univ of Cambridge Faculty of Divinity, Project Ctee Sadler's Wells Theatre; pres Friends of Museum of Empire and Commonwealth 1996; Order of Sacred Treasure (third class) Japan 1975; hon fell Clare Coll Cambridge 1993; fell Royal Asiatic Soc, FRSA 1984; *Recreations* drawing, theatre; *Clubs* Athenaeum, Royal Cwlth Soc; *Style*— Sir Nicholas Barrington, KCMG, CVO; ✉ Clare College, Cambridge CB2 1TL

BARRINGTON, Raymond Lewis; s of Walter Lewis Barrington (d 1990), of Redland, Bristol, and Muriel, *née* Adams (d 1980); *b* 25 July 1928; *Educ* St Brendan's Coll Bristol; *m* 14 March 1953, Shirley, da of George William Yarwood (d 1981), of Hilperton, Wilts; 1 da (Katharine b 1958); *Career* Nat Serv Glos Regt 1946–48; mgmnt conslt Peat Marwick Mitchell & Co 1957–81 (consultancy ptnr 1963–81), chm Fairford Electronics Ltd 1982–, chm Dartmouth Golf and Country Club plc 1991–93, chm South Hams Environment Tst 1993–; hon treas Kingsbridge Cons Club 1982–, town cncllr Kingsbridge 1982–87, dist cncllr South Hams 1983–91 (chm Housing Ctee 1988–91); Freeman City of London 1977, Liveryman Worshipful Co of Wheelwrights 1977; FCA 1963, FCMA 1966, Hon FBCS (pres 1973–74); *Recreations* golf, crossword solving; *Clubs* Thurlestone Golf; *Style*— Raymond Barrington, Esq; ✉ Lukes Farm, Kingsbridge, Devon (☎ 01548 853933); Fairford Electronics Ltd, Coombe Works, Derby Rd, Kingsbridge, Devon (☎ 01548 857494, fax 01548 853118)

BARRINGTON-CARVER, John; *b* 8 Dec 1941; *Educ* Britannia Royal Naval Coll Dartmouth; *m* 2 Jan 1965, Judith Rosemary, da of Douglas Arthur Garrett (d 1981); 1 da (Nicola Wyn Louise b 30 Sept 1965); *Career* RN: Seaman Offr, seagoing appts 1962–68, seconded RN Trg Team Kenya as Cmdg Offr KNS Chui 1966, ret at own request 1968; metals analyst and commodity and fin futures broker 1968–85; dir Streets Financial Communications 1985, dir and sr conslt Ogilvy Adams & Rinehart 1988–91, princ Public Relations and Marketing 1991–; MIPR; *Recreations* shooting, sailing, riding, antique restoration; *Clubs* Special Forces, Guards' Polo, Hurlingham, Press; *Style*— John Barrington-Carver, Esq; ✉ 10 Paultons Square, Chelsea, London SW3 5AP (☎ 0171 351 3409, fax 0171 352 8222)

BARRINGTON-WARD, Dr Edward James; s of Sir Lancelot Barrington Ward, KCVO, FRCS (d 1953), of Bury St Edmunds, and Catherine (Mamie), *née* Reuter (d 1984); *b* 19 July 1942; *Educ* Eton, Gonville and Caius Coll Cambridge, St Bartholomew's Hosp (MA, MB BChir, MRCS, LRCP); *m* 24 July 1969, Brigid, da of William J Concannon of Tuam, of Co Galway; 2 da (Elaine b 1971, Catherine b 1973); *Career* GP Bury St Edmunds 1970–87; med dir: St Nicholas Hospice Bury St Edmunds 1986–87, Highland Hospice Inverness 1987–94; cncl memb BASC 1975–82, fndr chm research/conservation Ctee BASC, memb Disciplinary Ctee BASC 1977; tstee Youth & The Countryside Educn Tst, vice pres Fenland Wildfowlers' Assoc; *Recreations* shooting, fly fishing, stalking; *Style*— Dr Edward J Barrington-Ward; ✉ Balfreish, Wester Galcantray, by Cawdor, Nairn IV12 5XY (☎ and fax 01667 493526)

BARRINGTON-WARD, Simon; *see:* Coventry, Bishop of

BARRIT, Desmond; s of Samuel Islwyn Brown, and Gwyneth, *née* West (d 1970); *b* 19 Oct 1944; *Educ* Garw GS; *Career* actor; organiser of charity events incl: Samaritans, The Lighthouse, Children in Need, Children North East; *Theatre* Brogard in Scarlet Pimpernel (Chichester and Her Majesty's); Cliton in The Liar (Old Vic); RNT incl: Archille Blond in The Magistrate, chauffeur in Jacobowsky, Charlie in 3 Men on a Horse (also at Vaudeville), Toad in Wind in the Willows, Brazen in The Recruiting Officer, Cotrone in The Mountain Giants; RSC 1988– incl: Trinculo in Tempest, Gloucester in King Lear, Porter/Ross in Macbeth, Tom Errand in Constant Couple, Banjo in The Man Who Came to Dinner 1990–91, Antipholus in Comedy of Errors; recent RSC prodns: Bottom in A Midsummer Night's Dream 1995, Malvolio in Twelfth Night 1995; *Television* incl: Boon, The Bill, Homer and his Pidgeons, Poirot; *Films* incl: Lassiter, Rebecca's Daughters, Fierce Creatures, A Midsummer Night's Dream; *Awards* Clarence Derwent Award for Trinculo, Olivier Award for Best Comedy Performance in Comedy of Errors 1988; nominations for A Midsummer Night's Dream incl: Critics' Circle Award and Fany Award; *Recreations* antiques, cooking, travel; *Style*— Desmond Barrit, Esq; ✉ c/o Sally Hope Associates, 108 Leonard Street, London EC2A 4RH (☎ 0171 613 5353)

BARRON, Brian Munro; s of Albert Barron (d 1986), and Norah, *née* Morgan; *b* 28 April 1940; *Educ* Bristol GS; *m* Jan 1974, Angela Lee Barron; 1 da (Fleur b 1982); *Career* jr reporter Western Daily Press Bristol 1956–59, Evening World Bristol 1960–61, Daily Mirror 1962, BBC External Servs 1965; BBC Radio: Aden corr 1967, Cairo corr 1968, SE Asia corr (Singapore) 1969–71; reporter BBC TV London 1972; BBC TV: Far East corr (Hong Kong) 1973, Africa corr (Nairobi) 1977–81, Ireland corr 1982, Washington corr 1983–86, Asia Bureau chief (TV and Radio) 1987–94, New York corr 1994–; *Awards* Journalist of the Year UK (RTS) 1980, Int Reporting Award (RTS) 1985; *Recreations* cinema, opera, theatre, tennis, jogging, post-war British/Irish art; *Clubs* Oriental; *Style*— Brian Barron, Esq; ✉ c/o BBC Television, 1995 Broadway, Suite 505, New York, NY 10023, USA

BARRON, Derek Donald; s of Donald Frederick Barron (d 1967), of Beckenham, Kent, and Hettie Barbara, *née* McGregor; *b* 7 June 1929; *Educ* Beckenham GS, Univ Coll London; *m* 16 June 1963, Rosemary Ingrid, da of Lionel George Brian (d 1984); 2 s (Andrew b 1965, Adam b 1968); *Career* served Intelligence Corps 1947–49; Ford Motor Co: joined Ford Motor Co Sales 1951, Tractor Gp 1961, tractor mangr Ford Italiana 1963–70, mktg assoc US 1970–71, gen sales mangr overseas mkts Ford US 1971–73, md Ford Italiana 1973–77, gp dir Southern Euro sales Ford Europe 1977–79, sales and mktg dir Ford Brazil 1979–82, vice pres Ford Motor de Venezuela 1982–85, dir and vice pres ops Ford Brazil 1985–86, chm Ford Motor Credit Co Ltd 1986–91, chm and chief exec Ford Motor Co Ltd 1986–91; SMMT: pres 1990–91, dep pres 1991; Hon DUniv Essex 1989; *Style*— Derek Barron, Esq; ✉ c/o National Westminster Bank, Warley, Essex

BARRON, Sir Donald James; kt (1972), DL (N Yorks 1971); s of Albert Gibson Barron, of Edinburgh, and Elizabeth, *née* Macdonald; *b* 17 March 1921; *Educ* George Heriot's Sch Edinburgh, Univ of Edinburgh; *m* 1956, Gillian Mary, da of John Saville, of York; 3 s, 2 da; *Career* CA (Scot); Rowntree Mackintosh Ltd: joined 1952, dir 1961, vice chm 1965, chm 1966–81; Midland Bank plc: dir 1972, vice chm 1981–82, chm 1982–87; chm: CLCB 1983–85, Ctee of London and Scottish Bankers 1985–87; dir: Investors in Industry Group plc (subsequently 3i Group) 1980–91, Canada Life Assurance Co of GB Ltd 1980–96 (chm 1991–94), Canada Life Unit Tst Managers Ltd 1980–96, Canada Life Assurance Co Toronto 1980–96, Clydesdale Bank 1986–87; memb Bd of Banking Supervision 1987–89, dir BIM Fndn 1977–80 (memb Cncl 1978–80); tstee Joseph Rowntree Fndn 1966–73 and 1975–96 (chm 1981–96); memb: Cncl CBI 1966–81 (chm CBI Educn Fndn 1981–85), SSRC 1971–72, UGC 1972–81, Cncl Policy Studies Inst 1978–85, Cncl Inst of CAs of Scotland 1980–81, NEDC 1983–85; a pro-chllr Univ of York 1982–94 (treas 1966–72), govr London Business Sch 1982–88; Hon Doctorates: Loughborough 1982, Heriot-Watt 1983, CNAA 1983, Edinburgh 1984, Nottingham 1985, York 1986; *Recreations* golf, tennis, gardening; *Clubs* Athenaeum; *Style*— Sir Donald Barron, DL; ✉ Greenfield, Sim Balk Lane, Bishopthorpe, York (☎ 01904 705675)

BARRON, Iann Marchant; CBE (1994); s of William A Barron (d 1974), and Lilian E Barron (d 1969); *b* 16 June 1936; *Educ* Univ Coll Sch, Christ's Coll Cambridge (MA); *m* 1962 (m dis 1989), Jacqueline Rosemary, da of Arthur W Almond (d 1978); 2 s (Marc b 1965, Simon b 1967), 2 da (Clare b 1963, Sian b 1969); *Career* Elliott Automation 1961–65; md: Computer Technology Ltd 1965–72, Microcomputer Analysis Ltd 1973–78, INMOS Ltd 1981–88; chief strategic offr INMOS International plc 1984–89 (dir 1978–89); chm Division Limited 1989–; visiting prof Westfield Coll London 1976–78, visiting industl prof Univ of Bristol 1985–; visiting fell: QMC London 1976, Sci Policy Res Unit Univ of Sussex 1977–78; hon fell Bristol Poly 1986, distinguished fell Br Computer Soc 1986; RW Mitchell Medal 1983, J J Thompson Medal IEE 1986, IEE Achievement Medal for Computing and Control 1996; memb Cncl Univ Coll Sch 1983–; tstee The Exploratory 1990– (exec tstee 1992–), dir Bristol 2000 1995–; Hon DSc: Bristol Poly 1988, Univ of Hull 1989; FBCS 1971, FIEE 1994; *Publications* The Future with Microelectronics (with Ray Curnow, 1977), technical papers; *Style*— Iann M Barron, Esq, CBE; ✉ Barrow Court, Barrow Gurney, Bristol BS19 3RW

BARRON, Prof John Penrose; s of George Barron (d 1984), and Minnie Leslie, *née* Marks (d 1994); *b* 27 April 1934; *Educ* Clifton Coll, Balliol Coll Oxford (Thomas Whitcombe Greene prize, scholar, Barclay Head prize, MA, DPhil); *m* 1 Sept 1962, Caroline Mary, da of late William David Hogarth, OBE; 2 da (Catherine Alice Penrose b 25 Nov 1970, Helen Mary Hogarth 19 July 1973); *Career* lectr in Latin Bedford Coll London 1961–64 (asst lectr 1958–61), reader in archaeology and numismatics UCL 1967–71 (lectr in archaeology 1964–67), prof of Greek language and literature KCL 1971–91 (head Dept of Classics 1972–84); Univ of London: dean Faculty of Arts 1976–80, public orator 1978–81 and 1986–88, dir Inst of Classical Studies 1984–91, dean Insts for Advanced Study 1989–91, pro-vice chllr 1987–89; master St Peter's Coll Oxford 1991–; chm Conf of Colls Univ of Oxford 1993–95; visiting memb Inst for Advanced Study Princeton 1973, Blegen distinguished visiting prof Vassar Coll Poughkeepsie NY 1981, T B L Webster visiting prof Stanford Univ Calif 1986; Crown rep and vice-chm SOAS 1993–; memb UFC 1989–93, FKC 1988, memb Academia Europaea 1990, pres Soc for the Promotion of Hellenic Studies 1990–93 (tstee 1970–, hon sec 1981–90), tstee Prince of Wales's Inst of Architecture 1990–; FSA 1967; *Books* Greek Sculpture (1965, revd edn 1981), Silver Coins of Samos (1966); *Recreations* travel, gardens; *Clubs* Athenaeum, United & Oxford & Cambridge Univ; *Style*— Prof John Barron, FSA; ✉ St Peter's College, Oxford OX1 2DL (☎ 01865 278862, fax 01865 278855)

BARRON, Kevin John; MP (Lab) Rother Valley (majority 17,222); s of Richard Barron; *b* 26 Oct 1946; *m* 1969; 1 s, 2 da; *Career* NCB 1962–83 (NUM exec for Maltby Colliery), pres Rotherham and District TUC; MP (Lab) Rother Valley 1983–, memb Energy Select Ctee 1983–85, PPS to Neil Kinnock 1985–88, shadow energy min 1988–92, memb Environment Select Ctee 1992–93, shadow employment min 1993–95, shadow health min 1995–96, shadow min for public health 1996–; chair Yorkshire Gp of Lab MPs 1987–; vice pres Combined Heat and Power Assoc; *Style*— Kevin Barron, Esq, MP; ✉ House of Commons, London SW1A 0AA (☎ 0171 219 3000)

BARRON, Prof Laurence David; s of Gerald Landon Barron, of Southampton, and Stella, *née* Gertz; *b* 12 Feb 1944; *Educ* King Edward VI GS, Northern Poly (BSc), Lincoln Coll Oxford (DPhil); *m* 10 Aug 1969, Sharon Aviva, da of Denis Harris Wolf; 1 da (Susannah Mira b 23 Sept 1971), 1 s (Daniel Morris 17 May 1973); *Career* Ramsay Meml fell Univ Cambridge 1974–75 (research asst 1969–74); Univ of Glasgow: lectr 1975–80, reader 1980–84, prof of chemistry 1984–; G M J Schmidt Meml lectr Weizmann Inst of Sci Israel 1984, F L Conover Meml lectr Vanderbilt Univ USA 1987, visiting Miller Research prof Univ of California Berkeley 1995, sr fell EPSRC 1995–; Corday-Morgan Medal and Prize Chemical Soc 1979, Sir Harold Thompson Award for Spectroscopy 1993; memb: RSC, APS, ACS; MInstP, FRSE 1992; *Books* Molecular Light Scattering and Optical Activity (1982); *Recreations* music, walking, watercolour painting, radio controlled model aircraft; *Style*— Prof Laurence Barron, FRSE; ✉ Chemistry Department, The University, Glasgow G12 8QQ (☎ 0141 330 5168, fax 0141 330 4888)

BARRON, (Solomon) Leonard; *b* 29 Sept 1926; *Educ* St Thomas' Hosp Med Sch London (entrance scholar, MB BS, Sutton Sam prize); *m* 1959, Elizabeth Eleanor, *née* Evans; 1 da (b 1981), 1 s (b 1983); *Career* conslt obstetrician and gynaecologist: Prince of Wales Hosp Tottenham London 1962–67, Princess Mary Maternity Hosp and Royal Infirmary Newcastle upon Tyne 1967–91; lectr Univ of Newcastle upon Tyne 1967–91; conslt WHO 1977–80, memb, non-exec dir and chm Gateshead HA 1981–94, chm Freeman Gp of Hosps NHS Tst 1994–; Galton lectr 1992; past pres N of England Medico-Legal Soc; hon fell Faculty of Family Planning and Reproductive Health RCOG 1994; FRCS(Eng) 1955, FRCOG 1970 (MRCOG 1959); *Books* Obstetrical Epidemiology (with A M Thomson, 1983), Issues in Fetal Medicine (with D F Roberts, 1995); various chapters in textbooks related to obstetrics and ethics; *Style*— Leonard Barron, Esq; ✉ Freeman Group of Hospitals NHS Trust, Freeman Hospital, Freeman Road, High Heaton, Newcastle upon Tyne NE7 7DN (☎ 0191 284 3111, fax 0191 213 1968)

BARRON, Steve; *Career* film and video dir/prodr; chm Limelight (London) Ltd 1996–; early career experience as camera asst on films incl Superman 1 and 2, A Bridge Too Far (dir Richard Attenborough) and Duellists (dir Ridley Scott), concurrently experimented in early music video (The Jam and Sham 69) 1977, conceived and directed multi award winning promo Billy Jean (Michael Jackson) 1982, other promos incl Take on Me (A-HA, over 40 awards) 1985 and Money for Nothing (Dire Straits, MTV Video of Yr) 1986, subsequently dir of various commercials incl Motorcycle Chains (D&AD award) and others in UK and USA for clients incl Pepsi, Coca-Cola, Ford and Renault, dir Electric Dreams (first feature film, Best Dir Madrid Film Festival and Best Film Award Avoriaz Fantastique Film Festival) 1984, dir Hans my Hedgehog (Emmy Award), Fearnot and Sapsorrow (Storyteller episodes for NBC TV) 1987, dir Teenage Mutant Ninja Turtles (highest grossing ind film, CBS TV Award for Best Family Entertainment Film of Yr) 1990, subsequently dir of music promos Calling Elvis (Dire Straits, Grammy nomination) 1991, Unforgettable (Natalie Cole, Billboard Best Dir Award) 1991 and Let's Get Rocked (Def Leppard, MTV nomination) 1992, dir feature film Coneheads 1993, exec prodr The Specialist (feature with Sylvester Stallone and Sharon Stone) 1994, exec prodr ReBoot (animated TV show, ABC TV 1994, UK 1995), exec prodr While You Were Sleeping 1995, dir The Adventures of Pinocchio 1996; *Style*— Steve Barron, Esq; ✉ Limelight (London) Ltd, 3 Bromley Place, London W1P 5HB (☎ 0171 255 3939, fax 0171 436 4334)

BARROS D'SA, Aires Agnelo Barnabé; s of Inaçio Francisco Purificação Saude D'Sa (d 1978), of London, and Maria Eslinda Inez D'Sa, *née* Barros; *b* 9 June 1939; *Educ* Duke of Gloucester Sch, The Queen's Univ of Belfast (MB BCh, BAO, MD), ECFMG cert USA; *m* 12 May 1972, Elizabeth Anne, da of Hugh Austin Thompson (d 1984), of Belfast; 4 da (Vivienne, Lisa, Miranda, Angelina); *Career* formerly: house offr Royal Victoria Hosp Belfast, demonstrator Dept of Anatomy The Queen's Univ of Belfast, registrar and sr registrar appts in gen surgery and surgical specialities in teaching and dist gen hosps; sr tutor Dept of Surgery The Queen's Univ of Belfast 1974, Calvert lectr Royal Victoria Hosp 1975 (res fell in surgery 1973), vascular surgn and researcher Reconstructive Cardiovascular Res Centre Int, Providence Med Center Seattle USA 1977–78, conslt vascular surgn Royal Victoria Hosp Belfast 1978, Hunterian prof RCS 1979, 77th James IV surgical traveller (representing Br Isles) to N America, Australia and SE Asia 1983, Rovsing and Tcherning lectr Denmark 1987, jt lectureship RCS Edinburgh and Acad of Med Singapore 1989, examiner FRCS (Edinburgh) 1984, hon lectr in surgery Dept of Surgery The Queen's Univ of Belfast 1989, Gore visitor and hon memb Vascular Section Royal Australasian Coll of Surgeons 1994; memb: Cncl Vascular Surgical Soc of GB & I 1986–89, Clinical Res Awards Advsy Ctee DHSS NI 1986–91, Editorial Bd Euro Jl of Vascular and Endovascular Surgery 1987 (reviewer for several jls of surgery), Grant-giving Ctee Br Vascular Fndn 1994; regnl advsr RCS 1988 (regnl vascular advsr 1991), memb Faculty of Med The Queen's Univ of Belfast 1988, RCSE rep on NI Cncl for Post Grad Med Educn 1989; prodr Carotid Endarterectomy Teaching Film (Merit award Assoc of Surgns); memb: Assoc of Surgns of GB & I 1973, Ulster Med Soc 1973, Euro Soc for Surgical Res 1974, Surgical Res Soc 1975, BMA 1976, Vascular Surgery Soc of GB & I 1978, Ulster Surgery Club 1981, Venous Forum RSM 1982, Jt Vascular Res Gp UK 1983, Euro Soc of Cardiovascular Surgery 1984, Euro Soc for Vascular Surgery 1987, Forum of Angiology RSM 1987, Int Union of Angiology 1992, Int Soc of Pathophysiology 1992, Int Soc of Surgery 1995, Environmental Investigation Agency, Int Coll of Surgeons 1995, Earth Life Assoc, Friends of the Earth, Greenpeace; FRSM, FRCS, FRCSEd; *Books* Vascular Surgery - Current Questions (co-ed, 1991), Emergency Vascular Practice (co-ed, 1996); author of papers and chapters on varied clinical and research subjects in vascular and gen surgery; *Recreations* music, reading, travel, painting, environmental protection; *Style*— Aires Barros D'Sa, Esq; ✉ Vascular Surgery Unit, Royal Victoria Hospital, Belfast BT12 6BA (☎ 01232 240503 ext 3680, fax 240899, telex 747578 QUBMED G)

BARROS D'SA, Alban Avelino John; s of Inaçio Francisco Purificação Saude D'Sa (d 1978), of London, and Maria Eslinda Inez, *née* Barros; *b* 25 Oct 1937; *Educ* Teacher Training Coll Nairobi Kenya, West Ham Coll London, Univ of Bristol (MB ChB, LRCP, MRCS, FRCSEdin); *m* 22 July 1972, Gwenda Anne, da of Richard Arthur Davies, of Coventry; 1 s (Ian James b 30 April 1976), 1 da (Sonia Helen b 4 Sept 1974); *Career* house surgn and physician Bristol Royal Infirmary 1967–68, memb staff Faculty of Anatomy Univ of Bristol 1968–69, sr house offr in surgery (renal transplantion, orthopaedic, general, traumatic and cardio-thoracic surgery) Bristol Hosps 1969–71, registrar in surgery and urology Musgrove Park Hosp Taunton 1971–74, Pfizer res fell (also tutor in surgery and hon sr registrar) Royal Postgrad Med Sch and Hammersmith Hosp 1974–75, sr registrar in surgery Univ Hosp of Wales Cardiff and Singleton Hosp Swansea, conslt surgn Walsgrave Hosp Coventry and St Cross Hosp Rugby 1979–, clinical dir Surgery St Cross Hosp Rugby 1990–93, surgical tutor RCS England 1987–93; examiner (FRCS) in gen surgery for RCS Edinburgh 1990–, tutor in laparoscopic surgery for RCS England 1995–, memb Ct Univ of Bristol 1969–; memb: Soc of Minimally Invasive Gen Surgns, Midland Vascular Soc, Br Soc of Gastroenterology, Midland Gastroenterology Assoc, Midland Surgical Soc, Rugby and Dist Med Soc; Fell Assoc of Surgns GB and Ireland; memb: Warwicks Medico-legal Soc, BMA; *Books* Rhoads Textbook of Surgery (contrib chapter 5 edn, 1977); author of numerous pubns in med jls on oesophageal, gastric, pancreatic and vascular surgery; *Recreations* travel, golf; *Style*— Alban Barros D'Sa, Esq; ✉ 40 Nightingale Lane, Westwood Gardens, Coventry CV5 6AY (☎ 01203 675181); Walsgrave Hospital, Coventry (☎ 01203 602020); St Cross Hospital, Rugby (☎ 01788 545192); 5 Davenport Road, Coventry; 56 Regent Street, Rugby (☎ 01203 677838, fax 01788 578115, 01203 713822)

BARROTT, Michael Anthony Cooper; s of Brian Robert James Barrott (d 1963), and Betty Doreen, *née* Berryman; *b* 9 Dec 1954; *Educ* Reading Sch, St John's Coll Oxford (MA), Open Univ (MBA); *m* 29 May 1982, Elizabeth Jelisaveta, da of Stojan Stosic (d 1994); 1 s (William b 12 Aug 1996); *Career* Price Waterhouse 1976–87, gp financial controller The Private Capital Gp 1987–89, md Private Capital (Financial Services) Ltd 1989–90, fin dir Mortgage Trust Ltd 1990–95, chief exec Strategy, Finance & Control 1995–; non-exec and chm Fin Ctee Thames Valley Housing Assoc 1992–; FCA 1990 (ACA 1979), MIMgt 1987, MInstD 1992; *Recreations* music, skiing, golf, history, restoring Georgian houses; *Clubs* IOD; *Style*— Michael Barrott, Esq; ✉ Strategy, Finance & Control, 126 Kennington Road, London SE11 6RE (☎ 0171 582 2453)

BARROW, Andrew James; s of Gerald Ernest Barrow, MBE, of Gustard Wood, Wheathampstead, Herts, and Angela Eileen, *née* Frank; *b* 17 May 1954; *Educ* King's Sch Canterbury, Univ of Nottingham (LLB); *m* 16 April 1983, Helen Elizabeth, da of Brian Carter; 3 s (Charles Andrew b 24 May 1984, Frederick Nicholas b 26 May 1986, Joshua Barnaby b 9 April 1993), 1 da (Clementine Elizabeth b 17 March 1988); *Career* slr; Travers Smith Braithwaite: articled clerk 1976–78, asst slr 1978–83, ptnr 1983–; memb City of London Slrs' Co; memb: Law Soc, Int Bar Assoc, Inter-Pacific Bar Assoc; *Recreations* family, golf, tennis; *Clubs* City of London, Royal Wimbledon, Royal County Down; *Style*— Andrew Barrow, Esq; ✉ 10 Snow Hill, London EC1A 2AL (☎ 0171 248 9133, telex 887117, fax 0171 236 3728, car 0831 386119)

BARROW, Anthony John Grenfell; s and h of Capt Sir Richard John Uniacke Barrow, 6 Bt; *b* 24 May 1962; *Educ* Dulwich Coll, Univ of Edinburgh (MA); *m* 21 April 1990 (m dis 1996), Rebecca Mary Long; 1 da (Bryony Helen Ann Lambert b 22 Jan 1996); *Career* DHSS 1986–88, Nat Audit Office 1988–; CIPFA 1993; *Style*— Anthony Barrow, Esq; ✉ 37 Gleneldon Road, London SW16 2AX

BARROW, Dame Jocelyn; DBE (1992, OBE 1972); *b* 15 April 1929; *Educ* Univ of London (BA); *m* Henderson Downer; *Career* dep chm Bdcasting Standards Cncl (and chm of its Complaints Ctee) 1985–92; govr: BBC 1981–88, Farnham Castle (centre for training Third World workers), Cwlth Inst (and chair of its Educn Ctee), Cwlth of Learning; gen sec Campaign Against Racial Discrimination 1964–69, vice chm International Human Rights Year Ctee 1968, memb Community Relations Cmmn 1968–72, national vice pres Nat Union of Townswomen's Guilds 1978–80 and 1987–, memb EC Econ and Social Ctee 1990–; fndr (now pres) Community Housing Assoc Camden, vice chm E London Housing Assoc; govr and patron Goldsmiths' Coll (memb Equal Opportunities Ctee), patron Caribbean Centre (and its Caribbean Int Studies network); former sr lectr in educn Furzedown Teachers Coll, seconded to Univ of London Inst of Educn; Hon DLitt Univ of E London 1992; FRSA; *Style*— Dame Jocelyn Barrow, DBE; ✉ c/o Broadcasting Standards Council, 5–8 The Sanctuary, London SW1P 3JS (☎ 0171 233 0408, fax 0171 233 0397)

BARROW, Prof John David; s of Walter Henry Barrow (d 1979), of London, and Lois Miriam, *née* Tucker; *b* 29 Nov 1952; *Educ* Ealing GS, Van Mildert Coll Durham (BSc), Magdalen Coll Oxford (DPhil); *m* 13 Sept 1975, Elizabeth Mary, da of James William East (d 1978), of London; 2 s (David Lloyd b 1978, Roger James b 1981), 1 da (Louise Elizabeth b 1984); *Career* jr res lectr ChCh Oxford 1977–80; Univ of Sussex: lectr 1981–89, prof of astronomy 1989–, dir Astronomy Centre 1995–; Lindemann fell English Speaking Union Cwlth 1977–78, Miller fell Univ of California Berkley 1980–81, Nuffield fell 1986–87, Gifford lectr Univ of Glasgow 1988, Samuel Locker Award 1989, Scott meml lectr Leuvan 1989, Collingwood meml lectr Univ of Durham 1990, Sigma-Tau-Laterza lectures Milan Univ 1991, Leverhulme fell Royal Soc 1992, George Darwin lecture RAS 1992, PPARC sr fell 1994, Templeton Award 1995; external examiner Open Univ, memb various ctees SERC; FRAS, memb Int Astronomical Union; *Books* The Left Hand of Creation (1983), The Anthropic Cosmological Principle (1986), L'Homme et Le Cosmos (1984), The World Within the World (1988), Theories of Everything (1991), Perchè il mondo è matematico? (1992), Pi in the Sky (1992), The Origin of the Universe (1994), The Artful Universe (1995); *Recreations* athletics; *Style*— Prof John D Barrow; ✉ Astronomy Centre, University of Sussex, Falmer, Brighton BN1 9QH (☎ 01273 678574, fax 01273 678097, telex 877159 BHVTXS G)

BARROW, Julian Gurney; s of G Erskine Barrow (d 1979), and Margaret Armine MacInnes (d 1977); bro of Simon Hoare Barrow, *qv*; *b* 28 Aug 1939; *Educ* Harrow; *m* 1971, Serena Catherine Lucy, da of Maj John Harington (d 1983); 2 da; *Career* landscape and portrait painter; pres Chelsea Art Soc; *Recreations* painting, travel; *Style*— Julian Barrow, Esq; ✉ 33 Tite St, London SW3 4JP (☎ 0171 352 4337)

BARROW, Capt Sir Richard John Uniacke; 6 Bt (UK 1835), of Ulverstone, Lancs; s of Maj Sir Wilfrid John Wilson Croker Barrow, 5 Bt (d 1960); *b* 2 Aug 1933; *Educ* Beaumont; *m* 1961 (m dis 1974), (Alison) Kate, da of late Capt Russell Grenfell, RN; 1 s (Anthony John Grenfell b 1962), 2 da (Nony Mary Louise (Mrs Simon Kerr-Smiley) b 1963, Frances Teresa Catherine b 1971); *Heir* s, Anthony John Grenfell Barrow b 24 May 1962; *Career* served Irish Gds 1952–60; with Int Computers and Tabulators Ltd until 1973 (resigned); *Style*— Capt Sir Richard Barrow, Bt

BARROW, Robert; s of Frederick Barrow, of Congleton, and Hannah, *née* Carless; *b* 27 Dec 1949; *Educ* Sandbach Sch, Univ of Warwick, Univ of Staffs (BSc); *m* 14 Oct 1972, Pamela, da of Kenneth Stuart Snelgrove; 1 da (Alethea Mary Fiona b 20 June 1980); *Career* on mgmnt staff Computing Div British Railways Bd 1972–77, conslt ICL Ltd 1977–82, co-fndr and chief exec JSB Computer Systems Ltd 1982–; winner Design Cncl award for JSB Multiview computer windowing product 1989, nominated for Duke of Edinburgh's special designers prize 1989; MBCS 1976, CEng 1990; *Style*— Robert Barrow, Esq; ✉ JSB Computer Systems Ltd, Riverside, Mountbatten Way, Congleton, Cheshire CW12 1DY (☎ 01260 296200, fax 01260 296201, car 0860 736959)

BARROW, Simon Hoare; s of G Erskine Barrow (d 1979), of IOM, and Margaret Armine MacInnes (d 1977); bro of Julian Gurney Barrow, *qv*; *b* 4 Nov 1937; *Educ* Harrow, Ch Ch Oxford, Hill Sch Pennsylvania ESU Exchange; *m* 1, 1964 (m dis 1977), Caroline Peto Bennett; 1 s (Thomas), 3 da (Sasha, Emmeline, Rebecca); m 2, 1983, Sheena Margaret, da of Maj-Gen Sir John Anderson, KBE; 2 da (Kate, Florence); *Career* 2 Lt Scots Gds 1956–58; dir Charles Barker Group (now BNB Resources plc) 1978–92; chief exec: Ayer Barker 1978–86, Barkers Human Resources 1987–92; chm: People In Business Mgmnt Communication Conslts 1992–, The Recruitment Soc 1992–, Human Resource Interest Gp Market Research Soc 1995–; memb: Advsy Cncl European Movement 1992–, City Disputes Panel 1995–; FRGS; *Recreations* sailing; *Clubs* Brooks's; *Style*— Simon Barrow, Esq; ✉ 16 Chelsea Embankment, London SW3 4LA (☎ 0171 352 7531); Cowton House, Sudbourne, Suffolk IP12 2HB (☎ 01394 450737); People In Business, 10 Bowling Green Lane, London EC1R 0BD (☎ 0171 336 7790)

BARROWCLOUGH, Sir Anthony Richard; kt (1988), QC (1974); s of Sidney Barrowclough, of 28 Albion St, W2; *b* 24 June 1924; *Educ* Stowe, New Coll Oxford; *m* 1949, Mary Agnes, yr da of Brig Arthur Francis Gore Pery-Knox-Gore, CB, DSO (d 1954); 1 s (Richard b 1953), 1 da (Claire b 1956); *Career* called to the Bar Inner Temple 1949, bencher 1982, recorder of the Crown Ct 1972–84; Parly cmmr for Admin and Health Serv cmmr for England Wales and Scotland 1985–90; memb Cncl on Tribunals (and memb Scottish Ctee) 1985–90; *Recreations* country pursuits; *Style*— Sir Anthony Barrowclough, QC; ✉ The Old Vicarage, Winsford, nr Minehead, Somerset TA24 7JE

BARRY, Prof Brian Michael; *b* 1936; *Educ* Queen's Coll Univ of Oxford (Southampton exhibitioner, MA, DPhil); *m*; *Career* Lloyd-Muirhead res fell Dept of Philosophy Univ of Birmingham 1960–61, asst lectr Dept of Moral amd Political Philosophy Univ of Keele 1962–63, lectr Dept of Politics Univ of Southampton 1963–65, tutorial fell Univ Coll Oxford 1965–66, official fell Nuffield Coll Oxford 1966–69 and 1972–75 (sr tutor 1968–69), prof of govt Univ of Essex 1969–72 (dean of social studies 1970–72), prof of political science Univ of Br Columbia 1975–77; Univ of Chicago: prof of political science and philosophy and memb Ctee on Public Policy 1977–81, distinguished serv prof 1981–82, dir of graduate placement 1981–82; Calif Inst of Technol: prof of philosophy 1982–83, Edie and Lew Wasserman prof of philosophy 1983–86; prof (A3) in Dept of Social and Political Science Euro Univ Inst Florence 1986–87, prof of political science LSE 1987–, convenor LSE 1992–94; visiting assoc prof of political science Univ of Pittsburgh 1967, John Hinckley prof Dept of Political Science John Hopkins Univ Baltimore 1974, Olmsted visiting prof Yale Univ 1995, Tanner lectr Harvard Univ 1980; fndr ed The British Journal of Politcal Science 1971–72, section ed Political Theory 1973–75; Ethics - An International Journal of Social, Political and Legal Philosophy: ed 1979–82, manuscript ed 1982–86, assoc ed 1986–90; memb Editorial Bds of 13 jls; Rockefeller fell in legal and political philosophy and fell Harvard Coll 1961–62, fell Center for Advanced Study in the Behavioral Sciences Stanford Univ 1976–77, visiting fell Dept of Politics Australian Nat Univ 1977, Rockefeller Fndn Humanities fell 1979–80, American Cncl of Learned Socs fell 1980, Leverhulme sr fell (admin by Br Acad) 1991–92; Hon DSc Univ of Southampton 1989; FAAAS 1976, FBA 1988; *Books* Political Argument (1965, revised edn 1990), Sociologists, Economists and Democracy (1970), The Liberal Theory of Justice (1973), Power and Political Theory - Some European Perspectives (ed, 1976), Obligations to Future Generations (ed with Richard Sikora, 1978), Rational Man and Irrational Society? An Introduction and Source Book (ed with Russell Hardin, 1982), Theories of Justice (vol I of A Treatise on Social Justice, 1989), Democracy, Power and Justice - Essays in Political Theory (1989), Does Society Exist? The Case for Socialism (Fabian Soc tract, 1989), Democracy and Power - Essays in Political Theory 1 (1991), Liberty and Justice - Essays in Political Theory 2 (1991), Free Movement - Ethical Issues in the Transnational Migration of People and of Money (ed with Robert Goodin, 1992), Justice as Impartiality (vol II of A Treatise on Social Justice, 1995); author of numerous articles in various jls; *Style*— Prof Brian Barry, FBA; ✉ Department of Government, London School of Economics, Houghton Street, London WC2A 2AE (☎ 0171 955 7175, fax 0171 831 1707)

BARRY, Prof Brian William; s of William Paul Barry (d 1982), and Jean, *née* Manson (d 1959); *b* 20 April 1939; *Educ* Univ of Manchester (BSc, DSc), Univ of London (PhD); *m* 26 March 1966, Betty Barry, da of John Hugh Boothby, of Portsmouth; 1 s (Simon John b 1967); *Career* community and industl pharmacist 1960–62, asst lectr and lectr Univ of London 1962–67, sr lectr and reader Portsmouth Poly 1967–77, prof Univ of Bradford 1977– (dean of Natural and Applied Sciences 1991–94); FRSC 1976; fell: Royal Pharmaceutical Soc 1982, American Assoc of Pharmaceutical Scientists 1990; *Books* Dermatological Formulations: Percutaneous Absorption (1983); author of numerous research papers and book chapters; *Recreations* swimming, walking, golf; *Style*— Prof Brian Barry; ✉ School of Pharmacy, University of Bradford, Bradford BD7 1DP (☎ 01274 384760)

BARRY, Colin Campbell; s of Adm Sir Claud Barry, KBE, CB, DSO (d 1951), of Beaulieu, Hants, and Marsali Eleanor Mary, *née* Campbell (d 1974); *b* 2 Feb 1936; *Educ* Marlborough, Millfield; *m* 9 Sept 1967, Caroline Anne Vaughan, da of late Llewelyn Bevan; 1 da (Victoria b 20 Oct 1969), 1 s (Alexander b 21 Nov 1971); *Career* formerly with: International Thomson Corporation plc, Dorland Advertising Group; fndr and md Overton Shirley & Barry Ltd (int search conslts) 1976–95, vice chm and md Knight Wendling Executive Search 1995–; Liveryman Worshipful Co of Broderers 1989; *Recreations* sailing; *Clubs* City of London, Royal Cruising, RNSA; *Style*— Colin Barry, Esq; ✉ Knight Wendling Executive Search Ltd, 140 Park Lane, London W1Y 3AA (☎ 0171 355 1455)

BARRY, Dr David Walter; *b* 19 July 1943, Nashua, New Hampshire; *Educ* Yale (BA), Sorbonne, Yale Univ Sch of Med (MD); *m*; 2 c; *Career* research assoc Rockefeller Fndn Yale Arbovirus Research Unit 1967–69, med resident Yale-New Haven Hosp 1969–72 (med intern 1969–70), cmmnd offr (sr surgn) US Public Health Serv 1972–77; Bureau of Biologics Federal Drug Administration: staff assoc Viral Pathogenesis Branch Div of Virology 1972–73, dir Gen Virology Branch Div of Virology 1973–77, actg dep dir Div of Virology 1973–77, dir Influenza Vaccine Task Force 1976–77; Burroughs Wellcome Co: head Dept of Clinical Investigation Med Div 1978–85 (head Anti-Infectives Section 1977–78), head Dept of Virology Wellcome Research Laboratories 1983–89, dir Div of Clinical Investigation 1985–86, vice pres research Wellcome Research Laboratories 1986–89, memb Bd of Dirs Burroughs Wellcome Fund 1986–94, memb Bd of Dirs Burroughs Wellcome Co 1989–94, vice pres of research, devpt and med affrs Wellcome Research Laboratories 1989–94, memb Bd of Dirs Family Health International 1990–, gp dir research devpt and med Wellcome Research Laboratories The Wellcome Foundation Ltd (Wellcome plc) 1994–95, chm and chief exec offr Triangle Pharmaceuticals 1995–; visiting fell in infectious diseases Univ of Maryland Baltimore 1975–76, adjunct prof of med Duke Univ Sch of Med 1977–, Elisha Atkins visiting prof of med Yale Univ 1988; memb: AIDS Task Force and AIDS Program Advsy Ctee US Nat Insts of Health 1986, AIDS Task Force Pharmaceutical Mfrs' Assoc 1990, various other US anti-AIDS bodies and confs, Industry Liaison Panel Inst of Med 1992, Dean's Advsy Cncl Yale Med Sch, Research in Human Subjects Ctee Bureau of Biologists FDA, Med and Scientific Section Pharmaceutical Mfrs' Assoc, Scientific Affrs Ctee Nat Pharmaceutical Cncl, N Carolina Med Soc, N Carolina Industl (Vaccine) Cmmn, American Soc for Virology, American Soc for Microbiology, American Fedn for Clinical Research, American Assoc for the Advancement of Science, American Med Assoc; memb Editorial Bd: AIDS Research and Human Retroviruses, AIDS Patient Care, Jl of Infectious Diseases (also ad hoc reviewer); Wellcome Scientist Lecture 1981, Peter A Leermakers Symposium Wesleyan Univ 1986, Harold Brun Soc Lecture San Francisco 1987; jt holder of numerous pharmaceutical patents, author of approx 100 papers in med jls; *Style*— Dr David Barry; ✉ Triangle Pharmaceuticals Inc, 1810 South Lakeshore Drive, Chapel Hill, NC 27514, USA (☎ 001 919 929 3102, fax 001 919 932 6668)

BARRY, Sir (Lawrence) Edward Anthony Tress; 5 Bt (UK 1899), of St Leonard's Hill, Clewer, Berks, and Keiss Castle, Wick, Caithness-shire; Baron de Barry of Portugal, Lord of the Manors of Ockwells and Lillibrooke, Berks; s of Maj Sir Rupert Rodney Francis Tress Barry, 4 Bt, MBE (d 1977); *b* 1 Nov 1939; *Educ* Haileybury; *m* 1, 1968 (m dis 1991), Fenella, da of Mrs Hilda Hoult, of Knutsford, Cheshire; 1 s (William Rupert Philip Tress b 1973), 1 da (Alexandra Diana Frances Louise b 1977); m 2, 1992, Elizabeth Jill, da of G Bradley, of Fishtoft, Boston; *Heir* s, William Rupert Philip Tress Barry b 13 Dec 1973; *Career* former Capt Grenadier Gds; *Style*— Sir Edward Barry, Bt; ✉ 4 The Gables, Argos Hill, Rotherfield, East Sussex TN6 3QJ

BARRY, His Hon Judge; James Edward; s of James Douglas Barry (d 1971), of Southgate, Glamorgan, and Margaret Agnes, *née* Thornton; *b* 27 May 1938; *Educ* Merchant Taylors' Crosby, Brasenose Coll Oxford (MA); *m* 11 June 1963, (Ann) Pauline; 3 s (Matthew b 28 Sept 1967, David b 23 Jan 1972, William b 23 Dec 1976); *Career* Nat Serv RASC and Intelligence Corps 1957–59; called to the Bar Inner Temple 1963, practiced NE circuit 1963–85, pt/t chm Industl Tribunals 1983–85, stipendiary magistrate South Yorks 1985–94, recorder of the Crown Ct 1985–94, circuit judge (NE Circuit) 1994–; *Recreations* reading, home life; *Style*— His Hon Judge Barry; ✉ Leeds Combined Court Centre, Court House, 1 Oxford Row, Leeds LS1 3BQ

BARRY, Dr Michael; s of Maj Francis Patrick Barry, MC, TD (d 1964), and Margaret Julia, *née* Hunter (d 1996); *b* 9 March 1934; *Educ* Repton, Pembroke Coll Cambridge, The London Hosp (BA, MB BChir, MD); *m* 4 July 1964, Helen Margaret, da of Capt Hector Lloyd Price, MC (d 1979); 1 s (Timothy b 14 April 1965), 1 da (Susannah b 3 May 1967); *Career* Nat Serv Capt RAMC 1960–63, Maj Ghana Armed Forces 1961–62; The London Hosp 1958–60: house physician, house surgeon registrar in pathology, fell in gastroenterology Cornell Med Centre NY Hosp 1968–69, sr registrar in med the Royal Free Hosp 1969–74 (registrar in med 1963–65, hon lectr in med 1966–68), conslt physician Taunton and Somerset Hosp 1974–; chm SW Gastroenterology Group; MRCP 1960, FRCP 1979; *Recreations* gardening, photography, ornithology; *Style*— Dr Michael Barry; ✉ Pitlands Farm, Hillfarrance, Taunton, Somerset (☎ 01823 461338); Taunton and Somerset Hospital, Taunton, Somerset (☎ 01823 342126)

BARRY, Michael; *see:* Bukht, Michael

BARRY, Rt Rev (Noel) Patrick; OSB; 2 s of Dr T St J Barry (d 1962), of Wallasey, Cheshire, and Helen Agnes, *née* Walsh (d 1977); *b* 6 Dec 1917; *Educ* Ampleforth, St Benet's Hall Oxford (MA); *Career* headmaster Ampleforth 1964–79 (housemaster 1954–64), abbot of Ampleforth 1984–97; chm: Conf of Catholic Colls 1973–75, HMC 1975, Union of Monastic Superiors 1989–95; *Style*— The Rt Rev Patrick Barry, OSB; ✉ Ampleforth Abbey, York YO6 4EN

BARRY, Quintin; DL (E Sussex); s of Garrett Wright Barry (d 1967), of Worthing, and Elizabeth, *née* Ash (d 1962); *b* 7 March 1936; *Educ* Eastbourne Coll, Open Univ (BA); *m* 1, 1959 (m dis 1974), Ann, *née* Wilcox; 2 da (Sarah b 3 June 1960, Josephine b 8 June 1962), 1 s (John b 5 April 1965); m 2, 1975, Diana, *née* Pelling; 3 step c (Clara, Katherine, Oliver); *Career* slr; articled to H C Mileham of Mileham Scatliff & Allen 1953–58, asst slr Cronin & Son 1959–60, ptnr Mileham Scatliff & Allen 1962–70 (asst slr 1960–62), ptnr Donne Mileham & Haddock 1970–; pt/t chm Induatrial Tbnl; memb: Law Soc, Sussex Law Soc, Employment Lawyers' Assoc, Legal Aid Practitioners' Gp; chm Southern Sound plc; dep chm S Downs Health NHS Trust; *Recreations* history; *Style*— Quintin Barry, Esq, DL; ✉ 9 Mill Lane, Shoreham-by-Sea, West Sussex BN43 5AG (☎ 01273 455753); Donne Mileham & Haddock, 42–46 Frederick Place, Brighton, East Sussex BN1 1AT (☎ 01273 744268, fax 01273 202105)

BARRYMORE, Michael; s of George Parker, and Margaret, *née* O'Reilly; *b* 4 May 1952; *Educ* St Michael's RC Sch, LAMDA; *m* 10 June 1976, Cheryl Carlisa, da of Edward Charles Cocklin; *Career* TV personality; Russ Abbot's Madhouse (LWT) 1981–82, The

Michael Barrymore Show (series, Thames) 1983, host Strike It Lucky (Thames) 1986 (ITV Nat TV Award for Best Quiz Show 1995), The Michael Barrymore Special (Thames) 1988, The Michael Barrymore Show (series, BBC) 1988 and 1989, Barrymore (series, LWT) 1991 (Best Entertainment Prog RTS Awards and Br Comedy Awards 1994, ITV Nat TV Awards for Best Family Show and Best Presenter 1995), Strike It Rich 1996; Royal Variety Performance 1983, 1987 and 1993, Forty Years On (in presence of HRH Princess Anne, LWT) 1986, Children's Royal Variety Performance 1988 and 1990; Br Comedy Award for Best ITV Entertainment Presenter 1995; numerous star appearances in UK theatres incl: London Palladium, Apollo, Dominion, Opera House Blackpool, The Palace Manchester, Bournemouth Int Centre; *Recreations* classic cars, cooking, fishing, antique toys; *Style—* Michael Barrymore, Esq; ✉ c/o Norman Murray and Anne Chudleigh, First Floor, Regent House, 235/241 Regent Street, London W1R 5DD (☎ 0171 629 4817, fax 0171 629 5668)

BARSHAI, Rudolph; s of Benjamin Barshai, and Maria Alexeeva Barshai; *b* 28 Sept 1924; *Educ* Moscow Conservatory; *m* Helena, da of Sergey Raskov; *Career* viola player and conductor; memb Borodin String Quartet 1946–53, fndr and music dir Moscow Chamber Orch 1955–77, music dir New Israel Orch 1977–79, princ conductor Bournemouth Symphony Orch 1981–88, music dir Vancouver Symphony Orch 1985–88, princ guest conductor Orchestre National de France 1987–89; conducted all major orchs in USSR before emigration 1977, conducted numerous leading Euro orchs 1979–; instrumentations and arrangements incl: Prokofiev's Visions Fugitives 1960, Shostakovich Chamber Symphonies nos 1 and 2 1968, Symphony for Strings and Woodwinds 1988, Chamber Symphonie op 83 1990, J S Bach's Das Musikalische Opfer 1970 and Art of Fugue 1985, Eine Kleine Symphonie op 49a 1995; pres Jury Arturo Toscanini Int Conductors Competition Parma Italy 1990–; winner L'Orphee d'Or de l'Academie National de Disque Lyrique 1968, Grand Prix du Disque 1970; Hon DMus Univ of Southampton; *Recordings* incl: Bach Brandenburg Concertos, various Haydn, Mozart, Beethoven, Mahler and Shostakovich symphonies, other works by Tchaikovsky, Lokshin, Prokofiev, Bartok and Tippet; *Style—* Rudolph Barshai, Esq; ✉ c/o Allied Artists Agency, 42 Montpelier Square, London SW7 1JZ (☎ 0171 589 6243, fax 0171 581 5269)

BARSTOW, Dame Josephine Clare; DBE (1995, CBE 1985); da of Harold Barstow, of Sussex, and Clara Edith, *née* Shaw; *b* 27 Sept 1940; *Educ* Univ of Birmingham (BA), London Opera Centre; *m* 1, 1964 (m dis 1967), Terry Hands, *qv*; m 2, 1969, Ande Anderson (d 1996); *Career* soprano; debut with Opera for All 1964, studied at London Opera Centre 1965–66, Opera for All 1966, Glyndebourne Chorus 1967; contract principal: Sadler's Wells 1967–68, WNO 1968–70; freelance 1971–; US debut as Lady Macbeth in Miami 1977; has appeared with ENO, SNO, WNO, Glyndebourne, Opera North; has appeared at numerous international venues incl: Covent Garden, Vienna Staatsoper, Aix-en-Provence Festival, Bayreuth Festival, Salzburg, Munich, Zurich, Toulouse, San Francisco, Met Opera NY, Houston, Chicago, Adelaide, Bolshoi Moscow, Riga and Tbilisi; Hon DMus Univ of Birmingham; *Roles* with WNO incl: Violetta in La Traviata, Fiordiligi in Cosi fan Tutte, Amelia in Simon Boccanegra, Elisabeth de Valois in Don Carlos 1973, Jenufa 1975, Ellen Orford in Peter Grimes 1978 and 1983, Tatyana in Eugene Onegin 1980, title role in Tosca 1985, Amelia in Un Ballo in Maschera 1986; at Covent Garden incl: Alice Ford in Falstaff 1975, title role in Salome 1982, Santuzza in Cavalleria Rusticana 1982, Ellen Orford in Peter Grimes 1988, Attila 1990, Fidelio 1993; with Glyndebourne Festival Opera incl: Lady Macbeth in Macbeth (for TV) 1972, Elektra in Idomeneo 1974, Leonore in Fidelio 1981; with ENO incl: various in The Tales of Hoffman, Emilia Marty in The Makropoulos Case, Natasha in War and Peace, Violetta in La Traviata, Octavian and The Marschallin in Der Rosenkavalier 1975 and 1984, title role in Salome 1975, Elisabeth in Don Carlos 1976 and 1986, Tosca 1976 and 1987, Leonora in La Forza del Destino 1978 and 1992, title role in Aida 1979, Leonore in Fidelio 1980, Senta in Der Fliegende Holländer 1982, Mimi in La Boheme 1982, Sieglinde in Die Walküre 1983, Donna Anna in Don Giovanni 1986, Lady Macbeth of Mtsensk 1987 and 1991; appearances in world première performances incl: Denise in Tippett's The Knot Garden 1970, Marguerite in Crosse's The Story of Vasco 1974, Gayle in Tippett's The Ice Break 1977, Benigna in Penderecki's Die Schwarze Maske (Salzburg) 1986; other performances incl: Gudrun in Götterdämmerung (Bayreuth) 1983, title role in Katya Kabanova, Elizabeth I in Britten's Gloriana (Opera North Leeds and Covent Garden) 1994, Kostelnicka in Jenufa (Opera North) 1995, Medea and Marie in Wozzeck (Opera North) 1996; *Recreations* breeding Arabian horses (stud farm in Sussex); *Style—* Dame Josephine Barstow, DBE; ✉ c/o John Coast, 31 Sinclair Road, London W14 0NS (☎ 0171 603 4600, fax 0171 603 4233)

BARSTOW, Stan; s of Wilfred Barstow (d 1958), and Elsie, *née* Gosnay (d 1990); *b* 28 June 1928; *Educ* Ossett GS; *m* 1951, Constance Mary, da of Arnold Kershaw (d 1935); 1 s (Neil), 1 da (Gillian); *Career* draughtsman engrg indust 1944–62; novelist, short story-writer, script writer for TV; winner Best Br Dramatisation Writers' Guild of GB 1974; hon fell Bretton Coll, Hon MA Open Univ; *Books* A Kind of Loving 1960, The Desperadoes 1961, Ask Me Tomorrow 1962, Joby 1964, The Watchers on the Shore 1966, A Raging Calm 1968, A Season with Eros 1971, The Right True End 1976, A Brother's Tale 1980, The Glad Eye 1984, Just You Wait and See 1986, B-Movie 1987, Give Us This Day 1989, Next of Kin 1991; *Plays* Ask Me Tomorrow (with Alfred Bradley, 1966), Listen for the Trains Love 1970, A Kind of Loving (with Alfred Bradley, 1970), Stringer's Last Stand (with Alfred Bradley, 1972), An Enemy of the People 1978; *Television* dramatisations: A Raging Calm 1974, South Riding 1974 (RTS Writer's Award 1975), Joby 1975, The Cost of Loving 1977, Travellers 1978, A Kind of Loving 1982, A Brother's Tale 1982, The Man Who Cried 1993; scripts: Joby 1977, The Human Element 1984, Albert's Part 1984; *Style—* Stan Barstow, Esq; ✉ c/o Lemon, Unna & Durbridge Ltd, 24 Pottery Lane, London W11 4LZ (☎ 0171 727 1346)

BART, Lionel; *b* 1 Aug 1930; *Career* songwriter, composer, lyricist; lyrics written incl: Lock Up Your Daughters (1959), Fings Ain't Wot They Used t'Be (and music, 1959), Oliver! (and music and book, 1960), Blitz! (and music and direction, 1962), Maggie May (and music, 1964); film scores incl: Serious Charge, In the Nick, Heart of a Man, Let's Get Married, Light Up the Sky, The Tommy Steele Story, The Duke Wore Jeans, Tommy the Toreador, Sparrers Can't Sing, From Russia with Love, Man in the Middle; writer of many hit songs; awards incl: Ivor Novello Awards 1957, 1959 and 1960, Variety Silver Heart for Show Business, Personality of the Year Broadway USA 1960, Antoinette Perry Award (Tony) for Oliver! 1962, Gold Disc Award for the soundtrack of Oliver! 1969, Ivor Novello Jimmy Kennedy Award 1985, Ivor Novello Award for Best Theme from a Radio/TV Commercial (Abbey National) 1989, Golden Break Award 1990; *Style—* Lionel Bart, Esq; ✉ c/o 8–10 Bulstrode St, London W1M 6AH

BART-WILLIAMS, Chris; *b* 16 June 1974; *Career* professional footballer; clubs: Leyton Orient 1990–91 (36 appearances), transferred to Sheffield Wednesday for £350,000 1991–95, transferred to Nottingham Forest FC for £2.5m 1995–; England: memb Youth team, under 21; *Style—* Chris Bart-Williams, Esq; ✉ c/o Nottingham Forest FC, City Ground, City Road, Nottingham NG2 5FL

BARTER, Ian Stuart; s of John Wilfred Barter (d 1977), of Chipping Campden, Glos, and Catherine Cross, *née* Gray (d 1984); *b* 9 March 1933; *Educ* Cranleigh Sch, Gonville and Caius Coll Cambridge (open exhibitioner, BA, LLB); *m* 1 June 1960, Gillian Frances, da of Cowper Frederick Ide; 2 s (Charles Stuart John b 5 April 1962, William Iain b 1 November 1966), 1 da (Charlotte Catherine Jill b 9 Jan 1964); *Career* law supervisor Cambridge 1957–60; called to the Bar Gray's Inn 1958, in practice as barr 1958–60, mangr Cow & Gate Ltd 1960–68; Unigate plc: joined 1968, chm Int Div 1976–86, bd dir 1976–89; fell and first bursar King's College Cambridge 1989–; memb and pres Int Confedn of Infant Food Industries 1975–80, independent chm of pension funds 1986–, memb Monopolies and Mergers Cmmn 1990–96; *Recreations* collecting, charitable work; *Style—* Ian Barter, Esq; ✉ King's College, Cambridge CB2 1ST (☎ 01223 331217, fax 01223 331315)

BARTHOLOMEW, Prof David John; s of Albert Bartholomew, and Joyce Bartholomew; *b* 6 Aug 1931; *Educ* Bedford Modern Sch, UCL (BSc, PhD); *m* 1955, Marian Elsie, *née* Lake; 2 da (Ruth b 1963, Ann b 1966); *Career* scientist Field Investigation Gp NCB 1955–57, lectr in statistics Univ of Keele 1957–60, lectr then sr lectr in statistics UCW Aberystwyth 1960–67, prof of statistics Univ of Kent 1967–73; LSE: prof of statistics 1973–96 (prof emeritus 1996–), convener Statistics Dept 1976–78, vice chm Appts Ctee 1982–86, pro-dir 1988–91; visiting appts: Harvard 1964–65, Univ of Calif 1969, Technion Haifa Israel 1972, Univ of Melbourne 1977 and 1986, Univ of Alberta Canada 1982, Univ of Indiana 1987, Oregon State Univ 1987; consultancies incl: Civil Serv Dept 1969–80, DHSS 1976–82, statistical advsr BDA 1982–88 and BMA 1984–88; memb: Statistics Ctee SSRC 1970–74 (vice chm 1972–74), Orgn and Manpower Planning Ctee IPM 1970–72, Assessments Bd MOD 1973–76, Fellows Ctee Inst of Mathematical Statistics 1976–78, Advsy Ctee for Med Manpower Planning 1982–83 and 1985–88, Med Manpower Standing Advsy Ctee 1991–95, Statistics Advsy Ctee of Assessment of Performance Unit DES 1986–88; Royal Statistical Soc: memb Cncl 1970–74, Guy Medal in Bronze 1971, chm Gen Applications Section 1974–76, hon sec 1976–82, treas 1989–93, pres 1993–95; vice pres Manpower Soc 1987–94 (memb Cncl and chm 1970–76), memb Cncl Goldsmiths' Coll; memb Editorial Bd Br Jl of Mathematical and Statistical Psychology; memb: Int Statistical Inst 1967, Manpower Soc 1970; FIMS 1964, FBA 1986, CStat 1993; *Books* incl: Backbench Opinion in the House of Commons (jtly, 1961), Stochastic Models for Social Processes (1967, 3 edn 1982), Let's Look at the Figures: the quantitative approach to human affairs (with E E Bassett, 1971), Statistical Inference under Order Restrictions (jtly, 1972), Statistical Techniques for Manpower Planning (jtly 1979, 2 edn 1991), Mathematical Methods in Social Science (1981), God of Chance (1984), Latent Variable Models and Factor Analysis (1987), Uncertain Belief (1996), The Statistical Approach to Social Measurement (1996); author of numerous papers and chapters in books; *Recreations* gardening, steam railways, theology; *Style—* Prof David Bartholomew, FBA; ✉ The Old Manse, Stoke Ash, Suffolk IP23 7EN (☎ 01379 678197, fax 01379 678089, e-mail 101545.2512@Compuserve.Com)

BARTLAM, Thomas Hugh; s of Howard Bennett Bartlam (d 1970), and Mary Isobel Bartlam, *née* Lambert; *b* 4 Dec 1947; *Educ* Repton, Selwyn Coll Cambridge (MA); *m* 4 June 1977, Elizabeth Gabriel, da of Andrew David Arthur Balfour, of Beech House, Shalford, Surrey; 2 s (Edward b 1979, Henry b 1985), 1 da (Harriet b 1981); *Career* merchant banker; dir: Charterhouse Bank 1984–89, Charterhouse Venture Capital Fund, Charterhouse Buy-Out Fund, Charterhouse Business Expansion Fund; md Intermediate Capital Group plc 1989–; *Recreations* opera, gardening; *Clubs* MCC, City of London; *Style—* Thomas H Bartlam, Esq; ✉ Blounce House, South Warnborough, nr Basingstoke, Hants (☎ 01256 862234); 14 Addisland Court, Holland Villas Road, London W14; Intermediate Capital Group plc, 62 Threadneedle Street, London EC2 (☎ 0171 628 9898)

BARTLE, Ronald David; s of Rev George Clement Bartle (d 1993), of Surrey, and Winifred Marie Bartle; *b* 14 April 1929; *Educ* St John's Sch Leatherhead, Jesus Coll Cambridge (MA); *m* 1981, Hisako, da of Shigeo Yagi (d 1983), of Japan; 1 s (Nicholas b 1967), 1 da (Elizabeth b 1968) (both by former m); *Career* Nat Service 1947–49, RAEC 1948, army athletic colours 1954; called to the Bar Lincoln's Inn, practised in leading criminal chambers 1956–72; dep circuit judge 1974–78; Parly candidate 1958 and 1959; met stipendary magistrate 1972–, chm Inner London Juvenile Cts 1973–79; memb: HO Advsy Cncl on Drug Abuse 1987–, HO Ctee on Magistrates' Cts Procedure 1989–; patron The Pathway-to-Recovery Tst; Freeman City of London 1976; elected Steward of Worshipful Co of Basket Makers 1987; memb: Royal Soc of St George, Lawyers' Christian Fellowship; *Books* Introduction to Shipping Law (1958), The Police Officer in Court (1984), Crime and the New Magistrate (1985), The Law and the Lawless (1987); *Recreations* reading, walking, travel, relaxing at home; *Clubs* Lansdowne, Garrick; *Style—* Ronald D Bartle, Esq; ✉ c/o Bow St Magistrates' Court, London WC2 (☎ 0171 434 5270)

BARTLES-SMITH, Ven Douglas Leslie; s of Leslie Charles Bartles-Smith (d 1975), of Shrewsbury, and Muriel Rose Bartles-Smith (d 1993); *b* 3 June 1937; *Educ* Shrewsbury Sch, St Edmund Hall Oxford (MA), Wells Theol Coll; *m* 1967, Patricia Ann, da of James Garlick Coburn (d 1971), of Derbyshire; 2 s (Andrew James b 1969, Peter Nathaniel b 1976), 1 da (Sarah Elizabeth b 1971); *Career* Nat Serv 1956–58, 2 Lt RASC 1957, Lt 1958; curate St Stephen's Westminster 1963–68, priest i/c St Michael and All Angels and All Souls 1968–72 (vicar 1972–75), vicar St Lukes Battersea 1975–85 (rural dean 1981–85), archdeacon of Southwark 1985–; chaplain to HM The Queen 1996–; *Books* Urban Ghetto (co-author 1976), Opportunities for a Strong Church (1993); *Recreations* Shrewsbury Town football, travel, reading; *Style—* The Ven the Archdeacon of Southwark; ✉ 1A Dog Kennel Hill, E Dulwich, London SE22 8AA (☎ 0171 274 6767)

BARTLETT, Adrian; s of Alan Baskerville Bartlett (d 1981), and Marjorie Jesse, *née* Launder; *b* 31 March 1939; *Educ* Bedales, Camberwell Sch of Art, Univ of Durham; *m* 17 July 1962, Victoria Anne Bartlett, *qv*, *née* Howitt; 2 da (Zoë b 27 March 1965, Eve b 9 Feb 1967); *Career* artist; head of printmaking Morley Coll; visiting lectr Univ of Oxford, Wimbledon Sch of Art; *Solo Exhibitions* British Cncl Athens 1985, Oxford Gallery 1987, Blenheim Gallery 1988, Tsikalioti Museum Greece 1989, and others; *Group Exhibitions* numerous RA Summer Exhbns, 6th Int Art Fair London 1991; *Public Collections* Ashmolean Museum Oxford, British Museum, British Cncl, Berlin Graphotek, Dept for Educn, Herbert Art Gallery Coventry, McNay Inst Texas, Oldham City Art Gallery, St Thomas's Hospital, Surrey Educn Authy; UK rep Florence Biennale 1976; finalist Hunting/Observer Prize 1992; pres London Gp 1993 (memb 1979); *Books* Drawing and Painting the Landscape (1982), British Art in the Eighties (1983); *Clubs* Chelsea Arts; *Style—* Adrian Bartlett, Esq

BARTLETT, Andrew Vincent Bramwell; QC (1993); *Educ* Whitgift Sch, Univ of Oxford (BA); *Career* called to the Bar Middle Temple 1974; FCIArb; *Style—* Andrew Bartlett, Esq, QC; ✉ One Paper Buildings, Temple, London EC4Y 7EP (☎ 0171 583 7355, fax 0171 353 2144)

BARTLETT, Anthony David (Tony); s of Clifford Sydney McDonald Bartlett, of Ash, Surrey, and Sylvia Patricia, *née* Samson; *b* 21 Feb 1951; *Educ* Stamford Sch Lincs; *m* 1; 1 s (Joshua b 1984), 1 da (Melissa b 1982); m 2, 19 Aug 1993, Alison McNeill Kerr, da of late William Kerr; *Career* CA; Neville Russell & Co 1971–74, ptnr Coopers & Lybrand 1984–95 (joined 1975), dir and head of corp fin Beeson Gregory 1995–; *Recreations* golf, fishing, sailing, theatre; *Clubs* RAC; *Style—* Tony Bartlett, Esq; ✉ 19 Tedworth Square, London SW3 4DR (☎ 0171 352 2880); Beeson Gregory, The Registry, Royal Mint Court, London EC3N 4EY (☎ 0171 488 4040, fax 0171 481 3762)

BARTLETT, (Harold) Charles; s of Charles Henry Bartlett, and Frances Kate; *b* 23 Sept 1921; *Educ* Eastbourne GS, Eastbourne Sch of Art, RCA (ARCA); *m* 1, 1950 (m dis), Elizabeth, *née* Robertson; 1 s (Dr Charles Bartlett b 1956); m 2, 1970, Olwen Elizabeth Jones; *Career* WWII served RCS 1942–45; artist; many one man exhibitions in London, exhibited widely in UK and abroad, work in private and public collections; official purchases incl: V&A, Arts Cncl of GB, Nat Gallery of S Australia, Albertina Collection Vienna; pres Royal Soc of Painters in Watercolours, fell of the Royal Soc of Painters Etchers and Engravers; RWS 1970, RE 1961; *Recreations* music, sailing; *Style*— Charles Bartlett, Esq; ✉ St Andrews House, Fingringhoe, Colchester, Essex CO5 7BG (☎ 01206 729406)

BARTLETT, Prof Christopher John; s of Sqdn-Ldr Reginald George Bartlett (d 1977), and Winifred Kathleen, *née* Luther (d 1978); *b* 12 Oct 1931; *Educ* Univ Coll Exeter (BA), LSE (PhD); *m* 7 Aug 1958, Shirley Maureen (d 1988), da of Alfred Briggs (d 1957); 3 s (Paul b 1960, d 1962, Roger b 1963, Nigel b 1965); *Career* asst lectr Univ of Edinburgh 1957–59; lectr: Univ of the W Indies Jamaica 1959–62, Queen's Coll Dundee 1962–68; prof Univ of Dundee 1978–96 (reader 1968–78, emeritus prof 1996–); memb Scottish Examination Bd 1984–92; FRHistS 1967, FRSE 1989; *Books* Great Britain and Sea Power 1815–53 (1963), Castlereagh (1966), The Long Retreat 1945–70 (1972), The Rise and Fall of the Pax Americana (1974), History of Postwar Britain (1977), British Foreign Policy in the Twentieth Century (1989), The Special Relationship since 1945 (1992), Defence and Diplomacy 1815–1914 (1993), The Global Conflict 1880–1990 (revised edn, 1994), Peace, War and the European Powers, 1814–1914 (1996); contrib Annual Register (1987–); *Style*— Prof Christopher Bartlett, FRSE; ✉ History Department, The University, Dundee DD1 4HN (☎ 01382 223181 ext 4511)

BARTLETT, George Robert; QC (1986); s of Cdr Howard Volins Bartlett, RN (d 1988), of Putney, and Angela Margaret, *née* Webster; *b* 22 Oct 1944; *Educ* Tonbridge, Trinity Coll Oxford (MA); *m* 6 May 1972, Dr Clare Virginia, da of Gordon Chalmers Fortin (d 1995), of Castle Hedingham; 3 s (William b 1973, Frederick b 1979, Charles b 1982); *Career* called to the Bar Middle Temple 1966, bencher 1995; recorder of the Crown Court 1990–, asst parly boundary cmmr 1992–, dep judge of the High Ct 1994–; *Books* Ryde on Rating (ed, 1991–); *Recreations* cricket and other games; *Style*— George R Bartlett, Esq, QC; ✉ The Court House, East Meon, Petersfield, Hants GU32 1NJ; 2 Mitre Court Buildings, Temple, London, EC4Y 7BX (☎ 0171 583 1380, telex 28916)

BARTLETT, James Michael Gilbert; s of Maj Michael George Bartlett, TD, and Elizabeth Marjorie, *née* Grieve; *b* 21 March 1947; *Educ* Bromsgrove; *m* 20 Sept 1975, (Patricia) Anne, da of Ronald Dean Cranfield (d 1976); 1 s ((James) Michael Ronald b 1981), 1 da (Catherine Anne b 1978); *Career* princ Bartlett & Co CAs 1983–89, sr ptnr Bartlett Hall CAs 1989–96, managing ptnr Bartlett Kershaw Trott CAs 1996–; dir of several private cos; formerly: chm Winchcombe Deanery Synod, memb Glos Diocesan Synod, dir Glos Diocesan Bd of Fin; treas Glos Branch Cncl for Preservation of Rural England 1987–93, vice chm UK National Cadet Class Assoc 1996– (treas 1992–96); Freeman City of London 1979, Liveryman Worshipful Co of Builders Merchants; FCA 1971, FIMgt 1988; *Recreations* sailing, riding; *Clubs* Royal Ocean Racing, Royal Northumberland Yacht, South Cerney Sailing (cdre 1991–94), Royal Torbay Yacht; *Style*— James Bartlett, Esq; ✉ Cleeve House, West Approach Drive, Cheltenham, Gloucestershire GL52 3AD (☎ 01242 575000); Bartlett Kershaw Trott, 4 Pullman Court, Great Western Rd, Gloucester GL1 3ND (☎ 01452 527000, fax 01452 304585)

BARTLETT, Sir John Hardington David; 4 Bt (UK 1913), of Hardington-Mandeville, Somerset; ggs of Sir Herbert Henry Bartlett, 1 Bt (d 1921); s as 4 Bt 1989; *b* 11 March 1938; *Educ* St Peter's Guildford; *m* 1, May 1966, Susan Elizabeth (d 1970), da of Norman Waldock, of Gt Bookham, Surrey; 1 da (Nicola Jane b 20 April 1969); m 2, 19 June 1971, Elizabeth Joyce, da of George Thomas Raine, of Kingston; 2 s (Andrew Alan b 26 May 1973, Stephen b 5 July 1975); *Heir* s, Andrew Alan Bartlett b 26 May 1973; *Career* co dir, engr electrical and gen engrg; Freeman Worshipful Co of Pattenmakers, Freeman City of London; FRSA; *Recreations* construction design and model making, fine wines; *Style*— Sir John Bartlett, Bt; ✉ Hardington House, Ermyn Way, Leatherhead, Surrey KT22 8TW

BARTLETT, John Vernon; CBE (1976); s of late Vernon Ferdinand Bartlett, and Olga Beatrice Margareta, *née* Testrup (d 1992); *b* 18 June 1927; *Educ* Stowe, Trinity Coll Cambridge (MA); *m* 1951, Gillian, da of late Philip Hoffmann, of Sturmer Hall, Essex; 4 s; *Career* consulting engr; formerly sr ptnr and chm Mott Hay & Anderson, conslt Mott MacDonald Group (formerly Mott Hay & Anderson) 1988–95; pres Inst of Civil Engrs 1982–83; memb Governing Body Imperial Coll London 1991–95; Master Worshipful Co of Engrs 1992–93; FEng 1978, FICE, FASCE, FIEAust; *Recreations* sailing; *Clubs* Royal Engrs Yacht; *Style*— John Bartlett, Esq, CBE, FEng

BARTLETT, Maj-Gen (John) Leonard; CB (1985); s of Frederick Bartlett (d 1941), of Liverpool, and Eva, *née* Woods (d 1984); *b* 17 Aug 1926; *Educ* Holt GS; *m* 1952, Pauline, da of James Waite (d 1979); 2 s (Nigel, David); *Career* cmmnd RAPC 1946, served Hong Kong, Singapore, BAOR, War Office, Washington, Malta, Libya, HQ MELF 1966–67 (despatches), staff paymaster and offr i/c FBPO Berlin 1968–69, GS01 (Sec) NATO Military Agency for Standardisation 1969–71, cmmnd paymaster Hong Kong 1972–74, Col GS MOD 1974–76, chief paymaster ADP and Station Cdr Worthy Down 1976–79, chief paymaster BAOR 1980–82, paymaster-in-chief and inspr of Army Pay Servs 1983–86, ret; mgmnt conslt; Col Cmdt RAPC 1987–90; Freeman City of London 1984; MBCS, FIMgt; *Recreations* golf; *Clubs* Lansdowne, Royal Winchester Golf; *Style*— Maj-Gen Leonard Bartlett, CB; ✉ Chiphall Cottage, Droxford Road, Wickham, Hants PO17 5AZ

BARTLETT, Neil; *b* 23 Aug 1958; *Educ* Magdalen Coll Oxford; partner James Gardiner; *Career* performer, dir, translator and writer; artistic dir Lyric Theatre Hammersmith 1994–; recent prodns incl: The Picture of Dorian Gray 1994, Splendid's 1995, The Letter 1995, Romeo and Juliet 1995, Mrs Warren's Profession 1996, Lady into Fox 1996; fndr memb Gloria; *Stage Plays* incl: A Vision of Love Revealed in Sleep (1989), Sarrasine (1990), A Judgement in Stone (1992), Night After Night (1993), The Picture of Dorian Gray (1994), Lady into Fox (1996); *Translations* The Misanthrope (Molière), The School for Wives (Molière), Bérénice (Racine), The Game of Love and Chance (Marivaux), Splendid's (Genet); *Films and TV* That's What Friends Are For (1988), Where is Love? (1988), That's How Strong My Love Is (1989), Pedagogue (with Stuart Marshall, 1988), Now That It's Morning (1992); *Biography* Who Was that Man - A Present for Mr Oscar Wilde (1988); *Novels* Ready to Catch Him Should He Fall (1990), Mr Clive & Mr Page (1996); *Style*— Neil Bartlett, Esq; ✉ c/o Lyric Theatre Hammersmith, King Street, London W6 0QL (☎ 0181 741 0824, fax 0181 741 7694)

BARTLETT, Victoria Anne; da of Edgar Howitt; *b* 25 March 1940; *Educ* Camberwell Sch of Art, Univ of Reading; *m* 17 July 1962, Adrian Bartlett, *qv*; 2 da (Zoë b 27 March 1965, Eve b 9 Feb 1967); *Career* artist; currently tutor at Morley Coll London; visiting lectr Goldsmiths' Coll Univ of London; *Solo Exhibitions* The Egg & The Eye Gallery LA 1974, Van Doren Gallery San Francisco 1975, Morley Gallery London 1976, Edward Totah Gallery London 1981, Camden Arts Centre 1981, Galerie Simoncini Luxembourg 1985, Benjamin Rhodes Gallery London 1987 and 1991, Peralta Pictures 1994; *Group Exhibitions* incl: (Young Artists) NYC 1975, Flowers Gallery London 1977, The London Group (RCA) 1978, Galerie Etienne de Causans Paris 1980, Central Museum of Textiles Lodz Poland 1986, Oxford Gallery 1987, RA Summer Exhibition 1973, 1979, 1989, 1992 and 1993, The London Group (Barbican Concourse Gallery) 1993 and 1994, Morley Gallery 1992, 1993, 1994 and 1995, Michael Parkin Gallery 1994, Browse and Darby 1995; various work in public and private collections in UK and abroad; *Style*— Ms Victoria Bartlett; ✉ Morley College, 61 Westminster Bridge Road, London SE1 (☎ 0171 928 8501)

BARTOLO, David Charles Craig; s of Albert Edward Bartolo (d 1993), of Malta, and (Evelyne Valerie) Jean, *née* Callie; *b* 21 July 1949; *Educ* Queen Elizabeth GS Carmarthen, St Mary's Hosp Med Sch Univ of London (MB BS, MS); *m* 20 April 1974, Lesley Anne, da of Raymond Jeremy; 1 s (James b 1985), 2 da (Victoria b 1979, Rebecca b 1980); *Career* sr registrar S Western RHA 1982–86, sr registrar St Mark's Hosp London 1985, hon conslt surgn Bristol Royal Infirmary 1987–90, conslt sr lectr Univ of Bristol 1987–90, conslt surgn Royal Infirmary of Edinburgh Lothian Health Bd 1990–; Hunterian prof RCS 1984–85, Moynihan travelling fell Assoc of Surgns of GB and Ireland 1987, jt winner Patey Prize SRS 1988, jt winner New England surgical prize American Soc of Colon and Rectal Surgns 1988; memb Cncl Assoc of Coloproctology UK and Ireland, past memb Cncl Surgical Res Soc, memb Br Soc of Gastroenterology; FRCS 1976; *Style*— David Bartolo, Esq; ✉ Easter Hatton House, Kirknewton, Edinburgh EH27 8EB (☎ 0131 333 3797); The Royal Infirmary of Edinburgh, Edinburgh EH2 9YW (☎ 0131 536 1610)

BARTON, Alan Burnell; s of Charles Henry Barton (d 1976), and Rose Edith Barton (d 1976); *b* 2 May 1943; *Educ* Glyn GS Ewell, Univ of Bristol (BSc); *m* 1969, Jirina, *née* Klapstova; 1 s, 1 da; *Career* VSO in Sierra Leone 1965–66, operational res exec NCB 1966–73; asst sec DHSS 1978–90 (princ 1973–78); Dept of Health: dir Medical Devices Directorate 1990–93, head of resource mgmnt and fin div 1993–; *Recreations* jazz, theatre, country houses; *Style*— Alan Barton, Esq; ✉ Department of Health, Richmond House, 79 Whitehall, London SW1A 2NS (☎ 0171 210 4907)

BARTON, Prof (Barbara) Anne; *née* Roesen; da of Oscar Charles Roesen (d 1955), of New York, and Blanche Godfrey Williams (d 1968); *b* 9 May 1933; *Educ* Bryn Mawr Coll Pennsylvania USA (BA), Univ of Cambridge (PhD); *m* 1, 1957 (m dis 1968), William Harvey Righter; m 2, Aug 1969, John Bernard Adie Barton, s of the late Sir Harold Montagu Barton, of London; *Career* Girton Coll Cambridge: Rosalind Lady Carlisle res fell 1960–62, offical fell in English 1962–72, dir of studies in English 1963–72; Hildred Carlile prof of English and head of dept Bedford Coll London 1972–74, fell and tutor in English New Coll Oxford 1974–84, Grace II prof of English Univ of Cambridge 1984–, fell Trinity Coll Cambridge 1986–; memb Editorial Bds: Shakespeare Survey 1972–, Shakespeare Quarterly 1981–, Studies in English Literature 1976–; hon fell: Shakespeare Inst Univ of Birmingham 1982, New Coll Oxford 1989, Academia Europaea 1995; FBA 1991; *Books* Shakespeare and the Idea of the Play (1962), Introductions to the Comedies, The Riverside Shakespeare (1974), Ben Jonson, Dramatist (1984), The Names of Comedy (1990), Byron: Don Juan (1992), Essays, Mainly Shakespearean (1994); *Recreations* travel, opera, fine arts; *Style*— Prof Anne Barton, FBA; ✉ Leverington Hall, Wisbech, Cambridgeshire PE13 5DE; Trinity College, Cambridge CB2 1TQ (☎ 01223 338466)

BARTON, Dr David Garbutt; s of James Richard Barton (d 1983), of York, and Marion Joyce, *née* Garbutt; *b* 29 Jan 1937; *Educ* St Peter's Sch York, Emmanuel Coll Cambridge, Univ Coll Hosp Med Sch Univ of London (MA, MB BChir, MRCS, LRCP, DCH, DObstRCOG, FPCert); *m* 2 April 1961, Bernice Ann, da of George Birnie Banton (d 1995), of Wallasey; 2 s (Sebastian b 1963, Hugo b 1968); *Career* 2 Lt 5 W Yorks Regt (TA) 1958, Lt 1960, resigned cmmn 1962; GP Herne Bay Kent 1968–, sr ptnr Dr Barton and Partners; hon med offr Kent County Agricultural Soc, co surgn St John Ambulance Kent, memb St John Cncl for Kent; OStJ 1990; Freeman City of London 1977, Liveryman Worshipful Soc of Apothecaries 1977; FRCSEd 1969, FRCGP 1976, MFFP 1993; *Books* Child Care in General Practice (contrib, 2 edn 1982); *Recreations* theatre, ballet, opera (memb Glyndebourne); *Clubs* BMA London, Kent and Canterbury, Kent CCC; *Style*— Dr David Barton; ✉ 64 Western Esplanade, Herne Bay, Kent CT6 8DN; The Park Surgery, Herne Bay, Kent CT6 5RE (☎ 01227 742200, fax 01227 742277)

BARTON, Derek; s of Ronald Pascoe Barton (ka 1944), and Hetty Iris Barton; *b* 16 Oct 1934; *Educ* Henry Thornton GS; *m* 24 Aug 1956, Angela Mary, da of Patrick O'Connell, of Oxford; 2 da (Julie Ann b 3 Sept 1957, Deborah b 19 March 1963); *Career* RAF Police 1952–55; advertisement rep TV Times 1957–60, advertisement mangr IPC 1960–67; Farming Press: advertisement mangr 1967–70, advertisement dir 1970–74, jt md 1974–76, chm and md 1976–; *Recreations* travel, golf, DIY; *Style*— Derek Barton, Esq; ✉ Pleasant View, 12 Norman Close, Felixstowe, Suffolk IP11 9NQ

BARTON, Eric James; s of James Barton (d 1957), and Robina Edith, *née* Beveridge; *b* 2 Nov 1953; *Educ* Cumbernauld HS, Univ of Glasgow (MA), Univ of Strathclyde (LLB); *m* 13 July 1978, Heather, da of George Kennedy, of Cumbernauld; 3 s (Iain b 1980, Stuart b 1982, Graeme b 1989); *Career* slr; tstee and co sec Cumbernauld and Kilsyth Enterprise Trust Ltd 1985–, sr ptnr Barton & Hendry Slrs; chm Sch Bd Stirling HS 1994–; *Recreations* literature, historical reading; *Style*— Eric J Barton, Esq; ✉ 60 Grampian Rd, Stirling; Barton & Hendry Slrs, Fleming House, Tryst Rd, Cumbernauld (☎ 01236 735446, fax 01236 735451); 28 Murray Place, Stirling (☎ 01786 445441, fax 01786 445502)

BARTON, Maj-Gen Eric Walter; CB (1983), MBE (1966); s of Reginald John Barton (d 1968), and Dorothy, *née* Bradfield (d 1965); *b* 27 April 1928; *Educ* St Clement Danes Sch, Royal Mil Coll of Sci (BSc), UCL (Dip in Photogrammetry); *m* 1, 1963 (m dis 1983), Margaret Ann, *née* Jenkins; 2 s; m 2, 1984, Pamela Clare Frimann, da of late Reginald D Mason, of Winchelsea; *Career* RE 1948, served Middle East 1948–52, E Africa 1957–59, Middle East 1965–67; asst survey dir MOD 1967–70, dep dir Ordnance Survey 1972–74, geographic advsr HQ AFCENT 1974–76, dir surveys and prodn Ordnance Survey 1977–80, Maj-Gen 1980, dir of Mil Survey 1980–84, Col Cmdt RE 1982–87, Hon Col TA 1984–89; pres Field Survey Assoc 1991– (chm 1984–86); memb: Cncl Photogrammetric Soc 1979–82, Nat Ctee for Photogrammetry 1979–84, Cncl RGS 1980–83, Cncl Br Schs Exploring Soc 1980–84, Nat Ctee for Geography 1981–84; dir Caravan Club 1984–93; FIMgt, FRGS; *Recreations* water sports, numismatics; *Clubs* Geographical; *Style*— Maj-Gen Eric Barton, CB, MBE; ✉ c/o Barclays Bank, Lewes, E Sussex BN7 2JP

BARTON, Glenys; da of Alexander James Barton, and Gertrude Elizabeth, *née* Farmer; *b* 24 Jan 1944; *Educ* RCA (MA); *m* Martin Hunt; 1 s (Felix b 1982); *Career* artist; *Solo Exhibitions* Museum of Decorative Art Copenhagen 1973, Sculpture and Drawings (Angela Flowers Gall 1974, Galerie Het Kapelhuis 1976, Germeenttelijk Museum Het Princessehof 1976), Sculpture and Reliefs (Angela Flowers Gall) 1981 and 1983, Glenys Barton at Wedgewood (Crafts Cncl Gall) 1977, Heads: Sculpture and Drawings (Angela Flowers Gall) 1986, Artists and Green Warriors (Flowers East) 1990, Northern Centre for Contemporary Art 1991, New Sculpture (Flowers East) 1993, Portraits (Angela Flowers Gall) 1994, New Sculpture (Flowers East at London Fields) 1996; *Group Exhibitions* Images of Man (ICA) 1980, Sculptures in Clay (Yorkshire Sculpture Park) 1980, Nudes (Angela Flowers Gall) 1980–81, Art into the Eighties (Walker Art Gall and The Fruitmarket) 1981, A Taste of British Art Today (Contemporary Art Soc Brussels) 1982, South Bank Show (Arts Cncl) 1982, Small Is Beautiful - Part 3 (Angela Flowers Gall) 1983, Black and White (Angela Flowers Gall) 1985, Small Is Beautiful - Part 4 (Angela Flowers Gall) 1985, Sixteen Years Sixteen Artists (Angela Flowers Gall) 1986, Multiplemedia (Nicholson Gall) 1986, Sixteen Artists - Process and Product (Turnpike Gall) 1987, Contemporary Portraits (Flowers East) 1988 and 1990, Figure 11 Naked (Aberystwyth Arts Centre and tour) 1988, The Face (Arkansas Arts Centre) 1988, Out of Clay (Manchester City Art Gall) 1988, Small Is Beautiful - Part 6 (Flowers East) 1988, Angela Flowers Gallery 1990 (Barbican Centre) 1989, Badge Art 11 (Flowers East) 1989, Colours of the Earth (Arts Cncl tour) 1990, Small Is Beautiful - Part 8 The Figure (Flowers East) 1990, Angela Flowers Gallery 1991 (Flowers East) 1991, Nudes (Watermans Arts Centre) 1991, Artist's Choice (Flowers East) 1992, Small Is Beautiful

- Part 10 Animals (Flowers East) 1992, Portrait of the Artist's Mother Done From Memory (Flowers East) 1992, Decouvertes (Grand Palais Paris) 1993, The Portrait Now (National Portrait Gall) 1993, The Contemporary Print Show (Barbican) 1995, Contemporary Sculpture (Collyer Bristow) 1995, The Twenty Fifth Anniversary Exhibition (Flowers East) 1995, Flowers at Koplin (Koplin Gallery, Los Angeles) 1995, Methods and Materials of Sculpture (Nat Portrait Gallery, London) 1995; *Work in Public Collections* incl: Birmingham Museum and Art Gall, Contemporary Art Soc, Crafts Cncl, Leeds Museum and Art Gall, National Gall of Victoria, Princessehoff Museum, Royal Scottish Museum, Manchester Museum and Art Gall, Stockholm Museum, Pennsylvania State Univ Museum of Modern Art, V & A, National Portrait Gall, Scottish National Portrait Gall; pt/t lectr: Portsmouth Poly 1971–74, Camberwell Sch of Arts and Crafts 1971–87; *Style*— Ms Glenys Barton; ✉ c/o Flowers East Contemporary Art Gallery, 199–205 Richmond Road, London E8 3NJ

BARTON, The Rev Prof John; s of Bernard Arthur, and Gwendolyn Harriet Barton; *b* 17 June 1948; *Educ* Latymer Upper Sch London, Keble Coll Oxford (MA, DPhil, DLitt); *m* 16 July 1973, Mary, da of Alfred Burn; 1 da (Katherine Rachel b 26 June 1975); *Career* ordained priest C of E 1973; Univ of Oxford: jr res fell Merton Coll 1973–74, jr chaplain Merton Coll 1973–76, univ lectr in theology 1974–89, reader in Biblical studies 1989–91, Oriel & Laing prof of the interpretation of Holy Scripture 1991–, fell St Cross Coll 1974–91 (emeritus 1991), fell Oriel Coll 1991–; Canon Theologian Winchester Cathedral 1991–; Bampton lectr Oxford 1988, Hulsean lectr Cambridge 1990; *Books* Amos's Oracles Against the Nations (1980), Reading the Old Testament - Method in Biblical Study (1984), Oracles of God - Perceptions of Ancient Prophecy in Israel after the Exile (1986), People of the Book? The Authority of the Bible in Christianity (Bampton lectures, 1988), Love Unknown - Meditations on the Death and Resurrection of Jesus (1990), What is the Bible? (1991), Isaiah 1–39 (1995), The Spirit and the Letter: Studies in the Biblical Canon (1997); *Style*— The Rev Prof John Barton; ✉ Oriel College, Oxford OX1 4EW (☎ 01865 276537)

BARTON, John Bernard Adie; CBE (1981); s of Sir Harold Montagu Barton (d 1963), and Joyce, *née* Wale (d 1988); *b* 26 Nov 1928; *Educ* Eton, King's Coll Cambridge (BA, MA); *m* 1968 (Barbara) Anne Righter (Prof Anne Barton, *qv*), da of Oscar Charles Roesen; *Career* drama director and adaptor; fell King's Coll Cambridge 1954–60; RSC: joined 1960, assoc dir 1964–91, advsy dir 1991–; dir and co-dir of numerous plays for RSC incl: Othello 1972, Richard II 1973, Dr Faustus 1974–75, King John 1974–75, Cymbeline 1974–75, Much Ado about Nothing 1976, Winter's Tale 1976, Troilus & Cressida 1976, King Lear 1976, Midsummer Night's Dream 1977, Pillars of the Community 1977, The Way of the World 1977, The Merchant of Venice 1978, Love's Labour Lost 1979, The Greeks 1980, Hamlet 1980, Titus Andronicus 1981, Two Gentlemen of Verona 1981, La Ronde 1982, Life's a Dream 1983, The Devils 1984, Dream Play 1985, The Rover 1986, The Three Sisters 1988, Coriolanus 1989, Peer Gynt 1994, Cain 1995; other prodn incl: School for Scandal (Haymarket) 1983, own adaption of The Vikings (Den Nat Scene Bergen Norway) 1983, Peer Gynt (Oslo) 1990; wrote and presented Playing Shakespeare (LWT 1982, Channel Four 1984), narrated Morte d'Arthur (BBC2) 1984; *Books* The Hollow Crown (1962, 1971), The War of The Roses (1970), The Greeks (1981), La Ronde (1981), The Greeks (1983), Playing Shakespeare (1984), The Rover (1986); *Recreations* travel, chess, work; *Style*— John Barton, Esq, CBE; ✉ 14 De Walden Court, 85 New Cavendish Street, London W1 (☎ 0171 580 6196)

BARTON, Ven (Charles) John Greenwood; s of Charles William Greenwood Barton, and Doris Lilian, *née* Leach; *b* 5 June 1936; *Educ* Battersea GS, London Coll of Divinity (ALCD); *children* 1 s (Matthew John Greenwood b 1972); *Career* jr in Sales Office London 1953–54, Nat Serv RAF 1954–56, commercial sales 1956–60; asst curate St Mary Bredin Church Canterbury 1963–66; incumbent: Whitfield and West Langdon Dio of Canterbury 1966–75 (and Guston 1974–75), St Luke South Kensington 1975–83 (area dean Chelsea 1980–83), chief broadcasting offr for C of E 1983–90, archdeacon of Aston and canon residentiary Birmingham Cathedral 1990–; memb Cncl of the Corp of Church House 1990–, chm BBC W Midlands Advsy Ctee 1990–, tstee St Peter's Urban Village Tst; *Clubs* Nat Liberal; *Style*— The Ven the Archdeacon of Aston; ✉ Birmingham Diocesan Office, 175 Harborne Park Road, Birmingham B17 0BH (☎ 0121 454 5525, fax 0121 455 6085, office ☎ 0121 427 5141, fax 0121 428 1114)

BARTON, Marcia Christine Eleanor; da of Horace Arthur Barton (d 1982), and Beatrice Florence, *née* Brown; *b* 29 Dec 1943; *Educ* Walthamstow County HS for Girls Essex; *Career* admin offr in various posts LCC and GLC 1963–69, various posts local Govt Mgmnt Bd 1969–90 (asst sec to Bd 1986–90), gen sec ACPO 1990–; *Recreations* gardening, walking, entertaining family and friends; *Style*— Miss Marcia Barton; ✉ General Secretary, Association of Chief Police Officers, Room 311, Wellington House, 67–73 Buckingham Gate, London SW1E 6BE (☎ 0171 230 7184, fax 0171 230 7212)

BARTON, Martin; s of Walter Barton, of 215 Cyncoed Rd, Cardiff, and Sadie, *née* Shipman (d 1990); *b* 7 May 1944; *Educ* Quakers Yard GS nr Cardiff, Co GS Merthyr Tydfil S Wales; *m* 6 May 1969, Jeanette, da of Arran Lermon (d 1988), of Cardiff; 1 s (David b 1970), 1 da (Susannah b 1972); *Career* articled clerk Leyshon & Lewis CAs Merthyr Tydfil 1963–68, ptnr Curitz Berg & Co 1971 (joined 1970), formed own practice Barton Felman & Co 1979 (Barton Felman & Cotsen 1981, Barton Cotsen & Co 1983, Bartons 1990); memb: Cardiff Utd Synagogue, Cardiff Bridge Club; ACA 1968, FCA 1976; *Recreations* bridge, badminton; *Style*— Martin Barton, Esq; ✉ 15 Ty Gwyn Crescent, Cyncoed, Cardiff (☎ 01222 481471); Bartons, Lermon Court, Fairway House, Links Business Park, St Mellons, Cardiff (☎ 01222 777756)

BARTON, Nicholas James; s of Sqdn Ldr Ronald Cecil Nicholson Barton (d 1986), and Mary Carty, *née* Farrell; *b* 28 May 1935; *Educ* Westminster, Univ of Cambridge (MA, MB BChir); *m* 13 Aug 1960, Margaret Anne Joyce, da of Sgt Leslie Holman Rowe, DFM (d 1978); 2 s (Neil b 1961, David b 1972), 3 da (Katherine b 1963, Jane b 1963, Clare b 1966); *Career* conslt hand surgn Nottingham Univ Hosp and Harlow Wood Orthopaedic Hosp 1971–95, civilian consIt in hand surgery to the RAF 1980–95, ed Jl of Hand Surgery 1987–91; chm Nomenclature Ctee Int Fedn of Socs for Surgery of the Hand; hon memb: S African Soc for Surgery of the Hand, Brazilian Soc for Surgery of the Hand, Hong Kong Soc for Surgery of the Hand, NZ Soc for Surgery of the Hand; corresponding memb American Soc for Surgery of the Hand, pres Br Soc for Surgery of the Hand 1989; FRCS, FBOA; *Books* The Lost Rivers of London (1962), Fractures of the Hand and Wrist (ed, 1988); *Recreations* walking, reading, watching cricket; *Style*— Nicholas Barton, FRCS; ✉ 34 Regent Street, Nottingham NG1 5BT (☎ 0115 956 1305)

BARTON, (Malcolm) Peter Speight; s of Michael Hugh Barton (d 1996), and Diana Blanche, *née* Taylor; *b* 26 March 1937; *Educ* St Edward's Sch Oxford, Magdalen Coll Oxford (MA); *m* 7 Sept 1963, Julia Margaret, da of Hon James Louis Lindsay; 2 s (Henry (Harry) b 1967, Christopher b 1970), 1 da (Fenella (Mrs Nicholas Clements) b 1965); *Career* Nat Serv 2 Lt Oxford and Bucks LI (later 1 Greenjackets) 1955–56, Capt London Rifle Bde Rangers TA 1960–63; admitted slr 1964; ptnr Travers Smith Braithwaite 1967–86; md corp fin Lehman Bros 1986–95; dir: Robert Fleming & Co Ltd 1995–, Robert Fleming Holdings Ltd 1996–; memb: Law Soc, Int Bar Assoc, Cncl Br Inst of Int and Comparative Law, The Pilgrims (hon sec); MSI (memb Stock Exchange 1986); *Recreations* walking, shooting, skiing; *Clubs* Brooks's, City of London, City Law; *Style*— Peter Barton, Esq; ✉ 3 Aubrey Road, London W8 7JJ (☎ 0171 221 7888); Robert Fleming Holdings Ltd, 25 Copthall Avenue, London EC2R 7DR (☎ 0171 382 8379, fax 0171 638 5858)

BARTON, Roger; MEP (Lab) Sheffield (majority 50,288); *b* 6 Jan 1945; *Career* MEP (Lab) Sheffield 1989–; *Style*— Roger Barton, Esq, MEP; ✉ 2nd Floor, Barkers Pool House, Burgess Street, Sheffield S1 2HF (☎ 0114 2753431, fax 0114 2739666)

BARTON, Stephen James; s of Thomas James Barton, of Birkenhead, Merseyside (d 1996), and Vera Margaret, *née* Francis (d 1983); *b* 4 May 1947; *Educ* Birkenhead Sch, Jesus Coll Cambridge (MA), Coll of Law; *m* 20 April 1974, Catherine Monica Lloyd, da of Arthur Frederick Buttery (d 1986); 2 da (Tamsin b 1975, Claire b 1977); *Career* admitted slr 1971; Herbert Smith Slrs: articled 1969, asst slr 1971–78, ptnr 1978–97, conslt 1997–; fell commoner Jesus Coll Cambridge 1996–; memb: UK Energy Lawyers' Gp, Insolvency Lawyers' Assoc, Soc of Practitioners of Insolvency, Law Soc, IBA; Freeman City of London Slrs' Co; *Books* contributing ed Butterworths Co Law Serv 1985–; *Recreations* photography, gardening, walking, reading; *Style*— Stephen Barton, Esq; ✉ Jesus College, Cambridge CB5 8BL (☎ 01223 339339)

BARTRAM, Dr Clive Issell; s of Henry George Bartram, of Oxford, and Muriel Barbara, *née* Partridge; *b* 30 June 1943; *Educ* Dragon Sch Oxford, St Edward Sch Oxford, Westminster Hosp Med Sch (MB BS); *m* 29 Oct 1966, Michele Juliette Francois, da of John Anthony Beeston Clark (d 1988), of Bath; 2 s (Damian b 1970, Guy b 1974); *Career* conslt radiologist Bart's 1974–94; St Mark's Hosp: conslt radiologist 1974, dean of postgraduate studies 1985–88 (subdean 1976), chm Radiology Div 1987; radiologist King Edward VII Hosp 1978; FRCR 1972, FRCP 1985; *Books* Clinical Radiology in Gastroenterolgoy (1981), Radiology in Inflammatory Bowel Disease (1983); *Recreations* walking, theatre, music; *Style*— Dr Clive Bartram; ✉ Pelhams, Maplefield Lane, Chalfont St Giles, Bucks HP8 4TY (☎ 01494 766303); St Mark's Hosp, Northwick Park, Harrow HA1 3JU (☎ 0181 235 4081)

BARTTELOT, Col Sir Brian Walter de Stopham; 5 Bt (UK 1875), of Stopham, Sussex, OBE (1983), DL (W Sussex 1988); s of Brig Sir Walter de Stopham Barttelot, 4 Bt, DSO (ka 1944), and Sara Patricia, da of late Lt-Col Herbert Valentine Ravenscroft, JP, of The Abbey, Storrington, Sussex; *b* 17 July 1941; *Educ* Eton, Sandhurst, Staff Coll Camberley; *m* 1969, Hon Fiona, *née* Weld-Forester; 4 da (Isabel Emily b 1971, Sophie Rosalind b 1973, Ursulina May b 1978, Emma Amelia b 1981); *Heir* bro, Robin Ravenscroft Barttelot b 15 Dec 1943; *Career* cmmnd Coldstream Gds 1961, temp equerry to HM the Queen 1970–71, Camberley Staff Coll 1974, GSO2 Army Staff Duties Directorate MOD 1975–76, 2 i/c 2 Bn Coldstream Gds 1977–78, Mil Sec to Maj-Gen cmdg London Dist and Household Div 1978–81, GSO1 MOD 1981–82, CO 1 Bn Coldstream Gds 1982–85, GSO1 HQ BAOR 1985–86, Regimental Lt-Col cmdg Coldstream Gds 1987–92, Col Foot Gds 1989–92, ret; High Sheriff W Sussex 1997, HM Vice Lord-Lt W Sussex 1994–; dir Parham Park Ltd 1993–; Hon Col Sussex Army Cadet Force 1996–; pres W Sussex Scouts 1993–; memb HM Body Guard of the Hon Corps of Gentlemen at Arms 1993–; Liveryman Worshipful Co of Gunmakers 1980; *Clubs* Cavalry and Guards', Pratt's, Farmers'; *Style*— Col Sir Brian Barttelot, Bt, OBE, DL; ✉ Stopham Park, Pulborough, W Sussex RH20 1EB (office ☎/fax 01798 865861)

BARTTELOT, Robin Ravenscroft; s of Lt-Col Sir Walter Barttelot, 4 Bt (d 1944), and Sara, *née* Ravenscroft; bro and h of Col Sir Brian Barttelot, 5 Bt; *b* 15 Dec 1943; *Educ* Seaford Coll, Perth Univ W Aust; *m* 1987, Teresa, er da of late Kenneth Greenlees; 1 s (Hugo Ravenscroft b 7 April 1990), 1 da (Emily Rose b 1 May 1988); *Career* stockbroker; *Style*— Robin Barttelot, Esq

BARTY-KING, Mark Baxter; MC (1958); s of George Ingram Barty-King (d 1981), and Barbara Baxter Barty-King (d 1979); *b* 3 March 1938; *Educ* Winchester; *m* 1, 1963, Margild Bolten; 2 s (Daniel b 11 May 1964, Dominic Alexis b 20 June 1967); m 2, 1976, Marilyn Scott; 2 s (Sam Baxter b 10 April 1978, Mark Benedict b 2 Jan 1980); *Career* Nat Serv Capt 13/18 Royal Hussars (Aden, Oman, Malaya) 1957–61; Abelard Schuman NY 1962–64, John Howell Books San Francisco 1964–65; William Heinemann Ltd London 1966–74: dir Peter Davies Ltd 1969–74, dir 1970–74; editorial dir Granada Publishing 1974–84; Transworld Publishers: dir 1984–, fndr Bantam Press 1984, md Bantam Press, Doubleday London and Partridge Press, dep md publishing Transworld Publishers until 1995, md 1995–; Under Renter Warden Worshipful Company of Merchant Taylors 1992 (Liveryman 1971, memb Ct of Assts 1992); FRSA 1993; *Recreations* countryside, books, music; *Clubs* Groucho, Lansdowne; *Style*— Mark Barty-King, Esq, MC; ✉ Transworld Publishers Ltd, 61–63 Uxbridge Road, London W5 5SA (☎ 0181 579 2652, fax 0181 231 6710)

BASHMET, Yuri Abramovich; *b* 24 Jan 1953; *Educ* Moscow Conservatoire; *m* Natalia, *née* Timofeevna; 1 da (Ksenya b 15 July 1980), 1 s (Alexander b 17 May 1986); *Career* viola player; studied with Vadim Borisovsky and Feodor Druzhinin, winner first prize Munich Int Viola Competition 1976; made youngest ever professor at Moscow Conservatoire, first ever viola soloist at various international venues incl La Scala Milan and the Concertgebouw Amsterdam; appeared with numerous major artists incl Sviatoslav Richter, Natalia Gutman and the Borodin Quartet; worked with numerous orchs incl: Berlin Philharmonic, Concertgebouw Orch, Boston, Chicago and Montreal Symphony Orchs, Los Angeles Philharmonic and Philharmonia, LSO, Moscow Soloists; viola concerti written for him by various composers incl Alfred Schnittke (premièred Amsterdam Concertgebouw 1986), Giya Kancheli (premièred Berlin Festival 1990) and John Tavener The Myrrh Bearer (premièred LSO at the Barbican 1994); soloist UK première Poul Ruders Concerto for Viola and Orchestra (with Danish Radio Symphony Orch) BBC Proms 1995; *Recordings* various with RCA Victor Red Seal incl: Schnittke Viola Concerto (with LSO and Rostropovich), twentieth century viola concerti and two chamber music recordings with Moscow Soloists, various recital recordings incl works by Schubert and Schumann; *Style*— Yuri Bashmet, Esq; ✉ c/o Katherine Wolfenden, Van Walsum Management Ltd, 26 Wadham Road, London SW15 2LR (☎ 0181 874 6344, fax 0181 877 0077)

BASIL, Victor; *b* 3 Aug 1933; *Educ* Liverpool Coll, Univ of Liverpool (BArch, MCD); *m* 14 Sept 1963, Susan Julia Taylor; 1 s (Philip David b 18 Dec 1964), 1 da (Sarah Louise b 14 March 1966); *Career* architect; ptnr Holford Associates; RIBA 1958, MRTPI 1963, memb Assoc of Project Mangrs; *Recreations* sailing, shooting, classic cars; *Style*— Victor Basil, Esq; ✉ Holford Associates, Barnett House, 53 Fountain Street, Manchester M2 2AN (☎ 0161 228 3566, fax 0161 228 3569)

BASING, 5 Baron (UK 1887); Neil Lutley Sclater-Booth; s of 4 Baron Basing (d 1983), and his 1 w Jeanette (d 1957), da of late Neil Bruce MacKelvie, of New York; *b* 16 Jan 1939; *Educ* Eton, Harvard (BA); *m* 1967, Patricia Ann, da of George Bryan Whitfield (d 1967), of New Haven, Conn, USA; 2 s (Hon Stuart, Hon Andrew b 1973); *Heir* s, Hon Stuart Whitfield Sclater-Booth b 18 Dec 1969; *Clubs* Harvard, Meadow Brook; *Style*— The Rt Hon the Lord Basing

BASINGSTOKE, Archdeacon of; *see:* Knight, Ven Alexander Frances

BASINGSTOKE, Bishop of 1994–; Rt Rev (Douglas) Geoffrey Rowell; s of Cecil Victor Rowell, of Gavin Astor House, Aylesford, Kent, and lat Kate, *née* Hunter; *b* 13 Feb 1943; *Educ* Eggar's GS Alton Hampshire, Winchester (Hampshire CC bursar), Corpus Christi Coll Cambridge (MA, PhD, George Williams prize in liturgy), MA, DPhil (Oxon) by incorporation, Cuddesdon Theological Coll; *Career* ordained: deacon 1968, priest 1969; asst chaplain and Hastings Rashdall student New Coll Oxford 1968–72, hon curate St Andrew's Headington 1968–71; Univ of Oxford: fell and chaplain Keble Coll 1972–94, emeritus fell 1994–, tutor in theol Keble Coll 1976–94, univ lectr in theol 1976–94; Wiccamical canon and preb Bargham Chichester 1981–; memb C of E: Liturgical Cmmn 1981–91, Doctrine Cmmn 1991–96; hon dir Archbishop's Examination in Theol 1985–, conservator Mirfield Cert in Pastoral Theol 1988–; memb: Anglican-Oriental Orthodox Int Forum 1985– (Anglican co-chm 1996–), Ctee of Mgmnt St Stephen's House Oxford 1986–; tstee Scott-Holland Lectureship 1979– (chm 1993–); govr: Posey House Oxford 1979– (pres 1995–), Eggar's Sch Alton 1994–; almoner Christ's Hosp 1979–89; visiting prof The Chichester Inst 1996–; Hon DD Nashotah House Wisconsin USA 1996; *Books* Hell and the Victorians (1974), Rock-Hewn Churches of Eastern Tigray (ed with B E Juel-Jensen, 1976), The Liturgy of Christian Burial (1977), The Vision Glorious (1983 and 1991), Tradition Renewed (ed, 1986), To the Church of England (ed and contrib, 1988), Confession and Absolution (ed with M Dudley and contrib, 1990), The English Religious Tradition and the Genius of Anglicanism (ed, 1992), The Oil of Gladness: Anointing in the Church (ed with M Dudley and contrib, 1993), A Speaking Life: the legacy of John Keble (contrib, 1995), From Oxford to the People: reconsidering Newman and the Oxford Movement (contrib), By Whose Authority? Newman, Manning and the Magisterium (contrib, 1996); contrib theol and historical jls; *Style*— The Rt Rev the Bishop of Basingstoke; ✉ Little Acorns, Boyneswood Road, Medstead, Alton, Hants GU34 5EA (☎ 01420 562925, fax 01420 561251)

BASKERVYLE-GLEGG, John; MBE (1974); s of John Baskervyle-Glegg (d 1972), of London, and Ethne, *née* Woollan (d 1969); *b* 10 Nov 1940; *Educ* Eton; *m* 1974, Jane, *née* Van der Noot; *Career* joined Army 1960, served UK, Europe, Far East, Middle East, Africa, psc 1974, CO 1 Bn Grenadier Gds Berlin and UK 1980–82, Directing Staff RCDS 1982–84, cmd 24 Infantry Bde UK 1984–86, cmd Br Mil Advsy and Trg Team Zimbabwe 1987–89, Arabic course 1989–90, Sr Br Loan Serv Offr Oman 1990–93, ret as Maj-Gen 1994; FIMgt; *Recreations* all sport, music, travel, gardening; *Clubs* Cavalry and Guards'; *Style*— Maj-Gen John Baskervyle-Glegg, MBE

BASKETT, Dr Peter John Firth; s of Sir Ronald Gilbert Baskett, OBE (d 1972), and Joan Shirley Staples, *née* Firth (d 1982); *b* 26 July 1934; *Educ* Belfast Royal Acad, Campbell Coll Belfast, Queens' Coll Cambridge (BA, MB BCh), Queen's Univ Belfast (MB BCh, BAO); *Career* TA RAMC (V) 1982–: Capt 1982–84, Maj 1984–87, Lt-Col 1988–92, Col 1992–95, Hon Col 1996–; hon civilian conslt in resuscitation to the Army and RN; conslt anaesthetist emeritus Royal Infirmary and conslt anaesthetist Frenchay Hosp Bristol 1966–, sr clinical lectr Univ of Bristol 1966–; author of numerous chapters and articles in books and med jls; hon sec Assoc of Anaesthetists 1978–80, hon sec RSM Anaesthesia 1980–82, fndr memb Resuscitation Cncl UK 1983–, chm Br Assoc for Immediate Care 1984–86, memb Bd Faculty of Anaesthetists 1984–88, vice pres Assoc of Anaesthetists 1985–88, chm Monospecialist Ctee Union of Euro Med Specialists 1985–88 (UK rep 1982–), academician Euro Acad of Anaesthesiology 1985–, pres Euro Section World Fedn of Socs of Anaesthesiology 1986–90 (hon sec 1982–86), memb Cncl Royal Coll of Anaesthetists 1988–, chm Euro Resuscitation Cncl 1988–94; pres: World Assoc for Emergency and Disaster Med 1989–93 (hon sec 1979–89), Assoc of Anaesthetists 1990–92, Int Trauma and Critical Care Soc 1995–; Liveryman Worshipful Soc of Apothecaries 1990 (memb 1986); hon memb: Aust Soc of Anaesthetists, Ugandan Soc of Anaesthetists, Romanian Soc for Emergency and Disaster Medicine; FFARCS 1963, MRCP 1994; *Books* Immediate Care (with Dr J Zorab, 1976), Pre Hospital Immediate Care (1981), Medicine for Disasters (with Dr R Weller, 1988), Cardiopulmonary Resuscitation (1989), Resuscitation Handbook (1989, 2 edn 1993), Practical Procedures in Anaesthesia and Critical Care (1994); also author of over 120 papers relating to anaesthesia and resuscitation in scientific jls; *Clubs* RSM; *Style*— Dr Peter Baskett; ✉ Stanton Court, Stanton St Quinton, nr Chippenham, Wilts SN14 6DQ (☎ 01666 837210, fax 01666 837775); Department of Anaesthesia, Frenchay Hospital, Bristol BS16 1LE (☎ 0117 970 1212/702020, fax 0117 957 4414)

BASRA, Dev; s of Bishan Singh Basra, and Harbans, *née* Kaur; *b* 9 Jan 1942; *Educ* Col Brown Sch Dehra Dun India, Medical Coll Amritsar (MB BS, Best Artist); *m* 1, 1966; 2 c (Sukhdev, Devina); m 2, 25 Nov 1989, Sara Victoria, da of Harold James Hill; 1 s (Dev Santini b 3 June 1992); *Career* surgn various NHS hosps 1966–76, private practice aesthetic plastic surgery 1977–; professional sculptor 1986– (studied under Martine Vaugel New York Acad of Art); exhibitions: International Contemporary Art Fair (Shore Gallery) 1989, Maclaurin Art Gallery Ayr 1989, The Atrium Gallery London 1993; vice pres Federation Europèene des Societes Nationales de Chirurgie Esthetique, pres Indian Assoc of Cosmetic Surgns, charter memb Int Soc of Aesthetic Surgery; memb: Int Acad of Cosmetic Surgery, Japanese Assoc of Aesthetic Surgns; former sec Br Assoc of Cosmetic Surgns; FRCS 1976, FRSM; *Books* The Ageing Skin (1986); *Recreations* sculpture, photography, painting, design; *Style*— Dev Basra, Esq; ✉ 111 Harley St, London W1N 1DG (☎ 0171 486 8055 and 0171 487 4654)

BASS, Dr John Charles; CBE (1988); *b* 29 July 1929; *Educ* Farnham GS, Univ of Southampton (BSc), King's Coll London (MSc), Univ of Sheffield (PhD); *m* June 1954, Jean Edith Bass; 2 s (Stephen Michael John b 6 May 1958, David Nicholas John b 26 June 1960); *Career* AEI Research Laboratory Aldermaston Court 1954–63, researcher Univ of Sheffield Staff 1963–66, corp dir of research and memb Bd Plessey until 1990 (joined Plessey Research Caswell 1966), chm Phoenix VSLI Ltd 1990–; non-exec dir Argyll Consultancies plc; hon prof of engrg Univ of Warwick; memb various governmental and EU scientific and engrg ctees 1980–; author of numerous publications on electronic materials and devices; FIEE 1975, FEng 1982; *Recreations* gardening, natural philosophy; *Style*— Dr John Bass, CBE, FEng; ✉ Phoenix VLSI Ltd, Towcester Mill, Towcester, Northants NN12 6AD

BASS, Dr Neville M; s of Arthur Bass, of Manchester; *b* 8 June 1938; *Educ* Manchester GS, Univ of Manchester, Turner Dental Sch (LDS, BDS), Eastman Dental Inst (DipOrth, FDSRCS); *m* 6 Jan 1968, Mona; 2 s (Alexander b 1970, Anthony b 1973); *Career* house surgn Manchester Dental Hosp 1960–61, Eastman Dental Hosp London 1961–62 (registrar Orthodontic and Paedodontic Depts 1962–63), gen dental practice 1964–65, conslt orthodontist USAF London 1965–69, private orthodontic practice 1969–, postgrad teaching staff Royal Dental Hosp London 1972–76, postgrad orthodontic teaching staff Royal London Hosp Med Coll Dental Sch 1989–; Angle Soc of Europe: memb 1974–, sec 1978–81, memb Scientific Ctee 1988–94, chm Scientific Ctee 1994; certification Br Orthodontic Cert Bd 1984 (memb Mgmnt Ctee 1985–), memb Tweed Orthodontic Fndn USA; *Recreations* sculpting, jogging, golf, skiing, reading, jazz and classical music, wind surfing, sailing; *Style*— Dr Neville Bass; ✉ 4 Queen Anne St, London W1 (☎ 0171 580 8780)

BASSET, Lady Elizabeth; *née* Legge; DCVO (1989, CVO); 2 da of 7 Earl of Dartmouth, GCVO (d 1958); *b* 5 March 1908; *Educ* at home; *m* 1931, Ronald Lambart Basset (d 1972, whose mother Rebecca was da of Sir William Salusbury-Trelawny, 10 Bt); 1 s (*see* Lady Carey Basset) and 1 s decd; *Career* extra woman of the bedchamber to HM Queen Elizabeth the Queen Mother 1958–82, full time woman of the bedchamber 1982–94, extra woman of the bedchamber 1994–; *Books* anthologies: Love is My Meaning (1973, 2 edn 1988), Each in His Prison (1978), The Bridge is Love (1981), Interpreted by Love (1994); *Recreations* reading, writing; *Style*— The Lady Elizabeth Basset, DCVO; ✉ 67 Cottesmore Court, Stanford Rd, London W8 (☎ 0171 937 1803)

BASSET, Gerard Francis Claude; s of Pierre Rene Basset (d 1976), and Marguerite, *née* Conorton; *b* 7 March 1957; *Educ* Lycee Albert Camus Firminy France, Ecole Hoteliere de Dardilly Lyon France; *Partner* Nina Howe; *Career* commis de cuisine Frantel Hotel Marseille 1981–83, head waiter The Crown Hotel Lyndhurst Hants 1984–85 (chef de rang 1983–84), head waiter Morel's Haslemere 1985–86, Manley's Storrington W Sussex 1986–87, head waiter The Crown Hotel Lyndhurst 1987–88, chef sommelier Chewton Glen Hotel New Milton Hants 1988–94, co-proprietor Hotel du Vin & Bistro Winchester 1994–; fell Acad of Food and Wine Service (tech dir 1997), vice chm Ct of Master Sommeliers; memb: 3 Ceps St Bris 1989, Cava Inst 1993, Cognac Inst 1994, Sommeliers Club of GB 1994, Academie Culinaire de France 1995; *Awards* Best Sommelier for french wines and spirits in UK 1988 and 1992, Wine Waiter of the Year 1989 and 1992, winner Southern Sommelier Competition 1989, Calvet Cup of Acad of Wine Service (for overall outstanding achievement in wine knowledge and service) 1989, 1990 and 1993, Bronze Medal Best Sommelier in Euro Competition Reims 1990 and 1992, Champagne Travel Bursary 1990, winner Ruinart UK Selection for Euro 1990, winner Int Sommelier Competition Paris 1992, Silver Medal World Championship Rio de Janeiro 1992, Courvoisier Best of the Best Sommelier 1992, Marques de Caceres Food & Wine Person of the Year 1993, Rame d'Honneur (for servs given to wine) 1993, winner Euro Trophee Ruinart Reims 1996; for Hotel du Vin: Egon Ronay Cellnet Guide Newcomer of the Year 1996, Catey Award Newcomer of the Year 1996; *Recreations* chess, ice-skating; *Style*— Gerard Basset, Esq; ✉ Hotel du Vin Ltd, 14 Southgate Street, Winchester, Hampshire SO23 9EF (☎ 01962 841414, fax 01962 842458)

BASSETT, David Thomas (Dave); s of Harold Thomas Bassett, and Joyce Mary, *née* Spicer; *b* 4 Sept 1944; *Educ* Roxeth Manor Secdy Sch; *m* 8 July 1972, Christine, da of Thomas Edward Carpenter; 2 da (Carly Dawn b 12 July 1979, Kimberley Anne b 12 Feb 1982); *Career* professional football manager; amateur player Walton & Hersham 1970–75; Wimbledon: semi-professional player 1975–78, professional player 1978–79 with 36 league appearances in Wimbledon's first season in the Football League, asst mangr and coach 1978–81, mangr 1981–87; mangr: Watford 1987–88, Sheffield Utd 1988–95, Crystal Palace 1996–; 10 England amateur caps 1972–75; capt Walton & Hersham Amateur Cup Winners 1973; achievements as mangr: Wimbledon promoted to Div 3 1981, Div 4 Championship 1983 (after relegation 1982), promoted to Div 2 1984 and Div 1 1986, Sheffield Utd promoted to Div 2 1989 and Div 1 1990, Crystal Palace losing finalists Div 1 play offs 1996; 9 Mangr of the Month Awards, Bells Whiskey and LWT Special Merit Awards (for taking Wimbledon into Div 1), Barclays Bank League Managers Special Achievement Award 1991–92; *Style*— Dave Bassett, Esq

BASSETT, Prof Douglas Anthony; s of Hugh Bassett, and Annie Jane Bassett; *b* 11 Aug 1927; *Educ* Llanelli GS for Boys, Univ Coll of Wales Aberystwyth (BSc, PhD); *m* 1954, Elizabeth Menna, da of Gwylim Roberts; 3 da (Sarah, Sian, Rhian); *Career* lectr Dept of Geology Univ of Glasgow 1954–59, dir Nat Museum of Wales 1977–85 (keeper Dept of Geology 1959–77); chm: Ctee for Wales Water Resources Bd 1968–73, Royal Soc Ctee on History of Geology 1972–82, Advsy Ctee for Wales Nature Conservancy Cncl 1973–85; The Assoc of Teachers of Geology: fndr chm 1967, pres 1969, ed 1969–74; fndr memb and dir Nat Welsh-American Fndn 1980–87 and 1990–; memb: Ordnance Survey Review Ctee 1978–80, Ctee for Wales Br Cncl 1983–90; ed Manual of Curatorship Museums Assoc 1983–; Officier de l'Ordre des Art et des Lettres 1984, Silver Medal Czechoslovak Soc for Int Relations 1985, Aberconway Medal Instn of Geologists 1985; hon professorial fell Univ of Wales Coll of Cardiff 1977–, hon res fell Nat Museum of Wales 1986–; *Books* Bibliography and Index of Geology and Allied Sciences for Wales and the Welsh Borders 1897–1958 (1961), A Source-book of Geological Geomorphological and Soil Maps for Wales and the Welsh Borders (1800–1966) (1967); contribs to various geological, museum and historical jls; *Recreations* bibliography, chronology; *Style*— Prof Douglas Bassett; ✉ 4 Romilly Rd, Canton, Cardiff CF5 1FH (☎ 01222 227823); National Museum of Wales, Cardiff CF1 3NP (☎ 01222 397951)

BASSINGTHWAIGHTE, His Hon Judge Keith; s of Reginald Hugh Bassingthwaighte, of Egham, Surrey, and Barbara Joan, *née* Fludder; *b* 19 Jan 1943; *Educ* Ashford Co GS Mddx, Coll of Law London and Guildford; *m* 7 May 1966, Olwyn, da of James Storey Burn; *Career* articled clerk to R W Bennett, Esq, of Messrs Herrington and Carmichael Aldershot Hants 1961–66, admitted slr 1967, asst slr Clifford Cowling & Co Farnborough Hants 1967–68; RAF Legal Branch: Flt Lt 1968–73, Sqdn Ldr 1973–77, Wing Cdr 1977–81, Gp Capt 1981–84; asst recorder and pt/t chm Industrial Tbnls (London Central) 1984, chm Industrial Tbnls (London Central) 1985–87 and (London South) 1987–91, recorder 1987–91, circuit judge (SE Circuit) 1991–; pres Social Security, Med, Disability and Child Support Appeal Tbnls and of Vaccine Damage Tbnls 1994–, judge Employment Appeal Tbnl 1996–; memb Law Soc 1967; *Recreations* golf, tennis, bridge, scuba diving; *Clubs* RAF, Worplesdon Golf (Woking); *Style*— His Hon Judge Bassingthwaighte; ✉ Independent Tribunal Service, City Gate House, 39–45 Finsbury Square, London EC2A 1PX (☎ 0171 814 6514)

BASSNETT, Peter; s of Herbert Bassnett, and Emma, *née* Bacon; *b* 6 Dec 1940; *Educ* Stand GS Manchester; *m* 12 March 1965, Gabrielle Charlotte, *née* Hall; 2 da (Samantha Jane b 1970, Annabelle b 1972); *Career* dir field ops Abbey Life 1982–86 (agency mangr 1971–82), sales dir Aetna Life Insurance Co Ltd 1986–, md Westminster Ltd 1989; memb Judging Panel Br Quality Assoc; FLIA; *Recreations* sailing; *Clubs* Royal Motor Yacht; *Style*— Peter Bassnett, Esq, QFSM; ✉ 21 Branksome Towers, Westminster Rd, Poole, Dorset BH13 6JT

BASTABLE, Arthur Cyprian; OBE (1984); s of Herbert Arthur Bastable (d 1943), and Edith Ellen, *née* Allen (d 1954); *b* 9 May 1923; *Educ* St Georges Sch Harpenden, Univ of Manchester (BSc); *m* 3 April 1946, Joan, da of David Cardwell (d 1990); 1 s (Roger b 1952), 1 da (Susan b 1955); *Career* served WWII RNVR; chartered electrical engr; Fielden Electronics Ltd 1947–50, Ferranti plc 1950–88, sales mangr Vac Physics Dept Scot Gp Ferranti 1957–71, gen mangr Ferranti Dundee 1971–86, dir Ferranti Astron Ltd 1983–86, dir Ferranti Industrial Electronics Ltd 1984–86; memb: Dundee Port Authy 1967–92, Scot Cncl CBI 1980, Dundee and Tayside C of C (pres 1970–71); CEng, FIEE, FIMgt; *Recreations* sailing, skiing, hill-walking; *Clubs* Danish, Royal Tay Yacht, Scottish Ornithologists; *Style*— Arthur C Bastable, Esq, OBE; ✉ Hunters Moon, 14 Lorne Street, Monifieth, Dundee DD5 4DU (☎ 01382 532 043)

BASTIN, Prof John Andrew; s of Arthur Edward Bastin (d 1930), of London, and Emma Lucy Price, *née* Dunk (d 1955), of Essex; *b* 3 Jan 1929; *Educ* Sir George Monoux GS, CCC Oxford (BA), Univ of London (PhD); *m* 1, 1959 (m dis 1982); 1 s (Richard Edward b 28 Feb 1964), 1 da (Claire Damaris b 2 Jan 1962); m 2, 1985, Aida Baterina, da of Felicano Delfino (d 1985), of Sala Cabuyao, Laguna, Luzon; *Career* Nat Serv Leading Seaman RN 1948–49; lectr Univ of Nigeria Ibadan 1952–56, res fell Univ of Reading 1956–59, Queen Mary Coll Univ of London 1959–84 (lectr, reader in astrophysics, prof, head of dept, now emeritus prof); initiated res gp in Far Infrared Astronomy 1960–75 (discovered solar enhancements at these wavelengths assoc with sunspots, lunar dumbbel formation and seismic propagation, the liquification model and limitations of earths atmosphere for astronomy), princ investigator NASA US Lunar Samples prog (for infrared and other measurements made with lunar rock) 1969–76, Leverhulme emeritus fell (light scattering applied to landscape) 1985–88; landscape painting currently exhibited in several London and provincial galleries; Hon MA Oxon 1956; FRAS (former memb Cncl); *Recreations* architecture, music, tennis; *Style*— Prof John Bastin; ✉ 27 Endwell Road, Brockley, London SE4 2NE (☎ 0171 635 8501)

BASU, Himansu Kumar; s of Sudhangsu Kumar Basu (d 1992), and Rajlaxmi, *née* Ghosh (d 1950); *b* 10 April 1934; *Educ* Gopalpur Acad and Calcutta Med Coll Univ of Calcutta (MB BS), Univ of Liverpool (PhD); *m* Lynda Ann, da of Ronald Sanders, of Rochester, Kent; 1 da (Maya Louise b 1979), 1 s (Christopher Kumar b 1984); *Career* lectr in obstetrics and gynaecology Univ of Liverpool 1965–72, conslt obstetrician and gynaecologist Dartford and Gravesham NHS Tst 1972–; SE Gynaecological Soc: sec 1976–82, vice pres 1984–86, treas 1987–91, pres 1991–; RCOG: memb Cncl 1977–83, 1988–91 and 1993–, memb Fin and Exec Ctee 1980–83, memb Examination Ctee 1981–84; Section of Obstetrics and Gynaecology RSM: memb Cncl 1979–88 and 1994–, hon sec 1983–84, vice pres 1985–88, pres 1995–96; chm Osprey's Gynaecological Soc 1981–84; examiner for MB ChB, DRCOG and MRCOG; Ethel Boyce fell Univ of Liverpool 1967, William Blair Bell lectr RCOG 1969, Catherine Bishop Harman prize BMA 1969, Eden fell RCOG 1970; memb: Br Fertility Soc, American Fertility Soc, Br Soc of Gynaecological Endoscopy, American Assoc of Gynaecological Endoscopists; FRCSEd, FRCOG; *Recreations* travel, photography, good food; *Clubs* Rotary Club of Northfleet (pres 1989–90); *Style*— Himansu Basu, Esq; ✉ Glengarry, Woodlands Lane, Shorne, Gravesend, Kent DA12 3HH (☎ 01474 822294, fax 01474 824019, mobile 0374 181289)

BASUROY, Dr Ratish; s of Ramesh Basuroy (d 1947), of Calcutta, India, and Chinmoyee Basuroy; *b* 27 April 1937; *Educ* Univ of Calcutta (MB BS); *m* 16 Jan 1971, Namita, da of Tarapada Biswas (d 1985); 3 s (Raja b 6 July 1974, Rono b 6 Sept 1976, Robin b 15 May 1981); *Career* IA 21 Bengal Med NCC sr under offr, Capt 93 NCC Co Calcutta India 1963–64; demonstrator in anatomy Calcutta Nat Med Coll 1963–64, surgical registrar various hosps in UK 1965–70, registrar in genito-urinary med St Thomas's Hosp London 1971, sr registrar Bournemouth and Southampton gp of hosps 1971–73, physician in charge conslt i/c Dept of Genito-Urinary Med E Dorset Health Authy 1973–92; conslt in genito-urinary med: W Dorset 1973–90, E Dorset 1973–, Univ of Southampton Gp of Hosps; clinical tutor of gen practitioners Dorset Health Authy 1973–90, conslt surgn Br Pregnancy Advsy Serv Bournemouth 1974–90; Univ of Southampton: clinical tutor in genito-urinary med 1974–, conslt advsr Inst of Modelling for Health Care Faculty of Med 1993–; HIV/AIDS physician Dorset; memb Wessex Regnl Aids Expert Ctee 1986–89; memb Conslt and Sr Registrar Appts Ctee WRHA 1973–: memb Cncl: BMA 1982–89, Med Soc for the Study of Veneral Diseases 1982–85 and 1989–92; memb SAC in Genito-Urinary Med JCHMT RCP 1982–86, memb/chm SAC Visiting Team RCP 1983–; memb Central Audit Gp in Genito-Urinary Med RCP London 1995–96; former chm Wessex Genito-Urinary Physicians Sub-Ctee Wessex RHA; BMA: dep chm Genito-Urinary Med Sub-Ctee 1984–92, dep chm Dermato-Venereology Sub-Ctee 1992–94; memb CCHMS Ctee: BMA 1991–94, CCSC 1991–95; pres MSSVD 1995–97 (treas 1993–95); contrib articles to: BMJ, Genito-Urinary Med Jl, Br Jl of Clinical Practice, Br Jl of Sexual Med, Lancet; reviewer of books for The Br Jl Genito-Urinary Med 1986–; memb Bournemouth and Poole Med Soc; FRCS 1968, FRCPE 1989 (MRCPE 1986), FRCP 1995; *Recreations* photography, philately, numismatics, reading, finance; *Style*— Dr Ratish Basuroy; ✉ Pannel Suite, Royal Bournemouth Hospital, Castle Lane East, Bournemouth BH7 7DW (☎ 01202 704918, fax 01202 704481)

BATCHELLER, Catherine; *Educ* Washington Sch of Ballet; *Career* ballet dancer; San Francisco Ballet 1981–85, Stuttgart Ballet 1985–94, princ Birmingham Royal Ballet 1994–; toured USA, Germany, France; performed The Nutcracker pas de deux at Olivier Awards 1995; *Roles* with San Francisco Ballet: Titania in Balanchine's Midsummer Night's Dream, white couple in Jiri Kylian's Forgotten Land, Sugar Plum Fairy and Snow Queen in The Nutcracker, Fairy Godmother in Michael Smuin's Cinderella, cr pas de deux Romanze, Robbins's In The Night, Tommason's Menuetto, Balanchine's Chaconne; with Stuttgart Ballet: Aurora and Lilac Fairy in The Sleeping Beauty, Odette/Odile in Swan Lake, Juliet in John Cranko's Romeo and Juliet, Myrtha in Marcia Haydee's Giselle (for television), Gsovsky's Grand pas Classique, Manon in John Neumeier's Lady of the Camelias, Holberg pas de deux, princ role in Maurice Bejart's Bolero, Queen of the Night in The Magic Flute, cr princ role in Jiri Kylian's Stepping Stones, Forsythe's In the Middle, Some What Elevated, Van Manen's Grosse Fuge, princ role in Five Tangos, McMillan's Requiem, Song of the Earth, My Brother My Sister; with Birmingham Royal Ballet: Lady Mary in Sir Frederick Ashton's Enigma Variations, Galanteries, Choreartium, Theme and Variations, princ role in Birthday Offering, cr role Fortuna in Bintley's Carmina Burana; *Style*— Miss Catherine Batcheller; ✉ c/o The Birmingham Royal Ballet, Birmingham Hippodrome, Thorp Street, Birmingham B5 4AU (☎ 0121 622 2555, fax 0121 622 5038)

BATCHELOR, Andrew Goolden Grant; s of Lt-Col Hugh Thomas Nicolas Batchelor (d 1976), and Margaret Irene, *née* Grant; *b* 28 Aug 1951; *Educ* Whitchurch HS, St Mary's Hosp Med Sch Univ of London (BSc, MB BS); *m* 3 Nov 1973, Rosemary Marion, da of Horace William Gibson, of Melksham, Wilts; 1 s (Thomas b 18 April 1980), 1 da (Elizabeth b 6 Oct 1982); *Career* surgical res King Edward VII Hosp Paget Bermuda 1978–79, sr house offr in gen surgery St Mary's Hosp London 1979–80, registrar in gen surgery Queen Elizabeth II Hosp Welwyn Gdn City 1980–81, sr house offr in plastic surgery Wexham Park Hosp Slough 1981–82, registrar in plastic surgery Nottingham City 1982–84, sr registrar W of Scotland Regnl Plastic Surgery Unit 1984–86, sr clinical lectr in surgery Univ of Leeds 1986–; conslt plastic surgn: St James's Hosp Gen Infirmary Leeds 1986–, S York Dist Hosp 1988– (clinical dir plastic surgery 1993–); memb Cncl British Assoc of Plastic Surgns 1993– (memb 1986); memb: Br Microsurgical Soc 1982, Br Soc of Head and Neck Oncologists 1986, Br Assoc of Aesthetic Plastic Surgns 1988; FRCS, FRCS (Plastic Surgns); *Books* contrib: Essential Surgical Practice (1988), Tissue Expansion (1989), Excision and Reconstruction in Head and Neck Cancer (1993); *Recreations* sailing, shooting; *Style*— Andrew Batchelor, Esq; ✉ Field House, 10 Sicklinghall Road, Wetherby, W Yorks LS22 6AA (☎ 01937 583654); Department of Plastic Surgery, St James's University Hospital, Beckett St, Leeds LS8 1DF (☎ 0113 283 6901)

BATCHELOR, Prof Bruce Godfrey; s of Ernest Walter Batchelor (d 1982), of Rugby, Warwickshire, and Ingrid Maud, *née* Wells; *b* 15 May 1943; *Educ* Lawrence Sherrif Sch Rugby, Univ of Southampton (BSc, PhD); *m* 21 Aug 1968, Eleanor Gray, da of Percy William Pawley (d 1993), of Cardiff; 2 c (Helen b 1969, David b 1972); *Career* engr Plessey Co Ltd 1968–70, lectr Univ of Southampton 1971–80, prof Univ of Wales Cardiff 1980–; conslt: Br Robotic Systems Ltd 1980–86, 3M Co USA 1984–92, Vision Dynamics Ltd 1987–91; visiting prof Dublin City Univ 1993–; author of over 200 tech articles; chm 9 int confs; CEng 1972, FRSA 1983, FIEE 1993 (memb 1972), fell SPIE 1994 (memb 1983), FBCS 1994, fell SME 1995 (sr memb 1994); *Books* Practical Approach Pattern Classification (1975), Pattern Recognition, Ideas In Practice (ed, 1978), Automated Visual Inspection (ed, 1985), Intelligent Image Processing in Prolog (1991), Interactive Image Processing for Machine Vision (1993), Industrial Machine Vision Systems (ed, 1994); *Recreations* Presbyterian Church, walking, swimming, photography; *Style*— Prof Bruce Batchelor; ✉ Department of Computer Science, University of Wales, Cardiff, PO Box 916, Cardiff CF2 3XF (☎ 01222 874390, fax 01222 874598, e-mail bruce.batchelor@cs.cf.ac.uk)

BATCHELOR, Prof Sir Ivor Ralph Campbell; kt (1981), CBE (1976); s of Ralph C L Batchelor, and Muriel, *née* Shaw; *b* 29 Nov 1916; *Educ* Edinburgh Acad, Univ of Edinburgh (MB ChB), Univ of London (DPM); *m* 1941, Honor Wallace Williamson; 1 s, 3 da; *Career* RAFVR 1941–46, Sqdn Ldr, Cmd Neuro-psychiatrist CMF; asst physician and dep physician supt Royal Edinburgh Hosp and sr lectr in psychiatry Univ of Edinburgh 1947–56, physician supt Dundee Royal Mental Hosp 1956–62; prof of psychiatry: Univ of St Andrews 1962–67, Univ of Dundee 1967–82 (now emeritus); chm Ctee on Staffing Mental Deficiency Hosps 1967–70; memb: Med Servs Review Ctee (Porritt Ctee) 1958–62, Gen Nursing Cncl for Scotland (chm Educn Ctee) 1964–71, Standing Med Advsy Ctee Scot 1967–74, Advsy Ctee on Med Res Scot 1969–73, Ctee on Nursing (Briggs Ctee) 1970–72, Scot Cncl for Postgrad Med Educn 1970–79, Ctee on the Working of the Abortion Act (Lane Ctee) 1971–74, MRC 1972–76 (chm Clinical Res Bd 1973–74, chm Neuro-Scis Bd 1974–75), Chief Scientist Ctee Scot 1973–82, Royal Cmmn on the NHS 1976–79, Ind Sci Ctee on Smoking and Health 1980–86, UK Central Cncl for Nursing, Midwifery and Health Visiting 1980–83, MRC Health Servs Res Panel 1981–82, Scot Hosp Endowments Res Tst 1984–90; chm Tstees Orchar Art Gallery Dundee 1980–87; FRSE 1960, FRCPE, Hon FRCPsych 1984 (FRCPsych 1971); *Recreations* field natural history; *Clubs* Athenaeum, Royal and Ancient Golf; *Style*— Prof Sir Ivor Batchelor, CBE, FRSE

BATCHELOR, Paul Anthony; s of Joseph John Batchelor (d 1963), of Little Chart, Ashford, and Irene Margaret, *née* Shoobridge; *b* 4 July 1946; *Educ* Ashford GS, St John's Coll Cambridge (College scholar, MA, Dip in Devpt Economics, Philip Lake Prize, Hughes and Wright Prizes, Larmor Award, David Richards travelling scholar); *m* 5 July 1969, Janet, da of Jack Rowden King; 1 da (Emma Jane b 16 May 1972), 1 s (Jonathan Mark b 12 Feb 1976); *Career* vol teacher Miny of Educn Zambia 1965, supervisor of studies in geography St John's Coll Cambridge 1968–69, govt economist Swaziland 1969–72, acting chief economist Office of the President & Cabinet Malawi 1973–74 (sr economist 1972–73); Coopers & Lybrand: joined as econ conslt 1974, ptnr 1982–, chm Int Mgmnt Consulting Servs Exec 1989–95, ptnr i/c Mgmnt Consulting Servs Europe 1990–94, exec ptnr in charge Coopers & Lybrand Europe 1994–; Liveryman Guild of Management Consultants 1994; FIMC 1980; *Recreations* classical music, gardening, mountain walking; *Clubs* Reform, Hever Golf; *Style*— Paul Batchelor, Esq; ✉ 3 Burntwood Grove, Sevenoaks, Kent TN13 1PZ (☎ 01732 452358); Les Chalets de la Beune 1, La Beunaz, St Paul en Chablais 74500, France; Coopers & Lybrand, Executive Office, avenue de Tervuren 2 Bte 3, 1040 Brussels, Belgium; Coopers & Lybrand, European Executive Office, 1 Embankment Place, London WC2N 6NN (☎ 0171 213 4509, fax 0171 213 2407)

BATCHELOR, Prof (John) Richard; s of Basil William Batchelor, CBE (d 1956), of Pembury, Kent, and Esme Clare, *née* Cornwall; *b* 4 Oct 1931; *Educ* Marlborough, Emmanuel Coll Cambridge, Guy's Hosp Med Sch; *m* 23 July 1955, Dr Moira Ann Batchelor, da of William McLellan (d 1987), of Tadworth, Surrey; 2 s (Andrew b 1957, Simon b 1962), 2 da (Annabel b 1959, Lucinda b 1964); *Career* Nat Serv MO RAMC 1957–59; lectr then sr lectr Dept of Pathology Guy's Hosp Med Sch 1962–67; prof of: transplantation res RCS 1967–79, tissue immunology Royal Postgrad Med Sch 1979–82, immunology Royal Postgrad Med Sch Hammersmith Hosp 1982–94; dir Blond McIndoe Res Centre Queen Victoria Hosp E Grinstead; memb: MRC Grants Ctees and Cell Bd 1972–78, UK Transplantation Support Servs Authy 1991–96; chm: Arthritis & Rheumatism Cncl Grants Ctee 1986–88, Scientific Co-ordinating Ctee 1988–96; pres: Int Transplantation Soc 1988–90, British Soc of Histcompatibility of Immunogenetics 1992–94; Euro ed Transplantation 1964–; memb Court Worshipful Co of Skinners (Master 1984–85); FRCPath, FRCP, FRSM, FIBiol; *Recreations* tennis, skiing; *Clubs* Brooks's, Queen's; *Style*— Prof Richard Batchelor; ✉ Little Ambrook, Nursery Rd, Walton-on-the-Hill, Tadworth, Surrey KT20 7TU (☎ 01737 812 028); c/o Department of Immunology, Royal Postgraduate Medical School, Hammersmith Hospital, Du Cane Rd, London W12 0NN (☎ 0181 740 3225)

BATE, Anthony; s of Hubert George Cookson Bate (d 1986), and Cecile Marjorie, *née* Canadine (d 1973); *b* 31 Aug 1927; *Educ* King Edward VI Sch Stourbridge Worcs, Central Sch of Speech & Drama; *m* 22 May 1954, Diana Fay, da of Kenneth Alfred Charles Cawes Watson (d 1939), of Seaview, IOW; 2 s (Gavin Watson b 25 Feb 1961, Mark Hewitt b 23 Sept 1963); *Career* actor; Nat Serv RNVR 1945–47; entered professional theatre 1953, first West End appearance Inherit the Wind (St Martin's) 1960; memb BAFTA; *Theatre* incl: Treasure Island (Mermaid) 1960, Happy Family (Hampstead) 1966, Much Ado About Nothing and Silence (RSC Aldwych) 1969, Find Your Way Home (Open Space Theatre) 1970, Eden End (tour) 1972, Economic Necessity (Haymarket Leicester) 1973, Getting Away with Murder (Comedy) 1976, Shadow Box (Cambridge) 1979, The Old Jest (tour) 1980, A Flea in her Ear (Plymouth Theatre Co) 1980, Little Lies (Wyndhams) 1983, Master Class (tour) 1984, The Deep Blue Sea (Theatre Royal Haymarket) 1988, Relative Values (Chichester Festival Theatre and Savoy) 1993–94; *Television* first TV appearance 1955; numerous appearances incl: Philby Burgess and Maclean 1976, The Dutch Train Hijack 1976, The Seagull 1977, An Englishman's Castle 1978, The Trial of Uri Urlov 1978, Tinker Tailor Soldier Spy 1978, Crime and Punishment 1979, 'Tis A Pity She's A Whore 1979, The Human Crocodile 1980, Smiley's People 1981, A Woman Called Golda 1981, Artists and Models 1983, War and Rememberance 1986, Game Set and Match 1987, Countdown to War 1989, Medics 1991 and 1992, Prime Suspect 1994, Rebecca, A Touch of Frost 1996; *Films* incl: The Set Up 1961, Stopover Forever 1963, Act of Murder 1964, Davey Jones' Locker 1964, Ghost Story 1973, Bismark 1975, Give My Regards to Broad Street 1982, Exploits at West Poley 1985, Eminent Domaine 1990; *Recreations* listening to music, painting; *Clubs* Garrick; *Style*— Anthony Bate, Esq; ✉ c/o Ken McReddie Ltd, 91 Regent Street, London W1 7TB (☎ 0171 439 1456, fax 0171 734 6530)

BATE, David Christopher; QC (1994); s of Robert Leslie Bate (d 1954), of Mill Hill, London, and Brenda Mabel, *née* Price; *b* 2 May 1945; *Educ* Hendon Co GS, Univ of Manchester (LLB); *m* 28 July 1973, Patricia Joan, da of David Alan Bailey; 3 s (Tristan David Leslie b 1 June 1976, Simeon James Jonathan b 13 Nov 1978, Diccon Mark Julian b 30 March 1983), 1 da (Wendy Jeanne Alison b 3 Feb 1981); *Career* called to the Bar Gray's Inn 1969, VSO 1969–71, crown counsel Protectorate British Solomon Islands 1971, asst recorder 1989, recorder of the Crown Court 1992–; memb Criminal Bar Assoc; *Recreations* trying to sing in tune with St Albans Bach Choir, the Seven Deadly Sins, tennis; *Style*— David Bate, Esq, QC; ✉ Hollis Whiteman Chambers, Queen Elizabeth Building, Temple, London EC4Y 9BS (☎ 0171 583 5766, fax 0171 353 0339)

BATE, Jennifer Lucy; da of Horace Alfred Bate, and Dorothy Marjorie, *née* Hunt; *b* 11 Nov 1944; *Educ* Tollington GS, Univ of Bristol (BA); *Career* asst organist St James Muswell Hill 1955–78, superintendent Shaw Library LSE 1966–69, became a full time professional musician 1969–, specialist in eighteenth century Eng organ music, frequently appears with Dolmetsch Ensemble at Haslemere Festival of Early Music; world authy on works of the composer Olivier Messiaen, soloist at Br première of Messiaen's Livre du Saint Sacrement at Westminster Cathedral, opened a series on the complete organ works of Messiaen on Radio France in the presence of the composer; designed (with N P Mander Ltd) portable pipe organ and (with Wyvern Organs) a new type of computer organ; collaborator with many British composers; works written for her incl: Blue Rose Variations (by Peter Dickinson), Fenestra (by William Mathias); memb: Royal Soc of Musicians, Royal Philharmonic Soc, Br Music Soc, Incorporated Soc of Musicians; FRCO, LRAM (organ performer), ARCM (organ performer); *Awards* GLAA Young Musician 1972, Personnalité de l'Année (France) 1990; Silver plaque for services to music: Alassio (Italy) 1996, Garbagna (Italy) and hon citizenship for servs to music; *Recordings* over 30 incl: From Stanley to Wesley (6 Vols, winner Retailers' Assoc Award for Early Music 1991), Liszt & Schumann, Elgar and his English Contemporaries, complete organ works of Franck and Messiaen (awarded Grand Prix du Disque for Livre du Saint Sacrement); *Music Published* Introduction and Variations on an Old French Carol, Four Reflections, Hommage to 1685, Toccata on a Theme of Martin Shaw, Grove's Dictionary of Music & Musicians (contrib); *Recreations* gardening, cooking, philately; *Style—* Miss Jennifer Bate; ✉ 35 Collingwood Ave, Muswell Hill, London N10 3EH (☎ 0181 883 3811, fax 0181 444 3695); Bureau de Concerts Maurice Werner, 7 Rue Richepance, 75008 Paris, France (☎ 00 331 40 15 92 80, fax 00 331 42 60 30 49)

BATE, Prof (Andrew) Jonathan; s of Ronald Montagu Bate (d 1978), and Sylvia Helen, *née* Tait; *b* 26 June 1958; *Educ* Sevenoaks Sch, St Catharine's Coll Cambridge (T R Henn English scholar, Charles Oldham Shakespeare scholar, MA, PhD); *m* 1, 1984 (m dis 1995), Hilary Lorna, da of Prof Maxwell Gaskin; m 2, 1996, Paula Jayne, da of Timothy Byrne; *Career* Harkness fell Harvard Univ 1980–81; research fell St Catharine's Coll Cambridge 1983–85, fell Trinity Hall and lectr Girton Coll Cambridge 1985–90; King Alfred prof of Eng lit Univ of Liverpool 1991–; research reader The British Academy 1994–; *Books* Shakespeare and the English Romantic Imagination (1986), Lamb's Essays (ed, 1987), Shakespearean Constitutions (1989), Romantic Ecology (1991), The Romantics on Shakespeare (ed, 1992), Shakespeare and Ovid (1993), The Arden Shakespeare: Titus Andronicus (ed, 1995), Shakespeare: An Illustrated History (ed, 1996); *Recreations* cricket, tennis, walking, music; *Style—* Prof Jonathan Bate; ✉ Department of English, University of Liverpool, PO Box 147, Liverpool L69 3BX (☎ 0151 794 2704, fax 0151 794 2730)

BATE, Kenneth James (Ken); s of Maj Ernest James Bate, MBE, of Dudley, West Midlands, and Mary Joyce Adelaine, *née* Morgan (d 1970); *b* 20 June 1943; *Educ* Oldswinford Hosp Sch Stourbridge, Univ of Aston Birmingham (BSc, Dip Arch); *m* 26 Sept 1968, Susan Kay (d 1982); 2 s (Simon b 1972, Matthew b 1975); *Career* princ architect Wolverhampton Borough Cncl 1975–79, regnl architect Tarmac Construction Ltd 1979–84, ptnr Quest International Group Practice 1984–90, dir Tweedale Planning and Design Group Ltd and md Bloomer Tweedale Project Management Services Ltd 1991–93, own practice Kenneth J Bate Chartered Architect and Project Managers 1993–; memb: Assoc of Project Managers 1993, W Midlands branch The Arbitration Club; memb RIBA 1976; *Recreations* sailing; *Style—* Kenneth J Bate, Esq; ✉ Mount Pleasant, Hilton, nr Bridgnorth, Shropshire WV15 5PD (☎ and fax 01746 716627)

BATE, Terence Charles; s of Harry James Bate (d 1975), of Preston, Lancs, and Annie Evelyn, *née* Gore (later Graffy) (d 1993); *b* 3 Oct 1930; *Educ* Hele's Sch Exeter, Univ of Liverpool (BVSc), Lancashire Poly (LLB); *m* 24 Feb 1961, Mary Evelyn, da of Capt Herbert Edgar Newth (d 1964); 2 s (Anthony John b 1961, Christopher David b 1962), 2 da (Carolyn Mary b 1964, Nicola Anne b 1967 d 1969); *Career* vet surgn; ptnr practice 1955–85, former vet advsr Assoc of District Cncls, vet surgn W Lancs DC 1979–85; RSPCA: asst chief vet offr 1987–92 chief vet offr RSPCA 1992–95, conslt 1995–; former pt/t lectr: Manchester Poly, Lancs Coll of Agric; called to the Bar Lincoln's Inn 1986; memb: Cncl BVA 1978–90, Cncl Vet Public Health Assoc (former pres); Cert Dip AF; MRCVS; *Recreations* cycling, running, walking; *Clubs* Cyclists' Touring; *Style—* Terence C Bate, Esq; ✉ Fernside, West Street, Billingshurst, West Sussex RH14 9LG (☎ 01403 784149); RSPCA Headquarters, Causeway, Horsham, West Sussex RH12 1HG (☎ 01403 264181, fax 01403 241048)

BATE-WILLIAMS, John Robert Alexander; yr s of Maj Michael Thomas Jerome Bate-Williams, RA (ret), of Wootra Brook, Bindoon, Western Australia, and Rosemary Suzanne, *née* Bate (d 1979); *b* 25 Sept 1951; *Educ* private tuition, Whitefriars Sch, Stoke-on-Trent Coll of Building and Commerce, Univ of Wales (LLB); *m* 4 Aug 1984, Elizabeth Anne, da of Richard Lippiatt; 1 s (Rory b 1987), 1 da (Rosemary b 1989); *Career* called to the Bar Inner Temple 1976; memb Hon Soc of Inner Temple 1976; *Recreations* travel, rowing, tennis; *Clubs* Jokers; *Style—* John Bate-Williams, Esq; ✉ 4 Swan Studios, 69 Deodar Rd, London, SW15 2NU (☎ 0181 874 5739); Tie Cross Cottage, Murcott, nr Malmesbury, Wilts SN16 9EX (☎ 01666 577617); 1 Temple Gardens, Temple, London EC4Y 9BB (☎ 0171 583 1315, fax 0171 353 3969)

BATELY, Prof Janet Margaret; da of Alfred William Bately, TD (d 1985), and Dorothy Maud, *née* Willis (d 1988); *b* 3 April 1932; *Educ* Somerville Coll Oxford (Dip Comparative Philology, MA); *m* 20 Aug 1964, Leslie John, s of John Summers (d 1965), of Bromley, Kent; 1 s (Michael b 23 Aug 1966); *Career* Birkbeck Coll Univ of London: asst lectr 1955–58, lectr 1958–69, reader in English 1970–76; King's Coll London: prof of Eng language and medieval lit 1977–95, head Dept of English 1980–95, Sir Israel Gollancz research prof 1995–; memb: Cncl Early English Text Soc 1980–, Advsy Ctee Int Soc of Anglo-Saxonists 1985–90, Exec Ctee Fontes Anglo-Saxonici (formerly Sources of Anglo-Saxon Literature) 1985–, Exec Ctee Sources of Anglo-Saxon Lit and Culture 1987–, Humanities Res Bd 1994–95; govr: Cranleigh Sch 1982–88, King's Coll Sch Wimbledon 1991–94; gen ed King's Coll London Medieval Studies 1987–; FKC 1986, FBA 1990; *Books* incl: The Old English Orosius (1980), The Anglo Saxon Chronicle - MS.A (1986), The Tanner Bede (1992), The Anglo-Saxon Chronicle - Texts and Textual Relationships (1991), Anonymous Old English Homilies: A Preliminary Bibliography of Source Studies (1993), A Palaeographer's View (ed with M Brown and J Roberts, 1993); *Recreations* music, gardening; *Style—* Prof Janet Bately, FBA; ✉ 86 Cawdor Crescent, London W7 2DD (☎ 0181 567 0486); King's College, University of London, Strand, London WC2 R2LS (☎ 0171 873 2594)

BATEMAN, Barry Richard James; *b* 21 June 1945; *Educ* Univ of Exeter (BA); *m* Christine; 1 s (James b 1980); *Career* res dir Hoare Govett 1972–75 (investmt analyst 1967–72), mktg dir Datastream 1975–81, sr mktg dir Fidelity International Management Ltd 1981–86, md Fidelity Investment Services Ltd 1986–, pres Fidelity International Ltd 1991–; chm Unit Tst Assoc 1991–93; AMIIMR; *Recreations* photography, music, E Type Jaguars, writing; *Clubs* Jaguar Drivers; *Style—* Barry Bateman, Esq; ✉ Fidelity Investment Services Ltd, Oakhill House, 130 Tonbridge Rd, Hildenborough, Tonbridge, Kent TN11 9DZ (☎ 01732 361144, fax 01732 777441, telex 957 344 FIMLO)

BATEMAN, Dr Christopher John Turner; s of Sir Geoffrey Hirst Bateman, *qv*, of Thorney, Graffham, W Sussex, and Margaret, *née* Turner; bro of Dr Nigel Turner Bateman, *qv*; *b* 3 June 1937; *Educ* Marlborough, Univ Coll Oxford (MA, BM BCh), St Thomas's Hosp Med Sch; *m* 1, 1961, Hilary (d 1984), da of James Stirk, of Worcester; 1 s (Alastair b 1963), 2 da (Jennifer b 1964, Caroline b 1966); m 2, 1986, Joan Valerie, da of Dr J Cann, of Southampton; *Career* conslt haematologist: Chichester Health Authy 1973–92, King Edward VII Hosp Midhurst 1975–96; med dir Royal West Sussex Tst Chichester 1994–96; chm St Wilfrids Hospice Chichester, tstee Dunhill Med Tst, memb Cncl Shipwrecked Mariners Soc; Freeman City of London 1961, Warden Worshipful Co of Haberdashers; FRCPath 1982; *Recreations* fishing, tennis, golf, shooting; *Style—* Dr Christopher Bateman; ✉ Waterleas, West Ashling, Chichester, W Sussex PO18 9LE (☎ 01243 575484, fax 01243 576302)

BATEMAN, Cynthia (Mrs Norman Livesey); da of Harry Bateman (d 1985), of Eccleston, Chorley, Lancs, and Bessie, *née* Gray; *b* 24 April 1940; *Educ* Ormskirk GS; *m* 5 Oct 1963, Norman Livesey; *Career* French translator Leyland Motors Ltd 1959–60; Lancashire Evening Post 1960–76: joined as news reporter 1960, subsequently feature writer then travel ed, news ed until 1976; The Guardian: feature writer and sub ed Manchester Office 1976–88, sports writer specialising in soccer 1988–96; freelance writer 1996–; Willie Clissett Prize for Newspaper Practice Nat Cncl for Trg of Journalists 1963, Thomson Travel Award 1969, IPC Press Award commendation 1969; hon memb 12 LI RA, memb RSPCA; *Recreations* Spain, travel, walking (English Setter); *Style—* Ms Cynthia Bateman; ✉ Puerto de la Infanta, Riogordo, 29180, Malaga, Spain

BATEMAN, Derek; s of Thomas Bateman, of Ellesmere Port, and Millicent, *née* Blackburn; *b* 8 Feb 1949; *Educ* Stanney Secdy Modern Tech Sch; *m* 5 Aug 1978, Jenny, da of Samuel Howarth (d 1986), of Gateshead, Tyne and Wear; 4 step s (Hilton b 1960, Sean b 1965, Wayne b 1967, Craig b 1971), 1 step da (Jaqualine b 1962); *Career* machinist and fitter Vauxhall Motors 1970–82 (engr 1965–70); borough cncllr Ellesmere Port and Neston 1974–78; Cheshire CC: memb 1977–, dep ldr 1985–91 and 1992–93, chm Environment Servs Ctee; chm 1981–93: Manchester Ship Canal Steering Ctee, Nat Public Tport Forum, int authy Getting The Best From The Channel Tunnel representing all local govt assocs; Assoc of CCs: vice chm Planning and Tport Ctee 1986–88, chm Public Tport Sub-Ctee 1987–88, Lab ldr Environment Ctee 1989–93 (chm 1993–); conslt in politics 1993–; chm Shires Public Tport Consortium of Non-Metropolitan Counties 1987–; NW Regnl Assoc of Local Authorities: chm Transportation Working Pty 1992–94 (vice chm 1995–), chm Local Agenda 21 Steering Gp 1995–; *Recreations* Lab Pty; *Style—* Derek Bateman, Esq; ✉ 168 Cambridge Rd, Ellesmere Port, Cheshire (☎ 0151 355 6575, fax 0151 357 4057); County Hall, Chester (direct ☎ 01244 602194, fax 01244 602206)

BATEMAN, Derek Walls; s of David Charteris Graham Bateman, of Selkirk, and Mary Ann, *née* Walls; *b* 10 May 1951; *Educ* Selkirk HS, Edinburgh Coll of Commerce; *m* 11 Nov 1972, Alison, *née* Edgar; 2 da (Eilidh b 24 March 1975, Lucy b 11 Nov 1978); *Career* trainee journalist Scotsman Publications 1968–71; reporter: Edinburgh Evening News 1971–73, Glasgow Herald 1973–86; reporter and presenter BBC TV (Scotland) 1986–88, political ed Scotland on Sunday 1988–91, ed Bateman Associates (freelance journalism) 1991–; currently contrib: Radio Scotland, The Sunday Times; finalist Young Journalist of the Year Edinburgh Evening News 1973, runner-up Reporter of the Year Glasgow Herald 1986, USIA journalism participant 1991; dir Graduate Art Gallery; memb: Selkirk Merchant Co, NUJ 1968; *Books* Unfriendly Games (with Derek Douglas, 1986); *Style—* Derek Bateman, Esq; ✉ Ty Mawr, Boggs Farm Steading, Pencaitland, Tranent, East Lothian EH34 5BD (☎ 01875 340 538)

BATEMAN, Sir Geoffrey Hirst; kt (1972); s of Dr William Hirst Bateman, JP (d 1959), of Rochdale, Lancs, and Ethel Jane, *née* Scrimgeour (d 1964); *b* 24 Oct 1906; *Educ* Epsom Coll, Univ Coll Oxford (Theodore Williams scholar in anatomy, BA, BM BCh); *m* 1931, Margaret, da of Sir Samuel Turner (d 1955); 3 s (*see* Dr Nigel Turner Bateman and Dr Christopher John Turner Bateman), 1 da; *Career* George Herbert Hunt travelling scholar Univ of Oxford 1933; RAFVR Wing Cdr 1939–45; surgn ENT Dept St Thomas' Hosp London 1939–71; formerly hon conslt on oto-rhino-laryngology to the Army, conslt advsr in otolaryngology DHSS; memb: Bd of Govrs St Thomas' Hosp 1948, Collegium Otolaryngologica Amicitae Sacrum 1949, Cncl RCS 1963–67; ed Jl of Laryngology and Otology 1961–77; pres Br Assoc of Otolaryngologists 1970–71 (vice pres 1967–70); hon corresponding memb American Laryngological Assoc 1960; FRCS 1933, Hon FRSM 1978; *Books* Diseases of the Nose and Throat (asst ed to V E Negus, 6 edn 1955); contribs to various jls; *Recreations* golf, fishing; *Style—* Sir Geoffrey Bateman; ✉ Thorney, Graffham, Petworth, W Sussex GU28 0QA (☎ 01798 867314)

BATEMAN, Dr Nigel Turner; s of Sir Geoffrey Hirst Bateman, *qv*, and Margaret, *née* Turner; bro of Dr Christopher John Turner Bateman, *qv*; *b* 3 April 1943; *Educ* Marlborough, Univ Coll Oxford, St Thomas' Hosp (BM BCh); *m* 10 Dec 1966, Susannah Christian, da of Cdr A Denis Bulman, of The Old Manse, Midlem, by Selkirk, Scotland; 4 s (Thomas Andrew b 1969, Patrick Edward b 1971, Colin David b 1972, Michael Geoffrey b 1981); *Career* War Memorial scholarship Univ Coll Oxford 1962, assoc prof of preventive med Univ of Wisconsin 1978–79; conslt physician: St Thomas' Hosp 1980–93, Guy's and St Thomas' Hosp Tst 1993–; UMDS Guy's and St Thomas' Hosp: hon sr lectr 1992–, asst clinical dean 1993–; Liveryman Worshipful Soc of Apothecaries 1985, Freeman City of London 1985; FRCP 1985; *Books* Respiratory Disorders (with I R Cameron, 1983); *Recreations* tennis, golf, fishing, hill walking; *Style—* Dr Nigel Bateman; ✉ St Thomas' Hospital, London SE1 7EH (☎ 0171 928 9292, fax 0171 922 8206)

BATEMAN, Paul Terence; s of Nelson John Bateman (d 1983), and Frances Ellen, *née* Johnston; *b* 28 April 1946; *Educ* Westcliff HS for Boys, Univ of Leicester (BSc); *m* 18 Jan 1969, Moira; 2 s (Michael b 1973, Timothy b 1977); *Career* Save and Prosper Group Ltd: graduate in secretarial dept 1967–68, asst to gp actuary 1968–73, mktg mangr 1973–75, gp mktg mangr 1975–80, gp mktg and devpt mangr 1980–81, exec dir mktg and devpt 1981–88, chief exec 1988–95; exec dir Robert Fleming Holdings Ltd (parent co of Save & Prosper) 1988–, exec chm Robert Fleming Asset Management 1995–; dir: Lautro Ltd 1988–94, Personal Investment Authy 1993–94; chm Bd of Govrs Westcliff HS for Boys 1988–95; *Recreations* yachting, squash, golf, skiing; *Clubs* Royal Burnham Yacht; *Style—* Paul Bateman, Esq; ✉ 95 Thorpe Bay Gardens, Thorpe Bay, Essex SS1 3NW (☎ 01702 587152); Robert Fleming Holdings, 25 Copthall Avenue, London EC2R 7DR (☎ 0171 382 8475, fax 0171 382 8907)

BATEMAN, Peter Leonard Goodchild; s of Albert Henry Bateman (d 1963), and Mabel Margaret, *née* Goodchild (d 1967); *b* 8 May 1935; *Educ* Whitgift Sch Croydon, Regent Street Poly, Coll for the Distributive Trades (DipCAM, Lord Leverhulme essay award); *m* 27 July 1963, Joan Hilary, da of John Lockyer; 3 da (Rachel Helen b 2 April 1965, Kathleen Margaret b 19 April 1967, Claire Judith b 30 Dec 1973), 1 s (Richard Michael b 6 Feb 1971); *Career* Nat Serv Queen's Royal Regt; buying asst Unilever Ltd 1954–58, advtg asst Craigmillar & British Creameries Ltd (Unilever) 1958–62; Rentokil Ltd: asst publicity/advtg mangr 1962–63, PR mangr 1963–64, gen mangr/dir Advice & Action Ltd (PR subsid) 1964–74, dir of PR 1975–95; conslt in PR, reputation mgmnt and pest control 1995–; *Awards* Int Cncl of Industrial Editors' Award 1965, BAIE National House Jl Award of Merit 1967, 1970, 1983 and 1984, winner IPR Sword of Excellence (public affairs category) 1986, Keith Cleverly Award for services to BPCA 1991; hon advsr Academic Bd Coll for the Distributive Trades 1980–83; memb: Cncl IPR 1981–83, Cncl Soc of Food Hygiene Technol 1984–89, Speak Out panel Chemical Industries Assoc; chm: Educn Ctee IPR 1981, PR and Conf Ctee BPCA 1983–93; pres British Pest Control Assoc 1983–84, former govr and chief examiner CAM Fndn, tstee PR Educn Tst 1981–83; MCIM 1963, fell Entomological Soc 1964, FIPR 1981, fell Br Assoc of Industrial Editors 1988, fell Soc of Food Hygiene Technology 1991, FRSA 1994; *Books* Household Pests (1979); author of numerous articles and papers on PR; *Recreations* natural history, theatre, music, writing, keeping up with the family, local church and parish council affairs; *Style—* Peter Bateman, Esq; ✉ Poynings, The Limes, Felbridge, East Grinstead, W Sussex RH19 2QY (☎ 01342 325615)

BATEMAN, Richard Harrison; s of Herbert F A Bateman (d 1991), of Southborough, Kent, and Minnie, *née* Harrison (d 1986); *b* 21 April 1945; *Educ* Hampton Sch; *m* 1 April 1967, Maureen Winifred, da of Michael Devaney; 1 s (Stephen Harrison b 7 April 1968), 1 da (Kate Mary b 12 May 1970); *Career* with Coutts & Co 1963–67, Charles Fulton & Co int money brokers 1967–70; dir: Kirkland Whittaker Group Ltd and subsids 1978–89 (joined 1970), Prebon Yamane (UK) plc (formerly Babcock Fulton Prebon plc) 1989–95 (ret); England rugby football trials 1966; *Recreations* sports, metaphysical poetry; *Clubs* Richmond RFC; *Style—* Richard Bateman Esq; ✉ c/o Prebon Yamane (UK) plc, 155 Bishopsgate, London EC2 (☎ 0171 522 2222)

BATEMAN, Richard Montague; s of Gordon Montague Bateman, of Bournemouth, and late Joan Rhoda, *née* Puddifoot; *b* 27 Nov 1943; *Educ* Lyme Regis GS; *m* 5 Sept 1970, Gillian Elizabeth, da of Noel Leslie Costain; 1 da (Genevieve Tara Elizabeth b 10 Aug 1986); *Career* Civil Serv: joined 1964, MOD 1965–69, asst sec Chamber of Shipping of UK 1973–75, Gen Cncl of Br Shipping 1975–80; exec sec Geological Soc 1980–, sec Assoc of Euro Geological Socs 1987–92; environment cncllr 1994–; assoc memb IOD 1989; *Recreations* maritime history, classical music; *Clubs* Anchorites; *Style—* Richard

Bateman, Esq; ✉ The Geological Society, Burlington House, Piccadilly, London W1V 0JU (☎ 0171 434 9944, fax 0171 439 8975)

BATES, Alan Arthur; CBE (1995); s of Harold Arthur Bates (d 1976), of Bradbourne, Derbyshire, and Florence Mary, *née* Wheatcroft; *b* 17 Feb 1934; *Educ* Herbert Strutt GS Belper Derbys, RADA; *m* 1970, Victoria Valerie (d 1992), da of Roland Ward (d 1980); 2 s (Tristan b Nov 1970 d 1990, Benedick (twin)); *Career* actor; RAF 1952–54; *Theatre* English Stage Co (Royal Court): The Mulberry Bush, Cards of Identity, Look Back in Anger, The Country Wife, In Celebration; West End: Long Day's Journey into Night, The Caretaker, The Four Seasons, Hamlet, Butley (also NY (Evening Standard Best Actor Award 1972, Antoinette Perry Best Actor Award 1973)); other roles incl: Poor Richard (NY), Richard III and The Merry Wives of Windsor (Stratford, Ontario), Venice Preserved (Bristol, Old Vic), Taming of the Shrew (Stratford-on-Avon) 1973, Life Class 1974, Otherwise Engaged (Queen's (Variety Club of GB Best Stage Award)) 1975, The Seagull (Duke of York's) 1976, Stage Struck (Vaudeville) 1979, A Patriot for Me (Chichester, Haymarket) 1983, Victoria Station and One for the Road (Lyric Studio) 1984, The Dance of Death (Riverside Studios) 1985, Yonadab (NT) 1985, Melon (Haymarket) 1987, Much Ado About Nothing and Ivanov (double bill, Strand) 1989, Stages (RNT) 1992, The Showman (Almeida) 1993, The Master Builder (Theatre Royal) 1995, Simply Disconnected (Chichester) 1996, Fortune's Fool (Chichester) 1996; *Television* incl: Plaintiff and Defendant, Two Sundays, The Collection 1977, The Mayor of Casterbridge 1978, Very Like a Whale, The Trespasser 1980, A Voyage Round My Father, Separate Tables, An Englishman Abroad 1983 (BAFTA Best TV Actor Award 1984), Dr Fisher of Geneva 1984, The Dog It Was That Died 1988, 102 Boulevard Haussmann 1990, Secret Friends 1991, Unnatural Pursuits 1992, Hard Times 1993, Oliver's Travels 1994; *Films* incl: The Entertainer, Whistle Down the Wind, A Kind of Loving, The Running Man, The Caretaker, Zorba the Greek, Nothing but the Best, Georgie Girl, King of Hearts, Far from the Madding Crowd, The Fixer (Oscar Nomination), Women in Love, The Three Sisters, A Day in the Death of Joe Egg, The Go-Between, Second Best (prodr), Impossible Object, Butley, In Celebration, Royal Flash, An Unmarried Woman, The Shout, The Rose, Nijinsky, Quartett, The Return of the Soldier, The Wicked Lady, Duet for One, Prayer for the Dying, Pack of Lies, We think the World of You, Mr Frost, Dr M, Hamlet 1990, Shuttlecock 1990, Losing Track 1991, Secret Friends 1992, Silent Tongue 1992, The Grotesque 1995; *Awards* for Best Actor incl: Evening Standard 1973, Tony 1973, Drama Desk 1973, Drama League 1973, Variety Club 1975 and 1983, BAFTA, NCTA (USA) 1983 and 1985; *Recreations* driving, swimming, riding; *Style*— Alan Bates, Esq, CBE; ✉ c/o Chatto & Linnit, Prince of Wales Theatre, Coventry Street, London W1V 7FE (☎ 0171 930 6677, fax 0171 930 0091)

BATES, Christopher; s of Alan Douglas Bates, of Gedling, Nottingham, and Alma, *née* Atkins; *b* 10 Oct 1962; *Educ* Carlton Le Willows Sch Gedling Nottingham; *m* Alison Elaine; *Career* oarsman; Newark Rowing Club 1973–81, Nottingham Boat Club and Notts County Rowing Assoc 1981–; 68 caps England and GB 1983–; Nat Championships: represented Newark 1980, Silver medal lightweight coxless fours 1982, Gold medal 1983, 1984, 1988 (2), 1990 (2) and 1992, 1995 and 1996 (2), Silver medal 1985; World Championships: Silver medal 1983, 1986 and 1987, 1995, Bronze medal 1984 and 1990, Gold medal Vienna 1991, Montreal 1992, Indianapolis 1994; medals won at other int events incl: 7 Gold Henley Royal Regatta, Gold Tokyo Henley, 5 Gold, 2 Silver and 1 Bronze unofficial Euro Championships Lucerne, Gold Cwlth Games 1986, 2 Gold German Int Duisburg, 2 Gold German International Berlin, 3 Gold French International Paris; records: Lightweight four Cwlth Games 1986, Ladies Plate Henley Royal Regatta 1989, world lightweight eight 1990, world lightweight coxless fours 1991 (first lightweight four to row 2000m int course under 6 mins); employed in family firm; *Recreations* motor boats, classic sports cars; *Style*— Christopher Bates, Esq; ✉ 6 Paget Crescent, Ruddington, Nottingham NG11 6FD (☎ 0115 921 3480); Nottinghamshire County Rowing Association, National Water Sports Centre, Nottingham (☎ 0115 982 1212)

BATES, Christopher; s of Derek Roland Bates, of Windsor, Berks, and Cora Mary, *née* Pemberthy, of Penzance, Cornwall; *b* 16 Nov 1951; *Educ* Royal Free Secdy Sch, Windsor GS, Univ of Keele (BA); *m* Jenny Bates; *Career* PA Harry South Associates 1975–76, company admin Second City Theatre Co 1976–78, mktg mangr Charles Vance Promotions 1978–79, touring mangr then positions until asst dir South East Arts 1979–88, chief exec South West Arts 1990–95 (asst dir 1988–90), princ ptnr Butler Bates Associates (arts and media consits) 1995–; *Style*— Christopher Bates; ✉ Butler Bates Associates, 1 Courtney Terrace, Moretonhampstead, Devon TQ13 8NJ (☎ 01647 440995)

BATES, Prof Colin Arthur; s of Ralph Mehew Bates (d 1965), and Annie Kathleen, *née* Cooper (d 1993); *b* 7 May 1935; *Educ* City of Norwich Sch, Univ of Nottingham (BSc, PhD); *m* 29 July 1961, Margaret, da of Edmund Green, of Nottingham; 2 s (Julian Michael b 1967, Richard Daniel b 1971), 1 da (Karen Nicola b 1965); *Career* sr res asst Stanford Univ California USA 1961; Univ of Nottingham: demonstrator 1958, res assoc 1959, lectr in physics 1962, sr lectr in physics 1970, reader in theoretical physics 1974, prof 1984, prof and head of dept 1987–, dean of science 1996–; FInstP, CPhys; *Publications* author of various scientific articles; *Recreations* aquarist, sport, garden; *Style*— Prof Colin Bates; ✉ 26 Lime Grove Ave, Chilwell, Nottingham NG9 4AR (☎ 0115 925 5568); Physics Department, The University, Nottingham NG7 2RD (☎ 0115 951 5127, fax 0115 951 5187, telex 37345 UNINOT G)

BATES, Corinne Andree Reppin; da of Jameson Reppin Bates, of S Benfleet, Essex, and Andree Josephine Amand Eugenie, *née* Eyskens; *b* 18 March 1961; *Educ* Queenswood Sch; *Career* dir Co-ordinated Properties Ltd, trainee asst buyer Harrods 1979–84, conslt Ligne Roset (UK) Ltd 1984–86, sales mangr Van Cleef and Arpels 1987, sales dir Elizabeth Gage 1987–89, md Chaumet (UK) 1989–90, vice pres DeAranda & Associates 1991–; *Recreations* skiing, music; *Clubs* Annabel's, Harry's Bar; *Style*— Corinne Bates

BATES, Air Vice-Marshal David Frank; CB (1983); s of S F Bates (d 1977), and N A Bates, *née* Story; *b* 10 April 1928; *Educ* RAF Coll Cranwell; *m* 1954, Margaret Winifred, *née* Biles; 1 s, 1 da; *Career* RAF; cmmnd 1950, served Egypt, UKSLS Aust, HQ Tport Cmd, RAF Tech Coll, Staff Coll Lyneham, El Adem, Jt Servs Coll Innsworth and RCDS 1950–73; Station Cdr Uxbridge 1974–75, dir of Personnel Ground 1975–76, dir of Personnel Mgmnt (ADP) 1976–79, air offr admin HQ RAF Support Cmd 1979–82; bursar Warwick Sch 1983–85; *Recreations* cricket, most sports, gardening, model railways; *Clubs* RAF, MCC; *Style*— Air Vice-Marshal David Bates, CB; ✉ c/o Lloyds Bank Ltd, 73 Parade, Leamington Spa, Warwickshire CV32 4BB

BATES, Sir (John) Dawson; 2 Bt (UK 1937), of Magherabuoy, Co Londonderry, MC (1943); s of Rt Hon Sir Dawson Bates, 1 Bt, OBE (d 1949), and Muriel (d 1972), da of Sir Charles Cleland, KBE, MVO; *b* 21 Sept 1921; *Educ* Winchester, Balliol Coll Oxford; *m* 30 April 1953, Mary Murray, da of late Lt-Col Joseph Murray Hoult, RA, of Norton Place, Lincoln; 2 s (Richard Dawson Hoult b 1956, Charles Joseph Dill b 1959), 1 da (Drusilla Mary Cynthia (Mrs Gervase Belfield) b 1954); *Heir* s, Richard Dawson Hoult Bates b 12 May 1956; *Career* WWII Maj Rifle Brigade; regnl dir Nat Tst, ret 1981; FRICS; *Style*— Sir Dawson Bates, Bt, MC; ✉ Butleigh House, Butleigh, Glastonbury, Somerset

BATES, Edward Robert; s and h of Sir Geoffrey Bates, 5 Bt, MC, *qv*; *b* 4 July 1946; *Educ* Gordonstoun; *Style*— Edward Bates, Esq; ✉ Gyrn Castle, Llanasa, Holywell, Clwyd (☎ 0174 585 3500)

BATES, Sir Geoffrey Voltelin; 5 Bt (UK 1880), of Bellefield, Co Lancaster, MC (1942); o s of Maj Cecil Robert Bates, DSO, MC (d 1935), and Hylda Madeleine (d 1960), da of Sir James Heath, 1 Bt; suc unc, Sir Percy Elly Bates, 4 Bt, GBE (d 1946); *b* 2 Oct 1921; *Educ* Radley; *m* 1, 12 July 1945, Kitty (d 1956), da of Ernest Kendall-Lane, of Saskatchewan; 2 s (Edward Robert b 1946, Richard Geoffrey b 1948); m 2, 31 July 1957, Hon Olivia Gwyneth Zoë FitzRoy (d 1969), da of 2 Viscount Daventry; 1 da (Celina Zoë (Mrs Timothy Radcliffe) b 1958) and 1 da decd; m 3, 1971, Mrs Juliet Eleanor Hugolyn Whitelocke-Winter, da of late Cdr G Whitelocke, RN, and wid of Edward Winter; *Heir* s, Edward Robert Bates, *qv*; *Career* High Sheriff Flintshire 1969; Maj (ret) Cheshire Yeomanry; *Recreations* hunting, shooting, fishing; *Style*— Sir Geoffrey Bates, Bt, MC; ✉ Gyrn Castle, Llanasa, Holywell, Clwyd (☎ 01745 853500)

BATES, (Michael) Jeremy; s of Samuel Bates, of Solihull, West Midlands, and Marjorie, *née* Bourne; *b* 19 June 1962; *Educ* Strodes GS, Tudor Grange Comp Sch Solihull, Solihull Sixth Form Coll; *m* 1992, Ruth, *née* Leech; *Career* tennis player; turned professional 1980; nat champion: under 12 1974, under 18 1979 and 1980, sr 1985, 1988 and 1990; county champion various levels 1973–80; represented GB: int events at various levels, Galea Cup, Euro Youth Championships, Coupe Jean Beeker, King's Cup 1980–84, Euro Cup 1985–90, Davis Cup 1984–95; achievements incl: mixed doubles champion Wimbledon 1987, mens doubles runner-up Aust Open 1988, doubles champion Queen's Club 1990, mixed doubles champion Aust Open 1991 (semi-finalist mens doubles), reached last 16 of singles Wimbledon 1992, winner Korean Open 1994, reached quarter-finals Stella Artois Championships 1994; former Br number one; ret after Wimbledon 96; various LTA awards incl Sr Player of the Year; *Recreations* golf, guitar, karate; *Style*— Jeremy Bates, Esq; ✉ c/o IMG, The Pier House, Strand on the Green, Chiswick, London W4 3NN (☎ 0181 994 1444)

BATES, Malcolm Rowland; s of late Rowland Bates, of Waterlooville, Hants; *b* 23 Sept 1934; *Educ* Portsmouth GS, Univ of Warwick (MSc), Harvard Grad Sch of Business Admin; *m* 1960, Lynda, da of Maurice Price, of Bristol; 3 da; *Career* jt md Wm Brandt's & Sons 1972–75; GEC plc: joined 1976, main bd dir 1980–, dep md 1985–; chm: Picker International Inc, General Domestic Appliances Ltd, Pearl Assurance Group plc; dir: A B Dick Inc, GEC Inc, GEC Alsthom NV, GPT Ltd, Associated Electrical Industries Ltd, English Electric Co Ltd, Canadian Marconi Co, Videojet Systems International Inc; chm Business in the Arts, non-exec dir Industl Devpt Advsy Bd, govr Univ of Westminster; FCIS, FRAeS, CIMgt; *Recreations* classical music, reading, tennis; *Style*— Malcolm Bates, Esq; ✉ Mulberry Close, Croft Rd, Goring-on-Thames, Oxon RG8 9ES (☎ 01491 872214); General Electric Company plc, 1 Stanhope Gate, London W1A 1EH (☎ 0171 493 8484, fax 0171 491 1788)

BATES, Michael; MP (C) Langbaurgh (majority 1,564); s of John Bates, and Ruth Bates; *b* 26 May 1961; *Educ* Heathfield Sr HS Gateshead, Gateshead Coll; *m* 25 June 1983, Carole, *née* Whitfield; 2 s; *Career* jr ptnr J M Bates & Co 1979–83, inspr Clerical Medical Investment Group 1983–86, conslt Hogg Robinson (benefit consits) 1986–88, investmt advsr Joseph Nelson (fund mangrs) 1988–91, asst dir Godwins Ltd (pensions consits and actuaries) 1991–; Parly candidate (C) Tyne Bridge 1987, MP (C) Langbaurgh 1992– (also contested by-election 1991); PPS to: Rt Hon Nicholas Scott MBE, MP as Min of State Dept of Social Security 1992–93, Rt Hon Sir John Wheeler, MP as Min of State Northern Ireland Office May-July 1994: asst govt whip July 1994–95, Lord Cmmr HM's Treasy (sr Govt whip) 1995–96, Paymaster Gen December 1996–; chm Northern Area Young Conservatives 1985–87, memb YC Nat Advsy Ctee 1984–89; pres: Gateshead Cons Assoc, Northern Area YCs 1993–; *Recreations* family, football (Middlesbrough FC), reading; *Style*— Michael Bates, Esq, MP; ✉ House of Commons, London SW1A 0AA

BATES, Michael Charles (Mike); OBE (1994); s of Stanley Herbert Bates, of Sandy, Beds, and Winifred, *née* Watkinson; *b* 9 April 1948; *Educ* Stratton GS Biggleswade; *m* 29 May 1971, Janice Kwan Foh Yin, da of late Kwan Fui Kong, MBE; 1 da (Antonia b 14 March 1977), 1 s (Christopher b 23 Dec 1978); *Career* entered HM Dip Serv 1966, attaché New Delhi 1971–74, third sec Moscow 1974–77, FCO 1977–79, second later first sec Singapore 1979–83, first sec Brussels 1983–87, press offr PM's Office 1987–89, head of Parly Rels Unit FCO 1989–91, dep head of mission Riga 1991–92, chargé d'affaires Bratislava 1993–94, ambass to the Slovak Republic 1994–95, dep head of news FCO 1995–96, dep high cmmr Bombay 1996–; *Recreations* music, reading, travel; *Style*— Mike Bates, Esq, OBE; ✉ c/o Foreign & Commonwealth Office (Bombay), King Charles Street, London SW1A 2AH

BATES, Peter Edward Gascoigne; CBE (1987); s of James Edward Bates (d 1952), and Esme Grace Gascoigne, *née* Roy (d 1960); *b* 6 Aug 1924; *Educ* Kingston GS, SOAS Univ of London, Lincoln Coll Oxford; *m* 15 Dec 1947, Jean Irene Hearn, da of Brig W Campbell Grant, MC, RA (d 1966); 2 s (Jeremy b 3 March 1949, Nigel b 23 Feb 1953), 1 da (Deborah b 13 Feb 1957); *Career* cmmnd Intelligence Corps 1944, served India, Burma, Malaya, Japan 1944–46, released 1946 with rank of Capt; Malayan Civil Serv 1947–55, Aero Engine Div Rolls-Royce Ltd 1955–57, Bristol Aircraft Ltd (later British Aircraft Corp) 1957–64 (special dir 1963); Plessey Co plc (formerly Ltd): joined 1964, gen mangr Plessey Radar 1967–71 (md Radar Div 1971–76), dep chm Plessey Electronic Systems Ltd 1976–86; chm British Defence Market Intelligence Ltd 1986–92, dir General Technology Systems Ltd 1986–92; memb: Cncl Electronic Engrg Assoc 1973–85 (pres 1976), Cncl SBAC 1978–86 (pres 1983–84), Overseas Ctee CBI 1981–86, Br Overseas Trade Bd 1984–87; pres Association Européenne des Constructeurs de Matériel Aérospatial 1985–86; FRSA 1988; *Recreations* golf, theatre, gardening; *Clubs* Army and Navy, Royal Wimbledon Golf; *Style*— Peter Bates, Esq, CBE; ✉ 22 Haygarth Place, Wimbledon, London SW19 5BX (☎ 0181 946 0345)

BATES, Peter Francis; s of Lt-Col Charles Donald Bates (d 1979), and Gladys Elizabeth, *née* Wilson; *b* 12 Aug 1934; *Educ* Friends Sch Lisburn NI, Royal GS Lancaster, Gonville and Caius Coll Cambridge (MA, MB BChir), St Mary's Hosp London, FRCSI 1967, FRCS(Eng) 1969; *m* 1, Aug 1964 (m dis 1970), Cynthia Joan, da of Leslie Herbert Trace, of Twickenham, Middx; m 2, June 1971 (m dis 1980), Maggie, da of Bernard Wright; *Career* W Middx Hosp 1961–64, surgical registrar Hillingdon Hosp 1965–68; hon tutor: Royal Coll of Surgeons 1974–83, Guy's Hosp 1981; conslt gen surgn Dartford and Gravesham Health Dist 1974–91; memb: Hosp Conslt Specialists' Assoc, Br Assoc of Surgical Oncology, Euro Soc of Oncology, Br Soc of Gastroenterology, Br Assoc of Surgns of GB and Ireland, Br Computer Assoc, World Medical Assoc, BMA; chm Lunchtime Comment Club 1992–93; memb: Aldersgate, United and Basingstoke Ward Clubs, St Paul's PCC Covent Garden 1983– (churchwarden 1990–); Freeman City of London 1983, memb Guild of Freemen of the City of London 1988; memb Worshipful Soc of Apothecaries 1983 (Liveryman 1990–93), Liveryman Worshipful Co of Loriners 1991; *Recreations* theatre, skiing, books, collecting pictures, sculpture; *Clubs* United Oxford and Cambridge Univ, Arts, Wig and Pen, Rugby, City Livery, Royal Over-Seas League; *Style*— Peter F Bates, Esq

BATES, Robert Alexander; s of Richard William Bates, of Haywards Heath, Sussex, and Barbara Joan, *née* Gully (d 1990); *b* 20 Sept 1941; *Educ* Emanuel Sch; *m* 1966, Susan Margaret, da of Geoffrey; 1 s (Richard Alexander b 1970), 1 da (Emma Lucy b 1967); *Career* chartered accountant 1965; ptnr Moore Stephens 1971–94; conslt 1995–; Freeman of the City of London, Liveryman Worshipful Co of Upholders; *Recreations* reading, golf, gardening; *Clubs* The Royal Soc of St George; *Style*— Robert Bates, Esq; ✉ 24 Lucastes Avenue, Haywards Heath, West Sussex RH16 1JX

BATES, His Hon Stewart Taverner; QC (1970); s of John Bates (d 1946), of Greenock; *b* 17 Dec 1926; *Educ* Univ of St Andrews, CCC Oxford; *m* 1950, Anne Patricia, da of David West, of Pinner; 2 s, 4 da; *Career* Offrs' Trg Sch Bangalore 1946, cmmnd Argyll and Sutherland Highlanders; called to the Bar Middle Temple 1954, bencher 1975, recorder 1981–89, Lent reader 1992, circuit judge 1989–95, ret; memb Bar Cncl 1962–66, chm Barrs' Benevolent Assoc 1983–89; memb: Goodman Ctee on Charity Law and Voluntary Orgns 1976, Ctee of Mgmnt Inst of Urology Univ of London 1978–89; chm St Peter's Hosp Special Ctee 1986–89; *Recreations* theatre, sailing, skiing; *Clubs* Garrick; *Style*— His Hon Stewart Bates, QC; ✉ Horsington Grange, Templecombe, Somerset (☎ 01963 370521)

BATES, Dr Thelma Dorothy; da of William Cyril Johnson (d 1970), and Dorothy Florence, *née* Proudman (d 1986); *b* 18 Aug 1929; *Educ* Orme Girls Sch Staffs, Univ of Birmingham (MB ChB); *m* 23 July 1960, (Sidney Edward) Mills Bates (d 1996); 1 da (Anne b 1961), 2 s (Richard b 1963, Charles b 1964 d 1991); *Career* conslt radiotherapist and oncologist St Thomas' Hosp 1968–94, dir SE London Radiotherapy Centre 1986–93, conslt oncologist St Christopher's Hospice; vice pres Royal Coll of Radiologists 1988–90, memb GMC 1989– (chm Health Ctee 1994–), pres Radiology Section RSM 1991–92; FRACR, FRCR, FRSA 1986; *Style*— Dr Thelma Bates; ✉ Saxonwood, Albany Cl, Blackhills, Esher, Surrey KT10 9JR (☎ 01372 464851)

BATESON, Fergus Dingwall; MBE (1995); s of Owen Latham Bateson, KC (d 1947), of Berkhamsted, Herts, and Eileen Mary Havelock, *née* Collins (d 1965); *b* 26 April 1930; *Educ* Westminster, Hertford Coll Oxford (BA); *m* 11 April 1957, Ann Margaret, da of Dr Jared Totten (d 1959), of Lochnell, Northchurch, Berkhamsted, Herts; 3 s (James b 1961, Alexander b 1962, Charles b 1965), 1 da (Lucinda b 1960); *Career* admitted slr 1956; conslt Thomas Cooper and Stibbard 1990–96 (ptnr 1959, sr ptnr 1986–90), princ Fergus Bateson Slrs 1990–; chm CPC Ctee Cons Party Eastern Area 1967–70, memb Runciman Advsy Ctee on Historic Wreck Sites 1974–96, tstee Nautical Museums Tst 1983–; Liveryman Worshipful Co of Solicitors 1970, Freeman City of London 1970; memb Law Soc; *Books* Digest of Commercial Laws of the World (contrib 1966); *Recreations* amateur theatre, bridge; *Clubs* Law Soc, Mitre; *Style*— Fergus Bateson, Esq, MBE; ✉ 18 Fishpool St, St Albans, Herts AL3 4RT (☎ 01727 859340, fax 01727 847696)

BATESON, Lynne; *b* 16 Aug 1952; *Educ* Univ of London (external student, BSc); *Career* gen reporter Pudsey News 1973–77, feature writer Yorkshire Evening Post 1978–81; city writer: Utd Newspapers 1981–84, Thomson Regnl Newspapers 1984–86; personal fin writer Daily Express 1986–87, features ed Money Magazine 1987–88; Sunday Express: personal fin ed 1988–94, fin ed 1994–95, asst ed 1995–; special commendation Bradford & Bingley's Personal Fin Journalist of the Year award 1990, Br Insurance and Investment Brokers' Assoc Consumer Journalist of the Year (tabloid) 1993; *Recreations* mystery and history books, Wagner, Puccini, Debussy and soul, Oriental food, hot baths; *Style*— Ms Lynne Bateson; ✉ Assistant Editor, Sunday Express, Ludgate House, 245 Blackfriars Rd, London SE1 9UX (direct ☎ 0171 922 7679)

BATESON, Prof Paul Patrick Gordon; s of Capt Richard Gordon Bateson (d 1956), and Solvi Helene, *née* Berg (d 1987); *b* 31 March 1938; *Educ* Westminster, King's Coll Cambridge (BA, PhD, ScD); *m* 20 July 1963, Dusha, da of Kenneth Matthews, of Halesworth, Suffolk; 2 da (Melissa b 1968, Anna b 1972); *Career* Harkness fell Stanford Univ Med Center California 1963–65; Univ of Cambridge: sr asst in res Sub-Dept of Animal Behaviour 1965–69, lectr in zoology 1969–78, dir Sub-Dept of Animal Behaviour 1976–88, reader in animal behaviour 1978–84, prof of ethology 1984–, provost King's Coll 1988– (professorial fell 1984–88); pres: Assoc for the Study of Animal Behaviour 1977–80, Cncl Zoological Soc of London 1989–92; tstee Inst for Public Policy Studies 1988–95; Scientific Medal Zoological Soc of London 1976; FRS 1983; *Books* Growing Points of Ethology (ed with R A Hinde, 1976), Perspectives in Ethology Vols 1–9 (ed with P H Klopfer, 1972–91), Mate Choice (ed, 1983), Defended to Death (with G Prins & Others, 1984), Measuring Behaviour (with P Martin, 1986, 2 edn 1993), The Domestic Cat: The Biology of its Behaviour (ed with D Turner, 1988); *Style*— Prof Patrick Bateson, FRS; ✉ Provost's Lodge, Kings College, Cambridge CB2 1ST (☎ 01223 355949)

BATEUP, John Brian; s of John Maynard Bateup (d 1971), of Horsmonden, Kent, and Dorothy Nellie, *née* Rose; *b* 22 Aug 1949; *Educ* The Judd Sch Tonbridge Kent; *m* 5 Jan 1974, Christine Anne, da of Rev William Preston, of Horsmonden, Kent; 3 s (Matthew b 1983, Timothy b 1986, Andrew b 1989), 2 da (Helen b 1975, Anne b 1977); *Career* actuary; md: Reliance Mutual Insurance Society Ltd 1982–, The British Life Office Ltd, Reliance Fire and Accident Insurance Corporation Ltd, Reliance Unit Managers Ltd, Reliance Pension Scheme Trustee Ltd; FIA; *Recreations* sport, especially table-tennis; *Clubs* IOD, Actuarial Dining; *Style*— John B Bateup, Esq; ✉ Reliance House, Tunbridge Wells, Kent TN4 8BL (☎ 01892 510033, fax 01892 532374)

BATH, 7 Marquess of (GB 1789); Sir Alexander George Thynn (*sic*, reverted to this spelling); 10 Bt (E 1641); also Viscount Weymouth and Baron Thynne of Warminster (E 1682); s of 6 Marquess of Bath, ED (d 1992), and his 1 w, Hon Daphne Winifred Louise (*see* Hon Mrs Fielding), da of 4 Baron Vivian; *b* 6 May 1932; *Educ* Eton, Christ Church Oxford (MA); *m* 1969, Anna, da of Laszlo Izsak Gyarmathy, originally of Budapest but latterly of Los Angeles (Anna Gael, the actress, journalist and novelist); 1 s, 1 da (Lady Lenka Abigail b 1969); *Heir* s, Ceawlin Henry Laszlo, Viscount Weymouth b 6 June 1974; *Career* late Lt Life Gds & Royal Wilts Yeo; contested: Westbury (Feb 1974) and Wells (1979) in Wessex Regionalist Pty's interest, Wessex (Euro elections 1979) Wessex Regionalist and European Fed Pty; Lib Dem whip House of Lords 1993–; painter; opened perm exhibition of murals in private apartments of Longleat 1973; dir Longleat Enterprises (incl Cheddar Caves) 1964–, planted first of the mazes within 'the Labyrinths of Longleat' 1975, opened Center Parcs Village Longleat Forest 1994; *Books* (as Alexander Thynne before 1976, Thynn thereafter); The Carry Cot (1972), Lord Weymouth's Murals (1974), A Regionalist Manifesto (1975), The King is Dead (1976), Pillars of the Establishment (1980); *Record* I Play the Host (1974, singing own compositions); *Style*— The Most Hon the Marquess of Bath; ✉ Longleat, Warminster, Wilts BA12 7NN (home ☎ 01985 844300, fax 01985 844888, business ☎ 01985 844400, fax 01985 844885)

BATH, Archdeacon of; *see:* Evens, Ven Robert John Scott

BATH AND WELLS, Bishop of 1991–; Rt Rev James Lawton Thompson; s of Bernard Isaac Thompson, and Marjorie May Thompson; *b* 11 Aug 1936; *Educ* Dean Close Sch Cheltenham, Emmanuel Coll Cambridge (MA), Cuddesdon Coll Oxford; *m* 1965, Sally Patricia; 1 s (Ben), 1 da (Anna); *Career* Nat Serv 2 Lt 3 RTR 1959–61; ordained deacon 1966, curate East Ham 1966–68, chaplain Cuddesdon Coll Oxford 1968–71, rector Thamesmead and ecumenical team ldr 1971–78, examining chaplain to the Bishop of Southwark 1974–78, suffragan then area bishop of Stepney 1978–91; co-chm Inter Faith Network 1987–92; chm: Br Cncl of Churches Ctee for Rels with People of Other Faiths 1983–90, London Diocesan Bd for Social Responsibility 1979–87, Tower Hamlets Assoc for Racial Justice 1979–85, The Urban Learning Fndn 1983–91, Social Policy Ctee for the Gen Synod Bd for Social Responsibility 1990–95, Social, Economic and Industl Affrs Ctee for the Gen Synod Bd for Social Responsibility 1996–; memb House of Bishops Gen Synod of the C of E 1985–; commissary for the Bishop of Namibia, reg broadcaster on radio and TV; jt winner (with Rabbi Gryn) Sir Sigmund Sternberg Award for Christian-Jewish Rels 1987; ICA Founding Societies' Centenary Award 1994; Companion Honour of Orthodox Hospitallers 1987; hon fell Queen Mary Coll London 1986, Hon DLitt E London Poly 1989, Hon DD Univ of Exeter 1995; FCA 1959; *Publications* Origins of Love and Hate (1983), Half Way: Reflections in Midlife (1986), First Aid in Pastoral Care (contrib, 1987), Trevor Huddleston's Essays on His Life and Work (contrib, 1988), The Lord's Song (1990), Stepney Calling (1991), Why God? (1996); *Recreations* painting, horses, sport; *Style*— The Rt Rev the Bishop of Bath and Wells; ✉ The Palace, Wells, Somerset BA5 2PD (☎ 01749 672341)

BATHO, Prof Gordon Richard; s of Walter Batho (d 1955), of Ealing, W London, and Harriet Emily, *née* Dymock (d 1988); *b* 27 Feb 1929; *Educ* Ealing GS for Boys, UCL (BA), Inst of Educn London (PGCE), Royal Holloway Coll London (MA); *m* 5 Sept 1959, Hilary, da of Alfred Crowson (d 1963), of Bakewell, Derbyshire; 2 s (Richard b 1965, Paul b 1969); *Career* sr history master Ilfracombe GS 1953–55, sr lectr in educn Univ of Sheffield 1966–74 (asst lectr 1956, lectr 1958), emeritus prof of educn Univ of Durham 1988 (prof 1975–88); visiting lectr: McMaster Univ 1963, Univ of BC 1963–64 and 1966, Carleton Univ 1964; Thomas Harriot lectr Oriel Coll Oxford 1991; reviews ed British Journal of Educational Studies 1990–95; vice pres History Assoc, lately chm Standing Conf on Studies in Educn, chm Durham Thomas Harriot Seminar 1977–; memb Cncl: Church Schs Co 1991–92, Governing Bodies of Girls' Schools Assoc 1992–95; hon dir: Young Historian Prizes 1988–, Nat Conf Historical Assoc 1993; FRHistS 1956 (assoc 1954); *Books* Household Papers of Henry Percy (1564–1632) Royal Historical Society (1962), Calendar of the Talbot Papers, Historical MSS Commission (1972) Political Issues In Education (1989), The Advice to His Son by Henry Percy, 9th Earl of Northumberland (Roxburgh Club vol for The Lord Egremont, 1996); *Recreations* gardening, historical visiting; *Style*— Prof Gordon Batho; ✉ 3 Archery Rise, Durham DH1 4LA (☎ 0191 386 8908); School of Education, University of Durham, Leazes Rd, Durham DH1 1TA (☎ 0191 374 3497, fax 0191 374 3506)

BATHO, Sir Peter Ghislain; 3 Bt (UK 1928), of Frinton, Essex; s of Sir Maurice Benjamin Batho, 2 Bt (d 1990), and Antoinette Marie, da of Baron Paul d'Udekem d'Acoz, of Ghent, Belgium; *b* 9 Dec 1939; *Educ* Ampleforth, Writtle Farm Inst; *m* 29 Oct 1966, Lucille Mary, da of late Wilfrid Francis Williamson, of The White House, Saxmundham, Suffolk; 3 s (Rupert Sebastian Ghislain b 1967, Alexander Francis Ghislain b 1970, Hugh Charles Ghislain b 1973); *Heir* s, Rupert Sebastian Ghislain Batho b 26 Oct 1967; *Career* career in agriculture; cncllr Suffolk CC 1989–93; *Style*— Sir Peter Batho, Bt; ✉ Park Farm, Saxmundham, Suffolk IP17 1DQ

BATHURST, Adm of the Fleet Sir (David) Benjamin; GCB (1991, KCB 1987), DL (Somerset); s of late Gp Capt Peter Bathurst, and Lady Ann Bathurst, qv; *b* 27 May 1936; *Educ* Eton, Britannia RN Coll Dartmouth; *m* 1959, Sarah, *née* Peto; 1 s, 3 da; *Career* joined RN 1953; qualified: pilot 1960, helicopter instr 1964; Fleet Air Arm appts incl: 2 years exchange with 723 and 725 Sqdns RAN, sr pilot 820 Naval Air Sqdn, CO 819 Naval Air Sqdn, HMS Norfolk 1971, naval staff 1973, CO HMS Ariadne 1975, naval asst to First Sea Lord 1976, Capt 5 Frigate Sqdn HMS Minerva 1978, RCDS 1981, dir Naval Air Warfare 1982, flag offr 2 Flotilla 1983–85, dir gen Naval Manpower and Trg 1985–86, Chief of Fleet Support 1986–89, Cdr in Chief Fleet, Cdr in Chief Eastern Atlantic Area, Allied Cdr in Chief Channel 1989–91, Vice Chief of Defence Staff 1991–93, Chief of Naval Staff and First Sea Lord 1993–95; Liveryman Guild of Air Pilots and Air Navigators; yr bro Trinity House; FRAeS, CIMgt; *Recreations* gardening, shooting, fishing; *Clubs* Boodle's, Army and Navy, MCC; *Style*— Admiral of the Fleet Sir Benjamin Bathurst, GCB, DL; ✉ c/o Coutts and Co, 440 Strand, London WC2

BATHURST, Lady (Joan) Caroline; *née* Petrie; da of James Alexander Petrie (d 1977), of London, and Adrienne Johanna, *née* van den Bergh; *b* 2 Nov 1920; *Educ* Wycombe Abbey Sch, Newnham Coll Cambridge (BA, MA); *m* 8 Aug 1968, Sir Maurice Edward Bathurst, CMG, CBE, QC, *qv*, s of Edward John James Bathurst (d 1978), of East Horsley, Surrey; 1 step s (Adrian Edward b 1948); *Career* HM Dip Serv: FO 1947–48, second sec The Hague 1948–50, FO 1950–54 (first sec 1953), UK High Cmmn and Embassy Bonn 1954–58, FO (later FCO) 1958–71, cnsllr 1969, head Euro Communities Info Unit FCO 1969–71, ret 1972; memb UK Delgn to Colombo Plan Consultative Ctee Jogjakarta 1959, advsr Br Gp Inter-Parly Union 1962–68; Offr Order of Leopold (Belgium) 1966; *Recreations* genealogy, gardening, music; *Clubs* Utd Oxford and Cambridge; *Style*— Lady Bathurst; ✉ Airlie, The Highlands, East Horsley, Surrey KT24 5BG (☎ 01483 283269)

BATHURST, 8 Earl (GB 1772); Henry Allen John Bathurst; DL (Glos 1960); also Baron Bathurst (GB 1711) and Baron Apsley (GB 1771); s of Lt-Col Lord Apsley, DSO, MC, TD, MP (k on active serv 1942) and late Lady Apsley, CBE; suc gf (7 Earl) 1943; *b* 1 May 1927; *Educ* Eton, Ch Ch Oxford, Ridley Coll Canada; *m* 1, 1959 (m dis 1976), Judith Mary, da of late Amos Christopher Nelson, of Fosse Corner, Cirencester; 2 s, 1 da; m 2, 1978, Gloria Wesley, da of Harold Edward Clarry, of Vancouver, and wid of David Rutherston; *Heir* s, Lord Apsley; *Career* Lt 10 Royal Hussars 1946–48, Royal Glos Hussars 1948–59, Capt TA; master VWH (Earl Bathurst's) Hounds 1950–64, jt master VWH Hounds 1964–66; hon sec Agricultural Ctee (Cons) House of Lords 1957, a Lord-in-Waiting 1957–61, jt Parly under sec of state Home Office 1961–62; govr Royal Agricultural Coll, pres Glos Branch Cncl for the Protection of Rural England until 1989, chllr Primrose League 1959–61; memb: Cncl CLA 1965 (chm Glos Branch CLA 1968–71), Cncl Timber Growers' Orgn 1966; pres: Royal Forestry Soc 1976–78, Inst of Sales & Mktg Mgmnt 1981–92, Assoc of Professional Foresters 1983–86 and 1995–; dir Forestor Group 1986–92; *Clubs* White's, Cavalry and Guards'; *Style*— The Rt Hon the Earl Bathurst, DL; ✉ Manor Farm, Sapperton, nr Cirencester, Glos GL7 6LE

BATHURST, Sir Maurice Edward; kt (1984), CMG (1953), CBE (1947), QC (1964); o s of late Edward John James Bathurst, of E Horsley, Surrey, and late Annie Mary Bathurst; *b* 2 Dec 1913; *Educ* Haberdashers' Aske's Hatcham, King's Coll London (LLB, LLD), Columbia Univ New York (LLM), Gonville and Caius Coll Cambridge (PhD); *m* 1, 1941 (m dis 1963), Dorothy Eunice, da of late W S Stevens, of Gravesend, Kent; 1 s; m 2, 1968, Joan Caroline, da of James Alexander Petrie; *Career* slr 1938–56, called to the Bar Gray's Inn and Inner Temple 1957, bencher Gray's Inn 1970; legal advsr Br Info Services NY 1941–43, legal advsr Br Embassy Washington 1943–46, legal memb UK Delgn to UN 1946–48, dep legal advsr Control Cmmn Germany 1949–51, legal advsr to UK High Cmmn for Germany 1951–55, judge Supreme Court Br Zone 1953–55, legal advsr to Br Embassy Bonn 1955–57, Br judge Arbitral Cmmn Germany 1968–69; memb UK Delgns: UNRRA, WHO, UN Gen Assembly, NATO Status of Forces Conf; memb: Panel of Arbitrators Int Centre for Settlement of Investment Disputes 1968–87, Panel of Presidents Arbitral Tbnls Int Telecommunications Satellite Orgn 1974–78, UK Ctee UNICEF 1959–84; hon visiting prof of int law King's Coll London 1967–77 (hon fell); judge Arbitral Tbnl and Mixed Cmmn for the Agreement on German External Debts 1977–88; memb: Gen Cncl of the Bar 1970–71, Senate of Inns of Court 1971–73, Senate of Inns of Court and the Bar 1974–77; pres Br Insur Law Assoc 1971–75; vice pres: Br Inst of Int and Comparative Law 1986–, Br Acad of Experts 1988–92 (hon fell); Master Worshipful Co of Haberdashers 1980–81 (chm Bd of Govrs Haberdashers' Aske's Hatcham Schs 1972–80); Freeman: City of London, City of Bathurst New Brunswick; Hon DCL Sacred Heart New Brunswick 1946; *Clubs* Garrick; *Style*— Sir Maurice Bathurst, CMG, CBE, QC; ✉ Airlie, The Highlands, East Horsley, Leatherhead, Surrey KT24 5BG (☎ 01483 283269)

BATISTE, Spencer Lee; MP (C) Elmet (majority 3,261); s of late Samuel Batiste, and late Lottie Batiste; *b* 5 June 1945; *Educ* Carmel Coll, Sorbonne, Univ of Cambridge; *m* 1969, Susan Elizabeth, da of late Ronald William Atkin; 1 s, 1 da; *Career* slr in private practice 1970–; Euro Parly candidate (C) Sheffield, Chesterfield and NE Derbyshire 1979,

MP (C) Elmet 1983–; PPS to Min of State for: Indust and Info Technol 1985–87, Def Procurement 1987–89; PPS to Sir Leon Brittan as Vice Pres of EC Cmmn 1989–; memb Select Ctees: on Energy 1985, on Sci and Technol 1992–, on Info 1992–; vice chm: Cons Space Ctee 1986– (sec 1983–85), Cons Trade and Indust Ctee 1989–94, Small Business Bureau 1983–92; pres Cons Trades Unionists 1987–92 (chm Yorks Area 1984–87), chm Cons Academic Liaison Prog 1988–; law clerk to the Guardians of the Standard of Wrought Plate within the Town of Sheffield 1973–92; memb: Cncl Univ of Sheffield 1982–92, British Hallmarking Cncl 1988–; *Recreations* gardening, reading, photography; *Style—* Spencer Batiste, Esq, MP; ✉ House of Commons, London SW1A 0AA (☎ 0171 219 4054)

BATLEY, John Geoffrey; OBE (1987); s of John William Batley (d 1971), of Keighley, W Yorks, and Doris, *née* Midgeley (d 1985); *b* 21 May 1930; *Educ* Keighley GS; *m* 1953, Cicely Anne, da of William Bean Pindar, of Bradford; 1 s (John), 1 da (Janet); *Career* BR: trained and qualified as chartered engr NE Region 1947–53, asst divnl engr Leeds 1962, mgmnt servs offr BR HQ London 1965, dep princ Br Tport Staff Coll Woking 1970, divnl mangr Leeds 1976, dep chief sec BRB London 1982, sec BR Bd 1984–87; conslt Dan-Rail Copenhagen 1988–, tport conslt Carl Bro Leeds 1993–96, World Bank/Tanzanian Railway Corp project coordinator Tanzania 1988–92; Liveryman Worshipful Co of Loriners; CEng, MICE, MCIT; *Recreations* walking, golf, gardening; *Clubs* Savile, Farmers'; *Style—* John Batley, Esq, OBE; ✉ c/o Savile Club, 69 Brook St, London W1Y 2ER (☎ 0171 629 5462)

BATTEN, Sir John Charles; KCVO (1987); s of Raymond Wallis Batten, JP (d 1979), of Worthing, Sussex, and Kathleen Gladys, *née* Charles (d 1982); *b* 11 March 1924; *Educ* Mill Hill Sch, St Bartholomew's Med Coll London (MB BS, MD, FRCP); *m* 14 Oct 1950, Anne Mary Margaret, da of John Augustus Oriel, CBE, MC; 1 s (Mark b 1957), 3 da (Elizabeth b 1951, Sarah b 1953 d 1955, Clare b 1957); *Career* Surgn Capt RHG 1947–49; jr hosp appts St George's and Brompton Hosps 1946–57; physician: St George's Hosp 1958–79 (now hon physician), Royal Brompton Hosp 1959–87 (now hon physician), King Edward VII Hosp for Offrs 1968–89; physician to HM the Queen 1974–89, head HM Med Household 1981–89; sr censor RCP 1980–81 (censor 1977–78), vice pres RCP 1980–81; pres: Cystic Fibrosis Res Tst 1986–, Br Lung Fndn 1987–95, Med Protection Soc 1988–; memb: Bd of Govrs Brompton Hosp 1966–69, St George's Hosp Med Sch Cncl 1969, Cncl RSM 1970; Hon Freeman Worshipful Soc of Apothecaries; memb: Assoc of Physicians, Br Thoracic Soc; FRSM; *Recreations* music, sailing, plants; *Style—* Sir John Batten, KCVO; ✉ 7 Lion Gate Gardens, Richmond, Surrey TW9 2DF

BATTEN, Miriam; da of Christopher John Batten, of Ditchling, E Sussex, and Madella, *née* Thomas; *b* 4 Nov 1964; *Educ* St Mary's Hall Brighton, Dauntsey's Sch nr Devizes, Univ of Southampton (BSc); *Career* amateur rower; memb: Thames Rowing Club, GB squad 1990–96; achievements incl: Bronze medal pairs World Championships Vienna (with Fiona Freckleton, *qv*) 1991, first ever Br womens's crew to win World Championship medal, fifth place pairs Olympic Games Barcelona 1992, seventh place eight Olympic Games Atlanta 1996; Sunday Times Sports Woman of the Year team award 1991; systems trainer Burton Group 1987–; *Recreations* sailing and most water sports, greasy cafes for breakfast, sportswear; *Style—* Miss Miriam Batten; ✉ 5 South Worple Way, Mortlake, London SW14 8SD (☎ 0181 876 7679); Thames Rowing Club, Putney Embankment, Putney, London SW15 (☎ 0181 788 0676)

BATTEN, Stephen Duval; QC (1989); s of Brig Stephen Alexander Holgate Batten, CBE (d 1957), and Alice Joan, *née* Royden, MBE (d 1990); *b* 2 April 1945; *Educ* Uppingham, Pembroke Coll Oxford (BA); *m* 5 June 1976, Valerie Jean, da of George Ronald Trim (d 1982); 1 s (Henry b 1978), 1 da (Sarah b 1980); *Career* called to the Bar Middle Temple 1968, recorder of Crown Court 1988–; *Recreations* golf, sheep farming; *Style—* Stephen Batten, Esq, QC; ✉ 3 Raymond Buildings, Gray's Inn, London WC1R 5BH (☎ 0171 831 3833, fax 0171 242 4221)

BATTERBURY, His Hon Judge; Paul Tracy Shepherd; TD 1972 (and 2 bars 1978 and 1984), DL (Greater London 1986); s of Hugh Basil John Batterbury (d 1986), of Sidcup, and Inez, *née* Shepherd; *b* 25 Jan 1934; *Educ* St Olave's GS, Univ of Bristol (LLB); *m* 11 April 1962, Sheila Margaret, da of John Arthur Watson (d 1991); 1 s (Simon b 1963), 1 da (Sarah b 1967); *Career* RAF 1952–55, Maj RA (TA) 1959–85; called to the Bar Inner Temple 1959, dep circuit judge 1975–79, recorder 1979–83, circuit judge 1983–; cncllr: Sidcup and Chislehurst UDC 1960–62, Greenwich BC 1968–71 (chm Housing Ctee 1970–71); rep DL London Borough of Havering 1989–95; fndr tstee St Olave's Prep Sch New Eltham 1969–, fndr chm Gallipoli Meml Lectures 1985, vice pres SE London St John Ambulance 1988–91; Liveryman Worshipful Co of Plumbers 1985; *Recreations* walking, caravanning; *Clubs* Civil Service; *Style—* His Hon Judge Batterbury, TD, DL; ✉ 5 Paper Buildings, Temple, London EC4 (☎ 0171 583 9275)

BATTERSBY, Prof Sir Alan Rushton; kt (1992); s of William Battersby (d 1967), and Hilda, *née* Rushton (d 1972); *b* 4 March 1925; *Educ* Leigh GS, Univ of Manchester (BSc, MSc), Univ of St Andrews (PhD), Univ of Bristol (DSc), Univ of Cambridge (ScD); *m* 18 June 1949, Margaret Ruth, da of Thomas Hart (d 1965); 2 s (Martin b 29 July 1953, Stephen b 24 April 1956); *Career* asst lectr in chemistry Univ of St Andrews 1948–53, Cwlth Fund fell at Rockefeller Inst NY 1950–51 and Univ of Illinois 1951–52, lectr in chemistry Univ of Bristol 1954–62; second chair of organic chemistry Univ of Liverpool 1962, elected to chair of organic chemistry Univ of Cambridge 1969–92 (elected to 1702 chair 1988), fell St Catharine's Coll Cambridge; conslt AgrEvo Ltd; memb Cncl Royal Soc 1973–75, pres Bürgenstock Conf 1976, chm Exec Cncl Ciba Fndn 1983–90 (tstee 1992–); Chemical Soc: Corday-Morgan Medal 1959, Tilden Medal and lectr 1963, Hugo Müller Medal and lectr 1972, Flintoff Medal 1975, Award in Natural Product Chemistry 1978, Longstaff Medal 1984, Robert Robinson lectr and Medal 1986; Paul Karrer Medal and lectr Zürich Univ 1977; Royal Soc: Davy Medal 1977, Royal Medal 1984; Roger Adams Award in Organic Chemistry ACS 1983, Havinga Medal Holland 1984, Antoni Feltrinelli Int Prize for Chemistry Rome 1986, Varro Tyler lectr and Award Purdue 1987, Adolf Windaus Medal Göttingen 1987, Wolf Prize Israel 1989, Arun Guthikonda Meml Award Univ of Columbia 1991, August Wilhelm von Hofmann Meml Medal Gesellschaft Deutscher Chemiker 1992, Tetrahedron Prize 1995; Hon DSc: Rockefeller Univ NY 1977, Univ of Sheffield 1986, Heriot-Watt Univ 1987, Univ of Bristol 1994, Univ of Liverpool 1996; Hon LLD Univ of St Andrews 1977; FRS 1966; memb: Deutsche Akademie der Naturforscher Leopoldina (Germany) 1967, Soc Royal de Chimie (Belgium) 1987; hon memb American Acad of Arts and Sci (USA) 1988, foreign fell Nat Acad of Scis India 1990, foreign fell Indian Nat Sci Acad 1993; *Recreations* music, camping, sailing, gardening, fly-fishing; *Style—* Prof Sir Alan Battersby, FRS; ✉ 20 Barrow Rd, Cambridge CB2 2AS (☎ 01223 363799); University Chemical Laboratory, Lensfield Rd, Cambridge CB2 1EW (☎ 01223 336400, fax 01223 336362)

BATTERSBY, Robert Christopher; CBE (1990, MBE 1971); s of late Maj Robert Luther Battersby, MM, RFA, late IA, and Dorothea Gladys, *née* Middleton; *b* 14 Dec 1924; *Educ* Edinburgh Univ, Cambridge Univ (BA, MA), Sorbonne, Toulouse Univ; *m* 1, 1949 (m dis), June Scriven; 1 da; *m* 2, 1955, Marjorie Bispham; 2 s, 1 da; *Career* served RA (Field) and Intelligence Corps 1942–47 (Italian Campaign, Greece and Crete 1944), Central and Western Macedonia 1945–47), TA until 1952, Lt RARO; with Dowsett Gp of shipbuilding cos 1953–63, mangr Eastern Trade Dept Glacier Metal Co Ltd 1963–66; sales dir: Associated Engineering Services Ltd 1966–71, GKN Contractors Ltd 1971–73; export, fin and commercial advsr to various UK and USA cos, memb CBI and Soc of Br Engrs delgns to China, Poland, Yugoslavia and Singapore, memb Exec Cncl Russo-Br C of C and Russian and Polish Sections London C of C 1968–73, advsr to E Euro Trade Cncl 1969–71; princ admin: Credit and Investmts Directorate-Gen EEC Cmmn Luxembourg 1973–75, Agriculture Directorate-Gen 1975–76, Fisheries Directorate-Gen Brussels 1976–79; memb 1st EEC Vice-Presidential Delgn to Poland 1977; MEP (C) Humberside 1979–89, memb Agriculture and Budgetary Control Ctees 1979, chm Fisheries Working Gp 1979–84; vice chm: Fisheries Sub-Ctee 1984–87, Budgetary Control 1984–89; vice pres: Euro Parl Delgn to China 1981, 1984 and 1987, Euro Parl Delgn to USSR 1987–89; chief whip EDG 1987–89; Euro Parl candidate (C) Humberside 1989; special advsr on Eastern Europe Cons Pty 1990–93, conslt on Eastern Europe, former Soviet Union and Central Asia 1995–; vice pres Yorks and Humberside Devpt Assoc 1980–87, pres (former chm) Friends of Poland Assoc Euro Parl; occasional lectr at Farnham Castle on E/W trade and in Poland and USSR on automotive component mfrg technol; Liveryman Worshipful Co of Gunmakers; memb: RIIA, Anglo-Hellenic Soc; Silver Medal for Euro Merit Luxembourg 1981; FIL 1958, FIMgt 1982; KSG 1990; *Recreations* politics, Euro and Oriental languages, history, opera, music, travel; *Clubs* Carlton; *Style—* Robert Battersby, Esq, CBE; ✉ 7 South Close Green, Merstham, Surrey RH1 3DU (☎ 01737 643783)

BATTIE, David Anthony; s of Donald Charles Battie (d 1988), of Woking, and Peggy Joan Battie; *b* 22 Oct 1942; *Educ* King James I Sch; *m* 1 Jan 1972, Sarah, da of Philip James Francis (d 1987), of Merstham, Surrey; 2 da (Henrietta Victoria b 17 Aug 1977, Eleanor Harriet b 4 June 1980); *Career* dir Sotheby's 1976–; expert BBC TV Antiques Roadshow 1977–; *Books* Price Guide to 19th Century British Pottery (1975), Price Guide to 19th Century British Porcelain (1979), Sotheby's Encyclopedia of Porcelain (ed, 1990), Sotheby's Encyclopedia of Glass (co-ed, 1991), Readers' Digest Treasures in Your Home (conslt ed, 1992), Understanding 19th Century British Porcelain (1994); *Recreations* book binding; *Style—* David Battie, Esq; ✉ Sotheby's, 34/35 New Bond St, London W1A 2AA (☎ 0171 408 5366)

BATTISCOMBE, HE Christopher Charles Richard; CMG (1992); s of Lt-Col Christopher Robert Battiscombe (d 1989), and Karin Sigrid, *née* Timberg (d 1983); *b* 27 April 1940; *Educ* Wellington Coll, New Coll Oxford (BA); *m* 1972, Brigid Melita Theresa, da of Peter Northcote Lunn; 1 s (Max b 1977), 1 da (Antonia b 1975); *Career* HM Dip Serv: MECAS 1963, second sec FO (later FCO) 1963, third sec Kuwait 1965, asst private sec to Chllr of Duchy of Lancaster 1969, UK del OECD Paris 1971, first sec UK mission to UN New York 1974, asst head Eastern Euro and Soviet Dept FCO 1978, cnsllr (commercial) Cairo 1981, cnsllr (commercial) Paris 1984, cnsllr FCO 1986–90, HM ambass to Algeria 1990–94, asst under sec (Public Depts) FCO 1994–April 1997, HM ambass Jordan April 1997–; *Recreations* golf, tennis, skiing; *Clubs* Kandahar; *Style—* HE Mr Christopher Battiscombe, CMG; ✉ c/o Foreign & Commonwealth Office (Amman), King Charles Street, London SW1A 2AH

BATTISCOMBE, (Esther) Georgina; da of George Harwood, MP (d 1912), and Ellen, *née* Hopkinson (d 1965); *b* 21 Nov 1905; *Educ* St Michael's Oxford, Lady Margaret Hall Oxford (BA); *m* 1 Oct 1932, Lt-Col Christopher Francis Battiscombe, OBE, FSA (d 1964), s of Christopher William Battiscombe; 1 da (Aurea (Mrs Morshead) b 1935); *Career* biographer; reviews and articles in: The Times, Country Life, Times Literary Supplement, many other periodicals; memb: Diocesan Ctee for Care of Churches 1950–80, Redundant Churches Ctee 1977–80; county organiser St John Red Cross Hosp Libraries 1947–52; FRSL 1964; *Books* Charlotte Mary Yonge (1943), Two on Safari (1946), English Picnics (1949), Mrs Gladstone (1956), John Keble (1963, James Tait Black Meml Prize for Best Biography of the Year), Queen Alexandra (1969), Lord Shaftesbury (1974), Reluctant Pioneer (Elizabeth Wordsworth) (1978), Christina Rossetti (1981), The Spencers of Althorp (1984), Winter Song (1992); *Recreations* looking at churches, bird watching; *Style—* Mrs Georgina Battiscombe, FRSL; ✉ 40 Phyllis Court Drive, Henley-on-Thames, Oxon RG9 2HU (☎ 01491 574830)

BATTISHILL, Sir Anthony Michael William; GCB (1997, KCB 1989); s of William George Battishill (d 1994), and Kathleen Rose, *née* Bishop (d 1989); *b* 5 July 1937; *Educ* Taunton Sch, Hele's Sch Exeter, LSE (BSc Econ); *m* 1961, Heather Frances, *née* Lawes; 1 da (Sarah b 1966); *Career* 2 Lt RAEC 1958–60; Civil Service: Inland Revenue 1960–63, HM Treasy 1963–65, Inland Revenue 1965–76, Central Policy Review Section Cabinet Office 1976–77, PPS to Chancellor of the Exchequer 1977–80, under sec HM Treasy 1980–82, under sec Inland Revenue 1982–83, under sec HM Treasy 1983–85, chm Inland Revenue 1986– (dep chm 1985–86); memb Ct of Govrs LSE; chm Civil Serv Sports Cncl Sports and Leisure; CIMgt; *Recreations* gardening, old maps; *Style—* Sir Anthony Battishill, GCB; ✉ Inland Revenue, Somerset House, London WC2R 1LB (☎ 0171 438 7711, fax 0171 438 6494)

BATTLE, John Dominic; MP (Lab) Leeds W (majority 13,828); s of John Battle, and Audrey, *née* Rathbone (d 1982); *b* 26 April 1951; *Educ* Upholland Coll, Univ of Leeds (BA); *m* 12 April 1977, Mary Geraldine, da of Jerry Meenan; 1 s (Joseph b 1978), 2 da (Anna b 1981, Clare b 1982); *Career* trg for RC priesthood 1969–73, res Univ of Leeds 1973–79, res offr to Derek Enright MEP 1979–83, nat co-ordinator Church Action on Poverty 1983–87, MP (Lab) Leeds W 1987–, shadow min of housing and planning 1992–94, shadow min of sci and technol 1994–95, shadow energy min 1995–; vice chm All Pty Gp on Overseas Devpt; cncllr Leeds CC 1980–87 (chm Housing Ctee 1983–85); *Recreations* poetry; *Style—* John Battle, Esq, MP; ✉ 26 Victoria Park Avenue, Leeds LS5 3DG (☎ 0113 231 0258); House of Commons, London SW1A 0AA (☎ 0171 219 5954)

BATTY, Andrew James; s of Francis Leslie Batty (d 1971), and Pamela, *née* Ball; *b* 12 April 1956; *Educ* Roundhay GS, Jacob Kramer Coll Leeds; *m* 24 Oct 1992, Rachel Jane, *née* Sharman; 1 s (James Mark b 1995); *Career* copywriter Charles Walls Advertising 1975–79, creative dir Severn Advertising 1979–81, dir MCS Robertson Scott Yorks 1981–82, chm and md Creative Marketing Services 1982–; chm: Publicity Assoc of Bradford, Yorkshire Advertising and Communications Training, National CAM Graduates Assoc; registered marketer 1996; MSIAD 1978, MCAM 1979, MInstM 1981 (chm Leeds Branch), MIMgt 1984, FInstSMM 1987; *Recreations* voluntary activities in advertising training, local history; *Style—* Andrew Batty, Esq; ✉ Larks Rise, Keswick Grange, East Keswick, West Yorkshire LS17 9BX (☎ 01937 574692); Creative Marketing Services, CMS House, 4 Spring Bank Place, Bradford, W Yorkshire BD8 7BX (☎ 01274 820444, fax 01274 822800)

BATTY, David; *b* 2 Dec 1968; *Career* professional footballer (midfielder); with Leeds United 1987–93 (over 200 games); Blackburn Rovers FC 1993–96: transferred (for £2.75m) 1993–, winners FA Premier League 1994/95; transferred to Newcastle United (for £4m) 1996–; honours: League Championship 1992 and 1995; England: 19 full caps (as at Jan 1997); *Style—* David Batty; ✉ Newcastle United FC, St James' Park, Newcastle-upon-Tyne NE1 4ST

BATTY, Paul Daniel; QC (1995); s of Vincent Batty (d 1973), of Seaham Harbour, and Catherine, *née* Kane; *b* 13 June 1953; *Educ* St Aidan's GS, Univ of Newcastle upon Tyne (LLB); *m* 30 Sept 1986, Angela Jane; 1 da (Sarah Georgina b 2 Nov 1987); *Career* called to the Bar Lincoln's Inn 1974, mess jr Newcastle Bar 1980–83, jr North Eastern Circuit 1984, recorder of the Crown Court 1994– (asst recorder 1989–94); *Recreations* swimming, boating, angling; *Style—* Paul D Batty, Esq, QC; ✉ Broad Chare Chambers, 33 Broad Chare, Quayside, Newcastle upon Tyne NE1 3DQ (☎ 0191 232 5597, fax 0191 261 0043)

BATTY, Peter Wright; s of Ernest Faulkner Batty (d 1986), of Surrey, and Gladys Victoria, *née* Wright (d 1979); *b* 18 June 1931; *Educ* Bede GS Sunderland, Queen's Coll

Oxford (MA); *m* 1959, Anne Elizabeth, da of Edmund Stringer, of Devon; 2 s (David, Richard), 1 da (Charlotte); *Career* feature writer Financial Times 1954–56, freelance journalist 1956–58, prodr BBC TV 1958–64, memb original Tonight team (ed 1963–64); other BBC prodns incl: The Quiet Revolution, The Big Freeze, The Katanga Affair, Sons of the Navvy Man; exec prodr and assoc head of Factual Programming ATV 1964–68; prodns include: The Fall and Rise of the House of Krupp (Grand Prix for Documentary Venice Film Festival 1965, Silver Dove Leipzig Film Festival 1965), The Road to Suez, The Suez Affair, Vietnam Fly-in, Battle for the Desert; chief exec Peter Batty Productions 1970–; recent programmes directed, produced and scripted for BBC TV, ITV and Channel 4 incl: The Plutocrats, The Aristocrats, Battle for Cassino, Battle for the Bulge, Birth of the Bomb, Farouk Last of the Pharaohs, Operation Barbarossa, Superspy, Spy Extraordinary, Sunderland's Pride and Passion, A Rothschild and his Red Gold, Search for the Super, The World of Television, Battle for Warsaw, The Story of Wine, The Rise and Rise of Laura Ashley, The Gospel According to St Michael, Battle for Dien Bien Phu, Nuclear Nightmares, A Turn Up In a Million, Il Poverello, Swindle!, The Algerian War, Fonteyn and Nureyev The Perfect Partnership, The Divided Union, A Time for Remembrance, Swastika Over British Soil; contrib to The World at War series; life memb Kingston Soc; *Books* The House of Krupp (1966), The Divided Union (1987), La Guerre d'Algerie (1989); *Recreations* walking, reading, listening to music; *Clubs* Garrick; *Style—* Peter Batty, Esq; ✉ Claremont Ho, Renfrew Rd, Kingston, Surrey KT2 7NT (☎ 0181 942 6304, fax 0181 336 1661)

BATTY, Dr Vincent Bernard; s of Henry Joseph Batty, of London, and Ena Violet, *née* Cavenagh; *b* 8 June 1951; *Educ* St Aloysius Coll Highgate, Middx Hosp Med Sch (BSc, MB BS, DMRD, MSc, FRCR); *m* 21 Feb 1987, Dr Wilma Westensee, da of Rolf Westensee, of Grahamstown, SA; 1 s (Adam b 1980), 2 da (Louise b 1980, Anke b 1989); *Career* house physician Watford Gen Hosp 1977, house and casualty surgn Middx Hosp 1978, GP Hythe Hants 1979, conslt in radiology and nuclear med Southampton Gen Hosp 1984– (registrar in radiology 1979, sr registrar in radiology 1982), sr registrar in ultrasound and nuclear med Royal Marsden Hosp 1984; FRCR; memb: Br Inst of Radiology, Br Nuclear Med Soc, Worshipful Soc of Apothecaries; *Books* Nuclear Medicine In Oncology (ed, 1986); *Recreations* squash, gardening, music, photography; *Style—* Dr Vincent Batty; ✉ Denny Cottage, Denny Lodge, Lyndhurst, Hants SO43 7FZ (☎ 01703 292918); Department of Nuclear Medicine, Southampton General Hospital, Tremona Rd, Southampton SO16 6YD (☎ 01703 796201, fax 01703 796927)

BATTY, Sir William Bradshaw; kt (1973), TD (1946); s of Rowland Batty, and Nellie Batty; *b* 15 May 1913; *Educ* Hulme GS Manchester; *m* 1946, Jean Ella Brice; 1 s (and 1 s decd), 1 da; *Career* served WWII RASC, Lt-Col; Ford Motor Co Ltd: apprentice toolmaker Trafford Park Manchester 1930, co trainee 1933, press liaison Advertising Dept 1936, Serv Dept 1937, Tractor Sales Dept 1945, asst mangr Tractor Dept 1948, mangr Tractor and Implement Product Planning 1953, mangr Tractor Div 1955, gen mangr Tractor Gp 1961, dir Tractor Gp 1963, dir Car and Truck Gp 1964, md 1968–73, chm 1972–75; chm: Ford Motor Credit Co Ltd 1968 (dir 1963–), Automotive Finance Ltd 1970–75; dir: Henry Ford & Son Ltd Cork 1965–75, Ford Lusitana SARL Portugal 1973–75; memb Engrg Industs Cncl 1975–76, pres SMMT 1975–76; Hon LLD Manchester 1976; FIMgt; *Recreations* golf, sailing, gardening; *Clubs* Royal Western Yacht; *Style—* Sir William Batty, TD; ✉ Glenhaven Cottage, Riverside Rd West, Newton Ferrers, Plymouth, Devon PL8 1AD

BATTY SHAW, Patricia Dorothy Mary; CBE (1982), JP (Norfolk 1968), DL (Norfolk 1989); da of Dr Graham Heckels, of Norwich, and Dorothy Clark (d 1980); *b* 18 Nov 1928; *Educ* Wimbledon HS for Girls, Univ of Southampton; *m* 1954, Dr Anthony Batty Shaw, s of Dr Harold Batty Shaw (d 1936); 1 da (Susan Elizabeth (Mrs Francis J B Corrie)); *Career* tax cmmr Wymondham 1975– (chm 1987–), nat chm Nat Fedn of Women's Inst 1977–81, dep chm Norfolk Magistrates' Ctee 1985–87, pres Royal Norfolk Agricultural Assoc 1993–; memb: UEA Cncl 1978–85, Devpt Cmmn 1981–90, AG Wages Bd England and Wales 1984–91, Eng Advsy Ctee on Telecommunications 1985–88, Archbishop's Cmmn of Rural Affrs 1988–90; chm Bd of Govrs Norwich HS for Girls 1981–94, chm and vice pres Norfolk Rural Community Cncl 1991–, vice pres ACRE; tstee: Theatre Royal Norwich 1982–88, Charities Aid Fndn 1983–90; AMIA; *Style—* Mrs Anthony Batty Shaw, CBE, JP, DL; ✉ Appleacre, Barford, Norwich NR9 4BD (☎ 01603 545 268)

BATY, Clifford John; s of Herbert Thomas Baty (d 1937), and Ethel Beatrice, *née* Garrod (d 1989); *b* 6 Nov 1934; *Educ* Haberdashers' Aske's, Hampstead Sch, North Western Poly; *m* 19 March 1960, Brenda Anne, da of Edward Laurie Fonceca (d 1955); 1 da (Helen Jane b 1967); *Career* ATV Network Ltd: accountant 1963–74, fin controller 1974–77, fin dir 1977–81; Central Independent Television plc: dir of fin 1982–88, commercial dir 1988–91; non-exec dir Central Television Enterprises Ltd 1988–94; ACMA; *Recreations* golf, bridge; *Style—* Clifford Baty, Esq; ✉ Dormers, 27 Bellemere Road, Hampton-in-Arden, Solihull, W Midlands B92 0AN (☎ 01675 442872)

BAUDINO, Dr Catherine Anne; da of Jean Rene Baudino, and Anne-Marie, *née* Camus; *b* 26 Oct 1952; *Educ* Lycee Francais de Londres, UCL (BA, PhD); *m* May 1994, Alastair Ian Alexander Garrow; *Career* dir Institutional Investor 1980–87; chief exec: Maxwell Satellite Communications Ltd 1987–89, Baudino Enterprises Ltd 1989–; non-exec dir VideoLink Business Communications Ltd 1992–94; cncllr to the French C of C 1991–95, pres The Franco-Br Construction Indust Gp 1992–94, business devpt dir The NASDAQ Stock Market 1994–95; *Recreations* opera, theatre, wine and food; *Clubs* Reform; *Style—* Dr Catherine A Baudino; ✉ Baudino Enterprises, 217A Ashley Gardens, Emery Hill St, London SW1P 1PA (☎ 0171 828 2449, fax 0171 233 6268)

BAUER, Eran Nicodemus; s of Dr Jacob Bauer (d 1961), and Gitta, *née* Gaal; *b* 25 Feb 1954; *Educ* King's GS Grantham; *m* 27 Aug 1994, Penelope Jane, da of Terence Griffiths, of Pudsey, West Yorkshire; 2 da (Florence Eloise and Charlotte Amelia (twins) b 10 April 1995); *Career* Parachute Regt 16 Ind Co (V) 1973–78; dir: Universal Cleaning Services (historic bldgs restoration conslt), Civil Defence Supply 1980–; co-designer, patentee and inventor of military and police special ops equipment, patented first interlocking riot shield, introduced new side-handled batons and trg to UK police, chemical warfare civil def advsr to Saudi Arabian Govt during Gulf War, contrib pubns on police technol, security conslt to UK Goct depts, tech advsr to TV and films; memb RUSI for Def Studies, MRAeS; *Recreations* architecture, architectural drawing and rendering, flying (operator of 3 ex-RAF flight simulators), sports sponsorship, writing; *Clubs* Special Forces; *Style—* Eran Bauer, Esq; ✉ Civil Defence Supply, Wellingore, Lincoln LN5 0JF (☎ 01522 810388, fax 01522 811353, telex 56472 CIVDEF G)

BAUER, Baron (Life Peer UK 1983), of Market Ward in the City of Cambridge; Prof Peter Thomas Bauer; s of Aladar Bauer (d 1944), of Budapest, Hungary; *b* 6 Nov 1915; *Educ* Scholae Piae Budapest, Gonville and Caius Coll Cambridge (MA, DSc); *Career* reader in agric economics Univ of London 1947–48, economics lectr Univ of Cambridge 1948–56, Smuts reader Cwlth Studies Univ of Cambridge 1956–60, prof of economics LSE 1960–83 (now emeritus); fell Gonville and Caius Coll Cambridge 1946–60 and 1968–; FBA; *Publications* The Rubber Industry (1948), West African Trade (1954), The Economics of Underdeveloped Countries (with B S Yamey, 1957), Economic Analysis and Policy in Underdeveloped Countries (1958), Indian Economic Policy and Development (1961), Markets, Market Control and Marketing Reform (with B S Yamey, 1968), Dissent on Development (1972), Aspects of Nigerian Development (1974), Equality, the Third World and Economic Delusion (1981), Reality and Rhetoric: Studies in the Economics of Development (1984), The Development Frontier (1991); *Clubs* Garrick, Beefsteak; *Style—* The Rt Hon the Lord Bauer, FBA; ✉ House of Lords, Westminster, London SW1A 0AA

BAUER, Willy Benedikt (*né* Gegen-Bauer); s of Willy Gegen-Bauer (d 1990), of Stuttgart, Germany, and Maria, Elizabeth, *née* Schuhbauer (d 1965); *b* 8 Nov 1937; *Educ* GS and HS Biberach Germany, Hotel Sch Heidelburg (Diploma); *Career* hotelier; mgmnt trg Hotel Rad Biberach Germany 1957–60; hotel trg: Lausanne and Geneva Switzerland 1961–62, Grand Hotel Eastbourne 1962–63, Grand Metropolitan Hotel London 1963–65; banqueting mgmnt trg Hilton International London 1965; various mgmnt positions Trust Houses 1965–69; gen mangr Trust House Forte: Red Lion Colchester 1969–71, Cairn Hotel Harrogate 1971–72, St George's Hotel Liverpool 1972–75, Hyde Park Hotel 1975–80; exec dir and gen mangr Grosvenor House Park Lane 1980–81, gen mangr The Savoy London 1982–83, md The Savoy Management Ltd (The Savoy, The Lygon Arms, Wiltons Restaurant) 1983–89, chief exec Wentworth Group 1989–; dir: The Berkeley Scott Group, Messenger Group Ltd, Molton Brown, Wiltons Restaurant, The Vanderbilt Racquet Club, Mosimann's Ltd; European Hotelier of the Year 1985, Hotel of the Year Award 1988; Freeman City of London 1987; memb: Master Innholders 1987, Chaine de Rotisseurs, Reunion des Gastronomes, Savoy Gastronomes, Bd of Friends Univ of Surrey Food & Wine Soc 1986, RAGB 1990; FHCIMA 1987, FRSA 1993; *Recreations* music, theatre, sport, gardening, architecture, design, antiques; *Clubs* The Duke's 100–1990, Wentworth Golf, One Ninety Queens Gate; *Style—* Willy Bauer, Esq; ✉ Wentworth Group Holdings, Wentworth Drive, Virginia Water, Surrey GU25 4LS (☎ 01344 845216, fax 01344 845415)

BAUGHAN, Julian James; QC (1990); s of Prof Edward Christopher Baughan, CBE (d 1995), and Jacqueline Baughan; *b* 8 Feb 1944; *Educ* Eton, Balliol Coll Oxford (scholar, BA); *Career* called to the Bar Inner Temple 1967 (Profumo scholar, Philip Teichman scholar, maj scholar); prosecuting counsel DTI 1983–90, recorder of the Crown Court 1985–; *Style—* Julian Baughan, Esq, QC; ✉ 13 Kings Bench Walk, Temple, London EC4Y 7EN (☎ 0171 353 7204)

BAUGHAN, Michael Christopher; s of Prof Edward Christopher Baughan, CBE (d 1995), and Jacqueline Fors, *née* Hodge (d 1986); *b* 25 April 1942; *Educ* Westminster; *m* 1975, Moira Elizabeth, da of Percy Reginald Levy, MBE; 2 s (James b 1977, Nicholas b 1979); *Career* N M Rothschild & Sons 1959–66; Lazard Brothers & Co Ltd: joined 1966, dir 1979–86, md 1986–; non-exec dir: Goode Durrant plc 1987–, Scapa Group plc 1994–, Independent Insurance Group 1996–; memb: Bd of Govrs Westminster Sch 1980–, Slrs Disciplinary Tbnl 1990–; *Clubs* Brooks's; *Style—* Michael C Baughan, Esq; ✉ Lazard Brothers & Co Ltd, 21 Moorfields, London EC2P 2HT (☎ 0171 588 2721, fax 0171 628 2485)

BAUGHEN, Rt Rev Michael Alfred; s of Alfred Henry Baughen (d 1956), and Clarice Adelaide Baughen (d 1986); *b* 7 June 1930; *Educ* Bromley Co GS, Univ of London, Oak Hill Theol Coll (BD); *m* 1956, Myrtle Newcomb Phillips; 2 s, 1 da; *Career* served in Royal Signals 1948–50; with Martins Bank 1946–48 and 1950–51; ordained: deacon 1956, priest 1957; curate: Nottingham 1956–59, Reigate 1959–61; candidates sec Church Pastoral Aid Soc 1961–64, rector Holy Trinity Rusholme 1964–70, vicar All Souls Langham Place 1970–75 (next to Broadcasting House and whence BBC transmitted daily services), rector 1975–82, area dean St Marylebone 1978–82, prebendary St Paul's 1979–82, bishop of Chester 1982–96, ret; memb Gen Synod 1975–; Hon LLD Univ of Liverpool 1994; *Style—* The Rt Rev Michael Baughen; ✉ 99 Brunswick Quay, London SE16 1PX

BAUM, Prof (John) David; s of Isidor Baum (d 1980), and Mary, *née* Rosenberg (d 1974); bro of Prof Harold Baum, *qv*, and Prof Michael Baum, *qv*; *b* 23 July 1940; *Educ* Univ of Birmingham (MB ChB, MD), Univ of Glasgow (DCh), Univ of London (MSc), Univ of Oxford (MA); *m* 5 Jan 1967, Angela Rose Goschalk; 4 s (Benjamin b 1970, Joshua b 1971, Jacob b 1974, Samuel Alexander b 1980); *Career* RMO Birmingham Children's Hosp 1965; Hammersmith Hosp: neonatal resident 1967, paediatric registrar 1968, sr registrar paediatrics 1970; Univ of Oxford: lectr 1972, clinical reader in paediatrics 1974–85, professorial fell St Catherine's Coll 1977; hon conslt in paediatrics Oxfordshire Health Authy; Univ of Bristol: prof of child health 1985–, founding dir Inst of Child Health 1988–; visiting prof: Univ of Colorado Med Center 1969, Med Coll of S Africa 1982, Hadassah Hosp and Med Sch Jerusalem and West Bank Hosps Israel 1985, Royal Children's Hosp and Monash Med Centre Melbourne Australia 1987; Dozor professorship Ben Gurion Univ of the Negev Israel 1988–89, Frolich professorship Royal Soc of Med NY USA 1989; external examiner med schs in England, Ireland, Sweden, Hong Kong and Addis Ababa, Ethiopia since 1976; pres Coll of Paediatrics and Child Health (formerly British Paediatric Assoc) 1997– (dir Res Unit 1993–); founding chm Nat Assoc for Care of Children with Life Threatening Diseases and their Families 1990–; chm: British Assoc of Community Child Health 1991–94, Research Advsy Ctee Winnicott Research Unit 1992– (chm 1993–); tstee Bristol Family Conciliation Serv, guardian Helen House Oxford, patron Children's Hospice South West; memb numerous nat and int ctees and scientific socs; inventor: Silver Swaddler 1968, Human Milk Pasteuriser 1976; BPA Guthrie medal 1976, Prix de la Vulgarisation Medicale 1981; FRCP 1977 (MRCP 1966); *Books* Clinical Paediatric Physiology (with S Godfrey, 1979), Human Milk Processing, Fractionation and Nutrition of the Low Birth Weight Baby (with A F Williams, 1984), Care of the Child with Diabetes (with A L Kinmonth, 1985), Child Health - The Complete Guide (with S Graham-Jones, 1989), Listen - My Child has a lot of Living to Do (with Mother F Dominica and R Woodward, 1990); memb editorial bds and contrib numerous papers to learned jls; *Recreations* visual arts, environmental affairs; *Style—* Prof David Baum; ✉ 19 Charlotte Street, Bristol BS1 5PZ (☎ 0117 926 0448); Institute of Child Health, Royal Hospital for Sick Children, St Michael's Hill, Bristol BS2 8BJ (☎ 0117 928 5383, fax 0117 925 5051)

BAUM, Prof Harold; s of Isidor Baum (d 1980), and Mary, *née* Rosenberg (d 1974); bro of Prof Michael Baum, *qv*, and Prof David Baum, *qv*; *b* 14 Nov 1930; *Educ* Halesowen GS Worcs, Univ of Birmingham (BSc, PhD); *m* 30 Oct 1962, Patricia Glenda, da of late Maj George Magrill, OBE, JP; a direct desc of The Marahil, Jacob Moelln, a great 14 C Rabbi; 1 s (David b 1964), 2 da (Mandy b 1967, Alison b 1969); *Career* prof of biochemistry Chelsea Coll London 1968–85; King's Coll London: head of Dept of Biochemistry and dean of Faculty of Life Scis 1987–89, head Sch of Life Basic Med and Health Scis 1989–94, prof emeritus and visiting prof 1996–; dir Taylor and Francis Group Ltd; radio and TV broadcaster; chm Professional and Educnl Ctee Biochemical Soc 1981–95, chm of govrs S Thames Coll 1983–87, memb Cncl Glynn Research Fndn, tstee Nuffield Chelsea Curriculum Tst, memb Prog Ctee Edinburgh Int Science Festival 1992–; treas Internal Fedn of Scientists for Soviet Refuseniks, govr Ben Gurion Univ Israel; FRSC, CChem, FIBiol (memb Cncl 1993–), CBiol, FKC 1994; *Recreations* grandchildren, travel, fishing, songwriting, bridge; *Clubs* Roehampton, Royal Society of Medicine; *Style—* Prof Harold Baum; ✉ Yew Trees, 356 Dover House Rd, London SW15 5BL (☎ 0181 789 9352, 0181 788 2471); King's College London; Campden Hill Rd, London W8 7AH (☎ and fax 0171 333 4103, e-mail harold.baum@kcl.ac.uk)

BAUM, Louis Clarence; s of Rudolf Josef Baum (d 1984), and Heather, *née* Shulman; *b* 15 March 1948; *Educ* SA Coll Sch, Univ of Cape Town (BA); *m* 1971 (m dis 1982), Stephanie, *née* Goodman; 1 s (Simon b 1979); *Career* author of children's books; journalist Cape Times 1979–84; The Bookseller: ed 1980–, journalist 1986–; dir J Whitaker & Sons; *Books* JuJu and the Pirate (1983), I Want to see the Moon (1984), After Dark (1984), Are We Nearly There? (1986), Joey's Coming Home Today (1989);

Recreations writing; *Clubs* The Groucho (dir 1984–); *Style*— Louis Baum, Esq; ✉ J Whitaker & Sons Ltd, 12 Dyott St, London WC1A 1DF (☎ 0171 420 6000, fax 0171 836 6381)

BAUM, Prof Michael; s of Isidor Baum (d 1980), and Mary, *née* Rosenberg (d 1974); bro of Prof Harold Baum, *qv*, and Prof David Baum, *qv*; *b* 31 May 1937; *Educ* George Dixon's GS Birmingham, Univ of Birmingham Medical Sch (MB ChB, ChM); *m* 12 Sept 1965, Judith, da of Reuben Marcus, of Newcastle upon Tyne; 1 s (Richard b 20 Sept 1966), 2 da (Katie b 19 April 1969, Suzanne b 22 March 1973); *Career* lectr in surgery King's Coll London 1969–72, sr lectr in surgery (later reader) Welsh Nat Sch of Medicine 1972–79, prof of surgery King's Coll Sch of Medicine and Dentistry 1980–90, hon dir Cancer Res Campaign Clinical Trials Centre 1980–, prof of surgery Inst of Cancer Res Royal Marsden Hosp 1990–95, visiting prof UCL 1995–; memb: UK Coordinating Ctee for Cancer Res 1989– (chm Breast Cancer Sub Ctee), Advsy Ctee on Breast Cancer Screening Dept of Health 1987–95; chm SE Thames Regnl Cancer Orgn 1988–90, vice pres Euro Society of Mastology 1991–, pres Br Oncological Assoc 1996–; past chm: Br Breast Gp, Higher Degrees Ctee Univ of London (vice chm Bd of Studies in Surgery); Skinner medal Royal Coll of Radiologists 1990; Hon Doctorate of Medicine Univ of Gotenberg 1986; FRCS 1965, Int Master Surgn Int Coll of Surgns 1994; *Books* Breast Cancer The Facts (1984, 3 edn 1994); *Recreations* painting, sculpture, theatre, literature, philosophy, food, wine, skiing; *Clubs* Athenaeum, Royal Soc of Medicine, Chelsea Arts; *Style*— Prof Michael Baum; ✉ Consultant Surgeon, Royal Marsden Hospital, Fulham Road, London SW3 (☎ 0171 352 8171, fax 0171 351 5410)

BAVIDGE, Elizabeth Mary (Liz); OBE (1997), JP (1979); da of Walter Robert Ashton (d 1972), and Mary Newton, *née* Donaldson (d 1986); *b* 24 Aug 1945; *Educ* Carlisle & Co HS for Girls, Univ of Newcastle upon Tyne (BA); *m* 1972, Nigel Patrick Bavidge, s of Dr Kenneth George Scott Bavidge (d 1972); 2 c (Gabrielle Mary b 1972, Fintan Nicholas Ashton b 1975); *Career* graduate trainee Shell-Mex & BP Ltd 1967–72, pt/t lectr in English language and literature Percival Whitley Coll 1980–87, asst princ Airedale & Wharfedale Coll Leeds 1992 (lectr in flexible learning opportunities 1987–92); nat pres Nat Cncl of Women 1990–92 (nat vice pres 1988–90), currently co-chair Women's Nat Cmmn; dir EM Associates (orgn devpt conslts); chair Yorks and Humberside Fair Play Consortium; FRSA (memb Working Gp on Early Educn); *Books* Let's Talk to God (1980); *Recreations* playing the piano, making bread, speaking French, eating; *Style*— Mrs Liz Bavidge, OBE, JP; ✉ 22 Savile Park, Halifax, W Yorkshire HX1 3EW (☎ 01422 353955, fax 01422 330586)

BAVIN, Rt Rev Timothy John; s of Edward Sydney Durrance Bavin, RASC (d 1979), and Marjorie Gwendoline, *née* Dew; *b* 17 Sept 1935; *Educ* St George's Sch Windsor Castle, Brighton Coll, Worcester Coll Oxford, Cuddesdon Coll Oxford; *Career* Nat Serv RASC 1957–59, cmmnd 1958, Platoon Offr (2 Lt) 90 Co Aden 1958–59; curate St Alban's Cathedral Pretoria SA 1961–63, chaplain St Alban's Coll Pretoria 1963–69, curate Uckfield with Little Horsted 1969–71, vicar Parish of the Good Shepherd Brighton 1971–73, dean of Johannesburg and rector of the Cathedral Parish 1973–74, bishop of Johannesburg 1974–84, bishop of Portsmouth 1985–95, resigned; postulant OSB 1996; memb Oratory of the Good Shepherd 1987; Hon FRSCM 1991; *Books* Deacons in the Ministry of the Church (ed, 1988); *Recreations* music, victoriana, country life; *Style*— The Rt Rev Timothy Bavin

BAVISTER, Edward John; CBE (1988); s of Aubrey John Bavister (d 1974), of Herts, and Ethel, *née* Dennis; *b* 19 April 1933; *Educ* Berkhamsted Sch, St John's Coll Cambridge (MA); *m* 1958, Barbara Jean, da of Harold Foster (d 1973), of Cumbria; 3 da (Heather Jane b 1960, Anne Kirsten b 1962, Gillian Fiona b 1965); *Career* chartered engr; dep md John Brown plc 1987–93 (dir 1982–93); chm Morris Mechanical Handling Ltd 1992–; FEng 1989, FIChemE (pres 1992–93); *Recreations* sailing, walking, opera; *Clubs* Oriental; *Style*— Edward Bavister, Esq, CBE, FEng; ✉ Top Lock Cottage, Long Buckby Wharf, Northampton NN6 7PW (☎ 01327 843063, fax 01327 843817); Morris Mechanical Handling Ltd, PO Box 7, North Road, Loughborough LE11 1RL (☎ 01509 643200)

BAWDEN, Nina Mary (Mrs Austen Kark); *née* Mabey; CBE (1995); da of Cdr Charles Mabey (d 1976), and Ellaline Ursula May, *née* Cushing (d 1986); *b* 19 Jan 1925; *Educ* Ilford County HS for Girls, Somerville Coll Oxford (MA); *m* 1 Oct 1946 (m dis 1954), Henry Walton Bawden, s of Victor Bawden; 2 s (Robert Humphrey Felix b 1951, Nicholas Charles b 1948 d 1982); m 2, 5 Aug 1954, Austen Steven Kark, *qv*, s of Maj Norman Benjamin Kark, of East India Club, St James's Square, London; 1 da (Perdita Emily Helena b 1957); *Career* novelist; pres Soc of Women Writers & Journalists; JP Surrey 1969–76; memb: Video Appeals Ctee, PEN, Soc of Authors; FRSL; *Books* Devil by the Sea (1955), Just Like a Lady (1960), In Honour Bound (1961), Tortoise by Candlelight (1963), Under the Skin (1964), A Little Love, A Little Learning (1965), A Woman of My Age (1967), The Grain of Truth (1969), The Birds on the Trees (1970), Anna Apparent (1972), George Beneath a Paper Moon (1974), Afternoon of a Good Woman (1976, Yorkshire Post Novel of the Yr), Familiar Passions (1979), Walking Naked (1981), The Ice House (1983), Circles of Deceit (1987, Booker Shortlist 1987), Family Money (1991); *Autobiography* In My Own Time (1994); *For Children* The Secret Passage, On The Run, The Witch's Daughter, The White Horse Gang, A Handful of Thieves, Squib, Carrie's War (Phoenix Award 1994), The Peppermint Pig, The Finding, Keeping Henry, The Outside Child, Humbug (1992), The Real Plato Jones (1994, WH Short List - Mind Boggling Read, Young Telegraph Short List), Granny the Pag (Carnegie Medal Shortlist, 1996); *Recreations* food, films, theatre, travel, politics, garden croquet; *Clubs* Groucho, Oriental; *Style*— Miss Nina Bawden, CBE, FRSL; ✉ 22 Noel Road, London N1 8HA (☎ 0171 226 2839); 19 Kapodistriou, Nauplion, Greece

BAXANDALL, Prof Michael David Kighley; s of David Kighley Baxandall (d 1993), and Sarah Isobel Mary, *née* Thomas (d 1990); *b* 18 Aug 1933; *Educ* Manchester GS, Downing Coll Cambridge (MA), Univ of Pavia, Univ of Munich, Warburg Inst Univ of London (jr fell); *m* 1963, Katharina Dorothea, da of late Sir Francis Simon; 1 da (Sarah Lucy b 1963), 1 s (Thomas David Franz b 1968); *Career* asst keeper Dept of Architecture and Sculpture V&A Museum 1961–65; Warburg Inst: lectr in renaissance studies 1965–72, reader in history of the classical tradition 1973–80, prof of history of the classical tradition 1981–88; prof of history of art Univ of California at Berkeley 1986–; Slade prof of fine art Univ of Oxford 1974–75, A D White prof-at-large Cornell Univ 1982–88, fell Wissenschaftskolleg Berlin 1992–93; hon fell Warburg Inst 1988, Aby M Warburg prize City of Hamburg 1988, fell MacArthur Fndn 1988–93; FAAAS 1990, FBA 1982; *Books* Giotto and the Orators (1971), Painting and Experience in Fifteenth-Century Italy (1972), The Limewood Sculptors of Renaissance Germany (1980), Patterns of Intention (1985), Tiepolo and the Pictorial Intelligence (with Svetlana Alpers, 1994), Shadows and Enlightenment (1995); *Style*— Prof Michael Baxandall, FBA

BAXENDALE, Thomas Dawtrey; s of Hugo Lloyd Baxendale, JP (d 1957), of Chidmere House, Chidham, W Sussex, and Eleanor Sibyl Mitford, *née* Oliver (d 1968); *b* 7 April 1937; *Educ* Eton; *Career* 2 Lt Welsh Gds 1957–58; called to the Bar Inner Temple 1962; in practice in Chancery 1963–, barr Lincoln's Inn 1967, underwriting memb Lloyd's 1970–, memb Syndicate 89 Ctee 1984–89, memb Syndicate 384 Ctee 1992–; memb Ct Corp of Sons of the Clergy 1972– (treas 1994–); *Recreations* gardening, art, travel; *Clubs* Pratt's; *Style*— Thomas Baxendale, Esq; ✉ Chidmere House, Chidham, Chichester, West Sussex; 24 Old Buildings, Lincoln's Inn, London WC2A 3UJ (☎ 0171 404 0946, fax 0171 405 1360)

BAXENDELL, Sir Peter Brian; kt (1981), CBE (1972); s of Lesley Wilfred Edward Baxendell (d 1968), and Evelyn Mary, *née* Gaskin; *b* 28 Feb 1925; *Educ* St Francis Xavier's Liverpool, Royal Sch of Mines (ARSM, BSc); *m* 1949, Rosemary, da of Herbert Leo Lacey; 2 s, 2 da; *Career* dir Shell Transport and Trading Co plc 1973–95 (chm 1979–85), chm Ctee of Managing Dirs Royal Dutch Shell Gp of Cos 1982–85; dir: Hawker Siddeley Group plc 1984–91 (chm 1986–91), Inchcape PLC 1986–93, Sun Life Assurance Co of Canada 1986–; memb Univ Grants Ctee 1983–89; Cdr of the Order of Orange-Nassau 1985; Hon DSc: Heriot-Watt Univ 1982, Queen's Univ of Belfast 1986, Univ of London 1986, Loughborough Univ of Technology 1987; FEng 1978, fell Imperial Coll London 1983; *Recreations* tennis, fishing; *Clubs* Hurlingham; *Style*— Sir Peter Baxendell, CBE, FEng

BAXI, Vibhaker Kishore; s of Kishore Jayantilal Baxi (d 1967), and Indira Kishore Baxi; *b* 25 Dec 1947; *Educ* Brooklands Co Tech Coll Surrey, Univ of Surrey Guildford (BSc), Brunel Univ Uxbridge (PGCE), Manchester Business Sch (MBA); *m* 12 Nov 1978, Hina, da of Indulal Vaikunthrai Vaidya, of India; 1 da (Mamta b 1982); *Career* fin inst account offr Citibank Dubai 1975–76, asst treas Citibank NA Dubai 1976–78; treas: Citibank NA Bahrain 1979–80, Chemical Bank Hong Kong 1981–85; head and md Money Mkt & Securities Trading Chemical Bank London 1985–89, sr risk mangr (interest rates) Hongkong & Shanghai Banking Corpn London 1989, jt md James Capel Gilts Ltd (HSBC subsid) 1991–92, global mangr money markets (UK, North and South America, Japan) HongkongBank/Midland Group 1992–93; chm and md Navras Records (PVT) Ltd 1992–, risk mgmnt conslt and investment mangr; *Style*— Vibhaker Baxi, Esq; ✉ 22 Sherwood Rd, London NW4 1AD (☎ 0181 203 1503, fax 0181 203 2553)

BAXTER, Glen; s of Charles Bertie Baxter (d 1993), of Leeds, and Florence Mary, *née* Wood (d 1988); *b* 4 March 1944; *Educ* Cockburn HS Leeds, Leeds Coll of Art (NDD); *m* Carole Agis; 1 s (Harry b 1978), 1 da (Zoë b 1975); *Career* artist; pt/t lectr Goldsmiths' Coll London 1974–87, Glen Baxter Ceramics launched (by Poole Pottery) 1996; exhibitions: Gotham Book Mart Gallery NY 1974, 1976 and 1979, Fuller Goldeen San Francisco 1986, ICA London 1981, Museum of Modern Art Oxford 1981, Nigel Greenwood 1981, 1983, 1987 and 1990, Galleria Del Cavallino Venice 1984, Royal Festival Hall 1984, Holly Solomon Gallery NY 1985 and 1988, Sydney Biennale 1986, Saouma Gallery Paris 1987 1989 and 1993, Musée de L'Abbaye Sainte-Croix Les Sables D'Olonne 1987, MUHKA Antwerp 1988, DC Art Sydney Australia 1990, Adelaide Festival 1992, Michael Nagy Gallery Sydney 1992, Anthony Wilkinson Fine Art London 1994, Ginza Art Space Tokyo 1994, Artothèque de Caen France 1995, Michael Nagy Fine Art Sydney 1996, Le Salon d'Art Brussels 1996, Anthony Wilkinson Fine Art London 1996; *Books* The Impending Gleam (1981), Atlas (1982), His Life (1983), Jodhpurs in the Quantocks (1987), Charles Malarkey and the Belly Button Machine (with William and Bren Kennedy), Welcome to the Weird World of Glen Baxter (1989), The Billiard Table Murders - A Gladys Babbington Morton Mystery (1990), Glen Baxter Returns to Normal (1992), The Collected Blurtings of Baxter (1993), The Wonder Book of Sex (1995); *Recreations* croquet, marquetry and stump work; *Clubs* Chelsea Arts, Groucho, Ale and Quail; *Style*— Glen Baxter, Esq; ✉ Aitken & Stone, 29 Fernshaw Road, London SW10 0TG (☎ 0171 351 7561)

BAXTER, Dr (William) Gordon; OBE (1964), DL (Morayshire 1985); s of William Alexander Baxter (d 1973), of Fochabers, Moray, and Ethelreda, *née* Adam (d 1963); *b* 8 Feb 1918; *Educ* Ashville Coll Harrogate, Univ of Aberdeen (BSc); *m* 26 Sept 1952, Euphemia Ellen (Ena), da of Thomas William Robertson (d 1955), of Castlepark, Huntly; 2 s (Andrew b 1958, Michael b 1962), 1 da (Audrey b 1961); *Career* res and devpt mangr ICI Explosives Ltd 1940–45; returned to family business W A Baxter & Sons Ltd: prodn dir 1946, md 1947, chm and md 1973; pres: W A Baxters & Sons Ltd, Scottish International Register Ltd (part of SBAAT); former chm Grampian Food Technology Centre Ltd, former dir Grampian Regnl Bd of Bank of Scotland; memb: Scot Cncl for Devpt and Indust, Cncl Royal Warrant Holders' Assoc, Aberdeen Assoc of Royal Warrant Holders, Cncl Food Mfrs' Fedn, N American Advsy Gp to the BOTB; Hon LLD: Univ of Strathclyde 1987, Univ of Aberdeen 1995; Hon DBA Napier Univ 1994; MInstD 1970, FIGD 1983; *Recreations* fishing; *Clubs* Caledonian; *Style*— Dr Gordon Baxter, OBE, DL; ✉ Speybank House, Fochabers, Morayshire IV32 7HH (☎ 01343 821234); W A Baxter & Sons Ltd, Fochabers, Morayshire IV32 7LD (☎ 01343 820393, fax 01343 820286, telex 73327)

BAXTER, Maj-Gen Ian Stuart; CBE (1982, MBE 1973); s of Charles Henry Baxter (d 1972), of Pendle, nr Nelson, Lancs, and Edith May, *née* Trinder; *b* 20 July 1937; *Educ* Ottershaw Sch; *m* 19 Aug 1961, Meg Lillian, da of Ronald Bullock, of Pensnett, Brierly Hill, Staffs; 3 da (Deborah b 1962, Louise b 1964, Marianna b 1971); *Career* cmmnd RASC 1958, regtl duty in UK, Kenya, India, NI (2 Lt, Capt) 1958–69, Staff Coll Camberley (Maj) 1970, DAA and QMG 8 Inf Bde Londonderry 1971–73, OC 60 Sqdn RCT 1973–74, NDC 1974–75, GSO 1 DS Staff Coll Camberley (Lt-Col) 1975–78, CO 2 Armd Div Tport Regt RCT 1978–80, Col AQ Commando Forces RM and Col Station Cdr Plymouth (incl Falklands campaign) 1980–84, RCDS 1984, Brig dir army recruiting MOD 1985–87, Maj-Gen ACDS (L) MOD 1987–90; chm Euro Log/Euro Group 1987–90; Col Cmdt RCT 1989, ret 1990, representative Col Cmdt RCT 1992–93; antique dealer 1990–; non-exec dir Cornwall Community Health Care Tst 1991–93, vice chm Cornwall Healthcare Tst 1993–95, mangr Mental Health Act (Cornwall) 1995–; chm RASC/RCI Inst 1993–; *Recreations* antique restoration, gardening; *Style*— Maj-Gen Ian S Baxter, CBE; ✉ c/o Barclays Bank, 50 Fore St, Callington, Cornwall PL17 7AQ

BAXTER, John Stephen; s of George Arthur Baxter (d 1972), and Constance Muriel, *née* Firman (d 1989); *b* 7 Sept 1939; *Educ* Magdalen Coll Sch Oxford, Grey Coll Durham (Univ Hockey, memb GB Olympic Hockey squad, capt English Univs cricket), Merton Coll Oxford; *m* 7 Aug 1965, Priscilla, da of Percival George Candy; 2 s (Jonathan Mark b 14 May 1967, Mark Simon b 25 Oct 1969); *Career* asst master: Cranleigh Sch Surrey 1964–67, Christ's Coll Christchurch NZ 1967–70; Westminster Sch: asst master 1971–86, head of history 1974–79, housemaster 1979–86; headmaster Wells Cathedral Sch 1986–; res asst House of Commons 1971–79, reader in history for Edward Arnold 1971–86, memb Admiralty Interview Bd 1988–; chm Choir Schools' Assoc 1995–; Korea Fndn fell 1993, Frank Fisher scholar 1993; Freeman City of London 1991, memb Worshipful Co of Musicians 1992; MIMgt 1991, FRSA 1990; *Books* Lords and Commons Cricket (contrib, 1989); *Recreations* music, cricket, Cornwall, fine wine; *Clubs* MCC, Vincent's (Oxford), East India, St Enodoc Golf; *Style*— John Baxter, Esq; ✉ Wells Cathedral School, Wells, Somerset BA5 2ST (☎ 01749 672117, fax 01749 670724)

BAXTER, Keith; s of Capt Stanley Baxter-Wright (d 1960), of Swansea, and Emily Marian, *née* Howell (d 1972); *b* 29 April 1933; *Educ* Newport HS, Barry GS, RADA (Bronze medal); *Career* actor; *Theatre* Oxford Repertory Co (Playhouse Oxford) 1956, London debut as Ralph in Tea & Sympathy (Comedy Theatre) 1957, Hippolytus in Phedre (Stephen Joseph's in the Round) 1957, Jean Pierre in Change of Tune (Strand) 1959, Prince Hal in Chimes at Midnight (Opera House Belfast) 1960, Roger in Time and Yellow Roses (St Martin's) 1961, King Henry VIII in A Man for All Seasons (Anta Theatre NY) 1961, Howard in The Affair (Henry Miller's Theatre NY) 1962, Gino in Where Angels Fear To Tread (St Martin's) 1963, Inspector in Torpe's Hotel (Yvonne Arnaud Theatre Guildford) 1965, Valentine in You Can Never Tell (Haymarket) 1966, Bob Acres in The Rivals (Haymarket) 1966, Baldo in Avanti (Booth Theatre NY) 1968, Horner in The Country Wife (Chichester) 1969, Octavius Caesar in Antony & Cleopatra (Chichester) 1969, Milo in Sleuth (St Martin's and Music Box Theatre NY) 1970, title role in Macbeth (Birmingham Repertory 1972, Vershinin in Three Sisters (Greenwich) 1973, Benedick in Much Ado About Nothing (Lyceum Edinburgh) 1973, Rico in Tonight We Improvise (Chichester) 1974, Antony in Antony & Cleopatra and Witwoud in The Way of the World and Vershinin in Three Sisters (Stratford Ontario) 1976, King in Red Devil Battery Sign (Phoenix) 1977, Lord Illingworth in A Woman of No Importance and Dorante in The Inconstant Couple (Chichester) 1978, Patrick in A Meeting By the River (Palace Theatre NY) 1979, Bill in Home and Beauty (Kennedy Centre) 1979, title role in Hamlet (Citadel Theatre Edmonton Canada) 1979, Ken in Whose Life is it Anyway? (US tour) 1979, Sherlock Holmes in the Penultimate Case of Sherlock Holmes (Hudson Guild NY) 1980, Jason Carmichael in Romantic Comedy (Barrymore Theatre NY) 1980, Frederick in Undiscovered Country and Antony in Antony & Cleopatra and Kean in Kean (Hartford Stage Co) 1981, Gwilym in 56 Duncan Terrace (Citadel Theatre Edmonton Canada) 1982, Narrator in Oedipus Rex (Philadelphia Opera) 1982, Antony in Antony & Cleopatra (Young Vic) 1983, Evelyn and Rupert in Corpse (Apollo 1984, Helen Hayes Theatre NY 1985 and Footbridge Theatre Sydney Aust 1986), Carleton in Light Up the Sky (Globe) 1987, Dafydd in Barnaby and The Old Boys (Vaudeville) 1989, Elyot in Private Lives (Aldwych) 1990, Cassius in Julius Caesar (Hartford Stage Co USA) 1991, The Duke in Measure for Measure (Shakespeare Theatre Washington DC) 1992, Louis Jouvet in Elvira 40 (Chichester) 1993; dir: Red Devil Battery Sign 1977, Time and The Conways 1988, Rope (Chichester) 1993 and (Wyndhams) 1994, Dangerous Corner (Chichester 1994, Whitehall 1995 (also acted role of Robert), Gaslight (tour) 1995, Measure for Measure (Shakespeare Theatre Washington DC) 1996; author of plays: 56 Duncan Terrace (1982), Cavell (1982), Barnaby & The Old Boys (1989); *Television* Young May Moon 1958, Man and Superman 1958, Incident at Echo Six 1958, Dead Secret 1959, Sweet Poison 1959, After the Party 1960, Square Dance 1960, Jealousy 1962, Rewards of Silence 1963, For Tea on Sunday 1963, Nobody Kills Santa Claus 1964, I've Got A System 1964, Curtains For Sheila 1965, St Joan 1966, Love Story 1966, Shakespeare 1976, Six Characters in Search of an Author 1992; *Films* The Barretts of Wimpole St 1956, Peeping Tom 1958, Chimes At Midnight 1967, Love in Mind 1968, Ash Wednesday 1973, La Regenta 1974, Berlin Blues 1989; *Radio* King Arthur in Arthur the King 1990; *Awards* Theatre World Award NY 1961, Drama Desk Award NY 1972, NY Outer Circle Critics' Award 1972; *Recreations* the sea; *Style*— Keith Baxter, Esq; ✉ c/o ICM Ltd, Oxford House, 76 Oxford Street, London W1N 0AX (☎ 0171 636 6565, fax 0171 323 0101)

BAXTER, Margaret Eleanor (Maggie); da of Charles Frank Alexander Baxter, JP, of Shaftesbury, Dorset, and Eleanor Frances Mary, *née* Bloomer; *b* 7 July 1947; *Educ* Godolphin Sch Wiltshire, Open Univ (BA); *m* 1 (m dis); *ptnr* (common law husband), George Sean Baine, s of Roney Baine (d 1988), of Belfast; 1 s (Alex b 13 May 1981), 1 da (Holly b 30 Jan 1985), 2 step s (Jack b 10 Feb 1972, Kieran b 25 May 1974); *Career* project dir Action Res Centre 1972–75, dir Dame Colet House Settlement Stepney 1975–80, vol orgns offr London Borough of Camden 1982–89, advsr Baring Fndn 1989–91; Charity Projects: grants dir (UK) 1991–94, grants dir (UK & Africa) 1994–; tstee and chair Tst for London, tstee City Parochial Fndn, govr Beckford Sch; *Recreations* family, theatre, cinema, tennis; *Style*— Ms Maggie Baxter; ✉ 40 Hillfield Rd, London NW6 1PZ (☎ 0171 794 2636); Charity Projects - Comic Relief, 74 New Oxford Street, London WC1A 1EF (☎ 0171 436 1122)

BAXTER, Prof Murdoch Scott; s of John Sawyers Napier Baxter (d 1977), and Margaret Hastie, *née* Murdoch; *b* 12 March 1944; *Educ* Hutchesons' Boys' GS, Univ of Glasgow (BSc, PhD); *m* 3 Aug 1968, Janice, da of James Henderson (d 1990), of Shawlands, Glasgow; 1 foster s (John b 1969); *Career* visiting res fell (Apollo 11 Lunar Res) NY State Univ 1969–70, sabbatical res conslt IAEA International Laboratory of Marine Radioactivity Monaco (radioactive waste disposal) 1981–82; Univ of Glasgow: lectr in environmental radiochemistry Dept of Chemistry 1970–85, prof 1985–, dir Scottish Univ Res and Reactor Centre 1985–90; dir IAEA Marine Environment Laboratory Monaco 1990–; memb: Challenger Soc, Scottish Assoc for Marine Science, NERC COGER Ctee, various IAEA expert gps, Editorial Bd Journal of Radioanalytical and Nuclear Chemistry; fndr ed Journal of Environmental Radioactivity (Elsevier Sci Pubn); author of more than 160 res papers in scientific lit; CChem, FRSC 1984, FRSE 1989; *Recreations* sports, walking; *Clubs* Queens Park FC, Auld Alliance; *Style*— Prof Murdoch Baxter, FRSE; ✉ IAEA, Marine Environment Laboratory, BP 800, Principality of Monaco, MC 98012 (☎ 00 377 92 05 22 22, fax 00 377 92 05 77 44, telex 479378 ILMR, e-mail BAXTER@UNICE.FR)

BAXTER, Dr Roger George; s of Rev Benjamin George Baxter (d 1994), and Gweneth Muriel, *née* Causer (d 1989); *b* 21 April 1940; *Educ* Handsworth GS Birmingham, Univ of Sheffield (BSc, PhD); *m* 1967, Dorothy Ann, da of Albert Leslie Cook (d 1949); 1 s (Philip b 1968), 1 da (Fiona b 1972); *Career* lectr Dept of Applied Mathematics Univ of Sheffield 1966–70 (jr res fell 1965–66), under master Winchester Coll 1976–81 (asst mathematics master 1970–81), headmaster Sedbergh Sch 1982–95, conslt in educn (Select Consultants, Select Education) 1995–; govr: Bramcote Sch Scarborough 1982–95, Hurworth House Sch Darlington 1982–95, Mowden Hall Sch Northumberland 1984–, The Cathedral Choir Sch Ripon 1984–95, Cundall Manor Sch York 1988–, Durham Sch 1995–; memb: HMC Academic Policy Ctee 1985–90, Common Entrance Bd 1989–94, Cartmel Priory PCC and Deanery Synod 1996–; Freeman City of London 1992, Liveryman Worshipful Co of Gunmakers 1992; FRAS; *Publications* author of various papers on numerical studies in magnetoplasm diffusion with applications to the F-2 layer of the ionosphere, incl contrib to Proceedings of the Royal Society; *Recreations* production of opera, opera, music, cooking, wine; *Clubs* Royal Scottish Automobile; *Style*— Dr Roger Baxter; ✉ The Rivelin, Lindale, Grange-over-Sands, Cumbria LA11 6LJ (☎ and fax 01539 535129)

BAXTER, (Andrew) Travis; s of Bill Baxter, of E Coker, Somerset, and Anne, *née* Whittaker; *b* 26 Sept 1957; *Educ* Yeovil GS, Yeovil Coll, Plymouth Poly; *Career* bdcaster Capital 604 Radio S Africa 1979–80, bdcaster Devonair Radio Exeter 1980–82, prodr BBC Local Radio and BBC Radio 2 1982–87; Atlantic 252: gen mangr 1987–92, md 1992–, chm Atlantic 252 UK; md: CLT UK Radio Ltd, Talk Radio UK Ltd; *Style*— Travis Baxter, Esq; ✉ CLT UK Radio Ltd, 74 Newman Street, London W1P 3LA (☎ 0171 436 6363, fax 0171 436 4017)

BAXTER-WRIGHT, Keith; *see:* Baxter, Keith

BAYFIELD, Rabbi Anthony Michael (Tony); s of Ronald David Bayfield, of 45 Vista Drive, Redbridge, Ilford, Essex, and Sheila Queenie, *née* Mann; *b* 4 July 1946; *Educ* Royal Liberty Sch Gidea Park, Magdalene Coll Cambridge (MA), Leo Baeck Coll London (Rabbinic ordination); *m* 3 Aug 1969, Linda Gavinia, da of Hyman Rose (d 1976); 1 s (Daniel b 1975), 2 da (Lucy b 1972, Miriam b 1979); *Career* rabbi NW Surrey Synagogue 1972–82; chief exec Reform Synagogues of Great Britain and The Reform Movement 1994–; lectr Leo Baeck Coll 1973–; dir: The Sternberg Centre for Judaism 1983–, Manor House Tst 1983–, Advancement of Jewish Educn Tst 1986–; cnsllr Spelthorne MGC 1973–82; chm: Assembly of Rabbis Reform Synagogues of GB 1980–81, Cncl of Reform and Lib Rabbis 1983–85; tstee Michael Goulston Educnl Fndn; fndr ed Manna (quarterly jl) 1983–; *Books* Prejudice (1974), Churban - The Murder of the Jews of Europe (1982), Dialogue with a Difference (ed with Marcus Braybrooke, 1992), Sinai, Law and Responsible Autonomy: Reform Judaism and the Halakhic Tradition (1993); *Recreations* family, reading, walking, watching cricket and football; *Style*— Rabbi Tony Bayfield; ✉ The Sternberg Centre for Judaism, The Manor House, 80 East End Road, Finchley, London N3 2SY (☎ 0181 346 2288, fax 0181 343 0901)

BAYFIELD, Stephen Peter; s of Stanley William Henry Bayfield, of Harlow, and Eileen Lilian, *née* Sears; *b* 21 May 1954; *Educ* Brays Grove Harlow; *m* 20 July 1974, Margaret Anne, da of Edwin Stanley Barrett, of Brockholes, nr Huddersfield; 2 s (Richard b 1981, Mark b 1986), 1 da (Sarah b 1983); *Career* Inland Revenue 1976–78, Frazer Whiting & Co CA's 1978–81, ptnr Robson Rhodes 1985–94 (joined 1981), dir British Bus plc 1994–; memb Inst of Taxation 1979; *Recreations* athletics, swimming; *Style*— Stephen Bayfield, Esq; ✉ British Bus plc, 54 Endless Street, Salisbury, Wiltshire SP1 3UH (☎ 01722 413323, fax 01722 326590)

BAYLEY, Prof Frederick John (Fred); s of Frederick John Bayley (d 1974), of Greenhithe, Kent, and Kate, *née* Dalley (d 1967); *b* 30 July 1928; *Educ* Gravesend GS, King's Coll Newcastle, Univ of Durham (BSc, MSc, PhD, DSc); *m* 1 April 1950, Norma June, da of Robert Ferguson (d 1969), of Whitley Bay, Northumberland; 2 s (Robert b 1952, Keith b 1963), 1 da (Janette (Mrs Clark) b 1956); *Career* scientific offr Nat Gas Turbine Estab Farnborough 1948–51, res engr Pametrada Res Station Wallsend 1951–53; Univ of Durham (later Newcastle): James Clayton res fell in mechanical engrg 1953–55, lectr then reader in mechanical engrg 1955–65; Univ of Sussex: prof of mechanical engrg 1966–93, dean of engrg 1979–80, pro vice chllr (sci) 1980–85, sr pro vice chllr 1988–92, prof emeritus 1993–; memb: Aeronautical Res Cncl 1965–75, Def Scientific Advsy Ctee 1977–81; FIMechE 1966; *Books* Introduction to Fluid Dynamics (1958), Heat Transfer (with J M Owen and A B Turner, 1972), numerous scientific and tech papers; *Recreations* photography, walking; *Clubs* Athenaeum; *Style*— Prof Fred Bayley; ✉ Camberley, Firle Rd, Seaford, E Sussex (☎ 01323 490024); University of Sussex, Falmer, Brighton, E Sussex (☎ 01273 606755)

BAYLEY, Gordon Vernon; CBE (1976); s of Capt Vernon Bayley (d 1949), and Gladys Maud, *née* Sharp (d 1985); *b* 25 July 1920; *Educ* Abingdon Sch Oxon; *m* 25 Aug 1945, (Miriam Allenby) Theresa, da of Frederick Walter Ellis (d 1959); 1 s (Mark b 1960), 2 da (Angela b 1946, Susan b 1948); *Career* joined HM Forces 1940, cmmnd RA, Maj 1945; asst actuary Equitable Life Assurance Society 1949, ptnr Duncan C Fraser & Co 1954–57; National Provident Institution: asst sec 1957, jt sec 1959, gen mangr and actuary 1964–85, dir 1970–94; chm: Swiss Reinsurance Co (UK) Ltd 1985–92, Life Offices Association 1969–70; memb: Occupational Pensions Bd 1973–74, Steering Bd Companies House 1988–91, Ctee to Review Functioning of Fin Institutions 1977–80; chm Bd Govrs Abingdon Sch 1979–83; Freeman Worshipful Co of Insurers 1979; FIA 1946 (pres 1974–76, Gold Medal 1985), FSS 1947, FIMA 1976, CIMgt 1980; *Recreations* sailing; *Clubs* Athenaeum, English Speaking Union, Sea View Yacht; *Style*— Gordon Bayley, Esq, CBE; ✉ The Old Manor, Witley, Surrey GU8 5QW (☎ and fax 01428 682301)

BAYLEY, Hugh; MP (Lab) York (majority 6,342); s of Michael Bayley, and Pauline Bayley; *b* 9 Jan 1952; *Educ* Haileybury, Univ of Bristol (BSc), Univ of York (BPhil); *m* 1984, Fenella, *née* Jeffers; 1 s, 1 da; *Career* nat offr NALGO 1977–82 (dist offr 1975–77), gen sec International Bdcasting Tst 1982–86, res fell in health economics Univ of York 1987–92 (lectr in social policy 1986–87), MP (Lab) York 1992– (also contested 1987); memb House of Commons Select Ctee on Health; sometime freelance TV prodr; cncllr London Borough of Camden 1980–86 (chm Lab Gp 1982–85), memb York DHA 1988–90, chm Yorks Region Fabian Soc; memb RMT; *Publications* The Nation's Health (Fabian Soc, 1995); *Recreations* family; *Style*— Hugh Bayley, Esq, MP; ✉ 59 Holgate Road, York YO2 4AA; c/o House of Commons, London SW1A 0AA

BAYLEY, Prof Peter Charles; s of William Charles Abell Bayley (d 1939), and Irene Evelyn Beatrice, *née* Heath (d 1962); *b* 25 Jan 1921; *Educ* The Crypt Sch Gloucester, Univ Coll Oxford (MA); *m* 30 June 1951 (m dis), Patience, da of Sir George Norman Clark; 1 s (Nicholas), 2 da (Rosalind, Clare); *Career* served RA and Intelligence Corps India 1941–46; Univ Coll Oxford: jr fell 1947, fell and praelector in English 1949–72 (now emeritus), univ lectr in English 1952–72, proctor 1957–58; Oxford corr The Times 1960–63; master Collingwood Coll and lectr Dept of English Univ of Durham 1971–78, Berry prof and head of English Univ of St Andrews 1978–85 (now emeritus); visiting reader Birla Inst Pilani Rajasthan India 1966, visiting lectr Yale Univ and Robert Bates visiting fell Jonathan Edwards Coll 1970, Brown distinguished visiting prof Univ of the South Sewanee Tennessee 1978, Brown distinguished visiting lectr in Br studies Vanderbilt Univ, Sewanee, Rhodes, Birmingham-Southern, Millsaps etc 1985; *Books* The Faerie Queene (ed, vol 1 1966, vol 2 1965), Edmund Spenser, Prince of Poets (1971), Loves and Deaths (ed, 1972), A Casebook on The Faerie Queene (ed, 1977), On Selected Poems of John Milton (1982), An ABC of Shakespeare (1985), University College Oxford: A Guide and Brief History (1992); *Style*— Prof Peter Bayley; ✉ 63 Oxford St, Woodstock, Oxon OX20 1TJ (☎ 01993 812300)

BAYLEY, Prof Peter James; s of late John Henry Bayley, of Portreath, Cornwall, and Margaret, *née* Burness; *b* 20 Nov 1944; *Educ* Redruth GS, Emmanuel Coll Cambridge (MA, PhD), Ecole Normale Supérieure Paris; *Career* fell: Emmanuel Coll Cambridge 1969–71, Gonville and Caius Coll Cambridge 1971–; Drapers prof of French Univ of Cambridge 1985– (lectr in French 1978–85), hon sr res fell Inst of Romance Studies Univ of London 1990; vice pres Assoc of Univ Profs of French 1989–97, pres Soc for French Studies 1990–92; Officier des Palmes Académiques (France) 1988; *Books* French Pulpit Oratory 1598–1650 (1980), The Equilibrium of Wit: essays for Odette de Mourgues (ed with D Coleman, 1982), Selected Sermons of the French Baroque (1983); contrib: Critique et création littéraires en France (ed Fumaroli, 1977), Bossuet: la Prédication au XVIIe siècle (ed Collinet and Goyet, 1980), Catholicism in Early Modern History: a guide to research (ed O'Malley, 1988), Convergences: rhetoric and poetic in seventeenth-century France (ed Rubin and McKinley, 1989), Dictionnaire des littératures (ed Didier, 1994), Oxford Companion to Literature in French (ed France, 1995); contrib: Cambridge Review, Dix-Septième Siècle, French Studies, Modern Language Review; *Recreations* Spain, wine and food, gardening; *Style*— Prof Peter Bayley; ✉ Gonville and Caius College, Cambridge CB2 1TA (☎ 01223 332439)

BAYLEY, Stephen Paul; s of Donald Sydney Bayley, of Staffs, and Anne, *née* Wood; *b* 13 Oct 1951; *Educ* Quarry Bank Sch Liverpool, Univ of Manchester (BA), Univ of Liverpool (MA); *m* 29 Sept 1981, Flo, da of Richard Ernest Fothergill, of London; 1 s (Bruno b 3 June 1985), 1 da (Coco b 9 March 1987); *Career* history and theory of art lectr: Open Univ 1974–76, Univ of Kent 1976–80; dir Boilerhouse Project 1981–86; princ: Eye-Q Limited 1990–95, Redwood & Bayley 1995–; chief exec The Design Museum 1981–90, commissioning ed GQ 1991–; former memb Design Policy Ctee LRT, govr History of Advertising Tst 1985–96; awarded Columnist of the Year PPA 1995; FRSA; Chevalier des Arts et des Lettres 1989; *Books* In Good Shape (1979), Albert Memorial (1981), Harley Earl (1983), Conran Directory of Design (1985), Sex, Drink and Fast Cars (1986), Commerce and Culture (1989), Taste: The Secret Meaning of Things (Faber & Faber, 1991), The Beefeater Two-Day Guide to London (Bloomsbury, 1993), The Paris Style Guide (Ford Motor Co, 1994); *Recreations* words, pictures, food, drink, travel, sport; *Clubs* Savile, Hurlingham; *Style*— Stephen Bayley, Esq; ✉ Redwood & Bayley Ltd, 30 Chelsea Wharf, London SW10 0QJ (☎ 0171 351 5084, fax 0171 351 5128)

BAYLEY, Trevor John; *b* 22 Sept 1951; *Educ* Newcastle-under-Lyme HS; *m*; 5 c; *Career* articled clerk Alex G Duncan & Co 1970–74, PA to ptnr L George Fetzer & Co 1974–76, gp accountant Alfred Clough Ltd 1976–79; Britannia Building Society: financial accountant 1979–85, chief accountant 1985, dep gen mangr 1986, gen mangr (finance) 1987–88, finance dir 1988–94, gp fin dir 1994–, also dir various subsid companies; FCA

(ACA 1974); *Recreations* clay pigeon shooting, sport, music; *Style*— Trevor Bayley, Esq; ✉ Britannia Building Society, Britannia House, Leek, Staffs ST13 5RG (☎ 01538 399399, fax 01538 399261)

BAYLIS, Rear Adm Robert Goodwin (Bob); CB (1984), OBE (1964); s of Harold Goodwin Baylis (d 1963), and Evelyn May, *née* Whitworth (d 1961); *b* 29 Nov 1925; *Educ* Highgate Sch, Univ of Cambridge (MA); *m* 1949, Joyce Rosemary (d 1995), da of Lawrence Dyer Churchill (d 1952); 2 s (Mark, Nicholas), 1 da (Rachel); *Career* joined RN 1943, Fleet Weapons Engr Offr 1973–75, Capt RN Engrg Coll 1975–78, staff of Vice Chief of Def Staff 1979–80; chief exec R G Baylis & Associates (mgmnt and engrg conslt) 1984–, dir British Maritime Technology Reliability Consultants Ltd 1988–, conslt Solen, Burns and King; pres Ordnance Bd 1980–84; chm Bd Nuffield Theatre Tst 1988–, memb Bd Solent Maritime 1994–, assoc memb (emeritus) Aust Ordnance Cncl; CEng, MRAeS, FIEE (memb Cncl 1984–86); *Recreations* windsurfing, theatre, tennis; *Clubs* Lansdowne, Owls (Cape Town), SeaVets; *Style*— Rear Adm Bob Baylis, CB, OBE; ✉ Broadwaters, 4 Cliff Rd, Hill Head, Fareham, Hants PO14 3JS (☎ 01329 319838)

BAYLISS, Dr Christopher Richard Butler; s of Sir Richard Bayliss, KCVO, *qv*, and Margaret Joan Hardman, *née* Lawson (d 1994); *b* 10 Oct 1945; *Educ* Rugby, Clare Coll Cambridge (MA, MB BChir); *m* 20 May 1978, (Felicity) Nicola, da of Ivor Adye (d 1972); 1 s (Timothy Richard b 1985), 2 da (Clare Alexandra b 1982, Lucy Margaret b 1988); *Career* sr registrar X-ray Dept Royal Postgrad Med Sch Hammersmith Hosp London 1976–79, conslt med diagnostic imaging Royal Devon and Exeter Hosp 1979–; chm: Radiology Sub-Ctee BMA 1993–, SW Regnl Conslts and Specialists Ctee 1994–; memb Central Conslts and Specialists Ctee; FRCR; *Recreations* skiing, golf; *Clubs* East Devon Golf (Budleigh Salterton); *Style*— Dr Christopher Bayliss; ✉ Royal Devon & Exeter Hospital, Exeter, Devon (☎ 01392 402325)

BAYLISS, Eur Ing David; OBE (1991); s of Herbert Bayliss (d 1968), of Blackpool, and Annie Ester, *née* Roper (d 1988); *b* 9 July 1938; *Educ* Arnold Sch Blackpool, UMIST (BSc Tech), Univ of Manchester (DipTP); *m* 25 Aug 1961, Dorothy Christine, da of Eric Algernon Carey Crohill; 2 s (Mark Andrew b 22 Dec 1963, Jason Peter b 14 Feb 1966), 1 da (Ruth Abigail b 12 Aug 1968); *Career* asst planning offr Manchester City Cncl 1963–66 (grad engr 1961–63), res offr GLC 1966–68, princ sci offr Centre for Environmental Studies 1968–69, asst divnl engr rising to chief tport planner GLC 1969–84, dir of planning London Transport 1984–; chm Regnl Studies Assoc 1978–81; pres: Br Parking Assoc 1987–89, Tport Studies Assoc 1989–90; Freeman City of London 1993; CEng 1968, FICE 1980 (MICE 1978), fell Inst of Transportation Engrs 1984 (memb 1977), FIHT 1972 (MIHT 1972), FCIT 1977; Eur Ing 1992, FEng 1993, FRSA 1994; *Recreations* writing, travel, wine; *Style*— Eur Ing David Bayliss, OBE, FEng; ✉ 37 Ledborough Lane, Beaconsfield, Buckinghamshire HP9 2DB (☎ 01494 673313); London Transport, 55 Broadway, London SW1H 0BD (☎ 0171 918 3457, fax 0171 222 6016)

BAYLISS, Jeremy David Bagot; s of Edmund Bayliss (d 1990), of Guernsey, and Marjorie Clare Thompson (d 1983); *b* 27 March 1937; *Educ* Harrow, Sidney Sussex Coll Cambridge (MA); *m* 1962, Hon Mrs Mary Selina Bayliss, 3 da of 2 Viscount Bridgeman, KBE, CB, DSO, MC (d 1982); 3 s (Jonathan Andrew Bagot b 2 Jan 1964, Richard Charles b 11 Dec 1965, Patrick Thomas Clive b 6 March 1968); *Career* Nat Serv 2 Lt Coldstream Gds 1956–57; Gerald Eve: joined 1960, ptnr 1967, jt sr ptnr 1988, sr ptnr 1990–; chm Gerald Eve Financial Services Ltd 1989–96; RICS: memb Gen Cncl 1987–, pres Planning and Devpt Div 1989–90, sr vice pres 1995, pres 1996; memb Rating Surveyors' Assoc 1976, FRICS 1971 (ARICS 1962); *Recreations* gardening, shooting, reading, tapestry work; *Clubs* Boodle's; *Style*— Jeremy Bayliss, Esq; ✉ Sheepbridge Court, Swallowfield, nr Reading, Berkshire RG7 1PT (☎ 0118 988 3218); 2 Park Steps, St George's Fields, London W2 2YQ (☎ 0171 262 9349, fax 0171 491 1825)

BAYLISS, Sir Richard Ian Samuel; KCVO (1978); s of late Frederick William Bayliss, of Tettenhall, and late Muryel Anne Bayliss; *b* 2 Jan 1917; *Educ* Rugby, Clare Coll Cambridge, St Thomas' Hosp London (MD, FRCP, FRCPath); *m* 1, 1941 (m dis 1956), Margaret Joan Hardman Lawson (d 1994); 1 s, 1 da; m 2, 1957, Constance Ellen, da of Wilbur J Frey, of Connecticut; 2 da; m 3, 1979, Marina de Borchgrave d'Althena, wid of Charles Rankin; *Career* formerly: casualty offr, house physician, registrar and resident asst physician St Thomas' Hosp 1941–45, offr i/c Med Div RAMC India 1945–48, sr med registrar and tutor Hammersmith Hosp 1948–50, Rockefeller fell in med Columbia Univ New York 1950–52, lectr in med and physician Postgrad Med Sch of London; consulting physician: Westminster Hosp 1954–81 (dean Westminster Med Sch 1960–64), King Edward VII's Hosp for Offrs 1964–86; med dir Swiss Reinsurance Co 1969–85, physician to HM The Queen 1970–82, head of HM's Med Household 1973–82, civilian conslt in med RN 1975–82, dir and vice chm Private Patients Plan plc 1979–89, dir J S Pathology plc 1980–90, hon med advsr Nuffield Hosps 1981–88, asst dir RCP Res Unit London 1982–88, conslt physician/endocrinologist Lister Hosp 1981–; second vice pres RCP 1983–84; chm Med Advsy Panel ITC 1983–, conslt Biotechnology Investments Ltd 1981–; Liveryman Worshipful Soc of Apothecaries; hon fell Clare Coll Cambridge; *Books* Thyroid Disease: The Facts (1982, 2 edn 1991), Practical Procedures in Clinical Medicine (3 edn); *Recreations* skiing, photography, music; *Clubs* Garrick; *Style*— Sir Richard Bayliss, KCVO; ✉ Flat 7, 61 Onslow Square, London SW7 3LS (☎ 0171 589 3087, fax 0171 581 5937); Lister Hospital, Chelsea Bridge Road, London SW1W 8RH (☎ 0171 730 3417)

BAYLISS, Valerie J; *Educ* Univ of Wales (MA); *Career* res student LSE 1966–68; Dept of Employment (now Education and Employment): asst princ 1968–72, princ 1972–78, asst sec 1978–85, involved in establishment of Youth Trg Scheme 1982–85, dir Field Ops 1985–87, dir Resources and Personnel Manpower Servs Cmmn, currently dir Youth and Educn Policy; memb Governing Body Univ of Sheffield; FRSA; *Style*— Mrs Valerie J Bayliss; ✉ Department of Education and Employment, Moorfoot, Sheffield S1 4PQ (☎ 0114 259 4573, fax 0114 259 4746)

BAYLY, Vice Adm Sir Patrick Uniacke; KBE (1968), CB (1965), DSC (1944, and two bars 1944, 1951); 2 s of Lancelot Francis Sanderson Bayly (d 1952), and Eileen Maude, *née* Bayly (d 1961); *b* 4 Aug 1914; *Educ* Aravon Bray Co Wicklow, RNC Dartmouth; *m* 4 April 1945, Moyra Gourlay (Moy), da of Robert Gourlay Jardine, of Newtonmearns, Scotland; 2 da (Caroline, Jennifer); *Career* midshipman 1932, combined ops 1941–43, Lt Cdr 1943, HMS Mauritius 1944, Cdr 1948, Korean War 1952–53, Capt 1954, IDC 1957, Capt (D) 6 Destroyer Sqdn 1958, staff SACLANT Norfolk Va 1960, C of S Med 1962, Rear Adm 1963, Flag Offr Sea Trg 1963, Adm pres RNC Greenwich 1965, Vice Adm 1967, C of S COMNAVSOUTH Malta 1967, ret 1970; dir The Maritime Tst 1971–88, chm Falklands Appeal 1983–89; *Style*— Vice Adm Sir Patrick Bayly, KBE, CB, DSC; ✉ Dunning House, Liphook, Hants (☎ 01428 723116)

BAYNE, Brian Leicester; s of John Leonard Bayne, and Jean Leicester Bayne; *b* 24 July 1938; *Educ* Ardingly Coll, Univ of Wales (BSc, PhD); *m* 1961, Marianne, *née* Middleton; 2 da; *Career* post-doctoral fell Univ of Copenhagen 1963–65, visiting res fell Univ of Sao Paulo Brazil 1965–66, sr res fell Shellfish Res Laboratory Conwy N Wales 1966–68, lectr in zoology Sch of Biological Scis Univ of Leicester 1968–73, Nuffield fell in tropical marine biology Univ of Kuala Lumpur Malaysia and Phuket Biological Laboratory Thailand 1972; IMER Plymouth: princ scientific offr 1973, sr princ scientific offr 1977, dep dir 1978, dir 1983, dir Plymouth Marine Laboratory (following merger of IMER and Marine Biological Assoc) 1988–94; dir NERC Centre for Coastal and Marine Sciences 1994–; visiting lectr: Marine Biological Laboratory Woods Hole USA 1976, State Univ of NY Stony Brook USA 1980; hon prof: of marine sci Plymouth Poly 1983, of zoology Univ of Wales Swansea; professorial fell in zoology Univ of Sheffield 1984; chm Int Oceanographic Cmmn Gp of Experts on the Effects of Pollution 1984–94; memb: Br Nat Ctee on Problems of the Environment (SCOPE) 1985–93, Royal Soc Study Gp on Priorities in Pollution Control 1987–93, NERC Scientific Steering Gps on Marine Genetics, N Sea Water Quality and Biogeochemical Ocean Flux Studies, Exec Ctee Euro Soc for Comparative Physiology and Biochemistry 1988–, Bd of Govrs Poly of the South West 1989–93; memb Editorial Bd: Marine Ecology Progress Series Marine Pollution Bulletin Jl of Applied Ecology 1981–, Jl of Functional Ecology 1986–; managing ed Jl of Experimental Marine Biology and Ecology, author of numerous scientific papers; FIBiol 1983, FZS 1985, FSA 1987; *Books* incl Marine Mussels - Ecology and Physiology (ed, 1976); *Recreations* sailing; *Style*— Brian Bayne, Esq, FSA; ✉ Centre for Coastal and Marine Sciences, Plymouth Marine Laboratory, Prospect Place, The Hoe, Plymouth, Devon PL1 3DH (☎ 01752 633100, fax 01752 269011)

BAYNE, HE Sir Nicholas Peter; KCMG (1992, CMG 1984); s of Capt Ronald Bayne, RN (d 1978), and Elisabeth Margaret, *née* Ashcroft; *b* 15 Feb 1937; *Educ* Eton, ChCh Oxford (MA, DPhil); *m* 1961, Diana, da of Thomas Wilde, of Bideford, N Devon; 2 s (and 1 decd); *Career* HM Dip Serv: served at Br Embassies Manila 1963–66 and Bonn 1969–72, seconded to HM Treasy 1974–75, fin consllr Paris 1975–79, head of Fin then Economic Rels Dept FCO 1979–82, attached RIIA 1982–83, ambass Zaire 1983–85, non-resident ambass Congo, Rwanda and Burundi 1984–85, UK perm rep OECD Paris 1985–88, dep under sec of state FCO 1988–92, high cmmr Canada 1992–96, ret; *Books* Hanging Together: the Seven-Power Summits (with R D Putman, 1984, revised edn 1987); *Clubs* Travellers'; *Style*— Sir Nicholas Bayne, KCMG; ✉ 2 Chetwynd House, Hampton Court Green, Molesey, Surrey KT8 9BS

BAYNE-JARDINE, Colin Charles; s of Brig Christian West Bayne-Jardine, CBE, DSO, MC (d 1959), and Isabel Anna, *née* Forman (d 1991); *b* 8 Jan 1932; *Educ* Marlborough, Univ Coll Oxford (MA), Univ of Bristol (MEd); *m* 7 Sept 1957, (Helen) Elizabeth, da of Arthur Douglas Roberts, OBE (d 1979); 4 s (John b 1958, Charles b 1960, Thomas b 1962, Andrew b 1963); *Career* 2 Lt RA BAOR; Capt RA TA; teacher: St Paul's Sch Concord New Hampshire USA 1956–57, Upper Canada Coll Toronto Canada 1957–58, Glasgow Acad 1958–61, Blundell's Sch 1961–65, Henbury Sch Bristol 1966–69, Univ of Bristol 1969–70; headmaster: Culverhay Sch Bath 1970–76, Henbury Sch Bristol 1976–85; sr inspr (secdy) Staffs 1986–88, princ co inspr Hereford and Worcester 1988–94, princ educn offr 1994–96; chm of govrs Downs Sch Wraxall, memb Local Review Ctee Bristol Prison, memb Cncl Cheltenham Coll; *Books* Mussolini and Italy (1966), World War Two (1968), World War Two and Its Aftermath (1986); *Style*— Colin Bayne-Jardine, Esq; ✉ The Half Timbered Barn, Church Lane, Eldersfield, Glos GL19 4NP

BAYNES, Christopher Rory; s and h of Sir John Christopher Malcolm Baynes, 7 Bt, *qv*; *b* 11 May 1956; *Educ* Winchester, Univ of Bristol; *m* 1992, Sandra Merriman; 1 s (Alasdair William Merriman b 1993); *Career* ACA 1982; *Style*— Christopher Baynes, Esq; ✉ Greywalls, High Street, Findon, Worthing, Sussex

BAYNES, Lt-Col Sir John Christopher Malcolm; 7 Bt (UK 1801), of Harefield Place, Middlesex; s of Lt-Col Sir Rory Malcolm Stuart Baynes, 6 Bt (d 1979), and Ethel Audrey, *née* Giles (d 1947); *b* 24 April 1928; *Educ* Sedbergh, RMA Sandhurst, Univ of Edinburgh (MSc); *m* 1955, Shirley Maxwell, o da of Robert Allan Dodds, of Foxbury House, Lesbury, Alnwick, Northumberland (d 1952); 4 s (Christopher Rory Baynes, *qv*, b 1956, Timothy Peter b 1957, Simon Robert Maurice b 1960, William John Walter b 1966); *Heir* s, Christopher Rory Baynes, b 11 May 1956; *Career* Lt-Col (ret); Cameronians (Scot Rifles) 1948–68, Malaya 1952 (despatches), Aden 1966, def fell Univ of Edinburgh 1968–69, cmd 52 (L) Vols TAVR 1969–72; Queen's Own Highlanders 1968–72; writer; Order of the Sword 1 Class (Sweden) 1965; *Publications* Morale: A Study of Men and Courage (1967 and 1987), The Jacobite Rising of 1715 (1970), The Soldier in Modern Society (1971), Vol IV of The History of The Cameronians (Scot Rifles) (1971), Soldiers of Scotland (1988), The Forgotten Victor: The Life of General Sir Richard O'Connor (1989), A Tale of Two Captains (1990), No Reward But Honour? (1991), Urquhart of Arnhem (1993), Far from a Donkey: Life of General Sir Ivor Maxse (1995); *Recreations* shooting, fishing, reading; *Clubs* Army and Navy; *Style*— Lt-Col Sir John Baynes, Bt; ✉ Talwrn Bach, Llanfyllin, Powys SY22 5LQ (☎ 01691 648 576)

BAYNES, Pauline Diana; da of Frederick William Wilberforce Baynes, CIE, and Jessie Harriet Maud Cunningham; *b* 9 Sept 1922; *Educ* Beaufront Sch Camberley, Farnham Sch of Art, Slade Sch of Art; *m* 1961, Fritz Otto Gasch; *Career* designer and book illustrator; memb Women's Int Art Club 1938; vol worker Camouflage Devpt and Trg Centre RE 1940–42, Hydrographic Dept Admty 1942–45; designer of world's largest crewel embroidery Plymouth Congregational Church Minneapolis 1970; Kate Greenaway medal Library Assoc 1968; *Books* illustrated: Farmer Giles of Ham (and subsequent books and posters by J R R Tolkien, 1949), The Lion, the Witch and the Wardrobe (and subsequent Narnia books by C S Lewis, 1950), The Arabian Nights (1957), The Puffin Book of Nursery Rhymes (by Iona and Peter Opie, 1963), Recipes from an Old Farmhouse (by Alison Uttley, 1966), Dictionary of Chivalry (1968), Snail and Caterpillar (1972), A Companian to World Mythology (1979), The Enchanted Horse (1981), Frog and Shrew (1981), All Things Bright and Beautiful (1986), The Story of Daniel (by George MacBeth, 1986), Noah and the Ark (1988), numerous other children's books; written and illustrated: Victoria and the Golden Bird (1948), How Dog Began (1985), King Wenceslas (1987); *Recreations* walking with dogs; *Style*— Miss Pauline Baynes; ✉ Rock Barn Cottage, Dockenfield, Farnham, Surrey (☎ 01428 713306)

BAYNHAM, Dr (Alexander) Christopher; s of Alexander Baynham (d 1965), of Stroud, Glos, and Dulcie Rowena, *née* Rees (d 1959); *b* 22 Dec 1935; *Educ* Marling Sch, Univ of Reading (BSc), Univ of Warwick (PhD), RCDS; *m* 5 Aug 1961, Eileen May, da of George Wilson, of Tadcaster, Yorks; 2 s (Andrew b 27 April 1965, Peter b 13 Oct 1966), 1 da (Sharon b 8 March 1968); *Career* Civil Serv: joined RSRE 1955, head Optics and Electronics Gp 1976, dep dir 1980–83, dir 1984–86, dir RARDE 1986–89; prof and princ Cranfield Univ RMCS Campus 1989–96, conslt 1996–; *Books* Plasma Effects in Semi-conductors (1971), assorted papers in learned jls; *Recreations* local church activities, music; *Style*— Dr Christopher Baynham; ✉ Cranfield University RMCS, Shrivenham, Swindon, Wilts SN6 8LA (☎ 01793 785437)

BAYNHAM, Dr John William; CBE (1994); s of Rev Albert John Baynham (d 1980), of Euphemia, *née* Sell; *b* 20 Jan 1929; *Educ* Bathgate Acad, Univ of Aberdeen (BSc, PhD), Imperial Coll London (DIC); *m* 1959, Marcella Bridget (Marié), *née* Friel; 1 da (Sioban Janet); *Career* Scottish Agricultural Industries: R&D chemist 1955–62, technol/commercial 1962–64, prodn commissioning/mgmnt 1964–69, prodn planning/trade union negotiating 1970–74, gen mgmnt 1974–80, dir of sales and mktg 1980–84, overall agribusiness dir 1984–87; fndr dir Leith Enterprise Tst 1984– (chm 1987–90), chm Bd of Govrs Moray House Coll 1991–95 (govr 1987–), govr Queen Margaret Coll 1995–; chm: Lothian Health Bd 1990– (bd memb 1987–90), Scottish Health Bd Chairmen's Gp 1995–; Hon DUniv Edinburgh 1995; *Recreations* golf, good food and wine, grandchildren; *Clubs* Caledonian (Edinburgh); *Style*— Dr John Baynham, CBE; ✉ 2/18 Succoth Court, Succoth Park, Edinburgh EH12 6BZ (☎ 0131 337 2813, fax 0131 337 7955); Lothian Health Board, Deaconess House, 148 Pleasance, Edinburgh EH8 9RS (☎ 0131 536 9002, fax 0131 536 9011)

BAZALGETTE, Rear-Adm Derek Willoughby; CB (1976); yr s of Harry L Bazalgette (d 1953); *b* 22 July 1924; *Educ* RNC Dartmouth; *m* 1, 1947, Angela Hilda Vera (d 1991), da of Sir Henry Hinchliffe (d 1980); 4 da (Louise, Caroline, Emma, Olivia); m

2, 14 April 1994, (Helen) Ann, da of Henry Lingard (d 1935), of Chiengmai, Thailand, and widow of Adm Sir Peter Maxwell Stanford, GCB, LVO; *Career* joined RN 1938, served WWII, specialised in gunnery 1949, HMS Centaur 1952–54, HMS Birmingham 1956–58, SO 108 Minesweeping Sqdn and in cmd HMS Houghton 1958–59, HMS Centaur 1963–65, dep dir Naval Ops 1965–67, cmd HMS Aurora 1967–68, idc 1969, chief staff offr to Cdr Br Forces Hong Kong 1970–72, cmd HMS Bulwark 1972–74, Adm Pres RNC Greenwich 1974–76; Cdr 1958, Capt 1965, Rear-Adm 1974, ADC 1974; HQ cmmr for water activities Scout Assoc 1976–87, princ Netley Waterside House 1977–83, ind inquiry inspr 1983–92, lay canon and chm of tstees Portsmouth Cathedral 1984–, memb Gen Synod 1985–90, sr treas Corp of Sons of the Clergy 1992–94, chm Portsmouth Housing Tst 1989–; Freeman City of London 1976, Liveryman Worshipful Co of Shipwrights 1986; FIMgt 1976; *Clubs* Lansdowne; *Style*— Rear-Adm Derek Bazalgette, CB; ✉ Park House, Hambledon, Waterlooville, Hants (☎ 01705 632782)

BAZALGETTE, Peter Lytton; s of Paul Bazalgette, and Diana, *née* Coffin (d 1995); *b* 22 May 1953; *Educ* Dulwich, Fitzwilliam Coll Cambridge (MA Law, pres Cambridge Union 1975); *m* 1985, Hilary Jane, *née* Newiss; 1 da (Emily b 1986), 1 s (Felix b 1990); *Career* BBC News trainee 1977, researcher That's Life 1978, reporter Man Alive and Out of Court (BBC 2) 1980–81, creator and prodr TV Bridge (BBC 2's Grand Slam) 1981, head of corp video EPIC 1982 (prodr of interactive videos for IBM, BT, Shell, Smith Kline French during 1980's), prodr and creator Food and Drink (BBC 2) 1983–, prodr and creator People (BBC 1) 1988; creator: Ready Steady Cook (BBC 2) 1995, Can't Cook Won't Cook (BBC 1) 1995, Going Going Gone (BBC 2) 1995, Changing Rooms (BBC 2) 1996; md Bazal Productions 1987–90 (sold to Broadcast Communications (TV arm of Guardian Media Group) 1990), dir of facutal progs Broadcast Communications plc 1995–; memb GMTV bid team 1991, exec prodr The Sunday Prog (GMTV) 1994; Glenfiddich TV Food Prog of the Yr 1986, Glenfiddich (overall) Award 1986, Argos Award for Consumer Journalists 1990, Indi Award for Best Factual 1993, AMSO Research Effectiveness Award (for Ready Steady Cook) 1995; chm Bd Acad of Gastronomes; memb: Govt's Health of the Nation Task Force 1992–95, ESU's Centre for Int Debate; tstee: Crossness Engines Tst, Good Food Fndn; treas Caroline Walker Tst (nutritional charity); *Books* co-author: BBC Food Check (1989), The Food Revolution (1991), The Big Food and Drink Book (1994), You Don't Have to Diet (1993); occasional contrib to The Spectator, The Sunday Times and Good Food Magazine; *Recreations* gastronomy, cricket; *Clubs* Hurlingham, BBC Mishits Cricket; *Style*— Peter Bazalgette, Esq; ✉ Broadcast Communications plc, 48 Bedford Square, London WC1B 3DP (☎ 0171 255 2551, fax 0171 436 3975)

BAZLEY, Thomas John Sebastian; s and h of Sir Thomas Bazley, 3 Bt, *qv*; *b* 31 Aug 1948; *Style*— Thomas Bazley, Esq

BAZLEY, Sir Thomas Stafford; 3 Bt (UK 1869), of Hatherop, Co Gloucester; s of late Gardner Sebastian Bazley, o s of 2 Bt; suc gf, Sir Thomas Sebastian Bazley, 2 Bt, 1919; *b* 5 Oct 1907; *Educ* Harrow, Magdalen Coll Oxford; *m* 1945, Carmen, o da of James Tulla, of 11 Stanley Gardens, London W11; 3 s (Thomas John Sebastian b 1948, Anthony Martin Christopher b 1958, John Francis Alexander b 1961), 2 da (Catherine b 1950, Virginia b 1953); *Heir* s, Thomas John Sebastian Bazley, *qv*, b 31 Aug 1948; *Style*— Sir Thomas Bazley, Bt; ✉ Eastleach Downs Farm, Eastleach Turville, Cirencester, Glos GL7 3PX

BEACH, Sir (William Gerald) Hugh; GBE (1980, OBE 1966, MBE 1956), KCB (1976), MC (1944); s of Maj-Gen William Henry Beach, CB, CMG, DSO (d 1952), and Constance Maude, *née* Cammell; *b* 20 May 1923; *Educ* Winchester, Peterhouse Cambridge (MA), Univ of Edinburgh (MSc); *m* 1951, Estelle Mary (d 1989), da of Gordon Henry, of Ewell, Surrey; 3 s, 1 da; *Career* served WWII RE, NW Europe and Far East, Lt-Col 1963, Brig 1968, Cdr 12 Inf Bde BAOR 1968–71, Maj-Gen 1971, dir Army Staff Duties MOD 1971–74, Cmdt Staff Coll Camberley 1974–75, Lt-Gen 1976, dep C-in-C UK Land Forces 1976–77, Gen 1977, master-gen of the Ordnance 1977–81, Hon Col Cambridge Univ OTC 1979–89; Vice Lord Lt Gtr London 1981–87 (DL 1981); warden St George's House Windsor 1981–86, memb Security Cmmn 1982–91, Chief Royal Engr 1982–87, chm Study Gp on Censorship to Protect Mil Info 1983, dir The Cncl for Arms Control 1986–89; chm: Gordon's Sch Fndn 1988–93, Rochester 2000 1986–, Winchester Diocesan Advsy Ctee for the Care of Churches 1988–, Govrs of Bedales Sch 1991–96, Governing Body of the Church Army 1990–95, Governing Body of SPCK 1994–; patron Venturers Search and Rescue 1985–, pres Sheffield Branch CPRE, memb Fabric Advsy Ctee Winchester Cathedral, memb Southampton Univ Devpt Tst; Hon DCL Univ of Kent 1990, hon fell Peterhouse Cambridge, hon fell CIBSE; CIMgt, FRSA; *Recreations* sailing, skiing; *Clubs* Farmers', Royal Lymington Yacht; *Style*— Sir Hugh Beach, GBE, KCB, MC; ✉ The Ropeway, Beaulieu, Hants SO42 7YG (☎ 01590 612269); Flat 3, 107 Queen's Gate, London SW7 5AG (☎ 0171 370 0893)

BEACHAM, Stephanie; *b* 28 Feb 1947; *Educ* Convent of the Sacred Heart Whetstone, QEGGS, RADA, Mime School Paris; *m* 2 da (Phoebe b 1974, Chloe b 1977); *Career* actress; spokesperson American Speech Language and Hearing Assoc; *Theatre* incl: Tea Party and The Basement (Duchess) 1969, London Cuckolds (Royal Court) 1977, Venice Preserved (NT) 1985, The Rover (RSC) 1988; *Television* incl: Tenko 1982, Connie 1984, The Colbys and Dynasty (ABC TV USA) 1985–87 and 1988–89, Sister Kate (NBC TV USA) 1989; other credits incl: The Picnic (BBC), The Silent Preacher (BBC), All The World's A Stage (BBC), French and Saunders (series II), To Be The Best, Riders (Anglia), Seaquest (Amblin/NBC), Dorothea Grant in No Bananas (BBC); *Films* incl: The Games, Tam Lyn, The Nightcomers, Movie Blackmail, Fengriffen, And now the Screaming Starts, The Confessional, Inseminoid, The Wolves of Willoughby Chase, The Lilac Bus, Foreign Affairs; *Style*— Ms Stephanie Beacham; ✉ c/o Peters Fraser & Dunlop Ltd, 503 The Chambers, Chelsea Harbour, Lots Road, London SW10 0XF (☎ 0171 352 4446, fax 0171 352 7356)

BEALBY, Walter; s of Harry Bealby, of Nottingham, and Heulwen, *née* Morris; *b* 8 Jan 1953; *Educ* Henry Mellish GS Nottingham, Univ of Bristol (BA); *m* 22 Nov 1980, Finnula Leonora Patricia, da of Daniel O'Leary, of Abingdon, Oxon; 1 s (Thomas Henry b 21 Jan 1985), 1 da (Polly Megan b 5 July 1988); *Career* called to the Bar Middle Temple 1976; Blackstone scholarship 1977; *Recreations* motor cycling, opera; *Clubs* Nat Lib; *Style*— Walter Bealby, Esq; ✉ 5 Fountain Court, Steelhouse Lane, Birmingham B4 6DR (☎ 0121 606 0500, fax 0121 606 1501)

BEALE, Prof Hugh Gurney; s of Charles Beale, TD, of Birmingham, and Anne Freeland, *née* Gurney-Dixon (d 1953); *b* 4 May 1948; *Educ* The Leys Sch Cambridge, Exeter Coll Oxford (BA); *m* 18 July 1970, Jane Wilson, da of Nathan Cox (d 1980), of Clarkton, N Carolina; 2 s (Ned b 1977, Thomas b 1979), 1 da (Martha b 1981); *Career* lectr Univ of Connecticut 1969–71, called to the Bar Lincoln's Inn 1971, lectr UCW Aberystwyth 1971–73, reader Univ of Bristol 1986–87 (lectr 1973–86), prof of law Univ of Warwick 1987–; memb Commission for Euro Contract Law 1987–; *Books* Remedies for Breach of Contract (1980), Contract Cases and Materials (with W D Bishop and M P Furmston, 1985, 1990 and 1995), Principles of European Contract Law, Part 1 (ed with O Lando 1995); *Recreations* fishing, music, walking; *Style*— Prof Hugh Beale; ✉ School of Law, University of Warwick, Coventry CV4 7AL (☎ 01203 523185, fax 01203 524105)

BEALE, (Alfred) James; s of Alfred James Beale (d 1950), of Edinburgh, and Thomasina Wilkie, *née* Robertson (d 1990); *b* 12 July 1935; *Educ* George Heriot's Sch, Univ of Edinburgh (MA); *m* 30 Aug 1958, Kathleen, da of George Edward McHugh; 1 s (David Alistair b 31 Jan 1963), 1 da (Susan Carole b 4 Dec 1960); *Career* Nat Serv 2 Lt 1 Bn Royal Scots 1957–59; brand mangr Procter & Gamble Ltd 1959–64; P A Consulting Group: mktg conslt 1964–68, mktg supervisor 1968–72, regnl mangr NI 1972–77, dir in charge NE Eng 1978–91, chief exec P A Cambridge Economic Consultants 1987–90; dir: Marketing House Publishers Ltd 1989–95, Marketing Business Ltd 1989–95, College of Marketing Ltd 1989–95, Marketing Training Ltd 1989–95, The Marketing Fndn 1989–95, Quality Street Ltd 1991–, CIM Holdings Ltd 1991–95; pres: NI Chamber of Commerce and Indust 1977–78, European Marketing Confedn 1993–94, nat chm Chartered Inst of Mktg 1990–91 (chm NI branch 1975–76, chm NE branch 1983–84); chm: Northumbria branch BIM 1983–85, Rail Users' Consultative Ctee for NE England 1995–; govr: Ulster Coll 1974–77, Centre for Info on Language Teaching and Res 1990–; chm Chartered Inst of Mktg Charitable Tst 1991–; memb: Lead Body for Accounting 1987–, Languages Lead Body 1990–, Mktg Standards Bd 1991–, Product Devpt Ctee Business and Tech Educn Cncl 1989–95 (chm Languages Panel), Prog Advsy Gp Poly and Colls Funding Cncl 1989–91; FCIM, CIMgt, FIMC, FInstD; *Books* Irish Salesmen Under The Microscope (1971); *Recreations* golf (playing), rugby and cricket (watching); *Style*— James Beale, Esq; ✉ Hallbankfield, Newcastle Road, Corbridge, Northumberland NE45 5LN (☎ 01434 632158)

BEALE, Nicholas Clive Lansdowne; s of Prof Evelyn Martin Lansdowne Beale, FRS (d 1985), and Violette Elizabeth Anne, *née* Lewis; *b* 22 Feb 1955; *Educ* Winchester (scholar), Trinity Coll Cambridge (scholar, MA Maths); *m* 16 July 1977, Christine Anne, da of Peter McPoland, of Bedford; 1 s (Rupert Christopher Lansdowne b 1977), 2 da (Rebecca Merryn Elizabeth b 1980, Rose Theodora Elizabeth b 1991); *Career* mgmnt conslt; md Beale Electronic Systems Ltd 1977–85, exec vice chm Beale International Technology Ltd 1985–88, conslt McKinsey & Co 1988–89; chm: Beale Holdings 1988–, Sciteb 1989–; dir: First Film Foundation 1991–, Sector Dialogue Teams project 1992–; author of Sciteb/Sunday Times Poll of R & D Effectiveness, Intellectual Assets (in Professional Investor) and various technical articles and speeches at int confs on computer communications; project ldr City Science and Technology Dialogue 1995; Freeman of Worshipful Co of Information Technologists 1995; Oblate Alton Abbey 1994–; FRSA 1991; *Books* R & D Short-Termism? (published in cooperation with CBI, 1991), Engineering Consensus (ed) and Good Disclosure Practice Code (ed, both published in cooperation with DTI); *Recreations* piano, music; *Clubs* Royal Inst, IOD; *Style*— Nicholas Beale, Esq; ✉ Sciteb, 1 Hay Hill, Berkeley Square, London W1X 7LF (☎ 0171 381 1481, fax 0171 491 4811)

BEALE, Lt-Gen Sir Peter John; KBE (1992); s of Basil Hewett Beale (d 1987), of Romford, Essex, and Eileen Beryl, *née* Heffer; *b* 18 March 1934; *Educ* St Paul's Cathedral Choir Sch, Felsted, Gonville & Caius Coll Cambridge (BA), Westminster Hosp (MB BChir, DTM & H); *m* 22 Aug 1959, Julia Mary, da of John Clifton Winter; 4 s (Simon Russell b 12 Jan 1961, Timothy John b 17 Jan 1962, Andrew Mark (twin) b 17 Jan 1962, Matthew James Robert b 25 Jan 1974), 2 da (Katie Louise b 28 June 1964, Lucy Ann b 10 Dec 1967, d 1971); *Career* RMO 34 LAA Regt RA 1960–63, trainee and specialist physician 1963–71, conslt physician 1971–, cmd Med 2 Div 1981–83, Col Armd 3 1983–84, cmd Med 1 Br Corps 1984–87, cmd Med UKLF 1987–90, Surgn-Gen and DG Army Med Servs 1991–94; chief med advsr British Red Cross 1994–; author of various articles in med jls on mil med matters; QHP 1988–94; memb: BMA, RIPHH, RSTM&H; FRCP, FFCM, FFOM, MRCS; *Recreations* golf, squash, tennis, music (conducting and singing); *Clubs* Tidworth Golf (pres); *Style*— Lt-Gen Sir Peter Beale, KBE; ✉ HQ British Red Cross Society, 9 Grosvenor Crescent, London SW1X 7EJ (☎ 0171 235 5454)

BEALE, Trevor Howard; s of Thomas Edward Beale, CBE, JP, of Hadley Wood, Herts, and Beatrice May, *née* MacLaughlin (d 1986); *b* 28 Nov 1934; *Educ* Westminster, Trinity Coll Cambridge (MA); *m* 5 May 1962, Susan Jane, da of Philip Reginald Brierley, of Chalfont St Peter, Bucks; 3 s (Andrew b 30 Nov 1963, Christopher b 20 Nov 1967, Nicholas b 30 Dec 1969), 1 da (Philippa b 5 Nov 1965); *Career* called to the Bar Gray's Inn 1960; chm Beales Ltd (hoteliers) 1990– (md 1970); churchwarden St Michael's Highgate 1979–82; memb Ct of Assts Worshipful Co of Bakers (Master 1993); FHCIMA 1990, FRSA 1993; *Recreations* music; *Style*— Trevor Beale, Esq; ✉ Bunkers House, Gaddesden Row, nr Hemel Hempstead, Herts; West Lodge Park, Hadley Wood, Herts (☎ 0181 440 8311)

BEALES, Prof Derek Edward Dawson; s of Edward Beales (d 1984), and Dorothy Kathleen, *née* Dawson (d 1993); *b* 12 June 1931; *Educ* Bishop's Stortford Coll, Sidney Sussex Coll Cambridge (BA, MA, PhD, LittD); *m* 14 Aug 1964, Sara Jean (Sally), da of Francis Harris Ledbury (d 1971); 1 s (Richard Derek b 1967), 1 da (Christina Margaret (Kitty) b 1965); *Career* Nat Serv Sgt RA 1949–50; Univ of Cambridge: univ asst lectr 1962–65, lectr 1965–80, prof of modern history 1980–, chm Bd of History 1979–81; Sidney Sussex Coll Cambridge: res fell 1955–58, fell 1958–, vice master 1973–75; visiting lectr Harvard Univ 1965, visiting prof Central European Univ Budapest 1995–; fndr's meml lectr St Deiniol's Library Hawarden 1990, Stenton lectr Univ of Reading 1992, Birkbeck lectr Trinity Coll Cambridge 1993; chm Editorial Bd Historical Journal 1990– (ed 1971–75), chm Mgmnt Ctee Centre of Int Studies 1993–95; memb: Univ Library Syndicate Cambridge 1981–89, Gen Bd of the Faculties 1987–89, Standing Ctee for Humanities Euro Science Fndn 1994–; author articles in learned jls; FRHistS (memb Cncl 1984–88), FBA (memb 1989); *Books* England and Italy 1859–60 (1961), From Castlereagh to Gladstone (1969), The Risorgimento and the Unification of Italy (1971), History and Biography (1981), History Society and the Churches (ed with Geoffrey Best, 1985), Joseph II - in the Shadow of Maria Theresa 1741–80 (1987), Mozart and the Habsburgs (1993), Sidney Sussex College Cambridge: Historical Essays in Commemoration of the Quatercentary (ed with H B Nisbet, 1996); *Recreations* music, walking, bridge; *Style*— Prof Derek Beales, FBA; ✉ Sidney Sussex Coll, Cambridge CB2 3HU (tel 01223 338800)

BEALES, Ian Michael; *b* 16 July 1944; *Educ* The Sweyne Sch Rayleigh Essex; *Career* trainee reporter Southend Standard 1961–65, trainee sub-ed South Wales Echo 1966 (joined as reporter and feature writer 1965); Western Daily Press: joined 1967, dep ed 1970–80, ed 1980–; Guild of Eds Nat Award for best all-round candidate, RSPCA Award for campaigning in journalism 1977; chm Parly and Legal Ctee Guild of Br Newspaper Eds 1989–91 (former chm and sec Western Region); *Recreations* gardening; *Style*— Ian Beales; ✉ Western Daily Press, Bristol United Press, Temple Way, Old Market, Bristol BS99 7HD (☎ 0117 934 3202 ext 2530, fax 0117 934 3574)

BEALEY, Prof Frank William; s of Ernest Bealey (d 1951), of Netherton, Dudley, and Nora, *née* Hampton (d 1982); *b* 31 Aug 1922; *Educ* King Edward VI GS Stourbridge, LSE (BScEcon, DScEcon); *m* 2 July 1960, Sheila, da of James Hurst (d 1955); 1 s (William b 20 Nov 1968), 2 da (Rachel b 14 Sept 1963, Rosalind b 11 March 1967); *Career* seaman RN 1941–46; Finnish Govt scholar at Univ of Helsinki 1948–49, res asst for Passfield Tst LSE 1950–51, extra-mural lectr Univ of Manchester (Burnley area) 1951–52, asst lectr, lectr then sr lectr Univ of Keele 1952–64, prof of politics Univ of Aberdeen 1964–90 (prof emeritus 1990–); visiting fell Yale 1980; tstee Jan Hus Educnl Fndn 1981–96, organiser Parly All-Party Gp Social Sci and Policy 1984–89, co-ordinator Jt European Project 0276 for TEMPUS (EC) in Czechoslovakia 1990–93; FRHistS 1971; Order of the Blyskiwicka (Poland) 1979; *Books* Labour and Politics (with Henry Pelling 1958, 2 edn 1982), Constituency Politics (with J Blondel and W P McCann, 1965), The Social and Political Thought of the British Labour Party (1970), The Post Office Engineering Union (1976), The Politics of Independence (with John Sewel, 1981), Democracy in the Contemporary State (1988); *Recreations* watching football and cricket, swimming, darts;

Clubs Economicals Assoc Football and Cricket; *Style—* Prof Frank Bealey; ✉ 2 Morag House, Oyne, Aberdeenshire AB52 6QT (☎ 01464 851457); Department of Politics, The University, Aberdeen AB9 2UB (☎ 01224 273490)

BEAMENT, Sir James William Longman; kt (1980); o s of Tom Beament (d 1958), of Crewkerne, Somerset; *b* 17 Nov 1921; *Educ* Crewkerne GS, Queens' Coll Cambridge (MA, ScD), London Sch of Tropical Med (PhD); *m* 1962, (Sara) Juliet, yst da of Prof Sir Ernest Barker (d 1959); 2 s; *Career* princ scientific offr Agric Res Cncl to 1961; Univ of Cambridge: fell and tutor Queens' Coll 1962–67, reader 1967–69, head Dept of Applied Biology 1969–89, emeritus prof of agric and life fell Queens' Coll 1989–; memb: Composers' Guild of GB 1967, Advsy Bd for the Res Cncls 1977; chm NERC 1978–81 (memb 1970–83); Scientific Medal Zoological Soc 1963; FRS 1964; *Recreations* composing music, playing music, DIY; *Style—* Sir James Beament, FRS; ✉ 19 Sedley Taylor Rd, Cambridge CB2 2PW (☎ 01223 562433)

BEAMISH, HE Adrian John; CMG (1988); s of Thomas Charles Constantine Bernard Beamish (d 1948), and Josephine Mary, *née* Lee (d 1968); *b* 21 Jan 1939; *Educ* Prior Park Coll Bath, Cambridge Univ (BA); *m* 1, 1965, Caroline (m dis), da of Dr John Lipscomb, of Chilham, Kent; 2 da (Catherine b 1966, Antonia b 1968); m 2, 1994, Antonia, da of Cdr Cyril Patrick Cavanagh, RN (d 1987); 1 da (Mary-Rose Guadalupe b 1996), 1 step da (Emma b 1980), 1 step s (James b 1983); *Career* HM Dip Serv: third then second sec Tehran 1963–66, second sec FO 1966–69, first sec UK Delgn OECD Paris 1970–73, dir Br Info Servs New Delhi 1973–76, dep head Personnel Operations FCO 1978–80 (returned 1976), cnsllr Bonn 1981–85, head Falklands Islands Dept FCO 1985–87, ambass Lima 1987–89, under sec for Americas FCO 1989–94, ambass to Mexico 1994–; *Recreations* books, plants; *Clubs* United Oxford and Cambridge Univ; *Style—* HE Mr Adrian Beamish, CMG; ✉ c/o Foreign and Commonwealth Office (Mexico City), King Charles Street, London SW1A 2AH

BEAMISH, Sally; da of William Anthony Alten Beamish, of Sussex, and Ursula Mary, *née* Snow; *b* 26 Aug 1956; *Educ* Camden Sch for Girls, Trinity Coll of Music (jr), RNCM; *m* 1988, Robert Irvine, s of Joseph Irvine; 2 s (Laurence George b 3 Jan 1989, Thomas Stuart b 2 June 1990), 1 da (Stephanie Rose b 1 Oct 1995); *Career* composer; studied under Anthony Gilbert and Sir Lennox Berkeley; viola: Raphael Ensemble, London Sinfonietta, Lontano; artistic dir and co-fndr Chamber Group of Scotland 1991–, co-host composers' course Scottish Chamber Orch Hoy (with Sir Peter Maxwell Davies) 1994 & 1995; appearances on: Radio Manchester BBC, Radio Scotland, BBC TV, Scottish TV, Channel 4; works incl: Sonata for violin and piano 1976, Three Ladies Met in a Garden 1982, Mr & Mrs Discobollos 1983, Capriccio for bassoon and piano 1988, Seven Songs 1990, The Lost Pibroch 1991, Symphony 1992, Into the Furnace 1993, Tam Lin for oboe and orch 1993, Concerto Grosso for strings 1993, Concerto for violin and orch 1994, Walking Back 1994, Gala Water for solo cello 1994, Shadow and Silver 1995, Concerto for Viola and Orchestra (premiered BBC Proms) 1995, Sule Skerrie 1995; Arts Cncl Composer's Bursary 1989, Paul Hamlyn Award 1993; memb: Performing Rights Soc, APC; *Style—* Ms Sally Beamish; ✉ c/o Scottish Music Information Centre, 1 Bowmont Gardens, Glasgow G12 9LR (☎ 0141 334 6393, fax 0141 337 1161)

BEAMONT, Wing Cdr Roland Prosper; CBE (1965, OBE 1953), DSO (1943 and bar 1944), DFC (1941, and bar 1942), DFC (USA 1945), DL (Lancashire 1977); s of Lt-Col E C Beamont, of Summersdale, Chichester (d 1957), and Dorothy Mary, *née* Haynes (d 1950); *b* 10 Aug 1920; *Educ* Eastbourne Coll; *m* 1, 1942, Shirley (d 1945), da of Bernard Adams, of Chelsea; 1 da (Carol); m 2, 1946, Patricia, da of Capt Richard Galpine Raworth, of Harrogate; 1 step s (Richard), 2 da (Patricia, Elizabeth); *Career* author, aviation consl; cmmnd RAF 1939, served WWII Fighter Cmd, RAF, BEF, Battle of Britain (despatches), Battle of France and Germany; attached as test pilot to Hawker Aircraft Ltd during rest periods in 1941–42 and in 1943–44, experimental test pilot Gloster Aircraft Co Ltd 1946, chief test pilot English Electric Co 1947–61 (1st Br pilot to fly at speed of sound (USA) May 1948, 1st flight of Britain's 1st jet bomber (the Canberra) May 1949, holder of Atlantic record Belfast-Gander (4 hrs 18 mins in a Canberra) Aug 1951, 1st two-way Atlantic record Belfast-Gander-Belfast (10 hrs 4 mins, in a Canberra) Aug 1952, first flight of P1 (Britain's 1st fully supersonic fighter) 1954, 1st Br pilot in Br aircraft to fly faster than sound in level flight 1954 and first to fly at twice the speed of sound Nov 1958, first flight of Lightning supersonic all-weather fighter 1957, 1st flight of TSR2 (Britain's 1st supersonic bomber) Sept 1964), special dir and dep chief test pilot BAC 1961–64; dir of flight ops: BAC Preston (later British Aerospace Warton Div) 1965–78, Panavia (Tornado testing prog) 1971–79; Britannia Trophy 1953, Derry and Richards Meml Medal 1955, R P Alston Meml Medal RAeS 1960, Br Silver Medal for Aeronautics 1965; memb Battle of Britain Fighter Assoc; pres: Popular Flying Assoc 1979–84, 609 (WR) Sqdn Assoc RAuxAF 1993; DL Lancs 1977–81; Master Pilot and Liveryman Guild of Air Pilots and Air Navigators; hon fell Soc of Experimental Testpilots USA 1985, FRAeS; *Books* Phoenix into Ashes (1968), Typhoon and Tempest at War (1979), Testing Years (1980), English Electric Canberra (1982), Fighter Test Pilot (1986), English Electric P1 Lightning (1984), My Part of the Sky (1988), Testing Early Jets (1990), Tempest Over Europe (1994), Flying to the Limit (1996); *Recreations* fishing, aviation; *Clubs* RAF, Bustard Flying (hon memb); *Style—* Wing Cdr Roland Beamont, CBE, DSO, DFC, DL; ✉ Cross Cottage, Pentridge, Salisbury SP5 5QX

BEAN, Basil; CBE (1985); s of Walter Bean (d 1976), of York, and Alice Louise Chambers (d 1978); *b* 2 July 1931; *Educ* Archbishop Holgate Sch York; *m* 1956, Janet Mary, da of Frederick Cecil Rex Brown (d 1961), of West Bromwich; 1 da (Rachel); *Career* York City Cncl 1948–53, West Bromwich BC 1953–56, London Borough of Sutton 1957–62, Skelmersdale Devpt Corp 1962–66, London Borough of Havering 1967–69, Northampton Devpt Corp 1969–80 (gen mangr 1977–80); chief exec: Merseyside Devpt Corp 1980–85, Nat House Bldg Cncl 1985–94; chm Admiral Homes Ltd 1995– (dep chm 1994–95); memb: Chartered Inst of Public Finance and Accountancy, Br Waterways Bd 1985–88; hon fell Assoc of Building Engineers; *Recreations* travel, walking, bridge; *Clubs* Northampton and Co, Cheyne Walk; *Style—* Basil Bean, Esq, CBE; ✉ 4 Paget Close, Great Houghton, Northampton NN4 7EF (☎ 01604 765135)

BEAN, Hugh Cecil; CBE (1970); s of Cecil Walter Claude Bean, MBE (d 1975), and Gertrude Alice, *née* Chapman (d 1982); *b* 22 Sept 1929; *Educ* Beckenham GS, RCM; *m* 16 April 1963, Mary Dorothy, da of Henry Unwin Harrow (d 1981); 1 da (Fiona b 8 May 1969); *Career* Grenadier Gds 1949–51; prof of violin RCM 1954–91, ldr Philharmonia Orchestra 1956–67, assoc ldr BBC Symphony Orchestra 1967–69, ldr LSO 1969–71, co ldr Philharmonia Orchestra 1989–; memb: Bean-Parkhouse Duo, Music Gp of London 1951–88; recordings: Elgar Violin Concerto (EMI), Vivaldi's Seasons (Decca), numerous works of chamber music for various cos; memb Royal Philharmonic Soc; FRCM 1968 (Hon ARCM 1961); *Recreations* model aircraft, steam railways, record collecting; *Style—* Hugh Bean, Esq, CBE; ✉ 30 Stone Park Ave, Beckenham, Kent BR3 3LX (☎ 0181 650 8774)

BEAN, Rev Canon John Victor; s of Albert Victor Bean (d 1961), and Eleanor Ethel Bean (d 1975); *b* 1 Dec 1925; *Educ* Gt Yarmouth GS, Univ of Cambridge (MA), Salisbury Theological Coll; *m* 1955, Nancy Evelyn, da of Capt Thomas Allen Evans, MC (d 1964); 2 s (Simon, Martin), 2 da (Judith d 1961, Rosalind); *Career* war serv RNVR; ordained: deacon 1950, priest 1951; various appts in diocese of Portsmouth, vicar St Mary Cowes 1966–91, canon emeritus Portsmouth Cathedral 1991– (hon canon 1970–91), priest i/c All Saints Gurnard 1978–91; chaplain to HM The Queen 1980–95; *Recreations* boatwatching, photography, tidying up; *Clubs* Gurnard Sailing, Cowes Rotary, Ryde Golf; *Style—* Rev Canon John Bean; ✉ 23 Seldon Avenue, Ryde, Isle of Wight PO33 1NS (☎ 01983 812516)

BEAN, Robert Malcolm; s of Gerald Thomas Bean, and Maria Rosaria, *née* Silvestro (d 1986); *b* 26 Sept 1959, Salvador, Brazil; *Educ* British Sch of Rio de Janeiro, Ardingly Coll; *m* 1986, Rose Victoria (Tori), da of Richard Hardy (d 1984); 2 s (Daniel Jay b 6 May 1987, Gabriel Thomas Sebastian b 31 Aug 1993); *Career* prodn asst Benton & Bowles advtg 1978–79, prodn & traffic mangr Lonsdale Advertising 1979–81; account mangr: Lintas 1981–83, Doyle Dane Bernbach 1983–85; account dir Lowe Howard-Spink 1985–88, new business dir Edwards Martin Thornton 1988, gp dir WCRS 1988–91, head of advtg & media quality British Telecom 1991–94; fndr ptnr: Bean MC (advtg) 1994–96, Bean Andrews Norways Cramphorn (brand devpt and communications); memb Communications Panel Red Cross; *Recreations* all sport, music; *Style—* Robert Bean, Esq

BEAN, Sean; *Career* actor; *Theatre* Romeo in Romeo and Juliet (RSC Stratford/Barbican), Spencer in Fair Maid of the West (RSC Stratford/Mermaid), Starvling in A Midsummer Night's Dream, Who Knew Mackenzie & Gone (Royal Court), Lederer in Deathwatch (Young Vic Studio), Last Days of Mankind (Citizens' Theatre Glasgow); *Television* BBC incl: Mellors in Lady Chatterley's Lover 1993, Fools Gold, Clarissa, Prince, Tell Me That You Love Me, Wedded, Small Zones, My Kingdom For A Horse; Central incl: title role in Sharpe's: Rifles, Gold, Company, Eagle, Enemy, Honour, Battle, Sword, Regiment, Seige, Mission (seperate progs 1993–96); Channel 4 incl: The Loser, The Border Country; other credits incl: A Woman's Guide to Adultery (ITV) 1993, Inspector Morse (Thames), Troubles (LWT), 15 Streets (World Wide/Tyne Tees), War Requiem (Anglo-Int Films), Winter Flight (Enigma), Samson & Delilah (Flamingo Films), The True Bride (TVS Films), Fenton in Scarlett, Esav in Jacob; *Radio* title role in The True Story of Martin Guerre (Radio 4) 1992; *Audio* Sharpe's Devil; *Film* Sean Miller in Patriot Games, Rannucio in Caravaggio 1986, Carver Doone in Lorna Doone, Tadgh in The Field 1990, Brendan in Stormy Monday (Channel 4) 1987, Windprints 1989, Black Beauty, Shopping, Jimmy Muir in When Saturday Comes 1995, 006 in Goldeneye 1995; *Style—* Sean Bean, Esq; ✉ c/o ICM Ltd, Oxford House, 76 Oxford Street, London W1N 0AX (☎ 0171 636 6565, fax 0171 323 0101)

BEANEY, Linda Margaret; da of Kenneth Ashley Beaney, of Gidea Park, Essex, and Kathleen Margaret, *née* Stainforth; *b* 1 Dec 1952; *Educ* Coborn Sch for Girls London; *Career* trainee property sales negotiator Edward Erdman & Co Mayfair London 1969; Hampton & Sons: joined 1976, ptnr 1981, md London 1989–91; dir Hornchurch Theatre Trust Ltd 1985–90, dir P H Gillingham Investments 1986–, jt chief exec Hamptons Residential Developments 1989–91, sr ptnr Beaney Pearce 1992–; Freeman City of London 1984; memb Land Inst 1988, FInstD 1991, FNAEA 1992; *Recreations* theatre, tennis, golf and skiing; *Clubs* Queen's; *Style—* Ms Linda Beaney; ✉ Beaney Pearce, 14 Culford Gardens, Sloane Square, London SW3 2ST (☎ 0171 589 1333, fax 0171 589 1171)

BEARCROFT, (Joseph) Peter; s of Arthur William Bearcroft (d 1975), of Scarborough, N Yorks, and Elizabeth Jane, *née* McKinley (d 1982); *b* 15 July 1923; *Educ* St Mary's GS Hummersknott nr Darlington, Queensland Univ Brisbane Aust, Balliol Coll Oxford (MA); *m* 14 June 1952, Dr Rosalind Irene Bearcroft, da of Victor Albert Chamberlain, MBE (d 1978); 1 s (Philip b 13 March 1964), 2 da (Charlotte b 5 June 1962, Emma b 19 May 1968); *Career* flying cadet Fleet Air Arm 1942, flying trg with US Navy 1943–44, Sub Lt RNVR, flying control offr Fleet Air Army HQ for the Normandy Landings 1944, TAMY I and MONAB 5 Aust SE Asia Cmd 1945, demob Lt RNVR 1946; jr commercial asst ICI Ltd Distribution Centre Billingham, trainee London and Manchester Assurance Co Ltd 1949, trainee tech asst Howards & Sons (Ilford) Ltd 1950, Horlicks Ltd 1950–63 (mgmnt trainee, market res offr, asst to co sec, head of Mktg Div), dir Pristine Products Ltd and Airwick Ltd; British Railways Bd: dir of mktg (HQ) 1963–65, freight mktg and sales mangr, chief freight mangr Western Region (Paddington) HQ, freight mktg advsr (HQ) 1978–83, ret 1983; business cnsllr DTI and Dept of Employment 1983–86, currently private industl mktg consl and business advsr; underwriting memb Lloyd's 1981; fndr chm: Railway Mktg Soc 1971–83, Tport and Distribution Gp Inst of Mktg (memb Nat Cncl); memb Ctee for Terotechnology with DTI 1973–78; fndr memb SDP 1981; Catholic Union: memb Cncl 1995–, memb Issues Ctee 1995–; memb: Advsy Panel Kent Fndn, Prince's Youth Business Tst, govr's Ctee of two state primary schs since 1994 and one independent private sch since 1985; Catenian Assoc: memb 1979, pres Maidstone Circle 1982, provincial pres Province 7 1990; Knight of the Equestrian Order of the Holy Sepulchre of Jerusalem 1991; Freeman City of London, Liveryman Worshipful Co of Marketors 1976; FILog, FCIT, FCIM; *Recreations* swimming, golf, reading, travelling; *Clubs* MCC, Cricketers; *Style—* Peter Bearcroft, Esq; ✉ Barming Place, Maidstone, Kent ME16 9ED (☎ and fax 01622 727844)

BEARD, Allan Geoffrey; CB (1979), CBE (1994); s of Maj Henry Thomas Beard (d 1969), and Florence Mercy, *née* Baker (d 1954); *b* 18 Oct 1919; *Educ* Ormskirk GS; *m* 21 June 1945, Helen Matthews, da of Michael James McDonagh (d 1956); 1 da (Mary Taylor); *Career* clerical offr Air Miny 1936, successively exec offr, higher exec offr then asst princ Assistance Bd 1938–47; Capt RE 1940–46; princ Nat Assistance Bd 1950, asst sec 1962, under sec DHSS 1968–79; hon treas Motability 1985–; *Recreations* gardening; *Clubs* RAC; *Style—* Allan Beard, Esq, CB, CBE; ✉ 51 Rectory Park, Sanderstead, Surrey CR2 9JR (☎ 0181 657 4197)

BEARD, Andrew; s of Richard Geoffrey Beard, of Sheffield, and Constance Lorna, *née* Booth; *b* 17 July 1943; *Educ* Rishworth Sch; *m* 23 Oct 1982, Barbara Anne, da of Ralph Gordon Bristow; 3 s (Matthew Andrew b 11 Feb 1972, Duncan Edward b 9 June 1973, Jonathan Charles b 14 Nov 1983), 1 da (Harriet Emma Kate b 30 March 1988); *Career* articled clerk Knox Burbidge Henderson Sheffield 1960–65, ptnr Pannell Kerr Forster 1972– (following a series of mergers), nat dir of Business Servs Pannell Kerr Forster 1985–89, managing ptnr Pannell Kerr Forster S Yorks 1992–; non exec dir: Sheffield Enterprise Agency Ltd, Business Link Sheffield, Knowle House Services Ltd, Class Quest Ltd; pres Sheffield and Dist Soc of CAs 1991–92; FCA (ACA 1965); *Recreations* DIY, sailing; *Style—* Andrew Beard, Esq; ✉ Pannell Kerr Forster, 4 Norfolk Park Road, Sheffield S2 3QE (☎ 0114 276 7991, fax 0114 275 3538)

BEARD, Michael (Mike); s of Joseph Beard (d 1995), of Stockport, Cheshire, and Harriet Louvain, *née* Holmes (d 1990); *b* 18 Aug 1942; *Educ* St Bede's Coll Manchester; *m* 1966, Jennifer, da of John Robert Marr; 1 da (Katherine Louise b 1979); *Career* political organiser Cons Pty 1960–73, PRO then mangr British Leyland 1973–77, mktg servs mangr The Pilkington Group 1977–79, dir of public affrs, advtg and promotion The Perkins Engines Group 1979–83, md Burson-Marsteller Singapore 1983–84, head of PR The Wiggins Teape Group 1984–86; dir of corp communications: Delta plc 1987–88, Taylor Woodrow plc 1989–95; dir of communication Lucas Varity (formerly Lucas Industries plc) 1995–96; IPR: memb 1979, fell 1991, treas 1992, pres 1994; *Recreations* sport, current affairs, travel, rock music; *Clubs* RAC; *Style—* Mike Beard, Esq

BEARD, (Christopher) Nigel; s of Albert Leonard Beard (d 1958), of Castleford, Yorks, and Irene, *née* Bowes (d 1968); *b* 10 Oct 1936; *Educ* Castleford GS Yorks, UCL (BSc); *m* 1969, Jennifer Anne, da of Thomas Beckerleg Cotton, of Guildford, Surrey; 1 s (Daniel b 1971), 1 da (Jessica b 1973); *Career* supt land ops and reinforcement policy studies Def Operational Analysis Estab 1968–73, chief planner strategy GLC 1973–74, dir London Docklands Devpt Orgn 1974–79, sr mangr New Business Devpt ICI Millbank 1979–92, gp mangr Res and Devpt Planning ZENECA 1992–; Parly candidate (Lab):

Woking 1979, Portsmouth North 1983, Erith and Crayford 1992, Bexleyheath and Crayford (prospective Parly candidate); memb: SW Thames RHA 1978–86, Royal Marsden Cancer Hosp and Inst of Cancer Res 1981–90, Nat Constitutional Cncl Lab Party 1995–; FRSA; *Recreations* reading, theatre, talking; *Clubs* Athenaeum, Royal Inst; *Style*— Nigel Beard, Esq; ✉ Lanquhart, The Ridgway, Pyrford, Woking, Surrey (☎ 01932 348630); ZENECA plc, 15 Stanhope Gate, London W1Y 6LN (☎ 0171 304 5000)

BEARD, Prof Richard William; s of Brig William Horace Gladstone Beard, OBE (d 1989), and Irene, *née* Foote; *b* 4 May 1931; *Educ* Westminster, Christ's Coll Cambridge (MA, MB BChir), Bart's London (MD); *m* 1, 28 Aug 1957 (m dis 1979), Jane Elizabeth, *née* Copsey; 2 s (Charles b 3 Sept 1959, Nicholas b 27 March 1962); m 2, 24 Feb 1979, Irène Victoire Marie, da of Comte de Marotte de Montigny (d 1973), of Chateau de Libois, Belgium; 1 s (Thomas b 14 Dec 1979); *Career* obstetrician and gynaecologist RAF Changi Singapore 1957–60 (Malaya Medal 1958); house surgn Chelsea Hosp for Women 1961–62, asst obstetrician Univ Coll Hosp 1963–64; sr lectr and hon conslt: Queen Charlotte's and Chelsea Hosps 1967–68, King's Coll Hosp 1968–72; prof and head Dept of Obstetrics and Gynaecology St Mary's Hosp Med Sch 1972–96, dir Pelvic Pain Clinic Northwick Park and St Marks Hosp 1996–; visiting prof St George's Hosp London 1993; advsr to Social Servs Select Ctee House of Commons 1978–90, civilian conslt advsr in obstetrics and gynaecology RAF 1983–, conslt advsr in obstetrics and gynaecology Chief Med Offr DHSS 1984–92; RCOG: chm Scientific and Pathology Ctee 1983–86, chm Birthright Res Ctee 1987–90, central assessor Confidential Enquiry into Maternal Death 1984–92, memb Cncl 1988–92; pres Euro Bd and Coll of Obstetrics and Gynaecology 1996–; praelector Univ of Dundee 1991, govr Downe House Sch Newbury Berks 1993–; memb Académie Royale de Medécine de Belgique 1983; FRCOG 1972, FRGS 1996; *Books* Fetal Medicine (1974), Fetal Physiology and Medicine (1976, 2 edn 1983); *Recreations* tennis, sailing, classical music; *Clubs* Garrick; *Style*— Prof Richard Beard; ✉ 64 Elgin Crescent, London W11 2JJ (☎ 0171 221 1930, fax 0171 727 1416); Lough Ine House, Lough Ine, nr Skibbereen, Co Cork, Eire; Pelvic Pain Clinic, Department of Obstetrics and Gynaecology, Northwick Park and St Marks Hospital, Watford Road, Harrow, Middx (☎ 0181 869 2919)

BEARDMORE, Prof John Alec; s of George Edward Beardmore, of Burton on Trent, and Anne Jean, *née* Warrington; *b* 1 May 1930; *Educ* Burton on Trent GS, Birmingham Central Tech Coll, Univ of Sheffield (BSc, PhD); *m* 26 Dec 1956, Anne Patricia, da of Frederick William Wallace (d 1951); 3 s (James b 1960, Hugo b 1963, Charles b 1965), 1 da (Virginia b 1957); *Career* radar operator RAF 1948–49; res demonstrator Univ of Sheffield 1954–56, Cwlth Fund fell (Harkness) Columbia Univ NY 1956–58, visiting asst prof of plant breeding Cornell Univ 1958, lectr in genetics Univ of Sheffield 1958–61, prof of genetics and dir Genetics Inst Univ of Groningen The Netherlands 1961–66, sr fell Nat Sci Fndn Pennsylvania State Univ 1966; Univ of Wales Swansea: prof of genetics 1966–, head of dept 1966–87, dean of sci 1974–76, vice princ 1977–80, dir Inst of Marine Studies 1983–87, head Sch of Bio Sci 1988–95; chm Univ of Wales Validation Bd 1994–; hon sec Inst of Biology 1980–85 (vice pres 1985–87); memb: NERC Aquatic Life Sci Ctee 1982–87 (chm 1984–87), Br Nat Ctee for Biology 1983–87, Cncl Linnean Soc 1989–93; chm: CSTI Bd 1984–85, UK Heads of Biological Scis 1992–94; md Fishgen Ltd; Univ of Helsinki medal 1980; FIBiol, FRSA, FLS; *Books* Marine Organisms: Genetics Ecology and Evolution (co ed with B Battaglia, 1977); *Recreations* bridge, hill walking; *Style*— Prof John A Beardmore; ✉ 153 Derwen Fawr Road, Swansea SA2 8ED (☎ 01792 206232); School of Biological Sciences, University of Wales Swansea, Swansea SA2 8PP (☎ 01792 295382, fax 01792 295447, telex 48149)

BEARDSLEY, Peter Andrew; MBE (1995); *b* 18 Jan 1961; *married*; *Career* professional footballer; clubs: Carlisle Utd 1979–82 (102 appearances, 22 goals), Manchester Utd 1982–83, Newcastle Utd 1983–87 (147 appearances, 61 goals), transferred to Liverpool for £1.9m 1987–91 (131 appearances, 46 goals), Everton 1991–93 (81 appearances, 25 goals), rejoined Newcastle Utd for £1.5m 1993–; honours with Liverpool: League champions 1987–88 and 1989–90, winners FA Cup 1989; England: over 50 full caps, ret from int football 1996 (prior to Euro Championships); *Books* Peter Beardsley - My Life Story (1995); *Style*— Peter Beardsley, Esq, MBE; ✉ Newcastle United FC, St James's Park, Newcastle upon Tyne NE1 4ST (☎ 0191 232 8361)

BEARDSWORTH, Maj-Gen Simon John; CB (1984); s of Paymaster Capt Stanley Thomas Beardsworth, RN (ka 1941), and Pearl Sylvia Emma (Biddy), *née* Blake (d 1976); *b* 18 April 1929; *Educ* St Edmund's Coll, RMA Sandhurst, Royal Mil Coll of Science (BSc); *m* 1954, Barbara Bingham, da of Brig James Bingham Turner, RA (d 1963), and Norah Beryl, *née* Clayton (d 1969); 3 s (Jonathan Paul Bingham b 1955, James Thomas Blake b 1957, Simon Anthony De Aula b 1962); *Career* cmd 1 Royal Tank Regt 1970–71, Project Mangr 1973–77 (Col), Dir of Projects 1977–80 (Brig), Dep Cmdt Royal Mil Coll of Science 1980–81, Maj-Gen 1981, Vice Master Gen of the Ordnance 1981–84, ret; self employed conslt in defence procurement; non-exec dir OMI International plc 1993–95; *Recreations* game shooting, helping out at horsey events, writing a book, travel, garden; *Clubs* Army & Navy; *Style*— Maj-Gen S J Beardsworth, CB; ✉ c/o Lloyds Bank plc, 37 Market Square, Crewkerne, Somerset TA18 7LR

BEARMAN, Garth Russell; s of Russell Legerton Bearman (d 1986), and Barbara Maye Fester, *née* Limb (d 1971); *b* 3 Oct 1946; *Educ* Harrow; *m* 26 Jan 1972, Diana Jane, da of Clair Morrel Waterbury, of Virginia Water, Surrey; 1 s (Christian), 1 da (Katherine); *Career* chief exec The Swire Fraser Group Ltd (formerly chief exec Robert Fraser Insurance Brokers Ltd); *Recreations* polo, tennis, squash; *Clubs* Turf, Naval and Military, City, Cowdray Park Polo, Lloyd's Saddle; *Style*— Garth Bearman, Esq; ✉ Swire Fraser Ltd, 32/38 Leman Street, London E1 (☎ 0171 481 0111, fax 0171 481 2232)

BEARSTED, 5 Viscount (UK 1925); Sir Nicholas Alan Samuel; 5 Bt (UK 1903); er s of 4 Viscount Bearsted, MC, TD (d 1996), and his 2 w, Hon Elizabeth Adelaide (d 1983), da of Baron Cohen, PC (Life Peer, d 1973); *b* 22 Jan 1950; *Educ* Eton, New Coll Oxford (BA); *m* 1975, Caroline Jane, da of Dr David Sacks; 1 s (Hon Harry Richard b 23 May 1988), 4 da (Hon Eugenie Sharon b 1977, Hon Natalie Naomi b 1979, Hon Zöe Elizabeth b 1982, Hon Juliet Samantha b 1986); *Heir* s, Hon Harry Richard Samuel b 23 May 1988); *Career* chief exec offr Hulton Deutsch Collection Ltd; chm Cncl Royal Free Hosp Med Sch; *Style*— The Rt Hon the Viscount Bearsted; ✉ 9 Acacia Road, London NW8 6AB; Farley Hall, Farley Hill, Berks RG7 1UL

BEASANT, Dave; s of Cecil Hugh Beasant, of Willesden, Brent, and May Edith, *née* Timms; *b* 20 March 1959; *Educ* Willesden HS; *m* Sandra Dawn, da of Victor Albert Harris; 2 s (Nicholas David b 23 Oct 1985, Samuel James b 8 April 1988), 1 da (Sophie Charlotte b 20 June 1991); *Career* professional footballer; 340 league appearances Wimbledon 1980–88, 20 league appearances Newcastle Utd 1988–89 (joined for a fee of £850,000), over 100 appearances Chelsea 1989–93 (joined for a fee of £725,000), with Southampton FC 1993–; England: 7 B caps, 2 full caps, memb World Cup squad Italy 1990; first goalkeeper to captain FA Cup Final team Wimbledon 1988, first goalkeeper to save penalty in FA Cup Final; honours with Wimbledon: Div 4 Championship 1983, FA Cup 1988; honours with Chelsea: Div 2 Championship 1989, Zenith Data Systems Cup 1990; memb: Variety Club of GB Golf Soc, Charity Assoc, Bunbury's and Lord's Taverners Cricket; *Books* Tales of the Unexpected: The Dave Beasant Story; *Recreations* golf; *Style*— Dave Beasant, Esq; ✉ Southampton FC, The Dell, Milton Road, Southampton SO9 4XX

BEASHEL, His Hon Judge; John Francis; s of Nicholas Beashel (d 1983), of Bradford-on-Avon, Wilts, and Margaret Rita, *née* McGurk; *Educ* Trowbridge Commercial Inst, Coll of Law; *m* 1966, Kay, *née* Dunning; 3 s (Mark Nicholas b 12 March 1968, Simon John b 26 Oct 1969, Jeremy Peter b 29 Sept 1973), 1 da (Caroline Natasha b 11 July 1985); *Career* called to the Bar: Gray's Inn 1970, NSW 1989; dep clerk to the Justices Ipswich 1970–73, practising barr 3 Paper Buildings Temple London and Annexe Bournemouth 1973–93, recorder 1989– (asst recorder 1983–89), circuit judge Western Circuit 1993–; *Recreations* golf, travel, reading, walking, cycling, photography; *Style*— His Hon Judge Beashel; ✉ Courts of Justice, Deansleigh Road, Bournemouth, Dorset BH7 7DS (☎ 01202 502800)

BEASLEY, Alan Walter; s of Frederick Hancock Beasley (d 1980); *b* 10 Feb 1935; *Educ* King Edward VI GS Nuneaton; *m* 1960, Margaret, da of Frederick Payne (d 1990); 3 s (Andrew b 1961, Nigel b 1963, Stephen b 1969); *Career* dir: Charrington Industrial Holdings 1974–77 (when taken over by Coalite Group), Coalite Group plc Bd 1979–90 (ret); chief exec Great Central Merchants Ltd 1990– (dir 1986–); Midland Region CBI: memb 1981–87 and 1988–90, memb Nat Cncl 1988–90, regnl vice chm 1988–90; chm Bolsover Enterprise Agency Ptnrship 1991– (dep chm 1988–91); pres Rotary Club 1990–91; FCA; *Recreations* sport, reading, travel, theatre, home and garden, family, rotary; *Style*— Alan Beasley, Esq; ✉ 694 Chatsworth Rd, Brookside, Chesterfield, Derbys S40 3PB (☎ 01246 568785, fax 01246 569891)

BEASLEY-MURRAY, Rev Dr Paul; s of Rev Dr George Raymond Beasley-Murray, of Hove, East Sussex, and Ruth, *née* Weston; *b* 14 March 1944; *Educ* Trinity Sch of John Whitgift Croydon, Jesus Coll Cambridge (MA), Univ of Zurich, Univ of Manchester (PhD), N Baptist Coll, Int Baptist Theol Seminary Switzerland; *m* 26 Aug 1967, Mrs Caroline Wynne Beasley-Murray, JP, da of Arthur Maelor Griffiths, of Wrexham, North Wales; 3 s (Jonathan Paul b 6 Aug 1969, Timothy Mark b 19 Nov 1971, Benjamin James b 6 March 1976), 1 da (Susannah Caroline Louise b 21 Sept 1973); *Career* prof of New Testament Nat Univ of Zaire at Kisangani (in assoc with Baptist Missionary Soc) 1970–72, pastor Altrincham Baptist Church Altrincham Cheshire 1973–86, princ Spurgeons Coll London 1986–92, sr min Victoria Road South Baptist Church Chelmsford 1993–; chm Richard Baxter Inst for Ministry; ed Ministry Today 1994–; memb: Theol and Academic Ctee Baptist World Alliance, Studiorum Novi Testamenti Societas; *Books* Turning the Tide (with Alan Wilkinson, 1980), Pastors Under Pressure (1989), Dynamic Leadership (1990), Mission to the World (ed, 1991), Faith and Festivity (1991), Radical Believers (1992), Anyone For Ordination? (ed 1993), Prayers For All Peoples (co-ed, 1993), A Call to Excellence (1995), Radical Leaders (1996); *Recreations* walking, music, cooking; *Style*— The Rev Dr Paul Beasley-Murray; ✉ 12 Beach's Drive, Chelmsford, Essex CM1 2NJ (☎ office 01245 347095, home 01245 352996, fax 01245 347016)

BEASTALL, John Sale; CB (1995); s of Howard Beastall, and Marjorie Betty, *née* Sale; *b* 2 July 1941; *Educ* St Paul's, Balliol Coll Oxford (BA); *Career* HM Treasy: asst princ 1963–66, asst private sec to Chllr of Exchequer 1966–67, princ 1967–68 and 1971–74; princ Civil Serv Dept 1968–71; HM Treasy: private sec to Paymaster Gen 1974–75, asst sec 1975–79 and 1981–85; asst sec: Civil Serv Dept 1979–81, DES 1985–87; Treasy Offr of Accounts 1987–93, head of Local Govt, Housing and Environment Gp 1993–95; receiver Met Police 1995; *Recreations* Christian youth work; *Clubs* Utd Oxford and Cambridge Univ; *Style*— John Beastall, Esq, CB

BEATON, James Wallace; GC (1974), CVO (1992, LVO 1987); s of J A Beaton, and B McDonald; *b* 16 Feb 1943; *Educ* Peterhead Acad Aberdeenshire; *m* 1965, Anne C Ballantyne; 2 da; *Career* Metropolitan Police: joined 1962, Notting Hill 1962–66, sgt Harrow Rd 1966–71, station sgt Wembley 1971–73, royalty protection offr 'A' Div 1973, police offr to HRH Princess Anne 1973–79, inspr 1974, chief inspr 1979–83, chief superintendent (Queen's Police Offr) 1983–92, ret; Dir's Honor Award US Secret Serv 1974; *Recreations* reading, keeping fit; *Style*— James Beaton, Esq, GC, CVO; ✉ 1 Kingswells View, Westhill, Skene, Aberdeenshire (☎ 01224 744361)

BEATSON, Prof Jack; s of John James Beatson (d 1961), and Miriam, *née* White (d 1991); *b* 3 Nov 1948; *Educ* Whittingehame Coll Brighton, Univ of Oxford (BCL, MA); *m* 1973, Charlotte, da of Lt-Col John Aylmer Christie-Miller, CBE, of Bourton-on-the-Hill, Glos; 1 s (Samuel J b 1976), 1 da (Hannah A b 1979); *Career* called to the Bar Inner Temple 1972, hon bencher 1993, law lectr Univ of Bristol 1972–73, hon fell Merton Coll Oxford 1994– (fell 1973–94), law cmmr England and Wales 1989–94, memb Editorial Bd Law Quarterly Review; memb Civil and Family Ctee Judicial Studies Bd 1994–, memb Monopolies and Merges Cmmn 1995–; Univ of Cambridge: Rouse Ball prof of English Law 1993–, fell St John's Coll 1994–; visiting prof: Osgoode Hall Law Sch Toronto 1979, Univ of Virginia 1980 and 1983; *Books* Administrative Law - Cases and Materials (jtly 1983, 2 edn 1989), The Use and Abuse of Unjust Enrichment (1991), Chitty on Contracts (jt ed, 1994), Good Faith and Fault in Contract Law (jtly 1995); *Recreations* travelling, gardening; *Style*— Prof Jack Beatson; ✉ St John's College, Cambridge CB2 1TP

BEATTIE, Alexander Montgomery Greaves; s of Matthew Pool Beattie, of Newbie House, Dumfriesshire, and Clare Evelyn Henrietta, *née* Gibbs; *b* 1919; *Educ* Shawnigan Lake Coll BC, RMA Sandhurst; *m* 1953 (m dis 1962), Lady Frederica Rozelle Ridgway Pierrepont, da of 6 and last Earl Manvers MC; *Career* painter; Major Coldstream Guards WWII; one man exhibitions: London, Brussels, Paris, The Hague, Florence, Nassau, USA, Canada; formerly artist in residence and lectr in painting Univ of Louisville Kentucky; City of London Guildhall Prize 1956; Hon Col Cwlth of Kentucky; *Recreations* foreign travel, shooting, cooking; *Clubs* Guards', Pratt's; *Style*— Alexander Beattie, Esq; ✉ 11 Sherford Street, Bromyard, Herefordshire HR7 4DL (☎ 01885 482803)

BEATTIE, Dr Alistair Duncan; s of Alexander Nicoll Beattie (d 1965), of Paisley, and Elizabeth McCrorie, *née* Nisbet (d 1961); *b* 4 April 1942; *Educ* Paisley GS, Univ of Glasgow (MB ChB, MD); *m* 29 Oct 1966, Gillian Margaret, da of Dr James Thomson McCutcheon (d 1964); 3 s (Duncan b 16 Feb 1970, Douglas b 30 April 1975, Neil b 26 Aug 1979), 2 da (Charlotte b 23 May 1968, Deirdre b 25 May 1972); *Career* res fell Scottish Home and Health Dept 1969–73, lectr materia medica Univ of Glasgow 1973–76, res fell MRC Royal Free Hosp 1974–75, conslt physician S Gen Hosp Glasgow 1976–; chm W of Scotland Bd for Postgraduate Med Educn, hon treas Med and Dental Def Union of Scotland; MRCP 1973, FRCPGlas 1983, FRCP 1985, FFPM 1989; *Books* Emergencies in Medicine (jt ed, 1984), Diagnostic Tests in Gastroenterology (1989); *Recreations* golf, music; *Clubs* Douglas Park Golf; *Style*— Dr Alistair Beattie; ✉ 228 Queen Victoria Drive, Glasgow G13 1TN (☎ 0141 959 6639); Southern General Hospital, Glasgow G51 4TF (☎ 0141 201 1100)

BEATTIE, (George) Anthony; s of James Ellison Beattie (d 1973), of Highgate, London, and Christine, *née* Mayman (d 1995); *b* 17 April 1944; *Educ* Stationers' Co's Sch London, Trinity Coll Cambridge (MA); *m* 1973, Janet Frances, da of Douglas Dring; 1 s (Matthew James b 4 Nov 1990); *Career* Econ Planning Div Office of the Pres Malawi 1966–69; ODA: memb Econ Planning Staff 1969–78, memb Admin Gp 1978–86; dir Tropical Devpt and Resources Inst 1986–87, dir Overseas Devpt Natural Resources Inst 1987–90, chief exec Natural Resources Inst 1990–96, Efficiency and Effectiveness Cabinet Office (Office of Public Serv) 1996–; *Recreations* music, pottering in the country, Border terriers; *Style*— Anthony Beattie, Esq; ✉ Cabinet Office (OPS), Horse Guards Road, London SW1P 3AL (☎ 0171 270 5074, fax 0171 270 6243)

BEATTIE, Basil; *b* 1935; *Educ* Royal Acad Schs; *Career* artist; teacher Goldsmith' Coll London; *Solo Exhibitions* Greenwich Theatre Gallery London 1968, Mayfair Gallery

London 1971, Consort Gallery London 1973, Hoya Gallery London 1974, New 57 Gallery Edinburgh 1978, Newcastle Poly 1979, Goldsmiths' Gallery London 1982, Minories Gallery Colchester 1982, Bede Gallery Jarrow 1984, Gray's Art Gallery Hartlepool 1986, Curwen Gallery London 1987 and 1990, Drawing on the Interior (installation at The Eagle Gallery London) 1991, Castlefield Gallery Manchester 1993, MAAK Gallery London 1993, Todd Gallery London 1994 and 1995, Ikon Gallery 1994, Angel Row Gallery Nottingham 1995, Path Gallery Aalst Belgium 1996, Todd Gallery London 1996; *Group Exhibitions* incl: John Moores Exhbn 4 (Liverpool) 1965, Large Paintings (Hayward Gallery) 1970, London Now in Berlin (Germany) 1970, Four Painters (Museum of Modern Art Oxford) 1971, British Painting (Hayward Gallery) 1974, Hayward Annual (Hayward Gallery) 1980, Hayward Annual - British Drawing (Hayward Gallery) 1982, European Painting (Trier Germany) 1984, British Art Show (Arts Cncl travelling exhbn) 1984, John Moores Exhbn 15 (Liverpool) 1987, Presence of Painting (Mappin Gallery Sheffield) 1988, Three British Painters (Northern Centre for Contemporary Art Sunderland) 1988, John Moores Exhbn 16 (Liverpool) 1989, The Abstract Connection (Flowers East Gallery London) 1989, John Moores Exhbn 17 (Liverpool) 1991, Painting and Sculpture at the MAAK Gallery 1992, (Pomeroy Purdy Gallery London) 1992, Moving into View (Royal Festival Hall London) 1993, Summer Exhibition (Royal Academy London) 1993, (Morgan Stanley Bank) 1994, Painters and Prints (Curwen Gallery London) 1994, Lead and Follow (Bede Gallery Jarrow and Atlantis Gallery London) 1994, Summer Exhibition (Royal Academy London) 1994, Paintmarks (Kettles Yard Cambridge) 1994, British Abstract Art Part 1 (Flowers East Gallery London) 1994, Monotypes (Art Space Gallery London) 1995, Green on Red Gallery Dublin 1995, Ace! Arts Cncl Collection (travelling exhbn) 1996–97; works in the collections incl: Tate Gallery, Arts Cncl Collection London, Contemporary Arts Soc and other public and private collections in the UK and overseas; cmmns incl mural for Manors Station Newcastle Metro for Northern Arts; Awards: major Arts Cncl Award 1976, Athena Awards winner 1986, John Moores second prize winner 1989; *Style—* Basil Beattie, Esq; ✉ Flat 1, 3 Drakefield Road, Tooting, London SW17 8RT (☎ 0181 767 7728)

BEATTIE, David; CMG (1989); s of George William David Beattie, and Norna Alice, *née* Nicolson; *b* 5 March 1938; *Educ* Merchant Taylors' Sch Crosby, Lincoln Coll Oxford (MA); *m* 1966, Ulla Marita, da of Allan Alha (d 1987), of Helsinki, Finland; 2 da; *Career* Nat Serv RN 1957–59; RNR: Sub Lt 1959–62, Lt 1962–67; Dip Serv 1963–97: FO 1963–64, Moscow 1964–66, FO 1966–70, Nicosia 1970–74, FCO 1974–78, cnsllr then dep head UK delgn to negotiations on mutual reduction of forces and armaments and associated measures in Central Europe (Vienna) 1978–82, cnsllr (commercial) Moscow 1982–85, head of Energy Sci Space Dept FCO 1985–87, min and dep UK permanent rep to NATO Brussels 1987–92, ambass to Switzerland and (non-resident) ambass to Liechtenstein 1992–97; Freeman City of London 1989; FIL 1990; *Recreations* walking, bridge, history of the House of Stuart; *Clubs* Travellers'; *Style—* David Beattie, Esq, CMG; ✉ c/o Foreign & Commonwealth Office, King Charles Street, London SW1A 2AH

BEATTIE, Hon Sir David Stuart; GCMG (1980), GCVO (1981) QSO (1985); s of Joseph Nesbitt Beattie; *b* 29 Feb 1924; *m* 1950, Norma, da of John Macdonald; 3 s, 4 da; *Career* barr, slr; QC 1965; judge Supreme Ct (now High Ct) of NZ 1969–80, govr-gen of NZ 1980–85; dir of several public companies incl: National Bank of New Zealand, Independent News Ltd, New Zealand Meat Industry Assoc (chm), Hewlett Packard (NZ), Ericsson Communications (NZ) 1989, Sedgwick's (Aust) 1991, Trans Tasman Properties Ltd 1992; chm: Sedgwicks (NZ), Sedgwicks (Fiji), Royal Cmmn on the Cts 1978–79, Ministerial Ctee on Sci and Technol 1986, NZ Int Festival of the Arts 1987–; pres NZ Olympic and Cwlth Games Assoc; patron: NZ Rugby Football Union, NZ Squash Raquets; sole cmmr Fijian Court System 1992; Hon LLD Auckland 1983; *Style—* The Hon Sir David Beattie, GCMG, GCVO, QSO; ✉ 18 Golf Rd, Heretaunga, Upper Hutt, New Zealand

BEATTIE, Jennifer Jane Belissa (Mrs Geoffrey Luckyn-Malone); da of Maj Ian Dunbar Beattie (d 1987), of Brighton, Sussex, and Belissa Mary Hunter Graves, *née* Stanley; *b* 20 July 1947; *Educ* Queen Anne's Sch Caversham; *m* 11 July 1992, Maj William Geoffrey Luckyn-Malone, late Argyll and Sutherland Highlanders; *Career* solicitor; ptnr: Blacket Gill & Langhams 1973–77 (joined 1972), Blacket Gill & Swain 1977–85, Beattie & Co 1985–; Women's Nat Cancer Control Campaign: dep chm 1983–86, vice pres 1986–92, dir 1992–; memb Law Soc 1972; *Recreations* skiing, tennis, reading, dog walking; *Clubs* Naval & Military; *Style—* Mrs Geoffrey Luckyn-Malone; ✉ 41 Great Percy St, London WC1X 9RA (☎ 0171 278 5203); Miss Jennifer Beattie, Beattie & Co, 9 Staple Inn, Holborn, London WC1V 7QH (☎ 0171 831 1011, fax 0171 831 8913)

BEATTIE, Trevor Stephen; s of John Vincent Beattie (d 1980), and Ada Alice, *née* Page; *b* 24 Dec 1958; *Educ* Moseley Art Sch Birmingham (BA), Wolverhampton Poly; *Career* copywriter Allen Brady & Marsh advtg agency 1981–83, dep creative dir Ayer Barker 1983–87, gp head Boase Massimi Pollitt 1987–90, creative dir TBWA (formerly TBWA Holmes Knight Ritchie) 1993– (joined 1990); *Awards* Best Radio Commercial ILR Awards 1984, Silver TV Advtg Awards 1989, Silver Cannes Advtg Festival 1985 and 1992, World's Best Poster Award Vienna Festival 1992, Gold Best Campaign Campaign Press Awards 1993; *Recreations* film making, flying, tourism; *Style—* Trevor Beattie, Esq; ✉ TBWA, 8 Crinan Street, Battle Bridge Basin, London N1 9UF (☎ 0171 833 5544, fax 0171 833 8751)

BEATTY, 3 Earl (UK 1919); David Beatty; also Viscount Borodale and Baron Beatty (UK 1919); s of 2 Earl Beatty, DSC (d 1972); *b* 21 Nov 1946; *Educ* Eton; *m* 1, 23 June 1971 (m dis 1983), Anne, da of A Please, of Wokingham; 2 s (Viscount Borodale, Hon Peter Wystan b 28 May 1975); m 2, 18 June 1984, Anoma Corinne, da of Ray Wijewardene, of Colombo, Sri Lanka; *Heir* s, Viscount Borodale, *qv*; *Career* photographer and writer; FRGS; *Style—* The Rt Hon the Earl Beatty; ✉ 2 Larkhall Place, Larkhall, Bath

BEATTY, Col Michael Philip Kenneth; CBE (1990), TD (1971, and Bars 1977, 1987 and 1994), DL (Staffs 1980); s of Col George Kenneth Beatty, MC, MRCS, LRCP (d 1962), of Upland Grange, Kidderminster; *b* 9 June 1941; *Educ* St Edward's Sch Oxford; *m* 13 Dec 1969, Frances Elizabeth, JP, o da of Richard Nathaniel Twisleton-Wykeham-Fiennes (ggs of 16 Baron Saye and Sele); 4 da (Geraldine, Zazie, Katie, Caroline); *Career* Glynwed International 1965–84; company dir 1985–; cmmnd Queen's Own Mercian Yeomanry 1978–80; TA Col: Western District 1985–90, UKLF 1990–92, MOD 1992–; Hon Col 35 Signal Regt (Vols) 1986–91; ADC to HM The Queen 1987–90; gen cmmr of taxes; High Sheriff of Staffordshire 1994–95; tstee Lichfield Cathedral; *Recreations* restoring old houses, gardening; *Clubs* Royal Over-Seas League; *Style—* Col Michael Beatty, CBE, TD, DL; ✉ Tixall Hall Farmhouse, Tixall, Stafford ST18 0XT (☎ 01785 661098, fax 01785 664756)

BEATY, Prof Robert Thompson (Bob); s of Laurence Beaty, of Ayrshire, and Elizabeth Todd, *née* Beattie; *b* 13 Oct 1943; *Educ* Hamilton Acad, Univ of Glasgow (Hoover scholar, BSc); *m* Anne Veronica, da of George Gray Gillies (d 1990); 2 s (Kenneth Robert b 23 Dec 1968, Steven Gillies b 5 Oct 1971); *Career* trainee then test engr Hoover Cambuslang 1966–68; IBM: quality engr Greenock Plant 1968–69, Uithoorn Devpt Laboratory Holland 1969–71, World Trade HQ White Plains NY 1973–74, second level mgmnt 1974 (mgmnt 1971), functional mangr quality assurance 1976–78, mangr PCB Business Unit 1978–80, various sr mgmnt positions 1980–87, asst plant mangr 1987–89, dir of ops European HQ Paris 1989–92, dir technol prod ops 1992, dir of manufacturing ops and location exec 1993, dir IBM Greenock 1994–96; chief exec Scottish Electronics Forum (SEF) 1996–; md: Scottish Electronics Technol Gp (SETG) 1996–, RTB Professional Services 1996–; non-exec dir: Turnkey Holdings Ltd 1996–, Calluna plc 1996–; dir Greenock Tall Ships 1999 Ltd 1996–; visiting prof of product design Univ of Glasgow 1996–; dir: Renfrewshire Enterprise Coy 1994–, Quality Scotland Fndn (QSF) 1995–; FIEE 1985, FIProdE 1987, FEng 1989; *Recreations* golf, jogging, hillwalking, cycling, car restoration, DIY; *Style—* Prof R T Beaty, FEng; ✉ Glenside, 89 Newton St, Greenock, Renfrewshire PA16 8SG (☎ 01475 722027, ☎ and fax 01475 726266); Scottish Electronics Forum, 120 Bothwell St, Glasgow G2 7JP (☎ 0141 228 2546, fax 0141 228 2237)

BEAUCHAMP, *see:* Proctor-Beauchamp

BEAUCHAMP, Vernon John; s of Herbert George Beauchamp (d 1952), of Waterlooville, Hants, and Vera Helena, *née* Daly; *b* 19 Sept 1943; *Educ* Portsmouth GS; *m* 27 Nov 1971, Annemarie, da of Evind Teunis Van Den Born (d 1982), of Renkum, Holland; 2 s (Mark b 9 Dec 1972, Dominic b 16 Oct 1975); *Career* commissioned Royal Warwickshire Fusiliers 1963, transferred 2 Gurkha Rifles 1969, served in Germany, UK, Borneo, HK, Brunei, Malaysia, Army Staff Coll 1976, Brigade Maj 20 Armoured Brigade 1977–79, Nat Defence Coll 1981, Cmdt 2 Bn 2 Gurkha Rifles 1981–84, sr staff appts MOD and HQ BAOR 1984–87, Cdr 48 Gurkha Infantry Brigade 1987–89, RCDS 1990; currently chief exec Royal Hospital for Neuro-Disability; FIMgt; *Recreations* golf, running; *Clubs* Fadeaways; *Style—* Vernon Beauchamp; ✉ Royal Hospital for Neuro-Disability, West Hill, London SW15 3SW (☎ 0181 780 4512, fax 0181 780 4501)

BEAUCLERK-DEWAR, Peter de Vere; RD (1980, bar 1990), JP (Inner London 1983); s of James Dewar, MBE, GM, AE (d 1983), and Hermione de Vere (d 1969), yr da and co-heir of Maj Aubrey Nelthorpe Beauclerk, of Little Grimsby Hall, Lincs (d 1916, heir-in-line to Dukedom of St Albans); recognised by Lord Lyon King of Arms 1965 in additional surname and arms of Beauclerk; *b* 19 Feb 1943; *Educ* Ampleforth; *m* 4 Feb 1967, Sarah Ann Sweet Verge, elder da of Maj Lionel John Verge Rudder, DCLI, of Cirencester, Glos; 1 s (James William Aubrey de Vere b 30 Sept 1970), 3 da (Alexandra Hermione Sarah b 1 Aug 1972, Emma Diana Peta b 6 Sept 1973, Philippa Caroline Frances b 8 Aug 1982); *Career* Lt Cdr RNR 1977 (cmmnd London Div 1966), Intelligence Branch 1979–92, ret 1992; genealogist: Falkland Pursuivant Extraordinary 1975, 1982, 1984, 1986, 1987, 1991, 1994 and 1996; usher: (Silver Stick) Silver Jubilee Thanksgiving Serv 1977, (Liaison) HM Queen Elizabeth The Queen Mother's 80th Birthday Thanksgiving Serv 1980; heraldry conslt to Christie's Fine Art Auctioneers 1979–, chm Assoc of Genealogists and Record Agents 1982–83, vice pres Royal Stuart Soc 1995 (hon treas 1985–94), tstee Inst of Heraldic and Genealogical Studies 1992– (hon treas 1979–94); chief accountant Archdiocese of Westminster 1982–85; dir: Mgmnt Search International Ltd 1985–87, Five Arrows Ltd 1986–87, Clifton Nurseries (Holdings) Ltd 1986–88, Room Twelve Ltd 1987–88; princ and fndr Peter Dewar Associates 1988–, sr conslt Sanders and Sidney plc 1990–; court chm Family Proceedings Court (Inner London) 1991–, vice chm Inner London Magistrates' Assoc 1994–95, dep chm East Central Petty Sessional Div 1995–; govr More House Sch SW1 1986–95 (dep chm 1991–95); memb Queen's Body Guard for Scotland (Royal Co of Archers) 1981–; kt of Hon and Devotion SMO Malta 1971 (Dir of Ceremonies Br Assoc 1989–95), kt of Justice Sacred Mil Order of Constantine St George 1981; OStJ 1987; Cdr of Merit with Swords 'Pro Merito Melitensi' 1989; Liveryman Haberdashers' Co 1968; Hon FHG 1982, FIMgt, FFA, FSA Scot, FMAT; *Books* The House of Nell Gwyn 1670–1974 (co-author), The House of Dewar 1296–1991, The Family History Record Book 1991, contributor to many pubns; *Clubs* Puffin's, New (Edinburgh); *Style—* Peter Beauclerk-Dewar, Esq, RD, JP; ✉ 22 Faroe Road, Brook Green, London W14 0EP (☎ 0171 371 1365, fax 0171 610 4163, mobile 0860 614817); Coln Cottage, Marston Meysey, Cricklade, Wilts SN6 6LQ (☎ 01285 810126); Holm of Huip, By Stronsay, Orkney Islands

BEAUFORT, 11 Duke of (E 1682); David Robert Somerset; also Baron Herbert of Raglan, Chepstow and Gower (E 1506), Earl of Worcester (E 1513), Marquess of Worcester (E 1642) and hereditary keeper of Raglan Castle; s of Henry Somerset, DSO (d 1965; ggs of 8 Duke), and Bettine (d 1978), yr da of Maj Charles Malcolm (bro of Sir James Malcolm, 9 Bt); suc kinsman, 10 Duke of Beaufort, KG, GCVO, PC, 1984; *b* 23 Feb 1928; *Educ* Eton; *m* 1950, Lady Caroline Jane Thynne (d 1995), da of 6 Marquess of Bath (d 1992); 3 s, 1 da; *Heir* Marquess of Worcester, *qv*; *Career* late Lt Coldstream Gds; chm Marlborough Fine Art 1977–; pres Br Horse Soc 1988–90; *Clubs* White's; *Style—* His Grace the Duke of Beaufort; ✉ Badminton House, North Somerset GL9 1DB

BEAUMAN, Christopher Bentley; s of Wing Cdr Eric Bentley Beauman (d 1989), of London, and Katharine Burgoyne, *née* Jones; *b* 12 Oct 1944; *Educ* Winchester, Trinity Coll Cambridge, John Hopkins Sch of Advanced Int Studies and Columbia Univ (Harkness fell); *m* 1, 1966 (m dis 1976), Sally, *née* Kinsey-Miles; m 2, 1976, Nicola, da of Dr Francis Mann (d 1991), of London; 1 s, 1 da, 3 step c; *Career* corp fin exec Hill Samuel 1968–72; dir: Guinness Mahon 1973–76, FMC Ltd 1975–81; advsr to Chm: BSC 1976–81, Central Policy Review Staff 1981–83, Morgan Grenfell Group 1983–91 (planning dir 1989–91), sr advsr European Bank for Reconstruction and Development 1995– (sr banker 1991–95); Centre for Economic Performance LSE 1994–; *Recreations* reading, family, London; *Style—* Christopher Beauman, Esq; ✉ 35 Christchurch Hill, London NW3 (☎ 0171 435 1975)

BEAUMONT, His Hon (Herbert) Christopher Beaumont; MBE (1948); s of Maj Gerald Beaumont, MC and bar (d 1933), of Woolley Moor House, Wakefield, and Gwendolene, *née* Haworth; *b* 3 June 1912; *Educ* Uppingham, Worcester Coll Oxford; *m* 1940, Helen Margaret Gordon, da of William Mitchell Smail, of Edinburgh; 1 s, 2 da (*see* (Arthur) David Bowyer and Sir Mark Waller); *Career* Indian Civil and Political Servs 1936–47, private sec to Lord Radcliffe chm Indo-Pakistan Boundary Cmmn 1947, FO 1948–52, called to the Bar Inner Temple 1951 (in practice 1951–62), Met magistrate 1962–72, chm London Juvenile Cts 1964, dep chm N Riding QS 1966–71, circuit judge 1972–85, temp resident judge Cyprus 1986; memb Parole Bd 1974–76, a chm Police (Disciplinary) Appeal Tbnl 1988–96; *Recreations* European travel; *Clubs* Brooks's; *Style—* His Hon Christopher Beaumont, MBE; ✉ Minskip Lodge, Boroughbridge, N Yorks (☎ 01423 322365)

BEAUMONT, Christopher Hubert; s of Hubert Beaumont, MP (d 1948), and Beatrix Beaumont (d 1982); *b* 10 Feb 1926; *Educ* W Monmouth Sch Pontypool, Balliol Coll Oxford (MA); *m* 1, 31 Aug 1959, Catherine (d 1971), da of Eric Clark (d 1982); 2 s (Simon b 1962, Guy b 1964); m 2, 28 June 1972, Sara Patricia, da of Cdr William Magee, RN (d 1976); 1 da (Justine b 1973); *Career* served RN 1944–47 (Sub Lt RNVR); called to the Bar Middle Temple 1950, recorder of the Crown Court 1981–; chm Agric Land Tbnl Eastern Area 1985– (dep chm 1979–85); asst dep Coroner Inner W London 1963–81; *Books* Law Relating to Sheriffs (1968), Town and Country Planning Act 1968 (1969), Town and Country Planning Acts 1971 and 1972 (1972), Land Compensation Act 1973 (with W G Nutley, 1973), Community Land Act 1975 (with W G Nutley, 1976), Planning Appeal Decisions (jt ed with W G Nutley, in series since 1986); *Style—* Christopher H Beaumont, Esq; ✉ White Lodge, Crescent Road, Alverstoke, Gosport, Hants PO12 2DU (☎ and fax 01705 583184); 2 Harcourt Buildings, Temple, London EC4Y 9DB (☎ 0171 353 8415, fax 0171 353 7622)

BEAUMONT, HE David Colin Baskcomb; s of late Colin Baskcomb Beaumont, and late Denise Heather, *née* Smith; *b* 16 Aug 1942; *Educ* St Benedict's Sch Ealing; *m* Barbara, da of Edward Morris; 1 da (Diana b 29 Oct 1970), 2 s (Ben b 15 May 1972, Nick b 17 Aug 1973); *Career* HM Dip Serv; asst private sec to Perm Under-Sec Cwlth

Rels Office 1964–65, private sec to Rt Hon Malcolm MacDonald, Special Rep in E and Central Africa Nairobi 1965–67, third sec (political) Bahrain 1967–70, second sec FCO 1970–73, second sec (commercial) Accra 1974–77, first sec FCO 1977–81, first sec (devpt) Kathmandu 1981–82, dep head of mission Addis Ababa 1983–86, first sec later head of Protocol Dept and First Asst Marshal of the Diplomatic Corps 1987–94, high cmmr Botswana 1995–; *Recreations* tennis, walking, cooking; *Clubs* MCC; *Style*— HE Mr David Beaumont; ✉ 42 Harvey Road, Guildford, Surrey GU1 3SE (☎ 01483 39577); c/o Foreign and Commonealth Office (Gaborone), King Charles Street, London SW1A 2AH

BEAUMONT, Sir George Howland Francis; 12 Bt (E 1661), of Stoughton Grange, Leicestershire; s of Sir George Arthur Hamilton Beaumont, 11 Bt (d 1933); *b* 24 Sept 1924; *Educ* Stowe; *m* 1, 1949 (m annulled 1951), Barbara, da of William Singleton; m 2, 1963 (m dis 1985), Henrietta Anne, da of late Dr Arthur Weymouth; 2 da (Georgina Brienne Arabella (Mrs Patrick Beaumont-Fay) b 1967, Francesca Renée Henrietta (Mrs John Beaumont-Clarke) b (twin) 1967); *Heir* none; *Career* formerly warrant offr Australian Army; Coldstream Gds, Lt 60 Rifles WW II; *Clubs* Lansdowne; *Style*— Sir George Beaumont, Bt; ✉ Stretton House, Stretton-on-Fosse, nr Moreton in Marsh, Glos GL56 9SB

BEAUMONT, John Richard; s of Stanley Beaumont (d 1992), of Denmead, Hampshire, and Winifred Louise, *née* Williams (d 1984); *b* 22 June 1947; *Educ* Wolverhampton GS, Merton Coll Oxford (MA); *m* 18 Oct 1986, Susan Margaret, da of Ivan Stanley Blowers, of Oulton Broad, Suffolk; 2 da (Anna Jane b 1988, Rosemary Clare b 1990), 1 s (Andrew James b 1994), 1 step s (Christopher Jones b 1983); *Career* schoolmaster Buckingham Coll Harrow 1969–71; Shelter National Campaign for the Homeless Ltd: regnl organiser W Mids 1971–73, nat projects dir 1973–74; legal offr: Alnwick DC Northumberland 1974, Thurrock Borough Cncl 1974–75; called to the Bar Inner Temple 1976, memb Northern Circuit, full-time chm Industrial Tribunals 1994– (pt/t chm 1992), formerly pt/t legal advsr Assoc Newspapers plc; former memb Mgmnt Ctees of: Bradford Housing and Renewal Experiment (SHARE), North Islington Housing Rights Project; *Recreations* walking, reading history and Victorian literature, having picnics; *Style*— John Beaumont, Esq; ✉ Carlton House, Seymour Chase, Knutsford, Cheshire (☎ 01565 633419); Regional Office of Industrial Tribunals, Alexandra House, 18–22 The Parsonage, Manchester (☎ 0161 833 0581)

BEAUMONT, Prof John Richard; s of Jim Beaumont, of Leeds, and Betty Marie, *née* Jarratt; *b* 24 June 1957; *Educ* Temple Moor Leeds, Univ of Durham (BA); *m* 1, 21 July 1979 (m dis), Margret, da of Prof R Payne; 2 da (Judith Alison b 23 Nov 1980, Claire Marie b 27 Aug 1982); m 2, 19 June 1987 (m dis), Jeanne Ann, da of A Magro; *Career* res asst Univ of Leeds 1978–80, lectr Univ of Keele 1980–83, sr conslt Coopers & Lybrand London and NYC 1983–85, jt md Pinpoint Analysis Ltd 1985–87, ICL prof Univ of Stirling 1987–90, prof of mgmnt Univ of Bath 1990–92, md StrataTech Ltd 1993, dir of strategy and business devpt Energis Communications Ltd 1993–; non-exec dir Office for Nat Statistics 1996–; memb Cncl Economic and Social Res Cncl 1989–93; hon prof: Queen's Univ Belfast 1990–93, City Univ 1994–; FRGS 1985, MIMgt 1987, FRSA 1989; *Publications* Future Cities (1982), Projects in Geography (1983), Introduction to Market Analysis (1992), Information Resources Management (1992), Managing Our Environment (1993); *Recreations* writing, sport, food, wine and travel; *Clubs* Athenaeum; *Style*— Prof John Beaumont; ✉ 92 Lauderdale Tower, Barbican, London EC2Y 8BY; Energis Communications Ltd, Carmelite, 50 Victoria Embankment, London EC4Y 0DE (☎ 0171 936 5504)

BEAUMONT, Martin Dudley; s of Patrick Beaumont, JP, DL, of Donadea Lodge, Clwyd, and (Doreen Elizabeth) Lindesay, *née* Howard; *b* 6 Aug 1949; *Educ* Stowe, Magdalene Coll Cambridge (MA); *m* 12 June 1976, Andrea Evelyn, da of John Wilberforce, of The Red House, Corbridge; 3 da (Alice b 11 July 1980, Jessica b 22 Dec 1981, Flora b 4 Oct 1989); *Career* ptnr KPMG (formerly Thomson McLintock) 1983–87 (dir 1980–87), gp fin dir Egmont Publishing Group 1987–90; dir: World International Publishing Ltd 1987–90, Ward Lock Ltd 1987–89; chief exec: Children's Best Sellers Ltd 1989–90, United Norwest Cooperatives Ltd 1992– (fin controller and sec 1990–92); dir: Norpak Ltd 1991–, Co-operative Press Ltd 1994–, North Staffordshire and South Cheshire Broadcasting Ltd 1995–96, Cooperative Wholesale Society Ltd 1996–, Cooperative Bank plc 1996–; FCA 1977; *Recreations* shooting, fishing, tennis; *Style*— Martin Beaumont, Esq; ✉ Beech Cottage, Hand Green, Tarporley, Cheshire CW6 9SN (☎ 01829 732994)

BEAUMONT, Mary Rose; da of Charles Edward Wauchope (d 1969), and Elaine Margaret, *née* Armstrong-Jones (d 1965); *b* 6 June 1932; *Educ* Prior's Field Godalming Surrey, Courtauld Inst Univ of London (BA); *m* 1955, Timothy Wentworth Beaumont (Baron Beaumont of Whitley, *qv*), s of Michael Wentworth Beaumont; 2 s (Hubert Wentworth b 1956, Alaric Charles Blackett b 1958, d 1980), 2 da (Atalanta Armstrong b 1961, Ariadne Grace b 1963); *Career* fndr Centre for the Study of Modern Art at ICA 1972; writer and art critic for newspapers and periodicals incl: Financial Times, Sunday Telegraph, Art International, Arts Review, Art and Design; author of numerous catalogue introductions for individual artists, teacher at art schs and polys, lectr at Tate Gallery and National Gallery; exhibition curator: for Br Cncl in E Europe and Far East 1983–87, The Human Touch (Fischer Fine Art) 1986, The Dark Side of The Moon (Benjamin Rhodes Gallery) 1990, Three Scottish Artists (Pamela Auchincloss Gallery NY) 1990; Picker Fellowship at Kingston Poly; exec and memb Cncl Contemporary Arts Soc 1980–90, memb Advsy Ctee Govt Art Collection 1994; *Recreations* listening to opera and reading novels; *Clubs* Chelsea Arts; *Style*— Ms Mary Rose Beaumont; ✉ 40 Elms Road, London SW4 9EX (☎ 0171 498 8664)

BEAUMONT, (John) Michael; Seigneur of Sark (cr 1565) 1974–; s of late Lionel (Buster) Beaumont, and Enid, *née* Ripley; gs of Dame Sibyl Mary Hathaway, DBE, Dame of Sark, whom he suc on her death; *b* 20 Dec 1927; *Educ* Loughborough Coll; *m* 1956, Diana, *née* La Trobe-Bateman; 2 s; *Heir* s, Christopher Beaumont; *Career* aircraft design engineer 1952–70, chief tech engr Beagle Aircraft 1969–70, design engr BAC GW Div 1970–75; Seigneur of Sark 1974–; *Style*— Michael Beaumont, Esq; ✉ La Seigneurie, Sark, Channel Islands (☎ 0148183 2017)

BEAUMONT, Capt the Hon (Edward) Nicholas Canning; KCVO (1994, CVO 1986, MVO 1976), DL (Northumberland 1996); 3 s of 2 Viscount Allendale, KG, CB, CBE, MC (d 1956); *b* 14 Dec 1929; *Educ* Eton; *m* 1953, Jane Caroline Falconer, da of Alexander Lewis Paget Falconer Wallace, JP, of Candacraig, Strathdon, Aberdeen; 2 s (Thomas b 1962, Henry b 1966, a page of honour to HM Queen Elizabeth The Queen Mother 1979–82); *Career* joined Life Gds 1948, Capt 1956, ret 1960; asst to clerk of the course Ascot 1964–69, clerk of the course and sec Ascot Authy 1969–94; dir High Gosforth Park 1994–96; KStJ 1996 (SBStJ 1982, OStJ 1988), pres Berkshire St John 1988–94, Vice Lord Lt Berkshire 1989–94 (DL 1982); *Style*— Capt the Hon Sir Nicholas Beaumont, KCVO, DL; ✉ Low Shield House, Sparty Lea, Allendale, Northumberland NE47 9UW (☎ 01434 685037)

BEAUMONT, Sir Richard Ashton; KCMG (1965, CMG 1955), OBE (1949); s of A R Beaumont (d 1962), of Uppingham, Rutland, and Evelyn Frances, *née* Rendle; *b* 29 Dec 1912; *Educ* Repton, Oriel Coll Oxford; *m* 1, 1942, Alou (d 1985), da of M Camran, of Istanbul; 1 da; m 2, 24 Feb 1989, Mrs Melanie E M Anns, da of H Brummell; *Career* served WWII; joined HM Consular Serv 1936, served Beirut and Damascus; FCO: re-joined 1945, served various posts in Middle East and Latin America, head of Arabian Dept 1959, ambass Morocco 1961–65, ambass Iraq 1965–67, dep under-sec of state 1967–69, ambass Egypt 1969–72; chm: Anglo-Arab Assoc 1979–, Arab-Br C of C 1980–; tstee Thomson Fndn 1974–; *Clubs* United Oxford & Cambridge Univ; *Style*— Sir Richard Beaumont, KCMG, OBE; ✉ 82 Peterborough Road, London SW6 3EB

BEAUMONT, Hon Richard Blackett; CVO (1995); 2 s of 2 Viscount Allendale, KG, CB, CBE, MC (d 1956); *b* 13 Aug 1926; *Educ* Eton; *m* 1971, Lavinia Mary (sometime Governess to HRH The Prince Edward), da of late Lt-Col Arnold Keppel (ggs of Rt Rev Hon Frederick Keppel, sometime Bishop of Exeter and 4 s of 2 Earl of Albemarle); *Career* joined RNVR 1944, Sub Lt 1946; PA to Sir Walter Monckton Hyderabad 1947–48, joined James Purdey and Sons 1949 (dir 1952), ADC to Sir Donald MacGillivray Malaya 1954–55, chm James Purdey and Sons 1971–95; memb Ct of Assts Gunmakers' Co (Master 1969 and 1985); *Books* Purdey's, The Guns and the Family (1984); *Recreations* shooting, travel; *Clubs* White's, Turf, Pratt's; *Style*— The Hon Richard Beaumont, CVO; ✉ Flat 1, 13–16 Embankment Gardens, London SW3 4LW (☎ 0171 376 7164)

BEAUMONT, Rupert Roger Seymour; s of Robert Beaumont, of Hampshire, and Peggy Mary Stubbs, *née* Bassett (d 1988); *b* 27 Feb 1944; *Educ* Wellington Coll, Univ of Grenoble France; *m* 24 Feb 1968, Susie Diane, da of Noel Sampson James Wishart; 1 s (James b 1971), 1 da (Juliet b 1972); *Career* articled clerk Beaumont & Son 1962–68, admitted slr 1968, with Appleton Rice and Perrin NY USA 1968–69, ptnr Slaughter and May 1974– (joined 1969, Hong Kong office 1976–81); author various articles for learned jls; hon fell ACT, memb Law Soc 1973; *Recreations* tennis, fishing, carpentry; *Clubs* Cavalry and Guards; *Style*— Rupert Beaumont, Esq; ✉ Slaughter and May, 35 Basinghall Street, London EC2V 5DB (☎ 0171 600 1200, fax 0171 726 0038/0171 600 0289)

BEAUMONT, Hon Wentworth Peter Ismay; s and h of 3 Viscount Allendale, *qv*; *b* 13 Nov 1948; *Educ* Harrow; *m* 1975, Theresa Mary Magdalene, da of Frank More O'Ferrall (d 1977); 1 s, 3 da; *Career* landowner; chm of Northumberland Assoc of Boys' Clubs; *Recreations* shooting, skiing, horseracing; *Clubs* Jockey, Northern Counties, White's; *Style*— The Hon Wentworth Beaumont; ✉ Bywell Castle, Stocksfield-on-Tyne, Northumberland (☎ 01661 842450, office 01661 843296, fax 01661 842838); Flat 7, 8 Draycott Place, London SW3 2SB (☎ 0171 584 6826)

BEAUMONT, William Anderson; CB (1986), OBE (Mil 1961), AE (1958); s of William Lionel Beaumont, of Nesbit Hall, Pudsey, W Yorks (d 1956), and Ivy Mima, *née* Anderson (d 1990); *b* 30 Oct 1924; *Educ* Moorlands Sch Leeds, Terrington Hall York, Cranleigh, ChCh Oxford (MA, DipEd); *m* 1, 24 Aug 1946, Kythé, *née* Mackenzie (d 1988); 1 da (Kythé Victoria b 1958); m 2, 3 June 1989, Rosalie Jean Underhill, *née* Kinloch, wid of Judge Michael Underhill, QC; *Career* navigator RAF 1942–47, 355 Sqdn, 232 Sqdn, SEAC (Flt Lt); RAuxAF 3507 (Co of Somerset) Fighter Control Unit 1948–54, 3609 (W Riding) Fighter Control Unit 1954–61 (Wing Cdr CO 1958–61), Observer Cdr No 18 (Leeds) Gp Royal Observer Corps 1962–75 (ROC Medal 1975); asst master Bristol GS 1951–54; md: Beaumont and Smith Ltd Pudsey Yorks (textile mfrs) 1954–66, Henry Mason (Shipley) Ltd (textile mfrs) 1966–76; asst sec Welsh Office Cardiff 1976–82, Speaker's sec House of Commons 1982–86; ret; active in various official and semi-official bodies incl: dir St David's Forum (Fforum Dewi Sant) 1986–92, memb Panel of Chairmen Civil Serv Selection Bd 1988–93, pres RAF Club Dining Soc 1991–, vice chm Franco-Br Soc 1991–, chm Sub-Ctee RAF Benevolent Fund, rep Offrs' Assoc; *Recreations* inland waterways; *Clubs* RAF, Civil Service, United Services (Cardiff); *Style*— W A Beaumont, Esq, CB, OBE, AE; ✉ 28 Halford Rd, Richmond, Surrey TW10 6AP (☎ 0181 940 2390)

BEAUMONT, William Blackledge (Bill); OBE (1982); s of Ronald Walton Beaumont, of Croston, Lancs, and Joyce, *née* Blackledge; *b* 9 March 1952; *Educ* Ellesmere Coll; *m* 1977, Hilary Jane, da of Kenneth Seed, of Iken House, Freckleton, Preston, Lancs; 2 s (Daniel b 1982, Samuel b 1985); *Career* co dir J Blackledge and Son Ltd 1981; dir: Red Rose Radio 1981, Chorley and District Bldg Soc 1983; England Rugby capt 1977–82, Br Lions capt SA 1980, Barbarians capt, Lancashire capt, capt England to Grand Slam 1980; BBC sports analyst: Grandstand, Rugby Special; team capt A Question of Sport (BBC 1) until 1996; *Books* Thanks to Rugby (autobiography, 1982); *Recreations* golf, boating; *Clubs* E India, Royal Lytham Golf, Fylde RUFC; *Style*— Bill Beaumont, Esq, OBE

BEAUMONT-DARK, Sir Anthony Michael; kt (1992); s of Leonard Cecil Dark; *b* 11 Oct 1932; *Educ* Birmingham Coll of Arts and Crafts, Univ of Birmingham; *m* 1959, Sheelagh Irene, da of R Cassey; 1 s, 1 da; *Career* investmt analyst and company dir, memb Birmingham Stock Exchange 1958–; Smith Keen Cutler: ptnr 1959–85, sr ptnr 1970–80, conslt 1985–95; conslt Brewin Dolphin Holdings PLC 1995–; contested (C) Birmingham Aston 1959 and 1964, MP (C) Birmingham Selly Oak 1979–92; dir: Wigham Poland (Midlands) Ltd 1960–82, National Exhibition Centre Ltd 1971–73, J Saville Gordon PLC 1989– (dep chm 1994–), TR High Income Trust PLC 1990– (chm 1994–), Cope Allman International Ltd 1972–89; Birmid Qualcast PLC 1983–89, chm Birmingham Executive Airways PLC 1983–86; memb: Central Housing Advsy Ctee DOE 1970–76, Treasy Civil Serv Select Ctee 1979–92, Birmingham City Cncl 1956–73 (chm Fin Ctee 1969–73), W Midlands County Cncl 1973–87 (chm Fin Ctee 1977–83); govr: Univ of Aston 1980–94, Univ of Birmingham 1984–92; tstee Birmingham Copec Housing Tst 1975–80; Alderman City of Birmingham 1967–74, Hon Alderman City of Birmingham 1976–, Freeman City of London 1982–, Liveryman Worshipful Co of Glovers 1982–; MSI 1989–, AIIMR 1965–, FRSA 1993; *Clubs* Carlton; *Style*— Sir Anthony Beaumont-Dark; ✉ 124 Lady Byron Lane, Knowle, Solihull, West Midlands B93 9BA

BEAUMONT OF WHITLEY, Baron (Life Peer UK 1967); Timothy Wentworth Beaumont; o s of late Maj Michael Wentworth Beaumont, TD (d 1958, gs of 1 Baron Allendale) by 1 w, Hon Faith Muriel, *née* Pease (d 1935), da of 1 Baron Gainford; *b* 22 Nov 1928; *Educ* Eton, Gordonstoun, ChCh Oxford, Westcott House Camb; *m* 13 June 1955, Mary Rose Beaumont, *qv*, yr da of Lt-Col Charles Edward Wauchope, MC (d 1969); 2 s (Hubert Wentworth b 1956, Alaric Charles Blackett b 1958, d 1980), 2 da (Atalanta Armstrong b 1961, Ariadne Grace b 1963); *Career* vicar of Christ Church Kowloon Hong Kong 1957–59 (resigned Holy Orders 1979, resumed 1984); proprietor various periodicals incl Time and Tide, Prism and New Christian 1960–70; pres Lib Pty 1969–70 (head of orgn 1965–66), del to Parly Assembly Cncl of Europe and Western Euro Union 1974–77; chm Studio Vista Books 1963–68; dir Green Alliance 1977–79; memb: Nat Exec Church Action on Poverty (CAP) 1982–86 and 1991–94, Lib Dem Federal Policy Ctee 1992–95; Lib spokesman House of Lords on educn, arts and the environment 1967–85, Lib Dem spokesman House of Lords Conservation and the Countryside 1993–; vicar of St Luke's and St Philip's (The Barn Church) Kew 1986–91, co-organiser Southwark Diocese Spiritual Directors Course 1994–96; *Books* Where Shall I Place My Cross? (1987); *Recreations* gardening; *Style*— The Rev the Rt Hon Lord Beaumont; ✉ 40 Elms Rd, London SW4 9EX

BEAVEN, John Lewis; CMG (1986), CVO (1983, MVO 1974); s of Charles Beaven (d 1967), and Margaret Beaven (d 1973); *b* 30 July 1930; *Educ* Newport HS Gwent; *m* 1, 1960 (m dis), Jane Beeson; 1 s, 1 da; m 2, 1975, Jean McComb Campbell; *Career* Flying Offr RAF Res 1948–50; BOT 1947; HM Dip Serv 1956–90; dep consul-gen New York and dir Br Trade Devpt Off NY 1978–82, consul-gen San Francisco 1982–86, ambass Khartoum 1986–90 (ret); US rep Save the Children Fund 1990–; *Recreations* computing, music, tennis, walking; *Style*— John Beaven, Esq, CMG, CVO; ✉ Scannell Rd, Ghent, NY 12075, USA (☎ 518 392 2152, fax 518 392 9418)

BEAVEN, Philip Edwin; s of Edwin George Beaven, of Pembrey, Dyfed, and Gwyneth, *née* Phillips; *b* 4 March 1946; *Educ* Dulwich, Queen's Coll Oxford (MA); *m* 2, 7 Sept 1984, Anna Margaret, *née* Marshall; 1 s (Jonathan Edwin b 4 June 1985); *Career* actuarial trainee Mercantile & General Reinsurance Co Ltd 1967–70, various positions rising to mangr investmt policy Hill Samuel Life Assurance Ltd 1970–83; Hill Samuel Investment Management Ltd: sr mangr UK Fixed Interest 1983–87, dir UK Fixed Interest 1987–90, dir of UK ops 1990–91, md 1991–; AIA 1972; *Recreations* travel, flying, theatre, rugby; *Clubs* RAF (hon memb); *Style—* Philip Beaven, Esq; ✉ Hill Samuel Investment Management Ltd, 10 Fleet Street, London EC4M 7RH (☎ 0171 203 3000, fax 0171 203 3038)

BEAVERBROOK, 3 Baron (UK 1917); Sir Maxwell William Humphrey Aitken; 3 Bt (UK 1916); s of Sir Max Aitken, 2 Bt, DSO, DFC (d 1985; suc as 2 Baron Beaverbrook 1964, which he disclaimed for life 1964) by his 3 w, Violet (*see* Lady Aitken); *b* 29 Dec 1951; *Educ* Charterhouse, Pembroke Coll Cambridge; *m* 1974, Susan Angela (Susie), da of Francis More O'Ferrall and Angela (niece of Sir George Mather-Jackson, 5 Bt, and da of Sir Anthony Mather-Jackson 6 Bt, JP, DL, by his w, Evelyn, da of Lt-Col Sir Henry Stephenson, 1 Bt, DSO); 2 s (Maxwell b 1977, Alexander Rory b 1978), 2 da (Charlotte 1982, Sophia b 1985); *Heir* s, Hon Maxwell Francis Aitken, b 17 March 1977; *Career* dir Ventech Ltd 1983–86, chm and pres Ventech Healthcare Corporation Inc 1988–92 (chm 1986); govt whip House of Lords 1986–88; treas: Cons Party 1990–92 (dep treas 1988–90), Euro Democratic Union 1990–92; tstee Beaverbrook Fndn 1974– (chm 1985–); memb Cncl Homeopathic Tst 1989–92, chm Nat Assoc of Boys' Clubs 1989–92; *Clubs* White's; *Style—* The Rt Hon the Lord Beaverbrook; ✉ House of Lords, London SW1

BEAVIS, Air Chief Marshal Sir Michael Gordon; KCB (1981), CBE (1977, OBE 1969), AFC (1962); s of Walter Erle Beavis (d 1972), of Haverhill, and Mary Ann, *née* Sarjantson (d 1990); *b* 13 Aug 1929; *Educ* Kilburn GS; *m* 9 Dec 1949, Joy Marion, da of Arthur Olwen Jones (d 1974); 1 s (Simon Anthony b 1 Jan 1960), 1 da (Lynn Alison Deborah b 16 April 1956); *Career* joined RAF 1947, cmmnd 1949, served Fighter Cmd Sqdns 1950–54, RNZAF 1954–56, flew Vulcan aircraft Bomber Cmd 1958–62, Staff Coll 1963, MOD 1964–66, OC No 10 Sqdn (VC10s) 1966–68, Gp Capt Flying Akrotiri Cyprus 1968–71, asst dir Def Policy MOD 1971–73, RCDS 1974, RAF Germany 1975–77 (SASO 1976–77), DG RAF Trg 1977–80, Cmdt RAF Staff Coll 1980–81, Air Marshal 1981, AOC-in-C RAF Support Cmd 1981–84, Air Chief Marshal 1984, Dep C-in-C Allied Forces Central Europe 1984–86, ret 1987; non-exec dir: Black & Edgington Group 1989–95 (latterly dep chm), SkyePharma Group plc 1996–; Freeman City of London 1980, Liveryman Guild of Air Pilots and Air Navigators 1982; CIMgt; *Recreations* golf, skiing, travel; *Clubs* RAF; *Style—* Air Chief Marshal Sir Michael Beavis, KCB, CBE, AFC; ✉ c/o Lloyds Bank Ltd, 202 High Street, Lincoln LN5 7AP

BEBB, Maureen Mary; da of Carl Burcham Bebb, of 16 Compton Place Rd, Eastbourne, Sussex, and Mary Ethel, *née* Barnes; *b* 16 Sept 1938; *Educ* St Maur's Convent Weybridge Surrey, Rosslyn House Weybridge Surrey; *Career* BBC World Service: sec 1956, studio mangr 1961, prog planner World Serv 1966, sr then chief prog planner World Serv 1973, chief asst directorate World Serv 1983–; *Recreations* opera, theatre, travel, food, wine, bridge; *Clubs* Ski Club of GB; *Style—* Miss Maureen Bebb; ✉ BBC World Service, Bush House, Strand, London WC2B 4PH (☎ 0171 257 2097, fax 0171 379 6841)

BECHER, *see:* Wrixon-Becher

BECK, Rev Brian Edgar; s of Alfred George Beck (d 1992), of Tooting, London, and Cicely Annie, *née* Roots (d 1987); *b* 27 Sept 1933; *Educ* City of London Sch, Corpus Christi Coll Cambridge, Wesley House Cambridge (MA); *m* 9 Aug 1958, Margaret Elizabeth Christie, da of William Ernest Ludlow (d 1952), of Basingstoke, Hants; 3 da (Eleanor (Mrs Cribb) b 1961, Julia (Mrs Ingram) b 1963, Marian b 1966); *Career* asst tutor Handsworth Coll 1957–59, ordained Methodist minister 1960, E Suffolk Circuit 1959–62, St Paul's United Theol Coll Limuru Kenya 1962–68, princ Wesley House Cambridge 1980–84 (tutor 1968–80), sec Methodist Conf 1984– (pres 1993–94); *Books* Reading the New Testament Today (1977), Christian Character in the Gospel of Luke (1989); contrib to: Christian Belief: A Catholic-Methodist Statement (1970), Unity the Next Step? (1972), Suffering & Martyrdom in the New Testament (1981); *Recreations* walking, DIY; *Style—* The Rev Brian E Beck; ✉ 76 Beaumont Road, Purley, Surrey CR8 2EG (☎ and fax 0181 645 9162); 25 Marylebone Road, London NW1 5JR (☎ 0171 486 5502, fax 0171 224 1510)

BECK, Charles Theodore Heathfield; s of Richard Theodore Beck, and Margaret Beryl, *née* Page; *b* 3 April 1954; *Educ* Winchester, Jesus Coll Cambridge (MA); *m* 19 Sept 1992, Nathakan Piyawannahong, da of Wan Saklor; *Career* Bank of England 1975–79; J M Finn & Co stockbrokers: joined 1979, ptnr 1984, fin ptnr 1988–91, 1993–; Freeman City of London 1980, Liveryman Worshipful Co of Broderers 1981; AIIMR 1980, MSI; *Recreations* fencing, Japanese fencing, archaeology; *Style—* Charles Beck, Esq; ✉ c/o J M Finn & Co, Salisbury House, London Wall, London EC2M 5TA (☎ 0171 628 9688, fax 0171 628 7314, telex 887281)

BECK, Clive; s of Sir Edgar Charles Beck, CBE, and his 1 wife, Mary Agnes, *née* Sorapure; *b* 12 April 1937; *Educ* Ampleforth; *m* 28 April 1960, Philippa Mary, da of Dr Philip Flood (d 1968), of Wimbledon; 3 s (David b 28 July 1962, Andrew b 22 Sept 1964, Simon b 30 Dec 1965), 3 da (Nicola b 17 Feb 1961, Emma b 19 Dec 1967, Sarah b 16 July 1971); *Career* 2 Lt The Life Guards 1955–57; John Mowlem & Co 1957, joined SGB Gp plc 1967 (dir 1968, chm 1985); rejoined John Mowlem & Co plc as dep chm and jt md (on acquisition of SGB by Mowlem 1986) until 1992; dir Pioneer Concrete Holdings plc; chm: UK Detention Services Ltd, London Management Ltd; Freeman of City of London 1960, Liveryman Worshipful Co of Plaisterers; *Recreations* fishing, golf; *Clubs* Royal Wimbledon Golf, Swinley Forest Golf; *Style—* Clive Beck, Esq; ✉ 2 Parkside Gdns, Wimbledon, London SW19 5EY (☎ 0181 946 5076, fax 0181 241 7723)

BECK, David Clive; s of Clive Beck, and Philippa, *née* Flood; *b* 28 July 1962; *Educ* Ampleforth, Univ of Kent at Canterbury (BA); *m* 18 July 1992, Katherine, *née* Millar; *Career* Lowe Bell Financial (PR consultancy): joined 1986, dir 1992–, dep md 1995–; *Recreations* golf, fishing, tennis; *Clubs* Swinley Forest Golf; *Style—* David Beck, Esq; ✉ 33 St Stephen's Terrace, London SW8 1DL; Lowe Bell Financial Ltd, 1 Red Lion Court, London EC4A 3EB (☎ 0171 353 9203, fax 0171 583 5207, mobile 0836 293383)

BECK, Dr Eric Robert; s of Dr Adolf Beck (d 1986), of London, and Helen, *née* Marhold (d 1992); *b* 26 Aug 1934; *Educ* St Paul's, UCL (BSc, MB BS); *m* 1, 18 Aug 1956, Patricia Chapman (d 1975); 1 s (Martin b 1963), 1 da (Helen Carol b 1959); m 2, 29 Feb 1980, Pamela Mary, da of Francis Leonard Bretherton (d 1987), of Kempsey, Worcs; 1 da (Lucy Claire b 1985); *Career* conslt physician Whittington Hosp London 1969–, hon sr clinical lectr in med UCH and Middx Hosp 1971–, fell UCL 1993; recognised teacher Univ of London 1971–, chm Part 2 Examination Bd MRCP(UK) 1995–; fndr memb and former treas NHS Conslts Assoc, cncl memb Mayer-Lismann Opera Workshop; memb BMA; MRCP 1961, FRCP 1974; *Books* Whittington Postgraduate Medicine (1974), Tutorials in Differential Diagnosis (1974, 1982, 3 edn 1992), In the Best of Health? (1992); *Recreations* opera, squash, hill walking; *Style—* Dr Eric Beck; ✉ 59 Glasslyn Rd, London N8 8RJ (☎ 0181 340 1564); Whittington Hospital, London N19 5NF (☎ 0171 288 5410); Royal College of Physicians, St Andrew's Place, Regents Park, London NW1 4LE (☎ 0171 935 1174)

BECK, Prof John Swanson; s of John Beck (d 1976), of Glasgow, and Mary, *née* Barbour (d 1976); *b* 22 Aug 1928; *Educ* Glasgow Acad, Univ of Glasgow (BSc, MB, MD), Univ of Dundee (DSc); *m* 10 June 1960, Marion Tudhope, da of Lt Cdr John Clendinning Paterson, DSO (d 1970), of Glasgow; 1 s (John b 1962), 1 da (Patricia Mary Swanson b 1965); *Career* lectr Univ of Glasgow 1958–63, sr lectr Univ of Aberdeen 1963–71, prof of pathology Univ of Dundee 1971–93 (emeritus 1993); fndn dean Int Med Coll Kuala Lumpur Malaysia 1992–; MRC: memb Cell Bd 1978–82, chm Breast Tumour Panel 1979–91; chm Clinical and Biomed Res Ctee Scot Home and Health Dept 1983–93; memb: Tayside Heath Bd 1983–91, Chief Scientist Ctee Scottish Home & Health Dept 1983–93, Cncl RSE 1986–89 (convenor Grants Ctee 1991–93), Med Advsy Bd LEPRA 1987–93, Nat Biol Standards Bd 1988–93 (chm Scientific Policy Advsy Ctee 1991–93); memb Incorporation of Masons Glasgow 1960, Bonnetmaker Craftsman Incorporated Trades Dundee 1973; FRCPG 1965, FRCPE 1966, FRCPath 1975, FRSE 1984, FIBiol 1987, CBiol 1987, EurBiol 1996, FRSA 1991; *Recreations* DIY work; *Clubs* Clyde Canoe, Royal Cwlth Soc, Bukit Kiara (Kuala Lumpur); *Style—* Prof John Beck, FRSE; ✉ Unit 30–3–3 Jamnah View, Jl Buluh Perindu, 59000 Kuala Lumpur, Malaysia (☎ 00 60 3 253 7242); International Medical Coll, 21 Jl Selangor, Petaling Jaya 46050, Malaysia (☎ 00 60 3 758 4244, fax 00 60 3 758 4239)

BECK, Lesley Susan Barron; da of Laurence Barron Beck, and Marjorie Stewart, *née* Reid; *b* 10 July 1964; *Educ* Jordanhill Coll Sch, Perth Coll of Further Educn, Motherwell Coll of Further Educn, Université de Savoie, Strathclyde Graduate Business Sch; *Career* slalom skier; Br jr champion 1980 and 1982, Br sr champion 1982, 1984–87 and 1992, Br dry slope champion 1987, 1989–92, Le Sauze Grand Prix winner 1984, Bronze medallist N American series 1986, 10 place World Slalom Championships 1987; memb: Br World Championship Team 1982, 1985–89 and 1991, Br Olympic Team 1984 and 1988; athletes' rep to Br Olympic Ctee 1984–88; memb: Alpine Exec Ctee Br Ski Fedn 1991–, Ladies Alpine Ctee Int Ski Fedn 1994–; *Recreations* other sports, rock climbing, grass skiing, cycling, photography, reading non-fiction; *Clubs* Scottish Ski, Bearsden Ski, Lang Craigs Climbing; *Style—* Ms Lesley Beck; ✉ 9 Kings Wark Court, 42 The Shore, Leith EH6 6QU; British Ski Federation, 258 Main St, East Calder, West Lothian EH53 0EE (☎ 01506 884343)

BECK, Dr Michael Hawley; s of William Hawley Beck, of Crewe, Cheshire, and June Aldersey, *née* Davenport; *b* 20 Oct 1948; *Educ* Sandbach Sch, Univ of Liverpool (MB ChB); *m* 18 March 1978, Gerralynn (Lynn), da of John Harrop (d 1986), of Worsley, Manchester; 2 s (Jamie b 1979, Robin b 1981); *Career* sr house offr: Clatterbridge Hosp Wirral 1972–74, neurosurgery Walton Hosp 1974; registrar in med Trafford Health Authy 1976–77, registrar and sr registrar in dermatology Salford Health Authy 1977–81 (sr house offr gen med 1974–76), conslt dermatologist NW RHA 1981–; Univ of Manchester: hon assoc lectr in dermatology 1981–92, hon clinical lectr in dermatology and occupational health 1992–; dermatological advsr to the Ileostomy Assoc of UK and Ireland 1982–, chm NW Regnl Sub-Ctee on Dermatology 1985–88, chm Br Contact Dermatitis Gp 1992–95; memb Steering Gp Epi-Derm 1994–; memb: Euro Contact Dermatitis Soc, Int Contact Dermatitis Computer Gp, American Contact Dermatitis Soc, Dowling Club 1977; author of various articles in med jls and books relating to clinical dermatology and contact dermatitis; MRCP 1977, FRSM 1981, FRCP 1991; memb: NEDS 1981, BAD 1981; *Recreations* genealogy; *Style—* Dr Michael Beck; ✉ 23 St John St, Manchester M3 4DT (☎ 0161 832 3080)

BECK, Sir (Edgar) Philip; kt (1988); s of Sir Edgar Charles Beck, CBE, and his 1 wife Mary Agnes, *née* Sorapure; *b* 9 Aug 1934; *Educ* Ampleforth, Jesus Coll Cambridge (MA); *m* 1, 1957 (m dis), Thomasina Joanna Jeal; 2 s (Adam, Thomas); m 2, 7 Feb 1991, Bridget Alexandra, da of Brig Roderick Heathcoat-Amory, MC, and formerly w of Michael R L Cockerell; *Career* chm John Mowlem and Co plc 1979–95 (dir 1963–95), former dir of various associated cos; non-exec dir: Siebe plc 1991–, Kitagawa Europe Ltd, Delta plc 1994–, Yorkshire Electricity Group plc 1995–, Railtrack Group plc 1995–; chm Federation of Civil Engrg Contractors 1982–83; *Recreations* sailing, flying; *Clubs* Royal Yacht Sqdn; *Style—* Sir Philip Beck; ✉ 67–68 Jermyn Street, London SW1Y 6NY (☎ and fax 0171 839 6763)

BECK-COULTER, (Eva Maria) Barbara; da of Wilhelm Beck (d 1979), of Hameln/Weser, Germany, and Clara Herta Edith Ursula Kothe (d 1989); *b* 14 Oct 1941; *Educ* Victoria-Luise Gymnasium Hameln Germany, Munich Univ, Univ of London (BSc); *m* 1971, Ian Coulter, s of William Coulter; 2 s (William Angus b 29 Sept 1974, Benjamin Ian b 19 June 1976), 1 da (Catherine Barbara b 10 Sept 1978); *Career* The Economist: researcher 1965–69, writer on business affairs 1969–74, ed Euro Community Section 1974–78, Euro ed 1978–81, asst ed 1980–81, surveys ed 1995–; sec gen Anglo-German Fndn for the Study of Industl Soc 1981–91, ed International Management Magazine (part of Reed International) 1991–94, head of public affairs (Europe) Andersen Consulting 1994; memb Cncl RIIA 1984–90 (memb Exec Ctee 1989–90), memb Academic Cncl Wilton Park (FCO Conf Centre) 1984–91, memb Steering Ctee Königswinter Conf 1982–91, memb Int Cncl Sci Centre Berlin (Social Sci Res) 1990–94, memb Cncl Federal Tst 1993–94; broadcaster, writer and lectr on current affairs in English and German; FRSA 1990; *Recreations* my children, music, walking, food; *Clubs* Reform (chm 1992–93, tstee 1995–); *Style—* Mrs Barbara Beck-Coulter; ✉ c/o The Economist, 25 St James's Street, London SW1A 1HG (☎ 0171 830 7168, fax 0171 839 2968)

BECKERMAN, (Claire) Deborah (Debbie); da of Wilfred Beckerman, of Balliol Coll, Oxford, and Nicole Geneviève, *née* Ritter (d 1979); *b* 5 Sept 1961; *Educ* Oxford HS For Girls, Somerville Coll Oxford (BA, tennis blue); *m* 29 June 1991, Keith Jones; 1 s (Nicholas b 12 Dec 1993), 1 da (Natasha b 13 Jan 1996); *Career* publisher; sec International Management Group 1984, ed of four book clubs Book Club Associates 1986–88 (grad trainee 1985), publishing mangr sporting imprint Partridge Press Transworld Publishers 1988–96; *Recreations* tennis, skiing, cinema, theatre, good food; *Clubs* David Lloyd Tennis; *Style—* Ms Debbie Beckerman; ✉ 20 Southwood Lane, Highgate, London N6 5EE (☎ 0181 348 7524)

BECKET, Michael Ivan H; *b* 11 Sept 1938; *Educ* Wynyard Sch Ascot, Sloane Sch Chelsea, Open Univ; *Career* Nat Serv 1957–59; lathe operator Elliot Bros (London) Ltd 1956–57, exhibition organiser Shell International Petroleum 1959–61, journalist Electrical & Radio Trading 1961, market res Young & Rubicam 1962; civil serv 1962–68 (Bd of Trade, Nat Bd for Prices and Incomes, Nat Econ Devpt Office); Daily Telegraph 1968–; dir Flame Books; *Books* Computer by the Tail (1972), Economic Alphabet (1976), Bluff Your Way in Finance (1990), Office Warfare: The Executive Survival Guide to Office Warfare (1993); *Style—* Michael Ivan H Becket, Esq; ✉ 9 Kensington Park Gardens, London W11 3HB (☎ 0171 727 6941); Daily Telegraph, 4 Fore Street, London EC2Y 5DT (☎ 0171 538 5000)

BECKETT, Allan Harry; MBE; s of George William Harry Beckett, MM (d 1949), of Belvedere, Kent, and Emma Louise, *née* Stokes (d 1983); *b* 4 March 1914; *Educ* East Ham Secdy Sch, London Univ (BSc); *m* 25 June 1949, Ida Gwladys, da of Kenbryd Morris James, DCM (d 1983), of Keston, Kent; 2 s (Michael b 1950, Timothy b 1953), 1 da (Sian b 1957); *Career* engrg asst: A J Bridle 1934–35, HM Office of Works 1935–37; bridge designer Br Steelwork Assoc 1937–38, asst site engr Woolwich Arsenal Chief Architects Dept 1938–39; RE 1940, 142 OCTU 1940, cmmnd 2 Lt 1941, Capt 1942, Staff Maj 1942, tech advsr in field 21 Army RE 1944, seconded to BAOR 1945; formerly sr engr Sir Bruce White; Wolfe Barry and Partners Conslting Engrs: sr engr 1946–57, ptnr 1957–83, sr ptnr 1983–88; conslt Beckett Rankine Partnership 1988–; FICE, MIConsE; *Books* numerous tech papers on engrg; *Recreations* sailing; *Clubs* St Stephens and Erith Yacht; *Style—* Allan Beckett, Esq, MBE; ✉ Thistledown, Wood Way, Farnborough Park, Kent;

83 Abbey St, Faversham, Kent (☎ 01689 852193); Beckett Rankine Partnership, 270 Vauxhall Bridge Road, Westminster, London SW1V 1BB (☎ 0171 233 6423, fax 0171 834 7265)

BECKETT, Bruce Probart; s of Capt James Donald Lancaster Beckett (d 1969), and Florence Theresa, *née* Probart (d 1983); *b* 7 June 1924; *Educ* Rondebosch Boys' HS Cape Town, Cape Town Univ (BArch), UCL (DipTP); *m* 9 May 1957, Jean, da of William Low McDonald (d 1949); 2 s (John, Malcolm), 3 da (Elizabeth, Janet, Margaret); *Career* sea cadet RNVR SA Div 1938–42 (later cadet petty offr RNVR), WWII SANF seconded RN 1943, Midshipman 1943, Sub Lt 1944; active serv: S Atlantic, W Africa, Med, Western Approaches; Lt Indian Ocean 1946, Antarctic Expdn SANR 1948, escort to HM King George VI and Royal Family Visit to South Africa 1948 in HMS Nigeria, Lt Cdr 1950, resigned cmmn 1960; architect: Lightfoot Twentyman-Jones & Kent Cape Town 1951–59, Arthur Kenyon & Ptnrs 1960–61; Civil Serv: sr architect WO 1961–64, supt architect Directorate-Gen of Res Devpt MPBW 1964–67, chief architect and under sec Scottish Office 1967–84; ptnr Hutchison Locke & Monk 1984–86; in private practice as chartered architect, town and country planner and building conslt; hon sec Cape Town Architectural Assoc, sr vice pres Edinburgh Architectural Assoc; memb Cncl: Royal Incorporation of Architects (Scotland) 1970–86, RIBA 1972–78 (vice pres 1972–76), ARCUK 1968–92; MIA 1966, FRIBA, FRIAS, FRTPI, FCIOB; *Recreations* gardening, drawing, watercolour painting, DIY; *Clubs* New (Edinburgh), Arts (London), Kelvin (Cape Town); *Style—* Bruce Beckett, Esq; ✉ Summerfield, Vines Cross Rd, Horam, nr Heathfield, E Sussex TN21 OHE (☎ 01435 812042); 7/6 Ettrickdale Place, Edinburgh EH3 5JN (☎ 0131 556 2867)

BECKETT, Maj-Gen Denis Arthur; CB (1971), DSO (1944), OBE (1960); s of Archibald Edward Beckett (d 1976), of Radlett, Herts, and Margery Mildred, *née* Robinson (d 1954); *b* 19 May 1917; *Educ* Forest Sch Essex, Chard Sch Somerset; *m* 1, 1946, Elizabeth, da of Col Guy Edwards, DSO, MC (d 1962), of Rockcliffe House, Upper Slaughter, Glos; 1 s (Nigel Robert b 1954); m 2, 1978, Nancy Ann, da of Charles Bradford Hitt (d 1957), of Grosse Pointe, Michigan, USA; *Career* Maj-Gen (late Parachute Regt), COS Far East Land Forces 1966–68, dir Personal Servs (Army) 1968–71; tstee Airborne Forces Museum 1985–95, govr Forest Sch 1985–95; Freeman City of London, Liveryman Worshipful Co of Coopers; FIMgt; *Clubs* Army and Navy, Lansdowne; *Style—* Maj-Gen Denis Beckett, CB, DSO, OBE; ✉ 12 Wellington House, Eton Rd, London NW3 4SY

BECKETT, Hon Edward John; s and h of 4 Baron Grimthorpe, OBE, DL, *qv*; *b* 20 Nov 1954; *Educ* Hawtreys, Harrow; *m* 20 May 1992, Mrs Carey Elisabeth McEwen, yr da of Robin Graham; 1 s (Harry Maximillian b 28 April 1993); *Style—* The Hon Edward Beckett

BECKETT, Maj-Gen Edwin Horace Alexander; CB (1988), MBE (1974); s of William Alexander Beckett (d 1986), of Sheffield, and Doris, *née* Whitham (d 1989); *b* 16 May 1937; *Educ* Henry Fanshawe Sch, RMA Sandhurst; *m* 1963, Micaela Elizabeth Benedicta, yr da of Col Sir Edward Malet (d 1990); 3 s (Simon b 1965, Alexander b 1979, Thomas b 1980), 1 da (Diana b 1964); *Career* cmmnd West Yorks Regt 1957; regtl serv: Aden (despatches 1968), Gibraltar, Germany, NI; DAA and QMG 11 Armd Bde 1972–74, CO 1 PWO 1976–78 (despatches 1977), GSO1 (DS) Staff Coll 1979, Cmdt Jr Div Staff Coll 1980, Cdr UKMF and 6 Field Force 1981, Cdr UKMF 1 Inf Bde and Tidworth Garrison 1982; dir: Concepts MOD 1983–84, Army Plans and Progs MOD 1984–85; chief of staff HQ BAOR 1985–88, head of Br Def Staff and def attaché Washington DC 1988–91; dir of corporate affairs International Distillers and Vintners Ltd 1992–96; fndr chm Br Producers and Brand Owners Group 1993–95, chm British Brands Group 1995–, dir Southern Africa Business Assoc 1995–; *Recreations* fishing, golf; *Clubs* Cavalry and Guards, Woodroffe's, Pilgrims; *Style—* Maj-Gen Edwin Beckett, CB, MBE

BECKETT, Frances Mary (Fran); da of Josephine Godwin, *née* Beckett; *b* 20 Nov 1951; *Educ* CSQW, Cert in Biblical Studies, MSc Vol Sector Orgn; *Career* trainee mental welfare offr Somerset CC 1969–71, professional social work trg Trent Poly Nottingham 1971–73, rejoined Somerset CC as social worker 1973–75, religious educn studies ANCC Herts 1975–77, student counselling 1977–81, community worker and advice centre mangr 1981–86; Shaftesbury Society: social work advsr 1986–90, community care coordinator 1990–92, urban action dir 1992–95, chief executive 1995–; memb Bd of Govrs London Bible Coll, dir Christian Impact; memb Cncl: Evangelical Alliance, Reference/Pioneer Tst Links Int, Social Workers Christian Fellowship; memb ACENVO 1995; *Books* Called to Action (1989), Love in Action (1993); also author of various articles in religious and professional jls; *Recreations* local church involvement, jazz, cinema, theatre; *Style—* Ms Fran Beckett; ✉ Shaftesbury Society, 16 Kingston Road, London SW19 1JZ (☎ 0181 239 5580, fax 0181 239 5555)

BECKETT, Frank Blair; s of Frank Beckett (d 1967), and Janet Catherine, *née* Blair (d 1981); *b* 30 Oct 1941; *Educ* Glasgow Acad, Univ of Glasgow; *m* 7 Sept 1972, Sandra Margaret, da of Percy John Green (d 1966); 1 s (Graham Frank b 20 Dec 1974), 2 da (Julie Margaret b 7 Dec 1976, Sally Jane b 5 Jan 1979); *Career* accountant; Kerr Macleod & MacFarlan (now Coopers & Lybrand): joined as apprentice 1960, mangr 1968, ptnr 1974– (merged with Deloitte Haskins & Sells 1974, with Coopers & Lybrand 1990); lectr to students and membs of Scot Inst of CAs 1969–73, memb Rep Ctee Deloitte Haskins & Sells 1987–90; govr: Glasgow Acad 1983–89, Forest Sch Knaresborough 1988–95 (dep chm 1990–95); MICAS, ACA; *Clubs* Glasgow Academical, Golf House (Elie), Harrogate Golf; *Style—* Frank B Beckett, Esq; ✉ Alverthorpe, 29 Wheatlands Rd East, Harrogate, North Yorkshire HG2 8QS (☎ 01423 502525); Coopers & Lybrand, Albion Court, 5 Albion Place, Leeds LS1 6JP (☎ 0113 243 1343, fax 0113 242 4009)

BECKETT, Keith Austin; s of Frank Austin James Beckett (d 1967), and Evelyn Amelia, *née* Clarke; *b* 20 April 1934; *Educ* Lowestoft GS, Univ of Leicester (BSc London); *m* 1; 2 s (Douglas Keith b 1959, Stephen John b 1962); m 2, 1982, Mary Catherine, da of Sam Sharpe (d 1967); *Career* Nat Serv Flying Offr RAF Signals Branch 1957–59; process engr Matthew Hall and Co Ltd 1957–62; ICI: process design section mangr Agric Div 1962–67, engrg conslt Central Mgmnt Servs 1967–69, process engrg mangr Organics Div 1969–74; dir Tech Div Burmah Oil 1974–76, dir and gen mangr Burmah Petrocarbon 1976–81, dir of project mgmnt Building Design Partnership 1981–82, gp chief engr Pilkington plc 1982–92, dir (Europe) Pilkington PLC 1991–, vice-pres engrg Pilkington PLC 1994–, dir Pilkington Properties Ltd 1987–; visiting prof Dept of Industl Studies Univ of Liverpool, chm North West Engrg Educn Club, co-inventor (with Prof S P S Andrew, FRS) patented process for producing methanol at low pressure; FIChemE 1972 (MIChemE 1964), FEng 1992; *Books* Plant Layout (IChemE, jtly, 1969); *Recreations* golf, music, travel, cricket, theatre; *Style—* Keith Beckett, Esq, FEng; ✉ Pilkington PLC, Prescot Road, St Helens, Merseyside WA10 3TT (☎ 01744 692634)

BECKETT, Rt Hon Margaret Mary; MP (Lab) Derby S (majority 6,936), PC (1993); da of Cyril Jackson, and Winifred Jackson; *b* 15 Jan 1943; *Educ* Notre Dame HS, Manchester Coll of Sci and Technol; *m* 1979, Lionel A Beckett; *Career* sometime metallurgist; MP (Lab, TGWU sponsored): Lincoln Oct 1974–79 (also contested Feb 1974), Derby South 1983–; PPS to Min of Overseas Devpt 1974–75, asst Govt whip 1975–76, min DES 1976–79; princ researcher Granada TV 1979–83; oppn front bench spokesman on social security 1984–89, shadow chief sec to the Treasy 1989–92, dep ldr of the opposition July 1992–94 (ldr May-July 1994), shadow ldr of the House of Commons and Lab campaign co-ordinator 1992–94, candidate Lab Pty leadership and dep leadership elections 1994, shadow sec of state for health 1994–95, shadow sec of state for trade and indust 1995–; memb: Lab Pty NEC 1980–81, 1985–86 and 1988–, Tribune Gp, Fabian Soc, CND; *Style—* Rt Hon Margaret Beckett, MP; ✉ House of Commons, London SW1A 0AA

BECKETT, Martin; s of Vernon Beckett, of New Milton, Hants, and Dorothy Evelyn, *née* Heywood (d 1993); *b* 5 May 1954; *Educ* Ludlow GS, Manchester Poly; *partner* Janet Ibbotson; *Career* photographer; formerly asst to many photographers incl David Swan, Alan Dunn and Chris Holland; Silver Award 1989 and Merit Award 1995 Assoc of Photographers; work exhibited in exhibitions throughout Europe and featured in Art Dirs' Awards NY; chm Assoc of Photographers 1994–95 (vice chm 1993–94), vice pres Pyramide Europe 1995–; ed Image Magazine, Fuji Times columnist Br Jl of Photography and Amateur Photographer; *Recreations* cuisine; *Style—* Martin Beckett, Esq; ✉ c/o Germaine Walker, 38a Canonbury Square, London N1 2AN (☎ 0171 837 4586, fax 0171 837 4605, mobile 0850 287206)

BECKETT, Sir Martyn Gervase; 2 Bt (UK 1921), of Kirkdale Manor, Nawton, N Riding of Yorkshire, MC (1945); s of Hon Sir William Gervase Beckett, 1 Bt (d 1937), bro of 2 Baron Grimthorpe, and Lady Marjorie (d 1964), da of 5 Earl of Warwick and wid of 2 Earl of Feversham; *b* 6 Nov 1918; *Educ* Eton, Trinity Coll Cambridge (BA); *m* 1941, Hon Priscilla Léonie Helen Brett, da of 3 Viscount Esher, GBE (d 1964); 2 s (Richard Gervase b 1944, Jeremy Rupert b 1952), 1 da (Lucy Caroline (Mrs John Warrack) b 1942); *Heir* s, Richard Gervase Beckett b 27 March 1944; *Career* Capt Welsh Gds 1944–45; architect; tstee: Wallace Collection 1972– (chm 1976–92), Br Museum 1978–88; chm Yorkshire Regnl Ctee Nat Tst 1980–85; memb Cncl of Mgmnt Chatsworth House Tst 1981–; tstee: CPRE Tst 1983–90, D'Oyly Carte Charitable Tst 1985–; memb Cncl RSPB 1985–87; ARIBA 1952, FRSA 1982; *Recreations* painting, piano; *Clubs* Brooks's, MCC; *Style—* Sir Martyn Beckett, Bt, MC; ✉ 3 St Alban's Grove, London W8 5PN (☎ 0171 937 7834); Kirkdale Farm, Nawton, Yorks (☎ 01751 431301)

BECKETT, Richard Gervase; QC (1988); s and h of Sir Martyn Beckett, 2 Bt, MC, *qv*; *b* 27 March 1944; *Educ* Eton; *m* 1976, Elizabeth Ann, da of Maj (Charles) Hugo Waterhouse; 1 s (Walter Gervase b 16 Jan 1987), 3 da; *Career* called to the Bar Middle Temple 1965; *Recreations* walking; *Clubs* Pratt's, Portland; *Style—* Richard Beckett, Esq, QC; ✉ 33 Groveway, London SW9 (☎ 0171 735 3350)

BECKETT, Sir Terence Norman; KBE (1987, CBE 1974), kt (1978), DL (Essex 1991); s of Horace Norman Beckett, MBE, and Clarice Lillian, *née* Allsop; *b* 13 Dec 1923; *Educ* engrg cadet 1943–45 (GIMechE), LSE (BSc(Econ)); *m* 1950, Sylvia Gladys Asprey; 1 da (Alison b 1960); *Career* served WWII Capt REME (UK, India, Malaysia); RARO 1949–62; Ford Motor Co Ltd: co trainee 1950, gen mangr product planning staff 1955–63 (responsible for Cortina, Transit Van and D series truck), exec dir 1966, md and chief exec 1974–80, chm 1976–80; dir ICI 1976–80, DG CBI 1980–87 (memb Cncl 1976–80); pt/t memb CEGB 1987–90 (dep chm 1990), conslt Milk Mktg Bd and Dairy Trade Fedn 1987–94, pres IVCA 1987–91; memb: Top Salaries Review Body 1987–92, Engrg Industs Cncl 1975–80, Cncl BIM 1976–80 (Gold medal 1980), Cncl Automotive Div IMechE 1979–80, NEDC 1980–87; vice pres Conf on Schs Science and Technol 1979–80; memb Court Cranfield Inst of Technol 1977–82, govr Nat Inst of Econ and Social Res 1978–, govr and memb Court LSE 1978– (hon fell 1995), chm Governing Body London Business Sch 1979–86 (hon fell 1987), memb Ct and Cncl Univ of Essex 1986– (chm Cncl 1989–95, pro-chllr 1989–); memb Cncl BTO 1986–90, govr Chigwell Sch 1986–; Hon DSc: Cranfield 1977, Heriot-Watt 1981; Hon DSc (Econ) London 1982; Hon DTech: Brunel 1991, Wolverhampton 1995; Hon DUniv Essex 1995; Businessman of the Year 1978; Stamp lectr Univ of London 1982, Pfizer lectr Univ of Kent 1983; hon fell Sidney Sussex Coll Cambridge 1981, hon memb REME Instn 1990; FEng 1980, FIMechE, CIMgt, FIMI (vice pres 1974–80); *Recreations* ornithology, music; *Clubs* Athenaeum; *Style—* Sir Terence Beckett, KBE, DL, FEng; ✉ c/o Barclays Bank plc, 74 High St, Ingatestone, Essex CM4 9BW

BECKLAKE, Dr (Ernest) John Stephen; s of Ernest Becklake, of Weare Gifford, Devon, and Evelyn Beatrice, *née* Stevens; *b* 24 June 1943; *Educ* Bideford GS, Univ of Exeter (BSc, PhD, rugby colours); *m* 21 Aug 1965, Susan Elizabeth, da of Norman Buckle; 2 s (Peter Julian b 23 Nov 1972, Robin Edward b 22 April 1977); *Career* sr scientist EMI Electronics Wells 1967–69, post-doctoral fell Univ of Victoria BC Canada 1969–70, sr engr Marconi Space and Def Systems Frimley Surrey 1970–72; Science Museum London: asst keeper (curator of space technol collection) 1972–80, head of engrg 1980–90, head of technol (dir of curatorial activities of all technol collections) 1990–94, sr res fell in astronautics 1994–, managing ed DERA History Project; dir of numerous exhbn projects at Science Museum incl: Exploration (1977), Telecommunications (1982), Exploration of Space (1986), Robotics Japan (1991); memb and tstee Int Acad of Astronautics 1989–; MIEE 1987, FRAeS 1996; *Books* incl: Man and the Moon (1980), The Population Explosion (1990), Pollution (1991); author of over twenty papers on history of rocketry and spaceflight; *Recreations* sport (particularly rugby and golf), gardening and reading; *Clubs* Puttenham Golf, Farnborough RFC; *Style—* Dr John Becklake; ✉ Treewood, Robin Hood Lane, Sutton Green, Guildford, Surrey GU4 7QG (☎ and fax 01483 766931)

BECKMAN, Michael; QC (1976); s of Nathan Beckman, and Esther, *née* Sonabend; *b* 6 April 1932; *Educ* King's Coll London (LLB); *m* 1, 1966 (m dis), Sheryl Robin, *née* Kyle; 2 da (Amanda, Natasha); m 2, 1990, Jennifer Johnson, *née* Redmond; *Career* called to the Bar Lincoln's Inn 1954, head of Chambers; *Recreations* tennis, food, wine, cinema, reading, travel, people, animals; *Style—* Michael Beckman, Esq, QC; ✉ Bullards, Widford, Herts SG12 8SG; St Germaine de Talloires, 74290 Veyrier du Lac, France; chambers: 11 Stone Buildings, Lincoln's Inn, London WC2A 3TG; 3 East Pallants, Chichester (☎ 01243 784538)

BECKWITH, Rev Canon John Douglas; o s of William Albert Beckwith (d 1977), of Leeds, and Gladys Rubery, *née* Barley (d 1989); *b* 6 July 1933; *Educ* Leeds Modern, King's Coll London (AKC); *Career* Nat Serv War Office 1951–53; ordained: deacon 1958, priest 1965; sr tutor Ijebu-Igbo GS and lectr Molusi Coll W Nigeria 1960–62, tutor Eltham Coll 1964–69, chaplain Gothenburg 1969–70, chaplain to Bishop of Edmonton 1970–77 (hon chaplain 1977–84), dir of ordinands 1970–77, vicar St Anne Highgate 1977–88, canon Gibraltar Cathedral 1984, commissary Diocese in Europe 1984–94, priest i/c Bladon-cum-Woodstock 1988–93; memb Br Factory Gothenburg 1969, tstee Highgate Cemetery 1979–87, chm Church Needlework News 1979–92; Freeman City of London 1979, Liveryman Worshipful Co of Broderers 1979; Order of Thyateira and GB (First Class) 1974; *Recreations* graphic and applied arts, writing, pilgrimages; *Clubs* City Livery, Nikaean; *Style—* The Rev Canon John Beckwith; ✉ 1–16 Northwood Hall, Hornsey Lane, London N6 5PG (☎ 0181 340 0626)

BECKWITH, Peter Michael; s of Col Harold Andrew Beckwith (d 1966), of Hong Kong, and Agnes Camilla McMichael, *née* Duncan (d 1980); *b* 20 Jan 1945; *Educ* Harrow, Emmanuel Coll Cambridge (MA); *m* 19 Oct 1968, Paula, da of late Robin Stuart Bateman, of Cliftonville, Kent; 2 da (Tamara Jane b 1970, Clare Tamsin b 1972); *Career* admitted slr 1970; chm: London & Edinburgh Trust plc 1992, PMB Holdings Ltd 1992–; *Recreations* association football, tennis, skiing, theatre, opera, gardening, dogs; *Clubs* Riverside Racquets (chm 1989–95), Old Harrovian AFC, Chelsea FC, Downhill Only (Wengen), Covent Garden First Night, Harbour (London and Milano); *Style—* Peter Beckwith, Esq; ✉ PMB Holdings Ltd, Hill Place House, 55a High Street, Wimbledon, London SW19 5BA (☎ 0181 944 1288, fax 0181 944 1054)

BECTIVE, Earl of; Thomas Michael Ronald Christopher Taylour; s and h of 6 Marquess of Headfort, *qv*; *b* 10 Feb 1959; *Educ* Harrow, Royal Agric Coll Cirencester;

m 17 Oct 1987, Susan Jane, da of Charles Anthony Vandervell (d 1987), of Burnham, Bucks; 2 s (Thomas Rupert Charles Christopher, Lord Kenlis b 18 June 1989, Hon Henry James Anthony Christopher b 18 April 1991); *Heir* s, Hon Thomas Rupert Charles Christopher; *Career* Bective Davidson independent property consltѕ; *Style*— Earl of Bective; ✉ 1 Cadogan Street, London SW3 2PP (☎ 0171 589 6677)

BEDDARD, Dominic Anthony Hamilton; s of Terence Elliot Beddard (d 1966), and Ursula Mary Howard, *née* Gurney Richards, BEM (d 1985); *b* 14 May 1937; *Educ* Cheam Sch, Eton; *m* 17 Sept 1966, Susan Claire, da of Leslie Leo Stevens, of E Sussex; 1 s (Matthew b 1968), 2 da (Emma b 1969, Henrietta b 1971); *Career* KRRC (60 Rifles) 1955–56, cmmnd 1955, served Libya and Cyprus, TA (Queen Victorias Rifles, Queens Royal Rifles, 4 Bn Royal Green Jackets) 1958–69, Capt 1961, Major 1964; NSU (GB) Ltd 1957–62; Wilson Smithett and Co tea brokers: joined 1962, ptnr 1968–, chm 1993–; church warden St Thomas á Becket Brightling 1979–84, sec Brightling Village Tst 1985, chm Tea Brokers Assoc of London 1986 and 1988; *Recreations* golf, gardening; *Clubs* Lansdowne, Royal Green Jackets London; *Style*— Dominic Beddard, Esq; ✉ Wyland Wood, Robertsbridge, E Sussex; Wilson Smithett & Co, Sir John Lyon House, Upper Thames St, London EC4V 3LS (☎ 0171 236 0611, fax 0171 236 4976, telex 888627)

BEDDARD, His Hon Judge; Nicholas Elliot; s of Terence Elliot Beddard (d 1966), of Kensington, London, and Ursula Mary Hamilton Howard, *née* Gurney-Richards, BEM (d 1985); *b* 26 April 1934; *Educ* Cheam Sch, Eton; *m* 25 Apr 1964, Gillian Elisabeth Vaughan, da of Llewelyn Vaughan Bevan (d 1987), of Cambridge; 2 s (James b 1966, Benedict b 1968), 1 da (Emily b 1974); *Career* Royal Sussex Regt 1952–54, cmmnd 1953, TA 1955–64; mgmnt trainee United Africa Co 1955–58, asst public policy exec RAC 1958–68, called to the Bar Inner Temple 1967, practiced SE Circuit 1968–86, recorder Crown Ct 1986, circuit judge (SE Circuit) 1986–; memb Cncl HM Circuit Judges 1986–; fndr memb Barnsbury Singers; Freeman City of London, Liveryman Worshipful Co of Skinners 1957; *Recreations* choral singing, squash, golf; *Clubs* Lansdowne, Orford Sailing; *Style*— His Hon Judge Beddard; ✉ Farrar's Building, Temple, London EC4Y 7BD (☎ 0171 583 9241); Ipswich Crown Court, The Court House, Civic Drive, Ipswich IP1 2DX

BEDDOES, Edward William; OBE (1996); s of James Ronald Beddoes (d 1989), of Bristol, and Elizabeth Phyllis, *née* Owen; *b* 3 May 1937; *Educ* Llanelli Boys' GS, Preston Road GS London, Borough Poly (HNC Electrical Engrg); *m* 1, Sept 1963, Yvonne; 1 da (Louise Caroline b July 1965); m 2, Dec 1972, Jane Priscilla; 1 da (Sarah Jane b Jan 1973), 2 s (Thomas James b Oct 1977, Jonathan Edward b June 1985); *Career* trainee MOD (Air) 1953–55 and 1957–59 (Nat Serv RAF 1955–57), research and devpt gp ldr Radio Systems Elliott Bros London Ltd (taken over by GEC) 1959–69, Racal Research/Redac 1970–76, chief engr rising to tech mangr Racal Communications Security 1976–82, tech dir Vodafone Ltd 1986– (tech mangr 1982–86); FIEE 1985 (MIEE 1965), FEng 1995; *Recreations* music, antiques; *Style*— Edward Beddoes, Esq, OBE, FEng; ✉ Vodafone Ltd, The Courtyard, 2–4 London Road, Newbury, Berks RG14 1JX (☎ 01635 33251, mobile 0385 200191)

BEDDOW, Anthony John; s of Walter Matthew Beddow, of Kingswinford, W Mids, and Mabel, *née* Tennant; *b* 28 Nov 1947; *Educ* Brierley Hill GS, Bournemouth Coll of Technol (BScEcon); *m* 11 Nov 1972, Susan Dorothy, da of Phillip Francis Gilbey Jarrold; 1 da (Louise Anne b 19 Dec 1973); *Career* nat trainee 1969–71, dep hosp sec Queen Elizabeth Hosp Birmingham 1971–74, actg personnel mangr Utd Birmingham Hosps 1974–75, sector admin Kidderminster Gen Hosp 1975–78, asst dist admin N Devon Health Dist 1978–82; chief exec: W Glamorgan Health Authy 1991–96 (dist planning offr 1982–91), Morriston Hosp NHS Tst 1996–; Nuffield travelling fellowship to NZ 1991; MIHSM 1977; *Recreations* folk music, theatre; *Clubs* Swansea Rotary; *Style*— Anthony Beddow, Esq; ✉ Morriston Hospital NHS Trust, Morriston Hospital, Swansea SA6 6NL (☎ 01792 702222)

BEDDOW, (Frank) Howard; s of late Frank Harold Beddow, and late Ethel, *née* Urmson; *b* 8 May 1927; *Educ* Birkenhead Sch, Univ of Liverpool (MB ChB, MChOrth); *m* 31 July 1964, Ann Lilian, da of late Albert Edward Collins; *Career* RAMC, Lt 1951, Capt 1952–53; conslt orthopaedic surgn: Whiston and Rainhill Hosp 1962–72, Royal Liverpool Univ Hosp Tst (formerly Liverpool Royal Infirmary), Sefton Gen Hosp, Sir Alfred Jones Meml Hosp 1972–92; univ appts: memb Med Appeal Tbnl 1969–, pt/t clinical lectr in orthopaedic surgery, examiner for MB ChB and MChOrth 1972–92, memb of Bd of Orthopaedic Studies 1972–92, chm Regnl Sub-Ctee in Orthopaedic Surgery 1986–88, memb Regnl Med Ctee 1986–88, chm Postgrad Advsy Panel in Orthopaedic Surgery 1989–92; memb Cncl Br Orthopaedic Assoc 1984–86 (fell 1963–), vice pres Liverpool Med Inst 1985–86 (cncl memb 1976–87, memb 1954–); RCS: regnl advsr in orthopaedic surgery 1986–92, rep on Physiotherapy Bd 1988–95; memb Hoylake Civic Soc; FRCSE 1956, FRCS 1988; *Books* The Surgical Management of Rheumatoid Arthritis (1988); *Recreations* gardening, canal boating, photography, organist; *Clubs* Nantwich & Border Counties Yacht; *Style*— Howard Beddow, Esq; ✉ 72 Rodney St, Liverpool L1 9AF (☎ 0151 709 2177)

BEDELIAN, Haro Moushegh; OBE (1986); s of Moushegh Haroutune Bedelian (d 1974), and Annig, *née* Nigogosian; *b* 6 March 1943; *Educ* English Sch Nicosia Cyprus, St Catharine's Coll Cambridge (MA); *m* 1970, Yvonne Mildred, da of Stephen Gregory Arratoon (d 1993), of London; 1 s (Stepan b 1973), 2 da (Lisa b 1975, Claire b 1978); *Career* dep chief exec Balfour Beatty Ltd 1992– (dir 1988–), chief exec Transmanche Link (TML) 1993–, pres and chief exec offr Balfour Beatty Inc 1996–; visiting prof of civil engrg Univ of Portsmouth 1993–; pres Export Gp for Constructional Industries (EGCI) 1995–; memb Cncl: Inst of Civil Engrs 1987–90, Fedn of Civil Engrg Contractors 1989–93, Royal Acad of Engrg 1991–94; FEng 1989; *Recreations* squash, golf; *Clubs* RAC, Kingswood; *Style*— Haro Bedelian, OBE, FEng; ✉ Bryn Stoke, 30 Downs Way, Tadworth, Surrey KT20 5DZ (☎ 01737 813261); Balfour Beatty, 1 Angel Square, Torrens Street, London EC1V 1SX (☎ 0171 216 6800, fax 0171 216 6933)

BEDELL, Geraldine Claire; da of Bert Bedell (d 1982), and Iris Wright; *Educ* Wanstead HS, Lady Margaret Hall Oxford; *children* 1 da (Henrietta b 20 July 1983), 2 s (Freddie b 31 June 1987, Harry b 12 April 1995); *Career* features writer and columnist The Independent On Sunday 1992–96, features writer Night & Day (Mail on Sunday) 1996–; *Books* Party Tricks (1997); *Recreations* family; *Style*— Ms Geraldine Bedell; ✉ Night & Day, Mail on Sunday, Northcliffe House, 2 Derry Street, Kensington, London W8 5TS (☎ 0171 938 7051, fax 0171 241 5070)

BEDELL-PEARCE, Keith Leonard; s of Leonard Bedell-Pearce, of Purley, Surrey, and Irene, *née* Bedell; *b* 11 March 1946; *Educ* Trinity Sch of John Whitgift, Univ of Exeter (LLB), Univ of Warwick, Graduate Business Sch (MSc); *m* 2 Oct 1971, Gaynor Mary, da of Frederick Charles Penberthy Trevelyan, of Exeter, Devon; 1 s (Jack b 1980), 2 da (Olivia b 1976, Harriet b 1988); *Career* systems analyst: Plessey 1969–70, Wiggins Teape 1970–72; Prudential Assurance Co Ltd: computer projects mangr 1972–75, Legal Dept 1975, slr 1978, gen mangr field operations 1986 (additional responsibility for mktg 1987), dir 1988–; chief exec and dir Prudential Financial Services Ltd 1991–95; dir: Prudential Portfolio Managers Ltd 1985, Prudential Unit Trust Managers Ltd 1986, various Prudential subsid cos, Staple Nominees Ltd 1991–, Prudential Corporation plc 1992– (md UK Div 1995–96); memb Law Soc, fell Mktg Soc; *Books* Checklists for Data Processing Contracts (1978), Computers & Information Technology (1979, 2 edn 1982); *Recreations* shooting, squash, tennis; *Style*— Keith Bedell-Pearce, Esq; ✉ Prudential Corporation plc, 142 Holborn Bars, London EC1N 2NH (☎ 0171 334 4447, fax 0171 334 6875, telex 266431)

BEDFORD, Alan Frederick; s of Frederick Thomas Bedford (d 1967), of London, and Muriel Evelyn, *née* Sampson (d 1996); *b* 14 May 1947; *Educ* Strand GS, Westminster Med Sch (MB BS, FRCS, MChOrth); *m* 11 Dec 1971, Janine Wendy, da of Kenneth Charles Smithson, of Thurston, Suffolk; 2 s (Mark b 1981, Nicholas b 1985), 1 da (Anna b 1984 d 1984); *Career* conslt in traumatic and orthopaedic surgery to West Suffolk Hosp 1982–; memb: Br Orthopaedic Assoc, BMA; *Recreations* wine, photography, horticulture; *Clubs* Nibblers, Busted, West Suffolk Headway (vice-pres), Rotary; *Style*— Alan Bedford, Esq; ✉ Hydene Cottage, Hawkedon, Bury St Edmunds, Suffolk IP29 4NP (☎ 01284 789483); West Suffolk Hospital, Hardwick Lane, Bury St Edmunds, Suffolk (☎ 01284 713000); St Edmunds Hospital, St Mary's Square, Bury St Edmunds (☎ 01284 701371)

BEDFORD, Anthony Peter; s of Philip Derek Bedford (d 1962), and Jean Rachel, *née* Whyman; *b* 30 Sept 1951; *Educ* King's Sch Canterbury, St Catherine's Coll Oxford (MA), Univ of London (MPhil); *m* 14 March 1974, Anita Susan (d 1992), da of Charles Hamilton-Matthews, of Cornwall; 1 s (Tobias b 1974), 1 da (Anouska b 1977); *Career* chartered clinical psychologist; head of Psychology Dept St Andrew's Hosp Northampton 1974–84; dir: Psychiatric and Psychological Consultant Services Ltd 1981–, PPCS Properties Ltd 1988–; dir of psychological servs AMI Psychiatric Div 1984–87; dir: Centre for Occupational Res 1984–94, The Rehabilitation Group 1989–92; assoc fell Br Psychological Soc; *Recreations* riding; *Style*— Anthony P Bedford, Esq; ✉ Flat 1, 14 Devonshire Place, London W1N 1PB

BEDFORD, David Vickerman; s of Leslie Herbert Bedford, CBE (d 1989), and Lesley Florence Keitley, *née* Duff (d 1987); *b* 4 Aug 1937; *Educ* Lancing, RAM; *m* 1, 4 Sept 1958 (m dis 1968), Maureen, *née* Parsonage; 2 da (Tamara b 1959, Chloe b 1962); m 2, 27 Sept 1970 (m dis 1986), Susan, da of Gordon Pilgrim; 2 da (Sarah b 1969, Emily b 1971); m 3, 30 Dec 1994, Allison, *née* Powell; 1 s (Thomas b 1995); *Career* composer of over 100 published musical pieces to date; assoc visiting composer Gordonstoun Sch 1984–88, youth music dir English Sinfonia 1986–93 (composer in assoc 1993–), pres Br Music Info Centre Friends 1988, chm Assoc of Professional Composers 1991–93; *Recreations* cricket, squash, film; *Style*— David Bedford, Esq; ✉ 39 Shakespeare Rd, London NW7 4BA (☎ 0181 959 3165)

BEDFORD, (Charlotte) Gaby; *née* Martin-Langley; da of Charles Harold Martin-Langley (d 1977), and Ruby, *née* Middleton Rowe; *b* 14 June 1943; *Educ* St Monica's Sch for Girls, Falmouth County HS for Girls; *m* 1, 1965 (m dis 1966), Raymond Argent; m 2, 18 May 1974, Piers Errol James Bedford, s of Errol Bedford, of London; 2 s (James Simon b 12 May 1966, Timothy Piers James b 15 Sept 1975); *Career* film prodr Eyeline Films Ltd 1970–74, dir and prodr Piers Bedford Productions Ltd 1974–90; fndr and dir: Component Editing Ltd 1984–89, Component TV Productions Ltd 1987– (clients incl BP, Memorex Computers, Telstar Records, Royco Varia Investment); dir Bedford Properties; *Recreations* skiing, gardening; *Style*— Mrs Piers Bedford; ✉ 31 Barrowgate Road, Chiswick, London W4 4QX (☎ 0181 747 0069, fax 0181 995 0137)

BEDFORD, Bishop of 1994–; Rt Rev John Henry Richardson; s of Ven John Farquhar Richardson, Archdeacon of Derby (d 1991), and Elizabeth Mary, *née* Dean; *b* 11 July 1937; *Educ* Winchester, Trinity Hall Cambridge (MA), Cuddesdon Coll Oxford; *m* 1963, Felicity-Anne, *née* Lowes; 3 da (Emma b 1964, Nicki b 1965, Pippa b 1969); *Career* Nat Serv cmmnd RA Malaya 1956–58 (despatches 1958); Trinity Hall Cambridge 1958–61, Cuddesdon Coll Oxford 1961–63; ordained deacon 1963, priest 1964; asst curate Stevenage then curate Eastbourne 1966–68; vicar: Chipperfield 1968–75, Rickmansworth 1975–86; rural dean Rickmansworth 1977–86, vicar Bishop's Stortford 1986–94, hon canon St Albans Abbey 1987–94; chaplain Michael Sobell House; *Recreations* rowing, walking, gardening, windsurfing, bird watching, fishing, music; *Clubs* RAC; *Style*— The Rt Rev the Bishop of Bedford; ✉ 168 Kimbolton Road, Bedford MK41 8DN (☎ 01234 357551, fax 01234 218134)

BEDFORD, 13 Duke of (E 1694); John Robert Russell; also Baron Russell (E 1539), Earl of Bedford (E 1550), Baron Russell of Thornhaugh (E 1603), Marquess of Tavistock (E 1694), Baron Howland (E 1695); s of 12 Duke (d 1953); *b* 24 May 1917; *m* 1, 1939, Mrs Clare Gwendolen Hollway (d 1945), da of late John Bridgman; 2 s; m 2, 1947 (m dis 1960), Hon Lydia Yarde-Buller, da of 3 Baron Churston, MVO, OBE (d 1930), and late Duchess of Leinster, and wid of Capt Ian Archibald de Hoghton Lyle, Black Watch; 1 s; m 3, 1960, Mme Nicole Milinaire, da of Paul Schneider, of Paris; *Heir* s, Marquess of Tavistock, *qv*; *Career* Coldstream Gds WW II (invalided out); *Style*— His Grace the Duke of Bedford; ✉ Les Ligures, 2 Rue Honoré Labande, MC98000 Monaco

BEDFORD, Prof Peter George Courtney; *b* 2 June 1943; *Educ* King James's GS, RVC London (BVetMed, PhD); *Career* RVC Univ of London: Wellcome clinical fell Dept of Surgery 1971–71, Guide Dog for the Blind Assoc prof of canine med and surgery 1992–, head Dept of Small Animal Med and Surgery 1996–; visiting prof in veterinary ophthalmology Univ of Illinois 1991; author of over 140 pubns; William Hunting award BVA 1983; BSAVA: Simon award 1977, Bourgelat award 1986, Blaine award 1995; David Cole fellowship Br Glaucoma Gp 1988; RCVS fndn diplomate in veterinary ophthalmology 1982, diplomate French Veterinary Ophthalmology Coll 1990, diplomate Euro Coll of Veterinary Ophthalmologists 1993; pres: BSAVA 1982–83, Euro Soc for Veterinary Ophthalmology 1987–91, World Small Animal Veterinary Assoc 1994–96; memb Exec Bd Euro Coll of Veterinary Ophthalmologists; FRCVS 1977; *Recreations* sailing; *Style*— Prof Peter Bedford; ✉ Royal Veterinary College, Hawkeshead Lane, Hatfield, Herts AL9 7TA (☎ 01707 666229, fax 01707 652090)

BEDFORD, Peter Wyatt; s of David Edwin Wyatt Bedford (d 1979), of Hampshire, and Ruth Lakin, *née* Jackson (d 1993); *b* 9 March 1935; *Educ* Spyway Sch Langton Matravers Dorset, Marlborough; *m* 1959, Valerie Clare, da of John Walton Collins (d 1989), of IOW; 4 s (Rupert b 1960, Julian b 1962, Mark b 1963, Hugo b 1970); *Career* chm Collard & Partners Ltd; non-exec dir: Minories Underwriting Agencies Ltd, Guinness Mahon Insurance and Risk Managers Ltd; chm Royal Humane Soc, govr Haberdashers' Aske's Sch Elstree; *Recreations* golf, shooting, horseracing; *Clubs* MCC, Sunningdale, Swinley Forest; *Style*— Peter Bedford, Esq; ✉ Elderfield House, Herriard, Basingstoke, Hampshire RG25 2PY (☎ 01256 381339)

BEDFORD, Sybille; OBE (1982); da of Maximilian von Schoenebeck (d 1923), and Elizabeth, *née* Bernard (d 1937); *b* 16 March 1911; *Educ* privately educated Italy, France and England; *Career* author and literary journalist; vice pres English Centre PEN 1981; memb Soc of Authors; CLit 1994 (FRSL 1964); *Books* A Visit to Don Otavio The Sudden View (1953), A Legacy (1956), The Best We Can Do: The Trial of Doctor Bodkin Adams (1958), The Faces of Justice (1960), A Favourite of the Gods (1962), A Compass Error (1968), Aldous Huxley: A Biography (Vol I 1973, Vol II 1974, new edn 1993), Jigsaw (1989), As It Was (1990); *Recreations* reading, wine, cookery; *Style*— Mrs Sybille Bedford, OBE, CLit

BEDFORD, (John Leslie) William; s of Walter Bedford, and Florence Winifred, *née* Sarjeant, of Humberston, Lincs; *b* 9 Dec 1943; *Educ* Univ of Sheffield (BA, Moore Smith prize, Gibbons prize, PhD); *m* 13 Jan 1978, Fiona Mary, da of Rev Frederick William Hartland White, MBE, QHC; 1 da (Rachael Mary b 27 Jan 1987), 1 s (Thomas William b 3 Feb 1989); *Career* writer and poet; claims and new business broker with various Lloyds brokers 1963–71, postgrad tutor Univ of Sheffield 1977–79, lectr Middlesex Poly

1980–81, tutor Open Univ 1981–82, freelance feature writer with Punch, Harpers, Independent, Telegraph and others 1978–92; ed Delta 1978–79, occasional ed Agenda 1980, 1988 and 1989; *Awards* Arts Cncl Major Bursary 1978, runner up Guardian Fiction Prize 1990, Soc of Authors Award 1993, Yorkshire and Humberside Arts Award 1993; *Books* Annual Bibliography of English Language and Literature (contrib, 1974, 1975 and 1976); *Poetry* The Hollow Landscapes (1977), Journeys (1988), Imaginary Republics (1993); *Fiction* Happiland (1990), Golden Gallopers (children's, 1991), All Shook Up (1992), Nightworld (1992), Catwalking (1993), The Lost Mariner (1995), Jacob's Ladder (1996), The Freedom Tree (1997); *Recreations* music, walking, swimming; *Style*— William Bedford, Esq; ✉ c/o Rogers Coleridge & White Ltd, 20 Powis Mews, London W11 1JN (☎ 0171 221 3717)

BEDINGFELD, Sir Edmund George Felix Paston-; 9 Bt (E 1661), of Oxburgh, Norfolk; co-heir to Barony of Grandison (abeyant since *temp* Edward III); s of Sir Henry Edward (Paston-)Bedingfeld, 8 Bt (d 1941), and Sybil, *née* Lyne-Stephens (d 1985 aged 101); *b* 2 June 1915; *Educ* Oratory Sch, New Coll Oxford; *m* 1, 1942 (m dis 1953), Joan Lynette (d 1965), da of Edgar G Rees, of Llwyneithin, Llanelly; 1 s (Henry Bedingfeld, *qv*), 1 da; m 2, 1957, Agnes Kathleen Susan Anne Danos (d 1974), da of late Miklos Gluck, of Budapest, Hungary; m 3, 1975, Mrs Peggy Hannaford-Hill (d 1991), of Fort Victoria, Rhodesia (now Zimbabwe); m 4, 15 Feb 1992, Mrs Sheila Riddell, eld da of late John Douglas, of Edinburgh; *Heir* s, Henry Edgar (Paston-)Bedingfeld, *qv*; *Career* Maj Welsh Gds, served WW2 (wounded, despatches), Palestine 1945–46; under sec (Agriculture and Forestry) RICS 1964–69, md Handley Walker (Europe) Ltd 1969–80; Freeman City of London 1988, Liveryman Worshipful Co of Bowyers; *Recreations* ornithology, heraldry, painting, fly fishing; *Clubs* Naval and Military; *Style*— Sir Edmund Bedingfeld, Bt; ✉ The Old Stables, Livermere Road, Great Barton, Bury St Edmunds, Suffolk (☎ 01284 878160); Oxburgh Hall, kings Lynn, Norfolk

BEDINGFELD, Henry Edgar Paston-; s and h of Sir Edmund Bedingfeld, 9 Bt, *qv*, and his 1 w, Joan Lynette, *née* Rees (d 1965); *b* 7 Dec 1943; *Educ* Ampleforth; *m* 7 Sept 1968, Mary Kathleen, da of Brig Robert Denis Ambrose, CIE, OBE, MC (d 1974); 2 s (Richard Edmund Ambrose b 8 Feb 1975, Thomas Henry b 6 Sept 1976), 2 da (Katherine Mary b 4 Oct 1969, Charlotte Alexandra b 6 May 1971); *Career* chartered surveyor 1968; vice pres Norfolk Heraldry Soc 1980– (fndr chm 1975–80); Rouge Croix Pursuivant of Arms 1983–93, York Herald of Arms 1993–; sec Standing Cncl of the Baronetage 1984–88; memb Cncl: Norfolk Record Soc, The Heraldry Soc; vice pres: Cambridge Univ Heraldic and Genealogical Soc, Suffolk Family History Soc; rep of the Duke of Norfolk Commission d'Information et de Liaison des Associations Nobles d'Europe 1994–; Freeman City of London 1985, Liveryman Worshipful Cos of Scriveners and Bowyers; Knight of Sov Mil Order of Malta 1975 (genealogist Br Assoc 1995–); *Books* Oxburgh Hall - The First 500 years (1982), Heraldry (jtly, 1993); *Recreations* redecorating; *Clubs* Boodle's; *Style*— Henry Bedingfeld, Esq, York Herald; ✉ Oxburgh Hall, Norfolk PE33 9PS (☎ 01366 328269); The College of Arms, Queen Victoria St, London EC4V 4BT (☎ 0171 236 6420, fax 0171 248 4707)

BEDSER, Sir Alec Victor; kt (1997), CBE (1982, OBE 1964); yr twin s of Arthur Bedser (d 1978), and Florence Beatrice, *née* Badcock (d 1989); *b* 4 July 1918; *Educ* Monument Hill Secdy Sch Woking; *Career* RAF 1939–46, served in France with BEF 1939–40, evacuated S of Dunkirk 1940, Flt Sgt served N Africa, Sicily, Greece, Italy and Austria 1942–46; cricket player: Surrey CCC 1946–60 (County Championship winners 7 consecutive years 1952–59), played for England in First Test after war at Lord's v India 1946, record test debut taking 22 wickets in first two matches, total 51 test matches (21 v Aust) taking 236 wickets; memb England tours to: Aust and NZ 1946–47, SA 1948–49, Aust and NZ 1950–51, Aust and NZ 1954–55; asst mangr to The Duke of Norfolk Aust and NZ 1962–63; mangr England team: to Aust and NZ 1974–75, to Aust and India 1979–80; journalist and TV commentator England Tour of Aust 1958–59; memb: England Test Team Selection Panel 1962–85 (chm 1969–82), MCC Ctee 1982–85; Surrey CCC: memb Ctee 1961–, vice pres, pres 1987–88; fndr own office equipment and supplies co (with Eric Bedser) 1955; Freeman City of London 1968, Liveryman Worshipful Co of Environmental Cleaners 1988; *Books* Our Cricket Story (with E A Bedser, 1951), Bowling (1952), Following On (with E A Bedser, 1954), Cricket Choice (1981), Twin Ambitions (autobiography, 1986); *Recreations* golf, gardening, cricket, charities; *Clubs* MCC (hon life), Surrey CCC (hon life), East India and Sports, West Hill Golf; *Style*— Sir Alec Bedser, CBE; ✉ c/o Surrey County Cricket Club, Kennington Oval, London SE11 5SS

BEECH, Brian Philip; s of Geoffrey Ewart Beech, of Salford, Greater Manchester, and Hilda, *née* Povah (d 1965); *b* 7 Sept 1954; *Educ* Worsley Wardley GS, Eccles Sixth Form Coll, Univ of Warwick (BA), Edge Hill Teacher Trg Coll Ormskirk; *m* 14 Nov 1994, Rebecca Elizabeth, da of Ernest Want; *Career* teacher of English and drama Deane Sch Bolton 1977–79, head of promotional devpt Piccadilly Radio 1983–86 (successively researcher, sports prodr, features presenter and prodr then sr prodr 1979–83), account dir Greenwood Tighe Public Relations 1986–88, estab Piccadilly First Ltd (Piccadilly Radio) 1988–89; Greenwood Tighe Public Relations: md Manchester Office 1990–93, md i/c NW, Leeds and Edinburgh Offices 1993–96; jt md Communique Public Relations Manchester 1996–; Sony Award for Best Educnl Prog, PRCA Award for Outstanding Consultancy Practice; memb NW Ctee IPR; memb NW Ctee Lord's Taverners'; memb PRCA, MPA; *Recreations* Manchester United, squash, golf; *Clubs* Mere Golf and Country; *Style*— Brian Beech, Esq; ✉ Communique Public Relations, Waterside, 1 Canal Street, Manchester (☎ 0161 228 6677, fax 0161 228 7391, mobile 0976 272255)

BEECH, Sydney John; s of Sydney Beech, of Stoke-on-Trent, Staffs, and Ruth, *née* Baskeyfield; *b* 6 Feb 1945; *Educ* Hanley HS, Univ of Sheffield (BA); *m* 6 Sept 1969, Jean Ann, da of Bertram Gibson, of Gillow Heath, Biddulph, Staffs; *Career* grad trainee Peat Marwick Mitchell & Co 1966–69, lectr in accounting taxation and quantitative techniques 1969–72; Lyon Griffiths and Co PA to ptnr 1972–74, ptnr 1974–86, sr ptnr 1986–; memb of Clark Whitehill Assocs (memb Exec Ctee, chm W Midland region); FCA, ATII; *Recreations* golf, weightlifting, music; *Clubs* Hill Valley Golf, Dabbers Golf Soc; *Style*— S J Beech, Esq; ✉ 8 Woodland Ave, Nantwich, Cheshire; Lyon Griffiths & Co, 63–67 Welsh Row, Nantwich, Cheshire (☎ 01270 624445, fax 01270 623916)

BEECHAM, Alan; *b* 12 June 1935; *Educ* Boston GS, Open Univ (BA); *m* (m dis); 2 s (Jonathan b 1967, Christopher b 1969); *Career* Nat Serv Royal Lincolnshire Regt Malaya 1955–57; journalist 1951–62; newspapers: Lincs Standard Series, Southern Times, Southern Journal, Surrey Comet, News Chronicle, Daily Express; external news serv BBC 1961–62; radio news and current affrs BBC 1962–89: chief sub ed 1967–69, duty ed 1969–70, sr duty ed 1970–78, asst ed radio news 1978–87, news output ed 1987–89; for radio: general election, Euro election, referenda, budget, local and by-election news progs, Falklands War coverage, Royal Weddings 1964–89; created modern BBC internal news agency and news serv between London and local radio; currently media conslt and freelance journalist; FRSA (Silver Medal, advanced English); *Recreations* media, theatre, cinema, writing, Italy and France; *Style*— Alan Beecham, Esq; ✉ 7 Thalia Close, Greenwich, London SE10 9NA (☎ 0181 858 7887)

BEECHAM, Sir Jeremy Hugh; kt (1994), DL (Tyne and Wear 1995); s of Laurence Beecham (d 1975), of Newcastle upon Tyne, and Florence, *née* Fishkin (d 1986); *b* 17 Nov 1944; *Educ* Royal GS Newcastle upon Tyne, Univ Coll Oxford (MA); *m* 7 July 1968, Brenda Elizabeth, da of Dr Sidney Woolf; 1 s (Richard b 1973), 1 da (Sara b 1972); *Career* admitted slr 1968; ptnr Allan Henderson Beecham & Peacock 1968–; memb: Local & Regnl Govt Sub Ctee Lab Pty NEC 1971–83, Lab Pty Jt Policy Ctee 1992–, Lab Pty Domestic and Int Policy Ctee 1992–, Theatre Royal Tst 1985–, Cncl Neighbourhood Energy Assoc 1987–89, President's Ctee Business in the Community 1988–; dir N Devpt Co Ltd 1986–91; Newcastle upon Tyne City Cncl: cncllr 1967–, chm Social Serv Ctee 1973–77, chm Policy and Resources Ctee 1977–94, leader 1977–94, chm Fin Ctee 1979–8, Devpt Ctee 1995–; AMA: dep chm 1984–86, vice chm 1986–91, chm 1991–; cmmr English Heritage 1983–87; Parly candidate (Lab) Tynemouth 1970; chm Local Govt Assoc 1995–, vice chm Northern Regnl Cncls Assoc 1985–91, memb Cncl Common Purpose 1989–, pres Age Concern Newcastle 1995–; hon fell Newcastle upon Tyne Poly 1989, Hon DCL Univ of Newcastle upon Tyne 1992, Hon Freeman Newcastle upon Tyne 1995; *Recreations* reading (esp novels and history), music; *Clubs* Manors Social (Newcastle upon Tyne); *Style*— Sir Jeremy Beecham, DL; ✉ 39 The Drive, Gosforth, Newcastle upon Tyne (☎ 01912 851 888); 7 Collingwood St, Newcastle upon Tyne (☎ 01912 325 048);

BEECHAM, Sir John Stratford Roland; 4 Bt (UK 1914), of Ewanville, Huyton, Co Palatine of Lancaster; s of Sir Adrian Beecham, 3 Bt (d 1982), and gs of Sir Thomas Beecham, 2 Bt, the conductor; *b* 21 April 1940; *Educ* Winchester, The Queen's Coll Oxford; *Heir* bro, Robert Adrian Beecham b 6 Jan 1942; *Recreations* walking; *Style*— Sir John Beecham, Bt; ✉ Shalom, Station Road, Shipston-on-Stour, Warwicks CV36 4BT

BEECHAM, Shirley, Lady; Shirley Jean; da of Albert George Hudson; *m* 1959, as his 3 w, Sir Thomas Beecham, 2 Bt, CH (d 1961) internationally renowned conductor, composer, author and wit; *Career* dir and tstee Sir Thomas Beecham Tst Ltd, formerly admin RPO; *Style*— Shirley, Lady Beecham; ✉ Denton House, Denton, Harleston, Norfolk IP20 OAA (☎ 01986 788780)

BEECHEY, Prof (Ronald) Brian; s of Albert Ernest Beechey, of Heckmondwike, Yorks, and Edna Beechey; *b* 24 April 1931; *Educ* Whitcliffe Mount GS, Cleckheaton, Univ of Leeds (BSc, PhD); *Career* Scientific Staff MRC 1956–58, lectr Univ of Southampton 1958–63, princ scientist Shell Research Ltd 1963–83, currently prof Inst of Biological Sciences Univ of Wales Aberystwyth; author of articles in scientific jls; treas Biochemical Soc; FRSC 1970; *Clubs* Lensbury; *Style*— Prof Brian Beechey; ✉ Institute of Biological Sciences, University of Wales, Aberystwyth, Dyfed SY23 3DD (☎ 01970 622291, fax 01970 622307, telex 35181 ABYUCW G)

BEECROFT, (Paul) Adrian Barlow; s of Thomas Ford Beecroft (d 1989), of E Yorkshire, and Jean Margaret, *née* Barlow; *b* 20 May 1947; *Educ* Hymers Coll Hull, Queen's Coll Oxford (Hastings exhibitioner, MA), Harvard Business Sch (Harkness fell, Baker scholar, MBA); *m* 13 May 1972, Jacqueline Ann, *née* Watson; 2 da (Claire Damaris Watson Beecroft b 14 June 1977, Imogen May Watson Beecroft b 8 Feb 1991), 1 s (James Nicholas Watson Beecroft b 4 March 1980); *Career* account exec ICL 1968–73, project exec Ocean Transport and Trading 1973–74, vice pres Boston Consulting Group 1976–84, dir Apax Partners & Co Ventures Ltd 1984– (also chm Operating Ctee); non-exec dir various cos incl: Break for the Border Group plc, National Telecommunications plc, The BTS Group plc; chm Br Venture Capital Assoc 1991–92, memb Royal Instn; MSI 1992; *Recreations* cricket, theatre, travel; *Clubs* MCC, CCC, Incogniti CC; *Style*— Adrian Beecroft, Esq; ✉ Apax Partners & Co Ventures Ltd, 15 Portland Place, London W1N 3AA (☎ 0171 872 6300, fax 0171 636 6475)

BEEDHAM, Brian James; CBE (1989); s of James Victor Beedham (d 1973), of Nottingham, and Nina Florence Grace, *née* Zambra (d 1964); *b* 12 Jan 1928; *Educ* Leeds GS, Queen's Coll Oxford (MA); *m* 1960, (Ruth) Barbara, da of Werner Zollikofer (d 1975), of Zurich; *Career* Royal Artillery 1950–52; journalist; assoc ed The Economist 1989– (foreign ed 1964–89); *Recreations* music, walking; *Clubs* Travellers'; *Style*— Brian Beedham, Esq, CBE; ✉ 9 Hillside, London SW19 4NH (☎ 0181 946 4454); The Economist, 25 St James's St, London SW1 (☎ 0171 830 7000)

BEEDHAM, Trevor; s of Herbert Victor Beedham (d 1955), of Nottingham, and Olive Mildred, *née* Spikings; *b* 30 July 1942; *Educ* High Pavement GS Nottingham, Univ of London (BDS, MB BS (Hons)); *m* 21 May 1966, Anne, da of Maj James Darnbrough-Cameron (d 1977); 2 s (Robin b 28 July 1971, Martyn b 29 June 1973), 1 da (Erica b 11 April 1969); *Career* sr registrar The London Hosp 1979; conslt obstetrician and gynaecologist The Royal Hosps Tst 1981–; examiner: MB BS London, MRCOG; RCOG: NE Thames regnl advsr 1991–94, careers offr 1994–; chm NET Specialist Higher Trg Ctee 1991–93, memb United Examining Bd and Examinations Ctee 1993–; Freeman City of London 1984, Liveryman Worshipful Soc of Apothecaries 1988; FRSM, MIBiol 1979, FRCOG 1989 (memb 1977); *Books* Treatment and Prognosis in Obstetrics and Gynaecology (with J G Grudzinskas, 1988), The Examination of Women (in Hutchison's Clinical Methods, 1989); *Recreations* swimming, skiing; *Clubs* City Livery; *Style*— Trevor Beedham, Esq; ✉ 127 Harley St, London W1 1DJ (☎ 0171 935 8157, fax 0171 935 1427)

BEEKE, Peter James; s of Leonard James Beeke (d 1966), of London, and Violet Ruth Beeke (d 1985); *b* 2 May 1942; *Educ* Erith GS, UCL; *m* 14 Aug 1970 (m dis 1987), Gillian Mary, da of John Patterson Irvine, of London; 1 s (James b 1977), 1 da (Eleanor b 1975); *Career* programmer W H Smith & Son 1962, chief programmer Br Euro Airways 1964, mgmnt conslt Peat Marwick Mitchell 1967, gen mangr Woolwich Bldg Soc 1984 (formerly data processing mangr and asst gen mangr), gen mangr Pearl Assurance until 1992, dir Bristol & West Building Society 1992–; MBCS 1970, FCBSI 1987; *Recreations* rugby football, golf, music, personal counselling; *Style*— Peter Beeke, Esq; ✉ Bristol & West Building Society, Broad Quay, Bristol BS99 7AX (☎ 0117 943 2250, fax 0117 943 2317)

BEELEY, Sir Harold; KCMG (1961, CMG 1953), CBE (1946); s of Frank Arthur Beeley (d 1966), of Southport, Lancs, and Ada, *née* Marsh; *b* 15 Feb 1909; *Educ* Highgate Sch, Queen's Coll Oxford; *m* 1, 1933 (m dis 1953), Millicent Mary; 2 da; m 2, 1958, Patricia Karen; 1 da, 1 step s, 2 step da; *Career* lectr: Queen's Coll Oxford 1935–38, UC Leicester 1938–39; wartime orgn of RIIA (later FO Res Dept) 1939–45; Foreign Serv: entered 1946, ambass Saudi Arabia 1955, asst under sec FO 1956–58, dep UK rep to UN 1958–61, ambass UAR 1961–64 and 1967–69, UK rep Disarmament Conf Geneva 1964–67, lectr QMC 1969–75; pres Egypt Exploration Soc 1969–88; chm: World of Islam Festival Tst 1973–, Egyptian-Br C of C 1981–92; *Clubs* Reform; *Style*— Sir Harold Beeley, KCMG, CBE; ✉ 38 Slaidburn St, London SW10 (☎ 0171 351 0997)

BEER, Andrew Michael Salisbury; s of Adolphus Sharman Beer (d 1983), of Thame, Oxford, and Elsie Margaret Emily, *née* Williams; *b* 26 Aug 1939; *Educ* Shrewsbury; *m* Elizabeth Julia, *née* Dawes; 2 c; *Career* ptnr Wilde Sapte 1969–95 (joined 1968, conslt 1995–), ptnr Ivor Fitzpatrick & Co 1995–; memb: City of London Slrs Co, Law Soc; *Recreations* rugby; *Clubs* Law Soc RFC; *Style*— Andrew Beer, Esq; ✉ Wilde Sapte, 1 Fleet Place, London EC4M 7WS (☎ 0171 246 7000, fax 0171 246 7777); Ivor Fitzpatrick & Co Solicitors, Peffer Chanister House, Mount Street Crescent, Dublin 2 (☎ 00 3531 661 1385, fax 00 3531 661 3650)

BEER, Prof Gillian Patricia Kempster; da of Owen Thomas, and Ruth Winifred Bell, *née* Burley; *b* 27 Jan 1935; *Educ* Bruton Sch for Girls, St Anne's Coll Oxford (Charles Oldham scholar, BA, MA, BLitt), Univ of Cambridge (LittD); *m* 7 July 1962, John Bernard Beer, s of Jack Beer; 3 s (Daniel b 1965, Rufus b 1968, Zachary b 1971); *Career* asst lectr Bedford Coll London 1959–62, pt/t lectr Univ of Liverpool 1962–64; Univ of Cambridge: fell Girton Coll 1965–94, asst lectr 1966–71, lectr then reader in literature and narrative 1971–89, prof of English 1989–, King Edward VII prof 1994–, pres Clare Hall 1994–; vice pres British Academy 1994–96 (res reader 1987–89); chair Poetry Book Soc 1993–96; memb: Bd of Tstees of British Museum, Cwlth Scholarship Cmmn 1987–94, Lab Party; Hon LittD Univ of Liverpool 1996; hon fell: St Anne's Coll Oxford, Girton

Coll Cambridge, Univ of Wales Cardiff; FBA, FRSA; *Books* Meredith: A Change of Masks (1970), The Romance (1970), Darwin's Plots (1983), George Eliot (1986), Arguing with the Past (1989), Forging the Missing Link (1992), Open Fields (1996), Virginia Woolf: the Common Ground (1996); *Recreations* music, travel, conversation; *Style*— Prof Gillian Beer, FBA; ✉ Clare Hall, Cambridge CB3 9AL (☎ 01223 332370)

BEER, Ian David Stafford; CBE (1992), JP (Glos 1991); s of William John Beer (d 1976), of Surrey, and Doris Ethel, *née* Rose; bro of Prof (Anthony) Stafford Beer, *qv*; *b* 28 April 1931; *Educ* St Catharine's Coll Cambridge (MA, PGCE); *m* 1960, Angela Felce, 2 da of Lt-Col Eric Spencer Gravely Howard, MC, RA (d 1977); 2 s (Martin b 1962, Philip b 1965), 1 da (Caroline b 1967); *Career* 1 Bn Royal Fusiliers Berlin 1949–51; bursar Ottershaw Sch 1955, housemaster Marlborough Coll 1957–61 (asst master 1955–57); headmaster: Ellesmere Coll Shropshire 1961–69, Lancing Coll Sussex 1969–81, Harrow Sch 1981–91; res govr Br Sch Sri Lanka 1996–; chm: HMC 1980, Physical Educn Working Gp on the Nat Curriculum 1990–92, Advsy Ctee ISJC 1988–91; vice chm: Governing Bodies Assoc 1994–, Independent Schools Jt Cncl 1994–; govr Malvern Coll, pres RFU 1993–94 (memb Exec Ctee 1985–95); JP: Shropshire 1962–69, West Sussex 1969–81, Middlesex 1981–91, Glos 1991–; tstee: Welfare Tst, RMC, Churchill Meml Tst; memb Cncl Buckingham Univ 1991–, chm designate England Sports Cncl 1992–94; Hon FCP 1991; *Recreations* rugby football, gardening, natural history; *Clubs* Hawks (Cambridge), East India and Sports; *Style*— Ian D S Beer, Esq, CBE, JP; ✉ c/o East India and Sports Club, 16 St James's Square, London SW1Y 4LH

BEER, Prof John Bernard; s of late John Bateman Beer, and late Eva, *née* Chilton; *b* 31 March 1926; *Educ* Watford GS, St John's Coll Cambridge (MA, PhD, LittD); *m* 7 July 1962, Gillian Patricia Kempster, *née* Thomas; 3 s (Daniel, Rufus, Zachary); *Career* RAF 1946–48; lectr Univ of Manchester 1958–64; Univ of Cambridge: res fell St John's Coll 1955–58, fell Peterhouse 1964–93 (emeritus fell 1993), univ lectr 1964–78, reader 1978–87, prof of English lit 1987–93 (emeritus prof 1993), Leverhulme emeritus fell 1995–96; pres Charles Lamb Soc 1989–; FBA 1994; *Books* Coleridge the Visionary (1959), The Achievement of E M Forster (1962), Coleridge's Poems (ed, 1963 and 1993), Milton Lost and Regained (1964), Blake's Humanism (1968), Blake's Visionary Universe (1969), Coleridge's Variety: Bicentenary Studies (ed, 1974), Coleridge's Poetic Intelligence (1977), Wordsworth and the Human Heart (1978), Wordsworth in Time (1979), E M Forster - A Human Exploration (ed with G K Das, 1979), A Passage to India - Essays in Interpretation (ed, 1985), Coleridge's Writings (general ed, 1990–), Aids to Reflection - Collected Coleridge (ed, 1993), Romantic Influences: Contemporary - Victorian - Modern (1993), Against Finality (1993), Questioning Romanticism (ed, 1995); *Recreations* walking in town and country, listening to music; *Clubs* Royal Over-Seas League; *Style*— Prof John Beer, FBA; ✉ Peterhouse, Cambridge CB2 1RD (☎ 01223 356384, fax 01223 337578)

BEER, Prof (Anthony) Stafford; s of William John Beer (d 1976), of Surrey, and Doris Ethel, *née* Rose (d 1993); bro of Ian David Stafford Beer, CBE, JP, *qv*; *b* 25 Sept 1926; *Educ* Whitgift Sch, UCL, Univ of Manchester (MBA); *Career* WWII Gunner RA, cmmnd Royal Fus, Co Cdr 9 Gurkha Rifles 1945, Staff Capt Intelligence Punjab, army psychologist 1947, Capt Royal Fus; prodn controller Samuel Fox 1949–56, head of operational res and cybernetics United Steel 1956–61, fndr and md SIGMA (Science in General Management) Ltd 1961–66 (and dir parent co Metra International), devpt dir International Publishing Corporation 1966–70; freelance conslt: Ernst & Whinney 1970–87, Govt of Chile 1971–73, Presidential Offices of Mexico, Venezuela and Uruguay; fndr and dir Metapraxis Ltd 1984–87; academic career: visiting prof of cybernetics Univ of Manchester 1969–94, prof of gen systems Open Univ 1970–71, adjunct prof of social systems scis Wharton Sch Univ of Pennsylvania 1981–87 (adjunct prof of statistics and operations res 1972–81), research prof of managerial cybernetics Euro Business Management Sch Univ Coll Swansea 1990–; visiting prof: Concordia Univ Montreal 1982, Univ of British Columbia 1982, Business Sch Univ of Durham 1990–94; distinguished cybernetician in res McCluhan Prog Univ of Toronto 1984, adjunct prof of educn Univ of Toronto 1990–; Silver medal Royal Swedish Acad for Engrg Scis 1958, Lanchester prize Operations Res Soc of America 1966, Resolution of the United States House of Representatives for Wise and Objective Counsel 1970, McCulloch plaque American Soc of Cybernetics 1970, Life Membership plaque Austrian Soc for Cybernetics 1984; memb: Operational Res (memb Cncl 1958–62 and 1969–72, pres 1970–71), Operations Res Soc of America, Société Française de la Recherche Operationelle, Royal Inst of Philosophy, Soc for Gen Systems Res (govr and pres 1971–72), Teilhard Centre for the Future of Man 1975; pres World Orgn of Systems and Cybernetics, govr Int Cncl for Computer Communication; hon prof of organisational transformation Liverpool John Moores Univ 1990; fell RSS (regnl chm and memb Industl Relations Ctee 1953–59); hon fell: Int Inst of Social Invention, St David's Univ of Wales 1989, Liverpool John Moores Univ 1996; Freeman City of London 1970; Hon LLD Concordia Univ Montreal 1988; FREconS, FWA, FRSA; *Books* Cybernetics and Management (1959), Decision and Control (1966), Management Science (1968), Brain of the Firm (1 edn 1972, 2 edn 1981), Designing Freedom (1974), Platform for Change (1975), Transit (poems, 1977, 2 edn 1983), The Heart of Enterprize (1979), Diagnosing the System for Organisations (1985), Pebbles to Computers - The Thread (1986); Requiem - installation of paintings in Metropolitan Cathedral Liverpool 1992/93, How Many Grapes Went Into the Wine? - the Art and Science of Holistic Management (1994), Beyond Dispute: the Invention of Team Syntegrity (1994); *Recreations* staying put; *Clubs* Athenaeum; *Style*— Prof Stafford Beer; ✉ 34 Palmerston Square, Toronto, Ontario, Canada M6G 257 (☎ and fax 00 1 416 535 0396); Cwarel Isaf, Pont Creuddyn, Llanbedr Pont Steffan, Dyfed SA48 8PG

BEERLING, John William (Johnny); s of Raymond Starr Beerling, and May Elizabeth Julia, *née* Holden; *b* 12 April 1937; *Educ* Sir Roger Manwood's GS Sandwich Kent; *m* 1, (m dis); 1 s (David John b 1965), 1 da (Julie Margaret b 1963); m 2, 1993, Celia Margaret, *née* Potter; *Career* Nat Serv wireless fitter RAF 1955–57; BBC: joined 1957, studio mangr 1958, prodr 1963, head Radio 1 Programmes 1983, controller Radio 1 1985–93; chm Unique Special Projects 1995–; pres Television and Radio Industs Club (TRIC) 1992–93, govr BRITS Sch for Performing Arts and Technol 1994–; *Publications* Emperor Rosko's DJ Handbook (1976); *Recreations* photography, skiing, angling; *Style*— Johnny Beerling; ✉ Unique Broadcasting, 50 Lisson Street, London NW1 5DF (☎ 0171 402 1011, fax 0171 723 6132)

BEESLEY, Sonia; *see:* Hornby, Lady Sonia Margaret

BEESON, Andrew Nigel Wendover; s of Capt Nigel Wendover Beeson (d 1944), and Ann Margaret, *née* Sutherland; *b* 30 March 1944; *Educ* Eton; *m* 1, 1971 (m dis 1983), Susan Roberta Caroline, da of Guy Standish Gerard (d 1981); 1 s (James Gerard b 26 March 1976), 1 da (Susanna Caroline b 27 June 1973); m 2, 12 July 1986, Carrie Joy, da of Norman Joseph Martin, of Majorca; 1 da (Christabel Alexandra Robina Martin b 4 Sept 1989); *Career* stockbroker; ptnr Capel-Cure-Carden 1972–85; dir: ANZ Merchant Bank 1985–87, ANZ McCaughan 1987–89; chief exec Beeson Gregory Ltd 1989–; *Recreations* real tennis, rackets, shooting, collecting; *Clubs* White's, Pratt's, MCC, Swinley; *Style*— Andrew N W Beeson, Esq; ✉ 21 Warwick Square, London SW1V 2AB (☎ 0171 834 2903); Beeson Gregory Ltd, The Registry, Royal Mint Court, London EC3N 4EY (☎ 0171 488 4040, fax 0171 481 3762, car tel 0836 202374)

BEESON, Headley Thomas; s of Thomas Benjamin Beeson (d 1942), of Headley Park, Headley, nr Epsom, Surrey, and Elizabeth, *née* Brezovits; *b* 20 Aug 1942; *Educ* Clark's GS Surbiton; *m* 7 Sept 1968, Lesley Ann, da of Roland Conrad Wontner (d 1993), of Heathlands, Woodside Rd, Cobham, Surrey; 1 s (Miles b 1973), 1 da (Caroline b 1975); *Career* Fenn & Crosthwaite stockbrokers 1962–67, investmt mgmnt and mktg Barclays Bank Group 1967–81; dir: N M Schroder Unit Trust Managers Ltd 1981–88, Schroder Investment Management Ltd 1988–; AIIMR 1972; *Recreations* rowing, motor sports; *Style*— Headley Beeson, Esq; ✉ Courtlands, 14 The Ridings, Cobham, Surrey KT11 2PU (☎ 01372 843 230); Schroder Investment Management Ltd, 33 Gutter Lane, London EC2V 8AS (☎ 0171 382 6000 or 0171 382 6498, fax 0171 382 3827, telex 885029)

BEESON, Very Rev Trevor Randall; OBE (1997); s of Arthur William Beeson (d 1979), and Matilda Beeson (d 1980); *b* 2 March 1926; *Educ* King's Coll London, St Boniface Coll Warminster (MA); *m* 1950, Josephine Grace, da of Ernest Joseph Cope (d 1974); 2 da (Jean, Catherine); *Career* dean of Winchester 1987–96 (dean emeritus 1996); FKC; *Books* The Church of England in Crisis (1973), Discretion and Valour (1974), A Vision of Hope (1984); *Recreations* gardening, cricket; *Style*— The Very Rev Trevor Beeson, OBE

BEETHAM, Marshal of the RAF Sir Michael James; GCB (1978, KCB 1976), CBE (1967), DFC (1944), AFC (1960), DL (Norfolk 1989); s of Maj George C Beetham, MC (d 1953), of Broadstairs, Kent; *b* 17 May 1923; *Educ* St Marylebone GS; *m* 1956, Patricia Elizabeth, da of Henry Lane, of Christchurch, NZ; 1 s, 1 da; *Career* joined RAF 1941, Bomber Cmd 1943–46 (flying 30 combat missions in Lancaster bombers of 50 Sqdn), psa 1952, idc 1967, Dir Ops (RAF) MOD 1968–70, Cmdt RAF Staff Coll 1970–72, ACOS (plans and policy) SHAPE 1972–75, Dep C-in-C Strike Cmd 1975–76, C-in-C RAF Germany and Cdr 2 Allied Tactical Air Force 1976–77, Chief of the Air Staff 1977–82, Air ADC to HM the Queen 1977–82, Marshal of the RAF 1982; dir: Brixton Estate plc 1983–93, GEC Avionics Ltd 1984–91 (chm 1986–90); pres: Bomber Command Assoc 1987–, RAF Historical Soc 1992–, RAF Club 1993–; chm of Tstees RAF Museum 1983–; govr: Cheltenham College 1983–90, Wymondham Coll 1991–; Hon Air Cdre RAuxAF 1983–; Liveryman Guild of Air Pilots and Air Navigators; FRAeS; *Clubs* RAF; *Style*— Marshal of the RAF Sir Michael Beetham, GCB, CBE, DFC, AFC, DL; ✉ c/o RAF Club, Piccadilly, London W1

BEETHAM, Roger Campbell; CMG (1993), LVO (1976); s of Henry Campbell Beetham (d 1986), of Burnley, Lancashire, and Mary, *née* Baldwin (d 1978); *b* 22 Nov 1937; *Educ* Peter Symonds Sch Winchester, BNC Oxford (MA); *m* 1, 1965 (m dis 1986), Judith, *née* Rees; m 2, 1986, Christine Marguerite, da of Adrien Malerme, of Callas, S France; *Career* HM Dip Serv 1960–: UK Delgn to Disarmament Conf Geneva 1962–65, Washington 1965–68, FCO 1969–72, Helsinki 1972–76, FCO 1976–77, EC Cmmn 1977–81, cnsllr (econ & commercial) New Delhi 1981–85, head Maritime Aviation & Environment Dept FCO 1985–90, ambass Senegal (also non-resident Cape Verde, Guinea, Guinea-Bissau and Mali) 1990–93, ambass and perm rep Cncl of Europe Strasbourg 1993–; Order of the White Rose of Finland 1976; *Recreations* travel, cooking, wine; *Clubs* Travellers'; *Style*— Roger Beetham, Esq, CMG, LVO; ✉ c/o Foreign & Commonwealth Office (Strasbourg), King Charles St, London SW1A 2AH

BEETON, David Christopher; s of Ernest Walter Beeton, and Ethel Louise, *née* Lemon; *b* 25 Aug 1939; *Educ* Ipswich Sch, King's Coll London (LLB); *m* 6 July 1968, Elizabeth Brenda; 2 s (Thomas b 1970, Samuel b 1972); *Career* admitted slr 1966; chief exec Bath City Cncl 1973–85, sec The Nat Tst 1985–89, chief exec Historic Royal Palaces 1989–; *Recreations* classical music, historic buildings, cooking; *Style*— David Beeton, Esq; ✉ Historic Royal Palaces, Hampton Court Palace, Surrey KT8 9AU (direct ☎ 0181 781 9751, fax 0181 781 9754)

BEEVERS, Prof (David) Gareth; s of Rev Charles Edward Beevers, CBE (d 1973), sometime rector of The Lophams, Norfolk, and Mabel, *née* Charlton (d 1991); *b* 4 June 1942; *Educ* Dulwich, The Royal London Hosp Med Coll (MB BS, MD), MRCP; *m* 30 Sept 1967, Michèle, da of Peter Barnett, of Royston, Herts; 1 s (Robert Charles Josiah b 15 Feb 1976), 2 da (Hellen Elizabeth Michèle b 7 June 1969, Rachel Victoria b 30 Nov 1972); *Career* clinical scientist MRC Blood Pressure Unit Western Infirmary Glasgow 1972–77, prof of med Univ of Birmingham 1977–, hon conslt physician City Hosp Birmingham 1977–; ed in chief Jl of Human Hypertension, pres Br Hypertension Soc; FRCP (London) 1981; memb: BMA, Int Soc of Hypertension, Euro Soc of Hypertension, Int Soc for the Study of Hypertension in Pregnancy; *Books* Hypertension in Practice (with G A MacGregor, 1987, 2 edn 1995); *Recreations* collecting medical postage stamps and old toy soldiers; *Style*— Prof D G Beevers; ✉ Department of Medicine, City Hospital, Birmingham B18 7QH (☎ 0121 554 3801)

BEEVOR, Antony Romer; s of Miles Beevor (d 1994), of Mill Lane, Welwyn, Herts, and Sybil, *née* Gilliat (d 1991); *b* 18 May 1940; *Educ* Winchester, New Coll Oxford; *m* 1970, Cecilia, da of John Hopton (d 1969); 1 s, 1 da; *Career* slr Ashurst Morris Crisp 1962–72, exec dir Hambros Bank 1982– (joined 1974, on secondment dir gen Panel on Takeovers and Mergers 1987–89), dir Hambros plc 1990–; non-exec dir: Rugby plc 1993–, Gerrard and National Holdings plc 1995–, Croda International plc 1996–; *Style*— Antony Beevor, Esq; ✉ 20 Radipole Rd, London SW6 (☎ 0171 731 8015); Hambros Bank Ltd, 41 Tower Hill, London EC3N 4HA (☎ 0171 480 5000, fax 0171 702 4424)

BEEVOR, (Thomas) Hugh Cunliffe; s and h of Sir Thomas Beevor, 7 Bt; *b* 1 Oct 1962; *Educ* Radley, Pembroke Coll Cambridge, RAC Cirencester; *m* 27 Aug 1988, Charlotte Louise, da of Keith Ernest Harvey, of Nuthall, Nottingham; 2 s (Thomas William Harvey b 15 April 1990, Joshua Peter Hugh b 19 May 1992), 1 da (Georgina Emily Clare b 17 April 1995); *Style*— Hugh Beevor, Esq; ✉ Hall Farmhouse, Hargham, Norwich NR16 2JW

BEEVOR, Sir Thomas Agnew; 7 Bt (GB 1784); s of Cdr Sir Thomas Lubbock Beevor, 6 Bt, RN (d 1943), and Edith Margaret, *née* Agnew (d 1985, having m 2, 1944, Rear Adm Robert Alexander Currie, CB, DSC); *b* 6 Jan 1929; *Educ* Eton, Magdalene Coll Cambridge; *m* 1, 1957 (m dis 1965), Barbara Clare, yst da of Capt Robert Lionel Brooke Cunliffe, CBE, RN (ret); 1 s (Thomas Hugh Cunliffe b 1962), 2 da (Bridget Anastasia (Mrs Matthew Porteous) b 1958, Juliana Clare (Mrs Roderick Marrs) b 1960); m 2, 1966 (m dis 1975), Carola, da of His Hon Judge Jesse Basil Herbert, MC, QC; m 3, 1976, Mrs Sally Elisabeth Bouwens, da of Edward Madoc, of White Hall, Saham Toney, Thetford, Norfolk; *Heir* s, Thomas Hugh Cunliffe Beevor b 1 Oct 1962; *Style*— Sir Thomas Beevor, Bt; ✉ Hargham Hall, Quidenham, Norwich, Norfolk

BEGBIE, David John; s of Donald Begbie, of London, and Gwendoline Mary, *née* Potter; *b* 30 April 1955; *Educ* Hereson Co Secdy Sch for Boys, Thanet Tech Coll, Winchester Sch of Art, Gloucestershire Coll of Art and Design (BA), Slade Sch of Fine Art (HDFA); *m* 1980 (m dis 1994), Katherine Frances, da of Maj Michael Everitt; 1 da (Rosalind Ruth b 1987); *partner* Tracy Irene, da of Edward George Coleman; *Career* sculptor; *Solo Exhibitions* Brompton Gallery London 1984, 1985 and 1986, Forum Zurich 1986, Navy Pier Chicago 1986, Savacou Fine Art Toronto 1986, Salama-Caro Gallery 1987, 1989 and 1990, ICAF Olympia 1987, Crucifix (Winchester Cathedral) 1988, Henley Festival 1988, Wates City Tower 1990, City Place House London (permanent installation) 1991, Tower Bridge Piazza 1992–93, Gallery Differentiate London 1993–96, Catto Gallery London 1993, Fire Station Gallery Sydney 1994, Cannons City Gym London (permanent installation) 1994, Emporio Armani London 1994, Joel Kessler Fine Art Miami Beach 1994–95, Magidson Fine Art Aspen Colorado USA 1995, Posner Fine Art Santa Monica USA 1995, Artopia Gallery New York 1996, Hannah Peschar Gallery and Sculpture Garden Surrey 1996; *Group Exhibitions* incl: Tristan (MOMA, Mallorca) 1986, Mandelzoom (CANINO, Italy) 1986, The Rachael Papers (Serpentine Gallery) 1987, Australian Fashion: The Contemporary Art Show (V & A) 1989, Philip Samuels Fine

Art St Louis 1992, The Inventive Spirit (Autodrome, Brussels) 1992, Charles Whitchurch Gallery California 1993, Arij Gasiunasen Fine Art Palm Beach 1993, 1994 and 1995, The Olympian Art Exhbn (Centre Point) 1993, Masks Exhbn (West Soho Gallery) 1993, Joel Kessler Fine Art (Int Art Fair, Miami) 1994 and 1995, Bruce R Lewin Gallery NY 1994 and 1995, SeaJapan Exhbn Yokohama 1994, Olympian Arts Charity Auction (Fine Art Soc Galleries) 1994, The Inaugural Grosvenor Place Fine Arts Exhbn Sydney 1994, The Meridian Gallery Melbourne 1994, Gallerie Pierre Nouvion Monte Carlo 1994, FIAC Crane Kalman Gallery Paris 1994 and 1995, Hang Up Gallery Sarasota Florida 1995, Gallery K London 1995, London Contemporary Art London 1995, Midsummer Art Fair Galleries Tower Bridge London 1995, Weiss Sori Fine Art Coral Gables Florida USA 1995, Miriam Sheil Fine Art Toronto Canada 1995, Margaret Lipworth Fine Art Bocca Raton Florida USA, The Associates Gallery London 1995, Howard Russeck Fine Art Philadelphia 1995, Jorge M Sori Fine Art (Int Art Fair) Miami 1996, The Tresors Int Fine Art & Antiques Fair Singapore 1996; *Work in Collections* Natural History Museum 1993, Primates Gallery 1993, Galleria Nationali de Arte Moderna Rome, National Gallery Canberra Australia, Museum Beelden aan Zee Holland, Southwark Bridge Office Devpt 1989, City Place House London 1991, Hyatt Carlton London 1993–96, Natural History Museum Primates Gallery London 1993, Royal Carribean Cruise Lines 1996; *Awards* Gane Travel Scholarship 1979, Elizabeth Greenshields Award 1980; Assoc RSBS 1993; *Recreations* gym, swimming, travel; *Clubs* Soho House; *Style*— David Begbie, Esq; ✉ c/o Tracy Coleman, Differentiate Ltd, 45 Shad Thames, Tower Bridge Piazza, London SE1 2NJ (☎ 0171 357 8909)

BEGG, Prof David Knox Houston; s of Robert William Begg, of Glasgow, and Sheena Margaret, *née* Boyd; *b* 25 June 1950; *Educ* Kelvinside Acad Glasgow, Univ of Cambridge, Univ of Oxford (MPhil), Massachusetts Inst of Technol (PhD); *Career* Lloyd's fell in econs Worcester Coll Oxford 1977–86, visiting prof Princeton Univ 1979, res dir Centre Econ Forecasting London Business Sch 1981–83, res fell Centre Econ Policy Res 1983–, founding managing ed of Economic Policy 1984–, advsr econ policy res Bank of England 1986, prof of econs Birkbeck Coll Univ of London 1987–; memb: Academic Panel HM Treasy 1981–, Res Awards Advsy Ctee Leverhulme Tst 1987–93; specialist advsr: Treasy and Civil Serv Ctee House of Commons 1983, House of Lords Euro Communities Ctee 1988–89, Commission of the Euro Cmmn 1989–90, Federal Govt of Czechoslovakia 1990–91, Internation Monetary Fund 1995–; *Books* The Rational Expectations Revolution in Macroeconomics (1982), Economics (with S Fischer and R Dornbusch, 1984, 4 edn 1994), Monitoring European Integration: The Impact of Eastern Europe (1990), Monitoring European Integration: The Making of Monetary Union (1991), Monitoring European Integration: The Economics of EC Enlargement (1992), Monitoring European Integration: Making Sense of Subsidiarity (1993); *Recreations* travel, eating, gambling; *Style*— Prof David Begg; ✉ Department of Economics, Birkbeck College, 7 Gresse St, London W1P 1PA (☎ 0171 631 6414, fax 0171 613 6416)

BEGG, Prof Hugh MacKemmie; s of Hugh Alexander Begg (d 1978), of Glasgow, and Margaret Neil, *née* MacKemmie (d 1994); *b* 25 Oct 1941; *Educ* HS of Glasgow, Univ of St Andrews, Univ of BC, Univ of Dundee; *m* 20 July 1968, Jane Elizabeth, da of Charles Wilfred Harrison (d 1995), of Salt Spring Island, BC; 2 da (Mary Margaret b 26 April 1970, Susan Morven b 28 Sept 1973); *Career* asst lectr Univ of St Andrews 1966–67, res fell Tayside Study 1967–69, lectr Univ of Dundee 1969–76, asst dir Tayside Regnl Cncl 1976–79, head Sch of Town and Regnl Planning Duncan of Jordanstone Coll Univ of Dundee 1981–93 (sr lectr 1979–81), conslt economist and chartered town planner in private practice 1993–; pt/t reporter Scottish Office Inquiry Reporters Unit 1994–; convener RTPI Scotland 1991; FRSA 1988, FRTPI 1989; *Recreations* hill walking, puppy walking guide dogs; *Clubs* Monifieth and Dist Rotary; *Style*— Prof Hugh Begg; ✉ 4 Esplanade, Broughty Ferry, Dundee DD5 2EL (☎ 01382 779642)

BEGG, Dr Robert William; CBE (1977); s of David Begg (d 1968), and Elizabeth Young Thomson; *b* 19 Feb 1922; *Educ* Greenock Acad, Univ of Glasgow (MA); *m* 1948, Sheena Margaret, da of Archibald Boyd (d 1958), of Largs; 2 s (David b 1950, Alan b 1954); *Career* CA; tstee Nat Galleries of Scot 1974–91, memb Ct Univ of Glasgow 1986–90, exec memb Nat Tst for Scot 1986–90, pres Glasgow Inst of Fine Arts 1987–90, memb Museums and Galleries Cmmn 1988–91; Hon DUniv Glasgow 1990; *Recreations* painting; *Clubs* Glasgow Art; *Style*— Dr Robert Begg, CBE; ✉ 3 Colquhoun Drive, Bearsden, Glasgow G61 4NQ (☎ 0141 942 2436)

BEGGS, Roy J; MP (UU) Antrim East (majority 7,422); *b* 20 Feb 1936, Belfast; *Educ* Ballyclare HS, Stranmillis Training Coll; *m* Wilma; 2 s, 2 da; *Career* teacher/vice princ Larne HS 1957–82; MP (UU) Antrim E 1983–; memb House of Commons Public Accounts Cmmn 1983–; memb Larne Borough Cncl 1973–, Mayor of Larne 1978–83; elected to NI Assembly at Stormont 1982, chm Economic Devpt Ctee 1982–84; memb NE Educn and Library Bd 1973–, pres Assoc Educn and Library Bds NI 1984–85; dir Larne Enterprise and Development Co; farmer and landowner; vice pres Gleno Valley Young Farmers' Club; memb Ulster Farmers' Union; *Recreations* fishing; *Style*— Roy Beggs, Esq, MP; ✉ House of Commons, London SW1A 0AA (☎ 0171 219 6305, fax 0171 219 3889); office: 41 Station Road, Larne, County Antrim BT40 3AA (☎ and fax 01574 273258)

BEGLEY, Kim Sean Robert; s of William Begley (d 1989), of Birkenhead, and Elizabeth, *née* Cooke; *b* 23 June 1952; *Educ* Rock Ferry HS Birkenhead, Wimbledon Sch of Art, Guildhall Sch of Music and Drama, National Opera Studio; *m* 20 Oct 1986, Elizabeth Mary, da of Charles Collier; 2 s (Edward Charles William b 29 Jan 1988, William George b 17 May 1991); *Career* tenor; princ tenor Royal Opera House Covent Garden 1983–89, has also performed with numerous other opera cos and all major Br orchs; former actor, with Liverpool Playhouse and Watermill Theatre Newbury (also West End and tours of England and Canada), with RSC in Stratford and London 1977–78; fndr Broomhill Tst; *Performances* over thirty roles with Royal Opera incl: Lysander in A Midsummer Night's Dream, Achilles in King Priam, Prince in Zemlinsky's Florentine Tragedy, Cassio in Otello, Froh in Das Rheingold, Walther von der Vogelweide in Tannhäuser, Tichon in Katya Kabanova; others incl: Don Ottavio in Don Giovanni (Glyndebourne Touring Opera 1986, Opera Northern Ireland 1988, ENO 1991), Boris in Katya Kabanova (Glyndebourne Touring Opera 1989, Glyndebourne Festival Opera 1990), Graf Elemer in Arabella (Glyndebourne Festival) 1989, High Priest in Idomeneo (Glyndebourne Festival) 1991, Pellegrin in Tippett's New Year (Glyndebourne Festival and Touring) 1991, Laca in Jenufa (Glyndebourne Festival and Touring) 1992, Tanzmeister in Ariadne auf Naxos (Frankfurt Opera), title role in Lohengrin (Frankfurt Opera), Alfred in Die Fledermaus (Frankfurt Opera), Nadir in The Pearl Fishers (Scottish Opera), Prince Shuisky in Boris Godunov (Opera North), Fritz in Der Ferne Klang (Opera North), Satavyan in Savitri (Rome Opera), Vaudemont in Yolanta (Opera North), Dr Caius in Falstaff (Salzburg Easter Festival) 1993, Narraboth in Salome (Salzburg Summer Festival) 1993, Grigori in Boris Godunov (under Edo de Wart, Geneva) 1993, Male Chorus in Rape of Lucretia (ENO) 1993, Golitsin in Khovanshchina (ENO) 1994, Albert Gregor in The Makropoulos Case (WNO 1994, Glyndebourne 1995, Chicago Lyric Opera 1995/96), Jimmy Mahoney in the Rise and Fall of the City of Mahagonny (Opéra de la Bastille Paris) 1995, Skuratov in From the House of the Dead (Opéra de Nice) 1995, Loge in Das Rheingold (under James Conlon, Cologne) 1995, Albert Gregor in The Makropoulos Case (with LPO under Andrew Davis at Glyndebourne) 1995, Florestan in Leonore (Salzburg and BBC Proms under John Eliot Gardiner) 1996; recital engagements incl: Don Basilio in The Marriage of Figaro (with LPO under Sir Georg Solti in London, Paris, Frankfurt and Cologne), Alfred in Die Fledermaus (with RPO under Andre Previn), Dream of Gerontius (with the Philharmonia under Vernon Handley), Tippett's New Year (with LPO), Beethoven Ninth Symphony and Haydn Nelson Mass (with BBC Symphony Orch), Verdi Requiem (with Bournemouth Symphony Orch), Beethoven Ninth (with Cleveland Symphony Orch under Dohnanyi), Janacek Glagolitic Mass (with London Philharmonic), Tambour Major in Wozzeck (with Cleveland Orch under Dohnanyi, Carnegie Hall NY) 1995, Mahler 8th Symphony (with Cleveland Orch under Dohnanyi) 1995, Mahler 8th Symphony (with LPO under Andrew Davis at BBC Proms) 1995, Britten War Requiem (Zurich Opera) 1995; *Recordings* audio incl: Turandot, Der Rosenkavalier, Falstaff (under Solti, Decca), Das Rheingold (under Dohnanyi, Decca), Salome (under Dohnanyi, Decca), Florestan in Leonore (under John Eliot Gardiner, Deutsche Grammophon) 1996; video incl: Norma (with Dame John Sutherland and Richard Bonynge), La Traviata (with Carlo Rizzi); *Style*— Kim Begley, Esq; ✉ c/o IMG Artists Europe, Media House, 3 Burlington Lane, Chiswick, W4 2TH (☎ 0181 747 9977, fax 0181 747 9131)

BEHAN, Prof Peter Oliver; s of Patrick Behan (d 1985), and Mary Ellen, *née* Ryan; *b* 8 July 1935; *Educ* Christian Brothers Schs Authy, Univ of Leeds (MB ChB, MD), Nat Univ of Ireland (DSc); *m* 23 Aug 1968, Dr Wilhelmina Behan, da of Dr William Hughes (d 1981); 2 s (Miles b 1973, Edmund b 1977), 1 da (Charlotte b 1969); *Career* demonstrator in pathology Univ of Cambridge, res fell in psychiatry and special res fell neurology Univ of Harvard, special res fell in neurology Univ of Oxford, asst prof of neurology Univ of Boston; Univ of Glasgow: lectr, sr lectr, reader, prof of neurology; med patron Scot Motor Neurone Disease Assoc; memb: Neuroimmunology Res Gp World Fedn of Neurology, Rodin Acad for Dyslexia Res; pres Ramsay Soc; Pattison Medal for Research, Dutch Int Award for Study of Fatigue States 1994; FRCP, FRCPG, FRCPI, FACP, fell American Neurological Assoc, hon fell Norwegian Neurological Assoc; *Books* Clinical Neuroimmunology (with S Curie, 1978), Clinical Neuroimmunology (with W Behan and J Aarli, 1987); *Recreations* salmon fishing, gardening; *Clubs* Savile, Flyfishers'; *Style*— Prof Peter Behan; ✉ 17 South Erskine Park, Bearsden, Glasgow G61 4NA (☎ 0141 942 5113); Department of Neurology, Institute of Neurological Sciences, Southern General Hospital, Glasgow G51 4TF (☎ 0141 445 2466 or 0141 445 2466 ext 4334)

BEHARRELL, Steven Roderic; s of late Douglas Wells Beharrell, TD, and Pamela, *née* Pearman Smith; *b* 22 Dec 1944; *Educ* Uppingham; *m* 1, 10 June 1967, Julia Elizabeth (d 1994), da of Canon William Wilson Powell, DL; 2 da (Victoria Jane b 5 Aug 1971, Rebecca Clare b 9 Oct 1973); m 2, 1 Sept 1995, Mary Rebecca Mortimer; *Career* admitted slr 1969; ptnr Denton Hall Burgin & Warrens 1973–90, fndr ptnr Beharrell Thompson & Co 1990–93, ptnr Coudert Brothers 1993–; Freeman Worshipful Co of Drapers; memb: Law Soc, Int Bar Assoc; *Style*— Steven Beharrell, Esq; ✉ Coudert Brothers, 20 Old Bailey, London EC4M 7JP (☎ 0171 248 3000, fax 0171 248 3001)

BEHRENS, James Nicholas Edward; s of Col William Edward Boaz Behrens (d 1989), of Homegarth, Swinton Grange, Malton, N Yorks, and Dulcie Bella, *née* Mocatta; *b* 22 Dec 1956; *Educ* Eton, Trinity Coll Cambridge (scholar, MA), Univ Coll of Cardiff (LLM 1996); *m* 6 Sept 1986, Sally, da of Michael Templeton Brett, of Harpsden Hill, Harpsden, Henley-on-Thames, Oxfordshire; 2 da (Deborah b 1987, Emma-Jane b 1991); *Career* called to the Bar Middle Temple 1979 (Astbury scholar 1978); memb Bar Cncl 1991–94; churchwarden St Luke's Church Redcliffe Square London SW10 1994–; *Books* WordPerfect for the Legal Profession (1991), Confirmation, Sacrament of Grace: The theology, practice and law of the Roman Catholic Church and the Church of England (1996); *Recreations* music, photography; *Clubs* Lansdowne; *Style*— James Behrens, Esq; ✉ 13 Old Square, Lincoln's Inn, London WC2A 3UA (☎ 0171 242 6105, fax 0171 405 4004)

BEHRENS, John Stephen; JP (1970); s of Edgar Charles Behrens, CBE, JP (d 1975), of Norwood House, Ilkley, Yorks, and Winifred Wrigley, *née* Luckhurst (d 1976); *b* 9 July 1927; *Educ* Rugby; *m* 1964, Kathleen Shirley, da of Richard Alfred Leicester Billson, JP (d 1949); 2 s (Charles, James), 1 da (Philippa); *Career* Nat Serv Rifle Bde 1945, cmmnd 1946, served 2 KRRC N Africa and Palestine, completed serv at Rifle Bde Depot Winchester 1948; dir Sir Jacob Behrens and Sons Ltd and subsidiary cos; chm: Francis Willey (British Wools 1935) Ltd and subsidiary cos, John Smith and Sons (Shrewsbury) Ltd, Craig Home for Children, Bradford Tradesmen's Homes and assoc charities; pres Country Wool Merchants' Assoc, pres Friends of Bradford Art Galleries and Museums; High Sheriff of West Yorkshire 1996–97; *Recreations* shooting, tennis; *Style*— John Behrens, Esq, JP; ✉ Park Green, Littlethorpe, Ripon, N Yorks (☎ 01765 677262); Ravenscliffe Mills, Calverley, Pudsey, W Yorks (☎ 01274 612541)

BEILL, Air Vice-Marshal Alfred; CB (1986); s of Gp Capt Robert Beill, CBE, DFC (d 1970), and Sophie, *née* Kulczycka (d 1991); *b* 14 Feb 1931; *Educ* Rossall, RAF Coll Cranwell; *m* 1953, Vyvian Mary, da of Dr Basil Crowhurst-Archer (d 1981); 4 da (Francesca b 1956, Jacqueline b 1957, Anna-Louise b 1961, Miranda b 1962); *Career* cmmnd RAF 1952; serv in: UK, Aden, Singapore, Cyprus; student RAF Staff Coll 1964, Joint Servs Staff Coll 1968 and on staff 1970–73, RCDS 1978, ADC to HM The Queen 1974–75, Air Vice Marshal 1984, dir gen of Supply (RAF) 1984–87, ret 1987; appeals sec King Edward VII's Hosp for Offrs 1987–, pres RAF Swimming Assoc 1982–87 (life vice pres 1987–); *Clubs* RAF; *Style*— Air Vice-Marshal Alfred Beill, CB; ✉ c/o Lloyds Bank plc, Cox's and King's Branch, 7 Pall Mall, London SW1Y 5NA; Appeals Office, King Edward VII's Hospital for Officers, 6 Buckingham Place, London SW1E 6HR (☎ 0171 828 4454)

BEISHON, Dr (Ronald) John; s of Arthur Robson Beishon (d 1991), of Brighton, and Irene, *née* Westerman; *b* 10 Nov 1930; *Educ* Battersea Poly, Birkbeck Coll London (BSc), Univ of Oxford (DPhil); *m* 25 March 1955, Gwenda Jean; 2 s (Marc, Daniel), 2 da (Jessica, Judith); *Career* Nat Serv marine engr RASC 1951–53; tech offr ICI 1954–58, section ldr BICC 1958–61, sr res offr Univ of Oxford 1961–64, lectr Univ of Bristol 1964–68, reader Univ of Sussex 1968–71, prof Open Univ 1971–80; dir: South Bank Poly 1980–85, North London Poly 1985–87, Assoc for Consumer Res 1987–94, Trading Standards Services Ltd 1992–94, Euroconsumer Publications Ltd 1992–94; publisher European Bookseller 1995–; chief exec Consumers' Assoc 1987–94; hon sec Int Orgn of Consumer Unions (IOCU) 1991–94, govr Brighton Univ, chm Audit Cmmn 1990–92, chm Bd of Mgmnt Int Co-operative Coll 1994–, memb HRH Duke of Edinburgh's Design of the Year Judging Panel 1989–93; Hon DUniv Central England; hon fell: South Bank Univ, Univ of North London; CEng, CPsychol, FRSA, MIM, MWeldI, AFBPsS; *Recreations* squash; *Clubs* Wig and Pen; *Style*— Dr John Beishon; ✉ 421 Ditchling Rd, Brighton BN1 6XB (☎ 01273 562945, fax 01273 884506)

BEITH, Rt Hon Alan James; PC (1992), MP (Lib Dem) Berwick-upon-Tweed (majority 5,043); o s of James Beith (d 1962), of Poynton, Cheshire, and Joan Beith; *b* 20 April 1943; *Educ* King's Sch Macclesfield, Balliol and Nuffield Colls Oxford; *m* 1965, Barbara Jean Ward; *Career* lectr Dept of Politics Univ of Newcastle upon Tyne 1966–73; MP (Lib, now Lib Dem) Berwick-upon-Tweed 1973– (also contested 1970), Lib chief whip 1976–85, Lib dep ldr and foreign affrs spokesman 1985–87, Treasy spokesman Lib Democrats 1988–94, home affairs spokesman Lib Democrats 1994–, memb House of Commons Cmmn, dep ldr of Liberal Democrats 1992–, memb Intelligence and Security Ctee 1994–; tstee Historic Chapels Tst 1993–; *Recreations* walking, music, boating; *Clubs* Nat Liberal; *Style*— The Rt Hon Alan Beith, MP; ✉ House of Commons, London SW1A 0AA

BEITH, Ian Mark; s of Sir John Greville Stanley Beith, KCMG, of Winchester, and Diana, *née* Gilmour (d 1987); *b* 2 Dec 1950; *Educ* Univ of Cambridge (MA), Harvard Univ; *m* 18 Oct 1975, Mary Jane, da of late Harry Selwyn Spicer Few; 2 s (Mark b 9 Jan 1983, Nick b 29 Jan 1985); *Career* Citibank: Energy Dept UK Corp Bank 1972–75, Metals and Mining Dept NY 1975–80, team head Oil and Mining Dept London 1980–82, dir Euro Training Centre London 1982–84, head N Euro Shipping Gp 1984–86, head of UK corp banking 1986–88; Charterhouse Bank Ltd: dir of mktg debt related servs 1988, md and head of debt servs 1988–; *Recreations* shooting, films, theatre; *Clubs* Whites; *Style*— Ian Beith, Esq; ✉ Charterhouse Bank Ltd, 1 Paternoster Row, St Paul's, London EC4M 7DH (☎ 0171 522 3756, fax 0171 522 3767, mobile 0385 280275)

BEKER, Prof Henry Joseph; s of Jozef Beker (d 1960), and Mary, *née* Gewaid; *b* 22 Dec 1951; *Educ* Kilburn GS, Univ of London (BSc, PhD), Open Univ (BA); *m* 30 Oct 1976, Mary Louise, *née* Keilthy; 2 da (Hannah Louise b 1979, Josephine Tamara b 1988); *Career* sr res asst Dept of Statistics Univ Coll Swansea 1976–77, princ mathematician Racal Comsec Ltd 1977–80 (chief mathematician 1980–83), dir of res Racal Research Ltd 1983–85, dir of systems Racal-Chubb Security Systems Ltd 1985–86, md Racal-Guardata Ltd 1986–88, chm and chief exec Zergo Holdings plc 1988–; visiting prof IT Westfield Coll Univ of London 1983–84, visiting prof IT Royal Holloway Univ of London 1984–; Freeman Worshipful Co of Information Technologists 1995, Freeman City of London (by redemption) 1996; FIS, CStat, MIEE, CEng, FIMA (vice-pres 1988–89), CMath; *Books* Cipher Systems (with Prof F C Piper, 1982), Secure Speech Communications (with Prof F C Piper, 1985), Cyrptography and Coding (with Prof F C Piper, 1989); *Recreations* music, opera, natural history, mycology; *Style*— Prof Henry Beker; ✉ Zergo Holdings plc, The Square, Basing View, Basingstoke, Hants RG21 4EG (☎ 01442 342600, fax 01256 812901, e-mail beker@zergo.com)

BELCHAMBER, Peter John; s of John Belchamber (d 1983), of Derbyshire, and Sheila, *née* Warwick; *b* 5 Sept 1943; *Educ* Monkton Combe Sch, Nottingham People's Coll, Alexander Hamilton Inst (Dip Business Admin); *m* 2 Sept 1972, Margaret Anne Elizabeth, da of George William Bowes (d 1968), of Hutton Mount, Essex; 1 s (James), 2 da (Emma, Fiona); *Career* journalist Nottingham Evening Post 1962–66, ed Nottingham Observer 1965–67, account mangr Ogilvy and Mather 1967–71, account dir J Walter Thompson 1971–74, dir Charles Barker Lyons 1976–86, md Charles Barker Traverse-Healy 1986–88; dir: College Hill Associates 1988–92, Christopher Bosanquet 1992–93; dir of PR and mktg The Papworth Tst 1994–96, chief exec Cardiomyopathy Assoc 1996–; fndr memb Exec Ctee Br Assoc of Cancer United Patients 1986–96; vice chm Friends of Green Hedges Sch 1995–; *Books* East Midlands Airport (1965); *Recreations* opera, reading, music, cricket, tennis; *Clubs* Scribes; *Style*— Peter Belchamber, Esq; ✉ Oakwood, High Street, Whittlesford, Cambridge (☎ 01223 833729); Cardiomyopathy Association, 40 The Metro Centre, Tolpits Lane, Watford, Herts WD1 8SB (☎ 01923 249977)

BELCHAMBERS, Anthony Murray; s of Lyonel Eustace Belchambers (d 1981), of Ashburton, Devon, and Dorothy Joan, *née* Wylie; *b* 14 April 1947; *Educ* Christ Coll Brecon; *m* Joanna Anthonia Vestbirk; *Career* called to the Bar Inner Temple, in practice Western Circuit 1972–75; lawyer: DTI 1975–82, Dir of Public Prosecutions 1982–84, Treasy 1984–86; co sec and gen counsel Assoc of Futures Brokers and Dealers 1986–89, gen counsel Jt Exchanges Ctee 1989–93, exec dir The Futures and Options Assoc 1993–; memb various City ctees concerning financial services; *Publications* incl: Soviet Financial Services: The Need for Technical Assistance and Training (1991), The British Derivatives Markets Handbook (1993); *Recreations* tennis, riding, bridge; *Clubs* HAC; *Style*— Anthony Belchambers, Esq; ✉ The Futures and Options Association, Aldgate House, 33 Aldgate High Street, London EC3N 1EA (☎ 0171 426 7250)

BELCHER, Anthony Dennis (Tony); s of Dennis Frederick Belcher, of Chertsey, and Kathleen Patricia, *née* Backhouse; *b* 26 Feb 1957; *Educ* Salesian Coll Chertsey, Poly of the South Bank (BSc); *m* 16 May 1981, Andrea Margaret, da of Victor Ernest Whatley; 2 s (Nicholas Anthony b 8 July 1983, Shaun Anthony b 21 Feb 1987), 1 da (Justine Emma b 22 Oct 1991); *Career* Mellersh & Harding: trainee surveyor 1975, salaried ptnr 1985, equity ptnr 1990–; FRICS 1981, DipArb 1994, FCIArb, MAPM, FBEng, ABIFM; *Recreations* skiing, badminton, squash, fishing, restoration of French house, golf, travel; *Clubs* English Setter Assoc; *Style*— Tony Belcher, Esq; ✉ Mellersh & Harding, 43 St James's Place, London SW1A 1PA (☎ 0171 499 0866, fax 0171 799 2010, car 0468 372368)

BELCHER, John Leonard; s of Leonard Charles Belcher, and Hannah Joan, *née* Collins; *b* 27 Oct 1949; *Educ* Kesteven Coll, Univ of Nottingham (BEd), Univ of London (MA); *Career* educationalist; lectr Open Univ 1974–75, asst prof of sociology American Coll of Switzerland 1975–80, various academic appts in US 1980–83, dir external rels Queen Mary and Westfield Coll London 1983–90, chief of public affrs The United Nations Univ 1990–92, pro rector Univ of Westminster 1992–; memb various ctees concerning educn incl: Editorial Bd International Education, Exec Ctee Compostela Gp, Dep Assoc Int Universities; dir various cos; *Recreations* music, gardening, swimming, skiing, reading, travel; *Style*— John Belcher, Esq; ✉ The Garden Flat, 9 Belsize Avenue, London NW3 4BL; The Rectorate, University of Westminster, 309 Regent Street, London W1R 8AL (☎ 0171 911 5000, fax 0171 911 5103, telex 25964)

BELDAM, Robert Geoffrey; CBE (1975); s of late Ernest Asplan Beldam, and Ethel Mary Lang, *née* Whiteaway; *b* 3 Jan 1914; *Educ* Repton, Corpus Christi Coll Cambridge (MA); *Career* chm and md: Beldam Lascar Seals Ltd, Auto-Klean Filtration Ltd; memb: CBI Cncl 1965–86, CBI Smaller Firms Cncl 1965–79 (chm 1965–74), CBI London Regnl Cncl 1952–80 and 1981–87, SE Econ Planning Cncl 1966–73 (acting chm 1971), Woking UDC 1947–70 (chm 1954–55); Brunel Univ: life memb Ct 1966, memb Cncl representing CBI 1962–87, memb Fin Ctee and Sites Bldgs (chm 1982–87), Dr (hc) 1995; hon fell Corpus Christi Coll Cambridge 1993, Fndn benefactor Repton Sch 1996; FCA, CEng, FIMarE; *Recreations* travel, gardening, historic buildings, education; *Clubs* MCC, Carlton; *Style*— Robert Beldam, Esq, CBE; ✉ Rocombe, Grange Road, Horsell, Woking, Surrey GU21 4DA (☎ 01483 761400)

BELDAM, Rt Hon Lord Justice; Rt Hon Sir (Alexander) Roy Asplin; kt (1981), PC (1989); s of George William Beldam (d 1937), of Brentford and Shiness Lodge, Lairg, and Margaret Frew Shettle, formerly Beldam, *née* Underwood; *b* 29 March 1925; *Educ* Oundle, BNC Oxford; *m* 1953, Elisabeth Bryant, da of Frank James Farr (d 1969), of Hong Kong; 2 s (Rufus, Royston), 1 da (Alexandra); *Career* served WWII Sub-Lt RNVR Air Branch 1943–46; called to the Bar 1950, QC 1969, recorder of the Crown Court 1972–81, bencher 1977, High Court judge (Queen's Bench) 1981–89, presiding judge Wales and Chester circuit 1985, a Lord Justice of Appeal 1989–; chm The Law Cmmn 1985–89; *Style*— The Rt Hon Lord Justice Beldam; ✉ Royal Courts of Justice, Strand, London WC2 2LL

BELFAST, Earl of; (Arthur) Patrick Chichester; s and h of 7 Marquess of Donegall, *qv*; *b* 9 May 1952; *Educ* Harrow, RAC Cirencester; *m* 14 Oct 1989, Caroline Mary, er da of Maj Christopher Roland Philipson, of Elmdon, Saffron Walden, Essex; 1 s (James, Viscount Chichester b 19 Nov 1990), 1 da (Lady Catherine Gabrielle b 18 Dec 1992); *Heir* s, Viscount Chichester b 19 Nov 1990; *Career* Lt Coldstream Gds, ret 1977; entered Cater Allen (Bill Brokers), resigned 1986; *Recreations* shooting, racing (horses); *Style*— Earl of Belfast

BELHAVEN, Master of; Hon Frederick Carmichael Arthur Hamilton; s and h of 13 Lord Belhaven and Stenton; *b* 27 Sept 1953; *Educ* Eton; *m* 1, 1981 (m dis), Elizabeth Anne, da of S V Tredinnick, of Naldretts Court, Wisborough Green, W Sussex; 2 s (William Richard b 30 Dec 1982, James Frederick b 25 Dec 1984); m 2, 1991, Philippa Martha Gausel, da of Sir Rowland John Rathbone Whitehead, 5 Bt, and former wife of Brian James Douglas Collins; 1 da (Olivia Martha b 1993); *Style*— The Master of Belhaven

BELHAVEN AND STENTON, 13 Lord (S 1647); Robert Anthony Carmichael Hamilton; s of 12 Lord Belhaven and Stenton (d 1961), and Heather Mildred Carmichael, *née* Bell (d 1993); *b* 27 Feb 1927; *Educ* Eton; *m* 1, 1952 (m dis 1973), (Elizabeth) Ann, da of late Col Arthur Henry Moseley, DSO, of NSW; 1 s, 1 da; m 2, 1973 (m dis 1986), Rosemary (d 1992), da of Sir Herbert Williams, 1 Bt, MP (d 1954), sis of Sir Robin Williams, 2 Bt, *qv*, and formerly w of Sir Ian Mactaggart, 3 Bt; 1 adopted da; m 3, 1986, Malgorzata Maria, da of Tadeusz Pobog Hruzik-Mazurkiewicz, Advocate, of Krakow, Poland; 1 da (Alexandra Maria b 1987); *Heir* s, Master of Belhaven; *Career* Army 1945–48, cmmnd Cameronians 1947; farmer 1950–72, hotelier 1972–80; sits as Cons in House of Lords; awarded Commander Cross of Order of Merit of the Republic of Poland 1995; *Recreations* writing children's stories; *Clubs* Army and Navy; *Style*— The Rt Hon the Lord Belhaven and Stenton; ✉ 16 Broadwater Down, Tunbridge Wells, Kent TN2 5NR

BELL, Alan Scott; s of late Stanley Bell, of Sunderland, and late Iris, *née* Scott; *b* 8 May 1942; *Educ* Ashville Coll, Selwyn Coll Cambridge (MA), Univ of Oxford (MA); *m* 1966, Olivia, da of late Prof J E Butt, FBA; 1 s (Nicolas), 1 da (Julia); *Career* asst registrar Royal Cmmn on Historical Manuscripts 1963–66, asst keeper Nat Library of Scotland 1966–81, visiting fell All Souls Coll Oxford 1980, librarian Rhodes House Library Univ of Oxford 1981–93, librarian The London Library 1993–; advsy ed New Dictionary of National Biography 1993–; FSA 1995; *Books* Sydney Smith (1980), Leslie Stephen's Mausoleum Book (ed, 1976), Lord Cockburn (ed, 1979); *Clubs* Beefsteak, Brooks's; *Style*— Alan Bell, Esq, FSA; ✉ The London Library, 14 St James's Square, London SW1Y 4LG (☎ 0171 930 7705, fax 0171 930 0436)

BELL, Maj Alexander Fulton; s of Harry Bell, OBE (d 1984), of Viewpark, St Andrews, Fife, and Sophia McDonald, *née* Fulton (d 1991); *b* 20 Jan 1937; *Educ* Shrewsbury, RMA Sandhurst, Dundee Coll of Technol and Commerce; *m* 1, 4 Jan 1969, Sophia Lilian Elizabeth Morgan (d 1971), da of Cdr Donald Hugh Elles, RN, of N Tullich, Inveraray, Argyll; 2 s (Harry b 7 Dec 1969, Thomas b 25 Feb 1971); m 2, 23 April 1984, Alison Mary, da of John Cole Compton, MBE, of Ward of Turin, Forfar, Angus; *Career* cmmnd Argyll and Sutherland Highlanders 1957, Capt HM The Queen's Gd Balmoral 1963, Adj 1 Bn Singapore/Borneo 1964–65, served Cyprus, BAOR, Malaya, Borneo, Berlin; ADC to GOC 51 Highland Div 1966, ret 1969; Maj 1/51 Highland Vols TAVR 1972–74, Home Serv Force 1982–83; sales exec Assoc of Br Maltsters 1969; ABM (parent Dalgety plc): sales mangr 1971, dir of sales 1973–87; dir of mktg Pauls Malt (parent Harrisons and Crossfield plc) 1987–89, dir of sales J P Simpson & Co (Alnwick) Ltd 1989–; chm and pres Inst of Mktg (Tayside branch) 1975–77, memb Advsy Cncl Dundee Coll of Commerce 1976–78, govr Ardvreck Sch Crieff 1982–86; MIBrew 1970, MInstM 1972, MIMgt 1975, MCIM 1989; *Recreations* golf, fishing, shooting, skiing, walking; *Clubs* Royal & Ancient (St Andrews), The Hon Co of Edinburgh Golfers, MCC, Highland Bde; *Style*— Maj Alexander Bell; ✉ Drumclune, By Forfar, Angus DD8 3TS (☎ 01575 572074, fax 01575 573477); Simpsons Malt Ltd, Berwick-Upon-Tweed TD15 2UZ (☎ 01289 330033, car 0860 113180)

BELL, Alexander Gilmour; CB (1991); s of Edward William Bell (d 1976), of Glasgow, and Daisy, *née* Peat (d 1933); *b* 11 March 1933; *Educ* Hutcheson's GS Glasgow, Univ of Glasgow (BL); *m* 2 Aug 1966, Mary Brigid Ann, da of William Andrew Chisholm (d 1977), of New Eltham; 4 s (Andrew William b 1967, David Graham b 1969, Ian Peter b 1971, Roderick Alexander b 1979); *Career* admitted slr 1954, bank offr in Far East The Chartered Bank 1956–64, slr Messrs Maclay Murray & Spens Glasgow 1965–67; Scottish Office: sr legal offr 1967–73, dep chief reporter 1973–79, chief reporter 1979–93; session clerk St Mary's Church Haddington, tstee E Lothian Music Therapy Tst; memb Law Soc of Scotland 1965; *Books* The Laws of Scotland - Stair Memorial Encyclopaedia (contrib, 1991); *Recreations* golf, casual outdoor pursuits, choral music; *Style*— Alexander Bell, Esq, CB; ✉ Woodend, Goatfield, Haddington, East Lothian EH41 3PL (☎ 01620 823514)

BELL, Sheriff Andrew Montgomery; s of James Montgomery Bell (d 1953), of Edinburgh, and Mary, *née* Cavaye (d 1975); *b* 21 Feb 1940; *Educ* The Royal HS, Univ of Edinburgh (BL); *m* 3 May 1969, Ann Margaret, da of William Robinson (d 1956), of Darlington, Durham; 1 s (James b 1972), 1 da (Lucy b 1970); *Career* slr 1961–74; Sheriff of: S Strathclyde, Dumfries and Galloway at Hamilton 1979–84, Glasgow and Strathkelvin at Glasgow 1984–90, Lothian and Borders 1990–; memb Faculty of Advocates 1975; *Recreations* reading, listening to music; *Clubs* New (Edinburgh); *Style*— Sheriff Andrew Bell; ✉ Sheriffs' Chambers, Sheriff Court House, 27 Chambers Street, Edinburgh EH1 1LB (☎ 0131 225 2525)

BELL, Ann Forrest (Mrs Robert Lang); da of Dr John Forrest Bell (d 1966), and Marjorie, *née* Byrom (d 1984); *b* 29 April 1940; *Educ* Birkenhead HS (GPDST), RADA; *m* 23 Dec 1971, Robert Lang, s of Robert Lang (d 1962); 1 da (Rebecca Catherine b 1974), 1 s (John Stephen Jervis b 1975); *Career* actress; *Theatre* incl: The Provoked Wife, So What About Love, Othello, Lady with the Dog, Twelfth Night, The Seagull, She Stoops to Conquer, Veterans, The Philanderer, Eclipse; *Television* incl: Jane Eyre, For Whom the Bell Tolls, Three Sisters, Uncle Vanya, The Lost Boys, Double First, Tumbledown, Tenko, Company of Five, The Road, Inspector Morse, Head over Heels, Poirot, Anna Lee, Dr Finlay's Casebook; *Films* incl: The Reckoning, Till Saturday Comes; *Recreations* reading, swimming, walking dogs; *Style*— Ms Ann Bell; ✉ c/o Julian Belfrage Associates, 46 Albemarle Street, London W1X 4PP (☎ 0171 491 4400, fax 0171 493 5460)

BELL, Anne Margaret; *see:* Jobson, Anne Margaret

BELL, Anthony Holbrook (Tony); s of late Alan Brewis Bell, of Abergele, Clwyd, and Kathleen Burton, *née* Holbrook, of Waco, Texas; *b* 7 Nov 1930; *Educ* Haberdashers' Aske's; *m* 15 Sept 1956, Lorraine Every, da of Leslie Charles Wood (d 1956), of Stanmore, Middx; 1 s (Ian Charles b 1958), 1 da (Susan Nicola (Mrs Auden) b 1960); *Career* Nat Serv cmmnd 2 Lt RA 1949, Lt 1950; chm A H Bell & Co (Holdings) Ltd; dir: Derbyshire Building Society, Derby Grammar School Trust Ltd, Birchover Assured Ltd; former pres Insur Inst of Derby; pres Derby RFC 1987–89; ACII 1961, ACIArb 1971, FBIBA 1974; *Recreations* golf, rugby football; *Clubs* Chevin Golf (past capt), Bridport and West Dorset Golf, Derby RFC; *Style*— Tony Bell, Esq; ✉ Hob Hill Cottage, Hazelwood, Derbyshire DE56 4AL (☎ 01332 840747); A H Bell and Co (Insurance Brokers) Ltd, Marlborough House, 2 Charnwood St, Derby DE1 2GT (☎ 01332 372111, fax 01332 290786)

BELL, Prof (Ernest) Arthur; CB (1988); s of Albert Bell (d 1975), of Newcastle upon Tyne, and Rachel Enid, *née* Williams (d 1957); *b* 20 June 1926; *Educ* Dame Allan's Sch Newcastle upon Tyne, Univ of Durham (BSc), Trinity Coll Dublin (MA, PhD); *m* 3 Sept 1952, Jean Swinton, da of James Dall Ogilvie (d 1975), of Belfast, NI; 2 s (Alasdair Gordon Simon b 1955, Robin Andrew b 1958), 1 da (Victoria Jane b 1953); *Career* res chemist ICI 1946–47, asst lectr in biochemistry Trinity Coll Dublin 1949–53; King's Coll London: lectr then reader 1953–68, prof of biology 1972–81, chm Biology Div 1974–80, dean of natural sciences 1980–81; prof of botany Univ of Texas at Austin 1968–72, dir Royal Botanic Gardens Kew 1981–88; visiting appts: Univ of Kansas 1966–67, Univ of

Sierra Leone 1978, Instituto Technologico y de Estudios Superioes de Monterrey Mexico 1979, Japan Soc for Promotion of Sci 1986, Univ of Br Columbia 1987, Univ of Texas at Austin 1988–90, Univ of Manitoba 1991; visiting prof King's Coll London 1980–, adjunct prof Univ of Texas at Austin 1990–; memb Phytochemistry Editorial Bd; tstee: Thomas Phillips Price Tst, Third World Med Res Fndn; memb Royal Mint Advsy Ctee 1992–; author of over 130 academic papers and pubns; hon memb Phytochemical Soc of Europe (formerly chm); fell King's Coll, hon fell Trinity Coll Dublin, hon Leverhulme fell 1991–93; CChem, FRSC, CBiol, FIBiol, FLS (formerly vice pres); *Recreations* travel, natural history, watching rugby football; *Clubs* Athenaeum; *Style—* Prof E Arthur Bell, CB; ✉ Pharmacology Group, King's College London, Manresa Road, London SW3 6LX (☎ 0171 333 4932, fax 0171 333 4739)

BELL, Dr Catherine; *Educ* Balshaw's GS, Girton Coll Cambridge (BA), Univ of Kent (PhD); *Career* DTI: admin trainee 1975–81, princ 1981–84, asst sec 1984–89, under sec 1989–, head Competition Policy Div 1991–93, maternity leave 1993–94, on secondment to Cabinet Office as resident chm Civil Serv Selection Bd 1994–95, head of DTI Central Policy Unit 1995–; *Style—* Dr Catherine Bell; ✉ Department of Trade and Industry, 1 Victoria Street, London SW1H 0ET (☎ 0171 215 5000, fax 0171 222 2629)

BELL, Christopher Charles; s of Lendon Bell (d 1986), and Dorothea Anne, *née* Preston (d 1989); *b* 31 Dec 1945; *Educ* Marlborough, Pembroke Coll Cambridge (BA); *m* 1, 1969 (m dis 1976), Caroline Robey; 1 s (Edward b 5 Feb 1975), 1 da (Clarissa b 11 June 1973); m 2, 1977, Dinah, da of Col John Erskine Nicholson; 2 da (Rowena b 3 April 1981, Octavia b 9 Dec 1982); *Career* slr; articled clerk Crossman Block & Keith 1969–71; Travers Smith Braithwaite: asst slr 1971, ptnr 1975–, currently head Corp Dept; *Style—* Christopher Bell, Esq; ✉ Travers Smith Braithwaite, 10 Snow Hill, London EC1A 2AL (☎ 0171 248 9133)

BELL, David Charles Maurice; s of R M Bell (d 1992), and M F Bell (d 1973); *b* 30 Sept 1946; *Educ* Worth Sch, Trinity Hall Cambridge (BA), Univ of Pennsylvania (MA); *m* 30 Dec 1972, Primrose Frances, da of E S Moran (d 1973); 2 s (Charles Alexander b 1977, Thomas George b 1981), 1 da (Emma Theodora b 1975); *Career* Oxford Mail and Times 1970–72; Financial Times: news ed, int ed 1978–80, asst ed feature 1980–85, managing ed 1985–89, advertisement and mktg dir 1989–93, chief executive 1993–96, chm 1996–; dir Pearson plc (parent co of FT) 1996–; chm: Islington SDP 1981–86, Common Purpose Europe 1996–; dir Ambache Chamber Orch 1987–, tstee Common Purpose 1994–, memb Bd Int Youth Fndn 1996–; *Recreations* theatre, cycling, family, Victorian social history; *Style—* David Bell, Esq; ✉ 35 Belitha Villas, London N1 1PE (☎ 0171 609 4000); Financial Times, No 1 Southwark Bridge, London SE1 9HL; Pearson plc, 3 Burlington Gardens, London W1X 1LE

BELL, David Mackintosh; s of David L Bell (d 1974), of Ayr, and Kathleen, *née* McBurnie (d 1985); *b* 2 Aug 1939; *Educ* Ayr Acad, Univ of Glasgow (MA), Jordanhill Coll of Educn; *m* 1, 1963 (m dis 1996), Ann Adair; 1 s (Michael David b 25 Nov 1969), 1 da (Suzanne Louise b 10 June 1976); m 2, 1996, Dominique van Hille; 1 s (Thomas Dominic b 29 July 1995); *Career* HM Dip Serv: joined Cwlth Relations Office 1960, Karachi 1961–63, Enugu Nigeria 1963–65, second sec Havana 1966–68, Olympic attache Mexico City 1968, FCO 1969–71, Budapest 1971–74, first sec FCO 1974–77, commercial consul NYC 1977–81, FCO 1981–86, press sec Bonn 1986–90, cnsllr/HM consul-gen Lille France 1990–95, DG Br Export Promotion in Switzerland and consul-gen Zurich 1995–; *Recreations* golf, reading; *Style—* David M Bell, Esq; ✉ HM Consul-General, British Consulate-General, Dufourstrasse 56, 8008 Zurich (☎ 00 41 1 2611520, fax 00 41 1 2528351)

BELL, Derek Reginald; MBE (1986); s of Albert Reginald Bell (d 1985), of Farnham, Surrey, and Dorothy Beryl, *née* Wheeler; *b* 31 Oct 1941; *Educ* King's Sch Worcester, Royal Agric Coll Cirencester; *Children* 1 s (Justin b 23 Feb 1968), 1 da (Melanie b 16 May 1969); *Career* motor racing driver; first race in Lotus 7 at Goodwood 1964, Formula 2 and Formula 1 debuts 1968; achievements incl: winner 23 races World Sportscar Championships 1971–87 (champion 1985 and 1986), winner 22 races in Int Motor Sports Assoc Championship 1979–89, winner Le Mans 24–hr race 1975, 1981, 1982, 1986 and 1987 (competed annually 1970–92, except 1984), winner Daytona 24–hr race 1986, 1987 and 1989; awards: Driver of the Year Br Guild of Motoring 1982 and 1985, winner BRDC Gold Star 1984, 1986 and 1987, RAC Plaque d'Honneur 1985; only driver ever to have won eight 24hr int races; runs Derek Bell Precision Driving Days in UK; *Books* Derek Bell - My Racing Life (with Alan Henry, 1988); *Recreations* deep sea diving, boating, hockey, motor cross, tennis; *Style—* Derek Bell, Esq, MBE; ✉ c/o David Mills, Planners International, Upton Lodge, Upton, Tetbury, Glos GL8 (☎ 01666 503776, fax 01666 504386)

BELL, Diane; da of William Bell (d 1991), and Joan, *née* Teasedale (d 1985); *b* 11 Oct 1963; *Educ* Ryton Comp Sch; *Career* judoist; *Honours* Euro Championships: Gold medal 1984, 1986 and 1988, Silver medal 1990 and 1994, Bronze medal 1985, 1987 and 1989; World Championships: Gold medal 1986 and 1987, Silver medal 1991, Bronze medal 1982 and 1993; Gold medal Olympic Games 1988, Bronze medal Tournoi de Paris 1995, two times Commonwealth champion, two times Young Women's German Open champion, three times Jr Nationals champion; *Recreations* crosswords and any sport; *Style—* Ms Diane Bell; ✉ c/o Crawcrook Judo Club, 3 Horsley Avenue, West Burn Estate, Crawcrook, Tyne and Wear (☎ 0191 413 3020)

BELL, Dr Donald Atkinson; s of Robert Hamilton Bell (d 1989), and Gladys Mildred, *née* Russell (d 1979); *b* 28 May 1941; *Educ* Royal Belfast Acad Inst, Queen's Univ Belfast (BSc), Univ of Southampton (PhD); *m* 25 March 1967, Joyce Louisa, da of James Conroy Godber (d 1996); 2 s (Alistair b 1971, Richard b 1973); *Career* res asst King's Coll London 1962–66, princ sci offr Nat Physics Laboratory 1966–77, dep chief sci offr DTI 1978–82, dir Nat Engrg Laboratory 1983–90, head of R & D Strathclyde Inst 1990–91, dir Marchland Consulting Ltd 1991–; visiting prof Univ of Strathclyde 1992–95; MIEE 1978, FIMechE 1987, FBCS 1988; *Style—* Dr Donald Bell; ✉ Marchland Consulting Ltd, 108 East Kilbride Road, Busby, Glasgow G76 8JF (☎ 0141 644 2000, fax 0141 644 2856, e-mail donald@marchcon.demon.co.uk)

BELL, Dr (Geoffrey) Duncan; s of Sqdn Ldr Robert Charles Bell, of 20 Linden Rd, Gosforth, Newcastle upon Tyne, and Phyllis Pearl Hunter Codling (d 1992); *b* 19 June 1945; *Educ* Royal GS Newcastle upon Tyne, St Bartholomew's Hosp Med Coll, Univ of London (MB BS, MRCS, LRCP, MRCP, MSc, MD); *m* 21 June 1969, Joanna Victoria, da of Capt Joseph Henry Patterson (d 1981); 2 s (Jonathan b 8 March 1970 d 1994, Robert b 13 Oct 1977), 2 da (Anne Hélène b 30 Oct 1973 d 1975, Karen b 7 May 1980); *Career* lectr in med St Bartholomew's Hosp Med Sch 1973–76, sr lectr in therapeutics Univ of Nottingham 1976–83, conslt gastroenterologist Ipswich Hosp 1983–; developer (with BT) of virtual reality remote surgery; memb Assoc of Physicians 1979, chm working party on endoscopic safety and monitoring Br Soc of Gastroenterology, fndr memb Suffolk Branch Br Digestive Fndn, Hunterian prof RCS 1990; FRCP 1985; *Recreations* canoeing, boxing, rowing; *Style—* Dr Duncan Bell; ✉ Swiss Farm, Falkenham, Ipswich, Suffolk IP10 0QU (☎ 01394 448249); Department of Medicine, The Ipswich Hospital, Ipswich, Suffolk IP4 5DP (☎ 01473 712233)

BELL, (Edward) Eddie; s of Edward and Jean Bell; *b* 2 Aug 1949; *Educ* Airdrie HS, Cert of Business Studies; *m* 1969, Junette, da of Malcolm Bannatyne; 2 da (Catherine b 22 Oct 1969, Joanne b 24 May 1973), 1 s (Edward b 19 June 1984); *Career* Hodder & Stoughton 1970–85 (latterly dep md), md Collins Gen Div 1985–89 (dep md Fontana William Collins 1985), fndr Harper Paperbacks USA 1989–90; HarperCollins UK: dep chief exec and publisher 1990–91, chief exec and publisher 1991–92, exec chm and publisher 1992–; *Recreations* reading, golf, supporting Arsenal, opera, collecting old books; *Clubs* Naval & Military, RAC, Annabel's, Autowink (Epsom); *Style—* Eddie Bell, Esq; ✉ HarperCollins Publishers, 77–85 Fulham Palace Road, Hammersmith, London W6 8JB (☎ 0181 307 4362, fax 0181 307 4249)

BELL, Eric Gairdner; s of Richard Bell (d 1965), of Belfast, and Barrie, *née* Price (decd); *b* 23 April 1944; *Educ* Methodist Coll Belfast; *m* 3 Aug 1968, Eileen Marie, da of Maj George Roy; 2 s (Richard b 18 May 1972, Christopher b 27 May 1973); *Career* articled to Oughton Boyd McMillan & Co CAs (now part of KPMG Peat Marwick), auditor then audit mangr Cooper Brothers (now Coopers & Lybrand); BDO Binder Hamlyn: joined as mangr 1971, ptnr 1973, insolvency practitioner, regnl managing ptnr 1986–94, sr ptnr Belfast Office (following merger with Grant Thornton 1994) 1994–; FCA Ireland 1969; *Recreations* watching rugby at all levels, developing youth in sport and enterprise; *Clubs* Collegians Rugby Football, Belvoir Park Golf; *Style—* Eric Bell, Esq; ✉ Grant Thornton, Water's Edge, Clarendon Dock, Belfast BT1 3BH (☎ 01232 315500)

BELL, Gavin Paterson; s of Gavin Bell, and Annie, *née* Gribbin; *b* 29 July 1947; *Educ* Hutcheson's Boys' GS Glasgow; *Career* journalist and author; Scottish Daily Mail and Daily Record 1966–71, Agence France-Presse Paris 1971–73, National Enquirer Florida 1973–75, Reuters (based in London, Beirut and Paris) 1975–86, The Times (based in London, Delhi, Seoul and Johannesburg) 1986–92, The Herald (Glasgow) 1995–; carried Olympic torch at Seoul Games Korea 1988; Thomas Cook/Daily Telegraph Travel Book Award 1995; *Publications* In Search of Tusitala: Travels in the Pacific After Robert Louis Stevenson (1994); *Recreations* running, tennis, supporting Motherwell FC; *Clubs* Bellahouston Harriers Glasgow; *Style—* Gavin Bell, Esq; ✉ The Cottage, 12 Farm Road, Dumbreck, Glasgow G41 5BP (☎ 0141 427 7366)

BELL, Howard James; *b* 28 March 1944; *Educ* Univ of Bradford (MBA); *m* 5 June 1969, Susan Vivienne; 1 da (Amanda Jayne b 1972 d 1993), 1 s (Nicholas James b 26 Jan 1976); *Career* gp md Provident Financial plc; dir Bradford and District TEC, chm Bradford and District Business Link Ltd; *Style—* Howard Bell, Esq; ✉ Provident Financial plc, Colonnade, Sunbridge Road, Bradford, West Yorkshire BD1 2LQ (☎ 01274 731111, fax 01274 393369)

BELL, Rear Adm John Anthony; CB (1977); s of Mathew Bell (d 1948), of Dundee, and Mary Ann Ellen, *née* Goss (d 1979); *b* 25 Nov 1924; *Educ* St Ignatius Coll, Univ Coll of the South West (BA, BSc, LLB); *m* 1946, (Eileen) Joan, da of Daniel Woodman (d 1934); 3 da; *Career* RM 1943–45, RAN 1948–52, SACLANT USA 1961–64, dir Naval MET 1973–75, Rear Adm 1975, dir Naval Educn Serv 1975–78, Chief Naval Instr Offr 1978–79; called to the Bar Gray's Inn 1970; educn sec BBC 1979–83; dep chm: Police Complaints Bd 1983–85, Police Complaints Authy (Discipline) 1985–86; memb: BEC Educn Ctee 1975–79, City & Guilds Policy Ctee 1975–79, TEC 1976–79; govr SOAS 1975–79; vice chm Bd of Govrs London Guildhall Univ (formerly City of London Poly) 1984–95; ed in chief Educational Media Int 1986–; vice pres United Servs Catholic Assoc 1979–, chm RNLI Wellington 1988–, dep pres RN Assoc 1996– (nat vice pres 1983–96); vice chm SW Gp Chairs of FE Colls 1993–95, memb SW Ctee Further Educn Funding Cncl 1993–; chm: Kent Ecumenical Cmmn 1982–84, Somerset Ecumenical Cmmn 1993–; govr: Somerset Coll of Arts and Technol 1987–95 (vice chm Bd of Govrs 1989–95), London Coll of Furniture 1988–90; Hon LLD London Guildhall Univ 1996; KSG 1983; *Recreations* swimming, travel, France; *Style—* Rear Adm John Bell, CB; ✉ Farthingdown House, Holywell Lake, Wellington, Somerset TA21 0EH (☎ and fax 01823 672555)

BELL, Prof John Irving; *b* 1 July 1952; *Educ* Ridley Coll Canada, Univ of Alberta (Province of Alberta scholar, BMedSci), Magdalen Coll Oxford (Rhodes scholar, Cwlth scholar, BA, BM BCh, DM, Radcliffe Infirmary prize in surgery, Spray prize in clinical biochemistry); *Career* house offr John Radcliffe Hosp Oxford (Nuffield Dept of Clinical Med and Regnl Paediatric Surgery Serv) 1979–80; sr house offr: to Dept of Clinical Cardiology Hammersmith Hosp London 1980–81, to Renal Unit Guy's Hosp London 1981, in neurology Nat Hosp for Neurological Diseases Queen Square London 1981–82; res fell Nuffield Dept of Clinical Med Univ of Oxford 1982, clinical fell Dept of Med and postdoctoral fell Dept of Med Microbiology Stanford Univ 1982–87, Wellcome sr clinical fell and hon conslt physician Nuffield Dept of Clinical Med and Surgery John Radcliffe Hosp Oxford 1987–89, Nuffield prof of clinical med Univ of Oxford 1992– (univ lectr 1989–92); memb: Assoc of Physicians of GB and I 1990, Human Genome Orgn 1990, Br Soc of Rheumatology 1991, Int T Cell Receptor Nomenclature Ctee 1991, Sci Sub-ctee Br Soc of Allergy and Clinical Immunology 1992; fndr memb Oxford Experimental Med Club 1992; Norbert Freinkel lectr American Diabetes Assoc 1991; professorial fell Magdalen Coll Oxford 1992 (non-stipendiary fell 1990), FRCP 1992; *Books* Genetics and Human Nutrition (jt ed with P J Randle and J Scott, 1990), T Cell Receptor Genes (jt ed with E Simpson and M Owen, 1993); *Recreations* sport (skiing, rowing, golf); *Style—* Prof John Bell; ✉ Nuffield Department of Clinical Medicine, John Radcliffe Hospital, Headington, Oxford OX3 9DU (☎ 01865 221340)

BELL, Sir John Lowthian; 5 Bt (UK 1885), of Rounton Grange, Co York, and of Washington Hall, Co Durham; s of Sir Hugh Francis Bell, 4 Bt (d 1970), and his 2 w, Mary, *née* Howson; *b* 14 June 1960; *Educ* Glenalmond, RAC Cirencester; *m* 22 June 1985, Venetia Mary Frances, 2 da of J A Perry, of Taunton, Somerset; 1 s (John Hugh b 1988), 1 da (Sophia Amelia Bridget b 10 April 1990); *Heir* s, John Hugh Bell b 29 July 1988; *Career* farmer; *Recreations* fishing, shooting; *Style—* Sir John Bell, Bt; ✉ Arncliffe Hall, Ingleby Cross, Northallerton, N Yorks (☎ 01609 882202)

BELL, John Nicholson; s of John Joseph Bell (d 1973), and Mary Annie, *née* Wills (d 1994); *b* 14 Dec 1947; *Educ* Nelson Thomlinson GS Wigton, Univ of Manchester (BA); *m* 10 Aug 1979, Jeanette Wynn, da of Thomas Arthur Jones; 1 s (John Alexander b 9 Feb 1987), 1 da (Emma Jane b 18 Aug 1980); *Career* bowls player; memb: Wigton Throstle Nest Bowling Club 1960–70, Wigton Bowling Club 1970–, England Outdoor Int team (54 caps) 1978–, England Indoor Int team (39 caps) 1983–, 5 man England team World Bowls Championships (Melbourne 1980, Aberdeen 1984, Auckland 1988, Worthing 1992, Cwlth Games team 1994); minor championship wins: 10 Outdoor Club Singles, 4 Cumbria Indoor Singles, 3 Cumbria Champion of Champions Singles; runner up: Granada Superbowl Singles 1984, EIBA Nat Singles 1984, Hong Kong Int Singles 1983 and 1984, EBA Nat Triples 1985; Bronze medallist EBA Gateway Masters 1985; major titles incl: EBA Triples champion 1976 and 1991, EBA Singles champion 1983, Gold medallist (World Fours) 1984, Br Isles Singles champion 1984, Gold medallist (world team) 1980 and 1988; Bronze medallist (World Fours & Triples) 1988, EIBA Nat Triples 1991, EBA Top Four 1983 and 1995, EBA Nat Pairs 1991, EIBA Nat Fours 1992, Br Isles Pairs and Triples 1992, BIIBC Fours 1993; commentator BBC TV bowls events; played rugby for Cumbria (full-back) 1972–75; currently tourism and mktg mangr Economic Devpt Unit Carlisle City Cncl (joined 1970); Cumbria Sports Personality of Year 1979, pres of Cumbria County Bowling Assoc 1981, winner Vaux Silver Star award 1979, 1980 and 1984; *Recreations* music, humour (after dinner speaking); *Style—* John Bell, Esq; ✉ Bangla, Cross Lane, Wigton, Cumbria (☎ 016973 43124)

BELL, John Sydney; s of Percy Bell (d 1970), of Northampton, and Florence Annie, *née* Jones; *b* 5 Oct 1930; *Educ* Northampton GS, St Catharine's Coll Cambridge (MA); *m* 5 March 1966, Margot Diana, da of Wing Cdr Cedric Alfred Wright, of Worlebury, Weston-super-Mare; 2 s (Stuart b 1967, Edward b 1971), 1 da (Caroline b 1969); *Career* Nat Serv RAF Pilot Offr 1949–50; admitted slr 1957, ptnr Aplin Stockton Fairfax 1968–

(sr ptnr 1987–), Notary Public, clerk to Cmmrs of Income Tax; chm N Oxfordshire Cons Assoc 1980–85 (vice pres 1986–92, pres 1992–), pres Banbury C of C 1986–87, vice chm Bucks & Oxon East Euro Cons Assoc 1993–; memb Law Soc 1957; *Recreations* horticulture, model engineering; *Style*— John Bell, Esq; ✉ The Manor House, Overthorpe, Banbury, Oxon (☎ 01295 710005); Aplin Stockton Fairfax, 36 West Bar, Banbury, Oxon (☎ 01295 251234)

BELL, Joshua; *b* 1967, Indiana; *Career* violinist; studied with Josef Gingold, int debut with the Philadelphia Orch under Riccardo Muti 1981; appeared with orchs incl: London Philharmonic, Royal Philharmonic, BBC Symphony, The Philharmonia, Chicago Symphony, Boston Symphony, Cleveland Orch, NY Philharmonic, LA Philharmonic, Orchestre de la Suisse Romande, RAI Rome, Orchestre Philharmonique, Acad of St Martin in the Fields, Czech Philharmonic, City of Birmingham Symphony; worked with conductors incl: Vladimir Ashkenazy, Paavo Berglund, Charles Dutoit, John Eliot Gardiner, James Levine, Andrew Litton, André Previn, Esa-Pekka Salonen, Leonard Slatkin, Yuri Temirkanov, Michael Tilson Thomas, Lorin Maazel, Sir Neville Marriner, Roger Norrington; gave premiere of Nicholas Maw violin concerto written specially for him 1993; regular guest at summer festivals incl: Tanglewood, Mostly Mozart, Edinburgh, BBC Proms, Ravinia; *Recordings* Mendelssohn and Bruch violin concertos, Tchaikovsky Violin Concerto and Wieniawski D Minor Violin Concerto, Lalo Symphonie Espagnole and Saint-Saëns Violin Concerto No 3, two recital and chamber music albums of French repertoire, Poeme (album of virtuoso classics, with RPO under Andrew Litton), Mozart Concertos Nos 3 and 5 (with Eng Chamber Orch under Peter Maag), Prokofiev Violin Concertos (with Montreal Symphony Orch under Charles Dutoit), Prokofiev Recital Disc (with Olli Mustonen), Kreisler Pieces (with Paul Coker), Brahms and Schumann Concertos (with Cleveland Orch under Dohnanyi); formerly under exclusive contract to Decca, currently with Sony; *Style*— Joshua Bell, Esq; ✉ c/o Nicola Eaton, IMG Artists (Europe) Ltd, Media House, 3 Burlington Lane, Chiswick, London W4 2TH (☎ 0181 233 5800, fax 0181 233 5801, telex 291009 McMARK G)

BELL, Kevin; s of Ronald Bell, of Durham, and Sylvia, *née* Hampton; *b* 24 Sept 1957; *Educ* Washington GS, Univ of Reading (BA); *Career* public affrs/PR conslt; advsr to MPs and PA to Cons Pty candidates 1979, 1983, 1987 and 1992 gen elections; account exec K H Publicity 1979–80, dir Michael Forsyth Associates 1980–84; The Grayling Company: dir 1984–86 and 1990–94, md 1991–93; Westminster Strategy: dir 1986–94, dep md 1990–93, md 1993–94; dir: St James's Corporate Communications 1991–94, Pagette Communications 1991–94; md Lowe Bell Political 1994–, dir Lowe Bell Communications 1994–; *Recreations* keeping fit, gardening, opera, eating and drinking well, teasing my friends; *Clubs* YMCA; *Style*— Kevin Bell, Esq; ✉ Lowe Bell Communications Ltd, 7 Hertford Street, London W1V 7DY (☎ 0171 495 4044, fax 0171 629 1279)

BELL, (Caithleen) Maeve; da of John McKeown (d 1968), of Armagh, and Olive Kathleen, *née* Sadd (d 1983); *b* 25 April 1944; *Educ* St Louis GS Kilkeel, The Queen's Univ Belfast; *m* Adrian Kennedy Bell; *Career* research offr The Queen's Univ Belfast 1968–77, sr educn and info offr Equal Opportunities Commission for NI 1977–83, dir Autographics Software (NI) Ltd 1983–85, dir Gen Consumer Council for NI 1985–; vice chm Sports Cncl for NI 1979–81 (memb 1975–85); memb: Higher Educn Review Gp 1979–82, Broadcasting Cncl for NI 1981–85, Standing Advsy Cmmn on Human Rights 1984–86; *Clubs* Irish Cruising; *Style*— Mrs Maeve Bell; ✉ The General Consumer Council for Northern Ireland, Elizabeth House, 116 Holywood Road, Belfast BT4 1NY (☎ 01232 672488, fax 01232 657701)

BELL, Margaret; *Career* former teacher; subsequently: systems analyst Lucas Aerospace, head of Computer Based Learning Unit Coventry CC, mangr Distance Learning BT; currently chief exec National Cncl for Educational Technology; chm Forum for Technology Based Training; memb: Exec Parly IT Ctee, Bd of Dirs RSA Examinations and Assessment Fndn, Cncl Inst of IT Trg (chair Educn Sub Gp), COMMITT (Ctee on Multimedia in Teacher Trg) Netherlands, Multimedia Advsy Bd Univ of Wolverhampton, Cncl Univ of Warwick, Tile Hill FE Coll Corp; Freeman City of London, memb Worshipful Co of Info Technologists; MInstD, FRSA; *Style*— Ms Margaret Bell; ✉ National Council for Educational Technology, Milburn Hill Road, Science Park, Coventry CV4 7JJ (☎ 01203 416994, fax 01203 411418)

BELL, Martin; OBE (1992); s of Adrian Bell (d 1980), and Marjorie, *née* Gibson (d 1991); *b* 31 Aug 1938; *Educ* The Leys Sch Cambridge, King's Coll Cambridge; *m* 1, 1971, Nelly, *née* Gourdon; 2 da (Melissa b 1972, Catherine b 1974); m 2, 1985 (m dis 1993), Rebecca, *née* Sobel; *Career* BBC: news asst BBC Norwich 1962–64, gen reporter BBC London and overseas 1964–76, dip corr 1976–77, chief N American corr 1977–89, Berlin corr BBC TV News 1989–93, Vienna corr 1993–94, foreign affrs corr (based London) 1994–; reported from 70 countries, covered wars in Vietnam, Middle East 1967 and 1973, Angola, Rhodesia, Biafra, El Salvador, Gulf 1991, Nicaragua, Croatia and Bosnia (wounded 1992); RTS Reporter of the Year 1976 and 1992, Television and Radio Industries Club Newscaster of the Year 1995, IPR President's Medal 1996; Hon Doctorate Univ of Derby 1996; *Books* In Harm's Way (1995); *Style*— Martin Bell, Esq, OBE; ✉ BBC TV News and Current Affairs, BBC Television Centre, Wood Lane, London W12 7RJ (☎ 0181 576 4613)

BELL, Martin George Henry; s of Leonard George Bell (d 1968), of Loughton, and Phyllis, *née* Green; *b* 16 Jan 1935; *Educ* Charterhouse; *m* 2 Jan 1965, Shirley, da of William Henry Wrightson (d 1960), of Bournemouth; 2 s (Thomas b 1966, Jeremy b 1969); *Career* admitted slr 1961, sr ptnr Ashurst Morris Crisp 1986–92 (ptnr 1963–92); dir The Laird Group plc; Freeman City of London, memb Worshipful Co of Slrs; memb Law Soc; *Style*— Martin Bell, Esq; ✉ Mulberry, Woodbury Hill, Loughton, Essex IG10 1JB (☎ 0181 508 1188)

BELL, Martin Irvine; MBE (1985); s of George Alfred Bell (d 1975), and Margaret Martin, *née* Young; *b* 9 Dec 1938; *Educ* King's Park Sr Secdy Sch, Univ of Glasgow (BSc); *m* 5 Sept 1962, Joyce Hislop, da of John Shearer (d 1972); 1 s (Adrian b 1971), 1 da (Fiona b 1965); *Career* engrg dir Barr and Stroud Ltd 1984–85 (asst md operations 1985, chief exec 1988–90), chm and non-exec dir A and S Engineering Designs 1985–90; md Proctor & Schwartz Ltd 1991–94, md Zynocyte Ltd 1994–95; chm Photocraft Ltd 1994–95; memb IOD 1992–95; *Recreations* sailing, skiing, squash, music, reading; *Clubs* Clyde Cruising, Helensburgh Sailing; *Style*— Martin Bell, Esq, MBE; ✉ 7 Lower Sutherland Crescent, Helensburgh, Argyll & Bute G84 9PG (☎ 01436 72606)

BELL, Martin Neil; s of Flt Lt Arthur Rodney Bell, RAF, of Harrogate, and Dorothy Jean, *née* Little; *b* 6 Dec 1964; *Educ* George Watson's Coll Edinburgh, Internatsschule für Skisportler Stams Austria; *children* 1 da (Imogen Louisa b 1 Aug 1994); *Career* journalist and broadcaster; skier (ret); British champion: jr 1978–80, Slalom 1981, 1987 and 1989, Giant Slalom 1980 and 1986, Downhill 1981, 1986 and 1995, Super G 1992; Australia and NZ Cup winner 1981, Australian Slalom champion 1981, FIS Downhill winner Italy 1985, fifth World Cup Downhill Sweden 1986, FIS Super G winner Canada 1986, eighth Olympic Downhill Canada 1988, FIS Giant Slalom winner France 1991, Scottish champion 1994; ski conslt to Daily Mail Ski Magazine and Daily Mail Ski & Snowboard Shows; contrib The Times, The Financial Times and The Guardian, expert commentator BBC Olympic Grandstand, presenter Ski-Time (Meridian TV); Br Ski Fedn rep British Olympic Athlete's Cmmn; *Books* The British Ski Federation Guide to Better Skiing (contrib, 1986), Let's Go Skiing (1990); *Recreations* tennis, squash, football, volleyball, grass skiing; *Clubs* Kandahar, Scottish Ski, Ski Club of GB, Riverside Racquet Centre; *Style*— Martin Bell, Esq; ✉ 51 Avondale Rd, London SW14 8PU (☎ 0181 876 1254); MTC (UK) Ltd, 10 Kendall Place, London W1H 3AH (☎ 0171 935 8000, fax 0171 935 8066)

BELL, (William) Michael; s of William Bell (d 1993), and Hilda, *née* Taylor (d 1984); *b* 16 Sept 1944; *Educ* Berwick upon Tweed GS; *m* 4 Oct 1969, Helen Robina, da of William John Brown (d 1978), of Langleeford, Wooler, Northumberland; 3 da (Alison b 1971, Sarah b 1974, Lesley b 1977); *Career* CA; Thornton Baker & Co 1967–70; Wheeler & Co Wisbech: joined 1970, ptnr 1972–, sr ptnr 1991–; memb Wisbech Rotary 1982–94 (hon asst sec 1985–87, hon sec 1987–90), clerk to and govr St Peter's Junior Sch Wisbech 1971–91, memb St Peter and St Paul PCC 1972–85 (hon treas 1972–85); FCA; *Recreations* golf; *Clubs* Sutton Bridge Golf (capt 1989–90, hon treas 1983–94), Kings Lynn Golf, Thetford Golf; *Style*— Michael Bell, Esq; ✉ Apple Acre, Park Lane, Leverington, Wisbech, Cambs PE13 5EH (☎ 01945 870736); Wheeler & Co, 16 North St, Wisbech, Cambs PE13 1NE (☎ 01945 582547)

BELL, Michael Jaffray de Hauteville; s of Capt C L de Hauteville Bell, DSC, RD, RNR (d 1972); *b* 7 April 1941; *Educ* Charterhouse; *m* 1965, Christine Mary, *née* Morgan; 1 s, 4 da; *Career* conslt ptnr R Watson and Sons 1993– (ptnr 1967–93), actuary to various life assurance cos in UK and overseas, chm Century Life plc; non-exec dir: Prior plc, Lombard International Assurance SA; FIA 1964, ASA, FPMI; *Style*— Michael Bell, Esq; ✉ Century Life plc, 5 Old Bailey, London EC4M 7BA

BELL, Michael John Vincent; CB (1992); s of Christopher Richard Vincent, OBE, and Violet Irene Edith Lorna (Jane) Bell, MBE (d 1989), of Ditchling, Sussex; *b* 9 Sept 1941; *Educ* Winchester, Magdalen Coll Oxford; *m* 3 Sept 1983, Mary, da of John William Shippen (d 1957), of Shiremoor, Northumberland; 1 s (John b 1985), 2 da (Julia b 1987, Jane b 1989); *Career* res assoc Inst for Strategic Studies 1964–65, asst princ MOD 1965, asst private sec to Sec of State for Def 1968–69, princ MOD 1969, private sec to Perm Under Sec MOD 1973–75, asst sec MOD 1975, on loan to HM Treasy 1977–79, asst under sec MOD 1982, asst sec gen def planning and policy NATO 1986–88, dep under sec of state (Fin) MOD 1988–92, dep under sec of state (Defence Procurement) 1992–95 (post re-titled dep chief of def procurement (Support) 1995–96), on secondment as project dir European Consolidation British Aerospace plc 1996–; *Recreations* motor cycling, mil history; *Style*— Michael Bell, Esq, CB; ✉ British Aerospace, Farnborough, Hants GU14 6YU (☎ 01252 384607)

BELL, Michael Leopold Wentworth; s of Brian Raymond Wentworth Bell, of Moreton-in-Marsh, Glos, and Fiona Daphne, *née* Menzies; *b* 10 Oct 1960; *Educ* Stowe; *m* 27 April 1988, Georgina Patricia, da of Alan Lillingston; 1 s (Alexander Luke Wentworth b 30 April 1990), 1 da (Amy Kitty Wentworth b 30 Dec 1991); *Career* flat racehorse trainer and amateur jockey; *Recreations* golf, tennis, shooting, fox hunting; *Style*— Michael Bell, Esq; ✉ Fitzroy House, Newmarket, Suffolk CB8 0JT (☎ 01638 666567)

BELL, Dr Patrick Michael; s of Benjamin Jonathan Bell (d 1982), and Jane, *née* McIllveen; *b* 9 March 1953; *Educ* Friends' Sch Lisburn Co Antrim, Queen's Univ Belfast (MB BCh, BAO, MD); *m* 28 June 1979, (Dorothy Lavina) Patricia, da of Canon Leslie Walker, of Ballylesson, Co Down; 1 s (Jonathan b 1987), 2 da (Jane b 1980, Katie b 1982); *Career* DHSS res fell Royal Victoria Hosp and Belfast City Hosp 1981–82, sr registrar Royal Victoria Hosp 1982–84, Mayo Fndn fell in endocrinology (as Fulbright scholar) Mayo Clinic USA 1984–85, sr registrar Belfast City Hosp 1985–86, conslt physician Royal Victoria Hosp 1986–, hon lectr Queens' Univ Belfast 1992–; Central Exec Ctee Alliance Pty of NI 1987–94, chm NI Ctee Br Diabetic Assoc 1992–; numerous articles in learned jls on glucose metabolism; memb Assoc of Physicians of GB and Ireland 1994; FRCP (Glas) 1988, MRCPI 1989, FRCP (Edin) 1992, FRCPI 1992, FRCP (Lond) 1995; *Books* Multiple Choice Questions in Medicine (1981); *Style*— Dr Patrick Bell; ✉ 14 Clonevin Park, Lisburn, Co Antrim BT28 3BL (☎ 01846 674703); Wards 9 and 10, Royal Victoria Hospital, Grosvenor Rd, Belfast BT12 6BA (☎ 01232 240503 ext 3423)

BELL, Peter Christopher Alexander; s of Brian Talbot Bell (d 1988), of Woking, Surrey, and Rosemary, *née* Boswell; *b* 2 Dec 1948; *Educ* King's Coll Sch Wimbledon (head of sch), Exeter Coll Oxford (BA); *m* 19 Dec 1970, Jennifer Gay, da of Air Cdre William Henry Pope, OBE; 2 da (Catherine Susan b 9 Feb 1973, Alice Jane b 17 Nov 1976); *Career* graduate trainee Thomson Regional Newspapers 1970, reporter Reading Evening Post 1971–73; BBC: news prodr BBC Radio Brighton 1973–75, prodr BBC Radio Current Affrs 1975–77 (on The World at One and The World Tonight), prodr then sr prodr BBC TV Current Affrs 1977–87 (on Tonight, Nationwide, Newsnight and Panorama), asst ed, managing ed then ed BBC television news progs 1988–93, head of news progs BBC News and Current Affrs Directorate 1994–; *Recreations* racing; *Style*— Peter Bell, Esq; ✉ BBC News & Current Affairs Directorate, Room 6202, BBC Television Centre, Wood Lane, London W12 7RJ (☎ 0181 576 1472, fax 0181 743 7882)

BELL, Prof Peter Frank; s of late Frank Bell, of Sheffield, and late Ruby, *née* Corks; *b* 12 June 1938; *Educ* Marcliffe Secdy Sch Sheffield, High Storrs GS Sheffield, Univ of Sheffield (MB ChB, MD); *m* 26 Aug 1961, Anne, da of Oliver Jennings (d 1981), of Dewsbury, Yorks; 1 s (Mark b 1967), 2 da (Jane Marie b 1962, Louise b 1963); *Career* registrar in surgery Sheffield Health Bd Sheffield Yorks 1963–65, Sir Henry Wellcome travelling fell Wellcome Fndn Denver Coll USA 1968–69, sr lectr in surgery Univ of Glasgow 1969–74 (lectr 1963–68), fndn prof of surgery Univ of Leicester 1974–; formerly memb: Cell Bd MRS, Transplant Mgmnt Ctee DHSS, Advsy Panel Br Cwlth Fellowship, Bd of Govrs De Montfort Univ; currently memb Leicester Orgn for Relief of Suffering; memb: Int Transplantation Soc (past sec), Surgical Research Soc (past hon sec and pres), American Soc of Transplant Surgns, Br Soc of Immunology and Transplantation (past Ctee memb), Royal Med Chirurgical Soc of Glasgow, Vascular Surgical Soc (past Ctee memb and chm Vascular Advsy Ctee), Collegium Internationale Chirurgiae, Br Transplantation Soc, Euro Soc for Vascular Surgery (past pres), Assoc of Profs of Surgery (currently chm); FRCS 1965 (past memb Surgical Advsy Ctee, currently memb Cncl), FRCSGlas 1969; *Books* Operative Arterial Surgery (1983), Surgical Aspects of Haemodialysis (1985), Vascular Surgery (ed and contrib, 1985), Arterial Surgery of the Lower Limb (1991), Surgical Management of Vascular Disease (ed jtly and contrib, 1991); author of numerous articles in academic jls; past ed Euro Jl of Vascular Surgery, past cncl memb and hon treas British Journal of Surgery Society Ltd; *Recreations* painting, gardening, woodwork; *Style*— Prof Peter Bell; ✉ University of Leicester, Department of Surgery, Robert Kilpatrick Building, Leicester Royal Infirmary, Leicester LE2 7LX (☎ 0116 252 3142)

BELL, Peter John Marshall; JP (1969, supplemental list 1984); s of Edwin Bell (d 1990), and Eleanor Sybil, *née* Marshall; *b* 31 May 1933; *Educ* Bradford GS, Bradford Tech Coll (Harlow Meml medal and prize, dip in textiles); *m* 21 March 1959, Mary Susan, da of John Arthur Richardson; 1 da (Alison Frances Mary b 1 March 1960), 1 s (Dr Andrew John Edward b 4 Feb 1963); *Career* Nat Serv Sgt RAOC 1954–56; Robt Jowitt & Sons Ltd Bradford: trainee 1956–58, sales mangr 1958–63, prodn dir 1963–67, md 1967–74; dir of raw wool servs International Wool Secretariat 1974–83; Australian Wool Corp: dir Europe 1983–85, dir of tech servs 1985–89; wool textile conslt 1989–; non-exec memb Airedale Health Authy 1990–92, chm Airedale NHS Trust 1991–; FRSA 1964, FCIS 1973, FTI 1981; *Recreations* reading, travel, golf; *Clubs* Bradford, Craven, Keighley Golf; *Style*— Peter J M Bell, Esq, JP; ✉ Park Gate, Park Road, Cross Hills, Keighley, W Yorks BD20 8BG (☎ and fax 01535 636595); Airedale NHS Trust, Airedale General

Hospital, Skipton Road, Steeton, Keighley, W Yorks BD20 6TD (☎ 01535 652511, fax 01535 655129)

BELL, Quentin Ross; s of Ross Bell, and Violet Martha, *née* Douglas; *b* 24 June 1944; *Educ* Presentation Coll Reading; *m* Hilary Sian, da of Vernon Jones; 2 da (Verity Ross, Henrietta Ross); *Career* various appts: Reading Standard, Thomson Newspapers, Haymarket Publishing; chm The Quentin Bell Organisation plc 1973–; chm PRCA 1994–96; PR Professional of the Year (PR Week PR Awards) 1995 and 1996; MInstD, FCIM, FIPR; *Books* The PR Business: an insider's guide to real life public relations, Win that Pitch!; *Recreations* collecting art, clocks, watches, parrots, cars, wine and compliments, walking; *Clubs* RAC; *Style*— Quentin Bell, Esq; ✉ The Quentin Bell Organisation plc, 22 Endell St, Covent Garden, London WC2H 9AD (☎ 0171 379 0304, fax 0171 379 5483); Eggesford Mill, Eggesford, Chulmleigh, Devon; Domaine de Villeneuve, Villeneuve-sur-Vere 81130, Tarn, France

BELL, Sir (George) Raymond; KCMG (1973), CB (1967); eldest s of William Bell (d 1954), of Bradford, and Christabel, *née* Appleton; *b* 13 March 1916; *Educ* Bradford GS, St John's Coll Cambridge; *m* 1944, Joan Elizabeth, o da of William George (d 1951), of London, and Christina Coltham; 2 s, 2 da; *Career* WWII Lt RNVR; entered Civil Serv 1938, sec Fin Office of UK High Cmmr (Canada) 1945–48, dep sec HM Treasy 1966–72 (asst sec 1951, under sec 1960), memb UK delgn to Brussels Conf 1961–62 and 1970–72, vice pres Euro Investmt Bank 1973–78, ret 1978; hon vice pres EIB 1978–; *Style*— Sir Raymond Bell, KCMG, CB; ✉ Quartier des Bories, Aouste-sur-Sye, 26400 Crest, Drôme, France (☎ 00 33 4 75 25 26 94)

BELL, (John) Robin Sinclair; s of Ian Cardean Bell, OBE, MC (d 1967), of Edinburgh, and Cecile, *née* Rutherford (d 1980); *b* 28 Feb 1933; *Educ* The Edinburgh Acad, Loretto Sch, Worcester Coll Oxford (BA), Univ of Edinburgh (LLB); *m* 27 April 1963, Patricia, da of Edward Upton, of Whitby, N Yorkshire; 4 s (Charles b 1965 d 1969, Patrick b 1967, Peter b 1970, Jonathan b 1972); *Career* Nat Serv cmmnd Royal Scots Berlin 1951–53, Capt TA 1953–63; slr and WS; Coward Chance slrs 1961–62, sr ptnr Tods Murray WS Edinburgh 1987–94 (ptnr 1963); non-exec dir: Edinburgh Financial Trust plc 1983–87, Upton and Southern Holdings plc 1984–93; Law Soc of Scotland: memb Cncl 1975–78, memb Co Law Ctee 1975–94; memb Co Law Ctee of Cncl Bars & Law Socs of EU 1976–94, memb East of Scotland Water Authy 1995–, Scottish Charities nominee 1995–; vice chm Edinburgh Central Citizens Advice Bureau 1995–; memb Scottish Cncl Salmon & Trout Assoc 1994–; *Recreations* salmon fishing, gardening; *Clubs* New (Edinburgh), The Royal Scots (Edinburgh); *Style*— Robin Bell, Esq; ✉ 7 Heriot Row, Edinburgh EH3 6HU (☎ 0131 556 2983)

BELL, Hon Mr Justice; Hon Sir Rodger; kt (1993); s of John Thornton Bell (d 1974), and Edith Bell (d 1994); *b* 13 Sept 1939; *Educ* Brentwood Sch, BNC Oxford; *m* 27 Sept 1969, (Sylvia) Claire, only survg da of William Eden Tatton Brown, CB, by his w Aileen Hope Johnston; 1 s (Benjamin b 1970), 3 da (Natasha b 1972, Lucinda b 1975, Sophie b 1982); *Career* called to the Bar Middle Temple 1963; recorder of the Crown Ct 1980, QC 1982, bencher Middle Temple 1989, legal memb Mental Health Review Tbnl 1983–93, memb Parole Bd 1990–93, chm NHS Tbnl 1991–93, judge Employment Appeal Tbnl 1994–; judge of the High Court of Justice (Queen's Bench Div) 1993–; *Style*— The Hon Mr Justice Bell; ✉ Royal Courts of Justice, Strand, London WC2A 2LL

BELL, (Alexander) Scott; s of William Scott Bell (d 1978), of Falkirk, Scotland, and Catherine Irene, *née* Traill (d 1994); *b* 4 Dec 1941; *Educ* Daniel Stewart's Coll Edinburgh; *m* 12 Oct 1965, Veronica Jane, da of James Simpson (d 1985), of Edinburgh; 2 s (Scott b 1968, David b 1970), 1 da (Victoria b 1974); *Career* gp md Standard Life Assurance Co 1994– (joined 1958); dir: Bank of Scotland 1988–96, Hammerson plc 1988–, Scottish Financial Enterprise 1989–95; Hon Canadian consul in Scotland 1994–; FFA 1966, FPMI 1978; *Recreations* golf, travel, reading; *Clubs* New (Edinburgh), Bruntsfield Links Golfing Soc; *Style*— Scott Bell, Esq; ✉ Standard Life Assurance Co, 3 George St, Edinburgh EH2 2XZ (☎ 0131 245 6011, fax 0131 245 6010, telex 72530)

BELL, Stuart; MP (Lab) Middlesbrough (majority 15,784); s of Ernest and Margaret Rose Bell; *Educ* Hookergate GS Durham; *m* 1, 1960, Margaret, da of Mary Bruce; 1 s, 1 da; m 2, Margaret, da of Mary Allan; 1 s; *Career* called to the Bar Gray's Inn, sometime journalist; joined Lab Pty 1964, Parly candidate (Lab) Hexham 1979, MP (Lab) Middlesbrough 1983–, PPS to Rt Hon Roy Hattersley 1982–84, oppn front bench spokesman on NI 1984–87, oppn front bench spokesman on trade and industry 1992–; cncllr Newcastle City Cncl 1980–83; legal advsr Trade Unions for Lab Victory N Region, fndr memb Br-Irish Parly Body 1990, vice chm Br Gp Inter-Parly Union 1992–, memb Police and Criminal Evidence Bill Ctee 1986 and Children's Bill Ctee 1989; memb: Soc of Labour Lawyers, Fabian Soc, Co-operative Soc, Gen and Municipal Boilermakers and Allied Trades Union; *Publications* Paris 69, Days That Used To Be, When Salem Came to the Boro, How to Abolish the Lords (Fabian tract), The Principles of US Customs Valuation (legal pubn), Annotation of the Children Act (legal pubn, 1989); *Recreations* short story and novel writing; *Style*— Stuart Bell, Esq, MP; ✉ House of Commons, London SW1A 0AA

BELL, Sir Timothy John Leigh (Tim); kt (1990); s of Arthur Leigh Bell (d 1963), of SA, and Greta Mary, *née* Findlay; *b* 18 Oct 1941; *Educ* Queen Elizabeth's GS Barnet Herts; *m* 11 July 1988, Virginia Wallis, da of Dr John Wallis Hornbrook, of Sydney, Aust; 1 s (Harry Leigh b 22 April 1991), 1 da (Daisy Alicia Wallis b 1988); *Career* ABC TV 1959–61, Colman Prentis & Varley 1961–63, Hobson Bates 1963–66, Geers Gross 1966–70, chm and md Saatchi & Saatchi Compton 1975–85 (md 1970–75), gp chief exec Lowe Howard-Spink Cambell Ewald 1985–87, dep chm Lowe Howard-Spink & Bell 1987–89; currently chm: Lowe Bell Communications, Chime Communications plc; special advsr to Chm NCB 1984–86; former dir Centre for Policy Studies; memb: PR Ctee Gtr London Fund for the Blind 1979–86, Public Affrs Ctee WWF 1985–88, Indust Ctee Save the Children Fund; pres Charity Projects 1993– (chm 1984–93); memb: Cncl Royal Opera House 1982–85, S Bank Bd 1985–86; govr BFI 1983–86; FIPA; *Recreations* golf, politics; *Clubs* Mark's, Harry's Bar, RAC, St Edward Yacht (Sydney); *Style*— Sir Tim Bell; ✉ Chime Communications plc, 7 Hertford St, London W1Y 8LP (☎ 0171 495 4044, fax 0171 491 9860)

BELL, William Archibald Ottley Juxon; s of William Archibald Juxon Bell (d 1970), late of Pendell Court, Bletchingley, Surrey, and Mary Isabel Maude, *née* Ottley (d 1969); *b* 7 July 1919; *Educ* Eton, Trinity Coll Oxford (MA); *m* 19 July 1947, Belinda Mary, da of Geoffrey Dawson (d 1944), of Langcliffe Hall, Settle, and late Hon Cecilia, *née* Lawley; 2 s (Robert b 1950, Nicholas b 1952), 3 da (Georgiana (Mrs Jeffrey Heskins) b 1948, Caroline (Mrs Henry Llewellyn) b 1955, Joanna (Mrs John Goodwin) b 1958); *Career* WWII Temp Capt Welsh Gds 1940–45; served: N Africa, Italy, Austria; FO: entered 1945, Egyptian Dept 1945–46, political private sec to High Cmmr India 1946–47; private sec to exec dirs Br South Africa Company 1947–50, dir King & Shaxson plc (Bill-brokers) 1950–89 (md 1950–70); memb Chelsea GLC & ILEA 1970–86; chm: Diocesan Bd of Fin Oxfordshire 1974–75, GLC Historic Bldgs Ctee 1977–81, Oxfordshire Bldgs Tst 1986–93; memb London Advsy Ctee English Heritage 1986–90, chm English Heritage London Blue Plaques Panel 1990–95; pres: Oxfordshire Historic Churches Tst 1995, Heritage of London Tst 1996–; High Sheriff Oxfordshire 1978–79; *Recreations* shooting, golf tennis, painting; *Clubs* White's, Pratt's; *Style*— William Bell, Esq; ✉ 165 Cranmer Ct, London SW3 3HF (☎ 0171 589 1033); Jasmine House, The Green, Kingham, Oxfordshire OX7 6YD (☎ 01608 658030)

BELL, William Edwin; CBE (1980); s of Cuthbert Edwin Bell (d 1961), and Winifred Mary, *née* Simpson; *b* 4 Aug 1926; *Educ* Univ of Birmingham, Royal Sch of Mines; *m* 1952, Angela Josephine, da of Flt Lt E Vaughan, MC (d 1931); 2 s, 2 da; *Career* formerly exec Royal Dutch/Shell Gp, dir Shell International 1980–84, non-exec dir Costain Group plc 1980–92, chm Enterprise Oil plc 1984–91 (non-exec dep chm 1991–); CIMgt, FInstPet; *Recreations* golf, sailing; *Clubs* Nevill Golf; *Style*— William Bell, Esq, CBE; ✉ Fordcombe Manor, nr Tunbridge Wells, Kent TN3 0SE

BELL, William Lewis; CMG (1970), MBE (1945); s of Frederick Robinson Bell (d 1957), of Cheltenham, and Kate Harper, *née* Lewis (d 1984); *b* 31 Dec 1919; *Educ* Hymers Coll Hull, Oriel Coll Oxford; *m* 1 Sept 1943, Margaret, da of William Giles (d 1957), of Carmarthen; 1 s (Richard Jeremy Giles), 1 da (Rosalind Margaret (Mrs N S Bowlby)); *Career* Glos Regt 1940–46: Capt and Adj 2 Bn 1942, Maj and DAAG 49 WR Inf Div 1943–46; HM Colonial Admin Serv Uganda: dist offr 1946–54, asst fin sec 1954, dep sec to Treasy 1956, perm sec to Min of Educn 1958–62; dir Cox & Danks Ltd (MI Group) 1963–64, sec Westfield Coll Univ of London 1964–65, founding head Br Devpt Div for Caribbean Miny of Overseas Devpt 1966, UK dir Caribbean Devpt Bank 1970–72, founding dir gen Tech Educn & Trg Orgn Miny of Overseas Devpt 1972–77, info offr Univ of Oxford 1977–84; chm Uganda Nat Parks 1962, pres Uganda Sports Union 1961–62; fell Econ Devpt Inst World Bank 1958; *Recreations* watching cricket, Caribbeana, gardening; *Clubs* MCC, Vincent's; *Style*— William Bell, Esq, CMG, MBE; ✉ Hungry Hatch, Fletching, East Sussex TN22 3SH (☎ 0182 572 3415)

BELL BURNELL, Prof (Susan) Jocelyn; da of George Philip Bell (d 1982), of Solitude, Lurgan, N Ireland, and Margaret Allison Bell, MBE, JP, *née* Kennedy; *b* 15 July 1943; *Educ* The Mount Sch York, Univ of Glasgow (BSc), New Hall Cambridge (PhD); *m* 21 Dec 1968 (m dis 1989), Martin Burnell, s of Arnold Burnell, of London; 1 s (Gavin b 1973); *Career* Univ of Southampton: SRC fell 1968–70, jr teaching fell 1970–73; Mullard Space Sci Laboratory UCL: pt/t graduate programmer 1974–76, pt/t assoc res fell 1976–82; Royal Observatory Edinburgh: pt/t sr res fell 1982–86, astronomer i/c Visitor Centre 1985–86, pt/t sci offr and head of James Clerk Maxwell Telescope Section 1986–89, pt/t grade 7 and head of James Clerk Maxwell Telescope Section 1989–91; prof of physics The Open Univ 1991– (tutor, conslt, guest lectr 1973–88); ed The Observatory 1973–76; vice-pres RAS 1995– (memb Cncl 1978–81 and 1992–), memb various bds, ctees and panels PPARC and SERC 1978– (incl vice chm Astronomy 1 Ctee 1983–84), chair EC Physics TMR-TTR Panel 1996– (vice chair 1995); hon fell: Univ of Edinburgh 1988–91, New Hall Cambridge 1996–; memb Bd Edinburgh Int Sci Festival 1991–; memb: Br Cncl of Churches Assembly 1978–90, Scottish Churches Cncl 1982–90 (Exec Ctee 1984–88); Michelson medal Franklin Inst Philadelphia 1973, J Robert Oppenheimer meml prize Center for Theoretial Studies Miami 1978, Beatrice Tinsley prize American Astronomical Soc (first recipient) 1987, Herschel medal RAS London 1989; Hon DSc: Heriot-Watt Univ 1993, Univ of Warwick 1995, Univ of Newcastle 1995, Univ of Cambridge 1996; Hon DUniv York 1994; FRAS 1969, memb Int Astronomical Union 1979, FInstP 1992, memb American Astronomical Soc 1992; *Recreations* swimming, learning languages, knitting and sewing, Quaker activities; *Style*— Prof Jocelyn Bell Burnell; ✉ Physics Department, The Open University, Walton Hall, Milton Keynes MK7 6AA (☎ 01908 653229, fax 01908 654192)

BELL DAVIES, Vice Adm Sir Lancelot Richard; KBE (1977); s of Vice Adm Richard Bell Davies, VC, CB, DSO, AFC (d 1966), and Mary Pipon Bell Davies, *née* Montgomery (d 1975); f VC Gallipoli Campaign one of the first RNAS pilots; *b* 18 Feb 1926; *Educ* Boxgrove Sch Guildford, RNC Dartmouth (13 year old entry); *m* 1949, Emmeline Joan, da of Prof G J H Molengraaff (d 1961), of Holland; 1 s (Richard William b 1955), 2 da (Emmeline Anne b 1950, Daphane Alexandra b 1956); *Career* Midshipman HMS Norfolk 1943 Battle of North Cape, joined submarines 1944; cmd: HMS Subtle 1953, HMS Explorer 1955, HMS Leander 1962, HMS Forth 1967; Dir Naval Warfare 1969, Capt HMS Bulwark 1972–73, Naval Attaché Washington DC 1973–75, Supreme Allied Cdr Atlantic Rep Europe 1975–78, Cmdt NATO Def Coll Rome 1978–81; chm Sea Cadet Cncl 1983–92; CIMgt; *Recreations* sailing, gardening; *Clubs* Royal Yacht Sqdn, Naval and Military, RNSA; *Style*— Vice Adm Sir Lancelot Bell Davies, KBE; ✉ Wessex Bungalow, Satchell Lane, Hamble, Hampshire SO31 4HS (☎ 01703 457415)

BELLAK, John George; *b* 19 Nov 1930; *Educ* Rose Hill Sch Tunbridge Wells, Uppingham, Haute Ecole Commerciale Lausanne Switzerland, Clare Coll Cambridge (MA); *m* Mary Prudence (Pru); 3 s (Max b 1962, Leo b 1966, Benjy b 1968), 1 da (Maria b 1964); *Career* J Whittingham & Sons Ltd 1952–58, A Hoffmann & Co Ltd 1958–68, Doulton & Co Ltd 1968–83 (sales dir (fine china), commercial dir Tableware Ltd, mktg dir 1972, dep md, Euro distributive NV Royal Doulton (Belgium) SA, md Royal Doulton Tableware Ltd 1980); chm: Royal Crown Derby Porcelain Co Ltd, Lawleys Ltd 1968–83, Severn Trent plc (formerly Severn Trent Water Authy) 1983–94, Abtrust High Income Trust 1994–, The Celebrated Group plc; pres: Br Ceramic Mfrs' Fedn 1982–83, Fedn Europeene des Industries de Porcelaine et de Faience de Table et d'Ornementation 1982–83, Euro Waste Water Gp 1992–94; chm Water Servs Assoc 1991; memb Ct Univ of Keele; Parly candidate (Cons): Kingston upon Hull West 1964, Keighley 1966; treas Ripon Div Cons Assoc 1967; FRSA; *Recreations* politics, shooting, ornithology, wild life, conservation, ancient Chinese artefacts; *Clubs* Carlton, Beefsteak; *Style*— John Bellak, Esq; ✉ 1 Council House Court, Shrewsbury SY1 2AU (☎ 01743 233765)

BELLAMY, Andrew James; *b* 19 Sept 1949; *Educ* Spalding GS Lincolnshire, Univ of Wales Coll of Cardiff (BSc(Econ)), DipHSM; *m* Nicola; 1 da (Jane), 2 s (Ian, Richard); *Career* nat admin trainee SE Metropolitan Regnl Health Bd 1971–73, dep hosp sec Birkenhead Hosp Mgmnt Ctee/Wirral AHA 1973–75, princ admin Planning and Resources Sefton AHA 1975, sector admin Liverpool AHA 1975–79; asst dist admin: E Cumbria HA 1979–83, S Tees HA 1983–85; W Glamorgan HA: unit gen mangr 1985–90, asst gen mangr 1990–92 (secondment to Welsh Office 1991–92), unit gen mangr E Unit 1992–95; chief exec Glan-y-Môr NHS Tst 1995–; *Recreations* watching sport, golf, theatre, foreign travel; *Style*— Andrew Bellamy, Esq; ✉ Glan-y-Môr NHS Trust, 21 Orchard Street, Swansea, W Glamorgan SA1 5BE (☎ 01792 651501, fax 01792 458730, mobile 0374 974772)

BELLAMY, Judge; Christopher William; s of Dr William Albert Bellamy, TD (d 1960), of Waddesdon, Bucks, and Vyvienne Hilda, *née* Meyrick; *b* 25 April 1946; *Educ* Tonbridge, BNC Oxford; *m* 1 (m dis 1982); m 2, 1989, Deirdre Patricia, da of Alexander Turner (d 1961); 1 s (Edward Alexander William), 2 da (Charlotte Elizabeth, Alexandra Anne); *Career* called to the Bar Middle Temple 1968, bencher 1994; in practice specialising in EEC, competition, public law and related matters 1970–92, QC 1986, asst recorder Crown Ct 1989–92, judge of the Ct of First Instance of European Communities 1992–; govr Ravensbourne Coll of Design and Communication 1988–92; *Books* Common Market Law of Competition (ed V Rose, 4 edn, 1993); *Recreations* history, walking, family life; *Clubs* Athenaeum; *Style*— Judge Bellamy; ✉ Court of First Instance of the European Communities, L2925, Luxembourg (☎ 352 4303 3494)

BELLAMY, Prof David James; OBE (1994); s of Thomas James Bellamy (d 1988), and Winifred May, *née* Green (d 1979); *b* 18 Jan 1933; *Educ* Sutton County GS, Chelsea Coll of Sci and Technol (BSc), Bedford Coll London (PhD); *m* 3 Jan 1959, (Shirley) Rosemary, da of Frederick Herbert Froy (d 1959); 2 s (Rufus b 8 June 1966, Eoghain b 9 May 1975), 3 da (Henrietta b 14 Feb 1970, Brighid b 7 March 1972, Hannah b 24 June 1978); *Career* Univ of Durham: lectr in botany 1960–68, sr lectr in botany 1968–82, hon prof of adult educn 1982–; special prof of botany Univ of Nottingham 1987–, visiting prof of natural heritage studies Massey Univ NZ 1989; dir: Botanical Enterprises Ltd, David Bellamy Assocs, (fndr) Natural Heritage Conservation Fndn NZ, Conservation Fndn London; memb various professional ctees, recipient of many awards incl UNEP Global 500 1990; Hon DUniv Open Univ, Hon DSc CNAA; FLS, FIBiol, FRGS, fell Inst of Environmental Sci; Order of the Golden Ark (Netherlands) 1988, Commemoration medal (NZ) 1990; *Television* for BBC incl: Life in Our Sea 1970, Bellamy on Botany 1973, Bellamy's Britain 1975, Bellamy's Europe 1977, Up a Gum Tree 1980, Backyard Safari 1981, The Great Seasons 1982, Bellamy's New World 1983, You Can't See The Wood 1984, Seaside Safari 1985, Blooming Bellamy 1993, Bellamy Rides Again; for ITV incl: Botanic Man 1979, The End of the Rainbow Show 1986, Bellamy's Bugle 1986, Turning the Tide 1986, Bellamy's Birds Eye View 1988, Don't Ask Me, It's Life, It's More Life, The Gene Machine, Swallow, Bellamy on Top of the World, Paradise Ploughed, The Owl and the Woodsman, England's Lost Wilderness 1991, England's Last Wilderness 1992, Routes of Wisdom 1993; Moa's Ark (TVNZ) 1990; *Books* Bellamy on Botany (1972), Peatlands (jtly, 1973), Bellamy's Britain (1974), Life Giving Sea (1975), Green Worlds (jtly, 1975), The World of Plants (1975), It's Life (1976), Bellamy's Europe (1976), Botanic Action (1978), Botanic Man (1978), Half of Paradise (1979), Forces of Life (1979), Bellamy's Backyard Safari (1981), The Great Seasons (jtly, 1981), Il Libro Verde (1981), Discovering the Countryside (1982 and 1983), The Mouse Book (jtly, 1983), Bellamy's New World (1983), The Queen's Hidden Garden (jtly, 1984), Bellamy's Ireland (1986), Turning the Tide (jtly, 1986), Bellamy's Changing Countryside (1987), England's Last Wilderness (jtly, 1989), England's Lost Wilderness (jtly, 1990), Wetlands (jtly, 1990), Wilderness Britain (jtly, 1990), How Green are You (jtly, 1991), Tomorrow's Earth (jtly, 1991), World Medicine: Plants Patients and People (jtly, 1992), Blooming Bellamy (1993), Trees of the World (jtly, 1993); *Style—* Prof David Bellamy; ✉ Mill House, Bedburn, Bishop Auckland, Co Durham DL13 3NN

BELLAMY, Stephen Howard George Thompson; QC (1996); s of George Bellamy (d 1976), of Birstall, and Clarice, *née* Thompson; *b* 27 Sept 1950; *Educ* The GS Heckmondwike Yorkshire, Trinity Hall Cambridge (MA Law); *m* 15 Oct 1988, Rita James; 1 da (Georgina Claudia Carla (Nina) b 6 Nov 1991); *Career* called to the Bar Lincoln's Inn 1974; in practice SE Circuit, specialist in family law (especially children); memb Ctee Family Law Bar Assoc 1989–, memb Gen Cncl of the Bar 1993–96; memb Br Inst of Int and Comparative Law; ACIArb 1990; *Recreations* music, opera, gardening, tennis, skiing; *Style—* Stephen Bellamy, Esq, QC; ✉ 1 King's Bench Walk, Temple, London EC4Y 7DB (☎ 0171 936 1500, fax 0171 936 1568, mobile 0802 782981)

BELLANY, Prof Ian; s of James Bellany (d 1984), of Sheffield and Bristol, and Jemima, *née* Emlay; *b* 21 Feb 1941; *Educ* Preston Lodge, Prestonpans, Firth Park Sheffield, Balliol Coll Oxford (BA, MA, DPhil); *m* 7 Aug 1965, Wendy Ivey, da of Glyndwr Thomas (d 1978), of Gilwern, Abergavenny; 1 s (Alastair b 1968), 1 da (Alison b 1971); *Career* asst princ FCO 1965–68, res fell Aust Nat Univ Canberra 1968–70; Univ of Lancaster: lectr in politics (sr lectr 1974–79), prof of politics 1979–, dir of the Centre for the Study of Arms Control and Int Security 1979–90; founding ed Arms Control, memb Advsy Panel on Disarmament FCO; external examiner in: Int Rels LSE 1985–88, Int Studies Univ of Birmingham 1989–92, Int Rels Univ of Aberdeen; *Books* Australia in the Nuclear Age (1972), Anti-Ballistic Missile Defence in the 1980s (ed 1983), The Verification of Arms Control Agreements (ed 1983), The Nuclear Non Proliferation Treaty (ed 1985), New Conventional Weapons and Western Defence (ed 1987), A Basis for Arms Control (1991), Reviewing Britain's Defence (1994), The Environment in World Politics (1996); *Recreations* broadcasting, carpentry and computing; *Style—* Prof Ian Bellany; ✉ University of Lancaster, Bailrigg, Lancaster LA1 4YL (☎ 01524 65201)

BELLANY, Dr John; CBE (1994); s of Richard Weatherhead Bellany (d 1985), of Port Seton, E Lothian, and Agnes Craig Maltman Bellany; *b* 18 June 1942; *Educ* Cockenzie Sch E Lothian, Preston Lodge Prestonpans, Edinburgh Coll of Art (DA), RCA (MA); *m* 1, 19 Sept 1964 (m dis 1974), Helen Margaret, da of late Harold Percy, of Golspie, Sutherland; 2 s (Jonathan b 22 Dec 1965, Tristan b 21 Aug 1968), 1 da (Anya b 30 Sept 1970); m 2, 1980, Juliet Gray, *née* Lister (d 1985); m 3, 1986, his first wife Helen Margaret; *Career* lectr in fine art Winchester Sch of Art 1969–73, head Faculty of Painting Croydon Coll of Art 1973–78, visiting lectr in painting RCA 1975–84, lectr in fine art Goldsmiths' Coll London 1978–84, artist in residence Victorian Coll of the Arts Melbourne Aust 1983, fell commoner Trinity Hall Cambridge 1988; Maj Arts Cncl Award 1981, jt first prize Athena Int Award 1985, Korn Ferry Int Award RA 1993; Hon Doctorate Univ of Edinburgh; Hon RSA 1987, RA 1991 (elected ARA 1986); *Exhibitions* maj solo exhbns: Drian Gallery London 1970, 1971, 1972, 1973 and 1974, Aberdeen City Art Gallery 1975, Acme Gallery London 1977 and 1980, Scottish Arts Cncl Gallery 1978, 3rd Eye Centre Glasgow 1979, Southampton Art Gallery, Rosa Esman Gallery NY 1982, 1983 and 1984, Beaux Arts Gallery Bath 1989 and 1990, Fischer Fine Art London 1986, 1987, 1989 and 1991, Scot Nat Gallery of Modern Art 1986 and 1989, Raab Gallery Berlin 1989, Fitzwilliam Museum Cambridge 1991, Fischer Fine Art London 1991; Arts Cncl touring exhibition 1983: Ikon Gallery Birmingham, Walker Art Gallery Liverpool, Graves Art Gallery Sheffield; Arts Cncl touring exhibition 1984: Christine Abrahams Gallery Melbourne, Dusseldorf Gallery Perth Aust, Roslyn Oxley Gallery Sydney Aust, Nat Portrait Gallery 1986, Galerie Kirkhaar Amsterdam; retrospective exhbns: Scot Nat Gallery of Modern Art 1986, Serpentine Gallery London, RCA Gallery 1987, Kunsthalle Hamburg 1989, Roslyn Oxley Gallery Aust, Butler Gallery Kilkenny Castle, Hendrix Gallery Dublin, 3rd Eye Centre Glasgow (prints) 1988, Ruth Siegel Gallery NY 1988 and 1990, The Renaissance of John Bellany (Nat Gallery of Modern Art) 1988, Fisher Fine Art London 1988 and 1991, Raab Gallery Berlin 1990, Fitzwilliam Museum Cambridge 1991, A Long Night's Journey into Day: The Art of John Bellany (Kelvingrove Art Gallery and Museum, Glasgow) 1992, Berkeley Square Gallery London 1993; maj gp exhbns: British Romantic Painting (Madrid), El Greco - Mystery and Illumination (Nat Gallery), Every Picture tells a Story (Br Cncl touring exhibition Singapore and Hong Kong), Eros in Albion (House of Messaccio Italy), Scottish Art since 1990 (Nat Gallery of Scotland and Barbican London), Scotland Creates 1990, The Great British Art Show 1990; *Public Collections* Aberdeen Art Gallery, Arts Cncl of GB, Br Cncl, Br Govt Collection Whitehall, Contemporary Arts Soc, Hatton Art Gallery, Kelvingrove Art Gallery, Leeds Art Gallery, Leicester Art Gallery, Middlesborough Art Gallery, Nat Gallery of Poland Warsaw, Nat Library of Congress Washington USA, Museum of Modern Art NY, Met Museum NY, Nat Portrait Gallery, Nat Gallery of Modern Art Scotland, Gulbenkian Museum Lisbon, J F Kennedy Library Boston USA, V & A, Br Museum, Tate; *Clubs* Chelsea Arts, Scottish Arts (Edinburgh); *Style—* Dr John Bellany, CBE, RA; ✉ 2 Windmill Drive, Clapham Common, London SW4 9DE; 19 Great Stuart St, Edinburgh, Scotland; c/o Berkley Square Gallery, 23A Bruton Street, London W1X 7DA (☎ 0171 493 7939); represented by Angela Flowers Gallery plc, 199–205 Richmond Road, London E8 3NJ (☎ 0181 985 3333, fax 0181 985 0067)

BELLAS, Moira Aileen; da of Norman Spencer Bellas, of Worthing, and Catherine Winifred, *née* Whysall (d 1986); *b* 21 March 1950; *Educ* Woodfield Secondary Modern Sch Hounslow; *m* Dec 1974, Clive Alan Banks; 1 da (Kelly May b May 1987); *Career* jr clerk Pye Records 1965–67, press office asst Paragon Publicity 1967–68, press offr EMI Records 1968–70, press offr Three's Company (PR co) 1970–71; WEA Records (formerly Kinney Records): sec/PA 1971–73, press offr 1973–86, dir Artistic Devpt and Mktg 1986–92, md 1992–; winner Leslie Perrin Publicity Award; *Style—* Ms Moira Bellas; ✉ WEA Records, The Warner Building, 28 Kensington Church Street, London W8 4EP (☎ 0171 938 0005)

BELLE, Pamela Dorothy Alice; da of Brian Henry Belle, of Nacton, Suffolk, and Sylvia Catherine Victoire, *née* Wilkinson; *b* 16 June 1952; *Educ* Ipswich GPDST HS, Univ of Sussex (BA); *m* 1, 1976 (m dis 1983), Alan David Fincher; m 2, 6 Aug 1990, Stephen John Thomas; 2 s (Hugh Nicholas Belle Thomas b 21 April 1990, Patrick Luke Belle Thomas b 3 June 1993); *Career* teacher St Mary's CE First Sch Northchurch Berkhamsted Herts 1978–85, full time author 1985–; memb Soc of Authors; *Books* The Moon in the Water (1983), The Chains of Fate (1984), Alathea (1985), The Lodestar (1987), Wintercombe (1988), Herald of Joy (1989), A Falling Star (1990), Treason's Gift (1992), The Silver City (1994), The Wolf Within (1995), Blood Imperial (1996); *Recreations* reading, pottery, gardening, Burmese cats and Labrador dogs, country walks, history, architecture, archaeology, just lazing about; *Style—* Ms Pamela Belle; ✉ c/o Vivienne Schuster, Curtis Brown Group Ltd, 4th Floor, Haymarket House, 28–29 Haymarket, London SW1Y 4SP (☎ 0171 396 6600)

BELLENGER, Rev Dom Dominic Aidan; s of Gerald Bellenger, of London, and Kathleen Patricia, *née* O'Donnell; *b* 21 July 1950; *Educ* Finchley GS, Jesus Coll Cambridge (Lightfoot scholar, MA, PhD), Angelicum Univ Rome; *Career* asst master St Mary's Sch Cambridge 1975–78; Downside Abbey: Benedictine monk 1982, priest 1988; Downside Sch: asst master 1978–82, housemaster 1989–91, head master 1991–95, dir of historical research 1995–; memb: Ctee Ecclesiastical History Soc 1982–85, Ctee English Benedictine Historical Cmmn 1987–, Cncl Catholic Record Soc 1990–; tstee Catholic Family History Soc 1990–; pres English Catholic History Gp 1991–; govr: Moor Park Sch Ludlow 1991–, St Anthony's Leweston Dorset 1991–93, St Mary's Sch Shaftesbury 1992–, Moreton Hall Sch Suffolk 1994–; Leverhulme Res Award 1986; English corr Revue d'Histoire de l'Eglise de France 1982–85, ed South Western Catholic History 1982–; FRHistS, FRSA; *Books* English and Welsh Priests 1558–1800 (1984), The French Exiled Clergy (1986), Opening the Scrolls (ed, 1987), Les Archives du Nord, Calender of 20 H (jt ed, 1987), St Cuthbert (1987), Mélanges Charles Mollette (1989), Letters of Bede Jarrett (jt ed, 1989), Fathers in Faith (ed, 1991), The Great Return (ed, 1994); author of articles in jls, newspapers and periodicals; *Recreations* books, church architecture, travel, the visual arts, writing; *Clubs* Stratton-on-the-Fosse CC (pres 1991–95); *Style—* Rev Dom Aidan Bellenger; ✉ Downside School, Stratton-on-the-Fosse, Bath BA3 4RJ (☎ 01761 232206, fax 01761 233575)

BELLEW, Hon Bryan Edward; s and h of 7 Baron Bellew, *qv*; *b* 19 March 1943; *Educ* Eton, RMA Sandhurst; *m* 1968, Rosemary Sarah, er da of Maj Reginald Kilner Brasier Hitchcock, of Meers Court, Mayfield, Sussex; 2 s (Patrick Edward b 1969, Anthony Richard Brooke b 1972); *Career* Maj (ret) Irish Gds; *Style—* Maj the Hon Bryan Bellew

BELLEW, 7 Baron (I 1848); Sir James Bryan Bellew; 13 Bt (I 1688); s of 6 Baron Bellew, MC; suc f 1981; *b* 5 Jan 1920; *m* 1, 1942, Mary Elizabeth (d 1978), er da of Rev Edward Hill, of West Malling; 2 s, 1 da; m 2, 1978, Gwendoline, da of Charles Redmond Clayton-Daubeny, of Bridgwater, Somerset, and of Bihar, India, and formerly w of Maj P Hall; *Heir* s, Hon Bryan Bellew, *qv*; *Career* late Capt Irish Gds, served WW II; *Style—* The Rt Hon the Lord Bellew

BELLI, Dr Anna-Maria; da of Bartolomeo Antonio Luigi Belli, of Cwmgyn, Swansea, West Glam, and Carmen, *née* Lombardelli; *b* 5 Aug 1957; *Educ* Glanmôr Sch for Girls, Univ of London, Middx Hosp Med Sch (MB BS); *Career* sr registrar in radiology St George's Hosp 1985–87 (registrar 1982–85); sr lectr and hon conslt in radiodiagnosis: Univ of Sheffield 1987–90, Royal Postgraduate Medical School Hammersmith Hospital London 1990–92; currently conslt St George's Hosp London; memb Cncl BSIR 1993; fell CIRSE 1994, FRCR 1985; *Books* An Imaging Atlas of Human Anatomy (contrib 1 edn, 1992), Vascular Diseases in the Limbs (contrib 1 edn, 1993), Practical Interventional Radiology of the Peripheral Vascular System (contrib and ed, 1993); *Style—* Dr Anna-Maria Belli; ✉ Department of Radiology, St George's Hosp, Blackshaw Road, London SW17 0QT (☎ 0181 725 1481, fax 0181 725 2936)

BELLINGER, Christopher Henry; s of Clifford Bellinger (d 1992), of Cardiff, S Wales, and Margaret Joy, *née* Boddington; *b* 20 Feb 1943; *Educ* Abingdon Sch Berkshire; *m* 24 June 1972, Diana Penelope Margaret, da of Maj Frank Albert Bowater (d 1982), of London; *Career* BBC TV: Film Dept Wales 1964–70, TV presentation 1971–78, prodr Multi-Coloured Swap Shop, ed Saturday Superstore 1982, ed Going Live! 1986–93, ed Live and Kicking 1993–; *Books* Saturday Superstore Book (2 edns), The Going Live! Book (1988); *Style—* Christopher Bellinger, Esq; ✉ BBC Television Centre, London W12 7RJ (☎ 0181 576 1979, fax 0181 740 8835)

BELLINGER, Sir Robert Ian; GBE (1967), kt (1964); s of David Morgan Bellinger, of Cardiganshire, by his w Jane Ballantine Deans; *b* 10 March 1910; *Educ* Church of England Sch; *m* 1962, Christiane Marie Louise, da of Maurice Clement Janssens, of Brussels; 1 s, 1 da; *Career* chm: Kinloch (PM) Ltd 1964–75, Nat Savings Ctee 1970–75 (pres 1972–75), Danish Trade Advsy Bd 1977–82; dir Rank Organisation 1971–83; Lord Mayor of London 1966–67; one of HM Lieutenants City of London 1976–; pres Arsenal FC 1966– (dir 1960–), chm Fin Ctee BBC, govr BBC 1968–71; memb Ct of Assts Worshipful Co of Broderers; Gentleman Usher of the Purple Rod Order of the Br Empire 1969–85, KStJ 1966; *Style—* Sir Robert Bellinger, GBE; ✉ Penn Wood, Fulmer, Bucks (☎ 01753 662029)

BELLINGHAM, Prof Alastair John; CBE (1997); s of Stanley Herbert Bellingham, of Ewell, Surrey, and Sybil Mary, *née* Milne (d 1996); *b* 27 March 1938; *Educ* Tiffin Boys' Sch Kingston upon Thames, UCH Med Sch London; *m* 24 May 1963, (Valerie) Jill, da of Kenneth Morford (d 1971); 3 s (James b 24 April 1964, Richard b 14 April 1969, Paul b 5 Feb 1973); *Career* Mackenzie-Mackinnon Streatfeild fell RCP 1968–69, res fell Univ of Washington USA 1969–70, sr lectr in haematology UCH Med Sch London 1971–74; prof of haematology: Univ of Liverpool 1974–84, King's Coll London 1984–; pres Br Soc for Haematology 1991–92 (sec 1984–87), vice pres Euro African Div Int Soc of Haematology 1992–, chm Haematology Ctee RCP 1992; memb Cncl RCPath 1987–90; FRCP (London) 1976, FRCPath 1986 (vice pres 1990–93, pres 1993–96), FRCPGlas 1995; *Publications* author of papers on red cell genetic disorders and red cell function, incl enzymopathies and sickle cell disease; *Recreations* photography, oenology, viticulture; *Clubs* Savage; *Style—* Prof Alastair Bellingham, CBE; ✉ 13 Barnmead Rd, Beckenham, Kent BR3 1JF (☎ 0181 778 0730); Department of Haematological Medicine, King's College School of Medicine & Dentistry, Bessemer Rd, London SE5 9RS (☎ 0171 346 3080, fax 0171 346 3514)

BELLINGHAM, Anthony Edward Norman; s of Sir Roger Bellingham, 6 Bt (d 1973); bro and hp of Sir Noel Bellingham, 7 Bt; *b* 24 March 1947; *Educ* Rossall; *m* Denise Marie, da of Henry Calvin Moity, of New Orleans, USA; 1 s (William Alexander Noel Henry b Aug 1991); *Career* recruitment conslt; *Style—* Anthony Bellingham, Esq

BELLINGHAM, Henry Campbell; MP (C) North West Norfolk (majority 11,564); s of (Arthur) Henry Bellingham (d 1959), and June Marion, *née* Cloudesley Smith; *b* 29 March 1955; *Educ* Eton, Magdalene Coll Cambridge, Cncl of Legal Educn; *Career* called to the Bar Middle Temple 1978; MP (C) Norfolk North West 1983–, vice chm Cons Backbench Smaller Business Ctee 1987–90 (jt sec 1983–87), memb Environment Select Ctee 1987–90, chm Cons Cncl on Eastern Europe 1989–93, PPS to Rt Hon Malcolm Rifkind 1990–; memb British-Irish Parly Body 1992–; *Clubs* White's; *Style—* Henry Bellingham, Esq, MP; ✉ House of Commons, London SW1

BELLINGHAM, Kate; da of Roger Bellingham, of Pocklington, York, and Barbara, *née* Stapleton; *b* 7 July 1963; *Educ* Mount Sch York, Queen's Coll Oxford (BA); *Career* science and technology broadcaster; computer programmer CAP Alderley Edge 1984–87 (concurrently pt/t sound crew asst Royal Exchange Theatre Manchester), trainee electronic engr BBC Radio (London) 1987–90; presenter: BBC/IEE Faraday lecture tour 1988–89, Techno (BBC Schs TV) 1989, Tomorrow's World (BBC TV) 1990–94, The Acid Test (BBC Radio 5 Live) 1994–, Showcase (BBC Schs TV) 1995–, The Big Bang (ITV) 1996–; media advisor to Young Engineers 1995–; BBC Engrg Trg Standing Instructions qualification 1990; memb Women's Engrg Soc; *Recreations* music, crosswords, rambling; *Style*— Ms Kate Bellingham; ✉ c/o Dave Winslett, 6 Kenwood Ridge, Kenley, Surrey CR8 5JW (☎ 0181 668 0531, fax 0181 668 9216)

BELLINGHAM, Lynda (Mrs Nunzio Peluso); da of Capt D J Bellingham, and Ruth Bellingham; *b* 31 May 1948; *Educ* Convent GS, Central Sch of Speech and Drama; *m* 22 July 1981, Nunzio Peluso; 2 s (Michael b 1983, Robert Ciro b 1988); *Career* actress; *Theatre* appearances: Noises Off, Look No Hans, Double Double, The Sisters Rosensweig (Old Vic) 1994, The Sisters Rosensweig 1995; *Television* appearances incl: Billy Liar 1973, Mackenzie, Dr Who (BBC), Funny Man, All Creatures Great and Small (BBC), Second Thoughts (LWT), Faith in the Future (LWT) 1995 and 1996; star of Oxo adverts; *Style*— Ms Lynda Bellingham; ✉ William Morris Agency (UK) Ltd, 31/32 Soho Square, London W1V 6DG (☎ 0171 434 2191, fax 0171 437 0238)

BELLINGHAM, Sir Noel Peter Roger; 7 Bt (GB 1796), of Castle Bellingham, Co Louth; s of Sir Roger Carroll Patrick Stephen Bellingham, 6 Bt (d 1973), and Mary, *née* Norman; *b* 4 Sept 1943; *Educ* Lindisfarne Coll; *m* 1977, Jane, da of Edwin William Taylor, of Sale, Cheshire; *Heir* bro, Anthony Edward Norman Bellingham, *qv*; *Career* accountant; *Style*— Sir Noel Bellingham, Bt; ✉ 20 Davenport Park Rd, Davenport, Stockport, Cheshire SK2 6JS (☎ 0161 483 7168)

BELLIS, Michael John; s of Herbert Henry Bellis (d 1976), of Sherborne, Dorset, and Marjorie Dudley, *née* Charlton; *b* 28 April 1937; *Educ* Bancrofts Sch Woodford Green, College of Law; *Career* Nat Serv RCS 1956–58; admitted slr 1968, cmmr for oaths 1973, sr ptnr Edward Oliver and Bellis 1975–90 (conslt 1991–96); md Heritage Heirlooms (UK) Ltd 1990–; chm Med Serv Ctee FPC London Boroughs of Redbridge and Waltham Forest 1978–89, lay serv ctee memb Norfolk Family Health Serv Authy 1991–96, chm Discipline Panel E Norfolk Health Authy 1996–, memb Mgmnt Ctee The Intaglio Fndn Norwich 1996–; former vice pres W Essex Law Soc; hon slr and hon memb Rotary Club Ilford (former pres), Rotary Int Paul Harris fell; tstee, fundraising chm and memb Exec Ctee Redbridge Community Tst 1992–95, tstee London NE Community Fndn 1996–; Freeman City of London, Liveryman Worshipful Co of Bakers (memb Ct 1994); memb Law Soc 1968; *Recreations* collecting rare books, travel in the USA, growing and eating asparagus; *Clubs* Norfolk (Norwich), Law Society; *Style*— Michael John Bellis, Esq; ✉ Beck Farm Coach House, The Street, Kelling, Holt, Norfolk NR25 7EL (☎ 01263 588435); Baron Art, The Old Reading Room Gallery, The Street (at the War Memorial) Kelling, Holt, Norfolk NR25 7EL (☎ 01263 588227, fax 01263 588133)

BELLMAN, Dr Susan Caroline; *b* 27 April 1947; *Educ* Erdington GS Birmingham, Univ of Cambridge and (clinical at) St Mary's Hosp London (MB BChir, MA, Swimming blue); *Career* house surgn Middx Hosp 1971–72, house physician in gen med and neurology, locum SHO Mount Vernon Hosp and SHO in thoracic surgery Harefield Hosp 1972–73, locum SHO in gen surgery Barnet Gen Hosp and SHO in plastic surgery Hammersmith Hosp 1973–74, SHO Royal Devon and Exeter Hosp 1974–75, registrar Bart's 1975–76, sr registrar in audiological med Nuffield Speech and Hearing Centre Royal Nat Throat, Nose and Ear Hosp 1981–83 (registrar 1979–81), conslt audiological physician Great Ormond St Hosp for Children NHS Tst 1983–; ed Bulletin Int Assoc of Physicians in Audiology 1988–96, memb Editorial Bd Br Jl of Audiology 1992–96; memb: BMA, Med Women's Fedn, RSM, Br Soc of Audiology (memb Cncl 1991–), Br Assoc of Audiological Physicians, Br Soc of Otolaryngologists, Br Cochlear Implant Gp, Otorhinolaryngological Research Soc, Br Soc for Paediatric Otorhinolaryngology, Int Assoc of Physicians in Audiology, Int Soc of Audiology, Soc for Ear, Nose and Throat Advances in Children; DLO 1974, FRCS 1981; author of numerous book chapters and articles in med jls; *Recreations* gardening, machine knitting and creative embroidery; *Style*— Dr Susan Bellman; ✉ Great Ormond Street Hospital for Children NHS Trust, Great Ormond Street, London WC1N 3JH

BELLOS, Prof David Michael; s of Nathaniel Bellos, of London, and Katharine Mabel, *née* Shapiro; *b* 25 June 1945; *Educ* Westcliff HS, Univ of Oxford (BA, MA, DPhil); *m* 1, 31 Dec 1966 (m dis 1985), Ilona, da of Sandor Roth (d 1945); 1 s (Alexander b 1969), 2 da (Amanda b 1971, Olivia b 1974); m 2, 1 July 1989 (m dis 1995), Susan Esther Currie, da of Prof A C Lendrum; m 3, 25 June 1996, Pascale Voilley, da of Jean Voilley; *Career* fell Magdalen Coll Oxford 1969, lectr in French Univ of Edinburgh 1972, prof of French Univ of Southampton 1982, prof and head Dept of French Studies Univ of Manchester 1985–96, prof of French and comparative literature Princeton Univ 1997–; Chevalier de l'Ordre des Palmes Académiques France 1988, Prix Goncourt de la biographie France 1994; *Books* Balzac Criticism in France, 1850–1900 (1976), Georges Perec - Life A User's Manual (trans, 1987), Georges Perec - A Life in Words (1993), Ismail Kadure - The Pyramid (trans, 1996); *Recreations* cycling; *Style*— Prof David Bellos; ✉ Department of Romance Languages and Literature, Princeton University, Princeton, NJ 08544–5264, USA (☎ 00 1 609 258 4500, fax 00 1 609 258 4535)

BELLWIN, Baron (Life Peer UK 1979); Irwin Norman Bellow; JP (Leeds 1969), DL (W Yorks 1991); s of Abraham and Leah Bellow; *b* 7 Feb 1923; *Educ* Leeds GS, Univ of Leeds (LLB); *m* 1948, Doreen Barbara Saperia; 1 s, 2 da; *Career* alderman Leeds CC 1968–, ldr Leeds City Cncl 1975–79; Parly under sec of state DOE 1979–83, min of state for Local Govt 1983–84; bd memb New Towns Cmmn 1985–; chm N Hull Housing Action Tst 1993–; *Recreations* golf; *Clubs* Moor Allerton (hon pres); *Style*— The Rt Hon The Lord Bellwin, JP, DL; ✉ Woodside Lodge, Ling Lane, Scarcroft, Leeds LS14 3HX (☎ 0113 289 2908, fax 0113 289 2213)

BELMORE, 8 Earl (I 1797); John Armar Lowry-Corry; also Baron Belmore (I 1781) and Viscount Belmore (I 1789); s of 7 Earl Belmore, JP, DL (d 1960), and Gloria Anthea Harker; *b* 4 Sept 1951; *Educ* Lancing; *m* 1984, Lady Mary Jane Meade, 2 da of 6 Earl of Clanwilliam (d 1989); 2 s (Viscount Corry b 1985, Hon Montagu G G Lowry-Corry b 1989), 1 da (Lady Martha Catherine b 27 May 1992); *Heir* s, Viscount Corry, *qv*; *Career* farmer; *Recreations* art; *Clubs* Kildare Street Dublin; *Style*— The Rt Hon the Earl of Belmore; ✉ The Garden House, Castle Coole, Enniskillen, N Ireland BT74 6JX (☎ 01365 322463)

BELOFF, Baron (Life Peer UK 1981), of Wolvercote, Co Oxfordshire; Sir Max Beloff; kt (1980); er s of Simon Beloff, and Mary Beloff; *b* 2 July 1913; *Educ* St Paul's, CCC Oxford (MA, DLitt); *m* 1938, Helen, da of Samuel Dobrin; 2 s; *Career* sits as Cons in House of Lords; fell CCC Oxford 1937–39, asst lectr Univ of Manchester 1939–46; Univ of Oxford: Nuffield reader in comparative study of instns 1946–56 (Nuffield fell 1947–57), Gladstone prof of govt and public admin 1957–74, fell All Souls Coll 1957–74 (emeritus fell 1980–); princ UC Buckingham 1974–79, supernumerary fell St Antony's Coll Oxford 1975–84; hon fell: Mansfield Coll Oxford 1989–, CCC Oxford 1993–; hon prof Univ of St Andrews 1993–; memb Wilton Park Academic Cncl until 1983; Hon LLD: Univ of Pittsburgh, Univ of Manchester; Hon DCL Bishop's Canada; Hon DLitt: Bowdoin USA, Univ of Buckingham; Hon DUniv Aix-Marseille; FBA, FRHistS, FRSA; *Style*— The Rt Hon the Lord Beloff, FBA; ✉ Flat 9, 22 Lewes Crescent, Brighton BN2 1GB (☎ 01273 688622)

BELOFF, Hon Michael Jacob; QC (1981); er s of Baron Beloff (Life Peer), *qv*; *b* 19 April 1942; *Educ* Eton, Univ of Oxford (MA); *m* 1969, Judith Mary Arkinstall; 1 s, 1 da; *Career* called to the Bar Gray's Inn 1967, bencher 1988; former lectr Trinity Coll Oxford; former legal corr: New Society, The Observer; recorder of the Crown Court 1985–95, dep judge of the High Court 1989–96, jt head of chambers, judge of the Ct of Appeal of Guernsey and Jersey; memb Cncl of Arbitrators for Sport; emeritus chm Admin Law Bar Assoc; pres Trinity Coll Oxford 1996–; FRSA; *Style*— The Hon Michael Beloff, QC; ✉ 38 Park Town, Oxford; 4–5 Gray's Inn Square, Gray's Inn, London WC1R 5AY (☎ 0171 202 5252, fax 0171 242 7803); from Sept 1996: The President's Lodging, Trinity College, Oxford

BELOFF, Nora (Mrs Clifford Makins); da of Simon Beloff (d 1964), and Marie Katzin Beloff; *b* 24 Jan 1919; *Educ* King Alfred Sch London, Lady Margaret Hall Oxford (BA); *m* 10 March 1977, Clifford George Makins; *Career* Political Intelligence Dept FO UK and Paris 1941–45; Reuters News Agency Paris Office 1945–46, Paris corr The Economist 1946–50, editorial staff The Observer 1948–77 (chief political corr 1964–76, corr Paris, Washington, Moscow and Brussels); *Books* The General Says No (1963, French translation 1964), Transit of Britain (1973), Freedom Under Foot (1976), No Travel Like Russian (1979, USA edn Inside the Soviet Empire: Myth Reality 1980), Tito's Flawed Legacy (1985, USA 1986, Italian translation 1987, Slovene translation 1990); *Recreations* walking, conversation; *Clubs* Chatham House, London Library; *Style*— Miss Nora Beloff; ✉ 11 Belsize Rd, London NW6 4RX (☎ 0171 586 0378)

BELPER, 4 Baron (UK 1856); (Alexander) Ronald George Strutt; s of 3 Baron (d 1956), by 1 w, Hon Dame Eva Bruce, DBE, JP, da of 2 Baron Aberdare; bro of Lavinia, Duchess of Norfolk; *b* 23 April 1912; *Educ* Harrow; *m* 1940 (m dis 1949), Zara Sophie Kathleen Mary, da of Sir Harry Mainwaring, 5 Bt; 1 s; *Heir* s, Hon Richard Strutt; *Career* formerly Maj Coldstream Gds; *Style*— The Rt Hon The Lord Belper; ✉ c/o Withers Solicitors, 12 Gough Square, London EC4A 3DE (☎ 0171 936 1000, fax 0171 936 2589)

BELSHAW, Prof Deryke Gerald Rosten; s of Leonard Gerald Belshaw (d 1987), of Ash Vale, nr Aldershot, Hants, and Phyllis Guiver, *née* Rosten; *b* 9 Sept 1932; *Educ* Hampton GS, Selwyn Coll Cambridge (MA), Hertford Coll Oxford (Dip in Agric Econ); *m* 15 Aug 1959, Audrey Gladys, da of John Newell, MBE, VMH (d 1984), of Ringwood, Hants; 1 s (Jeremy b 1960), 2 da (Sarah b 1962, Anna b 1963); *Career* Nat Serv RA seconded to RWAFF Nigeria, gunner 1954, 2 Lt 1955, Lt 1956; res offr Sch of Agric Univ of Cambridge 1958–60, sr lectr then reader in agric economics Makerere Coll Univ of E Africa 1964–70 (lectr 1960–64), prof of rural devpt Sch of Devpt Studies Univ of E Anglia 1985– (sr lectr then reader in agric economics 1970–85, dean 1981–84); IBRD/UNDP visiting prof of economics Makerere Univ Uganda 1992–94, FAO food strategy advsr Govt of Ethiopia on secondment from Overseas Development Group Ltd Univ of E Anglia 1986–89, ODA economic advsr Govt of Kenya 1970–72, UNDP and FAO regnl devpt advsr Govt of Tanzania 1974–77, conslt UN Centre for Regnl Devpt 1995–; memb: Editorial Bd of Rural Development Abstracts, Bd of Dirs World Vision UK; tstee Traidcraft Foundation; fell Oxford Centre for Mission Studies; *Books* Farm Finance and Agricultural Development (1988), Towards a Food and Nutrition Strategy for Ethiopia (1989); *Recreations* vinous evaluation; *Style*— Prof Deryke Belshaw; ✉ School of Development Studies, University of E Anglia, Norwich NR4 7TJ Norfolk (☎ 01603 56161, fax 01603 593382)

BELSHAW, Kenneth John Thomas; s of John Everton Belshaw, and Lilian Elizabeth, *née* Stewart; *b* 14 May 1952; *Educ* Orangefield Sch for Boys Belfast; *m* 24 Nov 1979, Iris Elizabeth, da of Sydney Miller McKeown, of Shanliss, Stewartstown, Co Tyrone, N Ireland; 1 s (Stephen John Doran b 1987), 3 da (Maeve Elizabeth b 1983, Barbara Ruth and Jennifer Mary (twins) b 1 Aug 1992); *Career* recruitment conslt; md: Grafton Recruitment Ltd (Ireland's largest employment agency), Grafton Recruitment UK Ltd 1982–; *Recreations* fine wines, reading; *Clubs* Kildare St and Univ (Dublin), Holywood Golf; *Style*— Kenneth Belshaw, Esq; ✉ SherryGroom, 10 My Lady's Mile, Holywood, Co Down, Northern Ireland BT18 9EW; Grafton Recruitment, 35–37 Queens Square, Belfast BT1 3FG (☎ 01232 242824, fax 01232 242897)

BELSKY, Franta; s of Josef Belsky (d 1963), and Martha Grunbaum (d 1973); *b* 6 April 1921; *Educ* Acad of Fine Arts Prague, RCA London; *m* 1944, Margaret, da of Albert Edward Owen, DSO (d 1959); *Career* sculptor; gunner France 1940, Normandy 1944; taught in art schs 1950–55, pres Soc of Portrait Sculptors 1963–68 and 1994–, govr St Martin's Sch of Art 1967–88; work in: Nat Portrait Gallery, collections in USA and Europe, numerous CC's, industl shipping and private cos and educn authorities; works incl: Paratroop Meml Prague 1947, statue of Cecil Rhodes Bulawayo 1953, Triga Knightsbridge 1958, Astronomer Herschel Meml Slough 1969, Jamestown Harbour Docklands fountain 1988, Euro Shell Centre fountain, RAF Meml Prague 1995; portraits include: HM The Queen Mother 1962, HM The Queen 1981, Prince Andrew 1963 and 1984, Prince Philip 1979, Prince William 1985, Sir Winston Churchill (statue for Churchill Meml and Library in US, bust in Churchill Archives Cambridge 1971 and sculpture for Prague 1992), Harry S Truman, Lord Cottesloe, Queen Mother 80th Birthday Crown coin; Jean Masson Davidson award for distinction in portrait sculpture; FRBS; *Books* Franta Belsky Sculpture (monograph, 1992); illustrations and contributions in various books and journals; *Recreations* skiing, gardening, amateur archaeology; *Style*— Franta Belsky, Esq; ✉ 4 The Green, Sutton Courtenay, Abingdon, Oxfordshire OX14 4AE

BELSON, Dorrien Berkeley Euan; s of Frederic Charles Belson (d 1952), of Southsea, and Hilda Carlyon, *née* Euan-Smith (d 1954); *b* 10 Feb 1917; *Educ* St Edmund's Sch Canterbury; *m* 1948, Mary, da of Charles Deane Cowper (d 1956); 3 s, 1 da; *Career* 2 Lt Glos Regt 1939, POW Germany Poland and Austria 1940–45; dir John Harvey & Sons Ltd 1950–61, vice-chm Hedges & Butler Ltd London 1962–63, dir International Distillers & Vintners Ltd 1963–78; chm: IDV Export Ltd 1969–78, Justerini & Brooks Ltd 1971–78 (dir 1963–78, Queen's Award for Export Achievement 1974, 1977 and 1978), Gilbeys Ltd 1971–78; lay rep Gen Cncl of the Bar: Professional Conduct Ctee 1983–89, Professional Standards Ctee 1989–; chm The Spastics Soc (England & Wales, now Scope) 1973–80; High Sheriff of Bucks 1981–82; Steward Worshipful Co of Distillers 1972– (Liveryman 1965–); Knight of Honour and Devotion Br Assoc of SMOM 1977, Knight of Obedience BASMOM 1991; FInstD 1954–84; *Recreations* fly fishing, association croquet, wine, photography; *Clubs* Leander (chm 1981–83), Phyllis Court; *Style*— Dorrien Belson, Esq; ✉ 15 New Street, Henley-on-Thames, Oxon RG9 2BP (☎ 01491 571694)

BELSTEAD, 2 Baron (UK 1938); Sir John Julian Ganzoni; 2 Bt (UK 1929), PC (1983), JP (Ipswich); s of 1 Baron Belstead, JP, DL (d 1958), sometime MP Ipswich and PPS to Postmaster-Gen 1924; *b* 30 Sept 1932; *Educ* Eton, Christ Church Oxford; *Heir* none; *Career* Parly sec: DES 1970–73, NI 1973–74, Home Office 1979–82; min of state: FCO 1982–83, MAFF 1983–87, Environment Countryside and Water DOE 1987–88; Lord Privy Seal and Ldr of House of Lords 1988–90; paymaster gen and dep to Sec of State Northern Ireland Office 1990–92; chm: Governing Bodies Assoc 1974–79, Parole Bd for England and Wales 1992–; Hon Freeman City of London 1990; DL Suffolk 1979, Lord-Lt for Co of Suffolk 1994; *Clubs* Boodle's, MCC, All England Lawn Tennis and Croquet (Wimbledon); *Style*— The Rt Hon the Lord Belstead, PC, JP; ✉ House of Lords, London SW1A 0PW (☎ 0171 219 3000)

BELSTEAD, John Sydney; s of Eric Kenneth, and Kathleen Phyllis, *née* Curling (d 1985); *b* 16 Sept 1945; *Educ* Univ of Leeds (MB ChB); *m* 14 July 1969, Dr Susan Margaret Goord, da of Austin Arthur Goord; 3 da (Philippa b 1972, Stephanie b 1974, Anna b 1976); *Career* surgn Manorom Christian Hosp Thailand 1978–85, conslt Accident and Emergency Ashford Hosp 1985–; memb: Br Assoc of Accident & Emergency Med, Christian Med Fellowship; fell British Orthopaedic Assoc, FRCS Ed 1972, FRCS Ed Orth 1981; *Books* Aids to Post Graduate Surgery (1978); *Recreations* church, DIY; *Style*— John Belstead, Esq; ✉ A & E Dept, Ashford Hospital, London Rd, Ashford, Middx TW15 3AA (☎ 01784 258712, fax 01784 258712)

BELTRAMI, Joseph; s of Egidio Beltrami (d 1971), and Isabel, *née* Battison; *b* 15 May 1932; *Educ* St Aloysius Coll Glasgow, Univ of Glasgow (BL); *m* 18 Jan 1958, Brigid, da of Edward Fallon; 3 s (Edwin Joseph b 23 Sept 1962, Adrian Joseph b 8 Nov 1964, Jason Joseph b 23 Sept 1967); *Career* Intelligence Corps 1954–56: attached to Br Mil Delgn to Euro Def Community at Br Embassy Paris, Detachment Cdr Field security SW Dist Taunton; admitted slr 1956, ptnr Beltrami & Co (slr in cases of only two Royal pardons in Scotland this century: Maurice Swanson 1975, Patrick Meehan 1976); instructed in more than 350 murder trials; formerly: pres Bothwell Bowling Club, mangr and coach Bothwell AFC; memb Scottish Law Soc; *Books* The Defender (1980), Glasgow - A Celebration (contrib, 1984), Tales of the Suspected (1988), A Deadly Innocence (1989); *Style*— Joseph Beltrami, Esq; ✉ Blenio, Bothwell, Scotland (☎ 01698 852374); Beltrami & Co, 93 West Nile St, Glasgow (☎ 0141 221 0981)

BEMROSE, (William) Alan Wright; s of Col William Lloyd Bemrose, OBE, TD (d 1980), of Umtali, Zimbabwe, and Lucy Mabel Lewis (d 1982); *b* 13 June 1929; *Educ* Repton; *m* 1, 21 July 1952 (m dis 1984), (Elizabeth) Anne, da of John William Rose (d 1955), of Duffield; 1 da (Sarah b 15 July 1959); m 2, 31 Aug 1985, Elizabeth (Nibby), da of Reginald William Melling, of Downderry, Cornwall; *Career* served Sherwood Foresters (Notts & Derby), RCS, Selous Scouts Rhodesia; fndr chm Derbyshire Historic Tst 1974–, memb Historic Bldgs Cncl for England 1979–84, princ conslt bldgs at risk Historic Bldgs and Monuments Cmmn (memb Advsy Ctees Bldgs and Areas 1984–93), chief exec Buildings at Risk Tst 1992–; tstee Chatsworth House Tst 1982–; Derbyshire CC: memb 1964, alderman 1967, chm of fin 1967–74, ldr 1968–74, vice chm 1977–79; govr Sir John Port's Charity (Repton Sch) 1965–; Freeman and Liveryman Worshipful Co of Stationers and Newspaper Makers 1952 (memb Ct of Assts 1979–87, currently emeritus memb Ct); FRSA 1985; *Recreations* hunting, equestrian sports; *Style*— Alan Bemrose, Esq; ✉ Tinkersley Farm, Great Rowsley, Derbyshire DE4 2NJ (☎ 01629 732424, fax 01629 826390)

BEN-DAVID, Zadok; s of Moshe Ben-David, of Israel, and Hana Ben-David; *b* 1949; *Educ* Bezalel Acad of Art and Design Israel, Univ of Reading, St Martin's Sch of Art; *Career* asst to N H Azaz 1974, sculpture teacher St Martin's Sch of Art 1977–82, teacher Ravensbourne Coll of Art and Design 1982–85, visiting artist Stoke-on-Trent Museum 1987; sculptor; public cmmns: Runcorn Shopping City 1977, Tel-Hai Museum Israel 1983, Harlow Essex 1984, Villa Nova de Cerviera Portugal 1986, Forest of Dean Sculpture Project Glos 1988, Tel Aviv Promenade Israel 1989, Keren Karev Jerusalem 1990, ORS Building Tel Aviv 1990, Heaven and Earth (public sculpture) Tel Aviv 1995; solo exhibitions incl: AIR Gallery London 1980, Woodlands Art Gallery London 1982, 121 Gallery Antwerp 1984, Benjamin Rhodes Gallery London 1985, 1987, 1990 and 1992, Art and Project Amsterdam 1986, Albert Totah Gallery NY 1987, Newcastle Poly Gallery 1988, Luba Bilu Gallery Melbourne 1989, Collins Gallery Glasgow 1990, Annandale Gallery Sydney 1991, Albrecht Gallery Munich Germany 1991, Galerie im Happacher Esslingen 1993, Ecke Galerie Augsburg, Castlefield Gallery Manchester 1994, Jason Rhodes Gallery London 1995; gp exhibitions incl: Atlantis Gallery London 1983, 80 Years of Sculpture (Israel Museum Jerusalem) 1984, Who's Afraid of Red Yellow & Blue? (Arnolfini Gallery Bristol) 1985, From Two Worlds (Whitechapel Art Gallery) 1986, IV Int Biennale Portugal 1986, Ek'ymose Art Contemporain Bordeaux 1987, Israeli Artists (Brooklyn Museum NY) 1988, Fresh Paint (Israel Museum Jerusalem) 1988, Museum of Israeli Art Ramat Gan Israel 1988, Galerie Albrecht Munich (with Joel Fisher and Franz Bernhard) 1989, Gimmel Gallery Jerusalem 1990, Kunst Europa Germany 1991, Places and Mainstream (Museum Hara Tokyo) 1991, The New Metaphysics (Ivan Dougherty Gallery Sydney) 1992, Nat Museum of Contemporary Art Seoul 1992, A Collaboration of Music and Art (with Peter Gabriel, Land Mark Tower Yokahama Japan) 1993, Anti Patos (Israel Museum Jerusalem) 1993, Locus (Fisher Gallery Los Angeles) 1993, Public Art (Annadale Gallery Sydney Australia) 1994, VIII Biennale Portugal 1995; various collections in: UK, Europe, Israel, USA, Aust; jointly represented Israel Venice Biennale 1988 (with Moti Mizrachi); *Style*— Zadok Ben-David, Esq; ✉ 65 Warwick Avenue, London W9 2PP (☎ 0171 266 0536, fax 0171 266 3892, studio ☎ 0181 691 5323)

BENAMMAR, Julia Mary; da of Bernard Feighney, of Manchester, and Margaret, *née* McGowan; *b* 7 Sept 1954; *Educ* Adelphi House GS Manchester, Univ of Leeds (BA), Univ of Lille (LèsL, MèsL); *m* 19 July 1980, Rachid Benammar; 2 da (Alice b 2 Jan 1983, Emily b 14 Dec 1984); *Career* English teacher Lycée Georges Clemenceau Montpellier 1975–76; jr lectr: Univ of Valenciennes 1977–78 and 1979–81, Univ of Lille III 1978–79 and (Law and Tport Faculties) 1979–81; post grad research 1981–82, teacher modern languages Wellington Coll Berks 1982–92 (housemistress of only girls' house 1986–92), headmistress Heathfield Sch 1992–; memb GSA 1992; FRSA 1994; *Recreations* sport (most), walking in the Pyrenees, theatre, music, choral singing; *Clubs* Lansdowne; *Style*— Mrs Julia Benammar; ✉ Headmistress's House, Heathfield School, London Road, Ascot, Berkshire SL5 8BQ (☎ 01344 882955, fax 01344 890689)

BENARDOUT, Raymond; s of Nissim Benardout, of London, and Betty, *née* McInnes (d 1967); *b* 27 March 1942; *Educ* St Vincent's, John Perryn, The Elms; *m* 10 March 1966, Linda Susan, da of Al Berlin (d 1979); 1 s (Marc Nissim 1 Feb 1967), 1 da (Nicola Bettina b 5 Sept 1968); *Career* estab Raymond Benardout purveyors of antique rugs tapestries and textiles 1961–; dir: Benni Ltd, Raymond Benardout Ltd; chm Knightsbridge Group, memb Ctee Knightsbridge Assoc; curator Acor 3 exhbn Woven Stars; memb: IOD, BADA; *Books* author numerous books and articles incl: Turkoman Rugs (1974), Turkish Rugs (1975), Tribal Rugs (1976), Nomadic Rugs (1977), Caucasian Rugs (1978), Antique Rugs (1983), and also of published book collections of Southern Calirornian rugs and textiles; *Recreations* golf, travel; *Clubs* RAC; *Style*— Raymond Benardout, Esq; ✉ 17 Empire House, Thurloe Place, London SW7 2RU

BENAUD, Richard (Richie); OBE (1961); *b* 6 Oct 1930; *Educ* Parramatta HS; *m* Daphne; *Career* cricket commentator; former cricketer, capt Aust 1958–63 (without losing a series), toured Eng 1953, 1956 and 1961, first test cricketer to score 2,000 runs and take 200 wickets, also scored 10,000 and took 500 first class wickets; commentator BBC 1960– and Nine Network (Aust) 1977–; int sports conslt; *Books* Way of Cricket (1960), Tale of Two Tests (1962), Spin Me a Spinner (1963), The New Champions (1965), Willow Patterns (1972), Benaud on Reflection (1984), The Appeal of Cricket (1995); *Recreations* golf; *Style*— Richie Benaud, Esq, OBE; ✉ c/o Sue Freathy, Curtis Brown, 4th Floor, Haymarket House, 28–29 Haymarket, London SW1Y 4SP (☎ 0171 396 6600)

BENBOW, Michael; s of Arthur Benbow, of Cowbridge, Mid Glamorgan, and Sylvia, *née* Bailey; *b* 22 Feb 1957; *Educ* Trinity Secdy Modern Sch Bradord-on-Avon, Trowbridge Tech Coll, Salisbury Coll of Art, Cardiff Coll of Art (Dip Industl Design Engrg); *m* 19 Sept 1981, Christine, da of Peter Collier; *Career* design consultant; staff designer Gnome Photographic Products Ltd 1978–80, design mangr Bissell Appliances Ltd 1980–88, sr designer and business devpt mangr Ogle Design Ltd 1988–90, business devpt mangr Grey Matter Design Consultants plc 1990, design conslt 1990–; to date cmmnd to design attractive products for high volume manufacture; injection moulded plastics expertise; projects incl electronic consumer products, nursery equipment and housewares; first prize industl design Eisteddfod Festival 1978; SIAD: working pty leader Diploma Members' Gp 1983, memb Product Gp 1986–90; corp MCSD 1985; *Recreations* lawn tennis, squash; *Clubs* Woodford Wells; *Style*— Michael Benbow, Esq; ✉ 28 Brook Road, Loughton, Essex IG10 1BP (☎ 0181 508 4457, fax 0181 508 5642)

BENCE, John Douglas; *b* 18 June 1932; *Educ* King Edward Sch Birmingham; *m* Jennifer Patricia; 5 children; *Career* sr vice pres Euro Packaging Operations Stone Container Corp; vice pres Inst of Packaging Ltd; dir: Touring Club of GB and I, The Caravan Club Ltd, Europa Carton AG; chm Cartomills SA; chm: Societé Emballages des Cevennes, Financiere Carton Papier; hon treas the Caravan Club; *Recreations* sailing, caravanning; *Clubs* Royal Thames Yacht, Royal Lymington Yacht; *Style*— John Bence, Esq; ✉ Boundary Ford, Adlams Lane, Sway, nr Lymington, Hants SO41 6EG (☎ 01590 683896, fax 01590 683854); Stone Container Corp, 195 Knightsbridge, London SW7 1RG (☎ 0171 589 6381, fax 0171 589 6514)

BENDALL, David Vere; CMG (1966), MBE (1945); s of John Manley Bendall (d 1970), and Pearl Vere Dando (d 1967); *b* 27 Feb 1920; *Educ* Winchester, King's Coll Cambridge (BA); *m* 1941, Eve Stephanie Merrilees, da of Charles Galpin (d 1928), of Colombo; 1 da (Fern Evelyn (Mrs Alfred Elbrick) b 1942); *Career* Grenadier Guards 1941–46; HM Dip Serv 1946–71, asst under sec of state 1969–71; merchant banker 1971–94; chm: Morgan Grenfell Italy 1978–94, Banque Morgan Grenfell en Suisse 1978–90, Morgan Grenfell Int 1982–94, Banca Nazionale de Lavoro Investment Bank plc 1986–93; Br Red Cross Soc 1981–85; OStJ 1986; *Recreations* tennis, golf, shooting; *Clubs* Boodle's; *Style*— David Bendall, Esq, CMG, MBE; ✉ 3 Eaton Terrace Mews, London SW1 (☎ 0171 730 4229); Ashbocking Hall, Ipswich, Suffolk (☎ 01473 890262)

BENDALL, Dr (Michael) John; s of Edward Lewis Bendall (d 1987), of Risca, Gwent, and Edna May, *née* Williams (d 1983); *b* 7 June 1943; *Educ* Pontwaun GS Risca Gwent, Univ of London (BSc, MB BS), Univ of Nottingham (DM); *m* 4 Jan 1969, Patricia, da of Herbert Wyndham Jenkins (d 1980), of Newport, Gwent; 2 s (David b 1975, Thomas b 1977), 2 da (Megan b 1973, Elinor b 1983); *Career* conslt physician in geriatric med Colchester 1974–78, sr lectr and conslt physician in health care of the elderly Nottingham 1978–94, clinical dir of Health Care of the Elderly Queen's Medical Centre Nottingham 1991– (conslt physician 1994–); memb: Br Geriatrics Soc, BMA, Br Assoc of Med Mangrs; FRCP 1986; *Recreations* music, theatre, reading, photography, golf; *Style*— Dr John Bendall; ✉ Directorate of Health Care of the Elderly, Queen's Medical Centre, Nottingham NG7 2UH (☎ 0115 924 9924)

BENDALL, Vivian Walter Hough; MP (C) Ilford North (majority 9,071); s of Cecil Aubrey Bendall (d 1963), and Olive Alvina, *née* Hough (d 1980); *b* 14 Dec 1938; *Educ* Broad Green Coll Croydon; *m* 1969 (m dis); *Career* former surveyor and valuer; MP (C) Ilford N 1978–, vice chm Cons Backbench Employment and Tport Ctees, sec Cons Backbench Foreign and Cwlth Affrs Ctee; *Recreations* cricket, motor sport; *Clubs* Carlton, Essex CC; *Style*— Vivian Bendall, Esq, MP; ✉ 25A Brighton Rd, South Croydon, Surrey

BENDER, Brian Geoffrey; s of Arnold Eric Bender, of Leatherhead, Surrey, and Deborah, *née* Swift; *b* 25 Feb 1949; *Educ* Greenford GS, Imperial Coll London (BSc, PhD); *m* 1974, Penelope Gay, *née* Clark; 1 da (Laura Ann b 1979), 1 s (Russell Paul b 1983); *Career* DTI: admin trainee 1973–77, private sec to Sec of State for Trade (The Rt Hon Edmund Dell) 1976–77, first sec (Trade Policy) Office of UK Perm Rep to the EC 1977–82, princ Minerals and Metals Div 1982–84, cnsllr (Indust and Energy) Office of UK Perm Rep to the EC 1985–89, asst sec Mgmnt Servs and Manpower Div 1989–90, under sec and dep head of European Secretariat Cabinet Office 1990–93, head of Regnl Devpt Div DTI 1993–95, dep sec and head Euro Secretariat Cabinet Office 1994–; *Recreations* my family, theatre; *Style*— Brian Bender, Esq; ✉ Cabinet Office, 70 Whitehall, London SW1A 2AS (☎ 0171 270 0044, fax 0171 270 0112)

BENDER, Lee; *Educ* Kensington HS for Girls, London Coll of Fashion, St Martin's Sch of Art; *Career* fashion designer; designer and toilemaker for various wholesale ateliers Paris 1965–67, fndr designer Bus Stop chain of clothes shops 1969–80 (first opened Kensington Church Street, subsequently sited in Glasgow, Edinburgh, Newcastle, Leeds, Manchester, Liverpool, Birmingham, Nottingham, Bristol, Brighton and Southampton UK and within various dept stores in North America, Singapore and Hong Kong), various projects and consultancies 1980–83 (incl mens and womenswear for boatwear clothing specialists Norway), fndr of shop under own name (also mfr/buyer) Brompton Arcade Knightsbridge 1983–, market wholesale business 1988–; UN/EEC advsr on design and mktg to fashion industries of various developing countries incl: Mauritius and China 1993–, Pakistan 1994–, India/Botswana/Thailand and Nepal 1996–; advising and designing rental stores and clothing cos in Romania for EC and BR Govt; *Style*— Ms Lee Bender; ✉ The Kiln House, 22 Hippodrome Mews, London W11 4NN (☎ 0171 221 9697, fax 0171 221 9545)

BENEDICTUS, David Henry; s of Henry Jules Benedictus (d 1990), of Cookham Dean, Berkshire, and Kathleen Constance, *née* Ricardo (d 1992); *b* 16 Sept 1938; *Educ* Eton, Balliol Coll Oxford (BA), State Univ of Iowa; *m* 1971, Yvonne Daphne, da of late Harvey Antrobus; 1 s (Leo b 1977), 1 da (Chloe b 1979); *Career* author, critic, prodr, dir; story ed and dir BBC1 Wednesday Play 1965–66, Thames TV trainee dir 1968, asst dir RSC 1971, antiques corr Evening Standard 1980–82, commissioning ed Channel 4 Drama Series 1984–86, readings ed BBC 1989–94, fndr and dir Kingston Books, numerous TV and theatre credits; chm 28 Gp Amnesty Int; *Books* author of more than 25 incl: several books on London, Antiques and Meteorology; novels incl: The Fourth of June, The Rabbi's Wife, A Twentieth Century Man, Floating Down to Camelot, The Stamp Collector; *Recreations* chess, golf, piano playing, food, bank managers, dogs; *Style*— David Benedictus, Esq; ✉ 19 Oxford Rd, Teddington, Middx TW11 0QA (☎ 0181 977 6522)

BENFIELD, James Richard; *b* 22 April 1949; *Educ* Leamington Coll for Boys, Univ of Birmingham (BA); *m*; *Career* Marks & Spencer plc: mgmnt trainee 1970–73, merchandiser various food buying depts from 1973 then mgmnt and exec divnl positions rising to divnl dir 1986–93, buying gp dir 1993–; non-exec dir Whittington Hospital Trust; *Recreations* ballet, theatre, scuba diving; *Style*— James Benfield, Esq; ✉ Marks and Spencer plc, Michael House, Baker Street, London W1A 1DN (☎ 0171 268 8138, fax 0171 268 2688)

BENFIELD, John; s of George Frederick Turner, of Lancing, Sussex, and Phyllis Joan, *née* White; *b* 9 Nov 1951; *Educ* Loughton Sch, Univ of Nottingham (BA), Webber Douglas Drama Sch; *m* 6 May 1989, Lilian, da of George Lees; 1 s (Frederick George b 18 Oct 1989); *Career* actor; *Theatre* incl: Glengarry Glen Ross (Donmar Warehouse), Grafters (Hampstead), Macbeth (Newcastle), Twelfth Night (London); *Television* incl: Tears for George (Channel Four), Eurocops (Channel Four), Prime Suspect (Granada), Calling the Shots (BBC), The Secret Agent (BBC), Floodtide (Granada), No Further Cause for Concern (BBC), Lenny Henry Show (BBC), Deliberate Death of a Polish Priest (Channel Four), Sharpe (ITV); *Films* incl: In the Name of the Father, Hidden Agenda, Treasure Island, Buster, Cousin Bette; *Recreations* classical music, chess; *Clubs* The Brittania; *Style*— John Benfield, Esq; ✉ c/o Markham & Froggatt, 4 Windmill Street, London W1P 1HF (☎ 0171 636 4412, fax 0171 637 5233)

BENGER, Patrick; s of Harold Albert Benger (d 1978), of Worcester, and Mildred Nancy, *née* Freeman (d 1988); *b* 29 Sept 1939; *Educ* Farnborough GS, Royal Aircraft Estab Tech Coll; *m* 20 Oct 1966, Frances Ann, *née* Finch; 1 da (Georgina Anne (Mrs Andrew Morgan) b 1968); *Career* asst experimental offr RAE Farnborough, seconded as tech offr E African Meteorological Dept Tanganyika 1962–64; conslt meteorologist to offshore indust: Middle East 1965–71, N Sea and Europe 1972–88; management systems conslt 1988–; md Seaplace Ltd 1985–90, dir Chaucer Group Ltd 1991–, currently project servs co-ordinator UK-Continent Gas Interconnector Project; scientific advsr Hampshire Co Emergency Planning Orgn; FRMetS; author of technical papers and articles on meteorological aspects of offshore installation techniques; *Recreations* antique collecting; *Style*— Patrick Benger, Esq; ✉ Cold Ash House, Liphook, Hampshire GU30 7SR

BENGOUGH, Col Sir Piers Henry George; KCVO (1986), OBE (1973), DL (Hereford and Worcs, 1987); s of Nigel Crosbie Bengough (d 1980), of Hereford, and Alice, *née* Albu (d 1982); *b* 24 May 1929; *Educ* Eton; *m* 1952, Bridget Shirley Adams; 2 s (Andrew Nigel Crosbie b 13 Feb 1954, Jonathan Fiennes b 17 April 1955); *Career* cmmnd 10 Royal Hussars (PWO) 1948, cmd Royal Hussars (PWO) 1971–73 (Hon Col 1985–91); memb The Jockey Club 1965– (steward 1974–77 and 1990–92), Jockey Club rep Horserace Betting Levy Bd 1978–81; dir: Cheltenham Steeplechase Co 1977–91, Hereford Racecourse 1974–, Ludlow Race Club 1979–; chm Compensation Fund for Jockeys 1981–89; tstee: Br Racing Sch 1982–92, Ascot Authy 1972; Her Majesty's rep at Ascot 1982–; former amateur jockey; winner 4 Grand Mil Gold Cups 1960 and 1970–72, rode in 4 Grand Nationals 1957 and 1965–67; memb Hon Corps of Gentlemen at Arms 1981; *Recreations* farming, shooting, fishing; *Clubs* Cavalry, Pratt's; *Style*— Col Sir Piers Bengough, KCVO, OBE, DL; ✉ Great House, Canon Pyon, Herefordshire HR4 8PD

BENHAM, David Hamilton; s of George Frederick Augustus Benham (d 1980), and Pamela Ruth, *née* Kellond; *b* 7 Jan 1942; *Educ* King Edward VI Sch, Charterhouse, Univ of Southampton; *m* 1968 (m dis 1991), Ann Pyta, da of Sqdn Ldr L L Thomas, DFC (d 1975); 1 s (Nicholas Hamilton b 18 March 1971), 1 da (Fiona-Jane Teresa b 1 Oct 1973); *Career* admitted slr 1970; ptnr: Bischoff and Co 1975–92, Blick & Co 1992–; Freeman City of London 1980, Liveryman City Livery Co 1980; memb Law Soc; *Recreations* squash, photography, collecting antiques, power boating; *Clubs* Lambs, Colets, Royal Southampton Yacht; *Style*— David H Benham, Esq; ✉ Blick & Co, Sophia House, 32/35 Featherstone Street, London EC1Y 8QX (☎ 0171 253 6250, fax 0171 251 3519)

BENHAM, Keith Peter; s of Peter Gray Benham (d 1995), and (Susan) Phoebe, *née* Brown (d 1995); *b* 10 March 1943; *Educ* Marlborough; *m* 26 Nov 1969, Merilyn Anne, da of Maj Philip Norman Holbrook (d 1990); 3 da (Samantha b 1972, Lucy b 1974, Henrietta b 1978); *Career* slr; ptnr Linklaters & Paines 1973– (articled clerk 1963, asst slr 1968–73); memb Southern Region Bd of BR 1989–92, govr St Mary's Sch Calne 1989–, govr Lord Wandsworth Coll 1995–; memb: City of London Law Soc 1963–, The Law Soc 1963–; Freeman City of London 1968; memb: Worshipful Co of Skinners, Worshipful Co of Slrs (memb Co Law Sub Ctee 1976–85); *Recreations* gardening, sailing, skiing, shooting, tennis, opera, national hunt racing; *Clubs* City Law, Sea View Yacht, Bembridge Sailing; *Style*— Keith Benham, Esq; ✉ Linklaters & Paines, Barrington House, 59/67 Gresham St, London EC2V 7JA (☎ 0171 606 7080, fax 0171 606 5113, telex 884349, 888167)

BENINGTON, Prof Ian Crawford; s of George Crawford Benington (d 1980), of Tunbridge Wells, Kent, and Edith, *née* Green; *b* 24 Feb 1938; *Educ* Dalriada Sch Ballymoney Co Antrim, Queen's Univ Belfast (BDS); *m* 10 July 1967, Eileen Agnes, da of Thomas Irwin (d 1988), of Belfast; 1 s (David b 28 May 1974), 1 da (Fiona b 3 April 1973); *Career* served Army Cadet Force N Irish Horse 1950–58; dental staff Queen's Univ Belfast 1961–62, sr registrar Eastman Dental Hosp and Inst of Dental Surgery London 1965–72, conslt Glasgow Dental Hosp and Sch 1972–78, dir Sch of Clinical Dentistry Royal Victoria Hosp Belfast 1989– (sr lectr and conslt 1978–83, prof of dental prosthetics and head of Dept of Restorative Dentistry 1985–90); chm Specialist Advsy Ctee for Higher Trg in Restorative Dentistry RCS, memb Eastern Health and Social Servs Bd in NI, memb Central Dental Advsy Ctee of Jt Ctee for Higher Trg in Dentistry; chm: Dental Alumni Assoc Queen's Univ of Belfast 1992–, Dental Technicians' Educn and Trg Advsy Bd Educn Ctee; pres British Soc for the Study of Prosthetic Dentistry 1995–96, memb Bd Faculty of Dental Surgery RCS England 1994; FDSRCS, FFDRCSI; memb: BDA, RSM, Gen Dental Cncl; *Recreations* music, hill walking; *Clubs* East India, Stephen's Green (Dublin); *Style*— Prof Ian Benington; ✉ 20 Killynure Road West, Carryduff, Belfast BT8 8EA (☎ 01232 813696); Department of Restorative Dentistry, School of Dentistry, Royal Victoria Hospital, Grosvenor Rd, Belfast BT12 6BA (☎ 01232 240503 ext 2107, fax 01232 438861)

BENJAMIN, George; s of William Benjamin, and Susan, *née* Bendon; *b* 31 Jan 1960; *Educ* Westminster, Paris Conservatoire, King's Coll Cambridge, IRCAM Paris; *Career* composer, conductor, pianist; prof composition RCM 1985–, dir Ensemble Musique Oblique Paris 1989–93, princ guest artist Hallé Orch 1993–; princ works incl: Ringed by the Flat Horizon 1980, A Mind of Winter for soprano and orch 1981, At First Light (cmmnd by London Sinfonietta) 1982, Three Studies for solo piano 1982–85, Jubilation for orch and children's gps 1985, Antara for computerised keyboards and ensemble (cmmnd for 10 anniversary of Pompidou Centre Paris) 1987, Upon Silence for mezzo-soprano and 5 viols (written for Fretwork) 1990 (new version for mezzo-soprano and string ensemble 1991), Sudden Time (written for London Philharmonic Orch) 1989–93, Three Inventions for Chamber Orch (cmmnd for 75 Salzburg Festival) 1993–95, Sometime Voices for baritone, chorus and orchestra (cmmnd for the opening of the Bridgewater Hall, Manchester); conductor of orchs in: UK, France, Belgium, Switzerland, Austria, Holland, Germany, Italy, Spain, USA, Canada, Australia; artistic dir of new contemprary music festivals with: San Francisco Symphony and Opera Bastille Paris 1992, Meltdown Festival South Bank 1993; awards incl: Lili Boulanger award Boston 1985, Koussevitsky Int Record award 1987, Grand Prix du Disque Paris 1987, Gramophone Contemporary Music award 1990; Chevalier dans l'Ordre des Arts et Lettres 1996; FRCM 1994; *Style*— George Benjamin, Esq; ✉ c/o Faber Music, 3 Queen Square, London WC1N 3AU (☎ 0171 833 7900, fax 0171 278 3817)

BENJAMIN, Prof Irving Stuart; s of Isidore Benjamin (d 1969), of Manchester, and Elsie, *née* Dennerley (d 1971); *b* 22 June 1946; *Educ* Hutchesons' Boys' GS, Univ of Glasgow (BSc, MB ChB, MD); *m* Barbara Anne, da of Paul Anthony Breton (d 1994); 1 s (Matthew Stuart b 2 Aug 1972), 2 da (Lucie Katherine b 26 Oct 1973, Frances Joanna b 7 March 1977); *Career* Hall tutorial res fell Univ Dept of Surgery Glasgow 1972–73, Scottish Home and Health Dept res fell 1973–74, lectr in surgery Glasgow Royal Infirmary 1975–79, visiting fell and jr conslt surgn Groote Schuur and Univ of Cape Town 1978–79, Wellcome Tst then CRC research fell and lectr in surgery 1980–83, sr lectr in surgery and hon conslt surgn Royal Postgrad Med Sch and Hammersmith Hosp (concurrently fell in transplantation surgery for one yr Nuffield Dept of Surgery Oxford) 1983–90, reader in surgery Royal Postgrad Med Sch 1990, prof of surgery and head Academic Dept of Surgery King's Coll Sch of Med and Dentistry 1990–; memb: Br Soc of Gastroenterology (memb Cncl 1990–93), Surgical Research Soc, RSM, Pancreatic Soc of GB and I, Br Assoc for the Study of the Liver, Br Transplantation Soc, Assoc of Surgns of GB and I, Soc for Minimally Invasive Surgery, Christian Med Fellowship, Amnesty Int, Int Hepatopancreatobiliary Surgery Assoc (formerly treas UK Chapter and memb Scientific Ctee World Assoc fo HPB Surgery), Br Assoc of Surgical Oncology; FRCSGlas 1976, FRCS 1991; *Publications* author of numerous pubns in med and scientific jls on the subject of hepatic and biliary surgery and research in these fields; *Recreations* church activities, sailing, music (playing the guitar), photography, personal computing; *Style*— Prof Irving Benjamin; ✉ Academic Department of Surgery, King's College School of Medicine and Dentistry, Denmark Hill, London SE5 9RS (☎ 0171 346 3017, fax 0171 346 3438)

BENJAMIN, John Circus; s of Bernard Benjamin, and Doris, *née* Mindel; *b* 15 Jan 1955; *Educ* John Lyon Sch Middx; *m* 27 June 1986, Patricia Adele Ruane, da of Sqdn Ldr Michael Joseph Francis Burgess, of Hale, Cheshire; *Career* Phillips Auctioneers: former cataloguer then sr cataloguer, mangr 1976–, dir Jewellery Dept 1986–, dir 1990–; broadcaster & regular lectr on history of jewellery; FGA 1975, DGA 1976; *Style*— John Benjamin, Esq; ✉ Phillips, 101 New Bond Street, London W1Y 0AS (☎ 0171 468 8240, fax 0171 465 0222, telex 298855 BLEN G)

BENJAMIN, Leanne; *b* 1964; *Educ* Royal Ballet Upper Sch (Adeline Genée Gold Medal); *Career* ballet dancer; Birmingham Royal Ballet (formerly Sadler's Wells Royal Ballet): joined 1983, soloist 1985–87, princ 1987–88; princ dancer English Nat Ballet (formerly London Festival Ballet) 1988–90, Deutsche Oper Ballet Berlin 1990–92, princ Royal Ballet 1993– (first soloist 1992–93); *Roles* princ roles with Birmingham Royal Ballet: Swan Lake, Giselle, La Fille mal Gardée, The Sleeping Beauty, Tchaikovsky Pas de Deux, Las Hermanas, Quartet, Concerto, Elite Syncopations, Five Tangos, cr role of Greta in Metamorphosis, cr role of Gerda in The Snow Queen, Flowers of the Forest; English Nat Ballet: Juliet and Livia in Rome and Juliet, lead in The Nutcracker, Olga in Onegin, Sphinx, Third Movement in Symphony in C, Swannhilda in Coppelia, lead girl in Etudes, Symphony in Three Movements, Odette/Odile in Swan Lake; Deutsche Oper Ballet incl: A Folktale, Apollo, First and Fourth Movement Symphony in C, Carmen, Giselle, Who Cares?, Twilight, Paquita, Pas de Trois, Different Drummer, Cinderella, Brunhilda in The Ring; Royal Ballet incl: Mary Vetsera and Mizti Caspar in Mayerling, Gloria, The Woman in The Judas Tree, Kitri in Don Quixote, Odette/Odile in Swan Lake, Titania in The Dream, The Autumn Fairy in Cinderella, First Section in Herman Schmerman, Caught Dance, Sugar Plum Fairy in The Nutcracker, Ballet Imperial, Danses Concertantes, Irina in Winter Dreams, Marie in Different Drummer, Thais pas de deux, Parlourmaid in La Ronde, Manon, Side Show, Mr Worldy Wise, The Invitation, Anastasia; guest appearance with Dresden Ballet 1991; gala appearances: World Festival Tokyo 1985, pas de deux from La Fille mal Gardée with Australian Ballet Bicentennial celebrations 1988, Peter Wright's Mirrors Walkers pas de deux in honour of Sir Frederick Ashton Royal Opera House 1988, Madrid 1989, Le Corsaire pas de deux with Peter Schaufuss Saville 1990, CRUSAID charity gala 1991, Kirov Theatre 1991, Spain 1991, Tchaikovsky Gala Royal Opera House 1994; *Television* The Snow Queen (Birmingham Royal Ballet), BBC Masterclass, BBC documentary about David Bintley and making of Metamorphosis, Swan Lake (English Nat Ballet), Royal Ballet's new prodn Sleeping Beauty; *Style*— Ms Leanne Benjamin; ✉ c/o The Royal Ballet, Royal Opera House, Covent Garden, London WC2E 9DD; c/o Birdsong Public Relations, 12 Penzance Place, London W11 4PA (☎ 0171 229 9166, fax 0171 221 5042)

BENJAMIN, Prof Ralph; CB (1980); s of Charles Benjamin (d 1944), and Claire, *née* Stern (d 1944); *b* 17 Nov 1922; *Educ* Ludwig Georg's Gymnasium Darmstadt Germany, Rosenberg Coll St Gallen Switzerland, St Oswald's Coll Ellesmere Salop, Imperial Coll London (BSc, ACGI, PhD, DSc); *m* 1951, Kathleen Ruth, *née* Bull; 2 s (John b 28 June 1956, d 1987, Michael b 30 Dec 1959); *Career* joined RN Scientific Serv 1944, head of res and dep chief scientist Admiralty Surface Weapons Estab: 1960–64, dir Admiralty Underwater Weapons Estab (and dir MOD HQ) 1964–71, dir of sci and technol GCHQ 1971–82, head communications techniques and networks Supreme HQ Allied Powers in Europe Tech Centre 1982–87; visiting prof: Imperial Coll London 1988–, UCL 1988–, Open Univ 1991–96, Cranfield Univ 1992–96, Univ of Bristol 1993–; IEE Marconi Premium 1965, Heinrich Hertz Premium 1980 and 1984, Judo Black Belt, RN Diving Offrs Cert, first ascent North Face Cima di Moro; FIEE 1976, FCGI 1981, FEng 1983 (CEng 1962), FRSA 1984; *Books* Modulation, Resolution and Signal Processing (1966), Five Lives in One (autobiography, 1996); numerous articles in learned jls; *Recreations* hill-walking, skiing, watersports, work; *Clubs* Athenaeum; *Style*— Prof Ralph Benjamin, CB, FEng; ✉ 13 Bellhouse Walk, Rockwell Park, Bristol BS11 0UE (☎ 0117 982 1333)

BENJAMIN, Victor Woolf; s of Harry Benjamin, and Dorothy, *née* Cooper; *b* 2 March 1935; *Educ* Malvern; *m* 1; 3 s (Daniel John, Bruce Adam, Harry), 2 da (Lucy Ann, Ruth Miranda); m 2, 1990, Judith, *née* Powell; 1 step s; *Career* leading coder (special) RN 1956–58; admitted slr 1956, conslt Berwin Leighton; dep chm: Lex Service plc, Tesco plc 1993–96 (pt/t exec dir 1982–93); non-exec chm Tesco Pension Tstees Ltd 1996–, chm Beazer Homes plc 1994–, non-exec dir Gartmore PLC until 1996; memb Law Soc; *Recreations* sailing, skiing, opera; *Clubs* City of London, Savile; *Style*— Victor W Benjamin, Esq; ✉ Berwin Leighton, Adelaide House, London Bridge, London EC4R 9HA (☎ 0171 623 3144, fax 0171 860 9597, telex 886420, car 0860 286 896)

BENN, Rt Hon Anthony Neil Wedgwood (Tony); PC (1964), MP (Lab) Chesterfield (majority 6,414); s of 1 Viscount Stansgate, DSO, DFC, PC (d 1960), and Margaret Eadie, *née* Holmes (d 1991); suc as 2 Viscount 1960, but made it known that he did not wish to claim the Viscountcy; disclaimed his peerage for life 31 July 1963, having unsuccessfully attempted to renounce his right of succession 1955 and 1960; *b* 3 April 1925; *Educ* Westminster, New Coll Oxford; *m* 1949, Caroline Middleton, da of late James Milton De Camp, of Cincinnati, USA; 3 s, 1 da; *Career* WW RAFVR 1943–45, RNVR 1945–46; joined Lab Pty 1943; MP (Lab): Bristol SE 1950–60 and 1963–83, Chesterfield 1984–; memb Nat Exec Ctee Lab Pty 1959–60 and 1962–94 (chm 1971–72), candidate for Lab Pty leadership 1976 and 1988 (for dep leadership 1971 and 1981); postmaster-gen 1964–66, min of: technol 1966–70, power 1969; oppn spokesman on trade and indust 1970–74, sec of state for indust and min for post and telecommunications 1974–75, sec of state for energy 1975–79; chm Lab Home Policy Ctee 1974–82, pres EEC Council of Energy Mins 1977, memb Labour-TUC Liaison Ctee until 1982, pres Socialist Campaign Gp 1990–; *Books* The Privy Council as a Second Chamber (1957), The Regeneration of Britain (1964), The New Politics (1970), Speeches (1974), Arguments for Socialism (1979), Arguments for Democracy (1981), Writings on the Wall - A Radical and Socialist Anthology 1215–1984 (ed 1984), Fighting Back - Speaking Out for Socialism in the Eighties (1988); Out of the Wilderness - Diaries 1963–67 (1987), Office Without Power - Diaries 1968–72, Against the Tide - Diaries 1973–76, Conflicts of Interest - Diaries 1977–80, A Future for Socialism (1991), The End of an Era - Diaries 1980–90 (1992), Common Sense (with Andrew Hood, 1993), Years of Hope - Diaries 1940–62 (1994), Benn Diaries 1940–90 (1995); Speaking Up in Parliament (video, 1993), The Benn Tapes (Vol 1, 1994, Vol II, 1995); *Style*— The Rt Hon Tony Benn, MP; ✉ House of Commons, London SW1A 0AA (☎ 0171 219 3000)

BENN, Sir (James) Jonathan; 4 Bt (UK 1914), of The Old Knoll, Metropolitan Borough of Lewisham; s of Sir John Andrews Benn, 3 Bt (d 1984), and Hon Lady (Ursula Helen Alers) Benn, da of 1 Baron Hankey; bro of Timothy Benn, *qv*; *b* 27 July 1933; *Educ* Harrow, Clare Coll Cambridge (BA, MA); *m* 2 July 1960, Jennifer Mary, eldest da of Dr Wilfred Vivian Howells, OBE (d 1987), of The Ferns, Clun, Shropshire; 1 s, 1 da (Juliet Clare (Mrs Simon Erridge) b 1966); *Heir* s, Robert Ernest Benn, *qv*; *Career* dir Reedpack Ltd 1988–90, chm and chief exec Reed Paper and Bd (UK) Ltd 1978–90, chm J & J Maybank Ltd 1988–90, dir The Broomhill Tst, chm SCA Pension Tstees Ltd; pres Br Paper and Board Industs Fedn 1985–87; Liveryman Worshipful Co of Stationers &

Newspaper Makers; *Style*— Sir Jonathan Benn, Bt; ✉ Fielden Lodge, Tonbridge Rd, Ightham, nr Sevenoaks, Kent TN15 9AN

BENN, Nigel Gregory; s of Dixon Benn, of Ilford, Essex, and Loretta Benn; *b* 22 Jan 1964; *Educ* Loxford Comp Sch; *m* 22 Jan 1991, Sharon Crowley; 2 s (Dominic, Reece), 1 da (Sade); *Career* served 1 Bn RRF W Germany and N Ireland 1980–85; professional middleweight boxer; began fighting career whilst in the Army; amateur career: memb West Ham ABC Club, London ABA Middleweight champion 1986, Nat ABA Middleweight champion 1986, winner 48 fights (1 defeat); professional boxing debut v Graeme Ahmed 1987; *Major Titles* Cwlth Middleweight Title: won v Abdul Umuru Sanda (Muswell Hill) April 1988, defended v Anthony Logan (Kensington) Oct 1988 (Fight of the Year Br Boxing Bd of Control 1988, Int Fight of the Year Boxing News 1988), defended v David Noel (Crystal Palace) Dec 1988, defended v Mike Chilambe (Kensington) Feb 1989, lost v Michael Watson (Finsbury Park) May 1989 (Fight of the Year Br Boxing Bd of Control, Domestic Fight of the Year Boxing News); WBO Middleweight Title: won v Doug de Witt (Atlantic City) April 1990, defended v Iran Barkley (Las Vegas) Aug 1990, lost v Chris Eubank (NEC Birmingham) Nov 1990 (British Fight of the Year Boxing Weekly, Fight of the Year Br Boxing Bd of Control, Domestic Fight of the Year Boxing News); WBC Super-Middleweight Title: won v Mauro Galvano (Rome) Oct 1992, defended v Juan Carlos (Paraguay) 1994, defended v Gerald McClellan (London) 1995, lost v Sugar Boy Malinga 1996; lost to Steve Collins (WBO Super-Middleweight champion) 1996; *Awards* Best Young Boxer (Boxing Writers' Club) 1987, British Fighter of the Year (Boxing Weekly readers) 1990, Best Middleweight Puncher of 1990 (The Ring), fourth Most Destructive Puncher in the World 1990 (KO Magazine); debut single Stand and Fight released 1990; *Recreations* music, keep fit, all sports; *Style*— Nigel Benn, Esq; ✉ Sports Network Ltd, Centurion House, Bircherley, Hertford, Herts SG14 1AP (☎ 01992 505550, fax 01992 505552)

BENN, Robert Ernest (Robin); s and h of Sir Jonathan Benn, 4 Bt, and Jennifer Mary, da of Dr Wilfred Vivian Howells, OBE; *b* 17 Oct 1963; *Educ* Judd Sch, Tonbridge, CCC Cambridge (MA); *m* 1985, Sheila Margaret, 2 da of Dr Alastair Macleod Blain, of Braco Lodge, Elgin, Moray; 1 s (Alastair Frederick b 28 Feb 1995); *Career* CA; with: Touche Ross & Co London 1985–91, FGL-Deloitte & Touche Luxembourg 1991–; *Recreations* music, walking, photography; *Style*— Robin Benn, Esq; ✉ 22 Rue Jean-Baptiste Fresez, L-1542 Luxembourg, Luxembourg (☎ 00 352 473353)

BENN, Stephen Michael Wedgwood; s of Rt Hon Tony Benn PC, MP, *qv*, and h to Viscountcy of Stansgate, which was disclaimed by his f for life 1963; *b* 21 Aug 1951; *Educ* Holland Park Sch, Keele Univ (DUniv 1984); *m* 1988, Ishika Nita, da of Stuart Ashley Bowes, of Tel Aviv Univ, Ramat Hasharon, Israel; 1 s (Daniel b 10 Dec 1991), 1 da (Emily b 4 Oct 1989); *Career* memb ILEA 1981–90 (chm Gen Purposes Ctee 1986–90); parly affairs offr for Royal Soc of Chemistry 1988–; *Books* The White House Staff (1984), Politics and International Relations (1979); *Style*— Stephen Benn, Esq

BENN, Timothy John; s of Sir John Andrews Benn, 3 Bt (d 1984), and Hon Ursula Lady Benn, *née* Hankey; bro of Sir Jonathan Benn, 4 Bt, *qv*; *b* 27 Oct 1936; *Educ* Harrow, Clare Coll Cambridge (MA), Princeton, Harvard Business Sch USA; *m* 1982, Christina Grace Townsend; *Career* served HM Forces 2 Lt Scots Gds 1956–57; Benn Brothers Ltd: memb Bd 1961–82, md 1972–82, dep chm 1976–81; chm Benn Brothers plc 1981–82; Ernest Benn: memb Bd 1967–82, md 1973–82, chm and md 1974–82; chm: Timothy Benn Publishing 1983–, Bouverie Publishing Co 1983–, Buckley Press 1984–, Bouverie Data Services 1986–, Henry Greenwood and Co 1987–, Dalesman Publishing Co 1989–, Stone & Cox 1989–; pres Tonbridge Civic Soc 1982–87; Liveryman Worshipful Co of Stationers & Newspaper Makers; *Books* The (Almost) Compleat Angler (1985); *Recreations* writing, toymaking; *Style*— Timothy Benn, Esq; ✉ The Priory, Bordyke, Tonbridge, Kent TN9 1NN

BENNER, Patrick; CB (1975); s of Henry Grey Benner (d 1971), of Ipswich, and Gwendolen May, *née* Freeman (d 1974); *b* 26 May 1923; *Educ* Ipswich Sch, Univ Coll Oxford (BA); *m* 1952, Joan Christabel, da of John Godfrey Beresford Draper (d 1972); 2 da (Lucy, Mary); *Career* admin civil servant 1949–84; dep sec: Cabinet Office 1972–76, DHSS 1976–84; chm Rural Dispensing Ctee 1987–91; memb: Exec Cncl Hosp Saving Assoc 1984–, Exec Ctee Musicians Benevolent Fund 1986– (dep chm 1996–); *Style*— Patrick Benner, Esq, CB; ✉ 12 Manor Gardens, Hampton, Middlesex TW12 2TU (☎ 0181 783 0848)

BENNET, Rev the Hon George Arthur Grey; s of 8 Earl of Tankerville (d 1971), and hp of n, 10 Earl of Tankerville; *b* 12 March 1925; *Educ* Radley, CCC Cambridge, Clifton Theol Coll; *m* 1957, Hazel (Jane) Glyddon, da of late Ernest W G Judson, of Bishopswood, Chard, Somerset; 2 s, 1 da; *Career* sr physics master Clifton Coll; ordained 1969, vicar Shaston Team Ministry 1973–80, rector Redenhall Harleston Wortwell and Needham 1980–90; *Books* Electricity and Modern Physics (1965), Progress through Lent - A Course for Pilgrims (1993); One Fold, One Shepherd - The Challenge to the post-Reformation Church (1996); with T B Akrill and C J Millar: Physics (1979, 2 edn 1994), Practice in Physics (1979, 2 edn 1994); *Style*— The Rev the Hon George Bennet; ✉ 112 Norwich Rd, Wymondham, Norfolk NR18 0SZ (☎ 01953 601284)

BENNET, George Charters; s of George Charters Bennet (d 1968), and Euphemia, *née* Igoe; *b* 8 Aug 1946; *Educ* Holy Cross Acad, Univ of Edinburgh Med Sch (BSc, MB ChB); *m* 17 June 1978, (Kathryn) Louise, da of Dr Bernard Gwillam Spilbury; 3 s (George b 1979, Simon b 1982, Matthew b 1987); *Career* former med appts London, Oxford, Southampton and Toronto; currently: conslt surgn Royal Hosp for Sick Children Glasgow, hon clinical sr lectr Univ of Glasgow; FRCS, FBOA; *Books* Paediatric Hip Disorders (1987); chapters and res papers on children's orthopaedic surgery; *Recreations* hill walking, game fishing, gardening; *Style*— George C Bennet, Esq; ✉ Tamarack House, Moor Rd, Strathblane, Stirlingshire (☎ 01360 770233); Royal Hospital For Sick Children, Yorkhill, Glasgow G3 8SJ (☎ and fax 0141 201 0275)

BENNET, Hon Ian; s of 8 Earl of Tankerville (d 1971), and his 2 w, Violet; *b* 16 April 1935; *Educ* Radley, CCC Cambridge (MA Agric); *Career* Lt RNR; farmer and land agent; mangr Chillingham Estates 1961–83; chm Northumbria Region Historic Houses Assoc 1982–85, vice chm Duke's Sch Alnwick (govr 1983–); memb (C) Berwick-upon-Tweed Borough Cncl 1983– (Cons Gp ldr 1987–), pres Berwick-upon-Tweed Constituency Cons Assoc 1993–; memb River Tweed Cmmn 1983–, pres Governing Cncl Chillingham Wild Cattle Assoc 1990– (memb 1967–, vice pres 1988–90); *Recreations* shooting, forestry; *Style*— The Hon Ian Bennet; ✉ Estate House, Chillingham, Alnwick, Northumberland NE66 5NW (☎ 01668 215213)

BENNETT, Alan; *b* 9 May 1934; *Educ* Leeds Modern Sch, Exeter Coll Oxford (BA); *Career* dramatist and actor; Hon DLitt Univ of Leeds 1990; hon fell Exeter Coll Oxford 1987, tstee Nat Gallery 1993; *Theatre* incl: Beyond the Fringe (Royal Lyceum Edinburgh 1960, Fortune London 1961, NYC 1962); Forty Years On (Apollo) 1968, Getting On (Queen's) 1971, Habeas Corpus (Lyric) 1973, The Old Country (Queen's) 1977, Enjoy (Vaudeville) 1980, Kafka's Dick (Royal Court) 1986, Single Spies (NT, double bill of A Question of Attribution (BPG TV & Radio Writer's Award 1992)), An Englishman Abroad (also dir, NT) 1988, Wind in the Willows (adaptation, RNT) 1990, The Madness of George III (RNT) 1991–93, Getting On 1995; *Television* incl: On the Margin (series) 1966, A Day Out 1972, Sunset Across the Bay 1975, A Little Outing, A Visit from Miss Prothero 1977, Doris and Doreen 1978, The Old Crowd 1978, Me! I'm Afraid of Virginia Woolf 1978, All Day on the Sands 1979, Afternoon Off 1979, One Fine Day 1979, Intensive Care, Say Something Happened, Our Winnie, Marks, A Woman of No Importance, Rolling Home, An Englishman Abroad 1983, The Insurance Man 1986, Talking Heads (series) 1988, 102 Boulevard Haussmann 1991, A Question of Attribution 1992; TV documentaries: Dinner at Noon 1988, Portrait or Bust 1994; *Films* A Private Function 1984, Prick Up Your Ears 1987, The Madness of King George (Evening Standard Award for Best Screenplay) 1995; *Books* Beyond the Fringe (with Peter Cook, Jonathan Miller and Dudley Moore, 1962), Forty Years On (1969), Getting On (1972), Habeas Corpus (1973), The Old Country (1978), Enjoy (1980), Office Suite (1981), Objects of Affection (1982), A Private Function (1984), The Writer in Disguise (1985), Prick Up Your Ears (screenplay, 1987), Two Kafka Plays (1987), Talking Heads (1988), Single Spies (1989), The Lady in the Van (1990), The Wind in the Willows (adaptation, 1991), The Madness of George III (1991), Writing Home (1994, Bowater Book of the Year British Book Awards 1995); *Style*— Alan Bennett, Esq; ✉ c/o Peters Fraser & Dunlop Ltd, 503 The Chambers, Chelsea Harbour, Lots Road, London SW10 0XF (☎ 0171 376 7676, fax 0171 352 7356)

BENNETT, Andrew Francis; MP (Lab) Denton and Reddish (majority 12,084); *b* 9 March 1939; *Educ* Univ of Birmingham; *m* 2 s, 1 da; *Career* teacher, NUT official, memb Oldham Borough Cncl 1964–74; Parly candidate (Lab) Knutsford 1970; MP (Lab): Stockport North Feb 1974–83, Denton and Reddish 1983–; chm Select Ctees on: Statutory Instruments (Jt Standing Ctee), Violence in the Family (former Standing Ctee), Members' Interests 1979–83, Social Services 1979–83, Environment 1995– (memb 1992–); sec PLP Civil Liberties Gp, oppn front bench spokesman on educn 1983–88; *Style*— Andrew Bennett, Esq, MP; ✉ House of Commons, London SW1

BENNETT, Andrew John; s of Leonard Charles Bennett (d 1994), and Edna Mary, *née* Harding (d 1984); *b* 25 April 1942; *Educ* St Edward's Sch Oxford, Univ Coll N Wales Bangor (BSc), Univ of W Indies Trinidad, Univ of Reading (MSc); *Career* Lt 6/7 Bn Royal Welch Fus TA 1961–66; VSO Kenya 1965–66, agric res offr Govt of St Vincent W Indies 1967–69, maize agronomist Govt Republic of Malawi 1971–74, chief res offr (agric) Regnl Miny of Agric Southern Sudan 1976–80; Overseas Devpt Admin FCO London: agric advsr 1980–83, nat resources advsr SE Asia Devpt Div Bangkok 1983–85, head Br Devpt Div in the Pacific Fiji 1985–87, chief nat res advsr 1987–; memb: Cncl RASE, TAA; *Recreations* walking, boating; *Style*— Andrew Bennett, Esq; ✉ Overseas Development Administration, 94 Victoria St, London SW1E 5JL (☎ 0171 917 0513)

BENNETT, Dr Anna Teresa Natalie; da of Sydney Bennett (d 1974), and Ardene Hilton, of Devon; *b* 20 May 1959; *Educ* Lycée Franç de Londres, Inst of Archaeology Univ of London (BSc), Inst of Archaeology UCL (PhD, Br Acad scholar); *m* 1991, Kevin Warren Conru; 1 s (Maximilian b 1996); *Career* asst conservator English Heritage London 1978–79, antiquities conservator J Paul Getty Museum Los Angeles 1982–84, post-doctoral res fell Univ of London 1988–89, commercial art conservation and analytical practice at Univ of London 1989– (clients incl Nat Tst, English Heritage, Cncl for the Care of Churches, numerous museums and commercial and private orgns); project admin for conservation of Uppark contents on behalf of Nat Tst; author of numerous papers and lectrs on archaeology and conservation (incl The Sevso Treasure 1994); hon fell Univ of London 1989–; registered with The Conservation Unit; memb: Int Inst for Conservation of Works of Art (IIC), Int Cncl of Museums (ICCOM); *Style*— Dr Anna Bennett; ✉ Conservation and Technical Services Ltd, Birkbeck College, Malet Street, London WC1E 7HX (☎ 0171 631 6899, fax 0171 631 6898, mobile 0836 577725)

BENNETT, Chris John Arthur; s of Stanley Arthur Bennett (d 1973), and Beatrice Rose, *née* Helsdon (d 1990); *b* 22 Aug 1947; *Educ* Ewell Castle Sch; *m* 1, 25 Jan 1975 (m dis 1985), Barbara Lois, da of Michael Burn, of Somerset; 1 s (Benjamin James b July 1980); m 2, 2 April 1988, Jennifer Margaret, da of Herbert Edward Dabnor, of Macclesfield, Cheshire; *Career* sales dir Autochem Instruments Ltd 1978–79, sr ptnr Bennett & Co 1979–81; md: C B Scientific Ltd 1981–, Bennett & Co Ltd 1985–, Biopack Ltd 1989–, Ismatec UK Ltd 1994–; *Style*— Chris Bennett, Esq; ✉ Elborough House, Banwell Road, Locking, Weston-super-Mare, N Somerset BS24 8PB (☎ 01934 822201, office ☎ 01934 823823, fax 01934 823331); Ismatec UK Ltd (☎ 01934 822000, fax 01934 823331)

BENNETT, Clive Frank; s of Oswald Bartram Tom Bennett, of Budleigh Salterton, Devon, and Olive Helena, *née* Archer; *b* 28 Aug 1945; *Educ* The Dragon Sch Oxford, St Lawrence Coll Ramsgate; *m* 22 Feb 1969, Jill, da of Ken Alexander Woodward (d 1993); 2 s (Patrick Martin b 2 Nov 1971, Graham Neal b 24 Sept 1973), 1 da (Kim Sara b 11 Aug 1975); *Career* auditor Peat Marwick Mitchell London 1968–69 (auditor Johannesburg 1969–71); Grant Thornton Oxford: articled clerk 1963–67, mangr 1972–73, client service ptnr 1973–80, office managing ptnr 1980–88, memb Nat Policy Bd 1985–87, regnl managing ptnr Central Region 1989–95, head of int client servs 1995–, memb Int Policy Bd 1995–; Freeman City of Oxford; FCA (ACA 1968); *Recreations* yachting, canoeing, swimming, squash, skiing, walking, reading, travelling; *Clubs* Royal Dart Yacht; *Style*— Clive Bennett, Esq; ✉ Grant Thornton, Grant Thornton House, 22 Melton Street, London NW1 2EP (☎ 0171 383 5100, fax 0171 728 2744)

BENNETT, David Anthony; s of Albert Henry Bennett, of Solihull, West Midlands, and Doris May, *née* Ward; *b* 4 Oct 1948; *Educ* Harold Malley GS Solihull, Portsmouth Univ, Johns Hopkins Univ, Sch of Advance Int Studies (scholar, BSc Econ, Dip Int Affrs, MIPR); *Career* stagiaire and admin Euro Cmmn 1973–74, Econ Planning Div Br Gas 1976–84, dir public affairs Eurofi 1984–87, md Powerhouse Europe 1987–92, chm and md Beaumark Ltd 1993–; chm Nat Assoc of Mutual Guarantee Socs 1993–; conslt speaker for Euro Cmmn, alternate memb Econ and Social Ctee of Euro Communities 1982–84 (expert 1990–91); sec Labour Econ Fin and Taxation Assoc (LEFTA) 1979–81; Parly candidate (SDP/Alliance) 1983 and 1987, Euro Parly candidate 1984, chm Lib Democrats Euro Gp 1991–; *Books* The European Economy in 1975 (1975); *Recreations* tennis, skiing, walking, travel, theatre; *Style*— David Bennett, Esq; ✉ 1 The Vat House, 27 Regent's Bridge Gardens, London SW8 1HD (☎ and fax 0171 735 0241); Beaumark Ltd, 10 Little College Street, Westminster, London SW1P 3SH (☎ 0171 222 1371, fax 0171 222 1440)

BENNETT, His Hon Judge; Dudley Paul; s of late Patrick James Bennett, of Bognor Regis, and Mary, *née* Edmondson; *b* 4 Aug 1948; *Educ* Bradfield, Univ of London (LLB); *m* 24 May 1986, Patricia Anne, da of James Kinnear Martin, of Notts; 2 da (Olivia Mary b 4 Feb 1988, Emma Jayne b 5 Oct 1989); *Career* called to the Bar Inner Temple 1972; recorder Crown Ct 1988–93, circuit judge (Midland & Oxford Circuit) 1993–; *Recreations* gardening, travel; *Style*— His Hon Judge Bennett; ✉ Nottingham Crown Court, Canal Street, Nottingham

BENNETT, Dr (Albert) Edward; s of Albert Edward Bennett (d 1973), and Frances Anne, *née* Owen (d 1971); *b* 11 Sept 1931; *Educ* Univ Coll Sch, The London Hosp Medical Coll (Arnold Thompson prize for Medical and Surgical Diseases of Children); *m* 1 Feb 1957, Jean Louise, da of Lawrence Dickinson (d 1980); 2 s (Mark Edward Hurley b 1957, Neil Edward Francis Bennett, *qv* b 1965); *Career* Surgeon Lt RN 1957–60; medical offr The Wellcome Fndn 1960–64, sr lectr Dept of Clinical Epidemiology and Social Medicine St Thomas's Hosp Medical Sch Univ of London 1964–70, dir Health Servs Evaluation Gp Univ of Oxford 1970–77, prof and head Dept of Clinical Epidemiology and Social Medicine St George's Hosp Medical Sch Univ of London 1974–81; dir Euro Cmmn: Directorate of Health and Safety 1981–87, Directorate of Nuclear Safety Industry and Environment and Civil Protection 1987–95, Nuclear Safety Assistance Co-ordination Centre 1992–95, ret; FFPHM 1972, FFOM 1984; *Books* Questionnaires in Medicine (1975), Recent Advances in Community Medicine (ed, 1978), Communications Between Doctors and Patients (1976); *Recreations* music, cinema, gardening; *Clubs* Athenaeum; *Style*— Dr Edward Bennett; ✉ The Walled Garden, Liston, Sudbury, Suffolk CO10 7HT

BENNETT, Francis Ernest Herman; CBE (1963); s of Sir Ernest Nathaniel Bennett (d 1947), of Cwmllecoediog, Aberangell, Machynlleth, and Marguerite, *née* Kleinwort; bro of Rt Hon Sir Frederic Mackarness Bennett, *qv*; *b* 5 Nov 1916; *Educ* Westminster, New Coll Oxford; *m* 1947, Hon Ruth Gordon, da of 1 Baron Catto, CBE (d 1959); 2 s (David b 1948, Adam b 1954), 1 da (Olivia b 1950); *Career* WWII Capt 1939–46; third sec to HM Legation Bucharest 1947–49; sec-gen Lib Int 1951–52; called to the Bar 1953, chm WJ Cox Ltd 1959–74, dep chm Cons GLC 1975–76 (chief whip 1959, alderman and chief whip 1965–79), chm and cmmr Advsy Ctee on Gen Cmmrs of Income Tax 1978–91; former govr London Festival Ballet; Hon DUniv Brunel; *Recreations* skiing, shooting, travelling, entomolgy; *Clubs* Reform, Carlton; *Style*— Francis Bennett, Esq, CBE; ✉ c/o The Carlton Club, 69 St James's Street, London SW1A 1PJ

BENNETT, Rt Hon Sir Frederic Mackarness; kt (1964), DL (Greater London 1990), PC (1985); 2 s of Sir Ernest Nathaniel Bennett (d 1947), of Cwmllecoediog, Aberangell, Machynlleth, and Marguerite, *née* Kleinwort; bro of Francis Ernest Herman Bennett, *qv*; *b* 2 Dec 1918; *Educ* Westminster; *m* 1945, Marion Patricia, da of late Maj Cecil Burnham, OBE, of Manor Farm, Rustington, Sussex; *Career* serv WWII RA, commended for gallantry 1940, Lt Col 1945, released to reserve 1946, permanent rank of Major; called to the Bar Lincoln's Inn 1946; contested (C) Burslem 1945, MP (C) Reading North 1951–55, Torquay 1955–87; ldr Br Delegation to Cncl of Europe and WEU 1979–87 (vice pres 1979–87); pres: Anglo-Turkish Soc, Baltic Cncl, Anglo-Polish Soc (London Branch), Anglo-Jordanian Soc; vice-pres British Moroccan Soc, Pakistan Soc, Anglo-Polish Soc, Estonian Assoc; Cdr Order of Phoenix (Greece) 1963, Star of Pakistan (Sithari, Pakistan) 1964, Cdr Polonia Restituta (Poland) 1977, Grand Cdr's Cross 1984, Order of Al-Istiqlal (Jordan) 1980, Cdr Isabel la Catolica (Spain) 1982, Hilal-i-Quaid-i-Azam (Pakistan) 1983, cdr Order of Merit (Germany) 1989, Grand Cross Order of Polonia Restituta (First Class) 1990, Knight Commander The Knightly Order of Vitez (Hungary) 1990, Order of Maarjamaa Risti (First Class) 1996; Hon LLD Univ of Istanbul 1984; Freeman City of London 1984; Lord of the Manor of Mawddwy; *Books* Reds under the Bed, or the Enemy at the Gate - and Within (1979, 3 edn 1982); *Recreations* shooting, sailing; *Clubs* Carlton, Beefsteak, Royal Anglo-Belgian, Royal Torbay Yacht; *Style*— The Rt Hon Sir Frederic Bennett, DL; ✉ Cwmllecoediog, Aberangell, nr Machynlleth, Powys SY20 9QP (☎ 01650 511430, fax 01650 511469); Oswego Island, St Davids, Bermuda; Flat 1, 24 Old Buildings, Lincoln's Inn, London WC2A 3UP (☎ 0171 242 3900, fax 0171 831 8455)

BENNETT, Dr Gerald Charles Joseph; *b* 28 July 1951; *Educ* Welsh Nat Sch of Med Cardiff (MB BCh, FRCP); *Career* lectr in geriatric med St George's Hosp 1980–84, currently reader in health care of the elderly London Hosp Med Coll and med dir Tower Hamlets Healthcare NHS Tst; author of numerous articles and chapters in books/various TV and radio appearances concerning: pressure sores, living wills, elder abuse; chair Action on Elder Abuse 1992; memb Br Geriatrics Soc; *Books* Alzheimer's Disease and Other Causes of Confusion (1989 and 1994), Essentials of Health Care of the Elderly (1992 and 1995), Elder Abuse: Concepts, Theories and Interventions (1993), Wound Care for Health Professionals (1995); *Recreations* ballet, travel; *Style*— Dr Gerald Bennett; ✉ 46 Gerrard Rd, London N1 8AX (☎ 0171 359 9320); The London Hospital Medical College, Department of Health Care of the Elderly, Royal London Hosp (Mile End), Bancroft Rd, London E1 4DG (☎ 0171 377 7843, fax 0171 377 7844)

BENNETT, (Jeffery) Graeme; *b* 30 May 1942; *Educ* Univ of Queensland (MB BS); *Career* cardiac surgn Royal Brompton Hospital, sr lectr Nat Heart and Lung Inst; FRCS, FRCSEd; *Recreations* golf, art; *Clubs* Hurlingham, MCC, Royal Wimbledon Golf; *Style*— Graeme Bennett, Esq; ✉ Royal Brompton Hospital, Sydney Street, London SW3 6NP (☎ 0171 351 8566, fax 0171 351 8566)

BENNETT, Guy Patrick de Courcy; s of Patrick John de Courcy Bennett, of Thames Ditton, and Pamela Mary Ray, *née* Kirchner; *b* 27 Oct 1958; *Educ* Wimbledon Coll, Manchester Univ (BSc); *m* 5 Nov 1988, Monica Beatrice, da of Alfred Cecil Francis Brodermann (d 1974); 3 da (Emily b 1990, Olivia b 1991, Beatrice b 1994); *Career* investmt analyst Equity & Law Life 1980–83; dir: Marketable Securities Div CIN Management 1984–96, EFM Japan Trust 1992–, Genesis Malaysia Maju Fund 1992–, Taiwan Capital Fund 1994–, Goldman Sachs Asset Management 1996–; *Recreations* golf, tennis, squash; *Style*— Guy Bennett, Esq; ✉ 20 Hendham Road, London SW17 7DQ (☎ 0181 767 2098); Goldman Sachs Asset Management, Peterborough Court, 133 Fleet Street, London EC4A 2BB

BENNETT, Sir Hubert; kt (1970); s of Arthur Bennett, JP, and Eleanor, *née* Peel; *b* 4 Sept 1909; *Educ* Victoria Univ, Manchester Sch of Architecture; *m* 1938, Louise F C Aldred; 3 da (Louise, Elizabeth, Helen); *Career* architect in private practice; chief architect to LCC and GLC 1956–71, exec dir English Property Corp 1971–79; assessor: Vauxhall Cross Competition, City Poly Hong Kong 1982; conslt architect for guest palace for HM Sultan of Oman 1982, architect to UNESCO Paris 1982; memb RIBA Cncl 1952–55, 1957–62, 1965–66 and 1967–69; recipient of various architectural and design awards; FRIBA; *Recreations* golf; *Style*— Sir Hubert Bennett; ✉ Broadfields, Ripsley Park, Liphook, Hants GU30 7JH (☎ 01428 724176)

BENNETT, Hon Mr Justice; Hon Sir Hugh Peter Derwyn; kt (1995); s of Peter Ward Bennett, OBE (d 1996), and Priscilla Ann, *née* Troughton; *b* 8 Sept 1943; *Educ* Haileybury and ISC, Churchill Coll Cambridge (MA); *m* 6 Dec 1969, Elizabeth, da of James Whittington Landon, DFC; 1 s (Vivian Hugh James b 16 Nov 1974), 3 da (Ursula Ann (Mrs H J F S Cholmeley) b 29 Jan 1971, Henrietta Mary b 1 July 1973, Rosamond Elizabeth b 13 Sept 1976); *Career* called to the Bar Inner Temple 1966 (bencher 1993), QC 1988, recorder of the Crown Court 1990–95 (asst recorder 1987), judge of the High Court of Justice (Family Div) 1995–; memb Supreme Ct Rule Ctee 1988–92; hon legal advsr Sussex Co Playing Fields Assoc 1988–95, pt/t chm Horserace Betting Levy Appeal Tbnl 1989–95; govr Lancing Coll 1981–95, fell SE Div Woodard Corp 1987–; *Recreations* cricket, tennis, shooting and fishing; *Clubs* MCC, Sussex, Pilgrims; *Style*— The Hon Mr Justice Bennett; ✉ The Royal Courts of Justice, Strand, London WC2A 2LL

BENNETT, District Judge; Ivor; s of Abraham Bennett (d 1971), of Liverpool, and Flora, *née* Heilbron; *b* 6 Sept 1937; *Educ* Liverpool Coll, Univ of Liverpool (LLB, Liverpool Bd of Legal Studies Equity Prize); *m* 26 Oct 1966, Valerie Gwen, da of Samuel Polak (d 1989); 2 s (Nigel Myles b 16 March 1968, Roger James b 14 Sept 1970), 1 da (Amy Laura b 24 Oct 1982); *Career* slr; articled to Stuart Rayner of Rayner and Wade Liverpool 1957–61, ptnr Bell & Joynson Liverpool & Wallasey (Bell Lamb & Joynson since 1988) 1963–91 (joined 1961), district judge at Liverpool and St Helens 1991–; memb: No 15 Legal Aid Area Gen Ctee 1971–91, Law Soc; Lancashire Co hockey team 1961–62 (colours 1962); *Recreations* golf, bridge, photography; *Clubs* Lee Park Golf, Liverpool; *Style*— District Judge Bennett; ✉ St Helens County Court, Rexmore house, Cotham Street, St Helens, Merseyside; Liverpool Combined Court Centre, Queen Elizabeth II Law Courts, Derby Square, Liverpool L2 1XA

BENNETT, James Douglas Scott; s of Andrew Carmichael Bennett, (d 1983), of Edinburgh, and Margaret Catherine, *née* Nelson; *b* 1 March 1942; *Educ* Fettes, Univ of Edinburgh (MA); *m* 14 June 1969, Lorna Elizabeth Margaret, da of John Trevor William Peat (d 1974); 2 s (Hamish b 1974, Fraser b 1977); *Career* dir: Anglo Continental Tst 1972–5, Chloride Alcad Ltd 1978–81, Quayle Munro Holdings plc (formerly East of Scotland Industrial Investments plc) 1984–; grp finance dir John Menzies plc 1981–; memb: Accounts Commission for Scot 1983–94, Scot Provident Inst 1989–; MICAS, FIMgt, FRSA; *Recreations* golf, reading; *Clubs* New (Edinburgh), Royal and Ancient, Hon Co of Edinburgh Golfers, Denham Golf, IOD, Luffness New, Murrayfield; *Style*— James Bennett, Esq; ✉ John Menzies plc, 108 Princes Street, Edinburgh EH2 3AA (☎ 0131 225 8555)

BENNETT, Jeremy James Balfe; s of Arthur Henry Bennett (d 1968), and Anne Gladys Bennett (d 1976); *b* 20 Jan 1934; *Educ* Repton; *m* 24 April 1965, Shelagh Winifred, da of Robert Jones (d 1968); 3 da (Sarah b 1962, Charlotte b 1967, Jane b 1967); *Career* cmmnd Sherwood Foresters, Cheshire Yeomanry (TA); dir Grants of St James's Ltd 1975–91, md Grants Wine & Spirit Merchants 1978–82, dir European Cellars Ltd 1987–91; chm: London Wine Importers 1981–87, Wine & Spirit Educn Tst 1988–91; chm and chief exec Acad of Wine Service 1991– (chm 1988–); govr Enham Alamein Tst 1995–, vice chllr Wine Guild of the UK 1996–; sec The Old Codgers Assoc 1992–; *Recreations* photography, music, reading, walking; *Clubs* Army and Navy; *Style*— Jeremy Bennett, Esq; ✉ The Vine House, Rookery Lane, Broughton, nr Stockbridge, Hants SO20 8AZ (☎ 01794 301219, fax 01794 301784)

BENNETT, Prof John Roderick; s of William Henry Bennett (d 1966), and Janet Elizabeth, *née* Earl (d 1990); *b* 15 Sept 1934; *Educ* Wallasey GS, Univ of Liverpool (MB ChB, MD); *m* 1963, Helen, da of Rt Rev Clifford Martin (d 1977); 2 s (Paul b 3 Aug 1964, Mark b 17 Dec 1965), 1 da (Sarah b 10 Aug 1969); *Career* conslt physician Hull Royal Infirmary 1964–97, hon prof of clinical med Univ of Hull 1994–97; memb GMC 1978–; FRCP 1976 (vice pres 1995–96, treas 1996–); *Books* Therapeutic Endoscopy and Radiology of the Gut (1980, 2 edn 1988), Practical Gastroenterology (1986); *Recreations* sailing, walking, gardening, music, literature; *Clubs* Athenaeum; *Style*— Prof John Bennett; ✉ Remenham House, 197 Westella Road, Westella, Humberside HU10 7RP (☎ 01482 653781, fax 01482 652850); Royal College of Physicians, 11 St Andrews Place, Regent's Park, London NW1 4LE (☎ 0171 935 1174, fax 0171 487 5218)

BENNETT, Lilian Margery; *née* Barnett; OBE (1993); da of Maurice Sydney Barnett (d 1981), of London, and Sophia Levy (d 1975); *b* 22 Aug 1922; *Educ* West Ham Secdy Sch; *m* 2 Nov 1952, Ronald Bennett, s of Alec Bennett (d 1974), of London; 1 s (Jonathan b 1954); *Career* dir: Thermo-Plastics Ltd 1957–68, Girlpower Ltd 1968–, Overdrive plc 1968–; chm Manpower plc (dir 1968–); memb: The Parole Board 1984–87, Community Serv Volunteers Employment Panel, Butler Tst Panel; FRSA; *Recreations* reading, music, community work; *Style*— Mrs Lilian Bennett, OBE; ✉ 67 Porchester Terrace, London W2 3TT (☎ 0171 262 4001); Manpower plc, 66 Chiltern St, London W1M 1PR (☎ 0171 224 6688, fax 0171 224 4904)

BENNETT, Linda Margaret; da of Norman James Turner (d 1981), of Swanage, Dorset, and Margaret Doris, *née* Kneller; *b* 28 Aug 1950; *Educ* Sutton HS GPDST, UCW Aberystwyth (BSc); *m* 28 Aug 1982, Thomas John Paterson, s of Thomas Bennett, of Amesbury, Wilts; *Career* regnl mangr Angus Fire Armour 1972–78, dir Rayner Advertising 1978–81, md Eros Marketing Support Services 1987–95 (client servs dir 1982–87), dir In Touch Services 1986–; non-exec dir Frimley Hosp NHS Tst 1995–; MInstM, FInstD; *Recreations* water skiing, snow skiing, golf; *Style*— Mrs Linda Bennett; ✉ In Touch Services Ltd, 30 Quince Tree Way, Raven Meadow, Hook, Basingstoke, Hampshire RG27 9SG (☎/fax 01256 764320)

BENNETT, Prof Michael David; OBE (1996); s of Stanley Roland Bennett, and Marion, *née* Woods; *b* 6 Oct 1943; *Educ* Gravesend Boys' GS, Univ Coll Wales Aberystwyth (BSc, PhD); *m* 28 Aug 1971, Anita Lucy, da of Harry Ring, of Northfleet, Kent; 1 s (Nathan b 1980), 2 da (Michelle b 1976, Danielle b 1977); *Career* res scientist (cytogeneticist) Plant Breeding Inst Cambridge 1968–87, BP Venture res fell 1986–92, keeper of Jodrell Laboratory Royal Botanic Gardens Kew 1987–; FLS 1988; *Recreations* gardening, reading, bible study; *Style*— Prof Michael Bennett, OBE; ✉ 2 Kew Palace Cottages, Royal Botanic Gardens, Kew, Richmond, Surrey TW9 3AQ (☎ 0181 332 5857); Jodrell Laboratory, Royal Botanic Gardens, Kew, Richmond, Surrey TW9 3DS (☎ 0181 332 5311, fax 0181 332 5310, telex 296694 KEWGAR)

BENNETT, Neil Edward Francis; s of (Albert) Edward Bennett, *qv*, of Liston, Long Melford, Suffolk, and Jean Louise, *née* Dickinson; *b* 15 May 1965; *Educ* Westminster, UCL (BA), City Univ London (Postgrad Dip in Journalism); *m* 19 Sept 1992, Carole, da of William Kenyon, of Allestree, Derby; 1 da (Violet Xanthe b 30 Oct 1995); *Career* feature writer Investors' Chronicle 1987–89; The Times 1989–95: City reporter 1989–90, banking corr 1990–93, ed Tempus column 1993, dep ed Business News until 1995; City ed Sunday Telegraph 1995–; Wincott Jr Financial Journalist of the Year 1992; *Recreations* antiquarian book collecting, long-distance running; *Clubs* London Capital; *Style*— Neil Bennett, Esq; ✉ Sunday Telegraph City Office, Salters' Hall, 4 Fore Street, London EC2Y 5DT (☎ 0171 538 5000, fax 0171 513 2504)

BENNETT, Prof (Stanley) Neville; s of late Stanley Bennett, of Preston, Lancs, and Gladys, *née* Welch; *b* 25 July 1937; *Educ* Kirkham GS, Univ of Lancaster (BEd, PhD); *m* 18 March 1961, Susan Gail, da of Peter Umney, of Foyers, Scotland; 1 s (Neil b 1961), 2 da (Louise b 1963, Sara b 1964); *Career* radio offr Mercantile Marine 1956–61, radio engr Br Aerospace 1961–64, prof of educnl res Univ of Lancaster 1978–85 (res offr 1969–72, lectr and sr lectr 1972–78), dir Centre for Res on Teaching and Learning Univ of Exeter 1987– (prof of educn 1985–); memb: Br Educnl Res Assoc, American Educnl Res Assoc, Euro Assoc for Res on Learning and Instruction (pres elect); ed Teaching and Teacher Educn; *Books* Teaching Styles and Pupil Progress (1976), Focus on Teaching (1979), Open Plan Schools (1980), The Quality of Pupil Learning Experiences (1984), A Good Start (1989), From Special to Ordinary Schools (1989), Talking and Learning in Groups (1990), Managing Classroom Groups (1992), Learning to Teach (1993), Class Size in Primary Schools (1994), Teaching Through Play (1997); *Recreations* gardening, travel, DIY, walking, reading; *Style*— Prof Neville Bennett; ✉ School of Education, University of Exeter, St Luke's, Exeter, Devon (☎ 01392 264796, fax 01392 264792)

BENNETT, Dr Peter Norman; s of Norman Bennett (d 1989), and Elizabeth Jane, *née* Ogston; *b* 25 Nov 1939; *Educ* Nairn Acad, Univ of Aberdeen (MB ChB, MD); *m* 31 Aug 1963, Jennifer Mary, da of Eric Arthur Brocklehurst, of Hull, N Humberside; 2 s (Michael John b 1965, Neil Robert b 1968), 1 da (Sally Ann Elizabeth b 1972); *Career* lectr in med Univ of Aberdeen 1967–71, Wellcome res fell UCH London 1971–73, lectr Royal Postgrad Med Sch 1973–76, conslt physician in clinical pharmacology and dir of Clinical Pharma Unit Royal United Hosp Bath 1976–; School of Postgrad Med Univ of Bath: sr lectr in clinical pharmacology 1976–90, dir Centre for Med Studies 1978, assoc dean 1989, reader in clinical pharmacology 1990; memb Br Pharmacological Soc (treas Clinical Section 1982–87), chm WHO (Euro) Working Gp on Drugs and Breast Feeding 1983–, memb Bd Euro Ethical Review Ctee 1990–; *Books* Clinical Pharmacology (with D R Laurence, 5 edn 1980, 6 edn 1987, 7 edn 1992, 8 edn 1997), Multiple Choice Questions on Clinical Pharmacology (with D R Laurence and F Stokes, 1 edn 1983, 2 edn 1988), Drugs and Human Lactation (ed, 1988, 2 edn 1996), Ethical Responsibilities in European Drug Research (ed, 1991), Good Clinical Practice and Ethics in European Drug Research (ed, 1994); *Recreations* fly-fishing; *Clubs* Royal Soc of Med; *Style*— Dr Peter Bennett; ✉ Denmede, Southstoke Rd, Combe Down, Bath BA2 5SL (☎ 01225 824536, fax 01225 825520)

BENNETT, Prof Philip Anthony; s of George Joseph Bennett, of Brigg, and Rita, *née* Skelton (d 1984); *b* 1 Sept 1947; *Educ* PhD; *m* 20 Sept 1969 (m dis 1996), Kathryn Margaret, da of Sidney French (d 1977); 2 s (Lance Andrew b 3 Jan 1972, Robin Michael b 3 Jan 1980); *Career* apprenticeship Richard Thomas & Baldwin (later part of British

Steel) 1963–69, sr engrg positions British Steel 1969–81; md and chm: The Centre for Software Engineering Ltd 1984–, York Software Engineering Ltd 1995–; prof of safety critical systems Dept of Computer Science Univ of York 1993–; chm The Hazards Forum 1993–; scouting 1977–91 (Cmmr); Freeman Ciy of London 1990, Liveryman Worshipful Co of Engrs 1991; FIQA 1985, FIEE 1989, FEng 1991, FICE 1995; *Books* Safety Aspects of Computer Control (ed, 1992), Software Engineers Reference Book (contrib, 1991); ed High Integrity Systems Jl; *Recreations* fly-fishing, horse riding, reading; *Clubs* Athenaeum, Royal Over-Seas League; *Style*— Prof P A Bennett, FEng; ✉ 2 Brigg Road, Broughton, Brigg, South Humberside DN20 0JW (☎ 01652 652649); The Centre for Software Engineering Ltd, Glanford House, Bellwin Drive, Flixborough, Scunthorpe, South Humberside DN15 8SN (☎ 01724 862169, fax 01724 846256)

BENNETT, His Hon Judge; Raymond Clayton Watson; s of Harold Watson (Church Army Capt, d 1941), and Doris Helena, *née* Edwards (d 1988); *b* 20 June 1939; *Educ* Glasgow Acad, Bury GS, Univ of Manchester (LLB); *m* 24 April 1965, Elaine Margaret, da of William Haworth, of Clitheroe; 1 s (John b 1966), 1 da (Jane b 1969); *Career* slr Blackburn 1964–72; called to the Bar Middle Temple 1972; Northern Circuit 1972–, recorder of the Crown Ct 1988, circuit judge (Northern Circuit) 1989–; memb Hon Soc of Middle Temple; *Recreations* tennis, sailing, cycling; *Style*— His Hon Judge Bennett; ✉ c/o The Crown Court, Burnley, Lancs

BENNETT, Dr Sir Reginald Frederick Brittain; kt (1979), VRD (1944); s of Samuel Robert Bennett (d 1964), and Gertrude, *née* Brittain (d 1946); *b* 22 July 1911; *Educ* Winchester, New Coll Oxford (MA, BM BCh, Sailing blue), LMSSA, Inst of Psychiatry London (DPM); *m* 1947, Henrietta, da of Capt Henry Berwick Crane, CBE, RN (d 1987); 1 s (Timothy), 3 da (Antonia, Medina, Belinda); *Career* Surgn Lt Cdr RNVR and Fleet Air Arm Pilot 1939–46; sr psychiatric registrar Maudsley Hosp 1948–49; MP (Cons) Gosport and Fareham 1950–79; PPS to: Sir David Maxwell Fyfe (Home Sec) 1951–53, Iain Macleod 1954–63; chm: Parly and Scientific Ctee 1959–61, Parly Anglo-Italian Ctee 1969–79, Catering Sub Ctee 1970–79; vice pres Parly Franco-British Ctee 1972–79, memb Servs Ctee; wine conslt and co dir; chm Nadder Wine Co Ltd 1985–92, dir Italian General Shipping Co Ltd 1977–96; memb Cncl of Mgmnt Int Nutrition Fndn Oxford 1978–96; chm: Amateur Yacht Research Soc 1972–90, World Sailing Speed Record Cncl (IYRU) 1980–, RYA Speed Sailing Ctee 1980–92, RYA Nat Match-Racing Championship 1989–94; Liveryman Worshipful Soc of Apothecaries; Grande Officiale Italian Order of Merit 1977; *Recreations* yacht racing, foreign travel, painting (exhibited Royal Acad 1995), basking in the sun; *Clubs* incl: White's, Imperial Poona Yacht (Cdre), Sea View Yacht; *Style*— Dr Sir Reginald Bennett, VRD; ✉ 19 Elm Lodge, River Gardens, London SW6 6NZ (☎ 0171 386 5490)

BENNETT, Richard Rodney; CBE (1977); s of H Rodney and Joan Esther Bennett; *b* 29 March 1936; *Educ* Leighton Park, Royal Acad of Music; *Career* composer; memb Gen Cncl Performing Right Soc 1975–, vice pres London Coll of Music 1983–; author of various music articles in magazines and jls; *Works* operas: The Mines of Sulphur 1965 and A Penny for a Song 1968 (both cmmnd by Sadler's Wells), All The King's Men (children's opera) 1969, Victory 1970 (cmmnd by Royal Opera Covent Garden); music for films incl: Indiscreet, The Devil's Disciple, Only Two Can Play, The Wrong Arm of the Law, Heavens Above, Billy Liar, One Way Pendulum, The Nanny, Far from the Madding Crowd, Billion Dollar Brain, The Buttercup Chain, Figures in a Landscape, Lady Caroline Lamb, Voices, Murder on the Orient Express (SFTA award, Academy Award nomination, Performing Right Soc Ivor Novello award), Permission to Kill, Equus (BAFTA nomination), The Brinks Job, Yanks (BAFTA nomination), Return of the Soldier; music for TV incl: The Christians, L P Hartley Trilogy, The Ebony Tower, Tender is the Night, The Charmer, Poor Little Rich Girl, The Hiding Place, The Story of Anne Frank; other works incl: Guitar Concerto 1970, Spells (choral work) 1975, various chamber, orchestral and educational music works; *Recreations* cinema, modern jazz; *Style*— Richard Rodney Bennett, Esq, CBE; ✉ c/o Novello & Co Ltd, 8–9 Frith Street, London W1V 5TZ (☎ 0171 434 0066, fax 0171 287 6329)

BENNETT, Robert (Bob); s of late Robert Bennett, and Emily, *née* Clegg; *b* 16 June 1940; *Educ* Rossall; *m* 5 Oct 1963, Alice Mary, da of late George William Ormerod; 1 s (Robin b 1964 d 1966), 2 da (Georgina b 1967, Jill b 1968); *Career* chm Lancs CCC 1987– (cricketer 1962–66); mangr England A Team to Zimbabwe and Kenya 1990, mangr England A Team to Pakistan and Sri Lanka 1991, mangr England A Team to S Africa 1993/94; mangr England team: to NZ and World Cup Aust and NZ 1991/92, to India and Sri Lanka 1992/93; *Style*— Bob Bennett, Esq; ✉ Pippin Bank, Braaid Rd, Marown Douglas, Isle of Man

BENNETT, Prof Robert John; s of Thomas Edward Bennett, of Southampton, and Kathleen Elizabeth, *née* Robson; *b* 23 March 1948; *Educ* Taunton's Sch Southampton, St Catharine's Coll Cambridge (BA, MA, PhD); *m* 5 Nov 1971, Elizabeth Anne, da of William Allen, of Eastrington, Humberside; 2 s (Phillip Stewart Edward b 1982, Richard John Charles b 1986); *Career* lectr UCL 1973–78, visiting prof Univ of California Berkeley 1978, lectr Univ of Cambridge 1978–85 (fell, tutor and dir of studies Fitzwilliam Coll 1978–85); LSE: prof of geography 1985–96, Leverhulme prof 1996–; prof of geography Univ of Cambridge 1996–; gen ed Government and Policy 1982–; memb: Govt and Law Ctee ESRC 1982–87, Cncl Inst of Br Geographers 1985–87 (treas 1990–); memb Cncl Royal Geographic Soc 1995– (vice pres 1993–95); chm Election Studies Advsy Ctee ESRC 1987–88, conslt to House of Commons Employment Ctee 1988–89 and Scottish Affrs Ctee 1994–95; FRGS 1982, FBA 1991; *Books* incl: Environmental Systems - Philosophy, Analysis and Control (with R J Chorley, 1978), Local Business Taxes in Britain and Germany (with G Krebs, 1988), Enterprise and Human Resource Development: local capacity building (with A McCoshan, 1993); *Recreations* craft work, the family; *Style*— Prof Robert Bennett, FBA; ✉ University of Cambridge, Department of Geography, Downing Place, Cambridge CB2 3EN

BENNETT, Eur Ing Robert Michael; s of Frederick William Bennett (d 1980), of Friern Barnet, London, and Doris Annie, *née* Mallandaine (d 1990); *b* 29 Nov 1944; *Educ* Woodhouse GS Finchley, Northampton Coll of Advanced Technol (first and second year Dip Tech), Enfield Tech Coll (HND, IEE part III); *m* 1969, Norma, *née* Baldwin; 1 s (Simon Michael b 1971); *Career* apprenticeship trg Eastern Electricity Bd Wood Green 1963–68; design/contracts engr Christy Electrical Ltd Chelmsford 1969–72, electrical design engr Posford Pavry & Ptnrs London (civil structural & building servs consltg engrs) 1972–73, sr electrical engr James R Briggs & Associates Hampstead (building servs consltg engrs) 1973–76, electrical assoc Donald Smith Seymour & Rooley London 1981–86 (exec sr electrical engr 1976–81); electrical engrg ptnr: Building Design Partnership London 1986–91, Frederic J Whyte & Ptnrs 1991–93; regnl/business devpt dir YRM Engineers 1994–; chm South Bucks Area IEE 1984–85; DipEE 1968, CEng 1978, FCIBSE 1985, FIEE 1987, Eur Ing 1988; *Books* Electricity and Buildings (jt author, 1984), CIBSE Applications Manual AM8 - Private and Standby Generation of Electricity (jtly, 1992); *Recreations* golf, theatre-going; *Clubs* Hazlemere Golf (Bucks), Beaconsfield 41; *Style*— Eur Ing Robert Bennett; ✉ YRM Engineers Ltd, 24 Britton Street, London EC1M 5NQ (☎ 0171 253 4311, fax 0171 250 1688)

BENNETT, Sir Ronald Wilfrid Murdoch; 3 Bt (UK 1929), of Kirklington, Co Nottingham; o s of Sir (Charles) Wilfrid Bennett, 2 Bt, TD (d 1952), and Marion Agnes, OBE (d 1985), da of James Somervell, of Sorn Castle, Ayrshire; *b* 25 March 1930; *Educ* Wellington Coll, Trin Coll Oxford; *m* 1, 1953, Audrey Rose-Marie Patricia, o d of Maj A L J H Aubépin; 2 da (Anne-Marie Julia (Mrs Stephen Hickman) b 1954, Georgina Marion b 1956); m 2, 1968, Anne, da of late Leslie George Tooker; m 3; *Heir* kinsman, Mark Edward Francis Bennett b 5 April 1960; *Style*— Sir Ronald Bennett, Bt

BENNETT, Roy Grissell; CMG (1971), TD (1946); s of Charles Ernest Marklew Bennett (d 1962), and Lilian, *née* Bluff (d 1972); *b* 21 Nov 1917; *Educ* privately, RMC Sandhurst; *Career* served WWII Maj 17/21 Lancers; 24 Lancers D Day, 2 Lothian Border Horse 2 in Cmd; chm: Singapore Anti Tuberculosis Assoc 1958–62, Maclaine Watson and Co Singapore 1960–72 (dir 1956–72), Singapore Int Chamber of Commerce 1968–70, Pilkington SEA Pte Ltd 1972–89, Fibre Glass Pilkington Malaysia 1972–89, Racehorse Spelling Station (Malaya) 1976–, Beder Malaysia Sdn Bhd (current); ctee memb and chm: Rubber Assoc Singapore 1960–72, Singapore Chamber of Commerce Rubber Assoc 1960–72; fndr chm: Utd World College SEA 1970–78 (now memb bd), Riding for the Disabled Assoc of Singapore (now patron); dir Vavasseur and Co Penang 1948–52; patron Singapore Polo Club (chm 1958–70), dep chm Singapore Turf 1966–88; FZS 1996; *Recreations* polo (5 handicap 1967–78), racing, swimming, shooting, travelling, gardening, photography, people of all races, building projects; *Clubs* Cavalry and Guards', IOD, Tanglin (Singapore), Turf (Singapore), Polo (patron, Singapore), Polo (Penang), Swimming (Penang), Victoria Racing (Melbourne); *Style*— Roy Bennett, Esq, CMG, TD; ✉ Oak Tree House, S Holmwood, Surrey RH5 4NF (☎ 01306 889414, fax 01306 877604); Taman Indera, 22 Jalan Perdana, Johoru Bharu 80300, Johor, Malaysia (☎ 00 607 2 234505, fax 00 607 2 249006)

BENNETT, Stephen Scott; s of Montague Bennett (d 1976), and Rachel, *née* Lopez-Dias, of Sutton; *b* 6 Dec 1946; *Educ* Rutlish Sch Merton; *m* 22 June 1969, Bobbi, da of Leon Hanover (d 1992); *Career* qualified CA 1968, tax specialist Fuller Jenks Beecroft 1968–70, ptnr Accountancy Tuition Centre 1970–78; Coopers & Lybrand Deloitte: dir of educn 1978–82, ptnr 1982–90, head of M & A until 1990; currently chm and chief exec Princedale Group plc; FCA 1968, FCCA 1973, ATII 1970; *Recreations* golf, squash, rugby, drama; *Style*— Stephen Bennett, Esq; ✉ Princedale Group Plc, 78 Buckingham Gate, London SW1E 4PE (☎ 0171 222 6040)

BENNETT, Tracie; da of Ronald Bennett, and Marjorie Bennett; *b* 17 June 1961; *Educ* Leigh Girls' GS, Italia Conti Acad of Theatre Arts, Royal Northern Coll of Music; Advanced Ballet (RAD, BBO Hons), Advanced Tap (ISTD Hons); *Career* actress; *Theatre* Crucible Theatre Sheffield: Rita in Educating Rita, Wendla in Spring Awakening; Library Theatre Manchester: Katalin in Chicago, Mary in Grease, Jemima in Working Class Hero, Ten Tiny Fingers, Mary in Merrily we Roll Along; other credits incl: Pauline in One for the Road (Palace Theatre Watford), Kate in She Stoops to Conquer (Haymarket Leicester), Angie in Putting on the Ritz (Haymarket Leicester), Sandra in Breezeblock Park (Forum Manchester), Mrs Johnstone in Blood Brothers (Dublin Olympia), Linda in Blood Brothers (Forum Manchester), Amid the Standing Corn (Joint Stock Theatre Co), Carrie in Carousel (Royal Exchange Manchester), Ilona Ritter in She Loves Me (Savoy), Lisa in Terry Jonson's Dead Funny (nat tour), Linda in Ray Cooney's Cash on Delivery (Whitehall); *Television* for BBC: Liz in Next of Kin (2 series), Tracy in Joking Apart (2 series), Sally in Casualty, Norma in Making Out (3 series), Miss Wilson in Brush Strokes, Alas Smith & Jones (5 episodes), Connie Fazakerly in The Bretts, Black Silk, Knock Knock; for YTV: Stella in The Gingerbread Girl, Nicky in Rich Tea and Sympathy, June in The Refuge; for Central: Michelle in The Upper Hand, Cheryl in Unnatural Causes, Patsy in Boon; for TVS: The Bill, Marilyn in Ruth Rendell's Mystery, Relative Strangers, The Rector of Stifkey, Going Out, Shame; for Granda: Monica in Made in Heaven, Sharon Gaskell in Coronation Street; *Films* incl: Milandra in Shirley Valentine (Paramount), Anna in Deep Red Instant Love (Channel 4), Tina in Knights and Emeralds (Enigma Films); *Awards* Manchester Evening News Drama Awards for Best Actress (Carousel and Merrily we Roll Along) 1984, Olivier Award for Best Supporting Performance (She Loves Me) 1995; *Recreations* qualified PADI scuba-diver, classically trained pianist; *Style*— Miss Tracie Bennett; ✉ c/o Conway van Gelder Robinson Ltd, 18–21 Jermyn Street, London SW1Y 6HP (☎ 0171 287 0077, fax 0171 287 1940)

BENNETT-JONES, Peter; s of Dr N Bennett-Jones, of Rhosneigr, Anglesey, and Ruth H Bennett-Jones; *b* 11 March 1955; *Educ* Winchester Coll, Magdalene Coll Cambridge (MA); *m* 29 June 1990, Alison, *née* Watts; 2 s (Ludovic Robin Devereux b 1991, Albert George (Bertie) b 1994), 1 da (Matilda Emma b 1992); *Career* dir OCSC Ltd 1977–79, freelance prodn mangr 1979–81 (projects incl Bubble Theatre UK, Chung Ying Theatre Hong Kong, course dir City Univ London), dir Pola Jones Associates 1982–, md Talkback Productions 1983–86, md Corporate Communication Group Ltd 1986–88; chm: Tiger Television 1988–, PBJ Management 1988–, Tiger Aspect Productions 1993–; dir TEAM plc 1993–; Tiger Aspect prodns incl: Mr Bean (ITV, winner numerous awards incl Int Emmy and Golden Rose of Montreux), The Vicar of Dibley (BBC1) 1994, Harry Enfield and Chums (BBC1) 1994, Clive Anderson's Great Railway Journey and Our Man in... series (BBC2) 1994–, The Thin Blue Line (BBC1) 1995; *Recreations* numerous; *Clubs* United Oxford & Cambridge Univ, Savile, Groucho; *Style*— Peter Bennett-Jones, Esq; ✉ Tiger Aspect Productions/PBJ Management, 5 Soho Square, London W1V 5DE (☎ 0171 434 0672, fax 0171 287 1448, car 0370 306065)

BENNETTS, Rt Rev Colin James; *see:* Buckingham, Bishop of

BENNEWITH, Anthony John (Tony); Catford Secdy Boys' Sch; s of Frank Bennewith, of Catford, and Elsie, *née* Poll; *b* 14 Jan 1946; *m* 8 June 1968, Babs, da of Jack Connolly; 4 da (Christine b 9 Jan 1971, Ruth b 4 June 1992, Heather b 8 Sept 1974, Antonia b 12 May 1988), 1 s (Graham b 15 Jan 1979); *Career* articled clerk 1962–67, Internal Audit Castrol Oil 1968–69; mangr: Griffin Stone Mosscrop 1969–72, Neville Russell London 1972–73; ptnr Neville Russell Guildford 1974–86, own practice 1986–; memb Cncl ICAEW 1996–; deacon Godalming Baptist Church, treas Guildford Hospice; FCA 1978 (ACA 1968); *Recreations* opera, squash, philately; *Style*— Tony Bennewith, Esq; ✉ Elmfield, Tuesley Lane, Godalming, Surrey GU7 1SJ (☎ 01483 415107); A J Bennewith & Co, Hitherbury House, 97 Portsmouth Road, Guildford, Surrey GU2 5DL (☎ 01483 39777, fax 01483 576235, mobile 0374 479676)

BENNEY, (Adrian) Gerald Sallis; CBE (1995); s of Ernest Alfred Sallis Benney, and Aileen Mary, *née* Ward; *b* 21 April 1930; *Educ* Brighton GS, Brighton Coll of Art (Nat Dip), Royal Coll of Art (DesRCA); *m* 4 May 1957, Janet, da of Harold Neville Edwards, of Rawlins Farm, Ramsdell, nr Basingstoke, Hants; 3 s (Paul b 1959, Jonathan b 1961, Simon b 1966), 1 da (Genevieve b 1962); *Career* REME 1949–51; designer and maker of domestic and liturgical silver; started workshop in London in 1955, conslt designer to Viners Ltd 1957–59; holder of Royal Warrants to: HM The Queen 1974–, HRH The Duke of Edinburgh 1975–, HM Queen Elizabeth The Queen Mother 1975–, HRH The Prince of Wales 1980–; memb: Govt's Craft Advsy Ctee 1972–77, Advsy Ctee UK Atomic Energy Ceramics Centre 1979–83; metalwork design advsr to Indian Govt 1977–78, chm Govt of India Hallmarking Survey 1981, memb Br Hallmarking Cncl 1983–88, export advsr and conslt designer to Royal Selangor Pewter Co Kuala Lumpur 1986–; commenced Reading Civic Plate 1960; Freeman: City of London 1957, Borough of Reading 1984; Liveryman Worshipful Co of Goldsmiths 1964; Hon MA Univ of Leicester 1963; RDI 1971, FRSA 1971; *Recreations* walking, landscape gardening, painting; *Style*— Gerald Benney, Esq, CBE; ✉ Beenham House, Beenham, nr Reading, Berks (☎ 0118 974 4370, fax 0118 974 5020); 73 Walton Street, London SW3 2HT (☎ 0171 589 7002/3, fax 0171 581 2573)

BENNINGTON, Prof Geoffrey Peter; s of Jonathan Bennington, of Empsay, N Yorkshire, and Lilian, *née* Lowther; *b* 24 July 1956; *Educ* Chesterfield Sch, St Catherine's

Coll Oxford (jr and sr Heath Harrison travelling scholar, MA, DPhil); m 1, 1987 (m dis 1991), Rachel, *née* Bowlby; *partner* Susan Patricia Collard, da of Peter Ward; 1 step s (Louis Collard b 8 July 1986), 1 da (Alice b 15 Aug 1992); *Career* Laming fell Queen's Coll Oxford 1980–82, prof of French Univ of Sussex 1992– (lectr 1983–89, sr lectr 1989–92); *Books* Sententiousness and the Novel (1985), Lyotard: Writing the Event (1988), Jacques Derrida (1991), Dudding: des noms de Rousseau (1991), Legislations (1994); *Recreations* chess, computing, cricket, music (violin); *Style*— Prof Geoffrey Bennington; ✉ School of European Studies, University of Sussex, Falmer, Brighton BN1 9QN (☎ 01273 678542, fax 01273 623246)

BENNION, Francis Alan Roscoe; s of Thomas Roscoe Bennion (d 1968), of Hove, Sussex, and Ellen Norah, *née* Robinson (d 1986); *b* 2 Jan 1923; *Educ* John Lyon's Sch Harrow, Univ of St Andrews, Balliol Coll Oxford (MA); *m* 1, 28 July 1951 (m dis 1975), Barbara Elizabeth, da of Harry Arnold Braendle (d 1964), of Little Hadham, Herts; 3 da (Sarah, Carola, Venetia); m 2, 2 Nov 1977, Mary Anne, wid of William Field, da of Patrick Lynch (d 1962), of Limerick; *Career* WWII Flt Lt Pilot RAFVR 1941–46; called to the Bar Middle Temple (Harmsworth scholar) 1951, in practice 1951–53 and 1985–94, now full-time writer; lectr and tutor in law St Edmund Hall Oxford 1951–53, Parly counsel 1953–65 and 1973–75, sec-gen RICS 1965–68, research assoc Oxford Univ Centre for Socio-Legal Studies 1984–; constitutional advsr: Pakistan 1956, Ghana 1959–61, Jamaica 1969–71; govr Coll of Estate Mgmnt 1965–68, co-fndr and first chm Professional Assoc of Teachers 1968–72, fndr and first chm World of Property Housing Tst (now Sanctuary Housing Assoc) 1968–72 (vice pres 1986–); fndr: Statute Law Soc 1968 (chm 1978–79), Freedom Under Law 1971, Dicey Tst 1973, Towards One World 1979, Statute Law Tst 1991; co-fndr Areopagitica Educnl Tst 1979; chm Oxford City FC 1988–89; *Books* Constitutional Law of Ghana (1962), Professional Ethics (1969), Tangling With The Law (1970), Consumer Credit Control (1976–), Consumer Credit Act Manual (1978, 3 edn 1986), Statute Law (1980, 3 edn 1990), Statutory Interpretation (1984, 3 edn 1997), Victorian Railway Days (1989), The Sex Code: Morals for Moderns (1991); *Recreations* cricket, Victoriana, old railways; *Clubs* MCC; *Style*— Francis Bennion, Esq

BENSON, Sir Christopher John; s of late Charles Woodburn Benson and Catherine Clara, *née* Bishton; *b* 20 July 1933; *Educ* Worcester Cathedral Kings Sch, The Incorporated Thames Nautical Training Coll HMS Worcester; *m* 1960, Margaret Josephine (Lady Benson, OBE, JP), da of Ernest Jefferis Bundy; 2 s; *Career* Sub Lt RNVR; chartered surveyor and agricultural auctioneer Worcs, Herefordshire, Wilts, Dorset and Hants 1953–64; dir Arndale Developments Ltd 1965–69; fndr chm: Dolphin Developments 1969–71, Dolphin Property Ltd 1969–72, Dolphin Farms Ltd 1973; asst md The Law Land Co Ltd 1972–74; MEPC plc: dir 1974–93, md 1976–88, chm 1988–93; Royal & Sun Alliance Insurance Group plc (formerly Sun Alliance Group plc): dir 1988–, dep chm 1992–93, chm 1993–; chm: LDDC 1984–88, Reedpack Ltd 1989–90, The Boots Company plc 1990–94, The Housing Corporation 1990–94, Costain plc 1993– Dec 96, Albright and Wilson 1995–; dep chm Thorn Lighting Group plc 1994–; dir: House of Fraser plc 1982–86, Royal Opera House Covent Garden Ltd 1984–92; pres Br Property Fedn 1981–83, hon vice pres Nat Fedn of Housing Assocs 1994–; chm: Civic Tst 1985–90, Property Advsy Gp to the Dept of the Environment 1988–90, Funding Agency for Schools 1994–, Steering Ctee British Red Cross Soc 1994–95; memb: Investment Ctee BP Pension Fund 1979–84, Cncl Marlborough Coll 1982–90, Advsy Bd RA 1987–90, Advsy Cncl Prince's Youth Business Tst 1994; lay memb The Take Over Panel 1994–; tstee: Metropolitan Police Museum 1986–, Westminster Christmas Appeal 1989–95, Joy to the World 1991–95; vice pres: Royal Soc of Arts 1992–, Cancer Relief Macmillan Fund 1992–; pres Nat Deaf Children's Soc 1994–; patron Changing Faces 1993–, lay govr Royal London Hosp Med Coll 1993–95; underwriting memb Lloyd's 1979–; Freeman Worshipful Co of Watermen and Lightermen; Liveryman: Guild of Air Pilots and Air Navigators, Worshipful Co of Gold and Silver Wyre Drawers; hon bencher Middle Temple 1984, hon fell Wolfson Coll Cambridge 1990, Hon FRCPath 1992, Hon FCIOB 1992; FRICS, FRSA 1987; *Recreations* farming, aviation, opera, swimming (Wilts Co diving champion 1949); *Clubs* Garrick, City Livery, Naval, RAC, MCC, Australian (Sydney); *Style*— Sir Christopher Benson; ✉ 111 Westminster Bridge Road, London SE1 7UE (☎ 0171 705 8511); Royal & Sun Alliance Insurance Group plc, 1 Bartholomew Lane, London EC2N 2AB (☎ 0171 588 2345, fax 0171 588 1159)

BENSON, Clifford George; s of George Benson, of Grays, Essex, and Doris Lilian, *née* Jennings; *b* 17 Nov 1946; *Educ* RCM; *m* 1 Sept 1973, Dilys Morgan, da of Robert Davies, of Llysfaen, nr Colwyn Bay, Clwyd; 2 da (Sarah b 22 July 1975, Emily b 8 Aug 1977); *Career* concert pianist; first prize with Levon Chilingirian on violin BBC Beethoven Duo Competition 1969, Royal Festival Hall debut playing Rachmaninov 3 Piano Concerto 1970, first prize with Levon Chilingirian Int Duo Competition Munich 1971, recital with Thea King and Peter Pears Aldeburgh Festival 1975, performed Constant Lambert Piano Concerto 1975, world premiere of Richard Rodney Bennett's Three Romantic Pieces for BBC Pebble Mill Howard Ferguson 80th birthday concert 1988; performed solo piano and chamber music recitals and concertos world-wide incl: Canada, Middle and Far East, USA, Czechoslovakia, Europe; regular broadcaster BBC Radio 3; recordings with: Deutsche Grammophon, CBS, Hyperion, Chandos, CRD, Camerate (Tokyo); compositions incl: Au Revoir Sylvie 1979, Three Pieces for Piano 1983, Mozart goes to Town (piano duet) 1985, A Song for Wibb 1986, Tango Variations 1991; currently visiting prof of chamber music RAM London; memb ctee Tonbridge Music Club; life memb RCM Student's Union, memb ISM; *Style*— Clifford Benson, Esq

BENSON, David Holford; s of Lt-Col Sir Reginald (Rex) Lindsay Benson, DSO, MVO, MC (d 1968), of Cucumber Farm, Singleton, nr Chichester, Sussex, and Leslie, *née* Foster (d 1981); *b* 26 Feb 1938; *Educ* Eton, Madrid; *m* 1964, Lady Elizabeth Mary, *née* Charteris, da of 12 Earl of Wemyss and (8 of) March, KT, JP; 1 s, 2 da; *Career* merchant banker; Kleinwort Benson Group plc: joined 1963, vice chm 1989–92, non-exec dir 1992–; chm Kleinwort Charter Investment Trust plc 1992–; also non-exec dir: British Gas plc, Wemyss and March Estate Co, Marshall Cavendish, The Rouse Co and Dover Corporation (both NYSE listed cos); tstee Charities Official Investment Fund (COIF) 1985–; *Recreations* painting; *Clubs* White's, ESU; *Style*— David Benson, Esq; ✉ Kleinwort Benson Group plc, 20 Fenchurch St, London EC3P 3DB (☎ 0171 623 8000)

BENSON, David Wilbert; s of Wilbert Thomas Benson (d 1956), of South Africa, and Lilian Ethel, *née* Verner (d 1980); *b* 25 July 1929; *Educ* King Edward VII Sch Johannesburg, Univ of Witwatersrand (DNF, BSc); *m* Feb 1968, Vera Evelyn (d 1994), da of Sydney Coking, formerly Mrs Sugg; 1 step da (Penelope Jennifer Ann Sugg b 1948); *Career* sales engr G H Langler Johannesburg 1949–52; actor in UK incl experience at Old Vic, Manchester Library Theatre, Birmingham Repertory, Westminster Theatre 1952–57; freelance journalist 1957–60, journalist Today Magazine 1961–64, dep ed Motor Magazine 1964–65; Daily Express: feature writer 1965–70, motoring corr 1970–80, motoring ed 1980–94; motoring ed Sunday Express 1987–94; motoring conslt Express Newspapers Group 1993–; tstee dir Express Newspapers Pension Fund 1988–; Conoco Motoring Writer of the Year 1984, Conoco Special award 1985, British Press Awards Campaigning Journalist of the Year 1985, Special Award Society of Motor Manufacturers and Traders 1994; memb Guild of Motoring Writers 1961 (chm 1976, life memb 1995); *Books* Hunt v Lauda; *Recreations* swimming; *Clubs* BRDC, BARC, Wig and Pen; *Style*— David Benson, Esq; ✉ 28 St George's Square, Narrow Street, London E14 8DL (☎ 0171 791 0906); Express Newspapers plc, Ludgate House, 245 Blackfriars Rd, London SE1 9UX (☎ 0171 928 8000, fax 0171 620 1654)

BENSON, (John) Graham; s of Marshall Benson, of Stanmore, Middx, and Beatrice, *née* Stein; *b* 29 April 1946; *Educ* Central Foundation Boys' GS London; *m* 13 May 1978, Christine Margaret, *née* Fox; 1 da (Fay Cecily b 1 Nov 1983); *Career* stage mangr in theatre 1965–68, TV prodn mangr and assoc prodr Drama Plays Dept BBC 1968–76; prodr: Premiere Films, BBC and other TV drama 1976; Fox for Euston Films 1979; Euro prodn exec The Robert Stigwood Group 1980–82, freelance/independent prodr 1982–86, md Consolidated Productions 1986, controller of drama for TVS and dir Telso Communications 1987–92, chm and chief exec Blue Heaven Productions Ltd (prodrs of The Ruth Rendell Mysteries) 1992–; freelance prodr many films including: Thank You Comrades (BBC1) 1978, A Hole in Babylon (BBC1) 1978, Outside Edge (LWT) 1982, Red Monarch (theatrical feature, Channel 4) 1982, Meantime (Central/Channel 4) 1983, Charlie (Central) 1983, Honest Decent and True (BBC2) 1984, Coast to Coast (BBC1) 1984; chm: BAFTA 1985–87 (memb Cncl 1980–93), PACT 1995– (formerly Exec Ctee Br Film and TV Prodrs Assoc, memb 1981–90, memb Cncl 1991–); dep chm Bd of Mgmnt BAFTA 1993–94; FRSA 1987; *Recreations* food, drink, literature, opera, cricket, travel, walking; *Clubs* Savile, Surrey CCC, Ventnor CC; *Style*— Graham Benson, Esq; ✉ Blue Heaven Productions Ltd, 3 The Quarterdeck, Port Solent, Hants PO6 4TP (☎ 01705 200200, fax 01705 200205)

BENSON, James; s of Henry Herbert Benson and Olive, *née* Hutchinson; *b* 17 July 1925; *Educ* Bromley GS, Emmanuel Coll Cambridge (MA); *m* 1950, Honoria Margaret, da of Patrick Hurley (d 1952), of Dublin; 1 da; *Career* served WWII RNVR, N Atlantic and East Indies, midget submarines and minesweepers; with Kemsley Newspapers 1948–58; Mather and Crowther (subsequently Ogilvy & Mather advtg): joined 1959, dir 1960, md 1967, chm 1970–78; Ogilvy & Mather International: dir 1966, vice chm 1970–87; pres James Benson Associates Inc 1987–; dir: Duffy Design Group Inc 1988–91, Scali McCabe Sloves Inc 1989–93; govr Brasilinvest SA 1977–87 (memb Advsy Bd 1984–87); chm Bd of Tstees American Assocs of the Royal Acad Tst 1983–; FIPA; *Books* Above Us The Waves (1953), The Admiralty Regrets (1956), Will Not We Fear (1961), The Broken Column (1966); *Recreations* writing, travelling, painting, music, reading; *Style*— James Benson Esq; ✉ Box 271, Sheffield, Mass 01257, USA

BENSON, Jane Elliott; LVO (1981), OBE (1991); da of Frank Elliott Allday, DL, TD (d 1970), and Agnete, *née* Kuhn; *b* 19 Dec 1937; *Educ* St James West Malvern, St Hilda's Coll Oxford (MA); *m* 23 July 1964, Robin Stephen Benson, s of Col Sir Rex Benson, DSO, MC, MVO (d 1969); 2 da (Lucinda b 1965, Camilla b 1968); *Career* Lady in Waiting to Princess Margaret 1963–; Courtauld Inst of Art: hon sec of friends 1972–84, appeal organiser 1983–90, sponsorship conslt 1990–; memb centenary appeal ctee St Hilda's Coll 1989–94; tstee Nat Portrait Gallery 1992–; patron Friends of Thomas Coram Fndn; *Recreations* tennis, gardening, travelling; *Clubs* Queens, Vanderbilt; *Style*— Mrs Jane Benson, LVO, OBE; ✉ 11 Kensington Gate, London W8 5NA

BENSON, Hon Michael D'Arcy; yr s of Baron Benson, GBE (Life Peer; d 1995), and Anne Virginia, *née* Macleod; *b* 23 May 1943; *Educ* Eton; *m* 1969, Rachel Candia Woods; 1 s (Charles D'Arcy b 1976), 2 da (Catherine Rachel b 1971, Harriet Anne b 1974); *Career* memb Research Dept L Messel & Co (Stockbrokers) 1965–67 (clerk on dealing floor 1963–65); Lazard Brothers & Co Ltd: joined 1967, dir Lazard Securities Ltd 1978 (head Private Client Dept and admin dir 1980), dir Lazard Brothers 1980–85, jt md Lazard Securities Ltd 1980, dir Lazard Securities (Jersey) Ltd 1981–85, dir Lazard Bros & Co (Jersey) Ltd 1981–85, dir Lazard Securities (HK) Ltd 1984–85, dir Lazard Bros & Co (Guernsey) Ltd 1984–85; md Scimitar Asset Management Ltd (London) 1985–92; dir: Standard Chartered Merchant Bank Ltd 1985, Gracechurch Nominees Ltd 1985–92, Scimitar Global Asset Management Ltd 1986–92, Scimitar Asset Management Asia Ltd 1986–92, Scimitar Asset Management (CI) Ltd 1986, Scimitar Worldwide Selection Fund Ltd 1986–92, Scimitar Asset Management (Singapore) Ltd 1988–92; chm: Scimitar Unit Trust Managers Ltd 1989–92, Scimitar Asset Management Ltd 1985–91; dir: Chartered Financial Holdings Ltd 1990, Capital House Investment Management 1992–93, Capital House Asia 1992–93, Capital House (Singapore) Ltd 1992–93; chief exec: Asia Pacific Region Invesco Group 1994–96, Invesco Global Asset Management 1996–; dir Invesco plc 1994–; *Style*— The Hon Michael Benson; ✉ 34 St John's Avenue, London SW15 6AN (☎ 0181 788 3828); Flat 28A, Tower Two, Tregunter Towers, Mid Levels, Hong Kong (☎ 00 852 2530 4274)

BENSON, Neil; s of Eric Benson, of Sheffield, and Vera, *née* Mower (d 1976); *b* 22 Oct 1954; *Educ* City GS Sheffield; *m* Joan Philippa; 2 s (Joseph Samuel b 29 Oct 1992, Rory Christopher b 15 March 1994), 1 da (Meredith Hope b 12 May 1995); *Career* The Star Sheffield 1974–79 (trainee reporter, sr reporter, news desk asst, news sub ed), Daily Express Manchester 1979–85 (features sub ed, sr news sub ed), Telegraph & Argus Bradford 1985–88 (features ed, asst ed), dep ed Chronicle & Echo Northampton Jan-June 1989, dep ed Telegraph & Argus Bradford 1989–91, ed and dir Coventry Evening Telegraph 1991–93, ed Newcastle Evening Chronicle 1993–96, exec ed daily newspapers Newcastle Chronicle & Journal Ltd 1996–; dep chm Guild of Eds Northern Region 1991–; *Recreations* golf, road running, supporting Leeds RLFC; *Style*— Neil Benson, Esq; ✉ Newcastle Evening Chronicle, Thomson House, Groat Market, Newcastle upon Tyne NE1 1ED (☎ 0191 232 7500, fax 0192 221 0172)

BENSON, Peter Charles; s of Robert Benson (d 1970), of The Anchorage, Baildon, Yorks, and Dorothy, *née* Cartman; *b* 16 June 1949; *Educ* Bradford GS, Univ of Birmingham (BSocSc); *Career* called to the Bar Middle Temple 1975; in practice NE Circuit 1975–; junior of NE Circuit 1979–80, recorder of the Crown Court 1995– (asst recorder 1991–95); tstee Henry Scott Fund; *Recreations* golf, reading, conversation; *Clubs* Ilkley Golf, Ilkley Bowling, Ganton Golf; *Style*— Peter Benson, Esq; ✉ Bygreen Cottage, Parish Ghyll Drive, Ilkley, Yorkshire (☎ 01943 601245); Fifth Floor, St Paul's House, Park Square, Leeds LS1 2ND (☎ 0113 245 5866, fax 0113 245 5807, car 0973 799708)

BENSON, Hon Peter Macleod; er s of Baron Benson, GBE (Life Peer; d 1995), and Anne Virginia, *née* Macleod; *b* 1940; *Educ* Eton, Univ of Edinburgh (MA); *m* 1, 1970 (m dis 1987), Hermione Jane Boulton; 1 s (Edward Henry b 1975), 2 da (Candida Jane b 1972, Hermione Emily b 1980); m 2, 3 Aug 1989, Señora Maria de los Angeles Martin, da of Don Victoriano Martinez Latasa; *Career* CA; ptnr Coopers & Lybrand; memb Bd of Mgmnt Royal NT 1991–; *Recreations* shooting, golf, theatre; *Clubs* Brooks's, Hurlingham, MCC, Tandridge Golf; *Style*— The Hon Peter Benson; ✉ 51 Riverside One, 22 Hester Road, London SW11 4AN (☎ and fax 0171 924 6200); Coopers & Lybrand, 1 Embankment Place, London WC2N 6NN (☎ 0171 583 5000, fax 0171 213 8600)

BENSON, Richard; s of Gordon Benson, of Doncaster, Yorkshire, and Pauline, *née* Hollingworth; *b* 13 Feb 1966; *Educ* Driffield Secdy Sch Yorkshire, King's Coll London (Gilbert & Levison Prize, BA, AKC), City Univ London (Dip Jour); *Career* on staff Independent 1990–91, freelance journalist 1991–92, ed The Face 1995– (assoc ed 1992–95); memb Press Ctee Br Fashion Cncl 1995–; memb Amnesty Int; *Books* Night Fever: Club Culture in The Face 1980–1997 (1997); *Recreations* football (Leeds Utd); *Style*— Richard Benson, Esq; ✉ The Face, Exmouth House, Pine Street, London EC1R 0JL (☎ 0171 837 7270, fax 0171 837 3906, e-mail RichardBenson@TheFace.co.uk)

BENSON, Richard Anthony; QC (1995); s of Douglas Arthur Benson (d 1983), and Muriel Alice, *née* Fairfield (d 1984); *b* 20 Feb 1946; *Educ* Wrekin Coll, Inns of Court Sch of Law; *m* 15 Sept 1967 (m dis 1996), Katherine Anne, da of Tom Anderson Smith, of Highfield, Whiteway, Gloucestershire; 1 s (Jake Alexander Fairfield b 22 Feb 1970), 2 da (Amy Rebecca b 26 April 1972, Chloe Kate b 25 Aug 1981); *Career* called to the Bar Inner Temple 1974, in practice Midland & Oxford Circuit 1974–, recorder 1995–;

Recreations flying, offshore cruising, drama, after dinner speaking; *Clubs* Northampton & County, British Airways Flying, Bar Yacht; *Style*— Richard Benson, Esq, QC; ✉ 36 Bedford Row, London WC2R 4JH (☎ 0171 421 8000)

BENSON, His Hon Judge; Richard Stuart Alistair; *b* 23 Nov 1943; *Educ* Univ of Nottingham (BA Politics); *Career* called to the Bar Gray's Inn 1968, in practice Midland & Oxford Circuit 1968–93, recorder 1991–93, circuit judge (Midland and Oxford Circuit) 1993–; *Style*— His Hon Judge Benson; ✉ 1 High Pavement, Nottingham NG1 1HF (☎ 0115 941 8218)

BENSON, Ross; s of Stanley Ross Benson, of St John's Wood, London, and Mabel, *née* Greaves; b 29 Sept 1948; *Educ* Sydney GS, Gordonstoun; *m* 1, 1968 (m dis 1974), Beverly Jane, da of K A Rose; 1 s (Dorian Ross b 1974); m 2, 1975 (m dis 1986), Zoë, da of G D Bennett; 1 da (Anouchka b 1975); m 3, 27 Nov 1987, Ingrid, da of Dr Eric Canton Seward; 1 da (Arabella b 1989); *Career* journalist and broadcaster; dep diary ed: Daily Mail 1968–71, Sunday Express 1971–72; Daily Express: joined 1973, foreign news ed 1975–76, specialist writer 1976–78, US W Coast corr 1978–82, chief foreign corr 1982–87, chief feature writer 1987–88, diary ed 1988–96, sr writer and columnist 1996–; Int Reporter of the Year Br Press Awards 1983; *Books* The Good, the Bad and the Bubbly (with George Best), Paul McCartney: Behind the Myth, Charles: The Untold Story; *Recreations* skiing, motor racing, fishing; *Style*— Ross Benson, Esq; ✉ c/o Daily Express, Ludgate House, 245 Blackfriars Road, London SE1 9UX (☎ 0171 928 8000)

BENSON, Stephen; s of A Benson; *b* 7 June 1943; *Educ* Highgate, Magdalen Coll Oxford; *m* 1966, Jacqueline, *née* Russell; 3 da; *Career* dir: Davidson Pearce 1974–89, Dewe Rogerson 1989–90; head corp fundraising ActionAid 1990–92, dir of Appeal Trinity Hospice Clapham 1992–; *Recreations* music, running; *Style*— Stephen Benson, Esq; ✉ 8 Laurier Rd, London NW5 (☎ 0171 485 0287)

BENT, Dr Margaret Hilda; da of Horace Bassington, and Miriam, *née* Simpson; *b* 23 Dec 1940; *Educ* Haberdashers' Aske's, Girton Coll Cambridge (Organ scholar, MusB, MA, PhD); *Career* sr lectr Goldsmiths' Coll London 1974–75 (lectr 1972–74), prof Brandeis Univ 1976–81 (visiting prof 1975–76, chm Dept of Music 1978–79 and 1980–81), prof Princeton Univ 1981–92 (chm Dept of Music 1986–90), sr res fell All Souls Coll Oxford 1992–; Fowler Hamilton visiting res fell Christ Church Coll Oxford 1990–91, Guggenheim fell 1983–84, Dent medal Int Musicological Soc 1979; hon memb American Acad of Arts and Sciences 1994, memb American Musicological Soc (pres 1984–86); FBA 1993; author of numerous pubns and articles on late-medieval music; *Style*— Dr Margaret Bent, FBA; ✉ All Souls College, Oxford OX1 4AL (☎ 01865 279379, fax 01865 279299)

BENTALL, (Leonard) Edward; s of (Leonard Edward) Rowan Bentall, DL (d 1993), and his 1 w, Adelia Elizabeth, *née* Hawes (d 1986); ggs of Frank Bentall, Fndr of Bentalls (d 1923); *b* 26 May 1939; *Educ* Stowe; *m* 1964, Wendy Ann, *née* Daniel; 3 da; *Career* articled clerk Dixon Wilson Tubbs & Gillett 1958–64, CA 1964; Bentalls PLC: joined 1965, merchandise controller 1968, merchandise dir Household and Furnishing Gp 1972, merchandise dir 1974, jt md 1977, md 1978, chm and md 1982, chief exec 1990–92, chm 1990–; non-exec dir: Associated Independent Stores Ltd 1979–82, Kingston Hosp Tst 1991–, Radio Riverside Ltd 1996–; govr: Brooklands Tech Coll 1981–90 (vice chm Governing Body and chm Fin Ctee 1989–90), Kingston Coll of FE, Kingston GS; tstee and memb Exec Ctee Kingston and Dist Steadfast Sea Cadet Corps (chm 1993–); vice pres Surrey PGA, pres Textile Benevolent Assoc 1991–95; FInstD; *Clubs* MCC, Surrey CCC, Saints and Sinners, Winnowing, Naval; *Style*— Edward Bentall, Esq; ✉ Bentalls PLC, Anstee House, Wood Street, Kingston upon Thames, Surrey KT1 1TS (☎ 0181 546 2002); Runnymede, Sandpit Hall Road, Chobham, Surrey GU24 8AN (☎ 01276 858256)

BENTALL, John Anthony Charles (Tony); s of Frank Bentall (d 1975), of Beckenham, Kent, and Freda, *née* Hooper (d 1964); *b* 16 Jan 1929; *Educ* Dulwich, Lincoln Coll Oxford (BA Jurisprudence, MA); *m* 23 March 1963, Brenda Kathryn, da of Francis Scaife; 2 c (Andrew Christopher b 17 Feb 1969, Suzanna Kathryn b 20 July 1972); *Career* Nat Serv RA 2 Lt 1947–49; qualified chartered accountant 1956, audit mangr Layton-Bennett Billingham & Co 1961–63; ptnr: Viney Price & Goodyear 1963–70, Viney Merretts 1970–80 (following merger), Binder Hamlyn 1980–89 (following merger); ret 1989; memb Appeal Ctee (Disciplinary Scheme) ICAEW 1980–; Freeman City of London 1978, memb Worshipful Co of Chartered Accountants in England and Wales; memb second XI Kent CCC 1947–48; FCA 1966 (ACA 1956); *Recreations* charitable matters, golf, theatre going, hill walking, gardening; *Clubs* East India, Vincent's (Oxford), MCC; *Style*— Tony Bentall, Esq; ✉ 5 Briary Lodge, 56 The Avenue, Beckenham, Kent BR3 5ES (☎ 0181 658 0827)

BENTATA, (Morris) David Albert; s of Robert Victor Bentata (d 1961), of Didsbury, Manchester, and Joyce Ethel, *née* Weinberg; *b* 22 Oct 1913; *Educ* Blundell's, ChCh Oxford (BA, MA); *m* 20 Feb 1964, Alison Jessica, da of Christopher Henley Boyle Gilroy, of Boundstone, nr Farnham, Surrey; 1 s (Robert b 5 Nov 1968), 1 da (Victoria b 10 Feb 1966); *Career* Nat Serv: enlisted N Staffs Regt 1957, OCS Eaton Hall and Mons 1957–58, cmmnd 2 Lt Intelligence Corps 1958, serv BAOR 1958–59, cmmnd Lt Intelligence Corps (TA) 1959, RARO 1963; md M Bentata & Son Ltd 1962–67, fndr int mangr Hill Samuel & Co Ltd 1969–72 (investmt analyst 1968–69), int investmt mangr Charterhouse Japhet Ltd 1972–79, dir Charterhouse Investment Management Ltd 1986–88 (int dir 1979–86), md Charterhouse Portfolio Managers Ltd 1986–88, fndr chm Bentata Associates Ltd 1988–; dir: Pegasus Financial Holdings Ltd 1989–92, Murray European Investment Trust plc (formerly European Project Investment Trust plc) 1990–, Newport Capital Ltd 1991–, Marcher Diagnostics plc 1996–; chm: Sage Partners Ltd 1991–95, Marine & Mercantile Securities plc 1996– (dir 1994–), MMS Petroleum Services Ltd (formerly Gandalf Explorers International Ltd) 1996– (fndr fin dir 1989); elected Lloyd's underwriter 1976; vice chm and chm Stoke d'Abernon Residents' Assoc 1969–77, memb Ctee Oxshott Cons Assoc 1969–72; memb The Sherlock Holmes Soc of London (memb Cncl 1992); Liveryman Worshipful Co of Feltmakers 1983 (Steward 1989–91, memb Ct of Assts 1993), Freeman City of London 1984; AIIMR 1969, FInstD 1988, FRGS 1988, FRSA 1995; *Recreations* full-bore rifle shooting, travel, dancing the minuet (Covent Garden Minuet Co); *Clubs* City of London; *Style*— David Bentata, Esq

BENTHALL, Jonathan Charles Mackenzie; s of Sir (Arthur) Paul Benthall, KBE (d 1992), and Mary Lucy, *née* Pringle (d 1988); *b* 12 Sept 1941; *Educ* Eton (King's scholar), King's Coll Cambridge (MA); *m* 23 Oct 1975, Hon Zamira Menuhin, da of Rt Hon the Lord Menuhin, OM, KBE, *qv*; 2 s (Dominic b 1976, William b 1981); *Career* sec ICA 1971–73, dir RAI 1974–; ed Anthropology Today 1985– (RAIN 1974–84), hon research fell Dept of Anthropology UCL 1994–; Save the Children Fund: former memb UK Child Care Ctee, memb Cncl, memb Assembly 1990–, memb Overseas Advsy Ctee 1990–; memb Bd Int Broadcasting Tst 1991–95; Anthropology in Media Award American Anthropological Assoc 1993; Chevalier de l'Ordre des Arts et des Lettres France 1973; memb Assoc of Social Anthropologists 1983; *Books* Science and Technology in Art Today (1972), The Body Electric - Patterns of Western Industrial Culture (1976), Disasters, Relief and the Media (1993); *Recreations* listening to music, swimming, mountain-walking; *Clubs* Athenaeum; *Style*— Mr Jonathan Benthall; ✉ 212 Hammersmith Grove, London W6 7HG; RAI, 50 Fitzroy St, London W1P 5HS (☎ 0171 387 0455, fax 0171 383 4235)

BENTHAM, Howard Lownds; QC (1996); s of William Foster Bentham (d 1982), and Elsie, *née* Lownds (d 1982); *b* 26 Feb 1948; *Educ* Malvern, Univ of Liverpool (LLB); *m* Elizabeth, da of Robert Pickering Owen; 1 s (Robert b 29 Dec 1982); *Career* called to the Bar Gray's Inn 1970, recorder 1996– (asst recorder 1985); *Recreations* watching wildlife, rebuilding, driving, racing Lotus cars; *Style*— Howard Bentham, Esq, QC; ✉ Peel Court Chambers, 45 Hardman Street, Manchester M3 3HA (☎ 0161 832 3791)

BENTHAM, Prof Richard Walker; s of Richard Hardy Bentham (d 1980), of Woodbridge, Suffolk, and Ellen Walker, *née* Fisher (d 1983); *b* 26 June 1930; *Educ* Campbell Coll Belfast, Trinity Coll Dublin (BA, LLB, Julian Prize); *m* 16 May 1956, Stella Winifred, da of Henry George Matthews (d 1969), of Hobart, Tasmania; 1 da (Stella); *Career* called to the Bar Middle Temple 1955; lectr in law: Univ of Tasmania Hobart 1955–57, Univ of Sydney NSW 1957–61; visiting scholar UCL 1961–62, BP Legal Dept 1961–83 (dep legal advsr 1979–83); Univ of Dundee: prof of petroleum and mineral law until 1991 (prof emeritus 1991), dir Centre for Petroleum and Mineral Law Studies 1983–90; pubns in learned journals in the UK and Overseas; govr Heatherton House Sch Amersham 1969–83; memb: Bd Scot Cncl for International Arbitration 1988–, Cncl ICC Inst of Int Business Law and Practice 1988–95; Br nominated memb IEA Dispute Settlement Centre's Panel of Arbitrators 1989–; tstee: Petroleum and Mineral Law Educn Tst 1991–, Russian Oil and Gas Law Project 1991–; memb: Int Law Assoc (memb Cncl 1980–90), Int Bar Assoc 1978; FRSA 1986; *Books* State Petroleum Corporations (with W G R Smith, 1987), Precedents in Petroleum Law (with W G R Smith, 1988); *Recreations* cricket, military history; *Clubs* Dundee Univ; *Style*— Prof Richard Bentham; ✉ Centre for Petroleum and Mineral Law and Policy, The University of Dundee, Park Place, Dundee, Scotland (☎ 01382 344300, fax 01382 322578)

BENTLEY, (Henry) Brian; s of John Clarence Hayes Bentley (d 1967), and Emily Mary, *née* Church; *b* 9 Aug 1933; *Educ* Castleford GS, Open Univ (BA), CNAA (MPhil), Univ of Leeds (MEd); *m* 30 Nov 1957, Sylvia Mary, da of William Drabble (d 1984), of Thrybergh, Rotherham; 1 s (Phillip John Henry b 1971), 2 da (Alison Deborah (Mrs Clark) b 1960, Susan Lesley (Mrs Jackson) b 1965); *Career* Nat Serv RAF served various RAF hosps 1955–57; trained nurse Rotherham Hosp 1951–55, RGN 1954; princ Sch of Radiography Gen Infirmary at Leeds 1968–90 (radiographer 1957–68, Archibald Reid medal 1964, Stanley Melville Meml lectr 1979, Coll and Soc of Radiographers Gold medal (75th anniversary celebrations) 1995); Univ of Leeds: hon lectr Faculty of Med 1989–, pt/t res offr Academic Unit of Public Health Med 1994–96, head Div of Imaging and Radiotherapy Sci Sch of Health Scis Faculty of Med 1996–; pt/t res fell Div of Imaging and Radiotherapy S Bank Univ London 1996–; memb: NETRHA Working Paper 10 Implementation Gp, DOH Working Party Coll of Health, Ctee Yorks Branch Soc of Radiographers (chm 1972–74 and 1978–80), Cncl Coll of Radiographers 1974–84 (pres 1981–82); res fell Royal Coll of Radiologists and Kodak 1984–87; external examiner Univ of Dublin, examiner Coll of Radiographers (various bds); examiner: MSc degree in Imaging Technology Univ of Liverpool, BSc (Hons) Radiography South Bank Univ and Guy's Hospital London, PhD City Univ London 1994; dir of education NETRHA Charterhouse Coll of Radiography 1990–93; memb: Cncl and Senate City Univ 1992–93, Mgmnt Bd St Bartholomew's and Royal London Hosps Schs of Nursing and Midwifery 1992–93; ed-in-chief Radiography int jl of diagnostic imaging and radiation therapy 1994–; memb Garforth St Mary's PCC 1985–90 (lay chm 1994–); FCR 1966, FRIPHH 1985, MSPH 1994; *Books* A Textbook of Radiographic Science (editor 1986); contrib many papers to learned jls and has presented numerous papers at scientific confs; *Recreations* traction engine rallying, gardening, church choir; *Style*— H Brian Bentley, Esq; ✉ Fairfield, Aberford Rd, Garforth, Leeds LS25 1PZ (☎ 0113 286 2276, fax 0113 287 6100); Academic Unit of Public Health Medicine, The University of Leeds, 30–32 Hyde Terrace, Leeds LS2 9LN (☎ 0113 233 4828)

BENTLEY, David Edward; *see:* Gloucester, Bishop of

BENTLEY, His Hon Judge David Ronald; QC (1984); s of Edgar Norman Bentley (d 1982), and Hilda, *née* Thirlwall (d 1959); *b* 24 Feb 1942; *Educ* King Edward VII Sch Sheffield, Univ Coll London (LLB, LLM), Univ of Sheffield (PhD); *m* 1978, Christine Elizabeth, da of Alec Stewart (d 1978); 2 s (Thomas b 1985, David b 1989); *Career* called to the Bar Gray's Inn 1969 (Macaskie scholar), recorder of the Crown Ct 1985–88, circuit judge (NE Circuit) 1988–; *Recreations* legal history, literature, cinema, dogs; *Style*— His Hon Judge David Bentley, QC; ✉ c/o North Eastern Circuit Office, West Riding House, Albion St, Leeds LS1 5AA

BENTLEY, The Ven Frank William Henry; s of Nowell James Bentley (d 1945), and May Sophia, *née* Gribble (d 1991); *b* 4 March 1934; *Educ* Yeovil Boys GS, King's Coll London (AKC); *m* 1, 28 Sept 1957, Muriel (d 1958), da of Maj Lionel Stewart Bland (d 1983); 1 s (Michael b 1958); m 2, 29 Oct 1960, Yvonne Mary, da of Bernard Henry Wilson (d 1991); 2 s (Stephen b 1962, Richard b 1971), 1 da (Frances b 1964); *Career* curate Shepton Mallet 1958–62, rector Kingsdon with Podymore Milton 1962–66; curate in charge: Yeovilton 1962–66, Babcary 1964–66; vicar Wiveliscombe 1966–76, rural dean Tone 1973–76, vicar St John in Bedwardine 1976–84; rural dean Martley and Worcester West 1979–84, hon canon Worcester Cathedral 1981–84, archdeacon of Worcester (and residentiary cathedral canon) 1984–; chaplain to HM The Queen 1994–; memb General Synod 1986–95; *Recreations* gardening, motoring; *Style*— The Ven the Archdeacon of Worcester; ✉ Archdeacon's House, 56 Battenhall Rd, Worcester WR5 2BQ (☎ 01905 764446); Diocesan Office, The Old Palace, Deansway, Worcester WR1 2JE (☎ 01905 20537)

BENTLEY, Prof George; s of George Bentley (d 1964), and Doris, *née* Blagden; *b* 19 Jan 1936; *Educ* Rotherham GS, Univ of Sheffield (MB ChB, ChM); *m* 4 June 1960, Ann Gillian, da of Herbert Hutchings (d 1953); 2 s (Paul b 4 March 1964, Stephen b 2 March 1966), 1 da (Sarah b 2 Dec 1962); *Career* lectr in anatomy Univ of Birmingham 1961–62, surgical registrar Sheffield Royal Infirmary 1963–65, orthopaedic registrar Orthopaedic Hosp Oswestry 1965–67, sr orthopaedic registrar Nuffield Orthopaedic Centre Oxford 1967–69, instr in orthopaedics Univ of Pittsburgh USA 1969–70, Univ of Oxford 1970–76 (lectr, sr lectr, clinical reader in orthopaedics); prof of orthopaedics: Univ of Liverpool 1976–82, Univ of London 1982–, Inst of Orthopaedics; hon conslt orthopaedic surgeon Royal Nat Orthopaedic and Middx Hosps 1982–, dir Inst of Orthopaedics UC and Middx Sch of Med 1992–; pres Br Orthopaedic Assoc 1991–92 (vice pres 1990–91), memb Cncl RCS 1992–; FRCS 1968; *Books* Mercer's Orthopaedic Surgery (jt ed, 1983, new edn 1996), Rob and Smith Operative Surgery - Orthopaedics Vols I and II (conslt ed, 1991); *Recreations* music, tennis, horology; *Style*— Prof George Bentley; ✉ 120 Fishpool St, St Albans, Herts AL3 4RX (☎ 01727 51600); University Department of Orthopaedics, Institute of Orthopaedics, Royal National Orthopaedic Hospital, Stanmore, Middlesex HA7 4LP (☎ 0181 954 2300 ext 531/532, fax 0181 954 3036)

BENTLEY, Michael John; s of Leopold John Bentley (d 1987), and Ann Margaret, *née* MacGillivray (d 1968); *b* 23 Nov 1933; *Educ* Morrisons Acad Crieff Perthshire; *m* 24 June 1961, Sally Jacqueline, da of Stanley Bertram James Hogan, of Bexhill-on-Sea, Sussex; 4 s (Jeremy b 26 March 1963, Rupert b 29 April 1966, Andrew b 4 March 1968, David b 27 Aug 1970); *Career* Lehman Brothers (investmt bankers NY) 1959; S G Warburg & Co Ltd: joined 1962, dir 1968–76; dir Mercury Securities Ltd 1974–76, dir and exec vice pres Korea Merchant Banking Corporation Seoul 1977–79, dir Lazard Bros & Co Ltd 1977–80, jt vice chm J Henry Schroder Wagg & Co Ltd 1980–85, dir Schroders plc 1980–83 (gp md corp fin 1983–85), chm Electra Management Services Ltd 1986–90, dep chm and chief exec Electra Investment Trust plc 1986–89 (jt dep chm 1989–91); dep chm Electra Kingsway Managers Holdings Ltd 1989–90; dir: Campbell Lutyens Hudson & Co Ltd 1991–94, Campbell Lutyens International Ltd 1994–, Celltech Group plc 1991–,

Mezzanine Management Ltd 1991–, M A Media Ltd 1994–; chm: Environment Investment Co Ltd (Jersey) 1994–, TSG Investment Management Ltd (Bermuda) 1993–, M J Bentley & Co Ltd 1991–; chm: Fin Ctee London Borough of Islington 1968–71, Islington Nat Savings Ctee 1968–71; FCA 1963 (ACA 1958); *Recreations* music, opera, sailing, gardening; *Clubs* Links (New York); *Style*— Michael Bentley, Esq; ✉ Campbell Lutyens & Co Ltd, 5 Clifford St, London W1X 1RB (☎ 0171 439 7191, fax 0171 437 0153)

BENTLEY, Sir William; KCMG (1985, CMG 1977); s of Lawrence Bentley, and Elsie Jane Bentley; *b* 15 Feb 1927; *Educ* Bury HS, Univ of Manchester, Wadham Coll Oxford, Coll of Europe Bruges; *m* 1950, Karen Ellen, *née* Christensen; 3 da, 2 s; *Career* joined FO 1952, head Far Eastern Dept FCO 1974–76, ambass to The Philippines 1976–81, high cmmr to Malaysia 1981–83, ambass to Norway 1983–87; chm: Coflexip Stena Offshore Holdings Ltd, Duco Ltd, Soc of Pensions Conslts; *Recreations* fly fishing; *Clubs* Brook's, Roehampton; *Style*— Sir William Bentley, KCMG; ✉ 48 Bathgate Rd, London SW19; Les Terriers, Landivy, 53190, France

BENTON, Joseph Edward (Joe); JP, MP (Lab) Bootle (majority 29,442); s of Thomas Benton, and Agnes Benton; *b* 28 Sept 1933; *Educ* St Monica's Secdy Sch, Bootle Tech Coll; *m* Doris; 4 da; *Career* apprentice fitter 1949, Nat Serv RAF 1955; sometime personnel mangr Pacific Steam Navigation Co, with Girobank 1982–90; MP (Lab) Bootle Nov 1990–, memb Select Ctee on Energy 1991–, NW regional Lab whip 1994–; cncllr Derby Ward Sefton Borough Cncl 1970–90 (ldr Lab Gp 1985–90), chm Bd of Govrs Hugh Baird Coll of Technol; memb Inst of Linguists, affiliate memb Inst of Personnel Mgmnt; *Recreations* reading, listening to classical music, squash, swimming; *Style*— Joe Benton, Esq, JP, MP; ✉ House of Commons, London SW1A 0AA

BENTON, Kenneth Carter; CMG (1966); s of William Alfred Benton (d 1944), and Amy Adeline, *née* Kirton; *b* 4 March 1909; *Educ* Wolverhampton GS, London Univ; *m* 1938, (Winifred) Peggie (d 1992), da of Maj Gen Charles Pollock, CB, CBE, DSO (d 1929); 1 s, 2 decd step s; *Career* HM Foreign Serv: Vienna, Riga, Madrid (twice), Rome (twice), Lima, cncllr Rio 1966–68, ret; *Books* eleven thrillers, two historical novels; *Recreations* painting, writing; *Clubs* Detection; *Style*— Kenneth Benton, Esq, CMG; ✉ 2 Jubilee Terrace, Chichester, W Sussex PO19 1XL (☎ 01243 787148)

BENTON, Peter Faulkner; s of Shirley Faulkner Benton (d 1985), of India and Haslemere, Surrey, and Hilda Dorothy Benton (d 1994); *b* 6 Oct 1934; *Educ* Oundle, Queens' Coll Cambridge (MA); *m* 1959, Ruth Stansfeld, da of Robert Stanley Cobb, MC, of Nairobi and Kidlington, Oxon; 2 s (Robert, Thomas), 3 da (Sarah, Juliet, Katherine); *Career* co dir and business conslt specialising in strategy and IT; special advsr on IT to EEC 1983–85; chm Euro Practice Nolan Norton and Co 1984–87; dir: Turing Inst 1985–, Singer and Friedlander Ltd 1983–89, Tandata Hldgs 1983–89; md then dep chm Br Telecom 1978–83; memb: Bd PO 1978–81, Gp Bd Gallaher Ltd 1973–77, Bd McKinsey & Co London and Chicago 1964–71; chm: Identica Ltd 1992–93, Enterprise Support Group 1993–; dir gen BIM (now Inst of Mgmnt) 1987–92, chm Enfield Health Authy 1986–92, ind memb Br Library Advsy Cncl 1988–93; memb: Indust Devpt Advsy Bd 1988–94, Supervisory Bd Hiross Holdings AG (Vienna) 1992–94, Bd Woodside Communications Ltd 1995–; advsr Arthur Andersen 1992–; gen chm World Bank Confs on Catastrophe 1988–89, chm Visiting Gp Inst of Systems Engineering and Informatics (Ispra) 1993, chm EFS & T Seminar Science in European Public Policy 1994; Olin lectr Univ of Oxford 1991, Adam Smith lectr Kirkcaldy 1991; CIMgt; *Publications* Riding the Whirlwind (1990), articles on science, information technology and management; *Recreations* reading, conversation; *Clubs* Athenaeum, United Oxford and Cambridge Univ, The Pilgrims, Horatian, Blythe Sappers, Highgate Literary and Scientific, Highgate Golf; *Style*— Peter Benton, Esq; ✉ Northgate House, Highgate Hill, London N6 5HD (☎ 0181 341 1122, fax 0181 341 1133)

BENTOVIM, Dr Arnon; s of Zvi Harry Bentovim (d 1989), and Gladys Rachel, *née* Carengold (d 1985); *b* 24 July 1936; *Educ* St Thomas' Hosp London (MB BS, DPM); *m* 1, 2 April 1958 (m dis 1987), Cecily Anne; 1 da (Ayalah b 1970); m 2, 1989, Marianne; *Career* psychoanalyst, family and child psychiatrist; registrar Maudsley Hosp 1962–66, sr registrar and conslt child psychiatrist Hosps for Sick Children Gt Ormond St 1966–94, conslt Tavistock Clinic 1975–94, conslt specialist advsr to House of Commons Select Ctee 1978–79, conslt Huntercombe Manor Hosp; fndr: CIBA Fndn Study Gp, Trg Advsy Gp for the Sexual Abuse of Children, first sexual treatment prog in UK at Hosps for Sick Children 1981–; pubns on: child psychiatry, family therapy, aspects of child abuse; fndr memb: Assoc for Family Therapy, Br Assoc for the Prevention of Child Abuse and Neglect, Inst of Family Therapy; FRCPsych 1966; *Books* Family Therapy, Complimentary Frameworks of Theory and Practice (1984–89), Child Sexual Abuse within the Family - Assessment & Treatment (ed, 1988), Trauma Organised Systems - Physical & Sexual Abuse in the Family (1993); *Recreations* music (particularly jazz), theatre, opera, travel; *Style*— Dr Arnon Bentovim; ✉ Great Ormond Street Children's Hospital, 34 Great Ormond St, London WC1N 3JH (☎ 0171 405 9200); London Child & Family Consultation Service, 10 Harley Street, London W1N 1AA (☎ 0171 467 8322)

BENYAMINA, HE Ahmed; *b* 4 Jan 1953; *Educ* Ecole Nationale d'Administration Algiers; *m*; 2 c; *Career* Algerian diplomat; desk offr Strategic Affrs and Disarmement Political Affrs Dept UN 1979–81 (desk offr Int Orgn Dept 1978–79), first sec Algerian Embassy Havana 1981–84, cnsllr Perm Mission of Algeria in NY 1984–89, advsr to Min for Foreign Affrs Jan-Nov 1990, head of Policy and Planning Dept 1990–92; ambass: to Pakistan 1992–96, to Ct of St James's 1996–; *Style*— HE Mr Ahmed Benyamina; ✉ Algerian Embassy, 54 Holland Park, London W11 3RS (☎ 0171 221 7800, fax 0171 221 0448)

BENYON, Thomas Yates; s of Capt Thomas Yates Benyon (d 1958, s of Capt Thomas Yates Benyon (d 1893) and Hon Christina Philippa Agnes, OBE, da of 11 Baron North, JP), and his 2 wife, Joan Ida Walters (d 1982); *b* 13 Aug 1942; *Educ* Wellington Sch Somerset, RMA Sandhurst; *m* 1968, (Olivia) Jane, da of Humphrey Scott Plummer by his w, Hon Pamela, *née* Balfour, da of 2 Baron Kinross, KC; 2 s, 2 da; *Career* former Lt Scots Gds, served Kenya, Muscat; MP (C) Abingdon 1979–83; dir Bucks Purchasing Authy; chm: Assoc of Lloyd's Membs 1982–86, Milton Keynes Health Authy 1990–; dir Soc of Names; chm Guild of Shareholders; *Recreations* hunting, music; *Clubs* RAC, Pratt's; *Style*— Thomas Benyon, Esq; ✉ The Old Rectory, Adstock, Buckingham, Bucks MK18 2HY (☎ 01296 714255)

BENYON, Sir William Richard; kt (1994), DL (1970); s of Vice Adm Richard Benyon, CB, CBE (d 1968, 2 s of Sir John Shelley, 9 Bt, JP, DL, a distant cous of the Shelley Bts who produced the poet, and Marion, da of Richard Benyon), and Eve (d 1995), twin da of Rt Rev Lord William Cecil, sometime Bp of Exeter (2 s of 3 Marquess of Salisbury); the Adm changed his name to Benyon by Deed Poll on inheriting the Benyon estates of his cous Sir Henry Benyon, Bt; *b* 17 Jan 1930; *Educ* RNC Dartmouth; *m* 1957, Elizabeth Ann, da of Vice Adm Ronald Hallifax, CB, CBE (d 1943), of The Red House, Shedfield, Hants; 2 s (Richard, Edward); 3 da (Catherine, Mary, Susannah); *Career* served RN 1947–56; Courtaulds Ltd 1957–67; MP (C): Buckingham 1970–83, Milton Keynes 1983–92; PPS to Paul Channon as Min for Housing 1972–74, oppn whip 1974–77, memb Exec 1922 Ctee 1982–89; JP Berks 1962–77; chm: Peabody Tst 1992, Ernest Cook Tst 1992; High Sheriff for Co of Berks 1995; *Clubs* Boodle's, Pratt's, Beefsteak; *Style*— Sir William Benyon, DL; ✉ Englefield House, Englefield, Reading, Berks RG7 5EN (☎ 0118 930 2221, fax 0118 930 3226)

BENZIE, Alan Athol Emslie; s of Athol Emslie Benzie (d 1976), of Wilmslow, and Helen Margaret, *née* Ritchie (d 1980); *b* 5 May 1947; *Educ* Lindisfarne Coll N Wales; *m* 3 June 1971, Penny Jane, da of Albert Victor Maynard; 2 s (Toby b 11 Aug 1976, Ollie b 22 Sept 1984), 1 da (Annie b 13 April 1973); *Career* articled clerk Thornton Baker 1964–69; Peat Marwick Mitchell: Manchester 1969–71, Johannesburg 1971–74, London 1974–75; KPMG 1975–: ptnr 1977, head NW region corp fin 1984–95, managing ptnr Manchester 1989–95, memb UK Planning and Strategy Ctee, UK gen ptnr 1995–, sr regnl ptnr 1996– (dep sr regnl ptnr 1995–96); former bd memb Manchester YMCA (former hon treas), memb East Manchester Partnership; licensed insolvency practitioner; FCA (ACA 1970); *Recreations* fishing, shooting, golf, gardening; *Clubs* St James's, Knutsford Golf, Birdsgrove Fly Fishing; *Style*— Alan Benzie, Esq; ✉ KPMG, St James' Square, Manchester M2 6DS (☎ 0161 838 4000)

BERESFORD, Bruce; s of Leslie Beresford (d 1989), of Sydney, Aust, and Lona Doreen, *née* Warr (d 1987); *b* 16 Aug 1940; *Educ* The Kings Sch Parramatta NSW, Sydney Univ (BA); *m* 1, 1965, Rhcisin Harrison; 2 s (Benjamin b 22 Feb 1967, Adam b 2 Sept 1971), 1 da (Cordelia b 14 April 1969); m 2, 1988, Virginia Duigan; 1 da (Trilby b 9 June 1986); *Career* film director; formerly with Australian Broadcasting Commission (ABC) Sydney 1957–59, film ed Enugu Nigeria 1963–65, prodn offr BFI 1966–71; *Theatre* stage direction incl: Girl of the Golden West (Spoleto Festival) 1985, Elektra (South Australian Opera Co) 1991; *Films* features incl: Adventures of Barry Mckenzie (co-scriptwriter) 1971, Barry Mckenzie Holds His Own (co-scriptwriter) 1973, Side By Side 1975, Don's Party 1975, Getting of Wisdom 1977, Money Movers 1978, Breaker Morant (scriptwriter) 1979, Puberty Blues 1981, The Club 1981, Tender Mercies 1982, King David 1985, Fringe Dwellers (scriptwriter) 1986, Crimes of the Heart 1987, Her Alibi 1988, Driving Miss Daisy 1989, Mister Johnson 1990, Black Robe 1991, Rich in Love 1991, A Good Man in Africa 1992; *Awards* Aust Film Inst Awards: for best dir Don's Party and Breaker Morant, for best script Fringe Dwellers and Breaker Morant; Academy Awards: nominations for Tender Mercies and Breaker Morant, winner of four awards incl best picture for Driving Miss Daisy; *Recreations* skiing, surfing; *Style*— Bruce Beresford, Esq; ✉ c/o William Morris Agency, 151 El Cimino Drive, Beverly Hills, CA 90212, USA

BERESFORD, Christopher Charles Howard; s of (Richard) Marcus Beresford (d 1968), of Oundle, and Diana Katharine, *née* Howard; *b* 9 July 1946; *Educ* The Dragon Sch, Rugby, Trinity Coll Cambridge (MA); *m* 5 May 1973, (Philippa) Susan, da of Dennis Yates (d 1968); 1 s (Nicholas b 1979), 2 da (Antonia b 1975, Fiona b 1977); *Career* CA; ptnr KPMG 1981–; treas Inst of Business Ethics 1993–; Liveryman Worshipful Co of Grocers; FCA, MSI; *Recreations* skiing, tennis, shooting, badminton, bridge; *Clubs* City Livery, Ski Club of GB; *Style*— Christopher Beresford, Esq; ✉ KPMG, 8 Salisbury Square, London EC4Y 8BB (☎ 0171 311 8997, fax 0171 311 8748, telec 8811541 KPMGLO)

BERESFORD, Elisabeth; da of J D Beresford (the novelist), and Beatrice, *née* Roskams; *b* Paris; *Educ* St Mary's Hall Brighton, Brighton & Hove HS; *m* 1 s (b 1956), 1 da (b 1951); *Career* author; formerly: shorthand typist CCO, ghost writer, reporter/interviewer Today and Woman's Hour (BBC Radio 4); creator: The Wombles (books and BBC TV series) 1973, The Adventures of Dawdle (ITV series) 1996; numerous other children's books published; Tokyo video award (for film Rosebud), Puffin award (for selling a million copies); dir: Walker Books, Craigie Robertson Ltd; chm Aurignoco Ltd Media Services; fndr The Alderney Youth Tst 1982; *Recreations* gardening, entertaining, filming; *Style*— Ms Elisabeth Beresford; ✉ Alderney, CI; c/o Juvenilia, Avington, Winchester, Hants SO21 1DB (☎ 01962 78656)

BERESFORD, Marcus de la Poer; s of Anthony de la Poer Beresford, TD, of Harrow-on-the-Hill, Middx, and Mary, *née* Canning; *b* 15 May 1942; *Educ* Harrow, St John's Coll Cambridge (MA); *m* 25 Sept 1965, Jean, da of H T Kitchener, of Shepreth, Cambs; 2 s (Thomas, William); *Career* Smiths Industs 1960–83 (operating gp md 1979–83), dir and gen mangr Lucas Electronics & Systems 1983–85, md Siemens Plessey Controls Ltd 1985–92, dir Siemens plc 1991–92, dir GKN plc and md GKN Industrial Servs 1992–; non-exec dir CAMAS plc; Freeman City of London 1963, Liveryman Worshipful Co of Skinners; CIMgt, FIEE, MIMechE, CEng; *Recreations* golf; *Style*— Marcus Beresford, Esq; ✉ GKN plc, 7 Cleveland Row, London SW1A 1DB (☎ 0171 930 2424, fax 0171 930 3255)

BERESFORD, Lord Patrick Tristram de la Poer; s of 7 Marquess of Waterford (d 1934); *b* 16 June 1934; *Educ* Eton, RMA Sandhurst; *m* 1964 (m dis 1971), Mrs Julia Carey, da of Col Thomas Cromwell Williamson, DSO (d 1987); 1 s, 1 da; *Career* Capt RHG (ret); bloodstock agent; Chef d'Équipe Br 3 Day Event Team 1985–92, equestrian tour dir Abercrombie and Kent 1993–; *Clubs* White's; *Style*— The Lord Patrick Beresford; ✉ Fairview Cottage, Wicks Green, Binfield, Berks RG42 5PF (☎ 01344 860976, fax 01344 55413)

BERESFORD, Sir (Alexander) Paul; kt (1990), MP (C) Croydon Central (majority 9,650); *b* 6 April 1946; *Educ* Waimea Coll Richmond NZ, Otago Univ Dunedin NZ; *m* Julie Haynes; 3 s, 1 da; *Career* dental surgeon; London Borough of Wandsworth: cncllr 1978–, former chm various ctees, ldr 1983–92; MP (C) Croydon Central 1992–; Parly under-sec of state Dept of Environment 1994–; prospective Parly candidate Mole Valley; *Recreations* DIY, reading; *Style*— Sir Paul Beresford, MP; ✉ House of Commons, London SW1A 0AA

BERESFORD, Dr Richard Charles; s of Eric Beresford, of Whychford, Warks, and Barbara, *née* Gatenby (d 1989); *b* 25 Feb 1958; *Educ* Uppingham, Courtauld Inst of Art (BA, PhD); *Career* research asst rising to curator of paintings pre-1800 The Wallace Collection 1982–94, curator Dulwich Picture Gallery 1995–; *Publications* A Dance to the Music of Time by Nicolas Poussin (1995); *Style*— Dr Richard Beresford; ✉ Dulwich Picture Gallery, College Road, London SE21 7AD (☎ 0181 693 5254, fax 0181 693 0923)

BERESFORD-PEIRSE, Sir Henry Grant de la Poer; 6 Bt (UK 1814), of Bagnall, Waterford; s of Sir Henry Campbell Beresford-Peirse, 5 Bt, CB (d 1972), and Margaret, *née* Grant (d 1995); *b* 7 Feb 1933; *Educ* Eton, Ontario Agric Coll; *m* 1966, Jadranka, da of Ivan Njerš, of Zagreb; 2 s; *Heir* s, Henry Beresford-Peirse, *qv*; *Career* investment mgmnt; *Recreations* tennis, golf, country homes in Yorkshire and Portugal; *Style*— Sir Henry Beresford-Peirse, Bt; ✉ Bedall Manor, Bedale, N Yorks DL8 1EP (☎ 01677 422811); 34 Cadogan Square, London SW1X 0JL (☎ 0171 589 1134)

BERESFORD-PEIRSE, Henry Njerš de la Poer; s and h of Sir Henry Grant de la Poer Beresford-Peirse, 6 Bt, *qv*; *b* 25 March 1969; *Educ* Harrow; *Career* TV and radio reporter/journalist; UN (MIBH), head UNMIBH Radio, editor-in-chief 'efm' Sarajevo, Bosnia and Hercegovina; *Recreations* cricket, golf, tennis; *Style*— Henry Peirse, Esq; ✉ c/o Bedall Manor, Bedale, N Yorks

BERESFORD-WEST, Michael Charles; QC (1975); s of Arthur Charles West OBE, and Ida Dagmar West; *b* 3 June 1928; *Educ* St Peter's, Portsmouth GS, Brasenose Coll Oxford (MA); *m* 1956 (m dis), Patricia Eileen, *née* Beresford; 2 s, 1 da; m 2, 1986, Sheilagh Elizabeth Davies; *Career* Intelligence Serv Middle East; called to the Bar 1952, Western Circuit 1953–65, South Eastern Circuit 1965, recorder of the Crown Court 1975–83; chm Ind Schools Tbnl 1974–80; *Recreations* music, golf, swimming; *Clubs* Oxford and Cambridge, MCC (1949–79), Hampshire Hogs, Aldeburgh Golf, Aldeburgh Yacht, Bar Yacht; *Style*— Michael Beresford-West, Esq, QC; ✉ Goldsmith Chambers, Goldsmith's Building, Temple, London EC4Y 7BL (☎ 0171 353 6802, fax 0171 583 5255)

BERG, Adrian; s of Charles Berg, and Sarah, *née* Sorby; *b* 12 March 1929; *Educ* Charterhouse, Gonville and Caius Coll Cambridge (MA), Trinity Coll Dublin (HDipEd),

St Martin's Sch of Art, Chelsea Sch of Art (NDD), RCA; *Career* Nat Serv 1947–49; artist; *Solo Exhibitions* incl: five at Arthur Tooth & Sons Ltd 1964–75, three at Waddington Galleries 1978–83, Waddington Galleries Montreal and Toronto 1979, Hokin Gallery Inc Chicago 1979, Paintings 1955–1980 (Rochdale Art Gallery) 1980, five at The Piccadilly Gallery 1985–93, Paintings 1977–1986 (Serpentine Gallery London and Walker Art Gallery Liverpool) 1986, Adrian Berg: A Sense of Place (Barbican and touring) 1993–94; work in permanent collections incl: Arts Cncl of GB, Br Cncl, Br Museum, Euro Parl, Govt Art Collection, Hiroshima City Museum of Contemporary Art, The Tate Gallery, Tokyo Metropolitan Art Museum; RA 1992; *Style*— Adrian Berg, Esq, RA; ✉ c/o The Piccadilly Gallery, 16 Cork St, London W1X 1PF (☎ 0171 629 2875)

BERG, Robert Vivian Nathaniel; s of Bernard Berg (d 1975), of London, and Zena Berg; *b* 4 June 1947; *Educ* St Paul's, Magdalen Coll Oxford; *m* 1989, Gillian Margaret, da of John Thorn; *Career* KPMG: CA 1973, ptnr 1981–, memb bd 1989–; *Recreations* architecture, art; *Clubs* Athenaeum; *Style*— Robert Berg, Esq; ✉ KPMG, 8 Salisbury Square, London EC4Y 8BB (☎ 0171 311 1000, fax 0171 311 8735)

BERGENDAHL, (Carl) Anders; s of Carl Johan Bergendahl (d 1995), of Djursholm, Sweden, and Ingrid Bergendahl (d 1964); *b* 20 March 1952; *Educ* Djursholm's Samskola Sweden, Stockholm Sch of Econs; *m* 18 March 1984, Maria, da of Stephen Heineman (d 1967); 2 s (David b 11 Sept 1985, Alexander b 18 June 1987); *Career* assoc Merrill Lynch 1977–, md Merrill Lynch & Co 1985–96, co-head Global Dept Capital Mkts Merrill Lynch & Co Inc; pres Minna-James-Heineman Stifung 1993; memb Bd of Dirs: Heineman Medical Research Inc 1992, Heineman Fndn for Research, Educational, Charitable and Scientific Purposes Inc 1994; *Recreations* sailing, tennis, squash, skiing; *Clubs* Sallskapet, RAC; *Style*— Anders Bergendahl, Esq; ✉ Merrill Lynch International Ltd, 25 Ropemaker St, Ropemaker Place, London EC2Y 9LY (☎ 0171 867 2800, fax 0171 867 4455)

BERGER, Herbert; s of Herbert Berger, and Hedwig; *b* 19 April 1953; *Educ* Catering Coll Salzburg; *m* 16 Feb 1989, Jane, *née* Crawford; 1 da (Annie b 2 April 1990); *Career* apprentice Grand Hotel Zell/See Austria 1968–71, seasonal work various hotels Switzerland 1971–75, chef de partie then sous chef Fredericks Restaurant 1975–76, head chef Le Connoisseur Restaurant London (Michelin Star) 1977–79, various positions rising to sous chef Connaught Hotel 1980–85, premier sous chef Claridges Hotel 1985–86, head chef Mirabelle Restaurant Curzon Street 1986–88, owner Keats Restaurant Hampstead (Michelin Red M within 6 months of opening) 1988–91, ptnr Berger & Sawyer Restaurant Ltd 1988–91, ptnr Restaurant Partnership 1991–, exec chef Café Royal 1992–; subject of various magazine articles; guest appearances: The Good Food Show (BBC), The Restaurant Show, Telegraph House & Garden Food Show, Masterchef, Nat Museums & Galleries of Wales, Nat Gallery Washington DC, Trimbach Food and Wine Masterclass, Marco Polo Cruise Liner, The Big Breakfast, After Five Dilly Dines Out; guest chef: The Restaurateurs Dinner, Assoc Culinaire de France Dinner, SOS Charity Dinner, Fundraising Acad Dinners; memb: Academie Culinaire de France UK 1986–, Euro Togue 1995, Assoc Culinaire de France, Club des Amis Connaught Hotel; *Awards* mention d'honneur Prix Pierre Taittinger 1983, AA 3 Rosettes, Egon Ronay Star, Michelin Star (Grill Room Café Royal), Eros Award 1995, Mumm Stars of Gastronomy; *Recreations* travel, gastronomic tours, eating out, music, the arts, skiing; *Clubs* The Tabasco; *Style*— Herbert Berger, Esq; ✉ Café Royal, 68 Regent Street, London W1R 6EL (☎ 0171 437 9090, fax 0171 439 7672)

BERGER, Vice Adm Sir Peter Egerton Capel; KCB (1979), LVO (1960), DSC (1949); s of Capel Colquhoun Berger (d 1941), and Winifred Violet, *née* Levett-Scrivener (d 1981); *b* 11 Feb 1925; *Educ* Harrow; *m* 1956, June Kathleen, da of Cdr Frederick Arthur Pigou, RN (d 1979); 3 da (Sarah b 1959, Louisa b 1961, Katy b 1964); *Career* joined RN 1943, Normandy and S of France landings in HMS Ajax 1944, Lt 1946, Yangtse Incident in HMS Amethyst 1949, Lt Cdr 1953, Cdr 1956, Fleet Navigating Offr Home Fleet 1956–58, Navigating Offr HM Yacht Britannia 1958–60, i/c HMS Torquay 1962–64, Capt 1964, i/c HMS Phoebe 1966–68, Cdre Clyde 1971–73, Rear Adm 1973, Asst Chief of Naval Staff (Policy) 1973–75, COS to C-in-C Fleet 1976–78, Flag Offr Plymouth, Port Adm Devonport, Cdr Centl Sub Area E Atlantic and Cdr Plymouth Sub Area Channel 1979–81; bursar and fell Selwyn Coll Cambridge 1981–91; Hon MA Cambridge 1984; *Recreations* reading history, shooting, fishing; *Style*— Vice Adm Sir Peter Berger, KCB, LVO, DSC; ✉ Linton End House, Linton Road, Balsham, Cambs CB1 6HA; Selwyn College, Cambridge CB3 9DQ

BERGIN, Prof Joseph; s of late Cornelius Bergin, and late Brigid, *née* Phelan; *b* 11 Feb 1948; *Educ* Rockwell Coll Co Tipperary Eire, Univ Coll Dublin (BA, MA), Peterhouse Cambridge (PhD); *m* 1978, Sylvia Papazian; 1 s (Edward b 1981), 1 da (Olivia b 1985); *Career* lectr in history Maynouth Coll Eire 1976–78; Univ of Manchester: lectr in history 1978–88, sr lectr 1988–92, reader 1992–96, prof 1996–; winner Prix Richelieu 1995; FRHistS 1988, FBA 1996; *Books* Cardinal Richelieu: Power and the Pursuit of Wealth (1985), The Rise of Richelieu (1991), The Making of the French Episcopate 1589–1661 (1996); *Recreations* sports, book-hunting; *Style*— Prof Joseph Bergin, FBA; ✉ Department of History, University of Manchester, Oxford Road, Manchester M13 9PL (☎ 0161 275 3084)

BERGNE, (Alexander) Paul A'Court; OBE (1984); s of Villiers A'Court Bergne (d 1989), and Diana, *née* Holman-Hunt (d 1993); *b* 9 Jan 1937; *Educ* Winchester, Trinity Coll Cambridge, Sch of Oriental and African Studies London (MA 1993); *m* 25 March 1963, Suzanne Hedwig Judith, da of Wilhelm Karl Wittich (d 1973); 1 da (Theresa Rebecca A'Court b 15 Oct 1963), 1 s (Sebastian Karl David A'Court b 12 Nov 1966); *Career* cameraman Krasicki Iran Expdn 1958–59; HM Dip Serv: entered FO 1959, third sec Vienna 1961–63, FCO 1963–64, SOAS London 1964–65, Faculty of Literature Univ of Isfahan 1965–66, second then first sec Tehran 1966–68, FCO 1968–70, MECAS 1970–72, first sec Abu Dhabi 1972–75, first sec Cairo 1975–77, FCO 1977–80, first sec Athens 1980–84, cnsllr HQ Br Forces Hong Kong 1985–87, FCO 1987–93, Br ambass Uzbekistan (Tashkent) 1993–95, ret; conslt BBC World Service; *Recreations* hill-walking, numismatics, gardening; *Clubs* Brooks's; *Style*— Paul Bergne, Esq, OBE; ✉ c/o St Antony's College, Oxford OX2 6JF

BERGSTROM, Prof (Albert) Rex; s of Albert Victor Bergstrom (d 1945), of Christchurch, NZ, and Lily, *née* Markland (d 1976); *b* 9 July 1925; *Educ* Christchurch Boys' HS NZ, Univ of NZ (MCOM), Univ of Cambridge (PhD); *m* 12 Dec 1960, Christine Mary, da of Basil Egmont Arnold (d 1968), of Auckland, NZ; 1 s (Carl b 1961); *Career* RNZAF 1945–46; reader in economics LSE 1962–64, prof of econometrics Univ of Auckland 1965–70, prof of economics Univ of Essex 1971–92 (emeritus prof 1992); fell Econometric Soc; *Books* The Construction and Use of Economic Models (1967), Statistical Inference in Continuous Time Economic Models (ed, 1976), Stability and Inflation (jt ed, 1978), Continuous Time Econometric Modelling (1990); *Recreations* music, opera; *Style*— Prof Rex Bergstrom; ✉ 46 Regency Lodge, Avenue Rd, St John's Wood, London NW3 5ED (☎ 0171 586 6259)

BERINGER, Guy; *b* 12 Aug 1955; *Educ* Campbell Coll Belfast, St Catharine's Coll Cambridge (MA); *m* 1979, Margaret Catherine, *née* Powell; 3 da; *Career* ptnr Allen & Overy 1985– (asst 1980–85); memb Law Soc; *Style*— Guy Beringer, Esq; ✉ Allen & Overy, One New Change, London EC4M 9QQ (☎ 0171 330 3000, fax 0171 330 9999)

BERIOSOVA, Svetlana; da of Nicolas Beriozoff (d 1996), of Zurich, and his 1 w, Maria Beriosova (d 1942); *b* 24 Sept 1932; *Educ* Vilzak Schollar Sch of Ballet; *m* 1959 (m dis 1974) Mohammed Masud Khan (d 1989); *Career* ballet dancer; joined Grand Ballet de Monte Carlo 1947; danced with: Metropolitan Ballet 1948–49, Sadler's Wells Theatre Ballet 1950–52, Sadler's Wells Ballet (now The Royal Ballet); cr leading roles in: Designs for Strings, Fanciulla delle Rose, Trumpet Concerto, Pastorale, The Shadow, Armida, Prince of the Pagodas, Antigone, Baiser de la Fee, Diversions, Persephone, Images of Love; classical roles in ballets incl: Le Lac des Cygnes, The Sleeping Beauty, Giselle, Coppelia, Sylvia, Cinderella, The Nutcracker; has danced with Royal Ballet in: USA, France, Italy, Aust, SA, Russia; guest: Belgrade, Granada, Milan (La Scala), Stuttgart, Bombay, Paris, Vienna, NZ, Zurich; film The Soldier's Tale 1966, numerous tv appearances, currently teaches worldwide; *Recreations* the arts; *Style*— Ms Svetlana Beriosova

BERKELEY, Andrew Wilson Atkins; s of Andrew Berkeley, JP (d 1952), of Cookstown, Co Tyrone, NI, and Mabel Berkeley; *b* 15 July 1936; *Educ* Rainey Sch Co Derry, Queen's Univ Belfast (BSc), Harvard Business Sch (AMP), King's Coll London (MSc); *m* 30 Nov 1968, Carolyn Blyth Hinshaw Ross, of Milngavie, Glasgow, Scotland; 2 da (Kirsten b 16 Nov 1972, Iona b 27 April 1978); *Career* HAC Inf Bn TA 1966–67; int commercial lawer and registered arbitrator; called to the Bar Gray's Inn 1965 (readmitted 1995), admitted slr 1980; Legal Dept ICI Ltd 1966–78, dir ICI Petroleum Ltd 1978–81, sec The British National Oil Corporation 1981–84, dir of legal corp affrs STC plc 1984–87, gp gen counsel and sec Laporte plc 1987–92; currently conslt ICC (UK); vice chm Section for Energy and Nat Resources Law Int Bar Assoc 1979–83; Law Soc: memb Standing Ctee on Revenue Law, chm Ctee on Petroleum Taxation 1980–84; memb: Cncl and Exec Ctee Inst of Industl and Commercial Law and Practice, Int C of C Paris; FCIArb; *Recreations* riding; *Clubs* Athenaeum; *Style*— Andrew Berkeley, Esq; ✉ 49 Arden Rd, London N3 3AD (☎ 0181 343 4050, fax 0181 343 1762)

BERKELEY, 18 Baron (E 1421); Anthony FitzHardinge Gueterbock; OBE (1989); o s of Brig Ernest Adolphus Leopold Gueterbock, late RE (d 1984), and Hon Cynthia Ella Foley (d 1991); suc aunt Mary Lalle Foley Berkeley, Baroness Berkeley (d 1992); *b* 20 Sept 1939; *Educ* Eton, Trinity Coll Cambridge (MA); *m* 10 July 1965 (sep 1994), Diana Christine, er da of Eric William John Townsend, MRCS, LRCP; 2 s (Hon Thomas FitzHardinge b 1969, Hon Robert William b 1970), 1 da (Hon Philippa Louise b 1975); *Heir* s, Hon Thomas FitzHardinge Gueterbock b 5 Jan 1969; *Career* engrg, construction and planning Sir Alexander Gibb and Partners 1961–67, construction, planning and business devpt George Wimpey plc 1967–85, public affrs mangr Eurotunnel plc 1985–95 (public affrs advsr 1995–); chm: The Piggyback Consortium 1993–, Discover Kent; sits as Lab whip and spokesman on tport House of Lords; Hon DSc Univ of Brighton 1996; CEng, MICE, FRSA; *Recreations* sailing, skiing; *Clubs* Ski Club of GB, Leander; *Style*— The Rt Hon the Lord Berkeley, OBE; ✉ House of Lords, London SW1A 0PW

BERKELEY, David James; s of Aubrey William Grandidier Berkeley, of Reigate, Surrey, and Sheena Elsie, *née* Turner; *b* 7 Aug 1944; *Educ* Rugby; *children* 2 da (Georgina b 1972, Louisa b 1975); *Career* chm and md: Standard Bank Jersey Ltd, Standard Bank Offshore Group Ltd; dir: Standard Bank Stockbrokers (CI) Ltd, Standard Bank Stockbrokers (Isle of Man) Ltd; chm: Standard Bank Trust Company (Jersey) Ltd, Standard Bank Trust Company (Isle of Man) Ltd, Standard Bank Isle of Man Ltd; MSI, FCA; *Recreations* lawn tennis, English watercolours, English drinking glasses; *Clubs* Public Schools Old Boys', LTA; *Style*— David J Berkeley, Esq; ✉ La Rocque, La Rue du Crocquet, St Aubin, Jersey JE3 8BZ, CI (☎ 01534 46530); Standard Bank Jersey Ltd, PO Box 583, 1 Waverley Place, St Helier, Jersey JE4 8XR, CI (☎ 01534 881188)

BERKELEY, (Robert) John Grantley; TD (1967), JP (Glos 1960), DL (Glos 1982, Hereford and Worcester 1983); s of Capt Robert George Wilmot Berkeley (d 1969, himself 13 in descent from Hon Thomas Berkeley (4 s of 1 Baron Berkeley cr 1421, gs of 4 Baron Berkeley cr 1295, and descended in direct male line from Eadnoth the Staller, pre-Conquest Anglo-Saxon nobleman at Court of King Edward the Confessor) by his 2 w Isabel, da and co-heir of Thomas Mowbray, 1 Duke of Norfolk and Hon Myrtle, da of 14 Baron Dormer; *b* 24 July 1931; *Educ* Oratory Sch, Magdalen Coll Oxford; *m* 25 Jan 1967, Georgina Bridget, eld da of Maj Andrew Charles Stirling Home Drummond Moray (d 1971), of Easter Ross, Comrie, Perthshire; 2 s (Robert Charles b 1968, Henry John Mowbray b 1969); *Career* Maj Queen's Own Warwicks Yeo 1963; jt master Berkeley Hunt 1960–84; High Sheriff: Worcs 1967, Glos 1982–83; *Clubs* Cavalry and Guards'; *Style*— R J Berkeley, Esq, TD, JP, DL; ✉ Berkeley Castle, Glos (☎ 01453 810 202); Spetchley Park, nr Worcester (☎ 01905 345224)

BERKELEY, Michael Fitzhardinge; s of Sir Lennox Randolph Francis Berkeley, CBE (d 1989), of 8 Warwick Ave, London, and Elizabeth Freda, *née* Bernstein; *b* 29 May 1948; *Educ* Westminster Cathedral Choir Sch, The Oratory, Royal Acad of Music (ARAM), postgrad work with Richard Rodney Bennett, *qv*; *m* 19 Nov 1979, Deborah Jane Coltman, da of Guy Coltman Rogers (d 1976), of Stanage Park, Knighton, Powys; 1 da (Jessica Rose b 28 June 1986); *Career* composer and broadcaster; phlebotonist St Bartholomew's Hosp 1969–71, announcer BBC Radio 1974–79, regular broadcaster on music and the arts BBC radio and TV 1974–; music panel advsr Arts Cncl of GB, artistic dir Cheltenham Int Festival of Music 1995–; memb: Central Music Advsy Ctee BBC 1986–89, Gen Advsy Cncl BBC 1990–95, Bd of Dirs Royal Opera House 1996– (memb Opera Bd 1994–); co-artistic dir Spitalfields Festival 1995–; assoc composer Scottish Chamber Orch 1979; pres Presteigne Festival, govr National Youth Orch of GB; compositions incl: Meditations (Guinness prize for composition) 1977, Primavera 1979, Uprising 1980, Wessex Graves 1981, Oratorio Or Shall We Die? 1982, Music from Chaucer 1983, Fierce Tears 1984, Pas de Deux 1985, Songs of Awakening Love 1986, Organ Concerto 1987, The Red Macula 1989, Gethsemane Fragment 1990, Entertaining Master Punch 1991, Clarinet Concerto 1991, Baa Baa Black Sheep 1993, Viola Concerto 1994, Magnetic Field 1995, Winter Fragments 1996; memb: Composers' Guild of GB, APC; author of various articles in The Observer, The Guardian, The Listener, The Sunday Telegraph and Vogue; FRAM 1996; *Recreations* contemporary painting, walking, hill farming in Mid Wales; *Style*— Michael Berkeley, Esq; ✉ c/o Rogers, Coleridge & White Ltd, 20 Powis Mews, London W11 1JN

BERKOFF, Steven; *b* 3 Aug 1937; *Career* writer, actor and director; fndr London Theatre Group 1968 (first professional prodn In The Penal Colony); *Theatre* adapted/dir/toured: The Trial, Metamorphosis, Agamemnon, The Fall of the House of Usher; dir/toured: Hamlet, Macbeth, own one man show (GB, USA, Aust); dir: Coriolanus (NY and West Yorkshire Playhouse (also title role, 1995)), Kvetch, Richard II (NY); *Television* appearances incl: Sins, Beloved Family, Knife Edge, The Professionals, War and Remembrance, Michaelangelo - Season of Giants; TV prodns incl: West (Channel 4) 1984, Metamorphosis (BBC 2) 1989, Harry's Christmas, Silent Night (Channel 4) 1991, Tell Tale Heart (Channel 4) 1991; *Radio* prodns incl: title role in Macbeth (Radio 4) 1995, the MC in Cabaret (musical debut, Radio 2) 1996; *Films* appearances incl: The Clockwork Orange, Barry Lyndon, The Passenger, McVicar, Outlands, Octopussy, Beverly Hills Cop, Rambo, Underworld, Revolution, Under the Cherry Moon, Absolute Beginners, Prisoner of Rio, The Krays, Fair Game, Decadence, Flynn and Love in Paris; *Original Plays* East (first original play presented at Edinburgh Festival 1975), Decadence (1982), Greek (1982), West (1985), Harry's Christmas (1985), Lunch (1985), Sink The Belgrano (1987), Massage (1987), Kvetch (1987), Acapulco (1987), Sturm und Drang, Brighton Beach Scumbags; other publications incl: The Trial (play adaptation, 1978), Gross Intrusion (1979), America (poetry and prose, 1988), A Prisoner of Rio (film journal, 1989), I am Hamlet (prodn diary, 1989), The Theatre of Steven Berkoff (photographic history),

Meditations on Metamorphosis (1995), Free Association (autobiography, 1996); *Style*— Steven Berkoff, Esq; ✉ c/o Rosica Colin Ltd, 1 Clareville Grove Mews, London SW7 5AH (☎ 0171 370 1080, fax 0171 244 6441)

BERKOVITS, Dayan Rabbi Bernard; s of Rabbi David Berkovits (d 1977), and Joana, *née* Adler; *b* 3 June 1949; *Educ* Hasmonean GS London, Gateshead Talmudical Coll, Talmudical Coll of Mir Jerusalem Israel, LSE (LLB, Hughes Parry prize, scholarship to Int Ct of Justice); *m* 16 June 1981, Zelda Ruth, da of late Lionel Gillis; 4 s (Elliot Lionel b 10 Oct 1982, David b 26 May 1985, Joseph b 5 May 1987, Nathan b 19 April 1996); *Career* lectr in family law, criminal law, torts and int human rights Univ of Buckingham 1977–83, registrar Ct of the Chief Rabbi London 1984–90, dayan Beth Din of the Fedn of Synagogues 1990–; *Books* Nachmanides' Commentary on The Torah Vols 2–4 (ed and trans, 1972–75), Oxford Dictionary of Law (ed and contrib, 1983), Quest (1984), Pesach in the Modern Home (1988); *Recreations* reading, travelling, astronomy; *Style*— Dayan Rabbi Bernard Berkovits; ✉ Federation of Synagogues, 65 Watford Way, London NW4 3AQ (☎ 0181 202 2263, fax 0181 203 0610)

BERKSHIRE, Archdeacon of; *see:* Hill, Ven Michael Arthur

BERLIAND, David Michael; s of Jasha Berliand (d 1976), and Phyllis, *née* Doresa; *b* 17 Dec 1935; *Educ* Charterhouse; *m* 1961, Diana Jill, da of Antony Maynard Puckle (d 1989), of Hants; 1 s (Richard b 1962), 2 da (Louise b 1964, Penelope Sarah (Mrs Charles Edward Philip Otton) b 1967); *Career* Nat Serv Lt RA Germany 1955; dir Bain Hogg International Ltd insurance brokers 1987–; Freeman Worshipful Co of Insurers; *Recreations* tennis, golf; *Clubs* MCC, Sunningdale Golf, St George's Hill Lawn Tennis; *Style*— David Berliand, Esq; ✉ Bridgefoot Farm, Ripley, Surrey (☎ 01483 224354); Bain Hogg Ltd, 15 Minories, London EC3N 1NJ (☎ 0171 680 4000, fax 0171 301 4647, telex 8813411)

BERLIN, Sir Isaiah; OM (1971), kt (1957), CBE (1946); s of Mendel and Marie Berlin, of London; *b* 6 June 1909; *Educ* St Paul's CCC Oxford; *m* 1956, Aline, da of Baron Pierre de Gunzbourg, of Paris and formerly w of Dr Hans Halban; *Career* served WWII with Miny of Info and Foreign Office; Chichele prof of social and political theory Oxford Univ 1957–67, visiting prof of humanities City Univ NY 1966–71, pres Wolfson Coll Oxford 1966–75; pres Br Acad 1974–78; fell: New Coll Oxford 1938–50, All Souls Coll Oxford; memb bd of dirs Royal Opera House Covent Garden 1954–65 and 1974–87; tstee Nat Gallery 1975–85; awarded: Lippincott Prize 1977, Erasmus Prize for promoting European culture 1983, Jerusalem Prize 1983, Agnelli Prize 1990; Commandeur de l'Ordre des Arts et des Lettres 1990; hon doctorates from twenty five British, Israeli and American Univs; hon fell Univ of Oxford: Corpus Christi Coll, New Coll, St Antony's Coll, Wolfson Coll; FBA; *Books* Karl Marx (1939, 1978), First Love by I A Turgenev (translation, 1950), The Age of Enlightenment (1956), Four Essays on Liberty (1969), Vico and Herder (1976), Concepts and Categories (1978), Russian Thinkers (1978), Against the Current (1979), Personal Impressions (1980), The Crooked Timber of Humanity (1990), Hamann, The Magus of the North (1993); *Clubs* Brooks's, Athenaeum, Garrick, Century (New York); *Style*— Sir Isaiah Berlin, OM, CBE, FBA; ✉ All Souls College, Oxford

BERMAN, Edward David (ED); MBE (1979); s of Jack Berman, of America, and Ida, *née* Webber; *b* 8 March 1941; *Educ* Harvard (BA), Exeter Coll Oxford (Rhodes Scholar); *Career* playwright, theatre director and producer, actor and educationalist; theatre direction credits incl: Dirty Linen (premieres London and Broadway) 1976, The Dogg's Troupe Hamlet 1976 (filmed same yr), The Irish Hebrew Lesson 1976, Samson and Delilah 1978, Dogg's Hamlet, Cahoot's Macbeth 1979; prodr of various plays for adults and for children 1967–95, artistic dir of annual public art profects 1968–95; editor of: 2 anthologies of plays 1976–78, various community arts and action handbooks; maker of educnl films: The Head 1971, Two Wheeler 1972, Farm in the City 1977, Marx for Beginners cartoon (co-prodr) 1978; fndr chief exec, artistic dir and tstee Inter-Action Tst 1968–; Labrys tst 1969–; dir and fndr various companies/gps/tsts concerning constructive leisure incl: Prof Dogg's Troupe for Children 1968–, Inter-Action Advsy Serv 1970, Infilms 1970, The Almost Free Theatre 1971, Inprint Publishing Unit 1972, City Farm 1 1972, Alternative Educn Project 1973–84, Ambiance Inter-Action Inc 1976, City Farm Movement 1976, Talacre Centre Ltd 1977, Weekend Arts Coll 1979; co-fndr: Inter-Action Housing Tst Ltd 1970, Community Design Centre (NUBS) 1974, Sport-Space 1976, Beginners Books Ltd 1978, London and Commonwealth Youth Ensemble 1981; chm: Save Piccadilly Campaign 1971–80, Talacre Action Gp 1972, Nat Assoc of Arts Centres 1975–79; dir Islington Bus Co 1974–76; fndr and co-dir: Int Inst for Social Enterprise 1980, Social Property Developments Ltd; fndr and tstee: Inter-Action Social Enterprise Tst Ltd, Social Enterprise Fndn of Inter-Action 1984; fndr and dir: Network Inter-Action, Youth-Tech, Learning Domes; special advsr on inner city matters to Sec of State for the Environment 1982–83; Cdre Ships-in-the-City 1988; *Publications* Prof R L Dogg's Zoo's Who I and II (1975), Selecting Business Software (1984), Make a Real Job of It, Breaks for Young Bands (1985), How to Set Up a Small Business (1987), Healthy Learning Songs and Activities (1989), New Game Songs and Activities (1989), Early Learning Maths Songs and Activities (1991), The Democracy Handbook (1995); *Style*— ED Berman, Esq, MBE; ✉ Inter-Action Trust, HMS President (1918), Victoria Embankment, London EC4Y 0HJ (☎ 0171 583 2652)

BERMAN, Sir Franklin Delow; KCMG (1994, CMG 1987); s of Joshua Zelic Berman, of Cape Town, and Gertrude, *née* Levin; *b* 23 Dec 1939; *Educ* Rondebosch Boys' HS, Univ of Cape Town (BA, BSc), Wadham and Nuffield Colls Oxford (MA); *m* 24 July 1964, Christine Mary, da of Edward Francis Lawler (d 1978); 2 s (Jonathan b 1966, Stefan b 1968), 3 da (Katharine b 1972, Judith b 1972, Victoria b 1972); *Career* called to the Bar Middle Temple 1966; joined HM Dip Serv 1965, asst legal advsr FCO 1965–71, legal advsr Br Mil Govt Berlin 1971–72, legal advsr Br Embassy Bonn 1972–74, legal cnsllr FCO 1974–82, cnsllr UK Mission UN 1982–85, legal advsr FCO 1991– (dep legal advsr 1988–91); J C Smith visiting fell Univ of Nottingham 1993; chm: Dip Serv Assoc 1979–82, Staff Tbnl Int Oil Pollution Compensation Fund 1985–, Bd Inst of Advanced Legal Studies Univ of London 1991–, Cncl British Inst of Int and Comp Law 1992–; memb: Cncl Br Branch Int Law Assoc 1992–, Appeals Bd Western EU 1994–96, Editorial Bd Br Yearbook of Int Law 1994–; tstee Edward Fry Memorial Library 1991–; hon QC 1992, hon fell Wadham Coll 1995; *Recreations* reading, walking, choral singing, gardening; *Style*— Sir Franklin Berman, KCMG, QC; ✉ Foreign and Commonwealth Office, King Charles St, London SW1A 2AH (☎ 0171 270 3000)

BERMANT, Chaim Icyk; s of Azriel Bermant (d 1962), of Glasgow, and Feiga, *née* Daets (d 1971); *b* 26 Feb 1929; *Educ* Queens Park Sch Glasgow, Univ of Glasgow (MA, MLitt), LSE (MSc); *m* 16 Dec 1962, Judy, da of Fred Weil, of Jerusalem; 2 s (Azriel b 1968, Daniel b 1972), 2 da (Alisa b 1963, Evie b 1966); *Career* staff writer: Scottish TV 1957–59, Granada TV 1959–61; journalist Jewish Chronicle 1961–66, author; *Books* Jericho Sleep Alone (1964), Berl Make Tea (1965), Ben Preserve Us (1965), Diary of an Old Man (1966), Israel (1967), Swinging in the Rain (1967), Troubled Eden (1969), The Cousinhood (1971), Here Endeth the Lesson (1969), Now Dowager (1971), Roses are Blooming in Picardy (1972), The Last Supper (1973), The Walled Garden (1974), Point of Arrival (1975), The Second Mrs Whitberg (1976), Coming Home (1976, Wingate-Jewish Chronicle Book Award), The Squire of Bor Shachor (1977), The Jews (1978), Now Newman was Old (1978), Belshazzar (1979, with Dr M Weitzman), Ebla (1979), The Patriarch (1981), On the Other Hand (1982), The House of Women (1983), Dancing Bear (1984), What's the Joke (1986),Titch (1987), The Companion (1987), Lord Jacobovits - The Authorised Biography of the Chief Rabbi (1990), Murmurings of a Licensed Heretic (1990); *Recreations* walking, sermon tasting; *Style*— Chaim Bermant, Esq

BERMINGHAM, Gerald Edward; MP (Lab) St Helens South (majority 18,209); s of late Patrick Xavier Bermingham and Eva Terescena Bermingham; *b* 20 Aug 1940; *Educ* Cotton Coll, Wellingborough GS, Univ of Sheffield; *m* 1, 1964 (m dis), Joan; 2 s; m 2, 1978, Judith; *Career* barr, formerly slr; cncllr Sheffield City Cncl 1975–79, Parly candidate (Lab) Derbyshire SE 1979, MP (Lab) St Helens South 1983–; *Style*— Gerald Bermingham, Esq, MP; ✉ House of Commons, London SW1A 0AA

BERNARD, Sir Dallas Edmund; 2 Bt (UK 1954), of Snakemoor, Co Southampton; s of Sir Dallas Gerald Mercer Bernard, 1 Bt (d 1975); *b* 14 Dec 1926; *Educ* Eton, CCC Oxford (MA); *m* 1, 1959 (m dis 1979), Sheila Mary, er da of Arthur Gordon Robey; 3 da (Juliet Mary b 1961, Alicia Elizabeth b 1964, Sarah Jane b 1968); m 2, 1979, Mrs Monica J Montford, da of late James Edward Hudson; 1 da (Olivia Louise b 1981); *Heir* none; *Career* dir: Morgan Grenfell and Co Ltd 1964–77, Morgan Grenfell Holdings Ltd 1970–79, Italian International Bank plc 1978–89; memb Monopolies and Mergers Cmmn 1973–79; chm: Nat and Foreign Securities Trust Ltd 1981–86, Thames Trust Ltd 1983–86; dir: Dreyfus Intercontinental Investment Fund NY 1970–91, Dreyfus Dollar International Fund NY 1982–91; int fin conslt 1986–; memb Cncl Girls' Public Day Sch Tst 1988–93; *Clubs* Lansdowne; *Style*— Sir Dallas Bernard, Bt; ✉ Stow, 106 Cheyne Walk, London SW10 0DG

BERNARD, Jeffrey Joseph; s of Maj Oliver Bernard, OBE, MC, (d 1939); *b* 27 May 1932; *Educ* Pangbourne; *m* 1978, Susan; 1 da (by previous m); *Career* journalist and columnist; formerly with New Statesman, Sporting Life, Daily Mirror, Pacemaker; feature writer Sunday Times Mag, reviewer Punch, racing columnist Harpers and Queen, columnist Private Eye; writer 'Low Life' column The Spectator for the past 20 years; subject of play by Keith Waterhouse 'Jeffrey Bernard is Unwell'; *Recreations* cooking, music, racing, drinking with friends; *Clubs* Colony Room, Chelsea Arts, Groucho; *Style*— Jeffrey Bernard, Esq; ✉ c/o The Spectator, 56 Doughty Street, London WC1N 2LF

BERNARD, (Francis) William Wigan; s of Brig Ronald Playfair St Vincent Bernard, DSO, MC, IA (d 1943), and Katharine Etheldreda, *née* Wigan (d 1978); *b* 5 June 1924; *Educ* Bedford Sch, BNC Oxford (MA); *m* 7 Feb 1958, Margaret Renee, da of Capt Wilfrid Dowman, RNVR (d 1936), and Catharine, *née* Courtauld, of Weymouth; 1 s (James b 1959), 4 da (Catherine b 1960, Antonia b 1961, Frances (twin) b 1961, Sarah b 1964); *Career* Capt RA 1942–47; ADC to Govr Gen of Fedn of Rhodesia and Nyasaland (Lord Llewellin) 1953–57, Maj Rhodesia and Nyasaland Defence Staff 1955–58, dir Central African Bldg Soc; tstee: Nat Museums of Zimbabwe 1962–69, The Nat Gallery Zimbabwe 1964–69; memb Governing Bd Coll of Music Harare 1964–69; cncllr Salisbury 9 yrs, chm Cncl St John in Jersey 1992–96 and Cdr Brigade for Jersey 1987–93; KStJ 1995 (CStJ 1990); *Recreations* ornithology, tennis; *Clubs* Boodle's; *Style*— William Bernard, Esq; ✉ Herupe House, St John, Jersey JE3 4YA, CI (☎ 01534 865358)

BERNAYS, Richard Oliver; s of Robert Hamilton Bernays, MP (MP for Bristol North 1931–45, ka 1945), and Nancy, *née* Britton (d 1987); *b* 22 Feb 1943; *Educ* Eton, Trinity Coll Oxford (MA); *m* 1, 12 Feb 1972 (m dis 1993), Karen Forney, of New Castle, PA, USA; 3 da (Lucy b 1975, Mary b 1977 d 1993, Amy b 1979); m 2, 22 Feb 1996, Rosamund Horwood-Smart, QC, *qv*; *Career* formerly: vice chm Mercury Asset Management plc, dir Mercury Fund Managers Ltd, chief exec Hill Samuel Investment Management Group; formerly dep chm Jupiter Asset Management until 1996; *Recreations* golf, fishing; *Clubs* Brooks's, Swinley Forest and Rye Golf; *Style*— Richard Bernays, Esq; ✉ 82 Elgin Crescent, London W11 2JL; Jupiter Asset Management, 197 Knightsbridge, London SW7 1RB (☎ 0171 412 0703, fax 0171 581 3857)

BERNBAUM, Prof Gerald; s of Benjamin Bernbaum (d 1967), of London, and Rebecca; *b* 25 March 1936; *Educ* Hackney Downs GS for Boys, LSE (BSc(Econ)), London Inst of Educn (PGCE); *m* 1959 (m dis 1987), Pamela Valerie, *née* Cohen; 2 s (Kevin Barry b 1962, Anthony David b 1965); *Career* asst master Mitcham County GS for Boys 1958–62; head of dept Rutherford Sch 1962–64; Univ of Leicester: lectr in educn 1964–70, sr lectr 1970–74, prof of educn 1974–93, dir Sch of Educn 1976–85, pro-vice chllr 1985–87, exec pro-vice chllr and registrar 1987–93; vice chllr and chief exec South Bank Univ 1993–; conslt OECD 1970–75; FRSA 1984; *Books* Social Change and the Schools 1918–44 (1967), Knowledge Ideology and Education (1977), Schooling in Decline (1978); *Recreations* professional sport, music, reading, walking in London, public affairs; *Style*— Prof Gerald Bernbaum; ✉ South Bank University, 103 Borough Rd, London SE1 0AA (☎ 0171 815 6004, fax 0171 815 6099)

BERNERS, Baroness (E 1455; 16 holder of Barony); Pamela Vivien Kirkham; er da of Vera Ruby, Baroness Berners (15 holder of the Barony; d 1992), and Harold Williams, JP (d 1971); suc on termination of abeyance 1995; *b* 30 Sept 1929; *m* 1952, Michael Joseph Sperry Kirkham; 2 s (Hon Rupert William Tyrwhitt b 1953, Hon Robin Raymond Tyrwhitt b 1958), 1 da (Hon Caroline Rosemary Tyrwhitt (Hon Mrs Gordon) b 1956); *Heir* s, Hon Rupert William Tyrwhitt Kirkham b 18 Feb 1953; *Style*— The Rt Hon Baroness Berners; ✉ Ashwellthorpe, 103 Charlton Lane, Cheltenham, Glos GL53 9EE

BERNEY, Sir Julian Reedham Stuart; 11 Bt (E 1620), of Parkehall in Reedham, Norfolk; s of Lt John Berney (ka Korea 1952), and Hon Jean Davina Stuart (who m 2, Percy William Jesson; and 3, Michael D Ritchie), da of 1 Viscount Stuart of Findhorn, CH, MVO, MC, PC; suc gf 1975; *b* 26 Sept 1952; *Educ* Wellington, N E London Poly; *m* 1976, Sheena Mary, da of Ralph Day, of Driftwood, Elm Green Lane, Danbury, Essex; 2 s (William Reedham John b 1980, Hugo Ralph b 1987), 1 da (Jessica Mary b 1982); *Heir* s, William Reedham John Berney b 29 June 1980; *Career* chartered surveyor; FRICS; *Recreations* sailing, hill walking; *Clubs* Royal Ocean Racing, Royal Automobile; *Style*— Sir Julian Berney, Bt; ✉ Reeds House, 40 London Rd, Maldon, Essex CM9 6HE (☎ 01621 853420)

BERNS, Richard Michael; s of Leonard Berns (d 1978), of Cobham, Surrey, and Elizabeth Grace, *née* Turner; *b* 16 Aug 1947; *Educ* Dulwich; *m* 16 Dec 1972, Roberta, da of Robert Dunlop Fleming (d 1978), of Perth, Scotland; 1 s (Ashley b 1969), 1 da (Antonia b 1974); *Career* slr; jt sr ptnr Piper Smith and Basham; dir Grange Park Securities Ltd; life govr Imperial Cancer Res Fund; memb Law Soc; *Recreations* sailing, skiing, tennis; *Style*— Richard M Berns, Esq; ✉ Leigh Hill House, Leigh Hill Rd, Cobham, Surrey (☎ 01932 862284); Piper Smith and Basham, 31 Warwick Square, London SW1V 2AF (☎ 0171 828 8685, fax 0171 630 6976, mobile 0836 227 653)

BERNSTEIN, Prof Basil Bernard; s of Percival Bernstein (d 1972), and Julia Bernstein (d 1931); *b* 1 Nov 1924; *Educ* Christ Coll Finchley, LSE (BScEcon), Univ of London (PhD); *m* 22 Nov 1955, Marion, da of Samuel Black (d 1955), of Manchester; 2 s (Saul b 17 Nov 1959, Francis b 24 Aug 1965); *Career* RAF 1942–46; teacher City Day Coll 1954–60; hon res asst UCL 1960–62; Inst of Educn Univ of London: reader sociology of educn 1963–67, prof sociology of educn 1967–79, Karl Mannheim prof in sociology of educn 1979, sr pro dir 1983–90, pro dir (res) 1983–90; emeritus prof of sociology of educn Univ of London 1990–; Hon DLitt Univ of Leicester 1974, Hon FilHDr Univ of Lund 1980, Hon DUniv Open Univ 1983, Hon DLitt Univ of Rochester USA 1989, Hon PhD Univ of Athens; *Books* Peoder, Education y Conciencia (1988), Class, Codes and Control (vol I 1971, vol II 1973, vol III 1975, vol IV 1990), Selection and Control (with W Brandis, 1974), Macht Kontroll och Pedagogic Liber Forlag Lund (ed with U Lundgrun, 1983), Pedagogy, Symbolic Control and Identity: theory, research and critique (1995), Children

Research & Policy (ed with J Brannen, 1996); *Style—* Prof Basil Bernstein; ✉ Institute of Education, University of London, 20 Bedford Way, London WC1 (☎ 0171 580 1122)

BERNSTEIN, Dr Robert Michael; s of Dr Fred Julian Bernstein (d 1986), and Dr Emilie Ellen Bernstein, *née* Guthmann (d 1995); *b* 31 Dec 1947; *Educ* Highgate Sch, King's Coll Cambridge (MA, MD, BChir), UCH Med Sch; *m* 29 Sept 1978, Frances Jane Northcroft, da of Dr Christopher Tibbits Brown, of North Mill, Wareham; 3 s (Jonathan b 1979, Nicholas b 1983, Jeremy b 1993), 3 da (Laura b 1981, Alice b 1986, Clare b 1991); *Career* sr registrar Royal Postgrad Med Sch Hammersmith Hosp 1981–85, visiting scientist Cold Spring Harbor Laboratory USA 1983–84, conslt rheumatologist and clinical lectr Univ of Manchester and Manchester Royal Infirmary 1985–; late memb Specialty Advsy Ctee in Rheumatology, chm Fibromyalgia Assoc UK; late members' columnist RCP, memb Editorial Bd Clinical and Experimental Immunology; late memb Nat Ctee Lupus UK, late bd memb Br Assoc for Performing Arts Medicine; memb Cncl Reform Synagogues of GB; FRCP 1990 (MRCP 1975); *Recreations* mountains, music; *Style—* Dr Robert Bernstein; ✉ Private Rooms: 23 Anson Rd, Manchester M14 5BZ (☎ 0161 225 1135, fax 0161 256 4717)

BERNSTEIN, Ronald Harold; DFC (1944), QC (1969); s of Mark Bernstein, and Fanny, *née* Levinson; *b* 18 Aug 1918; *Educ* Swansea GS, Univ Coll Swansea, Balliol Coll Oxford; *m* 4 Jan 1955, Judy, da of David Levi; 3 s (Mark b 1959, John b 1961, Daniel b 1965), 1 da (Sarah b 1963); *Career* cmd: 654 Air Op Sqdn RAF 1944–45, 661 Air Op Sqdn RAuxAF 1948–55; called to the Bar Middle Temple 1948, bencher 1975; recorder of the Crown Court 1975–90, dep official referee 1982–90; chm Panel of Arbitrators SFA 1992–94; FCIArb 1983 (vice pres emeritus), Hon ARICS, Hon FSVA; *Books* Handbook of Rent Review (1982–), Handbook of Arbitration Practice (jtly, 2 edn 1992), Essentials of Rent Review (with Kirk Reynolds, QC, 1995); *Clubs* Athenaeum; *Style—* Ronald Bernstein, Esq, QC; ✉ Falcon Chambers, Falcon Court, London EC4Y 1AA (☎ 0171 353 2484, fax 0181 348 7676)

BERRAGAN, Maj-Gen Gerald Brian; CB (1988); s of William James Berragan (d 1982), of York, and Marion Beatrice Berragan (d 1996); *b* 2 May 1933; *Educ* various schs in India and UK; *m* Anne Helen, da of David Boyd Kelly (d 1971), of York; 3 s (Howard Neil b 1959, Nigel Boyd b 1962, Nicholas Jeremy b 1967); *Career* cmmnd REME 1954, Lt attached 7 Hussars, trans RAOC 1956, Capt UK Belgium and Germany, Staff Coll 1966, served Maj York & BAOR, Nat Def Coll 1972–73, Lt Col 1972, Nat Def Coll 1972–73; Cmd: RAOC 3 Div 1976–78, AQMG HQ NI 1978–80; Col 1978, HQ DGOS 1978–80, Brig 1980, Cmd COD Chilwell 1980–82, Cmd COD Bicester 1982–83, Dir Supply Ops Army 1983–85, Maj Gen DGOS 1985–88; Col cmdt: RAOC 1988–93, RLC 1993–; chief exec Inst of Packaging 1988–, UK dir World Packaging Orgn; FCIPs; *Recreations* tennis; *Clubs* Athenaeum, Army and Navy; *Style—* Maj-Gen Gerald Berragan, CB; ✉ Institute of Packaging, Sysonby Lodge, Nottingham Road, Melton Mowbray, Leicestershire LE13 0NU (☎ 01664 500055)

BERRIDGE, Prof Michael John; s of George Kirton Berridge and Stella Elaine, *née* Hards; *b* 22 Oct 1938; *Educ* Univ Coll of Rhodesia and Nyasaland (BSc), Univ of Cambridge (PhD); *m* 5 March 1965, Susan Graham, *née* Winter; 1 s (Paul b 19 March 1969), 1 da (Rozanne b 4 June 1967); *Career* post doctoral fell Univ of Virginia 1965–66, res assoc Case Western Res Univ 1967 (post doctoral fell 1966–69); Univ of Cambridge: sr scientific offr Unit of Invertebrate Chemistry and Physiology 1969, chief sci offr Unit of Insect Neurophysiology and Pharmacology 1987–90; Agric Food Res Cncl Laboratory of Molecular Signalling 1990–94, The Babraham Inst Laboratory of Molecular Signalling 1994–; hon prof of cell signalling Univ of Cambridge 1994–; fell Trinity Coll Cambridge 1972; awards incl: Feldberg Prize 1984, The King Faisal Int Prize in Sci 1986, Louis Jeantet Prize in Med 1986, William Bate Hardy Prize (Cambridge Philosophical Soc) 1987, Abraham White Scientific Achievement Award (George Washington Univ Sch of Med) 1987, Gairdner Fndn Int Award 1988, Baly Medal (RCP) 1989, Albert Lasker Basic Med Res Award 1989, Heineken Prize Royal Netherlands Acad of Arts and Sciences 1994, The Wolf Fndn Prize in Med 1995; FRS 1984 (Royal Medal); *Recreations* golf, gardening; *Style—* Prof Michael Berridge, FRS; ✉ Dept of Zoology, Downing St, Cambridge CB2 3EJ (☎ 01223 336603, fax 01223 324387)

BERRIDGE, (Donald) Roy; CBE (1980); s of (Alfred) Leonard Berridge (d 1966), of Peterborough, and Pattie Annie Elizabeth, *née* Holloway (d 1986); *b* 24 March 1922; *Educ* King's Sch Peterborough; *m* 1945, Marie, da of Harold Kinder (d 1958), of Leicester; 1 da; *Career* chm South of Scotland Electricity Board 1977–82, dir Howden Group plc 1982–88; memb CBI (Scottish Council) 1977–83; FEng 1979, FIMechE; *Style—* Roy Berridge, Esq, CBE, FEng; ✉ East Gate, Chapel Square, Deddington, Oxford OX15 0SG (☎ 01869 338400)

BERRIGAN, Frances (Mrs Berrigan-Taplin); *b* 1943; *Educ* Santa Maria Ladies' Coll W Australia, Univ of W Australia (BA, Dip Ed); *m*; 2 c; *Career* television prodr/dir; teacher Australia 1964–65, prodr educnl progs Australian Broadcasting Cmmn 1965–66, researcher children's and higher educn progs BBC TV 1969–70, prodr educn and community progs BBC Radio London 1970–72, freelance bdcaster and journalist Paris 1973–75 (features contrib BBC Radio 4 progs incl The World Tonight, World at One and Today, contrib TES and THES, media conslt and writer for UNESCO), research fell Middx Poly 1976–77, lectr in media research methods Open Univ 1976–78, prodr/dir and co-ordinating ed BBC Open Univ Prodn Centre 1979–84; Cicada Films: joined 1984 (after producing Nature in Focus series), md and prodr/dir 1987–, latterly md and sole proprietor; Cicada prodns incl: Blue Eye of Siberia (for Channel 4 Fragile Earth strand, NY Film Festival Silver Medal, Channel 4 entry in Prix D'Italia), Birds as Prey (for Fragile Earth), Unnatural Disasters, China: An Environment in Crisis, The Great White Shark Hunt (for Fragile Earth strand), Making the Grade (for BBC Forty Minutes strand) and Soviet co-prodns Philby and The Krogers, Cutting Edge (Channel 4), The Club (Channel 4, finalist BAFTA Awards, 1995), various other wildlife and environmental films for Channel 4, BBC and others; *Style—* Ms Frances Berrigan; ✉ Cicada Films, 26 Great Western Road, London W9 2NX (☎ 0171 266 4646, fax 0171 289 2599)

BERRILL, Geoffrey William; s of William George Berrill (d 1969), of Cheam, Surrey, and Ada Alice, *née* Martin; *b* 4 June 1948; *Educ* Uppingham; *m* 10 June 1972, Karen Peta, da of Peter Frank (d 1974), of Tadworth, Surrey; 2 da (Victoria b 6 April 1977, Charlotte b 3 Oct 1979); *Career* dir: Alexander Howden Insurance Brokers Ltd 1980–83, Alexander Howden Ltd 1983–85, Halford Shead & Co Ltd 1984–86, HSBC Gibbs (HCA) Ltd (formerly Hartley Cooper Associates Ltd) 1986–; Freeman City of London 1969, Liveryman Worshipful Co of Glass Sellers 1969 (apprentice 1962); *Recreations* walking, gardening; *Style—* Geoffrey Berrill, Esq; ✉ Rook Hall, Kelvedon, Essex CO5 9DB; HSBC Gibbs (HCA) Ltd, Bishop's Court, 27–33 Artillery Lane, London E1 7LP (☎ 0171 247 5433, fax 0171 377 2139, telex 8950791)

BERRILL, Sir Kenneth; GBE (1988), KCB (1971); s of Stanley Berrill, of London; *b* 28 Aug 1920; *Educ* LSE, Trinity Coll Cambridge; *m* 1, 1941 (m dis), Brenda West; 1 s; m 2, 1950 (m dis), June, da of Arthur Phillips, of London; 1 s, 1 da; m 3, 1977, Jane Marris; *Career* served WWII REME; economist; former fell and bursar: St Catharine's Coll Cambridge, King's Coll Cambridge; prof MIT 1962, special advsr Treasy 1967–69, chief econ advsr 1973–74, head CPRS Cabinet Office 1974–80, govt nominee on Review Bd for Govt Contracts 1981–85, pro-chllr Open Univ (chm Governing Body) 1983–96; memb Stock Exchange London 1981–85, nominated memb Cncl of Lloyds 1983–88, chm Securities & Investmt Bd 1985–88; dep chm: Univs Superannuation Scheme 1980–85, General Funds Investment Trust 1982–85; chm: Vickers da Costa 1981–85 (joined 1980), NIESR 1987–96, Robert Horne Group plc 1987–90, Commonwealth Equity Fund 1990–95, Moneda Chile Fund 1995–; advsr Nippon Credit Bank 1988–; tstee London Philharmonic 1987–; *Style—* Sir Kenneth Berrill, GBE, KCB; ✉ Salt Hill, Bridle Way, Grantchester, Cambs CB3 9NY (☎ 01223 840335, fax 01223 845939)

BERRIMAN, Sir David; kt (1990); s of late Algernon Edward Berriman, OBE, and late Enid Kathleen, *née* Sutcliffe; *b* 20 May 1928; *Educ* Winchester, New Coll Oxford (MA), Harvard Business Sch (PMD course); *m* 1, 1955 (m dis 1969), Margaret Lloyd, *née* Owen (d 1995); 2 s; m 2, 1971, Shirley Elizabeth, *née* Wright (d 1993); m 3, 4 Aug 1995, Patricia Ann, widow of Dr Adrian Salter, of Sevenoaks; *Career* Citibank 1952–56, Ford Motor Co UK 1956–60, AEI Hotpoint 1960–63, United Leasing Corp 1963; dir: Morgan Grenfell Holdings (formerly Morgan Grenfell) 1963–73, Guinness Mahon 1973–87, Cable and Wireless plc 1975–88, Bahrain Telecom Co 1982–88, Britannia Building Society 1983–93, British Screen Finance Ltd 1985–91, Videotron Holdings Ltd 1989–, Sky Television plc (formerly Satellite Television plc) 1981–89 (chm 1981–85), East European Development Ltd 1990–92, EED Property Ltd 1990–94, Kent Community Housing Trust 1990–, KDB Bank (UK) Ltd 1991–, ALM Ltd 1993– (chm 1994–); chm: Bunzl Textile Holdings Ltd 1978–88, Alban Communications Ltd 1983–90, NE Thames RHA 1984–90, Knightstone Group Ltd 1992–93, Privatised Pension Tst 1995–; dep chm Nat Film and TV Sch 1989–92 (govr 1977–92), memb Br Screen Advsy Cncl (formerly Interim Action Ctee on Future of Br Film Indust) 1977–91, former memb Govt Ctee on Harland and Wolff Diversification; chm govrs MacIntyre Fndn (for the Mentally Disabled) 1972–95; govr United Med and Dental Schs of St Thomas' and Guy's Hosps 1982–84, tstee New Coll Oxford Devpt Fund 1989–95; FCIB, CIMgt; *Books* XYZ Case; *Recreations* golf, tennis; *Clubs* RAC, Royal St George's Golf, Valderrama Golf, Wildernesse Golf; *Style—* Sir David Berriman; ✉ Winwick House, Red Hill, Wateringbury, Kent ME18 5NN

BERRINGTON, Prof Hugh Bayard; s of William Majilton Berrington (d 1986), of Ewell, Surrey, and Grace Constance, *née* Smith (d 1931); *b* 12 Dec 1928; *Educ* Ewell Castle Sch Surrey, Nuffield Coll Oxford, Univ of London (BSc Econ); *m* 9 Aug 1965, Catherine Margaret, da of JC Llewellyn Smith, of W Bagborough, Somerset; 1 s (Andrew William b 25 Jan 1967), 3 da (Lucy Margaret b 20 Feb 1969, Sarah Constance b 2 April 1971, Mary Edith b 23 July 1974); *Career* Nat Serv RAF 1947–49; jr clerk Barclay's Bank Ltd 1944–47, Divnl Health Office and Co Educn Dept Surrey CC 1949–53, admin asst Divnl Health Office Wimbledon 1953–54, lectr Univ of Keele 1959–65 (asst lectr 1956–59), prof of politics Univ of Newcastle upon Tyne 1970–94 (prof emeritus 1994–, reader 1965–70); formerly memb SDP, vice pres Political Studies Assoc of UK; *Books* Backbench Opinion in the House of Commons 1955–59 (jtly, 1961), Backbench Opinion in the House of Commons 1945–55 (1973), Change in British Politics (ed, 1984); *Recreations* walking; *Style—* Prof Hugh Berrington; ✉ c/o Department of Politics, University of Newcastle upon Tyne, Newcastle upon Tyne NE1 7RU (☎ 0191 222 7530, fax 0191 222 5069)

BERRY, Hon Adrian Michael; s of Baron Hartwell, MBE, TD (Life Peer), *qv*; *b* 15 June 1937; *Educ* Eton, ChCh Oxford; *m* 1967, Marina Beatrice, da of Cyrus Sulzberger, of Paris; 1 s, 1 da; *Career* sci corr Daily Telegraph 1977–; FRAS, FRGS, FBIS; *Publications* The Next Ten Thousand Years (1974), The Iron Sun (1977), From Apes to Astronauts (1980), High Skies and Yellow Rain (1983), The Super-Intelligent Machine (1983), Ice With Your Evolution (1986), Koyama's Diamond (fiction, 1984), Labyrinth of Lies (fiction, 1986), Harrap's Book of Scientific Anecdotes (1989), Eureka: The Book of Scientific Anecdotes (1993), The Next 500 Years (1995), Galileo and the Dolphins (1996); *Style—* The Hon Adrian Berry; ✉ 11 Cottesmore Gardens, London W8 5PR

BERRY, Lady Anne Sophia; *née* Walpole; da of 5 and last Earl of Orford (d 1931; fifth in descent from bro of Sir Robert Walpole, the 1 PM & 1 Earl of Orford of 1 cr, and 1 cous four times removed of the litterateur Horace Walpole, 4 and last Earl of Orford of the 1 cr); *b* 11 Dec 1919; *m* 1, 1939, Col Eric Palmer, CBE, TD, DL (d 1980); 2 s; m 2, 1990, Robert James Berry, of Gisborne, New Zealand; *Career* horticulturist; awarded Victoria Medal of Honour (highest award conferred by RHS), hon fell RHS 1988; Hon DSc Univ of Exeter 1990; *Style—* The Lady Anne Berry; ✉ Hackfalls Arboretum, PO Box 3, Tiniroto, via Gisborne, New Zealand (☎ 00 64 6 863 7091, fax 00 64 6 863 7083)

BERRY, Anthony Charles; QC (1994); s of Geoffrey Vernon Berry (d 1983), and Audrey Millicent, *née* Farrar; *b* 4 Oct 1950; *Educ* Downside, Lincoln Coll Oxford (BA); *m* Susan Carmen, da of Derek Traversi, CBE; 3 s (Edward Paul b 8 Jan 1983, James Andrew b 15 Aug 1985, Richard John b 15 Aug 1988), 1 da (Tessa Jane b 17 March 1990); *Career* called to the Bar 1976; sec Criminal Bar Assoc 1991–93, memb Bar Cncl 1994–; *Recreations* golf, tennis; *Style—* Anthony Berry, Esq, QC; ✉ 4 Brick Court, Temple, London EC4Y 9AD (☎ 0171 583 8455, fax 0171 353 1699)

BERRY, Brig Anthony Edward; OBE (1982); s of Edward Joseph Berry, and Jean, *née* Larkin; *b* 4 Dec 1938; *Educ* RMA Sandhurst; *m* 3 Dec 1966, Sally, da of Lt-Col John Cairnes (ka 1943), of Dublin; 1 s (Nicholas Anthony b 1968), 1 da (Suzanna Claire b 1972); *Career* cmmnd KRRC 1958, Staff Coll 1970, CO 4 Bn Royal Green Jackets 1977–79, asst defence attaché Washington 1986–88, defence advsr Br High Cmmn Islamabad 1989–92; director Cancer Relief Macmillan Fund 1993–; memb Cncl (Pakistan) Br Cmmn Ex-Services League; Freeman City of London; KStJ 1993 (Dir of Ceremonies 1994); *Recreations* fishing; *Clubs* Army and Navy; *Style—* Brig Anthony Berry, OBE; ✉ c/o Army and Navy Club, Pall Mall, London SW1Y 5JN

BERRY, Dr (Anne) Caroline; da of Charles Rushton Elliott (d 1989), of Jersey, CI, and Evelyn Anne, *née* Le Cornu (d 1986); *b* 1 April 1937; *Educ* Bedgebury Park Sch, The Middlesex Hosp London (MB BS, PhD); *m* 13 June 1958, (Robert James) Sam Berry; 1 s (Andrew b 1963), 2 da (Alison b 1963, Susan b 1965); *Career* conslt clinical geneticist Guy's Hosp 1979–; FRCP 1991 (MRCP 1987); *Books* Rites of Life: Christians & Biomedical Decision Making (1987); *Style—* Dr Caroline Berry; ✉ South East Thames Regional Genetics Centre, 8th Floor, Guy's Tower, Guy's Hospital, London SE1 9RT (☎ 0171 955 4648)

BERRY, Claude de Pomeroy; s of Capt Paul Berry (d 1965), of St Helier, Jersey, CI, and Violet Ellen Patricia, *née* Lysaght; *b* 15 Aug 1938; *Educ* Wellington Coll, RMA Sandhurst, RAC Cirencester; *m* 1, 30 March 1961 (m dis 1983), Caroline Stafford Robinson, da of Capt Christopher Scott-Nicholson (ka 1945), of Whitecroft, Annan, Dumfriesshire; 2 s (Dominic b 18 Dec 1963, John b 7 June 1966); m 2, 5 June 1986, Meg (d 1994), da of Edward Gerald Hart Jackson (d 1963), of Filgrave, Bucks; *Career* cmmnd 16/5 Lancers 1958–61; farmer Scotland 1962–78, ptnr John Sale and Ptnrs (chartered surveyors) 1975–78, dir Tryon Gallery Ltd 1980– (joined 1978); ARICS 1973; *Books* Collecting Sporting Art (contrib, 1988), The Racehorse in Twentieth Century Art (1989); *Recreations* racing, hunting, ornithology, reading; *Style—* Claude Berry, Esq; ✉ 13 Colet Gardens, London W14 9DH (☎ 0181 741 5496); Mill Farm, Cadeleigh, Tiverton, Devon EX16 8HJ (☎ 01884 855245); Tryon Gallery Ltd, 23/24 Cork St, London W1X 1HB (☎ 0171 734 6961/2256, fax 0171 287 2480)

BERRY, Colin Derrick; s of Cecil Charles Ernest Berry (d 1968), of Kenton, Harrow, Middx, and Nellie Elsie Linda, *née* Young (d 1995); *b* 29 Jan 1946; *Educ* Wembley GS; *m* 4 July 1981, Sandra June, da of Arthur Albert Barker; 1 s (Jonathan Andrew b 19 June 1987), 1 da (Marina Jayne b 16 Jan 1985); *Career* broadcaster; former admin Granada TV, Westward TV and Radio Caroline (latterly newsreading and presenting sponsored programmes), freelance for Radio Medway (now Radio Kent) 1970–73 (also recorded on-air promotions for Radio 1 and announcer for HTV summer 1971), joined

Radio 2 1973; programmes presented incl: Night Ride, The Late Show, Music Through Midnight, Radio 2 Top Tunes, The Early Show, Band Parade, Two's Best, Europe 70/80, European Pop Jury, You and the Night and the Music, Gala Night, Happy Hour, Hogmanay Special, Sequence Time; writer and presenter various music series for BFBS and Inflight (programmes for airlines); TV appearances incl: Generation Game 1970's, Top of the Pops 1980, Wogan 1987, Going Live and Blankety Blank 1989; spokesman/chm London Jury on BBC TV's Rising Stars and Song for Europe, spokesman/chm UK Jury for Eurovison Song Contest; commentator for Barry Humphries Variety Club lunch 1988; *Recreations* Isle of Wight, country/coastal walks, Wimbledon fortnight, Victoria Wood, Thai and Peking/Szechuan cuisine, oysters and real ale; *Clubs* BBC; *Style*— Colin Berry, Esq; ✉ Radio Two Presentation, BBC Broadcasting House, London W1A 1AA (☎ 0171 765 3436/4695 (for messages))

BERRY, Prof Francis; s of James Berry (d 1952), of Malay States and Cheltenham, and Jane, *née* Ivens (d 1915); *b* 23 March 1915; *Educ* Hereford Cathedral Sch, Dean Close Sch, Univ of London (BA), Univ of Exeter (MA); *m* 1, 4 Sept 1947, Nancy Melloney (d 1967), da of Cecil Newton Graham (d 1929); 1 s (Scyld Berry, *qv*), 1 da (Melloney Poole); m 2, 1969 (m dis 1971), Patricia Tyler, da of John Gordon Thomson; m 3, 9 April 1979, Eileen Marjorie, da of Charles Eric Lear; *Career* 4 Bn Devonshire Regt 1939–46, Malta 1940–44; Univ of Sheffield 1947–70: asst lectr, lectr, sr lectr, reader, prof of English lit; prof of English Royal Holloway Coll Univ of London 1970–80 (emeritus prof 1980–); visiting appts: Carleton Coll Minnesota 1951–52, Jamaica 1957, India 1966–67; visiting fell Aust Nat Univ Canberra 1979; visiting prof: Malawi 1980–81, Japan 1983, NZ 1988; FRSL 1969; *Books* Gospel Of Fire (1933), Snake in the Moon (1936), The Iron Christ (1938), Murdock and Other Poems (1947), The Galloping Centaur (1952), Herbert Read (1953), Poets' Grammar (1958), Poetry and the Physical Voice (1958), Morant Bay (1961), The Shakespeare Inset (1965), Ghosts of Greenland (1967), I Tell of Greenland (1977), From the Red Fort (1984), Collected Poems (1994); *Recreations* following first class cricket; *Style*— Prof Francis Berry, FRSL; ✉ 4 Eastgate St, Winchester, Hants SO23 8EB (☎ 01962 854439)

BERRY, Dr Hedley; s of Edward Basil Berry, and Mathilde Josephine Berry (d 1982); *b* 18 Feb 1943; *Educ* Reading Sch, Wadham Coll Oxford (MA, DM); *m* 27 June 1974, Sonia, da of Joseph Tchoudy; 1 s (Michael b 1976); *Career* conslt physician and rheumatologist King's Coll Hosp 1976–; memb: Br Soc of Rheumatology, RSM; FRCP; *Books* Rheumatology and Rehabilitation (1985); *Recreations* music, travelling, eating, theatre; *Style*— Dr Hedley Berry, Esq; ✉ 21 Dorset Drive, Edgware, Middx HA8 7NT; 96 Harley St, London (☎ 0171 486 0967, fax 0171 935 1107); King's Coll Hospital, London SE5 (☎ 0171 346 6194)

BERRY, Ian Andrew; s of W S Berry, and Shirley, *née* Mackay; *b* 10 Jan 1953; *Educ* Univ of Toronto (BA); *m* 30 April 1983, Helen; *Career* trg Canadian Imperial Bank of Commerce 1976–80; Fixed Income Dept: Eliott and Page Fin Conslts 1980–82, Canada Permanent Tst 1982–84; currently md ScotiaMcLeod (formerly McLeod Young & Weir) 1987– (trader 1984–87, dir 1987–); *Style*— Ian Berry, Esq; ✉ ScotiaMcLeod, 33 Finsbury Square, London EC2A 1BD (☎ 0171 256 5656)

BERRY, Jack; s of Harry Berry (d 1989), and Nancy, *née* Potter (d 1953); *b* 7 Oct 1937; *Educ* Leeds and Boston Spa Secdy Modern Sch; *m* 30 Oct 1962, Josephine Mary Thames; 2 s (Alan Warwick b 30 May 1963, Martin Stratford b 13 April 1965); *Career* racehorse trainer; apprentice flat race jockey, nat hunt jockey for 16 years (first winner 1954); set record for a northern trainer with 143 flat winners in a season 1991, record holder for fastest 50 and fastest 100 flat winners in 1991, leading northern trainer for past six years; *Books* It's Tougher at the Bottom (1991), A Year in Red Shirts (1993); *Style*— Jack Berry, Esq; ✉ Moss Side Racing Stables, Crimbles Lane, Cockerham, Lancashire (☎ 01524 791179)

BERRY, Jamie Alistair Jagoe; s of Raymond Berry, of Dower House, Stonor, Oxon, and Phyllis, *née* Pegg; *b* 22 Dec 1955; *Educ* Harrow; *m* 2, 25 June 1992, Oonagh Mary Dode Patricia, da of U Alen-Buckley; 1 s (George Michael Jagoe b 3 Aug 1995), 1 da (Venetia Marina Patricia b 22 April 1993), 3 step c (Orlaith, Cian, Sorcha); *Career* GT Management plc 1973–81, md Berry Asset Management plc 1981–, chm Perpetual UK Smaller Companies Investment Trust; FIMBRA (memb Cncl 1984–87); *Recreations* sailing, shooting; *Clubs* City of London, Royal Thames Yacht; *Style*— Jamie Berry, Esq; ✉ The Chambers, Chelsea Harbour, London SW10 0XF (☎ 0171 376 3476)

BERRY, Dr John; CBE (1968), DL (Fife 1969); s of William Berry, OBE, DL (d 1954), of Tayfield, Fife; *b* 5 Aug 1907; *Educ* Eton, Trinity Coll Cambridge (BA, MA), Univ of St Andrews (PhD); *m* 20 Aug 1936, Hon Bride Faith Louisa, *née* Fremantle, (see Burke's Landed Gentry for Berry, Debrett for Fremantle), da of 3 Baron Cottesloe, CB, VD, TD (d 1956); 2 s (William, Peter, *qqv*), 1 da (Margaret); *Career* salmon res offr Fishery Bd for Scotland 1930–31, dir Biological Res Station Univ Coll Southampton 1936–39 (res offr 1932–36), chief press censor Scotland 1940–44, biologist and info offr N of Scotland Hydro-Electric Bd 1944–49, dir Nature Conservation in Scotland 1949–67; environmental conservation and fisheries advsr: N of Scotland Hydro-Electric Bd 1968–89, S of Scotland Electricity Bd 1973–89; environmental conservation advsr to Scottish Landowners' Fedn 1984–87; dir Br Pavillion Expo '71 Budapest 1971; fndr memb Int Union for Conservation of Natural Resources 1948; Cmmn on Ecology Int Union for Conservation of Natural Resources: pres 1954–56, vice pres 1956–60, memb 1966–72; memb: Court Univ of Dundee 1970–78, delegate to Cwlth Univs Congress, various Ct Appt Bds and Ctees incl Tay Estuary Res Centre (Int), Scottish Marine Biological Assoc 1947–71 (memb Cncl 1947–54 and 1957–66); UK rep Exec Bd Int Waterfowl Res Bureau 1963–72; chm Interdepartmental Salmon Res Gp (UK and Ireland) 1971–82; vice pres RZS Scotland 1959–82 (hon life fell and hon vice pres 1982), hon vice pres Scottish Wildlife Tst 1980; vice pres and memb Cncl Wildfowl Tst 1969– (hon life fell 1983), life memb Salmon & Trout Assoc 1926, life fell RSPB 1984; Br official rep Int Symposium on Hydropower and the Environment Guyana 1976, invited prof 'Cursurile de Vara Internationale' held in Al I Cuza Un Moldavia 1980; conslt on water impoundment biology (specialist on environmental and wildlife conservation and in water projects and their environmental and sociological impacts); Hon LLD Univ of Dundee 1970, Hon DSc Univ of St Andrews 1991; FRSE 1936; *Studies* Future Power Generation having regard to environmental conservation (financed by New Zealand Conservation Cncl, 1970 and 1975), Hydropower and the Environment, the Upper Mazaruni Devpt Project (UK Miny of Overseas Devpt, Nat Sci Res Cncl Guyana, 1976), Nature Reserves and Conservation in Iran (Iranian Miny for the Environment and the Br Cncl, 1975); *Recreations* natural history (especially wild geese and insects), music; *Clubs* New (Edinburgh); *Style*— Dr John Berry, CBE, DL, FRSE; ✉ The Garden House, Tayfield, Newport-on-Tay, Fife DD6 8HA (☎ 01382 543118)

BERRY, John Richard; s of Richard William Berry, of Cooden, E Sussex, and Margaret, *née* Hilliard; *b* 5 Aug 1948; *Educ* Berkhamsted Sch, Univ of Glasgow; *m* Anne Sarah, *née* Ronchetti; 1 s (Paul Mark), 1 da (Rachel Kathryn); *Career* Abbey National: joined 1969, trainee St Albans, various asst mangr appointments, branch mangr Putney and Ludgate Circus, nat sales mangr 1979–82, regnl dir London NE 1982–84, regnl dir Kent and S London 1984–87, regnl dir Central London 1987–88, field ops dir 1988–90, mktg dir 1990–93, European dir 1993–, dir Bd Abbey National France, Abbey National Bank (Italy) and Abbey National Bank (Spain); memb: Marketing Soc, Cncl Building Socs Inst; FIB, MIMgt; *Recreations* family, travel, gardening, DIY, politics, sport as spectator; *Style*— John Berry, Esq; ✉ Abbey National plc, Abbey House, Baker Street, London NW1 6XL (☎ 0171 612 4000)

BERRY, June; da of Edwin Norman Reeve, and Jessica, *née* Dibb Smith; *b* 10 Aug 1924; *Educ* Boston HS for Girls Lincs, Slade Sch of Fine Art (Dip in Fine Art London, design prize, awarded postgrad year), Wimbledon Sch of Art (Nat Dip in Design); *m* 1954, John Berry; 2 da (Harriet b 1958, Kate b 1963), 1 s (James b 1960); *Career* artist; RE 1986 (ARE 1982), RWS 1993 (ARWS 1989), NEAC 1990, RWA 1993; *Exhibitions* one and two person exhibitions incl: AIA Gallery London 1968, Fringe Soc Edinburgh 1968, Bangor Art Gallery 1969, Glynn Vivian Art Gallery Swansea 1969, Univ of Sussex 1969, Univ of Surrey 1970, Greenwich Theatre 1972, Univ of Southampton 1972, Bear Lane Gallery Oxford 1973, Massilon Museum and others Ohio 1975, Ogle Fine Art Cheltenham 1981 and 1985, Printmakers Cncl Gallery London 1981, Amalgam London 1987, 1990 and 1993, Bankside Gallery London 1987, Oriel 31 Newtown Powys 1987, Terrace Gallery Worthing 1991, Wherry Quay Gallery Ipswich 1992, Royal Exchange Theatre Gallery Manchester 1994, Alresford Gallery 1996, Alpha House Gallery Sherborne 1996; group exhibitions incl: RA Summer Exhbn 1982, 1988, 1990, 1992, 1993, 1995 and 1996, Singer & Friedlander/Sunday Times Watercolour Exhbn annually 1988–, Bath Contemporary Art Fair (Ogle Fine Art) 1984 and 1988–90, Art '90 and Art '91 (Business Design Centre London), Gorstella Gallery Chester 1991, 1992, 1994 and 1995, Open Print Exhbn Bristol 1991, International Waters (RWS touring exhbn UK, Canada and USA) 1991, Basque Int Exhbn of Watercolour (Seville, Bilbao and Barcelona 1992, Bilbao and Madrid 1995), Art Mart '92 Business Design Centre, Malcolm Innes Gallery Edinburgh 1993, Patterson's Gallery London 1993, 1994, 1995 and 1996), New Ashgate Gallery Farnham 1993, Nat Print Exhbn (Mall Galleries London 1994 and 1995), Our Environment in Watercolour (Christies London) 1994, Malta in Watercolour (Bankside Gallery London) 1994, Contemporary British Watercolours (Brian Sinfield Gallery Burford Oxon 1994; *Awards* first prize Watercolours of the North Whitworth Art Gallery/Coloroll 1987, Brandler Gallery Prize for Watercolour NEAC exhbn 1989, Kathleen Tronson Prize NEAC exhbn 1990, St Cuthbert's Mill Prize for Watercolour RWA 1991; *Collections* work in numerous private and public collections incl: Ashmolean Museum Oxford, Fitzwilliam Museum Cambridge, RWA Permanent Collection, Nat Museum of Wales, HM Treasy, Oldham Museum and Art Gallery, Kettering Art Gallery, Die Graphotek Berlin, All Union Soc of Bibliophiles Moscow, Wooster Art Centre and Museum Ohio, Univs of Sussex, Southampton and Cardiff, Kent CC, E Sussex, Herts, Lancs and Glamorgan Educn Ctees, Paintings in Hospitals Collection, St Cuthbert's Paper Mill (Inveresk Ltd); *Recreations* music, gardening, travel; *Style*— Mrs June Berry; ✉ 45 Chancery Lane, Beckenham, Kent BR3 2NR (☎ 0181 658 0351)

BERRY, Michael Robert William; s of William Berry (d 1976), and Lilian Gretton, *née* Buckley; *b* 8 May 1930; *Educ* Mill Hill Sch; *m* 1, 19 June 1954 (m dis); 2 s (Simon Frederick Michael b 23 Sept 1959, Timothy Robert James b 26 May 1961); m 2, 6 Sept 1991, Jean, *née* Kelso; *Career* Capt RAPC attached to 1 Bn KOSB 1955–56; CA; accountant Rack Engineering Ltd 1957–58, fin dir Sulzer Bros UK Ltd 1959–72, chm NW Region Best Western Hotels 1980–89, currently chm and md English Lakes Hotels Ltd; dir Cumbria Trg and Enterprise Cncl 1989–, dep chm Business Link Rural Cumbria (formerly Cumbria Rural Enterprise Agency) 1995– (dir 1991–); memb Commercial Membs Ctee Cumbria Tourist Bd 1972– (chm 1983–84), pres Ambleside Sports Ctee 1979–, vice chm and minister's nominee Northern Cncl for Sport and Recreation 1986–95, memb NW Regnl Advsy Ctee Nat Rivers Authy 1992–96, memb NW Chambers of Commerce Economic Ctee 1996–; tstee and dir Armitt Tst Ambleside 1966–, chm/sec St Bees Old Millhillians Assoc 1991–; FCA; *Recreations* walking, dogs, gardening, Cumbrian bibliophile; *Clubs* Old Millhillians; *Style*— Michael Berry, Esq; ✉ Pool Garth, Cartmel Fell, Grange-Over-Sands, Cumbria LA11 6NS (☎ 01539 531571, fax 01539 530106); English Lakes Hotels Ltd, Low Wood, Windermere, Cumbria LA23 1LP (☎ 01539 433773, fax 01539 434275, telex 65273)

BERRY, Norman Stevenson McLean; s of James Stevenson Berry, of Glasgow, and Mary Jane, *née* Oliver; *b* 23 Jan 1933; *Educ* Shawlands Acad Glasgow, Univ of Glasgow (BSc), Univ of Strathclyde (BSc); *m* 20 Oct 1965, Sheila Margaret, da of John Allan McMillan, DSO (d 1967), of Glasgow; 2 s (David John b 1969, Andrew James b 1970), 1 da (Ruth Margaret b 1966); *Career* student then asst engr Hugh Fraser & Partners 1952–57, Public Works Dept Eastern Nigeria 1957–61 (exec engr Roads Dept 1957, zone engr for Rural Water Supplies Programme 1958–61), water and sewerage engr Public Works Dept Solomon Is 1967–71; Babtie Shaw & Morton: asst engr water supply 1961–67, projects engr 1967, assoc 1975, ptnr 1977 (responsible for the Kielder Transfer Works incl 30km of hard rock tunnelling), md Water Div, dir Babtie Group 1993, sr conslt Babtie Group 1994–; *Awards* Telford Medal for paper on Kielder Transfer Works ICE 1983, Telford Premium for paper on Kielder Experimental Tunnel Final Results ICE 1984, Inst Medal for paper on Large Diameter Flexible Steel Pipes for the Transfer Works of the Kielder Water Scheme IWES 1986; treas Findlay Meml Church Glasgow; FICE, FCIWEM; memb American Soc of Civil Engrs; *Clubs* Royal Scot Automobile; *Style*— Norman Berry, Esq; ✉ 2 Fintry Gardens, Bearsden, Glasgow G61 4RJ (☎ 0141 942 0637); Babtie Group, 95 Bothwell St, Glasgow G2 7HX (☎ 0141 204 2511, fax 0141 226 3109, telex 77202)

BERRY, Very Rev Peter Austin; s of Austin James Berry, of Worcs, and Phyllis Evelyn Brettell; *b* 27 April 1935; *Educ* Solihull Sch, Keble Coll Oxford (BA, MA); *Career* Capt Intelligence Corps (Nat Serv and TA); bishop's chaplain Coventry Cathedral 1963–70, midlands regnl offr Community Relations Cmmn 1970–73, vice-provost of Coventry 1977–86 (canon residentiary 1973–86, canon emeritus 1986), provost of Birmingham 1986–; chm: Pre-Raphaelite Soc, Birmingham Int Cncl, Birmingham Standing Advsy Ctee for Religious Educn; memb General Synod (representing Deans and Provosts); rector Royal Birmingham Soc of Artists, govr Birmingham Blue Coat Sch; fell Univ of Coventry 1985–; church cmmr; chm Birmingham/Mirpur Friendship Soc 1994–; hon citizen Dallas USA 1994; *Recreations* theatre, architecture; *Clubs* St Paul's (Birmingham); *Style*— The Very Rev Peter A Berry; ✉ Provost's House, 16 Pebble Mill Road, Birmingham B5 7SA (☎ 0121 472 0709); The Round House, Ilmington, Warwickshire (☎ 01608 682518); Birmingham Cathedral, Colmore Row, Birmingham B3 2QB (☎ 0121 236 6323)

BERRY, Peter Fremantle; s of Dr John Berry, CBE, DL, FRSE, *qv*, of Newport-on-Tay, Fife, and Hon Bride Faith Louisa, *née* Fremantle (*see* Burke's Landed Gentry for Berry, Debrett for Fremantle); bro of William Berry, WS, *qv*; *b* 17 May 1944; *Educ* Eton, Lincoln Coll Oxford (MA); *m* 1972, Paola, da of Giovanni Padovani (d 1951); 1 s (Richard b 1979), 2 da (Sara b 1974, Anna b 1977); *Career* mgmnt appts Harrisons & Crosfield plc SE Asia 1967–73, dir Anglo-Indonesian Corp plc 1974–82; dir assocs and subsids notably: Anglo-Asian Investments Ltd, Ampat Rubber Estate Ltd Sumatra, Central Province Ceylon Tea Holdings Ltd, Colman & Co (Agric) Ltd, Walker Sons & Co Ltd, Anglo-Eastern Plantations plc 1990–93; Crown Agents For Oversea Govts and Admins: dir Asia and Pacific (res Singapore) 1982–84, dir ME Asia and Pacific 1984, md and Crown Agent 1988, dir various subsids and assocs; dir: Thomas Tapling & Co Ltd, T R Pacific Investment Trust plc, Scottish Eastern Investment Trust Plc; memb UK-Japan 2000 Gp; FRSA; *Recreations* international development, wildlife, country pursuits, Italy; *Clubs* RAC; *Style*— Peter Berry, Esq; ✉ Crown Agents, St Nicholas House, Sutton, Surrey (☎ 0181 643 3311, telex 916205, fax 0181 643 6518)

BERRY, Prof Robert James; s of Albert Edward James Berry (d 1952), of Preston, Lancs, and Nellie, *née* Hodgson (d 1956); *b* 26 Oct 1934; *Educ* Shrewsbury, Gonville and Caius Coll Cambridge (BA, MA), Univ Coll London (PhD, DSc); *m* 13 Jun 1958, Anne Caroline, da of Charles Rushton Elliott; 1 s (Andrew b 11 July 1963), 2 da (Alison (Mrs Glyn Jarvis) b (twin) 11 July 1963, Susan b 26 June 1965); *Career* lectr, reader then prof Royal Free Hosp of Med 1962–78, prof of genetics UCL 1978–; govr Monkton Coombe Sch 1979–92; memb: Gen Synod of C of E 1970–90, Cncl NERC 1981–87; pres: Linnean Soc 1982–85, British Ecological Soc 1987–89, Euro Ecological Fedn 1990–92, Christians in Science 1992–95, Mammal Soc 1995– (treas 1981–87); vice pres Zoological Soc of London 1988–90, memb Human Fertilization and Embryology Authy 1990–, tstee Nat Museums and Galleries on Merseyside 1986–94; FIBiol 1974, FRSE 1981; *Publications* Teach Yourself Genetics (1965, 3 edn 1977), Adam and the Ape (1975), Natural History of Shetland (jtly, 1980), Neo Darwinism (1982), Free to be Different (jtly, 1984), Natural History of Orkney (1985), God and Evolution (1988); ed: Biology of the House Mouse (1981), Evolution in the Galapagos (1984), Encyclopaedia of Animal Evolution (1986), Nature, Natural History and Ecology (1987); Evolution, Ecology and Environmental Stress (1989), Real Science, Real Faith (1991 and 1995), Genes in Ecology (jtly, 1992), Environmental Dilemmas (1992); *Recreations* walking, resting; *Style*— Prof Robert Berry, FRSE; ✉ Quarfseter, Sackville Close, Sevenoaks, Kent TN13 3QD; Department of Biology, Medawar Building, University College London, Gower St, London WC1E 6BT (☎ 0171 380 7170, fax 0171 380 7096)

BERRY, Prof Roger Julian; RD (1986); s of Sidney Norton Berry (d 1975), of NY, USA, and Beatrice, *née* Mendelson (d 1989); *b* 6 April 1935; *Educ* Stuyvesant HS NY, New York Univ (BA), Duke Univ Durham N Carolina (BSc, MD), Magdalen Coll Oxford (DPhil, MA); *m* 25 Sept 1960, (Joseline) Valerie Joan Berry, da of John Henley Butler, of Ramsey, Isle of Man; *Career* RNR 1971–92; PMO (Reserves) 1987–88, Capt Med Trg (Reserves) 1989–90; MRC external staff and head Radiobiology Laboratory Churchill Hosp Oxford 1965–74, clinical lectr in radiobiology Univ of Oxford 1969–76, hon conslt med radiobiologist United Oxford Hosps 1970–76; head of Neutron and Therapeutic Effects Gp MRC Radiobiology Unit Harwell 1974–76, Sir Brian Windeyer prof of oncology Middx Hosp Med Sch 1976–87, dir health and safety and environmental protection BNF PLC 1987–92, dir Westlakes Research Institute Cumbria 1992–95, ret; QHP 1987–89; visiting prof: Univ of Lancaster and UCL 1993–; Borden award for med res Duke Univ 1958, Roentgen prize Br Inst of Radiology 1970, Knox lectr RCR 1981, Florence Blair-Bell meml lectr Liverpool Med Inst 1982, Stanley Melville Meml lectr Coll of Radiographers 1987, Finzi lectr Radiology Section RSM 1989, Silvanus Thompson meml lectr Br Inst of Radiology 1991, Douglas Lea meml lecture Inst of Physical Sciences in Med 1993; memb: Nat Radiological Protection Bd 1982–87, Radioactive Waste Management Advsy Ctee DOE 1984–87, Ctee on Med Aspects of Radiation in the Environment Dept of Health 1985–87, Main Cmmn of Int Cmmn on Radiological Protection 1985–89, Advsy Ctee on Safety of Nuclear Installations Health and Safety Cmmn 1992–; chm Br Ctee on Radiation Units and Measurements 1995– (vice chm 1984–95), pres Br Inst of Radiology 1986–87 (hon sec 1970–73, vice-pres 1983–86); Freeman City of London 1982, Liveryman Worshipful Soc of Apothecaries 1984 (Yeoman 1981); FRCP 1978 (MRCP 1971), FRCR 1979, Hon FACR 1983, FFOM 1993 (MFOM 1988); OStJ 1990; *Publications* Manual on Radiation Dosimetry (with NW Holm); contrib chapters to: Oxford Textbook of Medicine, Florey's Textbook of Pathology, Hunter's Diseases of Occupation; *Recreations* sailing, music; *Clubs* Naval and Military, Royal Naval Sailing Assoc; *Style*— Prof Roger Berry, RD; ✉ Well Cottage, Parkgate Rd, Mollington, Chester CH1 6NE (☎ and fax 01244 851367)

BERRY, Roger Leslie; MP (Lab) Kingswood (majority 2,370); s of Sydney Berry, and Mary Joyce Berry; *b* 4 July 1948; *Educ* Huddersfield New Coll, Univ of Bristol (BSc), Univ of Sussex (DPhil); *Career* temp lectr in economics Sch of African and Asian Studies and assoc fell Inst of Devpt Studies Univ of Sussex 1973–74; lectr in economics: Univ of Papua New Guinea 1974–78, Univ of Bristol 1978–92; Avon CC: cncllr 1981–92, chm Fin and Admin Ctee 1983–86, dep ldr 1985–86, ldr Lab Gp 1986–92; Parly candidate (Lab) Weston-super-Mare 1983, Euro Parly candidate Bristol 1984, MP (Lab) Kingswood 1992– (also contested 1987), sec All Pty Disablement Gp 1995–; chair Full Employment Forum 1994–; vice pres Bristol Action for South Africa, memb MSF; *Clubs* Kingswood Labour; *Style*— Roger Berry, MP; ✉ House of Commons, London SW1A 0AA (☎ 0117 956 1837, fax 0117 970 1363)

BERRY, Hon Lady; Sarah Anne; *née* Clifford-Turner; da of Raymond Clifford-Turner, and Zöe, *née* Vachell; *b* 9 March 1939; *m* 5 April 1966, as his 2 w, Hon Sir Anthony George Berry (k in the IRA bomb explosion at the Grand Hotel, Brighton, 1984), yst s of 1 Viscount Kemsley (d 1968); 1 s, 1 da; *Style*— The Hon Lady Berry; ✉ Fox's Walk, Shurlock Row, Reading, Berks RG10 OPB

BERRY, (Anthony) Scyld Ivens; s of Prof Francis Berry, *qv*, of Winchester, and Nancy Melloney, *née* Graham (d 1967); *b* 28 April 1954; *Educ* Westbourne Sch Sheffield, Ampleforth, Christ's Coll Cambridge (MA); *m* 2 April 1984, Sunita, da of Brig M K Ghosh; 1 s (Sceaf b 17 Apr 1993), 1 da (Freya b 3 July 1991); *Career* cricket corr: The Observer 1978–89, Sunday Correspondent 1989–90, Independent on Sunday 1991–93, Sunday Telegraph 1993–; *Books* Cricket Wallah (1982), Train to Julia Creek (1984), The Observer on Cricket (ed, 1988), Cricket Odyssey (1988); *Recreations* village cricket; *Clubs* Hinton Charterhouse CC; *Style*— Scyld Berry, Esq; ✉ The Telegraph plc, 1 Canada Square, Canary Wharf, London E14 5DT

BERRY, (Roger) Simon; QC (1990); s of Kingsland Jutsum Berry, of Bristol, and Kathleen Margaret, *née* Parker; *b* 9 Sept 1948; *Educ* St Brendan's Coll Bristol, Univ of Manchester (LLB); *m* 1974, Jennifer Jane, da of Jonas Birtwistle Hall; 3 s (Richard James b 27 Nov 1979, Nicholas Peter b 25 June 1981, William Patrick b 17 Aug 1986); *Career* admitted slr 1973, ptnr Stanley Wasbrough (now Veale Wasbrough) 1975–77; called to the Bar Middle Temple 1977, asst recorder 1996–; memb: Middle Temple, Lincoln's Inn, Western Circuit, Chancery Bar Assoc, Ctee Chancery Bar Assoc 1984 and 1985, Professional Negligence Bar Assoc; *Recreations* family, the performing arts, cycling, skiing, keeping fit; *Clubs* Ski Club of GB, Riverside; *Style*— Mr Simon Berry, QC; ✉ 9 Old Square, Ground Floor, Lincoln's Inn, London WC2A 3SR (☎ 0171 405 4682, fax 0171 831 7107)

BERRY, William; WS; s of Dr John Berry, CBE, DL, FRSE, *qv*, of Newport-on-Tay, Fife, and Hon Bride Faith Louisa, *née* Fremantle (see Burke's Landed Gentry for Berry, Debrett for Fremantle); bro of Peter Fremantle Berry, *qv*; *b* 26 Sept 1939; *Educ* Eton, Univ of St Andrews (MA), Univ of Edinburgh (LLB); *m* 1973, Elizabeth, da of Sir Edward Warner, KCMG, OBE, of Blockley, Glos; 2 s (John b 1976, Robert b 1978); *Career* sr ptnr Murray Beith & Murray WS Edinburgh, chm Scottish Life Assurance Co 1993– (formerly dep chm), dep chm Inchcape Family Investments Ltd; dir: Scottish American Investment Co, Fleming Continental European Investment Trust, Alliance Trust, Second Alliance Trust, Dawnfresh Seafoods Ltd, various other cos; memb Royal Co of Archers (Queen's Body Guard for Scotland); dep chm Edinburgh Int Festival 1985–89, chm New Town Concerts Soc Edinburgh, tstee Royal Botanic Garden Edinburgh 1986–94; NP, FRSA; *Recreations* music, shooting, forestry; *Clubs* New (Edinburgh); *Style*— William Berry, Esq, WS; ✉ 39 Castle St, Edinburgh EH2 3BH; Tayfield, Newport-on-Tay, Fife DD6 8HA

BERRY OTTAWAY, Peter; s of Cecil Berry Ottaway (d 1986), of Sutton St Nicholas, Hereford, and Myfanwy, *née* Thomas; *b* 17 Feb 1942; *Educ* Steyning GS, Univ of London (BSc), Univ Coll of Rhodesia and Nyasaland; *m* 21 Dec 1963, Andrea, da of Richard Sampson, ED, of South Carolina, USA; 2 s (Gareth b 10 July 1965 (decd), Charles b 9 Oct 1986), 2 da (Samantha b 30 April 1969, Georgina b 17 Jan 1981); *Career* cmmnd Trg Branch RAFVR 1968–95 (Sqdn Ldr); res scientist Zambian Govt WHO 1963–65; res mgmnt: Unilever Ltd 1965–67, General Foods Ltd 1967–74; int consultancy in food technol, food sci and nutrition 1974–81, dir of sci and technol (Europe) Shaklee Corporation California USA 1981, md Berry Ottaway & Associates Ltd, dir Mercia Testing Laboratories Ltd, consulting scientist 1987–; memb Duke of Edinburgh's Award Ctee Herefordshire, treas Sports Nutrition Fndn; CBiol, FRSH 1974, MIBiol 1978, FIFST 1981, FRIPHH; *Books* Food for Sport (1985), Nutrition in Sport (ed with Dr D H Shrimpton, 1986), Preservatives in Food (1988), Nutritional Enhancement of Food (jtly, 1989), The Technology of Vitamins in Food (ed, 1992), The Harmonisation of European Union Food Legislation (1995), The Sanyati Survival Expedition (1996); *Recreations* light aviation, hill walking, art; *Clubs* RAF; *Style*— Peter Berry Ottaway, Esq; ✉ The Cedars, St Margaret's Road, Hereford HR1 1TS (☎ 01432 276 368); Berry Ottaway & Associates Ltd, Plough Lane, Hereford HR4 0EL (☎ 01432 270 886, fax 01432 270 808)

BERTHON, Vice Adm Sir Stephen Ferrier; KCB (1979); s of Rear Adm Charles Pierre Berthon, CBE (d 1965), of Deddington, Oxon, and Ruth, *née* Ferrier; *b* 24 Aug 1922; *Educ* RNC Dartmouth; *m* 1948, Elizabeth, da of Henry Leigh-Bennett; 2 s, 2 da; *Career* served WWII RN, Dep Chief Def Staff (Operational Requirements) 1978–80, ret 1981; *Recreations* riding, hunting, gardening, walking; *Clubs* Army and Navy; *Style*— Vice Adm Sir Stephen Berthon, KCB; ✉ Garden House, Stert, Devizes, Wilts

BERTHOUD, Anne Dorothy; da of George Esmond Berthoud (d 1943), and Dorette Edmee, *née* Oswald; *b* 5 Sept 1942; *Educ* Lyce'e de Jeunes Filles de Rabat Morocco, Lausanne Univ Switzerland (MA); *Career* gallery owner; publishing editions Rencontre Lausanne 1966–68, Linguistic Dept Mexico Olympic Games 1968, sec to Del in Athens of Int Ctee of the Red Cross (Geneva) 1969–71, head Film Dept of French Inst (London) 1971–76, Douglas Rae Management (lit agency) 1976–78, Hester Van Royen Gallery (Covent Garden) 1978–81, Anne Berthoud Gallery 1981–; *Style*— Ms Anne Berthoud; ✉ 4A Stanley Crescent, London W11 2NB (☎ 0171 229 8400, 0171 221 8185)

BERTHOUD, Prof Jacques Alexandre; s of Rev Alexandre Léon Berthoud (d 1962), of Neuchatel, Switzerland, and Madeleine, *née* Bourquin (d 1989); *b* 1 March 1935; *Educ* Collège de Genève Switzerland, Maritzburg Coll Natal SA, Witwatersrand Univ (BA); *m* 1958, Astrid Irene, da of Maj Eugene Titlestad, of Qudeni, Zululand; 1 s (Tristan Alexandre b 1964), 2 da (Dr Mireille Christine Berthoud b 1958, Josephine Madeleine (Mrs Berthoud-Dubreuil) b 1960); *Career* lectr Dept of Eng Univ of Natal Pietermaritzburg 1961–67, lectr then sr lectr Dept of Eng Univ of Southampton 1967–80; Univ of York: prof and head Dept of English and Related Lit 1980–, dep vice chllr 1987–90; visiting fell Trinity Coll Cambridge 1990–91; nat chm Br Section Amnesty Int 1978–80, pres Int Assoc of Univ Profs of Eng 1987; memb: Cncl Joseph Conrad Soc, Laurence Sterne Tst; *Books* Uys Krige (jtly, 1966), Joseph Conrad (1978); *Style*— Prof Jacques Berthoud; ✉ 30 New Walk Terrace, Fishergate, York YO1 4BG (☎ 01904 629212); Department of English and Related Literature, University of York, Heslington, York YO1 5DD

BERTHOUD, Sir Martin Seymour; KCVO (1985), CMG (1985); s of Sir Eric Berthoud, KCMG (d 1989), and Ruth Tilston (d 1988); *b* 20 Aug 1931; *Educ* Rugby, Magdalen Coll Oxford (BA, Capt Oxford Rugby Fives and Half Blue); *m* 10 Dec 1960, Marguerite Joan Richarda, da of Col Desmond Phayre, of Collatons, Bow, Crediton, Devon; 3 s (Colin b 1962, Charlton b 1963, Christopher b 1967), 1 da (Isabella b 1968); *Career* HM Dip Serv; third sec Tehran 1956–58, first sec Manila 1961–64, first sec Pretoria/Cape Town 1968–71, first sec Tehran 1971–74, cnsllr Helsinki 1974–77, head N American Dept FCO 1977–79 (inspectorate 1979–82), cnsllr and consul gen Sydney 1982–85, high cmmr Port of Spain 1985–91; dir Wates Fndn 1993–; memb Nat Tst; Cdr Order of the Lion Finland (1976); *Recreations* tennis, squash, golf, bird-watching, photography; *Clubs* Utd Oxford & Cambridge Univs; *Style*— Sir Martin Berthoud, KCVO, CMG; ✉ Gillyflower, Stoke by Nayland, Suffolk CO6 4RD (☎ 01206 263 237)

BERTIE, HMEH Prince and Grand Master of the Sovereign Military Hospitaller Order of St John of Jerusalem, of Rhodes and of Malta; Frà Andrew Willoughby Ninian; er s of Lt Cdr the Hon James Willoughby Bertie, RN (d 1966; yst s of 7 Earl of Abingdon), and Lady Jean Crichton-Stuart (d 1995), yr da of 4 Marquess of Bute, KT; *b* 15 May 1929; *Educ* Ampleforth, ChCh Oxford (MA), Sch of Oriental and African Studies Univ of London; *Career* Lt Scots Guards 1948–50; with City Press 1954–57, Ethicon 1957–59, Worth Sch 1960–83; elected Prince and Grand Master of the Sovereign Military Hospitaller Order of St John of Jerusalem, of Rhodes and of Malta 1988; *Recreations* reading, gardening, judo, fencing; *Clubs* Turf, RAC, Caccia (Rome), Scacchi (Rome), Casino (Malta); *Style*— His Most Eminent Highness the Prince and Grand Master of the Sovereign Military Hospitaller Order of St John of Jerusalem, of Rhodes and of Malta; ✉ Via Condotti 68, 00187 Rome, Italy (☎ 00 39 6 675 811, fax 00 39 6 679 7202, telex 612622 SMOM)

BERTIE, (Charles) Peregrine Albemarle; s of Lt Cdr the Hon James Willoughby Bertie, RN (d 1966, yst s of 7 Earl of Abingdon), and Lady Jean Crichton-Stuart (d 1995), yr da of 4 Marquess of Bute, KT; bro of the Prince and Grand Master SMOM (Andrew Willoughby Ninian Bertie), *qv*; *b* 2 Jan 1932; *Educ* Ampleforth; *m* 20 April 1960, Susan Griselda Ann Lyon, da of Maj John Lycett Wills, of Allanbay Park, Binfield, Berks; 1 s (David Montagu Albemarle b 12 Feb 1963), 1 da (Caroline Georgina Rose (Mrs Andrew Carrington) b 16 March 1965); *Career* Capt Scots Gds 1950–54; High Sheriff of Berkshire 1986–87; Kt of Obedience SMOM; pres The British Assoc 1995; memb Queen's Body Guard for Scot (Royal Co of Archers), Liveryman Worshipful Co of Armourers and Brasiers; KStJ 1996; Kt Cdr Order of St Gregory the Great 1983, Cdr of Merit with Swords Order Pro Merito Melitensi; *Clubs* Turf, White's, Pratt's; *Style*— Peregrine Bertie, Esq; ✉ Frilsham Manor, Hermitage, Newbury, Berks RG18 9UZ (☎ 01635 201291)

BERTRAM, Dr Brian Colin Ricardo; s of Dr George Colin Lawder Bertram, of Graffham, Sussex, and Dr Cicely Kate Ricardo Bertram; *b* 14 April 1944; *Educ* Perse Sch Cambridge, St John's Coll Cambridge (BA, PhD, TH Huxley Award Certificate of Commendation); *m* 3 May 1975, Katharine Jean, da of Francis Blaise Gillie, CBE (d 1981); 1 s (Nicholas Blaise Ricardo b 1983), 2 da (Joanna Mary Ricardo b 1981, Felicity Kate Ricardo (twin) b 1983); *Career* res fell Serengeti Res Inst Tanzania 1969–73, sr res fell King's Coll Cambridge 1976–79, curator of mammals Zoological Soc of London 1980–87, dir gen The Wildfowl & Wetlands Tst 1987–92; freelance zoological advsr 1993–; co-ordinator overseas conservation prog Federation of Zoological Gardens 1994–, special projects co-ordinator Bristol Zoo 1995–; vice pres World Pheasant Assoc 1990–, memb Cncl Zoological Soc of London 1993–; FIBiol 1979; *Books* Pride of Lions (1978), The Ostrich Communal Nesting System (1992); *Recreations* family, animals, garden, friends; *Clubs* Zoological; *Style*— Dr Brian Bertram; ✉ Fieldhead, Amberley, Stroud, Glos GL5 5AG (☎ 01453 872796)

BERTRAM, Claus-Werner; s of Ernst-Werner Bertram (d 1988), of Munich, and Maria Bertram; *b* 7 July 1945; *Career* Deutsche Bank AG: Munich 1963–69, Head Office Frankfurt 1969–75, Tokyo 1975–79, New York 1979–83, Frankfurt 1983–91, md London 1991–; memb IOD; *Clubs* Foxhills; *Style*— Claus-Werner Bertram, Esq; ✉ Deutsche Bank AG London, 6–8 Bishopsgate, London EC2P 2AT (☎ 0171 971 7555, fax 0171 971 7529, mobile 0385 387039)

BERTRAM, Peter John Andrew; s of Capt George Robert Bertram (d 1936), and Ann Mary, *née* Regan (d 1984); *b* 26 April 1930; *Educ* Henry Mellish Sch Nottingham, Göttingen Univ Germany; *m* 14 Sept 1957, Winifred Rita, da of Wilfred Henry Parr (d 1974); 2 s (Christopher b 1958, Timothy b 1964), 1 da (Nicola b 1961); *Career* CA in own practice Bertram & Co; md Old Market Square Securities Ltd 1984–; dir: Ryland Group plc, Longcliffe Golf Co Ltd, Tullett and Tokyo Forex International Ltd, Edinburgh Mortgage Corporation Ltd until 1996; sec The Shand Tst, chm Friends of Charnwood Forest; FCA, FCMA, FCT; *Recreations* golf, bridge, music, literature, travel; *Clubs* Royal Over-Seas League, Longcliffe Golf; *Style*— Peter Bertram, Esq; ✉ Cedar House, Nanpantan, Loughborough, Leics (☎ 01509 239253, fax 01509 217743); 89 Thomas More House, Barbican, London EC2 (☎ 0171 588 8431)

BERTRAM, Robert David Darney; WS (1969); s of David Noble Stewart Bertram (d 1981), of Edinburgh, and Angela Jean Weston, *née* Devlin; *b* 6 Oct 1941; *Educ* Edinburgh Acad, Oriel Coll Oxford (MA), Edinburgh Univ (LLB); *m* 23 Sept 1967, Patricia John, da of John Laithwaite, formerly of Prescot, Lancashire; 2 s (Andrew b 1972, Nicholas b 1975); *Career* ptnr Dundas and Wilson CS Edinburgh 1969–92, ptnr Corp Dept Shepherd & Wedderburn WS 1992–; non-exec dir The Weir Group plc 1983; memb: VAT Tbnl, Tech Ctee Inst Taxation 1986, Scottish Law Cmmn 1978–86, examiner Law Soc Scotland, memb Scottish Review Panel on Reform of Law on Security over Moveables 1986; ATII; *Recreations* books; *Clubs* Scottish Arts, Edinburgh Univ Staff; *Style*— R D Bertram, Esq, WS; ✉ Shepherd & Wedderburn, WS, Saltire Court, 20 Castle Terrace, Edinburgh EH1 2ET (☎ 0131 228 9900)

BERTRAM, (Charles) William; s of Lt-Col Richard Bertram, of Shenington, nr Banbury, and Elizabeth Florence Oriana, *née* Bedwell (d 1991); *Educ* Sherborne, Architectural Assoc (AADipl); *m* 16 Nov 1963, Victoria Harriette, da of Reginald Addington Ingle, of Timsbury, nr Bath; 1 s (Robert William b 1970), 2 da (Clare Victoria Harriette b 1965, Josephine Alice b 1967); *Career* fndr architectural practice William Bertram and Fell Bath 1969 (cons architects to Abbotsbury 1972), fndr William Betram Consultant Architects 1996; converted: Royal Crescent Hotel into 5 star hotel, Cliveden into hotel 1986–89; personal architect to HRH the Prince of Wales at Highgrove Glos 1987–, conslt to Eastern Region Duchy of Cornwall 1989, designer of Cavendish Lodge Bath; received: UK Cncl Euro Architectural Heritage Year Award 1975, Civic Tst Award for conservation of Abbotsbury Village Dorset, Civic Tst award for Dower House Bath 1986, Bath Conservation Area Advsy Ctee Environmental Award 1987, award for environmental design St Ann's Place and Environs; tstee Bath Preservation Tst 1966–68, listed in Architects Registration Cncl of UK; memb Br Soc of Architects, RIBA; *Books* An Appreciation of Abbotsbury (1973); *Recreations* tennis, landscape design, sketching, gardens; *Style*— William Bertram, Esq; ✉ Woodrising, Loves Hill, Timsbury, nr Bath BA3 1EU (☎ 01761 470718); 5 Gay St, Bath BA1 2PH (☎ 01225 337273)

BERTRAM-BROWN, Harvey; s of Dennis H Brown, of London, and Sandra M, *née* Finklestein; *b* 9 Jan 1966; *Educ* Haberdasher's Askes', St Martin's Sch of Art, Ravensbourne Coll of Art & Design (BA), RCA (MA); *Career* fndr memb The New RenaisCAnce (multi media co specialising in fashion and accessory design, display, styling and video prodn) 1991–; exhbns incl: Fouts and Fowler Gallery London 1991, Liberty London 1991, Premiere Classe Paris 1991, The World of The New RenaisCAnce (Royal Festival Hall and Parco Gallery Tokyo) 1992, Crafts in Performance (Crafts Cncl touring exhbn) 1993, In the Swim (Bremmerhaven Germany) 1993; TV and video work incl title sequences for BBC1, Ch4, S4C and Carlton, advtg work for British and Scottish Rail, W H Smith, TSB and Cusson's 'Pearl', window design for Liberty and Harvey Nichols London; *Style*— Harvey Bertram-Brown, Esq; ✉ The New RenaisCAnce, The Hall Studio, 23B Grove End Road, St John's Wood, London NW8 9BD (☎ 0171 266 2536, fax 0171 286 9280)

BESANT, Prof Colin Bowden; s of William Henry Besant (d 1949), of Plymouth, and Sarah Grace, *née* White (d 1975); *b* 4 April 1936; *Educ* Plymouth Coll, Plymouth Coll of Technol (BSc), Imperial Coll London (DIC, PhD); *m* (m dis); 1 s (Simon Bowden b 2 Jan 1968), 1 da (Christine Tanzi b 23 March 1963); *Career* scientific offr UKAEA 1960–64; Imperial Coll London: lectr 1964–75, reader in mechanical engrg 1975–89, prof of computer-aided manufacture 1989–; chm Turbo Genset Inc; HNC prizes IMechE and IEE; FEng 1988, FIMechE, FIEE, FINucE, FRSA; *Books* Computer-Aided Design and Manufacture (1986), Parallel Processing and Artificial Intelligence (1989); *Recreations* music, cricket; *Style*— Prof Colin Besant, FEng; ✉ Department of Mechanical Engineering, Imperial College, Exhibition Rd, London SW7 2BX (☎ 0171 594 7045)

BESLEY, Crispian George; s of Christopher Besley, of Wimbledon, London, and Pamela Geraldine Margaret Edgeworth, *née* David; *b* 21 Nov 1958; *Educ* Wellington; *m* 1, 1988 (m dis 1992), Elizabeth Charlotte (Libby), da of Thomas Bridger; m 2, 13 Aug 1994, Sarah (Sally) Helen Catherine, da of Stanley Morris; 1 s (Hugo Alexander Edgeworth b 14 Nov 1996); *Career* formerly dir Prudential Bache Securities Japan 1987; dir: Smith New Court Int 1987–95, Schroder Securities 1996–, Schroder Japan 1996–; *Recreations* motor racing and collecting classic cars; *Clubs* City Univ, Landsdowne, Annabel's, The Tasting Club, Raffles, Ferrari Owners Club; *Style*— Crispian Besley, Esq; ✉ Schroders, 120 Cheapside, London EC2V 6DS (☎ 0171 382 3000, fax 0171 382 3079, telex LONDON 885209)

BESSBOROUGH, 11 Earl of (I 1739); Arthur Mountifort Longfield Ponsonby; also Baron Bessborough (I 1721), Viscount Duncannon (I 1723), Baron Ponsonby of Sysonby (GB 1749), and Baron Duncannon (GB 1834); s of Maj the Hon Cyril Myles Brabazon Ponsonby, MVO, Grenadier Gds (ka 1915, 2 s of 8 Earl of Bessborough) and his 1 w, Rita Narcissa (d 1977), da of late Lt-Col Mountifort John Courtenay Longfield; suc his cousin 10 Earl of Bessborough (d 1993); *b* 11 Dec 1912; *Educ* Harrow, Trinity Coll Cambridge (BA); *m* 1, 1939, Patricia (d 1952), da of Col Fitzhugh Lee Minnigerode, of Virginia, USA; 1 s (Viscount Duncannon, *qv*), 1 da (Lady Sarah b 1943); m 2, 1956 (m dis 1963), Anne-Marie Galitzine; m 3, 1963, Madeleine Lola Margaret, *qv*, da of Maj-Gen Laurence Douglas Grand, CB, CIE, CBE (d 1975), of Delaford Manor, Iver, Bucks; 2 s (Hon Matthew Douglas Longfield b 1965, Hon Charles Arthur Longfield b 1967); *Heir* s, Viscount Duncannon, *qv*; *Career* served Welsh Gds 1940–46, Capt; company dir, ret; *Style*— The Rt Hon Earl of Bessborough; ✉ Roche Court, East Winterslow, nr Salisbury, Wilts (☎ 01980 862204)

BESSBOROUGH, Countess of; Madeleine Lola Margaret Ponsonby; da of Maj-Gen Laurence Douglas Grand, CB, CIE, CBE (d 1975), of Delaford Manor, Iver, Bucks, and Irene, *née* Mathew (d 1971); *b* 8 Nov 1935; *Educ* St Mary's Sch St Leonards-on-Sea, Priors Field Godalming; *m* 1963, as his 3 w, 11 Earl of Bessborough, *qv*; 2 s (Hon Matthew Douglas Longfield b 1965, Hon Charles Arthur Longfield b 1967); *Career* fndr The New Art Centre London 1957–, held over 200 exhibitions of British and Euro art, group shows incl St Ives 1946–56 and British Sculpture of the 1950s & 1960s, Roche Court Sculpture Garden opened as addition to gallery 1986–; memb Cncl RCA 1963–72; hon fell RCA 1973; *Recreations* gardening; *Style*— The Rt Hon Countess of Bessborough; ✉ New Art Centre, Sculpture Park, Roche Court, East Winterslow, Salisbury, Wilts SP5 1BG (☎ 01980 862244, fax 01980 862447)

BESSELL, Dr Eric Michael; s of William Henry Bessell, and Doris Mabel, *née* Willson (d 1992); *b* 17 Dec 1946; *Educ* Radcliffe Sch Wolverton Milton Keynes, Univ of Bristol (BSc), Inst of Cancer Research London (PhD), St Mary's Hosp Med Sch London (MB BS, MRCP); *m* 31 July 1971, Deborah Jane; 1 da (Laura Elizabeth b 29 Dec 1976), 1 s (Andrew Thomas b 29 Sept 1979); *Career* registrar in clinical oncology Royal Postgrad Med Sch Hammersmith Hosp London 1980–83, sr registrar in clinical oncology Royal Marsden Hosp London 1983–85, conslt in clinical oncology Nottingham Health Authy 1985–, clinical dir Dept of Clinical Oncology Nottingham 1986–96; FRCR 1984, FRCP 1993; *Recreations* mountain walking, piano playing, opera; *Style*— Dr Eric Bessell; ✉ Department of Clinical Oncology, Nottingham City Hospital NHS Trust, Hucknall Road, Nottingham (☎ 0115 969 1169)

BESSER, Prof (Gordon) Michael; *b* 22 Jan 1936; *Educ* St Bartholomew's Med Coll London (BSc, MB BS, MD, FRCP, DSc); *Career* house offr posts Bart's, Hammersmith and Brompton Hosps 1961–63, lectr in med Bart's 1966–68 (jr lectr in therapeutics 1963–66), NIH post doctoral fell Dept of Endocrinology Vanderbilt Univ Sch of Med Nashville Tennessee 1968–69; Bart's: sr lectr in med and hon conslt physician Med Professorial Unit 1970–74, prof of endocrinology (Univ of London) and hon conslt physician 1974–92, dir of Med Directorate 1990–92, prof of med 1992–, chief exec Bart's NHS Gp 1992–92; civilian endocrinologist RN 1989–, hon conslt endocrinologist Maltese Govt 1989–; RCP: second censor 1992–93, sr censor and sr vice pres 1995–97; review ed Clinical Endocrinology and Metabolism 1975–79; numerous int lectureships and professorships; Goulstonian lectr RCP 1974, Lumlean lectr RCP 1993, Sommer Meml lectr Portland Oregon 1977, Soc for Endocrinology Medal 1978, Chinese Acad of Med Scis Medal 1982, Clinical Endocrinology Prize 1986, Serbian Acad of Sci Medal 1987; Hon MD Univ of Turin 1985; memb/fell: RSM, Soc for Endocrinology 1969, Endocrine Soc USA 1971, Assoc of Physicians 1972, Euro Thyroid Assoc 1974, Thyroid Club 1975, Ovarian Club 1975, Physiological Soc 1978; William Julius Mickle fell for the advancement of med sci Univ of London 1976, scientific fell RZS 1978–92, hon memb: Assoc of American Physicians 1985, Royal Soc of Arts 1994; FRCP 1973; *Books* incl: Clinical Endocrinology: An Illustrated Text (jtly, 1 edn 1986, jtly, 2 edn 1994), Clinical Diabetes (jtly, 1988), Fundamentals of Clinical Endocrinology (jtly, 4 edn 1989); numerous published papers in learned jls; *Recreations* early Chinese ceramics, opera, ballet, theatre; *Clubs* Garrick; *Style*— Prof Michael Besser; ✉ St Bartholomew's Hospital, West Smithfield, London EC1A 7BE (☎ 0171 601 8342/3/4, fax 0171 601 8505)

BESSEY, Peter John Harvey; s of Cyril Leonard Bessey, of Twickenham, Middx, and Catherine Elizabeth, *née* Drury; *b* 17 May 1944; *Educ* Gunnersbury GS, Ealing Sch of Art, Central Sch of Art & Design (RSA bursary, industl and furniture design DipAD); *m* 18 Aug 1990, Joanna Mary Pokorski, da of Eric Bransby Gideon; 1 s (Matthew John Harvey b 1991); *Career* res and analytical chemistry BP Sunbury 1961–66; assoc: Keith Townend Associates 1970–78, Satherley Design Associates 1978–85; sr product engr PA Design (later Brand New Product Development Ltd) 1985–89, fndr ptnr Hothouse Product Development Partners 1989–; projects incl: Xenotron XVC3 Graphic Workstation/Terminal 1985 (COID Design Award), Esselte Meto System 2500 retail anti-theft system 1989–90 and System 2600 1994, Gerry Baby Products Co nursery monitor 1994, Kimberley-Clark handy pack wipes dispenser 1995; fndr memb SIAD Alternative Design Gp 1974, chm CSD Product Gp 1986–88, CSD rep Cncl Camberwell Sch of Art 1987–89, visiting tutor Central St Martin's Sch of Art 1988–; FCSD (1985, MSIAD 1977); *Recreations* dinghy racing, board sailing, photography, archaeology, travel; *Style*— Peter Bessey, Esq; ✉ Hothouse Product Development Partners, Merton Abbey Mills, London SW19 2RD (☎ 0181 543 0034, fax 0181 543 2250)

BEST, Gary Martin; s of Charles William Best, of South Shields, and Doreen, *née* Wright; *b* 6 Oct 1951; *Educ* South Shields Grammar Tech Sch, Exeter Coll Oxford (MA), Oxford Dept of Educn (PGCE); *m* 9 Aug 1975, Frances Elizabeth, da of Edward Albert Rolling, of Redruth; 1 da (Claire Frances b 1981); *Career* asst history teacher King Edward's Sch Bath 1974–80, head of Sixth Form Newcastle under Lyme Sch 1983–87 (head of history 1980–83), headmaster Kingswood Sch 1987–; Methodist local preacher; *Books* Seventeenth-Century Europe (1980), Wesley and Kingswood (1988); *Recreations* painting, music, reading, walking; *Style*— Gary Best, Esq; ✉ Summerfield, College Road, Bath BA1 5SD (☎ 01225 317907); Kingswood School, Bath BA1 5RG (☎ 01225 311627)

BEST, Dr Geoffrey Francis Andrew; s of Frederick Ebenezer Best (d 1940), and Catherine Sarah Vanderbrook, *née* Bultz; *Educ* St Paul's Sch, Trinity Coll Cambridge (BA, PhD), Harvard Univ (Joseph Hodges Choate fell); *m* 9 July 1955, (Gwenllyan) Marigold, da of Reginald Davies, CMG; 2 s (Simon Geoffrey b 1956, Edward Hugh b 1958), 1 da (Rosamund Margaret b 1961); *Career* 2 Lt RAEC 1946–47; asst lectr Univ of Cambridge 1956–61; Univ of Edinburgh: lectr 1961–66, Sir Richard Lodge prof of history 1966–73; Univ of Sussex: prof of history 1974–85, dean Sch of European Studies 1980–82; visitor and res fell LSE 1982–88; sr assoc memb St Antony's Coll Oxford 1988–; visiting fell: All Souls Coll Oxford 1969–70, Woodrow Wilson Center Washington DC 1978–79, Aust Nat Univ 1984; BRCS: chm Principles and Law Ctee 1980–84, hon conslt on Humanitarian law 1985–91; *Books* incl: Temporal Pillars (1964), Mid-Victorian Britain (1971), Humanity in Warfare (1980), Honour Among Men and Nations (1982), War and Society in Revolutionary Europe (1982), The Permanent Revolution (1988), War and Law since 1945 (1994); *Style*— Dr Geoffrey Best; ✉ 19 Buckingham St, Oxford OX1 4LH (☎ 01865 722793)

BEST, George; s of Richard Best, of Belfast, and Anne, *née* Withers (d 1978); *b* 22 May 1946; *m* 1, 24 Jan 1978 (m dis), Angela Macdonald Janes; 1 s (Calum Milan b 6 Feb 1981); m 2, 24 July 1995, Alexandra Jane, da of Adrian John Macadam Pursey; *Career* former professional footballer; Manchester United: joined 1963, FA Youth Cup Champions 1964, League Champions 1964/65 and 1966/67, European Cup winners 1968, 361 League appearances (137 goals), 46 FA Cup competition appearances (21 goals), 25 League Cup competition appearances (9 goals), 34 appearances Euro competitions (11 goals); rep Northern Ireland 37 times; honours: Irish Footballer of the Year 1967, Euro Footballer of the Year 1968, Br Footballer of the Year 1968, Sportswriters' Footballer of the Year 1968, Sportsman of the Year 1969 and 1971; Sky TV Award for Greatest Sportsman 1995, Greatest Sportsman of All Time Total Sport Magazine; currently after dinner speaker, sports commentator Sky TV and varied TV and radio work incl commercials; *Recreations* reading, crosswords, travelling, watching movies and all sports; *Style*— George Best, Esq

BEST, His Hon Giles Bernard; s of Hon James William Best, OBE, VD (d 1960), of Bridport, Dorset, and Florence Mary Bernarda, *née* Lees (d 1961); *b* 19 Oct 1925; *Educ* Wellington, Jesus Coll Oxford; *Career* Lt RM 1944–48; called to the Bar Inner Temple 1951, dep chm Dorset QS 1967–72, recorder 1972–75, circuit judge 1975–91; *Style*— His Hon Giles Best

BEST, Hon John Philip Robert; only s and heir of 8 Baron Wynford, MBE, *qv*; *b* 23 Nov 1950; *Educ* Radley, Keele Univ (BA), RAC Cirencester; *m* 10 Oct 1981, Fenella Christian Mary, o da of Capt Arthur Reginald Danks, MBE, TD (d 1996), and Hon Serena Mary, da of 4 Baron Gifford; 1 s (Harry Robert Francis b 9 May 1987), 1 da (Sophie Hannah Elizabeth b 1985); *Career* ARICS land agency div 1979; *Recreations* music, reading, shooting, bridge; *Style*— The Hon John Best; ✉ The Manor, Wynford Eagle, Dorchester, Dorset DT2 0ER (☎ 01300 320763)

BEST, Keith Howard; OBE (1983); s of Herbert Henry Best (d 1958), of Sheffield, and Margaret, *née* Appleyard (d 1925); *b* 16 Jan 1923; *Educ* High Storrs GS, Univ of Sheffield (BEng); *m* 5 April 1947, Maire Raymonde, da of George Ernest Lissenden (d 1965); 2 s (Jonathan b 1949, Clive b 1952), 1 da (Sarah b 1947); *Career* served WWII 1942–46, parachute sqdns RE France and Germany, Lt 1944, Palestine 1945, Capt; Husband and Co: asst engr Sheffield 1947–54, princ engr Ceylon 1954–57, ptnr London 1957–70; Bullen and Partners (now Bullen Consultants): ptnr Croydon 1970–81, ptnr Durham 1981–88, sr ptnr 1988–89, conslt 1989–; memb Cncl Inst of Structural Engrs 1968–71, pres Br Section Société des Ingenieurs et Scientifiques de France 1976, memb EDC (civil engrg) 1978–84; chm: Maritime Engrg Gp ICE 1981–84, Assoc of Consulting Engrs 1987–88, N region Engrg Cncl 1988–90; Freeman City of London, Liveryman Worshipful Co of Engrs 1985; FICE 1958, FIStructE 1957, FEng 1983; *Books* Best Endeavours (1992); *Recreations* sailing; *Clubs* Army and Navy, Royal Engr Yacht; *Style*— Keith Best, Esq, OBE, FEng; ✉ 7 Chessingham Gardens, York YO2 1XE (☎ 01904 701744); Bullen Consultants, Neville Court, Nevilles Cross, Durham DH1 4ET (☎ 0191 384 8594, fax 0191 384 6082)

BEST, Keith Lander; TD; s of Peter Edwin Wilson Best (d 1984), of Beeches, Pitt Lane, Hurstpierpoint, West Sussex, and Margaret Louisa, *née* Ambrose (d 1991); *b* 10 June 1949; *Educ* Brighton Coll, Keble Coll Oxford (BA, MA); *m* 28 July 1990, Elizabeth Margaret Gibson; 2 da (Phoebe b 22 Oct 1991, Ophelia b 2 Aug 1993); *Career* Maj 289 Parachute Battery RHA (V) and Commando Forces, served on HMS Bulwark 1976, naval gunfire liaison offr; called to the Bar Inner Temple 1971, barr in Old Steine Brighton 1971–87; borough cncllr Brighton 1976–80, MP (Cons) Anglesey Ynys Môn 1979–87, PPS to Sec of State for Wales 1981–84, direct mail conslt Nat Children's Home 1987, dir Prisoners Abroad 1989–93, chief exec Immigration Advisory Service 1993–; pres The Holyhead Festival Ltd, chm World Federalist Movement and Assoc of World Federalists, chm Cons Action for Electoral Reform; Freeman City of London, Liveryman Worshipful Co of Loriners; FRSA; *Books* Write Your Own Will (1978), The Right Way to Prove a Will (1980); *Recreations* walking, skiing, photography, being useful; *Style*— Keith Best, Esq, TD; ✉ 15 St Stephen's Terrace, London SW8 1DJ (☎ 0171 735 7699); 7 Alderley Terrace, Holyhead, Anglesey, Gwynedd LL65 1NL (☎ 01407 762972); Immigration Advisory Service, 190 Great Dover Street, London SE1 4YB (☎ 0171 357 6917, mobile 0385 323200)

BEST, Dr Michael Howard; s of Benjamin Frederick Best (d 1989), of Sidcup, Kent, and Betty Noreen, *née* Crawley (d 1970); *b* 6 Aug 1948; *Educ* Chislehurst and Sidcup GS for Boys, Univ of Newcastle upon Tyne (MB BS); *m* 4 July 1981, Sylvia Renée Martina, da of Hermann Rolf Pabst; *Career* house physician Dryburn Hosp Durham and house surgeon in paediatrics Newcastle Gen Hosp 1973–74, registrar Dept of Psychological Med Royal Victoria Infirmary Newcastle upon Tyne 1974–77, sr registrar Bethlem Royal and Maudsley Hosps London 1977–82; conslt psychiatrist: Frenchay Hosp and Glenside Hosp Bristol 1982–86, Charter Nightingale Hosp London 1987–89; in private practice 1989–; MRCPsych 1977; *Recreations* swimming, fell walking, antiquarian medical books, history of spa medicine; *Style*— Dr Michael H Best; ✉ 18 Upper Wimpole St, London W1M 7TB (☎ 0171 935 3940)

BEST, Norman Alexander; CBE (1980), DL (Hants 1992); s of Harold Ernest Best (d 1954), and Emily, *née* Webster (d 1990); *b* 5 May 1924; *Educ* St Gregory's Luton, Eggars GS Alton; *m* 11 Sept 1948, (Valerie) Mary Best, JP, da of Frank Archibald Appleton (d 1968); 1 s (Nicholas b 1964), 3 da (Julia b 1949, Hilary b 1953, Vivienne b 1954); *Career* WWII Dorset Regt and Queen's Own Royal W Kent Regt, serv with 8 Army N Africa and Italy 1943–47; legal profession 35 years (ret); Southampton City Cncl: cncllr 1967–94, leader 1972 and 1976–84, leader Cons Gp 1972–88, hon alderman 1994, memb various ctees (incl Policy and Resources, Strategy and Economic Devpt); Hampshire CC: cncllr 1973–, vice chm Cons Gp 1973–, vice chm Cncl 1992 and 1995, chm Cncl 1996; memb various Ctees incl: Policy and Resources, Public Protection (chm 1973–93); ACC: memb exec 1974–93, memb Consumer Service Ctee 1974–90 (chm 1974–79 and 1986–88), memb Fire and Emergency Planning Ctee 1974–93 (vice chm 1988–90 and 1992–93); memb: Nat Jt Cncl for Local Authy Fire Bdes 1974–93, Advsy Ctee on control of pollution of the sea 1974–90, LACOTS (fndr chm 1979), Univ of Southampton Ct and Cncl 1976–90, Mayflower Theatre Tst, Salvation Army Advsy Bd Southampton; Sheriff and Dep Mayor of Southampton 1988–89 (Mayor 1989–90); pres Southampton Test Cons Assoc 1981–96, memb Wessex Area Cons Local Govt Advsy Ctee; pres Age Concern Southampton 1987–96; vice pres: Inst of Trading Standards Admin, Hants CCC, Hursley Park CC, Southampton Musical Soc, Southampton Operatic Soc; Freeman City of London; FInstLEx; *Recreations* cricket, photography; *Style*— Norman A Best, Esq, CBE, DL; ✉ 1 Bassett Ct, Bassett Ave, Bassett, Southampton, Hants SO16 7DR (☎ 01703 769320)

BEST, Hon Patrick George Mathew; yst s of 7 Baron Wynford (d 1943), and Evelyn Mary Aylmer, *née* May (d 1929); *b* 5 Oct 1923; *Educ* Wellington Coll; *m* 29 March 1947, Heather Elizabeth, yr da of Hamilton Alexander Gardner (d 1952), of London and Assam; 4 s (Christopher b 1948, Michael b 1951 d 1952, David b 1953, Philip b 1960), 1 da (Clare b 1955); *Career* Lt RNVR, Channel, Atlantic, Med 1941–46; chm Wiggins Teape Group 1979–84; dir: BAT Industries 1979–84, BAT US Inc 1980–84; non-exec dir Ranks Hovis Macdougal 1984–88; Master Worshipful Co of Ironmongers 1985–86 (memb Ct of Assts); FRSA, CIMgt; offr Ordre de la Couronne (Belgium) 1982; *Recreations* skiing, golf; *Clubs* Boodle's; *Style*— The Hon Patrick Best; ✉ Monk's House, Durford Wood, Petersfield, Hants (☎ 01730 893176)

BEST, Sir Richard Radford; KCVO (1990), CBE (1989, MBE 1977); s of Charles Ronald Best (d 1960), and Frances Mary, *née* Raymond; *b* 28 July 1933; *Educ* Worthing HS, Univ Coll London (BA); *m* 1, 1957, Elizabeth Vera, *née* Wait (d 1968); m 2, 18 Jan 1969, Mary Kathleen Susan, da of Ernest Harry Wait (d 1977); 1 s (John Radford b 1973), 2 da (Anne Elizabeth Mary b 1961, Clare Caroline Frances b 1964); *Career* Home Office 1957–66; Dip Serv 1966–91: second sec (info) Lusaka 1969, first sec (econ) Stockholm 1972, first sec (commercial) New Delhi 1979, actg dep high cmmr Calcutta 1982, asst head Personnel Ops Dept FCO 1983, dep high cmmr Kaduna 1984, ambass Iceland 1989–91; ret 1991; memb Patching Parish Cncl 1993–; BBC 'Brain of Britain' 1966; Grand Cross Order of of the Icelandic Falcon; *Clubs* Royal Over-seas League, Nigeria Britain Assoc (life memb); *Style*— Sir Richard Best, KCVO, CBE; ✉ Holly Howe, The Street, Patching, W Sussex BN13 3XF (☎ 01903 871370)

BEST, Richard Stuart; OBE (1988); s of Walter Stuart Best, JP, DL (d 1984), and Frances Mary, *née* Chignell (d 1967); *b* 22 June 1945; *Educ* Shrewsbury, Univ of Nottingham (BA); *m* 1, 1970 (m dis 1976), Ima Akpan; 1 s (Peter b 1971), 1 da (Lucy b 1974); m 2, 1978, Belinda Janie Tremayne, da of Geoffrey Eustace Stemp, DFC, of Neill's Cottage, Lamberhurst, Kent; 1 s (William b 1984), 1 da (Jessica b 1981); *Career* dir: Br Churches Housing Tst 1970–73, Nat Fedn of Housing Assocs 1973–88, Joseph Rowntree Fndn 1988–; sec Duke of Edinburgh's Inquiry into Br Housing 1984–91, cmmr Rural Devpt Cmmn 1989–; chm: RDC Social Advsy Panel 1990–, UK Nat Cncl UN City Summit 1995–; memb: Social Policy Ctee of C of E Bd for Social Responsibility 1986–91, BBC/IBA Central Appeals Advsy Ctee 1988–91, Exec Ctee Assoc Charitable Fndns 1989–92, Community Advsy Panel IBM UK Ltd 1990–93; advsr Environment Ctee House of Commons 1993; *Clubs* Travellers'; *Style*— Richard Best, Esq, OBE; ✉ Director, Joseph Rowntree Foundation, The Homestead, 40 Water End, York YO3 6LP (☎ 01904 629241, fax 01904 620072)

BEST-SHAW, Sir John Michael Robert; 10 Bt (E 1665), of Eltham, Kent; s of Cdr Sir John Best-Shaw, 9 Bt, RN (d 1984), and Elizabeth Mary Theodora, eld da of late Sir Robert Heywood Hughes, 12 Bt of East Bergholt; *b* 28 Sept 1924; *Educ* Lancing, Hertford Coll Oxford (MA), Univ of London (CertEd); *m* 1960, Jane Gordon, 2 da of Alexander Gordon Guthrie, of Hampton Court House, Farningham, Kent; 2 s (Thomas Joshua b 1965, Samuel Stevenson b 1971), 1 da (Lucy Ann b 1961), and 1 child decd; *Heir* s, Thomas Joshua Best-Shaw, *qv*; *Career* late Capt Queen's Own Royal W Kent Regt, served WWII NW Europe; with Fedn Malaya Police 1950–58, church work 1959–71, teaching 1972–82, social work 1982–; Liveryman Worshipful Co of Vintners; *Recreations* bridge, writing; *Clubs* Cwlth Tst; *Style*— Sir John Best-Shaw, Bt; ✉ Belmont, 104 High Street, West Malling, Maidstone, Kent ME19 6NE (☎ 01732 843823)

BEST-SHAW, Thomas Joshua; s and h of Sir John Michael Robert Best-Shaw, 10 Bt, *qv*; *b* 7 March 1965; *Educ* Maidstone GS, Univ of Reading (BSc); *m* 19 Sept 1992, Emily Susan, da of Vivian Rubin, of Wateringbury, Kent; 1 s (Joshua John Kirkland b 17 Jan 1995); *Career* surveyor; Freeman of the City of London, Liveryman Worshipful Co of Vintners; *Recreations* piano, sketching, golf; *Style*— Thomas Best-Shaw, Esq; ✉ 4 The Terrace, Hadlow, Tonbridge, Kent TN11 0DL (☎ 01732 850036)

BESTERMAN, Prof Edwin Melville Mack; s of Theodore Besterman (d 1976), of Thorpe Mandeville, and Evelyn, *née* Mack (d 1964); *b* 4 May 1924; *Educ* Stowe, Trinity Coll Cambridge (BA, MA, MB BChir), Guy's Hosp (MB), Univ of Cambridge (MD, Raymond Horton Smith prize); *m* 23 Sept 1944 (m dis 1955), Audrey, *née* Heald; m 2, 9 July 1955 (m dis 1978), Eleanor, *née* Till; 4 s (Harvey, Tristram Besterman, *qv*, Adam, Gregory) from foregoing marriages; m 3, 7 July 1987, Perri Marjorie, da of Roy Burrowes, of Kingston, Jamaica; *Career* MO Outpatient Dept Guy's Hosp 1947, house physician Br Post-graduate Med Sch Hammersmith 1948, registrar Rheumatic Unit Canadian Red Cross Memorial Hosp 1949–52, lectr Inst of Cardiology and Nat Heart Hosp 1953–55, sr registrar Middlesex Hosp 1956–62; conslt cardiologist: St Mary's Hosp, Paddington Green Children's Hosp 1962–85; visiting cardiologist Malta Govt 1966–85; hon conslt cardiologist: Royal Post-graduate Med Sch Hammersmith 1981–85, Univ of W Indies Jamaica 1986–; FRCP, FACC; *Books* Paul Woods Diseases of Heart and Circulation (contrib, 1968), author of numerous articles on cardiological topics in learned journals; *Recreations* photography, breeding German Shepherd dogs, gardening; *Clubs* Liguanea (Jamaica); *Style*— Prof Edwin Besterman; ✉ Airy View, Stockfarm Road, Golden Spring, St Andrew, Jamaica, WI (☎ (Jamaica) 942 2308); PO Box 340, Stony Hill, Kingston 9, Jamaica; Dept of Medicine, Univ of West Indies, Mona, Kingston 7, Jamaica, WI (☎ (Jamaica) 9271707)

BESTERMAN, Tristram Paul; s of Prof Edwin Melville Mack Besterman, *qv*, of Stony Hill, Jamaica, and Audrey, *née* Heald; *b* 19 Sept 1949; *Educ* Stowe (music scholar), Univ of Cambridge (MA); *m* 1977, Peregrine Mary Louise, da of Gilbert Garceau; 2 s (Julius b 12 July 1979, Hugo b 9 Oct 1980), 1 da (Anna b 21 April 1983); *Career* BBC Radio 1971–73, res and design Geological & Mining Mus Sydney 1974, jackaroo on cattle station Queensland 1974, educn offr Sheffield City Mus 1974–78, dep curator and keeper of geology Warwickshire Museums 1978–85, curator Plymouth City Museums & Art Gall 1985–93, dir Manchester Museum 1994–; numerous articles in scientific and museological jls; FGS 1979, FMA 1985 (AMA 1979); *Recreations* music, cellist in chamber orchestras and quartets; *Style*— Tristram Besterman, Esq; ✉ The Manchester Museum, Oxford Road, Manchester M13 9PL

BESWICK, David John; s of David Beswick (d 1991), and Winifred Anne, *née* Davies (d 1985); *b* 30 Nov 1944; *Educ* Longton HS for Boys Stoke-on-Trent, Birmingham Coll of Food and Drink (Nat Dip Hotel Keeping); *m* 1 April 1967, Pauline Ann, da of late Arthur John Bayliss; 2 da (Allison Jane b 7 Aug 1968, Amanda Louise b 8 March 1971); *Career* mgmnt trainee Grosvenor House Park Lane 1963–65, asst mangr Grosvenor House Sheffield 1965–67, gen mangr Gulf Hotel BOAC Bahrain 1967–74, res mangr Sheraton Heathrow Hotel 1974–76, gen mangr Holiday Inns Inc Lagos Tel Aviv and Bermuda 1976–82, dir and gen mangr Broughton Park Hotel Preston 1982–89; gen mangr: Dalmahoy Hotel Golf and Country Club 1989, St Pierre Hotel Golf & Country Club until 1994, Redwood Lodge Hotel Bristol 1994–95, Cardiff Marriott Hotel 1995–; Master Innholder 1989–, Freeman City of London 1989; FHCIMA 1975, MInstD 1992; *Recreations* golf, gardening, study of wine; *Clubs* Rotary; *Style*— David Beswick, Esq; ✉ General Manager, Cardiff Marriott Hotel, Mill Lane, Cardiff CF1 1EZ (☎ 01222 399944)

BESWICK, Rev Esme Christiana; da of Nathan Coleman (d 1973), of Jamaica, and Ambroline Coleman (d 1980); *b* 9 April 1938; *Educ* Wyma HS Kingston Jamaica, West Ham Coll, Central Bible Inst (DipTh), Univ of London (extra mural studies); *m* 2 Nov 1962, Hubert George Beswick; 2 s (Derick Paul b 14 Feb 1964, Mark Anthony b 21 July 1965), 2 da (Michelle Marcia b 15 Oct 1969, Sharon Deborah b 24 June 1971); *Career* trainee nurse Queen Mary Hosp Sidcup and St Leonard's Hosp Bromley 1961–63; ordained Pentecostal Church Jamaica 1961, pastor of The New Testament Assembly Brixton 1965, hosp chaplain Whipps Cross Hosp 1986–91, gen sec Jt Cncl for Anglo Carribbean Churches 1989–; memb: British Cncl of Churches 1980–89, Cncl of Churches for Britain and Ireland 1989–; currently ecumenical borough dean; *Recreations* reading, swimming, cricket; *Style*— The Rev Esme Beswick; ✉ The Joint Council for Anglo Carribbean Churches, 141 Railton Road, London SE24 0LT (☎ 0171 737 6542)

BESWICK, Walter; s of Walter Beswick, of Draycott, Derbys, and Mary Elizabeth, *née* Skidmore; *b* 26 Sept 1933; *Educ* Long Eaton GS, Univ of Glasgow Vet Sch (BVMS); *m* 2 Sept 1957, Hazel (d 1992), da of Dr Alexander Shanks Bisset; 1 s (Walter Alastair Bisset b 7 Feb 1959), 1 da (Moira Carolyn (Mrs Syme) b 17 Jan 1961); *Career* asst in mixed vet practice Fakenham Norfolk 1957–60, princ in small animal practice Glasgow 1960–94; chm Scottish Region BSAVA 1970–72; BVA: pres W of Scotland Div 1967–68, pres Scottish Branch 1984–86, memb Cncl BVA 1983–94, chm Highlands and Islands Vet Servs Ctee 1984–94, pres BVA 1988–89; chm W of Scotland Med, Vet and Environmental Health Gp 1979–82, patron Scottish Pet Fostering Serv 1992– (chm of tstees 1985–92), hon vice pres Soc for Companion Animal Studies 1992– (memb Cncl 1989–92), co-ordinator VETCPD 1993– (dir 1990–93); Victory Medal (Central Vet Soc) 1989; MRCVS (memb Cncl 1990–); SBStJ 1984; *Recreations* field sports; *Clubs* St John House; *Style*— Walter Beswick, Esq; ✉ Imersay, 22 Boclair Crescent, Bearsden, Glasgow G61 2AG (☎ 0141 942 5188)

BETHEL, David Percival; CBE (1983); s of William George Bethell (d 1982), of Lydney, Glos, and Elsie Evelyn Gladys, *née* Cossins (d 1984); *b* 7 Dec 1923; *Educ* King Edward VI Sch Bath & Crypt GS, West of England Coll of Art, Univ of Bristol (NDD, ATD); *m* 1943, Margaret Elizabeth, da of Alexander John Dent-Wrigglesworth (d 1957); 1 s (Paul), 1 da (Ruth); *Career* designer and educator; lectr Stafford Sch of Art 1951–54, vice princ Coventry Coll of Art 1955–56 (princ 1965–69), dep dir Leics Poly 1969–73 (dir 1973–87); pres Nat Soc for Art Educn 1965–66; memb: Cncl Int Soc for Educn through Art 1970–77, Cncl for Educnl Technol 1974–80, Cncl CNAA 1975–81 (chm Ctee for Art and Design Res Degrees 1975–81), Hong Kong Univ and Poly Grants Ctee 1982–92, Nat Advsy Body for Public Sector Higher Educn 1982–87; chm: Design Cncl Educn Ctee 1981–89, Chartered Soc of Designers Educn Ctee 1987–91, Planning Ctee for Academic Awards Hong Kong 1986–87, Hong Kong Provisional Cncl for Academic Awards 1987–89, Hong Kong Cncl for Academic Awards 1989–92, East Midlands Regnl Advsy Cncl for Further Educn Academic Bd 1977–81, Ctee of Dirs of Polys 1975–81, Study of Primary Health Care Serv in E Midlands 1987–88, Cwlth of Australia Visiting Fellowship 1979–, Cyril Wood Tst, Jt NAB/UGC/SED Gp for Town & Country Planning 1985–; vice chm Inter-Univ Cncl for Higher Educn Overseas 1981–83; conslt: on tech educn South Africa CERTEC 1989, OECD/CERI on performance indicator for univs 1989–92, on research strategy to Columbian Govt 1990; assessor The Partnership Tst (industl design) 1991–93, co-ordinator Cons Academic Liaison Forum (Midlands) 1993, patron The Sir Richard Stapley Educnl Tst 1993, advsr Dept of Textiles and Fashion

Manchester Metropolitan Univ 1995–; Freeman City of London 1976, memb and steward Worshipful Co of Framework Knitters 1976 (chm Bursary Awards Ctee 1991–), memb Cncl Literary and Philosophical Soc Leicester 1995, Hon LLD Leics 1979, Hon DLitt Loughborough 1987; RWA (memb Cncl 1994–), FSAE, FSTC, FRSA, FCSD; *Recreations* travel, genealogy; *Clubs* Athenaeum; *Style*— Dr David Bethel, CBE; ✉ Stoke Lodge, 48 Holmfield Road, Stoneygate, Leics LE2 1SA (☎ 0116 270 4921)

BETHEL, Martin; QC (1983); s of Rev Ralph Arnold Bethel (d 1946), and Enid Ambery, *née* Smith (d 1996); *b* 12 March 1943; *Educ* Kingswood Sch, Fitzwilliam Coll Cambridge (MA, LLM); *m* 14 Sept 1974, Kathryn Jane, da of Isaac Allan Denby, of Riddlesden, Keighley, Yorkshire; 2 s (Thomas b 1980, William b 1981), 1 da (Sarah b 1976); *Career* called to the Bar Inner Temple 1965; recorder of the Crown Court (NE Circuit) 1979–, dep judge of the High Ct 1995–; head of chambers; *Recreations* sailing, skiing; *Style*— Martin Bethel, Esq, QC; ✉ Park Lane Chambers, 19 Westgate, Leeds LS1 (☎ 0113 245 2702, fax 0113 242 0683)

BETHEL, Dr Robert George Hankin; s of Horace Hankin Bethel (d 1961), of London and Eastbourne, and Eileen Maude (Mollie), *née* Motyer (d 1996); *b* 7 June 1948; *Educ* Eastbourne GS, Pembroke Coll Cambridge (BA, MA, MB BChir), St Mary's Hosp Med Sch; *Career* med practitioner; house physician Queen Elizabeth II Hosp London 1972, house surgn Nottingham Gen Hosp 1973, SHO Northwick Park Hosp and Clinical Res Centre Harrow 1974, registrar W Middx Univ Hosp 1974–76, gen med practitioner Englefield Green and Old Windsor 1976–; course tutor The Open Univ 1979–80, hosp practitioner in geriatrics 1980–91, pt/t rheumatologist Heatherwood Hosp Ascot 1976–92, trainer for GP (Oxford region) 1984–, assoc teacher Imperial Coll of Sci, Technol and Med (formerly St Mary's Hosp Med Sch) 1989–; med memb Ind Tbnl Serv (Disability) 1991–, med offr Brunel Univ 1993–; author of various scientific papers in med jls with particular interest in rheumatological and gen practice topics; advsy ed Horizons 1988–91; memb Exec Ctee E Berks BMA 1977–93 (divnl sec 1983–85), SW Thames Faculty Bd memb RCGP 1983–92, vice pres Section of Gen Practice RSM 1995– (hon sec 1993–95); The Cambridge Soc: memb Cncl 1991–, vice pres Surrey Branch 1995– (sec 1982–85, chm 1988–95); wandsman St Paul's Cathedral 1988–, vice chm Old Windsor Day Centre 1989–94; memb Soc of Genealogists; Freeman City of London 1977, memb Guild of Freemen City of London 1979, Liveryman Worshipful Soc of Apothecaries 1981 (Freeman 1977), memb United Wards Club of the City of London; fell Med Soc of London 1995; FRSM 1975, MRCGP 1979, FRSH 1989; *Recreations* genealogy, books, gardening; *Clubs* United Oxford & Cambridge Univ; *Style*— Dr Robert Bethel; ✉ Newton Court Medical Centre, Burfield Rd, Old Windsor, Berkshire SL4 2QF (☎ 01753 863642, fax 01753 832180)

BETHELL, Dr Hugh James Newton; MBE (1995); s of Brig Richard Brian Wyndham Bethell, DSO (d 1990), of Pilton House Barn, Pilton, nr Shepton Mallet, Somerset, and Jackomina Alice, *née* Barton (d 1979); *b* 31 March 1942; *Educ* Tonbridge, St John's Coll Cambridge (BA), Guy's Hosp (MB BChir, DObstRCOG, MRCP, MRCGP), FRCGP 1991, MD 1995, FRCP 1996; *m* 1, 1968, Astrid Jill, *née* Short (d 1979); 2 da (Katharine Emma b 25 Dec 1969, Christina Louise b 12 April 1973); m 2, 1984, Lesley, *née* Harris; *Career* cardiac registrar Charing Cross Hosp 1969–72, dermatology registrar Guy's Hosp 1972–74, princ in gen practice 1974–; dir Basingstoke and Alton Cardiac Rehabilitation Unit 1976–; chm Advsy Ctee on Coronary Rehabilitation to the Coronary Prevention Gp 1987–, founding pres British Assoc for Cardiac Rehabilitation, memb Br Cardiac Soc; fndr chm Alton Joggers; author of various articles; *Books* Exercise Based Cardiac Rehabilitation (1996); *Recreations* running, cinema; *Clubs* Hawks; *Style*— Dr Hugh Bethell, MBE; ✉ Farringdon Hurst, Nr Alton, Hants GU34 3DH (☎ 01420 588592); The Health Centre, Alton, Hants (☎ 01420 84676)

BETHELL, Prof Leslie Michael; s of Stanley Bethell (d 1969), and Bessie, *née* Stoddart; *b* 12 Feb 1937; *Educ* Cockburn HS Leeds, UCL (BA, PhD); *m* 1961 (m dis 1983); 2 s (Ben b 1966, Daniel b 1967); *Career* lectr in history: Univ of Bristol 1961–66, UCL 1966–74 (reader 1974–86); prof of Latin American history Univ of London 1986–92, dir Inst of Latin American Studies Univ of London 1987–92, fell St Antony's Coll Univ of Oxford 1993–; visiting prof: IUPERJ Rio de Janeiro 1979, Univ of Calif San Diego 1985, Univ of Chicago 1992–93; fell Wilson Center Washington DC 1986 and 1996; chm Bloomsbury Theatre 1977–86; author of numerous articles and chapters on Latin American history, the slave trade and slavery, the Paraguayan war, Brazilian history and politics, Britain and Latin America and the US and Latin America; ed Jl of Latin American Studies 1987–89; Cdr Order of the Southern Cross (Brazil) 1994; *Books* The Abolition of the Brazilian Slave Trade (1970), Latin America Between the Second World War and the Cold War 1944–48 (with Ian Roxborough, 1992); ed: The Cambridge History of Latin America - Colonial Latin America (vol I & II 1984), From Independence to c 1870 (vol III 1985), From c 1870 to 1930 (vol IV & V 1986), Mexico, Central America and the Caribbean since 1930 (vol VII 1990), Spanish South America since 1930 (vol VIII 1991), Latin America since 1930: Economy, Society and Politics (vol VI parts 1 and 2, 1994), Latin America since 1930: Ideas, Culture and Society (vol X 1995), Bibliographical Essays (vol XI 1995); *Style*— Prof Leslie Bethell; ✉ 2 Keats Grove, London NW3 2RT (☎ and fax 0171 431 5706)

BETHELL, 4 Baron (UK 1922) Nicholas William Bethell; 4 Bt (UK 1911); s of Hon William Gladstone Bethell (d 1964), 3 s of 1 Baron Bethell; suc cous 1967; *b* 19 July 1938; *Educ* Harrow, Pembroke Coll Cambridge (PhD); *m* 1, 1964 (m dis 1971), Cecilia Mary Lothian (d 1977), da of Prof Alexander Mackie Honeyman (d 1988), of Oldtown, Ardgay, Ross-shire; 2 s (Hon James Nicholas, Hon William Alexander b 18 March 1969); m 2, 13 July 1992, Bryony Lea Morgan, da of Bryan David Griffiths, of Llanrhystyd, Dyfed; 1 s (Hon John Andrew Rowland b 18 Aug 1992); *Heir* s, Hon James Nicholas Bethell b 1 Oct 1967; *Career* takes Cons Whip in House of Lords; chm Freedom of the Skies Campaign (lobby gp against Europe airline fares cartel); sub-editor TLS 1962–64, script editor BBC Radio Drama 1964–67; a govt whip 1970–71, nominated MEP 1975–79, elected MEP (Cons) London NW 1979–94; Order of Merit (Poland) 1991; *Books* Gomulka, The War Hitler Won, The Last Secret, Russia Besieged, The Palestine Triangle, The Great Betrayal, Spies and Other Secrets; trans: Cancer Ward (by Alexander Solzhenitsyn), Elegy to John Donne (by Joseph Brodsky), Six Plays (by Slawomir Mrozek); *Recreations* poker, cricket; *Clubs* Pratt's, Garrick, MCC; *Style*— The Rt Hon the Lord Bethell; ✉ Manor Farm, Brill, Bucks HP18 9SL

BETHELL, The Hon Richard Nicholas; MBE (1979); s and h of 5 Baron Westbury, MC; *b* 29 May 1950; *Educ* Harrow, RMA Sandhurst; *m* 1, 1975 (m dis 1991), Caroline, da of Richard Palmer, JP, of Swallowfield, Berks; 1 s, 1 da; m 2, 1993, Charlotte, *née* Bruce; *Career* Maj Scots Gds 1982 (despatches twice, NI and Falkland Islands); company dir 1988–; Officer Brother Order of St John; *Style*— The Hon Richard Bethell, MBE

BETHELL-JONES, Richard James Stephen; s of Geoffrey Bethell-Jones (d 1977), and Nancy Hartland, *née* Martin; *b* 16 Sept 1945; *Educ* St John's Leatherhead, Univ of Cambridge; *m* 15 Sept 1973, Sarah Landells, da of Lt-Col Felix Hodson (d 1989); 2 da (Jessica b 1977, Harriet b 1979); *Career* admitted slr 1970, ptnr Wilde Sapte 1975–; memb Worshipful Co of Slrs 1984, memb Banking Law Sub-Ctee City of London Law Soc; *Recreations* tennis, dinghy sailing; *Clubs* Hurlingham, Overy Staithe Sailing, Burnham Market Tennis; *Style*— Richard Bethell-Jones, Esq; ✉ Wilde Sapte, 1 Fleet Place, London EC4M 7WS (☎ 0171 246 7000, fax 0171 246 7777)

BETHENOD, Gilles Marie Nicolas; s of Maurice Bethenod (d 1980), of Paris, and Solange Salteur de la Serraz; *b* 28 Sept 1948; *Educ* Ecole Des Roches, Paris Univ; *m* 26 Oct 1974, Sylvie Paule Jeanne, da of Yvon Colin (d 1988); 2 s (Alexis b 18 Oct 1975, Nicolas b 20 Jan 1977), 1 da (Marie Astrid b 10 Oct 1979); *Career* Offr French Navy (reserve); Banque Nationale de Paris 1975–86, Yamaichi Int Europe Ltd 1986–92, IBJ International plc 1993–; *Recreations* tennis, skiing; *Clubs* Lansdowne; *Style*— Gilles Bethenod, Esq; ✉ 9 Route de Gambais, 78490 Gambaiseuil, France (☎ 00 33 1 34 86 36 80); IBJ International plc, Bracken House, 1 Friday Street, London EC4M 9JA (☎ 0171 236 1090, fax 0171 236 0484)

BETHUNE, Sir Alexander Maitland Sharp; 10 Bt (NS 1683), of Scotscraig, Co Fife; s of Sir Alexander Sharp Bethune, 9 Bt, JP (d 1917), by Elisabeth (d 1935), da of Frederick Maitland-Heriot; *b* 28 March 1909; *Educ* Eton, Magdalene Coll Cambridge; *m* 11 Jan 1955, (Ruth) Mary, da of James Hurst Hayes, of Marden House, East Harting, Sussex; 1 da (Lucy Elizabeth b 1959); *Heir* none; *Career* with: Quaker Oats Co USA 1932–34, Lord & Thomas advtg agency 1935–38, Walter Briggs Ltd sports mfrs 1938–40; FO 1940–43, Capt Army Intelligence Corps 1943–46; self-employed co dir in property and photocopying 1948–82; ret; *Recreations* golf, bridge, Scottish history; *Style*— Sir Alexander Sharp Bethune, Bt; ✉ 21 Victoria Grove, London W8 5RW

BETHUNE, Hon Sir (Walter) Angus; kt (1979); s of Frank Pogson, and Laura Eileen Bethune; *b* 10 Sept 1908; *m* 1936, Alexandra, da of P A Pritchard; 1 s, 1 da; *Career* premier and treas of Tasmania 1969–72; ldr Lib Pty 1960–72, oppn ldr 1960–69; pastoralist; *Clubs* Tasmanian, Naval Military and Air Force, Royal Automobile Club of Tasmania; *Style*— The Hon Sir Angus Bethune; ✉ 553 Churchill Avenue, Sandy Bay, Tasmania 7005

BETT, Sir Michael; kt (1995), CBE (1990); s of Arthur Bett, OBE, and Nina, *née* Daniells; *b* 18 Jan 1935; *Educ* Aldenham, Pembroke Coll Cambridge (MA); *m* 3 Oct 1959, Christine Angela Bett, JP, da of Maj Horace Reid, JP; 1 s (Timothy Mark b 1961), 2 da (Sally Maria b 1963, Lucy Ann b 1965); *Career* dir Industl Rels Engrg Employers' Fedn 1970–72; personnel dir: GEC 1972–77, BBC 1977–81; British Telecom: main bd dir 1981–96 (non-exec 1993–96), personnel dir 1981–85, md Local Communications Servs Div 1985–87, md UK Communications 1987–88, md BT UK 1988–91, dep chm BT plc 1991–94; chm Cellnet 1991–; First Civil Service Cmmr 1995–; memb: Pay Bd 1973–74, May Ctee of Inquiry into UK Prison Serv 1978–79, Ctee of Inquiry into Water Dispute 1983, Griffiths Inquiry into NHS Mgmnt 1983, Armed Forces Pay Review Body 1983–87, Manpower Servs Cmmn 1985–89; chm: Nurses Pay Review Body 1990–95, TEC Nat Cncl 1994–95, Social Security Advsy Ctee 1993–95, Armed Forces Ind Review on Manpower 1994–95; memb Cncl Cranfield Inst of Technol 1982–87, pro-chllr Aston Univ 1993–; pres Inst of Personnel and Devpt 1993–; chm: The Save the Children Fund, Govrs Cranbrook Sch, Inspectorate of the Security Indust; former vice pres Royal TV Soc, former Hon Col 81 Sqdn (V) RCS; Hon DBA Liverpool John Moores Univ, Hon DSc Aston Univ; CIMgt, CIPD, FRSA; *Style*— Sir Michael Bett, CBE; ✉ Colets Well, The Green, Otford, Kent TN14 5PD

BETT, Nigel; s of Philip Bett, of Rochester, Kent, and Molly, *née* Robertson; *b* 2 Sept 1949; *m* 1, 1977; 2 s (Philip b 11 March 1981, George b 30 Dec 1985); m 2, 12 Dec 1992, Barbara Kathryn, *née* Nierinck; *Career* club cricket: The Band of Brothers, The Mote CC, The Blue Mantles, The Oundle Rovers; mktg mangr Kent CCC 1978–87 (joined as head Gateman 1977), sec Sussex CCC 1987–; memb Mktg Ctee TCCB 1992–; *Recreations* all sports, collecting ties; *Clubs* MCC, Kent CCC, Lord's Taverners; *Style*— Nigel Bett, Esq; ✉ Sussex County Cricket Club, County Ground, Eaton Rd, Hove, East Sussex BN3 3AN (☎ 01273 732161, fax 01273 771549)

BETTINSON, John Richard; s of Harold Richard Bettinson, MC (d 1986), of Edgbaston, and Barbara, *née* Keene (d 1984); *b* 27 June 1932; *Educ* Haileybury, Univ of Birmingham (LLB); *m* 1 Nov 1958, (Margaret) Angela, da of Richard Good (d 1955), of Edgbaston; 1 s (Richard b 1961), 1 da (Hayley b 1963); *Career* Lt 3 Carabiniers 1955–57; admitted slr 1955; chm: Birmingham Area Health Authy 1973–82, Nat Assoc of Health Authys 1976–79, Age Concern England 1989–92, Birmingham Heartlands Hosp NHS Tst 1992–94, Victoria Carpet Holdings plc 1986–95, Assay Office Birmingham, Birmingham Research Park Ltd, National Windscreens Ltd; dep pro-chllr Univ of Birmingham; dep chm Concentric plc, pres W Midland Rent Assessment Panel; gen cmmr for Income Tax 1970–; Freeman Worshipful Co of Glaziers & Painters of Glass; memb Law Soc; *Recreations* theatre, bricklaying, reading; *Clubs* Cavalry and Guards'; *Style*— John Bettinson, Esq; ✉ Storey House, 4 Pritchatts Rd, Edgbaston, Birmingham B15 2QT (☎ 0121 455 7588, fax 0121 454 9316)

BETTISON, Paul David; s of Kenneth Henry David Bettison, of Worcester Park, Surrey, and Ona Patricia, *née* Ratcliffe; *b* 18 April 1953; *Educ* Tiffin Boys' Sch Kingston upon Thames; *m* 15 May 1976, Jean Margaret, da of Kenneth Charles Bradshaw, of Ewell, Epsom, Surrey; 2 da (Clare Louise b 1983, Emily Margaret b 1985); *Career* memb mgmnt Rockwell Graphic Systems Ltd 1978–87, md Graphic Systems International Ltd 1987–; dir: Factistel Ltd 1988–, Tolerans Ingol (UK) Ltd 1990–93, Topefa Limited 1990–95, Pizza De Action Ltd 1995–, Pizza Cake Ltd 1995–; memb (Cons) Sandhurst Town Cncl 1991– (dep mayor 1992–93, mayor 1993–95), memb Bracknell Forest Borough Cncl 1992– (chm Health and Safety Ctee 1993–95, vice chm Personnel Ctee 1993–95, ldr Cons Gp 1996–); govr: New Scotland Hill Primary Sch 1991–, Uplands County Primary Sch 1992–; CInstSMM 1996 (FInstSMM 1979); *Recreations* politics, flying light aircraft, travel, cars, wine; *Style*— Paul Bettison, Esq; ✉ Longdown House, Mickle Hill, Little Sandhurst, Berkshire GU47 8QL; Graphic Systems International Ltd, Caxton House, 23 Vicarage Rd, Blackwater, Camberley, Surrey GU17 9AX (☎ 01276 37337, fax 01276 37319, mobile 0836 287050)

BETTON, David John William; s of John Clifford Betton (d 1993), of Milverton, Taunton, Somerset, and Evelyn Naomi, *née* Byatt; *b* 30 Dec 1947; *Educ* Dulwich Coll, Emmanuel Coll Cambridge (BA, MA); *m* 1, 6 Jan 1970 (m dis 1975), Christine Judith Patey, da of Very Rev Edward Patey, Dean of Liverpool, Merseyside; m 2, 5 Sept 1980 (m dis 1994), Nicola Mary Mallen, da of John McGregor Carter (d 1983); 1 s (Jack David McGregor), 3 da (Victoria Christine Naomi, Polly Nicola, Nancy Evelyn Mary); m 3, 19 Jan 1996, Baroness Gillian van Overstraeten, da of Rylance John Taylor; *Career* called to the Bar 1972; sr legal advsr HM Customs and Excise 1976–86, nat dir of VAT Clark Whitehill CAs 1986–91, senior VAT conslt KPMG CAs 1991–; Freeman City of London, Liveryman Worshipful Co of Plumbers; *Recreations* cricket, theatre, walking; *Clubs* MCC; *Style*— David Betton, Esq; ✉ KPMG, PO Box 486, 1 Puddle Dock, Blackfriars, London EC4V 3PD (☎ 0171 311 2677, fax 0171 311 2943)

BETTON, Michael; s of Very Rev John Richard Betton, Dean of Bocking (d 1985), and Marjorie Phyillis, *née* Paine; *b* 4 Feb 1962; *Educ* Ipswich Sch, St Edmund Hall Oxford (BA, MA); *m* 29 June 1985, Margaret Claire, da of Reginald Seal (d 1990), of Langley Mill, Derbyshire; 1 da (Charlotte Hannah b 1988), 1 s (Sebastian Michael b 31 Aug 1992); *Career* mgmnt trainee Suffolk Group Radio 1984–85, station co ordinator Saxon Radio 1985–86; Ocean Sound: prog controller 1986–89, prog dir 1989, prog dir and dep md 1989–90, md 1990; md Lincs FM 1991–; *Recreations* travel, food and drink; *Style*— Michael Betton, Esq; ✉ Lincs FM, Witham Park, Waterside South, Lincoln LN5 7JN (☎ 01522 549900, fax 01522 549911)

BETTS, Charles Valentine; s of Harold Blair Betts, of S Harting, Sussex, and Mary Ellis, *née* France (d 1990); *b* 10 Jan 1942; *Educ* Seaford Coll Worthing, Lysses Sch Fareham, Ryde Sch Isle of Wight, Merchant Taylors' Crosby, St Catharine's Coll Cambridge (MA, capt of boats 1962–63), RNC Greenwich (Cert in Naval Architecture), UCL (MPhil); *m* 20 April 1965, Rev Patricia Joyce Betts (ordained deacon 1996), er da of William Gordon Bennett, of Great Crosby, Liverpool; 2 s (Christopher Jeremy b 3 April 1968, Richard Anthony b 25 March 1970); *Career* postgrad trg for RCNC: RNEC Manadon Plymouth 1963–64, RNC Greenwich 1964–66; asst constructor FE Fleet 1966–67, constructor MOD Foxhill Bath 1971 (asst constructor 1967–70), seconded as lectr in naval architecture UCL 1971–74, constructor HM Dockyard Portsmouth 1974–77; chief constructor: MOD Foxhill Bath 1979–83 (constructor 1977–79), MOD London 1983–85; seconded as prof of naval architecture UCL 1985–89; MOD Foxhill Bath: dir Surface Ships B 1989–92, DG Surface Ships 1992–94, DG Submarines 1994–; dep controller RN 1994–, head RCNC 1992–; memb Cncl RINA 1985–; CEng 1968, FRINA 1981 (MRINA 1968), FEng 1991, FRSA 1992; *Books* The Marine Technology Reference Book (Butterworth Scientific, contrib, 1990); *Recreations* sailing, music, Christian activities; *Clubs* RNSA; *Style—* Charles Betts, Esq, FEng; ✉ Ministry of Defence, Ash 2B, MOD Abbey Wood, PO Box 702, Bristol BS12 7DX (☎ 0117 913 5000, fax 0117 913 5908)

BETTS, Clive James Charles; MP (Lab) Sheffield Attercliffe (majority 15,480); s of Harold Betts (d 1992), of Sheffield, and Nellie, *née* Ellis (d 1991); *b* 13 Jan 1950; *Educ* King Edward VII Sch Sheffield, Pembroke Coll Cambridge (BA); *Career* economist TUC 1971–72; local govt offr: Derbyshire 1973–74, South Yorks 1974–86, Rotherham 1986–91; Parly candidate: Sheffield Hallam 1974, Louth 1979; MP (Lab) Sheffield Attercliffe 1992–; former chm Treasy Departmental Ctee Lab Pty, former memb Treasy Select Ctee, memb Lab Ldr's Campaign Team with responsibility for Environment and Local Govt, appointed Lab Pty whip 1996–; Lab Pty Sheffield City Cncl: cncllr (Lab) 1976–92, chm Housing Ctee 1980–86, chm Fin Ctee 1986–88, dep ldr 1986–87, ldr 1987–92; vice pres Assoc of Met Authys (chm Housing Ctee 1985–89, dep chm 1988–91); pres: Organising Ctee XVI Universiade 1990–91, Mosborough CAB; patron: Mosborough Township Youth Project, Nat Assoc for Therapeutic Educn; vice pres Energy from Waste Assoc; memb Lab Pty 1969–; *Recreations* Sheffield Wednesday FC, squash, cricket, walking, real ale; *Style—* Clive Betts, Esq, MP; ✉ 1 Plumbley Hall Mews, Mosborough, Sheffield S19 5BF; Barkers Pool House, Burgess Street, Sheffield S1 2HF (☎ 0114 273 4444, fax 0114 273 9666); House of Commons, London SW1A 0AA (☎ 0171 219 3588/5114)

BETTS, Air Vice-Marshal (Charles) Stephen; CBE (1962); s of Herbert Charles Betts (d 1971), of Nuneaton, Warwicks, and Edith Whiting, *née* French (d 1979); *b* 8 April 1919; *Educ* King Edward VI Sch Nuneaton, Sidney Sussex Coll Cambridge (MA); *m* 1, 1943 (m dis 1964), Pauline Mary (d 1965) da of Lt-Col P Heath, IA; 2 da (Susan, Stephanie); m 2, 1964, Margaret Doreen (d 1993), da of Col Walter Herbert Young, DSO (d 1941), of Farnham, Surrey; m 3, 1996, Denys Mary, da of William de Montigny Clarke, of Salisbury, Wilts; *Career* Engr Offr RAF 1941–74, Asst Cmdt RAF Coll Cranwell 1971, Air Offr cmdg No24 Gp Rudloe Manor 1972–74; head Inspection and Control Div The Armaments Control Agency Western Euro Union Paris 1974–84; ret; *Recreations* travel, music; *Clubs* RAF; *Style—* Air Vice-Marshal Stephen Betts, CBE; ✉ Cranford, Weston Rd, Bath BA1 2XX (☎ 01225 310995)

BETZ, Charles John Paul; s of Col Francis Betz (d 1949), of California, and Martha Abusdal Flannery (d 1988); *b* 8 Sept 1946; *Educ* American Grad Sch of Int Management (MIM), Univ of Stanford (Cert), California State Univ (BS), Univ of Uppsala Sweden (Cert); *m* 6 Dec 1969, Birgitta, da of Erik Gideon Thorell, of Solleron, Sweden; 2 s (Christian Michael b 1977, Clark Paul Erik b 1982), 2 da (Anika Ingrid b 1975, Martina Mary b 1980); *Career* dir customer serv Transworld Airlines NY 1970–72, regnl vice pres Bank of America London 1979–86 (various appts San Francisco 1973–76, vice pres NY 1976–79), md Carre Orban and Ptnrs 1986–91, European Bank for Reconstruction and Devpt 1991–92, chm Int Acad for Educn and Devpt 1993–; dep md: Bridge Information Systems, Bridge Int Brokering 1995–; chm and organizer Champion Polo Benefit; *Recreations* polo; *Clubs* Buck's, Salskopet (Sweden), Ham Polo, West Wycombe Park; *Style—* Charles Betz, Esq; ✉ Atkins Farm, Great Missenden, Buckinghamshire (☎ 01494 86 3762) 2809 Raccoon Trail, Pebble Beach, California, USA (☎ 408 372 2429)

BEUTHIN, Allan John Elrick; s of Prof R C Beuthin, of Johannesburg, S Africa, and Beryl Ada, *née* Bray; *b* 19 Jan 1944; *Educ* St Stithians Coll, Parktown Boys HS S Africa; *m* 15 April 1968, Sharon Alice, da of Lawrence John Landey; 1 s (Charles Lawrence b 1975), 1 da (Teresa b 1971); *Career* dir Menell Jack Hyman & Co 1962–78, memb Johannesburg Stock Exchange 1969–78, memb The Stock Exchange London 1980–, dir Merrill Lynch Ltd 1985–88, exec dir Deutsche Bank Capital Markets 1988–91, sr gen mangr Nedcor Bank London 1991–; *Recreations* golf, flying, theatre; *Clubs* Inanda Country; *Style—* Allan Beuthin, Esq; ✉ 48 Flask Walk, Hampstead, London NW3 1HE

BEVAN, *see:* Evans-Bevan

BEVAN, Anthony Richard Van (Tony); s of Adrian Van Cruiskerken Bevan, of Harbury, Warwicks, and Margaret Betty, *née* Pemberton; *b* 22 July 1951; *Educ* Bradford Sch of Art, Goldsmiths' Coll of Art and Design London, Slade Sch of Art London; *ptnr* Glenys, da of William Johnson; 1 da (Rosa Elizabeth Donna Johnson Glen Bevan b 25 Jan 1991); *Career* artist; *Solo Exhibitions* incl: Robert Self Gallery London 1976, Caius Coll Gallery Cambridge 1976, Matt's Gallery London 1981, 1982 and 1986, Tony Bevan Portraits and Emblems (Galeria Akumulatory 2 Poznan Poland) 1983, Chapter Arts Centre Cardiff Wales 1984, Tony Bevan, Bilder (Galerie Wittenbrink Regensburg Germany) 1984, The Honest Portrait (Nat Portrait Gallery London) 1985, Emblems (Riverside Studios London) 1985, Tony Bevan Neue Bilder (Galerie Wittenbrink) 1986, Tony Bevan - Paintings 1980–87 (ICA London touring Orchard Gallery Derry, Kettles Yard Cambridge and Cartwright Hall Bradford) 1987–88, Ronald Feldman Gallery NY 1988, Tony Bevan Neue Bilder (Kunsthalle Kiel Germany) 1988, Tony Bevan (Galerie Wittenbrink Munich Germany) 1988, Tony Bevan (Staatsgalerie Moderner Kunst Haus der Kunst Munich Germany) 1989, Tony Bevan - Paintings (LA Louver Venice Calif) 1989, Tony Bevan (Kunstverein Lingen Germany) 1990, Tony Bevan Neue Bilder (Galerie Wittenbrink Munich Germany) 1990, Louver Gallery NY 1991, Galerie Zink Baden Baden Germany 1991, The Meeting: and Other Recent Paintings (LA Louver Venice Calif) 1992, The Meeting and Related Works (Louver Gallery NY) 1993, Tony Bevan New Paintings (Galerie Wittenbrink Munich Germany and Frith Street Gallery London) 1993, Tony Bevan Whitechapel Art Gallery 1993, Head and Other Recent Paintings (LA Louver Gallery Venice Calif) 1995, Kopf Bilder (Galerie Wittenbrink Munich) 1995; *Gp Exhibitions* incl: Lisson Gallery London 1981, Problems of Picturing (Serpentine Gallery London) 1984, Private Symbol, Social Metaphor (Sydney Biennial Aust) 1984, The Br Art Show (touring Birmingham, Edinburgh, Sheffield and Southampton) 1984–85, Hand Signals (Ikon Gallery Birmingham, Milton Keynes Exhibition Gallery and Chapter Gallery Cardiff) 1985, Human Interest (Manchester Arts Centre) 1985, Cries and Whispers (paintings from the Br Cncl Collection touring Aust) 1987–88, Aperto 88 (Venice Biennale Italy) 1988, Prospect '89 (Schirn Kunsthalle Frankfurt Germany) 1989, Picturing People - Figurative Art in Britain 1945–1984 (Br Cncl travelling exhibition to Nat Gallery Kuala Lumpur, Museum of Art Hong Kong and Nat Gallery Harare Zimbabwe) 1989–90, Inconsolable (Louver Gallery NY) 1990, Cuatro Pintores de Londres (Colegio de Arquitectos de Malaga Spain) 1991, Out of Limbo (De La Fundacion Luis Cernuda Sevilla Spain) 1991, British Figurative Painting of the 20th Century (Museum of Israel Jerusalem) 1992–93, The Man, The Form and the Spirit (Connaught Brown London) 1992, The Portrait Now (Nat Portrait Gallery London) 1993, British Painting Since 1970 (Serpentine Gallery) 1994, Psychological Self Portrait (Aldrich Museum Connecticut USA) 1995; *Style—* Tony Bevan, Esq; ✉ c/o Galerie Wittenbrink, Jahnstrasse 18, München 5, Germany (☎ 00 4989 260 5580, fax 00 4989 260 5868); c/o L A Louver, 55N Venice Blvd, Venice, California CA 90291, USA (☎ 001 310 822 4955, fax 001 310 821 7589)

BEVAN, Rear Adm Christopher Martin; CB (1978); s of Humphrey Charles Bevan (d 1982), and Mary, *née* Mackenzie; *b* 22 Jan 1923; *Educ* Stowe, Victoria Univ Wellington NZ; *m* 1948, Patricia Constance, da of Rev Arthur William Bedford (d 1950); 1 s, 3 da; *Career* joined RN 1942, ADC to HM The Queen 1976, Flag Offr Medway and Port Adm Chatham 1976–78; under-treas Gray's Inn 1980–89; *Recreations* theatre, music, photography; *Clubs* Boodle's, Hurlingham; *Style—* Rear Adm Christopher Bevan, CB; ✉ c/o C Hoare & Co, 37 Fleet St, London EC4P 4DQ (0171 353 4522)

BEVAN, John Penry Vaughan; s of Llewelyn Vaughan Bevan (d 1987), and Hilda Molly, *née* Yates; *b* 7 Sept 1947; *Educ* Radley, Magdalene Coll Cambridge (BA); *m* 1, 1971 (m dis 1976), Dinah, *née* Nicholson; 2 da (Amelia b 1972, Lucinda b 1975); m 2, 12 May 1978, Veronica, *née* Aliaga-Kelly; 1 s (Henry b 1981), 1 da (Charlotte b 1985); *Career* called to the Bar Middle Temple 1970, sr prosecuting counsel to the Crown at Central Criminal Ct, recorder of the Crown Ct 1987–; *Recreations* sailing, tennis; *Clubs* Leander, Aldeburgh Yacht, Orford Sailing; *Style—* John Bevan, Esq; ✉ 2 Harcourt Buildings, Temple, London EC4Y 9DB

BEVAN, John Stuart; OBE (1995); s of Frank Oakland Bevan, of Stour Row, Dorset, and Ruth Mary, *née* Sadler; *b* 19 Nov 1935; *Educ* Eggar's GS, Jesus Coll Oxford (MA), Bart's Med Coll (MSc); *m* 30 July 1960, Patricia Vera Beatrice, da of Alfred Charles William Joyce, of Bude, Cornwall; 2 s (David b 16 Nov 1961, Robin b 14 Aug 1966), 2 da (Elizabeth b 19 Dec 1962, Sally b 22 March 1965); *Career* Harefield Hosp (Pathology Lab) 1954–56, physicist UKAEA 1960–62, lectr and sr lectr S Bank Poly (previously Borough Poly, now Univ of the S Bank) 1962–73, dir of educn ILEA 1979–82 (asst then sr asst educn offr 1973–76, dep educn offr 1977–79), sec NAB 1982–88, dir Educn Servs LRB 1989–92, chief exec ACFHE 1992–93, sec AFC 1993–95, Ombudsman FEFC 1996–; dep co cmmr Kent and nat chm Prog & Trg Scout Assoc; memb Exec Ctees: ATTI 1968–73 (pres 1972–73), NUT 1970–73, AEO 1977–82 (chm 1981–82); hon fell: S Bank Univ 1988, Westminster Coll Oxford 1990; Hon DUniv Surrey 1990, Hon LLD CNAA 1992; FInstP 1972; *Books* The Space Environment (jtly, 1969); *Recreations* scouting, mountaineering; *Style—* John Bevan, Esq, OBE; ✉ 4 Woodland Way, Bidborough, Tunbridge Wells, Kent TN4 0UX (☎ 01892 527461)

BEVAN, Jonathan Stuart Vaughan; s of Dr Edward Vaughan Bevan, TD, DL, (d 1988), and Joan Margot, *née* Goddard; *b* 15 June 1940; *Educ* St Faiths Cambridge, Bedford Sch; *m* 17 Sept 1960 (m dis 1986), Victoria Judith Helen, da of Hugh Leycester (d 1952), of Hilton, Hunts; 3 da (Charlotte Victoria (Mrs Mark Pearson) b 1961, Francesca (Hon Mrs Harry Herbert) b 1963, Tiffany Alice (Mrs William Rook) b 1965); *Career* dep export dir and PA to chm Pye of Cambridge 1959–66, joined Grievson Grant and Co 1966–85 (assoc memb 1968, ptnr 1970); dir: Kleinwort Benson Securities 1985–88, Alexander Laing and Cruikshank Securities 1988–90, Maximize Media plc 1994–; chm Atmospherics 1994–; int conslt 1990–; memb Stock Exchange 1970–; chm and memb Exec Ctee local Cons Assoc 1963–72, memb Cambridge Rowing Soc, dist cmmr Cambridgeshire Pony Club 1981–85, life pres St Moritz Sporting Club 1984–, chm and chief exec SMOMC 1984–; FRGS; *Books* Very Large Numbers (1984); *Recreations* tobogganning, art, walking; *Clubs* St Moritz Tobogganning; *Style—* Jonathan Bevan, Esq; ✉ 1 Eaton Gate, London SW1W 9BA (☎ 0171 730 3344, fax 0171 824 8801); La Forge Les Houches, Mont Blanc, France

BEVAN, (Edward) Julian; QC (1991); s of Capt Geoffrey Bevan (d 1994), and Barbara, *née* Locke (d 1991); *b* 23 Oct 1940; *Educ* Eton; *m* 17 Sept 1966, Bronwen Mary, da of Brig James Windsor Lewis, DSO, MC; 2 s (David, Dickon), 2 da (Anna, Henrietta); *Career* called to the Bar Gray's Inn 1962; standing cncl Inland Revenue 1973–77, first sr treasy cncl Central Criminal Court 1989 (jr treasy cncl 1977–84, sr treasy cncl 1984), master of the bench Gray's Inn 1989; *Clubs* Garrick; *Style—* Julian Bevan, Esq, QC; ✉ Queen Elizabeth Buildings, Temple, London EC4 (☎ 0171 583 5766)

BEVAN, Nicolas; CB (1991); s of Dr Roger Bevan (d 1973), formerly Lt-Col RAMC (despatches), and Diana Mary, *née* Freeman (d 1982); *b* 8 March 1942; *Educ* Westminster (Queen's scholar), CCC Oxford (Open scholar, MA); *m* 11 Dec 1982, (Helen) Christine, da of Norman Athol Berry, of Rhyl; *Career* MOD: asst princ 1964–69, princ 1969–76, private sec to Chief of Air Staff 1970–73, seconded to Cabinet Office 1973–75, asst sec 1976–84, RCDS 1981, asst under sec of state 1985–93, seconded to Cabinet Office 1992–93; Speaker's sec 1993–; *Recreations* gardening; *Style—* Nicolas Bevan, Esq, CB; ✉ Speaker's Office, House of Commons, London SW1A 0AA

BEVAN, (John) Peter; s of George Bevan (d 1986), of Liverpool, and Eileen Bevan (d 1975); *b* 29 Oct 1942; *Educ* Liverpool Inst HS; *m* 1966, Susan Jane, da of Sir Harold McDonald Steward; 1 s (Nicholas John b 9 March 1971), 1 da (Amanda Jayne b 8 June 1968); *Career* chartered accountant; articled clerk 1959–64, ptnr 1971, managing ptnr Grant Thornton Liverpool office 1990–; ACA 1964; *Recreations* golf, football; *Clubs* Woolton Golf (former capt), Liverpool Lyceum (pres 1989–90); *Style—* Peter Bevan, Esq; ✉ Grant Thornton, 1–3 Stanley St, Liverpool L1 6AD (☎ 0151 224 7200, fax 0151 224 7212)

BEVAN, Prof Peter Gilroy; CBE (1983); s of Rev Thomas John Bevan (d 1944), and Norah Gilroy (d 1974); bro of (Andrew) David Gilroy Bevan; *b* 13 Dec 1922; *Educ* King Edward's HS Birmingham, Univ of Birmingham Med Sch (MB ChB, ChM), Univ of London (MRCS, LRCP), FRCS, FRCSI (Hon); *m* 1, 1949, Patricia Joan (d 1985), da of Maj-Gen Rufus Henry Laurie (d 1960); 1 s (Jonathan), 1 da (Deirdre); m 2, Beryl Margaret Chempin, da of Arthur Harold Jordan Perry (d 1944); *Career* RAMC (Capt) BAOR 1947–49; conslt surgn Dudley Rd Hosp Birmingham 1958–87, advsr in gen surgery to the CMO 1975–84, postgrad dir Univ of Birmingham Med Sch 1978–87 (emeritus prof of surgery and postgrad medical educn 1988), postgrad tutor Birmingham Med Inst 1988–94 (pres 1994–); author of various papers on surgery and surgical trg; memb Cncl RCS 1971–83 (vice pres 1980–81), fndr chm W Midlands Oncology Assoc 1974–79, vice pres Br Assoc of Surgical Oncologists 1975–78, pres Pancreatic Soc of GB 1977, UK rep to EEC on Med Trg Advsy Ctee 1980–85 (on Monospecialist Section of Surgery 1975–84), advsr in gen surgery to the RN 1983–88; pres: Br Inst of Surgical Technols 1983–, Assoc of Surgns of GB and I 1985; pres W Midlands Surgical Soc 1986, chm Joint Planning Advsy Ctee 1990–, dir Overseas Doctors' Trg Scheme (RCS) 1987–90, med memb Pensions Appeal Tbnls 1987–89, chm DHSS Steering Gp on Operating Theatres 1989, memb Med Appeals Tbnls 1989–, pres Nat Assoc of Theatre Nurses 1991–94; *Books* Reconstructive Procedures in Surgery (1981), Handbook of General Surgery (1992); *Recreations* music, painting, inland waterways, golf, photography; *Clubs* Edgbaston Golf, Royal Navy Medical Club; *Style—* Prof Peter Gilroy Bevan, CBE; ✉ 10 Russell Rd, Moseley, Birmingham B13 8RD (☎ 0121 449 3055)

BEVAN, Rev Canon Richard Justin William; s of Rev Richard Bevan (vicar of St Harmon Radnorshire, d 1928), and Margaret Mabel, *née* Pugh; *b* 21 April 1922; *Educ* St Edmund's Sch Canterbury, St Augustine's Coll Canterbury, St Chad's Coll Durham (BA, LTh), Lichfield Theol Coll; *m* 4 Sept 1949, Sheila Rosemary, da of Thomas Barrow (d 1963), of Fazakerley, Liverpool; 4 s (Roderick, Nicholas, Timothy, Christopher b 1967 d 1968), 1 da (Rosemary); *Career* ordained Lichfield Cathedral: deacon 1945, priest 1946; asst curate Stoke-on-Trent 1945–49, chaplain Aberlour Orphanage Scotland 1949–51, asst master Towneley Tech HS Burnley 1951–60, licence to officiate Diocese of Blackburn 1951; hon asst curate: Church Kirk 1951–56, Whalley 1956–60; rector St Mary-le-Bow Durham 1964–74, vicar United Benefice St Oswald with St Mary-le-Bow

Durham 1964–74; chaplain: Univ of Durham 1961–74 (convenor of chaplains 1966–74), Durham Girls' HS 1966–74, St Mary's Coll Univ of Durham 1961–72, St Cuthbert's Soc Univ of Durham 1966–74, St Aidan's Soc Univ of Durham 1960–64, Trevelyan Coll Durham 1966–72; examining chaplain to Bishop of Carlisle 1970–, govr St Chad's Coll Durham 1969–89, rector Grasmere 1974–82, canon residentiary Carlisle Cathedral 1982–89 (treas and librarian 1982–89, vice dean 1986–89), chaplain to HM The Queen 1986–92; first pres and fndr memb Grasmere Village Soc; theol conslt Churchman Publishing Ltd 1986–; Hon ThD Geneva Theol Coll 1972, Hon PhD Columbia Pacific Univ 1980, Hon ThD Univ of Greenwich USA 1990; *Books* Steps to Christian Understanding (ed, 1959), The Churches and Christian Unity (ed, 1964), Durham Sermons (ed, 1964), Unfurl the Flame (poetry, 1980), A Twig of Evidence: Does Belief in God Make Sense? (1986); *Recreations* poetry, reading, musical appreciation, train travel; *Clubs* Victory Services; *Style*— The Rev Canon Richard Bevan; ✉ Beck Cottage, Burgh by Sands, Carlisle, Cumbria CA5 6BT; The Cathedral, Carlisle, Cumbria

BEVAN, Sir Timothy Hugh; kt (1984); yr s of late Francis Hugh Bevan, of Warehead House, Halnaker, Chichester, Sussex, and Pleasance Mary Vidal, *née* Scrutton; *b* 24 May 1927; *Educ* Eton; *m* 12 July 1952, Pamela Murray, da of late Norman Smith; 2 s (Mark b 1960, Hugh b 1961), 2 da (Nicola b 1955, Fiona b 1957); *Career* called to the Bar Middle Temple 1950; Barclays Bank: joined 1950, dir 1966–93, dep chm 1973–81, chm 1981–87; chm BET plc 1988–91, dep chm Foreign and Colonial Investment Trust 1993– (dir 1988–); *Clubs* Cavalry and Guards'; *Style*— Sir Timothy Bevan; ✉ c/o Barclays Bank plc, 54 Lombard St, London EC3V 9EX

BEVAN-THOMAS, Philip Morgan; s of William Ewart Thomas (d 1970), of Worthing, and Doris Winifred, *née* Morgan (d 1966); *b* 2 Dec 1934; *Educ* Cheltenham, St Edmund Hall Oxford (MA); *m* 18 June 1962, Janet Mary, da of Eric Walter Ward (d 1979), of Havant; 2 s (Giles b 1965, Oliver b 1967); *Career* Nat Serv 2 Lt RA 1953–55, Capt TA RHA (Para) 1958–63; slr; ptnr: Francis and Parkes 1964–86, Field Seymour Parkes 1987–; pres Berks, Bucks and Oxford Law Soc 1982–83, chm Shiplake Parish Council 1985; memb Law Soc 1963–; *Recreations* sailing, golf; *Clubs* Huntercombe Golf, Leander, Sea View Yacht; *Style*— Philip Bevan-Thomas, Esq; ✉ The Barns, Shiplake Rise, Shiplake, Oxford RG9 4DP (☎ 0118 948 2142); The Old Coroners Ct, 1 London St, Reading RG1 4QW (☎ 0118 939 1011, fax 0118 950 2704)

BEVERIDGE, Brian Francis; s of Maj-Gen Arthur J Beveridge, CB, OBE, MC (d 1959), of Dublin, and Sheila, *née* Macnamara (d 1952); *b* 7 May 1933; *Educ* St Conleth's Coll Dublin, Ampleforth, Univ Coll Dublin (MB BCh); *m* 20 July 1968, Victoria, da of Ronald Barton-Wright, of Northampton; 3 s (Richard b 1969, Dominic b 1972, Edward b 1975); *Career* cmmnd Capt 155 (L) Field Ambulance RAMC (TA) 1963, ret 1990; ret ophthalmologist: Whipps Cross Eye Unit, Holly House, BUPA Roding and BUPA Hartswood Hosps; memb: Hunterian Soc, Medact; FRCOphth 1988, FRSM 1980, FRCSEd 1970; *Recreations* swimming, Irish history, travel; *Style*— Brian Beveridge, Esq; ✉ 8 The Charter Rd, Woodford Green, Essex IG8 9QU (☎ 0181 504 2301); 42 The Old Dock, Little Ship Street, Dublin 8, Ireland

BEVERIDGE, Crawford William; CBE (1995); s of William Wilson Beveridge, and Catherine Crawford Beveridge; *b* 3 Nov 1945; *Educ* Univ of Edinburgh (BSc), Univ of Bradford (MSc); *Career* various appts Hewlett Packard 1968–77, Digital Equipment Corp 1977–81, vice pres corp resources Sun Microsystems 1985–90, chief exec Scottish Enterprise 1991–; *Style*— Crawford W Beveridge, Esq, CBE; ✉ Scottish Enterprise, 120 Bothwell Street, Glasgow G2 7JP (☎ 0141 248 2700, fax 0141 221 2250)

BEVERIDGE, George William; s of George Beveridge (d 1978), of Saline, Fife, and Margaret Patricia, *née* McLeod; *b* 23 Feb 1932; *Educ* Dollar Acad, Univ of Edinburgh (MB ChB); *m* 16 March 1962, Janette, da of John Millar, CBE (d 1978), formerly Lord Provost of Edinburgh; 2 s (Iain George b 25 Sept 1966, Alastair John b 13 March 1969), 2 da (Carolyn Janette b 1 May 1963, Susan Patricia b 7 Dec 1964); *Career* Nat Serv RAMC 1957–59, Capt RMO 2 Royal Tank Regt; conslt dermatologist The Royal Infirmary Edinburgh and pt/t hon sr lectr Univ of Edinburgh 1965–; author of articles in jls on acne, drug reactions and skin tumours; pres Scot Dermatological Soc 1982–85, elder Church of Scot; FRCPEd 1970 (MRCPEd 1961); *Recreations* gardening, golf; *Style*— George Beveridge, Esq; ✉ 8 Barnton Park View, Edinburgh EH4 6HJ (☎ 0131 336 3680); Dept of Dermatology, The Royal Infirmary, Edinburgh EH3 9YW (☎ 0131 536 6100 ext 62050, fax 0131 229 8769)

BEVERIDGE, Sir Gordon Smith Grieve; kt (1994); s of Victor Beattie Beveridge (d 1983), and Elizabeth Fairbairn, *née* Grieve (d 1971); *b* 28 Nov 1933; *Educ* Inverness Royal Acad, Univ of Glasgow (BSc), Royal Coll of Sci and Technol Glasgow (ARCST), Univ of Edinburgh (PhD); *m* 1963, Geertruida Hillegonda Johanna, da of Gerrit Hendrik Bruijn (d 1944), and Johanna Breyaen (d 1957); 2 s (Norman b 1965, Stuart b 1968), 1 da (Catriona b 1971); *Career* lectr in chem engrg Univ of Edinburgh 1962–67, sr lectr and reader in chem engrg Heriot-Watt Univ 1967–71, prof of chem engrg Univ of Strathclyde 1971–86, pres and vice chllr Queen's Univ Belfast 1986–Oct 1997; memb: Cncl Soc of Chem Indust 1978–88 (vice pres 1985–88), Engrg Cncl 1981–95, Engrg Bd of SERC 1983–86, Chem Econ Devpt Ctee NEDO 1983–87; chm Radioactive Waste Mgmnt Advsy Ctee 1995–98; Harkness fell the Cwlth Fund (NY), resident at Univ of Minnesota 1960–62; dir and chm Cremer & Warner Ltd 1985–90; Hon LLD: Dublin 1992, Nat Univ of Ireland 1995, Limerick 1995; Hon DSc: Ulster 1994, Connecticut 1995, Kingston 1995; Hon DAppSc Lodz Poland 1995; CEng, FEng 1984 (memb Cncl 1981–95), FIChemE 1969 (memb Cncl 1975–86, pres 1984–85), FRSE 1974, FRSA 1988, MRIA 1989, CIMgt 1990, Hon FRCSI 1995, hon memb City & Guilds Inst 1996; *Books* Optimization - Theory and Practice (with R S Schechter, 1970); *Recreations* Scottish, Irish and Dutch history, Marlburian war games, family golf, walking; *Clubs* Caledonian; *Style*— Sir Gordon Beveridge, FEng, FRSE; ✉ 4/18 Succoth Court, Edinburgh EH12 6BZ; until Oct 1997: The Vice-Chancellor's Lodge, 16 Lennoxvale, Belfast BT9 5BY (☎ 01232 245133 ext 3131, fax 01232 330808)

BEVERIDGE, John Caldwell; QC (1979); s of Prof William Ian Beardmore Beveridge, of Canberra, and Patricia Dorothy Nina, *née* Thomson (d 1996); *b* 26 Sept 1937; *Educ* Jesus Coll Cambridge (MA, LLB); *m* 1, 2 Aug 1973 (m dis 1989), Frances Ann Clunes Grant Martineau, da of Dr John Sutherland, of Edinburgh; m 2, 7 July 1989, Lilian Moira Weston, da of John Weston Adamson (d 1977), of Oldstead Hall, N Yorkshire; *Career* barr; recorder of the Crown Court (Western Circuit) 1975–, bencher Inner Temple 1987; QC NSW Australia 1980; Freeman City of London 1965, Liveryman Worshipful Co of Goldsmiths; *Recreations* hunting, shooting; *Clubs* Beefsteak, Brooks's, Pratt's, Turf; *Style*— John Beveridge, Esq, QC; ✉ Yeo Farm, Waterrow, Taunton TA4 2PT (☎ 01984 624611); 9 St James's Chambers, Ryder Street, London SW1Y 6QA (☎ 0171 930 1118)

BEVERLEY, Lt-Gen Sir Henry York La Roche; KCB (1991), OBE (1979); s of Vice Adm Sir York Beverley, KBE, CB (d 1982), and Maria Theresa Matilda, *née* Palazio (d 1957); *b* 25 Oct 1935; *Educ* Wellington; *m* 3 Aug 1963, Sally Anne, da of Alistair Maclean (d 1973); 2 da (Lucy Anne b 15 Nov 1965, Sara Elizabeth b 13 March 1968); *Career* ADC to Govr Gen NZ 1961–62, exchange offr US Marine Corps 1965–66, Staff Coll Camberley 1968, Jt Servs Staff Coll 1971, staff of SNO W Indies 1971–73, BM HQ 3 Commando Bde RM 1973–75, DS Camberley 1975–77, CO 42 Commando RM 1978–80, Cmdt CTC RM 1980–82, dir RM Personnel MOD 1982–84, Cmd 3 Commando Bde RM 1984–86, Maj-Gen TRF RM 1986–88, COS CGRM 1988–90, Cmdt Gen RM 1990–93; dir gen Winston Churchill Memorial Tst 1993–; Liveryman Worshipful Co of Plaisterers; *Recreations* golf, cross country skiing; *Clubs* RTYC; *Style*— Sir Henry Beverley, KCB, OBE; ✉ c/o Barclays Bank, 20 High Street, Exeter EX4 3LL

BEVERLEY, Bishop of 1994–; Rt Rev John Scott Gaisford; s of Joseph Gaisford, and Margaret Thompson, *née* Scott; *b* 7 Oct 1934; *Educ* Burnage GS, Univ of Durham (BA, MA, DipTheol); *m* 6 Oct 1962, Gillian, da of Francis Murdo Maclean; 1 s (Giles Gregory John b 6 July 1972), 1 da (Sophia Elizabeth Eve b 9 July 1970); *Career* Sr Aircraftsman RAF 1953–55; asst curate: St Hilda Audenshaw 1960–62, Bramhall 1962–65; vicar St Andrew Crewe 1965–86, rural dean Nantwich 1974–85, archdeacon of Macclesfield 1986–94; York provincial episcopal visitor 1994; hon asst bishop Dio of Ripon 1996–; memb: Gen Synod 1975–95, C of E Pensions Bd 1982–; hon canon Chester Cathedral 1980–86; church cmmr 1986–94, tstee Redundant Churches Fund (now Churches Conservation Tst) 1989–; *Recreations* fell walking, caravanning; *Clubs* Athenaeum; *Style*— The Rt Rev the Bishop of Beverley; ✉ 3 North Lane, Roundhay, Leeds LS8 2QJ (☎ 0113 273 2003, fax 0113 273 3002, mobile 0860 289550, e-mail 101740,2725@compuserve.com)

BEVERLEY, Michael; s of George Kenneth Beverley (d 1977), and Emily, *née* Wood; *b* 28 June 1947; *Educ* Univ of Leeds (BA); *m* 28 March 1970, Jennifer Anne, da of Leslie Farrar (d 1974); 1 da (Rachel b 12 Nov 1972), 1 s (James Leslie b 5 Jan 1974); *Career* Arthur Andersen: articled clerk Manchester 1973–76, CA 1976, mangr Leeds 1979, ptnr 1985–, head Tax Div 1986–93, office managing ptnr 1991–, regnl office (North of England) managing ptnr 1994; chm Devpt Ctee and dir of Opera North, chm Leeds Philharmonic, memb Ctee Leeds Int Piano Competition; govr Leeds Metropolitan Univ; FCA 1981 (ACA 1976); *Recreations* opera, keeping fit, shooting, farming; *Clubs* Leeds United (vice pres); *Style*— Michael Beverley, Esq; ✉ Arthur Andersen, St Paul's House, Park Square, Leeds, W Yorks LS1 2PY (☎ 0113 243 8222, fax 0113 245 9240)

BEVERLEY, Nigel; s of Jack Beverley, of Salhouse, Norfolk, and Amelia, *née* Hartley; *b* 22 June 1952; *Educ* High Storrs GS Sheffield, Univ of Nottingham (BSc); *m* Mary Elizabeth; 1 da (Katherine b 7 Dec 1983), 1 s (James b 25 May 1987); *Career* nat mgmnt trainee NE Thames RHA 1973–75, asst sector admin UCH 1975–77, sector admin Hammersmith Hosp 1977–80, asst dist admin Havering Dist Barking and Havering AHA 1980–82, unit gen mangr Colchester Gen Hosp 1985–88 (unit admin 1982–85), dist gen mangr Southend HA 1988–90, chief exec Southend Healthcare NHS Tst 1990–91, head Reforms Gp and head NHS Tst Unit NHS Mgmnt Exec 1991–92, tst unit dir NHS Exec (N Thames) 1992–96, chief exec Wellhouse NHS Tst 1996–; MHSM (DipHSM), MInstD; *Recreations* squash, golf, skiing; *Style*— Nigel Beverley, Esq; ✉ Wellhouse NHS Trust, Barnet General Hospital, Wellhouse Lane, Barnet, Herts EN5 3DJ (☎ 0181 732 4924, fax 0181 732 4954, mobile 0370 266438, e-mail nbeverley@ Wellhouse-tr.nthames.nhs.uk)

BEVES, Brian Montague; s of Montague Hebb Beves (d 1943), of Hove, and Dorothy Hamlyn, *née* Lawrence-Smith (d 1960); cous of Maj Alexander Greenwood, *qv*; *b* 8 Jan 1924; *Educ* Haileybury, King's Coll Cambridge (MA); *m* 28 Sept 1957, Carolyn Langworthy, da of Rear-Adm Cecil Ramsden Langworthy Parry, CB, DSO (d 1977), of Coachmans, Westbourne, Sussex; 2 da (Lucy b 1959, Frances b 1963); *Career* temp admin appt FO 1945–47; special corr The Times on Antarctic Expedn 1948; served in Sudan Political Serv 1951–54; broker and underwriter Lloyd's (Sedgwick Collins) 1955–73, ret 1973; chm: Hereford Diocesan Bd of Fin 1980–90, Friends of Hereford Cathedral 1993–; lay chm Ledbury Deanery Synod 1983–, memb Gen Synod and Central Bd of Fin C of E 1990–95 (memb Exec Ctee 1991–95), head House of Laity and vice chm Hereford Diocesan Synod 1991–95; *Recreations* gardening, music; *Style*— Brian Beves, Esq; ✉ Abbey House, Ledbury, Herefordshire HR8 1BP (☎ 01531 632762)

BEVINGTON, Christian Veronica; da of Michael Falkner Bevington (d 1993), of St Neots, Cambs, and his 1 w, Dulcie Marian, *née* Gratton (d 1979); *b* 1 Nov 1939; *Educ* St James's West Malvern; *m* 7 Oct 1961 (m dis 1974), Frederick David Andrew Levitt, OBE, s of late Frederick Charles Levitt; 1 s (Aldhun b 1965), 2 da (Alison b 1963, Evelyn b 1966); *Career* called to the Bar Inner Temple 1961, Lincoln's Inn (ad eundem) 1971; head of Chambers 1981–, recorder SE Circuit, bencher Inner Temple 1994; subscriber Hampstead Soc, subscribing memb Justice; memb: Criminal Bar Assoc, Family Law Bar Assoc; *Recreations* music (organ and harpsichord); *Style*— Ms Christian Bevington; ✉ New Court, Temple, London EC4Y 9BE (☎ 0171 583 5123, fax 0171 353 3383, DX LDE 0018)

BEVINS, Anthony John; s of Rt Hon John Reginald Bevins (d 1996), and Mary Leonora, *née* Jones; *b* 16 Aug 1942; *Educ* Liverpool Collegiate GS, LSE (BSc(Econ)); *m* 1965, Ruchira Mishtuni, da of Kshitis Roy, of Santiniketan, West Bengal, India; 1 s (Robert b 1968), 1 da (Nandini b 1972); *Career* VSO 1964–66; political corr: Liverpool Daily Post 1970–73 (sub ed 1967–70), Sunday Express 1973, The Sun 1973–76, Daily Mail 1976–81, The Times 1981–86; political ed: The Independent 1986–93 and 1996–, The Observer 1993–96; *Style*— Anthony Bevins, Esq; ✉ Press Gallery, House of Commons, London SW1A 0AA (☎ 0171 219 4700)

BEVINS, Kenneth Milton; CBE (1973), TD (1951); s of John Milton Bevins (d 1928), of Liverpool, and Grace Eveline Bevins, bro of Rt Hon John Reginald Bevins (d 1996); *b* 2 Nov 1918; *Educ* Liverpool Collegiate Sch; *m* 1, 1940, Joan Harding (d 1969); 2 da; m 2, 1971, Diana, da of the late Godfrey J Sellers, of Keighley; *Career* WWII: 136 Field Regt RA 1939–46 incl with 14 Army Burma 1943–46, Maj RA (TA); Royal Insurance Co: sec 1957, gen mangr 1963, dep chief gen mangr 1966, chief gen mangr 1970–80, dir 1970–89; dir Fire Protection Assoc 1963–77 (chm 1966–68), dir Trade Indemnity Co 1970–80 (chm 1975–80), dep chm Br Insur Assoc 1967–71 (chm 1971–73), dir Mutual & Federal Insurance Co Ltd 1971–80, dir British Aerospace PLC 1981–87; memb: Jt Fire Res Orgn Steering Ctee 1966–68, Home Sec's Standing Ctee on Crime Prevention 1967–73, Exec Ctee City Communications Centre 1976–80, Bd British Aerospace 1980–81, Govt Ctee to review Export Credit Guarantee Dept 1983–84; *Recreations* travel, gardening, reading, photography, painting, handiwork; *Clubs* Army and Navy, Oriental; *Style*— Kenneth Bevins, Esq, CBE, TD; ✉ Linton, The Drive, Sevenoaks, Kent TN13 3AF (☎ 01732 456909)

BEVIS, Prof Michael John; s of Bernard John Bevis, of Jersey, Channel Islands, and Kathleen Mary Balston; *b* 25 April 1940; *Educ* De La Salle Coll Jersey CI, Univ of London (BSc, PhD); *m* 23 May 1964, Diana, da of Edgar Holloway; 1 s (Andrew John b 12 Jan 1968), 2 da (Katie Ann b 30 April 1965, Sarah Jane b 11 March 1972); *Career* lectr rising to reader Dept of Metallurgy and Materials Sci Univ of Liverpool 1965–77; Brunel Univ: joined 1977, prof and head Dept of Non-Metallic Materials 1977–84, prof and head Dept of Materials Technol 1984–87, research prof and dir Wolfson Centre 1987–94, conslt dir Wolfson Centre 1994–; awarded A A Griffith Medal and Prize of Inst of Metals 1988, Swinburne Medal and Prize of Plastics and Rubber Inst 1990; FInstP 1971, fell Inst Metals 1977, FPRI 1980, FEng 1986; *Style*— Prof Michael Bevis, FEng; ✉ Wolfson Centre for Materials Processing, Brunel Univ, Uxbridge, Middlesex UB8 3PH (☎ 01895 274000, fax 01895 203376)

BEVITT, Paul Antony; s of Geoffrey Bevitt, of Horsforth, Yorks, and Betty, *née* Ibbotson; *b* 5 May 1951; *Educ* Ropewalk Secdy Modern, Wakefield Art Coll; *m* 30 July 1983, Diane, da of David Owen Fowles; 2 s (Christopher b 9 May 1984, Samuel b 30 July 1987); *Career* photographer's asst London 1969–74, Toronto Canada 1974–75, freelance photographer specialising in studio advtg London 1975–; *Awards* D&AD Silver 1986, Campaign Poster Silver 1987 and Gold 1988, Creative Circle Silver 1990, USA Art Dirs' Club Merit 1990, Ilford B&W Award 1990, 2 Campaign Poster Silvers

1990, USA Advtg Annual Award 1992, Assoc of Photographers Merit 1994; memb: Assoc of Photographers, D&AD; *Recreations* tennis, music, cinema, swimming, football; *Clubs* Highgate Lawn Tennis; *Style—* Paul Bevitt; ✉ Studio 5, Ivory Place, 20a Treadgold Street, London W11 4BX (☎ 0171 221 3599)

BEWES, Michael Keith; s of Rev Canon Thomas Francis Cecil Bewes (d 1993), and (Nellie) Sylvia Cohu, *née* De Berry; bro of Rev Prebendary Richard Thomas Bewes, *qv*; *b* 4 March 1936; *Educ* Marlborough, Emmanuel Coll Cambridge (MA); *m* 10 Oct 1964, (Patricia) Anrõs, *née* Neill; 3 s (Jonathan b 1965, Nicholas b 1967, Anthony b 1971), 1 da (Rebecca b 1973); *Career* Nat Serv 2 Lt RA 1954–56; BR 1959–66, Royal Exchange Assurance 1966–68, Guardian Royal Exchange plc 1968–96 (positions in personnel, field servs, corp affrs and corporate planning rising to asst gen mangr), chm The Willis Partnership 1996–; The Chartered Insurance Inst: treas 1985–87, dep pres 1987–88, pres 1988–89; chm Insurance Indust Training Cncl 1982–88; memb Governing Cncl Business in the Community 1983–96, chm of Cncl Scripture Union 1988–94; chm of govrs The Coll of Insurance, pres Insurance Benevolent Fund, tstee Dio of Central Tanganyika, govr Stowe Sch, chm Stowe Sch Educational Services Ltd; Freeman City of London 1990, Liveryman Worshipful Co of Insurers; FIPD 1983, FRSA 1989; *Recreations* fly fishing, heraldic painting, photography, music, Napoleon commemorative medals, various sports - lawn tennis and hockey at county level; *Clubs* RAC, Hawks' (Cambridge); *Style—* Michael Bewes, Esq; ✉ Clifton House, Church Lane, Lexden, Colchester, Essex CO3 4AE (☎ 01206 42710); The Willis Partnership, 23 Buckingham Gate, London SW1E 6LB (☎ 0171 821 6543, fax 0171 828 9967)

BEWES, Rev Prebendary Richard Thomas; s of Rev Canon Thomas Francis Cecil Bewes (d 1993), and (Nellie) Sylvia Cohu, *née* De Berry; bro of Michael Keith Bewes, *qv*; *b* 1 Dec 1934; *Educ* Marlborough, Emmanuel Coll Cambridge (MA), Ridley Hall Theol Coll Cambridge; *m* 18 April 1964, Elisabeth Ingrid, da of Lionel Jaques; 2 s (Timothy b 1966, Stephen b 1971), 1 da (Wendy b 1968); *Career* vicar: St Peter's Harold Wood Essex 1965–74, Emmanuel Northwood Middx 1974–83; rector All Souls Langham Place London 1983–, prebendary St Paul's Cathedral 1988–; chm: C of E Evangelical Cncl 1992, Anglican Evangelical Assembly 1992; Freedom of the City of Charlotte N Carolina USA 1984; memb Guild of Br Songwriters 1975; *Books* God in Ward 12 (1973), Advantage Mr Christian (1975), Talking About Prayer (1979), The Pocket Handbook of Christian Truth (1981), John Wesley's England (1981), The Church Reaches Out (1981), The Church Overcomes (1983), On The Way (1984), Quest For Life (1985), Quest For Truth (1985), The Church Marches On (1986), When God Surprises (1986), The Resurrection (1989), A New Beginning (1989), Does God Reign? (1995); *Recreations* tennis, photography, broadcasting, reading, writing; *Style—* The Rev Prebendary Richard Bewes; ✉ 12 Weymouth St, London W1N 3FB (☎ 0171 580 6029); All Souls Church, 2 All Souls Place, London W1N 3DB (☎ 0171 580 3522, fax 0171 436 3019)

BEWES, Rodney; s of Horace Bewes (d 1973), of Lancaster, and Bessie Bewes (d 1990); *b* 27 Nov 1937; *Educ* RADA; *m* 1972, Daphne; 3 s (Joe, Tom, Billy (triplets) b 1976), 1 da (Daisy b 1973); *Career* actor; formerly child actor (incl children's hour plays on radio and TV); Nat Serv RAF; subsequently 5 years appearing in rep throughout UK; Freeman: City of London 1991, Worshipful Co of Watermen and Lightermen of the River Thames 1991; *Theatre* incl: A Night Out (Comedy Theatre), Little Malcolm (Garrick), Middle Age Spread (Lyric and Apollo), William Blore in And Then There Were None (dir Kenneth Alan Taylor, Duke of York's), Flute in A Midsummer Night's Dream (with Sir Ralph Richardson as Bottom, int tour), Big in Brazil (with Timothy West and Prunella Scales, Old Vic), Love All and Jack and the Beanstalk (Thorndike); more recently: Wait Until Dark (dir Bill Kenwright, tour) 1990, Run For Your Wife (tour) 1991, An Awfully Big Adventure (Liverpool Playhouse) 1992, Widow Twanky in Alladin (Leatherhead) 1992, Three Men In A Boat (one man show, Kenton Theatre and tour) 1993–95, Funny Money (Playhouse) 1995, Odd Course (Theatre Royal) 1996; *Television incl* Bob in The Likely Lads (series with James Bolam, also film, repeated 1995) 1964–74, Dear Mother...Love Albert (also writer, prodr), The Camera Club (dir Nick Renton, BBC), 'Tis a Pity She's a Whore (dir Roland Joffe, BBC), Spender (BBC) 1992, Come Snow Come Blow 1994; *Films incl* Arthur in Billy Liar (film debut, dir John Schlesinger), Spring and Port Wine, The Gothick Chimney, We Joined the Navy, The Spaceman and King Arthur, Decline and Fall, Alice in Wonderland, The Wildcats of St Trinians, Saint Jack (dir Peter Bogdanovich); *Recreations* rowing (twice winner Chaplin Trophy Henley for boat restoration); *Clubs* London Rowing, Garrick; *Style—* Rodney Bewes, Esq; ✉ c/o Michelle Braidman Associates, 3rd Floor, 10/11 Lower John Street, London W1R 3PE (☎ 0171 437 0817, fax 0171 439 3600)

BEWLEY, Dr Beulah Rosemary; da of John B Knox (d 1975), of Lurgan, N Ireland, and Ina, *née* Charles (d 1995); *b* 2 Sept 1929; *Educ* Trinity Coll Dublin (MB BCh, MA, MD), Univ of London (MSc); *m* 20 April 1955, Dr Thomas Henry Bewley, CBE, *qv*, s of Dr A G Bewley (d 1980), of Dublin; 1 s (Henry John b 1963), 4 da (Susan Jane b 1958, Sarah Elizabeth b 1959, Louisa Mary b 1961, Emma Caroline b 1966); *Career* emeritus reader in public health med St George's Hosp Med Sch London; former SWTRA reg post-grad tutor in public health med; memb GMC; former pres Med Women's Fedn; FFCM 1980, FRCP 1992; *Recreations* music, travel, food; *Clubs* RSM, Reform; *Style—* Dr Beulah R Bewley; ✉ 11 Garrads Rd, London SW16 1JU (☎ 0181 769 1703)

BEWLEY, Dr Thomas Henry; Hon CBE (1988); s of Dr Geoffrey Bewley (d 1980), and Victoria Jane, *née* Wilson (d 1953); *b* 8 July 1926; *Educ* Rugby, St Columbus Coll Dublin, Trinity Coll Dublin (BA, MB, MA, MD); *m* 20 April 1955, Dr Beulah R Bewley, *qv*, da of John Knox (d 1975); 1 s (Henry b 1963), 4 da (Susan b 1958, Sarah b 1959, Louisa b 1961, Emma b 1966); *Career* conslt psychiatrist 1961–88: St Thomas's Hosp, St George's Hosp, Tooting Bec Hosp; hon sr lectr St George's Hosp Med Sch 1988–96, WHO expert Advsy Panel on Drug Dependence and Alcohol Problems 1988–96, pres Royal Coll of Psychiatrists 1984–87 (dean 1977–82), physician memb Social Security and Med Appeal Tbnls 1987–, memb Parole Bd 1988–91; memb GMC 1988–96; Hon MD Univ of Dublin 1987; FRCPI 1963, FRCPsych 1972, FRCP (London) 1988; *Style—* Dr Thomas Bewley, CBE; ✉ 11 Garrads Rd, London SW16 1JU (☎ 0181 769 1703)

BEXON, Roger; CBE (1985); s of MacAlister Bexon, CBE (d 1976), of High Wycombe, and Nora Hope, *née* Jenner (d 1976); *b* 11 April 1926; *Educ* St John's Coll Oxford (MA), Univ of Tulsa Oklahoma (MS); *m* 1951, Lois Loughran Walling; 1 s, 1 da; *Career* geologist and petroleum engr Trinidad Petroleum Devpt Co Ltd 1946–57; British Petroleum Company: E Africa 1958–59, Libya 1959–60, Trinidad 1961–64, London 1964–66, mangr N Sea Ops 1966–68, gen mangr Libya 1968–70, regnl coordinator ME London 1971–73, gen mangr Exploration and Prodn London 1973–76; md: BP Exploration Co Ltd London 1976–77, BP Co 1981–86 (dep chm 1983–86); chm: Laporte plc 1986–95, Goal Petroleum plc 1990–; dir: Standard Oil Co 1977–80 and 1982–86 (sr vice pres 1977–80), BP Canada Inc 1983–87, BICC 1985–92, Lazard Bros 1986–91, JH Fenner (Holdings) 1986–89, Cameron Iron Works 1987–89, Astec (BSR) 1989–; *Recreations* golf, reading, Times crosswords; *Style—* Roger Bexon, Esq, CBE; ✉ c/o 22 Hill Street, London W1X 7FB (☎ 0171 496 4423)

BEXSON, Peter James; s of Thomas William Bexson (d 1984), of E Molesey, Surrey, and Elsie Constance, *née* Cox (d 1986); *b* 2 May 1926; *Educ* Glasgow Acad, Gonville and Caius Coll Cambridge (BA Econ), Coll of Estate Mgmnt Univ of London (FRICS); *m* 7 Feb 1953, Edna May, da of Harold Glover, of Hartley, Dartford, Kent; 2 s (Robert b 9 July 1956, William b 18 May 1961); *Career* WWII cadet pilot Canada and USA 1944–45, instr PT Branch Germany 1946–47; chief surveyor Greencoat Properties 1956–63, ptnr Graves Son & Pilcher 1963–86, ptnr Stiles Harold Williams 1986–91, sole practitioner 1991–; past memb Gen Cncl RICS (chm Conduct Investigation Ctee), divnl pres Int Real Estate Fedn Paris, memb London Rent Assessment Panel DOE, former pres Soc of London Ragamuffins; Freeman City of London; Liveryman: Worshipful Co of Tallow Chandlers, Worshipful Co of Painter Stainers, Worshipful Co of Chartered Surveyors; FRICS 1961; *Recreations* walking, travel; *Clubs* RAC, Sloane, London Scottish FC; *Style—* Peter J Bexson, Esq; ✉ 1 Paxton Terrace, London SW1V 3DA (☎ 0171 834 4565); c/o P J Broomhall & Partners, 61 Petty France, London SW1H 9EZ (☎ 0171 222 1324)

BEYFUS, Drusilla Norman (Mrs Milton Shulman); da of late Norman Beyfus, and late Florence Noël Barker; *Educ* RN Sch, Channing Sch; *m* 1956, Milton Shulman, *qv*; 1 s (Jason), 2 da (Alexandra Shulman, *qv*, Nicola); *Career* assoc ed Queen Magazine 1958–63, home ed The Observer 1963–64, assoc ed Daily Telegraph colour supplement 1964–70, ed Brides Magazine 1971–79, assoc ed British Vogue Magazine Condé Nast 1979–86, ed Harrods Magazine 1987–88, columnist Daily Mail magazine 1988–89, contributing ed Telegraph Magazine 1990–, weekly columnist You magazine (Mail on Sunday) 1994–; visiting tutor Central St Martin's Coll of Art 1989–; author and broadcaster; *Books* Lady Behave (co-author), The English Marriage, The Bride's Book, The Art of Giving, Modern Manners (1992); The Done Thing: Courtship, Parties (1992), Business, Sex (1993); *Style—* Miss Drusilla Beyfus; ✉ 51G Eaton Square, London SW1 (☎ 0171 235 7162, fax 0171 823 1366)

BEYNON, David William Stephen; s of William Henry Beynon (d 1983), and Eileen Beynon (d 1992); *b* 14 March 1934; *Educ* King Edward VII Sch Sheffield, Trinity Hall Cambridge (MA); *m* 23 Sept 1961, Joyce Noreen, da of George Trevor Richards, of Wallasey, Ches; 2 s (Stephen b 1965, Daniel b 1971), 1 da (Jane b 1962); *Career* Nat Serv RA 1952–54; ICI: joined 1954, commercial appts Petrochemicals Div 1954–77, head Policy Gps Dept London 1977–79, dep chm Plastics Div 1979–81, gp dir Petrochemicals and Plastics Div 1981–87, dir ICI Chemicals & Polymers Ltd 1987–90, dir ICI Resources Ltd 1987–90, chm ICI Europe 1990–92; dir Holliday Chemical Holdings plc 1992–; pres: Br Plastics Fedn 1987–88 (memb Cncl 1980–89), Assoc of Euro Plastics Mfrs (APME) 1990–92 (memb Cncl 1987–92); memb: Ctee Euro Petrochem Assoc (EPCA) 1985–91, Cncl Assoc of Euro Petrochem Mfrs (APPE) 1988–91; visiting prof Univ of Herts 1993–; dir Apex Charitable Trust Ltd 1993–; capt Gt Ayton CC 1971–76, chm Welwyn Garden City CC 1980–86 and 1993–, ctee memb Herts County Cricket Assoc 1993–; Freeman City of London 1984, Ct Asst Worshipful Co of Horners 1993 (Liveryman 1984); *Recreations* family, cricket, golf; *Clubs* Forty, Hanbury Manor Golf, MCC; *Style—* David Beynon, Esq; ✉ 1 Downfield Court, Hanbury Drive, Thundridge, Nr Ware, Herts SG12 0SB (☎ 01920 484614)

BEYNON, Dr John David Emrys; s of John Emrys Beynon (d 1973), and Elvira, *née* Williams; *b* 11 March 1939; *Educ* Pontywaun GS Risca Gwent, Univ of Wales (BSc), Univ of Southampton (MSc, PhD); *m* 28 March 1964, Hazel Janet, da of Albert Hurley (d 1983); 2 s (Graham b 1968, Nigel b 1968), 1 da (Sarah b 1966); *Career* scientific offr DSIR Radio and Space Res Station Slough 1962–64, reader Dept of Electronics Univ of Southampton (lectr, sr lectr) 1964–77, prof of electronics UWIST Cardiff 1977–79; Univ of Surrey: prof of electrical engrg 1979–90, head Dept of Electronic and Electrical Engrg 1979–83, pro vice chllr 1983–87, sr pro vice chllr 1987–90; princ King's Coll London 1990–92; memb ITC 1995–; FIEE 1979 (MIEE 1968), FIERE 1979, FRSA 1982, FEng 1988; *Books* Charge Coupled Devices and Their Applications (1980); *Recreations* music, photography, travel; *Style—* Dr John D E Beynon, FEng; ✉ Chalkdene, Great Quarry, Guildford, Surrey (☎ 01483 503458)

BEYNON, Timothy George (Tim); s of George Beynon (d 1976), of Mumbles, Swansea, and Fona Inanda, *née* Smith; *b* 13 Jan 1939; *Educ* Swansea GS, King's Coll Cambridge (MA); *m* 1 March 1973, Sally Jane, da of John Wilson, of Little Gaddesden, Berkhamsted, Herts; 2 da (Sorrel b 1974, Polly b 1976); *Career* asst master City of London Sch 1962–63; Merchant Taylors' Sch: joined 1963, housemaster 1970–78, sr master 1977–78; headmaster: Denstone Coll 1978–86, The Leys Sch 1986–90; sr warden Saltwells LNR 1992–; expdns: Petra (overland) 1961, Spain, Hungary, Austria, Romania (ornithological); Denstone Expdn to Inaccessible Island 1982/83; memb: Eng Cncl 1986–89, Oxford and Cambridge Sch Examination Syndicate Appts Ctee; FRGS 1973, memb HMC 1978; *Recreations* ornithology, fishing, shooting, music, expeditions; *Style—* Tim Beynon; ✉ The Croft, College Road, Denstone, Uttoxeter, Staffs ST14 5HR

BHAN, Dr Girdari Lal; s of Arjun Nath Bhan (d 1955), and Laxmi Bhan; *b* 25 Dec 1943; *Educ* Med Coll Srinagar India (MB BS); *m* 31 Aug 1968, Supriya, da of Varkie Cherian; 2 da (Archana b 7 Oct 1969, Kanchan b 25 Nov 1975); *Career* sr house offr: med East Birmingham Hosp 1974–75, neurology Midland Centre for Neurosurgery and Neurology 1976; registrar med East Birmingham Hosp 1977–79, sr registrar North West RHA 1980–81, conslt physician Royal Oldham Hosp 1982–; memb: BMA, BGS; MRCP, FRCPI (MRCPI), FRCP (London); *Recreations* classical music, gardening; *Style—* Dr Girdari Bhan; ✉ Consultant Physician, Royal Oldham Hospital, Rochdale Road, Oldham, Lancashire OL1 2JH (☎ 0161 627 8480)

BHARUCHA, Dr Chitra; da of George Gnanadickam, of Madras, India, and Mangalam, *née* Ramaiya; *b* 6 April 1945; *Educ* Christian Med Coll Vellore India (MB BS); *m* 18 Jan 1967, Hoshang Bharucha, s of Kaikusru Bharucha, of Bombay, India; 2 da (Anita b 3 June 1972, Tara b 8 Jan 1974); *Career* currently dep dir NI Blood Transfusion Service and conslt haematologist Belfast City Hosp; past pres Med Women's Fedn, memb Expert Ctee WHO; FRCPath; *Recreations* opera, concerts, hillwalking, experimental cookery; *Clubs* Reform; *Style—* Dr Chitra Bharucha; ✉ Northern Ireland Blood Transfusion Service, Lisburn Road, Belfast BT9 7TS (☎ 01232 321414); Belfast City Hospital, Lisburn Rd, Belfast BT9 7AD

BHATT, Kanakrai (Kanak); s of Ramanlal Bhatt (d 1966), and Kanta Bhatt (d 1974); *b* 30 March 1939; *Educ* Menengai HS Nakuru Kenya, Univ of Poona (BCom); *m* Christine Lesley, da of Leonard Halstead (d 1986); 2 da (Anjlee b 19 Aug 1976, Sunita b 29 July 1978); *Career* British Vita plc: gp internal auditor 1966–70, dep chm fin Fibres Div 1970–71, dep chm fin Industl Div 1971–75, gp chief accountant 1975–85, gp treas 1985–91, fin dir 1991–96, currently main bd dir; MCT, FRSA 1992; *Recreations* sailing; *Style—* Kanak Bhatt, Esq; ✉ British Vita plc, Soudan St, Middleton, Manchester M24 2DB (☎ 0161 643 1133)

BHATT, Sujata; da of Pravin N Bhatt, of New Haven, USA, and Indu, *née* Pathak; *b* 6 May 1956, India; *Educ* Goucher Coll USA (BA), Univ of Iowa USA (MFA); *m* 5 Sept 1988, Michael Augustin, s of Jürgen Augustin; 1 da (Jenny Mira Swantje b 1 Feb 1989); *Career* writer and poet; currently visiting prof/writer in res Univ of Victoria BC Canada; Alice Hunt Bartlett prize 1988, Cwlth Poetry prize (Asian section) 1989, Cholmondeley award 1991, Poetry Book Soc recommendation 1991; Verband Deutscher Schriftsteller 1991; *Books* incl: Brunizem (poems, 1988), Monkey Shadows (poems, 1991); *Recreations* running; *Style—* Ms Sujata Bhatt; ✉ c/o Carcanet Press Ltd, Conavon Court, 12–16 Blackfriars Street, Manchester M3 5BQ (☎ 0161 834 8730)

BHATTACHARYYA, Mukti Nath; s of Manju Gopal Bhattacharyya (d 1981), of Calcutta, and Santilata Mukherjee (d 1936), of Calcutta; *b* 22 Jan 1935; *Educ* Univ of Calcutta (MB BS, Dip Gynaecology and Obstetrics), FRCOG London 1983 (MRCOG 1964); *m* 18 Oct 1969, Brenda Kathleen, da of L Evans Esq, of Wolverhampton; 2 s (Neil b 27 Nov 1972, Robin b 10 Dec 1973); *Career* Int R G Kar Med Coll Calcutta 1959–61; Teaching Hosp Calcutta: res in surgery, med, obstetrics and gynaecology 1959–62; registrar in obstetrics and gynaecology Wisbech Hosp 1963–64, sr house offr obstetrics and gynaecology Huddersfield Hosp 1964, registrar in obstetrics and gynaecology Stockport 1965–67, registrar in diagnostic radiology Manchester 1967–70, conslt in genito-urinary med Royal Infirmary Sheffield 1973–79 (sr registrar in venereology 1971–73), conslt physician Manchester Royal Infirmary 1979–, hon lectr Univ of Manchester 1979–; memb and chm Manchester BMA 1987–90 (sec 1984–87); govr William Hulme's GS Manchester 1993–; memb: Genito Urinary Med Advsy Subctee NW Region, Manchester Med Soc, Med Soc for Study of Venereal Diseases, Int Soc for Study of Vulvar Diseases, Int Soc Venereal Diseases and Treponematoses, Int Soc for Res into Sexually Transmitted Diseases, North of Eng Obstetrics and Gynaecological Soc; *Publications* incl numerous papers in professional med jls; *Recreations* astronomy, music, sports, travel; *Clubs* Manchester Rotary; *Style*— Mukti Bhattacharyya, Esq; ✉ 56 Green Pastures, Heaton Mersey, Stockport SK4 3RA (☎ 0161 432 3832); Manchester Royal Infirmary, Oxford Rd, Manchester M13 9WL (☎ 0161 276 1234)

BHOPAL, Prof Rajinder S (Raj); *b* 10 April 1953; *Educ* Shawlands Acad Glasgow, Univ of Edinburgh (BSc, MB ChB, MD), Univ of Glasgow (MPH, MacKinlay prize 1983), MRCP 1982, MFPHM 1987 (Littlejohn Gairdner prize 1986); *m*; 4 c; *Career* surgical/house offr 1978–79, med house offr 1979, SHO in accident and emergency 1979–80, trainee GP 1980–81, SHO in general med 1981–82, SHO in infectious and tropical diseases 1982, sr registrar in community med 1985 (registrar 1983–85), lectr and hon sr registrar in community med Univ of Glasgow 1985–88; Univ of Newcastle upon Tyne: sr lectr 1988–91, conslt in public health med 1988–, prof of epidemiology and public health 1991–; visiting prof Dept of Epidemiology Sch of Public Health Univ of North Carolina Aug 1996–June 1997; non-exec dir Newcastle Health Authy 1992–94, vice chm and non-exec dir Newcastle and N Tyneside Health Authy 1994–96, non-exec dir Health Educn Authy England 1996–; visiting worker MRC Med Sociology Unit Glasgow 1986–, memb Advsy Bd Int Respiratory Infection Taskforce Schering Plough 1993–96; assoc ed: Jl of Public Health Med 1989–90, Jl of Edidemiology and Community Health 1993–; Soc of Public Health: Maddison Research Prize 1992, J T Neech Prize 1994; memb GMC 1994; author of numerous pubns, papers and book chapters on the health and health care of ethnic minorities, infectious diseases and environmental health, epidemiology and public health; *Recreations* chess, hill climbing, photography, travel, bridge, jogging, cycling, tennis and walking; *Style*— Prof Raj Bhopal; ✉ Department of Epidemiology and Public Health, School of Health Care Sciences, The Medical School, Framlington Place, Newcastle upon Tyne NE2 4HH (☎ 0191 222 7372, fax 0191 222 8211, e-mail R.S.Bhopal@Ncl.ac.uk)

BIBBY, Sir Derek James; 2 Bt (UK 1959), of Tarporley, Co Palatine of Chester; MC (1945), DL (Cheshire 1987); s of Maj Sir (Arthur) Harold Bibby, 1 Bt, DSO, DL (d 1986), and Marjorie Guthrie, *née* Williamson (d 1985); *b* 29 June 1922; *Educ* Rugby, Trinity Coll Oxford (MA 1941); *m* 11 Jan 1961, Christine Maud, da of Rt Rev Frank Jackson Okell, Bishop of Stockport (d 1950); 4 s (Michael James b 2 Aug 1963, Geoffrey Frank Harold b 18 Feb 1965, Peter John b 26 March 1969, David Richard b 10 Aug 1970), 1 da (Jennifer Margaret b 3 March 1962); *Heir* s, Michael James Bibby b 2 Aug 1963; *Career* WWII as Capt RA 1942–46 (wounded, MC); ptnr Bibby Bros & Co 1950 (joined 1946); chm: Bibby Bros & Co (Management) Ltd 1978–92, Bibby Line Ltd (became Bibby Line Group Ltd in 1988) 1969–92, Renray Group Ltd 1987–92 (dir 1986); pres Bibby Line Group Ltd 1992–; chm Birkenhead Boys' Club (pres North West Coast Branch 1996–); MIOD; Chev de l'Ordre du Merite Maritime (France) 1978; *Recreations* gardening, tennis, shooting; *Clubs* Royal Cwlth Soc; *Style*— Sir Derek Bibby, Bt, MC, DL; ✉ Willaston Grange, Hadlow Rd, Willaston, S Wirral, Cheshire L64 2UN (☎ 0151 327 4913); Bibby Line Group Ltd, 105 Duke Street, Liverpool L1 5JQ (☎ 0151 708 8000, fax 0151 794 1099, telex 629241)

BICESTER, 3 Baron (UK 1938); Angus Edward Vivian Smith; s of late Lt-Col the Hon Stephen Edward Vivian Smith, 2 s of 1 Baron by Lady Sybil McDonnell (da of 6 Earl of Antrim); 4 cous once removed to 6 Baron Carrington, *qv*; suc unc 1968; *b* 20 Feb 1932; *Educ* Eton; *Heir* bro, Hugh Charles Vivian Smith; *Style*— The Rt Hon The Lord Bicester; ✉ c/o House of Lords, SW1A 0PW

BICHAN, Dr (Herbert) Roy; *b* 5 Nov 1941; *Educ* Univ of Aberdeen (BSc), Univ of Leeds (PhD); *m* Fiona Keay; 1 s (Michael Roy b 8 May 1969), 2 da (Inga Jane b 16 Feb 1967, Susan Elizabeth b 1 Aug 1971); *Career* chm The Robertson Group plc 1988–91, formerly dep chm Simon-Robertson; memb Cncl CBI 1991– (chm Wales 1993–95), chm Welsh Industl Devpt Advsy Bd, dep chm Welsh Development Agency 1993–; Adrian fell Univ of Leicester 1988–90; FIMM (pres 1988–89), MIGeol, FEng 1989; *Recreations* golf; *Style*— Dr Roy Bichan, FEng

BICHARD, Michael George; s of George Bichard (d 1981), and Nora, *née* Reeves (d 1971); *b* 31 Jan 1947; *Educ* King Edward VI GS Southampton, Univ of Manchester (LLB), Univ of Birmingham (MSocSci); *m* Christine; 1 s (Philip Michael), 2 da (Charlotte Emma Christine, Emma-Louise Christine); *Career* articled clerk, slr then sr slr Reading BC 1969–73, county liaison officer Berkshire CC 1973–77, head of Chief Exec's Office Lambeth BC 1977–80; chief exec: Brent BC 1980–86, Glos CC 1986–90, Benefits Agency 1990–95; perm sec Dept for Education and Employment 1995–; hon doctorate Leeds Metropolitan Univ; FRSA, CIMgt; *Recreations* food, wine, music, walking, Manchester Utd; *Style*— Michael Bichard, Esq; ✉ The Department for Education and Employment, Sanctuary Buildings, Great Smith Street, London SW1P 3BT (☎ 0171 925 5000, fax 0171 925 6000)

BICK, David Robert; s of Roy Leslie Samuel Bick, and Vera Grace, *née* Collis; *b* 9 April 1957; *Educ* Glyn GS Epsom, Univ of Essex; *m* 21 July 1984, Susan Christine, da of Joseph Esmond Stobbs (d 1979); 2 s (Charles b 1991, Henry b 1994), 2 da (Antonia b 1987, Harriet b 1989); *Career* PA to David Atkinson MP 1979–80; exec: KH Publicity Ltd 1980–81, Shandwick Conslts Ltd 1981–83; account dir Good Relations City Ltd 1984–85 (account mangr 1983–84), dir and jt fndr Lombard Communications plc 1985–93; dir: Buchanan Communications Ltd 1993–95, Financial Dynamics Feb 1995–; cncllr London Borough of Lambeth 1980–86 (chm Amenity Servs 1982); *Recreations* English cricket, Scottish football, sleep; *Style*— David R Bick, Esq; ✉ Financial Dynamics, 30 Furnival Street, London EC4A 1JE (☎ 0171 831 3113)

BICKERDIKE, Mark; s of Allan Bickerdike, of Dewsbury, and Margaret June, *née* Vasey (d 1990); *b* 15 Feb 1966; *Educ* Dewsbury and Batley Tech and Art Coll (BTEC dip in photography), Stradbroke Coll Sheffield (NCTJ certificate in photojournalism); *Career* Barry Wilkinson Picture Agency Bradford 1987–88, Yorkshire Evening Post Leeds 1988–; *Awards* Picture of the Year Yorks & Humberside Sports Cncl 1989, Picture of the Year British Sports Assoc for the Disabled 1990, Picture of the Year (Sport for All category) Nat Sports Cncl 1990, Regnl Photographer of the Year UK Press Gazette 1990, runner up Ilford Sports Picture of the Year 1991, Regnl Sports Photographer of the Year UK Press Gazette 1991; *Recreations* skiing, squash, fitness training, golf; *Style*— Mark Bickerdike, Esq; ✉ Yorkshire Evening Post, Wellington Street, Leeds, West Yorkshire LS1 1RF (☎ 0113 243 2701, fax 0113 244 3430)

BICKERS, Patricia Evelyn; da of Norman Sefton Reece Bickers, and N Evelyn, *née* Hill; *b* 26 Dec 1950; *Educ* Sch of Saints Helen & Katharine Abingdon Berks, Univ of Sussex (BA); *Career* sr lectr in art history: Harrow Sch of Art 1978–89 (lectr 1974–78), Univ of Westminster (formerly Poly of Central London) 1989–; Art Monthly: assoc ed 1989–91, dep ed 1991–92, ed 1992–; co-selector BT New Contemporaries 1993–94; broadcaster Kaleidoscope (BBC Radio 4) 1994–; memb Mgmnt Ctee Matt's Gallery 1992–, tstee Serpentine Gallery 1995–; memb Assoc of Art Historians 1978; *Books* The Brit Pack: Contemporary British Art, the view from abroad (1995); *Clubs* Lansdowne; *Style*— Miss Patricia Bickers; ✉ Art Monthly, Suite 17, 26 Charing Cross Road, London WC2H 0DG (☎ and fax 0171 240 0389)

BICKERSTETH, Rt Rev John Monier; KCVO (1989); yr s of Rev Canon Edward Monier Bickersteth, OBE (d 1976); *b* 6 Sept 1921, *Educ* Rugby, ChCh Oxford (MA), Wells Theological Coll; *m* 1955, Rosemary, yr da of Edward Cleveland-Stevens (d 1962), of Gaines, Oxted; 3 s, 1 da; *Career* Buffs and RA 1941–46; ordained deacon 1950, priest 1951; curate St Matthew Moorfields Bristol 1950–54, min i/c St John Hurst Green Southwark 1954–62, vicar St Stephen Chatham Rochester 1962–70, hon canon Rochester Cath 1968–70; bishop of: Warrington 1970–75, Bath and Wells 1975–87; chaplain and sub prelate Order of St John 1977–96; Clerk of the Closet to HM The Queen 1979–89, took seat in House of Lords 1981; memb Cncl: Marlborough Coll 1980–91, Wiltshire Wildlife Trust 1990–95; chm: Bible Reading Fellowship 1978–90, Royal Sch of Church Music 1977–89; Freeman City of London 1978, Liveryman Worshipful Co of Gunmakers; *Books* Clerks of the Closet - 500 Years of Service to the Crown (co-author, 1991), The Bickersteth Diaries 1914–1918 (ed, 1995); *Recreations* country pursuits; *Style*— The Rt Rev John Bickersteth, KCVO; ✉ Beckfords, Newtown, Tisbury, Wilts SP3 6NY (☎ 01747 870479)

BICKERTON, Peter W; *b* 4 July 1940; *Educ* Abbotsholme Sch Derbyshire, Univ of Durham (BSc), INSEAD, Univ of Grenoble; *m* 1967, Anne, da of John Mitchell, of Cheltenham; *Career* Koch-Light Laboratories Ltd 1962–65, new products devpt exec Miles Laboratories 1965–68, Fisons plc 1968–75; Sime Darby Group: gp treas 1975–80, fin dir Western Div 1980–83; Manufacturers Hanover Ltd: assoc dir 1983–84, exec dir 1984–87, md 1987–91; princ MTM Partnership 1992–94; dir: Gresham Computing plc 1992–, Cedef Structured Finance Ltd 1994–; FCT; *Recreations* classical music; *Style*— Peter Bickerton, Esq; ✉ 23 Wilton Crescent, London SW1X 8SA

BICKFORD, (James) David Prydeaux; CB (1995); s of William Alfred John Prydeaux Bickford, of London, and Muriel Adelyn, *née* Smythe (d 1973); *b* 28 July 1940; *Educ* Downside; *m* 24 April 1965, Carolyn Jane, da of Maj William Arthur Richard Sumner (d 1943); 3 s (Nicholas b 1966, James b 1967, Peter John b 1972); *Career* slr of the Supreme Ct 1963, in practice with J J Newcombe & Co Devon 1963–69, crown counsel and legal advsr to Turks and Caicos Island Govt 1969–71, asst legal advsr then counsellor to the FCO 1971–87, legal advsr Br Military Govt Berlin 1979–82, under sec of state and legal advsr to the Security and Intelligence Agencies 1987–95; visiting prof of law Cleveland-Marshall Coll of Law Cleveland State Univ USA 1995–96; currently: chm Bickford Associates, dep chm Straegy International Ltd; memb Panel of Legal Experts Int Telecommunications Satellite Orgn, chm Assembly Maritime Satellite Orgn 1985–87; Prof Ben C Green lectr in nat security law Case Western Univ Ohio USA; hon memb Nat Security Ctee American Bar Assoc; memb Law Soc; *Books* Land Dealings Simplified in the Turks and Caicos Islands (1971); *Recreations* the family, fishing; *Style*— David Bickford, Esq, CB; ✉ c/o National Westminster Bank, Torrington, Devon

BICKFORD SMITH, John Roger; CB (1988), TD (1950); er s of late Leonard W Bickford Smith, of Camborne, Cornwall, and Anny Grete, *née* Huth (d 1986); *b* 31 Oct 1915; *Educ* Eton, Hertford Coll Oxford; *m* 1, 1939 (m dis), Cecilia Judge, er da of W W Heath, of Leicester; 2 s; m 2, 1972, Baroness (Joaise) Miranda et Omnes Sancti von Kirchberg-Hohenheim; *Career* called to the Bar Inner Temple 1942, bencher 1984; master of the Supreme Ct Queen's Bench Div 1967–88; sr master and Queen's Remembrancer 1983–88; Master Worshipful Co of Bowyers 1986–88; *Clubs* Garrick; *Style*— John Bickford Smith, Esq, CB, TD; ✉ 65 Gibson Square, London N1 ORA

BICKFORD-SMITH, Peter Michael; s of Michael George Bickford-Smith (d 1975), of Helston, Cornwall, and Joyce Mallileu Bickford-Smith, MBE, *née* Coates (d 1984); *b* 23 April 1947; *Educ* Harrow, RAC Cirencester; *m* 15 May 1971 (m dis 1995), Margaret Mary, da of Lt Cdr David Verney (d 1992), of Truro; 1 s (Michael Rupert David b 27 March 1984), 3 da (Sacha Ann Mary b 21 March 1975, Charlotte Ann Bertha b 22 Feb 1977, Stephanie May b 1 May 1989); *Career* memb Stock Exchange 1974; pres BRCS Cornwall 1988–96; chm Cornwall Garden Soc 1989–96, county chm Game Conservancy Cornwall, pres Royal Cornwall Show 1990; memb Cncl BRCS 1993–96; co-author scientific papers on woodcock 1980–86; memb Worshipful Co of Clockmakers 1974; *Recreations* shooting, fishing, gardening, sailing; *Style*— Peter Bickford-Smith, Esq; ✉ Trelin, Chynhale, Helston, Cornwall TR13 0RX (☎ 01326 572022)

BICKHAM, Edward Sidney Côver; s of Eric Edward Bickham (d 1987), of Ringwood, Hants, and Frances Agnes, *née* Potter, of Reading, Berks; *b* 10 Aug 1956; *Educ* Brockenhurst GS, St John's Coll Oxford (MA Jurisprudence); *Career* asst to the Chairman Macmillan Publishers Ltd 1977–80, Euro affrs desk offr Cons Research Dept 1980–83; special advsr: to Sec of State for NI 1983–85, to Home Sec 1985–88; exec dir Corp Communications British Satellite Broadcasting 1988–90, special advsr to Foreign Sec 1991–93, md Corp Policy and Public Affrs Hill & Knowlton (UK) Ltd 1993–; pres Univ of Oxford Cons Assoc 1976; contested (Cons) Vauxhall ILEA Seat 1986, vice chm Cons Gp for Europe 1995–; memb Communications Advsy Gp ESRC; Robert Schuman Silver Medal for Servs to Euro Unity 1983; MIPR 1995; *Publications* various pamphlets incl Raising Kane? Preserving Diversity in Media Ownership (1996); *Recreations* cinema, theatre, tennis, horse racing; *Clubs* Carlton; *Style*— Edward Bickham, Esq; ✉ Hill & Knowlton (UK) Ltd, 5–11 Theobalds Road, London WC1X 8SH (☎ 0171 413 3050, fax 0171 413 3113)

BICKMORE, Peter Christopher; s of Lt-Col Lawrence Hyde Neild Bickmore, OBE, of Kensington, and Anne Windsor Lewis, *née* Drummond (d 1985); *b* 4 April 1943; *Educ* Charterhouse; *m* 22 July 1975, Isabel Margaret, da of Maj-Gen Lord Michael Fitzalan Howard, KCVO, MC, of Fovant House, Fovant, nr Salisbury, Wiltshire; 2 s (Andrew Ralph b 1979, Rupert Nicholas b 1985), 1 da (Fiona Clare b 1981); *Career* Lt short serv cmmn Life Gds 1962–68; md: Pegasus Insurance Services Ltd 1979–88, BBA Insurance Services Ltd 1989–96 (currently dir), British Bloodstock Agency plc 1992–95; sports conslt to Stuart Canvas Products; memb Insur Brokers' Registration Cncl 1986; Freeman City of London 1964, Liveryman Worshipful Co of Skinners 1969; *Recreations* tennis, golf, shooting; *Clubs* White's, Pratt's; *Style*— Peter Bickmore, Esq; ✉ PO Box 24, Watlington, Oxon OX9 5YX (☎ 01491 614100, fax 01491 613452, mobile 0860 964545)

BICKNELL, Claud; OBE (1946); s of Raymond Bicknell (d 1927), of Newcastle upon Tyne, and Phillis Ellen, *née* Lovibond (d 1957); *b* 15 June 1910; *Educ* Oundle, Queens' Coll Cambridge (MA, pres Univ Mountaineering Club 1930–31); *m* 1, 15 Dec 1934, Esther Irene (d 1958), da of Rev Kenneth Norman Bell (d 1951), of Oxford; 1 s (Mark Bicknell b 1936), 3 da (Meriel (Mrs Mastroyannopoulou) b 1939 d 1977, Clare (wife of Dr John Richard Shelley, *qv*) b 1943, Phillis (wife of Professor Christopher Jones) b 1949); m 2, 7 May 1960, Christine Betty, CBE, da of Walter Edward Reynolds (d 1940), of Dulwich; *Career* WWII Auxiliary Fire Serv Newcastle upon Tyne 1939–41, Nat Fire Serv 1941–45, sr fire staff offr Home Office 1943–45; admitted slr 1934; Stanton Atkinson & Bird Newcastle upon Tyne 1934–70, law cmmr 1970–75, chm of industl tbnls 1975–83; dir Northern Corp Ltd 1939–53, memb Planning Bd Lake Dist Nat Park 1951–70 (chm Devpt Control Ctee 1957–70), memb Lord Jellicoe's Ctee on Water Resources in the NW 1963, pres Newcastle upon Tyne Incorporated Law Soc 1969, chm Newcastle upon Tyne Housing Improvement Tst Ltd 1966–70; *Clubs* Garrick, Alpine; *Style*— Claud Bicknell, Esq, OBE; ✉ Aikrigg End Cottage, 115 Burneside Road, Kendal, Cumbria LA9 6DZ

BICKNELL, Darren John; s of Melvyn Bicknell, and Valerie, *née* Gorman (now Mrs Roper); bro of Martin Bicknell; *b* 24 June 1967; *Educ* Robert Haining Co Secdy Sch

Camberley Surrey, Guildford Co Coll of Technol; *m* 26 Sept 1992, Rebecca Hilsden; 1 da (Lauren Elizabeth b 21 Oct 1993), 1 s (Samuel Jack b 9 Nov 1995); *Career* professional cricketer Surrey CCC 1987– (awarded county cap 1990); toured with England A Team: Kenya and Zimbabwe 1988–89, Pakistan and Sri Lanka 1990, Bermuda and W Indies 1991; *Recreations* snooker, football, golf; *Style—* Darren Bicknell, Esq; ✉ c/o Surrey CCC, The Oval, Kennington, London SE11 5SS (☎ 0171 582 6660)

BICKNELL, John; s of Peter Barrie Bicknell, and Lorna Mary Graham, *née* Farmer; *b* 28 July 1958; *Educ* Sir Winston Churchill Co Secdy Sch Surrey, Ottershaw Sch Surrey, NE London Poly (BA), Slade Sch of Fine Art Univ of London (Boise travelling scholar, HDip, Slade prize); *m* Christina, da of Manthos Dorees; 1 da (Ariadne); *Career* artist; solo exhibitions: Paintings Drawings and Prints (Carlile Gallery London) 1987, Painting and Prints (Pomeroy Purdy Gallery London) 1990, Pomeroy Purdy Gallery London (1992); gp exhibitions incl: Sainsbury Centre for Visual Arts UEA 1980, Stowells Trophy (Royal Acad of Arts) 1983, New Graduate Art (Christies Contemporary Art) 1983, Leicester exhibition for schs and colls (Beaumanor Hall Loughborough) 1984, Athens International Awards (Mall Galleries) 1985, Open Studio exhibition (Wapping) 1985, XXV Joan Miró (Barcelona and touring Spain) 1986, Drawings (Carlile Gallery) 1986, John Moores 15 Liverpool Exhibition (Walker Art Gallery) 1987, South Bank Picture Show (Royal Festival Hall) 1987, For Sale (Minories Gallery) 1988, Art '89 (Islington Centre) 1989, Summer Exhibition (Pomeroy Purdy Gallery) 1989, New Talent (Schuster Gallery Florida) 1989, Christies New Contemporaries (RCA Galleries) 1989, Ninth Bath Fair 1989, Painting and Sculpture (Leeds Poly Gallery) 1990, Gallery Artists (Pomeroy Purdy Gallery) 1990, Fifth Br Int Contemporary Art Fair (Olympia) 1990, A View of the New (Br Over-Seas League) 1990, John Moores 17 Liverpool Exhibition (Walker Art Gallery) 1991, 10th Cleveland Int Drawing Bienale (Cleveland Gallery and nat tour) 1991; works in collections: Slade Collection, Boise Scholarship Collection, Leicester Collection for Schs and Colls, County National Westminster Bank, Reed International, private collections in England, Europe, Israel and USA; theatre work: asst designer studio ATA (Athens) prodn of White Nights by Fyodor Dostoevsky 1988, designer The Night is Not Dark by Peter Bicknell (Gate Theatre London) 1990; awards: Greater London Arts award, 1986, prizewinner John Moores Liverpool Exhibition 1987, second prize South Bank Bd, Leeds Metropolitan Univ research awards 1993 and 1994; Henry Moore Printmaking fellowship Leeds Poly 1989–90, assoc lectr Leeds Metropolitan Univ 1992–, tutor Wimbledon Sch of Art 1992–; *Style—* John Bicknell, Esq; ✉ Pomeroy Purdy Gallery, Jacob Street Studios, Mill Street, London SE1 2BA (☎ 0171 237 6062)

BICKNELL, Julian; s of Wing Cdr Nigel Bicknell, DSO, DFC (d 1990), and Sarah Greenway, *née* Leith; *b* 23 Feb 1945; *Educ* Winchester, King's Coll Cambridge (MA, DipArch); *m* 18 Nov 1967, Treld, da of Arthur K O Pelkey (d 1979), of West Hartford, Connecticut, USA; 1 s (Titus P b 1971), 1 da (Poppaea E b 1982); *Career* architect and teacher; asst later ptnr Edward Cullinan 1966–72; tutor and dir of Project Office RCA 1973–80: The Old Gaol Abingdon (RIBA award 1976), The Garden Hall and Library, Castle Howard (Carpenters' award 1984); staff architect Arup Assocs 1981–84 (reconstruction of Bedford Sch); in private practice 1984–: Henbury Rotonda, HM Ambassador's Residence Moscow, Upton Viva, Nagara Country Club Japan, High Corner, The Georgian Club Tokyo; external examiner Leeds Metropolitan Univ Sch of Architecture 1990–94, memb Advsy and Academic Bd and tutor Prince of Wales Inst of Architecture 1991–; RIBA 1971, memb AA 1987, FRSA 1988, elected to Art Workers' Guild 1995; *Books* The Design for Need Papers (1979), Hiroshige in Tokyo (1994); *Recreations* architecture, music, the countryside; *Style—* Julian Bicknell, Esq; ✉ 29 Lancaster Park, Richmond, Surrey (☎ 0181 940 3929); The White Cottage, Fontmell Magna, Dorset; (office) 20 Bedford St, London WC2E 9HP (☎ 0171 836 5875, fax 0171 836 8290)

BICKNELL, Stephen Alan; s of late Alan Bicknell, and Vivienne, *née* Colwell; *b* 30 Sept 1951; *Educ* Andover; *m* 19 July 1980, Karen Wendy, da of Edward Shotnik; 2 da (Kirstie b 24 Nov 1982, Susannah b 7 Aug 1984), 1 s (Christopher b 4 Sept 1986); *Career* trained in industl photography with Walter Gardiner of Worthing 1968–72, freelanced London 1972–76, started own studio business Horsham 1976– (specialised in creative industl photography at Billingshurst 1985); Industrial Ilford award 1987, highly commended Ilford Folio 1988, 1989, 1991 and 1993; FBIPP 1986, FRPS 1992; *Style—* Stephen Bicknell, Esq; ✉ Ashley House, Swan Corner, Pulborough, W Sussex (☎ 01798 872324); Steve Bicknell Photography, Unit 7 Eagle Industrial Estate, Brookers Rd, Billingshurst, West Sussex RH14 9RZ (☎ 01403 784311, fax 01403 785368, car 0860 610758)

BIDDISS, Prof Michael Denis; s of Daniel Biddiss (d 1984), of Orpington, and Eileen Louisa, *née* Jones (d 1984); *b* 15 April 1942; *Educ* St Joseph's Acad Blackheath, Queens' Coll Cambridge (MA, PhD), Centre des Hautes Études Européennes Univ of Strasbourg; *m* 8 April 1967, Ruth Margaret, da of Dr Frederick Fox Cartwright, of Swallowfield, Berks; 4 da (Clare b 1969, Kate b 1972, Sarah b 1974, Beth b 1977); *Career* fell and dir of studies in history and social and political sciences Downing Coll Cambridge 1966–73, lectr and reader in history Univ of Leicester 1973–79, prof of history Univ of Reading 1979– (dean of the Faculty of Letters and Social Sci 1982–85); visiting professorships: Univ of Victoria BC Canada 1973, Univ of Cape Town SA 1976 and 1978, Monash Univ Aust 1989; chm History at the Univs Defence Gp 1984–87; memb Cncl: Historical Association 1985– (pres 1991–94), Royal Historical Soc 1988–92 (jt vice pres 1995–); hon fell Faculty of History of Med Worshipful Soc of Apothecaries 1986– (pres 1994–, Osler medal 1989, Locke medal 1996); FRHistS 1974; *Books* Father of Racist Ideology (1970), Gobineau - Selected Political Writings (ed, 1970), Disease and History (jtly, 1972), The Age of the Masses - Ideas and Society in Europe since 1870 (1977), Images of Race (ed, 1979), Thatcherism - Personality and Politics (jt ed, 1987), The Nuremberg Trial and the Third Reich (1992); *Recreations* cricket, mountain walking, music and opera; *Style—* Prof Michael Biddiss; ✉ Department of History, University of Reading, Whiteknights, Reading RG6 6AA (☎ 0118 931 8146)

BIDDLE, Donald Frank; s of Kenneth Barrington Biddle, of Poole, Dorset, and Judy Hill, *née* Downie (d 1964); *b* 6 March 1933; *Educ* Uppingham; *m* 3 Oct 1963, Anne Muriel, da of Maj Charles Deane Cowper; 2 s (Justin b 1968, Mark b 1971), 2 da (Georgina b 1973, Anne-Marie (twin) b 1973); *Career* CA; 2 Lt RA Germany 1956–57, HAC 1957–63; Price Waterhouse 1957–62, ptnr Smith and Williamson 1962–93, gen cmmr of Taxation 1970–87 and 1989–; tstee: English Language Servs Int (Int House) 1963–, Ada Lewis Housing Tst 1967–82 (chm 1978–80), Samuel Lewis Housing Tst 1978–94, Southern Housing Gp 1993–94; involved with Cons Pty at local and area levels, sec Int Dragon Assoc 1982–89, treas Cncl Order of St John of Jerusalem (Dorset) 1993–; memb Olympic Yachting Ctee 1964–74; FCA; *Recreations* yachting, skiing, wine; *Clubs* Carlton, Boodle's, Royal Yacht Sqdn; *Style—* Donald F Biddle, Esq; ✉ The Old House, Milton-on-Stour, Gillingham, Dorset (☎ 01747 823487, fax 01747 825938)

BIDDLE, Howard William; s of Kenneth Howard Biddle, of Leicester, and Margaret Evelyn Biddle; *b* 11 Feb 1949; *Educ* Alderman Newton's Boys' Sch Leicester, QMC London (BSc), RCA (MDesRCA); *m* Hilary May, da of Hayden John; 1 s (Jonathan Howard b 19 April 1979), 1 da (Eleanor Catherine b 27 April 1981); *Career* devpt engr Cambridge Consultants Ltd 1972–75, student RCA 1975–78, currently md Cambridge Consultants Ltd (rejoined 1978, successively fndr Product Design Gp, mktg mangr Mech Engrg Div, dir then dep md); *Recreations* skiing, mountian biking, walking; *Style—* Howard Biddle, Esq; ✉ Cambridge Consultants, Science Park, Milton Road, Cambridge CB4 4DW (☎ 01223 420024, fax 01223 423373, mobile 0374 704262)

BIDDLE, Prof Martin; OBE (1997); s of Reginald Samuel Biddle (d 1971), and Gwladys Florence, *née* Baker (d 1986); *b* 4 June 1937; *Educ* Merchant Taylors', Pembroke Coll Cambridge (BA, MA), Univ of Oxford (MA); *m* 1, 9 Sept 1961 (m dis 1966), Hannelore Bäcker; 2 da (Joanna b 1962, Barbara b 1965); m 2, 19 Nov 1966, Birthe, da of Landsretssagfører Axel Th Kjølbye (d 1972), of Sønderborg, Denmark; 2 da (Signe b 1969, Solvej b 1971); *Career* 2 Lt 4 RTR 1956, Ind Sqdn RTR Berlin 1956–57; asst inspr of ancient monuments Miny of Public Bldg and Works 1961–63, lectr in medieval archaeology Univ of Exeter 1963–67, visiting fell All Souls Coll Oxford 1967–68, dir Winchester Res Unit 1968–, dir Univ Museum and prof of anthropology and history of art Univ of Pennsylvania 1977–81, lectr of the house ChCh Oxford 1983–86, Astor sr res fell in medieval archaeology and tutor in archaeology Hertford Coll Oxford 1989–; author of numerous books and articles; excavations with: Sir Mortimer Wheeler St Albans and Stanwick 1949 and 1952, Dame Kathleen Kenyon Jericho 1957–58; fieldwork: Nonsuch Palace 1959–60, Winchester 1961–71, St Albans 1978, 1982–84, 1991 and 1994–95, Repton 1974–88 and 1993, Holy Sepulchre Jerusalem 1989–93, Qasr Ibrim Nubia Egypt 1989–90, 1992 and 1995; archaeological conslt: Canterbury Cathedral, St Albans Abbey and Cathedral Church, Eurotunnel, British Telecom, etc; chm: Rescue The Trust for Br Archaeology 1971–75, Winchester in Europe (Nat Referendum 1975); served Cons Pty Ctees in: Winchester 1973–77, Oxford 1982–; cmmr Royal Cmmn on the Historical Monuments of England 1984–95; pres Soc for Medieval Archaeology 1995–; Hon Knight of the Hon Soc of Knights of the Round Table 1971; Freeman: Worshipful Co of Merchant Taylors 1963, City of London 1963; Univ of Pennsylvania: Hon MA 1977, Hon Phi Beta Kappa 1978; FSA 1964, FRHistS 1970, FBA 1985; *Books* Future of London's Past (1973), Winchester in the Early Middle Ages (ed, 1976), Object and Economy in Medieval Winchester (1990); *Recreations* travel, especially Hellenic and Middle East, reading; *Clubs* Athenaeum; *Style—* Prof Martin Biddle, OBE, FBA, FSA; ✉ Hertford College, Oxford OX1 3BW (☎ 01865 279422, fax 01865 279437); research office (☎ and fax 01865 559017)

BIDDLE, Neville Leslie; s of Walter Alan Biddle, of Nannerch Lodge, Nannerch, N Wales, and Beryl Mary, *née* Meadows; *b* 24 April 1951; *Educ* Wrekin, Univ Coll Wales Aberystwyth (BSc); *m* 2 Oct 1976, Sheila Ruth, da of Parimal Kumar Sen (d 1972); 4 da (Caroline b 22 Nov 1980, Josephine b 27 July 1982, Rebecca b 2 June 1986, Charlotte b 15 July 1991); *Career* called to the Bar Gray's Inn 1974; elected to Northern Circuit 1975, currently in practice Liverpool, asst recorder 1995–; non-exec dir R S Clare & Co Liverpool; *Style—* Neville Biddle, Esq; ✉ Peel House, Harrington St, Liverpool L2 9QA (☎ 0151 236 4321)

BIDDLE, Paul; *b* 11 Sept 1952; *Educ* art sch; *m* Aug 1972, Pamela, *née* Blanchflower; *Career* qualified teacher of art and photography Dartington 1977–86, photographer (advtg and design cmmns) 1986–; memb: Assoc of Photographers 1989, RSP 1991; *Awards* Assoc of Photographers Annual Awards Gold 1989/Merit 1989 and 1990, RSP Annual International Gold 1991 and 1992 (awards judge 1993), Kodak Triple Exposure winner 1991, Br Jl of Photography Annual 1990 and 1993, NY 3D Illustrators Awards Bronze 1993/Gold and 6 Bronzes 1994; *Recreations* guitar, walking, reading; *Style—* Paul Biddle, Esq; ✉ agent: Louise Fennell (☎ and fax 0171 352 5091)

BIDDULPH, Sir Ian D'Olier; 11 Bt (E 1664); s of Sir Stuart Royden Biddulph, 10 Bt (d 1986), and Muriel Margaret, *née* Harkness (d 1995); *b* 28 Feb 1940; *Educ* Slade Sch Warwick Queensland; *m* 1967, Margaret Eleanor, o da of late John Gablonski, of Oxley, Brisbane; 1 s (Paul William b 1967), 2 da (Julie Denise b 1969, Roslyn Mary b 1971); *Heir* s, Paul William Biddulph b 30 Oct 1967; *Career* grazier; *Style—* Sir Ian Biddulph, Bt; ✉ Mail Service 23, Mount Walker, via Rosewood, Queensland 4340, Australia

BIDDULPH, 5 Baron (UK 1903); (Anthony) Nicholas Colin Maitland Biddulph; er s of 4 Baron Biddulph (d 1988), and Lady Mary Maitland, da of Viscount Maitland, s of 15 Earl of Lauderdale; *b* 8 April 1959; *Educ* Cheltenham, RAC Cirencester; *m* 28 Aug 1993, Hon Sian Diana Gibson-Watt, yr da of Baron Gibson-Watt, MC, PC, *qv*; 1 s (Hon Robert Julian b 1994); *Heir* s, Hon Robert Julian Maitland Biddulph b 8 July 1994; *Career* interior designer and farmer; Liveryman Worshipful Co of Armourers and Brasiers; *Recreations* shooting, fishing, racing, skiing; *Clubs* Raffles, Cavalry and Guards; *Style—* The Rt Hon Lord Biddulph; ✉ Makerstoun, Kelso, Roxburghshire TD5 7PA (☎ 01573 460234); 8 Orbel St, London SW11 3NZ (☎ 0171 228 9865)

BIDE, Sir Austin Ernest; kt (1980); o s of Ernest Arthur Bide (d 1918), and Eliza, *née* Young (d 1976); *b* 11 Sept 1915; *Educ* Acton County Sch, Birkbeck Coll and Chelsea Poly Univ of London (BSc); *m* 1941, Irene, da of Ernest Auckland Ward (d 1953); 3 da; *Career* Maj 21 Army Gp Germany (CIOS); Dept of Govt Chemist until 1940; joined Glaxo Laboratories Ltd (Res Dept) 1940, consecutively head Chem Investigation and Devpt Dept, PA to dep md Glaxo Laboratories Ltd 1946, head of patents and trademarks; first factory mangr Montrose 1951, dep sec Glaxo Laboratories Ltd 1954 (sec 1959–65), dir Glaxo Group 1963, dep chm Glaxo Holdings 1971–73 (chm and chief exec 1973–80, chm until 1985, hon pres 1985–), non-exec dir J Lyons & Co Ltd 1977–78, non-exec chm BL 1982–86 (non-exec dir 1977–82); currently chm: CGEA (UK) Ltd, Onyx UK Ltd; admin Compagnie des Transports et Services Publiques France; dir Oxford Consultancy Ltd 1988–; CBI: chm Res and Technol Ctee 1977–86, memb Cncl 1976–85, memb Cos Ctee 1974–80, memb Pres Ctee 1983–86, memb Univs Polys and Indust Ctee 1984–85, memb Industl Performance Steering Gp 1985; chm: Nat Appeal Ctee Salisbury Cathedral 1986–92 (cnsllr Confraternity of Benefactors 1992–), Nat AIDS Tst 1987–91, Ct Shippers' Cncl (now Freight Transport Assoc) 1989–, World Humanity Action Tst 1993–, Bd Adam Smith Inst; memb: Cncl Imperial Soc for Knights Bachelor 1980–, Advsy Ctee on Indust to the Vice Chllrs and Princs of Univs of UK 1984–87, Cncl Inst of Manpower Studies 1985–, body to review the affrs of the Univ Grants Ctee 1985 (report published 1987); chm Visiting Ctee Open Univ 1982–89, tstee Br Motor Indust Heritage Tst 1983–86; memb MRC 1987–90 (chm Investments and Pensions Sub-Ctee, memb AIDS Sub-Ctee); former vice pres Inst of Industrial Managers; Br Inst of Mgmnt: memb Cncl 1976–88, memb Cos Ctee 1974–84, chm Fin Ctee and dir BIM Fndn 1977–79; vice pres Inst of Mgmnt (merger of Inst of Industrial Managers and Br Inst of Mgmnt) 1993–; winner: BIM Gold medal (for outstanding achievements in mgmnt of Glaxo Group 1982), Duncan Davies medal Research and Devpt Soc 1990; hon fell: Inst for Biotechnology Studies 1985 (memb Bd and fell Membership Ctee 1987–89), St Catherine's Coll Oxford 1987; Hon DSc: Queen's Univ Belfast, CNAA; Hon DUniv Open Univ 1991; CIMgt, FRSC, CChem, CIEx, FInstD 1989, FIIM, FIDS, Hon FIChemE 1983, Hon FICE 1983; *Publications* Biotechnology - A Report of a Joint Working Party (1980); *Clubs* Hurlingham, 1900; *Style—* Sir Austin Bide

BIDEN, Michael; s of John William Biden, and Erica Margaret, *née* Marsh; *Educ* Altrincham GS, Windermere GS, The Lakes Sch, Chargrin Falls HS Ohio, UMIST (BSc, RSA Silver medal); *m* Alison; 1 s (Edward), 1 da (Stephanie); *Career* BP Chemicals 1970–73, Pedigree Petfoods 1973–82, various positions rising to ops dir Four Square Div Mars GB 1982–89, vice pres global mktg Mars Electronics International 1989–93 (Euro gen mangr 1989–91), chief exec ITS Group plc 1993–94, personal communcations mktg and sales dir British Telecommunications plc 1994–96, exec dir Hays business servs gp 1996–; MInstD, FRSA; *Recreations* family, skiing, sailing, golf, reading; *Style—* Michael Biden, Esq

BIDWELL, Sir Hugh Charles Philip; GBE (1989); s of Edward Bidwell, and late Elizabeth Bidwell; *b* 1 Nov 1934; *Educ* Stonyhurst; *m* 1962, Jenifer Celia Webb; 2 s, 1 da; *Career* Nat Serv 1953–55, cmmnd E Surrey Regt, seconded to 1 Bn KAR Nyasaland; dir Viota Foods Ltd 1962–70 (joined 1957), dir Robertson Foods 1968–70; chm: Pearce Duff & Co Ltd 1970–84, Gill & Duffus Foods 1984–85; non-exec dir: Argyll Group plc 1990–95, Rothschild Asset Management Ltd 1992, Fleming Geared Income & Assets Investment Trust plc 1993–, Alpha Airports Group plc 1994–; non-exec chm: Applied Distribution Group plc 1993–, Julius Group Ltd 1993–; non-exec chm British Invisibles 1992–94; memb: Exec Ctee Food Manufacturers' Fedn 1973–86, Cncl London C of C and Indust 1976–85, Food from Britain Cncl 1983–89 (chm Export Bd 1983–86); pres Br Food Export Cncl 1980–87, dep pres Food and Drink Fedn 1985 and 1986; memb: Euro Trade Ctee 1989–91, Chamber of Commerce 1989–92, China-Britain Trade Gp 1989–94, BOTB 1992–94; Lord Mayor of London 1989–90, Alderman Billingsgate Ward 1979–96, Sheriff City of London 1986–87, memb Worshipful Co of Grocers (Master 1984–85), Hon Liveryman Worshipful Co of Marketors; pres: Billingsgate Ward Club, Fishmongers' & Poulterers' Inst; *Recreations* golf, fishing, tennis, cricket, shooting; *Clubs* Boodle's, City of London, MCC, Denham Golf, Royal St George's, Royal & Ancient; *Style—* Sir Hugh Bidwell, GBE; ✉ Five Arrows House, St Swithin's Lane, London EC4N 8NR (☎ 0171 280 5000)

BIELCKUS, Colin David; s of Louis Reginald Bielckus, of Thornhill, Southampton, and Lorna Elizabeth Mary Bielckus; *b* 17 June 1956; *Educ* King Edward VI Sch Southampton, Univ of E Anglia (BSc); *m* 11 Oct 1981, Lorraine, da of Reginald Alexander, of Southampton; 1 da (Penelope Louise b 18 May 1995); *Career* CA; audit mangr Alliott Wingham (formerly Alliott Millar) Fareham 1985–90, audit ptnr Alliott Millar Fareham 1990–; *Recreations* railways, collecting books, collecting beermats, collecting cacti and other succulent plants; *Style—* Colin Bielckus, Esq; ✉ 72 The Avenue, Fareham Hants PO14 1PB (☎ 01329 284728); Alliott Wingham, Kintyre House, 70 High St, Fareham, Hants (☎ 01329 822232, fax 01329 822405)

BIENKOWSKI, Jan Stanislaw; s of Zygmunt Witymir Bienkowski (d 1978) Polish Air Force Col, and Halina Wita Bienkowska, *née* Grzybowska; *b* 7 Nov 1948; *Educ* Salesian Coll, Univ of Surrey (BSc Eng), AA Sch of Architecture (AADip); *m* 21 Sept 1974, Zofia Joanna, da of Leszek Jozef Rybicki, Maj 15 Lancers (Polish Cavalry); 1 s (Andrzej b 1984), 2 da (Lidia b 1977, Monika b 1978); *Career* founding ptnr Spiromega Partnership (architects and designers) 1980–, jt md Blythe Projects plc 1985–89; dir: Myriad Ltd 1986–89, H and B Projects Ltd 1989–90; md Tolclose Ltd 1990–93; chm Bienkowski & Co Ltd 1990–, pres D W BB&P SA Poland 1992–, dir D W "Filipinka" Sp ZO.O Poland 1992–; MCSD, RIBA; *Recreations* landscape painting; *Style—* Jan S Bienkowski, Esq; ✉ Spiromega Partnership, Unit 3B Westpoint, 39–40 Warple Way, London W3 0RG (☎ 0181 743 0058, fax 0181 743 0736)

BIERBRIER, Dr Morris Leonard; s of Harry Arthur Bierbrier (d 1986), of Montreal, and Dorothy Greta, *née* Yachnin; *b* 30 March 1947; *Educ* McGill Univ Montreal (open fellowship, Quebec gold medal in history, BA), Univ of Toronto (Woodrow Wilson fell, open fellowship, MA), Univ of Liverpool (Canada Cncl fell, PhD); *m* 30 Dec 1974, Lydia Collins, *qv*, da of Joel Collins; *Career* Egyptologist; lectr Dept of Extra-Mural Studies Univ of London 1975–76, asst keeper Dept of Egyptian Antiquities Br Museum 1976– (res asst 1975–76); memb Ctee Egypt Exploration Soc 1985–88, 1989–92 and 1994– (hon librarian and reviews ed 1985–94), Br rep Int Assoc of Egyptologists 1985–88; ed Who was Who in Egyptology; Soc of Genealogists: memb Exec Ctee 1978–86, sometime vice chm Exec Ctee, sometime chm Library and Pubns Ctees; FSA 1984, FSG 1993; *Books* The Late New Kingdom in Egypt (1975), The British Museum Hieroglyphic Texts from Egyptian Stelae etc (pt 10, 1982, pt 11, 1987, pt 12, 1993), The Tomb-Builders of the Pharaohs (1982), Who was Who in Egyptology (3 edn, 1995); *Recreations* genealogy; *Style—* Dr Morris Bierbrier, FSA; ✉ Department of Egyptian Antiquities, British Museum, London WC1B 3DG (☎ 0171 323 8682, fax 0171 323 8303)

BIFFEN, Rt Hon (William) John; PC (1979), DL (1993 Shropshire), MP (C) Shropshire North (majority 16,211); s of Victor W Biffen, of Otterhampton, Somerset; *b* 3 Nov 1930; *Educ* Dr Morgan's GS Bridgwater, Jesus Coll Cambridge (BA); *m* 1979, Mrs Sarah Wood, *née* Drew; 1 step s, 1 step da; *Career* with Tube Investments Ltd 1953–60, Economist Intelligence Unit 1960–61; MP (C): Oswestry 1961–83, Shropshire North 1983–; chief sec to the Treasy 1979–81, sec of state for trade 1981–82, Lord Pres of the Cncl 1982–83, ldr House of Commons 1982–87, Lord Privy Seal 1983–87; dir: Glynwed International plc 1987–, J Bibby & Sons plc 1988–, Rockware Group plc 1988–91; tstee The London Clinic 1995–; *Style—* The Rt Hon John Biffen, DL, MP; ✉ c/o House of Commons, London SW1A 0AA

BIGGAR, (Walter) Andrew; CBE (1979, OBE 1967), MC (1945), TD; s of Walter Biggar (d 1949), of Grange, Castle Douglas, and Margaret, *née* Sproat (d 1965); *b* 6 March 1915; *Educ* Sedbergh, Univ of Edinburgh (BSc); *m* 11 June 1945, Patricia Mary Irving, da of William Elliot (d 1949), of Middletoun, Stow, Midlothian; 1 s (Michael b 1949), 1 da (Susan b 1947); *Career* cmmnd Royal Signals 1939 (POW Germany 1940–45); Rowett Res Inst 1935–54; farmer 1956–89; memb Agric Res Cncl 1969–79, vice chm Scottish Agric Devpt Cncl 1971–81; govr Grassland Res Inst 1961–80; dir and tstee: Scottish Soc for Crop Res 1958–88, Animal Diseases Res Inst 1960–; chm: Animals Bd Jt Consultative Orgn for Res in Agric 1973–80, Moredun Animal Health Tst 1988–; govr St Margaret's Sch Edinburgh 1959–79; hon fell Animal and Grassland Res Inst 1980; FRAgS 1969; *Recreations* photography, rugby football; *Style—* W Andrew Biggar, Esq, CBE, MC, TD; ✉ Magdalene Hall, St Boswells, Roxburghshire, Scotland (☎ 01835 823741)

BIGGART, Alastair Ross; OBE (1996); s of Thomas Biggart (d 1985), and Mary Gladys Biggart, of Bromley, Kent; *b* 13 Aug 1933; *Educ* Canford Sch, Univ of Loughborough (BSc, pres Univ Boat Club); *m* 1 Sept 1962, Mary Margaret Neill, da of James William Roxburgh Murray; 1 s (Iain William Murray b 13 Nov 1969), 3 da (Fiona Margaret b 11 Sept 1963, Kirsty Mary b 16 Dec 1964, Alison Elizabeth b 7 Nov 1967); *Career* Nat Serv pilot RAF 1956–58; asst engr on a number of civil engrg projects 1958–65; dir: Mitchell Brothers 1965–70, Edmund Nuttall Ltd 1972–80 (contracts mangr 1970–71); md R L Priestley Ltd 1981–82 (part of Nuttall Group); Lilley Construction: tunnel mangr 1983–84, dir with responsibility for tunnelling projects 1984–85, tech dir (Cairo) 1985–87, asst construction dir for all tunnelling and precast work on the Channel Tunnel Transmanche-Link 1987–89 (ops dir 1989–92); project dir on Storebaelt Tunnel Denmark 1992–95, project mangr and chief exec offr JMA Jr Red Line North Hollywood Project 1995–; holder of Br patent for Double Gate Valve for use with slurry machines; Gold Medal ICE 1995; FICE 1971, FEng 1990; *Publications* The Bentonite Tunnelling Machine (Proceedings ICE, 1973, awarded Telford Gold medal), The Bentonite Tunnelling Machine at Warrington (jtly, Symposium Tunnelling '76, 1976), Slurry Face Machine Tunnelling (Proceedings RETC, 1979), The Channel Tunnel (Channel Tunnel Conf Paris, 1989), Channel Tunnel: Design and Construction (Proceedings ICE, 1992), The Changing Face of Tunnelling (Proceedings IMM 1994), Storebaelt Tunnel-Construction (Proceedings ICE, 1996); *Recreations* sailing, shooting, converting old buildings; *Clubs* RAF; *Style—* Alastair Biggart, Esq, OBE, FEng; ✉ JMA Joint Venture, 4640 Lankershim Boulevard, North Hollywood, California 91602, USA (☎ 00 1 818 505 1770, fax 00 1 818 755 4460)

BIGGART, (Thomas) Norman; CBE (1984); o s of Andrew Stevenson Biggart, JP, and his w Marjorie Scott; *b* 24 Jan 1930; *Educ* Morrisons Acad Crieff, Univ of Glasgow (MA, LLB); *m* 1956, Eileen Jean Anne Gemmell; 1 s, 1 da; *Career* RN 1954–56, Sub Lt RNVR; ptnr Biggart Baillie & Gifford slrs Glasgow & Edinburgh 1959–95; dir: Clydesdale Bank plc 1985–, Independent Insurance Group plc (formerly New Scotland Insurance Group plc) 1986– (chm 1989–93); chm: Beechwood Glasgow plc 1989–; Law Soc of Scotland: memb Cncl 1977–86, vice pres 1981–82, pres 1982–83; pres Business Archives Cncl Scot 1977–86; memb: Scot Tertiary Educn Advsy Cncl 1984–87, Exec Scot Cncl Devpt and Indust 1984–94, Cncl on Tbnls (chm Scot Ctee) 1990–, Scot Records Advsy Cncl 1985–91; tstee Scottish Civic Tst 1989–; hon memb American Bar Assoc 1982; OStJ 1968; memb WS Soc; *Recreations* golf, hill-walking; *Clubs* Western (Glasgow); *Style—* Norman Biggart, Esq, CBE, WS; ✉ Gailes, Kilmacolm, Renfrewshire PA13 4LZ (☎ 0150 587 2645)

BIGGINS, Christopher; s of William Biggins, of Salisbury, Wilts, and Pamela Parsons; *b* 16 Dec 1948; *Educ* St Probus Salisbury, Bristol Old Vic Theatre Sch; *Career* actor, dir and personality; govr St Dunstan's Coll Catford, tstee All Hallows by the Tower; Freeman City of London; *Recreations* eating, swimming, enjoying life; *Clubs* RAC; *Style—* Christopher Biggins, Esq; ✉ c/o Jonathan Altaras Associates Ltd, 27 Floral Street, London WC2E 9DP (☎ 0171 836 8722, fax 0171 836 6066)

BIGGLESTONE, John George; s of John Bigglestone (d 1992), and Lillian Bigglestone (d 1978); *b* 10 Aug 1934; *Educ* Bablake Sch Coventry, Coventry Coll of Art, Wolverhampton Poly; holder City & Guilds Full Technol Cert, BIPP Final Cert and Cert in Educn (FE); *m* 22 Dec 1984, Annette Vivian, da of Kenneth and Audrey Bull, of Devizes; *Career* professional photographer (jt prop Wharf Studios, Devizes), journalist and lectr; sr lectr in photography: Salisbury Coll of Art 1966–93, Guildford Coll 1993–; nat examiner photographic courses City & Guilds of London Inst, nat inspr FEFC; contrib to photographic magazines; photographic clients incl many leading industl cos; sponsored seminar presenter to professional photographers and colls; memb: Inst of Journalists, Royal Photographic Soc; *Recreations* learning; *Style—* John Bigglestone, Esq; ✉ The Gables, Potterne Park, Devizes, Wiltshire SN10 1QT (☎ 01380 725709)

BIGGS, Bryan George; MBE (1996); s of late George William Biggs, of Barnet, Herts, and Barbara Anne, *née* Bonner; *b* 13 Oct 1952; *Educ* Queen Elizabeth's GS for Boys Barnet, Barnet Coll of Art (fndn course), Liverpool Poly (BA); *m* 12 May 1979, Christine, da of John Edward Landells; 2 s (Michael William b 22 May 1982, Jonathan Richard b 7 July 1988), 1 da (Laura Frances b 1 May 1985); *Career* admin asst Bluecoat Soc of Arts 1975–76; dir: Bluecoat Gallery 1976–94, Bluecoat Arts Centre 1994–; organiser of numerous exhibitions at Bluecoat and other venues in UK and abroad incl: Duncan Grant - Designer 1980, Derek Boshier - Drawings 1983, Liverpool/Cologne Exchange Programme 1987–, Trophies of Empire 1992, Mal Dean Cartoons 1993; author of numerous articles and reviews on art and popular music; catalogue essays incl: Ray Walker Murals (Bluecoat) 1987, New North (Tate Gallery Liverpool) 1990; memb: Performance Art Advsy Panel Arts Cncl of GB 1986–87, Bd Merseyside Moviola 1990–95 (acting chair 1994–95); *Style—* Bryan Biggs, Esq, MBE; ✉ 5 Elmbank Rd, Mossley Hill, Liverpool L18 1HR (☎ 0151 733 8546); Bluecoat Arts Centre, School Lane, Liverpool L1 3BX (☎ 0151 709 5297)

BIGGS, Lewis; s of Ian Biggs, of Culachy, Fort Augustus, Inverness-shire, and Penelope, *née* Torr; *b* 22 April 1952; *Educ* Wellington, New Coll Oxford (BA, scholar), Courtauld Inst Univ of London (MA); *m* 1983, Ann, da of Michael Compton; 1 s (Nicholas b 1989), 1 da (Alison b 1987); *Career* gallery co-ordinator Arnolfini Bristol 1979–84, exhibition offr Fine Art Dept Br Cncl 1984–87, curator of exhibitions Tate Gallery Liverpool 1987–90 (curator 1990–); dir Art Transpennine Ltd 1996–; memb: Visual Arts Advsy Ctee Br Cncl 1992–, Fabric Advsy Ctee Liverpool Cathedral 1995–, Visual Arts Panel Arts Cncl of England 1996–; fell Univ of Liverpool 1992–; memb ICOM 1983–, CIMAM; *Style—* Lewis Biggs, Esq; ✉ Tate Gallery Liverpool, Albert Dock, Liverpool L3 4BB (☎ 0151 709 3223, fax 0151 709 3122)

BIGGS, Brig Michael Worthington; CBE (1962, OBE 1944); s of Lt Col Charles William Biggs, OBE (d 1965), of Montpellier Grove, Cheltenham, Glos, and Winifred Jesse Bell, *née* Dickinson (d 1932); *Educ* Cheltenham, RMA Woolwich, Pembroke Coll Cambridge (MA); *m* 1940, Katharine Mary, da of Sir Walter Harragin, CMG, KC (d 1966); 2 da (Patricia, Hilary); *Career* mil serv RE (cmmnd 1931) and King's African Rifles, incl active serv in Palestine, Abyssinia (BM) and Burma (GSO1 & CRE), COS E Africa Cmd 1960–63, dir of Quartering (Army) 1963–66; gp bldg exec Forte's Holdings 1966–67; mangr Welwyn Garden City and Hatfield Cmmn for the New Towns 1967–78, pres KAR & EAF Offrs Dinner Club 1972–, chm Herts Bldg Preservation Tst 1978–86, memb Cncl Town & Country Planning Assoc 1978–84, memb Exec Ctee Herts Conservation Soc 1978–93; Freeman City of London 1985; CEng, MICE; *Recreations* tennis, golf; *Clubs* Army & Navy; *Style—* Brig Michael Biggs, CBE; ✉ 1 Mildmay Court, Odiham, Hampshire RG29 1AX (☎ 01256 702715)

BIGGS, Neil William; s of Sir Lionel Biggs (d 1985), of Bournemouth, and Doris Rose, *née* Davies (d 1989); *b* 29 March 1939; *Educ* Shrewsbury; *m* 1 Sept 1969, Shirley Evelyn, da of Albert Harfield Simpson (d 1957); *Career* slr; ptnr: Withington Petty & Co (Manchester) 1962–73, Masons (London) 1973–; NP; involved in CEDR and other legal and artistic socs; memb Law Soc; *Recreations* swimming, theatre, literature; *Clubs* RAC; *Style—* Neil Biggs, Esq; ✉ 40 South Hill Park, London NW3 2SJ; Masons, 30 Aylesbury St, London EC1R 0ER (☎ 0171 490 4000, fax 0171 490 2545, telex 8811117)

BIGGS, Prof Norman Linstead; s of Joseph John Biggs (d 1965), and Dorothy Linstead (d 1982); *b* 2 Jan 1941; *Educ* Harrow County GS, Selwyn Coll Cambridge (MA), Univ of London (DSc); *m* 1, 1968 (m dis 1975), Rita Elizabeth, *née* Kelly; m 2, 20 March 1975, Christine Mary, da of Eric Richard Farmer, of Bromley, Kent; 1 da (Juliet b 1980); *Career* lectr Univ of Southampton 1963–70, reader in pure mathematics Royal Holloway Coll Univ of London 1976–88 (lectr 1970–76); LSE: prof of mathematics 1988–, govr 1995–, dir Centre for Discrete and Applicable Mathematics 1995–, vice chm Appointments Ctee 1993–96; memb London Mathematical Soc (chm Computer Sci Ctee 1985–89, memb Cncl 1979–85), chm Royal Soc Mathematical Instruction Ctee 1991–94; memb Br Numismatic Soc; *Books* Finite Groups of Automorphisms (1971), Algebraic Graph Theory (1974, 2 edn 1993), Graph Theory 1736–1936 (jtly 1976), Interaction Models (1977), Permutation Groups and Combinatorial Structures (jtly 1979), Discrete Mathematics (2 edn 1989), Introduction to Computing With Pascal (1989), Computational Learning Theory (jtly, 1992), English Weights (1993), Mathematics for Economics and Finance (jtly, 1996); *Recreations* metrology and numismatics; *Style—* Prof Norman Biggs; ✉ LSE, Houghton St, London WC2A 2AE (☎ 0171 955 7640, fax 0171 955 6877)

BIGGS, Sir Norman Parris; kt (1977); s of John Gordon Biggs, and Mary Sharpe Dickson; *b* 23 Dec 1907; *Educ* John Watson's Sch Edinburgh; *m* 1936, Peggy Helena Stammwitz (d 1990); 2 s (Nigel, Alastair), 1 da (Lindsay); *Career* Bank of England 1927–46; dir: Kleinwort Sons & Co 1946–52, Esso Petroleum 1952–66 (chm 1968–72), Gillet Bros Discount 1963–71; chm: Williams & Glyn Bank 1972–76, United Int Bank 1970–79; dep chm Privatbanken Ltd 1980–83; dir: Royal Bank of Scotland 1974–76, Banco de Bilbao 1981–87; memb Bullock Ctee Industl Democracy 1976; *Style—* Sir Norman Biggs; ✉ Northbrooks, Danworth Lane, Hurstpierpoint, Sussex (☎ 01273 832022)

BIGGS, Prof Peter Martin; CBE (1987); s of (George) Ronald Biggs (d 1985), and Cécile Agnes, *née* Player (d 1981); *b* 13 Aug 1926; *Educ* Bedales Sch, Cambridge Sch Mass USA, RVC (BSc), Univ of Bristol (PhD), Univ of London (DSc); *m* 9 Sept 1950, Alison Janet, da of late Malcolm Christian Molteno; 2 s (Andrew b 20 May 1957, John b 15 Nov 1963), 1 da (Alison (Mrs Stanley) b 27 May 1955); *Career* RAF; univ short course

Queen's Univ 1944–45, air crew undertraining, remustered Corp, demobbed 1948; lectr in veterinary clinical pathology Univ of Bristol 1955–59 (res asst 1953–55); Houghton Poultry Res Station: head Leukosis Experimental Unit 1959–73, dep dir 1971–73, dir 1974–86; visiting prof RVC Univ of London 1982–, dir AFRC Inst for Animal Health 1986–88, Andrew D White prof-at-large Cornell Univ USA 1988–94; pres Inst of Biology 1990–92, chm Scientific Advsy Ctee Animal Health Tst; memb: Vet Prods Ctee, Meds Cmmn 1973–, Advsy Ctee on Dangerous Pathogens 1988–91; Hon DVM Maximillian Univ Munich Germany, Hon DUniv Liège Belgium, Wolf Fndn Prize in Agric 1989; FRCVS, FRCPath, FIBiol, CBiol, FRS; *Recreations* music, boating, photography; *Clubs* Athenaeum, Farmers'; *Style*— Prof Peter Biggs, CBE, FRS; ✉ Willows, London Rd, St Ives, Huntingdon, Cambs PE17 4ES (☎ and fax 01480 463471)

BIGHAM, (Derek) Alastair; s of Capt Robert Alexander Bigham (d 1968), and Dorothy May, *née* Bowyer (d 1963); *b* 7 March 1926; *Educ* Whitgift Sch, Trinity Hall Cambridge, Univ Coll Oxford (MA); *m* 1, 22 Aug 1952 (m dis 1983), June Diana, da of Lt Col John Grenville Fortescue (d 1964), of Stowford Grange, Lewdown, N Devon; 2 da (Diana Susan (Mrs W Grundy) b 1954, Julia Rosemary b 1959); m 2, 3 April 1984, Mary Elizabeth, *née* Gregory; 2 step da (Nichola Mary Wild b 1967, Kirsty Elizabeth Wild b 1969), 1 step s (Edward John Wild b 1973); *Career* war serv RM then Lt Seaforth Highlanders 1944–48; called to the Bar 1952, legal advsr/PA to Lloyd's brokers, PA to sec RIBA, chartered land agent (estate mgmnt) and chartered surveyor (Planning and Devpt Div) partnership in practice Bath 1959–69, bar practice specialising in environmental and real property Middle Temple 1969–82; chm: Rent Assessment Panel 1971–82, Industrial Tribunals (full-time) 1982–91; fndr ptnr Environmental Control Consultants Sheffield and London 1991–; chm: UK Ministerial Delegation at Conf on the Environment Bern 1976, Ctee of Agric Law Assoc (UK) 1973–82, Cncl Inst of Environmental Science 1974–77; conslt to: Euro Cmmn 1979–, Cmmn Permanente Droit et Technique of Int Union of Advocates 1979–; memb Cmmn on Enviromental Law of Int Union for Conservation of Nature and Natural Resources (IUCN) 1980–; memb International Council of Environmental Law 1984–, visiting fell Univ of Sheffield 1986; cncllr: Windsor BC 1954–58, Somerset CC 1967–70 (chm Co Planning Ctee 1969–70); FCIArb 1965, FRICS 1972, MIEnvSc 1974, FRSA 1980; *Books* The Law and Administration Relating to Protection of the Environment (1973, supplement 1975), The Impact of Marine Pollution (with others, 1980), Aviation, the Environment and Planning Law (1995); *Recreations* natural history, history, visual arts, fly fishing, shooting; *Style*— Alastair Bigham, Esq; ✉ 1 Simon Court, Graham Rd, Ranmoor, Sheffield S10 3GR (☎ 0114 230 7392); Environmental Control Consultants, Sheffield (☎ 0114 230 7392)

BIGHAM, Hon Edward John Hallam; s and h of 4 Viscount Mersey; *b* 23 May 1966; *Educ* Eton, Balliol Coll Oxford; *m* 26 May 1994, Claire L, da of David Haigh, of Woking, Surrey; *Career* music producer; *Style*— The Master of Nairne; ✉ 32 Bloemfontein Road, London W12 7BX

BIGSBY, Prof Christopher William Edgar; s of Maj Edgar Edward Leo Bigsby (d 1968), and Ivy May, *née* Hopkins; *b* 27 June 1941; *Educ* Sutton GS, Univ of Sheffield (BA, MA), Univ of Nottingham (PhD); *m* 9 Oct 1965, Pamela Joan, da of Stephen Joseph Lovelady; 2 s (Gareth Christopher b 1968, Ewan James b 1976), 2 da (Kirsten Rebecca b 1972, Bella Juliet Natasha b 1974); *Career* prof of American studies UEA; writer and broadcaster; TV with Malcolm Bradbury: The After Dinner Game 1975, Stones 1976; BBC radio: Patterson (with Malcolm Bradbury) 1983, Fictions 1984, Long Day's Journey 1988, Kaleidoscope, Third Ear, Meridian; *Books* Confrontation and Commitment 1967, Albee 1969, Three Negro Plays (1969), The Black American Writer (2 vols, 1971), Dada and Surrealism (1972), Edward Albee (1975), Superculture (1975), Approaches to Popular Culture (1976), Tom Stoppard (1980), The Second Black Renaissance (1980), Contemporary English Drama (1981), A Critical Introduction to 20th Century American Drama (3 vols, 1982), Joe Orton (1982), The Radical Imagination and the Liberal Tradition (1982), David Mamet (1985), Cultural Change in the United States since World War II (1986), Plays by Susan Glaspell (1987), File on Miller (1987), Arthur Miller and Company (1990), American Drama 1945–1990 (1992), Nineteenth Century American Short Stories ed, 1995), The Portable Arthur Miller (ed, 1995); *Novels* Hester (1994), Pearl (1995), Still Lives (1996); *Recreations* so far undiscovered; *Style*— Prof Christopher Bigsby; ✉ 3 Church Farm, Colney, Norwich NR4 7TX, (☎ 01603 456048); School of English and American Studies, University of East Anglia, Norwich NR4 7TJ (☎ 01603 456161)

BILK, Bernard Stanley (Acker); s of William John Bilk (d 1941), of Pensford, Somerset, and Lillian Lydia Amanda, *née* Paske (d 1970); *b* 28 Jan 1929; *Educ* Pensford Sch Somerset; *m* 23 October 1954, Jean, da of Walter Lewis Hawkins; 1 s (Peter b 9 Jan 1959), 1 da Jenny (b 24 March 1960); *Career* jazz musician, composer and bandleader; Nat Serv Royal Engrs Canal Zone; clarinettist with Ken Colyer's Band London, fndr Bristol Paramount Jazz Band 1951; singles incl: Somerset, Stranger on the Shore 1961 (first no 1 simultaneously in England and America), Aria 1976; albums incl: The One For Me, Sheer Magic, Evergreen, Chalumeau - That's My Home 1994, Three in the Morning 1995 (with Humphrey Lyttelton, John Barnes, Dave Green, Dave Cliff and Bobby Worth); 1995 tours incl: Europe with Kenny Ball and Papa Bue, New Orleans with Kenny Colyer Trust Band, Isle of Bute with Paramount Jazz Band, Denmark, UK with Chris Barber; *Recreations* painting in oils; *Style*— Acker Bilk, Esq; ✉ c/o Acker's International Jazz Agency, 53 Cambridge Mansions, Cambridge Road, London SW11 4RX (☎ 0171 978 5885/5886, fax 0171 978 5882)

BILLETT, John Anthony; s of Ernest Edward Billett (d 1981), of Middlesex, and Angelina Christina Billett, *née* Martinelli; *b* 22 June 1945; *Educ* Ealing County GS, Dartmouth Royal Naval Coll; *m* 3 July 1971, Carole Elizabeth, da of Harold Edward Jarvis; 1 s (Christian b 1976), 1 da (Elizabeth b 1986); *Career* RN pilot 1962–71; insur broker princ 1971–72, American International Group 1972–81 (UK production mangr, dep regnl dir E Africa, dep regnl dir ME, gen mangr Netherlands, dir of ops Caribbean), vice pres The Continential Corporation (regnl dir Europe, Africa and ME) 1981–85, chm Continental Hellas; dir: Continental Life, Continental Pensions; dir and conslt Tillinghast Nelson and Warren Ltd 1985–87, chm and chief exec Barkers Finance Services Ltd 1987–92, md Bankers Insurance Co Ltd 1992–96, vice pres Life Ops Europe, Africa and ME CIGNA International 1996–; *Recreations* riding, shooting, sailing, golf; *Clubs* RAC, Glyfada Golf; *Style*— John A Billett, Esq; ✉ Barkers Farmhouse, Little Chalfont, Buckinghamshire HP7 9JY (☎ 01494 762026); CIGNA International Life Operations, 2 Minster Court, Mincing Lane, London EC3R 7XA (☎ 0171 560 8000)

BILLINGHAM, Angela Theodora; MEP (Lab) Northants and Blaby (majority 26,085); da of Theodore Vincent Case (d 1941), and Eva, *née* Saxby (d 1964); *b* 31 July 1939; *Educ* Aylesbury GS, Univ of London, Depts of Educn Oxford; *m* 1962, Anthony Peter Billingham (d 1992), s of late Cyril Billingham; 2 da (Zoë Ann b 31 Dec 1964, Caroline Lucy b 12 July 1967); *Career* numerous teaching posts most recently at Banbury Sch, former examiner for an examinations bd; cncllr: Banbury BC 1970–74, Cherwell DC 1974–84, Oxfordshire CC 1993–94; mayor of Banbury 1976; magistrate 1976–; contested gen election (Lab) Banbury 1992, MEP (Lab) Northants and Blaby 1994; memb Economic and Monetary Affairs Ctee; substutute memb Agric and Rural Devpt Sec Sports Inter Gp; *sporting achievements* tournament and county tennis player for 25 years and currently capt Oxfordshire Co Tennis team, co hockey and badminton player; *Recreations* tennis, gardening, cinema, bridge; *Style*— Mrs Angela Billingham, MEP; ✉ Ivy House, The Green, Oxford Road, Adderbury, nr Banbury, Oxon OX17 3NG (☎ 01295 810004); The Labour Party, Waterloo House, 21 Market Square, Northampton NN1 2DL (☎ 01604 27803, fax 01604 27805)

BILLINGHAM, Jeremy Ellis; s of Maj Gilbert Ellis Billingham, RA (ret), MC, TD (d 1981), late of 651 Air Op Sqdn, and Pearl, *née* Baker; *b* 19 Sept 1948; *Educ* Tonbridge; *m* 24 March 1973, Juliet Sarah, da of Wilfred William Archibald, *qv*, of Deakes Manor, Cuckfield, W Sussex; 2 da (Sacha Emma b 7 Dec 1975, Georgina Laura b 12 Nov 1978); *Career* Johnson Matthey Bankers 1969–71, Alexanders Discount plc 1971–84, Hill Samuel Wood Mackenzie 1984–86, dir Chase Investment Bank 1986–89, corp treasy conslt to Southern Water plc 1990; estab: Business Finance Bureau (corp treasy and int fin conslts) 1991, Terra Firma (land devpt advsr) 1994, Stonegate Village Garage (classic cars) 1995; Freeman City of London 1988; *Recreations* vernacular architecture, property renovation, performance cars; *Style*— Jeremy Billingham, Esq; ✉ The Jetty House, The Acorns, Stonegate, East Sussex TN5 7EY (☎ 01580 200643)

BILLINGTON, Dr (William) David; *b* 26 Feb 1938; *Educ* MA, BSc, PhD; *Career* vice dean Faculty of Med Univ of Bristol; *Style*— Dr David Billington; ✉ Department of Pathology and Microbiology, School of Medical Sciences, University of Bristol, Bristol BS8 1TD (☎ 0117 928 7882, fax 0117 928 7896)

BILLINGTON, Guy; s of Reginald Arthur Billington (d 1960), of 1 Arterberry Rd, London, and Constance May, *née* Riches; *b* 12 Nov 1946; *Educ* King's Coll Sch Wimbledon, St John's Coll Cambridge (MA); *m* 5 July 1966, Christine Ellen, da of Rev Frederick Charles Bonner, of Upton upon Severn, Worcs; 2 da (Nicole b 13 Dec 1966, Suzanne b 21 Jan 1971); *Career* articled clerk Lovell White & King 1969–72, ptnr McKenna & Co 1977– (asst slr 1972–77); memb City of London Slrs' Co; memb Law Soc; *Recreations* rugby, music, scuba diving; *Clubs* Rosslyn Park Football, BSAC; *Style*— Guy Billington, Esq; ✉ 16 Belvedere Grove, London SW19 7RL (☎ 0181 946 4889); McKenna & Co, Mitre House, 160 Aldersgate St, London EC1A 4DD (☎ 0171 606 9000, fax 0171 606 9100, telex 27251 CDE Box 724)

BILLINGTON, (Edward) John; CBE (1996), RD, DL; s of Edward Billington, and Nesta, *née* Boxwell; *b* 21 Dec 1934; *Educ* Uppingham; *m* 5 Dec 1964, Fenella, da of Dr Hamilton-Turner; 2 s (Edward b 1966, Richard b 1970), 1 da (Suzetta b 1968); *Career* RNR 1953–86; commodity broker; chm Edward Billington & Son Ltd; High Sheriff of Mersyside 1990–91; memb: NW Bd DTI, Cncl Univ of Liverpool; chm Mersey Partnership 1991–92, tstee Nat Museums and Galleries on Merseyside, dir Royal Liverpool Philharmonic Orch, dir Park Foods PLC; CIMgt; *Style*— John Billington, Esq, CBE, RD, DL; ✉ Edward Billington & Son Ltd, Cunard Building, Liverpool L3 1EL (☎ 0151 236 5371)

BILLINGTON, Kevin; s of Richard Billington (d 1987), and Margaret, *née* Hennessy; *b* 12 June 1934; *Educ* Bryanston Sch, Queens' Coll Cambridge; *m* 13 Dec 1967, Lady Rachel Billington, *qv*; 2 s (Nathaniel b 1970, Caspar b 1979), 2 da (Catherine Rose b 1973, Chloe b 1975); *Career* theatre/television/film director and producer; teacher British Centre in Sweden 1957–58, Economist Intelligence Unit London 1958–59, BBC Radio prodr Leeds 1959–60, BBC TV prodr Manchester 1960–61, prodr BBC Tonight 1961–64, documentary prodr BBC and ATV 1964–67, freelance dir 1968–95; co-owner Billington-Scott 1979–86, manager and owner Court House Films 1982–88; memb Cncl IPPA 1982–84, memb Fulbright Panel 1993–95; BAFTA: memb Cncl 1983, vice-chm 1986–89, chm 1989–91, dep chm 1991–94; *Theatre* credits incl: Find Your Way Home (world premiere, Open Space Theatre) 1971, Me (world premiere, Citizen's Theatre Glasgow) 1972, The Birthday Party (first London revival, Shaw Theatre) 1974, Bloody Neighbours (world premiere, NT at ICA) 1975, Emigres (world premiere, NT at The Old Vic) 1976, The Caretaker (London revival, Shaw Theatre) 1976, The Homecoming (first London revival, Garrick and Jerusalem Festival) 1979, The Deliberate Death of a Polish Priest (Almeida) 1985, The Lover, A Slight Ache (both Vienna English Theatre and The Young Vic) 1987, The Breadwinner (nat tour) 1989, Veteran's Day (Haymarket) 1989, Quartermaine's Terms (nat tour) 1992, Old Times (Gate Theatre Dublin) 1993; *Television and Film* documentaries 1964–67 incl: The English Cardinal, Twilight of Empire, Madison Avenue, All the Queen's Men, Matador (numerous awards incl: Encyclopaedia Brittanica Prize, Screenwriters' Guild Awards, RTS Award, BAFTA Awards); other credits incl: Interlude (Columbia) 1968, The Rise and Rise of Michael Rimmer (Warner Bros) 1970, The Light at the Edge of the World (Nat General) 1971, And No One Could Save Her (ABC) 1972, Voices (Hemdale) 1973, Once Upon a Time is Now (NBC) 1977, Henry VIII (BBC/Time-Life) 1979, Echoes of the Sixties (NBC) 1979, The Jail Diary of Albie Sachs (BBC) 1980, The Good Soldier (Granada) 1981, Outside Edge (LWT) 1981, Shakespeare's Sonnets (Court House Films prodn for Channel 4) 1983, Reflections (Film on Four) 1984, Heartland (BBC Wales) 1989, Smith and Jones in Small Doses 1989, A Time to Dance (BBC Scotland) 1992, Handling Complaints and Managing Complaints (both Video Arts) 1994; *Recreations* swimming, football (QPR FC); *Clubs* Garrick; *Style*— Kevin Billington, Esq; ✉ c/o Judy Daish Associates, 2 St Charles Place, London W10 6EG (☎ 0181 964 8811, fax 0181 964 8966)

BILLINGTON, Lady Rachel Mary; *née* Pakenham; da of 7 Earl of Longford, KG, PC, *qv*, and Countess of Longford, CBE, *qv*; *b* 11 May 1942; *Educ* Univ of London; *m* 13 Dec 1967, Kevin Billington, *qv*; 2 s (Nathaniel b 1970, Caspar b 1979), 2 da (Catherine Rose b 1973, Chloe b 1975); *Career* author of 13 novels and 5 children's books; memb: PEN, Soc of Authors; *Novels* incl: A Women's Age, Occasion of Sin, Loving Attitudes, Theo and Matilda, Bodily Harm, Magic and Fate, Perfect Happiness; *Non-Fiction* incl: The Family Year, The Great Umbilical - Mother Daughter Mother, the Unbreakable Bond, The Life of Jesus (for children); *Style*— Lady Rachel Billington; ✉ The Court House, Poyntington, nr Sherborne, Dorset DT9 4LF

BILLIS, Dr David; s of Harry Billis (d 1982), of London, and Anne, *née* Jacobson (d 1967); *b* 10 April 1934; *Educ* Hackney Downs GS, LSE (BSc(Econ), PhD); *m* 1957, Jacqueline Nahoma, *née* Ludwig; 2 s (Neeve Joseph b 1960, Tal b 1962); *Career* latterly i/c fin and cost accounts Kibbutz Zikkim 1957–66; Brunel Univ: successively research fell, sr research fell then fndr and dir Programme of Research and Training into Voluntary Action (PORTVAC); currently reader in social serv orgn and fndr dir Centre for Voluntary Orgn LSE; co-fndr and int ed NonProfit Management and Leadership; memb: Royal Inst of Public Admin 1968–73, Social Policy Assoc 1975–, Assoc for Research on Non Profit Organisations and Voluntary Action 1985–; American Assoc for Research on Nonprofit Organizations and Voluntary Action (ARNOVA) Distinguished Lifetime Achievement Award 1995; *Books* Social Services Departments (with R W Rowbottom and A M Hey, 1974), Organising Social Services Departments (with G Bromley, A M Hey and R W Rowbottom, 1980), Welfare Bureaucracies (1984), Organising Voluntary Agencies (with M Harris, 1986), Organisational Design (with R W Rowbottom, 1987), Organising Public and Voluntary Agencies (1993), Voluntary Agencies (with M Harris, 1996); *Recreations* gardening, walking, yoga; *Style*— Dr David Billis; ✉ Centre for Voluntary Organisation, London School of Economics and Political Science, Houghton Street, Aldwych, London WC2 2AE (☎ 0171 955 7360)

BILLS, David James; s of Nigel Carey Bills (d 1994), and Susan, *née* Thompson, of Hobart, Tasmania; *b* 9 Feb 1948; *Educ* Hobart Matriculation Coll Tasmania, Australian Nat Univ (BSc), BC Inst of Tech (Dip), MIT USA (sr Myte Programme); *m* Michele, da of Gilbert Ellis; 2 da (Jessica b Feb 1977, Amy b July 1985), 1 s (Thomas b Sept 1978); *Career* research scientist CSIRO Australia 1970–73, Dept of Agriculture Australia 1976, forest mangr Associated Pulp and Paper Mills Australia 1983, gen mangr North Forest Products, currently DG and accounting offr Forestry Commission; vice pres AFDI

Australia 1983–86, pres Nat Assoc of Forest Industries Australia 1993–95, warden Hobart Marine Bd; author various scientific articles; memb Inst of Foresters in Australia (MIFA) 1970; *Recreations* tennis, music, skiing, sailing, classic cars; *Clubs* Edinburgh Sports; *Style—* David Bills, Esq; ✉ Forestry Commission, 231 Corstorphine Road, Edinburgh EH12 7AT (☎ 0131 334 0363, fax 0131 334 1903, mobile 0468 403800)

BINDER, Alan Naismith; OBE (1974); s of Frederick John Binder (d 1961), of Hampshire, and Kathleen Mary, *née* Darker (d 1967); *b* 4 Aug 1931; *Educ* Bedford Sch, Magdalen Coll Oxford (MA); *m* 1958, Gillian Patricia, da of George Francis Wilson, of Sussex; 1 s (Jonathan b 1962), 2 da (Jennifer b 1958, Stephanie b 1959); *Career* dir Shell International Petroleum Co Ltd 1984, pres Shell International Trading Co 1987–91; chm: United Communications Ltd 1991–, Expro International Group 1992–; dir: The Housing Finance Corporation 1993–, RJB Mining PLC 1995–; *Recreations* tennis, skiing, reading, music; *Clubs* Carlton, Leander, MCC, Mosimann's; *Style—* Alan Binder, Esq, OBE; ✉ Old Place, Speldhurst, Kent TN3 0PA (☎ 01892 863227, fax 01892 861478); United Communications Ltd, Summit House, 27 Sale Place, London W2 1YR (☎ 0171 262 5000)

BINDING, Paul; s of Leonard Hubert Binding (d 1972), of Devon, and Muriel Hope, *née* Middleton (d 1965); *b* 7 Jan 1943; *Educ* Berkhamsted Sch, New Coll Oxford (open scholar, BA, BLitt); *Career* lectr in Eng literature Umeå Sweden 1970–72, a managing ed Oxford Univ Press 1974–77, dep literary and arts ed New Statesman 1979–81, writer in residence (Arts Cncl fellowship) St John's Sch Epping 1984, Eudora Welty visiting prof of Southern studies Millsaps Coll Jackson Mississippi 1985–86, lectr in Eng literature Univ of Macerata Italy 1987–89; lectr on works of Lorca, American Southern literature, animal issues, Swedish culture, and other literary and cultural matters in US, UK, Sweden and Netherlands; contribs literary reviews to various pubns and articles on animal rights and Swedish politics to New Statesman, author of various introductions to works published by Virago Modern Classics and Gay Modern Classics; memb: League Against Cruel Sports, Br Union Against Vivisection, Animal Aid, Fox Project, Movement for Compassionate Living, PEN; *Books* Separate Country (1979, revised edn 1988), Harmonica's Bridegroom (novel, 1984), Lorca - The Gay Imagination (1985), Dreams and Speculations (poems, with John Horder, 1986), Kingfisher Weather (novel, 1989), St Martin's Ride (autobiographical novel, 1990, J R Ackerley prize), Eudora Welty: Portrait of a Writer (1994), Sweden: A Destination (1997); *Recreations* listening to music, exploring Britain and Sweden, houseplants, the company of animals, 'Brookside'; *Style—* Paul Binding, Esq; ✉ Llanfair House, Bucknell, Shropshire SY7 6AA (☎ 01547 530634); c/o A M Heath, 79 St Martin's Lane, London WC2N 4AA (☎ 0171 836 4271)

BINDMAN, Geoffrey Lionel; s of Dr Gerald Bindman (d 1974), and Lena Bindman (d 1989); *b* 3 Jan 1933; *Educ* Royal GS Newcastle upon Tyne, Oriel Coll Oxford; *m* 1961, Lynn Janice; 2 s, 1 da; *Career* slr; Bindman & Partners London (sr ptnr); chm Legal Action Gp 1976–78, legal advsr Cmmn for Racial Equality 1977–83, hon visiting prof of law UCL 1990–, hon visting fell in civil legal process Univ of Kent 1991–; chm Discrimination Law Assoc 1995–; *Books* Race and Law (co-author, 1972), South Africa: Human Rights and the Rule of Law (ed, 1988); *Recreations* book collecting, music, walking; *Clubs* Law Society; *Style—* Geoffrey Bindman; ✉ 275 Gray's Inn Road, London WC1X 8QF (☎ 0171 833 4433, fax 0171 837 9792)

BINFIELD, Dr (John) Clyde Goodfellow; OBE (1991); s of Edward John Binfield, DSC (d 1976), and Margaret Florence, *née* Goodfellow (d 1976); *b* 5 Dec 1940; *Educ* Dover GS, Emmanuel Coll Cambridge (minor scholar, exhibitioner, Bachelor scholar, MA, PhD); *m* 1969, Noreen Helen, da of late William Henry Maycock; 2 da (Emma Victoria (Mrs James Stone) b 1970, and Anna Alexandra (Mrs John Eagles) b 1972); *Career* Univ of Sheffield: asst lectr in modern history 1964–67, lectr 1967–74, sr lectr 1974–84, reader 1984–, head Dept of History 1988–91; memb Exec Ctee World Alliance of YMCAs 1981–91 (chm of two ctees), chm Nat Cncl of YMCAs 1992– (vice chm 1982–90); pres: Ecclesiastical History Soc 1990–91, Chapels Soc 1992–, Friends of Dr Williams's Library 1993–; chm Voluntary Action Sheffield 1990–93; govr: Stocksbridge Coll of Further Educn 1975–88, Northern Coll Manchester 1976– (memb Educn Ctee), Silcoates Sch Wakefield 1977– (vice chm 1982–83, chm of govrs 1983–93), Dunford (YMCA) Coll Sussex 1981–87, Loxley Tertiary Coll 1988–90; memb Cncl YMCA George Williams Coll 1991–; tstee: Yorkshire Historic Churches Tst 1993–, South Yorkshire Historic Buildings Tst 1994–; FRHistS 1983, FSA 1987; *Books* George Williams and the YMCA: a Study in Victorian social attitudes (1973), So Down to Prayers: Studies in English Nonconformity 1780–1920 (1977), Pastors and People: The Biography of a Baptist Church: Queen's Road Coventry (1984), This Has Been Tomorrow: The World Alliance of YMCAs since 1955 (1991); ed of various books and jls and author of numerous articles, book chapters and reviews; *Recreations* travel, architecture, opera; *Clubs* Royal Over-Seas League; *Style—* Dr Clyde Binfield, OBE; ✉ Whitecliffe, 22 Whiteley Wood Road, Sheffield S11 7FE (☎ 0114 230 5256); Department of Modern History, University of Sheffield, Sheffield S10 2TN (☎ 0114 222 2000, fax 0114 278 8304)

BING, Peter John; OBE (1974); s of William Leslie Bing, of Crowborough, Sussex; *b* 30 Aug 1925; *Educ* Felsted, RNC Dartmouth, RNEC Plymouth; *m* 1954, Hon Christian Keith, da of 15 Viscount of Arbuthnott, CB, CBE, DSO, MC; 3 s, 1 da; *Career* midshipman HMS Berwick 1945, Lt Cdr 806 Seahawk Sqdn, HMS Centaur 1955, cdr DAEO HMS Hermes 1963–64, Jt Servs Staff Coll 1964, dir RN Air Engrg Sch 1968–71 (ret 1974); mangr first Offshore Trg Centre for the Oil Indust 1975–82, bd sec OPITB Montrose 1983–90, mgmnt conslt 1990–; dir Montrose C of C, chm Fedn of Dundee and Angus C of C 1994–, dir Humberside Offshore Trg Assoc Hull 1987–90; CEng, FIMechE, FCIS, FIMgt, FInstPet; *Recreations* gardening, hockey (Devon & RN), cricket (RN); *Clubs* Army and Navy; *Style—* Peter Bing, Esq, OBE; ✉ The Lodge, Church Street, Edzell, Brechin, Angus DD9 7TQ (☎ 01356 648566)

BING, Robert Fill; s of Alec George Bing (d 1994), of 23 Harcourt Drive, Canterbury, Kent, and Kate Isobel, *née* Theobald; *b* 9 Feb 1945; *Educ* Simon Langton GS, Canterbury, Univ of Sheffield (MB ChB); *m* 11 Oct 1969, Ann, da of Philip Walter Grunsell (d 1987); 2 s (Andrew b 1971, Simon b 1977), 1 da (Emma-Jane b 1974); *Career* res registrar in hypertension United Sheffield Hosps 1972–74 (med training rotation 1969–72), clinical res fell MRC Univ of Sussex 1974–76; currently: conslt physician Leics Health Authy, sr lectr in med Univ of Leicester (lectr 1976–81), hon conslt physician Leics Health Authy; memb Exec Ctee Br Hypertension Soc, govr Alderman Newtons Sch Leicester, memb Assoc of Physicians of GB and Ireland 1984; FRCP 1984 (memb 1971); *Style—* Robert Bing, Esq; ✉ University of Leicester, Department of Medicine, University Road, Leicester LE1 7RH (☎ 0116 252 2522, fax 0116 252 2200)

BINGHAM, Charlotte; *see:* Brady, Hon Mrs (C M T)

BINGHAM, Dr Elizabeth; da of Clifford Douglas Bingham (d 1993), and Ada Jane, *née* Bentley; *b* 8 Jan 1941; *Educ* King Edward's Sch Camp Hill Birmingham, Univ of Birmingham (BSc, MB ChB), DCH (London); *m* 1965, Raymond John Heitzman, PhD; 2 da (Catherine Anne b 27 March 1968, Jacqueline Sarah b 21 Nov 1969); *Career* house surgn Birmingham Gen Hosp 1965, house physician The Children's Hosp Birmingham 1966, clinical asst Dept of Paediatrics Royal Berkshire Hosp 1967–81 (SHO in paediatrics Sept-Dec 1966), asst gen practitioner 1968–69, princ in gen practice Berkshire Health Cmmn 1969–96, GP advsr to the Ombudsman 1996–; gen practice trainer 1986–96 (assoc course organiser Reading Vocational Trg Scheme 1993–96); examiner for MRCGP 1989–; memb Thames Valley Faculty Bd RCGP 1984– (chm Faculty Bd 1990–93); FRCGP 1991 (MRCGP 1984); *Recreations* golf, skiing, gardening, embroidery; *Style—* Dr Elizabeth Bingham; ✉ The Boundary House, 1 Churn Road, Compton, nr Newbury, Berkshire RG20 6PP (☎ 01635 578925, fax 01635 578428); 13th Floor, Millbank Tower, Millbank, London SW1P 3BW (☎ 0171 217 4963, fax 0171 217 4000)

BINGHAM, Lord; George Charles Bingham; s and h of 7 Earl of Lucan, *qv*; *b* 21 Sept 1967; *Educ* Eton, Trinity Hall Cambridge; *Career* with Kleinwort Benson; *Style—* Lord Bingham

BINGHAM, Dr James Stewart; TD (1982); s of Dr William Bingham, of Malone, Belfast, and Norah Mary, *née* Beckett; *b* 31 July 1945; *Educ* Campbell Coll Belfast, Queen's Univ Belfast (MB BCh, BAO, DObstRCOG, FRCOG, FRCPE); *m* 21 Sept 1974, Elizabeth Eleanor, da of Charles Arnold Stewart; 1 s (Stewart Mark b 20 Jan 1983); *Career* Univ Offrs' Trg Corp 1963–69, 253 (NI) Field Ambulance and 217 (L) Gen Hosp RAMC 1969–83, resigned as Lt-Col, currently Maj RARO; house physician and surgn The Royal Victoria Hosp Belfast 1969–70; training posts rising to sr registrar in obstetrics and gynaecology in Belfast, Salisbury (Rhodesia) and Vancouver (Canada) 1970–75; The Middlesex Hosp London: sr registrar in genitourinary med 1975–77, conslt 1977–92, dir of serv 1983–91; conslt in genitourinary med St Thomas' Hosp London 1992–; Med Soc for Study of Venereal Diseases: memb Cncl 1979–82 and 1983–86, hon treas 1986–93, pres 1993–95; hon treas Br HIV Assoc, memb Exec Ctee and hon treas Int Union Against Venereal Diseases and Treponematosis 1995–; memb: Bd of Examiners for Dip in Genitourinary Med Soc of Apothecaries of London 1982– (convenor of examiners 1992–95), Working Party on Med Audit in Genitourinary Med RCP 1989–94, Dermatovenereology Sub Ctee CCSC BMA 1992–, Genitourinary Sub Ctee CCSC BMA 1986–92 (rep Sub Ctee on CCSC 1989–91); rep RCOG on Specialist Advsy Ctee in Genitourinary Med RCP 1988– (sec 1990–93, chm 1993–95), rep Middx and Univ Coll Hosp on Univ Hosp Assoc 1989–90; memb Editorial Bd: International Journal of STD and AIDS 1990–, Genitourinary Med 1993–95; ed Continuing Med Educn 1995–; memb: BMA, RSM, Med Soc for the Study of Venereal Disease, Soc for the Study of Sexually Transmitted Diseases in Ireland, Int Union Against the Venereal Diseases and Treponematoses, Euro Acad of Dermatology and Venereology, Br Soc for Colposcopy and Cervical Pathology; *Books* Sexually Transmitted Diseases (1984, 2 edn 1990); *Recreations* British military history with particular emphasis on the Anglo-Irish contribution, reading military and political biographies, gardening; *Style—* Dr James Bingham, TD; ✉ Harrison Wing, St Thomas' Hospital, London SE1 7EH (☎ 0171 928 5485, 0171 928 9292 ext 1696, fax 0171 922 8291)

BINGHAM, John Temple; o s of Rear Adm the Hon Edward Barry Stewart Bingham, VC, OBE (d 1939), and Vera Maud Temple, *née* Patterson; kinsman and hp of 8 Baron Clanmorris, *qv*; *b* 22 Feb 1923; *m* 28 April 1949, Joan Muriel Bown (d 1955); *Career* fundraiser for Greater London Fund for the Blind 1989–; *Style—* John Bingham, Esq; ✉ Flat 1, 48 Holland Road, London W14 8BB

BINGHAM, Judith Caroline; da of Jack Bingham (d 1993), and Peggy, *née* MacGowan; *b* 21 June 1952; *Educ* High Storrs GS for Girls Sheffield, Royal Acad of Music; *Career* composer; studied under Hans Keller; singer BBC Singers 1983–95; works incl: Cocaine Lil Songmakers' Almanac 1977, A Hymn Before Sunrise in the Vale of Chamouni 1982, Cradle Song of the Blessed Virgin 1983, Just Before Dawn 1985, A Cold Spell 1987, I Have a Secret to Tell 1990, Unpredictable but Providential 1991, The Uttermost 1992–93, The Ghost of Combermere Abbey 1993, O Magnum Mysterium (cmmnd by Lichfield Cathedral Choir) 1994, Evening Canticles (choir and organ) King's Coll Cambridge 1995; instrumental works incl: Into the Wilderness 1982, Scenes from Nature 1983, Brazil 1985, Christmas Past, Christmas Present 1988, Chartres 1988, Dove Cottage by Moonlight 1989, Four Minute Mile 1991, The Stars Above: The Earth Below 1991, Santa Casa 1994, Beyond Redemption 1994–95, Salt in the Blood 1995 (premiered BBC Proms 1995), The Red Hot Nail (educn project for LSO), Prague 1995; winner BBC Young Composers' Forum 1977; *Recreations* bird watching, cinema; *Style—* Miss Judith Bingham; ✉ c/o Maecenas Music Ltd, 5 Bushey Close, Old Barn Lane, Kenley, Surrey CR8 5AU (☎ 0181 660 4766, fax 0181 668 5273)

BINGHAM, Prof Nicholas Hugh; s of Robert Llewelyn Bingham (d 1972), of Dolgellau, and Blanche Louise, *née* Corbitt; *b* 19 March 1945; *Educ* Tadcaster GS, Trinity Coll Oxford (MA), Churchill Coll Cambridge (PhD, ScD); *m* 13 Sept 1980, Cecilie Ann, da of Ralph William Gabriel (d 1973), of Leigh-on-Sea; 2 s (James b 1982, Thomas b 1993), 1 da (Ruth b 1985); *Career* Univ of London: lectr then reader Westfield Coll 1969–84, reader 1984–85, prof of mathematics Royal Holloway and Bedford New Coll 1985–95, prof of statistics Birkbeck Coll 1995–; ed book reviews 1981–90; memb London Mathematical Soc, Inst of Mathematical Statistics; RSS; *Books* Regular Variation 1987; *Recreations* running, gardening; *Style—* Prof Nicholas Bingham; ✉ 13 Woodside Grange Rd, London N12 8SJ (☎ 0181 445 5779); Department of Statistics, Birkbeck College, Senate House North Block, Malet Street, London WC1E 7JG (☎ 0171 631 6346)

BINGHAM, Stephen Denis; OBE; s of Cdr Francis Bingham, RN (d 1986); *b* 28 June 1934; *Educ* Ampleforth, St Catharine's Coll Cambridge (BA); *m* 1962, Elizabeth, da of Cdr G Paine, RN (d 1980); 3 s (Benedict, Thomas, Patrick), 2 da (Emma, Catherine); *Career* Lt Irish Gds; md Johnson & Johnson Benelux BV 1964–74, md and vice chm Sodastream Ltd 1974–78, gp md Servotomic Ltd 1986–88, memb Bd Peterborough Devpt Corpn, nat dir PLAN International UK 1988–96, currently business devpt dir PLAN International; tstee: NCVO, St Joseph's Soc; *Recreations* sailing, indifferent golf, painting; *Style—* Stephen Bingham, Esq, OBE; ✉ Geeston, Ketton, Stamford, Lincs PE9 3RH (☎ 01780 720135)

BINGHAM OF CORNHILL, Baron (Life Peer UK 1996); Sir Thomas Henry Bingham; kt (1980), PC (1986); s of Dr Thomas Henry Bingham, of Reigate, Surrey, and Catherine, *née* Watterson; *b* 13 Oct 1933; *Educ* Sedbergh, Balliol Coll Oxford; *m* 1963, Elizabeth Patricia, o da of Peter Noel Loxley (d 1945); 2 s (Hon Thomas Henry b 1967, Hon Christopher Toby b 1969), 1 da (Hon Catherine Elizabeth b 1965); *Career* called to the Bar 1959, jr counsel Dept of Employment 1968–72, QC 1972, High Ct judge (Queen's Bench Div) 1980–86, Lord Justice of Appeal 1986–92, Master of the Rolls 1992–96; Lord Chief Justice of England 1996–; ldr of investigations into: Supply of Petroleum and Petroleum Prods to Rhodesia 1977–78, Bank of Credit and Commerce International (BCCI) 1991–92; fell: King's Coll London 1992, Queen Mary and Westfield Coll 1993; visitor: Balliol Coll (and hon fell), Royal Postgrad Med Sch, Nuffield Coll Oxford, UCL, London Business Sch; hon fell American Coll of Trial Lawyers; hon bencher Inn of Court of Northern Ireland; Hon LLD Univ of Birmingham 1993, Hon DCL Oxford 1994; *Style—* The Rt Hon Lord Bingham of Cornhill; ✉ Royal Courts of Justice, Strand, London WC2A 2LL

BINNEY, Ivor Ronald; s of Ronald Frederick Binney (d 1979), and Ethel Alice, *née* Dredge (d 1990); *b* 11 Oct 1929; *Educ* Haberdashers' Aske's; *m* 1957, Susan Mary Campbell, da of Capt John Calendar Ritchie (d 1939); 1 s (Hugo), 3 da (Emma, Lucy, Sara); *Career* dir: CT Bowring & Co Ltd 1970–87 (dep chm), Terra Nova Insurance Co Ltd 1970–87, Marsh & McLennan Cos Inc 1980–87, Archer Group Holdings plc 1987–; chm: Syndicate Underwriting Management Ltd (formerly AUA4) 1987–92, Benfield Reinsurance Company Ltd 1993–; Lloyd's: memb Ctee 1978–81 and 1984–87, memb Cncl 1984–87; *Recreations* golf; *Clubs* MCC, Pilgrims', RAC; *Style—* Ivor Binney, Esq; ✉ 175 Cranmer Court, Whiteheads Grove, London SW3 3HF

BINNEY, Marcus Hugh Crofton; OBE (1983); s of late Lt Col Francis Crofton Simms, MC, and Sonia (d 1985), da of Rear Adm Sir William Marcus Charles Beresford-Whyte, KCB, CMG (she m 2, 1955, as his 2 wife, Sir George Binney, DSO, who d 1972); *b* 21 Sept 1944; *Educ* Eton, Magdalene Coll Cambridge (BA); *m* 1, 1966 (m dis 1976), Hon

Sara Anne Vanneck (d 1979), da of 6 Baron Huntingfield; m 2, 1981, Anne Carolyn, da of Dr T H Hills of Merstham, Surrey; 2 s (Francis Charles Thomas b 1982, Christopher Crofton b 1985); *Career* writer; Country Life: architectural writer 1968–77, architectural ed 1977–84, ed 1984–86; ed Landscape 1987, freelance architecture corr The Times 1991–; sec UK Ctee Int Cncl on Monuments and Sites 1972–81, dir Railway Heritage Tst 1984–; pres: Save Britain's Heritage 1984– (chm 1975–84), Save Europe's Heritage 1995–; co-organiser: The Destruction of the Country House (exhibition V & A) 1974, Change and Decay: The Future of our Churches (V & A) 1977; *Books* Change and Decay: The Future of our Churches (with Peter Burman, 1977), Chapels and Churches: Who Cares? (with Peter Burman, 1977), Preservation Pays (with Max Hanna, 1978), Railway Architecture (ed jtly, 1979), Our Past Before Us (ed jtly, 1981), The Country House: To Be or Not to Be (with Kit Martin, 1982), Preserve and Prosper (with Max Hanna, 1983), Sir Robert Taylor (1984), Our Vanishing Heritage (1984); contrib: Satanic Mills (1979), Elysian Gardens (1979), Lost Houses of Scotland (1980), Taking the Plunge (1982), SAVE Gibraltar's Heritage (1982), Vanishing Houses of England (1983), Time Gentlemen Please (1983), Great Railway Stations of Europe (1984); *Style*— Marcus Binney, Esq, OBE; ✉ Domaine des Vaux, St Lawrence, Jersey JE3 1JG, CI (☎ 01534 864424)

BINNEY, (Harry Augustus) Roy; CB (1950); s of Harry Augustus Binney (d 1960), of Churston, Devon; *b* 18 May 1907; *Educ* Royal Dockyard Sch Devonport, Univ of London (BSc(Eng)); *m* 1944, Barbara (d 1975), da of Jeffrey Poole (d 1952), of Harborne, Birmingham; 3 s (Robert b 1945, James b 1950, George b 1953), 1 da (Frances b 1946) (and 1 da decd); *Career* entered Bd of Trade 1929, under sec BOT 1947–51, dir-gen BSI 1951–72, memb Cncl Int Standards Orgn Geneva 1951–72 (vice pres 1964–69), chm CEN (ctee for Euro standards) 1963–65, UN advsr on standards Cyprus 1974–77; hon life fell Standards Engineering Soc of America, hon life memb American Soc for Testing and Materials; FKC, FRSA; *Recreations* gardening; *Style*— Roy Binney, Esq, CB; ✉ Hambutts Orchard, Edge Rd, Painswick, Glos (☎ 01452 813718)

BINNIE, Ann; da of Jeffrey Wyatt, of Weston-super-Mare, and Doreen Eugenie, *née* Manley; *b* 10 March 1953; *Educ* Brentwood Co HS for Girls, Univ of Bradford (BSc, MSc); *m* 8 Sept 1973, David John Binnie, s of late Harold F Binnie; 1 da (Isla Jane b 28 Sept 1987), 1 s (Jamie Joe b 24 July 1990); *Career* staff: Br Inst of Mgmnt 1975–77, Rex Stewart Group 1977–79, W S Crawford 1979–80; various positions rising to bd planning dir DMB&B (formerly DMM) 1980–87, bd planning dir/head of planning KHBB 1987–90, planning conslt with retainers Ernest & Julio Gallo and Malcolm Gluck of PM&G 1990–92, bd planning dir/head of planning Arc Advertising 1992–94; planning conslt to ad hoc clients and retained by: Group X (for Royal Mail and Budgens), Arc Advertising (for BBC Network Radio) 1994–; fndr Ann Binnie Brand Planning 1996– (planning conslt to clients incl Arc Advertising, Clark & Taylor and Ogilvy and Mather); memb Judging Panel DBA Effectiveness Awards 1990 and 1992; memb: MRS, Mktg Soc; *Recreations* reading, theatre, tapestry, (observing) drag racing, enjoying my children; *Style*— Mrs Ann Binnie; ✉ Ann Binnie Brand Planning, Catalyst House, 1 Hempstead Road, Kings Langley, Hertfordshire WD4 8BJ (☎ 01923 261000, fax 01923 261100)

BINNIE, Prof Christopher Jon Anthony; s of Lt Cdr William Anthony Charles Binnie (d 1947), of Minehead, Somerset, and Barbara Kathleen, *née* Goddard-Jackson; *b* 20 June 1938; *Educ* Stowe, Univ of Cambridge (MA), Imperial Coll London (Dip); *m* 14 Sept 1968, Deryn, da of Lt Col Ian Harry Keith Chauvel; 2 s (Anthony b 25 Feb 1974, Jeremy b 20 Dec 1975); *Career* Nat Serv midshipman RN 1957–58; student 1958–63, graduate trainee Binnie & Partners 1963–64, project engr NCB 1964–66, civil engr GEO Wimpey 1967–68, resident engr Durban Reservoir Murray & Roberts 1968–69; Binnie & Partners: sr engr (water resources) Malaysia 1969–71, project engr Marchlyn Dam 1972–78; dir Water Unit W S Atkins Consultants 1984–95 (chief engr Water Dept 1978–84), dir W S Atkins plc (formerly W S Atkins Group Ltd) 1994–; chm WSA Water and Environment Gp 1992; CIWEM: fndr chm Expert Panel on Water Resources 1991–94, chm Int Ctee 1992–, pres 1995–96; memb Cncl: British Water Industries Gp 1984–92, Fndn for Water Research 1989–95; visiting prof of design Univ of Kingston 1995–; memb Co of Water Conservators 1988 (memb Ct 1989–), Freeman City of London 1991; memb: British Dams Soc 1974, British Geotechnical Soc 1979, Assoc of Consulting Engrs 1986; FICE 1976, FCIWEM 1976, FEng 1994; *Publications* Water Supplies in the UK in the 1990's and Beyond (1991) and 20 others; *Recreations* sailing, riding; *Clubs* RYA; *Style*— Prof Christopher Binnie, FEng; ✉ Westpoint, Reigate Hill Close, Reigate, Surrey RH2 9PG (☎ 01737 247459); W S Atkins plc, Woodcote Grove, Epsom, Surrey (☎ 01372 726140, fax 01372 740055)

BINNIE, Prof Colin David; s of Horace David Binnie, of Leigh-on-Sea, Essex, and Doris Amy, *née* Read (d 1966); *Educ* Felstead, Univ of Cambridge (MD, MA, BCh), Guy's Hosp Med Sch, MRCS, MRCP, FRCPGlas; *m* 31 Oct 1964, (Florence) Margaret, da of George Shields (d 1980); 1 s (Jonathan Nicholas b 1968), 1 da (Caroline b 1965); *Career* physician i/c Dept of Clinical Neurophysiology Bart's and Southend Hosp 1972–76, head of clinical neurophysiology serv Inst Voor Epilepsie Bestrjding Heemstede Netherlands 1976–86, conslt clinical neurophysiologist Bethlem Royal Hosp and Maudsley Hosp 1986–, clinical dir of neurosciences 1991–95, prof of clinical neurophysiology King's Coll Hosp Sch of Med and Dentistry London 1995–; pres British Soc for Clinical Neurophysiology, chm Neurosurgical Cmmn of International League against Epilepsy; memb: Int League Against Epilepsy, Electroencephalography and Clinical Neurophysiology Educnl Bd, Electrophysiological Tech Assoc, RSM 1965, Assoc Br Clinical Neurophysiologists 1970, Br Assoc for Neuropsychiatry 1988, Assoc of British Neurologists; *Books* A Manual of Electroencephalographic Technology (1982), Biorhythms and Epilepsy (1986), Clinical Neurophysiology (1994), numerous pubns on Electroencephalography and Epilepsy; *Recreations* opera, computing, languages; *Style*— Prof Colin Binnie; ✉ Department of Clinical Neurophysiology, Maudsley Hospital, Denmark Hill, London SE5 8AZ (☎ 0171 919 2150, fax 0171 919 2171)

BINNIE, Frank Hugh; s of Dr Hugh Lawson Binnie, of Leicester (d 1972), and Isobel, *née* Nairn; *b* 1 March 1950; *Educ* Oadby GS, Leicester Poly; *children* 3 s (Christopher Hugh b 1974, Jonathon Stuart b 1976, Edward Stanley b 1985); *Career* design mgmnt trainee Design and Product Devpt Leicester 1970–73, factory mangr Floreal Mfrg Mauritius 1973–76, sales mangr Kemptons Knitwear Leicester 1976–79, gen mangr Sales and Mktg Unilever Texport Heathrow 1979–82, mfrg mangr Kilspindie Knitwear Edinburgh 1982–85, dir and Co sec Midlothian Enterprise 1985–88, md H & G Perkins Mfrg Glasgow 1988–90, dir Design Cncl Scotland Glasgow 1990–94 and UK team ldr Clothing and Textiles Initiative 1990–95, chief exec offr Scottish Design (formerly Design Cncl Scotland) 1994–96, chief exec Caledonian Fndn 1996–; visiting prof Univ of Strathclyde; founder pres Midlothian Business Club; memb Cncl: Esk Valley Coll, Textile Inst; chm: Fashion Design Product Mktg Ctee, Glasgow Int Festival of Design; MInstD, FRSA; *Recreations* yacht sailing, yachtmaster running, running half marathons; *Clubs* Round Table 41; *Style*— Frank Binnie, Esq; ✉ Caledonian Foundation, 9 Lynedoch Crescent, Glasgow G3 6EQ (☎ 0141 332 5668, fax 0141 332 5673)

BINNING, Kenneth George Henry; CMG (1976); s of Henry Binning (d 1976), of Wivenhoe, Essex, and Hilda, *née* Powell (d 1987); *b* 5 Jan 1928; *Educ* Bristol GS, Balliol Coll Oxford (MA); *m* 28 Feb 1953, Pamela Dorothy, da of Alfred Edward Pronger (d 1963), of Streatham, London; 3 s (Simon Kenneth b 1955, Julian Charles b 1957, Marcus Adam b 1963), 1 da (Susanna Clare b 1960); *Career* Nat Serv Capt RAEC 1950–52; HM Treasy 1952–59 (private sec to Fin Sec 1956), UK AEA 1959–65, seconded Miny of Technol 1965–67 and 1969, asst dir Progs Analysis Unit 1967–69, DG Concorde Prog (UK) 1973–76, cr Invest in Britain Bureau 1976–80, govt dir BSC 1980–82; dir of govt rels: NEI plc 1983–90, Rolls Royce plc 1991–93; dir Public Policy Unit Ltd 1993–; *Recreations* music, gardening; *Clubs* Reform; *Style*— Kenneth Binning, Esq, CMG; ✉ 12 Kemerton Road, Beckenham, Kent BR3 2NJ (☎ 0181 650 0273); Public Policy Unit Ltd, 50 Rochester Road, London SW1P 1HU (☎ 0171 828 6088)

BINNINGTON, Bernard Thomas; OBE (1994); s of Richard Binnington (d 1963), of Jersey, and Florence Mary, *née* Quenault; *b* 23 Nov 1930; *Educ* Victoria Coll Jersey; *m* 28 Sept 1953, Elizabeth Rowley, da of James Davidson (d 1979), of Edinburgh; 1 s (Alan Richard), 1 da (Anne Elizabeth); *Career* exec dir: Chelsea Hotels Ltd 1955–94, Pioneer Coaches Ltd 1965–94; dir Samuel Montagu & Co (Jersey) Ltd 1979–87, chm Jersey Electricity Co Ltd 1982–88 (dir 1976–82), dir A Degruchy & Co Ltd 1987–; St Helier Jersey Parliament: dep 1969 and 1972, senator 1975, 1982 and 1987; pres: Jersey Hotel and Guest House Assoc 1966–68, States of Jersey Harbours and Airport Ctee 1981–95; chm Jersey Tport Authy 1981–95; *Recreations* sailing, music; *Style*— Bernard Binnington, Esq, OBE; ✉ La Rochelle, St Aubin, Jersey, CI (☎ 01534 43303)

BINNS, Christopher; s of Herbert Chester Binns (d 1988), of Norwich, and Winifred Ann Binns (1991); *b* 28 June 1941; *Educ* Birmingham Coll of Food & Domestic Art; *m* 5 July 1969, Brenda Margaret, da of Leslie Flowers; 2 s (Gregory Haston b 22 Oct 1970, Adam James b 16 Nov 1977), 1 da (Sarah Marie b 13 May 1972); *Career* Strand Hotels Ltd 1960–70: trainee mangr London hotels, devpt of provincial hotels in Birmingham 1963 and Nottingham 1969, latterly asst gen mangr Albany Hotel Nottingham; Property Partnerships (Hotels) Ltd: mangr Hotel Nelson Norwich 1970–72, gen mangr Hotels Div 1972–75, md 1975–89 (also dir Property Partnership PLC); md Waveney Inns Group Diss Norfolk 1990–91, proprietor The Greens Norwich 1992–; chm: E Anglia Branch BHRCA 1974–75 and 1987–90, E Anglia Branch HCIMA 1974–75, Best Western E Anglia Region 1977–78; fndr chm: Norwich & Dist Hoteliers Assoc 1977–78, Norwich Tourist Assoc 1980–82: memb: Dist MSC 1977–79, Exec Ctee E Anglia Tourist Bd 1978–82; dir Norwich Area Tourism Agency 1982–92, govr Norwich City Coll 1988–92; Freeman City of London 1981; FHCIMA (HCIMA 1960), Master Inn Holder 1980 (vice chm 1989–91), CIMgt 1988; *Recreations* wine, badminton, mountain climbing, conservation; *Style*— Christopher Binns, Esq

BINNS, Colin; s of Arthur Thomas Binns, and Amy Evelyn Binns; *b* 20 April 1942; *Educ* Arnold Sch, Leeds Sch of Architecture (DipArch); *m* 25 Feb 1967 (m dis 1994), Pamela, da of Kenneth Crook, of Dugvesta De Espana, Torremolinos; 2 da (Joanna b 1969, Nina b 1971); *Career* head of fine and applied arts Preston Coll, environmental conslt, artist and interior designer; main projects incl: Fort Regent Leisure and Conference Centre Jersey 1970, ICI Petrochemicals HQ Wilton 1976, housing assoc projects 1976–82, indust projects 1982–85, leisure projects 1985–90, Dept of Health and DSS Quarry House 1990–92, private housing 1992–96; RIBA Design Prize 1966, RIBA Award 1976, BDA Award 1976, Civic Tst Award 1979; chm: Art and Design Educn Advsy Panel Preston Coll, NW Contemporary Design Collective; former memb Ctee Lancs Region CPRE; RIBA, ARCUK; *Recreations* sculpture, photography, artworks; *Clubs* Fylde Fencing; *Style*— Colin Binns; ✉ 116 Preston Old Road, Freckleton, Preston, Lancashire PR4 1HD (☎ 01772 635122, fax 01772 635055)

BINNS, David John; CBE (1989); s of Henry Norman Binns, OBE (d 1959), of Grimsby, and Ivy Mary, *née* Baker (d 1981); *b* 12 April 1929; *Educ* Rossall Sch, Univ of Sheffield (LLB); *m* 6 July 1957, Jean Margaret, da of Lt Cdr Frank Newton Evans, DSC (d 1968), of Hoylake; 1 s (Jonathan b 1964), 1 da (Caroline b 1959, d 1962); *Career* admitted slr 1954; Warrington Co Borough: asst slr 1954–55, chief asst slr 1955–58, dep town clerk 1958–69; gen mangr: Warrington Devpt Corp 1969–81, Warrington and Runcorn Devpt Corp 1981–89; memb Warrington Health Authy 1990–92, sec Bd Halton Gen Hosp NHS Tst 1995– (non-exec dir 1992–94); *Recreations* gardening, walking, swimming, music; *Clubs* Warrington; *Style*— David Binns, Esq, CBE; ✉ 4 Cedarways, Appleton, Warrington, Cheshire WA4 5EW (☎ 01925 262169)

BINNS, Prof Kenneth John; s of Harold Gladstone Binns (d 1972), of Withington, Manchester, and Helen Cecilia, *née* Moss (d 1975); *b* 4 Aug 1934; *Educ* Xaverian Coll Manchester, Univ of Manchester (BSc), Univ of Southampton (DSc); *m* 5 May 1962, Patricia Ann, da of James Patrick McGrath (d 1979); 2 da (Louise, Jane); *Career* reader Univ of Southampton 1972–83, prof of electrical engrg Univ of Liverpool 1983–93 (professorial fell 1993–); hon ed IEE Proceedings Part B; FIEE, FRSA; *Books* Analysis and Computation of Electric and Magnetic Field Problems (jtly, 1973), Vibration and Audible Noise in A C Machines (jtly, 1986), The analytical and numerical solution of electric and magnetic fields (jtly, 1992); *Recreations* gardening, badminton; *Style*— Prof Kenneth Binns; ✉ The University of Liverpool, Department of Electrical Engineering and Electronics, PO Box 147, Brownlow Hill, Liverpool L69 3BX (☎ 0151 794 4500, fax 0151 794 4540, telex 627095)

BINNS, Lorna Emily; da of Harold John Harrison (d 1968), of Sheffield, and Rebecca Louise, *née* North (d 1958); *b* 23 Oct 1914; *Educ* Abbeydale Girls GS, Sheffield Coll of Art, RCA (free studentship, ARCA, fourth year scholar, silver medal); *m* 4 March 1940, John Dawson Binns, s of Frank Binns; 2 da (Jacqueline Ree Dawson b 19 Sept 1945, Maryanne Dawson b 28 June 1950); *Career* artist; RWS: memb Selection Panel for first Open Exhbn, memb Cncl 1977–85, sr membs' rep on Cncl; gp exhbns incl: RA Summer Exhbns RA, RWS Spring Exhbns (featured artist 1995), Bath Festival, Barbican, Royal W of England Acad, RBA and FBA Galleries, Guildhall, special RWS exhbn Bankside Gallery 1987, Int Exhbn of Watercolours (tour of Spain) 1992–93, Middlesbrough Art Gallery 1993, Malta in Colour (Malta and London) 1994, also tours of Canada and USA; work in numerous collections; RWS 1977 (ARWS 1973, sr memb 1985); *Style*— Mrs Lorna Binns; ✉ 7 Egmont Avenue, Surbiton, Surrey KT6 7AU

BINNS, Malcolm; s of Douglas Priestley Binns (d 1988), of Keighley, Yorkshire, and May, *née* Walker; *b* 29 Jan 1936; *Educ* Bradford GS, RCM; *Career* prof RCM 1961–65; concert pianist: London debut 1959, debut Promenade Concerts 1960, regular performances at Proms 1962–, Royal Festival Hall debut 1961, has appeared in London Philharmonic seasons 1962–; soloist with all major Br orchs, over 30 recordings, first complete recording of Beethoven Piano Sonatas on original instruments, played Far E and toured with Scot Nat Orch and Limbourg Orch 1987–88; ARCM; *Recreations* gardening; *Style*— Malcolm Binns, Esq; ✉ Michael Harrold Artist Management, 223 Kingston Road, Leatherhead, Surrey KT22 7PE (☎ 01372 375728)

BINT, Dr Adrian John; s of Arthur Herbert Bint, of Birmingham, and Lily, *née* Naylor; *b* 3 April 1948; *Educ* Moseley GS Birmingham, Univ of Birmingham (MB ChB); *m* 12 June 1971, Marilyn Joyce, da of Charles Bourne Wathes, of Kingsbury nr Tamworth, Staffs; 1 s (Alastair Halford b 1974), 1 da (Nicola Sarah b 1975); *Career* conslt microbiologist Royal Victoria Infirmary Newcastle 1979–; meetings sec Br Soc for Antimicrobial Chemotherapy 1980–83; chm Clinical Servs Ctee Assoc of Med Microbiologists 1994–; memb: Cncl Assoc of Clinical Pathologists 1983–86, Editorial Bd Jl of Clinical Pathology 1988–93; ed Jl of Antimicrobial Chemotherapy 1994–96; FRCPath 1989 (MRCPath 1977); *Recreations* fell walking, badminton; *Style*— Dr Adrian Bint; ✉ Department of Microbiology, The Royal Victoria Infirmary, Newcastle-upon-Tyne NE1 4LP (☎ 0191 232 5131)

BINTLEY, David Julian; s of David Bintley, of Honley, Huddersfield, and Glenys, *née* Ellinthorpe; *b* 17 Sept 1957; *Educ* Holme Valley GS, Royal Ballet Upper Sch; *m* 12 Dec 1981, Jennifer Catherine Ursula, da of Bernard Mills, of San Diego, California; 2 s

(Michael b 21 March 1985, Gabriel b 7 Sept 1995); *Career* Sadler's Wells Royal Ballet 1976–86: debut The Outsider 1978, resident choreographer and princ dancer 1983–86; resident choreographer and princ dancer Royal Ballet 1986–93, freelance 1993–95, artistic dir Birmingham Royal Ballet 1995–; other works incl: Galanteries 1986, Allegri Diversi 1987, Hobson's Choice 1989, Edward II 1995, Carmina Burana 1995; *Awards* incl: Evening Standard Award for Choros and Consort Lessons 1983, Olivier Award for performance in Petrushka (title role) 1984, Manchester Evening News Award for Still Life at the Penguin Café 1988; *Style*— David Bintley, Esq; ✉ Birmingham Royal Ballet, Hippodrome Theatre, Thorp Street, Birmingham B5 4AU

BION, Dr Julian Fleetwood; s of Dr Wilfred Ruprecht Bion, DSO (d 1979), of Oxford, and Francesca, *née* Purnell; *b* 30 July 1952; *Educ* Harrow, Charing Cross Hosp, Univ of London (MB BS); *m* 15 June 1985, Nitaya, da of Sanit Tangchurat (d 1979), of Bangkok, Thailand; *Career* previous appts in anaesthesia, gen med and cardiology, sr anaesthetist Red Cross surgical team Thai-Cambodian border 1983, sr lectr in intensive care Univ of Birmingham 1989–; memb Editorial Bds: British Jl of Hosp Med, Clinical Intensive Care, Intensive Care Med, Intensive and Critical Care Nursing; author of numerous publications on aspects of intensive care med, audit, infection-prevention, outcome prediction and scoring systems; BUPA Med Fndn Dr of the Year award 1985; memb: Intensive Care Soc UK (memb Cncl 1993–), Cncl Euro Soc of Intensive Care Medicine, Assoc of Anaesthetists, BMA; sec Scientific Sub-Ctee Intensive Care Soc UK, advsr Commonwealth Scholarships Cmmn; MRCP 1980, FFARCS 1982, FRCA 1988, MD 1991, FRCP 1996; *Style*— Dr Julian Bion; ✉ Senior Lecturer in Intensive Care Medicine, University of Birmingham, Queen Elizabeth Hospital, Birmingham B15 2TH (☎ 0121 627 2060, fax 0121 627 2062)

BIRCH, Prof Bryan John; s of Arthur Jack Benjamin Birch, and Mary Edith, *née* Buxton; *b* 25 Sept 1931; *Educ* Shrewsbury, Trinity Coll Cambridge (BA, PhD); *m* 1 July 1961, Gina Margaret, da of late Digby Henry Christ; 2 s (Colin b 1962, Michael b 1964), 1 da (Alison b 1968); *Career* fell: Trinity Coll Cambridge 1956–60, Churchill Coll Cambridge 1960–62; sr lectr and reader Univ of Manchester 1962–65, fell of BNC and prof of arithmetic Univ of Oxford 1985– (reader 1966–85); del OUP 1988–; FRS 1972; *Recreations* theoretical gardening, opera, admiring marmots; *Style*— Prof Bryan Birch, FRS; ✉ Mathematics Institute, 24–29 St Giles, Oxford (☎ 01865 273528)

BIRCH, Carol; da of Frederick Fidler (d 1981), and Nancy, *née* Rowe (d 1989); *b* 3 Jan 1951; *Educ* Manchester Central GS for Girls, Univ of Keele (BA); *m* 1, 1981 (m dis 1990), Leonard William Birch; m 2, 1990, Martin Lucas Butler, s of Arthur Butler; 2 s (Joseph Lucas b 1989, Richard Lyman b 1991); *Career* author; memb Soc of Authors 1988; *Books* Life in the Palace (1988, David Higham Prize for Best First Novel), The Fog Line (1989, Geoffrey Faber Meml Award 1991), The Unmaking (1992), Songs of the West (1994); *Recreations* reading, research, drawing, music, theatre; *Style*— Ms Carol Birch; ✉ c/o Mic Cheetham Agency, 138 Buckingham Palace Road, London SW1W 9SA (☎ 0171 703 3027)

BIRCH, Cherry Janet; da of Edward James Pinniger (d 1978), of Salisbury, Wilts, and Eileen Nancy, *née* Perkins; *b* 26 Aug 1955; *Educ* Godolphin Sch Salisbury, Bristol Poly; *m* 8 June 1991 (m dis); *Career* CA; sr Ball Baker Carnaby Deed 1978–79 (trainee 1974–78), supervisor Fraser Threlford 1979–80, audit sr and supervisor Ernst & Whinney 1980–83 (latterly in Training Dept), Internal Audit Dept Manufacturers Hanover Trust 1983–85; Finnie & Co: nat training mangr 1985–88, ptnr responsible for training 1988–91, ptnr London Office until 1991; mgmnt devpt conslt Sundridge Park Mgmnt Centre (part of PA Consulting Gp) 1991–95, on secondment PA Consulting Gp Kuala Lumpur 1995–; FCA 1988 (ACA 1978); *Recreations* wine, walking, sailing, theatre; *Clubs* International Exhibition Cooperative Wine Soc Stevenage (co-opted memb Mgmnt Ctee 1989–90); *Style*— Mrs Cherry Birch; ✉ PA Consulting Group, 5th Floor, Bangunan Getah Asli (Menara), 148 Jalan Ampang, 50450 Kuala Lumpur, Malaysia (☎ 00 60 3 261 2322, fax 00 60 3 261 8231)

BIRCH, Clive Francis William; s of Raymond William Birch, CBE (d 1980), and (Olive Edith Charlton) Valerie, *née* Fry; *b* 22 Dec 1931; *Educ* Uppingham; *m* 1, 1957 (m dis 1961), Gillian May, *née* Coulson; m 2, 1961 (m dis 1978), Penelope Helen, *née* Harman; 1 s (James b 1962), 1 da (Emma b 1964), 1 adopted s (Richard b 1957), 1 adopted da (Cally b 1959); m 3, 16 April 1983, Carolyn Rose, da of Thomas Desborough (d 1978); 1 step s (Jamie b 1974), 1 step da (Katie b 1970); *Career* Nat Serv radar RAF 1950–52; office jr Stretford Telegraph 1952, reporter Stockport Express 1952, dist reporter Kent and Sussex Courier 1953, chief reporter Herts Newspapers 1954, ed Bucks Examiner 1956, press offr Frigidaire Div General Motors Ltd 1958, product devpt Metro-Cammell Weyman Ltd 1959, gp advertisement mangr Modern Transport Publishing Co Ltd 1965, mangr Electrical Press Ltd 1966; dir: Birch Bros Ltd 1966–, Illustrated Newspapers Ltd 1969; ed Illustrated London News 1970, dir Northwood Publications Ltd 1971, md designate Textile Trade Pubns Ltd 1972, publishing dir Mercury House Ltd 1973, fndr chm Barracuda Books Ltd 1974–92, dir Quotes Ltd 1985–, princ Radmore Birch Associates 1991–, dir TLC Pharmacies Ltd 1995–; hon life memb Chiltern Car Club 1956–; fndr chm Buckingham and Dist Chamber of Trade Commerce and Indust 1983, hon life memb Inst of the Royal Corps of Tport 1985–, fndr chm Buckingham Heritage Tst 1985–; govr Royal Latin Sch Buckingham 1989–93, former memb Cncl Chesham Round Table; Freeman City of London 1960–; Worshipful Co of Carmen: Freeman and Liveryman 1960, memb Ct of Assts 1966, Master 1984–85, Dep Master 1988–89; memb Carmen's Awards Ctee 1969– (sometime vice chm), fndr chm Carmen's Charity Ball 1985 (jt chm 1988–) chm Carmen's Press Rels Ctee 1994–; FRSA 1980, FSA 1981; Chevalier Confrérie des Chevaliers du Trou Normand 1991–; *Books* incl: The Book of Chesham (1974), The Book of Aylesbury (1975), The Freedom-History and Guilds of the City of London (jtly, 1982), Buckingham in Camera (1987), Chiltern Thames in Camera (1990), Yesterday's Town: Amersham (jtly, 1991), Old Milton Keynes in Camera (1992), On the Move - The Road Haulage Association 1945–94 (jtly, 1995); *Style*— Clive Birch, FSA; ✉ Radmore Birch Associates, The Book Barn, Whittlebury, Northants NN12 8SX (☎ 01327 858301, fax 01327 858302)

BIRCH, Dennis Arthur; CBE (1977), DL (W Midlands 1979); s of George Howard Birch (d 1960), of Wolverhampton, and Leah, *née* Draycott; *b* 11 Feb 1925; *Educ* Wolverhampton Municipal GS; *m* 1948, Mary Therese, da of Bernard Lyons (d 1964); 1 da (Imelda); *Career* draughtsman and estimator John Thompson Ltd Wolverhampton 1942–64, PR exec George Wimpey and Co Ltd Birmingham 1966–77; mktg mangr: C Bryant and Son Birmingham 1978–83, E Manton Ltd Birmingham 1983–90; *Style*— Dennis Birch, Esq, CBE, DL; ✉ 3 Tern Close, Wolverhampton Road East, Wolverhampton (☎ 01902 883837); Manton Estates Ltd, 195 Bradford Road, Castle Bromwich, Birmingham B36 9AQ (☎ 0121 776 7333)

BIRCH, Frank Stanley Heath; s of late John Stanley Birch, CEng, and Phyllis Edna Birch, *née* Heath; *b* 8 Feb 1939; *Educ* Weston-super-Mare GS for Boys, Univ of Wales (BA), Univ of Birmingham (Inst of Local Govt Studies); *m* 1963, Diana Jacqueline, *née* Davies; 1 da; *Career* entered local govt service 1962, City Treas and Controller's Dept Cardiff 1962–69, chief internal auditor Dudley 1969–73, asst chief exec West Midlands CC 1974–76 (asst co treas 1973–74), chief exec Lewisham 1976–82, town clerk Croydon 1982–90, hon clerk Gen Purposes Ctee London Boroughs Assoc 1982–90; advsr to Assoc of Met Authorities 1976–90, dir Croydon Business Venture Ltd 1983–92, chm Lifecare NHS Tst 1994–; St John Ambulance London District: vice pres 1988–90, dep cdr 1990–92, cdr 1992–; sec London Co-ordinating Ctee 1985–86, memb London Cncl 1986–; Freeman City of London 1980; FRSA 1980, IPFA, MIMgt; CStJ 1992 (OStJ 1988); *Recreations* music, walking, caravanning, the countryside; *Style*— Frank Birch, Esq; ✉ St John Ambulance, London (Prince of Wales's District), Edwina Mountbatten House, 63 York St, London W1H 1PS (☎ 0171 258 3794, fax 0171 258 3793)

BIRCH, Sir John; KCVO (1993), CMG (1987); s of Dr C Allan Birch (d 1983); *b* 24 May 1935; *Educ* Leighton Park Sch, CCC Cambridge (MA); *m* 5 March 1960, Primula Haselden; 3 s (James b 1962, Alexander b 1963, Henry b 1969), 1 da (Melanie (Mrs James Pinkney) b 1967); *Career* Nat Serv Army 1954–56; joined HM Dip Serv 1959; serv: Paris, Singapore, Bucharest, Geneva, Kabul, Budapest; RCDS 1977; ambass and Br dep perm rep to UN 1986–89, ambass Hungary 1989–95; dir Br Assoc for Central and Eastern Europe 1995–; *Recreations* skiing, tennis; *Clubs* Athenaeum; *Style*— Sir John Birch, KCVO, CMG; ✉ 50 Hans Crescent, London SW1X 0NA

BIRCH, Dr John Anthony; s of Charles Aylmer Birch (d 1966), of Leek, Staffs, and Mabel, *née* Greenwood (d 1971); *b* 9 July 1929; *Educ* Trent Coll Notts, RCM (RCO 'Pitcher' scholar); *Career* Nat Serv RCS 1949–50; organist and choirmaster St Thomas's Church Regent St 1950–53, accompanist St Michael's Singers 1952–58, organist and choirmaster All Saints Church Margaret St London 1953–58, sub-organist HM Chapels Royal 1957–58, organist and master of the choristers Chichester Cathedral 1958–80, prof RCM 1959–, re-established the Southern Cathedrals Festival with Cathedral Organists of Salisbury and Winchester 1960, musical advsr Chichester Festival Theatre 1962–80, choirmaster Bishop Otter Coll Chichester 1963–69, accompanist Royal Choral Soc 1965–70 (organist 1966–), md CA Birch Ltd Staffs 1966–73 (rep 1950–66), univ organist Univ of Sussex 1967–94 (visiting lectr in music 1971–83), special cmmr Royal Sch of Church Music, organist and dir of choir Temple Church 1982–, organist of Royal Philharmonic Orchestra 1983–, curator-organist Royal Albert Hall 1984–; concert appearances: France, Belgium, Austria, Germany, Italy, Switzerland, Netherlands, Spain, Portugal, Scandinavia, Japan, USA, Far E; recital tours: Canada and US 1966 and 1967, Aust and NZ 1969, SA 1978; examiner Assoc Bd Royal Schs of Music 1958–77, a gen ed Novello & Co 1967–77, fell Corpn of SS Mary and Nicolas (Woodard Schs) 1973–; govr Hurstpierpoint Coll 1974–93, memb Cncl Corp of the Cranleigh and Bramley Schs (govr St Catherine's Bramley 1981–89); tstee Ouseley Trust 1989–; pres RCO 1984–86 (memb Cncl 1964–); Hon MA Univ of Sussex 1971, DMus Lambeth 1989; Freeman City of London 1991; ARCM, LRAM, FRCM 1981, FRCO (dipCHM), FRSA; *Recreations* gardening, collecting pictures; *Clubs* Garrick, New (Edinburgh); *Style*— Dr John Birch; ✉ 13 King's Bench Walk, Temple, London EC4Y 7EN (☎ and fax 0171 353 5115); Fielding House, The Close, Salisbury, Wilts SP1 2EB

BIRCH, Peter Gibbs; CBE (1992); s of William Birch (d 1971), and Gladys, *née* Gibbs (d 1971); *b* 4 Dec 1937; *Educ* Allhallows Sch; *m* 17 March 1962, Gillian Heather, da of Leonard Brace Sale Benge; 3 s (James b 1964, Simon b 1967, Alexander b 1970), 1 da (Sophie b 1972); *Career* Nat Serv 2 Lt Royal West Kent Regt 1956–58, seconded to Jamaica Regt; with Nestlé in UK, Switzerland, Singapore and Malaysia 1958–65; Gillette: with Gillette UK 1965–68, Gillette Australia (Melbourne) 1969–71, gen mangr Gillette NZ 1971–73, gen mangr Gillette SE Asia 1973–75, gp gen mangr Gillette Africa, Middle E and Eastern Europe 1975–81, md Gillette (UK) 1981–84; chief exec Abbey National plc (formerly Abbey National Building Society) 1984–; non-exec dir: Argos plc 1990–, Dalgety plc 1992–; chm Cncl of Mortgage Lenders 1991; pres Middx Young People's Clubs; *Recreations* swimming, wind surfing, cycling, skiing; *Style*— Peter G Birch, Esq, CBE; ✉ Abbey National plc, Baker St, London NW1 6XL (☎ 0171 612 4131)

BIRCH, Robin Arthur; CB (1995), DL (Oxfordshire 1996); s of Arthur Birch, and Olive Birch; *b* 12 Oct 1939; *Educ* King Henry VIII Sch Coventry, ChCh Oxford (MA); *m* 15 Dec 1962, Jane Marion Irvine, da of Vivian Sturdy (d 1965); 2 s (David b 1965, Michael b 1967); *Career* Civil Serv: princ Miny of Health 1966–69 (asst princ 1961–66), seconded Interdepartmental Social Work Gp 1969–70, Home Office 1970–72, asst sec DHSS 1973, princ private sec to Ldr of House of Commons 1980–81, under sec DHSS 1982, seconded NAO as asst auditor gen (under sec) 1984–86, dir of regnl orgn DSS 1988–90, dep sec (grade 2) and head Policy Group DSS 1990–95, ret; nat chm Age Concern England 1995–; hon sec Friends of Christ Church Cathedral Oxford 1978–; chm Oxford Gp Homes Orgn 1995–, tstee Oxfordshire Community Fndn, memb Mgmnt Ctee Oxford CAB, also involved in various other voluntary activities in Oxford city and county; *Recreations* family and friends, books, listening to music; *Clubs* Oxford Union; *Style*— Robin Birch, Esq, CB, DL; ✉ c/o The Cathedral, Christ Church, Oxford OX1 1DP

BIRCH, Sir Roger; kt (1992), CBE (1987), QPM (1980); s of John Edward Lawrence Birch (d 1981), and Ruby Birch; *b* 27 Sept 1930; *Educ* Teignmouth GS, Torquay GS, King's Coll Taunton; *m* Jeanne Margaret, da of Herbert Ernest Head (d 1976); 1 s (Steven); *Career* cadet RNC Dartmouth 1949–50, Pilot Offr RAF Canada 1950–52; joined Devon Police 1954, served in CID and Uniform Branch rising to chief supt 1954–72, asst chief constable Mid Anglia Constabulary 1972, dep chief constable Kent 1974; chief constable: Warwickshire 1978–83, Sussex 1983–93; dir of Police Extended Interviews 1983–91, chm Traffic Ctee ACPO 1983–86, pres ACPO 1987–88 (vice-pres 1986–87), chm and fndr Int Advsy Ctee 1988–92, int vice pres Int Assoc of Chief Police Offrs 1992–94; pres Chief Constable's Club 1991–92; UK vice pres Royal Life Saving Society (and chm SE Region) 1983–93; memb Cncl: Order of St John for Sussex 1983–93, Inst of Advanced Motorists 1983–93; Hon LLD Univ of Sussex 1991, hon fell Centre for Legal Studies 1994; *Recreations* walking, swimming; *Clubs* RAF; *Style*— Sir Roger Birch, CBE, QPM; ✉ c/o National Westminster Bank, Uckfield, East Sussex

BIRCH REYNARDSON, William Robert Ashley; CBE (1995); s of Lt-Col Henry Thomas Birch Reynardson, CMG (d 1972), and his 1 w Diana Helen, *née* Ponsonby (d 1962); *b* 7 Dec 1923; *Educ* Eton, Ch Ch Oxford; *m* 30 Nov 1950, (Pamela) Matnika, da of Lt-Gen Sir (Edward) Thomas Humphreys, KCB, CMG, DSO; 1 s (Thomas), 2 da (Juliet (Mrs R Stewart-Brown), Clare (Mrs A Hopkinson)); *Career* cmmnd 9 QR Lancers 1941, served in N Africa and Italy; called to the Bar Inner Temple 1950; sr ptnr and chm Thomas Miller, ret 1987; dir Graham Miller & Co, ret 1994; vice pres: Br Maritime Law Assoc, Comitè Maritime Int; High Sheriff of Oxfordshire 1974–75; past memb Bullingdon RDC; *Recreations* hunting, shooting, painting, gardening; *Clubs* Cavalry and Guards', Pratt's, City of London; *Style*— William Birch Reynardson, Esq, CBE; ✉ Adwell House, Tetsworth, Oxfordshire OX9 7DQ (☎ 01844 281204, fax 01844 281300); 111 Marsham Court, Marsham Street, London SW1 (☎ 0171 630 1191)

BIRCHALL, Adrian Philip; s of Wilfred Birchall (d 1977), and Mona Winifred, *née* Hibbert (d 1996); *b* 11 Oct 1946; *Educ* Up Holland GS, Univ of Birmingham (BSocSci); *m* 1 (m dis), 6 July 1968, Jacqueline Mullis; m 2, 9 Oct 1981, Elizabeth Anne, da of Harold Lowe (d 1979); 1 s (Andrew Philip Lowe b 24 Oct 1983), 1 da (Jessica Elizabeth Anne b 1 March 1985); *Career* advertising exec; teacher in mathematics Croydon and Wimbledon Secdy Sch, media res mangr and planning gp head Lintas Ltd 1969–73, media gp mangr McCann-Erickson 1973–75, media dir BBDO 1975–79, media dir and dep md Geers Gross 1979–85, vice chm DMB & B 1986–90, chm and chief exec The Media Centre 1991–; FIPA 1981; *Recreations* theatre, music, sport; *Style*— Adrian Birchall, Esq; ✉ The Media Centre, 123 Buckingham Palace Road, London SW1W 9DZ (☎ 0171 233 5678)

BIRD, Harold Dennis (Dickie); MBE (1986); s of James Harold Bird (d 1969), and Ethel, *née* Smith (d 1978); *b* 19 April 1933; *Educ* Raley Sch Barnsley; *Career* cricket umpire; only man to umpire 3 World Cup finals (W Indies v Australia Lord's 1975, W Indies v England Lord's 1979, W Indies v India Lord's 1983); other major matches umpired incl: World Cup India 1987, Queen's Silver Jubilee Test Match (England v Aust Lord's 1977), Centenary Test Match (England v Aust Lord's 1980), Bi-centenary Test Match (MCC v Rest of World Lord's 1987); only umpire of both men's and women's World Cup Finals (women's World Cup NZ 1982), umpire of 68 test matches and 92 one-day internationals (world record) and many other cricketing events (incl Gillette, Nat West, Benson and Hedges and Refuge Assurance Cup Finals, int tournaments Sharjah (EAE), Best Batsman in the World, World Double Wicket and Best All-Rounder in the World competitions), umpire of 159 int matches (world record), other matches umpired incl: Ashia Cup in Sri Lanka 1984, ind umpire Zimbabwe v India and NZ 1992, ind umpire test series West Indies v Pakistan 1993, test series Zimbabwe v New Zealand 1993, test series New Zealand v Pakistan 1994, test match Pakistan v Aust 1994, test match India v W Indies 1994, test series Australia v Pakistan 1996; ret as test umpire 1996; qualified MCC advanced cricket coach, former player Yorkshire and Leicestershire CCCs; hon life memb Yorks CCC and Leicestershire CCC; Yorkshire Personality of the Year 1977 and Carlesberg-Tetley Yorkshireman of the Year 1996, subject of This is your Life 1992 and Through The Keyhole, appeared on Breakfast with Frost (BBC TV), Desert Island Discs (Radio 4), Songs of Praise (BBC TV); Hon Dr Sheffield Hallam Univ 1996; *Books* Not Out (1978), That's Out (1985), From The Pavillion End (1988); *Clubs* Lord's Taverners', MCC (hon life memb); *Style*— Dickie Bird, Esq, MBE; ✉ White Rose Cottage, 40 Paddock Rd, Staincross, Barnsley, Yorks S75 6LE (☎ 01226 384491); Test and County Cricket Board, Lord's Cricket Ground, London NW8 8QN (☎ 0171 286 4405)

BIRD, John Alfred William; s of John William Bird (d 1978), and Elsie Louisa, *née* Hallett (d 1945); *b* 4 Feb 1924; *Educ* Bushbury Hill Secdy, Wolverhampton and Staffordshire Coll of Technol; *m* 21 Sept 1946, Gwendoline, da of Robert Davies (1971), of New Broughton, Wrexham, North Wales; 2 s (David John b 1 April 1948, Julian Robert b 18 June 1954); *Career* army serv Infantry 1943–47; Wolverhampton Borough PC 1947–49, gear cutter Henry Meadows Ltd 1949–51, personnel HM Hobson Ltd and Lucas Aerospace 1963–82 (turner 1951–63), MEP (Lab) Midlands West 1987–94 (Hon MEP 1994–), chair Euro Parly Lab Pty 1989–90; memb: Wolverhampton Borough Cncl 1962–88 (chm Educn Ctee 1972–80, ldr 1973–87), W Midlands CC 1973–81, vice pres AMA 1988– (Educn Ctee 1972–80, Cncl 1972–87), AEC 1972–75, EC 1974–75, W Midlands Econ Planning Cncl 1974–79, chm W Midlands Cncls 1986–87; chm of Dirs Temple Training Agency 1994–; pres Norwest Chartered Inst of Mktg 1990–91; hon fell Sci and Technol Wolverhampton Poly; *Recreations* sport, soccer, brass band music; *Style*— John Bird, Esq; ✉ 5 Giffard Road, Bushbury, Wolverhampton WV10 8EG (☎ 01902 782830)

BIRD, Michael George; s of George Bird, and Margaret, *née* Stephens; *b* 5 Jan 1960; *Educ* Bedales (scholar), Emmanuel Coll Cambridge (senior scholar, MA), Voronezh Univ (British Cncl scholar), Harvard Univ (Kennedy scholar); *m* 31 July 1988, Dr Delia da Sousa Correa; *Career* British Council: London 1985–87, Moscow 1987–91, UK Research and HE Liaison Office Brussels 1991–93, regional dir St Petersburg and North-West Russia 1993–; *Style*— Michael Bird, Esq; ✉ c/o FCO (St Petersburg), King Charles Street, London SW1A 2AH; The British Council, 46 Fontanka River Embankment, St Petersburg, Russia (☎ 00 7 812 325 6074, fax 00 7 812 325 6073)

BIRD, Richard; s of Desmond Bird, and Betty, *née* Brookman; *b* 12 Feb 1950; *Educ* King's Sch Canterbury, Magdalen Coll Oxford (MA, represented Britain at fencing); *m* July 1973, Penelope Anne, da of Dennis and Joan Frudd; 1 s (Martin b Sept 1977), 1 da (Eleanor b Feb 1980); *Career* DOE: admin trainee 1971–73, asst private sec to Min of Planning and Local Govt 1974–75; Dept of Tport: princ 1975–78, first sec UK Perm Representation to EC Brussels 1978–82, princ private sec to Sec of State for Tport 1982–83, asst sec 1983–90, under sec and head of Road Safety Directorate 1990–92; under sec Cabinet Office 1992–94, dir Personnel Dept of Tport 1994–; *Recreations* choral singing, summer sports; *Style*— Richard Bird, Esq; ✉ Department of Transport, 76 Marsham Street, London SW1P 4DR

BIRD, Sir Richard Geoffrey Chapman; 4 Bt (UK 1922), of Solihull, Co Warwick; s of Sir Donald Geoffrey Bird, 3 Bt (d 1963); *b* 3 Nov 1935; *Educ* Beaumont; *m* 1, 1957, Gillian Frances (d 1966), da of Bernard Haggett, of Solihull; 2 s (John Andrew b 1964, Mark Richard b 1965), 4 da (Cecilia Mary b 1957, Frances Bernadette b 1959, Brigitte Ann b 1960, Rowena Clare b 1962); m 2, 1968, Helen Patricia, o da of Frank Beaumont, of Pontefract; 2 da (Catherine Veronica b 1970, Denise Helen b 1972); *Heir* s, John Andrew Bird b 19 Jan 1964; *Style*— Sir Richard Bird, Bt; ✉ 39 Ashleigh Road, Solihull, W Midlands B91 1AF

BIRDWOOD, 3 Baron (UK 1938), of Anzac and of Totnes, Devon; Sir Mark William Ogilvie Birdwood; 3 Bt (UK 1919); s of 2 Baron, MVO (d 1962), and (Elizabeth) Vere Drummond, CVO, da of Lt-Col Sir George Drummond Ogilvie, KCIE, CSI; *b* 23 Nov 1938; *Educ* Radley, Trinity Coll Cambridge; *m* 27 April 1963, Judith Helen, er da of Reginald Gordon Seymour Roberts; 1 da (m 1987 Earl of Woolton, *qv*); *Career* former 2 Lt RHG; J Walter Thompson Cambridge Consits, vice pres Boyden Int, Wrightson Wood, chm Martlet Ltd 1986–; dir: Scientific Generics Ltd, Toy Options plc, Fiortho plc; chm Worthington & Co; Liveryman Worshipful Co of Glaziers & Painters of Glass; *Clubs* Brooks's; *Style*— The Rt Hon the Lord Birdwood; ✉ Russell House, Broadway, Worcs WR12 7BU; 5 Holbein Mews, London SW1W 8NW

BIRDWOOD, Baroness; (Elizabeth) Vere Drummond; CVO (1972, MVO 1958); da of Lt-Col Sir George Drummond Ogilvie, KCIE, CSI (d 1966); *b* 7 Aug 1909; *m* 7 March 1931 (m dis 1954), 2 Baron Birdwood, MVO (d 1962); 1 s, 1 da; *Career* private sec to Govr of Sind 1942–45, administrator King Edward VII's Hosp for Offrs 1950–72, ed Public Record Office 1972–95, vice chm Provident Assoc for Med Care 1977–82 (bd memb 1958–82); memb AHA: Westminster, Kensington, Chelsea 1973–76; memb Chelsea Borough Cncl 1954–60; *Books* So Dearly Loved, So Much Admired: Letters to Hester Pitt, Lady Chatham 1744–1801 (1994); *Style*— Vere, Lady Birdwood, CVO; ✉ 11 Whitelands House, Cheltenham Terrace, London SW3 4QX

BIRKBECK, John Oliver Charles; yr s of Lt-Col Oliver Birkbeck (d 1952), of Little Massingham House, King's Lynn, Norfolk, and Lady (Mary) Joan Wilhelmina Cator, *née* Fitzclarence, sis of 5 Earl of Munster; *b* 22 June 1936; *Educ* Gordonstoun, RAC Cirencester; *m* 2 May 1964, Hermione Anne, o da of Maj D'Arcy Dawes (d 1967), of Leacon Hall, Warehorne, Ashford, Kent; 1 s (Oliver Benjamin b 1973), 2 da (Lucy Claire (Mrs Leitao) b 1966, Rosanna Mary b 1974); *Career* chm: Breckland Dist Cncl 1987–88 (memb 1969–95), Norfolk County Cncl 1989 (memb 1970–93, chm Planning Ctee), Norfolk Historic Buildings Tst 1987–, Norfolk Windmills Tst 1988–, Norfolk Churches Tst 1992–95 (vice chm 1990–92); Norfolk rep Tennants of Yorkshire Auctioneers, church warden Litcham All Saints 1980–; High Sheriff for Co of Norfolk 1995; *Recreations* shooting, gardening, looking at old buildings; *Clubs* Norfolk (Norwich), All Sorts; *Style*— John Birkbeck, Esq; ✉ Litcham Hall, King's Lynn, Norfolk PE32 2QQ (☎ 01328 701389, fax 01328 701164)

BIRKBY, Roger; s of John Robert Howarth Birkby (d 1978), and Vera Mary, *née* Hirst; *b* 21 Nov 1945; *Educ* Bradford GS, Christ's Coll Cambridge (MA, LLB); *m* 1974, Wendy, *née* Godfree; 2 da (Miranda b 1985, Olivia b 1987); *Career* articled clerk Lovell White & King 1969–71; Norton Rose: joined 1971, ptnr 1976–, resident ptnr Bahrain Office 1982–84, Hong Kong Office 1985–88, managing ptnr Norton Rose 1994–; memb City of London Slrs' Co; memb: Law Soc, Int Bar Assoc; *Recreations* golf, tennis, walking, music; *Style*— Roger Birkby, Esq; ✉ Norton Rose, Kempson House, Camomile Street, London EC3A 7AN (☎ 0171 283 6000, fax 0171 283 6500)

BIRKENHEAD, Brian; *Career* fin dir Shell UK Oil 1983–87, fin dir Johnson Matthey plc 1987–89; National Power plc: joined National Power Div CEGB 1989, gp fin dir National Power plc until 1996; non-exec dir De La Rue plc 1994–; chm 100 Gp of Finance Dirs 1995–; *Style*— Brian Birkenhead, Esq; ✉ 14 President's Quay, St Katharine's Way, London E1 9UF

BIRKENHEAD, Bishop of 1993–; Rt Rev Michael Laurence Langrish; s of Douglas Frank Langrish, of Southampton, and Brenda Florence, *née* Passingham; *b* 1 July 1946; *Educ* Univ of Birmingham (BSocSci, Chllr's prize, postgrad cert in educn), Fitzwilliam Coll Cambridge (MA), Ridley Hall Cambridge; *m* 10 Aug 1968, Esther Vivien, da of Rev John William Rudd; 1 s (Richard Michael John b 8 Sept 1970), 2 da ((Rachel) Emma b 31 Oct 1973, Kathryn Jane b 31 Oct 1979); *Career* lectr in educn Mid-West State Coll of Educn Nigeria 1969–71, asst curate Holy Trinity Stratford-upon-Avon 1973–76, chaplain Rugby Sch 1976–81, diocesan dir of ordinands and lay min advsr, CME offr and vicar of Offchurch 1981–87, examining chaplain to the Bishop of Coventry 1982–87, dir diocesan Exploring Christian Miny scheme 1982–87, chaplain Hosps of St Cross and St Luke Rugby 1984–87, team rector Rugby Team Miny 1987–93, hon canon Coventry Cathedral 1990–93; diocesan memb Crown Appointments Cmmn 1985; memb: Gen Synod 1985–93, Cncl ACCM 1986–91; chm Chester Diocesan Bd of Educn 1993; govr: The Bishops' HS Chester 1993–, Birkenhead Sch 1993–; rep Cncl of Churches for Br and Ireland (CCBI) on UK Round Table on Sustainable Devpt; *Recreations* walking, gardening, Rotary, local history, railways (history, modelling, steam preservation), reading, theatre going, music (especially opera, classical and jazz); *Clubs* Royal Commonwealth Soc; *Style*— The Rt Rev the Bishop of Birkenhead; ✉ Bishop's Lodge, 67 Bidston Road, Oxton, Birkenhead, Merseyside L43 6TR (☎ 0151 652 2741, fax 0151 651 2330)

BIRKENSHAW, Jack; s of John Ward Birkenshaw, of Rothwell, Leeds, Yorks, and Edith, *née* Simpson; *b* 13 Nov 1940; *Educ* Rothwell GS; *m* 16 March 1963, Gloria, da of Ernest Jenkins; 1 s (Mark Howard b 9 Dec 1966); *Career* professional cricketer: Yorks CCC 1956–60, Leics 1961–80, Worcs 1981; umpire 1982–88; mangr/coach: Somerset 1989–90, Leics 1991–, Orange Free State Cricket Club 1993/94 and 1995/95; played 5 tests for Eng (touring WI, India, Pakistan and Sri Lanka); *Recreations* golf, music; *Clubs* MCC; *Style*— Jack Birkenshaw, Esq; ✉ Leicestershire CCC, County Ground, Grace Road, Leicester LE2 8AD (☎ 0116 283 2128, fax 0116 244 0363)

BIRKETT, 2 Baron (UK 1958); Michael Birkett; s of 1 Baron Birkett (d 1962); *b* 22 Oct 1929; *Educ* Stowe, Trinity Coll Cambridge; *m* 1978, Gloria, da of Thomas Taylor, of Queen's Gate, London; 1 s; *Heir* s, Hon Thomas Birkett b 25 July 1982; *Career* film prodr 1961–; prodns incl: The Caretaker, Marat/Sade, A Midsummer Night's Dream, King Lear; dep dir Nat Theatre 1975–77, conslt to Nat Theatre on films, TV and sponsorship 1977–79, dir Recreation and the Arts GLC 1979–86; chm of govrs BRIT Sch for Performing Arts and Technol Croydon 1980; Master Worshipful Co of Curriers' 1975–76; *Recreations* the arts; *Style*— The Rt Hon the Lord Birkett; ✉ House of Lords, London SW1

BIRKETT, Peter Philip; s of Philip Walker Birkett (d 1945), of Lincoln, and Kathryn, *née* Tidy; *b* 19 Aug 1944; *Educ* Dauntsey's Sch Devizes Wilts; *m* Christine Sally; 2 da (Alice Emily, Rosamund Kate); *Career* reporter: Kent Messenger Maidstone Kent 1965–68, Daily Sketch 1968–70, Sunday Telegraph 1970–74, Daily Telegraph 1974–75, Daily Mail 1975–79; news ed Daily Telegraph 1980–84, ed Peterborough Column in Daily Telegraph 1984–89, foreign ed Daily Mail 1989–93, freelance 1993–95, features ed Sunday Express 1995–; *Recreations* fishing, gardening; *Style*— Peter Birkett, Esq; ✉ Sunday Express, Ludgate House, 245 Blackfriars Road, London SE1 9UX (☎ 0171 928 8000, fax 0171 922 7599)

BIRKETT, Peter Vidler; QC (1989); s of Neville Lawn Birkett, JP, of Kendal, Cumbria, and Marjorie Joy, *née* Vidler; *b* 13 July 1948; *Educ* Sedbergh Sch Yorkshire, Univ of Leicester (LLB); *m* 11 Dec 1976, Jane Elizabeth, da of Robert Hall Fell, MBE (d 1981); 2 s (Nicholas Robert b 12 Dec 1984, Michael Peter Vidler b 20 Dec 1986); *Career* called to the Bar Inner Temple 1972, barr N Circuit 1972–, recorder of the Crown Court 1989–; memb Hon Soc of the Inner Temple; *Recreations* golf, skiing, music; *Clubs* Wilmslow Golf; *Style*— Peter Birkett, Esq, QC; ✉ 18 St John St, Manchester M3 4EA (☎ 0161 834 9843)

BIRKETT-JONES, Michael Phillip; adopted s of Harold Ernest Birkett (d 1992), and Marion Jane, *née* Booth (d 1972); *b* 30 May 1948; *Educ* Burton upon Trent GS, Leeds Poly (BA Hons), RCA (MA); *m* 1977, Denise Patricia, da of Leaster Greenwood (d 1983); 1 s (Jeremy Michael b 1978), 2 da (Rowena Claire b 1980, Georgina Cicely b 1983); *Career* Paris Biennale 1969, Purcell Miller Tritton 1970–72, Replicards Ltd 1972–73, Purcell Miller Tritton 1973–77, lectr London Coll of Furniture 1978–83, Gordon Bowyer & Partners 1980–81, princ lectr Bournemouth & Poole Coll of Art & Design 1983–85, SPS Consultancy Group plc 1985–88, ptnr Purcell Miller Tritton & Partners 1988–95, conslt 1996–; BTEC moderator 1985–90, external assessor Chelsea Sch of Art 1989–90; FCSD; *Style*— Michael Birkett-Jones, Esq; ✉ Purcell Miller Tritton & Partners, No 1 Tideway Yard, Mortlake High St, London SW14 8SN (☎ 0181 392 1277)

BIRKIN, Sir (John) Derek; kt (1990), TD (1965); s of Noah Birkin, and Rebecca, *née* Stranks; *b* 30 Sept 1929; *Educ* Hemsworth GS; *m* 1 April 1952, Sadie, da of Ernest Wade-Smith; 1 s (Michael b 16 April 1957), 1 da (Alison (Mrs Lear) b 16 July 1958); *Career* Nat Serv 2 Lt RA Nat Serv 1948–50, Maj TA; James Williamson 1950–66; md: Velmar Ltd 1966–67, Nairn Williamson Ltd 1967–70; chm and md Tunnel Holdings Ltd 1975–83 (md 1971–83); The RTZ Corporation PLC (now RTZ-CRA plc): dir 1982–, dep chief exec 1983–85, chief exec and dep chm 1985–91, chm 1991–96 (non-exec chm 1994–96); chm elect Watmoughs plc 1996–; dir: Smiths Industries Ltd 1977–84, British Gas Corporation 1982–85, George Wimpey plc 1984–92, CRA Ltd (Aust) 1985–96 (unified with RTZ Dec 1995), Rio Algom Ltd (Canada) 1985–92, British Steel plc (formerly British Steel Corporation) 1986–92, The Merchants Trust plc 1986–, Barclays Plc 1990–94, Carlton Communications plc 1992–, Merck & Co Inc (USA) 1992–, Unilever plc (advsy dir) 1993–; memb: Cncl The Industrial Soc 1985–, Top Salaries Review Bd 1986–89; dir Royal Opera House 1993–; CIMgt 1980, FRSA 1988; *Recreations* opera, rugby, cricket; *Clubs* Athenaeum, MCC, Harlequins; *Style*— Sir Derek Birkin, TD; ✉ Watmoughs plc, Jason House, Hillam Road, Bradford, W Yorks BD2 1QN (☎ 01274 735663, fax 01274 734206)

BIRKIN, Sir John Christian William; 6 Bt (UK 1905), of Ruddington Grange, Ruddington, Notts; o s of Sir Charles Lloyd Birkin, 5 Bt (d 1985), and Janet Ramsay, *née* Johnson; *b* 1 July 1953; *Educ* Eton, Trinity Coll Dublin, London Film Sch; *m* 25 June 1994, Emma Louise, da of Roger Leonard Gage, of Chantry House, Aveton Gifford, nr Kingsbridge, S Devon; 1 s (Benjamin Charles b 6 Nov 1995); *Heir* s, Benjamin Charles Birkin b 4 Nov 1995; *Career* freelance television director, dir Compound Eye Productions Ltd; *Style*— Sir John Birkin, Bt; ✉ Barn Cottage, Church Street, Micheldever, Hants SO21 3DB

BIRKMYRE, Sir Archibald; 3 Bt (UK 1921), of Dalmunzie, Co Perth; s of Sir Henry Birkmyre, 2 Bt (d 1992), and Doris Gertrude, *née* Austen Smith (d 1992); *b* 12 Feb 1923; *Educ* Radley; *m* 1953, Gillian Mary, o da of late Eric Mytton Downes, OBE, of Dorndon House, Hurst, Berks; 1 s (James b 1956), 2 da (Alison Mary (Lady De Ramsey) b 1954, Serena Jane (Mrs Hugo E S Jackson) b 1960); *Heir* s, James Birkmyre b 29 Feb 1956; *Career* Capt RA Burma 1942–45; ptnr George Henderson & Co, dir Henderson Crosthwaite Ltd 1976–88; memb London Stock Exchange 1960–88; *Recreations* golf, shooting, fishing; *Clubs* Boodle's, Huntercombe Golf; *Style—* Sir Archibald Birkmyre, Bt; ✉ The Old Presbytery, Buckland, Faringdon, Oxon SN7 8QW (☎ 0136 787253)

BIRKS, Dr Jack; CBE (1975); s of Herbert Horace Birks (d 1950), and Ann Birks; *b* 1 Jan 1920; *Educ* Ecclesfield GS, Univ of Leeds (BSc, PhD); *m* 1948, Vere Elizabeth, da of Barnard Burrell-Davis (d 1960); 2 s, 2 da; *Career* md BP 1978–82 (ret); chm: Charterhouse Petroleum plc 1982–86, NMI Ltd 1982–85, British Maritime Technology Ltd 1985–95, Mountain Petroleum 1988–91 (dir 1985–91), North American Investment Trust 1989–95, Midland and Scottish Resources 1994– (dir 1982–94); dir: Wimpey Gp 1982–90, Petrofina (UK) 1986–89, Bellwether Exploration Co 1988–, BP Minerals International 1982–85, London American Energy NV 1982–88; memb: SRC 1976–80, Meteorological Ctee 1977–82, Cncl Univ of Surrey 1982–87, Maritime League 1982–86, Royal Inst 1982–85 and 1988–91; pres: Soc for Underwater Technol 1974–75, Pipeline Industs Guild 1979–81, Inst of Petroleum 1984–86; Hon LLD: Univ of Aberdeen 1981, Univ of Surrey 1981; CEng, FEng 1978, FIMM, FInstPet, FIMechE; *Recreations* golf, tennis; *Clubs* Athenaeum, Norfolk; *Style—* Dr Jack Birks, CBE, FEng; ✉ High Silver, High St, Holt, Norfolk (☎ 01263 712847); High Bank, Laceys Lane, Niton, Isle of Wight (☎ 01983 730282)

BIRKS, His Hon Michael; s of Falconer Moffat Birks, CBE (d 1960), and Monica Katherine Lushington, *née* Mellor (d 1957); *b* 21 May 1920; *Educ* Oundle, Trinity Coll Cambridge (MA); *m* 1947, Ann Ethne, da of Capt Henry Stafford Morgan; 1 da; *Career* Lt 22 Dragoons; slr 1946, asst registrar Chancery Div of High Ct 1953, asst County Ct registrar 1960; registrar Birkenhead and Chester Gp of County Cts 1961–66, West London County Ct 1966–83, recorder 1979, circuit judge S Eastern Circuit 1983–93; advsy ed Atkins Ct Forms 1966–91; *Books* Gentlemen of the Law (1960), contrib to fourth edn Halsbury's Laws of England; *Recreations* painting; *Style—* His Hon Michael Birks

BIRKS, Prof Peter Brian Herrenden; Hon QC (1995); s of Dr Peter Herrenden Birks, and (Maud) Mary, *née* Morgan; *b* 3 Oct 1941; *Educ* Trinity Coll Oxford (MA), UCL (LLM), Univ of Oxford (DCL), Univ of Edinburgh (LLD); *m* 29 Oct 1984, Jacqueline Susan, *née* Stimpson; *Career* lectr UCL 1967–71, law fell Brasenose Coll Oxford 1971–81, prof of civil law Univ of Edinburgh 1981–88, prof of law Univ of Southampton 1988–89, visiting prof Aust Nat Univ 1989, Regius prof of civil law Univ of Oxford and professorial fell All Souls Coll Oxford 1989–; memb: Lord Chllr's Advsy Ctee on Legal Educn 1989–91, SEAC Ctee on Social Sciences 1989–91; hon sec Soc of Public Teachers of Law 1989–96, sec Standing Conf on Legal Educn 1991–94, tstee Oxford Inst of Legal Practice 1994–; memb: Academic Consultative Ctee Law Soc 1991–93, Editorial Bd Lloyd's Maritime and Commercial Law Quarterly 1993–, Humanities Research Bd British Acad 1996–; conslt ed Restitution Law Review 1993–; DJur (hc) Regensburg Univ; FBA 1989, FRSA 1992; *Books* The Legal Mind (ed with N MacCormick), The Institutes of Justinian (with G McLeod, 1986), Introduction to the Law of Restitution (1989), New Perspectives in the Roman Law of Property (ed, 1989), Restitution - The Future (1992), The Life of the Law (ed, 1993), The Frontiers of Liability, Vols 1 and 2 (ed, 1994), Reviewing Legal Education (ed, 1994), Laundering and Tracing (ed, 1995), What are law schools for? (ed, 1996), Wrongs and Remedies in the 21st Century (ed, 1996); *Clubs* Athenaeum; *Style—* Prof Peter Birks, QC, FBA; ✉ Oak Trees, Sandy Lane, Boars Hill, Oxford OX1 5HN (☎ 01865 735625); All Souls College, Oxford OX1 4AL (☎ 01865 279379, fax 01865 279 299)

BIRLEY, Richard Yvon; s of Stephen Harvey Yvon Birley, of Br Columbia (d 1941), and Erica Pressey (d 1971); *b* 16 Jan 1928; *Educ* RNC Dartmouth; *m* 1, April 1953 (m dis 1958), Constance, da of Richard Rheem, of San Francisco (d 1975); m 2, August 1958, Maureen Ann, da of James McNicol, of Perth, Scot; 4 s (Richard b 1954, Jeremy b 1959, Mark b 1962, Stephen b 1965), 1 da (Nicolette b 1956); *Career* RN Lt Submarines 1944–55; Shell International (London, Hague, S Africa, Iran) 1957–66; dir: Wm Brandts and Sons Ltd 1969–72, Edward Bates 1972–75; md KCA Drilling Ltd 1975; chm: Rea Bros Leasing 1976–91, TLS Range plc 1988–92, P C Security Ltd 1989–; non-exec dir: Salop Sand and Gravel 1989, Birkby Group Plc 1988–93, Falmouth Oil Services (1994) Ltd 1995–; *Style—* Richard Birley, Esq; ✉ Argyll House, 6–13 Chamber Street, London E1 8BW (☎ 0171 480 5516, fax 0171 480 5830)

BIRLEY, Prof Susan Joyce (Sue); *Educ* Univ Coll London (BSc), Harvard Univ (Int Teachers Prog scholar), Univ of London (PhD); *Career* advanced and scholarship mathematics teacher Dunsmore Sch 1964–66, lectr in quantitative aspects Dept of Economics and Mgmnt Lanchester Poly 1966–68, sr lectr in business policy Mgmnt Sch Poly of Central London 1970–72 (lectr in quantitative methods 1968–70), sr res fell City Univ 1972–74, London Business Sch: lectr in small business 1974–79, sr res fell Inst of Small Business 1979–82, dir New Enterprise Prog 1979–82; assoc prof of strategy and entrepreneurship Coll of Business Univ of Notre Dame USA 1982–85 (adjunct assoc prof 1978–82); Cranfield Sch of Mgmnt Cranfield Inst of Technology: Philip & Pauline Harris prof of entrepreneurship 1985–90, also dir of research and dir Cranfield Entrepreneurship Research Centre; dir of res and prof of mgmnt in the field of entrepreneurship The Management School Imperial College of Science, Technology and Medicine 1990–; visiting prof INSEAD 1991 (visiting lectr 1978); fndr dir: The Guidehouse Group plc 1980–85, Greyfriars Ltd 1982–85, Newchurch & Co (chm) 1986–; non-exec dir National Westminster Bank plc 1996–; advsr Dept of Econ Devpt N Ireland 1985–88, academic dir Euro Fndn for Entrepreneurship Research 1988–90, vice chm Exec Ctee Br Acad of Mgmnt 1988–89, govr Harris City Technol Coll 1990–92, bd memb Local Enterprise Devpt Unit (LEDU) N Ireland 1991–93 (advsr 1988–89), currently conslt advsr Grant Thornton; memb: Postgrad Bd CNAA 1979–82, Steering Ctee UK Nat Small Firms Policy and Res Conf 1985–90, Adjudication Ctee Prince of Wales' Award for Innovation 1986–, Bd of Dirs Strategic Mgmnt Soc 1987–90, Cncl N Ireland Econ Cncl 1988–94, Deregulation Advsy Bd DTI 1988–90, Polytechnics and Colls Funding Cncl 1988–93, E European Links Advsy Bd British Cncl 1990–91, Advsy Cncl Sheffield Business Sch 1990–93, Growing Business Target Team Business in the Community 1990–91, Enterprise and Econ Devpt Leadership Team Business in the Community 1992–93; convenor: Conf of Teachers of Mgmnt 1986 (also chm), Tenth UK Nat Small Firms Policy and Res Conf 1987, Annual Global Conf on Entrepreneurship Research (jtly) 1990–; author of numerous jl articles, conf papers, reports, case studies and books; Freeman City of London; *Books* The Small Business Casebook (1979), New Enterprises (1982), The British Entrepreneur (jtly, 1990), Building European Ventures (ed, 1990); *Style—* Prof Sue Birley; ✉ Imperial College of Science, Technology and Medicine, The Management School, Exhibition Rd, London SW7 2BP (☎ 0171 589 5111)

BIRMINGHAM, Bishop of 1987–; Rt Rev Mark Santer; s of Rev Canon Eric Arthur Robert Santer (d 1979), of The Chaplain's Lodge, St Cross, Winchester, Hants, and Phyllis Clare, *née* Barlow (d 1978); *b* 29 Dec 1936; *Educ* Marlborough, Queens' Coll Cambridge (MA), Westcott House Cambridge; *m* 3 Oct 1964, Henriette Cornelia (d 1994), da of Willem Antonie Gerard Weststrate (d 1987), of Driebergen; 2 da (Hendrika b 1966, Miriam b 1967), 1 s (Diederick b 1969); *Career* ordained: deacon 1963, priest 1964; asst curate Cuddesdon and tutor Cuddesdon Theol Coll Oxford 1963–67, fell and dean Clare Coll Cambridge 1967–72, asst lectr in divinity Univ of Cambridge 1968–72, princ Westcott House Cambridge 1973–81, bishop of Kensington 1981–87; co-chm Anglican-Roman Catholic Int Cmmn 1983–; hon fell: Clare Coll Cambridge 1987, Queens' Coll Cambridge 1991; memb Cncl Nat Assoc for Care and Resettlement of Offenders 1985–; Freeman City of London 1984; *Books* The Phenomenon of Christian Belief (contrib, 1970), Documents in Early Christian Thought (1975), Their Lord and Ours (contrib, 1982), The Church and State (contrib, 1984), Dropping the Bomb (contrib, 1985); *Style—* The Rt Rev the Bishop of Birmingham; ✉ Bishop's Croft, Old Church Rd, Harborne, Birmingham B17 0BG (☎ 0121 427 1163, fax 0121 426 1322)

BIRMINGHAM, 7 Archbishop of (RC) 1982–; Most Rev Maurice Noël Léon Couve de Murville; s of Noël Couve de Murville, and Marie, da of Sir Louis Souchon; 4 cous once removed of Maurice Couve de Murville, French PM 1968–69; *b* 27 June 1929, in France; *Educ* Downside, Trinity Coll Cambridge (MA), Institut Catholique Paris (STL), Sch of Oriental and African Studies Univ of London (MPhil); *Career* ordained priest 1957, curate St Anselm's Dartford 1957–60, priest i/c St Francis Moulsecoomb 1961–64; Catholic chaplain: Univ of Sussex 1961–77, Univ of Cambridge 1977–82; Hon DUniv Open Univ 1994, Hon DD Univ of Birmingham 1996; *Clubs* Birmingham, Lansdowne; *Style—* The Most Rev the Archbishop of Birmingham; ✉ Archbishop's House, 8 Shadwell Street, Birmingham B4 6EY (☎ 0121 236 9090, fax 0121 212 0171)

BIRNBAUM, Edwin Jerome; s of Salomon Birnbaum, of Antwerp, Belgium, and Leone, *née* Krieger; *b* 18 Feb 1961; *Educ* Koninklijke Atheneum Berchem, Free Univ of Brussels (BSc, MSc), Catholic Univ of Leuven (MBA); *m* 25 Aug 1991, Sandra, *née* Dwek; *Career* brand mangr Procter & Gamble Benelux 1984–89, sr strategy conslt Bain & Co London 1989–91; mktg dir: Dixons Stores Group 1991–93, Wickes Building Supplies 1993–95; md Wickes Continental 1995–; *Style—* Edwin Birnbaum, Esq; ✉ Dennenlaan 20, 2020 Antwerpen, Belgium; Wickes Continental, Takkebijsters 57a, 4817 BL Breda, The Netherlands (☎ 00 31 76 716111, fax 00 31 76 716717)

BIRNBERG, Benedict Michael; s of Jonas Birnberg (d 1970), and Naomi Hilda, *née* Bentwich (d 1988); *b* 8 Sept 1930; *Educ* Minehead GS, King's Sch Canterbury, Corpus Christi Coll Cambridge (BA); *m* 29 April 1968, Triantafyllia (Felitsa), da of Kyriakos Matziorinis (d 1946); 1 da (Ariadne b 1971); *Career* admitted slr 1958; sr ptnr B M Birnberg and Co; chm NCCL 1974; chm Lewisham CAB 1979–84; govr Greenwich Theatre Ltd 1974–78; *Recreations* music, theatre, politics; *Style—* Benedict Birnberg, Esq; ✉ 4 Eliot Place, Blackheath, London SE3 (☎ 0181 852 1937); B M Birnberg, 103 Borough High St, London SE1 (☎ 0171 403 3166, fax 0171 378 1856)

BIRO, Val Balint Stephen; s of Dr Balint Biro (d 1944), of Budapest, Hungary, and Margaret, *née* Gyulahazi (d 1982); *b* 6 Oct 1921; *Educ* Cistercian Sch Budapest, Central Sch of Art and Design London; *m* 1, 1945 (m dis), Vivien, da of A H Woolley; 1 da (Melissa b 1951); m 2, 1970, Marie-Louise Ellaway, da of P Christofas; 1 step s (Philip b 1956), 1 step da (Caroline b 1961); *Career* author and illustrator; memb AFS London 1942–45, studio mangr Sylvan Press London 1944–46, prodn mangr C & J Temple London 1946–48, art dir John Lehmann Ltd London 1948–53; cncllr 1966–70, memb/chm governing bodies Amersham Coll of Art & Design 1974–84, vice chm Bosham Assoc 1989–91; contrib weekly illustrations Radio Times 1951–72; named among Top Hundred Authors in list from PLR 1990; memb Soc of Authors; *Books* author and illustrator of numerous children's books incl: series of 35 Gumdrop books (about his vintage car) since 1965, Hungarian Folktales (1981), The Magic Doctor (1982), The Hobyahs (1985), Tobias and the Dragon (1989), Look-and-Find ABC (1990), Miranda's Umbrella (1990), Rub-a-Dub-Dub Nursery Ryhmes (1991), Three Billy Goats Gruff (1993), Jasper's Jungle Journey (1995), Lazy Jack (1995), Bears Can't Fly (1996), Hansel and Gretel (1996); illustrator of over 300 books incl: Worlds Without End (Denys Val Baker, 1945), The Prisoner of Zenda (Anthony Hope, 1961), Wizard of Oz books (L Frank Baum, 1965–67), The Good Food Guide (1971), The Wind in the Willows (Kenneth Grahame, 1983), The King's Jokes (Margaret Mahy, 1987), When I Was Your Age (Ken Adams, 1991), What's Up The Coconut Tree? (A H Benjamin, 1991), The Show-off Mouse (A H Benjamin, 1993), My Oxford Picture Word Book (OUP, 1994), The Dinosaur's Egg (Christina Butler, 1994), The Flying Boot Reading Scheme (Ted Wragg, 1994/95), The Landleagers (Trollope, 1995), The Father Brown Stories (2 Vols, Chesterton, 1996), The Dinosaur's Dinner (Christina Butler, 1997); *Recreations* vintage car motoring; *Clubs* Vintage Sports Car, Vintage Austin Register; *Style—* Val Biro, Esq; ✉ Bridge Cottage, Brook Avenue, Bosham, West Sussex PO18 8LQ (☎ 01243 574195)

BIRRELL, James Gibson; WS (1979); s of late James Adamson Birrell, of Edinburgh, and Louisa Elizabeth, *née* Silvester; *b* 10 June 1948; *Educ* Loretto, Queen Mary Coll, Univ of London (BA); *m* 15 Aug 1970, Angela Hilary, da of Eric Robert Soame, of Abingdon, Oxon; 2 s (Gordon b 1976, David b 1978), 1 da (Jane b 1982); *Career* slr 1972; ptnr: Brodies 1976–85, Dickson Minto 1985–; external examiner in commercial law Univ of Edinburgh, memb Insolvency Practitioners Adjudication Panel (Scot); memb Law Soc: Eng and Wales 1972, Scotland 1975; *Books* Stair Memorial Encylopaedia (contrib, 1987); *Recreations* music, photography, skiing, squash, golf; *Style—* James Birrell, Esq, WS; ✉ 26 Kinnear Rd, Edinburgh EH3 5PE (☎ 0131 552 1077); 11 Walker St, Edinburgh EH3 7NE (☎ 0131 225 4455, fax 0131 225 2712); Royal London House, 22/25 Finsbury Square, London EC2A 1DS (☎ 0171 628 4455, fax 0171 628 0027)

BIRSE, Peter Malcolm; s of Peter Alexander McCauley Birse, of 7 MacKenzie St, Carnoustie, Scotland, and Margaret Cumming, *née* Craib; *b* 24 Nov 1942; *Educ* Arbroath HS, Univ of St Andrews (BSc); *m* 25 Jan 1969, Helen, da of Paul Stanley Searle, of Bishopston, Bristol; 2 s (James Peter Alexander b 1971, Robert Archibald b 1975), 1 da (Bridget b 1969); *Career* engr John Mowlem Ltd 1963–65, engr and project mangr Gammon Ghana Ltd 1965–67, contract mangr Gammon (UK) Ltd 1967–70, established Birse Gp plc (construction gp) 1970– (currently chm); chm Peter Birse Charitable Tst; MICE 1971; *Recreations* sailing, skiing, tennis, golf, fishing; *Clubs* Royal Ocean Racing; *Style—* Peter Birse, Esq; ✉ Birse Group plc, Humber Rd, Barton-on-Humber, North Lincolnshire, DN18 5BN (☎ 01652 633222, fax 01652 633360)

BIRT, John; s of Leo Vincent Birt, of Richmond, Surrey, and Ida Birt; *b* 10 Dec 1944; *Educ* St Mary's Coll Liverpool, St Catherine's Coll Oxford (MA); *m* 14 Sept 1965, Jane Frances, da of James Harris Lake (d 1982, 2 Lt US Navy), of Chevy Chase, Maryland, USA; 1 s (Jonathan b 1968), 1 da (Eliza b 1971); *Career* prodr Nice Time 1968–69, jt ed World in Action 1969–70, prodr The Frost Programme 1971–72, exec prodr Weekend World 1972–74, head of current affairs LWT 1974–77, co prodr The Nixon Interviews 1977, controller of features and current affairs LWT 1977–81, dir of programmes LWT 1982–87; BBC: dep dir gen 1987–92, DG 1992–; memb: Wilton Park Academic Cncl 1980–83, Media Law Gp 1983–, Working Pty on the New Technols Broadcasting Res Unit 1981–83 (memb Exec Ctee 1983–87), Opportunity 2000 Target Team 1991–; visiting fell Nuffield Coll Oxford 1991–; hon fell St Catherine's Coll Oxford; Hon Doctorate Liverpool John Moores Univ; winner Emmy (for outstanding contrib to int TV) Nov 1995; FRTS (vice pres); *Style—* John Birt, Esq; ✉ BBC, Broadcasting House, London W1A 1AA (☎ 0171 580 4468)

BIRTS, Peter William; QC (1990), QC (NI, 1996); s of John Claude Birts (d 1969), of Sussex, and Audrey Lavinia, *née* McIntyre; *b* 9 Feb 1946; *Educ* Lancing, St John's Coll Cambridge (choral scholar, MA); *m* 24 April 1971, Penelope Ann, da of Wing Cdr Anthony Eyre, DFC (d 1946); 1 s (William b 1979), 2 da (Melanie b 1972, Charlotte b 1975); *Career* called to the Bar Gray's Inn 1968; recorder of the Crown Court 1989–; memb: Bar Cncl 1990–95, Judicial Studies Bd 1991–96, County Ct Rule Ctee 1991–; chm Bar Cncl Legal Aid and Fees Ctee 1994–95; asst cmmr Parly Boundary Cmmn for England 1992–, legal memb Mental Health Review Tbnls 1994–; govr Benenden Sch 1990–93; Freeman of City of London 1967, Liveryman Worshipful Co of Carpenters 1967; *Books* Trespass: Summary Procedure for Possession of Land (with Alan Willis, 1987), Remedies for Trespass (1990); author of numerous articles on trespass and countryside law; *Recreations* music, shooting, fishing, tennis, walking; *Clubs* Hurlingham; *Style—* Peter Birts, Esq, QC; ✉ Farrar's Building, Temple, London EC4Y 7BD (☎ 0171 583 9241, fax 0171 583 0090)

BIRTWISTLE, Maj-Gen Archibald Cull; CB (1983), CBE (1976, OBE 1971), DL (N Yorkshire 1991); s of Walter Edwin Birtwistle, and Eila Louise, *née* Cull; *b* 19 Aug 1927; *Educ* St John's Coll Cambridge (MA); *m* 1956, Sylvia Elleray; 2 s, 1 da; *Career* cmmnd RCS 1949, serv Korea (despatches), Dep Cmdt RMCS 1975–79, Chief Signal Offr BAOR 1979–80, Signal Offr-in-C (Army) 1980–83, ret; Col Cmdt RCS 1983–, Hon Col 34 (Northern) Signal Regt (Volunteers) 1988–90; Master of Signals and Col Cmdt RCS 1990–; CEng, MIEE; *Recreations* gardening; *Style—* Maj-Gen Archibald Birtwistle, CB, CBE, DL; ✉ c/o Nat West Bank plc, 97 High St, Northallerton, N Yorks DL7 8PS

BIRTWISTLE, Sir Harrison; kt (1988); s of Frederick Birtwistle (d 1985), and Margaret, *née* Harrison (d 1970); *b* 15 July 1934; *Educ* Royal Manchester Coll of Music, RAM London (LRAM); *m* 4 Jan 1958, Sheila Margaret Wilhelmina, da of George Duff (d 1986); 3 s (Adam b 1959, Silas b 1963, Thomas b 1965); *Career* composer; associate dir music Nat Theatre London 1976–88, Henry Purcell prof of composition King's Coll London, composer-in-res LPO; visiting fell Princeton Univ USA 1968, visiting prof of music Swarthmore Coll Pennsylvania USA 1975, Slee visiting prof NY State Univ at Buffalo USA 1977, Harkness fell Univ of Colorado Boulder USA 1969; retrospective Secret Theatres South Bank Centre 1996; Hon FRMCM and ARMCM 1986, Hon FRAM, hon fell Akademie der Kunst Berlin; Chevalier des Arts et des Lettres (France) 1986; *Works* incl: Secret Theatre (1965), Tragoedia (1965), Punch and Judy (first staged Aldeburgh Festival 1967), Meridian (1971), The Mask of Orpheus, Ritual Fragment, The Triumph of Time (1972), Earth Dances (1986), Gawain (1991), Antiphonies, Nomos, An Imaginary Landscape, The Second Mrs Kong (premiered Glyndebourne 1994), Panic (saxophone concerto premiered BBC Proms 1995), Slow Frieze 1996; *Awards* Evening Standard Award for Opera 1986, Grawemeyer Award Univ Louisville Kentucky USA 1986, Royal Philharmonic Soc Award for large scale composition 1992 (for Gawain), Siemens Prize 1995; *Recreations* fishing, walking; *Style—* Sir Harrison Birtwistle; ✉ c/o Allied Artists Agency, 42 Montpelier Square, London SW7 1JZ (☎ 0171 589 6243, fax 0171 581 5269)

BIRTWISTLE, Sue Elizabeth; da of Frank Edgar Birtwistle (d 1987), of Northwich, Cheshire, and Brenda Mary, *née* Higham; *m* 14 July 1973, Sir Richard Charles Hastings Eyre, CBE, *qv*, s of Cdr Richard Galfredus Hastings Giles Eyre; 1 da (Lucy b 25 Sept 1974); *Career* theatre dir: Royal Lyceum Theatre in Educn Co 1970–72, Nottingham Playhouse Roundabout Co 1973–78, freelance 1978–80; freelance TV prodr 1980–; work incl: Hotel du Lac (BBC, BAFTA Award 1987, ACE Award 1988), Scoop (LWT), 'v' (Ch4, Royal TV Soc Award), Or Shall We Die? (Ch4), Dutch Girls (LWT), Ball-Trap on the Côte Sauvage (BBC), Anna Lee (LWT) 1993, Pride and Prejudice (BBC, 4 BAFTA nominations, 4 Emmy nominations, 2 ACE Award nominations, TRIC Awad, VVL Award 1995/96) 1995, Emma (ITV) 1996; memb Arts Cncl Drama Panel 1975–77; memb ACTT 1979; *Books* The Making of Pride and Prejudice (1995), The Making of Jane Austen's Emma (1996); *Recreations* the countryside, books, theatre, music, croquet; *Style—* Miss Sue Birtwistle; ✉ c/o Peter Murphy, Curtis Brown, 4th Floor, Haymarket House, 28–29 Haymarket, London SW1Y 4SP (☎ 0171 396 6600)

BISCHOFF, Winfried Franz Wilhelm (Win); s of late Paul Helmut Bischoff, and Hildegard, *née* Kühne; *b* 10 May 1941; *Educ* Marist Bros Inanda Johannesburg SA, Univ of the Witwatersrand Johannesburg (BCom); *m* 1972, Rosemary Elizabeth, da of Hon Leslie John Leathers; 2 s; *Career* md Schroders Asia Ltd Hong Kong 1971–82; J Henry Schroder & Co Ltd: dir 1983–, chm 1983–94; Schroders plc: dir 1983–, gp chief exec 1984–95, chm 1995–; dir Schroder Wertheim Holdings NYC 1986–; non-exec dir Cable and Wireless plc 1991– (dep chm 1995–); *Recreations* opera, music, golf; *Clubs* 300 Club (Japan), Frilford Heath Golf (Woking); *Style—* Win Bischoff, Esq; ✉ Schroders plc, 120 Cheapside, London EC2V 6DS (☎ 0171 382 6000)

BISCOE, Michael; s of Guy Biscoe (d 1967), of London, and Sheila Mary, *née* Seymour Chalk; *b* 4 May 1938; *Educ* Westminster, Selwyn Coll Cambridge (MA, DipArch); *m* 28 Jan 1967, Kari Jetten, da of Edward Beresford Davies, MD, of Cambridge, and late Hendriette Marie, *née* Fuglesang; 1 s (Guy b 14 May 1970), 1 da (Henrietta b 5 Jan 1968); *Career* Nat Serv Royal Artillery, served Cyprus 1956–58; sr ptnr Biscoe & Stanton 1977– (ptnr 1967–); govr Colfe's Sch 1996–; Liveryman: Worshipful Co of Leathersellers 1972 (Fourth Warden 1993), Worshipful Co of Chartered Surveyors 1975; RIBA, FRICS; *Recreations* music, rowing, shooting, fishing; *Clubs* Boodle's, Chelsea Arts; *Style—* Michael Biscoe, Esq; ✉ Biscoe & Stanton Architects, 35 Alfred Place, London WC1E 7DP (☎ 0171 580 9484, fax 0171 580 9487)

BISCOE, Prof Timothy John; s of Rev W H Biscoe, TD (d 1969), and M G A Biscoe, *née* Middleton (d 1989); *b* 28 April 1932; *Educ* Latymer Upper Sch, London Hosp Med Coll (BSc, MB BS), DSc (London) 1993, FRCP 1993; *m* 17 Sept 1955, Daphne Miriam, da of W P Gurton; 1 s (Max), 2 da (Sarah, Mandy); *Career* short serv cmmn RAMC 1958–61; Inst of Animal Physiology Babraham Cambridge 1962–65, Inst of Advanced Studies Canberra 1965–66, Cardiovascular Research Institute San Francisco Med Center 1966–68; Dept of Physiology Univ of Bristol: research assoc 1969–70, prof 1970–79, head of dept 1975–79; UCL: Jodrell prof Dept of Physiology 1979–92, head Dept of Physiology 1979–88, vice provost 1990–92; dep vice-chllr Univ of Hong Kong 1992–95, pro-provost UCL 1996–; pubns in scientific jls and books on neurobiology; memb Academia Europaea 1991; *Recreations* reading, writing, looking; *Clubs* Garrick; *Style—* Prof Timothy Biscoe; ✉ University College London, Gower Street, London WC1E 6BT (☎ 0171 380 7022, fax 0171 813 2812)

BISHOP, Alan Henry; CB (1989); s of Robert Dick Bishop (d 1968), and May Douglas, *née* Watson (d 1968); *b* 12 Sept 1929; *Educ* George Heriot's Sch Edinburgh, Univ of Edinburgh (MA); *m* 30 March 1959, Marjorie Anne, da of Joseph Henry Conlan (d 1988); 1 s (Keith b 1961), 1 da (Susan b 1960); *Career* asst princ Dept of Agric 1954–59, private sec to Lord John Hope (Lord Glendevon) and G Leburn (jr mins SO) 1958–59, princ Dept of Agric and Fisheries Scotland 1960–63 and 1967–68, first sec Food and Agric Copenhagen and The Hague 1963–66; asst sec: Scot Devpt Dept 1968–69, Royal Cmmn on the Constitution 1969–73, SO 1973–80; asst under sec of state SO 1980–84; princ estab offr 1984–89, HM Chief Inspr of Prisons for Scotland 1989–94; *Recreations* contract bridge, theatre, golf, reading; *Clubs* New (Edinburgh), Murrayfield Golf (Edinburgh), Melville Bridge (Edinburgh); *Style—* Alan Bishop, Esq, CB; ✉ Beaumont Court, 19/8 Wester Coates Gardens, Edinburgh EH12 5LT (☎ and fax 0131 346 4641)

BISHOP, (William) Archie; s of Evelyn Archie Bishop (1979), and Gertrude, *née* Pocock (1988); *b* 21 July 1937; *Educ* Thames Nautical Training Coll, Sir John Cass Coll, Coll of Law; *m* 1961 (m dis 1996); 1 s (Mark b 14 Feb 1966), 1 da (Paula b 24 Feb 1963); *Career* deck offr P & O Line 1954–60; slr in UK and Hong Kong; Holman Fenwick & Willan: mangr Admiralty Dept 1960–70, ptnr 1970–89, sr ptnr 1989–; legal advsr to the International Salvage Union, examiner in Admiralty; Freeman: City of London, Worshipful Co of Watermen and Lightermen, City of London Solicitors Co; memb Law Soc; *Recreations* golf, horse riding, hunting, fishing, painting; *Clubs* IOD, RAC, Hurlingham; *Style—* Archie Bishop, Esq; ✉ Holman, Fenwick & Willan, Marlow House, Lloyds Avenue, London EC3N 3AL (☎ 0171 488 2300, fax 0171 481 0316)

BISHOP, Christopher Charles Rigby; s of Michael Bishop, and Beatrice, *née* Villemer; *b* 17 Nov 1952; *Educ* Stonyhurst, Magdalene Coll Cambridge (MA), St Thomas' Hosp Med Sch (MB BChir, MChir); *m* 17 Sept 1977, Anthea Jane, *née* Tilzey; 2 s (Charles Alexander Rigby b 17 May 1983, Hugo Guy Pierre b 8 July 1984), 2 da (Lucie Marie Henrietta b 11 Sept 1986, Gabrielle Marie Susanna (twin) b 11 Sept 1986); *Career* surgical registrar Southampton Univ Hosps 1980–82, sr surgical registrar St Thomas' Hosp 1987–90 (surgical registrar 1982–84, lectr in surgery 1984–87), conslt surgn Middx, UC and Whittington Hosps 1991–; vascular fell Scripps Clinic and Research Fndn Calif USA 1989, Hunterian prof RCS 1991; *Recreations* yachting, skiing; *Style—* Christopher Bishop, Esq; ✉ 149 Harley Street, London W1 (☎ 0171 235 6086, mobile 0831 631007)

BISHOP, Christopher David; s of Joseph Charles Bishop (d 1992), and Zephyr Ethel, *née* Breese; *b* 8 Sept 1938; *Educ* Eastbourne Coll; *m* 22 July 1961, Judith, da of Harry Leonard Wise (d 1986); 3 s (David Charles b 1962, Simon Christopher b 1965, Guy Elliott b 1970), 1 da (Lucinda b 1968); *Career* articled clerk then mangr Baker Sutton and Co 1956–71, co sec GR Merton (Agencies) Ltd 1971–74, princ Christopher Bishop and Co 1974–85, ptnr Ernst and Whinney (now Ernst & Young) 1985–; FCA; *Recreations* hunting, equestrian sports, golf; *Clubs* City of London; *Style—* Christopher Bishop, Esq; ✉ Ernst & Young, Becket House, 1 Lambeth Palace Rd, London SE1 7EU (☎ 0171 928 2000, fax 0171 928 1345, telex 885234)

BISHOP, (Thomas) David; s of Thomas Challis Bishop (d 1981), and Mary, *née* Simmons; *b* 22 Aug 1934; *Educ* Charterhouse; *m* 20 Sept 1966, Josephine Anne, da of Lionel Mitchell Robinson, of Rodney, Brockenhurst, Hants; 1 s (Jeremy b 1970), 1 da (Belinda b 1973); *Career* Nat Serv RA 1955–56; admitted slr 1960, ptnr Hunters 1961–; dir Slrs' Benevolent Assoc 1972–; Liveryman Worshipful Co of Masons 1988– (clerk 1986–87); *Recreations* cricket, tennis, skiing, shooting, classical music, travelling; *Clubs* Boodle's, MCC; *Style—* David Bishop, Esq; ✉ Hunters, 9 New Square, Lincoln's Inn, London WC2A 3QN (☎ 0171 412 0050, fax 0171 412 0049)

BISHOP, David Broughton Gibson; s of Col A W G Bishop, MC (d 1979); *b* 1 Feb 1933; *Educ* Wellington, Jesus Coll Cambridge; *m* 1974, Judith, *née* Brown; 1 s, 1 da; *Career* solicitor; ptnr Baileys Shaw & Gillett 1961– (sr ptnr 1979–88); dir Syndicate Administration Ltd, Devoran Trustees Ltd and other cos; *Recreations* cricket, skiing, shooting, gardening, antiques; *Clubs* South Winchester Golf, Lowtonian Soc, Hawks; *Style—* David Bishop, Esq; ✉ Old Rectory, Easton, nr Winchester, Hants (☎ 01962 779205); Baileys Shaw and Gillett, 17 Queen Square, London WC1N 3RH (☎ 0171 837 5455, fax 0171 837 0071)

BISHOP, David Charles; s of Kenneth Charles Bishop, MBE, of Sedbergh, Cumbria, and Margaret Cecilia Bishop, JP, *née* Birtwistle; *b* 6 April 1947; *Educ* Sedbergh, Gonville and Caius Coll Cambridge (MA); *m* 6 June 1980, Ann Winifred, da of Leslie Brian Tallon (d 1984), of Blundellsands; 1 s (Michael b 1983), 1 da (Julia b 1984); *Career* admitted slr 1972; ptnr Laces & Co, Notary Public 1984, ptnr Lace Mawer Slrs 1988–; chm Liverpool Branch Soc of Tst and Estate Practitioners 1991, assoc Assoc of Pension Lawyers 1990, memb Law Soc, memb Int Tax Planning Assoc 1995; *Recreations* ornithology; *Style—* David Bishop, Esq; ✉ 27 Victoria Road, Freshfield, Liverpool L37 7AQ (☎ and fax 01704 873819); Lace Mawer, Solicitors, 43 Castle St, Liverpool L2 9SU (☎ 0151 236 2002, fax 0151 236 2585, mobile 0385 901782)

BISHOP, Sir Frederick Arthur; kt (1975), CB (1960), CVO (1957); s of late A J Bishop, of Bristol, and Mary Shaw; *b* 4 Dec 1915; *Educ* Colston's Hosp, Univ of London (LLB); *m* 1940, Elizabeth Finlay, da of Samuel Stevenson, of Belfast; 2 s, 1 da; *Career* Miny of Food 1947, PPS to Min of Food 1949–52, asst sec to Cabinet Office 1952–55, PPS to PM 1956–59; dep sec: Cabinet 1959–61, MAFF 1961–64; perm sec Miny of Land and Natural Resources 1964–65; dir: S Pearson and Sons Ltd 1966–70, Pearson Longman Ltd 1970–77; dir-gen Nat Tst 1971–75; dir: English China Clays, Lloyds Bank Ltd (Devon and Cornwall) 1975–86; *Style—* Sir Frederick Bishop, CB, CVO; ✉ Manor Barn, Bramshott, Liphook, Hants

BISHOP, Sir George Sidney; kt (1975), CB (1958), OBE (1947); s of late Joseph Bishop, of Wigan, Lancs; *b* 15 Oct 1913; *Educ* Ashton-in-Makerfield GS, LSE; *m* 1, 1940 (m dis 1961), Marjorie, da of C H Woodruff, of Illingworth; 1 da; m 2, 1961, Una, da of late C F C Padel, of Inkpen, Berks; *Career* joined Civil Serv 1940, under-sec MAFF 1949 (dep sec 1959–61), vice chm Int Wheat Cncl 1959, memb Panel for Civil Serv Manpower Review 1968–70, chm West India Ctee 1969–71; Booker McConnell Ltd: dir 1961–82, vice chm 1970–71, chm 1972–79, chm Bookers International Holdings Ltd 1964–70, dir IBEC (agribusiness assoc of Booker McConnell) to 1983; dir: Nigerian Sugar Co Ltd 1966–70, Barclays Bank International 1972–83, Barclays Bank 1974–83, Ranks Hovis McDougall 1976–84, International Basic Economy Corpn USA 1980–83; memb Cncl CBI 1973–80; *Style—* Sir George Bishop, CB, OBE; ✉ Brenva, Egham's Wood Rd, Beaconsfield, Bucks (☎ 01494 673096)

BISHOP, James Drew; s of Sir (Frank) Patrick Bishop, MBE, MP (d 1972), and his 1 wife Vera Sophie, *née* Drew (d 1953); *b* 18 June 1929; *Educ* Haileybury, CCC Cambridge; *m* 1959, Brenda, da of George Pearson; 2 s; *Career* The Times: foreign corr 1957–64, foreign news ed 1964–66, asst ed features 1966–70; ed Illustrated London News 1971–87; dir: Illustrated London News and Sketch Ltd 1971, International Thomas Publishing Ltd 1980–85; ed in chief Illustrated London News Pubns 1987–95; chm Assoc of Br Editors 1987–95; memb Advsy Bd Annual Register 1970–; *Books* A Social History of Edwardian Britain (1977), A Social History of the First World War (1982), The Story of the Times (with Oliver Woods, 1983), Illustrated Counties of England (ed, 1985); *Recreations* reading, walking; *Clubs* Oxford and Cambridge, MCC; *Style—* James Bishop, Esq; ✉ 11 Willow Rd, London NW3 (☎ 0171 435 4403, fax 0171 435 0778)

BISHOP, John Andrew; s of Sidney Bishop (d 1978), and Winnie Bishop; *b* 1 Aug 1946; *Educ* London GS; *m* 20 March 1972, Bernadette; 2 s (Sebastian Luke b 11 April 1974, Oliver Sam b 30 Jan 1977); *Career* photographer; worked regularly for: Vogue, Elle (Br, French, Italian), Harpers, Tatler, Marie Claire; also worked for major advertisers including: L'Oreal, Max Factor, Harrods, Next, Austin Reed, Laura Ashley; *Recreations* sports; *Style—* John Bishop, Esq; ✉ Studio, 126 Shirland Rd, London W9 2BT (☎ 0171 286 8136)

BISHOP, John Anthony Fremantle; s of Evan Winfrid Bishop, OBE, of Lymington, Hants, and Mary, *née* Godwin-Smith (d 1983); *b* 17 Feb 1949; *Educ* Warminster Sch, LAMDA; *Career* BBC TV: floor asst 1971, asst floor mangr, then prodn mangr 1974, dir light entertainment 1980, prodr light entertainment 1984, exec prodr 1988, asst head of variety and light entertainment 1988–91; controller of entertainment Carlton Television 1991–; *Recreations* theatre and swimming; *Style—* John Bishop, Esq; ✉ Carlton UK Television Ltd, 101 St Martin's Lane, London WC2N 4AZ (☎ 0171 240 4000)

BISHOP, Dr John Edward; s of Reginald John Bishop, and Eva, *née* Lucas; *b* 23 Feb 1935; *Educ* Cotham Sch Bristol, St John's Coll Cambridge (MA, MusB), Univ of Reading, Univ of Edinburgh (DMus); *Career* asst dir then sr dir of music Worksop Coll 1958–72; Birmingham Sch of Music 1972–86: dir of studies, head of sch, head of admissions, then head of organ studies; freelance concert organist and pianist 1986–; former pres Birmingham, Sheffield and Bristol Organists' Assocs, former govr of City of Birmingham Poly; memb: Cncl Incorporated Soc of Musicians, Kingsdown Duo (violin and piano); hon fell Birmingham Sch of Music 1986; FRCO (chm), ADCM; *Recreations* walking, savouring the countryside, railways; *Style—* Dr John Bishop; ✉ 98 High Kingsdown, Bristol BS2 8ER (☎ 0117 942 3373)

BISHOP, His Hon Judge; John Edward; s of Albert George Bishop (d 1988), of Banstead, and Frances Marion, *née* Clericetti (d 1984); *b* 9 Feb 1943; *Educ* St Edward's Sch Oxford; *m* 29 June 1968, Elizabeth Ann, da of Frank Grover; 2 da (Caroline Jane b

20 Nov 1970, Sally Ann b 22 Feb 1973); *Career* articled to Peter Carter-Ruck Messrs Oswald Hickson Collier & Co London WC2 1962–66, admitted slr 1966, ptnr Messrs Copley Clark & Co Sutton Surrey 1969–81, ptnr Messrs Tuck & Mann Epsom Surrey 1981–85; registrar: Woolwich Co Ct 1985–88, Croydon Co Ct 1988–93; recorder 1990–93 (asst recorder 1987–90), district judge 1992–93, circuit judge (SE Circuit) 1993–; memb The Law Soc 1966, pres Mid Surrey Law Soc 1980–81; *Recreations* golf, walking, music, reading, garden, family; *Clubs* Walton Heath Golf; *Style*— His Hon Judge Bishop; ✉ Kingston County Court, St James' Road, Kingston-upon-Thames, Surrey KT1 2AD

BISHOP, John Maurice; s of Edwin Maurice Bishop, of Paignton, Devon, and Joyce Emily, *née* Edmunds; *b* 6 May 1947; *Educ* Sherborne, Queen Mary Coll Univ of London (LLB); *m* 1, 30 March 1970 (m dis 1985), Maureen, *née* Maloney; 1 s (Edward b 19 Dec 1973), 4 da (Laura b 6 March 1976, Sophie b 10 Nov 1979, Alice b 26 July 1982, Chloe (twin) b 26 July 1982); m 2, 18 April 1986, Virginia, *née* Welsh; 1 step da (Sophie b 22 April 1980); *Career* slr; Masons: articled clerk 1969–71, asst slr 1971, salaried ptnr 1972, equity ptnr 1973, managing ptnr 1987–90, sr ptnr 1991–; official referee Solicitors' Assoc (chm 1990–94, pres 1995–); memb Law Soc 1969, admitted slr Hong Kong 1983, MFB 1975, ACIArb 1980; *Recreations* golf, horse riding, shooting; *Clubs* Aldrburgh Golf, Rye Golf; *Style*— John Bishop, Esq; ✉ Masons (Solicitors), 30 Aylesbury Street, London EC1R 0ER (☎ 0171 490 4000, fax 0171 490 2545)

BISHOP, John Michael; s of Lt Wilfred Charles John Michael Bishop (d 1988), of Whitstable, Kent, and Margery Bains, *née* Emmerson (d 1990); *b* 1 March 1947; *Educ* Kent Coll Canterbury, LSE (LLB); *m* 12 Aug 1982, Laurie Marie, da of Lyman Charles Harris (d 1980), of Virginia Beach, Virginia, USA; 2 da (Heather Virginia, Lucy Cecilia); *Career* Kent and Co of London Yeomanry (TA) 1965–67; head of chambers at 7 Stone Buildings 1986; memb Hon Soc Middle Temple; *Recreations* photography, antiquarian books; *Style*— John Bishop, Esq; ✉ Greenfields, Pean Hill, Whitstable, Kent; 7 Stone Buildings, Lincoln's Inn, London WC2A 3SZ (☎ 0171 242 0961, fax 0171 405 7028)

BISHOP, Kevin John; s of Lindsay Bishop, and Mary Inez, *née* King; *Educ* South Bromley Coll, Plymouth Poly Coll of Art (BA); *Career* televison director and producer; dir: Wogan 1984–86, Paul Daniels Magic Show 1987, French and Saunders 1987–88, Victoria Wood 1989, HM Queen Mother's 90th Birthday Gala; prodr: Michael Barrymore's Saturday Night Out 1988–89, Rory Bremner 1990–91, Rita Rudner 1991, The Children's Royal Variety Performance 1991, 1993 and 1994, A Bit of Fry and Laurie 1991, The Royal Variety Performance 1992, 1994 and 1996, Showstoppers 1995; *Style*— Kevin Bishop, Esq; ✉ BBC TV, Wood Lane, London W12 (☎ 0181 743 8000)

BISHOP, Martin Egerton; s of Louis Egerton Bishop (d 1973), of Worthing, Sussex; *b* 8 June 1929; *Educ* St Edward's Sch Oxford, Univ of St Andrews; *m* 22 April 1961, Ann, da of Keith Ernest Thurley (d 1980), of Padstow, Cornwall; 2 da (Samantha b 1966, Georgina b 1968); *Career* RA 1947–49; Int Stock Exchange 1959–94; Greig, Middleton & Co 1988–94, Batten & Co Slrs 1994–96, investment conslt 1996–; memb The Bow Gp; memb Securities Inst; *Recreations* photography, music; *Style*— M E Bishop, Esq; ✉ The Thatched Cottage, Mawgan-in-Meneage, Helston, Cornwall TR12 6AB (☎ 01326 221306)

BISHOP, Sir Michael David; kt (1991), CBE (1986); s of Clive Leonard Bishop (d 1980), and Lilian, *née* Frost (d 1989); *b* 10 Feb 1942; *Educ* Mill Hill; *Career* chm: Airlines of Britain Holdings plc, Manx Airlines 1982–, Loganair 1983–, British Midland Airways (joined 1964); dir Airtours plc 1987–; chm Channel 4 Television 1993– (dep chm 1991–93), dir Williams Holdings plc 1993–; memb: E Midlands Electricity Bd 1980–83, E Midlands Bd Central Ind TV plc 1981–90; chm D'Oyly Carte Opera Tst; *Recreations* music; *Clubs* Brooks's, St James's (Manchester); *Style*— Sir Michael Bishop, CBE; ✉ Donington Hall, Castle Donington, nr Derby (☎ 01332 854000, telex 37172)

BISHOP, Patrick Joseph; s of Ernest Bishop, of Wimbledon, and Kathleen, *née* Kelly; *b* 17 Oct 1952; *Educ* Wimbledon Coll, CCC Oxford (exhibitioner, BA); *m* 1989 (m dis), Marie, da of William Colvin, of Oyster Bay, NY; *Career* journalist; training scheme Mirror Group Newspapers 1974–76, freelance 1976–78, news reporter Evening Standard 1978–79, The Observer 1979–84 (news reporter, NI corr, corr with Br Forces in Falklands War), reporter ITN Channel Four News 1984–85, reporter and diplomatic corr The Sunday Times 1985–87; The Sunday Telegraph: sr corr 1987–88, Middle East corr 1988–92, sr foreign corr 1992–95, foreign ed 1995–; chm Medécins sans Frontières (UK) 1995– (dir 1992–95); *Books* The Winter War (with John Witherow, 1982), The Provisional IRA (with Eamonn Mallie, 1987), Famous Victory (1992); *Style*— Patrick Bishop, Esq; ✉ The Daily Telegraph, 1 Canada Square, Canary Wharf, London E14 5DT (☎ 0171 538 5000)

BISHOPP, Michael; s of Dennis George Bishopp, of Shrewsbury, and Vivienne Anne Mortimer, *née* Patton; *b* 7 May 1950; *Educ* Ludlow GS, Priory Sch Shrewsbury, Wadham Coll Oxford (MA Jurisprudence); *Career* chartered accountant; Price Waterhouse: joined 1971, ptnr 1983–, head executive & benefit servs 1990–93, head personal tax 1993–95, dir of operations 1995–; FCA 1980 (ACA 1974); *Recreations* travel, architecture, cars, food; *Style*— Michael Bishopp, Esq; ✉ Price Waterhouse, Southwark Towers, 32 London Bridge Street, London SE1 9SY (☎ 0171 939 3000)

BISS, Adele; *b* 18 Oct 1944; *m* Roger Davies; *Career* grad trainee Consumer Product Mktg Unilever 1968–70, head of Winter Holiday Div then head of Mktg Communications and PR Thomson Holidays 1970–78, dir Biss Lancaster until 1990 (fndr 1978, sold to WCRS, now Aegis Gp Plc); chm BTA and English Tourist Bd 1993–96, fndr chm A S Biss & Co (political and public affrs) 1996–; non-exec dir: Bowthorpe plc, Eurostar (UK) Ltd, Harry Ramsden's plc; *Style*— Ms Adele Biss; ✉ A S Biss & Co, 8 Wilfred Street, London SW1E 6PL (☎ 0171 828 3030, fax 0171 931 7871)

BISSELL, Frances Mary; da of Robert Maloney, and Mary, *née* Kelly; *b* 19 Aug 1946; *Educ* Goyt Bank HS Cheshire, Cape Town HS, Allerton HS Leeds, Univ of Leeds (BA); *m* 12 Dec 1970, Thomas Emery Bissell, s of Thomas Wilson Bissell (d 1975), of Pittsburgh, USA; 1 step da (b 1958); *Career* VSO Nigeria 1965–66, asst Ecole Normale 1968–69, The British Cncl 1970– (leave of absence 1987–), freelance writer, author, broadcaster and conslt on cookery and food 1983–, The Times Cook 1987–; fndr memb Guild of Food Writers 1985; guest cook: Mandarin Oriental Hong Kong 1987 and 1990, Intercontinental Hotel London 1987 and 1988, Manila Peninsula 1989, Dusit Thani Bangkok 1992, Café Royal 1994–95; television: Frances Bissell's Westcountry Kitchen 1995, Frances Bissell's Westcountry Christmas; *Awards* Glenfiddich Cookery Writer of the Year 1994, James Beard Fndn Award 1995; *Books* A Cooks Calendar (1985), The Pleasures of Cookery (1986), Ten Dinner Parties for Two (1988), The Sainsbury's Book of Food (1989), Oriental Flavours (1990), The Real Meat Cookbook (1992), The Times Cookbook (1993), Frances Bissell's Westcountry Kitchen (1996); *Recreations* writing and cooking; *Style*— Mrs Thomas Bissell; ✉ c/o Peters Fraser and Dunlop, 5th Floor, The Chambers, Chelsea Harbour, Lots Road, London SW10 0XF (☎ 0171 376 7676, fax 0171 352 7356)

BLACH, Rudolf Karl (Rolf); s of Paul Samuel Blach (d 1940), and Hedwig Jeanette Blach (d 1968); *b* 21 Jan 1930; *Educ* Berkhamsted Sch, Trinity Coll Cambridge, St Thomas's Hosp London (MA, MB BChir, MD); *m* 26 March 1960, Lynette Cecilia (Lyn), da of Jaffray Andrew Conynghame Sceales; 2 s (Thomas b 1962, Richard b 1968), 1 da (Catherine b 1964); *Career* Lt RAMC 1956 (Capt 1957); conslt ophthalmic surgn St Mary's Hosp Paddington 1963–70, hon conslt ophthalmologist Royal Postgrad Med Sch Hammersmith 1967–74, conslt ophthalmologist St Dunstans 1967, conslt surgn Moorfields Eye Hosp 1969–95, dean Inst of Ophthalmology Univ of London 1985–91; hon conslt ophthalmologist KCH London, vice chm Br Cncl for the Prevention of Blindness; memb (formeer dep master) Oxford Congress; Freeman City of London 1967, Liveryman Worshipful Soc of Apothecaries; FRCS, FRCOphth, FRSM; *Clubs* RSM; *Style*— Rolf Blach, Esq; ✉ Lister House, 11/12 Wimpole St, London W1M 7AB (☎ 0171 636 3407, fax 0171 436 2870)

BLACK, Alan William; s of William Black, of Styvechale, Coventry, and Agnes Whyte Buchanan, *née* Wilson; *b* 21 Feb 1952; *Educ* King Henry VIII Sch, King's Coll London (LLB); *Career* slr; ptnr Linklaters & Paines 1983–; Freeman Worshipful Co of Slrs 1983; memb Law Soc; *Recreations* tennis, golf, opera and early music, Far East, searching for Schrodinger's cat; *Clubs* The Second Eleven, The Inner Theatre; *Style*— Alan Black, Esq; ✉ 16 Marryat Road, London SW19; Linklaters & Paines, Barrington House, 59–67 Gresham St, London EC2

BLACK, Alastair Kenneth Lamond; CBE (1989), DL (Gtr London 1978); s of late Kenneth Black, and Althea Joan, *née* Hanks (d 1984); *b* 14 Dec 1929; *Educ* Sherborne, Law Soc Sch of Law; *m* 1955, Elizabeth Jane (d 1995), da of Sir Henry Darlington, KCB, CMG, TD (d 1959); 1 s (Rupert), 2 da (Sarah, Susan); *Career* admitted slr 1953; Nat Serv Lt Intelligence Corps 1953–55; ptnr Messrs Burchell and Ruston 1953–94; Dep Sheriff Co of London then Gtr London 1953–74, Under Sheriff Gtr London 1974–94, Dep Sheriff Co of Surrey 1978–94; clerk to the Gen Cmmrs of Income Tax for the Divs of Holborn, Finsbury, St Paul's and Covent Garden 1966–94, clerk to the Bowyers Co 1985–94; memb House of Laity Gen Synod for Guildford Dio 1982–, lay reader 1983–, chm Gen Synod 1991, memb Bd of Social Responsibility 1992–96; pres Under Sheriffs Assoc 1987–93 (vice pres 1985–87), memb Cncl Shrievalty Assoc 1985–91; Liveryman: City of London Solicitors' Co, Worshipful Co of Bowyers; *Books* contrib to: Halsbury's Laws of England (4 edn vol 25 1978 and vol 42 1983, revised edn 1994), Atkins Court Forms (3 edn vol 19 1972 (revised edn 1985), vol 22 1968 and vol 36 1977 (revised edn 1988)), Enforcement of a Judgment, Longman Practice Notes (6 edn 1979, 7 edn 1986, 8 edn 1993); *Recreations* horse racing, gardening, travel; *Style*— Alastair Black, Esq, CBE, DL; ✉ South Lodge, Guildford Road, Effingham, Surrey (☎ 01372 452862)

BLACK, Anthony Edward Norman (Tony); OBE (1981); s of Arthur Norman Black (d 1973), of Hove, Sussex, and Phyllis Margaret, *née* Ranicar (d 1989); *b* 20 Jan 1938; *Educ* Brighton Coll, RMA Sandhurst, Army Staff Coll Camberley; *m* 1 Oct 1963, Susan Frances, da of Maj John Watt Copeland (d 1965), of Ilkley, W Yorks; 2 s (Simon b 12 July 1965, Michael b 13 March 1968); *Career* cmmnd RE 1957, served Kenya, Aden, Germany and Cyprus, Army staff course Camberley 1970, GSOI Ghana Armed Forces Staff Coll 1976–78, CO 36 Engr Regt 1978–80, Col GS MGO Secretariat 1980–82, cmd Engrs Falkland Is 1983, Cmdt Army Apprentices Coll Chepstow 1983–86, ret as Col 1987; chief exec cmmr The Scout Assoc 1987–95, ret; *Recreations* driving Ferraris, walking, gardening, Thames cruising; *Style*— Tony Black, Esq, OBE; ✉ c/o National Westminster Bank, 50 High Street, Egham, Surrey TW20 9EU

BLACK, Barrington; s of Louis L Black, and Millicent, *née* Brash; *b* 16 Aug 1932; *Educ* Roundhay Sch, Univ of Leeds (LLB); *m* 19 June 1962, Diana Heller, JP, da of Simon Heller; 2 s (Matthew b 1965, Jonathan b 1968), 2 da (Harriette b 1963, Anna b 1971); *Career* admitted slr 1956; cmmnd RASC 1956–58; met stipendiary magistrate 1984–93, chm Inner London Juvenille Court 1986–93, recorder of the Crown Ct 1991–93, circuit judge (SE Circuit) 1993–; memb Br Acad of Forensic Science 1976–; former pres Univ of Leeds Union, memb Court and Cncl Univ of Leeds, vice pres NUS, chm Family Ct 1991–93; *Recreations* music, opera, ski-bobbing; *Style*— His Hon Judge Black; ✉ Harrow Crown Court, London HA1 4TU

BLACK, Colin Hyndmarsh; s of Robert Black, and Daisy Louise, *née* Morris; *b* 4 Feb 1930; *Educ* Ayr Acad, Fettes, Univ of St Andrews (MA), Univ of Edinburgh (LLB); *m* 1955, Christine Fleurette, *née* Browne; 1 s, 1 da; *Career* ptnr i/c investmt mgmnt Brander and Cruickshank Aberdeen 1957–71, dep chm Globe Investment Trust 1983–90 (joined 1971); chm: Scottish Widows' Fund and Life Assurance Society 1987–95 (dir 1968–95), Association of Investment Trust Companies 1987–89, Kleinwort Benson Investment Management Ltd 1988–95, The Merchants Trust plc 1993– (dir 1992–), Advsy Ctee ABC Property Fund 1993–, Govett Asian Smaller Companies Investment Trust Ltd 1994–; non-exec dir: Temple Bar Investment Trust 1963–, Electra Investment Trust 1975–94, Clyde Petroleum 1976–96, Kleinwort Benson Group plc 1988–95, Scottish Power plc 1990–95, The East German Investment Trust 1990–, The Wisley Golf Club plc 1994–96, Postern Fund Management Ltd 1996–; advsr to Chm and Managing Ptnr UK Ptnrship of Richard Ellis 1989–95; *Recreations* golf, gardening, reading, watching cricket, walking labradors; *Clubs* New (Edinburgh), Wisley Golf; *Style*— Colin Black, Esq; ✉ The Merchants Trust plc, PO Box 191, 10 Fenchurch St, London EC3M 3LB (☎ 0171 956 6600, fax 0171 929 0296, telex 9413545)

BLACK, Hon Conrad Moffat; PC (Canada, 1992), OC (1990); *b* 25 Aug 1944; *Educ* Carleton Univ (BA), Laval Univ (LLL), McGill Univ (MA); *m* 1, 1978 (m dis 1992), (Shirley) Joanna Catherine Louise; 2 s, 1 da; m 2, 21 July 1992, Barbara Amiel, newspaper columnist; *Career* chm The Telegraph plc 1987– (dir 1985–); chm and chief exec: Hollinger Inc 1987– (chm 1985–), Argus Corporation Ltd 1985– (chm 1979–), The Ravelston Corporation Ltd 1985– (chm 1979–); chm Saturday Night Magazine Ltd 1987, dep chm American Publishing Company 1987–, dep chm John Fairfax Holdings Ltd (dir 1992–), chief exec offr Southam Inc 1994–, co-chm The Sun-Times Company 1994–; dir: Eaton's of Canada Ltd 1976–, Canadian Imperial Bank of Commerce 1977–, Brascan Ltd 1986–, The Financial Post Company Ltd 1988–, The Spectator (1828) Ltd 1990–, Unimédia Inc 1990– (chm 1988–90), Key Publishers Co Ltd 1991–; memb: Advsy Bd The National Interest Washington DC, Chm's Cncl of the Americas Soc, The Int Inst for Strategic Studies, The Trilateral Cmmn, Steering Ctee Bilderberg Meetings, Advsy Bd St Mary's Hosp West Palm Beach Florida, Advsy Bd Gulfstream Aerospace Corp 1994–; patron The Malcolm Muggeridge Fndn; Hon LLD: Carleton Univ 1989, St Francis Xavier 1979, McMaster Univ 1979; Hon LittD Univ of Windsor 1979; *Books* Duplessis (1977), A Life in Progress (1993); *Clubs* Everglades (Palm Beach), Toronto, Toronto Golf, York (Toronto), University, Mount Royal (Montreal), Athenaeum, Beefsteak, White's; *Style*— The Hon Conrad Black, PC, OC; ✉ c/o 10 Toronto St, Toronto, Ont M5C 2B7, Canada (☎ 00 1 416 363 8721); The Telegraph plc, 1 Canada Square, Canary Wharf, London E14 5DT (☎ 0171 538 6219)

BLACK, Sir (Robert) David; 3 Bt (UK 1922), of Midgham, Co Berks, DL (Caithness 1991); s of Sir Robert Andrew Stransham Black, 2 Bt, ED (d 1979); *b* 29 March 1929; *Educ* Eton; *m* 1, 1953 (m dis 1972), Rosemary Diana, da of Sir Rupert John Hardy, 4 Bt; 2 da (Diana Sarah (Mrs Mark Newton) b 1955, Joanna Rosemary (Mrs Christopher R C Wild) b 1966), and 1 da decd; m 2, 1973, (Dorothy) Maureen, da of Maj Charles Robert Eustace Radclyffe, and wid of Alan Roger Douglas Pilkington; *Career* formerly Maj Royal Horse Gds and Maj Berks and Westminster Dragoon Yeo 1964–67; jt MFH Garth and S Berks Hunt 1964–72; vice chm Berks Eastern Wessex TAVR 1985–92; Hon Col 94 (Berks Yeo) Signal Sqdn 1988–; High Sheriff Oxfordshire 1993–94; *Clubs* Cavalry and Guards', Flyfishers'; *Style*— Sir David Black, Bt, DL; ✉ Beech Farm House, Woodcote, nr Reading, Berks RG8 0FX (☎ 01491 872160); Shurrery Lodge, Shebster, Thurso, Caithness (☎ 01847 81252)

BLACK, Don; s of Morris Blackstone (d 1979), of Hackney, London, and Betsy, *née* Kersh (d 1966); *b* 21 June 1938; *Educ* Cassland Rd Sch Hackney; *m* 7 Dec 1958, Shirley Kitty, da of James Berg; 2 s (Grant Howard b 28 Jan 1961, Clive Darren b 24 Aug 1963); *Career* lyricist; office jr New Musical Express 1955, music publisher, professional comedian, agent and mangr for Brian Epstein's NEMS co; chm Br Acad of Songwriters Composers and Authors 1986–, frequent broadcaster and chm of the Vivien Ellis prize held at the Guildhall Sch of Music; worked with well known composers incl: Andrew Lloyd Webber, John Barry, Henry Mancini, Elmer Bernstein, Charles Aznavour, Quincy Jones, Jule Styne, Charles Strouse; *Musicals* incl: Tell Me on Sunday, Billy, Aspects of Love, Song and Dance, Sunset Boulevard; *Films* incl: Born Free, To Sir With Love, Diamonds are Forever, Ben, The Man With The Golden Gun, Thunderball, True Grit; *Awards* Oscar Award (for Born Free 1966), Golden Globe Award, 4 Ivor Novello Awards, 3 Tony Nominations, numerous Platinum, Gold and Silver discs; *Recreations* swimming, snooker; *Clubs* RAC, Groucho, St James's; *Style—* Don Black, Esq; ✉ c/o John Cohen, Clintons Solicitors, 55 Drury Lane, London WC2B 5SQ (☎ 0171 379 6080, fax 0171 240 9310)

BLACK, Donald Sinclair; s of Frank Charles Briscoe Black (d 1988), of 26 Learmonth Terrace, Edinburgh, and Anne Betty Hirst, *née* Sinclair (d 1989); *b* 4 July 1941; *Educ* Merchiston Castle Sch Edinburgh, Univ of Edinburgh (LLB); *m* 30 Sept 1972, (Evelyn) Bronwen Louise, da of William Kennedy, of Sidmouth, Devon; 3 s (Roderick b 1975, Graeme b 1979, Alistair b 1982), 1 da (Tamara b 1973); *Career* CA; articled Deloittes (Edinburgh) 1963–67, Investmt Dept Royal Bank of Scotland 1967–68, Edinburgh Fund Managers Fund 1968–70, dir Panmure Gordon & Co Ltd 1975–96 (joined 1970), Leafe City Consultancy 1996–; chm London Ctee Scottish Chamber Orchestra; MICAS 1966; *Recreations* skiing, tennis; *Style—* Donald Black, Esq; ✉ Leafe City Consultancy, 19 Little Russell Street, London WC1A 2HN (☎ 0171 419 0994)

BLACK, Dr (Ann) Dora; *b* 2 July 1932; *Educ* Univ of Birmingham (MB ChB), Inst of Psychiatry (DPM); *m* 4 Dec 1955, Jack Black, *qv*; 2 s (David b 1960, Andrew b 1961), 1 da (Sophie b 1963); *Career* conslt child and adolescent psychiatrist: Edgware Gen Hosp 1968–84, Royal Free Hosp 1984–95; dir Traumatic Stress Clinic 1995–; author of chapters and papers on: bereavement and traumatic bereavement in childhood, family therapy, liaison psychiatry; lately assoc ed British Journal of Psychiatry; chm Inst of Family Therapy London 1989–92, memb Cncl Cruse (nat charity for bereavement care) 1969–95; Winston Churchill travelling fell 1993; MCPCH 1996; FRCPsych 1979 (MRCPsych 1971); *Books* Child Psychiatry and the Law (jtly, 1989), Child and Adolescent Psychiatry (with D Cottrell, 1993), When Father Kills Mother (jtly, 1993), Psychological Trauma: a developmental approach (jtly, 1996); *Recreations* travel, theatre, friends; *Style—* Dr Dora Black; ✉ Traumatic Stress Clinic, 73 Charlotte Street, London W1P 1LB (☎ 0171 530 3666, fax 0171 530 3677, e-mail chtrauma@ptsd.demon.co.uk)

BLACK, Sir Douglas Andrew Kilgour; kt (1973); s of Rev Walter Kilgour Black (d 1951), and Mary Jane, *née* Crichton; *b* 29 May 1913; *Educ* Forfar Acad, Univ of St Andrews; *m* 1948, Mollie, da of Edward Thorn (d 1962); 1 s, 2 da; *Career* served WWII in RAMC as Maj (India); prof of med Univ of Manchester 1959–78, chief scientist DHSS 1973–77; chm Working Pty on: Inequalities in Health 1977–80, Childhood Leukaemia in W Cumbria 1983–84; pres: RCP 1977–83, BMA 1984–85; KStJ 1989; *Books* Invitation to Medicine (1987), Recollections and Reflections (1987); *Recreations* reading, writing; *Clubs* Athenaeum; *Style—* Sir Douglas Black; ✉ The Old Forge, Duchess Close, Whitchurch-on-Thames, nr Reading RG8 7EN (☎ 0118 984 4693)

BLACK, Air Vice-Marshal George Philip; CB (1987), OBE (1967), AFC (1962, and bar 1971); s of William Black, and Elizabeth Edward, *née* Philip; *b* 10 July 1932; *Educ* Aberdeen Acad, Jt Servs Staff Coll, RCDS; *m* 1954, Ella Ruddiman, da of Edwin Stanley Walker (d 1961); 2 s (Stuart Douglas b 1955, Ian Craig b 1959); *Career* joined RAF 1950, flying trg Canada 1951, serv fighter pilot, carrier pilot (on exchange to FAA), flying instr, HQ Fighter Command, Cdr No 111 (Fighter) Sqdn 1964–66, ldr Lightning Aerobatic Team 1965, Cdr Lightning Operational Conversion Unit 1967–69, Cdr No 5 (Fighter) Sqdn 1969–70, jssc 1970, air plans MOD 1971–72, Station Cdr RAF Wildenrath 1972–74, Harrier Field Force Cdr RAF Germany 1972–74, Gp Capt Ops HQ 38 Gp 1974–76, RCDS 1977, Gp Capt Ops HQ 11 (Fighter) Gp 1978–80, Cdr Allied Air Defence Sector One 1980–83, Commandant ROC 1983–84, DCS (Ops), HQ AAFCE 1984–87, Air ADC to HM The Queen 1981–83; sr def advsr Ferranti Defence Systems Edinburgh 1987–92, dir of mil business GEC Marconi Defence Systems 1993–; FIMgt 1977; *Recreations* military aviation, model railways, philately; *Clubs* RAF; *Style—* Air Vice-Marshal George Black, CB, OBE, AFC; ✉ GEC Marconi Defence Systems Ltd, The Grove, Warren Lane, Stanmore, Middlesex HA7 4LY (☎ 0181 420 3944, fax 0181 420 3969)

BLACK, Jack; *b* 9 Jan 1932; *Educ* Towcester GS, Hendon County Sch, UCL (LLB); *m* 4 Dec 1955, Dr (Ann) Dora Black, *qv*, *née* Braham; 2 s (David b 1960, Andrew b 1961), 1 da (Sophie b 1963); *Career* Nat Serv RASC 2 Lt, Battalion Courts Martial Offr and Asst Adjutant 1954–56; admitted slr 1954; sr ptnr Heald Nickinson 1984–91 (ptnr 1956), conslt Radcliffes Crossman Block 1991–; memb: Cncl Int Copyright Soc, Legal Ctee German Chamber of Indust and Commerce UK 1984–94; chm: Intellectual Property Cmmn Union Internationale des Avocats 1988–94, The Bentham Club UCL 1994–; dep chm Cncl Intellectual Property Inst (formerly Common Law Inst of Intellectual Property) 1995–; vice chm Br Literary and Artistic Copyright Assoc 1994– (chm 1985–93); former chm of Cncl King Alfred Sch Hampstead; memb Law Soc; fndr memb: British-German Jurists Assoc 1970–, Slrs Euro Gp 1970–; FRSA; *Books* An Introduction to EEC Law (contrib, 1972), Halsbury's Laws of England EC vols (contrib 5 edn, 1986), Merkin and Black Copyright and Designs Law (jtly 1993), Holding The Ring - The UK Performing Right Tribunal and Copyright Tribunal (Intellectual Property Inst, with M Freegard, 1995); *Recreations* the Arts, travel; *Clubs* Reform, Groucho; *Style—* Jack Black, Esq; ✉ c/o Radcliffes Crossman Block, 5 Great College St, Westminster, London SW1P 3SJ (☎ 0171 222 7040, fax 0171 222 6208, telex 919302 RADLEX G)

BLACK, James Edward (Ted); s of James Craig Black (d 1987), and Catherine Robertson, *née* Glass; *b* 6 July 1942; *Educ* Eastwood HS; *m* 1 Sept 1966, Dorothy Dow; 2 da (Sharon McCallum b 7 March 1969, Tracey Louise b 19 Nov 1973); *Career* trainee banker Commercial Bank of Scotland Ltd 1958–62, sales exec commercial fin Lloyds & Scottish Finance Ltd 1962–63, regnl dir of leasing Forward Trust Group Ltd 1963–85, md asset fin subsid of TSB Scotland Ltd 1985–87, md EFT Finance Ltd (subsid of EFT Group plc) 1987–92, md EFT Group plc 1992– (dir 1987–92); ACIB; *Recreations* contract bridge, golf; *Style—* Ted Black, Esq; ✉ EFT Group PLC, 7 John Street, Glasgow G1 1HP (☎ 0141 552 5552, fax 0141 552 2272, mobile 0374 153065)

BLACK, Prof Sir James Whyte; kt (1981); *b* 14 June 1924; *Educ* Beath HS, Univ of St Andrew's (MB ChB); *m* 16 April 1994, Prof Rona McLeod MacKie, FRSE, *qv*, da of Prof J Norman Davidson, FRS (d 1972); *Career* prof and head of Dept of Pharmacology Univ Coll London 1973–77; dir of therapeutic research Wellcome Research Laboratories 1978–84; prof of analytical pharmacology King's Coll Hosp Med Sch Univ of London 1984–; chllr Univ of Dundee 1992–; awarded Nobel Prize for Medicine 1988; FRCP, FRS; *Style—* Prof Sir James Black, FRS; ✉ Analytical Pharmacology Unit, Rayne Institute, 123 Coldharbour Lane, London SE5 9NU (☎ 0171 274 7437)

BLACK, Adm Sir (John) Jeremy; GBE (1991, MBE 1963), KCB (1987), DSO (1982); s of Alan Henry Black, and Gwendoline, *née* Westcott; *b* 17 Nov 1932; *Educ* RNC Dartmouth; *m* 1958, Alison Pamela, da of Col Philip Thomas Barber, MC (d 1965), Baluch Regt; 2 s (Simon b 1967, Julian b 1968), 1 da (Carolyn b 1965); *Career* served in HMS Belfast (Korean War, Malaysian Emergency) 1950, specialized in naval gunnery 1958, CO HMS Fiskerton (Borneo confrontation) 1962, CO HMS Decoy (Far E and Mediterranean) 1968, Naval Staff Appts 1970, 1975, 1980 and 1984, RCDS 1979; elected yr bro of Trinity House; CO HMS Invincible (Falklands War) 1982, Flag Offr 1 Flotilla 1983, Asst Chief Naval Staff 1984, Dep Chief of Def Staff (Systems) 1986, C-in-C Naval Home Cmd 1989–91, Flag ADC to HM The Queen 1989–91; non-exec chm Remy and Associates UK Ltd 1992–96; dir: Devonpost Management Ltd 1992–, Macallan Glenlivet 1993–96, Global Emerging Markets (Europe) 1993–, International Aluminium Products 1993–; Cdre RNSA 1989–91, memb Cncl RUSI 1987–89, chm Race Ctee Whitbread Round The World Race 1990–94, tstee Imperial War Museum 1992–; govr: Wellington Coll 1992–, Ocean Youth Club 1991–; Liveryman Worshipful Co of Shipwrights; Order of Royal Star of Brunei 1963; *Recreations* history, sailing; *Clubs* Boodles, Royal Yacht Sqdn, RN Sailing Assoc (Cdre 1989–91), RN Club of 1765 and 1785 (pres 1992–95), St Barbara Assoc (pres 1990–93); *Style—* Adm Sir Jeremy Black, GBE, KCB, DSO; ✉ Crabtree Farmhouse, Durley, Southampton SO32 2AB

BLACK, Jill; da of Austin Hemingsley (d 1969), of Dulwich, and Veronica Elizabeth, *née* Smith; *b* 30 Oct 1930; *Educ* Gardenhurst Sch Burnham-on-Sea Somerset, Westfield Coll London (BA); *m* 1, 28 April 1960 (m dis 1982), Neil Cathcart Black, s of Dr Harold Black, of Edgbaston, Birmingham; 1 s (James Murray b 3 July 1964), 2 da (Katharine b 9 Sept 1961, Alison Louise b 14 May 1966); m 2, 20 Aug 1983, (Reginald) Wyndham Lloyd-Davies, *qv*, s of Dr A W Lloyd-Davies, of Wolverhampton; *Career* educational asst Edward Arnold (Publishers) Ltd 1951–57, children's book ed Abelard-Schuman Ltd 1957–58; The Bodley Head Ltd: children's book ed 1958–73, adult books ed 1973–76, dir 1976–89, editorial dir 1989–91, editorial conslt 1991–93; memb Ctee Romantic Novelists' Assoc 1989–94, memb Ctee Royal Literary Fund 1990–, administrator Catherine Cookson Fiction Prize Transworld Publishers Ltd 1991–; *Recreations* reading, gardening, cooking, opera, English furniture and watercolours; *Style—* Mrs Jill Black; ✉ 53 Harley St, London W1N 1DD (☎ 0171 631 4617)

BLACK, Jill Margaret; QC (1994); da of Dr James Irvine Currie, of Leeds, and Margaret Yvonne, *née* Rogers; *b* 1 June 1954; *Educ* Penrhos Coll Colwyn Bay, Trevelyan Coll Durham (BA); *m* 10 June 1978, David Charles Black, s of Norman John Black; 1 da (Charlotte Louise b 14 Sept 1982), 1 s (Andrew Michael Charles b 14 June 1986); *Career* called to the Bar Inner Temple 1976; fell Br-American Project; FRSA; *Books* The Working Mother's Survival Guide (1988), Divorce: The Things You Thought You'd Never Need to Know (latest edn 1993), A Practical Approach to Family Law (jtly, 4 edn 1994), The Family Court Practice (jtly, latest edn 1996); *Style—* Mrs Jill Black, QC; ✉ 30 Park Square, Leeds LS1 2PF (☎ 0113 243 6388, fax 0113 242 3510)

BLACK, John Alexander; CBE (1983); s of Arthur Alexander Black (d 1958); *b* 8 July 1923; *Educ* Cheltenham Coll, Univ of Birmingham; *m* 1950, Joan, da of Henry Knight (d 1954); 2 da; *Career* dir: AA Black Ltd 1948–63, Charles Barker Gp Ltd 1976–83, Birmingham Convention and Visitor Bureau Ltd 1982–87, Task Undertakings Ltd 1988–89; gen cmmr for Income Tax 1966–72; chm: Bd of Mgmnt Birmingham Cncl of Social Serv 1964–67 (memb 1960–74), S Birmingham Hosp Mgmnt Ctee 1972–74 (memb 1971–72), Longleys & Hoffmann Ltd 1972 (dir 1963–72, vice chm and md 1970–72), Charles Barker Black & Gross Ltd 1976–83 (vice chm 1972–75, dep chm 1975–76), Solihull AHA 1977–82, Charles Barker Scotland Ltd 1980–83, Solihull Health Authy 1982–88, Birmingham Venture 1985–88; pres: Birmingham Jr C of C 1956–57, Birmingham Publicity Assoc 1974–75, Birmingham Chamber of Indust & Commerce 1981–82 (hon treas 1974–78); FIPA; *Recreations* gardening, woodturning, walking, photography; *Style—* John A Black, Esq, CBE; ✉ 2 Old Hay Gardens, Dore, Sheffield S17 3HG (☎ 0114 235 0182)

BLACK, Michael Jonathan; QC (1995); s of Samuel Black (d 1971), and Lillian, *née* Ruben (d 1988); *b* 31 March 1954; *Educ* Stand GS, UCL (LLB); *m* 1984, Ann, da of late Keith Pentol; 2 s (Samuel Simon Joshua b 25 July 1985, Benjamin David Louis b 30 Jan 1989); *Career* pupillage 1977–79, called to the Bar Middle Temple 1978, in practice Deans Court Chambers Manchester 1979–95, trained as mediator Harvard Law Sch 1992, barr, arbitrator and mediator (commercial disputes especially in construction indust) Byrom Chambers Manchester and London 1995–, asst recorder of the Crown Court 1995–; visiting research fell Univ of Manchester Inst of Sci and Technol 1996–; memb: American Bar Assoc, Forum on Construction Indust (USA), Official Referees' Bar Assoc, Professional Negligence Bar Assoc, Union Internationale des Advocats, Int Cncl for Building Studies Res and Documentation (Netherlands); FCIArb 1991; *Books* The Sanctuary House Case: an Arbitration Workbook (contrib, 1996); *Style—* Michael Black, Esq, QC; ✉ Byrom Chambers, 25 Byrom Street, Manchester M3 4PE (☎ 0161 829 2100, fax 0161 829 2101, mobile 0860 795187, e-mail 100307.1554@compuserve.com); Byrom Chambers, 61 Fleet Street, London EC4Y 1JU (☎ 0171 353 4363, fax 0171 583 1491)

BLACK, Moira Elizabeth; da of Hugh Kenneth Black (d 1990), and Margaret Mary, *née* Healey (d 1986); *b* 20 April 1950; *Educ* The Lady Eleanor Holles Sch (scholar), Somerville Coll Univ of Oxford (Beilby scholar, MA, half blue badminton); *m* 1976, Dr Robert Christopher Gurd, s of Raymond Gurd; *Career* Price Waterhouse: joined 1972, ptnr 1984–93, specialist Corp Tax 1977–93, ptnr Price Waterhouse Privatisation Servs 1988–92; chm: Riverside Community Health Care NHS Tst, English Advsy Ctee on Telecommunications, Forum UK; former chm City Women's Network; memb: Panel Financial Services Tbnl, Cncl of Mgmnt Fndn for Mgmnt Educn; govr Univ of N London; FCA 1982 (ACA 1976), FIMgt 1985; *Recreations* tennis umpiring, gardening, architecture, music, travel; *Style—* Miss Moira Black; ✉ 60 Beaufort Road, London W5 3EA

BLACK, (Francis) Peter; s of Francis Raymond Black (d 1985), and Rosina Mary, *née* De Burgh; *b* 20 Aug 1932; *Educ* Gunnersbury GS, Hammersmith Coll of Art; *m* 15 March 1958, Jillian Elsie; 2 da (Susan b 1961, Caroline b 1964); *Career* architect with Norman and Dawbarn for 4 years designing Imperial Coll building; joined Scott Brownrigg and Turner 1961 (ptnr 1970–); bldgs include Sport City Dubai and three airports in Iraq, also responsible for biothermal waste to energy plants in Redhill and Cambridge; dir: Building Design Services (BDS) Ltd 1992–, Consolidated Development Group 1992–; conslt Internation Banking Group responsible for devpt of infrastructure in Myanmar, Laos and CIS; pres Chertsey Agric Assoc 1990; govr St Paul's Sch (grant maintained); Ecclesia et Pontifici (Vatican) 1990; RIBA, FSIAD, FCSD, FRSA, MIMgt; *Recreations* runs a small farm at Englefield Green specialising in breeding and showing Dexters, short-legged rare breed of British cattle; *Style—* Peter Black, Esq; ✉ Sandylands Home Farm, Wick Road, Englefield Green, Surrey TW20 0HJ (☎ 01784 32782); Barlow Black Partnership, Rivers Suite, Fairoaks Airport, Chobham, Surrey GU24 8HU (☎ 01276 858771, fax 01276 858811)

BLACK, Prof Robert; QC (Scot 1987); s of James Little Black, of Lockerbie, Scot, and Jeannie Findlay, *née* Lyon; *b* 12 June 1947; *Educ* Lockerbie Acad, Dumfries Acad, Univ of Edinburgh (LLB), McGill Univ Montreal (LLM); *Career* advocate of the Scot Bar 1972, sr legal offr Scot Law Cmmn 1975–78, in practice Scot Bar 1978–81, prof of Scots Law Univ of Edinburgh 1981– (lectr 1972–75); Temp Sheriff 1981–94; gen ed The Laws of Scotland: Stair Meml Encyclopaedia 1988–96 (dep then jt gen ed 1981–88); memb: Exec Cncl Scot Nat Dictionary Assoc, Legal Ctee RSSPCC; FRSA 1991, FRSE 1992; *Books* An Introduction to Written Pleading (1982), Civil Jurisdiction: The New Rules (1983); *Recreations* beer, wine, tea (not always in that order); *Clubs* Sloane, University Staff (Edinburgh); *Style—* Prof Robert Black, QC, FRSE; ✉ 6/4 Glenogle Rd, Edinburgh EH3 5HW (☎ 0131 557 3571); Department of Private Law, Old College, South Bridge, Edinburgh EH8 9YL (☎ 0131 650 2017, fax 0131 662 4902, telex 727442)

BLACK, Sir Robert Brown (Robin); GCMG (1962, KCMG 1955, CMG 1953), OBE (1949, MBE (Mil) 1948); s of Robert Black (d 1929), of Blair Lodge, Stirlingshire, and Catherine Black; *b* 3 June 1906; *Educ* George Watson's Coll Edinburgh, Univ of Edinburgh (MA); *m* 1937, (Elsie) Anne, da of Allan Stevenson (d 1960), of Edinburgh; 2 da; *Career* Capt Intelligence Corps (Special Ops) Far East, 43 Special Mil Mission, POW Japan; Colonial Admin Serv; govr and C-in-C: Singapore 1955–57, Hong Kong 1958–64; cmmr Cwlth War Graves Cmmn 1964–82; pres Int Social Serv (GB) 1973–82 (chm 1965–73); chm Clerical, Medical and General Life Assurance Soc 1975–78; Hon LLD Hong Kong Univ, Chinese Univ of Hong Kong; KStJ 1955; Grand Cross Order of Merit (Peru) 1962; *Recreations* fishing, walking; *Clubs* E India Sports, Devonshire and Public Schools; *Style*— Sir Robin Black, GCMG, OBE; ✉ Mapletons House, Ashampstead Common, nr Reading, Berks RG8 8QN (☎ 01635 201254)

BLACK, Robert William; s of Robert G Black (d 1966), of Aberdeen, and Nell, *née* Gray; *b* 6 Nov 1946; *Educ* Robert Gordon's Coll Aberdeen, Univ of Aberdeen (MA Economics), Heriot Watt Univ (MSc Town Planning), Univ of Strathclyde (MSc Public Policy); *m* 1970, Doreen Mary, da of George Riach; 1 da (Emily Doreen b 1971), 3 s (Angus Robert George b 1974, Duncan Riach b 1978, Colin David William b 1984); *Career* planner Notts CC 1971–73, supervisory planner Glasgow Corp 1973–75, sr exec Strathclyde Regnl Cncl 1975–85; chief exec: Stirling Dist Cncl 1985–90, Tayside Regnl Cncl 1990–95; controller of Audit for Scotland 1995–; clerk to the Lord Lieut of Stirling and Falkirk 1985–90; memb Soc of Local Authy Chief Execs 1985, FRSS 1984; *Recreations* the Arts, swimming, golf; *Clubs* New (Edinburgh); *Style*— Robert Black, Esq; ✉ The Accounts Commission for Scotland, 18 George Street, Edinburgh EH2 2QU (☎ 0131 477 1234)

BLACK, Roger Anthony; MBE (1992); s of David Harrison Black, and Thelma Royds, *née* Culshaw; *b* 31 March 1966; *Educ* Portsmouth GS; *Career* athlete; represented UK 1985–; honours incl: Gold medal 400m and 4 x 400m Euro Jr Championships 1985, Gold medal 400m and 4 x 400m Cwlth Games 1986, Gold medal 400m and 4 x 400m Euro Championships 1986 and 1990, Silver medal 4 x 400m World Championships 1987, Gold medal 4 x 400m and Silver medal 400m World Championships Tokyo 1991, Bronze medal 4 x 400m Olympic Games Barcelona 1992, Gold medal 4 x 400m and Silver medal 400m Euro Championships 1994, Gold medal 4 x 400m World Cup 1994, Silver medal 400m and 4 x 400m Olympic Games Atlanta 1996; Br 400m record 1996; Male Athlete of the Year Br Athletic Writers' Assoc 1986 and 1996; Freeman of Gosport (Hants) 1996; *Recreations* guitar, song writing, tennis, arts; *Style*— Roger Black, Esq, MBE; ✉ c/o British Athletic Federation, 225A Bristol Road, Edgbaston, Birmingham B5 7BR

BLACK, Prof Samuel (Sam); MBE (1969); s of Lionel Black (d 1960), of London, and Sophia, *née* Divinsky (d 1968); *b* 6 Jan 1915; *Educ* Owens Sch, Northampton Engrg Coll, Univ of London; *m* 1, 24 June 1939, Muriel Cecilia Emily (d 1982), da of Cornelius George Snudden (d 1924), of Woodford, Essex; 1 s (Christopher), 1 da (Patricia); m 2, 27 Sept 1986, (Lucy) Gwendoline, da of George Bowles (d 1969), of Northampton; *Career* RAMC 1941–46; head of PR: Assoc of Optical Practitioners 1946–55, Br Electrical and Allied Mfrs Assoc 1955–60; PR advsr London C of C 1965–72, PR cnsllr 1961–, memb: Ophthalmic Optical Advsy Ctee Miny of Health, Optical Whitley Cncl; chm Inst Public Relations, pres Int Public Relations Assoc, sec Finchley Chess Club; hon prof of public relations Univ of Stirling 1988–, visiting prof of public relations Coll of St Mark and St John Plymouth 1989–; Freeman City of London 1956, Liveryman Worshipful Co of Spectacle Makers 1956; FIMgt, FRSA, FBCO, FSMC; Hon FIPR; *Books* Practical Public Relations (1962), Exhibiting Overseas (1971), Role of Public Relations in Management (1972), Businessman's Guide to The Centrally Planned Economies (1972), Public Relations in the 1980's (1979), Exhibitions and Conferences from A-Z (1989), Introduction to Public Relations (1989), Public Relations Revision Workbook (1993), International Public Relations Case Studies (1993), The Essentials of Public Relations (1993), The Practice of Public Relations (1995), The Commitment to Excellence - IPRA the first 40 years (1995); *Recreations* chess, travel; *Clubs* Reform; *Style*— Prof Sam Black, MBE; ✉ Keswick House, 3 Greenway, London N20 8EE (☎ 0181 445 5256, fax 0181 446 9108)

BLACK, Sheila Psyche; OBE (1986); da of Clement Johnston Black, and Mildred Beryl Black; *b* 6 May 1920; *Educ* Dorset, Switzerland and RADA; *m* 1, 1939 (m dis 1951), Geoffrey Davien; 1 da (and 1 s decd); m 2, 1951 (m dis 1973), L A Lee Howard; *Career* woman's ed Financial Times 1959–72, specialist feature writer for national newspapers and magazines, author of several books; dir MAI plc 1976–92, chm MAI Pension Fund Trustees Ltd 1992–95; memb: Liquor Licensing Law Reform Ctee 1967–70, Price Cmmn 1973–77, Cncl IOD 1975–91, Nat Consumer Cncl 1981–91, Ctee on Privacy and Related Matters 1989–90; chm Gas Consumers' Cncl 1980–89; Freeman City of London 1985; *Style*— Miss Sheila P Black, OBE; ✉ 12A Earl's Court Gardens, London SW5 0TD (☎ 0171 373 3620, 0171 912 0530)

BLACK, Virginia; da of (Morice) William Black, of Birmingham, and Mabel Florence, *née* Jones; *b* 1 Oct 1943; *Educ* King's Norton GS Birmingham, RAM; *m* 1965, Howard Davis, s of Howard Davis; 2 s (Guy b 25 Sept 1969, Oliver b 6 Jan 1972); *Career* solo harpsichordist specialising in the virtuoso repertoire; tours abroad incl: USA, NZ, Aust, France, Germany, Austria, Poland, Sweden; appearances at major early music festivals incl: Göttingen Handel Festival, Herne, York, Carmel Bach Festival; major venues incl: South Bank, Carnegie Hall, NY, Vienna's Konzerthaus; half of duo with Howard Davis (baroque violin); many live broadcasts and TV appearances in UK and abroad; concerts with Eng Chamber Orch and Ancient Acad of Music, professor of harpsichord RAM; recordings incl: Scarlatti Sonatas (1985), Soler Sonatas (1987), J C Bach (1987), Mozart Violin and Keyboard Sonatas (with Howard Davis, 1988), Brandenburg 5 with Consort of London (1989), The Essential Harpsichord (1989), J S Bach - Goldberg Variations (1990), First Choice in Gramophone (1992), Collector's Choice in Classic CD (1992), Soler Scarlatti (1993), 3 Suites by Rameau (1995); Gramophone's Critics Choice of the Year for Soler Sonatas; FRAM; *Recreations* interior design, creative cookery; *Style*— Virginia Black; ✉ 123 Sheering Rd, Old Harlow, Essex CM17 0JP (☎ 01279 431337); Melanie Turner Management

BLACKADDER, Elizabeth Violet; OBE (1982); da of Thomas Blackadder (d 1941), of Falkirk, and Violet Isabella, *née* Scott (d 1984); *b* 24 Sept 1931; *Educ* Falkirk HS, Univ of Edinburgh, Edinburgh Coll of Art; *m* 1956, John Houston, *qv*, s of Alexander Anderson Houston (d 1947); *Career* artist; lectr Sch of Drawing and Painting Edinburgh Coll of Art 1962–86; numerous solo exhibitions since 1960 (Mercury Gallery 1965–), shows regularly at Royal Scottish Acad and Royal Acad, Tapestry designs (woven by Dovecot Studios) in private collections Robert Fleming Holdings Ltd, Reckitt & Colman plc; solo exhibitions incl: Retrospective (Scottish Arts Cncl & touring) 1981–82, Retrospective (Aberystwyth Arts Centre & touring) 1989; works in the collections of: Scottish Arts Cncl, Scottish Nat Gallery of Modern Art, Scottish Nat Portrait Gallery, Nat Portrait Gallery, Govt Art Collection, Kettle's Yard Univ of Cambridge, Univ of Edinburgh, Hunterian Art Gallery Univ of Glasgow, Univ of St Andrews, Univ of Stirling, Nat Museum of Women in the Arts Washington DC, McNay Art Museum San Antonio Texas, Heriot-Watt Univ, Robert Fleming Holdings Ltd; Guthrie award Royal Scottish Acad 1963, Pimms award Royal Acad 1983, Watercolour Fndn Royal Acad 1988; memb: Soc of Scottish Artists, Royal Glasgow Inst of the Fine Arts, Royal Scottish Soc of Painters in Watercolours; hon memb: Royal W of Eng Acad, RWS, Royal Soc of Painter-Printmakers; hon fell RIAS; Hon DLitt Heriot-Watt Univ 1989, Hon Doctorate Univ of Edinburgh 1990; Hon FRSE, RSA 1972, RA 1976; *Recreations* gardening and golf; *Style*— Ms Elizabeth Blackadder, OBE, RA; ✉ 57 Fountainhall Rd, Edinburgh EH9 2LH (☎ 0131 667 3687)

BLACKADDER, Dr Eric Sutton; RD (1968, clasp 1978); s of John Williamson Blackadder (d 1946), of Falkirk, and Phoebe Euodia, *née* Sutton (d 1973); *b* 25 Nov 1927; *Educ* Falkirk HS, Univ of Edinburgh (MB ChB); *m* 28 July 1955, Jean, da of William Law Gordon (d 1985), of Sunningdale; 2 s (Mark b 1956, John b 1957), 1 da (Averil b 1959); *Career* Nat Serv Surgn Lt RNVR 1953–55; RNR 1958–81: Surgn Lt Cdr 1960, Surgn Cdr 1965, ret 1981; jr hosp appts 1952–58, princ in gen practice 1958–68, fell in med admin Scottish Home and Health Dept 1968–70, med inspr of factories 1970–71, dep dir of med servs Health and Safety Exec 1977–80 (sr employment med advsr 1972–77), chief med offr BBC 1980–84, gp med dir BUPA 1984–90; govr BUPA Med Fndn Ltd 1986–95, exec govr BUPA 1986–90; dir: BUPA Health Insurance 1986–90, BUPA International 1986–90, Foundation Health Ltd 1993–; hon lectr Dept of Gen Practice Univ of Edinburgh 1963–68, hon clinical lectr in community med Univ of Glasgow 1975–77, guest lectr Dept of Social Med Univ of Edinburgh and Dept of Occupational Med Univ of Dundee 1968–77; memb Rotary Club of London 1986–94 and of Anstruther 1994–, vice pres Int Med Assoc for Radio and TV 1980–84, hon treas Int Assoc of Physicians for Overseas Servs 1986–90, chm Fin Ctee Royal Inst of Public Health and Hygiene 1986–92; contrib numerous articles to medical and scientific jls; memb BMA; MRCGP 1961, MFCM 1974, FRCPGlas 1983 (MRCPGlas 1980), FRCPEd 1988 (MRCPEd 1985), FFOM 1984 (MFOM 1978), FRSM, fell Royal Inst of Public Health and Hygiene; *Recreations* sailing, golf; *Clubs* Royal and Ancient Golf (St Andrews), Royal Naval Sailing Assoc, Royal Yachting Assoc; *Style*— Dr Eric Blackadder, RD; ✉ 65 Thames Close, Hampton, Middx TW12 2ET; 14 East Shore, Pittenweem, Anstruther, Fife KY10 2NH (☎ 01333 310038, fax 01333 310038)

BLACKBURN, Bishop of 1989–; Rt Rev Alan David Chesters; s of Herbert Chesters (d 1982), of Huddersfield, W Yorks, and Catherine Rebecca, *née* Mountfort (d 1984); *b* 26 Aug 1937; *Educ* Elland GS, St Chad's Coll Durham (BA), St Catherine's Coll Oxford (MA), St Stephen's House Oxford; *m* 23 July 1975, Jennie, da of Thomas Davison Garrett (d 1973), of Sunderland, Tyne and Wear; 1 s (David b 1977); *Career* curate St Anne Wandsworth London 1962–66, chaplain Tiffin Sch Kingston upon Thames 1966–72, hon curate St Richard Ham 1967–72, dir of Educn Dio of Durham 1972–85, rector of Brancepeth 1972–85, hon canon Durham Cathedral 1975–55, archdeacon Halifax 1985–89; C of E Gen Synod: memb 1975–, memb Standing Ctee 1985–89 and 1990–95, vice chm Bd of Educn 1984–90, chm Bd of Educn Schs Ctee 1984–90, memb Bd of Govrs 1992–; church cmmr 1982–; memb Bd of Govrs St Chad's Coll Durham 1980–89; chm: Bd of Govrs St Martin's Coll Lancaster 1991–, HEFCE Advsy Ctee for Church Colleges 1993–96; pres Woodard Corp 1993–, memb Countryside Cmmn 1995–; took seat in House of Lords 1995; *Recreations* railways, walking; *Style*— The Rt Rev the Bishop of Blackburn; ✉ Bishop's House, Ribchester Road, Blackburn BB1 9EF (☎ 01254 248234, fax 01254 246668)

BLACKBURN, Rear Admiral (David) Anthony James; LVO (1978); s of late Lt J Blackburn, DSC, RN, and late Mrs M J G Pickering-Pick; *b* 18 Jan 1945; *Educ* Taunton Sch, RNC Dartmouth; *m* 1973, Elizabeth Barstow; 3 da; *Career* cmd HMS Kirkliston 1972–73, Equerry-in-Waiting to HRH The Duke of Edinburgh 1976–78, exec offr HMS Antrim 1978–81; Cmd: HMS Birmingham 1983–84, Capt Third Destroyer Sqdn HMS York 1987–88; Cdre and Naval Base Cdr Clyde 1990–92, OC HMS Cornwall and Capt Second Frigate Sqdn 1992–93, Defence Attaché and Head British Defence Staff Washington DC 1994–; *Style*— Rear Admiral Anthony Blackburn, LVO

BLACKBURN, Archdeacon of; *see:* Marsh, Ven Dr (Francis) John

BLACKBURN, Barrie; s of Harold Blackburn (d 1995), of Blewbury, Oxfordshire, and Kathleen May, *née* King (d 1984); *b* 23 June 1948; *Educ* Marling Sch Stroud, Univ of Leeds (BCom); *m* 9 Jan 1971, Julie Maureen, da of Phillip Ronald Baker, of Abingdon, Oxon; 2 s (David Charles b 1971, Luke b 1979), 1 da (Jane b 1984); *Career* articled clerk Touche Ross & Co 1970–75, taxation mangr Davy Corporation plc 1975–84, gp taxation controller The Plessey Co Plc 1984–87, gp dir of taxation TI Group Plc 1987–92, conslt 1992–; FCA, ATII; *Recreations* skiing, reading, watching sport, gardening; *Style*— Barrie Blackburn Esq; ✉ Yew Trees, Wantage Road, Streatley-on-Thames, Berkshire, RG8 9LD (☎ 01491 874221, fax 01491 874221)

BLACKBURN, David Michael; s of Rudolph Isaac Blackburn, of London, and Esther Sybil, *née* Levy; *b* 23 Dec 1937; *Educ* City of London Sch, St John's Coll Cambridge (MA, LLM); *m* 1, 11 Jan 1962 (m dis 1969), Louise Joy, da of Louis Courts, of London; 1 s (James b 1964), 1 da (Deborah b 1963); m 2, 30 April 1970, Janice, da of Louis Brown (d 1987); 2 s (Oliver b 1971, Joshua b 1973); *Career* solicitor; ptnr Courts & Co 1962–81; dir: Rosehaugh plc 1979–85, Rosehaugh Stanhope Developments plc 1983–92, Blackburn Associates Ltd 1986–; property project conslt 1985–; bd memb Nat Opera Studio 1994–; memb Law Soc 1962; *Style*— David M Blackburn, Esq; ✉ 6 Rosslyn Mews, London NW3 1NN (☎ 0171 431 3467, fax 0171 435 0332)

BLACKBURN, Frank Victor; s of John Martin Blackburn (d 1975), and Mabel Gregg (d 1951); *b* 29 Oct 1931; *Educ* numerous schs; *m* 1, 27 Sept 1952 (m dis 1969), Dorothea, da of Franz Schibitschek; 2 s (Mark b 1954, Fraser b 1957), 1 da (Susan b 1955); m 2, 3 Sept 1969, Gwendoline, da of Cecil Jones; *Career* photographer; served RE 1949–54; md Frank V Blackburn (Printers) Ltd 1955–70, freelance wildlife photographer 1970–, chm Nature Photographers Ltd 1980–86; major contrib of natural history photographs to leading pubns worldwide; *Books* Natural History Photography (jtly, 1974); *Recreations* darkroom activities, bird watching, natural history, good music, reading, hill walking, fishing; *Style*— Frank Blackburn, Esq; ✉ 15 Dolley's Hill, Normandy, Guildford, Surrey GU3 2AJ (☎ 01483 811569)

BLACKBURN, Julia Karen Eugénie; da of Thomas Blackburn (d 1977), of London and N Wales, and Rosalie, *née* De Meric; *b* 12 Aug 1948; *Educ* Putney HS, Univ of York (BA); *m* 1978 (m dis 1996), Hein Bonger; 1 da (Natasha b Aug 1978), 1 s (Martin Thomas b Nov 1983); *Career* writer; *Books* The White Men (1978), Charles Waterton - Traveller and Conservationist (1989), The Emperor's Last Island (1991), Daisy Bates in the Desert (1994), The Book of Colour (1995); stories in PN Review 1990–91; *Style*— Ms Julia Blackburn; ✉ c/o Toby Eady, Third Floor, 9 Orme Court, London W2 4RL (☎ 0171 792 0092, fax 0171 792 0879)

BLACKBURN, (Jeffrey) Michael; *b* 16 Dec 1941; *Career* chief exec: Joint Credit Card Co Ltd 1983–87, Leeds Permanent Building Society 1987–93, Halifax Building Society 1993–; FCIB, CIMgt, FRSA; *Style*— Michael Blackburn, Esq; ✉ Halifax Building Society, Trinity Road, Halifax, West Yorkshire HX1 2RG (☎ 01422 333333)

BLACKBURN, Michael John; s of Francis Blackburn (d 1970), and Ann Elizabeth, *née* Thornley (d 1973); *b* 25 Oct 1930; *Educ* Kingston GS; *m* 19 March 1955, Maureen Beatrice, da of Arnold Dale; 1 s (Alastair b 1957), 2 da (Fiona b 1958, Anna b 1966); *Career* Touche Ross: ptnr 1960–92, managing ptnr 1984–90, chm 1990–92; chm GEI International plc 1990–95; non-exec dir: Blue Arrow Holdings 1992–96, Aerostructures Hamble Holdings 1992–95, William Hill Group 1992–, Chubb Security plc 1992–, Steel Burrill Jones Group plc 1992–; chm Voices for Hospices 1990–; FCA 1953; *Recreations* horse racing, the garden; *Style*— Michael Blackburn, Esq; ✉ Chubb Security plc, Richmond Court, 309 Fleet Road, Fleet, Hampshire GU13 8BV

BLACKBURN, Peter Hugh; s of Hugh Edward Blackburn, of Bradford, Yorkshire (d 1964), and Sarah, *née* Moffatt; *b* 17 Dec 1940; *Educ* Douai Sch, Univ of Leeds (BA), Univ of Poitiers (Dip French), Harvard Business Sch (AMP); *m* 17 Aug 1967, Gillian Mary, da of William Francis Popple, of Yorkshire; 3 da (Joanna Clare b 1968, Catherine Elizabeth b 1970, Louise Mary b 1973); *Career* articled clerk RS Dawson & Co Chartered Accountants 1962–66, fin controller John Mackintosh & Sons Ltd Norwich 1967–72 (works accountant Halifax 1966–67); Rowntree Mackintosh: fin dir Overseas Div 1972–75, asst md Europe rising to md 1975–84, gp bd dir 1982–88, chm UK and Eire Region 1985–88; Nestle SA (following takeover): md Rowntree UK 1988–91, dir int chocolate & confectionery strategy 1989–90, chm and chief exec Nestle UK Ltd 1991–96, pres and dir gen Nestle France SA 1996–; dep pres Food and Drink Fedn 1993–95; memb Worshipful Co of Merchant Adventurers York 1989; Hon DLitt Univ of Bradford 1991; Hon FIL 1989, CIMgt, FIGD, FCA 1976 (ACA 1966), FRSA; *Recreations* fell walking, swimming, photography; *Style*— Peter H Blackburn, Esq; ✉ Nestle UK Ltd, St George's House, Croydon CR9 1NR (☎ 0181 686 3333)

BLACKBURN, Provost of; *see:* Frayne, Very Rev David

BLACKBURN, Richard John; s of Tom Binks Blackburn (d 1973), and Mabel, *née* Cleal (d 1992); *b* 22 Feb 1938; *Educ* Eastbourne Coll, Worcester Coll Oxford (MA); *m* 3 Sept 1966, Jennifer Ann Yelland; 1 s (Alistair b 1971), 2 da (Joanna b 1968, Sophie b 1974); *Career* Nat Serv 2 Lt RASC 1956–58; Deloitte & Touche: articled 1961–64, qualified 1965, ptnr 1969–, London 1961–81 and 1986–, Glasgow 1981–86, various mgmnt appts 1979–86; memb Cncl: Roedean Sch Brighton 1987–, Hazelwood Sch Oxted 1981–96; Freeman City of London 1988, Liveryman Worshipful Co of Turners 1993; FCA 1975; *Recreations* sailing, skiing; *Clubs* City of London, United Oxford and Cambridge University, Royal Southampton Yacht; *Style*— Richard Blackburn, Esq; ✉ Deloitte & Touche, Stonecutter Court, 1 Stonecutter Street, London EC4A 4TR (☎ 0171 303 5309, fax 0171 303 5775)

BLACKBURN, Thomas; s of Thomas Blackburn (d 1987), of Preston; *b* 22 July 1932; *Educ* Oundle; *m* 1955, Diana Christine, da of William Ascough Lillico (d 1983), of Barnet; 1 s, 2 da; *Career* engr; chm: C Seward & Co Holdings 1960–95, Shard Bridge Co 1984–95 (dir 1980), C Seward (Properties) Ltd 1989–95; *Recreations* shooting, fishing; *Style*— Thomas Blackburn, Esq; ✉ Hill Top Farm, Thornley with Wheatley, Longridge, Preston, Lancs PR3 2TY (☎ 01772 783353)

BLACKBURN, William Howard; s of Thomas Cather Johnston Blackburn (d 1960), and Elizabeth, *née* Jones (d 1978); *b* 23 Dec 1932; *Educ* Holt Sch, Univ of Liverpool (LLB); *m* 1, 9 April 1960, Marie-Therese (d 1983), da of Gen André Dorange (d 1985); m 2, 23 July 1985, Chloë Marya Tickell, da of Sir James Gunn (d 1964); 2 s (Alexander b 1963, James b 1965); *Career* ptnr Theodore Goddard Paris 1957–62, IBM 1962–84 (mangr legal dept, co sec, md Euro office SA), chm Legal Exchange & Development Corporation; non-exec dir: Chelsea Building Society, OCE (UK) Ltd; pres Franco-British Lawyers' Soc; memb: Cncl Law Soc 1979–95, Br Cncl Law Advsy Ctee, Franco-British Cncl; *Recreations* golf; *Clubs* RAC, Royal Mid-Surrey Golf; *Style*— William Blackburn, Esq; ✉ 18 Alma Square, London NW8 9QA (☎ 0171 286 5273, fax 0171 266 2627)

BLACKER, Dr Carmen Elizabeth; da of Carlos Paton Blacker, and Helen Maud, *née* Pilkington; *b* 13 July 1924; *Educ* Benenden Sch, SOAS Univ of London (BA, PhD), Somerville Coll Oxford (BA), Radcliffe Coll USA, Keio Univ Tokyo; *Career* univ lectr in Japanese Univ of Cambridge 1958–91 (fell Clare Hall 1965–), prof Ueno Gakuen Coll Tokyo 1991; visiting prof: Columbia Univ 1965, Princeton 1979; pres Folklore Soc 1982–84; hon fell Somerville Coll Oxford 1991; Order of the Precious Crown (Japan); FBA 1989; *Books* The Japanese Enlightenment: A Study of the Writings of Fukuzawa Yukichi (1964), The Catalpa Bow: A Study of Shamanistic Practices in Japan (1975, revised edn 1986); articles in Monumenta Nipponica, Folklore, Trans of Asiatic Soc of Japan, Asian Folklore Studies; *Recreations* walking, comparative mythology; *Style*— Dr Carmen Blacker, FBA; ✉ Willow House, Grantchester, Cambridge CB3 9NF (☎ 01223 840196); Faculty of Oriental Studies, Sidgwick Ave, Cambridge

BLACKER, Gen Sir Cecil Hugh; GCB (1975, KCB 1969, CB 1967), OBE (1960), MC (1944); s of Col Norman Valentine Blacker, DSO, MC (d 1958), and Olive Georgina, *née* Hope (d 1978); *b* 4 June 1916; *Educ* Wellington, RMC Sandhurst; *m* 26 Feb 1947, Felicity Mary, da of Maj Ivor Buxton, DSO, TD (d 1969), and wid of Maj John Rew (ka 1943); 2 s; *Career* 2 Lt Royal Inniskilling Dragoon Gds 1936, GOC-in-C Northern Cmd 1969–70, vice CGS 1970–73, Adj-Gen 1973–76, ret 1976; ADC to HM The Queen 1962–64, ADC (Gen) to HM The Queen 1974–76; pres: Br Showjumping Assoc 1976–80, Br Equestrian Fedn 1980–84; chm Racecourse Security Servs Ltd 1980–83; memb Horserace Betting Levy Bd 1980–83; dep sr steward Jockey Club 1984–86; FIMgt 1973; *Recreations* painting, growing orchids; *Clubs* Jockey; *Style*— Gen Sir Cecil Blacker, GCB, OBE, MC

BLACKER, Jacob (Jac); s of Benjamin Blacker (d 1968), of Cape Town, SA, and Rosa Blacker (d 1983); *b* 13 Oct 1933; *Educ* Matriculation Wynberg Boys' HS Cape Town, Univ of Cape Town (BArch); *m* 14 Jan 1962, Delores Ramona (Del), da of Donald Reynolds (d 1981), of Brisbane, Aust; 3 s (Amos b 1966, Ben b 1968, Adam b 1970); *Career* job architect Chrysos Daneel SA 1957, assoc Ernö Godlinger Architects & Planners 1958–65, fndr Jacob Blacker Architects Designers Planners 1965–; buildings designed and constructed incl: Islamic Art Museum, Jerusalem City Museum; tutor UCL Architecture Sch 1975–79; Furnival site devpt for housing 1989; fndr Intro Course for Overseas Students 1986–; memb: London Regnl Ctee RIBA, Bd of Govrs Building Centre; chm: Educn Gp RIBA, chm Camden Soc Architects; RIBA 1961, memb RSA 1989; *Books* Building Owners Maintenance Manual & Job Diary (1966–82); *Recreations* singing opera, descriptive geometry, drawing, painting, the mathematics of perception; *Clubs* Chelsea Arts; *Style*— Jac Blacker, Esq; ✉ 5 Shepherds Walk, Hampstead, London NW3 5UE (☎ 0171 431 1776); Jacob Blacker Architects, 5 Shepherds Walk, Hampstead, London NW3 5UE (☎ 0171 431 1776, fax 0171 435 9739)

BLACKER, Gen Sir (Anthony Stephen) Jeremy; KCB (1992), CBE (1987, OBE 1979); s of Kenneth Anthony Blacker, CBE, and Louise Margaret, *née* Band (d 1985); *b* 6 May 1939; *Educ* Sherborne; *m* 30 June 1973, Julia Mary, da of John Trew (d 1942); 2 da; *Career* joined Army 1957, RMA Sandhurst 1957–59, cmmnd 1 RTR 1959, served Hong Kong and BAOR 1959–61, in-Service degree course Corpus Christi Coll Cambridge (BA) 1961–64, re-joined 1 RTR serving BAOR, Bahrain, Aden and UK 1964–68, instr Royal Armd Corps Signal Sch 1968–70, Army Staff Course Royal Mil Coll of Sci at Shrivenham 1970 and at Camberley 1971 (Maj), Directorate of Mil Ops (MO1) MOD 1971–74, Sqdn Ldr 1 RTR 1974–76 (served NI, Cyprus and Tidworth), mil asst (Lt-Col) to Vice Chief of Gen Staff MOD 1976–79, cmd 1 RTR BAOR 1979–81, mil dir of studies (Col) RMCS Shrivenham 1981, cmd (Brig) 11 Armd Bde Minden BAOR 1982–85, princ staff offr to Chief of Def Staff MOD 1985–87, Cmdt (Maj Gen) RMCS 1987–89, Asst Chief of Def Staff Operational Requirements (Land Systems) 1989–91, Lt Gen 1991, Master Gen of the Ordnance 1991–95, Gen 1994; Col Cmdt: RAC 1993–95, RTR 1987–95 (REME 1987–92); FIMechE; *Recreations* most sports especially skiing and tennis; *Style*— Gen Sir Jeremy Blacker, KCB, CBE

BLACKETT, Capt (John) Beauchamp; s of Maj (Christopher) William Stewart Blackett (d 1985), of Arbigland by Dumfries, and Kathleen Charlotte, *née* Williams-Wynn (d 1991); *b* 6 May 1939; *Educ* Eton; *m* 1, 15 Jan 1964 (m dis 1977), Sarah Jennifer, da of James Withycombe (d 1984), of Bury Farm, Studham, Dunstable; 2 s (James b 1964, Edward b 1969), 1 da (Annabel b 1966); m 2, 1977, Susan Elizabeth, da of Michael Badger, of Chilson, Charlbury, Oxon; 2 da (Flora b 1978, Letitia b 1983); *Career* Coldstream Gds 1957–70; chm: Ashdown (Leadenhall) Ltd 1970–90, Ashdown (Leadenhall) plc 1990–, Beauchamp's Restaurant 1989; Co pres SSAFA Dumfries; chm: Dumfries Prison Visiting Ctee 1982–85, Congregational Bd Kirkbean Church; tstee and chm Fishmongers' and Poulterers' Charitable Inst; Freeman City of London 1989, Freeman and Liveryman Worshipful Company of Fishmongers 1994; FInstD 1970; *Recreations* polo, shooting, fishing, gardening; *Clubs* Pratt's, Beauchamp's Tap; *Style*— Capt Beauchamp Blackett; ✉ Arbigland, Dumfries DG2 8BQ (☎ 0138788 283); 4/261 South Lambeth Road, London SW8 (☎ 0171 582 1852); Quinta da Escocia, Pincho, Bensafrim, Lagos, Algarve; Ashdown (Leadenhall) plc, 23–25 Leadenhall Market, London EC3 (☎ 0171 626 1949/0178, fax 0171 626 5889)

BLACKETT, David John; s of Capt Frederick Herbert Blackett, of Edinburgh, and Mary, *née* Watson (d 1982); *b* 22 Aug 1950; *Educ* Dollar Academy Scotland, Univ of Edinburgh (BCom); *m* 1979, Anita Mary, da of Gareth Evans; 1 s (Matthew Gareth b 9 March 1988), 1 da (Sarah Louise b 12 Dec 1983); *Career* trainee CA Graham Smart & Annan 1970–73, N M Rothschild & Sons Ltd: joined 1973, seconded to venture in Malaysia with Bumiputera Merchant Bankers 1975–77, md N M Rothschild & Sons (Singapore) Ltd 1979–86, dir N M Rothschild & Sons Ltd 1983–, md N M Rothschild & Sons (Hong Kong) Ltd 1986–; MICAS 1975; *Recreations* polo, sailing, golf, tennis, photography; *Clubs* Oriental (London), Guards' Polo, Royal Hong Kong Yacht, Jurong Golf & Country, Shek-O Golf; *Style*— David Blackett, Esq; ✉ N M Rothschild & Sons (Hong Kong) Ltd, 16th Floor, Alexandra House, Central, Hong Kong (☎ 00 852 525 5333)

BLACKETT, Sir Hugh Francis; 12 Bt (E 1673), of Newcastle, Northumberland; s of Maj Sir Francis Hugh Blackett, 11 Bt (d 1995), and his 1 w Elizabeth Eily (d 1982), *née* Dennison; *b* 11 Feb 1955; *Educ* Eton; *m* 1982, Anna Margaret, yr da of James St George Coldwell, of Somerton, Oxon; 1 s (Henry Douglas b 1992), 3 da (Amelia b 1984, Isabella b 1986, Flora b 1988); *Heir* s, Henry Douglas Blackett b 2 Feb 1992; *Style*— Sir Hugh Blackett, Bt; ✉ Halton Castle, Corbridge, Northumberland

BLACKETT-ORD, His Hon (Andrew) James; CVO (1988); 2 s of John Reginald Blackett-Ord, JP (d 1967), of Whitfield Hall, Hexham, Northumberland, and Lena Mary, *née* Blackett-Ord (d 1961); *b* 21 Aug 1921; *Educ* Eton, New Coll Oxford (MA); *m* 9 June 1945, Rosemary, da of Edward William Bovill (d 1966), of Brook House, Moreton, Essex; 4 s (Christopher b and d 13 Feb 1946, Charles b 6 Feb 1948, Mark, *qv*, b 10 May 1950, Benjamin James b 12 Feb 1963), 1 da (Nicola Mary Lena (Mrs George St Leger Granville) b 25 Oct 1961); *Career* Lt Scots Guards, served in UK, N Africa and Italy 1941–46 (prisoner (Anzio) 1944–45); called to the Bar Inner Temple 1947, Lincoln's Inn 1948; County Court judge 1971; vice chllr Co Palatine of Lancaster, memb Cncl Duchy of Lancaster and circuit judge (Chancery Div) Northern Area 1973–87; chllr Dio of Newcastle-upon-Tyne 1971–; bencher Lincoln's Inn 1985; *Recreations* rural life, reading, travel; *Clubs* Garrick, Lansdowne; *Style*— His Honour A J Blackett-Ord, CVO; ✉ Helbeck Hall, Brough, Kirkby Stephen, Cumbria (☎ 017683 41323)

BLACKETT-ORD, Mark; s of His Hon (Andrew) James Blackett-Ord, CVO, *qv*, and Rosemary, *née* Bovill; *b* 10 May 1950; *Educ* Eton, New Coll Oxford; *m* 2 Dec 1981, Carol Theresa Anne, da of Sir David Scott-Fox, KCMG (d 1984); 3 da (Katherine b 1983, Elinor b 1986, Constance b 1988); *Career* called to the Bar Lincoln's Inn 1974; *Books* Hell-Fire Duke (1981), ed Partnership Law in Halsbury's Laws of England (1981); *Recreations* old books, old buildings; *Style*— M Blackett-Ord, Esq; ✉ Warcop Hall, Warcop, Appleby, Cumbria CA16 6NX; 5 Stone Buildings, Lincoln's Inn, London WC2A 3RU (☎ 0171 242 6201, fax 0171 831 8102)

BLACKHAM, Rear Adm Jeremy Joe; s of Rear Adm Joseph Leslie Blackham, CB, DL, of Bembridge, Isle of Wight, and Coreen Shelford, *née* Skinner; *b* 10 Sept 1943; *Educ* Bradfield Coll Berks, BRNC Dartmouth, Open Univ; *m* 18 Dec 1971, Candy, da of George Carter (d 1992), of Durban, S Africa; *Career* entered RN 1961; CO HMS Beachampton 1969–70, CO HMS Ashanti 1975–77, promoted Cdr 1977, Capt 1984, CO HMS Nottingham 1984–85; Comdt RN Staff Coll Greenwich 1987–89, Dir of Naval Plans and Progs 1989–92, CO HMS Ark Royal 1992–93 and CO RN Task Force in Adriatic 1993, Rear Adm 1993, DG Naval Personnel Strategy and Plans 1993–95, Asst Chief of Naval Staff 1995–; memb Cncl Royal Utd Inst for Defence Studies 1990–94, memb RIIA; author of numerous articles for professional jls, regular lectr at Staff Colls; Freeman City of London 1995; FRSA; *Recreations* cricket, music, walking, reading, writing, theatre, travel, languages; *Clubs* MCC; *Style*— Rear Adm Jeremy Blackham; ✉ Ministry of Defence, Main Building, Whitehall, London SW1A 2HB (☎ 0171 218 6534)

BLACKHURST, Christopher Charles (Chris); s of Donald Blackhurst, of Barrow-in-Furness, Cumbria, and Rose Bestwick, *née* Wood; *b* 24 Dec 1959; *Educ* Barrow-in-Furness GS, Trinity Hall Cambridge (MA); *m* 2 Aug 1986, Lynette Dorothy Wood, da of Philip Grice; 2 s (Harry Max Thomas b 20 Sept 1987, Barnaby Samuel b 15 April 1992), 1 da (Daisy Natasha b 25 Dec 1988); *Career* articled clerk Cameron Markby 1982–84, asst ed International Financial Law Review (Euromoney Publications) 1985–86, sr writer Business Magazine 1987–88 (staff writer 1986–87), dep ed Insight The Sunday Times 1990 (business reporter 1989–90), city ed Sunday Express 1990–92, sr business writer The Independent on Sunday 1992–93, Westminster corr The Independent 1993–94, sr journalist The Observer 1994–95, Westminster corr The Independent 1995–; TSB/PIMS Fin Journalist of the Year 1988, Highly Commended British Press Awards 1993; *Recreations* golf, tennis, playing with the children; *Clubs* Fulwell Golf, Sigi Cornish Tennis; *Style*— Chris Blackhurst; ✉ The Independent, One Canada Square, Canary Wharf, London E14 5DL (☎ 0171 293 2000)

BLACKIE, Prof John Walter Graham; s of Walter Graham Blackie (d 1972); *b* 2 Oct 1946; *Educ* Uppingham, Peterhouse Cambridge, Harvard Univ, Merton Coll Oxford, Univ of Edinburgh; *m* 1972, Jane; *Career* advocate 1974, lectr in Scots law Univ of Edinburgh 1975 (sr lectr 1988–93), visiting lectr Univ of Göttingen 1981 and 1990, prof of law Univ of Strathclyde 1991–; dir Blackie & Son Ltd (Publishers) 1970–93; *Recreations* sailing, playing wind instruments; *Style*— Prof John Blackie; ✉ 17 Parsonage Square, Glasgow G4 0TA (☎ 0141 552 8286); University of Strathclyde, The Law School, Stenhouse Building, 173 Cathedral Street, Glasgow G4 0RQ (☎ 0141 552 4400, fax 0141 553 1546)

BLACKISTON, Galton Benjamin; s of B L J Blackiston, of Morston Hall Hotel, Norfolk, and Anne, *née* Skerrett-Rogers; *b* 13 Aug 1962; *Educ* Homewood Sch Tenterden Kent; *m* 12 Dec 1987, Tracy Jane Rowe; 2 s (Sydney, Harry Galton); *Career* restaurateur and hotelier; weekly Galtons Goodies stall on Rye Market 1979, trained under John Tovey of Miller Howe 1980–86, head chef Miller Howe 1986–90 (involved with public demonstrations for TV and radio and work in USA, SA and Canada), proprietor Morston Hall Hotel Holt Norfolk 1991–; *Awards* AA Best Newcomer Award 1992, Independent Newspaper Country Hotel of the Year, Catey Award for Best Newcomer, 2 Red AA Stars and Rosettes, Michelin Red M; *Recreations* cricket, eating out, wine, reading cookery books old and new, golf; *Style*— Galton Blackiston, Esq; ✉ Morston Hall, Morston, nr Holt, Norfolk NR25 7AA (☎ 01263 741041, fax 01263 740419)

BLACKLEDGE, Michael Glyn; s of Edward John Blackledge (d 1981), of Bromley, Kent, and Winifred May, *née* Hemsley; *b* 24 Oct 1954; *Educ* Colfe's GS Lee London, South Bank Poly (Dip Estate Mgmnt), Garnett Coll (Cert Ed), Coll of Estate Management (Dip Arbitration, David Lawrence Prize 1995); *m* 21 Aug 1976, Janet May, da of Edward Arthur Connell, of Seaview, Isle of Wight; 2 s (Jonathan b 1984, Alexander b 1990); *Career* surveyor Thames Water Authy 1974–78; valuer: City of Westminster 1978–79, London Borough of Croydon 1979–81; sr lectr: Vauxhall Coll of Bldg and Further Educn 1981–88, Thames Poly 1988–89; sr surveyor King & Co 1989–91; sr lectr: Portsmouth Poly 1991–92, Univ of Portsmouth 1992–; sole princ conslt 1992–; tutor Coll of Estate Mgmnt 1989–; Freeman City of London, memb Worshipful Co of Feltmakers; FRICS

1990 (ARICS 1978); *Recreations* writing, golf, soccer, wargaming and computing; *Style*— Michael Blackledge, Esq; ✉ 34 Horestone Drive, Seaview, Isle of Wight, PO34 5DD (☎ 01983 567577, fax 01983 616534)

BLACKLEY, Emma Clare; da of John Barney Blackley (d 1988), and Cecily Clare Coales, *née* Stuart-Prince; *b* 11 June 1956; *Educ* Berkhamsted Sch for Girls, Lady Margaret Hall Oxford (BA); *m* 10 Dec 1988, Dr (Alan) Nicholas Spoliar, s of Stanislas Vjekoslav Spoliar; 1 s (Frederick Francis Blackley b 21 Dec 1992), 1 da (Anna Lucy Faithful b 18 Jan 1995); *Career* sec to Dir Old Master Drawings Dept P & D Colnaghi & Co Ltd 1979–80, PA to Editorial Dir Cassell Ltd 1980–81; Octopus Books Ltd: asst ed Fiction Dept 1981–82, ed Children's and Fiction Depts 1982–84, publishing mangr Children's and Fiction Depts 1984–86, dep publisher Children's and Fiction Depts 1986–87, dep publisher New Edns Div 1987–89, publisher New Edns Div 1989–90; publishing dir Octopus Illustrated Publishing (div of Reed Consumer Books Ltd) 1990–92, divnl md Reed Illustrated Books 1992–93, gp publishing devpt dir Reed Consumer Books 1993–July 1995; publishing conslt 1995– (clients incl Ryland Peters & Small Ltd and Phaidon Press Ltd); *Recreations* walking, tennis, squash, opera, cinema, literature, wine, travel; *Style*— Ms Emma Blackley; ✉ 26 Baxendale Street, Shoreditch, London E2 7BY (☎ 0171 729 0993)

BLACKLEY, Neil Ramsay; s of (Samuel) Ramsay Blackley, OBE, of Beetley, Norfolk, and Deirdre, *née* Wilson; *b* 30 Aug 1955; *Educ* Malvern, Imperial Coll London (BSc), London Business Sch (MBA); *Career* shipping analyst Lindsay Blee (chartering) Ltd 1979–82; investmt/media analyst: Esso Pension Fund 1982–83, James Capel 1983–93, Goldman Sachs 1993–96, Merrill Lynch 1996–; memb Business Graduates Assoc; ACGI 1977, MSI, MBIM; *Publications* incl: The Design Consultancy Marketplace, The Global Advertising Marketplace, Electronic Retailing, Pay TV in Europe, UK Cable Book; *Recreations* squash; *Style*— Neil Blackley, Esq; ✉ Merrill Lynch International Ltd, 20 Farringdon Road, London EC1M 3NH (☎ 0171 772 1000, fax 0171 772 2614)

BLACKMAN, Dr Lionel Cyril Francis; s of Ernest Albert Cecil Blackman (d 1949), of Grange Hill, Essex, and Amy McBane (d 1979); *b* 12 Sept 1930; *Educ* Wanstead Co High, Univ of London (BSc, PhD, DIC); *m* 15 Oct 1955 (m dis 1983), Susan Hazel, da of Leonard Edward Arthur Peachey (d 1978), of Western Lullingfields; 1 s (Stuart b 1956), 1 da (Suzanne b 1959); *Career* sr res fell Royal Naval Scientific Serv 1955–57, ICI res fell and lectr Imperial Coll London 1957–60, asst dir and dir of chem res BR 1960–64, dir and dir gen Br Coal Utilisation Res Assoc 1964–70, dir of res Fibreglass Ltd 1971–78; dir: Compocem Ltd 1975–78, Cemfil Corp (US) 1975–78; vice pres Cementos y Fibres SA (Spain) 1976–78, gen mangr and dir of res British American Tobacco Co Ltd 1978–84; memb: Parliamentary and Scientific Ctee, UN Industl Liaison Gp for Sci and Technol, Non-Metallic Materials and Chemicals Ctee DTI, Bd of Studies Univs of Sheffield and Surrey; fndr chm Epping Forest Wine Soc 1960 (pres 1971), chm Hockering Residents' Assoc 1995–; FRSC 1960, SFInstE 1965, CEng 1972, CChem 1975; *Books* Modern Aspects of Graphite Technology (1970), Athletic World Records (1988); *Recreations* garden, music, wine; *Style*— Dr Lionel Blackman; ✉ Griffin House, Knowl Hill, The Hockering, Woking GU22 7HL (☎ 01483 766328)

BLACKMORE, John Ashurst; s of Harold Ashurst (d 1961), and Iris, *née* Tandy; *b* 20 Jan 1941; *Educ* Whitgift Sch, Univ of Hull (BSc), Univ of Manchester (post grad dip); *m* 12 Aug 1970, Stella Christine, da of William Tolley; 2 da (Rachel Justine b 20 Sept 1974, Kate Marie b 20 March 1978); *Career* theatre director; marketing exec Garland-Compton Advtg Agency 1963–66; Library Theatre Manchester: actor and asst dir 1967–72, co-dir of prodns 1969–72; co-dir of prodns New Forum Theatre Manchester 1971–72, dir of prodns Midlands Arts Theatre Co Midlands Arts Centre Birmingham 1972–74, co fndr and dir Second City Theatre Co Birmingham 1974, assoc dir Phoenix Theatre Leicester 1974, artistic dir The Duke's Playhouse Lancaster 1975–78, dir Tynewear Theatre Co Newcastle Playhouse 1983–87 (co-fndr and artistic dir 1983–87), dir Tyne Theatre Co Newcastle 1987–88, dir Fay Weldon's adaption of Ibsen's A Doll's House Oxford Stage Co 1988, dir The Arts Centre Univ of Warwick 1989–90, exec prodr English Shakespeare Co (with artistic dirs Michael Bogdanov and Michael Pennington, *qqv*) 1990–92, chief exec Leicester Haymarket Theatre 1992–; has directed over 100 professional prodns incl: West End (Strippers and Bring Me Sunshine), nat tours and regnl repertory; memb: Lab Party Arts Study Gp 1974–76, Northern Arts Drama Panel 1978–80, Arts Cncl Touring Bd 1989–92, CNAA Validation Panel for BA Hons English Sunderland Poly 1988, BA Performing Arts and Arts Mgmnt De Montfort Univ 1992; *children's plays* Merlin the Wizard (co author, 1969), Billy Bodger's Magic Circus (1974); *Recreations* sport, cooking, music; *Style*— John Blackmore, Esq; ✉ Leicester Haymarket Theatre, Belgrave Gate, Leicester LE1 3YQ (☎ 0116 253 0021, fax 0116 251 3310)

BLACKMORE, Lady Pamela Maxwell; *née* Fyfe; da of 1 and last Earl of Kilmuir, GCVO, PC (d 1967); *b* 14 Oct 1928; *Educ* Crofton Grange, LMH Oxford; *m* 1, 24 May 1950, Clive Wigram (d 1956), o s of late Nathan Graham Wigram; 1 da; m 2, 26 Oct 1957, Courtenay Thomas Gardner Blackmore (d 1992), 2 s of late Rev Canon Alfred T G Blackmore, of Apple Trees, Steeple Ashton, Wilts; 1 s, 2 da; *Career* chm S Eastern Greenwich and Woolwich Div Inner London Bench 1983–86 (dep chm 1976–83 and 1986–94), memb Inner London Probation Ctee 1986–90, memb David Isaac Ctee 1980–89, chm Ilderton Project 1989–93; JP Inner London; Freeman City of London; *Style*— The Lady Pamela Blackmore; ✉ 61 Riverview Gardens, Castelnau, London SW13 9QZ

BLACKMORE, Prof Stephen; s of Edwin Arthur Blackmore, and Josephine, *née* Henwood; *b* 30 July 1952; *Educ* Cheltenham GS, St George's Sch Hong Kong, Univ of Reading (BSc, PhD); *m* 7 July 1973, Patricia Jane Melrose, *née* Hawley; 1 da (Elizabeth Jane b 27 Oct 1979), 1 s (Roger Arthur b 20 June 1982); *Career* botanist Royal Soc Aldabra Res Station Seychelles 1976–77, lectr in botany and head Nat Herbarium Univ of Malawi 1978–80; Natural History Museum: head of palynology Dept of Botany 1980–90, keeper of botany 1990–, assoc dir of life sciences 1992–95; chm UK Systematics Forum 1993, pres Systematics Assoc 1994–; Trail Crisp medal Linnean Soc 1987, Bicentenary medal Linnean Soc 1992; FLS 1976, FIBiol 1993; author of over 70 scientific papers and 7 botanical books; *Recreations* photography, blues guitar music; *Style*— Prof Stephen Blackmore; ✉ Natural History Museum, Cromwell Road, London SW7 5BD (☎ 0171 938 8992, fax 0171 938 9232)

BLACKSHAW, Alan; OBE (1992), VRD (1970); s of Frederick William Blackshaw (d 1983), of Blundellsands, Liverpool, and Elsie, *née* MacDougall (d 1978); *b* 7 April 1933; *Educ* Merchant Taylors' Sch Crosby, Wadham Coll Oxford (MA); *m* 1, 1956 (m dis 1983), Jane Elizabeth Turner; 1 da (Sara); m 2, 1984, Dr Elspeth Paterson, da of late Rev Gavin C Martin; 1 s (Alasdair b 1985), 2 da (Elsie b 1987, Ruth b 1990); *Career* RM 1954–56, RMR 1954–74, Capt; business conslt and author; HM Civil Serv: joined 1956, under sec Dept of Energy 1974–79 (dir gen Offshore Supplies Office 1976–78, head of Coal Div 1978–79); pres Br Mountaineering Cncl 1973–76 (patron 1976–); memb: Scot Cncl for Devpt and Indust 1974–78, Scot Sports Cncl 1990–95, Scot Natural Heritage 1991–, Adventure Activities Licensing Authy 1996–; conslt dir Strategy International Ltd 1979–91, dir Paths for All Partnership Ltd 1996–, assoc Oakwood Environmental Ltd 1991–; hon advsr Mountaineering Cncl of Scot 1994–, sec (Edinburgh Branch) Oxford Soc 1989–; chm: Br Ski Fedn 1984–86, Nat Mountain Centre Plas y Brenin 1986–95, Mountaineering Cmmn Union Internationale des Associations d'Alpinisme (UIAA) 1990–, UK Mountain Trg Bd 1991–94, Scot Nat Ski Cncl 1991–94 (pres 1994–), Access and Conservation Group UIAA 1995–; Freeman City of London 1966; FRGS, FInstPet; *Books* The Alpine Journal (ed 1968–70), Mountaineering (3 edn, 1975); *Recreations* mountaineering, skiing, sailing; *Clubs* Alpine, Ski Club of GB (hon memb), Royal Forth Yacht; *Style*— Alan Blackshaw, Esq, OBE, VRD; ✉ 2 Clark Rd, Edinburgh EH5 3BD (☎ 0131 467 3366, fax 0131 467 3367); Les Autannes, Le Tour, F74402 Argentière, France (☎ 00 33 04 50 54 12 20)

BLACKSHAW, Ian Stewart; s of late William Parkington Blackshaw, of Derbys; *b* 18 Dec 1943; *Educ* King Edward VII Sch Lytham St Anne's, Univ of London, Madrid Univ; *m* 1970, Christine, da of late Thomas Haworth, of Lytham St Anne's; 2 s; *Career* admitted slr 1967, private practice in NW England, London and Madrid and corp practice with Coca-Cola and GKN 1967–80, sec of Bd and legal advsr Monsanto plc 1980–81, counsel for int affrs Gomez-Acebo & Pombo Madrid 1981–86; legal advsr: Br Embassy Madrid 1981–86, Br Chamber of Commerce Spain 1981–86, Europe Middle East Africa Div RJR Nabisco Geneva 1986–90, vice pres (legal affrs) ISL Marketing Group AG Lucerne 1990–91; ptnr Co and Commercial Dept Bird & Bird Slrs London and Brussels 1991–92, ptnr Intellectual Property Dept Field Fisher Waterhouse Slrs London, Brussels and Beijing 1992–93, int counsel De La Rosa & Asociados (Abogados) Seville and Marbella Spain 1994–95; visiting prof of int business law Inst of Int Legal Studies Salzburg; memb: Int Bar Assoc, LES Int; author of several books and articles on legal subjects; *Recreations* music, travel, family pursuits; *Clubs* Travellers', Baur au Lac (Zurich); *Style*— Ian S Blackshaw, Esq; ✉ New Cottage, Eversley, Hants (☎ 0118 973 2213); Chalet Suisse, Les Crys, La Roche-sur-Foron, France (☎ 00 33 50 25 11 73)

BLACKSTONE, Baroness (Life Peeress UK 1987), of Stoke Newington, Greater London; Tessa Ann Vosper Blackstone; *née* Blackstone; er da of late Geoffrey Vaughan Blackstone, CBE, GM (d 1989), of Bures, Suffolk, and Joanna, *née* Vosper; *b* 27 Sept 1942; *Educ* Ware GS for Girls, London Sch of Economics and Political Science (BSc, PhD); *m* 1963 (m dis), Thomas Charles Evans (d 1985); 1 s (Hon Benedict Evans, *qv*), 1 da (Hon Liesel); *Career* assoc lectr in sociology Enfield Coll of Technol 1965–66, asst lectr then lectr in social admin LSE 1966–75, fell Centre for Studies in Social Policy 1972–74, advsr Central Policy Review Staff Cabinet Office 1975–78, prof of educational administration Univ of London Inst of Education 1978–83, dep education offr (Resources) ILEA 1983–86, clerk to the Authy and dir of education ILEA April-Nov 1986, Rowntree special res fell Policy Studies Inst 1986–87, master Birkbeck Coll Univ of London 1987–; chm: Fabian Soc 1984–85, General Advsy Cncl BBC 1987–91, Inst for Public Policy Res 1988–; memb: Arts Cncl Planning Bd 1986–90, Bd Royal Opera House 1987– (chm Ballet Bd 1991–), Mgmnt Ctee King Edward's Hosp Fund for London 1990–95; dir: Fullemploy Group 1984–91, Br Assoc for Central and Eastern Europe 1987–, Thames Television 1991–92; tstee Natural History Museum 1992–; *Books* Students in Conflict: The LSE in 1967 (co-author, 1970), A Fair Start: The Provision of Pre-School Education (1971), The Academic Labour Market: Economic and Social Aspects of a Profession (co-author, 1974), Disadvantage and Education (co-author, 1982), Testing Children: Standardised Testing in Local Education Authorities and Schools (co-author, 1983), Response to Adversity (co-author, 1983), Inside the Think Tank: Advising the Cabinet 1971–83 (co-author, 1988), Prisons and Penal Reform (1990); *Style*— The Rt Hon Baroness Blackstone; ✉ 2 Gower St, London WC1; Birkbeck College, Malet St, London WC1 (☎ 0171 631 6274)

BLACKTOP, Rev Graham Leonard; s of Leonard Blacktop (d 1981), and Grace Ivy May, *née* Evans (d 1988); *b* 21 July 1933; *Educ* Christ's Coll Finchley; *m* 9 May 1959, Alison Margaret, da of Kenneth Campbell; 3 da (Louise b 1960, Catherine b 1962, Ruth b 1965); *Career* cmmnd Royal Fusiliers (City of London Regt) and Royal W African Frontier Force 1951–54, TA Middx Regt (Duke of Cambridge's Own) and Herts Regt 1954–61; jr clerk Standard Bank of S Africa 1949–51, md Alexanders Discount plc 1983–91 (joined 1954); contrib articles to: Euromoney, American Banker, Jl of the Inst of CAs in Scotland, Jl of the Cricket Soc; non-stipendary Anglican priest (ordained 1985); Liveryman: Worshipful Co of Painter-Stainers 1969 (Hon Chaplain 1991, Renter Warden 1994–95), Worshipful Co of Parish Clerks 1980 (Master 1996–97); *Publications* Thou shalt not lend upon usury (1992), The Background to the New Testament - four addresses (1996); *Recreations* Dorset interregna, watching cricket, travel; *Clubs* MCC, Army & Navy; *Style*— The Rev Graham Blacktop; ✉ Dairy House, Wolfeton, Dorchester, Dorset DT2 9QN (☎ 01305 262184)

BLACKWELL, Sir Basil Davenport; kt (1983); s of late Alfred Blackwell, and late Hilda Kathleen Sophia Bretherick (later Mrs Lloyd); *b* 8 Feb 1922; *Educ* Leeds GS, St John's Coll Cambridge (MA), Univ of London (BSc); *m* 1948, Betty, da of Engr Capt Meggs, RN; 1 da (Susan); *Career* chm: Westland Group of Cos 1985 (dep chm and chief exec 1984–85, vice chm and chief exec 1974–84), Westland Helicopters Ltd 1976–85, British Hovercraft Corporation 1979–85, Normalair-Garrett Ltd 1979–85; memb Cncl Bath Univ 1986–; chm Astrid Tst 1986–93; Liveryman Worshipful Co of Coachmakers & Coach Harness Makers; Hon DSc Bath 1984; FEng 1978, FIMechE, FRAeS (Gold Medal 1982); *Recreations* gardens, gardening; *Clubs* United Oxford and Cambridge Univ; *Style*— Sir Basil Blackwell, FEng; ✉ High Newland, Newland Garden, Sherborne, Dorset DT9 3AF (☎ 01935 813516)

BLACKWELL, Colin Roy; s of John Harris (d 1931), of Witheridge, and Marjorie Grace Blackwell (d 1982); *b* 4 Sept 1927; *Educ* West Buckland, Univ of Bristol (BSc); *m* 1979, Susan Elizabeth, da of Brig Cecil Hunt, CBE (d 1985), of Chichester; *Career* cmmnd 83 LAA Regt RA served ME 1946–48; Freeman Fox and Ptnrs Conslt Engrs: joined 1951, site engr Gold Coast (later Ghana) 1955–57, sr engr 1957–68, princ engr 1969–82; dir Freeman Fox Ltd 1983–87, int conslt on telescopes and observatories Hyder Consulting Ltd (formerly Acer Freeman Fox then Acer Consultants Ltd) 1987–; memb: CIRIA Res Ctee 1976–79, Br Cncl Mission to Saudi Arabia 1985, BSI CSB Ctee 1986–91; FICE, FASCE, FRAS; *Clubs* Athenaeum; *Style*— Colin Blackwell, Esq; ✉ 34 Drayton Gardens, London SW10 9SA (☎ 0171 370 1145, fax 0171 835 1351); Hyder Consulting Ltd, 29 Bressenden Place, London SW1E 5DZ (☎ 0171 316 6000, fax 0171 316 6215)

BLACKWELL, Dr John Charles; CBE (1988); s of Charles Arthur Blackwell (d 1989), and Louisa Amy, *née* Sellers; *b* 4 Nov 1935; *Educ* Glynn GS Ewell Surrey, Dudley Coll of Educn (CertEd), Univ of Bristol (BA, MEd, PhD); *m* 1, 3 Aug 1961 (m dis 1973), Julia, *née* Rose; 1 s (Mark Frazer Charles b 23 Aug 1963); m 2, 1978, Inger Beatrice Lewin; 1 step s (Patrick Richard b 23 Oct 1967); *Career* Met Police Cadet 1952–53, RAF 1954–56; teacher Dempsey Secdy Sch London 1958–60; British Cncl: asst rep Tanzania 1966–70, educn offr Calcutta India 1971–72, asst educn offr New Delhi India 1973–75, head Schs and Teacher Educn Unit London 1976–78; asst cultural attaché Br Embassy Washington DC 1979; British Cncl: dir Educn Contracts Dept London 1980–83, rep Indonesia 1983–89, devpt advsr Educn and Sci Div Manchester 1993–95 (dir 1989–92), ret; chm Educn and Trg Export Ctee 1989–95; memb: Bd Bd Br Accreditation Cncl 1990–95, Bd Int Agric Trg Prog 1990–95; *Recreations* angling, boating; *Style*— Dr John Blackwell, CBE

BLACKWELL, Nigel Stirling; s of Richard Blackwell, DSC (d 1980), and Marguerite, *née* Holliday; *b* 18 March 1947; *Educ* Winchester, St Edmund Hall Oxford (MA); *m* 22 Sept 1984, Eliza Pumpelly (d 1995), da of Frank Mauran III, of Rhode Island; 1 s (Richard Raphael Holliday b 17 June 1989), 1 da (Georgina Stirling b 27 July 1986); *Career* dep chm and chief exec offr Blackwell N America 1979–86, jt md BH Blackwell 1980–83 (dir 1974), md The Blackwell Gp 1983–89, chm and md Blackwell Retail Gp 1983–89; chm: Blackwell Publisher Ltd (formerly Basil Blackwell Ltd) 1985–, Blackwell Publishing 1989–, Blackwell Science (formerly Blackwell Scientific) 1990– (dir 1980–), Munksgaard Publishers Copenhagen 1992– (dir 1987–); dir Western Provident Assoc

1990–; chm Richard Blackwell Scholarship Tst; *Recreations* country pursuits; *Clubs* Brooks's, Leander (Henley-on-Thames), Dunes (Narragansett RI), Vincent's, White's; *Style*— Nigel Blackwell, Esq; ✉ The Blackwell Publishing Companies, 50 Broad Street, Oxford OX1 3BQ (☎ 01865 791638, fax 01865 791638)

BLACKWELL, Dr Norman Roy; s of Albert Edward Blackwell (d 1972), and Frances Evelyn, *née* Lutman; *b* 29 July 1952; *Educ* Latymer Upper Sch Hammersmith, Royal Acad of Music (jr exhibitioner), Trinity Coll Cambridge (MA), Wharton Business Sch Univ of Pennsylvania (Thouron Scholar, MBA, PhD); *m* 1974, Brenda, da of Thomas Clucas; 2 da (Jane b 1979, Sarah b 1983), 3 s (Simon b 1981, Richard b 1987, William b 1989); *Career* strategic planning Plessey Co 1976–78, with McKinsey & Co 1978–86, special advsr Prime Minister's Policy Unit 1986–87, ptnr McKinsey & Co 1988–95, head Prime Minister's Policy Unit 1995–; *Recreations* classical music, walking, gardening; *Clubs* Carlton, RAC; *Style*— Dr Norman Blackwell; ✉ Prime Minister's Policy Unit, 10 Downing Street, London SW1A 2AA

BLACKWOOD, Brian; s of George Blackwood (d 1971), of Reigate, Surrey, and Eva Blanche, *née* French (d 1964); *b* 4 Feb 1926; *Educ* Holmesdale Sch Reigate, Redhill Tech Coll, Inverness HS, Tunbridge Wells Sch of Art, Architectural Assoc, Northern Poly, Univ Coll London (Dip TP), Dept of History of Art Birkbeck Coll Univ of London, Univ of York Inst of Advanced Architectural Studies (Dip Conservation Studies), Courtauld Inst of Art Univ of London, Hertfordshire Coll of Art and Design St Albans, Chelsea Coll of Art; *m* 1950 (m dis 1974); 1 s (Hugh Brian b 7 Jan 1955), 2 da (Jane Blanche (Mrs Mark Massey) b 22 Sept 1952, Jill Ann (Mrs Ed Branch) b 11 April 1962); *Career* artist, photographer, architect, conservationist, town planner and leading authy on lives and works of architects Smith and Brewer (contrib on them to Catalogue of the Drawings Collection of RIBA and The Dictionary of Art); local govt 1945–70; Tunbridge Wells Borough Cncl 1951–62, Stevenage Devpt Corp 1962–66, head of design and conservation Herts Co Planning Dept 1966–70; architectural advsr The Victorian Soc 1974–75; memb: St Albans Diocesan Advsy Ctee for the Care of Churches 1972–77, William Morris Soc Ctee 1974–77, City of Cambridge Listed Bldgs Panel 1974–, Cncl Ancient Monuments Soc 1982–, Cases Ctee Herts Conservation Soc 1987– (Exec Ctee 1992–), N Herts Crime Prevention Panel 1977–89; fndr memb: Royal Tunbridge Wells Civic Soc 1959, Cncl for Ind Archaeology 1990; with Surrey Special Constabulary 1950; Honours Cert Royal Drawing Soc 1935; Freeman City of London 1979, Liveryman Worshipful Co of Painter-Stainers 1984; FRSA 1947, FRIBA 1968 (ARIBA 1961), FRTPI 1974 (AMTPI 1968), FSAScot 1972, ARHistS 1976, FSAI 1976, FRGS 1983, fell Cambridge Philosophical Soc 1986, FLS 1990, memb Soc of Architect Artists 1993; *Recreations* archaeology, researching for a Dictionary of Architects of Cambridge Buildings 1800–1940, listening to music, writing; *Clubs* Art Workers' Guild, Cambridge University Cricket Club (CUCC), Cambridge University Rugby Union Football Club (CURUFC); *Style*— Brian Blackwood, Esq; ✉ Ebony House, Whitney Drive, Stevenage, Herts SG1 4BL (☎ 01438 725111)

BLAGG, Nikola Kate; da of Cedric Charles Blagg, of Peterborough, and Enid, *née* Hancock; *b* 27 Sept 1955; *Educ* Stewards Comp Harlow Essex, UCL (BSc); *m* Kevin Michael O'Connell; 1 s (Sam b 25 Oct 1988), 1 da (Ellen b 4 Nov 1993); *Career* media trainee Albany Advertising International 1979–80, media exec rising to assoc dir managing Int Media Dept D'Arcy MacManus & Masius (now DMB&B) 1980–85; Carat International (int media planning and buying) 1985–: joined 1985, subseqeuntly media dir then md, currently commercial dir; dir Carat UK 1991–96; memb Int Advtg Assoc 1980; *Style*— Ms Nikola Blagg; ✉ Carat International, Broadway House, 2–6 Fulham Broadway, London SW6 1AA (☎ 0171 381 8010, fax 0171 385 3233)

BLAGG, Dr Thomas Frederick Colston; s of Lt-Col Thomas Colston Blagg (d 1983), of Brunsell Hall, Car-Colston, Notts, and Loys Willis, *née* Cope (d 1989); *b* 10 Aug 1942; *Educ* Oakham, Keble Coll Oxford (BA, MA), Inst of Archaeology Univ of London (PhD); *Career* admitted slr 1967, in practice 1967–70; freelance archaeologist 1970–78, memb Educn Serv Br Museum 1978, sr lectr in archaeology Univ of Kent 1991– (lectr 1978–91); FSA 1983; *Books* The Roman Riverside Wall and Monumental Arch in London (jtly, 1980), Papers in Iberian Archaeology (jtly, 1984), Military and Civilian in Roman Britain (jtly, 1984), Excavations at Hal Millieri, Malta (jtly, 1990), The Early Roman Empire in the West (jtly, 1990); *Recreations* travel (wine and ruins), shooting, London; *Style*— Dr Thomas Blagg; ✉ Darwin College, The University, Canterbury, Kent CT2 7NY (☎ 01227 764000)

BLAHNIK, Manolo; s of E Blahnik (d 1986), and Manuela, *née* Rodrigo-Acosta; *b* 28 Nov 1943; *Educ* Univ of Geneva, Louvre Art Sch Paris; *Career* designer of shoes and furniture; co proprietor 1973–; *Awards* Fashion Cncl of America Award 1988, Hispanic Inst Washington Autonio Lopez Award 1990, Br Fashion Cncl Award 1990, Fashion Cncl of America Award 1991 (won for second time), American Leather New York Award 1991; *Recreations* travel and painting; *Style*— Manolo Blahnik, Esq; ✉ 49–51 Old Church St, London SW3 5BS (☎ 0171 352 8622 and 0171 352 3863)

BLAIR, Sir Alastair Campbell; KCVO (1969, CVO 1953), TD (1950), WS (1932); 2 s of late William Blair, WS, of Edinburgh, and late Emelia Mylne Campbell; *b* 16 Jan 1908; *Educ* Charterhouse, Clare Coll Cambridge (BA), Univ of Edinburgh (LLB); *m* 1933, Catriona Hatchard, o da of late Dr William Basil Orr, of Edinburgh; 4 s (incl Robin Orr Blair and Michael Campbell Blair, *qqv*); *Career* former ptnr Dundas & Wilson, CS; sec Royal Co of Archers (Queen's Body Guard for Scotland) 1946–59, Capt 1982–84, Purse Bearer to The Lord High Cmmr to the Gen Assembly of the Church of Scotland 1961–69; JP Edinburgh 1954; *Style*— Sir Alastair Blair, KCVO, TD, WS; ✉ 7 Abbotsford Court, Colinton Rd, Edinburgh EH10 5EH (☎ 0131 447 3095)

BLAIR, Dr Alastair William; s of Dr Lyon Blair (d 1941), and Isobel, *née* Breen; *b* 11 Aug 1936; *Educ* Harris Acad, Univ of St Andrews (MB ChB); *m* 16 Oct 1970, Irene Elizabeth Greenhill Blair; 2 s (Oliver b 1972, Roderick b 1975); *Career* house offr and registrar posts Maryfield and King's Cross Hosps Dundee and Gt Ormond St Hosp London, lectr in child health Univs of Dundee and Aberdeen, Wellcome Swedish res fell Sweden, sr registrar paediatrics Southmead Hosp Bristol; currently: conslt paediatrician Kirkaldy Acute Hosps NHS Tst, hon sr lectr in child health Univs of St Andrews and Edinburgh; memb: Hosp Conslts and Specialists Assoc, Nat Assoc of Clinical Tutors; sec and treas Scottish Paediatric Soc 1987–94; *Books* Prenatal Paediatrics: a Handbook for Obstetricians and Paediatrician (1971); *Recreations* sailing, private flying, jazz; *Style*— Dr Alastair Blair; ✉ Paediatric Unit, Victoria Hospital, Kirkcaldy, Fife KY2 5AH (☎ 01592 261155, fax 01592 202248)

BLAIR, Rt Hon Anthony Charles Lynton (Tony); PC (1994), MP (Lab) Sedgefield (majority 14,859); s of Leo Charles Lynton Blair and late Hazel Blair; *b* 6 May 1953; *Educ* Durham Choristers Sch, Fettes, St John's Coll Oxford; *m* 1980, Cherie Booth, QC, *qv*, da of Tony Booth, the actor; 2 s (Euan Anthony b 19 Jan 1984, Nicholas John b 6 Dec 1985), 1 da (Kathryn Hazel b 2 March 1988); *Career* called to the Bar Lincoln's Inn 1976; Parly candidate Beaconsfield by-election 1982, MP (Lab) Sedgefield 1983–; memb Shadow Cabinet 1988–, chief oppn spokesman on energy 1988–89, chief oppn spokesman on employment 1989–92, chief oppn spokesman on home affrs 1992–94, ldr Lab Pty and ldr of HM Opposition 1994–; *Style*— The Rt Hon Tony Blair, MP; ✉ House of Commons, London SW1A 0AA

BLAIR, Lt-Gen Sir Chandos; KCVO (1972), OBE (1962), MC (1941, and Bar 1944); s of Brig-Gen Arthur Blair, DSO (KOSB, d 1947), and Elizabeth Mary, *née* Hoskyns; *b* 25 Feb 1919; *Educ* Harrow and RMC Sandhurst; *m* 1947, Audrey Mary, da of F Guy Travers; 1 s, 1 da; *Career* 2 Lt Seaforth Highlanders 1939, served WWII 2 and 7 Seaforth Highlanders, Lt-Col 1957, CO 4 Kings African Rifles 1959–61, Brig 1964, GOC 2 Div BAOR 1968–70, Maj-Gen 1968, Defence Servs Sec MOD 1970–72, GOC Scotland and govr of Edinburgh Castle 1972–76, Lt-Gen 1972; *Clubs* Naval and Military; *Style*— Lt-Gen Sir Chandos Blair, KCVO, OBE, MC

BLAIR, David Hetherington; s of late George Tallantyre Blair, of Penrith, and late Mary Isobel, *née* Hetherington; *b* 22 Dec 1943; *Educ* Queen Elizabeth GS Penrith; *m* Vanessa, da of late Albert George Taylor; 2 da (Maxine b 1965, Zoe b 1968), 1 s (Joshua b 1986); *Career* John Laing Construction Ltd: joined 1962, dir 1988–95, chm 1995–; chm Laing Construction plc 1995–, main bd dir John Laing plc 1994–; FCIOB, FRICS; *Style*— David H Blair, Esq; ✉ John Laing plc, Page Street, London NW7 2ER (☎ 0181 906 5691, fax 0181 906 5617)

BLAIR, Prof Gordon Purves; CBE (1995); s of Gordon Blair (d 1984), and Mary Helen, *née* Purves (d 1994); *b* 29 April 1937; *Educ* Larne GS, The Queen's Univ of Belfast (BSc, PhD, DSc); *m* 23 July 1964, Norma Margaret, da of James Millar (d 1979); 2 da (Rosemary b 15 June 1969, Alison b 2 March 1973); *Career* asst prof New Mexico State Univ 1962–64; The Queen's Univ of Belfast: lectr in mechanical engrg 1964–71, sr lectr 1971–73, reader 1973–76, prof 1976–, head of dept 1982–89, pro vice chllr 1989–94; chm Automobile Div IMechE 1991–92, FIMechE 1976, FSAE 1979, FEng 1982; *Books* The Basic Design of Two-Stroke Engines (1990), Design and Simulation of Two-Stroke Engines (1996); *Recreations* fishing, golf; *Clubs* Cairndhu Golf, Royal Portrush Golf; *Style*— Prof Gordon Blair, CBE, FEng; ✉ 9 Ben Madigan Park South, Newtownabbey, Co Antrim NI BT36 7PX (☎ 01232 773280); Department of Mechanical & Manufacturing Engineering, School of Mechanical and Process Engineering, Ashby Building, The Queen's University of Belfast BT9 5AH (☎ 01232 245133, fax 01232 661729)

BLAIR, Isla Jean; da of Ian Baxter (d 1981), of Blair Hill, Horsham, Sussex, and Violet Barbara Skeoch; *Educ* St Marays Dunblane Scotland, W Preston Manor Rustington Sussex, RADA; *m* 1968, Julian Glover, *qv*; 1 s (Jamie Blair Glover b 1969); *Career* actress; *Theatre* Prospect Theatre Co: The Padlock, Geraldine in What the Butler Saw, Miss in Her Teens, title role in Miss Julie, Regan in King Lear, Lydia Languish in The Rivals, Viola in Twelfth Night, Fanny Burney in Boswell's Life of Johnson, Thieves Carnival; Yvonne Arnaud Theatre Guildford: Amanda in Private Lives (and tour), Nora in A Doll's House (and tour); Bristol Old Vic: Kate in Kiss Me Kate, Heloise in Abelard and Heloise, Maggie in Hobson's Choice, Varya in The Cherry Orchard, Mary in Vivat Regina, Dotty in Jumpers, Desdemona in Othello, Clea in Black Comedy, Millie in The Browning Version; Triumph Prodns: Sarah in Say Who Your Are, Myra in Hay Fever; Palace Theatre Watford: Ruth in So Long on Lonely Street, Linda/Maud in Suite in Two Keys, Mrs Erlynne in Lady Windermere's Fan; RSC: Aglaya in Subject Fits, Emilia in The Man of Mode; others incl: Mad, Bad and Dangerous to Know (Ambassadors and Doolittle Theater USA), Belise in The Sisterhood (Minerva Chichester), Marchesa Matilde Spina in Henry IV (Wyndham), Jenny in The Health Farm (King's Head), Regan in King Lear (Compass), Gilda in Design for Living (Nottingham Playhouse), Lydia Languish in The Rivals (American tour), Lady Teazle in The School for Scandal (Thorndike Leatherhead), Philia in A Funny Thing Happened on the Way to the Forum (Strand), Nora in A Doll's House (Thorndike Leatherhead), Rhoda in Popkiss (Globe), Irene Molloy in The Matchmaker (Chichester Theatre), Keyboard Skills (Southampton), Mrs Prentice in What the Butler Saw (RNT), The Verge (Orange Tree); *Television* roles for BBC incl: Caroline in A Legacy, Lady Caroline in When the Boat Comes In, title role in Jean Brodie (Open Univ), title role in 'Alexa' Love Story, Flora in The History Man, Jenny in The Beggars' Opera, Ruth in Mother Love (series), In Your Dreams, True Tilda; other credits incl: Sarah in The Liars (Granada), Daphne in Present Laughter (LWT), Linda in The Doctors, Elizabeth in Off Peak (STV), Laura in The Bounder (series Yorkshire), Caroline in Boon VI (Central), Maggie in The Good Guys (Havahall Pictures), Jenny in 'Cherubim and Seraphim' Inspector Morse VI (Central), Katherine Dunbar in The Advocates (series STV), The Office (Carlton); BBC appearances incl: Blake's Seven, An Englishman's Castle, Forgotten Love Songs, Doctor Who, The Final Cut; other appearances incl: The Avengers, Space 1999, Only When I Laugh, Six Centuries of Verse (Thames), C.A.T.S. Eyes (TVS), Taggart (STV), Bookie (series, STV), Haggard (Yorkshire), The Darling Buds of May, Medics, Dr Finlay, Hellfire, In Suspicious Circumstances; *Radio* incl: Mary Bannister in The House (series), Titania in A Midsummer Night's Dream; *Films* incl: The Tennis Court, Real Life, Lucy in Taste the Blood of Dracula, Battle of Britain, Mrs Donovan in Indiana Jones and The Last Crusade, Mrs Hawkins in Treasure Island, The Baroness in Valmont, Mother Agatha in The Monk; *Style*— Ms Isla Blair; ✉ c/o Chris Neil, ICM Ltd, Oxford House, 76 Oxford Street, London W1N 0AX (☎ 0171 636 6565, fax 0171 323 0101)

BLAIR, John Garde; s of Douglas Granville Blair (d 1976), of Melbourne, Aust, and Isobel Nora, *née* MacNamara (d 1989); *b* 1 Feb 1932; *Educ* Christian Brothers Coll St Kilda Melbourne, Melbourne Univ (BDSc); *m* 15 April 1961, Catherine Ann, da of John Edwin Marriott; 3 s (Matthew b 1962, Richard b 1965, David b 1973); *Career* dentist; in practice: Melbourne 1956–58 and 1961–63, London 1959–61 and 1963–65, Sunningdale 1965–88, Harley St 1982– (private 1970–); *Recreations* cars, cinema, theatre, 78 records, restoring period houses; *Clubs* Royal Society of Medicine; *Style*— John Blair, Esq; ✉ 100 Harley St, London W1N 1AF (☎ 0171 935 3668)

BLAIR, Lionel; *b* 12 Dec 1936; *m* 21 March 1967, Susan; 2 s (Daniel Mark b 6 Aug 1968, Matthew James b 26 June 1982), 1 da (Lucy Jane b 18 July 1971); *Career* boy actor in Watch on the Rhine (Stratford and the West End); choreography for and appearing with (on ATV): Dave King, Arthur Askey, Roy Castle, Jo Stafford, Harry Secombe, Bob Hope and Sammy Davis Jr; appeared in Royal Variety Performance 1968; TV shows incl: Give Us A Clue, Name That Tune; recent work incl: Jim in Mr Cinders, cameo role in Absolute Beginners, Seasons Greetings (with Marti Caine), starred in There's a Girl in my Soup, Don't Dress for Dinner (with sue Pollard and Les Dennis) (Bournmouth) 1993 and (Jersey) 1994; dir and starred in pantomime: Norwich Theatre Royal 1992 and 1993, Bath Theatre Royal 1994; chm: Help the Aged (Stage for Age), Grand Order of Water Rats; *Books* Stage Struck (autobiog); *Style*— Lionel Blair, Esq; ✉ c/o Peter Charlesworth Ltd, 2nd Floor, 68 Old Brompton Road, London SW7 3LQ (☎ 0171 581 2478, fax 0171 589 2922)

BLAIR, Louise Caroline Marian; da of Donald A Blair, of Brighton and the Outer Hebrides, and Alexandria, *née* Mackenzie-Macarthur; *b* 10 May 1958; *Educ* Canterbury Coll of Art, Hornsey Sch of Art (BA), Chelsea Sch of Art (MA); *m* 1981 (m dis 1989), Simon Edmonson; *Career* artist; lectr in fine art Univ of Newcastle 1980–81; *Solo Exhibitions* incl: Cockpit Theatre London 1981, Nicola Jacobs Gallery London 1983, 1985, 1986 and 1989; *Gp Exhibitions* incl: Young Contemporaries (ICA London) 1977, 1978 and 1980, Stowells Trophy (Royal Acad London) 1977 and 1978, Summer Exhibition (Royal Acad London) 1980, Sets for Station House Opera (Waterloo Gallery London) 1982, Passion and Power (Gracie Mansion Gallery NY) 1985, Heads (Nicola Jacobs Gallery London) 1986, Winter '89 (Nicola Jacobs Gallery London) 1989; work in The Contemporary Art Soc's public collection, designer of clothes for various commercials; *Recreations* dress design, writing, gardening; *Clubs* Chelsea Arts; *Style*— Miss Louise Blair; ✉ Nicola Jacobs Gallery

BLAIR, Michael Campbell; Hon QC (1996); s of Sir Alastair Campbell Blair, KCVO, TD, WS, *qv*; *b* 26 Aug 1941; *Educ* Cargilfield Sch Edinburgh, Rugby, Clare Coll Cambridge (MA, LLM), Yale Univ USA (MA); *m* 1966, Halldóra Isabel, da of late Richard

Anthony Conolly Tunnard, DL, of Lincs; 1 s (Alastair Magnus b 1974); *Career* called to the Bar Middle Temple 1965, bencher 1995; circuit admin Midland and Oxford Circuit 1982–86, under sec Lord Chllr's Dept 1982–87 (joined 1966, private sec to Lord Chllr and dep Sjt at Arms House of Lords 1968–71), Cabinet Office Top Mgmnt Prog 1986; The Securities and Investments Bd: dir legal servs 1987–91, gen counsel 1991–93, head Policy and Legal Affairs 1993–95, dep chief exec 1996–; memb Gen Cncl of the Bar 1989– (chm Professional Standards Ctee 1994, treas 1995–96), chm Bar Assoc for Commerce Fin and Indust 1990–91, memb Cncl of Legal Educn 1992–, chm Bar Conf 1993; FRSA 1993; *Books* Sale of Goods Act 1979 (1980), Financial Services: the New Core Rules (1991), Butterworth's European Law Service (vol on Banking and Financial Services, conslt ed 1992); *Recreations* family life; *Clubs* Athenaeum; *Style*— Michael Blair, Esq, QC; ✉ The Securities and Investments Board, Gavrelle House, 2–14 Bunhill Row, London EC1Y 8RA

BLAIR, Nicholas Peter; s of Maj Peter Blair, TD, and Ann de Quincey, *née* Walker; *b* 22 Feb 1949; *Educ* Wood Tutorial Coll; *Career* Collett Dickenson Pearce and Ptnrs Ltd (advtg) 1967–71; Bates Dorland Ltd (formerly BSB Dorland): gp md 1989–96, vice chm 1995–96, conslt 1996–; dir High Flyer Ltd 1994–; chm Eyden Construction Ltd 1989–; Freeman: City of London 1970, Worshipful Co of Dyers 1970; MIPA, MInstM; *Recreations* shooting, horseracing; *Clubs* Buck's; *Style*— Nicholas Blair, Esq; ✉ 41 Southwood Park, Highgate, London N6 5SG (☎ 0181 348 5730, fax 0181 347 9932); Bates Dorland Ltd, 121–141 Westbourne Terrace, London W2 6JR (☎ 0171 262 5077, fax 0171 724 3845, car 0836 311111, telex 27778)

BLAIR, Robin Orr; WS (1965); s of Sir Alastair Campbell Blair, KCVO, *qv*; *b* 1 Jan 1940; *Educ* Rugby, Univ of St Andrews (MA), Univ of Edinburgh (LLB); *m* 20 May 1972, (Elizabeth) Caroline McCallum, da of Ian McCallum Webster (d 1973), of Walberswick, Suffolk; 2 s (Matthew b 1974, Benjamin b 1976), 1 da (Alice b 1980); *Career* ptnr Davidson & Syme WS 1967–74, non-exec dir Tullis Russell & Co Ltd 1978–, chm Top Flight Leisure Group 1987– (non-exec dir 1977–), managing ptnr Dundas & Wilson CS 1988–91 (ptnr 1974, managing ptnr 1976–83), chm Scottish Solicitors' Staff Pension Fund 1985–91; Purse Bearer to the Lord High Cmmr to the Gen Assembly of the Church of Scotland 1988–; sec Assoc of Edinburgh Royal Tradesmen 1966–91, memb Queen's Bodyguard for Scotland (Royal Co of Archers) 1970–; memb Law Soc of Scotland 1965; *Recreations* skiing, hill walking; *Clubs* New (Edinburgh), Hon Co of Edinburgh Golfers; *Style*— Robin Blair, Esq, WS; ✉ 2 Greenhill Park, Edinburgh EH10 4DW (☎ 0131 447 4847); Dundas & Wilson, Saltire Court, 20 Castle Terrace, Edinburgh EH1 2EN (☎ 0131 228 8000, fax 0131 228 8888)

BLAIR, (Nicholas) Sean Patrick; *b* 23 Sept 1965; *Educ* Newcastle Poly (BA Design for Indust), Durham Univ Business Sch; *Career* Atkinson Design Associates Leicester May-Sept 1987, Pitney Bowes Corporate Industrial Design Connecticut June-July 1988, princ octo industrial design Newcastle upon Tyne 1989–95, design dir Design Cncl 1995–; visiting lectr Design Faculty Univ of Northumbria at Newcastle (formerly Newcastle Poly) 1989–95; awards incl: Redheads Advtg Design Award (jtly) 1990, Livewire Young Entrepreneur of the Yr 1990, first prize Young Business category Northern Business Awards 1990, Tyne & Wear Business Club Award 1993, Shell Livewire Significant Progress Award 1993, Business to Business Strategic Mktg scholar Kellogg Grad Sch of Mgmnt Illinois 1994; featured in pubns incl: Telegraph, Independent, Sunday Times, Design, Design Week; featured on TV: Tomorrows World (BBC 1) 1990, The Shadow (BBC 2) 1990, Design for Effective Marketing (MTVI and BBC Select) 1992 (writer and presenter); assoc memb RSA, MCSD; *Recreations* rock climbing, playing the clarinet; *Style*— Sean Blair, Esq; ✉ The Design Council, Haymarket House, 1 Oxendon Street, London SW1Y 4EE (☎ 0171 208 2121, fax 0171 839 6033)

BLAIR-GOULD, John Anthony; s of Ralph Blair-Gould (d 1984), and Lydia, *née* Geneen (d 1974); *b* 25 Jan 1942; *Educ* Sherborne; *m* 11 Sept 1982, Margaret Anne, da of Joseph Lewis Bryan, of Oakham, Rutland; *Career* admitted slr 1965, called to the Bar Inner Temple 1970, recorder of the Crown Court 1986–; inspr DTI 1988–89; asst Parly Boundary Cmmr 1992–95; *Recreations* music; *Style*— John Blair-Gould, Esq; ✉ 3 Raymond Buildings, Gray's Inn, London WC1R 5BH (☎ 0171 831 3833, fax 0171 242 4221)

BLAKE, Sir Alfred Lapthorn; KCVO (1979, CVO 1975), MC (1945), DL; s of late Leonard Nicholson Blake, and Nora Woodfall, *née* Lapthorn; *b* 6 Oct 1915; *Educ* Dauntsey's Sch, Univ of London (LLB); *m* 1, 1940, Beatrice Grace Nellthorp (d 1967); 2 s (Carey b 11 May 1943, David b 4 Oct 1945); m 2, 1969, Alison Kelsey Dick, of Boston, USA; *Career* served WWII RM (latterly Lt-Col cmdg 45 RM Commando, H Ops Commando); slr and Notary Public; former sr ptnr Blake Lapthorn Slrs Portsmouth and South Hampshire (conslt 1985–); memb Portsmouth CC 1950–67 (chm Educn Ctee 1952–58); Lord Mayor of Portsmouth 1958–59, memb Nat Youth Serv Devpt Cncl 1960–67, dir and tstee The Duke of Edinburgh's Award Scheme 1967–78; lay canon Portsmouth Cathedral 1962–72; patron: Elizabeth Fndn, Portsmouth Family Welfare; pres Portsmouth Youth Activities Ctee and other local community organisations; hon fell Portsmouth Univ; *Recreations* golf; *Style*— Sir Alfred Blake, KCVO, MC, DL; ✉ 21 Lombard Court, Lombard Street, Portsmouth PO1 2HU (☎ 01705 755099)

BLAKE, Andrew Nicholas Hubert; s of John Berchmans Blake, of Clitheroe, Lancs, and Beryl Mary, *née* Murphy; *b* 18 Aug 1946; *Educ* Ampleforth, Hertford Coll Oxford (MA); *m* 7 July 1978, Joy Ruth, da of Ronald Shevloff (d 1986), of Southport; 1 s (Ben b 4 June 1980); *Career* called to the Bar Inner Temple 1971, recorder of the Crown Court 1988–; *Recreations* skiing, the Turf, fishing; *Style*— Andrew Blake, Esq; ✉ 18 St John Street, Manchester M3 4EA (☎ 0161 834 9843)

BLAKE, Anthony Martin; s of David Alick Blake, of Croydon, and Joan Irene, *née* Powell; *b* 18 Aug 1946; *Educ* Whitgift Sch; *m* 1 Aug 1970, Marion Celia, da of Frederick George Davey (d 1993); 2 da (Clare Elizabeth b 1973, Sarah Louise b 1975); *Career* articled clerk Jacob Cavenagh & Skeet Chartered Accountants 1964–68, ptnr Neville Russell 1974– (joined 1969); licensed reader Southwark Diocese; FCA 1978 (ACA 1968); *Recreations* chess, cricket; *Clubs* Surrey CCC; *Style*— Anthony Blake, Esq; ✉ Neville Russell, 24 Bevis Marks, London EC3A 7NR (☎ 0171 377 1000, fax 0171 377 8931)

BLAKE, Anthony Teilo Bruce; s of Maj Charles Anthony Howell Bruce Blake (ka Korea 1951); hp to baronetcy of kinsman, Sir Richard Blake, 17 Bt; *b* 5 May 1951; *Educ* Wellington Coll, Lanchester Poly; *m* 1988, Geraldine, da of Cecil Shnaps, of Cape Town, South Africa; 1 s (Charles Valentine Bruce b 1994), 2 da (Sarah Elizabeth Bruce b 1990, Rachael Louise Bruce b 1991); *Career* engr; *Style*— Anthony Blake, Esq; ✉ Woodlands, Higher Lane, Lymm, Cheshire WA13 0AZ

BLAKE, Prof Christopher; CBE (1991); s of George Blake (d 1961), of Glasgow, and Eliza Malcolm, *née* Lawson (d 1983); *b* 28 April 1926; *Educ* Dollar Acad, Univ of St Andrews (MA, PhD); *m* 25 July 1951, Elizabeth, da of John Easson McIntyre, of Broughty Ferry (d 1947); 2 s (Duncan b 1952, Neil b 1954), 2 da (Catriona b 1959, Janet b 1960); *Career* Sub Lt RNVR 1944–47, served Med; Bonar prof of applied economics Univ of Dundee 1974–88; dir Alliance Trust plc 1974–94; chm: William Low & Co plc 1985–90, Glenrothes Devpt Corp 1987–96; memb Royal Cmmn on Environmental Pollution 1980–85, treas Royal Soc of Edinburgh 1985–89; FRSE 1978; *Recreations* golf, reading; *Clubs* New (Edinburgh), Royal and Ancient (St Andrews); *Style*— Prof Christopher Blake, CBE, FRSE; ✉ Westlea, 14 Wardlaw Gardens, St Andrews, Fife KY16 9DW (☎ 01334 473840)

BLAKE, Eur Ing David Charles; s of Walter David John Blake (d 1989), and Ellen Charlotte, *née* Wood; *b* 23 Sept 1936; *Educ* SE Essex Tech Sch and Coll; *m* 1, 17 Oct 1959 (m dis 1996), Della Victoria, *née* Stevenson; 2 s (Kean Nigel b 6 Aug 1960, Jeremy David b 3 Oct 1962); m 2, 28 May 1996, Christine Emmett; 1 da (Charlotte Catherine May); *Career* British Rail: various engrg appts 1953–69, electrification construction engr 1969–74, area maintenance engr Motherwell 1974–75, area maintenance engr Glasgow 1975–77, rolling stock engr Scot 1977–78, electrical engr Eastern 1978–80, chief mech and electrical engr Southern 1980–82, project mangr orgn 1982–83, mech and electrical engr London and SE 1983–84, dir of mfrg and maintenance policy 1984–87, dir of mech and electrical engrg 1987–91, md King's Cross Projects 1991–93, md Vendor Unit 1993–96, ret; ptnr Bees Services 1997–; vice chm Railway Div IMechE; CEng, FIMechE; *Recreations* gardening, hill walking; *Style*— Eur Ing David Blake; ✉ The Woolbarn, Cross Lane, Preston, Rutland LE15 9NQ; Bee Services, The Woolbarn, Cross Lane, Preston, Rutland LE15 9NQ (☎ and fax 01572 737581)

BLAKE, Prof David Leonard; s of Leonard Arthur Blake (d 1979), of London, and Dorothy Violet, *née* Bristow (d 1992); *b* 2 Sept 1936; *Educ* Latymer Upper Sch Hammersmith, Gonville and Caius Coll Cambridge (BA, MA), Deutsche Akademie der Künste East Berlin; *m* 24 Sept 1960, Rita Mary, da of Frank Adolphus Muir (d 1976); 2 s (Andrew b 23 Aug 1961, Daniel b 11 July 1964), 1 da (Claire b 24 Nov 1962); *Career* Nat Serv RAF 1955–57; teacher; prof of music Univ of York 1976– (lectr 1964, sr lectr 1971, head of dept 1981–84); composer: Chamber Symphony 1966, Lumina (cantata) 1969, Violin Concerto 1976, Toussaint Opera in 3 acts 1977, From the Mattress Grave song cycle 1978, Clarinet Quintet 1980, Rise Dove for bass and orchestra 1983, The Plumber's Gift opera in two acts 1988, Cello Concerto 1992, The Griffin's Tale for baritone and orchestra 1994; *Books* Hanns Eisler - a miscellany (1995); *Style*— Prof David Blake; ✉ Mill Gill, Askrigg, Leyburn, N Yorks DL8 3HR (☎ 01969 650364), Department of Music, University of York (☎ 01904 432451)

BLAKE, David William John; s of William Morley Blake (d 1985), and Winifred Juliet, *née* Virgo (d 1975); *b* 19 Oct 1946; *Educ* King Henry VIII GS Abergavenny, Univ of Sussex (BSc); *m* 1972 (m dis 1992), Marianne Neville-Rolfe, *qv*; *Career* journalist; roving European economic reporter Sunday Times 1970–72; The Times: joined 1973, foreign ed Business News, economics corr 1977–78, economics ed 1978–82, home ed 1982–86, managing ed Business News 1986–87; fndr then dep ed Sunday Correspondent 1987–91, assoc ed The European 1991–94, exec dir Goldman Sachs 1994–; parly candidate (Lab) East Grinstead 1974, local cncllr 1974–78; *Books* The Economics of Prosperity (ed with P Ormerod, 1980); *Recreations* cinema, music, travel; *Clubs* Reform; *Style*— David Blake, Esq; ✉ c/o Goldman Sachs Ltd, Peterborough Court, 133 Fleet Street, London EC4A 2BB (☎ 0171 774 1000, fax 0171 774 1181)

BLAKE, Howard David; OBE (1994); s of Horace Claude Blake (d 1985), of Brighton, and Grace, *née* Benson (d 1990); *b* 28 Oct 1938; *Educ* Brighton GS, RAM (LRAM); *Career* composer, conductor, pianist; dir Performing Right Soc 1978–87, fndr memb Assoc of Professional Composers 1980, visiting prof of composition RAM 1992; FRAM 1989; *Film and Theatre* film scores incl: The Duellists 1977, The Riddle of the Sands 1978, The Snowman 1982, The Lords of Discipline 1983, A Month in the Country 1986, Granpa 1989, A Midsummer Night's Dream 1996; theatre: Henry V RSC 1984, As You Like It RSC 1985; stage works: The Annunciation 1979, The Station 1987; ballet: The Annunciation, Reflections, Diversions, Court of Love, The Snowman 1993, Eva (Sweden) 1995; *Orchestral works* Toccata 1976, The Snowman 1982, Concert Dances 1984, Concerto for Clarinet and Orchestra 1984, Nursery Rhyme Overture 1984, Suite, The Up And Down Man 1985, The Conquest of Space 1988, Granpa 1988, Diversions 1989, The Bells 1991, Piano Concerto (cmmnd by The Philharmonia for the birthday of HRH The Princess of Wales) 1991, Violin Concerto (cmmnd by City of Leeds) 1993, The Land of Counterpane 1994, La Belle Dame Sans Merci 1994, Agatha Suite 1994, All God's Creatures 1995; chamber music: Reflections 1974, The Up and Down Man 1974, Concert Dances (wind band) 1988, Serenade for Wind Octet 1991; piano and instrumental music: Penillion 1975, Eight Character Pieces 1976, Dances for Two Pianos 1976, Prelude for Solo Viola 1979; brass ensemble and brass band: Sinfonietta 1981, Fusions 1986; *Vocal works* Three Sussex Songs 1973, A Toccata of Gallupi's 1978, Walking in the Air, Shakespeare Songs 1987, Make Believe; choral music: The Song of St Francis 1976, The New National Songbook 1976, Benedictus 1979, Festival Mass 1987, Four Songs of the Nativity 1991, Song of St Francis (revised, premiered at The Three Choirs Festival Hereford) 1991, Charter for Peace (cmmnd for UN fiftieth anniversary celebrations) 1995; *Recordings* The Snowman 1982, Clarinet Concerto 1986, Benedictus 1988, Granpa 1988, Piano Concerto 1990, Violin Concerto 1993; *Recreations* reading, walking, swimming; *Clubs* Groucho's; *Style*— Howard Blake, Esq, OBE; ✉ c/o Faber Music, 3 Queen Square, London WC1N 3AU (☎ 0171 833 7911/2, fax 0171 278 3817, telex 299633); c/o Sean Rourke, 296 Hughenden Road, High Wycombe, Bucks HP13 5PE (☎ 01494 461177, fax 01494 461188)

BLAKE, Jeremy Michael; s of Norman Edward Blake (d 1994), of Faversham, Kent, and Betty Mary, *née* Whiting; *b* 10 April 1953; *Educ* Sir Roger Manwood's GS Sandwich, Univ of Newcastle-upon-Tyne (H B Saint scholarship, BA, BArch), British Sch at Rome (Rome scholar in Architecture); *m* 1 Sept 1984, (Eleanor) Katharine Margaret, da of Rev (Francis) John Bacon; 3 s (Matthew David b 8 Feb 1986, Jonathan Paul b 22 April 1989, Timothy Stephen b 4 June 1992); *Career* architect; L J Couves & Partners Newcastle-upon-Tyne 1972–77, APP Horsham 1978–80, EPR London 1980, own practice Sussex 1980–84, Erith & Terry Dedham 1984–87, Fitzroy Robinson Ltd Cambridge 1987– (currently dir); memb: RIBA 1980, Faculty of Architecture Br Sch at Rome 1980, Soc of Architectural Historians of GB 1979; *Books* La Falsa Prospettiva in Italian Renaissance Architecture (1982); *Recreations* classical music, painting, swimming, gardening, reading; *Style*— Jeremy Blake, Esq; ✉ Director, Fitzroy Robinson Ltd, Grafton House, 64 Maids Causeway, Cambridge CB5 8DD (☎ 01223 361221, fax 01223 460285)

BLAKE, John Michael; s of Maj Edwin Francis Blake, MBE (d 1972), of London, and (Evelyn) Joyce, *née* Meadows; *b* 6 Nov 1948; *Educ* Westminster City GS, NW London Poly; *m* 29 June 1968, Diane Sutherland, da of Peter John Campbell (d 1973), of London; 1 s (Adam b 1985), 2 da (Emma b 1969, Charlotte b 1971); *Career* reporter: Hackney Gazette 1965–68, Evening Post Luton 1968–69, Fleet Street News Agency 1969–71; columnist: London Evening News 1971–80, London Evening Standard 1980–82, The Sun 1982–84; asst ed Daily Mirror 1984–88, ed The People 1988–89, prodr Sky Television 1990, md Blake Publishing 1991–; *Books* Up And Down With The Rolling Stones (1979), All You Needed Was Love (1981); *Recreations* sailing, skiing, distance running, travel; *Style*— John Blake, Esq; ✉ Blake Publishing, 3 Bramber Court, 2 Bramer Road, London W14 9PB

BLAKE, Jonathan Elazar; s of Asher Blake, of London, and Naomi, *née* Dūm; *b* 7 July 1954; *Educ* Haberdashers' Aske's, Queens' Coll Cambridge (MA, LLM); *m* 3 Aug 1980, (Marion) Isabel, da of Joseph Horovitz, of London; 1 da (Lucy Esther b 1984), 3 s (David Edward b 1987, Simon Andrew b 1989, Michael Alexander b 1993); *Career* slr; Stephenson Harwood 1977–82, ptnr SJ Berwin Co 1982– (currently head Private Equity); memb: Law Soc, Inst of Taxation, Br Venture Capital Assoc, Euro Venture Capital Assoc; *Books* Venture Capital Fund Structures in Europe, Venture Capital in Europe (contrib), AIM and EASDAQ in the New Enterprise Markets; *Recreations* family, theatre, walking, skiing; *Style*— Jonathan Blake, Esq; ✉ SJ Berwin & Co, 222 Grays Inn Rd, London WC1X 8HB (☎ 0171 533 2222, fax 0171 833 2860)

BLAKE, Sir (Francis) Michael; 3 Bt (UK 1907), of Tillmouth Park, Cornhill-on-Tweed, Co Northumberland; s of Sir (Francis) Edward Colquhoun Blake, 2 Bt (d 1950); *b* 11 July 1943; *Educ* Rugby; *m* 1968, Joan Ashbridge, o da of Frederic Cecil Ashbrige Miller, of Ramsay Lodge, Kelso; 2 s (Francis Julian b 1971, Nicholas Winston b 1974); *Heir* s, Francis Julian Blake b 17 Feb 1971; *Career* stockbroker; *Style*— Sir Michael Blake, Bt; ✉ The Dower House, Tillmouth Park, Cornhill-on-Tweed, Northumberland TD12 4UR (☎ 01890 882443)

BLAKE, Nicholas John Gorrod; QC (1994); s of Leslie Gorrod Blake (d 1960), and Jean Margaret, *née* Ballinger; *b* 21 June 1949; *Educ* Cranleigh, Magdalene Coll Cambridge (exhibitioner, MA), Inns of Court Sch of Law; *m* 5 July 1986, Clio, da of Chris Whittaker; 4 c (Lydia Beatrice b May 1986, Harrison b and d May 1987, Sophia Isobel b Oct 1988, Sebastian Patrick b June 1991); *Career* called to the Bar Middle Temple 1974; specialist in immigration law and in criminal, civil and admin law concerning human rights; former sec Haldane Soc of Socialist Lawyers, current chm Immigration Law Practitioners' Assoc; *Publications* Police, the Law and the People (1978), Wigs and Workers (1980), Policing the Miners' Strike (contrib, 1983), Jury Trial Under Attack (contrib, 1985), The New Nationality Law (with Ian Macdonald, 1983), Immigration Law and Practice (with Ian Macdonald, 1990 and 1995); *Style*— Nicholas Blake, Esq, QC; ✉ First Floor, 2 Garden Court, Middle Temple, London EC4Y 9BL (☎ 0171 353 1633, fax 0171 353 4621)

BLAKE, Prof Quentin Saxby; OBE (1988); s of William Blake, and Evelyn Blake; *b* 16 Dec 1932; *Educ* Downing Coll Cambridge (MA); *Career* freelance artist and illustrator; head of Dept of Illustration RCA 1978–86 (visiting prof 1989–); RDI, FCSD, sr fell RCA 1988; *Style*— Prof Quentin Blake, OBE, RDI; ✉ 30 Bramham Gardens, London SW5

BLAKE, Richard John Bowden; s of Frederick Milman Blake (d 1989), of Guildford, and Ida Mary (Mollie), *née* Wood; *b* 12 March 1936; *Educ* Aldenham Sch; *m* 1, 23 April 1960, Gillian Mary Wagner (d 11 July 1986); 1 s (Jonathan Rupert Bowden b 23 July 1962), 2 da (Annabelle Clare b 28 Feb 1965, Sophie Alexandra (twin) b 28 Feb 1965); m 2, 12 Aug 1988, Shirley Anne Virginia Edwards, da of Gerald Lee; *Career* Baker Todman: articled clerk 1954, chartered accountant 1960, ptnr 1964–93, chm London Mgmnt Ctee Baker Rooke 1981–82, staff ptnr 1973–76, sr ptnr 1986–93; chm Baker Tilly 1988–94; dir: Filtronic Comtek plc, Attenborough Holdings Group; chm Parkside Sch Tst; FCA; *Recreations* golf, theatre, racing, cricket; *Clubs* MCC, Turf, Saints & Sinners, Lucifers, Surbiton Hockey, Royal Porthcawl Golf; *Style*— Richard Blake, Esq; ✉ c/o Baker Tilly, 2 Bloomsbury St, London WC1B 3ST (☎ 0171 413 5100, fax 0171 413 5101)

BLAKE, Sir (Thomas) Richard Valentine; 17 Bt (I 1622), of Menlough, Galway; s of Sir Ulick Temple Blake, 16 Bt, of Saltergill, Yarm-on-Trees, Yorkshire (d 1963), and Elizabeth Longley-Cook (d 1978); *b* 7 Jan 1942; *Educ* Bradfield; *m* 1, 1976, Jacqueline, da of late Desmond E Daroux, and formerly w of Peter Alers Hankey; m 2, 1982 (m dis 1986), as her 3 husband, the singer Bertice Reading; m 3, 1991, Wendy, wid of late Anthony Ronald Roberts, and da of Edward William Gough (d 1965), of Richmond, Surrey; *Heir* kinsman, Anthony Teilo Bruce Blake b 5 May 1951; *Career* joined motor trade 1959; formerly car sales mangr Lavant Motor Centre; dir: Sir Richard Blake & Assocs 1967–75, City Chase Ltd 1980–84 (specialists in Rolls-Royce, Bentley and Gordon-Keeble cars); proprietor Autobart 1988–92, sales assoc Taylor's of Birdham 1995– (Rolls-Royce and Bentley specialists); *Recreations* gardening, three day eventing, vintage cars; *Clubs* Gordon-Keeble Owners' (hon life memb), Rolls-Royce Enthusiasts', Goodwood Racecourse, Cowdray Park Polo, Chiddingfold, Leconfield, Cowdray Hunt; *Style*— Sir Richard Blake, Bt; ✉ Old Janes, River, nr Petworth, W Sussex GU28 9AY (☎ 01798 861717, mobile 0831 855331); Lou Kalinou Lotissment 14, Cavalaire La Croix-Valmer, 83420 France (☎ 00 33 94 79 69 94); Menlough Castle, Co Galway, Republic of Ireland; (work ☎ 01243 513222)

BLAKE, Baron (Life Peer UK 1971); Robert Norman William Blake; er s of William Joseph Blake (d 1964), of Brundall, Norfolk, and Norah Lindley Daynes; *b* 23 Dec 1916; *Educ* King Edward VI Sch Norwich, Magdalen Coll Oxford (DLitt, MA); *m* 1953, Patricia Mary (d 1995), eldest da of Thomas Richard Waters (d 1983), of Great Plumstead, Norfolk; 3 da (Hon Deborah b 1955, Hon Letitia b 1960, Hon Victoria b 1963); *Career* sits as Conservative in House of Lords; served WWII Capt RA (POW Italy 1942–44, escaped 1944; despatches), MI6 1944–46; Christ Church Oxford: lectr 1946–47, student and tutor in politics 1947–68, censor 1950–55, sr proctor 1959–60, Ford's lectr in Eng history 1967–68, hon student 1977; provost Queen's Coll Oxford 1968–87, pro-vice chllr Univ of Oxford 1971–87; hon fell: Queen's Coll Oxford, Pembroke Coll Cambridge; Hon DLitt: Glasgow, Buckingham and E Anglia Univs, Westminster Coll Fulton Missouri; ed Dictionary of National Biography 1980–90; chm: Royal Cmmn on Historical Manuscripts 1982–89, Rhodes Tst 1983–87; tstee Br Museum 1978–88, dir Channel Four Television Co 1983–87; high bailiff Westminster Abbey 1988–89 (high steward 1989–); memb City Cncl Oxford 1957–64, JP Oxford 1964–86; memb Ct of Assts Worshipful Co of Dyers; FBA 1967; *Books* The Private Papers of Douglas Haig (ed, 1952), The Unknown Prime Minister, Bonar Law (1955), Disraeli (1966), The Conservative Party from Peel to Churchill (1970, 2nd edn The Conservative Party from Peel to Thatcher 1985), The Office of Prime Minister (1975), A History of Rhodesia (1977), The English World (ed, 1982), Disraeli's Grand Tour (1982), The Decline of Power 1915–1964 (1985), Churchill (ed with Roger Louis, 1993); *Recreations* reading and writing; *Clubs* Beefsteak, Brooks's, United Oxford and Cambridge, Norfolk County, Pratt's; *Style*— The Rt Hon the Lord Blake; ✉ Riverview House, Brundall, Norwich NR13 5LA (☎ 01603 712133)

BLAKEMORE, Prof Colin Brian; s of Cedric Norman Blakemore (d 1987), of Kidlington, Oxford, and Beryl Ann, *née* Smith; *b* 1 June 1944; *Educ* King Henry VIII Sch Coventry, Corpus Christi Coll Cambridge (BA, MA), Univ of California Berkeley (PhD), MA Oxon, ScD Cantab, DSc Oxon; *m* 28 Aug 1965, Andrée Elizabeth, da of Ronald George Washbourne (d 1995), of Coventry; 3 da (Sarah Jayne b 1974, Sophie Ann b 1976, Jessica Katy b 1979); *Career* Univ of California Berkeley Harkness fell of the Cwlth Fund 1965–67; Univ of Cambridge: demonstrator in physiology 1967–72, lectr in physiology 1972–79, Royal Soc Locke res fell 1976–79, official fell and dir of med studies Downing Coll 1971–79; Waynflete prof of physiology Univ of Oxford and professorial fellow Magdalen Coll Oxford 1979–; dir: McDonnell-Pew Centre for Cognitive Neuroscience 1990–, Med Res Cncl Interdisciplinary Research Centre for Cognitive Neuroscience 1996–; visiting prof: Dept of Psychology NY Univ USA 1970, Dept of Psychology Mass Inst of Tech USA 1971; visiting scientist Salk Inst San Diego California USA 1982, 1983 and 1992, McLaughlin visiting prof McMaster Univ Hamilton Ontario 1992, Regents' prof Univ of Calif Davis 1995–96; memb: BBC Sci Consultative Gp 1975–79, Scientific Advsy Bd Cognitive Neuroscience Inst NY 1981–, Sci Ctee Bristol Exploratory 1983–, Professional Advsy Ctee Schizophrenia: A National Emergency (SANE) 1989–, Exec Ctee Dana Alliance for Brain Initiatives NY and Washington DC 1996–; patron CORPAL (support gp for families affected by ageneis of the corpus callosum and Aicardi's Syndrome) 1989–, tstee Brain Child (charity supporting research into the developmental neuropsychology of cognitive disorders 1991–; numerous named lectures, hon appointments and awards incl: BBC Reith lectr 1976, Lethaby prof RCA 1978–79, Royal Soc Michael Faraday Award and Medal 1989, Osler Medal (RCP) 1993, Ellison-Cliffe Medal (RSM) 1993, Royal Soc lectr 1995, Physiological Soc Prize Review Lecture 1995, Leverhulme Research Grant 1995–96; Hon DSc: Univ of Aston 1992, Univ of Salford 1994; hon fell Corpus Christi Coll Cambridge 1994; memb: Brain Res Assoc 1968 (memb Nat Ctee 1973–77), Physiological Soc 1968, Experimental Psychological Soc 1968, Euro Brain and Behaviour Soc 1972 (memb Ctee 1974–76), Int Brain Res Orgn 1973 (memb Governing Cncl 1973–, memb Exec Ctee 1979–91), Cambridge Philosophical Soc 1975–79, Euro Neuroscience Assoc 1977 (memb Nominating Ctee 1988), Soc for Neuroscience 1981, Oxford Med Soc 1986, Child Vision Res Soc 1986 (memb Organising Ctee 1986–), Nat Conf of Univ Profs 1989, Br Assoc for the Advancement of Science 1990 (vice pres 1990–, pres-elect for 1997–98), Euro Biomedical Research Assoc (fndr memb) 1994, Academia Europaea 1995; foreign memb Royal Netherlands Acad of Arts and Sciences 1993, fell World Economic Forum 1994 and 1995; FRS 1992; *Books* Handbook of Psychobiology (1975), Mechanics of the Mind (1977), Mindwaves (1987), The Mind Machine (1988), Images and Understanding (1990), Vision: Coding and Efficiency (1990); *Publications* varied editorial work incl: memb Editorial Bds Vision Research and Int Review of Neurobiology, ed-in-chief Oxford Companion to the Body (OUP) 1996–; *Recreations* running, the arts; *Clubs* Chelsea Arts; *Style*— Prof Colin Blakemore, FRS; ✉ University Laboratory of Physiology, Parks Rd, Oxford OX1 3PT (☎ 01865 272470, fax 01865 272488)

BLAKEMORE, Michael Howell; s of Dr Conrad Howell Blakemore (d 1976), and Una Mary, *née* Litchfield (later Mrs Heyworth, d 1982); related through American paternal gm Maud Howell to US presidents John Quincey Adams and John Adams; *b* 19 June 1928, Sydney, NSW; *Educ* Cranbrook Sch, The King's Sch, Univ of Sydney, RADA; *m* 1, 1960 (m dis 1986), Shirley Mary Bush; 1 s (Conrad); m 2, 1986, Tanya, da of Clement McCallin (actor, d 1978); 2 da (Beatrice b 1981, Clementine b 1984); *Career* stage and film dir (occasional writer and actor); co-artistic dir Glasgow Citizen's Theatre 1966–68, assoc dir NT 1971–76, resident dir Lyric Theatre Hammersmith 1980; freelance dir of prize winning prodns: A Day in the Death of Joe Egg 1968, Arturo Ui 1969, Forget-Me-Not-Lane 1971; also dir of: The National Health 1969, Plunder 1975, Long Day's Journey Into Night 1971, The Front Page 1972 (Plays and Players Best Dir award for the latter two prodns), The Wild Duck, Make and Break, Noises Off, Design for Living, Knuckle, Candida, Separate Tables, Privates on Parade (also the film), Deathtrap, All My Sons, Benefactors (London and Broadway), Made in Bangkok, Lettice and Lovage (London and Broadway), Uncle Vanya, After The Fall, City of Angels (Broadway and London), Noises Off (London and Broadway, received Drama Desk Award 1984), The Sisters Rosensweig (Old Vic); film A Personal History of the Australian Surf (also wrote and acted in the latter, Peter Seller's Award for Comedy in the Standard Film Awards); actor The Last Bastion for Channel 10 television in Australia 1984; film actor, writer, dir Country Life (Australia) 1994; *Books* Next Season (1969); *Clubs* RAC; *Style*— Michael Blakemore, Esq; ✉ 18 Upper Park Rd, London NW3 2UP (☎ 0171 483 2576, fax 0171 483 2676)

BLAKEMORE, William Graham (Bill); s of Norman S Blakemore, of Wheatley Hill, Co Durham, and Mary, *née* Graham; *b* 26 Dec 1947; *Educ* The Johnston GS, St John's Coll York (CertEd), Univ of Leeds (BEd), Keele Univ (MEd); *m* 1969, Susan Patricia, da of Arthur Pexton; 1 da (Zōe Claire b 4 June 1976), 2 s (Kieron James b 11 April 1978, Liam Martyn b 17 April 1981); *Career* asst English teacher Wellington Boys' GS Salop 1971–75, second head of English dept The Grove Sch Market Drayton Salop 1975–78, head of English and head of house Minsthorpe HS and Community Coll South Elmsall W Yorks 1978–81, first dep head teacher Stirchley Upper Sch (now The Lord Silkin Sch) Telford 1982–1987, headteacher North Cumbria Technology Coll (formerly Harraby Sch) Carlisle 1988–; memb: NAS/UWT 1967–85, SHA 1985–; sec Cumbria Assoc of Secdy Headteachers 1990–94, chm NE Cumbria Secdy Headteachers 1990–95; *Recreations* rugby union, squash, gardening, target shooting, wild life protection, reading; *Clubs* Carlisle Rugby (hon vice pres), Carlisle South Rotary; *Style*— Bill Blakemore, Esq; ✉ North Cumbria Technology College, Edgehill Road, Carlisle, Cumbria CA1 3SL (☎ 01228 31435, fax 01228 810962)

BLAKENHAM, 2 Viscount (UK 1963); Michael John Hare; s of 1 Viscount Blakenham, OBE, PC, VMH (d 1982, 3 s of 4 E of Listowel), and (Beryl) Nancy, *née* Pearson, da of 2 Viscount Cowdray; *b* 25 Jan 1938; *Educ* Eton, Harvard (AB Econ); *m* 12 Jan 1965, his 1 cous, Marcia Persephone, da of Maj Hon Alan Victor Hare, MC (d 1995); 1 s, 2 da; *Career* 2 Lt The Life Gds 1956–57; English Electric 1958, Lazard Bros 1961–63, Standard Industrial Group 1963–71, Royal Doulton 1972–77, CE Pearson plc 1978–83; chm: Pearson plc 1983–, Financial Times Group Ltd 1983–93, MEPC plc 1993– (dir 1990–); ptnr Lazard Ptnrs 1984– (dir 1975–); dir: Sotheby's Holdings Inc 1987–, UK-Japan 2000 Gp 1990–; memb: Int Advsy Bd Lafarge 1979–, House of Lords Select Ctee on Sci and Technol 1985–88, Nature Conservancy Cncl 1986–90, House of Lords Select Ctee on Sustainable Development 1994–95; pres Sussex Wildlife Tst 1983–, vice-pres Royal Soc for the Protection of Birds 1986– (chm 1981–86); tstee Royal Botanic Gardens Kew and Wakehurst Place 1991–; *Style*— The Rt Hon Viscount Blakenham; ✉ Pearson plc, 3 Burlington Gardens, London W1X 1LE (☎ 0171 411 2000, fax 0171 411 2390)

BLAKER, Sir John; 3 Bt (UK 1919), of Brighton, Sussex; s of Maj Sir Reginald Blaker, 2 Bt, TD (d 1975), and Sheila Kellas, *née* Cran; *b* 22 March 1935; *m* 1, 1960 (m dis 1965), Catherine Ann, da of late Francis John Anselm Thorold; m 2, 1968, Elizabeth Katherine, da of Col John Tinsley Russell, DSO; *Heir* none; *Style*— Sir John Blaker, Bt; ✉ Stantons Farm, E Chiltington, nr Lewes, Sussex

BLAKER, Michael; *b* 19 Jan 1928; *Educ* Brighton Hove and Sussex GS, Heversham Sch, Brighton Coll of Art (NDD); *m* 1977, Catriona McTurk; *Career* artist, printmaker; proprietor own gallery New Bond St London 1951–53; ed and designer Printmakers' Jl 1983–93, memb Editorial Bd Printmaking Today; sr fell RE; *Exhibitions* solo and small gp exhbns: Hove Library 1949 and 1951, Foyles Gallery 1951, Bedford Coll London 1976, St Edmunds Art Centre Salisbury 1981, Medici Gallery 1986, Nevill Gallery Canterbury 1990, Four Thanet Artists (Broadstairs Library Gallery 1989, 1990 and 1992, Margate Library Gallery 1991 and 1992), The Thanet Group (Margate Library Gallery) 1995; larger gp exhbns incl: RA Summer Exhbns regularly, RE exhbn Bankside Gallery (featured artist 1992); *Collections* work in numerous public and private collections incl: Tate Gallery, V&A, S London Art Gallery, Brighton Gallery, Bedford Coll London, Ashmolean Museum Oxford, Fitzwilliam Museum Cambridge; *Books* The Autobiography of a Painter-Etcher (1985), A Beginner's Guide to Oil Painting (1994); *Style*— Michael Blaker, Esq; ✉ 122 Grange Road, Ramsgate, Kent CT11 9PT (☎ 01843 596401)

BLAKER, Lt-Col (Guy) Peter; s of Guy Stewart Blaker (d 1969), of Rotherfield Greys, Henley-on-Thames, and Dawn Laetitia Prudence, *née* Watson (gda of Gen Sir John Watson, VC, GCB); *b* 10 Nov 1936; *Educ* Lancing, Jesus Coll Cambridge (MA, LLB); *m* 18 Jan 1969, Hiltegund Maria, da of Dr Hermann Bastian (d 1945), of Freiburg-im-Breisgau; 2 s (Dominic b 1971, Nicholas b 1975), 1 da (Alexandra b 1970); *Career* Nat Serv, cmmnd W Yorks Regt 1957, Royal Green Jackets 1961–84, served Malaya, Borneo, Singapore, Cyprus, UK, Germany, Belgium (SHAPE); Army Aviation Pilot 1964–67, Staff Coll 1968, cmd Cambridge Univ Offrs Trg Corps 1979–82; Queen's Messenger 1984–85; gen mangr Newdata Publishing 1985–86, sec Gen Cncl and Register of Osteopaths 1987–95, sec Blackie Fndn Tst 1996–; lay chm Rotherfield Greys PCC; chm Berkshire Automobile Club; *Recreations* classical music, history, languages, ornithology, fly-fishing, bee-keeping, rowing; *Clubs* Naval and Military, MCC; *Style*— Lt-Col Peter Blaker;

✉ Greys Piece, Rotherfield Greys, Henley-on-Thames, Oxfordshire RG9 4QG (☎ 01491 628308)

BLAKER, Baron (Life Peer UK 1994), of Blackpool in the County of Lancashire and of Lindfield in the County of West Sussex; Sir Peter Allan Renshaw Blaker; KCMG (1983), PC (1983); s of Cedric Blaker, CBE, MC, ED (d 1965), of Scaynes Hill, Sussex, and Louise Douglas, *née* Chapple (d 1985); *b* 4 Oct 1922; *Educ* Shrewsbury, Trinity Coll Toronto (BA), New Coll Oxford (MA); *m* 1953, Jennifer, er da of Sir Pierson John Dixon, GCMG, CB (d 1965); 1 s (Hon Adam Pierson Renshaw b 1963), 2 da (Hon Antonia Helena Renshaw b 1957, Hon Candida Juliet Renshaw b 1961); *Career* WWII Capt Argyll and Sutherland Highlanders Canada (wounded); admitted slr 1948, called to the Bar 1952; Foreign Serv 1953–64; MP (C) Blackpool S 1964–92; Parly under sec Army 1972–74 and FCO 1974, min of state FCO 1979–81, min of state for Armed Forces 1981–83; chm Cons Pty Foreign and Cwlth Affairs Ctee 1983–92 (vice chm 1974–79); *Recreations* tennis, sailing, swimming, opera; *Clubs* Garrick; *Style—* The Rt Hon Lord Blaker, KCMG, PC

BLAKEWAY, (Arthur) John; s of Francis Lett Blakeway (d 1949), of Staverton, Cheltenham, Glos, and Bernice Marinda, *née* Matthews (d 1949); *b* 5 July 1925; *Educ* The Crypt GS Gloucester; *m* 1, 24 April 1946, Joyce Cynthia, da of Horace Forty; 3 s (Philip John b 1950, Francis Mark b 1952, Richard Clive b 1959), 1 da (Gillian Bridget b 1948); m 2, 8 April 1986, Rosemary Catherine de Courcy, da of Cdr Henry Leslie Spofforth Baker, RN, of Carrowduff House, Ballymacurley, Co Westmeath; *Career* served RN 1943–46; former chm and md of family co (started by father in 1925) Francis Blakeway Ltd fruit merchants; formerly farmer; chm BSJA 1976–83; MFH: Croome 1961–68, Belvoir (Duke of Rutland's Hounds) 1983–91; show dir and chm Horse of Year Show 1987–94; *Recreations* hunting; *Style—* John Blakeway, Esq; ✉ Blacklains Farm, Birdlip, Gloucester (☎ 01452 862355); 2B Eastbrooke Rd, Eastern Ave, Gloucester (☎ 01452 303376)

BLAKEY, Chief Constable David Cecil; QPM (1992); s of Cecil Blakey, and Elsie Blakey (d 1987); *b* 24 Nov 1943; *Educ* Jarrow GS, Univ of Newcastle upon Tyne (MBA (pt/t)); *m* 1966, Wendy Cartwright; 1 s (Stephen b 1967), 1 da (Kerris b 1970); *Career* VSO Sarawak 1962–63, police constable rising to supt Durham Constabulary 1963–84, chief supt Northumbria 1984–86, asst chief constable West Mercia (Hereford, Worcester, Shropshire) 1986–89, Royal Coll of Def Studies 1989, dep chief constable Leics Constabulary 1990–91, chief constable West Mercia 1991– (joined as dep chief constable 1991); pres ACPO 1997–98 (second vice pres 1995–96, first vice pres 1996–97); vice pres Hereford and Worcester Scouts, pres Hereford and Worcester RLSS (chm Midlands Region); *Clubs* Royal Over-Seas League; *Style—* Chief Constable David Blakey, QPM; ✉ West Mercia Constabulary HQ, PO Box 55, Hindlip Hall, Hindlip, Worcester WR3 8SP (☎ 01905 723000, fax 01905 454226)

BLAKEY, Ian Johnston; s of Walter James Blakey, BEM, of Cottingham, N Humberside, and Freda Blakey, *née* Johnston; *b* 25 Aug 1932; *Educ* Hull GS; *m* 9 June 1956, Pamela Mary, da of late George Edward McMurran; 1 s (Jeremy Sean b 1961), 1 da (Zelda Rebecca b 1965); *Career* Nat Serv RN 1950–52; dir: Robertson Dale Transport Co Ltd 1952–62, Rediffusion Singapore (PTE) Ltd, Consultco Ltd, Nisa Today Central Distribution Ltd 1986–, The Health Scheme 1987–; chm: I J Blakey Haulage Co Ltd 1962–, Minster Sound Radio plc 1995–, Humberside Wishing Well Appeal, Royal Hull Hospitals NHS Tst 1996–; Liveryman Worshipful Co of Carmen; FCIT 1981, FInstTA 1976; OStJ; *Recreations* golf, horse racing, charity fund raising; *Style—* Ian Blakey, Esq; ✉ Beech House, Northgate, Cottingham, North Humberside HU16 5QL (☎ 01482 846131); Consultco Ltd, Fleet House, Woodhouse Street, Hedon Road, Hull (☎ 01482 327359, fax 01482 216489)

BLAKEY, Richard John; s of Brian Blakey, of Huddersfield, and Anne Pauline Blakey; *b* 15 Jan 1967; *Educ* Rastrick GS; *Career* professional cricketer; Yorkshire CCC 1984– (debut 1985), Waverley CC Melbourne Australia 1985–86 and 1986–87, Mount Waverley CC Melbourne Australia 1987–88, Bionics CC Zimbabwe 1989–90; England: memb A tours to Zimbabwe 1990 and Pakistan 1991, tour to India and Sri Lanka 1992–93, full debut one day int v Pakistan Lord's 1992; *Recreations* eating out, any sport, DIY, music; *Style—* Richard Blakey, Esq; ✉ c/o Yorkshire County Cricket Club, Headingley Cricket Ground, Headingley, Leeds LS6 3BU (☎ 0113 278 7394)

BLAKISTON, Caroline; da of Noel Blakiston, OBE (d 1984) and (Rachel) Georgiana, *née* Russell (d 1995); *Educ* RADA (Bronze Medal, Liverpool Playhouse Award); *children* 1 s (Adam Hunter b 2 Oct 1969), 1 da (Charlotte Hunter b 14 March 1972); *Career* actress; fndr memb Actors Co; *Theatre* incl: A Midsummer's Night Dream (Regents Park), Look Back in Anger, King Lear (both Prospect Theatre Co), The Cocktail Party (Theatre Royal Windsor), A Suite in Two Keys (Palace Theatre Watford and Yvonne Arnaud Theatre Guilford), Hand Over Fist (Theatre Royal Windsor), Les Parents Terribles (Orange Tree), Ripping Them Off (The Warehouse Croydon), The Cherry Orchard (Moscow Art Theatre, Taganrog, Yalta and Vladimir Fests), Division Belle (Theatre Royal Margate), The Importance of Being Earnest (Theatr Clwyd and Theatre Royal Brighton), Turners Crossing (Croydon Warehouse); RSC 1994–97: Volumina in Coriolanus, Mrs Friendall in The Wives Excuse, Mistress Overdone in Measure for Measure, Cornelia in The White Devil, Philaminte in The Learned Ladies; West End appearances incl: Everything in the Garden, Poor Bitos, The Real Inspector Hound, Murderer, Knots, Women All Over, Particular Friendships, one woman show Black Bread and Cucumber (also writer, London, NY and Moscow); *Television* for ITV: The Avengers, The Saint; for BBC: The Forsyte Saga, Wives and Daughters, Shoestring, Not So Much A Programme, Private Schultz, Nanny, Life After Death, The Last Song, Charters and Chaldicott, Bertram's Hotel, Rides; for Granada: The Caesars, The Mallens, Crown Court, Brass; for YTV: Racing Game, The Refuge, Till We Meet Again; other credits incl: Mr Palfrey of Westminster (Thames), Lovejoy (Witsend Television), Shrinks (Euston Films); *Films* incl: The Trygon Factor, Magic Christian, Sunday Bloody Sunday, Yanks, Knots, The Return of the Jedi, The Fourth Protocol; *Awards* Fringe Best Actress Award (for Particular Friendships) 1987, Golden Globe (for Black Bread and Cucumber) 1994; *Recreations* seaside; *Style—* Caroline Blakiston; ✉ c/o Caroline Dawson Associates, Apartment 9, 47 Courtfield Road, London SW7 4DB (☎ 0171 370 0708, fax 0171 835 1403)

BLAKISTON, Sir Ferguson Arthur James; 9 Bt (GB 1763), of the City of London; s of Sir (Arthur) Norman Hunter Blakiston, 8 Bt (d 1977); *b* 19 Feb 1963; *Educ* Lincoln Coll New Zealand (DipAg); *m* 3 April 1993, Linda Jane, da of late Robert John Key, of Queenstown, NZ; *Heir* bro, Norman John Balfour Blakiston, *qv*; *Career* farmer; *Style—* Sir Ferguson Blakiston, Bt; ✉ 28 McKenzie St, Geraldine, S Canterbury, New Zealand

BLAKISTON, Lt Col John Alan Cubitt; s of John Francis Blakiston, CIE (d 1965), of Anelog, Aberdaron, Pwllheli, Gwynedd, and Margaret Dora, *née* Ward-Jackson (d 1991); descended from Sir Matthew Blakiston, Lord Mayor of London 1760; *b* 15 July 1938; *Educ* Wellington, Univ of London; *m* 30 May 1975, Sally Ann, da of Lt-Col J D L Dickson, MC (d 1958); 1 s (Matthew b 11 Nov 1982), 2 da (Caroline b 22 Nov 1979, Emma b 1 July 1981); *Career* RNVR 1956–60, cmmnd 13/18 Royal Hussars (QMO) 1961, seconded to 4 Royal Tank Regt in Borneo 1965, seconded to UN Forces Cyprus 1966–67, Staff Coll RMCS and Camberley 1969–71, regtl duty in NI 1972, cmd Demonstration Sqdn Sch of Infantry 1972–74, SO2 (W) Def Intelligence Staff 1974–76, regtl duty in BAOR and NI 1976–78, German Staff Coll 1979–81, SO1 Def Intelligence Staff 1981–85, SO1 Ops HQ AFCENT 1985–88; sr mil rep AWE Aldermaston, chm NATO and FINABEL (Euro) Nuclear Defence Ctees 1988–93; *Recreations* riding, hunting; *Clubs* Cavalry and Guards'; *Style—* Lt Col John A C Blakiston; ✉ Grove House, Lydiard Millicent, Swindon, Wilts SN5 9LP (☎ 01793 770450)

BLAKISTON, Norman John Balfour; s of Sir (Arthur) Norman Hunter Blakiston, 8 Bt (d 1977); hp to baronetcy of bro, Sir Ferguson Blakiston, 9 Bt, *qv*; *b* 7 April 1964; *Style—* Norman Blakiston, Esq

BLAKSTAD, Michael Björn; s of Gabriel Clifford Clark Blakstad, and Alice Blakstad; *b* 18 April 1940; *Educ* Ampleforth, Oriel Coll Oxford (MA); *m* 1965, Patricia Marilyn, da of Robert Andrew Wotherspoon, DL (d 1977); 1 s, 2 da (twins); *Career* prodr: Papa Doc, The Black Sheep (ITV) 1970, Children in Crossfire (BBC) 1974; ed BBC 1974–80 (Tomorrow's World, The Risk Business), dir of progs Television South plc 1981–84; chm and chief exec 1988–90: Chrysalis Television Ltd, Workhouse Productions Ltd; dir 1988–90: Chrysalis Group plc, Blackrod Interactive Servs; chm Workday Ltd 1988–90; dir 1991: Televison Enterprise and Asset Management plc, Winchester Theatre Royal Ltd; chm and chief exec Workhouse Ltd; chm Winchester Independent Local Radio Ltd 1995; prizes incl: BAFTA/Shell 1975, John Player 1975, RTS best science prog 1975, 1977 and 1979; Hon MSc Univ of Salford 1983; FRTS 1990, FRSA, FRI; *Books* The Risk Business, Tomorrow's World Looks to the Eighties, The Communicating Organisation; *Recreations* golf, opera, theatre, writing; *Clubs* Reform, RSA, Royal Inst; *Style—* Michael Blakstad, Esq; ✉ Workhouse Ltd, Granville House, St Peter St, Winchester, Hants SO23 9AF; Flat 3, 16 Floral Street, London WC2

BLAMEY, Norman Charles; s of Charles Henry Blamey (d 1965), of London, and Ada, *née* Beacham (d 1980); *b* 16 Dec 1914; *Educ* Holloway Sch, Regent St Poly Sch of Art, Univ of London Inst of Educn; *m* 26 Oct 1948, Margaret (d 1989), da of late Peter Kelly; 1 s (Stephen b 1950); *Career* Nat Serv Army 1941–46; art lectr and painter; lectr Regent St Poly Sch of Art 1946–63, sr lectr Chelsea Sch of Art 1963–79, painter mural cmmn Lutheran Church of St Andrew Ruislip Manor 1964 (Anglican Church of St Luke Leagrave 1956), visitor Ruskin Sch of Drawing and Fine Arts Univ of Oxford 1978; Royal Acad Summer Expo Awards: Roy Miles 1978, Rowney Bi-centenary 1983, Charles Woolaston 1984, Korn/Ferry Carré/Orban 1995; permanent collections incl: Municipal Gallery Port Elizabeth SA, Victoria and Albert Museum, Tate Gallery, Government Art Collection, Pennsylvania State Univ Museum of Art, Towner Art Gallery Eastbourne, Southampton Art Gallery; cmmnd portraits incl: Sir Robert Bellinger, GBE 1984, Rt Hon Bernard Weatherill, MP (Speaker House of Commons) 1985, Lord Rees-Mogg 1988; RA 1975 (ARA 1970); *Recreations* walking; *Style—* Norman Blamey, Esq, RA; ✉ 39 Lyncroft Gardens, London NW6 1LB (☎ 0171 435 9250)

BLANC, Raymond René Alfred; s of Maurice Blanc, and Anne-Marie, *née* Tournier; *b* 19 Nov 1949; *Educ* Besançon Coll France (Dip BEPC); *m* 1, 14 Jan 1974 (m dis 1986), Jennifer Colbeck; 2 s (Olivier b 18 Oct 1974, Sebastien b 15 April 1981); m 2, 18 Dec 1990 (sep), Katalin Szoke; *Career* chef; chef/patron: Quat'Saisons Oxford 1977, Maison Blanc 1978–88, Le Manoir Aux Quat'Saisons 1984–, Le Petit Blanc 1996–; patron and chm Blanc Restaurants Ltd 1984–; TV appearances incl: Food and Drink 1987, In At the Deep End 1989, Chef's Apprentice 1989; own TV series Blanc Mange (BBC 2) 1994; memb: Academie Culinaire de France, Syndicat de l'Haute Cuisine Française, Relais Chateaux Tradition Qualité; Personalité de l'année 1990; 5 out of 5 Good Food Guide 1996; Cdr de l'Assoc Int des Maîtres Conseils en Gastronomie Française; *Books* Le Manoir Aux Quat'Saisons (1988), Cooking for Friends (1991), Blanc Mange (1994), A Blanc Christmas (1996); *Recreations* reading, music, tennis, swimming; *Style—* Raymond Blanc, Esq; ✉ Le Manoir Aux Quat'Saisons, Church Road, Great Milton, Oxford OX44 7PD (☎ 01844 278881, fax 01844 278847)

BLAND, Sir (Francis) Christopher Buchan; kt (1993); eldest s of James Franklin MacMahon Bland, of Co Down, and Jess Buchan, *née* Brodie; *b* 29 May 1938; *Educ* Sedbergh, Queen's Coll Oxford; *m* 1981, Jennifer Mary Denise, elder da of late Rt Hon William Morrison May, MP, of Co Down, and formerly w of Viscount Enfield (now 8 Earl of Strafford); 1 s; *Career* chm: Sir Joseph Causton & Sons 1977–85, LWT Holdings plc 1984–94, Life Sciences International, NFC plc 1995–, Bd of Govrs BBC April 1996–; dep chm Independent Bdcasting Authy (IBA) 1972–79; *Recreations* fishing, skiing; *Clubs* Beefsteak; *Style—* Sir Christopher Bland; ✉ NFC plc, 66 Chiltern Street, London W1M 2LT (☎ 0171 317 0123, fax 0171 224 2378)

BLAND, Prof David Edward; s of Rev Albert Edward Bland, of Blackburn, and Lily, *née* Simmons; *b* 9 Dec 1940; *Educ* Queen Elizabeth GS Blackburn, Univ Coll Durham (BA, M Litt), Univ of Sheffield (PhD); *m* 27 Sept 1986, Christine, da of Keith Holliday, of King's Lynn, Norfolk; *Career* warden of Sorby Hall and pro vice chllr Univ of Sheffield 1964–89, dir gen The Chartered Insurance Inst 1989–; visiting prof City Univ 1994–; memb Ct of Assts Worshipful Co of Insurers, Renter Warden Co of Firefighters; fell Inst of Co Accountants 1970 (pres 1990–91), FSCA, FIPD 1991, FCII 1994; *Books* Can Britain Survive? (with KW Watkins, 1971), Managing Higher Education (1990), Principles and Practice of Insurance (1994); *Recreations* walking, music; *Style—* Prof David Bland; ✉ 31 Dundee Court, 73 Wapping High St, London E1 9YG (☎ 0171 481 8234); Western View, Sunny Bank, Great Longstone, Derbyshire DE45 1TL; The Chartered Insurance Institute, 20 Aldermanbury, London EC2V 7HY (☎ 0171 417 4401, fax 0171 972 0157, telex 957017)

BLAND, Gladys Kathleen; da of John Bland (d 1990), and Grace, *née* Roberts, of Otley, W Yorks; *b* 3 Nov 1937; *Educ* Tottenham HS, Queen Mary Coll London BA (Draper's Co Arts scholarship, Goldsmiths Co Travel Award), Somerville Coll Oxford (state studentship); *Career* asst history mistress Casterton Sch by Carnforth Lancs 1961–65, asst history mistress Manchester HS 1965–69; Malvern Girls' Coll: head of History Dept 1969–76, sr house tutor 1974–76, sr mistress 1976–78; headmistress Stamford HS Lincs 1978–; GSA: memb Educn Sub-Ctee 1986–89, memb Exec Ctee 1989–92, chm Memb Ctee; memb: SHA, ESU, Historical Assoc, Wine Guild of the UK; FRSA; *Recreations* travel, reading and book collecting, art appreciation, food; *Clubs* The Arts; *Style—* Miss Gladys Bland; ✉ Stamford High School, St Martin's, Stamford, Lincolnshire PE9 2LJ (☎ 01780 62330)

BLAND, Hamilton Edwin; s of Alice Bland; *b* 4 June 1943; *Educ* Folds Rd Sch Bolton, Hayward Sch Bolton, Loughborough Coll (DLC); *m* 1, 26 March 1967, Hazel, da of Leslie Gear; 1 da (Anna Danielle b 16 Aug 1978); m 2, 26 August 1989, Nicola Clare, da of Arthur May; 2 s (David Hamilton b 14 June 1990, Jack Kingsley b 24 April 1992), 1 da (Jodie Charlotte b 12 May 1994); *Career* master Rugby Sch 1965–67, nat tech offr Amateur Swimming Assoc 1967–72, dir of swimming Coventry 1972–81, chm and md Hamilton Bland (Prods) Ltd 1981–86, proprietor Hamilton Bland Conslts 1987–, BBC TV swimming commentator 1975–; formerly: memb Coventry Round Table, chm Coventry Mentally Handicapped Soc; Winston Churchill fell 1969; *Books* Waterpolo, Swimming To Win; *Recreations* swimming; *Style—* Hamilton Bland, Esq; ✉ Honiley Hall, Honiley, Kenilworth, Warwicks CV8 1NP

BLAND, Jeff; s of Albert Bland, and Marjory Bland; *b* 17 Aug 1953; *Educ* Carlton GS Bradford, Bradford Tech Coll (City & Guilds, Student of the Year); *partner* Jill Hepburn; *Career* various positions rising to sous chef Gleneagles Hotel 1973–77, relief chef Br Transport Hotels 1978–80, chef Station Hotel Inverness 1980–82; exec chef: Gosforth Park Newcastle 1982–87, Caledonian Edinburgh 1987–90, Cameron House Hotel Alexandria 1990–; demonstrator Good Food Show 1995; guest appearances: Square Meals, Junior Masterchef; guest chef fundraising dinner Michigan USA (raised 1 million dollars); memb: Craft Guild of Chefs 1974, Academie Culinaire de France 1988; *Awards*

Craft Guild Chef of the Year 1995, Chefs of GB Chef of the Year 1995; Cameron House Hotel: Scottish Hotel of the Year 1991, 3 AA Rosettes, Egon Ronay Award, Macallan Decanter Restaurant of the Year 1992, RAC Blue Ribbon 1994, Michelin Star 1995 and 1996, AA Hotel of the Year 1995; *Recreations* eating out, wine, entertaining friends, running (completed various half marathons and London marathon); *Style*— Jeff Bland, Esq; ✉ Cameron House Hotel, Loch Lomond, Alexandria, Dunbartonshire G83 8QZ (☎ 01389 755565)

BLAND, Peter; s of Joseph Whalley Bland (d 1951), and Doris, *née* Simpson (d 1949); *b* 12 May 1934; *Educ* Alleynés GS Staffs, Victoria Univ of Wellington NZ; *m* 1956, Beryl Matilda, *née* Connolly; 1 s (Carl b 1960), 2 da (Karen b 1956, Joanna b 1958); *Career* freelance actor and writer; radio prodr NZ Bdcasting Co and journalist NZ Listener 1958–64, co-fndr and artistic dir Downstage Theatre Co Wellington 1964–68; McMillan-Browne Prize for Creative Writing Univ of NZ 1958, Melbourne Arts Festival Literary Award 1960, Br Soc of Authors Cholmondely Award for Poetry 1977, QEII Arts Cncl Drama fellowship 1968, Observer/Arvon Foundation Poetry Competition winner 1980 and 1990, Best Film Actor Award Guild of Film and TV Arts 1986; memb PEN (NZ); *Theatre* Bristol Old Vic Co 1969–72; credits incl: Prahda Singh in Conduct Unbecoming (Queen's) 1970, Shut Your Eyes and Think of England (Apollo) 1974, Chichester Festival 1975, Peter Pan (London Palladium) 1976; *Television* appearances incl: Hammer House of Horror, The Les Dawson Show, The Old Curiosity Shop, Heart of the High Country, The Victoria Wood Show, Lazarus and Dingwall, Cribb; *Films* Don't Just Lie There, Say Something 1974, Came a Hot Friday 1984; *Poems* My Side of the Story (1964), The Man with the Carpet Bag (1972), Mr Maui (1976), Stone Tents (1981), The Crusoe Factor (1985), Selected Poems (1987), Paper Boats (1991); *Plays* Father's Day (1967), George the Mad Ad Man (1967); *Recreations* tennis, travel, contemporary art; *Style*— Peter Bland, Esq; ✉ c/o Peters Fraser & Dunlop Ltd, 503 The Chambers, Chelsea Harbour, Lots Road, London SW10 0XF (☎ 0171 352 4446, fax 0171 352 7356)

BLAND, Lt-Col Sir Simon Claud Michael; KCVO (1982, CVO 1973, MVO 1967); s of Sir (George) Nevile Maltby Bland, KCMG, KCVO (d 1972), and Portia Christabel Irene, *née* Ottley (d 1968); *b* 4 Dec 1923; *Educ* Eton; *m* 1954, Beatrice Olivia, da of late Maj William Blackett; 1 s, 3 da; *Career* WWII Scots Gds (served Italy), Br Jt Servs Mission Washington DC 1948–49, 2 Bn Scots Gds Malaya 1949–51, asst mil advsr UK High Cmmn Karachi 1959–60; comptroller, and asst private sec to: HRH late Duke of Gloucester 1961–74, Private Sec to HRH late Prince William 1968–72; comptroller private sec and equerry to HRH Princess Alice, Duchess of Gloucester and to TRHs the Duke and Duchess of Gloucester 1972–89 (extra equerry 1989–); dir West End Hand-in-Hand Bd Commercial Union; pres: Friends of Edenbridge Hosp, Lingfield and Area Branch Riding for the Disabled; vice pres: Nat Assoc of Boys' Clubs, Raleigh International, Homelife DGAA; chm Cncl The Coll of St Barnabas; memb Cncl: St John Ambulance Bde Kent, Pestalozzi Children's Village Tst; tstee Grant Maintained Schs Tst; CStJ 1978, KStJ 1987; *Recreations* shooting; *Clubs* Buck's; *Style*— Lt-Col Sir Simon Bland, KCVO; ✉ Totties Mill Hill, Edenbridge, Kent (☎ and fax 01732 862340)

BLANDFORD, Marquess of; (Charles) James (Jamie) Spencer-Churchill; s and h (by 1 w, *see* Mrs John Gough), of 11 Duke of Marlborough, JP, DL, *qv*; *b* 24 Nov 1955; *Educ* Pinewood, Harrow, RAC Cirencester; *m* 24 Feb 1990, Rebecca Mary, da of Peter Few Brown and Mrs John Winnington-Ingram; 1 s (George, Earl of Sunderland b 28 July 1992); *Career* insurance broker and helicopter pilot; PR dir Brodie Brittain Racing; *Recreations* skiing, flying, shooting; *Clubs* Turf, Annabel's; *Style*— Marquess of Blandford; ✉ Gate Farm, Kiddington, Woodstock, Oxon (☎ 01608 677558); 16 Lawrence Street, London SW3 (☎ 0171 351 2730, mobile 01385 300145); Brodie Brittain Racing, Brackley, Northants NN13 7DY (☎ 01280 702389)

BLANDFORD, Prof Roger David; s of Jack George Blandford, and Janet Margaret Blandford; *b* 28 Aug 1949; *Educ* King Edward's Sch Birmingham, Magdalene Coll Cambridge (BA, Charles Kingsley Bye Fell, MA, PhD); *m* 1972, Elizabeth Denise Kellett; 2 s; *Career* res fell St John's Coll Cambridge 1973–76, memb Inst for Advanced Study Princeton 1974–75; California Inst of Technol: asst prof 1976–79, prof 1979–88, Richard Chace Tolman prof of theoretical astrophysics 1989–; Alfred P Sloan res fell 1980–84, Guggenheim fell 1988–89; FRS, FRAS, FAAAS; *Style*— Prof Roger Blandford, FRS; ✉ 130–133 Caltech, Pasadena, California 91125, USA (☎ 00 1 818 395 4200)

BLANDY, Prof John Peter; CBE (1995); s of Sir Edmond Nicolas Blandy, KCIE, CSI, ICS (d 1942), of Calcutta, and Dorothy Kathleen, *née* Marshall (d 1985); *b* 11 Sept 1927; *Educ* Clifton, Balliol Coll Oxford (MA, DM, MCh), The London Hosp Med Coll; *m* 6 Aug 1953, Anne, da of the late Henry Hugh Mathias, of Tenby; 4 da (Susan, Caroline, Nicola, Kitty); *Career* Nat Serv RAMC 1953–55 (Lt, Capt, Actg Maj), Maj 22 London Gen Hosp (TA), Maj RARO; conslt surgn: London Hosp 1964, St Peter's Hosp 1968; prof of urology Univ of London 1969 (prof emeritus 1992), vice pres Urology Section RSM 1973 (hon fell 1995); pres: Br Assoc of Urological Surgns 1985–86, Euro Assoc of Urology 1986–88, European Bd of Urology 1991–92; cncl memb RCS 1982, vice pres RCS 1992–94; memb General Medical Cncl 1992–96; govr Clifton Coll 1992; St Peters Medal 1982; hon fell Balliol Coll Oxford 1992; Hon FRCSI 1992, FRCS 1956, FAC 1980; *Books* Tumours of the Testicles (1970), Transurethral Resection (1970), Lecture Notes on Urology (1976), The Prostate (1986), Operative Urology (1978), Urology (1976, 2 edn 1995); translations into Italian, Spanish, Portuguese; *Recreations* painting, sculpture; *Clubs* The Royal Society of Medicine; *Style*— Prof John Blandy, CBE; ✉ 362 Shakespeare Tower, Barbican, London EC2Y 8NJ (☎ 0171 638 4095)

BLANE, Michael Lawrence; *b* 17 Aug 1938; *Educ* Washington and Lee Univ, Case Western Reserve Univ (BA, LLB); *Career* enforcement counsel US Securities and Exchange Cmmn 1967–70, vice pres and asst gen counsel Dean Witter Reynolds Inc 1973–81, sr counsel Merrill Lynch Europe Ltd 1981–90, dir Int Securities Regulatory Orgn 1985–86, gp compliance offr Banque Nationale de Paris 1990–; dir Securities Assoc 1986–88: Rules Ctee, Enforcement Ctee, Authorisation Ctee Bd; memb: 1992 Ctee Int Stock Exchange, Nat Assoc of Securities Dealers, American Arbitration Assoc, Commodity Futures Indust Assoc; *Style*— Michael L Blane, Esq; ✉ Banque Nationale de Paris London, 8–13 King William St, London EC4P 4HS (☎ 0171 895 7216, fax 0171 895 7013)

BLANK, (Maurice) Victor; s of Joseph Blank, and Ruth, *née* Levey; *b* 9 Nov 1942; *Educ* Stockport GS, St Catherine's Coll Oxford (MA); *m* 29 June 1977, Sylvia Helen, *née* Richford; 2 s (Simon b 1 May 1978, Robert b 23 June 1984), 1 da (Anna b 16 Sept 1979); *Career* ptnr Clifford-Turner (solicitors) 1969–81; Charterhouse plc: chief exec 1985–96, chm 1991–, chm Charterhouse Bank Ltd 1985–, chm Charterhouse European Holding Ltd 1993–; non-exec dir: Coats Viyella plc 1989–, The Great Universal Stores plc 1993– (dep chm 1996–), Williams Holdings plc 1994–; chm WellBeing (formerly Birthright) 1991–, chm of Govrs Univ Coll Sch; memb: Business in the Community, Campaign for Oxford, RSA, Advsy Cncl Orch of the Age of Enlightenment; advsr to Oxford Environmental Change Unit; Freeman City of London, memb City of London Slrs Co; memb Law Soc, CIMgt; *Books* Weinberg and Blank on Takeovers and Mergers; *Recreations* family, cricket, tennis, theatre; *Clubs* IOD; *Style*— Victor Blank, Esq; ✉ Charterhouse plc, 1 Paternoster Row, St Paul's, London EC4M 7DH, (☎ 0171 248 4000, fax 0171 522 3799)

BLANKSTONE, Michael David; s of Solomon Julius Blankstone (d 1981), of Liverpool, and Isabel, *née* Franklin (d 1979); *b* 20 Nov 1936; *Educ* Quarry Bank HS Liverpool; *m* 17 June 1963, Anne, *née* Harrison; 2 s (Mark Lewis b 13 April 1964, Neil Simon b 6 Jan 1968); *Career* with family furniture mfrg business 1953–59, trainee then stockbroker Hornby Tobin & Ockleston 1959–66, ptnr Neilson Hornby Crichton 1966–75, sr ptnr Blankstone Sington & Co 1975–89 (co-fndr), chm and chief exec Blankstone Sington Ltd 1989–; chm: Blankstone Investments Ltd, BS Advisory Services Ltd; chm The Stock Exchange Liverpool 1988–90 (vice chm 1986–88), memb Stock Exchange NW Advsy Gp, chm Liverpool Stock Exchange Benevolent Fund; memb Cncl Liverpool Sch of Tropical Med, memb Nat Museums and Galleries on Merseyside Devpt Tst; tstee: Hillsborough Disaster Appeal, Liverpool Jewish Youth & Community Centre, Royal Liverpool Philharmonic Soc Jubilee Fndn Tst; MSI (memb Stock Exchange 1964), FInstD 1975; *Recreations* golf, holidays in the sun, reading, charity work; *Clubs* Lee Park Golf; *Style*— Michael D Blankstone, Esq; ✉ Blankstone Sington Ltd, 91 Duke St, Liverpool L1 5AA (☎ 0151 707 1707, fax 0151 707 1247)

BLANNING, Prof Timothy Charles William; s of Thomas Walter Blanning, and Gwendolyn Marchant, *née* Jones; *b* 21 April 1942; *Educ* King's Sch Bruton Somerset, Sidney Sussex Coll Cambridge (BA, MA, PhD); *m* 1988, Nicky Susan Jones; *Career* Univ of Cambridge: asst lectr in history 1972–76, lectr in history 1976–87, reader in modern Euro history 1987–92, prof of modern Euro history 1992–; fell Sidney Sussex Coll Cambridge 1968– (res fell 1965–68); FBA 1990; *Books* Joseph II and Enlightened Despotism (1970), Reform and Revolution in Mainz 1740–1803 (1974), The French Revolution in Germany (1983), The Origins of the French Revolutionary Wars (1986), The French Revolution: Aristocrats versus Bourgeois? (1987), Joseph II (1994), The Oxford Illustrated History of Modern Europe (ed, 1996), The French Revolutionary Wars 1787–1802 (1996), The Rise and Fall of the French Revolution (ed, 1996), History and Biography: Essays in Honour of Derek Beales (ed, 1996); *Recreations* gardening, music; *Style*— Prof Timothy Blanning, FBA; ✉ Sidney Sussex College, Cambridge CB2 3HU (☎ 01223 338800)

BLASHFORD-SNELL, Col John Nicholas; OBE (1996, MBE 1969); s of Alderman the Rev Prebendary Leland John Blashford-Snell, MBE, TD (d 1978), of Angmering-on-Sea, Sussex, and Gwendolen Ives, *née* Sadler (d 1968); *b* 22 Oct 1936; *Educ* Victoria Coll Jersey, RMA Sandhurst, The Staff Coll Camberley; *m* 27 Aug 1960, Judith (Frances), da of Lt-Col Beresford Thomas Sherman, OBE (d 1982), of Tivoli Court, Westbourne, Dorset; 2 da (Emma b 1964, Victoria b 1967); *Career* cmmnd RE 1957, Trg Adj 33 Ind Field Sqdn RE Cyprus 1959–62 (Troop Cdr 1958–59), Troop Cdr Junior Leaders Regt RE 1962–63, Instr & Adventure Trg Offr RMA Sandhurst 1963–66, Adj 3 Div Engrs 1966–67, leader Gt Abbai (Blue Nile) Expdn 1968, Staff Coll (RMCS and Camberley) 1968–69, GSO2 MOD 1970–72, leader Br Trans-Americas Expdn 1972, OC 48 Field Sqdn RE (Belize, Oman, N Ireland) 1972–74, leader Zaire River Expdn 1974–75, GSO1 MOD 1975–76, CO Junior Leaders Regt RE 1976–78, Cdr Operation Drake 1978–81, ACPR MOD 1981–82, Cdr Fort George Volunteers 1983, Cdr Operation Raleigh 1984–89 (dir gen 1989–91); lectr MOD 1991–; dir Starting Point Appeal The Merseyside Youth Assoc 1993–; leader: Kalahari Quest Expdn 1990, Karnali Quest Expdn 1991, Karnali Gorge Expdn 1992, Mongolia Amarsana Expdn 1992 and numerous other expeditions since; chm: The Scientific Exploration Soc, Br Chapter Explorers Club; co-chm Operation New World; pres Galley Hill Gun Club; Freeman of the City of Hereford 1984; Hon DSc Durham 1986; Darien Medal (Colombia) 1972, Livingstone Medal RSGS 1975, Patron's Medal RGS 1993, Gold Medal Inst of Royal Engrs 1994; FRSGS 1976; *Books* Weapons and Tactics (with Tom Wintringham, 1973), Where the Trails Run Out (1974), In the Steps of Stanley (1975), A Taste for Adventure (1978), Expeditions the Experts Way (with Alistair Ballantine, 1977), In the Wake of Drake (with Mike Cable, 1980), Operation Drake (with Mike Cable, 1981), Mysteries, Encounters with the Unexplained (1983), Operation Raleigh - the Start of an Adventure (1987), Operation Raleigh, Adventure Challenge (with Ann Tweedy, 1988), Operation Raleigh, Adventure Unlimited (with Ann Tweedy), Something Lost Behind the Ranges (1994), Mammoth Hunt (with Rula Lenska, 1996); *Recreations* shooting, travel, food and wine, diving, photography; *Clubs* Explorers, Wig and Pen, Little Ship; *Style*— Col John Blashford-Snell, OBE; ✉ c/o Scientific Exploration Society, Expedition Base, Motcombe, Dorset SP7 9PB (☎ 01747 854456, fax 01747 855411)

BLATCH, Baroness (Life Peer UK 1987), of Hinchingbrooke in the county of Cambridgeshire; Emily May Blatch; *née* Triggs; PC (1993), CBE (1983); da of late Stephen Joseph Triggs, and late Sarah Ann, *née* Carpenter; *b* 24 July 1937; *Educ* Prenton Secdy Girls Sch, Huntingdonshire Coll; *m* 7 Sept 1963, John Richard Blatch, AFC, s of George Henry Blatch (d 1968); 3 s (David b 1964 d 1979, Hon James b 1967, Hon Andrew b 1968), 1 da (Hon Elizabeth b (twin) 1968); *Career* WRAF 1955–59; govt whip 1990–, parly under sec of state DOE 1990–91, min of state: DOE 1991–92, Dept for Educn 1992–94, Home Office 1994–; cncllr Cambs 1977–89 (ldr of the Cncl 1981–85); pres Nat Benevolent Inst 1989–; memb: Euro Economic and Social Ctee 1986–87, Assoc of Co Cncls 1981–85, Sch's Cncl 1981–83; bd memb Peterborough Devpt Corp 1984–88, chm Anglo American Community Relations Ctee RAF Alconbury 1985–91; Paul Harris fell 1992; Baroness in Waiting to HM The Queen 1990; FRSA 1983; *Recreations* reading, theatre, music; *Clubs* RAF; *Style*— The Rt Hon the Lady Blatch, PC, CBE; ✉ House of Lords, Westminster, London SW1A 0AA (☎ 0171 219 3000)

BLATCHFORD, Brian; s of Brian Geoffrey Blatchford, MBE (d 1985), of Sherborne St John, Basingstoke, and May Joyce, *née* Faulkner; *b* 7 Dec 1959; *Educ* St Edward's Sch Oxford, St Catherine's Coll Oxford (BA, MSc); *m* 22 March 1986, Caroline Mary, da of Colin Greenwood, Sutton, Macclesfield, Cheshire; *Career* IBM Laboratories Ltd Hursley 1979, tech offr in office automation ICL 1983–85, md Chas A Blatchford and Sons Ltd 1986– (mgmnt trainee 1985–86), chm Possum Controls Ltd 1994–95, non-exec dir Redrice Ltd 1994–; govr London Sch of Prosthetics 1986–92, chm Prosthetics Section British Surgical Trades Assoc 1988–; memb: Basingstoke C of C, Basingstoke and Andover Enterprise Centre, Biological Engrg Soc 1986–93, Int Soc of Prosthetics and Orthotics 1986–; *Recreations* badminton, computers, wine tasting, reading; *Clubs* IOD, Dummer Golf; *Style*— Brian Blatchford, Esq; ✉ The Oast House, Pitt Lane, Dockenfield, Farham, Surrey GU10 3EF (☎ 01252 793063); Chas A Blatchford and Sons Ltd, Lister Rd, Basingstoke, Hampshire RG22 4AH (☎ 01256 465771, fax 01256 331164)

BLATHERWICK, HE David Elliott Spiby; s of late Edward S Blatherwick; *b* 13 July 1941; *Educ* Lincoln Sch, Wadham Coll Oxford; *m* 1964, (Margaret) Clare, *née* Crompton; 1 da (b 1969), 1 s (b 1972); *Career* HM Dip Serv; MECAS 1964, third later second sec Foreign Office 1966–68, second sec Kuwait 1968–70, first sec Dublin 1970–73, first sec FCO 1973–77, first sec and head of Chancery Cairo 1977–81, cnsllr and head of Political Affrs Div Northern Ireland Office 1981–83, head of Energy, Sci and Space Dept 1983–85, on leave to Stanford Univ California 1985–86, cnsllr and head of Chancery UK Mission to UN NY 1986–89, princ fin offr and chief inspector FCO 1989–91: HM ambass: Dublin 1991–95, Cairo 1995–; *Clubs* Athenaeum; *Style*— HE Mr D E S Blatherwick, CMG, OBE; ✉ c/o Foreign and Commonwealth Office (Cairo), King Charles Street, London SW1A 2AH

BLATT, Nina Joy; da of Samuel Blatt (d 1980), of Hendon, and Rose, *née* Meisler (d 1978); *b* 19 April 1934; *Educ* The Skinners Co Sch for Girls, City of London Coll Moorgate; *m* 17 Sept 1973 (m dis 1986), (Joseph) Peter Roden, s of Gregory Roden (d 1974), of Brinscall, Lancs; *Career* PA to Head of Publicity Hulton Press (Picture Post) 1949–56, freelance writer travel features for various magazines, PA to First Sec HM Embassy Paris 1956–58, prodr ATV Network Ltd 1958–71 (formerly prodn asst, asst prodr, assoc prodr), dir Nina Blatt Ltd (representing prodrs and dirs in media) 1977–92, dir Consultancy (Media) Company 1992–; fndr memb The Samaritans, memb BAFTA 1971; *Recreations* theatre, music, writing, literary pursuits; *Style—* Mrs Nina Roden; ✉ The Coach House, 1A Larpent Ave, Putney, London SW15 6UP (☎ 0181 788 9971, fax 0181 788 5602)

BLAU, Dr Joseph Norman; s of Abraham Moses Blau (d 1942), and Reisla, *née* Vogel (d 1942); *b* 5 Oct 1928; *Educ* Dame Alice Owens Sch, St Bartholomew's Hosp Univ of London (MB BS, MD); *m* 19 Dec 1968, Jill Elise, da of Geoffrey C Seligman; 2 s (Justin b 15 Jan 1970, Adrian b 27 April 1972), 1 da (Rosie b 9 Sept 1975); *Career* Nat Serv Lt and Capt RAMC 1953–55; med offr: SW Dist HQ Taunton 1954, Army Neurological Unit Wheatley Oxon 1955; sr registrar London and Maida Vale Hosp 1960–61, Nuffield Med Res Fellowship Mass Gen Hosp Boston USA 1962; conslt neurologist: Nat Hosps for Neurology and Neurosurgery Queen Square and Maida Vale 1962–93, Royal Nat Throat Nose and Ear Hosp 1965–93, Northwick Park Hosp Harrow Middx 1972–93; hon sr lectr Histopathology Dept Guy's Med Sch 1970–89, jt hon dir and conslt neurologist City of London Migraine Clinic 1980–, hon conslt neurologist Nat Hosp for Neurology and Neurosurgery Queen Square 1993–; chm Soc of Authors Writer Gp (Med Writers Gp) 1989–91, former pres London Jewish Med Soc, hon med advsr Br Migraine Assoc 1980–; memb: Cncl Neurological Section RSM 1984–87 and 1994–, Scientific Advsy Ctee Migraine Tst 1989–92, Professional and Linguistic Assessment Bd General Med Cncl 1990–93, Assoc of Br Neurologists, Advsy Cncl Br Soc of Music Therapy, Cncl Br Assoc for Performing Arts Med 1993–; memb Editorial Bd: Cephalalgia, Headache Quarterly; FRCP, FRCPath; *Publications* Migraine - Clinical, Therapeutic, Conceptual and Research Aspects (ed and contrib, 1987), Migraine (with J F Drummond, Office of Health Economics, 1991), Behaviour During a Cluster Headache (1993); author of chapters in books and original articles on Headache, Migraine and other neurological topics; *Recreations* cello playing, history of ideas; *Clubs* Royal Soc of Med; *Style—* Dr J N Blau; ✉ 5 Marlborough Hill, London NW8 0NN (☎ 0171 586 3804); Private Consulting Rooms, National Hospital for Neurology and Neurosurgery, Queen Square, London WC1N 3BG (☎ 0171 829 8742, fax 0171 833 8658)

BLAUG, Prof Mark; s of Bernard Blaug (d 1949), and Sarah, *née* Toeman (d 1974); *b* 3 April 1927; *Educ* Queen's Coll NY (BA), Univ of Columbia NY (MA, PhD); *m* 1, 1946 (m dis 1951), Rose Lapone; m 2, 1954 (m dis 1960), Brenda M Ellis; 1 s (David Ricardo b 1956); m 3, 26 March 1969, Ruth Marilyn, da of Ronald Towse (d 1971); 1 s (Tristan Bernard b 1971); *Career* asst prof Yale 1954–62, Univ of London Inst of Educn 1963–84 (sr lectr, reader, prof), lectr London Sch of Economics 1963–78; prof emeritus: Univ of London 1984, Univ of Buckingham 1984; visiting prof Univ of Exeter 1989–; conslt 1964–90 (World Bank, UNESCO, ILO, Ford Fndn), editorial conslt Edward Elgar Publishing 1986–; memb: American Econ Assoc, Royal Econ Soc; Hon DSc Univ of Buckingham 1994; FBA 1989; foreign hon memb Royal Netherlands Acad of Arts and Scis 1986, distinguished fell History of Economics Soc 1990; *Books* Ricardian Economics (1958), The Causes of Graduate Employment in India (1969), Education and The Employment Problem in Developing Countries (1973), Economic History and the History of Economics (1986), John Maynard Keynes, Life, Ideas, Legacy (1990), The Methodology of Economics (1992), Economic Theory in Retrospect (1996); *Recreations* talking, walking, sailing; *Style—* Prof Mark Blaug, FBA; ✉ Langsford Barn, Peter Tavy, Tavistock, Devon PL19 9LY (☎ 01822 810562); Department of Economics, University of Exeter, Exeter EX4 4RJ (☎ 01392 263237, telex 42894)

BLAUSTEN, Cyril; JP; *b* 1916; *m* 1944, Norma Marion Cinnamon; 4 s (Richard, Douglas, Simon, Peter); *Career* underwriting memb Lloyds; dir: New Islington and Hackney Housing Assoc, JBG Housing Soc; cmmr of taxes; vice pres: Jewish Care, Maccabi Assoc; Freeman City of London, Liveryman Worshipful Co of Glaziers and Painters of Glass; fell Surveyors' and Valuers' Assoc, memb Royal Soc of Health, FZS; *Clubs* City Livery, United University, MCC; *Style—* Cyril Blausten, Esq, JP; ✉ 5 Linnell Close, Meadway, London NW11; office: 25 Gilbert Street, Grosvenor Square, London W1Y 2EJ

BLAXTER, Prof John Harry Savage; s of Kenneth William Blaxter, CMG (d 1964), and Janet Hollis (d 1981); *b* 6 Jan 1929; *Educ* Berkhamsted Sch, Oxford Univ (MA, DSc); *m* 20 Dec 1952, Valerie Ann, da of Gerald McElligott; 1 s (Timothy b 1958), 1 da (Julia b 1955); *Career* sci offr then sr sci offr Marine Lab Aberdeen 1952–64, lectr Zoology Dept Univ of Aberdeen 1964–69; Scot Marine Biological Assoc Dunstaffnage Marine Lab Oban: princ sci offr 1969–74, sr princ sci offr special merit 1974–85, dep chief sci offr special merit 1985–91, res fell 1991–; pres Fisheries Soc of the Br Isles 1992–; emeritus fell The Leverhulme Tst 1991–93, hon prof Dept of Molecular and Biol Sci and Inst of Aquaculture Univ of Stirling 1986–, hon prof Dept of Biology and Preclinical Med Univ of St Andrews 1990–; Hon DUniv Stirling 1994; FIBiol, FRSE 1974; *Books* Advances in Marine Biology (ed); over 130 papers in learned journals on fish behaviour and physiology, ed ICES Journal of Marine Science; *Recreations* sailing, gardening, golf; *Style—* Prof John H S Blaxter, FRSE; ✉ Dems Lodge, Barcaldine, Oban, Argyll PA37 1SF (☎ 01631 720228); Scottish Association for Marine Science, Dunstaffnage Marine Laboratory, Oban, Argyll PA34 4AD (☎ 01631 562244)

BLAYNEY, Robert Hamilton; s of Lt-Col Owen Geoffrey Blayney, MC (d 1957), and Olive Agar, *née* Lazenby (d 1962); *b* 23 June 1934; *Educ* Uppingham; *m* 16 Jan 1965, Ann, da of James Francis Angus Turner; 2 s (Andrew Owen b 1966, David James b 1969); *Career* Lt Royal Northumberland Fusiliers TA; wine trade; dir: Blayney & Co Ltd 1956–68, Blayneys Park Hotels Ltd 1957–68, Leslie Rankin Ltd St Helier 1969–78, La Mare Vineyards Ltd Jersey; memb Cncl Wine and Spirit Assoc GB 1961–68; Freeman City of London, Liveryman Worshipful Co of Vintners; *Recreations* gardening, genealogy, wine with friends; *Clubs* Royal Over-Seas League; *Style—* Robert H Blayney, Esq; ✉ Elms Farm, St Mary, Jersey JE3 3BA, CI (☎ 01534 481491); La Mare Vineyards, Jersey, CI (☎ 01534 481178)

BLEAKLEY, Rt Hon David Wylie; CBE (1984), PC (NI 1971); s of John Wesley Bleakley, of Belfast, and Sarah, *née* Wylie; *b* 11 Jan 1925; *Educ* Ruskin Coll Oxford, Queen's Univ Belfast (MA); *m* 1949, Winifred, da of Alfred Wason (d 1931); 3 s; *Career* MP (Lab) Victoria (Belfast) NI Parly 1958–65, memb NI Assembly 1973–75, NI Convention 1975–76, min Community Rels NI Govt 1972, chm Standing Advsy Ctee on Human Rights 1980–84; chief exec Irish Cncl of Churches 1980–92, pres Church Mission Soc London 1983–, lectr in industl rels Kivukoni Coll (Dar es Salaam) 1967–69; memb: Ctee of Inquiry on UK Police 1979, Press Cncl 1988–91; delegate NI Peace Talks Forum 1996; Hon MA Open Univ; *Books* Irish Peacemaker (1980), In Place of Work (1981), Work-Shadow & Substance (1983), Beyond Work Free to Be (1985), Will the Future Work (Symposium, 1987), Peace Together (Symposium, 1987), Europe - A Christian Vision (1992), Ireland - Two States, One People (1995); *Style—* The Rt Hon David Bleakley, CBE; ✉ 8 Thornhill, Bangor, Co Down, N Ireland BT19 1RD (☎ 01247 454898, fax 01247 274274); Church Mission Society, 157 Waterloo Rd, London SE1 (☎ 0171 928 8681)

BLEASDALE, Cyril; OBE (1988); s of Frederick Bleasdale, and Alice Bleasdale (d 1976); *b* 8 July 1934; *Educ* Stanford Business Sch; *m* 1970, Catherine Valerie; 2 da (Jane b 1970, Emma b 1972); *Career* md Freightliner 1975–82, dir BR Intercity 1982–86, gen mangr BR LM 1986–89, dir Scotrail 1990–94; chm: Management Transport Consultancy 1994–, Riverside Bakeries 1994–; FCIT, FIMgt, FRSA; *Recreations* squash, keep fit; *Style—* Cyril Bleasdale, Esq, OBE; ✉ 7102 Dalhousie Court, 42 West Graham Street, Glasgow G4 9LH (☎ and fax 0141 332 3979)

BLEASDALE, Prof John Kenneth Anthony; CBE (1988); s of John Henry Bleasdale (d 1958), and Helen, *née* Rushworth (d 1960); *b* 17 May 1928; *Educ* Manchester GS, Univ of Manchester (BSc, PhD); *m* 24 Sept 1953, Zoë Patricia, da of Frederick Vivian Wallis (d 1962); 2 s (Richard b 1956, Robert b 1959); *Career* cmmnd fighter controller RAF 1952–54; dir Nat Vegetable Res Station Wellesbourne Warwicks 1977–88 (joined 1954, head of Plant Physiology Section 1961–77), head of crop prodn Inst of Horticultural Res 1985–88; former nat pres: Assoc of Applied Biologists, Agric Section of Br Assoc for the Advancement of Sci, The Inst of Horticulture; govr Pershore Coll; special prof Univ of Nottingham 1977–92, hon prof Univ of Birmingham 1977– (emeritus prof 1988); Research Medal RASE 1973, Veitch Gold Medal RHS 1989, Pres's Medal Inst of Horticulture 1993; FIBioL 1976, FIHort 1985; hon memb Assoc of Applied Biologists 1988; *Books* Plant Physiology in Relation to Horticulture (1973, 2 edn 1979), Know and Grow Vegetables (co-ed and contrib vol 1 1979, vol 2 1982); *Style—* Prof John Bleasdale, CBE

BLEASE, Hon (William) Victor; eldest s of Baron Blease, JP (Life Peer), *qv*; *b* 1942; *m* 1969, Rose Mary, da of Alan Seaton; 2 s, 2 da; *Career* chief exec NI Housing Exec; *Style—* The Hon W Victor Blease; ✉ Chief Executive, Northern Ireland Housing Executive, 2 Adelaide Street, Belfast BT2 8PB (☎ 01232 240588)

BLEASE, Baron (Life Peer UK 1978), of Cromac, City of Belfast; William John Blease; JP (Belfast 1974); s of late William John Blease, and Sarah Blease; *b* 28 May 1914; *Educ* Belfast Tech, New Univ of Ulster; *m* 1939, Sarah Evelyn (d 1995), da of William Caldwell; 3 s, 1 da; *Career* industl rels conslt, former union official; memb IBA 1974–79; Hon DLitt Univ of Ulster 1972, Hon LLD Queen's Univ Belfast 1982; *Recreations* reading, DIY; *Style—* The Rt Hon Lord Blease; ✉ House of Lords, Westminster, London SW1A OPW

BLECH, Harry; CBE (1984, OBE 1962); *b* 2 March 1910; *Educ* Trinity Coll of Music, Manchester Coll of Music; *m* 1, 1935, Enid Marion Lessing (d 1977); 1 s, 2 da; m 2, 1957, Marion Manley, pianist; 1 s, 3 da; *Career* fndr and ldr Blech String Quartet 1934–50, musical dir Haydn-Mozart Soc; fndr and conductor London Mozart Players 1949–84, ret 1984; conductor laureate; memb RSA; fell: Trinity Coll of Music, Royal Manchester Coll of Music; FRAM; *Style—* Harry Blech, Esq, CBE; ✉ The Owls, 70 Leopold Rd, London SW19 (☎ 0181 946 8135)

BLEDISLOE, 3 Viscount (1935 UK); Christopher Hiley Ludlow Bathurst; QC (1978); s of 2 Viscount Bledisloe, QC (d 1979); *b* 24 June 1934; *Educ* Eton, Trinity Coll Oxford; *m* 1962 (m dis 1986), Elizabeth Mary, da of late Sir Edward Thompson; 2 s (Hon Rupert, Hon Otto Benjamin Charles b 16 June 1971), 1 da (Hon Matilda Blanche (Hon Mrs Clark) b 16 Feb 1967); *Heir* s, Hon Rupert Bathurst b 13 March 1964; *Career* called to the Bar Gray's Inn 1959; *Clubs* Garrick; *Style—* The Rt Hon the Viscount Bledisloe, QC; ✉ Fountain Court, Temple, London EC4Y 9DH (☎ 0171 583 3335)

BLEEHEN, Prof Norman Montague; CBE (1994); s of Solomon Bleehen (d 1972), of London, and Lena, *née* Shlosberg; b 24 Feb 1930; *Educ* Manchester GS, Haberdashers' Aske's, Univ of Oxford (MA, BSc, MB BCh), Middx Hosp Med Sch; *m* 14 Dec 1969, Tirza, da of Arnold Loeb, of Sydney, Aust; *Career* Nat Serv BAOR 1957–59, med specialist Br Military Hosp and Berlin MO to Spandau Military Gaol 1958–59; prof of radiotherapy Middx Hosp Med Sch 1969–75, prof of clinical oncology Univ of Cambridge 1975–95, hon dir MRC Clinical Oncology and Radiotherapeutics Unit 1975–95, chm Br Assoc Cancer Res 1977–80, pres Int Soc of Radiation Oncology 1985–89, vice pres Int Assoc Study of Lung Cancer 1987–90; hon fell American Coll of Radiologists 1973, hon doctorate Bologna 1990; Liveryman Worshipful Soc of Apothecaries 1973; FRCR 1964, FRCP 1970; *Books* Tumours of the Brain (1986), Radiobiology in Radiotherapy (1988); *Recreations* reading, gardening; *Clubs* Athenaeum; *Style—* Prof Norman Bleehen, CBE; ✉ 21 Bentley Rd, Cambridge CB2 2AW (☎ 01223 354320); St John's College, Cambridge CB2 1TP (☎ 01223 338762, fax 01223 377720)

BLENNERHASSETT, Sir (Marmaduke) Adrian Francis William; 7 Bt (UK 1809), of Blennerville, Co Kerry; s of Lt Sir Marmaduke Charles Henry Joseph Casimir Blennerhassett, 6 Bt, RNVR (d 1940), and Gwenfra Mary, *née* Harrington-Morgan; *b* 25 May 1940; *Educ* Michael Hall, McGill Univ Montreal Canada (BSc), Imperial Coll London (MSc), Cranfield Business Sch (MBA); *m* 1972, Carolyn Margaret, da of late Gilbert Brown; 1 s (Charles b 1975), 1 da (Celina Mary Charlotte b 1973); *Heir* s, Charles Henry Marmaduke Blennerhassett b 18 July 1975; *Clubs* Royal Ocean Racing; *Style—* Sir Adrian Blennerhassett, Bt; ✉ 54 Staveley Rd, Chiswick, London W4 3ES (☎ 0181 994 4908, fax 0181 742 7162)

BLESSED, Brian; s of William Blessed, of Bolton-on-Dearne, S Yorks, and Hilda, *née* Wall; *b* 9 Oct 1936; *Educ* Bolton-on-Dearne Secondary Modern; *m* 28 Dec 1978, Hildegard Neil *née* Zimmermann; 1 da (Rosalind Josephine b 16 April 1975); *Career* actor; tstee Bowles Rocks Tst; patron: Michael Elliott Tst, Dearne Community Miners' Welfare Scheme, VIGIL; fund-raiser: Royal Marsden Cancer Fund, Frimley Park Hosp Childrens Ward Appeal; *Theatre* RSC: Claudius in Hamlet, Hastings in Richard III, Exeter in Henry V; RNT: Maxim Gorky in State of Revolution, John Freeman in Metropolis, Old Deuteronomy in Cats, Henry II in The Lion in Winter; An Evening with Brian Blessed (one man show) 1992–93 & 1995–96; *Television* PC Fancy Smith in Z Cars, Augustus Caesar in I Claudius, Albert in George's Sand, King Guthram in Churchill's People, Porthos in The Three Musketeers, Pepone in The Little World of Don Camillo, Spiro in My Family and Other Animals, King Richard in Blackadder (first series), Kemble in Sweeney, Freddie Dyer in Minder, The Boy Dominic, Boon, Prof Atticus in Magyver - Lost Treasure of Atlantis, Bestuzhev in Catherine The Great, William Stickers in Johnny & the Dead; *Films* Prince Vultan in Flash Gordon, Long John Silver in Return to Treasure Island, Talthybius in Trojan Women, Pedro in Man of La Mancha, Exeter in Henry V, General Zukov in War and Remembrance, Lord Locksley in Robin Hood Prince of Thieves, General Gonse in Prisoners of Honour, Antonio in Much Ado About Nothing, The Ghost in Hamlet; *Books* The Turquoise Mountain, The Dynamite Kid, Nothing's Impossible, Blessed Everest; *Style—* Brian Blessed, Esq; ✉ c/o William Morris Agency (UK) Ltd, 31/32 Soho Square, London W1V 6DG (☎ 0171 434 2191, fax 0171 437 0238)

BLETHYN, Brenda; *Educ* Guildford Sch of Dance and Drama; *Career* actress; *Theatre* NT incl: Beaux Stratagem (Best Actress nomination), Troilus and Cressida, Tambourlaine, Tales From the Vienna Woods, Madras House, The Passion, Bedroom Farce, The Double Dealer, Fruits of Enlightenment, Strife, A Midsummer Night's Dream, The Guardsman, The Provoked Wife, Dalliance; other roles incl: Steaming (Comedy Theatre, Best Supporting Actress Award), Benefactors (Vaudeville, Best Actress nomination), Crimes of the Heart (Bush), A Doll's House (Royal Exchange), Born Yesterday (Royal Exchange Manchester), An Ideal Husband (Royal Exchange Manchester), The Dramatic Attitudes of Miss Fanny Kemble (Southampton), Absent Friends (Manhattan Theater NY, Theater World Award for Outstanding Performance), Wildest Dreams (RSC), The Bed Before Yesterday (Almeida), Habeas Corpus (Donmar); *Television* incl: The Labours of Erica (2 series), Death of An Expert Witness (3 series), A Chance in a Million (Comedy Award), Alas Smith and Jones, Tales of the Unexpected, The Shawl, All Good Things, Bedroom Farce, Play for Today (Grown Ups), The Richest Woman In The World, Yes Minister, King Lear, Henry VI, The Story Teller, The Bullion Boys, The Buddah of Suburbia, Sleeping with Mickey, Outside Edge (3 series, Best Comedy Actress Award); *Films* incl: The Witches, A River Runs Through It, Secrets and Lies (Best Actress Award Cannes 1996); *Style—* Miss Brenda Blethyn; ✉ c/o Sally

Long-Innes, ICM Ltd, Oxford House, 76 Oxford Street, London W1N 0AX (☎ 0171 636 6565, fax 0171 323 0101)

BLEWITT, Maj Sir Shane Gabriel Basil; GCVO (1996, KCVO 1989, CVO 1987, LVO 1981); s of late Col Basil Blewitt; *b* 25 March 1935; *Educ* Ampleforth, ChCh Oxford; *m* 1969, Julia, da of late Robert Henry Calvert, and wid of Maj John Morrogh-Bernard, late of the Irish Gds; 1 s (and 1 step s), 1 da (and 1 step da); *Career* Army Service Irish Gds 1956–74 (BAOR, Germany, Aden, Hong Kong); Antony Gibbs & Sons Ltd 1974; Keeper of the Privy Purse and Treasurer to HM The Queen 1988–96 (Dep Keeper 1985–87, Asst Keeper 1975–85), Extra Equerry to HM The Queen 1996–; *Recreations* shooting, gardening; *Clubs* White's; *Style*— Maj Sir Shane Blewitt, GCVO

BLIGH, (Peter) Robin; s of Barry Anstey Bligh (d 1996) and Mary Irene, *née* Floyd; *b* 1 Feb 1940; *Educ* Ardingly College Sussex, Bedford School; *m* 4 April 1964, Kathleen Mary, da of late John A Nicholson; 1 s (Andrew William b 3 Dec 1966), 1 da (Helen Mary b 26 Sept 1968); *Career* formerly with Holloway Blount Duke slrs 1956; Spicer and Pegler Chartered Accountants: articled clerk 1957–62, Cambridge 1972, ptnr 1973–; ptnr Touche Ross (following merger, now Deloitte & Touche); dir Ely Diocesan Bd of Fin, former govr The Perse Sch and chm Fin and Gen Purposes Ctee; Freeman City of London, Liveryman Worshipful Co of Wheelwrights 1986; ACA 1962; *Recreations* golf, skiing, wines, antiques; *Clubs* The Gog Magog Golf; *Style*— Robin Bligh, Esq; ✉ April House, 2 Penarth Place, Cambridge CB3 9LU (☎ 01223 566630); Deloitte & Touche, Leda House, Station Road, Cambridge CB1 2RN (☎ 01223 460222, fax 01223 350839)

BLIGHT, Catherine Montgomery; da of Murdo Montgomery (d 1969), and Catherine A Montgomery (d 1995); *Educ* Laxdale Sch Isle of Lewis, George Watson's Ladies' Coll Edinburgh, Univ of Edinburgh (BL, MSc); *m* 28 Oct 1961, David Philip Blight, s of Frank Blight (d 1971); 2 da (Josephine (Mrs J Truscott) b 1964, Charlotte b 1966); *Career* slr and economist in private and commercial practice; academic res Edinburgh until 1990; memb: Gas Consumers Cncl 1988–96, MMC 1990–96, Cornwall & Isles of Scilly Health Authys 1992–96; chm Cornwall Healthcare Tst 1996–; govr St Austell Coll 1994–; author of many pubns on law and economics in learned jls; memb Commun na Gaidhlig Inverness 1989–91, tstee and non-exec dir David Hume Inst Edinburgh, memb Mont Pelerin Soc; Euro Parly candidate Lothians 1989; memb Law Soc of Scotland; *Recreations* growing camellias, collecting books, starting up new organisations; *Clubs* Farmers', Whitehall Court; *Style*— Mrs Catherine M Blight; ✉ Parc Mead, Retanning Lane, Sticker, St Austell, Cornwall PL26 7HH (☎ and fax 01726 73613)

BLIN, Raymond Ellis; s of Arnold Blin, of Newton Mearns, Glasgow, and Helen, *née* Shenken; *b* 6 Oct 1950; *Educ* Hutchesons' GS, Univ of Aberdeen; *m* 3 Aug 1982, Shoana Marshall, da of John Marsh; 1 da (Francesca Anna Kimberley b 28 May 1990); *Career* articled clerk Kerr McLeod & Co (now Deloitte & Co) 1969–76, CA 1976, ptnr Insolvency Douglas Laing and Jackson CA's 1977–81; Pannell Kerr Forster: local managing ptnr 1981–89, regnl managing ptnr Scotland 1990–92, exec ptnr Nat Firm 1992–; dir Inside Out Devpt Ltd 1993–; ICAS, IPA, MCIM, SPI; *Recreations* breeding and showing German Shepherds and St Bernards, showjumping and breeding horses, bridge; *Style*— Raymond Blin, Esq; ✉ Pannell Kerr Forster, 78 Carlton Place, Glasgow, Scotland G5 9TH (☎ 0141 429 5900, fax 0141 429 5901)

BLIN-STOYLE, Prof Roger John; s of Cuthbert Basil St John Blin-Stoyle (d 1978), and Ada Mary, *née* Nash (d 1983); *b* 24 Dec 1924; *Educ* Alderman Newton's Boys' Sch Leicester, Wadham Coll Oxford (MA, DPhil); *m* 30 Aug 1949, Audrey Elizabeth, da of Joseph Clifford Balmford (d 1977); 1 s (Anthony b 1955), 1 da (Helena b 1952); *Career* WWII served RCS 1943–46, cmmnd 1944; res fell Pressed Steel Co Univ of Oxford 1951–53, lectr in mathematical physics Univ of Birmingham 1953–54, sr res offr in theoretical physics Univ of Oxford 1954–62, fell and lectr in physics Wadham Coll Oxford 1956–62 (hon fell 1987), visiting assoc prof of physics MIT 1959–60; Univ of Sussex: prof of theoretical physics 1962–90, emeritus prof 1990, founding science dean 1962–68, pro vice chllr 1965–67, deputy vice chllr 1970–72, pro vice chllr (science) 1977–79; chm Sch Curriculum Devpt Ctee 1983–88, memb or chm of various ctees incl SERC and Royal Soc; pres: Inst of Physics 1990–92, Assoc for Science Educn 1993–94; Hon DSc Univ of Sussex 1990; FInstP 1962, FRS 1976; *Books* Theories of Nuclear Moments (1957), Fundamental Interactions and the Nucleus (1973), Nuclear and Particle Physics (1991); *Recreations* making music; *Style*— Prof Roger Blin-Stoyle, FRS; ✉ 14 Hill Rd, Lewes, E Sussex BN7 1DB (☎ 01273 473640); Physics Building, The University of Sussex, Brighton, E Sussex BN1 9QH (☎ 01273 678088, fax 01273 678335)

BLISS, Prof Christopher John Emile; s of John Llwelyn Bliss of London (d 1978), a founder of the BBC TV service from 1936, working as a "boffin" designer, etc, and Patricia Paula, *née* Dubern; *b* 17 Feb 1940; *Educ* Finchley Catholic GS, King's Coll Cambridge (BA, PhD); *m* 1, 1964, Heather, da of Cyril Midmer, of Dublin; 1 s (John Benet b 1966), 2 da (Anna Katharine b 1968, Madeline Frances b 1974); m 2, 1983, Ghada, da of Adel Saqf El Hait, of Kuwait; *Career* fellow Christ's College Cambridge 1965–71, asst lecturer 1965–67, lecturer 1967–71; prof of economics Univ of Essex 1971–77; fell Econometric Soc 1978; ed Review of Economic Studies 1967–71; Nuffield Coll Oxford: fell 1977–, Nuffield reader in economics 1977–92, Nuffield prof of economics 1992–; *Books* Capital Theory of the Distribution of Income (1975), Palanpur: the Economy of an Indian Village (with N H Stern); *Recreations* music; *Style*— Prof Christopher Bliss, FBA; ✉ Tamarisk Cottage, South Street, Steeple Aston, Oxon OX6 3RT; Nuffield College, Oxford OX1 1NF (☎ 01865 278573)

BLISS, Dr Timothy Vivian Pelham; s of late Cdr Pelham Marryat Bliss, RN, and Elizabeth Cotton, *née* Sproule; *b* 27 July 1940; *Educ* Dean Close Sch Cheltenham, McGill Univ Montreal (BSc, PhD), Imperial Coll London, Hatfield Poly (BSc); *m* 1, 1975 (m dis 1994), Virginia Catherine Morton-Evans; 2 step da (Clara, Catherine), 1 step s (James); m 2, 1994, Isabel Frances Vasseur; 2 step s (Roman, Blaise); 1 da by Katherine Sarah Clough (Linnea Ann Susan b 4 Feb 1981); *Career* memb scientific staff MRC 1967–, head Div of Neurophysiology Nat Inst for Medical Research 1988–; visiting prof: Dept of Physiology UCL 1993–, Univ of Paris Sud Orsay 1996; Bristol Myers Squibb Award for neuroscience (with E R Kandel) 1991, Feldberg Prize 1994; memb: Brain Research Assoc 1967–, Physiological Soc 1968–, European Neuroscience Assoc (memb Scientific Program Ctee 1994–); FRS 1994; *Recreations* cooking, travelling; *Style*— Dr T V P Bliss, FRS; ✉ National Institute for Medical Research, Mill Hill, London NW7 1AA (☎ 0181 959 3666, fax 0181 906 4477, e-mail t-bliss@nimr.mrc.ac.uk)

BLOCH, (Andrew Charles) Danby; s of late Prof Moishe Rudolf Bloch, and Mary Hall Bloch; *b* 19 Dec 1945; *Educ* Tonbridge, Wadham Coll Oxford (MA); *m* 1968, Sandra, da of late William Wilkinson; 1 s (Adam b 1972), 1 da (Hester b 1974); *Career* researcher Oxford Centre for Mgmnt Studies (now Templeton Coll) 1968–70; dir: Grosvenor Advisory Services Ltd 1971–74, Oxford Fine Arts Ltd 1975–85, Raymond Godfrey & Partners Ltd 1974–, Taxbriefs Ltd 1975–; regular weekly column on taxation (and related topics): The Times 1979–82 and 1986–88, The Sunday Times 1988–91; regular fin column in The Daily Telegraph 1982–86; dep chm Bd of Govrs Oxford Brookes Univ (formerly Oxford Poly) 1990, memb Cncl Museum of Modern Art Oxford 1990, memb Tstees Oxford Inst of Legal Practice (chm 1994–95), memb Steering Ctee for Investment Advsrs' Cert of Securities Inst, memb Soc of Fin Advsrs; *Books* Providing Financial Advice, Financial Advice, Planning for School and College Fees (co-author); ed: Taxation and Trusts, Personal Investment Planning, Corporate Financial Planning, Pensions; *Style*— Danby Bloch, Esq; ✉ 17 Norham Rd, Oxford OX2 6SF (☎ 01865 55308); 193 St John Street, London EC1 (☎ 0171 250 0967, fax 0171 251 8867)

BLOCH, Prof Maurice E F; *b* 21 Oct 1939, Caen, France; *Educ* sch in Paris, LSE (BA), Univ of Cambridge (PhD); *m*; 2 c; *Career* lectr Univ of Wales Swansea 1967–68, lectr LSE 1968–76, reader Univ of London 1976–83, prof of anthropology Univ of London 1983–; convenor Anthropology Dept LSE 1985–88 and 1990–; visiting prof: Univ of Calif at Berkeley 1974–75, Univ of Paris Nanterre 1979, Univ of Stockholm 1980–81, Nat Ethnology Museum of Japan 1984; dir d'etudes associe Ecole des Hautes Etudes en Sciences Sociales France 1982–83; Rivers Medal Royal Anthropological Inst 1983; fell Danish Centre for the Humanities Copenhagen 1988; FBA 1990; *Books* Placing the Dead: Tombs, Ancestral Villages and Kinship Organization in Madagascar (1971), Political Laguage, Oratory and Traditional Society (ed, 1975), Marxist Analyses and Social Anthropology (ed, 1975), Death and the Regeneration of Life (ed, 1982), Marxism and Anthropology: The History of a Relationship (1983), From Blessing to Violence: History and Ideology in the Circumcision Ritual of the Merina of Madagascar (1986), Ritual, History and Power - Selected Papers in Anthropology (1989), Money and the Morality of Exchange (ed, 1989), Prey into Hunter: The Politics of Religious Experience (1991); author of numerous articles in publications and jls; *Style*— Prof Maurice Bloch, FBA; ✉ Department of Anthropology, London School of Economics, Houghton Street, London WC2A 2AE (☎ 0171 405 7686, fax 0171 242 0392)

BLOCH, Michael Anthony; s of Richard Bloch, and Ruth, *née* Grant; *b* 24 Sept 1953; *Educ* Portadown Coll, St John's Coll Cambridge (MA, LLB); *Career* called to the Bar Inner Temple 1978; assisted Maître Suzanne Blum of Paris with affairs of the Duchess of Windsor and her Estate 1979–88; author; *Books* The Duke of Windsor's War (1982), Operation Willi (1984), Wallis and Edward (1986), The Secret File of the Duke of Windsor (1988), The Reign and Abdication of Edward VIII (1990), Ribbentrop (1992), The Duchess of Windsor (1996); *Recreations* eating, bridge, playing Chopin; *Clubs* Savile, Cambridge Union Soc, Players Theatre, Green Street Bridge; *Style*— Michael Bloch, Esq; ✉ 2 Strathearn Place, London W2 2NQ (☎ and fax 0171 723 2220, e-mail padders@dircon.co.uk); c/o Curtis Brown Ltd, 28 Haymarket, London SW1Y 4SP (☎ 0171 396 6600)

BLOCK, Simon Anthony Allen; s of Gerald Allen Block (d 1969), of Battle, E Sussex, and Eileen Marjorie, *née* Handley (d 1982); *b* 19 July 1935; *Educ* Marlborough, Pembroke Coll Cambridge (MA); *m* 16 Aug 1958, Patricia Ann, da of Gen Sir Rodney Moore, GCVO, KCB, CBE, DSO (d 1985), Chief Steward of Hampton Court Palace; 3 s (Adam b 1960, Robert b 1962, Justin b 1964); *Career* 2 Lt 1 Bn Queen's Royal West Surrey Regt 1952–54; slr; sr ptnr Crossman Block and Keith 1977–88, ptnr Withers Crossman Block 1988–89, sr ptnr Crossman Block 1989–95, conslt Radcliffes Crossman Block 1995–; memb Common Cncl City of London 1983–; Liveryman: Worshipful Co of Broderers (Master 1979–80), Worshipful Co of Weavers (Renter Bailiff 1995–96), City of London Solicitors' Co 1988; memb Ct Guild of Freeman City of London; Sheriff of the City of London 1988–89, pres The Embroiderers' Guild 1986–93, hon sec King George's Fund for Sailors 1993–; *Recreations* fine wines, field sports; *Clubs* Leander, City Livery, The Grannies; *Style*— Simon A A Block, Esq; ✉ Radcliffes Crossman Block, 5 Great College Street, Westminster, London SW1P 3SJ (☎ 0171 222 7040, fax 0171 222 6208)

BLOCKLEY, Prof David Ian; s of Harold Gwynne Blockley (d 1972), of Derby, and Olive Lydia Blockley (d 1979); *b* 18 Sept 1941; *Educ* Bemrose Sch Derby, Univ of Sheffield (BEng, PhD 1967), Univ of Bristol (DSc 1987); *m* 6 Aug 1966, Karen Elisabeth Blockley; 1 s (Andrew David b 1968), 1 da (Alison Mary b 1973); *Career* devpt engr BCSA Ltd London 1967–69; Univ of Bristol: lectr 1969–82, reader 1982–89, prof 1989–, head Dept of Civil Engrg 1989–95, dean of engrg 1994–; corresponding memb: Argentinian Acad of Engrs, Argentinian Acad of Science; Telford Gold Medal Inst of Civil Engrs 1978, George Stephenson Medal Inst of Civil Engrs 1981, Oscar Faber dip Inst of Structural Engrs 1986; FEng 1992, FICE, FIStructE, FRSA; *Books* The Nature of Structural Design and Safety (1980), Engineering Safety (1992); *Recreations* reading, gardening, swimming, golf, watching sport (esp soccer and cricket); *Style*— Professor D I Blockley, FEng; ✉ Dean of Engineering, University of Bristol, Bristol BS8 1TR (fax 0117 925 1154)

BLOFELD, Hon Mr Justice; Hon Sir John Christopher Calthorpe; kt (1990), DL (Norfolk 1991); s of late Thomas Robert Calthorpe Blofeld, CBE, JP (d 1986; High Sheriff of Norfolk 1953, and chm CGA), and Grizel Blanche, *née* Turner (d 1992); *b* 11 July 1932; *Educ* Eton, King's Coll Cambridge; *m* 1961, Judith Anne, elder da of late Dr Alan Mohun, and Mrs James Mitchell; 2 s, 1 da; *Career* called to the Bar Lincoln's Inn 1956, recorder of the Crown Court 1975, QC 1975, circuit judge (SE) 1982–90, judge of the High Court of Justice (Queen's Bench Div) 1990–, presiding judge SE Circuit until 1997; chllr Diocese of St Edmundsbury 1973; chm CGA 1977; Liveryman Worshipful Co of Mercers; *Recreations* gardening; *Clubs* Boodle's, Norfolk County; *Style*— The Hon Mr Justice Blofeld, DL

BLOIS, Sir Charles Nicholas Gervase; 11 Bt (E 1686), of Grundisburgh Hall, Suffolk; er s of Capt Sir Gervase Blois, 10 Bt, MC (d 1968), and Audrey Winifred, *née* Johnson; *b* 25 Dec 1939; *Educ* Harrow, Trinity Coll Dublin, Royal Agricultural Coll; *m* 8 July 1967, Celia Helen Mary, o da of late Cyril George Francis Pritchett, CBE, of Aldeburgh, Suffolk; 1 s, 1 da (Helen Janet b 1974); *Heir* s, Andrew Charles David Blois b 7 Feb 1971; *Career* farmer and landowner; chm Access & Justice Ltd; FRGS; *Recreations* yacht cruising (yacht 'Caleta'), travel, shooting; *Clubs* Cruising Assoc, Ocean Cruising; *Style*— Sir Charles Blois, Bt; ✉ Red House, Westleton, Saxmundham, Suffolk (☎ 01728 648200)

BLOM-COOPER, Sir Louis Jacques; kt (1992), QC (1970); s of Alfred Blom-Cooper (d 1964), and Ella, *née* Flesseman (d 1932); *b* 27 March 1926; *Educ* Seaford Coll, King's Coll London (LLB), Municipal Univ of Amsterdam (Dr. Juris), Fitzwilliam House Cambridge; *m* 1, 7 July 1952 (m dis 1970), Miriam Eve, da of Daniel Swift (d 1988); 2 s (Jeremy Rupert Louis b 25 Jan 1961, Keith Sebastian Daniel (twin) b 25 Jan 1961), 1 da (Alison Jeanette b 13 April 1958); m 2, 16 Oct 1970, Jane Elizabeth, da of Maurice Douglas Smither; 1 s ((Samuel) George Abbott b 8 July 1979), 2 da (Martha Clare Justine b 6 Jan 1971, Hannah Jane Notcutt b 13 Nov 1972); *Career* joined army 1944, 2 Lt E Yorks Regt 1945, Capt 1946, demobbed 1947; called to the Bar Middle Temple 1952, bencher 1978, memb Home Sec's Advsy Cncl on the Penal System 1966–78; Northern Ireland independent cmmr for the Holding Centres 1992–; chm: Advsy Cncl BBC London Local Radio 1970–73, Ind Ctee for the Supervision of Standards of Telephone Info Servs 1986–93, Mental Health Act Cmmn 1987–94, Press Cncl 1989–90, Inquiry into Ashworth Hosp 1991–92; chm Victim Support 1995–, vice pres Howard League for Penal Reform 1984– (chm 1973–84), tstee Prison Reform Tst; jt dir Legal Res Unit Bedford Coll Univ of London 1967–82; visiting prof: QMC Univ of London 1983–86, Univ of Loughborough 1993–95; tstee Scott Tst (The Guardian Newspaper) 1982–89; jt ed Common Market Law Reports; JP Inner London 1966–79 (transferred City of London 1969); Hon DLitt: Loughborough 1991, Univ of Ulster 1995; FRSA 1964; *Books* Bankruptcy in Private International Law (1954), The Law as Literature (anthology, 1962), The A6 Murder (A Semblance of Truth) (1963), A Calender of Murder (with TP Morris, 1964), Language of the Law (anthology, 1965), Separated Spouses (with O R McGregor and Colin Gibson, 1970), Final Appeal: A Study of the House of Lords in its Judicial Capacity (with G Drewry, 1972), Progress in Penal Reform (ed, 1975), Law and Morality (ed with G Drewry, 1976); *Recreations* watching and reporting on association football, reading, music, writing, broadcasting; *Clubs* MCC, Athenaeum; *Style*— Sir Louis Blom-Cooper, QC; ✉ 2 Ripplevale Grove, London N1 1HU (☎ 0171 607 8045, fax 0171 609 3350);

Glebe House, Montgomery, Powys SY15 6QA (☎ 01686 668458 or 01686 668079); Doughty Street Chambers, 11 Doughty Street, London WC1 (☎ 0171 404 1313)

BLOMEFIELD, Sir (Thomas) Charles Peregrine; 6 Bt (UK 1807), of Attleborough, Co Norfolk; s of Sir Thomas Edward Peregrine Blomefield, 5 Bt (d 1984), and Ginette, *née* Massart; *b* 24 July 1948; *Educ* Wellington, Mansfield Coll Oxford; *m* 1975, Georgina Geraldine, da of late Cdr Charles Over, RN, of Lugger End, Portscatho, Cornwall; 1 s (William), 2 da (Emma Georgina b 1980, Harriet Elizabeth b 1986); *Heir* s, Thomas William Peregrine Blomefield b 16 July 1983; *Career* fine art conslt; Christies 1970–75, Wildenstein and Co 1975–76; dir: Lidchi Art Gallery Johannesburg 1976–78, Thomas Heneage and Co 1981–87, Fleetwood-Hesketh Ltd 1982–; md Charles Blomefield and Co 1980–; *Recreations* travel; *Style*— Sir Charles Blomefield, Bt; ✉ Attlepin Farm, Chipping Campden, Glos GL55 6PP

BLOOD, Peter Bindon; o s of Brig William Edmund Robarts Blood, CBE, MC (d 1976), and Eva Gwendoline Olive Clarisse Mends, *née* Harrison (d 1981); collateral descendant of Col Thomas Blood who attempted to steal the Crown Jewels on 9 May 1671, later pardoned and pensioned by Charles II; *b* 24 Sept 1920; *Educ* Imperial Service Coll, Windsor; *m* 20 June 1953, Elizabeth Ann, da of Harold Drummond Hillier, MC, of Sudbury, Suffolk; 1 s (Anthony b 1956), 1 da (Jennifer b 1954); *Career* served RE 1941–46 (despatches), regular cmmn RE 1948, Staff Coll Camberley 1951, sec Army Bd NATO Mil Agency for Standardisation 1952–53, invalided from serv 1953; intelligence co-ordination staff FO 1953–58; fndr and md: Isora Integrated Ceilings Ltd, Clean Room Construction Ltd, Mitchel and King Sales Ltd 1959–71; dir gen Inst of Marketing 1972–84, chm Industrial Market Research Ltd 1984–87, govr and former chm Berks Coll of Art and Design 1981–89, cnsllr DTI Enterprise Initiative; Hon Liveryman Worshipful Co of Marketors; FRSA, FInstM; *Recreations* local community activities, photography, travel, music, furniture restoration; *Style*— Peter Blood, Esq; ✉ 8 Woodhurst South, Raymead Road, Maidenhead, Berks SL6 8NZ (☎ and fax 01628 26600)

BLOOM, Anthony Herbert; s of Joseph Bloom, and Margaret Roslyn Bloom; *b* 15 Feb 1939; *Educ* King Edward VII HS S Africa, Univ of Witwatersrand (BCom, LLB), Harvard Law Sch (LLM), Stanford Univ Graduate Sch of Business (Sloan fell); *m* 10 Jan 1972, Gisela; 2 s (Andrew Martin b 7 Sept 1965, Nicholas Peter b 10 Dec 1973), 2 da (Rosemary Claire b 24 Jan 1963, Alexis Monica b 27 May 1975); *Career* with Hayman Godfrey & Sanderson 1960–64; Premier Group Ltd: joined 1966, dir 1969, dep chm 1975, chm 1979–87; Barclays Nat Bank and First Nat Bank of Southern Africa Ltd 1980–88, Liberty Life Association 1982–88, The South African Breweries Ltd 1983–89, CNA Gallo Ltd 1983–89, currently: dir RIT Capital Partners plc, chm Cine-UK Ltd, non-exec dir Sketchley plc, dir Ballet Rambert, bd memb British Library; *Recreations* karate, opera, ballet, theatre, music; *Style*— Anthony Bloom, Esq; ✉ 8 Hanover Terrace, London NW1 4RJ (☎ 071 723 3422); RIT Capital Partners plc, 27 St James's Place, London SW1A 1NR (☎ 0171 493 8111)

BLOOM, Charles; QC (1987); s of Abraham Barnet Bloom (d 1973), of Manchester, and Freda, *née* Craft (d 1994); *b* 6 Nov 1940; *Educ* Manchester Central GS, Manchester Univ (LLB); *m* 16 Aug 1967, Janice Rachelle, da of Reuben and Lily Goldberg, of Crumpsal, Manchester; 1 s (David Benjamin b 31 Aug 1972), 1 da (Sarah Rebecca b 10 July 1969); *Career* called to the Bar Gray's Inn 1963, dep circuit judge 1979, recorder of the Crown Court 1983–, head of chambers; chm Med Appeal Tbnls 1979; *Recreations* gardening, tennis; *Clubs* Friedland Postmusaf Tennis, Larner Viniflora Appreciation Society; *Style*— Charles Bloom, Esq, QC; ✉ 28 St John Street, Manchester M3 4DJ (☎ 0161 834 8418, fax 0161 835 3929)

BLOOM, Claire; da of late Edward Bloom and Elizabeth Bloom; *b* 15 Feb 1931; *Educ* Badminton, USA and privately; *m* 1, 1959 (m dis 1969), Rod Steiger; 1 da (Anna Steiger b 1960); m 2, 1969 (m dis 1976), Hillard Elkins; *Career* actress; *Theatre* The Condemned of Altona (Royal Court), Duel of Angels (Globe), The Lady's Not For Burning (Globe), Ring Around the Moon (Globe), various Shakespeare, Ivanov, A Doll's House (NY and London), The Cherry Orchard (Chichester Festival Theatre), A Streetcar Named Desire, Hedda Gabler, Vivat! Vivat Regina!, The Turn of the Screw (NY), Till We Awaken the Dead (Almeida), King John, Hamlet and A Winter's Tale (Stratford); *Television* Henry VIII, Hamlet, Cymbeline and King John (BBC Shakespeare series), Brideshead Revisited, Time and the Conways, Shadowlands (BAFTA Best Actress Award), Oedipus the King, The Ghost Writer, Anne & Debbie, The Belle of Amhurst (Int Emmy Award), Intimate Contact, Queenie, Anastasia, Liberty, The Camomile Law (Channel 4), Miss Marple - The Mirror Cracked (BBC); *Films* Limelight, The Man Between, Alexander the Great, Richard III, Look Back in Anger, The Spy Who Came in From the Cold, The Outrage, The Brother Karamazov, The Buccaneer, Charly, The Brothers Grimm, A Doll's House, Islands in the Stream, Clash of the Titans, Sammie & Rosie Get Laid, Crimes and Misdemeanours; *Books* Limelight and After; *Style*— Miss Claire Bloom; ✉ c/o Conway van Gelder Robinson Ltd, 18–21 Jermyn Street, London SW1Y 6HP (☎ 0171 287 0077, fax 0171 287 1940)

BLOOM, Dr Victor Roy; s of Froim Bloom (d 1961), of Westbourne, and Jesse Selina Tomson, *née* Parker (d 1989); *b* 13 March 1932; *Educ* Bembridge Sch, Univ of Oxford (MA, BM BCh); *m* 1, 1964 (m dis 1976), Chloe Ann, da of Frederick Jack Rich; 1 s (Marston), 1 da (Emma); m 2, 16 April 1994, Vanessa Lee, da of Frank Gale; *Career* UCH 1957–58, Bristol Royal Infirmary 1958–59, Hosp for Sick Children Gt Ormond St 1959–60, Nat Heart Hosp 1960, Hammersmith Hosp 1960–62, Central Middx Hosp 1962–64, physician Harley House 1964–; ed jl of RSM 1976–88; chm: Harley Street Consultants Ltd, Harley Street Health Care Centre Ltd; chm Health and Safety UK Ltd 1993–; vice pres Hornsby Educnl Tst; memb: Nichiren Shoshu of the UK, Advsy Panel Pro-Dogs, Dartmoor Preservation Soc, Torquay Pottery Collectors Soc, Med Soc London, Assur Med Soc; Freeman City of London 1979, Liveryman Worshipful Soc of Apothecaries 1978; MRCP 1964, MFOM RCP 1982; *Recreations* opera, theatre, ceramics, cricket, assoc football; *Clubs* United Oxford & Cambridge Univ; *Style*— Dr Victor Bloom; ✉ 40 Harley House, Marylebone Rd, London NW1 5HF (☎ 0171 935 1411, fax 0171 224 0178, car 0836 203783)

BLOOMER, Jonathan William; *b* 23 March 1954; *Educ* Imperial Coll London (BSc, ARCS); *m* Sept 1977, Judy; 3 c; *Career* Arthur Andersen: joined 1974, ptnr Fin Mkts Div Audit and Business Advsy Practice 1987–91, managing ptnr Euro Insur Practice 1991–94; gp fin dir Prudential Corporation plc 1995–; FCA; *Recreations* sailing, rugby; *Style*— Jonathan Bloomer, Esq; ✉ The Prudential Corporation plc, 142 Holborn Bars, London EC1N 2NH (☎ 0171 548 3100, fax 0171 548 3930)

BLOOMER, Robin Howard; s of Arthur Hugh Bloomer (d 1972), of Grimsby, Humberside, and Elizabeth Kathleen, *née* Watson (d 1964); *b* 6 May 1930; *Educ* Shrewsbury; *m* 24 May 1958, Edith Alice (d 1994), da of Charles William Green (d 1954); 1 s (Charles b 1961), 1 da (Susan b 1966); *Career* admitted slr 1956, princ H K & H S Bloomer & Co slrs 1964–; pres Grimsby and Cleethorpes Law Soc 1978, jt vice chm No 10 Legal Aid Area 1988–91; *Style*— Robin Bloomer, Esq; ✉ 1 Bargate Avenue, Great Grimsby (☎ 01472 343251); 28 Hainton Avenue, Great Grimsby, S Humberside DN32 9BG (☎ 01472 350711)

BLOOMFIELD, Barry Cambray; s of Clifford Wilson Bloomfield (d 1981), and Eileen Elizabeth Bloomfield (d 1953); *b* 1 June 1931; *Educ* East Ham GS, Univ Coll Exeter (BA), Birkbeck Coll London (MA); *m* 29 Dec 1958, Valerie Jean, da of George Philpot (d 1964); *Career* Nat Serv 1952–54; asst Nat Central Library 1955, librarian Coll of St Mark & St John 1956–61, asst librarian LSE 1961–63, librarian Sch of Oriental and African Studies 1972–78 (dep librarian 1963–72), dir India Office Library & Records FCO 1978–85 (concurrently keeper Dept of Oriental Manuscripts and Printed Books 1983–85), dir Collection Devpt Br Library 1985–90; tstee Shakespeare Birthplace Tst 1985–90; memb: Cncl Britain-Burma Soc 1979–90, Cncl Royal Asiatic Soc 1980–84 and 1996–, Cncl Br Assoc for Cemeteries in S Asia 1980–90, Exec Ctee Friends of the Nat Libraries 1981–96, Bibliographical Soc (vice pres 1979–90, pres 1990–92), Oxford Bibliographical Soc, Cambridge Bibliographical Soc, Philip Larkin Soc (vice pres 1995–); hon memb Darwin Coll Univ of Kent 1982; FLA 1965; *Books* W H Auden: a bibliography (2 edn, with E Mendelson, 1972), An Author Index to Selected British Little Magazines (1976), Philip Larkin: a bibliography (1979), Middle East Studies and Librarianship (1980); *Recreations* reading, music; *Clubs* Civil Serv; *Style*— Barry Bloomfield, Esq; ✉ Brambling, 24 Oxenturn Road, Wye, Ashford, Kent TN25 5BE (☎ 01233 813038)

BLOOMFIELD, Janet Elizabeth; da of Roy Hood (d 1969), and Eileen, *née* Johnson, of Sheffield; *b* 10 Oct 1953; *Educ* Abbeydale Grange Sch Sheffield, Univ of Sussex (BA); *m* 24 July 1976, Richard John Bloomfield, s of Raymond John Bloomfield; 1 da (Lucy Elizabeth b 29 April 1980), 1 s (Robin John b 31 Jan 1982); *Career* staff mgmnt trg scheme Marks & Spencer PLC 1975–77, admin asst N Yorks AHA 1977–78; CND: memb Nat Cncl and Exec Ctee 1978, co-organiser W Mids 1986–91, chair 1993–96 (vice chair 1991); vice pres: Int Peace Bureau 1994–, Nat Peace Cncl 1995–; author of various articles in peace movement and gen magazines; chair of govrs Grange Farm Primary Sch Coventry 1988–92, memb Relgious Soc of Friends; joined Green Party 1996; *Recreations* family, listening to and playing music, reading, gardening, birdwatching, travel, entertaining friends; *Style*— Ms Janet Bloomfield; ✉ c/o Campaign for Nuclear Disarmament, 162 Holloway Road, London N7 8DQ (☎ 0171 700 2350, fax 0171 700 2357, e-mail cnd@gn.apc.org, WWW http://www.mcb.net./cnd)

BLOOMFIELD, Sir Kenneth Percy; KCB (1987, CB 1982); s of Harry Percy Bloomfield (d 1993), of Belfast, and Doris, *née* Frankel (d 1991); *b* 15 April 1931; *Educ* Royal Belfast Academical Inst (John Morton scholar), St Peter's Coll Oxford (NI State exhibitioner); *m* 7 Sept 1960, (Mary) Elizabeth, da of Cncllr Robert Ramsey, JP (d 1990); 1 s (Timothy b 1970), 1 da (Caroline b 1966); *Career* Miny of Finance NI 1952–59, dep dir Br Industl Devpt Office NY 1960–63, Cabinet Secretariat NI 1963–72, under sec NI Office 1972–73; perm sec: Office of the Executive NI 1974–75, Dept of Housing Local Govt and Planning NI 1975–76, Dept of the Environment NI 1976–81, Dept of Commerce NI 1981–82, Dept of Econ Devpt NI 1982–84; head NI Civil Serv and second perm under sec NI Office 1984–91; nat govr BBC for NI and chm NI Broadcasting Cncl 1991–; chm: Chief Execs Forum 1991–, Children In Need Tst 1992–, NI Higher Educn Cncl 1993–; bd memb: Co-operation North 1991–93, Opera NI 1991–, NI Advsy Bd Bank of Ireland 1991–; memb Navan at Armagh, patron Belfast Improved Houses, senator Queen's Univ Belfast 1992–93, govr Royal Belfast Academical Inst; Hon LLD Queen's Univ Belfast 1991, hon fell St Peter's Coll Oxford 1991; *Publications* Stormont in Crisis (1994); contrib: Parliamentary Brief, Fortnight, etc; *Recreations* swimming, reading history and biography; *Clubs* United Oxford and Cambridge Univ; *Style*— Sir Kenneth Bloomfield, KCB; ✉ c/o BBC, Broadcasting House, Ormeau Avenue, Belfast BT2 (☎ 01232 338000)

BLOOMFIELD, Richard Campbell; s of William Lovat Bloomfield, and Margaret Coulson, *née* Nelson; *b* 8 July 1944; *Educ* Charterhouse, Neuchatel Univ Switzerland; *m* June 1969, Denise Ann Scovell, da of Derek Lowe (d 1990); 1 s (Toby b 6 March 1975), 1 da (Lucy Jane b 15 April 1972); *Career* trainee rising to account dir Lintas Overseas advtg agency 1965–74, account dir McCann Erickson 1974–78, bd dir Harrison McCann 1978–79; md: Legon Bloomfield Associates 1979–86, Brooks Legon Bloomfield 1986–89; managing ptnr and client servs dir FCA London (now Impact FCA) 1989–; memb Mktg Soc 1987; *Recreations* horse racing, running (completed 2 NY marathons), reading; *Clubs* Naval and Military; *Style*— Richard Bloomfield, Esq; ✉ Impact FCA, 110 St Martin's Lane, London WC2N 4DY (☎ 0171 240 0888)

BLOOMFIELD, Robin Russell Clive; CBE (1993); s of Cyril George Bloomfield (d 1984), of Aldenham, Watford, and Gwendolen Lucy, *née* Hall; *b* 2 Oct 1933; *Educ* Univ Coll Sch, Shuttleworth Agric Coll (NDA); *m* 1, 1968, Janet Cecily (d 1991); 2 da (Justine Anne b 9 Dec 1971, Philippa Lucy b 8 March 1975), 1 s (Russell George b 2 May 1976); m 2, 1994, Angela Rae; *Career* began farming 1953, fndr Oakridge Farms 1958, variously farming up to 1,700 acres (currently 600); built own golf course Aldenham 1973 (also designed three others); chm Eastern Counties Farmers 1979–84, memb Cncl NFU HQ 1974–88 (memb SE Planning Cncl 1971–76), chm Eastern Region MAFF 1986–93, memb Govt Deregulation Task Force 1994; memb: Royal Agric Assoc of England, Nat Inst of Agric Botany, Agric Research Inst Assoc; parish cncllr 1968–77, JP Watford Bench 1972–85; Master Worshipful Co of Barbers 1996–97, memb Ct of Assts Worshipful Co of Farmers, Freeman City of London; memb NFU 1953; *Recreations* fishing, shooting, golf, walking; *Clubs* Farmers'; *Style*— Robin Bloomfield, Esq, CBE; ✉ Oakridge Farms Ltd, Hill Farm, Radlett, Herts WD7 7HP (☎ 01923 854681, fax 01923 854148, mobile 0468 010255)

BLOSSE, *see:* Lynch-Blosse

BLOUNT, Sir Walter Edward Alpin (Jasper); 12 Bt (E 1642), of Sodington, Worcs; DSC (1943 and two bars 1945); s of Sir Edward Robert Blount, 11 Bt (d 1978), and Violet Ellen, *née* Fowler (d 1969); *b* 31 Oct 1917; *Educ* Beaumont Coll, Sidney Sussex Coll Cambridge (MA 1943); *m* 1954, Eileen Audrey, da of late Hugh Blasson Carritt; 1 da (Nicola Jane Eileen (Mrs Charles Glanville) b 1955); *Heir* none; *Career* Lt RNVR; slr; farmer; *Recreations* sailing; *Clubs* Bembridge Sailing, Seaview Yacht, CUCC, RNVR Yacht; *Style*— Sir Walter Blount, Bt, DSC; ✉ Tilkhurst, Imberhorne Lane, East Grinstead, W Sussex RH19 1TY (☎ 01342 323018); Regent House, Seaview, Isle of Wight (☎ 01983 613326)

BLOW, Prof David Mervyn; *b* 27 June 1931; *Educ* Kingswood Sch Bath, Corpus Christi Coll Cambridge (entrance scholar, Boyd scholar, BA, PhD); *m* 1955, Mavis, *née* Sears; 1 da (Elizabeth b 1958), 1 s (Julian b 1961); *Career* Nat Serv RAF 1949–51; Fulbright fell Nat Inst of Health Bethesda Maryland 1957–58 and MIT 1958–59; MRC: Unit for Molecular Biology Cavendish Lab 1959–61, Lab of Molecualr Biology 1961–77; fell and lectr in crystallography Trinity Coll Cambridge 1969–77; Imperial Coll of Science and Technol London: prof of biophysics 1977–94, dean Royal Coll of Science 1981–84, memb Governing Body 1987–94, head Dept of Physics 1991–94, memb Audit Ctee 1993–94, sr research fell 1994–; visiting prof: Dept of Computer Science Univ of N Carolina 1985, Dept of Physics Univ of Grenoble 1989, Dept of Chemistry Univ of Exeter 1995–; memb: European Molecular Biology Orgn, British Crystallographic Assoc (fndr memb, pres 1984–87) Biochemical Soc, British Biophysical Soc (memb Ctee 1968–71); membre associé étranger Académie des Sciences Paris 1992–; CIBA Medal Biochemical Soc 1967, jt winner Prix Leopold Mayer French Acad of Sciences 1979, jt winner Wolf Prize for Chemistry Jerusalem 1987; FInstP 1971, FRS 1972; *Style*— Prof David Blow, FRS; ✉ Blackett Laboratory, Imperial College of Science, Technology and Medicine, London SW7 2BZ (☎ 0171 594 7683, fax 0171 589 0191)

BLOW, Joyce (Mrs Anthony Darlington); OBE (1994); da of Walter Blow (d 1962), and Phyllis, *née* Grainger (d 1961); *b* 4 May 1929; *Educ* Bell-Baxter Sch Cupar Fife, Univ of Edinburgh (MA); *m* 27 March 1974, (John) Anthony Basil Darlington (ret Lt-Col RE), s of Lt-Col Arthur James Darlington, DSO, JP (d 1960); *Career* princ Bd of Trade 1965–67, M & MC 1967–70, asst sec DTI 1972–77, under sec OFT 1977–80, under sec DTI 1980–84; chm: Mail Order Publishers Authy 1985–92, Authy of the Direct Mktg Assoc 1992–; memb Money Mgmnt Cncl 1985–90, vice pres Inst of Trading Standards

Admin 1985–, memb Bd Br Standards Instn (chm Consumer Policy Ctee 1986–93) 1986–, dir Arts Club 1987–90; chm: E Sussex Family Health Servs Authy 1990–96, Child Accident Prevention Tst 1996–; tstee Univ of Edinburgh Devpt Tst 1990–94, pres AQH 1991–94, chm PR Educn Tst 1992–; Freeman City of London; FIPR 1964, FIMgt 1977; *Recreations* music, the arts, travel, France; *Clubs* Arts, Reform; *Style*— Miss Joyce Blow, OBE; ✉ 17 Fentiman Rd, London SW8 1LD (☎ 0171 735 4023); 9 Crouchfield Close, Seaford, E Sussex

BLOW, Sandra; *Educ* St Martin's Sch of Art, RA Schs London, L'accademia di Belle Arti Rome; *Career* artist; RA; *Exhibitions* incl: ICA London 1951, Gimpel Fils London regularly (solo and gp exhbns) 1951–65, Adams, Blow, Paolozzi and Pasmore (Galleria Origine Rome) 1953, New Trends in British Art (Art Fndn Rome (also NY)) 1957, Young British Painters (Art Club Chicago, 2–year US tour, Rotterdam, Zürich and Düsseldorf) 1957–58, Young Artists Section XXIV Venice Biennale 1958, John Moores Exhbn Liverpool 1959, 1961 (second prize) and 1965, Vitalita nell'Arte (Palazzo Grassi Venice, Kunsthalle Recklinghausen, Stedelijk Museum Amsterdam, Louisiana Humblebaek Denmark) 1959–60, International Guggenheim Award (Guggenheim Museum NY) 1960, Carnegie Inst 1961, Painting in the '60s (Contemporary Art Soc Tate Gallery) 1962, Contemporary British Painting (Albright Knox Art Gallery Buffalo NY) 1964, RA Summer Exhbn annually 1971–, British Painting '74 (Hayward Gallery) 1974, Hayward Annual 1978, St Ives 1939–64: Twenty Five Years of Painting (Tate Gallery London) 1985, Exhibition Road (RCA) 1988, solo exhbn Francis Graham-Dixon Gallery London 1991, Sandra Blow Retrospective (Sackler Galleries RA) 1994, Porthmeor Beach: A Century of Images (Tate Gallery St Ives) 1995, Sandra Blow: Contours of Ideas from the Studio (Newlyn Art Gallery Newlyn Cornwall) 1995; *Works* recent cmmns incl glass screen for Heathrow Airport (BAA plc) 1995, illustrations for book Waves on Porthmeor Beach (by Alaric Sumner, Words Worth Books) 1995; work in public collections incl: Tate Gallery, V&A, Arts Cncl of GB, Museum of Modern Art NY, Albright-Knox Gallery Buffalo NY, Contemporary Arts Soc London, Br Cncl, Fitzwilliam Museum Cambridge, Arts Cncl of Northern Ireland, Walker Art Gallery Liverpool, Felton Bequest Melbourne Australia, Arts Cncl Purchase Award (1965), Nuffield Fndn, Nuffield Pictures for Hospitals for Children, Peter Stuyvesant Collection, Dept of the Environment, Dept for Educn, Leeds City Art Gallery, Univ of Liverpool, Chelsea and Westminster Hosp; *Style*— Ms Sandra Blow, RA; ✉ c/o The Secretary, The Royal Academy of Arts, Piccadilly, London W1V 0DS (☎ 0171 439 7438)

BLOWERS, Dr Anthony John; CBE (1985), JP (Surrey 1970), DL (Surrey 1986); s of Geoffrey Hathaway Blowers (d 1973), of Chertsey, Surrey, and Louise, *née* Jux; *b* 11 Aug 1926; *Educ* Sloane GS Chelsea, Sir John Cass Coll Univ of London, Univ of Surrey (PhD); *m* 4 Sept 1948, Yvonne, da of Capt Alan Victor Boiteux-Buchanan (d 1986); 2 s (Colin b 1953, Christopher b 1955), 1 da (Anne (Mrs Ricketts) b 1951); *Career* RCS 1944–45, RAMC 1945–46, RWAFF (served Nigeria) 1946–48; experimental offr Miny of Agric 1953–59 (sr sci asst 1949–53); Sandoz Pharmaceuticals: joined 1959, sr res offr 1973–87, conslt in psychopharmacology 1987–91; conslt in bacteriology Mansi Laboratories 1973–95, dir of corp affrs Magellan Medical Communications 1990–; vice chm Surrey AHA 1976–77 (memb 1973–80), memb SW Thames RHA 1980–81, chm W Surrey and NE Hants HA 1981–86; memb Mental Health Review Tbnl 1975–, cmmr Mental Health Act Cmmn 1987–96, Mental Health Act mangr Heathlands Mental Health NHS Tst 1994–; memb Cons Policy Gp on Mental Health 1978–81, admin sec Parly Gp for Research and Devpt in Fertility and Contraception 1994–; vice pres: Hosp Saving Assoc 1994–, Parkinson's Disease Soc 1995– (actg chief exec 1995); chm Surrey Drugs Action Team 1995–; memb: Scientific Bd Worthing Mental Health Fndn, Cncl Psychiatry Research Tst 1986– (tstee 1995–), Health Servs Ctee CNAA 1989–94, Devpt Gp MA/MSc in in Drugs Policy, Prevention and Educn Roehampton Inst 1995–; cncllr: Chertsey UDC 1964–74 (chm 1969–70 and 1973–74), Surrey CC 1970–85 (vice chm Social Servs Ctee 1973–77), Runnymede BC 1973–84 (chm 1973–74); memb Bd of Visitors Coldingley Prison 1978–92; chm Surrey Police Authy 1981–85 (memb 1973–90), vice chm Farnham Police Community Liaison Ctee 1985–94; chm: Runnymede and Elmbridge Police Community Liaison Ctee 1983–94, SW Surrey Crime Prevention Ctee 1986–92, Surrey Ctee Police Convalescence and Rehabilitation Tst 1986–88, London and SE Young Offenders Working Gp 1991–95, Runnymede and Elmbridge Ctee Wishing Well Appeal; Duke of Edinburgh Award: vice chm Woking Ctee 1987–92, chm SE Region 1990–, memb Nat Advsy Cncl 1990–; memb Cncl Magistrates' Assoc 1986–91, chm Surrey Magistrates' Soc 1988–94; memb: Surrey Magistrates' Club, Middlesex and Surrey Soc; govr: Fullbrook Sch 1967–85 (chm 1981–85), Ottershaw Sch 1975–81 (chm 1979–81); memb Court Univ of Surrey 1986–; pres Runnymede Scout Cncl 1970–84; St John Ambulance: cdr Surrey 1987–91, asst dir gen 1985–91, dir gen 1991–94; Order of St John: memb Chapter-Gen 1990–, chm St John Fellowship 1995–; High Sheriff of Surrey 1990–91; Freeman: Borough of Runnymede 1985, City of London 1983; Liveryman Worshipful Soc of Apothecaries 1988 (Yeoman 1983–88); CBiol 1983, FIMLS 1983; KStJ 1991; *Books* The Isolation of Salmonellae (1978), Tardive Dyskinesia (1982); numerous contributions to science books and jls; *Recreations* fund raising, gardening; *Style*— Dr Anthony Blowers, CBE, JP, DL; ✉ Westward, 12 Birch Close, Boundstone, Farnham, Surrey GU10 4TJ (☎ 01252 792769); Magellan Medical Communications, 40–42 Osnaburgh St, London NW1 3ND (☎ 0171 546 1546, fax 0171 546 1515)

BLUCK, Duncan Robert Yorke; CBE (1990, OBE 1984); s of Thomas Edward Bluck, and Ida Bluck; *b* 19 March 1927; *Educ* Taunton Sch; *m* 1952, Stella Wardlaw Murdoch; 1 s, 3 da; *Career* served RNVR 1944–47; dir John Swire & Sons Ltd 1984– (joined 1948); chm: Hong Kong Aircraft Engineering Co Ltd 1970–84 (dir 1984–89 and 1994–), Cathay Pacific Airways 1980–84 (dir 1970–, md 1971–84), Swire Pacific Ltd 1980–84 (dir 1970–), John Swire & Sons (HK) Ltd 1980–84 (dir 1970–), Br Tourist Authy 1984–90, English Tourist Bd 1984–90, Kent Econ Devpt Bd 1985–90; JP Hong Kong 1976–84; chm English Schs Fndn (Hong Kong) 1976–84; memb Ct Univ of Kent 1990–; *Recreations* sailing, swimming; *Clubs* Brooks's; *Style*— Duncan Bluck, Esq, CBE; ✉ Elfords, Hawkhurst, Kent TN18 4RP (☎ 01580 752153); John Swire & Sons Ltd, Swire House, 59 Buckingham Gate, London SW1E 6AJ (☎ 0171 834 7717)

BLUE, Rabbi Lionel; OBE (1994); s of Harry Blue (d 1965), and Hetty Blue; *b* 6 Feb 1930; *Educ* Westminster City Sch, Hendon Co Sch, Balliol Coll Oxford (MA), UCL (BA), Leo Baeck Coll (Rabbinical Dip); *Career* minister Settlement Synagogue 1957, rabbi Middx New Synagogue 1959, religious dir for Euro Bd World Union for Progressive Judaism 1963–66, lectr Leo Baeck Coll 1963–, convener Ecclesiastical Ct Reformed Synagogues of GB 1969–89; broadcaster: Prayer for the Day, Thought for the Day, Pause for Thought, In Search of Holy England; writer, columnist The Tablet, co-ed Forms of Prayer 1969–, retreat leader; memb Rabbinical Assembly Reformed Synagogues of GB, vice chm Standing Conf of Jews, Christians and Moslems in Europe; *Books* To Heaven with Scribes and Pharisees (1975), Forms of Prayer Vols 1 and 2 (1977), A Backdoor to Heaven (1978), Kitchen Blues (1985), Bright Blue (1985), Blue Heaven (1987), Guide to Here and Hereafter (jtly, 1988), Blue Horizons (1989), Bedside Manna (1991), How to get up when life gets you down (jtly, 1992), The Little Blue Book of Prayer (jtly, 1993), Tales of Body and Soul (1994), Kindred Spirits (jtly, 1995); *Recreations* monasteries, charity shops, painting, travelling; *Style*— Rabbi Lionel Blue, OBE; ✉ Leo Baeck College, 80 East End Road, London N3 2SY (☎ 0181 349 4525)

BLUETT, David Frederick; s of Frederick Dawson Bluett (d 1977), of Beckenham, Kent, and Muriel Emma, *née* Fells (d 1982); *b* 5 Dec 1937; *Educ* Cranleigh; *m* (m dis), Gillian Lalage, da of Richard Travis Harris; 2 s (James Edward Nutcombe b 3 Oct 1974, Charles Piers b 28 June 1978); *Career* CCF Artillery Section Cranleigh Sch 1951–55, HAC 1955–56, Nat Serv RA 1956–58, cmmnd 1957, Kent Yeo 1958–63; Royal Insurance Co 1955–56; Bluett Smith & Company Ltd: joined 1959, md 1968, chm 1972–; chm: Sunset Cleaning Group 1975–89, subsids of TKM plc 1980–83, Saunders Abbott 1987; formerly: capt, sec, chm and vice pres and pres Old Cranleighan RFC, chm Old Cranleighan Soc, capt Old Cranleighans Golf Soc; involved with St Christopher's Hospice; Liveryman: Worshipful Co of Skinners 1968 (Freeman 1961), Worshipful Co of Carmen 1979 (memb Court); *Recreations* golf, previously tennis, squash and rugby; *Clubs* City Livery, E India, RAC, HAC, Royal Cinque Ports, Old Cranleighan Rugby (pres 1994–), Harlequin RFC, Offrs Dining (Kent), County of London Yeo; *Style*— David Bluett, Esq; ✉ Fairfield, Furze Hill, Kingwood, Tadworth, Surrey KT20 6HB (☎ 017373 51867); Bluett Group, Bluett House, 189–195 High St, Beckenham, Kent BR3 1BA (☎ 0181 658 2222 or 0181 658 0915, fax 0181 650 1017, car 0831 343852, telex 946254)

BLUGLASS, Prof Robert Saul; CBE (1995); s of Henry Bluglass (d 1973), and Fay, *née* Griew (d 1987); *b* 22 Sept 1930; *Educ* Warwick Sch, Univ of St Andrews (MB ChB, DPM, MD); *m* 24 Aug 1961, Dr Jean Margaret Kerry, *née* Montgomery; 1 s (Charles Edward b 1963), 1 da (Amanda Clare b 1967); *Career* Nat Serv RAF 1948–49; house offr appts 1957–58, registrar in psychiatry Dundee 1958–61, sr registrar in psychiatry Royal Dundee Liff Hosp 1961–67, conslt in forensic psychiatry W Mids RHA and Home Office 1967–95, prof of forensic psychiatry Univ of Birmingham 1979–, regnl advsr in psychiatry (formerly dep regnl advsr) 1986–92, chm Postgraduate Trg Ctee in Psychiatry W Mids 1991–94, clinical dir Reaside Clinic 1986–95, civil conslt advsr to RAF 1992–, med dir South Birmingham Mental Health NHS Trust 1995–96; external examiner: Univ of London, Queen's Univ of Belfast; memb: Mental Health Review Tbnl 1979–, Mental Health Act Cmmn 1983–85, Steering Ctee on Servs for Mentally Abnormal Offenders DOH 1990–93; chm (former sec) Midlands Soc of Criminology 1983–95; specialist advsr: House of Commons Social Servs Ctee 1984–85, Mental Health Servs and Correction Health Servs NSW Aust 1996; memb Bd of Inquiry on death of Christopher Edwards 1996–; RCPsych: vice pres 1984–85, former chm Forensic Psychiatry Special Section, chm Midlands Div 1986–91, Cncl memb; MRCPsych 1971, FRCPsych 1976, FRSM, MRCP 1994; memb: Br Acad of Forensic Sci, BMA, Soc of Authors; *Books* A Guide to the Mental Health Act 1983 (1983), Psychiatry, Human Rights and the Law (with Sir Martin Roth, 1985), Principles and Practice of Forensic Psychiatry (with Dr Paul Bowden, 1990, awarded highly commended category, Glaxo prize 1990); *Recreations* watercolour painting, swimming, listening to music; *Clubs* RSM; *Style*— Prof Robert Bluglass, CBE; ✉ Reaside Clinic, Bristol Road South, Birmingham B45 9BE (☎ 0121 453 6161, fax 0121 453 7181)

BLUMBERG, Prof Baruch Samuel; s of Meyer Blumberg; *b* 28 July 1925; *Educ* Union Coll Schenectady NY (BS), Columbia Univ NYC Graduate Sch, Coll of Physicians and Surgeons Columbia Univ NYC (MD), Balliol Coll Oxford (DPhil); *m* 4 April 1954, Jean Liebesman; 2 s (George b 4 Aug 1958, Noah b 30 March 1965), 2 da (Anne b 18 April 1957, Jane b 9 Sept 1960); *Career* Mil Serv: Nat Serv USN 1943–46, Ensign (Deck) 1946, CO USS (L) 36 1946, Lt USNR 1946–55, Col med dir US Public Health Serv 1955–64, US Public Health Serv Reserve 1964–; intern and asst res First Columbia Med Div Bellevue Hosp NY 1951–53, research fell Dept of Med Coll of Physicians and Surgns 1953–55; Univ of Oxford: Dept of Biochemistry 1955–57, visiting fell Trinity Coll 1972–73, George Eastman visiting prof Balliol Coll 1983–84, master Balliol Coll 1989–94; chief Geographic Med and Genetics Section Nat Inst of Health Bethesda Maryland USA 1957–64, assoc prof in clinical med Georgetown Univ Sch of Med Washington DC 1962–64; Fox Chase Cancer Center Philadelphia USA: assoc dir for clinical res Inst for Cancer Res 1964–86, vice pres for population oncology 1986–89, sr advsr to the Pres 1989–, Fox Chase distinguished scientist 1989–; Univ of Pennsylvania: attending physician 1965–82, prof of human genetics 1970–75, univ prof of med and anthropology 1977–; conslt physician Pennsylvania Hosp Philadelphia 1965–, sr attending physician Philadelphia Gen Hosp 1975–76; Raman visiting prof Indian Acad of Sci Bangalore 1986, Ashland visiting prof Univ of Kentucky Lexington Kentucky USA 1986–87, clinical prof Dept of Epidemiology Sch of Public Health Univ of Washington Seattle USA 1983–88, Lee Kuan Yew distinguished visitor Nat Univ of Singapore 1992, William Evans prestige visitor Univ of Otago NZ 1994; conslt: The Franklin Inst Philadelphia 1980–, Office of Surgn Gen Office of Asst Sec for Health Rockville Maryland USA 1989–; research collaborator Brookhaven Nat Labs Upton LI NY 1960; memb: Scientific Advsy Bd Leonard Wood Meml and the Inst for Tropical Health 1977, Scientific Advsy Bd American Ctee for the Weizmann Inst 1979–, Advsy Bd Vittal Mallya Scientific Research Fndn Bangalore 1986–, Scientific Advsy Bd Stazione Zoologica Naples 1987 and 1990, Scientific Advsy Bd Fogarty Int Center Nat Insts of Health Bethesda Maryland 1989–93, Bd of Dirs Inst for Scientific Info Philadelphia 1989–92, Bd of Dirs Zoological Soc of Philadelphia (memb emeritus) 1989–, Tech Scientific Ctee Italian Inst Fernando de Ritis for the Prevention of Hepatic Diseases (WHO Collaborating Centre) Naples 1991–, External Advsy Ctee Univ of Illinois at Chicago Specialised Cancer Center Chicago 1991–, Advsy Bd Evy Lessin Fund for Ovarian Cancer Research Philadelphia 1991–, Sci Bd Santa Fe Inst New Mexico 1995–, Bd of Govrs Gtr Philadelphia Philosophy Consortium; memb Advsy Bd Perspectives in Biology and Med 1979–; memb Editorial Bd: Jl of Viral Hepatitis 1993–, American Jl of Human Biology 1995–; numerous awards incl: Grand Scientific Award Phi Lambda Kappa Med Fraternity 1971, Nobel Prize in Physiology or Med 1976, John P McGovern Award American Med Writers' Assoc 1988, James Blundell Award Br Blood Transfusion Soc 1989, Showa Emperor Award Japan Red Cross Soc 1994; numerous hon degrees incl: Hon DSc Univ of Pittsburgh 1977, Hon DLitt Jewish Theol Seminary of America NY 1977, Hon DUniv Paris 1978, Hon DSc Univ of Pennsylvania 1990, Hon DSc Columbia Univ NY 1990, Hon DSc McMaster Univ Ontario 1993; hon fell: Balliol Coll Oxford 1976, American Gastroenterological Assoc 1979, American Coll of Gastroenterology 1979, Royal Coll of Physicians 1984, Royal Soc of Med 1984, Indian Acad of Sci Bangalore 1987, Korean Med Assoc Seoul 1988, Royal Coll of Pathologists 1993; memb: Nat Acad of Scis USA (and its Inst of Med), American Philosophical Soc, American Acad of Arts and Scis, Assoc of American Physicians, American Soc for Clinical Investigation, American Soc of Human Genetics, American Assoc of Physical Anthropologists, The John Morgan Soc Univ of Pennsylvania, Interurban Clinical Club, Alpha Omega Alpha Coll of Physicians and Surgns Columbia Univ, Molecular Med Soc; fell American Coll of Physicians, fell Coll of Physicians of Pennsylvania; *Publications* Proceedings of the Conference on Genetic Polymorphisms and Geographic Variations in Disease, February 23–25 1960 (ed, 1961), New Developments in Medicine (ed with HM Rawnsley, 1970), Australia Antigen and Hepatitis (jtly, 1972), Hepatitis B - The Virus, The Disease and the Vaccine (ed jtly, 1984); *Recreations* rock climbing, canoeing, bicycle touring, cattle raising, trekking; *Clubs* Athenaeum, Explorers' (NYC); *Style*— Prof Baruch S Blumberg; ✉ Fox Chase Cancer Centre, 7701 Burholme Avenue, Philadelphia, PA 19111, USA (☎ 00 1 215 728 3164, fax 00 1 215 728 5310)

BLUMENTHAL, Dr Ivan; *b* 16 Jan 1947; *Educ* Queen's Coll Queenstown South Africa, Univ of Cape Town (MB ChB); *m* 16 Dec 1973, Janet Helen; 2 s (Morris b 4 Oct 1974, Toby b 3 Sept 1976); *Career* med trg in paediatrics: S Africa, UK, USA; currently conslt paediatrician Royal Oldham Hosp; contrib med jls; MRCP 1975, DCH 1974; *Books* Your Child's Health (1987), Child Abuse - A Handbook for Health Care Practitioners (1994);

Recreations bridge; *Style—* Dr Ivan Blumenthal; ✉ 38 Norford Way, Bamford, Rochdale OL11 5QS (☎ 01706 358954); The Royal Oldham Hospital, Rochdale Rd, Oldham OL1 2JH (☎ 0161 6278308, fax 0161 6278309)

BLUMSOM, John David; TD (1964); s of Thomas George Blumsom, of Chalfont St Giles, Bucks, and Joan, *née* Dixon; *b* 7 Dec 1932; *Educ* Merchant Taylors, London Business Sch; *m* 23 Feb 1957, Gillian Mary, da of Russell Paul, of Berkhamsted; 3 s (Giles, David, William), 2 da (Alexandra, Elizabeth); *Career* Nat Serv cmmnd Queen's Royal Regt 1951–53; TA: Queen's Royal Regt 1953–59, Beds and Herts Regt 1960–69, ret as Maj; articled clerk Moore Stephens & Co CAs 1953–59, commercial mangr Electrolux Ltd 1967–69, gen mangr Electrolux Commercial Equipment Ltd 1969–71 (joined 1959), dir Hambros Bank Ltd 1986–92 (joined 1971), non-exec dir Hemmington Scott Publishing Ltd 1986–; chm Herts Ctee Army Benevolent Fund 1986–, fundraiser Fairbridge 1993–; FCA; *Recreations* golf, squash, walking; *Style—* John Blumsom, Esq, TD; ✉ 25 Shrublands Rd, Berkhamsted, Herts HP4 3HX (☎ and fax 01442 384058)

BLUNDELL, Prof Derek John; s of Frank Herbert Blundell (d 1978), and Irene Mary, *née* Davie (d 1963); *b* 30 June 1933; *Educ* East Grinstead GS, Univ of Birmingham (BSc), Imperial Coll London (PhD, DIC); *m* 15 Sept 1960, Mary Patricia, da of Archibald James Leonard (d 1968); *Career* lectr in geology Univ of Birmingham 1959–70, reader in geophysics Univ of Lancaster 1971–75 (sr lectr 1970–71), prof of environmental geology Univ of London 1975–; head Dept of Geology: Chelsea Coll 1975–85, Royal Holloway Coll 1992– (dean of Research and Enterprise 1995–); pres Geological Soc 1988–90; memb Academia Europaea; Coke Medal Geological Soc 1994; FGS 1956, CGeol 1990; *Publications* A Continent Revealed - The European Geotraverse (Cambridge Univ Press, 1992), Salt Tectonics (Geological Soc Special Pubn 100, 1996), Tectonic Evolution of Southeast Asia (Geological Soc Special Pubn 196, 1996); contrib to various jls on seismic exploration, earthquake hazards and mountain building; *Recreations* skiing, cycling, golf; *Clubs* Athenaeum; *Style—* Prof Derek Blundell; ✉ Geology Department, Royal Holloway, University of London, Egham, Surrey TW20 0EX (☎ 01784 443811, fax 01784 471780, e-mail d.blundell@gl.rhbnc.ac.uk)

BLUNDELL, John Durham; s of late John Charles Blundell, and Mary Elizabeth, *née* Verrill; *b* 26 July 1938; *Educ* Wigan GS, Bolton Co GS, Univ of Liverpool (BSc); *m* 1963, Barbara Edna, *née* Hodson; *Career* museum asst Bolton Museum & Art Gallery 1960–62, science teacher Fleetwood GS 1962–65, asst to dep curator Blackburn Museum & Art Gallery 1966–71, curator Towneley Hall Art Gallery & Museum Burnley 1971–72, co museum offr Lancs Co Cncl 1974– (museum offr 1972–74); museum advsr Assoc of Co Cncls 1986–, memb Cncl Br Assoc of Friends of Museums 1990–, past pres NW Fedn of Museums & Art Galleries, chm Soc of Co Museum Directors 1979–82; FGS 1961, FMA 1980 (AMA 1968); *Recreations* walking, camping, amateur dramatics; *Clubs* Rotary; *Style—* John D Blundell, Esq; ✉ Lancashire County Museum Service, Stanley Street, Preston, Lancs PR1 4YP (☎ 01772 264061, fax 01772 264079)

BLUNDELL, Mark; s of Danny Blundell, of Royston, Herts, and Christine, *née* Rayner; *b* 8 April 1966; *Educ* Bassingbourn Village Coll nr Royston; *m* 1995, Deborah Tracy, *née* Jones; 2 s (Mark Junior b 27 Feb 1987, Callum Daniel b 25 Nov 1993); *Career* motor racing driver; began racing 1984, turned professional 1989; categories: Formula Ford 1600 1984–85, Formula Ford 2000 1985–86, Formula 3000 1987–89, Formula 3 1988, World Sports Prototype Championship 1989 and 1990; Formula 1: official test driver Williams-Judd/Williams-Renault 1989, official reserve and test driver Williams-Renault 1990, 14 grand prix starts Brabham Yamaha 1991 test driver Honda Marlboro McLaren 1992, official driver Ligier 1993 driver Tyrrell Yamaha 1994, driver McLaren-Mercedes 1995; joined Indy Car circuit with PacWest team 1995, driver PacWest Racing 1997; winner Le Mans 24–hr race for Peugeot 1992; 1995 Grand Prix Season: sixth Brazil 1995, fifth Monaco, Silverstone and Spa; winner Golden Helmet and Grovewood Award 1984; former: car dealer, roofer, labourer; *Recreations* music, keep fit, golf, squash; *Style—* Mark Blundell, Esq; ✉ The Malt House, 27 Kneesworth Street, Royston, Herts SG8 5AB (☎ and fax 01763 246598)

BLUNDELL, Prof Richard William; *b* 1 May 1952; *Educ* Univ of Bristol (BSc), LSE (MSc); *Career* lectr in econometrics Univ of Manchester 1975–84, prof of economics UCL 1984–; dir of res Inst for Fiscal Studies 1986–; dir: Society for Economic Analysis Ltd 1988–93, ESRC Centre for Micro-Economic Analysis of Fiscal Policy 1991–; visiting assoc prof Univ of British Columbia 1980; visiting prof: Massachusetts Inst of Technol 1993, Univ of Calif Berkeley 1994; memb Cncl Royal Economic Soc 1990–; memb Advsy Bd: Dept of Applied Economics Univ of Cambridge, Br Household Panel Study Univ of Essex; memb Ed Bd: The Manchester School 1983–, Jl of Applied Econometrics 1985–89, Fiscal Studies 1986–, Ricerche Economiche 1993–, Int Jl of Taxation 1993–; ed Jl of Econometrics 1991–, assoc ed Econometric Reviews 1991–; Jrjö Jahnsson Prize 1995; fell Econometric Soc 1991; *Books* Unemployment, Search and Labour Supply (with I Walker, 1986), The Measurement of Household Welfare (with I Preston and I Walker, 1994); author of numerous articles in books and jls; *Style—* Prof Richard Blundell; ✉ Department of Economics, University College London, Gower Street, London WC1E 6BT (☎ 0171 380 7863, fax 0171 916 2773, e-mail r.blundell@ucl.ac.uk)

BLUNDELL, Prof Sir Thomas Leon (Tom); kt (1997); s of Horace Leon Blundell, of Sussex, and Marjorie, *née* Davis; *b* 7 July 1942; *Educ* Steyning GS, Brasenose Coll Oxford (BA, DPhil); *m* 1, 1964 (m dis 1973), Lesley; 1 s (Ricky b 19 Nov 1969); m 2 (m dis); m 3, 22 May 1987, Lynn Bancinyane, da of Phineas Sibanda, of Zimbabwe; 2 da (Sichelesile 5 Jan 1988, Samkeliso b 25 June 1989); *Career* postdoctoral res fell Molecular Biophysics Laboratory Univ of Oxford 1967–72 (jr res fell Linacre Coll 1968–70), lectr in biological sci Univ of Sussex 1973–76, prof of crystallography Birkbeck Coll London 1976–90 (govr 1985–89), dir gen Agric and Food Res Cncl 1991–94, chief exec Biotechnology and Biological Sciences Research Cncl 1994–96, Sir William Dunn prof of biochemistry Univ of Cambridge 1996–; professorial fell Sydney Sussex Coll Cambridge 1995–; chm Biofabrica 1989–91; industl conslt: CellTech 1981–86, Pfizer Central Research 1984–90, Abingworth Management Ltd 1988–90; hon dir Imperial Cancer Research Fund Structural Molecular Biology Unit 1989–96, dir Int Sch of Crystallography Erice Italy 1982–, chm Biological Sci Ctee SERC 1983–87 (memb Cncl 1989–); memb: Cncl AFRC 1985–90, Advsy Cncl on Science and Technol 1988–90, Advsy Bd Res Cncls 1991–94, Euro Sci and Technol Assembly (ESTA) 1995–; memb Editorial Advsy Bd: Biochemistry 1986–89, Protein Engineering 1986–, Protein Science 1992–; jt ed Progress in Biophysics and Molecular Biology 1979–; cncllr Oxford CBC 1970–73 (chm Planning Ctee 1972–73); Hon DSc: Univ of Edinburgh 1993, UEA 1993, Univ of Sheffield 1994, Univ of Strathclyde 1994, Univ of Warwick 1995, Univ of Antwerp 1995, Univ of Nottingham 1996; Alcon Award 1985, Gold Medal Inst of Biotechnological Studies 1987, Sir Hans Krebs Medal Fedn of Euro Biochemical Socs 1987, Ciba Medal UK Biochemical Soc 1988, Feldberg Prize in biology and medicine 1988, Gold Medal Soc for Chem Indust 1995; hon fell: Birkbeck Coll London 1989, Brasenose Coll Oxford, Linacre Coll Oxford 1991, Royal Agric Soc of England 1993; fell Indian Nat Acad 1994; memb: EMBO 1984, Academia Europea 1993; FRS 1984; *Books* Protein Crystallography (1976); *Recreations* playing jazz, listening to opera, walking; *Style—* Prof Sir Tom Blundell, FRS; ✉ Department of Biochemistry, University of Cambridge, Tennis Court Road, Cambridge CB2 1QW (☎ 01223 333628, fax 01223 333629, e-mail tom@ cryst.bioc.cam.ac.uk)

BLUNDELL-HOLLINSHEAD-BLUNDELL, Brig Dermot Hugh; s of Maj Christian Victor Richard Blundell-Hollinshead-Blundell (d 1971), of London SW7, and Helen Kate, *née* Guthrie (d 1989); *b* 18 Oct 1935; *Educ* Eton, Sandhurst, Staff Coll Camberley; *m* 1, 16 Feb 1966 (m dis 1973), Princess Stephanie, da of Prince Franz Joseph Windischgraetz (d 1983); 2 s (Henry Victor William b 3 Nov 1967, Alexander Otto b 7 Aug 1969); m 2, 11 March 1976, Sally Anne Veronique, da of Victor Charles Hamish Creer, of Liphook, Hampshire; 1 s (Victor Richard Dermot b 1 Dec 1978), 2 step s (Charles Donald Greville Leigh b 2 Nov 1969, Thomas William Elliott Leigh b 28 Nov 1971); *Career* cmmnd Grenadier Guards 1955, ADC to Govr Gen NZ 1960–62, cmd 2 Battalion Grenadier Guards 1976–78 (despatches 1978), COS London Dist 1984–86, cmd 56 London Brigade 1986–88, sec to COS SHAPE 1988; *Recreations* military history, country pursuits; *Clubs* Pratt's, Army and Navy; *Style—* Brig Dermot Blundell-Hollinshead-Blundell; ✉ Laughern Hill, Wichenford, Worcester WR6 6YB

BLUNDEN, George Patrick; s of Sir George Blunden, of Hindringham, Norfolk, and Anne, *née* Bulford; *b* 21 Feb 1952; *Educ* St Edward's Sch Oxford, Univ Coll Oxford (BA); *m* 8 July 1978, Jane Rosemary, da of Gp Capt Charles Eric Hunter (d 1986); 1 s (George Edward Paul b 4 Aug 1982), 2 da (Victoria Jane b 10 Sept 1980, Eleanor Louise b 18 Sept 1985); *Career* dir: Seccombe Marshall & Campion 1983–86, S G Warburg Securities 1986–92, S G Warburg Discount 1989–92; chief exec Union plc 1992–; dir Beazley Furlonge Ltd 1994–; memb: Family Welfare Assoc Almshouse Ctee, Sir Abraham Dawes Almshouses; chm and stee Southern Housing Group; Freeman City of London 1988; Liveryman Worshipful Co of Goldsmiths; *Clubs* Reform, MCC; *Style—* George Blunden, Esq; ✉ The Union plc, 39 Cornhill, London EC3V 3NU (☎ 0171 623 1020)

BLUNDEN, Hubert Chisholm; er s and h of Sir Philip Overington Blunden, 7 Bt, *qv*; *b* 9 Aug 1948; *Educ* Avoca Sch Blackrock; *m* 1975, Allish O'Brien; 1 s (Edmond b 31 July 1982), 1 da (Amelia b 1977); *Career* 1 Bn Irish Guards; *Style—* Hubert Blunden Esq

BLUNDEN, Sir Philip Overington; 7 Bt (I 1766), of Castle Blunden, Kilkenny; s of Sir John Blunden, 5 Bt (d 1923); suc bro Sir William Blunden, 6 Bt (d 1985); *b* 27 Jan 1922; *Educ* Repton; *m* 1945, Jeanette Francesca Alexandra (WRNS), da of Capt Duncan Macdonald, RNR, of Portree, Isle of Skye; 2 s (Hubert Chisholm b 1948, John Maurice Patrick b 1955), 1 da (Marguerite Eugenie b 1967); *Heir* s, Hubert Chisholm Blunden, *qv*; *Career* served RN 1942–45; estate mangr Castle Blunden 1948–62, mktg of industl plastics 1962–83, engaged in fine art restoration and painting 1976–; *Recreations* gardening, fishing, field sports, reading, painting; *Clubs* Royal Dublin Soc (life memb); *Style—* Sir Philip Blunden, Bt; ✉ 60 The Drive, Castletown, Celbridge, Co Kildare, Ireland

BLUNKETT, David; MP (Lab) Sheffield Brightside (majority 22,681); s of Arthur Blunkett (d 1960), and Doris Matilda Elizabeth, *née* Williams (d 1983); *b* 6 June 1947; *Educ* Univ of Sheffield (BA), Huddersfield Holly Bank Coll of Educn (PGCE); *m* (m dis 1990); 3 s (Alastair Todd b 27 March 1977, Hugh Sanders b 13 July 1980, Andrew Keir b 31 Oct 1982); *Career* clerk typist 1967–69, lectr and tutor in industl rels and politics Barnsley Coll of Technol 1973–81, on secondment 1981–87, dep chm AMA 1984–87; Sheffield City Cncl: memb 1970–88, chm Family and Community Servs Ctee 1976–80, ldr 1980–87; memb Lab Pty NEC 1983–, chm Lab Pty Ctee on Local Govt 1984–92, MP (Lab) Sheffield Brightside 1987–, oppn front bench spokesman on the environment 1988–92, memb Shadow Cabinet 1992–; chief oppn spokesman on: health 1992–94, educn 1994–95, educn and employment 1995–; chm Labour Party 1993–94; *Books* jtly: Local Enterprise and Workers' Plans (1981), Building from the Bottom: the Sheffield Experience (1983), Democracy in Crisis: the town halls respond (1987), On a Clear Day (1995); *Recreations* poetry, walking, music, sailing, being with friends; *Style—* David Blunkett, Esq, MP; ✉ Town Hall Chambers, 1 Barkers Pool, Sheffield S1 1EN; House of Commons, London SW1A 0AA (☎ 0171 219 4043)

BLUNOS, Martin Lauris; s of Leon Karl Blunos, of Thornbury, Bristol, and Venita, *née* Kalnins; *b* 11 April 1960; *Educ* Castle Sch Thornbury Bristol, Gloucestershire Coll of Arts and Technol Cheltenham (City & Guilds), Cambridge Catering Coll (City & Guilds); *m* 27 April 1989, Siân Eulyned, da of William Gilbert Williams; 2 s (Leon William Lauris b 12 Dec 1989, Max Elwyn Harijs b 2 Nov 1991); *Career* restaurateur; early catering experience working in Switzerland (Rorschach and Zurich) and on private yacht in Athens, subsequent experience working in hotels and restaurants in London, fndr proprietor Lettonie 1988–; *Awards* for Lettonie: 4*/5 Good Food Guide 1997, Restaurant of the Year 1997, 4 AA Rosettes, 2 Michelin stars, 1 Egon Ronay star; *Recreations* family; *Style—* Martin Blunos, Esq; ✉ Restaurant Lettonie, 9 Druid Hill, Stoke Bishop, Bristol BS9 1EW (home ☎ 0117 968 6943, restaurant ☎ 0117 968 6456)

BLUNT, David John; QC (1991); s of Vernon Egerton Rowland Blunt (d 1990), of Staunton on Wye, Herefordshire, and Catherine Vera, *née* Jones; *b* 25 Oct 1944; *Educ* Farnham GS, Trinity Hall Cambridge (MA), Inns of Court Sch of Law (Colombos Prize for Public Int Law); *m* 28 Feb 1976, Zaibonisa, da of Isaak Ebrahim (d 1962), of Capetown, SA; 1 s (Joseph Isaac b 1987), 1 da (Nadia Shaida b 1980); *Career* called to the Bar Middle Temple 1967, asst recorder 1985–90, recorder of the Crown Court 1990–; memb Lib Dem Pty; Parly candidate (Lib): Lambeth Central 1978 and 1979, Cornwall SE 1983; *Recreations* reading, writing, running, cycling, gardening, old cars; *Clubs* Thames Hare and Hounds; *Style—* David Blunt, Esq, QC; ✉ 4 Pump Court, Temple, London EC4Y 7AN (☎ 0171 353 2656)

BLUNT, Sir David Richard Reginald Harvey; 12 Bt (GB 1720), of London; s of Sir Richard David Harvey Blunt, 11 Bt (d 1975); *b* 8 Nov 1938; *m* 1969, Sonia Tudor Rosemary, da of late Albert Edward Day; 1 da (Davina Angela Rosemary b 1972); *Heir* kinsman, Robin Anthony Blunt b 2 Feb 1926; *Style—* Sir David Blunt, Bt; ✉ 74 Kirkstall Rd, SW2 4HF

BLUNT, Oliver Simon Peter; QC (1994); s of Maj-Gen Peter John Blunt, CB, MBE, GM, of Harefield House, Ramsbury, Wilts, and Adrienne, *née* Richardson; *b* 8 March 1951; *Educ* Bedford Sch, Univ of Southampton (LLB); *m* 29 Sept 1979, Joanna Margaret, da of Robert Dixon (d 1985); 3 da (Felicity b 1981, Emily b 1983, Susannah b 1991), 1 s (Sebastian b 1989); *Career* called to the Bar Middle Temple 1974, asst recorder 1991, recorder 1995; *Recreations* cricket, squash, golf; *Clubs* Roehampton, Barnes Sports; *Style—* Oliver Blunt, Esq, QC; ✉ 106 Priory Lane, Roehampton, London SW15 5JL (☎ 0181 876 3369); Furnival Chambers, 32 Furnival Street, London EC4A 1JQ (☎ 0171 405 3232)

BLUNT, Maj-Gen Peter; CB (1978), MBE (1955), GM (1959); s of Albert George Blunt (d 1952), and Claudia Wintle (d 1972); *b* 18 Aug 1923; *m* 5 March 1949, Adrienne, da of General T W Richardson; 3 s (Oliver, Robin, Crispin); *Career* joined army 1937, cmmnd Royal Fus, served DCLI and Royal Scots Fus 1946, Foreign Serv 1946–49, Staff Coll 1957, Jt Serv Staff Coll 1963, cmd 26 Regt Bridging 1965, GSO 1 Def Plans FARELF 1968, Cdr RCT 1 Corps 1970, RCDS 1972, dep tport offr-in-chief (Army), later tport offr-in-chief 1973, Asst CPL (Army) MOD 1977–78, ACDS (Personnel and Logistics) MOD 1978–79; md Earls Court Ltd 1979–80, exec vice chm Brompton and Kensington Special Catering Co Ltd 1979–80, jt md Angex-Watson 1980–83, chm and md Angex Ltd 1983–88 (non-exec chm 1988–89), dir Associated Newspaper Holdings plc 1984–89, chm and md Market Sensors 1986–88, non-exec chm Argus Shield Ltd 1988–89; Col cmd RCT 1974–89, specially appointed cmmr Royal Hosp Chelsea 1979–88; Liveryman Worshipful Co of Carmen 1973; exec memb Caravan Club 1989; *Recreations* sea fishing, caravanning; *Clubs* RCT Luncheon (pres); *Style—* Maj-Gen Peter Blunt, CB, MBE, GM; ✉ Harefield House, Crowood Lane, Ramsbury, Marlborough, Wiltshire SN8 2PT

BLYTH, 4 Baron (1907 UK); Sir Anthony Audley Rupert Blyth; 4 Bt (1895); s of 3 Baron Blyth (d 1977); *b* 3 June 1931; *Educ* St Columba's Coll Dublin; *m* 1, 1954 (m dis 1962), Elizabeth Dorothea, da of Robert T Sparrow, of Vancouver, BC, Canada; 1 s (Hon Riley Audley John b 4 March 1955, d June 1996), 2 da (Hon Marcia Edna Dorothea b 1956, Hon Alexandra b 1957); m 2, 1963, Oonagh Elizabeth Ann, yr da of late William Henry Conway, of Dundrum, Dublin; 1 s (Hon James Audley Ian b 1970), 1 da (Hon Lucinda Audley Jane b 1966); *Heir* s, Hon James Audley Ian Blyth b 1970; *Style*— The Rt Hon the Lord Blyth; ✉ Blythwood Estate, Athenry, Co Galway, Republic of Ireland

BLYTH, Charles (Chay); CBE (1972), BEM (1967); s of Robert Blyth (d 1971), and Jessie Pat, *née* Patterson (d 1965); *b* 14 May 1940; *Educ* Hawick HS; *m* 1, 1962 (m dis 1992), Maureen Margaret, da of Albert Morris (d 1956); 1 da (Samantha b 1967); m 2, 1995, Felicity Rayson; *Career* served 3 Bn Para Regt 1958–67, Sgt; Cadbury Schweppes 1968–69, dir Sailing Ventures (Hampshire) Ltd 1969–73; md: Rainbow Charters Ltd 1974–, South West Properties Ltd 1978–94, The Challenge Business Ltd 1989–; conslt Hill & Knowlton Ltd 1983–92; rowed N Atlantic with Capt John Ridgeway 1966, circumnavigated world westwards solo in yacht British Steel 1970–71, circumnavigated world eastwards with crew of paratroopers in yacht Great Britain II Whitbread Round the World Yacht Race 1973–74 (winner Elapsed Time prize), Atlantic sailing record Cape Verde to Antigua 1977, winner Round Britain Race in yacht Great Britain IV (crew Robert James) 1978, winner Observer/Europe 1 Doublehanded Transatlantic Race in record time (crew Robert James) 1981, captained yacht United Friendly (first British yacht home) Whitbread Round the World Race 1981/82, in yacht Brittany Ferries GB came 2nd overall and first in Class I Round Britain and Ireland Race 1982 and first in Class Plymouth Vilamoura Plymouth Race 1983, in trimaran Beefeater II (with Eric Blunn) capsized off Cape Horn during NY-San Francisco record attempt and spent 19 hours in water before rescue 1984, co-skiiper Virgin Atlantic Challenger I 1985, co-skipper Virgin Atlantic Challenge II on the successful Blue Riband 1986; chm: Silk Cut Awards Ctee 1983–92, British Steel Challenge Round the World Yacht Race 1992–93, BT Global Challenge Round the World Yacht Race 1996/97; Man of the Year 1966; Yachting Journalists' Assoc: Yachtsman of the Year 1971, Special Award for Outstanding Servs to Yachting 1994; Chichester Trophy RYS 1971; Hon DTech Univ of Plymouth 1994; *Books* A Fighting Chance (1966), Innocent Aboard (1968), The Impossible Voyage (1971), Theirs is the Glory (1974), Challenge (1993); *Recreations* horse riding, skiing; *Clubs* Royal Southern Yacht, Royal Western Yacht, Royal Ocean Racing, Special Forces; *Style*— Chay Blyth, Esq, CBE, BEM; ✉ Trepen House, Menheniot, Liskeard, Cornwall PL14 3PN (☎ 01579 348387, fax 01579 347255)

BLYTH, Kenneth William; OBE (1993); s of Rev Canon Arthur Cecil Blyth (d 1961), of Cambridge, and Lorna Marjorie Iveson, *née* Campbell (d 1991); *b* 6 Sept 1933; *Educ* Marlborough, St John's Coll Cambridge (MA, PhD); *m* 18 July 1964, Ena, da of Roy Franey (d 1959), of London; 2 s (Thomas b 1966, Stephen b 1967); *Career* DSIR res studentship 1958–61, scientific staff Nat Inst of Industl Psychology 1961–62, asst dir Nuffield Fndn 1964–72 (joined 1962); sec IBA 1988–90 (joined 1972, chief asst to dir gen 1979–88), ITC 1990–93; *Style*— Kenneth Blyth, Esq, OBE; ✉ 27 Laurier Road, London NW5 1SH

BLYTH, (William) Michael; s of William Paterson Blyth (d 1993), and Bertha Margaret, *née* Roxburgh; *b* 12 May 1950; *Educ* Sedbergh, Univ of St Andrews (BSc); *m* 1972, Carolyn Winifred, da of Samuel Alexander Haig Haddow; 2 s (Christopher Michael b 1974, Mark Alexander b 1978); *Career* Thomson McLintock & Co (now KPMG): apprentice 1972–76, audit mangr 1977–79; S Easton Simmers & Co: audit mangr 1979–81, ptnr 1981–86; Kidsons Impey: ptnr 1986–, nat dir Staff Resources 1990–93, office managing ptnr (Glasgow) 1991–96, regnl managing ptnr (Scotland) 1994–; memb Incorporation of Bakers (Glasgow) 1963; MICAS 1976; *Recreations* skiing, tennis, gardening, hobby farming; *Style*— Michael Blyth, Esq; ✉ Low Borland, Dunlop, Ayrshire KA3 4BU (☎ 01560 484846); Kidsons Impey, Breckenridge House, 274 Sauchiehall Street, Glasgow G2 3EH (☎ 0141 307 5000, fax 0141 307 5005)

BLYTHE, Dr John Hosking; s of Harry Stanley Blythe (d 1956), and Emily Letitia Alice, *née* Hibbard (d 1982); *b* 21 April 1932; *Educ* Romford Royal Liberty Sch, Christ's Coll Cambridge (MA, PhD, Soccer blue); *m* 1 Sept 1958, Margaret Grace, da of Ralph Wilfred Webb; 1 da (Sarah Louise b 27 Feb 1960), 1 s (James Stanley b 10 Aug 1964); *Career* GEC-Marconi Res Centre: joined 1956, gp chief Propagation Gp 1968–78, mangr Communications Lab 1978–86, chief engr (communications) 1986–88, mangr Communications and Computing Lab 1988–95, chief engr (communications) 1995–; chm AGARD EPP (electromagnetic wave propagation panel of NATO's advsy gp for aerospace R & D) 1983–85, memb Cncl IEE 1984–87; FIEE 1974, FEng 1986; *Recreations* squash, gardening, family history; *Style*— Dr John Blythe, FEng; ✉ Communications and Computing Laboratory, GEC Marconi Research Centre, Great Baddow, Essex CM2 8HN (☎ 01245 242193, fax 01245 242124)

BLYTHE, Ronald George; s of Albert George Blythe (d 1957), of Sudbury, Suffolk, and Matilda Elizabeth Elkins (d 1976); *b* 6 Nov 1922; *Educ* St Peter's and St Gregory's Sch Sudbury Suffolk; *Career* writer; reference librarian until 1954, full-time writer 1955–; memb Centre of E Anglian Studies UEA 1972–76, chm Essex Festival 1981–83, pres The John Clare Soc 1981–; Hon MA Univ of E Anglia 1990; memb Soc of Authors, memb Eastern Arts Lit Panel, memb Mgmnt Ctee Soc of Authors 1970–79; FRSL 1969; *Awards* Heinemann Award 1969, Angel Prize 1985; *Films* A Painter in the Country (BBC2) 1968, Constable Observed 1969, Akenfield 1974; *Books* incl: A Treasonable Growth (1960), Immediate Possession: Short Stories (1961), The Age of Illusion (history, 1963), Components of the Scene: Poems, Essays and Stories of the Second World War (1965), Akenfield (1969), Aldeburgh Anthology (1972), The View in Winter (1979), From the Headlands (1982), The Stories of Ronald Blythe (1985), Divine Landscapes (1986), The Pleasure of Diaries (1989), Private Words: Letters and Diaries of the Second World War (1991), Word from Wormingford (1997), First Friends: Paul and Bunty, John and Christine and Carrington (1997), The Papers of the Late Lieutenant (novel, 1997); author of essays, stories, poems, reviews in newspapers and magazines and critical studies of: Jane Austen, Leo Tolstoy, Henry James, J C Powys, William Hazlitt, Thomas Hardy; *Recreations* gardening, walking, looking at architecture, plants and landscape; *Style*— Ronald Blythe; ✉ Bottengoms Farm, Wormingford, Colchester, Essex (☎ 01206 271308); Deborah Rogers Literary Agency, 20 Powis Mews, London W11 1JN (☎ 0171 221 3717, fax 0171 229 9084)

BLYTON, Carey; s of Hanly Harrison Blyton, and Florence Maud, *née* Pullen; *b* 1932; *Educ* Beckenham GS Kent, UCL, Trinity Coll of Music London (BMus), Royal Danish Acad of Music Copenhagen; *m* Mary Josephine Mills; 2 s (Matthew James, Daniel Carey); *Career* music ed: Mills Music Ltd 1958–63, Faber Music Ltd 1963–74, Universal Edition 1975–; music lectr 1963–; prof of harmony, counterpoint and orchestration Trinity Coll of Music 1963–73, visiting prof of composition for film, TV and radio GSM London 1972–83, composer, short story writer and nonsense poet; piano music incl: Six Epigrams (1951), Three Impressions (1963–64); madrigals and partsongs incl: What Then is Love? (1956), The Silly Flea (1962), In Lighter Mood (1972), A Nursery Song Suite (1985); song cycles incl: The Poetry of Dress (1956), Prayers from the Ark (1964–65); voice and chamber ensemble: Moresques (1952), The Maiden Deceived (1982); music for schs: Mixed Bag (1962–63), Sweeney Todd the Barber (1977), Dracula! (1983), Frankenstein! (1987); chamber music: Scherzo (1949), For the Delight of Shiva (1986); music for saxophone quartet incl: In Memoriam Scott Fitzgerald (1971), Suite Carolina (1984); music for brass: Eilgut-Galopp (1980), Sweet and Sour Rag (1983), Pasticheries (1987); music for orchestra: Cinque Port (1957–58), Overture: The Hobbit (1967), The Birds of the Air (1971), The Golden Road to Samarkand (1991); memb: The Composers' Guild of GB, The Performing Right Soc Ltd, Mechanical-Copyright Protection Soc Ltd; *Books* The Faber Book of Nursery Songs (1968), Bananas in Pyjamas (1972), Noah & the Unicorns (1979); *Clubs* The Aborigine; *Style*— Carey Blyton, Esq; ✉ Hawthornden, 55 Goldsel Rd, Swanley, Kent BR8 8HA (☎ 01322 664380)

BNINSKI, Dr Kazimierz Andrzej; s of Count Charles Felix Bninski-Mizgalski (d 1983), Lt Cdr Polish Navy (and POW), of Sopot, Poland, and Countess Sophie, *née* de Saryusz-Woyciechowska (descends from ancient Polish Jelita clan, and descendant of Floryan Saryusz who fought against the Teutonic Knights in the Battle of Plowce in 1331); paternal gggf Count Pawel Bninski (b 1773, s of Count Lucas Victor Bninski) was a distinguished cavalry officer who fought against the Russian army of Catherine II in 1792; *b* 28 Feb 1939; *Educ* Univ of Gdańsk Poland (MD); *m* 2 July 1988, Teresa Maria, da of Baron Adam Andrzej Maria de Gallen-Bisping, and a cous of King Juan Carlos of Spain; 2 s (Paul Charles b 11 Oct 1989, Adam Charles b 9 June 1994), 1 da (Maria Elizabeth Sophie b 17 Oct 1992); *Career* sr house offr: Nelson Hosp London 1967–68, St Mary Abbots Hosp London 1969–71; registrar in med St Mary's Hosp and St Charles' Hosp London 1972–76, physician 7 US Army Germany 1977–80, jr ptnr gen practice 1981–87; dir i/c Polish Clinic Harley St London 1988–; *Style*— Dr Kazimierz Bninski; ✉ The Polish Clinic, 131 Harley Street, London W1 (☎ 0171 580 4693)

BOADEN, Prof Noel Thomas; s of William Alfred Boaden (d 1960), of York, and Mabel Gladys, *née* Winspear (d 1981); *b* 19 Dec 1934; *Educ* LSE (BSc), Univ of Essex (MA), Univ of Liverpool (PhD); *m* 1, 31 Dec 1955 (m dis 1984), June Margaret, da of Percy Till, of York; 1 da (Jane b 22 May 1959); m 2, 14 Dec 1985, Margaret Elizabeth Hierons; *Career* Nat Serv RAPC 1956–58; lectr: Ipswich Civic Coll 1959–63, Chesterfield Tech Coll 1963–65; Univ of Liverpool: res fell 1967–71, lectr 1971–75, sr lectr 1975–85, prof of continuing educn 1985–91, emeritus prof 1991; visiting prof Univ of Leeds 1991–95; educn advsr to Regnl Advsr in Gen Practice Mersey Region 1992–; FRSA 1988; *Books* Urban Policy Making (1971), Public Participation in Planning (1980), Participation in Local Services (1981); *Style*— Prof Noel Boaden; ✉ 12 Bell Meadow Court, Tarporley, Cheshire CW6 0DT (☎ 01829 733098)

BOAITEY, Charlotte; da of Kwaku Yentumi Boaitey (d 1944), and Lydia, *née* Sarpong (d 1989); *b* 21 March 1944; *Educ* Aburi Girls' Sch Ghana, Univ of London (LLB), Lady Margaret Hall Oxford (MPhil Social Anthropology); *m* 19 Oct 1972, Alfred Kwasi Kwarteng, s of Kodua Kwarteng; 1 s (Kwasi Addob b 26 May 1975); *Career* barrister; fndr memb Legal Dept of Community Relations Cmmn (now Cmmn for Racial Equality) 1972–75, called to the Bar Middle Temple 1976, currently head of Chambers 12 Old Square; conslt anthropologist Granada TV series Disappearing World 1982; chm Queensbury Methodist Home and Overseas Mission; tstee of various charities; *Recreations* swimming, gardening, house keeping and visiting friends; *Style*— Mrs Charlotte Boaitey; ✉ 12 Old Square, 1st Floor, Lincoln's Inn, London WC2A 3TX (☎ 0171 404 0875)

BOAL, His Hon Judge; (John) Graham; QC (1993); s of Surgn-Capt Jackson Graham Boal (d 1958), and Dorothy Kenley, *née* Hall (d 1984); *b* 24 Oct 1943; *Educ* Eastbourne Coll, King's Coll London (LLB); *m* 28 June 1978, Elizabeth Mary, da of Col L C East, DSO, OBE; 1 s (Thomas Henry b 1980); *Career* called to the Bar Gray's Inn 1966 (bencher 1991), jr Treasury counsel 1977–85, sr prosecuting counsel to Crown at Central Criminal Ct 1985–91, first sr Treasury counsel Central Criminal Court 1991–93; recorder of the Crown Court 1985–96, circuit judge (SE Circuit) 1996–; vice chm Criminal Bar Assoc 1991–93; *Recreations* golf, theatre, watching sport; *Clubs* Garrick, Royal Wimbledon Golf, MCC; *Style*— His Hon Judge Boal, QC; ✉ Central Criminal Court, Old Bailey, London EC4

BOAM, Maj-Gen (Thomas) Anthony; CB (1987), CBE (1978, OBE 1973); s of Lt-Col T S Boam, OBE; *b* 14 Feb 1932; *Educ* Bradfield Coll, RMA Sandhurst; *m* 1961, Penelope Christine Mary, da of Cyril Alfred Roberts, CBE, DL; 1 s, 2 da; *Career* cmmnd Scots Gds 1952; served: NI, Canal Zone Egypt, Kenya, Malaysia, W Germany (BAOR); cmd Br Army Trg Team Nigeria 1976–78, Dep Cdr and COS Hong Kong 1979–81, head Br Def Staff Washington and def attaché 1981–84, Cdr Br Forces Hong Kong and Maj-Gen Bde of Gurkhas 1985–87; memb Hong Kong Exec Cncl 1985–87; dir Br Conslts Bureau 1988–95; chm Leonard Cheshire Fndn Servs in W Sussex 1996–; govr: Hayes Dashwood Fndn 1989–, Queen Alexandra Hospital Home 1995; *Recreations* fishing, shooting, gardening, sport, bridge; *Clubs* MCC, Army and Navy; *Style*— Maj-Gen Anthony Boam, CB, CBE; ✉ Bury Gate House, Pulborough, West Sussex RH20 1HA (☎ 01798 831440)

BOARD, Prof Kenneth; s of George Herbert Board, of Llanelli, and Beryl, *née* Roberts; *b* 15 April 1941; *Educ* Llanelli Boys' GS, Univ of Wales (BSc, MSc, DSc), Univ of Bangor (PhD); *m* 30 July 1966, Meriel, da of Gwilym Leonard Jones, of Bynea, Llanelli, Dyfed; 2 s (Meirion b 1973, Alun b 1976); *Career* research scientist: GEC Hirst Research Centre, Philips Research Lab 1969–75; Dept of Electrical Engrg Univ of Wales Swansea: lectr 1975–82, sr lectr 1982–84, reader 1984–86, prof 1986–, head of Dept 1992–; dir Rockfield Software Ltd; MIEE 1976, MIEEE 1982; *Books* Introduction to Semiconductor Microtechnology (1983); *Recreations* squash, running, music; *Clubs* Clyne Golf; *Style*— Prof Kenneth Board; ✉ 51 Westport Avenue, Mayals, Swansea SA3 5EQ; Department of Electrical Engineering, University of Wales Swansea, Singleton Park, Swansea SA2 (☎ 01792 205678, fax 01792 295686)

BOARDMAN, Christopher Miles (Chris); MBE (1993); s of Keith Boardman, and Carol, *née* Lindfield; *b* 26 Aug 1968; *Educ* Hilbre Secdy Sch, Withens Coll; *m* 22 Oct 1988, Sally-Anne, *née* Edwards; 3 s (Edward Thomas b 11 March 1989, George Douglas b 15 Jan 1994, Oscar Miles b 13 July 1995), 1 da (Harriet Lydia b 1 June 1991); *Career* cyclist (individual); int debut Jr World Championships Stuttgart 1985; achievements incl: Bronze medal Cwlth Games Edinburgh 1986, 2 Bronze medals Cwlth Games Auckland 1990, Gold medal 4,000m individual pursuit Olympic Games Barcelona 1992, Double World champion 1994 (individual pursuit and individual time trial), Bronze medal individual time trial Olympic Games Atlanta 1996; professional cyclist; with French Gan Team (world rank number 12), winner Tour de France Prologue and holder Yellow Jersey 1994; competed in 9 World Championships, world champion and world record holder; dir: Beyond Level Four Ltd, NWV Racing Team (GB); vice pres: Sports Aid Fndn NW, Claire House Charity; memb English Sports Cncl; *Recreations* swimming, family; *Style*— Chris Boardman, Esq, MBE; ✉ c/o Beyond Level Four Ltd, Lindfield House, Station Approach, Meols L47 8XA (☎ 0151 632 3383)

BOARDMAN, Faith Rosemary; *Educ* Univ of Oxford; *m*; 2 c; *Career* HM Customs and Excise: various policy and mgmnt positions incl private sec to chm of Customs and Excise 1972–77, VAT Policy Directorate 1978–79; Fiscal Policy Div HM Treasy 1979–82, pt/t position Tobacco Policy HM Customs and Excise 1982–86, project ldr Consumer Credit Tax Policy Team 1986–87, Personnel Dept HM Customs and Excise 1987–89, chief exec HM Customs & Excise London Central 1989–95, chief exec Contributions Agency Newcastle upon Tyne 1995–; Financial Services Woman of the Year Award; *Style*— Mrs Faith Boardman; ✉ Contributions Agency, Room C1828, DSS Longbenton, Newcastle-upon-Tyne NE98 1YX (☎ 0191 225 4106, fax 0191 225 4198)

BOARDMAN, Sir John; kt (1989); s of Frederick Archibald Boardman (d 1938), and Clare, *née* Wells (d 1975); *b* 20 Aug 1927; *Educ* Chigwell Sch, Magdalene Coll Cambridge (BA, MA, Walston student); *m* 26 Oct 1952, Sheila Joan Lyndon Stanford; 2 c (Julia b

1955, Mark b 1957); *Career* Mil Serv 2 Lt Intelligence Corps 1950–52; asst dir Br Sch of Athens 1952–55 (tstee), asst keeper Ashmolean Museum Oxford 1955–59, reader in classical archaeology Univ of Oxford 1959–78, Lincoln prof of classical archaeology and art Univ of Oxford 1978–94; Merton Coll Oxford: fell 1963–78, subwarden 1975–78, hon fell 1978; Geddes-Harrower prof Univ of Aberdeen 1974; visiting prof: Columbia Univ 1965, Aust Inst of Archaeology 1987; prof of ancient history Royal Acad of Arts 1990–; ed: Jl of Hellenic Studies 1958–65, Lexicon Iconographicum 1972–; conducted excavations on: Chios 1953–55, Crete, Tocra in Libya 1964–65; del OUP 1979–89; Cromer Greek prize Br Acad 1959, Kenyon Medal British Acad 1995; corr fell Bavarian Acad of Sciences 1969; fell: Inst of Etruscan Studies Florence 1983, Austrian and German Archaeological Insts; hon fell: Magdalene Coll Cambridge 1984, Lincoln Coll Oxford 1995; Hon Doctorate: Univ of Athens 1991, Univ of Paris (Sorbonne) 1994; foreign memb Royal Danish Acad 1979, membre associé Académie des Inscriptions et Belles Lettres Institut de France 1991; Hon MRIA 1986; FSA 1957, FBA 1969; Hon RA; *Publications* incl: Cretan Collection in Oxford (1961), Island Gems (1963), Archaic Greek Gems (1968), Athenian Black Figure Vases (1974), Harari Collection of Finger Rings (with D Scarisbrick, 1978), The Greeks Overseas (1980), Escarabeos de Piedra de Ibiza (1984), The Oxford History of the Classical World (jtly 1986), Athenian Red Figure Vases, Classical Period (1989), The Oxford History of Classical Art (jtly 1993), The Diffusion of Classical Art in Antiquity (1994), Greek Art (1996); articles in various learned jls; *Clubs* Athenaeum; *Style*— Sir John Boardman, FBA; ✉ 11 Park St, Woodstock, Oxford OX20 1SJ (☎ 01993 811259, fax 01865 278082)

BOARDMAN, Hon Nigel Patrick Gray; s of Baron Boardman (Life Peer), *qv*; *b* 1950; *Educ* Ampleforth, Univ of Bristol; *m* 1975, Sarah, da of T A Coslett, of Cambridge; 1 s (Hugo b 1990), 6 da (Tamsin b 1980, Charlotte b 1981, Rebecca b 1984, Victoria b 1985, Cordelia b 1987, Elizabeth b 1992); *Career* admitted slr 1975; ptnr Slaughter and May; *Style*— The Hon Nigel Boardman; ✉ Slaughter and May, 35 Basinghall Street, London EC2V 5DB (☎ 0171 600 1200, fax 0171 600 0289)

BOARDMAN, Peter Charles (Pete); s of James Boardman, and Ethel, *née* Yates; *b* 8 April 1956; *Educ* Hesketh Fletcher Secdy Sch; *m* 17 April 1987, Margaret Murray, da of John Blair Rice; *Career* entered RAF Photographic Trade as aircraftsman 1974, ret Corpl 1989; driver's mate 1972–74, fndr Pete Boardman Photography (industl, commercial, aerial and advtg photography) 1990–; photographs published incl: numerous in military and non-military magazines, 18 in British Air Power in the Eighties, front cover Hamish McInnes's Sweep Search; Photographer of the Year RAF 1983 (runner-up 1982 and 1985); FBIPP 1989 (ABIPP 1986, LBIPP 1984); *Recreations* photography, swimming, motor sports, DIY; *Style*— Pete Boardman, Esq; ✉ 50 Pitreuchie Place, Forfar, Angus, Scotland DD8 2DG (☎ 01307 466172); Pete Boardman Photography, Unit 7, Riverside Court, Riverside Drive, Airport Enterprise Zone, Dundee DD2 1XD (☎ 01382 642279, fax 01382 642279)

BOARDMAN, Peter Laird; s of Dr Hedley Boardman, of London W8, and Patricia, *née* Laird (d 1954); *b* 24 Feb 1934; *Educ* Wrekin Coll Wellington Shropshire, Queens' Coll Cambridge (MA), Westminster Hosp Med Sch (MD); *m* 21 Sept 1963, Hilary Barbara, da of Dr Ronald Jones, of Thorndon Hill, nr Eye, Suffolk; 1 s (Alan b 1969), 2 da (Hannah b 1966, Laura b 1968); *Career* sr registrar Westminster Hosp 1964–67, Buswell fell and res instr in med State Univ of NY Buffalo 1967–68, conslt physician Royal Shrewsbury Hosp 1968–95, ret; ex pres Midland Rheumatology Soc; FRCP; *Recreations* hill walking, golf, reading, wine; *Style*— Peter Boardman, Esq; ✉ 3 Mayfield Park, Shrewsbury SY2 6PD (☎ 01743 232768)

BOARDMAN, Royston James (Roy); MBE (1990); s of Herbert James Boardman (d 1969), of London, and Alice Pauline (d 1967); *b* 2 Feb 1937; *Educ* Walworth Secdy Sch, Borough Rd Training Coll Univ of London, Univ of Essex (MA); *m* Nov 1975, Saverina, da of Dr Aniello Curzio; 2 s (Michael b 21 Dec 1962, Arthur b 17 Aug 1964), 1 da (Luisa b 25 Sept 1973); *Career* Nat Serv RAPC 1955–57; jr librarian Islington Public Libraries 1953–55, head of English Sandon Secdy Sch Essex 1961–65 (joined 1959), lectr in English language & lit The British Council Naples and Istituto Universitario Orientale Naples 1965–69, linguistic and cultural researcher Naples 1969–71, lector Univ of Bari 1972–75; The British Council Naples: English language offr South Italy 1975–80, dir 1980–; practical assessor TEFL RSA 1979–88; *Awards* Premio Calabria 1987 (for cultural rels), Premio Sebetia-Ter 1992; *Books* In the Web (poems, 1961), Over to You (1978), Variety (1982), Springboard 1 (1982), Springboard 2 (1982), Approaching Springboard (1984), Reading Between the Lines (with John McRae, 1984), My Generation (1994), Literature in Foreign Language Education (1995), Naples and its Environs (1995); *Recreations* reading, poetry, travel, theatre; *Style*— Roy Boardman, Esq, MBE; ✉ 4 Old Way, Bletsoe, Bedford MK44 1QG (☎ 01234 782263); The British Council, Palazzo d'Avalos, Via dei Mille 48, 80121 Naples, Italy (☎ 00 39 081 4037591, fax 00 39 081 426962)

BOARDMAN, Baron (Life Peer UK 1980); Thomas Gray Boardman; MC (1944), TD (1952), DL (Northants 1977); s of John Clayton Boardman (d 1944), of Daventry, Northants, and Janet, *née* Houston (d 1940); *b* 12 Jan 1919; *Educ* Bromsgrove Sch; *m* 1948, (Norah Mary) Deirdre, da of Hubert Vincent Gough, of Pangbourne, and wid of John Henry Chaworth-Musters, of Annesley Park, Nottingham; 2 s, 1 da; *Career* sits as Cons peer in House of Lords; served WWII Northants Yeo, cmdg 1956; admitted slr 1947; MP (C): Leicester SW 1967–74, Leicester S Feb-Sept 1974; min for indust DTI 1972–74, chief sec to Treasy 1974; chm: Chamberlain Phipps Ltd 1958–72, The Steetley Co Ltd 1978–83 (dir 1975–83), National Westminster Bank 1983–89 (dir 1979–89), Heron International NV 1993–95; dir: Allied Breweries Ltd 1968–72 and 1974–77 (vice chm 1975–76), MEPC Ltd 1980–89; memb Advsy Bd The LEK Partnership 1990–; pres Assoc of Br Chambers of Commerce 1977–80, treas Cons Pty 1981–82, memb Exec Assoc of Cons Peers 1981–84 and 1991–95, chm Ctee of London and Scottish Bankers 1987–89, tstee Prince's Youth Business Tst 1989–93; High Sheriff Northants 1979, HM Lieutenant City of London; *Recreations* riding; *Clubs* Cavalry and Guards'; *Style*— The Rt Hon Lord Boardman, MC, TD, DL; ✉ The Manor House, Welford, Northants NN6 6HX (☎ 01858 575235); Flat 29, Tufton Court, Tufton St, London SW1P 3QH (☎ 0171 222 6793); House of Lords, Westminster, London SW1A 0PW (☎ 0171 219 3000)

BOAS, (John) Robert Sotheby; s of Edgar Henry Boas, of Teddington, Middx, and Mary Katherine, *née* Beattie; *b* 28 Feb 1937; *Educ* Clifton, Corpus Christi Coll Cambridge; *m* 25 Sept 1965, (Karen) Elisabeth, da of Gunnar Gersted, of Copenhagen; 2 s (Christopher b 1972, Nicholas b 1975), 1 da (Helena b 1970); *Career* S Lt Royal Signals 1955–57; merchant banker Price Waterhouse 1960–64, ICI 1964–65, S G Warburg & Co Ltd 1965–95, md SBC Warburg 1995–; non-exec dir Chesterfield Properties 1978–; bd memb Securities Assoc (now Securities and Futures Authy) 1988–; cncl memb The English Stage Co 1978–83, dir English National Opera 1990–; FCA; *Recreations* opera, theatre, reading; *Style*— Robert Boas, Esq; ✉ 5 Longwood Drive, London SW15 5DL (☎ 0171 788 9667); SBC Warburg, 2 Finsbury Ave, London EC2M 2PA (☎ 0171 606 1066)

BOASE, Martin; s of Prof Alan Martin Boase (d 1982), of Inverleith Place, Edinburgh, and Elizabeth Grizelle, *née* Forster (d 1977); *b* 14 July 1932; *Educ* Rendcomb Coll, New Coll Oxford (MA); *m* 1, Dec 1960 (m dis 1971), Terry-Ann, *née* Moir; 1 s (Daniel b 1962), 1 da (Rachel b 1964); m 2, 1974, Pauline Valerie, da of Lt-Col Philip Henry Akerman Brownrigg, CMG, DSO, OBE, TD, of Checkendon, nr Reading, Berks; 1 s (Luke b 1981), 1 da (Hannah b 1976); *Career* Russian interpreter Intelligence Corps 1951–53; exec London Press Exchange Ltd 1958–60, md Pritchard Wood & Partners Ltd 1967–68 (joined 1961), fndr ptnr The Boase Massimi Pollitt Partnership Ltd 1968; chm: Boase Massimi Pollitt plc 1979–89 (jt chm 1977–79), Omnicom UK plc 1989–95, Kiss FM 1993–, Maiden Outdoor plc 1993–, Herald Investment Trusts 1994–, Investment Trust of Investment Trusts 1995–; dir: Omnicom Group Inc 1989–94, EMAP plc 1991–, Matthew Clark plc 1995–; chm: Advertising Assoc 1987–92, British Television Advertising Awards Ltd 1993–; dir Oxford Playhouse Tst 1991–; FIPA 1976; *Recreations* the Turf; *Style*— Martin Boase, Esq; ✉ 12 Bishops Bridge Road, London W2 6AA (☎ 0171 258 3979, fax 0171 706 3854)

BOATENG, Paul Yaw; MP (Lab) Brent South (majority 9,705); s of Kwaku Boateng, of Ghana and England, and Eleanor, *née* McCombie; *b* 14 June 1951; *Educ* Accra Acad, Apsley GS, Univ of Bristol (LLB); *m* 1980, Janet, da of Leonard Alleyne; 3 da (Mirabelle b 1980, Beth b 1982, Charlotte b 1983), 2 s (Benjamin b 1984, Seth b 1987); *Career* admitted slr 1976, slr Paddington Law Centre 1976–79, slr and ptnr BM Birnberg & Co 1979–87; called to the Bar Gray's Inn 1989; legal advsr Scrap Sus Campaign 1977–81, memb (Lab) for Walthamstow GLC 1981–85 (chm Police Ctee 1981–85, vice chm Ethnic Minorities Ctee 1981–85); Parly candidate (Lab) Hertfordshire West 1983, MP (Lab) Brent South 1987–; memb House of Commons Environment Ctee 1987–89, oppn spokesman on Treasy and Economic Affairs 1989–92, oppn spokesman on Legal Affairs (Lord Chllr's Dept) 1992–; broadcaster; presenter Looking Forward to the Past (BBC Radio 4); chm Afro-Caribbean Educn Resource Project 1978–86; memb: Exec NCCL 1980–86, World Cncl of Churches Cmmn Prog to Combat Racism 1984–91; chm of govrs Priory Park Sch 1978–84, govr Police Staff Coll Bramshill 1981–84; memb Bd: ENO 1984–, English Touring Opera 1993–; *Books* Reclaiming the Ground (contrib with Rt Hon John Smith, QC, MP), contrib foreword to Sense and Sensibility (in Complete Works of Jane Austen, HarperCollins); *Style*— Paul Boateng, Esq, MP; ✉ House of Commons, London SW1A 0AA

BOBB, (Louise) Gabrielle; *see:* Gabrielle

BOBROW, Prof Martin; CBE (1995); s of Joe Bobrow, of Ontario, Canada, and Bessie Leah, *née* Rosin; *b* 6 Feb 1938; *Educ* Johannesburg, Univ of Witwatersrand (BSc, MB BCh, DSc); *m* 1963, Lynda Geraldine, *née* Strauss; 3 da (Catherine, Gina, Jennifer); *Career* clinical scientific offr MRC Population Genetics Res Unit 1965–72, res offr Dept of the Regius Prof of Med and Genetics Laboratory Univ of Oxford 1972–74, jt appts as conslt in clinical genetics Dept of Med Genetics Oxford AHA, hon lectr Univ of Oxford and memb MRC External Scientific Staff Univ Genetics Laboratory 1974–81, prof of human genetics Univ of Amsterdam 1981–82, Prince Philip prof of paediatric res Utd Med and Dental Schs of Guy's and St Thomas's Hosps Univ of London 1982–95, dir SE Thames Regnl Genetics Centre Guy's Hosp 1982–93, prof of medical genetics Univ of Cambridge 1995–; memb Editorial Bd: Cytogenetics and Cell Genetics 1974–81, Jl of Med Genetics 1976–89 and 1995– (asst ed 1979–81, ed 1995–), Genetica 1981–90, Prenatal Diagnosis 1984–, Jl of Intellectual Disability Res 1986–, Bulletin of Med Ethics 1990–92; series ed: Monographs in Med Genetics 1984–, Human Mutation 1991–; author of numerous book chapters and articles on clinical and molecular genetics; memb: Cell Bd MRC 1980–81 and 1985–88, Res Ctee Muscular Dystrophy Gp of GB and NI 1981–, Med Advsy Ctee The Spastics Soc (now Scope) 1983–89, Academic Bd Br Paediatric Assoc 1983–87, Ctee on Clinical Genetics RCP 1984–92, Cncl MRC 1988–92, Ctee to Examine the Ethical Implications of Gene Therapy and Gene Therapy Advsy Ctee Dept of Health 1989–95, Cncl Clinical Genetics Soc 1989–92, Med Advsy Ctee Cystic Fibrosis Res Tst 1990–91, Central Res and Devpt Ctee Dept of Health 1991–, MRC Human Genome Mapping Project 1989–95, Wellcome Tst's Genetic Interest Gp 1992–95, Nat Cncl Muscular Dystrophy Gp of GB and NI 1993–, Cncl MRC 1993–94, Nat Radiological Protection Bd 1994–95; non-exec memb Lewisham NHS Tst Bd 1993–95; chm: Ctee on the Med Aspects of Radiation in the Environment Dept of Health 1985–92, Standing Advsy Ctee on Clinical Cytogenetics and Molecular Genetics RCPath 1987–90, Unrelated Living Transplant Regulatory Authy 1990–, Steering Ctee Cochrane Centre Oxford 1992–, Molecular and Cellular Med Bd MRC 1992–94, Res Ctee Muscular Dystrophy Gp of GB and NI 1993–96, Nat Cncl Muscular Dystrophy Gp 1995–; pres Clinical Genetics Soc 1993–94 (vice pres 1992–93 and 1995–96); FRCPath 1990 (MRCPath 1978), FRCP; *Style*— Prof Martin Bobrow, CBE; ✉ Department of Medical Genetics, Box 238, Addenbrooke's Hospital, Cambridge CB2 2QQ (☎ 01223 331154, fax 01223 331206)

BOBROWSKI, Dr Jan Jozef; s of Aleksander Bobrowski (d 1987), of Poland, and Antonina, *née* Kandefer (d 1978); *b* 31 March 1925; *Educ* Univ of London, Battersea Coll of Advanced Technol (BSc), ACT (Battersea), Univ of Surrey (PhD); *m* 28 Aug 1954, Zofia, da of Boleslaw Kowalski (d 1972), of Poland; 1 da (Izabella Cecylia Antonina b 3 June 1957); *Career* Polish Corps 1942–47, Lt 1945; practical design trg with Twisteel Reinforcement Ltd 1952–53, pt/t lectr Battersea Coll of Advanced Technol 1952–58, engrg asst C J Pell & Partners 1953–58; chief engr: Pierhead Engrg Div Unit Construction Co 1958–59, Pierhead Ltd 1959–62, Unit Construction Co 1961–62, Jan Bobrowski and Partners 1962–; medal for contribs to pre-stressed concrete 1978, currently holds record for longest span concrete shell constructed at the Olympic Saddledome Calgary; visiting prof Imperial Coll of Sci and Technol 1981; pres Concrete Soc 1986–87; vice pres: Inst of Structural Engrs 1985–86, (UK) Fedn Internationale Precontrainte, Univ of Surrey Soc; memb Euro-International Du Beton Econ Devpt Ctee; Freeman City of London 1977, Liveryman Worshipful Co of Constructors 1977; FEng 1983, FICE 1962, FIStructE 1973, MCSCE, Hon FICT, MConsE, MSocIS (France), PEng (Alberta BC); Sovereign Military Order of St John of Jerusalem Knights of Malta 1984, Polish Army Medal 1945, Cross of Monte Cassino 1945, Polish Defence Medal 1945; *Publications* author of numerous articles to tech jls; *Recreations* equestrianism, fishing; *Style*— Dr Jan Bobrowski, FEng; ✉ Jan Bobrowski and Partners Consulting Engineers, Grosvenor House, Grosvenor Road, Twickenham, Middlesex TW1 4AA (☎ 0181 892 7627, fax 0181 891 3151, telex 8954665 VBSTLX G JBP)

BODDINGTON, (Robert) Christopher Hance; s of Lt Robert Evelyn Boddington, RN (ka 1942), of Peterchurch, Herefordshire, and Heather Elizabeth Bryant, *née* Hance (d 1989); *b* 4 May 1941; *Educ* Rugby, The Queen's Coll Oxford (MA); *m* 1, 21 Sept 1963 (m dis 1983), (Mary) Jane, da of John Baughn Wiggs (d 1973), of Bournemouth; 2 da (Naomi b 1964, Lucia b 1965); m 2, 2 March 1991, Ruth Dianne, da of Guy Rogers Naylor III (d 1968), of Westwood, Maryland, USA; *Career* admitted slr 1966; slr: Western Sons & Neave 1966–69, McKenna & Co 1969–72; ptnr: Ziman and Co 1972–77, Nabarro Nathanson 1977– (commercial lawyer in field of corp fin, head Eastern Europe Group); dir: British Consultants Bureau 1994–, Brooke Industrial Holdings plc 1996–; memb Law Soc 1966; *Recreations* travel, opera, food; *Clubs* Brooks's; *Style*— Christopher Boddington, Esq; ✉ Nabarro Nathanson, 50 Stratton St, London W1X 6NX (☎ 0171 493 9933, fax 0171 629 7900, telex 8813144)

BODDINGTON, Ewart Agnew; JP (Macclesfield 1959), DL (Cheshire 1993); s of (Charles) Geoffrey Boddington (d 1982), and Edith Norah, MBE, *née* Agnew (d 1990); *b* 7 April 1927; *Educ* Stowe, Trinity Coll Cambridge (MA); *m* 1954, (Vine) Anne, da of Louis Arthur Hubert Clayton (d 1989); 2 s, 1 da; *Career* Boddington Group plc (formerly Boddingtons' Breweries Ltd): chm 1970–88, pres and non-exec dir 1989–92, pres 1992–95; chm Brewers' Soc 1984–85, pres Inst of Brewing 1972–74, dir Northern Bd National Westminster Bank 1977–92; High Sheriff of Cheshire 1978–79; Hon MA Univ of Manchester 1977; Liveryman Worshipful Co of Brewers 1980; *Recreations* shooting, fishing, golf; *Style*— Ewart A Boddington, Esq, JP, DL; ✉ Fanshawe Brook Farm, Henbury, Macclesfield, Cheshire SK11 9PP (☎ 01260 244387)

BODDY, Dr (Francis) Andrew; s of William Boddy (d 1966), and Janet Hogg, *née* Noble (d 1991); *b* 1 March 1935; *Educ* Prince Henry's GS Otley Yorks, Univ of Edinburgh (MB ChB); *m* 1965, Adele, da of Arnold Wirszubski; 2 da (Kasia b 1966, Janet b 1969); *Career* asst lectr Dept of Public Health and Social Med Univ of Edinburgh 1960–63, research assoc NY City Dept of Health 1963–65, lectr Dept of Social Med Univ of Aberdeen 1966–69; Univ of Glasgow: sr lectr Dept of Community Med 1969–78, dir Social Paediatric and Obstetric Research Unit 1978–91, dir Public Health Research Unit 1991–; convenor Scottish Affrs Ctee Faculty of Public Health Med 1991–94; Soc for Social Med: memb 1963, hon sec 1982–87, chm 1996; author of pubns on socio-medical and public health topics; FFPHM 1976, FRCPEd 1981; *Recreations* fishing, photography; *Style*— Dr Andrew Boddy; ✉ 26 Rowallan Gardens, Glasgow G11 7LJ (☎ 0141 339 4644); Public Health Research Unit, University of Glasgow, 1 Lilybank Gardens, Glasgow G12 8RZ (☎ 0141 330 5075, fax 0141 337 2776)

BODDY, Prof Keith; OBE (1989); *b* 1 Nov 1937; *Educ* Univ of Liverpool (BSc), Univ of London (MSc), Univ of Glasgow (PhD), Univ of Strathclyde (DSc); m; 2 s; *Career* radiation protection offr and head Health Physics Section Res Laboratory Associated Electrical Industries Ltd 1959–63, sr lectr and head Health Physics and Nuclear Med Unit Scottish Universities Research and Reactor Centre 1967–78 (lectr 1963–67), head Regnl Med Physics Dept Gateshead and South Tyneside HA 1978–, prof of med physics Univ of Newcastle 1978–; currently memb: Radioactive Waste Mgmnt Advsy Ctee, Ctee on Medical Aspects of Radiation in the Environment, Ionising Radiations Advsy Ctee Health and Safety Cmmn; pres: Hosp Physicists' Assoc 1986–88, Inst of Physical Sciences in Med 1986–88, Int Orgn for Med Physics 1994–; pres elect Int Union of Physical and Engrg Scis in Medicine; hon memb: RCR, Br Nuclear Med Soc; FInstP 1969 (Glazebrook medal and prize 1991), FRSE 1980, FIPSM 1988; author of over 200 papers; *Recreations* walking, gardening, crosswords, logic puzzles, music, family activities; *Style*— Prof Keith Boddy, OBE, FRSE; ✉ Regional Medical Physics Department, Newcastle General Hospital, Newcastle upon Tyne NE4 6BE (☎ 0191 273 8811 ext 22513, fax 0191 226 0970)

BODEN, Kenneth Henry Edmund; s of Henry James Randolph Boden (d 1982, formerly 4QOH and Inspr Palestine Police), and Ada Dorothy, *née* Hazle; *b* 15 Dec 1941; *Educ* Southend HS for Boys' Southend on Sea; *m* 20 Sept 1969, June Irene, da of Harold Gibbs, of London; *Career* underwriters clerk Gardner Mountain D'Ambrumenil and Rennie Lloyd's Insur Brokers 1958, marine cargo surveyor Insur Co of N America 1966–68, dep marine underwriter at Lloyd's for Laurence Philipps Agencies (now Eastgate Gp) 1968–80, active underwriter 1980–95, cargo underwriter for syndicate 902 at Lloyd's (PB Coffey and others) 1993–; memb: Round Table until 1982, Assoc of Ex-Tablers Club; ACII 1968; memb Lloyd's 1979; *Recreations* skiing, travel, gardening, cage birds; *Clubs* 41; *Style*— Kenneth Boden, Esq; ✉ Box 068(B), Lloyd's, London (☎ 0171 623 7100 ext 3765)

BODEN, Leonard; *Educ* Sedbergh Sch, Sch of Art Glasgow, Heatherley's Sch of Art London; *m* Margaret Tulloch, PS, FRSA, portrait painter; 1 da (Daphne, ARCM, FRSA); *Career* portrait painter; portraits incl: nineteen Royal portraits (incl ten of HM Queen Elizabeth II and five of HRH The Duke of Edinburgh, KG, HM Queen Elizabeth The Queen Mother and HRH The Prince of Wales), Pope Pius XII (only portrait he ever sat for), Baroness Thatcher (now hangs in Carlton Club), Boris Christoff (Theatre Museum Covent Garden), Tito Gobbi, Donald Sinden, Lord Wakefield of Kendal, Field Marshal Lord Slim, awards incl Gold Medal (Hors Concours) Paris Salon; vice-pres Artists' Gen Benevolent Inst (memb 1965–, hon sec), Freeman City of London, Liveryman Worshipful Co of Painter-Stainers 1966; RP 1973, FRSA; *Clubs* Arts, Savage, Chelsea Arts (chm 1961); *Style*— Leonard Boden, Esq, RP; ✉ 36 Arden Road, London N3 3AN (☎ and fax 0181 346 5706)

BODEN, Prof Margaret Ann; da of Leonard Forbes Boden, OBE (d 1986), of London, and Violet Dorothy, *née* Dawson (d 1967); *b* 26 Nov 1936; *Educ* City of London Sch for Girls, Newnham Coll Cambridge (MA), Harvard Graduate Sch for Arts and Scis (AM, PhD); *m* 24 June 1967 (m dis 1981), John Raymond Spiers; 1 s (Ruskin b 1968), 1 da (Jehane b 1972); *Career* lectr in philosophy Univ of Birmingham 1959–65, prof in philosophy and psychology Univ of Sussex 1980– (lectr and reader 1959–65), founding dean Sch of Cognitive and Computing Sci Univ of Sussex 1987–; visiting scientist Yale Univ 1979; Duijken lecture Amsterdam 1985, Templeton lecture Sydney 1994, Dacre lecture Peterhouse Cambridge 1994; co fndr dir Harvester Press Ltd 1968–85 (sec 1968–79); chm Cncl and vice pres Royal Inst of GB 1993–95 (memb Cncl 1992–95), pres General Section BAAS 1992–93; memb: Mind Assoc, Aristotelian Soc, Royal Inst of Philosophy (memb Cncl 1988–), Br Psychological Soc, Br Soc for Philosophy of Science, Advsy Bd Res Cncls 1989–91, Soc of Authors, Animal Procedures Ctee (Home Office) 1994–; tstee Cncl for Science and Society (chm Working Pty on Benefits and Dangers of Knowledge-Based Systems 1987–88); memb: Academia Europaea 1993, New York Acad of Sciences 1994; ScD Univ of Cambridge 1990; FBA 1983 (memb Cncl 1988–, vice pres 1989–91), FRSA 1992, fell American Assoc for Artificial Intelligence 1993 (memb); *Books* Purposive Explanation in Psychology (1972), Artificial Intelligence and Natural Man (1977), Piaget (1979), Minds and Mechanisms (1981), Computer Models of Mind (1988), Artificial Intelligence in Psychology (1989), The Philosophy of Artificial Intelligence (ed, 1990), The Creative Mind (1990), Dimensions of Creativity (ed, 1994), The Philosophy of Artificial Life (ed, 1996), Artificial Intelligence (ed, 1996); *Recreations* dressmaking, travel; *Clubs* Reform; *Style*— Prof Margaret Boden; ✉ School of Cognitive and Computing Sciences, University of Sussex, Falmer, Brighton, E Sussex BN1 9QH (☎ 01273 678386, fax 01273 671320)

BODEY, David Roderick Lessiter; QC (1991); s of Reginald Augustus Bodey (d 1987), and Betty Frances Ada, *née* Lessiter (d 1987); *b* 14 Oct 1947; *Educ* King's Sch Canterbury, Univ of Bristol (LLB); *m* 28 Feb 1976, Ruth, da of Dr Denis MacAdorey, of Healing, Lincs; 1 s (Simon Christopher b 13 Jan 1980), 1 da (Katherine Sarah b 29 April 1982); *Career* called to the Bar Middle Temple (Harmsworth scholar) 1970; legal assessor to UK Central Cncl for Nursing Midwifery and Health Visiting 1983; recorder of the Crown Court 1993– (asst recorder 1989–93), dep judge of the High Ct (Family Div) 1995; sec Family Law Bar Assoc 1995; fell Int Acad of Matrimonial Lawyers 1995; *Recreations* music, marathon running; *Clubs* Lansdowne; *Style*— David Bodey, Esq, QC; ✉ 2nd Floor, Queen Elizabeth Building, Temple, London EC4Y 9BS (☎ 0171 797 7837, fax 0171 797 5422)

BODILLY, Lt Cdr Sir Jocelyn; kt (1969), VRD; s of Cdr Ralph Burland Bodilly, RN, of Trenarren, Alverton, Penzance, Cornwall, and Sybil Bodilly; *b* 15 Sept 1913; *Educ* Munro Coll Jamaica, Schloss Schule Salem Baden Germany, Wadham Coll Oxford; *m* 1, 1936, Phyllis Maureen (d 1963), da of Thomas Cooper Gotch; m 2, 1964, Marjorie (d 1996), da of Walter Fogg, of St Helens, Lancs; *Career* RNVR 1937–56, Lt Cdr (S), served WWII; called to the Bar Inner Temple 1937; judge High Court Sudan 1946–55, crown counsel Hong Kong 1955, princ crown counsel Hong Kong 1961, law draftsman Hong Kong 1964, chief justice Western Pacific 1965–75, chm Industrial Tbnls for London (S) 1976–86; *Clubs* Royal Ocean Racing; *Style*— Lt Cdr Sir Jocelyn Bodilly, VRD, RNVR, Ret; ✉ Myrtle Cottage, St Peter's Hill, Newlyn, Penzance, Cornwall TR18 5EQ

BODIWALA, Gautam Govindlal; JP; s of Dr Govindlal R Bodiwala (d 1983), of Ahmedabad, India, and Sumanben, *née* Parikh; *b* 11 Oct 1943; *Educ* Univ of Gujarat (MB BS, MS); *m* 28 Dec 1969, Gita, da of Prabhulal G Thanawala, of Thana, India; 1 s (Dhaval b 1973), 1 da (Janki b 1977); *Career* conslt and head of Accident and Emergency Serv Leicester 1977–; hon treas British Assoc for Accident and Emergency Med, memb Rotary Int, fndr pres Leics Medico-Legal Soc; memb: BMA, American Coll of Emergency Physicians; founding fell and treas Faculty of Accident and Emergency Med; fell: Int Coll of Surgns, Int Coll of Angiology; FRSM; *Recreations* music and reading; *Clubs* Rotary (Oadby); *Style*— Gautam Bodiwala, Esq, JP; ✉ Lykkebo, 7 Blackthorn Lane, Oadby, Leicester LE2 4FA (☎ 0116 271 8899); Accident and Emergency Department, Leicester Royal Infirmary, Infirmary Close, Leicester LE1 5WW (☎ 0116 258 5274)

BODLENDER, Jonathan A; CBE (1995); s of Leonard Bodlender (d 1958), of Harrogate, and Renie Frieze (d 1982); *b* 29 Nov 1938; *Educ* Bootham Sch York, LSE; *m* 18 Jan 1979, Catherine Genevieve, da of Albert Schmitt; *Career* Horwath Consulting (formerly Horwath & Horwath (UK) Ltd): progressively md, exec chm, chm 1968–94; chm Horwath Consulting Europe and chm Horwath UK Ltd 1994–; also special advsr on tourism investmt to The World Tourism Orgn; major assignments incl: London's Tourist Accommodation in the 1990's (for Br Govt agencies) 1986, Hotels of the Future (report for Int Hotel Assoc) 1987–88, The Future of Swiss Tourism (for Swiss Govt) 1990; bd memb Eng Tourist Bd 1979–82, vice-chm World Tourism Orgn Affiliate Members 1983–91 and 1992–94 (co-chm 1991); fndr chm Univ of London Wine and Food Soc 1957–59, sec of debates LSE 1957–58; has given speeches in over 50 countries; ACA 1962, FTII 1962, FHCIMA 1977, fell Tourism Soc 1979; memb: Confrerie des Chevaliers du Tastevin (Bourgogne), Confrerie des Hospitaliers du Haut d'Andlau (Alsace); *Publications* Profile of Government Financial and Grant Aid to Tourism (with E J G Davies, 1984), An Examination of Tourism Investment Incentives (with T J Ward, 1987), Tourism: A Portrait (1988), Horwath Book of Tourism (contrib, 1990), Guidelines to Hotel and Leisure Project Financing (with T J Ward and M Dillon, 1991), Investment and Privatisation in International Tourism (with M W Gerty, 1995); also author of numerous published articles; *Recreations* wines, snuff bottles, tennis, gardening; *Clubs* Reform, Hurlingham, RAC; *Style*— Jonathan A Bodlender, Esq, CBE; ✉ 3 Sterling Street, Montpelier Square, Knightsbridge, London SW7 (☎ and fax 0171 589 4164); Horwath UK Ltd, 25 New Street Square, London EC4A 3LN (☎ 0171 353 5380, fax 0171 583 1720)

BODMER, Sir Walter Fred; kt (1986); s of Dr Ernest Julius Bodmer (d 1968), and Sylvia Emily, *née* Bodmer; *b* 10 Jan 1936; *Educ* Manchester GS, Univ of Cambridge (BA, PhD); *m* 1956, Julia Gwynaeth, da of William Gwyn Pilkington (d 1976); 2 s (Mark, Charles), 1 da (Helen); *Career* Univ of Cambridge: research fell Clare Coll 1958–60, official fell 1961, demonstrator Dept of Genetics 1960–61; prof Dept of Genetics Stanford Univ Sch of Med 1968–70 (asst prof 1962–66, assoc prof 1966–68), prof of genetics Univ of Oxford 1970–79; Imperial Cancer Research Fund: dir of research 1979–91, dir gen 1991–96; non-exec dir Fisons plc 1990–96; princ Hertford Coll Oxford 1996–; chm: Ctee on Public Understanding of Sci 1990–93, Science Consultative Gp BBC 1981–87; pres: Royal Statistical Soc 1984–85, Br Assoc for the Advancement of Sci 1987–88, Assoc for Science Educn 1989, Br Soc for Histocompatibility and Immunogenetics 1990–91, Human Genome Orgn 1990–92, Int Fedn of Assocs for the Advancement of Science and Technol 1992 (first pres); tstee: Natural History Museum (formerly Br Museum (Natural History)) 1983–93 (chm 1988–93), Sir John Soane's Museum, Gtr Manchester Museum of Sci and Indust 1989–90; vice pres Royal Instn 1981–82, memb Advsy Bd for the Research Cncls 1983–88, memb Orgn of Euro Cancer Insts 1990–93; memb Bd of Patrons St Mark's Hosp and Academic Inst London 1996; chllr Univ of Salford 1995–; hon fell: Keble Coll Oxford 1981, Clare Coll Cambridge 1989, Green Coll Oxford 1993; hon memb: American Assoc of Immunologists, St Mark's Assoc London 1995; Liveryman Worshipful Co of Scientific Instrument Makers; William Allan Meml Award 1980, Conway Evans Prize 1982, Rabbi Shai Shacknai Meml Prize Lectureship in Immunology and Cancer Res 1983, John Alexander Meml Prize Lectureship 1984, Rose Payne Distinguished Scientist Lectureship 1985, Michael Faraday Award (Royal Soc) 1994, Harveian orator Royal Coll of Physicians 1996; Laurea Honoris Causa in Medicine and Surgery Univ of Bologna 1987; Hon DSc: Univ of Bath 1988, Univ of Oxford 1988, Univ of Edinburgh 1990, Univ of Hull 1990, Univ of Bristol 1991, Loughborough Univ of Technol 1993, Univ of Lancaster 1994, Univ of Aberdeen 1994, Univ of Plymouth 1995, Univ of Salford 1996, Univ of London 1996; Hon MD Birmingham 1992, Dr Honoris Causa Univ of Leuven 1992, Hon LLD Univ of Dundee 1993, Dr Honoris Causa Masaryk Univ Brno 1994; foreign memb American Philisophical Soc USA 1989; foreign hon memb American Acad of Arts and Scis, foreign assoc US Nat Acad Scis; CBiol, FIBiol, FRCPath, Hon FRCP, Hon FRCS, Hon FRSE 1992, Hon FRSM 1994, FRS; *Books* The Genetics of Human Populations (with L Cavalli-Sforza, 1971), Our Future Inheritance: Choice or Chance? (with A Jones, 1974), Genetics, Evolution and Man (with L Cavalli-Sforza, 1976), The Book of Man (with Robin McKie, 1994); *Recreations* playing the piano, riding, swimming; *Clubs* Athenaeum; *Style*— Sir Walter Bodmer, FRS; ✉ Hertford College, Oxford OX1 3BW (☎ 01865 279405, e-mail walter.bodmer@hertford.ox.ac.uk)

BODMIN, Archdeacon of; *see:* Whiteman, Ven Rodney David Carter

BODSWORTH, Prof Colin; s of George William Bodsworth (d 1971), of Sheffield, and Daisy Mary, *née* Gregory; *b* 10 Aug 1924; *Educ* Univ of Sheffield (BMet, MMet, PhD); *m* 9 July 1949, Muriel, da of William Henry Ashforth (d 1984); 1 s (David Gordon b 15 Nov 1957); *Career* WWII Somerset Light Inf and RCS 1944–47; mgmnt apprentice United Steel Cos Ltd 1940–44, lectr in metallurgy Univ of Liverpool 1950–64, chief physical metallurgist Richard Thomas & Baldwins Ltd 1964–65; Brunel Univ: head Dept of Metallurgy 1965–82, vice princ 1973–75, dean Faculty of Technology 1982–88, research prof 1988–90, prof emeritus 1990; Inst of Metals: memb Cncl 1977–80, vice pres 1980–83, chm Accreditation Ctee 1987–90, editorial conslt 1995–; memb Engrg Ctee 4 and Coordinating Ctee of Engrg Cncl; CEng, FIM 1958; *Books* Physical Chemistry of Iron and Steel Making (1963), Problems in Applied Thermodynamics (1965), The Extraction and Refining of Metals (1994); *Recreations* gardening, walking, archeology; *Style*— Prof Colin Bodsworth; ✉ 52 Mayflower Way, Farnham Common, Bucks SL2 3UB (☎ 01753 643172); Department of Materials Technology, Brunel University, Uxbridge, Middx UB8 3PH (☎ 01895 274000, fax 01895 32806, telex 261173 G)

BODY, Sir Richard Bernard Frank Stewart; kt (1986), MP (C) Holland with Boston (majority 13,831); s of Lt-Col Bernard Richard Body, of Donnington, Berkshire, and Daphne Mary Eleanor, *née* Corbett; *b* 18 May 1927; *Educ* Reading Sch; *m* 1959, (Doris) Marion, da of late Maj Harold John Graham, OBE, of Midhurst Sussex; 1 s, 1 da; *Career* called to the Bar Middle Temple 1949; contested (C): Rotherham 1950, Abertillery by-election 1950, Leek 1951; MP (C): Billericay 1955–59, Holland with Boston 1966–; memb Commons Select Ctee on Agric 1979–87 (chm 1986–87); chm Open Seas Forum 1971–, jt chm Cncl Get Britain Out referendum campaign 1975; Lloyd's underwriter 1979–, dir New European Publications Ltd 1986–; *Books* Agriculture - The Triumph and the Shame (1982), Farming in the Clouds (1984), Red or Green for Farmers (and the Rest of Us) (1987), Europe of Many Circles (1990), Our Food, Our Land (1991); *Recreations* hunting with his bloodhounds; *Clubs* Carlton, Reform, Athenaeum; *Style*— Sir Richard Body, MP; ✉ Jewell's Farm, Stanford Dingley, Reading, Berks (☎ 0118 974 4295)

BOE, Norman Wallace; s of Alexander Thomson Boe, of Edinburgh, and Margaret Wallace, *née* Revans; *b* 30 Aug 1943; *Educ* George Heriot's Sch, Univ of Edinburgh

(LLB); *m* 9 Aug 1968, Margaret Irene, da of Alexander McKenzie; 1 s (Douglas), 1 da (Sheila); *Career* legal apprentice Lindsays WS 1965–67, admitted slr 1967, legal asst Menzies & White WS 1967–70; Office of Slr to Sec of State for Scotland: legal asst 1970–73, sr legal asst 1973–82, divnl slr 1982–87, dep slr 1987–; *Recreations* golf, dog walking; *Clubs* Edinburgh Univ Staff; *Style*— Norman Boe, Esq; ✉ Solicitor's Office, Scottish Office, New St Andrew's House, Edinburgh, Lothian (☎ 0131 244 4884)

BOEVEY, *see:* Crawley-Boevey

BOGAN, Anthony Robert Liam; s of Col Robert Bogan, of London, and Patricia, *née* Knight; *b* 30 Oct 1958; *Educ* St George's Coll Weybridge, Univ of Keele (BA); *m* 1994, Julia Gilson; 1 da (Alexandra b 2 Nov 1995); *Career* admitted slr 1985, ptnr Saunders & Co 1987, in private practice with Bogan Gilson; memb Cncl Law Soc 1995–, memb Ctee Surrey Law Soc, co-fndr and chm Slrs' Assoc 1996; FRSA; *Recreations* rowing, gardening, writing; *Style*— Anthony Bogan, Esq; ✉ Bogan Gilson, 35 Petersham Road, Richmond-upon-Thames, Surrey TW10 6UH (☎ 0181 940 6457)

BOGARDE, Sir Dirk; kt (1992); *né* Derek Niven van den Bogaerde; er s of Ulric van den Bogaerde, first art ed of The Times (d 1972), and Margaret (d 1980), da of Forest Niven; *b* 28 March 1921; *Educ* Univ Coll Sch, Allan Glen's Scotland; *Career* actor and author; serv WWII, Queen's Royal Regt 1940–46; Hon DLitt St Andrews Univ 1985; Commandeur de l'Ordre des Arts et des Lettres 1990 (Chevalier 1982); *Theatre* incl: Cliff in Power Without Glory 1947, Orpheus in Point of Departure 1950, Nicky in The Vortex 1953, Alberto in Summertime 1955–56, Jezebel (Oxford Playhouse) 1958; *Television* incl: The Patricia Neal Story (film, USA) 1981, May We Borrow Your Husband? (play) 1986, The Vision (film) 1987; *Films* incl: Hunted 1947, Appointment in London, They Who Dare, The Sleeping Tiger, Doctor in the House, Doctor at Sea, Doctor at Large, Simba, The Spanish Gardener, Cast a Dark Shadow, Ill Met by Moonlight, The Blue Lamp, So Long at the Fair, Quartet, Sidney Carton in A Tale of Two Cities, The Wind Cannot Read, The Doctor's Dilemma, Libel, Song Without End, The Angel Wore Red, The Singer Not the Song, Victim, HMS Defiant, The Password is Courage, The Lonely Stage, The Mindbenders, The Servant, Doctor in Distress, Hot Enough for June, The High Bright Sun, King and Country, Darling ..., Modesty Blaise, Accident, Our Mother's House, Mister Sebastian, The Fixer, Oh! What A Lovely War, Götterdämmerung, Justine, Death in Venice, Upon This Rock, Le Serpent, The Night Porter, Permission to Kill, Providence, A Bridge Too Far, Despair; *Autobiographical Books* A Postillion Struck by Lightning (1977), Snakes and Ladders (1978), An Orderly Man (1983), Backcloth (1986), A Particular Friendship (1989), Great Meadow - An Evocation (1992), A Short Walk From Harrods (1993); *Novels* A Gentle Occupation (1980), Voices in the Garden (1981), West of Sunset (1984), Jericho (1992); *Style*— Sir Dirk Bogarde; ✉ c/o Jonathan Altaras Associates Ltd, 27 Floral Street, London WC2E 9DP (☎ 0171 836 8722, fax 0171 836 6066)

BOGDANOR, Prof Vernon; s of Harry Bogdanor (d 1971), of Uxbridge, and Rosa, *née* Weinger (d 1987); *b* 16 July 1943; *Educ* Queen's Coll Oxford (BA, MA); *m* 23 July 1972, Judith Evelyn, da of Frederick Beckett (d 1985), of Oxford; 2 s; *Career* fell Brasenose Coll Oxford 1966– (sr tutor 1979–85), reader in govt Univ of Oxford 1990–96, prof of govt and politics Univ of Oxford 1996–; special advsr: House of Lords Select Ctee on Euro Communities 1982–83, House of Commons Public Service Ctee; memb: Political Studies Assoc 1966–, Cncl Hansard Soc for Parly Govt, Nat Ctee for Electoral Reform 1981–, Court Univ of Essex 1982–84, UK delgn CSCE Conf Oslo 1991, Cncl Inst of Jewish Affairs 1991–, Cncl Euro Movement 1994–; FRSA 1992; *Books* incl: The Age of Affluence 1951–64 (jt ed, 1970), Devolution (1979), The People and the Party System (1981), Liberal Party Politics (ed, 1983), Multi-Party Politics and the Constitution (1983), Science and Politics (ed, 1984), The Blackwell Encyclopaedia of Political Institutions (ed, 1987), Comparing Constitutions (jtly, 1994), The Monarchy and the Constitution (1995), Essays on Politics and the Constitution (1996); *Recreations* music, walking, talking; *Style*— Prof Vernon Bogdanor; ✉ Brasenose College, Oxford OX1 4AJ (☎ 01865 277830, fax 01865 277822)

BOGDANOV, Prof Michael; s of Francis Benzion Bogdin (d 1962), and Rhoda, *née* Rees (d 1988); *b* 15 Dec 1938; *Educ* Lower Sch of John Lyon, Harrow, Trinity Coll Dublin (MA), Univ of Munich, Sorbonne; *m* 17 Dec 1966, Patricia Ann, da of Walter Stanley Warwick (d 1985); 2 s (Jethro Rhys Warwick b 1968, Malachi Taplin b 1969), 1 da (Ffion b 1971); *Career* director and producer; prodr/dir Radio Telifis Eireann (RTE) 1966–69; artistic dir: Phoenix Theatre Leicester 1973–77, Young Vic 1978–80; assoc dir National Theatre 1980–88, artistic dir and fndr English Shakespeare Co 1986–, artistic dir/exec prodr Deutsches Schauspielhaus Hamburg 1989–92; Dir of the Year: SWET Awards 1979, Laurence Olivier Awards 1989; outstanding achievement Drama Awards 1987, Melbourne Spoleto Golden Pegasus Award 1988, BAFTA nomination and RTS Award (for Shakespeare on the Estate, BBC documentary) 1994; awarded Sr Academic Fellowship by: Leicester Poly (now De Montfort Univ) 1992, Univ of Wales Cardiff 1993; fell Welsh Coll for Music and Drama; *Recreations* sport, music, Celtic languages, wine; *Clubs* Lord's Taverners, MCC; *Style*— Prof Michael Bogdanov; ✉ English Shakespeare Company, 95 Palewell Park, London SW14 8JJ (☎ 0181 392 1958, fax 0181 392 1993)

BOGGIS-ROLFE, Richard; s of Paul Boggis-Rolfe (d 1988), of Paris, France, and (Anne) Verena, *née* Collins; *b* 5 April 1950; *Educ* Eton, Trinity Coll Cambridge (MA), London Business Sch; *m* 7 March 1987, Lucy Elisabeth, da of Lt-Col Stephen Jenkins, MC, DL, of Ballingers House, Hampnett, Glos; 1 s (James Edward b 22 Jan 1994), 2 da (Elisabeth Verena b 8 Jan 1988, Alice Catherine b 30 Aug 1990); *Career* cmmnd Coldstream Gds 1970, ADC to Lt Gen Sir Richard Worsley (GOC 1 (Br) Corps) 1975–77, Co Cdr 1977–79, Staff Capt QMG MOD 1979–80, ret Hon Maj 1980; dir: Russell Reynolds Associates 1983, Norman Broadbent International Ltd 1984–; md Norman Broadbent (Hong Kong) 1986; chm NB Selection Ltd 1995– (chief exec 1987–95), gp md BNB Resources plc 1995– (dir 1992–), chm Barkers Human Resource Advertising Ltd 1992–; Freeman City of London, Liveryman Worshipful Co of Pewterers; *Recreations* hunting, gardening, travel; *Clubs* Brooks's, Beefsteak, Pratt's; *Style*— Richard Boggis-Rolfe, Esq; ✉ The Glebe House, Shipton Moyne, Tetbury, Glos (☎ 01666 880441); 15 Brechin Place, London SW7 (☎ 0171 373 5910); L'Hermitage, Basse Nouailette, Hautefort, Dordogne, France (☎ 00 33 53 50 43 71); BNB Resources plc, 30 Farringdon Street, London EC4A 4EA (☎ 0171 634 1110, fax 0171 489 9330)

BOGIE, Sheriff David Wilson; s of Robert T Bogie (d 1978), of Edinburgh, and Isobel, *née* Wilson (d 1994); *b* 17 July 1946; *Educ* George Watson's Coll, Grenoble Univ, Edinburgh Univ (LLB), Balliol Coll Oxford (MA); *m* 1, April 1983 (m dis 1987), Lady Lucinda Louise Mackay, da of 3 Earl of Inchcape (d 1994); m 2, 1 July 1996, Mrs Margaret Jean Innes Leith, yr da of late Prof John Lothian, of Aberdeen Univ; *Career* admitted memb of Faculty of Advocates 1972, Temp Sheriff 1981; Sheriff of Grampian, Highland and Islands at Aberdeen and Stonehaven 1985–; hon lectr Faculty of Law Univ of Aberdeen 1986–; FSA (Scot); *Recreations* architecture, antiquities, heraldry; *Clubs* Brooks's, Royal Northern and Univ (Aberdeen); *Style*— Sheriff D W Bogie; ✉ 22 Forest Road, Aberdeen; Sheriff's Chambers, Sheriff Court House, Aberdeen AB9 1AP (☎ 01224 648316)

BOGLE, Joanna Margaret; da of Herbert Eric Nash, of Wallington, Surrey, and Ursula Mary, *née* Campbell; *b* 7 Sept 1952; *Educ* St Philomena's Sch Carshalton Surrey; *m* 20 Sept 1980, James Stewart Lockhart Bogle, s of Brig Bruce Lockhart Bogle; *Career* journalist, author and broadcaster; cncllr London Borough of Sutton 1974–82, Conservative Res Dept 1978–79; regular contrib to: BBC, Catholic Times, various US and Australian papers; lecture tours USA 1976, 1977, 1986 and 1987; Women of the Year speaker 1975 (as Britain's youngest borough cncllr); FRSA 1988; *Books* The First Croydon Airport, The Great Days - Croydon Airport 1928–39, Croydon Airport and the Battle for Britain, A Book of Feasts and Seasons (1986), Celebrating Our Heritage (1988), Who Lies Where (1989), A Heart for Europe - a Life of Emperor Charles and Empress Zita of Austria-Hungary (with James Bogle, 1991), When the Summer Ended (with Cecylia Wolkowinska, 1992), Caroline Chisholm - The Emigrant's Friend (1993), Come on in - It's Awful (ed, 1994), numerous political and religious pamphlets; *Recreations* family life: nieces and nephews; eating chocolate cake, walking in rain; *Style*— Mrs Joanna Bogle; ✉ 34 Barnard Gardens, New Malden, Surrey KT3 6QG

BOGOJEVIĆ, HE Rajko; s of Branislav Bogojević (d 1987), and Marija, *née* Tomić; *b* 29 Feb 1948; *Educ* Eight Belgrade Gimnasium, Faculty of Political Sciences Belgrade; *m* 1968, Mirjana, da of Dobrota Ljubomir; 1 s (Mario b 1969), 1 da (Bojana b 1974); *Career* Yugoslav diplomat; Miny of Foreign Affairs of Yugoslavia: attaché N American Dept 1973–74, third sec W European Dept 1974–76, second sec Embassy Guyana 1976–80, first sec N American Dept 1980–83, first sec Embassy Finland 1983–87, cnsllr Int Orgns Dept 1987–89, chief of gp for GB, Ireland and Nordic Countries W European Dept 1989–91; head of W European/N American Dept Miny for Foreign Affairs of Serbia 1991–92, Miny for Foreign Affairs of Yugoslavia 1992, Yugoslav min cnsllr-chargé d'affaires to the Ct of St James's 1992–; *Style*— HE Mr Rajko Bogojevic; ✉ Embassy of the Federal Republic of Yugoslavia, 5 Lexham Gardens, London W8 5JJ (☎ 0171 370 6105, fax 0171 370 3838)

BOHM, Nicholas David Frederick; s of Franz Bohm (d 1993), and Johanna Cecilia, *née* Bauer; *b* 12 July 1943; *Educ* Leighton Park Sch Reading, St John's Coll Cambridge (MA); *m* Carola Ann, *née* Freeman; 5 c; *Career* asst slr Gregory Rowcliffe & Co 1968–70 (articled clerk 1966–68); ptnr: Edward Moeran & Partners 1970–72, Norton Rose 1975–94 (asst slr 1972–75); independent conslt slr 1994–; Freeman City of London, memb City of London Solicitors' Co; *Recreations* computers, rough gardening; *Style*— Nicholas Bohm, Esq; ✉ Salkyns, Great Canfield, via Takeley, Bishop's Stortford CM22 6SX (☎ 01279 870285, fax 01279 870215)

BOHT, Jean; da of Thomas Herbert Dance (d 1970), of Birkenhead, and Edna May, *née* McDonald (d 1989); *b* 6 March 1936; *Educ* Wirral GS for Girls Bebington, Hilary Burrow's Ballet Sch Liverpool; *m* 1 (m dis 1970), William P Boht (d 1975); m 2, 1971, Carl Davis, *qv*, s of Irving Davis (d 1988); 2 da (Hannah Louise b 1 Jan 1972, Jessie Jo b 3 May 1974); *Career* actress; patron: Br Homoeopathic Assoc, CMV Fndn, Health Unlimited, Clare's Children's Hopice, Thornberry Animal Sanctuary, SOS, Hoylake Cottage Hosp, Parents for Safe Food, Tommy's Campaign, Lung Cancer Appeal, Merseyside Kidney Fndn, Vera Gray Tst; hon Lady Taverner; hon fell John Moores Univ 1992; *Theatre* Liverpool Playhouse 1962–64, Bristol Old Vic Co 1964, Royal Court 1965–66, Library Theatre Manchester 1966–67, NT 1968 and 1971, Lincoln Theatre Royal 1969, Joan Littlewood's Theatre Workshop 1969–71, Chichester Festival 1992–94; credits incl: St Joan of the Stockyards (Queens) 1964, Steel Magnolias (Lyric) 1990, Bread (Dominion) 1990–91, Dangerous Corner (Whitehall) 1995, Kindertransport (Vaudeville) 1996; fringe incl: Kennedy's Children (Kings Head Islington) 1974, Mecca (Open Space) 1977, Wednesday (Bush) 1979, Touched and To Come Home To This (Royal Court) 1980, Birds of Passage (Hampstead) 1983, Lost (Bush) 1986; tours incl: Dangerous Corner 1994–95, Pride and Prejudice 1995; *Television* plays incl: Where Adam Stood, Cranford, Eskimos Do It; series incl: Funny Man, Spyship, Sons and Lovers, Boys From The Black Stuff, Scully, I Woke Up One Morning, Bread, Brighton Belles; many guest appearances in comedy series, game shows, charity TV shows and radio plays; *Recordings* The Pigeon (by Carla Lane) 1990; *Films* incl: Meddle Not With Change, Distant Voices, Girl On A Swing, Arthur's Hallowed Ground, The Big Game, Jim's Gift; *Awards* incl: BBC TV Personality 1988 (Variety Club of GB), Top Comedy Television Actress 1990 (The Br Comedy Awards), Top Television Personality 1990 (Whitbread Scouseology Awards); *Recreations* fndr Barnes Theatre Co (an amateur gp for teenagers formed in 1985); *Style*— Miss Jean Boht; ✉ c/o Derek Webster, AIM, 5 Denmark Street, London WC2H 8LP (☎ 0171 836 2001, fax 0171 379 0848)

BOILEAU, Lt-Col Sir Guy Francis; 8 Bt (UK 1838), of Tacolnestone Hall, Norfolk; s of Sir Edmond Charles Boileau, 7 Bt (d 1980), and Marjorie Lyle, *née* D'Arcy; *b* 23 Feb 1935; *Educ* Xavier Coll Melbourne, RMC Duntroon Aust; *m* 1962, Judith Frances, da of Sen George Conrad Hannan, of Glen Iris, Canberra; 2 s (Nicholas Edmond George b 1964, Christopher Guy b 1969), 3 da (Simone Teresa b 1963, Caroline Virginia b 1968, Antonia Josephine b 1975); *Heir* s, Nicholas Edmond George Boileau b 17 Nov 1964; *Career* Lt-Col Australian Army; co dir, sports administrator; *Recreations* boating, fishing, tennis; *Clubs* The Heroes (Victoria); *Style*— Lt-Col Sir Guy Boileau, Bt; ✉ 14 Faircroft Ave, Glen Iris, Victoria 3146, Australia

BOILING, James; s of Graham Boiling, and Geraldine, *née* Currie; *b* 8 April 1968; *Educ* Rutlish Sch Merton, Univ of Durham (BA); *Career* professional cricketer; Surrey CCC 1988–94, Durham CCC 1995–; rep: Combined Univs 1988–90, Young England in Youth World Cup Aust 1988 (8 caps), England A Team Aust 1993; off-seasons: Treasy Div Lloyd's Bank 1990–91, player and coach Bionics CC Harare Zimbabwe 1991–92, player and coach St Augustine's CC Cape Town SA 1992–93; NCA sr coaching award, Daily Telegraph Under 19 Bowler of the Year 1986; *Recreations* travel, theatre, history, blues and jazz music, walking, most sports; *Style*— James Boiling, Esq; ✉ Durham CCC, Riverside Ground, Chester-Le-Street, Co Durham

BOISSIER, Roger Humphrey; CBE (1992); 3 and yst s of Ernest Gabriel Boissier, DSC, CEng, FIEE (d 1976), of Derby, and Doris Mary, *née* Bingham (d 1958), of Bingham's Melcombe, Dorset; descended from Gaspard Boissier (d 1705), of Geneva, whose grandson Jean-Daniel Boissier (d 1770), settled in England at Lime Grove, Putney (*see* Burke's Landed Gentry, 18 edn, vol I, 1965); *b* 30 June 1930; *Educ* Harrow; *m* 30 Oct 1965, (Elizabeth) Bridget (Rhoda), eldest da of Sir Gerald Gordon Ley, 3 Bt, TD (d 1980); (see Debrett's Peerage & Baronetage, 1980); 1 s (Rupert John b 25 May 1967), 1 da (Clare Louise b 16 Nov 1968); *Career* md Aiton & Co Ltd 1975–83 (joined 1955), exec dir Whessoe plc 1975–83; chm Pressac Holdings plc 1990– (dir 1984–, dep chm 1989–90); non-exec dir: Derbyshire Building Society 1972–81, Simmonds Precision NV (Holland) 1976–82, Ley's Foundries and Engineering plc 1977–82, British Gas plc (formerly British Gas Corporation) 1981–96, Severn Trent plc (formerly Severn Trent Water Authy) 1986–, T & N plc 1987–, Edward Lumley Holdings Ltd 1988–, Kalon Group plc 1992– (chm 1992–95), AMEC Power Ltd 1992–94, AMEC Mechanical and Electrical Services Ltd 1994–96, Allott & Lomax 1996– (advsr 1984–96); a vice pres Br Jr Chambers of Commerce 1961–64, memb Br Nat Ctee (now Br Energy Assoc) World Energy Cncl 1971– (chm 1977–80); High Sheriff of Derbyshire 1987–88; govr: Harrow Sch 1976–96 (dep chm 1988), Landau Forte City Technol Coll Derby 1995–; memb Ct and Cncl Loughborough Univ 1991–; Freeman City of London, Master Worshipful Co of Tin Plate Workers alias Wire Workers 1988–89; CIGasE 1983, FInstD 1984, FRSA 1987, CInstE 1991; *Recreations* cars, reading, foreign travel, meeting people; *Clubs* Brooks's, MCC, Surrey CCC, County (Derby); *Style*— Roger Boissier, Esq, CBE; ✉ Easton House, The Pastures, Repton, Derby DE65 6GG (☎ 01283 702274, fax 01283 701489); Pressac Holdings plc, Park House, 104 Derby Road, Long Eaton, Nottingham NG10 4LS (☎ 0115 946 2525, fax 0115 946 2481)

BOIZOT, Peter James; MBE (1986); s of Gaston Charles Boizot, and Susannah, *née* Culshaw; *b* 16 Nov 1929; *Educ* King's Sch Peterborough (chorister Peterborough

Cathedral 1940–44), St Catharine's Coll Cambridge (MA, fell commoner 1996); *Career* Nat Serv 1948–50, cmmnd RASC; capt MV YARVIC 1951; various sales jobs 1953–64; PizzaExpress: fndr 1965, chm and md 1965–93, chm PizzaExpress plc (following flotation) 1993–96, pres 1996–; proprietor: Pizza on the Park 1976–, Kettners Restaurant 1980–, Great Northern Hotel (Peterborough) 1993–; dir Connoisseur Casino 1970–82; publisher: Jazz Express magazine 1983, Boz magazine 1994, Hockey Sport, World Hockey; pres Hampstead & Westminster Hockey Club 1986, a vice pres Hockey Assoc 1990; fndr memb Soho Soc, fndr chm Soho Restaurateurs' Assoc 1980, dir Soho Jazz Festival 1986–96; chm Westminster Chamber of Commerce 1992–94, memb Cncl London Chamber of Commerce 1992–; Parliamentary candidate (Lib) Peterborough Gen Elections Feb and Oct 1974, former pres Eastern Region Liberal Party; Bolla Award 1983, Hotel and Caterer Food Service Award 1989, Hon LLD Westminster Univ 1995; Cavaliere Ufficiale Al Merito della Repubblica Italiana 1983; FHCIMA 1989; *Books* Pizza Express Cook Book (1976, new edn 1991); *Recreations* hockey, jazz, eating out; *Clubs* RAC, National Liberal; *Style—* Peter Boizot, Esq, MBE; ✉ 10 Lowndes Square London SW1X 9HA (☎ 0171 235 9100); Kettners Restaurant, 29 Romilly Street, London W1V 6HP (☎ 0171 437 6437, fax 0171 434 1214)

BOKSENBERG, Prof Alexander; CBE (1996); s of Julius Boksenberg, and Ernestina Steinberg; *b* 18 March 1936; *Educ* Stationers' Co Sch, Univ of London (BSc, PhD); *m* 1960, Adella Coren; 1 s, 1 da; *Career* Dept of Physics and Astronomy UCL: SRC res asst 1960–65, lectr in Physics 1965–75, head of Optical and Ultraviolet Astronomy Res Gp 1969–81, reader in Physics 1975–78, SRC sr fell 1976–81, prof of physics 1978–81, visiting prof 1981–; dir: Royal Greenwich Observatory 1981–93, Royal Observatories (Royal Greenwich Observatory Cambridge, Royal Observatory Edinburgh, Isaac Newton Gp of Optical Telescopes Canary Islands, Jt Astronomy Centre Hawaii) 1993–; exec ed Experimental Astronomy 1995–; Sherman Fairchild distinguished scholar Calif Inst of Technol 1981–82, visiting prof Univ of Sussex 1981–89, hon prof of experimental astronomy Univ of Cambridge 1991–; pres W London Astronomical Soc 1978–, pres and memb Int Scientific Ctee Canary Islands Observatories 1981–; hon pres Astronomical Soc of Glasgow; chm: New Industrial Concepts Ltd 1969–81, SRC Astronomy Ctee 1980–81, Int Expert Ctee Gemini Telescopes Project 1992, UK Gemini Telescopes Steering Ctee; memb and dep chm Anglo-Aust Telescope Bd 1989–92; memb: Instrument Definition Team Hubble Space Telescope Euro Space Agency 1973–, Advsy Ctee South African Astronomical Observatory 1978–85, Science Advsy Ctee Br Cncl 1987–91, Hubble Space Telescope Users Ctee 1990–91, Fachbeirat Max-Planck-Institut für Astronomie 1991–, USA Gemini Telescopes Oversight Ctee 1993–94, Visiting Ctee Euro Southern Observatory 1993–, Cncl Royal Society; memb and or chm of more than 30 other bds or ctees; memb Court Worshipful Co of Clockmakers 1994 (Freeman 1984, Liveryman 1989); Dr hc l'Observatoire de Paris 1982, Hon DSc Univ of Sussex 1991; asteroid (3205) Boksenberg named 1988; memb Academia Europaea 1989, fell UCL 1991; FRAS 1965, FRS 1978, FRSA 1984; *Books* Modern Technology and its Influence on Astronomy (jt ed, 1990); contrib to various learned jls; *Recreations* skiing; *Clubs* Athenaeum; *Style—* Prof Alexander Boksenberg, CBE, FRS; ✉ Royal Greenwich Observatory, Madingley Road, Cambridge CB3 0EZ (☎ 01223 374886, fax 01223 374778)

BOLAM, Simon; s of Alexander Crossman Bolam (d 1963), of Berwick-upon-Tweed, and Elizabeth Mary, *née* Drybrough (d 1990); *b* 5 Sept 1942; *Educ* St Mary's Sch Melrose, Glenalmond Coll; *m* 6 July 1968, Sylvia Forsyth, da of Sidney Dawson Ranson; 2 da (Caroline b 5 March 1970, Valerie b 5 May 1971); *Career* with Royal Insurance Edinburgh then Liverpool 1961–70; E H Ranson & Co Insurance Brokers: joined 1970, ptnr 1971, owner 1972–; Insurance Soc of Edinburgh: sec 1986, dep pres 1988, pres 1989, a vice pres 1990–; Chartered Insurance Inst: memb Cncl 1988–, chm Mktg and Pubns Ctee and hon ed CII Jl 1989, chm Educn Ctee and a govr CII's Coll of Insurance 1992, dep pres 1993, pres 1994–95; Br Insurance and Investmt Brokers' Assoc: chm Scottish Ctee 1986, chm Motor Ctee 1986, chm Educn and Employment Policy Ctee 1996–, dep chm Gen Insur Broking Ctee 1996–, memb Nat Bd 1996–; memb Nat Exec Round Table 1981–83; underwriting memb Lloyd's 1989; Liveryman Worshipful Co of Insurers 1990; High Constable City of Edinburgh; FCII 1971 (ACII 1961), FRSA 1995; *Recreations* hillwalking, cycling; *Style—* Simon Bolam, Esq; ✉ 14 Ramsay Garden, Edinburgh EH1 2NA (☎ 0131 225 1849); E H Ranson & Co, 11 Coates Crescent, Edinburgh EH3 7AT (☎ 0131 225 9136, fax 0131 220 6149)

BOLD, Alan Norman; s of William Bold (d 1956), of Edinburgh, and Marjorie Urquhart Wilson (d 1983); *b* 20 April 1943; *Educ* Broughton Secdy Sch, Univ of Edinburgh; *m* 29 June 1963, Alice, *née* Howell; 1 da (Valentina b 5 April 1964); *Career* journalist The Times Educational Supplement Scotland 1965–66, full time writer and visual artist 1966–; contribs to The Sunday Times, The Times Higher, TLS, Observer, currently reviewer The Glasgow Herald; hon pres Auchinleck Boswell Soc 1992; exhibitions of illuminated poems: Univ of Boston, Nat Library of Scotland, Cheltenham Festival, Poetry Soc London, Demarco Gallery, City Arts Centre Edinburgh; illuminated poems in public collections incl: Scottish Nat Gallery of Modern Art, Scottish Arts Cncl; received Annual Arts Award Royal Philosophical Soc of Glasgow 1990; *poetry incl* Society Inebrious (1965), A Perpetual Motion Machine (1969), The Auld Symie (1971), A Pint of Bitter (1971), This Fine Day (1979), Summoned by Knox (1985), Bright Lights Blaze Out (1986); stories: Hammer and Thistle (1975), The Edge of the Wood (1984); *novel* East is West (1991); *non-fiction incl* Thom Gunn & Ted Hughes (1976), The Sensual Scot (1982), MacDiarmid The Terrible Crystal (1983), MacDiarmid A Critical Biography (1988, awarded McVitie's Prize 1989, Scottish Writer of the Year), Scotland A Literary Guide (1989), A Burns Companion (1990); *books edited incl* The Penguin Book of Socialist Verse (1970), Making Love The Picador Book of Erotic Verse (1978), The Sexual Dimension in Literature (1983), Byron Wrath and Rhyme (1983), The Poetry of Motion (1984), Auden The Far Interior (1985), The Quest for Le Carré (1988), Rhymer Rab (1993); *Recreations* gardening, playing the saxophone; *Style—* Alan Bold, Esq; ✉ Balbirnie Burns East Cottage, nr Markinch, Glenrothes, Fife KY7 6NE (☎ and fax 01592 757216)

BOLD, Simon Mercer; s of Thomas George Mercer Bold (d 1996), and Joyce Mary, *née* Denny (d 1993); *b* 19 July 1945; *Educ* Hampton GS, Woking County GS; *m* 1, 1969, Jacqueline Ann, da of Kenneth Camp; 1 s (Benjamin Nicholas Mercer b 1972), 1 da (Victoria Jane b 1974); m 2, 1987, Anna Olive, da of Edward George Pocknell; 1 da (Sophie Louise b 1987); *Career* articled clerk Harvey Preen & Co 1963–68 (tax mangr 1969–72); Coopers & Lybrand: tax supervisor 1972–73, tax mangr 1973–74, gp sr tax mangr 1975–77; tax ptnr Slater Chapman & Cooke 1977–80; sr tax mangr Arthur Andersen 1981–83 (head of tax Reading 1984–86); tax ptnr: Grant Thornton Reading 1987–90, Pannell Kerr Forster Nottingham 1990–; FCA 1970; *Recreations* sailing, shooting; *Style—* Simon Bold, Esq; ✉ Pannell Kerr Forster, Regent House, Clinton Avenue, Nottingham NG5 1AZ (☎ 0115 960 8171, fax 0115 960 3665)

BOLÉAT, Mark John; s of Paul John Boléat, and Edith Maud, *née* Still; *b* 21 Jan 1949; *Educ* Victoria Coll Jersey, Coventry Univ (BA), Univ of Reading (MA); *m* 13 May 1991, Elizabeth Ann, *née* Barker; *Career* asst master Dulwich Coll 1972, economist Indust Policy Gp 1973; Building Societies Assoc: asst sec 1974–76, under sec 1976–79, dep sec 1979–81, dep sec gen 1981–86, sec gen 1986–87, dir gen 1987–93; sec gen Int Union of Housing Finance Instns 1986–89; dir gen: Cncl of Mortgage Lenders 1989–93, Assoc of Br Insurers 1993–; chm: Govrs Eastbury Farm Sch 1989–92, Circle 33 Housing Tst 1990–93; memb: Bd Housing Corp 1988–93, Cncl Assoc of Soc Execs 1995–; author of various articles on housing and housing finance; *Books* The Building Society Industry (1982, 2 edn 1986), National Housing Finance Systems - A Comparative Study (1985), The Mortgage Market (with Adrian Coles, 1987), Building Societies - The Regulatory Framework (1992), Housing in Britain (1993), Trade Association Strategy and Management (1996); *Recreations* squash, golf, reading; *Clubs* Carlton, Moor Park Golf; *Style—* Mark Boléat, Esq; ✉ 26 Westbury Rd, Northwood, Middx HA6 3BU; Association of British Insurers, 51 Gresham St, London EC2V 7HQ (☎ 0171 600 3333, fax 0171 216 7302)

BOLES, Sir Jeremy John Fortescue; 3 Bt (UK 1922), of Bishop's Lydeard, Somerset; s of Capt Sir Gerald Fortescue Boles, 2 Bt (d 1945); *b* 9 Jan 1932; *Educ* Stowe; *m* 1, 1955 (m dis 1970), Dorothy Jane, yr da of James Alexander Worswick, of Enmore, Somerset; 2 s (Richard Fortescue b 1958, David Hastings Fortescue b 1967), 1 da (Sarah Jane (Mrs Paul Bird) b 1956); m 2, 1970 (m dis 1981), Elisabeth Gildroy, yr da of Edward Phillip Shaw, of Englefield Green, Surrey, and wid of Oliver Simon Willis Fleming; 1 da (Jessica Blanche Mary b 1971); m 3, 1982, Marigold Aspey, eld da of Donald Seckington, of Clevedon, Avon; *Heir* s, Richard Fortescue Boles b 12 Dec 1958; *Style—* Sir Jeremy Boles, Bt; ✉ Buttys, Stogumber, Taunton, Somerset TA4 3TD (☎ 01984 656300)

BOLES, Sir John Dennis (Jack); kt (1983), MBE (1960), DL (Devon 1991); s of Cdr Geoffrey Coleridge Boles (d 1976), and Hilda Frances, *née* Crofton; *b* 25 June 1925; *Educ* Winchester; *m* 1, Benita (d 1969), da of Maj Leslie Graham Wormald; 2 s, 3 da; m 2, 1971, Lady Anne Hermione Waldegrave, 4 da of 12 Earl Waldegrave, KG, GCVO, TD (d 1995); *Career* served Rifle Bde 1943–46; Colonial Serv N Borneo 1947–64; National Trust: asst sec 1965–68, sec 1968–75, dir gen 1975–83, memb Devon and Cornwall Regnl Ctee 1985–95; dir SW Regnl Bd Lloyds Bank 1984–91; tstee Ernest Cook Tst; High Sheriff Devon 1993–94; *Clubs* Army and Navy; *Style—* Sir Jack Boles, MBE, DL; ✉ Rydon House, Talaton, nr Exeter, Devon EX5 2RP (☎ 01404 850225)

BOLES, Richard Fortescue; s and h of Sir Jeremy John Fortescue Boles, 3 Bt, *qv*, and Dorothy Jane, *née* Worswick; *b* 12 Dec 1958; *m* 26 May 1990, Allison Beverley, da of Brian MacDonald; 1 s (James Alexander Fortescue b 25 May 1993), 1 da (Samantha Jane b 1 July 1996); *Style—* Richard Boles, Esq; ✉ 3 Orchard Close, Lower Cross, Clearwell, Coleford, Glos GL16 8LX (☎ 01594 834414); Forestry Authority, Wye and Avon Conservancy, Bank House, Bank Street, Coleford, Glos GL16 8BA (☎ 01594 810983)

BOLES, Timothy Coleridge; s of Vernon Coleridge Boles, and Elizabeth Ann, *née* Spence-Thomas; *b* 27 Nov 1959; *Educ* Eton, RMC Sandhurst; *Career* cmmnd into RHG/D (Blues & Royals), Capt 1982–86, special reserve cmmn 1987; Sedgwick Underwriting Agencies 1986–88; dir: Gardner Mountain and Capel Cure Agencies Ltd 1989–94, Harrison Brothers 1994–; GSM Northern Ireland, UN Peacekeeping Medal 1982; FRGS 1983, memb Chartered Insurance Inst 1988; *Recreations* winter sports, shooting, poetry, theatre (acting); *Clubs* Shikar, Cavalry & Guards, City; *Style—* Timothy Boles, Esq; ✉ Old Clune Lodge, Tomatin, Inverness-shire (☎ 01808 511208); 9 Cabul Rd, Battersea, London SW11

BOLGER, Dermot; s of Roger Bolger, of Dublin, and Bridie, *née* Flanagan (d 1969); *b* 6 Feb 1959; *Educ* St Canice's Boys' Sch, Nat Sch Finglas, Beneavin Coll Finglas; *m* 17 Dec 1988, Bernadette, da of Vincent Clifton; 2 s (Donnacha b 30 Nov 1990, Diarmuid b 1 May 1992); *Career* writer; factory hand 1978–79, library asst 1979–84, ed and fndr Raven Arts Press 1979–92, exec ed New Island Books 1992–; memb: Arts Cncl of Ireland 1989–93, Aosdána 1991–; ed of numerous poetry and prose anthologies incl The Picador Book of Contemporary Irish Fiction (1993); *Novels* Night Shift (1985, A E Meml prize 1986), The Woman's Daughter (1987, extended version 1991, Macaulay fell 1987, shortlisted Hughes Fiction prize 1988), The Journey Home (1990, shortlisted Irish Times/Aer Lingus prize 1992, shortlisted Hughes Fiction prize 1990), Emily's Shoes (1992), A Second Life (1994), Father's Music (1997); *Poetry* The Habit of Flesh (1979), Finglas Lilies (1980), No Waiting America (1981), Internal Exile (1986), Leinster Street Ghosts (1989); *Plays* The Lament for Arthur Cleary (first staged Dublin Theatre Festival 1989, Samuel Beckett award, Stewart Parker BBC award, Edinburgh Fringe First), Blinded by the Light (Abbey Theatre Dublin 1990, A Z Whitehead prize), In High Germany (Dublin Theatre Festival 1990, filmed for RTE TV) 1993, The Holy Ground (Gate Theatre Dublin) 1990, One Last White Horse (Dublin Theatre Festival and Abbey Theatre) 1992, April Bright (Abbey Theatre) 1995; *Film* The Disappearance of Finbar (C4) 1996; *Recreations* soccer, golf; *Style—* Dermot Bolger, Esq; ✉ c/o A P Watts, 20 John Street, London WC1N 2DR (☎ 0171 405 6774, fax 0171 831 2154)

BOLINGBROKE AND ST JOHN, 7 Viscount (GB 1712); Sir Kenneth Oliver Musgrave St John; 11 Bt (E 1611); also Baron St John of Lydiard Tregoze (GB 1712), Viscount St John and Baron St John of Battersea (GB 1716); s of Capt Geoffrey St John, MC (d 1972); suc kinsman 1974; *b* 22 March 1927; *Educ* Eton; *m* 1, 1953 (m dis 1972), Patricia Mary, da of B J McKenna, of Christchurch, NZ; 1 s; m 2, 1972 (m dis 1987) Jainey Anne, da of late Alexander Duncan McRae, of Timaru, NZ; 2 s (Hon Oliver b 1972, Hon Nicholas b 1974); *Heir* s, Hon Henry St John b 18 May 1957; *Career* patron of one living; pres of Travel Agents Assoc of NZ 1966–68, dir of World Assoc of Travel Agencies 1967–75; chm: Atlantic & Pacific Travel Gp of Cos 1958–76, Australian Cncl of Tours Wholesalers 1972–75; dir Bolingbroke and Ptnrs Ltd; fell of Aust Inst of Travel; *Recreations* tennis, history, cricket; *Clubs* Christchurch Club (Christchurch); *Style—* The Rt Hon The Viscount Bolingbroke and St John; ✉ 15 Tonbridge Mews, Shrewsbury St, Christchurch, New Zealand

BOLLAND, Alexander; QC (1992); s of James Bolland, of Kilmarnock, and Agnes Elizabeth, *née* Anderson; *b* 21 Nov 1950; *Educ* Kilmarnock Acad, Univ of St Andrews (BD), Univ of Glasgow (LLB); *m* 4 July 1973, Agnes Hunter Pate, da of George Pate Moffat; 2 da (Hilary Louise b 11 Sept 1980, Sophia Francesca b 1 Sept 1984), 1 s (Miles Louis James b 6 Aug 1991); *Career* apprentice Maclay, Murray & Spens 1976–77, pupil advocate 1977–78, admitted Scottish Bar 1978, capt Army Legal Services (later Army Legal Corps) BAOR and UKLF 1978–80, procurator fiscal depute 1980–82, in private practice Scottish Bar 1982–, standing jr counsel to Dept of Employment 1988–92, temp sheriff 1989–; pt/t chm Industl Tbnls 1992–; *Recreations* reading, hellenistics; *Clubs* Naval and Military, RSAC; *Style—* Alexander Bolland, Esq, QC; ✉ 60 North Street, St Andrews, Fife KY16 9AH (☎ 01334 474599); Advocates' Library, Parliament House, Edinburgh EH1 1RF

BOLLAND, Sir Edwin; KCMG (1981, CMG 1971); s of George Bolland, of Morley, Yorks; *b* 20 Oct 1922; *Educ* Morley GS, Univ Coll Oxford; *m* 1948, Winifred, da of William Mellor, of Morley, Yorks; 1 s, 3 da; *Career* HM Dip Serv: entered FO 1947, head Far Eastern Dept 1965–67, cnsllr Washington 1967–71, ambass Bulgaria 1973–76, head Br Delgn to Negotiate Mutual and Balanced Force Reductions (MBFR) 1976–80, ambass Yugoslavia 1980–82; *Recreations* walking, gardening; *Style—* Sir Edwin Bolland, KCMG; ✉ Lord's Spring Cottage, Godden Green, Sevenoaks, Kent TN15 0JS

BOLLAND, Mark William; s of Robert Arthur Bolland (d 1993), and Joan, *née* Barker; *b* 10 April 1966; *Educ* King's Manor Sch Middlesbrough, Univ of York (BSc); *Career* public affairs exec Public Affairs Int Ltd Toronto 1986–87, mktg exec IBM (UK) Ltd 1987–88, advsr to DG Advtg Standards Authy 1988–91; Press Complaints Cmmn: exec asst to Chm 1991–92, dir 1992–96; asst private sec to HRH The Prince of Wales 1996–; MInstD; *Recreations* reading, theatre, music, walking; *Style—* Mark Bolland, Esq

BOLLERS, Hon Sir Harold Brodie Smith; kt (1969); s of late John Bollers; *b* 5 Feb 1915; *Educ* Queen's Coll Guyana, King's Coll London; *m* 1, 1951, Irene Mahadeo (d 1965); 2 s, 1 da; m 2, 1968, Eileen Indrani, da of James Hanoman; 1 s; *Career* called to the Bar

Middle Temple 1938, sr magistrate Guyana 1949 (magistrate 1946), puisne judge Guyana 1960, chief justice of Guyana 1966–81, chm Elections Cmmn 1982–91; *Recreations* reading, walking; *Style*— The Hon Sir Harold Bollers; ✉ c/o Chief Justice's Residence, 245 Vlissengen Rd, Georgetown, Guyana; 252 South Rd, Bounda, Georgetown

BOLONGARO, Michael Francis; s of Louis Harold Bolongaro (d 1969), of Tapley, Fleetwood Rd, Fleetwood, Lancs, and Millicent Dorcus, *née* Wrathall (d 1963); *b* 22 Feb 1930; *Educ* St Joseph's Coll Blackpool; *m* 30 Dec 1958, Anne June, da of John Frederick Dodding (d 1981), of The White Hart Hotel, Exeter; 3 s (Gregory John b 1966, Dominic Louis b 1972, Guy Francis b 1978), 4 da (Clare Celeste b 1962, Lucy Anne b 1965, Catherine Emma b 1968, Emma Louise b 1971); *Career* chartered surveyor; estates surveyor Shell-Mex and BP 1955–65, chief valuer of Dublin City & Co 1970–73, fine art conslt and connoisseur of old master paintings 1975–; FRICS; *Recreations* mountain walking, historical and art study; *Style*— Michael Bolongaro, Esq; ✉ Woodlands, Queens Rd, Kendal, Cumbria (☎ 01539 727934), La Tuilerie, Montalembert, 79190 Sauzé Vaussais, France (☎ 00 33 49 07 77 55)

BOLSOVER, John Derrick; s of Dr G D Bolsover, MBE (d 1987), and Yoma Constance, *née* Stephens (d 1993); *b* 21 June 1947; *Educ* Repton, McGill Univ Canada (BA); *m* (m dis 1994); 2 s (Michael b 1976, Lincoln b 1978), 1 da (Jacqueline b 1974); *Career* chm and chief exec offr Baring Asset Management Ltd 1985–; *Recreations* golf, shooting; *Clubs* Boodle's, Sunningdale Golf, Valderrama Golf; *Style*— John Bolsover, Esq; ✉ Baring Asset Management Ltd, 155 Bishopsgate, London EC2M 3XY (☎ 0171 628 6000, fax 0171 638 7928)

BOLT, Roderick Langston; s of late Lt Cdr Geoffrey Peter Langston Bolt, and Mrs Margaret Elmslie Ashley Hall, *née* Brebner; *b* 14 Oct 1943; *Educ* Sedbergh; *m* 20 July 1968, Gillian Rosamond, da of late Lt-Col and Mrs J R Palmer; 1 s (Charles Henry Langston b 8 Jan 1971), 1 da (Amabel Margaret Langston b 27 May 1972); *Career* 13/18 Royal Hussars (Queen Mary's Own) 1962–67, medically discharged; asst agent for Earl of Harewood 1969–74, sr asst Cluttons 1974–77, resident agent for Lord St Oswald Wakefield 1977–79, princ land agent Hampshire CC 1979–82, factor for the Crown Estate Cmmrs Glenlivet and Auchindoun Estates with Smiths Gore 1983–86, Defence Lands Service Catterick Garrison 1986–95; FRICS 1983; *Recreations* shooting, fishing, politics; *Style*— Roderick Bolt, Esq; ✉ Graystone Lodge, Maunby, Thirsk, N Yorks YO7 4HA

BOLT, William Norris; s of William Clayton Bolt (d 1984), of Hadley Wood, Herts, and May Gertrude, *née* Norris (d 1973); *Educ* Queen Elizabeth's Sch Barnet Herts, Univ of London (BSc); *m* 1962, Judy Rae, da of John Hanson Greville-Williams; 1 da (Lucinda Jane (Lucy) b 9 June 1969); *Career* ptnr Chesterton International plc (formerly Chesterton & Sons) 1960–91 (joined 1955); dir: Fairview New Homes plc, Dwyer Estates plc; govr Suttons Hosp Charterhouse, chm Hanover Housing Assoc 1989–94; Renter Warden Worshipful Co of Wheelwrights; FRICS 1965; *Recreations* gardening, fishing, shooting, books; *Clubs* Flyfishers, Brooks's; *Style*— William Bolt, Esq; ✉ Lodkin, Lodkin Hill, Hascombe, Godalming, Surrey GU8 4JP

BOLTER, John Reginald; s of Reginald Thomas Bolter (d 1975), and Edith, *née* Wright; *b* 22 May 1928; *Educ* Manchester GS, Univ of Manchester (William Kirtley engrg scholar, BSc); *m* 1952, Vera, da of William Longworth; 2 s (Jonathan Paul b 1956, Jeremy David b 1958); *Career* C A Parsons and Co Ltd (now Parsons Power Generation Systems Ltd): graduate apprentice 1949–51, res engr Gas Turbine Dept 1951–59, asst chief engr Blower and Gas Turbine Dept 1960–64, chief designer of steam turbines 1965–66, asst chief turbine engr 1967–70, chief turbine engr 1970–73, chief mechanical engr 1974–81, engrg mangr 1982–83, engrg dir 1984–87, engrg devpt dir 1987–91, conslt 1991–; IMechE: memb Ctee Steam Plant Gp 1977–87, chm N Eastern Branch 1984–85, chm Power Industs Bd 1995–; FIMechE 1978, FEng 1987; *Recreations* rowing (currently umpire), gardening, photography, model engineering; *Style*— John Bolter, Esq, FEng

BOLTON, Anthony Hale; s of Eric Hale Bolton (d 1986), and Betty Maude (d 1986), of New Barnet, Herts; *b* 8 Aug 1942; *Educ* St Albans Sch Herts; *m* 12 May 1962, Olive Muriel, da of Thomas Brian O'Loughlin, of Brookmans Park; 1 s (David b 1968), 1 da (Jenny b 1971); *Career* chm and chief exec CT Bowring & Co (Insurance) 1993–, dep chm The Bowring Group Ltd 1996–; dir Marsh & MacLennan Inc USA 1994–; chm Aviation Ctee Lloyd's Insurance Brokers Ctee; *Recreations* golf, music, theatre, ballet; *Clubs* Brookmans Park Golf; *Style*— Anthony Bolton Esq; ✉ C T Bowring & Co (Insurance) Ltd, The Bowring Building, Tower Place, London EC3P 3BE (☎ 0171 357 5200)

BOLTON, Archdeacon of; *see:* Davies, Ven Lorys Martin

BOLTON, Bishop of 1991–; Rt Rev David Bonser; s of George Frederick Bonser (d 1981), of Huddersfield, and Alice, *née* Roe (d 1995); *b* 1 Feb 1934; *Educ* Hillhouse Secdy Sch Huddersfield, Huddersfield Tech Coll, King's Coll London (AKC), Univ of Manchester (MA); *m* 22 Aug 1960, Shirley, da of Irving Wilkinson (d 1965), of Huddersfield; 1 s (Simon b 8 March 1965), 2 da (Jane b 21 June 1963, Elizabeth b 26 April 1967); *Career* Nat Serv SAC (RAF) 1955–57; textile mangr 1958; curate St James' Heckmondwike 1962–65, asst chaplain Univ of Sheffield and curate St George's Sheffield 1965–68, rector St Clement's Chorlton-cum-Hardy Manchester 1968–82, canon Manchester Cathedral 1980–, area dean Hulme 1981–82, archdeacon of Rochdale 1982–91, team rector Rochdale Team Miny 1982–91 (vicar St Chad's 1982–86); *Recreations* golf, painting, reading, theatre; *Clubs* Commonwealth Tst; *Style*— The Rt Rev the Bishop of Bolton; ✉ 4 Sandfield Drive, Lostock, Bolton BL6 4DU (☎ 01204 843400, fax 01204 849652)

BOLTON, Prof Eric James; CB (1987); s of James Bolton (d 1951), and Lilian Bolton (d 1983); *b* 11 Jan 1935; *Educ* Wigan GS, Chester Coll, Univ of Lancaster (MA); *m* 13 Aug 1960, Ann, da of late William Charles Edward Gregory; 1 s (Benjamin b 1962), 2 da (Emma b 1966, Charlotte (twin) b 1966); *Career* Nat Serv 1953–55; teacher of English Lancs Secdy Sch 1957–67, lectr in teacher trg Chorley Coll of Higher Educn 1967–70, LEA inspr of schs Outer London Borough of Croydon 1970–73; HM Inspectorate: HM inspr of schs 1973–79, staff inspr educnl disadvantage 1979–81, chief inspr 1981–83, sr chief inspr and head 1983–91; prof for teacher educn Inst of Educn Univ of London 1991–96; FRSA 1982; *Books* Verse Writing In Schools (1964); *Recreations* reading, music and opera, fly-fishing; *Style*— Prof Eric Bolton, CB; ✉ 50 Addington Road, Sanderstead, South Croydon, Surrey CR2 8RB (☎ and fax 0181 657 6368)

BOLTON, Sir Frederic Bernard; kt (1976), MC (1945); s of Louis Hamilton Bolton (d 1953), of Woodford Halse, nr Rugby, and Beryl (d 1977), da of Dr Bernard Shirley Dyer (d 1948); *b* 9 March 1921; *Educ* Rugby; *m* 1, 1950, Valerie Margaret (d 1970), da of George Short Barwick (d 1937); 2 s; m 2, 1971, Vanessa Mary Anne, da of Lt-Col Anthony Vere Cyprian Robarts (d 1981); 2 s, 2 da; *Career* served Welsh Gds 1940–46, Maj N Africa and Italy, Northants Yeo 1952–56; shipowner; chm F Bolton Group 1953–91, Atlantic Steam Navigation Co and subsids 1960–71; dir BP Tanker Co 1968–82; pres: Chamber of Shipping 1966–67, Inst of Marine Engrs 1968–70, Br Shipping Fedn 1972–75, General Cncl of Br Shipping 1975–76, Int Shipping Fedn 1973–82, Br Maritime League 1985–91; chm Dover Harbour Bd 1983–88 (memb 1957–62 and 1980–88), Br Ports Assoc 1985–88; FIMarE; Hon FNI; *Recreations* country sports; *Clubs* City of London; *Style*— Sir Frederic Bolton, MC; ✉ Pudlicote, nr Charlbury, Oxon OX7 3HX (☎ 01608 76427)

BOLTON, Ivor; *b* 17 May 1958; *Educ* Clare Coll Cambridge, RCM, Nat Opera Studio; *m* Dr T Knighton (musicologist, journalist and broadcaster); 1 s (Sam b 26 June 1991); *Career* conductor Schola Cantorum Oxford, fndr St James's Baroque Players 1984, music dir Glyndebourne Touring Opera 1992– (joined 1982); reg conductor Bayerische Staatsoper Munich, music dir Eng Touring Opera 1991 and 1992, chief conductor Scottish Chamber Orch 1994–96; conducting debut ENO 1992 (Handel's Xerxes), debut BBC Proms 1993 (with St James's Baroque Players); *Opera* Glyndebourne Festival incl: Gluck's Orfeo 1989, Don Giovanni 1994, Le Nozze di Figaro 1994; with Glyndebourne Touring Opera: Il Barbiere di Siviglia, The Magic Flute, The Rake's Progress, La Clemenza di Tito, Eugene Onegin, Owen Wingrave; work for other cos incl: La Cenerentola and Carmen (English Touring Opera), Rossini's La Gazza Ladra (Opera North), Mozart's La Finta Giardinera (WNO), Ariadne (Garsington), Giulio Cesare and Serse (Bayerische Staatsoper), Poppea (Teatro Communale Bologna with Graham Vick), Iphigenie en Tauride (Teatro Colon Buenos Aires), Il Barbiere di Siviglia (Australian Opera), Ariadne (Opera Zuid Netherlands), Goehr's Arianna (world première Royal Opera House), Paisiello's La Molinara (Bologna), Ariodante (ENO, to be televised by BBC); *Concert performances* with LSO, BBC Scottish Symphony Orch, London Mozart Players, English Chamber Orch, English Northern Philharmonia, Bournemouth Sinfonietta, Ulster Orch, BBC Symphony Orch (recording), Montreal Symphony, Nat Arts Centre Orch Ottawa, Netherlands Chamber Orch (series Concertgebouw Amsterdam); *Recordings* with St James's Baroque Players: all Bach Harpsichord Concertos, Purcell's Dido and Aeneas, Baroque Music from Bologna; Brahms and Mendelssohn violin concertos (with London Philharmonic and Xue Wei), Popular Operatic Arias (with Lesley Garrett), Saxophone Concerti (with John Harle), Vivaldi's Stabat Mater (for Thames TV); *Style*— Ivor Bolton, Esq; ✉ 171A Goldhurst Terrace, London NW6 3ES

BOLTON, Lucinda Carol; da of Gordon Gustav-Adolf Winter, TD (d 1993), and Elspeth Kerr, *née* Bone; *b* 3 Dec 1952; *Educ* Benenden Sch, St Hugh's Coll Oxford (MA); *m* 12 June 1982, (Francis) Edward Kennaway Bolton, s of Martin Alfred Butts Bolton, DL, JP, of Croxden Abbey, Nr Uttoxeter, Staffordshire; 1 da (Camilla b 1985); *Career* dir: Guinness Mahon & Co Ltd 1987–89, Best Peninsular Homes plc 1989–96; cncllr London Borough of Hammersmith and Fulham 1980–82, memb Bd Tower Hamlets Housing Action Tst; *Style*— Mrs Lucinda Bolton; ✉ 33 St Maur Rd, London SW6

BOLTON, Lyndon; s of Brig Lyndon Bolton, DSO (d 1995), of Denwick, Alnwick, Northumberland, and Elizabeth Inglis, *née* Cran (d 1985); *b* 24 Jan 1937; *Educ* Wellington Coll, RMA Sandhurst; *m* Rosemary Jane Toler, *née* Mordaunt; 2 s; *Career* Nat Serv RA 1955–57; Deloitte Plender Griffiths & Co London 1957–63; md Alliance Trust plc and Second Alliance Trust plc until April 1995 (joined 1964); dir: General Accident Fire and Life Assurance Corp plc 1982–, TSB Group 1983–95 (trustee TSB 1970–79, bd memb 1979–83); chm TSB Group Pension Trust Ltd 1991–; govr: Dundee Coll of Educn 1980–85, Culford Sch Bury St Edmunds 1995–; memb Ct Univ of Dundee 1985–92; DL Angus 1993–95; FRSA 1993; *Recreations* sailing, golf, fishing, painting; *Clubs* New (Edinburgh); *Style*— Lyndon Bolton, Esq; ✉ Burcott, Herrings Lane, Burnham Market, Kings Lynn, Norfolk PE31 8DP

BOLTON, 7 Baron (GB 1797); Richard William Algar Orde-Powlett; s of 6 Baron Bolton (d 1963) and Victoria, da of late Henry Montagu Villiers, MVO, gn of 4 Earl of Clarendon; *b* 11 July 1929; *Educ* Eton, Trinty Coll Cambridge; *m* 1, 1951 (m dis 1981), Hon Christine Helena Weld Forester, da of 7 Baron Forester, and Marie, CStJ, da of Sir Herbert Perrott, 6 Bt, CH, CB; 2 s, 1 da; m 2, 1981, Masha Anne, da of Maj Francis Edward Hudson, of Hornby, Bedale, Yorks; m 3, 24 July 1991, Mrs Lavinia Fenton, da of late William Edward Wright; *Heir* s, Hon Harry Orde-Powlett; *Career* dir: Yorkshire Insurance Co 1964–70, General Accident Life Assurance Ltd 1970–; former chm: Waterers Group, Yorks Soc of Agric; chm: Richmond Div Cons Assoc 1957–60, Yorks Branch Royal Forestry Soc 1963–64; memb Cncl Timber Growers' Orgn; JP N Riding of Yorks 1957–78; FRICS; *Clubs* Sloane; *Style*— The Rt Hon the Lord Bolton; ✉ Bolton Hall, Leyburn, Yorks DL8 4UF (☎ 01969 622303)

BOLTON, Roger John; s of Harold Bolton, and Olive Yarker, *née* Buck; *b* 13 Nov 1945; *Educ* Carlisle GS, Univ of Liverpool (BA); *m* 1 (m dis); 2 s (Alexander b 1970, Giles b 1973); m 2, 1987, Julia Helene McLaren; 2 da (Olivia b 1988, Jessica b 1989); *Career* BBC TV: gen trainee 1967, ed Tonight Prog 1977–79, ed Panorama 1979–81, ed Nationwide 1981–83, head of Manchester Network Prodn Centre 1983–86; Thames TV: ed This Week 1986–89, controller of network factual progs 1989–92; ind prodr BBC's Heart of the Matter series 1992–; *Books* Death on the Rock and Other Stories (1990); *Recreations* reading history, visiting churches, walking, five-a-side football; *Style*— Roger Bolton, Esq; ✉ Roger Bolton Productions, The Manor House, Little Gaddesden, nr Berkamsted, Herts (☎ 01442 843718)

BOLTON, Roger William; s of William John Bolton (d 1986), of London, and Nora, *née* Dillon (d 1994); *b* 7 Sept 1947; *Educ* St Paul's, St Thomas More Sch; *m* Elaine Elizabeth, da of Harold Lewis; 1 da (Sally b 3 April 1977); *Career* photographic sales asst 1964–69, photographer BBC 1969–79, TU offr 1979–93, gen sec BECTU 1993–; *Recreations* walking, cinema, theatre, reading; *Style*— Roger Bolton, Esq; ✉ BECTU, 111 Wardour Street, London W1V 4AY (☎ 0171 437 8506, fax 0171 437 8268)

BOLTON, Prof Thomas Bruce; *b* 14 Nov 1941; *Educ* Woodhouse Grove Sch (State scholar), RVC Univ of London (BSc, BVetMed, biology, physiology, biochemistry and pharmacology medals, 2 centenary prizes, Thomson prize, Cecil Aldin prize), Univ of London (PhD), Univ of Oxford (MA), MRCVS; *m*; 3 c; *Career* veterinary surgn; lectr RVC 1965–66, Royal Soc Locke res fell Brasenose Coll Univ of Oxford 1969–76, prof St George's Hosp Med Sch 1980– (sr lectr 1976–80); memb Int Interest Gp Wellcome Tst 1992–94 (Physiology and Pharmacology Panel 1985–90), memb and vice chm Horserace Scientific Advsy Ctee for British Racing 1971–85, chm and memb Cncl Academic Bd St George's Hosp Med Sch 1989–91 and 1995–, chm Basic Med and Dental Sciences Assessment Panel UFC 1992 and HEFCE 1996; memb: EC Biomed Panel 1995, Chairs and Programme Grants Ctee British Heart Fndn 1995–; ed: British Jl of Pharmacology 1975–81, Jl of Physiology 1985–92; memb: British Pharmacological Soc 1970, Research Defence Soc 1971, Univ Fedn of Animal Welfare 1971, Physiological Soc 1971, British Biophysical Soc 1974, Biochemical Soc 1987, American Biophysical Soc 1988; *Books* Biography of Edith Bülbring (with A F Brading, 1992), Smooth Muscle Exploitation (with T Tomita, 1996); *Recreations* sport and building; *Style*— Prof Thomas B Bolton; ✉ Department of Pharmacology and Clinical Pharmacology, St George's Hospital Medical School, Cranmer Terrace, Tooting, London SW17 0RE (☎ 0181 725 5617)

BOMFORD, Nicholas Raymond; s of Ernest Raymond Bomford (d 1962), and Patricia Clive, *née* Brooke; *b* 27 Jan 1939; *Educ* Kelly Coll, Trinity Coll Oxford (MA); *m* 1966, Gillian Mary, da of Maj Peter Beckingham Reynolds (ka 1943); 2 da (Kate b 1967, Rebecca b 1969); *Career* memb academic staff: BRNC Dartmouth 1964–68, Wellington Coll 1968–76 (housemaster 1973–76); headmaster: Monmouth Sch 1977–82, Uppingham Sch 1982–91, Harrow 1991–; chm Jt Standing Ctee HMC/IAPS 1986–89, nat rep HMC Ctee 1990–91; govr: Roedean Sch 1992–, Sherborne Sch for Girls 1993–; Freeman Worshipful Co of Haberdashers 1992; FRSA 1989; *Books* Documents in World History 1914–70 (1973); *Recreations* shooting, fishing, music, gardening; *Style*— Nicholas Bomford, Esq; ✉ Peel House, Football Lane, Harrow on the Hill, Middx HA1 3EA

BOMPAS, Donald George; CMG (1966); s of Rev Edward Anstie Bompas (d 1956), of London; *b* 20 Nov 1920; *Educ* Merchant Taylors', Oriel Coll Oxford; *m* 1946, Freda Vice, da of Fred Milner Smithyman (d 1969), of Malawi; 1 s, 1 da; *Career* formerly with Overseas Audit Serv; auditor-gen: Malaya 1960–63, Malaysia 1963–66; sec: Guy's Hosp Med and Dental Schs 1969–82, United Med and Dental Schs of Guy's and St Thomas's Hosps 1984–86; managing exec: Philip & Pauline Harris Charitable Tst 1986–;

Liveryman Worshipful Co of Merchant Taylors 1951–; Hon JMN (Malaya) 1961; *Clubs* Royal Cwlth Soc; *Style*— Donald Bompas, Esq, CMG; ✉ 8 Birchwood Rd, Petts Wood, Kent BR5 1NY (☎ 01689 821661)

BOMPAS, (Anthony) George; QC (1994); s of Donald George Bompas, and Freda Vice, *née* Smithyman; *b* 6 Nov 1951; *Educ* Merchant Taylors', Oriel Coll Oxford (scholar, MA); *m* 16 Jan 1981, Donna Linda, da of John Oscar Schmidt; 2 s (Samuel Henry b 13 July 1983, Caleb George b 6 Aug 1989), 1 da (Abra Mae b 8 Aug 1985); *Career* called to the Bar Middle Temple 1975, jr counsel to DTI (Chancery) 1989–94; Liveryman Worshipful Co of Merchant Taylors 1982; *Style*— George Bompas, Esq, QC; ✉ 4 Stone Buildings, Ground Floor, Lincoln's Inn, London WC2A 3XT (☎ 0171 242 5524, fax 0171 834 7907)

BONA, HE Sir Kina; KBE (1993); *b* 14 Feb 1954, Kwato Mission, Milne Bay Province, Papua New Guinea; *Educ* secdy schs in Papua New Guinea and NSW Aust, Univ of Papua New Guinea (LLB), Univ of Clermont France (Dip in French Language); *m*; 1 c; *Career* Papua New Guinea diplomat, barr and slr; legal offr Public Prosecutor's Office 1976–78, teaching fell Law Faculty Univ of Papua New Guinea 1979, sr state prosecutor 1980–85, asst sec for justice Dept of Justice 1986–87, Public Prosecutor of Papua New Guinea 1988–94, barr and slr (assisting Min for Justice Dept of Attorney Gen) Jan-Oct 1995, high cmmr to Ct of St James's and NI Nov 1995– (concurrently ambass accredited to Israel, Egypt and Zimbabwe); Long Serv Medal (Public Serv of Papua New Guinea); memb Papua New Guinea Law Soc; *Recreations* legal and political history, international relations; *Style*— HE Sir Kina Bona, KBE; ✉ Papua New Guinea High Commission, 14 Waterloo Place, London SW1R 4AR (☎ 0171 930 0922, fax 0171 930 0828)

BONALLACK, Michael Francis; OBE (1971); s of Col Sir Richard Frank Bonallack, CBE (d 1996), and (Winifred) Evelyn Mary, *née* Esplen (d 1986); *b* 31 Dec 1934; *Educ* Chigwell Sch, Haileybury; *m* 8 Feb 1958, Angela, da of Harry Vivian Ward, of Birchington, Kent; 1 s (Robert Richard Ward b 1967), 3 da (Glenna (Mrs Beasley) b 1959, Jane (Mrs Baker) b 1961, Sara (Mrs Stocks) b 1965); *Career* Nat Serv 2 Lt RASC 1953–55; dir: Bonallack & Sons Ltd (later Freight Bonallack Ltd) 1962–74 (joined 1955), Miller Buckley and Buckley Investments Ltd 1976–84; chm: Cotton (CK) Pennink & Ptnrs Ltd 1980–83, Miller Buckley Leisure Ltd 1980–83; sec Royal and Ancient Golf Club St Andrews 1983–; 5 times Br Amateur Golf Champion, 5 times Eng Amateur Golf Champion, 4 times Eng Amateur Stroke Play Champion, twice Leading Amateur in Open Golf Championship, played for Eng 1957–74 (Capt 1962–67), played for Br Walker Cup Team 1957–73 (Capt 1969–71), awarded Bobby Jones Trophy by US Golf Assoc 1972; chm: Golf Fndn 1977–83, PGA 1976–82; pres Eng Golf Union 1982; Freeman City of London, Liveryman Worshipful Co of Coachmakers and Coach Harness Makers 1962; Hon Doctorate Univ of Stirling 1994; *Recreations* all sports, reading; *Clubs* Chantilly (France), Pine Valley (USA), Royal and Ancient (sec); *Style*— Michael Bonallack, Esq, OBE; ✉ Clatto Lodge, Blebo Craigs, Cupar, Fife KY15 5UF (☎ 01334 850600); Royal and Ancient Golf Club, St Andrews, Fife KY16 9JD (☎ 01334 472112, fax 01334 477580, telex 76348)

BONAS, Ian George; DL (Co Durham 1985); s of Harry Bonas (d 1984), and Winifred Bonas; *b* 13 July 1942; *Educ* Harrow, Univ of Oxford (MA, DipEcon); *m* 23 Sept 1967, Katharine Anne, *née* Steel; 2 s (James Henry b 19 April 1972, William Ian b 7 June 1978), 2 da (Anna Katharine b 25 May 1969, Sophie Katharine b 23 May 1971); *Career* Ferguson International Holdings plc 1988–95; chm and md: Bonas Machine Co Ltd 1973–84 (md 1969–73), Bonas Griffith Ltd 1985–88; chm: Bentley Group Ltd 1989–, Crane Electronics Ltd 1992–; memb: Northern Econ Planning Cncl 1973–79, Ctee in Fin for Indust NEDC 1978–, Cncl Univ of Durham 1983–89; dir Washington Devpt Corp 1979–83, chm Northern Region CBI 1981–83 (memb Nat Ctee 1973–84), dir Civic Tst for NE 1980–89, chm Durham Family Health Servs Ctee 1989–96; chm N E Region REPAC 1996–; High Sheriff Co Durham 1987–88; *Recreations* music, books, painting, forestry, gardening, skiing, machine building, joinery; *Clubs* Northern Counties; *Style*— Ian Bonas, Esq, DL; ✉ Bedburn Hall, Hamsterley, Bishop Auckland, Co Durham DL13 3NN

BOND, Anthony Hugh; s of Lt-Col James Hugh Bond, MC (d 1983), of Shepton Mallet, Somerset, and Joan Winifred Dodman, *née* Goodall (d 1989); *b* 7 July 1951; *Educ* Radley; *m* 27 July 1974, Caroline Mary, da of Brig Frederick Manus De Butts, CMG, OBE, DL, of Great Gaddesden, Hemel Hempstead, Herts; 2 s (Jonathan James Hugh b 16 Aug 1977, Rupert Charles b 23 April 1980), 1 da (Victoria Jane b 3 Oct 1984); *Career* trainee CA Moore Stephens London, qualified CA 1977; KPMG: joined 1977, ptnr i/c Bahrain and Qatar 1982–84, ptnr London, nat co-ordinator for business servs 1987–89, ptnr SE region based in Milton Keynes office 1987–94 (ret); dir Broadgate Wine Shippers plc 1995–; chm: Milton Keynes and N Bucks Disability Employment Network 1993–95 (patron 1995), Milton Keynes Special Needs Advancement Project 1993; govr Milton Keynes Coll 1990–96, hon treas and vice chm Br Wheelchair Sports Fndn 1995–; ACA 1977, FCA 1983; *Recreations* golf, tennis, skiing; *Style*— Anthony Bond, Esq; ✉ The Granary, Cublington, Leighton Buzzard, Beds LU7 OLE (☎ 01296 682176)

BOND, Bruce R; *b* Ohio; *Educ* Colorado State Univ, MIT (Sloan Mgmnt Degree), Univ of Dayton Ohio (MBA); *Career* with Ohio Bell 1969–75, various planning and mktg appts AT&T 1975–85, with US West 1985–89 (latterly corp vice pres strategic planning); British Telecommunications plc: joined as dir of corp strategy 1989, i/c Products and Servs Mgmnt Div 1990–94, md BT National Business Communications 1994–96, memb Gp Managing Dir's Ctee, Quality Cncl and Gp Strategy Ctee until 1996; pres and chief exec offr ANS (subsid of American Online) USA 1996–; *Style*— Bruce Bond, Esq

BOND, Christopher Michael; s of Lt-Col James Hugh Bond, MC (d 1983), of Somerset, and Winifred Dodman, *née* Goodall (d 1989); *b* 28 June 1943; *Educ* Wellington, Trinity Hall Cambridge (BA); *m* 19 Feb 1966, Lindsay, da of late Arthur Lewis Cruickshank, of Bedford; 1 s (Neil Alexander), 1 da (Lara Marianne); *Career* admitted slr 1969, asst co sec Reuters Ltd 1972–76, ptnr Field Fisher Waterhouse 1979–; lectr int law confs in: America, Japan, Korea; UK memb Br Invisibles Missions to Korea and Taiwan; memb Law Soc 1969–; *Books* Investing in the United Kingdom (1986), Investing in the United Kingdom - The Basic Issues (1987); *Recreations* music, hill walking, reading, gardening; *Style*— Christopher Bond, Esq; ✉ Richmond, Surrey; Shepton Mallet, Somerset; Field Fisher Waterhouse, 41 Vine Street, London EC3N 2AA (☎ 0171 481 4841, fax 0171 488 0084)

BOND, Rt Rev (Charles) Derek; s of Flt Lt Charles Norman Bond, RAF (d 1985), and Doris, *née* Rosendale; *b* 4 July 1927; *Educ* Bournemouth Sch, King's Coll London (AKC); *m* 4 July 1951, (Joan) Valerie, da of Capt Ralph Meikle, RAOC (d 1988), of Bournemouth; 2 s (Stephen b 1957, Andrew b 1965), 2 da (Fiona b 1955, Elizabeth b 1963); *Career* Mids area sec SCM in Schs 1955–58; vicar: Harringay 1958–62, Harrow Weald 1962–71; archdeacon of Colchester 1971–76, bishop of Bradwell 1976–92, ret; *Recreations* travel; *Style*— The Rt Rev C D Bond; ✉ Ambleside, 14 Worcester Road, Evesham, Worcs WR11 4JU (☎ 01386 446156)

BOND, Edward; *b* 18 July 1934; *m* 1971, Elisabeth Pablé; *Career* playwright and director; Northern Arts literary fell 1977–79, George Devine award 1968, John Whiting award 1968; Hon DLitt Yale 1977; *Plays* Saved (1965), Narrow Road to the Deep North (1968), Early Morning (1968), The Pope's Wedding (1971), Passion (1971), Black Mass (1971), Lear (1972), The Sea (1973), Bingo (1974), The Fool (1976), A-A-merica! (1976), Stone (1976), The Woman (1978), The Bundle (1978), Theatre Poems and Songs (1978), The Worlds and The Activist Papers (1980), Restoration (1981), Summer: a play for Europe (1982), Derek (1983), Human Cannon (1984), The War Plays (1985), Jackets (1989), In The Company of Men (1990), September (1990), Olly's Prison (TV, 1990), Tuesday (TV, 1993), Coffee: A Tragedy (1994), At the Inland Sea (a play for young children, 1996); *Opera Libretti* We Come to the River (1976), The English Cat (1983); *Ballet Libretto* Orpheus (1982); *Translations* Chekhov's The Three Sisters (1967), Wedekind's Spring Awakening (1974), Lùlù (with Elisabeth Bond-Pablé, 1992); *Publications* Collected Poems 1978–85 (1987), Notes on Post-Modernism (1990), Letters (4 Vols, 1994 and 1995); *Style*— Edward Bond, Esq; ✉ c/o Casarotto Ramsay Ltd, National House, 4th Floor, 60–66 Wardour Street, Londo W1V 3HP (☎ 0171 287 4450, fax 0171 287 9128)

BOND, Prof Geoffrey Colin; s of Capt William Henry Bond, MC (d 1982), and Kate, *née* Digby; *b* 21 April 1927; *Educ* King Edward VI GS Stratford-upon-Avon, Univ of Birmingham (BSc, PhD, DSc); *m* 29 Aug 1953, (Angela) Mary, da of Arthur Lovatt Ingram (d 1981); 3 s (Richard b 1954, Martin b 1956, Andrew b 1959), 1 da (Rosemary b 1961); *Career* lectr Univ of Hull 1955–62, head Catalysis Res Gp Johnson Matthey & Co Ltd 1962–70; Brunel Univ: prof of applied chemistry 1970–71, prof and head Dept of Industl Chemistry 1971–82, vice princ 1979–81, dean Faculty of Mathematics and Sci 1982–84, head Dept of Chemistry 1984–90, prof of chemistry 1990–92, emeritus prof 1992–; FRSC, CChem; *Books* Catalysis by Metals (1962), Principles of Catalysis (1963), Heterogeneous Catalysis (2 edn, 1987), Catalysis by Metals and Alloys (with V Ponec, 1995); *Recreations* philately, gardening; *Style*— Prof Geoffrey Bond; ✉ Flint Cottage, Deadmans Ash Lane, Sarratt, Herts WD3 6AL (☎ 01923 263561); Department of Chemistry, Brunel University, Uxbridge UB8 3PH (☎ 01895 274000, fax 01895 256844, telex 261173 G)

BOND, Cdr Geoffrey Leonard; MBE (1970); *b* 5 Sept 1928; *Educ* Devizes GS, Univ of Bristol (BA, PGC); *m* 7 June 1952, Catherine Jean, *née* Healey; 2 s (Richard Patrick b 1959, Crispin Nicholas b 1964), 2 da (Caroline Nicola (Mrs C Wadkin) b 1956, Elizabeth May (Mrs de Lacy) b 1961); *Career* Nat Serv 2 Lt Wiltshire Regt 1950–52; extended serv cmmn to 1956; RN 1956–84: Commando Trg Centre RM 1957–60, HMS Raleigh 1960–62, Depot RM 1962–64, HMS Ark Royal 1969–71, HMS St Angelo 1971–74, MOD 1965–69 and 1975–84; appointed first chief exec The English Vineyards Assoc 1985, ed The Grape Press, writer and lectr on history of wine in England, contrib works on landscape and English wine; *Recreations* exploring and studying the British land & townscape and their traditions; *Clubs* Royal British Legion, St James's; *Style*— Cdr Geoffrey Bond, MBE; ✉ 38 West Park, London SE9 4RH (☎ 0181 857 3306/0452)

BOND, Godfrey William; s of William Niblock Bond, MC (d 1955), and Emily Janet, *née* Godfrey (d 1955); *b* 24 July 1925; *Educ* Campbell Coll, Royal Belfast Acad Inst, Trinity Coll Dublin (scholar, BA, Berkeley medal, Classics Gold medal), St John's Coll Oxford (MA); *m* 19 Sept 1959, Shirley Alison, da of Mr Justice T C Kingsmill Moore (d 1979); 1 s (Kingsmill b 1967), 2 da (Catherine b 1960, Elwyn b 1962); *Career* Foreign Office (GCHQ) 1943–45; fell and classical Tutor Pembroke Coll Oxford 1950–92, lectr in classics Univ of Oxford 1952–92, sr tutor Pembroke Coll 1962–72, sr proctor Univ of Oxford 1964–65, visitor of Ashmolean Museum 1972–81, dean of Pembroke Coll 1979–92 (emeritus fell 1992–), public orator Univ of Oxford 1980–92; memb: Inst for Advanced Study Princeton NJ 1969–70, Gen Bd of Faculties Univ of Oxford 1970–76; *Books* Euripides Hypsipyle (ed, 1963), Euripides Heracles (ed, 1981); *Recreations* opera, dining, swimming; *Clubs* Athenaeum, Kildare Street and University (Dublin); *Style*— Godfrey Bond, Esq; ✉ c/o Pembroke College, Oxford (☎ 01865 276444)

BOND, Graham; s of Thomas Carlile (d 1980), of Blackburn, and Mary, *née* Dixon; *Educ* Queen Elizabeth's GS Blackburn, RCM (exhibition scholar, various prizes); *Career* repetiteur London Opera Centre 1970; London Festival Ballet/Eng Nat Ballet: conductor 1970–76, princ conductor 1976–94, music dir 1983–94; chief conductor Royal Danish Ballet 1994–; tours incl: Aust, France, Spain, Italy, Germany, Yugoslavia, Greece, Denmark, Venezuela, Turkey, China, USA; orchs worked with incl: Monte Carlo Philharmonic, Tivoli Symphony Copenhagen, Stanislavsky Theatre Moscow, Opera House Turin, Hong Kong Philharmonic 1987, Danish Radio 1988, Royal Opera Copenhagen 1988, Opera Teatro Massimo Sicily 1988, Cairo Symphony 1988; guest conductor: Stuttgart Ballet, San Carlo Opera Orch Naples, Metropolitan Opera NY 1989, Deutsche Oper Berlin 1990–93, Bolshoi Ballet tour of Eng 1990, Opera House Budapest 1992, Palacio de Bella Artes Mexico 1993, Sofia Opera Orch Bulgaria 1993; memb conducting staff RCM 1985–94; *Awards incl* Worshipful Co of Musicians medal for a Distinguished Student RCM, Adrian Boult scholarship for study at the Accademia Chigiana Siena; Hon RCM 1994; *Recreations* theatre, reading, walking; *Style*— Graham Bond, Esq; ✉ 21a Esmond Gardens, South Parade, London W4 1JT (☎ 0181 995 8743); c/o Royal Theatre, Copenhagen, Denmark (☎ 00 45 33 32 20 20)

BOND, Ian Charles Winsor; s of Charles Walter Bond (d 1961), and Beryl Irene Bond (d 1961); *b* 15 June 1938; *Educ* King Edward VI Sch Camp Hill; *m* 28 July 1962, Audrey Kathleen, da of William Edward Robinson (d 1965), of Thornton Clevely, S Lancs; 2 s (Richard b 1965, Andrew b 1967), 2 da (Jane b 1963, Catherine b 1968); *Career* CA; sr ptnr Midlands Offices Baker Tilly 1988– (ptnr constituent firm 1964–); farmer breeding Charolais cattle; memb: Fin Ctee CRUSE, Gen Cncl Stonehouse Gang; FCA 1960; *Recreations* shooting, farming; *Style*— Ian Bond, Esq; ✉ Baker Tilly, 154 Great Charles Street, Birmingham B3 3HN (☎ 0121 233 2323, fax 0121 236 9720, car 0860 531103)

BOND, Jane Alison Mary; da of Geoffrey Macdonald Mallock Bond (d 1984), of Budleigh Salterton, Devon, and Louise Margurite, *née* Houssemayne du Boulay; *b* 1 April 1939; *Educ* Kinnaird Park Sch Bromley, St Martin's Sch of Art, City and Guilds Sch of Art (Rodney Burns drawing award), RA Schs (Henfield figure painting award, S J Soloman Bronze medal, Duff Greet prize); *Career* TV, theatre and film costume designer for WNO, ENO, Wexford Opera Festival, Goldcrest Films and many LWT prodns until 1978, currently full time artist; *Exhibitions* Costume Designs (Phoenix Theatre Gall) 1980, Imperial Tobacco Award (Nat Portrait Gall) 1981, British Drawing (Hayward Gall) 1982, Spirit of London (Royal Festival Hall) 1982 and 1986, Cleveland Int Drawing Biennale 1983, The Pick of New Graduate Art (Christie's) 1984, Riverside Open (Riverside Studios) 1985 and 1987, The Human Figure (Business Art Galls) 1986, Drawings 1978–87 (Holland Gall) 1987, Themes and Variations (New Academy Gall) 1988, Highgate Gall 1988, The Discerning Eye (Mall Galls) 1991 and 1992, A Critics' Choice 11 & 111 (Cooling Gall) 1992, Selected Drawings (Glyndebourne Opera House) 1992, Making A Mark (Mall Galls) 1993; exhibits regularly at New English Art Club, Royal Soc of Portrait Painters and Royal Academy of Arts Summer Exhbns; Ernest Kleinwort Meml prize New English Art Club 1989, House & Garden Interior prize RA Summer Exhbn 1993; memb Riverside Artists Gp 1986; elected memb: New English Art Club 1989, Royal Soc of Portrait Painters (RP) 1992; *Recreations* travel, opera, antique dolls houses; *Clubs* Arts; *Style*— Miss Jane Bond, RP; ✉ 8 Ceylon Road, London W14 0PY (☎ 0171 603 8308)

BOND, John David; MVO (1988); s of Arthur Henry Bond (d 1968), and Agnes Mary, *née* Peters (d 1984); *b* 14 June 1932; *Educ* St Mary's Welwyn; *m* 18 Jan 1958, Edna, da of William Samuel Reeves (d 1975); 1 s (Christopher John b 1962), 1 da (Susan Mary b 1959); *Career* keeper of the gardens The Gt Park Windsor 1970–; memb Cncl RHS 1985– (chm Rhododendron and Camelia Ctee 1987–); Victoria Medal of Honour in Horticulture RHS 1981; fell Inst of Hort 1984; *Recreations* horticulture, natural history, travel, railways; *Style*— John Bond, Esq, MVO; ✉ Verderers, Wick Rd, Englefield Green, Egham, Surrey TW2 0HL (☎ 01784 432168); Crown Estate Office, The Great Park, Windsor, Berks (☎ 01753 860222)

BOND, John Reginald Hartnell; s of Cdre Reginald Harold Arthur Bond, OBE (d 1978), of Hampshire, and Edith Christine Alice, *née* Powell; *b* 22 July 1941; *Educ* Tonbridge Sch Kent, Cate Sch Calif (ESU scholar); *m* 27 April 1968, Elizabeth Caroline, da of John Anthony Parker; 2 da (Annabelle Sarah b 12 July 1969, Lucy Candida b 18 Dec 1972), 1 s (Jonathan Simon b 13 Nov 1976); *Career* Hongkong and Shanghai Banking Corporation: joined Hongkong Bank 1961, chief exec Wardley Ltd (HSBC subsid) Hong Kong 1983–87 (dep md 1982–83), exec dir and chief exec Americas Regnl Office USA 1988–90 (gen mangr and chief exec 1987–88), exec dir banking Gp Head Office Hong Kong 1990–91, pres and chief exec Marine Midland Banks Inc Buffalo 1991–92, gp chief exec HSBC Holdings plc London 1993–; non-exec dir: British Steel plc 1994–, London Stock Exchange, Visa International, Orange plc; FCIB 1983, CIMgt 1993; *Recreations* skiing, golf and reading biography; *Clubs* MCC, Hong Kong, Royal Ashdown Forest Golf, John's Island (Florida); *Style—* John R H Bond, Esq; ✉ Group Chief Executive, HSBC Holdings plc, 10 Lower Thames Street, London EC3R 6AE (☎ 0171 260 0497, fax 0171 260 6686)

BOND, Maj Gen (Henry) Mark Garneys; OBE (1993), DL (Dorset 1977); s of William Ralph Garneys Bond (d 1952), of Moigne Combe, and Evelyn Isabel, *née* Blake (d 1954); *b* 1 June 1922; *Educ* Eton; *Career* enlisted Rifle Bde 1940, cmmnd 1941, served Western Desert 1942–43, Italy 1943, POW 1943, seconded Parachute Regt 1947–50, ADC to Field Marshal Viscount Montgomery of Alamein 1950–52, Staff Coll psc 1953, DS Staff Coll 1958–60, Brevet Lt Col 1961, served Kenya, Malaya, Aden, Cyprus, Malaysia and Borneo, cmd 12 Bde 1967–68, idc 1969, Chief of Staff Hong Kong 1970, Asst Chief of Def Staff (Ops and Plans) 1971–72, ret 1972; JP 1972–92 (chm Wareham Bench 1984–89), Vice Lord Lt Dorset 1982; memb Dorset CC 1973–85 (vice chm 1981–85), chm Dorset Police Authy 1980–92; pres: Community Cncl of Dorset 1978–97, Dorset Branch CPRE 1975–96, Dorset Assoc of Parish and Town Cncls 1985–97; visitor Milton Abbey Sch (chm Bd of Govrs 1981–94); tstee Dorset Co Museum 1970–; *Style—* Maj Gen H M G Bond, OBE, JP, DL; ✉ Moigne Combe, Dorchester, Dorset DT2 8JA (☎ 01305 852265)

BOND, Prof Sir Michael Richard; kt (1995); s of Frederick Richard Bond, of 10 Falstone Ave, Newark on Trent, Notts, and Dorothy, *née* Gardner (d 1988); *b* 15 April 1936; *Educ* Magnus GS Newark Notts, Univ of Sheffield (MB ChB, MD, PhD); *m* 24 June 1961, Jane, da of Charles Issitt (d 1962); 1 s (Matthew b 9 Aug 1970), 1 da (Lucy b 2 June 1975); *Career* lectr in psychiatry Univ of Sheffield 1964–67 (asst lectr and res registrar surgery 1961–64); Univ of Glasgow: sr house offr, registrar then sr registrar in neurosurgery 1967–71, lectr then sr lectr in neurosurgery 1971–73, prof of psychological med 1973–, vice princ 1986–, admin dean Faculty of Med 1991–; memb: Universities Funding Cncl 1991–93 (on dissolution), London Inquiry Gp 1992–93; memb Cncl Higher Educn Funding Cncl for Scotland 1993–96, chm Jt Med Advsy Ctee of Higher Educn Funding Cncls for England, Scotland and Wales 1993–95; memb Cncl: St Andrews Ambulance Assoc, Prince and Princess of Wales Hospice Glasgow; govr Glasgow HS, chm Head Injury Tst Scotland; Hon DSc Univ of Leics 1996; FRCSEd 1969, FRCPsych 1981, FRCPS 1981, FRSA; *Books* Pain: Its Nature Analysis Treatment (2 edns 1979, 1984); *Recreations* painting, forest walking, physical fitness, antique book collecting; *Clubs* Athenaeum; *Style—* Prof Sir Michael R Bond; ✉ 33 Ralston Rd, Bearsden, Glasgow G61 3BA (☎ 0141 942 4391); Department of Psychological Medicine, Gartnavel Royal Hospital, Great Western Rd, Glasgow (☎ 0141 334 9826); Vice Principal and Administrative Dean, Faculty of Medicine, University of Glasgow, Glasgow G12 8QQ (☎ 0141 307 8014, fax 0141 330 5440)

BOND, Nigel Graham; s of (Peter) Graham Bond, of Matlock, Derbyshire, and Ann, *née* Marshall; *b* 15 Nov 1965; *Educ* Ernest Bailey GS Matlock, Chesterfield Coll of Technol; *Career* professional snooker player 1989–; represented England as amateur Home Int Championships 1987 and 1988, English Amateur champion 1989; winner King's Cup Bangkok; finalist: Rothmans Grand Prix 1990 (test v Stephen Hendry), Embassy World Championship 1995 (v Stephen Hendry); semi-finalist: BCE International 1989, Rothmans Grand Prix 1991, Mercantile Credit Classic 1992, Regal Welsh Open 1992, Strachan Open 1992, European Open 1994; quarter-finalist: European Open 1990, Stormseal UK Championship 1990, Royal Liver Assurance UK Championship 1993, British Open 1994, Embassy World Championship 1994; Best Newcomer of the Year (World Professional Billiards and Snooker Assoc) 1990; *Recreations* golf; *Clubs* Matlock Golf; *Style—* Nigel Bond, Esq; ✉ c/o Ian Doyle, Cuemasters Ltd, Kerse Rd, Stirling FK7 7SG (☎ 01786 462634, fax 01786 50068)

BOND, Paul; *see:* Fielding, David

BOND, Richard Douglas; s of Douglas Charles Bond, and Vera Eileen, *née* Richards; *b* 23 July 1946; *Educ* Berkhamsted Sch, London Coll of Law; *m* 27 Oct 1973, Anthea Mary (d 1996), da of Harold Francis Charrington, GC; 2 da (Charlotte Emma b 3 May 1976, Suzanne Claire b 1 Sept 1980); *Career* articled clerk Halsey Lightly & Hemsley 1964–69, ptnr Herbert Smith 1977– (joined as slr 1969), seconded to British National Oil Corporation 1976–78; memb Worshipful Co of Solicitors; memb: Law Soc, Int Bar Assoc; *Clubs* MCC, Lansdowne; *Style—* Richard Bond, Esq; ✉ Herbert Smith, Exchange House, Primrose St, London EC2A 2HS (☎ 0171 374 8000, fax 0171 496 0043)

BOND, Richard Henry; s of Lt-Col Ashley Raymond Bond, MBE, DL, JP (d 1975), of Creech Grange, Wareham, Dorset, and Mary, *née* Bowles (d 1952); *b* 15 April 1947; *Educ* Sherborne; *m* 25 April 1987, (Annabel) Susan, da of Brig John Henry Peter Curtis, MC, of Inshriach House, nr Aviemore, Invernessshire; 1 s (Henry b 30 Oct 1988), 1 da (Annabel b 27 Feb 1990); *Career* called to the Bar Inner Temple 1970, recorder of the Crown Ct 1995–; *Recreations* shooting, gardening, walking; *Clubs* Travellers, RAC; *Style—* Richard Bond, Esq; ✉ 1 Mitre Court Buildings, Temple, London EC4 (☎ 0171 797 7070, fax 0171 797 7435)

BOND, Steven John; s of John George Bond (d 1995), of Virginia, USA, and Frances Irene, *née* Jones; *b* 20 Aug 1954; *Educ* Swayne GS Rayleigh Essex, Univ of Southampton (LLB); *Career* articled clerk Masons 1978–80; asst slr: Denton Hall 1980–81, Marriott & Co (London and Hong Kong) 1981–83; Masons: rejoined 1984, ptnr Hong Kong 1984–86, ptnr London 1986–; memb Law Soc 1980; *Recreations* tennis, swimming, travel; *Clubs* RAC; *Style—* Steven Bond, Esq; ✉ Masons, 30 Aylesbury Street, London EC1R 0ER (☎ 0171 490 4000, fax 0171 490 2545)

BOND GUNNING, Rufus Gordon; s of Col John Trehane Hamilton Gunning, and Beatrice Ibea Burton, *née* Todd (d 1973); the Gunnings are an old county family, and were seated at Tregonning in Cornwall during the reign of Henry IV, AD 1400; *b* 24 Sept 1940; *Educ* Harrow, RMA Sandhurst; *m* 1967, Lilah Mary, da of Capt John Bowen McKay, OBE (d 1971), of Laguna, Brightwalton Holt, nr Newbury, Berkshire; 1 s (Heyrick b 1971), 1 da (Annastasia b 1974); *Career* 9/12 Royal Lancers (POW) 1961, Capt, ret 1967; trg and personnel mangr Chubb Alarms Ltd 1967–72, dir and gen mangr Chubb Alarms Hong Kong Ltd 1972–74, md Chubb Hong Kong Ltd 1974–80, dir Chubb Cash 1980; chm: Chubb Alarms Ltd 1981–87, Guardal Ltd 1981–84, ICC Ltd 1981–82, Chubb Wardens Ltd 1981–87; exec memb Chubb & Son plc 1981–84, dir Chubb Racal Ltd 1986–87 (exec memb 1984–86), md Kalamazoo plc 1989 (resigned May 1989), md Sketchley Vending PLC (converted to Provend Services Limited following buy-out) 1991–; govr Tower Hamlets Coll of Further Educn 1970–72, tstee Royal Armouries 1989–; FIOD, MIPD, memb IBM; *Recreations* tennis, swimming, walking, skiing; *Clubs* Cavalry and Guards'; *Style—* R G Bond Gunning, Esq; ✉ Hopton Court, Alfrick, Worcestershire WR6 5HP

BONDI, Prof Sir Hermann; KCB (1973); s of Samuel Bondi (d 1959), and Helene Bondi (d 1960); *b* 1 Nov 1919; *Educ* Realgymnasium Vienna, Trinity Coll Cambridge (MA); *m* 1947, Christine M, da of Henry Watson Stockman, CBE (d 1982); 2 s, 3 da; *Career* lectr in maths Univ of Cambridge 1948–54 (asst lectr 1945–48), prof of mathematics King's Coll London 1954–85 (leave of absence 1967–71, titular prof 1971–85, prof emeritus 1985–), Master Churchill Coll Cambridge 1983–90; chm Space Ctee MOD 1964–65, dir-gen Euro Space Research Orgn 1967–71, chief scientific advsr MOD 1971–77, chief scientist Dept of Energy 1977–80; chm: Advsy Cncl Energy Conservation 1980–82, Natural Environment Research Cncl (and chief exec) 1980–84, Advsy Cncl Royal Naval Engrg Coll 1988–94, Advsy Panel on Environmental Change, Cmmn of the Euro Communities and Euro Science Fndn 1989–95; pres: Inst of Mathematics and its Applications 1974–75, Assoc of Br Science Writers 1981–83, Soc Research into Higher Educn 1981–, Br Humanist Assoc 1982–; memb: Rationalist Press Assoc, Science Policy Fndn; FKC 1968; fell: Trinity Coll Cambridge 1943–49 and 1952–54, Churchill Coll 1990–; Hon DSc: Univ of Sussex 1974, Univ of Bath 1974, Univ of Surrey 1974, Univ of York 1980, Univ of Southampton 1981, Univ of Salford 1982, Univ of Birmingham 1984, Univ of St Andrews 1985, Univ of Vienna 1993, Univ of Plymouth 1995; G D Birla Award for Humanism New Delhi 1990, Gold Medal IMA 1989; FRS 1959, FRAS, Hon FIEE 1979, Hon FInstP 1991, Hon FIMA 1992; *Books* Cosmology (1952, 2 edn 1960), The Universe at Large (1961), Relativity and Common Sense (1964), Assumption and Myth in Physical Theory (1968), Magic Squares of Order Four (with Dame Kathleen Ollerenshaw, 1982), Science, Churchill and Me (autobiography, 1990); *Recreations* walking, talking; *Style—* Prof Sir Hermann Bondi, KCB, FRS; ✉ 60 Mill Lane, Impington, Cambridge CB4 4XN (☎ 01223 565180)

BONE, Charles William Henry; s of William Stanley Bone (d 1966), and Elizabeth, *née* Burfoot; *b* 15 Sept 1926; *Educ* Farnham Coll of Art, Royal Coll of Art; *m* 1950, Sheila Mary, da of Lionel Mitchell (d 1956); 2 s (Richard, Sebastian); *Career* artist; lectr Brighton Coll of Art 1950–86, conslt COSIRA 1952–70; craft advsr Malta Industs Assoc 1952–78, designer Stourhead Ball 1959–69, dir RI Galleries Piccadilly 1965–70; critic for Arts Review; memb Cncl RI 1964 (vice pres 1974), govr Fedn of Br Artists 1976–81 and 1983– (memb Exec Cncl 1983–84 and 1986–88), pres Royal Inst of Painters in Water Colours 1979–89 (vice pres 1974–79); Hunting Gp Prize for the Most Outstanding Watercolour by a Br Artist 1984; hon memb: Botanical Artists, Medical Art Soc, Fedn of Canadian Artists; ARCA, FRSA; *Exhibitions* oils and water colours in exhibitions: Medici Gallery 1950–, London Gp, NEAC, RBA 1950–, RA 1950–; 35 one man exhibitions 1950–; *Works in Private Collections* France, Italy, Malta, America, Canada, Japan, Aust, Norway, Sweden, Germany; *Other Work* incl: ceramic mural on the history of aerial photography, other murals in Italy and Spain, film on painting for Castle Communications plc 1990, book on Waverley Surrey 1991; *Clubs* Chelsea Arts; *Style—* Charles Bone, Esq; ✉ Winters Farm, Puttenham, Guildford, Surrey GU3 1AR (☎ 01483 810226); 17 Carlton House Terrace, London SW1

BONE, Prof (James) Drummond; s of William Drummond Bone (d 1979), and Helen, *née* Yuill (d 1973); *b* 11 July 1947; *Educ* Ayr Acad, Univ of Glasgow (Snell exhibitioner), Balliol Coll Oxford; *m* 1970, Vivian Clare, *née* Kindon; *Career* lectr Dept of English and Comparative Literary Studies Univ of Warwick 1972–80; Univ of Glasgow Dept of English Literature: lectr then sr lectr 1980–95, prof of English literature 1995–; Univ of Glasgow: dean Faculty of Arts 1992–95, vice-princ 1995–; academic ed The Byron Jl 1978–88, ed Romanticism 1995–, author of many articles on Romanticism and also the occasional short story; FRSA 1995; *Recreations* music, skiing, Maseratis (memb Maserati Club); *Clubs* Glasgow Art; *Style—* Prof Drummond Bone; ✉ The Old Manse, Bow-of-Fife, Nr Cupar, Fife KY15 4NH; Vice-Principal, University of Glasgow, Glasgow G12 8QQ (☎ 0141 330 8026, fax 0141 330 8019, e-mail JDBOARTS.GLA.AC.UK)

BONE, Rt Rev John Frank Ewan; s of Jack Bone (d 1944), and Herberta Blanche, *née* Ewan (d 1984); *b* 28 Aug 1930; *Educ* Monkton Combe Sch, St Peter's Hall Oxford (MA), Ely Theol Coll, Whitelands Coll of Educn; *m* 26 June 1954, Ruth Margaret, da of Wilfrid John Crudgington (d 1968); 2 da (Sarah b 1955, Elizabeth b 1958), 3 s (Nicholas b 1961, Stephen b 1964, Patrick (adopted) b 1972); *Career* asst curate: St Gabriel's Pimlico 1956–60, St Mary's Henley-on-Thames 1960–63; vicar St Mary's Datchet 1963–76, rural dean Burnham 1974–77, rector St Mary's Slough 1976–78, archdeacon of Buckingham 1978–89, bishop of Reading 1989–97; memb General Synod 1980–85; *Style—* The Rt Rev J F E Bone; ✉ 4 Grove Road, Henley-on-Thames, Oxon

BONE, Dr Quentin; JP; s of Stephen Bone (d 1958), and Sylvia Mary, *née* Adshead (d 1995); *b* 17 Aug 1931; *Educ* Warwick Sch, St John's Coll and Magdalen Coll Oxford (DPhil); *m* 9 Aug 1958, Susan Elizabeth, da of Sidney Smith (d 1963), of Witney, Oxon; 4 s (Matthew b 5 June 1959, Oliver b 2 Jan 1961, Alexander b 13 Aug 1963, Daniel b 21 Nov 1965); *Career* Plymouth Lab of the Marine Biological Assoc UK: zoologist 1959–, dep chief scientific offr 1987–91, emeritus res fell 1992–; ed Philosophical Transactions Royal Soc of Biological Sciences 1988–94; FRS 1984; *Books* Biology of Fishes (with N B Marshall and J S Blaxter, 1994); *Recreations* botany, travel, repairing machines; *Style—* Dr Quentin Bone, FRS, JP; ✉ Marchant House, Church Rd, Plymstock, Plymouth PL9 9BG; The Marine Lab, Citadel Hill, Plymouth (☎ 01752 633100)

BONE, HE Roger Bridgland; CMG (1996); s of Horace Bridgland Bone (d 1979), and Dora Rose, *née* Tring; *b* 29 July 1944; *Educ* Palmer's Sch Grays Essex, St Peter's Coll Oxford (MA); *m* 3 July 1970, Lena Marianne, da of Georg Bergman (d 1975); 1 s (Christopher b 1977), 1 da (Marianne b 1980); *Career* HM Dip Serv: UK Mission to UN 1966, FCO 1967, 3 sec Stockholm 1968–70, 1 sec Moscow 1973–75, 1 sec UK Representation to the Euro Communities Brussels 1978–82, asst private sec to Sec of State for Foreign and Cwlth Affrs 1982–84, visiting fell Harvard Center for Int Affrs 1984–85, cnsllr Washington 1985–89 (head of Chancery 1987–89), cnsllr FCO 1989–91, asst under sec of state FCO 1991–95, UK ambass Sweden 1995–; *Recreations* wine, music; *Style—* HE Mr Roger Bone, CMG; ✉ c/o Foreign and Commonwealth Office (Stockholm), London SW1A 2AH

BONE, Prof Thomas Renfrew (Tom); CBE (1987); s of James Renfrew Bone, and Mary, *née* Williams (d 1984); *b* 2 Jan 1935; *Educ* Port Glasgow HS, Greenock HS, Univ of Glasgow (MA, MEd, PhD); *m* 31 July 1959, Elizabeth, da of William Stewart (d 1972); 1 s (David James b 1960), 1 da (Hazel Jeanette b 1963); *Career* Eng teacher Paisley GS 1957–62, lectr educn Univ of Glasgow 1963–67; Jordanhill Coll of Educn: lectr in educn 1962–63, head Dept of Educn 1967–71, princ 1972–92; dep princ Univ of Strathclyde 1992–; chm: Scottish Cncl for Educn Technology 1981–87, Standing Conf on Studies in Educn 1982–84, IBA's Educnl Advsy Cncl 1986–87, CNAA's Ctee for Teacher Educn 1987–89; vice chm: Scottish Examination Bd 1977–84, Scottish Tertiary Educn Advsy Cncl 1984–87, Gen Teaching Cncl 1987–90 and 1991–92 (chm 1990–91); fell Cwlth Cncl for Educnl Admin 1984; *Books* Studies in the History of Scottish Education 1872–1939 (ed, 1967), School Inspection in Scotland 1840–1966 (1968), The Changing Role of the Teacher Unesco (ed, 1987), Teacher Education in Europe: The Challenges Ahead (jt ed, 1990), contrib to various educnl books; *Recreations* golf; *Clubs* Western Gailes Golf, Paisley Burns; *Style—* Prof Tom Bone, CBE; ✉ University of Strathclyde, Richmond Street, Glasgow G1 1XQ (☎ 0141 552 4400, fax 0141 553 1521)

BONE, Vivian Clare; da of Keith Dudley Kindon (d 1958), and Matilda Mary, *née* Nash; *b* 15 May 1946; *Educ* Channing Sch Highgate, Univ of Sussex (BSc); *m* 1970, (James) Drummond Bone, s of William Drummond Bone; *Career* publishing; maths and physics ed Academic Div Oxford University Press 1968–79; Edinburgh University Press: sr ed and asst sec 1980, acting sec 1990, publisher 1991–96, md 1992–96, non-exec dir and conslt 1996–; memb Scottish Publishers Assoc (cncl memb 1992–); *Recreations* publishing; *Style*— Mrs Vivian Bone; ✉ Edinburgh University Press, 22 George Square, Edinburgh, Scotland EH8 9LF (☎ 0131 650 4219, fax 0131 662 0053)

BONEY, Guy Thomas Knowles; QC (1990); s of Lt-Col Thomas Knowles Boney (d 1975), of Llandudno, and Muriel Hilary Eileen, *née* Long (d 1984); *b* 28 Dec 1944; *Educ* Winchester, New Coll Oxford (MA); *m* 4 Dec 1976, Jean Ritchie, QC, *qv*, da of Walter Ritchie (d 1979), of Solihull; 2 s (R Oliver b 21 Jan 1979, Christian V K b 29 March 1981); *Career* called to the Bar Middle Temple 1968; in practice Western Circuit 1969–, recorder of the Crown Court 1985–; head Pump Court Chambers 1992–; contrib to horological jls; *Books* The Road Safety Act 1967 (1971), Halsbury's Laws of England vol 40 (contrib); *Recreations* horology, music, amateur drama; *Clubs* Reform, Hampshire; *Style*— Guy Boney, Esq, QC; ✉ 3 Pump Court, Temple, London EC4 (☎ 0171 353 0711, fax 0171 353 3319); 31 Southgate Street, Winchester, Hants SO23 9EE (☎ 01962 868161, fax 01962 867645)

BONFIELD, Sir Peter Leahy; kt (1996), CBE (1989); s of George Robert Bonfield (d 1975), of Baldock, Herts, and Dora Patricia, *née* Talbot; *b* 3 June 1944; *Educ* Hitchin Boys' GS, Loughborough Univ of Technol (BTech, DTech); *m* 9 March 1968, Josephine, da of George Houghton, of Whitton, Humberside; *Career* div mangr Texas Instruments Inc Dallas 1966–81, exec dir and gp mktg dir International Computers Ltd London 1981–84, chm STC International Computers 1986–90 (md 1984–90), dep chief exec STC plc 1987–90, chm and chief exec ICL plc 1990–96 (non-exec chm 1996–), chief exec BT plc 1996–; non-exec dir Zeneca Group plc 1995–; vice pres Br Quality Fndn; memb: Trilateral Cmmn, Euro Round Table, CBI, Worshipful Co of Technologists; Freeman City of London; recipient hon doctorates from Univs of Loughborough, Surrey and Mid Glamorgan; FIEE, FCIM, FBCS, FRSA, FEng 1993, CIMgt; *Recreations* music, sailing, jogging; *Clubs* RAC; *Style*— Sir Peter Bonfield, CBE, FEng; ✉ British Telecommunications plc, 81 Newgate Street, London EC1A 7AJ (☎ 0171 356 5000, fax 0171 356 5520)

BONFIELD, Prof William; s of Cecil William Bonfield, of Baldock, Herts, and Ellen Gertrude, *née* Hawkes (d 1981); *b* 6 March 1937; *Educ* Imperial Coll London (Perry Meml medal, Bessemer medal, Ernest Edward Glorney prize, BSc(Eng), PhD, ARSM, DIC); *m* 18 June 1960, Gillian Winifred Edith, da of John Hamilton Cross; 1 s (Peter William b 25 June 1963), 2 da (Stephanie Jane b 10 Sept 1965, Astrid Elizabeth b 21 May 1969); *Career* Honeywell Res Center Minnesota: sr res scientist 1961–63, princ res scientist 1963–65, sr princ res scientist 1965–68; ed: Jl of Materials Science 1973–, Jl of Materials Science Letters 1981–, Materials in Medicine 1990–; Queen Mary and Westfield Coll: head Dept of Materials 1980–90, chm Sch of Engrg 1981–88, govr 1984–87, dean of Engrg 1985–89, currently prof of materials and dir Interdisciplinary Res Centre in Biomedical Materials; distinguished visiting prof Univ of Toronto 1990, visiting prof Henry Ford Hosp Detroit 1992, hon prof Univ of Sichuan China 1992–, adjunct prof Univ of Naples 1993–; memb: Biological Engrg Soc, Bone and Tooth Soc, Euro Soc of Biomechanics, Euro Soc for Biomaterials, Euro Soc for Engrg and Med; hon memb: Canadian Orthopaedic Res Soc 1984, Indian Materials Res Soc 1993; A A Griffith Silver Medal Inst of Medals 1991, Royal Soc Armourers and Brasiers' Co Medal 1991, George Winter Award Euro Soc for Biomaterials 1994, Kelvin Medal Instn of Civil Engrs 1995; Freeman Worshipful Co of Armourers and Brasiers 1994; CEng 1972, FIM 1972, FEng 1993, founding fell in biomaterials and engrg (FBSE) Euro Soc for Biomaterials 1995; *Books* Bioceramics (with G W Hastings and K E Tanner, 1991); author of over 180 scientific papers; *Recreations* cycling (qualified coach British Cycling Coaching Scheme), gardening; *Clubs* Athenaeum, North Road Cycling, Gosling Sports Park; *Style*— Prof William Bonfield, FEng; ✉ Interdisciplinary Research Centre in Biomedical Materials, Queen Mary and Westfield College, Mile End Road, London E1 4NS (☎ 0171 975 5285, fax 0181 983 1799, e-mail W.Bonfield@qmw.ac.uk)

BONGERS, Paul Nicholas; s of Henry Ernest Bongers, and Marjorie Hines, *née* Luxton (d 1989); *b* 25 Oct 1943; *Educ* Bradfield Coll, New Coll Oxford (BA, MA), Univ of London (DPA external); *m* 3 Sept 1968, Margaret Jean, da of Frederick William Collns (d 1994); 2 s (Nicholas Julian Huddleston b 1982, Matthew Rupert Huddleston b 1985), 2 da (Georgina Margaret Huddleston b 1976, Alexandra Mary Huddleston b 1979); *Career* admin trainee Southampton City Cncl 1965–68, PA to Town Clerk Nottingham City Cncl 1968–69, admin Cncl of Europe Strasbourg 1969–71; asst sec: Assoc of Municipal Corporations 1971–74, Assoc of Met Authys 1974–78; exec sec Br Sections Int Union of Local Authys/Cncl of Euro Municipalities and Regions 1978–88, dir Local Govt Int Bureau 1988–95, special advsr Int Union of Local Authys 1995–, int local govt conslt Bongers de Roth 1995–; memb: Nat Tst, Wadhurst Area Soc for Protection and Preservation, Euro Movement, Euro Atlantic Gp; *Books* European Communities Information (contrib, 1985), Local Government and 1992 (1990, 2 edn Local Government and the Single European Market, 1992), Subsidiarity (contrib, 1993); *Recreations* family, music, countryside, travel, the arts; *Clubs* Reform, Rotary; *Style*— Paul N Bongers, Esq; ✉ Saxonhurst House, Durgates, Wadhurst, E Sussex TN5 6RT (☎ and fax 01892 783417)

BONHAM, Sir Antony Lionel Thomas; 4 Bt (UK 1852); DL (Glos 1983); s of Maj Sir Eric Henry Bonham, 3 Bt, CVO, JP (d 1937), and Ethel (d 1962), da of Lt-Col Leopold Seymour (s of Rt Hon Sir George Seymour, GCB, GCH, PC, and Hon Gertrude, da of 21 Baron Dacre; Sir George Seymour was s of Lord George Seymour, MP, s of 1 Marquess of Hertford); Sir Samuel George Bonham, 1 Bt, KCB, was govr and C-in-C Hong Kong and chief supt Br Trade in China 1847–53; *b* 21 Oct 1916; *Educ* Eton, RMC Sandhurst; *m* 19 Feb 1944, Felicity, o da of Col Frank Lionel Pardoe, DSO (d 1947), of Bartonbury, Cirencester; 3 s ((George) Martin Antony b 1945, Simon Philip b 1947, Timothy Eric b 1952); *Heir* s, (George) Martin Antony Bonham, *qv*; *Career* serv Royal Scots Greys 1937–49, Maj; dir wine merchants 1950–70, ret; *Style*— Sir Antony Bonham, Bt, DL; ✉ Ash House, Ampney Crucis, Cirencester, Glos (☎ 01285 851391)

BONHAM, Derek C; *Career* Hanson plc: joined as dep fin controller 1971, dir 1981–, chief exec 1992–, dep chm 1993–; non-exec dir: Glaxo Wellcome plc 1995–, US Industries Inc; former memb: Fin Accounting Standards Advsy Cncl (USA), Accounting Standards Ctee (UK); memb Ct of Assts Worshipful Co of Feltmakers; FCA, FCT; *Style*— Derek Bonham, Esq; ✉ Hanson plc, 1 Grosvenor Place, London SW1X 7JH (☎ 0171 245 1245)

BONHAM, (Arthur) Keith; DL (Bristol 1996); s of George Bonham, of Plymouth, and Phyllis Ann, *née* Hammond; *b* 28 March 1939; *Educ* Plymouth Coll, Univ of Keele (BA); *m* 4 July 1964, Gillian Ann, da of William Ortelli Vokins (d 1981), of Bristol; 1 s (Adrian b 25 Sept 1970), 1 da (Tracy b 6 Aug 1968); *Career* CA 1966; Ernst & Whinney: ptnr 1975–, managing ptnr Bristol office 1985–89, ptnr in charge of audit Ernst & Young 1989–90, managing ptnr Bristol office 1990–92, sr client ptnr 1992–, memb Cncl Ernst & Young 1989–92; pres W of Eng Soc of CAs 1987–88; treas and vice pres Clifton RFC 1967–; memb: President's Gp Bristol C of C and Initiative, SW Regnl Cncl CBI 1992–, Ctee Fairbridge in Avon; dir Empire Museum Ltd; tstee: Bristol Energy and Environment Trust, St Peter's Hospice Ltd; vice chm Manor Farm Boys' Club; Master of the Guild of Guardians of Bristol 1994–95; memb: Dolphin Soc, Bristol Soc; FCA; *Recreations* rugby, running, squash, swimming; *Clubs* Clifton RFC; *Style*— Keith Bonham, Esq, DL; ✉ Ernst & Young, One Bridewell St, Bristol BS1 2AA

BONHAM, (George) Martin Antony; s and h of Sir Antony Lionel Thomas Bonham, 4 Bt, *qv*; *b* 18 Feb 1945; *Educ* Eton, Aston Univ Birmingham; *m* 1979 (m dis 1992), Nenon Baillieu (b 1948), eldest da of Robert Ruttan Wilson, of Petersfield (whose gggf in the male line, the Rev George Wilson, was bro of 9 and 10 Barons Berners), and Hon Yvette Baillieu, da of 1 Baron Baillieu; 1 s (Michael Francis b 24 May 1980), 3 da (Lucie Nenon b 1982, Camilla Felicity b 1984, Sarah Yvette b 1987); *Recreations* sailing, skiing, golf, tennis, squash; *Clubs* Bembridge Sailing; *Style*— Martin Bonham, Esq; ✉ 15 St James Street, Castle Hedingham, Essex CO9 3EN

BONHAM, Nicholas; s of the late Leonard Charles Bonham and Diana Maureen, *née* Magwood (d 1995); *b* 7 Sept 1948; *Educ* Trent Coll; *m* 7 April 1977, Kaye Eleanor, da of John Robert Ivett, of Brisbane, Aust; 2 da (Katie b 1981, Jessica b 1982); *Career* dir Bonhams Group Ltd 1970–, dep chm W & F C Bonham & Sons Ltd 1987– (dir 1970, md 1975–87); Freeman City of London 1970, memb Worshipful Co of Pewterers; *Recreations* sailing, tobogganing, golf, skiing, elephant polo; *Clubs* South West Shingles Yacht, Acton Turville Bobsleigh, St Moritz Sporting, Royal Thames Yacht, Seaview Yacht, Kennel; *Style*— Nicholas Bonham, Esq; ✉ W & F C Bonham & Sons Ltd, Montpelier St, London SW7 1HH (☎ 0171 393 3900, fax 0171 393 3905)

BONHAM CARTER, Helena; da of The Hon Raymond Bonham Carter, and Elena, *née* Propper de Callejon; *b* 26 May 1966; *Educ* S Hampstead HS, Westminster; *Career* actress; *Theatre* incl: Woman in White (Greenwich), The Chalk Garden (Windsor), The House of Bernarda Alba (Nottingham Playhouse), Rosine in the Barber of Seville (Palace Theatre Watford) 1992, Trelawney of the Wells (Triumph, Guildford, Brighton and West End); *Television* incl: The Vision (BBC) 1987, Arms and the Man (BBC) 1988, Beatrix Potter 1989, Dancing Queen (Granada) 1993, A Dark Adapted Eye (BBC) 1993, Absolutely Fabulous (BBC), Jo Brand Through the Cakehole (Noel Gay TV); *Radio* incl: The Reluctant Debutant, Marie Antoinette, The Seagull; *Films* incl: Lady Jane (Paramount) 1985, A Room with a View (Merchant Ivory) 1986, A Hazard of Hearts 1987, Francesco 1988, Hamlet (Nelson Ent) 1990, Where Angels Fear to Tread (Merchant Ivory) 1990, Howard's End (Merchant Ivory) 1990, Fatal Deception (Eliott Friedgen & Co) 1992, Frankenstein 1993, Butter (Sundial Pictures), The Gallery (Talking Pictures), Margaret's Museum (Glace Bay Pics Inc), Mighty Aphrodite (Sweetheart Prodn) 1995, Chinese Portraits (IMA Prodn) 1995, Twelfth Night 1996; *Style*— Miss Helena Bonham Carter; ✉ c/o Conway van Gelder Robinson Ltd, 18–21 Jermyn Street, London SW1Y 6HP (☎ 0171 287 0077, fax 0171 287 1940)

BONHAM-CARTER, Norman Albert; s of late Air Cdre David William Frederick Bonham-Carter, CB, DFC, and Joyce Angela Bonham-Carter; *b* 28 May 1928; *Educ* St Johns Coll and Gordon Bell HS Winnipeg Manitoba Canada, Charterhouse; *m* 1, 14 April 1956 (m dis 1974), Dorothy Lorna, da of late Samuel Harcombe; 2 s (David b 1963, Henry b 1965), 1 da (Miranda b 1962); m 2, 6 March 1974, Eirian Whittington, da of late Daniel Jenkins, and formerly w of (Brian) Ashley Barker, OBE, *qv*; *Career* National Provincial Bank (now National Westminster) 1947–50; admitted slr 1956; ptnr: Thorold Brodie Bonham-Carter & Mason 1959–73, Radcliffes & Co (following merger) 1973–90 (conslt 1990–94); hon slr Anglo Belgian Soc 1968– (vice pres), hon memb City of Westminster Law Soc (former pres and sec), former pres and chm Slrs' Wine Soc; chm Old Gownbay Assoc 1983–; memb Law Soc (memb Cncl 1980–89); Officier Ordre de Coteaux de Champagne; *Recreations* wine, food, sport; *Clubs* Anglo Belgian; *Style*— Norman Bonham-Carter, Esq; (☎ and fax 0181 741 3900)

BONINGTON, Sir Christian John Storey (Chris); kt (1996), CBE (1976); s of Charles Bonington (d 1983), and Helen Anne, *née* Storey; *b* 6 Aug 1934; *Educ* Univ Coll Sch London, RMA Sandhurst; *m* 1962, (Muriel) Wendy, da of Leslie Marchant; 2 s (and 1 s decd); *Career* cmmnd RTR 1956, served in N Germany, Army Outward Bound Sch (mountaineering instr); mgmnt trainee Unilever 1961–62; freelance writer, photographer and mountaineer 1962–; first ascent: Annapurna II (26,041 feet) Nepal with Dick Grant 1960, Nuptse (25,850 feet), third peak of Everest with Sherpa Ang Pemba 1961, Central Pillar of Freney Mont Blanc with Whillans, Clough and Djuclosz 1961; first Br ascent North Wall of the Eiger with Clough 1962; first ascent: Central Tower of Paine Patagonia with Whillans 1963, Old Man of Hoy with Patey and Bailey 1966; ascent Sangay in Ecuador (highest active volcano in the world) 1966; ldr: Annapurna South Face Expdn 1970, Br Everest Expdn 1972; first ascent: Brammah (21,036 feet) Kashmir with Estcourt 1973, Changabang Garhwal Himalaya with Boysen, Haston, Scott and Sandhu 1974; ldr Br K2 Expdn 1978, climbing ldr Br Mount Kongur Expdn 1981 (first ascent with Boardman, Rouse and Tasker 1981), ldr Br Everest Expdn NE Ridge 1982, first ascent W Summit of Shivling (21,330 feet) Gangotri with Fotheringham 1983, first Br ascent (solo) Mount Vinson (highest in Antarctica) 1983, ascent of Mount Everest (29,028 feet) as a memb of 1985 Norwegian Everest Expdn, ldr Norwegian-Br Menlungtse Expdn 1987, ldr Tibet Expdn 1988 which made first ascent West Summit Menlungtse, first ascent W Ridge Panch Chuli II Kumona Himalayas 1992, first ascent Meslin in Lemon Mountains 1993, first ascent Rangrik Rang Kinnaur Himalayas 1994, first ascent Drangnag-Ri 1995; memb Advsy Bd Outward Bound Mountain Sch Eskdale; pres: LEPRA 1983, Br Orienteering Fedn 1985–, Br Mountaineering Cncl 1988–91 (vice pres 1976–79 and 1985–88), Nat Tst Lake Dist Appeal, Cncl for National Parks 1992–; vice pres: Army Mountaineering Assoc 1980–, Young Explorer's Trust Youth Hostels Assoc, Br Lung Fndn; tstee: Calvert Tst Outdoor Activity Centre for the Disabled, Himalayan Adventure Tst; Hon MA Univ of Salford 1973, hon fell UMIST 1976; Hon DSc: Univ of Sheffield 1976, Univ of Lancaster 1983; FRGS (Founder's medal 1974), Lawrence of Arabia medal RSAA 1986, David Livingston medal RSGS 1991; *Books* I Chose to Climb (autobiography, 1966), Annapurna South Face (1971), The Next Horizon (autobiography, 1973), Everest South West Face (1973), Changabang (jt author), Everest the Hard Way (1976), Quest for Adventure (1981), Kongur - China's Elusive Summit (1982), Everest - The Unclimbed Ridge (with Dr Charles Clarke, *qv*, 1983), The Everest Years (1986), Mountaineer - Thirty Years of Climbing on the World's Great Peaks (autobiography, 1989), The Climbers (1992), Sea, Ice and Rock (with Robin Knox-Johnston, *qv*, 1992), Great Climbs (gen ed, 1994); *Recreations* skiing, orienteering; *Clubs* Alpine (pres 1996–), Climbers', Fell & Rock, Climbing, Army & Navy; *Style*— Sir Chris Bonington, CBE; ✉ Badger Hill, Hesket Newmarket, Wigton, Cumbria CA7 8LA (☎ 016974 78286, fax 0196974 78238)

BONN, Michael Walter; s of Maj Walter Basil Louis Bonn, DSO, MC (d 1973), of Oaklands, St Peter, Jersey, CI, and Lena Theodora, *née* Davidson (d 1974); *b* 12 Jan 1927; *Educ* Eton; *m* 16 June 1951, Elizabeth Mary, da of Maj Anthony Buxton, DSO (d 1970), of Horsey Hall, Gt Yarmouth, Norfolk; 1 s (Simon b 1953), 3 da (Sara b 1952, Mary b 1956, Theresa b 1959); *Career* Lt Welsh Gds 1944–48, cmmnd 1945; joined Willis Faber & Dumas Ltd 1949 (dir 1965–76, md Willis Faber & Dumas (Agencies) Ltd 1967–76); dir: Anglo American Securities Ltd 1972–75, N Atlantic Securities Ltd 1972–75, Morgan Grenfell (CI) Ltd 1976–93, Jersey Electricity Co Ltd 1980–, Fleming Ventures Ltd 1987–, Equity Capital for Industry Ltd 1987–95 (chm 1994–95), ECI Management (Jersey) Ltd 1987– (chm 1994–), ECI International Management Ltd 1988– (chm 1994–), Beauport Trustees Ltd 1989–, ECNG (Jersey) Ltd 1990–95, Deutsche Morgan Grenfell Holding Co BV 1993–; memb: Ctee Men of the Trees 1976–88, Jersey Assoc of Youth & Friendship (treas 1976–78, chm 1984–88), Ctee Société Jersiaise 1985–88, Cncl Int Dendrology Soc (chm 1993–); chm Eric Young Orchid Fndn 1992–; dep for St Peter in States of Jersey 1978–84, Jurat of the Royal Court of Jersey 1985–; Liveryman Worshipful Co of Fishmongers; Knight of Magistral Grace SMOM 1979; *Recreations* gardening; *Clubs* United; *Style*— Michael Bonn, Esq; ✉ Oaklands, St Peter, Jersey JE3 7DT, CI (☎ 01534 481481, fax 01534 483925)

BONNAR, Prof John; s of John Bonnar, of St Mary's Hosp Lanark, and Mary, *née* Breen (d 1986); *b* 12 July 1934; *Educ* Our Lady's HS Motherwell, Univ of Glasgow (MB ChB, MD, Boxing blue, pres Athletic Club, capt Scottish Univ Boxing Team); *m* Dr Eliz Bonnar, da of James Murray; 3 s (John Paul b 1 Sept 1961, Christopher Matthew b 1 June 1964, Peter James b 3 Oct 1969), 1 da (Clare Elizabeth b 29 March 1966); *Career* SHO Bellsmill Maternity Hosp 1959–60, registrar Victoria Infirmary Glasgow 1961–63, sr registrar Royal Maternity Hosp Glasgow 1964–69, reader and conslt obstetrician and gynaecologist Nuffield Dept of Obstetrics and Gynaecology Univ of Oxford John Radcliffe Hosp 1969–75, prof of obstetrics and gynaecology Trinity Coll Dublin 1975– (dean Faculty of Health Scis 1983–87); conslt obstetrician and gynaecologist: Rotunda Hosp 1975–85, St James's and Coombe Women's Hosps 1986–; memb Cncl Med Protection Soc 1990–; fell Trinity Coll 1976, FRCOG (memb Cncl 1991–); *Recreations* fishing, golf; *Clubs* University and Kildare St (Dublin); *Style*— Prof John Bonnar; ✉ 58 Deerpark Road, Castleknock, Dublin (☎ 00 353 1 821 3854) Trinity College Department of Obstetrics and Gynaecology, Trinity Centre, St James's Hospital, Dublin 8 (☎ 00 353 1 453 1888, fax 00 353 1 453 1614, car 0871 573231)

BONNER, Frederick Ernest; CBE (1974); s of George Frederick Bonner (d 1983), of London, and Edith May, *née* Luckhurst (d 1951); *b* 16 Sept 1923; *Educ* St Clement Danes Holborn Estate GS, Univ of London (BSc, DPA); *m* 1, 1957, Phyllis (d 1976), da of Henry Holder (d 1957), of Cobham, Surrey; m 2, 24 Sept 1977, Ethel Mary, da of John Beardon (d 1952), of Harberton, Devon; *Career* fin appts in local govt 1940–48, asst fin offr Central Electricity Authy 1950–58 (sr accountant 1949–50); CEGB: asst chief fin offr 1958–61, dep chief fin offr 1961–65, chief fin offr 1965–69, memb Bd 1969–75, dep chm 1975–86; memb Electricity Cncl 1969–86, pt/t memb UKAEA 1977–86, chm BA Helicopters 1983–85, memb Bd Public Fin Fndn 1985–, chm Uranium Inst 1985–86 (vice chm 1984 and 1987), pt/t memb Monopolies and Mergers Cmmn 1987–93, memb Tech Advsy Ctee SE Soc of CA's 1987–; hon treas: BIEE 1989–, Chichester Counselling Services 1994–; non-exec dir Nuclear Electric plc 1990–93; Freeman City of London 1983; IPFA 1946, FCA 1949, CIMgt 1976, FRSA 1984; *Recreations* music, gardening, reading; *Style*— Frederick Bonner, Esq, CBE; ✉ Joya, 20 Craigweil Manor, Aldwick, Bognor Regis, W Sussex PO21 4DJ (☎ 01243 267329, fax 01243 262815)

BONNER, Hilary Mary (Mrs Gunnell); da of Cecil Raymond Bawden (d 1980), of Bideford, North Devon, and Hilda May, *née* Keen; *b* 2 Aug 1949; *Educ* Edgehill Coll Bideford Devon; *m* 1969 (m dis), Geoff Bonner; m 2, 1987, Clive Gunnell; *Career* journalist and author; Daily Mirror Training Scheme Devon 1967–71, The Sun 1972–82 (news reporter, showbusiness reporter, feature writer and chief showbusiness writer); showbusiness ed: The Mail on Sunday 1982–86, The Daily Mirror 1986–90, The People (and asst ed) 1990–91, The Daily Mirror 1991–93; *Books* Rene and Me, The Story of Actor Gorden Kaye (1989), Benny - The True Story (1991), Heartbeat - The Real Life Story (1994), The Cruelty of Morning (1995); *Recreations* scuba diving, horse riding, films, gardening, backgammon, books, boats; *Clubs* Soho House, Lansdowne; *Style*— Ms Hilary Bonner; ✉ c/o The Lansdowne Club, 9 Fitzmaurice Place, London W1X 6JD

BONNER, John Albert Gordon; s of Gordon Pearson Bonner (d 1976), of Whitley Bay, Tyne & Wear, and Kathlyn Elizabeth, *née* Bygott (d 1983); *b* 26 Oct 1942; *Educ* Hymers Coll Hull, Darlington GS, Univ of Birmingham (Open Scholar, BSc); *m* 25 March 1967, Judith, da of Walter Culton; 2 da (Catherine Louise b 30 Dec 1971, Elizabeth Sarah b 7 Sept 1974); *Career* prodn control engr C A Parsons & Co Ltd Newcastle upon Tyne 1966–68 (graduate apprentice 1964–66), sr economist North Eastern Electricity Bd 1968–70, sr engr Midlands Electricity Bd 1970–73; South Western Electricity: tariffs and economics mangr 1973–88, dir of privatisation 1988–89, contracts and tariffs dir 1989–92, commercial dir 1992–; dir: Teesside Power Ltd 1990–, Western Gas Ltd 1992–; chm South Western Power Ltd 1990–; *Recreations* distance swimming; *Style*— John Bonner, Esq; ✉ South Western Electricity plc, 800 Park Avenue, Aztec West, Almondsbury, Bristol BS12 4SE (☎ 01454 201101, fax 01454 617912)

BONNER, Paul Max; s of Frank Max Bonner (d 1985), and Lily Elizabeth Marchant, *née* Jupp; *b* 30 Nov 1934; *Educ* Felsted; *m* 26 July 1956, (Nora) Jenifer, da of Dr George Raymond Hubbard; 2 s (Neil b 6 Jan 1957, Mark b 27 May 1959), 1 da (Alison b 27 June 1962); *Career* Nat Serv 1953–55, cmmnd 2 Lt RASC 1953, Acting Capt 1955, served in Egypt; BBC: radio studio mangr Bristol 1955–57, TV prodn Bristol 1957–59, current affairs prodr Lime Grove 1960–62, documentary producer 1962–74, ed community progs 1974–77, head of sci and feature progs 1977–80; Channel Four TV: channel controller 1980–83, exec dir and prog controller 1983–87; dir of Programme Planning Secretariat ITVA 1987–92, dir of secretariat ITV Network Centre 1992–94; memb: Bd Children's Film Unit 1989–, Ctee for Public Understanding of Sci 1986–92; chm COPUS Broadcast 1995–; dir: Broadcasting Support Services 1987–94, House of Commons Broadcasting Unit Ltd 1989–94; govr Nat Film and TV Sch 1983–88; FRTS 1989; *Books* The Third Age of Broadcasting (jtly); *Recreations* walking, photography, sailing; *Clubs* Chelsea Arts Club, Reform; *Style*— Paul Bonner, Esq; ✉ 5 North View, Wimbledon Common, London SW19 4UJ

BONNET, Maj-Gen Peter Robert Frank; CB (1991), MBE (1975); s of James Robert Bonnet (d 1970), and Phyllis Elsie, *née* Lumsden (d 1985); *b* 12 Dec 1936; *Educ* RMA Sandhurst, Univ of London (BSc), Allahabad Univ (MPhil); *m* 29 Dec 1961, Sylvia Mary, da of George William Coy (d 1964); 2 s (Gavin b 21 Oct 1962, Timothy b 6 June 1964); *Career* cmmnd 2 Lt Royal Regt of Artillery 1958, regtl duty Parachute Bde 1962–64, Capt 17 Trg Regt RA 1964–66, 3 Regt RHA 1966–68, Maj Royal Mil Coll of Sci 1969, Staff Coll Camberley 1970, GS02 Intelligence Centre Ashford 1971–72, Battery Cdr 40 Field Regt RA 1973–75, Lt-Col HQ Dir RA 1975–78, CO 26 Regt RA 1978–81, Brig Cdr RA 2 Div 1982–84, Nat Def Coll New Delhi India 1984–85, Maj-Gen Dir RA 1986–89, GOC Western Dist 1989–91; Col Cmdt Royal Regt of Artillery, Hon Col 26 Field Regt RA, vice pres Nat Artillery Assoc; gen sec Officers' Pensions Soc 1995–; dir OPS Investment Co 1995–, managing tstee OPS Widows' Fund 1995–; memb: Exec Ctee Army Benevolent Fund (chm Grants Ctee), Bd of Mgmnt RA Charitable Fund, Cncl Legal Practice Course Central Applications Bd; *Books* International Terrorism: Its Nature and Ways (1985), A Short History of the Royal Regiment of Artillery (1993); *Recreations* painting and sculpture; *Clubs* Army & Navy; *Style*— Maj-Gen Peter Bonnet, CB, MBE

BONNET, Robert (Rob); s of Harold Geoffrey Bonnet (d 1990), of Beckenham, Kent, and Margaret Mary, *née* Beevers; *b* 27 Sept 1952; *Educ* Dulwich, Univ of Sussex (BA); *m* 1980, Margaret Suzanne, *née* Harvey; 2 da (Clare Louise b 1981, Eleanor Jane b 1983); *Career* media buyer Benton and Bowles advtg agency 1976–77, disc jockey Evian-les-Bains 1977; BBC: station asst BBC Radio Brighton 1978–80, prodr BBC Radio Norfolk 1980–82, prodr BBC Radio Sport 1982–85, sports reporter BBC East (Norwich) 1985–87, sports corr BBC TV News 1989–95 (sports reporter 1987–89), sports presenter/reporter BBC TV News and Radio Sport 1995–; RTS Sports Report of the Year (for 9 O'Clock News coverage of Sydney winning Olympics for 2000) 1993; *Recreations* golf, travel; *Clubs* Studley Wood Golf; *Style*— Rob Bonnet, Esq; ✉ BBC TV News and Current Affairs, Television Centre, London W12 7RJ

BONNETT, Prof Raymond; s of Harry Bonnett (d 1955), of Lakenheath, and Maud, *née* Rolph; *b* 13 July 1931; *Educ* Bury St Edmunds Co GS, Imperial Coll London (BSc), Univ of Cambridge (PhD), Univ of London (DSc); *m* 24 Aug 1956, Shirley, da of Samuel James Rowe (d 1959), of Bewdley; 2 s (Paul b 1962, Alastair b 1964), 1 da (Helen b 1960); *Career* served RAF 1949–51, cmmnd PO 1950, RAF Lyneham 1950, RAF Mauripur 1951 (air movements); Salters fell Cambridge 1957–58, res fell Harvard 1958–59, assoc prof of chemistry UBC 1959–61; QMC (now Queen Mary and Westfield Coll) London: lectr in organic chemistry 1961–66, reader 1966–74, prof 1974–76, chm of organic chemistry 1976–94, head Dept of Chemistry 1982–87, Scotia research prof 1994–; friend of: Tate Gallery, William Morris Gallery, Globe Theatre; life memb: Royal Inst, NACF, National Tst; FRSC, CChem; *Recreations* theatre, private press books, gardening; *Style*— Prof Raymond Bonnett; ✉ Chemistry Department, Queen Mary and Westfield College, Mile End Rd, London E1 4NS (☎ 0171 975 5024, fax 0181 981 8745)

BONNEVILLE, Hugh Richard (né Williams); s of John Pritchard Williams, FRCS, of West Sussex, and Patricia Adèle, *née* Freeman; *b* 10 Nov 1963; *Educ* Sherborne Sch Dorset, CCC, Webber Douglas Acad; *Career* actor; theatrical prodr: Beautiful Thing (Duke of York's Theatre), Half Time (Donmar Warehouse); *Theatre* RNT roles incl: The Devil's Disciple, School for Scandal, Juno and the Paycock, School for Wives, Entertaining Strangers, Yerma; RSC (nominee Ian Charleson Award) incl: Hamlet, Amphibians, The Alchemist, 'Tis Pity She's a Whore, Two Gentlemen of Verona, The Virtuoso; other credits incl: Beatrice and Benedict (Royal Festival Hall), Habeas Corpus (Donmar), The Handyman (Chichester); rep work at Leicester Haymarket and Colchester Mercury; *Television* incl: The Man Who Made Husbands Jealous (Anglia), The Vet (Ikona Films), Stick with Me Kid (Buena Vista), Between the Lines (BBC), Peak Practice (Central), Sherlock Holmes (Granada), Cadfael (Central), Stalag Luft (Yorks); *Radio* incl: The Double Dealer, Weekending, People Like Us; *Films* incl: Frankenstein; *Recreations* studying jobsworths in their natural habitat; *Clubs* Garrick, Green Street, Peg's; *Style*— Hugh Bonneville, Esq; ✉ c/o Marina Martin Associates, 12–13 Poland Street, London W1V 3DE (☎ 0171 734 4818, fax 0171 734 4832)

BONNEY, Barbara; *b* 14 April 1956; *Educ* Mt Ararat Sch, Univ of New Hampshire, Univ of Salzburg, Mozarteum Salzburg; *m* Maurice Whitaker; *Career* soprano; studied under Hanna Ludwig, Walter Raninger, Liselotte Egger and Connie Prestel; memb: Franziskaner Kirche Choir, Salzburg ORF Radio Choir, Salzburger Kammerchor under Rupert Huber, Staatstheater Darmstadt 1979–83, Ensemble Städtischen Bühnen Frankfurt 1983–84; freelance singer 1984–; resident teacher Tanglewood USA 1995; numerous works recorded on Decca, Deutsche Grammophon, Philips, EMI, Teldec, Sony and Hyperion labels; video Der Rosenkavalier, Mozart C minor Mass; festivals incl: Munich Summerfestival 1984, Salzburg 1991 and 1992, Tanglewood 1993, 1994 and 1995; tours incl: Vienna Staatsoper Japan 1989 and 1994; *Concert appearances* incl: Brahms Requiem (Vienna Philharmonic) 1986, Die Fledermaus (Metropolitan Opera) 1989, Mozart C minor Mass (Berlin Philharmonic) 1990, Acis & Galatea (with Trevor Pinnock and English Concert Orch) 1991, Mahler Symphony No 4 (with Seiji Ozawa) 1993 and 1994, music by Handel (Drottningholm Theater) 1994, Orfeo (Geneva) 1995, The Marriage of Figaro (Covent Garden) 1995, Grieg songs (BBC Proms) 1996; *Solo roles* Pergolesi Stabat Mater (under Walter Raninger), Helena in Odysseus, Anna in Die Lustige Weiber von Windsor 1979, Sophie in Der Rosenkavalier (Munich and Covent Garden) 1984, Pamina in Die Zauberflöte (La Scala Milan 1985 and Zurich Opera 1986), Nyade in Ariadne auf Naxos (Metropolitan Opera) 1987, Susanna in The Marriage of Figaro (Zurich Opera) 1989; *Style*— Ms Barbara Bonney; ✉ c/o Tom Graham, IMG, 3 Burlington Lane, Chiswick, London W4 2TH (☎ 0181 233 5000, fax 0181 233 5801)

BONNEY, George Louis William; s of Dr Ernest Henry Bonney (d 1938), of London, and Gertrude Mary, *née* Williams; *b* 10 Jan 1920; *Educ* Eton, St Mary's Hosp Med Sch (MB, MS); *m* 26 Dec 1950, Margaret, da of Thomas William Morgan, of Nelson, Glamorgan; 2 da (Mary b 1952, Victoria b 1954); *Career* Surgn Lt RNVR 1945–47, RNR 1949–53; travelling fellowship postgrad Med Fedn 1950–51, registrar and clinical res asst Inst of Orthopaedics 1947–54; orthopaedic surgn: Southend-on-Sea Gp of Hosps 1953–55, St Mary's Hosp Paddington 1954–84 (consulting surgn 1984–); Watson-Jones lectr RCS 1976, Henry Floyd lectr Inst of Orthopaedics 1977; assoc ed Jl of Bone and Joint Surgery 1960–68; chm: St Mary's Hosp Med Ctee 1972–74, Dist Hosp Med Ctee and Mgmnt Team Paddington and N Kensington Health Dist 1978–80; memb: Cncl Med Def Union 1964–88 (hon fell), Bd of Govrs St Mary's Hosp 1972–74, SICOT; pres Old Etonian Med Soc 1989–92; FRSM, FRCS, FBOA; *Publications* chapters in: British Surgical Practice (1957), Clinical Surgery (1966), Operative Surgery (1977), Clinical Orthopaedics (1983 and 1995), Microreconstruction of Nerve Injuries (1987), Current Therapy in Neurologic Disease (1987), Medical Negligence (1990 and 1994), Clinical Neurology (1991); *Recreations* fishing, reading, photography, listening to music; *Clubs* Leander; *Style*— G L W Bonney, Esq; ✉ 6 Wooburn Grange, Grange Drive, Wooburn Green, Bucks HP10 0QU (☎ 01628 525598)

BONO, (Paul Hewson); s of Robert (Bobby) Hewson, and Iris Hewson; *b* 10 May 1960; *Educ* Mount Temple Sch; *m* Alison (Ali); 2 da (Jordan b 10 May 1989, Eve); *Career* lead singer and fndr memb U2 1978– (with The Edge, *qv*, Adam Clayton, *qv* and Larry Mullen, Jr, *qv*); first U2 release U23 (EP) 1979; *Albums* Boy 1980, October 1981, War 1983 (entered UK chart at no 1), Under A Blood Red Sky (live album) 1983, The Unforgettable Fire 1984 (entered UK charts at no 1), The Joshua Tree 1987 (entered UK charts at no 1, fastest selling album ever in UK), Rattle & Hum 1988 (entered UK charts at No 1), Achtung Baby 1991, Zooropa 1993 (No 1 in 18 countries); *Singles* incl: Fire 1981, New Year's Day (first UK Top Ten hit) 1983, Pride (In the Name of Love) 1984, Unforgettable Fire 1985, With or Without You 1987, I Still Haven't Found What I'm Looking For 1987, Where The Streets Have No Name 1987, Desire (first UK no 1 single) 1988, Angel of Harlem 1988, When Love Comes to Town 1989, All I Want Is You 1989, Night & Day (for AIDS benefit LP Red Hot & Blue) 1990, The Fly (entered UK charts at no 1) 1991, Stay 1993; also duet with Frank Sinatra I've Got You Under My Skin 1993; *Film* Rattle & Hum 1988; *Tours* incl: UK, US, Belgium and Holland 1980, UK, US, Ireland and Europe 1981–83, Aust, NZ and Europe 1984, A Conspiracy of Hope (Amnesty International Tour) 1986, world Joshua Tree tour 1987, Rattle & Hum tour 1988, Zoo TV world tour (played to 5m people) 1992–93; also appeared at: Live Aid 1985 (Best Live Aid Performance Rolling Stone Readers' Poll 1986), Self Aid Dublin, Smile Jamaica (Dominion Theatre, in aid of hurricane disaster relief) 1988, New Year's Eve concert Dublin (broadcast live to Europe and USSR) 1989; performed at venues incl: Wembley Stadium, Madison Square Garden NY, Longest Day Festival Milton Keynes Bowl, Croke Park Dublin, Sun Devil Stadium Arizona; *Awards* Grammy awards: Album of the Year (The Joshua Tree) 1987, Best Rock Performance (Joshua Tree tour) 1987, Best Rock Performance (Desire) 1989, Best Video (Where The Streets Have No Name) 1989, Best Alternative Album (Zooropa) 1993; others incl: Best Band Rolling Stone Readers' Poll 1986 (also jt winner Critics' Poll), Band of the Year Rolling Stone Writers' Poll 1984, Best International Act BPI Awards 1989 and 1990, Best Live Act BPI Awards 1993; *Style*— Bono; ✉ c/o Regine Moylett Publicity, First Floor, 145a Ladbroke Grove, London W10 6HJ (☎ 0171 221 0554, fax 0171 221 8532)

BONSALL, Sir Arthur Wilfred; KCMG (1977), CBE (1957); s of Wilfred Cook Bonsall (d 1963), of Beck House, Seathwaite, Broughton-in-Furness, and Sarah Bonsall; *b* 25 June 1917; *Educ* Bishop's Stortford Coll, St Catharine's Coll Cambridge; *m* 1941, Joan Isabel (d 1990), da of late G C Wingfield, of Bournemouth; 4 s, 3 da; *Career* joined Air Miny 1940, transferred to FO 1942, IDC 1962, dir Govt Communications HQ 1975–78; *Recreations* coarse gardening; *Style*— Sir Arthur Bonsall, KCMG, CBE; ✉ 1 Coxwell Court, Coxwell St, Cirencester, Gloucestershire GL7 2BQ

BONSALL, David Charles; s of Leonard Dale Bonsall (d 1984), and Nellie Bonsall; *b* 26 July 1956; *Educ* Winchester, St John's Coll Cambridge (MA, LLM); *m* 11 Oct 1980, Margaret Ruth, da of Arthur George Shaw, OBE, of St Albans, Herts; 2 da (Philippa

Ruth b 25 Sept 1989, Kathryn Penelope b 20 June 1992); *Career* admitted slr 1981; ptnr Freshfields 1987–93 (articled clerk 1979–81), md Euro Asset Backed Fin UBS Ltd 1993–; Freeman Worshipful Co of Slrs; *Books* Securitisation (1990); *Recreations* golf, skiing, music; *Clubs* The Royal St George's Golf, The Royal and Ancient Golf, Rye Golf; *Style*— David Bonsall, Esq; ✉ 49 Scarsdale Villas, London W8 6PU (☎ 0171 937 4063); UBS Ltd, 100 Liverpool Street, London EC2M 2RH (☎ 0171 901 3792, fax 0171 901 4890)

BONSALL, Richard James (Rick); s of Geoffrey Holtham (d 1972), and Gladys Elizabeth Catherine, *née* Tait; *b* 6 Nov 1955; *Educ* Westlake Boys HS Auckland NZ, Univ of Auckland (BA), Osaka Univ of Foreign Studies (postgrad dip), Tokyo Univ of Fine Arts (MA); *m* 1985, Julia, da of Roland Jesse; 1 s (James Joseph Holtham b 3 April 1990); *Career* press offr Japan Nat Tourist Orgn London 1979, mgmnt trainee and PR mangr Matsushita Electric London 1980–83, account dir Charles Barker Lyons 1983–85, assoc dir Rowland Company London 1985, dir and head of International Business Unit Hill and Knowlton London 1986–91, md and chief exec offr Hill and Knowlton Japan Ltd 1991–95, sr vice pres and regnl dir Hill and Knowlton Asia Ltd Hong Kong 1995–96, sr md Hill and Knowlton Inc NY 1996–; assoc Trinity Coll London (Dip Piano Teaching); memb: Japan Soc (London), Br C of C in Japan, American C of C in Japan; MIPR, MInstD; *Recreations* skiing, tennis, health and fitness, music, antiques; *Clubs* City (Tokyo), Foreign Correspondents' (Tokyo); *Style*— Richard Bonsall, Esq; ✉ Hill & Knowlton Inc, 466 Lexington Avenue 3F, New York, NY 10017, USA (☎ 00 1 212 885 0345, e-mail rbonsall@hillandknowlton.com)

BONSER, Rt Rev David; *see:* Bolton, Bishop of

BONSOR, Anthony Miles; s of David Victor Bonsor, of Herts, and Sheila Valerie, *née* Graham; *b* 3 May 1948; *Educ* Eton, Univ of Southampton (LLB); *m* 1980, Frances Elizabeth, da of David Bankes; 1 s (Miles David b 12 Sept 1984), 2 da (Sophie Elizabeth b 27 Aug 1982, Laura Frances b 17 June 1988); *Career* articled clerk Farrer & Co 1971–73, admitted slr 1974, Richards Butler & Co 1975–76; Denton Hall (formerly Denton Hall Burgin & Warrens): London Office 1976–79, Hong Kong Office 1979–83, ptnr London Office 1983–; memb Law Soc; *Recreations* sailing, shooting; *Style*— Anthony Bonsor, Esq; ✉ Denton Hall, Five Chancery Lane, Clifford's Inn, London EC4A 1BU (☎ 0171 242 1212, fax 0171 404 0087)

BONSOR, Sir Nicholas Cosmo; 4 Bt (UK 1925), of Kingswood, Epsom, Surrey; MP (C) Upminster (majority 13,821); s of Sir Bryan Cosmo Bonsor, 3 Bt, MC, TD (d 1977), and Elizabeth, *née* Hambro (d 1995); *b* 9 Dec 1942; *Educ* Eton, Keble Coll Oxford (MA); *m* 4 Sept 1969, Hon Nadine Marisa Lampson, da of 2 Baron Killearn (d 1996); 2 s (Alexander Cosmo b 1976, James Charles b 1983), 3 da (Sacha Henrietta b 1975, Elizabeth Nadine b 1987, Mary Catherine b (twin) 1987); *Heir* s, Alexander Cosmo Bonsor b 8 Sept 1976; *Career* served The Royal Bucks Yeo (RA TA) 1964–69; called to the Bar Inner Temple 1967, in practice 1967–75; MP (C): Nantwich 1979–83, Upminster 1983–; min of state FCO 1995–; vice chm Tourism Sub-Ctee 1980–83, vice chm Cons Parly Foreign Affrs Ctee 1981–83, vice chm Cons Parly Defence Ctee 1987–90, chm Commons Select Ctee on Defence 1992–95, memb Select Ctee on Bdcasting 1992–95, memb Liaison Ctee 1992–95, vice chm Cons Parly Constitutional Ctee 1992–95; chm: Food Hygiene Bureau Ltd 1986–95, The Cyclotron Tst for Cancer Treatment 1984–92 (pres 1992–95), The Br Field Sports Soc 1988–94, The Baronets' Tst 1993–95; memb Cncl of Lloyd's 1987–92; chm Standing Cncl of the Baronetage 1990–93 (vice chm 1987–89); FRSA 1970; *Recreations* sailing, military history, shooting; *Clubs* White's, Royal Yacht Sqdn, House of Commons Yacht (commodore 1985–86), Pratt's, Beefsteak; *Style*— Sir Nicholas Bonsor, Bt, MP; ✉ c/o House of Commons, London SW1A 0AA

BONSOR, (Angus) Richard; s of Sir Bryan Cosmo Bonsor, 3 Bt, MC, TD (d 1977), of Liscombe, Leighton Buzzard, Beds, and Elizabeth, *née* Hambro (d 1995); *b* 3 Feb 1947; *Educ* Eton, Keble Coll Oxford (BA); *m* 14 Jan 1971, Susan Anne, da of David Henry Lewis Wigan, of Thorpe Abbotts Place, Diss, Norfolk; 2 s (Rupert James b 26 Sept 1974, Edward Richard b 16 July 1976), 1 da (Clare Lucinda b 3 Sept 1981); *Career* ptnr Rowe & Pitman 1978 (joined 1968); dir: S G Warburg Securities 1986, associated to Matheson Securities 1989–92, UBS Ltd 1992–95, J O Hambro Investment Management 1995–; MSI; *Recreations* golf, racquets; *Clubs* White's, Turf, Pratts, Sunningdale, Royal West Norfolk Golf; *Style*— Richard Bonsor, Esq; ✉ J O Hambro Investment Management, 10 Park Place, London SW1A 1LP (☎ 0171 222 2020, car 0860 212204)

BONYNGE, Richard; AO (1983), CBE (1977); s of C A Bonynge, of Epping, NSW; *b* 29 Sept 1930; *Educ* Sydney HS, Sydney Conservatorium; *m* 1954, Dame Joan Sutherland, *qv*; 1 s; *Career* opera conductor; official debut as conductor Santa Cecilia Orch Rome 1962; artistic dir: Sutherland/Williamson Int Grand Opera Co Aust 1965, Vancouver Opera Assoc 1974–78, Aust Opera 1975–85; conducted many operas in: Metropolitan Opera, San Francisco, Chicago Lyric Opera, Teatro Liceo, Barcelona, Royal Opera House Covent Garden, San Diego Opera, Sydney Opera; has made numerous recordings of opera and ballet; *Style*— Richard Bonynge, Esq, AO, CBE; ✉ c/o Australian Opera, PO Box 291, Strawberry Hills, NSW 2012, Australia

BOOK, Anthony; JP (1987); s of Alec Book (d 1987), of Newcastle upon Tyne, and Betty Book (d 1957); *b* 19 June 1946; *Educ* Newcastle Royal GS, Univ of Bristol (BSc); *m* 1, 5 Aug 1969, Susan Lynn (d 1985), da of Irving Brand, of Long Beach, California; 1 s (Jeffrey Adam b 1971), 2 da (Jennifer Beth b 1973, Juliette Hiliary b 1977); m 2, 1989, Miriam, da of Walter Newton, of London; *Career* brand mangr and market res Lever Brothers Ltd 1969–78, dir of Consumer Servs American Express Europe Ltd 1978–84, currently md Finesse Ltd and Riomay Ltd; winner: Br Computer Soc Award (for Applications) 1982, Int Direct Mktg Symposium (for Tech Innovation in Mktg) 1984; speaker on direct mktg and electronic media at major confs in UK and overseas; FIMgt 1986, MIDM 1994; *Recreations* flying, DIY, gardening, philately, travel; *Style*— Anthony Book, Esq, JP; ✉ Riomay Ltd, 1 Birch Road, Eastbourne, E Sussex BN23 6PL (☎ 01323 648641, fax 01323 720682)

BOOKER, (Gordon) Alan; s of Frederick William Booker, and Beryl Booker; *b* 17 Feb 1938; *Educ* Dronfield GS, Univ of Sheffield (BEng); *m* 1957, Anne Christine, *née* Pike; 2 s, 1 da; *Career* Sheffield Water 1960–65, Birmingham Water 1965–70, W Glamorgan Water 1970–74, Welsh Water 1974–80, chief exec E Worcester Water 1980–89, md Biwater Supply 1987–90, Bournemouth and W Hants Water Cos 1989–90, dep DG Water Servs 1990–; cncl memb Water Res Centre 1985–90, chm several water indust ctees on automation and leakage control; MICE 1963, FIWEM 1966; *Books* Water Distribution Systems (1984), Telemetry and Control (1986), author of numerous articles in jls; *Recreations* walking, painting; *Style*— Alan Booker, Esq; ✉ 106 The Holloway, Droitwich, Worcs WR9 7AH (☎ 01905 772432); Sheplegh Court, Blackawton, Devon TQ9 7AH (☎ 01803 712577); Ofwat, Centre City Tower, 7 Hill Street, Birmingham B5 4UA (☎ 0121 625 1304, fax 0121 625 1311)

BOOKER, Christopher John Penrice; s of late John Mackarness Booker, of Shillingstone, Dorset, and Margaret Booker (d 1991); *b* 7 Oct 1937; *Educ* Shrewsbury, CCC Cambridge; *m* 1, 1963 (m dis), Hon Mrs Emma C Tennant, *qv*; m 2, 1972, Christine Verity (m dis); m 3, 1979, Valerie, da of late Dr M S Patrick, OBE; 2 s; *Career* author, journalist and broadcaster; Liberal News 1960, jazz critic Sunday Telegraph 1961, ed Private Eye 1961–63 (contrib 1965–); resident scriptwriter: That Was The Week That Was 1962–63, Not So Much A Programme 1963–64; former contrib: Spectator, Daily Telegraph (Way of the World column as Peter Simple II 1987–90); columnist: Sunday Telegraph 1990–, Daily Mail 1995–; wrote extensively on property devpt, planning and housing 1972–77, TV prog City of Towers: the Rise and Fall of a Twentieth Century Dream (1979); memb Cowgill Enquiry into post-war repatriations from Austria 1986–90; *Books* The Neophiliacs: A Study of the Revolution in English Life in the 50's and 60's (1969), Goodbye London (with Candida Lycett-Green, 1973), The Booker Quiz (1976), The Seventies (1980), The Games War: A Moscow Journal (1981), Repatriations from Austria in 1945 (jtly, 1990), The Mad Officials (with Richard North, 1994), The Castle of Lies: Why Britain Must Get Out of Europe (1996); *Recreations* the psychology of storytelling, nature, music, following Somerset CCC; *Style*— Christopher Booker, Esq; ✉ The Old Rectory, Litton, Bath, Somerset (☎ 01761 241263)

BOOKER, Michael William; s of Donald Booker, of Great Longstone, Derbyshire, and Mary Elizabeth, *née* Trickett; *b* 5 Oct 1955; *Educ* King Edward VII Sch Sheffield, Univ of Liverpool Med Sch (BM BCh, MRCOG); *m* 1, 1979 (m dis 1991), Judith Anne, da of Donald Ryder; 2 da (Laurie Anne b 15 Sept 1982, Chloe Maxine b 5 June 1985); m 2, 1994, Elizabeth Mary, da of Gordon Ball; *Career* research fell then lectr in obstetrics and gynaecology King's Coll Sch of Med and Dentistry 1984–89; conslt in obstetrics and gynaecology: Singapore Gen Hosp 1989–90, Mayday Univ Hosp Croydon 1990– (estab centre for reproductive med and in-vitro fertilization and embryo transfer clinic (transport IVF prog) 1992); district tutor (Croydon Health Dist) RCOG; author of numerous contribs to med jls; memb: BMA 1978, RSM 1988, AFS 1988, BFS 1991, ESHRE 1994; *Recreations* windsurfing, scuba diving, jazz; *Style*— Michael Booker, Esq; ✉ 235 Banstead Road, Banstead, Surrey SM7 1RB; Mayday Hospital, Mayday Road, Croydon, Surrey CR7 7YE (☎ 0181 657 6155, fax 0181 657 0755)

BOOKER, Russell Stuart; s of Wilfred Bryan Booker, of Maidstone, Kent, and Irene, *née* Netherton; *b* 21 Aug 1957; *Educ* Maidstone GS, Univ of Birmingham; *m* 23 March 1985 (m dis 1988), Hilary Margaret Curley; *Career* slr and ptnr: Booth & Blackwell 1981–86, Masons 1986–; *Books* Buying & Selling a Business (with L Kane, 1990); *Recreations* golf, sailing, gardening; *Style*— Russell Booker, Esq; ✉ Masons, 30 Aylesbury St, London EC1R 0ER (☎ 0171 490 4000, fax 0171 490 2545)

BOOLELL, HE Sir Satcam; kt (1977); s of Sahadewoo Boolell (d 1940), of Mauritius, and Cossilah, *née* Choony (d 1985); *b* 11 Sept 1920; *Educ* LSE (LLB (Hons)); *m* 1, 1948, Premila K, *née* Indurjeet (decd); m 2, 1987, Myrtha Eugenia, *née* Poblete; *Career* called to the Bar Lincoln's Inn 1952, admitted Mauritian Bar 1952; Mauritian diplomat; elected memb Legislative Assembly 1953, 1959, 1963, 1967, 1976, 1984 and 1987; min of agriculture and natural resources 1959–67 and 1968–82, min of educn 1967–68, elected pres and ldr Mauritius Lab Pty 1983, min of economic planning and devpt 1984–86, dep PM, attorney-gen, min of justice and min of external affrs and emigration 1986–90; Mauritian high cmmr to the Ct of St James's 1996–; rep Mauritius at numerous int confs; independent dir Jardine Fleming Ltd (India Fund) 1993–96; memb Soc of the Prevention of Cruelty to Animals; Hon DCL Mauritius 1986; Cdr de la Legion d'Honneur (France) 1990; *Books* The Untold Stories (1996); author of various press articles on social, political and economic subjects 1993–95; *Recreations* travelling, reading, walking in the countryside; *Clubs* Turf (Mauritius); *Style*— HE Sir Satcam Boolell, QC; ✉ 4 Bis Bancilhon Street, Port Louis, Mauritius (☎ 00 230 208 0079); Mauritius High Commission, 32/33 Elvaston Place, London SW7 5NW (☎ 0171 581 0294, fax 0171 823 8437)

BOON, Dr Nicholas Antony; s of Capt John Nicholas Boon, MC, of Loudwater, nr Rickmansworth, Herts, and Doreen Myrtle, *née* Francke; *b* 31 Dec 1950; *Educ* Canford, Gonville and Caius Coll Cambridge (MA, MB BChir), Middx Hosp Med Sch (MD); *m* 19 May 1979, (Grace) Anne, da of Prof W B Robertson, of Wimbledon, London; 2 da (Victoria b 11 Aug 1982, Sarah Jane b 15 March 1984); *Career* clinical lectr and sr registrar John Radcliffe Hosp Oxford 1983–86, conslt cardiologist Royal Infirmary of Edinburgh 1986–, hon sr lectr Univ of Edinburgh 1986–; FRCP 1988; *Publications* author of numerous scientific pubns and contrib to various med textbooks incl Davidson's Principles and Practice of Medicine and Oxford Textbook of Medicine; *Recreations* golf, skiing; *Clubs* Dalmahoy Country; *Style*— Dr Nicholas Boon; ✉ 7 Cobden Crescent, Edinburgh EH9 2BG (☎ 0131 667 3917); Department of Cardiology, Royal Infirmary of Edinburgh, Lauriston Place, Edinburgh (☎ 0131 536 2006, fax 0131 536 2021)

BOON, Sir Peter Coleman; kt (1979); s of Frank and Evelyn Clara Boon; *b* 2 Sept 1916; *Educ* Felsted; *m* 1940, Pamela; 1 s, 1 da; *Career* Stock Exchange 1933–34, Lloyds & National Provincial Foreign Bank 1934–35, Dennison Manufacturing Co USA 1936–39; served WWII 1939–46; Hoover Ltd: joined 1946, md (Australia) 1955–65, md 1965–75, chm 1975–78; chm: Highclere Investment Tst 1979, Hoover Administrative Services Brussels 1978; jt dep chm London Sound 1982; Goodyear prof of business admin Kent State Univ USA 1983–86; Hon LLD Univ of Strathclyde 1978; FIMgt, FRSA 1980; Chevalier de l'Ordre de la Couronne (Belgium) 1976; *Recreations* horses, swimming, golf, theatre, economics, boys clubs, education; *Clubs* Hurlingham, Western Racing (Ayr), Australia Jockey, American National (Sydney), Royal Sydney Yacht Sqdn; *Style*— Sir Peter Boon

BOORD, Antony Andrew; s of Sqdn Ldr Sir Richard William Boord, 3 Bt (d 1975), and Yvonne Swingler, *née* Bird (d 1991); bro and hp of Sir Nicolas John Charles Boord, 4 Bt, *qv*; *b* 21 May 1938; *Educ* Charterhouse; *m* 1960, Anna Christina von Krogh; 1 s (Andrew Richard b 1962), 1 da (Tamsin Katrina b 1961); *Career* dir Planned Packaging Ltd; *Clubs* Special Forces; *Style*— Antony Boord, Esq; ✉ Higher Spring Grove Lodge, Milverton, nr Taunton, Somerset TA4 1NW

BOORD, Sir Nicolas John Charles; 4 Bt (UK 1896), of Wakehurst Place, Ardingly, Sussex; s of Sqdn Ldr Sir Richard William Boord, 3 Bt (d 1975), and Yvonne Swingler, *née* Bird; *b* 10 June 1936; *Educ* Eton, Sorbonne, Societa Dante Alighieri Italy, Univ of Santander Spain; *m* 1, 1960 (m dis 1965), Françoise, da of Giuseppe Tempra; m 2, 1965, Françoise Renée Louise, da of Marcel Clovis Mouret, of Marseilles; *Heir* bro, Antony Andrew Boord, *qv*; *Career* scientific translator/English trg specialist; jt translator: The History of Physics and The Philosophy of Science (1972), numerous scientific papers for English and American scientific and tech jls; *Recreations* English and French literature and linguistics; *Style*— Sir Nicolas Boord, Bt; ✉ 61 Traverse le Mée, 13009 Marseilles, France

BOORMAN, Sir Derek; KCB (1986, CB 1982); s of late N R Boorman, MBE, and Mrs A L Boorman, *née* Patman; *b* 13 Sept 1930; *Educ* Wolstanton, Sandhurst; *m* 1, 1956, Jennifer Jane Skinner (d 1991); 1 s (decd), 2 da; m 2, 1992, Nicola Caroline Cox; *Career* Public Rels Army 1978–79, Dir Military Ops 1980–82, Cdr Br Forces Hong Kong 1982–85, Chief of Defence Intelligence 1985–88, attained rank of Lt-Gen; Col The Staffordshire Regt (Prince of Wales) 1985–90, Col 6 Gurkha Rifles 1983–89; chm: Camberwell Health Authy and King's Coll Hosp 1989–93, Bart's, Royal London and London Chest Hosp Tst 1993–; dir: Tarmac Construction Ltd 1988–95, Crown House Engineering Ltd 1990–; memb The Security Cmmn 1991–; Lt of the Tower of London 1989–92; memb Cncl Univ of Kent 1997; *Recreations* gardening, music, tennis; *Clubs* Naval and Military; *Style*— Sir Derek Boorman, KCB

BOORMAN, Edwin Roy Pratt; s of Henry Roy Pratt Boorman, CBE (d 1992), and his 1 w, Enid Margaret, *née* Starke; *b* 7 Nov 1935; *Educ* Rydal Sch, Queens' Coll Cambridge (MA); *m* 1 (m dis 1982), Merrilyn Ruth Pettit; 4 da; m 2, 1983, Janine Mary, of William Craske, of Penenden Heath, Maidstone; 1 s; *Career* Kent Messenger Group: joined 1959, ed South Eastern Gazette 1960–62, ed Kent Messenger 1962–65, md 1965–86, chm and chief exec 1986–; chm Messenger Print Ltd 1972–; chm: Kent Assoc of Boys' Clubs 1988–, Kent Branch IOD 1993–96, North Kent Success 1993–96; pres Loose Amenities Assoc 1989–, fin chm Sutton Valence Sch 1990–, vice chm Royal British Legion

Industries 1995–; tstee: Kent Air Ambulance Appeal 1993–, Chatham Historic Dockyard 1992–; Kent county dir St John Ambulance Assoc 1993–; High Sheriff in nomination for Kent 1996–97; memb Ct of Assts Worshipful Co of Stationers and Newspapermakers 1986; *Recreations* sailing (yacht 'Messenger'); *Clubs* Ocean Cruising, Medway Yacht, Kent CCC, Carlton; *Style*— Edwin Boorman, Esq; ✉ Redhill Farm, 339 Redhill, Wateringbury, Kent; Kent Messenger, Messenger House, New Hythe Lane, Larkfield, Kent ME20 6SG (☎ 01622 717880, fax 01622 710937)

BOORMAN, John; CBE (1994); s of George Boorman, and Ivy, *née* Chapman; *b* 18 Jan 1933; *Educ* Salesian Coll Chertsey; *Career* film director; contrib articles to Manchester Guardian and various magazines 1950–54, successively broadcaster, critic BBC radio, film ed ITN London 1955–58, dir/prodr Southern TV 1958–60, head of documentaries BBC TV Bristol (dir The Citizens series and The Newcomers documentaries) 1960–64; *Films* Catch us if you can 1965, Point Blank 1967, Hell in the Pacific 1968, Leo the Last 1969, Deliverance 1970, Zardoz 1973, The Heretic 1976, Excalibur 1981, The Emerald Forest 1985, Hope and Glory 1987, Where the Heart is 1989, I Dreamt I Woke Up 1991, Beyond Rangoon 1994; *Books* The Legend of Zardoz (1973), Money into Light (1985), Hope and Glory (1987), Projections 1 1992 (2 1993, 3 1994); *Style*— John Boorman, Esq, CBE; ✉ c/o ICM Ltd, 8942 Wilshire Boulevard, Beverly Hills, Los Angeles, CA 90211, USA

BOOSEY, Georgina Caroline; da of Dr Donald Harden, CBE, FSA (archaeologist and museum dir, d 1994), and Cecil Ursula, *née* Harriss (d 1963); *b* 3 Jan 1936; *m* 1960, Anthony Leslie Marchant Boosey (vice pres The Hawk and Owl Tst), s of Leslie Boosey (sometime chm of Boosey and Hawkes, d 1979); *Career* magazine ed, food, wine and restaurant journalist; managing ed Vogue Magazine 1979–93; assessor for the food category The André Simon Memorial Fund 1994 Book Awards; dir Friends of the Earth Tst, tstee Br Ptnrs of the World (sister orgn of the Léger Fndn of Canada); *Style*— Mrs Anthony Boosey; ✉ Annings, Chardleigh Green, Wadeford, nr Chard, Somerset TA20 3AJ (☎ 01460 64805, London ☎ 0171 284 0934)

BOOT, David Henry; s of Henry Matthews Boot (d 1974); *b* 15 Sept 1931; *Educ* Uppingham, Loughborough Univ of Technol (DLC); *m* 1956, Gillian Mary, da of Reeves Charlesworth, OBE (d 1974); 4 s; *Career* non-exec dir (formerly chm) Henry Boot & Sons plc; *Recreations* photography, golf, walking; *Style*— David Boot, Esq; ✉ Henry Boot & Sons PLC, Banner Cross Hall, Sheffield S11 9PD (☎ 0114 255 5444, fax 0114 258 5548)

BOOT, Edward James (Jamie); s of (Edward) Hamer Boot, OBE, MM (d 1987), and Joan Margaret, *née* Denniff; *b* 19 Nov 1951; *Educ* Rossall Sch; *m* Susan Philippa (Sue), da of John Humphrey Gowers (d 1988); 2 s (Hamer b 1981, William b 1987), 1 da (Georgina b 1984); *Career* md Henry Boot & Sons plc 1986–; *Recreations* shooting; *Style*— Jamie Boot, Esq; ✉ Henry Boot & Sons plc, Banner Cross Hall, Ecclesall Road South, Sheffield S11 9PD (☎ 0114 2 555 444)

BOOTE, Barbara Mary; da of Arthur Boote (d 1989), of Colehill, Wimborne, Dorset, and Joan, *née* West (d 1980); *b* 8 June 1954; *Educ* Bromley GS; *Career* sec and editorial asst: Coronet Books 1973–77, Magnum Books 1977–80; Macdonald Sphere: editorial mangr 1981–86, editorial dir 1986–89, publishing dir 1989–92; editorial dir Little Brown and Co (UK) Ltd 1992–; *Style*— Barbara Boote; ✉ Little Brown and Company (UK) Ltd, Brettenham House, Lancaster Place, London WC2 7EN (☎ 0171 911 8000, fax 0171 911 8100)

BOOTE, Charles Richard Michael; TD (1971, and two clasps 1978 and 1983), DL (Staffs 1988); s of Col (Charles Geoffrey) Michael Boote, MBE, TD, JP, DL, and Elizabeth Gertrude, *née* Davies (d 1980); *b* 7 Aug 1939; *Educ* Cheltenham; *m* 9 Oct 1965, Alison Brookes, da of Charles Kenneth Stott (d 1979), of Stafford; 1 s (James b 1974), 2 da (Vanessa b 1967, Emma b 1970); *Career* Maj TA cmd B (Staffs Yeo), The Queen's Own Mercian Yeo 1974–78, 2 i/c The Queen's Own Mercian Yeo 1978–80; md Armitage Shanks Integrated Systems 1988–90, corp devpt dir Home Products Div Blue Circle Industries plc 1987–89, currently independent mgmnt conslt and distributor; chm: Staffs Ctee of the Rural Devpt Cmmn 1984– (memb Cmmn's Econ Advsy Panel 1988–96), Staffs Ambulance Serv NHS Tst 1991–93; dir: Staffs Trg and Enterprise Cncl 1989–94, Stafford Enterprise Ltd 1990–; memb: Exec Ctee Staffs Devpt Assoc 1991–94, Staffs Ctee Country Landowners Assoc 1988–95; gen cmmr of taxes Stafford Div 1993–; vice chm and treas Staffs Assoc of Boys Clubs 1976–, employers rep W Midlands TAVR Assoc Ctee 1983–; High Sheriff of Staffs 1990–91; FCA, FCMA, CMI; *Recreations* skiing, salmon fishing, stalking, tennis, squash; *Style*— Charles Boote, Esq, TD, DL; ✉ Enson Moor House, Sandon, Stafford ST18 9TA (home ☎ 01889 508223, office ☎ 01889 508008, fax 01889 508405)

BOOTE, Gervase William Alexander; s of Col (Charles Geoffrey) Michael Boote, MBE, TD, JP, DL, of Tomatin, Inverness-shire, and Elizabeth Gertrude Boote, *née* Davies (d 1980); *b* 2 April 1944; *Educ* Cheltenham; *m* 1967 (m dis 1987), Janet, da of Alan Stott (d 1990); 1 s (Richard b 1969), 1 da (Caroline b 1972); *Career* Peat Marwick Mitchell & Co 1962–72; dir corp fin HSBC Samuel Montagu (formerly Samuel Montagu & Co Ltd) 1972–; FCA; *Recreations* golf, tennis, salmon fishing; *Clubs* Hurlingham, Worplesdon Golf, Hankley Common Golf; *Style*— Gervase Boote, Esq; ✉ 2A Hurlingham Court, Ranelagh Gardens, London SW6 3UL (☎ 0171 736 6530); HSBC Samuel Montagu, Vintner's Place, 68 Upper Thames Street, London EC4V 3BJ (☎ 0171 336 9000)

BOOTE, Robert Edward; CVO (1971); s of Ernest Haydn Boote (d 1983), and Helen Rose (d 1941); *b* 6 Feb 1920; *Educ* Hanley HS Stoke-on-Trent, Univ of London (BSc, DPA); *m* 2 April 1948, Vera, da of Ernest Badian; 1 s (Anthony Robert b 1953), 1 da (Karin Verli b 1949); *Career* Army 1939–46, actg Lt-Col, demobbed with hon rank of Maj; admin offr City of Stoke-on-Trent 1946–48, chief admin offr Staffs Co Planning and Devpt Dept 1948–54; Nature Conservancy Cncl: princ 1954–64, dep dir 1964–73, first DG 1973–80; chm Broadland Report 1965; memb: Govt Ctee on Pesticides 1958–73, Govt Countryside Review Ctee 1977–79; IUCN: fndr and chm UK Ctee 1974–80, treas and vice pres 1975–81, election offr 1984; UK del to Cncl of Europe Ctee for Conservation of Nature and Natural Resources 1963–71, chm Euro Ctee 1969–71, chm Organising Ctees for Euro Year and Conservation Conf 1970 (conf vice pres); various posts in meetings of UN, UNESCO, EEC and OECD 1968–81, chm UN Habitat Symposium 1970, chm Anglo American Environmental Gp Ditchley 1970, helped to prepare and appeared in film Pacemaker 1970, judge Agro Environmental TV and Films Berlin 1970, 1972, 1974 and 1980, speaker Eurogespräch Vienna 1970, IUCN rep Int Conf on Antarctica Marine Living Resources 1984 (chm Resolution 1981); memb Cncl: FFPS 1979–83, WWF 1980–86, Ecological Parks Tst 1980–85, Ctees for UK Conservation and Devpt Prog 1980–83, Friends of ENO 1980–87, Common Ground Int 1981–85, HGTAC Foresty Cmmn 1981–87, FRGS 1983–86; vice pres: BTCV 1980–, RSNC 1980–, Age Concern 1990–; conservator Wimbledon and Putney Commons 1981–, memb Seychelles Appeal Ctee Royal Soc 1980–87, chm and initiator Age Resource 1988–; advsr: Euro Architectural Heritage Year 1975, House of Lords Select Ctee on Euro Community 1980–81, Macmillan Guide to Br Nature Reserves 1980–93, Shell Better Britain Campaign 1980–90; a chief marshal to HM The Queen 1970; memb Editorial Bds: International Journal of Environmental Studies 1975–, Town Planning Review 1979–85, International Journal of Environmental Education and Information 1981–83; chm Instn of Environmental Sciences 1981–84; Hon ALI 1971, Hon MRTPI 1978; FREconS 1953–61, AIPR 1957–61, FCIS 1960–81, FRSA 1971, FRGS 1982; *Awards* Greek Distinguished Serv Medal 1946, BBC Man of Action 1977, van Tienhoven European Prize 1980, Merit Award IUCN 1984, Special Alfred Toepfer Prize for the protection of nature in Europe (Euro Nature Conservation Prize, Cncl of Europe) 1995; *Books* Man and Environment (as Robert Arvill, 1967, 5 edn 1984); *Recreations* travel, theatre, music, dancing; *Style*— Robert Boote, Esq, CVO; ✉ 3 Leeward Gardens, Wimbledon, London SW19 7QR (☎ 0181 946 1551)

BOOTH, *see also:* Gore-Booth

BOOTH, His Hon Alan Shore; QC (1975); 4 s of Parkin Stanley Booth, and Ethel Mary, *née* Shore; *b* 20 Aug 1922; *Educ* Shrewsbury, Univ of Liverpool (LLB); *m* 1954, Mary Gwendoline, da of John Hilton; 1 s, 1 da; *Career* served RNVR Fleet Air Arm (despatches 1944), Sub-Lt 1942, HMS Illustrious 1943–45, Lt 1944; called to the Bar Gray's Inn 1949; recorder Crown Ct 1972–76, circuit judge 1976–92; memb Cncl of Mgmnt Hoylake Cottage Hosp Trust Ltd 1995; govr Shrewsbury Sch 1969; *Recreations* golf, grandchildren; *Clubs* Royal Liverpool Golf, Royal and Ancient (St Andrews), Liverpool Ramblers AFC (pres); *Style*— His Hon Alan Booth, QC; ✉ 18 Abbey Rd, West Kirby, Wirral L48 7EW (☎ 0151 625 5796)

BOOTH, Rt Hon Albert Edward; PC (1976); s of Albert Henry Booth, of Scarborough, and Janet, *née* Mathieson; *b* 28 May 1928; *Educ* St Thomas's Winchester, South Shields Marine Sch, Rutherford Coll of Technol; *m* 1957, Joan, da of Josiah Amis, of North Shields; 3 s; *Career* election agent 1951 and 1955, contested (Lab) Tynemouth 1964; MP (Lab) Barrow-in-Furness 1966–83; chm Select Ctee on Statutory Instruments 1970–74, min of state Dept of Employment 1974–76, sec of state for employment 1976–79, oppn spokesman on transport 1979–83, treas Lab Pty 1984; contested (Lab): Barrow and Furness 1983, Warrington S 1987; dir S Yorks Passenger Transport Exec 1983–87; CIMechE 1985; *Style*— The Rt Hon Albert Booth

BOOTH, Anthony John; CBE (1993); s of Benjamin Booth, and Una Lavinia, *née* Cumberpatch; *b* 18 March 1939; *Educ* Bungay GS, Univ of London (BSc (Eng)), Ealing Coll (DMS); *m* 4 Sept 1965, Elspeth Marjorie, da of Rev Francis Stewart Gordon Fraser, MBE, TD (d 1962); 1 s (Richard Mark b 1970), 1 da (Caroline Ruth b 1968); *Career* British Telecom (formerly GPO): scientific asst Res Dept PO 1957, exec engr then sr exec engr Telecom HQ 1965–71, asst staff engr Central HQ Appts 1971–74, head of section and div External Telecom Exec 1974–78, head of div Telecommunications HQ 1978–79, dir of int networks 1979–80, regnl dir London Region 1980–83, md British Telecom International 1983–91, corp dir British Telecommunications plc 1984–94, md BT Worldwide Networks 1991, md BT Business Communications 1991–92, md BT Special Businesses and International Affairs 1992–94; chm Ericsson Ltd 1994–; memb: Regnl Affairs Ctee C of C and Indust 1980–84, London Regnl Ctee CBI 1982–84, Overseas Ctee CBI 1984–94; govr Ealing Coll 1989–91, chm Bd Govrs Thames Valley Univ 1992–96 (govr when Poly of W London 1991–92), memb Bd HEFCE; memb Guild of Freemen of the City of London 1982; CEng 1985, FIEE 1985, MInstD 1985, CIMgt 1986, FRSA 1991; *Recreations* opera, golf, philately; *Clubs* Camberley Heath Golf; *Style*— Anthony Booth, Esq, CBE; ✉ Ericsson Ltd, Telecommunications Centre, Ericsson Way, Burgess Hill, West Sussex RH15 9UB (☎ 01444 234525, fax 01444 234551)

BOOTH, Brian George; JP (Preston 1987); s of George Booth, and Ada Booth; *b* 6 Sept 1942; *Educ* Univ of Manchester (BA), Brunel Univ (MTech); *m* 1965, Barbara Ann, *née* Wright; 2 da (Alison Jane, Susan Margaret); *Career* High Wycombe Coll of Technol (asst lectr, lectr in statistics) 1965–68, Kingston Poly (lectr, sr lectr, princ lectr and subject leader in economic statistics) 1968–73; Univ of Central Lancashire (formerly Lancashire Poly): head Dept of Business & Admin 1974–78, dean Faculty of Business and Mgmnt 1978–82, dep dir 1982–89, seconded as actg dir of progs Polys and Colls Funding Cncl 1988–89, rector and chief exec 1989–95, vice-chllr 1995–; memb Governing Body: Lancs Coll of Agric and Hort 1990–, Preston Coll 1990–; reg speaker at educnl confs and professional assocs; chm: Preston Business Venture 1983–92, Preston Promotion and Guild Consultative Ctee 1985–92, Tstees Preston Postgrad Med Centre 1990–96; vice chm Lancs Centre for Med Studies 1992–; non-exec dir Preston Acute Hosps NHS Tst 1993–; CIMgt 1992; FSS 1968, FRSA 1990; *Recreations* golf, watching Preston North End FC; *Style*— Brian Booth, Esq, JP; ✉ 9 Moorfield Close, Fulwood, Preston, Lancs PR2 9SW (☎ 01772 864243); University of Central Lancashire, Preston, Lancs PR1 2HE (☎ 01772 892500)

BOOTH, Charles Leonard; CMG (1978), LVO (1961); s of Charles Leonard Booth (d 1987), and Marion, *née* Lawton (d 1981); *b* 7 March 1925; *Educ* Heywood GS, Pembroke Coll Oxford (MA); *m* 1 Aug 1958, Mary Gillian, da of Archibald George Emms (d 1975); 2 s (Charles b 1959, James b 1962), 2 da (Lydia b 1960, Rachel b 1964); *Career* WWII Capt RA 1943–47; HM Dip Serv; third sec (later second sec) Rangoon 1950–55, FO 1955–60 (private sec to Parly Under Sec 1958–60), first sec Rome 1960–63; head of chancery: Rangoon 1963–64, Bangkok 1964–67, FO 1967–69; dep high cmmr Kampala 1969–71; cnsllr and consul gen Washington 1971–73, cnsllr Belgrade 1973–77, ambass Burma 1978–82, high cmmr Malta 1982–85, FCO 1985–90; Offr of the Order of Merit of the Italian Republic 1961; *Recreations* opera, reading; *Clubs* Travellers'; *Style*— Charles Booth, Esq, CMG, LVO; ✉ 7 Queen St, Southwold, Suffolk IP18 6EQ

BOOTH, Cherie; QC (1995); da of Anthony George Booth, of Broadbottom via Hyde, Gtr Manchester, and Gale, *née* Smith; *b* 23 Sept 1954; *Educ* Seafield Convent GS Liverpool, LSE (LLB); *m* 29 March 1980, Anthony Charles Lynton (Tony) Blair, *qv*, s of Leo Charles Lynton Blair; 2 s (Euan Anthony b 19 Jan 1984, Nicholas John b 6 Dec 1985), 1 da (Kathryn Hazel b 2 March 1988); *Career* called to the Bar Lincoln's Inn 1976 (Hardwicke & Kennedy scholar, winner Ede & Ravenscroft Prize for highest bar finals' results); in practice: Alexander Irvine (now Baron Irvine of Lairg, QC, *qv*) 1976–77, New Court Chambers 1977–91, Gray's Inn Square Chambers 1991–; Parly candidate (Lab) Thanet North Gen Election 1983; chair IT Ctee Bar Cncl 1991, vice chair (IT) Bar Services and Information Technology Ctee 1995–96; govr: LSE, St Joan of Arc Roman Catholic Sch Highbury; memb: Sadler's Wells, Bd of Mgmnt Refuge, Mgmnt Ctee Citizenship Fndn; vice pres Kids Club Network; *Recreations* keeping fit, the arts, spending as much time as possible with my children, reading; *Style*— Ms Cherie Booth, QC; ✉ 4–5 Gray's Inn Square, Gray's Inn, London WC1R 5AY (☎ 0171 404 5252)

BOOTH, Sir Christopher Charles; kt (1982); s of Lionel Barton Booth and Phyllis Petley, *née* Duncan; *b* 22 June 1924; *Educ* Sedbergh Sch, St Andrew's Univ (MB, MD); *m* 1, 1959, Lavinia Loughridge, of Belfast; 1 s, 1 da; m 2, 1970, Soad Tabaqchali; 1 da; *Career* formerly med tutor, lectr then sr lectr London Postgrad Medical Sch, prof and dir Dept of Medicine RPMS London Univ 1966–77, dir Clinical Research Centre MRC 1978–88; Harveian librarian Royal Coll of Physicians 1989–; memb: Advsy Bd to Res Cncls 1976–78, MRC 1981–84; chm: Med Advsy Ctee Br Cncl 1979–85, Royal Naval Personnel Ctee 1985–92; pres: Br Soc of Gastroenterology 1978–79, BMA 1986–87, RSocMed 1988, Johnson Soc 1987–88; FRCP 1964, FRCPEd 1967, Hon FACP 1973, Hon FRSM 1991; Dr hc: Paris 1975, Poitiers 1981, Bologna 1991; Hon LLD Univ of Dundee 1982; Chevalier de l'Ordre National du Mérite (France) 1977; *Books* Chain of Friendship: Letters of Dr John Fothergill of London 1735–1780 (with Betsy C Corner, 1971), Disorders of the Small Intestine (with G Neale, 1985), Doctors in Science and Society (1987); *Recreations* fishing, history; *Style*— Sir Christopher Booth; ✉ 9 Kent Terrace, London NW1 4RP (☎ 0171 724 3379)

BOOTH, Dr Clive; s of Henry Booth and Freda Frankland; *b* 18 April 1943; *Educ* King's Sch Macclesfield, Trinity Coll Cambridge (MA), Univ of California Berkeley (Harkness fell, MA, PhD); *m* 1969, Margaret Sardeson; *Career* joined DES 1965, princ private sec to Sec of State for Educn and Sci 1975–77, asst sec 1977–81; dep dir Plymouth Poly

1981–84, memb HM Inspectorate DES 1984–86, vice-chllr Oxford Brookes Univ (formerly Oxford Poly) 1986–; asst cmmr Nat Cmmn on Educn 1992–; memb: Governing Cncl SRHE 1981–90, Advsy Ctee Brunel Univ Educn Policy Centre 1986–90, Computer Bd for Univs and Res Cncls 1987–92, CNAA Ctee for Info and Devpt Servs 1987–91, Fulbright Academic Administrators Selection Ctee 1988–, Br Cncl Ctee for Int Cooperation in Higher Educn 1988–, Cncl for Indust and Higher Educn 1990, Fulbright Cmmn 1992–, Oxford Inst of Nursing Bd 1991–, Cwlth Scholarships Cmmn 1992–, UK ERASMUS Cncl 1992–, Br Cncl Bd 1995–; dir: Thames Action Resource Gp for Educn and Trg 1986–, Thames Valley Technol Centre 1989–, Oxfordshire Business Link 1995–; vice chm Ctee of Vice-Chllrs and Princs 1992–94; Leverhulme res fell 1983; govr Headington and Wheatley Park Schs, jt ed Higher Educn Quarterly 1986, memb Ed Bd Oxford Review of Educn 1990–; *Recreations* cycling, walking, bridge, opera; *Style*— Dr Clive Booth; ✉ Oxford Brookes University, Gipsy Lane, Headington, Oxford OX3 0BP (☎ 01865 484801)

BOOTH, Dr Derek Blake; s of Sir Philip Booth, 2 Bt (d 1960); h to Btcy of bro, Sir Douglas Booth, 3 Bt, *qv*; *b* 7 April 1953; *Educ* Hampshire Coll, Univ of California, Stanford Univ, Univ of Washington; *m* 1981, Elizabeth Dreisbach; 1 s (Colin b 1982), 1 da (Rachel b 1986); *Career* geologist; *Style*— Dr Derek Booth

BOOTH, Sir Douglas Allen; 3 Bt (UK 1916), of Allerton Beeches, City of Liverpool; s of Sir Philip Booth, 2 Bt (d 1960), and his 2 w, Ethel, *née* Greenfield; *b* 2 Dec 1949; *Educ* Gaspar de Portolà Junior HS, Beverly Hills HS California, Harvard Univ; *m* 17 Nov 1991, Yolanda Marcella, *née* Scantlebury; 1 da (Zahra Jessica b 13 Aug 1993); *Heir* bro, Derek Blake Booth b 7 April 1953; *Career* TV and film writer/prodr; *Recreations* music, backpacking; *Style*— Sir Douglas Booth, Bt; ✉ 22933 Portage Circle Drive, Topanga, CA 90290, USA

BOOTH, Sir Gordon; KCMG (1980, CMG 1969), CVO (1976); s of Walter Booth, of Bolton, Lancs, and Grace Booth; *b* 22 Nov 1921; *Educ* Canon Slade Sch, Univ of London (BCom); *m* 1944, Jeanne Mary, da of James Herbert Kirkham, of Bolton; 1 s, 1 da; *Career* served WWII Capt RAC and 13/18 Royal Hussars; HM Dip Serv: cnsllr Copenhagen 1965–69, consul gen Sydney 1971–74, consul gen NY 1975–80, DG of Trade Devpt USA 1975–80; dir Hanson PLC 1981–89 (advsr 1990–), vice chm Bechtel Ltd 1986–91, dir City of London Heliport Ltd 1989–; dir Allders International Ltd 1992–, chm I-FAX Ltd 1992–, chm London Clubs International plc 1992–95 (dir 1995–); advsr on int trade and investmt; chm Simplification of Int Trade Procedures Bd 1980–86, memb BOT 1981–85; *Recreations* golf, bridge; *Clubs* Walton Heath Golf; *Style*— Sir Gordon Booth, KCMG, CVO; ✉ Glade Lodge, The Glade, Kingswood, Surrey KT20 6LL (☎ 01737 832156, fax 01737 832526)

BOOTH, (Vernon Edward) Hartley; MP (C) Finchley (majority 6,388); s of Vernon William Hartley Booth, and Eilish, *née* Morrow; *b* 17 July 1946; *Educ* Queens Coll Taunton, Univ of Bristol (LLB), Downing Coll Cambridge (LLM, Dip in Int Law, PhD); *m* 30 July 1977, Adrianne Claire Cranefield, da of Knivett Garton Cranefield, DFC; 2 s (Peter Toby Hartley b 1985, Thomas Edward Hartley b 1988), 1 da (Emily Claire Hartley b 1982); *Career* called to the Bar Inner Temple, practising 1970–84, special advsr to PM and memb 10 Downing St Policy Unit 1984–88, chief exec and md Br Urban Devpt Ltd 1988–90, vice pres British Urban Regeneration Assoc 1992–94 (chm 1990–92), dir British Urban Development Ltd 1990; Parly candidate (C) Hackney and Stoke Newington 1983, MP (C) Finchley 1992–, PPS to Rt Hon Douglas Hogg, QC, MP 1992–94, PPS to Eric Forth, MP 1996–; memb: Select Ctee on European Legislation 1992, Select Ctee on Home Affairs 1992, Euro Standing Ctee 1995–; chm: Urban Affrs Ctee 1994–, All Pty Central Asia Ctee 1995–; former leader writer Daily Telegraph; vice pres: OCU, Royal Life Saving Soc; sch govr; FInstD; *Books* British Extradition Law and Procedure (volume I 1980, volume II 1981), Victims of Crime (1992), Into the Voids (1993), There Goes the Neighbourhood (1994), Return Ticket (1994); *Style*— Hartley Booth, Esq, MP; ✉ House of Commons, London SW1A 0AA

BOOTH, John Aidan; s of Sidney Booth (d 1953), and Ruth, *née* Traylor (d 1977); *b* 7 Dec 1926; *Educ* Selby Abbey Sch, Selby Tech Inst, Univ of Goettingen, Univ of Bristol; *m* 21 Oct 1947, Pamela Jean, *née* Olivant; 3 da (Dorinda b 1949, Kathryn b 1954, Joanne b 1961); *Career* WWII dep chief clerk RE 1944–48, chief engr 5 Div BAOR 1947; univ extramural lectr in fine art, freelance author, publisher Cambridge House Books; fndr: Univ of Bristol Bowman 1950, Royal Leamington Spa Canoe Club 1954; fndr memb West Wilts Youth Sailing Assoc 1966; FRSA 1977; *Books* Antique Maps of Wales (1977), Looking at Old Maps (1979), Looking at Old Prints (1983), Day War Broke Out (St Dunstan's Charity Book, 1984), Our Forgotten History (filmscript, 1986), The Loss of the Titanic (ed, 1991), Titanic - Signals of Disaster (1993), Church, Crown and Commonwealth (1994); *Recreations* collecting, chess, brass band music, power boating; *Style*— John Booth, Esq; ✉ 30 Edenvale, Westbury, Wiltshire BA13 3NY (☎ 01373 823 271)

BOOTH, John Barton; s of (Percy) Leonard Booth (d 1972), of Bournemouth, and Mildred Amy, *née* Wilson (d 1975); *b* 19 Nov 1937; *Educ* Canford, King's Coll London (AKC), King's Coll Hosp Med Sch (MB BS); *m* 18 June 1966, Carroll, da of (James) Ivor Griffiths (d 1983), of Peel, IOM; 1 s (James b 29 Aug 1972); *Career* conslt ENT surgn Royal Hosp of St Bartholomew's and Royal London Hosp (formerly London Hosp) 1972–, conslt surgn Royal Nat Throat Nose and Ear Hosp 1973–78, Hunterian prof RCS 1980–81, hon conslt ENT surgn St Luke's Hosp for the Clergy 1983–, civil conslt otologist RAF 1983–; hon conslt laryngologist: Musicians Benevolent Fund 1974–, RCM 1974–, Newspaper Press Fund 1982–, Royal Opera House Covent Garden 1983–, Royal Soc of Musicians of GB 1987–; hon chm IXth Br Academic Conf in Otolaryngology 1995; RSM: memb Cncl 1980–88 and 1993–, memb Sci and Exec Ctee 1984–87, memb Educn Ctee 1989–94, pres Section of Otology 1996–97, hon sec 1996–; Fedn of Univ Cons: vice chm 1960–61, chm 1961–62, vice pres 1962–63; memb Gen Purposes and Exec Ctees Cons Pty 1961–62; ed Jl of Laryngology and Otology 1987–92 (asst ed 1979–87); Freeman City of London 1972, Liveryman Worshipful Soc of Apothecaries 1969; hon corresponding memb American Otological Soc, assoc memb American Neurolological Soc; FRCS 1968, FRSM 1967, MRAeS 1989, FZS; *Books* The Ear (vol 3, ed 6 edn) Scott Brown's Otolaryngology (1996); *Recreations* golf, the arts; *Clubs* MCC, RAC, United and Cecil; *Style*— John Booth, Esq; ✉ 18 Upper Wimpole St, London W1M 7TB (☎ 0171 935 5631, 0171 935 1304, fax 0171 224 1645)

BOOTH, Laurie; *Educ* Dartington Sch of Arts; *Career* work with various experimental theatre gps incl Triple Action Theatre and Cardiff Laboratory Theatre 1979; ind choreographer and performer; works incl: Yip Yip Mix in the 20th Century 1985, Totally Successful Amnaesia 1986, Euroshima 1986, Andi (Deutsche Schauspielhaus Hamburg) 1987, Suspect Terrain (NY) 1989, Terminus Terminux (Dance Umbrella London) 1989, Well-known Worlds 1990, Spatial Decay 1990, New Text, New Kingdom (Laurie Booth & Co) 1991, Completely Birdland (Rambert Dance Co) 1991, River Run 1992, Deep Field Line (Dutch Nat Ballet) 1993, Wonderlawn (Laurie Booth & Co) 1994, Tango Variations 1995, Condition Red 1995, Storm Garden 1996, ACT/ual f/ACT/ual 1997; for TV: TV Dante (Channel 4) 1990, Dance House (BBC) 1991, Close to the Ground Tate Gallery (BBC) 1991; awarded numerous public awards incl Greater London Arts Dance and Mime award 1984, Time Out award 1990/91, Digital Dance award 1991, Barclays New Stages 1993; *Style*— Laurie Booth, Esq; ✉ c/o Lianne Jarrett Associates, 35 Queens Gardens, Brighton BN1 4AR (☎ 01273 622403, fax 01273 696067)

BOOTH, Dame Margaret Myfanwy Wood; DBE (1979); da of late Alec Wood Booth and Lillian May Booth; *b* 1933; *Educ* Northwood Coll, UCL (LLM); *m* 1, 1982, Joseph Jackson, QC, s of Samuel Jackson (d 1987); m 2, 1993, Peter Glucksmann; *Career* called to the Bar Middle and Inner Temples 1956, QC 1976, bencher Middle Temple 1979, High Court judge 1979–94; visiting prof of law Univ of Liverpool 1994–; govr Northwood Coll 1975–95; memb Cncl UCL 1980–84; chm: Family Law Bar Assoc 1976–78, Lord Chllr's Advsy Ctee Inner London Justices 1990–93, Lord Chllr's Advsy Ctee (Children Act 1989) 1990–93, Bd of Govrs UK Coll of Family Mediators 1996–; pres Family Mediators' Assoc 1994–95, tstee Joseph Rowntree Fndn 1996–; Hon LLD Univ of Liverpool 1992; fell UCL 1982; *Books* Rayden on Divorce (co-ed 10–13 and 15–16 edns), Clarke Hall and Morrison on Children (co-ed 9 edn, 1977); *Clubs* Reform; *Style*— Dame Margaret Booth, DBE; ✉ 15 Wellington House, Eton Road, London NW3 4SY

BOOTH, Neil Douglas; s of Charles Douglas Booth, of Hartlepool (d 1990), and Greta, *née* Sylvester (now Mrs Lawrence); *b* 11 Feb 1942; *Educ* Keighley Boys' GS, St John's Coll Durham; *m* 1, Barbara Ann, da of Edwin Cullerton, of Bradford; 2 da (Heidi Amanda b 1971, Christy Elizabeth b 1974); m 2, 22 July 1978, Yvonne Margaret, da of Peter Holdsworth Kennedy, of Bradford; *Career* managing ptnr JWM Thompson & Co Keighley 1969–73; ordinand in trg for Anglican Miny 1973–76; various accountancy posts 1976–81, ptnr Rawlinsons Bradford 1981–83, sr ptnr Booth & Co Bradford 1983–89, ptnr Ernst & Young and nat dir NI Consultancy 1989–92, ptnr KPMG Peat Marwick 1992–94, ret; ed Booth's NIC Brief 1988–94; Inst of Taxation Thesis prize 1985; chm Nat Insur Ctee ICAEW 1984–94; FCA 1964, FTII 1985; *Books* Social Security Contributions (1982), Tolley's National Insurance Contributions (annually 1984–94), DHSS Official Contribution Guides (1985), NIC Legislation and Cases (1986), Residence, Domicile and UK Taxation (1987); *Recreations* reader in diocese of Bradford, reading, water colourpainting, computer programming, cooking; *Style*— Neil Booth, Esq; ✉ Rivendell, 1114 Bolton Rd, Bradford, W Yorks BD2 4HS (☎ 01274 631154)

BOOTH, Peter John Richard; s of Eric Albert Booth, and Edith, *née* Brown; *b* 27 March 1949; *Educ* Benton Park Secdy Modern Sch; *m* 27 July 1970, Edwina Ivy; 3 s (Peter Tristan b 24 Jan 1971, Jonathen Richard b 11 Sept 1972, James Lee b 19 Sept 1978); *Career* Dyers Operative 1964; Nat Union of Dyers Bleachers and Textile Workers: dist offr 1973, nat res offr 1975, nat organiser 1980; TGWU: joined 1982, nat trade gp organiser 1982, textile nat gp sec 1986–93; pres Int Textile Garment & Leather Workers' Fedn 1996– (memb Exec Ctee); vice pres Br Textile Confedn 1989–, vice pres Euro Trade Union Ctee of Textiles Clothing and Leather; dir: Apparel Knitting and Textiles Alliance 1989–, Man-Made Fibres Indust Trg Advsy Bd 1986–, Nat Textile Trg Gp 1988–; chm Carpet Indust Trg Cncl 1986–; memb: Presidium 1982–96, Textiles Clothing and Footwear Industs Ctee TUC 1976–, Confedn of Br Wool Textiles Trg Bd 1986–, Health and Safety Ctee Cotton and Allied Textiles Industs Advsy Ctee, Health and Safety Cmmn Texile Indust Advsy Ctee, Textiles Industry Advsy Cmmn (TEXIAC); *Books* The Old Dog Strike (1985); *Recreations* walking, gardening, dominoes, chess; *Clubs* Yeadon Trades Hall; *Style*— Peter Booth, Esq; ✉ Dye House, St John's Court, Yeadon, Leeds (☎ 0113 250 0543)

BOOTH, Robert Michael; s of Robert Noel Wylde Booth, of South Harting, W Sussex, and Joan Poole, *née* Hanson; *Educ* Bedales, King's Coll Cambridge, LAMDA; *m* 15 July 1989, Suzie, da of late Vivian Holmes Watkins; 1 s (Theo Robert Lawrence b 11 Feb 1991), 1 da (Francesca Lucy b 31 Oct 1992); *Career* broadcaster and writer; presenter BBC Radio 4 and World Service: Just Three Wishes, Could Do Better, The Needle's Tale, A Priest At The Altar of Literature, Looking Forward To The Past, and others; presenter Classic FM 1992–; *Recreations* reading, the 1890's, Venice, talking, food and wine; *Clubs* Chelsea Arts, The Academy, Garrick; *Style*— Robert Booth, Esq; ✉ c/o Classic FM, 24–28 Oval Road, London NW1 7DQ (☎ 0171 284 3000)

BOOTH, Robin Godfrey; s of Frank Booth (d 1990), of York, and Dorothy, *née* Johnson; *b* 11 Aug 1942; *Educ* Winchester, King's Coll Cambridge (DipArch, MA), Univ of Edinburgh (MSc); *m* 10 July 1971, Katherine, da of Arthur Middleton, of Lynchburg, Virginia, USA; 1 s (Richard b 1977), 1 da (Emily b 1974); *Career* architect and town planner; master planner and job architect Devpt Dept of Architecture and Civic Design GLC 1965–71, architect planner for South West Area Traffic and Devpt Branch GLC 1971–72, project architect for New County HQ for Hereford-Worcester (RIBA commendation 1978) Robert Matthew Johnson-Marshall & Partners 1972–76, sr architect concerned with design of various projects overseas and in London John S Bonnington Partnership 1976–80, project architect then ptnr for Standard Chartered Bank's HQ (special award Marble Architectural Awards West Europe 1987), Fitzroy Robinson Ltd 1980– (formerly ptnr now dir Thames Exchange and Scottish Widows London Wall projects and dir i/c of works on the Union Bank of Switzerland in London and Barclaycard HQ Northampton); author of various articles in Architects Journal and RIBA Journal; Plasterers' trophy for fibrous plasterwork 1985, Br Assoc of Landscape Industries principal award for interior landscaping 1986; tstee County Houses Assoc; memb: RIBA 1970 (memb Eastern Regions Competitions Ctee 1979–80), Royal Town Planning Inst 1978; *Books* Neufert: Architectural Data (contrib 1980 edn); *Recreations* music, theatre, travel, photography; *Clubs* Baconian Society (St Albans); *Style*— Robin Booth, Esq; ✉ Fitzroy Robinson Ltd, 77 Portland Place, London W1N 4EP (☎ 0171 636 8033, fax 0171 580 3996)

BOOTH, Sarah Ann (Sally); CBE (1995); da of Eric David Booth, of St Newlyn East, Cornwall, and Mary, *née* Moore (d 1981); *b* 28 March 1950; *Educ* Kendal HS, Callington GS, Girton Coll Cambridge (exhibitioner, Charity Reeves Prize, BA, MA); *m* 1980 (m dis); 1 s (William Booth Dorling, b 17 Sept 1982); *Career* civil servant; DOE: joined 1974, private sec to Permanent Sec 1980–81, princ 1981–86, asst sec 1987, head Central Policy and Planning Unit 1987–88; dir of fin and resources Historic Royal Palaces 1989–92; Dept of Nat Heritage: dir of fin and head Nat Lottery Div 1992–94, head Broadcasting Policy Div 1994–95, under sec 1995, head Libraries Galleries and Museums Gp 1995–; *Recreations* family, books, walking; *Style*— Ms Sally Booth, CBE; ✉ Department of National Heritage, 2–4 Cockspur Street, London SW1Y 5DH (☎ 0171 211 6193, fax 0171 211 6195)

BOOTH, Scott; *b* 16 Dec 1971; *Career* professional footballer; with Aberdeen 1988–; 5 full caps Scotland; *Style*— Scott Booth, Esq; ✉ c/o Aberdeen FC, Pittodrie Stadium, Aberdeen AB2 1QH

BOOTH-JONES, Charles Vernon Colville; s of Major Thomas Vernon Booth-Jones JP, DL (d 1966), of Hale Park, Fordingbridge, Hampshire, and Margaret Wallace, *née* Colville (d 1984); *b* 5 Feb 1928; *Educ* Eton, Sandhurst; *m* 1, 2 Oct 1951 (m dis 1973), Louise Anne, 2 da of Col Guy Janion Edwards, DSO; 1 s (Roderick Vernon b 1954), 1 da (Thalia Jane b 1952); m 2, 19 Jan 1974, Pauline Celia, 3 da of Sir James Gunn, RA; *Career* RHG 1946, Sqdn Ldr 1957–64 (despatches 1959), 2 i/c 1965, Maj MOD DOAE, HQ RAC 3 Div ret 1970; with Picture Gallery 1972, dealer in paintings of the 17–20 centuries, now conservator of paintings; memb Int Inst for Conservation of Art, listed by Museums and Galleries Cmmn; *Recreations* all country sports, painting; *Style*— Charles Booth-Jones, Esq; ✉ Hill Barn, Monkton Deverill, Wiltshire BA12 7EY; Fox Conservation Studio (☎ 01985 844479)

BOOTHBY, Sir Brooke Charles; 16 Bt (1660), of Broadlow Ash; s of Sir Hugo Boothby, 15 Bt (d 1986); *b* 6 April 1949; *Educ* Eton, Trinity Coll Cambridge (BA); *m* 1976, Georgiana Alexandra, da of Sir John Wriothesley Russell, GCVO, CMG (d 1984), and Lady (Aliki) Russell; 2 da; *Heir* kinsman, George William Boothby; *Career* Fontygary

Parks Ltd: md 1979–95, vice-chm 1995–; chm: Tourism Quality Services Ltd 1990–, Associated Quality Services 1994–, TQS (1994) Ltd 1994–, TQS (Ireland) 1995–; chm: Historic Houses Assoc Inheritance Ctee 1984–86, Nat Caravan Cncl Parks Div 1987–90, Adventure Activities Licensing Authy 1996–; pres Glamorgan Branch Country Landowners Assoc 1991–94; High Sheriff S Glamorgan 1986–87; *Recreations* shooting, gardening; *Style*— Sir Brooke Boothby, Bt; ✉ Fonmon Castle, Barry, S Glam CF62 3ZN (☎ 01446 710206, fax 01446 711687)

BOOTHBY, Richard Charles Brooke; s of George William Bernard Boothby (d 1972), and Avril Alice, *née* Innell; *b* 16 Dec 1955; *Educ* Barry Boys' Comp Sch, Univ of Manchester (MusB, postgrad study with David Fallows), Salzburg Mozarteum (with Nikolaus Harnoncourt); *m* 23 May 1992, Fiona Clare, da of Peter Padfield; *Career* viola da gamba player and 'cellist; fndr and memb: Purcell Quartet 1984–, Purcell Simfony 1992–; fndr memb Fretwork 1985–; regularly tours Europe, Japan and US with these ensembles, has also played with other ensembles incl Taverner Players, and as soloist; prof of viola da gamba RCM, prof of viola da gamba and baroque cello RNCM and RSAMD; *Recordings* with Purcell Quartet on Hyperion: Vivaldi solo and trio sonatas, Corelli solo and trio sonatas, C P E Bach trio sonatas and viola da gamba sonata, two Scarlatti cantatas (with Lynne Dawson), Francesco Geminiani solo and trio sonatas and two concerti grossi, Marin Marais' Pièces en trio, Suite in D major and Les Folies d'Espagne; with Purcell Quartet on Chandos: 3 vols of Purcell sonatas, 2 vols of Vivaldi sonatas, 4 vols of Corelli trio sonatas, William Lawes' Fantasy Suites, H I F Biber's Harmonia Artificiosa-Ariosa; with Fretwork on Virgin Classics Veritas: Heart's Ease (late Tudor and early Stuart), Armada (Elizabethan), Night's Black Bird (works by John Dowland and William Byrd), Cries and Fancies (works by Orlando Gibbons), Go Nightly Cares (Dowland and Byrd), For ye Violls (works by William Lawes), William Byrd - Complete Consort Music, A Play of Passion (music for the Elizabethan theatre); with Fretwork on Amon Ra: In Nomine (16 Century viol music incl complete consort music of Thomas Tallis); *Style*— Richard Boothby, Esq

BOOTHMAN, Clive Nicholas; s of Thomas Hague Boothman (d 1996), and Margaret, *née* Knox; *b* 28 May 1955; *Educ* Charterhouse, Trinity Coll Oxford (BA); *m* 28 May 1983, Anne, da of Wace Philo; 2 s (Alexander b 4 July 1986, Harry b 9 July 1988), 1 da (Georgina b 1 Aug 1990); *Career* Arthur Young McClelland Moores Jersey CI 1976–81, accountant Moore Stephens & Butterfield Bermuda 1982–83; Schroder Group: joined 1983, asst dir J Henry Schroder Wagg & Co Ltd 1986–87 (mangr 1985–86, investmt res 1983–85), md Schroder Unit Trusts Ltd 1988–, dir Schroder Investment Management Ltd 1992–; chm Assoc of Unit Tsts and Investmt Funds; ACA 1980, AIIMR 1984; *Recreations* sailing, windsurfing, tennis, vintage cars; *Style*— Clive Boothman, Esq; ✉ Schroder Unit Trusts Ltd, Senator House, 85 Queen Victoria Street, London EC4V 4EJ (☎ 0171 382 6000, fax 0171 288 2106)

BOOTHROYD, Rt Hon Betty; PC (1992), MP (Lab) West Bromwich W (majority 7,830); da of Archibald Boothroyd (d 1948), of Dewsbury, Yorks, and Mary Boothroyd (d 1982); *b* 8 Oct 1929; *Educ* Dewsbury Coll of Commerce and Art; *Career* Parly candidate (Lab): Leicester SE (by-election) 1957, Peterborough 1959, Nelson and Colne (by-election) 1968, Rossendale 1970; MP (Lab): West Bromwich 1973–74, West Bromwich West 1974–; asst Govt whip 1974–76, UK memb Euro Parl 1975–77, former memb Select Ctee on Foreign Affrs, memb Speaker's Panel of Chairmen 1979–87, Lab Pty Nat Exec Ctee 1981–87, House of Commons Cmmn 1983–87, second dep chm Ways and Means and dep speaker 1987–92; elected Speaker House of Commons 1992–; memb Hammersmith Borough Cncl 1965–68; memb Ct Univ of Birmingham 1982–; Hon LLD: Birmingham, Leeds Metropolitan, Leicester South Bank, Cambridge, North London, Oxford; chllr Open Univ 1994–; Liveryman Worshipful Co of Feltmakers; The Spectator Parliamentarian of the Year Award 1992; *Recreations* reading, walking and gardening; *Style*— The Rt Hon Betty Boothroyd, MP; ✉ Speaker's House, House of Commons, London SW1A 0AA (☎ 0171 219 4136)

BOOTLE, Michael James; s of Richard James Bootle, of Felpham, Sussex, and Olive Mary, *née* Childs; *b* 19 April 1947; *Educ* Chichester HS for Boys, KCL (BA, Jelf medal); *m* 16 June 1973, Baudine Petra Maria Elisabeth Nieuwenhuizen, da of Prof Steven Vandenberg (d 1993); 3 s (Alexander Michael Boudewyn b 7 Sept 1977, Oliver James Martyn b 11 Sept 1979, Robin Joost Richard b 13 Jan 1981); *Career* British Council: Kuwait 1969–71, Netherlands 1971–76, UK 1976–78, cultural attaché Greece 1978–83, India 1983–85, UK 1985–90, dir Mauritius, Madagascar and The Seychelles and cultural attaché Madagascar 1990–97; *Recreations* walking, tennis, gardening, politics, people; *Clubs* Mauritius Gymkhana; *Style*— Michael Bootle, Esq; ✉ The British Council, Royal Road, PO Box 111, Rose Hill, Mauritius

BOOTLE, Roger Paul; s of David Bootle, MBE (d 1972), and Florence Ethel, *née* Denman (d 1982); *b* 22 June 1952; *Educ* Downer GS, Merton Coll Oxford (BA), Nuffield Coll Oxford (MPhil); *Career* lectr in economics St Anne's Coll Oxford 1976–78, with Citibank 1978–79, dep head economic policy CBI 1979–81; chief economist: Capel Cure Myers 1982–86, Lloyds Merchant Bank 1986–87 (dir 1986–87); conslt 1987–89; chief economist and dir of research HSBC Greenwell (formerly Greenwell Montagu Gilt Edged) 1989–96, gp chief economist HSBC Holdings plc 1996–; visiting prof Manchester Business Sch 1995–; memb HM Treasy ind panel of economic forecasting advsrs 1996–; contrib: Financial Times, Times, numerous pubns; various TV and radio appearances as commentator on economic affairs; *Books* Theory of Money (jtly, 1978), Index-Linked Gilts (1986, 2 edn 1991), The Death of Inflation (1996); *Recreations* bridge, squash, horseracing, classical music, theatre; *Style*— Roger Bootle, Esq; ✉ HSBC Holdings plc, 10 Queen Street Place, London EC4R 1BL (direct ☎ 0171 336 3888, fax 0171 220 7113)

BOOTON, Dr Paul; s of Arthur Terence Booton, and Jean Brunhilde Mary, *née* Price; *b* 11 May 1955; *Educ* Hornchurch GS, The London Hosp Med Coll Univ of London (BSc, MB BS); *Career* physician to Prof J M Ledingham London Hosp 1980, MO to Kaitak and Sham Shui Po refugee camps UN High Cmmn on Refugees 1981, sr house offr and registrar med Oldchurch Hosp Romford 1982–86, lectr gen practice United Med and Dental Schs 1988–90; King's Coll Sch of Med and Dentistry: lectr Dept of Gen Practice 1990–94, curriculum sub-dean 1991–94, sr lectr in med educn 1994–, undergrad sub-dean 1994–; memb: Lab Pty, CND; MRCPUK 1984, MRCGP 1988; *Recreations* walking, skiing, cycling, theatre, music; *Style*— Dr Paul Booton; ✉ Department of General Practice and Primary Care, King's College School of Medicine and Dentistry, Bessemer Road, London SE5 9PJ (☎ 0171 346 3209, fax 0171 737 3556, e-mail P.Booton@kcl.ac.uk)

BORALESSA, Harsha Shanta; *b* 1 July 1943; *Educ* Visakha Girls' Sch Colombo Sri Lanka, Univ of Ceylon Sri Lanka (MB BS); *m* 2 Dec 1968, Harischandra Boralessa; 2 da (Harsha b 29 Oct 1970, Anoosha b 5 march 1972); *Career* registrar in anaesthetics: St Mark's Hosp City Rd London 1974–75, UCH Golder St London 1975–77, Moorfields Eye Hosp City Rd London 1977–78; sr registrar in anaesthetics 1978–83: Eastman Dental Hosp Gray's Inn Rd London, Hammersmith Hosp, Royal Postgrad Med Sch; conslt in anaesthesia and dir Intensive Care Oldchurch Hosp Romford Essex 1983–; memb: BMA, Assoc of Anaesthetists GB, Intensive Care Soc; FFARCS; *Style*— Mrs Harsha Boralessa; ✉ Oldchurch Hospital, Romford, Essex (☎ 01708 746090)

BORAN, David Frank; s of William Frank Boran (d 1985), of London, and Jessie, *née* Green; *b* 7 Aug 1957; *Educ* Battersea GS; *Career* Lloyds Bank: joined 1975, branch service 1975–81, seconded to National Bank of NZ 1981, PA to chief mangr Lloyds Bank City office 1982–85, asst in Corp Banking Div 1985–87, training mangr (with responsibility for lending skills) 1987–89, mktg and sales mangr (with responsibility for Small Business Sector) 1989–92, sr mangr Lloyds Bank Commercial Service 1992–; ACIB; *Recreations* golf, squash, eating out; *Style*— David Boran, Esq; ✉ Lloyds Bank Commercial Service, The Gables, 17 Massetts Road, Horley, Surrey RH6 7DQ (☎ 01293 785660)

BORBÓN, HE Jorge; s of Jorge Borbón (d 1981), of San José, Costa Rica, and Eugenia Ma Zeller (d 1980); *b* 8 May 1933; *Educ* Liceo de Costa Rica San José Costa Rica, Cornell Univ NY USA (BArch); *m* Maria Cecilia Beeche, da of Capt Luciano Beeche-Titzck; 1 s (Alfredo b 20 Aug 1957), 2 da (Maristella b 8 Nov 1958, Juliana b 14 April 1961); *Career* Costa Rican diplomat and architect; ambass of Costa Rica to Ct of St James's 1982–86 and 1994– (non-resident ambass to Portugal, Finland and Norway 1983–86); architectural designer Arguedas Dobles y Soto 1956–58, proprietor and gen mangr Sociedad Agricola Ganadera de Ujarrás Ltda (coffee plantation) 1956–, ptnr and vice pres Edica Ltda (construction firm) 1958–90, ptnr and gen mangr Arquitectura Moderna Ltda (architectural consulting firm) 1958–, co-proprietor and gen mangr Hacienda El Retiro Ltda (cattle farm) 1981–90, proprietor and vice pres Macebee SA (real estate firm) 1980–, proprietor and pres Torrejón SA (real estate firm); proprietor and gen mangr: Borbón Edificadora Ltda (construction firm) 1990–, Borbec Ltda (real estate firm) 1990–; prof of architecture Univ of Costa Rica 1980–82; perm dir Costa Rican C of C 1972–; memb Costa Rican: Chamber of Construction 1975–, Chamber of Architecture and Engrg 1980–; judging architect Second Biennial of Architecture and Urbanism for Costa Rica 1994; memb: Hon Architectural Socs L'Ogive and Gargoyle 1956, Costa Rican Assoc of Architects 1964, Federated Coll of Architects and Engrs of Costa Rica 1969, Colegio de Arquitectos Costa Rica 1980; *Style*— HE Mr Jorge Borbon; ✉ Embassy of Costa Rica, Flat 1, 14 Lancaster Gate, London W2 3LH (☎ 0171 706 8844, fax 0171 706 8655)

BORDELL, Gerald Jacob; s of Gabriel Bordell, and Eve, *née* Gavelber (d 1980); *b* 3 April 1934; *Educ* City of London Sch; *m* 20 March 1960, Valerie Joyce, da of John Alick (d 1967); 2 s (Keith Stephen b 1963, Jonathan David b 1967); *Career* md Little Lady (London) Ltd 1967–1987; chm Mermaid Theatre Assoc 1977–81, fndr and hon organiser the Friends of the RSC 1982–87, memb Cncl of Mgmnt Royal Shakespeare Theatre Tst 1984–87; md London Theatre Tours Ltd 1987; admin Friends of the Br Theatre 1987, chm Friends of the Br Theatre (Charitable Tst) Ltd 1988–; Freeman City of London 1973, Liveryman Worshipful Co of Basketmakers 1975; *Recreations* theatre, gardening; *Clubs* The City Livery, ESU; *Style*— Gerald Bordell, Esq; ✉ 5 Abbotswood Gardens, Clayhall, Ilford, Essex IG5 0BG (☎ 0181 550 0576)

BOREEL, Jonkheer Sir Francis David; 13 Bt (E 1645), of Amsterdam, Holland; s of Jonkheer Sir Alfred Boreel, 12 Bt (d 1964), and Countess Reiniera Adriana (d 1957), da of Count Francis David Schimmelpenninck; *b* 14 June 1926; *Educ* Univ of Utrecht; *m* 1964, Suzanne, da of Willy Campagne; 3 da (Reiniera Adriana b 1965, Christina Wilhelmina b 1966, Titia Florence b 1973); *Heir* kinsman, Jonkheer Stephan Gerard Boreel, *qv*, b 9 Feb 1945; *Career* cnsllr Netherlands Foreign Serv 1956–86, ret; *Recreations* tennis, sailing; *Style*— Jonkheer Sir Francis Boreel, Bt; ✉ Kapellestraat 25, 4351 Al Veere, Netherlands

BOREEL, Jonkheer Stephan Gerard; s of Jonkheer Gerard Lucas Boreel (d 1970), and Virginia Rae, *née* Bright (d 1972); hp to Btcy of kinsman, Jonkheer Sir Francis David Boreel, 13 Bt, *qv*; *b* 9 Feb 1945; *m* Francien P Kooijman; 1 s (Jacob Lucas Cornelis b 29 Sept 1974); *Style*— Jonkheer Stephan Boreel; ✉ Elzenoord 30, Vaassen, Holland

BOREHAM, Sir Leslie Kenneth Edward; kt (1972); *m* 1 s, 1 da; *Career* called to the Bar Lincoln's Inn 1947, bencher 1972; QC 1965, recorder Margate 1968–71, chm E Suffolk QS 1965–71 (dep chm 1962–65), judge of the High Court Queen's Bench Division 1972–92, presiding judge North Eastern Circuit 1974–79; dep chm Agric Lands Tbnl; *Recreations* gardening, golf; *Style*— Sir Leslie Boreham; ✉ c/o Royal Courts of Justice, Strand, London WC2A 2LL

BOREHAM, Michael Bryant; s of Harold Leslie Boreham, of Beach Hotel, Worthing, Sussex (d 1971), and Irene Ethel, *née* Bryant (d 1967); *b* 7 June 1928; *Educ* Highgate Sch, Univ of London (LLB); *m* 21 Jan 1956, Alison Jane, da of Douglas Archibald Clarke (d 1993), of St John's Wood Park NW8, and Shardeloes, Old Amersham, Bucks; 2 da (Jane Caroline b 13 March 1959, Penelope Lucy b 18 Dec 1962); *Career* Lt 16/5 Lancers 1947; slr; conslt Frere Cholmeley Bischoff, sr ptnr Frere Cholmeley 1979–90; dir: Knowles Electronics Co, The Material World Charitable Fndn Ltd; *Recreations* reading, theatre, shooting, fishing; *Clubs* Brooks's; *Style*— Michael B Boreham, Esq; ✉ The Old Rectory, Sutton, nr Pulborough, W Sussex RH20 1PS (☎ 01798 869258, fax 01798 869457); 225 Nell Gwynn House, Sloane Avenue, London SW3 3AZ (☎ 0171 581 3151)

BORENIOK, Heinrich Robert; s of Hans Peter Boreniok (d 1984), and Helga Margarete, *née* Rupp; *b* 6 July 1957; *Educ* Ratskeller Frauenaurach Bavaria; *m* 7 May 1988, Dorothy Patricia, da of Frederick Scroggie; *Career* Nat Serv German Air Force 1976–78; German diplommaster chef (Kuechen meister); first commis chef Great Western Royal Hotel 1978–79, chef de partie saucier Steigenberger Kurhaus Hotel Bad Kissingen Germany summer 1979, chef de partie saucier La Riva Lenzerheide Switzerland winter 1979, jr sous chef Dunloe Castle Co Kerry summer 1980 (joined as chef gardemanger), sous chef Hotel Forsthaus Furth Bavaria 1980–83, sous chef rising to premier sous chef The Savoy London 1983–86, maitre chef de cuisine A l'ecu de France London 1986–89, chef de cuisine Staple Ford Park Leicestershire 1989, exec chef Berkshire Hotel London 1990, exec chef de cuisine Edwardian Int until 1992, exec chef de cuisine Naval and Military Club 1992–; memb Assoc Culinaire Francaise UK 1983, memb Acad Culinaire de France GB 1994, memb Scotch Beef Club 1995; *Books* Readers Digest Cooks Scrapbook (contrib, 1995); *Recreations* cooking, reading, music, the outdoors, travelling, spectating and following equestrian and motor racing sports; *Style*— Heinrich Boreniok, Esq; ✉ Naval and Military Club, In and Out Ltd, 94 Piccadilly, London W1V 0BP (☎ 0171 499 5163)

BORG, Dr Alan Charles Nelson; CBE (1991); s of Charles John Nelson Borg (d 1986), and Frances Mary Olive, *née* Hughes (d 1985); *b* 21 Jan 1942; *Educ* Westminster, BNC Oxford (MA, Fencing blue 1961 and 1962), Courtauld Inst of Art London (MA, PhD); *m* 1, 1964; 1 s (Giles b 1965), 1 da (Emma b 1970); m 2, 1976, Lady Caroline Sylvia Hill (raised to the rank of a Marquess's da 1992), da of Lord Francis Hill and sister of 8 Marquess of Downshire; 2 da (Leonora b 1980, Helen b 1982); *Career* lectr in English Univ d'Aix-Marseille 1964–65, lectr in history of art Univ of Indiana 1967–69, asst prof of history of art Princeton Univ 1969–70, asst keeper of the armouries HM Tower of London 1970–78, keeper Sainsbury Centre for Visual Arts Univ of East Anglia 1978–82, dir-gen Imperial War Museum 1982–95, dir V & A Museum 1995–; FSA, hon fell RCA 1991; *Books* Architectural Sculpture in Romanesque Provence (1972), European Swords and Daggers in the Tower of London (1974), Torture and Punishment (1975), Heads and Horses (1976), Arms and Armour in Britain (1979), War Memorials (1991); *Recreations* music, travel; *Clubs* Special Forces; *Style*— Dr A C N Borg, CBE, FSA; ✉ Telegraph House, 36 West Square, London SE11 4SP (☎ 0171 582 8122); Victoria & Albert Museum, South Kensington, London SW7 2RL (☎ 0171 938 8504, fax 0171 938 8477)

BORINGDON, Viscount; Mark Lionel Parker; s and h of 6 Earl of Morley, *qv*; *b* 22 Aug 1956; *Educ* Eton; *m* 12 Nov 1983, Carolyn Jill, da of Donald McVicar, of Meols, Wirral, Cheshire; 3 da (Hon Alexandra b 1985, Hon Olivia b 1987, Hon Helena Georgia b 1991); *Career* cmmnd Royal Green Jackets 1976, Lt 1982; *Style*— Viscount Boringdon; ✉ Pound House, Yelverton, South Devon

BORMAN, Dr Edwin Miles; s of David Bevil Borman (b 1936), of Cape Town, SA, and Sophia, *née* Miller; *b* 9 Sept 1961; *Educ* Theodor Herzl HS Port Elizabeth SA, Univ of Cape Town Med Sch (MB ChB); *Career* house offr Groote Schuur Hosp Cape Town 1985; registrar posts in anaesthetics and intensive care: Plymouth Health Authy 1990–91 (SHO posts in surgical and med specialities 1986–90), S Birmingham Health Authy 1991–94; sr registrar posts in anaesthetics and intensive care (Coventry and Birmingham rotation) 1995–; BMA: chm Jr Doctors Ctee 1991–94, memb Cncl 1991–, memb Jt Consits Ctee 1991–94; memb: Ministerial Gps on 'Achieving a Balance' and 'The New Deal' 1991–94, Chief Med Offr's Working Gps on Specialist Med Trg 1992–93 and on Overseas Doctors in the UK 1994, Perm Working Gp of Euro Jr Hosp Doctors 1993–, GMC 1994–, Euro Bd of Anaesthesiology and Reanimation 1995–; memb BMA 1986, FFARCSI 1993, FRCA 1994; *Recreations* classical music, Eastern art; *Style—* Dr Edwin Borman; ✉ 30 Clover Drive, Bartley Green, Birmingham B32 3DJ (☎ 0121 426 5760); Anaesthetic Department, Walsgrave Hospital, Coventry CV2 2DX (☎ 01203 602020)

BORNER, John; *b* 11 July 1947; *Educ* Haileybury, Univ of London (BSc Estate Mgmnt, Cricket purple); *m* Geneviève, *née* Betis; 1 da (Catherine b 1979); *Career* ptnr Richard Ellis property consits (specialist in hotel and leisure work); memb Tech Ctee Br Assoc of Hotel Accountants; Master Worshipful Co of Farmers 1995–96; FRICS (ARICS 1972); *Publications* Law and Valuation of Leisure Property (jtly); *Recreations* playing cricket and hockey; *Clubs* Farmers', MCC; *Style—* John Borner, Esq; ✉ Richard Ellis, Berkeley Square House, London W1Y 6AX (☎ 0171 629 6290, fax 0171 493 3734)

BORODALE, Viscount; Sean David Beatty; s and h of 3 Earl Beatty, *qv*; *b* 12 June 1973; *Style—* Viscount Borodale

BORRETT, (Jack Geoffrey) Kingsley; s of Capt J T Borrett, OBE (d 1969), and Mary Edith Joy, *née* Symonds-Tayler (d 1981); *b* 25 April 1938; *Educ* Nautical Coll Pangbourne; *m* 1, 1 May 1962 (m dis 1990), Caroline Ann, da of K P Herron (d 1961); 2 da (Juliette Patricia b 1964, Lucinda Jane b 1967); m 2, 19 July 1991, Jacqueline Munro Morris, *née* Gibb; *Career* RNR 1951–56; broker Lloyd's 1956–95; Bevington Vaizey and Foster Ltd 1956–80; pres Berks, Bucks and Oxon Golf Union 1996; memb Lord's Taverners; Freeman: Worshipful Co of Insurers 1987, City of London 1987; ACII 1967, memb CIP 1989; *Recreations* golf, racing (horses and greyhounds), charity, travel; *Clubs* Royal & Ancient, Denham Golf, Chorleywood Golf, Quinta do Lago Golf, Lloyd's Golf; *Style—* Kingsley Borrett, Esq; ✉ Templars Barn, Wapseys Lane, Hedgerley Green, Bucks SL2 3XG (☎ 01753 890178)

BORRETT, Neil Edgar; s of Edgar Edward Borrett (d 1975), and Winifred, *née* Mowbray (d 1992); *b* 10 March 1940; *Educ* Dartford GS, Woolwich Poly, Coll of Estate Management Kensington; *m* 1965, Jane, da of Francis Wallace Chapman; 2 da (Deanna Jane b 31 July 1966, Joanne Emma b 23 July 1971); *Career* sarious positions in Reconstruction and Purchasing Depts NCB 1958–62, Alliance Property Co Ltd (later Argyle Securities) 1963–77, md Morgan Grenfell Property Servs 1977–87, ptnr Vigers 1987–90, dir of Property Holdings DOE 1990–96, chief exec Property Advisors to the Civil Estate (PACE) 1996–; FRICS 1968; *Recreations* golf, boating, photography; *Clubs* Bramley Golf; *Style—* Neil Borrett, Esq; ✉ Property Advisors to the Civil Estate, St Christopher House, Southwark Street, London SE1 0TE

BORRIE, Baron (Life Peer UK 1995), of Abbots Morton in the County of Hereford and Worcester; Sir Gordon Johnson Borrie; kt (1982), QC (1986); s of Stanley Borrie, of Croydon, Surrey; *b* 13 March 1931; *Educ* John Bright GS Llandudno, Univ of Manchester (LLB, LLM); *m* 1960, Dorene, da of Herbert Toland, of Toronto, Canada; *Career* Nat Serv Army Legal Servs, HQ Br Cwlth Forces Korea 1952–54; called to the Bar Middle Temple 1952, bencher 1980, in practice 1954–57, lectr then sr lectr Coll of Law 1957–64; Univ of Birmingham: sr lectr 1965–68, prof of Eng law and dir Inst of Judicial Admin 1969–76, dean Law Faculty 1974–76; dir-gen Office of Fair Trading 1976–92, chm Commission on Social Justice 1992–94, pres Inst of Trading Standards Admin 1992–; dir: Woolwich Building Society 1992–, Three Valleys Water Services plc 1992–, Mirror Group Newspapers plc 1993–, Telewest plc 1994–; govr Birmingham Coll of Commerce 1966–70; former memb Law Cmmn Advsy Panel for Contract Law; memb: Parole Bd 1971–74, Cncl Consumers' Assoc 1972–75, Equal Opportunities Cmmn 1975–76; contested: (Lab) Croydon NE 1955, Ilford South 1959; Hon LLD: City of London Poly (now City of London Univ) 1989, Univ of Manchester 1990, Univ of Hull 1991, Univ of Dundee 1993; hon memb SPTL 1989, FRSA 1982; *Books* Commercial Law (1962, 6 edn 1988), The Development of Consumer Law and Policy (1984), others in joint authorship; *Recreations* gastronomy, piano playing, travel; *Clubs* Reform, Garrick; *Style—* The Rt Hon Lord Borrie, QC; ✉ Manor Farm, Abbots Morton, Worcestershire (☎ 01386 792330); 1 Plowden Buildings, Temple, London EC4 (☎ 0171 353 4434)

BORRIE, Michael Anthony Frederick; OBE (1994); s of Douglas Armitage Borrie (d 1964), of London, and Lucy Mary, *née* White (d 1981); *Educ* The Salesian Colls London and Oxford, King's Coll London (BA), Inst of Historical Res; *m* 24 March 1974, Gillian Elizabeth, da of Clifford John Pollard, of Ipswich; 2 s (George b 1980, Thomas b 1981); *Career* asst keeper Dept of MSS Br Museum 1960, manuscripts librarian Br Library 1987; author of articles and reviews in: The Spectator, Journal of the British Archaeological Assoc, Journal of the Soc of Archivists, Library History, British Museum Quarterly, Literary Review; treas Plainsong and Medieval Music Soc 1966–79; First Div Assoc: sec Museums Sub Ctee 1968–75, nat exec memb 1971–79; sec Friends of the Nat Libraries 1995; memb: Cncl Br Records Assoc 1972, Ctee for Establishing the Museum of London 1973–76, Comité de Sigillographie Conseil International Des Archives 1974–88, Ctee Friends of the Geffrye Museum 1985; FRHistS 1969, FSA 1984; *Books* Magna Carta (1976), Vocabulaire International de Sigillographie (1984), Catalogue of the Yelverton Manuscripts in the British Library (ed 1994); *Recreations* gardening, reading, walking; *Clubs* Academy; *Style—* Michael Borrie, Esq, OBE, FSA; ✉ Friends of the National Libraries, c/o British Library, London WC1B 3DG (☎ 0171 412 7749, fax 0171 412 7745, telex 21462)

BORTHWICK, Antony Thomas; s and h of Sir John Thomas Borthwick, 3 Bt, MBE, *qv*; *b* 12 Feb 1941; *Educ* Eton; *m* 1, 1966, Gillian Deirdre Broke, twin da of late Nigel Vere Broke Thurston, RN; 1 s (Matthew Thomas Thurston b 1968), 2 da (Suzanna Claire Irene b 1970, Camilla Fay Broke b 1973); m 2, 1985, Jenny, eldest da of George Lanning; *Style—* Antony Borthwick, Esq; ✉ c/o Midland Bank, 31 Holborn, London EC1

BORTHWICK, (William) Jason Maxwell; DSC (1942); s of Hon William Borthwick (d 1958), bro of 1 and last Baron Whitburgh (their f Thomas, chm and sr ptnr Thos Borthwick & Sons, was nominated a Peer 1912 but d before the patent passed the Great Seal); *b* 1 Nov 1910; *Educ* Winchester, Trinity Coll Cambridge (BA); *m* 1937, Elizabeth Cleveland, *née* Elworthy (d 1978); 1 s, 3 da; *Career* called to the Bar Inner Temple 1932; cmmnd RNVR 1940, Cdr (QO) 1945; dir: Thomas Borthwick & Sons Ltd 1946–76 (joined 1934), International Commodities Clearing House Ltd 1952–83; memb Central Cncl of Physical Recreation 1950–, dir Cwlth Devpt Corpn 1971–77; *Recreations* shooting, sailing; *Clubs* United Oxford and Cambridge, Royal Thames Yacht; *Style—* Jason Borthwick, Esq, DSC; ✉ North House, Brancaster Staithe, King's Lynn, Norfolk PE31 8BY (☎ 01485 210475)

BORTHWICK, 24 Lord (S 1450); John Hugh Borthwick of that Ilk; Baron (territorial) of Heriotmuir, Borthwick and Lockerwart; er (twin) s of 23 Lord Borthwick, TD, JP, DL (d 1996), and Margaret, *née* Cormack (d 1976); *b* 14 Nov 1940; *Educ* Gordonstoun, Edinburgh Sch of Agric (SDA, NDA); *m* 1974, Adelaide, o da of Archy Birkmyre, of Lower Dalchonzie, Comrie, Perthshire; 2 da (Hon Georgina b 18 Dec 1975, Hon Alexandra b 25 Aug 1977); *Heir* twin bro, James Henry Alexander Borthwick of Glengelt b 14 Nov 1940; *Career* farmer and landowner; *Recreations* trout fishing, stalking; *Clubs* New (Edinburgh); *Style—* The Rt Hon the Lord Borthwick; ✉ The Neuk, Heriot, Midlothian EH38 5YS (☎ 01875 835236)

BORTHWICK, Sir John Thomas; 3 Bt (UK 1908), of Whitburgh, Humbie, Co Haddington, MBE (1945); s of late Hon James Alexander Borthwick, 2 s of 1 Bt; suc to Btcy of unc, 1 Baron Whitburgh, formerly Sir Thomas Banks Borthwick, 2 Bt, who d 1967, when Barony became ext; *b* 5 Dec 1917; *Educ* Eton, Trinity Coll Oxford; *m* 1, 1939 (m dis 1961), Irene (d 1978), o da of Joseph Heller, of 2 Buckingham Place, London SW1; 3 s (Antony Thomas Borthwick, *qv* b 1941, Peter Richard John b 1943, Patrick James Joseph b 1945); m 2, 1962, Irene, da of late Leo Fink, of Paris XVI; 2 s (Mark George Alexander b 1962, John Kelly Leo b 1965); *Heir* s, Antony Thomas Borthwick, *qv*; *Career* late Major Rifle Bde (TA); dir Thomas Borthwick & Sons Ltd until 1983 (vice chm 1979–83); Liveryman Worshipful Co of Butchers; *Style—* Sir John Borthwick, Bt, MBE; ✉ 41 Mizzentop, Warwick, Bermuda (☎ 001 809 236 0018)

BORTHWICK, Kenneth White; CBE (1979), JP (1966), DL (Edinburgh 1980); s of Andrew Graham Borthwick; *b* 4 Nov 1915; *Educ* George Heriot Sch Edinburgh; *m* 1942, Irene Margaret, da of John Graham Wilson, of Aberdeen; 2 s, 1 da; *Career* Flying Offr RAF WWII; memb: Edinburgh Town Cncl 1963, Lothian Regnl Cncl 1974–77, Edinburgh DC 1976; judge of police 1972–75; Rt Hon Lord Provost of City of Edinburgh and Lord-Lt of City and Co of Edinburgh 1977–80; memb: Lothians River Bd 1969–73, Organising Ctee Cwlth Games Edinburgh 1970, Edinburgh and Lothian Theatre Tst 1975–76, Lothian and Borders Police Bd 1975–77, BAA Consultative Ctee 1977–80, Convention of Scot Local Authorities 1977, Scot Cncl for Devpt and Indust 1977; chm: Edinburgh Dist Licensing Ct 1975–77, Edinburgh Int Festival Soc 1977–80, Edinburgh Mil Tattoo Policy Ctee 1977–80, Organising Ctee Cwlth Games Edinburgh (1986) 1983–86; govr George Heriot Sch 1965–73, curator of patronage Univ of Edinburgh 1977–80; Hon Consul for Malawi in Scotland 1982, Hon Consul Gen for Malawi in Scotland 1993, dean Edinburgh and Leith Consular Corps 1991; cdr of the Order of the Lion (Malawi) 1993, OStJ; *Recreations* golf, gardening; *Clubs* Caledonian (hon memb); *Style—* Kenneth Borthwick, Esq, CBE, JP, DL; ✉ 17 York Rd, Edinburgh EH5 3EJ (☎ 0131 552 2519)

BORTHWICK, Stephen Robert; s of Sidney Borthwick, and Edna, *née* Robinson; *b* 23 Sept 1951; *Educ* Strode's GS Egham Surrey, UNCW Bangor (open scholar, BSc), CCC Cambridge (PGCE); *m* 1974, Glynis Hannah, da of J A Francis (d 1987); *Career* asst master: Bloxham Sch 1974–80, Rugby Sch 1980–84; head Depts of Physics and Technology Marlborough Coll 1984–89, dep headmaster and dir of studies Bishop's Stortford Coll 1989–94, headmaster Aldenham Sch 1994–; memb: Secdy Heads Assoc 1989–, HMC 1994–; MInstP 1974, CPhys 1977; *Books* Revised Nuffield A Level Physics Course (co-author, 4 vols 1980); *Recreations* photography (landscape, portrait), collector of gramophone music, golf; *Clubs* East India, Cilgwyn Golf; *Style—* Stephen Borthwick, Esq; ✉ The Headmaster's House, Aldenham School, Elstree, Herts WD6 3AJ (☎ 01923 854419); Aldenham School, Elstree, Herts WD6 3AJ (☎ 01923 858122, fax 01923 854410)

BORWICK, Geoffrey Robert James (Jamie); s of Hon Robin Sandbach Borwick, *qv*, of Bosham, W Sussex, and Hon Patricia Borwick, *née* McAlpine; *b* 7 March 1955; *Educ* Eton; *m* 1981, Victoria Lorne Peta, da of R Dennis Poore (d 1987), of London; 2 s (Edwin b 1984, Thomas b 1987), 1 da (Alexandra b 1990); *Career* chief exec Manganese Bronze Holdings plc 1984–; chm: Finsbury Tst plc 1985–, London Taxis International Ltd 1984–, Manganese Bronze Components Ltd 1988–; *Recreations* travel; *Clubs* Garrick; *Style—* Jamie Borwick, Esq; ✉ Manganese Bronze Holdings plc, 1 Love Lane, London EC2V 7HJ (☎ 0171 606 0088)

BORWICK, 4 Baron (UK 1922); Sir James Hugh Myles Borwick; 4 Bt (UK 1916); MC (1945); s of 3 Baron Borwick (d 1961), and his 1 w, Irene Phyllis, *née* Patterson; *b* 12 Dec 1917; *Educ* Eton, RMC Sandhurst; *m* 14 Sept 1954, Hyllarie Adalia Mary, yr da of late Lt-Col William Hamilton Hall Johnston, DSO, MC, DL, of Bryn-y-Groes, Bala, N Wales; 4 da; *Heir* half-bro, Hon Robin Sandbach Borwick b 1927; *Career* Highland Light Infantry: cmmnd 2 Lt 1937, Capt 1939, Maj 1941, ret 1947; *Recreations* field sports, sailing; *Clubs* Royal Ocean Racing; *Style—* The Rt Hon the Lord Borwick, MC; ✉ The Leys, Bircher, Leominster, Hereford HR6 0AZ (☎ 01568 780367)

BORWICK, Hon Robin (Sandbach); s of 3 Baron Borwick (d 1961); hp to half-bro 4 Baron; *b* 22 March 1927; *Educ* Eton; *m* 1950, Hon Patricia, only da of Baron McAlpine of Moffat (Life Peer, d 1990); 2 s (Jamie, *qv*, Richard) 1 da (Judith (Mrs P D Curry-Towneley-O'Hagan)); *Career* Lt The Life Gds 1946–52; fndr Donkey Breed Soc 1967 (former first chm, now vice pres), pres Br Mule Soc 1978–; *Books* People With Long Ears (1965), Donkeys (1970), Esel, Freunde der Kinder (1970), The Book of the Donkey (1981), Esel Halten (1984), A Brief Guide to Lihou Island (1986), Never At Half Moon (1989); *Recreations* horses, donkeys, all equines; *Clubs* Cavalry and Guards'; *Style—* The Hon Robin Borwick; ✉ Neptune House, Newells Lane, Bosham, Sussex PO18 8PS (☎ 01243 576900, fax 01243 575541)

BOSANQUET, (Samuel) Anthony John Pierre; JP (1982), DL (Gwent 1991); s of Samuel John Anson Bosanquet (ka 1944), and Muriel Daphne, *née* Griffith; *b* 11 Jan 1944; *Educ* Eton, Keble Coll Oxford (MA, ARCM, ARCO); *m* 1975, Helen Margaret, da of William Hanbury Saumarez Smith, OBE; 2 s, 1 da; *Heir* Samuel David Saumarez Bosanquet (b 1977); *Career* music master Eton 1970–74, head of music King Henry VIII Sch Abergavenny 1974–79, asst music master Monmouth Sch 1979–93; landowner; memb: Home Grown Timber Advsy Ctee 1994–, Regional Advsy Ctee to the Forestry Cmmn in Wales 1995–; CLA: chm Gwent Branch 1988–90, chm Welsh Ctee 1990–93, chm Taxation Ctee 1991–93, chm Agric and Rural Economy Ctee 1993–, vice pres Europe 1994–; chm: Merlin Music Soc 1990–, Historic Houses Assoc in Wales 1991–94, Monmouth Operatic Soc 1995–; High Sheriff Co of Gwent 1994–95; *Recreations* gardening, country pursuits, music; *Clubs* United Oxford and Cambridge Univ; *Style—* Anthony Bosanquet, Esq, JP, DL; ✉ Dingestow Court, Monmouth, Gwent NP5 4YD (☎ 01600 740238)

BOSANQUET, Prof Nicholas Francis Gustavus; s of Lt-Col Neville Richard Gustavus Bosanquet, of Wiltshire, and Nancy Bosanquet, *née* Mason; *b* 17 Jan 1942; *Educ* Winchester, Clare Coll Cambridge, Yale Univ, LSE; *m* 31 Aug 1974 (m dis 1993), Anne Connolly; 2 da (Kate b 1978, Helen b 1981); *Career* sr res fell Centre for Health Econ Univ of York, lectr in econs LSE and the City Univ, prof of health policy Royal Holloway and Bedford New Coll Univ of London 1988–93, prof of health policy St Mary's Medical Sch Imperial Coll 1993–; former special advsr to Social Servs Select Ctee of The House of Commons; econ advsr: Nat Bd for Prices and Incomes, Royal Cmmn on Distribution of Income and Wealth; conslt: World Bank, OECD, health authys and cos in Britain; arbitrator ACAS; contrib to Economic Journal, British Medical Journal; *Books* Industrial Relations in the NHS: The Search for a System (1980), After the New Right (1983), Family Doctors and Economic Incentives (1989); *Recreations* collecting books on WWI, running; *Style—* Prof Nick F G Bosanquet; ✉ Health Policy Unit, Imperial College, University of London, Norfolk Place, London W2 1PG (☎ 0171 725 1550)

BOSCAWEN, Hon Evelyn Arthur Hugh; s and h of 9 Viscount Falmouth; *b* 13 May 1955; *Educ* Eton, RAC Cirencester; *m* 1977 (m dis 1995), Lucia Caroline, da of Ralph Vivian-Neal, of Poundisford Park, Somerset; 1 s ((Evelyn George) William b 1979), 1 da

(Laura Frances b 1982); m 2, 1995, Katharine Helen, eldest da of Mark Maley, of Nayland, Suffolk; 1 s (Frederick Mark b 1996); *Career* dep chm Goonvean & Rostowrack China Clay Co 1979–, Goonvean Ceramic Materials; chm Cornish Grain; chm Kent branch CLA; Liveryman Worshipful Co of Clockmakers; *Recreations* shooting, sailing; *Clubs* Whites', Athenaeum; *Style*— The Hon Evelyn Boscawen; ✉ c/o Tregothnan Estate Office, Truro, Cornwall (☎ 01872 520310)

BOSCAWEN, Rt Hon Robert Thomas; PC (1992), MC (1944); s of 8 Viscount Falmouth; *b* 17 March 1923; *Educ* Eton, Trinity Coll Cambridge; *m* 1949, Mary Alice Boscawen, JP, er da of Sir Geoffrey Codrington, KCVO, CB, CMG, DSO, OBE, TD; 1 s (Hugh), 2 da (Dozmary, Karenza); *Career* served NW Europe 1941–45, Capt Coldstream Gds 1945; attached to Br Red Cross Civilian Relief Orgn in occupied Europe 1946–47, memb London Exec Cncl NHS 1954–65; Parly candidate (C) Falmouth and Camborne 1964 and 1966; MP (C): Wells 1970–83, Somerton and Frome 1983–92; memb Select Ctee on Expenditure 1974, vice chm Cons Parly Health and Soc Security Ctee 1974; memb Parly Delgn to: Soviet Union 1978, Nepal 1981, UN Assembly 1988, Falkland Is 1990, Canada 1991; asst govt whip 1979–81, Lord Cmmr of the Treasy (govt whip) 1981–83, vice chamberlain of HM's Household 1983–86, comptroller HM Household 1986–88; Lloyd's underwriter 1952–; Liveryman Worshipful Co of Clockmakers; *Recreations* sailing, shooting; *Clubs* Pratt's, Royal Yacht Sqdn; *Style*— The Rt Hon Robert Boscawen, MC

BOSEL, Charles Henry; s of Douglas Henry Bosel (d 1985), of Brisbane, Aust, and Edith May, *née* Bouel (d 1987); *b* 4 July 1937; *Educ* Univ of Queensland (BArch), Univ of Liverpool (Master of Civic Design), Academica Britannica Rome (Rome Scholar in Architecture); *m* 6 Feb 1960, (Betty) Eunice, da of Cyril Allan Asplin (d 1977), of Tully, Aust; 2 s (Michael Charles b 1964, Stuart Allan b 1966), 2 da (Juliet Ann b 1971, Nicole Betty b 1975); *Career* architect and town planner; chm: Claverton House (Avon) Ltd 1984, St George's Hill Ltd 1981, SSC Overseas Ltd 1986, Ecinue Holdings Ltd 1987, Claverton House (Bridgwater) Ltd 1993, Avalon Homes (Minehead) Ltd 1993; dir Al Marzouk and Abi Hanna 1980–; pres Cor-Dor Group Holdings NV 1986–; memb: Royal Town Planning Inst, RIBA, Royal Inst Aust Architects, Royal Aust Planning Inst, Soc of Rome Scholars, Kuwait Soc of Engrs; fell IOD; *Recreations* tennis, squash; *Style*— Charles Bosel, Esq; ✉ Arnolds, Nursery Lane, Fairwarp, East Sussex TN22 3BD (☎ 01825 712997, fax 01825 713444)

BOSHOFF, (Louis) Leon; *b* 12 May 1940; *Educ* Rondebosch Sch Capetown SA, Stellenbosch Univ (BA, LLB); *m* 1, 1966 (m dis 1985), Heléne Steyn; 1 s (Andrew b 9 Dec 1967), 1 da (Alison b 18 June 1970); m 2, 1986, Aggy Kooper; 1 da (Kate b 2 May 1988); *Career* attorney and advocate SA 1965, in private practice Cape Bar 1965–72; admitted slr England 1975; Clifford Chance (Clifford-Turner until merger 1987): articled clerk 1972–75, ptnr 1975–, Riyadh Office 1982–84, Hong Kong Office 1986–89; admitted slr Hong Kong 1986, admitted advocate and slr Brunei 1986; vice chm Int Litigation Ctee Int Bar Assoc 1988–92; Freeman City of London Slrs' Co; *Clubs* Arts, Royal St George's Golf; *Style*— Leon Boshoff, Esq; ✉ Clifford Chance, 200 Aldersgate Street, London EC1A 4JJ (☎ 0171 600 1000, fax 0171 600 5555)

BOSOMWORTH, (Albert) John; JP (1991); s of John Bosomworth, of Beamsley, Skipton, and Agnes Mary, *née* Searle; *b* 28 Nov 1945; *m* 17 Sept 1977, Anne Caroline Mary, da of Charles Michael Dennison Roberts, OBE; *Career* farmer and landowner; dir: John Bosomworth (Holdings), Estate Properties, CC Yacht Charter, Shooting Sch, Arms Dealing (JB); *Recreations* shooting (ex Br and English shooting teams), hunting, fishing, yachting, motor racing; *Clubs* CA, RYA, CPSA, CLA; *Style*— John Bosomworth, Esq, JP; ✉ Beamsley Estate, Beamsley, Skipton, N Yorkshire (☎ 01756 710344, fax 01756 710554, car 0387 267007)

BOSSOM, Bruce Charles; s and h of Hon Sir Clive Bossom, 2 Bt, and Lady Barbara, *née* North, of 97 Cadogan Lane, London SW1; *b* 22 Aug 1952; *Educ* Eton, Coll of Estate Mgmnt, Harvard Business Sch (PMD); *m* 1985, Penelope Jane, da of Edward Holland-Martin (d 1981), of Overbury Court, Glos; 1 s (George Edward Martin b 21 Feb 1992), 2 da (Rosanna Emily b 1986, Amanda Lucy b 1988); *Career* chartered surveyor; Jones Lang Wootton 1972–86 (ptnr 1981); dir: Mountleigh Group plc 1989–93, Phoenix Properties & Finance plc 1986–89, LaSalle Partners 1993–; Liveryman Worshipful Co of Grocers; FRICS, FRSA; *Clubs* Pilgrims, Bath & Racquet, White's; *Style*— Bruce Bossom, Esq; ✉ Overbury Court, nr Tewkesbury, Glos GL20 7NP (☎ 01386 725312, fax 01386 725528); 34 Princedale Rd, London W11 (☎ 0171 727 5127); LaSalle Partners, Regent Arcade House, 19–25 Argyll Street, London W1V 1AA (☎ 0171 734 0055, fax 0171 734 1155)

BOSSOM, Hon Sir Clive; 2 Bt (UK 1953), of Maidstone, Kent; s of Baron Bossom (Life Peer and 1 Bt), by his 1 w Emily, *née* Bayne (d 1932); Sir Clive suc to Btcy 1965; *b* 4 Feb 1918; *Educ* Eton; *m* 1951, Lady Barbara Joan Bossom, *née* North, da of late Lord North and sis of 9 Earl of Guilford; 3 s (Bruce Charles b 1952, Andrew Clive b 1954, James Edward b 1962), 1 da (Arabella Emily b 1968); *Heir* s, Bruce Charles Bossom, *qv*; *Career* Maj Europe and Far East (regular soldier The Buffs 1939–48); cncllr Kent CC 1949–51; MP (C) Leominster 1959–74; PPS to: Jt Parly Secs of Mins of Pensions 1960, Sec of State for Air 1962–64, Home Sec 1970–72; chm Europ Assistance Ltd 1972–88, dir Vosper Ltd 1973–83; chm Br Motor Sports Cncl 1975–82, vice chm Br Road Fedn 1975–82, int pres Int Social Service for Refugees 1984–89; pres: IFPA 1969–81, Anglo-Netherlands Soc 1978–89, Anglo-Belgian Soc 1983–85; vice pres: (d'honneur) FIA, Iran Soc (past pres); chm Ex-Servs War Disabled Help Ctee 1973–88, vice chm Jt Ctee Red Cross and St John 1987–92; KStJ 1961, Almoner OStJ 1987–93; Cdr of Leopold II (Belgium), Cdr Order of Crown (Belgium), Kt Cdr Order of Orange Nassau (Netherlands), Order of Homayoun (Iran); memb Ct of Assts Worshipful Co of Grocers (Master 1979–80); FRSA, FRGS; *Recreations* travel; *Clubs* Carlton, RAC (chm 1975–78), BRDC, BARC (pres 1984–90); *Style*— The Hon Sir Clive Bossom, Bt; ✉ 97 Cadogan Lane, London SW1X 9DU (☎ 0171 245 6531); Rotherdown, Petworth, Sussex GU28 0BT (☎ 01798 342329)

BOSTELMANN, Michael John; s of Martin Horst Bostelmann; *b* 16 Nov 1947; *Educ* Bradfield; *m* 1973, Gillian, da of Allan Vickery; 2 s; *Career* sr ptnr Arnold Hill & Co CAs London; gp md Fandstan Electric Gp; dir: Quadrem Hope Ltd, British Paper Co, Quadrem Buildings Ltd; FCA; *Recreations* long distance running (fastest marathon 2 hrs 39 mins), squash, gardening; *Clubs* Thames Hare and Hounds, Hurlingham; *Style*— Michael Bostelmann, Esq; ✉ 33 West Temple Sheen, East Sheen, London SW14 7AP; Arnold Hill & Co, Craven House, 16 Northumberland Ave, London WC2N 5AP (☎ 0171 306 9100)

BOSTOCK, *see:* Ashton-Bostock

BOSTOCK, James Edward; s of William George Bostock (d 1948), and Amy, *née* Titley (d 1976); *b* 11 June 1917; *Educ* Borden GS Sittingbourne, Medway Sch of Art, RCA London; *m* 20 Dec 1939, Gwladys Irene, *née* Griffiths; 3 s (Philip b 1946, Michael b 1950, Christopher b 1959); *Career* teacher, painter and engraver; served Durham LI and RCS 1940–46; sr lectr Ealing Sch of Art 1946–60, head of dip studies Stoke on Trent Coll of Art 1960–65, vice princ West of England Coll of Art 1965–70, academic devpt offr Bristol Poly 1970–78; has exhibited watercolours, engravings, etchings and drawings worldwide; one-man shows incl: Mignon Gallery Bath, Univ of Bristol, Bristol Poly, Margate Library Gallery, Broadstairs Library Gallery, Deal Library Gallery, Folkestone Library Gallery, Phillip Maslen Gallery Canterbury; group exhibitions incl: RA Summer Exhibitions, NEAC, RBA, RE, RI; works acquired by: V&A Museum, Ashmolean Museum, Br Museum, Br Cncl, Hunt Botanical Library Pittsburgh, Hereford Museum, private collectors; work commissioned by: ICI Ltd, Br Museum, Odhams Press; contrib to: TES, Manchester Guardian, Studio magazine, Artist magazine; memb: Royal Soc of Painter-Etchers 1947, Soc of Wood Engravers 1950, E Kent Art Soc; RE 1961 (ARE 1947), ARCA 1939; *Books* Roman Lettering for Students (1959), Woodengraved Illustrations to Poems of Edward Thomas (Folio Soc, 1988); *Style*— James Bostock; ✉ 80 Lindenthorpe Rd, Broadstairs, Kent CT10 1DB (☎ 01843 869782)

BOSTOCK, Nicholas Stephen Godfrey; DL (Staffordshire 1988); s of Godfrey Stafford Bostock, of Tixall House, Tixall, Stafford, and Diana, *née* Heywood; *b* 8 July 1942; *Educ* Eton; *m* 9 Aug 1968, Marise Cynthia, da of Rupert Thomas Bebb; 1 s (Richard b 1969), 1 da (Tania b 1972); *Career* CA and farmer; dir Econ Estate Planning Co Ltd 1978–; underwriting memb Lloyd's 1968–; High Sheriff of Staffordshire 1987–88; memb S Staffordshire Health Authy 1989– (currently vice chm), chm Ingestre with Tixall Parish Cncl (memb 1983); FCA 1979; *Recreations* shooting, inland waterways; *Style*— Nicholas Bostock, Esq, DL; ✉ Tixall Lodge, Tixall, Stafford ST18 0XS (☎ 01785 661 713); Kennels Farm, Tixall, Stafford ST18 0XT (☎ 01785 662 626, fax 01785 660 780)

BOSTON, David Merrick; OBE (1976); s of Dr Hugh Merrick Boston (d 1980), of Salisbury, Wilts, and Jessie Mary, *née* Ingham (d 1979); *b* 15 May 1931; *Educ* Bishop Wordworth's Sch Salisbury Wilts, Selwyn Coll Cambridge (BA, MA), Univ of Cape Town; *m* 12 Aug 1961, Catharine Mary, da of Rev Prof E G S Parrinder, of Orpington, Kent; 1 s (Peter b 1966), 2 da (Janet b 1963, Andrea b 1969); *Career* Nat Serv 1950–51, Adj Marine Craft Trg Sch RAF Calshot, Flying Offr RAFRO 1951–55; Field Survey South African Inst of Race Relations 1955, keeper of ethnology (formerly special offr) Liverpool Museums 1956–62, asst keeper Dept of Ethnography Br Museum 1962–65, curator then dir Horniman Public Museum and Public Park Tst 1965–93 (formerly Horniman Museum and Library), vice pres Friends of the Horniman 1995–; conslt Programme for Belize 1994–, hon curator Quebec House 1996–; visiting scientist: Nat Museum of Man Ottawa 1970, Japan Fndn Tokyo 1986; chm Br Nat Ctee of the Int Cncl of Museums 1976–80; Royal Anthropological Inst: vice pres 1972–75, 1977–80 and 1995–, hon sec 1985–88, hon librarian 1993–; vice pres Dulwich Decorative and Fine Arts Soc 1987–, vice chm Int Ctee for Museums and Ethnography 1989–95; tstee: Photographers Gallery 1982–91, Haslemere Educnl Museum 1996–; govr Dolmetsch Fndn 1983–; FMA, FRAI, FRGS, FRSA; Ordenom Jugoslavenske Zastave sa zlatnom zvezdom na ogrlici (Yugoslavia) 1981; *Books* Pre-Columbian Pottery of the Americas (1980); *Recreations* travel; *Style*— David Boston, Esq, OBE; ✉ Quebec House, Westerham, Kent TN16 1TD (☎ 01959 562206)

BOSTON, Richard; s of Frank and Janet Boston; *b* 29 Dec 1938; *Educ* Stowe, Regent St Poly Sch of Art, King's Coll Cambridge (MA); *Career* writer; sometime memb editorial staff: Peace News, TLS, New Society; columnist and feature writer The Guardian; fndr ed: The Vole 1977–80, Quarto 1979–82; *Books* The Press We Deserve (ed, 1969), An Anatomy of Laughter (1974), The Admirable Urquhart (1975), Beer and Skittles (1976), Baldness Be My Friend (1977), The Little Green Book (1979), C O Jones's Compendium of Practical Jokes (1982), Osbert: a Portrait of Osbert Lancaster (1989), Boudu Saved from Drowning (1994); *Recreations* procrastination; *Style*— Richard Boston, Esq; ✉ The Old Sch, Aldworth, Reading, Berks (☎ 01635 578 587)

BOSTON, 10 Baron (GB 1761); Sir Timothy George Frank Boteler Irby; 11 Bt (E 1704); s of 9 Baron, MBE (d 1978), by his 2 w Erica; *b* 27 March 1939; *Educ* Clayesmore Sch Dorset, Univ of Southampton (BSc Econ); *m* 1967, Rhonda Anne, da of Ronald Albert Bate, of Balgowlah, NSW, Australia; 2 s (Hon George b 1971, Hon Jonathan b 1975), 1 da (Hon Rebecca b 1970); *Heir* s, Hon George William Eustace Boteler Irby b 1 Aug 1971; *Style*— The Rt Hon the Lord Boston; ✉ Cae'r Borth, Moelfre, Anglesey LL72 8NN

BOSTON OF FAVERSHAM, Baron (Life Peer UK 1976); Terence George; QC (1981); s of George Thomas Boston (d 1986), and Kate, *née* Bellati (d 1995); *b* 21 March 1930; *Educ* Woolwich Polytechnic Sch, King's Coll London; *m* 1962, Margaret Joyce, da of Rowley Henry Jack Head (d 1932), of Aust; *Career* sits as a cross-bench Peer in Lords; Flt Lt RAF 1950–52; called to the Bar Inner Temple 1960 (Gray's Inn 1973); news sub-ed BBC External Services 1957–60, sr prodr BBC (current affairs) 1960–64, chm TVS (later TVS Entertainment plc) 1980–90; MP (Lab) Faversham Kent 1964–70; PPS to: Min of Public Bldg and Works 1964–66, Min of Power 1966–68, Min of Tport 1968–69; asst govt whip 1969–70; min of state Home Office 1979; oppn front bench spokesman on: Home Office Affrs 1979–84, Defence 1984–86; princ dep chm of ctees House of Lords 1992–94, chm Select Ctee on the European Communities House of Lords 1992–94, chm of Ctees House of Lords 1994–; *Recreations* opera, fell walking; *Style*— The Rt Hon The Lord Boston of Faversham, QC; ✉ House of Lords, London SW1A 0PW

BOSVILLE MACDONALD OF SLEAT, Sir Ian Godfrey; 17 Bt (NS 1625), of Sleat, Isle of Skye; also 25 Chief of Sleat; s of Sir (Alexander) Somerled Angus Bosville Macdonald of Sleat, 16 Bt, MC (24 Chief of Sleat, d 1958), and Mary Elizabeth, *née* Gibbs; *b* 18 July 1947; *Educ* Pinewood Sch, Eton, RAC Cirencester; *m* 1970, Juliet Fleury, o da of late Maj-Gen John Ward-Harrison, OBE, MC; 1 s (Somerled Alexander b 1976), 2 da (Deborah Fleury b 1973, Isabel Mary b 1983); *Heir* s, Somerled Alexander Bosville Macdonald, yr of Sleat, b 30 Jan 1976; *Career* chartered surveyor; memb: Royal Soc of Health 1972, Economic Research Cncl 1979–; memb (for Bridlington S) Humberside CC 1981–85; pres: Humberside Branch Br Red Cross 1988–96, Hull and East Riding Branch Br Red Cross 1996–, Br Food and Farming Humberside 1989, Humberside Young Farmers; chm Rural Devpt Cmmn Humberside 1988–95, High Sheriff of Humberside 1988–89; FRICS 1986 (ARICS 1972), MRSH 1972; *Recreations* ornithology; *Clubs* White's, Puffin's; *Style*— Sir Ian Bosville Macdonald of Sleat, Bt; ✉ Thorpe Hall, Rudston, Driffield, E Yorkshire (☎ 01262 420239)

BOSWALL, *see:* Houstoun-Boswall

BOSWELL, Timothy Eric; MP (C) Daventry (majority 20,274); s of Eric New Boswell (d 1974), of Lower Aynho Grounds, Banbury, and Joan Winifred Caroline, *née* Jones; *b* 2 Dec 1942; *Educ* Marlborough, New Coll Oxford (MA, post grad dip); *m* 2 Aug 1969, Helen Delahay, da of the Rev Arthur Delahay Rees (d 1954), of Pennard Vicarage, Swansea; 3 da (Victoria b 1971, Emily b 1975, Caroline b 1978); *Career* head of Economic Section Cons Research Dept 1970–73 (agric and economics advsr 1966–73); managed family farm from father's death in 1974; MP (C) Daventry 1987–, memb Commons Select Ctee on Agriculture 1987–89, PPS to fin sec to the Treasy 1989–90, asst govt whip 1990–92, a Lord Cmmr of the Treasury (sr whip) 1992; Parly under sec of state: Dept for Education 1992–95, MAFF 1995–; chm: Daventry Constituency Cons Assoc 1979–83 (treas 1976–79), Northants Leics and Rutland Counties branch NFU 1983, Parly Charity Law Reform Panel 1988–90; memb: Cncl Perry Fndn for Agric Research 1966–90 (pres 1984–90), Agric and Food Research Cncl 1988–90; *Recreations* shooting, countryside, snooker, poetry; *Clubs* Farmers'; *Style*— Timothy Boswell, Esq, MP; ✉ House of Commons, London SW1A 0AA (☎ 0171 219 3000)

BOSWOOD, Anthony Richard; QC (1986); s of Noel Gordon Paul Boswood, of Radnage, Bucks, and Cicily Ann, *née* Watson; *b* 1 Oct 1947; *Educ* St Paul's, New Coll Oxford (BCL, MA); *m* 4 Jan 1973, Sarah Bridget, da of Sir John Lindsay Alexander; 3 da (Eleanor b 1976, Louise b 1978, Grace b 1983); *Career* called to the Bar Middle Temple 1970; *Recreations* opera, riding, tennis, gardening; *Style*— Anthony Boswood, Esq, QC; ✉ Fountain Court, Temple, London EC4Y 9DH (☎ 0171 583 3335, fax 0171

353 0329/1794, mobile 0580 771148, telex 8813408 FONLEG G); Podere Casanuova, Pieveasciata, Castelnuovo Berardenga (SI), Italy

BOSWORTH, Sir Neville Bruce Alfred; kt (1987), CBE (1982); s of late William Charles Neville Bosworth, of Birmingham, and late Nellie Ada Lawton, *née* Wheeler; *b* 18 April 1918; *Educ* King Edward's Sch Birmingham, Univ of Birmingham (LLB); *m* 22 Aug 1945, Charlotte Marian, da of late William Jacob Davis, of Birmingham; 1 s (Simon b 1946), 2 da (Jane b 1949, Josephine b 1950); *Career* admitted slr 1941; sr ptnr Bosworth Bailey Cox & Co until 1989, conslt Grove Tompkins Bosworth 1989–; a fndr and dir Nat Exhibition Centre 1969–96, dir several private cos; Birmingham City Cncl: memb (Cons) 1950–96, chm Gen Purposes Ctee 1966–69, Lord Mayor 1969–70, dep mayor 1970–71, ldr Cons Gp 1972–87, ldr of oppn 1972–76 and 1980–82, ldr 1976–80 and 1982–84, chm Fin Ctee 1976–80 and 1982–84, hon Alderman 1996–; West Midlands CC: memb (Cons) Edgbaston Ward 1973–86, chm Legal and Property Ctee 1977–79, vice chm Fin Ctee 1980–81; chm West Midlands Police Authy 1985–86 (memb 1985–95); former memb Univ of Birmingham Cncl, former govr King Edward's Sch (past tstee), former chm and tstee Hook Memorial Homes, vice chm Assoc of Municipal Authorities 1979–80, pres Edgbaston Supper Club 1974–; Hon Freeman City of Birmingham 1982; *Recreations* bridge, football; *Style*— Sir Neville Bosworth, CBE; ✉ Hollington, 8 Luttrell Rd, Four Oaks, Sutton Coldfield, Birmingham B74 2SR (☎ 0121 308 0647); 54 Newhall Street, Birmingham B3 3QG (☎ 0121 236 9341, fax 0121 236 5169)

BOSWORTH, Simon Charles Neville; s of Sir Neville Bruce Alfred Bosworth, CBE, and Lady Charlotte Marian Bosworth, *née* Davis; *b* 6 Aug 1946; *Educ* Stouts Hill Gloucester, Bradfield; *m* 2 Feb 1979, Evelyn Fay, da of William Leslie Wallace (d 1984); 1 da (Claudia b 1984); *Career* dir: W H Cutler (Midlands) Ltd 1968–70, Sutton (Wine Bars) Ltd 1972–74, Hill Alveston & Co Ltd 1973–, Luttrell Park Investments Ltd 1974–, Berkswell Properties Ltd 1983–, Berkswell Investments Ltd 1984–; *Recreations* football, gardening; *Style*— Simon C N Bosworth, Esq; ✉ Hill Alveston Group of Companies, Willowbrook House, Preston Road, Lowsonford, nr Henley-in-Arden, Solihull, West Midlands B95 5EZ (☎ 01926 842995)

BOTHAM, Brian William; s of William Botham (d 1979), of Staffs, and Ellen, *née* Burgess (d 1983); *b* 13 Feb 1932; *Educ* HS Newcastle-under-Lyme; *m* 14 Oct 1966, Christine, da of Wilfred Lord, of Bagnall Hall, Staffs; 1 s (Richard b 1968); *Career* slr; sr ptnr Clyde Chappell & Botham Slrs (Tunstall Meir and Biddulph Staffs); *Style*— Brian W Botham, Esq; ✉ The Retreat, Farley, nr Oakamoor, Staffs ST10 3BQ (☎ 01538 702230); Inverdart, Kingswear, S Devon (☎ 01803 752465); Clyde Chappell & Botham Solicitors, 99 Weston Rd, Meir, Stoke-on-Trent (☎ 01782 599577)

BOTHAM, Ian Terence; OBE (1992); s of Les Botham, and Marie Botham; *b* 24 Nov 1955; *Educ* Buckler's Mead Secdy Sch Yeovil; *m* 31 Jan 1976, Kathryn; 1 s (Liam James b 26 Aug 1977), 2 da (Sarah Lianne b 3 Feb 1979, Rebecca Kate b 13 Nov 1985); *Career* former professional cricketer; Somerset CCC: second XI 1971, first class debut 1974, awarded county cap 1976, capt 1984–85, benefit 1984; Worcestershire CCC 1987–91 (capped 1987), Queensland Aust off-season 1987–88, Durham CCC 1992–93 (capped 1992); England: 116 one day ints, 102 test matches 1977–92, capt 12 tests 1980–81, highest score 208 v India Oval 1982, best bowling 8 for 34 v Pakistan Lord's 1978; tours: Pakistan/NZ 1977–78, Aust 1978–79, Aust and India 1979–80, W Indies 1980–81, India 1981–82, Aust/NZ 1982–83, W Indies 1985–86, Aust 1986–87, NZ/Aust 1991–92; pt/t technical advsr England squad Zimbabwe and New Zealand 1996–97; test records incl: scored 1000 runs and took 100 wickets in fewest matches, first player to score a century and take 8 wickets in an innings (v Pakistan Lord's 1978), scored third fastest double century by Englishman (200 in 272 minutes v India Oval 1982); BBC TV Sporting Personality of the Year 1981; team capt Question of Sport (BBC 1) until 1996, currently cricket commentator Sky TV, various appearances in pantomime, raised over £3m for Leukaemia Research through long-distance walks; *Books* incl: Botham Down Under, High, Wide and Handsome, It Sort of Clicks (with Peter Roebuck), Cricket My Way (with Jack Bannister), The Incredible Tests (with late Peter Smith), Botham: My Autobiography (with Peter Hayter, 1994); *Recreations* golf, shooting, salmon and trout fishing, flying; *Style*— Ian Botham, Esq, OBE; ✉ c/o Vallance Lickfolds, 300 High Holborn, London WC1V 7JH (☎ 0171 404 0707)

BOTSFORD, Keith; s of Willard Hudson Botsford (d 1947), and Carolina Romani, *née* Rangoni-Machiavelli-Publicola-Santacroce (d 1995); *b* 29 March 1928; *Educ* Portsmouth Abbey Sch, Univ of Iowa (AB), Yale Univ (AM), Columbia Univ, Manhattan Sch of Music, Holborn Coll of Law, Strasbourg Univ; *m* 1, 1949 (m dis), Ann Winchester; 3 s (Aubrey b 1957, Giannandrea b 1960, Josue b 1962), 2 da (Clarissa b 1959, Flora b 1964); m 2 (m dis), Sally Elwina Weekes; 1 s (Matthew b 1968), 1 da (Polly b 1972); m 3, Nathalie Favre-Gilly, da of Paul Favre-Gilly; 1 s (Thomas b 1987), 1 da (Xenia b 1987 (decd)); *Career* writer, ed, prof and newspaper corr; 970 Counter Intelligence 1945–47; reporter France-Amerique 1945; instr in French: Yale Univ 1948–49, Univ of Iowa 1949–50; translator Human Relations Area Files 1949–51, asst prof Bard Coll 1953–56; asst prodr: CBS TV 1955–57, Stratford Shakespeare Festival 1958; assoc prof Univ of Puerto Rico 1958–61 (asst to Chllr 1958–61), Latin American corr New Leader 1962–65, dep sec Int PEN 1965–66, dir Nat Translation Centre and prof of English Univ of Texas 1966–71, chm Kolokol Press 1971–, writer in residence Deutsche Austauch Dienst Berlin 1973, corr The Sunday Times 1973–86; Boston Univ: prof of journalism and lectr in history 1978–81 and 1988–, asst to Pres 1978–81, dir public affrs publications 1989–; ed in chief Grand Prix International 1981–83, pres Int Racing Press Assoc 1981–84, corr and columnist The Independent 1987–, publisher and ed in chief Bostonia Magazine 1989–94, corr La Stampa 1992–; ed: Yale Poetry Review, Poetry New York, The Noble Savage, Delos, Anon, Kolokol; awarded Translation Medal City of Rimini, Ravenna Translation Medal, PEN Translation Prize; grantee: Ford Fndn 1961–65, Rockefeller Fndn, Moody Fndn; memb Soc of Editors, Magazine Publishers' Assoc; *Books* Novels: The Master Race (1955), The Eighth-best-dressed Man in the World (1957), Benvenuto (1961), The March-Man (1964), The Search for Anderson (as I I Magdalen, 1982), Ana P (as I I Magdalen, 1985), Cockpits (as Liam Frey, 1987); Non-Fiction: Dominguin (1972), Driving Ambition (1981), Keke (1985), Champions of Formula One (1988), Michelet, History of the French Revolution (trans, 1975–); *Recreations* law, musical composition; *Style*— Keith Botsford, Esq; ✉ 120 Cushing Ave, Dorchester, Mass 02125, USA; 17 Quai Louis Pasteur, Sète 34200, France (☎ 00 33 67 46 00 30); College of Communication, 640 Commonwealth Avenue, Boston, Mass 02215, USA (☎ 00 1 617 353 5804, fax 00 1 617 265 7186)

BOTT, Alan John; OBE (1996); s of Albert Henry John Bott, and Eileen Mary, *née* Spiers; *b* 30 March 1935; *Educ* King's Coll Sch Wimbledon, Merton Coll Oxford (MA, postmaster, memb SCR 1993–); *m* 10 Sept 1966, Caroline Gaenor, da of Frank Leslie Williams (d 1943); 2 s (Jonathan b 3 April 1968, Simon b 26 June 1970), 1 da (Alison b 24 March 1972); *Career* dir: The NZ Shipping Co 1971 (joined 1956), P & O Containers Ltd (formerly Overseas Containers Ltd) 1976–96; chm: The Aust and NZ Shipping Confs 1978–94, The Europe Southern Africa Shipping Conference 1990–96, NZ/UK C of C and Indust 1990–96; dir ECSA, dir and vice chm CENSA until 1996; extra mural univ lectr in architecture 1962–; churchwarden Godalming Parish Church 1979–, tstee Godalming Museum 1986– (chm 1994–); FSA 1965; FCIT 1990; *Books* Monuments in Merton College Chapel (1964), Sailing Ships of The NZSCO (1973), Baptisms and Marriages at Merton College Oxford (1981), Godalming Parish Church (1988), Rake Manor, Godalming (1990), Merton College, A Short History of the Buildings (1993); *Recreations* tennis, gardening, writing and lecturing on the history of European architecture; *Clubs* Travellers'; *Style*— Alan Bott, Esq, OBE; ✉ Rake Court, Milford, Godalming, Surrey GU8 5AD (☎ 01483 416546)

BOTT, Dennis Adrian Roxby; s of Frederick William Roxby Bott (d 1985), of Milford, Surrey, and Marie Therese, *née* Danger; *b* 29 April 1948; *Educ* Forest Sch Snaresbrook, Colchester Sch of Art, Norwich Sch of Art (Dip AD); *Career* artist; exhbns: Gallery 33 Billingshurst, The Ogle Galleries Eastbourne and Cheltenham, Bourne Gallery Reigate, Canon Gallery Chichester, Lannards Gallery Billingshurst; works incl: Fittleworth Station (Towner Gallery Eastbourne) 1976, Fittleworth Station (Hove Museum Purchase) 1977, Athina B on Brighton Beach (Brighton Museum purchase) 1979, Gatehouse at Ightham Moat (National Tst cmmn) 1987, HMY Britannia (Wardroom of HMY Britannia cmmn) 1990; prizewinner Discerning Eye Exhbn 1992; RWS 1983 (ARWS 1981), memb Art Workers' Guild 1989; *Recreations* walking, antiques; *Clubs* Arts; *Style*— Dennis Roxby Bott, Esq; ✉ School House, Bucks Green, Horsham, West Sussex RH12 3JP (☎ 01403 822189, fax 01403 823089)

BOTT, Ian Bernard; s of Edwin Bernard Bott (d 1979), and Agnes, *née* Hansell (d 1990); *b* 1 April 1932; *Educ* Nottingham HS, Southwell Minster GS, Stafford Tech Coll, Univ of Manchester (BSc); *m* 1955, Kathleen Mary, da of James Henry Broadbent; 1 s (Douglas James Bernard b 1961), 1 da (Mary Fiona b 1957); *Career* Nat Serv RAF 1953–55; Nottingham lace industry 1949–53, Research Laboratory English Electric (now part of GEC) 1955–57; MOD: research scientist Royal Radar Establishment Malvern (later head of Electronics Group) 1960–75, cnsllr Defence Research and Devpt Br Embassy Washington 1975–77, dep dir Underwater Weapon Systems Admty Underwater Weapon Establishment Dorset 1977–79, asst chief scientific advsr MOD HQ 1979–81, dir gen Guided Weapons and Electronics Army Controllerate 1981–82, princ dep dir Atomic Weapons Research Establishment Aldermaston 1982–84, dir Admty Research Establishment 1984–88; conslt engr 1988–; hon chm Portsmouth Area Hospice 1989–94; Freeman City of London 1985, Liveryman Worshipful Co of Engrs 1985; FInstP 1967, FIEE 1972, FEng 1985 (memb Cncl 1987–90); *Publications* Advances in Microwaves (vol 3, jtly), author of various articles in learned jls; *Recreations* horology, music, golf, computing, bricklaying; *Clubs* RAC; *Style*— Ian Bott, Esq, FEng

BOTT, Prof Martin Harold Phillips; s of Harold Bott (d 1958), and Dorothy, *née* Phillips (d 1970); *b* 12 July 1926; *Educ* Clayesmore Sch Dorset, Magdalene Coll Cambridge (MA, PhD); *m* 17 April 1961, Joyce Cynthia, da of Flying Offr John William Hughes (d 1969), of Lewes, Sussex; 2 s (Andrew Martin b 28 Aug 1962, Nicholas John b 6 Jan 1964), 1 da (Jacqueline Joyce Dorothy b 16 Jan 1966); *Career* Nat Serv Lt RCS 1945–48; Univ of Durham: Turner and Newall res fell Dept of Geology 1954–56, lectr in geophysics 1956–63, reader 1963–66, prof 1966–88, pt/t res prof 1988–91, emeritus prof 1991; memb Cncl Royal Soc 1982–84, Anglican reader St Nicholas Church Durham; Wollaston medallist Geological Soc of London 1992; FRS 1977, FRAS, FGS; *Books* The Interior of the Earth (1982), ed of other pubns; *Recreations* mountain walking; *Style*— Prof Martin Bott, FRS; ✉ 11 St Mary's Close, Shincliffe, Durham DH1 2ND (☎ 0191 386 4021); Department of Geological Sciences, University of Durham, South Road, Durham DH1 3LE (☎ 0191 374 2511)

BOTTENHEIM, Michael Charles; s of Jack Charles Bottenheim (d 1972), and Caryl Rosemary Squires, *née* Baring-Gould (d 1978); *b* 1 Nov 1947; *Educ* Leiden Univ (Netherlands Doctorate in Law), Michigan State Univ (MBA); *m* 1981, Yvonne Maria Josephina, da of Edwin Eugen Meile; 2 c; *Career* Pierson Heldring & Pierson Amsterdam NL 1972–76; asst mangr: Citicorp International Bank Ltd London 1976–79, Citicorp International Finance SA Zurich 1979–80; exec dir: Citicorp International Bank Ltd 1980–85, Lazard Bros & Co Ltd London 1985– (md); *Style*— Michael C Bottenheim; ✉ Lazard Bros & Co Ltd, 21 Moorfields, London EC2P 2HT (☎ 0171 588 2721)

BOTTING, (Elizabeth) Louise; CBE (1993); da of Robert Young (d 1956), and Edith, *née* Roberts (d 1981); sis of John R C Young, *qv*; *b* 19 Sept 1939; *Educ* Sutton Coldfield HS, LSE (BSc Econ); *m* 1, 1964 (m dis 1986), Douglas Botting; 2 da (Catherine b 1966, Anna b 1967); m 2, 23 May 1989, Leslie Carpenter, *qv*; *Career* broadcaster and financial journalist; investmt analyst Kleinwort Benson 1961–65, columnist Daily Mail 1970–75, Br Forces Broadcasting 1971–83; Douglas Deakin Young fin consultancy: joined 1975, md 1982–88, chm 1988–; presenter Money Box (BBC Radio 4) 1977–92; non-exec dir: Trinity International Holdings 1991–, London Weekend Television (Holdings) plc 1992–94, General Accident 1992–; memb Senior Salaries Review Body 1987–94; *Style*— Louise Botting, CBE; ✉ Douglas Deakin Young Ltd, 22–25a Sackville Street, London W1X 2DH (☎ 0171 439 3344)

BOTTOMLEY, Alan Ingham; TD; s of George R Bottomley (d 1980), and Olive, *née* Ingham (d 1989); *b* 14 Nov 1931; *Educ* Shrewsbury; *m* 25 March 1961, Jane Susan, da of Robert Werner (d 1973), of Harrogate; 1 s (Simon b 1962), 1 da (Anabel b 1964); *Career* slr; Maj RA (TA), ret 1965; sr ptnr Hammond Suddards Leeds, London, Manchester, Bradford and Brussels; *Recreations* sailing, opera, theatre, travel; *Clubs* Army and Navy, Bradford (pres 1993–94); *Style*— Alan I Bottomley, Esq, TD; ✉ Dormy Lodge, Kent Rd, Harrogate, N Yorks HG1 2LJ; 68 Walton St, London SW3; Hammond Suddards, 2 Park Lane, Leeds W Yorks LS3 1ES; Moor House, 119 London Wall, London EC2Y 5ET

BOTTOMLEY, Baroness; Dame Bessie (Ellen) Bottomley; *née* Wiles; DBE (1970); da of Edward Charles Wiles, of Walthamstow, and Ellen, *née* Estall; *b* 28 Nov 1906; *Educ* Maynard Rd Girls' Sch, N Walthamstow Central Sch; *m* 1936, Rt Hon Arthur George Bottomley, OBE, MP (cr a Life Peer as Baron Bottomley, of Middlesbrough in the Co of Cleveland 1984) (d 1995); *Career* on staff of NUT 1925–36; memb Walthamstow Borough Cncl 1945–48, Essex CC 1962–65; chm Lab Party Women's Section: E Walthamstow 1946–71, Chingford 1973–; memb: Forest Group Hosp Mgmnt Ctee 1949–73, W Roding Community Health Cncl 1973–76; chm Walthamstow Nat Savings Ctee 1949–65, vice pres Waltham Forest Nat Savings Ctee 1965, chm 1975; Mayoress of Walthamstow 1945–46; memb WVS Regional Staff (SE England) 1941–45, past memb Home Office Advsy Ctee on Child Care; chm of govrs: of two secdy mod schs 1948–68, gp of primary and infant schs, of high schools; memb Whitefield Tst; JP 1955–76, Juvenile Bench 1955–71, dep chm Waltham Forest Bench; *Recreations* theatre, gardening; *Style*— The Rt Hon the Lady Bottomley, DBE; ✉ 19 Lichfield Rd, Woodford Green, Essex IG8 9SU

BOTTOMLEY, Eur Ing Brian Rogers; s of Harry Bottomley (d 1958), of Sale, Cheshire, and Ivy, *née* Wragg (d 1974); *b* 14 Dec 1927; *Educ* Sale Central Sch; *m* 1950, Kathleen, da of Thomas Neville, of Altrincham; 1 s (Nigel Rogers); *Career* chartered engr; tech dir Churchill Machine Tool Co Ltd 1968–73; md: TI Matrix Ltd 1973–81, Staveley Machine Tools 1981–84; chm md and owner of Kearns-Richards Ltd and KRS Ltd 1984–89, chm Munslow Precision Engineering Ltd, dir Pen Associates 1991–93; mgmnt conslt; CEng, FIMechE, FIEE; *Recreations* sailing, shooting (Br short range pistol champion 1969); *Style*— Eur Ing Brian Bottomley; ✉ 28 Shavington Way, Kingsmead, Northwich, Cheshire

BOTTOMLEY, Sir James Reginald Alfred; KCMG (1973, CMG 1965); s of Sir (William) Cecil Bottomley, KCMG, CB, OBE (d 1954), and Alice Thistle, *née* Robinson, JP; *b* 12 Jan 1920; *Educ* King's Coll Sch Wimbledon, Trinity Coll Cambridge; *m* 1941, Barbara Evelyn (d 1994), da of Henry Vardon, of Market Drayton; 2 s (incl Peter Bottomley, MP, *qv*) and 1 s decd, 2 da; *Career* Inns of Court Regt NW Europe 1940–46; HM Dip Serv: CRO 1946, SA 1948–50, Pakistan 1953–55, USA 1955–59, UN NY 1959, dep high cmmr Malaysia 1963–67, dep under sec of state FCO 1970, ambass SA 1973–76, perm UK rep to UN at Geneva 1976–78; dir Johnson Matthey plc 1979–85; *Recreations* golf; *Style*— Sir James Bottomley, KCMG; ✉ 22 Beaufort Place, Thompson's Lane, Cambridge CB5 8AG

BOTTOMLEY, Dr Malcolm Brooke; s of John Reginald Bottomley (d 1988), of Sheffield, and Mary, *née* Evans; *b* 4 June 1933; *Educ* King Edward VII GS Sheffield, Univ of Sheffield (MB ChB); *m* 1, 1959 (m dis 1990), Paula Dorothy; 3 da (Caroline Mary b 1960, Sally Ann b 1962, Louisa Kate b 1965); m 2, 1991, Hilary Joyce; *Career* hon med offr: FA of Wales 1981–84, British Athletic Fedn (formerly British Amateur Athletic Board) 1984–; Bath Rugby Club 1989–91; med offr to GB team: IAAF World Marathon Cup Seoul 1987, World Athletics Championships Rome 1987, Track and Field Squad Seoul Olympics 1988; GP Yorkshire and Shropshire 1960–83, med offr Univ of Bath 1984–93, med dir Univ of Bath distance learning course in sports med for doctors 1992–, med dir European Youth Olympic Days 1994–95; *Books* Sports Injury Clinic (contrib, 1987), Medicine Sport and the Law (contrib, 1990), Soft Tissues - Trauma and Sports Injuries (contrib, 1992), Men's Health (contrib, 1993); *Recreations* outdoor activities; *Style*— Dr Malcolm Bottomley; ✉ Brunswick Cottage, 42 Combe Rd, Combe Down, Bath BA2 5HY (☎ 01225 833757); Centre for Continuing Education, University of Bath, Claverton Down, Bath BA2 7AY (☎ 01225 826453)

BOTTOMLEY, Peter James; MP (C) Eltham (majority 1,666); s of Sir James Bottomley, *qv*; *b* 30 July 1944; *Educ* Westminster, Trinity Coll Cambridge (MA); *m* 1967, Virginia Bottomley, MP, *qv*, da of John Garnett, CBE, *qv*; 1 s, 2 da; *Career* MP (C): Greenwich, Woolwich W June 1975–83 (also contested both 1974 gen elections), Eltham 1983–; PPS to: Min of State FCO 1982–83, Sec of State for Social Servs 1983–84, Sec of State for NI 1990; Parly under sec of state: Dept of Employment 1984–86, Dept of Transport (min for roads) 1986–89, NI Office (min for agriculture and for environment) 1989–90; chm: Br Union of Family Orgns 1973–80, Family Forum 1980–82, C of E Children's Soc 1983–84; tstee Christian Aid 1978–84; memb Ct of Assts Worshipful Co of Drapers; *Recreations* children; *Style*— Peter Bottomley, Esq, MP; ✉ House of Commons, London SW1 (☎ 0171 219 3000)

BOTTOMLEY, Stephen John; s of Frederick John Bottomley, of Barbican, London, and Jean Mary, *née* Moore; *b* 23 Oct 1954; *Educ* Sutton Valence Sch, Univ of East Anglia (BA); *m* 8 June 1984, Gail Barbara, da of Grenville Herbert Ryder (d 1989), of Crosby, Liverpool; 1 s (Charles b 1991), 2 da (Clare b 1987, Emma b 1989); *Career* admitted slr 1980; ptnr Bartletts De Reya 1984–88, dir Johnson Fry Corporate Finance Ltd 1988, ptnr Rowe & Maw 1988–; Freeman Worshipful Co of Slrs; memb Law Soc; *Recreations* squash, hockey, golf; *Style*— Stephen Bottomley, Esq; ✉ 10 Stradella Road, London SE24 9HA (☎ 0171 274 1258); Rowe & Maw, 20 Black Friars Lane, London EC4V 6HD (☎ 0171 248 4282, fax 0171 248 2009, telex 262787 MAWLAWG)

BOTTOMLEY, Rt Hon Virginia Hilda Brunette Maxwell; PC (1992), MP (C) Surrey South-West (majority 14,975); da of John Garnett, CBE, *qv*; *b* 12 March 1948; *Educ* Putney HS, Univ of Essex (BA), LSE (MSc); *m* 1967, Peter James Bottomley, MP, *qv*; 1 s, 2 da; *Career* res for Child Poverty Action Gp and further educn lectr 1971–73, psychiatric social worker Brixton and Camberwell Child Guidance Units 1973–84, chm Lambeth Juvenile Ct 1981–84; Parly candidate (C) IOW 1983, MP (C) Surrey South West 1984–; sec Cons Backbench Employment Ctee 1985; PPS to: Min of State for Educn and Sci 1985–86, Min for Overseas Devpt 1986–87, Sec of State for Foreign and Cwlth Affrs 1987–88; Parly under sec of state DOE 1988–89, min of state Dept of Health 1989–92, sec of state for Health 1992–95, sec of state for Nat Heritage 1995–; vice chm Nat Cncl of Carers and their Elderly Dependants 1982–88, memb Ct of Govrs LSE 1985–, JP Inner London 1975–84, dir Mid Southern Water Co 1987–88, memb MRC 1987–88, fell Industry and Parliament Tst 1987, govr Ditchley Fndn 1991–, govt chm Women's Nat Cmmn 1991–92; Freeman City of London 1989; *Recreations* family; *Style*— The Rt Hon Virginia Bottomley, MP; ✉ House of Commons, London SW1A 0AA

BOTTONE, Bonaventura; s of Bonaventura Bottone, of Harrow, and Kathleen, *née* Barnes; *b* 19 Sept 1950; *Educ* Lascelles Secdy Modern Sch Harrow, Royal Acad of Music London; *m* 28 April 1973, Jennifer, da of Ralph Dakin (d 1973); 2 s (Benjamin Nicholas b 13 Jan 1978, Jonathan Samuel b 16 March 1984), 2 da (Francesca Louise, Rebecca Charlotte (twins) b 23 Nov 1979); *Career* tenor; appeared at numerous international venues incl: Royal Opera House Covent Garden, London Coliseum, Glyndebourne Festival, Nice Opera, Batignano Festival Opera, Houston Opera, Met Opera NY, Munich Bavarian State Opera; frequent BBC broadcaster; ARAM; *Roles* with ENO incl: David in Die Meistersinger, The Duke of Mantua in Rigoletto, Alfred in La Traviata, Beppe in I Pagliacci, Nanki-Poo in The Mikado, Sam Kaplan in Street Scene, Truffaldino in The Love for Three Oranges, Lenski in Eugene Onegin 1994; with Royal Opera Co incl: the Italian Tenor in Der Rosenkavalier (Covent Garden debut), Alfredo in Die Fledermaus, the Italian Tenor in Capriccio, Raoul de Nanzis in Les Hugenots, Comte Liebenskof in Viaggio am Rhiems; with Scottish Opera incl: Governor General in Candide, Loge in Das Rheingold, Narraboth in Salome; others incl: Italian Tenor in Capriccio (Glyndebourne Festival Opera) 1990, Alfredo in La Traviata (Opera North) 1990, title role in Le Comte Ory (WNO) 1992, Pedrillo in Die Entführung aus dem Serail (Houston Opera, US debut), Fernando in La Favorita (WNO) 1993, Dream of Gerontius (Royal Festival Hall) 1994, the Italian Tenor in Capriccio (Chicago Lyric Opera debut) 1994, Governor General in Candide (Lisbon debut) 1994, BBC Proms 1996, Turiddu in Cavelleria Rusticana (WNO) 1996; *Recordings* incl: Cassio in Otello (EMI), Arturo in Lucia di Lammermoor (EMI), Nanki-Poo in The Mikado (with ENO (highlights), also with D'Oyly Carte), The Student Prince, Orpheus In The Underworld (with ENO), Sondheim's A Little Night Music, Weill's Street Scene, Tippett's The Ice Break, Vaughan Williams' Hugh the Drover (Hyperion); *Recreations* gardening, cycling, boating; *Style*— Bonaventura Bottone, Esq; ✉ c/o Stafford Law Associates, 6 Barham Close, Weybridge, Surrey KT13 9PR (☎ 01932 854489, fax 01932 858521)

BOUCH, Dr (Dennis) Clive; s of Tom Bouch (d 1967), of Aspatria, Cumbria, and Elizabeth Anderson, *née* Errington; *b* 12 Sept 1939; *Educ* Nelson Thomlinson GS, Wigton Cumbria, Univ of Edinburgh (BSc, MB ChB); *m* 12 Sept 1968, (Valerie Alexander) Sandra, da of Alexander Lamb (d 1983), of Edinburgh; 2 s (David Christopher b 1972, Jeremy Clive b 1973), 2 da (Caroline Anne b 1975, Katharine Mary b 1978); *Career* lectr in pathology Univ of Edinburgh 1966–75, conslt pathologist to Leics Health Authy 1976–, head of dist pathology serv 1985–94, Home Office pathologist 1984–, dir of forensic pathology Univ of Leicester 1990–; chm: Dist Hosps Med Staff Ctee Leics Health Authy 1984–88, Dist Med Advsy Ctee Leics Health Authy 1990–94; conslt memb Policy Advsy Gp Leics Health Authy 1990–94; FRCPath 1985; *Style*— Dr Clive Bouch; ✉ Dept of Pathology, The Leicester Royal Infirmary, Leicester LE1 5WW (☎ 0116 254 7198)

BOUCHER, Prof Robert Francis (Bob); s of Robert Boucher (d 1987), of London, and Johanna, *née* Fox (d 1982); *b* 25 April 1940; *Educ* St Ignatius Coll Stamford Hill, Borough Poly London, Univ of Nottingham (PhD); *m* 16 Aug 1965, Rosemary Ellen, *née* Maskell; 3 s (Jeremy Robert Philip b 4 Sept 1968, Jonathan Francis b 26 Jan 1971 (decd), Timothy James b 19 June 1972), 1 da (Justine Louise Julia b 20 Nov 1974); *Career* ICI post-doctoral fell Univ of Nottingham 1966, lectr Queen's Univ Belfast 1968–70 (res fell 1966–68); Univ of Sheffield: lectr 1970–76, sr lectr 1976–85, prof 1985–95, pro-vice-chllr 1992–95; princ and vice-chllr UMIST 1995–; dir: Higher Educn Quality Cncl 1995–, Univs and Colls Staff Devpt Agency 1995–; chm: Engrg Professors' Cncl 1993–95, DTI Action for Engrg Task Force 1994–96, HEQC Quality Enhancement Gp 1995–, HEQC Graduate Standards Programme 1995–; memb Senate Engrg Cncl; author of various articles for engrg jls, confs and papers; MASME 1983, MIEEE 1986, FRSA 1987, FIMechE 1992, FEng 1994; *Recreations* hill walking, music, exercise; *Clubs* Athenaeum; *Style*— Prof Bob Boucher, FEng; ✉ UMIST, PO Box 88, Manchester M60 1QD (☎ 0161 200 4010, fax 0161 236 7219)

BOUCHERAT, Dr Rosemary; da of Joseph Hayes Fairweather (d 1959), of Clitheroe, and Mary Helen Fergusson, *née* Lawson, (d 1960); *b* 29 July 1936; *Educ* Clitheroe GS, Queenswood Sch Hatfield, St Mary's Hosp Univ of London (MB BS, DRCOG, DA, DCH, DPM); *m* 30 April 1966, Robert Jean-Marie Boucherat, s of Lucien Boucherat; 2 s (Ben b 28 May 1967, Mark b 11 Sept 1969); *Career* Civilian Med Offr RCAF 1965–66; sr registrar child psychiatry Sheffield Central Health Authy, conslt child psychiatrist Doncaster Royal Infirmary 1977–; memb: Amnesty Int, MIND, Greenpeace, People of Sheffield; MRCPsych 1975, Assoc Family Therapists 1980; *Recreations* walking, travelling; *Style*— Dr Rosemary Boucherat; ✉ 69 Church St, Bawtry, Doncaster, S Yorks DN10 6HR (☎ 01302 710951); Doncaster Royal Infirmary, Armthorpe Rd, Doncaster DN2 (☎ 01302 366666)

BOUCHIER, Prof Ian Arthur Dennis; CBE (1990); s of Edward Alfred Bouchier, of Cape Town, SA, and May, *née* Simons; *b* 7 Sept 1932; *Educ* Rondebosch Boys' HS, Cape Town Univ, Univ of London, Boston Univ Med Sch USA (MB ChB, MD); *m* 5 Sept 1959, Patricia Norma, da of Thomas Henshilwood (d 1985), of Cape Town, SA; 2 s (Anthony James b 1962, David Ian b 1964); *Career* med registrar Groote Schuur Hosp 1958–61; various res posts 1961–65: Royal Free Hosp London, Boston Univ Med Sch; reader in med Univ of London 1970–73 (sr lectr 1965–70); prof of medicine: Univ of Dundee 1973–86 (dean Faculty of Med and Dentistry 1982–86), Univ of Edinburgh 1986–; chief scientist in Scotland 1992–; memb: MRC 1982–86, Cncl RCPE 1984–90, Tenovus-Scotland Advsy Ctee; Br Soc of Gastroenterology: memb Cncl 1987–90, chm Educn Ctee 1987–90, pres 1994–95; chm Health Serv Res Ctee, vice chm Scot AIDS Res Appeal, pres World Orgn of Gastroenterology 1990– (sec gen 1982–90); hon memb S African, Italian and Japanese Socs of Gastroenterology; FRCP 1970, FRCPE 1973, FRSE 1985, FIBiol 1988, FRSA 1991, Hon FCP (SAF) 1992, FFPHM 1993; *Books* Gastroenterology (1973, 1977, 1982), Recent Advances in Gastroenterology (1976, 1980, 1983), Clinical Investigation of Gastrointestinal Function (1969, 1981, 1988), Gastroenterology: Clinical Science and Practice (1984, 1993); *Recreations* gardening, history of whaling, music; *Clubs* New (Edinburgh), Edinburgh Angus; *Style*— Prof Ian Bouchier, CBE, FRSE; ✉ Department of Medicine, Royal Infirmary, Edinburgh EH3 9YW (☎ 0131 536 2234, fax 0131 229 2948, telex 727 442 UNIVED G)

BOUCHIER HAYES, Dr Thomas Anthony Ivan; s of Thomas Adrian Bouchier Hayes (d 1962), of Dublin, and Mona, *née* Graham; *b* 10 June 1937; *Educ* Clongowes Wood Coll, RCSI (DObstRCOG); *m* 16 Sept 1964, Winifred Heather, da of Alfred Coulthard (d 1978); 1 s (Tommy Adrian b 5 Oct 1966), 1 da (Alexandra Siobhan b 29 Aug 1968); *Career* joined RAMC 1965; MO: Singapore 1965–70, BAOR 1970–73, Bridge of Guards 1975–80; tutor to Army Gen Practice 1975–80, SMO RMA Sandhurst 1980–83, Colchester 1983–85, Gp Practice Queen Elizabeth Mil Hosp B Woolwich 1985–87, prof of Army gen practice RAMC Millbank 1987–94, ret with rank of Col; currently MO Royal Military Sch of Music Medical Centre 1995–; FRCGP 1980, fell London Soc of Med 1988, FRSM 1988, LAM; *Books* MRCGP tutor (1980), Beecham Manual of General Practice (1981), MRCGP Study Book (1892), MCQ Tutor (1982), Guide to PLAB (1983), Emergencies in General Practice (1983); *Recreations* tennis, bridge, watching sports; *Clubs* London Irish Rugby Football, Southfields Lawn Tennis; *Style*— Dr Thomas Bouchier Hayes; ✉ 57 Brixton Water Lane, Brixton, London SW2 1PH (☎ 0171 274 9140); Medical Centre, Royal Military School of Music, Kneller Hall, Twickenham, London TW2 7DU (☎ 0181 898 5533 ext 8653)

BOUGH, Francis Joseph (Frank); s of Austin Joseph Bough (d 1963), of Oswestry, Shropshire, and Annie Tyrer, *née* Moulton; *b* 15 Jan 1933; *Educ* Oswestry Boys' HS, Merton Coll Oxford (BA, soccer blue); *m* 25 July 1959, Nesta, *née* Howells; 3 s (David b 1961, Stephen b 1963, Andrew b 1965); *Career* Nat Serv Cmmn 2 RTR 1955–57; ICI Billingham 1957–62; BBC presenter (joined 1962): Sportsview 1964–69, Grandstand 1969–82, 6 Olympic Games 1964–82, 6 World Cups, Nationwide 1972–83, Breakfast TV 1983–87, Holiday prog 1986–88; The Frank Bough Interview (Sky TV) 1989–90, presenter Six O'Clock Live (LWT) 1989–, presenter Moneywise (TVS), anchorman Rugby World Cup (ITV) 1991; Richard Dimbleby BAFTA award 1976, 3 awards for presenting sport, news and current affrs TV and Radio Industs Club; *Books* Cue Frank (autobiography, 1980), The Frank Bough Breakfast Book (1984); *Recreations* cricket, golf, hockey, drama, singing; *Style*— Frank Bough, Esq; ✉ c/o Jon Roseman Associates Ltd, 46 Sutton Court Road, London W4 4NL (☎ 0181 742 0552)

BOUGHEY, James Richard; s of Sir Richard James Boughey, 10 Bt, JP, DL (d 1978), and his 1 w, Davina Julia, *née* Wright (now Baroness Loch); h to Btcy of bro, Sir John Boughey, 11 Bt; *b* 29 Aug 1960; *Educ* Eton, Royal Agricultural Coll Cirencester; *m* 1989, Katharine Mary, o da of Capt (Geoffrey Thomas) Warren Fenwick-Clennell; 2 s (George Richard Douglas b 27 March 1992, William James b 28 June 1995), 1 da (Victoria Rose b 12 Nov 1990); *Career* agriculture; *Recreations* cricket, hunting, shooting, fishing; *Clubs* Cavalry & Guards', MCC; *Style*— James Boughey, Esq; ✉ The Manor House, Piddletrenthide, Dorchester, Dorset DT2 7QX

BOUGHEY, Dr Sir John George Fletcher; 11 Bt (GB 1798), of Newcastle-under-Lyme, Staffordshire; s of Sir Richard James Boughey, 10 Bt, JP, DL (d 1978); *b* 12 Aug 1959; *Educ* Eton, Univ of Zimbabwe; *Heir* bro, James Richard Boughey, *qv*; *Career* medical; MRCPI 1994; *Clubs* Boodle's; *Style*— Dr Sir John Boughey, Bt; ✉ Bratton House, Westbury, Wilts BA13 4RN

BOUGHTON, Stephen David; s of Gerald Leslie Grantham Boughton, and Marjorie Hilda, *née* Johns (d 1986); *b* 29 Sept 1955; *Educ* George Abbot Boys' Sch Guildford, Trinity Hall Cambridge (MA); *m* 30 June 1989, Tracey Howcroft; 1 s (Samuel James Alexander b 1990), 1 da (Alice Marjorie Rose b 1991); *Career* slr; assoc Sullivan & Cromwell NY 1982–83, ptnr Linklaters & Paines 1986– (slr 1980–82 and 1983–86); memb: Law Soc, City of London Slrs' Co, Hong Kong Law Soc; *Recreations* sport, travel, theatre, cinema; *Clubs* Hong Kong; *Style*— S D Boughton, Esq; ✉ Linklaters & Paines, Barrington House, 59/67 Gresham Street, London EC2V 7JA (☎ 0171 606 7080, fax 0171 606 5113)

BOUKAMEL, Bassam; s of Rafic Yusuf Boukamel (d 1989), and Vasima, *née* Kazou; *b* 2 June 1948; *Educ* International Coll Beirut, American Univ of Beirut (BA), Fordham Univ NY (MA); *Career* economist and investment advsr 1975–86, dir Raab Boukamel Galleries Limited 1986– (promoter of contemporary artists and publisher of art books); *Recreations* racquet sports and reading; *Style*— Bassam Boukamel, Esq; ✉ Raab Boukamel Galleries Limited, 9 Cork Street, London W1X 1PD (☎ 0171 734 6444, fax 0171 287 1740)

BOULAY, *see:* Houssemayne du Boulay

BOULDING, Philip Vincent; QC (1996); s of Vincent Fergusson Boulding, of Cambridge, and Sylvia Boulding; *b* 1 Feb 1954; *Educ* Downing Coll Cambridge (scholar, MA, LLM, rugby blue, pres CU Amateur Boxing Club); *m* Helen Elizabeth, da of Joseph William Richardson; 1 s (Joseph William b 1993), 1 da (Harriet Helen b 1995); *Career* called to the Bar Gray's Inn 1979 (Holker Entrance Award 1978, Sr Holker Award 1979), in practice SE Circuit; memb Ctee Official Referees' Bar Assoc; memb London Common Law and Commercial Bar Assoc; played rugby for England (at under 23 level) 1977;

Recreations sport generally; *Clubs* Hawks' (Cambridge); *Style*— Philip Boulding, Esq, QC; ✉ Keating Chambers, 10 Essex Street, Outer Temple, London WC2R 3AA (☎ 0171 240 6981)

BOULIS, Dr Zoser; s of Fouad Boulis (d 1976), and Irene Grais, *née* Wassif; *b* 1 Jan 1944; *Educ* Camboni Coll Khartoum Sudan, Univ of Khartoum (MB BS, ECFMG, DMRD), LRCP, MRCS; *m* 20 July 1974, Afaf Hanna, da of Ayoub Girgis (d 1989); 1 s (Michael Menes b 9 April 1975), 1 da (Sandra Anne b 23 April 1976); *Career* sr house offr Royal Marsden Hosp 1973, registrar in gen surgery Barking Hosp Essex 1973–76, sr registrar in diagnostic radiology Royal Free Hosp 1976–83, conslt radiologist Bromley Health Tst 1983–; contrib to Journal of Radiology; memb: BMA, Hosp Med Advsy Ctee; FRCS 1973, FRCSEd 1974, FRCSGlas 1975, FRCR 1982; *Style*— Dr Zoser Boulis; ✉ Consultant Radiologist, Farnborough Hospital (Ultrasound Department), Farnborough Common, Orpington, Kent BR6 8ND (☎ 01689 814140)

BOULOS, Paul Bernard; s of Bernard Boulos (d 1964), of Khartoum, and Evelyn, *née* Haggar; *b* 10 March 1944; *Educ* Comboni Coll Khartoum Sudan, Univ of Khartoum (MB BS); *m* 1 March 1979, Marilyn Lesley, da of Ronald Robert Went (d 1994), of Highgate, London; 1 s (Mark Ronald b 22 Aug 1980), 2 da (Sarah-Jane b 15 Sept 1981, Paula Louise b 28 Dec 1984); *Career* surgical registrar UCH 1970–73; lectr in surgery Faculty of Med Univ of Khartoum 1973–76, res fell Dept of Surgical Studies Middx Hosp 1976–77, sr surgical registrar UCH 1977–80 and St Mark's Hosp 1980–81; UCL: sr lectr in surgery 1981–92, reader in surgery 1992–; conslt surgn: UCH 1981–, The Middlesex Hosp 1993–; memb: RSM (memb Cncl Coloproctology Section), Assoc of Surgns of GB and I, Br Soc of Gastroenterology, Assoc of Coloproctology of GB and I, Surgical Res Soc, BMA; RCSEng surgical tutor; RCSEd examiner; NE Thames college rep, college tutor Hong Kong, Univ of London examiner; MS, FRCS, FRCSEd; *Style*— Paul Boulos, Esq; ✉ St Anne, 15 Richmond Road, New Barnet, Herts EN5 1SA (☎ 0181 449 6552); Department of Surgery, University College London Medical School, 67–73 Riding House Street, London W1P 7LD (☎ 0171 380 9317, fax 0171 636 5176)

BOULTER, Prof Donald; CBE (1991); s of George Boulter (d 1953), and Vera Annabelle, *née* Medland; *b* 25 Aug 1926; *Educ* Portsmouth GS, ChCh Oxford (MA, DPhil); *m* 1 Sept 1956, (Margaret) Eileen, da of William Kennedy (d 1952); 4 da (Susan (Mrs Stafford), Sara (Mrs Wilson), Catherine, Vanessa (Mrs Zhang)); *Career* RAF VR UT pilot, vocational advice offr RAF 1945–48; asst lectr King's Coll London 1955–57, sr lectr Univ of Liverpool 1957–66 (formerly lectr); Univ of Durham: prof of botany and head Dept of Botany 1966–88 (prof emeritus 1988), head Dept of Biological Sciences 1988–91, dir Botanic Garden 1966–91; visiting prof Univ of Texas Austin 1967; AFRC: memb 1985–89, memb Plants and Environmental Res Ctee 1985–91, sr scientific conslt 1991–; memb: Biological Scis Sub-Ctee UFC 1988–89, Exec Cmmn Horticulture Res Inst 1990–96; govr: Scot Crop Res Inst 1986–92, Inst of Plant Sci Res Cambridge 1989–92; chm Plant Science Research Ltd 1992–94, tstee John Innes Fndn 1994–97; FIBiol 1970, FRSA 1972; *Books* Chemotaxonomy of the Leguminosae (ed, 1971), Qualitas Plantarum: Plant Foods for Human Nutrition (assoc ed, 1980–93), Encyclopedia of Plant Physiology, Vol 14B (ed, 1982); various papers in scientific jls on molecular evolution, genetic engrg of crops and molecular biology of seed devpt; *Recreations* travel, reading; *Style*— Prof Donald Boulter, CBE; ✉ 5 Crossgate, Durham City DH1 4PS (☎ 0191 386 1199); c/o Department of Biological Sciences, University of Durham, South Rd, Durham DH1 3LE (☎ 0191 374 2420, fax 0191 374 2417, telex 537351 DURLIB G)

BOULTER, Prof Patrick Stewart; s of Frederick Charles Boulter, MC (d 1961), of Annan, Scotland, and Flora Victoria, *née* Black (d 1965); *b* 28 May 1927; *Educ* King's Coll Sch, Carlisle GS, Guy's Hosp Med Sch (MB BS, Gold medal); *m* 7 March 1946, (Patricia) Mary Eckersley, da of Samuel Gordon Barlow (d 1966), of Lowton, Lancs; 2 da (Jennifer (Mrs Bond), Anne (Mrs Wood)); *Career* registrar Dept of Surgical Studies Middx Hosp 1957–59, sr surgical registrar Guy's Hosp 1959–62, conslt surgn Guildford Hosps and Regnl Cancer Unit 1962–91, emeritus conslt oncological and gen surgn Royal Surrey Co Hosp and Regnl Radiotherapy Centre; visiting prof Univ of Surrey 1986– (hon reader 1968–80); RCS (England): surgical tutor 1964, regnl advsr 1975, Penrose-May teacher 1985–; RCS (Edinburgh): examiner 1979, memb Cncl 1984–, vice pres 1989–91, pres 1991–94, regent 1995; hon citizen State of Nebraska 1967; Hon DUniv Surrey 1996; memb Br Breast Gp and hon memb Surgical Res Soc; hon memb: Assoc of Surgns India 1993, Soc of Surgns of Nepal 1994; hon fell Royal Aust Coll of Surgns 1984, Hon FCS South Africa 1992, Hon FCS Sri Lanka 1992, Hon FRCSI 1993, Hon FCSHK 1993; memb Acad of Med of Malaysia 1993; fell Assoc of Surgns of GB and I (former chm Educnl Ctee), FRCS, FRCS (Edinburgh), FRCP (Edinburgh), FRCPS (Glasgow) 1993, FCPS (Pakistan) 1994, fell Acad of Med Singapore 1994, Int Master Surgn (Int Coll of Surgns) 1994; *Publications* articles and chapters on surgical subjects incl breast disease, surgical oncology and endocrine surgery; *Recreations* mountaineering, skiing, fishing, gardening; *Clubs* Alpine, Caledonian, Swiss Alpine, New (Edinburgh); *Style*— Prof Patrick Boulter; ✉ Quarry Cottage, Salkeld Dykes, Penrith, Cumbria CA11 9LL (☎ and fax 01768 898822); 8 Waterden Road, Guildford, Surrey; Royal College of Surgeons, Nicolson Street, Edinburgh EH8

BOULTING, Roy A C; s of Walter Arthur Boulting (d 1957), and Rose Bennett (d 1980); *b* 21 Nov 1913; *Educ* HMS Worcester, Reading Sch; *m* 1, 1936 (m dis 1941), Angela, da of Rt Hon Edmond Warnock, KC, Home Sec NI (d 1971); m 2, 1942 (m dis 1951), Mrs Jean Capon, da of Eric Gamage; 2 s (Jonathan Eric Shaw b 1944, Laurence Roy Oliver b 1945); m 3, 1951 (m dis 1964), Mrs Enid Munnik, da of Pieter Groenwald, of S Africa (she m 1970, 9 Earl of Hardwicke); 3 s (Fitzroy Linde b 1951, Rupert Alan Francis David b 1952, Edmund Charles Alexander (twin) b 1952); common-law-wife (until 1967), Victoria, da of James Vaughan; 1 s (Fitzroy William Humphrey Rufus b 1965); m 4, 1971 (m dis 1978), Hayley Mills, *qv*, the actress, da of Sir John Mills, CBE, *qv*; 1 s (Crispian b 1973); m 5, 1978 (m dis 1984), Sandra, da of Gilbert Spencer Payne; *Career* film producer and director; fndr ind film prodn co with late twin bro John 1937; served RAC WWII, Capt; dir: British Lion Films Ltd 1958–72, Shepperton Studios Ltd 1964–70; prodr and jt md Charter Film Productions Ltd 1973–; prodr: Brighton Rock 1947, Seven Days to Noon 1950, Lucky Jim 1957, I'm All Right Jack, Heavens Above! 1962; dir: Thunder Rock 1942, Desert Victory (American Acad Award) 1942, Fame is the Spur 1946, The Guinea Pig 1948, Carlton-Browne of the FO 1958–59, Twisted Nerve 1968; memb: Exec Ctee Assoc of Cine Technicians 1946–47, Cncl Dirs' and Prodrs' Rights Soc 1987, Cncl Local Radio Assoc 1965, Advsy Cncl Directors' Guild of GB 1990; hon doctorate RCA 1990, Directors' Guild of GB Award for Outstanding Contribution to Cinema 1995; *Recreations* film making; *Clubs* Lord's Taverners; *Style*— Roy Boulting, Esq

BOULTING, Sydney Arthur Rembrandt; *see:* Cotes, Peter

BOULTON, Prof Andrew James Michael; s of Prof James Thompson Boulton, and Margaret Helen, *née* Leary; *b* 21 Feb 1953; *Educ* Nottingham HS, Univ of Newcastle upon Tyne (MB BS, MD); *m* 3 July 1976, Helen Frances, da of Dr Mark Charlton Robson, of Maple House, The Green, Hurworth on Tees, County Durham; 1 s (Jonathan David b 1 July 1978), 2 da (Caroline Helen b 14 Sept 1979, Sarah Elizabeth b 24 July 1985); *Career* sr med registrar Royal Hallamshire Hosp 1981–86 (diabetes res fell 1979–81), visiting asst prof of med Univ of Miami Florida 1983–84, conslt and prof in med Manchester Royal Infirmary 1995– (conslt and sr lectr 1986–91, reader and conslt 1991–95); R D Lawrence lectr Br Diabetic Assoc 1990, Sri Prakash Endowment Lecture Madras 1990; ed Diabetic Medicine 1991–95 (formerly dep ed); chm Postgrad Educn Euro Diabetic Assoc 1995–; author numerous papers on diabetic complications; memb Med and Sci Section Ctee and Patient Servs Ctee of Br Diabetic Assoc; FRCP 1992 (MRCP 1979); *Books* The Foot In Diabetes (jtly, 1987, 2 edn 1994), Diabetes In Practice (jtly, 1989); *Recreations* campanology, classical music; *Style*— Prof Andrew Boulton; ✉ Department of Medicine, Manchester Royal Infirmary, Oxford Rd, Manchester M13 9WL (☎ 0161 276 4452, fax 0161 274 4740)

BOULTON, Sir Clifford John; GCB (1994, KCB 1990, CB 1985); s of Stanley Boulton, and Evelyn, *née* Hey, of Cocknage, Staffs; *b* 25 July 1930; *Educ* Newcastle-under-Lyme HS, St John's Coll Oxford (MA); *m* 1955, Anne, da of Rev E E Raven, of Cambridge; 1 adopted s (Richard Boulton, *qv*), 1 adopted da; *Career* Nat Service RAC 1949–50, Lt Staffs Yeomanry TA; clerk in House of Commons 1953–94: clerk of Select Ctees on Procedure 1964–68 and 1976–77, Public Accounts 1968–70, Parly Questions 1971–72, Privileges 1972–77, clerk Overseas Office 1977–79, princ clerk Table Office 1979–83, clerk asst 1983–87, clerk of the House of Commons 1987–94; tstee Industry and Parliament Tst 1991–95; memb Nolan Ctee on Standards in Public Life 1994–; sch govr then bd memb Church Schs Co 1965–79; Hon LLD Univ of Keele 1993; *Publications* Erskine May's Parliamentary Practice (ed 21 edn), Halsbury's Laws of England (contrib, 4 edn), contrib various Parly jls; *Style*— Sir Clifford Boulton, GCB; ✉ The Elms, Lyddington, Oakham, Rutland, Leics LE15 9LT (☎ 01572 823487)

BOULTON, Prof Geoffrey Stewart; s of George Stewart Boulton, of Forsbrook, Staffs, and Rose Boulton (d 1990); *b* 28 Nov 1940; *Educ* Longton HS, Univ of Birmingham (BSc, PhD, DSc); *m* Denise Bryers, da of Joseph Lawns; 2 da (Katherine Elisabeth b 7 March 1973, Olivia Frances b 28 April 1976); *Career* Br Geological Survey 1962–64, Univ of Keele 1964–65, Univ of Birmingham 1965–67, Water Dept Nairobi Kenya 1968, lectr then reader Sch of Environmental Science UEA 1968–86, prof Univ of Amsterdam 1980–86; Univ of Edinburgh: regius prof of geology and mineralogy 1986–, provost and dean Faculty of Science 1994–; chm: NERC Polar Science Bd until 1994, NERC Earth Science and Technol Bd, Royal Soc Section Ctee for Earth Science and Astronomy; memb: Natural Environment Res Cncl, Nature Conservancy Cncl for Scotland Science Bd until 1992, Royal Cmmn on Environmental Pollution; contrib to numerous books and papers in Glaciology, Polar Science, Global Environmental Change; awarded Kirk Bryan Medal of The Geological Soc of America; FRS 1991, FRSE 1989, FGS; *Recreations* climbing, violin, sailing; *Style*— Prof Geoffrey Boulton; ✉ 19 Lygon Road, Edinburgh EH16 5QD (☎ 0131 667 2531); Department of Geology & Geophysics, Grant Institute, Kings Buildings, University of Edinburgh, Edinburgh EH9 3JW (☎ 0131 650 4844, fax 0131 668 3184)

BOULTON, Prof James Thompson; s of Harry Boulton, MM (d 1951), of Pickering, Yorks, and Annie Mary Penty, *née* Thompson (d 1974); bro of Rev Canon Peter Boulton, *qv*; *b* 17 Feb 1924; *Educ* Univ Coll Durham (BA), Lincoln Coll Oxford (BLitt), Univ of Nottingham (PhD); *m* 6 Aug 1949, Margaret Helen, da of Arthur Haydn Leary (d 1966), of Stockton-on-Tees; 1 s (Prof Andrew Boulton b 1953), 1 da (Prof Helen Wilcox b 1955); *Career* RAF Flt Lt pilot 1943–46; Univ of Nottingham: lectr, sr lectr, reader in English 1951–64, prof 1964–75, dean Faculty of Arts 1970–73; John Cranford Adams prof of English Hofstra Univ NY 1967; Univ of Birmingham: prof of English studies and head of dept 1975–88, dean Faculty of Arts 1981–84, public orator 1984–88, emeritus prof 1988, dir Inst for Advanced Res in the Humanities 1988–; Hon DLitt: Univ of Durham 1991, Univ of Nottingham 1993; FRSL, FBA; *Books* Burke's Sublime and Beautiful (ed 1958, 1987), The Language of Politics In The Age of Wilkes and Burke (1963, 1975), Letters of D H Lawrence, Vols 1–7 (ed 1979–93), Selected Letters of D H Laurence (1997); *Recreations* gardening; *Style*— Prof James Boulton, FBA, FRSL; ✉ Institute for Advanced Research in the Humanities, University of Birmingham, Edgbaston, Birmingham B15 2TT (☎ 0121 414 5850)

BOULTON, Rev Canon Peter Henry; s of Harry Boulton (d 1951), of Pickering, N Yorks, and Annie Mary Penty, *née* Thompson (d 1974); bro of Prof James Boulton, FBA, FRSL, *qv*; *b* 12 Dec 1925; *Educ* Lady Lumley's GS Pickering, St Chad's Coll Durham (BA), Ely Theol Coll Cambridge, Cardiff Law Sch (LLM in Canon Law); *m* 1955, Barbara Ethelinda, da of Arthur Davies, of Cheshire; 3 s (Timothy Peter b 1956, Michael John b 1958, Christopher David b 1962); *Career* served RN 1942–46 (1939–45 Star, Atlantic Star with France and Germany Bar, Defence Medal and Victory Medal); ordained (Chester Dio): deacon 1950, priest 1951; asst curate: St Michael Coppenhall Crewe 1950–54, St Mark Mansfield Notts 1954–55; vicar: All Saints Clipstone Notts 1955–60, St John Baptist Carlton Nottingham 1960–67, Priory Church of Our Lady and St Cuthbert Worksop Notts 1967–87; hon canon of Southwell Minster 1975–87, canon residentiary of Southwell Minster 1987–92 (canon emeritus 1992–), granted permission to preach in Chester Dio 1992–, chaplain to HM The Queen 1991–95; dir of educn Dio of Southwell 1987–92; proctor for the clergy of Southwell Dio in York Convocation, Church Assembly and Gen Synod 1959–92; C of E del to Anglican Consultative Cncl 1972–80, del to WCC Assembly Nairobi 1975; memb: Lord Howick Cmmn 1962–64, Gen Synod Standing Ctee 1974–90, Churches Cncl for Covenanting 1978–82, Crown Appts Cmmn 1982–92, Legal Advsy Cmmn 1986–91, Notts Co Educn Ctee 1987–92, Gen Synod Bd of Educn 1991–92; memb Ecclesiastical Law Soc and Gen Ctee 1992–; author of articles in church and learned jls; *Recreations* crosswords, swimming, gardening, bridge, reading; *Style*— The Rev Canon Peter Boulton; ✉ 3 Grasmere Drive, Holmes Chapel, Cheshire CW4 7JT

BOULTON, Richard Edward Stanley; s of Sir Clifford Boulton, GCB, *qv*, and Anne, *née* Raven; *b* 3 May 1959; *Educ* Marlborough Coll (Wedgwood scholar), Oriel Coll Oxford (half blue); *m* 23 July 1994, Fiona Jane, da of Michael H Lockton; *Career* Arthur Andersen: trainee CA 1981–84, mangr 1985–90, ptnr i/c of Litigation Servs Gp 1990–, head of Econ and Fin Consulting Gp 1994–, head of Business Consulting Div 1995–; advsr to Office of Rail Regulator 1994, conslt to Scott Inquiry 1995; FAE 1994, FCA 1996 (ACA 1984); *Recreations* golf, tennis, travel, wine; *Clubs* MCC; *Style*— Richard Boulton, Esq; ✉ Waterton, Cleardown, Woking, Surrey GU22 7HH (☎ 01483 760258); Arthur Andersen, 1 Surrey Street, London WC2R 2PS (☎ 0171 438 3638, fax 0171 438 5582)

BOURDEAUX, Rev Canon Michael Alan; s of Richard Edward Bourdeaux, and Lillian Myra, née Blair; *b* 19 March 1934; *Educ* Truro Sch, St Edmund Hall Oxford (MA, BD), Moscow State Univ, DD Lambeth 1996; *m* 1, 1960, Gillian Mary Davies (d 1978); 1 s (Mark), 1 da (Karen); m 2, 1979, Lorna Elizabeth, da of John Waterton, of Sudbury, Suffolk; 1 s (Adrian), 1 da (Lara Clare); *Career* ordained: deacon 1960, priest 1961; res assoc Centre de Recherches Geneva Switzerland 1965–68, res fellow Univ of London 1968–70, visiting prof St Bernard's Seminary Rochester NY 1969, res fellow Royal Inst of Int Affairs 1970–72, Kathryn C Davis prof of Slavic studies Wellesley Mass 1981, Templeton prize 1984, visiting fell St Edmund Hall Oxford 1989–90, sr assoc memb St Antony's Coll Oxford 1989–; Hon Canon Rochester Cathedral 1990; memb Philharmonia Chorus 1961–91, fndr and dir Keston Coll (now Keston Inst) 1969–, memb Br Tennis Umpires Assoc 1974–, bd of Cornish Gorsedd 1985–; *Books* Opium of the People (1965, 2 edn 1977), Religious Ferment in Russia (1968), Patriarch and Prophets (1970, 2 edn 1975), Faith on Trial in Russia (1971), Land of Crosses (1979), Risen Indeed (1983), Ten Growing Soviet Churches (1987), Gorbachev, Glasnost and the Gospel (1990), The Gospel's Triumph Over Communism (1991), The Politics of Religion in Russia and of the New Eurasia (ed, 1995); *Clubs* Athenaeum; *Style*— The Rev Canon Dr Michael

Bourdeaux; ✉ 101 Church Way, Iffley, Oxford OX4 4EG (☎ 01865 777276, fax 01865 311280)

BOURDILLON, Mervyn Leigh; JP (1970); s of Prebendary Gerard Leigh Bourdillon (d 1971), and Cara Phyllis Evan-Thomas (d 1971); *b* 9 Aug 1924; *Educ* Haileybury; *m* 1961, Penelope Anne, da of Peter Wellesbourne Kemp-Welch, OBE (d 1964); 1 s (Patrick), 3 da (Tatiana, Sarah (Mrs Nicholas Allan), Lucinda (Mrs Simon Miesegaes)); *Career* served RNVR 1943–46; memb Breconshire CC 1962–73, forestry cmmr 1973–76; High Sheriff Breconshire 1970, Lord-Lt Powys 1986– (Vice Lord-Lt 1978–86, DL 1962–78); KStJ 1994; *Clubs* Army and Navy; *Style—* Mervyn Bourdillon, Esq, JP; ✉ Llwyn Madoc, Llanwrtyd Wells, Powys LD5 4TU

BOURDILLON, Dr Peter John; QHP (1996); s of John Francis Bourdillon, of Bradford-on-Avon (d 1992), and Pamela Maud, *née* Chetham (d 1992); *b* 10 July 1941; *Educ* Rugby, Middlesex Hospital Med Sch (MB, BS); *m* 1964, Catriona Charmian Cecil, da of Brig Walter Glencairn-Campbell OBE; 2 da (Charmian Xenia (Mrs Andrew H Findlay) b 4 Feb 1968, Helena Maude b 30 April 1974), 1 s (Paul Charles Chetham b 14 April 1972); *Career* house physician and surgeon posts in London 1965–68, med registrar Middlesex Hosp 1969–70; Hammersmith Hosp: med registrar 1970–72, sr registrar in cardiology 1972–74, pt/t conslt in clinical physiology (cardiology) 1975–; Dept of Health (formerly DHSS): pt/t med offr 1975–81, pt/t sr med offr 1981–91, head of Medical Manpower and Educn Div NHS Mgmnt Exec 1991–93, head Health Care Medical Div 1993–95, head Specialist Clinical Services Div 1995–; hon sr lectr Univ of London 1979–; numerous articles in med jls; memb: BMA 1965, RSM 1970, British Cardiac Soc 1972; FRCP 1983 (MRCP 1968); *Recreations* writing software, golf, skiing; *Clubs* Highgate Golf; *Style—* Dr Peter Bourdillon, QHP; ✉ 13 Grove Terrace London NW5 1PH (☎ 0171 485 6839); Hammersmith Hospital, Du Cane Road, London W12 0HS (☎ 0181 383 3951); Department of Health, Wellington House, 133 Waterloo Road, London SE1 8UG (☎ 0171 972 4339, fax 0171 972 4681)

BOURDIN, Michel Armand; s of Maurice Bourdin (d 1981), and Simone, *née* Leroux (d 1982); *b* 6 June 1942; *m* 1965, Mireille Monique, *née* Letournelle; 2 s (Olivier b 8 June 1966, Charles b 9 May 1967); *Career* chef; apprentice (Ecole Hoteliere Jean Drouant Paris) 1958–61: successively commis de cuisine Potel Etoile Paris, commis de cuisine Grand Hotel Dinard Brittany, chef in the service of the Prime Minister (Mil Serv), commis de cuisine rising to chef de partie Restaurant Ledoyen Champs Elysees Paris; Restaurant Maxim's de Paris: chef de partie 1964–69, sous chef de cuisine 1969–73; chef de cuisine: Pavillon Royal Paris 1973–75, The Connaught Hotel London 1975– (5th chef de cuisine since hotel estab 1887); recipient first Caterer & Hotelkeeper Catey Award (chef category) 1984; Academie Culinaire de France: memb 1968, fndr pres UK branch 1980, currently chllr UK branch; Maitre Cuisinier de France 1975; Chev du Merite Agricole (France), Chev dans l'Ordre du Merite National (France); *Style—* Michel Bourdin, Esq; ✉ The Connaught Hotel, Carlos Place, Mayfair, London W1A 6AL (☎ 0171 499 7070, fax 0171 495 3262)

BOURKE, Dr Brian Eamonn; s of Edmund Egan Bourke (d 1961), of Lines End, Winchelsea, Sussex, and Joan Eileen, *née* Kiernan; *b* 29 April 1948; *Educ* Beaumont Coll, King's Coll and King's Coll Hosp Univ of London (MB BS); *m* 25 March 1972, Elisabeth Janie, da of Brig Christopher Percy Sibthorpe Bright, CBE (d 1988), of Henley-on-Thames, Oxfordshire; 2 s (Henry Edmund b 12 April 1976, Piers Christopher b 18 Aug 1978), 2 da (Serena Katherine b 15 March 1974, Imogen Elisabeth b 6 July 1984); *Career* house surgn KCH London 1972, house physician Royal Berks Hosp Reading 1972, sr house offr in med The London Hosp 1972–74, med registrar St Stephen's Hosp London 1974–76, registrar and sr registrar Charing Cross Hosp London 1976–81, conslt physician and hon sr lectr St George's Hosp and Med Sch London 1981–; hon sec Br Soc for Rheumatology, memb BR Soc for Immunology; FRSM, MRCP 1974, FRCP 1989; *Recreations* tennis, swimming, skiing; *Clubs* Hurlingham, Queens; *Style—* Dr Brian Bourke; ✉ 152 Harley St, London W1N 1HH (☎ 0171 935 2477); St George's Hospital, London SW17 0QT (☎ 0181 672 1255)

BOURKE, Martin; s of Robert Martin Bourke, of Stockport, Cheshire, and Enid Millicent, *née* Love; *b* 12 March 1947; *Educ* Stockport GS, UCL (BA), KCL (MA); *m* 23 Aug 1973, Anne Marie Marguerite, da of Armand Gaston Ghislain Hottelet; 4 s (Robert b 25 April 1974, Simon b 20 Oct 1977, Adam b 12 Dec 1979, Neil b 13 Jan 1983); *Career* HM Dip Serv: joined FCO 1970, third sec Brussels 1971–74, second sec Singapore 1974–76, FCO 1976–78, first sec Lagos 1978–80, on loan to DTI 1980–84, HM consul (commercial) Johannesburg 1984–88, FCO 1988–93, govr Turks and Caicos Islands 1993–96, on secondment as business advsr to the Prince's Youth Business Trust 1996–; *Recreations* tennis, walking, amateur dramatics, reading; *Clubs* Royal Over-Seas League; *Style—* Martin Bourke, Esq

BOURN, Sir John Bryant; KCB (1991, CB 1986); s of Henry Thomas Bryant Bourn, of London, and Beatrice Grace, *née* Pope (d 1979); *b* 21 Feb 1934; *Educ* Southgate County GS, London Sch of Economics (BSc, PhD); *m* 21 March 1959, Ardita Ann, da of Maurice Wilfred Fleming (d 1940); 1 s (Jonathan b 1967), 1 da (Sherida b 1962); *Career* Air Miny 1956–63, HM Treasy 1963–64, private sec to Permanent Under Sec MOD 1964–69, asst sec and dir of programmes Civil Serv Coll 1969–72, asst sec MOD 1972–74, under sec N Ireland Office 1974–77, asst under sec of state MOD 1977–82, dep sec N Ireland Office 1982–84, dep under sec of state (Defence Procurement) MOD 1985–88, comptroller and auditor gen 1988–; visiting prof London Sch of Economics 1983–; *Recreations* swimming; *Style—* Sir John Bourn, KCB; ✉ National Audit Office, 159–197 Buckingham Palace Road, Victoria, London SW1W 9SP

BOURN, Prof (Alan) Michael; s of Ernest James Bourn (d 1988), and Frances Mary, *née* Fones (d 1977); *b* 10 June 1934; *Educ* Southgate County GS London, LSE (BSc); *m* 4 April 1960 (m dis 1986), (Karoline) Sigrid, *née* Hegmann; 2 s (Alexander b 1961, Jeremy b 1962); *Career* Nat Serv 2 Lt RAPC 1958–60; professional accounting 1954–58, IBM UK Ltd 1960–61; various academic appts 1962–69: London, Liverpool, Manchester; prof of industl admin Univ of Canterbury NZ 1969–72, prof of business studies Univ of Liverpool 1972–80, chm Liverpool University Press 1976–80; Univ of Southampton: prof of accounting 1980–, dean Faculty of Social Sciences 1983–86, dep vice chllr 1986–90; pres Assoc of Univ Teachers of Accounting 1982–83, chm Conf of Profs of Accounting 1987–90, memb Bd Nuffield Theatre Tst 1991–94, chm Multicosm Ltd 1995–; FCA 1968 (ACA 1958); *Books* Shipping Enterprise and Management 1830–1939 (with F E Hyde and J R Harris, 1967), Studies In Accounting for Management Decision (1969), Favell's Book-keeping & Accounts (7 edn, 1980), Industrial Development In Merseyside (with P Stoney, 1984), Management Accounting in Healthcare (with C M S Sutcliffe, 1996); *Recreations* trumpet-playing, jazz, racquet sports; *Style—* Prof Michael Bourn; ✉ University of Southampton, Southampton SO17 1BJ (☎ 01703 592545, fax 01703 593844); Multicosm Ltd, 2 Venture Road, Chilworth Research Centre, Southampton SO16 7NP (☎ 01703 742401, fax 01703 767665, e-mail M.Bourn@Multicosm.com)

BOURNE, Edward Owen (Teddy); s of Dr Jack Bourne, MBE (d 1993), and Mary, *née* Myers; *b* 30 Sept 1948; *Educ* Brentwood Sch Essex, King's Coll London (LLB); *m* 1976, Marcy Leavitt; 1 step s (Owen Thomas); *Career* articled clerk Linklaters & Paines 1970–72, ptnr Commercial Property Dept Clifford Chance (formerly Clifford-Turner) 1981– (joined 1972); chm Investment Property Forum Working Party on Streamlining Commercial Property Transactions 1995–96; tstee Hampstead Wells & Campden Tst, memb Tst Cncl Hampstead Garden Suburb Tst; memb Br Olympic Fencing Team 1968, 1972 and 1976, Br Épée champion 1966, 1972, 1974 and 1976–78; *Publications* Handbook of Conveyancing Searches (1984, 2 edn 1986); *Recreations* Kendo, tennis, films, Punch & Judy; *Clubs* Menorca Cricket; *Style—* Mr Teddy Bourne; ✉ Clifford Chance, 200 Aldersgate Street, London EC1A 4JJ (☎ 0171 600 1000, fax 0171 600 5555, e-mail teddybourne@cliffordchance.com)

BOURNE, Henry; s of Prof Kenneth Bourne (d 1992), and Eleanor Anne, *née* Wells; *b* 10 May 1963; *Educ* City of London Sch, Crown Woods Sch; *Career* photographer; photographic asst to Michael Joseph 1982–84, freelance photographic asst 1984–86, freelance editorial photographer of portraits, fashion, interiors, still life and reportage; cmmns incl contribs to: Elle, Elle Decoration, Esquire, GQ, The Guardian, The Independent, The Independent Magazine, Vogue, The World of Interiors; *Style—* Henry Bourne, Esq; ✉ 1 Lily Place, Saffron Hill, London EC1N 8JY (☎ 0171 242 1494, fax 0171 242 1495)

BOURNE, (Margaret) Janet; OBE (1982); da of Thomas William Southcott (d 1947), and Nora Annie, *née* Pelling (d 1977); *b* 18 Aug 1931; *Educ* Twickenham GS, Royal Holloway Coll London (BSc); *m* 29 Nov 1960, (George) Brian Bourne, s of George Stanley Bourne (d 1978); *Career* Fairey Engineering 1954–62; MOD: Army Operational Res Estab 1962–65, DOAE 1965–76, asst dir Scientific Advsy Gp (Army) 1976–80, head Weapon Dept Admty Surface Weapons Estab 1982–84 (head Assessment Div 1980–82), dep dir (above water) Admty Res Estab 1984–87, asst chief scientific advsr (capabilities) 1987–91; chm CORDA 1992–; MRAeS 1962; *Recreations* early music, gardening; *Style—* Mrs Janet Bourne, OBE; (☎ and fax 01428 714329)

BOURNE, Prof (Frederick) John; CBE; s of Sydney John Bourne (d 1960), of Evesham, Worcs, and Florence Beatrice, *née* Craven (d 1988); *b* 3 Jan 1937; *Educ* Prince Henry's GS Evesham, RVC (BVetMed, MRCVS), Univ of Bristol (PhD); *m* 12 Sept 1959, Mary Angela, da of William Reginald Minter (d 1990); 2 s (Stephen b 1962, Nigel b 1964); *Career* asst in gen vet practice Cornwall 1961–62, jr ptnr in 2-man vet practice Glos 1962–66; Univ of Bristol: lectr in animal husbandry 1966–74, reader in animal husbandry 1974–80, prof and head Dept of Vet Med 1980–88, BBSRC prof of animal health 1988–; visiting prof Univ of Reading 1988–; dir BBSRC Inst for Animal Health 1988–, memb Technol Interaction Bd BBSRC, memb Agric and Veterinary Ctee Br Cncl, foreign memb Polish Acad of Scis; CBiol, FIBiol; *Books* Advances in Veterinary Immunology (1984 and 1985); chapters in over 20 books; *Recreations* golf, fishing; *Style—* Prof John Bourne, CBE; ✉ Institute for Animal Health, Compton, Newbury, Berks RG16 0NN (☎ 01635 578411, fax 01635 578844)

BOURNE, Prof John Russell; *b* 27 Nov 1932; *Educ* Univ of Birmingham (PhD, DSc); *Career* tech offr Fibres Div ICI Ltd 1959–62, lectr then sr lectr Univ of Nottingham 1962–68, prof Eidgenössische Technische Hochschule (ETH) 1968–95, ret; Moulton Medal Inst of Chemical Engrs 1984; FIChemE, FEng 1994; *Style—* Prof John Bourne, FEng

BOURNE, Matthew Christopher; s of Harold Jeffrey (Jim) Bourne, of London, and June Lillian, *née* Handley; *b* 13 Jan 1960; *Educ* Sir George Monoux Sch London, The Laban Centre (BA); *Career* dancer Transitions Dance Co 1986, fndr, artistic dir, resident choreographer and performer Adventures In Motion Pictures (AMP) 1987; *Choreography* incl: Overlap Lovers 1987, Buck and Wing 1988, Spitfire 1988, The Infernal Galop 1989 (revived 1992), Green Fingers 1990, Town and Country 1991, Deadly Serious 1992, Nutcracker (co-prodn with Opera North 1992, revived 1993), The Percys of Fitzrovia 1992, Highland Fling 1994, Swan Lake 1995 (TV 1996); performed with choreographers incl: Jacob Marley, Brigitte Farges, Ashley Page; fndr memb Lea Anderson's Featherstonehaughs 1988; choreography for theatre incl: As You Like It (RSC, Stratford and Barbican) 1989, Singer (RSC, Stratford and Barbican) 1989, Leonce and Lena (Crucible Sheffield) 1989, Children of Eden (Prince Edward Theatre) 1991, A Midsummer Night's Dream (Aix-en-Provence Opera Festival) 1991, The Tempest (Nat Youth Theatre 1991, revived 1993), Show Boat (Malmö Stadsteater Sweden) 1991, Peer Gynt (Ninagawa Co Oslo, Barbican and World Tour) 1994, Watch with Mother (Nat Youth Dance Co) 1994, Oliver! (Palladium) 1994, Boutique (Images of Dance) 1995, Watch Your Step (Irving Berlin Gala) 1995; *Television* incl: Late Flowering Lust (BBC/Ecosse Films) 1993, Drip: A Self-Love Story (BBC) 1993, Roald Dahl's Little Red Riding Hood (BBC) 1995; *Awards* incl: Place Portfolio Award 1989, Bonnie Bird Choreography Award 1989, Barclays New Stages Award 1990, nominated for Most Outstanding Achievement in Dance Olivier Award 1992, nominated for Best New Dance Prodn (The Nutcracker) Olivier Awards 1994; *Recreations* theatre, cinema, the choreography of Frederick Ashton and Fred Astaire, the music of Percy Grainger, Ella Fitzgerald and most pre-1950 singers; *Style—* Matthew Bourne, Esq; ✉ Adventures In Motion Pictures, AMP House, 396 St John Street, London EC1V 4NJ (☎ 0171 833 5803, fax 0171 713 6040); agent: John Wood, London Management, Noel House 2/4 Noel Street, London W1V 3RB (☎ 0171 287 9000, fax 0171 287 3036)

BOURNE, (Rowland) Richard; s of late Arthur Brittan Bourne and Edith Mary (Mollie) Bourne (d 1991); *b* 27 July 1940; *Educ* Uppingham, BNC Oxford; *m* 1966, Juliet Mary, da of John Attenborough, CBE; 2 s, 1 da; *Career* Cwlth admin, journalist and author; educn corr The Guardian 1968–72, asst ed New Society 1972–77, dep ed and columnist London Evening Standard 1977–78, ed Learn Magazine 1979, freelance writer and conslt 1980–83, dep dir Cwlth Inst 1983–89; dir: Cwlth Human Rights Initiative 1990–93, Cwlth Non-Governmental Office for SA 1995–, Cwlth Values in Educn London Univ Inst of Educn; *Recreations* gardening, fishing, the theatre; *Clubs* RAC; *Style—* Richard Bourne, Esq; ✉ 36 Burney St, London SE10 8EX (☎ 0181 853 0642)

BOURNE, Valerie (Val); OBE (1991); *Educ* Elmhurst Ballet Sch, Royal Ballet Sch (also with Cleo Nordi, Anna Northcote and Andrew Hardie); *Career* performed with: Royal Ballet and Opera Ballet in final year at Royal Ballet Sch 1960–61, Sadlers Wells Opera Ballet 1961–63; Wilfred Stiff Assocs PR (clients incl: Ballet Rambert, Owen Brannigan, Daniel Barenboim, John Ogden, Cyril and Phyllis Sellick); press and publicity offr: London Festival Ballet 1967, Ballet Rambert 1968–76; asst to offr i/c dance Music Dept Arts Cncl of GB 1976–77, dance offr Gtr London Arts 1977–80, artistic dir Dance Umbrella 1980– (organised first Dance Umbrella Festival 1978); *Awards* Digital Dance Premier Award 1989, Int Theatre Inst's Award 1990, Chevalier dans l'Ordre des Arts et des Lettres 1996; *Style—* Ms Val Bourne, OBE; ✉ Dance Umbrella, 20 Chancellor's Street, London W6 9RN (☎ 0181 741 4040, fax 0181 941 7902)

BOURNE, Vanessa Jane; da of Rev Gordon Taylor, and Audrey, *née* Rowse (d 1981); *b* 23 May 1949; *m* 1974, Merfyn Russell Howard Bourne, s of late Dr Geoffrey H Bourne; 1 s (Gordon b 1977), 2 da (Georgina (twin) b 1977, Diana b 1981); *Career* proprietor The Welsh House 1986–90; memb E Dyfed HA 1986–90; chm: Dyfed Family Health Servs Authy 1990–95, Dyfed HA 1995–96, Dyfed Powys HA 1996–; vice-chm The Patients' Assoc, memb HA Cncl NAHAT; chm Welsh Assoc of Health Authorities and Tsts 1992–94; memb Exec Ctee CONCAH (continuing care at home); *Clubs* Lansdowne; *Style—* Mrs Vanessa Bourne; ✉ Dyffryn, Caio, Carmarthenshire SA19 8RA (☎ and fax 01558 650419); Dyfed Powys Health Authority, PO Box 13, Carmarthen SA31 3YH (☎ 01267 234501, fax 01267 228520, mobile 0374 224856)

BOURNE, Sir (John) Wilfrid; KCB (1979, CB 1975), QC (1981); s of Capt the Rt Hon Robert Croft Bourne, MP (d 1938), and Lady Hester Margaret Bourne, *née* Cairns (d 1985); *b* 27 Jan 1922; *Educ* Eton, New Coll Oxford; *m* 2 Aug 1958, Elizabeth Juliet, da of George Romney Fox (d 1969), of Trewardreva, Constantine, Falmouth, Cornwall; 2 s (William b 1959, John b 1960); *Career* Rifle Bde 1941–45, Lt and Actg Capt Western Desert, Tunisia, Italy, NW Europe; called to the Bar Middle Temple 1948, Lord

Chancellor's Office 1956–82 (dep clerk of crown 1975–77, clerk of crown and permanent sec 1977–82), bencher 1977; *Recreations* gardening; *Clubs* Leander; *Style—* Sir Wilfrid Bourne, KCB, QC; ✉ Povey's Farm, Ramsdell, Tadley, Hants (☎ 01256 850158)

BOURNE-ARTON, Simon Nicholas; QC (1994); s of Maj Anthony T Bourne-Arton, MBE (d 1996), of W Tanfield, Ripon, N Yorks, and (Margaret) Elaine, da of W Denby Arton, of Sleningford Park, Ripon; *b* 5 Sept 1949; *Educ* Harrow, Teesside Poly (HND), Univ of Leeds (LLB); *m* 1974, Diana Carr-Walker; 2 s (James b 3 Aug 1977, Tom b 9 March 1980), 1 da (Isabel b 15 Aug 1983); *Career* called to the Bar Inner Temple 1975, in practice NE Circuit, recorder of the Crown Court 1993–; *Recreations* golf, tennis, walking, wine, family and friends; *Style—* Simon Bourne-Arton, Esq, QC; ✉ Park Court Chambers, 40 Park Cross Street, Leeds LS1 2QH (☎ 0113 243 3277)

BOURSNELL, Clive; s of Raymond Robert Morgan, of Sunningdale, Berks, and Vera, *née* Kossick; *b* 2 June 1942; *Educ* Corona Stage Sch; *Career* professional photographer (initially working in fashion, currently specialising in portraits and feature work); child actor appearing on TV and in films: Hunted (with Dirk Bogarde) 1952, The Beggar's Opera (with Laurence Olivier) 1952; woodman Windsor Great Park Berks 1958–60; extensive travelling throughout Canada 1960–64: successively dairy farmer, pit labourer in uranium and gold mines, door-to-door magazines salesman, prospector for natural gas and oil then asst glaciologist Geography Dept McGill Univ Montreal; fashion photographer's asst London 1964–66, photographic printer 1966–67, staff photographer Ambassador Magazine 1968–69, freelance photographer 1969–; work featured in various pubns incl: The Observer, Vogue and Honey magazines, Sunday Times and Telegraph magazines, Independent on Sunday, Illustrated London News, Country Living, Country Life; fndr memb Photographers Assoc 1968 (variously memb Cncl); *Books* Covent Garden Market (1977), The Royal Opera House (1982), English Herb Gardens (1986), English Water Gardens (1987), Making of the English Garden (1989); *Recreations* photography, opera, dance, walking, climbing (lone attempt of Mt McKinley Alaska, mountaineer on Arctic expedition to Alex Wieberg), being me; *Style—* Clive Boursnell, Esq; ✉ 15 Provost Court, Eton Road, London NW3 4SR (☎ 0171 722 1998, fax 0171 483 1432, mobile 0831 647244), The Old Chapel, Bucks Mill, nr Bideford, Devon EX39 5DY

BOUTTELL, Brian; s of Robert Bouttell (d 1992), of Middlesbrough, and Gertrude, *née* Page (d 1986); *b* 12 May 1944; *Educ* Middlesbrough HS; *m* 28 Sept 1963, Glenda Lee, *née* Jackson; 1 s (Gary b 19 Oct 1965 d 1990), 2 da (Janet b 6 May 1967, Laura b 4 Dec 1970); *Career* CA; articled clerk George C Wilkinson & Co 1960–66; Peat Marwick Mitchell Darlington: joined 1966, ptnr 1977, transferred to Leeds 1985, office managing ptnr Leeds 1987; sr regnl ptnr KPMG 1990–; dir West Yorkshire Playhouse; FCA 1966; *Recreations* squash, running, bridge, theatre; *Style—* Brian Bouttell, Esq; ✉ Rockwell, 25 Margerison Rd, Ben Rhydding, Ilkley, W Yorks LS29 8QY (☎ 01943 602952); KPMG, 1 The Embankment, Neville St, Leeds LS1 4DW (☎ 0113 231 3000, fax 0113 231 3200)

BOUTWOOD, Nigel Peter Ralph; s of Peter Ralph Wood Boutwood, and Roberta May, *née* Pool; *b* 12 May 1951; *Educ* Lancing Coll; *m* 2 April 1977, Jeanette Elsma, da of Jeffery Warner Etherington; 1 s (Charles Peter Warner b 1991), 2 da (Emma Jane Elsma b 1980, Tiffany Roberta b 1982); *Career* J Walter Thompson 1970, Thames TV 1971–78, Southern TV 1978–82, TVS 1982–85, chm and md Boutwood Advertising Ltd 1985–; chm of tstees Charlie's Challenge Charity (raising funds for research into children's brain tumours) 1995–; *Recreations* sailing, skiing, tennis; *Style—* Nigel Boutwood, Esq; ✉ Boutwood Advertising Ltd, 37 Terminus Rd, Eastbourne, East Sussex BN21 3QL (☎ 01323 640212, fax 01323 411999)

BOVEY, Barry William Vincent; OBE (1979); s of William Vincent Bovey (d 1965), of Worcester, and Irene Ida, *née* Holderness (d 1982); *b* 29 Oct 1929; *Educ* Haileybury, Univ of London; *m* 1, 23 June 1954 (m dis 1978), Daphne Joan, da of Cdr Arthur Gordon Marshall, RNR (d 1981), of Hampton Court; 2 s (Michael b 1957, Nigel b 1961); m 2, 22 Dec 1979, Jean Christine, da of Ronald Yeardley Goddard (d 1991), of Sheffield; *Career* Nat Serv cmmnd RA 1951–53, Capt RA (TA) 1953–57; gp sales dir Robert Jenkins Ltd 1967–72, chm Orbit Valve plc 1974– (md 1972–74), chm Energy Industries Cncl 1980–84 and 1993– (vice pres 1984–93); Process Plant EDC: memb Nat Econ Devpt Office 1980–87, chm Int Mktg Gp 1981–87; Freeman City of London, jr memb Ct of Assts Worshipful Co of Glovers; FCIM 1980, FIEx 1987, FInstD 1979; *Recreations* yachting, golf, tennis; *Clubs* Royal Thames Yacht; *Style—* Barry Bovey, Esq, OBE; ✉ Chadmore House, Willersey, Broadway WR12 7PH (☎ 01386 858 922); Orbit Valve plc, Orbit House, Alexandra Way, Ashchurch, Glos GL20 8NB (☎ 01684 274444, fax 01684 274822, car 0860 746630, telex 43317)

BOVEY, Dr Leonard; s of Alfred Bovey (d 1968, twice Mayor of Exeter), and Gladys, *née* Brereton; *b* 9 May 1924; *Educ* Hele's Sch Exeter, Emmanuel Coll Cambridge (BA, PhD); *m* Nov 1943, Constance (d 1987), da of Thomas Hudson (d 1960); 1 s (Christopher b 1951), 1 da (Jennifer b 1955); *Career* post doctoral fell Nat Res Cncl Ottawa 1950–52, AERE Harwell 1952–65; dir: W Midlands Regnl Office Miny of Tech 1966–70, Yorks & Humberside DTI 1970–73; cnsllr scientific and technol affrs High Cmmn Ottawa 1974–77, head Technol Requirements Branch DTI 1977–84; ed Materials & Design (Butterworth Heinemann) 1985–; CPhys, FInstP; *Recreations* theatre, music; *Clubs* Civil Service; *Style—* Dr Leonard Bovey; ✉ 32 Radnor Walk, London SW3 4BN (☎ 0171 352 4142); Butterworth Heinemann, Oxford OX2 8DP (☎ 01865 310366, fax 01865 310898)

BOVEY, Philip Henry; s of Cdr Norman Henry Bovey, OBE, DSC, VRD, of Killock House, Laughton, Lutterworth, Leics, and Dorothy Yvonne, *née* Kent Williams; *b* 11 July 1948; *Educ* Rugby, Peterhouse Cambridge (BA, MA); *m* 14 Sept 1974, Jenet Alison, da of Canon James Mitchell McTear (d 1973); 2 c (Katherine b 1976, Stephen b 1978); *Career* FCO 1970–71; admitted slr 1974; Slaughter & May 1972–75, DTI 1976–77, Cabinet Office 1977–78, DTI 1978– (under sec 1985–); inspr Companies Act 1984–88; *Recreations* photography; *Style—* Philip Bovey, Esq; ✉ 102 Cleveland Gardens, Barnes, London SW13 0AH (☎ 0181 876 3710); Department of Trade and Industry, 10–18 Victoria St, London SW1 (☎ 0171 215 5000)

BOWACK, Michael Hamilton; s of Norman Hamilton Bowack (ka 1942), and Vera Marion Ives, *née* Franklin; *b* 26 July 1942; *Educ* Uppingham; *m* 6 Aug 1983, Ann Jennifer Bowack, JP, da of Frank Charles Sherwill (d 1988); 1 da (Claire b 1985); *Career* Blease Lloyd & Co 1960–66, Touche Ross & Co 1966–67; various appts: Imperial Group plc 1967–74, The RTZ Corp plc 1974–85, The Plessey Co plc 1985–88, GEC Plessey Telecommunications Ltd 1988–90, Civil Serv 1990–93, The Chartered Inst of Tport 1994–; FCA, FCT; *Recreations* cricket, rugby football, gardening, music; *Clubs* MCC; *Style—* Michael Bowack, Esq; ✉ Pathways, 53 Fairmile Lane, Cobham, Surrey KT11 2DH (☎ 01932 865451)

BOWATER, Sir John Vansittart; 4 Bt (UK 1914), of Hill Crest, Borough of Croydon; s of Capt Victor Spencer Bowater (d 1967), 3 s of 1 Bt; suc unc, Sir (Thomas) Dudley (Blennerhassett) Bowater, 3 Bt, 1972; *b* 6 April 1918; *m* 1943, Joan Kathleen (d 1982), da of Wilfrid Ernest Henry Scullard (d 1963), of Boscombe; 1 s (Michael Patrick b 1949), 1 da (Penelope Ann (Mrs Martin Doughty) b 1954); *Heir* s, Michael Patrick Bowater b 18 July 1949; *Career* dir Oswald Bailey Gp of Cos; cncllr Bournemouth Town Cncl 1983–91; *Style—* Sir John Bowater, Bt; ✉ 214 Runnymede Ave, Bearwood, Bournemouth, Dorset (☎ 01202 571782)

BOWDEN, Sir Andrew; kt (1994), MBE (1961), MP (C) Brighton Kemptown (majority 3,056); s of William Victor Bowden, of Brighton, and Francesa Wilson; *b* 8 April 1930; *Educ* Ardingly; *m* 1970, Benita, da of B A Napier, of Brighton; 1 s, 1 da; *Career* worked in paint indust 1955–68, personnel conslt 1967–; memb Wandsworth BC 1950–62, nat chm Young Cons 1960–61; Parly candidate (C): N Hammersmith 1955, N Kensington 1964, Kemptown Brighton 1966; MP (C) Brighton Kemptown 1970; memb Select Ctees on: Expenditure 1973–74, Abortion 1975, Employment 1979–; jt chm All-Party Parly Gp for Pensioners 1971–, int chm People to People 1981–83, memb Cncl of Europe 1987–, nat pres Captive Animals Protection Soc; *Recreations* chess, golf; *Clubs* Carlton; *Style—* Sir Andrew Bowden, MBE, MP; ✉ House of Commons, London SW1A 0AA (☎ 0171 219 5047); Ashdene, 4 Carden Avenue, Brighton, Sussex BN1 8NA

BOWDEN, Rev Canon (Robert) Andrew; s of Charles Victor Bowden (d 1951), and Miriam Frances Howard, *née* Tripp, of Stroud, Glos; *b* 13 Nov 1938; *Educ* St Dunstan's Burnham-on-Sea Somerset, Clifton Coll Bristol (scholar, capt Shooting VIII), Worcester Coll Oxford (scholar, MA, DipTh, BD (Qualifying)), Cuddesdon Theol Coll; *m* 10 Sept 1966, Fiona Susan Elizabeth, er da of Kenneth Palmer Humpidge, CMG; 3 da (Emma Caroline b 16 Nov 1967, Henrietta Lucy b 11 June 1969, Polly Elizabeth Helena b 14 Sept 1975); *Career* cmmnd 1st King's Dragoon Gds (later 1st Queen's Dragoon Gds) 1958–59, Lt Shropshire Yeo 1959–63; Cuddesdon Theol Coll 1963–65; curate: St George's Wolverhampton 1965–69, St Luke's Duston Northampton 1969–72; rector: of Byfield Northants 1972–79, of Coates Rodmarton and Sapperton with Frampton Mansell 1979–; rural advsr to Dio of Glos 1981–93, vice chm Glos Rural Community Cncl 1985–88, memb Archbishop's Cmmn on Rural Areas (ACORA) 1987–90; chaplain to: RAC Cirencester 1979–93, The Worshipful Co of Drapers 1989, HM The Queen 1992–; hon canon Gloucester Cathedral 1990–; local miny offr Dio of Glos 1993–; hon research fell Centre for Theology Trinity Coll Carmarthen 1995–; *Books* Ministry in the Countryside (1994); *Recreations* the breeding of old breeds of poultry, walking, writing, music; *Style—* The Rev Canon Andrew Bowden; ✉ Coates Rectory, Cirencester, Glos GL7 6NR (☎ 01285 770235, fax 01285 770988)

BOWDEN, Francis William; s of Stanley Bowden (d 1951), of Stockport, and Ruth Grant, *née* Jenson (d 1996); *b* 21 May 1944; *Educ* Manchester GS, Christ's Coll Cambridge (MA); *m* 2 May 1970, Bridget Elizabeth, da of Randle Leigh Smith (d 1975), of Solihull; 1 s (John b 1973), 1 da (Susanna b 1974); *Career* actuary Godwins Ltd 1970–73, actuary and dir Fenchurch Gp 1973–84, ptnr Hymans Robertson 1985–95, independent pension conslt 1995–; FIA 1968, FPMI 1978; *Recreations* gardening, philately; *Style—* Francis Bowden, Esq; ✉ 55 Somerset Road, New Barnet, Herts EN5 1RF (☎ and fax 0181 441 4080)

BOWDEN, Sir Frank Houston; 3 Bt (UK 1915), of City of Nottingham; s of Sir Harold Bowden, 2 Bt, GBE (d 1960), and his 1 w Vera, *née* Whitaker; *b* 10 Aug 1909; *Educ* Rugby, Merton Coll Oxford (BA, MA); *m* 1, 28 April 1934 (m dis 1936), Marie-José, o da of Charles Stiénon, of Paris, and Comtesse Laure de Messey; 1 s (Nicholas Richard b 1935); m 2, 3 March 1937, Lydia Eveline (d 1981), da of Jean Manolovici, of Bucharest; 3 s (Adrian Harold Houston b 1938, d 1996, Aubrey Francis Houston b 1940, Gregory Andrew Houston b 1948); m 3, 1989, Oriol Annette Mary, o da of Charles Hooper Bath, of London; *Heir* s, Nicholas Richard Bowden b 13 Aug 1935; *Career* memb Br team Olympic Games Los Angeles 1932; Paymaster Lt RNVR 1939–44; ret industrialist and landowner; vice chm Japan Soc 1970–75, 1979–82 and 1984–87 (hon vice pres 1990–), pres British Kendo Assoc 1969–, hon vice pres World Kendo Championships 1976; pres University Hall Buckland 1967–71, vice pres Oxfordshire County Scout Cncl; pres: Thame Branch Royal Naval Assoc, Merton Soc 1975–80; collector of and writer and lectr on Japanese swords and armour; *Recreations* Kendo, bird-watching; *Clubs* White's, Royal Thames Yacht; *Style—* Sir Frank Bowden, Bt; ✉ The Old Vicarage, Winkfield, Windsor, Berks SL4 4SE (☎ 01344 886310)

BOWDEN, Gerald Francis; TD; s of Frank Albert Bowden, and Elsie, *née* Burrill; *b* 26 Aug 1935; *Educ* Battersea GS, Magdalen Coll Oxford, Coll of Estate Mgmnt; *m* 1967, Heather Elizabeth Hill, *née* Hall (d 1984); 2 da, 1 step s, 1 step da; *Career* called to the Bar Gray's Inn 1963, chartered surveyor; cncllr Dulwich Div GLC 1977–81, MP (C) Dulwich 1983–92; in practice as barrister 1992–; univ lectr 1992–; chm Leasehold Valuation Tbnl and Rent Assessment Panel 1994–; princ lectr in law Dept of Estate Mgmnt S Bank Univ (formerly S Bank Poly) 1972–83; *Style—* Gerald Bowden, Esq, TD; ✉ c/o 2 Paper Buildings, 1st Floor, Temple, London EC4Y 7ET

BOWDEN, Nicholas Richard; s and h of Sir Frank Houston Bowden, 3 Bt, *qv*; *b* 13 Aug 1935; *Educ* Millfield; *Career* Nat Serv, former trooper Life Gds; farmer; *Recreations* riding; *Style—* Nicholas Bowden, Esq; ✉ 4 Hensting Farm Cottages, Hensting Lane, Fishers Pond, nr Eastleigh, Hants SO5 7HH (☎ 01962 777260)

BOWDEN, Dr Paul Michael Anthony; *b* 1 April 1941; *Educ* Guy's Hosp London (LRCP, MRCS, MRCP, MRCPsych, MPhil); *Career* registrar in psychiatry Maudsley Hosp 1970–73, sr registrar in gen psychiatry Hammersmith Hosp 1973–74, hon lectr and res worker in forensic psychiatry Inst of Psychiatry and hon sr registrar Maudsley Hosp Sept 1974; conslt in forensic psychiatry: SW Thames RHA 1977–79, Bethlem Royal and Maudsley Hosps and to Home Office 1979–; tutor in psychiatry Social Sci Studies Chiswick Poly 1973–74, hon lectr Inst of Psychiatry 1975–76, hon sr lectr St George's Hosp 1977–78; conslt to Alcoholics Recovery Project 1971–73, conslt psychiatrist to and exec memb of the Circle Tst (providing facilities and support for prisoners and their families) 1974–79, res registrar in neuro-ophthalmology Royal Eye Hosp Unit Lambeth Hosp, awarded DHSS grant to study need for facilities to treat mentally abnormal offenders 1975–78; memb: DHSS Gp providing a comprehensive dist serv for the adult mentally ill, DHSS Working Party studying the provision of Nat Alcohol Detoxification Facilities 1974, Sec of State's Working Gp on Regnl Secure Units 1977–85, SE Thames RHA Working Party on Detoxification Facilites 1974–75, SE Thames RHA Working Party on provision of a Regnl Intensive Care and Assessment Unit 1975–77; chm: Forensic Psychiatry Specialist Section Exec Ctee RCPsych 1982–86 (sec 1978–82, memb 1976–78), Forensic Psychiatry Specialist Advsy Sub-Ctee Jt Ctee on Higher Psychiatric Trg RCPsych 1980–82 (sec 1978–80); ex-officio memb: Journal Ctee RCPsych 1977–84, Programmes and Meetings Ctee RCPsych 1978–80, Res Ctee RCPsych 1977–83; memb: Cncl RCPsych 1980–84, Special Ctee on the Mental Health Act 1959 White Paper RCPsych 1979–85, Ct of Electors RCPsych 1983–87; psychiatrist Mental Health Act Cmmn 1983–87; memb: Organising Ctee Br Soc of Criminolgy 1973–79, Cncl Howard League for Penal Reform 1974–80, Advsy Cncl Albany Tst 1978–79, Acad of Forensic Scis 1979–; examiner parts B and C Dip in Psychological Med 1980–83, memb Bd of Examiners RCPsych 1984–89; FRCPsych 1983; *Books* Principles and Practices of Forensic Psychiatry (ed jtly, 1990); fndr ed Jl of Forensic Psychiatry; author of numerous articles in various learned jls; *Style—* Dr Paul Bowden; ✉ Maudsley Hospital, Denmark Hill, London SE5 8AZ

BOWDEN, Prof Ruth Elizabeth Mary; OBE (1980); da of Sqdn Ldr Frank Harold Bowden (d 1959), and Louise Ellen, *née* Flick (d 1976); *b* 21 Feb 1915; *Educ* St Paul's Girls' Sch, Univ of London (MB BS, DSc); *Career* graduate asst Nuffield Dept of Orthopaedic Surgery Peripheral Nerve Injury Unit 1942–45; Royal Free Hosp Sch of Med Univ of London: lectr 1945–49, reader 1949, Rockefeller travelling fell 1949–50, prof of anatomy 1951–80, emeritus prof 1980–; hon res fell Inst of Neurology 1980–, Sir William Collins prof of anatomy RCS 1984–89; WHO conslt in anatomy Sudan 1970, 1972 and 1974; former pres: Anatomical Soc of GB and Ireland, Med Women's Fedn, Inst of Sci and Technol; life vice pres Chartered Soc of Physiotherapy (former chm); N London Hospice Gp: cncl memb, exec ctee memb, former chm Professional Sub Ctee; former convener Academic Awards Ctees of Int Fedns of Univ Women, former convener

Academic Awards Ctee Br Fedn of Women Graduates, former memb Exec Ctee Women's Nat Cmmn, memb Exec Ctee and Med Advsy Bd Lepra, vice pres Riding For the Disabled, life memb Anatomical Soc of GB and Ireland; memb: Zoological Soc, Royal Instn, Med Women's Fedn; Freeman by redemption City of London, Liveryman Worshipful Soc of Apothecaries; Jubilee Medal 1977, Wheatley Medal (jtly) Librarian's Assoc, Wood Jones Medal RCS; *Recreations* photography, painting, carpentry, reading; *Clubs* RSM, Br Fedn of Women Graduates; *Style—* Prof Ruth Bowden, OBE; ✉ 6 Hartham Close, Hartham Rd, London N7 9JH (☎ and fax 0171 607 3464)

BOWE, David Robert; MEP (Lab) Cleveland and Richmond (majority 57,568); *b* 19 July 1955; *Educ* Heathfield Sr HS Gateshead, Sunderland Poly, Univ of Bath, Teesside Poly; *m* 1977, Helena Margaret; 1 s (James), 1 da (Emily Anne); *Career* sci teacher 1977–89; memb Middlesbrough Cncl 1983–89; MEP (Lab): Cleveland and Yorkshire North 1989–94, Cleveland and Richmond 1994–; Euro Parl: memb Ctee on Environment, Public Health and Consumer Protection, substitute memb Economic and Monetary Affairs Ctee, chm Ctee of Inquiry into spread of organised crime linked to drug trafficking in the community; *Recreations* swimming, reading, walking; *Style—* David Bowe, Esq, MEP; ✉ 10 Harris St, Middlesbrough, Cleveland TS1 5EF (☎ 01642 247722, fax 01642 247804)

BOWE, John; s of William Wilson, of Wirral, Merseyside, and Evelyn Florence Wilson; *b* 1 Feb 1950; *Educ* Calday Grange GS, Bretton Hall Coll, Bristol Old Vic Theatre Sch; *children* 1 s (Joseph b 1 Nov 1981), 2 da (Maddie Florence b 1 Dec 1994, Aimee May b 12 Aug 1996); *Career* actor; *Theatre* RSC: Tinman in The Wizard of Oz, Tranio in The Taming of the Shrew, Blackwill in Arden of Faversham, Orlando in As You Like It; other roles incl: Observe the Sons of Ulster Marching Towards the Somme (Hampstead), Le Bret in Cyrano de Bergerac (LA Olympic Arts Festival, NY Broadway and Washington DC), Iago in Othello (New Shakespeare Co), Dunois in St Joan (Old Vic), title role in Henry V (Prospect Theatre Co); *Television* BBC: Paul Taylor in Testimony of a Child, Kester Woodseaves in Precious Bane, DCI Reynolds in Wall of Silence; other roles incl: Ross Poldark in Poldark (HTV), Daniel Stern in Body & Soul (Red Rooster Prodns), Voroshilov in Stalin (HBO), George Marlow in Prime Suspect (Granada), Leonard Ansen in Capital City (Euston Films), Jack Booker in Class Act (Carlton), Lord Hertford in the Prince and the Pauper (BBC); *Films* incl The Living Daylights; *Style—* John Bowe, Esq; ✉ c/o Conway van Gelder Robinson Ltd, 18–21 Jermyn Street, London SW1Y 6HP (☎ 0171 287 0077, fax 0171 287 1940)

BOWEN, Anthony James George; JP (1972); s of Howard James Bowen (d 1976), of Saundersfoot, Dyfed, and Georgina Ann, *née* Morris; *b* 29 Jan 1941; *Educ* Narbeth GS, Loughborough Coll of Advanced Tech (DLC); *m* 1 June 1973, Patricia Ann, da of Douglas Edward Watson Hutchinson (d 1964), of Nottingham; 1 step s (Simon Miles Barrett b 30 April 1967), 1 step da (Lisa Ellen Barrett b 29 April 1970); *Career* chm and md Green Bower Garages Ltd (BMW main dealers Dyfed) 1963–, ptnr Slebech Finance Co 1970–, chm Pembrokeshire NHS Trust 1992–95; sub prior Priory for Wales Order of St John 1991–, chm Mid and W Wales Area Ctee The Prince's Trust 1984–, former memb Round Table, memb Rotary Int; FIMI 1984; KStJ 1988; *Recreations* golf, skiing, walking; *Style—* Anthony Bowen, Esq, JP; ✉ St Giles, Uzmaston Rd, Haverfordwest, Pembrokeshire SA61 1TZ (☎ 01437 762792); Green Bower Garages Ltd, Slebech, Haverfordwest, Pembrokeshire SA62 4PD (☎ 01437 751251, 01437 751373)

BOWEN, Charles John; *b* 11 Dec 1941; *Educ* Brockenhurst County HS, Univ of Exeter (BA); *Career* mkt research assoc ICI 1965–67, product mangr Flora and Blue Band Van Den Berghs (subsid of Unilever Group) 1967–73; General Foods Corporation UK: mktg mangr coffee then devpt dir desserts 1973–78, gen mangr Puerto Rico 1978–82, gen mangr Main Meals Div USA 1982, gp vice pres General Foods and pres Meals Div until 1988; Hillsdown Holdings: exec dir processed food and distribution 1988–89, chm Premier Brands 1989–92, pres and chief exec offr Maple Leaf Foods 1992–93; chief exec Booker PLC 1993–; non-exec dir Legal & General plc 1996–; FRSS; *Clubs* Travellers'; *Style—* Charles Bowen, Esq; ✉ Booker PLC, 85 Buckingham Gate, London SW1E 6PD

BOWEN, Christopher Richard Croasdaile; s of Christopher James Croasdaile Bowen (ka 1944), and Helen Florence Anderton, *née* Lyons; *b* 7 Oct 1944; *Educ* Rugby; *m* 22 April 1972, Janet Margaret, da of Capt Alexander Francis Matheson, RN; 1 da (Nicola Frances b 26 March 1976), 1 s (Robert James Croasdaile b 28 April 1978); *Career* Royal Tank Regt 1963–68; IBM (UK) 1969–79; chartered accountant 1983; Saffery Champness: joined 1980, ptnr 1983–, dep chm 1993–95, chm 1995–; FCCA 1979; *Recreations* the countryside, light aviation; *Clubs* New (Edinburgh); *Style—* Christopher Bowen, Esq; ✉ Kinellan House, Strathpeffer, Ross-shire IV14 9ET (☎ 01997 421476); Saffery Champness, Fairfax House, Fulwood Place, Gray's Inn, London WC1V 6UB (☎ 0171 405 2828, fax 0171 405 7887); Saffery Champness, Hill Place House, Inverness, Scotland IV2 3AD (☎ 01463 224660, fax 01463 243273)

BOWEN, Prof David Aubrey Llewellyn; s of Thomas Rufus Bowen, JP (d 1946), and Catherine, *née* Llewellyn (d 1973); *b* 31 Jan 1924; *Educ* Caterham Sch Surrey, Univ of Wales, Univ of Cambridge (MA, MB); *m* 1, 1950, Joan Rosemary, *née* Davis (d 1973); 2 s (Mark b 1952, Roderic b 1966), 1 da (Diana b 1953); m 2, 21 Jan 1975, Helen Rosamund, da of Ralph Landcastle, of Haddenham, Bucks; *Career* Capt RAMC 1947–49; house offr: W Middx Hosp 1947, London Chest Hosp 1949–50, Bristol Royal Infirmary 1950–51; registrar: London Chest Hosp (Pathology) 1951–52, Nat Hosp for Nervous Diseases 1952–55, Royal Marsden Hosp 1955–56; forensic med lectr St George's Hosp 1956–66, emeritus prof of forensic med Univ of London, prof Charing Cross Hosp Med Sch 1977–90 (sr lectr 1966–73, reader 1973–77), lectr in forensic med Univ of Oxford 1974–90; chm Med Ctees Charing Cross Hosp and Med Sch; memb: Med Legal Soc (vice pres 1977–), Br Assoc Forensic Med (pres 1977–79), Int Academy Legal and Social Med 1976–, Br Academy Forensic Sci; vice pres Old Caterhamians Assoc 1987–88, pres W London Medico Chirurgical Soc 1987–88; Freeman City of London, Liveryman Worshipful Soc of Apothecaries; FRCP (London and Edinburgh), FRCPath, DPath, DMJ; *Recreations* hockey, running (jogging); *Style—* Prof D A L Bowen; ✉ 19 Letchmore Rd, Radlett, Herts WD7 8HU (☎ 01923 856936)

BOWEN, David Ian Henry; s of Ivor Llewelyn Bowen, of Mumbles, Swansea, and Marjorie, *née* Abbay; *b* 8 June 1950; *Educ* Dynevor GS Swansea, Swansea Coll of Technol; *m* 16 Nov 1983, Elizabeth Mary; 1 s (James b 9 Dec 1984); *Career* presenter/prodr Swansea Sound 1974–80, journalist/presenter Hereward Radio 1980–83, prog controller Radio Aire 1983–84, gp head of music GWR Group plc 1984–90, md Bowen-Sklar Programming 1990–93, gp prog controller West Country Broadcasting (WCB) 1993–95, chief exec offr The Executive Network North America; *Recreations* tennis, cycling, squash, golf; *Style—* David Bowen, Esq; ✉ 510 Mumbles Road, Mumbles, Swansea SA3 4BU (☎ 01792 366856, fax 01792 361372, e-mail 100637.504@compuserve.com)

BOWEN, Prof David Quentin; s of William Esmond Bowen (d 1984), of Heddlys, Glasfryn, Llanelli, and Jane, *née* Wiliams (d 1992); *b* 14 Feb 1938; *Educ* Llanelli GS, UCL (BSc, PhD); *m* 18 Sept 1965, Elizabeth, da of David Islwyn Williams (d 1989); 2 s (Huw b 1966, Wyn b 1969); *Career* prof of physical geography UCW Aberystwyth 1983–85, prof of geography Univ of London Royal Holloway 1985–88; prof and dir Inst of Earth Studies UCW 1988–93, prof of quaternary geology Univ of Wales Cardiff 1994–; ed in chief Quaternary Sci Review 1982–94, pres Quaternary Res Assoc (UK) 1979–81, pres INQUA Stratigraphy Cmmn (Int Union for Quaternary Res) 1991–93; memb: Natural Environment Res Cncl Ctees 1978–96, UGC Earth Sci Review 1988, Nature Conservancy Cncl 1986–91, Jt Nature Conservation Ctee (GB) 1990–, American Geophysical Union, Dutch Univs Earth Sci Review 1996; dep chm Countryside Cncl for Wales 1990–, chm Llanelli Millennium Coastal Park Forum 1996–; BBC Wales Annual Lecture 1996; FGS 1988; *Books* Quaternary Geology (1978, Russian edn 1982), The Llanelli Landscape (1980), Glaciations in the Northern Hemisphere (1986); *Recreations* music, rugby, cricket; *Style—* Prof David Bowen; ✉ Department of Earth Sciences, University of Wales, Cardiff CF1 3YE (☎ 01222 874337, fax 01222 874326, e-mail BowenDQ@cardiff.ac.uk)

BOWEN, Edward Farquharson; TD (1977), QC (Scot 1992); s of Stanley Bowen, CBE; *b* 1 May 1945; *Educ* Melville Coll Edinburgh, Univ of Edinburgh (LLB); *m* 1975, Patricia Margaret, da of Rev Robert Russell Brown, of Gowanbank, Isla Rd, Perth; 2 s (James, David), 2 da (Helen, Alexandra); *Career* admitted slr 1968, passed advocate 1970; advocate depute 1979–83, Sheriff of Tayside Central and Fife at Dundee 1983–90, ptnr Thorntons WS 1990–91, resumed practice at Scottish Bar 1991; memb Criminal Injuries Compensation Bd 1996; *Recreations* golf; *Clubs* New (Edinburgh), Hon Co of Edinburgh Golfers, Panmure Golf, Royal & Ancient Golf (St Andrews); *Style—* Edward Bowen, Esq, TD, QC; ✉ The Old Manse, Lundie, Angus (☎ 01382 581230)

BOWEN, John; s of John Thomas Bowen (d 1964), and Marjorie Mabel, *née* George (d 1973); *b* 7 June 1937; *Educ* Aberdare Boys' Co GS, Univ Coll of Wales (LLB); *m* 6 Sept 1969, Helen Margaret, da of Dudley Guildford Keay; 1 s (Thomas Huw David b 1 July 1975); *Career* slr; articled clerk Marchant Harries & Co Slrs Aberdare 1957–60; asst slr: G Houghton & Son London EC2 1960, Gamlen Bowerman & Forward Lincoln's Inn London 1960–64; Morgan Bruce: asst slr 1964–66, ptnr 1966–, chm Mgmnt Bd 1989–; memb Law Soc 1960, memb and past chm Area Ctee Legal Aid Bd (S Wales), dep chm Inst of Welsh Affairs, memb Exec Ctee Tenovus Cancer Appeal; *Recreations* English literature, music, industrial history, contract bridge; *Style—* John Bowen, Esq; ✉ Morgan Bruce Solicitors, Bradley Court, Park Place, Cardiff CF1 3DP (☎ 01222 233677)

BOWEN, John Griffith; s of Hugh Griffith Bowen (d 1988), and Ethel May, *née* Cooke; *b* 5 Nov 1924; *Educ* Queen Elizabeth's GS Crediton, Pembroke Coll Oxford (MA), St Anthony's Coll Oxford, Ohio State Univ; *Career* writer/producer/dir of television drama and stage plays; author of various reviews and articles; Capt Mahratha LI 1943–47; *Novels* The Truth Will Not Help Us (1956), After the Rain (1958), The Centre of the Green (1959), Storyboard (1960), The Birdcage (1962), A World Elsewhere (1965), Squeak (1983), The MacGuffin (1984), The Girls (1986), Fighting Back (1988), The Precious Gift (1992), No Retreat (1994); *Plays* incl: I Love You, Mrs Patterson (St Martin's Theatre) 1964, After the Rain (Duchess Theatre) 1966, Fall and Redemption (Pitlochry) 1967, Little Boxes (Duchess) 1968, The Disorderly Women (Manchester) 1969, The Corsican Brothers (Greenwich) 1970, The Waiting Room (Soho Poly) 1970, Heil, Caesar (Birmingham) 1974, Which Way Are You Facing? (Bristol Old Vic) 1976, Singles (Greenwich) 1977, Bondage (Soho Poly) 1978, The Inconstant Couple (adaptation of Marivaux, Chichester Festival Theatre) 1978, Uncle Jeremy (Newcastle) 1981, The Geordie Gentleman (adaptation of Molière, Newcastle Playhouse) 1987; *Television* various plays for BBC, LWT, Associated Television, Yorkshire Television, Central Television (incl Heil, Caesar, winner of Tokyo prize); *Radio* plays for BBC incl The False Diaghilev 1987; *Style—* John Bowen, Esq; ✉ Old Lodge Farm, Sugarswell Lane, Edgehill, Banbury OX15 6HP (☎ 01295 680401, fax 01295 688003)

BOWEN, Kenneth John; s of Hector John Bowen (d 1980), of Llanelli, Carmarthenshire, and Sarah Ann (Sally), *née* Davies (d 1939); *b* 3 Aug 1932; *Educ* Llanelli GS, Univ Coll of Wales Aberystwyth (BA), St John's Coll Cambridge (MA, MusB), Inst of Educn Univ of London; *m* 31 March 1959, Angela Mary, da of George Stanley Evenden, of Morecambe, Lancs; 2 s (Geraint, Meurig); *Career* Flying Offr Educn Branch RAF 1958–60; head of vocal studies RAM 1987–91 (prof of singing 1967–); conductor: London Welsh Chorale 1983–, London Welsh Festival Chorus 1987–90; former concert and operatic tenor (ret 1988); debut Tom Rakewell New Opera Co Sadler's Wells 1957; appeared: Promenade concerts, Three Choirs Festival, Aldeburgh and other maj festivals; performed at: Royal Opera, House ENO, WNO, Glyndebourne Touring Opera, English Opera Gp, English Music Theatre, Kent Opera, Handel Opera Soc; numerous recordings and int appearances (Europe, USA, Canada, Israel, Far East), winner first prize Munich Int Competition and Queen's prize; adjudicator Royal Nat Eisteddfod of Wales and Llangollen In Eisteddfod; memb: Gorsedd of Bards, Cncl Br Youth Opera; vice pres Guild for Promotion of Welsh Music; hon memb RAM, FRSA; *Recreations* golf, walking, cinema, theatre, wine; *Style—* Kenneth Bowen, Esq; ✉ 61 Queens Crescent, London NW5 3QS (☎ and fax 0171 267 4700); Royal Academy of Music, Marylebone Rd, London NW1 5HT

BOWEN, Sir Mark Edward Mortimer; 5 Bt (UK 1921), of Colworth, Co Bedford; o s of Sir Thomas Frederic Charles Bowen, 4 Bt (d 1989), and Jill Claude Murray, *née* Evans; *b* 17 Oct 1958; *Educ* Wellington Coll; *m* 1983, Kerry Tessa, da of Michael John Moriarty, of The Grey House, Links Road, Worthing, Sussex; 1 s (George Edward Michael), 1 da (Grace Francesca b 3 March 1989); *Heir* s, George Edward Michael Bowen b 27 Dec 1987; *Career* Lloyd's broker 1978–; *Recreations* swimming, golf; *Style—* Sir Mark Bowen, Bt; ✉ Jardine Insurance Services Ltd, Jardine House, 6 Crutched Friars, London EC3

BOWEN, Most Rev Michael George; *see:* Southwark, Archbishop and Metropolitan of (RC)

BOWEN, Dr (John) Myles; OBE (1977); s of Cdr Harold Townshend Bowen, OBE (d 1971), and Cicely Frances Anne, *née* Cooper (d 1996 in her 100th year); *b* 23 Aug 1928; *Educ* Sherborne, Lincoln Coll Oxford (BA), Univ of Edinburgh (PhD); *m* 7 Jan 1961, Margaret Compton, da of James Guthrie (d 1938); 3 da (Frances Belinda b 1963, Joanna Marion b 1964, Jennifer Isabel b 1968); *Career* cmmnd RA 1946; worked as exploration geologist for Royal Dutch Shell Group 1954–84 (Africa, S America, Europe), exploration dir Enterprise Oil London 1984–91 (dir N Sea exploration when 10 oil and 5 gas fields discovered), petroleum exploration conslt 1991–; hon memb PESGB, FGS, AAPG, EAPG (past pres); *Recreations* sailing, skiing, rough shooting; *Clubs* Little Ship, OCC; *Style—* Dr Myles Bowen, OBE; ✉ Rudge, Lustleigh, Newton Abbot, Devon TQ13 9SL (☎ and fax 01647 277336)

BOWEN, (William) Neville; s of Maj-Gen William Oswald Bowen, CB, CBE (d 1961), of Winchester, and Ethel Gwenllian, *née* Davies; *b* 16 March 1935; *Educ* Shrewsbury, New York Univ Grad Sch of Business Admin; *m* 1960, Rosemary Rowena, da of Trevlyn Acheson-Williams-Flanagan; 2 da (Suzanne b 1963, Joanna b 1966); *Career* investment banker and advsr NY and Toronto 1957–72, md Hill Samuel Unit Trust Mangrs Ltd 1973–76, chief exec Bank von Ernst & Cie AG (Switzerland) 1976–80; chm: Hill Samuel Investment Management Ltd 1982–92 (joined 1980), Investment Advisers Inc (USA) 1986–92, Hill Samuel Fagan Investment Management Ltd (Ireland) 1988–92, Atlanta Capital Management (USA) 1990–92; chief exec: Hill Samuel Investment Management Group Ltd 1986–92, Citibank Global Asset Management 1992–; dir: Irish Life plc 1992–, Citibank International plc 1994–; CIMgt; *Recreations* skiing, scuba diving, music, gardening; *Clubs* Brooks's; *Style—* Neville Bowen, Esq; ✉ Citibank Global Asset Management, PO Box 200, Cotton's Centre, 4th Floor, Hay's Lane, London SE1 2QT (☎ 0171 500 5579)

BOWEN, Roderic Huw Mellows; s of Jonathan David Maxwell Bowen, and Jane, *née* Mellows; *b* 25 March 1958; *Educ* Kings Coll Taunton, Univ of Bristol (BSc); *Career* articled clerk Price Waterhouse CAs 1978–79, account exec SSC & B Lintas advtg 1979–81; account dir: Young & Rubicam 1981–85, BSB Dorland 1985–86; gp bd dir

Grey London Ltd 1986–95 (new business dir 1990–92), managing ptnr Bayntun Bowen 1995–; memb IAA, MIPA; *Recreations* golf, music, fly-fishing, skiing; *Clubs* Huntercombe Golf, Lansdowne, Old Aluredians, Rags, Hooligani; *Style*— Roderic Bowen, Esq

BOWEN-SIMPKINS, Peter; s of Horace John Bowen-Simpkins (d 1969), and Christine Dulce, *née* Clarke; *b* 28 Oct 1941; *Educ* Malvern, Selwyn Coll Cambridge (MA, MB, BChir), Guy's Hosp; *m* 19 Aug 1967, Kathrin, da of Karl Otto Ganguin (d 1987), of Chelmsford, Essex; 2 da (Emma Jane b 6 Nov 1969, Philippa b 28 Dec 1971); *Career* resident MO Queen Charlotte's Maternity Hosp London 1971, resident surgical offr Samaritan Hosp for Women London 1972, sr registrar and lectr in obstetrics and gynaecology Middx Hosp and Hosp for Women 1972–78, conslt gynaecologist and obstetrician Singleton Hosp Swansea 1979–, inspr of nullity for Wales, lectr in family planning Margaret Pyke Centre London; broadcaster and lectr; contrib chapters in various books on obstetrics and gynaecology, and author of papers and pubns in med jls incl: Br Med Jl, Br Jl of Obstetrics and Gynaecology; examiner: Royal Coll of Obstetricians and Gynaecologists, Univ of Wales, GMC; memb Cncl RCOG 1993–, memb Fndn Bd Faculty Family Planning RCOG; Handcock Prize for Surgery RCS 1966; co-fndr Victor Bonney Soc, ldr Cambridge Expedition to Eritrea 1963; Freeman City of London, Liveryman Worshipful Soc of Apothecaries 1976, Liveryman Welsh Livery Guild (Urdd Lifrai Cymru) 1995; LRCP 1966, MRCS 1966, MRCOG 1973, FRCOG 1985; *Books* Pocket Examiner in Obstetrics & Gynaecology (1983); *Recreations* fly fishing, skiing, golf, sailing, tennis; *Clubs* Pennard Golf, Royal Over-Seas League; *Style*— Peter Bowen-Simpkins, Esq; ✉ Bosco's Knoll, 73 Pennard Rd, Southgate, Swansea SA3 2AJ; 38 Walter Rd, Swansea SA1 5NW (☎ 01792 655600, fax 01792 232170)

BOWER, Michael James Eills Graham; s of James Graham Bower (d 1968), of Hants, and Sybil Galilee, *née* Eills (d 1971); *b* 14 June 1938; *Educ* Eton, ChCh Oxford (MA); *m* 23 June 1967, Carolyne Patricia Sherwell, da of Derek Frank Sherwell Clogg (d 1986), of London; 1 s (Michael b 3 Nov 1968); *Career* dir: Rea Bros Ltd 1974– (joined 1961), Rea Brothers Group plc 1987–, Rea Bros Investment Management 1988–; *Recreations* golf, bridge; *Clubs* White's, Royal and Ancient Golf, Royal St George's Golf; *Style*— Michael Bower, Esq; ✉ Stuart House, Sandwich, Kent; Rea Bros Ltd, House, Aldermans Walk, London EC2 (☎ 0171 623 1155)

BOWERING, Christine; da of Kenneth Soper (d 1978), and Florence Evelyn Winifred, *née* Kruse (d 1982); *b* 30 June 1936; *Educ* St Bernard's Convent Westcliff, Newnham Coll Cambridge; *m* 23 July 1960, The Rev (John) Anthony Bowering, s of John Bowering; 1 s (John Robert b 1962), 1 da (Eleanor Jane (Mrs Wray) b 1964); *Career* teacher: St Bernard's Convent Westcliff 1959–60, Ursuline Convent Brentwood 1960–62; various pt/t occupations 1962–72, teacher then second mistress Sheffield HS for Girls GPDST 1972–84, headmistress Nottingham HS for Girls GPDST 1984–96; memb: Engrg Cncl 1988–91, Cncl GSA, Ind Schs Curriculum Ctee 1990–94 (chm 1992–94), Educn Ctee Goldsmiths' Co 1992–; non-exec dir Queens' Med Centre Hosp Tst Nottingham 1993–; govr Nottingham Trent Univ (formerly Nottingham Poly) 1989–96, memb Educn Ctee GSA 1989–96 (chm 1989–93), memb Cncl Standing Conf on Schools Sci and Technol (SCSST), assoc memb Newnham Coll Cambridge 1991–, hon memb GSA 1996–; Hon DLitt Univ of Nottingham; FRSA; *Recreations* holidaying in France, church and family activities; *Clubs* University Women's; *Style*— Mrs Christine Bowering; ✉ The Vicarage, 2 Sunderland Street, Tickhill, Doncaster DN11 9QJ (☎ 01302 742224)

BOWERING, Ven Michael Ernest; s of Hubert James Bowering (d 1961), of Barnstaple, and Mary Elizabeth, *née* Tucker (d 1982); *b* 25 June 1935; *Educ* Barnstaple GS, Kelham Theol Coll; *m* 18 Aug 1962, Aileen, da of Joseph William Fox (d 1979), of Middlesbrough; 1 s (Paul b 1963), 2 da (Alice b 1966, Joanne b 1967); *Career* curate: St Oswald Middlesbrough 1959–62, All Saints Huntington 1962–64; vicar St Wilfrid Brayton with Barlow 1964–72, rural dean Selby 1971–72, vicar Emmanuel Saltburn By The Sea 1972–81, canon residentiary York Minster 1981–87, sec for Mission and Evangelism York Dio 1981–87, archdeacon of Lindisfarne 1987–; *Recreations* photography, walking; *Style*— The Ven the Archdeacon of Lindisfarne; ✉ 12 Rectory Park, Morpeth, Northumberland NE61 2SZ (☎ 01670 513 207)

BOWERMAN, David William; JP (1970), DL (W Sussex 1992); s of Alfred Hosegood Bowerman (d 1982), of Champs Hill, Coldwaltham, and Margaret, *née* Vellacott; *b* 9 Jan 1936; *Educ* Monkton Combe Sch, Univ of Reading (BSc); *m* 9 Sept 1961, (Clarice) Mary Bowerman, da of Prof William Melville Capper (d 1975), of Clifton, Bristol; 3 da (Janet Mary (Mrs William Taylor) b 28 June 1962, Katharine Emma b 9 July 1964, Anna Margaret (Mrs Simon Downham) b 28 May 1966); *Career* farmer, property developer; chm: Arundel Bench 1985–89, Arundel Juvenile Bench 1980–85, Bd of Visitors HM Prison Ford 1979–82 (memb 1970–85), W Sussex Probation Ctee 1979–94, W Sussex Forum for Offender Accommodation 1979–94; vice chm Sussex Assoc for Rehabilitation of Offenders 1979–; chm Music at Boxgrove 1991–; tstee: Chichester Cathedral Trust, Mary How Trust, Bowerman Meml Trust; memb Cncl and Instn King Edward VII Hosp Midhurst; High Sheriff W Sussex 1990–91; *Recreations* music, fly-fishing; *Clubs* Mosimann's; *Style*— David Bowerman, Esq, JP, DL; ✉ Champs Hill, Coldwaltham, Pulborough, West Sussex (☎ 01798 831868/831205, fax 01798 831536)

BOWERMAN, John Ernest; s of Ernest James Bowerman (d 1973), and Irene May, *née* Partridge; *b* 13 March 1931; *Educ* Torquay GS, Dental and Med Schs Univ of Bristol (scholar, BDS, MB ChB, numerous prizes and awards, Badminton colours); *m* 20 March 1955, Hilary Winifred, da of Charles Frederick Hazlewood; 1 s (Martin John b 15 Aug 1959), 1 da (Sarah Jane b 2 May 1962); *Career* Lt RADC 1954–55, ret Capt 1956; house surgn Univ of Bristol Dental Sch 1954, in gen dental practice 1955–60, dental surgn Marlpitts Geriatric Hosp Honiton Devon 1958–59, registrar in dental surgery Univ of Bristol Dental Sch and Maxillofacial Unit Frenchay Hosp Bristol 1960–61, house physician in gen med Professorial Med Unit United Bristol Hosps 1965–66, house surgn in gen and ENT surgery Frenchay Hosp Bristol 1966; sr registrar in oral surgery 1967–69: Westminster Hosp and Queen Mary's Univ Hosp Roehampton (registrar in oral surgery 1966–67), UCH Dental Sch; hon conslt in oral and maxillofacial surgery Royal Dental Hosp of London and St George's Hosp Tooting London 1974–81; formerly conslt in maxillofacial surgery: Westminster Hosp 1969–91, Queen Mary's Univ Hosp 1969–94 Epsom Dist Hosp Surrey 1978–94; currently: hon consulting surgeon in maxillofacial surgery Chelsea and Westminster Hosp, Queen Mary's Univ Hosp, in private practice London; visiting prof: Univ of Cairo and Egyptian Air Force Hosp 1984, Univ of Alexandria and Maadi Armed Forces Hosp 1985, Univ Dental Sch Kenyatta Nat Hosp Kenya 1988; dental clinical tutor Roehampton Postgrad Med Centre 1977–93, examiner RCS 1983–89; memb: Euro Assoc for Cranio-Maxillofacial Surgery (memb Cncl 1986–92), Regional Hosp Dental Surgery Ctee SW Thames RHA (chm 1975–83); memb: BDA, BMA; FDS RCS 1964, FRCSEd 1985, fell BAOMS (memb Cncl 1983–84); *Books* Dental Manifestations of Systemic Disease (Radiology in Clinical Diagnosis Series, with D H Trapnell, 1973); contrib chapters to numerous med and dental textbooks, author of numerous published articles in learned jls; *Recreations* salmon fishing, skiing, DIY; *Style*— John Bowerman, Esq; ✉ Pond Cottage, Whitmore Vale, Grayshott, Hampshire GU26 6JB (☎ 01428 713314); Princess Grace Hospital, London W1 (☎ 0171 486 1234 ext 4646)

BOWERS, Daniel Selwyn (Danny); s of Philip Louis Bowers, and Iris, *née* Pash; *b* 13 Oct 1958; *Educ* Manchester Poly (BA), London Coll of Printing (Dip in Radio Journalism); *m* 12 March 1989, Elizabeth, da of Lawrence Abramson; 1 s (Adam Benjamin b 4 March 1992), 1 da (Emma Sarah b 19 Sept 1994); *Career* news reporter and prodr (Midlands) BBC Radio 1980–83, dep news ed and sports ed (Staffs and Cheshire) Signal Radio 1983–85, news/business reporter LBC/IRN 1985–86, fin corr LBC Radio 1986–90; freelance: Pink Section London Evening Standard 1990–91, Business Daily (C4) 1990–91; fin ed Independent Radio News (ITN Radio) 1991–95; co-fndr Electronic Media Relations 1989–91 (resigned as dir 1991), publisher MoneyWorld UK (formerly Lizdan Ltd) 1995– (dir 1991–); *Recreations* playing tennis, running and playing with the children, pony trekking; *Style*— Danny Bowers, Esq; ✉ MoneyWorld UK, Dome House, 48 Artillery Lane, London E1 7LS (☎ 0171 247 0200, fax 0181 343 3244, e-mail danny@moneyworld.co.uk, internet http://www.moneyworld.co.uk)

BOWERS, (John) Michael; OBE; s of F G Bowers, CB (d 1937), of Surrey, and Frances Bowers (d 1982); *b* 24 April 1927; *Educ* Dauntsey's Sch, Balliol Coll Oxford (BA); *m* 13 Sept 1958, Rosalind, da of Percy Bourdon Smith; 2 s (Philip b 1960, Robert b 1963), 2 da (Joanna b 1961, Valery b 1965); *Career* ptnr McKenna & Co Solicitors 1958–87; chm: CARE Britain, Copyright Tbnl, Fin Servs Tbnl, govrs Thomas Mills High Sch Framlingham; dir London Sinfonietta; formerly: dir Hyde Housing Assoc, founding dir Abbeyfield Soc, founding dir Greenwich Theatre, vice chm Nat Assoc of Citizen's Advice Bureaux; sailed across Atlantic 1982; *Recreations* sailing, music; *Clubs* Garrick; *Style*— Michael Bowers, Esq, OBE; ✉ Yew Tree Farm, Sweffling, Saxmundham, Suffolk IP17 2BU

BOWERS, His Hon Judge; Peter Hammond; s of Edward Hammond Bowers (d 1993), of Cleveland, and Elsie, *née* Wharton; *b* 22 June 1945; *Educ* Acklam Hall Sch Middlesbrough, Coll of Law London; *m* 26 Aug 1970, Brenda Janet, da of Alistair Gordon Burgess (d 1969); 2 s (Richard Peter b 8 Oct 1976, Martin James b 31 May 1978), 1 da (Jayne Elizabeth (twin) b 1978); *Career* articled clerk Alex Lauriston & Son Middlesbrough, admitted slr 1966, in private practice 1966–70, prosecuting slr 1970–72, transferred to the Bar (Inner Temple) 1972, recorder of the Crown Ct 1989–95 (asst recorder 1984), circuit judge (NE Circuit) 1995–; memb Law Soc 1966–72; *Recreations* golf, cricket and armchair spectator, paintings and antiques, aspiring artist; *Style*— His Hon Judge Bowers

BOWERS, Dr Peter John; s of Dr Arthur Clifford Bowers (d 1947), and Doris; *b* 2 June 1946; *Educ* Queen Elizabeth GS, Univ of London (BSc, AKC), Univ of Manchester (MB ChB, MSc, FRCPsych); *m* 1 Aug 1970, (Patricia) Lesley, da of Philip Bethell, of Darlington, Co Durham; 2 s (Jonathan b 1975, Anthony b 1982), 1 da (Juliet b 1974); *Career* house physician and surgn Central Manchester Hosps 1973–74, sr house offr in paediatrics Booth Hall Hosp 1974–75, sr registrar in child psychiatry S Manchester Hosp 1978–81 (registrar in psychiatry 1975–78), tutor Dept of Child Psychiatry Univ of Manchester 1981–82, conslt in child and adolescent psychiatry NW RHA 1983–94, conslt in child and adolescent psychiatry and med dir Tameside and Glossop Community and Priority Servs NHS Tst 1994–; expert witness for official slr in wardship of court cases 1984–; memb: Manchester Med Soc, Assoc of Family Therapists, Assoc of Child Psychology and Psychiatry, BAMM; *Recreations* amateur dramatics and operatics, theatre, jogging, travel; *Style*— Dr Peter Bowers; ✉ 6 Clifton Ave, Fallowfield, Manchester M14 6UB (☎ 0161 224 9508); Springhill Department of Child and Family Psychiatry and CPS Headquarters, Tameside General Hospital, Fountain St, Ashton-Under-Lyne (☎ 0161 331 5151)

BOWERS-BROADBENT, Christopher Joseph St George; s of Henry William Bowers-Broadbent (d 1965), of Ilfracombe, Devon, and Doris E, *née* Mizen; *b* 13 Jan 1945; *Educ* King's Coll Cambridge, Berkhamsted Sch, Royal Acad of Music (Recital Dip); *m* 17 Oct 1970, Deirdre Ann, da of Norman Cape, of Kimbolton, Cambs; 1 s (Henry William b 10 Jan 1975), 1 da (Tabitha Jane b 2 May 1971); *Career* int concert organist; organist and choirmaster St Pancras Parish Church 1965–88, concert organist debut Camden Festival 1966, organist W London Synagogue 1973–, prof Royal Acad of Music 1976–92, organist and choirmaster Gray's Inn 1983–; many sacred and secular compositions; operas incl: The Pied Piper 1972, The Seacock Bane 1979, The Last Man 1983; FRAM; *Recreations* sketching; *Style*— Christopher Bowers-Broadbent, Esq; ✉ 94 Colney Hatch Lane, Muswell Hill, London N10 1EA (☎ and fax 0181 883 1933)

BOWERY, Prof Norman George; s of George Bowery (d 1971), and Olga, *née* Beevers (d 1991); *b* 23 June 1944; *Educ* Christ's Coll Finchley, Univ of London (PhD, DSc); *m* 14 Feb 1970, Barbara Joyce, da of Eric Norman Westcott, of Goring, Sussex; 1 s (Andrew James b 1975), 2 da (Nicole Louise b 1973, Annette Jane b 1977); *Career* sr lectr St Thomas' Hosp London 1982–84 (lectr 1975–82), section ldr Neuroscience Res Centre MSD Harlow 1984–87, Wellcome prof of pharmacology Univ of London 1987–95, prof of pharmacology The Med Sch Univ of Birmingham 1995–, memb and vice chm Biological Cncl 1988–91; memb: MRC Neuroscience Ctee 1983–87 and 1995–, SERC Link Ctee 1988–90; memb and hon gen sec Br Pharmacological Soc; memb: American Neuroscience Assoc, Soc of Drug Res; Laurea honoris causa Univ of Florence; *Books* Actions and Interactions of GABA and Benzodiazepines (1984), GABAergic Mechanisms on the Periphery (1986), GABA Basic Research and Clinical Applications (1989), GABAB receptors in mammalian function (1990), The GABA Receptors (1996), GABA: Receptors, Transporters and Metabolism (1996); *Recreations* walking, gardening, socializing; *Style*— Prof Norman Bowery; ✉ The Medical School, University of Birmingham, Edgbaston, Birmingham B15 2TT (☎ 0121 414 4506)

BOWES, Roger Norman; s of Russell Ernest Bowes, and Sybil Caroline Rose, *née* Bell; *b* 28 Jan 1943; *Educ* Chiswick GS, Dorking GS; *m* 1 (m dis 1974), Denise Hume Windsor; 1 da (Virginia Lynsey b 1961); m 2 (m dis 1988), Ann Rosemary O'Connor, *née* Hamstead; *Career* sales mangr Mirror Group Newspapers 1970–75, media dir McCann Erickson Advertising 1976–78; Mirror Group Newspapers: advtg dir 1978–81, dep chief exec 1982–83, chief exec 1984; md Guinness Enterprises 1985, chief exec Express Group Newspapers 1985–86, chm Citybridge 1987–, chief exec ASLIB (Assoc for Information Management) 1989–; memb: Br Cncl Libraries and Information Advsy Ctee, Euro Cncl of Info Assocs; treas Int Fedn for Info and Documentation; *Recreations* political and military history, cookery, classic cars; *Style*— Roger Bowes, Esq; ✉ ASLIB, Information House, 20–24 Old Street, London EC1V 9AP (☎ 0171 253 4488, fax 0171 430 0514, e-mail rbowes@aslib.co.uk, World Wide Web http://www.aslib.co.uk/aslib/)

BOWES LYON, Hon (Michael) Albemarle; s of late Capt the Hon Michael Claude Hamilton Bowes Lyon, 5 s of 14 E of Strathmore and Kinghorne; bro of 17 E; raised to the rank of an E's s 1974; *b* 29 May 1940; *Educ* Eton, Magdalen Coll Oxford; *Career* dir Coutts & Co 1969–93; govr Peabody Tst 1982–, hon treas Family Serv Units 1976–; *Recreations* hill walking; *Clubs* Brooks's, White's; *Style*— The Hon Albemarle Bowes Lyon; ✉ 138 B Whitehall Court, London SW1A 2EP

BOWES-LYON, David James; DL (Midlothian, 1992); s of Maj-Gen Sir James Bowes-Lyon, KCVO, CB, OBE, MC (d 1977), and Mary, *née* De Trafford; *b* 21 July 1947; *Educ* Ampleforth; *m* 1976, Elizabeth Harriet Bowes-Lyon (Lady-in-Waiting to HRH the Princess Royal), da of Sir John Colville, CB, CVO, of Broughton, nr Stockbridge, Hants; 2 s (James b 1979 (Page of Honour to HM the Queen), Charles b 1989), 2 da (Georgina b 1977, Alexandra b 1986); *Career* Capt 14/20 Kings Hussars 1970–78 NI, W Germany, Cyprus, Zaire; The Union Discount Co of London 1979–92 (dir various subsid cos); dir: Scottish Business Achievement Tst 1981–, Aitken Campbell and Co Ltd 1987–, Lothian Racecourse Ltd (Edinburgh) 1987–, Independent Pension Trustees plc 1993–, Christies Scotland Ltd 1994–; memb the Queen's Body Guard for Scotland (The Royal Company of Archers); *Recreations* shooting, fishing, racing; *Clubs* White's; *Style*— David

Bowes-Lyon, Esq, DL; ✉ Heriot Water, Heriot, Midlothian (☎ 01875 835281); work: (☎ 0131 220 3131)

BOWES LYON, Simon Alexander; s of Hon Sir David Bowes Lyon, KCVO (d 1961), and Rachel Pauline, *née* Spender Clay (d 1996); *b* 17 June 1932; *Educ* Eton, Magdalen Coll Oxford; *m* 11 April 1966, Caroline Mary Victoria, er da of Rt Rev Victor Joseph Pike, CB, CBE, MA, DD, Bishop of Sherborne 1959–76; 3 s (Fergus b 1970, David b 1973, Andrew b 1979), 1 da (Rosie (Mrs David Glazebrook) b 1968); *Career* dir Dominion Insurance Co Ltd and other cos incl WRVS Tstees Ltd; Lord Lieut of Hertfordshire 1986–; FCA 1959; *Recreations* shooting, gardening, walking, music; *Clubs* Brooks's; *Style*— Simon Bowes Lyon, Esq; ✉ St Paul's Walden Bury, Hitchin, Herts SG4 8BP (☎ 01438 871218); 12 Morpeth Mansions, London SW1 (☎ 0171 834 8057, fax 01438 871218)

BOWETT, Prof Derek William; CBE (1983), QC (1978); s of Arnold William Bowett (d 1960), of Sale, Cheshire, and Marion, *née* Wood (d 1948); *b* 20 April 1927; *Educ* William Hulme's GS, Downing Coll Cambridge (MA, LLB, PhD, LLD); *m* 29 Dec 1953, Betty, da of William Sidney Northall (d 1983), of Rhyl, N Wales; 2 s (Richard William b 1956, Adam Northall b 1958), 1 da (Louise Marion b 1961); *Career* AB RNVR 1945–47; called to the Bar Middle Temple 1953, bencher 1976; lectr in law Univ of Manchester 1951–59; pres Queens' Coll Cambridge 1970–82 (fell 1960–70 and 1982–); Whewell prof of int law Cambridge 1981–91 (lectr then reader Law Faculty Cambridge Univ 1960–81); former memb Royal Cmmn on Environmental Pollution, memb Int Law Cmmn 1991–, memb UN Int Law Cmmn 1992–96; PhD Manchester; cdr Order of Dannebrog (Denmark) 1993, Grand Cross Order José Cecilio del Valle (Honduras) 1993; FBA 1985; *Books* Self-Defence in International Law (1957), Law of International Institutions (1964), United Nations Forces (1964), Search for Peace (1970), Legal Regime of Islands (1978); *Recreations* music, walking, gardening; *Style*— Prof Derek Bowett, CBE, QC, FBA; ✉ 228 Hills Road, Cambridge CB2 2QE (☎ 01453 210688, fax 01223 414617)

BOWIE, David (*né* David Robert Jones); *b* 8 Jan 1947; *Career* singer; formerly with: The Kon-Rads 1964, The Manish Boys 1964–65, The Lower Third 1965–66, Tin Machine 1989–92 (album Tin Machine 1989, UK no 3); 25 UK top ten singles incl 4 no 1's (Space Oddity 1975, Under Pressure 1981, Let's Dance 1983, Dancing in the Street 1985), 7 US top ten singles incl 2 no 1's (Fame 1975, Let's Dance 1983); solo albums incl: David Bowie (1967), The Man Who Sold the World (1971), Hunky Dory (1971), The Rise and Fall of Ziggy Stardust and the Spiders from Mars (1972, UK no 5), Hunky Dory (1972, UK no 3), Space Oddity (1972, UK no 26), Images 1966–67 (1973), Aladdin Sane (1973, UK no 3), Pin-Ups (1973, UK no 3), Diamond Dogs (1974, UK no 1, US no 5), David Live (1974, UK no 2, US no 8), Young Americans (1975, UK no 2, US no 9), Station to Station (1976, UK no 5, US no 3), Changesonebowie (compilation 1976, UK no 2, US no 10), Low (1977, UK no 2, US no 11), Heroes (1977, UK no 3), Stage (1978, UK no 5), Lodger (1979, UK no 4), Scary Monsters and Super Creeps (1980, UK no 10), The Very Best of David Bowie (1981, UK no 3), Let's Dance (1983, UK no 1, US no 4), Golden Years (compilation 1983, UK no 33), Ziggy Stardust-The Motion Picture (1983, UK no 17), Fame and Fashion (1984, UK no 40), Love You Till Tuesday (1984, UK no 53), Tonight (1984, UK no 1), Absolute Beginners (1986), Never Let Me Down (1987, UK no 6), Sound and Vision (1989), Changesbowie (1990, UK no 1), Black Tie White Noise (1993, UK no 1), Bowie: The Singles Collection (1993), Outside (1995, UK no 8), Earthling (1997); soundtrack for The Buddha of Suburbia (1993); *Awards* Ivor Novello Award (for Space Oddity) 1969, Best Male Singer UK Rock and Pop Awards 1981, Best British Male Artist BRIT Awards 1984, Int Hit of the Year and Best Rock Song (for Let's Dance) Ivor Novello Awards 1984, Best Album Package (for Sound and Vision) Grammy Awards 1990, Q Award (for Inspiration with Brian Eno) 1995, Outstanding Contribution BRIT Award 1996; album prodr for: Iggy Pop, Lou Reed, Mott the Hoople; actor; *Films* The Man Who Fell to Earth, The Hunger, Absolute Beginners, Labyrinth, The Last Temptation of Christ; exhibited installation art Florence Biennale 1996; *Style*— David Bowie, Esq; ✉ c/o Poole Edwards Ltd, Queens House, 180–182 Tottenham Court Road, London W1P 9LE (☎ 0171 436 3633, fax 0171 436 3632)

BOWIE, Rev (Alexander) Glen; CBE (1984); s of Alexander Bowie (d 1983), of Stevenston, Ayrshire, and Annie Robertson, *née* McGhie (d 1977); *b* 10 May 1928; *Educ* Stevenston HS, Irvine Royal Acad, Univ of Glasgow (BSc), Trinity Coll Univ of Glasgow (Dip Theol), Open Univ (BA); *m* 15 March 1952, Mary (d 1991), da of John McKillop (d 1945); 2 da (Alexandra b 8 March 1955, Jenifer b 12 Sept 1960); *Career* ordained minister Church of Scot 1954; inducted into RAF as chaplain 1954, chaplain RAF Henlow 1955, Padgate 1955–56, Akrotiri 1956–59, Stafford 1959–61, Butzweilerhof 1961–64, Halton 1964–67, Akrotiri 1967–70, RAF Coll Cranwell 1970–75, asst princ chaplain 1975, HQ Rheindahlen 1975–76, HQ RAFSC 1976–80, princ Chaplain Church of Scot and Free Churches 1980–84, Hon Chaplain to HM the Queen 1980–84, ret from RAF 1984; ed Scot Forces Bulletin 1985–95, moderator of Presbytery of England 1988–89; hon chaplain Royal Scot Corp 1981–, pres Scot Chaplains' Assoc 1987–88, actg London chaplain to Moderator Church of Scotland 1985–; *Recreations* painting, boating and leading holy land pilgrimages; *Clubs* RAF; *Style*— The Rev Glen Bowie, CBE; ✉ 16 Weir Road, Hemingford Grey, Huntingdon, Cambs PE18 9EH (☎ 01480 381425)

BOWIE, James; s of James Bowie (d 1991), of Leicester, and Olive May, *née* Elcock; *b* 22 Jan 1947; *Educ* Oakham Sch Rutland, Westminster Tech Coll London (HND Hotel Mgmnt); *m* 1, 1972 (m dis), Anne Margaret Stephens; 1 s (James b 15 Nov 1975); m 2, 1988, Susan Elizabeth, *née* Messenger; 1 s (Nicolas Edward b 24 June 1984), 1 da (Rosie Victoria b 27 Jan 1982); *Career* food service trg Hotel Normandie Le Havre 1964, food preparation and service Moëvenpick Zurich 1967, mgmnt trainee Plough & Harrow Birmingham then Vendage Pommerol 1968; Belmont Hotel (family business): joined 1969, gen mangr 1971, md 1975; mangr Hathersage Inn Hathersage; chm: Leicester Hoteliers 1974, 1977 and 1985, Best Western Hotels 1988–90 (memb 1971–); dir Leicester Promotions Ltd 1993; vice chm Leicester Tourism TDAP 1989–92; active in: BHA 1970–, Leicester Assoc of Hotels 1972–; chm Heart of Eng Divnl Ctee BHA 1993–94; FHCIMA 1980, Master Innholder 1986; *Recreations* hunting, eating, drinking, skiing, rugby, tennis; *Style*— James Bowie, Esq; ✉ Belmont House Hotel, Leicester LE1 7GR (☎ 0116 254 4773)

BOWIE, Prof Malcolm McNaughtan; *b* 5 May 1943; *Educ* Woodbridge Sch, Univ of Edinburgh (MA), Univ of Sussex (DPhil), MA Cantab 1969, MA Oxon 1992; *Career* asst lectr in French UEA 1967–69, lectr Univ of Cambridge 1972–76 (asst lectr 1969–72), fell and dir of studies Clare Coll Cambridge 1969–76 (tutor 1971–76); Univ of London: prof of French language and literature 1976–92, head Dept of French QMC 1976–89, fndr dir Inst of Romance Studies 1989–92 (hon sr research fell 1993); Marshal Foch prof of French Literature Univ of Oxford and fell All Souls Coll Oxford 1992–; visiting prof Univ of California at Berkeley 1983, visiting distinguished prof Grad Center City Univ NY 1989, Andrew W Mellon lectr Bucknell Univ 1990, visiting fell Centre for Research in Philosophy and Literature Univ of Warwick 1991; pres: Assoc of Univ Profs of French 1982–84, Soc for French Studies 1994–96; memb Exec Ctee UCML 1994; gen ed French Studies 1980–87, fndr gen ed Cambridge Studies in French 1980–95, ed Jl Inst of Romance Studies 1992; memb Academia Europaea 1989; Chevalier L'Ordre des Palmes Académiques (France) 1987; FBA 1993; *Books* Henri Michaux: a study of his literary works (1973), Mallarmé and the Art of Being Difficult (1978), Freud, Proust and Lacan: theory as fiction (1987), Lacan (1991), Psychoanalysis and the Future of Theory (1993); also author of contribs to learned jls; *Style*— Prof Malcolm Bowie, FBA; ✉ All Souls College, Oxford OX1 4AL (☎ 01865 279379, fax 01865 279299)

BOWIE, Norman Walter; s of Walter Stronach Bowie (d 1950), and Marion Louise, *née* Thomson (d 1956), of Beckenham; *b* 10 Oct 1914; *Educ* Stationers' Co's Sch, Coll of Estate Mgmnt; *m* 1947, Kathleen Cecelia, da of John Augustus Hannigan (d 1965), of Highgate; *Career* served WWII, Local Defence Vol June-Aug 1940, Sapper RE 1941, Maj RE 14 Army SE Asia Cmd until 1946; chartered surveyor; surveyor to Prudential Assurance Co 1934–59, ptnr Jones Lang Wootton chartered surveyors 1959–74 (conslt 1975–89), dir Town and City Properties 1962–73; memb Ctee of Mgmnt The Pension Fund Property Unit Tst 1966–79, dir Es Court 1967–72; property conslt: British Land plc 1974–84, Nat River Authy Superannuation Fund 1974–92, Crown Agents for Overseas Govts and Admins 1976–82; dir Imry Property Holdings 1965–86, chm RICS Assets Valuation Ctee 1973–76, chm Euro Gp of Valuers of Fixed Assets 1977–82, sec Int Assets Valuation Standards Ctee 1981–84, dir London Small Businesses Property Tst 1987–91, property conslt to chief exec Property Services Agency DOE 1982–83 and London Borough of Bromley 1982–84; vice pres Barnardos (memb Cncl 1981–89, chm 1984–87), patron Amateur Rowing Assoc 1977–93 (memb Ctee 1952–61), pres Chiswick Amateur Regatta 1982–94; chm Admin Bd Jones Lang Wootton Travelling Scholarship 1983–89 (memb 1983–94); ed: Statements of Asset Valuation Practice (RICS handbook), Asset Valuation Standards for The Int Assets Valuation Standards Ctee; hon fell Coll of Estate Mgmnt (Property Award 1988), hon memb Property Investment Forum 1990; FRICS; *Recreations* rowing, writing on property investment and valuation; *Clubs* Placemakers; *Style*— Norman Bowie, Esq; ✉ 1 Uplands Close, London SW14 7AS (☎ 0181 876 1434); office: 22 Hanover Square, London W1A 2BN (☎ 0171 493 6040, fax 0171 408 0220)

BOWIS, John Crocket; OBE (1981), MP (C) Battersea (majority 4,840); s of Thomas Palin Bowis (d 1957), of Brighton, and Georgiana Joyce Bowis, *née* Crocket; *b* 2 Aug 1945; *Educ* Tonbridge Sch, BNC Oxford (MA); *m* 1968, Caroline Taylor, of Oxon; 2 s (Duncan b 1972, Alistair b 1978), 1 da (Imogen b 1970); *Career* Cons Central Office 1972–80, public affrs dir Br Insur Brokers' Assoc 1981–86, cncllr Royal Borough of Kingston upon Thames 1982–86 (chm of educn 1984–86); MP (C) Battersea 1987–, memb Select Ctee on Membs Interests 1987–90; PPS to: Min for Inner Cities and Local Govt 1989–90, Sec of State for Wales 1990–93; jt Parly under-sec of state Dept of Health 1993–96, Parly under-sec of state Dept of Transport 1996–; pres Br Youth Cncl 1987–92, vice chm Int Soc for Human Rights 1989–92, chm Nat Cncl for Civil Protection 1990–93, pres Cons Trade Unionists 1990–; *Recreations* theatre, music, art, sport; *Style*— John Bowis, OBE, MP; ✉ House of Commons, London SW1A 0AA (☎ 0171 219 3535/6214, fax 0181 395 7463)

BOWKER, Prof John Westerdale; s of Gordon Westerdale Bowker, and Marguerite, *née* Burdick; *b* 30 July 1935; *Educ* St John's Sch Leatherhead, Worcester Coll Oxford (MA), Ripon Hall Oxford; *m* 1963, Margaret Roper; 1 s; *Career* Nat Serv RWAFF N Nigeria 1953–55; Henry Stephenson res fell Univ of Sheffield and deacon and curate of St Augustine's Brocco Bank 1961–62, fell, dir of studies and dean of chapel CCC Cambridge 1962–74, lectr Faculty of Theology Univ of Cambridge 1965–74, Wilde lectr Univ of Oxford 1972–75, prof of religious studies Univ of Lancaster 1974–85, fell, dir of studies and dean of chapel Trinity Coll Cambridge 1984–94, hon canon of Canterbury 1985–; Gresham prof Gresham Coll 1992–; Staley lectr Rollins Coll Florida 1978–79, public lectr Univ of Cardiff 1984, Riddell lectr Univ of Newcastle and Boutwood lectr Univ of Cambridge 1985, Philippa Harris lectr Ontario Cancer Inst 1986, adjunct prof N Carolina State Univ and Univ of Pennsylvania 1986, CIBA Fndn lectr in religion and embryo res 1986, Boardman lectr Univ of Pennsylvania and Bicentenary lectr Georgetown Univ 1988, Scott Holland lectr Univ of London and Montefiore lecture Univ of Southampton 1989; memb: Durham Cmmn on Religious Educn 1967–70, Root Cmmn on Marriage and Divorce 1967–71, Archbishops' Cmmn on Doctrine 1977–86; conslt Marriage Res Inst 1981; vice pres Culture and Animals Fndn 1986, pres Christian Action AIDS 1986; hon pres Stauros (Euro/American inst concerned with med ethics) 1980; Euro ed Zygon (jl of religion and sci) 1980; contrib numerous and varied documentary progs for BBC and ITV incl: The Nature of Religious Experience, AIDS - the Issues and the Actions, Evil (series awarded Sandford St Martin prize), Places of Poetry and Praise (BBC series), An Alphabet of Faith, The Poetry of Presence; *Books* The Targums and Rabbinic Literature: An Introduction to Jewish Interpretations of Scripture (1969 and 1979), Problems of Suffering in Religions of the World (1970, 3 edn 1990), Jesus and the Pharisees (1973, new edn 1995), The Sense of God: Sociological, Anthropological and Psychological Approaches to the Origin of the Sense of God (1973, 2 edn 1995), The Religious Imagination and the Sense of God (1978), Worlds of Faith: Religious Belief and Practice in Britain Today (1983), The Origins, Functions and Management of Aggression in Biocultural Evolution - Zygon (ed with introduction, 1983), Licensed Insanities: Religions and Belief in God in the Contemporary World (1987), The Meanings of Death (1991, HarperCollins Prize 1993), A Year to Live (1991), Hallowed Ground: The Religious Poetry of Place (1993), Is God a Virus? Genes, Culture and Religion (1995), Voices of Islam (1995), The Oxford Dictionary of World Religions (1997), Beyond Words - Religions and the Poetry of Presence (1997); for children: Uncle Bolpenny Tries Things Out (1973); *Recreations* walking, books, gardening, cooking, painting, poetry; *Style*— Prof John Bowker; ✉ 14 Bowers Croft, Cambridge CB1 4RP

BOWLBY, Sir Richard Peregrine Longstaff; 3 Bt (UK 1923), of Manchester Square, Borough of St Marylebone; s of (Edward) John Mostyn Bowlby, CBE, MD (d 1990), and Ursula, *née* Longstaff; s his uncle, Sir Antony Hugh Mostyn Bowlby, 2 Bt, 1993; *b* 11 Aug 1941; *Educ* Dauntsey's; *m* 27 April 1963, Xenia, o da of Roderick Paul Agnew Garrett, of London N6; 1 s (Benjamin b 1966), 1 da (Sophia b 1969); *Heir* s, Benjamin Bowlby b 2 Nov 1966; *Style*— Sir Richard Bowlby, Bt; ✉ Boundary House, Wyldes Close, London NW11 7JB (☎ 0181 458 8474)

BOWLES, Rt Rev Cyril William Johnston; s of late William C A Bowles, of Scotstoun, Glasgow; *b* 9 May 1916; *Educ* Brentwood Sch, Emmanuel Coll Cambridge, Jesus Coll Cambridge, Ridley Hall Cambridge; *m* 1965, Florence Joan, da of late John Eastaugh, of Windlesham, Surrey; *Career* ordained: deacon 1939, priest 1940; princ Ridley Hall 1951–63, hon canon of Ely Cathedral 1959–63, archdeacon of Swindon Dio of Bristol 1963–69, bishop of Derby 1969–87; president St John's Coll Durham 1970–84 (hon fell 1990–); memb House of Lords 1973–87, hon asst Bishop Dio of Glos 1987–; *Style*— The Rt Rev C W J Bowles; ✉ Rose Lodge, Tewkesbury Rd, Stow-on-the-Wold, Cheltenham, Glos GL54 1EN (☎ 01451 831965)

BOWLES, Godfrey Edward; s of Llewellyn Crowley Bowles (d 1978), of Swindon, Wilts, and Florence Jane, *née* Edwards (d 1946); *b* 21 Dec 1935; *Educ* Commonweal GS Swindon, Univ of Oxford (MA); *m* 9 Aug 1958, Elizabeth Madge, da of Reginald Charles Dunning; 2 s (Michael Edward b 6 Sept 1963, David Insull b 14 Sept 1965), 2 da (Jacqueline Elizabeth (Mrs Trevalyan) b 15 May 1961, Sarah Jane b 1 Dec 1968); *Career* Australian Mutual Provident Society: joined 1959, dep mangr Wellington NZ 1976–80, mangr Western Aust Branch Perth 1980–83, mangr Victoria Branch Melbourne 1983–86, chief mangr Corporate Servs Sydney 1986–88, gen mangr AMP Corporate Sydney 1988–89; md Pearl Group plc Peterborough (following takeover by Australian Mutual Provident Soc) 1989–94; non-exec dir Royal Liver Assurance 1995–; chm: Greater Peterborough Partnership 1995–, Assoc for Spina Bifida and Hydrocephalus 1995–; *Recreations* running, cycling, music, theatre, reading, cinema; *Clubs* Australian

(Melbourne); *Style*— Godfrey Bowles, Esq; ✉ Priory Gardens, Church Road, Ketton, Stamford, Lincs PE9 3RD (☎ and fax 01780 720545)

BOWLES, Hamish Philip; s of David Victor Bowles, of London, and Anne, *née* Burmester; *b* 23 July 1963; *Educ* Simon Langton Boys' GS Canterbury, William Ellis Sch Highgate, St Martin's Sch of Art; *Career* guest fashion ed Teenage Issue Harpers & Queen 1983, London and Paris ed Harpers' Bazaar Australia 1983–84, contributing ed 1983–84 (Harpers & Queen, The Face, Arena, GQ, Vanity Fair); Harpers & Queen: jr fashion ed 1985, fashion dir 1987, style dir 1989–92; style ed American Vogue 1992–; memb The Costume Soc 1976; *Recreations* collecting vintage couture, travel, theatre; *Style*— Hamish Bowles, Esq; ✉ Vogue, Condé Nast Publications Inc, 350 Madison Avenue, New York, NY 10017, USA (☎ 00 1 212 880 8800, fax 00 1 212 880 6878)

BOWLES, Peter John; s of Herbert Reginald Bowles, and Sarah Jane, *née* Harrison; *b* 16 Oct 1936; *Educ* High Pavement GS Nottingham, RADA (scholar, winner Kendal prize); *m* 8 April 1961, Susan Alexandra, da of David Cyril Bennett; 2 s (Guy Rupert b 24 Sept 1962, Adam Peter b 26 Jan 1964); 1 da (Sasha Jane b 12 Oct 1966); *Career* actor; *Theatre* London debut in Romeo and Juliet (Old Vic) 1956; other work incl: Happy Haven and Platonov (Royal Court) 1960, Afternoon Men (Arts Theatre) 1961, Absent Friends (Garrick) 1975, Dirty Linen (Arts Theatre) 1976, Born In the Gardens (Globe) 1980, Some of My Best Friends are Husbands (Haymarket Leicester and nat tour) 1985, The Entertainer (Shaftesbury) 1986, Canaries Sometimes Sing (Albery) 1987, Man of The Moment (Globe) 1990, Otherwise Engaged (nat tour) 1992, Seperate Tables (Albery) 1993, Pygmalion (Chichester) 1994, In Praise of Love (Apollo) 1995, Gangster No1 (Almeida) 1995, Present Laughter (Wyndhams) 1996; *Television* series incl: Rumpole of The Bailey 1976–, To The Manor Born 1979–82, Only When I Laugh 1979–82, The Bounder 1982–83, The Irish RM 1982–84, Lytton's Diary 1984–85 (devised series), Executive Stress 1987–88, Perfect Scoundrels 1989–92 (co-devised series), Running Late (TV film, also co-prodr, winner The Golden Gate Award San Francisco); *Films* incl: Blow Up 1966, The Charge of the Light Brigade 1967, Laughter In The Dark 1968, A Day in the Death of Joe Egg 1970; *Awards* Comedy Actor of the Year Pye Awards 1984, ITV Personality of the Year Variety Club 1984; *Recreations* motoring and physical jerks; *Clubs* Garrick, Chelsea Arts, Groucho; *Style*— Peter Bowles, Esq; ✉ c/o Dennis Selinger, ICM Ltd, Oxford House, 76 Oxford Street, London W1N 0AX (☎ 0171 636 6565, fax 0171 323 0101)

BOWMAN, James Thomas; s of Benjamin and Cecilia Bowman; *b* 6 Nov 1941; *Educ* Ely Cathedral Choir Sch, King's Sch Ely, New Coll Oxford; *Career* counter-tenor; operatic debuts incl: Glyndebourne Festival 1970, Scottish Opera 1971, Royal Opera House Covent Garden 1972, Sydney Opera 1978, Opéra Comique Paris 1979, Theatre du Châtelet Paris 1983, Badisches Staatstheater Karlsruhe 1984, ENO 1985, La Scala Milan 1987; prof of singing Guildhall Sch of Music; pres: Dorking Halls Concertgoers Soc 1994–, The Holst Singers 1995–; patron New Chamber Opera Oxford 1995–; Medal of Honour City of Paris 1992, Officier de l'Ordre des Arts et des Lettres 1995 (Chevalier 1992), Hon DMus Newcastle upon Tyne 1996; *Style*— James Bowman, Esq; ✉ 4 Brownlow Road, Redhill, Surrey RH1 6AW (☎ 01737 767520, fax 01737 779690)

BOWMAN, Sir Jeffery Haverstock; kt (1991); s of Alfred Haverstock Bowman (d 1974), and Doris Gertrude, *née* Beck (d 1983); *b* 3 April 1935; *Educ* Winchester, Trinity Hall Cambridge (MA); *m* 15 June 1963, Susan Claudia, da of Dr Oliver Hays Bostock (d 1982), of Guernsey; 1 s (Mark b 1970), 2 da (Caroline b 1964, Victoria b 1967); *Career* 2 Lt RHG 1953–55; Price Waterhouse: articled 1958–61, mangr 1964, ptnr 1966, memb firm's Policy Ctee 1972–91, dir Technical Servs 1973–76, dir London office 1979–81, sr ptnr 1982–91, chm Price Waterhouse Europe BV 1988–93, jt chm Price Waterhouse World Firm Ltd 1992–93; personal auditor Duchy of Cornwall 1971–93; chm: Masthead Insurance Underwriting plc 1993–, Mid Essex Hosp Servs NHS Trust 1993–; dir Gibbs Mew plc 1995–; memb: Accounting Standards Ctee 1982–87, Cncl ICAEW 1986–90; govr Brentwood Sch 1985–, tstee Royal Botanic Gardens Kew 1995–; Liveryman Worshipful Co of Chartered Accountants; FCA 1962; *Recreations* golf, opera, gardening, sailing; *Clubs* Garrick; *Style*— Sir Jeffery Bowman; ✉ The Old Rectory, Boreham, Chelmsford, Essex CM3 3EP (☎ 01245 467233); Mid Essex Hospitals, Broomfield Court, Pudding Wood Lane, Broomfield, Chelmsford, Essex CM1 7WE (☎ 01245 514563)

BOWMAN, Dr John Christopher; CBE (1986); s of Mark Christopher Bowman (d 1987), of Prestbury, and Clara Vera, *née* Simister; *b* 13 Aug 1933; *Educ* Manchester GS, Univ of Reading (BSc), Univ of Edinburgh (PhD), N Carolina State Univ; *m* 15 July 1961, Sheila Jean, da of James Lorimer (d 1953), of Bramhall; 3 da (Hilary b 1962, Jillian b 1964, Bernadette b 1968); *Career* geneticist rising to chief geneticist Thornber Bros Ltd 1958–66; Univ of Reading: prof of animal prodn (dir of Univ farms) 1966–81, dir Centre for Agric Strategy 1975–81; sec to NERC 1981–89, chief exec Nat Rivers Authy 1989–91, md Halliburton NUS Environmental Ltd 1991–93, environmental conslt 1994–; chm: Sonning Lawn Tennis Club, Sonning Parish Cncl; Hon DSc Cranfield Inst of Technol 1990; FIBiol 1970, FRSA 1976; *Books* Introduction to Animal Breeding, Animals for Man, Future of Beef Production in the EEC (with P Susmel), Hammonds Farm Animals (with J Hammond Jr); *Recreations* gardening, tennis, golf; *Style*— Dr John Bowman, CBE; ✉ Farmhouse, Charvil Lane, Sonning, Reading RG4 6TH (☎ 0118 969 3224)

BOWMAN, Maj-Gen John Francis (Jack); CB (1986); s of Francis Bowman (d 1985), and Gladys Rose Bowman (d 1985); *b* 5 Feb 1927; *Educ* Queen Elizabeth GS Penrith, Hertford Coll Oxford (MA); *m* 1956, Laura, da of John Moore (d 1952); 1 s (John b 1959), 1 da (Tessa b 1961); *Career* RN 1943–48, served Med, Atlantic and Antarctica, Maj-Gen Army; called to the Bar Gray's Inn; dir Army Legal Services 1983–86 (served Africa, Far, Near and Middle East, UK, BAOR); dir Concepts Financial Ltd; life vice pres Army Boxing Assoc; BRCS: memb Cncl 1988–91 and 1992–94, chm Principles and Law Panel 1988–94; *Recreations* sailing, mountain walking, skiing; *Clubs* Royal Naval Sailing Assoc; *Style*— Maj-Gen Jack Bowman, CB; ✉ c/o Midland Bank plc, Newmarket St, Ulverston, Cumbria LA12 7LH

BOWMAN, Sir Paul Humphrey Armytage; 5 Bt (UK 1884), of Holmbury St Mary, Co Surrey; s of Maj Humphrey Ernest Bowman, CMG, CBE (d 1965), and his 1 w Frances Guinevere, *née* Armytage (d 1923); suc his kinsman, Sir John Paget Bowman, 4 Bt, 1994; *b* 10 Aug 1921; *Educ* Eton; *m* 1, 1943 (m dis 1947), Felicité Anne Araminta, da of Sir Harold Alfred MacMichael, GCMG, DSO; m 2, 1947 (m dis 1974), Gabrielle May, formerly w of Lt-Col Walter Currie, US Army; 1 da (Amanda Caroline (Mrs David Levy) b 1947); m 3, 1974, Elizabeth Deirdre (d 1993), yr da of late Bruce R Campbell, of Goorianawa, NSW, and formerly w of Maj-Gen Thomas Bell Lindsay Churchill, CB, CBE, MC; *Heir* cousin, Martin Ramsay Bowman b 1928; *Career* Maj Coldstream Guards; dir Hill Samuel & Co Ltd 1962–78; *Clubs* White's, Royal Corinthian Yacht, The Brook (New York); *Style*— Sir Paul Bowman, Bt; ✉ 3/414 Edgecliff Road, Woollahra, NSW 2025, Australia

BOWMAN, William Archibald; s of Archibald George Bowman (d 1978), of Auchtermuchty, and Eleanor Little, *née* Ratcliff; *b* 30 May 1950; *Educ* George Watson's Coll Edinburgh, Univ of Edinburgh (BCom); *m* 10 April 1973, Helen Macaulay, da of Malcolm Macleod, of Strathkinness; *Career* CA; ptnr KPMG; *Clubs* Royal Northern, University (Aberdeen); *Style*— William A Bowman, Esq; ✉ c/o KPMG, 37 Albyn Place, Aberdeen AB10 1JB (☎ 01224 591000, fax 01224 590909)

BOWMAN, Prof William Cameron; s of John William Bowman (d 1976), of Carlisle, and Esther Reed, *née* Cameron (d 1980); *b* 26 April 1930; *Educ* Univ of London (BPharm, PhD, DSc); *m* 12 Aug 1972, Anne Wyllie, da of Frank Douglas Stafford (d 1968), of Sydney; 1 s (Ewen Cameron), 1 da (Alison); *Career* Nat Serv RAF 1955–57; lectr then reader Univ of London 1952–66; Univ of Strathclyde: prof of pharmacology and head of dept 1966–86 and 1990–94, dean Sch of Pharmaceutical Sciences 1974–77, dep princ then vice princ 1986–90; praelector Med Sch Univ of Dundee 1985, Litchfield lectr Med Sch Univ of Oxford 1986, visiting prof of anaesthesia McGill Univ Montreal 1987, visiting Sterling prof of pharmacology Cornell Univ NY 1989 and Ohio Coll of Med 1991; sec gen Int Union of Pharmacology 1994–98; author of numerous articles on res, served on twelve editorial bds of sci jls (currently on seven); memb: Nomenclature Ctee Br Pharmacopoeia Cmmn 1964–67, Biology Ctee MOD 1966–75, TCT and SEAR Sub Ctees of CSM 1972–82, Biomedical Res Ctee SHHD 1980–85, Physiological Soc, Br Pharmacological Soc, NY Acad of Sciences, Br Toxicological Soc, Scot Soc of Experimental Med; FRPharmS, FRSM, Hon FFARCS 1986, FIBiol, FRSE 1976, FRSA; *Books* ed of several books, author of Textbook of Pharmacology (with M J Rand, 1966, 2 edn 1980), Pharmacology of Neuromuscular Function (1980, 2 edn 1990), Dictionary of Pharmacology (with Anne Bowman and Alison Bowman, 1986); *Style*— Prof William C Bowman, FRSE; ✉ Department of Physiology & Pharmacology, University of Strathclyde, Glasgow G1 1XW (☎ 0141 552 4400, fax 0141 552 2562, telex 77472 UNSLIB G)

BOWMAN, William Powell; CBE (1995, OBE 1972); s of George Edward Bowman (d 1977), and Isobel Conyers Dix (d 1971); *b* 22 Oct 1932; *Educ* Uppingham; *m* 26 April 1956, Patricia Elizabeth, da of Wallace Normand McCoskrie, of Hemel Hempstead, Herts; 2 s (Jonathan b 1957, Edward b 1959); *Career* RAF 1951–53, Royal Aux Air Force 1953–58, Flying Offr (UK); gp personnel dir United Biscuits plc 1977–84 (md Int Div 1966–77); chm: Royds Advertising Group 1984–87, Royds-McCann Advertising 1987–88, Van der Haas BV Holland 1987–89; Trident Tst 1985–94, Occupational Counselling and Unemployment Services Ltd 1986–89, Covent Garden Market Authy 1988–, Br Food and Farming (Bucks Ctee) 1987–89, Flowers and Plants Assoc 1989–, Gibbson Blackthorn Ltd 1989–90, Extel plc 1984–87, Twynam and Fishlock Advertising Ltd 1987–88, Harvey Bergenroth Ptnrs Ltd (mgmnt conslts) 1987–89, Right Assocs Ltd 1989–94; dir Fresh Fruit Produce Assoc 1989–93; tstee London Zoological Devpt Soc Cncl 1986–91, chm St Peter's Tst 1990–92, chm Trident Transnational 1993–94, hon life vice pres Trident Tst 1994–; chm (UK) Euro Catering Assoc 1995–, vice pres Weston Spirit 1995–; hon Stanford Raffles fell; Freeman City of London 1989, memb Guild of Freemen 1989, Hon Asst Worshipful Co of Fruiterers (Liveryman 1990); FZS, FInstD, FInstM, FIPM, FRSA 1989; *Recreations* gardening, tennis, travel; *Clubs* RAF, Mosimann's; *Style*— William P Bowman, Esq, CBE; ✉ The Coach House, Shardeloes, Old Amersham, Bucks HP7 0RL (☎ 01494 724187); Covent Garden Market Authority, Covent House, New Covent Garden Market, London SW8 5NX (☎ 0171 720 2211, fax 0171 622 5307)

BOWMAN-SHAW, Sir (George) Neville; kt (1984); s of George Bowman-Shaw; *b* 4 Oct 1930; *Educ* privately; *m* 1962, Georgina, da of John Blundell; 3 s (Andrew, Justin, Fergus Neville (d 1996)), 1 da (Annabelle); *Career* exec chm Lancer Boss Group 1966–94; chm Lancer Boss subsids: Lancer Boss France 1967–94, Lancer Boss Austria 1966–94, Boss Trucks 1959–94, Lancer Boss International SA Lausanne 1962–94, Boss Engineers 1961–94, Boss France 1968–94, Boss Espana 1984–94, Boss Trucks España 1984–94, Steinbock GmbH Moosburg 1984–94, Tamefire Ltd 1983–94; also chm: Forexia Ltd 1994–, BMH Ltd 1994–, Stephensons BMH Ltd 1994–, Avanti BMH Ltd 1995–, Samuk Ltd 1995–; memb: Design Cncl 1979–84, Br Overseas Trade Bd 1982–85; Liveryman: Worshipful Co of Feltmakers, Worshipful Co of Coachmakers & Coach Harness Makers; *Recreations* shooting, farming, rare breeds and vintage tractors collections; *Clubs* Cavalry & Guards', Buck's; *Style*— Sir Neville Bowman-Shaw; ✉ Toddington Manor, Toddington, Beds LU5 6HJ (☎ 01525 872576)

BOWMONT AND CESSFORD, Marquess of; Charles Robert George Innes-Ker; s and h of 10 Duke of Roxburghe by Lady Jane Grosvenor, da of 5 Duke of Westminster; *b* 18 Feb 1981; *Style*— Marquess of Bowmont and Cessford

BOWN, Christopher Michael; s of Michael John David Bown, of Le Touquet, and Dora Winifred, *née* Horsfall; *b* 25 Aug 1956; *Educ* Haileybury Coll, Queens' Coll Cambridge (exhibitioner), Coll of Law; *m* 17 Oct 1987, Lorna Mary, da of Arthur Southcombe Parker; 2 s (Alexander b 27 April 1989, Dominic b 24 June 1995), 2 da (Sophia b 25 March 1991, Florence b 19 April 1993); *Career* Baker & McKenzie: articled clerk 1979, assoc London 1981–82 and 1984–87, seconded to Frankfurt 1983, ptnr 1987–; *Recreations* sailing; *Style*— Christopher Bown, Esq; ✉ Baker & McKenzie, 100 New Bridge Street, London EC4V 7JA (☎ 0171 919 1000, fax 0171 919 1999)

BOWN, Prof Lalage Jean; OBE (1977); da of Arthur Mervyn Bown, MC (d 1969), of Woolstaston Hall, Shropshire, and Dorothy Ethel, *née* Watson; *b* 1 April 1927; *Educ* Wycombe Abbey, Cheltenham Ladies' Coll, Somerville Coll Oxford (BA, MA); 2 foster da (Taiwo b 1956, Kehinde b 1956); *Career* resident tutor Univ Coll of the Gold Coast (now Univ of Ghana) 1949–55, res tutor Makerere Univ Coll of Uganda 1955–59, tutorial advsr, asst dir and dep dir Extra-Mural Dept Univ of Ibadan Nigeria 1960–66 (assoc prof 1962), dir of extra-mural studies and prof Univ of Zambia 1966–70, prof of adult educn Ahmadu Bello Univ Nigeria 1971–76, prof of adult educn Univ of Lagos 1977–80 (dean of educn 1979–80), dir and titular prof Dept of Adult and Continuing Educn Univ of Glasgow 1981–92 (currently emeritus prof), hon prof Dept of Continuing Educn Univ of Warwick 1992–; author of several academic books, monographs and articles; Cwlth visiting prof Univ of Edinburgh 1974, visiting fell Inst of Devpt Studies Univ of Sussex 1980–81, faculty fell Univ of Southampton 1981, distinguished visiting fell Curtin Univ of Technol Perth Australia 1995; jt sec Int Congress of Africanists 1961–67, sec Int Congress of Univ Adult Educn 1976–81; hon life memb People's Educn Assoc Ghana 1973, hon life memb African Adult Educn Assoc 1976; memb: Bd Int Cncl for Adult Educn 1975–79, Bd Br Cncl 1981–89, Scottish Community Educn Cncl 1982–89, Governing Body Inst of Devpt Studies 1982–91; pres Devpt Studies Assoc 1984–86; vice pres: Nat Union of Townswomen's Guilds 1984–, Workers' Educnl Assoc 1984–95; pres Br Comparative Int Educn Soc 1985–86, hon pres British Assoc for Literacy in Devpt 1992–, memb Bd of Tstees of Nat Museums of Scotland 1987–97, tstee Womankind Worldwide 1988–96, Br memb Cwlth Standing Ctee for Student Mobility and Higher Educn Co-operation 1989–, chair Scottish Museums Cncl 1993–96, memb Cncl Royal Soc of Edinburgh 1995–; William Pearson Tolley Medal Univ of Syracuse 1975; Hon DUniv: Open Univ 1975, Paisley 1993, Stirling 1994; Dr (hc) Edinburgh 1993; Hon FITD 1993, FRSA 1984, FEIS 1990, FRSE 1991; *Recreations* travel, entertaining friends; *Clubs* Royal Over-Seas League; *Style*— Prof Lalage Bown, OBE, FRSE; ✉ International Centre for Education in Development, Department of Continuing Education, University of Warwick, Coventry CV4 7AL (☎ 01203 523829, fax 01203 524223)

BOWN, Prof Stephen Glendening; s of Eric Inston Bown (d 1988), of Bexhill-on-Sea, and Olive Mary Kirkman, *née* Payne; *b* 13 Dec 1944; *Educ* St Dunstan's Coll Catford, Univ of Cambridge (MA, MB BChir, MD), Harvard Univ (AM); *m* 3 April 1982, Sheila Alyson, da of Peter Taylor (d 1991), of Bexhill-on-Sea; 2 da (Philippa Lucy b 1989, Sophie Elizabeth b 1991); *Career* Nat Med Laser Centre UCL Med Sch: dir 1986–, prof of laser med and surgery 1990–; conslt physician UCL Hosps NHS Tst 1987–; past pres Br Med Laser Assoc; over 200 sci pubns on med applications of lasers, past ed Lasers in Medical Science; Freeman City of London 1982; memb: Br Soc of Gastroenterology 1977, BMA 1974; MRCP 1974, FRCP 1991; *Recreations* squash, travel; *Style*— Prof Stephen Bown; ✉ 10 Watling St, St Albans, Herts AL1 2PX (☎ 01727 833701); National Medical Laser Centre, Department of Surgery, The Institute of Surgical Studies, Charles

Bell House, 67–73 Riding House Street, London W1P 7LD (☎ 0171 380 9917, fax 0171 813 2828)

BOWNESS, Sir Alan; kt (1988), CBE (1976); er s of George Bowness (d 1951), and Kathleen, *née* Benton (d 1973); *b* 11 Jan 1928; *Educ* Univ Coll Sch Hampstead, Downing Coll Cambridge (MA), Courtauld Inst of Art Univ of London; *m* 1957, Sarah, da of Ben Nicholson, OM (d 1982), the painter, and Dame Barbara Hepworth, DBE (d 1975), the sculptor; 1 s (Paul), 1 da (Sophie); *Career* reg arts offr Arts Cncl of GB 1955–57; Courtauld Inst of Art London: lectr 1957–67, reader 1967–78, prof of history of art and dep dir 1978–79; dir Tate Gallery 1980–88, dir Henry Moore Fndn 1988–94 (tstee 1984–88 and 1994–); Arts Cncl: memb 1973–75 and 1978–80, memb Art Panel 1960–80 (chm 1978–80), memb Arts Film Ctee 1968–77 (chm 1972–75); memb: Fine Arts Ctee Br Cncl 1960–69 and 1970–92 (chm 1981–92), Exec Ctee Contemporary Art Soc 1961–69 and 1970–86, Cncl RCA 1978–; govr Chelsea Sch of Art 1965–93, hon sec Assoc of Art Historians 1973–76, dir Barbara Hepworth Museum St Ives Cornwall 1976–88; tstee: Yorkshire Sculpture Park 1979, Handel House Museum 1994–; Hon DLitt: Univ of Liverpool 1989, Univ of Leeds 1995, Univ of Exeter 1996; hon fell: Bristol Poly 1980, RCA 1984, Courtauld Inst 1986, RIBA 1994; Chevalier de l'Ordre des Arts et des Lettres (France) 1973; *Books* William Scott Paintings (1964), Impressionists and Post Impressionists (1965); (ed) Henry Moore: Complete Sculpture 1955–64 (vol 3, 1965), 1964–73 (vol 5, 1977), 1974–80 (vol 4, 1983), 1949–54 (vol 2, 1987), 1980–86 (vol 6, 1988); Modern Sculpture (1965), Barbara Hepworth Drawings (1966), Alan Davie (1967), Recent British Paintings (1968), Gauguin (1971), Barbara Hepworth: Complete Sculpture 1960–70 (1971), Modern European Art (1972), Ivon Hitchens (1973), The Conditions of Success (1989), Bernard Meadows Sculpture (1995); contrib: Picasso 1881–1973 (ed R Penrose, 1973), The Genius of British Painting (ed D Piper, 1975); *Clubs* Athenaeum; *Style*— Sir Alan Bowness, CBE; ✉ 91 Castelnau, London SW13 9EL (☎ 0181 846 8520)

BOWNESS, Baron (Life Peer UK 1995), of Warlingham in the County of Surrey and of Croydon in the London Borough of Croydon; Sir Peter Spencer Bowness; kt (1987), CBE (1981), DL (Greater London 1982); s of Hubert Spencer Bowness (d 1981), of Cardiff, and Doreen (Peggy) Blundell, *née* Davies; *b* 19 May 1943; *Educ* Whitgift Sch Croydon; *m* 1, 27 July 1969 (m dis 1983), Marianne, da of Robert Hall, of Croydon; 1 da (Hon Caroline b 1978); m 2, 6 June 1984, Mrs Patricia Jane Cook, da of John Cullis, of Abergavenny; *Career* slr; ptnr Weightman Sadler Solicitors Purley 1970–; ldr Croydon Cncl 1976–79 and 1980–94, ldr Opposition Croydon Cncl 1994–, chm London Boroughs Assoc 1978–94, dep chm Assoc of Metropolitan Authorities 1978–80; memb: Audit Cmmn England & Wales 1983–, London Residuary Body 1985–93, Nat Trg Task Force 1989–92, Congress (formerly Standing Conf) of Local and Regnl Authys of Europe (Cncl of Europe) 1990–, UK Delgn Ctee of Regions Euro Union 1993–, Bureau COR 1993–; memb Bd London First/London Forum 1993–94; govr Whitgift Fndn; Freeman City of London 1987; Hon Col 151 (Greater London) Tport Regt (V) 1988–93; *Recreations* gardening, theatre; *Style*— The Rt Hon Lord Bowness, CBE, DL; ✉ Weightman Sadler, 1/2 The Exchange, Purley Road, Purley, Surrey CR2 2YY (☎ 0181 660 6455)

BOWRAN, Peter Anthony Graham (Tony); s of James Eric Bowran, of Heswall, Wirral, Merseyside, and Charlotte, *née* Peacock (d 1981); *b* 23 Aug 1953; *Educ* Calday Grange GS, London Coll of Printing; *partner* Linda Rosena Peryer; *Career* advertising photographer; early career experience as asst to various photographers 1976–78, work commissioned by advertising agencies; recent campaign work incl: TSB Bank campaign 1990, Burton campaign 1991, IBM campaign 1992, Cotton Cncl int campaign 1992, Philip Morris/Marlboro Reds campaign 1992, SIP Italy campaign 1993, AT&T Pan Asian campaign 1994; other cmmns for: Dunhill, Crookes Healthcare, Chesterfield Cigarettes, London Transport, Smirnoff, Peugeot; numerous D&AD, Creative Circle, Clio, Communication Arts and One Show awards and commendations; AFAEP awards incl: Gold, Silver and Merit 1991, Silver 1993; memb Assoc of Photographers (AFAEP); *fencing achievements* fenced for London 1991, 1994 and 1995, fenced for GB in the Fedn Int Escrime A Grade (sponsored by Martini) 1991, 1992 and 1994, memb Épée Weapon Ctee; *Clubs* Lansdowne Fencing (ctee memb), Haverstock Fencing Épée Club; *Style*— Tony Bowran, Esq; ✉ 5 Wandon Road, London SW6 2JF (☎ 0171 731 2689); studio: Studio 12, 39 Tadema Road, Chelsea, London SW10 (☎ 0171 351 3357)

BOWRING, Clive John; s of George Edward Bowring, of Guernsey, and Kathleen Elma (Jane), *née* Tyte (d 1993); *b* 1 Sept 1937; *Educ* Rugby; *Career* Nat Serv RN 1956–58; C T Bowring & Co Ltd 1958–80 (dir C T Bowring (Insurance) Holdings Ltd 1976); dir Robert Fleming Insurance Brokers Ltd 1980– (chm 1996–); chm: Robert Fleming Insurance Brokers (UK) Ltd, Robert Fleming Benefit Consultants Ltd; dir: Robert Fleming Marine Ltd, Robert Fleming Pension Trust Ltd, Robert Fleming Fox Craig Ltd, New Hurlingham Court Ltd; Freeman City of London 1984, Liveryman Worshipful Co of Insurers 1984; memb Lloyd's; *Recreations* sailing; *Clubs* City of London, Royal Ocean Racing, The Hurlingham, Poole Yacht; *Style*— Clive Bowring, Esq; ✉ Robert Fleming Insurance Brokers Ltd, Staple Hall, Stone House Court, London EC3A 7AX (☎ 0171 621 1263, fax 0171 623 6175)

BOWRING, Debra Louise (formerly Compton, Peter John); changed name by Deed Poll 1991; s of John Matthew Bowring Compton (d 1967), of Leigh-on-Sea, Essex, and Amy Gwendoline Lucas (d 1968); *b* 26 June 1938; *Educ* Belfairs HS Leigh-on-Sea Essex; *m* 25 May 1968 (m dis 1987), Mary Elisabeth, da of late Hubert William Jones, of Rayleigh, Essex; 3 da (Nicola b 1969, Stephanie b 1971, Andrea b 1973); *Career* film and sound editor and producer; asst Br Movietone News 1955, prodr and dir The Story of Torfaen for Pontypool (Gwent) Museum; co author screenplay and co prodr Goldie 1990, prodr and dir documentaries 1990, ed TV drama series Gateway for Cannes Prodns Finland 1991; currently working on autobiography; TV work incl The Sweeney; films incl: The Killing Fields, Brazil, White City, A Room with a View; memb BAFTA 1975, MBKS 1985; *Recreations* athletics, photography, theatre; *Style*— Ms Debra Bowring; ✉ 3 Upper Waun Street, Blaenavon, Torfaen, South Wales NP4 9QF

BOWRING, Edgar Rennie Harvey; MC (1945); yst s of Arthur Bowring (d 1960), of Goudhurst, Kent, and Margaret Harvey, *née* Beakbane (d 1944); *b* 5 Nov 1915; *Educ* Eastbourne Coll, Clare Coll Cambridge (MA), Berkeley Coll Yale (Mellon fell), Law Soc Sch of Law; *m* 6 April 1940, Margaret (Peggy) Grace, da of John Grant Brook (d 1938), of Goudhurst, Kent; 2 s (Anthony b 1941, Philip b 1942), 1 da (Clare b 1959); *Career* cmmnd Kent Yeo RA 1939, served Iceland 1940–42, Capt 1941, served UK 1942–44, Maj 1942, served France and Germany 1944–45 (despatches 1944), demobbed 1946, Actg Lt-Col; admitted slr 1949; ptnr Cripps Harries Hall 1950–55; dir C T Bowring & Co (Insurance) Ltd 1960 (joined 1956), chm and chief exec C T Bowring & Co Ltd 1973–78 (dir 1962), former chm C T Bowring (Insurance) Holdings Ltd (dep chm 1966–73); chm: English and American Insurance Co Ltd 1965–71, Bowmaker Ltd, Crusader Insurance Co Ltd and other cos 1973–77; dir Marsh & McLennan Cos Inc New York USA 1980–88 (advsy dir 1988–95); vice pres Corp of Insur Brokers 1970–77, pres Insurance Inst of London 1971–72 (dep pres 1970–71), chm City Ctee for Electoral Reform 1978–81, memb IBRC 1979–81; Cmdt W Kent Special Constabulary 1965–71; tstee Memorial Univ of Newfoundland Harlow Campus 1977–; FIMgt 1970; *Recreations* golf, gardening; *Clubs* City Univ, Rye Golf, Piltdown Golf; *Style*— Edgar Bowring, Esq, MC; ✉ Leopards Mill, Horam, Heathfield, East Sussex TN21 OPD (☎ 01435 812687)

BOWRING, Maj-Gen John Humphrey Stephen; CB (1968), OBE (1958), MC (1941); s of Maj Francis Stephen Bowring (ka 1915), and Helen Jessie, *née* McNabb (d 1945); *b* 13 Feb 1913; *Educ* Downside, RMA Woolwich, Trinity Coll Cambridge (MA); *m* 20 Oct 1956, Iona Margaret, da of Lenox Biggar Murray, OBE (d 1963), of Painswick Lodge, Painswick, Glos; 2 s (Charles b 1957, Michael b 1961), 2 da (Caroline (twin) b 1957, Camilla b 1959); *Career* 2 Lt RE 1933; served: Palestine 1936, India 1937–40; WWII: ME, India, Burma; BMM Greece 1947–49; GSO I Cabinet Offices 1949–51, CRE 17 Gurkha Div Malaya and Cmdt Gurkha Engrs 1956–58, chief engr Farelf (Brig) 1961–64, Brig GS MOD 1964–65 (Col 1959–60), engr in chief (Army) 1965–68 (Maj-Gen), Col Gurkha Engrs 1966–71, Col Cmdt RE 1968–73; dir: Consolidated Gold Fields 1969–82, Amey Roadstone Corp 1971–82; High Sheriff Wilts 1984; FICE 1965; Knight Sovereign Mil Order of Malta 1986; *Recreations* sailing, flying, riding; *Clubs* Army & Navy, Royal Ocean Racing; *Style*— Maj-Gen J H S Bowring, CB, OBE, MC; ✉ 4 The Manor, Coln St Aldwyns, Cirencester, Glos GL7 5AG (☎ 01285 750492)

BOWRING, Rev Lyndon; s of Arthur Bowing, of Caerphilly, Mid Glam, and Ellen May, *née* Gardner; *b* 15 Feb 1948; *Educ* Caerphilly GS, London Bible Coll; *m* 25 May 1974, Celia Joan, da of Capt Edward Ernest Bartholomew (d 1983), of Shoreham-by-Sea; 2 s (Daniel Alexander, Andrew Gareth), 1 da (Emma Charlotte); *Career* Elim pentecostal minister Kensington Temple 1972–80, chm NFOL 1981–83, exec chm CARE 1983–; vice chm: Luis Palau's Mission 1984, Billy Graham's Mission 1989; chm Maranatha Christian Tst, dir London and Nationwide Missions; public speaker; *Recreations* family, reading, walking, gardening, exploring London; *Style*— The Rev Lyndon Bowring; ✉ 22 Thornton Ave, Chiswick, London W4 (☎ 0181 747 3796); CARE, 53 Romney St, London SW1 (☎ 0171 233 0455, fax 017 233 0983)

BOWRING, Peter; CBE (1993); eld s of Frederick Clive Bowring (d 1965), and Agnes Walker, *née* Cairns (d 1961); *b* 22 April 1923; *Educ* Shrewsbury; *m* 1, 1946 (m dis), Barbara Ekaterina Brewis; 1 s (Antony), 1 da (Thérèsa); m 2, 1979 (m dis), Carol Hutchings; m 3, 1986, Carole M Dear; *Career* served WWII 1941–46, cmmnd Rifle Brigade 1942, served Egypt, N Africa, Italy, Austria (despatches); C T Bowring & Co Ltd: joined 1947, dir 1956–84, dep chm 1973–78, chm 1978–82; chm: C T Bowring Trading (Holdings) Ltd 1967–84, Bowmaker Plant Ltd 1972–83, Bowring Steamship Co Ltd 1974–82, Bowmaker Ltd 1978–82, C T Bowring UK Ltd 1980–84; vice chm Marsh & McLennan 1982–84 (dir 1980–84); memb Lloyd's 1968–; dir: Centre for Policy Studies 1983–88, Ind Primary and Secdy Educn Tst 1986–; pres Help the Aged 1988– (chm 1977–87); chm: Aldeburgh Fndn 1982–89, City Arts Tst 1987–94 (dep chm 1986–87), Inter-Action Social Enterprise Tst Ltd 1989–91, Bd of Govrs St Dunstan's Educnl Fndn 1977–90 (govr 1974–95); memb Bd of Govrs Shrewsbury Sch 1969–; tstee: Wakefield (Tower Hill, Trinity Square) Tst 1986–, Ironbridge Gorge Museum Devpt Tst 1989–93 (companion 1993), Upper Severn Navigation Tst 1989–, Third Age Challenge Tst 1991–; memb Guild of Freemen of City of London, Liveryman Worshipful Co of Insurers, Master Co of World Traders 1989–90 (sr warden 1988–89); FRSA, FInstD; *Recreations* sailing, motoring, listening to music, cooking, photography; *Clubs* Royal Thames Yacht, Royal Green Jackets, Little Ship; *Style*— Peter Bowring, Esq, CBE; ✉ 79 New Concordia Wharf, Mill St, London SE1 2BA (☎ 0171 237 0818)

BOWRING, Prof Richard John; s of Richard Arthur Bowring (d 1987), and Mabel, *née* Eddy; *b* 6 Feb 1947; *Educ* Blundell's, Downing Coll Cambridge (BA, PhD); *m* 30 Jan 1970, Susan, da of Wilfred Raymond Povey, of Stoke-on-Trent; 1 da (Imogen Clare b 17 May 1977); *Career* mgmnt trainee Cathay Pacific Airways 1968–70, lectr in Japanese Monash Univ Melbourne Aust 1976–78, asst prof of Japanese Columbia Univ NY USA 1978–79, assoc prof of Japanese Princeton Univ New Jersey USA 1979–84, prof of modern Japanese studies and fell Downing Coll Cambridge 1985– (lectr in Japanese 1984), readership British Acad 1995–97; tstee Cambridge Fndn 1989–, advsr to UFC 1991–92, Crown rep Governing Body SOAS 1994–; *Books* Mori Ogai and the Modernisation of Japanese Culture (1979), Murasaki Shikibu: Her Diary and Poetic Memoirs (1982), Murasaki Shikibu: The Tale of Genji (1988), Introduction to Modern Japanese (1992), Cambridge Encyclopedia of Japan (1993), The Diary of Lady Murasaki (1996); *Style*— Prof Richard Bowring; ✉ Faculty of Oriental Studies, University of Cambridge, Sidgwick Ave, Cambridge CB3 9DA (☎ 01223 335100, fax 01223 335110)

BOWRON, John Lewis; CBE (1986); s of John Henry Bowron (d 1944), and Lavinia, *née* Prosser (d 1967); *b* 1 Feb 1924; *Educ* Grangefield GS Stockton on Tees, King's Coll London (LLB); *m* 19 Aug 1950, Patricia, da of Arthur Cobby (d 1959), of Worthing; 2 da (Judith b 1952, Margaret b 1956); *Career* RAF 1943–46; slr 1950; sr ptnr Malcolm Wilson & Cobby (Worthing) 1964–74 (ptnr 1952–64); sec gen Law Soc 1974–87 (memb Cncl 1969–74), legal assessor to Insur Brokers' Registration Cncl Disciplinary Ctee 1987–89, pt/t chm Social Security Appeal Tbnl 1988–, pt/t agent Crown Prosecution Serv 1988–93; fell King's Coll London 1976; *Recreations* golf, listening to music; *Style*— John Bowron, Esq; ✉ Hurworth, Sanctuary Lane, Storrington, Pulborough, W Sussex RH20 3JD (☎ 01903 746949)

BOWSER OF ARGATY AND THE KING'S LUNDIES, David Stewart; JP (Perthshire 1956); s of Maj David Charles Bowser, CBE, (d 1979), and Maysie Murray, *née* Henderson (d 1974); in direct descent from William Bowser of Wharram le Street, Yorkshire, who lived in the mid 15 century; *b* 11 March 1926; *Educ* Harrow, Trinity Coll Cambridge (BA); *m* 1951, Judith, da of Col Sir John Gordon Crabbe, OBE, MC (d 1961), of Duncow, Dumfries; 1 s (Niall), 4 da (Emma, Susan, Fiona, Anna); *Career* Capt Scots Guards 1944–47; forestry cmmr 1974–82, tstee Scottish Forestry Tst 1983–89 (chm 1987–88); chm Scot Cncl The Br Deer Soc 1988–94, vice chm Assoc of Deer Mgmnt Gps 1995–; memb Queen's Body Guard for Scotland (Royal Company of Archers); elder Killin and Ardeonaig Parish Church, convener Property Ctee of the Presbytery of Stirling; *Recreations* shooting, fishing, stalking; *Style*— David Bowser, Esq, JP; ✉ Auchlyne, Killin, Perthshire FK21 8RG (☎ 01567 820506)

BOWSHER, Dr David Richard; s of Reginald William George Bowsher (d 1971), of Bishop's Cleeve, Glos, and Marion, *née* Scott (d 1966); *b* 23 Feb 1925; *Educ* Haileybury, Gonville and Caius Coll Cambridge (MA, MD), UCH, Univ of Liverpool (PhD), Harvard Med Sch Boston USA; *m* 1, 1952 (m dis 1959), (Anna) Meryl, *née* Reid; 1 s (Julian Michael Charles b 1953); m 2, 1 April 1969, Doreen, da of Laurence Arthur (d 1971); *Career* Cncl of Europe res fell: Oslo and Leyden 1958, Uppsala 1970; Royal Soc Euro fell: Paris 1968–69, Marseilles 1974; reader and hon conslt neurologist Faculty of Med Univ of Liverpool 1972–90 (res fell 1952–54, asst lectr 1954–56, lectr 1956–64, sr lectr 1964–72); professeur associé Faculté des Sciences: de Paris 1963–64, de Marseille 1986; currently dir of res and hon conslt neurologist Pain Res Inst and tstee Pain Relief Fndn; former pres: Br and Irish Chapter Int Assoc for the Study of Pain, North of England Neurological Assoc, Liverpool Div BMA; pres Burke and Hare Soc, Neuroscience ed Clinical Anatomy, former chm Merseyside and N Wales Pain Gp; author of over 200 articles in med and scientific jls; memb: Physiological Soc, Assoc des Physiologistes de Langue Française, Brain Res Assoc; FRCPEd, FRCPath; *Books* Cerebrospinal Fluid Dynamics in Health and Disease (1960), Mechanisms of Nervous Disorder: An Introduction (1978), Introduction to the Anatomy and Physiology of the Nervous System (5 edn, 1988), Pain: Management and Control in Physiotherapy (jtly, 1988), Neurological Emergencies in Medical Practice (1988), Pain Control in Nursing Practice (jtly, 1994); *Recreations* walking, language and languages, opera and music, history, uxoriousness; *Style*— Dr David Bowsher; ✉ Pain Research Institute, Walton Hospital, Liverpool L9 1AE (☎ 0151 523 1486, fax 0151 521 6155)

BOWSHER, His Hon Judge; Peter Charles; QC (1978); s of Charles Bowsher, and Ellen Bowsher; *b* 9 Feb 1935; *Educ* Ardingly, Oriel Coll Oxford (MA); *m* 1960, Deborah, da of Frederick Wilkins, of Vancouver; 2 s; *Career* cmmnd RA 1954; called to the Bar Middle Temple 1959, bencher 1985; recorder (SE Circuit) 1983–87, official referee and circuit judge (SE Circuit) 1987–; memb: Cncl Soc for Computers and Law 1990–95, Judicial Ctee Acad of Experts 1992–; FCIArb 1990; *Recreations* music, photography; *Clubs* Brooks's, RAC; *Style*— His Hon Judge Bowsher, QC; ✉ Royal Courts of Justice, Strand, London WC2A 2LL

BOWTELL, Ann Elizabeth; *née* Kewell; CB (1989); da of John Albert Kewell, of Hove, and Olive Rose, *née* Sims; *b* 25 April 1938; *Educ* Kendrick Girls' Sch Reading, Girton Coll Cambridge (BA); *m* 11 Feb 1961, Michael John Bowtell, s of Norman Bowtell; 2 s (Thomas, Samuel), 2 da (Sophie, Harriet); *Career* asst princ Nat Assistance Bd 1960–64; DHSS: princ 1964–73, asst sec 1973–80, under sec 1980–86, dep sec 1986–88; DSS 1988–90, princ estab and fin offr Dept of Health 1990–93 (on secondment), first civil serv cmmr Cabinet Office 1993–95, dep then perm sec DSS 1995–; memb Mgmnt Ctee Civil Serv Healthcare, tstee Windsor Leadership Tst; Hon DUniv Middx; FRSA; *Recreations* walking, bird watching, classical music; *Style*— Mrs Ann Bowtell, CB; ✉ Permanent Secretary, DSS, Richmond House, 79 Whitehall, London SW1A 2NS (☎ 0171 238 0701)

BOWYER, (Arthur) David; s of Sir Eric Blacklock Bowyer, KCB, KBE (d 1964), and Elizabeth Crane, *née* Nicholls (who m 2, Sir Sidney Caine, KCMG (d 1991), and d 1996); *b* 27 Aug 1940; *Educ* Tonbridge, Trinity Hall Cambridge (BA); *m* 6 Dec 1969, Ann Victoria, da of His Hon Herbert Christopher Beaumont, MBE, *qv*, of Minskip Lodge, Minskip, Boroughbridge, Yorks; 2 s (Edward Christopher b 1972, Andrew Mark b 1975), 1 da (Katharine Sarah b 1971); *Career* admitted slr 1965; ptnr Clifford Chance (formerly Clifford-Turner) 1968–91, ptnr Withers 1991–; memb: Law Society 1976, Int Acad of Estate and Tst Law (USA); *Recreations* skiing, golf, tennis, shooting; *Clubs* Boodle's, Huntercombe Golf; *Style*— David Bowyer, Esq; ✉ Ashe Warren House, Ashe Warren, Overton, Basingstoke, Hants RG25 3AW (☎ 01256 770215); Withers, 12 Gough Square, London EC4A 3DE (☎ 0171 936 1000)

BOWYER, (Arthur) William; s of Arthur Bowyer (d 1979), of Leek, Staffs, and Emma Bowyer (d 1983); *b* 25 May 1926; *Educ* Burslem Sch of Art, Royal Coll of Art (ARCA); *m* Vera Mary, da of William Norman Small (d 1986); 2 s (Francis David b 1951, Jason Richard b 1957), 1 da (Emma Jane b 1966); *Career* painter; Bevin Boy Sneyd Colliery Burslem 1942–44; teacher: Gravesend Sch of Art, Central Sch of Art, Walthamstow Sch of Art; Sir John Cass head of fine art Maidstone Coll of Art 1971–81, ret to paint; work in collections: Royal Acad, Royal Soc of Painters in Watercolour, Nat Portrait Gallery, Graves Gallery Sheffield, Arts Cncl of GB, many private collections; hon sec New English Art Club; RA 1981 (ARA 1974), RP, RBA, RWS; *Recreations* cricket, swimming; *Clubs* Arts; *Style*— William Bowyer, Esq, RA; ✉ 12 Cleveland Avenue, Chiswick, London W4 (☎ 0181 994 0346); Studio, 8 Gainsborough Rd, Chiswick, London W4

BOWYER-SMYTH, Sir Thomas Weyland; 15 Bt (E 1661), of Hill Hall, Essex; s of Capt Sir Philip Weyland Bowyer-Smyth, 14 Bt, RN (d 1978); *b* 25 June 1960; *m* 14 Aug 1992, Sara Louise, *née* Breinlinger; *Heir* kinsman, John Jeremy Windham, *qv*; *Style*— Sir Thomas Bowyer-Smyth, Bt

BOX, John Allan Hyatt; s of Allan Cyril Box (d 1974), of Sri Lanka, Ceylon and London, and Albertha, *née* Storey (d 1930); *b* 27 Jan 1920; *Educ* Sri Lanka, Lime House Sch Wetheral Carlisle, Highgate Sch London, Northern Poly Sch of Architecture (RIBA); *m* 1, 1944, Barbara Courtenay, *née* Linton; m 2, 1953, Doris, da of Thomas Lee; 2 da (Susan b 28 Dec 1955, Deborah b 3 July 1959); *Career* film production designer; served WWII RAC and RTR 1940–46, Maj (despatches 1944); entered film indust 1948; BAFTA Award for Special Contribution fo Film Making 1991; RDI 1992, FRSA 1993; *Film Credits* as prodn designer incl: The Million Pound Note (dir Ronald Neame) 1954, The Inn of the Sixth Happiness (dir Mark Robson) 1958, Our Man in Havana (dir Carol Reed) 1959, The World of Suzie Wong (dir Richard Quine) 1960, Lawrence of Arabia (dir David Lean, Oscar) 1962, Doctor Zhivago (dir David Lean, Oscar) 1965, A Man for All Seasons (dir Fred Zinnermann, BAFTA Award) 1966, Oliver! (dir Carol Reed, Oscar) 1968, Nicholas and Alexandra (dir Franklin Schaffner, Oscar) 1971, Travels with my Aunt (dir George Cukor, nominated Oscar) 1972, The Great Gatsby (dir Jack Clayton, BAFTA Award) 1974, Rollerball (dir Norman Jewison, BAFTA Award) 1975, The Keep (dir Michael Mann) 1983, A Passage to India (dir David Lean, nominated Oscar) 1984, Black Beauty (dir Caroline Thompson) 1995, The First Knight (dir Jerry Zucker) 1995, Farewell to the Barbarians (dir Robert Gardner) 1995; as prodr: The Looking Glass War (written by John Le Carré, dir Frank R Pierson) 1969; *Recreations* painting, visiting art galleries and exhibitions, interested in most sports, particularly cricket and rugby; *Style*— John Box, Esq; ✉ c/o William Morris (UK) Agency, 31–32 Soho Square, London W1V 5DG (☎ 0171 434 2191)

BOX, Stephen John; s of Ronald Tully Box (d 1981), and Mollie Rita, *née* Clarke; *b* 13 Sept 1950; *Educ* Ardingly Coll; *m* 25 April 1992, Christine Elisabeth, da of Robert Beevers (d 1989), of Rockhampton, Qld, Australia; *Career* CA; articled clerk Hilton Sharp & Clarke 1967–71; Coopers & Lybrand: senior 1971–73, mangr 1973–82, ptnr 1982–; FCA 1971; *Recreations* opera, theatre, travel, gardening, bridge, reading, swimming; *Style*— Stephen Box, Esq; ✉ Coopers & Lybrand, 1 Embankment Place, London WC2N 6NN (☎ 0171 213 1005, fax 0171 213 1330)

BOX, Stephen Thomas; s of Thomas George, of Nuneaton, and Edith Helen, *née* Reid; *Educ* Queen Elizabeth GS Atherstone, Univ of Salford (BSc), Physical Electronics City Business Sch (DipBA); *m* 8 Jan 1988 (m dis 1995), Sarah, da of Dennis Grimwood Roscow; 2 da (Daisy Philippa b 24 Aug 1988, Imogen Poppy b 9 Aug 1990); *Career* sci offr AERE Harwell 1968–74, computer conslt CSI Ltd 1974–76, systems analyst Chase Manhattan Bank 1976–78, head int systems devpt Citicorp 1978–80, freelance mgmnt conslt 1980–86, dir debt securities ops Kleinwort Benson Ltd 1987–89, mgmnt conslt and corp financier Stephen Box & Co 1989–90, co-fndr and dir Blue Skies Corporation plc 1990–94, dir UNIVEST Project Development Ltd 1995–; *Recreations* shooting, tennis, golf, music, opera; *Style*— Stephen Box, Esq; ✉ The Oasthouse, Petham Court, Swanley, Kent BR8 8DL (☎ 01322 665925, fax 01322 613238)

BOXER, Arabella; *see:* Stuart, Lady Arabella

BOXER, Prof David Howell; s of William H S Boxer, of Aberdare, and Sarah, *née* Davies; *b* 11 June 1947; *Educ* Aberdare Boys' GS, Univ of Bristol (Univ scholar, Lord Kitchener Nat Meml Fund scholar, BSc, PhD, CertEd); *m* Dr Maureen Boxer, da of Matthew McGuckin; 1 s (Iain b 6 Oct 1983); *Career* Univ of Dundee: Nuffield Fndn sci res fell 1982–83, head Dept of Biochemistry 1988–93, personal chair 1991, currently prof of microbial biochemistry, dean Science and Engrg Faculty 1994–; memb SERC: Molecular Recognition Initiative Ctee 1989–93, Biochemistry and Biophysics Sub Ctee (chm 1991–93); external examiner: Univ of Stirling 1992–, Univ of Edinburgh 1992–, Univ of Newcastle 1993–, Univ of Sheffield 1994–; ed: Molecular Microbiology 1986–91, Biochemical Jl 1989–90, Methods in Microbiology 1991–; author of numerous pubns in scientific jls, regular invited speaker at Univs and int meetings; memb: Biochemical Soc 1974–, Soc for General Microbiology 1980–, British Biophysical Soc 1980–, American Soc for Microbiology 1981–, Inorganic Biochemistry Discussion Gp 1983–, American Chemical Soc 1990–; *Recreations* walking, cycling, skiing; *Style*— Prof David Boxer; ✉ Department of Biochemistry, Medical Sciences Institute, University of Dundee, Dundee DD1 4HN (☎ 01382 344834, fax 01382 322558)

BOXER, Stephen Stanley; s of Alfred Henry Boxer, of Mosterton, Dorset, and Muriel Dorothy Elizabeth, *née* Page; *b* 19 May 1950; *Educ* Magdalen Coll Sch Oxford, Rose Bruford Coll of Speech and Drama; *m* 9 May 1993, Tamsin Oglesby; 1 s (Finn Gabriel b 21 January 1996); *Career* actor; Nat Youth Theatre 1966–68; composer of many pieces for theatre and radio; *Theatre* incl: The Brothers Karamazov (Fortune Edinburgh and Soviet Union) 1981, The Devil and the Good Lord (Lyric Hammersmith) 1984, The Cocktail Party (Phoenix) 1986, Portraits (Savoy) 1987, Rousseau's Tale 1991, Measure for Measure (Lyric Hammersmith) 1994, The Clearing (Bush (Best Actor London Fringe Awards 1994)); RSC: The Duchess of Malfi 1990, Richard III 1992, The White Devil, The Herbal Garden 1996; RNT: Once in a While the Odd Thing Happens 1990, The Shape of the Table 1990, White Chameleon 1991, Volpone 1995; *Television* incl: The Waterfall, co-presenter Mooncat and Co, Prime Suspect II, III & VI, The Best Man to Die, Under the Hammer 1994, Karaoke 1995; *Radio* Caesar in South China; *Recreations* tennis, squash, football, walking, playing piano and guitar; *Style*— Stephen Boxer, Esq; ✉ c/o Kerry Gardner Management, 15 High Street Kensington, London W8 5NP (☎ 0171 937 4478, fax 0171 376 2587)

BOYARS, Marion Ursula; da of Johannes Asmus (d 1966), and Herta, *née* Feiner (d 1943); *b* 26 Oct 1929; *Educ* Ecole Les Rayons Gland Switzerland, New York Univ, Univ of Keele (BA); *m* 1, 24 Nov 1950 (m dis 1962), George, s of Hans Lobbenberg (d 1969); 2 da (Susan (Mrs Quateman) b 13 March 1955, Catheryn (Mrs Kilgarriff) b 17 Jan 1957); m 2, 8 May 1964, Arthur Boyars; *Career* md Calder and Boyars publishers 1960–89: fiction (6 Nobel Prize winners), biography, poetry, music, theatre; md Marion Boyars Publishers London and NY 1975–: int fiction (4 Nobel Prize Winners), poetry, music, film, theatre, social scis; memb: Publishers Assoc (memb various ctees), various anti-censorship orgns; *Recreations* all the arts, travel, cooking, food & wine; *Clubs* Hurlingham; *Style*— Mrs Marion Boyars; ✉ 4 Hollywood Mews, London SW10 9HU (☎ 0171 352 6400); 24 Lacy Rd, London SW15 1NL (☎ 0181 788 9522, fax 0181 789 8122)

BOYCE, HE Graham Hugh; CMG (1991); s of Cdr Hugh Boyce, DSC, RN, and Madeline Millicent, *née* Manley; *b* 6 Oct 1945; *Educ* Hurstpierpoint Coll, Jesus Coll Cambridge (MA); *m* 11 April 1970, Janet Elizabeth, da of Rev Gordon Charles Craig Spencer, of Bath; 1 s (James b 1971), 3 da (Rachel b 1974, Sara b 1980, Josephine b 1984); *Career* VSO Antigua 1967; FCO: HM Dip Serv 1968, 3 then 2 sec Ottawa 1971, MECAS Shemlan 1972–74, 1 sec Tripoli 1974–77, FCO 1977–81, 1 sec Kuwait 1981–85, asst head ME Dept 1985–86, cnsllr and consul gen Stockholm 1987–90, HM ambass and consul gen Doha 1990–93, head Environment Science and Energy Dept 1993–96, HM ambass Kuwait 1996–; *Recreations* tennis, reading; *Style*— HE Mr Graham Boyce, CMG; ✉ c/o Foreign & Commonwealth Office (Kuwait), King Charles Street, London SW1A 2AH

BOYCE, John Leslie; s of late Sir (Harold) Leslie Boyce, 1 Bt, KBE; hp of nephew, Sir Robert Boyce, 3 Bt; *b* 16 Nov 1934; *Educ* Cheltenham Coll; *m* 1, 1957 (m dis 1975), Finola Mary, da of late James Patrick Maxwell, of Bansha, Co Tipperary; 1 s (Richard Allen b 1968), 3 da (Elizabeth Jane Leslie b 1958, Evelyn Mary b 1961, Suzanne Caroline b 1963); m 2, 1980, Fusako, da of Yonesaku Ishibashi, of Shinagawa-ku, Tokyo, Japan; 2 da (Miyo Maybery b 1981, Kyoko Jacqueline b 1983); *Career* apprentice aeronautical design engr Sir W G Armstrong Whitworth Aircraft Company Ltd (later Hawker Siddeley Dynamics (Coventry) Ltd, now part of British Aerospace) 1953–58, head Flight Instrumentation Section Missile Design Group 1956–64 (working on Seaslug Mk1 and Mk2), head all Electrical and Measurement Design Sections Missile Design Group 1964–67 (working on Seaslug Mk2 and SeaDart), Defence Standards Laboratories (Dept of Supply) Melbourne 1967–77, head Electronics Section 3AQUA (Dept of Defence) Aust Army 1977–78, Monash Univ Melbourne (studying physics and applied maths) 1978–79, electronics design and computer conslt 1979–; *Recreations* radio amateur (G3PZA/VK3AXF); *Style*— John Boyce, Esq; ✉ 182 Huntingdale Rd, Mt Waverley, Victoria 3149, Australia

BOYCE, Sir Robert Charles Leslie; 3 Bt (UK 1952), of Badgeworth, Co Gloucester; s of Sir Richard (Leslie) Boyce, 2 Bt (d 1968), and Jacqueline Anne Boyce-Dennis, *née* Hill; *b* 2 May 1962; *Educ* Cheltenham Coll, Univ of Salford (BSc); *m* 1985, Fiona Margaret, 2 da of John Savage, of Harborough Road, Coventry; 1 s (Thomas Leslie b 3 Sept 1993), 1 da (Amelia Moira b 23 March 1996); *Heir* s Thomas Boyce; *Career* electronics engr; *Clubs* IEE; *Style*— Sir Robert Boyce, Bt

BOYCOTT, Prof Brian Blundell; s of Percy Blundell Boycott (d 1953), of London, and Doris Eyton Boycott (d 1993); *b* 10 Dec 1924; *Educ* Royal Masonic Sch for Boys Bushey, Birkbeck Coll Univ of London; *m* 7 May 1950, Marjorie Mabel, da of late George Ernest Burchell, of Beaminster, Dorset; 2 s (Antony b 1 April 1951, Richard b 1956, d 1963); *Career* reserved occupation as res technician Nat Inst for Med Res 1942–46; UCL: asst in anatomy 1947–52, lectr in zoology 1952–62, reader in zoology 1962–68, prof of zoology 1968–70; sr scientific staff MRC 1971–89; King's Coll London: prof of biology 1971–89, dir Cell Biophysics Unit 1980–89; emeritus prof of biology and hon sr res fell Guy's Hosp Med Sch 1990–; 75 pubns in learned jls; memb Cncl: Royal Soc 1976–78, Open Univ 1975–87; memb: Academic Advsy Ctee Open Univ 1990–93, MRC Neuroscience and Mental Health Bd 1990–91; fell King's Coll London 1990, Hon DUniv Open Univ; FIBiol 1967, FRS 1971; *Style*— Prof Brian Boycott, FRS; ✉ Department of Anatomy and Cell Biology, Guy's Hospital, London Bridge, London SE1 9RT (☎ 0171 955 2991, fax 0171 955 4915)

BOYCOTT, Geoffrey (Geoff); OBE (1981); s of late Thomas Wilfred Boycott, and Jane, *née* Speight; *b* 21 Oct 1940; *Educ* Kinsley Secdy Mod, Hemsworth GS; *Career* former cricketer; played for: Yorkshire CCC 1962–86 (co cap 1963, capt 1971–78), England 1964–74 and 1977–82 (capt 1977–78, 4 tests); scored one hundredth first class century 1977 (England v Australia), scored one hundred and fiftieth century 1986, exceeded world record no of runs scored in Test Matches Delhi 1982; memb Yorks CCC (memb Gen Ctee 1984–92); currently commentator BBC; *Books* Geoff Boycott's Book for Young Cricketers (1976), Put to the Test: England in Australia 1978–79 (1979), Geoff Boycott's Cricket Quiz (1979), Boycott On Batting (1980), Opening Up (1980), In the Fast Lane: England in the West Indies (1981), Master Class (1982), Boycott, The Autobiography (1987), Boycott on Cricket (1990); *Videos* Boycott on Batting (1990), Geoff Boycott's Greatest England Team (1991); *Recreations* golf, tennis; *Style*— Geoff Boycott, Esq, OBE; ✉ Yorkshire County Cricket Club, Headingley Cricket Ground, Leeds, Yorkshire LS6 3BY

BOYCOTT, Rosel Marie (Rosie); da of Maj Charles Boycott, and Betty, *née* Le Sueur (d 1981); *b* 13 May 1951; *Educ* Cheltenham Ladies Coll, Univ of Kent; *m* David Leitch; 1 da (Daisy Anna b 9 Aug 1983); *Career* journalist and author; fndr: Spare Rib magazine 1972, Virago Press 1973; ed Osrati (Kuwaiti women's magazine) 1976–79, freelance contrib to various nat newspapers, full-time appts at Daily Mail, Daily Telegraph and Harpers & Queen, ed British Esquire 1992–96, ed Indpendent on Sunday 1996–; *Books* Loka: The Buddhist Journal of Naropa (ed, 1975), Batty, Bloomers and Boycott (1981), A Nice Girl Like Me (autobiography, 1983), All For Love (novel, 1985); *Recreations* sailing, tennis, riding; *Clubs* Globe, Groucho, Academy; *Style*— Ms Rosie Boycott; ✉ The Independent on Sunday, 1 Canada Square, Canary Wharf, London E14 5AP (☎ 0171 293 2000)

BOYD, Alan Robb; s of Alexander Boyd (d 1963), and Mary Herd, *née* Robb; *b* 30 July 1953; *Educ* Irvine Royal Acad, Univ of Dundee (LLB), Open Univ (BA); *m* 1973, Frances Helen, da of Joseph Donaldson; 2 da (Carol Jane b 10 Sept 1975, Fiona Anne b 22 March 1979); *Career* admitted slr 1976, princ legal asst Shetland Islands Cncl 1979–81, princ slr Glenrothes Development Corporation 1981–84, legal advsr Irvine Development

Corporation 1984–; pres Euro Co Lawyers' Assoc 1992–94, pres Law Soc of Scotland 1995–96 (vice pres 1994–95, memb Cncl 1985–); NP 1982, SSC; *Recreations* golf, music, gardening; *Clubs* Turnberry Golf; *Style*— Alan Boyd, Esq; ✉ 45 Craigholm Road, Ayr KA7 3LJ (☎ 01292 262542); Irvine Development Corporation, Perceton House, Irvine KA11 2AL (☎ 01294 214100, fax 01294 211467)

BOYD, Sir Alexander Walter; 3 Bt (UK 1916), of Howth House, Howth, Co Dublin; s of late Maj Cecil Anderson Boyd, MC, MD, late RAMC, 2 s of 1 Bt; suc unc, Sir Walter Herbert Boyd, 2 Bt, 1948; *b* 16 June 1934; *m* 1958, Molly Madeline, da of late Ernest Arthur Rendell, of Vernon, BC, Canada; 2 s (Ian Walter Rendell b 1964, Robert Alexander Rendell b 1966), 3 da (Heather Lynn b 1959, Susan Christine b 1961, Sandra Molly b 1967); *Heir* s, Ian Walter Rendell Boyd b 14 March 1964; *Style*— Sir Alexander Boyd, Bt; ✉ Box 261, Whistler, British Columbia V0N 1B0, Canada

BOYD, (Morgan) Alistair; CMG (1990); s of Preb Norman Robert Boyd (d 1945), of Bournemouth, Hants, and Muriel Katherine, *née* Humby (d 1984); *b* 1 May 1934; *Educ* Marlborough, Wadham Coll Oxford (BA, MA); *m* 26 May 1959, Judith Mary, da of Preb Henry Wilfred Lawrence Martin, of Christ Church, Jerusalem; *Career* Commonwealth Development Corporation: mgmnt trainee 1957, investigations exec Malaysia and rep Economist Intelligence Unit Liaison Office for the Fedn of Br Indust 1961, mangr E Caribbean Housing and related mortgage fin cos in the Caribbean 1967, attached to FO for mission to Turks and Caicos Islands 1970, gen mangr Tanganyika Development Finance Co Tanzania 1970–74, seconded as advsr on establishing Industrial Devpt Bank to Kenya Govt 1975, regnl controller Central Africa Lusaka 1976–80, regional controller E Africa Nairobi 1980–83, head of new business worldwide London 1983, dir of operations in Africa London 1985, dep chief exec 1991–94, advsr 1994–; memb Cncl Africa Centre 1995–, chm UK Southern Africa Business Assoc 1995–, vice chm Royal African Soc 1996–; bd memb: Hub Rivert Power Co Pakistan 1994–96, EDESA Managment AG Switzerland 1994–; memb: Ctee on S African Trade 1995–, Steering Ctee World Congress (1998) Land Ownership and Resource Mgmnt 1996–; tstee CDC Pension Fund 1995–; lectr for Maurice Frost Lecture Agency and ESU 1956–62 (USA tour 1961), Malaysia corr Far Eastern Economic Review 1963–66; FRGS 1959, memb RSA 1990; *Books* Royal Challenge Accepted (1961); *Recreations* sailing, music; *Clubs* Naval, ESU; *Style*— Alistair Boyd, Esq, CMG; ✉ c/o Commonwealth Development Corporation, One Bessborough Gardens, London SW1V 2JQ (☎ 0171 828 4488, fax 0171 828 6505, telex 21431 VELOP G/25849 VELOP G)

BOYD, HE Aquilino E; *b* 30 March 1921; *Educ* Univ of Panama (lawyer in human rights and political sci), Holy Cross Coll New Orleans; *m* Dora, *née* Brin; 5 c; *Career* Panamanian diplomat; first sec: Cuba 1945–46, Washington DC 1946–47; memb Nat Legislative Assembly 1948–62 (pres 1949, variously pres Foreign Affrs Ctee), min for foreign affrs 1956–58, ambass to Mexico 1958, perm rep to UN 1962–76, pres UN Security Cncl March 1973 (pres ad-hoc Ctee on Int Terrorism 1973), rep UN Security Cncl 1976, min for foreign affrs 1976–77 (invited to the new Carter admin to discuss the Panama Canal Treaty leading to Boyd-Vance declaration and subsequent signing of the Torrijos-Carter Treaty 1977), ambass to Washington DC and memb Panamanian Acad of Int Human Rights 1982–85, ambass to Ct of St James's Dec 1994–; Grand Cross: Order of Vasco Nuñez de Balboa (Panama), Order de Manuel Amador Guerrero (Panama); recipient of other decorations from Argentina, Brazil, Chile, Bolivia, Colombia, Dominican Republic, Cuba, China, Greece, Holland, Nicaragua and Guatemala; *Style*— HE Mr Aquilino Boyd; ✉ Embassy of the Republic of Panama, Ground Floor, 48 Park Street, London W1Y 3PD (☎ 0171 493 4646, fax 0171 493 4333)

BOYD, Arthur Merric Bloomfield; AO (1979), OBE (1970), AC (1992); *b* 24 July 1920, Murrumbeena, Victoria; *Educ* Nat Gallery of Victoria Sch Melbourne; *m* Yvonne; 1 s (Jamie b 1948), 2 da (Polly b 1946, Lucy b 1958); *Career* conscripted Aust Army 1940, Cartographic Dept 1941, demob 1943; artist; fndr The Arthur Merric Boyd Pottery Murrumbeena 1944–58, has lived/worked between Aust and Eng since 1959; *Solo Exhibitions* incl: Zwemmer Gall London 1961, Whitechapel Art Gall 1962, Adelaide Festival Nat Gallery of S Aust 1964, Terry Clune Galleries Sydney 1967, Arthur Boyd - The Complete Artist Adelaide Festival of Arts Exhibition 1968, Richad Demarco Gall Edinburgh 1969, Prints Maltzahn Gall London 1969, Tapestries Pastels and Drawings Hamet Gall London 1969, Suite of Etchings - Lysistrata Ganymed Gall London 1971, Paintings Ceramics Graphics and Tapestries Melville Hall Aust Nat Univ Canberra 1971, Recent Paintings Fischer Fine Art London 1972, 1977, 1981 and 1983, The Graphic Work of Arthur Boyd Municipal Gall of Modern Art Dublin 1972, Drawings 1934–70 Rudy Komon Gall Sydney 1975, Oils Ceramics Sculpture and Paintings, Watercolour Drawings Lithographs Rudy Komon Gall Sydney 1978, Paintings and Drawings 1944–1978 Inst of Modern Art Brisbane 1978, Landscapes and Portraits 1934–49, Bronze Castings of Four Ceramic Sculptures 1935–54, Paintings 1982 Aust Galleries Melbourne 1982, Bonython-Meadmore Gall Adelaide 1984, Drawings Paintings Prints and Ceramics (1940–1970) from the Collection Art Gall of S Aust Adelaide 1984, Fischer Fine Art London 1986, Pyramid Gall NY 1986, Adelaide Festival of Arts Exhibition BMG Fine Art Adelaide 1988, Mars Exhibition BMG Fine Art Sydney 1988, The XLIII Biennale of Venice 1988; *Retrospective Exhibitions*: Art Gall of New South Wales Sydney 1993–, Melbourne Nat Gall 1994–, Tasmania and Western Australia State Galls 1994–; cmmns incl tapestry for reception hall at new Parl House Canberra (for Parl House Authy) and 16 canvases (for State Theatre Melbourne) 1984; subject of documentary films incl: A Man in Two Worlds (BBC/ABC co-prodn) 1978, Figures in the Landscape (LWT) 1985; fell Aust Nat Univ 1971–72; *Style*— Arthur Boyd, Esq, AO, OBE, AC

BOYD, David Barclay; JP (Argyll and Bute); s of David Boyd, and Janet MacLennan Barclay; *b* 23 July 1933; *Educ* Dunoon GS, Edinburgh Univ (BSc); *m* 8 Nov 1958, Emily Margaret, da of James Wilson, of Dunoon; 2 s (David James b 1960, Andrew Wilson b 1968), 2 da (Kirsty (Mrs Reid) b 1959, Bryony (Mrs McFarlane) b 1964); *Career* cmmnd 2 Lt RE 1957, active serv Cyprus 1957–58; dist offr Forestry Cmmn, asst regnl offr Argyll 1960–62, factor Glencruitten Estate Oban 1962–66, factor Islay Estate Islay of Islay 1966–95; former chm Islay Farmers Ltd; memb Argyll and Bute Rating and Valuation Ctee; chm Islay Branch Ctee RNLI; crew memb Sceptre America's Cup Challenge at Newport Rhode Island 1958; fell Inst of Chartered Foresters; *Recreations* shooting, sailing; *Clubs* Royal Scottish Automobile, Trout Anglers'; *Style*— David Boyd, Esq, JP; ✉ 105 Hyndland Rd, Glasgow (☎ 0141 339 7641); Cnoc Na Daal, Bridgend, Islay, Argyll PA44 7NY (☎ 01496 810464)

BOYD, Dennis Galt; CBE (1988); s of Thomas Ayre Boyd (d 1968), and Minnie, *née* Galt (d 1962); *b* 3 Feb 1931; *Educ* S Shields HS; *m* 1953, Pamela Mary, da of John Moore McLean (d 1980); 1 s (Simon), 1 da (Angela); *Career* Nat Serv 1949–51; Miny of Supply/MOD 1951–66, Bd of Trade 1966–69, personnel offr Forestry Cmmn 1969–75, dir of corp servs Health and Safety Exec Dept of Employment 1975–80, chief conciliation offr ACAS 1980–92; FIPM; *Recreations* golf; *Clubs* Civil Serv; *Style*— Dennis Boyd, Esq, CBE; ✉ Dunelm, Silchester Rd, Little London, Tadley, Hants RG26 5EW

BOYD, Don; s of Donald John Boyd (d 1991), of Tollard Royal, Dorset, and Lubov Petrovna Drosdovo; *Educ* Loretto, London Film Sch; *m* 1, 1970 (m dis 1973), Vivien; 1 da (Amanda Cara b 6 May 1971); m 2, 21 July 1973, Hilary, da of Maj John Heale Sandeman-Allen; 2 da (Clare Sandeman b 1 July 1974, Katherine Robertson b 12 Aug 1977); *Career* film director and producer; fndr: Boyd's Co 1978, Lexington Films 1996; season of films presented at Nat Film Theatre 1982, deliverer of Guardian Lecture 1982; occasional contributor to The Guardian, The Observer and The Sunday Times; govr London Int Film Sch; Freeman: City of Mount Dora Florida 1981, State of Florida 1981; memb: Directors' Guild of GB, ACTT, BAFTA; FRSA; *Television* documentaries as dir (for Channel 4) incl: Man, God and Africa 1992, Vicars 1993, The Babe Business 1993, The Last Afrikaner 1994; other credits incl: Ruby's Health Quest (series, BBC) 1995, Ruby Does the Season (series, ITV, also prodr) 1995, Ruby With....(series, BBC) 1996, Sir Norman Foster (BBC) 1996; *Films* as dir incl: Intimate Reflections (starring Anton Rodgers) 1974, East of Elephant Rock (starring John Hurt, Christopher Cazenove and Anton Rodgers) 1975/76, The Four Seasons 1977; as exec prodr incl: Sweet William (with Sam Waterston & Jenny Agutter) 1978, Scum 1978, The Tempest (with Toyah Wilcox & Heathcote Williams, dir Derek Jarman) 1979, Hussy (with Helen Mirren & John Shea) 1979, Blue Suede Shoes 1979, The Great Rock'n'Roll Swindle 1980, Look Back in Anger (with Malcolm MacDowell, dir Lindsay Anderson) 1980, Anticlock 1980, An Unsuitable Job for Woman (with Billie Whitelaw) 1981; as prodr (with Boyd's Co) incl: Honky Tonk Freeway 1980/81 (with Hume Cronyn, Jessica Tandy & Beau Bridges, dir John Schlesinger), Scrubbers 1982, Captive (with Oliver Reed) 1985, Aria (closing night film Cannes Film Festival 1987) 1986/87; Anglo International Films, as prodr incl: The Last of England (dir Derek Jarman) 1987, War Requiem (featuring Laurence Olivier) 1988; as dir incl: Goldeneye (with Charles Dance) 1989, Twenty-One (with Patsy Kensit & Rufus Sewell) 1990, Kleptomania (with Amy Irving & Patsy Kensit) 1993; *Recreations* cinema and all other arts in particular opera and theatre; *Clubs* Groucho, Chelsea Arts; *Style*— Don Boyd, Esq; ✉ 12 Stafford Terrace, London W8 7BH; c/o ICM Ltd, Oxford House, 76 Oxford Street, London W1N 0AX (☎ 0171 636 6565, fax 0171 323 0101)

BOYD, Douglas; *Educ* RAM under Janet Craxton, studied with Maurice Bourgue in Paris; *Career* professional oboist; debut Salzburg Festival 1990; soloist in important musical centres of Europe, Far East and America; co-fndr Chamber Orch of Europe (princ oboist, leading memb Wind Soloists); prof RAM (Hon ARAM 1990); concerto appearances incl: Chamber Orch of Europe, Scottish Chamber Orch, Vienna Symphony Orch, BBC Scottish Symphony, Bournemouth Sinfonietta, Orch of St Johns Smith Square, Acad of St Martin in the Fields, Moscow Virtuosi, Hong Kong Philarmonic, Basle Radio Symphony, Nat Arts Centre Orch Ottawa, Royal Scot Nat Orchestra, Northern Sinfonia of England, Winterthur Orchestra (debut); work with conductors incl: Claudio Abbado, Paavo Berglund, Sir Yehudi Menuhin, Alexander Schneider, Michael Tilson Thomas; int festivals incl: Berlin, City of London, Edinburgh, Korsholm, Vancouver, Charleston, Spoleto; *Recordings* Bach Oboe Concerto (dir and soloist, Deutsche Grammaphon) 1990, Vivaldi Oboe Concerti (dir and soloist, Deutsche Grammaphon) 1992; Strauss Oboe Concerto (ASV) 1990; *Style*— Douglas Boyd, Esq; ✉ c/o Sue Lubbock Concert Management, 25 Courthope Road, London NW3 2LE (☎ 0171 485 5932, fax 0171 267 0179)

BOYD, Douglas Turner; s of David Findlay Boyd (d 1979), and Edith May, *née* Turner (d 1981); *b* 7 April 1939; *Educ* Hutchesons' GS; *m* 2 Sept 1968, Sheena Lynam Park, da of John Lynam Henderson (d 1970); 2 da (Catriona Henderson b 8 April 1970, Aileen Elizabeth b 30 Aug 1971); *Career* KPMG: joined as apprentice 1956, qualified CA 1961, ptnr 1974–, office managing ptnr (Glasgow) 1992–, head regnl human relations (Scotland) 1994–; memb Doctors and Dentists Pay Review Body 1987–95, memb Scottish Milk Mktg Bd 1994–; lay memb General Optical Cncl 1986–; memb: Incorporation of Gardeners (Glasgow) 1986, Incorporation of the Weavers of Anderston 1987, The Merchants House of Glasgow 1990; *Recreations* keep fit, golf; *Clubs* Western (Glasgow), Lenzie, Lenzie Golf; *Style*— Douglas Boyd, Esq; ✉ 5 Laurel Avenue, Lenzie, Kirkintilloch, Glasgow G66 4RX (☎ 0141 776 5625); KPMG, 24 Blythswood Square, Glasgow G2 4QS (☎ 0141 226 5511, fax 0141 204 1584)

BOYD, Fionnuala; da of Joseph Douglas Allen Boyd (d 1990), and Doreen, *née* Wilson; *b* 13 April 1944; *Educ* The Grammar Sch Welwyn Garden City, St Albans Art Sch, Univ of Leeds (BA); *m* 1965, Leslie Douglas Evans, *qv*, s of Leslie Edward Evans; 1 s (Jack Luis b 1969), 1 da (Ruby Rose b 1971); *Career* artist; began working with Leslie Evans 1968, Bi-Centennial fell USA 1977–78; artist in residence: Milton Keynes Devpt Corp 1982–84, Brunei Rainforest Project 1991–92; *Solo Exhibitions* (with Leslie Evans): Angela Flowers Gallery 1972, 1974, 1977, 1979, 1980, 1982, 1984, 1986, 1988, Park Square Gallery Leeds 1972, Boyd and Evans 1970–75 (Turnpike Gallery Leigh) 1976, Fendrick Gallery Washington DC 1978, Graves Art Gallery Sheffield 1978, Spectro Arts Workshop Newcastle 1980, Ton Peek Utrecht 1981, A Decade of Paintings (Milton Keynes Exhibition Gallery) 1982–83, Drumcroon Art Centre Wigan 1985, Bird (Flowers East, London) 1990, English Paintings (Brendan Walter Gallery Santa Monica) 1990, Angela Flowers (Ireland) Inc Rosscarberry Ireland 1990, Flowers East London 1991, Brunei Rain Forest (Flowers East) 1993; *Gp Exhibitions* incl: Postcards (Angela Flowers Gallery) 1970, British Drawing 1952–72 (Angela Flowers Gallery) 1972, Imagini Come Strumenta di Realta (Studio la Citta Verona) 1973, New Image Painting (First Tokyo Int Biennale of Figurative Art) 1974, Body and Soul (Peter Moores, Liverpool) 1975, British Realist Show (Ikon Gallery) 1976, Aspects of Realism (Rothmans of Pall Mall, Canada) 1976–78, The Real British (Fischer Fine Art) 1981, Black and White Show (Angela Flowers Gallery) 1985, Sixteen (Angela Flowers Gallery) 1986, State of the Nation (Herbert Gallery, Coventry) 1987, Contemporary Portraits (Flowers East) 1988, The Thatcher Years (Flowers East) 1989; Picturing People: British Figurative Art since 1945 (touring exhibition Far East) 1989–90, Art '90 London (Business Design Centre) 1990; work in public collections of: Arts Cncl of GB, Br Cncl, Museum of Modern Art NY, Metropolitan Museum NY, Sheffield City Art Gallery, Wolverhampton City Art Gallery, Leeds City Art Gallery, Contemporary Art Soc, Leicester Educn Authy, Manchester City Art Gallery, Unilever plc, Tate Gallery, Williamson Art Gallery, Borough of Milton Keynes; *awards* prizewinner Bradford Print Biennale, first prize 6th Festival Int de la Peinture Cagnes-sur-Mer; *Recreations* books, films, hills, friends, exercise, music; *Style*— Ms Fionnuala Boyd; ✉ Boyd & Evans, Flowers East, 199/205 Richmond Rd, London E8 3NJ (☎ 0181 985 3333, fax 0181 985 0067)

BOYD, Iain Edward; s of John Edward Boyd (d 1982), of Glasgow, and Sheena Dunkeld, *née* Buchanan; *b* 4 March 1937; *Educ* The HS of Glasgow, Univ of Glasgow (MB ChB); *m* 26 March 1964, Una Barrie, da of John Cameron, of Glasgow; 1 da (Susan b 1967); *Career* Physiology Dept Univ of Glasgow 1962–64, Univ of Chicago clinics 1964–68, UCH London 1968–69, Queen Charlotte's Maternity Hosp and Chelsea Hosp for Women 1969–73, Southampton Univ Hosps Tst 1974–; speciality regnl advsr Wessex Region, former sec S Western Obstetricians and Gynaecologists; memb Br Gynaecological Cancer Soc 1986; FRCS 1968, FRCOG 1982 (MRCOG 1968); *Recreations* skiing, dining out, theatre, sailing; *Clubs* Gynaecological Visiting Soc; *Style*— Iain Boyd, Esq; ✉ Forest Edge, Woodlands Crescent, Ashurst, Hants SO40 7AQ (☎ 01703 292324); Princess Anne Hospital, Coxford Rd, Southampton SO9 4HA (☎ 01703 796042)

BOYD, Ian Mair; s of John Telfer Boyd (d 1976), of Ayr, and Margaret Mair, *née* Murdoch; *b* 4 Sept 1944; *Educ* Ayr Acad, London Business Sch (MSc); *m* 20 Dec 1975, Theodora (Toody), da of Theodor Georgopoulos, of Athens; 2 s (Telfer, Fraser), 1 da (Amber); *Career* CA 1966, gp fin dir The Weir Group plc 1981–, dir Glasgow Income Trust plc 1990–, dir Inveresk plc 1993–; memb Cncl Inst of CAs of Scotland 1987–93, chm Gp of Scot Fin Dirs 1990–92; *Recreations* golf, hill-walking, skiing, bird watching, fishing; *Clubs* Prestwick Golf; *Style*— Ian M Boyd, Esq; ✉ 34 Newark Drive, Glasgow G41 4PZ (☎ 0141 429 1840); The Weir Group Plc, 149 Newlands Rd, Glasgow G44 4EX (☎ 0141 637 7111, fax 0141 637 2221, telex 77161 WPL CRT)

BOYD, James Edward (Teddy); s of Robert Edward Boyd, and Elizabeth Reid Sinclair; *b* 14 Sept 1928; *Educ* Kelvinside Acad, The Leys Sch Cambridge; *m* Judy Ann Christey Scott; 2 s, 2 da (1 decd); *Career* CA Scot (dist) 1951; ptnr McClelland Ker & Co 1953–61; fin dir: Lithgows Ltd 1962–69, Scott Lithgow Ltd 1970–78; dir and fin advsr Denholm Gp of Cos 1968–96; dir: Lithgows (Hldgs) Ltd 1962–87, Ayrshire Metal Products plc 1965–94 (dep chm 1989–91, chm 1991–94), Invergordon Distillers (Hldgs) plc 1966–88 (md 1966–67), Nairn & Williamson (Hldgs) Ltd 1968–75, GB Papers plc 1977–87, Carlton Industries plc 1978–84, James River UK Hldgs Ltd 1987–90, Jebsens Drilling plc 1978–85, Save & Prosper Gp Ltd 1987–89; Scottish Widows' Fund & Life Assurance Soc 1981–94 (dep chm 1988–93), Br Linen Bank Ltd 1983–94 (govr 1986–94), Shanks & McEwan Gp plc 1983–94, Scottish Exhibition Centre 1983–89, Civil Aviation Authority 1984–85, Bank of Scotland 1984–94, Bank of Wales 1986–88, dep chm BAA plc (formerly British Airports Authy) 1985–94; chm: Fairfield Shipbuilding & Engrg Co Ltd 1964–65, Gartmore European Investmt Tst plc 1978–91, English & Caledonian Investment plc 1981–91, Yarrow plc 1984–86; memb: Clyde Port Authority 1974–80, Cncl Inst of Chartered Accountants of Scotland 1977–83 (vice pres 1980–82, pres 1982–83), Exec Ctee Accountants Jt Disciplinary Scheme 1979–81; memb Cncl Glenalmond Coll 1983–92; *Recreations* tennis, golf, gardening, painting; *Style*— J E Boyd, Esq; ✉ Dunard, Station Road, Rhu, Dunbartonshire G84 8LW (☎ 01436 820441); The Denholm Group, Inter-City House, 80 Oswald Street, Glasgow G1 4PX (☎ 0141 204 1004, fax 0141 248 5647)

BOYD, Prof (Thomas) James Morrow; s of Thomas James Boyd (d 1979), and Isobel Cameron, *née* Morrow; *b* 21 June 1932; *Educ* Larne GS, Queen's Univ Belfast (BSc, PhD); *m* 5 Sept 1959, Marguerite Bridget, da of William Snelson (d 1980), of Drayton Manor, Dunston, Stafford; 2 da (Rebecca b 1964, Marguerite b 1968); *Career* res fell Univ of Birmingham 1957–59, asst res prof Univ of Maryland 1959–61, Ford fndn fell Princeton Univ 1962, sr res assoc UKAEA Culham Lab 1962–65, sr lectr Univ of St Andrews 1965–68; Univ of Wales Bangor: prof of applied mathematics and computation 1968–82, prof of theoretical physics 1982–90, dean Faculty of Sci 1981–85; prof of physics Univ of Essex 1990–; visiting prof of physics Univ of British Columbia 1975, Fulbright sr fell and visiting prof of physics Dartmouth Coll USA 1987–88; memb NY Acad of Sciences 1987, FInstP 1974 (chm Plasma Physics Gp 1975–77); *Books* Plasma Dynamics (with J J Sanderson, 1969), Electricity (with C A Coulson, 1979), The Physics of Plasmas (with J J Sanderson, 1997); *Recreations* skiing, climbing, travel; *Style*— Prof James Boyd; ✉ 6 Frog Meadow, Brook St, Dedham, Colchester CO7 6AD (☎ 01206 323170); The Roddens, Larne, Co Antrim BT40 1PN; Dept of Physics, University of Essex, Wivenhoe Park, Colchester CO4 3SQ (☎ 01206 872885, fax 01206 873598, e-mail tjmb@essex.ac.uk)

BOYD, (David) John; QC (1982); s of David Boyd (d 1964), and Ellen Jane, *née* Gruer (d 1953); *b* 11 Feb 1935; *Educ* Eastbourne Coll, St George's Sch Newport Rhode Island, Gonville and Caius Coll Cambridge (MA); *m* 1960, Raija Sinikka, da of Onni Lindholm (d 1952), of Finland, 1 s (Roderick b 1972), 1 da (Karin b 1969); *Career* called to the Bar Gray's Inn 1963, bencher 1988; sec asst ICI 1957–62, legal asst Pfizer 1962–66, legal offr Henry Wiggin and Co 1966–68; joined Inco Europe Ltd 1968, sec and chief legal offr Inco Europe Ltd 1972–86 (dir 1984–86); in private practice at Bar 1986; Digital Equipment Co: dir of legal servs 1986–93, dir of public affrs and communications 1993–95; dir: Digital Equipment Scotland Ltd 1987–95, AXXIA Systems Ltd 1995–; special immigration adjudicator 1995–; chm Competition Panel CBI 1988–93, dir Impala Platinum 1972–78, gen cmmr of Income Tax 1978–81, memb Senate of Inns of Ct and Bar 1978–81, chm Bar Assoc for Commerce Fin and Indust 1980–81, sec gen Assoc des Juristes d'Enterprise Européens 1983–84, legal advsr Review Bd for Govt Contracts 1984–91, memb Monopolies and Mergers Cmmn 1991–, dir Centre for Euro Dispute Resolution 1991–94; memb: Cncl Centre for Commercial Law Studies Queen Mary and Westfield Coll 1989–93, Exec Ctee Royal Acad of Dance 1991–; chm Contemporary Dance Tst and The Place theatre London 1995–, dir Oxford Orchestra da Camera 1996–; FCIArb; *Recreations* viticulture, France; *Clubs* Leander; *Style*— John Boyd, Esq, QC; ✉ Beeches, Upton Bishop, Ross-on-Wye, Herefordshire (☎ 01989 780214, fax 01989 780538, e-mail boydj@axxia.com)

BOYD, John; s of John Richardson Boyd, and Janet, *née* Anderson; *b* 5 April 1925; *Educ* Heriot-Watt Univ Edinburgh; *Career* WWII served RN 1942–45; Royal Milliner; *Style*— John Boyd, Esq; ✉ 16 Beauchamp Place, London SW3 1NQ (☎ 0171 589 7601)

BOYD, Sir John Dixon Iklé; KCMG (1992, CMG 1985); s of Prof James Dixon Boyd (d 1968), of Cambridge, and Amélie, *née* Lowenthal; *b* 17 Jan 1936; *Educ* Westminster, Clare Coll Cambridge (BA), Yale (MA); *m* 1, 28 Jan 1968 (m dis 1977), Gunilla Kristina Ingegerd, da of Gösta Rönngren, of Västeraås, Sweden; 1 s (Jonathan b 1969), 1 da (Emily b 1971); m 2, 11 Nov 1977, Julia Daphne, da of Capt Antony Edward Montague Raynsford, DL, RN (d 1993), of Milton Malsor Manor, Northampton; 3 da (Jessica b 1978, Alice b 1979, Olivia b 1981); *Career* HM Dip Serv: Hong Kong 1962–64, Peking 1965–67, FCO 1967–69, Washington 1969–73, Peking 1973–75, HM Treasy (on loan) 1976, Bonn 1977–81, UK Mission to UN 1981–84, political advsr Hong Kong 1985–87, dep under sec of state FCO 1987–89, chief clerk 1989–92, ambass to Japan 1992–96; hon fell Clare Coll Cambridge 1994; master Churchill Coll Cambridge 1996–; tstee Br Museum 1996–, govr RSC 1996–, chm of govrs Bedales Sch 1996–, vice chm Menuhin Prize 1996–; *Recreations* music, fly fishing; *Clubs* Hawks (Cambridge), Hong Kong; *Style*— Sir John Boyd, KCMG; ✉ Churchill College, Cambridge CB3 0DS

BOYD, John George; s of John Boyd (d 1980), of Corby, Northampton, and Christina Blair, *née* Wood; *b* 7 April 1940; *Educ* Mackie Acad Stonehaven Kincardineshire, Gray's Sch of Art Aberdeen (DA), Hospitalfield Coll of Art Arbroath, Jordanhill Coll of Educn Glasgow; *m* 1, 23 Oct 1965 (m dis 1975), Janet, *née* Binns; m 2, 10 June 1980 (m dis 1985), Marilyn, *née* Apps; m 3, 11 Nov 1985, Estrild, *née* Macdougall; *Career* artist; teacher 1963–78, pt/t lectr Glasgow Sch of Art 1967–88, pt/t lectr in further educn 1978–95; Latimer Award RSA 1972, Eastwood Publications Award RGI 1990, Armour Award RGI 1993; memb Cncl RGI 1984–90 (elected 1982); RP 1989; *Exhibitions* incl: New 57 Gallery Edinburgh 1967, Armstrong Gallery Glasgow 1970, Glasgow Art Club 1971, 1973, 1974, 1976 and 1980, Present Gallery Lanark 1975, Henderson's Gallery Edingburgh 1978 and 1980, Corners Gallery Glasgow 1985, Barclay Lennie Fine Art Glasgow 1988, Open Eye Gallery Edinburgh 1989, Graeme Mundy Fine Art Glasgow 1990, Conservation Management London 1992, Wm Hardie Ltd Glasgow 1994, Portland Gallery London 1995, Contemporary Fine Art Gallery Eton 1996; regular exhibitor at: Royal Academy, RSA, RGI; *Works in Collections* private collections: UK, USA, SA and Hong Kong, clients incl Earl of Moray, The Captain of Clanranald, Lord McFarlane, Robert Fleming Holdings and Bank of Ireland; public collections: People's Palace Glasgow, Paisley Art Gallery, Lillie Art Gallery Milngavie; *Recreations* reading, music, wine; *Clubs* Glasgow Art; *Style*— John G Boyd, Esq; ✉ Hayston, 26 Cleveden Rd, Glasgow G12 OPX (☎ 0141 357 2176)

BOYD, John MacInnes; CBE (1990), QPM (1984); s of late Duncan Campbell Boyd, and Catherine, *née* MacInnes; *b* 14 Oct 1933; *Educ* Oban HS; *m* 1957, Sheila, *née* MacSporran; 2 s (Peter, Alastair); *Career* Nat Serv with Gordon Highlanders 1954–56; Paisley Burgh Police 1956–67, Renfrew and Bute Constabulary 1967–75, Strathclyde Police 1975–84, Asst Chief Constable Strathclyde Police 1979–84, Chief Constable Dumfries and Galloway Constabulary 1984–89, HM Chief Inspr of Constabulary for Scotland Scottish Office 1993–96 (HM Inspr 1989–93); vice chm Scottish Assoc for the Study of Delinquency 1992–, chm Sec of State for Scotland's Crime Prevention Ctee 1984–87, pres ACPOS (chm Crime Ctee 1984–87) 1988–89; CIMgt; *Recreations* golf, gardening, reading; *Style*— John M Boyd, Esq, CBE, QPM; ✉ HM Inspectorate of Constabulary, The Scottish Offfice, 2 Greenside Lane, Edinburgh EH1 3AG (☎ 0131 244 5614, fax 0131 244 5616)

BOYD, Lawrence David; s of William Robert Boyd, of Bothwell, Glasgow, and Agnes Jane, *née* Armstrong; *b* 25 May 1949; *Educ* Hamilton Acad Lanarkshire, Univ of Glasgow (BSc), Imperial Coll London (MPhil, DIC); *m* 23 July 1977, Nicola Judith Ann, da of Norman Mahy, of Derby; 1 s (Neil b 30 Nov 1984), 1 da (Joanna b 16 April 1983); *Career* Alliance & Leicester Building Society: fin res offr 1976–80, corp planning mangr 1980–82, chief accountant 1982–83, mgmnt servs cncllr 1983–85, asst gen mangr mortgage admin 1985–87, asst gen mangr corp devpt 1987–90, gen mangr corp devpt and planning 1990–94; mgmnt conslt 1994–; ACBSI 1979, ACIS 1979, FCCA 1981; *Books* Accounting - Principles and Practice (1983); *Recreations* walking, fencing; *Style*— Lawrence Boyd, Esq; ✉ 28 Mallory Rd, Hove, E Sussex BN3 6TD (☎ 01273 504253)

BOYD, Michael Neil Murray; s of Lt Cdr Neil Kenneth Boyd, DSC, of New Milton, Hants, and Felicity Victoria, *née* Weston; *b* 17 Aug 1946; *Educ* Bryanston; *m* 30 May 1970, Belinda Rachel Elizabeth, da of Capt Basil Harry Lawrence (d 1973); 1 s (Ashleigh b 21 June 1980), 1 da (Zara b 18 Sept 1975); *Career* Ernst & Young (formerly Ernst & Whinney): ptnr London 1975, NY 1979–82, ptnr i/c London Audit Dept 1984–86, memb Exec and Firm's Cncl 1986–89 and 1992–, fin ptnr 1987–89, chm Int Extractive Industs Ctee 1988–92, chm Ernst & Young Eastern Europe 1988–90, nat audit ptnr 1989–92, managing ptnr London Office 1992–95; vice chm Auditing Practices Bd 1991–94; memb: Cncl Corp of Cranleigh Sch and St Catherine's Bramley 1975–, Oil Industry Accounting Ctee 1988–, Cncl E Euro Trade Cncl 1989–92; govr Cranleigh Sch 1975–79 and 1985–; MInstPet 1983, FCA 1975 (memb 1969); *Recreations* tennis, skiing, opera; *Clubs* City of London; *Style*— Michael Boyd, Esq; ✉ Pleasant Cottage, Chapel Lane, Pirbright, Surrey GU24 0LU (☎ 01483 475705); Ernst & Young, Becket House, 1 Lambeth Palace Rd, London SE1Y 7EU (☎ 0171 928 2000, 0171 928 9615, fax 0171 620 1612, telex 885234)

BOYD, Dr (John) Morton; CBE (1987); s of Thomas Pollock Boyd (d 1953), of Darvel, Ayrshire, and Jeanie Reid, *née* Morton (d 1955); *b* 31 Jan 1925; *Educ* Darvel Sch, Kilmarnock Acad, Univ of Glasgow (BSc, PhD, DSc, DLitt); *m* 18 Jan 1954, Winifred Isobel, da of John Rome (d 1971), of Kilmarnock, Ayrshire; 4 s (Alan Morton b 1955, Ian Lamont b 1957, Neil Rome b 1959, Keith John b 1963); *Career* Air Navigator, Station Adj RAF 1943–47, Flt Lt; ecologist; regnl offr West Scotland Nature Conservancy 1957–68, asst dir Nature Conservancy (Scotland) 1968–70, dir (Scotland) Nature Conservancy Cncl 1971–85; conservation conslt: Forestry Cmmn 1985–92 (hon conslt 1992), Nat Tst for Scotland 1985–, N Scotland Hydro Electric 1985–90, Scottish Hydro-Electric plc 1990–; memb Cncl: Royal Zoological Soc of Scotland 1964–72, 1980–83 and 1985–, Nat Tst for Scotland 1971–85, Royal Soc of Edinburgh 1978–81; memb Advsy Ctee on Sites of Special Scientific Interest Scottish Natural Heritage 1992–95; editorial conslt: Edinburgh Univ Press 1985–92, Mirror Publications Ltd 1989–90; guest lectr: Nat Tst for Scotland 1968–, Swan (Hellenic) Ltd 1972–93, Serenissima Travel Ltd 1990–91, Noble Caledonia Ltd 1992–; vice-pres: Scottish Conservation Projects Tst 1985, Scottish Wildlife Tst 1995 (memb Cncl 1971–78 and 1985–91); patron Woodland Tst 1995, Nuffield travelling fell (ME and E Africa) 1964–65; FRSE 1968 (Neill prize 1983), CBiol 1987, FIBiol 1987, FRSA 1985, Hon FRZS(Scot) 1985, Hon FRSGS 1987; *Books* St Kilda Summer (with K Williamson, 1960), Mosaic of Islands (with K Williamson, 1963), The Highlands and Islands (with F F Darling, 1964), Travels in the Middle East and East Africa (1966), Island Survivors (with P A Jewell and C Milner, 1974), The Natural Environment of the Outer Hebrides (ed, 1979), The Natural Environment of the Inner Hebrides (ed with D R Bowes, 1983), Fraser Darling's Islands (1986), The Hebrides - A Natural History (with I L Boyd, 1990), Fraser Darling in Africa (1992), The Hebrides - A Trilogy: A Habitable Land?, A Natural Tapestry, A Mosaic of Islands (with I L Boyd, 1996); *Recreations* travel, painting, photography; *Clubs* New (Edinburgh); *Style*— Dr J Morton Boyd, CBE, FRSE; ✉ 57 Hailes Gardens, Edinburgh EH13 0JH (☎ and fax 0131 441 3220); Balephuil, Isle of Tiree, Argyll PA77 6UE (☎ 018792 521)

BOYD, Prof Robert David Hugh; s of Prof James Dixon Boyd (d 1968), of Cambridge, and Dr Amélie Boyd; *b* 14 May 1938; *Educ* Univ of Cambridge, UCH London; *m* 1 April 1966, Meriel Cornelia, da of T G Talbot, CB, QC, of Falconhurst, Edenbridge, Kent; 1 s (Thomas b 1967), 2 da (Diana b 1969, Lucy b 1974); *Career* res med posts: UCH, Brompton Hosp, Gt Ormond St Hosp; res fell and sr lectr UCH 1967–80, Faculty of Med Univ of Manchester: prof of child health and paediatrics 1981–96, dean 1989–93; princ and prof of child health St George's Hosp Med Sch London 1996–; chair: Manchester Health Authy 1994–96, Nat Centre for Research and Development in Primary Care 1994–96; pubns on child health, gen practice and foetal physiology; FRCP; *Books* Placental Transfer-Methods and Interpretations (co-ed, 1981), Perinatal Medicine (co-ed, 1983), Paediatric Problems in Gen Practice (jtly, 1989); *Style*— Prof Robert Boyd; ✉ Stone House, Adlington, Cheshire SK10 4NU (☎ and fax 01625 872400); Greenacres, Balinoe, Tiree, Scotland PA77 6TZ (☎ 01879 220443); Principal's Office, St George's Hospital Medical School, Cranmer Terrace, London SW17 0RE (☎ 0181 725 5008, fax 0181 672 6940) (evenings ☎ 0171 383 2568)

BOYD, Prof Sir Robert Lewis Fullarton; kt (1983), CBE (1972); s of late Dr William John Boyd, of Sanderstead, Surrey; *b* 19 Oct 1922; *Educ* Whitgift Sch, Univ of London; *m* 1949, Mary (d 1996), da of late John Higgins; 2 s, 1 da; *Career* dir Mullard Space Sci Lab UCL 1954–83; prof of astronomy Royal Instn 1961–67, prof of physics Univ of London 1962–83; memb SRC 1977–81, tstee Nat Maritime Museum 1980–89; fell UCL 1989; FRS 1969; *Recreations* elderly Rolls Royce motor cars and live steam model engineering; *Style*— Prof Sir Robert Boyd, CBE, FRS; ✉ Roseneath, 41 Church St, Littlehampton, W Sussex BN17 5PU (☎ 01903 714438)

BOYD, Robert Nathaniel; CBE (1971); s of Peter Ferguson Boyd, and Annie Jane, *née* Newton; *b* 17 Nov 1918; *Educ* Boys' GS Suva Fiji, Churchers' Coll Petersfield; *m* 1947, Carrie, da of Harry Squires; 2 s; *Career* Lt-Col (ret) Br Somaliland 1940, Abyssinia, Madagascar and Burma, 30 years Territorial and Res Service; served Central Africa Civil Serv 1947–68; auditor gen Zambia 1966–68, sec and fin controller Air Tport and Travel Indust Trg Bd 1969–77; practising arbitrator and co dir; chm Dist Fin Ctee Wokingham Dist Cncl 1974–77 (memb Cncl 1972–77); vice pres United Soc for Propagation of Gospel 1992– (vice chm 1982–90, treas 1982–); Efficiency Decoration Zambia 1968, Order of the Epiphany Anglican Church in Central Africa 1968; FCIS, FCIArb, FIMgt; *Recreations* bowls; *Clubs* Hurst Bowling, Royal Cwlth Soc; *Style*— Robert Boyd, Esq, CBE; ✉ 7 Acorn Drive, Wokingham, Berks RG40 1EQ (☎ 0118 978 1122)

BOYD, Dr Roy Victor; s of Ernest Arthur Boyd (d 1965), and Olive, *née* Bachelor; *b* 14 Sept 1934; *Educ* Bromley Co GS, UCH London; *m* 1 (m dis 1966), Ann Esther, *née* Wright; 4 s (Andrew Charles b 22 Aug 1958, David John b 15 Jan 1960, Paul Nicholas (twin) b 15 Jan 1960, Simon James b 1 Sept 1965); m 2, Elizabeth Mary Jean, *née* Dalgleish (d 1986); 1 da (Rachel Jean b 1 Aug 1972); m 3, 12 July 1986, Jennifer; *Career* former conslt in geriatric med: Greenwich 1964–73, Plymouth 1973–77, Nottingham 1977–93; postgrad dean Univ of Nottingham Med Sch 1986–96, regnl postgrad dean Trent Regnl Health Authy 1992–96; FRCP 1979, FRCPE 1980; *Recreations* bridge, music, theology, woodwork; *Style*— Dr Roy Boyd; ✉ 65 Trowell Road, Nottingham NG8 2EJ (☎ 0115 928 8744)

BOYD, Stewart Craufurd; QC (1981); s of Leslie Balfour Boyd, OBE, of London, and Wendy, *née* Blake; *b* 25 Oct 1943; *Educ* Winchester, Trinity Coll Cambridge (MA); *m* 1970, Catherine (Hon Mrs Boyd), da of late Baron Jay, PC (Life Peer); 1 s (Matthew b 1975), 3 da (Rachel b 1972, Emily b 1973, Hannah b 1987); *Career* called to the Bar Middle Temple 1967, bencher 1990, recorder of the Crown Court; *Books* Scrutton on Charterparties and Bills of Lading (jt ed), Commercial Arbitration (jtly with The Rt Hon Lord Mustill); *Recreations* sailing, gardening, music; *Style—* Stewart Boyd, Esq, QC; ✉ 1 Gayton Crescent, London NW3 1TT (☎ 0171 431 1581); Wraxall Manor, Higher Wraxall, Dorchester, Dorset DT2 0HP (☎ 01935 83283); Essex Court Chambers, 24 Lincoln's Inn Fields, London WC2A 3ED (☎ 0171 813 8000, fax 0171 813 8080)

BOYD, Tommy; *b* 24 Nov 1965; *Career* professional footballer; over 250 appearances Motherwell 1983–91, transferred to Chelsea 1991, Celtic 1992–; Scotland: memb under 21 team, over 20 full caps; *Style—* Tommy Boyd, Esq; ✉ Celtic FC, Celtic Park, 95 Kerrydale Street, Glasgow G40 3RE

BOYD, William Andrew Murray; s of Alexander Murray Boyd (d 1979), and Evelyn, *née* Smith; *b* 7 March 1952; *Educ* Gordonstoun, Univ of Nice (Dip), Univ of Glasgow (MA), Jesus Coll Oxford; *m* Susan Anne, da of David Leslie Wilson, of Maxwell Park, Glasgow; *Career* lectr in English lit St Hilda's Coll Oxford 1980–83, TV critic New Statesman 1981–83; author; FRSL 1982, Chevalier de l'Ordre des Arts et des Lettres 1991; *Films* Good and Bad at Games (1983), Dutch Girls (1985), Scoop (adaptation from Evelyn Waugh novel, 1986), Stars and Bars (1988), Aunt Julia and the Scriptwriter (adaptation from Mario Vargas Llosa novel, 1990), Mister Johnson (adaptation from Joyce Cary novel, 1990), Chaplin (1992), A Good Man in Africa (1994); *Novels* A Good Man in Africa (1981, Somerset Maugham Award, Whitbread Prize first novel 1981), On the Yankee Station (1981), An Ice-Cream War (1982, John Llewelyn Rhys Prize 1982), Stars and Bars (1984), School Ties (1985), The New Confessions (1987), Brazzaville Beach (1990, James Tait Black Meml Prize 1991, McVitie's Prize 1991, Scottish Writer of the Year 1991), The Blue Afternoon (1993, Sunday Express Book of the Year 1993, Los Angeles Times Award for Fiction 1995), The Destiny of Nathalie 'X' (1995); *Clubs* Chelsea Arts, Two Brydges Place, Groucho; *Style—* William Boyd, Esq, FRSL; ✉ c/o The Agency, 24 Pottery Lane, Holland Park, London W11 4LZ

BOYD-CARPENTER, (Marsom) Henry; CVO (1994); s of Francis Henry Boyd-Carpenter (d 1984), of East Lambrook Manor, Somerset, and Nina, *née* Townshend (d 1982); *b* 11 Oct 1939; *Educ* Charterhouse, Balliol Coll Oxford (BA, MA); *m* 18 Sept 1971, Lesley Ann, da of William Henry Davies (d 1986), of Billericay, Essex; 1 s (William Henry Francis b 28 July 1975), 1 da (Alexandra Mary b 28 June 1979); *Career* admitted slr 1966; ptnr Farrer & Co 1968–, slr Duchy of Cornwall 1976–94, private slr to HM The Queen 1995–; hon auditor Law Soc 1979–81, hon steward Westminster Abbey 1980–, memb Governing Body Charterhouse Sch 1981–, memb Cncl Chelsea Physic Garden 1983–, memb Bd of Govrs Sutton's Hosp 1994–, hon legal advsr Canterbury Cathedral Appeal Fund 1994–, memb Cncl Prince of Wales Inst of Architecture 1995–; memb Law Soc 1966; *Recreations* reading, listening to music, hill walking; *Clubs* Brooks's; *Style—* Henry Boyd-Carpenter, Esq, CVO; ✉ Guardswell House, Brockenhurst Road, South Ascot, Berkshire SL5 9HA (☎ 01344 23993); Farrer & Co, 66 Lincoln's Inn Fields, London WC2A 3LH (☎ 0171 242 2022, fax 0171 831 9748, telex 24318)

BOYD-CARPENTER, Baron (Life Peer UK 1972) of Crux Easton, co Southampton; John Archibald Boyd-Carpenter; PC (1954), DL (Gtr London 1973); s of Maj Sir Archibald Boyd Boyd-Carpenter, MP (d 1937), of River House, Walton-on-Thames, and Annie, *née* Dugdale; gs of Rt Rev William Boyd-Carpenter, KCVO, DD, Bishop of Ripon (d 1918); *b* 2 June 1908; *Educ* Stowe, Balliol Coll Oxford (BA, Dip in Econ, pres Oxford Union Soc 1930); *m* 1937, Margaret Mary, da of Lt-Col George Leslie Hall, OBE, by his w, Dorothy, *née* Coventry, ggggda of 6 Earl of Coventry; 1 s, 2 da; *Career* WWII served Scots Gds 1939–45, Maj 1942; Harmsworth law scholar Middle Temple 1932, barr 1934, practised London and SE Circuit 1934–39, jr SE Circuit 1939; MP (C) Kingston-upon-Thames 1945–72; fin sec Treasury 1951–54; Min of Transport and Civil Aviation 1954–55, Min of Pensions and Nat Insur 1955–62, chief sec Treasury and Paymaster-Gen 1962–64, opposition front bench spokesman on housing & land 1964–66, chm Public Accounts Ctee 1964–70, sits as Conservative in House of Lords, pres Assoc of Cons Peers 1990– (chm 1981–90); chm: Orion Insur Co and CLRP Investmt Tst 1968–72, Civil Aviation Authority 1972–77, Rugby Portland Cement Co 1976–84; dir of other cos, dep chm Cncl Forte 1990– (memb 1977–); high steward The Royal Borough of Kingston-upon-Thames 1976–; *Books* Way of Life; *Recreations* swimming, tennis, walking, gardening; *Clubs* Carlton (chm 1979–86); *Style—* The Rt Hon Lord Boyd-Carpenter, PC, DL; ✉ 12 Eaton Terrace, London SW1 (☎ 0171 730 7765); Crux Easton House, Crux Easton, nr Highclere, Newbury, Berks (☎ 01635 253037)

BOYD-CARPENTER, (Lt-Gen the Hon) Sir Thomas Patrick John; KBE (Mil 1993, MBE (Mil) 1973); s of Baron Boyd-Carpenter, PC, DL (Life Peer); *b* 1938; *Educ* Stowe; *m* 1972, Mary Jean, da of John Elwes Duffield; 3 c; *Career* Scots Gds, Col GSAT3 MOD 1981, Cmd 24 Inf Bde 1983–84, D DEF Pol MOD 1985–87, COS HQ BAOR 1988–89, ACDS (Prog) MOD 1989–92, DCDS (P & P) MOD 1992–96; chm: Social Security Advsy Ctee 1995–, Kensington and Westminster HA 1996–; sr conslt People in Business 1996–; *Style—* Sir Thomas Boyd-Carpenter, KBE

BOYD MAUNSELL, Nevill Francis Wray; s of Col Cecil Robert Wray Boyd Maunsell (d 1961), of Worcester, and Elizabeth Frances, *née* Boyd; *b* 22 Dec 1930; *Educ* Winchester, Univ Coll Oxford (BA); *m* 5 Oct 1957, Lyghia, da of Dr Mihai Peterson (d 1954), of London; 1 s (Michael b 1958), 1 da (Indi b 1963); *Career* Nat Serv 2 Lt Royal Warwick Regt 1949–50; schoolmaster in UK and USA 1953–55; journalist: Reuters 1955–57, Financial Times 1957–60, Time and Tide 1960–61, Daily Sketch 1961–65, freelance 1965–73; The Birmingham Post: dep city ed 1973–86, city ed 1986–94, economics ed 1994–; *Recreations* gardening, reading, idle chatter; *Style—* Nevill Boyd Maunsell, Esq; ✉ The Birmingham Post, 11 Buckingham Street, London WC2N 6DF (☎ 0171 839 9090, fax 0171 839 6300)

BOYD OF MERTON, 2 Viscount (UK 1960); Simon Donald Rupert Neville Lennox-Boyd; s of 1 Viscount Boyd of Merton, CH, PC, DL (d 1983), and Patricia, Viscountess Boyd of Merton; *b* 7 Dec 1939; *Educ* Eton, ChCh Oxford (MA); *m* 1962, Alice Mary, JP (High Sheriff of Cornwall 1987), DL (Cornwall 1995), da of Maj Meysey George Dallas Clive (ka 1943); 2 s (Hon Benjamin b 21 Oct 1964, Hon Edward b 30 March 1968), 2 da (Hon Charlotte b 1963, Hon Philippa b 1970); *Heir* s, Hon Benjamin Alan Lennox-Boyd, *qv*; *Career* dep chm Arthur Guinness & Sons 1981–86, chm The Iveagh Tstees Ltd 1993– (dir 1967–); chm: Save the Children Fund 1987–92, Stonham Housing Assoc 1992–; vice chm Guinness Tst 1993– (tstee 1974–); Liveryman Worshipful Co of Goldsmiths; *Recreations* planting trees; *Style—* The Rt Hon the Viscount Boyd of Merton; ✉ 9 Warwick Square, London SW1V 2AA (☎ 0171 821 1618); Ince Castle, Saltash, Cornwall (☎ 01752 842672, fax 01752 842249); office: Iveagh House, 41 Harrington Gdns, London SW7 4JU (☎ 0171 373 7261, fax 0171 244 8281)

BOYDELL, Chancellor Peter Thomas Sherrington; QC (1965); s of late Frank Richard Boydell, JP, and late Frances Barton Boydell; *b* 20 Sept 1920; *Educ* Arnold Sch Blackpool, Univ of Manchester (LLB); *Career* Adj 17 Field Regt RA 1943, Bde Major RA 1 Armoured Div 1944, Bde Major RA 10 Indian Div 1945; admitted slr 1947, barr Middle Temple 1948, bencher 1970 (dep treas 1988, treas 1989), head of chambers; memb: Legal Bd of Church Assembly 1958–71, Advsy Bd Redundant Churches 1993–; Parly candidate (C) Carlisle 1964; chm Planning and Local Govt Ctee of the Bar 1973–86 (chm Local Govt and Planning Bar Assoc 1986–90), leader Parly Bar 1975–; chancellor Diocese of: Truro 1957–, Oxford 1958–, Worcester 1959–; ARICS 1982; *Recreations* mountaineering, travel, music; *Clubs* Garrick, RAC, Climbers'; *Style—* The Worshipful Chancellor Peter Boydell, QC; ✉ 2 Harcourt Buildings, Temple, London EC4 (☎ 0171 353 8415)

BOYER, Ernest Stanley; s of Walter Boyer (d 1981), of Holmstall, Quorn, Leics, and Evelyn, *née* Hudson (d 1976); *b* 30 Nov 1925; *Educ* Kingsbury GS, Regent St Sch of Architecture; *m* 27 March 1954, Patricia (d 1995), da of Montegue Cecil Cuthbertson (d 1950), of Hampstead, London; 1 s (Guy b 1959); *Career* architect; assoc ptnr Monro & Sons 1949–57; fndr: E S Boyer & Partners 1957, Boyer Design Group 1974; memb Cncl RIBA for Essex, Cambs and Herts 1961; memb: Worshipful Co of Bowyers, Worshipful Co of Constructors; RIBA 1957, FASI 1976; *Recreations* riding, painting, cricket; *Clubs* Les Ambassadeurs, Wig and Pen, MCC; *Style—* Ernest Boyer, Esq; ✉ Lone Pine, 100 Green Lane, Bovingdon, Herts HP3 OLA (☎ 01442 834365)

BOYES, (Charles) Robin; s of Norman Frank Boyes, of Huntingdon, Cambs, and Rose Margaret, *née* Slingsby; *b* 16 Nov 1939; *Educ* Oundle; *m* 20 April 1968, Carroll Anne, da of Raymond Elkerton (d 1972), of St Albans, Herts; 1 s (Christopher b 1969); *Career* slr; dir Argyle Building Soc 1966–85; ptnr: Grover Humphreys & Boyes 1965–75, Warrens 1976–85, Warrens Boyes & Archer 1985–; Liveryman Worshipful Co of Needlemakers; hon slr Royal Photographic Soc of GB, Fenton Medal 1980; *Recreations* cricket, golf, collecting old toy soldiers; *Clubs* East India; *Style—* Robin Boyes, Esq; ✉ Punch's Grove, Hilton, Huntingdon, Cambs (☎ 01480 830335); 20 Hartford Road, Huntingdon, Cambs (☎ 01480 411331, fax 01480 59012)

BOYES, Roger F; *Career* grp fin dir Fenner plc 1986–90; Leeds Permanent Building Society: fin dir 1990–93, actg chief exec 1990–94, chief exec 1994–95; grp fin dir Halifax Building Soc 1995–; FCMA, MInstD, FRSA; *Style—* Roger Boyes, Esq; ✉ Halifax Building Society, Head Office, Trinity Road, Halifax, West Yorkshire HX1 2RG (☎ 01422 333333, fax 01422 333000)

BOYES, Roland; MP (Lab) Houghton and Washington (majority 20,808); *b* 12 Feb 1937; *m* Patricia, *née* James; 2 s; *Career* former teacher and former asst dir of Social Servs; MEP (Lab) Durham 1979–84, MP (Lab) Houghton and Washington 1983–, front bench environment spokesman 1985–88, defence spokesman 1988–92, memb Speaker's Panel 1994–; memb GMB, chm Tribune Group 1985–86, chm All Pty Photography Gp 1987–; vice pres Hartlepool Utd AFC; *Recreations* photography, sports, brass bands; *Clubs* Peterlee CC (pres); *Style—* Roland Boyes, Esq, MP; ✉ 12 Spire Hollin, Peterlee, Co Durham (☎ 0191 586 3917); Constituency Office (☎ 0191 385 7825); House of Commons, London SW1A 0AA

BOYLAN, Clare Catherine; da of Patrick Francis Boylan (d 1989), of Dublin, and Evelyn, *née* Selby; *b* 21 April 1948; *Career* writer; journalist Irish Press Group Dublin 1968–69 and 1973–78, ed Image magazine Dublin 1981–84; contrib to: Sunday Times, The Guardian, Los Angeles Times; winner Benson & Hedges prize for outstanding work in Irish journalism 1974; judge Booker Prize 1978, international judge Irish Times Literature Prize 1993; *Novels* Holy Pictures (1983), Last Resorts (1984), Black Baby (1988), Home Rule (1992); *Short Stories* A Nail on the Head (1983), Concerning Virgins (1989), short story Some Retired Ladies on a Tour adapted into film (Oscar nomination 1988), That Bad Woman (1995); *Others* The Agony and The Ego (essays, ed, 1993), intro to Taking Chances (by M J Farrell), The Literary Companion to Cats (ed, 1994); *Recreations* collecting cats; *Clubs* Groucho; *Style—* Ms Clare Boylan; ✉ c/o Rogers Coleridge & White, Literary Agents, 20 Powis Mews, London W11 1JN (☎ 0171 221 3717)

BOYLE, Billy; s of Bill Boyle (d 1983), of Dublin, Ireland, and Kathleen, *née* Noone; *b* 24 Feb 1948; *Educ* O'Connell's Sch Dublin Ireland; *Career* actor; *Theatre* incl: Maggie May, Canterbury Tales, Hello Dolly, Billy, No Sex Please We're British, Playboy of the Western World, What's a Nice Country, The Fantastiks, The Rivals (NY), The Scheming Lieutenant (US), Boots for the Footless, Merman, Some Like it Hot, The Absolute Irishman, The Music Man; *Television* incl: EastEnders, Jackanory, The Professionals, Life at Stake, Frost Report, The Saturday Crowd, It's Billy Boyle, The Basil Brush Show, The Generation Game, Dance Crazy, The Kelly Monteith Show, The Bretts, Parnell, The Grass Arena, Father Ted; *Films* incl: Barry Lyndon, Side by Side, Groupie Girl, Sean, The Scarlet and the Black, The Predator, Wild Geese II; *Style—* Billy Boyle, Esq; ✉ c/o Billy Marsh Associates Ltd, 174–178 North Gower Street, London NW1 2NB (☎ 0171 388 6858, fax 0171 388 6848)

BOYLE, George Hamilton; DL (Leics 1980); s of Capt E M G L Boyle, RN (d 1982), and Maida Cecil, *née* Evans-Freke (d 1995); *b* 15 Sept 1928; *Educ* Canford, Univ of London (BSc); *m* 25 July 1953, Alathea Henriette Mary March Phillipps de Lisle; 3 s (Robert b 28 Sept 1954, Richard b 8 Jan 1959, Rupert b 19 Sept 1960); *Career* RTZ 1953–55; chm Leics and Rutland Branch CLA 1976–79; non-exec dir E Midland Electricity Bd 1980–90; memb Advsy Panel Environmental Devpt National Grid Co 1990–93; pres Friends of Rutland Co Museum and Record Soc 1973–93; High Sheriff Co of Rutland 1964 and Leics 1976; ARSM; *Style—* George Boyle, Esq, DL; ✉ Nozieres, 07270 Lamastre, France

BOYLE, (Samuel) Gerald; s of Samuel Joseph Boyle, of Belfast (d 1972), and Mary Alice, *née* Edgar; *b* 23 May 1937; *Educ* St Patrick's HS Downpatrick Co Down; *m* 5 Oct 1965, Kathleen Bernadette, da of Hugh Blaney Crossey (d 1983); 3 s (Gary b 1966, Jonathan b 1968, Nicholas b 1972); *Career* chartered insurer and gen insurance advsr; dir: Shield Insurance Co Ltd Dublin 1984–91, Europ Assistance Ltd Croydon 1987–89, Eagle Star Insurance Co Ltd 1991–96 (gen mangr 1985–87), Industl and Agric Safety Conslts 1988–96, Eagle Star Group Engineering Insurance Ltd 1991–96, Inspecting Engineers (Scotland) Ltd 1991–96, Inspecting Engineers Ltd 1991–96, Midland Assurance Ltd 1991–96, Eagle Star Pension Trustee Ltd 1994–, South African Eagle Insurance Company Ltd 1994–, Sorema UK Ltd 1996–; *Recreations* golf and rugby; *Clubs* Minchinhampton Golf (Glos), La Manga Golf (Spain), Northern FC (Newcastle upon Tyne); *Style—* Gerald Boyle, Esq; ✉ The Little House, Barnsley, Cirencester, Gloucestershire GL7 5EF (☎ 01285 740726)

BOYLE, Prof Iain Thomson; s of Dugald Thomson Boyle (d 1971), and Annie Ross, *née* MacPhail; *b* 7 Oct 1935; *Educ* Paisley GS, Univ of Glasgow; *m* 28 Aug 1964, Elizabeth Johnston, da of John Trew Carmichael, of Glasgow; 1 s (Douglas), 2 da (Catriona, Alison); *Career* Hartenstein res fell Univ of Wisconsin USA 1970–72, ed Scottish Medical Journal 1978–83, reader in med Univ of Glasgow and Glasgow Royal Infirmary 1984–96, med advsr Univ of Strathclyde 1991–; visiting prof Depts of Physiology and Pharmacology Univ of Strathclyde 1994–; pres: Caledonian Philatelic Soc 1983–84, Bone and Tooth Soc 1994–96 (treas 1989–93), Assoc of Scottish Philatelic Socs 1995–96; vice pres (medical) RCPGlas 1992–96 (hon librarian 1994–); chm: Bd of Mgmnt Scottish Medical Journal 1987–96, Sientific Advsy Ctee Tenovus-Scotland 1997–; hon sec: Scott Soc of Physics 1983–88, Scott Soc Experimental Med 1983–88; memb Assoc of Physicians of GB and Ireland; FRCP Glasgow 1974, FRCP 1978, FSA Scotland 1985; *Recreations* angling, social history, philately, golf, France and the French; *Style—* Prof Iain Boyle; ✉ Student and Occupational Health Service, University of Strathclyde, 26 Richmond Street, Glasgow (☎ 0141 548 3916)

BOYLE, John Godfrey (Geoff); OBE (1977); s of John Boyle (d 1980), of Edinburgh, and Maude Craven (d 1935); *b* 17 Nov 1928; *Educ* Daniel Stewart Coll Edinburgh; *m* 1955,

Sarah, da of G D Ward (d 1968), of Edinburgh; 1 s (Adrian), 1 da (Philippa); *Career* formerly: fin conslt and business cnsllr Lothian and Edinburgh Enterprise Ltd, enterprise cnsllr DTI, fin dir Burmah Oil Exploration Ltd; formerly dir: Oil India Ltd, Tinplate Co of India Ltd, Burmah Shell Oil Storage & Distribution Co of India Ltd, Bladite Holdings Ltd, Burmah Oil Co Pakistan Trading Ltd, Assam Oil Co Ltd, Burmah Oil Kenya Ltd, Burmah Oil Somalia Ltd, PS & S (Personnel) Ltd; currently: chm Scotprint Ltd, dir Amaising Publishing House Ltd, dir Glowworm Books Ltd; MICAS 1955; *Recreations* literature, music, yachting; *Clubs* East Lothian Yacht (North Berwick); *Style*— John G Boyle, Esq, OBE; ✉ 60A Forth Street, North Berwick, East Lothian EH39 4JJ (☎ 01620 893301)

BOYLE, Katie (Catherine Irene Helen Mary); da of Marchese Demetrio Imperiali dei Principi di Francavilla, and Dorothy Kate, *née* Ramsden; *b* 29 May 1926; *Educ* Switzerland and Italy; *m* 1, 1947 (m dis 1955), Viscount Boyle, now Earl of Shannon, *qv*; m 2, 1955, Greville Baylis (d 1976); m 3, 1979, Sir Peter Saunders, *qv*; *Career* TV/radio presenter and panellist, columnist and occasional actress; author of "Dear Katie" column TV Times 1970–88, frequent contributor to various publications, permanent agony aunt for Daily Mail off-shoot Dogs Today (now over 5 years), and for 8 years to Here's Health; broadcaster of wide variety of subjects (including Quite Contrary 1954, Golden Girl, Eurovision Song Contests, various Katie Boyle shows, Katie & Friends, currently on Radio 2 FM); various stage and film work; princ stage appearances: lead in Pardon My Claws 1955, Stella Manners, Silver Wedding (Cambridge Theatre, London) 1957; princ film appearances: Old Mother Riley Goes to School 1956, Not Wanted on Voyage 1957, Intent to Kill 1958; winner Europremio Award TV Personality of Europe 1964, Favourite Eurovision Personality from Eurovision Network Oscars 1992; memb Bd of Govrs Royal Homoeopathic Hosp 1990–92; memb Ctee Battersea Dogs' Home; *Recreations* animals and animal welfare, dog training, gardening, jigsaw puzzles, embroidery; *Style*— Miss Katie Boyle; ✉ Canons Close, London N2 0BH

BOYLE, Leonard Butler; CBE (1976); s of Harold Boyle, and Edith Boyle; *b* 13 Jan 1913; *Educ* Roundhay Sch Leeds; *m* 1938, late Alice Baldwin Yarborough; 2 s; *Career* dir and gen mangr Principality Building Society 1956–78; vice pres: Bldg Soc Assoc 1978 (chm 1973–75), Chartered Bldg Socs Inst 1978–94, Chartered Inst of Bankers 1994–; *Style*— Leonard Boyle, Esq, CBE; ✉ Northwick Cottage, Marlpit Lane, Seaton, Devon (☎ 01297 22194)

BOYLE, Capt Michael Patrick Radcliffe; DL (Hants 1982); s of Patrick Spencer Boyle (s of late Capt Hon E Spencer H Boyle, RN, 5 s of 5 Earl of Shannon, by his 2 w, Julia, da of Sir William Hartopp, 3 Bt); *b* 25 Jan 1934; *Educ* Eton; *m* 1, 1962 (m dis 1995), Lady Nell Carleton Harris, da of 6 Earl of Malmesbury, TD, DL, and Hon Diana Carleton, da of 2 Baron Dorchester; 2 s, 1 da; m 2, 1 June 1995, Mrs Alexandra Mary Hilda Seymour, da of Maj Sir Victor Basil John Seely, 4 Bt (d 1980); *Career* cmmnd Irish Gds 1953, Capt 1961, ret 1966; High Sheriff of Hants 1976–77; memb: Hants CC 1970–, Hants Police Authority 1970– (chm 1976–88); cmmr St John Ambulance Bde Hants 1969–75; Freeman City of London, Liveryman Worshipful Co of Gunmakers; CStJ; *Recreations* shooting, sailing; *Clubs* Boodle's, Pratt's, Royal Yacht Sqdn; *Style*— Capt M P R Boyle, DL; ✉ Saint Cross House, Whitchurch, Hampshire RG28 7AS (☎ 01256 895505)

BOYLE, Viscount; Richard Henry John Boyle; s (by 2 m) and h of 9 Earl of Shannon; *b* 19 Jan 1960; *Educ* Northease Manor Sch Lewes; *Style*— Viscount Boyle; ✉ Edington House, Edington, Bridgwater, Somerset TA7 9JS

BOYLE, Sir Stephen Gurney; 5 Bt (UK 1904), of Ockham, Salehurst, Sussex; er s of Sir Richard Gurney Boyle, 4 Bt (d 1983, s of Sir Edward Boyle, 2 Bt; suc to Btcy only of bro, Baron Boyle of Handsworth 1981), and Elizabeth Anne, yr da of Norman Dennes; *b* 15 Jan 1962; *Heir* bro, Michael Desmond Boyle b 16 Sept 1963; *Style*— Sir Stephen Boyle, Bt; ✉ 19 Gibb Croft, Harlow, Essex CM18 7JL

BOYLE, Thomas (Tommy); s of Thomas Boyle, of Motherwell, Strathclyde, and Agnes, *née* Kerr; *b* 21 May 1947; *Educ* Dalziel HS, Coatbridge Tech Coll, Motherwell Tech Coll (ONC); *m* 1, (m dis); 1 s (Mark Allen b 15 Dec 1980); m 2, Julie Blair; *Career* athletics coach; coach Bellshill YMCA Athletics Club 1968– (formerly competitor), involved with educn of other Scottish coaches 1978–86; coach to Yvonne Murray, *qv*, 1987–; currently working on jt project with North Lanarkshire Cncl to promote local athletics; BAF master coach qualification, Scottish Coach of the Year 1988, 1990 and 1994, BAAB Coach of the Year 1990, Coach of the Year Motherwell District 1993, 1994 and 1995; mechanical engr; Bull HN Computers Livingston 1967– (jr engr, engr, sr engr, engrg mangr, currently prodn mangr); *Recreations* gardening, my son, all sport; *Style*— Tommy Boyle, Esq; ✉ Lucozade Motherwell District Athletics, Westwind, 53 Harvest Drive, North Lodge, Motherwell, Scotland ML1 2RT (☎ 01698 731440)

BOYLE, William Russell; s of Charles Harry Boyle (d 1988), of Wimborne St Giles, Dorset, and Winifred Boyle (d 1967); *b* 15 Feb 1945; *m* 19 July 1969, Janet Elizabeth; 1 s (Matthew b 1974), 1 da (Joanne b 1971); *Career* insur broker; dir Bowring Marine Ltd, md Marsh and McLennan Incorporated; *Style*— William R Boyle, Esq; ✉ C T Bowring & Co (Insurance) Ltd, The Bowring Building, Tower Place, London EC3P 3BE (☎ 0171 357 5514, fax 0171 929 2705)

BOYLSTON, Prof Arthur William; s of George Arthur Boylston, and Marie, *née* Showers; *b* 16 Nov 1942; *Educ* Phillips Exeter Acad, Yale Univ (BA), Harvard Univ (MD); *m* 1 July 1978, Anthea, da of John Murray Phelps; 2 s (Thomas Arthur b 1980, Nicholas John b 1984); *Career* sr asst surgn US Public Health Serv 1970–72, lectr, sr lectr then reader St Mary's Hosp Med Sch London 1972–88, prof of pathology Univ of Leeds 1988–; FRCPath 1988; *Recreations* gardening, walking; *Clubs* Atheneaum; *Style*— Prof Arthur Boylston; ✉ Molecular Medicine Unit, Clinical Sciences Building, St James's Hospital, Leeds LS9 7TH (☎ 0113 283 7077, fax 0113 244 4475)

BOYNE, 11 Viscount (I 1717); Gustavus Michael Stucley (Tavie) Hamilton-Russell; also Baron Hamilton of Stackallen (I 1715) and Baron Brancepeth (UK 1866); sits as Baron Brancepeth; s of 10 Viscount Boyne, KCVO, JP (d 1995), and Rosemary Anne, *née* Stucley; *b* 27 May 1965; *Educ* Harrow, RAC Cirencester (Dip in Rural Estate Mgmnt); *m* 1 June 1991, Lucy, da of George Potter, of Foxdale, Bunbury, Cheshire; 1 da (Hon Emelia Rose b 25 Jan 1994); *Heir* great unc, Brig Hon Richard Gustavus Hamilton-Russell, DSO, LVO, *qv*; *Career* assoc RICS; *Recreations* cricket, skiing, travel; *Clubs* Turf; *Style*— The Rt Hon the Viscount Boyne; ✉ Dingle Leys, Burwarton, Bridgnorth, Shropshire WV16 6QG (☎ 01746 787221)

BOYNE, Sir Henry Brian (Harry); kt (1976), CBE (1969); 2 s of late Lockhart Alexander Boyne, of Inverness, and Elizabeth Jane Mactavish; *b* 29 July 1910; *Educ* HS and Royal Acad Inverness; *m* 1935, Margaret Little, da of John Templeton, of Dundee; 1 da; *Career* political corr: Glasgow Herald 1950–56, Daily Telegraph 1956–76; dir of communications Cons Central Office 1980–82; *Books* The Houses of Parliament (1981), Scotland Rediscovered (1986); *Recreations* reading, watching cricket; *Clubs* Victory; *Style*— Sir Harry Boyne, CBE; ✉ 122 Harefield Rd, Uxbridge, Middx UB8 1PN (☎ 01895 255211)

BOYNTON, Sir John Keyworth; kt (1979), MC (1944), DL (Cheshire 1975); s of Ernest Boynton (d 1940), of Hull; *b* 14 Feb 1918; *Educ* Dulwich Coll; *m* 1, 1947, Gabrielle (d 1978), da of G Stanglmaier, of Munich; 2 da; m 2, 1979, Edith Laane, of The Hague; *Career* slr; chief exec Cheshire CC 1974–79, election cmmr S Rhodesia 1979–80; *Books* Compulsory Puchase (7 edn, 1994), Job at the Top (1986); *Recreations* golf; *Clubs* Army and Navy; *Style*— Sir John Boynton, MC, DL; ✉ 40 High Sheldon, Sheldon Avenue, London N6 4NJ (☎ 0181 348 5234)

BOYNTON-WOOD, *see:* Wood

BOYS, John Philip; s of late Rev Stephen Philip Boys, and late Constance Rhoda Towns; *Educ* Glasgow and Dundee Colls of Art (DA); *m* 29 June 1963 (m dis 1988), Christine Bridget, da of late Cdr Jorgen Svend Jensen; 2 s (Adam b 1967, Jamie b 1970), 1 da (Amanda Jo b 1974); *Career* RAEC Egypt and Kenya 1946–48; former princ John Boys Architects (formerly Lothian Barclay, Jarvis & Boys then Boys Jarvis Partnership, joined 1960); firms awards and commendations incl: finalist Sydney Opera House Competition, finalist Financial Times Industl Architecture award 1974, Civic Tst commendations 1978 and 1988, Assoc for the Protection of Rural Scotland award 1978 and 1991, Saltire Soc commendations 1986 and 1988, RIBA/RIAS Scot regnl award 1989, GIA award (highly commended) 1990, Civic Tst award (diploma of excellence) 1990; formerly memb Cncl RIAS and Glasgow Inst of Architects, memb Royal Fine Art Cmmn for Scotland 1982–92; ARSA, FRIBA, FRIAS; *Recreations* painting, curling, sailing; *Clubs* Glasgow Art; *Style*— John Boys, Esq; ✉ San Makessan, Gartocharn, Dunbartonshire G83 8NQ (☎ 01389 830228)

BOYS, Penelope Ann; da of late Hubert John Boys, and Mollie, *née* Harnett; *b* 11 June 1947; *Educ* Guildford Co Sch for Girls; *m* 1977, David Charles Henshaw Wright; *Career* exec offr DES (now DFE) 1966–69, asst princ Miny of Power 1969–72, private sec to Min without Portfolio 1972–73; Dept of Energy: princ 1973–78, seconded to British Nat Oil Corp 1978–80, head of Int Unit 1981–85, seconded as head ST2 Div HM Treasy 1985–87, dir of personnel 1987–89, dep DG Office of Electricity Regulation 1989–93; head of personnel Dept of Trade and Industry 1993–; *Recreations* cooking, walking, racing; *Style*— Miss Penelope Boys; ✉ Department of Trade and Industry, 1 Victoria Street, London SW1H 0ET

BOYS SMITH, Stephen Wynn; s of John Boys Smith (d 1991), and Gwendolen Sara, *née* Wynn (d 1994); *b* 4 May 1946; *Educ* Sherborne, St John's Coll Cambridge (MA), Univ of British Columbia (MA); *m* 1971, Linda Elaine, da of Ronald Price; 1 s (Nicholas John b 16 Oct 1973), 1 da (Sarah Jane b 9 March 1977); *Career* teaching asst Univ of British Columbia 1967–68; Home Office: joined 1968, asst private sec to Home Sec 1971–73; Central Policy Review Staff Cabinet Office 1977–79, Home Office 1979–81, asst sec NI Office 1981, princ private sec to Sec of State for NI 1981–82, Home Office 1984, princ private sec to Home Sec 1985–87, under sec Home Office Police Dept 1989–92, under sec HM Treasy 1992–95, dep sec (head of Police Dept) Home Office 1995–96, dir of police policy Home Office 1996–; *Style*— Stephen Boys Smith, Esq; ✉ Home Office, Queen Anne's Gate, London SW1H 9AT (☎ 0171 273 3601)

BOYSON, Rt Hon Sir Rhodes; kt (1987), MP (C) Brent North (majority 10,131); s of Alderman William Boyson, MBE, JP, of Haslingden, Lancs, and Bertha Boyson; *b* 11 May 1925; *Educ* Haslingden GS, Univ of Manchester, Univ Coll Cardiff, LSE, CCC Cambridge (BA, MA, PhD); *m* 1, 1946 (m dis), Violet Burletson; 2 da; m 2, 1971, Florette, *née* MacFarlane; *Career* headmaster: Lea Bank Secdy Modern Rossendale 1955–61, Robert Montefiore Secdy Sch Stepney 1961–66, Highbury GS 1966–67, Highbury Grove Sch 1967–74; Parly candidate (C) Eccles 1970, MP (C) Brent N Feb 1974–, vice chm Cons Parly Educn Ctee 1975–76, oppn spokesman for educn 1976–79, Parly under sec DES 1979–83, min for social security DHSS 1983–84, dep sec for NI 1984–86, min for local govt 1986–87; chm Nat Cncl for Educnl Standards 1974–79; dir Blacks Leisure; conslt Arc International; *Recreations* gardening, sport, writing, talking; *Clubs* St Stephen's, Carlton; *Style*— Rt Hon Sir Rhodes Boyson, MP; ✉ c/o House of Commons, London SW1A 0AA

BRABAZON OF TARA, 3 Baron (UK 1942); Ivon Anthony Moore-Brabazon; DL (1993, IOW); s of 2 Baron Brabazon of Tara, CBE (d 1974, whose f, 1 Baron, was Min of Aircraft Production after Beaverbrook; the Bristol-Brabazon airliner was named after him); *b* 20 Dec 1946; *Educ* Harrow; *m* 8 Sept 1979, Harriet, da of Mervyn de Courcy Hamilton, of Harare, Zimbabwe, by his w, Lovell Ann, da of Rowland Cullinan, of Olifantsfontein, Transvaal; 1 s (Hon Benjamin Ralph b 1983), 1 da (Hon Anabel Mary b 1985); *Heir* s, Hon Benjamin Ralph Moore-Brabazon b 15 March 1983; *Career* memb London Stock Exchange 1972–84; a Lord in Waiting (government whip) 1984–86; spokesman for Dept of Transport 1984–85, and for Treasy, Dept of Trade and Industry, Energy 1985–86; Parly under-sec of state for Transport and min for Aviation and Shipping 1986–89, min of state Foreign and Commonwealth Office 1989–90, min of state Dept of Tport 1990–92; pres UK Warehousing Assoc 1992–, dep chm Fndn for Sport and the Arts 1992–, memb Cncl RAC Public Policy 1992–, memb Cncl Shipwrecked Mariners Soc 1993–; dir: Aurigny Air Services Ltd, Anglo Normandy Aeroengineering Ltd; chm Vehicle Security Installation Bd; *Recreations* sailing, Cresta Run, golf; *Clubs* White's, Royal Yacht Sqdn; *Style*— The Rt Hon the Lord Brabazon, DL; ✉ House of Lords, London SW1A 0PW

BRABBINS, Martyn Charles; s of Herbert Henry Brabbins (d 1985), and Enid Caroline, *née* Pope (d 1985); *b* 13 Aug 1959; *Educ* Sponne Sch Towcester Northants, Goldsmiths' Coll London, Leningrad State Conservatoire; *m* 31 August 1985, Karen Maria, da of John Christopher Evans; 2 s (Alexander John b 17 June 1989, Leo John b 30 June 1992), 1 da (Nina Pamela b 13 Sept 1994); *Career* conductor; winner Leeds Conductors Competition 1988; professional debut Scottish Chamber Orch 1986; assoc conductor BBC Scottish Symphony Orch 1992–, princ conductor Sinfonia 21 1994–; conductor: RPO, LPO, Philharmonia Orch, BBC Symphony Orch, Royal Liverpool Philharmonic Orch, BBC Nat Orch of Wales, Ulster Orch, North German Radio Orch, St Petersburg Philharmonic, Australian Youth Orch, English Chamber Orch, Northern Sinfonia, ENO, Opera North, Scottish Opera, English Touring Opera, Kirov Opera, Nash Ensemble; *Recordings* Henseldt Piano Concerto, Hindemith Viola Concertos, Britten War Requiem, Parry Piano Concerto, Stanford Piano Concerto, orchestral works by Mackenzie and Maccunn; *Recreations* cooking, running, travelling, reading, being with my family; *Style*— Martyn Brabbins, Esq; ✉ c/o Andrew Rosner, Allied Artists, 42 Montpelier Square, London SW7 1JZ (☎ 0171 589 6243, fax 0171 581 5269)

BRABHAM, Sir John Arthur (Jack); kt (1979), OBE (1966); s of Cyril Thomas Brabham; *b* 2 April 1926; *Educ* Hurstville Tech Coll Sydney; *m*; 3 s; *Career* racing driver 1947–1970; md: Jack Brabham (Ewell) Ltd, Jack Brabham (Worcester Park) Ltd, Engine Developements Ltd; three times World Motor Racing champion 1959, 1960 and 1966; *Books* When the Flag Drops; *Recreations* flying, boating, skindiving; *Clubs* BRDC, RAC; *Style*— Sir Jack Brabham, OBE; ✉ 5 Ruxley Lane, Ewell, Surrey KT19 0JB (☎ 0181 3941667)

BRABOURNE, 7 Baron (UK 1880); John Ulick Knatchbull; 16 Bt (E 1641); CBE (1993); s of 5 Baron Brabourne, GCSI, GCIE, MC, JP, MP (d 1939, sometime viceroy and actg govr-gen India) by his w, Lady Doreen Browne (Dowager Lady Brabourne, d 1979, da of 6 Marquess of Sligo); suc er bro, 6 Baron (d 1943, shot after escaping from a prison train in Italy and being recaptured); *b* 9 Nov 1924; *Educ* Eton, BNC Oxford; *m* 1946, Lady Patricia Edwina Victoria Mountbatten (Countess Mountbatten of Burma, *qv*), da of 1 Earl Mountbatten of Burma; 4 s (and 1 s decd), 2 da; *Heir* s, Lord Romsey; *Career* film and television producer; served WWII Capt Coldstream Gds (wounded NW Europe); dir: Mersham Productions Ltd 1970–, Thames Television plc 1978–95 (chm 1991–93), Euston Films Ltd 1979–95, Thorn EMI plc 1981–86; vice-chm Copyright Promotions Group plc 1987–; pro chllr Univ of Kent 1993– (memb Cncl 1968–); chm Govrs: Norton Knatchbull Sch 1955–95 (govr 1947–), Wye Coll 1994– (also provost, govr 1955–); govr: Gordonstoun Sch 1964–94, United World Coll of the Atlantic 1965–96, Nat Film and Television Sch 1981–96; tstee: BAFTA 1988–, Science Museum 1983–94, Nat

Museum of Photography Film and Television 1983–94; memb: Br Screen Advsy Cncl 1985–, Advsy Ctee British Library Nat Sound Archive 1990–; patron London International Film Sch 1977–, fell BFI 1979 (govr 1979–94); pres Kent Tst for Nature Conservation 1958–, vice pres Royal Soc of Nature Conservation 1988–; Liveryman Worshipful Co of Fishmongers; *Films* prodr/co-prodr: Harry Black and the Tiger 1958, Sink the Bismarck! 1960, HMS Defiant 1961, Othello 1966, Romeo and Juliet 1966, The Mikado 1967, Up the Junction 1968, The Dance of Death 1969, The Tales of Beatrix Potter 1971, Murder on the Orient Express 1974, Death on the Nile 1978, Stories from a Flying Trunk 1979, The Mirror Crack'd 1980, Evil Under the Sun 1982, A Passage to India 1984, Little Dorrit 1986; *Television* prodns incl: The Life and Times of Lord Mountbatten 1966, Royal Family (memb Advsy Ctee) 1969, Romantic Versus Classic Art 1973, The National Gallery - A Private View 1974, A Much Maligned Monarch 1976, Royal Heritage (memb Advsy Ctee) 1977, Leontine/Leontyne 1988; *Style*— The Rt Hon Lord Brabourne, CBE; ✉ Newhouse, Mersham, Ashford, Kent TN25 6NQ (☎ 01233 503636, fax 01233 512244); 41 Montpelier Walk, London SW7 1JH (☎ 0171 589 8829, fax 0171 584 0024)

BRACE, Robert P; *Career* joined Peat Marwick Mitchell (now KPMG) 1971, sr fin roles Unipart and Black & Decker; BT plc: joined 1989, gp fin dir 1993–; chm BT Welsh Advsy Forum; FCA; *Style*— Robert Brace, Esq; ✉ BT plc, 81 Newgate Street, London EC1A 7AJ (☎ 0171 356 5000)

BRACEWELL, Hon Mrs Justice; Hon Dame Joyanne Winifred (Dame Joyanne Bracewell); DBE (1990); da of Jack Bracewell, and Lilian Bracewell; *b* 5 July 1934; *Educ* Univ of Manchester (LLB, LLM); *m* 1963, Roy Copeland, s of late Jack Copeland; 1 s (Adam b 1965), 1 da (Philippa b 1967); *Career* recorder of the Crown Court (Northern Circuit) 1975–83, QC 1978, circuit judge Northern Circuit 1983–86 (Western Circuit 1986–90), judge of the High Court of Justice (Family Div) 1990–; chm Children Act Advsy Ctee 1993–; Hon LLD Univ of Manchester 1991; *Recreations* antiques, cooking, reading, walking, wildlife conservation; *Style*— The Hon Mrs Justice Bracewell, DBE

BRACEWELL-SMITH, Sir Charles; 4 Bt (UK 1947), of Keighley, Co York; s of Sir George Bracewell Smith, 2 Bt, MBE (d 1976); suc bro, Sir Guy Bracewell Smith, 3 Bt 1983; *b* 13 Oct 1955; *Educ* Harrow; *m* 1, 1977, Carol Vivien (d 1994), da of Norman Hough, of Cookham, Berks; m 2, 25 July 1996, Nina, da of Kuldip Kakkar, of New Delhi, India; *Heir* none; *Career* former dir: Park Lane Hotel, Mayfair Health Club; fndr: The Homestead Charitable Tst; *Books* The Song of Saints (as Francis O'Donovan); *Recreations* comparative religion, mystical theology, philosophy, psychology, Arsenal FC; *Clubs* RAC; *Style*— Sir Charles Bracewell-Smith, Bt; ✉ The Hermitage, 7 Clarence Gate Gardens, Glentworth Street, London NW1 6AY

BRACK, Peter Kenneth; s of Rev Martin Brack (d 1953), Rector of Wolviston, Co Durham 1906–50, private chaplain to Marquess of Londonderry 1908–14, and Dorothea, *née* Martin (d 1977); *b* 13 April 1922; *Educ* Trent Coll Derbyshire; *m* 1 April 1961, Nora, da of Francis Kilmartin, MM (d 1957), of Cheadle, Cheshire; *Career* Rolls Royce Ltd (Derby) 1940–71; engrg apprenticeship followed by various duties home and abroad: Cordoba Argentina 1950–52, Venezuela 1953–56, France and Italy 1957–59; md Rolls Royce De Espana SA Barcelona 1963–71; memb Ctee of Inspection Rolls Royce Ltd liquidation 1971–; dir: Bennett's Machine Co 1973–75, TTI Ltd (Translations Co) 1975–77; md Brack & Associates Ltd 1977–; memb Consultative Cncl Southern Derbyshire Chamber of Commerce, Trg and Enterprise 1996–; memb Derby Crime Prevention Panel 1994–; pres Br Club Barcelona 1966–71; CEng, FIMgt; *Recreations* philately (recognised authority on Venezuelan stamps), golf, chess, natural history; *Clubs* Canning, Naval and Military; *Style*— Peter Brack, Esq; ✉ Chrysalis, Windley, Belper, Derbyshire DE56 2LP (☎ 01773 550364); Brack & Associates Ltd, 66–66A Friar Gate, Derby DE1 1DJ (☎ 01332 360242, fax 01332 291551)

BRACK, Terence John; CB (1994); s of Noel Douglas John Brack, of Harlow, Essex, and Tertia Doreen, *née* Kennard (d 1987); *b* 17 April 1938; *Educ* Bradfield Coll Berks, Gonville and Caius Coll Cambridge (MA); *m* 29 Oct 1983, Christine Mary, da of late Douglas Ronald Cashin, of IOM; *Career* Nat Serv RAF (secretarial Branch) 1956–58; Air Miny 1961–64; MOD: private sec to Parly Under Sec of State for RAF 1964–66, princ 1966–73, seconded to Treasy 1968–72, asst sec 1973–85, head of fin and secretariat div for controller of the Navy 1975–78, head of defence secretariat for operational requirements and major equipments 1978–81, RCDS 1982–82, head of fin and secretariat Div of Air Launched Guided Weapons and Air Electronics 1983–84, asst under sec (Naval Personnel) 1985–89, asst under sec (General Fin) 1989–94, ret; *Recreations* walking, travel; *Style*— Terence Brack, Esq, CB

BRACKEN, Kyran Paul Patrick; s of Joseph Bracken, of Jersey, and Jane Martha Mary, *née* May; *b* 22 Nov 1971; *Educ* St Edward's Sch Liverpool, Stonyhurst, Univ of Bristol (LLB); *Career* Rugby Union scrum-half; clubs: Bristol RC 1992–94, currently with Saracens RFC; England: Schools 16 1987–88, Schools 18 1988–90 (capt 1990), England Students 1992–93 (capt 1993), Under 21 team, memb World Cup squad S Africa 1995, 11 full caps (debut v NZ); BBC West Country Player of the year; articled clerk Alsters Slrs 1994–; *Recreations* all sports; *Style*— Kyran Bracken, Esq; ✉ c/o Park Associates Ltd, Sports Management, 6 George Street, Nottingham NG1 (☎ 0115 948 3206, fax 0115 952 7203)

BRACKENBURY, Ven Michael Palmer; s of Frank Brackenbury (d 1959), and Constance Mary, *née* Palmer (d 1946); *b* 6 July 1930; *Educ* Norwich Sch, Lincoln Theol Coll; *m* 9 Apr 1953, Jean Margaret, da of Oscar Arnold Harrison (d 1966); *Career* RAF 1948–50; asst curate S Ormsby Gp 1966–69, rector Sudbrooke with Scothern 1969–77, rural dean Lawres 1973–78, diocesan dir of ordinands Lincoln 1977–87, personal asst to Bishop of Lincoln 1977–88, canon and prebendary of Lincoln 1979–95, diocesan lay ministry advsr Lincoln 1986–87, archdeacon of Lincoln 1988–95, archdeacon emeritus 1995–; memb Gen Synod 1989–95; memb Ecclesiastical Law Soc 1988–, chm Lincolnshire Ctee Princes' Tst 1996–; ACII 1956; *Recreations* music, travel; *Style*— The Ven Michael Brackenbury; ✉ 18 Lea View, Ryhall, Stamford, Lincolnshire PE9 4HZ (☎ 01780 52415)

BRACKLEY, Rt Rev Ian James; *see:* Dorking, Bishop of

BRADBEER, Sir (John) Derek (Richardson); kt (1988), OBE (1973), TD (1964), DL (1988); s of William Bertram Bradbeer (d 1992), of Hexham, Northumberland, and Winifred, *née* Richardson (d 1985); *b* 29 Oct 1931; *Educ* Canford, Sidney Sussex Coll Cambridge (MA); *m* 6 April 1962, Margaret Elizabeth, da of Gerald Frederick Chantler, TD, of Ponteland, Northumberland; 1 s (Jeremy b 1962), 1 da (Amanda b 1963); *Career* cmmnd RA 1951, CO 101 (N) Med Regt RA (V) 1970–73, Dep Cdr 21 and 23 Bdes 1973–77, Hon Col 101 (N) FD Regt RA (V) 1986–91; chm TAVR Assoc North of England 1990–; admitted slr 1959; ptnr Wilkinson Maughan Newcastle 1961–; memb Cncl Law Soc 1973–94, vice pres Law Soc 1986–87, pres 1987–88; pres Newcastle Law Soc 1980, govr Coll of Law 1983–, chm 1990–; UK vice pres Union Internationale des Avocats 1989–93; memb Criminal Injuries Compensation Bd 1988–, chm 1992–; dir: JT Dove Pensions Tst Ltd 1975–, Newcastle and Gateshead Water plc 1978–, North East Water plc 1990–, chm 1992–; memb Insurance Brokers Registration Cncl 1990–; *Recreations* gardening, reading, tennis, general sport; *Clubs* Army & Navy, Northern Counties; *Style*— Sir Derek Bradbeer, OBE, TD, DL; ✉ Wilkinson Maughan, Sun Alliance House, 35 Mosley St, Newcastle upon Tyne NE1 1XX (☎ 0191 261 1841, fax 0191 261 8267, telex 537477); 21 New Fetter Lane, London EC4A 1DL (☎ 0171 353 4100, fax 0171 353 3739)

BRADBEER, Richard Neil; *b* 30 Oct 1936; *Educ* Burnham-on-Sea Secondary Sch; *m* 11 Dec 1986, Patricia Ann; *Career* professional golfer; clubs: Taunton and Pickeridge 1959–63, Bristol and Clifton 1963–69, Burnham and Berrow 1969–79, The Royal Birkdale 1979–; capt European PGA Cup Team (against USA) 1990, capt PGA 1990, sr instructor PGA, English Golf Union coach NW England; designed 18 hole golf course at Garstang Lancs 1993; *Books* 100 Golfing Tips (1990), Ahead of the Game (1990), The Ultimate Golfer (1991); *Recreations* travel, good food and wine; *Style*— Richard Bradbeer, Esq; ✉ 19 Harrod Drive, Birkdale Southport, Merseyside PR8 2HA (☎ 01704 68594); The Royal Birkdale Golf Club, Waterloo Rd, Birkdale Southport, Merseyside (☎ 01704 68857)

BRADBURY, His Hon Judge Anthony Vincent; s of Alfred Charles Bradbury (d 1955), and Noreen, *née* Vincent Jones; *b* 29 Sept 1941; *Educ* Kent Coll Canterbury, Univ of Birmingham (LLB, Sir Henry Barber law scholar); *m* 22 Jan 1966, Rosalie Anne, *née* Buttrey; 1 da (Irene Jane b 18 Jan 1973); *Career* admitted slr 1965, asst slr Frere Cholmeley 1965–67 (articled clerk 1963–65), asst slr Abbot Thomas & Co 1967–70, princ Bradbury & Co 1970–81, dep registrar 1978–81, registrar Ilford Co Ct 1981–91, asst recorder 1985–90, recorder 1990–92, district judge Chelmsford Co Ct 1991–92, circuit judge (SE Circuit) 1992–; memb GLC and ILEA for Wandsworth 1967–70; Parly candidate (C): Battersea N 1970, Battersea S Feb 1974; contrib articles to Wisden's Cricketers Almanack and other cricket publications; *Recreations* long distance walking, travel, supporting Yorkshire cricket; *Clubs* MCC, Yorkshire CCC; *Style*— His Hon Judge Bradbury; ✉ Chelmsford Crown Court, PO Box 9, New Street, Chelmsford CM1 1EL

BRADBURY, Surgn Vice Adm Sir Eric Blackburn; KBE (1971), CB (1968); s of late A B Bradbury, of Orchard House, Maze, Co Antrim; *b* 2 March 1911; *Educ* Royal Belfast Academical Instn, Queen's Univ Belfast; *m* 1939, Elizabeth Constance (d 1991), da of late J C Austin, of Armagh; 3 da; *Career* RN Med Serv 1934, Surgn Capt 1959, Med Offr i/c RN Hosp Haslar 1966, Surg Rear Adm 1966, Surgn Vice Adm 1969, Med Dir Gen of the Navy 1969–72; chm Tunbridge Wells DHA 1981–84; FRCS 1972, Hon LLD Queen's Univ Belfast, CStJ, former QHP; *Style*— Surgn Vice Adm Sir Eric Bradbury, KBE, CB; ✉ 3 Lions Hall, St Swithun's Street, Winchester, Hampshire SO23 9HW

BRADBURY, 3 Baron (UK 1925); John Bradbury; s of 2 Baron Bradbury (d 1994), and his 1 w, Joan, *née* Knight; *b* 17 March 1940; *Educ* Gresham's and Univ of Bristol; *m* 1968 Susan, da of late W Liddiard, of East Shefford, Berks; 2 s (Hon John b 1973, Hon Ben b 1975); *Heir* s, Hon John Bradbury b 1973; *Style*— The Rt Hon the Lord Bradbury; ✉ 1 Irakli Street, Engomi, Nicosia, Cyprus

BRADBURY, John Howard Hullah; CBE (1986); s of Prof Fred Bradbury (d 1948), and Florence Jane, *née* Ratcliffe (d 1982); *b* 26 Feb 1940; *Educ* Friends' Sch Saffron Walden, Pomfret Sch Connecticut, Jesus Coll Cambridge; *m* 31 Aug 1963, Christine Annette J, da of Rev Christopher Augustine Kelly, of Gargrave, Skipton, Yorks; 1 s (Michael b 2 Jan 1973), 1 da (Elizabeth b 19 Mar 1970); *Career* factory supt AEI Rugby 1965–67 (prodn devpt engr 1964–65), raw materials buyer Mars Ltd 1968–75 (shift prodn mangr 1967–68), UK buying dir United Biscuits (UK) Ltd 1978–89 (dep buying dir 1975–78), dir Euro indust policy and purchasing United Biscuits (UK) Ltd 1989–94 (gp dir of commodities and corporate affrs 1991–92, gp dir of buying and corp affairs 1993–94); ind non-exec dir Security and Futures Authy Ltd 1991–96; Tower Capt St Mary's Farnham Royal; former pres Cake and Biscuit Alliance; *Recreations* fell walking, flying, skiing, amateur radio, shooting, campanology; *Style*— John Bradbury, Esq, CBE; ✉ c/o United Biscuits (UK) Ltd, Park Place, Church Road, West Drayton, Middx UB7 7PR (☎ 01895 432100, fax 01895 448848, telex 8954657)

BRADBURY, John Keith; s of Ronald Charles Bradbury (d 1996), of Knowle, Warwicks, and Gladys Marjorie, *née* Green (d 1971); *b* 18 Feb 1932; *Educ* King Henry VIII Sch Coventry; *m* 6 March 1954, Molly, da of Horace Reginald Woodbridge, of Coventry (d 1973); 2 s (Andrew John b 1955, Richard Anthony b 1963), 1 da (Jennifer Ann 1958); *Career* Nat Serv RAF 1950–52; dep ed The Birmingham Post 1975–80; ed: Sandwell Evening Mail 1980–84, Birmingham Post and Mail Weeklies 1984–85, Sunday Mercury Birmingham 1985–90; hon sec Birmingham Dist Newspaper Press Fund 1972–92, chm Nat Cncl for the Trg of Journalists 1987–88; former chm Birmingham Press Club, vice pres Walmley CC, former pres Wylde Green Bowling Club; Guild of Br Newspaper Eds: memb 1980, memb Cncl 1983–90, regnl chm 1983–84, nat sec 1990–93; *Recreations* theatre, music, travel, gardening, railways; *Clubs* Birmingham Press; *Style*— John Bradbury, Esq; ✉ Farriers Cottage, Ebrington, Chipping Campden, Glos (☎ 01386 593418)

BRADBURY, Julie Jane; da of Tony John Bradbury, of Southmoor, Oxon, and Sally Ann, *née* Burnhope; *b* 12 Feb 1967; *Educ* Northway Middle Sch Marston Oxford, Milham Ford Upper Sch Oxford, Oxford Coll of Further Educn; *m*, Stephen Naylor; *Career* badminton player; England debut v Canada 1991, currently 46 caps; achievements incl: nat singles champion 1991, team Bronze medal Euro Championships 1992, semi-finalist Taiwan Open 1992, nat ladies doubles champion (with Gillian Clark) 1992, quarter-finalist ladies doubles (with Gillian Clark) Olympic Games 1992, Bronze medal ladies doubles (with Gillian Clark) European Championships 1994, semi-finalist ladies doubles (with Gillian Clark) All-England Championships 1994, Gold medal team event Cwlth Games 1994, Silver medal ladies doubles and mixed doubles Cwlth Games 1994, semi-finalist ladies doubles (with Joanne Wright) and semi-finalist mixed doubles (with Simon Archer) All England Championships 1995, winner ladies doubles (with Joanne Wright) Malaysian Open 1995, runner up mixed doubles (with Simon Archer) World Cup 1995, runner up ladies doubles (with Joanne Wright) Hong Kong Open 1995, runner up mixed doubles (with Simon Archer) Korean Open 1996, Swiss Open 1996 and also All-England Championships 1996; also memb squads: World Championships 1991, 1993 and 1995, Uber Cup 1992, 1994 and 1996, Olympic Games 1992 and 1996, Silver medal mixed doubles, Bronze medal ladies doubles, Bronze medal team event Euro Championships 1996, winner English Nationals ladies doubles and mixed doubles 1996; Wyatt Trophy for outstanding performance of All England Championships 1992, Badminton Writers Player of the Year Award 1995/96; employment: sec Blackwells Publishing, legal sec Marshall & Galpin and Thomas Mallam slrs, pt/t admin asst Guardian Housing Assoc; *Recreations* reading, cooking, eating out, tennis, music; *Style*— Miss Julie Bradbury; ✉ 3a Meads Close, Drayton, Oxon OX14 4JN (☎ 01235 536239)

BRADBURY, Prof Malcolm Stanley; CBE (1991); s of Arthur Bradbury, and Doris, *née* Marshall; *b* 7 Sept 1932; *Educ* Univ of Leicester, Queen Mary Coll London (MA, hon fell 1984), Manchester Univ (PhD), Indiana Univ, Yale Univ; *m* 1959, Elizabeth Salt; 2 s (Matthew, Dominic); *Career* staff tutor in lit and drama Dept of Adult Educn Univ of Hull 1959–61, lectr in English language and lit Dept of English Univ of Birmingham 1961–65; UEA: lectr, sr lectr, then reader in English and American lit Sch of English and American Studies 1965–70, prof of American studies 1970–95, prof emeritus 1995–; visiting prof to Univs of: Zurich, Washington, St Louis, Queensland; visiting fell All Souls Coll Oxford 1969, visiting sr research fell St John's Coll Oxford 1994; chm of judges Booker McConnell Prize 1981, hon fell Queen Mary and Westfield Coll London 1984; Hon DLitt: Leicester 1986, Birmingham 1989, Hull 1994, Nottingham 1996; FRSL; *Television* ed: The After Dinner (TV plays, 1982); adapted: Blott on the Landscape (1985, by Tom Sharpe), Porterhouse Blue (1987, by Tom Sharpe, Int Emmy Award), Imaginary Friends (1987, by Alison Lurie), The Green Man (1990, by Kingsley Amis), Cold Comfort Farm (1994, by Stella Gibbons); writer of series: Anything More Would be Greedy (winner Monte Carlo Television Award), The Gravy Train, The Gravy Train Goes East; *Theatre* Inside Trading (stage play, Norwich, 1996); *Books* fiction incl: Eating People is Wrong (1959), Stepping Westward (1965), The History Man (1975), Who Do You Think You Are? (short stories, 1976), All Dressed Up and Nowhere To Go (1982), Rates of Exchange (shortlisted Booker Prize, 1982), Why Come to Slaka? (1986), Mensonge (1987), Cuts: a very short novel (1987), Doctor Criminale (1992); other publications incl: Evelyn Waugh (1962), What is a Novel? (1965), EM Forster: a collection of critical essays (ed 1965), A Passage to India: a Casebook (ed 1970), Penguin Companion to Literature Vol 3: American (with E Mottram, 1971), The Social Context of Modern English Literature (1972), Possibilities: essays on the state of the novel (1973), Modernism (with JW McFarlane, 1976), The Novel Today (ed 1977), An Introduction to American Studies (ed with H Temperley, 1981), Saul Bellow (1982), The Modern American Novel (1983), Penguin Book of Modern British Short Stories (ed 1987), The Modern World: Ten Great Writers (1987), New Writing (ed with Judy Cooke, 1992), New Writing 2 (ed, with Andrew Motion, 1993), The Modern British Novel (1993), Present Laughter (ed, 1994), Dangerous Pilgrimages: Transatlantic Mythologies and the Novel (1995), Class Work (ed, 1995), The Atlas of Literature (1996); also ed: Arnold Stratford upon Avon Studies series, Methuen Contemporary Writers series; *Recreations* farming; *Style*— Prof Malcolm Bradbury, CBE, FRSL; ✉ c/o EAS, University of East Anglia, University Plain, Norwich NR4 7TJ

BRADBURY, Michael Raymond; s of Arnold Needham Bradbury, of Wetherby, Yorkshire, and Rita Ann, *née* Fenwick; *b* 26 April 1952; *Educ* Leeds GS, Liverpool Univ Sch of Architecture (BA, BArch); *m* 17 Sept 1977, Susan Shepherd, da of Dr Alan Dawson; 1 s (Augustus William b 16 Oct 1978), 2 da (Sally Elizabeth Rose b 21 April 1983, Laura Jane b 26 Feb 1986); *Career* Poynton Bradbury Wynter (formerly R A Pounton & Associates): joined Robert A Poynton, RIBA as architectural asst 1976, qualified 1977, assoc 1979, equal ptnr 1983–; chm Cornwall Branch RIBA 1989–91, chm South Western Region RIBA 1993–95 (vice chm 1991–93), memb Exec Ctee Cornwall Branch CPRE 1991–92; winner various CPRE and RIBA awards; ARCUK 1977, RIBA 1977, MFB 1995; *Recreations* sailing, windsurfing, squash; *Clubs* St Ives Sailing, St Ives Leisure and Squash; *Style*— Michael R Bradbury, Esq; ✉ Poynton Bradbury Wynter, The Old Sail Lofts, Bethesda Hill, St Ives, Cornwall TR26 1PB (☎ 01736 797828, fax 01736 798464, car 0831 468479)

BRADBURY, Rear Adm Thomas Henry; CB (1979); s of Thomas Henry Bradbury (d 1970), and Violet, *née* Buckingham; *b* 4 Dec 1922; *Educ* Christ's Hospital; *m* 1, 1945 (m dis 1979), Beryl Doreen Evans; 1 s, 1 da; m 2, 1979, Sarah Catherine, da of Harley Hillier; 2 step s; *Career* Flag Offr Admty Interview Bd 1977–79; gp personnel dir Inchcape Group 1979–86, gp personnel exec Davy Corp 1987–91; non-exec memb Eastbourne Health Authy 1990–93; *Recreations* gardening in Sussex and Andalucia; *Style*— Rear Adm Thomas Bradbury, CB; ✉ Padgham Down, Dallington, Heathfield, Sussex TN21 9NS (☎ 01435 830208)

BRADFIELD, Dr John Richard Grenfell; CBE (1986); s of Horace Bradfield (d 1959), of Cambridge, and Ada Sarah, *née* Houghton (d 1952); *b* 20 May 1925; *Educ* Cambridgeshire Co HS for Boys, Trinity Coll Cambridge (MA, PhD); *m* 23 June 1951, Jane, da of Capt Edgar W Wood, MC (d 1974); 1 s (Robert Andrew Richard b 1952); *Career* Univ of Cambridge: res fell in cell biology Trinity Coll 1947, sr bursar Trinity Coll 1956–92 (jr bursar 1951–56), hon fell Darwin Coll 1973–; Cwlth Harkness fell Chicago 1948; dir: Cambridge Water Co 1965–95, Cambridge Building Society 1968–95; fndr and mangr Cambridge Science Park 1970–92, memb Bd Anglian Water Authy 1975–89; dir: Anglian Water plc 1989–93, Biotechnology Investments 1989–; chm: Abbotstone Agric Property Unit Tst 1975–, Addenbrooke's NHS Tst 1993–96, Cmmn for the New Towns 1995–; govr Leys Sch, former chm St Faith's Prep Sch Cambridge; Hon LLD Univ of Cambridge 1992; AIIMR 1970; *Recreations* walking, sailing, arboretum-visiting; *Style*— Dr John Bradfield, CBE; ✉ Trinity College, Cambridge CB2 1TQ (☎ 01223 338 400)

BRADFIELD, Prof John Walter; *Educ* Magdalen Coll Sch Oxford, Aylesbury GS Bucks, St Peter's Coll Oxford/St Mary's Hosp Med Sch London (MA, BM BCh, FRCPath), Univ of London (PhD); *Career* prof of histopathology Univ of Bristol 1985–; *Recreations* hill walking, squash; *Style*— Prof John Bradfield; ✉ 22 Beaconsfield Road, Clifton, Bristol BS8 2TS (☎ 0117 973 8837); Department of Pathology, Bristol Royal Infirmary, Bristol BS2 8HW (☎ 0117 928 2586, fax 0117 929 2440)

BRADFORD, Archdeacon of; *see:* Shreeve, The Ven David Herbert

BRADFORD, Barbara Taylor; da of Winston Taylor (d 1981), and Freda Walker Taylor (d 1981); *b* 10 May 1933; *Educ* Northcote Sch for Girls; *m* 24 Dec 1963, Robert Bradford; *Career* author and journalist; women's ed Yorkshire Evening Post 1951–53 (reporter 1949–51), fashion ed Woman's Own 1953–54, columnist London Evening News 1955–57, exec ed The London American 1959–62, ed National Design Center Magazine USA 1965–69; nationally syndicated columnist: Newsday (New York) 1968–70, Chicago Tribune/New York Daily News Syndicate 1970–75, Los Angeles Times Syndicate (New York) 1975–81; memb: Cncl The Authors' Guild Inc USA 1989, PEN USA; Hon DLitt Univ of Leeds 1992, Hon DLitt Univ of Bradford 1995; *Novels* A Woman of Substance (1980, Matrix Award for books from New York Women in Communications 1985), Voice of the Heart (1983), Hold the Dream (1985, screen adaptation 1986), Act of Will (1986), To Be The Best (1988), The Women in his Life (1990), Remember (1991), Angel (1993), Everything to Gain (1994), Dangerous to Know (1995), Love In Another Town (1995), Her Own Rules (1996); *Non-fiction* published in USA incl: Complete Encyclopedia of Homemaking Ideas (1968), How To Be The Perfect Wife (1969), How to Solve Your Decorating Problems (1976), Luxury Designs for Apartment Living (1981); *Style*— Mrs Barbara Taylor Bradford; ✉ Bradford Enterprises, 450 Park Ave, New York, NY 10022, USA (☎ 00 1 212 308 7390, fax 00 1 212 935 1636)

BRADFORD, Bishop of 1992–; Rt Rev David James Smith; s of Stanley James Smith (d 1965), and Gwendolen Emie, *née* Nunn (d 1960); *b* 14 July 1935; *Educ* Hertford GS, King's Coll London (AKC), St Boniface Coll Warminster; *m* 2 Dec 1961, Mary Hunter, da of Eric John Moult (d 1970); 1 s (Christopher Michael b 16 Sept 1966), 1 da (Rebecca Clare b 9 Feb 1965); *Career* asst curate: All Saints Gosforth 1959–62, St Francis High Heaton 1962–64, Longbenton 1964–68; vicar: Longhirst with Hebron 1968–75, St Mary Monkseaton 1975–81, Felton 1982–83; archdeacon of Lindisfarne 1981–87, bishop of Maidstone 1987–92, bishop to HM Forces 1990–92; *Recreations* walking, reading novels; *Style*— The Rt Rev the Bishop of Bradford; ✉ Bishopscroft, Ashwell Road, Heaton, Bradford, W Yorks BD9 4AU (☎ 01274 545414, fax 01274 544831)

BRADFORD, Prof Henry Francis; s of Henry Bradford, and Rose Bradford; *b* 8 March 1938; *Educ* Dartford GS, Univ Coll London (MB BS), Univ of Birmingham (BSc), Inst of Psychiatry London (PhD, DSc, FRCPath); *m* 28 March 1964, Helen, da of Benjamin Caplan (d Nov 1985); 1 s (Daniel Benjamin Alexander b 24 Aug 1969), 1 da (Sonya Helen b 25 Jan 1968); *Career* Imperial Coll London: lectr in biochemistry 1968–, reader in biochemistry 1975–, prof of neurochemistry 1979–, dir of undergraduate studies 1988–; ed: The Journal of Neurochemistry 1973–81, The Biochemist 1989–95; silver jubilee lectr Indian Inst of Chemical Biology Calcutta 1982, Sandoz lectr Inst of Neurology London 1976 and 1985, guest lectr Int Soc for Neurochemistry Japan 1985, 1995 and 1997, Harold Chaffer Meml lectr Univ of Otago NZ 1987; gen ed The Biochemist 1988–94, author of about 300 scientific papers, ed 3 vols of scientific reviews 1981–88; awarded £6 million in neuroscience res grants 1971–93; chm MRC Epilepsy Res Coordinating Ctee 1978–88 (memb Neuroscience Ctee and Bd 1973–82), scientific advsr Brain Res Tst 1985–90, hon archivist The UK Biochemical Soc 1988– (hon sec 1973–81), Bronze medal for contrib to neurochemistry Univ of Okayama Japan 1985; memb: UK Biochemical Soc, Int Soc Neurochemistry, Brain Res Assoc; *Books* Chemical Neurobiology (1985); *Recreations* natural history, music; *Style*— Prof Henry Bradford; ✉ Department of Biochemistry, Imperial College, South Kensington, London SW7 2AZ (☎ 0171 594 5246 ext 229/230)

BRADFORD, 7 Earl of (UK 1815); The Rt Hon Richard Thomas Orlando Bridgeman; 12 Bt (E 1660); also Baron Bradford (GB 1794) and Viscount Newport (UK 1815); s of 6 Earl of Bradford, TD (d 1981); *b* 3 Oct 1947; *Educ* Harrow, Trinity Coll Cambridge (MA); *m* 1979, Joanne Elizabeth, da of Benjamin Miller, of London W8; 3 s (Viscount Newport b 6 Sept 1980, Hon Henry Gerald Orlando b 18 April 1982, Hon Benjamin Thomas Orlando b 7 Feb 1987), 1 da (Lady Alicia Rose b 27 Dec 1990); *Heir* eld s, Viscount Newport; *Career* owner Porters Restaurant Covent Garden 1979–; chm: W Midlands Advsy Ctee Tidy Britain Group 1990–, Wrekin Heritage Assoc 1987–, Westminster Considerate Restaurateurs Assoc 1992–; pres: Stepping Stones Appeal for the Fndn for Conductive Educn 1991–94, Wrekin Tourism Assoc 1980–, Telford Victim Support 1986–, Newport Branch RNLI 1981–, Wolverhampton Friends of the Samaritans 1982–, Master Chefs of GB 1990–, Assoc of Conf Execs 1990–; vice pres Re-Solv (The Campaign Against Solvent Abuse) 1989– (pres 1984–89); tstee: The Weston Park Fndn 1988– (chm Weston Park Enterprises Ltd 1986–), Castle Bromwich Hall Gardens Tst; ctee memb: Midlands Ctee IOD 1989–, Restaurateurs Assoc of GB 1977–82 and 1992–, Great Britain Great Food Working Party 1990–, Policy and Advsy Ctee Tidy Britain Gp 1994–; memb Appeal Ctee Inst of Orthopaedics Oswestry 1992–; *Publications* My Private Parts and The Stuffed Parrot (compilation, 1984), The Eccentric Cookbook (1985), Stately Secrets (hardback 1994, paperback 1996); *Recreations* shooting, cooking, gardening; *Style*— The Rt Hon the Earl of Bradford; ✉ Woodlands House, Weston-under-Lizard, Shifnal, Shropshire TF11 8PX; Weston Park, Shifnal, Shropshire TF11 8LE (☎ 01952 850201, fax 01952 850430)

BRADFORD, Sarah Mary Malet (Viscountess Bangor); da of Brig Hilary Anthony Hayes, DSO, OBE (d 1984), and Mary Beatrice de Carteret Malet (who m 2, Keith Murray, and d 1995); *b* 3 Sept 1938; *Educ* St Mary's Convent Shaftesbury, Lady Margaret Hall Oxford (state scholarship, college history scholarship); *m* 1, 1959 (m dis), Anthony John Bradford, s of John Frank Bradford; 1 da (Annabella Mary b 1964), 1 s (Edward John Alexander b 1966); m 2, 1976, 8 Viscount Bangor, *qv*; *Career* author, reviewer and journalist; *Books* The Story of Port (1978, new edn 1983, first published as The Englishman's Wine 1969), Portugal and Madeira (1969), Portugal (1973), Cesare Borgia (1976), Disraeli (1982), Princess Grace (1984), King George VI (1989), Sacheverell Sitwell (1993), Elizabeth, A Biography of Her Majesty The Queen (1996); *Recreations* reading biographies, diaries and letters, gardening, travelling, watching Liverpool FC; *Style*— Sarah Bradford; ✉ 31 Britannia Road, London SW6 2HJ (☎ 0171 731 0699, fax 0171 736 1089)

BRADLEY, Anna Louise; da of Donald Ernest Bradley, of London, and Angela Lucy, *née* Bradley; *b* 29 July 1957; *Educ* Univ of Warwick (BA, MBA); *partner* Norman Howard Jones; 1 da (Natasha Storm b 11 March 1988), 1 s (Nathan Blaze b 12 Oct 1990); *Career* sr sub-ed Marshall Cavendish Partworks Ltd 1978–82; Consumers' Association: sr project ldr 1982–87, project mangr 1987–88, head of food and health 1988–91, dep res dir 1991–93; dir and co sec Institute for the Study of Drug Dependence 1993–; jt asst sec All Pty Parly Gp on Drug Misuse 1994–; memb: Ctee The Patients' Assoc 1985–88 and 1989–91, Nutrition Advsy Ctee Coronary Prevention Gp; *Books* Healthy Living (co-author, 1985), Understanding Additives (ed, 1988), Healthy Eating (1989), Caring for Someone with AIDS (contrib, 1990); author of numerous articles in jls and research papers; *Style*— Ms Anna Bradley; ✉ 17 Beverley Road, Colchester CO3 3NG (☎ 01206 578481); Institute for the Study of Drug Dependence, Waterbridge House, 32–36 Loman Street, London SE1 0EE (☎ 0171 928 1211, fax 0171 928 1771)

BRADLEY, Prof Anthony Wilfred; s of David Bradley (d 1970), of Dover, Kent, and Olive Margaret, *née* Bonsey (d 1964); *b* 6 Feb 1934; *Educ* Dover GS, Emmanuel Coll Cambridge (MA, LLM); *m* 5 Sept 1959, Kathleen, *née* Bryce; 1 s, 3 da; *Career* slr of the Supreme Ct 1960–89, fell Trinity Hall Cambridge 1960–68; Univ of Edinburgh: prof of constitutional law 1968–89, dean Faculty of Law 1979–82, emeritus prof 1990; ed Public Law 1986–92; called to the Bar Inner Temple 1989, in practice 1989–; memb: Ctee of Inquiry into Local Govt in Scotland 1980, Ctee to Review Local Govt in the Islands of Scotland 1983–84; chm Edinburgh Cncl for Single Homeless 1984–88; Hon LLD Univ of Staffordshire 1993; *Books* Justice Discretion and Poverty (with M Adler, 1976), Constitutional and Administrative Law (ed with K Ewing, 11 edn 1993), Governmental Liability (with J Bell, 1991), European Human Rights Law (with M Janis and R Kay, 1995); *Recreations* music; *Style*— Prof Anthony Bradley; ✉ Morland, Sheepstead, nr Marcham, Abingdon OX13 6QG (☎ 01865 390774); Cloisters, 1 Pump Court, Temple, London EC4Y 7AA (☎ 0171 583 0303, fax 0171 583 2254)

BRADLEY, Prof Benjamin Arthur de Burgh; *b* 17 Sept 1942; *Educ* Silcoates Sch Wakefield, Bilston GS, Univ of Birmingham Med Sch (MB ChB, MSc, PhD), Univ of Cambridge (MA); *m* 27 April 1968, Anne; 4 da (Rachel b 18 Oct 1970, Lucy b 4 Aug 1972, Elise b 8 July 1976, Nicola b 29 Jan 1979); *Career* house surgn and house physician United Birmingham Hosps 1965–66, MRC res scholar and latterly MRC jr res fell Dept of Experimental Pathology Univ of Birmingham 1966–70, asst dir of res Univ of Cambridge and hon sr registrar in transplantation immunology Addenbrooke's 1970–75, sr lectr Dept of Immunohaematology Rijksuniversiteit and pt/t clinical specialist Academisch Ziekenhuis Leiden 1975–79, dir United Kingdom Transplant Service 1979–92; Univ of Bristol: hon clinical lectr in haematology Faculty of Med 1979–92, hon prof of transplantation immunology Faculty of Med 1988–92, personal chair 1992–, prof of transplantation sciences 1992–, dir Dept of Transplantation Sciences 1992–; med dir British Bone Marrow Donor Appeal 1993–95; hon conslt: Southmead District Health Authy 1979–, United Bristol Healthcare Tst 1993–; memb Bd of Tstees Jenner Educnl Tst 1992–, fndr and memb Bd of Tstees Transplant Tst 1990–, chm Ed Bd Euro Jl of Immunogenetics 1989–; memb: British Soc for Immunology 1969–, British Transplantation Soc 1972– (memb Ctee 1987–89), Transplantation Soc 1975–, Dutch Soc for Immunology 1976–, Bristol Medico-Chirurgical Soc 1979–, Euro Soc for Organ Transplantation 1986–, RSM 1987–, Scientific Ctee Anthony Nolan Tst 1987–92, Euro Bone Marrow Transplant Gp 1989–, British Soc of Histocompatibility and Immunogenetics 1989–, Exec Ctee World Marrow Donor Assoc 1990–94, Scientific Policy Advsy Ctee Bd Nat Inst for Biological Standards and Control 1991–96, Euro Fndn for Immunogenetics 1991– (pres 1988–89), Assoc in Research and Vision Ophthalmology 1991–94; FRCPath 1986 (MRCPath 1974); *Recreations* yachting and dinghy racing; *Style*— Prof Benjamin Bradley; ✉ University of Bristol, Department of Transplantation Sciences, Professorial Unit, Southmead Health Services, Westbury-on-Trym BS10 5NB

BRADLEY, Christopher; s of Hugh Bradley (d 1968), of Glasgow, and Jean McQueen, *née* Dunn (d 1987); *b* 29 May 1950; *Educ* St Aloysius Coll, Blackpool and Fylde Coll (HND Hotel Mgmnt); *m* 3 May 1979, Judy Patricia, da of Robin Cousins; *Career* asst mangr Trust House Forte 1971–72, sales mangr Grand Metropolitan & Centre Hotels 1972–75, internal auditor Lord Chllr's Office 1975–78, systems conslt ICL and NCR 1978–80, chef/patron Mr Underhill's 1981– (Michelin star 1994, Etoiles Mondials de la

Gastronomie 1994, 4/5 Good Food Guide 1996); MHCIMA; *Recreations* motor racing, gardening, not cooking; *Style—* Christopher Bradley, Esq; ✉ Mr Underhill's, Stonham, Suffolk IP14 5DW (☎ 01449 711206)

BRADLEY, Clive; CBE (1996); s of Alfred Bradley (d 1970), and Annie Kathleen, *née* Turner (d 1990); *b* 25 July 1934; *Educ* Felsted, Clare Coll Cambridge (MA), Yale Univ; *Career* PO RAF 1953–55; called to the Bar Middle Temple 1961; BBC 1961–63 and 1965, bdcasting offr Lab Party 1963–64, political ed The Statist and broadcaster 1965–67, gp lab advsr IPC 1967–69, dep gen mangr Daily and Sunday Mirror and controller of admin IPC Newspapers 1969–71, project dir IPC 1971–73, dir The Observer 1973–76, chief exec The Publishers Assoc 1976–, dir Confederation of Information Communication Industries 1984–; author of various pubns on politics, econs, media, industl rels and law; dep chm Central London Valuation Panel; govr Felsted Sch Essex; Liveryman Worshipful Co of Stationers & Newspaper Makers; FRSA; *Clubs* Reform, Groucho, Elizabethan; *Style—* Clive Bradley, Esq, CBE; ✉ 8 Northumberland Place, Richmond upon Thames, Surrey TW10 6TS (☎ 0181 940 7172, fax 0181 940 7603); The Publishers Association, 19 Bedford Square, London WC1B 3HJ (☎ 0171 580 6321, fax 0171 636 5375, telex 267160)

BRADLEY, Dr (Charles) Clive; s of Charles William Bradley (d 1992), and Winifred, *née* Smith (d 1963); *b* 11 April 1937; *Educ* Longton HS, Univ of Birmingham (BSc), Univ of Cambridge (PhD); *m* 25 Sept 1965, Vivien Audrey, da of Charles Frederick Godley, of Hillsborough, Sheffield; 1 s (Daniel b 5 Sept 1969), 1 da (Abigail b 19 May 1973); *Career* sr scientific offr Nat Physical Laboratory 1961–67, res scientist MIT and Nat Bureau of Standards USA 1967–69, sr and princ scientific offr Nat Physical Laboratory 1972–75, sr princ scientific offr and dep chief scientific offr DTI 1975–82, cnsllr sci and technol Br Embassy Tokyo 1982–88, head Advsy Cncl on Sci and Technol Secretariat Cabinet Office 1988–90, md Sharp Laboratories of Europe Ltd 1990–; dep cmmr gen for UK Sci Expo Japan 1985, chm Industl Energy Conservation Ctee Int Energy Agency 1980–82; memb: SERC and EC Ctees 1978–82 and 1989–93, Technology and Innovation Ctee CBI 1993–, Cncl for Continuing Educn Univ of Oxford 1993–; *Books* High Pressure Methods in Solid State Research (1969); *Recreations* tennis, golf, gardening; *Clubs* Athenaeum; *Style—* Dr Clive Bradley; ✉ 8 Montrose Gardens, Oxshott, Surrey KT22 0UU (☎ 01372 843664); Sharp Laboratories of Europe Ltd, Edmund Halley Road, Oxford Science Park, Oxford OX4 4GA (☎ 01865 747711)

BRADLEY, Prof David John; s of late Harold Robert Bradley, and Mona Bradley; *b* 12 Jan 1937; *Educ* Wyggeston Sch Leicester, Selwyn Coll Cambridge, Univ Coll Hosp Med Sch (Atchison scholar, Magrath scholar, MB BChir, MA, Trotter medal in surgery, Liston gold medal in surgery, Frank Smart prize), Univ of Oxford (DM); *m* 1961 (m dis 1989), Lorne Marie, da of late Maj L G Farquhar; 2 s, 2 da; *Career* med res offr Bilharzia Res Unit Tanzania 1961–64, sr lectr Makerere Univ of East Africa Uganda 1966–69 (lectr 1964–66), Royal Soc tropical res fell Sir William Dunn Sch of Pathology Oxford 1969–73, sr res fell and Staines med fell Exeter Coll Oxford 1971–74, clinical reader in pathology Oxford Clinical Med Sch 1973–74, prof of tropical hygiene and research advsr London Sch of Hygiene and Tropical Med 1974–; dir Malaria Reference Laboratory PHLS 1974–, hon specialist community physician N Thames RHA 1974–, hon conslt in tropical and communicable diseases Bloomsbury DHA 1983; memb: WHO Expert Advsy Panel on Parasitic Diseases 1972–, Panel of Experts on Environmental Mgmnt 1981–; chm Div of Communicable and Tropical Diseases LSHTM 1982–88; ed: Jl of Tropical Med and Hygiene 1981–95, Tropical Med and Int Health 1995–; RSTM&H: Chalmers Medal 1980, Macdonald Medal 1996; foreign corresponding memb Royal Belgian Acad of Med 1984, corresponding memb German Tropenmedizingingesellschaft 1980; FIBiol 1974, FFPHM 1979, Hon FCIWEM 1981, FRCPath 1981, FRCP 1985; *Books* Drawers of Water (with G F and A U White, 1972), Problems and Perspectives in Tropical Diseases (in Russian with O V Baroyan, 1979), Health in Tropical Africa During the Colonial Period (with E E Sabben-Clare and B Kirkwood, 1980), Sanitation and Disease (jtly, 1983), Travel Medicine (jtly, 1992); *Recreations* landscape gardens, natural history, travel; *Style—* Prof David Bradley; ✉ 11 Selwyn House, Lansdowne Terrace, London WC1N 1DJ (☎ 0171 278 3918); Department of Epidemiology & Population Sciences, London School of Hygiene and Tropical Medicine, Keppel St, London WC1E 7HT (☎ 0171 927 2216, fax 0171 580 9075)

BRADLEY, David Rice; s of George Leonard Bradley, and Evelyn Annie Bradley; *b* 9 Jan 1938; *Educ* Christ Coll Brecon, St Catharine's Coll Cambridge (exhibitioner, MA), Univ of Edinburgh (Dip in Applied Linguistics); *m* 1962, Josephine Elizabeth Turnbull Fricker, *née* Harries; 2 s; *Career* Nat Serv cmmnd 24 Regt S Wales Borderers 1956–58, served UK, Malaya, Singapore and British N Borneo; British Council: gen servs offr England and Madrid 1961–62, asst educn offr Dhaka E Pakistan 1962–64, educn offr E Pakistan 1964–65, seconded as assoc prof to Eng Language Teaching Inst Allahabad India 1966–68, educn offr N India (temporarily chief educn offr India) 1968–69, dir of studies Br Inst Madrid, Eng language offr Spain and dir Br Cncl Eng Teaching Centre Madrid 1969–73; DOE: princ Directorate Gen of Res Secretariat 1973–76, Planning and Land Use Directorate Devpt Control Div 1976–78, Inner Cities Directorate 1978–79, study offr to devise MINIS (Mgmnt Info System for Ministers) in consultation with Lord Rayner 1979–80, Central Policy Planning Unit 1980–81, study offr (asst sec) Local Govt Fin 1981–82; Nuffield Coll Oxford: Gwilym Gibbon res fell (on leave from DOE) 1982–83, visiting fell Oct 1993–; head of fin Environmental Servs Div 1983–86, head London Urban Devpt Div 1986–88, dir (under sec) Merseyside Task Force 1988–90; chief exec London Borough of Havering 1990–95, memb Cncl Sch of Mgmnt Studies Univ of Oxford 1995–; *Recreations* gardening; *Style—* David R Bradley, Esq; ✉ 27 Clare Lawn Ave, London SW14 8BE

BRADLEY, Graham John; s of Norman Bradley, of Wetherby, W Yorkshire, and late Sheila, *née* Deacey; *b* 8 Sept 1960; *Educ* Wetherby HS; *Career* professional national hunt jockey 1979–; major races won: Hennessy Gold Cup 1982 (Bregawn), Sun Alliance Novice Hurdle 1983 (Sabin du Loir), Cheltenham Gold Cup 1983 (Bregawn), Welsh Grand Nat 1984 (Righthand Man), Irish Grand Nat 1985 (Rhyme 'n' Reason), Charlie Hall Chase 1985 (Wayward Lad), King George VI Chase 1985 (Wayward Lad), Grand Annual Chase 1986 (Pearlyman), Welsh Grand Nat 1987 (Stearsby), Sun Alliance Novice Chase 1987 (Kildimo), Long Walk Hurdle 1990 (Floyd), Italian Champion Hurdle 1991 (Bokaro), Grand Annual Chase 1992 (My Young Man), Martell Hurdle 1993 (Morley Street), Grand Annual Chase 1995 (Sound Reveille), Martell Chase 1995 (Merry Gale), Champion Hurdle 1996 (Collier Bay); Nat Hunt jr champion 1981–82, memb Br Jockey's team 1984–91; Ritz Club Charity Trophy for leading rider at Cheltenham Festival 1983 and Liverpool 1993; *Recreations* Leeds Utd FC, golf, snooker, good films; *Style—* Graham Bradley, Esq; ✉ Brook House, West Street, Sparsholt, Wantage, Oxon OX12 9PS (☎ 01235 751533, car 0850 350200); c/o Graeme James (☎ 01235 821250, 0831 547233)

BRADLEY, Jenny; da of John Shannon Kean, of Oxford, and Jean Smith, *née* Coburn; *b* 2 June 1947; *Educ* Headington Sch Oxford, Oxford Poly; *Career* served indentures as journalist Bracknell News Berkshire 1966–69, PR exec Joan Chesney Frost Publicity Services London 1969–71, pubns mangr Marks & Spencer Ltd 1971–74; ed: Thames & Chilterns Tourist Bd Oxon 1974–77, Milk Producer 1977–82; pubns mangr Milk Mktg Bd 1977–82, communications dir Dairy Crest Ltd Surrey 1982–90, public affrs dir Heathrow Airport Ltd 1990–; memb: Int Assoc of Business Communicators 1987, Assoc of Women in PR 1988; *Style—* Ms Jenny Bradley; ✉ Heathrow Airport Ltd, Heathrow Point, 234 Bath Road, Harlington, Middlesex UB3 5AP (☎ 0181 745 4108, fax 0181 745 5612)

BRADLEY, John Stirling; s of Ronald Day Bradley, of Colchester; *b* 2 Jan 1948; *Educ* King's Sch Ely; *m* 16 Aug 1975, Christine Madeleine, da of Edwin David Finch; 1 da (Alison b 6 Oct 1976), 2 s (Anthony b 10 April 1979, Edward b 28 June 1983); *Career* admitted slr 1971, slr Bischoff & Co 1971–74; RTZ Corporation plc: slr 1974–86, dep head Legal Dept 1986–92, co sec 1992–; memb Law Soc 1971; *Recreations* sailing, gardening, tennis, Christian life; *Clubs* RAC; *Style—* John Bradley, Esq; ✉ The RTZ Corporation plc, 6 St James's Square, London SW1Y 4LD (☎ 0171 930 2399, fax 0171 753 2268)

BRADLEY, Julia Anne (Mrs Keith Sharp); da of Herbert Bradley (d 1974), and Minnie Adelaide Amelia Doris, *née* King; *b* 22 Nov 1938; *Educ* Hove and Aldrington HS, Brighton Tech Coll; *m* 28 Sept 1963, Keith Lorenza Sharp, s of Frederick William Lorenza Sharp (d 1979); 2 s (Trevor b 1970, Martin b 1972); *Career* asst sec Atlas Homes Ltd 1959–64; ptnr Bradley Kempton & Co 1966–69, proprietor Julia A Bradley 1969–77, ptnr WA Honey & Co 1977–85, ptnr Bradley Soni & Co 1987–; sec: Br Engineerium 1985, Fedn of Sussex Industs 1986–87, Centre for Res Educn and Trg in Energy 1990–, Brighton and Hove Business Enterprise Agency 1988–; memb Cncl ICSA (chm Benevolent Fund and former chm Sussex Branch); admin Vega Science Tst; govr: Somerhill Jr Sch, Varndean Sch; former chm Sussex Branch Chartered Inst Taxation, former chm Sussex Professional and Mgmnt Orgns, sec Brighton and Hove Soc of Miniature Locomotive Engrs; former memb: Brighton and Hove Camera Club, Sussex Car Club, Locomotive Club GB; Freeman City of London 1980, Liveryman Worshipful Co Chartered Secs and Admins 1980; FCIS, ATII; *Recreations* railways, photography, gardening, travel; *Style—* Miss Julia Bradley; ✉ 64 Palmeira Ave, Hove, E Sussex BN3 3GF (☎ 01273 734236); Bradley Soni & Co, 86 South Coast Rd, Peacehaven, E Sussex BN10 8SL (☎ 01273 582605, fax 01273 587445)

BRADLEY, Keith John Charles; MP (Lab) Manchester Withington (majority 9,735); *m*; 2 s, 1 da; *Career* MP (Lab) Manchester Withington 1987–; shadow min: for social security 1991–96, for tport 1996–; Manchester City Cncl: cncllr 1983–88, chm Environmental Servs Ctee 1984–88; dir: Manchester Ship Canal Co 1984–87, Manchester Airport plc 1984–87; *Style—* Keith Bradley, Esq, MP; ✉ House of Commons, London SW1A 0AA (☎ 0171 219 5217, fax 0171 219 5901), constituency (☎ 0161 446 2047, fax 0161 445 5543)

BRADLEY, Michael John; CMG (1990), QC (Cayman Islands) 1983; *b* 1933; *Educ* Queen's Univ Belfast (LLB); *m*; 1 s; *Career* attorney gen: British Virgin Islands 1977–78, Turks and Caicos Islands 1980, Montserrat 1981, Cayman Islands 1982–87; govr Turks and Caicos Islands WI 1987–93, law revision cmmr Cayman Islands 1994–; memb Law Soc NI; *Style—* Mr Michael Bradley, CMG, QC; ✉ 25 Springfield, Bradford-on-Avon, Wiltshire BA15 1BA (☎ and fax 01225 865852); PO Box 907 GT, Grand Cayman, Cayman Islands, W Indies (☎ 00 1 345 5925)

BRADLEY, Patrick James; s of Gerard Bradley (d 1967), of Dublin, and Nan, *née* O'Leary (d 1990); *b* 10 May 1949; *Educ* Glenstal Abbey Sch Murroe Co Limerick Ireland, Univ Coll Dublin (MB BCh, BAO, DCH); *m* 17 May 1974, Sheena, da of Frank Kelly (d 1954), of Draperstown, Co Derry; 3 s (Darragh Francis b 19 Nov 1976, Cormac b 12 Dec 1978, Eoin Patrick b 16 Oct 1980), 2 da (Paula b 19 Nov 1975, Caitriona b 5 June 1984); *Career* Nottingham Health Authy: consIt otolaryngologist and head and neck oncologist 1982–, clinical dir Dept of Otolaryngology 1991–96, clinical dir of audit, risk and effectiveness 1996–, memb Theatre Users (former chm); vice chm Trent Regnl Advsy Ctee (Otolaryngology), former hon sec and memb Assoc of Head and Neck Oncologists GB; pres Young Otolaryngologist Head and Neck Surgeons 1993–94; chm: Nottingham Section BMA 1994–95, Clinical Practice Br Assoc of Otorhinolaryngologists Head and Neck Surgns 1995–; memb Cncl: Otorhinolaryngological Res Soc (treas 1993–), RSM (memb Section of Laryngology/Rhinology 1991–); corresponding memb: American Laryngological Assoc, Triological Soc, Assoc of Head and Neck Surgns; memb: Br Assoc of Surgical Oncologists, Br Assoc of Otorhinolaryngologists; DCH, FRCSI, FRCSEd; *Books* Ear, Nose and Throat Disease (1989), Robb and Smith (contrib, 1992), Scott-Brown's ORL (contrib, 1994 and 1995 edns), Mawson's Head and Neck (contrib, 1997); also author of various pubns on head and neck cancer diagnosis and mgmnt; *Recreations* skiing, golf; *Clubs* Nottingham RFC (vice-pres), Beeston Fields Golf; *Style—* Patrick Bradley, Esq; ✉ 32A The Ropewalk, Nottingham NG1 5EH (☎ 0115 947 2631, fax 0115 924 1653)

BRADLEY, Philip Herbert Gilbert; s of Herbert Bradley (d 1981), of S Ireland, and Phyllis Eleanor Josephine, *née* Marshall; *b* 11 Nov 1949; *Educ* Charterhouse, Trinity Coll Dublin (BA, BAI); *m* 3 Sept 1977, Charlotte Knollys Olivia, da of Lt-Col John Clairmont Wood, of Coombe Down, Beaminster, Dorset; 3 s (William b 6 Oct 1980, Piers b 9 Dec 1982, Timothy b 14 March 1985); *Career* Coopers & Lybrand chartered accountants 1974–78, Robert Fleming & Co Ltd bankers 1978–79, Jardine Fleming & Co Ltd bankers Hong Kong 1979–81, dir Robert Fleming & Co bankers London 1984–; ACA; *Recreations* music, opera, fishing, shooting, skiing; *Clubs* Kildare Street (Dublin), Lansdowne; *Style—* Philip Bradley, Esq; ✉ Robert Fleming & Co Ltd, 25 Copthall Avenue, London EC2R 7DR (☎ 0171 638 5858, fax 0171 638 9110, telex 297451)

BRADLEY, Roger Thubron; s of Ivor Lewis Bradley (d 1972), of Bournemouth, and Elizabeth, *née* Thubron; *b* 5 July 1936; *Educ* Lancaster Royal GS, Univ of Oxford (MA); *m* 19 Sept 1959, Ailsa Mary, da of Eric Walkden, of Bromley Cross; 1 s (Mark b 1963), 1 da (Julia b 1960); *Career* Forestry Cmmn: joined 1960, dist offr Argyll 1970, conservator N Wales 1977, sr offr Wales 1979, dir of harvesting and marketing 1983, forestry cmmr 1985, head of Forestry Authy 1992–95; pres Inst of Chartered Foresters 1996–, chm Edinburgh Centre for Tropical Forestry 1996–; FICFor, FIWSc; *Clubs* Cwlth Soc, Royal Over-Seas League; *Style—* Roger T Bradley, Esq; ✉ Easter Dullater, Callander, Perthshire FK17 8HQ (☎ 01877 331124)

BRADLEY, (Philip) Stephen; s of Robert Bradley, of St Annes on Sea, and Hilda, *née* Whalley; *b* 22 Aug 1949; *Educ* Queen Elizabeth's GS Blackburn Lancs; *m* 4 April 1976 (m dis 1985), Janet Elizabeth, da of Eric Hollingworth; 2 s (Richard b 26 Oct 1980, Alexander b 2 Sept 1982); m 2, 21 May 1993, Anne, da of Diana May Hill; *Career* CA; articled clerk Waterworth Rudd & Hare Blackburn Lancs 1967–71; Price Waterhouse: audit sr Manchester 1972–75, mgmnt consIt Manchester 1975–77, mgmnt consIt Nairobi 1978–84, ptnr 1980, mgmnt consIt ptnr London 1987–; FCA 1971, FIMC 1980, MILDM 1987; *Style—* Stephen Bradley, Esq; ✉ Price Waterhouse, 1 London Bridge, London SE1 9SY (☎ 0171 939 3000, fax 0171 638 1358)

BRADLEY, (Charles) Stuart; CBE (1990); s of Capt Charles Bradley, OBE (d 1959), of Penarth, Glamorgan, and Amelia Jane, *née* Ryan; *b* 11 Jan 1936; *Educ* Penarth Co Sch, Univ of Southampton, Sch of Navigation; *m* 7 April 1959, Kathleen Marina (Kate); 2 s (Philip b 1962, Patrick b and d 1964), 1 da (Bridget b 1967); *Career* deck offr P&O SNCO 1952–64; Associated British Ports Holdings plc (formerly Br Tport Docks Bd) 1964–: dock and harbour master Silloth 1968–70, dockmaster 1970–74, dock and marine supt Plymouth 1974–76, docks mangr Lowestoft 1976–78, port mangr Barry 1978–80, port mangr Hull 1980–87 (formerly dep port mangr), asst md resources 1987–88, md Assoc Br Ports 1988–95 (currently dir), chm Red Funnel 1989–; dep chm NAPE 1986–89, memb NDLB 1987–90; Yr Bro Trinity House; Master Mariner, FCIT 1978; *Recreations* cycling, walking, theatre, welsh rugby; *Clubs* Cardiff Athletic, Hon Co of Master Mariners, Oriental, Royal London Yacht; *Style—* Stuart Bradley, Esq, CBE;

✉ Associated British Ports Holdings plc, 150 Holborn, London EC1N 2LR (☎ 0171 430 1177, fax 0171 430 1384, telex 23913)

BRADLEY, Thomas George (Tom); s of George Henry Bradley (d 1953), and Agnes Mason (d 1993); *b* 13 April 1926; *Educ* Kettering Central Sch; *m* 15 Aug 1953, Joy Patricia (d 1993), da of George Stramer (d 1964); 2 s (David b 1961, Peter b 1963); *Career* cncllr (Lab): Northamptonshire CC 1952–74 (alderman 1964–74), Kettering BC 1956–61; pres Tport Salaried Staffs Assoc 1964–76 (actg gen sec 1977); memb Lab Pty Nat Exec Ctee 1966–81, chm Lab Pty 1976, MP Leicester E 1962–83 (Lab 1962–81, SDP 1981–83), fndr memb SDP, PPS to Roy Jenkins at Ministries of Aviation, Home Office and Treasy 1964–70, front bench oppn spokesman on Tport 1970–74, chm House of Commons Select Ctee on Tport 1979–83; dir Br Section European League for Econ Co-operation 1979–91; *Recreations* watching football, cricket; *Clubs* Savile; *Style*— Tom Bradley, Esq; ✉ The Orchard, 111 London Rd, Kettering, Northants (☎ 01536 513019)

BRADMAN, Godfrey Michael; s of William Isadore Bradman (d 1973), and Anne Brenda, *née* Goldsweig; *b* 9 Sept 1936; *m* 2, 1975, Susan, da of George Bennett, of Slough; 1 s (Daniel b 1977), 2 da (Camilla b 1976, Katherine b 1976), 1 step-s (Christian), 1 step-da (Sophie); *Career* CA 1961; chm: London Mercantile Corporation 1969, Rosehaugh plc 1979–91; chm and jt chief exec European Land and Property Corporation plc 1992–; chm European Land and Property Investments Co 1993–, Ashpest Finance 1993–, Pondbridge Europe Ltd 1994–; jt chm: Victoria Quay Ltd 1993–, Welbeck Land and European Property plc 1994–, Meco Investments Pondbridge Co 1994–; dir AIDS Policy Unit 1987–90; established: Parents Against Tobacco Campaign, Opren Victims Campaign; fndr CLEAR Campaign for Lead Free Air 1981–91, jt fndr and hon pres Campaign for Freedom of Information 1983–91, fndr Citizen Action 1983–91 (memb Cncl 1983–91), pres Soc for the Protection of Unborn Children Educnl Research Tst 1987–, chm Friends of the Earth Tst 1983–91; memb: Cncl UN Int Year of Shelter for the Homeless 1987, Governing Body LSHTM 1988–91; hon fell KCL; Hon DSc Univ of Salford; FCA; *Recreations* riding; *Style*— Godfrey Bradman, Esq; ✉ 15 Hanover Terrace, Regent's Park, London NW1 4RJ (☎ 0171 706 0189, fax 0171 723 5341)

BRADSHAW, Adrian; s of Sydney Bradshaw, of Wilmslow, and Nina, *née* Gerrand; *b* 24 Feb 1957; *Educ* Urmston GS, Birmingham Poly (BA Law); *m* 12 Sept 1984, Valerie Joy, da of Dr Ivor Citron; 1 s (Benjamin b 11 Oct 1989), 1 da (Charlotte b 16 Jan 1986); *Career* Citicorp Scrimgeour Vickers 1978–81, Bell Lawrie White 1981–82, corporate fin Nat West Markets 1982–83, dir Guidehouse Ltd 1983–89, md Corp Fin Div and bd memb Arbuthnot Latham Bank 1989–91, chm and chief exec Incepta Group plc fin mktg gp 1991–93, dir Bradmount Investments Ltd 1994–; MInstD; *Recreations* tennis, golf, skiing, theatre, cuisine, travel; *Clubs* Groucho, Riverside Racquet, Peak, IOD; *Style*— Adrian Bradshaw, Esq; ✉ Bradmount Investments Ltd, 51 Lincolns Inn Fields, London WC2 (☎ 0171 242 2517)

BRADSHAW, Sir Kenneth Anthony; KCB (1986, CB 1982); s of late Herbert Leo Bradshaw, and Gladys Margaret Bradshaw; *b* 1 Sept 1922; *Educ* Ampleforth, St Catharine's Coll Cambridge; *Career* clerk assistant House of Commons 1979–83, Clerk of the House 1983–87 (ret); pres Assoc of Secs Gen of Parliaments IPU 1986–87; administrator Compton Verney Opera and Ballet Project 1989–; *Books* Parliament and Congress (with David Pring 1982); *Recreations* music, theatre; *Clubs* Garrick; *Style*— Sir Kenneth Bradshaw, KCB

BRADSHAW, Stephen Paul; s of Eric Douglas Bradshaw, and Victoria, *née* Gibbons; *b* 26 Nov 1948; *Educ* Nottingham HS, Queens' Coll Cambridge (MA); *m* 27 May 1972, Jenny, da of Michael Richards; 2 s (Nicholas b 4 Oct 1973, Rusty b 2 May 1977), 1 da (Melissa b 17 Aug 1980); *Career* prodr BBC Radio London 1970–73; reporter and presenter: File on 4 (BBC Radio Four) 1977–80, Newsweek (BBC 2) 1980–83, People and Power (BBC 1) 1983, Newsnight (BBC 2) 1984–87; corr Panorama (BBC 1) 1987–97; *Books* Cafe Society (1978); *Recreations* work, children; *Style*— Stephen Bradshaw, Esq; ✉ 81 Charlotte Street, London W1P 1LB (☎ 0171 580 4886)

BRADSHAW, William Martin (Bill); s of Leslie Charles Bradshaw (d 1971), of Lobley Hill, Gateshead, and Vera, *née* Beadle; *b* 12 Dec 1955; *Educ* Gateshead GS and Saltwell HS, Darlington NCTJ Journalism Sch; *m* 13 June 1981, Fiona Judith, da of William MacBeth (d 1974); 1 s (Kit Leslie b 12 Nov 1990), 1 da (Holly b 15 Feb 1993); *Career* jr then sr reporter Halifax Courier 1975–77, news reporter Newcastle Evening Chronicle 1977–79, sports reporter (covering soccer and athletics) Newcastle Journal 1979–83, sports ed The People London 1990–94 (sports reporter Manchester 1983–85 and London 1985–89), ed The Journal Newcastle 1994–96; memb: Football Writers' Assoc 1981, SWA 1985; Sports Journalist of the Year 1990, Sports Reporter of the Year 1990; *Recreations* cricket, soccer, water skiing, reading, golf; *Style*— Bill Bradshaw, Esq; ✉ The Journal, Thomson House, Groat Market, Newcastle upon Tyne, Tyne and Wear NE1 1ED (☎ 0191 232 7500, fax 0191 232 2256)

BRADSHAW, Prof William Peter (Bill); s of Leonard Charles Bradshaw (d 1978), of Wargrave, Berks, and Ivy Doris, *née* Steele (d 1980); *b* 9 Sept 1936; *Educ* Slough GS, Univ of Reading (BA, MA); *m* 30 Nov 1957, Jill Elsie, da of James Francis Hayward, of Plastow Green, Hampshire; 1 s (Robert William b 1966), 1 da (Joanna b 1968); *Career* Nat Serv 1957–59; BR: mgmnt trainee 1959, div movements mangr Bristol 1967, div mangr Liverpool 1973, chief ops mangr London Midland Region 1976, dep gen mangr London Midland Region 1977, dir of ops BR HQ 1978, dir Policy Unit BR HQ 1980, gen mangr W Region 1983–85; sr res fell Centre for Socio Legal Studies Wolfson Coll Oxford 1985–, prof of tport mgmnt Univ of Salford 1986–92 (visiting prof Sch of Mgmnt 1992–); chm Ulsterbus 1987–93, dir Northern Ireland Transport Holding Co 1988–93; special advsr Tport Select Ctee House of Commons 1992–; FCIT 1986; *Recreations* growing hardy perennial plants, playing memb of brass band; *Clubs* Nat Lib; *Style*— Prof Bill Bradshaw; ✉ Centre for Socio-Legal Studies, Wolfson College, Oxford OX2 6UD (☎ 01865 284232, fax 01865 284221)

BRADSTREET, Philip Lionel Stanton; s of Arthur William Haywood Bradstreet (d 1987), and Catherine Margaret Patricia, *née* Brennan; *b* 14 Aug 1946; *Educ* Downside, Trinity Coll Cambridge (MA); *m* 5 June 1971, Marie Christine Francoise Dominique, da of Henri Coronat (d 1986); 3 s (Christophe b 1972, Matthieu b 1975, William b 1983), 1 da (Anne-Marie b 1976); *Career* expert Cmmn of the Euro Communities 1981–83, dir Euro Community Servs Price Waterhouse Brussels 1983–94, dir Bossard Consultants Brussels 1994–; memb: de L'Ordre des Experts-Compatables France, de L'Institut des Experts-Comptables Belgium; Freeman City of London 1970; FCA; *Recreations* tennis, rugby, music; *Clubs* Hawks (Cambridge); *Style*— Philip Bradstreet, Esq; ✉ 38 Avenue Maurice, 1050 Brussels, Belgium (☎ 00 322 647 7394); Bossard Consultants, 1 Avenue de la Joyeuse Entree, 1040 Brussels, Belgium (☎ 00 322 285 0035, fax 00 322 283 0024)

BRADWELL, Bishop of 1993–; Rt Rev Dr Laurence Alexander (Laurie) Green; s of Leonard Alexander Green, and Laura Elizabeth, *née* McKee; *b* 26 Dec 1945; *Educ* East Ham GS, KCL (BD, AKC), NY Theol Seminary (STM), New York State Univ (DMin), St Augustin's Coll Canterbury; *m* Victoria (Vicki); 2 da (Rebecca b 18 Sept 1974, Hannah b 6 June 1976); *Career* curate St Mark Kingstanding Birmingham 1970–73, vicar St Chad Erdington Birmingham 1973–83, princ Aston Trg Scheme 1983–89, team rector All Saints Poplar 1989–93; formerly: industl chaplain British Steel Corporation, asst youth offr Birmingham Dio; *Publications* Power to the Powerless (1987), Let's Do Theology (1990), God in the City (jtly, 1995); *Recreations* jazz piano and guitar, long distance running, interest in modern culture; *Style*— The Rt Rev the Bishop of Bradwell; ✉ Bishop's House, Orsett Road, Horndon-on-the-Hill, Essex SS17 8NS (☎ 01375 673806, fax 01375 674222, e-mail lauriegr@globalnet.co.uk)

BRADY, Hon Mrs (Charlotte Mary Thérèse); *née* Bingham; writes as Charlotte Bingham; da of 7 Baron Clanmorris (d 1988); *b* 29 June 1942; *Educ* The Priory Hayward's Heath, The Sorbonne; *m* 1964, Terence Joseph Brady, *qv*, s of Frederick Arthur Noel Brady (d 1985), of Montacute, Somerset; 1 s (Matthew b 1972), 1 da (Candida b 1965); *Career* playwright, novelist; *Books* Coronet Among the Weeds (1963), Lucinda (1965), Coronet Among the Grass (1972), Rose's Story (with husb Terence Brady 1973), Yes Honestly (1977), Belgravia (1983), Country Life (1984), At Home (1985), To Hear A Nightingale (1988), The Business (1989), In Sunshine or in Shadow (1991), Stardust (1992), By Invitation (1993), Nanny (1993), A Change of Heart (1994), Debutantes (1995), The Nightingale Sings (1996), Country Wedding (1996), Grand Affair (1997); *Plays* I Wish I Wish, Coming of Age; *TV Series* (with Terence Brady): Take Three Girls, Upstairs Downstairs, No Honestly, Yes Honestly, Play for Today, Thomas and Sarah, Nanny, Pig in the Middle; *TV Films* Love With A Perfect Stranger, This Magic Moment; *Recreations* horse breeding, riding, gardening, racing, swimming; *Style*— The Hon Mrs Brady; ✉ Peters Fraser & Dunlop, Literary Agents, 5th Floor, The Chambers, Chelsea Harbour, Lots Road, London SW10 0XF

BRADY, Janet Mary; *née* Mount; da of Allan Frederick Mount, MBE, of Oxford, and Doreen Margaret, *née* Hicks; *b* 26 Feb 1956; *Educ* Rochester GS, Medway and Maidstone Coll of Technol; *Career* legal asst Mobil Oil 1974–77, tax asst Marathon Oil 1977–81, account dir Sterling PR 1982–85, dir PR American Express (UK and Ireland) 1985–87, fndr dir Kinnear PR 1988–89, chief exec Cadogan Management Ltd 1994–95 (md 1989–94), chm Specialtours Ltd 1990–95, md The Albermarle Connection 1995–; chm Women in Mgmnt 1991–94, pres Soc of Consumer Affrs Professionals UK 1993; advsr Br Sports Assoc for the Disabled 1990–96; patron Himage - Women of Influence Exhibition 1993–95; FInstD; *Recreations* ballooning, stonemasonry, landscape gardening, writing; *Clubs* IOD; *Style*— Ms Janet Brady; ✉ Barcheston House, Northside, Steeple Aston, Oxon OX6 3SE (☎ 01869 347633); The Albermarle Connection, 99 Charterhouse Street, London EC1M 6HR (☎ 0171 251 5911, fax 0171 251 5912)

BRADY, (Helen) Joan; da of Robert Alexander Brady (d 1963), and Mildred Alice, *née* Edie (d 1965); *b* 4 Dec 1939; *Educ* Univ of Columbia (Phi Beta Kappa); *m* 23 Sept 1963, Dexter Wright Masters, s of Thomas Davis Masters; 1 s (Alexander Wright b 12 Oct 1965); *Career* author; formerly dancer: San Francisco Ballet 1955–57, New York City Ballet 1960; awarded Nat Endowment for the Arts (Washington) 1986; *Books* The Impostor (1979), The Unmaking of a Dancer (1982), Theory of War (1993, Whitbread Novel of the Yr 1993, Whitbread Book of the Yr 1994, trans into 8 foreign languages, French edn L'Enfant Loué, Prix du Meilleur Livre Etranger 1995), Prologue (1994), Death Comes For Peter Pan (1996); *Style*— Ms Joan Brady; ✉ c/o Laura Morris, Abner Stein, 10 Roland Gardens, London SW7 3PH (☎ 0171 373 0456, fax 0171 370 6316)

BRADY, Karren; da of Terry Brady, of Enfield, and Rita, *née* Chambers; *b* 4 April 1969; *Educ* Poles Convent Sch, Alderham Sch; *m* 1995, Paolo (Paul) Peschisolido; *Career* jr exec Saatchi & Saatchi 1987–88, sales exec London Broadcasting Company (LBC) 1988–89, mktg and sales dir Sport Newspapers Ltd 1989–93, md Birmingham City Football Club plc 1993–; *Style*— Miss Karren Brady; ✉ Birmingham City Football Club plc, St Andrews' Ground, Birmingham B9 4NH (☎ 0121 772 0101, fax 0121 766 7269)

BRADY, Prof (John) Michael; s of John Brady, OBE, and Priscilla Mansfield, *née* Clark; *b* 30 April 1945; *Educ* Prescot GS, Univ of Manchester (BSc, MSc), Aust Nat Univ (PhD); *m* 2 Oct 1967, Naomi, *née* Friedlander; 2 da (Sharon b 1971, Carol b 1973); *Career* sr lectr Univ of Essex 1978–80 (lectr 1970–78), sr res scientist MIT 1980–85, prof Univ of Oxford 1985–; memb Bd of Dirs: GCS, Intelligent Systems Solutions, Oxford Instruments, AEA, AEA Technology; memb Foresight Steering Gp, chm Info Technol Advsy Bd Technol Foresight Steering Gp Office of Science and Technol; founding ed International Journal of Robotics Research 1981–; MIEEE, FRSA, FIEE, FEng 1992; *Books* Theory of Computer Science (1976), Computer Vision (1981), Robot Motion (1983), Computational Models of Discourse (1983), Robotics (1985), Robotics Science (1989); *Recreations* windsurfing, squash, Dickens, wine, Everton FC; *Style*— Prof Michael Brady, FEng; ✉ Department of Engineering Science, University of Oxford, Parks Rd, Oxford OX1 3PJ (☎ 01865 273002, fax 01865 283310, telex 83295 NUCLOX G)

BRADY, Paul Joseph; s of Sean Brady, and Mollie, *née* McElholm; *b* 19 May 1947; *Educ* St Columb's Coll Derry, Univ Coll Dublin; *m* 14 March 1975, Mary Jacinta, da of William Elliott; 1 s (Colm Marcus b 14 March 1979), 1 da (Sarah Eavan b 2 Nov 1977); *Career* musician; memb bands The Kult and Rockhouse while at univ in Dublin 1965–66, professional debut with folk band The Johnstons at Nat Stadium Dublin, with folk band Planxty 1974–76, solo 1978–; has toured extensively with own band or solo, also toured with Eric Clapton 1983 and Dire Straits 1984; discs: Gold for Back to the Centre 1986, Platinum for Trick or Treat 1991; Hotpress Music Critics Awards: Best Single (Crazy Dreams) 1981, Best Song (Nothing But the Same Old Story) 1981, Best Songwriter 1985, 1986 and 1991, Best Male Vocalist 1986; other awards: Folk Album of the Year (Welcome Here Kind Stranger) Melody Maker 1978, Best Rock Artist Nat Entertainment Opel Awards 1986, Best Rock Artist EMA Arts Awards (NI) 1991; *Recreations* scuba diving, golf, theatre, photography, gardening; *Style*— Paul Brady, Esq; ✉ c/o Damage Management, 16 Lambton Place, London W11 2SH (☎ 0171 229 2992, fax 0171 229 0098)

BRADY, Terence Joseph; s of (Frederick Arthur) Noel Brady (d 1985), of Montacute, Somerset, and Elizabeth Mary Moore (d 1986); *b* 13 March 1939; *Educ* Merchant Taylors', Trinity Coll Dublin (BA); *m* 1964, Hon Charlotte Mary Thérèse Brady, *qv*, da of Lord Clanmorris, of London; 1 s (Matthew), 1 da (Candida); *Career* writer and actor; contrib: Daily Mail, Daily Express, Sunday Express, Mail on Sunday, Country Homes and Interiors, Punch, The Field; *Theatre* credits incl: I Wish I Wish (also writer), Glory Be!, The Dumb Waiter, Would Anyone Who Saw The Accident, Beyond The Fringe, In The Picture, A Present From The Corporation, Clope; *Television* series and plays with wife (as Charlotte Bingham) incl: Take Three Girls, Upstairs Downstairs, Play for Today, 6 Plays of Marriage, No Honestly, Yes Honestly, Thomas and Sarah, Nanny, Pig in the Middle, Take Three Women, Love with A Perfect Stranger, Father Matthew's Daughter, This Magic Moment, Riders, Polo; other TV incl: Dig This Rhubarb, Broad and Narrow, First Impressions, Z Cars, My Name is Dora, Cribbins, A Man For Today, N F Simpson Series, Time For The Funny Walk, Boy Meets Girl; *Films* incl: Baby Love, Foreign Exchange; *Books* Rehearsal (1972), The Fight against Slavery (1976), Roses Story (1973), Yes Honestly (1977), A History of Point-to-Pointing (1991); *Recreations* racing, training point-to-pointers, riding, music, painting; *Clubs* PEN; *Style*— Terence Brady, Esq; ✉ c/o Peters Fraser & Dunlop Ltd, 503 The Chambers, Chelsea Harbour, Lots Road, London SW10 0XF (☎ 0171 352 4446, fax 0171 352 7356)

BRAGG, (Henry) John; s of Henry Bragg, of Torquay; *b* 28 Nov 1929; *Educ* Torquay GS, Chelsea Poly, London Univ; MRPharmS, FRPharmS, DBA, FCIT; *m* 1, 1954, Jean, *née* Harris (d 1969); 1 s, 2 da; m 2, 1972, Anthea, da of Kew Shelley, QC; 1 step s, 1 step da; *Career* Nat Serv RAMC 1951–53; Glaxo Laboratories 1953–55, Pfizer Ltd 1955–70, md Calor Gas Ltd 1970–80, dir Imperial Continental Gas Assoc 1978–85, md Calor Group 1980–85, dir Advanced Petroleum Technology Ltd 1985–89; chm: Canterbury and Thanet Health Authy 1986–94, East Kent Health Authy 1994–96; memb Professions Allied to Medicine Whitley Cncl 1990–96, govr Christ Church Coll Canterbury 1991–; tstee: Kent Community Housing Tst 1992–, Sandwich Utd Charities

1992–; Mayor of Sandwich 1989–92; memb: Dover Dist Cncl 1989–, Sandwich Town Cncl 1985–; *Recreations* golf, books, maps; *Clubs* Royal St George's Golf; *Style—* John Bragg, Esq; ✉ Hideway House, St George's Road, Sandwich, Kent CT13 9LE

BRAGG, Melvyn; s of Stanley Bragg, of Wigton, Cumbria, and Mary Ethel, *née* Parks; *b* 6 Oct 1939; *Educ* Nelson Thomlinson GS Wigton, Wadham Coll Oxford (Open scholar, MA); *m* 1, 1961, Marie-Elisabeth Roche (decd); 1 da; m 2, 1973, Catherine Mary (see Cate Haste, *qv*), da of Eric Haste, of Crantock, Almondsbury, Avon; 1 da (Alice b 1977), 1 s (Tom b 1980); *Career* writer and broadcaster; general traineeship BBC 1961, prodr on Monitor (BBC) 1963; ed BBC 2 1964: New Release (arts magazine latterly called Review, then Arena), Writers World (documentary), Take It or Leave It (literary panel game); presenter: In The Picture (Tyne Tees) 1971, 2nd House (BBC) 1973–77, Start the Week (BBC Radio 4, TRIC Award 1990 and 1994); presenter and ed: Read All About It (BBC) 1976–77, South Bank Show (ITV) 1978– (Prix Italia thrice); dir LWT Productions 1992, controller Arts Dept LWT 1990– (head of arts 1982–90), chm Border Television 1990–96 (dep chm 1985–90); occasional contrib Observer, Sunday Times, New York Times and Guardian; memb RSL 1977–80, pres Nat Campaign for the Arts; Hon DUniv Open Univ 1988, Hon DLaw Univ of St Andrews 1993; Hon DLitt: Liverpool 1986, Lancaster 1990, CNAA 1990; Hon DCL Univ of Northumbria 1994; hon fell Lancashire Poly; Domus fell St Catherine's Coll Oxford 1990, hon fell Library Assoc 1994, hon fell Wadham Coll Oxford 1995, hon fell Univ of Wales Cardiff 1996; FRSL, FRTS; *Awards* John Llewellyn-Rhys Award and PEN Awards for Fiction, BAFTA Richard Dimbleby Award for Outstanding Contribution to TV 1987, RTS Gold Medal 1989, winner BAFTA Huw Wheldon Award for Best Arts Programme or Series (for An Interview with Dennis Potter) 1994; *Novels* For Want of a Nail (1965), The Second Inheritance (1966), Without a City Wall (1968), The Hired Man (1969), A Place in England (1970), The Nerve (1971), The Hunt (1971), Josh Lawton (1972), The Silken Net (1974), Autumn Manoeuvres (1978), Kingdom Come (1980), Love and Glory (1983), The Cumbrian Trilogy (1984, comprising The Hired Man, A Place in England and Kingdom Come), The Maid of Buttermere (1987), A Time to Dance (1991, BBC TV series 1992), Crystal Rooms (1992), Credo: An Epic Tale of Dark Age Britain (1996); *Non fiction* Land of the Lakes (1983), Laurence Olivier (1984), Rich (1988, biog of Richard Burton), Speak for England (oral history of England since 1900), Ingmar Bergman: The Seventh Seal; *Musicals* Mardi Gras, Orion (TV, 1976), The Hired Man (W End 1985, Ivor Novello Award 1985); *Screenplays* Isadora, Jesus Christ Superstar (with Ken Russell), The Music Lovers, Clouds of Glory; *Stage Play* King Lear in New York 1992; *Recreations* walking, books; *Clubs* Garrick; *Style—* Melvyn Bragg, Esq; ✉ 12 Hampstead Hill Gardens, London NW3; The South Bank Show, The London Television Centre, Kent House, Upper Ground, London SE1 9LT (☎ 0171 261 3128, fax 0171 261 3782, telex 918123)

BRAGG, Stephen Lawrence; eldest s of Sir (William) Lawrence Bragg, FRS (Nobel Laureate, d 1971), and Alice Grace Jenny Bragg, CBE, *née* Hopkinson (d 1989); *b* 17 Nov 1923; *Educ* Rugby, Trinity Coll Cambridge (MA), MIT (MSc); *m* 1951, Maureen Ann, da of Dr D Roberts (d 1953), of Darlington; 3 s; *Career* chartered engr, chief res engr Rolls-Royce 1963–70, vice-chllr Brunel Univ 1971–81, chm Cambridge Health Authy 1982–86, dir industl co-operation Univ of Cambridge 1984–87; admin American Friends of Cambridge Univ 1988–93, emeritus fell Wolfson Coll 1991–; FEng 1981, FIMechE, FRAeS; *Books* Rocket Engines (1962); *Recreations* railway history; *Clubs* Athenaeum; *Style—* Stephen Bragg, Esq, FEng; ✉ 22 Brookside, Cambridge CB2 1JQ (☎ 01223 362208)

BRAGGE, Nicolas William; s of Norman Hugh Bragge, of The Towers, Brabourne, nr Ashford, Kent, and Nicolette Hilda, *née* Simms (d 1989); *b* 13 Dec 1948; *Educ* S Kent Coll of Technol Ashford, Holborn Coll of Law London (LLB), Inns of Court Sch of Law; *m* 22 Dec 1974, Pamela Elizabeth Brett, LLB; 3 s (Thomas Hereward b 1976, Christopher Joseph b 1980, Alasdair Charles b 1986); *Career* visiting lectr in law Princeton Coll London 1970–73; called to the Bar Inner Temple 1972, admitted Gray's Inn 1972; in practice at Intellectual Property and Chancery Bars 1973–; pt/t chm: Social Security Appeal Tbnls 1990–, Disability Appeal Tbnls 1992–; a dep master High Ct (Chancery Div) 1993–, a dep social security cmmr 1996–; asst examiner in law Associated Examining Bd 1970–73, examiner of the Supreme Court 1978–88; author of various articles on legal and historical subjects; Freeman City of London 1970, Liveryman Worshipful Co of Cutlers 1973, Hon Clerk Worshipful Co of Horners 1979–81; memb: Patent Bar Assoc, Chancery Bar Assoc; *Recreations* family, history of detective fiction to 1950, visiting Switzerland; *Clubs* City Livery, Travellers'; *Style—* Nicolas Bragge, Esq; ✉ The Towers, Brabourne, nr Ashford, Kent; New Court, Temple, London EC4Y 9BE (☎ 0171 797 8994, fax 0171 583 5885)

BRAGGINS, Maj-Gen Derek Henry; CB (1986); s of Albert Edward Braggins (d 1988), of Pagham, Sussex, and Hilda Mary, *née* Pearce; *b* 19 April 1931; *Educ* Rothesay Acad, Hendon Tech Coll; *m* 10 April 1953, Sheila St Clair, da of George Stuart (d 1969), of Kirkwall, Orkney; 3 s (Geoffrey b 1953, Nigel b 1959, Mark b 1965); *Career* cmmnd RASC 1950, transferred RCT 1965; regtl and staff appts: Korea, Malaya, Singapore, Ghana, Aden, Germany, UK, Staff Coll Camberley 1962, Jt Servs Staff Coll Latimer 1970, CO 7 Regt RCT 1973–75, Col AQ Commando Forces RM 1977–80, cmd tport and movements BAOR 1981–83, dir gen tport and movements and head of RCT 1983–86; Col Cmdt RCT 1986–93, pres RASC and RCT Assoc 1988–95; Freeman City of London 1983, Liveryman Worshipful Co of Carmen 1983–; FIMgt 1979, FCIT 1983; *Recreations* running, shooting, fishing, gardening, country life; *Style—* Maj-Gen Derek Braggins, CB

BRAGGINS, Peter Charles; s of Lt Col Charles Braggins (d 1990), of Bedford, and Hilda, *née* Hayes; *b* 10 July 1945; *Educ* Bedford Sch, Christ's Coll Cambridge (BA), Univ of Southampton (PGCE); *m* 21 Aug 1968, Julia, da of Richard Harold Cox (d 1991); 3 da (Polly Jane b 9 June 1971, Lucy Claire b 2 April 1973, Emily Ruth b 11 March 1976); *Career* asst master Newcastle Royal GS 1968–72, head of history Bootham Sch York 1972–77, head of history Bedford Sch Bedford 1977–82, dep headmaster Wilson's Sch Wallington Surrey 1982–91, headmaster The Skinners' Company's Sch 1992–; memb SHA; *Recreations* various!; *Style—* Peter Braggins, Esq; ✉ The Skinners' Company's School, St Johns Road, Tunbridge Wells, Kent TN4 9PG

BRAHAM, Charles James; s of Charles Braham (d 1986), and Violet Alice Braham (d 1980); *b* 25 Sept 1931; *Educ* Haverfordwest GS, Millfield; *m* 1953, Maureen, da of George Mervyn Evans (d 1991); 1 s (Mark Richard Charles b 1962), 1 da (Alison b 1954); *Career* journalist and newspaper sub-ed 1954–57, md Llanelli Star Ltd 1957–74, chm Cardigan & Tivyside Advertiser Ltd 1965–88; Swansea Sound Ltd: md 1974–95, chm 1993–96; dir Independent Radio News Ltd 1992–; pres S Wales Newspaper Soc 1963–64 and 1987–88, memb Cncl Assoc of Ind Radio Contractors 1974–85 (tstee Pension Fund 1974–96), chm Ind Radio News Network Ctee 1980–82; pres Llanelli Rotary Club 1970–71; *Style—* Charles Braham, Esq; ✉ Winscott, Felinfoel Rd, Llanelli, Carms SA15 3NJ

BRAHAM, Philip John Cofty; s of Ronald Marcus Braham, of Klaus, Knockamillie Terrace, Innellan, Argyll, and Dorothy May, *née* Cofty; *b* 8 April 1959; *Educ* Bearsden Acad, Duncan of Jordanstone Coll of Art Dundee (Br Cncl scholar, Dip Fine Art), Royal Acad of Fine Art The Hague (Greenshields Award, special commendation for postgrad studies); *m* Barbara, *née* Campbell; 1 da (Robyn b 13 March 1987); *Career* artist; visiting artist Univ of Calif LA 1981–82; subject of various exhibition catalogues; *Solo Exhibitions* Main Fine Art Glasgow 1984, The Scottish Gallery Edinburgh 1985, Glasgow Art Centre 1987, The Scottish Gallery 1988, The Raab Gallery London 1989, 1992, 1994 and 1995, Compass Gallery Glasgow 1993, Galerie Christian Dam Copenhagen 1994; *Gp Exhibitions* incl: The Human Touch (Fischer Fine Art London) 1985, Artists at Work (Edinburgh Festival Event) 1986, The Vigorous Imagination (Nat Gallery of Modern Art Edinburgh) 1987, Metamorphosis (Raab Gallery, London & Berlin) 1989, Landscape and Cityscape (Raab Gallery London) 1990, Cimal (Lucas Gallery Valencia) 1990, Galerie Bureaux et Magasins Ostend 1991, Scottish Art in the 20th Century (Royal W of England Acad Bristol) 1991, Scottish Painters (Flowers East London) 1993, Visions of Albion - Aspects of British Landscape I, II and III (Collyer-Bristow Gallery London) 1992, 1993 and 1994, The Power of the Image (Martin Gropius Bau Berlin) 1995, Aspects of Landscape (Scottish Gallery) 1996, Love and Poetry (Tobias Hirschmann, Frankfurt) 1996; *Collections* incl: Scottish Arts Cncl, Scottish Nat Gallery of Modern Art, Aberdeen Art Gallery, BBC, The Contemporary Arts Soc, RCP (Edinburgh), Life Assoc of Scotland, Educnl Inst of Scotland, Fleming Holdings, Texaco Holdings, Rainbow GmbH; *Awards* incl: EIS Award 1985, SAC Award 1989, RSA Guthrie Award 1995; *Style—* Philip Braham, Esq; ✉ 20 Bryson Rd, Edinburgh, Scotland EH11 1EE; Raab Boukamel Gallery, 9 Cork Street, London W1X 1PD (☎ 0171 734 6444, fax 0171 287 1740)

BRAHAMS, Diana Joyce; da of Gustave Arnold, and Rita, *née* Rosenberg; *b* 18 Feb 1944; *Educ* Roedean SA, Queen's Coll Harley St London; *m* 14 June 1964, Malcolm Henry Brahams, s of Reginald Brahams; 2 s (Nigel Robert b 20 Aug 1966, Gareth Edmund b 25 April 1970), 1 da (Catherine Sophie b 16 July 1968); *Career* called to the Bar Middle Temple 1972; tenant in chambers of John Melville-Williams QC (specialising in med negligence, personal injuries and product liability suits); legal practitioner, freelance writer and lectr specialising in med and the law; contrib to: legal and property jls 1977–86, various medical and scientific jls 1981–; legal corr The Lancet 1981–, ed Medico-legal Jl 1983–; fndr memb: Concern, Health Watch; memb: Ethics Ctee RCGP, PNBA, PIBA, APIL; FRSM; *Books* contrib: The Law and You (1987), Encyclopaedia Britannica's Medical and Health Annual (1985, 1986, 1989 and 1990), No Fault Compensation in Medicine (1989), Benzodiazepines - Current Concepts (1990), Human Genetic Information, Science Law and Ethics (1990), Orthogeriatrics (1991), Pharmaceutical Medicine (1993), Oxford Medical Companion (1994), Nursing Law & Ethics (1995); *Recreations* theatre, travel, reading, antiques, paintings (esp Victorian), going to and having parties; *Style—* Mrs Diana Brahams; ✉ 1 Verulam Buildings, Gray's Inn, London WC1R 5LQ (☎ 0171 831 0801, fax 0171 405 1387)

BRAIDEN, Prof Paul Mayo; s of Isaac Braiden (d 1966), and Lilian, *née* Mayo; *b* 7 Feb 1941; *Educ* Dudley GS, Univ of Sheffield (BEng, MEng, PhD); *m* 30 Aug 1993, Lesley, *née* Howard; *Career* Speedicut res scholar Firth Brown Tool Ltd Sheffield 1965–68, asst prof and Ford Fndn fell Dept of Mechanical Engrg Carnegie-Mellon Univ Pittsburgh 1968–70, sr and princ sci offr AERE 1970–76, Univ of Durham 1976–83 (lectr and sr lectr Dept of Engrg Sci, tutor Trevelyan Coll); Univ of Newcastle upon Tyne: head Dept of Mechanical Materials and Manufacturing Engrg 1992–, Sir James Woodeson prof of mfrg engrg 1983–, John Holmes meml lectr 1989; chm: NE Sector Working Pty on Advanced Mfrg Technol DTI 1986–88, N Region IProdE 1988–90; SERC: chm Ctee of Engrg Design 1990–94, memb Electro-Mechanical Ctee 1989–91, memb Innovative Manufacturing Engrg Panel, memb Engrg Bd 1990–91, memb Engrg Res Ctee 1991–94; memb Nat Ctee Methodist Hymn Book Revision 1979–82; MInstP 1976, FIMechE 1979, FIProdE 1981, FEng 1994; *Recreations* music (especially opera and oratorio), trained tenor voice, cycling, skiing; *Style—* Prof Paul Braiden, FEng; ✉ Department of Mechanical Materials & Manufacturing Engineering, University of Newcastle upon Tyne, Stephenson Building, Claremont Rd, Newcastle upon Tyne NE1 7RU (☎ 0191 222 6210, fax 0191 222 8600, telex 53654 UNINEW G)

BRAILSFORD, (Sidney) Neil; QC (Scot 1994); s of Sidney James Brailsford, of Edinburgh, and Jean Thelma More, *née* Leishman; *b* 15 Aug 1954; *Educ* Daniel Stewart's Coll Edinburgh, Univ of Stirling (BA), Univ of Edinburgh (LLB); *m* 7 Sept 1984, Elaine Nicola, yr da of late John Mausie Robbie; 2 s (Sidney Joshua Lawrence b 25 Jan 1995, Nathaniel Oliver Robbie b 29 July 1996); *Career* apprentice Messrs Biggart Baillie & Gifford, WS Edinburgh and Glasgow 1979–80, admitted to Faculty of Advocates 1981, standing jr counsel Dept of Agric and Fisheries in Scot 1987–92, called to the English Bar Lincoln's Inn 1990; sec Advocates' Business Law Gp 1988–; *Recreations* swimming, travel, food and wine, history (particularly American history and politics), commercial aviation; *Clubs* New (Edinburgh); *Style—* Neil Brailsford, Esq, QC; ✉ 29 Warriston Crescent, Edinburgh EH3 (☎ 0131 556 8320); c/o Advocates' Library, Parliament House, Edinburgh EH1 1RF (☎ 0131 226 5071, fax 0131 225 3642)

BRAIN, 2 Baron (UK 1962); Sir Christopher Langdon Brain; 2 Bt (UK 1954); s of 1 Baron, DM, FRS, FRCP, FRCPI, FRCPE (d 1966), and Stella, *née* Langdon-Down (d 1993); *b* 30 Aug 1926; *Educ* Leighton Park Sch, New Coll Oxford (MA); *m* 1953, Susan Mary, da of George Philip Morris; 3 da (Hon Nicola Dorothy (Hon Mrs Bashforth) b 1955, Hon Fiona Janice (Hon Mrs Proud) b 1958, Hon Naomi Melicent (Hon Mrs Kemp) b 1960); *Heir* bro, Hon Michael Brain; *Career* mgmnt conslt; various posts in photographic indust; memb: British Copyright Cncl 1989–, British Photographers Liaison Ctee 1989– (chm 1991–); memb House of Lords: Euro Sub Ctee 1990–, Euro Select Ctee 1991–95; Liveryman Worshipful Co of Weavers (Upper Bailiff 1984–85); *Recreations* sailing, fly-fishing; *Clubs* Oxford and Cambridge Sailing Soc, Royal Photographic Soc (ARPS); *Style—* The Rt Hon the Lord Brain; ✉ The Old Rectory, Cross St, Moretonhampstead, Devon TQ13 8NL

BRAIN, Dr The Hon Michael Cottrell; s of 1 Baron Brain (d 1966), and hp of bro, 2 Baron; *b* 6 Aug 1928; *Educ* Leighton Park Sch, New Coll Oxford (MA, BCh, DM), London Hospital; *m* 1960, Hon Elizabeth Ann Brain, da of Baron Tangley, KBE (Life Peer); 1 s (Thomas Russell b 1965), 2 da (Hilary Catherine (Mrs Guido Dino DeLuca) b 1961, Philippa Harriet (Mrs Armando Teves) b 1963); *Career* Capt RAMC 1956–58; physician Hammersmith Hosp 1966–69, prof of medicine McMaster Univ Canada 1969–94 (now emeritus), hon prof of med Univ of Calgary Canada 1995–; FRCP, FRCP Canada; *Books* Current Therapy Hematology and Oncology (4 edn), Current Therapy of Internal Medicine (2 edn); *Recreations* tennis; *Style—* Dr the Hon Michael Brain; ✉ 3215 1st Street, SW, Calgary, Alberta, Canada T2S 1P9 (☎ 00 1 403 287 3386, fax 00 1 403 243 1468)

BRAIN, Sir (Henry) Norman; KBE (1963, OBE 1947), CMG (1953); s of Bert Brain, of Rushall, Staffs, and Ann Gertrude Swaffer; *b* 19 July 1907; *Educ* King Edward VI HS Birmingham, Queen's Coll Oxford; *m* 1939, Nuala Gertrude (d 1988), da of Capt Archibald W Butterworth, of Ryde, IOW; 1 s (and 1 s decd); *Career* ambass Cambodia 1956–58 and Uruguay 1961–66, pres Br-Uruguayan Soc 1973–; *Recreations* music, golf; *Clubs* Canning; *Style—* Sir Norman Brain, KBE, CMG; ✉ St Andrews, Abney Court, Bourne End, Bucks (☎ 01628 520509)

BRAIN, Prof Paul Fredric; s of Frederick Ernest Brain, of Manchester, and Ada, *née* Squirell; *b* 1 July 1945; *Educ* Stretford Coll Manchester, Univ of Hull (BSc, PhD); *m* 4 July 1975, Sonja, da of Johannes Antonius Quirinus Strijbos, of Rotterdam, Holland; 2 s (Vincent Fredric b 1976, Daniel Robert b 1983); *Career* fellowship Univ of Sheffield 1970–71; Dept of Zoology Univ of Wales Swansea: lectr 1971–78, sr lectr 1978–83, reader 1983–87, personal chair in zoology 1987–95; head Sch of Biology Univ of Wales Swansea 1995–; visiting prof in psychology Univ of Hawaii 1986–90, visiting prof in zoology Univ of Kebangsaan Malaysia 1987; vice pres: Laboratory Animal Science Assoc, Assoc for Study of Animal Behaviour; pres Int Soc for Res on Aggression; FIBiol; St Vincent

(Italy) Int Prize for Med 1980; FRSA; *Books* numerous incl: Hormones and Aggression Vol I (1977), Alcohol and Aggression (1986), Ethoexperimental Approaches to the Study Behaviour (with R J Blanchard and S Parmigiani, 1989), Fear and Defence (1989); *Recreations* travel, reading, photography, marathon running; *Clubs* Sospan Road Runners; *Style*— Prof Paul Brain; ✉ School of Biological Sciences, University of Wales Swansea, Swansea SA2 8PP (☎ 01792 295444, fax 01792 295447, telex 48358 ULSWAN G)

BRAIN, Rt Rev Terence John; s of Reginald John Brain, of Coventry, W Mids, and Mary, *née* Cooney; *b* 19 Dec 1938; *Educ* King Henry VIII GS Coventry, Cotton Coll N Staffs, Oscott Coll Birmingham; *Career* ordained RC priest (Birmingham) 1964; asst priest St Gregory's Longton Stoke-on-Trent 1964–65, on staff Cotton Coll 1965–69, hosp chaplain Birmingham 1969–71, private sec to Archbishop of Birmingham 1971–82; parish priest: Bentilee Stoke-on-Trent 1982–88, St Austin's Stafford 1988–91; aux bishop of Birmingham and titular bishop of Amudarsa 1991–, bishop for prisons 1994–; memb Staffordshire LEA Ctee 1982–91; chm Bishop's Social Welfare Ctee 1992–, episcopal advsr Union of Catholic Mothers 1993–; *Recreations* watercolour painting, crossword puzzles; *Style*— The Rt Rev Terence Brain; ✉ Roman Catholic Archdiocese of Birmingham, Cathedral House, St Chad's, Queensway, Birmingham B4 6EX (☎ 0121 236 5535)

BRAINE OF WHEATLEY, Baron (Life Peer UK 1992), of Rayleigh in the County of Essex; Sir Bernard Richard Braine; kt (1972), PC (1985), DL (Essex 1978); s of Arthur Ernest Braine (d 1933), of Kew Gdns; *b* 24 June 1914; *Educ* Hendon County GS; *m* 1935, Kathleen Mary (d 1982), da of late Herbert William Faun, of East Sheen; 3 s (Hon Richard Laurence b 15 April 1939, Hon Michael Rodney b 10 April 1942, Hon Brendan Timothy b 19 Feb 1945); *Career* entered Civil Service 1931 (Inland Revenue); cmmnd N Staffs Regt, served 1939–45 in W Africa, NW Europe, SE Asia, Camberley Staff Coll, Temp Lt-Col; Parly candidate (C) East Leyton 1945; MP (C): Billericay 1950–55, Essex SE 1955–83, Castle Point 1983–92 (Father of the House of Commons 1987–92); Parly sec Miny of Pensions and Nat Insur 1960–61, under-sec of state Cwlth Rels 1961–62, Parly sec Miny of Health 1962–64, Cons front bench spokesman on Cwlth Affairs and Overseas Aid 1967–70; ldr Parly Missions to: India 1963, Mauritius 1971, Ethiopia 1971, W Germany 1973, Greece 1982, Poland 1986, Australia 1988, also led human rights mission to Soviet Union 1991; chm: Parly Select Ctee on Overseas Aid 1970–74, Nat Cncl on Alcoholism 1974–82, Br-German Parly Gp 1970–92, Br-Greek Parly Gp 1979–92, Br Solidarity with Poland Campaign 1981, UK Chapter Soc for Int Devpt, Tibet Parly Gp 1989; former chm: All Party Ctee on the Misuse of Drugs, All Party Pro-Life Ctee dep chm Cwlth Parly Assoc 1963–64 and 1970–74 (treas 1974–78); vice-chm: All Party Parly Human Rights Gp, Health Visitors Assoc; pres UK Ctee for Defence of the Unjustly Prosecuted, tstee (and former govr) Cwlth Inst, assoc Inst of Devpt Studies Sussex Univ; nat vice chm Jr Imperial League (Cons youth movement) 1937–45; Europe Peace Medal 1979, Cdr Polonia Restituta (Polish Govt in Exile) 1983 (Grand Cross 1991), Kt Cdr Order of Merit (W Germany) 1984, KCSG (Papal) 1987, Grand Cdr Order of Honour (Greece) 1987; KStJ 1985; FRSA; *Recreations* reading history, gardening; *Style*— The Rt Hon Lord Braine of Wheatley, PC, DL; ✉ King's Wood, 67 Great Wheatley Road, Rayleigh, Essex SS6 7AW

BRAINSBY, Anthony Thomas John (Tony); s of Thomas John Brainsby (d 1990), of Teesdale Gardens, Isleworth, Middx, and Kathleen Mary, *née* French (d 1985); *b* 6 March 1945; *Educ* Spring Grove GS; *m* 1980 (m dis 1984), Jane, *née* Abbott; 1 da (Miranda Jane Mary b 6 July 1979); *Career* public relations company owner 1965–; clients incl: Jayne Mansfield 1966, Music Therapy Charity 1975–, Thin Lizzy 1972–87, Queen 1974–79, Paul McCartney 1974–84, Steve Strange 1980–84, HMV Stores 1983–85, Virgin Atlantic Airline 1984–86, Me and My Girl 1985–88, Hippodrome Club, Limelight Club 1986–88, Montreal Comedy Festival 1988, Pink Floyd 1988–90, Penthouse Magazine 1988–95, Chess, Knebworth Charity Concert 1990, David Essex 1991–95, Arbiter Karaoke 1991–95, Fender Guitars 1991–95, For Women Magazine 1992–95, Iceland (Tourism and Culture) 1992–95, Br Music Indust Award Charity Dinner 1992–, OK! Magazine 1993–95, Hendon Football Club 1994–95, English Heritage 10th Anniversary 1994, Chris de Burgh 1994–, Rock Circus 1994–, Knebworth Talent Ctee 1995–, Vanessa Mae 1995–, Russian All Stars Ice Ballet Tour 1995–96, AOL internet serv 1995–, Arbiter Music CD-Rom series 1996; Freeman City of London 1982; *Recreations* snooker, tennis, collector of music memorabilia, traveller; *Clubs* RAC, Pall Mall; *Style*— Tony Brainsby, Esq; ✉ Tony Brainsby PR, Flat 1, 12–14 De Vere Gardens, London W8 5AE (☎ home 0171 937 9876, ☎ office 0171 937 9376, car 0836 382111, fax 0171 937 8765, e-mail tbrainsby@aol.com, internet: http://home.aol.com/TBrainsby)

BRAITHWAITE, Althea; da of Air Vice-Marshal Francis Joseph St George Braithwaite (d 1956), and Rosemary, *née* Harris (Lady Earle (d 1978)); *b* 20 June 1940; *Educ* Felixtowe Coll; *m* 1, 1966 (m dis 1974), Malcolm Gordon Graham-Cameron; 1 s (Duncan Charles b 1968); m 2, 1979, Edward James Parker; *Career* writer and illustrator of about 200 books for children 1968–; specialises in information books covering numerous topics; fndr and managing ed Dinosaur Publications Ltd (sold to Collins 1984); *Style*— Ms Althea Braithwaite; ✉ Beechcroft House, Over, Cambridge CB4 5NE

BRAITHWAITE, His Hon Bernard Richard Braithwaite; s of Bernard Leigh Braithwaite, of Great House, Newchurch, Mon, and Emily Dora Ballard, *née* Thomas; *b* 20 Aug 1917; *Educ* Clifton, Peterhouse Cambridge; *Career* barr 1946, circuit judge 1971–88; ret; *Recreations* gardening, travelling; *Clubs* Boodle's; *Style*— His Hon B R Braithwaite; ✉ Summerfield House, Owlpen, Uley, Glos

BRAITHWAITE, Brian; s of Thomas Guy Braithwaite (d 1989), and Dorothea, *née* Swinbanks (d 1976); *b* 15 May 1927; *Educ* Mercers' Sch London; *m* 1, 6 June 1959 (m dis 1962), Patricia, *née* Moore; m 2, 1962, Gwendoline Phyllis, da of John Trevor Everson (d 1976); 2 s (Simon Guy b 1963, Christopher Brian b 1968), 1 da (Philippa Kate b 1964); *Career* Gordon Highlanders Trg Bn and Forces Broadcasting Serv, Italy and Austria 1945–48; Associated Newspapers 1948–53; advertisement exec: Hulton Press 1953–56, Harrison Raison 1956–64; advertisement and bd dir Stevens Press 1964–69; National Magazine Co: joined 1969, publisher Harpers Bazaar then Harpers & Queen, launch publisher Cosmopolitan 1972, dir Good Housekeeping 1979–91 (publishing dir 1984), launch publisher Country Living 1985, gp commercial dir 1991–92, ret; magazine conslt 1992–; festival chm Newsvendors Benevolent Inst 1993–94; vice pres Publicity Club of London until 1992; *Books* Business of Women's Magazines (1978, 2 edn 1988), Ragtime to Wartime (1986), Home Front (1987), The Christmas Book (1988), Food Glorious Food (1990), Things My Mother Should Have Told Me (1991), Childhood Memories (1991), Home Sweet Home (1992), Women's Magazines: The First 300 Years (1995); *Recreations* golf, theatre, cinema; *Style*— Brian Braithwaite; ✉ 1 Narbonne Avenue, London SW4 (☎ 0181 673 4100)

BRAITHWAITE, Sir (Joseph) Franklin Madders; kt (1980), DL (Cambs 1983); s of Sir John Braithwaite (d 1973, sometime chm Stock Exchange Cncl), and Martha Janette, *née* Baker; *b* 6 April 1917; *Educ* Bootham Sch, King's Coll Cambridge; *m* 1939, (Charlotte) Isabel, da of Robert Elmer Baker, of NY; 1 s (Peter Franklin b 1942), 1 da (Virginia Louise b 1940); *Career* dir Baker Perkins 1950– (joined 1946), chm Baker Perkins Holdings plc 1980–84 (md 1971–79), pres Process Plant Assoc 1977–79, dir East Co Regnl Bd Lloyds Bank 1979–87, dep chm Peterborough Devpt Corp 1982–88, chm Peterborough Independent Hospital plc 1981–87; *Recreations* music, golf; *Clubs* Army and Navy; *Style*— Sir Franklin Braithwaite, DL; ✉ 7 Rutland Terrace, Stamford, Lincs PE9 2QD (☎ 01780 51244)

BRAITHWAITE, Mary Anne; da of Brig K W Hervey (d 1973), DSO, JP, of East Bilney Hall, Norfolk, and Hope Marian, *née* Barclay; *b* 16 Aug 1932; *Educ* Downham Sch Hatfield Heath Bishops Stortford Herts; *m* 1, 29 July 1952, Flt Lt James W Duff (d 1953); m 2, 12 July 1955, William Arthur (Jim) Drysdale (d 1970); 4 s (James (Jim) b 30 April 1956, William (Bill) b 27 Oct 1957, Keith (twin) b 27 Oct 1957, d 1989, Robert b 13 Nov 1960); m 3, 18 Dec 1975, Maj (Cecil) Geoffrey Braithwaite (d 1987); *Career* thoroughbred racehorse breeder 1970–, Jockey Club permit trainer 1976–86, dist cmmr Pony Club 1981–85; winner Horse and Hound Buccleuch Cup twice with homebred brother and sister horses; memb: BHS, Pony Club, Permit Trainers Assoc, Thoroughbred Breeders Assoc; *Recreations* hunting, racing, grandmother; *Style*— Mrs M A Braithwaite; ✉ Lochmalony, Cupar, Fife KY15 4QF (☎ 01337 870238)

BRAITHWAITE, Michael; *b* 10 Dec 1937; *Educ* City Univ (BSc); *m* 4 Feb 1967, (Pamela) Margaret; 1 s (James b 7 Jan 1971), 1 da (Sally b 4 Oct 1969); *Career* UKAEA 1958–69, ptnr Deloitte & Touche (formerly Touche Ross) 1969–; Liveryman Worshipful Co of Info Technologists 1988; CEng, MBCS, FInstMC; *Recreations* skiing, gardening; *Style*— Michael Braithwaite, Esq; ✉ Thriplow, Royston, Herts; Deloitte & Touche, Stonecutter Court, 1 Stonecutter Street, London EC4A 4TR (☎ 0171 936 3000)

BRAITHWAITE, Sir Rodric Quentin; GCMG (1994, KCMG 1988); s of (Henry) Warwick Braithwaite (d 1971), and Lorna Constance, *née* Davies; *b* 17 May 1932; *Educ* Bedales, Christ's Coll Cambridge (BA); *m* 1 April 1961, Gillian Mary, da of Patrick Robinson (d 1975); 4 s (Richard b 1962, Julian b 1968, Mark (twin) b 1968, d 1971, David b 1972), 1 da (Katharine b 1963); *Career* Nat Serv 1950–52; HM Dip Serv: entered 1955, Djakarta 1958–59, Warsaw 1959–61, FO 1961–63, Moscow 1963–66, Rome 1966–69, FO 1969–72, Oxford 1973–75, UK perm rep to Euro Community Brussels 1975–78, FCO 1978–82, min commercial Washington 1982–84, dep under sec of state FCO 1984–88, ambass Moscow 1988–92, also ambass (non-resident) Republic of Armenia and Republic of Georgia 1992; foreign policy advsr to the Prime Minister 1992–93, sr advsr Deutsche Morgan Grenfell 1994–; visiting fell All Souls Coll Oxford 1972–73, hon fell Christ's Coll Cambridge; memb Bd: ENO, SSEES, RAM; *Recreations* music, sailing, walking, reading, Russia; *Clubs* Reform; *Style*— Sir Rodric Braithwaite, GCMG; ✉ c/o Morgan Grenfell Group plc, 23 Great Winchester Street, London EC2P 2AX (☎ 0171 588 4545, fax 0171 826 6155)

BRAITHWAITE, William Thomas Scatchard (Bill); QC (1992); s of John Vernon Braithwaite (d 1975), and Nancy Phyllis Scatchard (d 1995); *b* 20 Jan 1948; *Educ* Gordonstoun, Univ of Liverpool (LLB); *m* Sheila, *née* Young; 1 da (Dawn Plint), 1 s (Ross Thomas Vernon); *Career* called to the Bar Gray's Inn 1970, pupil to His Hon Judge Arthur, currently in personal injury litigation practice in Liverpool, recorder of the Crown Court; conslt ed The Quantum of Damages; memb: Euro Brain Injury Soc, Spinal Injuries Assoc, Headway, Nat Head Injury Fndn of America, Assoc of Personal Inuury Lawyers, Advsy Bd Kemsley Unit; author of articles and lectures on brain and spine litigation in England, Europe and America; *Recreations* cars and wine; *Style*— Bill Braithwaite, QC; ✉ Exchange Chambers, Pearl Assurance House, Derby Square, Liverpool L2 9XX (☎ 0151 236 7747, fax 0151 236 3433); 2 Crown Office Row, London EC4Y 7HJ

BRAKA, Ivor Isaac; s of Joseph Braka, and Margaret Elizabeth, *née* Dodds; *b* 19 Dec 1954; *Educ* Oundle, Pembroke Coll Oxford (BA); *m* 1991, Camilla Mary, da of Duncan Henry Davidson; 1 s (Joseph Duncan b 10 Nov 1996); *Career* art dealer; *Style*— Ivor Braka, Esq; ✉ 63 Cadogan Square, London SW1X 0DY (☎ 0171 235 0266)

BRAMALL, Sir (Ernest) Ashley; kt (1975), DL (Gtr London 1982); er s of Maj Edmund Haselden Bramall, RA (d 1964), of 2 Symons St, Chelsea, and Katharine Bridget, *née* Westby (d 1985); bro of Field Marshal Baron Bramall (Life Peer), *qv*; *b* 6 Jan 1916; *Educ* Westminster, Canford, Magdalen Coll Oxford (MA); *m* 1, 2 Sept 1939 (m dis 1950), Margaret Elaine, da of Raymond Taylor (d 1942), of Teddington, Middx; 2 s (Christopher b 1942, Richard b 1944); m 2, 23 Sept 1950, Germaine (Gery) Margaret, da of late Dr Victor Bloch (d 1968), of 48 Queen's Gate, London; 1 s (Anthony b 1957); *Career* served WWII 1940–46, Maj RAC 1943, psc; called to the Bar Inner Temple 1949; MP (Lab) Bexley 1946–50; cncllr (Lab): Westminster City Cncl 1959–68, LCC Bethnal Green 1961–65, GLC Tower Hamlets 1964–73, Bethnal Green and Bow 1973–86; chm: GLC 1982–83, ILEA 1984–86 (ldr 1970–81), Nat Cncl for Drama Trg 1981–89; dep chm Museum of London 1991, chm Westminster College Corporation 1992; Freeman City of London, Liveryman Worshipful Co of Skinners 1951; Grand Offr Order of Orange Nassau (Netherlands) 1982; *Recreations* opera; *Style*— Sir Ashley Bramall, DL; ✉ 2 Egerton House, 59/63 Belgrave Rd, London SW1V 2BE (☎ and fax 0171 828 0973)

BRAMALL, Field Marshal Baron (Life Peer UK 1987); Edwin Noel Westby; KG (1990), GCB (1979, KCB 1974), OBE (1965), MC (1945) JP (1986); yr s of Maj Edmund Haselden Bramall, RA (d 1964), and Katharine Bridget, *née* Westby (d 1985); bro of Sir Ashley Bramall, *qv*; *b* 18 Dec 1923; *Educ* Eton; *m* 1949, Dorothy Avril Wentworth, only da of Brig-Gen Henry Albemarle Vernon, DSO, JP (ggggs of Henry Vernon by his w Lady Henrietta Wentworth, yst da of 1 Earl of Strafford, Henry Vernon being himself 2 cous of 1 Baron Vernon); 1 s, 1 da; *Career* 2 Lt KRRC 1943, served NW Europe WWII, Japan 1946–47, Middle East 1953–58, Instr Army Staff Coll 1958–61, staff offr to Lord Mountbatten for re-organising MOD 1963–64, served Malaysia during Indonesian confrontation 1965–66 (CO 2 Greenjackets KRRC), cmd 5 Airportable Bde 1967–69, IDC 1970, GOC 1 Div BAOR 1971–73, Lt-Gen 1973, Cdr Br Forces Hong Kong 1973–76, Gen 1976, Col Cmdt 3 Bn Roy Green Jackets 1973–84, Col 2 Gurkhas 1976–86, C-in-C UKLF 1976–78, Vice-Chief Defence Staff (Personnel and Logistics) 1976–79, Chief General Staff 1979–82, ADC Gen to HM The Queen 1979–82, Field Marshal 1982, Chief of the Defence Staff 1982–85; pres Gurkha Bde Assoc 1987–, pres (Army) Not Forgotten Assoc; tstee Imperial War Museum 1983– (chm 1989); HM Lord Lt of Greater London 1986–; pres: MCC 1988–89, Greater London Playing Fields Assoc 1990–, London Age Concern, OStJ; *Books* The Chiefs: The Story of the UK Chiefs of Staff (co-author); *Clubs* MCC, Travellers', Pratt's; *Style*— Field Marshal the Lord; ✉ c/o House of Lords, London SW1A 0PW

BRAMBELL, Dr Michael Rogers; s of Prof F W Rogers Brambell, CBE, FRS (d 1970), of Bangor, and Margaret Lilian, *née* Adgie; *b* 2 Aug 1932; *Educ* Epsom Coll, Christ's Coll Cambridge (MA, VetMB), Univ of Edinburgh (PhD), MRCVS; *m* 1961, Patricia Margaret, da of James Robertson (d 1954); 2 s (William Rogers b 1963, David James b 1965); *Career* scientific then sr scientific offr Animal Diseases Research Assoc 1956–67, curator of mammals Zoological Soc of London 1967–78, dir North of England Zoological Soc Chester Zoo 1978–95; memb Cncl: Linnean Soc 1969–73, Fauna Preservation Soc 1973–78, World Owl Tst 1992–, Zoological Soc of London 1992–95 and 1996–; chm: Scientific Authy for Animals 1978–81, Int Ad Hoc Ctee Ranching CITES 1980–81, Animal Advsy Ctee Nature Conservancy Cncl 1981–85, London Zoo Bd Zoological Soc of London 1994–95; hon treas: Scottish Branch Inst of Professional Civil Servants 1966–67, Fedn of Zoological Gardens of Great Britain and Ireland 1989–94; Hon DVSc Univ of Liverpool 1996; *Books* Horse, Tapir and Rhinoceros (1976), Animals and Ethics (jtly, 1980); author of numerous papers in Zoological jls; *Recreations* sailing in Scotland, hill walking, naval history; *Style*— Dr Michael Brambell; ✉ 176 Liverpool Road, Chester CH2 1BD

BRAMBLE, Roger John Lawrence; DL (Greater London 1986); s of Courtenay Parker Bramble, CIE (d 1987), of Childer Thornton, Cheshire, and Margaret Louise Bramble, MBE (d 1989), da of Sir Henry Lawrence, KCSI; *b* 3 April 1932; *Educ* Eton, King's Coll Cambridge (MA); *Career* cmmnd Coldstream Gds 1951; dir: Bankers' Insurance Co Ltd, Sun International (UK) Ltd, English Nat Opera 1986–, English Nat Ballet 1986– (dep chm 1990–); cncllr City of Westminster 1968–, Lord Mayor of Westminster 1985–86; memb Lloyd's 1960–; chm Benesh Inst; tstee Serpentine Gallery 1990–, tstee Albert Memorial 1996–; FRSA 1989; Order of the Aztec Eagle Mexico 1985, Order of Merit Qatar 1985, Order of Southern Cross Brazil 1993; *Recreations* music, farming, languages; *Clubs* Turf; *Style*— Roger Bramble, Esq, DL; ✉ 2 Sutherland Street, London SW1V 4LB (☎ and fax 0171 828 2439); Sutton Hosey Manor, Long Sutton, Langport, Somerset TA10 9NA

BRAMLEY, Andrew; s of Peter Bramley (d 1989), of Ridgeway, Derbyshire, and Tessa Bramley, *qv*, *née* Hardwick; *b* 18 Jan 1966; *Educ* Henry Fanshawe Sch Derbyshire; *Career* mangr family business until 1985; converted Old Vicarage (family home) into restaurant 1985–87; owner and mangr Old Vicarage 1987–; awarded: Egon Ronay Star 1988–92, Good Food Guide Newcomer of the Year 1988, Derbyshire Restaurant of the Year Award 1988–90, Clover Leaf Award in Ackerman Guide 1990–92, Northern Restaurant of the Year Award Chef Magazine 1991; featured in major Food and Wine Guides; TV and radio appearances; memb: Restaurant Assoc of GB, Sheffield C of C; *Books* Women Chefs of Great Britain (with Tessa Bramley, 1990); *Recreations* cooking, writing, riding, motor sport, interior design; *Style*— Andrew Bramley, Esq; ✉ The Old Vicarage, Ridgeway Moor, Ridgeway, Nr Sheffield, Derbyshire S12 3XW (☎ 0114 247 5814, fax 0114 247 7079)

BRAMLEY, Barry David; s of David Scotson Bramley (d 1994), of Cranleigh, Surrey, and Marjorie Sutcliffe Duckett (d 1990); *b* 29 Sept 1937; *Educ* Stowe; *m* 18 July 1970, Margaret Helen, da of Kenneth Edmond Hansel; 1 da (Susan Elisabeth b 27 Aug 1971), 1 s (Justin Kenneth David b 10 March 1975); *Career* Nat Serv 3rd Carabiniers (Prince of Wales's Dragoon Gds) 1960–62; CA Cook & Co 1962–63 (trainee 1955–60); British-American Tobacco Co Ltd: joined 1963, internal auditor Nigeria, Sierra Leone, Belgium and Guatemala 1964–66, fin dir BAT Zaire SARL 1966–68, Fin Dept BAT Head Office London 1968–69; Corp Fin Dept NM Rothschild & Sons Ltd 1969–70; rejoined British-American Tobacco Co Ltd 1970, fin advsr non-tobacco BAT Head Office 1970–71, special assignment Amatil Ltd Australia 1971–72, corp fin advsr and planning co-ordinator non-tobacco Head Office 1972–81, md W D & H O Wills (New Zealand) Ltd 1981–83, territorial dir British-American Tobacco Co Ltd 1983–85, sr vice pres and chief admin offr BATUS Inc USA 1985–88, chm British-American Tobacco Co Ltd and dir BAT Industries plc 1988–96; non-exec dir: Premier Farnell Plc, Brown Forman Corporation (USA), Skandinavisk Tobakskompagni A/S; ACA 1960; *Recreations* golf, tennis; *Style*— Barry Bramley, Esq; ✉ Little Court, Beech Avenue, Effingham, Surrey KT24 5PJ (☎ and fax 01372 452027)

BRAMLEY, Dr John Vincent; s of George Vincent Bramley, and Kathleen Mary, *née* Phillips; *b* 4 July 1935; *Educ* Wyggeston GS Leicester, Imperial Coll London (BSc, PhD, DIC, ARSM); *m* 7 Jan 1961, Rosalind Mary Culhane, da of Maj George Pinckard Lathbury; 2 s (Robert George Vincent b 24 March 1964, Matthew John b 7 Nov 1967), 1 da (Katharine Susan b 31 Dec 1961); *Career* Laporte plc: joined 1959, mangr Glebe Mines 1969–76, gen mangr Laporte Minerals 1984–95; conslt 1996–; govr Imperial Coll of Science Technol and Medicine; Inst of Mining and Metallurgy: memb 1961, fell 1972, memb Cncl 1986, chm Exec Ctee 1990, vice pres 1991, pres 1993; memb Cncl Mineral Industries Research Organisation, pres Royal Sch of Mines Assoc 1996–97; CEng, FEng 1988; *Recreations* choral singing, walking; *Style*— Dr John Bramley, FEng; ✉ Marsham, Start Lane, Whaley Bridge, Stockport SK12 7BP (☎ 01663 732701, fax 01663 719997)

BRAMLEY, Prof Sir Paul Anthony; kt (1984); s of Charles Bramley (d 1962), and Constance Victoria Bramley (d 1983); *b* 24 May 1923; *Educ* Wyggeston Leicester, Univ of Birmingham (MB ChB, BDS); *m* 1952, Hazel Morag, da of Harold Arthur Boyd (d 1964), of Glasgow; 1 s, 3 da; *Career* Capt RADC 1946–48; MO Church of Scotland, Kenya, registrar Rooksdown House, conslt oral surgn Southwest Regnl Hosp Bd 1954–69; Univ of Sheffield: prof of dental surgery 1969–88 (now emeritus), dean Dental Sch 1972–75; Royal Cmmn NHS 1976–79, dean of faculty RCS 1980–83, chm Dental Protection Ltd, emeritus conslt RN; pres: Sands Cox Soc, BDA, Br Assoc of Oral and Maxillofacial Surgeons; memb Cncl Med Protection Soc, chm Cavendish DFAS; Hon DDS: Univ of Birmingham, Prince of Songkla Thailand; Hon MD Univ of Sheffield; FDSRCS, FRCS, Hon FRACDS; Bronze Medal Univ of Helsinki, Colyer Gold Medal RCS; *Books* The Temporomandibular Joint: Disease, Disorders, Surgery (1989); *Style*— Prof Sir Paul Bramley; ✉ Greenhills, Back Lane, Hathersage, Sheffield S30 1AR (☎ 01433 650502)

BRAMLEY, Robin Thomas Todhunter; s of E A Bramley (d 1991), of Gillingham, Norfolk, and Mary, *née* Todhunter; *b* 16 June 1950; *Educ* Ampleforth, Univ of Exeter (LLB); *m* 20 Oct 1973, Patricia Anne, da of Maj E S L Mason (d 1996), of Bungay, Suffolk; 1 s (George b 1982), 1 da (Henrietta b 1979); *Career* landowner and farmer Gillingham Estate, sr ptnr Francis Hornor chartered surveyors Norwich 1992– (ptnr 1976–); memb: The Broads Authy, Norfolk Police Authy, Ctee Norfolk Branch CLA; chm Broads Soc 1986–87, memb of Lord Chllr's Panel of Arbitrators 1992; JP; FRICS 1978; *Recreations* shooting, riding, fishing, history, conservation; *Clubs* Norfolk; *Style*— R T T Bramley, Esq; ✉ Gillingham Hall, Norfolk (☎ 01502 717247, fax 01502 716856); Old Bank of England Court, Queen St, Norwich (☎ 01603 629871, fax 01603 760756)

BRAMLEY, Tessa; da of Howard Hardwick (d 1990), of Coal Aston, nr Sheffield, and Irene, *née* Barber; *b* 3 April 1939; *Educ* Henry Fanshawe GS Derbyshire, High Storrs GS Sheffield, London Coll of Home Econ, Totley Hall Trg Coll Sheffield (Dip in Domestic Sci, DipEd); *m* 8 May 1965, Peter Bramley (d 1989), s of Francis Bramley; 1 s (Andrew Bramley, *qv*, b 18 Jan 1966); *Career* teacher and lectr in domestic sci 1963–75, sales and promotion in food business 1975–81, own restaurant (with husband) 1981–, opened Old Vicarage 1987 (Good Food Guide's Newcomer of Year 1988, Egon Ronay star 1988–94 (2 stars 1995), Clover Leaf in Ackerman Guide 1990–95, Northern Restaurant of the Year award Chef Magazine 1991, Derbyshire Restaurant of the Year 1988–90); memb Restaurant Assoc of GB, Sheffield C of C, Inst of Master Chefs; *Books* Women Chefs of Great Britain (with Andrew Bramley, 1990), The Instinctive Cook (1995), featured in Great British Chefs (II) (1995); *Recreations* literature and music; *Style*— Ms Tessa Bramley; ✉ Old Vicarage, Ridgeway Moor, Ridgeway, Nr Sheffield, Derbyshire S12 3XW (☎ 0114 247 5814, fax 0114 247 7079)

BRAMMA, Dr Harry Wakefield; s of Fred Bramma (d 1983), of Guiseley, W Yorks, and Christine, *née* Wakefield; *b* 11 Nov 1936; *Educ* Bradford GS, Pembroke Coll Oxford (MA); *Career* master King Edward VI GS E Retford 1961–63, asst organist Worcester Cathedral 1963–76, dir of music The King's Sch Worcester 1965–76; organist Three Choirs' Festival 1966, 1969, 1972 and 1975; conductor Kidderminster Choral Soc 1972–79; organist and dir of music: Southwark Cathedral 1976–89, All Saints Margaret St London 1989–; hon treas RCO 1987–, dir Royal Sch of Church Music 1989–, sec Cathedral Organists' Assoc 1989–; organ advsr Dio of Southwark 1976–93, pres Southwark and S London Soc of Organists; Liveryman Worshipful Co of Musicians; Hon DLitt Univ of Bradford 1995; FRCO; *Style*— Dr Harry Bramma; ✉ Addington Palace, Croydon, Surrey CR9 5AD (☎ 0181 654 7676, fax 0181 655 2542)

BRAMPTON, Sally Jane; da of Roy Reginald Brampton, of Sunbury on Thames, Middlesex, and Pamela Mary, *née* Ray; *b* 15 July 1955; *m* (m dis 1990), Nigel Cole; m 2, 29 Dec 1990, Jonathan Powell, *qv*; 1 da (Molly Elizabeth b 23 Jan 1992); *Career* fashion writer Vogue 1978–81, fashion ed Observer 1981–85, ed-in-chief Elle 1985–89, assoc ed Mirabella 1990–91, freelance journalist and novelist; dir Fashion Acts charity; visiting prof Central St Martin's Coll of Art and Design; *Books* Good Grief (1993), Lovesick (1995); *Recreations* gardening; *Clubs* Groucho; *Style*— Miss Sally Brampton

BRANCH, Prof Michael Arthur; s of Arthur Frederick Branch (d 1986), of Hornchurch, Essex, and Mahala, *née* Parker; *b* 24 March 1940; *Educ* Shene London, Univ of London Sch of Slavonic and E European Studies (BA, PhD), Univ of Helsinki; *m* 11 Aug 1963, (Ritva-Riitta) Hannele, da of Erkki Lauri Kari (d 1982), of Heinola, Finland; 3 da (Jane, Jean, Ann); *Career* Univ of London: lectr Finno-Ugrian Studies 1971–73 (asst lectr 1967–71), dir Sch of Slavonic and E Euro Studies 1980–, prof of Finnish 1986– (lectr 1973–77, reader 1977–86); govr: Britain-Russia Centre, Br Assoc for Central and E Europe; Hon DPhil Univ of Oulu Finland 1983; Commander of the Finnish Lion Finland 1980, Commander of the Order of Merit Poland 1993; *Books* A J Sjögren: Travels in the North (1973), Finnish Folk Poetry - Epic (jtly, 1977), Student's Glossary of Finnish (jtly, 1981), Kalevala - translated by W F Kirby (ed, 1985), Edith Södergran (jt ed, 1992), The Great Bear (jtly, 1993), Uses of Tradition (jt ed, 1994), Finland and Poland in the Russian Empire (jt ed, 1995); *Recreations* walking, gardening; *Clubs* Athenaeum; *Style*— Prof M A Branch; ✉ 33 St Donatt's Rd, New Cross, London SE14 6NU; Hämeentie 28 A3, 00530 Helsinki, Finland; School of Slavonic and East European Studies, University of London, Senate House, Malet St, London WC1E 7HU (☎ 0171 637 4934, fax 0171 636 6672)

BRAND, Gordon John; s of Peter Gordon Brand, of Baildon, W Yorks, and Mary, *née* Dellar; *b* 6 Aug 1955; *Educ* Woodend Secdy Sch Shipley W Yorks; *m* 16 July 1979, Lyn Margaret, *née* Ghent; 2 da (Marylyn Louise b 28 March 1983, Elizabeth Jane b 6 Oct 1987); *Career* professional golfer; amateur record: England rep Home Ints 1976, capt England youth team 1976, winner Yorks Amateur Championship 1976, GB rep v Europe 1976; turned professional 1976; professional record: winner 7 tournaments Safari Tour Africa 1981–90, played for Europe Ryder Cup 1983, runner-up British Open 1986, England rep Dunhill Cup 1986 and 1987 (won with Nick Faldo and Howard Clark), winner Belgium Open 1989; *Recreations* gardening, snooker, cars; *Style*— Gordon J Brand, Esq; ✉ c/o PGA European Tour, Wentworth Club, Wentworth Drive, Virginia Water, Surrey GU25 4LS

BRANDER, Robert William (Bob); s of William Brander, of Largs Ayrshire, and Thomasina, *née* Mallinson; *b* 27 May 1936; *Educ* N Kelvinside Sch Glasgow, Univ of Strathclyde (BSc), The Royal Coll of Science and Technol Glasgow (ARCST); *m* 1 July 1961, Janet, da of Ernest Alexander Hornsby; 1 s (Andrew William b 15 March 1964), 1 da (Alison Jane b 31 Jan 1966); *Career* GEC Hirst Res Centre: joined 1957, gp ldr Solid State Physics 1965–68, head Material Dept 1969–72; British Telecommunications plc: head Transistor Prodn 1972–75, head Bipolar and Hybrid Technols 1975–78, head Device Res Div 1978–80, dep dir Res & Advanced Technol 1981–83, dep dir Switching Devpt 1984, dir Systems Evolution & Standards Dept 1984–85, dir Technol Applications BT Res Labs Ipswich 1985–87, tech dir Communications Systems Div and Int Products Div 1987–90; tech dir Racal-Datacom Group Ltd 1990–92, tech and managerial conslt (telecommunications) 1992–; James Muir prize for Natural Philosophy; charter memb Int Ctee on Silicon Carbide; FEng 1987, FIEE 1972, FInstP 1970; *Recreations* sailing, golf, walking; *Clubs* Deben Yacht, Rushmere Golf; *Style*— Bob Brander, Esq, FEng; ✉ High Trees, Bucklesham Road, Foxhall, Ipswich, Suffolk IP10 0AA (☎ 01473 659291, fax 01473 659921)

BRANDON, Michael; s of Sol Feldman, and Miriam, *née* Tumen; *b* 20 April 1945; *Educ* Central HS NY, Nassau Community Coll, NY Univ, American Acad of Dramatic Arts; *m* 1, Dec 1976 (m dis 1978), Lindsay Wagner; m 2, 18 Nov 1989, Glynis Barber; 1 s (Alexander Max b 21 Nov 1992); *Career* actor and director; memb: Greenpeace, Children in Need, Screen Actors Guild, Equity (American and Br), Writers Guild, AFTRA, Academy of Motion Picture Arts and Sciences; *Television* incl: Dynasty (mini-series), Hypnotic Confession, The Marshall, James Dean, Queen of the Stardust Ballroom, Hitchhike, Red Alert, Third Girl from the Left, Dennis Potter's Visitors (BBC), Care of Time (ATV), Dempsey and Makepeace also dir, series for LWT, starring with Glynis Barber), Rock and Roll Mum, Moment of Truth, Shattering the Silence, Apocalypse Watch (mini-series); dir: rock videos, Monsters (Spelling TV); *Films* incl: Lovers and Strangers (with Diane Keaton), Jennifer On My Mind (with Robert De Niro), FM, Change of Seasons (with Shirley Maclaine and Anthony Hopkins), George Cukor's Rich and Famous (with Jacqueline Bisset), Dario Argento's Four Flies on Grey Velvet, Deja Vu (with Vanessa Redgrave); *Recreations* skiing, scuba-diving, horseback riding, photography (photo exhibition for Prince's Trust London 1986); *Clubs* Mossiman's, Tramp, Rest; *Style*— Michael Brandon, Esq; ✉ c/o London Management, 2–4 Noel Street, London W1V 3RB (☎ 0171 287 9000, fax 0171 287 3036); c/o David Shapira and Associates, Los Angeles, California 91403, USA (☎ 00 1 818 906 0322, fax 00 1 818 783 2562)

BRANDON, (David) Stephen; QC (1996); s of James Osbaldeston Brandon (d 1992), and Dorothy, *née* Wright; *b* 18 Dec 1950; *Educ* Univ of Nottingham (BA), Keele Univ (LLM); *m* 1987, Helen Beatrice, da of Frank Lee; 1 da (Arabella Beatrice May b 1989); *Career* lectr in law Keele Univ 1975–85, called to the Bar Gray's Inn 1978, in practice at Revenue Bar 1981; *Books* Taxation of Migrant and Non-Resident Companies (1989), Taxation of Non-UK Resident Companies and their Shareholders (1997); *Recreations* art (especially collecting early woodcuts), opera, nurturing woodlands, shooting; *Style*— Stephen Brandon, Esq, QC; ✉ Clopton Manor, Clopton, Northants; 24 Old Buildings, 1st Floor, Tax Chambers, Lincoln's Inn, London WC2A 3UU (☎ 0171 242 2744, fax 0171 831 8095)

BRANDON OF OAKBROOK, Baron (Life Peer UK 1981); Sir Henry Vivian; kt (1966), MC (1942), PC (1978); yr s of Capt Vivian Ronald Brandon, CBE, RN (d 1944), of Kensington, and Joan Elizabeth Maud, *née* Simpson (d 1979); *b* 3 June 1920; *Educ* Winchester (scholar), King's Coll Cambridge (scholar, John Stewart of Rannoch scholar); *m* 1955, Jeanette Rosemary, da of Julian Vivian Breeze Janvrin (d 1988), late Indian Police; 3 s, 1 da; *Career* served WWII RA, UK 1939–42, Madagascar 1942, India and Burma 1942–45 (Maj 1944); called to the Bar Inner Temple 1946 (Entrance and Yarborough Anderson scholar); QC 1961; High Court judge: Probate, Divorce and Admty Div 1966–71, Family Div 1971–78; judge of Admiralty Court 1971–78, judge of Commercial Court 1977–78; Lord Justice of Appeal 1978–81, Lord of Appeal in Ordinary 1981–91; Hon LLD Univ of Southampton 1984; *Recreations* watching cricket, travel, bridge; *Clubs* MCC; *Style*— The Rt Hon the Lord Brandon of Oakbrook, MC, PC; ✉ 6 Thackeray Close, Wimbledon, London SW19 4JL (☎ 0181 947 6344)

BRANDRAM, Lady Katherine; HRH Princess Katherine of Greece and Denmark; yst da of HM King Constantine I of the Hellenes (d 1923), and HM Queen Sophie, *née* HRH Princess Sophie of Prussia (d 1932), 3 da of Friedrich III, German Emperor and King of Prussia; ggda of HM Queen Victoria; granted the style, title and precedence of a Duke's da in Great Britain by Royal Warrant of HM King George VI 9 Sept 1947; *b* 4 May 1913; *m* 21 April 1947, Maj Richard Campbell Andrew Brandram, MC, TD, RA (d 1994), o s of late Richard Andrew Brandram, of The Well House, Bickley, Kent; 1 s (Paul); *Career* formerly HRH Princess Katherine of Greece and Denmark; Grand Cross

Order of SS Olga and Sophia (Greece); *Style*— The Lady Katherine Brandram; ✉ Croft Cottage, Pound Lane, Marlow, Bucks

BRANDRETH, Gyles Daubeney; MP (C) City of Chester (majority 1,101); s of Charles Daubeney Brandreth (d 1972), of London, and Alice, *née* Addison; *b* 8 March 1948; *Educ* Bedales, New Coll Oxford (MA); *m* 8 June 1973, Michele, da of Alec Brown; 1 s (Benet Xan b 1975), 2 da (Saethryd Charity b 1976, Aphra Kendal Alice b 1978); *Career* author, broadcaster, producer; MP City of Chester 1992–; PPS: to Fin Sec to the Treasy 1993–94, to Sec of State for Nat Heritage 1994–95, to Sec of State for Health 1995, govt whip 1995–; journalist and TV presenter 1973–; fndr: Nat Teddy Bear Museum Stratford upon Avon, Nat Scrabble Championships; vice pres National Playing Fields Assoc 1993– (appeals chm 1984–88, chm 1989–93); *Books* various incl: Created in Captivity (1972), Under the Jumper (autobiog, 1993), Who is Nick Saint? (novel, 1996); *Recreations* sometime holder of world record for longest-ever after-dinner speech (12 1/2 hours); *Style*— Gyles Brandreth, Esq, MP; ✉ House of Commons, London SW1A 0AA (☎ 0171 219 5233, fax 0171 219 2707)

BRANDSTRUP, Kim; s of Finn Brandstrup, of Denmark, and Tove Riis, *née* Mortensen; *b* 9 Jan 1957; *Educ* Univ of Copenhagen (BA), London Contemporary Dance Sch; *Career* Arc Dance Company: fndr 1985, artistic dir, Les Noces 1985, The Dybbuk 1987, Peer Gynt 1990, Antic 1992, Othello 1994 (with Irek Mukhamedov & Co, winner Evening Standard Award 1994), Crime Fictions 1996; White Nights 1992 (English National Ballet), Death In Venice (Royal Opera House Covent Garden 1992, Metropolitan Opera 1994), Eugene Onegin (Royal Opera House), Mysteries (for Royal Danish Ballet) 1995; London Contemporary Dance Theatre: Orfeo (1989, Olivier Award for Most Outstanding Contrib to Dance); choreographer for film Angels and Insects; *Style*— Kim Brandstrup, Esq; ✉ c/o Ms Loesje Sanders, 1 North Hill, Woodbridge, Suffolk IP12 1HH (☎ 01394 385260)

BRANDT, Peter Augustus; s of Walter Augustus Brandt, of Saffron Walden, and Dorothy Gray, *née* Crane; *b* 2 July 1931; *Educ* Eton, Trinity Coll Cambridge; *m* 1962, Elisabeth Margaret, da of Frans ten Bos, of Holland; 2 s, 1 da; *Career* chm Atkins Fulford Ltd 1977–, chief exec William Brandt's Sons & Co 1966–72; bd memb National Rivers Authy 1989–95, dir Corp of Argentine Meat Producers' London Cos; *Recreations* rowing, sailing, watercolours; *Clubs* Boodle's, Leander; *Style*— Peter Brandt, Esq; ✉ Spout Farm, Boxford, Suffolk CO10 5HA

BRANDT, Richard; s of Edmund Hubert Brandt (d 1965), of London, and Norah, *née* Toole (d 1971); *b* 7 Aug 1929; *Educ* Downside, Lincoln Coll Oxford (BA, MA); *m* 4 July 1964, Margaret, da of Philip Archibald Campbell Adamson (d 1977), of Broadstairs; 2 s (Edmund Richard Adamson b 1967, William Robert Aldhelm b 1973), 1 da (Charlotte Louise b 1968); *Career* Nat Serv 1948–49; articled to Annan Dexter & Co 1953–57; ptnr: G Dixey & Co 1957–61, Dearden Harper Miller & Co 1962–68; mangr Arthur Andersen & Co 1969–72, ptnr Grant Thornton (formerly Thornton Baker & Co) 1972–94; research fell Univ of Portsmouth 1994–; memb Cncl and Fin Ctee Save the Children Fund 1975–90 (treas 1982–87); FCA 1962 (ACA 1957), FRSA 1993; *Recreations* sailing, collecting antiques (particularly drinking glasses); *Clubs* Sea View Yacht; *Style*— Richard Brandt, Esq; ✉ The Anchorage, Ryde Rd, Seaview, Isle of Wight PO34 5AB (☎ 01983 613769)

BRANIGAN, Sir Patrick Francis; kt (1954), QC (Gold Coast 1949); eldest s of Daniel Branigan (d 1923), and Teresa Alice, *née* Clinton (d 1921); *b* 30 Aug 1906; *Educ* Newbridge Coll Co Kildare, Trinity Coll Dublin, Downing Coll Cambridge; *m* 1935, Prudence, da of Dr Arthur Avent (d 1953), of Seaton, Devon, 1 s, 1 da; *Career* barr; Colonial Legal Service 1931–54, attorney gen and minister of justice Gold Coast 1948–54, dep chm Devon QS 1958–71, recorder of the Crown Ct 1972–75; chm: Pensions Appeal Tbnl 1955–81, Agric Land Tbnl 1955–79, Med Appeal Tbnl 1960–78, Mental Health Review Tbnl 1960–78; former chm Suflex Ltd (ret 1983); *Style*— Sir Patrick Branigan, QC; ✉ 17 Pyndar Court, Newland, Malvern, Worcs WR13 5AX (☎ and fax 01684 567761)

BRANNAN, Tom; s of James Brannan, of Bargeddie, nr Glasgow, and Rebecca Brannan (d 1994); *b* 21 Aug 1951; *Educ* St Patrick's Secdy Sch Coatbridge, Univ of Strathclyde (BA Business Studies); *m* (m dis); 2 da (Kirsty b 14 Dec 1976, Sarah b 11 Aug 1979); *Career* export exec Black & Decker 1971–75, sales dir Hestair Group 1975–81, sales and mktg dir Shelvoke & Drewry 1981–82, mktg dir Lancer Boss 1982–84, client servs dir Primary Contact Advertising (Ogilvy Group) 1984–95; currently: freelance mktg conslt, sales and mktg dir Labfax Systems Ltd (pt/t proprietor), corp communications mangr UniChema (Unilever), strategic planning dir (pt/t) Primary Contact Advertising, chm Beyond Communications; mktg advsr and speaker for various charities, business gps and other bodies; nat chm CIM 1996; FCIM 1990 (MCIM 1983), FRSA 1996; *Books* The Effective Advertiser (1993), A Practical Guide to Integrated Marketing Communications (1995), Gower Handbook of Marketing (contrib), Profit from Strategic Marketing (contrib); *Recreations* fly fishing, reading, antiquities, antiques; *Style*— Tom Brannan, Esq; ✉ 20A Freegrove Road, London N7 9JN; office: (e-mail TBrannan@cityscape.co.uk)

BRANSBY, (Eur Ing) Dr Peter Leigh; s of Dr Ernest Roy Bransby, of Warlingham, Surrey, and Nancy Barbara, *née* Leigh-Smith; *b* 9 Oct 1942; *Educ* Caterham, Trinity Coll Cambridge (scholar, BA, PhD); *m* July 1965, Jillian Elizabeth, da of R Eric Dobson; 1 s (Mark Fraser b 25 Oct 1969), 1 da (Hilda Jane b 21 April 1971); *Career* post doctoral fell Univ of British Columbia 1968–69, demonstrator (later lectr) Dept of Engineering Univ of Cambridge 1969–76, fell Christ's Coll Cambridge 1970–76, head materials handling then dep dir Warren Spring Laboratory (DTI) 1976–85, memb Policy Planning Unit DTI 1985–86, dir gen Construction Industry Research and Information Association 1986–; Br Geotechnical Soc Prize 1970, Author's Prize Instn of Chemical Engrs 1982; MICE 1972, FICE 1987, FEng 1989; *Books* The Mechanics of Soils (with J H Atkinson, 1978); *Recreations* hill walking, tennis, folk dancing; *Style*— Dr Peter Bransby, FEng; ✉ Construction Industry Research and Information Association, 6 Storey's Gate, London SW1P 3AU (☎ 0171 222 8891, fax 0171 222 1708)

BRANSON, Richard Charles Nicholas; s of Edward James Branson, and Evette Huntley, *née* Flindt; bro of Vanessa Gay Devereux, *qv*; *b* 18 July 1950; *Educ* Stowe; *m* 1, 1969 (m dis), Kristen Tomassi; m 2, 20 Dec 1989, Joan Sarah Drummond, da of John Templeman (d 1988), of Glasgow, Scotland; 1 s (Sam Edward Charles b 12 Aug 1985), 1 da (Holly Katy b 20 Nov 1981); *Career* ed Student magazine 1968–69; fndr: Student Advsy Centre (now Help) 1970, Virgin Mail-Order Co 1969, Virgin Retail 1970, Virgin Records 1973, Virgin Atlantic Airways 1984, Voyager Group Ltd 1986; chm and chief exec: Virgin Management, Virgin Retail Group, Virgin Communications, Virgin Holdings, Virgin Radio 1993, Virgin Direct 1995, V2 Music 1996; life pres Virgin Music 1992–; tstee: Healthcare Fndn (fndr 1987), Charity Projects; patron: Nat Holiday Fund, Paul O'Gorman Fndn, Trevor Jones Tst, London Sch for Performing Arts & Technol; pres Br Disabled Water Ski Assoc, hon vice pres Operation Raleigh, hon memb Ctee The Friends of the Earth; capt Atlantic Challenger II, winner Blue Riband for fastest crossing of the Atlantic by boat 1986, world record crossings of Atlantic and Pacific by hot air balloon with Per Lindstrand 1987 and 1991; Excellent Hon Prof of Economics Miyazaki Sangyo Keiei Univ Japan, Key to the City of NY, hon Japanese citizen (City of Miyakanojo); Hon DTech Loughborough 1993; *Recreations* tennis, skiing, swimming, ballooning; *Clubs* Roof Garden, Br Balloon and Airship Club; *Style*— Richard Branson, Esq; ✉ Virgin Management Ltd, 120 Campden Hill Road, London W8 7AR (☎ 0171 229 1282, fax 0171 727 8200)

BRASHER, Christopher William; CBE (1996); s of (William) Kenneth Brasher, CBE (d 1972), and Katie, *née* Howe (d 1987); *b* 21 Aug 1928; *Educ* Rugby, St John's Coll Cambridge; *m* 1959, Shirley, *née* Bloomer; 1 s, 2 da; *Career* jr exec Mobil Oil Co 1951–57; Olympic Gold medallist (3,000m Steeplechase) 1956; sports ed The Observer 1957–61, BBC TV reporter Tonight 1961–65, ed Time Out and Man Alive 1964–65, head Gen Features BBC TV 1969–72, columnist The Observer 1961–91, md Fleetfoot Ltd 1979–95; race dir London Marathon 1981–95, fndr and tstee The London Marathon Charitable Tst 1981–, pres London Marathon Ltd 1995– (fndr and chm 1981–95); fndr and tstee John Muir Tst 1983–92 and 1996–; chm: Brasher Leisure Ltd 1977–, Chris Brasher Tst 1988–, Reebok UK Ltd 1990–93, The Brasher Boot Co Ltd 1992–, Berghaus Ltd 1993–; memb Cncl Racehorse Owners Assoc 1996–; Nat Medal of Honour Finland 1975; Hon DUniv Stirling 1989; OStJ 1995; *Recreations* mountains, horse racing, flyfishing, orienteering, social running; *Clubs* Alpine, Flyfishers', Hurlingham, Ranelagh Harriers, Thames Hare and Hounds, Travellers; *Style*— Christopher Brasher, Esq, CBE; ✉ The Navigator's House, River Lane, Richmond, Surrey TW10 7AG (☎ 0181 940 0296)

BRASON, Paul; s of John Ainsley Brason, and Audrey, *née* Wheldon; *b* 17 June 1952; *Educ* King James I GS Newport IOW, Camberwell Coll of Art; *m* 13 Feb 1978, Judy, da of late Louis Yudkin, tech dir Royal Opera House; 2 s (Oliver Louis b 11 April 1983, Simon Nicholas b 9 June 1987), 1 da (Anne Louise b 9 June 1987); *Career* artist, portrait painter; has exhibited regularly at Nat Portrait Gall, RA and Royal Soc of Portrait Painters; work in many private and public collections incl: Royal Collection Windsor Castle, Nat Portrait Gall, Balliol Coll Oxford, Trinity Coll Oxford, Eton Coll, Museums and Galleries Cmmn and others; RP 1994; *Recreations* early period houses and gardens; *Style*— Paul Brason, Esq, RP; ✉ Hinton House, 140 High Street, Marshfield, Chippenham, Wiltshire SN14 8LU (☎ 01225 891301)

BRASSEY, Hon Edward; s and h of 3 Baron Brassey of Apethorpe; *b* 9 March 1964; *Educ* Eton, RMA Sandhurst; *Career* Capt Grenadier Gds 1985–91; public affrs conslt Ludgate Communications 1992–; *Recreations* karate, cricket; *Style*— The Hon Edward Brassey; ✉ The Manor House, Apethorpe, Peterborough PE8 5DL

BRASSEY OF APETHORPE, 3 Baron (UK 1938); Sir David Henry Brassey; 3 Bt (UK 1922); OBE (1994), JP (Northants 1970), DL (1972); s of 2 Baron Brassey of Apethorpe, MC, TD (d 1967, whose maternal gf was 7 Duke of Richmond and Gordon); *b* 16 Sept 1932; *Educ* Stowe; *m* 1, 15 Oct 1958, Myrna Elizabeth (d 1974), da of Lt-Col John Baskervyle-Glegg, of Withington Hall, Cheshire; 1 s; m 2, 17 Oct 1978, Caroline, da of Lt-Col Godfrey Evill, TD, of Chepstow; and step-da of Sir George Duntze, CMG, 6 Bt; 2 da (Hon Zara b 29 Feb 1980, Hon Chloe b 26 Feb 1982); *Heir* s, Hon Edward Brassey b 9 March 1964; *Career* Gren Guards 1951–67, ret as Major; farmer 1967–; vice pres Wildfowl & Wetlands Tst; *Style*— The Rt Hon the Lord Brassey of Apethorpe, OBE, JP, DL; ✉ The Manor House, Apethorpe, Peterborough PE8 5DL (☎ 01780 470231)

BRATZA, Nicolas Dušan; QC (1988); s of Milan Bratza (concert violinist, d 1964), and Hon Margaret, *née* Russell (d 1981); *b* 3 March 1945; *Educ* Wimbledon Coll, Brasenose Coll Oxford (BA, MA); *Career* instr Univ of Pennsylvania Law Sch 1967–68, called to the Bar Lincoln's Inn 1969; jr counsel to the Crown, common law 1978–88, recorder of the Crown Court 1993–; bencher Lincoln's Inn 1993; UK memb Euro Cmmn of Human Rights 1993–; memb Cncl of Legal Educn 1988–92, vice chm Br Inst of Human Rights 1989–; *Books* Halsbury's Laws of England (4 edn, jt contrib of titles Contempt of Court and Crown Proceedings); *Recreations* music, cricket; *Clubs* Garrick, MCC; *Style*— Nicolas Bratza, Esq, QC; ✉ 1 Hare Court, Temple, London EC4Y 7BE (☎ 0171 353 3171, fax 0171 583 9127); European Commission of Human Rights, Council of Europe, F-67075 Strasbourg Cedex, France

BRAUER, Irving; s of Jack Brauer (d 1972), of Hackney, London, and Lily, *née* Croll (d 1978); *b* 8 Aug 1939; *Educ* Davenant Fndn, Northern Poly (Dip Arch); *m* 21 April 1964, Stephanie Margaret, da of Edwin Sherwood, of Florida; 1 s (Marlow b 1975), 1 da (Amelia b 1965); *Career* architect and designer, worked in London and NY 1960–63, partnership Beryl Gollins 1963–76, ptnr Brauer Associates 1976–; visiting tutor: Canterbury Sch of Architecture 1967–70, Central London Poly 1968–71; elected memb CSD 1967 (elected fell 1976); RIBA; *Recreations* house renovation, theatre, reading, travel; *Style*— Irving Brauer, Esq; ✉ Mount Stuart, Westgrove Lane, Greenwich, London SE10 8QP (☎ 0181 692 3210); Brauer Associates, 20 Dock St, London E1 8JP (☎ 0171 481 2184, fax 0171 481 3368)

BRAUN, Prof Edward; s of Cecil Arthur Braun (d 1952), of Bath, Somerset, and Stella Mabel, *née* Truscott (d 1956); *b* 28 Jan 1936; *Educ* City of Bath Boys' Sch, Univ of Cambridge (MA, PhD); *m* 18 Sept 1965, Sarah, da of John Brooke (d 1987), of Market Lavington, Wilts; 2 s (Felix b 1968, Joseph b 1970); *Career* Flying Offr RAF 1955–61; Univ of Bristol: lectr in drama 1969–, reader in drama 1980, head of Drama Dept 1985–92, prof of drama 1986–96; chm: Bristol Old Vic Tst 1987–92, Gulbenkian Enquiry into dir trg in Britain 1987–89; memb Assoc of Univ Teachers; *Books* Meyerhold on Theatre (1969), The Theatre of Meyerhold (1979), The Director and the Stage (1982), Meyerhold: A Revolution in Theatre (1995); *Recreations* cooking, wine, fishing on holiday; *Clubs* Labour Party, Friends of the Earth; *Style*— Prof Edward Braun; ✉ Department of Drama: Theatre, Film, Television, University of Bristol, Cantocks Close, Woodland Road B58 1UP (☎ 0117 942 4601)

BRAY, (Richard) Andrew; s of John Frederick Arthur Bray (d 1962), and Dorothy Agnes Bray (d 1981); *b* 5 Dec 1938; *Educ* Sandown Sch Bexhill-on-Sea Sussex, Canterbury Coll of Art (NDD), RCA Sch of Silversmithing and Jewellery Design (scholar); *m* 1965, Margaret Anne, da of James Norman Hope; 2 da (Emma Claire b 1970, Shuna Anne b 1974); *Career* silversmith; visiting tutor Dip AD Silversmithing: Canterbury Coll of Art 1965–67, Camberwell Sch of Art and Crafts 1963–73; head of Art Kent Coll Canterbury Kent 1976–77; Silversmithing and Metalwork Dept Camberwell Sch of Art and Crafts: lectr 1977, sr lectr 1983, princ lectr 1989–; design work 1965–89 (freelance for various firms, numerous cmmnd pieces of jewellery and silverplate for private and public bodies), involved in res 1983–85; participant in exhibitions at: The Commonwealth Institute London 1967, The Greewich Museum London 1968, Two Man Exhibitions Silver Plate London Wall 1969, The Fitzwilliam Museum Cambridge 1973, The Victoria and Albert Museum London 1977, The Goldsmiths Hall London 1982, The Rufford Craft Centre 1985, Twentieth Century European Silver Crafts Cncl 1993, selected designer/maker Nat Forum for New British Silver 1995; winner Ascot Gold Cup National Design Competition 1960; fell Soc Designer Craftsmen 1969; Freeman Worshipful Co of Goldsmiths 1989, Freeman City of London 1992; *Style*— Andrew Bray, Esq; ✉ Department of Silver Metals, Camberwell College of Arts, Peckham Road, London SE5 8UF

BRAY, Denis Campbell; CMG (1977), CVO (1975), JP (1960); s of Rev Arthur Henry Bray, and Edith Muriel Bray; bro of Jeremy William Bray, MP, *qv*; *b* 24 Jan 1926; *Educ* Chefoo Sch China, Kingswood Sch Bath, Jesus Coll Cambridge; *m* 1952, Marjorie Elizabeth, da of John Hubert Bottomley; 1 s (decd), 4 da; *Career* sec home affairs Hong Kong 1973–77 and 1980–84, Hong Kong cmmr London 1977–80; chm Denis Bray Consultants Ltd 1985–; *Clubs* Travellers', Royal Hong Kong Yacht; *Style*— Denis Bray, Esq, CMG, CVO, JP; ✉ 8A-7 Borrett Mansions, 8–9 Bowen Rd, Hong Kong (☎ 00 852 2526 3630, fax 00 852 2868 1884)

BRAY, Dr Jeremy William; MP (Lab) Motherwell South (majority 14,013); s of Rev Arthur Henry Bray and Edith Muriel Bray; bro of Denis Campbell Bray, CMG, CVO,

JP *qv*; *b* 29 June 1930; *Educ* Aberystwyth GS, Kingswood Sch, Jesus Coll Cambridge, Harvard Univ; *m* 1953, Elizabeth, da of Rev Dr Hubert Carey Trowell, OBE, MD, of Salisbury; 4 da; *Career* tech offr Wilton Works of ICI; contested (Lab) Thirsk and Malton 1959; MP (Lab): Middlesbrough West 1962–70, Motherwell and Wishaw 1974–83, Motherwell South 1983–; memb Select Ctee on: Nationalised Industs 1962–64, Treasury and Civil Service 1979–83 (chm sub-ctee 1981–82), Sci and Technol 1992–; chm: Lab Sci and Tech Gp 1964–66, Econ Affrs Estimates Sub-Ctee 1964–66; Parly sec Miny of Power 1966–67, jt Parly sec Miny of Tech 1967–69; oppn front bench spokesman on Sci and Technol 1983–92; vice pres Parliamentary and Scientific Ctee 1992–; vice chm: British-Chinese Parly Gp 1987–, Parliament Engineering Gp 1992–; chm All Pty Gp on Mental Health; memb: Advsy Cncl Save British Science 1993–, Bd Parly Office of Science and Technology 1993–; chm Fabian Soc 1971–72; dir Mullard Ltd 1970–73; conslt Battle Res Centre Geneva 1973, visiting prof Univ of Strathclyde 1975–79 (sr res fell 1974); dep chm Christian Aid 1972–84; *Publications* Decision in Government (1970), Production Purpose and Structure (1982); *Recreations* sailing; *Style*— Dr Jeremy Bray, MP; ✉ House of Commons, London SW1A 0AA (☎ 0171 219 6979)

BRAY, John Frederick; s of John Bray (d 1970), of Goosnargh, Lancs, and Doris Hilda, *née* Brewin (d 1995), of Preston, Lancs; *b* 5 Sept 1934; *Educ* Preston GS, Victoria Univ of Manchester (BA, Dip in Town and Country Planning), Univ of Illinois USA (MArch); *m* 1, 27 May 1958 (m dis 1988), Anne Christine Townley, da of Walter Kershaw (d 1980), of Preston; 2 s (Andrew b 1962, Anthony b 1966), 1 da (Susan b 1961); m 2, 19 Aug 1989, Mary-Rew, da of George Bryce Robertson (d 1965); *Career* RNVR 1954–57, dep launching authy RNLI 1976–79 and 1985–87 (launching authy and station sec 1979–85); asst architect and town planner London CC 1957–58; Central Mortgage and Housing Corpn (CMHC) Canada 1958–64; teaching asst Univ of Illinois USA 1959–60; sr architect and town planner in private practice 1964–65, princ and ptnr architectural practice 1965–83, princ and sr ptnr Bray Singleton Partnership 1983–; registered arbitrator, special referee IOM High Court, examiner in Professional Practice Univ of Manchester, examiner ARCUK, lectr and former dir Expert Witness Course and chm Exam Bd for CIArb; former Cdre Ribble Cruising Club; Freeman City of London 1981, Liveryman Worshipful Co of Arbitrators 1982, Liveryman Worshipful Co of Chartered Architects 1990; FRIBA 1970, FRTPI 1972, FCIArb 1981, FIMgt 1983, FAE 1995; *Recreations* golf, fly-fishing, reading, music, photography; *Style*— John Bray, Esq; ✉ Bray Singleton Partnership, 5 Eastway Business Village, Olivers Place, Fulwood, Preston, Lancs PR2 9WT (☎ 01772 702009, fax 01772 702010, mobile 0385 311633)

BRAY, Julian Charles; s of Flt Lt Reginald Charles Julian Bray, and Irene Audrey, *née* Stewart; *b* 23 May 1945; *Educ* Ayr Acad Ayr Scotland; *m* 1, 1971 (m dis 1981), Judith Marina; 2 s (Dominic Julian b 13 Oct 1977, Oliver William b 13 June 1980); m 2, 1985, Vivienne Margaret Carlton, *qv*, da of John Carlton; 1 s (William Charles b 18 Aug 1989); *Career* independent TV prodr and presenter, broadcaster, writer and journalist; md: Leadenhall Associates Ltd 1986–90, Alpha Strategy Management Ltd 1991–92; non-exec dir CNS (City News Service) 1986–90; dir: NTN TV News Ltd 1988, DTI Eureka Information Bureau 1990; dir business devpt Extel PR, head of media relations Welbeck PR Ltd; memb: NUJ, PACT, Magic Circle, Int Brotherhood of Magicians (Br Ring No 25); *Books* Information Technology in the Corporate Environment (1980); *Recreations* theatre, travel, magic; *Clubs* Magic Circle; *Style*— Julian Bray; ✉ South Lodge, Smalls Hill Road, Leigh, Reigate, Surrey RH2 8QB (☎ 01293 863310, fax 01293 862969)

BRAY, Kelvin Arthur; CBE (1990, OBE 1982); s of Arthur William Stretton Bray (d 1979), of Leicester, and Clarice May, *née* Perrin (d 1985); *b* 4 Feb 1935; *Educ* Leicester City Boys' Sch, King's Coll Cambridge (MA); *m* 1959, Grace Elizabeth, da of Dr Matthew Millar Tannahill (d 1981), of Lincoln; 2 s (Adam Kelvin b 9 March 1966, Julian Dominic b 27 February 1968); *Career* sales mangr (Gas Turbine Div) Ruston & Hornsby Ltd 1963; md: Ruston Gas Turbines Ltd 1969– (Queen's Award for Export 1969, 1977, 1978 and 1982, Queen's Award for Technol 1986), GEC Gas Turbines Ltd 1983–89, GEC Alsthom NV 1991–, GEC Alsthom Power Gen Div 1994–; assoc dir GEC 1985; chm: Napier Turbochargers Ltd, Euro Gas Turbines NV 1989; Royal Soc Esso Medal 1974, Mac Robert Award 1983, Gold Medal Inst of Gas Engrs 1994, Lincoln Civic Award 1995; FEng 1979, FIMechE; *Recreations* golf, swimming; *Style*— Kelvin Bray, Esq, CBE, FEng; ✉ 17 Cherry Tree Lane, Nettleham, Lincoln LN2 2PR; European Gas Turbines Ltd, PO Box 1, Lincoln LN2 5DJ (☎ 01522 583002, fax 01522 583195)

BRAY, Kenneth Rising (Ken); s of William Rising Bray, and Margaret Lees, *née* Alden; *b* 25 June 1929; *Educ* Buckhurst Hill Co HS, SW Essex Tech Coll (BSc, capt Coll Cross Country Team); *m* 25 April 1959, Brenda Anne, da of Arthur James Borkett; 1 s (Jonathan Alden b 18 May 1962), 2 da (Rowan Margaret b 14 Nov 1964, Sorrell Anne b 20 Feb 1972); *Career* photographer (specialising in portraits), founded own studio 1952; accredited photographer at Royal Investitures 1973–92; ARPS, assoc BIPP (pres 1992–93); *Recreations* running (Essex Steeplechase Champion 1954), mountaineering, photography; *Clubs* Woodford Green Athletic (past pres); *Style*— Ken Bray, Esq; ✉ Ken Bray Studios, 223 High Road, South Woodford, London E18 2PB (☎ 0181 504 8463, fax 0181 559 1068)

BRAY, Michael Peter; s of Sqdn Ldr William Charles Thomas Bray, DFC (d 1985), and Ivy Isobel, *née* Ellison (d 1986); *b* 27 March 1947; *Educ* Caterham Sch, Univ of Liverpool (LLB); *m* 25 July 1970, Elizabeth-Ann, da of Hubert John Harrington (d 1981); 2 da (Natasha Jane b 13 April 1977, Samantha Louise b 13 April 1984); *Career* slr; ptnr Clifford Chance 1976– (formerly Coward Chance, joined 1970); memb: Banking Law Sub Ctee City of London Slrs' Co, Jt Working Pty on Banking Law of the Law Reform Ctees of the Law Soc and Bar Cncl; Freeman City of London Slrs' Co 1976; memb Law Soc; *Recreations* theatre, reading, skiing, photography; *Style*— Michael Bray, Esq; ✉ Clifford Chance, 200 Aldersgate Street, London EC1A 4JJ (☎ 0171 600 1000, fax 0171 600 5555)

BRAY, Noreen; OBE (1996); *Educ* Heathfield House RC HS, Univ Coll Wales (BA); *children* 2 s; *Career* PR exec; grad trainee BBC 1971–73, TV and radio news and current affairs journalist BBC Wales 1976–89, bd dir Lowe Bell Good Relations Ltd (formerly Good Relations Ltd) 1989– (currently md Cardiff Office); cmmr for Wales Equal Opportunities Cmmn 1990–95, pres SCOPE (formerly Spastics Soc) Wales; MIPR, MInstD, FRSA; *Recreations* reading, music, exercise; *Style*— Ms Noreen Bray, OBE; ✉ Lowe Bell Good Relations Ltd, Caerwys House, Windsor Lane, Cardiff CF1 3DE (☎ 01222 344888)

BRAY, His Hon Judge; Richard Winston Atherton; s of Winston Bray, CBE, and Betty Atherton, *née* Miller; *b* 10 April 1945; *Educ* Rugby, CCC Oxford; *m* 6 Jan 1978, Judith Elizabeth Margaret, da of Maj C B Ferguson (d 1980); 1 s (Edward b 2 Oct 1984), 3 da (Hester b 24 May 1981, Miranda b 12 Sept 1986, Rosalind b 23 Aug 1989); *Career* called to the Bar Middle Temple 1970; recorder Midland and Oxford circuit 1987–93; circuit judge (Midland and Oxford Circuit) 1993–; *Recreations* cricket, real tennis, astronomy; *Clubs* MCC, Frogs, I Zingari; *Style*— His Hon Judge Bray; ✉ 36 Bedford Row, London WC1R 4JH (☎ 0171 421 8000, fax 0171 421 8080)

BRAYBROOKE, Rev Marcus Christopher Rossi; s of Lt-Col Arthur Rossi Braybrooke, of Cranleigh, Surrey, and Marcia Nona, *née* Leach; descended on female side from a brother of Robert Braybrooke, Bishop of London (d 1404); *b* 16 Nov 1938; *Educ* Cranleigh Sch, Magdalene Coll Cambridge (BA, MA), Univ of London (MPhil), Madras Christian Coll India, Wells Theological Coll; *m* 1964, Mary Elizabeth, da of Dr George Walker, of Cambridge; 1 s (Jeremy b 1966), 1 da (Rachel b 1965); *Career* curate St Michael's Highgate 1964–67, memb Strood Team Miny 1967–73, rector Swainswick with Langridge and Woolley 1973–79, dir of trg Dio of Bath and Wells 1979, priest i/c Christ Church Bath 1984–91, prebendary Wells Cathedral 1990–93, chaplain Magdalen Chapel Bath 1992–93, non-stipendary priest Marsh and Toot Baldon Dorchester Team Miny 1993–; research fell Westminster Coll Oxford 1994–; chm World Congress of Faiths 1978–83 and 1992–, pres Parliament of the World's Religions Chicago 1993, chm Int Interfaith Orgns Co-ordinating Ctee 1988–93; exec dir Cncl of Christians and Jews 1984–87, tstee Int Interfaith Centre Oxford 1993–; ed jl: World Faiths Insight 1976–91, Common Ground 1986–93; *Books* Together to the Truth, The Unknown Christ of Hinduism, Interfaith Organisations - A Historical Directory, Time to Meet - Towards a Deeper Relationship of Jews and Christians, Children of One God - A History of the Council of Christians and Jews, Pilgrimage of Hope - One Hundred Years of Interfaith Discovery, Wide Embracing Love, Be Reconciled, Love without Limit, Faith in a Global Age, How to Understand Judaism, A Wider Vision, Stepping Stones to a Global Ethic (ed), Dialogue with a Difference (ed with A Bayfield); *Recreations* gardening, travel, photography, local history; *Style*— The Rev Marcus Braybrooke; ✉ The Rectory, Marsh Baldon, Oxford, Oxon OX44 9LS (☎ 01865 343215, fax 01865 343575)

BRAYBROOKE, Neville Patrick Bellairs; s of Patrick Philip William Braybrooke (d 1966), and Lettice Marjorie, *née* Bellairs (d 1986); *b* 30 May 1925; *Educ* Ampleforth; *m* 5 Dec 1953, June Guesdon (the author Isobel English; d 1994), da of John Mayne Jolliffe (d 1962); 1 step da (Victoria Mary Guesdon Orr-Ewing b 1942); *Career* ed The Wind and the Rain Quarterly 1941–51, editorial staff Chambers Encyclopaedia 1947–48, literary ed Catholic Herald 1964–66; *Books* This is London (1953), London Green - The Story of Kensington Gardens, Hyde Park, Green Park and St James's Park (1959), London (1961), The Idler (1961), The Delicate Investigation (BBC Play, 1969), Four Poems for Christmas (1986), Dialogue with Judas (1989), Two Birthdays (1995); ed: T S Eliot A Symposium for his 70th Birthday (1958), A Partridge in a Pear Tree - A Celebration for Christmas (1960), Pilgrim of the Future - Teilhard de Chardin Symposium (1966), The Letters of J R Ackerley (1975), Seeds in the Wind - 20th Century Juvenilia from W B Yeats to Ted Hughes (1989); *Recreations* little reviews, hats, animals; *Clubs* PEN; *Style*— Neville Braybrooke, Esq; ✉ 10 Gardnor Rd, London NW3 1HA (☎ 0171 435 1851); Grove House, 29 Castle Rd, Cowes, Isle of Wight PO31 7QZ (☎ 01983 293950)

BRAYBROOKE, 10 Baron (GB 1788); Robin Henry Charles Neville; JP; hereditary visitor Magdalene Coll Cambridge; s of 9 Baron Braybrooke, JP, DL (d 1990), and his 1 w, Muriel Evelyn, *née* Manning (d 1962); *b* 29 Jan 1932; *Educ* Eton, Magdalene Coll Cambridge (MA), RAC Cirencester; *m* 1, 1955 (m dis 1974), Robin Helen, o da of late T A Brockhoff, of Rose Bay, Sydney, NSW, Australia; 4 da (Hon Amanda Muriel Mary (Hon Mrs Murray) b 1962, Hon Caroline Emma (Countess of Derby) b 1963, Hon Victoria (Hon Mrs Bromet) b 1970, Hon Arabella b (twin) 1970), and 1 da decd (Henrietta Jane b 1965, d 1980); m 2, 1974, Linda, 2 da of Arthur Norman, of Robblyns, Saffron Walden, Essex; 3 da (Hon Sara Lucy b 1975, Hon Emma Charlotte b 1979, Hon Lucinda Octavia b 1984); *Heir* kinsman, George Neville b 1943; *Career* cmmnd Rifle Bde 1951, served with 3 Bn King's African Rifles in Kenya and Malaya 1951–52; farmer and landowner; RDC cncllr 1959–69, CC for Stansted 1969–72; memb: Cncl of CLA 1965–83, Agric Land Tbnl Eastern Area 1975–; chm: Price Tst 1983–94, Rural Devpt Cmmn for Essex 1984–90; dir Essex and Suffolk Insur Co until taken over by Guardian Royal Exchange; HM Lord-Lt for Essex 1992–; KStJ; *Recreations* railways, motorcycling, photography; *Clubs* Boodle's, Farmers'; *Style*— The Rt Hon the Lord Braybrooke, JP; ✉ Abbey House, Audley End, Saffron Walden, Essex CB11 4JB (☎ 01799 522484, office 01799 541354/541956, fax 01799 542134)

BRAYE, Baroness (8 holder of the title); (Mary) Penelope Aubrey-Fletcher; *née* Verney-Cave; JP (Northants); da of 7 Baron Braye, DL (d 1985), and Dorothea, *née* Donoghue (d 1994); *b* 28 Sept 1941; *Educ* Assumption Convent, Hengrave Hall, Warwick Univ; *m* 1981, Lt-Col Edward Henry Lancelot Aubrey-Fletcher, DL, Gren Gds, s of Maj Sir Henry Lancelot Aubrey-Fletcher, 6 Bt, CVO, DSO, JP, HM Lord-Lieut for Bucks; *Heir* co-heiresses, Mrs Christopher Fothergill and Miss Tessa Browne; *Career* govr St Andrew's Hosp Northampton 1978–; JP South Northants 1981–86; High Sheriff Northants 1983; dep pres Northants Red Cross 1983–; govr Three Shires Hosp Northampton 1983–; pres Blaby Conservative Assoc 1986–; chm sch ctee St Andrew's Occupational Therapy Sch 1988–; *Style*— The Rt Hon Baroness Braye; ✉ Stanford Hall, Lutterworth, Leics LE17 6DH (☎ 01788 860250)

BRAYFIELD, Celia Frances; da of Felix Francis Brayfield (d 1975), and Ellen, *née* Jakeman (d 1995); *b* 21 Aug 1945; *Educ* St Paul's Girls' Sch, Universitaire de Grenoble; *children* 1 da (Chloe Elizabeth b 8 Oct 1980); *Career* writer and broadcaster; trainee Nova IPC Magazines 1968–69, asst to Women's ed The Observer 1969, feature writer Daily Mail 1969–71, TV critic Evening Standard 1974–82, TV critic The Times 1983–88, columnist Sunday Telegraph 1989–90, books ed She magazine 1990–91; memb: Ctee of Mgmnt Nat Cncl for One Parent Families 1990–, Mgmnt Ctee Soc of Authors 1995–; *Books* The Body Show Book (co-author, 1982), Pineapple Dance Book (co-author, 1984), Glitter - The Truth About Fame (1985), Pearls (1987), The Prince (1990), White Ice (1993), Harvest (1995), Bestseller (1996); *Recreations* family life, cinema, ballet, opera, fitness; *Clubs* Groucho, Chelsea Arts; *Style*— Ms Celia Brayfield; ✉ c/o John Johnson Agency, Clerkenwell House, Clerkenwell Green, London EC1R 0HT (☎ 0171 251 0125)

BRAYNE, Mark Lugard; s of Thomas Lugard Brayne, of Barney, Fakenham, Norfolk, and Audrey Diana, *née* Thompson; *b* 17 April 1950; *Educ* Gresham's, Wymondham Coll Norfolk, Univ of Leeds (BA); *m* 25 March 1977, Jutta, da of Fritz Hartung, of Ohlstadt, Germany; 2 s (Christopher b 1980, Alastair b 1982), 1 da (Katharine b 1987); *Career* Moscow and E Berlin Reuters News Agency 1973–78; BBC: German service corr Berlin 1979–81, Central Euro corr Vienna 1981–84, Peking corr China 1984–87; BBC World Service: dip corr 1988–92, dep head Central European Serv 1992–93, dep head Russian Serv 1993–94, regnl ed Europe 1994–; *Recreations* family, singing, cycling; *Style*— Mark Brayne, Esq; ✉ BBC World Service, Bush House, Strand WC2B 4PH (☎ 0171 240 3456, fax 0171 379 6841)

BRAYTON, Margaret Abigail; MBE (1989); da of Thomas George Brayton (d 1965), of Cumbria, England, and Sybella, *née* Little (d 1974); *b* 6 July 1919; *Educ* White House GS Brampton Cumbria, City of Carlisle GS Cumbria, Newcastle Gen Sch of Nursing (SRN), Simpson Meml Maternity Pavilion Royal Infirmary of Edinburgh (SCM), Hosp for Sick Children Great Ormond St (RSCN), Yale Univ, McGill Univ Montreal (Br Cwlth Nurses War Meml scholar), RCN (Br Red Cross and St John Jt Ctee scholar, NsgMD); *Career* Br Red Cross vol with Royal Naval Nursing Serv 1939–40, qualified nurse working with med relief teams in Europe 1944–45; nursing offr Paediatric Unit Newcastle Gen Hosp 1946–47, sister Nuffield Dept of Child Health Babies Hosp Royal Victoria Infirmary and Newcastle Gen Hosp 1949–53, assignments with WHO and UNICEF in India, Malaysia, Singapore, Hong Kong, Sri Lanka, Pakistan and Uganda 1949–55, James Mackenzie Child Health Unit Fife CC and Univ of St Andrews 1953–55, matron and princ of nursing educn Whitehaven and W Cumberland Hosp 1956–59, asst regnl nursing offr S Eastern Regnl Hosp Bd Edinburgh and Eastern Regnl Hosp Bd Dundee 1959–60, chief regnl nursing offr S Eastern Regnl Hosp Bd Edinburgh Scotland 1960–72, exec sec Commonwealth Nurses Fedn (and ed Newsletter) 1973–93; formerly: vice chm RCN Scotland, memb Cncl RCN London, vice pres Assoc of State Enrolled Nurses (now amalgamated with RCN), chm Extension Servs Scottish Nursing Servs Ctee, memb Advsy Ctee Nursing Degree Prog Dept of Nursing Studies Univ of

Edinburgh, pres Soroptimist Int of Edinburgh and Central London; fndr chm and memb Cwlth Professional Assoc Meetings (now Assoc of Cwlth Orgns); memb: Working Gp on Official and Unofficial Cwlth (for Cwlth Secretariat), Cwlth Fndn Gp to visit Zimbabwe; cncllr and vice pres Royal Cwlth Soc, former chairwoman Cwlth Countries League (and ed Newsletter), chm Women Speakers for Cwlth, pres Divnl Union Soroptimist Int S Scotland, dep pres Women's Corona Soc, patron Assoc of Guyanese Nurses and Allied Professionals (UK), memb Bd Govrs Friends of the Commonwealth Inst, hon sec Int Network Towards Smoke Free Hospitals 1993–; hon chiefdom title Western Samoa 1975, hon fell W African Coll of Nursing 1982, Distinguished Service award Trinidad and Tobago Registered Nurses Assoc 1990; Freeman City of London 1980; FRSA 1982; *Recreations* the Arts, archeological digs, hill climbing, unusual train journeys, sailing, reading; *Clubs* Royal Cwlth Soc, Soroptimist Int of Central London; *Style*— Miss Margaret Brayton, MBE; ✉ 43 Etloe House, 180 Church Rd, London E10 7DF (☎ 0181 539 7774)

BRAZENDALE, Alan Courtenay; s of Capt George William Ernest Brazendale (d 1970), of Greasby, Wirral, and Alice Annie, *née* Courtenay (d 1981); *b* 15 Dec 1924; *Educ* Birkenhead Sch; *m* 13 July 1946, Elizabeth Ewan (d 1992), da of William Stewart Carr (d 1969), of Stanley, Perthshire; 1 da (Elizabeth Ann b 1953); *Career* Fleet Air Arm 1943–47; CA; mayor of Gateshead MBC 1980–81, chm Gateshead Educn Ctee 1982–94; dir Alton Associates Ltd, chm Northern Cncl for Further Educn; chm of govrs Gateshead Coll; FCA, MIMgt, MInstAM; *Recreations* golf, local history, reading, writing, gardening; *Style*— Alan Brazendale, Esq; ✉ 8 The Orchard, Whickham, Newcastle upon Tyne NE16 4HD (☎ 0191 420 7149)

BRAZIER, Julian William Hendy; TD, MP (C) Canterbury (majority 10,805); s of Lt-Col Peter Hendy Brazier, and Patricia Audrey Helen, *née* Stubbs, ggda of Bishop Stubbs of Oxford noted lectr and author of the Stubbs Charters (Constitutional History of England); *b* 24 July 1953; *Educ* Dragon Sch Oxford, Wellington, BNC Oxford (scholar, MA), London Business Sch; *m* 21 July 1984, Katharine Elizabeth, da of Brig Patrick Blagden, CBE; 3 s (William, Alexander (twin), John b 3 Dec 1992); *Career* SSLC with RE and Capt TA in Airborne Forces; with Charter Consolidated Ltd (now plc) 1975–84 (sec to Exec Ctee of the Bd of Dirs 1981–84), H B Maynard International Management Consultants 1984–87; MP (C) Canterbury 1987–; PPS to Mrs Gillian Shepherd: as Min of State at the Treasy 1990–92, as Sec of State for Employment 1992–93; *Recreations* cross country running, history, science, philosophy; *Style*— Julian Brazier, Esq, TD, MP; ✉ House of Commons, London SW1A 0AA

BRAZIER, Paul; *b* 29 July 1962; *Career* advtg exec; art dir Cogent Elliott 1984–87, WCRS 1987–91; bd/art dir Abbott Mead Vickers BBDO 1991–; *Awards* D&AD: 1990 (Carling Black Label), 1993 (RSPCA), 1994 (Volvo and Economist) and 1995 (Queen Elizabeth Fndn for Disabled People); One Show: 1994 (Economist and RSPCA), 1995 (Queen Elizabeth Fndn for Disabled People); Hon Degree in Visual Arts (Graphics) Wolverhampton; *Style*— Paul Brazier, Esq; ✉ Abbott Mead Vickers BBDO Ltd, 191 Old Marylebone Road, London NW1 5DW (☎ 0171 402 4100, fax 0171 935 5883)

BRAZIER-CREAGH, Maj-Gen Sir (Kilner) Rupert; KBE (1962, CBE 1947), CB (1954), DSO (1944); s of Lt-Col Kilner Brazier-Creagh, TD (d 1956); *b* 12 Dec 1909; *Educ* Rugby, RMA Woolwich; *m* 1, 1938, Elizabeth Mary (d 1967), da of Edward Magor (d 1954); 1 s, 2 da; m 2, 1968, Marie, da of Edward O'Keeffe; *Career* served NW Europe 1944–45, Malayan Emergency 1952–55; Asst Cmdt Staff Coll 1955–57, COS E Cmd 1957–59, DSD War Office 1959–61; sec Horse Race Betting Levy Bd 1961–65; *Recreations* gardening, travel; *Style*— Maj-Gen Sir Rupert Brazier-Creagh, KBE, CB, DSO; ✉ Travis Corners Rd, Garrison, New York 10524, USA

BREACH, Peter John Freeman; s of Andrew Breach, CBE, LLD (d 1992), of Pensford, nr Bristol, and Christine Ruth, *née* Watson (d 1973); *b* 12 Jan 1942; *Educ* Clifton, Univ of Bristol (BA); *m* 17 Dec 1966, Joan, da of (William) Raymond Livesey, of Clitheroe, Lancashire; 3 s (Harry William Freeman b 1972, Christopher Andrew Talbot (Kit) b 1974, Alexander Robin Livesey b 1989); *Career* Coopers & Lybrand 1963–68, Hoare Govett 1968–69, County Bank Ltd 1969–70, JH Vavasseur & Co Ltd 1970–73, pres and chief exec offr Major Holdings & Developments Ltd 1972–73, divnl md Bath & Portland Group Ltd 1974–78, md James Dixon/Viners Ltd 1978–82, fin dir Bristol & West Building Soc 1988–91 (dir 1976–91, exec dir 1983–91); chm 1992: Hawksworth Securities plc (dir 1988), Principality Holdings Group (dir 1972), West Dock Estate Co Ltd (dir 1983), Surthurst Ltd (dir 1983); govr and chm Redland High Sch for Girls, memb Nat Bd of Governing Bodies of Girls Schs; Freeman: City of London, City of Bristol; Liveryman Worshipful Co of Basketmakers; memb Anchor Soc; FCA, ATII, MCT, AIIMR; *Recreations* sailing, skiing, gardening; *Clubs* Royal Dart; *Style*— Peter Breach, Esq; ✉ 7 Park St, Bristol BS1 5NF (☎ 0117 925 9494, fax 0117 927 2462, mobile 0836 728587)

BREADEN, Very Rev Robert William; s of Moses Breaden (d 1958), of Drummond, Magheracloone, Carrickmacross, Co Monaghan, and Martha Jane, *née* Hall (d 1988); *b* 7 Nov 1937; *Educ* The King's Hosp Dublin, Edinburgh Theol Coll; *m* 3 July 1970, Glenice Sutton, da of Douglas Martin (d 1990), of Dundee, and Joyce, *née* Sutton; 1 s (Patrick b 1971), 4 da (Sarah b 1973, Kathleen b 1979, Christina b 1981, Ann-Louise b 1987); *Career* ordained 1961, asst curate St Mary's Broughty Ferry 1961–65; rector: Church of the Holy Rood Carnoustie 1965–72, St Mary's Broughty Ferry 1972–; canon of St Paul's Cathedral Dundee 1977, dean of the Diocese of Brechin 1984–; *Recreations* gardening, horse-riding; *Clubs* Rotary of Abertay (pres 1979–80); *Style*— The Very Rev the Dean of Brechin; ✉ 46 Seafield Road, Broughty Ferry, Dundee DD5 3AN (☎ 01382 477477)

BREAKS, Michael Lenox; s of Cdr John Lenox Breaks, OBE, RN, of Denmead, Portsmouth, and Madeleine Henrietta, *née* Page; *b* 12 Jan 1945; *Educ* St George's Coll Weybridge Surrey, Univ of Leeds (BA), Univ Coll Aberystwyth (Dip Lib); *m* 12 April 1970, Barbara Monica, da of Charles Lawson (d 1984); 1 s (Jeremy Lenox b 1 March 1973), 1 da (Sarah Jessica b 15 May 1975); *Career* asst librarian: Univ Coll Swansea 1971–72, Univ of York 1972–73; social scis librarian Univ Coll Cardiff 1977–81, dep librarian Univ Coll Dublin 1981–85, univ librarian Heriot-Watt Univ 1985–; chm Joint Academic Network (JANET) Nat User Gp 1991–93, sec Int Assoc of Technological Univ Libraries 1992–; non-exec dir UK Education and Research Networking Assoc 1993–; memb: Advsy Ctee on Networking 1991–93, Advsy Ctee on Br Library Document Supply Centre 1992–96; ed New Review of Information Networking; memb: Cncl SCONUL 1993–, Research Sub-Ctee Library and Information Cmmn 1996–; *Recreations* gardening, horse riding, walking; *Style*— Michael Breaks, Esq; ✉ 2 Correnie Gardens, Edinburgh EH10 6DG (☎ 0131 447 7193); Heriot-Watt University, Riccarton, Edinburgh EH14 4AS (☎ 0131 451 3570, fax 0131 451 3164)

BREAKWELL, Prof Glynis Marie; da of Harold Breakwell, of Tipton, and Vera, *née* Woodhall (d 1993); *b* 26 July 1952; *Educ* Univ of Leicester (BA), Univ of Strathclyde (MSc), Univ of Bristol (PhD), Univ of Oxford (DSc); *Career* lectr in social psychology Univ of Bradford 1976–78, prize fell and tutor in social psychology Nuffield Coll Oxford 1978–82; Univ of Surrey: lectr in social psychology 1981–87, sr lectr in psychology 1987–88, reader 1988–91, prof of psychology 1991–, head Dept of Psychology 1990–95, pro-vice-chllr (staff devpt and continuing educn) 1994–95, pro-vice-chllr (research) 1995–; pres Psychology Section Br Assoc for the Advancement of Sci 1994– (vice-pres 1995–96); Br Psychological Soc: Young Social Psychologist Award 1978, assoc fell 1984, fell 1987, Meyers Award 1993, memb Social Psychology Section Ctee 1995–98; MA (by special resolution) Univ of Oxford 1978; CPsychol 1988; *Books* Social Work: The Social Psychological Approach (with C Rowett, 1982), The Quiet Rebel (1985), Coping with Threatened Identities (1986), Facing Physical Violence (1989), Interviewing (1990), Managing Violence at Work: Course Leader's Guide (with C Rowett, 1992), Managing Violence at Work: Workbook (with C Rowett, 1992), Careers and Identities (jtly, 1992), Basic Evaluation Methods (with L Millward, 1995), Social Psychology of Sexuality (with C R Fife-Schaw, 1996), Coping with Aggressive Behaviour (1996), Identity (1996); also author of numerous booklets, monographs and book chapters; *Recreations* tennis, raquet ball, squash, drawing and painting; *Clubs* The Bourne, Univ Women's; *Style*— Prof Glynis Breakwell; ✉ Department of Psychology, University of Surrey, Guildford, Surrey GU2 5XH (☎ 01483 259438, fax 01483 259512, e-mail g.breakwell@surrey.ac.uk)

BREALEY, Prof Richard Arthur; s of Albert Brealey (d 1974), and Irene Brealey; *b* 9 June 1936; *Educ* Queen Elizabeth's Sch Barnet, Exeter Coll Oxford (MA); *m* 10 Feb 1967, Diana Cecily, da of Derek Brown-Kelly, of Oddington, Glos; 2 s (David Andrew b 1970, Charles Richard b 1972); *Career* Investmt Dept Sun Life Assurance Co of Canada 1959–66, mangr computer applications Keystone Custodian Funds of Boston 1966–68; London Business Sch: dir Inst of Fin and Accounting 1974–84, memb Body of Govrs, dep princ and academic dean 1984–88, currently Tokai Bank prof of fin; visiting prof: Univ of California Berkeley, Univ of Br Colombia, Univ of Hawaii, Aust Graduate Sch of Mgmnt; dir: Sun Life Assurance Co of Canada UK Holdings Plc, Tokai Derivative Products; former: pres European Fin Assoc, dir American Fin Assoc; *Books* incl: Introduction to Risk and Return from Common Stocks (2 edn, 1983), Principles of Corporate Finance (with S C Myers, 5 edn, 1996), Fundamentals of Corporate Finance (jtly, 1994); *Recreations* rock climbing, skiing, horse racing; *Style*— Prof Richard Brealey; ✉ Haydens Cottage, The Pound, Cookham, Berks (☎ 01628 520143); London Business School, Sussex Place, Regent's Park, London NW1 (☎ 0171 262 5050, fax 0171 724 7875, telex 27461 LOND IS KOL)

BREAM, Julian; CBE (1985, OBE 1964); *b* 15 July 1933; *Educ* RCM; *m* 1, Margaret Williamson; 1 adopted s; m 2, 1980 (m dis), Isobel, *née* Sanchez; *Career* guitarist and lutanist; professional debut Cheltenham 1947, London debut Wigmore Hall 1950; fndr Julian Bream Consort 1960, organiser own summer arts festival, estab workshops in Wiltshire for manufacture of guitars, lutes and harpsichords; subject of biographical film A Life in the Country BBC TV 1976, gave series of masterclasses on BBC TV, made series of films on location on devpt of Spanish lute and guitar music 1984, made film of Elizabethan music and poetry with Dame Peggy Ashcroft for BBC TV 1987; performed with: BBC Symphony Orch, Scottish Chamber, London Symphony Orch, various string quartets and chamber ensembles, internationally known duo with John Williams; venues incl: Toronto, Boston, Chicago, Belgium, Concertgebouw Amsterdam, Musikverein Vienna, Milan, Rome, Venice, Berlin, Munich, Frankfurt, Zurich, Geneva, Japan, Hong Kong, Aust, NZ, Madrid, Athens, Paris, Bratislava, Prague, Warsaw, India, S America; performed at festivals incl: Aldeburgh, Bath, Three Choirs, Echternach, Ansbach, Ludwigsburg, Bergen, Prague Spring, Stresa, Helsinki; winner various int recording awards incl: six from Nat Acad of Recording Arts and Scis USA, two Edison Awards, various prizes from Gramophone magazine, platinum disc, various gold and silver discs for recordings made with John Williams; exclusive artist EMI 1990–; cmmnd new works from composers incl: Britten, Henze, Arnold, Walton, Brouwer; Hon DUniv Univ of Surrey 1968, Hon DMus Univ of Leeds 1984; Villa-Lobos Gold medal 1976; ARAM 1969, FRCM 1981, FRNCM 1983; *Performances* incl: first UK public performance of Brouwer's Concerto Elegiaco (written especially for him) St John's Smith Square 1986, Georg Malcolm's 70th Birthday Concert (with Dame Janet Baker and Sir Yehudi Menuhin) Wigmore Hall 1987, concert on centenary of Villa-Lobos' birth Wigmore Hall 1987, BBC Proms Concerts 1987, 1989, 1991 and 1993, recitals with Dame Peggy Ashcroft at Greenwich and Aldeburgh Festivals 1990, own 40th anniversary concert Wigmore Hall 1990, Japan Festival London 1991, 60th birthday season recitals Amsterdam and UK 1992/93; *Style*— Julian Bream, Esq, CBE; ✉ c/o Hazard Chase Ltd, Richmond House, 16–20 Regent Street, Cambridge CB2 1DB (☎ 01223 312400, fax 01223 460827)

BREARLEY, Dr Arthur; TD (1960); s of Leonard Brearley, of Lancs, and Mary Brearley; *b* 31 Aug 1931; *Educ* Queen Elizabeth I GS Middleton, Univ of Manchester (BSc, MSc, PhD); *m* 1955, Margaret, da of Ben Lee, of Manchester; 2 s (John b 1961, Mark b 1963); *Career* Lt RE then pilot RAuxAF, Maj RE (TA); various industl mgmnt appts and directorships; former professorial fell in mgmnt devpt Univ of Bradford, assoc Ernst & Young Manchester and 3i Manchester; currently chm: R L Martindale Liverpool, Huthwaite Research Group Rotherham, Crewdson & Co Kendal; vice chm Wrightington Hosp Trust; dir: Lord Street Properties Southport, Anne Shaw Consultants Bollington, Production Group Chelford; *Books* Management of Drawing and Design (1975), Control of Staff Related Overheads (1976), Ernst & Young Management Self Assessment System (1990), The Management Self Assessment Kit (1991); *Recreations* flying, fell walking; *Style*— Dr Arthur Brearley, TD; ✉ Sheringham House, Ladybrook Road, Bramhall, Stockport, Cheshire (☎ 0161 485 3944)

BREARLEY, Christopher John Scott; CB (1994); s of Geoffrey William Brearley (d 1968), and Winifred Marion, *née* Scott (d 1995); *b* 25 May 1943; *Educ* King Edward VII Sch Sheffield, Trinity Coll Oxford (MA, BPhil); *m* 1971, Rosemary Nanette, da of Lt-Col Wilfrid Sydney Stockbridge (d 1993), and Dorothea Stockbridge; 2 s (Thomas b 1973, William b 1976); *Career* civil servant; former dir: Scottish Servs, Property Servs Agency 1981–83; under sec Cabinet Office 1983–85; DOE: dir Local Govt Fin 1985–88, dir Planning and Devpt Control 1988–89, dep sec Local Govt 1990–93, dep sec Local Govt and Planning 1994–95, dep sec Local Devpt Gp 1996–; non-exec dir John Maclean & Son 1986–88; govr and tstee Watford GS for Boys 1988–; memb Bd Public Finance Fndn 1990–; FRSA; *Recreations* walking, crosswords; *Clubs* New (Edinburgh); *Style*— Christopher Brearley, Esq, CB; ✉ Department of the Environment, Eland House, Stag Place, London SW1E 5DU (☎ 0171 890 4040)

BREARLEY, Stephen; s of Roger Brearley, of Mossley Hill, Liverpool, and Joyce Mary, *née* Hewitt; *b* 17 March 1953; *Educ* Liverpool Coll, Gonville and Caius Coll Cambridge (MA), Middx Hosp Med Sch (MB BChir, MChir (Cantab), FRCS (England) 1981); *m* 1980, Margaret Faith, da of Edward Collier; 2 s (Jonathan Joshua b 5 March 1982, Samuel Sebastian James b 1 Dec 1985); *Career* research fell Birmingham Gen Hosp 1983–84, surgical sr registrar W Midlands Region 1988–91; conslt gen and vascular surgn: Whipps Cross Hosp London 1992–, BUPA Roding Hosp Ilford, Holly House Hosp Buckhurst Hill; RCS surgical tutor Whipps Cross Hosp, organiser Whipps Cross Advanced Surgery Course, memb Redbridge and Waltham Forest Research Ethics Ctee; memb: Jr Doctors' Ctee BMA 1979–91 (chm 1983–84), GMC 1984–, Standing Ctee on Postgraduate Med Educn 1989–92 (fndr memb), Permanent Working Gp of Euro Jr Hosp Doctors 1985–91 (chm Educn Sub-ctee); memb: Assoc of Surgns of GB and I, Vascular Surgical Soc, RSM; *Publications* author of articles on med educn, med manpower and medicine in Europe; *Recreations* playing, conducting and listening to music, flying, cricket, golf; *Style*— Stephen Brearley, Esq; ✉ Whipps Cross Hospital, London E11 1NR (☎ 0181 535 6670, mobile 0850 510650)

BREARS, Peter Charles David; s of Charles Henry, and Mary Theresa Margaret, Brears; *b* 30 Aug 1944; *Educ* Castleford Tech HS, Leeds Coll of Art (dipAD); *Career* keeper of folk life Hampshire Co Cncl 1967–69; curator: Shibden Hall Halifax 1969–72, Clarke Hall Wakefield 1972–75, Castle Museum York 1975–79; dir Leeds City Museums 1979–94, museum conslt and writer 1994–; pres Soc for Folk Life Studies 1992; FMA

1980, FSA 1980; *Books* The English Country Pottery (1971), Yorkshire Probate Inventories (1972), The Collectors' Book of English Country Pottery (1974), Horse Brasses (1981), The Gentlewoman's Kitchen (1984), Traditional Food in Yorkshire (1987), North Country Folk Art (1989), Of Curiosities and Rare Things (1989), Treasures for the People (1989), Images of Leeds (1992), Leeds Described (1993), Leeds Waterfront Heritage (1993), The Country House Kitchen (1996); numerous articles in Folk Life, Post-Medieval Archaeology and others; *Recreations* hill walking, drawing, cooking; *Style—* Peter Brears, Esq, FSA; ✉ 4 Woodbine Terrace, Headingley, Leeds LS6 4AF (☎ 0113 275 6537)

BREATHWICK, Leslie; s of R H Breathwick (d 1979), of Lincolnshire, and W M Breathwick (d 1973); *m*; 2 s (Richard Eliot b 26 Nov 1962, Martin Leslie b 23 Dec 1964), 1 da (Katherine Juliet b 15 Dec 1971); *Career* qualified accountant 1956, chm Cannoncourt Ltd Leicester; FCA 1965, FCCA 1956; *Recreations* hill walking and rambling, golf, bridge; *Clubs* Royal Automobile, Leicestershire Golf, Market Harborough Golf; *Style—* Leslie Breathwick, Esq; ✉ The Old Farmhouse, Mayns Lane, Burton Overy, Leics LE8 9DP (☎ and fax 0116 270 3890)

BRECHER, David John; s of William Brecher (d 1974), and Rachel, *née* Teitelbaum (d 1979); *b* 4 May 1927; *Educ* Haberdashers' Aske's, Trinity Coll Cambridge (MA); *m* 8 April 1953, Marjorie, da of Samuel Gordon; 1 s (Andrew Justin b 1965), 1 da (Valerie Zara b 1955); *Career* Nat Serv Army 1946–48; admitted slr 1952, fndr and sr ptnr Brecher & Co slrs 1952–95, currently conslt to Nicholson Graham & Jones; formerly chm Thompson Property Co, non-exec dir Alba PLC 1987–; memb Exec Cystic Fibrosis Res Tst; memb Worshipful Co of Blacksmiths, Freeman City of London 1963; memb Law Soc; *Recreations* golf, bridge, boating, reading; *Clubs* Estates Golfing Soc, Coombe Hill Golf, Mark's, Annabel's, Harry's Bar, Cambridge Union; *Style—* David Brecher, Esq; ✉ c/o Nicholson Graham & Jones, 110 Cannon Street, London EC4N 6AR (☎ 0171 648 9000, fax 0171 648 9001)

BRECHIN, Dean of; *see:* Breaden, Very Rev Robert William

BRECKENRIDGE, Prof Alasdair Muir; CBE (1995); s of Thomas Breckenridge (d 1973), of Arbroath, Scotland, and Jane, *née* Mackay (d 1986); *b* 7 May 1937; *Educ* Bell Baxter Sch Fife, Univ of St Andrews (MB ChB, MD); *m* 28 Feb 1967, Jean Margaret, da of Trevor Charles William Boyle, of E London, SA; 2 s (Ross Alexander b 1969, Bruce Gordon b 1971); *Career* surgn Dundee Royal Infirmary 1961–62 (house physician); Hammersmith Hosp and Royal Postgrad Med Sch London 1962–74: house physician, res fell, registrar, sr registrar, lectr, sr lectr; prof of clinical pharmacology Univ of Liverpool 1974–; memb: Ctee on Safety of Medicines, Cncl MRC, Drugs Advsy Ctee and Central R & D Ctee NHS; chm NW Regnl Health Authy; FRCP 1974, FRSE 1991; *Recreations* golf, stock market; *Style—* Prof Alasdair Breckenridge, CBE, FRSE; ✉ Cree Cottage, Feather Lane, Heswall, Wirral L60 4RL (☎ 0151 342 1096); Dept of Pharmacology and Therapeutics, Univ of Liverpool, PO Box 147, Liverpool L69 3BX (☎ 0151 794 5542, fax 0151 794 5540)

BRECKNOCK, Earl of; James William John Pratt; s and h of 6 Marquess Camden, *qv*; *b* 11 Dec 1965; *Educ* Eton, Univ of Edinburgh; *Style—* Earl of Brecknock

BRECON, Dean of; *see:* Harris, Very Rev John

BRECON, Baroness; Mabel Helen; CBE (1964), JP (1957); da of John McColville (d 1946), of Abergavenny, and Martha McColville (d 1944); *b* 8 May 1910; *Educ* St Alban's Convent; *m* 1933, 1 and last Baron Brecon, PC (d 1976), s of Alfred William Lewis (d 1955); 2 da (Hon Mrs Price, Hon Mrs Foss); *Career* cncllr Brecknock RDC 1949–74 (chm 1972), High Sheriff of Breconshire 1971–72; chm: Wales Women Cons Advsy Ctee 1955–62, Wales World Refugee Year 1959, Freedom from Hunger Campaign 1961–66; patron: Wales' Womens' Cons Assocs, Brecon & Radnor Cons Assocs; *Recreations* gardening, reading; *Style—* The Rt Hon the Lady Brecon, CBE, JP; ✉ Greenhill, Cross Oak, Brecon, Powys (☎ 0187 487 247)

BREDIN, James John; s of John Francis Bredin (d 1981), and Margaret Bredin; *b* 18 Feb 1924; *Educ* Finchley Catholic GS, Univ of London; *m* 1958, Virginia, da of John Meddowes; 1 s, 2 da; *Career* served WWII Sub-Lt Fleet Air Arm RNVR Europe, ME, Far East; prodr: BBC TV 1950–55, ITN 1955–59, Associated TV (documentaries) 1959–64; chm Guild of Televison Prodrs and Dirs 1961–64, dir ITN 1970–72, md Border Television Ltd 1964–82; specialist in television archives 1982–, London contrib ed Industry Week (USA) 1991–; press fellow Wolfson Coll Cambridge 1987; FRTS 1983; *Clubs* Beefsteak; *Style—* James Bredin, Esq; ✉ 25 Stack House, Cundy St, London SW1W 9JS (☎ 0171 730 2689)

BREEN, Geoffrey Brian; s of Ivor James Breen, of Cowbridge, S Wales, and Doreen Odessa Breen (d 1995); *b* 3 June 1944; *Educ* Harrow HS, Coll of Law; *m* 8 April 1978, Lucy, da of Serafin Cabrera (d 1984), of Bogota, Colombia; 1 s (Christopher b 1977), 1 da (Deborah b 1979); *Career* Stiles Breen & Partners: articled clerk 1962–67, admitted slr 1967, ptnr 1970–75, sr ptnr 1976–86; ptnr Blaser Mills & Newman 1976–86; appointed metropolitan stipendary magistrate 1986, recorder of the Crown Court 1993–, chm Youth Cts 1989–93; chm Family Proceedings Cts 1992; former memb Ctee: Central and S Middx Law Soc, London Criminal Cts Slrs' Assoc; fell and former memb Cncl Br Acad of Forensic Sciences; *Recreations* classical guitar, DIY, reading; *Style—* Geoffrey Breen, Esq; ✉ Horseferry Road Magistrates Court, 70 Horseferry Road, London SW1 2AX (☎ 0171 233 2000)

BREEZE, Alan Leonard; s of William John Richard Breeze (d 1994), and Ivy Lorretta, *née* Bird; *b* 11 Nov 1950; *Educ* Eastbourne GS; *m* 7 July 1973, Barbara Caroline (d 1993), da of Edwin Frederick Hope; 2 s (Jonathan b 1980, Thomas b 1983); *Career* CA 1973, currently sole practitioner Breeze Ralph & Co; *Style—* Alan L Breeze, Esq; ✉ 36 Ratton Drive, Eastbourne, East Sussex BN20 4NN; Breeze Ralph & Co, 5 Cornfield Terrace, Eastbourne BN21 4NN (☎ 01323 411416)

BREEZE, Prof David John; s of Reginald Coulson Breeze, of Blackpool, and Marian, *née* Lawson; *b* 25 July 1944; *Educ* Blackpool GS, Univ of Durham (BA, PhD); *m* 22 July 1972, Pamela Diane, da of Victor James William Silvester; 2 s (Simon David b 10 March 1976, Christopher John b 16 Jan 1979); *Career* pt/t lectr Dept of Archaeology Univ of Durham 1968–69, Miny of Public Building and Works 1969–89 (successively asst inspr of ancient monuments, inspr then princ inspr), chief inspr ancient monuments Historic Scotland 1989–; visiting prof Dept of Archaeology Univ of Durham 1994–, hon prof Univ of Edinburgh 1996–; memb: Int Ctee of the Congress of Roman Frontier Studies 1983–, Hadrian's Wall Advsy Ctee 1977–; corresponding memb German Archaeological Inst 1979; pres: South Shields Archaeological and Historical Soc 1983–85, Soc of Antiquaries of Scotland 1987–90 (vice pres 1984–87); tstee Senhouse Museum Trust 1985–; chm: Hadrian's Wall Pilgrimage 1989, British Archaeological Awards 1993–; FSAS 1970, FSA 1975, MIFA 1990, FRSE 1991; *Books* incl: The Romans in Scotland- An Introduction to the Collections of The National Museum of Scotland (with D V Clarke and G MacKay, 1980), The Northern Frontiers of Roman Britain (1982), Roman Forts in Britain (1983), Hadrian's Wall (with B Dobson, 1987), Hadrian's Wall- A Souvenir Guide to the Roman Wall (1987), A Queen's Progress (1987), Invaders of Scotland (with Anna Ritchie, 1991), Roman Officers and Frontiers (with B Dobson, 1993), Roman Scotland: Frontier Country (1996); author of many articles in British and foreign jls; *Recreations* reading, travel; *Style—* Prof David Breeze, FSA, FRSE; ✉ 36 Granby Road, Edinburgh EH16 5NL (☎ 0131 667 8876); Historic Scotland, Longmore House, Salisbury Place, Edinburgh EH9 1SH (☎ 0131 668 8724, fax 0131 668 8730)

BREMNER, Charles John Fraser; s of John Fraser Bremner, and Rosemary, *née* Ives; *b* 16 June 1951; *Educ* Blairmore Sch Aberdeenshire, St Peter's Coll South Australia, New Coll Oxford (BA), Univ Coll Cardiff (Dip in Journalism Studies); *m* 1, 1973 (m dis 1982), Valeria, *née* Gaidukowski; 1 da (Anna Lucy b 1977); m 2, 1987, Fariba, da of Abbas Shirdel, of Tehran; 1 s (James Charles Farhad b 1991), 1 da (Leila Jenny b 1993); *Career* Reuters: trainee 1975–77, Moscow corr 1977–79, Mexico City corr 1979–80, Paris corr 1981–83, bureau chief Moscow 1983–86; The Times: New York corr 1987–92, Paris corr 1992–95, Europe corr 1995–; *Recreations* flying, sailing, music; *Style—* Charles Bremner, Esq; ✉ The Times, 15 rue Philippe Le Bon, B-1040, Brussels, Belgium (☎ 00 32 2 230 7770, fax 00 32 2 230 8776)

BREMNER, Eric; s of Hamish Bremner, of Edinburgh, and Mary Wotherspoon Thomson, *née* Ross; *b* 9 July 1958; *Educ* Trinity Acad Edinburgh, Grays Sch of Art Aberdeen, Harrow Coll of Further Educn (Dip Fashion Design), RCA (MA); *m* 1 Sept 1979, Jane Catherine Mary, da of Donald Bruce Scott; 1 s (Hamish Scott b 10 May 1986), 1 da (Grace Francine b 5 March 1991); *Career* design asst Margaret Howell 1984; designer: Sportmax, Max Mara Italy 1984–94 (sr designer 1994–); design dir Laura Ashley 1993–94; design conslt: Marina Rinaldi Italy 1986–93, Prisma Commerciale Abbigliamento Italy 1987–93; pt/t tutor Fashion Sch RCA 1987–; external assessor: fashion (MDes) Edinburgh Coll of Art 1989–94, fashion (BA) Nat Coll of Art and Design Dublin 1989–94; *Recreations* cooking, music; *Style—* Eric Bremner, Esq; ✉ 9 High Street, Sutton Courtenay, Oxon OX14 4AW (☎ 01235 848620)

BREMNER, Rory Keith Ogilvy; s of Maj Donald Stuart Ogilvy Bremner (d 1979), of Merchiston, Edinburgh, and Anne Ulithorne, *née* Simpson; *b* 6 April 1961; *Educ* Wellington, King's Coll London (BA); *m* 8 Jan 1987 (m dis 1996), Susan Catherine, *née* Shackleton; *Career* satirical impressionist, writer and performer 1984–; tours and one-man shows 1985–, series BBC TV 1986–92, series Rory Bremner - Who Else? (Channel 4) 1992–; videos: Rory Bremner 1988, The Best of Rory Bremner 1989, Rory Bremner - Creased Up 1995; *Awards* winner Press Prize (Montreux) 1987, Top Male Comedy Performer (BCA) 1992, BAFTA 1994, 1995 and 1996, RTS Award 1995; *Recreations* cricket, travel, tennis; *Clubs* Lord's Taverners', Queen's; *Style—* Rory Bremner, Esq; ✉ The Richard Stone Partnership, 25 Whitehall, London SW1A 2BS (☎ 0171 839 6421, fax 0171 839 5002)

BRENCHLEY, (Thomas) Frank; CMG (1964); s of Robert Ballard Brenchley (d 1967), and Alice, *née* Brough (d 1974); *b* 9 April 1918; *Educ* Univ of Oxford (MA), Open Univ (BA); *m* 1946, Edith Helen (d 1980), da of Moritz Helfand (d 1938), of Vienna, Austria; 3 da (Hilary, Victoria, Clare); *Career* RCS 1939–46, ME cmd, Actg Lt-Col; first sec: Singapore 1950–53, Cairo 1953–56, FO 1956–58, MECAS 1958–60; cnsllr Khartoum 1960–63, charge d'affaires Jedda 1963, head of Arabian Dept FO 1963–67, under sec FCO 1967–68; ambass: Norway 1968–72, Poland 1972–74; dep sec, head of Oversea and def sec Cabinet Office 1975–76, ret HM Dip Serv 1976; chm: Inst for Study of Conflict 1984–89, Res Inst for Study of Conflict and Terrorism 1989–94; dir Center for Security Studies Washington DC 1988–90, pres Int Inst for Study of Conflict Geneva 1989–91; *Recreations* collecting books; *Clubs* Travellers (chm 1991–94); *Style—* Frank Brenchley, Esq, CMG; ✉ 19 Ennismore Gdns, London SW7 1AA (☎ 0171 584 7981)

BRENDEL, Alfred; Hon KBE (1989); s of Albert Brendel, of Graz, and Ida, *née* Wieltschnig; *b* 5 Jan 1931; *m* 1, 1960 (m dis 1972), Iris Heymann-Gonzala; 1 da (Doris); m 2, 1975, Irene, da of Dr Johannes Semler, of Munich; 1 s (Adrian), 2 da (Anna-Sophie, Katharina); *Career* pianist and writer; concert career since 1949; recordings for Vox, Turnabout, Vanguard, Philips; memb Acad of Arts and Sciences USA 1989; Hon RAM; fell Royal Northern Coll Manchester 1990, fell Exeter Coll Oxford; Hon DMus: London 1978, Sussex 1980, Oxford 1983, Warwick 1991, Yale 1992; winner Evening Standard Outstanding Artistic Achievement Award for 1995; Cdr of Arts and Letters France 1985, Ordre Pour le Merite Germany 1991; *Books* Musical Thoughts and Afterthoughts (essays, 1976), Music Sounded Out (essays, 1990), Fingerzeig (45 Texts, German, 1996); *Recreations* reading, theatre, films, unintentional humour, kitsch; *Style—* Alfred Brendel, Esq, KBE; ✉ c/o Ingpen & Williams, 14 Kensington Court, London W8 5ND (☎ 0171 937 5158)

BRENDON, John Patrick; *b* 27 March 1947; *Educ* Tonbridge Sch, Univ of Manchester (BA Economics); *m* (Grace) Esme Brendon; 1 da (Camilla b 4 Oct 1985), 1 s (Richard b 2 May 1987); *Career* Price Waterhouse: joined London office 1968, ptnr 1980–, New York office 1984–87, sr client ptnr 1993–; FCA (ACA 1972); *Clubs* Marylebone Cricket, Hever Golf; *Style—* John Brendon, Esq; ✉ Price Waterhouse, Southwark Towers, 32 London Bridge Street, London SE1 9SY (☎ 0171 939 3000)

BRENNAN, Daniel Joseph; QC (1985); s of Daniel Brennan, of Bradford (d 1969), and Mary, *née* Ahearne (d 1966); *b* 19 March 1942; *Educ* St Bede's GS Bradford, Univ of Manchester (LLB); *m* 21 Aug 1968, Pilar, da of Luis Sanchez Hernandez, of Madrid (d 1980), and Nieves Moya Dominguez; 4 s (Daniel b 1971, Patrick b 1972, Michael b 1977, Alexander b 1980); *Career* called to the Bar: Gray's Inn 1967, King's Inn Dublin 1990; recorder of the Crown Court 1982–; memb Criminal Injuries Compensation Bd 1989; bencher Gray's Inn 1993; chm Personal Injury Bar Assoc 1995–; *Publications* Provisional Damages (1986), Bullen & Leake on Pleadings (contrib 13 edn); *Style—* Daniel J Brennan, Esq, QC; ✉ 19 Royal Avenue, London SW3 4QE; 39 Essex St, London WC2R 3AT (☎ 0171 583 1111, fax 0171 353 3978)

BRENNAND-ROPER, Dr David Andrew; s of Dr John Hanson Brennand-Roper (d 1974), of Guernsey, CI, and Joyce Brennand-Roper, *née* Deans; *b* 22 Aug 1946; *Educ* Bryanston, BNC Oxford (MA), Guy's Hosp Med Sch (BM BCh); *m* Sheila Jane, *née* Boswell; 4 c (Tanya Alexandra b 8 June 1982, Anneka Louise b 18 June 1984, Alexander James Boswell b 4 Aug 1992, Giles William John b 24 Aug 1995); *Career* Sir Phillip Oppenheimer res fell in nuclear cardiology 1979–81, sr registrar in cardiology Guy's Hosp 1981–82, conslt cardiologist Guy's and St Thomas Tst and West Hill Hosps 1982–; lectr of the Br Heart Fndn; memb: Br Cardiac Assoc, American Coll of Cardiology, European Soc of Cardiology; Freeman City of London 1977, former Freeman Worshipful Co of Tobacco Pipe Makers 1977–82; memb BMA; FRCP; *Recreations* golf, photography, oenology; *Style—* Dr David Brennand-Roper; ✉ Suite 201, Emblem House, London Bridge Hospital, 27 Tooley Street, London SE1 2PR (☎ and fax 0171 357 8467); Cardiology Department Guy's and St Thomas Trust Hospitals, St Thomas Street, London SE1 9RT (☎ 0171 955 4930)

BRENNER, Sydney; CH (1987); *b* 13 Jan 1927; *Educ* Univ of Witwatersrand S Africa (MSc, MB BCh), Univ of Oxford (DPhil); *m* 3 c, 1 step s; *Career* Carnegie Corp fell USA 1954, Virus laboratory Univ of Calif Berkeley USA 1954, lectr in physiology Univ of Witwatersrand S Africa 1955–56, fell King's Coll Cambridge 1959–; MRC: memb scientific staff 1957–92, memb Cncl 1978–82 and 1986–90; dir Laboratory of Molecular Biology Cambridge 1979–86, dir Molecular Genetics Unit 1986–91; non-resident fell The Salk Inst San Diego Calif USA 1981–85, visiting fell Central Res and Devpt Dept E I du Pont de Nenours & Co Wilmington Delaware USA 1985–, visiting prof in med Royal Free Hosp Sch of Med Univ of London 1987–91, hon prof of genetic med Univ of Cambridge Clinical Sch 1989–, scholar in residence The Scripps Res Inst La Jolla USA 1989–91 (memb 1991–), research worker Dept of Med Univ of Cambridge Sch of Clinical Med 1992–, assoc The Neuroscience Res Program NY 1992–; *Awards* Warren Triennial prize 1968, Albert Lasker Medical Research award 1971, Royal medal Royal Soc of London 1974, Charles-Leopold Mayer prize (French Acad) 1975, Gairdner Fndn Int award Canada 1978 and 1991, Ciba medal (Biochemical Soc) 1981, Neil Hamilton Fairley medal (RCP) 1985, Croonian lectr Royal Soc of London 1986, Prix Louis Jeantet de Medicine (Fndn Louis Jeantet de Medicine Switzerland) 1987, Harvey prize Technion - Israel Inst of Technol 1987, Hughlings Jackson medal (Royal Soc of Med London) 1987, Waterford Bio-Medical Sci award (The Res Inst of Scripps Clinic, La Jolla, USA) 1988, Kyoto prize 1990, Copley medal Royal Soc of London 1991, King Faisal Int prize for Science King Faisal Fndn Saudi Arabia 1992, Bristol-Myers Squibb award for Distinguished Achievement in Neuroscience Res 1992; foreign hon memb American Acad of Arts and Scis 1965; Hon DSc: Trinity Coll Dublin 1967, Univ of Witwatersrand 1972, Univ of Chicago 1976, Univ of London 1982, Univ of Leicester 1983, Univ of Oxford 1985, Rockefeller Univ 1986; Hon DLitt National Univ of Singapore 1995; hon memb: Deutsche Akademie der Natursforscher Leopoldine Germany 1975, Soc for Biological Chemists 1975, The Chinese Soc of Genetics (Taiwan) 1989, Assoc of Physicians of GB and Ireland 1991; Hon LLD Univ of Glasgow 1981; hon fell: Exeter Coll Oxford 1985, Indian Acad of Scis 1989; Hon FRCPath 1990; foreign assoc: US Nat Acad of Scis 1977, Royal Soc of S Africa 1983; foreign memb: American Philosophical Soc 1979, Real Academia de Ciencias (Spain) 1985; external scientific memb Max Planck Soc 1988, memb Academia Europaea 1989, Correspondant Scientifique Emérite de l'INSERM Paris 1991, Associé Etranger Académie des Sciences Institut de France Paris 1992; FRS 1965, FRCP 1979, hon FRSE 1979; *Style—* Dr Sydney Brenner, CH, FRS

BRENT, Allan Arthur; s of Lawrence Arthur Brent (d 1975); *b* 10 Aug 1931; *Educ* Woodhouse Sch, City of London Coll; *m* 1, 1963 (m dis 1980), Sheila Moira, da of James Patrick Caird MacKinlay; 3 s, 1 da; m 2; *Career* md Grendon Trust Ltd 1969–71; chm: Monotype Corporation 1970–71, Camco (Machinery) Ltd 1975–80; sr conslt Alpha Beta Consultants Ltd 1975–, princ Alpha Beta Investments 1990–; gen cmmr of tax 1973–76; memb Bd of Visitors HM Prison Serv 1973–76; Liveryman Worshipful Co of Scriveners; Knight Govr Royal Soc of St George 1968; FCIS (memb Cncl 1974–80), FCIArb, FTII (memb Cncl 1966–81, pres 1969–70); *Recreations* tennis, sailing, bridge, travel; *Style—* Allan Brent, Esq; ✉ 1500 Quail Street, Suite 550, Newport Beach, Calif 92660, USA (☎ 00 1 714 581 8644, fax 00 1 714 581 2054)

BRENT, Prof Leslie; s of late Arthur Baruch, of Köslin, Germany, and late Charlotte, *née* Rosenthal; *b* 5 July 1925; *Educ* Bunce Court Sch Kent, Birmingham Central Tech Coll, Univ of Birmingham (BSc), UCL (PhD); *m* 16 April 1955, Joanne Elisabeth, da of Oates Manley, of Todmorden, Lancs; 1 s (Simon b 1956), 2 da (Susanna b 1958, Jennifer b 1963); m 2, 12 Oct 1991, Carol Pamela, da of Samuel Pritchard, of Newport, Gwent; *Career* served Inf UK, Italy and Germany 1943–47 (acting Capt); lectr in zoology UCL 1954–62, Rockefeller res fell 1956–57, scientist Nat Inst for Med Res 1962–65, prof of zoology Univ of Southampton 1965–69, prof of immunology St Mary's Hosp Med Sch London 1969–90, emeritus prof; ed: Transplantation 1962–67, Immunology Letters 1983–90; fndr chm Wessex Branch Inst of Biology 1966–68, memb WHO Expert Advsy Ctee on Immunology 1970–90, fndr sec Br Transplantation Soc 1972–75, pres The (Int) Transplantation Soc 1976–78; chm: Organising Ctee of 9 Int Transplantation Congress 1982, Fellowship Cmmn Inst of Biol 1979–85, Univ of London Jt Advsy Cmmn in Immunology 1987–90, British Univ Vietnam Orphans Appeal Fund 1967–69; convenor Res and Action Gp of the Social Serv Haringey Lab Pty 1970–79, treas Haringey Community Rels Cncl 1974–79 (chm 1979–80), fndr memb and vice chm Exec Ctee Haringey Cncl for Voluntary Serv 1974–79; fndr chm Haringey SDP 1981–83; memb SLD 1987; Vice Chllr Prize 1951, Scientific Medal Zoological Soc of London 1964, Peter Medawar Prize 1994; hon memb: Scandinavian and Polish Socs of Immunology, Assoc American Transplant Surgeons, S African Transplant Soc; memb: Br Soc for Immunology, Br Transplantation Soc (hon memb 1988), Hon MRCP 1986; FIBiol 1964; *Books* Progress in Immunology II (4 Vols, ed, 1974), Proceedings of the 9 Int Congress of The Transplantation Soc (2 vols ed, 1983), Organ Transplantation - Current Clinical and Immunological Concepts (ed, 1989), A History of Transplantation Immunology (Academic Press, 1996); *Recreations* formerly hockey (Br Univs and Staffs); fell walking, cricket, music, novels, singing (Crouch End Festival Chorus); *Style—* Emeritus Prof Leslie Brent; ✉ 30 Hugo Road, London N19

BRENT, Lucy Elizabeth; da of Allan Henry David George Brent (d 1978), and Irene Dorothy, *née* Jameson; *b* 7 Jan 1947; *Educ* Oak Hall; *Career* dep chm Trimite Ltd; FIMgt; *Recreations* skiing, bridge, golf, theatre, opera; *Clubs* Wentworth Golf; *Style—* Miss Lucy Brent; ✉ c/o Midland Bank, 28 High St, PO Box 41, Uxbridge, Middx UB8 1JN

BRENT, Michael Hamilton; s of Allan Henry David George Brent (d 1978), and Irene Dorothy, *née* Jameson; *b* 18 March 1943; *Educ* Charterhouse; *m* 1973, Janet, da of Irvine McBeath; 1 s, 2 da; *Career* chm and md Trimite Ltd 1975–; FCA; *Recreations* bridge, chess, golf, sailing, skiing, tennis; *Clubs* Carlton, Wentworth Golf; *Style—* Michael Brent, Esq; ✉ Trimite Ltd, Arundel Rd, Uxbridge, Middx UB8 2SD (☎ 01895 251234, fax 01895 256789); c/o Midland Bank, 28 High St, PO Box 41, Uxbridge, Middx

BRENT, Michael Leon; QC (1983); *b* 8 June 1936; *Educ* Manchester GS, Univ of Manchester (LLB); *m* 22 Aug 1965, Rosalind, *née* Keller; 2 da (Sasha b 1970, Ella b 1972); *Career* called to the Bar Gray's Inn 1961; practised: Northern Circuit 1961–67 (Circuit Jr 1964), Midland & Oxford Circuit 1967–; recorder of the Crown Court 1990–, dep High Ct judge 1994–, head of chambers; *Style—* Michael Brent, Esq, QC; ✉ 9 Gough Square, London EC4A 3DE (☎ 0171 353 5371, fax 0171 353 1344)

BRENTFORD, 4 Viscount (UK 1929), of Newick, Sussex; Sir Crispin William Joynson-Hicks; 4 Bt of Holmbury (UK 1919), 2 Bt of Newick (UK 1956); s of 3 Viscount Brentford, DL (d 1983) and Phyllis, *née* Allfrey (d 1979); *b* 7 April 1933; *Educ* Eton, New Coll Oxford; *m* 1964, Gillian Evelyn, OBE (1996), er da of late Gerald Edward Schluter, OBE, of Nairobi, Kenya; 1 s, 3 da (Hon Emma b 1966, Hon Rowena (Hon Mrs Banks) b 1967, Hon Amy b 1978); *Heir* s, Hon Paul William Joynson-Hicks b 1971; *Career* late Lt 9 Lancers; slr 1960; ptnr in legal firm of Taylor Joynson Garrett 1961–95; memb Ct of Assts Worshipful Co of Girdlers (Master 1983–84); *Style—* The Rt Hon the Viscount Brentford; ✉ Cousley Place, Wadhurst, East Sussex TN5 6HF (☎ 0189 278 3737)

BRENTON, Howard John; s of Donald Henry Brenton, and Rose Lilian, *née* Lewis; *b* 13 Dec 1942; *Educ* Chichester HS for Boys, St Catharine's Coll Cambridge (BA); *m* 31 Jan 1970, Jane Margaret, da of William Alfred Fry; 2 s (Samuel John b 23 Sept 1974, Harry William Donald b 6 Sept 1976); *Career* playwright; plays incl: Christie in Love (Portable Theatre) 1969, Revenge (Royal Court Theatre Upstairs) 1969, Hitler Dances (Traverse Theatre Workshop Edinburgh) 1972, Measure for Measure, after Shakespeare (Northcott Theatre Exeter) 1972, Magnificence (Royal Ct Theatre) 1973, Brassneck (with David Hare, Nottingham Playhouse) 1973, The Churchill Play (Nottingham Playhouse) 1974 and twice revived by the RSC in 1978 and 1988, Government Property (Aarhus Theatre Denmark) 1975, Weapons of Happiness (NT) 1976 (winner of the Evening Standard Best Play of the Year award), Epsom Downs (Jt Stock Theatre Co) 1977, Sore Throats (RSC) 1979, The Romans in Britain (NT) 1980, Thirteenth Night (RSC) 1981, The Genius (Royal Ct Theatre) 1983, Bloody Poetry (Folo Novo Theatre) 1984 and revived by the Royal Ct Theatre 1988, Pravda (with David Hare, NT) 1985 (winner of the Evening Standard Best Play of the Year award), Greenland (Royal Ct Theatre) 1988, Iranian Nights (with Tariq Ali, Royal Ct Theatre) 1989, HID - Hess is Dead (RSC and Mickery Theatre Amsterdam) 1989, Moscow Gold (with Tariq Ali, RSC) 1990, Berlin Bertie (Royal Court) 1992, Playing Away (opera libretto, Opera North) 1994, Faust (RSC) 1995; TV plays incl: A Saliva Milkshake (BBC) 1975, The Paradise Run (Thames) 1976, Desert of Lies (BBC) 1984, the four part series Dead Head (BBC) 1986; *Books* Diving for Pearls (1989), Hot Irons (1995); Freeman City of Buffalo NY State USA; *Recreations* painting; *Style—* Howard Brenton, Esq; ✉ c/o Casarotto Ramsay Ltd, National House, 60–66 Wardour Street, London W1V 3HP

BRENTON, Timothy Deane; s of Cdr Ronald William Brenton, MBE (d 1982), and Peggy Cecilia Deane, *née* Biggs; *b* 4 Nov 1957; *Educ* King's Sch Rochester, Britannia RNC, Univ of Bristol (LLB); *m* 29 Aug 1981, Annabel Louisa, da of Alan Harry Robson, of Sharrington, Norfolk; 1 s (Benjamin Alexander b 27 April 1993), 1 da (Louisa Elizabeth b 8 April 1990); *Career* RN 1975–79; lectr in law King's Coll London 1980, called to the Bar Middle Temple 1981; *Recreations* golf, fishing; *Clubs* Wrotham Heath; *Style—* Timothy Brenton, Esq; ✉ 4 Essex Court, Temple, London EC4Y 9AJ (☎ 0171 797 7970, fax 0171 353 0998, telex 8812528 ADROIT G)

BRENTWOOD, Bishop of (RC) 1980–; Rt Rev Thomas McMahon; *b* 17 June 1936; *Educ* St Bede's GS Manchester, St Sulpice Paris; *Career* ordained Wonersh Surrey 1959, asst priest Colchester 1959–64, priest Westcliff-on-Sea 1964–69, parish priest Stock 1969–, chaplain Univ of Essex 1972–80; formerly memb: Nat Ecumenical Cmmn, Liturgical Cmmn; chm: Brentwood Ecumenical Cmmn 1979, Ctee for Pastoral Liturgy 1983–, Essex Churches Consultative Cncl 1984–, Ctee for Church Music 1985–; memb London Church Leaders Gp; pres Essex Show 1992; Hon Doctorate Univ of Essex 1991; *Style—* The Rt Rev the Bishop of Brentwood; ✉ Bishop's House, Stock, Ingatestone, Essex CM4 9BU (☎ 01277 840268)

BRERETON, Donald; s of Clarence Vivian Brereton (d 1965), and Alice Gwendolin, *née* Galpin; *b* 18 July 1945; *Educ* Plymouth Coll, Univ of Newcastle upon Tyne (BA); *m* 12 April 1969, Mary Frances, da of William Turley (d 1967); 1 s (Samuel Edward b 21 Feb 1977), 2 da (Kathryn Vivian b 15 Nov 1972, Sally Clare b 21 Dec 1974); *Career* VSO Malaysia 1963–64, asst princ Miny of Health 1968–71, asst private sec to Sec of State for Social Servs 1971–72, private sec to Permanent Sec DHSS 1972–73, princ Health Servs Planning 1973–79, princ private sec to Sec of State for Social Servs 1979–82; asst sec: DHSS Policy Strategy Unit 1982–84, Housing Benefit 1984–89; under sec and head PM's Efficiency Unit 1989–93, under sec DSS 1993–; selector VSO; *Recreations* squash, holidays, books, bridge; *Style—* Donald Brereton, Esq; ✉ DSS, Room 11R1, The Adelphi, 1–11 John Adam Street, London WC2N 6HT (☎ 0171 962 8870, fax 0171 962 8867)

BRESLER, Fenton Shea; s of Herman Bresler (d 1972), and Bronia, *née* Tannenholtz (d 1968); *b* 22 Aug 1929; *Educ* Brighton Hove & Sussex GS, Sorbonne, King's Coll Univ of London (LlB); *m* Georgina Mary Bell (Gina), da of Capt George Bell Potts (d 1985); 1 s (Nicholas Joseph b 24 April 1961), 1 da (Katherine Celia (Mrs Sheppard) b 10 Aug 1959); *Career* called to the Bar Middle Temple 1951; also journalist and author (currently working on new biography of Napoleon III); extensive TV and radio work 1955–, currently contrib to (among others) Sky News, Daily Express, Daily Telegraph, BBC Radio and Readers Digest; *Books* 18 incl The Murder of John Lennon (1989), Interpol (hardback 1992, updated paperback 1993), Law Without a Lawyer (1995); *Recreations* squash until put out of action by a car crash, now reading, music and living; *Clubs* Reform; *Style—* Fenton Bresler, Esq; ✉ 3 Paper Buildings, Temple, London EC4Y 7EU (☎ 0171 797 7000, fax 0171 797 7100)

BRET DAY, Robin Carew; s of Lawrence Bret Day (d 1963), and Marguerite Jeanne, *née* Cros (d 1979); *b* 20 Aug 1926; *Educ* St Paul Sch France, Sorbonne; *m* 29 March 1952, Joan Hannah, da of Charles Henry Harding (d 1943); 2 s (Philip b 1954, Timothy b 1959), 1 da (Joanna b 1968); *Career* conslt oral and maxillofacial surgn; Edgware Hosp 1964–66, Hillingdon Hosp 1964–79, Guy's Hosp 1966–92; currently in private practice; past chm: Med and Dental Ctee Guy's Hosp, Academic Bd UMDS of Guy's and St Thomas' Hosp; govr UMDS of Guy's and St Thomas' Hosp (also hon conslt); FDS RCS, LRCP, MRCS; memb: BMA, BDA; *Recreations* tennis, shooting, reading; *Style—* Robin Bret Day; ✉ Oakwood, 12 North Park, Iver, Bucks (☎ 01753 653226); 84 Harley Street, London W1N 1AE (☎ 0171 935 8084/0171 486 2109)

BRETSCHER, Dr Mark Steven; s of Egon Bretscher (d 1973), and Hanna, *née* Greminger (d 1993); *b* 8 Jan 1940; *Educ* Abingdon Sch Berks, Gonville and Caius Coll Cambridge (minor scholar, major scholar, College Prize, MA, PhD); *m* 1978, Barbara Mary Frances Pearse; 1 s (Andrew Jonathan b 1981), 1 da (Nicola Katherine Pearse b 1978); *Career* research fell Gonville and Caius Coll Cambridge 1964–70 (research student 1961–64), head Div of Cell Biology MRC Laboratory of Molecular Biology Cambridge 1984–95 (resigned) (memb Scientific Staff 1965–); Jane Coffin Childs Meml fell Stanford Univ California 1964–65, visiting prof: Harvard Univ 1975–76, Stanford Univ 1984–85; memb Euro Molecular Biology Orgn; Friedrich Miescher prize Swiss Biochemical Soc 1979; FRS 1985; *Publications* papers in scientific jls on topics of: the genetic code and protein synthesis 1962–70; membrane structure 1971–, cell locomotion 1976–; *Recreations* planting and cultivating woodland, mountain walking; *Style—* Dr Mark Bretscher, FRS; ✉ Ram Cottage, Commerical End, Swaffham Bulbeck, Cambridge CB5 0ND (☎ 01223 811276); MRC Laboratory of Molecular Biology, Hills Road, Cambridge CB2 2QH (☎ 01223 248011, fax 01223 412142)

BRETT, Hon Christopher Lionel Baliol; eld s and h of 4 Viscount Esher; *b* 23 Dec 1936; *Educ* Eton, Magdalen Coll Oxford; *m* 1, 1962 (m dis 1970), Camilla Charlotte, da of Sir (Horace) Anthony Claude Rumbold, 10 Bt, KCMG, CB; 1 s (Matthew b 1963), 2 da (Miranda b 1964, Rebecca b 1966); m 2, 1971, F Valerie, da of Maxwell Maurice Harrington; 2 s (Oliver b 1972, William b 1982), twin da (Susannah and Clare b 1973); *Style—* The Hon Christopher Brett; ✉ Watlington Park, Watlington, Oxon (☎ 0149 161 2302)

BRETT, Nicholas Richard John; s of Reginald Sydney Brett (d 1993), and Urania Rhoda, *née* Morris; *b* 6 Feb 1950; *Educ* Abingdon Sch Oxon, Bedford Coll London (pres Students' Union, BA), Pennsylvania State Univ (MA); *m* 1 (m dis); m 2, 3 Dec 1981, Judith Anne, da of Norman Armitage Miller; 2 da (Camilla Beatrice Brett-Miller b 31 May 1980, Harriet Lucy Brett-Miller b 3 July 1983); *Career* news reporter then news ed East Ender (Stratford Express Series) 1977, chief reporter Camden Journal 1978–81, prodn ed Times Health Supplement 1981; The Times: sports sub-ed 1982, chief sub-ed Saturday section 1982, dep ed Saturday section 1983, ed Saturday section 1984, asst features ed 1985, dep features ed 1986, features ed 1986–88; ed Radio Times and editorial dir BBC Magazines 1988–96, publishing dir Radio Times 1996–; Radio Times winner Magazine of the Year Magazine Publishing Awards 1991, Ed of the Year Br Soc of Magazine Eds Awards 1993, Ed of the Year PPA Magazines Awards 1996; chm Br Soc of Magazine Editors 1992, pres European Assoc of TV Magazines 1993–95 (vice pres 1992–93); memb Code of Practice Ctee Press Standards Bd of Finance 1992–94; *Recreations* Arsenal, birdwatching, carpentry, walking; *Clubs* Groucho; *Style—* Nicholas Brett, Esq; ✉ Radio Times, Woodlands, 80 Wood Lane, London W12 0TT (☎ 0181 576 3120, fax 0181 576 3002)

BRETT, Simon Anthony Lee; s of Alan John Brett (d 1979), and Margaret, *née* Lee; *b* 28 Oct 1945; *Educ* Dulwich, Wadham Coll Oxford (maj scholar, BA, pres OUDS); *m* 27 Nov 1971, Lucy Victoria, da of late Alastair Dixon McLaren; 2 s (Alastair b 22 July 1977, Jack b 11 March 1981), 1 da (Sophie b 9 Oct 1974); *Career* writer; Father Christmas Toy Dept Shinners of Sutton Nov-Dec 1967; prodr light entertainment: BBC Radio 1968–77 (progs worked on incl: Week Ending, Frank Muir Goes Into..., The News Huddlines, Lord Peter Wimsey, The Hitch-Hikers Guide to the Galaxy), LWT 1977–79 (progs worked on incl: End of Part One, Maggie and Her, The Glums); full time writer 1979–; writing for TV incl After Henry (nominated for 1988 and 1989 BAFTA Awards),

How to be a Little S*D; writing for radio incl: Afternoon Theatre, Frank Muir Goes Into..., Semicircles, Molesworth, After Henry (BPG Award for Outstanding Radio Programme 1987), Dear Diary, No Commitments; Writers' Guild Award for Best Radio Feature Script (with Frank Muir) 1973; chm: Crime Writers' Assoc 1986–87, Soc of Writers 1995–; *Publications* incl: 16 crime novels featuring actor-detective Charles Paris (Cast, In Order of Disappearance, So Much Blood, Star Trap, An Amateur Corpse, A Comedian Dies, The Dead Side of The Mike, Situation Tragedy, Murder Unprompted, Murder in the Title, Not Dead Only Resting, Dead Giveaway, What Bloody Man is That?, A Series of Murders, Corporate Bodies, A Reconstructed Corpse, Sicken and so Die), 8 other crime novels (A Shock to the System (Best Novel Award nomination by Mystery Writers of America), Dead Romantic, A Nice Class of Corpse, Mrs Presumed Dead, Mrs Pargeter's Package, The Christmas Crimes at Puzzel Manor, Mrs Pargeter's Pound of Flesh, Singled Out), 2 crime novels for children (The Three Detectives and the Missing Superstar, The Three Detectives and the Knight-in-Armour), 1 volume of crime short stories (A Box of Tricks), various humorous books; *Style*— Simon Brett, Esq; ✉ c/o Michael Motley, Flat 4, 42 Craven Hill Gardens, London W2 3EA (☎ 0171 723 2973)

BRETT, Simon Baliol; s of Antony Reginald Forbes Baliol, MBE (d 1981), and Bay Helen, *née* Brownell (d 1989); *b* 27 May 1943; *Educ* Ampleforth, St Martin's Sch of Art; *m* 31 Aug 1974, Juliet Anne, da of Paul Hamilton Wood, OBE (d 1962); 1 da (Emily b 1977); *Career* wood engraver and artist illustrator; pt/t teacher Marlborough Coll Art Sch 1971–89, proprietor Paulinus Press 1981–; Francis Williams illustration award for The Animals of St Gregory, chm Soc of Wood Engravers 1987–92 (treas 1992–); RE 1991 (ARE 1987); *Books* written: Engravers - A Handbook for the Nineties (1987), Forty Nudes (1988), The Wood Engravings of Gwen Raverat (ed, 1989), Wood Engraving (1994); illustrated: Reader's Digest Illustrated Bible (1990), Clarissa, Jane Eyre (1991), The Confessions of St Augustine (1993), Amelia (1995); *Style*— Simon Brett, Esq; ✉ 12 Blowhorn St, Marlborough, Wilts SN8 1BT (☎ 01672 512905)

BRETT, Timothy Edward William; s of Reuben Brett (d 1982), of Gravesend, Kent, and Edna, *née* Waterman; *b* 28 March 1949; *Educ* Gravesend GS for Boys, Univ of Bristol (BSc), DipHSM, Grad IPD (Cabinet Office Top Mgmnt Prog 1995); *m* 1972, Barbara Jane, da of Joseph Lightfoot Turnbull; 3 s (Matthew b 1978 d 1982, Nicholas b 8 Dec 1983, Jonathan b 4 March 1989), 1 da (Deborah b 6 Dec 1985); *Career* teacher VSO Sierra Leone 1971–73, nat admin trainee Leeds Regnl Hosp Bd and Yorks RHA 1973–75, sr admin asst (planning and personnel) Leeds AHA 1975–76, business mangr Nixon Meml Hosp Segbwema Sierra Leone for Methodist Church Overseas Div 1976–78, community servs administrator Beverley Health Dist Humberside AHA 1978, dep administrator Derbys Royal Infirmary 1979–80, unit administrator Plymouth Gen Hosp 1981–85, unit gen mangr Dundee Gen Hosps Unit 1987–93 (unit administrator 1985–87), currently chief exec Dundee Teaching Hospitals NHS Tst; ldr Univ of Bristol expedition to Afghanistan 1970; Inst of Health Services Mgmnt: former chm S Western Branch, former memb Nat Cncl, former chm Scottish Div; FHSM (MHSM 1975); *Recreations* hill-walking, squash, swimming, theatre, church activities (presenter Reflections programme on Grampian TV); *Clubs* Claverhouse Rotary (Dundee), Grampian Climbing; *Style*— Timothy Brett, Esq; ✉ Dundee Teaching Hospitals NHS Trust, Level 10, Ninewells Hospital and Medical School, Dundee, Tayside DD1 9SY (☎ 01382 632598)

BRETT, District Judge Trevor Graham; s of Joseph Brett (d 1986), and Nellie Kathleen, *née* Dean (d 1994); *b* 26 Jan 1950; *Educ* Borden GS Sittingbourne Kent, Birmingham Poly (LLB London); *m* 5 April 1975, Gillian Margaret, da of Ernest Charles Fluck; 3 s (Mark Graham b 7 July 1978, Andrew Graham b 5 Dec 1980, Oliver Graham b 4 Nov 1985); *Career* articled 1972–74, admitted slr 1974; in private practice: Bradbury & Co Camberwell 1974–75, Basset & Boucher Rochester 1975–85, Dakers Green Brett Chatham 1985–92; district judge Uxbridge, Slough and Reigate Co Cts Apr 1992–Nov 1993; district judge Bromley Co Cts Nov 1993–; memb Law Soc 1974– (sec Rochester, Chatham and Gillingham Law Soc 1982–92); *Recreations* sport, especially golf, soccer and badminton, reading; *Style*— District Judge Brett

BRETT, William Henry (Bill); *b* 6 March 1942; *m* Janet, *née* Grose; 2 da (Judith, Hannah); *Career* former booking clerk British Rail and official Transport Salaried Staffs' Assoc, negotiator bank employees' union (now BIFU) 1966–68, divnl offr ASTMS 1968–74, also former presenter Union Scene (BBC Radio Nottingham); IPMS: joined as asst sec (environment and agric members) 1974–80, asst gen sec (private and public sectors) 1989, gen sec 1989–; memb Gen Cncl TUC 1989– (memb ctees: Fin and Gen Purposes, Int, Public Serv, Employment Policy and Organisation, Energy and Safety Health and Environment), memb Exec Ctee Public Servs Int (memb Steering Gp Euro Public Servs Ctee); cncllr (Lab) London Borough of Lewisham 1964–68; pres Workers' Gp and vice pres Governing Body ILO 1993; *Books* International Labour in the 21st Century (1994); *Style*— Bill Brett, Esq; ✉ IPMS, 79 York Road, London SE1 7AQ (☎ 0171 928 9951, fax 0171 928 5996)

BRETT-JONES, Anthony Tom (Tony); CBE (1979); s of Lt David Tom Jones, DCM (d 1969), of London, and Mary, *née* Brett Needham; *b* 4 March 1922; *Educ* Cranbrook Sch; *m* 30 Aug 1952, Ann, da of Sir Lionel Wray Fox, MC (d 1961); 1 s (Harry Anthony Lionel b 1964), 3 da (Lucy Katharine b 1955, Sarah Josephine b 1956, Jane Rosalind b 1959); *Career* WWII Flying Offr RAF Bomber Cmd 1942–46; chartered Quantity Surveyor, ptnr Dearle & Henderson 1957–87; RICS: memb Cncl 1952–90, memb QS Div Cncl 1955–93 (pres 1969–70), chm Educn Ctee 1973–78, govr Coll of Estate Mgmnt 1964–90 (chm govrs 1980–85); pres Cruising Assoc 1994– (vice pres 1985–88), ed Cruising Assoc Handbook 1982–; Freeman City of London 1977, memb Worshipful Co of Chartered Surveyors 1977; ARICS 1947, FRICS 1962, FCIArb, FRSA; *Books* 4 Aqua books (contrib 1960–); *Recreations* sailing; *Clubs* Reform; *Style*— Tony Brett-Jones, Esq, CBE; ✉ 13 Cumberland St, London SW1V 4LS (☎ 0171 834 7885)

BRETTEN, (George) Rex; QC (1980); s of Horace Victor Bretten (d 1954), and Kathleen Edna Betty Bretten; *b* 21 Feb 1942; *Educ* King Edward VII Sch, King's Lynn, Sidney Sussex Coll Cambridge (MA, LLM); *m* 1965, Maureen Gillian, *née* Crowhurst; 1 da; *Career* called to the Bar Lincoln's Inn 1965; *Style*— G R Bretten, Esq, QC; ✉ Stonehill House, Horam, Heathfield, East Sussex; 24 Old Buildings, 1 Floor, Tax Chambers, Lincoln's Inn, London WC2A 3UJ (☎ 0171 242 2744, fax 0171 831 8095)

BRETTLE, Robert Harvey Linton; s of Robert Edward Brettle (d 1974), and Mabel, *née* Linton, of Willingdon, nr Eastbourne, Sussex; *b* 3 April 1935; *Educ* Highgate Sch London, ChCh Oxford (MA); *m* 27 May 1964, Lindsay Mary, da of the late Sydney Howson; 3 s (Thomas b 1966, Oliver b 1969, Adrian b 1972); *Career* Nat Serv: cmmnd Middx Regt 1955, Royal West Africa Frontier Force 3 Bn Nigeria Regt (later Queen's Own Nigeria Regt) 1955–56, Intelligence and Recruitment Offr asst adj; admitted slr 1963 (insolvency practitioner); sr ptnr: Peard Son and Webster of Croydon 1983–86 (ptnr 1966–83), Peard Webster Pringle and John 1986–96 (conslt 1996–); dep registrar in bankruptcy, memb London Legal Aid Area Appeals Ctee, pres Croydon and Dist Law Soc 1972–73, chm of Govrs St Margaret's Sch for Spastics and Physically Handicapped Children 1972–84; memb Law Soc 1963; *Recreations* bridge, gardening, travel; *Clubs* RAC; *Style*— Robert Brettle, Esq; ✉ 42 Brownlow Rd, Croydon, Surrey CRO 5JT (☎ 0181 688 3307); Peard Webster Pringle and John, Suffolk House, College Rd, Croydon CR9 1DR (☎ 0181 680 5262, fax 0181 686 4560, telex 9180263 PWPJ G)

BREW, Richard Maddock; CBE (1981), DL (Greater London 1989); s of late Leslie Maddock Brew, of Suffolk, and Phyllis Evelyn, *née* Huntsman (d 1949); *b* 13 Dec 1930; *Educ* Rugby, Magdalene Coll Cambridge (BA); *m* 1953, Judith Anne, da of Dr Percy Ellis Thompson Hancock; 2 s (Antony b 1957, Timothy b 1961), 2 da (Charlotte b 1955 (first woman to ride in Grand National, 1977), Sophie b 1967); *Career* called to the Bar Inner Temple 1955; dep chm Brew Bros Ltd 1955–72, chm Monks Dormitory Ltd 1979–93, Budget Boilers Ltd 1984–, regnl dir (Eastern Counties) Lloyds Bank plc 1988–91; cncllr: Royal Borough of Kensington 1959–65, Royal Borough of Kensington and Chelsea 1964–70; GLC 1968–86: alderman 1968–73, vice chm Strategic Planning Ctee 1969–71, memb for Chingford 1973–86, dep ldr of Cncl and ldr Policy and Resources Ctee 1977–81, dep ldr Cons Pty and oppn spokesman on finance 1974–77 and 1981–82, ldr of the oppn 1982–83; chm Tower Hamlets Dist Health Authy 1990–93; memb: London Tourist Bd (London Visitor and Convention Bureau) 1970–88, Cncl Pony Club 1975–93, NE Thames RHA 1982–90 (vice chm 1982–86), Nat Theatre Bd 1982–86; special tstee Royal London Hosp 1990–93; High Sheriff Greater London 1988–89; *Recreations* The Pony Club, gardening; *Clubs* Carlton, MCC; *Style*— Richard Brew, Esq, CBE, DL; ✉ The Abbey, Coggeshall, Essex CO6 1RD (☎ 01376 561246)

BREWER, David; s of William Watson Brewer (d 1968), and Eileen, *née* Hall; *b* 24 July 1946; *Educ* Brigg GS, Emmanuel Coll Cambridge (BA); *m* 26 May 1973, Elizabeth Margaret, da of John William Ferguson (d 1986); 1 da (Jane b 1975); *Career* British Coal: area chief accountant South Midlands 1979–85, chief accountant 1985–87, head of fin servs 1987–91, fin controller 1991–93, head of fin 1993–95; fin and operations dir Scottish Coal 1995–; dir Mines Rescue Service Ltd 1996–; memb Consultative Ctee Euro Coal and Steel Community (ECSC) 1996–; tstee: Industry Wide Mineworkers' Pension Scheme, Industry Wide Staff Superannuation Scheme, Scottish Mining Museum; ACMA 1978; *Style*— David Brewer, Esq; ✉ 4 Westgarth Avenue, Edinburgh EH13 0BD (☎ 0131 441 6453); Scottish Coal Company Ltd, 160 Glasgow Road, Corstorphine, Edinburgh EH12 8LT (☎ 0131 317 3902, fax 0131 317 3913)

BREWER, David John; s of Raymond Bennett (d 1982), of Padstow, Cornwall, and Patricia Mary, *née* Key; *b* 29 Jan 1949; *Educ* Bodmin Co GS, Univ of Bath (BSc); *m* 31 March 1973, Kate, da of Mitchell Scatterty Milne; 1 da (Rebecca b 1977); *Career* CA; Deloitte Haskins and Sells: London 1970–78, Dubai UAE 1978–86, ptnr 1980, ptnr in charge Arabian Gulf Practice 1982–86, sr ptnr CI Firm 1986–90; dep chm CI Partnership Coopers and Lybrand 1990–94, md Abacus Financial Services Group Ltd (pt of Coopers and Lybrand International) 1994–; MInstD (Jersey Branch), FCA (ACA 1974); *Recreations* bridge, sailing, supporting amateur swimming; *Style*— David Brewer, Esq; ✉ Clos du Coin, La Haule, St Brelade, Jersey (☎ 01534 46432); Abacus Financial Services Group Ltd, La Motte Chambers, La Motte Street, St Helier, Jersey (☎ 01534 602000)

BREWER, Prof Derek Stanley; s of Stanley Leonard Brewer, and Winifred Helen, *née* Forbes; *b* 13 July 1923; *Educ* The Crypt GS, Magdalen Coll Oxford (MA), Univ of Birmingham (PhD), Univ of Cambridge (LittD); *m* 1951, Lucie Elisabeth Hoole; 3 s, 2 da; *Career* academic, author and academic publisher; Univ of Cambridge: master Emmanuel Coll 1977–90, prof of English 1983–90, emeritus prof 1990–; Seatonian prize 1969, 1972, 1979 (jtly), 1980 (jtly), 1983, 1986, 1988 1992 (jtly) and 1993; Hon: LLD Keio Univ 1982, LLD Harvard Univ 1983, LittD Univ of Birmingham 1985, DUniv York 1985, DUniv Sorbonne 1988, DLitt Williams Coll 1989, DUniv Liège 1990; hon memb Japan Acad 1981, corresponding fell Medieval Acad of America 1987; FSA 1977; *Style*— Prof Derek Brewer, FSA; ✉ Emmanuel College, Cambridge (☎ 01223 334200, fax 01223 334426)

BREWER, Rear Adm George Maxted Kenneth; CB (1981); s of Capt George Maxted Brewer (d 1954), of Dover, Kent, and Cecilia Victoria Jessie, *née* Clark (d 1987); paternal gf served in HMS Basilisk under the then Capt Moresby during his discoveries in New Guinea in 1873, hence Brewer Island shown on Admiralty Chart 1873; *b* 4 March 1930; *Educ* The Nautical Coll Pangbourne; *m* 1989, Betty Mary, o da of Cdr Claude Harold Welton, RN; *Career* cmd: HMS Carysfort (Home, Med and Far E) 1964–65, HMS Agincourt (Home) 1967, HMS Grenville (Home, Med and Far E) 1967–69, HMS Juno and Capt Fourth Frigate Sqdn (Home and Med) 1973–74; course student RCDS 1975; cmd: HMS Tiger (Far E deployment) and Flag Capt to the Flag Offr Second Flotilla 1978, appointed ADC to HM The Queen 1980, HMS Bulwark (NATO area) 1978–80; Flag Offr Medway and Port Adm Chatham 1980–82; *Recreations* watercolour painting; *Clubs* Royal Navy Club of 1765 and 1785; *Style*— Rear Adm George Brewer, CB; ✉ c/o National Westminster Bank, Portchester, Fareham, Hants

BREWER, Rt Rev John; *see:* Lancaster, Bishop of (RC)

BREWERTON, David Robert; s of Ernest John Brewerton (d 1980), and Violet Florence, *née* Smith; *b* 25 Feb 1943; *Educ* Coopers Company's Sch; *m* 25 May 1963, Patricia Ann, da of James Albert Driscoll, OBE; 2 s (Benjamin David b 27 March 1968, Jake David b 14 April 1970), 1 da (Sarah Ann Jane b 14 Sept 1973); *Career* Stock Exchange red button with Grieveson Grant 1959; sub ed: Extel Statistics 1964, Financial Times 1965; commercial property corr Daily Telegraph 1971 (reporter 1969), ed Policy Holder Insurance News 1977, Questor Daily Telegraph 1978, city ed The Independent 1986, exec ed finance and indust The Times 1988, dir Brunswick PR Ltd 1991–; *Awards* Financial Journalist of the Year 1986; *Recreations* sailing, cooking, travel; *Style*— David Brewerton, Esq; ✉ 82 Bickenhall Mansions, Bickenhall Street, London W1H 3LD (☎ 0171 486 0315); Brunswick Public Relations Ltd, 15 Lincoln's Inn Fields, London WC2A 3ED (☎ 0171 404 5959, fax 0171 831 2823, mobile 0860 219213)

BREWIN, Daniel Robert (Dan); s of John Stuart Brewin (d 1968), of Sheffield, and Elsie Mary Brewin, *née* Timm (d 1989); *b* 22 Aug 1946; *Educ* King Edward VII Sch Sheffield, Univ of Salford (BSc), Cranfield Sch of Mgmnt (MBA 1977); *m* 1, 1974 (m dis); 2 s (John b 1976, Timothy b 1980), 1 da (Anna b 1978); m 2, 1993, Lynne Joyce Pontet, da of Frank Harvey Manchester; *Career* British Airways: various appts 1964–81, dir of ops Manchester Airport 1981–84; gen mangr UK sales British Caledonian 1984–87 (sr gen mangr commerical 1987), sr gen mangr Gatwick British Airways plc 1991–93 (previously gen mangr catering), currently head UK sales British Airways; FInstTT (pres 1991–93); *Recreations* golf, cinema; *Style*— Dan Brewin, Esq; ✉ British Airways plc, 200 Buckingham Palace Road, London SW1A 9TA (☎ 0171 707 4035)

BREWIS, Dr (Robert) Alistair Livingston; s of Dr Ernest George Brewis, and Jean Elizabeth, *née* Livingston; *b* 16 Oct 1937; *Educ* Royal GS Newcastle, Univ of Durham, Univ of Newcastle upon Tyne (MB BS, MD); *m* 3 Nov 1962, Dr Mary Brewis, da of John William Burdus; 3 s (George b 1964, Robert b 1965, John b 1966); *Career* house offr: Royal Victoria Infirmary Newcastle, Hammersmith and Brompton Hosps London; registrar Charing Cross Hosp London, lectr in med Univ of Manchester 1966–70, currently conslt physician and med dir Royal Victoria Infirmary Newcastle upon Tyne; former pres Br Thoracic Soc; FRCP 1974; *Books* Lecture Notes on Respiratory Disease (4 edn, 1991), Respiratory Medicine (jt ed, 1990), Classic Papers in Asthma (1990); *Recreations* painting; *Style*— Dr Alistair Brewis; ✉ Royal Victoria Infirmary, Newcastle upon Tyne NE1 4LP (☎ 0191 232 5131, fax 0191 261 8505)

BREWSTER, David John; s of Dr Leslie George Brewster (d 1974), and Evangeline, *née* Creed (d 1976); *b* 16 June 1936; *Educ* Whitgift Sch, St John's Coll Cambridge (MA); *m* 9 May 1964, Christine, *née* Booth; 1 s (Jonathan b 27 March 1967), 3 da (Sarah b 6 March 1965, Louise b 10 Jan 1969, Emma b 22 Dec 1971); *Career* called to the Bar Gray's Inn 1961; practising barr in England 1961–63, ptnr Appleby Spurling and Kempe (barristers and attorneys) Bermuda 1964–74, dir Tyndall Gp 1974–86, legal and policy dir IMRO 1993– (sec 1986–88, legal dir 1989–93); chm St Peter's Hospice Bristol 1984–88;

Style— David Brewster, Esq; ✉ IMRO Ltd, Lloyds Chambers, 1 Portsoken Street, London E1 8BT (☎ 0171 390 5000)

BREWSTER, Martyn Robert; s of Robert Richard Frederick Brewster of Watford, Herts, and Doreen Violet, *née* Lilburn; *b* 24 Jan 1952; *Educ* Watford Boys GS, Hertfordshire Coll of Art, Brighton Poly (BA, Dip Painting and Printmaking, Art Teachers Cert); *m* 1988, Hilary Joy, da of Peter John Carter; 1 da (Sophie Roberta b 19 Aug 1988); *Career* artist; lectr in art East Herts Coll 1980–89; visiting lectr various arts schs 1980–89 incl: Winchester, Bournemouth, London Coll of Furniture; Space Studio in London 1983, studio in Dorset 1990; two-man exhibition Thumb Gallery Soho 1987–; one-man exhibitions incl: Peterborough City Museum and Art Gallery 1983, London Coll of Furniture 1984, Warwick Arts Tst London 1986, Winchester Gallery Hampshire 1986, Minories Essex 1986, Woodlands Gallery London 1987, Thumb Gallery (Shadows and Light 1987, Light Falls 1990), Atlanta USA 1991, Jill George Gallery 1992 (Nature Paintings 1994, Lowick Prints 1995); group exhibitions incl: Spirit of London (Festival Hall) 1983, English Expression (Warwick Arts Tst) 1984, Int Art Fair London 1985, Angela Flowers Gallery 1985–86, Int Art Fairs LA 1987–90, London Group (RCA) 1988, Art London (Thumb Gallery) 1989–90, Critics Choice (Air Gallery London and Ianetti Lanzone Gallery San Francisco) 1989; works in collection of: Warwick Arts Tst, The Open Univ, Wiltshire Educn Authy, various hosps, Peterborough Museum, various private collections worldwide; Eastern Arts Award 1977, awarded various Regnl Arts Association grants 1979–86, Br Cncl travel award 1991, Arts Cncl devpt grant 1994; memb Brighton Open Studios 1975–79; *Recreations* reading, jogging; *Style—* Martyn Brewster, Esq; ✉ c/o Jill George Gallery Ltd, 38 Lexington St, Soho, London W1R 3HR (☎ 0171 439 7319/7343, studio 01202 423300)

BREWSTER, Richard David; s of David Edward Brewster; *b* 5 Jan 1946; *Educ* Highgate; *m* Susan Ann; 2 s (Edward, William), 2 da (Emily, Rachel); *Career* CA; fin dir Giltspur plc until 1983; chief exec David S Smith (Holdings) plc 1983–91, Jarvis Porter Group PLC 1991–; formerly non-exec dir Welsh Devpt Agency, currently non-exec dir Bankers Investment Trust plc; vice pres RNIB; Liveryman Worshipful Co of Stationers and Newspaper Makers; FCA 1968; FInstD, fell Inst of Packaging (vice pres); *Recreations* sailing, tennis, skiing; *Clubs* Island Cruising, IOD, Anglo Belgium, Richmond Cricket and Tennis; *Style—* Richard Brewster, Esq; ✉ c/o Jarvis Porter Group PLC, Parkside Lane, Leeds LS11 5SZ (☎ 0113 270 3000, fax 0113 271 5233)

BREWSTER, Richard Philip; *b* 25 May 1952; *Educ* Leeds GS, Trinity Coll Oxford (Open scholar, BA, cross country running blue); *Career* various posts in commercial mgmnt ICI 1976–86, nat appeals mangr Oxfam 1986–89; SCOPE (formerly Spastics Soc): dir of mktg 1989–95, chief exec 1995–; memb ACENVO; *Style—* Richard Brewster, Esq; ✉ Chief Executive, SCOPE, 12 Park Crescent, London W1N 4EQ (☎ 0171 636 5020, fax 0171 637 3415)

BRIANCE, Richard Henry; o s of John Albert Perceval Briance, CMG (d 1989), and Prunella Mary, *née* Chapman; *b* 23 Aug 1953; *Educ* Eton, Jesus Coll Cambridge (BA); *m* 13 Oct 1979, Lucille, *née* de Zalduondo; 2 s (Henry b 1984, Frederick b 1989), 2 da (Zoe b 1982, Clementine b 1987); *Career* merchant banker; exec dir Credit Suisse First Boston Ltd until 1991, vice chm UBS Ltd 1991–; *Clubs* Hawks, City, Hurlingham, Royal Automobile; *Style—* Richard Briance, Esq; ✉ The Old House, Holland Street, London W8 4NA (☎ 0171 937 2113); UBS Ltd, 100 Liverpool Street, London EC2M 2RH (☎ 0171 901 1983)

BRIANT, (Anne) Gillian; da of Sir John Fletcher-Cooke, CMG (d 1989), and Alice Elizabeth, *née* Egner; *b* 12 Nov 1953; *Educ* Cheltenham, Univ of Bristol (BA), Univ of Oxford (PGCE); *m* 30 Sept 1978, Nicholas Adrian Briant, s of Donald William Briant, of Callow End, Worcs; 3 da (Genevieve Elizabeth b Sept 1985, Catherine Diana b Dec 1989, Susanna Jane b Nov 1991); *Career* admitted slr 1979; ptnr Denton Hall 1984– (legal trg ptnr 1988–); memb Law Soc, fell Cncl Land Inst; *Recreations* squash, cooking; *Clubs* Hurlingham, Wimbledon Squash & Badminton; *Style—* Mrs Gillian Briant; ✉ Denton Hall, 5 Chancery Lane, Cliffords Inn, London EC4 (☎ 0171 242 1212, fax 0171 404 0087, telex 263567 BURGI)

BRICE, Geoffrey James Barrington Groves; QC (1979); s of Lt Cdr John Edgar Leonard Brice, MBE (d 1971), and Winifried Ivy, *née* Field; *b* 21 April 1938; *Educ* Magdalen Coll Sch Brackley, UCL; *m* 1963, Ann Nuala, da of William Connor (d 1958); 1 s (Paul); *Career* called to the Bar Middle Temple 1960; arbitrator Lloyd's 1978–, wreck cmmr 1979–, recorder of Crown Court 1980–, master of the Bench 1986, head of chambers; visiting prof of maritime law Tulane Univ New Orleans USA 1989–; memb Gen Cncl of the Bar 1988–89; chm: London Common Law and Commercial Bar Assoc 1988–89, Direct Professional Access Ctee 1988–89; *Books* Maritime Law of Salvage (1983, 2 edn 1993); author of numerous articles in legal journals; *Recreations* listening to music; *Clubs* Athenaeum, Hampshire; *Style—* Geoffrey Brice, Esq, QC; ✉ 15 Gayfere St, Smith Square, London SW1P 3HP (☎ 0171 799 3807); Queen Elizabeth Building, First Floor, Temple, London EC4Y 9BS (☎ 0171 353 9153, fax 0171 583 0126)

BRICE, (Ann) Nuala; *née* Connor; da of William Connor (d 1957), of Manchester, and Rosaleen Gertrude, *née* Gilmartin (d 1991); *b* 22 Dec 1937; *Educ* Loreto Convent Manchester, UCL (LLB, LLM, PhD); *m* 1 June 1963, Geoffrey James Barrington Groves Brice, QC, s of Lt Cdr John Edgar Leonard Brice, MBE; 1 s (Paul Francis b 17 March 1964); *Career* admitted slr 1963 (awarded Stephen Heelis prize and John Peacock conveyancing prize); The Law Society: asst slr 1963, asst sec 1964, sr asst sec 1973, deptl sec 1982, asst sec-gen 1987–92; chm VAT and Duties Tbnls and dep special cmmr of taxes 1992–; visiting prof of law: Tulane Univ New Orleans 1990–, Univ of Natal 1996; Freeman City of London, Liveryman City of London Solicitors' Co; memb Law Soc 1963; *Recreations* reading, music, gardening; *Clubs* Univ Women's; *Style—* Mrs Nuala Brice; ✉ Yew Tree House, Spring Coppice, Lane End, Bucks HP14 3NU (☎ 01494 881810); 15 Gayfere Street, Smith Square, London SW1P 3HP (☎ 0171 799 3807)

BRICHTO, Rabbi Dr Sidney; s of Solomon Brichto (d 1991), of Jerusalem, and Rivka, *née* Frankel-Thomim (d 1972); *b* 21 July 1936; *Educ* NY Univ (BA, Phi Beta Kappa), Hebrew Union Coll NY (MA, MHL, DD), UCL (study fell); *m* 1, 1959, late Frances Goldstein; 1 da (Anne Eta b 11 Jan 1963), 1 s (Daniel S b 19 April 1966); m 2, 1971, Cathryn, da of Edward Goldhill; 2 s (Adam Haim b 20 May 1974, Jonathan James b 7 July 1978); *Career* assoc min Liberal Jewish Synagogue 1961–64, fndr princ Evening Inst for Study of Judaism 1962–65, exec vice pres and dir ULPS 1964–89, dir Joseph Levy Charitable Fndn 1989–; memb: Exec Cncl Leo Baeck Coll 1964–74, Exec and Forum Inst of Jewish Affrs 1992–; chm: Conf of Rabbis ULPS 1969–70 and 1974–75, Cncl of Reform and Liberal Rabbis 1974–76, Chief Rabbi's Consultative Ctee on Jewish-non-Jewish Rels 1976–78; fndr chm Advsy Ctee Israel Diaspora Tst 1982–, hon vice pres Nat Assoc of Bereavement Servs 1992–, govr Oxford Centre for Hebrew Studies 1994–; Hon DD Hebrew Union Coll Cincinnati Ohio 1984; *Books* Child's Bible (1957), Funny...You Don't Look Jewish - A Guide to Jews and Jewish Life (1994); *Recreations* reading and writing, writing letters to The Times, lunching; *Clubs* Athenaeum; *Style—* Rabbi Dr Sidney Brichto; ✉ The Joseph Levy Charitable Foundation, Pegasus House, 27–43 Sackville Street, London SW1 (☎ 0171 333 8111, fax 0171 333 0660)

BRICKWOOD, Prof Alan John; s of Robert James Brickwood (d 1988), of Hants, and Kathleen Agnes Brickwood (d 1978); *b* 16 Oct 1945; *Educ* Clapham Coll London, Central Sch of Art and Design (DipAD), Royal Coll of Art (MDes); *m* 4 Feb 1995, Dominique Ruth Louise, da of David Richard Nixon; 1 s from prev m (Benjamin James b 21 Nov 1971); *Career* research asst Human Scis and Advanced Technol Research Gp Loughborough Univ of Technol 1970–72, design and ergonomics conslt Loughborough Consultants 1972–74, fndr and co-dir Molehurst Ltd 1974–76, head of industl design Coventry Poly 1976–84, pro vice-chllr Staffordshire Univ 1993–95 (asst dir when Staffordshire Poly 1984–93), prof Dept of Design Brunel Univ 1996–, industl advsr Innovation Unit DTI 1996–; CNAA: chm Three Dimensional Design Bd 1981–84, memb Cncl and Gen Ctee 1984–87, chm Ctee for Art and Design 1984–90, chm CNAA/BTEC Art and Design Liaison Gp 1984–90, memb Strategy Gp 1986–87, memb Ctee for Academic Affrs 1987–90; HEFCE: memb Teaching Advsy Gp 1993–95, memb Advsy Gp on Continuing Vocational Educn 1994–95; chm Conf for Higher Educn in Art and Design (CHEAD) 1992–95; memb: Design Ctee RSA 1988–91, Cncl Polytechnics and Colls Funding Cncl (PCFC) 1988–93, Prince of Wales 'Partners in Innovation' Highgrove 1991, Educn and Trg Advsy Gp Design Cncl 1995, DTI Task Gp 'Action for Engrg' 1995–96, Staffordshire Mfrg Forum 1995–96; FRSA 1980, FCSD 1981; *Style—* Prof Alan Brickwood; ✉ Fortune House, New Road, Ham, Richmond upon Thames, Surrey TW10 7HZ; Innovation Unit, DTI, 151 Buckingham Palace Road, London SW1W 9SS (☎ 0171 215 1326, fax 0171 215 1997, compuserve 100437,1107)

BRICKWOOD, Sir Basil Greame; 3 Bt (UK 1927), of Portsmouth; s of Sir John Brickwood, 1 Bt; suc half bro, Sir Rupert Redvers Brickwood, 2 Bt, 1974; *b* 21 May 1923; *Educ* King Edward's GS Stratford, Clifton; *m* 1, 1947 (m dis), Betty Cooper; m 2, 1956, Shirley Anne, da of Richard Wallace Brown; 2 da (Tessa Anne b 1959, Gail Anne b 1963); *Heir* none; *Career* served WWII in RAF 1940–46; *Clubs* RAF; *Style—* Sir Basil Brickwood, Bt; ✉ c/o RAF Club, 128 Piccadilly, London W1V OPY

BRICKWOOD, Richard Ian; s of Basil Arthur Brickwood (d 1979), and Hilary Joan; *b* 22 Dec 1947; *Educ* Wesley Coll Dublin, Hele's GS Exeter Devon; *m* 6 March 1971, Susan Vanessa Mary, da of Donald Hugh Galpin (d 1971); 1 s (Stephen James b 1979), 1 da (Sarah Louise b 1977); *Career* Lloyds broker; md Marsh & McLennan Inc 1989; dir: CT Bowring (Insurance) Ltd 1985, Marsh & McLennan Finpro Ltd; *Recreations* sailing, gliding, canoeing, fishing; *Clubs* Lloyd's Yacht, Herts County Yacht, Cambridge Univ Gliding, Junior Offshore Group; *Style—* Richard I Brickwood, Esq; ✉ Swan House, Widford, Nr Ware, Herts SG12 8SJ (☎ 01279 842425, 0171 357 1202)

BRIDEN, Prof James Christopher; s of Henry Charles Timberlake Briden, of High Wycombe, and Gladys Elizabeth, *née* Jefkins; *b* 30 Dec 1938; *Educ* Royal GS High Wycombe, St Catherine's Coll Oxford (MA), Aust Nat Univ Canberra (PhD, DSc); *m* 20 July 1968, Caroline, da of Kenneth Gillmore (d 1988); 1 s (Benjamin b 1977), 1 da (Hannah b 1974); *Career* res fell Univs of: Rhodesia 1965–66, Oxford 1966–67, Birmingham 1967–68; Univ of Leeds: lectr 1968–73, reader 1973–75, prof of geophysics 1975–86, hon prof 1986–; Canadian Cwlth fell and visiting prof Univ of Western Ontario 1977–80, dir of Earth Sciences NERC 1986–94, NERC research prof Univ of Oxford 1994–; contrib over 80 geological and geophysical papers to learned jls; memb: Cncl Euro Geophysical Soc 1976–84, Cncl RAS 1978–79, Governing Cncl Int Seismological Centre 1979–83, NERC 1980–86, Cncl Geological Soc 1992–95; Murchison Medal Geological Soc 1984; FGS 1961, FRAS 1963, CGeol 1990, fell American Geophysical Union 1994; *Books* jt author of 2 books on past position of the continents; *Style—* Prof James Briden; ✉ Department of Earth Sciences, University of Oxford, Parks Road, Oxford OX1 3PR (☎ 01865 272049, fax 01865 376970)

BRIDGE, Andrew; s of Peter Bridge, and Roslyn Bridge; *b* 21 July 1952; *Educ* Port Regis Sch, Bryanston Sch, LAMDA, Theatre Projects London; *m* Susan Bridge; 2 s (Oliver b 1988, Alex b 1994), 1 da (Tessa (twin) b 1994); *Career* lighting designer; numerous projects incl: Siegfried and Roy spectacular (Mirage Hotel Las Vegas), Disneyland's Buffalo Bill's Wild West Show (France), Torvill and Dean, flood lighting Lloyds of London, designer to Shirley Bassey in Concert (for ten years); conslt Imagination (industrial and architectural lighting); memb: Assoc of Lighting Designers (Brit), United Scenic Artist (local 829, USA); *Theatre* UK credits incl: Carte Blanche, The Card, An Evening with Tommy Steele, Bing Crosby and Friends, Time, Oliver (also Broadway), The Boyfriend, Billy Bishop goes to War, Tomfoolery, Little Me, Blondel, The Hunting of the Snark, Five Guys Named Noe (also USA, Aust), Sunset Boulevard, Phantom of the Opera (also USA, Japan, Austria, Canada, Sweden, Germany, Aust, Switzerland, Holland), Joseph and the Amazing Technicolor Dreamcoat (also USA, Canada, Aust, Germany), Heathcliff; *Awards* for Phantom of the Opera incl: Tony Award, Drama Desk Award (NY), Outer Circle Critics' Award (NY), Dora Mavor Award (Canada), Los Angeles Critics' Award; for Sunset Boulevard incl: Tony Award, Los Angeles Critics' Award and Ovation Award; for Lloyds of London Nat Lighting Award; *Style—* Andrew Bridge, Esq; ✉ c/o Performing Arts Management, 6 Windmill Street, London W1P 1HF (☎ 0171 255 1362, fax 0171 631 4631)

BRIDGE, Very Rev Antony Cyprian (Tony); s of Cdr Cyprian Dunscomb Charles Bridge (d 1938), and Gladys, *née* Steel (d 1969); *b* 5 Sept 1914; *Educ* Marlborough, Royal Acad Sch of Art; *m* 1, 10 May 1937, Brenda Lois (d 1995), da of Dr Raymond Streatfeild; 1 s (Cyprian b 1955), 2 da (Victoria b 1944, Charlotte b 1946); m 2, 1 Dec 1995, Diana Joyce, da of Charles Readhead; *Career* served WWII, demobbed Maj 1945; subsequently artist and painter; ordained: deacon 1955, priest 1956; curate Hythe Kent 1955–58, vicar Christ Church Lancaster Gate London 1958–68, dean of Guildford 1968–86, dean emeritus 1986; FSA 1980; *Books* Images of God (1960), Theodora: Portrait in a Byzantine Landscape (1978), The Crusades (1980), Suleiman the Magnificent (1983), One Man's Advent (1985), Richard the Lionheart (1989); *Recreations* birdwatching; *Style—* The Very Rev A C Bridge, FSA; ✉ 34 London Rd, Deal, Kent CT14 9TE (☎ 01304 366792)

BRIDGE, Christopher John; s of Lt-Col J E Bridge, OBE, TD (d 1983), and Jeanne, *née* Pryor; *b* 30 April 1948; *Educ* Mount House Sch Tavistock, Prior Park Coll Bath, Univ of Aberdeen (LLB); *m* 1976, Caroline, da of John Perchard; 2 da (Claire b 7 Aug 1981, Helen b 13 Aug 1984); *Career* industl rels asst Rolls Royce Glasgow 1968–71, sr personnel offr BBC 1971–77; dist personnel offr: Kensington Chelsea and Westminster AHA 1977–82, Victoria Health Authy 1982–86; assoc gen mangr Charing Cross Hosp 1986–88, gen mangr Mental Health Unit North East Essex Health Authy 1988–91, chief exec NE Essex Mental Health NHS Tst 1991–; govr Colchester Inst of Higher and Further Educn 1990; MIPM 1971; *Recreations* cricket, golf, skiing; *Style—* Christopher Bridge, Esq; ✉ North East Essex Mental Health NHS Trust, Severalls Hospital, Boxted Rd, Colchester, Essex CO4 5HG (☎ 01206 852271, fax 01206 844435)

BRIDGE, Prof John William; s of Harry Bridge (d 1985), of Crewkerne, Somerset, and Rebecca, *née* Lilley (d 1983); *b* 2 Feb 1937; *Educ* Crewkerne Sch Somerset, Univ of Bristol (LLB, LLM, PhD); *m* 28 July 1962, Janet Faith, da of Horace George Attew Hearn (d 1985), of Crewkerne, Somerset; 1 da (Susan b 1968); *Career* visiting prof and sr Fulbright scholar Coll of William and Mary 1977–78; Univ of Exeter: lectr then sr lectr 1961–74, prof of public law 1974–, dean Faculty of Law 1979–82, head of Dept of Law 1983–88, dep vice-chllr 1992–94, sr dep vice-chllr 1994–96; visiting prof: Univ of Connecticut 1985 and 1991, Univ of Fribourg/Suisse 1990, Univ of Mauritius 1987; visiting fell All Souls Coll Oxford 1988–89; Fulbright scholar 1991–92; memb: Int Acad of Comparative Law, Hamlyn Tst, Cncl Int Assoc of Constitutional Law, Cncl of UK Nat Ctee for Comparative Law (chm 1992–), Editorial Bd Euro Law Review, Exec Ctee Int Assoc of Legal Science, Scientific Ctee Inst of Fedm Fribourg Switzerland; pres Exeter Musical Soc 1983–88; memb Soc of Public Teachers of Law 1961; *Books* European Legislation (with E Freeman, 1975), Law and Institutions of the European Union (with D Lasok, 6 edn 1994); *Recreations* singing in choirs, local history, gardening; *Clubs* Royal Over-Seas League;

Style— Prof John Bridge; ✉ 8 Pennsylvania Close, Exeter, Devon EX4 6DJ (☎ 01392 54576); Faculty of Law, University of Exeter, Amory Building, Rennes Drive, Exeter, Devon EX4 4RJ (☎ 01392 263370, fax 01392 263196, telex 42894 EXUNIV G, e-mail J.W.Bridge@exeter.ac.uk)

BRIDGE OF HARWICH, Baron (Life Peer UK 1980); Nigel Cyprian Bridge; kt (1968), PC (1975); s of Cdr Cyprian Dunscombe Charles Bridge, RN (d 1938); bro of Very Rev Antony Cyprian Bridge, *qv*, former Dean of Guildford; *b* 26 Feb 1917; *Educ* Marlborough; *m* 1944, Margaret, da of Leonard Heseltine Swinbank, of Weybridge, Surrey; 1 s, 2 da; *Career* barr 1947–68, High Court judge 1968–75, Lord Justice of Appeal 1975–80, Lord of Appeal in Ordinary 1980–92; chm Permanent Security Cmmn 1982–85; *Style*— The Rt Hon Lord Bridge of Harwich, PC; ✉ c/o House of Lords, London SW1A 0PW

BRIDGEMAN, Viscountess; (Victoria) Harriet Lucy; da of Ralph Meredyth Turton, TD (d 1988), of Kildale Hall, Whitby, N Yorks, and Mary Blanche, *née* Chetwynd-Stapylton; *b* 30 March 1942; *Educ* privately, St Mary's Sch Wantage, Trinity Coll Dublin (MA); *m* 10 Dec 1966, 3 Viscount Bridgeman, *qv*; 4 s; *Career* exec ed The Masters 1966–68; ed: Discovering Antiques 1968–70, series Going, Going, Gone (Sunday Times Colour Magazine) 1973; fndr and md The Bridgeman Art Library Ltd 1971–; company sec British Assoc of Picture Libraries and Agencies; *Books* author and ed of numerous books incl: The Encyclopaedia of Victoriana, The Illustrated Encyclopaedia of Needlework, The Last Word, Society Scandals, Guide to Gardens of Europe; *Recreations* reading, work, family, travelling; *Clubs* Chelsea Arts (hon memb); *Style*— The Viscountess Bridgeman; ✉ 19 Chepstow Rd, London W2 5BP (☎ 0171 727 4065/5400, fax 0171 792 8509); Watley House, Sparsholt, Winchester, Hants SO21 2LU (☎ and fax 01962 776297)

BRIDGEMAN, John Stuart; TD, DL (Oxon 1989); s of James Alfred George Bridgeman (d 1961), of Whitchurch, Cardiff, and Edith Celia, *née* Watkins (d 1994); *b* 5 Oct 1944; *Educ* Whitchurch Sch Cardiff, Univ Coll Swansea (BSc); *m* 1967, Lindy Jane, da of Sidney Fillmore, of Gidea Park, Essex; 3 da (Victoria b 1972, Philippa b 1974, Annabel b 1980); *Career* Alcan Industries 1966, Aluminium Co of Canada 1969, Alcan Australia 1970, commercial dir Alcan (UK) Ltd 1977–80, vice pres (Europe) Alcan Basic Raw Materials 1978–82, divnl md British Alcan Aluminium plc 1983–91 (divnl md Alcan Aluminium (UK) Ltd 1981–83), dir of corp planning Alcan Aluminium Ltd Montreal 1992–93, md British Alcan Aluminium plc 1993–95; memb Monopolies and Mergers Cmmn 1990–95, DG Office of Fair Trading 1995–; visiting prof of mgmnt Keele Univ 1992–; tstee Magnesium Indust Cncl 1976–80, chm Aluminium Extruders' Assoc 1987–88 (memb Cncl 1982–91), vice pres Aluminium Fedn 1995 (memb Bauxite Advsy Gp 1977–81); US Aluminium Association prize winner 1988; chm North Oxon Business Gp 1984–92, govr North Oxon Coll 1985– (chm 1989), chm Enterprise Cherwell Ltd 1985–91; memb Bd Heart of England TEC 1990–, tstee Oxon Community Fndn 1996–, dir Oxford Orchestra da Camera 1996–; vice pres Canada-UK C of C 1995–, memb Cncl Canada-UK Colloquia; TA and Reserve Forces: cmmnd 1978, QOY 1981–84, Maj REME (V) 1985–94, Staff Coll 1986, memb Oxon and E Wessex TAVRA 1985–, memb Nat Employer Liaison Ctee for Reserve Forces 1992–, Hon Col 5 (Queen's Own Oxfordshire Hussars) Sqdn 39 (Skinners) Signal Regt 1996; memb Def Sci Advsy Cncl 1991–94; High Sheriff for Co of Oxon 1995; CIMgt, FRGS, FRSA, FInstD, AMIPM; *Recreations* Oxfordshire affairs, Territorial Army, gardening, shooting, skiing; *Clubs* Glamorgan County Cricket; *Style*— John S Bridgeman, TD, DL; ✉ Director General, Office of Fair Trading, Field House, Bream's Buildings, London EC4A 1PR (☎ 0171 269 8920, fax 0171 269 8966)

BRIDGEMAN, June; CB (1990); da of Gordon Forbes, and Elsie, *née* Gibb; *b* 26 June 1932; *Educ* Bromley HS GPDST, Westfield Coll Univ of London (BA); *m* 1958, John Michael Bridgeman; 4 da (Anne Clare b 1959, Teresa Mary b 1961, Imogen Lucy b 1966, Cressida Alice b 1969), 1 s (Francis Michael b 1968); *Career* civil servant 1954–90: various positions in Bd of Trade, Dept of Econ Affairs, Prices and Incomes Bd, DOE, Central Policy Review Staff Cabinet Office, under sec Dept of Tport 1979–90; dep chair and cmmr Equal Opportunities Cmmn 1991–94; fell Queen Mary and Westfield Coll Univ of London 1994–; vice pres Fawcett Soc 1994–; memb Cncl: Nat Cncl for One Parent Families 1994–, Girls' Public Day Sch Tst (GPDST) 1994–; govr: The Skinners' Sch for Boys Tunbridge Wells 1984–95, Bromley HS for Girls 1992–; tstee Rees Jeffries Fund 1991–; FRSA 1991; *Recreations* Soroptimism, piano accordion, opera, gardening; *Style*— Mrs June Bridgeman, CB; ✉ Bridge House, Culverden Park Road, Tunbridge Wells, Kent TN4 9QX (☎ and fax 01892 525578)

BRIDGEMAN, 3 Viscount (UK 1929); Robin John Orlando Bridgeman; s of Brigadier Hon Geoffrey John Orlando Bridgeman, MC (d 1974, 2 s of 1 Viscount Bridgeman, sometime Home Sec & First Lord of the Admlty), and Mary Meriel Gertrude (d 1974), da of Rt Hon Sir George Talbot, a High Court Judge; suc his uncle, 2 Viscount 1982; *b* 5 Dec 1930; *Educ* Eton; *m* 10 Dec 1966, (Victoria) Harriet Lucy; 3 da of Ralph Meredyth Turton, TD (d 1988), of Kildale Hall, Whitby; 4 s; *Heir* s, Hon William Caspar Orlando b 15 Aug 1968; *Career* 2 Lt Rifle Bde 1950–51; CA 1958; ptnr Henderson Crosthwaite & Co Stockbrokers 1973–86; dir: Guinness Mahon & Co Ltd 1988–90, Nestor-BNA plc 1989–94, SPLIT PLC 1996–; dir The Bridgeman Art Library Ltd 1972–; chm Asset Management Investment Co PLC 1994–; Reed's Sch: pres Fndn Appeal 1992–93, govr 1994–, chm 1995–; special tstee Hammersmith Hospitals NHS Trust (formerly Hammersmith and Queen Charlotte's Special Health Authority) 1986–, chm Friends of Lambeth Palace Library; treasurer: Florence Nightingale Aid in Sickness Trust 1995–, New England Company 1996–; Knight SMO Malta; *Recreations* gardening, skiing, shooting, music; *Clubs* MCC, Beefsteak; *Style*— The Rt Hon the Viscount Bridgeman; ✉ 19 Chepstow Rd, London W2 5BP (☎ 0171 727 5400, fax 0171 792 9178); Watley House, Sparsholt, Winchester SO21 2LU (☎ and fax 01962 776297)

BRIDGER, David Wilson; s of Marcus Bridger, and Rosemary, *née* Wilson; *b* 15 Oct 1944; *Educ* Wyggeston Boys Sch, Univ of Bristol (BA); *m* 6 Jan 1968, Elizabeth Ann, da of Ernest Tapson; 1 s (Thomas Wilson b 6 Aug 1976), 2 da (Katherine Jane b 19 Sept 1972, Susanne Mary b 18 April 1975); *Career* accountant; Price Waterhouse: joined 1966, mangr 1972, ptnr 1978, ptnr i/c UK Litigation and Special Investigation Servs 1992–; auditing prize in ACA final exams; FCA 1980 (ACA 1970); *Recreations* church, watching sport; *Style*— David Bridger, Esq; ✉ Price Waterhouse, Southwark Towers, 32 London Bridge Street, London SE1 9SY (☎ 0171 939 3000, fax 0171 939 5550)

BRIDGER, Rev Canon Gordon Frederick; s of Dr John Dell Bridger (d 1955), and Hilda, *née* Piddington (d 1968); *b* 5 Feb 1932; *Educ* Christ's Hosp Horsham, Selwyn Coll Cambridge (BA, MA), Ridley Hall Cambridge; *m* 29 Sept 1962, Elizabeth Doris, da of Rev Canon Thomas Francis Cecil Bewes, of Southgate, London; 3 da (Rachel b 1963, Sarah b 1965, Mary b 1969); *Career* curate: Islington Parish Church 1956–60, Holy Sepulchre Church Cambridge 1960–62; vicar St Mary North End Fulham 1962–69, chaplain St Thomas's Episcopal Church Edinburgh 1969–76, rector Holy Trinity Church Heigham Norwich 1976–87, rural dean Norwich (South) 1981–86, examining chaplain to Bishop of Norwich 1981–86, emeritus canon Norwich Cathedral 1988– (hon canon 1984–87); princ Oak Hill Theol Coll 1987–96, dir Open Theological Coll 1993–; memb Principal's Conf 1987–; fell Coll of Preachers 1996–; *Books* The Man from Outside (1969), A Day that Changed the World (1975), A Bible Study Commentary (1985); *Recreations* music, sport, reading, walking; *Clubs* Christ's Hosp; *Style*— The Rev Canon Gordon Bridger; ✉ The Elms, 4 Common Lane, Sheringham, Norfolk NR26 8PL (☎ 01263 823522)

BRIDGES, Alan James Stuart; *b* 28 Sept 1927; *Educ* Holt HS Shrewsbury, Rhyl GS, RADA London (Dip RADA); *m* 31 July 1954, Eileen Middleton, da of Ridgeway Proctor Morton Brown (d 1965), of Newcastle and London; 1 s (Adam Patrick Ridgeway b 1965), 1 da (Emma Ann b 1962); *Career* film, theatre and television director; Army serv Capt; work incl The Edwardians (West End), Ghosts (RSC), Come As You Are (West End), The Father (BBC), The Intrigue, The Idiot, Great Expectations, Les Miserables, Let's Murder Vivaldi, The Lie (BAFTA Award), Traitor (BAFTA Award), Crown Matrimonial (BAFTA Award), Saturday Sunday Monday; films incl: The Hireling (Gold Palm Cannes Film Festival 1973), The Return of the Soldier (Golden Globe Award, USA), Puddinhead Wilson, Displaced Person (Emmy Award, USA), The Shooting Party, Pig Robinson (TV film); *Recreations* reading, music, theatre, film and sport; *Clubs* Garrick; *Style*— Alan Bridges, Esq; ✉ 2B High Street, Shepperton, Middlesex TW7 9AW

BRIDGES, Dewi Morris; *see:* Swansea and Brecon, Bishop of

BRIDGES, Prof James Wilfrid (Jim); s of Wilfrid Edward Seymour Bridges (d 1994), of Cuxton, nr Rochester, Kent, and Mary Winifred, *née* Cameron (d 1987); *b* 9 Aug 1938; *Educ* Bromley GS, King's Coll London (BSc), St Mary's Hosp Med Sch London (PhD), Univ of London (DSc); *Career* lectr St Mary's Hosp Med Sch London 1962–68; Univ of Surrey: reader in biochemistry 1968–78, dir Robens Inst of Industl and Environmental Health and Safety 1978–95, prof of toxicology 1979–, dean Faculty of Sci 1988–92, dir Euro Inst of Health Scis 1995–; visiting prof: Univ of Texas 1973 and 1979, Univ of Rochester NY 1974, Centro de Investigacion y de Estudios Avanzados Mexico 1991; visiting sr scientist Nat Inst of Environmental Health Sciences USA 1976; chm Br Toxicology Soc 1980–81, first pres Fedn of Euro Socs of Toxicology 1985–88, memb Exec Ctee Euro Soc of Biochemical Pharmacology 1983–89, fndr Euro Drug Metabolisms Workshops; memb: Veterinary Products Ctee MAFF 1982–, Advsy Ctee on Toxic Substances HSE 1986–89, Air Soil and Water Contaminants Ctee DHSS/DOE 1984–90, UK Shadow Gp on Toxicology DHSS 1984–, Watch Ctee HSE 1987–, Food Safety and Applied Res Consultative Ctee 1989–90, Advsy Ctee on Irradiated and Novel Foods MAFF 1982–88, Maj Hazards Ctee Working Party (HSE) 1982–84, Scientific Ctee on Animal Nutrition EEC 1990–, Corporation of Farnborough Coll of Technology 1992–; Inst of Biology: chm Food Policy Gp 1990–93, memb Policy Ctee 1993–; elected hon memb Soc of Occupational Med 1989, elected fell of Collegium Ramazzini 1990, MRCPath 1984, CChem, FRSC, FIBiol, CBiol 1981, MInstEnvSci 1980, FRSA 1989, FIOSH 1990; *Publications incl* Progress in Drug Metabolism (ed with Dr L Chasseaud, Vols 1–10), Watershed 89 The Future for Water Quality in Europe Vols I and II (ed with M L Richardson and D Wheeler), Animals and Alternatives in Toxicology (ed with M Balls and J Southee), Losing Hope: The Environment and Health in Russia (with Dr Olga Bridges, 1996); jt ed of 17 books and over 300 res pubns and reviews in scientific jls; *Recreations* running, theatre, concerts, travel; *Style*— Prof Jim Bridges; ✉ European Institute of Health and Medical Sciences, University of Surrey, Guildford, Surrey GU2 5XH (☎ 01483 259210, fax 01483 503517)

BRIDGES, Hon Mark Thomas; er s and h of 2 Baron Bridges, GCMG, *qv*; *b* 25 July 1954; *Educ* Eton, Corpus Christi Coll Cambridge; *m* 1978, Angela Margaret, da of J L Collinson, of Mansfield, Notts; 1 s (Miles Edmund Farrer b 1 July 1992), 3 da (Venetia Rachel Lucy b 21 Feb 1982, Camilla Frances Iona b 22 June 1985, Drusilla Katharine Anne b 12 July 1988); *Career* slr; dir The Abinger Hall Estate Company 1984–92, ptnr Farrer & Co 1985–; memb Cncl Royal Sch of Church Music 1989–, treas The Bach Choir 1992–, special tstee Middx Hosp 1992–; *Recreations* sailing (yacht 'Spirit of Man'), reading, music; *Clubs* Brooks's, House of Lords' Yacht; *Style*— The Hon Mark Bridges; ✉ 66 Lincoln's Inn Fields, London WC2A 3LH

BRIDGES, Dame Mary Patricia; DBE (1981); *m* 1951, Bertram Marsdin (d 1988); 1 s (1 da decd); *Career* nat chm Royal Br Legion Women's Section 1992–95; tstee and fndr: Exmouth Lympstone Hospice Care (currently pres), Exmouth Adventure Tst for Girls; fndr chm (now pres) Exmouth Cncl of Voluntary Serv, memb Exec St Loyes Coll Exeter, fndr pres Exmouth Ctee of Br Heart Fndn, pres The Abbeyfield (Exmouth) Soc Ltd, memb House Ctee Dunkirk Memorial House; hon life memb Devon Cricket League; *Recreations* cricket; *Clubs* Exmouth CC (pres), Retford CC (life memb); *Style*— Dame Mary Bridges, DBE; ✉ Walton House, 3 Fairfield Close, Exmouth, Devon EX8 2BN (☎ 01395 265317)

BRIDGES, Dr Paul Kenneth; TD (1977); s of Albert Charles Bridges (d 1955), of Stroud, Glos, and Alice Elizabeth, *née* Paul (d 1973); *b* 24 July 1931; *Educ* Marling Sch Stroud Glos, UCL, UCH (MB BS, MD, PhD, DPM, MRCS, LRCP, FRCPsych); *Career* RAMC 1957–60: Lt, Capt, Maj; sr psychiatric registrar KCH 1963–65, sr lectr in psychiatry The Royal Free Hosp 1965–70 (res fell and psychiatric registrar 1960–63), conslt psychiatrist Guy's Hosp 1975–96, sr lectr in psychiatry Utd Med and Dental Schs Guy's and St Thomas' Hosp Univ of London 1975–96; conslt psychiatrist: The Geoffrey Knight Nat Unit for Affective Disorders, Regnl Neurosurgical and Neurological Units at Brook Gen Hosp London 1970–95 (at Maudsley and King's Coll Hosps London 1995–); Liveryman Worshipful Soc of Apothecaries 1980, Freeman City of London 1986; memb BMA, FRSM 1961 (pres Section of Psychiatry 1983–84), memb Br Assoc for Psychopharmacology (hon treas 1974–79, hon sec 1981–83); *Books* Psychiatric Emergencies: Diagnosis and Management (1971), Psychiatry for Students (1989); *Recreations* visiting British country houses and classical sites abroad; *Clubs* Royal Automobile; *Style*— Dr Paul Bridges, TD; ✉ Keats House, Guy's Hospital, London SE1 9RT (☎ 0171 955 5000, fax 0171 955 4059)

BRIDGES, Sir Phillip Rodney; kt (1973), CMG (1967); eldest s of Capt Sir Ernest Arthur Bridges (d 1953), of Bedford, and Agnes Ida, *née* Conyers; *b* 9 July 1922; *Educ* Bedford Sch; *m* 1, 1951 (m dis 1961), Rosemary Ann, da of late Rev Canon Arthur Herbert Streeten, MC, of Bury St Edmunds; 2 s, 1 da; *m* 2, 1962, Angela Mary, da of Frederick George Dearden, of Appledore, and wid of James Huyton; *Career* Capt RA, served UK, W Africa, India and Burma 1941–47, Acting Maj TA (Beds Yeo) 1947–54; admitted slr England 1951, called to the Bar Gambia 1954; slr gen Gambia 1961, QC (Gambia) 1964, attorney gen Gambia 1964, chief justice Gambia 1968–83; *Clubs* Travellers'; *Style*— Sir Phillip Bridges, CMG; ✉ Weavers, Coney Weston, Bury St Edmunds, Suffolk IP31 1HG (☎ 01359 221316)

BRIDGES, Cdre Richard Antony Yeoward; s of Antony Gifford Bridges (d 1976), of Castletownsend, Co Cork, and Margaret Champernoune Denny, *née* Townsend (d 1976); *b* 14 Nov 1942; *Educ* Gordonstoun; *m* 23 Jan 1976, Helen Macgregor, da of James Gardner Struthers (d 1979), of Ardmaddy Castle, by Oban, Argyll; 1 s (Tom b 1977), 1 da (Lucy b 1979); *Career* RN 1960–95; HMS Eastbourne Far East Fleet 1962–64, HMS London 1964, Lt 1965, flying trg 1965, gained wings and joined 848 Naval Air Sqdn seeing serv in Aden 1966, qualified as helicopter instr 1968, Lt Cdr HMS Endurance 1972, RN Staff Course 1974, CO Univ of Aberdeen RN Unit 1975, CO 845 Naval Air Sqdn 1977–78, Cdr 1982, SO Ops FOST 1980–82, desk offr MOD 1982, CO HMS Jupiter involved in evacuation of UK and foreign nationals from Aden 1986, Capt 1986, asst dir Central Staff MOD, CO HMS Intrepid 1988–90, RCDS 1991–92, Cdre Amphibious Warfare 1992–94, Capt HMS Raleigh 1994–95, ret; project dir PSI Ltd 1996–; memb IISS 1976; Younger Brother Trinity House; Freeman City of London, Liveryman Worshipful Co of Farriers; *Recreations* equestrian (eventing), sailing, fishing; *Clubs* Farmers; *Style*— Cdre Richard Bridges, RN; ✉ Gears Mill, Shaftesbury, Dorset SP7 0LT (☎ and fax 01747 852825)

BRIDGES, 2 Baron (UK 1957), of Headley, Co Surrey and of St Nicholas-at-Wade, Co Kent; Sir Thomas Edward Bridges; GCMG (1988, KCMG 1983, CMG 1975); s of 1 Baron Bridges, KG, GCB, GCVO, MC (d 1969), and Hon Katherine, da of 2 Baron Farrer (d 1986); *b* 27 Nov 1927; *Educ* Eton, New Coll Oxford (MA); *m* 1953, Rachel Mary, da of Sir Henry Bunbury, KCB (d 1968), of Ewell, Surrey; 2 s, 1 da; *Heir* s, Hon Mark Bridges; *Career* entered HM Foreign Serv 1951; served: Bonn, Berlin, Rio de Janeiro, Athens, Moscow, Foreign Office; private sec (overseas affrs) to PM 1972–74, min (commercial) Washington 1975–79, dep sec FCO 1979–83, ambass to Italy 1983–87, ret 1987; memb Select Ctee on Euro Communities House of Lords 1988–92 and 1994–, ind bd memb The Securities and Futures Authority 1989–; chm: UK Nat Ctee for UNICEF 1989–, British-Italian Soc 1991–; *Style*— The Rt Hon the Lord Bridges, GCMG; ✉ 56 Church Street, Orford, Woodbridge, Suffolk IP12 2NT

BRIDGES-ADAMS, (John) Nicholas William; s of William Bridges-Adams, CBE (d 1965), and Marguerite Doris Wellsted (d 1963); *b* 16 Sept 1930; *Educ* Stowe, Oriel Coll Oxford (MA, DipEd); *m* 1962, Jenifer Celia Emily, da of David Hugh Sandell, FRCS; *Career* cmmnd RA 1949, RAFVR 1951; Flying Offr 2623 Sqdn RAuxAF Regt 1980–82; called to the Bar Lincoln's Inn 1958 (Gray's Inn 1979), recorder Crown Court 1972–, head of Chambers 1979–92; memb: Exec Ctee Soc of Cons Lawyers 1967–69 (chm Criminal Law Sub Ctee 1983–92), Ctee London Branch Chartered Inst of Arbitrators 1995–, London Court of Int Arbitration; supporting memb London Maritime Arbitrators' Assoc; Parly candidate (C) West Bromwich West Oct 1974; govr St Benedict's Upper Sch 1980–83; memb: RIIA, IISS; FCIArb; *Recreations* shooting, sailing, skiing; *Clubs* Savile, Garrick; *Style*— Nicholas Bridges-Adams, Esq; ✉ Fornham Cottage, Fornham St Martin, Bury St Edmunds, Suffolk IP31 1SP; 2 Field Court, Gray's Inn, London WC1R 5BB (☎ 0171 405 6114, fax 0171 831 6112)

BRIDGEWATER, Adrian Alexander; s of Maj Philip Alexander Clement Bridgewater (d 1980), of Southdown, Crease Lane, Tavistock, Devon, and Hon Ursula Vanda Maud Vivian (d 1984); *b* 24 July 1936; *Educ* Eton, Magdalene Coll Cambridge (MA); *m* 1, 11 April 1958 (m dis 1968), Charlotte, da of Rev Michael Ernest Christopher Pumphrey (d 1982); 1 s (Thomas Michael George b 12 Nov 1963), 2 da (Emma Mary b 23 Dec 1960, Sophy Charlotte b 31 July 1962); m 2, 7 Nov 1969, Lucy Le Breton, da of Sir Basil Bartlett, 2 Bt (d 1986); 1 s (Benjamin Hardington b 20 March 1979), 2 da (Nancy Le Breton b 10 Aug 1971, Daisy Maud b 27 Jan 1973); *Career* founder and dir CRAC 1963–74, founder and chm Hobsons Press Ltd 1974–87; chm: Hobsons Publishing PLC 1987–92, Johansens Ltd 1987–92, Homes Directories Ltd 1993–, Connect Publishing Ltd 1993–, ECCTIS 2000 Ltd 1991–; hon treas Papworth Gp 1989–; memb Cncl: Inst for Manpower Studies 1966–67, Open Univ 1974–80, RCA 1979–81, Nat Inst Careers Education and Counselling 1966–92, VSO 1980–82, Br Sch Osteopathy 1989–91, Careers Res and Advsy Centre (CRAC) 1993–, Ind Schs Careers Orgn 1994–; govr Kings Coll Choir Sch Cambridge 1988–92; *Recreations* walking, surfing, racing; *Clubs* Garrick, White's; *Style*— Adrian Bridgewater, Esq; ✉ Manor Farm, Great Eversden, Cambs CB3 7HW (☎ 01223 263229); 2 Carlton Mansions, Randolph Avenue, London W9 1NP

BRIDGEWATER, Allan; *b* 26 Aug 1936; *Educ* Wyggeston GS Leicester; *m* Janet; 3 da; *Career* Norwich Union Insurance Group: joined 1952, gen mangr Norwich Union Fire Insurance Society Ltd 1984–89 (dep gen mangr 1983–84), dir main group bds 1985–, gp chief exec 1989–; dir Riggs AP Bank Ltd; chm: Endeavour Trg, ABI 1993–95; pres Chartered Insur Inst 1989–90, tstee and treas Duke of Edinburgh's Study Conf, tstee Indust in Educn, govr Norwich HS; Liveryman Worshipful Co of Insurers; *Style*— Allan Bridgewater, Esq; ✉ Norwich Union Insurance Group, 8 Surrey Street, Norwich NR1 3PQ (☎ 01603 622200)

BRIDGWATER, Prof John; s of Eric Bridgwater, of Solihull, and Mabel Mary, *née* Thornley; *b* 10 Jan 1938; *Educ* Solihull Sch, Univ of Cambridge (MA, PhD, ScD), Princeton Univ (MSE); *m* 29 Dec 1962, Diane, da of Arthur Edgarton Tucker (d 1965); 1 s (Eric Arthur b 1966), 1 da (Caroline Mary b 1967); *Career* chemical engr Courtaulds Ltd 1961–64; Univ of Cambridge 1964–71: demonstrator and lectr in chemical engrg, fell St Catharine's Coll; visiting assoc prof Univ of BC 1970–71; Univ of Oxford 1971–80: fell Balliol Coll (former fell Hertford Coll), lectr in engrg sci; dean Faculty of Engrg Univ of Birmingham 1989–92 (prof 1980–93, head Sch of Chemical Engrg 1983–89); currently Shell prof of chemical engrg and head Dept of Chemical Engrg Univ of Cambridge (fell St Catharine's Coll); visiting prof Univ of Calif at Berkeley 1992–93; vice-pres Instn of Chemical Engrs; exec ed Chemical Engrg Sci 1983–; memb Engrg Bd SERC 1986–89; FIChemE 1974, FEng 1987; *Recreations* travel, gardening, walking; *Style*— Prof John Bridgwater, FEng; ✉ Department of Chemical Engineering, University of Cambridge, Pembroke Street, Cambridge CB2 3RA (☎ 01223 334799, fax 01223 334796)

BRIDLE, Prof Ronald Jarman; s of Raymond Bridle (d 1980), and Dorothy Ada, *née* Jarman (d 1968); *b* 27 Jan 1930; *Educ* Jones West Monmouth Sch for Boys, Univ of Bristol (BSc); *m* Beryl Eunice, *née* Doe; 2 da (Rachel Elizabeth b Oct 1956, Sian Isobel b Oct 1958); *Career* early career civil engrg works in UK and W Africa, project mangr Sheffield/Leeds Motorway 1962, dep county surveyor Cheshire 1966, dir Midland Road Construction Unit 1968, chief bridge engr MOT 1972, under sec (Highways) DOE, chief highway engr Dept of Tport 1977 (controller R & D 1980), dir of technol Mitchell Cotts plc 1983; hon prof Sch of Engrg Univ of Wales at Cardiff 1987–; former chm Building and Civil Engrg Cncl and memb Bd BSI, former memb Cncl ICE, memb Cncl Engrg Centre for Wales; former pres Inst of Highways and Transportation 1982 (Highways Award 1993), hon memb Br Nat Ctee PIARC; author of numerous publications in nat and int jls, keynote speaker S African and Aust nat confs; FICE 1968, FEng 1979; *Recreations* golf, oil painting; *Clubs* Pontypool Golf, Newport RFC; *Style*— Prof Ronald Bridle, FEng; ✉ Parsonage Farm, Kerrys Commander, Usk, Gwent NP5 1JU (☎ 01873 880929)

BRIDPORT, 4 Viscount (UK 1868); Alexander Nelson Hood; also Baron Bridport (I 1794) and 7 Duke of Brontë in Sicily (cr 1799 by Ferdinand IV, the 'Lazzarone' King of the Two Sicilies, largely for Nelson's role in exterminating the Parthenopean Republic). In 1801 a Br Royal Licence was issued to Admiral Lord Nelson allowing him to accept for himself and his heirs the Dukedom of Brontë; s of 3 Viscount (d 1969, fourth in descent from the union of 2 Baron Bridport (2 s of 2 Viscount Hood) and Lady Charlotte Nelson, da of 1 Earl and niece of the great Admiral), and Sheila Jeanne Agatha, *née* van Meurs (d 1996); *b* 17 March 1948; *Educ* Eton, Sorbonne; *m* 1, 1972 (m dis 1979), Linda Jacqueline, da of Lt-Col Vincent Rudolph Paravicini, of Nutley Manor, Basingstoke; 1 s (Hon Peregrine Alexander Nelson b 1974); m 2, 1979, Mrs Nina Rindt, da of Curt Lincoln; 1 s (Hon Anthony Nelson b 7 Jan 1983); *Heir* s, Hon Peregrine Alexander Nelson Hood b 30 Aug 1974; *Career* with Kleinwort Benson Ltd 1967–80, Robert Fraser & Ptnrs 1980–83, exec dir Chase Manhattan Ltd 1983–85, gen mangr Chase Manhattan Bank (Suisse) 1985–86, md Shearson Lehman Hutton Finance (Switzerland) 1986–90, managing ptnr Bridport & Cie SA 1991–; *Recreations* skiing, sailing; *Clubs* Brooks's, Royal Yacht Sqdn; *Style*— The Rt Hon the Viscount Bridport; ✉ Villa Jonin, 1261 Le Muids, Vaud, Switzerland (☎ 00 41 22 366 1705, fax 00 41 22 366 1898)

BRIEN, Alan; s of Ernest Brien, and Isabella, *née* Patterson; *b* 12 March 1925; *Educ* Bede GS Sunderland, Jesus Coll Oxford (BA); 2 previous m; m 3, 1973, Jill Sheila (d 1993), the writer Jill Tweedie, da of Patrick Graeme Tweedie, CBE (d 1990); *Career* served WWII Air Gunner RAF 1943–46; novelist and journlist; assoc ed Mini-Cinema 1950–52, courier 1952–53, film critic and columnist Truth 1953–54, TV critic The Observer 1954–55; film critic: New York corr Evening Standard 1954–58; drama critic and features ed The Spectator 1958–61; columnist: Daily Mail 1958–62, Sunday Dispatch 1962–63, Spectator 1963–65, New Statesman 1966–72, Punch 1972–84; political columnist Sunday Pictorial 1963–64, film critic Sunday Times 1976–84 (diarist 1967–75); regular broadcaster: radio 1952–, TV 1955–; IPC Critic of the Year 1966 and 1967; *Books* Domes of Fortune (essays, 1979), Lenin - The Novel (1988), And When Rome Falls (novel, 1995); *Style*— Alan Brien; ✉ 15 Marlborough Yard, Holloway Road London N19 4ND (☎ 0171 281 9640)

BRIEN, Nicolas Frederich; s of Hubert Barrie Brien, of London, and Ursula, *née* Pfaller; *b* 18 Jan 1962; *Educ* King's Coll Wimbledon, Coll for Distributive Trades London; *Career* Lerner & Grey June-Dec 1982, Grey Advertising 1983–84, Benton & Bowles 1984–85, WCRS 1985–89, BBJ Media Services 1989–92; Leo Burnett: exec media dir 1992–96, dep md 1994–96, md 1996–; memb Media Res Gp IPA; MInstD; *Recreations* polo, skiing, tennis, golf, squash, tae kwon do (former UK nat champion), theatre, ballet, opera, reading; *Clubs* RAC; *Style*— Nicolas Brien, Esq; ✉ Leo Burnett Ltd, The Leo Burnett Building, 60 Sloane Avenue, London SW3 3XB (☎ 0171 591 9111, fax 0171 591 9126/7)

BRIER, Norma; *b* 23 Dec 1949; *Educ* Henrietta Barnet Sch, Goldsmiths' Coll London (BA Sociology), LSE (MSc Social Policy and Social Admin, CQSW); *m* Sam Brier; 2 c; *Career* social worker and supervisor Student Unit London Borough of Camden 1971–76 (LSE 1973–74), pt/t lectr in social work and sociology and course organiser Counselling Skills for Teachers London Borough of Harrow 1976–83, charity work for learning-disabled children 1983–85; Ravenswood Fndn (now Norwood Ravenswood): joined as dir of community and social servs 1985, exec dir 1989–96, jt exec dir (following merger with Norwood) 1996–; memb Cncl SENSE; winner Prize for Leadership (Office for Public Mgmnt) 1994; *Recreations* cycling, tennis, gardening, theatre, cinema; *Style*— Mrs Norma Brier; ✉ Norwood Ravenswood, Broadway House, 80–82 Broadway, Stanmore, Middlesex HA7 4HB (☎ 0181 954 4555, fax 0181 420 6800)

BRIERLEY, Hon Mrs (Caroline); *née* Gordon Walker; da of Baron Gordon-Walker, CH, PC (d 1980); *b* 22 Dec 1937; *Educ* Cheltenham Ladies Coll, Lady Margaret Hall Oxford (BA); *m* 23 April 1960, David Brierley, *qv*, s of John Brierley (d 1965), of Durban, South Africa; 1 da (Margaret b 1970); *Career* economist; Int Sugar Cncl, Political and Economic Planning, head of Food and Services Unit Nat Economic Devpt Office, Henley Centre for Forecasting; lay asst Diocese of Gibraltar in Europe 1994–; *Books* Food Prices and The Common Market, The Making of European Policy, Textiles Industrial Review, Lifting Barriers to Trade, Work in the Countryside, Leisure Futures (ed), Chaplaincy of Aquitaine Report; *Recreations* travel, gardening, painting, making exotic jams and pickles; *Style*— The Hon Mrs Brierley; ✉ La Vieille Ferme, 24170 St Germain-de-Belvès, France (☎ 00 33 553 29 36 03)

BRIERLEY, Christopher Wadsworth; CBE (1987); s of Eric Brierley (d 1978), and Edna Mary, *née* Lister (d 1980); *b* 1 June 1929; *Educ* Whitgift Middle Sch Croydon; *m* 1, 24 Aug 1951 (m dis), Dorothy, da of Jack Scott (d 1987); 2 da (Lesley Jeanne b 1956, Alison Jane b 1958); m 2, 20 Nov 1984, Dilwen Marie, da of John Morgan (d 1969); *Career* Nat Serv 1947–49, Sgt RAEC, serv UK and BAOR; chief accountant: EMI Records Ltd 1960–68, British Gas E Midlands Region 1970–74; dir of fin: British Gas Eastern Region 1974–77, British Gas Corp 1977–80; dir of econ planning British Gas Corp 1980–82 (md 1982–87); dir: British Gas Corp 1984–86, British Gas plc 1986–89 (md resources and new business 1987–89); conslt World Bank 1990–94; *Recreations* music; *Style*— Christopher W Brierley, Esq, CBE; ✉ 6 Stobarts Close, Knebworth, Herts SG3 6ND (☎ 01438 814 988)

BRIERLEY, David; s of John Paul Brierley (d 1965), of SA, and Ruth Mary, *née* Richmond; *b* 30 July 1936; *Educ* Hilton Coll SA, Univ of Natal, Univ of Oxford (BA); *m* 23 April 1960, Caroline, see Hon Mrs Brierley, da of Baron Gordon-Walker, CH, PC (Life Peer, d 1980); 1 da (Margaret b 1970); *Career* teacher in France 1958–59, advertising 1960–75, author 1975–; *Books* Cold War (1979), Blood Group O (1980), Big Bear Little Bear (1981), Shooting Star (1983), Czechmate (1984), Skorpion's Death (1985), Snowline (1986), One Lives One Dies (1987), On Leaving a Prague Window (1995), The Horizontal Women (1996); *Style*— David Brierley, Esq; ✉ La Vieille Ferme, 24170 St Germain-de-Belvès, France (☎ 00 33 5 53 29 36 03)

BRIERLEY, David; CBE (1986); s of Ernest William Brierley (d 1982), of Romiley, Stockport, Cheshire, and Jessie, *née* Stanway (d 1991); *b* 26 July 1936; *Educ* Stockport GS, Clare Coll Cambridge (MA, CertEd); *m* 7 Dec 1962, Ann, da of Charles Rossell Fosbrooke Potter; 2 s (Benedict b 1964, Crispin b 1966); *Career* teacher 1959–61; Royal Shakespeare Theatre: stage mangr 1961–63, gen stage mangr 1963–66, asst to the dir 1966–68, gen mangr 1968–96, advsr dir 1996–; Hon DLitt; *Recreations* reading; *Style*— David Brierley, Esq, CBE; ✉ Tredenham Cottage, Tredenham Road, St Mawes, Truro, Cornwall TR2 5AN (☎ and fax 01326 270478); Royal Shakespeare Theatre, Stratford-upon-Avon, Warwicks CV37 6BB (☎ 01789 296 655, fax 01789 294 810)

BRIERS, Richard David; OBE (1989); s of Joseph Benjamin Briers (d 1980), and Morna Phyllis, *née* Richardson (d 1992); *b* 14 Jan 1934; *Educ* Ridgeways Co-Educnl Sch Wimbledon, RADA; *m* 24 Feb 1957, Ann Cuerton, da of Ronald Horace Davies (d 1980); 2 da (Katy Ann b 10 Aug 1963, Lucy Jane b 19 Aug 1967); *Career* actor 1955–; Nat Serv RAF 1951–53; London debut Gilt and Gingerbread (Duke of York's) 1959; *Theatre* incl: Arsenic and Old Lace 1965, Relatively Speaking 1966, The Real Inspector Hound 1968, Cat Among the Pigeons 1969, The Two of Us 1970, Butley 1972, Absurd Person Singular 1973, Absent Friends 1975, Middle Age Spread 1979, The Wild Duck 1980, Arms and the Man 1981, Run For Your Wife 1983, Why Me? 1985, The Relapse 1986, Twelfth Night 1987 (tv 1988), A Midsummer Night's Dream 1990, King Lear 1990, Wind in the Willows 1991, Uncle Vanya 1991, Home 1994; *Television* series incl: Brothers-in-Law, Marriage Lines, The Good Life, OneUpManShip, The Other One, Norman Conquests, Ever-Decreasing Circles, All In Good Faith; *Films* incl: Henry V 1989, Much Ado About Nothing 1992, Swansong 1993, Frankenstein 1994, In the Bleak Midwinter 1995, Hamlet 1996; *Books* Natter Natter (1981), Coward and Company (1987), A Taste of the Good Life (1995); *Recreations* gardening, reading; *Style*— Richard Briers, Esq, OBE; ✉ c/o Hamilton Asper Management, Ground Floor, 24 Hanway Street, London W1P 9DD (☎ 0171 636 1221, fax 0171 636 1226)

BRIGGS, Prof Anthony David Peach; s of Horace Briggs (d 1972), and Doris Lily, *née* Peach; *b* 4 March 1938; *Educ* King Edward VII Sch Sheffield, Trinity Hall Cambridge (BA, MA), Univ of London (PhD); *m* 28 July 1962, Pamela Anne, da of Harry Metcalfe, of Cookridge, Leeds; 1 s (Julian b 2 Jan 1974), 2 da (Fiona b 4 Nov 1966, Antonia 15 Aug 1970); *Career* Nat Serv 1956–58, trained as Russian interpreter CSC interpretership 1958; Univ of Bristol 1968–87: lectr in Russian, sr lectr, reader, head Russian Dept; prof of Russian language and lit Univ of Birmingham 1987–; memb Br Assoc for Slavonic and E Euro Studies; *Books* Mayakovsky, A Tragedy (1979), Alexander Pushkin: A Critical Study (1983), A Wicked Irony (Lermontov's A Hero of Our Time) (with Andrew Barratt, 1989), The Wild World (Pushkin, Nekrasov, Blok) (1990), Eugene Onegin (1992), Mikhail Lermontov: Commemorative Essays (1992); *Recreations* Mozart, housebuilding and restoration, country walking with large dogs; *Style*— Prof Anthony Briggs; ✉ Over Moreton, Breach Hill, Nempnett Thrubwell, Chew Stoke, Bristol BS18 8YA (☎ 01761 462143); Department of Russian Language & Literature, University of Birmingham, Edgbaston, Birmingham (☎ 0121 414 6043)

BRIGGS, Baron (Life Peer UK 1976); Asa Briggs; o s of William Walker Briggs (d 1952), of Keighley, and Jane Briggs; *b* 7 May 1921; *Educ* Keighley GS, Sidney Sussex Coll Cambridge (BA), LSE (BSc); *m* 1955, Susan Anne, da of Donald Ivor Banwell (d 1980), of Keevil, Wilts; 2 s, 2 da; *Career* served Intelligence Corps (Bletchley) 1942–45; historian and writer; prof of history Univ of Sussex 1961–76 (vice chllr 1967–76), provost Worcester Coll Oxford 1976–91, chllr Open Univ 1978–94; chm Cwlth of Learning 1988–93; Liveryman Worshipful Co of Spectacle Makers; FBA; *Awards* Marconi medal, French Academy of Architecture's medal for formation and teaching 1982, Snow medal 1991; *Recreations* travel; *Clubs* Beefsteak, Oxford and Cambridge; *Style*— The Rt Hon the Lord Briggs, FBA; ✉ The Caprons, Keere St, Lewes, E Sussex (☎ 01273 474704)

BRIGGS, David Muir; s of Maj Brian Ridsdale Briggs (d 1976), of Allt-Grianach Lochearnhead, and Elizabeth Hope, *née* Greenlees (d 1946); *b* 18 June 1944; *Educ* Ardvreck Sch Crieff Perthshire, Loretto Sch Musselburgh Midlothian; *m* 5 July 1974, Julie Marilyn, da of Milton George Webber, of 10 Sortie Port, Castlecrag, Sydney, Australia; 1 s (Ian b 6 Jan 1979), 1 da (Alison b 15 Nov 1976); *Career* qualified CA 1967, Peat Marwick Mitchell (Paris) 1967–70, ptnr Messrs Turner Hutton & Lawson 1977–77; dir: GN Fund Management Ltd 1977–82, J Rothschild Investment Management Ltd 1982–84, Murray Johnstone Ltd 1987–; *Recreations* fishing, golf, hill-walking, gardening, reading; *Clubs* Prestwick GC; *Style*— David Briggs, Esq; ✉ Claddoch, Gartocharn, Dunbartonshire G83 8NQ (☎ 0138 983 210); Murray Johnstone Ltd, 7 West Nile St, Glasgow (☎ 0141 226 3131, fax 0141 248 5420, telex 778667)

BRIGGS, Dr James Charles; s of Dering Thomas Briggs (d 1964), and Ivy Grace, *née* Muench; *b* 5 May 1933; *Educ* East Ham GS, St Thomas' Hosp Med Sch; *m* 14 Jan 1961, Waltraud Charlotte, da of Walter Schreck (d 1976), of Germany; 1 s (Robert James b 1963), 1 da (Nicola Charlotte b 1961); *Career* Nat Serv RAF 1951–53; lectr in clinical pathology St Thomas' Hosp 1960–66, conslt histopathologist Frenchay Hosp Bristol 1966–93, clinical teacher in pathology Univ of Bristol 1966–93; med referee City of Bristol 1985–; author of numerous pubns in jls; fell Hosp Conslts and Specialists Assoc, past hon sec UK Melanoma Study Gp, fndr and past coordinator UK Melanoma Histology Gp; *Recreations* flying radio controlled model aircraft; *Style*— Dr James Briggs; ✉ 194 Stoke Lane, Bristol BS9 3RU (☎ 0117 968 1415)

BRIGGS, (Frederick) John; s of Frederick John Briggs (d 1969), of Bournemouth, and Jessie Catherine, *née* Creighton; *b* 24 Oct 1923; *Educ* Christ Coll Finchley, William Hulme GS Manchester; *m* 1949, Margaret Jessie, da of Maj Percy Libbis Smout, MC (d 1960); 3 s (John, Norman, Stewart); *Career* served RAF 1942–46; chm: Manston Development Group Ltd 1978–81, Duckry Ltd 1980–93, Wiljay plc 1981–84, Pavion International plc 1982–87, Bullers plc 1983–89; dep chm: Wheway plc 1984–93, Reece plc 1986–91; dir: Norcros plc 1966–83, Reading FC Ltd 1978–83, Bunzl plc 1978–88, Blagden Industries plc 1980–89, Tudor plc 1982–, Erskine House plc 1983–93; memb BR Western Bd 1981–88; fndr pres World Packaging Orgn 1968–72; chm Organising Ctee: Pakex '77, Pakex '80, Pakex '83; memb: Cncl PIRA 1971–81, Euro Trade Ctee 1974–83; memb Ct and Liveryman: Worshipful Co of Tylers and Bricklayers 1954– (Master 1982–83), Worshipful Co of Marketors 1973–; FCIM (nat chm 1976, pres 1978–81), FIP (nat chm 1970, pres 1972–81), CIMgt (pres Reading Branch 1978–81, dir BIM Fndn 1980–83), FInstD; *Recreations* tennis; *Clubs* Carlton, City Livery, RAF, MCC; *Style*— John Briggs, Esq; ✉ 15 Ashdale Park, Wokingham, Berks RG40 3QS (☎ 01344 779317, fax 01344 762031)

BRIGGS, (Peter) John; s of Percy Briggs, CBE (d 1980), of Wansford, Peterborough, and Annie Maud (Topsy), *née* Folker (d 1994); *b* 15 May 1928; *Educ* King's Sch Peterborough, Balliol Coll Oxford (MA, BCL); *m* 24 July 1956, Sheila Phyllis, da of George Walton (d 1981), of Grimsby, Lincs; 1 s (Simon b 1963), 3 da (Ann b 1957, Abigail b 1960, Helen b 1961); *Career* RA and RAEC 1946–48, Warrant Offr; barr 1953–, dep circuit judge 1973, recorder of the Crown Court 1978–; legal memb: Mersey Mental Health Review Tbnl 1969–94 (dep chm 1971–79, chm 1979–94), North-West Mental Health Review Tbnl 1994–; *Recreations* music, especially amateur operatics, golf; *Clubs* Athenaeum (Liverpool); *Style*— John Briggs, Esq; ✉ Peel House, Harrington St, Liverpool L2 9XN (☎ 0151 236 0718, fax 0151 255 1085); Park Lodge, 107 Tarbock Rd, Huyton, Liverpool L36 5TD (☎ 0151 489 2664)

BRIGGS, Johnny Ernest; s of Ernest Briggs, and Rose, *née* Good; *b* 5 Sept 1935; *Educ* Singlegate Secdy Sch, Italia Conti Stage Sch; *m* 1, 1961 (m dis 1973), Caroline, *née* Hoover; 1 s (Mark b 1963), 1 da (Karen b 1965); m 2, 18 May 1977, Christine, da of Morris Allsop; 2 s (Michael b 1980, Anthony b 1989), 2 da (Jenifer b 1978, Stephanie b 1982); *Career* actor; Nat Serv 8 Royal Tank Regt 1953–55; *Theatre* began in Italian Opera at Cambridge Theatre 1947; rep: Amersham, Northampton, Dewsbury, Barrow-in-Furness, Bromley, Windsor; numerous tours and West End appearances; *Television* Mike Baldwin in Coronation Street (Granada) 1976–; *Films* over 50 incl: Carry On films, Cosh Boy, Light up the Sky, Wind of Change, HMS Defiant, The Last Escape; *Recreations* golf; *Clubs* Stourbridge Golf, Northandon Golf; hon memb: Mottram Hall Golf, Patshall Park Golf, St Pierre Golf, IOM Golf; *Style*— Johnny Briggs, Esq; ✉ c/o Marina Martin Associates, 12–13 Poland Street, London W1V 3DE (☎ 0171 734 4818, fax 0171 734 4832)

BRIGGS, Jon Peter; s of Dr Peter John Gold, of Bristol, and Julia Ruth Ballam; *b* 24 Jan 1965; *Educ* Magdalen Coll Sch Oxford, Univ of Bristol; *Career* presenter: BBC Radio Oxford, Morning Edition BBC Radio 5, Nightride BBC Radio 2, The Chip Shop, Breakaway and Going Places BBC Radio 4; newsreader BBC Radio's 1, 2, 4, and 5 and BFBS; TV presenter: C4, Homewise BBC 1, Ford Network Business TV; voice over artist for: BBC 1, C4, Carlton, Sky One, Sky Movies, Classic FM, Open Univ and many TV and radio advertising campaigns; owner and dir The Excellent Voice Company; *Recreations* motoring, flying, acting, anything with buttons to press, generally standing in the way of the hostess at dinner parties; *Style*— Jon Briggs, Esq; ✉ c/o Sara Cameron Management, 40 Redbourne Avenue, Finchley, London N3 2BS (☎ 0181 343 0433)

BRIGGS, Michael Townley Featherstone; QC (1994); s of Capt James William Featherstone Briggs, and Barbara Nadine, *née* Pelham Groom; *b* 23 Dec 1954; *Educ* Charterhouse, Magdalen Coll Oxford (MA); *m* 1981, Beverly Ann, da of late Gerald Alan Rogers; 3 s (Nicholas b 1984, James b 1986, Richard b 1988), 1 da (Jessica Molly b 1992); *Career* called to the Bar Lincoln's Inn 1978; *Recreations* sailing, singing, garden steam railways, cooking; *Clubs* Emsworth Sailing, Bar Yacht; *Style*— Michael Briggs, Esq, QC; ✉ 1st Floor, 13 Old Square, Lincoln's Inn, London WC2A 3UA (☎ 0171 242 6105)

BRIGGS, Dr (Michael) Peter; s of Hewieson Briggs (d 1992), and Doris, *née* Habberley; *b* 3 Dec 1944; *Educ* Abbeydale Boys' GS Sheffield, Univ of Sussex (BSc, DPhil); *m* 1969, Jennifer Elizabeth, da of late Donald Watts; 1 da (Alison Mary b 26 Jan 1976), 1 s (Andrew Peter b 30 July 1981); *Career* jr res fell Dept of Chemistry Univ of Sheffield 1969–71, res asst Dept of Architecture Univ of Bristol 1971–73, deputation sec Methodist Church Overseas Div 1973–77, area sec (Herts and Essex) Christian Aid Br Cncl of Churches 1977–80; Br Assoc for the Advancement of Science: educn mangr 1980–86, public affairs mangr 1986–88, dep sec 1988–90, exec sec 1990–; sec Assoc of Br Science Writers 1986–, chm Mgmnt Ctee Methodist Church Div of Social Responsibility 1983–86, exec memb Ctee on the Public Understanding of Sci 1986–, memb Prog Cncl Int Center for the Advancement of Scientific Literacy 1992–; FRSA 1990; *Recreations* walking; *Style*— Dr Peter Briggs; ✉ British Association for the Advancement of Science, 23 Savile Row, London W1X 2NB (☎ 0171 973 3054, fax 0171 973 3051)

BRIGGS, Raymond Redvers; s of Ernest Redvers Briggs, and Ethel, *née* Bowyer; *b* 18 Jan 1934; *Educ* Rutlish Sch Merton, Wimbledon Sch of Art, Slade Sch of Fine Art Univ of London (DFA); *m* 1963, Jean Patricia (d 1973), da of Arthur Taprell Clark; *Career* author, book illustrator and designer; *Books* Father Christmas (1973), Fungus the Bogeyman (1977), The Snowman (1978), When the Wind Blows (book, radio play and stage play, 1982–83), The Man (1992), The Bear (1994); *Clubs* Groucho's; *Style*— Raymond Briggs, Esq; ✉ Weston, Underhill Lane, Westmeston, nr Hassocks, Sussex

BRIGHT, Sir Graham Frank James; kt (1994), MP (C) Luton South (majority 799); s of late Robert Frank Bright, and Agnes Mary, *née* Graham; *b* 2 April 1942; *Educ* Hassenbrook Comp Sch, Thurrock Tech Coll; *m* 16 Dec 1972, Valerie, da of late Ernest Henry Wooliams; 1 s (Rupert b 1984); *Career* chm and md Dietary Foods Ltd 1977–; Parly candidate (C): Thurrock 1970 and 1973, Dartford 1974; MP (C): Luton East 1979–83, Luton South 1983–; PPS to: David Waddington QC MP and Patrick Mayhew QC MP as Mins of State Home Office March-June 1983, David Waddington and Douglas Hurd MP as Mins of State Home Office June-July 1983, David Waddington and Giles Shaw MP 1984–86, Earl of Caithness at DOE Oct 1988–July 1989 and as Paymaster Gen July 1989–90, John Major as Chllr of the Exchequer and as PM 1990–94; vice-chm Cons Pty 1994–; former dir Small Business Bureau Ltd 1989; memb: Thurrock Borough Cncl 1966–79, Essex CC 1967–70; sec Backbench Cons Smaller Business Ctee 1979–80 (vice chm 1980–83), sec Backbench Aviation Ctee 1980–83, memb Select Ctee on House of Commons Servs 1982–84, chm Cons Smaller Businesses Ctee 1983–84 and 1987–88, vice chm Cons Aviation Ctee 1983–85, sec Backbench Food and Drink Sub Ctee 1983–85; introduced Private Members Bills: Video Recordings Act 1984, Entertainments (Increased Penalties) Act 1990; jt sec Parly Aviation Gp 1984, vice chm Aviation Ctee 1987–88, former nat vice chm Young Cons; *Recreations* gardening and golf; *Clubs* Carlton; *Style*— Sir Graham Bright, MP; ✉ House of Commons, London SW1A 0AA (☎ 0171 219 5156)

BRIGHT, John William; *b* 6 May 1950; *Educ* Univ of Durham (BSc); *Career* qualified chartered surveyor; Grand Metropolitan: joined Norwich Brewery Co 1981, various sr mgmnt positions until 1987; Greenalls Group PLC: joined 1987, main bd dir 1992–, chm Tavern Wholesaling Ltd, chm Stretton Leisure, jt chm and md Greenalls Inns, chm and md Inn Partnership Div (pioneering pub franchising); memb Cncl and Exec Br Franchise Assoc; sometime memb Public Advsy Affrs Ctee Br Inst of Innkeeping; winner Pub Industry Award Caterer & Hotelkeeper Magazine 1996; *Style*— John Bright, Esq; ✉ Greenalls Group plc, Wilderspool House, Greenalls Avenue, Warrington WA4 6RH (☎ 01925 651234, fax 01925 402560)

BRIGHT, Michael John; s of John Thomas Bright (d 1984), and Alice Hearne (d 1990); *b* 10 Aug 1944; *Educ* Bromley GS Kent; *m* 15 July 1967, Catherine Ellen, da of Clifford Browne (ret silversmith), of Sheffield; 1 s (James Michael b 1972), 1 da (Victoria Jane b 1970); *Career* Orion Insurance Co Ltd 1967–82 (gp asst gen mangr 1980), dir and gen mangr Lombard Elizabethan Insurance Co plc (subsequently Lombard Continental Insurance plc) 1982–87; Independent Insurance Co Ltd: chief exec and md 1987–, chm 1991–; chief exec and md Independent Insurance Group plc; dir Lambert Smith Hampton 1990–; memb Lloyd's of London; memb Ct of Assts The Worshipful Co of Insurers; Freeman City of London; ACII; *Recreations* gardening, reading, holidays; *Clubs* MCC; *Style*— Michael J Bright, Esq; ✉ The Oasts, Biddenden Rd, Smarden, Kent (☎ 01233 77289); Independent Insurance Co Ltd, 5th Floor, 2 Minster Court, Mincing Lane, London EC3R 7BB (☎ 0171 623 8877, fax 0171 283 8275)

BRIGHTMAN, Baron (Life Peer UK 1982); John Anson Brightman; kt (1970), PC (1979); 2 s of William Henry Brightman (d 1951), of St Albans, Herts; *b* 20 June 1911; *Educ* Marlborough, St John's Coll Cambridge (MA, hon fellow 1982); *m* 1945, Roxane Gilda Hyacinth, da of Gerasimo Ambatielo (d 1958), of Cephalonia; 1 s (Dr the Hon Christopher Brightman); *Career* served WWII Able Seaman MN 1939–40; Lt Cdr RNVR Mediterranean and Atlantic, asst naval attaché Ankara, staff SEAC 1940–46; barr Lincoln's Inn 1932, QC 1961, attorney-gen Duchy Lancaster and attorney and serjeant within Co Palatine of Lancaster 1969–70, High Court judge (Chancery Div) 1970–79, judge Nat Industl Relations Court 1971–74, Lord Justice of Appeal 1979–82, Lord of Appeal in Ordinary 1982–86; chm Tancred's Fndn 1982–96; *Recreations* skiing, mountain trekking, Arctic travel; *Style*— The Rt Hon the Lord Brightman; ✉ Ibthorpe, Hants SP11 OBY

BRIGHTMAN, Sarah; da of Grenville Brightman, and Pauline, *née* Hall; *Career* actress and singer; former memb dance gps Pans People and Hot Gossip; operatic/musical roles incl: Victoria in I and Albert (music Charles Strouse, dir John Schlesinger), Jemima in premiere of Cats (New London Theatre, music Andrew Lloyd Webber, dir Trevor Nunn), title role in The Nightingale (Buxton Festival then Lyric Theatre Hammersmith, music Charles Strouse), premiered Requiem in New York and London (with Placido Domingo, music Andrew Lloyd Webber), Valencienne in The Merry Widow (for New Sadler's Wells Opera), Christine Dae in premiere of The Phantom of the Opera (Her Majesty's Theatre London and on Broadway, music Andrew Lloyd Webber, dir Trevor Nunn), Rose Vibert in Aspects of Love (on Broadway then Prince Edward Theatre London, music Andrew Lloyd Webber, dir Trevor Nunn), Rose in Trelawney of the Wells (Comedy Theatre London), Miranda Frayle in Relative Values (Chichester Festival then Savoy Theatre London, dir Tim Luscombe); appearances in live concerts and performances: The Metropolitan Opera House NY, The Tchaikovsky Hall Moscow, The Waldbuehne Berlin, The Orchard Hall Tokyo, The Olympic Games Barcelona 1992 (sang theme song with José Carreras at the closing ceremony); has performed worldwide in concerts of the music of Andrew Lloyd Webber; has recorded 5 top ten singles and 2 No 1 albums; nominated in: Grammy Awards for Best New Classical Artist in Requiem, Drama Desk Awards for Christine Dae in Phantom of the Opera NY; *Style*— Ms Sarah Brightman; ✉ c/o Sunhand Limited, 63 Grosvenor Street, London W1X 9DA (☎ 0171 493 7831)

BRIGHTMORE, Neil James John; s of James Joseph Edmund Brightmore (d 1964), of Stoke-on-Trent, Staffs, and Ethel Lettice Brightmore, MBE, *née* Goode (d 1986); *b* 21 Jan 1937; *Educ* The Lymes Sch Newcastle-under-Lyme, Stoke-on-Trent Coll of Art; *m* 1, 1961 (m dis), Sheila Charsley; 2 s (Adrian Neil b 1963, Roger Jason b 1967); m 2, 5 Sept 1979, Vivienne Brenda Margaret, da of John Anthony Augustus Ireson; 1 da (Verity Abigail b 1981); *Career* Nat Serv RAF, trained in photography; press photographer; most recent exhbns incl: Epcot Exhibition USA 1994, National BIPP Exhibition 1995–96; BIPP Fellow of the Year 1985, Peter Grugeon Jubilee award 1985, Patrick Lichfield Portfolio award 1985, Nat BIPP Portrait Photographer of the Year 1985, Kodak Portrait Photographer 1986 and 1988, Gold and Silver awards World Cncl of Professional Photographers 1989, three Kodak Gold awards World Travelling Exhibition 1989 (and eleven other Kodak Gold awards), Curzon Regnl BIPP Trophy (5 times winner), BIPP Trophy (pictorial and illustrative) 1996; memb: Nat Cncl BIPP 1984–86, Qualification Bd RPS 1986–; chm: BIPP NW Regn 1987–88, Qualifications for the MPA; FBIPP 1985, FRPS 1986, FRSA 1987, FMPA 1988; *Style*— Neil Brightmore, Esq; ✉ Elm Tree House, Garden St, Penkhull, Stoke-on-Trent, Staffs (☎ 01782 621839); 25 Ironmarket, Newcastle, Staffs ST5 1RH (☎ 01782 621839, fax 01782 611957)

BRIGHTON, Wing Cdr Peter; s of Henry Charles Brighton (d 1983), and Ivy Irene, *née* Crane (d 1987); *b* 26 March 1933; *Educ* Wisbech GS, Univ of Reading (BSc), RAF Tech Coll, RAF Flying Schs (graduated with special distinction), RAF Staff Coll; *m* 6 June 1959, (Anne) Maureen Lewis, da of Joseph Llewelyn Jones (d 1977); 1 s (Simon

Peter b 1968, d 1970), 1 da (Amanda Jane b 1963); *Career* RAF 1955–71 (pilot 26 Sqdn, engr offr and attaché South Vietnam, ret as Wing Cdr); md: Rockwell-Collins UK 1974–77, Plessey ME 1977–78, Cossor Electronics 1978–85; ops dir British Aerospace 1988 (divnl md 1985), dir gen Engrg Employers Fedn 1989–91; pres Electronic Engrg Assoc 1984–85 (memb Cncl 1979–87); currently chm Princess Alexandra Hosp NHS Tst; memb: Cncl Soc of British Aerospace Cos 1988, Round Table (Watton, Norfolk & Wokingham, Berks); Freeman City of London 1989, Liveryman Worshipful Co of Coachmakers and Coach Harness Makers 1989, CEng 1966, FRAeS 1981 (AFRAeS 1962), CIMgt 1984, FIEE 1980; *Recreations* flying (current pilot's licence), bridge, golf; *Clubs* Royal Air Force; *Style*— Wing Cdr Peter Brighton; ✉ St Andrew's Cottage, Church Lane, Much Hadham, Hertfordshire SG10 6DH (☎ 01279 842309)

BRIGHTWELL, Ann Elizabeth; *née* Packer; MBE (1965); da of Hector Frederick George Packer (d 1977), and Lilian Rosina, *née* Deacon; *b* 8 March 1942; *Educ* Moulsford C of E Sch, Wallingford Co GS, Didcot Girls' GS, Dartford Coll of Physical Educn; *m* 19 Dec 1964, Robbie Ian Brightwell, s of William Stanley Brightwell; 3 s (Gary Scott b 6 Oct 1965, Ian Robert b 9 April 1968, David John b 7 Jan 1971); *Career* former international athlete; represented GB: long jump, 100m, 4 x 100m, 200m, 400m, 800m, 80m hurdles; achievements incl: Bronze medal 4 x 100m Euro Championships Belgrade 1962, Silver medal 4 x 100m Cwlth Games Perth Aust 1962, Gold medal 800m Olympic Games Tokyo 1964 (Silver 400m); records: world 800m 1964, Euro 400m 1964, first Br woman to win track Gold medal Olympic Games; former hockey player: Southern Cos, Berks, Leics; teacher: Lady Edridge GS South Norwood 1962–64, New Malden Girls' Sch Croydon 1964–65; *Recreations* jogging, gardening, cooking, watching sons play football for Manchester City; *Style*— Mrs Ann Brightwell, MBE

BRIGHTY, HE (Anthony) David; CMG (1984), CVO (1985); s of C P J Brighty and Winifred, *née* Turner; *b* 7 Feb 1939; *Educ* Northgate GS Ipswich, Clare Coll Cambridge (BA); *m* 1, 1963 (m dis), Diana Porteous (decd); 2 s, 2 da; m 2, 1982 (m dis), Jane Docherty; *Career* entered Foreign Office 1961, Brussels 1962–63, Havana 1964–66, FO 1968–69, resigned, joined S G Warburg & Co 1969, rejoined FCO 1971, Saigon 1973–74, UK Mission to UN NY 1975–78, RCDS 1979, head of Personnel Operations Dept FCO 1980–83, cnsllr Lisbon 1983–86; dir of private office of Sec Gen of NATO 1986–87, res chm Civil Service Selection Bd 1988; HM ambass: to Cuba 1989–91, to Czech and Slovak Federal Republic 1991–93, to Czech Republic and Slovakia 1993–94, to Spain (concurrently non-resident ambass to Andorra) 1994–; *Style*— HE Mr David Brighty, CMG, CVO; ✉ c/o Foreign and Commonwealth Office (Madrid), King Charles Street, London SW1A 2AH

BRIGNELL, Prof John Ernest; s of Patrick John Brignell, and Marjorie Beatrice, *née* Acock; *b* 13 July 1937; *Educ* Stationers' Company's Sch Hornsey, Univ of London (BSc, PhD); *m* 1 July 1965, Gillian, da of Harry Wright (d 1985), of Nether Wallop; 1 da (Penelope b 1971); *Career* student apprentice STC Ltd 1955–59; City Univ London: res asst Northampton Coll 1959–64, res fell and res tutor 1964–67, lectr 1967–70, reader in electronics 1970–80; prof of industrial instrumentation Univ of Southampton 1985– (prof of electronics 1980–85); Goldsmiths travelling fell 1969: Grenoble, Gdansk, Geneva; Callendar Silver Medal (InstMC) 1994; FIEE, FInstP, FInstMC, FRSA; *Books* Laboratory on-line computing (1975), Intelligent sensor systems (1994); *Recreations* fly-fishing, horticulture; *Style*— Prof John Brignell; ✉ Chalk Bank Cottage, Broughton, Stockbridge, Hants SO20 8AN (☎ 01794 301420); Department of Electronics and Computer Science, University of Southampton, Highfield, Southampton SO17 1BH (☎ 01703 593580)

BRIGSTOCKE, Alexander Julian (Sandy); DL (Surrey 1990); s of Major Arthur Montagu Brigstocke (d 1928), and Doris Mamie, *née* Butler (d 1982); *b* 11 Nov 1922; *Educ* Wellington, Univ of London (BA); *m* 14 Dec 1949, Diana Mavis, da of John Arundel Evershed (d 1984); 1 s (Timothy b 1951), 2 da (Jennifer b 1953, Juliet b 1962); *Career* WWII Capt Rifle Bde, served N Africa and Italy 1941–45; jt headmaster Boxgrove Sch Guildford 1953–64; Surrey CC: elected 1970, vice chm Social Servs Ctee 1977–81, chm Planning Ctee 1981–85, vice chm Educn Ctee 1987–89, vice chm 1987–90, chm 1990–93; memb Exec Cncl Assoc of CCs 1989–93, pres Guildford Cons Assoc 1992– (chm 1978–81); chm: Nat Tst Winkworth Arboretum Mgmnt Ctee 1981–89, W Surrey Centre Nat Tst 1985–89, Surrey Historic Bldgs Tst 1985–93, Sports Aid Fndn (London and SE) 1993–97; govr: Kingston Poly, Guildford Coll of Technol, W Surrey Coll of Art and Design 1973–89, Guildford Sch of Acting 1984–96; gen cmmr of Taxes 1976–89, tstee Painshill Park Tst 1985–97; *Recreations* music, sport, travel; *Clubs* MCC, Surrey CCC; *Style*— Sandy Brigstocke, Esq, DL; ✉ Granton House, Shackleford, Godalming, Surrey GU8 6AX (☎ 01483 422545)

BRIGSTOCKE, Baroness (Life Peer UK 1990), of Kensington, in the Royal Borough of Kensington and Chelsea; Heather Renwick Brigstocke; da of Sqdn Ldr John Renwick Brown, DFC, and May Brown; *b* 2 Sept 1929; *Educ* Abbey Sch Reading, Girton Coll Cambridge; *m* 1952, Geoffrey Brigstocke (d 1974); 3 s (Hon David Hugh Charles b 1953, Hon Julian Renwick b 1955, Hon Thomas James Jefferson b 1961), 1 da (Hon Emma Persephone b 1957); *Career* classics mistress: Francis Holland Sch (Graham Terrace) 1951–53, Godolphin and Latymer Sch (pt/t) 1954–60; pt/t Latin teacher Nat Cathedral Sch Washington DC 1962–64; headmistress Francis Holland Sch (Clarence Gate) 1965–74; high mistress St Paul's Girls' Sch 1974–89; memb Cncl: London House for Overseas Graduates 1965– (vice-chm 1975–80), Middlesex Hosp Med Sch 1971–80, City Univ 1978–83, Royal Holloway Coll 1977–85, Royal Soc of Arts 1983–87; memb Ctee Automobile Assoc 1975–90; pres: Bishop Creighton Sch Settlement Fulham 1977–, Girls' Schools Assoc 1980–81; vice pres City and Guilds London Inst 1993–; govr: Wellington Coll 1975–87, The Royal Ballet Sch 1977–92, Forest Sch 1982–90, Museum of London 1986–92, Gordonstoun Sch 1991–93, Imperial Coll of Science Technol and Medicine 1991–; chm: Bd of Tstees Geffrye Museum 1990–, Thames LWT Telethon Tst 1990, The Menerva Educational Tst 1991–93, The English-Speaking Union, Landau Forte Coll Derby 1993– (govr 1992–); tstee: Nat Gallery 1975–82, Kennedy Meml Tst 1980–85, City Technol Colls Tst 1987–, Great Britain Sasakawa Fndn 1994–; memb Modern Foreign Languages Working Gp 1989–90; non-exec dir LWT 1982–90, ind nat bd dir Times Newspapers Holdings 1990–, memb Prog Advsy Bd LWT 1990–93, assoc dir Great Universal Stores plc 1993–96; non-exec dir: Health Educn Authority 1989–, Burberrys 1993–96; memb: Cncl St George's House Windsor 1984–90, Museums and Galleries Cmmn 1992–, European Cultural Fndn (UK Ctee) 1992–, Cncl Nat Literacy Tst 1993–; hon bencher Inner Temple 1992; *Style*— The Baroness Brigstocke; ✉ House of Lords, London SW1A 0PW (☎ 0171 219 3000)

BRIGSTOCKE, Dr Hugh; *Career* curator of Italian, French and Spanish pictures National Gall of Scotland 1968–83, ed in chief Macmillan Dictionary of Art 1983–87 (consulting ed 1987–); Sotheby's: conslt Old Master Paintings 1989, dir 1990, head Old Master Paintings Dept 1993 and 1994, sr expert 1994–95; freelance 1995– (ed The Oxford Companion to Art); *Publications* A Critical Catalogue to the Italian and Spanish Paintings in the National Gallery of Scotland (1978, 2 edn 1993), William Buchanan and the 19th Century Art Trade: 100 letters to his agent in London and Italy (1979), Poussin Bacchanals and Sacraments (exhbn catalogue National Gallery of Scotland, 1981), A Loan Exhibition of Drawings by Nicolas Poussin from British Collections (exhbn catalogue Ashmolean Museum, 1990), Masterpieces from Yorkshire Houses - Yorkshire Families at Home and Abroad 1700–1850 (jtly, exhbn catalogue York City Art Gallery, 1994), Italian Paintings from Burghley House (jtly, exhbn catalogue Frick Art Museum Pittsburgh, Indianapolis Museum of Art, Fresno Metropolitan Museum, Phoenix Art Museum, Mississipi Museum of Art and Richmond Museum USA, 1995); author of numerous articles on Italian and French painting in various jls incl Burlington Magazine, Apollo, Revue de l'Art, Revue du Louvre and Paragone; *Style*— Dr Hugh Brigstocke; ✉ 118 Micklegate, York YO1 1JX (☎ 01904 626013)

BRIGSTOCKE, Vice Adm John Richard; s of Canon G E Brigstocke (d 1971), and Mollie, *née* Sandford; *b* 30 July 1945; *Educ* Marlborough, Britannia Royal Naval Coll Dartmouth, Royal Naval Coll Greenwich, RCDS; *m* 21 April 1979, Heather, da of Dennis Day and Muriel Day, of Oxshott, Surrey; 2 s (Tom b 1981, Jamie b 1984); *Career* RN: joined 1962, Cdr 1977, Capt 1982, Rear Adm 1991, Vice Adm 1995; sea cmds: HMS Upton 1970–71, HMS Bacchante 1978–79, HMS York and 3rd Destroyer Sqdn 1986–87, HMS Ark Royal 1989–90, Flag Offr Flotilla Two 1991–92, Cdr UK Task Gp 1992–93, Flag Offr Surface Flotilla April 1995–; shore appts: Naval Plans MOD 1980–81 and 1982–84, Capt Britannia RNC Dartmouth 1987–88, Asst Chief of Naval Staff 1993–95; younger bro Trinity House; *Recreations* skiing, riding; *Style*— Vice Adm J R Brigstocke; ✉ Ministry of Defence, (c/o Naval Secretary), Victory Building, HM Naval Base, Portsmouth PO1 3LS

BRIGSTOCKE, Nicholas Owen; s of Mervyn Owen Brigstocke, of 12 Deep Acres, Chesham Bois, Amersham, Bucks, and Janet Mary, *née* Singleton; *b* 25 June 1942; *Educ* Summerfields Oxford, Epsom Coll; *m* 17 May 1969, Carol Barbara, da of Air Marshal Sir Walter Philip George Pretty, CB, KBE (d 1975), 2 s (Marcus b 1973, Henry b 1981), 1 da (Lucinda b 1971); *Career* Shell Mex and BP Ltd 1961–69, de Zoete and Gorton Ltd 1969–78, ptnr de Zoete and Bevan Ltd 1978–86; Barclays de Zoete Wedd Securities Ltd: dir and head of UK equity sales 1986–89, md corporate broking 1989–; chm de Zoete and Bevan Ltd 1994– (dep chm 1991–94); *Recreations* tennis, cricket; *Clubs* MCC, City of London, Escorts SRC, Twelve; *Style*— Nicholas Brigstocke, Esq; ✉ Linchmere House, Linchmere, nr Haslemere, Surrey GU27 3NG (☎ 01428 722 134); Barclays de Zoete Wedd Ltd, Ebbgate House, 2 Swan Lane, London EC4R 3TS (☎ 0171 623 2323, fax 0171 956 3286, car tel 0860 834485, telex 888221)

BRILL, John; s of late Eric William Brill, of Bramhall, Cheshire, and Barbara Brill; *b* 21 Aug 1935; *Educ* King's Sch Macclesfield, Jesus Coll Cambridge (MA); *m* 10 Sept 1960, Elizabeth, da of late David James Hughes-Morgan; 3 s (Timothy, Jonathon, James); *Career* Nat Serv RN 1956–59; mgmnt trainee and dep PR mangr Rank Organisation 1959–64, account exec London Press Exchange 1964–66, md Brian Dowling Ltd 1966–76; chm GCI London (formerly Sterling Public Relations) 1976–93, dir Hanson Green 1993–96; princ John Brill Consulting 1993–; FIPR; *Recreations* golf, tennis, pole vaulting; *Clubs* Savile; *Style*— John Brill, Esq; ✉ Rookhurst, Coast Hill Lane, Westcott, Dorking, Surrey (☎ 01306 882344); John Brill Consulting, The Clockhouse, 6 St Catherine's Mews, Milner Street, London (☎ 0171 838 1160, fax 0171 838 1161)

BRILL, Tony; *b* 1947; *Educ* Univ of Birmingham (LLB); *Career* admitted slr; mgmnt servs conslt United Glass 1970–73; Granada Television: mgmnt trainee 1973, prodn planning exec 1973–76, labour relations offr 1976–79, labour relations mangr 1979, drama planning mangr 1979–80, head of prodn planning 1980–83, head of prodn servs 1983–85, dep gen mangr 1985–87, gen mangr 1987–88, gp chm Industl Relations Ctee 1988 (chm Industry Sub-ctee 1988), dir 1988–94, md Granada Facilities Division 1988–94; gp dir of resources Yorkshire Television Ltd 1994–, md (broadcasting) Tyne Tees Television Ltd 1996–; *Style*— Tony Brill, Esq; ✉ Yorkshire Television Ltd, The Television Centre, Leeds LS3 1JS (☎ 0113 243 8283, fax 0113 244 5107)

BRIMACOMBE, Michael William; s of Lt-Col Winston Brimacombe, OBE (d 1995), of Torquay, Devon, and Marjorie Gertrude, *née* Ling; *b* 6 March 1944; *Educ* Kelly Coll Univ of London (LLB); *m* 8 April 1968, Pamela Jean, da of Charles Mark Stone, of Grouville, Jersey, CI; 1 s (John Mark b 1969), 2 da (Ruth Michelle b 1972, Helen Marie-Anne b 1976); *Career* sr ptnr Norman Allport & Co 1972–, ptnr Price Waterhouse (UK and Jersey) 1975–85; md Legal Tstees (Jersey) Ltd 1985–, chm CIK Holdings Ltd (trading as Pierre Sangan International) 1992–, chm Jobstream Group plc 1993–; FInstD, FCA 1968, FRSA 1987; *Recreations* reading, travelling, walking; *Clubs* Royal Western Yacht Club of England, Victoria, Arts; *Style*— Michael Brimacombe, Esq; ✉ Temple View, Rue des Marettes, Faldouet, St Martin, Jersey, CI (☎ 01534 851087); L T Group Ltd, PO Box 781, Norwich Union House, 8 Church St, St Helier, Jersey JE4 0SG, CI (☎ 01534 67766, fax 01534 69249)

BRIMACOMBE, Rodney John; JP (Plymouth 1992); s of Lt-Col Winston Brimacombe, OBE (d 1995), of Torquay, Devon, and Majorie Gertrude, *née* Ling; *b* 22 Dec 1940; *Educ* Kelly Coll Tavistock; *m* 16 Nov 1968, Susan Jane, da of John Stredwick, of Burrow Cottage, Livermead, Torquay; 2 s (Simon Rodney b 28 Jan 1970, Justin John b 22 May 1972); *Career* gen mangr Pophams Ltd Plymouth 1964–69, md Jolly Ltd Bath 1970–72, gp asst md E Dingle Co Plymouth 1972–79, non-exec dir Westward TV Ltd 1979–81, dir and gen mangr sales and devpt Harrods Ltd 1979–86; chm Knightsbridge Gp 1985–86, md MOR Advertising Ltd 1989–95, ptnr MOR Marketing 1995–; vice pres and cncllr French C of C 1986, sec 20 Club 1986, cncllr Plymouth C of C and Indust 1990–94; *Recreations* sailing; *Clubs* Royal Western Yacht (memb main ctee 1996–), Itchenor Sailing; *Style*— Rodney Brimacombe, Esq, JP; ✉ The Penthouse, 25 Dolphin House, Sutton Wharf, Sutton Harbour, Plymouth PL4 0DW (☎ 01752 201172, work ☎ 01752 201121, fax 01752 201173)

BRIMS, Charles David; s of David Vaughan Brims (d 1993), of Heddon, Northumberland, and Eve Georgina Mary, *née* Barrett; *b* 5 May 1950; *Educ* Winchester, Brasenose Coll Oxford; *m* 1973, Patricia Catherine, da of John Desmond Henderson, of Brimpton; 2 s (David b 1980, Edward b 1982); *Career* dir: Courage (Western) Ltd 1980–83, Imperial Inns and Taverns Ltd 1983–86, Imperial Leisure and Retailing Ltd 1985–86; chief exec Portsmouth and Sunderland Newspapers plc 1986–; non-exec dir George Gale & Co Ltd 1995–; govr Elstree Sch; *Recreations* cricket, tennis, golf, shooting; *Clubs* MCC, Vincent's (Oxford); *Style*— Charles Brims, Esq; ✉ Brimpton Lodge, Brimpton, Reading RG7 4TG; Buckton House, 37 Abingdon Rd, London W8 6AH (☎ 0171 938 3039, fax 0171 937 1479)

BRIMSON, Robert Charles; s of Henry John Robert Brimson (d 1977), of London, and Louisa Beatrice, *née* White; *b* 19 Sept 1947; *Educ* St Mary's Sch Hendon, Middx Poly, Southgate Coll, Harrow Sch of Art and Design; *m* 4 May 1979, Linda Anne Theresa, da of William George Bass; 1 s (Joseph William Robert b 11 Feb 1981); *Career* photographer; apprentice Eastern Electricity 1965–70, distribution engr 1970–71, photography student Harrow Coll 1971–74, freelance photographer 1974– (initially a record sleeve photographer, currently specialising in advtg campaigns); exhibitor Photographers Gallery London, recipient various Assoc of Photographers awards; memb Assoc of Photographers 1978 (chm 1989–91); *Recreations* skiing, watching my son grow, gallery-going, photography, theatre, opera, listening to Test Match Special; *Clubs* ET Cricket; *Style*— Robert Brimson, Esq; ✉ Robert Brimson Photography, 29 Waterside, 44–48 Wharf Road, London N1 7SH (☎ 0171 253 0157, fax 0171 253 0168, mobile 0860 747038)

BRIMSON LEWIS, Stephen John; s of David Raymond Lewis (d 1969), and Doris Agnes, *née* West; *b* 15 Feb 1963; *Educ* The Barclay Sch Herts, The Hertfordshire Coll of Art and Design, The Central Sch of Art and Design (BA); *Career* set and costume designer; memb Equity *Theatre* credits as designer incl: Once In A While The Odd Thing Happens (RNT), Uncle Vanya (RNT), Design for Living (Donmar Warehouse and Gielgud, winner Olivier Award 1995), Les Parents Terribles (RNT (Indescretions on Broadway, winner Olivier Award 1995, Tony nomination for set and costume)), A Little

Night Music (RNT) 1995; sets for: Otello (Vienna State Opera), Turn of the Screw (Aust Opera), Tales of Hoffman (Aust Opera), Dorian Gray (Monte Carlo Opera); costumes for: Mrs Klein (RNT), American Clock (RNT), Jeffrey Bernard Is Unwell (West End), Vanilla (West End), Bookends (West End), L'Elisir D'Amore (Dallas Opera), The Barber of Seville (The Royal Opera House); *Television* incls costumes for The Nightmare Years (TTN Cable USA); *Exhibitions* work incls Making Their Mark; *Films* Bent (Film Four Int) 1996; *Style*— Stephen Brimson Lewis, Esq; ✉ c/o Stephen Hatton Management, 1a Shepperton House, 83–93 Shepperton Road, London N1 3DF (☎ 0171 359 3593, fax 0171 354 2189)

BRINCKMAN, Sir Theodore George Roderick; 6 Bt (UK 1831), of Burton or Monk Bretton, Yorkshire; s of Col Sir Roderick Napoleon Brinckman, 5 Bt, DSO, MC, Grenadier Guards (d 1985), and his 1 w, Margaret Wilson (d 1977), da of Wilson Southam, of Ottawa, Canada; *b* 20 March 1932; *Educ* Millfield, Trinity Coll Sch Port Hope Ontario, ChCh Oxford, Trinity Coll Toronto Univ; *m* 1, 11 June 1958 (m dis 1983), Helen Mary Anne, da of late Arnold Elliot Cook, of Toronto, Canada; 2 s (Theodore Jonathan b 1960, Roderick Nicholas b 1964), 1 da (Sophia Theresa b 1963); m 2, 7 Dec 1983, Hon (Greta) Sheira Bernadette Grant-Ferris, da of Baron Harvington; *Heir* s, Theodore Jonathan Brinckman b 19 Feb 1960; *Career* publisher and antiquarian bookseller; *Clubs* White's, University (Toronto); *Style*— Sir Theodore Brinckman, Bt; ✉ Hazleton Manor, Cirencester, Glos GL7 6PG

BRIND, Bryony Jane Susan St John; da of Maj Roger Michael Atchley Brind, and Jenifer Mary St John, *née* Grey; *b* 27 May 1960; *Educ* Royal Ballet Sch White Lodge and Sr Sch; *Career* ballerina; Royal Ballet Co: joined 1978, soloist 1981, princ 1984, princ guest artiste 1991–; winner: Prix de Lausanne 1977, Olivier Award 1981; repertory of major classical ballets and created roles during career; *Style*— Miss Bryony Brind; ✉ The Royal Opera House, Covent Garden, Floral St, London WC2E 9DD (☎ 0171 240 1200)

BRIND, (Arthur) Henry; CMG (1973); o s of late Thomas Henry Brind, of Barry, and N W B Brind; *b* 4 July 1927; *Educ* St John's Coll Cambridge (MA); *m* 1954, Barbara, da of late George Frederick Harrison, of Bedford; 1 s, 1 da; *Career* HMOCS 1950–60; HM Dip Serv: joined 1960, actg high cmmr Uganda 1972–73, high cmmr Mauritius 1974–77, ambass Somalia 1977–80, high cmmr Malawi 1983–87; *Clubs* Reform; *Style*— Henry Brind, Esq, CMG; ✉ 20 Grove Terrace, London NW5 1PH (☎ 0171 267 1190)

BRINDLE, Ian; *b* 17 Aug 1943; *Educ* Rossall Sch, Blundells Sch, Univ of Manchester (BA Econ); *m* Elisabeth; 2 s (Michael, Andrew), 1 da (Jennie b 1977); *Career* chartered accountant; Price Waterhouse: articled in London 1965 (Toronto 1971), ptnr 1976–, memb Supervisory Ctee 1988–, dir Audit & Business Advsy Servs 1990–91, memb UK Exec 1990–, sr ptnr UK 1991–; memb: Auditing Practices Ctee 1986–90 (chm 1990), Urgent Issues Task Force Accounting Standards Bd 1991–93, Accounting Standards Bd 1993–, Cncl ICAEW; FCA; *Recreations* tennis and golf; *Style*— Ian Brindle, Esq; ✉ Price Waterhouse, Southwark Towers, 32 London Bridge Street, London SE1 9SY (☎ 0171 939 3000, fax 0171 378 0647)

BRINDLE, Michael John; QC (1992); s of John Arthur Brindle, and Muriel, *née* Jones (d 1975); *b* 23 June 1952; *Educ* Westminster, New Coll Oxford (BA, Ella Stephen scholar); *m* 5 Jan 1988, Heather Mary, *née* Pearce; 2 da (Alice Elizabeth b 3 Aug 1991, Antonia Claire b 28 Feb 1993), 1 s (Guy Francis b 7 May 1994); *Career* called to the Bar Lincoln's Inn (Hardwick scholar) 1975, pupillage with Denis Henry (now Lord Justice Henry) at 2 Crown Office Row Temple 1975–76, tenancy Fountain Court 1976–; *Recreations* classical music, travel, bridge; *Style*— Michael Brindle, Esq, QC; ✉ Fountain Court, Temple, London EC4 9DH (☎ 0171 583 3335)

BRINDLEY, John; CB (1996); s of Harold Brindley (d 1956), and Eva Brindley (d 1996); *b* 25 Sept 1937; *Educ* Leek HS Staffs; *m* 10 Sept 1960, Judith Ann; 1 da (Karen b 28 Feb 1968); *Career* civil servant; Lord Chancellor's Office: Stoke-on-Trent County Ct 1955, dep chief clerk Wolverhampton County Ct 1968–71, business offr Midland & Oxford Circuit Ct 1971–73, personnel offr Criminal Business Div Lord Chancellor's Dept 1973–81, ct admin Exeter Gp of Cts 1981–87, head Civil Business Div London HQ 1987–88, head Ct Serv Mgmnt Gp 1988–92, head Ct Serv Business Gp 1992–95, circuit admin SE Circuit 1995–; chm Inter-Agency Trial Issues Gp; hockey career: winner various county and nat championship medals, Midland League and London League medals, Euro Club Championship Gold Medal (as coach), sr coach Hockey Assoc; *Recreations* sport, amateur theatricals; *Clubs* Athenaeum; *Style*— John Brindley, Esq, CB; ✉ Circuit Administrator's Office, Lord Chancellor's Department, Cavendish House, 18 Maltravers Street, London WC2R 3EU (☎ 0171 936 7232)

BRINE, Roger Ernest William; s of Ernest Albert Brine, of West Malling, Kent, and Ivy, *née* Funnell (d 1993); *b* 13 Nov 1943; *Educ* Purley GS, Coll of Law; *m* 12 May 1973, Monica, da of Erich Bredenbrucher (d 1945), of Herdecke Germany; 1 s (Martin b 1974), 1 da (Katharine b 1977); *Career* admitted slr 1969; ptnr: Vallis and Struthers 1971–87, Amhurst Brown Colombotti 1988–; memb: Law Soc, City of Westminster Law Soc, Soc of Tst and Estate Practitioners, Soc for Computers and Law, Sevenoaks Round Table 1974–84; *Style*— Roger Brine, Esq; ✉ Amhurst Brown Colombotti, 2 Duke Street, St James's, London SW1Y 6BJ (☎ 0171 930 2366, fax 0171 930 2250, telex 261857)

BRINK, Prof André Philippus; s of Daniel Brink, of Potchefstroom, South Africa, and Aletta Wilhelmina, *née* Wolmarans; *b* 29 May 1935; *Educ* Potchefstroom Univ (MA), Rhodes University (DLitt); *m* 1, 1959 (m dis 1965), Estelle Naudé; 1 s (Anton b 1962); m 2, 1965 (m dis 1966), Salomina Louw; 1 s (Gustav b 1966); m 3, 1970 (m dis 1987), Sophia Albertina Miller; 1 s (Daniel b 1971), 1 da (Sonja b 1973); m 4, 16 Nov 1990, Marésa de Beer; *Career* Rhodes University: lectr 1961–73, sr lectr 1973–75, assoc prof 1976–79, prof 1980–90; prof Univ of Cape Town 1991–; memb Dutch Soc of Letters 1964–, pres Afrikaans Writers' Guild 1980–82; DLitt Univ of the Witwatersrand 1985; Martin Luther King Meml Prize 1980, Prix Médicis Etranger 1980; Chevalier de la Legion d'Honneur France 1982, Commandeur de l'Ordre des Arts et des Lettres France 1992; *Books* The Ambassador (1964, revised edn 1984), Looking on Darkness (1974), An Instant in the Wind (1976), Rumours of Rain (1978), A Dry White Season (1979), A Chain of Voices (1982), Mapmakers (1983), The Wall of the Plague (1984), States of Emergency (1988), An Act of Terror (1991), The First Life of Adamastor (1993), On The Contrary (1993), Imaginings of Sand (1996), Reinventing a Continent (1996); *Style*— Prof André Brink; ✉ University of Cape Town, Private Bag, Rondebosch 7700, South Africa (☎ 00 27 21 650 2836, fax 00 27 21 685 3945)

BRINTON, Michael Ashley Cecil; DL (Hereford and Worcester 1991); s of Maj Sir (Esme) Tatton Cecil Brinton, DL (d 1985), of Queen's Gate, London, and his 1 wife Mary Elizabeth, *née* Fahnestock (d 1960); bro of C Topham C Brinton, *qv*; *b* 6 Oct 1941; *Educ* Eton, Vienna, Perugia, Aix-en-Provence; *m* 1966, Angela, da of John Ludlow, of High Wycombe; 2 s, 1 da; *Career* Brintons Ltd: dir 1970–, mktg and sales dir 1988–, chm 1991–; pres: Confedn Int des Tapis et Tissus D'Ameublement 1987–91, Qualitas Furnishing Standards 1992–95, Chartered Inst of Mktg (Birmingham Branch) 1994–95, Furnishing Trades Benevolent Assoc 1995–96; High Sheriff Hereford and Worcester 1990–91; FRSA 1996; *Recreations* shooting, fishing; *Style*— Michael Brinton, Esq, DL; ✉ The Old Rectory, Pudleston, Leominster, Hereford HR6 0RA (☎ 01568 760234)

BRINTON, (Charles) Topham Cecil; s of Maj Sir (Esme) Tatton Cecil Brinton (d 1985), and Mary Elizabeth, *née* Fahnestock (d 1960); bro of Michael A C Brinton, *qv*; *b* 10 Sept 1939; *Educ* Eton, Brown Univ USA (BA); *m* 1, 26 June 1965 (m dis 1990), Rosemary Anna, da of Alfred Peter Wilson, 2 da (Catharine Elizabeth b 18 Aug 1966, Annabelle Mary b 4 Feb 1968); m 2, 2 Feb 1991, Carolyn Marion Pugh; *Career* Brintons Ltd: dir 1966, asst md 1977, vice chm 1978, chm 1981, chm and jt md 1988–91; memb Carpet Indust Trg Bd 1969–71, chm Nat Jt Advsy Cncl for the Carpet Indust 1972– (chm Dist Cncl 1972–84), pres Kidderminster and Dist C of C 1977–78, memb British Carpet Mfrs Assoc Ltd 1978–91 (pres 1981–86), chm Kidderminster Area Bd Young Enterprise 1981–83, tax cmmr Kidderminster Dist Carpet Mfrs and Spinners Assoc 1983– (chm 1981–83), vice chm W Midlands Region CBI 1988– (chm 1986–88); dir: W Midlands Devpt Agency 1990–91, CENTEC 1990–91; FRSA; *Recreations* shooting, tennis; *Style*— Topham Brinton, Esq; ✉ Gothersley Hall, Stourton, Stourbridge, Worcs DY7 5AZ (☎ 01384 873974)

BRISBOURNE, Richard; OBE (1971); s of Percy George Brisbourne (d 1957), of Uttoxeter, Staffs, and Beatrice Mabel, *née* Smith (d 1969); *b* 8 June 1920; *Educ* Alleynes GS Uttoxeter; *m* 17 June 1942, Joan, da of William Henry Smith (d 1959), of Uttoxeter, Staffs; 2 s (Richard Paul b 19 Nov 1943, Giles b 20 July 1948); *Career* Lt Leics Yeo 1942–46, served NW Europe; chm: Africa Timber and Plywood 1961–70, Ghana Timber Assoc 1961–65; pres Nigeria Timber Fedn 1965–70; conslt on tropical timber industs (Ind) to World Bank, FAO etc 1970–79, advsr on forest concessions (Sarawak Govt) and timber industs 1979–80; Bucks CC rep Chalfont St Giles 1981–93 (vice chm Bucks CC 1989–93), memb Thames Valley Police Authy 1989–93; Liveryman Worshipful Co of Loriners, Freeman City of London; *Recreations* golf, bridge, travel; *Clubs* Beaconsfield Golf; *Style*— Richard Brisbourne, OBE; ✉ c/o Lloyds Bank Plc, The Broadway, Wycombe End, Beaconsfield, Bucks

BRISBY, John Constant Shannon McBurney; QC (1996); s of Michael Douglas James McBurney Brisby (d 1965), of London, and Liliana, *née* Daneva; *b* 8 May 1956; *Educ* Westminster, Christ Church Oxford (MA); *m* 20 April 1985, Claire Alexandra Anne, da of Sir Donald Arthur Logan, KCMG, of 6 Thurloe St, London SW7; *Career* 2 Lt 5 Royal Inniskilling Dragoon Gds 1974, transferred Reserve 1975–77; called to the Bar Lincoln's Inn 1978; memb Exec Cncl Friends of Bulgaria (Charitable Orgn); *Style*— John Brisby, Esq, QC; ✉ 4 Stone Buildings, Lincoln's Inn, London WC2A 3XT

BRISBY, Stephen James Michael; s of Michael Douglas James McBurney Brisby (d 1965), and Liliana, *née* Daneva; *b* 31 Dec 1950; *Educ* Westminster, Trinity Hall Cambridge (MA); *m* 26 Jan 1989, Fritze, da of Hans Ole Klingenberg; 1 s (Michael Douglas James b 12 Jan 1990), 1 da (Georgina Rose b 19 April 1994); *Career* dir: J Henry Schroder Wagg & Co Ltd 1983–85 (joined 1971), Salomon Bros International Ltd 1985–88; vice chm UBS Ltd 1988–95, memb Int Investment Banking Ctee Société Générale 1996–; Freeman City of London, memb Worshipful Co of Blacksmiths; *Recreations* hunting, opera, music; *Style*— Stephen Brisby, Esq; ✉ 20 Thurloe Square, London SW7

BRISCO, Sir Campbell Howard; 9 Bt (GB 1782), of Crofton Place, Cumberland; s of Gilfred Rimington Brisco (d 1981), and Constance Freda, *née* Polson (d 1980); suc cousin, Sir Donald Gilfrid Brisco, 8 Bt (d 1995); *b* 11 Dec 1944; *m* 1969, Kaye Janette, da of Ewan William McFadzien, of 15 Russell Street, Winton, Southland, New Zealand; 2 s (Kent Rimington b 1972, Shannon Gregory b 1974), 1 da (Rebecca Kaye b 1978); *Heir* s, Kent Rimington Brisco b 24 Sept 1972; *Style*— Sir Campbell Brisco, Bt; ✉ 134 Park Street, Winton, Southland, New Zealand

BRISCOE, Edward Home; yr s of Sir John Leigh Charlton Briscoe, 4 Bt, DFC (d 1993), and Teresa Mary Violet, OBE, *née* Home (d 1995); hp to his nephew, Sir John Geoffrey James Briscoe, 6 Bt; *b* 27 March 1955; *m* 1, 1979 (m dis 1987), Anne Mary, da of Peter Vincent Lister, of Southside, Kingsash, The Lee, Great Missenden, Bucks; 1 s (Guy Home Sebastian b 1983), 1 da (Fay D'Arcy b 1981); m 2, 1994, Sandy Elizabeth King, 2 da of Victor Lloyd, of Seer Green, Bucks; *Style*— Edward Briscoe, Esq; ✉ Bank End Lodge, Forty Green Road, Beaconsfield, Bucks HP9 1XL

BRISCOE, Prof Eric Merrington; OBE; s of William Merrington Briscoe (d 1961), of Shrewsbury, and Gertrude Violet, *née* Edwards (d 1963); *b* 15 Nov 1924; *Educ* Coalbrookdale County HS, UCL (county scholarship, BSc); *m* 24 March 1951, Honor Mary, da of Col Theodore Browning; 3 s (Simon Jeremy b 27 Dec 1951, Charles William b 6 April 1954, Nigel James b 18 Sept 1955); *Career* postgrad trg A Reyrolle 1945–47, devpt engr Elecrical Res Assoc 1947–50, chief res devpt engr Crompton Parkinson 1950–57, dir of devpt Mawson Taylor 1957–62; Doulton Group 1962–86: divnl dir Doulton Industl Porcelains 1962–68, fndr md Doulton Industl Products, md Doulton Insulators, divnl dir Doulton Engineering Group, dir Advanced Materials Engineering, chm Doulton Aerospace Inc (USA), chm Hopyard Foundries, chm Fairey Tecramics; ret from indust 1987; proprietor Briscoe Assocs (consultancy) 1987–93; chm: Ceramic Indust Certification Scheme 1989–92, Staffordshire CBI, various govt ctees (DTI); ldr various export missions (DTI), pres Inst of Ceramics, memb Ct Univ of Keele; hon prof Univ of Sheffield 1989; FEng 1985, FIEE 1960, MIMechE 1960, FIM 1985; *Recreations* sailing; *Style*— Prof Eric Briscoe, OBE, FEng; ✉ Watersmeet, Fradley Junction, Alrewas, Nr Burton on Trent, Staffs DE13 7DN (☎ 01283 790256)

BRISCOE, Dr John Hubert Daly; s of Dr Arnold Daly Briscoe, TD, of Seckford Lodge, Woodbridge, Suffolk, and Doris Winifred, *née* Nicholson (d 1985); *b* 19 March 1933; *Educ* Winchester, St John's Coll Cambridge, St Thomas's Hosp London (BA, MB BChir, MA); *m* 1 Feb 1958, Janet Anne, da of James Douglas Earlam (d 1958), of Bayfield, Warlingham, Surrey; 1 s (James b 1964), 4 da (Sarah b 1959, Emma b 1960, Lucy b 1961, Martha b 1967); *Career* MO Overseas Civil Serv Basutoland 1959–62, asst in gen practice Aldeburgh Suffolk 1963–65, princ in gen practice Eton Berkshire 1965–; MO: Eton Coll 1965–, St George's Sch Windsor Castle 1976–; apothecary to: HM Household Windsor, HM The Queen Mother's Household Royal Lodge 1986–; memb Windsor and Dist Med Soc 1965–, Hon MO The Gds Polo Club 1966–83, bridgemaster Baldwin's Bridge Tst Eton 1988, pres MOs of Schools Assoc 1989–91 (hon sec 1980–85, hon tstee 1992–); hon auditor Euro Union of Sch and Univ Health and Med 1981–89; Liveryman City of London 1966, Asst Worshipful Soc of Apothecaries of London 1984– (Apprentice 1952, Yeoman 1956, Liveryman 1966); DObstRCOG 1959, MRCGP 1968, FRSM 1995; *Recreations* growing vegetables; *Clubs* Omar Khayyam; *Style*— Dr John Briscoe; ✉ Eton Court House, Eton, Windsor, Berkshire SL4 6AQ

BRISE, *see:* Ruggles-Brise

BRISTER, Graeme Roy; s of Royston George Brister, of Cambridge, and Eileen Gladys Brister; *b* 5 May 1955; *Educ* Forest Sch Essex, Phillips Exeter Academy Exeter New Hampshire USA, Brasenose Coll Oxford (MA); *m* 26 July 1986, Ashley Fiona, da of Frank Michael Ashley Hines (Wing Cdr RAF, ret), of Welton, Lincolnshire; 1 da (Leander b 1988), 1 s (Hugo b 1992); *Career* admitted slr 1979, ptnr Linklaters and Paines 1985–; memb: Law Soc 1979, American Bar Assoc, Lords Taverner; *Recreations* country weekends, sport, travel, wine; *Style*— Graeme R Brister, Esq; ✉ Hampstead, London NW3 1ST; Linklaters & Paines, Barrington House, 59–67 Gresham Street, London, EC2V 7JA (☎ 0171 606 7080, fax 0171 606 5113, telex 884 349)

BRISTOL, Archdeacon of; *see:* Banfield, Ven David John

BRISTOL, Bishop of 1985–; Rt Rev Barry Rogerson; s of Eric Rogerson (d 1986), and Olive Hooper; *b* 25 July 1936; *Educ* Magnus GS Newark Notts, Univ of Leeds (BA); *m* 1961, Olga May, da of Wilfred Gibson (d 1982); 2 da (Susan Claire b 1963, Deborah Jane b 1966); *Career* Nat Serv Corpl RAF 1955–57; Midland Bank 1952–57; curate: St Hilda with St Thomas South Shields 1962–65, St Nicholas Bishopwearmouth 1965–67; lectr Lichfield Theol Coll 1967–71, vice princ Lichfield Theol Coll 1971–72, lectr Salisbury/Wells Theol Coll 1972–75, vicar St Thomas Wednesfield 1975–79, team rector

Wednesfield Team 1979, Bishop Wolverhampton dio of Lichfield 1979–85; chm Melanesian Mission 1979–, chm Advsy Bd of Min 1987–93, memb Central Ctee World Cncl of Churches 1991– (memb Faith & Order Cmmn 1987–); Hon LLD Univ of Bristol 1993; *Recreations* cinema, stained glass, photography; *Clubs* Royal Cwlth Soc; *Style*— The Rt Rev the Lord Bishop of Bristol; ✉ Bishop's House, Clifton Hill, Clifton, Bristol BS8 1BW (☎ 0117 973 0222, fax 0117 923 9670)

BRISTOL, 7 Marquess of (UK 1826); (Frederick William) John Augustus Hervey; also Baron Hervey of Ickworth (E 1703), Earl of Bristol (GB 1714) and Earl Jermyn (UK 1826); Hereditary High Steward of the Liberty of St Edmund; patron of thirty livings; s of 6 Marquess of Bristol (d 1985), and his 1 w, Pauline Mary (now Mrs Edward G Lambton), da of late Herbert Coxon Bolton; *b* 15 Sept 1954; *Educ* Harrow, Univ of Neuchâtel Switzerland; *m* 1984 (m dis 1987), Francesca, formerly w of Phillip Jones, of USA, and da of Douglas H Fisher, of Marbella, Spain; *Heir* half-bro, Lord Nicholas Hervey; *Career* governing ptnr Jermyn Shipping; MInstD; *Recreations* horse racing, flying helicopters, snooker; *Clubs* Royal Thames Yacht, House of Lords Yacht, Travellers' (Paris); *Style*— The Most Hon the Marquess of Bristol; ✉ Ickworth, Bury St Edmunds, Suffolk (☎ 0128 488 285)

BRISTOL, Timothy Arnold Neil; s of Arnold Charles Verity Bristol (d 1984), of Wotton, Surrey, and Lillias Nina Maud, *née* Francis-Hawkins; *b* 21 Feb 1941; *Educ* Cranleigh Sch, Guildford Art Sch, RMA Sandhurst; *m* 7 Sept 1968, Elizabeth Olivia, da of John Gurney, *qv*, of Walsingham Abbey, Norfolk; 2 s (Benjamin b 7 Nov 1972, Samuel b 3 Sept 1983), 1 da (Arabella b 19 Aug 1970); *Career* 1 Bn KOSB 1960–67, service in the Radfan, Borneo, S Arabia and Dhofar campaigns, seconded to the Sultan of Muscat's Forces 1966–67, ret as Capt; diamond valuer De Beers, seconded to the Sierra Leone Govt Diamond Office 1967–70; publishing mangr Medici Society Ltd 1970–72, chm and chief exec Eastern Counties Printers and Publishing Gp 1972–85, dir Marlar International Ltd 1986–90, chief exec Sheffield International Ltd 1990–; *Recreations* riding, flying, travel; *Style*— Timothy Bristol, Esq; ✉ Sheffield International Ltd, 10–15 Queen Street, London EC4N 1TJ (☎ 0171 332 0032)

BRISTOW, Hon Sir Peter Henry Rowley; kt (1970); s of Walter Rowley Bristow (d 1947), of London, and Florence, *née* White; *b* 1 June 1913; *Educ* Eton, Trinity Coll Cambridge (MA); *m* 1, 1940, Josephine Noel (d 1969), da of Bertram Leney, of Wateringbury, Kent; 1 s, 1 da (decd); m 2, 1975, Elsa, da of Edwin Reynolds (d 1949), of Warwick, and wid of H B Leney; *Career* served WWII Sqdn Ldr RAF; called to the Bar Middle Temple 1936, QC 1964, dep chm Hants QS 1964–70, judge of Courts of Appeal of Guernsey and Jersey 1965–70, judge of the High Court Queen's Bench Div 1970–85, presiding judge Western Circuit 1979–82; *Books* Judge for Yourself; *Recreations* fishing, gardening; *Style*— The Hon Sir Peter Bristow; ✉ The Folly, Membury, Axminster, Devon EX13 7AG

BRITTAIN, Clive Edward; s of Edward John Brittain (d 1948), of Calne, Wilts, and Priscilla Rosalind, *née* Winzer (d 1990); *b* 15 Dec 1933; *Educ* Calne Secdy Mod Sch; *m* 23 Feb 1957, Maureen Helen, *née* Robinson; *Career* Nat Serv 1954–56; racehorse trainer 1972–; major races won incl: 1000 Guineas 1984, Eclipse Stakes, Dubai Champion Stakes and Breeders Cup Turf USA 1985 (Pebbles), Japan Cup Tokyo 1986 (Jupiter Island), St Leger 1978 (Julio Mariner), 2000 Guineas 1991 (Mystiko), Oaks Stakes Epsom, Irish Oaks, The Curragh, St Leger and Doncaster (User Friendly) 1992, 1000 Guineas 1993 (Sayyedati); *Recreations* shooting; *Clubs* Jockey Club Rooms; *Style*— Clive Brittain, Esq; ✉ Carlburg, 49 Bury Rd, Newmarket, Suffolk CB8 7BY (☎ 01638 663739); Carlburg Stables, 49 Bury Rd, Newmarket, Suffolk CB8 7BY (☎ 01638 664347, fax 01638 661744, mobile 0385 302121)

BRITTAIN, Nicholas John; s of Denis Jack Brittain, MBE (d 1977), of Hungerford, Berks, and Irene Jane Williams (d 1945); *b* 8 Sept 1938; *Educ* Lord Wandsworth Coll, Jesus Coll Oxford (MA); *m* 1964, Patricia Mary, da of Alan Francis John Hopewell (d 1957); 1 s (James b 1969), 2 da (Charlotte b 1971, Rebecca b 1973); *Career* Unilever plc 1960–82, head of gp fin Legal and General plc 1983–86, chief accountant Barclays plc, Barclays Bank plc and dir of various subsid cos 1986–96; govr Alexandra Tst 1980–; memb: Cncl ACCA 1988–, Mgmnt Ctee Providence Row Housing Assoc (chm Fin Ctee 1986–), Accounting Standards Bd FSOSIC 1994–, Common Purpose Nat Forum; chm Accounting Ctee BBA 1987–; Freeman City of London 1993, Liveryman Worshipful Co of Painter-Stainers; FCCA, FRSA; *Recreations* politics, singing, cricket, gardening; *Clubs* Cannons, MCC, Surrey CCC, Brook CC, Privateers CC, 59, Walbrook Ward, Royal Soc of St George, National; *Style*— Nicholas J Brittain, Esq; ✉ Churchfields, Church Lane, Witley, Godalming, Surrey GU8 5PP

BRITTAN, Lady; Diana; CBE (1995); da of Leslie Howell Clemetson (d 1964), and Elizabeth Agnes, *née* Leonard; *b* 14 Oct 1940; *Educ* Westonbirt Sch Tetbury, Univ of Grenoble, Hartwell House; *m* 1, 1965 (m dis 1980), Dr Richard Peterson; 2 da (Katharine b 10 Sept 1966, Victoria b 12 Sept 1968); m 2, 1980, The Rt Hon Sir Leon Brittan, QC, *qv*; *Career* managing ed EIBIS International (int tech press agency) 1977–88, non exec chair Rathbone CI 1992–; Equal Opportunities Commission (EOC): cmmr 1988–96, chair Legal Ctee 1994–96 (memb 1988–96), dep chair EOC 1994–96; magistrate City of London Magistrates' Court 1984– (chair of Bench 1990–), dep chair Human Fertilisation and Embryology Authy (HFEA) 1990– (also chair Licensing and Fees Ctee and Communications Working Gp); memb Bd of Mgmnt Br Sch of Brussels, patron Société Philharmonique de Bruxelles; tstee: Runnymede Tst, Action on Addiction, Open Univ Fndn 1995–, Open Univ Business Sch 1995–; pres Townwomen's Guilds 1995–; *Recreations* travel, walking, gardening, writing, keeping up with friends; *Style*— Lady Brittan, CBE; ✉ 18 Square du Val de la Cambre, 1050 Brussels, Belgium

BRITTAN, Rt Hon Sir Leon; kt (1989), PC (1981), QC (1978); s of Dr Joseph Brittan, and Rebecca, *née* Lipetz; yr bro of Sir Samuel Brittan *qv*; *b* 25 Sept 1939; *Educ* Haberdashers' Aske's, Trinity Coll Cambridge (MA, pres Cambridge Union 1960, chm Cambridge Univ Cons Assoc 1960), Yale Univ (Henry fell); *m* 1980, Diana Brittan, CBE, *qv*; 2 step da (Katharine b 10 Sept 1966, Victoria b 12 Sept 1968); *Career* called to the Bar Inner Temple 1962, bencher 1983; chm Bow Gp 1964–65, editor Crossbow 1966–67; Parly candidate (C) Kensington N 1966 and 1970; MP (C): Cleveland and Whitby Feb 1974–83, Richmond N Yorks 1983–88; oppn spokesman: Devolution and House of Commons Affrs 1976–78, Devolution and Employment 1978–79; min of state Home Office 1979–81, chief sec to Treasy 1981–83, sec of state for the Home Dept 1983–85, sec of state for Trade and Indust 1985–86; vice pres Cmmn of Euro Communities 1989–92 and 1995–; memb Ctee Br Atlantic Gp of Young Politicians 1970–78, vice chm Nat Assoc of Sch Govrs and Mangrs 1970–78, chm Soc of Cons Lawyers 1986–88, distinguished visiting fell Policy Studies Inst 1988, Hersch Lauterpacht Meml lectures Univ of Cambridge 1990; chllr Teeside Univ 1993; Hon DCL: Univ of Newcastle upon Tyne 1990, Univ of Durham 1992; Hon LLD: Univ of Hull 1990, Univ of Bath 1995; Hon DL Univ of Bradford 1992; Dr (hc) Edinburgh 1991; *Publications* incl: The Conservative Opportunity (contrib), Millstones for the Sixties (jtly), Rough Justice, Infancy and the Law, How to Save your Schools, A New Deal for Health Care (1988), Defence and Arms Control in a Changing Era (1988), Discussions on Policy (1989), Europe: Our Sort of Community (Granada Guildhall Lecture, 1989), Monetary Union: the issues and the impact (1989), European Competition Policy (1992), Europe: The Europe We Need (1994); *Clubs* White's, Carlton, Pratt's, MCC; *Style*— The Rt Hon Sir Leon Brittan, QC; ✉ Commission of European Communities, 200 rue de la Loi, 1049 Brussels, Belgium

BRITTAN, Sir Samuel; kt (1993); s of Dr Joseph Brittan and Rebecca, *née* Lipetz; er bro of Rt Hon Sir Leon Brittan, QC, *qv*; *b* 29 Dec 1933; *Educ* Kilburn GS, Jesus Coll Cambridge; *Career* with Financial Times 1955–61, economics ed Observer 1961–64, advsr Dept of Econ Affairs 1965, princ econ commentator Financial Times 1966–, asst ed Financial Times 1978–, visiting fell Nuffield Coll 1974–82, visiting prof Chicago Law Sch 1978; hon prof of politics Univ of Warwick 1987–92, hon fell Jesus Coll Cambridge 1988–; memb: Peacock Ctee on the Finance of the BBC 1985–86; *Awards* Sr Wincott Prize for Financial Journalism 1971, George Orwell Prize 1980, Ludwig Erhard Prize for Econ Writing 1988; Hon DLitt Heriot Watt Univ 1985, Hon DUniv Essex 1994; *Books* Left or Right - The Bogus Dilemma (1968), The Price of Economic Freedom - A Guide to Flexible Rates (1970), Steering the Economy (1971), Is There an Economic Consensus? (1973), Capitalism and the Permissive Society (1973, revised edn entitled A Restatement of Economic Liberalism, 1988), The Delusion of Incomes Policy (with Peter Lilley, 1977), The Economic Consequences of Democracy (1977), The Role and Limits of Government - Essays in Political Economy (1983), Capitalism with a Human Face (1995); *Style*— Sir Samuel Brittan; ✉ The Financial Times, Number One, Southwark Bridge, London SE1 9HL (☎ 0171 873 3000)

BRITTEN, Alan Edward Marsh; s of Robert Harry Marsh Britten (d 1987), and Helen Marjorie, *née* Goldson; *b* 26 Feb 1938; *Educ* Radley, Emmanuel Coll Cambridge (MA), Williams Coll Massachusetts, Princeton Univ NJ; *m* 23 Sept 1967, Judith Clare, da of Cdr Anthony Charles Akerman, OBE, DSC, RN, of Edinburgh; 2 da (Tamara b 22 July 1970, Sophie b 29 Feb 1972); *Career* Northamptonshire Regt 1956–57, 2 Lt Cheshire Regt 1957–58, served Malaya; md Mobil Oil Co Ltd UK 1987–89 (joined 1961), vice pres Mobil Europe Ltd 1990–, co assignments USA and Italy; md: Mobil Oil Kenya Group, Mobil Oil A/S Denmark, Mobil Oil Portuguesa SARL, Mobil Oil BV Group Rotterdam, Mobil Oil Co Ltd; memb: Cncl Aldeburgh Fndn, Cncl Royal Warrant Holders Assoc (vice-pres 1996–97), Advsy Bd 10 Days At Princeton, Cncl UEA; tstee dir Overseas Devpt Gp UEA; *Recreations* music, travel, gardening; *Clubs* Garrick, Noblemen and Gentlemen's Catch and Glee, Aldeburgh Golf; *Style*— Alan Britten, Esq; ✉ Mobil Europe Ltd, Mobil Court, 3 Clements Inn, London WC2A 2EB (☎ 0171 412 4000, fax 0171 412 2920, telex 8812411)

BRITTEN, Philip Stanley; s of Keith Stanley Britten, of Deal, Kent, and Kathleen Josephine, *née* Burton; *b* 29 Aug 1957; *Educ* Queen Elizabeth GS Faversham Kent, Ealing Tech Coll London (City & Guilds); *Career* chef; apprenticeship: Dorchester Hotel London 1973–78, Kulm Hotel St Moritz (2 seasons) and Victoria Jungfrau Interlaken (1 season) 1978–80; sous chef Hambleton Hall Leics 1980–82, head chef Dans Restaurant London 1982–83; Chez Nico London: sous chef 1983–85 (2 Michelin stars), chef patron 1985–87 (1 Michelin star); head chef Capital Hotel London 1988– (1 Michelin star, 4 out of 5 Good Food Guide 1996); md Oscar Samuel Ltd 1993–, dir Solstice Ltd 1996–; conslt Northern Foods (the recipe dish company) 1995–; *Recreations* driving/motor sports; *Style*— Philip Britten, Esq; ✉ Capital Hotel, 22 Basil Street, London SW3 1AT (☎ 0171 589 5171)

BRITTENDEN, (Charles) Arthur; s of late Tom Edwin Brittenden and Caroline, *née* Scrivener; *b* 23 Oct 1924; *Educ* Leeds GS; *m* 1, 1953 (m dis 1960), Sylvia Penelope Cadman; m 2, 1966 (m dis 1972), Ann Patricia Kenny; m 3, 1975, Val Arnison, *qv*; *Career* northern ed Daily Express 1962–63, dep ed Sunday Express 1963–64, ed Daily Mail 1966–71, dep ed The Sun 1972–81, dir of corp relations News International plc 1982–87, dir Times Newspapers Ltd 1982–87, sr conslt Lowe Bell Communications Ltd 1988–, dir Dowson-Shurman Associates Ltd 1990–; memb Press Cncl 1982–86 (jt vice chm 1983–86); *Style*— Arthur Brittenden, Esq; ✉ 22 Park St, Woodstock, Oxfordshire OX20 1SP (☎ 01993 811425); Lowe Bell Communications Ltd, 7 Hertford Street, London W1Y 8LP (☎ 0171 495 4044)

BRITTON, David George; *b* 3 Aug 1946; *Educ* The GS for Boys Weston-super-Mare; *m* 4 Nov 1967, Linda Diana; 1 s (Stephen b 7 May 1973), 1 da (Rachel b 11 Sept 1970); *Career* chief dealer: American Express International Banking Corporation London 1967–74, Nordic Bank Ltd 1975–78; dir: Banque Belge Ltd 1978–90, Quin Cope Ltd 1985–90, Belgian & Generale Investments 1989; currently int treas and risk mangr Merita Bank Ltd; memb: Membership and Rules Ctee London Int Fin Futures Exchange, Euro Advsy Ctee The Chicago Mercantile Exchange; chm Foreign Exchange Ctee Foreign Banks and Securities Houses Assoc; *Recreations* fell walking, Oriental antiques, sport; *Style*— David Britton, Esq; ✉ Merita Bank Ltd, 19 Thomas More Street, London E1 (☎ 0171 265 3173, telex 8601760)

BRITTON, Sir Edward Louis; kt (1975), CBE (1967); s of George Edwin Britton (d 1956), and Ellen Alice Britton; *b* 4 Dec 1909; *Educ* Bromley GS, Trinity Coll Cambridge (MA); *m* 1936, Nora, da of Thomas Gregory Arnald (d 1912); *Career* formerly teacher: Northmead Sch Guildford, Kingston Day Commercial Sch; headmaster Warlingham Co Secdy Sch 1952–60; pres Surrey Co Teachers' Assoc 1945; gen sec: Assoc of Teachers in Tech Instns 1960–68, Nat Union of Teachers 1969–75 (pres 1956); memb: General Cncl TUC 1970–74, Warnock Ctee of Special Educn 1974–78; sr res fell Univ of Sheffield 1975–79, lectr Christ Church Coll Canterbury 1979–86; hon fell Educnl Inst of Scotland; Hon DEd CNAA 1969; Hon FCP; *Style*— Sir Edward Britton, CBE; ✉ 40 Nightingale Rd, Guildford, Surrey GU1 1ER (☎ 01483 572084)

BRITTON, Jonathan; s of Gerald Percy Britton (d 1978), and Jean, *née* Bowler; *b* 23 May 1954; *Educ* King's Sch Worcester, Keble Coll Oxford (MA); *m* 21 Sept 1985, Dr Helen Florence Drake, da of Reginald George Drake; 2 s (Thomas Charles b 5 Nov 1987, Henry Robert b 31 July 1991), 2 da (Emma Katherine b 6 March 1990, Charlotte Rebecca b 28 Nov 1994); *Career* CA; Peat Marwick Mitchell & Co 1977–80, Financial Training Ltd 1980–82; mgmnt conslt: Arthur Andersen & Co 1982–84, Morgan Stanley International 1984–86; Swiss Bank Corporation London: fin dir 1986–90, chief operating offr Capital Markets and Treasy Div 1990–92, head of logistics Asia/Pacific Region Hong Kong 1993–95; global controller SBC Warburg London 1996– (chief operating offr Europe, Middle East and Africa 1995–96); memb ICAEW; *Recreations* opera, golf, sailing, running, DIY, wine; *Clubs* Vincents, Salcombe Yacht, Malden Golf, Piltdown Golf, Royal Ocean Racing; *Style*— Jonathan Britton, Esq; ✉ SBC Warburg, 1 High Timber Street, London EC4B 3SB (☎ 0171 329 0329, fax 0171 711 2770)

BRITTON, (Berry) Julian; s of Capt Gordon Berry Cowley Britton, CBE, RN (d 1979), of Southampton, and Vera, *née* Hyman (d 1988); *b* 9 Nov 1941; *Educ* Taunton Sch Southampton, Bart's Med Sch (MB BS, FRCS, MS, MA); *m* 20 April 1968, (Edith) Mona, da of Robert Cowans (d 1967), of Gateshead; 1 s (Jonathan b 1972), 1 da (Rachel b 1970); *Career* lectr in surgery Bart's 1972–74, reader in surgery Univ of Oxford 1976–80, conslt surgn Oxford Radcliffe Hosp 1980–; Green Coll Oxford: fell 1979–, sr tutor 1979–83, vice warden 1989–92; dir clinical studies Univ of Oxford 1985–88; memb: Int Hepato Pancreato Biliary Assoc, Assoc of Surgns of Great Britain and Ireland, British Soc of Gastroenterology, BMA, RSM; *Recreations* fly-fishing, carpentry; *Style*— Julian Britton, Esq; ✉ 89 Lonsdale Rd, Oxford OX2 7ET (☎ 01865 515404); Department of Surgery, John Radcliffe Hospital, Headington, Oxford OX3 9DU (☎ 01865 220929, fax 01865 60390)

BRITZ, Lewis; s of Alfred Britz (d 1963), and Hetty Britz (d 1948); *b* 7 Jan 1933; *Educ* Grocers Co Sch, Acton Tech Coll (OND), Univ of Nottingham (BSc); *m* 7 Dec 1960, Hadassah, da of Mendel Rosenberg (d 1987), and Libby Rosenberg; 4 da (Ruth b 1968, Miriam b 1972, Naomi b 1975, Hannah b 1978); *Career* Nat Serv Sgt RAOC 1951–53; exec cncllr Electrical, Electronic, Telecommunication and Plumbing Union (EETPU)

1984–95; memb: MMC 1986–92, Industl Tribunals 1989–; dir: London Electricity Bd 1976–86, British International Helicopters 1988–92, ESCA Services 1993–; *Recreations* philately; *Style—* Lewis Britz, Esq; ✉ c/o EETPU, Hayes Court, West Common Rd, Hayes, Bromley, Kent (☎ 0181 462 7755)

BRIXWORTH, Bishop of (First) 1989–; Rt Rev Paul Everard Barber; s of Cecil Arthur Barber (d 1981), and Marye (Mollie), *née* Hardingham; *b* 16 Sept 1935; *Educ* Sherborne, Univ of Cambridge (MA), Wells Theol Coll; *m* 1959, Patricia Jayne, da of Hubert Jack Walford, of Penygroes, Pen y Lan, Bassaleg, Gwent; 3 s (Andrew, Philip (decd), David), 2 da (Jane, Thi Lien Clare (adopted)); *Career* ordained: deacon 1960, priest 1961; asst curate St Francis Westborough Guildford 1960–66; vicar: St Michael's Yorktown Camberley 1966–73, St Thomas on the Bourne Farnham 1973–80; rural dean of Farnham 1974–79, archdeacon of Surrey 1980–89; Archbishop's advsr to the Headmasters' Conf 1993–; *Recreations* cricket, theatre, walking; *Style—* The Rt Rev the Bishop of Brixworth; ✉ 4 The Avenue, Dallington, Northampton NN5 7AN

BROACKES, Sir Nigel; kt (1984); s of late Donald Broackes, and Nan Alford; *b* 21 July 1934; *Educ* Stowe; *m* 1956, Joyce Edith Horne (d 1993); 2 s (Justin, Simon Broackes, *qv*), 1 da (Victoria); *Career* Nat Serv cmmnd 3 Hussars 1953–54; Stewart & Hughman Ltd Lloyd's underwriting agents 1952–55, various property devpts 1955–57; Trafalgar House Ltd (later Trafalgar House plc, taken over by Kvaerner ASA 1996): fndr 1956, md 1958, dep chm and jt md 1968, chm 1969–92, hon life pres 1992; chm Ship and Marine Technol Requirements Bd 1972–77, dep chm Offshore Energy Technol Bd 1975–77, chm designate then chm London Docklands Development Corporation 1979–84, Br chm EuroRoute 1984–86; non-exec dir: Distillers Co 1985–86, Eurotunnel plc 1986–87, Channel Tunnel Group Ltd 1986–87; dir Horserace Totalisator Bd 1976–81, hon treas Kensington House Tst 1963–69; vice chm: Mulberry Housing Tst 1965–69, London Housing Tst 1967–70; tstee: Royal Opera House Tst 1976–81, Nat Maritime Museum 1987–; memb: Cncl Nat Assoc of Property Owners 1967–73, Advsy Cncl V & A 1980–83; govr Stowe Sch 1974–81; chm Crafts Cncl 1991–; Freeman City of London, Liveryman Worshipful Co of Goldsmiths (memb Ct of Assts 1987–); Guardian Young Businessman of the Year 1978; *Books* A Growing Concern (1979); *Recreations* silversmith; *Style—* Sir Nigel Broackes; ✉ Checkendon Court, Checkendon, Oxon RG8 0SR

BROACKES, Simon Nigel; s of Sir Nigel Broackes, *qv*, of Berkley St, London, and late Joyce Edith, *née* Horn; *b* 31 July 1966; *Educ* Eton; *Career* quantity surveyor Trollope and Colls Ltd (awarded BEC mgmnt trg prize 1985), sr conslt to Sir Robert McAlpine Ltd incl mgmnt of special projects div 1987–95; exec dir SQ Group of Cos 1990–, dir London International Exhibition Centre Ltd; memb: Gen Cncl Westminster Property Owners' Assoc 1987–92, Lime St Ward Club 1986, Land Inst 1988, Met Special Constabulary 1986–90; *Recreations* classic cars, tennis; *Clubs* Lansdowne, Carlton; *Style—* Simon Broackes, Esq; ✉ Sir Robert McAlpine Ltd, 40 Bernard St, London WC1N 1LG (☎ 0171 480 5800, fax 0171 702 1695)

BROAD, (Charles) Peter; s of Charles Frederick Herbert Broad (d 1984), of Wimbledon, and Hilda Evelyn, *née* Cook; *b* 24 July 1930; *Educ* St Paul's Sch, King's Coll London, Westminster Med Sch (MB BS); *m* 25 April 1959, Dr Patricia Broad, da of David Ian Laird, of Keston, Kent; 1 s (Andrew St John), 2 da (Katharine Lucy, Rachel Victoria); *Career* house surgn Westminster Hosp 1956–57, lectr and tutor Dept of Anatomy King's Coll London 1959–62, registrar in orthopaedics Hammersmith Hosp and Postgrad Med Sch 1962–63, first asst in orthopaedics St Georges Hosp and The Rowley Bristow Orthopaedic Hosp, sr conslt orthopaedic surgn Bournemouth Dorset (ret); author of several articles on surgery and orthopaedics in med pubns; memb: Cons Party, Cons Med Soc; memb BMA, fell Br Orthopaedic Assoc, FRSM, FRCS; *Recreations* shooting and sailing; *Clubs* Old Pauline, Poole Harbour Yacht; *Style—* Peter Broad, Esq; ✉ Midwood, 14 Martello Rd, Canford Cliffs, Poole, Dorset BH13 7DH (☎ 01202 708550); Nuffield Private Clinic, 65 Lansdowne Rd, Bournemouth, Dorset BM1 1RN (☎ 01202 291866)

BROADBENT, Sir Andrew George; 5 Bt (UK 1893), of Brook Street, Co London, and Longwood, Yorkshire; o s of Sir George Walter Broadbent, 4 Bt, AFC (d 1992), and Valerie Anne, *née* Ward; *b* 26 Jan 1963; *Educ* Monkton Combe; *Heir* unc, Robert John Dendy Broadbent b 1938; *Career* late The Prince of Wales's Own Regt of Yorkshire, currently studying furniture restoration; *Style—* Sir Andrew Broadbent, Bt

BROADBENT, Prof Edward Granville; s of Joseph Charles Fletcher Broadbent (d 1963), and Lucetta, *née* Riley (d 1968); *b* 27 June 1923; *Educ* Huddersfield Coll, St Catharine's Coll Cambridge (MA, ScD); *m* 7 Sept 1949, Elizabeth Barbara, da of Percy Charles Puttick (d 1975); *Career* dep CSO RAE 1969–83 (govt scientist 1943–83), visiting prof Mathematics Dept Imperial Coll 1983–; author numerous scientific papers in learned jls on theory of aero-elasticity, aerodynamics, magnetohydrodynamics, acoustics and propulsion; FRAeS 1959, FIMA 1965, FRS 1977, FEng 1978; *Books* The Elementary Theory of Aeroelasticity (1953); *Recreations* gardening, theatre, concerts, bridge, chess; *Style—* Prof Edward Broadbent, FRS, FEng; ✉ 11 Three Stiles Rd, Farnham, Surrey GU9 7DE (☎ 01252 714621); Mathematics Department, Imperial College, Huxley Building, Queens Gate, London SW7 2BZ (☎ 0171 589 5111 ext 58604)

BROADBENT, Prof Geoffrey Haigh; s of Albert Broadbent (d 1962), and Florence, *née* Haigh (d 1962); *b* 11 June 1929; *Educ* Holme Valley GS, Univ of Manchester (BA); *m* 1, 25 June 1955, Anne Barbara (d 1985), da of Edgar Sheard; 2 s (Mark b 22 April 1960, Antony b 27 Feb 1962); m 2, 3 Aug 1991, Gloria Camino Maldonado, da of Guillermo Camino, of Cusco, Peru; *Career* asst architect Fairhursts 1956–59, lectr Univ of Manchester 1959–61, sec Inst of Advanced Architectural Studies Univ of York 1961–62, lectr Univ of Sheffield 1963–67, prof of architecture Univ of Portsmouth 1980–94 (head Sch of Architecture 1967–88); Br Cncl and other lecture tours to: USA, Canada, Central America, S America, Middle East, S Africa, Europe, SE Asia, Australasia, China; pres Portsmouth Soc 1973–88, memb Cncl ARCUK 1974–79 and 1981–86; Br Sch at Rome: memb Faculty of Architecture 1969–85, memb Appointing Bd Rome Scholar 1985–, chm 1992–; memb Cirque Int des Critiques d'Architecture 1986–; Prof Hon Univ de Santo Domingo 1975, Huesp de Honor Univ di Rosario 1981, Dr Hon Causa Univ di Tucuman 1981; Prof Visitante Univ Nac de Ingeniera Lima 1989, Dip d'Honor Univ de Arequipa 1989, Prof Hon Univ de Cusco 1989; ARIBA 1955, FRSA 1983; *Books* Design in Architecture (1973, 1987), Emerging Concepts in Urban Space Design (1990), Tómas Taveira I (1991), Deconstruction (1991); co-ed and contrib: Design Methods in Architecture (with A Ward, 1969), Signs, Symbols and Architecture (with C Jencks and R Bunt, 1980), Meaning and Behaviour in the Built Environment (with T Llorens and R Bunt, 1980), The New Free Spirits (with A Papadakis and M Toy, 1992), Miguel Angel Roca (1994), Tómas Taveira II (1994); *Recreations* music, fine arts, travel, photography; *Clubs* Architectural Assoc; *Style—* Prof Geoffrey Broadbent; ✉ 11 Hereford Rd, Southsea, Hants PO5 2DH (☎ 01705 828787, fax 01705 614973)

BROADBENT, John Michael (Mike); s of Ronald William Percy Broadbent (d 1979), of Huddersfield, Yorks, and Timperley, Cheshire, and Marion, *née* White (d 1963); *b* 24 Nov 1933; *Educ* Manchester GS; *m* 29 July 1961, Sandra Elizabeth, da of Lewis Phillips (d 1966), of Runcorn, Cheshire; 2 s (Adam b 1971, Simon b and d 1967), 3 da (Maryan b 1965, Jane b 1969, Philippa b 1971 d 1972); *Career* Nat Serv Bombardier RA 1953–55; journalist: Kemsley Newspapers 1950–57, Star Newspaper 1957–59; with BBC 1959–91: scriptwriter TV News, prodr (later ed) Westminster 1968–72, ed Nine O'Clock News, ed Sixty Minutes, founding ed One O'Clock News, ed Commons TV, asst to Head of BBC Westminster; freelance journalist, broadcasting conslt and lectr 1991–; accompanying offr FCO (OVIS) 1991–95; fndr and former chm Whitehill Ave Luton Res Assoc, memb Luton Town Supporters Club; *Recreations* supporting Luton Town FC, cinema; *Style—* Mike Broadbent, Esq; ✉ 1 Whitehill Ave, Luton, Beds LU1 3SP (☎ 01582 20494)

BROADBENT, (John) Michael; s of John Fred Broadbent (d 1973), of Chipping Campden, Glos, and Hilary Louise, *née* Batty; *b* 2 May 1927; *Educ* Rishworth Sch, Bartlett Sch of Architecture, UCL (Certificate in Architecture); *m* 19 June 1954, Mary Daphne, da of Edgar Lionel Joste (d 1985), of Dousland, Devon; 1 s (Bartholomew b 11 Jan 1962), 1 da (Emma b 9 Jan 1959); *Career* Nat Serv; RA 1945–48 (2 Lt and asst adj Dover Castle 1947–48); trainee Laytons Wine Merchants London 1952–53, Saccone and Speed London 1953–55, John Harvey and Sons Ltd 1955–66 (dir 1963–66), dir Christie Manson and Woods Ltd 1967–97 (head of Wine Dept 1966–97, conslt 1997–), dir Christie's Wine Course; chm Wine Trade Art Soc 1972–, pres Int Wine and Food Soc 1985–92; Master Worshipful Company of Distillers 1990–91 (Liveryman 1964, memb Ct of Assts 1969), Master of Wine 1960; memb Inst Masters of Wine (chm 1971–72), chm Wine & Spirit Trades' Benevolent Soc 1991–92; Membre d'Honneur l'Académie du Vin de Bordeaux (1973), Chevalier dans l'Ordre National du Mérite (1979), La Medaille de la Ville de Paris Echelon Vermeil (1989), Membre d'Honneur L'Académie International du Vin (1994); *Books* Wine Tasting (1968), The Great Vintage Wine Book (1980, II 1991), Pocketbook of Vintages (1992); *Recreations* drawing, piano playing; *Clubs* Brooks's; *Style—* Michael Broadbent, Esq; ✉ 87 Rosebank, London SW6 6LJ (☎ 0171 381 0858); Chippenham Lodge, Old Sodbury BS17 6RQ (☎ 01454 315712); Christie's, 8 King Street, St James's, London SW1Y 6QT (☎ 0171 389 2721, fax 0171 839 7869)

BROADBENT, Ven Peter Alan (Pete); *b* 31 July 1952; *Educ* Merchant Taylors' Sch Northwood Middx, Jesus Coll Cambridge (MA), Univ of Nottingham (DipTh), St John's Coll Nottingham (DPS); *m* 1974, Sarah; 1 s (Simon b 13 Nov 1978); *Career* ordained deacon 1977, priest 1978; asst curate: St Nicholas Durham City 1977–80 (concurrently asst chaplain HM Remand Centre Low Newton), Emmanuel Hornsey Rd Holloway 1980–83; Bishop of Stepney's chaplain for mission 1980–89; Anglican chaplain to the Poly of N London 1983–89 (concurrently hon curate St Mary Islington), vicar Trinity St Michael Harrow 1989–94, archdeacon of Northolt 1995–; memb London Diocesan: Synod 1985–, Bishop's Cncl 1988–89 and 1991–, Fin Ctee 1991–; chm London Diocesan Bd for Schs 1996–; memb Gen Synod (Proctor in Convocation London) 1985–; memb Gen Synod: Panel of Chairmen 1990–92, Standing Orders Ctee 1991–95, Standing Ctee 1992–, Appointments Sub-ctee 1992–95; chm Gen Synod: Business Sub-ctee 1996–, Election Review Gp 1996–; memb Dioceses Cmmn 1989–92, Diocesan rep on Crown Appts Cmmn 1990 and 1995; memb: Central Bd of Fin 1991–95 and 1996– (memb Exec Ctee 1991–95), Cncl Wycliffe Hall 1991–94, Archbishops' Advsy Gp on Fin Mgmnt and the Expectations of the Church 1993–; chm Vacancy in See Ctees Regulation Working Pty 1991–93; memb: C of E Evangelical Cncl 1984–95, London Diocesan Evangelical Cncl 1985–, Open Synod Gp Ctee 1994–, Evangelical Gp in Gen Synod Ctee 1996–; asst ed Anvil (theol jl) 1984–86; contrib: Third Way, Church of England Newspaper; Lab cncllr London Borough of Islington (chm Devpt and Planning Ctee) 1982–89, dep chm London Planning Advsy Ctee 1985–89, vice chm Planning and Tport Ctee Assoc of London Authorities 1985–89; chm: London Boroughs Tport Ctee 1986–89, London Road Safety Ctee 1987–89; memb S Eastern Regnl Planning Conf 1986–89; London Borough of Harrow: co-opted memb Educn Ctee 1990–96, chm Standing Advsy Cncl on RE 1990–95; chm Family Action Info and Rescue 1981–84, dir Homes for Islington Ltd 1992–; memb: Lab/Co-op Pty, ASTMS 1980–84, NUPE 1984–89; *Books* Hope for the Church of England? (contrib chapter The Political Imperative, 1986), Uncage the Lion (contrib, 1990), Church and Society in the 1990s (contrib 1990), Politics and the Parties (contrib chapter A Labour Party View, 1992), Restoring Faith in Politics (contrib, 1996); *Recreations* football (lifelong support of Tottenham Hotspur FC), theatre and film, railways, real ale, National Trust, popular music from the 1950s to the present day; *Style—* The Ven the Archdeacon of Northolt; ✉ 247 Kenton Road, Kenton, Harrow, Middx HA3 0HQ (☎ 0181 907 5941, fax 0181 909 2368)

BROADBENT, Simon Hope; s of Edmund Urquhart Broadbent, CBE, of Broughton, Hants, and Doris, *née* Hope; *b* 4 June 1942; *Educ* Univ Coll Sch, Hatfield Coll Durham (BA), Magdalen Coll Oxford (BPhil); *m* 2 Dec 1966, Margaret Ann, da of Herbert Franklin Taylor, of Thornbury, Avon; 2 s (Matthew b 1968, William b 1972), 1 da (Victoria b 1971); *Career* Malawi Civil Serv 1964; FCO: econ advsr 1971, 1 sec UK Treasy and Supply Delgn Washington 1974, seconded to Bank of England 1977, jt head of Economists Dept 1978, head of Econ Advsrs 1984, chief econ advsr 1988–93; visiting scholar Institut Universitaire de Hautes Etudes Internationales Geneva 1984, visiting fell Nat Inst of Economic and Social Research 1994–; tstee Anglo-German Fndn 1994–; *Style—* Simon Broadbent, Esq; ✉ 40 Parliament Hill, London NW3 2TN (☎ 0171 435 4159, fax 0171 435 0752)

BROADBENT, William Benedict; ERD (1959); s of William Keighley Benedict Broadbent (d 1949), of Gatesgarth, Huddersfield, and Gertrude, *née* Woodward (d 1961); *b* 10 Jan 1924; *Educ* Rugby; *m* 1, 1954 (m dis 1980), Joy Valerie, da of Ernest Wilkinson, CBE; 4 da; m 2, 1989, Cecelia Michèle, da of Wing Cdr Albert James Dudley Black; *Career* engr, mgmnt conslt, florist/nurseryman; Capt TA and Army Emergency Reserve UK; md Br Salt Ltd 1966–71, chm British Salt Manufacturers' Assoc 1968–72; Severn Valley Railway Holdings plc: dir 1972–92, chm 1975–87, vice pres 1992–; chm: Festiniog Railway Society Ltd 1957–81 (dir 1954–86), Staveley Lime Ltd 1966–71 (dir 1962–71), RD Nicol & Co Ltd 1966–71 (md 1960–66), Dial-a-Ride Ltd 1974–76; dir: Festinog Railway Co 1954–84, Festiniog Railway Society Sales Ltd 1965–, Staveley Industs Ltd 1968–71; chief ops exec Greater Manchester PTE 1972–76; tstee Festiniog Railway Co 1965–; pres British Lubricants Fedn 1968–69; *Recreations* hill climbing, cruise sailing; *Clubs* Mountain Rangers' Assoc; *Style—* William Broadbent, Esq, ERD; ✉ Pembroke Cottage, Long Compton, Warwicks CV36 5JN (☎ 01608 684644)

BROADBRIDGE, 3 Baron (UK 1945); Sir Peter Hewett Broadbridge; o s of 2 Baron Broadbridge (d 1972), and Mabel Daisy, *née* Clarke (d 1966); *b* 19 Aug 1938; *Educ* Hurstpierpoint, St Catherine's Coll Oxford (MA, BSc); *m* 1, 1 April 1967 (m dis 1980), Mary, o da of Wilhelm Otto Busch; 2 da (Hon Jemima Louise b 1970, Hon Sophie Mary b 1972); m 2, 14 Jan 1989, Sally Frances Finn; *Heir* cousin, Martin Broadbridge; *Career* former mangr Guild of Master Craftsmen; conslt Coopers & Lybrand, Peat Marwick Mitchell & Co; mktg appts with Gallaher, Colgate-Palmolive, Unilever; dep speaker House of Lords 1994–; Liveryman Worshipful Co of Goldsmiths; pres Nat Assoc of Allotment Gardeners 1977–80; FRSA; *Recreations* early English watercolours, old English silver, drawing and painting in watercolours, silversmithing, tennis, squash; *Style—* The Rt Hon the Lord Broadbridge; ✉ c/o House of Lords, London SW1A 0PW

BROADHURST, Dr Alan Desmond; s of Sydney Broadhurst (d 1980), of Thurmaston, Leicestershire, and Grace Ellen, *née* Kettle (d 1990); *b* 24 Feb 1926; *Educ* Wyggeston Sch Leicester, Univ of London, Univ of Sheffield, Univ of Cambridge (MB ChB), MRCS, LRCP, DPM, MIBiol, FRCPsych; *m* 11 Oct 1969, Lotte, da of Hans Zingrich, of Villigen, Kt Aargau, Switzerland; 2 s (Mark b 2 July 1970, Peter b 28 Dec 1971); *Career* Staff Capt ME Forces 1947–49; clinical pharmacologist 1955–60 (Geigy, Manchester, Basle), registrar in psychological med Fulbourn Hosp Cambridge 1960–62, sr res in med American Hosp of Paris 1963–64, med registrar Papworth Hosp Cambridge 1964–66, sr registrar in psychiatry and medicine Addenbrooke's Hosp Cambridge 1966–70, sr conslt psychiatrist W Suffolk Hosp Bury St Edmunds 1970–91, conslt physician Addenbrooke's Hosp Cambridge 1970–89; Univ of Cambridge: memb Faculty of Clinical

Med 1970–, clinical teacher in psychopharmacology 1984–; author of papers on psychopharmacology and the effects of drugs on human performance and in aviation medicine; memb: Royal Soc of Med, Exec Ctee Eastern Div RCPsych 1984–89, E Anglian Thoracic Soc, BMA, Aero-Med Int, Oxford Postgraduate Inst of Psychiatry; fndr memb British Assoc for Psychopharmacology; Freeman Worshipful Soc of Apothecaries 1993; *Recreations* motor cruising, sailing, travelling; *Style—* Dr Alan Broadhurst; ✉ Vicarage Grove, The Park, Great Barton, Suffolk IP31 2SU (☎ 01284 787288)

BROADHURST, John Charles; *see:* Fulham, Suffragan Bishop of

BROADHURST, Paul Andrew; s of Malcolm Thomas Henry Broadhurst, of Tamworth, Staffs, and Denise Evelyn Mary, *née* Bartlam (d 1982); *b* 14 Aug 1965; *Educ* Atherstone North Middle Sch, Atherstone Comp Sch; *m* 12 Jan 1991, Lorraine Mary, da of John Cyril Mansfield; 1 s (Alex b 4 Oct 1994), 1 da (Sophie (twin)); *Career* professional golfer; English Sch champion 1983, Lytham Trophy (amateur) 1988, memb English Amateur team 1985–88; turned professional 1988, winner Cannes Open 1989 and Motorola Classic 1990, Eng int 1987–89 (GB & Ireland 1989), runner up Euro Team Championship 1988, winner Euro Pro Celebrity 1991, winner Benson & Hedges Open 1993, winner French Open 1995; memb: Euro team Ryder Cup 1991, Dunhill Cup team 1991, Asahi Gloss Euro team 1991, World Cup team 1995; rookie of the year 1989, equalled lowest ever round (63) Br Open 1990; former employment: landscape gardener, delivery driver, glass fibre laminator; *Recreations* rock music, supporting Leeds Utd FC and Atherstone Utd FC; *Style—* Paul Broadhurst, Esq; ✉ c/o PGA European Tour, Wentworth Club, Virginia Water, Surrey GU25 4LX (☎ 01344 842881)

BROADIE, Prof Alexander; *Educ* Royal HS Edinburgh, Univ of Edinburgh (MA), Balliol Coll Oxford (BLitt), Univ of Glasgow (PhD, DLitt); *Career* prof of logic and rhetoric Univ of Glasgow; RSE Henry Duncan prize lectr in Scottish studies 1990–93; Gifford lectr in natural theology Univ of Aberdeen 1994; FRSE 1991; *Books* A Samaritan Philosophy (1981), George Lokert: Late Scholastic Logician (1983), The Circle of John Mair (1985), Notion and Object: Aspects of Late Medieval Epistemology (1989), The Tradition of Scottish Philosophy (1990), Paul of Venice: Logica Magna (1990), Robert Kilwardby OP: On Time and Imagination (1993), Introduction to Medieval Logic (2 edn, 1993), The Shadow of Scotus (1995); *Style—* Prof Alexander Broadie, FRSE; ✉ Department of Philosophy, University of Glasgow, Glasgow G12 8QQ (☎ 0141 339 8855 ext 4078 and 5692, fax 0141 330 4112, e-mail abr@arts.gla.ac.uk)

BROATCH, (Michael) Donald; s of Dr Alexander Donaldson Broatch (d 1982), of Folkestone, Kent; *b* 28 May 1948; *Educ* Felsted, QMC London (LLB, LLM); *m* 1 June 1974, Catherine Margaret, *née* Block; 2 s (Neil b 1978, Ian b 1980); *Career* called to the Bar Middle Temple 1971, in practice 1972–; *Style—* Donald Broatch, Esq; ✉ 5 Paper Buildings, Temple, London EC4Y 7HB (☎ 0171 353 8494, 0171 583 4555, fax 0171 583 1926)

BROCAS, Viscount; Patrick John Bernard Jellicoe; s (by 1 m) and h of 2 Earl Jellicoe, DSO, MC, PC; *b* 29 Aug 1950; *Educ* Eton; *m* 1971 (m dis 1981), Geraldine Ann FitzGerald Jackson; 2 s (Hon Justin Amadeus b 1970, Hon Jack b 13 March 1977); *Career* engineer; *Style—* Viscount Brocas; ✉ Pantglas, Llanwoda, Dyfed

BROCK, Prof David John Henry; s of John Fleming Brock (d 1983), of Cape Town, SA, and Ruth Mary, *née* Lomberg (d 1990); *b* 5 June 1936; *Educ* Univ of Oxford (BA), Univ of Cape Town (PhD); *m* 1, 30 July 1959, Sheila Margaret, da of Norman J Abercromby (d 1976), of Edinburgh; 4 s (Andrew b 1962, Graham b 1963, James b 1966, Martin b 1974); m 2, 15 May 1995, Moira Elizabeth, da of Lachlan B Young, of Perth; *Career* Univ of Edinburgh: lectr 1968–76, reader 1976–85, prof 1985–, chm Dept of Med 1994–; FIBiol, FRCPEd, FRCPath, FRSE 1983; *Books* Early Diagnosis of Foetal Defects (1982), Molecular Genetics for the Clinician (1992); *Recreations* walking; *Style—* Prof David Brock, FRSE; ✉ Human Genetics Unit, Western General Hospital, Edinburgh EH4 2XU (☎ 0131 651 1040, fax 0131 651 1059)

BROCK, John Hedley; OBE (1976); s of John Brock, JP (d 1949), of Kelly Bray, Cornwall, and Mary, *née* Priest (d 1960); *b* 18 Jan 1912; *Educ* Callington Sch; *m* 1, Vera Wonnacott (d 1972); 1 s; m 2, 1973, Ann Felicity, da of Harry Laity, JP (d 1980); *Career* served RN 1940–46, Lt-Cdr; mangr Lloyds Bank plc 1950–74, dir South Crofty Ltd 1972–85; chm: China Clay Cncl 1972–, Cornwall Indust Devpt Assoc 1975–83, Cornwall Industrial Research Assoc 1994–; pres Cornish Mining Devpt Assoc 1972–; Liveryman Worshipful Co of Tin Plate Workers; *Recreations* music; *Style—* John Brock, Esq, OBE; ✉ Chy an Mor, Coverack, Helston, Cornwall TR12 6SZ (☎ 01326 280417)

BROCK, Michael George; CBE (1981); s of Sir Laurence George Brock, CB (d 1949), and Ellen Margery, *née* Williams; *b* 9 March 1920; *Educ* Wellington, Corpus Christi Coll Oxford; *m* 1949, Eleanor Hope Morrison; 3 s; *Career* historian; pro vice chllr Univ of Oxford 1980–88; warden: Nuffield Coll Oxford 1978–88, St George's House Windsor Castle 1988–93; hon fell: Wolfson Coll Oxford 1977, Corpus Christi Coll Oxford 1982, Nuffield Coll Oxford 1988; Hon DLitt Univ of Exeter 1982; FRHistS, FRSL, FRSA; *Style—* Michael Brock, Esq, CBE, FRSL; ✉ 11 Portland Road, Oxford OX2 7EZ (☎ 01865 515075)

BROCKBANK, Mark Ellwood; s of John Ellwood Brockbank, of Westward Pk, Wigton, Cumbria, and Elizabeth, *née* Allen; *b* 2 April 1952; *Educ* Bootham Sch York; *Career* underwriter Lloyd's 1983–; chief exec Brockbank Group plc 1995– (dir 1988–); dir: Brockbank Syndicate Management Ltd 1982–, Energy Entertainment Co Ltd 1987–, Admiral Insurance Services Ltd 1992–; *Recreations* the arts, shooting, bridge; *Style—* Mark Brockbank, Esq; ✉ Brockbank Group plc, Fitzwilliam House, 10 St Mary Axe, London EC3A 8BS (☎ 0171 648 1000, fax 0171 648 1002)

BROCKBANK, Thomas Frederick; s of John Bowman Brockbank (d 1990), of Hilton, and Alice Margaret, *née* Parker (d 1987); *b* 6 March 1938; *Educ* Bootham Sch York, Loughborough Coll (DLC Mech Engrg); *m* 16 Dec 1967 (m dis 1992), Joan Emma, da of Martin Israelski, of Leamington; 3 da (Eleanor Clare b 1970, Laura Katherine b 1973, Harriet Elisabeth b 1975); *Career* merchant banker; Courtaulds Ltd 1960–65, mgmnt conslt Arthur Andersen & Co London 1965–68, RTZ Consultants (part of RTZ Corporation) 1968–73, Hill Samuel Bank Ltd 1973–93 (dir of corp fin 1985–93); currently: mgmnt conslt and expert witness, dep chm Computerised Financial Solutions plc, chm Nightingale Square Properties plc; author of numerous lectures and articles, particularly on finance for growing companies, flotation and general strategy; MIMC, MSI, FRSA; *Recreations* music, theatre, art, photography, travel; *Style—* Thomas Brockbank, Esq; ✉ Computerised Financial Solutions plc, CIS House, Intec Business Estate, Wade Road, Basingstoke, Hants RG24 8NE (☎ 01256 810100, fax 01256 55220)

BROCKES, Prof Jeremy Patrick; s of Bernard Arthur Brockes, of Stonor, Henley-on-Thames, and Edna, *née* Heaney (d 1959); *b* 29 Feb 1948; *Educ* Winchester, St John's Coll Cambridge (BA), Univ of Edinburgh (PhD); *Career* postdoctoral fell Harvard Medical Sch 1972–75, research assoc UCL 1975–78, assoc prof of biology California Inst of Tech 1981–83 (asst prof of biology 1978–81); memb MRC Biophysics Unit King's Coll London 1983–88, memb Ludwig Inst for Cancer Research 1988–, prof UCL 1991–; scientific medals: Zoological Soc of London 1985, Biological Cncl 1990; memb Soc for Neuroscience USA 1980; FRS 1994; *Recreations* saxophone, movies; *Style—* Prof Jeremy Brockes, FRS; ✉ Ludwig Institute for Cancer Research, 91 Riding House Street, London W1P 8BT (☎ 0171 878 4000)

BROCKET, 3 Baron (UK 1933); Sir Charles Ronald George Nall-Cain; 3 Bt (UK 1921); s of late Hon Ronald Charles Manus Nall-Cain, er s of 2 Baron; suc gf 1967; *b* 12 Feb 1952; *Educ* Eton; *m* 1982 (m dis 1995), Isabell (Isa) Maria, only da of Gustavo Lorenzo, of Long Island, NY, USA; 2 s (Hon Alexander Christopher Charles b 30 Sept 1984, Hon William Thomas Anthony b 8 July 1991), 1 da (Hon Antalya Stephanie Lauren b 2 Nov 1987); *Heir* s, Hon Alexander Christopher Charles Nall-Cain b 30 Sept 1984; *Career* late 14/20 King's Hussars, Gen Service Medal, UN Medal; prop Brocket Hall conference venue and golf club; pres Herts C of C and Indust 1992; chm: Br Motor Centenary Tst 1990, Tst for Information and Prevention (TRIP) (Drug Prevention Initiatives) 1993, Business Link Hertfordshire 1994; dir de Havilland Museum Tst 1992; patron Guild of Guide Lectrs 1992; *Style—* The Rt Hon The Lord Brocket

BROCKHURST, Rowan Benford; s of Geoffrey Thomas Brockhurst, of Ringwood, Hants, and Barbara, *née* Wickens (d 1994); *b* 23 June 1936; *Educ* Sutton Valence, Coll of Law London; *m* 1, 8 April 1961 (m dis 1984), Eve, da of Maj William Tristram (d 1942); 1 s (Nicholas b 1965), 1 da (Harriet b 1963); m 2, 13 May 1987, Fiona Daphne, da of John Cunningham (d 1985); *Career* Nat Serv 2 Lt RASC 1959–60, Capt Army Emergency Res of Offrs; admitted slr 1958; sr ptnr Meesons Ringwood & Fordingbridge Hants; pres Hants Inc Law Soc 1978–79, dir Slrs' Benevolent Assoc 1982–94, pres Ringwood and Dist Community Assoc 1992–95, vice chm Ringwood and Fordingbridge Footpath Soc, pres Ringwood Philatelic Soc, govr Holme Grange Sch Wokingham; memb Law Soc 1958; *Recreations* walking, gardening, reading, inland waterways; *Style—* Rowan Brockhurst, Esq; ✉ 78 Allen Water Drive, Fordingbridge, Hants (☎ 01425 653748); Meesons, New House Market Place, Ringwood, Hants (☎ 01425 472315, fax 01425 470912)

BROCKINGTON, Prof Ian Fraser; s of Prof Colin Fraser Brockington, of Ballasalla, IOM, and Joyce Margaret, *née* Furze; *b* 12 Dec 1935; *Educ* Winchester, Gonville and Caius Coll Cambridge, Univ of Manchester Med Sch; *m* 1 Aug 1969, Diana Hilary, da of Wilfred Joy Pink (d 1984); 2 s (Daniel b 1970, Samuel Fraser b 1978), 2 da (Alice Rose b 1972, Grace Ellen b 1976); *Career* house physician Hammersmith Hosp 1964, sr registrar UCH Ibadan 1964, Wellcome res fell Royal Postgrad Med Sch and Univ of Ibadan 1966, sr lectr Univ of Manchester 1975; visiting prof: Univ of Chicago 1980, Univ of Washington St Louis 1981; prof of psychiatry Univ of Birmingham 1983; pres Marcé Soc 1982; fndr and first chm ad hoc Section Women's Mental Health World Psychiatric Assoc; *Books* Motherhood and Mental Illness (vol 1 1982, vol 2 1988), Motherhood and Mental Health (1996); *Recreations* choral singing, French, Italian and German literature, family activities, house restoration; *Style—* Prof Ian Brockington

BROCKINGTON, Dr John Leonard; s of Rev Leonard Herbert Brockington (d 1978), and Florence Edith, *née* Woodward; *b* 5 Dec 1940; *Educ* Mill Hill Sch, Corpus Christi Coll Oxford (MA, DPhil); *m* 2 Aug 1966, Mary, da of Joseph Gascoigne Fairweather (d 1988); 1 s (Michael b 1971), 1 da (Anne b 1967); *Career* reader Univ of Edinburgh 1989– (lectr in Sanskrit 1965–82, head of dept 1975, sr lectr 1982–89); *Books* The Sacred Thread - Hinduism in its Continuity and Diversity (1981), Righteous Rama - The Evolution of an Epic (1985), Hinduism and Christianity (1992); *Style—* Dr John Brockington; ✉ 3 Eskvale Court, Penicuik, Midlothian EH26 8HT (☎ 01968 678709); Department of Sanskrit, University of Edinburgh, 7 Buccleuch Place, Edinburgh EH8 9LW (☎ 0131 650 4174)

BROCKLEBANK, Sir Aubrey Thomas; 6 Bt (UK 1885), of Greenlands, Co Cumberland and Springwood, Co Lancaster; s of Sir John Montague Brocklebank, 5 Bt, TD (d 1974), and Pamela Sue, *née* Pierce; *b* 29 Jan 1952; *Educ* Eton, Univ Coll Durham (BSc); *m* 1979 (m dis 1990), Dr Anna-Marie, da of Dr William Dunnet; 2 s (Aubrey William Thomas b 1980, Hamish John b 1987); *Heir* s, Aubrey William Thomas Brocklebank b 15 Dec 1980; *Career* financial conslt; chm: Café Inns plc, Select Holdings plc, Postes mobile plc, and dir of various other cos; *Clubs* Brooks's; *Style—* Sir Aubrey Brocklebank, Bt; ✉ Flat B, 120 Gloucester Terrace, London W2 6HP

BROCKLEBANK, Edward; s of Flt Lt Fred Brocklebank (d 1994), of Ballater, Grampian, and Agnes Mitchell, *née* Ainslie (d 1969); *b* 24 Sept 1942; *Educ* Madras Coll St Andrews Fife; *m* 21 Aug 1965 (m dis 1979), Lesley Beverley, da of Dr Ronald Beverley Davidson (d 1975), of Dundee; 2 s (Andrew Edward, Jonathan Ainslie); *Career* trainee journalist DC Thomson & Co Ltd Dundee 1960–63, freelance 1963–65, journalist Scot TV Glasgow 1965–70; Grampian TV: in vision journalist/presenter Aberdeen 1970–77, head of news and current affrs 1977–85, head of documentaries and features 1985–95; prodns incl: What Price Oil? (BAFTA Award 1974), Tale of Two Cities (TRICS Award 1977), Oil (8 pt series for Channel 4, AMANDA Award 1988); fndr and manager Greyfriars Productions 1995–; *Recreations* rugby football, golf, oil painting; *Clubs* New Golf (St Andrews); *Style—* Edward Brocklebank, Esq; ✉ Greyfriars Productions, Greyfriars Garden, St Andrews, Fife KY16 9GH

BROCKLEBANK-FOWLER, Christopher; s of Sidney Straton Brocklebank-Fowler (d 1954), of Oakham, Rutland; *b* 13 Jan 1934; *Educ* Perse Sch Cambridge; *m* 1, 1957 (m dis 1975), Joan, da of Louis Raymond Nowland (d 1961), of Kalgoorlie, W Australia; 2 s (see Simon Brocklebank-Fowler); m 2, 1975 (m dis 1985), Mary Berry; 1 step da; m 3, 13 January 1996, Mrs Dorothea Ann Joan Rycroft, yr da of late Robert William Nicholson Evans; *Career* served RN (submarines) 1952–54, Sub-Lt RNVR; farm mangr Kenya 1954–57; chm Datix International Ltd 1993–95; md: ACP Development Agency Ltd 1984–88, Cambridge Corporate Consultants Ltd 1985–87, Corporate Consultancy Network Ltd 1989–; dir: Creative Consultants Ltd 1966–92, Bow Publications 1968–71, SOS Children's Villages UK Trading 1981–84 (chm SOS Children's Villages UK 1978–84); contested (C) West Ham N 1964, MP (C) King's Lynn 1970–74, MP (C then SDP from 1981) Norfolk NW 1974–83; contested (SDP) Norfolk NW 1983 and 1987, contested (Lib Dem) Norfolk S 1992; memb Bow Gp 1961–81 (chm 1968–69); vice chm: Cons Parly Foreign and Cwlth Affrs Sub Ctee 1979–81, Cons Parly Trade Ctee 1979–81; chm UN Parly Gp 1979–83; memb Parly Select Ctee: on Overseas Devpt 1973–79, on Foreign and Cwlth Affrs and Overseas Devpt Sub Ctee 1979–83; SDP spokesman Agric and Foreign Affrs 1981–83, chm SDP Overseas Devpt Policy Ctee 1981–87; vice chm: SDP Agric Policy Ctee 1981–83, SDP Communications Ctee 1982–83; memb Cncl for Social Democracy 1982–83; govr Inst of Devpt Studies Univ of Sussex 1978–81 (hon fell); fell De Montfort Univ; MCAM, MCIM, MIMC, FIMgt, FInstD; *Recreations* swimming, shooting, fishing, painting; *Style—* Christopher Brocklebank-Fowler, Esq; ✉ The Long Cottage, Flitcham, King's Lynn, Norfolk PE31 6BU (☎ 01485 600255, fax 01485 601150)

BROCKLEBANK-FOWLER, Simon Edward; s of Christopher Brocklebank-Fowler, *qv*, of Norfolk, and Joan May, *née* Nowland; *b* 29 Sept 1961; *Educ* Westminster, Jesus Coll Cambridge (exhibitioner, MA); *m* 26 April 1993, Alexandra Katharine, da of Sir John Robson, KCMG (former ambass to Norway); *Career* FCO 1982–86, Kleinwort Benson Ltd 1986–91, dir Shandwick Consultants Ltd 1992–94, md Citigate Corporate Ltd 1995– (dir 1994–95); dir Investor Rels Soc 1994–; *Recreations* politics, music, shooting, skiing; *Clubs* Travellers', Leander; *Style—* Simon Brocklebank-Fowler, Esq; ✉ 10–12 Moreton Terrace Mews North, London SW1V 2NT; Citigate Corporate Ltd, 26 Finsbury Square, London EC4A 1DS (☎ 0171 282 8000, fax 0171 282 8060)

BROCKLEHURST, Aubrey Bernard; s of Clement George Bernard Brocklehurst, lithographic artist (d 1937), of Chorlton-cum-Hardy, Manchester, and Ellen, *née* Davies (d 1943); *b* 29 June 1913; *Educ* Chorlton HS Manchester; *m* 1, 23 Nov 1940 (m dis 1983), Joan, da of James Rowbotton (d 1945), of Woodland Way, Middleton, Lancs; 2 s (Kevin b 7 Nov 1943, Edwin (twin) b 7 Nov 1943), 1 da (Ruth b 14 Jan 1955); m 2, Hazel Victoria (d 1984), da of Henry James Bryan (d 1931), of Liverpool; m 3, 11 Dec 1987, Helen, da of Charles Lawrence Pryal (d 1940), of San Francisco; *Career* laboratory asst and observer in an experimental machinery laboratory Br Cotton Indust Res Assoc 1931–37, calculator in drawing office Henry Wallwork & Co Ltd 1937–38, mechanical designer Ferguson Pailin Ltd 1938–42, travel organiser for overseas workers Friends Relief Serv 1946–49 (warden FRS Staff Hostel 1946–), self employed watch and clock repairer 1950–63, proprietor (retailing and repairing) antique clock shop 1963–; chm London Section Fell and Rock Climbing Club 1986–88, chm North London Branch Br Horological Inst 1978–95, chm Nat Benevolent Soc of Watch and Clockmakers 1996–; Freeman City of London 1970, Liveryman Worshipful Co of Clockmakers 1973; FBHI 1960, memb Br Antique Dealers' Assoc 1973; *Recreations* walking, mountaineering, travel, DIY; *Clubs* Fell & Rock Climbing; *Style*— Aubrey Brocklehurst, Esq; ✉ Flat 1, 124 Cromwell Rd, S Kensington, London SW7 4ET (☎ 0171 373 0319); 12 Beaconsfield Rd, Hastings, E Sussex TN34 3TN;

BROCKLEHURST, Prof John Charles; CBE (1987); s of Harold John Brocklehurst (d 1981), and Dorothy, *née* Harrison; *b* 31 May 1924; *Educ* Glasgow HS, Ayr Acad, Univ of Glasgow (MB ChB, MD); *m* 27 July 1956, Gladys Florence (Susan); 2 s (Paul Harrison b 20 Aug 1958, Neil John b 20 June 1961), 1 da (Morag Jane b 1 May 1957); *Career* Maj RAMC 1949–51; Christine Hansen res fell Univ of Glasgow 1948–49, jr hosp appts 1951–55 and 1957–61, med offr Grenfell Mission N Newfoundland and Labrador 1955–57, conslt geriatrician Bromley Hosp Gp 1961–69, conslt in geriatric gen med Guy's Hosp 1969–70, hon conslt geriatrician NW Regnl Health Authy 1970–, prof of geriatric med Univ of Manchester 1970–89 (dir Unit for Biological Ageing Res 1974–89, prof emeritus 1990–), visiting prof and head Div of Geriatric Med Univ of Saskatchewan 1978–79, assoc dir Res Unit RCP 1989–; tstee CIBA Geigy Educnl Tst 1977–93, govr Res into Ageing 1980–, vice pres Age Concern England 1980– (vice chm 1971–73, chm 1973–77); tstee: Granada TV Telethon 1992–94, The Continence Fndn 1992–; pres: Age Concern Lancs 1977–88 (chm 1972–77), Manchester and Salford Med Engrg Club 1976–77, Soc of Chiropodists 1977–83, Br Geriatrics Soc 1983–85; Bellahouston Gold medal Univ of Glasgow 1951, Willard Thomson Gold medal American Geriatrics Soc 1977, Founders medal Br Geriatrics Soc 1990; Hon MSc Univ of Manchester 1974; MRCPS (Glasgow) 1959, FRCPS (Glasgow) 1972, MRCPE 1961, FRCPE 1970, FRCP 1984; *Books* Incontinence in Old People (1951), The Geriatric Day Hospital (1971), Textbook of Geriatric Medicine and Gerontology (jtly, 1973, 1978, 1985 and 1992), Geriatric Care in Advanced Societies (jtly, 1975), Geriatric Medicine For Students (jtly, 1976, 1981 and 1985), Progress in Geriatric Day Care (1980), Atlas of Geriatric Medicine (jtly, 1983 and 1992), Urology in Old Age (jtly, 1984), Geriatric Pharmocology and Therapeutics (jtly, 1984), British Geriatric Medicine in the 1980's (jtly, 1987), Case Studies in Medicine for the Elderly (jtly, 1987); *Recreations* painting; *Clubs* East India and Devonshire, RSM; *Style*— Prof John Brocklehurst, CBE; ✉ 59 Stanneylands Rd, Wilmslow, Cheshire SK9 4EX

BROCKMAN, Vice Adm Sir Ronald Vernon; KCB (1965), CSI (1947), CIE (1946), CVO (1979), CBE (1943), DL (Devon 1968); er s of Rear Adm Henry Stafford Brockman, CB (d 1958), and Edith Mary, *née* Sheppard (d 1974); *b* 8 March 1909; *Educ* Weymouth Coll; *m* 1932, Marjorie Jean (d 1994), da of Charles James Butt; 1 s (Peter), 3 da (Lalage, Penelope, Amanda); *Career* served RN 1927–65: private sec to Govr Gen of India 1947–48, princ SO to Chief of Def Staff Adm of The Fleet The Earl Mountbatten of Burma 1959–65; extra gentleman usher to HM The Queen 1979– (gentleman usher 1967–79); KStJ 1984; *Clubs* MCC, Royal Western Yacht of England, Naval (London); *Style*— Vice Adm Sir Ronald Brockman, KCB, CSI, CIE, CVO, CBE, DL; ✉ 3 Raleigh Court, Budleigh Salterton, Devon EX9 6HR (☎ 01395 442687)

BRODIE, Alan; s of Maxwell Brodie, of Glasgow, Scotland, and Judy, *née* Jacobson; *b* 11 Jan 1955; *Educ* HS of Glasgow, Univ of Edinburgh (BA, LLB); *m* 1, 15 Nov 1982 (m dis 1994), Rosemary Anne Squire; 1 s (Daniel Henry b 1987), 1 da (Jennifer b 1986); m 2, 20 Oct 1996, Caroline Louise Diprose; *Career* dir Michael Imison Playwrights Ltd (Literary Agents) 1981–89, fndr Alan Brodie Representation 1989–93 and 1996–, dir International Creative Management Ltd 1993–96; memb Down's Syndrome Assoc; *Style*— Alan Brodie, Esq; ✉ 211 Piccadilly, London W1V 9LD (☎ 0171 917 2871)

BRODIE, Sir Benjamin David Ross; 5 Bt (UK 1834), of Boxford, Suffolk; s of Sir Benjamin Collins Brodie, 4 Bt, MC (d 1971); *b* 29 May 1925; *Educ* Eton; *m* 19 Sept 1956 (m dis), Ludmilla Maria, da of August Adamer; 1 s (Alan Ross b 7 July 1960), 1 da (Sonja Mary Brodie-Fairhead); *Heir* s, Alan Ross Brodie b 7 July 1960; *Career* late Royal Signals; *Style*— Sir Benjamin Brodie, Bt

BRODIE, (James) Bruce; s of John Hobson Brodie (d 1979), of Graaff-Reinet, SA, and Edith Florence, *née* Murray; *b* 19 March 1937; *Educ* Union HS SA, Univ of Natal (BA), Fitzwilliam Coll Cambridge (MA); *m* 15 Dec 1962, (Amie) Louise, da of Kenneth Turner James, MBE (d 1964), of Fetcham, Surrey; 2 da (Sarah b 1964, Nicola b 1966); *Career* former slr and ptnr Frere Cholmeley (chm 1990–92), barr 1993–; FCIArb; *Recreations* cricket, fishing; *Clubs* Hawks (Cambridge), MCC; *Style*— Bruce Brodie, Esq; ✉ 39 Essex Street, London WC2R 3AT (☎ 0171 583 1111, fax 0171 353 3978)

BRODIE, Colin Alexander; QC (1980); s of Sir Benjamin Collins Brodie, MC, 4 Bt (d 1971); *b* 19 April 1929; *Educ* Eton, Magdalen Coll Oxford; *m* 1955, Julia Anne Irene, da of late Norman E Wates, of Elmore, Chipstead, Surrey; 2 s (Christian Norman b 1957, Alexander Colin b 1959); *Career* 2 Lt 8 KRI Hussars 1949–50; called to the Bar Middle Temple 1953, head of chambers, bencher Lincoln's Inn 1988, memb Bar Cncl 1989; Liveryman Worshipful Co of Skinners; *Recreations* polo; *Style*— C A Brodie, Esq, QC; ✉ 24 Old Buildings, Ground Floor, Lincoln's Inn, London WC2A 3UJ (☎ 0171 404 0946, fax 0171 405 1360)

BRODIE, Prof David Alan; s of William Brodie, and Margaret, *née* Blackwell; *b* 24 June 1946; *Educ* King's Sch Worcester, Univ of Nottingham (BEd), Univ of Loughborough (MSc, PhD); *m* 1971, Megan Elizabeth, da of Elvet Plummer; 1 da (Jo-Anne Beth b 1973), 1 s (Tom David b 1977); *Career* dir of physical welfare Abingdon Sch 1969–72, lectr in physical educn Saltley Coll 1972–74, sr res fell Carnegie Sch Leeds Poly 1974–81, prof and head Dept of Movement Sci and Physical Educn Univ of Liverpool 1990– (dir of physical educn and recreation 1981–90); memb Int Soc for the Advancement of Kinanthropometry 1991; *Books* Fitness Training for Rugby (jtly, 1978), Get Fit for Badminton (with J Downey, 1980), Microcomputing in Sport and Physical Education (with J J Thornhill, 1983), Citysport Challenge (jtly, 1992), Inner City Sport: who plays, what are the benefits? (with K Roberts, 1992), HE Departmental Leadership/Management - An Exploration of Roles and Responsibilities (with P Partington, 1992), Research Methods in Health Sciences (jtly, 1994), Health Matters at Work (1995); *Recreations* exercise, gardening, travel; *Clubs* Pensby Road Runners; *Style*— Prof David Brodie; ✉ Department of Movement Science and Physical Education, University of Liverpool, PO Box 147, Liverpool L69 3BX (☎ 0151 794 3221, fax 0151 794 3229)

BRODIE, Philip Hope; QC (Scot 1987); s of Very Rev Dr Peter Philip Brodie (d 1990), of Stirling, and Constance Lindsay, *née* Hope; *b* 14 July 1950; *Educ* Dollar Acad, Univ of Edinburgh (LLB), Univ of Virginia (LLM); *m* 16 April 1983, Carol Dora, da of Dr Ian Stanley McLeish, of Bearsden, Glasgow; 2 s (Alexander b 1984, Peter b 1986), 1 da (Alice b 1988); *Career* admitted Faculty of Advocates 1976; standing jr counsel (Scot) MOD (Procurement) Health and Safety at Work Exec 1983–87, pt/t chm Industl Tbnls 1987–91, pt/t chm Med Appeal Tbnls 1991–, memb Mental Welfare Cmmn for Scot 1985–, memb Faculty of Advocates; called to the Bar Lincoln's Inn 1991; *Style*— Philip H Brodie, Esq, QC; ✉ 2 Cobden Crescent, Edinburgh EH9 2BG (☎ 0131 667 2651); Advocates Library, Parliament House, Edinburgh (☎ 0131 226 5071)

BRODIE, Robert; CB (1990); s of Robert Brodie, MBE (d 1966), and Helen Ford Bayne, *née* Grieve; *b* 9 April 1938; *Educ* Morgan Acad Dundee, Univ of St Andrews (MA, LLB); *m* 26 Sept 1970, Jean Margaret, da of Sheriff Princ Thomas Pringle McDonald, QC (d 1969); 2 s (Robert b 1971, James b 1980), 2 da (Alison b 1973, Ruth b 1978); *Career* legal asst to Sec of State for Scotland 1965 (dep slr 1984–87, slr 1987–), dep dir of Scottish Cts admin 1975–82; memb: Sheriff Ct Rules Cncl 1975–82, Scottish Ctee on Jurisdiction and Enforcement 1977–80, Working Party on Divorce Procedure 1979–80; session clerk Wardie Parish Church 1981–91; memb Law Soc of Scotland; *Recreations* music, hill walking, making jam; *Style*— Robert Brodie, Esq, CB; ✉ 45 Stirling Rd, Edinburgh EH5 3JB (☎ 0131 552 2028); Solicitor's Office, The Scottish Office, Victoria Quay, Edinburgh EH6 6QQ (☎ 0131 244 0494)

BRODIE, Stanley Eric; QC (1975); s of Dr Abraham Brodie (d 1978), of Allerton, Bradford, and Cissie Rachel Garstein; uncle Sir Israel Brodie, former chief rabbi of GB and The Cwlth; *b* 2 July 1930; *Educ* Bradford GS, Balliol Coll Oxford (MA); *m* 1, 31 July 1956, Gillian Rosemary, da of Sir Maxwell Joseph; 2 da (Henrietta b 1957, Charlotte b 1960); m 2, 29 Oct 1973, Elizabeth Gloster, QC, *qv*, da of Peter Gloster; 1 da (Sophie b 1978), 1 s (Samuel b 1981); *Career* called to the Bar Inner Temple 1954, recorder Crown Court 1975, bencher Inner Temple 1984, memb Bar Cncl 1987; *Recreations* fishing, boating, opera, holidays; *Clubs* Flyfishers', Athenaeum; *Style*— Stanley Brodie, Esq, QC; ✉ 2 Hare Ct, Temple, London EC4Y 7BH (☎ 0171 583 1770, fax 0171 583 9269)

BRODIE-HALL, Sir Laurence Charles; kt (1982), AO (1993), CMG (1976); *b* 10 June 1910; *Educ* Sch of Mines Kalgoorlie (Dip Metallurgy, DipME); *m* 1, 1940, Dorothy Jolly (decd); 3 s, 2 da; m 2, 1978, Jean Verschuer; *Career* RAE; tech asst to md Western Mining Corporation 1950–51, gen supt Great Western Consolidated 1951–58; dir: Western Mining Corporation 1962–82 (gen supt 1958–62), Alcoa of Aust 1972–82; pres: Chamber of Mines WA 1970–75, AIMM 1974; chm: CSIRO State Ctee 1971–78, Central Norseman Gold Corporation 1974–82 (geologist 1948–49), Three Springs Talc 1974–82, Kalgoorlie Mining Associates, Gold Mines of Kalgoorlie 1974–85, Westintech Innovation Corporation 1984–87, Bd of Mgmnt W Aust Sch of Mines 1982–91, Fndn for Sci and Technol 1988–94; dir: Ansett WA 1983–93, Coolgardie Gold NL 1986–92; cncllr Curtin Univ of Technol 1982–90; Freeman City of Kalgoorlie/Boulder 1989; Hon DTech WA Inst of Technol 1978; Inst Medal Aust Inst of Mining and Metallurgy 1976 (former pres); fell Curtin Univ, Citizen of the Year award WA 1975; life memb: AIMM, Chamber of Mines WA, WASM Graduates' Assoc, Agricola Coll; *Style*— Sir Laurence Brodie-Hall, AO, CMG; ✉ 2 Cliff St, Perth, WA 6000, Australia (☎ 00 61 9 321 3250, fax 00 61 9 481 4618)

BRODIE OF BRODIE, (Montagu) Ninian Alexander; JP (Morayshire 1958), DL (Nairn 1970); 25 Chief of Clan Brodie; s of Ian Brodie of Brodie (d 1943); *b* 12 June 1912; *Educ* Eton; *m* 1939, Helena, da of Janssen Budgen, of Wendover; 1 s, 1 da (d 1972); *Heir* Alastair Brodie, younger of Brodie, *qv*; *Career* professional actor 1935–40 and 1945–50; market gardener and landowner 1953–80, ret; now involved in voluntary work (as a guide etc) at Brodie castle which has been owned by the Nat Tst for Scot since 1980; *Recreations* shooting, bridge, backgammon, bird watching; *Style*— Ninian Brodie of Brodie, JP, DL; ✉ Brodie Castle, Forres, Moray IV36 0TE (☎ 01309 641202)

BRODIE, YOUNGER OF BRODIE, Alastair Ian Ninian; s and h of Ninian Brodie of Brodie, JP, DL, *qv*; *b* 7 Sept 1943; *Educ* Eton, Balliol Coll Oxford; *m* 1968 (m dis 1986), Mary Louise Johnson; 2 s, 1 da; *Career* Turnkey Systems Pty, Sydney, Australia; *Recreations* squash, chess; *Style*— Alastair Brodie, yr of Brodie; ✉ c/o Ninian Brodie of Brodie, JP, DL, Brodie Castle, Forres, Moray IV36 OTE

BRODRICK, His Hon Judge; Michael John Lee; s of His Hon Norman John Lee Brodrick, QC, JP (d 1992), and Ruth Severn, da of Sir Stanley Unwin, KCMG, the publisher; *b* 12 Oct 1941; *Educ* Charterhouse, Merton Coll Oxford; *m* 1969, Valerie Lois, da of Gerald Max Stroud; 2 c; *Career* called to the Bar Lincoln's Inn 1965; memb Western Circuit; elected to Senate of Inns of Court and the Bar 1979–82, recorder 1981–87; memb Wine Ctee Western Circuit 1982–86, judicial memb Tport Tbnl 1986, circuit judge (Western Circuit) 1987–, liaison judge to SE Hants Magistrates 1989–93 and IOW Magistrates 1989–94, memb Lord Chllr's Advsy Ctee for Appt of Magistrates for SE Hants 1993 (Portsmouth 1990–93); cnsllr to the Dean and Chapter of Winchester Cathedral 1993; *Recreations* gardening; *Style*— His Hon Judge Brodrick; ✉ c/o Western Circuit Office, Bridge House, Sion Place, Clifton, Bristol BS8 4BN (☎ 0117 974 3763)

BRODWELL, John Shenton; s of Joseph Brodwell (d 1964), and Blanche Brodwell, *née* Shenton (d 1984); *b* 3 May 1945; *Educ* Woodhouse Grove Sch, Univ of Southampton (LLB); *Career* admitted slr 1970; ptnr: Harrisons 1973–87, Harrison Jobbings 1987–89, Blacks 1989–; dep coroner W Yorks (Eastern Dist) 1993– (asst dep 1990–93); Immigration adjudicator 1976–; govr: Woodhouse Grove Sch 1980–, Horsforth Sch 1974–80 and 1988– (vice chm 1978–80 and 1993–); chm Horsforth Civic Soc 1973–, hon sec Leeds Philharmonic Soc 1982–; memb: Bd Mgmnt of Methodist Schs 1987–91, Law Soc 1971, Leeds Law Soc 1971, Slrs Assoc of Higher Court Advocates 1995; *Recreations* music, choral singing, preservation of the environment; *Clubs* East India, Wig & Pen, Horsforth; *Style*— J S Brodwell, Esq; ✉ 30 Jackman Drive, Horsforth, Leeds LS18 4HS (☎ 0113 258 2744); 28 Park Square, Leeds LS1 2PH (☎ 0113 243 3311, fax 0113 242 0507)

BROERS, Prof Alec Nigel; s of Alec William Broers (d 1987), of Melbourne, Victoria, Aust, and Constance Amy, *née* Cox; *b* 17 Sept 1938; *Educ* Geelong GS, Melbourne Univ (BSc), Gonville and Caius Coll Cambridge (BA, PhD); *m* 1964, Mary Therese, da of Michael Phelan (d 1944); 2 s (Mark b 1965, Christopher b 1967); *Career* numerous managerial positions incl mangr Photon and Electron Optics IBM T J Watson Res Lab 1965–81; mangr: Lithography and Technology Tools 1981–82, Advanced Devpt IBM E Fishkill Lab 1983–84; prof of electrical engrg and head Electrical Div Engrg Dept Univ of Cambridge 1984–92 (head of dept 1992– Oct 1996), Master Churchill Coll Cambridge 1990– Oct 1996, vice chllr Univ of Cambridge Oct 1996–; IBM fell 1977, fell Trinity Coll 1985–90, memb IBM Corp Tech Ctee 1984; memb Cncl: Royal Acad of Engrg 1993–, EPSRC 1994–; IEEE Cledo Brunetti award 1985, American Inst of Physics prize for Industl Applications of Physics 1982; author of numerous papers, book chapters and patents on integrated circuit microfabrication and related subjects; ScD Univ of Cambridge 1991; Hon DEng Univ of Glasgow 1996; foreign assoc Nat Acad of Engrg USA; FIEE, FInstP, FEng 1985, FRS; *Recreations* music, sailing, skiing, tennis; *Style*— Prof Alec Broers, FRS, FEng; ✉ The Old Schools, Trinity Lane, Cambridge CB2 1TN (☎ 01223 332291, fax 01223 339669, e-mail broers@eng.cam.ac.uk)

BROKE, Adam Vere Balfour; s of Charles Vere Broke (d 1944), and Violet Rosemary, *née* Balfour; *b* 16 April 1941; *Educ* Eton; *m* 27 March 1965, Sarah Penelope, da of Norman Lanyon, DSC (d 1981); 3 da; *Career* CA; former pres Inst of Taxation; Freeman Worshipful Co of CAs; FCA 1964, FTII 1971; *Recreations* music, gardening, shooting; *Clubs* Boodle's; *Style*— Adam Broke, Esq; ✉ Adam Broke & Co, 29 Maiden Lane, London WC2E 7JS (☎ 0171 497 0105)

BROKE, Michael Haviland Adlington; s of Philip Adlington Broke, TD (d 1996), of 167 Broadway, Peterborough, and Jean Philippa, *née* Hiley; *b* 9 March 1936; *Educ* Eton, Corpus Christi Coll Cambridge (MA), London Business Sch; *m* 19 Aug 1961, Vera Antonjeta, da of Nikola Gjuracic (d 1972); 1 s (Philip Richard Vere b 9 Sept 1962), 1 da (Nicola b 17 June 1964); *Career* dir J Rothschild & Co Ltd 1975–84, chief exec Stockley plc 1984–87, dep chm Chelsfield plc 1987–; *Recreations* cricket, theatre, music; *Clubs* Buck's, MCC; *Style*— Michael Broke, Esq; ✉ Chelsfield plc, 67 Brook St, London W1

BROKE, Maj-Gen Robert Straton; CB (1967), OBE (1946), MC (1940); s of Rev Horatio George Broke (d 1931), and Mary Campbell, *née* Adlington (d 1949); *b* 15 March 1913; *Educ* Eton, Magdalene Coll Cambridge; *m* 1939, Ernine Susan Margaret, da of Rev William Henry Bonsey (d 1951); 2 s; *Career* RA 1933–66, served ME, N Africa, Europe, Maj-Gen 1964, Cdr Artillery Northern Army Gp 1964–66, Col Cmdt RA 1968–78; farmer; dir Wellman plc 1968–88; pres Metallurgical Plantmakers' Fedn 1977–79, hon treas Cancer Relief Macmillan Fund 1989–; *Recreations* country sports; *Clubs* Army and Navy; *Style*— Maj-Gen Robert Broke, CB, OBE, MC; ✉ Ivy Farm, Holme Hale, Thetford, Norfolk IP25 7DJ (☎ 01760 440225)

BROLLY, Brian Thomas; *b* 21 Oct 1936; *Educ* St Dunstan's Coll London; *m* 1 June 1963, Gillian Adams; 2 s (Sarsfield Kean b 1967, Tristan Patrick b 1970); *Career* MCA Inc/Universal Pictures USA 1957–73: fndr md MCA Records Ltd, MCA Films Ltd and Universal Pictures Television Ltd 1963–73, sr vice pres MCA Television, dir Universal Pictures Ltd; involved in prodn of various award winning television film dramas with MCA/Universal incl: Paul Gallico's The Snow Goose, Don Quioxte, Colditz, George Kauffman's The Man Who Came To Dinner, Hamlet, Test of Violence (art documentary, winner of awards at Venice Biennale, Moscow Film Festival and San Francisco); exec asst to DG Radio Telefis Eireann 1961–63; md and co-fndr: MPL Communications Ltd (with Paul McCartney) 1973–78, The Really Useful Group PLC (with Andrew Lloyd Webber) 1978–88; fndr and md Rosc Holdings Ltd (theatrical prodn co) 1988– prodns incl: Moscow Stations, Fascinating Aida, Valentine's Day, Freudiana; fndr and dir Freudiana Holdings Ltd 1989; fndr shareholder and dir: Classic FM, ABC Books Ltd (children's publishers), Priory Investments Holdings Ltd; *Style*— Brian T Brolly, Esq; ✉ Rosc Holdings Ltd, Broadmead House, 21–23 Panton Street, London SW1Y 4DR (☎ 0171 321 2299, fax 0171 321 0081)

BROME, Vincent; s of Nathaniel Gregory Brome, and Emily Brome; *Educ* Streatham GS, Elleston Sch; *Career* feature writer Daily Chronicle, ed Menu Magazines, Miny of Info, asst ed Medical World, memb Br Library Advsy Ctee 1975–82; play: The Sleepless One (1962) and six plays for TV and radio; *Publications* Anthology (1936), Clement Atlee (1947), H G Wells (1951), Aneurin Bevan (1953), The Last Surrender (1954), The Way Back (1956), Six Studies in Quarrelling (1958), Sometimes at Night (1959), Frank Harris (1959), Acquaintance With Grief (1961), We Have Come A Long Way (1962), The Problem of Progress (1963), Love in Our Time (1964), Four Realist Novelists (1964), The International Brigades (1965), The World of Luke Jympson (1966), Freud and His Early Circle (1967), The Surgeon (1967), Diary of a Revolution (1968), The Revolution (1969), The Imaginary Crime (1969), Confessions of a Writer (1970), The Brain Operators (1970), Private Prosecutions (1971), Reverse Your Verdict (1971), London Consequences (1972), The Embassy (1972), The Day of Destruction (1975), The Happy Hostage (1976), Jung - Man and Myth (1978), Havelock Ellis - Philospher of Sex (1981), Ernest Jones - Freud's Alter Ego (1983), The Day of the Fifth Moon (1984), J B Priestley (1989), The Other Pepys (1992); contrib: The Times, Sunday Times, Observer, Manchester Guardian, New Statesman, New Society, Encounter, Spectator, TLS; *Recreations* writing plays, talking; *Clubs* Savile; *Style*— Vincent Brome, Esq; ✉ 45 Great Ormond Street, London WC1 (☎ 0171 405 0550)

BROMET, Lady *see:* Conan Doyle, Dame Jean

BROMHEAD, Brig David de Gonville; CBE (1994, OBE 1988), LVO (1984); 2 s of Lt-Col Edmund de Gonville Hosking Bromhead (d 1976, himself yr bro of Sir Benjamin Bromhead, 5 Bt, OBE, and great nephew of Lt-Col Gonville Bromhead, VC, who defended Rorke's Drift in the Zulu War of 1879), and Joan, da of late Brig Sir Henry Scott, CB, DSO, MC; bro of John Edmund de Gonville Bromhead, *qv*; *b* 16 Sept 1944; *Educ* St Andrew's Grahamstown SA, RMA; *m* 1970, Susan, da of Cdr Richard Furley Fyson, DSC, JP, RN; 1 s (James Henry de Gonville b 1974), 2 da (Annabel Suzanne de Gonville b 1973, Antonia Diana de Gonville b 1978); *Career* Royal Regt of Wales, Gen Serv Medal (Clasps) S Arabia and NI; has taken part in expeditions under John Blashford-Snell down Blue Nile (1968) and led reconnaissance party through Darien Gap during Trans-America Expedition 1971; equerry to HRH The Prince of Wales 1982–84, Lt-Col 1983, cmd 1 Bn Royal Regt of Wales, Col 1987, Brig 1991; cmd Berlin Inf Bde 1990–94; Freeman of the Bezirk of Wilmersdorf Berlin; FRGS; *Recreations* fishing; *Style*— Brig David Bromhead, CBE, LVO

BROMHEAD, Sir John Desmond Gonville; 6 Bt (UK 1806), of Thurlby, Lincs; s of Col Sir Benjamin Denis Gonville Bromhead, 5 Bt, OBE (d 1981), and Nancy Mary, *née* Lough; *b* 21 Dec 1943; *Educ* Wellington, privately; *Heir* cous, John Edmund de Gonville Bromhead, *qv*, b 10 Oct 1939; *Style*— Sir John Bromhead, Bt; ✉ Thurlby Hall, Thurlby, nr Lincoln LN5 9EG

BROMHEAD, John Edmund de Gonville; s of late Lt-Col Edmund de Gonville Hosking Bromhead (d 1976), and Joan, da of late Brig Sir Henry Scott, CB, DSO, MC; bro of Brig David Bromhead, *qv*; first cous and hp of Sir John Bromhead, 6 Bt, *qv*; *b* 10 Oct 1939; *Educ* St Andrew's Coll Grahamstown S Africa, RAF Coll Cranwell; *m* 1965, Janet Frances, da of Henry Brotherton, of Moreton-in-Marsh, Glos; 1 s (Alistair John de Gonville b 1969), 1 da (Amanda-Jane de Gonville b 1965); *Career* served RAF, ret 1964; capt British Airways; *Style*— John Bromhead, Esq

BROMLEY, Archdeacon of; *see:* Norman, Ven Garth

BROMLEY, (Amey) Ida; MBE (1981); da of William Gordon Bromley (d 1967), and Amy Elizabeth, *née* Marsden (d 1973); *b* 18 July 1929; *Educ* Saxonholme Sch Birkdale Lancs, Royal Liverpool Hosps Sch of Physiotherapy; *Career* appts in various hosps in England and Royal N Shore Hosp Sydney Aust 1952–65; supt physiotherapist: Stoke Mandeville Hosp Aylesbury 1966–77, King's Coll Hosp London 1977–79; dir of physiotherapy services Hampstead Health Dist 1979–86; memb NHS Health Advsy Serv 1983–92; memb: Br Sports Assoc for the Disabled 1973–76, Soc for Res in Rehabilitation 1978–93 (fndr memb and former pres), Int Med Soc of Paraplegia, Editorial Bd Spinal Cord, Cncl of Chartered Soc of Physiotherapy 1972–83 (memb 1952, chm 1978–82), Cncl Bobath Centre 1980–; accompanied Br team to Olympic Games for the Paralysed in Japan, Israel, Germany; frequent lectr at nat and int confs; FCSP 1986; *Books* Paraplegia and Tetraplegia (1976, 4 edn 1991), International Perspectives in Physical Therapy (series ed 1984–93, 8 Vols); *Recreations* music, bridge, country pursuits, conservation, foreign travel, entertaining, bird watching; *Style*— Miss Ida Bromley, MBE; ✉ 6 Belsize Grove, London NW3 4UN (☎ 0171 722 1794)

BROMLEY, Sir Rupert Charles; 10 Bt (GB 1757), of East Stoke, Nottinghamshire; s of Maj Sir Rupert Howe Bromley, 9 Bt, MC (d 1966, fifth in descent from Sir George Bromley, 2 Bt, who changed his name to Bromley from Smith); *b* 2 April 1936; *Educ* Michaelhouse Natal, Rhodes Univ, ChCh Oxford; *m* 26 April 1962, Priscilla Hazel, o da of late Maj Howard Bourne, HAC; 3 s (Charles Howard b 1963, Philip Anthony b 1964, Henry Walford b 1970); *Heir* s, Charles Howard Bromley, b 31 July 1963; *Career* barrister at law Inner Temple 1959; dir Aggregate and Sand Producers' Assoc of S Africa 1991; diocesan registrar Dio of Johannesburg 1985; *Recreations* golf; *Clubs* Kelvin Grove, Johannesburg Country; *Style*— Sir Rupert Bromley, Bt; ✉ PO Box 249, Rivonia 2128, S Africa

BROMLEY-DAVENPORT, William Arthur; JP (Cheshire 1975); only s of Lt-Col Sir Walter Bromley-Davenport, TD, DL (d 1989), of Capesthorne Hall, and Lenette, *née* Jeanes (d 1989); *b* 7 March 1935; *Educ* Eton, Cornell Univ; *m* 29 Dec 1962, Elizabeth Boies, da of John Watts, of Oldwick, NJ, USA; 1 s (Nicholas Walter b 11 June 1964), 1 da (Liberty Charlotte b 25 Dec 1970); *Career* Nat Serv 2 Bn Grenadier Guards 1953–54, Hon Col 3 (Vol) Bn 22 Cheshire Regt 1985; vice pres TAVRA NW of Eng and IOM; landowner (UK and Norway); memb Ctee Cheshire Branch CLA 1962– (past chm); county pres: Cheshire Magistrates' Assoc 1990–, Cheshire & Wirral Fedn of Youth Clubs 1990–, Cheshire Branch Soldiers, Sailors and Airmen's Families Assoc and Forces Help Soc 1992–, Reaseheath Coll Tst 1991–; pres: Cheshire Scout Cncl 1990– (chm 1981–90), The Cheshire Agricultural Soc 1993–96, Quarry Bank Mill Trust Ltd 1993–; chm of Govrs King's Sch Macclesfield 1986–; High Sheriff of Cheshire 1983–84, Lord Lt of Cheshire 1990– (DL 1982); ACA 1966; *Style*— William A Bromley-Davenport, Esq, JP; ✉ The Kennels, Capesthorne, Macclesfield, Cheshire SK11 9LB; Fiva, 6300 Aandalsnes, Norway

BROMWICH, Prof Michael; s of William James Bromwich (d 1982), and Margery, *née* Townley (d 1977); *b* 29 Jan 1941; *Educ* Wentworth Secdy Modern Southend, LSE (BSc); *m* 10 Aug 1972, Dr Christine Margaret Elizabeth Whitehead, OBE, da of Edward Daniel Whitehead, MBE, of Tunbridge Wells; *Career* mangr Ford Motor Co Ltd 1965–66 (accountant 1958–62); lectr LSE 1966–70, prof UWIST 1970–77, prof Univ of Reading 1977–85, CIMA prof LSE 1985–; chm Bd of Accreditation of Educnl Courses 1987–89, pres CIMA 1987–88; memb: Indust and Employment Ctee SSRC/ESRC 1980–84, Accounting Standards Ctee 1981–84, Res Grants Bd ESRC 1992–; additional memb Monopolies and Mergers Cmmn; Hon DSc Lund Univ; FCMA (ACMA 1963), assoc memb CIPFA 1977; *Books* Economics of Capital Budgeting (1976), Economics of Accounting Standards (1985), Financial Reporting Information and Capital Markets (1992), Management Accounting: Pathways to Progress (1994); *Recreations* work, eating in restaurants; *Style*— Prof Michael Bromwich; ✉ London School of Economics and Political Science, Houghton St, London WC2A 2AE (☎ 0171 955 7323, fax 0171 955 7420, telex 24655 LSELON G)

BRON, Eleanor; da of Sydney Bron (d 1995), and Fagah Bron (d 1990); *b* 14 March 1938; *Educ* North London Collegiate Sch, Newnham Coll Cambridge (BA); *Career* actress and writer; with De La Rue Co 1961, subsequent revue work and appearances at Establishment Nightclub Soho 1962 and in NY 1963; *Theatre* incl: Jennifer Dubedat in The Doctor's Dilemma, 1966, title role in The Prime of Miss Jean Brodie 1967 and 1984, title role in Hedda Gabler 1969, Portia in The Merchant of Venice 1975, Amanda in Private Lives 1976, Elena in Uncle Vanya 1977, The Cherry Orchard (Charlotte 1978 and Varya 1985), Margaret in A Family 1978, On Her Own 1980, Goody Biddy Bean in The Amusing Spectacle of Cinderella and her Naughty, Naughty Sisters 1980, Betrayal 1981, Heartbreak House 1981, Duet for One 1982, The Duchess of Malfi 1985, The Real Inspector Hound and The Critic (double bill) 1985, Jocasta/Ismene in Oedipus and Oedipus at Colonus 1987, Infidelities 1987, The Madwoman of Chaillot 1988, The Chalk Garden 1989, Frosine in The Miser 1991, Isabella in The White Devil 1991, Gertrude in Hamlet 1993, Agnes in A Delicate Balance 1995; other performances incl: Façade by Walton Oral, Treason by Kagel (Almeida Festival of Contemporary Music) 1987, Die Glückliche Hand by Schönberg (Nederlandse Opera) 1990, Desdemona - If You Had Only Spoken (one-woman show, Almeida 1991, Edinburgh Festival 1992); *Music* composer of song-cycle with John Dankworth 1973 and verses for Saint-Saens' Carnival of the Animals 1975; *Television* appearances in Not So Much a Programme More a Way of Life (BBC) 1964 and several TV series written with John Fortune; other TV progs and series incl: Making Faces (by Michael Frayn) 1976, Pinkerton's Progress 1983, Inspector Alleyn 1992, Absolutely Fabulous 1992 and 1993; TV plays incl: Nina 1978, My Dear Palestrina 1980, A Month in the Country 1985, Quatermaine's Terms 1987, Changing Step 1989, The Hour of the Lynx 1990, The Strawberry Tree 1993 (Paris 1994), The Blue Boy 1994, The Saint Exupery Story 1994, Wycliffe 1995; *Films* Help!, Alfie, Two for the Road, Bedazzled, Women in Love, The National Health, The Day That Christ Died 1980, Turtle Diary 1985, Little Dorrit, Black Beauty 1993, Deadly Advice 1994, A Little Princess 1994; *Books* Is Your Marriage Really Necessary (with John Fortune, 1972), My Cambridge (contrib, 1976), More Words (contrib, 1977), Life and Other Punctures (1978), The Pillow Book of Eleanor Bron (1985), Desdemona - If You Had Only Spoken (by Christine Brückner, trans), Double Take (novel, 1996); *Style*— Miss Eleanor Bron; ✉ c/o Rebecca Blond Associates, 52 Shaftesbury Avenue, London W1V 7DE (☎ 0171 434 2010, fax 0171 434 2030)

BRONDER, Peter; s of Johann Bronder, and Gertrude, *née* Kastl; *b* 22 Oct 1953; *Educ* Letchworth GS, RAM; *Career* tenor; Bayreuth Festival Chorus 1983, Glyndebourne Festival Chorus 1985, princ tenor WNO 1986–90 (performances for WNO in NY and Milan 1989, Tokyo 1990), freelance 1991–, regular guest appearances with major UK Opera cos; debut: Royal Opera Covent Garden 1986, ENO 1989, Glyndebourne Festival 1990, Theâtre Champs Elysees Paris 1991, Bavarian State Opera 1995, Int Festival Istanbul 1995; live on BBC Radio 3: Snape Maltings Concert 1987, Richard Strauss' Salome 1988, Bellini's Somnambula 1989, Gluck's Iphigenie en Tauride 1992, Donizetti's Maria Stuarda 1994, Strauss' Der Rosenkavalier 1994, Beethoven's Choral Symphony 1995; recordings: Kiri Te Kanawa recital 1988, Adriana Lecouvreur Cilea 1988, Osud Janacek 1989, Weill's Street Scene 1991, Beethoven's Choral Symphony 1991, Rossini's Turco in Italia 1992; many appearances on TV and radio incl: BBC TV Laurence Olivier Awards 1985, Verdi's Falstaff (with WNO) 1989, Berg's Wozzeck (with ENO) 1990; ARAM, LRAM, LGSM; *Recreations* sports, photography, electronics, motorcyling; *Style*— Peter Bronder, Esq; ✉ c/o Allied Artists Agency, 42 Montpelier Square, London SW7 1JZ (☎ 0171 589 6243, fax 0171 581 5269)

BROOK, Anthony Donald; s of Donald Charles Brook (d 1976), and Doris Ellen, *née* Emmett (d 1987); *b* 24 Sept 1936; *Educ* Eastbourne Coll; *m* 18 March 1964, Ann Mary, da of Edwin Reeves (d 1991); 2 da (Clare b 30 June 1966, Joanne b 24 April 1970); *Career* CA Peat Marwick Mitchell CAs (now KPMG) 1960–65 (articled clerk 1955–60), mgmnt accountant Associated Television Ltd 1966–68, fin controller ATV Network Ltd 1969–74, dir external fin IBA 1975–77, fin dir and gen mangr ITC Entertainment Ltd 1978–80, dep chair and md TVS Entertainment plc and TVS Television Ltd 1981–93; dir: Independent Television Assoc Ltd 1991–92, Independent Television News Ltd 1991–93, Southern Radio plc 1984–94, Telemagination Ltd 1992–, Meridian Broadcasting 1993–95, AAB Management Ltd 1993–; chair: SelecTV plc 1993–95, Ocean Radio Group Ltd 1994–; FCA 1970; *Recreations* travel, sailing, golf; *Clubs* Royal Southern Yacht, Meon Valley Golf; *Style*— Anthony Brook, Esq; ✉ AAB Management Ltd, 18 Brookvale Road, Highfield, Southampton SO17 1QP (☎ and fax 01703 555689)

BROOK, Prof Charles Groves Darville; s of Air Vice-Marshal William Arthur Darville Brook, CB, CBE (d 1953), and Marjorie Jean Hamilton, *née* Grant; *b* 15 Jan 1940; *Educ* Rugby, Magdalene Coll Cambridge (BA, MA, MD), St Thomas's Hosp Med Sch (MB BChir); *m* 16 March 1963, Hon Catherine Mary, da of late Lord Hawke, of Northwich, Cheshire; 2 da (Charlotte b 1965, Henrietta b 1968); *Career* resident posts: St Thomas's Hosp 1964–68, Hosp for Sick Children Gt Ormond St 1968–74; Wellcome travelling res fell Kinderspital Zurich 1972–73, conslt paediatrician Middx Hosp 1974–, prof of paediatric endocrinology Univ of London 1989–; dir Endocrine Div London Centre of Paediatric Endocrinology and Metabolism Middx and Great Ormond St Hosps 1994–; chief examiner in med UCL Med Sch 1994–; chm Richmond Soc 1968–74, special tstee The Middx Hosp 1984–, tstee Richmond Parish Land Charity 1988–94; memb Ctee of Mgmnt: Royal Med Benevolent Fund 1976–96 (treas 1989), RSM; MRCP London 1967, FRCP 1979, DCH 1968; *Books* Clinical Paediatric Endocrinology (3 edn, 1995), All About

Adolescence (1985), Current Concepts in Paediatric Endocrinology (1988), The Practice of Medicine in Adolescence (1993), A Guide to the Practice of Paediatric Endrocrinology (1993); *Recreations* DIY, gardening, fishing; *Style*— Prof Charles Brook; ✉ 7 The Hermitage, Richmond, Surrey TW10 6SH (☎ 0181 940 2581); The Middlesex Hospital, Mortimer St, London W1N 8AA (☎ 0171 380 9455, fax 0171 636 9941, e-mail c.brook@med.ucl.ac.uk)

BROOK, Air Vice-Marshal David Conway Grant; CB (1990), CBE 1983); s of Air Vice Marshal William Arthur Darville Brook, CB, CBE (d 1953), and Marjorie Jean Hamilton, *née* Grant; *b* 23 Dec 1935; *Educ* Marlborough, RAF Coll Cranwell; *m* 14 Jan 1961, Jessica Rose, da of Col Michael Ronald Lubbock (d 1989), of Ottawa; 1 s (William b 1965), 1 da (Julie b 1961); *Career* Pilot Nos 263, 1 (Fighter) and 14 Sqdns (Hunter aircraft) 1957–62, ADC to AOC-in-C Near East Air Force 1962–64, CO No 1 (Fighter) Sqdn (Hunter MK 9) 1964–66, RN Staff Course 1967, RAF Advsr to Dir Land/Air Warfare (MOD Army) 1968–69, Wing Cdr Offensive Support (Jt Warfare Estab) 1970–72, CO No 20 (Army Cooperation) Sqdn (Harrier) 1974–76, Station Cdr RAF Wittering (Harrier) 1976–78, Royal Coll of Def Studies 1979, princ Staff Offr to Chief of Def Staff 1980–82, SASO HQ RAF Germany 1982–85, Air Offr Scot and NI 1986–89, ret 1989; appointed civil emergencies advsr Home Office 1989–93; *Recreations* golf, music, hill-walking; *Clubs* RAF; *Style*— D Brook, Esq; ✉ c/o Lloyds Bank, 19 High Street, Evesham, Worcs WR11 4DQ

BROOK, Dr Greville Bertram; s of Bertram Frederick Brook (d 1979), and Frances Emily, *née* Weldon (d 1975); *b* 30 July 1926; *Educ* Hipperholme GS, Scunthorpe GS, Univ of Sheffield (BMet); *m* 12 Sept 1953, Mary Rose, da of William Owen Saunders; 2 s (Adrian Kevin b 13 June 1958, Julian Simon William b 9 Jan 1963), 1 da (Deborah Clare Amanda b 2 Jan 1961); *Career* bursar Br Non-Ferrous Metals Res Assoc 1947–49; Fulmer Research Institute Ltd: investigator 1949–54, section head 1954–68, princ metallurgist 1968–75; dir: Fulmer Research Laboratories Ltd 1975–90, Yarsley Technical Centre Ltd 1982–90; metallurgical conslt 1990–; visiting reader Dept of Metallurgy Univ of Surrey 1974–86; Sir Robert Hadfield Medal Prize Inst of Metals 1988, TB Marsden Award Inst of Metals 1989; tstee Panasonic Tst 1992–95; MUniv Surrey 1980, DMet Univ of Sheffield 1992; fell Inst of Metals 1970 (memb 1946, memb Cncl 1983–87, treas Members' Tst 1993–), memb London Metallurgical Soc (chm 1980–81); FEng 1987, FRSA 1988; *Publications* Die Casting Handbook (contrib), Advanced Materials Technology (ed 1990, 2 edn 1991), Smithells Metals Reference Book (jt ed, 7 edn 1992); *Recreations* theatre, opera, photography, gardening, travel, music, wine; *Style*— Dr Greville Brook, FEng; ✉ 9 Whitfield Road, Hughenden Valley, High Wycombe, Bucks HP14 4NZ (☎ 01494 563570)

BROOK, Lady; Helen Grace Mary; CBE (1995); eldest da of John and Helen Knewstub, of Chelsea, SW3; *b* 12 Oct 1907; *Educ* Convent of Holy Child Jesus Mark Cross Sussex; *m* 2, 1937, Sir Robin Brook, CMG, OBE, *qv*; 2 da (and 1 da of previous m); *Career* voluntary work for Family Planning Assoc 1952, chm Islington Family Planning Clinic 1954, dir Marie Stopes Centre 1959, initiated first birth control sessions for the unmarried woman 1960, pres The Brook Advsy Centres for young people (fndr chm 1963–74), vice pres Family Planning Assoc 1974–, chm Family Planning Sales 1974–80; *Style*— Lady Brook, CBE; ✉ 31 Acacia Rd, London NW8 6AS (☎ 0171 722 5844); Claydene Garden Cottage, Cowden, Kent (☎ 01342 850 367)

BROOK, Irina Demetria Alexandra Jane; da of Peter Stephen Paul Brook, CBE, the director, of Paris, and Natasha, *née* Parry, actress; *Educ* Bedales, Stella Adler Sch NYC; *m* 19 June 1992, Neil Mullarkey; *Career* actress; *Theatre* incl: Irish Coffee (78th St Playhouse NYC) 1981, The Cherry Orchard 1982, Don Juan (both Theatre des Bouffes du Nord Paris) 1983, The Seagull (Watford Palace Theatre) 1986, More Light (Bush) 1986, La Chunga (Old Red Lion) 1988, Mrs Warren's Profession (Orange Tree) 1989, The Misunderstanding (Gate) 1990, The Importance of Being Earnest (Nottingham Playhouse) 1990, The Seagull 1991, Lady Windermere's Fan 1991, The Country Wife 1991, Violent Peace 1993, An Ideal Husband 1993, The Assassin (Chelsea Centre) 1994, Torquato Tasso (Edinburgh Festival) 1994, Lady Chatterley's Lover (tour) 1995; dir Beast on the Moon (bilingual rehearsed reading Paris and London 1995, prodr/dir BAC 1996); *Television* incl: The Bill, Inspector Morse, Bergerac, The Secret Garden, Last Days of General Patton, Zorro; *Films* The Girl in the Picture 1985, Captive 1985, Mashenka 1986, The Fool 1990; *Recreations* playing with Pushkin (my cat), travelling on Eurostar, walking, etymology; *Style*— Ms Irina Brook; ✉ c/o Hutton Management Ltd, 200 Fulham Road, London SW10 9PN (☎ 0171 352 4825, fax 0171 352 8579)

BROOK, Michael; s of John Brook (d 1981), and Mary, *née* Gilpin; *b* 1 Sept 1949; *Educ* Batley GS, Leeds Poly (BA); *m* 21 April 1973, Lynn, da of Leonard Sargeant Allan; 2 da (Alison Judith b 7 Feb 1976, Joanne Elizabeth b 25 May 1977); *Career* asst sales mangr British Jeffrey Diamond Wakefield 1972–73, asst mktg controller Yorkshire Electricity Bd 1974–76, brands mangr Thomas Eastham & Sons 1976–79; Graham Poulter Partnership: account mangr 1979–80, account dir 1980–82, assoc dir 1982–83, dir and ptnr 1983–91; md Ken Geddes Associates Ltd 1991–92, dir Lumley Warranty Services 1992–93; Creative Communications: account dir 1993–, md 1994–96; Internet 2 project dir On Demand Information 1996–; MCIM 1976; *Recreations* golf, cricket, photography, music; *Clubs* South Leeds Golf; *Style*— Michael Brook, Esq; ✉ 3 Woodkirk Gardens, Leeds Rd, Dewsbury, W Yorks WF12 7HZ (☎ 01924 475544); On Demand Information plc, 2 Burley Road, Leeds, W Yorks LS3 1NJ (☎ 0113 233 0000, fax 0113 233 0017)

BROOK, Nigel Geoffrey; s of Basil William Brook, of Coventry, and Dorothy, *née* Botting; *b* 13 Dec 1956; *Educ* Bablake Sch Coventry (Scholarship), St Catherine's Coll Oxford (David Blank Open Scholarship, BA Jurisprudence); *m* 28 April 1984, Ann, da of Edwin Carrington; 1 da (Emma Mary Carrington Brook b 2 March 1988); *Career* Clyde & Co: articled clerk 1979–81, ptnr 1985–; *Recreations* skiing; *Style*— Nigel Brook, Esq; ✉ Clyde & Co, 51 Eastcheap, London EC3M 1JP (☎ 0171 623 1244, fax 0171 623 5427)

BROOK, Sir Robin Ralph Ellis; kt (1974), CMG (1954), OBE (1945); s of Francis Brook, of Harley St, London W1; *b* 19 June 1908; *Educ* Eton, King's Coll Cambridge; *m* 1937, Helen, Grace Mary (Lady Brook, CBE, *qv*); 2 da; *Career* WWII Brig served W Europe 1945; dir Bank of England 1946–49; former chm: Gordon Woodroffe & Co, Leda Investment Trust, Jove Investment Trust, Ionian Bank Ltd, Truscon Ltd, Carclo Engineering Group, W E Sykes; dir: BP 1970–73, Northern Dairies; vice pres Assoc of Br Cs of C (formerly pres), président d'honneur Conf Permanente of EEC Cs of C; vice pres London C of C and Indust (formerly chm then pres); memb City and Hackney Health Authy (formerly City and E London HA) 1974–85; govr St Bartholomew's Hosp 1962–74 (treas and chm 1969–74), chm Special Tstees 1974–88, pres Medical Coll 1969–88, chm Res Tst; vice pres: Family Planning Assoc, Brook Advsy Centres; former chm Sports Cncl and Sport Devpt Ctee; govr Exec Ctee Sports Aid Fund; formerly memb: Cncl and Fin Ctee City Univ, Cncl and Mgmnt Ctee King's Fund; memb Cncl Festival of Britain 1951; former pres London Homes for the Elderly; High Sheriff London 1950; past Master and Wine Warden Worshipful Co of Haberdashers, Liveryman Worshipful Co of Spectacle Makers; Br sabre champion 1936 (Olympic Games 1936 and 1948); Hon DSc City Univ 1989; Cdr Legion of Merit, Legion of Honour, Croix de Guerre and bars, Offr Order of Leopold, Belgian Croix de Guerre; *Style*— Sir Robin Brook, CMG, OBE; ✉ 31 Acacia Rd, London NW8 (☎ 0171 722 5844); Claydene Garden Cottage, Cowden, Kent (☎ 0134 2850367)

BROOK, Rosemary Helen; da of Charles Rex Brook (d 1971), and Nellie Beatrice, *née* Yare; *b* 7 Feb 1946; *Educ* Gravesend Sch for Girls, Newnham Coll Cambridge (MA); *m* 1, 1970 (m dis 1979), Roger John Gross; m 2, 22 Sept 1984, Richard Winston Arbiter; 1 step da (Victoria b 1974); *Career* account mangr McCann Erickson Ltd 1975–77, head of public affrs Wiggins Teape Gp Ltd 1977–82 (Euro mktg coordinator 1968–75), chm and chief exec Edelman Public Relations Worldwide (UK) 1982–94, chm Brook Wilkinson 1994–; pres Inst of PR 1996; Freeman City of London 1985; FIPR 1977 (pres 1996), MIPRA 1979; *Recreations* opera, ballet, reading, gardening, swimming; *Clubs* Reform, Farmers'; *Style*— Miss Rosemary Brook; ✉ Brook Wilkinson, 87 Notting Hill Gate, London W11 3JZ (☎ 0171 229 9907, fax 0171 229 8809)

BROOK-PARTRIDGE, Bernard; s of Leslie Brook-Partridge (d 1933), and Gladys Vere, *née* Brooks, later Mrs Burchell (d 1989); *Educ* Selsdon Co GS, Cambs Tech Coll, Univ of Cambridge, Univ of London; *m* 1, 3 Nov 1951 (m dis 1965), (Enid) Elizabeth, da of Frederick Edmund Hatfield (d 1951), of Sanderstead; 2 da (Eva Katharine Helen (Mrs New) b 6 Dec 1952, Katrina Elizabeth Jane (Mrs Gannon) b 18 Aug 1954); m 2, 14 Oct 1967, Carol Devonald, da of Arnold Devonald Francis Lewis (d 1989), of Gower, S Wales; 2 s (Charles Gareth Devonald b 21 Dec 1969, James Edward Devonald b 4 June 1974); *Career* Nat Serv 1944–48; memb Bar Gray's Inn 1950, cashier and accountant Dominion Rubber Co Ltd 1950–51, asst export mangr British & General Tube Co Ltd 1951–52, asst sec Assoc of Int Accountants 1952–59, sec gen Inst of Linguists 1959–62, various teaching posts FDR 1962–66, special asst to md M G Scott Ltd 1966–68, business conslt (incl various directorships) 1968–72, memb Peterborough Devpt Corp 1972–88, ptnr Carsons Brook-Partridge & Co 1972–, dir and sec Roban Engineering Ltd 1975–96, chm Queensgate Management Services Ltd 1981–87; dir: Brompton Troika Ltd 1985–, Edmund Nuttall Ltd 1986–92, PEG Management Consultants plc 1988–92, Kyle Stewart Ltd 1989–92, St Albans Court Ltd, Lucarne International Ltd 1992–, Lucarne International (Bristol) Ltd 1994–, Lucknam Park Hotels Ltd 1994–95, Wilding Properties Ltd 1995–; chm: Dick Robson plc 1996–, Robson Dunk Ltd 1996–, Robsons of London Ltd 1996–; memb Cncl ICSA 1982– (pres 1986); local govt and political advsr Transmanche-Link 1988 and 1989; contested (C) St Pancras N LCC 1958, memb (C) St Pancras Met Borough Cncl 1959–62, prospective parly candidate (C) Shoreditch and Finsbury 1960–62, contested (C) Nottingham Central 1970; GLC: memb for Havering 1967–73, memb for Havering (Romford) 1973–85, chm of Cncl 1980–81; chm: Environmental Planning (NE) Area Ctee 1967–71, Town Devpt Ctee 1971–73, Arts Ctee 1977–79, Public Servs and Safety Ctee 1978–79; opposition spokesman: on arts and recreation 1973–74, on police matters 1983–85; memb: Exec Ctee Greater London Arts Assoc 1973–78, Exec Cncl Area Museums Serv for SE Eng 1977–78, Cncl and Exec Greater London and SE Cncl for Sport and Recreation 1977–78, GLC Leaders Ctee with special responsibility for law and order and police liaison matters 1977–79; dep ldr Recreation and Community Servs Policy Ctee 1977–79; memb: Exec Ctee Exmoor Soc 1974–79, BBC Radio London Advsy Cncl 1974–79, Gen Cncl Poetry Soc 1977–86 (treas 1982–86), London Orchestral Concert Board Ltd 1977–78, LCDT 1979–84; dir ENO 1977–79; tstee: London Festival Ballet 1977–79, Sadler's Wells Fndn 1977–79; chm: London Symphony Chorus Devpt Ctee 1981–88, The Young Vic Theatre 1983–87 (dir 1977–88), London Music Hall Trust Ltd 1983–, Royal Philharmonic Soc 1991–95; vice chm London Music Hall Protection Society Ltd (Wilton's Music Hall) 1983– (bd memb 1978–, chm 1981–83); chm: Samuel Lewis Housing Trust Ltd 1985–92 (tstee 1976–94), City & Coastal Housing Association Ltd 1991–94, St George's Housing Association Ltd 1985–92, Shipworkers Jubilee Housing Tst 1985–92 (both now part of Samuel Lewis Housing Trust Ltd), Spearhead Housing Tst 1986–92; govr and tstee SPCK 1976–; pres: Br Sch of Osteopathy Appeal Fund 1980–84, Witan Rifle Club 1979–92, City of London Rifle League 1980–, Gtr London Horse Show 1982–86, Gtr London Co Hall branch of the Royal Br Legion 1988–; Hon FIET, hon fell and Hon PhD Columbia Pacific Univ USA 1984; FCIS 1970, FCPU 1984, MIMgt 1978; Order of Gorkha Dakshina Bahu (2 class, Nepal) 1981; *Books* Europe - Power and Responsibility - Direct Elections to the European Parliament (with David Baker, 1972), author of numerous contribs to learned jls and periodicals on various subjects; *Recreations* conversation, opera, ballet, classical music, being difficult; *Clubs* Athenaeum, Leander, Sette of Odd Volumes; *Style*— Bernard Brook-Partridge, Esq; ✉ 28 Elizabeth Road, Henley-on-Thames, Oxon RG9 1RG (☎ 01491 575505)

BROOKE, Sir Alistair Weston; 4 Bt (UK 1919), of Almondbury, W Riding of Yorkshire; s of Sir John Weston Brooke, 3 Bt (d 1983), and his 1 w Rosemary, da of late Percy Llewelyn Nevill (gs of 4 Earl of Abergavenny); *b* 12 Sept 1947; *Educ* Repton, RAC Cirencester; *m* 1982, Susan Mary, o da of Barry Griffiths, of Church House, Norton, Powys; 1 da (Lorna Rosemary Weston b 1983); *Heir* bro, Charles Weston Brooke, *qv*; *Style*— Sir Alistair Brooke, Bt; ✉ Wootton Farm, Pencombe, Hereford; Fearn Lodge, Ardgay, Ross-shire

BROOKE, Charles Weston; s (by 1 m) of Sir John Weston Brooke, 3 Bt (d 1983); hp of bro, Sir Alistair Brooke, 4 Bt, *qv*; *b* 27 Jan 1951; *Educ* Repton; *m* 1984, Tanya Elizabeth, da of Antony Thelwell Maurice, of Lloran, Robertson, NSW, Aust; 1 s (John Weston b 23 Feb 1992), 2 da (Nicola Margery b 1985, Emily Grace b 1988); *Style*— Charles Brooke, Esq; ✉ Midfearn, Ardgay, Ross-shire

BROOKE, Prof Christopher Nugent Lawrence; CBE (1995); s of Prof Zachary Nugent Brooke (d 1946), of Cambridge, and Rosa Grace Stanton (d 1964); *b* 23 June 1927; *Educ* Gonville and Caius Coll Cambridge (BA, MA, DLitt); *m* 18 Aug 1951, Dr Rosalind Beckford Clark, da of Leslie Herman Septimus Clark; 3 s (Francis Christopher b 23 July 1953 d 1996, Philip David Beckford b 19 April 1956, Patrick Lawrence Harvey b 23 May 1959); *Career* Nat Serv 1948–50, RAEC temp Capt 1949–50; Univ of Cambridge: fell Gonville and Caius Coll 1949–56 and 1977–, asst lectr in history 1953–54, lectr in history 1954–56, praelector rhetoricus 1955–56, Dixie prof of ecclesiastical history 1977–94; prof of mediaeval history Univ of Liverpool 1956–67, prof of history Westfield Coll London 1967–77; vice pres Royal Historical Soc 1971–74; memb: Royal Cmmn on Historical Monuments 1977–84, Reviewing Ctee on Export of Works of Art 1979–82; pres Soc of Antiquaries 1981–84; vice pres: Cumberland and Westmorland Antiquarian and Archaeological Soc 1985–89, Northants Record Soc 1987–; corresponding fell Medieval Acad of America 1981, corresponding memb Monumenta Germaniae Historica 1988, fell Società Internazionale di Studi Francescani; Hon DUniv York; FSA, FBA 1970, FRHistS; *Books* The Letters of John Salisbury (with W J Millor and H E Butler, 1955 and 1979), Carte Nativorum - a Peterborough Abbey Cartulary of the fourteenth Century (with M M Postan, 1960), From Alfred to Henry III (1961), The Saxon and Norman Kings (1963), Gilbert Foliot and his Letters (with A Morey, 1965), Letters and Charters of Gilbert Foliot (with A Morey, 1967), The Twelfth Century Renaissance (1969–70), The Heads of Religious Houses, England and Wales, 940–1216 (with D Knowles and VCM London, 1972), The Monastic World 1000–1300 (with Wim Swaan, 1974), A History of Gonville and Caius Coll (1985), Oxford and Cambridge (with Roger Highfield and Wim Swaan, 1988), The Medieval Idea of Marriage (1989), David Knowles Remembered (jtly, 1991), A History of the University of Cambridge, IV, 1870–1990 (1993); *Style*— Prof Christopher Brooke, CBE; ✉ Gonville and Caius College, Cambridge CB2 1TA

BROOKE, (Richard) David Christopher; s and h of Sir Richard Neville Brooke, 10 Bt, *qv*, and his 1 w, Lady Mabel Kathleen, *née* Jocelyn (d 1985), da of 8 Earl of Roden; *b* 23 Oct 1938; *Educ* Eton; *m* 1, 1963 (m dis 1978), Carola Marion, eldest da of Sir Robert

Erskine-Hill, 2 Bt (d 1989); 2 s (Richard Christopher b 1966, Edward Marcus b 1970); m 2, 1979, Lucinda, o da of John Frederick Voelcker, of Happy Hill, Lidgetton, Natal, and formerly wife of William Barlow; *Career* Lt Scots Gds 1957–58; ptnr Rowe & Pitman 1968–86, dir S G Warburg Group plc and dep chm Warburg Securities 1986–90, pres and chm S G Warburg (USA) Inc 1988–90; dir: J O Hambro & Co 1990–, Govett Atlantic Investment Trust plc 1990–92, Contra Cyclical Investment Trust plc 1991–96, Exeter Preferred Capital Investment Trust plc 1991–, Gartmore American Securities plc 1991–95, Contra-Cyclical Trading Ltd 1992–96, Govett American Smaller Companies Investment Trust plc 1992–, HCG Lloyd's Investment Trust plc 1993–, Templeton Emerging Markets Investment Trust plc 1994–, Templeton Latin America Investment Trust plc 1994–, Mercury International Investment Trust plc 1995–, Fidelity Special Valves Investment Trust plc 1995–, Templeton Central & European Investment Co 1996–; chm: Armstrong International Ltd 1990–, North Atlantic Smaller Companies Investment Trust plc 1993–, Govett Global Smaller Companies Investment Trust plc 1994–; vice chm Avocet Mining plc 1995–; vice chm Bd of Govrs Nat Assoc of Securities Dealers Inc 1994–95; *Recreations* boating, fine art, travel; *Clubs* Boodle's, Pratt's, Port Royal (Naples), Taporley Hunt, Bond (NY), The Brook (NY); *Style*— David Brooke, Esq; ✉ c/o J O Hambro & Co Ltd, 10 Park Place, London SW1A 1LP (☎ 0171 629 6994)

BROOKE, Sir Francis George Windham; 4 Bt (UK 1903), of Summerton, Castleknock, Co Dublin; s of Sir George Cecil Francis Brooke, 3 Bt, MBE (d 1982), and Lady Melissa Eva Caroline Brooke; *b* 15 Oct 1963; *Educ* Eton, Univ of Edinburgh (MA); *m* 8 April 1989, Hon Katharine Elizabeth Hussey, o da of Baron Hussey of North Bradley, *qv*; 1 s (George Francis Geoffrey b 10 Sept 1991), 2 da (Olivia Nancy b 12 Jan 1994, Sarah Mary b 20 March 1996); *Heir* s, George Francis Geoffrey b 10 Sept 1991; *Career* AIIMR; *Clubs* Turf, White's; *Style*— Sir Francis Brooke, Bt; ✉ 65 Sterndale Road, London W14 OHU

BROOKE, Rt Hon Lord Justice; Rt Hon Sir Henry; kt (1988); yr s of Baron Brooke of Cumnor, CH, PC (Life Peer, d 1984), and Baroness Brooke of Ystradfellte, DBE (Life Peeress), *qv*; bro of Rt Hon Peter Brooke, CH, MP, *qv*; *b* 19 July 1936; *Educ* Marlborough, Balliol Coll Oxford (MA); *m* 16 April 1966, Bridget Mary, da of Wilfrid George Kalaugher, of Jesmond, Newcastle upon Tyne; 3 s (Michael John b 1967, Nicholas George b 1968, Christopher Robert b 1973), 1 da (Caroline Mary b 1973); *Career* Nat Serv 2 Lt RE 1955–57; called to the Bar Inner Temple 1963; jr counsel to the Crown (Common Law) 1978–81, QC 1981, counsel to Sizewell B Nuclear Reactor Inquiry 1983–85, recorder SE Circuit 1983–88, a judge of the High Court of Justice (Queen's Bench Div) 1988–96, a Lord Justice of Appeal 1996–; DTI inspr into the affairs of House of Fraser Holdings plc 1987–88, Master of the Bench (Inner Temple) 1987, chm Professional Standards Ctee Bar Cncl 1987–88, chm Law Commission 1993–95; chm Ethnic Minorities Advsy Ctee Judicial Studies Bd 1991–94, pres Soc for Computers and Law 1992–, tstee Wordsworth Tst 1995–; *Clubs* Brooks's; *Style*— The Rt Hon Lord Justice Brooke; ✉ Royal Courts of Justice, Strand, London WC2A 2LL

BROOKE, Martin Montague; s of Montague Brooke (d 1957), of Kew Gardens, Surrey, and Sybil Katharine, *née* Martin (d 1959); *b* 25 Aug 1923; *Educ* Eastbourne Coll, Magdalene Coll Cambridge (MA); *m* 1950, Judith Mary, da of Rev Truman Tanqueray (d 1960), of Peaslake, Surrey, late headmaster of Ipswich Sch; 2 s (Anthony, Samuel), 1 da (Katharine); *Career* Lt RNVR, served Atlantic and Indian Oceans 1942–45; banker; dir Guinness Mahon 1963–72, chm Druidale Securities 1972–; dir: Emperor Fund NV 1968–90, Cannon Assurance 1969–84, Cannon Lincoln Investment Management 1991–95; fund mangr M&G Investment Management 1996–; memb Cncl Distressed Gentlefolk's Aid Assoc 1969–94; *Recreations* gardening, walking; *Clubs* Naval; *Style*— Martin Brooke, Esq; ✉ Duxbury House, 53 Chantry View Rd, Guildford, Surrey GU1 3XT (☎ 01483 504777, fax 01483 453781); Johnson's Cottage, Druidale, Ballaugh, Isle of Man IM7 5JA (☎ 01624 897908); M&G Investment Management, 3 Minster Court, Great Tower Street, London EC3R 7XH (☎ 0171 626 4588)

BROOKE, Michael Eccles Macklin; QC (1994); s of Reginald Eccles Joseph Brooke (d 1978), and of Beryl Cicely, *née* Riggs (d 1988); *b* 8 May 1942, ; *Educ* Lycée Français de Londres, Univ of Edinburgh (LLB); *m* 1, 21 Oct 1972 (m dis 1985), Annie Sophie, da of André Vautier; 3 s (Nicholas b 1975, Anthony b 1977, Benjamin b 1979); m 2, 28 June 1996, Mireille, da of late Colin Colahan; *Career* called to the Bar Gray's Inn and in practice 1968–; admitted avocat a la Cour d'Appel de Paris and in practice 1987–; *Recreations* boating, England and France; *Style*— Michael Brooke, Esq, QC; ✉ 25 Molyneux Street, London W1 (☎ 0171 262 1739); 2 Crown Office Row, Temple, London EC4 (☎ 0171 797 8000, fax 0171 797 8001); 250 Bis Blvd St Germain, Paris 75007 (☎ 00 33 1 49 54 64 64, fax 00 33 1 45 44 44 13)

BROOKE, Patrick Thomas Joseph; s of Robert Samuel Brooke (d 1974), of Ross-on-Wye, and Mary Agnes, *née* Coleman (d 1987); *b* 4 Feb 1947; *Educ* Ross GS; *partner* Rosemary Elizabeth Joyce Shaw; 2 s (Daniel Patrick Coleman b 31 Oct 1983, Lewis Samuel Joseph b 9 Oct 1985); *Career* qualified CA 1970; ptnr Waugh Haines Rigby 1974 (merged Cheltenham office with Grant Thornton 1986), managing ptnr 1986–92, regnl mktg ptnr 1992–, nat ptnr responsible for Single Euro Market Servs 1989–; chm Tstees Cotswold Hosp Radio 1988–, chm Local Support Gp for Cotswold Nuffield Hosp 1992–, non-exec dir Glos Trg and Enterprise Cncl 1990– (dep chm 1994–); memb Devpt Ctee Cheltenham Arts Festivals 1996–; ATII 1972, FCA 1979 (ACA 1970); *Recreations* golf, tennis, music, reading; *Clubs* The New Cheltenham, East Gloucestershire, Cotswold Hills Golf; *Style*— Patrick Brooke, Esq; ✉ Grant Thornton, Chartered Accountants, The Quadrangle, Imperial Square, Cheltenham, Glos GL50 1PZ (☎ 01242 222900, fax 01242 222330, mobile 0385 908589)

BROOKE, Rt Hon Peter Leonard; CH (1992), PC (1988), MP (C) City of London and Westminster S (majority 13,369); s of Baron Brooke of Cumnor, CH, PC (Life Peer) (d 1984), and Baroness Brooke of Ystradfellte, DBE (Life Peeress), *qv*; bro of Rt Hon Lord Justice Brooke, *qv*; *b* 3 March 1934; *Educ* Marlborough, Balliol Coll Oxford (MA), Harvard Business Sch (MBA); *m* 1, 1964, Joan (d 1985), da of Frederick Smith, of São Paulo, Brazil; 3 s (and 1 s decd); m 2, 25 Jan 1991, Mrs Lindsay Allinson; *Career* Royal Engineers 1952–53 (invalided out); res assoc IMEDE Lausanne and Swiss corr Financial Times 1960–61, with Spencer Stuart Management Consultants 1961–79 (chm 1974–79); MP (C) City of London and Westminster S 1977–, asst Govt whip 1979–81, Lord Cmmr of the Treasy (Govt whip) 1981–83, under sec of state for Educn and Sci 1983–85, min of state Treasy 1985–87, Paymaster Gen Treasy 1987–89, chm Cons Pty 1987–89, sec of state for NI 1989–92, sec of state for Nat Heritage Sept 1992–94; chm: Cusichaca Project 1978–, Churches Conservation Tst 1995–, Conf on Trg for Architectural Conservation 1995–, Building Socs Ombudsman Cncl 1996–; pres Br Antique Dealers Assoc 1995–; sr fell Royal Coll of Art 1987, presentation fell King's Coll London 1989; Liveryman Worshipful Co of Drapers; *Recreations* cricket, walking; *Clubs* Beefsteak, Brooks's, City Livery, I Zingari, Lord's Taverners, MCC, St George's Conservative; *Style*— The Rt Hon Peter Brooke, CH, MP; ✉ House of Commons, London SW1A 0AA (☎ 0171 219 5041)

BROOKE, Piers Leighton; s of Sir Richard Neville Brooke, Bt, *qv*, and Lady Mabel Cheetham, *née* Jocelyn (da of Lord Roden) (d 1985); *b* 28 Dec 1940; *Educ* Eton; *m* 15 July 1967, Susan W, da of John Davenport of Middletown, New Jersey, USA (d 1987); 1 s (Sebastian b 1974), 1 da (Arabella b 1973); *Career* Lt Scots Gds 1960–63; regnl dir SE Asia Chase Manhattan Bank 1978–79 (dir merchant banking USA 1979–82), exec dir Lloyds Bank Int 1982–85, md Lloyds Merchant Bank 1985–88, gp asset and liability dir Midland Bank plc 1988–94, head of fin strategy NatWest Group 1995–; *Recreations* fishing, skiing, bridge, shooting; *Clubs* Boodle's; *Style*— Piers Brooke Esq; ✉ 37 Yeomans Row, London SW3 (☎ 0171 584 7823); NatWest Group, 41 Lothbury, London EC2P 2BP (☎ 0171 726 1985)

BROOKE, Richard; *Educ* Univ of Exeter (BA); *Career* mgmnt positions Oracle Teletext Ltd and MAI plc; treas BSB 1988–90, chief fin offr BSkyB 1992–95 (dir of treasy and planning (following merger) 1990–92), gp fin dir British Sky Broadcasting Group plc 1995–; *Style*— Richard Brooke, Esq; ✉ British Sky Broadcasting plc, Grant Way, Isleworth, Middx TW7 5QD (☎ 0171 705 3000, fax 0171 705 3030)

BROOKE, Sir Richard Neville; 10 Bt (E 1662), of Norton Priory, Cheshire; s of Sir Richard Christopher Brooke, 9 Bt (d 1981), and his 1 w, Marian Dorothea (d 1965), da of Arthur Charles Innes-Cross; *b* 1 May 1915; *Educ* Eton; *m* 1, 1937 (m dis 1959), Lady Mabel Kathleen Jocelyn (d 1985), da of 8 Earl of Roden; 2 s ((Richard) David Christopher Brooke, *qv* b 1938, Piers Leighton Brooke, *qv* b 1940); m 2, 1960, Jean Evison, da of late Lt-Col Arthur Cecil Corfe, DSO, and formerly w of Sir Nicolas John Cheetham, KCMG, *qv*; *Heir* s, (Richard) David Christopher Brooke b 23 Oct 1938; *Career* former Lt Scots Gds, serv WWII (POW escaped); sr ptnr Price Waterhouse & Co European Firms 1969–75, ret; FCA; *Recreations* racing, fishing; *Clubs* Boodle's; *Style*— Sir Richard Brooke, Bt; ✉ Pond Cottage, Crawley, nr Winchester, Hants (☎ 01962 776272)

BROOKE, Rodney George; CBE (1996), DL (1989); s of George Sidney Brooke (d 1967), of Morley, Yorks, and Amy, *née* Grant; *b* 22 Oct 1939; *Educ* Queen Elizabeth's GS Wakefield; *m* 2 Sept 1967, Dr Clare Margaret Brooke, da of William Martin Cox (d 1985), of Windermere Rd, Moseley, Birmingham; 1 s (Magnus b 1971), 1 da (Antonia b 1973); *Career* asst slr: Rochdale CBC 1962–63, Leicester City Cncl 1963–65; dir of admin Stockport CBC 1971–73 (sr asst slr 1965–67, asst town clerk 1967–69, dep town clerk 1969–71), chief exec and clerk W Yorks CC 1981–84 (dir of admin 1973–81), clerk to W Yorks Lieutenancy 1981–84, chief exec Westminster City Cncl 1984–89, hon sec London Boroughs Assoc 1984–90, clerk to Gtr London Lieutenancy 1987–89, chm Bradford Health Authy 1989–90, assoc Ernst and Young 1989–90, advsr Longman Group 1989–90, sec Assoc of Metropolitan Authorities 1990–; visiting res fell: Royal Inst of Public Admin 1989–91, Nuffield Inst for Health Service Studies Univ of Leeds 1989–; hon fell Inst of Local Govt Studies Univ of Birmingham 1987–; chm Durham Univ Public Serv Devpt Fndn 1994–, dir Dolphin Square Trust 1987–, dir Fndn for IT in Local Govt 1988–91; Freeman, City of London 1993; FRSA; OM (France) 1984, Order of Aztec Eagle (Mexico) 1985, Medal of Merit (Qatar) 1985, Order of Merit (Germany) 1986, Order of Merit (Senegal) 1988; *Books* Managing the Enabling Authority (1989), The Environmental Role of Local Government (1990), City Futures in Britain and Canada (jtly, 1991), The Handbook of Public Services Management (jtly, 1992); *Recreations* skiing, opera, Byzantium; *Clubs* Athenaeum, Ski of GB; *Style*— Rodney Brooke, Esq, CBE, DL; ✉ Stubham Lodge, Middleton, Ilkley, W Yorks LS29 0AX (☎ 01943 601869); 706 Grenville House, Dolphin Square, London SW1V 3LR (☎ 0171 798 8086); The Association of Metropolitan Authorities, 35 Great Smith Street, London SW1P 3BJ (☎ 0171 227 2828, fax 0171 222 0878)

BROOKE, (Christopher) Roger Ettrick; s of Maj Ralph Brooke, RAMC; *b* 2 Feb 1931; *Educ* Tonbridge, Trinity Coll Oxford; *m* 1958, Nancy; 3 s, 1 da; *Career* HM Dip Serv 1955–66; dep md IRC 1966–69, dir Pearson Group Ltd 1971–79, gp md EMI Ltd 1979–80; Candover Investments plc: chief exec 1981–91, chm 1991–; chm The Audit Cmmn 1995–; dir: Slough Estates plc, Lowndes Lambert Group Holdings plc, Tarmac plc, Wembley plc; *Recreations* tennis, theatre, golf; *Style*— Roger Brooke, Esq; ✉ Watermeadow, Swarraton, nr Alresford, Hampshire SO24 9TQ; Candover Investments plc, 20 Old Bailey, London EC4M 7LN (☎ 0171 489 9848, telex 928035, fax 0171 248 5483)

BROOKE-LITTLE, John Philip Brooke; CVO (1984, MVO 1969); s of Raymond Brooke-Little (d 1961), late of Unicorns House, Swalcliffe, Oxon, and Constance Marie, *née* Egan; *b* 6 April 1927; *Educ* Clayesmore Sch, New Coll Oxford (MA); *m* 1960, Mary Lee, o da of late John Raymond Pierce; 3 s (Philip b 1961, Leo b 1966, Merlin b 1968), 1 da (Clare b 1963); *Career* fndr Heraldry Soc (chm 1947–), hon ed The Coat of Arms 1950–, on Earl Marshal's Staff 1952–53, served as Gold Staff Offr Coronation 1953, Bluemantle Pursuivant 1956–67, Richmond Herald 1967–80, Norroy and Ulster King of Arms 1980–95, Clarenceux King of Arms 1995–, King of Arms, Registrar of and Knight Attendant on the Order of St Patrick 1980–95; Coll of Arms: registrar 1974–82, librarian 1974–94, treas 1978–; advsr on Heraldry: to Nat Tst 1983–, to Shrievalty Assoc 1988–; dir Herald's Museum 1991– (dep dir 1983–91); chm Harleian Soc 1984–, pres English Language Literary Tst 1985–; govr emeritus Clayesmore Sch 1983– (govr 1960–83, chm 1961–83); Liveryman Worshipful Co of Scriveners (Master 1985–86); Knight of Malta 1955, Knight Grand Cross of Grace and Devotion 1974 (chllr 1973–77), Cdr Cross of Merit Order of Malta 1964, Cruz Distinguida (1st class) Order of San Raimundo de Penafort (Spain) 1955, Knight Grand Cross of Grace Constantinian Order of St George (Naples) 1975; KStJ; hon fell Inst of Heraldic and Genealogical Studies; fell Soc of Genealogists 1969, FSA; *Books* Royal London, Pictorial History of Oxford, Boutell's Heraldry, Knights of the Middle Ages, Prince of Wales, Fox-Davies' Complete Guide to Heraldry, Kings and Queens of Great Britain, An Heraldic Alphabet, Beasts in Heraldry (co-author), The British Monarchy in Colour, Royal Arms, Beasts and Badges, Royal Ceremonies of State; *Clubs* Chelsea Arts; *Style*— John Brooke-Little, Esq, CVO, FSA, Clarenceux King of Arms; ✉ Heyford House, Church Lane, Lower Heyford, Bicester, Oxon OX6 3NZ (☎ 01869 340337); College of Arms, Queen Victoria St, London EC4V 4BT (☎ 0171 248 1310, fax 0171 248 6448)

BROOKE OF YSTRADFELLTE, Baroness (Life Peeress 1964); Barbara Muriel Brooke; *née* Mathews; DBE (1960); yst da of Rev Canon Alfred Augustus Mathews (d 1946), of Llanwern, Gwent, and Ethel Frances, *née* Evans (d 1951); *b* 14 Jan 1908; *Educ* Queen Anne's Sch Caversham, Glos Trg Coll of Domestic Sci; *m* 1933, Baron Brooke of Cumnor, CH, PC (d 1984); 2 s (The Rt Hon Peter Brooke, CH, MP, The Hon Sir Henry Brooke, QC, *qqv*), 2 da; *Career* memb Hampstead BC 1948–65, vice chm Cons Pty Orgn 1954–64, memb N W Met Regnl Hosp Bd 1955–66; chm: Governing Body of Godolphin and Latymer Sch 1960–78, Exec Ctee Queen's Inst of Dist Nursing 1961–71; memb Mgmnt Ctee King Edward's Hosp Fund for London 1967–70; *Style*— The Rt Hon the Lady Brooke of Ystradfellte, DBE; ✉ Romans Halt, Mildenhall, Marlborough, Wilts

BROOKE-ROSE, Prof Christine; da of Alfred Northbrook Rose (d 1934), and Evelyn Brooke (d 1984); *b* 16 Jan 1923; *Educ* St Stephen's Coll Folkestone, Univ of Oxford (BA, MA), Univ of London (PhD); *m* 1948 (m dis 1975), Jerzy Peterkiewicz; *Career* novelist and critic; Flt Offr WAAF 1941–45; freelance journalist 1955–68, prof of English language and lit Univ of Paris Vincennes 1975–88 (lectr 1968–75); Hon DLitt UEA 1988; travelling prize Soc of Authors 1964, James Tait Black Meml Prize 1966, translation prize Arts Cncl 1969; *Books* criticism: A Grammar of Metaphor (1958), A ZBC of Ezra Pound (1971), A Rhetoric of the Unreal (1981), Stories, Theories and Things (1991); novels: The Languages of Love (1957), The Sycamore Tree (1958), The Dear Deceit (1960), The Middlemen (1961), Out (1964), Such (1965), Between (1968), Thru (1975), Amalgamemnon (1984), Xorandor (1986), Verbivore (1990), Textermination (1991); also short stories and essays incl Go When You See the Green Man Walking (1969); *Recreations* people, travel; *Style*— Prof Christine Brooke-Rose; ✉ c/o Cambridge University Press, PO Box 110, Cambridge CB2 3RL

BROOKE-TAYLOR, Timothy Julian (Tim); s of Edward Mallalieu Brooke-Taylor (d 1953), of Buxton, Derbyshire, and Rachel Frances, *née* Pawson (d 1995); *b* 17 July

1940; *Educ* Winchester, Pembroke Coll Cambridge (MA); *m* 20 July 1968, Christine Margaret, da of Denis Wheadon; 2 s (Ben b 27 Nov 1969, Edward b 7 May 1971); *Career* actor; dir Derby County FC, rector Univ of St Andrews; Hon LLD Univ of St Andrews; *Theatre* West End: The Unvarnished Truth, Run For Your Wife, The Philanthropist; other: You Must Be The Husband (tour), My Fat Friend and Privates on Parade (Aust), Table Manners (Far and Middle East); *Television* The Braden Beat, At Last the 1948 Show, Broaden Your Mind, The Goodies, Me and My Girl, The Rough With The Smooth, You Must Be The Husband; *Films* 12 + 1, The Statue, Willy Wonka and the Chocolate Factory; *Radio* I'm Sorry I'll Read That Again, Hoax, I'm Sorry I Haven't A Clue; *Books* Rule Britannia, Tim Brooke-Taylor's Cricket Box, Tim Brooke-Taylor's Golf Bag; *Recreations* golf, skiing; *Clubs* Temple and Winter Hill Golf, Cookham Dean Nomads; *Style*— Tim Brooke-Taylor, Esq; ✉ c/o Jill Foster Ltd, 9 Barb Mews, London W6 7PA (☎ 0171 602 1263, fax 0171 602 9336)

BROOKE TURNER, Alan; CMG (1980); s of Capt Arthur Brooke Turner, MC (d 1953), of Bournemouth, and Ella Gladys, *née* Jackson, formerly Ella Gladys Rabone (d 1978); *b* 4 Jan 1926; *Educ* Marlborough, Balliol Coll Oxford; *m* 9 Oct 1954, Hazel Alexandra Rowan, da of Wilfred Alexander Henderson, CIE (d 1958), of Argyll; 2 s (Peter b 1958, James b 1960), 2 da (Prudence b 1955, Clarissa (Mrs Egon Vorfeld) b 1964); *Career* served in RAF 1944–48 (pilot offr); head of Southern European Dept FCO 1972–73, cnsllr HM Embassy Rome 1973–76, dir of studies and Dep Cmdt NATO Defence Coll Rome 1976–78, min HM Embassy Moscow 1979–82; ambass to Finland 1983–86; dir Br Assoc for Central and Eastern Europe (formerly GB/East Europe Centre) 1987–95; fell Center for Int Affairs Harvard Univ 1968–69, res assoc Int Inst for Strategic Studies 1978–79; memb: Working Gp on Peacemaking in a Nuclear Age (C of E Bd for Social Responsibility) 1986–88, Cncl of Anglican Centre Rome 1976–77, Cncl of Sch of Slavonic and E European Studies Univ of London 1987–95 (chm 1989–92); *Recreations* skiing, sailing; *Clubs* Travellers'; *Style*— Alan Brooke Turner, CMG; ✉ Poultons, Moor Lane, Dormansland, Lingfield, Surrey RH7 6NX (☎ 01342 832079)

BROOKEBOROUGH, 3 Viscount (UK 1952); Sir Alan Henry Brooke; 7 Bt (UK 1822), DL (Co Fermanagh 1987); er s of 2 Viscount Brookeborough, PC, DL (d 1987), and Rosemary, Viscountess Brookeborough; *b* 30 June 1952; *Educ* Harrow, Millfield; *m* 12 April 1980, Janet Elizabeth, o da of John Cooke, of Ballyvoy Lodge, Doagh, Co Antrim; *Heir* bro, Hon Christopher Arthur Brooke; *Career* cmmnd 17/21 Lancers 1972, transferred to UDR pt/t 1977, Co Cdr 4 Bn UDR 1980–83, transfer UDR pt/t 1983, Maj-Co Cdr UDR 1988–93, Lt Col Royal Irish Regt 1993–; non-exec dir Green Park Healthcare Tst 1992–; farmer; memb EEC Agric Sub-Ctee House of Lords 1988–; pres Army Benevolent Fund, N Ireland 1995–; chm Basel Internat (Jersey) 1996–; High Sheriff of Co Fermanagh 1995; *Recreations* riding, fishing, shooting, skiing; *Clubs* Cavalry and Guards'; *Style*— The Rt Hon the Viscount Brookeborough, DL; ✉ Colebrooke, Brookeborough, Co Fermanagh, NI (☎ 01365 531402)

BROOKER, Alan Bernard; JP (Essex 1972), DL (Essex 1982); s of Bernard John Brooker (d 1958), and Gwendoline Ada, *née* Launchbury (d 1975); *b* 24 Aug 1931; *Educ* Chigwell Sch Essex; *m* 23 March 1957, Diana, da of Colin Raymond Coles (d 1955); 1 s, 2 da; *Career* Nat Serv 2 Lt 2 RHA 1954–56; mangr Cole Dickin & Hills (chartered accountants) 1956–58 (articled clerk 1949–54), accountant Independent Dairies 1958–59, asst accountant Exchange Telegraph Co 1959–64, dir Extel Group plc 1964–87 (chm and chief exec 1980–87); vice chm: Provident Financial plc 1983–94, James Martin Associates 1987–89; non-exec dir: Pauls plc 1984–85, Aukett Associates plc 1988–, Plysu plc 1988–, PNA Holdings plc 1988–89, Addison Worldwide Ltd 1990–94, Eastern Counties Newspapers Ltd 1990–96; chm: Kode International plc 1988–, Serif plc (formerly Serif Cowells plc) 1990–93, E T Heron & Co Ltd 1991–96; memb Cncl CPU 1975–88; CBI: memb Companies Ctee 1979–83, memb Cncl London Region 1980–83; appeal chm Newspaper Press Fund 1985–86; govr: Chigwell Sch 1968– (chm 1978–), Felixstowe Coll 1986–94; churchwarden St Bride's Fleet Street 1986–; Freeman City of London, Liveryman Worshipful Co of Stationers and Newspapermakers (memb Court of Assts 1985, Master 1995–96); FCA, FInstD, FRSA 1980; *Recreations* golf, cricket; *Clubs* East India, MCC, Royal Worlington and Newmarket Golf; *Style*— Alan Brooker, Esq, JP, DL; ✉ Kode International plc, Station Road, Calne, Wiltshire SN11 0JT (☎ 01249 815247)

BROOKES, Beata Ann; CBE (1996); da of George Brookes, JP (d 1983), of Cwybr Farm, Rhyl, and Gwen Brookes; *b* 21 Jan 1931; *Educ* Lowther Coll Abergele, Univ of Wales Bangor, State Dept Scholarship USA; *m* (m dis 1963); *Career* formerly social worker Denbighshire CC, farmer and company secretary; contested (C): Widnes 1955, Warrington 1963, Manchester Exchange 1964; contested (C) N Wales Euro Parly Election 1989, MEP (EDG) N Wales 1979–89; currently chm Welsh Consumer Council; *Recreations* swimming, working; *Style*— Ms Beata Brookes, CBE; ✉ Welsh Consumer Council, Castle Buildings, Womanby Street, Cardiff CF1 2BN (☎ 01222 396056)

BROOKES, Brian Sydney; MBE (1982); s of Sydney Herbert Brookes (d 1967), and Edith, *née* Walker (d 1965); *b* 4 May 1936; *Educ* Beckenham GS, King's Coll London (BSc, PGCE), Univ of Dundee (MSc); *m* 30 Aug 1962 (m dis 1989), Margaret Mary; 3 s (David b 1967, Stephen b 1968, James b 1972), 1 da (Mary b 1970); *Career* teacher Forest Hill Sch and Sloane Sch 1958–65, asst warden Slapton Ley Field Centre Devon 1965–67, warden Kindrogan Field Centre Perthshire 1967–85, freelance biologist and environmental conslt 1985–; author of scientific papers; memb: cncls and ctee Nat Botanical Soc, various ctees Scottish Wildlife Tst, local community cncl, regnl advsy ctees Forestry Cmmn; CBiol, memb Inst of Biol; *Books* British Naturalists' Guide to Mountains and Moorlands (1985); *Recreations* beekeeping; *Style*— Brian Brookes, Esq, MBE; ✉ Borelick, Trochry, Dunkeld, Perthshire PH8 0BX (☎ and fax 01350 723222)

BROOKES, Bruno; s of Leslie Brookes, and Shelia Brookes; *b* 25 April 1959; *Educ* Bradwell HS, Seabridge HS; *m* 24 Sep 1994, Deborah Louise, da of Edward Brooker; *Career* radio DJ and television presenter; launched: Radio 5, Metropolitan Police Truancy Initiative, Police Nat Drug Line, Hertfordshire CC Lunch Club, Newspapers Deliverers Club of GB, The Post Office's new UK Anglers permit; prodr of records incl: Five Star (Shaft), Sam Fox and Frank Bruno (Come Outside), Liz Kershaw (Let's Dance and It Takes Two), The B Boys (Start Wrecken); also compliation album Meglomanio; supports numerous charities incl: Radio Lollipop (Hospital Radio), Prince's Tst, Nordoff Robbins Tst, Variety Club of GB, Leukamia Research, Happa; *Radio* numerous shows for BBC Radio 1 1984–95 incl: The Top 40, Roadshow, Live Aid; fndr The Independent Radio Network presenting Bruno at the Millhouse 1995–; also midmorning show for The New 96.3 Aire FM, drive time show 963 Liberty; *Television* presenter of numerous shows incl: Beat the Teacher (BBC), Love at First Sight (Sky), Top of the Pops (BBC), Tightlines (Sky Sports) 1995–; many appearances and voice overs; *Awards* incl: Virgin Atlantic Amateur Clay Shooting Trophy 1989, Smash Hits National DJ Award (5 times winner) 1989–94, Sony Awards 1990 and 1991, Daily Mirror Best DJ, Sun Best DJ, Best Dance DJ; *Books* Beat the Teacher, Half a Mind to Scream, What a Week with Bruno Brookes; *Recreations* fishing (especially trout), football, claypigeon shooting; *Style*— Bruno Brookes, Esq; ✉ c/o Fox Artist Management, Concorde House, 101 Shepherd's Bush Road, London W6 7LP (☎ 0171 602 8822, fax 0171 603 2352)

BROOKES, Harley Nigel Stephen; s of Albert Edwin Brookes (d 1994), and Dorothy Phyllis, *née* Bayliss; *b* 18 May 1938; *Educ* Univ of Birmingham (BA), Univ of London (PGCE), Univ of Essex (MA), Univ of Wales (MEd); *m* 1 (m dis); 1 s (Carl Ivan Oliver b 25 May 1964), 1 da (Luella b 4 July 1966); m 2, 28 March 1991, Maria Ida, *née* Testa; *Career* head of English: Ibo Union GS Kano 1962–64, Lucton Sch Herefordshire 1964–66, Lawrence Coll Murree Pakistan 1967–71; head EFL/linguistics United World Coll of the Atlantic 1972–76, CEC advsr Miny of Educn The Gambia 1976–78; British Council: dep English language offr Milan 1978–89, regnl language offr London 1984–86, English language offr Hong Kong 1986–89, dir Cameroon 1990–94, dir Israel 1994–; memb Mensa; FIL, FRSA; *Recreations* golf, bridge, travel, wines; *Clubs* Nat Liberal; *Style*— Harley Brookes, Esq; ✉ The British Council, 140 Hayarkon Street, PO Box 3302, Tel Aviv, Israel

BROOKES, Eur Ing James Robert (Jim); s of James Brookes, of Worsley, Lancs, and Hettie, *née* Colley; *b* 2 Sept 1941; *Educ* Manchester GS, Corpus Christi Coll Oxford (MA); *m* 30 May 1964, Patricia, da of John Gaskell, MBE, of Knutsford, Cheshire; 3 da (Diane (Mrs Chambers) b 9 Oct 1965, Gail b 28 June 1967, Maura (Mrs Grubb) b 8 July 1969); *Career* various posts in UK and USA as systems and applications programmer in devpt, tech support and sales; branch mangr Univ and Nat Res Region Ferranti Int Computers 1962–67, computer servs mangr Queen's Univ Belfast 1967–69, mangr Univ of Manchester Regnl Computer Centre 1969–75, dir SW Univs Regnl Computer Centre 1975–87, dir Univ of Bath Computer Servs 1983–87, chief exec Br Computer Soc 1986–91, chm BISL 1988–91; dir info servs Univ of Portsmouth 1992–95, head of information systems Avon and Somerset Constabulary 1995–; visiting prof Strathclyde Univ Business Sch 1991–95; Liveryman Worshipful Co of Info Technologists 1992 (memb 1988), Freeman City of London 1989; CEng, FBCS 1973, FRSA, Eur Ing 1991; *Recreations* sailing, fell walking, cycling, bridge, music, reading, badminton; *Clubs* United Oxford & Cambridge Univ; *Style*— Eur Ing Jim Brookes; ✉ 29 High St, Marshfield, Chippenham, Wilts SN14 8LR (☎ 01225 891294); Avon and Somerset Constabulary, Police HQ, PO Box 37, Valley Road, Portishead, Bristol BS20 8QJ

BROOKES, John A; s of Edward Percy Brookes (d 1982), and Margaret Alexandra, *née* Reid; *b* 11 Oct 1933; *Educ* Durham Sch, Durham Co Sch of Horticulture, UCL (DipLD); *Career* landscape designer; formerly apprentice with/to: Parks Dept Nottingham Corp, Brenda Colvin, Dame Sylivia Crowe; in private practice 1964–; work currently in progress incl private gardens in USA, GB, Japan and Argentina; formerly: lectr in landscape design Inst of Park Admin, asst lectr in landscape design Regent Street Poly, dir Inchbald Sch of Garden Design; lectr in landscape design Royal Botanical Gardens Kew; fndr: Inchbald Sch of Interior Design Teheran Iran 1978, Clock House Sch of Garden Design (within estab garden of Denmans W Sussex) 1980; regular lectr on garden design worldwide; FSGD; *Books* Room Outside (1969, reprint 1979), Gardens for Small Spaces (1970), Garden Design and Layout (1970), Living in the Garden (1971), Financial Times Book of Garden Design (1975), Improve Your Lot (1977), The Small Garden (1977, reprint 1984), The Garden Book (1984), A Place in the Country (1984), The Indoor Garden Book (1986), Gardens of Paradise (1987), The Country Garden (1987), The New Small Garden Book (1989), John Brookes' Garden Design Book (1991), Planting the Country Way (1994), John Brookes' Garden Design Workbook (1994); *Style*— John Brookes, Esq; ✉ Clock House, Denmans, Fontwell, nr Arundel, W Sussex BN18 0SU (☎ 01243 542808)

BROOKES, Mike; s of Lt-Col G K Brookes, MBE, RAMC; *b* 20 May 1940; *Educ* Univ of Exeter (BSc); *m* 1962, Maureen; *m*; 2 c; *Career* Ford of Europe 1962–94: various positions rising to dir of Euro gen servs 1977–90, dir of material planning and transportation 1990–94; chm Southend Health Care NHS Tst 1996–; MILog, FCIT; *Recreations* golf, rugby, cricket, reading; *Style*— Mike Brookes, Esq; ✉ Southend Healthcare NHS Trust, Southend Hospital, Prittlewell Chase, Westcliff on Sea, Essex SS0 0RY (☎ 01702 435555)

BROOKES, Nicola; da of Leon Bernard (d 1954), of Ruislip, and Violet Charlotte, *née* Farrar; *b* 25 Dec 1951; *Educ* Wycombe HS, Univ of Warwick (BSc); *m* 27 Sept 1980, Ian Thomas Burns, s of Thomas George Burns, of W Kirby, Wirral; 1 da (Laura Kathryn b 1988), 1 s (Thomas Leon Phillip b 1990); *Career* trainee accountant Arthur Andersen & Co 1973–76; Amari plc: joined 1976, corporate devpt dir 1984–86, fin dir 1986–89; dir Via International plc 1989– (formerly fin dir), dir Barnes Tst Media Ltd 1995–, mgmnt conslt Harrison Brookes; selected by Business magazine as one of Britain's Top 40 young leaders, finalist Business Woman of the Year 1988; FCA 1981; *Recreations* swimming, skiing, reading, music and opera; *Style*— Ms Nicola Brookes; ✉ Barnes Trust Media Ltd, 4 Old Park Lane, London W1Y 3LJ (☎ 0171 629 8000, fax 0171 221 9334)

BROOKES, Baron (Life Peer UK 1975); Raymond Percival Brookes; kt (1971); s of William Percival Brookes, of W Bromwich, Staffs, and Ursula Brookes; *b* 10 April 1909; *Educ* Kenrick Tech Coll W Bromwich; *m* 1937, Florence Edna, da of Isaac William Sharman; 1 s; *Career* former memb Cncl CBI; chm and chief exec Guest Keen & Nettlefolds Ltd 1965–74 (life pres 1975–); dir Plessey Co to 1989, memb Dubai Aluminium Authy 1981–86; *Style*— The Rt Hon the Lord Brookes; ✉ Mallards, Santon, Isle of Man (☎ 01624 822451)

BROOKES, Timothy Alastair Edward (Tim); s of Albert Edwin Brookes (d 1994), of Sutton Coldfield, and Dorothy Phyllis Brookes; *b* 16 June 1949; *Educ* Bishop Vesey's GS; *m* Ann Elizabeth; 1 s (James Alastair Bentley Russell), 2 da (Francesca Deborah Gale, Mellissa Claire Sintra); *Career* articled clerk then CA Peat Marwick Mitchell 1967–72, with British Enkalon 1973–74, ptnr Peat Marwick Mitchell (later KPMG Peat Marwick) 1974–86, dep chief exec Coline International plc 1986–87; chm: In Shops plc 1988–94, TAB Corporation plc 1994–, Take A Break Motorway Services plc 1994–, Jessop International Ltd 1996–; non-exec dir: Cheltenham & Gloucester plc, Lloyds Chemists plc, Eversheds, Birmingham C of C and Industry; memb: DTI Deregulation Panel 1989–94, CBI Smaller Firms Cncl 1990–93, CBI Birmingham Group 1990–94; Freeman City of London 1991; FCA, FCCA, FIPA, FSPI, FInstD; *Recreations* farming, archaeology, family; *Clubs* National Liberal; *Style*— Tim Brookes, Esq; ✉ Jessop International Ltd, Jessop House, Scudamore Road, Leicester LE3 1TZ (☎ 0116 232 0033)

BROOKES, Sir Wilfred Deakin; kt (1979), CBE (1972), DSO (1944), AEA (1945); s of Herbert Robinson Brookes, and Ivy, *née* Deakin; *b* 17 April 1906; *Educ* Melbourne GS, Melbourne Univ; *m* 1928, Bertha (Betty) (d 1968), da of Albert Henry Heal; 1 s; *Career* served RAAF Aust and overseas 1939–45, ret Gp Capt; former chm and dir various industrial, commercial and mining cos, ret; patron Deakin Univ Fndn, former chm Edward Wilson Charitable Tst; former govr Corps of Commissionaires; DLitt (hc) Deakin Univ; *Style*— Sir Wilfred Brookes, CBE, DSO, AEA; ✉ 20 Heyington Place, Toorak, Victoria 3142, Australia (☎ 00 61 9822 4553)

BROOKHOUSE, Graham Raymond; s of Raymond Nuttall Brookhouse, and Phyliss Adeline Teresa, *née* Hart; *b* 19 June 1962; *Educ* King Edward VI Camphill Sch for Boys Birmingham, Coll of St Paul and St Mary Cheltenham (BEd), LSSM (Dip); *m* May 1993, Jacky Harley; *Career* teacher of swimming Stowe Sch 1985–87; modern pentathlon: Br champion 1987–89, team Bronze Medal Seoul Olympics 1988, team Silver Medal Aust Cup Melbourne 1992, 8th Barcelona Olympics 1992, team Silver Medal World Championships 1994; chief Cheltenham Swimming Club 1994–, active memb Cheltenham Harriers; performance conslt, prog dir Br Olympic Assoc; *Recreations* horses, coaching, running, swimming, surfing; *Clubs* Spartan Modern Penthatlon; *Style*— Graham Brookhouse, Esq; ✉ 137 Village Rd, Cheltenham, Glos (☎ 01242 575353)

BROOKING, Alan; *b* 1928, Sydney, Australia; *Educ* England; *m* 1957, Margaret, *née* Yuill; 2 s; *Career* initial career concerned with design and construction of racing and sports cars, subsequently studied advtg design and typography under Arpad Elfer,

Klaus Friedeberger and Robert Harling amongst others, creative staff Collett Dickenson Pearce advtg 1961–66 (latterly sr art dir), independent advtg photographer 1966–; assignments for numerous worldwide advtg campaigns, numerous awards from D&AD, Association of Photographers (Chm's Award 1993), Campaign and Creative Circle; fndr memb: D&AD 1963 (former memb Exec Ctee and Awards Juries), Assoc of Photographers 1968 (former chm, memb Cncl and Awards Juries); originator IMAGE magazine; *Recreations* sailboat racing and cruising; *Style*— Alan Brooking; ✉ Wellington House, Bildeston, Suffolk IP7 7EB (☎ 01449 740305)

BROOKING, Barry Alfred; MBE (Mil, 1972), JP (Surrey 1985); s of Alfred Brooking, and Winifred Joan, *née* Morris; *b* 2 Feb 1944; *Educ* Milford Haven GS, Sir Joseph Williamson's Mathematical Sch Rochester, Univ of London (BA, MA); *m* (m dis 1993), Julia Irene, da of Maurice McBride; *Career* served RN 1965–81, BRNC Dartmouth 1965, HMS Pembroke 1966–67, HMS Diamond 1968–69, CTC RM Lympstone 1969, 41 Commando RM 1969–70, 40 Commando RM 1970–72, HMS Raleigh 1972–75, RN Sch of Educnl and Trg Technol 1976–78, ARE 1978–81, business admin Medical Protection Society 1981–91, regnl dir St John Ambulance 1992–95, chief exec Parkinson's Disease Soc of the UK 1995–; memb: Surrey Magistrates' Soc 1985–, Surrey Magistrates' Cts Ctee 1993–95, Surrey Probation Ctee 1993–95; dep chm North and East Surrey Parkinson's Disease Soc; chm Brooking Soc 1993– (memb 1980–); memb ACP 1970, MIPD 1977, MRTS 1978, MInstM 1981; *Publications* Naval Mathematics Self-Tuition Text (1966), Naval English Self-Tuition Text (1966), Naval Mathematics Programmed-Learning Text (1967), Royal Navy CCTV Production Techniques Handbook (1977), Educational Technology in a Changing World: Aspects of Educational Technology Vol XII (contrib, 1978); also author of various ARE reports and booklets and various articles in jls; *Recreations* travel, theatre, cinema, music, history, sport; *Clubs* Surrey Magistrates'; *Style*— Barry Brooking, Esq, MBE; ✉ Silver Birch Cottage, Fir Tree Close, Esher, Surrey KT10 9DS (☎ 01372 466062); Chief Executive, Parkinson's Disease Society of the UK, 22 Upper Woburn Place, London WC1H 0RA (direct ☎ 0171 391 6700, fax 0171 383 5754)

BROOKING, Maj-Gen Patrick Guy; CB (1988), CMG (1997), MBE (1975); s of Capt C A H Brooking, CBE, RN, and G M J White, *née* Coleridge; *b* 4 April 1937; *Educ* Charterhouse, Alliance Francaise Paris (Dip French Lang); *m* 11 April 1964, Pamela Mary, da of the late Lt-Col J E S Walford, MBE; 1 s (Jonathan b 1967), 1 da (Samantha b 1965); *Career* cmmnd 5 Royal Inniskilling Dragoon Gds 1956; served: Eng, W Germany, NI, Cyprus; Camberley Staff Coll 1969, Bde Maj 39 Bde Belfast 1974–75, Regtl Cdr 1975–77, instr Army Staff Coll 1978, COS 4 Armd Div 1979–80, RCDS 1981, Cdr 33 Armd Bde 1982–83, asst COS UK Land Forces 1984–85, Cmdt and GOC Br sector Berlin 1985–89, dir gen Army Manning and Recruiting 1989–90, ret 1990; Regtl Col: 5DG 1991–92, RDG 1992–94; sr exec worldwide subsidiaries of Krone AG (Berlin) 1990–; chm International Club Berlin (e.v) 1994–; Freeman City of London 1979, memb Worshipful Co of Broderers; *Recreations* tennis, golf, music (memb Berlin Philharmonic Choir 1986–); *Clubs* Cavalry and Guards; *Style*— Maj-Gen P G Brooking, CB, CMG, MBE; ✉ c/o National Westminster Bank, 42 Leicester Square, London WC2H 7LW

BROOKING, Trevor David; MBE (1981); *b* 2 Oct 1948; *m* 1970, Hilkka Helakorpi; 2 c; *Career* former professional footballer; with West Ham Utd 1965–84, over 500 appearances, FA Cup winners' medal 1975 and 1980; England: debut 1974, 47 caps, scored 5 goals, ret 1982; currently regular contrib Match of the Day (BBC) and memb football commentary team BBC Radio, columnist Evening Standard; vice chm Sports Council (memb 1989–), co-chm Lottery Sports Panel; *Style*— Trevor Brooking, Esq, MBE; ✉ c/o John Hockey Associates Ltd, 106 Gloucester Place, London W1H 3DB (☎ 0171 935 2506, fax 0171 935 0534)

BROOKMAN, (David) Keith; *b* 3 Jan 1937; *Educ* Nantyglo GS Gwent; *Career* Nat Serv RAF; crane driver Richard Thomas & Baldwin Ltd Ebbw Vale 1953–73; Iron and Steel Trades Confedn: divnl organiser 1973, asst gen sec 1985–93, gen sec 1993–; memb Exec Cncl Confedn of Shipbuilding and Engrg Unions 1989–96; chm Nat Steel Co-ordinating Ctee 1993 (memb 1991–93); TUC: memb Educn Advsy Ctee for Wales 1976–82, memb Steel Ctee 1985–90, memb Gen Cncl 1992–; British Steel: memb Jt Accident Prevention Advsy Ctee (JAPAC) 1985–93, memb Advsy Ctee on Educn and Trg (ACET) 1986–93, operatives' sec Long Products General Steels Jt Standing Ctee 1993–, operatives' sec Strip Trade Bd 1993–, bd dir British Steel (Industry) Ltd 1993–; Labour Pty: memb Exec Ctee Wales 1982–85, memb Nat Constitutional Ctee 1987–91, memb NEC 1991–92; International Metalworkers' Fedn: hon sec IMF British Section 1993–, pres IMF Iron and Steel and Non-Ferrous Metals Dept 1993–; operatives' sec Jt Industl Cncl for the Slag Indust 1985–93; memb: Exec Cncl European Metalworkers' Fedn 1985–95, Euro Coal and Steel Community Consultative Ctee 1993–; employees' sec Euro Works Cncl British Steel 1996–; govr Gwent Coll of HE 1980–84, tstee Julian Melchett Tst 1985–95; *Style*— Keith Brookman, Esq; ✉ Iron and Steel Trades Confederation, Swinton House, 324 Gray's Inn Road, London WC1X 8DD (☎ 0171 837 6691/2/3, fax 0171 278 8378)

BROOKNER, Dr Anita; CBE (1990); da of Newson Brookner, and Maude, *née* Schiska; *b* 16 July 1928; *Educ* James Allen's Girls' Sch, King's Coll London (BA), Courtauld Inst of Art (PhD); *Career* lectr then reader Courtauld Inst of Art 1964–88; FRSL; *Books* Watteau (1964), J B Greuze (1971), The Genius of the Future (1972), Jacques Louis David (1980), The Stories of Edith Wharton Vol I (ed, 1988) Vol II (ed, 1989); *Novels* A Start in Life (1981), Providence (1982), Look At Me (1983), Hotel du Lac (1984, Booker-McConnell prize, filmed for TV 1986), Family and Friends (1983), A Misalliance (1986), A Friend from England (1987), Latecomers (1988), Lewis Percy (1989), Brief Lives (1990), A Closed Eye (1991), Fraud (1992), A Family Romance (1993), Altered States (1996); many articles in Apollo, Burlington Magazine, TLS; *Recreations* walking, reading; *Style*— Dr Anita Brookner, CBE, FRSL; ✉ 68 Elm Park Gardens, London SW10 (☎ 0171 352 6894)

BROOKS, Charles Patrick Evelyn; s of Robert Noel Brand Brooks (d 1976), and Caroline Diana, *née* Todd; *b* 3 March 1963; *Educ* Cothill House, Eton; *Career* racehorse trainer; trained one hundred winners in first two seasons when England's youngest trainer; *Style*— Charles Brooks, Esq; ✉ Uplands, Lambourn, Newbury, Berks RG16 7QH (☎ 01488 72077, fax 01488 71206)

BROOKS, (Kathleen) Claire; OBE (1986); da of Arthur Graham (d 1969), of The Mains, Giggleswick, Settle, N Yorks, and Clara Grace, *née* Grisedale; *b* 20 June 1931; *Educ* Settle PS, Abraham Lincoln Sch NJ, Settle Girls HS, Skipton Girls HS, UCL (LLB); *m* 28 Sept 1963 (m dis 1971), Herbert Berwick Brooks, s of Herbert Berwick Brooks, Sr (d 1959), of Superior, Wisconsin, and Louisville, Kentucky; *Career* admitted slr 1956; S Kitching Walker & Co 1956–61, Medley Drawbridge & Co 1961–64, Victor D Zermansky & Co 1973–75; proprietor K Claire Brooks & Co Solicitors 1975–95 (conslt 1995–); dir former Settle Carlisle Joint Action Committee Ltd; tstee: Skipton & Craven Assoc for Disabled (pres 1988–89), Craven Museum, Petyt Library, Heap Parkinson Homes; former memb Ct and Cncl Univ of Lancaster; govr Skipton GHS and others; lifelong lib; memb: Craven DC 1976– (chm 1988–89), Skipton Town Cncl 1976– (Mayor 1985–86), Sub-Ctee Yorkshire and Humberside Tourist Bd; Parly candidate: 6 nat elections (4 Lib, 2 Alliance), 2 Euro elections; memb: Lib Pty Nat Exec Ctee 1975–88, Lib Pty Cncl 1973–88, Nat Exec Ctee Lib Movement 1988–90; memb: Law Soc, Br Legal Assoc; *Recreations* local history and archaeology, genealogy; *Clubs* Nat Lib; *Style*— Mrs Claire Brooks, OBE; ✉ c/o Mesdames K Claire Brooks & Co Solicitors, 43 Otley Street, Skipton, N Yorks BD23 1EL (☎ 01756 795069, fax 01756 798243)

BROOKS, (Francis) David; s of Francis Brooks (d 1945), of Great Haywood, Staffs, and Alice Ida, *née* Jones (d 1984); *b* 18 Jan 1934; *Educ* Ackworth Sch, Christ Church Oxford (BA, MA); *m* 19 July 1958, Jennifer Mary, da of Edward Line; 2 s (Julian Francis b 3 Nov 1961, Peter Edward b 15 Sept 1963), 2 da (Ruth Marguerite b 19 Jan 1967, Hilary Jennifer b 25 July 1969); *Career* Cadbury Bros/Cadbury Schweppes: personnel mangr Confectionery Gp 1974, Bournville Factory dir Cadbury Ltd 1976, vice pres tech Peter Paul Cadbury (USA) Inc 1982, sr vice pres confectionery ops Cadbury Schweppes (USA) Inc 1984, chm and md Cadbury Ltd 1990–94 (ops dir 1987, md 1989); memb: Exec Ctee Food & Drink Fedn 1990–93, President's Ctee Biscuit Cocoa Chocolate & Confectionery Alliance 1990–94; non-exec dir Birmingham Heartlands Development Corp 1993–; chm: Cncl Birmingham Common Purpose 1993, Groundwork Birmingham Ltd 1994–, Birmingham Settlement 1994–, Prince's Youth Business Tst (W Midlands & Warwickshire) 1996–; dir: Birmingham TEC 1992–94, Newtown/S Aston City Challenge Co 1995–, Aston Reinvestment Tst 1995–; FRSA 1992; *Recreations* music, history, countryside; *Style*— David Brooks, Esq; ✉ The Pond House, Hill Lane, Weatheroak, Alvechurch, nr Birmingham B48 7EG (☎ 01564 826529, fax 01564 822289)

BROOKS, Hon David Gerald; s of 3 Baron Crawshaw (d 1946); hp of bro, 4 Baron; *b* 14 Sept 1934; *Educ* Eton, RAC Cirencester; *m* 1970, Belinda Mary, da of G P H Burgess, of Sandringham, Melbourne, Australia; 4 da (Susanna b 1974, Amanda b 1975, Elisabeth b 1976, Katharine b 1978); *Style*— The Hon David Brooks; ✉ Little Riste Farm, Long Whatton, Loughborough, Leics (☎ 01509 842392)

BROOKS, Diana D; *Educ* Miss Porter's Sch Connecticut, Yale Univ; *m* Michael C Brooks; 1 da, 1 s; *Career* lending offr Nat Banking Gp Citibank NA 1973–79; Sotheby's North America: joined New York office 1979, sr vice pres and chief financial & admin offr 1982, exec vice pres 1984, chief operating offr 1985, pres 1987, chief exec offr 1990; pres and chief exec offr Sotheby's North and South America 1990–, pres and chief exec offr Sotheby's Holdings Inc 1994–; tstee: Yale Univ, Deerfield Acad Mass, Catalyst, Central Park Conservancy, Winterthur; memb Bd New York City Partnership; *Style*— Mrs Diana D Brooks; ✉ Sotheby's, 34–35 New Bond Street, London W1A 2AA (☎ 0171 408 5263, fax 0171 408 5969)

BROOKS, Donal Meredith; s of Edward Clive Brooks, of Dublin, and Kathleen Purdon, *née* Pollock; *b* 10 April 1917; *Educ* Repton, Trinity Coll Dublin; *m* 1947, Stephanie, da of Cyril W Mackworth-Praed, CBE; *Career* conslt orthopaedic surgn King Edward VII Hosp of Offrs London, emeritus civilian conslt orthopaedic surgn in hand surgery to RN, hon civilian conslt orthopaedic surgn in hand surgery RAF; conslt orthopaedic surgn: UCH, Royal Nat Orthopaedic Hosp London (surgn i/c peripheral nerve injury and hand unit); former chm of the Ct of Examiners RCS; former pres: orthopaedic section RSM, Chelsea Clinical Soc, Combined Servs Orthopaedic Soc; fell Br Orthopaedic Assoc (travelling fell 1954–), former memb Hand Club; memb: Br Soc for Surgery of the Hand, Groupe d'Etude de la Main; guest lectr: American Assoc of Neurosurgeons 1977, S African Soc for Surgery of the Hand 1978; Wattie visiting prof New Zealand 1983, Robert Jones lectr RCS 1979, fndr lectr of American Soc for Surgery of the Hand 1983; Jackson Burrows Lecture and Medal Award 1983; papers on peripheral nerve injuries and hand surgery in books and jls; *Recreations* farming, gardening, travelling; *Clubs* Landsdowne, Royal Irish Yacht; *Style*— Donal Brooks, Esq; ✉ Errislannan Manor, Clifden, Co Galway

BROOKS, Most Rev (Francis) Gerard; *see:* Dromore, Bishop of (RC)

BROOKS, Harry; Jr; eldest s of Harry Brooks Sr (d 1978), of Peover Hall, Knutsford, Cheshire, and Norah Brooks (d 1991); *b* 16 Feb 1936; *m* 23 July 1977, Mileva; 1 da (Milanka b 12 Sept 1983); *Career* actor, photographer, writer & prodr; writer of original screenplays: The Lady of Light, Disguise, Dance on Tap, Mice, Tea at the Palace, The Birth of Tomorrow; exec-prodr Harry Brooks Productions and Speakeazy/Danceazy (actors, actresses, writers, dancers, singers and models); fndr and chm: The MIDAS Academy - Multimedia Interactive Data Access Systems Ltd, rep Cybertran Light Rail Tport System; *Recreations* theatre & film, music, writing, languages, photography, swimming; *Style*— Harry Brooks, Jr; ✉ MIDAS Ltd, c/o Dale Cottage, Rostherne, nr Knutsford, Cheshire WA16 6QJ (☎ 07000 7000 11, fax 07000 7000 22, e-mail hbrmidas@dircon.co.uk)

BROOKS, Jermyn Paul; *b* 23 Feb 1939; *Educ* Northampton GS, Lincoln Coll Univ of Oxford (MA), Free Univ Berlin; *m* Val; 1 s (Robin b 1970), 1 da (Victoria b 1976); *Career* Price Waterhouse: joined 1962, Frankfurt office 1967, ptnr 1973–, ptnr i/c Iranian practice 1976–79, Frankfurt 1979–93, involved in establishment of Turkey office 1980–84, ptnr i/c Mgmnt Consultancy practice 1987–88 (Audit practice Frankfurt 1986–87), sr ptnr Germany 1989–93, memb Bd European Mgmnt, chm Eastern Europe Jt Venture Bd 1992–93, chm Price Waterhouse Europe 1993–, dep chm Price Waterhouse World Firm 1993–; former pres: Frankfurt Chapter, National Assoc of Accountants; memb Exec Ctee and treas American C of C Germany 1988–93; fell German Wirtschaftsprüfer, FCA; speaker at numerous seminars on bank accounting and auditing, author of 3 books on German banking law, private company law and the Accounting Directives Law; *Recreations* tennis, gardening, music; *Style*— Jermyn Brooks, Esq; ✉ Price Waterhouse, 32 London Bridge Street, London SE1 9SY (☎ 0171 939 3000)

BROOKS, Dr Nicholas Hugh; s of Lt-Col A Brooks, of Great Missenden, Bucks, and Mary, *née* Gerrard; *b* 6 July 1947; *Educ* Perse Sch Cambridge, St Bartholomew's Hosp Med Coll and Univ of London (MB BS, MD, MRCP); *m* 16 March 1974, Barbara Mary, da of Dr Robert Boal, of Southampton; 1 s (Alexander James b 1977), 1 da (Victoria Jane b 1979); *Career* St Bartholomew's Hosp: house surgn Surgical Professional Unit 1971, house surgn in cardiothoracic surgery then sr house offr in gen med 1972, registrar in cardiology 1973–74; house physician Southampton Gen Hosp 1971, Br Heart Fndn res fell St George's Hosp 1976–77 (registrar in med 1975), clinical lectr and hon sr registrar London Chest Hosp and London Hosp 1977, conslt cardiologist Wythenshawe Hosp Manchester 1984–; hon sec Cardiology Ctee RCP 1988–93, hon sec Br Cardiac Soc 1996– (hon asst sec 1994–96); FRCP 1990; *Books* Diseases of the Heart (contrib, 1989 and 1996); *Recreations* tennis, skiing, music; *Style*— Dr Nicholas Brooks; ✉ Oldcroft House, Elm Grove, Alderley Edge, Cheshire SK9 7PD (☎ 01625 582853); Regional Cardiac Centre, Wythenshawe Hospital, Manchester M23 9LT (☎ 0161 946 2387)

BROOKS, Prof Nicholas Peter; s of Dr (William) Donald Wykeham Brooks, CBE (d 1993), of Storrington, W Sussex, and Phyllis Kathleen, *née* Juler (d 1988); *b* 14 Jan 1941; *Educ* Winchester, Magdalen Coll Oxford (BA, MA, DPhil); *m* 16 Sept 1967, Chloë Carolyn, da of Rev Sidney C Willis (d 1978); 1 s (Crispin b 29 Dec 1970), 1 da (Ebba b 31 Jan 1969); *Career* sr lectr in medieval history Univ of St Andrews 1978–85 (lectr 1964–78); Univ of Birmingham: prof of medieval history 1985–, dean Faculty of Arts 1992–95; chm St Andrews Preservation Tst 1977–83; FBA, FRHistS, FSA; *Books* Latin and the Vernacular Languages in Early Medieval Britain (1982), The Early History of the Church of Canterbury (1984), St Oswald of Worcester: Life and Influence (1996); *Recreations* gardening, golf, walking; *Style*— Prof Nicholas Brooks, FBA, FSA; ✉ Department of Medieval History, University of Birmingham, Edgbaston, Birmingham B15 2TT (☎ 0121 414 5736)

BROOKS, Peter Malcolm; s of Roger Morrison Brooks (d 1968), of Winchester, and Phyllis Fuller, *née* Hopkinson; *b* 12 Feb 1947; *Educ* Marlborough, Univ of Southampton (LLB, Eng and Br Univs squash team rep); *m* 1, 1974 (m dis); 1 s (Matthew Harry Morrison b 21 July 1980); m 2, 1987, Patricia Margaret; 1 s (Nicholas John Morrison b

27 Nov 1987); *Career* VSO Sarawak 1965–66; admitted slr 1971; ptnr: Macfarlanes 1977–84, Clifford Chance 1984–, head of Corp Practice; memb Companies Ctee CBI; memb: City of London Slrs' Co, Law Soc 1971; *Recreations* real tennis, cricket, opera, theatre, travel; *Clubs* MCC; *Style—* Peter Brooks, Esq; ✉ Clifford Chance, 200 Aldersgate Street, London EC1A 4JJ (☎ 0171 600 1000, fax 0171 956 0143)

BROOKS, Richard John; s of Peter John Brooks, and Joan, *née* Maxwell (d 1965); *b* 5 Feb 1946; *Educ* Univ of Bristol (BA); *m* Jane Elizabeth; 2 da (Kate b 13 July 1981, Anna b 5 Dec 1984); *Career* journalist; Bristol Evening Post 1968–71, Daily Mail 1971, BBC 1971–79, The Economist 1979–80, Sunday Times 1980–85, media ed The Observer 1985–; *Recreations* watching films, playing sport; *Style—* Richard Brooks, Esq; ✉ The Observer, 119 Farringdon Road, London EC1R 3ER (☎ 0171 278 2332)

BROOKS, Robert; s of William Frederick Brooks, of Bishopswood House, Bishopswood, Herefordshire, and Joan Patricia, *née* Marshall; *b* 1 Oct 1956; *Educ* St Benedict's Sch Ealing; *m* 30 May 1981, Evelyn Rachel, da of Prof John William Durnford; 2 s (Charles b 24 Aug 1984, John b 21 June 1987), 1 da (Sarah b 11 May 1983); *Career* dir: Christie's S Kensington Ltd 1984–87 (joined 1975), Christie Manson and Woods Ltd 1987–89; estab Brooks (Auctioneers) Ltd 1989; *Recreations* flying; *Style—* Robert Brooks, Esq; ✉ Brooks (Auctioneers) Ltd, 81 Westside, London SW4 9AY (☎ 0171 228 8000, fax 0171 585 0830)

BROOKS, Robert Anthony (Bobby); s of Ronald Clifton Brooks (d 1980), and Iris Winifred, *née* Payne (d 1978); *b* 12 April 1931; *Educ* Eton; *m* 1955, Sally, da of Richard Burnie Armistead; 3 da (Amanda (Mrs Keegan) b 1956, Sarah (Mrs Dunbar) b 1959, Lucy (Mrs Nigel Burney) b 1966); *Career* articled clerk Viney Price & Goodyear 1951–57; CA: Coopers & Lybrand 1957–60, Robert Benson Lonsdale (now Kleinwort Benson Ltd) 1960–93 (dir 1967–93); dir: Commercial Union plc 1977–92, M & G Group plc 1979–96, Kleinwort Development Fund plc 1983–, The Securities Association Ltd (now The Securities and Futures Authy) 1989–93, CU Environmental Trust plc (chm 1992–), Syndicate Capital Trust plc 1993–; Freeman City of London, Liveryman Worshipful Co of Grocers; FCA; *Recreations* fishing, gardening, golf; *Clubs* City of London; *Style—* Bobby Brooks, Esq; ✉ Kleinwort Benson Limited, 20 Fenchurch St, London EC3 (☎ 0171 623 8000)

BROOKS, (Richard) Simon; s of Maj Richard Clement Brooks, TD, JP (d 1980), of Wrington, Nr Bristol, and Edith Mary, *née* Shellard (d 1950); *b* 29 March 1931; *Educ* Radley; *m* 8 Aug 1959, Helen Rosemary, da of Frederick James Weeks, of Wrington, Bristol; 1 s (Adam b 1965), 2 da (Victoria (Mrs Botsford) b 1961, Emma (Mrs Thompson) b 1962); *Career* Nat Serv RAF, PO Royal Auxiliary Air Force 1955 (Flying Offr 1959); CA 1954, former pres Br Textile Rental Assoc, chm Brooks Service Group plc, dir Bristol United Press plc; former memb W Eng Ctee IOD, chm Clifton Suspension Bridge Tst, govr Clifton Coll, former chm Clifton Club, former pres Anchor Soc; Freeman City of: Bristol 1969, London 1971; Liveryman Worshipful Co of: Dyers (Prime Warden) Launderers, Merchant Venturers; FCA 1965 (ACA 1954); *Recreations* reading, music, food and drink, motor sport, occasional squash, skiing, riding, sailing, golf, tennis, bridge, travel; *Clubs* Clifton; *Style—* Simon Brooks, Esq; ✉ Brooks Service Group plc, 210 Aztec West, Almondsbury, Bristol BS12 4SN (☎ 01454 614668)

BROOKS OF TREMORFA, Baron (Life Peer UK 1979), of Tremorfa in the County of South Glamorgan; John Edward Brooks; s of Edward George Brooks, and Rachel, *née* White; *b* 12 April 1927; *Educ* Coleg Harlech; *m* 1, 1948 (m dis 1956); 1 s, 1 da; m 2, 1958, Margaret Pringle; 2 s; *Career* sec Cardiff SE Lab Pty 1966–84, contested (Lab) Barry Feb and Oct 1974, Parly agent to Rt Hon James Callaghan, MP, at Gen Elections 1970 and 1979; S Glamorgan CC: memb 1973–93, leader 1973–77 and 1986–92, chm 1981–82; chm Lab Pty Wales 1978–79, oppn def spokesman 1980; dep chm Cardiff Bay Devpt Corp (memb 1987–); *Recreations* most sports, reading; *Style—* The Rt Hon the Lord Brooks of Tremorfa; ✉ 46 Kennerleigh Rd, Rumney, Cardiff, S Glamorgan CF3 9BJ (☎ 01222 791848)

BROOKSBANK, Sir (Edward) Nicholas; 3 Bt (UK 1919), of Healaugh Manor, Healaugh, W Riding of Yorks; Lord of the Manor of Healaugh; s of Lt-Col Sir (Edward) William Brooksbank, 2 Bt, TD, JP, DL (d 1983), and Ann, Lady Brooksbank; *b* 4 Oct 1944; *Educ* Eton; *m* 1970, Hon Emma Myrtle Mary Anne, o da of Baron Holderness, PC, DL, *qv*; 1 s (Florian Tom Charles b 1982), 1 da (Victoria Mary Grania b 1985); *Heir* s, Florian Tom Charles Brooksbank b 9 Aug 1982; *Career* Capt The Blues and Royals, ret; Christie's rep York; *Style—* Sir Nicholas Brooksbank, Bt; ✉ Ryton Grange, Malton, N Yorks (☎ Kirby Misperton (0165 386) 270)

BROOM, Prof Donald Maurice; s of Donald Edward Broom (d 1971), of Tatsfield, Surrey, and Mavis Edith Rose, *née* Thompson; *b* 14 July 1942; *Educ* Whitgift Sch, St Catharine's Coll Cambridge (MA, PhD); *m* 31 May 1971, Sally Elizabeth Mary, da of Thomas Edward Fisher (d 1969), of Ufton Nervet, Berkshire; 3 s (Oliver b 1973, Tom b 1976, Giles b 1981); *Career* lectr (later reader) Dept of Pure and Applied Zoology Univ of Reading 1967–86, Colleen Macleod prof of animal welfare Dept of Clinical Veterinary Med Univ of Cambridge 1986–; visiting asst prof Dept of Zoology Univ of Calif 1969, visiting lectr Dept of Biology Univ of WI Trinidad 1972, visiting scientist Div of Animal Prodn Cwlth Sci and Industl Res Orgn Perth 1983, memb NERC Ctee on Seals 1986–, invited advsr Cncl of Euro Standing Ctee on Welfare of Animals Kept for Farming Purposes 1987–, chm Euro Union Scientific Veterinary Ctee (Animal Welfare) 1990–, memb Farm Animal Welfare Cncl 1991–; hon res assoc Inst of Grassland and Environmental Res 1985–, tstee Farm Animal Care Tst 1986–, fell St Catharine's Coll Cambridge 1987–, hon treas Assoc for the Study of Animal Behaviour 1971–80 (cncl memb 1980–83); pres Int Soc for Applied Ethology 1987–89 (cncl memb 1981–84, vice pres 1986–87 and 1989–91); memb: Int Ethological Ctee 1976–79, Br Tst for Ornithology, Br Soc of Animal Sci, Zoological Soc of London, Assoc of Veterinary Teachers and Res Workers, Int Soc of Anthrozoology; winner of George Fleming prize for best paper in Br Veterinary Jl (1990); FIBiol 1986; *Books* Birds and their Behaviour (1977), Biology of Behaviour (1981), Encyclopaedia of Domestic Animals (ed, with P A Messent, 1986), Farmed Animals (ed, 1986), Farm Animal Behaviour and Welfare (with A F Fraser, 1990), Stress and Animal Welfare (with K G Johnson, 1993); *Recreations* squash, modern pentathlon, ornithology; *Clubs* Hawks' (Cambridge); *Style—* Prof Donald Broom; ✉ Department of Clinical Veterinary Medicine, University of Cambridge, Madingley Road, Cambridge CB3 OES; St Catharine's College, Cambridge CB2 1RL (☎ 01223 337697, fax 01223 337610)

BROOM, Douglas Philip; s of George Edward Shirley Broom, of Haxey, Lincolnshire, and Joyce Elizabeth, *née* Williams; *b* 27 Dec 1956; *Educ* Holy Trinity Sch Crawley, Highbury Coll Portsmouth (NCTJ course); *m* 20 Oct 1979, Susan Mary, da of Kenneth Dudley, of Harrold, Beds; 1 s (Thomas Edward b 16 Feb 1989), 1 da (Sophia Elizabeth b 22 July 1991); *Career* The News Portsmouth 1976–79 (joined as trainee, later dist chief reporter), dep news ed Bury Free Press Bury St Edmunds 1979–80, chief law courts reporter Cambridge Evening News 1980–82, law courts reporter Press Assoc 1982–86 (educn correspondent 1986–88); The Times: educn reporter 1988–90, local govt correspondent 1990–92, columnist 1992–; ed Public Finance magazine 1993– (asst ed 1992); memb: High Court Journalists' Assoc 1982–86 (chm 1985–86), Educn Correspondents' Gp 1986–90, Br Soc of Magazine Eds; FRSA 1995; *Recreations* reading, walking, opera; *Style—* Douglas Broom, Esq; ✉ Public Finance, 3 Robert Street, London WC2N 6BH (☎ 0171 543 5736, fax 0171 543 5793)

BROOM, Air Marshal Sir Ivor Gordon; KCB (1975, CB 1972), CBE (1969), DSO (1945), DFC (1942 and two bars 1944 and 1945), AFC (1956); s of Alfred Godfrey Broom, of Southport, and Janet Broom; *b* 2 June 1920; *Educ* W Monmouth Sch, Pontypridd GS; *m* 1942, Jess Irene, da of William Joseph Cooper, of Ipswich; 2 s, 1 da; *Career* served WWII bomber pilot, Cmdt Central Flying Sch 1968–70, controller of Nat Air Traffic Servs and bd memb CAA 1974–77, ret RAF 1977; int aerospace conslt 1977–94; chm Gatwick Handling Ltd 1982–93, dir Plessey Airports Ltd 1982–86, chm Farnborough Aerospace Devpt Corp 1985–92; *Recreations* golf; *Clubs* RAF, Moor Park Golf (pres); *Style—* Air Marshal Sir Ivor Broom, KCB, CBE, DSO, DFC, AFC; ✉ Cherry Lawn, Bridle Lane, Loudwater, Rickmansworth, Herts WD3 4JB (☎ 01923 778878)

BROOME, Ronald Frederick; OBE (1983), QPM (1989); s of Edgar Broome (d 1977), and Ida, *née* Richardson (d 1975); *b* 29 Dec 1932; *Educ* Hemsworth GS; *m* 2 Oct 1954, Kathleen, da of Jack Lyon (d 1962); 3 s (Christopher b 31 Oct 1956, Graham Mark b 21 Nov 1957, Michael Antony b 2 May 1964), 2 da (Deborah Elizabeth b 4 Aug 1960, Helen Lucy b 7 June 1968); *Career* RAF police 1950–54; joined W Riding Constabulary 1954, dep chief constable W Midlands Police 1980–83 (asst chief constable 1977–80), chief constable Avon and Somerset Constabulary 1983–89; vice pres: Police Athletic Assoc, Royal Life-Saving Soc; former memb Football Licensing Authy; *Recreations* tennis, badminton; *Clubs* Bristol Savages, Shakespeare; *Style—* Ronald Broome, Esq, OBE, QPM

BROOMFIELD, Graham Martin; s of Herbert Broomfield (d 1989), of W Sussex, and Muriel Joyce, *née* Robinson (d 1994); *b* 12 Feb 1945; *Educ* Dorking County GS, Chelsea Coll, Univ of London (BSc); *m* 5 Oct 1974, Wai Yu (Miranda), da of Leung Fu Ping (d 1972); 1 s (Lee b 1978), 1 da (Amy b 1981); *Career* CA; Charles Comins & Co 1967–72, Peat Marwick Mitchell & Co 1972–76, Warner Communications Inc 1977–81, Prager & Fenton 1981–87, Broomfield & Co 1983–; treas Friends of St James Norlands, govr St Clements & St James Sch; *Recreations* politics, squash; *Style—* Graham M Broomfield, Esq; ✉ 17 Cromwell Grove, London W6 (☎ 0171 603 4487, fax 0171 371 4908)

BROOMFIELD, Sir Nigel Hugh Robert Allen; KCMG (1993, CMG 1986); s of Col Arthur Allen Broomfield, OBE, MC (d 1970), and Ruth Sheilagh, *née* Anderson (d 1974); *b* 19 March 1937; *Educ* Haileybury, Trinity Coll Cambridge (BA); *m* 8 June 1963, Valerie, da of G Fenton, of Garden Court, Noirmont, Jersey, CI; 2 s (Alexander Allen b 29 April 1970, Nicholas Richard Allen b 2 Oct 1976); *Career* Maj 17/21 Lancers 1958–68; first sec: FCO 1969, Bonn 1970, Moscow 1973, FCO 1975; RCDS 1978, cnsllr and head of Chancery BMG Berlin 1979, head E Euro and Soviet Dept FCO 1981, dep high cmmr New Delhi 1986, ambass to GDR E Berlin 1988, dep under sec of state (Defence) FCO 1990; ambass to Germany 1993–97; Br Amateur Squash Champion 1957–58; *Recreations* reading, music, sport; *Clubs* MCC, RAC; *Style—* Sir Nigel Broomfield, KCMG; ✉ c/o FCO, Whitehall, London SW1A 2AA

BROPHY, Michael John Mary; s of Gerald Brophy, and Mary Brophy; *b* 24 June 1937; *Educ* Ampleforth, RN Coll Dartmouth; *m* 1962, Sarah Myrtle, da of Capt G B Rowe, RN; 3 s (James, Jonathan, Thomas), 1 da (Lucy); *Career* Lt Cdr RN 1953–66; assoc dir J Walter Thompson 1967–74, appeals dir The Spastics Soc (now Scope) 1975–81, chief exec Charities Aid Fndn 1982–; sec Cncl for Charitable Support 1986–, vice chm European Foundation Centre 1994; FRSA 1986, CIMgt 1994; *Recreations* travel, walking; *Clubs* Athenaeum; *Style—* Michael Brophy, Esq; ✉ 8 Oldlands Hall, Herons Ghyll, Uckfield, East Sussex TN22 3DA

BROTHERHOOD, James; s of Frederick Arthur Brotherhood (d 1974), and Isabel, *née* Bradley (d 1991); *b* 5 June 1946; *Educ* King's Sch Chester; *m* 1, 2 Aug 1969, Susan Elizabeth, da of Thomas Ian Jodrell Toler, of Cheshire; 3 s (Jonathan Alexander Jodrell b 1973, Philip Richard Thomas b 1975, Michael Rupert Benjamin b 1981), 2 da (Katherine Mary b 1978, Eleanor Elizabeth b 1984); m 2, 11 March 1989, Rosalind Ann, da of late Dr Robert Alan Blyth, of Cheshire; 1 da (Emily Victoria b 1991); *Career* architect; fndr James Brotherhood & Associates; pres Cheshire Soc of Architects 1978–80, chm NW Region RIBA 1983; Dip Arch (Hons) 1973, RIBA 1974; *Recreations* shooting, fishing; *Clubs* City (Chester), St James's (Manchester), Pitt; *Style—* James Brotherhood, Esq; ✉ James Brotherhood & Associates, The Steam Mill, Steam Mill St, Chester CH3 5AN (☎ 01244 347557)

BROTHERS, Air Cdre Peter Malam; CBE (1964), DSO (1944), DFC (1940, bar 1943); s of John Malam Brothers (d 1953), of Prestwich, Lancs, and Maude Elizabeth Owen (d 1969); *b* 30 Sept 1917; *Educ* North Manchester Sch; *m* 1939, Annette, da of James Wilson (d 1959), of Hutton House, Birmingham; 3 da (Caroline, Wendy, Hilary); *Career* Pilot Offr RAF 1936, Flt Lt 1939, served WW II, Battle of Britain 1940, Sqdn Ldr 1941, Wing Cdr 1942, Tangmere Wing Ldr 1942–43, Staff HQ No 10 Gp 1943, Exeter Wing Ldr 1944, US Cmd and Gen Staff Sch 1944–45, Central Fighter Estab 1945–46; dist offr (HM Colonial Serv): Meru 1947–48, Kisumu 1948–49; rejoined RAF 1949, cmd Bomber Sqdn 1949–52, HQ No 3 Gp 1952–54, RAF Staff Coll 1954, HQ Fighter Cmd 1955–57, Bomber Stn 1957–59, Gp Capt and staff offr SHAPE Paris 1959–62, Dir of Ops (overseas) Air Miny 1962–65, Air Cdre and AOC Mil Air Traffic Ops 1965–68, dir PR (RAF) MOD (AIR) 1968–73, ret 1973; chm and md Peter Brothers Consultants Ltd 1973–86; patron Spitfire Assoc Aust, vice pres Spitfire Soc, pres Devon Emergency Vols; Master Guild Air Pilots & Air Navigators 1974–75 (Freeman 1966, Liveryman 1968, Warden 1971), Freeman City of London 1967; *Recreations* flying, fishing, swimming; *Clubs* RAF, Honiton Golf; *Style—* Air Cdre Peter Brothers, CBE, DSO, DFC; ✉ c/o National Westminster Bank, Topsham, Devon

BROTHERSTON, Lez; s of Leslie Brotherston, of Liverpool, and Irene, *née* Richardson; *b* 6 Oct 1961; *Educ* Prescot GS, St Helens Sch of Art, Central Sch of Art and Design (BA); *Career* set and costume designer; *Theatre* for Greenwich Theatre: Northanger Abbey, The Last Romantics, Handling Bach, The Sisters Rosensweig (also Old Vic), Falling over England, Under the Stars, The Prisoner of Zenda, Schippel the Plumber (also Edinburgh Festival), The Government Inspector; for Actors' Touring Co: No Way Out, The Maids, The Triumph of Love, Hamlet, Princess Ivona, Dr Faustus, Heaven Bent Hellbound; for Oldham Coliseum: Wuthering Heights, Love on the Dole; other prodns incl: Hindle Wakes (Manchester Royal Exchange), Rosencrantz and Guildenstern are Dead (RNT), Enjoy (Nottingham Playhouse), Neville's Island (Apollo West End), The Schoolmistress (Chichester Festival Theatre), Jane Eyre (Playhouse West End), Comedians (West Yorkshire Playhouse and Lyric Hammersmith), Jane Eyre (Theatr Clwyd and Thorndike), Mystery Plays (Coventry Belgrade), The School for Wives (Belfast Arts), Jane Eyre (Derby Playhouse), A Midsummer Night's Dream (Royal Exchange), Speedking (Liverpool Playhouse), The Daughter-In-Law (Bristol Old Vic), The Little Foxes (Leeds Playhouse), The Beaux Stratagem (Stephen Joseph Theatre), The Man of Mode (Swan Theatre, Worcester), Pinocchio Boys (Paines Plough); *Musicals* incl: Camelot (BOC Covent Garden Festival), Face (Queen's Theatre Hornchurch and tour), Maria Friedman by Special Arrangement (Donmar Warehouse), Annie (Liverpool Playhouse), Cabaret (Sheffield Crucible), Closer than Ever (Manchester Library Theatre), High Society (West Yorkshire Playhouse), Songbook (Watermill Newbury); *Dance* for Northern Ballet Theatre: Dracula, The Brontes, A Christmas Carol (also BBC), Swan Lake, Romeo and Juliet (also BBC), Strange Meeting; for Adventures in Motion Pictures: Swan Lake (Olivier Award Winner for Best New Dance Prodn), Highland Fling; *Opera* for Opera North: Le Roi Malgre Lui, Madam Butterfly (set only), Masquerade, The Flying Dutchman; for Buxton Festival Opera: The Impresario, Il Sogno Di Scipione, David and Goliath, Sir Gawain and the Green Knight; for Opera Zuid: Hansel and Gretel,

A Cunning Little Vixon, Ariadne Auf Naxos, Werther; for Hong Kong Arts Festival: Der Rosenkavalier, The Marriage of Figaro; for Camden Festival: Silver Lake, The Tsar has his Photograph Taken, The Protagonists; other prodns incl: Falstaff (Teatro Bellini, Sicily), Dido and Aeneas/Venus and Adonis (Festwochen der Alten Musik, Innsbruck & De Vlaamse Opera, Antwerp), Cornet Christoph Rilke's Song of Love and Death (Glyndebourne Touring Opera), L'Italiana in Algeri (Dublin Grand Opera), Rigoletto (Opera Northern Ireland), Don Giovanni (Opera 80), Hansel and Gretel (set only, WNO), Die Fledermaus (Opera East), La Traviata (Phoenix Opera), Don Giovanni (Surrey Opera); *Films* Swan Lake (Thermal Pant Prodns), Letter to Brezhnev (Palace Pictures); *Costume & Props* for BBC: Dr Who, The Cleopatras, Richard III, Henry VI (parts I, II and III), King Lear, Antony and Cleopatra, The Merchant of Venice; for ITV: Deceptions (mini-series), The Far Pavilions; other prodns incl: Highlander, Bullshot Drummond, Brazil, Young Sherlock and the Pyramid of Fear, The Last Emperor; *Awards* Olivier Award nominations incl: Outstanding Achievement in Dance (for Northern Ballet Theatre Season at the Royalty Theatre) and Best Set Design (for Neville's Island); *Style*— Lez Brotherston, Esq; ✉ c/o Mayer & Eden Ltd, 34 Kingly Court, London W1R 5LE (☎ 0171 434 1242, fax 0171 287 5834)

BROTHERTON, Ven (John) Michael; s of Clifford Brotherton (d 1961), and Minnie, *née* Crowther (d 1946); *b* 7 Dec 1935; *Educ* Hipperholme Sch Yorks, St John's Coll Cambridge (MA), Cuddesdon Coll Oxford, Inst of Educn London (postgrad cert in educn in tropical areas); *m* 29 June 1963, Daphne Margaret Yvonne, da of Sir (Richard) Geoffrey Austin Meade, KBE, CMG, CVO (d 1992); 3 s (James Edward Meade b 26 July 1966, Peter Nicolas Meade b 13 Oct 1967, Mark Christian Meade b 22 June 1969), 1 da (Marianthe Elizabeth Meade b 14 Jan 1973); *Career* curate of St Nicolas Chiswick 1961–64, chaplain of Trinity Coll Port of Spain Trinidad 1965–69, rector of St Michael's Diego Martin Trinidad 1969–75, vicar of St Mary and St John Oxford 1976–81, chaplain of St Hilda's Coll Oxford 1976–81, rural dean of Cowley 1978–81, vicar of St Mary Portsea 1981–91, hon canon of Kobe Cathedral Japan 1986–, archdeacon of Chichester 1991–; proctor in convocation 1995–; memb: Sion Coll London, Soc for the Maintenance of the Faith; *Recreations* reading novels, walking; *Style*— The Ven the Archdeacon of Chichester; ✉ 4 Canon Lane, Chichester, West Sussex PO19 1PX (☎ 01243 779134, fax 01243 536452)

BROTHERTON, Paul; s of Neil Brotherton, of Leeds, and Kathleen, *née* Hampson; *b* 11 July 1966; *Educ* Counthill Comp Sch Oldham, Oldham Coll of Technol; *Career* yachtsman; began sailing 1970; clubs: Fairfield 1971–76, Glossop and Dist 1976; achievements incl: runner up Nat Schoolboy Championships 1978, rep UK sr team aged 15 World Championships 1982, runner up UK Youth Championship 1984 (joined UK youth squad 1980), Scottish Open champion 1984, nat champion 470 class 1991, Bronze medal 470 class World Championships 1991, sixth Olympic Games Barcelona 1992, second 505 Class World Championships 1993; mech engrg apprentice Cobden Chadwick 1982; mast rigger: Proctor Masts 1985–87, Racing Sailboats 1987–88, Owen Sails 1988–89, Hyde Sails 1989–95; racing coach Zap Sailing 1995–; Times/Minet Supreme Award for Sporting Excellence 1992; *Recreations* cycling, running, sailing; *Style*— Paul Brotherton, Esq; ✉ 19 Lindley Avenue, Southsea, Hampshire PO4 9NT

BROTZEN, David; *b* 27 May 1963; *Educ* BA Business Mgmnt and Psychology; *Career* former journalist; Issues and Crisis Unit Burson Marsteller 1988–93, dir of issues and crisis mgmnt Hill & Knowlton (UK) Ltd 1993–; speciality in providing strategic and tactical counsel to clients facing environmental disasters, hostage taking, transportation incidents, industl actions, death in service, consumer boycotts, serious fin irregularities and global recalls; fndr and co-ordinator PROMPT interactive crisis system; lectr in crisis mgmnt London Business Sch; IPR Sword of Excellence (for best overall PR campaign) 1987; MIPR 1992; *Style*— David Brotzen, Esq; ✉ Hill & Knowlton (UK) Ltd, 5–11 Theobalds Road, London WC1X 8SH (☎ 0171 413 3150, fax 0171 413 3202, mobile 0374 196114)

BROUCHER, David Stuart; s of Clifford Broucher, of Ewenny, Glamorgan, and Betty Elma, *née* Jordan; *b* 5 Oct 1944; *Educ* Manchester GS, Trinity Hall Cambridge (BA); *m* 25 Nov 1971, Marion Monika, da of Mr Wilkinson Gill, of Stagshaw, Northumberland; 1 s (Nicholas David b 1972); *Career* Foreign Office 1966–68, Br Mil Govt Berlin 1968–72, Cabinet Office 1972–75, Br Embassy Prague 1975–78, FCO 1978–83, UK perm rep to the EC 1983–85, cnsllr Jakarta 1985–89, cnsllr (econ) Bonn 1989–93, FCO 1994–; *Recreations* golf, music, sailing; *Style*— David Broucher, Esq; ✉ c/o FCO, King Charles St, London SW1

BROUGH, Michael David; s of (Kenneth) David Brough (d 1990), of Highgate, London, and Frances Elizabeth, *née* Davies (d 1996); *b* 4 July 1942; *Educ* Westminster, Christ's Coll Cambridge, Middx Hosp Med Sch (MA, MB BChir); *m* 8 June 1974, Dr Geraldine Moira Brough, da of Ernest Alfred Sleigh, of Sutton Coldfield; 2 s (Jonathan b 1977, Nicholas b 1983), 2 da (Charlotte b 1978, Veronica b 1981); *Career* med posts 1968–71: Middx Hosp, Central Middx Hosp; surgical trg posts Birmingham hosps 1971–74; plastic surgeon trg posts 1975–80: Mt Vernon Hosp London, Odstock Hosp Salisbury, Withington Hosp Manchester; conslt in plastic surgery: St Andrew's Hosp Billericay, Queen Elizabeth Hosp Hackney and Whipps Cross Hosp 1980–82, Royal Northern Hosp 1982–90, UCLH, Royal Free Hosp, Whittington Hosp 1982–; conslt King Edward VII Hosp for Officers and hon conslt St Luke's Hosp for the Clergy; fndr and hon sec Phoenix Appeal 1988–; author of specialist pubns on plastic and reconstructive surgery; Freeman City of London 1974; Liveryman: Worshipful Co of Tin Plate Workers (memb Ct of Assts), Worshipful Soc of Apothecaries; pres Plastic Surgery Section RSM 1990–91, FRCS; *Recreations* family, skiing; *Clubs* Hawks' (Cambridge); *Style*— Mr Michael Brough; ✉ The Consulting Suite, 82 Portland Place, London WIN 3DH (☎ 0171 935 8910)

BROUGHAM, Hon Charles William; s and h of 5 Baron Brougham and Vaux, *qv*; *b* 9 Nov 1971; *Educ* Summer Fields, Radley, Univ of Reading; *Style*— The Hon Charles Brougham; ✉ Highleaze House, Oare, nr Marlborough, Wilts

BROUGHAM, Christopher John; QC (1988); s of Lt Cdr Patrick Brougham, RN (ret, d 1991), and Elizabeth Anne, *née* Vestey; *b* 11 Jan 1947; *Educ* Radley, Worcester Coll Oxford (BA); *m* 28 Sept 1974, Mary Olwen, da of Timothy Traherne Corker; 1 s (William b 1977), 3 da (Emily b 1979, Miranda b 1982, Deborah b 1988); *Career* called to the Bar Inner Temple 1969, dep High Ct bankruptcy registrar 1984–, Sec of State for Trade and Indust inspr (under The Companies Act 1985) to investigate the affairs of BOM Holdings plc 1990–91; dep churchwarden Christ Church Kensington 1980–95; memb: Inner Temple 1966, Gray's Inn (ad eundem) 1989; *Recreations* listening to music, playing the piano, solving and setting crossword puzzles; *Style*— Christopher Brougham, Esq, QC; ✉ 3–4 South Square, Gray's Inn, London WC1R 5HP (☎ 0171 696 9900, fax 0171 696 9911)

BROUGHAM, Hon David Peter; s of 4 Baron Brougham and Vaux (d 1967); *b* 22 Aug 1940; *Educ* Sedbergh; *m* 1, 1969, Moussie Christina Margareta Hallström, da of Sven Hörnblad, of Stockholm, Sweden; 1 s (Henry, b 1971); m 2, 1977, Caroline Susan, only da of Lt-Col James Michael Heigham Royce Tomkin, MC, of Red House, Wissett, Halesworth, Suffolk (by his w Margaret Elinor, da of Sir Charles Henry Napier Bunbury, 11 B), and former w of Julian Dixon; 1 s (Oliver b 1978); *Career* dir Standard Chartered plc 1993– (joined as head of credit 1989, currently based Hong Kong), responsible for banking activities in Europe, America, Africa, ME and S Asia; *Style*— The Hon David Brougham; ✉ c/o Standard Chartered plc, 1 Aldermanbury Square, London EC2V 7SB (☎ 0171 280 7500, fax 0171 280 7791)

BROUGHAM AND VAUX, 5 Baron (UK 1860); Michael John Brougham; CBE (1995); s of 4 Baron (d 1967) by his 2 w, Jean (d 1992), da of late Brig-Gen Gilbert Follett, DSO, MVO, and Lady Mildred, *née* Murray (d 1992), da of 7 Earl of Dunmore, DL; *b* 2 Aug 1938; *Educ* Lycée Jaccard Lausanne, Millfield, Northampton Inst of Agric; *m* 1, 1963 (m dis 1968), Olivia Susan (d 1986), da of Rear Adm Gordon Thomas Seccombe Gray, DSC, of Midhurst; 1 da; m 2, 1969 (m dis 1981), Catherine (who m 1981 Rupert Edward Odo Russell, gs of Sir Odo Russell, KCMG, KCVO, CB, himself 2 s of 1 Baron Ampthill), da of William Gulliver; 1 s; *Heir* s, Hon Charles Brougham, *qv*; *Career* Parly consIt and co dir; pres ROSPA 1986–89; former chm Tax Payers' Soc; a dep chm House of Lords 1993; a dep Speaker House of Lords 1995; chm European Secure Vehicle Alliance (ESVA) 1993, pres Nat Health and Safety Groups Cncl 1994; *Recreations* rugger, tennis, photography; *Style*— The Rt Hon the Lord Brougham and Vaux, CBE; ✉ 11 Westminster Gardens, Marsham St, London SW1P 4JA

BROUGHSHANE, 3 Baron (UK 1945), of Kensington, Co London; (William) Kensington Davison; DSO (1945), DFC; yr s of 1 Baron Broughshane, KBE (d 1953), and his 1 w, Beatrice Mary, *née* Roberts (d 1971); suc bro 2 Baron Broughshane 1995; *b* 1914; *Educ* Shrewsbury, Magdalen Coll Oxford; *Heir* none; *Career* WWII Wing Cdr RAFVR; called to the Bar Inner Temple 1939; Liveryman Worshipful Co of Clothworkers; *Clubs* Garrick; *Style*— The Rt Hon the Lord Broughshane, DSO, DFC; ✉ 3 Godfrey St, London SW3 3TA (☎ 0171 352 7826)

BROUGHTON, Sir David Delves; 13 Bt (E 1660), of Broughton, Staffs; s of Lt Cdr Peter John Delves Broughton, RN (d 1963), and his 1 w, Nancy Rosemary, *née* Paterson; suc kinsman, Sir (Evelyn) Delves Broughton, 12 Bt (d 1993); *b* 7 May 1942; *m* 1969, Diane, da of Ronald Lindsay Nicol, of 29 Grange Road, Kew, Victoria 3101, Australia; (by Hildegard Weitzel) 1 da (Jennifer Zoë Weitzel b 1977); *Heir* half-bro, Geoffrey Delves Broughton b 1962; *Career* craftsman; *Style*— Sir David Broughton, Bt; ✉ 31 Mayfield Court, Sandy, Bedfordshire SG19 1NF (☎ 01767 691750)

BROUGHTON, Hon James Henry Ailwyn; s and h of 3 Baron Fairhaven, JP; *b* 25 May 1963; *Educ* Sunningdale, Harrow; *m* 22 March 1990, Sarah Olivia, da of Harold Digby Fitzgerald Creighton, of Upper Brook St, London W1; 2 da (Sophie Rose b 30 April 1992, Emily Patricia b 15 May 1995); *Career* Capt Blues and Royals 1984–94; Baring Asset Management Ltd 1994–; *Recreations* shooting, skiing, hunting, gardening; *Style*— The Hon James Broughton

BROUGHTON, Martin Faulkner; *b* 1947, London; *Educ* Westminster City GS; *m* 1974, Jocelyn Mary, *née* Rodgers; 1 s, 1 da; *Career* articled clerk then chartered accountant Peat Marwick Mitchell & Co; BAT Industries plc: joined British-American Tobacco as travelling auditor 1971, various financial positions London 1974–80, fin dir Souza Cruz Brazil 1984–85 (joined 1980), fin dir Eagle Star 1985–88, fin dir BAT Industries plc 1988–90, chm Wiggins Teape Group 1989–90, sr gp fin dir 1990–92, chm Eagle Star 1992–93, md fin servs 1992–, gp chief exec and dep chm 1993–; non-exec dir Whitbread plc 1993–; memb Urgent Issues Task Force Accounting Standards Bd 1991–95, chm CBI Companies Ctee 1995–, a vice pres Chartered Inst of Mktg 1996–, memb Takeover Panel 1996–; *Recreations* theatre, golf; *Style*— Martin Broughton, Esq; ✉ BAT Industries plc, Windsor House, 50 Victoria Street, London SW1H 0NL (☎ 0171 222 7979, fax 0171 222 0122)

BROUGHTON, Dr Peter; s of Thomas Frederick Broughton (d 1983), of Skipton, and Mary Theodosia, *née* Bracewell (d 1993); *b* 8 Sept 1944; *Educ* Univ of Manchester (BSc, PhD); *m* Aug 1968, Janet Mary, da of Ronald George Silveston; 2 s (Jonathan b 3 May 1971, Nicholas b 8 Jan 1974); *Career* research student then research asst in structural engrg Univ of Manchester 1966–71, structural engrg surveyor Lloyds Register of Shipping 1971–74, ptnr subsld of Campbell Reith and Partners (chartered engrs) 1974–75, soils/structural engr Burmah Oil Trading Ltd 1975–76, sr soils/structural engr rising to supervising structural engr British National Oil Corporation 1977–79; Phillips Petroleum Company: sr structural engr UK Div 1979–82, civil engrg supervisor UK Div 1982–86, princ project engr and co rep Norway Div 1986–90, princ project engr and co rep then engrg and procurement mangr UK Div 1990–93, engrg and construction project mangr for sub-structures Norway Div 1994–; visiting prof Dept of Civil Engrg Imperial Coll London 1991–; CEng, FICE, FIMarE, FIStructE, FRINA, FEng 1996; *Awards* Special Award Instn of Structural Engrs 1990, Stanley Gray Award Inst of Marine Engrs 1992, George Stephenson Medal ICE 1993; *Publications* The Ekofisk Protective Barrier (ICE, 1992), The Analysis of Cable and Catenary Structures (1994), The Effects of Subsidence on the Steel Jacket and Piled Foundation Design for the Ekofisk 2/4X and 2/4J Platforms (ICE, 1996); also author of numerous other pubns; *Recreations* gardening, walking, swimming, fishing; *Style*— Dr Peter Broughton, FEng; ✉ Phillips Petroleum Company Norway, PO Box 220, N-4056 Tananger, Norway (☎ 00 47 51694056, fax 00 47 51691120)

BROUN, Sir William Windsor; 13 Bt (NS 1686), of Colstoun, Haddingtonshire; s of William Arthur Broun (d 1925), and Marie Victoria, *née* McIntyre (d 1964); suc kinsman, Sir Lionel John Law Broun, 12 Bt (d 1995); *b* 11 July 1917; *m* 1952, D'Hrie, da of Frank R King, of Bingara, NSW; 2 da; *Heir* bro, Hulance Haddington Broun b 1919; *Career* vice pres Scottish Aust Heritage Cncl, fell Inst of Chartered Accountants in Aust; memb Royal Agric Soc of NSW; *Recreations* golf; *Clubs* Cromer Golf, Royal Automobile (Australia); *Style*— Sir William Broun, Bt; ✉ 12 Tamarisk Gardens, 2 Reed Street, Cremorne, NSW 2090, Australia

BROUWER, Egbert; CBE (1980); s of Jan Hendrick Brouwer, and Margaretha M E Dyjers; *b* 14 Feb 1927; *Educ* Nederlands Lyceum, The Netherlands Beatrix Coll Switzerland; *m* 14 Oct 1953, Dorine, da of Cornelis van Holst Pellekaan (d 1952); 3 s, 1 da; *Career* Capt Dutch Army 1947–49; branch mangr: Internatio NV in SE Asia 1949–56, Roosendaal Commodity Brokers Rotterdam 1957–65; gen mangr BP Nederland BV Amsterdam 1965–80, md BP Nutrition Ltd London 1978–87; memb: Cncl VNO 1973–78, Bd Govrs Maritime Ryksmuseum 1972–80; chm Supervisory Bd Atlas COPCO Amsterdam 1975–80; memb Bd: Atlas Copco (GB) Hemel Hempstead 1980–, Purina Mills Inc 1986–89, BP Nutrition Ltd 1987–89; memb Supervisory Bd: Merrem and Laporte 1974–80, JP Morgan Nederland 1977–90, BP Nederland 1980–89; chm Supervisory Bd Hendrix International 1979–89; Knight Netherlands Lion (1987); *Recreations* sailing, maritime history; *Clubs* Royal Netherlands Yacht; *Style*— Egbert Brouwer, Esq; ✉ Howick Farm, Balls Cross, nr Petworth, W Sussex GU28 9JY (☎ 01403 820548)

BROWETT, John Peter; s of Peter Harry James Browett, and Florence Margaret, *née* Kingdom; *b* 12 June 1946; *Educ* Wyggeston Boys' GS Leicester, Bart's Med Coll London; *m* 6 Sept 1969, Penelope Anne, da of Alan Ross Land; 1 s (Oliver Peter Ross), 1 da (Deborah Louise); *Career* consIt orthopaedic surgn Bart's (currently dir Sports Unit) 1980–95, orthopaedic consIt to Tottenham Hotspur FC 1980–94; Freeman City of London 1988; Liveryman: Worshipful Co of Barber Surgns 1989, Worshipful Co of Pattenmakers 1993; memb: Br Orthopaedic Assoc, BMA, Br Assoc Surgery of the Knee, Br Orthopaedic Sports Trauma Assoc, Int Arthroscopy Assoc; FRCS; *Recreations* skiing, wildlife, shooting, sailing; *Style*— John Browett, Esq; ✉ 95 Harley Street, London W1 (☎ 0171 486 9323)

BROWN, *see:* Holden-Brown

BROWN, Adrian James; s of Rev Stanley George Brown, of Ely, Cambs, and Gabrielle Mary, *née* Holmes; *b* 25 Nov 1946; *Educ* The Friends' Sch Saffron Walden Essex, Univ of Birmingham (BSc); *m* 21 Feb 1976, Jill, da of George Charles Harmsworth, of Rayleigh, Essex; 1 s (Gregory b 1985), 2 da (Hilary b 1980, Fiona b 1984); *Career* dir: MIM Ltd 1986–88, Britannia Asset Management Ltd 1985–86; sr investmt mangr Refuge Assurance PLC 1988–; *Recreations* sailing, reading; *Style*— Adrian Brown, Esq; ✉ Colts Pightle, Post Office Rd, Woodham Mortimer, Maldon, Essex (☎ 01245 225381); Refuge Assurance PLC, 66 Gresham St, London EC2V 7PQ (☎ 0171 600 0339, telex 295958)

BROWN, Prof Alan Geoffrey; s of Roy Brown (d 1943), and Edith Lillian, *née* Swift; *b* 20 April 1940; *Educ* Mundella GS Nottingham, Univ of Edinburgh (BSC, MB ChB, PhD); *m* 13 April 1963, Judith, da of Leonard Thomas Allen (d 1987); 1 s (Jeremy David b 1967), 1 da (Jessica Anne b 1968); *Career* Univ of Edinburgh: asst lectr in veterinary physiology 1964–65, lectr 1965–76, Beit meml fell for Medres 1968–71, res fell supported by MRC 1971–74, reader in veterinary physiology 1976–84, prof 1984–; memb Physiological Soc 1968; FRSE 1984, FIBiol 1987; *Books* Organization in the Spinal Cord (1981), Intracellular Staining of Mammalian Neurones (with R E W Fyffe, 1984), Nerve Cells and Nervous Systems (1991); *Recreations* music, gardening; *Style*— Prof Alan Brown, FRSE; ✉ Department of Preclinical Veterinary Sciences, University of Edinburgh, Summerhall, Edinburgh EH9 1QH (☎ 0131 650 6145, fax 0131 650 6576, telex 727442 UNIVED G)

BROWN, Alan Thomas; CBE (1978), DL (Oxon 1978); s of Thomas Henry Brown, of Cromer, and Lucy Lilian, *née* Betts; *b* 18 April 1928; *Educ* Wyggeston GS Leicester, Sidney Sussex Coll Cambridge; *m* 1962, Marie Christine, da of Hubert York East, late of Blackburn; 2 da; *Career* chief exec Oxon CC 1973–88, memb Audit Cmmn 1989–95; *Recreations* reading, chess, cliff walking; *Style*— Alan Brown, Esq, CBE, DL; ✉ 4 Malkin Drive, Beaconsfield, Bucks HP9 1JN (☎ 01494 677933)

BROWN, Rev Dr (James) Alistair; *b* 9 Sept 1950; *Educ* Bell Baxter Sr HS Cupar, Edinburgh Coll of Commerce (Journalism course), Univ of Edinburgh (BA, BD, PhD); *m* Alison; 4 c; *Career* reporter and sub-ed The Scotsman and Evening News (Glasgow and Edinburgh) 1967–70 (pt/t sub-ed Evening News while at univ 1970–78), clerical worker local govt 1974–75, student asst pastor Craigmillar Baptist Centre Edinburgh 1975–78; pastor: Livingston Baptist Church - Dedridge Congregation 1981–86 (pt/t pastor 1979–81), Gerrard Street Baptist Church Aberdeen 1986–96; gen dir Baptist Missionary Society Nov 1996–; accredited min Baptist Union of Scot (former memb Cncl and Exec), memb Tyndale Fellowship for Biblical and Theological Research; sometime pt/t lectr in New Testament studies Univs of Edinburgh and Aberdeen, former memb Scot Cncl of Interserve, former tstee Aberdeen Sch of Christian Studies, former baptist chaplain Univ of Aberdeen; *Books* To Illustrate That (1989), Late Night Extra (1991), Save Sam (1993), Worship: Adoration and Action (contrib, 1993), The Runaway (1994), Near Christianity (1996); *Recreations* golf, photography, hill-walking, advanced driving and motorcycling, lapidary; *Style*— Rev Dr Alistair Brown; ✉ Baptist Missionary Society, Baptist House, PO Box 49, 129 Broadway, Didcot, Oxon OX11 8XA (☎ 01235 512077, fax 01235 511265)

BROWN, Andrew William; s of Harry Eugene Brown (d 1971), of Ballygarvan House, Ballygarvan, Co Cork, and Geraldine, *née* O'Leary; *b* 3 March 1946; *Educ* St Edmund's Coll Ware Herts; *m* Shelby Ann, *née* Hill; *Career* J Walter Thompson Co Ltd: joined 1965, account planner 1973–76, head of trg 1980–86, bd dir 1982–93, head of account mgmnt 1986–88, gp dir 1987–93; DG Advertising Assoc 1993–; memb Cncl IPA 1991–93 (memb Trg Ctee 1980–93), chm CAM Fndn 1994–96; *Recreations* reading, theatre, sport; *Clubs* Reform, MCC, XL; *Style*— Andrew Brown, Esq; ✉ Advertising Association, Abford House, 15 Wilton Road, London SW1V 1NJ (☎ 0171 828 2771, fax 0171 931 0376)

BROWN, Anthony Nigel; s of Sydney Brown, of Birmingham, and Gene, *née* Laitner; *b* 12 June 1955; *Educ* Clifton Coll Bristol, Univ of Manchester (LLB); *m* 16 April 1989, Gail Denise, da of Dr Nathaniel Rifkind, of Glasgow; 1 s (Joshua Jack b 10 April 1991), 1 da (Sasha Jade b 14 Oct 1993); *Career* admitted slr 1980; voluntary asst Artlaw 1978–81, asst slr Janners 1980–84; fndr and md: Connaught Brown 1984–, The Affordable Art Company Ltd 1991–; exhibitions: Northern Spirit 1986, work of Oleg Tselkov 1990; organised Artlaw auction Royal Acad 1981 and Dulwich Art '90; memb: Soc of London Art Dealers, Educn Advsy Ctee Dulwich Art Gallery, Exec Ctee Patrons of New Art Tate Gallery 1994; *Recreations* looking at art, reading, swimming; *Clubs* RAC; *Style*— Anthony Brown, Esq; ✉ Connaught Brown, 2 Albemarle St, London W1X 3HF (☎ 0171 408 0362, fax 0171 495 3137)

BROWN, Prof Archibald Haworth (Archie); s of Rev Alexander Douglas Brown (d 1979), of Darvel, Ayrshire, and Mary, *née* Yates; *b* 10 May 1938; *Educ* Annan Acad, Dumfries Acad, City of Westminster Coll, LSE (BSc(Econ)), MA (Oxon); *m* 23 March 1963, Patricia Susan, da of Percival Walter Leslie Cornwell (d 1970); 1 da (Susan Woolford b 19 Jan 1969), 1 s (Alexander Douglas b 19 Oct 1971); *Career* reporter Annandale Herald and Annandale Observer 1954–56; Nat Serv 1956–58; lectr in politics Univ of Glasgow 1964–71 (Br Cncl exchange scholar Moscow Univ 1967–68); prof of politics Univ of Oxford 1989– (lectr in Soviet institutions 1971–89); St Antony's Coll Oxford: faculty fell 1971–89, professorial fell 1989–, sub-warden 1995–; visiting prof of political sci: Yale Univ and Univ of Connecticut 1980, Columbia Univ NY 1985; visiting prof (Frank C Erwin Jr Centennial Chair of Government) Univ of Texas at Austin 1990–91; dir Russian and East Euro Centre St Antony's Coll 1991–94; Henry L Stimson lectures Yale Univ 1980, Arnold Wolfers visiting fell lecture Yale Univ 1989; memb Cncl SSEES 1992–; memb: Political Studies Assoc, American Political Science Assoc, Int Political Science Assoc, British Assoc of Slavonic and East Euro Studies, American Assoc for the Advancement of Slavonic Studies, Assoc of Univ Teachers; FBA 1991; *Books* Soviet Politics and Political Science (1974), The Soviet Union Since the Fall of Khrushchev (co-ed and contrib, 1975), Political Culture and Political Change in Communist States (co-ed and contrib, 1977, 2 edn 1979), Authority, Power and Policy in the USSR: Essays dedicated to Leonard Schapiro (co-ed and contrib, 1980), The Cambridge Encyclopedia of Russia and the Former Soviet Union (co-ed and contrib, 1982, 2 edn 1994), Soviet Policy for the 1980s (co-ed and contrib, 1982), Political Culture and Communist Studies (ed and contrib, 1984), Political Leadership in the Soviet Union (ed and contrib, 1989), The Soviet Union: A Biographical Dictionary (ed and contrib, 1990), New Thinking in Soviet Politics (ed and contrib, 1992), The Gorbachev Factor (1996); *Recreations* novels and political memoirs, opera, ballet, watching cricket and football; *Style*— Prof Archie Brown, FBA; ✉ St Antony's College, Oxford OX2 6JF (☎ 01865 284748, fax 01865 310518)

BROWN, Prof Arthur Joseph; CBE (1974); s of Joseph Brown (d 1957), of Meliden, Prestatyn, Flintshire, and Adelene, *née* Lyles (d 1960); *b* 8 Aug 1914; *Educ* Bradford GS, Queen's Coll Oxford (BA, MA, DPhil); *m* 28 Dec 1938, Joan Hannah Margaret, da of Rev Canon Bertham Eustace Taylor (d 1961), of Walton Breck, Liverpool; 3 s (John Richard b 1940, d 1959, Henry Joseph b 1942, William Arthur b 1945); *Career* fell All Souls Coll Oxford 1937–46, lectr Hertford Coll Oxford 1937–40, Foreign Res and Press Serv 1940–43, FO Res Dept 1943–45, Cabinet Office Economic Section 1945–47, prof of economics Univ of Leeds 1947–79 (emeritus 1979); visiting prof: Columbia Univ NY 1950, Aust Nat Univ Canberra 1963; memb: East Africa Econ and Fiscal Cmmn 1960, Central Africa Office Sec of State's Advsy Gp 1962, Hunt Ctee on Intermediate Areas 1967–69, Univ Grants Ctee 1968–78 (vice chm 1977–78); pres Royal Econ Soc 1976–78; memb: Thoresby Soc, Leeds Civic Tst, Art Collections Fund; Hon DLitt: Univ of Bradford 1975, Univ of Kent 1979, Univ of Sheffield 1979; Hon LLD Univ of Aberdeen 1978, hon fell Queen's Coll Oxford 1985; memb RSS 1940, FBA 1972; *Books* Applied Economics (1948), The Great Inflation 1939–51 (1955), The Framework of Regional Economics in the UK (1972), World Inflation Since 1950 (1985); *Recreations* gardening, walking; *Clubs* Athenaeum; *Style*— Prof Arthur Brown; ✉ 24 Moor Drive, Leeds LS6 4BY (☎ 0113 275 5799)

BROWN, Dr Aubrey; MBE (1975); s of Robert Brown (d 1963), of Dunmurry, Co Antrim, and Emily, *née* Dillon; *b* 4 Dec 1927; *Educ* Huddersfield Tech Teachers' Trg Coll (pres Student Body), Univ of Leeds (CertEd), Univ of the Punjab (BA), Queen's Univ Belfast (BScEcon), Univ of Northern Colorado (MA), Columbia Pacific Univ (PhD); *m* 30 June 1962, Catherine, da of Francis McHugh (d 1973), of Blackrock, Co Louth; *Career* Colombo plan advsr on tech educn Pakistan 1963–65, sr inspr of schs (tech and commercial) Swaziland 1971–78, inspr of educn (tech) Transkei SA 1979, educn offr Southern Educn and Library Bd NI 1979–81, conslt on tech educn Univ of Papua New Guinea 1986–88; memb Coll of Handicraft 1952, fell Coll of Craft Educn 1966; *Books* A Technical Teachers' Training Manual (1988), The Training of Technical Teachers by Competency-Based Methods in Papua New Guinea; *Recreations* woodworking and history of furniture; *Style*— Dr Aubrey Brown, MBE; ✉ Tornabodagh Cottage, Drumaroan Rd, Ballycastle, County Antrim BT54 6QU (☎ 012657 63 685)

BROWN, Dr (James) Barry Conway; OBE (1978); s of Frederick Clarence Brown, of Stroud, Glos, and Alys Brown, *née* Bleackley; *b* 3 July 1937; *Educ* King's Coll Taunton, Clare Coll Cambridge (MA), Univ of Birmingham (MSc, PhD); *m* 7 Sept 1963, Anne Rosemary, da of Frederick Clough (d 1970); 2 s (Andrew b 1964, Phillip b 1967), 1 da (Clare b 1971); *Career* res offr CEGB 1963–67; British Cncl: sci offr London 1967–69, sci offr Spain 1969–72, sci offr France 1972–78, head Sci and Tech Gp London 1978–81, rep (head) Br Cncl and cultural cnsllr Br Embassy Mexico 1981–85, dep controller Higher Educn Div London 1985–89, dir Euro Cmmn Liaison Unit (Higher Educn) Brussels 1989–91, dir Br Cncl Poland 1992–94, ret; subject assessor Higher Educn Funding Cncl for England 1995–; memb: GB-Russia Assoc 1960, Soc for Research into Higher Educn 1995; *Recreations* singing, reading, foreign travel; *Style*— Dr Barry Brown, OBE; ✉ 42 Hazel Rd, Purley-on-Thames, Reading RG8 8BB (☎ 0118 941 7581)

BROWN, Ben Robert; s of Antony Victor Brown, of Smarden, Kent, and Sheila Mary, *née* McCormack; *b* 26 May 1960; *Educ* Sutton Valence Sch Kent, Keble Coll Oxford (open scholar, BA), Univ Coll Cardiff (Dip Journalism); *m* Geraldine Anne, *née* Ryan; 1 da (Ella Olivia b 31 Oct 1992); *Career* journalist; reporter: Radio Clyde Glasgow 1982–83, Radio City Liverpool 1983–85, Radio London 1985–86, Independent Radio News 1986–88; BBC TV News: gen reporter 1988–90, foreign affrs corr 1990–91, Moscow corr 1991–94, gen corr then foreign affrs corr 1994–; major assignments incl: fall of the Berlin Wall, Gulf War (from Riyadh and Kuwait), collapse of the Soviet Union; *Books* All Necessary Means - Inside the Gulf War (with David Shukman, 1991); *Recreations* theatre, cinema, soccer, reading novels and biographies; *Style*— Ben Brown, Esq; ✉ BBC Television News, BBC Television Centre, Wood Lane, London W12 7RJ (☎ 0181 743 8000)

BROWN, Bernard Joseph (Joe); CBE (1981), JP (1970); s of William Goulson Brown (d 1935), and Kate Alice Brown (d 1960); *b* 27 Feb 1916; *Educ* Ealing Co Sch, Southall Tech Coll; *m* 9 Sept 1939, Vera, da of Clarence Douglass (d 1918); 4 s (Peter b 1941, Christopher b 1945, Roger b 1949, Philip b 1955), 1 da (Felicity b 1947); *Career* WWII vol RA 1939 (cmmnd Survey 1941), Staff Capt Combined Ops 1942–46; asst Barry and Vernon Estate Agents London 1933–39, lands offr Air Miny Lands Branch 1946–49, fndr BJ Brown and Ptnrs Chartered Auctioneers and Estate Agents 1949–84; pres Ruislip Round Table 1961–63 (vice chm 1947, chm 1948), chm Ruislip Cons 1955–60 and 1965–70; memb Ruislip Northwood UDC 1949–55, Mayor London Borough of Hillingdon 1969–70 (Alderman 1964–74), vice chm GLC 1970–71 (memb 1967–77), memb Ct of Common Cncl City of London 1972–86, Sheriff City of London 1977–78, chief commoner Corp of London 1981, govr Christ's Hospital, pres City Livery Club 1984–85, former pres W Middx and S Bucks Assoc of Surveyors and Estate Agents; Master Worshipful Co of Fletchers 1986–87 (memb 1970); FAI 1939, FRICS 1970; Order of King Abdul al Aziz (Class 2) 1981; *Recreations* gardening, music; *Clubs* City Livery, United Wards; *Style*— Joe Brown, Esq, CBE, JP; ✉ 1 Lunsford Manor, Ninfield Rd, Bexhill-on-Sea, E Sussex (☎ 01424 892513)

BROWN, Brian Michael John; s of Arthur John Frederick Brown (d 1978), and Ethel Louise, *née* Redsull (d 1982); *b* 11 Feb 1937; *Educ* Sir Roger Manwoods GS Kent; *m* 1, 22 Feb 1960 (m dis 1989), Maureen Ivy Ticehurt; 2 s (Mark Stephen John b 12 March 1964, Timothy John Michael b 18 Jan 1967), 1 da (Rachel Suzanne b 17 March 1961); *m* 2, 20 April 1989, Elizabeth Charlotte, da of Maj Thomas John Saywell; *Career* serv Royal Hampshire Regt 1955–57, Intelligence Corps 1957–58; Trustee Savings Bank: London 1959–60, South Eastern 1960–67; TSB Trust Company Ltd: mktg mangr 1967–71, gen mangr 1971–83, dir 1976, md 1983–88, chief exec 1988–91; conslt and lectr in bancassurance Zebu Consultants 1991–; memb: Unit Trust Assoc Exec Ctee 1980–88, Lautro Selling Practices Ctee 1989–91, SIB Trg and Competence Panel 1992–94, Chartered Insurance Inst Accreditation Bd 1995–; chm Andover Dist Community Health Care NHS Tst 1992–; govr Cricklade Coll Andover 1989–94 (chm 1991), vice pres Winchester & Dist Macmillan Servs Appeal 1986–; FIMgt 1976, FCIB 1977; Allfinanz Without Limits (1991); *Recreations* railways, coin and stamp collecting, walking, reading, eating out; *Style*— Brian Brown, Esq; ✉ The Granaries, Chilbolton, Stockbridge, Hants SO20 6BE (☎ 01264 860127)

BROWN, Adm Sir Brian Thomas; KCB (1989), CBE (1983); s of Walter Thomas Brown (d 1984), and Gladys, *née* Baddeley (d 1989); *b* 31 Aug 1934; *Educ* Peter Symonds' Sch; *m* 1 Aug 1959, Veronica Mary Elizabeth, da of Wing Cdr J D Bird (d 1982); 2 s (Mark b 1960, Matthew b 1962); *Career* served RN 1952–91, RCDS 1983, Capt HMS Raleigh 1984–86, DGNPS 1986, Chief Naval S & S Offr 1986–88, DGNMT 1987–88, Second Sea Lord and Adm Pres RNC Greenwich 1988–91; non-exec dir: Cray Electronic Holdings 1991–, Lorien plc 1996–; chm P E International 1995–; pres Victory Services Assoc 1993–, chm King George Fund for Sailors 1993–; chm Exec Ctee Nuffield Tst for the Forces of the Crown 1996–; Freeman City of London 1989, Liveryman Worshipful Co of Gardeners 1991; Hon DEd; FIPD, CIMgt; *Recreations* cricket, gardening, fishing; *Clubs* Army and Navy; *Style*— Adm Sir Brian Brown, KCB, CBE; ✉ The Old Dairy, Stoner Hill House, Froxfield, Petersfield, Hants (☎ 01730 262041)

BROWN, Bryan Wyman; s of Lionel Bruce Brown (d 1967), and Rosina, *née* Puffet (d 1970); *b* 18 April 1947; *Educ* Cheney Sch Oxford, Oxford Sch of Art, Manchester Coll of Art and Design (DipAD, BA), INSEAD Business Sch Fontainebleau France; *m* 1970, Elizabeth Margaret, da of Richard Arthur Mills (d 1994); 2 s (Dominic b 1976, Peter b 1979), 1 da (Polly b 1974); *Career* graphic designer Graphic Display Unit 1969–70, art dir McGougan Bowler Associates 1970, sr designer Christian Brann Ltd 1970–71, sr designer then chm Allied International Designers Ltd and dir AIDCOM International plc (chm Design Div) 1971–86, dir Marketplace Design Partnership and associated businesses incl Marketplace Consultancy 1987– (projects incl corporate identities for Rover and Pearson TV, retail design for Burtons and Hamleys, leisure design for Rank, Granada and Wembley Stadium, new product devpt for Kodak and John Menzies); chm: Design Mgmnt Gp CSD 1986–, Design Gp CBI 1986–; memb: Design Bd RSA 1984–, Consumer Mktg Affairs Ctee CBI 1986–; formerly SIAD and CNAA assessor; lectr: numerous schs of art and design incl RCA and Eindhoven Sch of Design Holland 1974–, MBA Programmes London and Manchester Business Schs 1979–; memb Cncl and patron Sch of Communication Arts 1985–; estab 1986: Marketplace Design Partnership

Bursary with RSA, Design into Business Award Scheme; memb Victorian Soc; FRSA 1981, FCSD 1979; *Books* The England of Henry Taunt (1973); *Recreations* 19th Century history, conservation, natural history, ornithology, gardening and gardening design, walking, racquets; *Clubs* D&AD (UK), Oxford Unicorns; *Style*— Bryan Brown, Esq; ✉ Clanfield House, 16 Park Crescent, Abingdon-on-Thames, Oxfordshire OX14 1DF (☎ 01235 520278); Marketplace Design Partnership Ltd, Pulpit House, 1 The Square, Abingdon-on-Thames, Oxfordshire OX14 5SZ (☎ 01235 554499, fax 01235 532878)

BROWN, Cedric Harold; s of late William Herbert Brown, and Constance Dorothy, *née* Frances; *b* 7 March 1935; *Educ* Sheffield, Rotherham and Derby Coll of Technol; *m* 1956, Joan Hendry; 1 s, 3 da; *Career* East Midlands Gas Bd: pupil gas distribution engr 1953–58, various engrg posts 1958–75; engr asst Tunbridge Wells Borough Cncl 1959–60, dir of engr E Midlands Gas 1975–78; British Gas Corporation: asst dir ops and dir construction 1978–79, dir Morecambe Bay Project 1980–87, regnl chm British Gas West Midlands 1987–89; British Gas plc: dir of exploration and prodn 1989–90, memb Bd and md 1989–91, sr md 1991–92, chief exec 1992–96; proprietor C B Consultants Ltd 1996–; Freeman City of London 1989, Liveryman Worshipful Co of Engrs 1988; FEng 1990, CEng, FIGasE (pres 1996–), FICE; *Publications* author of various tech papers to professional bodies; *Recreations* sport, countryside, places of historic interest; *Style*— Cedric Brown, Esq, FEng; ✉ C B Consultants Limited, 1 Great Cumberland Place, London W1P 7PW

BROWN, Prof Charles Malcolm; s of Capt Charles Brown (d 1978), of Durham, and Beatrice Lily, *née* Haddrick (d 1988); *b* 21 Sept 1941; *Educ* Houghton-Le-Spring GS, Univ of Birmingham (BSc, PhD, DSc); *m* 16 July 1966, Diane Mary, da of Joseph Bryant (d 1962), of Birmingham; 3 da (Sara b 1969, Ann b 1971, Liz b 1976); *Career* lectr Univ of Newcastle upon Tyne 1966–73, sr lectr Univ of Dundee 1973–79; Heriot Watt Univ: prof 1979–, head of Dept of Biological Sciences 1988–93, dean of Science 1993–95, vice principal 1995–; dir: S Marine Biological Assoc 1975–81, Bioscot Ltd 1982–86, Fermentech Ltd 1983–85, ICBD 1988–90, CMIST 1992–, Microbiological Research Authy 1996–; FIBiol 1979, FRSE 1982, FIBrew 1993; *Books* Sediment Microbiology (jtly, 1981), Introduction to Biotechnology (jtly, 1987); *Recreations* music, walking, gardening; *Style*— Prof Charles Brown, FRSE; ✉ 19 Burnside Park, Balerno, Edinburgh EH14 7LY (☎ 0131 449 7125); Department of Biological Sciences, Heriot-Watt University, Riccarton, Edinburgh EH14 4AS (☎ 0131 451 3362, fax 0131 451 3009)

BROWN, Christina Hambley (Tina); da of George Hambley Brown, of St John's Wood, London, and Bettina Iris Mary, *née* Kohr; *b* 21 Nov 1953; *Educ* Univ of Oxford (MA); *m* 20 Aug 1981, Harold Matthew Evans, s of Frederick Albert Evans (d 1982); 1 s (George Frederick Evans b 26 Jan 1986), 1 da (Isabel Harriet Evans b 22 Oct 1990); *Career* columnist Punch 1978, editor Tatler 1979–83; editor-in-chief: Vanity Fair 1984–92, The New Yorker 1992–; Catherine Pakenham prize Most Promising Female Journalist (Sunday Times) 1973, Young Journalist of the Year 1978; *Books* Loose Talk (1979), Life as a Party (1983), Under the Bamboo Tree (play, 1973), Happy Yellow (play, 1977); *Style*— Ms Tina Brown; ✉ The New Yorker, 20 West 43 Street, New York, NY 10036, USA

BROWN, Rev Christopher; s of Reginald Frank Greenwood Brown (d 1970), and Margaret Eleanor, *née* Simmons (d 1988); *b* 21 June 1938; *Educ* Hertford GS, King's Coll London (AKC), St Boniface Coll Warminster, Green Coll Oxford; *m* 28 Sept 1968, Helen Margaret, da of George Arthur Woolsey, of Winchester; 3 s (Ian b 1974, Timothy b 1976, Joseph b 1984), 1 da (Lucy b 1973); *Career* ordained: deacon 1963, priest 1964; asst curate Diocese of Southwark 1963–67, probation offr Nottingham 1968–72, sr probation offr W Midlands 1972–74, asst dir Social Servs Dept Solihull 1974–76, asst chief probation offr Hereford and Worcester 1976–79; chief probation offr: Oxfordshire 1979–86, Essex 1986–89; dir and chief exec NSPCC 1989–95; memb Parole Bd England and Wales 1984–87, chm Social Issues Ctee Assoc of Chief Offrs of Probation 1985–88; memb: Br Assoc of Social Workers 1973, Cwlth Soc 1989; *Recreations* walking, conversation, gardening, reading; *Style*— The Rev Christopher Brown; ✉ 7 Baronia Croft, Highwoods, Colchester, Essex CO4 4EE

BROWN, Christopher David; s of Edward Kenneth Brown (d 1993), and Iris, *née* Hoddell (d 1995); *b* 8 July 1944; *Educ* Plymouth Coll, Fitzwilliam Coll Cambridge (MA); *m* 1972, Caroline, da of Dr Arthur Dunkerley (d 1980); 2 da (Katharine b 1979, Jennifer b 1981); *Career* head of Eng Radley Coll 1975–84, headmaster Norwich Sch 1984–; *Style*— Christopher Brown, Esq; ✉ 70 The Close, Norwich (☎ 01603 623194)

BROWN, Dr Christopher Paul Hadley; *b* 15 April 1948; *Educ* Merchant Taylors' Sch, St Catherine's Coll Oxford (BA, Dip in Art History), Courtauld Inst (PhD); *m*; 2 c; *Career* National Gallery London: asst keeper 1971–79, dep keeper 1979, curator Dutch and Flemish 17th c paintings, chief curator 1989–; undergraduate and postgrad teaching and external examiner Courtauld Inst and UCL; fell Netherlands Inst for Advanced Study in the Humanities and Social Scis Wassenaar 1993–94; lectures at: Univ of London, Univ of Cambridge, Univ of Oxford, Univ of Utrecht, Harvard Univ, Yale Univ, Princeton Univ, NY Inst of Fine Art; memb Ctee: Assoc of Art Historians 1978–81, Art Galls Assoc 1978–80; memb British Ctee of Comitè Int d'Histoire de l'Art; chm: Art History Seminar Centre for Low Countries Studies, Nat Loan Collection Trust; tstee Dulwich Picture Gall; *Books* Bruegel (1975), Dutch Painting (1976), Burgundy (co-author, 1977), Rembrandt - The Complete Paintings (2 vols, 1980), Carel Fabritius - Complete Edition with a Catalogue Raisonne (1981), A Chatelet - Early Dutch Painting (co-trans, 1981), Van Dyck (1982), Scenes of Everyday Life - Seventeenth-Century Dutch Genre Painting (1984), Anthony Van Dyck's Italian Sketchbook (1992); author of numerous exhbn catalogues and articles in The Times, TLS, Burlington Magazine, Apollo, Nat Gall Technical Bulletin and other jls; *Style*— Dr Christopher Brown; ✉ The National Gallery, Trafalgar Square, London WC2N 5DN (☎ 0171 839 3321)

BROWN, (Anthony) Clive Gordon; s of Robert Gordon Brown and Moya Gordon Brown; *b* 6 March 1944; *Educ* St John's Coll Johannesburg, Univ of Stellenbosch (BA, LLB), Univ of Cambridge (LLB); *m* 18 June 1969, Claire; 1 s (Crispian b 18 March 1972); *Career* ptnr Hewitt Woollacott & Chown 1977–89, managing ptnr Cameron Markby Hewitt 1994– (joined as ptnr 1989); *Recreations* sailing, flying; *Clubs* Sea Scamp Syndicate (cdre), Offshore Cruising, Marabu Syndicate, Little Ship; *Style*— Clive Brown, Esq; ✉ Cameron Markby Hewitt, Sceptre Court, 40 Tower Hill, London EC3N 4BB (☎ 0171 702 2345, fax 0171 702 2303)

BROWN, Colin; s of George Wilfred Brown (d 1970), and Gladys Lilian, *née* Carter (d 1963); *b* 8 April 1950; *Educ* Burscough Secdy Sch, Wigan Tech Coll; *m* Dorothy Amanda Golding; *Career* municipal corr: Southport Visiter 1968–73, Sheffield Star 1973–78; political corr: Yorkshire Post 1978–79, The Guardian 1978–86, The Independent 1986– (currently chief political corr); *Books* Fighting Talk; *Recreations* skiing, windsurfing; *Clubs* Ski Club of GB, Whitstable Yacht, RYA, Soho House; *Style*— Colin Brown, Esq; ✉ Chief Political Correspondent, The Independent, 1 Canada Square, Canary Wharf, London E14 5DL (☎ 0171 293 2000, fax 0171 293 2435)

BROWN, Colin Bertram; s of Prof Leslie Julius Brown (d 1981), of SA, and Adolfinna Anna, *née* Rose (d 1985); *b* 24 May 1942; *Educ* King David HS SA, Guy's Hosp Med Sch London (BSc, MB BS, MRCS, LRCP); *m* 22 Sept 1975, Jacquelynne Anne, *née* Baldwin; 2 s (Nicholas Daniel b 1966, Jason Peter b 1971), 2 da (Kate Victoria b 1978, Hannah Camilla Lester b 1982); *Career* res fell Harvard Med Sch Boston USA 1974–75, sr registrar Guy's Hosp 1973–78, conslt renal physician Sheffield Kidney Inst 1979–; chm Public Cmmn of Peritoneal Dialysis; memb: Ctee on Renal Diseases RCP, Section on Renal Disease MRC, Int Soc of Nephrology, Euro Dialysis and Transplant Assoc, Int Soc of Peritoneal Dialysis, Registry Ctee Renal Assoc of GB (sec); FRCP 1985; *Books* Manual of Renal Disease (1984); contrib incl: Guy's Hospital Reports (1965), Lancet (1970), British Journal of Urology (1972), American Journal of Physiology (1977), Cornell Seminars in Nephrology (1978), Journal of Infection (1983), British Medical Journal (1984), Transplantation (1986), Bone (1981), Clinica Chimica Acta (1988), Nephron (1989), Kidney International (1990), Nephrology Dialysis and Transplantation (1995); *Recreations* sailing, golf; *Style*— C B Brown, Esq; ✉ Sheffield Kidney Institute, Regional Renal Unit, Northern General Hospital, University of Sheffield Medical School, Herries Rd, Sheffield, S Yorks S5 7AU (☎ 0114 243 4343, fax 0114 256 2514)

BROWN, Craig Edward Moncrieff; s of Edward Peter Moncrieff Brown, of Duncton, W Sussex, and Hon Jennifer Mary, *née* Bethell, da of 2 Baron Bethell; *b* 23 May 1957; *Educ* Eton, Univ of Bristol; *m* 1987, Frances J M, *née* Welch; 1 s (Silas b 1990), 1 da (Tallulah b 1988); *Career* freelance journalist and columnist; articles for numerous newspapers and magazines incl: New Statesman, The Observer, TLS, Mail on Sunday, New York, Stern, Corriere della Serra; columnist The Times 1988– (Parly sketch writer 1987–88), restaurant critic Sunday Times 1988–93; columnist (as Wallace Arnold): The Spectator 1987–, Private Eye 1989–, The Independent on Sunday 1991–; columnist: Evening Standard (as Craig Brown) 1993–, The Guardian (as Bel Littlejohn) 1995–; *Books* The Marsh Marlowe Letters (1983), A Year Inside (1988), The Agreeable World of Wallace Arnold (1990), Rear Columns (1992), Welcome to My Worlds (1993), Craig Brown's Greatest Hits (1993), The Hounding of John Thenos (1994), The Private Eye Book of Craig Browm Parodies (1995); *Recreations* flower arrangement, needlework, tidying, deportment, macramé; *Clubs* The Academy; *Style*— Craig Brown, Esq; ✉ c/o The Evening Standard, Northcliffe House, 2 Derry Street, London W8 5EE

BROWN, David John Bowes; CBE (1982); s of Matthew Brown (d 1973), and Adelaide Helene, *née* Bowes (d 1990); *b* 2 Aug 1925; *Educ* King James Sch Knaresborough, Leeds Coll of Technol; *m* 1, 1954 (m dis 1982) Patricia; 2 s (David Patrick b 27 March 1955, John Bowes b 9 June 1958), 2 da (Angela (now Mrs Hall) b 31 July 1956, Janet (now Mrs Tough) b 9 April 1962); m 2, 24 Jan 1986, Eve Rose Watkinson; *Career* logging contractor UK and West Africa 1946–60, designer draftsman Hunslet Engine Co 1960–62, chief exec Chaseside 1962–65, md Muir Hill Ltd 1965–73, started DJB Engineering Ltd 1973, sold DJB Engineering Ltd product rights and formed Artix Ltd (currently world's largest prodr of heavy duty dump trucks) 1985 (now sold); purchased Bedford Trucks and formed AWD Ltd 1987 (chm 1987–92), formed Brown Design Engineering Ltd 1987 (now sold); currently chm Multidrive Ltd, Thirsk; FRSA, FCSD; *Style*— David J B Brown, Esq, CBE; ✉ Multidrive Ltd, Ravensthorpe Manor, Boltby, Thirsk, North Yorkshire YO7 2DX (☎ 01845 537137, fax 01845 537684)

BROWN, David Robert; s of David James Brown, of Winchester, Hants, and Carole Jean, *née* Cunningham; *b* 20 Sept 1962; *Educ* Peter Symonds Coll, Univ of Exeter (BSc Chemistry), DipM (CIM); *m* 4 May 1990, Patricia Ann, da of Ronald Cook; 1 s (James David b 26 Jan 1993), 1 da (Rebecca Louise b 12 Feb 1995); *Career* lab asst IBM Laboratories 1983–85, tech sales conslt Fospur Ltd 1985–87, business devpt exec Croxton & Garry Ltd 1988–92 (mktg asst 1987–88), mktg mangr Omya UK Ltd 1992–; MCIM 1992 (memb Nat Cncl 1995–); *Style*— David Brown, Esq; ✉ 34 Eggars Field, Bentley, nr Farnham, Surrey GU10 5LD (☎ 01420 23759); Omya UK Ltd, Curtis Road, Dorking, Surrey RH4 1XA (☎ 01306 886688, fax 01306 887780, mobile 0860 100752)

BROWN, Vice Adm Sir David Worthington; KCB (1984); s of Capt John Ronald Stewart Brown, RN (d 1989), of Cheltenham, and Mrs D M E Brown (d 1988); *b* 28 Nov 1927; *Educ* HMS Conway; *m* 1958, Etienne Hester, da of Col Dick Boileau, DSO (d 1978), of Bradford on Avon; 3 da; *Career* joined RN 1945; cmd HM Ships: MGB 5036, MTB 5020, Dalswinton, Chailey, Cavendish, Falmouth, Hermione, Bristol; dir Naval Ops and Trade 1971–72, dir of Offr Appts (Exec) 1976–78, ACDS (Ops) 1980–82, Vice Adm 1982, Flag Offr Plymouth, Port Admiral Devonport, Cdr Plymouth Sub Area Channel 1982–85; Yr Bro Trinity House; govr Rookesbury Park Sch Wickham; FIPM 1985; *Clubs* Army & Navy, Commodore Conway Club Cruising Association; *Style*— Vice Adm Sir David Brown, KCB

BROWN, Denise Jeanne Marie Lebreton (Mrs F Waters); da of Lt Frederick Peter Brown (d of wounds 1918), and Jeanne Marie Louise Lebreton (d 1974); *b* 8 Jan 1911; *Educ* Lyzeum Nonnenwerth im Rhein, RCA (ARCA); *m* 1938, Frank William Eric Waters (d 1986), s of Frank Waters (d 1922); 1 s (Peter); *Career* Br Inst scholarship in engraving 1932, RCA travelling scholarship 1936, proxime accessit Rome scholarship in engraving 1936; has exhibited regularly at: Royal Acad 1934–, Royal Soc of Painter-Etchers & Engravers 1941–, Royal West of England Acad 1979–; has also exhibited in Canada, USA and S Africa; works in collections incl: Br Museum, V&A, Ashmolean Museum, Sheffield Art Gallery, perm collection RWA; RE 1959 (ARE 1941), ARWA 1980 (elected cncl memb 1984), RWA 1986; *Books illustrated* many in the Famous Childhoods series, several gardening books; also illustrations for Farmers Weekly and designs for book jackets; *Recreations* music, gardening; *Clubs* RAF; *Style*— Miss Denise L Brown

BROWN, Sir Douglas Denison; kt (1983); s of Robert Brown (d 1968), and Alice Mary Brown; *b* 8 July 1917; *Educ* Bablake Sch Coventry; *m* 1941, Marion Cruickshanks (d 1992), da of James Emmerson (d 1935); 1 s, 1 da; *Career* served WWII RA: ME, N Africa, Italy, ret Maj; chm James Corson Co (ret 1988); chm: NW Leeds Cons Assoc 1961–74, Leeds and Northern Clothing Assoc 1975–77, Yorkshire Area Cons Assoc 1978–83 (treas 1971–78); govr: Leeds Coll of Art and Design (formerly Jacob Kramer Coll of Further Educn) 1975– (chm 1979–90, chair 1993), Cross Green HS 1988–96; chm Leeds Clothing and Textile Centre 1993, vice chm PCC St Edmund's Church Roundhay 1980–, vice chm Wool Textiles and Clothing Action Ctee Wooltac 1985–92 (memb 1982–), memb Bd Yorkshire Water Authy 1983–86, pres Water AID Yorks 1988, pres Leeds Allotment and Gardens Fedn 1991–94 (vice pres 1989–91); hon memb Br Clothing Industs Assoc 1990 (memb Exec Bd until 1989); *Recreations* gardening, golf, rugby, cricket; *Style*— Sir Douglas Brown; ✉ One Oak, 12 Elmete Grove, Leeds LS8 2JY (☎ 0113 273 5470)

BROWN, Capt Eric Melrose; CBE (1970, OBE 1945, MBE 1944), DSC (1942), AFC (1947); s of Robert John Brown (d 1947), of Edinburgh, and Euphemia Dorothy, *née* Melrose (d 1933); *b* 21 Jan 1919; *Educ* Royal HS Edinburgh, Univ of Edinburgh (MA); *m* 17 Jan 1942, Evelyn Jean Margaret, da of Robert Macrory (d 1946), of Belfast; 1 s (Glenn b 1 March 1948); *Career* Capt RN, serv WWII, Fleet Air Arm Fighter Pilot 1939–42, Naval Test Pilot 1942–44, Chief Naval Test Pilot 1944–49, resident Br Naval Test Pilot in USA 1951–52, CO No 804 (F) Sqdn 1953–54, Cdr (Air) RN Air Station Brawdy 1954–56, Head Br Naval Air Mission to Germany 1958–60, dep dir Gunnery Div Admiralty 1961, Naval Air Warfare Admiralty 1962–64, Naval Attachè Bonn 1965–67, CO RN Air Station Lossiemouth 1967–70; ADC to HM The Queen 1969–70; chief exec: Br Helicopter Advsy Bd 1970–87 (vice pres 1988–), European Helicopter Assoc 1980–92 (vice pres 1992–); pres: Royal Aeronautical Soc 1982–83, E Grinstead Branch Royal Naval Assoc; chm Exec Ctee Br Aviation Bicentenary 1983–84; hon fell Soc of Experimental Test Pilots 1984, elected to US Carrier Aviation Test Pilots Hall of Honor 1995; Freeman City of London 1975, Liveryman Guild of Air Pilots and Air Navigators 1978; Hon FEng Inst of Engrs Pakistan; FRAeS 1964; *Books* Wings on My Sleeve (1961, 2 edn 1978, paperback 1984 and 1993), Aircraft Carriers (jtly, 1969), Wings of the Luftwaffe (1977, 2 edn 1979, 3 edn 1987), Wings of the Navy (1980, 2 edn 1987), The Helicopter in Civil Operations (1981), Wings of the Weird and Wonderful Vol I

(1982) and Vol II (1985), Duels in the Sky (1989), Testing for Combat (1994); *Recreations* gardening, philately, bridge; *Clubs* Naval and Military, Explorers' (New York), City Livery; *Style*— Capt Eric Brown, CBE, DSC, AFC, RN; ✉ Carousel, New Domewood, nr Copthorne, W Sussex RH10 3HF (☎ 01342 712610)

BROWN, Prof Ewan; CBE (1996); s of John Moir Brown (d 1971), of Perth, and Isobel, *née* Crerar; *b* 23 March 1942; *Educ* Perth Acad, Univ of St Andrews (MA, LLB); *m* 1966, Christine Robertson, da of Hugh Douglas Robertson Lindsay; 1 s (Philip b 1968), 1 da (Kirsty b 1971); *Career* CA and merchant banker; exec dir Noble Grossart Ltd 1970–; princ dir: Scottish Business Sch 1972–80 (memb Exec Ctee 1974–80), Church of Scotland Tst 1981–87; dir: James Walker (Leith) Ltd 1972–, Pict Petroleum plc 1974–, Scottish Development Finance 1982–93, John Wood Group plc 1982–, Aberdeen Trust plc 1982–85, Scottish Transport Group 1983–87, Stagecoach Holdings plc 1988–, Lovegrove & Associates Ltd 1991–, Amicable Smaller Enterprises Trust plc 1992–; govr: Edinburgh Coll of Art 1986–88, George Watson's Coll 1989–91; treas Merchant Co of Edinburgh 1992–, session clerk Mayfield Salisbury Church 1983–88, memb Cncl Inst of CA's of Scotland 1989–92; hon prof Heriot-Watt Univ 1989–, tstee Carnegie Tst for the Univs of Scotland 1991–; FRSA; *Recreations* skiing, golf, music, mah jongg, family; *Clubs* Royal and Ancient (St Andrews), New (Edinburgh); *Style*— Prof Ewan Brown, CBE; ✉ Noble Grossart Ltd, 48 Queen Street, Edinburgh EH2 3NR (☎ 0131 226 7011, fax 0131 226 6032)

BROWN, Prof Fred; s of Fred Brown (d 1982), of Burnley, Lancs, and Jane Ellen, *née* Fielding (d 1975); *b* 31 Jan 1925; *Educ* Burnley GS, Univ of Manchester (BSc, MSc, PhD); *m* 1 May 1948, Audrey Alice, da of Ernest Doherty (d 1954); 2 s (Roger b 21 Nov 1949, David b 17 Oct 1953); *Career* asst lectr in chemistry Univ of Manchester 1946–48, lectr Univ of Bristol 1948–50, sr sci offr Hannah Dairy Res Inst 1950–53, sr sci offr Christie Hosp Manchester 1953–55; Animal Virus Res Inst Pirbright: sr sci offr 1955–58, princ scientific offr 1958–64, sr princ scientific offr 1964–71, dep chief scientific offr 1971–83, dep dir 1980–83; head Virology Dept Wellcome Biotechnology 1983–90, adjunct prof Dept of Epidemiology and Public Health Yale Univ 1990–95; visiting prof Queen's Univ of Belfast 1986–, visiting scientist US Dept of Agriculture Plum Island Animal Disease Center NY 1995–; hon memb Soc for Gen Microbiology, vice pres Inst of Biology 1988–90; Hon DSc Queen's Univ of Belfast 1992; FRS 1981; *Recreations* fell walking, watching cricket and association football; *Style*— Prof Fred Brown, FRS; ✉ Syndal, Glaziers Lane, Normandy, Guildford, Surrey GU3 2DF (☎ 01483 811107)

BROWN, Fred; s of late Wilfred Brown, and late Euphemia Logan, *née* Freeburn; *b* 4 Feb 1938; *Educ* Hamilton Acad, Univ of Glasgow Sch of Veterinary Med (BVMS, MRCVS); *m* 1984, Gunn Eriksen; *Career* hotelier; gen practitioner in veterinary med: Inverness 1966–72, Rogart Sutherland 1972–76; subsequent career experience in yacht chartering, proprietor Altnaharrie Inn Hotel Ullapool Ross-shire 1976–; *Recreations* sailing, hill walking, meeting challenges; *Style*— Fred Brown, Esq; ✉ Altnaharrie Inn, Ullapool, Ross-shire IV26 2SS (☎ 01854 633230)

BROWN, Prof Geoffrey; s of William Henry Brown (d 1981), of Kingston upon Hull, and Dorothy, *née* Shaw; *b* 26 June 1935; *Educ* Kingston HS, Univ of Leicester (MEd), Univ of Lancaster (PhD); *m* Christine Ann, da of William Bath (d 1982), of Stoke-on-Trent; 2 da (Helen b 21 May 1963, Clare 28 Dec 1965); *Career* Nat Serv RAF 1953–55; lectr in educnl psychology Anstey Coll of Physical Educn 1966–70, sr lectr in educnl psychology Univ of Lancaster 1970–81; UEA: prof of educn 1981–, dean of educn 1986–92, dir of graduate studies 1993–95, pro vice chllr 1995–96, professorial fell 1996–; FBPsS; *Books* Experiments in the Social Sciences (1975), Child Development (1977), Piaget's Theory: A Psychological Critique (1981); *Recreations* walking, music, woodturning; *Clubs* Liberal; *Style*— Prof Geoffrey Brown; ✉ School of Education, University of East Anglia, Norwich NR4 7TJ (☎ 01603 456161, fax 01603 593446, e-mail g.brown@uea.ac.uk)

BROWN, Rev Canon Geoffrey Harold; s of Harry Charles Brown, MBE (d 1972), and Ada Ethel, *née* Holliday; *b* 1 April 1930; *Educ* Monmouth, Trinity Hall Cambridge (MA); *m* 24 Aug 1963, (Elizabeth) Jane, da of Jack Watson Williams (d 1981), of Dudley, Worcs; 2 da (Frances b 14 May 1964, Alison (twin)); *Career* RA 1949–51; asst curate: St Andrew's Plaistow London 1956–60, St Peter's Spring Hill Birmingham 1960–63; rector: St George's Birmingham 1963–73, Grimsby 1973–85; vicar St Martin in the Fields 1985–95; chm Humberside Cncl on Alcoholism 1977–87, vice chm Humberside Local Radio Cncl 1983, exec memb Nat Cncl on Alcoholism 1980–83; FRSA 1991; *Recreations* theatre, photography, the countryside; *Style*— The Rev Canon Geoffrey Brown; ✉ 32 Church Street, Hagley, Stourbridge, West Midlands DY9 0NA (☎ 01562 883609)

BROWN, Geoffrey Howard; s of John Howard Brown (d 1983), of Coventry, and Nancy, *née* Fardoe (d 1996); *b* 1 March 1949; *Educ* King Henry VIII GS Coventry, Pembroke Coll Cambridge (BA), Sch of Film and TV RCA (MA); *m* 16 Sept 1985, Catherine Ann, da of Adolf Surowiec; *Career* contrib to Time Out 1974–81, contrib to Monthly Film Bulletin 1974–91, dep film critic Financial Times 1977–81, film critic Radio Times 1981–89, film critic The Times 1990– (dep film critic 1981–90); also contrib to Sight and Sound, Plays and Players and The Movie; *Books* Walter Forde (1977), Launder and Gilliat (1977), Der Produzent - Michael Balcon und der Englische Film (1981), Michael Balcon - The Pursuit of British Cinema (lead essay, 1984), The Common Touch - The Films of John Baxter (1989); *Recreations* music; *Style*— Geoffrey Brown, Esq; ✉ The Times, 1 Pennington Street, London E1 9XN (☎ 0171 782 5167, fax 0171 782 5748)

BROWN, Sir George Francis Richmond; 5 Bt (UK 1863), of Richmond Hill; s of Sir Charles Frederick Richmond Brown, 4 Bt, TD, DL (d 1995), and his 1 w, Audrey, *née* Baring (d 1996); *b* 3 Feb 1938; *Educ* Eton; *m* 1978, Philippa Jane, da of late Capt Edward Joseph W Willcox: 3 s (Sam George Richmond b 27 Dec 1979, Harry Richmond b 7 May 1982, Edward Richmond b 19 April 1987); *Heir* s, Sam George Richmond Brown b 27 Dec 1979; *Career* Maj Welsh Guards; extra equerry to HRH the Duke of Edinburgh 1961–63, ADC to Govr of Queensland 1963–65; *Style*— Sir George Richmond Brown, Bt; ✉ Mas de Sudre, 81600 Gaillac, France

BROWN, Maj George Gordon; s of Capt Arthur Frederick Brown (d 1963), and Evelyn Maude, *née* Lee (d 1974); *b* 17 Feb 1925; *Educ* Eastbourne Coll, Queen's Coll Oxford; *m* 16 Aug 1968, Wendy Margaret, da of Capt Thomas George Clark (d 1986), of Edinburgh; 1 s (Richard b 9 March 1973), 1 da (Melanie b 5 Oct 1969); *Career* 2 Lt 27 Lancers 1945, 1 RGH Austria 1945–46, ADC to Gen McCreery Germany 1946–48, 12 Royal Lancers Germany and Malaya 1948–60, 9/12 Royal Lancers Aden and Trucial Oman 1960–65, Staff Coll 1958, Maj 1960, ret 1965; called to the Bar Inner Temple 1966, divorce and family law practice in London and Western Circuit 1966–, dep judge 1978–85; chm res reports: Case for Family Courts (CPC, 1978), The Future of Marriage (CPC, 1981), Reconciliation and Conciliation in Divorce (Order of Christian Unity, 1982); chm Family Courts Ctee Soc of Cons Lawyers; memb Exec Ctee: Cons Family Campaign, Nat Campaign for Family; Freeman City of London 1946, Master Worshipful Co of Tylers and Bricklayers 1973; memb Family Law Bar Assoc; *Books* Getting a Divorce (1971), The New Divorce Laws (1971), Brown on Divorce (1974, 2 edn 1986), Brown on Separation (1981), Finding Fault in Divorce (1989), The Decay of Marriage (1991); *Recreations* golf, skiing, cricket; *Clubs* Cavalry and Guards', Hampshire; *Style*— Maj George Brown; ✉ 2 King's Bench Walk, Temple, London EC4Y 7DE (☎ 0171 353 1746, fax 0171 583 2051)

BROWN, Prof Gillian; CBE (1992); da of Geoffrey Rencher Read (d 1969), and Elsie Olive Read; *b* 23 Jan 1937; *Educ* Perse Sch for Girls Cambridge, Girton Coll Cambridge (exhibitioner, BA, MA), Univ of Edinburgh (PhD); *m* 21 Aug 1959, Prof (Edward) Keith Brown, s of Rev Reginald John Brown (d 1978); 3 da (Jane Caroline (Mrs Whitgift) b 1960, Katherine Victoria (Mrs Ruttle) b 1961, Sarah Harriett (Mrs Fleming) b 1962); *Career* lectr Univ Coll of Cape Coast Ghana 1962–64, reader Dept of Linguistics Univ of Edinburgh 1981–83 (lectr 1965–81), prof of applied linguistics Univ of Essex 1983–88; Univ of Cambridge: prof of English as an int language 1988–, dir Res Centre for English and Applied Linguistics 1988–, fell Clare Coll 1988–; memb: Ctee for Linguistics in Educn 1985–88, Kingman Ctee of Inquiry Into the Teaching of English Language 1987–88, ESRC Council 1987–90, Br Cncl English Teaching Advsy Ctee 1987–94, Univ Grants Ctee 1987–89, Univ Funding Cncl 1989–91, Cncl of the Philological Soc; chm: ESRC Res Grants Bd 1987–90, Bd Br Inst in Paris 1992–; Hon Doctorate Univ of Lyon 1987; *Books* Phonological Rules and Dialect Variation (1972), Listening to Spoken English (1977), Discourse Analysis (with G Yule, 1983), Teaching the Spoken Language (with G Yule, 1983), Speakers, Listeners and Communication (1995); *Style*— Prof Gillian Brown, CBE; ✉ Clare College, Cambridge CB2 1TL

BROWN, Prof Godfrey Norman; s of Percy Charles Brown (d 1957), of Croydon, Surrey, and Margaret Elizabeth, *née* Weller (d 1954); *b* 13 July 1926; *Educ* Whitgift Sch, Merton Coll Oxford (MA, DPhil); *m* 11 Jan 1960, Dr Freda Bowyer, da of Thomas Willis Bowyer (d 1976), of Huddersfield; 3 s (Denton Charles b 1961, Nigel Willis b 1963, Martin Giles b 1965); *Career* RAC Lt Intelligence Corps 1944–48; social affairs offr UN HQ NY 1953–54, sr history master Barking Abbey Sch Essex 1954–57, lectr in educn Univ Coll of Ghana 1958–61, visiting prof Univ Coll of Rhodesia and Nyasaland 1963, prof Univ of Ibadan Nigeria 1963–67 (sr lectr 1961), dir Inst of Educn Univ of Keele 1967–80, emeritus prof; dir Betley Court Gallery 1980–95, ed West African Journal of Education 1962–66; memb Exec Ctee and Bd of Dirs World Cncl for Curriculum and Instruction 1974–77, chm Assoc for Recurrent Educn 1976–77; vice pres: Cncl for Educn in World Citizenship, Community Cncl of Staffs; Newcastle under Lyme Civic award for Conservation 1990; *Books* An Active History of Ghana (2 vols, 1961 and 1964), Africa in the 19th and 20th Centuries (ed with J C Anene, 1966), Living History (1967), Towards a Learning Community (ed, 1971), Conflict and Harmony in Education in Tropical Africa (ed with M Hiskett, 1975), Apartheid, A Teacher's Guide (1981), Betley Through the Centuries (1985), This Old House - A Domestic Biography (1987); *Recreations* family life, art history, conservation; *Style*— Prof Godfrey Brown; ✉ Betley Court, Betley, nr Crewe, Cheshire CW3 9BH (☎ 01270 820652, fax 01270 820165)

BROWN, Rt Hon (James) Gordon; PC (1996), MP (Lab) Dunfermline East (majority 17,444); s of Rev Dr John Brown, and J Elizabeth Brown; *b* 20 Feb 1951; *Educ* Kirkcaldy HS, Univ of Edinburgh (MA, PhD); *Career* rector Univ of Edinburgh 1972–75 (temp lectr 1975–76), lectr in politics Glasgow Coll of Technol 1976–80, journalist then ed Current Affairs Dept Scottish TV 1980–83; memb Scottish Exec Lab Party 1977–83, Parly candidate (Lab) S Edinburgh 1979, MP (Lab) Dunfermline E 1983–, chm Lab Party in Scotland 1983–, oppn front bench spokesman on trade and indust 1985–87, memb Shadow Cabinet 1987–, shadow chief sec to the Treasy 1987–89, chief oppn spokesman on trade and indust 1989–92, chief oppn spokesman on Treasy and econ affrs (shadow chllr) 1992–; memb TGWU; *Books* Maxton (1986), Where There Is Greed (1989), John Smith: Life and Soul of the Party (1994), Values Visions and Voices: An Anthology of Socialism (1995); *Recreations* golf, tennis, reading; *Style*— The Rt Hon Gordon Brown, MP; ✉ House of Commons, London SW1A 0AA (☎ 0171 219 6345)

BROWN, Graham Alan; s of Sydney Brown, of Birmingham, and Gene Anne, *née* Laitner; *b* 29 March 1958; *Educ* Clifton, UC Cardiff (BA); *Career* trainee Broadcast Marketing Services 1981–82, various positions FCB London 1982–87, media dir FCB/Leber Katz NY 1987–90, client servs dir Aegis Group plc 1990–94, md Carat International 1995–96, int gp devpt dir Carat Group 1996–; *Recreations* tennis, skiing, jazz, blues, classical and rock music, walking; *Clubs* RAC; *Style*— Graham Brown, Esq; ✉ Carat International, 2–6 Fulham Broadway, London SW6 1AA (☎ 0171 381 8010, fax 0171 385 3233)

BROWN, Graham Stephen; s of Frank George John Brown, and Gwen, *née* Thompson; *b* 28 Nov 1944; *Educ* Farnborough Sch, Univ of Bristol (LLB), King's Coll London (LLM), Catholic Univ of Louvain Belgium; *m* 1972, Jacqueline, da of John Purtill, of Dublin; *Career* Payne Hicks Beach Solicitors: admitted slr 1969, ptnr 1972, sr ptnr 1994–; sometime memb: Capital Taxes Sub-Ctee and Fin Servs Act Working Party of Law Society, Ctee Holborn Law Soc; Liveryman Worshipful Co of Clockmakers; FRSA; *Recreations* music, theatre, fine arts and architecture; *Clubs* Arts, Farmers'; *Style*— Graham Brown; ✉ Payne Hicks Beach, 10 New Square, Lincoln's Inn, London WC2A 3QG (☎ 0171 465 4300, fax 0171 465 4429)

BROWN, Hamish Macmillan; s of William Dick Brown (d 1968), of Dollar and Kinghorn, and Effie Grace, *née* Swanson (d 1988); *b* 13 Aug 1934; *Educ* Dollar Acad; *Career* Nat Serv RAF Egypt and E Africa; asst Martyrs Meml Church Paisley 1958–59, outdoor educn Braehead Sch 1960–71, outdoor activities adviser Fife 1972–73; freelance author, photographer, lectr, poet, mountaineer, traveller and authority on Morocco 1974–; served SMLTB, dir SROW, creator Great Outdoors Challenge event; expeditions to: Morocco, Andes, Himalayas, Arctic, Africa, etc; contribs in over 100 pubns; *Books* Hamish's Mountain Walk (1978, SAC Award), Hamish's Groats End Walk (1981, shortlist for W H Smith Travel Prize), Poems of the Scottish Hills (1982), Speak to the Hills (1985), The Great Walking Adventure (1986), Travels (1986), Hamish Brown's Scotland (1988), The Island of Rhum (1988), Climbing the Corbetts (1988), Scotland Coast to Coast (1990), Walking the Summits of Somerset and Avon (1991), From the Pennines to the Highlands (1992), Fort William and Glen Coe Walks (1992), The Bothy Brew (Short Stories, 1993), The Fife Coast (1994), The Last Hundred (1994), 25 Walks, Fife (1995); *Recreations* skiing, canoeing, alpine flowers, gardening, music, books; *Clubs* Alpine, Swiss Alpine, Scottish Mountaineering; *Style*— Hamish M Brown, Esq; ✉ 26 Kirkcaldy Road, Burntisland, Fife KY3 9HQ (☎ 01592 873546)

BROWN, Harold Arthur Neville; CMG (1963), CVO (1961); s of Stanley Raymond Brown, of Penarth, and Gladys Maud Brown; *b* 13 Dec 1914; *Educ* Cardiff HS, Univ Coll Cardiff; *m* 1939, Mary McBeath (d 1994), da of late Alan Urquhart, of Cardiff; 1 s (Stephen), 1 da (Alison); *Career* entered Miny of Labour 1939; FO: joined 1955, ambass Liberia 1960–63, FO 1963, ambass Cambodia 1966–70, consul-gen Johannesburg 1970–73, min Pretoria/Cape Town 1973–74, ret 1975; *Style*— Harold Brown, Esq, CMG, CVO; ✉ 14 Embassy Court, King's Road, Brighton, Sussex BN1 2PX (☎ 01273 734623)

BROWN, Hilary Neilson; da of James Wilson Stanley, of Glasgow, and Irene Mignon Stanley; *b* 6 June 1952; *Educ* Hutchesons' Girls' GS, Glasgow and W of Scotland Coll of Domestic Sci (Dip Dom Sci), Jordanhill Coll (Dip Ed); *m* 27 Dec 1973, David Richard Brown, s of James Alexander Brown; *Career* restaurateur; teacher Bellarmine Sch Glasgow 1973–75, chef and proprietor La Potinière Gullane 1975–; *Awards* Good Food Guide Mortar & Pestle 1979–, AA Rosette 1977–, Egon Ronay Star 1985–, Michelin Star 1991–, 4/5 Good Food Guide 1990–; *Books* La Potinière and Friends (1990); *Recreations* France, Italy, cookery, films, health and nutrition, art; *Style*— Ms Hilary Brown; ✉ La Potinière, Gullane, East Lothian, Scotland (☎ 01620 843214)

BROWN, Howard Roger; s of Leslie John Brown (d 1975), of Portsmouth, and Ruth Ethel, *née* Smith; *b* 25 Feb 1945; *Educ* Portsmouth GS; *m* 17 Oct 1970, Elizabeth Jane, da of Sidney Douglas Hillyar (d 1985), of Emsworth, Hants; 3 da (Sally b 1974, Judith b 1976, Helen b 1979); *Career* trainee accountant Grant Thornton 1963–69; Ernst and Young: ptnr and sr ptnr 1969–, chm UK Banking Gp 1985–95, chm Int Banking Ctee 1986–; deacon Bloomsbury Central Church London 1981–; FCA 1969; *Books* Leasing, Accounting & Tax Implications (1978), International Bank Accounting (1987); *Recreations* badminton, tennis, reading; *Style*— Howard Brown, Esq; ✉ Ernst & Young, 1 Lambeth Palace Rd, London SE1 7EU (☎ 0171 928 2000, fax 0171 928 1345)

BROWN, Col Hugh Goundry; TD (1968), DL (1986); s of Charles Franc Brown, of Newcastle, and Edith Temple, *née* Smithson (d 1952); *b* 25 Feb 1927; *Educ* St Peter's Sch York, Univ of Durham (MB BS); *m* 26 Aug 1961, Ann Mary, da of Thomas Coburn Crump (d 1982); 1 s (Andrew b 1963), 2 da (Catherine b 1962, Elizabeth b 1967); *Career* Nat Serv RMO ATT 1(NY) BN KAR 1950–52; TA 1 (N) Gen Hosp 1952–75, OC 201 (N) Gen Hosp 1970–73, Hon Col 201 (N) Gen Hosp 1982–87; conslt plastic surgn and sr lectr 1968–; QHS 1972; pres: Br Soc for Surgery of the Hand 1985, Br Assoc of Plastic Surgns 1988, Br Assoc of Clinical Anatomists 1989; High Sheriff Tyne and Wear 1992–93, Vice Lord Lt Tyne and Wear 1994–; FRCS 1958; *Style*— Col Hugh Brown, TD, DL; ✉ Royal Victoria Infirmary, Newcastle upon Tyne, Tyne and Wear (☎ 0191 232 5131)

BROWN, Dr Iain Gordon; s of Reginald Sydney Brown (d 1982), of Durban, South Africa and Edinburgh, and Irene, *née* Young; *b* 10 Oct 1950; *Educ* George Watson's Coll, Univ of Edinburgh (MA), St John's Coll Cambridge (PhD); *Career* pt/t lectr Dept of Extra-Mural Studies Univ of Edinburgh 1975–76, asst keeper Dept of Manuscripts Nat Library of Scotland 1977–; curator of seven major and many smaller exhbns 1978–; author of approx 75 articles in learned jls, essays, exhbn catalogues and book chapters; Scottish rep Friends of the Nat Libraries 1985–, memb Advsy Ctee Yale Edns of the Private Papers of James Boswell 1987–, vice pres Edinburgh Antiques and Fine Arts Soc (NADFAS) 1990–; Old Edinburgh Club: memb Cncl 1989–93 and 1995–, memb Editorial Bd 1991–, vice-pres 1996–; chm James Craig Bicentenary Publications Ctee 1994–95; memb David Hume Commemoration Ctee Saltire Soc 1993–; tstee Penicuik House Preservation Tst; memb Incorporation of Hammermen of Edinburgh; FSA Scot (memb Cncl 1989–92, memb Editorial Bd of Soc's Proceedings 1992–), FRSA 1980, FSA 1985; *Books* Scottish Architects at Home and Abroad (with T A Cherry, 1978), The Hobby-Horsical Antiquary (1980), Poet and Painter: Allan Ramsay, Father and Son 1684–1784 (1984), The Clerks of Penicuik: Portraits of Taste and Talent (1987), History of Scottish Literature, vol II: 1660–1800 (contrib, 1987), Scott's Interleaved Waverley Novels: An Introduction and Commentary (ed and princ contrb, 1987), Building for Books: The Architectural Evolution of the Advocates' Library 1689–1925 (1989), For the Encouragement of Learning: Scotland's National Library (contrib, 1989), Monumental Reputation: Robert Adam and the Emperor's Palace (1992), The Role of the Amateur Architect (contrib, 1994), The Todholes Aisle (ed, 1994), Scottish Country Houses (contrib, 1995), James Craig 1744–1795 (contrib, 1995), Elegance and Entertainment in the New Town of Edinburgh (1995), Antonio Canova: The Three Graces (contrib, 1995), Witness to Rebellion (with H Cheape, 1996); *Recreations* travel, the Mediterranean world, looking at buildings, military history, books, antiquarian pursuits, buying ties, raking in skips; *Clubs* New (Edinburgh), Edinburgh Univ Staff; *Style*— Dr Iain G Brown, FSA; ✉ 46 Great King Street, Edinburgh EH3 6QY (☎ 0131 556 5196); National Library of Scotland, George IV Bridge, Edinburgh EH1 1EW (☎ 0131 226 4531, fax 0131 220 6662)

BROWN, Prof Ian James Morris; s of Bruce Beveridge Brown (d 1957), of Alloa, Scotland, and Eileen Frances, *née* Carnegie (d 1986); *b* 28 Feb 1945; *Educ* Dollar Acad, Univ of Edinburgh and Crewe and Alsager Coll (MA, DipEd, MLitt, PhD); *m* 8 June 1968, Judith Ellen, da of George Woodall Sidaway, of Adelaide; 1 s (Joshua b 1977), 1 da (Emily b 1972); *Career* playwright 1967–; sch teacher 1967–69 and 1970–71; lectr in drama: Dunfermline Coll Edinburgh 1971–76, Br Cncl Edinburgh and Istanbul 1976–78; princ lectr Crewe and Alsager Coll 1978–86 (seconded as sec Cork Enq into Professional Theatre 1985–86); drama dir Arts Cncl of GB 1986–94; prof and head Drama Dept Queen Margaret Coll Edinburgh 1995– (reader in drama 1994–95); programme dir Alsager Arts Centre 1980–86; chm Scot Soc of Playwrights 1973–75 and 1984–87; convenor N W Playwrights' Workshop 1982–85; chm: British Theatre Inst 1985–87 (vice chm 1983–85), Dionysia Chianti World Festival of Theatre 1991–93; FRSA 1991; *Plays* incl: Mother Earth 1970, The Bacchae 1972, Positively the Last Final Farewell Performance (ballet scenario) 1972, Carnegie 1973, Rune (choral work) 1973, The Knife 1973, Rabelais 1973, The Fork 1976, New Reekie 1977, Mary 1977, Runners 1978, Mary Queen and the Loch Tower 1979, Pottersville 1982, Joker in the Pack 1983, Beatrice 1989, First Strike 1990, The Scotch Play 1991, Bacchai 1991, Wasting Reality 1992; *Recreations* theatre, cooking, sport, travel; *Style*— Prof Ian Brown; ✉ Queen Margaret College, Clerwood Terrace, Edinburgh EH12 8TS (☎ 0131 317 3000)

BROWN, James Alan; s of Douglas R Brown, of Egham, Surrey, and Dulcie M Brown; *b* 4 Dec 1940; *Educ* Kingsbury Co GS London, Acton Hotel & Catering Sch Acton; *m* 28 Sept 1968, M Louise, da of Dudley James; 2 s (Rupert James Heathcliffe b 10 Feb 1970, Oliver James Quentin b 24 July 1972); *Career* trainee mangr Grand Metropolitan Hotels Ltd 1962–64, mangr De Vere Hotels 1964–66, advsr Cunard Line Ltd 1966–68; mangr: Rank Hotels Ltd 1968–70, Skyway Hotels (London) Ltd 1970–72; gen mangr: Post House Hotel Heathrow 1972–75, Royal Garden Hotel 1975–91, Athenaeum Hotel 1991–95, The Compleat Angler Hotel Marlow on Thames 1995–96; fndr IPS 1974; Freeman City of London, Master Innholder; FHCIMA 1962; *Style*— James Brown, Esq; ✉ 15 Riverside, Windsor Road, Egham, Surrey TW20 0AA

BROWN, James Clifford; s of Henry John Brown (d 1933), of Ipswich, Suffolk, and Lois, *née* Smith (d 1973); *b* 18 Aug 1923; *Educ* Northgate GS Ipswich, St John's Coll Cambridge (MA, MusB); *Career* Dept of Music Univ of Leeds: lectr 1948–72, univ organist 1948–83, sr lectr 1972–83, acting head of dept 1982; composed: piano sonata 1950, sonata for violin and piano 1956, serenade for chamber orch 1969, scena for organ The Burning Bush 1973, oratorio The Baptism of Christ 1979, cello concerto 1980, piano trio 1982, cantata The World of Light 1988, invocation for soprano, flute and piano 1988, Leeds Centenary Variations for organ 1993; ctee memb Leeds Philharmonic Soc 1972–95, pres Ipswich Choral Soc 1989–; FRCO 1948, memb Leeds Organists' Assoc 1963–; *Recreations* meeting friends; *Style*— James Brown, Esq; ✉ 29 Vesper Gate Drive, Leeds LS5 3NH

BROWN, Janet; *Educ* Gallowflat Sch, Rutherglen Acad; *m* Peter Butterworth (decd); 1 s (Tyler), 1 da (Emma); *Career* actress/impressionist; began career with amateur concerts in Glasgow, first engagement Children's Hour BBC Radio; *Theatre* incl: Mr Gillie (Garrick), The Bargain (St Martin's), Plaza Suite (Australia and Nottingham Playhouse), Fairy Godmother in Cinderella (Churchill Theatre Bromley) 1993, Hard Times (Good Co tour) 1996; *Television* incl: Who Do You Do (series, special for Thames TV), Just Janet (series, BBC) 1992, two series of Janet and Company 1983, Cats Eyes (BBC) 1994–95; guest appearances on: The Val Doonican Show, Parkinson, Aspel & Co, The Johnny Carson Show (USA), two Royal Command Performances, That's Life 1994 (guest presenter); subject of This is Your Life; *Films* incl: Folly to be Wise, For Your Eyes Only (as Margaret Thatcher); *Books* Prime Mimicker (autobiog, 1986); *Style*— Ms Janet Brown; ✉ c/o Peter Charlesworth, Peter Charlesworth Ltd, 68 Old Brompton Road, London SW7 3LQ (☎ 0171 581 2478, fax 0171 589 2922)

BROWN, Jeremy Ronald Coventry; s of Kenneth Coventry Brown, MBE (d 1987), of Durban, SA, and Mavis Kathleen, *née* Keal; *b* 2 May 1948; *Educ* Westville Boys HS SA, Univ of Natal (MSc, Chem Eng), Univ of SA (B Iuris); *Career* Spoor and Fisher (patent attorneys) South Africa 1971–78, Linklaters & Paines (solicitors) London 1978–; pres Licensing Execs Soc Int 1995–96; memb: Cncl Licensing Execs Soc Br and Ireland (pres 1991–92), Cncl AIPPI (British Gp); *Recreations* tennis, travel, the Arts; *Clubs* Roehampton; *Style*— Jeremy Brown, Esq; ✉ Linklaters & Paines, Barrington House, 59/67 Gresham St, London EC2V 7JA (☎ 0171 606 7080)

BROWN, Joe; MBE (1975); s of Joseph Brown (d 1930), and Mary, *née* Attwell (d 1983); *b* 26 Sept 1930; *Educ* Stanley Grove Sch Manchester; *m* 17 Feb 1957, Valerie Melville, da of Melville Gray (d 1947); 2 da (Helen Josephine b 1960, Zoe Melville b 1966); *Career* Nat Serv 1948–50; mountaineer; ascents: west face Petit Dru 1954, first ascent Kunchenjunga 1955, Mustagh Tower 1956, Mount Communism USSR 1962, Trango Tower 1976, Cataphaxi 1979, Mount Kenya 1984, Mount McInley 1986; other expdns: El Torro 1970, Bramah 1979, Thalaysaga 1982, north east ridge Mount Everest 1986 and 1988; retailer of climbing equipment Llanberis & Capel Curig North Wales 1965; film maker for cinema and TV; hon memb Climbers' Club (memb 1961–65); hon fell Manchester Poly 1970; *Recreations* mountaineering, fishing; *Style*— Joe Brown, Esq, MBE; ✉ Menai Hall, Llanberis, Gwynedd LL55 4HA (☎ 01286 870327)

BROWN, Joe Roger; s of John Vernon Brown (d 1953), and Nora Irene, *née* Rogers (d 1982); *b* 13 May 1941; *Educ* Plaistow GS, Pretoria Secdy Modern Sch; *m* 10 Dec 1963, Victoria Mary (d 1991), da of George Augustus Haseman; 1 s (Peter George Joseph b 6 Jan 1966), 1 da (Samantha b 7 Nov 1964); *Career* musician and entertainer; entered showbusiness professionally 1958; performed with: Johnny Cash, Eddie Cochran, Gene Vincent, Bill Haley, Jerry Lee Lewis, Little Richard, Chuck Berry, The Beatles; formed Joe Brown and the Bruvvers 1960 (numerous top ten hits), formed Brown's Home Brew mid 1970's; films incl: What A Crazy World, Three Hats for Lisa, Spike Milligan meets Joe Brown, Mona Lisa; numerous West End appearances incl: Charlie Girl (with Anna Neagle 1965, with Cyd Charisse 1986), Pump Boys and Dinettes (1985), Sleuth; participated in 3 Royal Command Performances; serving offr Grand Order of Water Rats; *Books* Brown Sauce (1986); *Recreations* flying, water sports, riding; *Clubs* Savage, West London Air; *Style*— Joe Brown, Esq; ✉ Joe Brown Productions, PO Box 272, London N20 0BY (☎ 0181 368 0340, fax 0181 368 8559, car 0836 279899)

BROWN, Prof John Campbell; s of John Brown, of Dumbarton, and Jane Livingstone Stewart, *née* Campbell; *b* 4 Feb 1947; *Educ* Dumbarton Acad, Univ of Glasgow (numerous undergraduate prizes and bursaries, Denny Medal, Kelvin Prize and Medal, BSc, PhD, DSc); *m* 18 Aug 1972, Dr Margaret Isobel Logan, da of Dr James Cameron Purse Logan; 1 s (Stuart John Logan b 30 June 1976), 1 da (Lorna Margaret b 9 May 1979); *Career* Univ of Glasgow: lectr in astronomy 1968–78, sr lectr 1978–80, reader 1980–84, prof of astrophysics 1984–96, Regius prof of astronomy 1996–; hon prof Univ of Edinburgh 1996–; visitorships: Harvard-Smithsonian Observatory Mass USA 1967 and 1969, Univ of Tübingen 1971–72, Univ of Utrecht 1973–74, Australian Nat Univ 1975, Ncar High Altitude Observatory Colorado USA 1977, Univ of Maryland 1980, Nuffield science research fell Univ of Amsterdam 1984 and Univ of California San Diego 1987, Brittingham prof Univ of Wisconsin Madison 1987, Univ of Sydney 1993; Astronomer Royal for Scotland 1995; FRAS 1973, FRSE 1984, FInstP 1996; *Books* Inverse Problems in Astronomy (with I J D Craig, 1986), The Sun: A Laboratory for Astrophysics (ed with J T Schmelz, 1993); *Recreations* oil painting, jewellery making, woodwork, magic, cycling, walking, photography, reading; *Style*— Prof John C Brown, FRSE; ✉ 21 Bradfield Avenue, Glasgow, G12 0QH (☎ 0141 339 1688); Astronomy and Astrophysics Group, Department of Physics and Astronomy, University of Glasgow, Glasgow G12 8QQ (☎ 0141 330 5182, fax 0141 330 5183)

BROWN, John David; s of Alfred Stanley Brown, Little Billing, Northampton, and Joan Mary, *née* Ogle; *b* 13 Oct 1942; *Educ* Northampton GS, Univ of Nottingham (BSc); *m* 24 Sept 1966, Diane Elaine, da of Eric Edmund Hatton (d 1987); *Career* entered patent agent profession 1964, qualified patent agent 1969, ptnr Forrester Ketley & Co London 1972–, fndr ptnr Forrester & Boehmert London, Munich, Bremen 1977–; memb: Kiwanis Club Welwyn, Cncl of the Chartered Inst of Patent Agents, Jt Examination Bd of the Chartered Inst of Patent Agents and the Inst of Trade Mark Agents; substitute memb Cncl of Euro Patent Inst; memb: SCI 1964, RSC 1964, CIPA 1969; *Recreations* walking, skiing; *Style*— John D Brown, Esq; ✉ Forrester Ketley & Co, Forrester House, 52 Bounds Green Rd, London N11 2EY (☎ 0181 889 6622, fax 0181 881 1088 or 0181 889 0131)

BROWN, Rt Rev John Edward; s of Edward and Muriel Brown; *b* 13 July 1930; *Educ* Wintringham GS Grimsby, Kelham Theol Coll (BD); *m* 1956, Rosemary, *née* Wood; 1 s; *Career* ordained priest (deacon 1955); formerly: master St George's Sch Jerusalem, curate St George's Cathedral Jerusalem; chaplain Amman Jordan 1954–57, curate i/c All Saints Reading 1957–60, missionary and chaplain All Saints Cathedral Khartoum Sudan 1960–64; vicar: Stewkley Buckingham 1964–69, St Luke's Maidenhead 1969–73, Bracknell Berks 1973–77; rural dean Sonning 1974–77, archdeacon of Berks 1978–86, episcopal canon St George's Cathedral Jerusalem 1987–95, bishop of Cyprus and The Gulf 1987–95, ret; asst bishop Dio of Lincoln 1995–; *Recreations* walking, Middle East and African studies; *Style*— The Rt Rev John E Brown; ✉ 130 Oxford Street, Cleethorpes, North East Lincolnshire DN35 0BP (☎ 01472 698840)

BROWN, Sir John Gilbert Newton; kt (1974), CBE (1966); s of John Brown, of Kent (d 1986), and Mary Edith, *née* Purchas (d 1974); *b* 7 July 1916; *Educ* Lancing, Hertford Coll Oxford (MA); *m* 1946, Virginia Helen Violet, da of late Darcy Braddell, of Holland Park, London W11; 1 s, 2 da; *Career* 2 Lt RA Malaya; publisher OUP 1956–80; chm: B H Blackwell 1980–83, Basil Blackwell Publishers 1983–85 (dep chm 1983–87); dir: John Brown Publishing Ltd, Blackwell Gp, Basil Blackwell Publishers until 1989, Book Tokens until 1989; chm Univ Bookshop Oxford until 1989; *Clubs* Garrick; *Style*— Sir John Brown, CBE; ✉ Milton Lodge, Great Milton, Oxford (☎ 01844 279217)

BROWN, Dr John Graham; s of Malcolm Brown, of York, and Doreen Ethel, *née* Calpin; *b* 3 March 1957; *Educ* Nunthorpe GS York, Queen Elizabeth Coll London (BSc, Helen R White prize in microbiology), Sch of Hygiene and Tropical Med London (PhD); *Career* MRC res fell Sch of Hygiene and Tropical Med London 1981–84, res and devpt offr Health Educn Cncl 1984–87; Burson-Marsteller Ltd (PR/Public Affrs): joined 1987, dir 1989–, memb Euro Bd 1995–; memb: Steering Ctee Food and Health Forum RSM, Cncl Br Nutrition Soc 1986–89 (memb 1975), MIMgt 1988, MIPR 1990; *Recreations* foreign travel, good food, numismatics; *Style*— Dr John Brown; ✉ Burson-Marsteller Ltd, 24–28 Bloomsbury Way, London WC1A 2PX (☎ 0171 831 6262, fax 0171 430 1033)

BROWN, John Granger; s of Frank Brown, of Birkenhead; *b* 24 Nov 1939; *Educ* Birkenhead Sch, Univ of Birmingham; *m* 1964, Averil, da of Arthur Jones, of Birkenhead; 2 da; *Career* CA; dir and co sec Bernard Matthews plc 1977–; *Recreations* golf, bridge; *Style*— John Brown, Esq; ✉ Rose Cottage, West End, Old Costessey, Norwich (☎ 01603 744477)

BROWN, John Morton; s of late James Brown, and Theresa Gilmour, *née* Cunningham; *b* Ayrshire; *Educ* Parkhouse Sch Newbury, Berkshire Coll of Art & Design Reading; *partner* Ann Cowling; 1 da (Isobel Sophie b 27 Dec 1986); *Career* early career as still-life photographer, subsequent experience in reportage, people and landscape photography, currently advtg and corp photographer; asst to various fashion, magazine and advtg photographers 1967–71; clients incl: Coca-Cola, Levi Strauss, IBM, Rank Xerox, British Airways, Air Canada, Quantas, Singapore Airlines, Lufthansa, American Cotton Club, J R Phillips; numerous gp exhbns incl Art and the Sea (ICA); numerous awards from professional bodies incl AFAEP and Br Design & Art Direction; memb Assoc of

Photographers (jury memb The Tenth Awards 1993); memb AFAEP; *Recreations* fly fishing, walking, swimming, sailing; *Style*— John Brown, Esq; ✉ c/o Ann Cowling, 90 Tyrwhitt Road, London SE4 1QB (☎ 0181 469 3000, fax 0181 469 2993)

BROWN, John Neville; CBE (1995); s of Alfred Herbert Brown (d 1978), of Tutbury, Staffordshire, and Jessie Wright (d 1991); *b* 18 Nov 1935; *Educ* Denstone Coll, Selwyn Coll Cambridge (MA); *m* 3 April 1965, Ann Hilliar, da of George William Hubert Edmonds; 1 s (Hamish John Benedict b 19 Dec 1968), 1 da (Sara Elizabeth Hilliar b 2 July 1966); *Career* articled clerk Shipley Blackburn Sutton & Co (Chartered Accountants) 1960–63; Ernst & Young (and predecessors): sr 1965, mangr 1968, ptnr 1986–94; princ VAT conslt Binder Hamlyn 1994–95; pres VAT Practitioners' Gp 1992–96; vice pres: World Pheasant Assoc, Old Denstonian Club; dir British Sports Assoc for the Disabled; fin advsr and ex officio memb Cncl Staffordshire Regt; hon treas The Leonard Cheshire Services in Berks; Liveryman Worshipful Co of Glovers; FCA 1964, AInsT 1966, FRGS 1988; *Recreations* photography, travel, beagling, reading, ornithology, conservation; *Clubs* United Oxford and Cambridge University, Royal Over-Seas League; *Style*— John Brown, Esq, CBE; ✉ 22 Wykeham Way, Haddenham, Aylesbury, Bucks HP17 8BX (☎ and fax 01844 290430)

BROWN, John Stevenson; s of Stanley Brown (d 1978), of Sanderstead, Surrey, and Agnes Campbell, *née* Stevenson; *b* 28 Dec 1929; *Educ* Whitgift Middle Sch Croydon, Coll of Estate Mgmnt; *m* 1953, Catherine Mary, da of Maurice Ludlam-Taylor (d 1981); 1 s, 1 da; *Career* Nat Serv RE UK, served E Africa 1948–49; vice chm and md Artagen Properties Ltd 1966–76, md Peachey Property Corporation plc 1977–88, chm Burton Property Trust Ltd 1991–95; non-exec dir Burton Group plc; pres: Br Chapter FIABCI 1975–76, Br Property Fedn 1986–87; Liveryman Worshipful Co of Paviors; FRICS; *Recreations* sailing (TSDY Galactic); *Clubs* Royal Thames Yacht, Royal Lymington Yacht; *Style*— John Brown, Esq; ✉ Burton Group plc, 10 Great Castle St, London W1N 7AD (☎ 0171 927 7642)

BROWN, Joseph Lawler; CBE (1977), TD (1953), DL (W Midlands 1975); s of Neil Brown, of Peebles; *b* 22 March 1921; *Educ* Peebles, Heriot-Watt Coll Edinburgh, Open Univ (BA); *m* 1950, Mabel, da of Alderman Pearson Smith, BEM; 1 s, 1 da; *Career* served WWII, Europe, Maj 7/9 The Royal Scots, TA 1939–57; dir: Coventry Newspapers 1960–69 (md 1964–69), BPM Holdings 1971–81, Reuters 1972–75; chm & md Birmingham Post and Mail 1971–77; memb Press Assoc 1968–75 (chm 1971); pres: Newspaper Soc 1976–77, Birmingham Chamber of Industry & Commerce 1979; warden Neidpath Castle Peebles 1983, memb The Guildry Corp of Peebles 1991, bailiff The Schs of King Edward VI in Birmingham 1987; FRSA 1975, FCIM 1976, CIMgt 1978; Cdr Order of Merit (Italy) 1973, Knight of Mark Twain Soc (USA) 1979; *Books* History of Peebles: 1850–1990 (1990); *Recreations* Japanese woodcuts; *Style*— Joseph Brown, Esq, CBE, TD, DL; ✉ 37 Mearse Lane, Barnt Green, Birmingham B45 8HH (☎ 0121 445 1234)

BROWN, Prof Judith Margaret (Mrs P J Diggle); da of Rev W G Brown (d 1968), of London, and Joan Margaret, *née* Adams; *b* 9 July 1944, India; *Educ* Sherborne Sch for Girls Dorset, Girton Coll Cambridge (exhibitioner, MA, PhD, research studentship); *m* 21 July 1984, Peter James Diggle, s of late J Diggle; 1 s (James Wilfred Lachlan b 9 Nov 1986); *Career* Girton Coll Cambridge: research fell 1968–70, official fell 1970–71, dir of studies in history 1969–71; Univ of Manchester: lectr in history 1971–82, sr lectr 1982–90, reader-elect 1990; Beit Prof of Cwlth History Univ of Oxford and fell Balliol Coll 1990–; FRHistS 1972; *Books* Gandhi's Rise to Power: Indian Politics 1915–22 (1972), Gandhi and Civil Disobedience. The Mahatma in Indian Politics 1928–34 (1977), Men and Gods in a Changing World (1980), Modern India. The Origins of an Asian Democracy (1984, 2 edn 1994), Gandhi. Prisoner of Hope (1989, Italian trans 1995), Migration. The Asian Experience (ed with Dr Rosemary Foot, *qv*, 1994), Gandhi and South Africa. Principles and Politics (1996), Hong Kong's Transitions, 1842–1997 (ed with Dr Rosemary Foot, *qv*, 1997); *Recreations* gardening, classical music; *Style*— Prof Judith M Brown; ✉ Balliol College, Oxford OX1 3BJ (☎ 01865 277736, fax 01865 277803)

BROWN, Karen; da of Leslie Gordon Brown, of Steyning, Sussex and Valerie Elizabeth, *née* Blyth; *b* 9 Jan 1963; *Educ* Oxted Co Sch; *Career* int hockey player; memb: Orpington Ladies Hockey Club 1977–87, Slough Ladies Hockey Club 1987–; England: jr 1979–81, under 21 1981–83, 109 full caps 1984–; 140 full caps GB 1984–; honours incl: Gold medal Euro Championships 1991, Silver medal Euro Championships 1987, Bronze medal Euro Indoor Championships 1982 and 1987, fourth place Olympic Games 1988, fourth place World Cup 1990, Bronze medal Olympic Games 1992, fourth place Olympics 1996; UK Player of the Year 1984 and 1994; official National Westminster Bank 1980; *Recreations* Manchester United FC; *Style*— Miss Karen Brown; ✉ 12 Parklands, Lynwood Rd, Redhill, Surrey (☎ 01737 778790); c/o All England Women's Hockey Assoc, 51 High St, Shrewsbury, Shropshire SY1 1ST

BROWN, Keith Clark; s of George Harold Brown (d 1970), and Sophie Eleanor, *née* Clark; *b* 14 Jan 1943; *Educ* Forest Sch, City of London Coll; *m* 16 April 1972, Rita Hildegard, da of Jack Stanley Rolfe (d 1977); 1 s (Timothy b 1979), 1 da (Lucy b 1976); *Career* stockbroker and investmt banker; ptnr W Greenwell & Co 1978–86; md: Greenwell Montagu Securities 1987, Morgan Stanley 1988–; MSI (Dp), AIIMR; bd memb London Regional Transport 1984–94, dir British Aerospace plc 1989–; cncllr: London Borough of Havering 1968–74, Brentwood DC 1976–86 (chm 1983–84); pres Brentwood and Ongar Cons Assoc; memb Racehorse Owners' Assoc, govr Brentwood Sch Essex; Liveryman Worshipful Co of Coopers; *Recreations* public and charitable affairs, horseracing; *Clubs* Carlton, Cordwainer; *Style*— Keith C Brown, Esq; ✉ Fryerning House, Ingatestone, Essex CM4 0PF (☎ 01277 352959, fax 01277 355051); Morgan Stanley, 25 Cabot Square, Canary Wharf, London E14 4QA (☎ 0171 513 6604)

BROWN, Keith John; JP (1979); s of Frederick Charles Brown, and Doris Lilian, *née* French; *b* 21 June 1949; *Educ* Forest Hill Sch, City and East London Coll, Univ of London; *Career* ocularist: Moorfields Eye Hosp 1970, Kent Co Ophthalmic and Aural Hosp Maidstone 1973, Kent and Sussex Hosp Tunbridge Well 1975; private practice ownership: Brown Poole & Ptnrs Tunbridge Wells 1972, Brown and Gimpel Southborough 1979; ind private practice: Southborough, Maidstone, W Malling 1981; conslt ocularist: Cromwell Hosp London 1984, Trotters Edinburgh 1986, Dolland and Aitchison Group 1987, Chaucer Hosp Canterbury 1988; chm Cranbrook and Dist Lib Democrat Pty 1990–96, cncllr (Lib Dem) Hawkhurst Ward Tunbridge Wells BC 1994–, prospective Parly candidate (Lib Dem) Tonbridge and Malling 1996–; Freeman: City of London, Worshipful Co of Spectacle Makers; fndn fell Br Assoc Dispensing Opticians 1986, assoc memb Inst of Ocular Prosthesists 1989; *Recreations* cooking, walking, shooting; *Clubs* Nat Lib; *Style*— Keith Brown, Esq, JP; ✉ Linnet House, Hawkhurst, Kent TN18 4AX (☎ 01580 753668, fax 01580 754254, e-mail 100043,1321@compuserve.com); 18–20 Swan St, West Malling, Kent ME19 6LP (☎ 01732 848384); 100 London Rd, Southborough Tunbridge Wells, Kent TN4 0PW (☎ 01892 535683); Cedex 11, Trois Monts, Evrecy 14210, France (☎ 00 33 2 31 79 16 62)

BROWN, Keith Robert; s of Kenneth William Brown, of Enfield, Middx, and Margaret Sonia, *née* Minns; *b* 18 March 1963; *Educ* Chace Boys' Sch Enfield; *m* 3 Nov 1984, Marie, da of Alec Barlow; 2 s (Zachary Joseph Keith b 24 Feb 1987, Alexander Kristian Miles b 29 Dec 1992), 1 da (Roseanna Seraphina Marie b 18 Dec 1989); *Career* professional cricketer; Middlesex CCC: joined 1983–, debut 1984, awarded county cap 1990, over 200 appearances, highest score 200 not out v Notts Lord's 1990; represented: South of England in Youth Tournament Denmark 1981, NCA v Young Indians; supporters' Player of the Year 1990, London Cricketer of the Year 1990; selected to play rugby for Essex 1986; also physical educn teacher and cricket coach, formerly builder's apprentice; *Style*— Keith Brown, Esq; ✉ Middlesex CCC, Lord's Cricket Ground, St John's Wood, London NW8 8QN (☎ 0171 286 4405)

BROWN, Kenneth Edward Lindsay; s of Col Thomas Pyne Brown, OBE (d 1957); *b* 17 Oct 1940; *Educ* Sherborne; *m* 1968, Mary Ruth, da of Thomas Forrester (d 1969); 3 s; *Career* chm A R Brown McFarlane & Co Ltd 1972– (dir 1967–); FCA; *Recreations* sailing, skiing; *Clubs* Royal Ocean Racing; *Style*— Kenneth Brown Esq; ✉ 65 St Andrews Drive, Glasgow G41 4HP (☎ 0141 423 8381); A R Brown McFarlane & Co Ltd, 239 Myreside St, Glasgow G32 6DR (☎ 0141 551 8281, fax 0141 551 1518)

BROWN, Prof Kenneth Joseph; s of Charles Brown, of Aberdeenshire, and Dorothy, *née* Duncan; *b* 20 Dec 1945; *Educ* Robert Gordon's Coll, Univ of Aberdeen (BSc), Univ of Dundee (PhD); *m* 6 Oct 1971, Elizabeth, da of James Lobban; 2 da (Sheila b 30 Jan 1975, Jenny b 29 March 1977), 1 s (Colin b 14 Aug 1980); *Career* Dept of Mathematics Heriot-Watt Univ: lectr 1970–81, sr lectr 1981–91, head of dept 1989–92, reader 1991–93, prof 1993–; memb: Inst for Mathematics and its Applications, American Mathematical Soc, Edinburgh Mathematical Soc; FRSE 1991; *Books* Reaction-Diffusion Equations (jt ed with A A Lacey, 1990); *Recreations* reading, coaching athletics; *Style*— Prof Kenneth Brown, FRSE; ✉ 3 Highlea Grove, Balerno, Edinburgh EH14 7HQ (☎ 0131 449 5314); Department of Mathematics, Heriot-Watt University, Riccarton, Edinburgh EH14 4AS (☎ 0131 451 3239, fax 0131 451 3249)

BROWN, Kenneth Thomas; s of Thomas Alfred Charles Brown (d 1966), and Lilian Florence, *née* Porter (d 1986); *b* 28 Nov 1928; *Educ* Christ's Coll Finchley; *m* 4 Feb 1956, Barbara Hooper; 3 s (Stephen b 9 Dec 1956, Martin b 11 July 1959, Julian b 16 Jan 1962); *Career* reporter Barnet Press 1945–47 and 1949–51, sub ed and picture ed Gloucestershire Echo 1951–54, features ed Birmingham Gazette 1954–56, sub ed London Evening News and News Chronicle 1956–58, asst night ed and gardening ed Daily Mail 1958–90, gardening editorial conslt 1991–; gardening tours conslt Royal Horticultural Soc 1995–; memb Garden Writers' Guild; *Recreations* gardening, travel; *Clubs* Farmers'; *Style*— Kenneth Brown, Esq; ✉ Parlour Farm House, Bisley, Stroud, Glos GL6 7BH (☎ and fax 01452 770878)

BROWN, Prof Lawrence Michael (Mick); s of Bertson Waterworth Brown, and Edith, *née* Waghorne (d 1989); *b* 18 March 1936; *Educ* Univ of Toronto (BASc), Univ of Cambridge (MA, DSc), Univ of Birmingham (PhD); *m* Dr Susan Drucker Brown, da of David Drucker, of Oronoque Village, Stratford, Wisconsin, USA; 1 s (Toby Solomon b 1974), 2 da (Sarah May b 1969, Isabel b 1972); *Career* Univ of Cambridge: W H Tapp fellowship Gonville and Caius Coll 1963, demonstrator 1965, lectr 1970, fndr fell and dir of studies in physical sci Robinson Coll 1977, reader 1982, prof 1990; awarded: Rosenhain Medal (Inst of Metals), R F Mehl Medal (Metals Soc and Inst of Metals); FRS 1981, FInstP, FIM; *Style*— Prof Mick Brown, FRS; ✉ Cavendish Laboratory, Madingley Rd, Cambridge CB3 0HE (☎ 01223 337291, fax 01223 63261)

BROWN, Maggie; da of Cecil Walter Brown and Marian, *née* Evans; *b* 7 Sept 1950; *Educ* Colston's Girls' Sch, Univ of Sussex, Univ of Cardiff (Dip in Journalism); *m* 22 June 1979, Charles John Giuseppe Harvey, s of Hon John Wynn Harvey, of Coed-y-Maen, Meifod, Powys (s of 1 Baron Harvey of Tasburgh); 3 da (Elena b 27 Dec 1982, Nina b 11 Aug 1985, Stephanie b 8 May 1989); *Career* trainee journalist Birmingham Post & Mail 1972–74; staff writer: Birmingham Post 1974–77, Reuters 1977–78; news editor: Financial Weekly 1979–80, Guardian 1980–86; media editor The Independent 1986; currently reg contrib: Guardian media pages, BBC radio; currently columnist: Daily Telegraph, PR Week; memb Victorian Soc; *Recreations* reading, gardening, being a mother; *Style*— Ms Maggie Brown; ✉ c/o PR Week, 22 Lancaster Gate, London W2 3LP

BROWN, Prof Sir (George) Malcolm; kt (1985); s of George Arthur Brown (d 1937), and Anne Brown (d 1986); *b* 5 Oct 1925; *Educ* Coatham Sch Redcar, Univ of Durham (BSc, DSc), Univ of Oxford (MA, DPhil), Princeton Univ, Univ of California, Univ of Berne; *m* 1, 1963 (m dis 1977); m 2, Sally Jane Marston, er da of Alan Douglas Spencer; 2 step da (Polly Marston b 1969, Verna Marston b 1971); *Career* served RAF (aircrew) 1944–47; Cwlth fell (Harkness) Princeton Univ 1954–55, coll lectr Lincoln New Coll, fell St Cross Coll Univ of Oxford 1955–66, sr res fell Geophysical Laboratory Washington DC USA 1966–67, prof of geology, dean of sci and pro vice chllr Univ of Durham 1967–79; princ investigator NASA Apollo Moon Exploration Prog 1967–75; dir: Br Geological Survey, Geological Museum, Geological Survey of NI 1979–85; conslt geologist 1985–, geological advsr ODA 1979–85; Hon DSc Univ of Leicester, Hon DUniv Open Univ; hon fell Geological Soc of America; FRS, FGS; *Books* Layered Igneous Rocks (1968), Origin of the Solar System (contrib, 1978), Planet Earth (contrib, 1977); *Recreations* exploration, classical guitar; *Clubs* Royal Over-Seas League; *Style*— Prof Sir Malcolm Brown, FRS; ✉ Rose Dene, Shipton Road, Milton under Wychwood, Oxon OX7 6JT (☎ 01993 830812)

BROWN, Malcolm Carey; s of Rev William George Brown (d 1978), and Bernice Nellie Cordelia, *née* Radcliffe (d 1978); *b* 7 May 1930; *Educ* Nelson GS Lancashire, Poole GS Dorset, St John's Coll Oxford (scholar, MA); *m* 1953, Beatrice Elsie Rose, da of Austin Albert George Light; 2 s (Martin John Carey b 1959, Michael Paul b 1961), 1 da (Catherine Mary b 1963); *Career* Nat Serv Midshipman RNVR 1953–54; BBC: gen trainee 1955–57, TV prodn asst 1957–60, documentary film prodr 1960–86; freelance writer 1986– (pt/t freelance writer 1968–86), freelance historian Imperial War Museum 1989–; *Television* documentary films as prodr/dir incl: T E Lawrence 1962, I'm a Stranger Here Myself 1963, Horseman Pass By 1966 (British entry in Cork Film Festival), Scapa Flow 1966, The World Turned Upside Down 1967, The Chalfont Profiles 1970–75, Battle of the Somme (short-listed for Int Emmy Award) 1976, Armistice and After 1978, Graf Spee 1979, Checkpoint Berlin 1981, Peace in No Man's Land 1981, Gordon of Khartoum 1983; *Books* Scapa Flow (jtly, 1968), Tommy Goes To War (1978), Christmas Truce (jtly, 1984, 1994), A Touch of Genius (jtly, 1988, short-listed NCR Non-Fiction Book Award 1989 and Nelson Hurst and Marsh Biography Award 1989), The Letters of T E Lawrence (ed, 1988), The Imperial War Museum Book of the First World War (1991), Secret Despatches from Arabia and Other Writings by T E Lawrence (ed, 1991), The Imperial War Museum Book of the Western Front (1993), The Imperial War Museum Book of the Somme (1996); *Recreations* walking, the making and keeping of friends; *Style*— Malcolm Brown, Esq; ✉ 4 Northbury Avenue, Ruscombe, Twyford, Reading, Berkshire RG10 9LG (☎ 0118 934 0370)

BROWN, Malcolm Ronald; s of Ronald Ernest Charles Brown, MBE (d 1988), of Orpington, Kent, and Peggy Elizabeth, *née* Mitchener; *b* 2 Aug 1946; *Educ* Quintin GS, Univ of London (BSc); *m* 3 Oct 1970, Lyntina Sydnie, da of Clinton Sydney Squire; 1 s (Philip Clinton b 18 May 1975), 1 da (Samantha Anne b 13 Feb 1972); *Career* construction analyst: de Zoete & Gorton 1968–72, James Capel & Co 1972– (ptnr 1981, sr exec 1984); chm Repair and Maintenance Gp Construction Indust Forecasting Body Nat Econ Devpt Office; author numerous specialist papers and pubns; AIIMR; *Recreations* ocean racing, chess, gardening; *Style*— Malcolm Brown, Esq; ✉ Carbery House, Carbery Lane, Ascot, Berks (☎ 01344 22620); James Capel House, Thames Exchange, 10 Queen Street Place, London EC4R 1BL (☎ 0171 621 0011 ext 2644)

BROWN, (Laurence Frederick) Mark; s of Rt Rev Ronald Brown, of Lathom, and Joyce, *née* Hymers (d 1987); *b* 16 March 1953; *Educ* Bolton Sch, Univ of Durham (BA);

m 5 Aug 1978, Jane Margaret, da of Rev Dr F H Boardman, of Gt Sankey, Cheshire; 1 s (Nicholas Edward b 29 April 1984); *Career* called to the Bar Inner Temple 1975; in practice Northern Circuit 1976–, pt/t tutor in law Univ of Liverpool 1976–83, counsel to Chief Constable Police Disciplinary Tbnls, asst recorder 1993; *Recreations* golf, gardening; *Clubs* The Royal Liverpool Golf; *Style*— Mark Brown, Esq; ✉ Holly Bank, Gayton Rd, Heswall Lower Village, Wirral (☎ 0151 342 2939); The Corn Exchange Building, Fenwick St, Liverpool L2 7QS (☎ 0151 227 1081, fax 0151 236 1120)

BROWN, Mark Finlay; *b* 16 March 1963; *Educ* Loughborough Univ of Technol (BScEcon); *Career* economist: CBI 1984, HM Treasy 1985–87, Phillips & Drew 1987–89; strategist UBS 1990–93, head of strategy and economics ABN AMRO Hoare Govett 1994–; *Recreations* rugby, mountaineering; *Style*— Mark Brown, Esq; ✉ ABN AMRO Hoare Govett Securities Ltd, 4 Broadgate, London EC2M 7LE (☎ 0171 374 7170, fax 0171 374 1778)

BROWN, Martin; s of Clarence Brown (d 1981), and Anne, *née* Gray; *b* 26 Jan 1949; *Educ* Bolton Sch, New Coll Oxford (MA); *m* 1971, Frances *née* Leithead; 2 s; *Career* civil servant; with HM Customs and Excise 1971–; postings incl: VAT liability HQ, anti-smuggling controls and excise duties, outfield operational mgmnt (Manchester Airport and Computer Audit Unit), various secondments (private sec to Treasy Min, customs advsr Barbados), dir Customs 1993–94, dir Central Ops 1994–96, dir VAT Policy 1996–; *Recreations* the arts, walking, travel, wine, cycling; *Clubs* Hale (Leigh Rd) Tennis; *Style*— Martin Brown, Esq; ✉ HM Customs and Excise, New King's Beam House, 22 Upper Ground, London SE1 9PJ (☎ 0171 865 5015, fax 0171 865 5892)

BROWN, Sir (Cyril) Maxwell Palmer (Max); KCB (1969, CB 1965), CMG (1957); s of Cyril Palmer Brown, of Wanganui, NZ; *b* 30 June 1914; *Educ* Wanganui Collegiate Sch, Victoria Univ NZ, Clare Coll Cambridge; *m* 1940, Margaret May, da of late W Edward Gillhespy, of Hathersage, Derbyshire; 3 s, 1 da; *Career* second perm sec BOT 1968–70, Dept of Trade 1970–74; dir: ERA Technology Ltd 1974–86, John Brown & Co 1975–82, Ransome Hoffman Pollard (later RHP Group) 1975–88; dep chm Monopolies Cmmn 1976–81; *Style*— Sir Max Brown, KCB, CMG; ✉ 20 Cottenham Park Rd, London SW20 0RZ (☎ 0181 946 7237)

BROWN, Sir Mervyn; KCMG (1981, CMG 1975), OBE (1963); s of William Brown, of Murton, Co Durham; *b* 24 Sept 1923; *Educ* Ryhope GS Sunderland, St John's Coll Oxford (MA); *m* 1949, Elizabeth, da of Harry Gittings, of Shipley, Derby; *Career* HM Foreign Serv in Buenos Aires, New York, Singapore and Vientiane 1949–83: ambass to Madagascar 1967–70 (non resident 1976–78), high cmmr Tanzania 1975–78, min and dep perm rep to UN 1978, high cmmr Nigeria and ambass to Benin 1979–83; chm: Visiting Arts of Great Britain 1983–89, Anglo-Malagasy Soc 1986–; *Books* Madagascar Rediscovered (1978), A History of Madagascar (1995); *Recreations* music, tennis, history, cooking; *Clubs* Royal Cwlth Soc, Hurlingham, All England Lawn Tennis; *Style*— Sir Mervyn Brown, KCMG, OBE; ✉ 195 Queen's Gate, London SW7 5EU

BROWN, Michael J (Mike); *Career* mgmnt trainee Seeboard 1964, mgmnt servs field until 1973, mgmnt servs and manpower offr Electricity Council 1978–82 (joined 1973); London Electricity plc (formerly London Electricity Board): joined as mgmnt servs dir 1982, mangr Southern Div 1984–87, Northern divnl mangr 1988–90, customer servs dir (after restructure) 1989–95, exec dir (i/c competitive supply, electricity purchasing and generation) 1995–; *Style*— Mike Brown, Esq; ✉ London Electricity plc, Templar House, 81–87 High Holborn, London WC1V 6NU (☎ 0171 242 9050, fax 0171 242 2815)

BROWN, Michael John; s of Lt Cdr S R Brown (d 1976), of Aylesbury, and Ada Phyllis, *née* Evett (d 1993); *b* 23 Sept 1932; *Educ* Berkhamsted Sch, New Coll Oxford (MA, fndr pres Oxford Univ Gymnastics Club); *m* 1, 20 Sept 1963, Margaret Jordan, JP (d 1988), da of William C Jordan; 4 s (Edward b 1964, Thomas b 1966, Robert b and d 1968, Adam b 1970); m 2, 24 May 1996, Valetta Radgosky, da of Edward Lucey; *Career* admitted slr 1957; ptnr Denton Hall and Burgin 1959–80, sr ptnr Brown Cooper 1981–96; dir: Urwick Orr and Partners Ltd (chm 1981–84), Channel TV 1972–77, Purcell Graham and Co 1978–88, Paulstra Ltd 1977–95; hon slr Variety Club of GB 1966–, chm Pooh Properties Trust 1972–; pres: Soc of Eng and American Lawyers 1989–93 (chm 1985–88), Copinger Soc 1992–93; memb: Arbitration Panel American Film Market Assoc 1990–, World Intellectual Property Orgn 1995–; *Recreations* diverse; *Clubs* Garrick; *Style*— Michael Brown, Esq; ✉ Lark Rise, Green End, Radnage, Bucks HP14 4BY

BROWN, Air Vice-Marshal Michael John Douglas; s of Norman Hillier Barnes Brown (d 1969), of Esher, Surrey, and Margaret Mary, *née* Nisbet (d 1981); *b* 9 May 1936; *Educ* Drayton Manor Sch, Trinity Hall Cambridge (MA); *m* 8 Sept 1961, Audrey Florence Woodward (d 1994); 1 s (Stephen b 1964); *Career* RAF: cadet entry Tech Coll Henlow 1953, cmmnd Tech (now Engr) branch 1954, pilot trg 1958–59, engrg duties Bomber Cmd 1959–61, signals duties Kenya 1961–64, advanced weapons course 1965–66, ops analyst MOD 1966–69, Staff Coll 1970, operational requirements MOD 1970–73, chief engr RAF Boulmer Radar Station 1973–75, USAF War Coll 1975–76, Gp Capt engrg co-ordination and plans HQ RAF Strike Cmd 1976–78, CO RAF North Luffenham 1978–80, RCDS 1981, dir air guided weapons MOD (PE) 1983–86, dir gen strategic electronic systems MOD (PE) 1986–91, ret RAF 1991; conslt engr and local public service 1991–; non-exec dir Centre for Software Engineering Ltd 1993–; vice-pres SSAFA Powys 1993–; CEng 1968, MRAeS 1968, MRIN 1981, CMath 1992, FIMA 1992; *Recreations* gardening, reading, music, archaeology; *Clubs* RAF; *Style*— Air Vice-Marshal M J D Brown; ✉ c/o RAF PMC, RAF Innsworth, Gloucester GL3 1EZ

BROWN, Michael Russell; MP (C) Brigg and Cleethorpes (majority 9,269); s of Frederick Alfred Brown, and Greta Mary Brown, OBE, *née* Russell; *b* 3 July 1951; *Educ* Littlehampton, Univ of York; *Career* memb Middle Temple; mgmnt trainee Barclays Bank 1972–74; lectr Swinton Cons Coll 1974–76, res asst to Michael Marshall MP 1975–77, Parly res asst to Nicholas Winterton MP 1977–79; MP (C): Brigg and Scunthorpe 1979–83, Brigg and Cleethorpes 1983–; sec Parly NI Ctee 1981–87 (vice chm 1987), PPS to Hon Douglas Hogg MP, min of state DTI 1989–90, min of state FCO 1990–92, PPS to Sec of State for N Ireland (Sir Patrick Mayhew) 1992–93, asst Govt whip 1993–94; *Style*— Michael Brown, Esq, MP; ✉ House of Commons, London SW1A 0AA

BROWN, Prof Morris Jonathan; s of Arnold Aaron Brown (d 1970), of London, and Irene Joyce, *née* Goodman; *b* 18 Jan 1951; *Educ* Edinburgh Acad, Harrow, Trinity Coll Cambridge (scholar, MA, MD), UCH Med Sch (scholar, MSc); *m* 31 July 1977, Diana Costa, da of Kostas Phylactou, of Cyprus; 3 da (Emily Irene Annie b 1981, Chrysothemis Celia Margaret b 1982, Ophelia Wendy Elizabeth b 1986); *Career* MRC sr fell Royal Postgrad Med Sch 1982–85, conslt physician Addenbrooke's Hosp Cambridge 1985–; Univ of Cambridge: prof of clinical pharmacology 1985–, fell Gonville & Caius Coll 1989–, dir of studies (clinical med); currently chm MRS; FRCP 1986; *Books* Advanced Medicine (1986), Clinical Pharmacology (jtly, 1996); papers on hypertension and vitamin E in heart disease; *Recreations* violin and oboe; *Clubs* RSM; *Style*— Prof Morris Brown; ✉ Clinical Pharmacology Unit, University of Cambridge, Level 2, F & G Block, Addenbrooke's Hospital, Cambridge CB2 2QQ (☎ 01223 336743, fax 01223 216893, car 0468 628137)

BROWN, Prof (Lionel) Neville; OBE; s of Reginald Percy Neville Brown (d 1978), of York Crescent, Wolverhampton, and Fanny, *née* Carver (d 1980); *b* 29 July 1923; *Educ* Wolverhampton GS, Pembroke Coll Cambridge (MA, LLM), Lyons Univ France (Dr en Droit); *m* 3 s (Roger b 1961, Simon b 1963, Adrian b 1965), 1 da (Rachel b 1967); *Career* WWII RAF 1942–45; admitted slr 1951; lectr in law Univ of Sheffield 1953–55; Univ of Birmingham: lectr 1955–57, sr lectr 1957–64, reader 1964–66, prof of comparative law 1966–90 (emeritus prof 1990–), dean Faculty of Law 1970–74; sr res fell Univ of Michigan 1960; visiting prof: Tulane Univ New Orleans 1968, Nairobi Univ 1974, Laval Univ Quebec 1975, 1979, 1983, 1987 and 1990, Limoges Univ 1987–88, Univ of Mauritius 1988–89; Cwlth Fndn Lectureship Caribbean 1976; memb Cncl on Tbnls 1982–88, chm Birmingham Social Security Appeal Tbnl 1988–96; reader C of E Lichfield Dio 1971–; Leverhume fellowship 1990–92; Docteur Honoris Causa: Limoges Univ France 1988, Laval Univ Quebec 1992; Officier Dans L'Ordre Des Palmes Académiques France 1987; memb Law Soc 1951; *Books* Amos & Walton's Introduction to French Law (3 edn with F H Lawson & Anton, 1967), French Administrative Law (4 edn with J S Bell, 1993), Court of Justice of European Communities (4 edn with T Kennedy, 1994, update 1995); *Recreations* landscape gardening, country walking, music; *Clubs* United Oxford and Cambridge; *Style*— Prof Neville Brown, OBE; ✉ 14 Waterdale, Compton, Wolverhampton WV3 9DY (☎ 01902 26666); Faculty of Law, University of Birmingham, Edgbaston, Birmingham B15 2TT (☎ 0121 414 6284)

BROWN, Nicholas (Anthony) Phelps; s of Prof Sir Henry Phelps Brown, of Oxford, and Dorothy Evelyn Mostyn, *née* Bowlby; *b* 5 May 1936; *Educ* Westminster, Trinity Coll Cambridge (Exhibition, MA, MD), Middlesex Hosp (DO); *m* 12 Dec 1960, Heather Mary, da of Ronald Hubert White; 1 s (Giles Nicholas b 22 May 1972), 2 da (Emily Sarah b 1 June 1967, Lucy Kate b 8 Oct 1969); *Career* Nat Serv 1955–57 (cmmnd RA); The Middlesex Hosp: house surgn 1964, house physician 1964, house offr 1965, clinical asst Univ Coll Hosp 1966–67; Moorfields Eye Hosp: out patient offr 1966–67, resident surgical offr 1967–70, chief clinical asst 1970–71, res fellow to Contact Lens Dept 1971–73, lectr then sr lectr Depts of Clinical Ophthalmology and Experimental Ophthalmology 1971–76 (and Inst of Ophthalmology), hon conslt 1975–76; clinical asst The Hammersmith Hosp 1971–75, private practice 1977–, pt/t teaching at Inst of Ophthalmology and with Univ Examination Postal Inst 1977–, hon conslt The Radcliffe Infirmary Oxford 1983–, dir Clinical Cataract Res Unit Nuffield Laboratory of Ophthalmology Oxford 1989– (res assoc 1983–); Kodak Res Award: slit-image camera devpt 1971, MRC Res Grant: study of the diabetic lens 1974–75, Nuffield Fndn Res Award: computerised analysis of the image of the lens of the eye 1987, Iris Fund for Eye Res: Glaucoma disc assessment by computerised image analysis 1989, Violt M Richards Charity: spoke cataract study 1990, Scheimpflug Award Osaka 1995; FRCS 1969, FCOphth; memb: RSM, BMA, Assoc for Eye Res, Oxford Ophthalmological Congress, Ophthalmological Soc of UK; *Publications* author of numerous papers and articles in ophthalmology journals; chapters in: Medical Ophthalmology, (ed Clifford Rose, 1975), Scientific Foundations of Ophthalmology (1977); Lens Disorders: A Clinical Manual of Cataract Diagnosis (with A J Bron, 1996); *Recreations* natural history, photography; *Style*— Nicholas Phelps Brown, Esq; ✉ 69 Harley St, London W1N 1DE (☎ 0171 636 7153, fax 0171 487 3901)

BROWN, Nicholas Hugh; MP (Lab) Newcastle upon Tyne East (majority 13,877); s of late R C Brown, and G K Brown, *née* Tester; *b* 13 June 1950; *Educ* Tunbridge Wells Tech HS, Univ of Manchester (BA); *Career* memb Newcastle upon Tyne City Cncl 1980– (memb Housing Sub Ctee on Slum Clearance); MP (Lab) Newcastle upon Tyne East 1983–, oppn frontbench dep spokesman on legal affrs 1985–87, oppn frontbench treasy spokesman 1987–94, dep to Margaret Beckett, MP as Shadow Ldr of the Commons 1992–94, oppn spokesman on health 1994–95, oppn dep chief whip 1995–; memb Select Ctee on Bdcasting 1994–95; *Style*— Nicholas Brown, Esq, MP; ✉ House of Commons, London SW1A 0AA

BROWN, (Mark) Nick; s of Henry Brown (d 1985), of Warrington, and Joan, *née* Horlock; *b* 3 Sept 1961; *Educ* English Martyrs RC HS; *m* 1, (m dis); m 2, 11 Aug 1994, Suzanne Charlton; *Career* professional tennis player and coach; GB under 18 rep World Team Cup Jr World Championships 1979, national under 21 champion 1980, memb GB Davis Cup team 1989–91, GB rep Euro Cup 1983, 1989 and 1990, ranked GB number 2 1990 and 1991; winner Indonesian Open 1989, winner Bangalore Open (doubles) 1992; runner-up: Bristol Grand Prix 1989, Manchester Grand Prix (doubles) 1990, World Series Tournament (doubles) 1991; GB team tennis champions with Heston Fiat 1987, US team tennis champions with LA Strings 1990; appointed LTA Laing Team coach 1991–94, LTA Nat Squad coach 1994–; TV and radio commentator, tennis journalist; *Recreations* steam trains, golf, squash, childrens charities; *Style*— Nick Brown, Esq; ✉ c/o The All England Club, Wimbledon, London SW19

BROWN, Prof Nigel Leslie; s of Leslie Charles Brown (d 1983), of Beverley, and Beryl, *née* Brown; *b* 19 Dec 1948; *Educ* Beverley GS, Univ of Leeds (BSc, PhD); *m* 7 Aug 1971, Gayle Lynnette, da of John Wallace Blackah, of Beverley; 2 da (Sally b 1975, Katie b 1977); *Career* lectr in biochemistry Univ of Bristol 1976–81, Royal Soc sr res fell 1981–88, visiting fell in genetics Univ of Melbourne Aust 1987–88; Univ of Birmingham: prof of molecular genetics and microbiology 1988–, head of biology 1994–; memb: Soc of Gen Microbiology, Biochemical Soc, Genetical Soc, American Soc of Microbiology; FIBiol 1989, FRSC 1990; *Recreations* science, travel, house renovation; *Style*— Prof Nigel Brown; ✉ 85 Oakfield Road, Selly Park, Birmingham B29 7HL; School of Biological Sciences, The University of Birmingham, Edgbaston, Birmingham B15 2TT (☎ 0121 414 5465, fax 0121 414 5907, telex 33893, e-mail N.L.Brown@bham.ac.uk)

BROWN, (Austen) Patrick; KCB (1995); *b* 14 April 1940; *Educ* Royal GS Newcastle upon Tyne, SSEES; *m* 1966, Mary; 1 da; *Career* Carreras Ltd until 1969: joined 1961, Cyprus office 1965–66, Belgium office 1967–68; mgmnt conslt Urwick Orr & Partners 1969–72, DOE 1972–76, asst sec Property Services Agency (PSA) 1976–80; Dept of Tport: asst sec 1980–83, under sec (fin and ports & buses privatisation) 1983–88; dep sec (privatisation of water indust) DOE 1988–90, chief exec PSA 1990–91, perm sec Dept of Tport 1991–; *Style*— Sir Patrick Brown, KCB; ✉ Department of Transport, Great Minster House, 76 Marsham Street, London SW1P 4DR (☎ 0171 271 5432)

BROWN, Paul; s of Alan Tertius Brown, of Wales, and Enfys Ann, *née* Jones; *b* 13 May 1960; *Educ* Univ of St Andrews; *Career* theatre designer; trained under Margaret Harris; *Theatre* designs for Royal Court, Traverse, Bush, Lincoln Centre NY; prodns 1985–87: A Lie of the Mind, Ourselves Alone, Road; *Opera* prodns incl: Mitridate (Covent Garden) 1991, Hamlet (Monte Carlo) 1993, L'Incoronzione di Poppea (Bologna) 1993, Zemire et Azor 1993, Don Giovanni (Israel) 1994, King Arthur (Paris Chatalet and ROH) 1995, Lady Macbeth of Mtsensk (Met NY) 1995, Tom Jones (Drottningholm Court Theatre Sweden) 1995, The Midsummer Marriage (ROH) 1996, Fidelio (ENO) 1996, Lulu (Glyndebourne) 1996; *Films* costumes for Angels and Insects 1995; *Style*— Paul Brown, Esq; ✉ c/o Performing Arts Management, 6 Windmill Street, London W1P 1HF (☎ 0171 255 1362, fax 0171 631 4631)

BROWN, Paul Gregorius; *Career* Lloyds Bank plc: joined 1960, main bd dir 1991–, dir of UK Retail Banking until 1996; dir of retail financial servs Lloyds TSB Group plc 1996–; *Style*— Paul Brown, Esq; ✉ Lloyds TSB Group plc, 71 Lombard Street, London EC3P 3BS (☎ 0171 626 1500)

BROWN, Paul Ray Beck; s of Sqdn Ldr Frederick Beck Brown, of Linslade, Beds, and Kathleen, *née* May; *b* 20 July 1944; *Educ* Churchers Coll Petersfield Hants; *m* 1964, Maureen Ellen Ann, da of Joseph Archibald McMillan (d 1982); 2 da (Lucy Elizabeth Beck b 10 Feb 1965, Clara Louise Beck b 20 Jan 1968); *Career* indentured: East Grinstead Courier 1963–65, Lincolnshire Standard 1965–66, Leicester Mercury 1966–68; investigative reporter Birmingham Post 1968–74, news ed Evening Post-Echo Hemel Hempstead 1980–81 (joined 1974), The Sun 1981–82, environment correspondent The

Guardian 1989– (joined 1982); Midlands Journalist of the Year 1974; *Books* The Last Wilderness, 80 Days in Antarctica (1991), Greenpeace (1993), Global Warming, Can Civilisation Survive (1996); *Recreations* badminton, travel; *Style*— Paul Brown, Esq; ✉ The Guardian, 119 Farringdon Rd, London EC1R 3ER (☎ 0171 239 9803)

BROWN, Peter Eric; s of Eric Henry Ibbetson Brown (d 1951), of King's Lynn, Norfolk, and Violet Mary, *née* Phipps (d 1931); *b* 3 Oct 1931; *Educ* Cheltenham; *m* 1, 23 Aug 1958, Sylvia Mary Ethel Watson (d 1991); 1 s (Richard Henry b 1967), 3 da (Vanessa Mary (Mrs Perkins) b 1960, Melanie Lucy (Mrs Conroy) b 1963, Camilla Susan (Mrs Hartley) b 1964); m 2, 1 Oct 1994, Margaret Temple Langstaff, *née* Saunders; *Career* Nat Serv Capt 1952, RAOC 1950–52; mktg dir Martin Cadbury Ltd 1966–70, dep chief exec Andercroft Ltd 1970–73, chm and md W S Cowell 1973–77, md Brown Knight & Truscott Ltd 1977–79, chm and md Claremont Press Ltd 1979–; Freeman City of London 1974, Liveryman Worshipful Co of Stationers and Newspaper Makers 1975; memb Inst of Printing 1977, FInstM 1985; *Recreations* golf, tennis, badminton, theatre; *Clubs* City Livery; *Style*— Peter Brown, Esq; ✉ Claremont Press Ltd, 23 Star Road, Partridge Green, Horsham, W Sussex RH13 8RA (☎ 01403 711474, fax 01403 711575)

BROWN, Peter Michael; s of Michael George Harold Brown (d 1969), of Sussex, and Dorothy Margaret, *née* Douty; *b* 11 July 1934; *Educ* Rugby; *m* 1963, Rosemary Anne, da of Hubert Simon (d 1979), of Geneva and Baden-Baden; 2 s (Hugo Michael Hubert b 1964, Dominic Peter b 1965); *Career* Nat Serv 2 Lt Somerset Light Infantry; dir: The Further Education Group, Enterprise Dynamics Ltd; chm: Synergy Holdings Ltd, Top Pay Research Group Ltd, Dawson Holdings plc, Surridge Dawson Holdings Ltd, Charity Appointments Ltd, Davis Laing & Dick, Gabbitas Educational Consultants Ltd; pres Thomas Coram Fndn; Liveryman Worshipful Co of Skinners; memb MRS, FInstD, FIPD, FRSA, FCA, FILog, FCIM; *Recreations* charity work, tennis, opera; *Clubs* Hurlingham, Lansdowne; *Style*— Peter Michael Brown, Esq; ✉ 12 Hyde Park Place, London W2 2LH; 1 Lancaster Place, London WC2E 7EB (☎ 0171 836 5831, fax 0171 379 3230)

BROWN, Peter Wilfred Henry; CBE (1996); s of Rev Wilfred George Brown (d 1968), and Joan Margaret, *née* Adams; *b* 6 June 1941; *Educ* Marlborough, Jesus Coll Cambridge (MA); *m* 29 March 1969 (m dis), Kathleen, da of Hugh Clarke, of Freetown (d 1982); 1 da (Sonya b 1971); *Career* asst master in classics Birkenhead Sch 1963–66, lectr in classics Fourah Bay Coll Univ of Sierra Leone 1966–68, asst sec SOAS Univ of London 1968–75, sec Br Acad 1983– (dep sec 1975–83, acting sec 1976–77); memb: Br Assoc for Central and Eastern Europe Governing Body 1983–96, Br Library Advsy Cncl 1983–89, Cncl Sch of Slavonic and E European Studies Univ of London 1984–92 and 1993–, Warburg Inst Univ of London 1987–93, Inst of Historical Research 1994–, Cncl Soc for the Protection of Sci and Learning 1996–; Hon DLitt Univ of Birmingham; *Recreations* sedentary pursuits, musical, bookish; *Style*— Peter Brown, Esq, CBE; ✉ 34 Victoria Road, London NW6 6PX; The British Academy, 20–21 Cornwall Terrace, London NW1 4QP (☎ 0171 487 5966, fax 0171 224 3807)

BROWN, Philip Nicholas; s of Reginald F Brown (d 1970), and Margaret E Gladwell, *née* Simmons (d 1988); *b* 24 June 1942; *Educ* Cheshunt GS, Albion HS, Hobart Coll (BA), Columbia Univ (LLB); *m* 27 Dec 1975, Geraldine Lynn, da of Frederick Grover, of New Malden, Surrey; 2 da (Naomi b 1982, Emily b 1983); *Career* Vol Serv Peace Corps 1966–68; worked on New Jersey Law Reform Project 1969–71, managing ptnr Wilde Sapte 1988–94 (ptnr 1975–95), sr conslt Hodgart Temporal & Co 1995–; memb: Law Soc 1975, NY Bar 1966, New Jersey Bar 1969; *Recreations* pottery; *Style*— Philip Brown, Esq; ✉ Hodgart Temporal & Company, 30 St James's Street, London SW1A 1HB (☎ 0171 460 4160, fax 0171 460 4161)

BROWN, Ralph; *b* 24 April 1928; *Educ* Leeds GS, Leeds Sch of Art, Hammersmith Sch of Art, RCA; *m* 1, 1952 (m dis 1962), Margaret Elizabeth Taylor; 1 s (Matthew b 1953), 1 da (Sara b 1955); m 2, Feb 1964, Caroline Ann, *née* Clifton-Trigg; 1 s (Jasper b 1965); *Career* sculptor; exhibited widely in UK and Europe 1953–, pt/t tutor RCA 1958–69; work purchased by many public collections incl: Tate Gallery, Leeds, Liverpool, Bristol, Arts Cncl of GB, RCA, Cardiff, Rijksmuseum, Kröller-Müller, Stuyvesant Fndn SA, Art Gallery of NSW, Contemporary Art Soc; ARA 1968, RA 1972, FRBS 1993; *Style*— Ralph Brown, Esq, RA; ✉ The Old House, Frampton on Severn, Glos GL2 7DY

BROWN, Rt Rev Mgr Ralph; s of John William Brown, and Elizabeth Josephine Brown; *b* 30 June 1931; *Educ* Highgate Sch, St Edmund's Coll, Old Hall Green Herts, Pontifical Gregorian Univ Rome (Dr in Canon Law JCD); *Career* Middx Regt 1949, served Korea 1950; ordained priest Westminster Cathedral 1959; Dio of Westminster: vice chllr, vice officialis 1964–69, officialis 1969–76 and 1987–, vicar gen 1976–; papal chamberlain 1972, sec Canon Law Soc of GB and I 1986–89 (pres 1980–86), nat co-ordinator for Papal visit to England and Wales 1982, prelate of honour to HH the Pope 1987, canonical advsr to Br Mil Ordinariate 1987–; sec Old Brotherhood of English Secular Clergy 1992 (memb 1987); Order of the Holy Sepulchre: Knight 1984, Knight Commander 1991, prior Westminster Section 1996; hon memb Canon Law Soc of: Aust and NZ 1975, Canada 1979, America 1979; *Books* Marriage Annulment (1969, 3 edn 1990), Matrimonial Decisions of Great Britain and Ireland (ed, 1969–), The Code of Canon Law in English Translation (co-translator, 1983), The Canon Law: Letter and Spirit (co-ed, 1995); various articles in Heythrop Jl, Studia Canonica, Theological Digest, The Jurist; *Clubs* Anglo-Belgian; *Style*— The Rt Rev Mgr Ralph Brown; ✉ 8 Morpeth Terrace, London SW1P 1EQ (☎ 0171 798 9020, fax 0171 798 9077)

BROWN, Hon Sir Ralph Kilner; kt (1970), OBE (Mil, 1945), TD (1952), DL (Warwicks 1956); s of Rev Arthur Ernest Brown, CIE (d 1952), of The Manor House, Churchdown, Glos, and E Gertrude, *née* Parsons (d 1971); *b* 28 Aug 1909; *Educ* Kingswood Sch, Trinity Hall Cambridge (MA); *m* 1943, Cynthia Rosemary, da of Lt-Col George Vernon Breffit, MC; 1 s, 2 da; *Career* TA private 1938, 2 Lt 1939, WWII Maj OC Coy and DAQMG 1941, Lt Col AQMG 1943, Normandy - Germany 1944–45 (despatches), Brig HQ 21 Army Gp 1945, Col TARO 1952; called to the Bar Middle Temple 1934 (Harmsworth scholar), QC 1958, bencher Middle Temple 1964, master reader 1982, recorder Lincoln 1962, recorder Birmingham 1964, chm Warwicks QS 1964–67, judge Central Criminal Ct 1965–67, recorder and judge Liverpool 1967–69, judge of the High Ct Queen's Bench Div 1970–84, judge Employment Appeal Tbnl 1976–84; *Books* Top Brass, No Brass; *Recreations* watching cricket and athletics (rep Univ of Cambridge, Eng and GB, AAA champion 440 yds hurdles 1934); *Clubs* Naval and Military, Hawks (Cambridge); *Style*— The Hon Sir Ralph Kilner Brown, OBE, TD, DL; ✉ 174 Defoe House, Barbican, London EC2Y 8ND

BROWN, Ralph William John Jules; s of John F W Brown, and Heather R Laming; *b* 18 June 1957; *Educ* LSE (LLB); *m* 25 July 1992, Jennifer Jules; *Career* actor, writer and director; *Theatre* incl: West 1985, Deadlines 1986, Panic 1987, Macbeth 1987, Earwig 1990; *Television* incl: West 1986, Christabel 1988, Rules of Engagement 1989, The Black & Blue Lamp 1989, Say Hello to the Real Dr Snide 1990, Requiem Apache 1993, Devil's Advocate 1994, Karaoke 1995, Place of the Dead 1995, Ivanhoe 1996; *Films* incl: Withnail and I 1986, Buster 1987, Diamond Skulls 1988, Impromptu 1989, Alien III 1991, The Crying Game 1991, Undercover Blues 1992, Psychotherapy 1992, Wayne's World II 1993; as writer: Sanctuary (Samuel Beckett Award for Best First Play) 1987, Drive Away the Darkness 1988, Sanctuary DC 1989, Zone 1991, The Passion 1992–94, New Year's Day 1995; dir: Danny and the Deep Blue Sea 1995; *Style*— Ralph Brown, Esq; ✉ c/o ICM Ltd, Oxford House, 76 Oxford Street, London W1N 0AX (☎ 0171 636 6565, fax 0171 323 0101)

BROWN, Rev (Robert) Raymond; s of Robert Brown (d 1939), of Stockport, and Elsie, *née* Dudson (d 1970); *b* 24 March 1936; *Educ* Stockport Sch, Univ of Leeds (BA), Univ of Manchester (BD), Hartley Victoria Coll Manchester; *m* July 1959, Barbara, da of James Johnson; 1 da (Sally Anne b 6 Nov 1960), 3 s (Stephen Timothy b 5 Jan 1962, Simon Jonathan b 26 Aug 1963, Adam Robert b 7 Nov 1967); *Career* asst min Luton Industl Coll and Mission 1959–64, ordained Methodist min 1961, min Heald Green and Handforth 1964–67; RAF chaplain 1967–94: RAF Locking 1967–69, Bahrein 1969–71, Cosford 1971–73, Cyprus 1973–75, W Germany 1975–78, vice princ RAF Chaplain's Sch 1978–83, asst princ chaplain 1983–90, princ chaplain 1990–94; lay trg and devpt offr Church Extension Prog Melton Mowbray 1995–; QHC 1990–94; *Recreations* drama and music (as performer), writing articles and stories, walking, foreign travel; *Clubs* RAF; *Style*— The Rev R Raymond Brown; ✉ Trinity Cottage, 6 Church Terrace, Melton Mowbray, Leicestershire LE13 0PW (☎ 01664 61179)

BROWN, Richard Francis; s of Francis Edwin Brown (d 1981), and Eileen Margaret Edith, *née* Searle (d 1992); *b* 5 June 1949; *Educ* Chingford Co HS, Poly of Central London (DipArch); *m* 10 Sept 1977, Sally Elizabeth, da of Ernest James Little (d 1967); 2 s (Timothy b 1979, Matthew b 1981); *Career* architect; ptnr ATP Group Partnership 1985– (joined 1973); chm W Essex Chapter RIBA 1986–87, pres Lions Club Chingford 1984–85 (memb 1975–88), memb Lions Club Billericay 1988–; RIBA 1975, memb Architects and Surveyors' Inst 1984; *Recreations* photography, archery; *Style*— Richard Brown, Esq; ✉ 28 Carson Rd, Billericay, Essex CM11 1SA (☎ 01277 631020); ATP Group Partnership, Mayflower House, The Walk, Billericay, Essex CM12 9YB (☎ 01277 658662, fax 01277 652312, mobile 0860 267957)

BROWN, His Hon Judge Richard George; s of late Arthur Lawson Brown, and Ivy Abigail, *née* Hathaway; *b* 10 April 1945; *Educ* Bournville Grammar/Tech Sch Birmingham, LSE (LLB), Inns of Ct Sch of Law (Blackstone entrance exhbn); *m* 1 Jan 1969, Ann Patricia, *née* Wade; 2 s (Lawrence Richard b 14 Sept 1977 d 18 Nov 1980, Jeremy Lawrence Richard b 19 July 1985), 1 da (Elizabeth Ann b 23 April 1982); *Career* insurance clerk 1961–62, shop asst 1962–63, bus conductor 1963–64, trainee radio offr Merchant Navy 1964–65, taxi driver 1965–66, asst in maladjusted sch 1966–67, driver of public serv vehicle 1967–68; called to the Bar Middle Temple 1972, in practice 1972–92, recorder 1990–92 (asst recorder 1986–90), circuit judge (SE Circuit) 1992–, resident and liaison judge Lewes Combined Ct Centre 1996–; chm Bd of Govrs Farney Close Sch Bolney Sussex 1984–86; *Recreations* travel, sport, being with the family; *Style*— His Hon Judge Richard Brown; ✉ c/o Lewes Crown Court, High Street, Lewes, Sussex (☎ 01273 480400)

BROWN, His Hon Judge Robert; s of Robert Brown (d 1966), and Mary Lily, *née* Pullen; *b* 21 June 1943; *Educ* Arnold Sch Blackpool, Downing Coll Cambridge (BA, LLB); *m* 1, 1964 (m dis 1971) Susan; 1 s (Andrew Juston b 20 June 1964), 1 da (Jocelyn Fiona 15 Sept 1970), m 2, 3 Nov 1973 Carole, *née* Tait; 2 step s (James Francis b 12 May 1965, Benjamin William b 1 May 1967); *Career* called to the Bar Inner Temple 1968, standing counsel to DHSS Northern Circuit 1983–88, recorder of the Crown Court 1983–88, circuit judge (Northern Circuit) 1988–; *Recreations* golf; *Clubs* Royal Lytham St Anne's Golf; *Style*— His Hon Judge Robert Brown; ✉ c/o The Preston Court Administrator's Office, 10 Winckley Square, Preston PR1 3JJ (☎ 01772 821451)

BROWN, Robert Burnett (Bob); s of David Brown (d 1973), and Isabella, *née* Dow; *b* 10 Aug 1942; *Educ* Kirkcaldy HS, Univ of Edinburgh (BSc); *m* 16 Sept 1972, Anne, da of Gino Boschetti, of Harrow, Middx; *Career* DHSS: various jobs as trainee graduate 1967–71, princ Policy on Radiotherapy and Cancer 1971–74, princ Servs for Physically Disabled People 1974–79, asst sec Policy on Benefits for Sick and Disabled People 1979–83, asst sec mgmnt and efficiency Mgmnt and Personnel Office of Cabinet Office 1983–87; DSS: asst sec Policy on Income Support 1987–89, head Corp Mgmnt Div (grade 3) 1989–93, head Policy Div D 1993–; *Books* Government Purchasing (1984), Office Accommodation (1985); *Recreations* jazz, football, Greece; *Style*— Bob Brown, Esq; ✉ Department of Social Security, The Adelphi, 1–11 John Adam Street, London WC1N 6HT

BROWN, Robert Edward; s of Albert Edward Brown, of Carlisle, and Joan, *née* Powton (d 1991); *b* 25 Dec 1947; *Educ* Gordon Schs Huntly Aberdeenshire, Univ of Aberdeen (LLB); *m* 8 Dec 1977, Gwen Wilson, *née* Morris; 1 da (Julie Elizabeth b 2 Jan 1979), 1 s (David Andrew b 17 Oct 1981); *Career* legal apprentice rising to legal asst Edmonds and Ledingham Aberdeen 1969–72, procurator fiscal depute Dumbarton 1972–74, ptnr Ross Harper and Murphy 1975– (legal asst 1974–75); memb Glasgow District Cncl (Lib then Lib Dem) 1977–92; Parly candidate (Lib) Rutherglen 1974, 1979, 1983 and 1987, vice chm Policy Ctee Scottish Lib Democrats 1995–; chm Rutherglen CAB; memb: Law Soc of Scot 1971, Scot Law Agents' Soc 1975, Glasgow Bar Assoc 1975, Royal Faculty of Procurators 1992; *Recreations* politics, history; *Style*— Robert Brown, Esq; ✉ 1 Douglas Avenue, Burnside, Rutherglen, Glasgow G73 4RA (☎ 0141 552 6343); Ross Harper & Murphy, 163 Ingram Street, Glasgow G1 1DW (☎ 0141 552 6343, fax 0141 552 8150)

BROWN, Roger Garrett; s of Norman Garrett Brown (d 1945), of Ipswich, Suffolk, and Molly Beryl, *née* Pawlyn; *b* 24 Feb 1943; *Educ* Ipswich Sch; *m* 1971, Bridget, *née* O'Sullivan; 1 s (Michael b 31 March 1975), 1 da (Laura b 22 Nov 1979); *Career* CA; articled clerk Ballam and Partners Ipswich 1962–67, Cooper Brothers 1967–76; ptnr: Dearden Farrow 1976–87, Binder Hamlyn (following merger with Dearden Farrow) 1987–; treas Nat Shearwater Club; FCA (ACA 1968); *Recreations* sailing, classic cars, photography; *Clubs* Elite and Reliant Scimitar Car, Stone Sailing, Nat Shearwater, RYA; *Style*— Roger Brown, Esq; ✉ Binder Hamlyn, 20 Old Bailey, London EC4M 7BH (☎ 0171 489 9000, fax 0171 489 6060, car 0860 213658)

BROWN, Roger Glendenning; s of Charles Henry Brown, of Cuddington, Northwich, Cheshire, and Gwendoline Irene, *née* Evans (d 1980); *b* 10 Oct 1932; *Educ* Bemrose Sch, Univ of Manchester (BA(Arch)); *m* 8 Aug 1956, Betty Joy, da of Wilfred Rimmington (d 1964), of Derby; 1 s (Andrew Ashleigh b 26 Sept 1957), 1 da (Rosamund Lindsey b 30 Jan 1961); *Career* dep regnl architect to Liverpool RHB 1971–75, regnl architect to North Western RHA 1975–87, private practice 1987–94, ret; chm Component Devpt Gp DHSS 1975–87, pres Manchester Soc of Architects 1989–90; MRIBA 1957 (memb Cncl 1983–86); *Recreations* walking, measured drawings, railway modelling; *Style*— Roger Brown, Esq; ✉ Norley, Warrington, Cheshire

BROWN, Ronald Hedley; OBE (1945); s of Reginald Hedley Brown (d 1967), and Lilian, *née* Howard (d 1963); *b* 2 Feb 1914; *Educ* Cambridgeshire HS, Univ of London (BSc, DipEd); *m* 1, 12 Aug 1939, Margaret Caroline Linforth (d 1982), da of Edward Clifford Pitman (d 1963), of Alpheton, Suffolk; 1 s (Richard Hedley b 1951), 1 da (Patricia Carol b 1947); m 2, Rosemary Dorothy, *née* Carter; *Career* RAF: educn offr 1938–39, intelligence offr 1939–46, Flt Lt Bircham Newton 1939–41, Sqdn Ldr Iceland 1941–42, Staff Coll 1942, Sqdn Ldr N Russia 1943, Gibraltar 1943–45 (despatches 4 times); Colonial Serv 1947–63 (dir educn N Rhodesia 1959–63); chief examiner Univ of Cambridge Syndicate GCE A Level (general studies) 1979–89; pres Devon Beekeepers' Assoc, former ed Beekeeping; *Books* 1000 Years of Devon Beekeeping (1973), Beeswax (1981), Beekeeping - A Seasonal Guide (1985), Honey Bees - A Guide to Management (1988), All Round the Compass (RAF stories, 1992), Great Masters of Beekeeping (1993), Ex Africa (1996); *Recreations* beekeeping, foreign travel; *Style*— Ronald Brown, Esq, OBE; ✉ 20 Parkhurst Rd, Torquay, Devon (☎ 01803 327563)

BROWN, Roy Drysdale; s of William Andrew Brown (d 1975), of Cambridge, and Isabelle Drysdale, *née* Davidson (d 1987); *b* 4 Dec 1946; *Educ* Tonbridge Sch, UCL (BSc Mech Engrg), Harvard Business Sch (MBA); *m* 1978, Carol Jane, da of Dr Keene Manning Wallace, of Charleston, S Carolina; 2 s (Alexander b 1980, Cameron b 1984); *Career* Univ Scholarship course GEC 1965–69, commercial gen mangr Vosper Thornycroft Ltd 1972–74; Unilever PLC: industl conslt 1975–77, mktg mangr Uracem Div 1978–80, commercial dir Food Industries Ltd 1981–82, chm Pamol Plantations Sdn Bhd 1982–86, chm PBI Cambridge Ltd 1987–88, tech dir Birds Eye Walls Ltd 1988–90, chm Lever Brothers Ltd 1991–92, regnl dir Africa, Middle E and Agribusiness and main bd dir Unilever PLC/NV 1992– (with additional responsibilty for Central and Eastern Europe 1994 and Turkey 1995, currently gp pres for food and beverages Europe); non-exec dir GKN plc 1996–; CEng 1983, FIME 1983, FIEE 1990; *Recreations* classical music, opera, golf, carpentry, photography, military history; *Style*— Roy Brown, Esq; ✉ Unilever PLC, Unilever House, PO Box 68, Blackfriars, London EC4P 4BQ (☎ 0171 822 6301); Hollybank, 44 Holmewood Ridge, Langton Green, Tunbridge Wells, Kent TN3 0ED (☎ 01892 862938)

BROWN, Russell Milton; s of Harry Louis Brown (d 1974), and Murielle Katherine, *née* Wartski (d 1983); *b* 20 May 1929; *Educ* Stowe; *Career* Nat Serv RAPC 1951–53; fin offr and clerk to the Govrs Sadler's Wells Theatre 1956–63, chief accountant and prodn controller RSC 1963–66, bursar RCA 1966–86; currently dir Scottish Ballet; tstee: Royal Ballet Benevolent Fund, Dancers Resettlement Fund, Areopagitica Educnl Tst; hon fell RCA 1986; memb Royal Acad of Dancing 1980, FRGS 1996, FCA; Chevalier de L'Ordre Nationale de Merite 1970; *Books* Sadler's Wells Theatre Ballet (ed, 1955); *Recreations* ballet, opera, music, theatre, foreign travel; *Style*— Russell Brown, Esq; ✉ Flat 8, 284 Old Brompton Rd, London SW5 9HR (☎ 0171 373 3141); Oak Tree Cottage, Thornborough, Bucks

BROWN, Prof Sally Ann; da of Fred Compigné-Cook (d 1962), and Gwen, *née* Barrett (d 1992); *b* 15 Dec 1935; *Educ* Bromley HS GPDST, UCL (state scholar, BSc), Smith Coll Mass USA (Fulbright scholar, English Speaking Union fell, elected Sigma Xi (US honour soc for sci), MA), Univ of Stirling (PhD), Jordanhill Coll (CertEd); *m* 21 March 1959, Charles Victor Brown (d 1991); 2 s (Keith b 19 June 1962, Ric b 7 Dec 1963); *Career* lectr in Physics Univ of Ife Nigeria 1960–64, princ teacher in sci St Bride's Sch Helensburgh 1964–70, sr research fell Univ of Stirling 1971–80, assessment and research advsr Scottish Educn Dept 1980–84, dir Scottish Cncl for Research in Educn 1986–90; Univ of Stirling: prof of educn 1990–, dep princ (pro-vice-chllr) 1996–; pres Br Educational Research Assoc 1990–91 (memb 1975–); chm: Ctee on a Nat Theatre Resource Scottish Arts Cncl 1994, Central Scotland Child Protection Ctee 1995–; memb: Scottish Educational Research Assoc 1975, American Educational Research Assoc 1982, General Teaching Cncl for Scotland 1990–94; fell Scottish Cncl for Research in Educn 1992, Cwlth fell Vice-Chllrs of Australia 1995; FRSA 1989, FRSE 1996; *Publications* author of over 100 pubns incl: What Do They Know? A Review of Referenced Assessment (1980), Making Sense of Teaching (1993), Research in Education: What Influence on Policy and Practice? (1994); *Recreations* squash, theatre, music; *Clubs* Commonwealth Trust; *Style*— Prof Sally Brown, FRSE; ✉ Department of Education, University of Stirling, Stirling FK9 4LA (☎ 01786 467600, fax 01786 467633, e-mail sab1@stirling.ac.uk)

BROWN, Dr (James) Scott; *b* 28 November 1954, Glasgow; *Educ* Queen's Univ Belfast (MB BCh, BAO, MD), DRCOG, DCH (RCPSI), FRCGP (London); *m* Anne; 2 da (Susan, Alison), 1 s (Finlay); *Career* SHO: in gen med Royal Victoria Hosp Belfast 1980–81 (jr house offr 1979–80), in paediatrics Royal Belfast Hosp for Sick Children 1981–82, in obstetrics and gynaecology Waveney Hosp Ballymena Co Antrim 1982–83; GP registrar Portglenone Health Centre Co Antrim 1983–84, princ in gen practice Coleraine Co Londonderry and MO to Univ of Ulster at Coleraine 1984–; GP trainer 1989–, GP postgrad tutor 1992–; Royal Coll of Gen Practitioners: NI Faculty rep on London Cncl 1989–, memb Clinical Research Div 1990–93, memb AIDS/HIV Working Pty 1991–93, chm Servs to Membs and Faculties Div 1992–93, chm Publishing Mgmnt Gp 1992–, chm Services Network 1993–, memb Central Exec Ctee 1993–, chm PR Gp 1993–94, memb RCGP/DOH Stress Fellowship Steering Gp 1995–, memb RCGP Reaccreditation Fellowship Steering Gp 1995–, vice chm RCGP 1996–; Astra/Shell Research Trg Fellowship (RCGP) 1988–90, Campbell Young Prize (NI Faculty RCGP) 1988 and 1990, hon research fell Dept of Gen Practice Queen's Univ Belfast 1988–; author of various articles in peer-reviewed jls; memb NI Medico-Legal Assoc; *Recreations* golf, choral music singing, theatre; *Style*— Dr Scott Brown; ✉ The Royal College of General Practitioners, 14 Princes Gate, Hyde Park, London SW7 1PU (☎ 0171 581 3232); Mountsandel Surgery, 4 Mountsandel Road, Coleraine, Co Londonderry BT52 1JB (☎ 01265 42650, fax 01265 321000)

BROWN, Rt Hon Lord Justice; Rt Hon Sir Simon Denis; kt (1984), PC (1992); s of Denis Baer Brown (d 1981), and Edna Elizabeth, *née* Abrahams; *b* 9 April 1937; *Educ* Stowe Sch, Worcester Coll Oxford (BA); *m* 31 May 1963, Jennifer, da of (Robert) Prosper Gedye Buddicom (d 1968); 1 da (Abigail b 1964), 2 s (Daniel b 1966, Benedict 1969); *Career* called to the Bar Middle Temple 1961 (Harmsworth scholar), recorder of the Crown Court 1979–84, first jr treas counsel Common Law 1979–84, master of the Bench Hon Soc of Middle Temple 1980–, judge of the High Court of Justice (Queen's Bench Div) 1984–92, Lord Justice of Appeal 1992–; hon fell Worcester Coll Oxford 1993; Liveryman Worshipful Co of Butchers; *Recreations* golf, skiing, theatre, reading; *Clubs* Denham Golf; *Style*— The Rt Hon Lord Justice Simon Brown; ✉ Royal Courts of Justice, Strand, London WC2A 2LL

BROWN, Simon John Saville; s of Ven Robert Saville Brown, and Charlotte, *née* Furber; *b* 6 July 1950; *Educ* Berkhamsted Sch, Selwyn Coll Cambridge (MA); *m*; 2 c; *Career* with Slaughter and May 1972–77 (admitted slr 1974), ptnr Denton Hall 1980– (joined 1977); *Recreations* jogging, impersonating Rev Gary Davis; *Style*— Simon Brown, Esq; ✉ Denton Hall, Five Chancery Lane, Clifford's Inn, London EC4A 1BU

BROWN, Sir (Frederick Herbert) Stanley; kt (1967), CBE (1959); s of Clement Brown, of Birmingham, and Annie S Brown; *b* 9 Dec 1910; *Educ* King Edward's Sch Birmingham, Univ of Birmingham; *m* 1937, Marjorie Nancy, da of William Astell Brown, of Sutton Coldfield; 2 da; *Career* chm CEGB 1965–72; FEng 1976 (founder fell), FIEE, FIMechE; *Style*— Sir Stanley Brown, CBE, FEng; ✉ Compton Suite, Northleach Court, High Street, Northleach, Glos GL54 3PQ (☎ 01451 860218)

BROWN, Sir (Arthur James) Stephen; KBE (1967); s of Arthur Mogg Brown, and Ada Kelk, *née* Upton; *b* 15 Feb 1906; *Educ* Taunton, Univ of Bristol; *m* 1935, Margaret Alexandra, da of late D L McArthur; 1 s, 1 da; *Career* former dir Fairey Co; dep chm Chloride Group 1965–73; chm: Stone-Platt Industries Ltd 1968–73, Molins Ltd 1971–78; dir Porvair Ltd 1971–78; fndr memb Export Cncl for Europe 1960; pres: Engrg Employers Fedn 1964–65, CBI 1966–68; memb Nat Econ Devpt Cncl 1969–71; *Style*— Sir Stephen Brown, KBE; ✉ Flat 20, Danny House, Hurstpierpoint, W Sussex (☎ 01278 833755)

BROWN, Rt Hon Sir Stephen; kt (1975), PC (1983); s of Wilfrid Brown (d 1972), of Longdon Green, Staffs, and Nora Elizabeth Brown; *b* 3 Oct 1924; *Educ* Malvern, Queens' Coll Cambridge; *m* 1951, Patricia Ann, da of Richard Good, of Tenbury Wells, Worcs; 2 s (twins), 3 da; *Career* served WWII as Lt RNVR; called to the Bar Inner Temple 1949, bencher 1974, dep chm Staffs QS 1963–71, recorder W Bromwich 1965–71, QC 1966, a recorder and hon recorder W Bromwich 1972–75, judge of the High Court of Justice (Queen's Bench) 1977–83 (Family Div 1975–77), presiding judge Midland and Oxford Circuit 1977–81, former memb Parole Bd England & Wales, Lord Justice of Appeal 1983–88, pres Family Div 1988–; memb Advsy Cncl on Penal System 1977; treas Inner Temple 1994; chm Cncl Malvern Coll 1976–94; *Recreations* sailing; *Clubs* Garrick, Birmingham; *Style*— The Rt Hon Sir Stephen Brown; ✉ President's Chambers, Royal Courts of Justice, Strand, London WC2A 2LL

BROWN, Prof Stephen Frederick; s of Francis Maurice Brown (d 1989), of Pembroke, and Ruth Audrey, *née* Swallow (d 1987); *b* 29 Sept 1939; *Educ* Pembroke GS, Univ of Nottingham (BSc, PhD, DSc); *m* 27 April 1963, Marie Josephe Maryse, da of Jean Jacques André la Hausse de Lalouvière; 3 s (Andrew Stephen Francis la Hausse b 9 March 1964, Timothy Peter la Hausse b 4 Jan 1966, Christopher Giles la Hausse b 15 Aug 1967), 1 da (Michelle Anne la Hausse b 22 Sept 1969); *Career* jr engr Sir Robert McAlpine (S Wales) Ltd 1960–61; jr asst engr: Dormon London (Africa) Ltd 1961–62, Scott Wilson Kirkpatrick and Partners 1962–63; Univ of Nottingham: sr res asst Dept of Civil Engrg 1963–65, lectr in civil engrg 1965–74, sr lectr 1974–78, reader 1978–82, prof of civil engrg 1982–, head of dept 1989–94, dean of engrg 1992–94, pro vice chllr 1994–; dir SWK Pavement Engineering Ltd 1985–, dir and pres SWK Pavement Engineering Inc 1993–; Br Geotechnical Soc: Prize 1976, Rankine lectr 1996; Instn of Highways and Tport Croda Award 1980, 1984 and 1989; FIHT 1979, FICE 1982, FEng 1992; *Publications* An Introduction to the Analytical Design of Bituminous Pavements (Univ of Nottingham, 1980), Cycling Loading of Soils (Univ of Nottingham, jt ed, 1991), over 160 technical papers on pavement engrg and soil mechanics; *Recreations* house maintenance, gardening, photography; *Clubs* Univ of Nottingham; *Style*— Prof Stephen Brown, FEng; ✉ Department of Civil Engineering, The University of Nottingham, University Park, Nottingham NG7 2RD (☎ 0115 951 3900, fax 0115 951 3909)

BROWN, Stephen Kenneth (Steve); s of Kenneth Alan Thomas Brown, of Wimbledon, London, and Valerie Ellen May, *née* Phillips; *b* 15 July 1962; *Educ* Wallington HS; *m* Aug 1993, Valerie Fish, of St Louis; *Career* professional darts player; county rep: Surrey 1978–80, London 1981–92; championship wins incl: BDO Mayday Festival 1986 and 1987, Thames TV Cockney Classic 1986 and 1987, Turnhout Open 1987, Antwerp Open 1988 and 1989, Dutch Open 1988, N American Open 1988 and 1989, Winmau Dutch Masters 1989, Rotterdam Open 1989, Flanders Open 1989, NDAGB Nat Pairs 1989, USA Int Challenge of Champions 1989, Malta Open Pairs 1989 and 1990, London Champion of Champions 1990, Limburg Open 1990, Venlo Open 1990, Swiss Open 1990 and 1991, Texas Open 1990 and 1991, Boston Open 1991, Cleveland Classic 1991, Little Rock Open 1991, Nashville Classic 1991, New Orleans Open 1991, Dallas Classic Pairs 1991, Swiss Open Pairs 1991; ranked number 4: World Darts Fedn 1990, World Darts Cncl 1994; memb: World Darts Fedn, American Darts Orgn, American Professional Dart Player's Assoc; *Recreations* astronomy, golf, photography, war poetry; *Style*— Steve Brown, Esq; ✉ c/o Sports Administration Services, 14 Melrose Tudor, Plough Lane, Wallington, Surrey SM6 8LR (☎ 0181 669 0471, fax 0181 401 2534)

BROWN, Prof Stewart Jay; s of Vernon George Brown, of St Charles, Illinois, USA, and Marion Eleanor, *née* Little; *b* 8 July 1951; *Educ* Glenbard West HS, Univ of Illinois (BA), Univ of Chicago (MA, PhD); *m* 2 Sept 1972, Teri Beth, da of Thomas Dorsey Hopkins (d 1981); 1 s (Adam b 1977), 1 da (Elizabeth b 1980); *Career* Whiting fell in humanities Univ of Chicago 1979–80, asst to Dean and lectr in history N Western Univ 1980–82, assoc prof and asst head Dept of History Univ of Georgia 1982–88, prof of ecclesiastical history and Senatus Assessor on Univ Ct Univ of Edinburgh 1988–; ed Scottish Historical Review 1993–; memb Cncl: Scot Church History Soc, Scot Catholic Historical Assoc; FRHistS; *Books* Thomas Chalmers and the Godly Commonwealth In Scotland (1982), Scotland in the Age of the Disruption (with M Fry, 1993), William Robertson and the Expansion of Empire (1997); *Recreations* swimming, hill-walking; *Style*— Prof Stewart J Brown; ✉ 160 Craigleith Hill Ave, Edinburgh EH4 2NB (☎ 0131 539 2863); Department of Ecclesiastical History, University of Edinburgh, New College, Mound Place, Edinburgh EH1 2LU (☎ 0131 650 8958)

BROWN, Stuart Christopher; QC (1991); s of Geoffrey Howard Brown (d 1960), of Middlesbrough, and Olive Lilian Baum, *née* Ford; *b* 4 Sept 1950; *Educ* Acklam HS Middlesbrough, Worcester Coll Oxford (BA, BCL); *m* 7 July 1973, Dr Imogen Brown, da of Edward Arthur Lucas, of Hitchin, Herts; 2 da (Sophie b 1976, Katherine b 1979); *Career* called to the Bar Inner Temple 1974, in practice N Eastern Circuit, asst recorder 1988–92, recorder of the Crown Court 1992–; memb Leeds & W Riding Medico-Legal Soc (pres 1988–90); *Recreations* theatre, windsurfing; *Style*— Stuart C Brown, Esq, QC; ✉ Pearl Chambers, 22 East Parade, Leeds LS1 5BU (☎ 0113 245 2702, fax 0113 242 0683)

BROWN, Terence Gibbin; s of Rex Brown (d 1990), of Peterborough, and Mary Kathleen, *née* Gibbin (d 1971); *b* 14 Sept 1943; *Educ* All Souls Roman Catholic Sch Peterborough, King's Sch Peterborough, Sch of Architecture Architectural Assoc (Mastic Asphalt Assoc scholar, AA Dipl, RIBA pt III); *m* 1, 10 June 1972 (m dis 1991), Jacqueline Lesley Chinnery; 1 da (Sophie Madelaine b 26 June 1975), 1 s (Edric Samuel b 29 Sept 1977); m 2, 29 Aug 1992, Lucille Julia Cooper, da of Thomas Higgins; *Career* worked for Howard V Lobb & Partners (before completion of AA course); GMW Partnership: joined 1969, assoc 1979, design ptnr 1984, a sr ptnr 1991–; highly commended Br Construction Indust Awards 1990, MIPIM Euro Shopping Centre of the Year (St Enoch Centre Glasgow) 1991; memb ARCUK 1971, RIBA 1971; memb: AA 1969, London Assoc of Conslt Architects 1989, Inst of Dirs 1990, Twentieth Century Soc 1993, Town & Country Planning Assoc 1993; friend of the Royal Acad 1993, fell RSA 1995; *Style*— Terence Brown, Esq; ✉ 24 West Hill Road, London SW18 1LN (☎ 0181 874 4505); Senior Partner, GMW Partnership, PO Box 1613, 239 Kensington High Street, London W8 6SL (☎ 0171 937 8020, fax 0171 937 5815)

BROWN, Sir Thomas; kt (1974); s of Ephraim Hugh and Elizabeth Brown; *b* 11 Oct 1915; *Educ* Royal Belfast Academical Inst; *m* 2 Sept 1988, Dr Eleanor A Thompson; *Career* admitted slr 1938; chm Eastern Health and Social Servs Bd NI (formerly NI Hosps Authy) 1967–84, ret; *Recreations* boating; *Style*— Sir Thomas Brown; ✉ Westgate, Portaferry, Co Down, Northern Ireland BT22 1PF (☎ 0124 77 28309)

BROWN, Timothy Colin; s of Peter Brindley Brown, of Isles Court, Ramsbury, Wilts, and Margaret Jean, *née* McIntosh; *b* 20 Sept 1957; *Educ* Eton, RMA Sandhurst; *m* 24 Jan 1987 (m dis 1995), Lady Vanessa Petronel Pelham, yst da of 7 Earl of Yarborough; *Career* 4/7 Royal Dragoon Gds 1976–82 (A/Capt 1980); City & Commercial Communications plc 1983–91 (dir 1987–91), jt chief exec Tavistock Communications Ltd 1992– (dir 1991–); *Recreations* skiing, shooting, backgammon; *Clubs* Cavalry and Guards', Lansdowne; *Style*— Timothy Brown, Esq; ✉ Tavistock Communications Ltd, 1 Angel Court, London EC2R 7HX (☎ 0171 600 2288)

BROWN, Timothy Frank (Tim); s of Frank Steel Brown, of The Furrows, Borstal, Rochester, Kent, and Katherine Mary, *née* Osenton; *b* 7 Nov 1944; *Educ* Sir Joseph Williamson's Mathematical Sch; *m* 1 July 1967, Kathleen Patricia, da of Frederick Geoffrey Smith (d 1975); 2 s (Matthew Philip b 1975, Michael James b 1980), 2 da (Karen Patricia b 1971, Amy Clare b 1978); *Career* CA; Larking & Larking 1963–68, Deloitte's 1968–69, Philips & Drew 1969–85 (until acquired by UBS Ltd in 1985), md UBS Ltd 1985–; FCA 1968, ATII 1969; *Style*— Tim Brown, Esq; ✉ Angley Lake, Cranbrook, Kent TN17 2PR (☎ 01580 714248); UBS Ltd, 100 Liverpool Street, London EC2M 2RH (☎ 0171 901 3333)

BROWN, Prof Tom; s of Tom Brown, of Barnsley, and Catherine, *née* Beardshall; *b* 10 Nov 1952; *Educ* Broadway GS Barnsley, Univ of Bradford (BTech, PhD, Griffin and George prize); *m* Dorcas Jemema Selverani, da of Jacob Samuel; 1 s (Tom b 23 Sept 1982), 1 da (Asha b 20 April 1984); *Career* postdoctoral res: Dept of Chemistry Univ of Nottingham 1978–79, Dyson Perrins Laboratory Univ of Oxford 1979–82, Chemical Laboratory Univ of Cambridge 1982–85; prof of nucleic acid chemistry Univ of Edinburgh 1985–94, prof of bio-organic chemistry Univ of Southampton 1995–; dir Oligonucleotide Service Wellcome Trust (OSWEL), conslt Chemistry Ctee SERC 1986; memb Ctee Edinburgh Centre for Molecular Recognition; Griffin and George Prize Univ of Bradford 1975, MakDougall-Brisbane Prize RSE 1992, Josef Loschmidt Award RSC 1992, Caledonian res fell RSE 1993; author of numerous pubns; CChem, FRSC, FRSE; *Style*— Prof Tom Brown, FRSE; ✉ Department of Chemistry, University of Southampton, Highfield, Southampton SO17 1BJ (☎ 01703 592974, fax 01703 592991)

BROWN, (Harold) Vivian Bigley; s of Alec Sidney Brown, of Leeds, and Joyce, *née* Bigley; *b* 20 Aug 1945; *Educ* Leeds GS, St John's Coll Oxford (BA), St Cross Coll Oxford (BPhil); *m* 25 July 1970, Jean Josephine, da of Sir Eric Blacklock Bowyer, KCB (d 1963); 2 s (Matthew b 1973, Oliver b 1974); *Career* entered Miny of Technol 1970, private sec to Perm Sec DTI 1972–74; commercial sec: Br Embassy Jedda 1975–79, DTI 1979–86 and 1989–, Cabinet Office 1986–89; dir Business Link DTI 1994–; *Books* Islamic Philosophy and The Classical Tradition (with S M Stern and A Hourani, 1972); *Recreations* cycling, canoeing, piano; *Style*— Vivian Brown, Esq; ✉ Department of Trade and Industry, 1 Victoria Street, London SW1H 0ET

BROWN, Prof William Arthur; s of Prof Arthur Joseph Brown, of Leeds, and Joan Hannah Margaret Brown; *b* 22 April 1945; *Educ* Leeds GS, Wadham Coll Oxford (BA); *Career* economic asst NBPI 1966–68, res assoc Univ of Warwick 1968–70; SSRC's Industl Res Unit Univ of Warwick: res fell 1970–79, dep dir 1979–81, dir 1981–85; Univ of Cambridge: Montague Burton prof of industl rels 1985–, fell Wolfson Coll 1985–; chm: Faculty of Economics and Politics 1992–, Sch of Humanities and Social Sciences 1993–; *Books* Piecework Bargaining (1973), The Changing Contours of British Industrial Relations (1981); *Recreations* gardening, walking; *Style*— Prof William A Brown; ✉ Wolfson College, Cambridge CB3 9BB; Faculty of Economics & Politics, Cambridge CB3 9DD (☎ 01223 335236)

BROWN, William Charles Langdon; CBE (1992, OBE 1982); s of Charles Leonard Brown (d 1952), and Kathleen May, *née* Tizzard (d 1988); *b* 9 Sept 1931; *Educ* John Ruskin Sch Croydon, Ashbourne GS Derbyshire; *m* 14 Feb 1959, Nachiko, da of Dr Eiji Sagawa (d 1952), of Tokyo, Japan; 1 s (Carl b 1959), 2 da (Lillian b 1963, Naomi b 1967); *Career* Nat Serv RAF 1949–51; Westminster Bank 1947–54; Standard Chartered Bank (formerly Chartered Bank of India, Aust and China): Tokyo 1954–59, Bangkok 1959–62, Hong Kong 1962–69, Singapore 1969–72, Bangkok 1972–75, area gen mangr Hong Kong 1975–87, sr gen mangr (London) for Asia Pacific Region 1987, dep chm 1989–91; Standard Chartered plc: exec dir 1987, md 1988, dep chm and dep gp chief exec 1988–91, non-exec dir 1991–94; non-exec dir: Hong Kong Investment Trust PLC 1991–, Kexim Bank (UK) Ltd 1992–, Arbuthnot Latham & Co Ltd 1993–; chm Atlantis Japan Growth Fund Ltd 1996–; unofficial memb of Legislative Cncl of Hong Kong 1980–85; Hon Doctorate in Social Science Chinese Univ Hong Kong 1987; FCIB, FInstD; *Recreations* mountain walking, skiing, yoga, philately, photography, clasical music; *Clubs* Oriental, RAC; *Style*— William Brown, Esq, CBE; ✉ Penthouse B, 15 Portman Square, London W1H 9HD (☎ 0171 487 5741, fax 0171 486 3005); Appleshaw, 11 Central Ave, Findon Valley, Worthing, Sussex BN14 ODS

BROWN, Dr William Christopher; OBE (1966); *b* 16 Sept 1928; *Educ* Univ of London (BSc), Imperial Coll London (PhD, DIC); *Career* chartered civil/consulting engr and designer; Freeman Fox & Partners 1951–85: asst designer to late Sir Gilbert Roberts and site engr 1951–56, princ designer 1956–70, ptnr 1970–85; i/c design and construction of bridges incl: Forth 1966, Severn and Wye 1966, Auckland Harbour 1969, Erskine 1971, Bosphorus 1973, Humber 1981; engr and project dir 2nd Bosphorus suspension bridge and nat motorway (Turkish Govt appt) 1985–87; fndr ptnr Brown Beech & Associates 1987–; lead designer Messina Strait road and rail bridge 1993, designer Dardanelles highway span 1994; additional experience in the design of special large and modern cranes and moving structures; holder of various patents; recipient: MacRobert Award for Innovation in Bridge Design (jtly) 1969, various British Constructional Steelwork Assoc and other design awards, various honours and awards from overseas instns; RSA: fell and vice pres, Master Faculty of Royal Design for Indust 1983–85; memb: Steel Cncl, Int Assoc of Bridge and Structural Engrg; fell Imperial Coll 1987; CEng, MICE, RDI 1977, Hon FRIBA 1978; *Publications* author of various technical papers in learned jls; *Style*— Dr William Brown, OBE, RDI; ✉ Brown Beech & Associates, Consultant Engineers, Orchard House, Adam & Eve Mews, 167–169 Kensington High Street, London W8 6SH (☎ 0171 938 3131, fax 0171 937 9776)

BROWNE, *see:* Gore Browne

BROWNE, Anthony George; s of Aloysious Browne, of London, and Frances, *née* Gurney; *b* 18 June 1950; *Educ* Downside, BNC Oxford (MA); *m* 15 Nov 1969, Monique Odette, da of Maxime Marnat (d 1965), of Paris; 2 da (Geraldine b 1970, Emily b 1972); *Career* CA 1974; Price Waterhouse: joined 1971, Exchequer and Audit Dept 1980–82, ptnr i/c privatisation servs 1983–89, ptnr i/c corp fin Australasia 1990–92, ptnr i/c corp fin and recovery UK 1992–94, memb UK Exec 1992–94, head of corp fin and recovery Europe 1994–, memb Euro Mgmnt Bd 1994–, world head of corp fin 1996–; memb Gen Cncl United World Coll of the Atlantic 1996–; FCA 1975; *Books* Guide to Evaluating Policy Effectiveness; *Recreations* sailing, opera, art, literature; *Clubs* Reform, Royal Cruising, Royal Southern Yacht; *Style*— Anthony Browne, Esq; ✉ Caley House, 74 Leopold Rd, Wimbledon, London SW19 7JQ (☎ 0181 946 8196); Price Waterhouse, Southwark Towers, 32 London Bridge St, London SE1 9SY (☎ 0171 939 3000, fax 0171 939 2528)

BROWNE, Benjamin Chapman; s of Benjamin Chapman Browne (d 1968), of Park House, Balsham, Cambs, and Marjorie Grace Hope, *née* Hope-Gill; *b* 18 May 1953; *Educ* Eton, Trinity Coll Cambridge (BA); *m* 28 July 1979, Sara Katharine, da of Brian Pangbourne, of Hythe, Hants; 2 s (Benjamin Chapman b 22 Dec 1982, Edward Pangbourne b 1 April 1985), 1 da (Rebecca Katharine b 24 April 1989); *Career* admitted slr 1978; Lovell White and King 1976–79, Morrell Peel and Gamlen Oxford 1979–81; Clyde and Co: joined 1981, ptnr London 1985, res ptnr Dubai 1989–90, currently ptnr Guildford; *Recreations* walking, tennis, gardening, family; *Style*— Benjamin Browne, Esq; ✉ The Old Vicarage, Church Road, Steep, nr Petersfield, Hants GU32 2DB (☎ 01730 233050); Clyde and Co, Beaufort House, Chertsey Street, Guildford, Surrey GU1 4HA (☎ 01483 31161, fax 01483 567330, telex 859477 CLYDE G)

BROWNE, Benjamin James; QC (1996); s of Percy Basil Browne, of Ford House, Silverton, Exeter, Devon, and Jenefer Mary, *née* Petherick; *b* 25 April 1954; *Educ* Eton, Christ Church Oxford (MA); *m* 30 May 1987, Juliet Mary, da of Maj Geoffrey Beresford Heywood; 1 s (Samuel James Timothy b 14 July 1992), 1 da (Matilda Jane b 4 Oct 1989); *Career* called to the Bar Inner Temple 1976; *Recreations* country pursuits, gardening; *Clubs* Boodle's; *Style*— Benjamin Browne, Esq, QC; ✉ 2 Temple Gardens, Temple, London EC4Y 9AY (☎ 0171 583 6041, fax 0171 583 2094)

BROWNE, (John) Colin Clarke; s of Ernest Browne, JP (d 1964), of Lisburn, Co Antrim, N Ireland, and Isobel Sarah, *née* McVitie; *b* 25 Oct 1945; *Educ* Wallace HS Lisburn, Trinity Coll Dublin (BA); *m* 3 March 1984, Karen Lascelles Barr, da of Ian Barr (d 1995), of Edinburgh; 1 s; *Career* joined Post Office 1969, head of Bd Secretariat Post Office 1977–80, dir Chm's Office BT 1981–85, chief exec Broadband Servs BT 1985–86; dir of corp relations: BT 1986–94, BBC 1994–; former dir MTV Europe and chm Children's Channel; non-exec dir Health Educn Authy 1996–; MIPR; *Recreations* sport, music, reading; *Clubs* Tulse Hill Hockey (pres); *Style*— Colin Browne, Esq; ✉ Stokenchurch Street, London SW6; BBC Corporate Affairs, Broadcasting House, London W1A 1AA (☎ 0171 765 5531)

BROWNE, Desmond John Michael; QC (1990); s of Sir Denis Browne, KCVO, FRCS (d 1967), of London, and Lady Moyra Browne, DBE, *née* Ponsonby; *b* 5 April 1947; *Educ* Eton, New Coll Oxford; *m* 1 Sept 1973, Jennifer Mary, da of Frank Wilmore, of Brierfield, Lancs; 2 da (Natasha b 1974, Harriet b 1976); *Career* called to the Bar Gray's Inn 1969, recorder of the Crown Court 1994–; *Recreations* Australiana, Venice, the South Downs; *Clubs* Brooks's, Beefsteak; *Style*— Desmond Browne, Esq, QC; ✉ 5 Raymond Buildings, Gray's Inn, London WC1R 5BP (☎ 0171 242 2902, fax 0171 831 2686)

BROWNE, Hon Dominick Geoffrey Thomas; s and h of 4 Baron Oranmore and Browne, *qv*, and his 1 w Mildred Helen (d 1980), da of Hon Thomas Egerton; *b* 1 July 1929; *m* 25 Oct 1957 (m dis 1974), Sara Margaret, da of late Dr Herbert Wright, of Dublin; *Career* poet, author; *Style*— The Hon Dominick Browne; ✉ 6 Kensington Square, London W8 5EB

BROWNE, (Harold) Godfree Rodan; s of Robert Hugh Browne (d 1994), of Augusta, Western Australia, and Jean Eleanor Douglas, *née* Rodan (d 1984); *b* 19 Sept 1940; *Educ* Uppingham, Univ of London (LLB); *m* 1, 18 Dec 1965 (m dis 1989), Frances Mary, da of late Francis Joseph Woods, of Luton; 1 s (Christopher), 1 da (Mary (Mrs Wood)); m 2, 11 April 1992, Rose Mairi Smither, da of late William Mortimer Zanoni Bailey, of Chelmsford; *Career* magistrates' cts S Rhodesian Civil Serv 1958–68, advocate Rhodesia 1968–70 (Botswana 1969), lectr Herts Educn Ctee 1970–71, practising barr 1972–; former chm Luton Churches Housing Ltd, memb Ctee Family Housing Assoc; regnl vol offr (Thames) Maritime Vol Serv 1995; FIMgt 1981, MRIN 1981; *Recreations* cruising and offshore racing; *Clubs* Royal Ocean Racing; *Style*— Godfree Browne, Esq; ✉ Serjeants' Inn, Temple, London EC4Y 1LT (☎ 0171 583 0659)

BROWNE, Henry; s of Henry Clarence Browne (d 1974), and Veva Helen, *née* Symons (d 1978); *b* 11 July 1944; *Educ* Felsted, Gstaad International Switzerland; *m* 30 May 1969, Marion Carole, da of Charles Anthony Wenninger (d 1991), of Poole, Dorset; 1 s (Stephen Henry b 15 Dec 1975), 1 da (Juliette Caroline b 30 Nov 1971); *Career* memb Lloyd's 1972, chm Falcon Holdings plc 1974–; Freeman City of London 1990, Liveryman Worshipful Co of Painter-Stainers 1991; *Recreations* golf; *Clubs* Moor Park Golf, RAC; *Style*— Henry Browne, Esq; ✉ Falcon Holdings plc, Walker House, Boundary St, London E2 7JG (☎ 0171 739 8456, fax 0171 729 5695)

BROWNE, John Ernest Douglas de la Valette; s of Col Ernest Coigny de la Valette Browne, OBE, of Woodside House, Freshford, nr Bath, and late Victoria Mary Eugene, *née* Douglas; *b* 17 Oct 1938; *Educ* Malvern, RMA Sandhurst, Cranfield Inst of Technol (MSc), Harvard Business Sch (MBA); *m* 1965 (m dis 1983), Elizabeth Jeannette Marguerite, *née* Garthwaite; m 2, 1986, Elaine Boylen, *née* Schmid; *Career* served Grenadier Gds Br Guyana (bn pilot), Cyprus, BAOR 1959–67, Capt 1963, TA Grenadier Gds (Vol) 1981–91, Maj 1986; associate: Morgan Stanley & Co NY 1969–72, Pember & Boyle London 1972–74; dir ME ops European Banking Co Ltd 1974–78; memb Westminster City Cncl 1974–78, MP (C) Winchester 1979–92; memb: Treasy Select Ctee 1982–87, Social Security Select Ctee 1990–92; chm Cons Backbench Smaller Business Ctee 1984–87 (vice-chm 1983–84); sec: Cons Backbench Fin Ctee 1981–84, Cons Backbench Def Ctee 1982–84, Anglo-Swiss Parly Gp 1987–92 (treas 1984–87); sponsor: Trades Description Act (Amendment) Bill 1988, Protection of Animals (Amendment) Act 1989, Protection of Privacy Bill 1989, Armed Forces (Liability for Injury) Bill 1991; UK del N Atlantic Assembly 1986–92, elected rapporteur on human rights 1989–92; md Falcon Finance Management 1978–, advsr Barclays Bank 1978–83; dir: The Churchill Clinic 1980–91, Worms Investment Ltd 1981–83, TV3 Broadcasting Gp Ltd 1987–92, Int Bd of World Paper 1988–, Tijari Finance Ltd 1989–, Scientific Component Systems NRG Inc 1990–91; tstee: Household Div Funds 1979–83, Winmall Community Assoc 1985–; memb Ct Univ of Southampton 1979–; govr Malvern Coll 1981–; Liveryman Worshipful Co of Goldsmiths 1982; OStJ; *Recreations* riding, sailing, skiing, shooting, golf; *Clubs* Boodle's, Turf; *Style*— John Browne, Esq

BROWNE, (E) John P; s of late Edmund Browne, and Paula Browne; *b* 20 Feb 1948, Hamburg; *Educ* King's Sch Ely, Univ of Cambridge (MA), Stanford Univ (MS); *Career* British Petroleum Company plc: joined as univ apprentice 1966, various exploration and prodn posts Anchorage, NY, San Francisco, London and Canada 1969–83, gp treas and chief exec BP Finance International 1984–86, exec vice pres and chief fin offr Standard Oil Co Ohio 1987–89 (chief fin offr 1986–87), chief exec and md BP Exploration Co Ltd 1989–95, main bd dir 1991–, gp chief exec 1995–; non-exec dir: Redland plc 1993–96, SmithKline Beecham plc 1996–; chm Advsy Bd Stanford Graduate Sch of Business (USA); tstee The British Museum 1995–; FIMM 1987, FEng 1993; *Recreations* ballet, opera, collecting pre-Columbian artefacts; *Style*— John Browne, Esq, FEng; ✉ The British Petroleum Company plc, 1 Finsbury Circus, London EC2M 7BA (☎ 0171 496 4000, fax 0171 496 4483)

BROWNE, Air Vice-Marshal John Philip Ravenscroft; CBE (1985); s of Charles Harold Browne (d 1965), and Lorna, *née* Bailey (d 1989); *b* 27 April 1937; *Educ* Brockenhurst Co HS, Univ of Southampton (BSc(Eng)); *m* 11 Aug 1962, Gillian Dorothy, da of Flt Lt Robert John Smith, MBE, RAF (d 1985); 2 s (Philip Michael Ravenscroft b 1964, Simon John Ravenscroft b 1967); *Career* RAF: cmmnd Airfield Construction Branch 1958, appts in Cyprus, N Africa and UK 1959–66, transferred to Engr Branch 1966, RAF Coll Cranwell 1966–67, Flt and Sqdn Cdr Engrg Wing RAF Valley 1967–70, aircraft engrg staff MOD 1970–71, RAF Staff Coll 1972, Sqdn Cdr Central Servicing Devpt Estab 1973, OC Engrg Wing RAF Valley 1973–75, trg staff MOD 1975–78, aircraft engrg staff HQ RAF Germany 1978–80, Dep Dir Aircraft Engrg 2 (RAF) MOD 1980–82, Asst Dir Harrier Projects MOD (PE) 1982–85, Dir Electronics (Radar) Airborne MOD (PE) 1985–86, Dir Airborne Early Warning MOD (PE) 1986–89, Dir Gen Support Servs (RAF) 1989–92, ret 1992; Nat Air Traffic Servs CAA: Dir Engrg 1992–95, Dir Systems 1995–96; engrg conslt 1996–; pres RAF Airfield Construction Offrs' Assoc, formerly pres UK Chapter Assoc of Old Crows; CEng 1966, FRAeS 1991 (MRAeS 1971), FIMgt 1991, FICE 1993 (MICE 1966); *Recreations* reading, military history, aviation, photography, music; *Clubs* RAF; *Style*— Air Vice-Marshal John Browne, CBE; ✉ c/o Lloyds Bank plc, New Milton, Hants BH25 6HU

BROWNE, (Matthew) Kennedy; OBE (1994); s of John Browne (d 1954), of Glasgow, and Mary Kennedy, *née* Goslan (d 1969); *b* 21 Nov 1929; *Educ* Whitehill Sr Secdy Sch, Univ of Glasgow (BSc, MB ChB, MD); *m* 15 July 1954, (Elspet Mary) Elma, da of Joseph Henry Walter Wood (d 1975), of Bothwell; 1 s (David b 29 Jan 1970), 2 da (Katy b 1964, Mandy b 1966); *Career* Flt Lt RAF Inst of Aviation Med Farnborough 1955–58; conslt surgn Glasgow Royal Infirmary 1963–77, hon clinical lectr Univ of Glasgow 1963–95 (sometime clinical sub-dean Faculty of Med), surgn Belvedere Hosp 1970–77, conslt surgn Monklands Dist Gen Hosp Airdrie, med dir Monkland and Bellshill Hosps Tst until 1995, ret; former memb W of Scotland Postgrad Med Ctee; FRCS Edinburgh 1961, FRCS Glasgow 1978; *Books* Clinical Gastroenterology (1972), Adult Surgery (1973), Taurolin, Ein Neues Konzept Zur Antimikrobiellen. Chemotherapie Chirugischer Infektionen (contrib, 1985); *Recreations* wandering in Europe, Spanish studies; *Clubs*

RAF; *Style*— Kennedy Browne, Esq, OBE; ✉ 7 Winton Drive, Glasgow G12 0PZ (☎ 0141 339 4926); 9 Finca La Nayca, Javea, Alicante, Spain; Consulting Rooms, Nuffield Hospital, 25 Beaconsfield Road, Glasgow G12 0PJ (☎ 0141 334 9441)

BROWNE, Brig Michael Edward; CBE (1994), TD (and three Bars), DL (1989); s of John Edward Stevenson Browne, CBE (d 1976), and Muriel May, *née* Lambert (d 1965); *b* 6 Dec 1942; *Educ* Uppingham; *m* 11 Dec 1970, Susan Elizabeth, da of James Hugh Neill, CBE; 2 da (Anna Jane b 27 April 1974, Nicola Catherine b 6 Sept 1975); *Career* TA 1961–94, cmd 3 WFR 1982–84, Brig TA UKLF 1991–94; admitted slr 1966, dep coroner Retford Dist 1970–80, dep dist judge Supreme Ct of Judicature 1986–; former chm Bassetlaw Cons Assoc; chm: Reserve Forces Assoc 1993–96, E Midlands TAVRA 1994–; pres CIOR (Interallied Confedn of Reserve Offrs) 1996–98; memb Law Soc 1966; *Recreations* squash, tennis, golf; *Clubs* Army and Navy; *Style*— Brig Michael Browne, CBE, TD, DL; ✉ Eel Pie Farm, Markham Moor, Retford, Notts DN22 0QX (☎ 01777 838581); 19 Churchgate, Retford, Notts DN22 6PF (☎ 01777 707401, fax 01777 709894, car 0374 233223)

BROWNE, Lady Moyra Blanche Madeleine; *née* Ponsonby; DBE (1977, OBE 1962); o da of 9 Earl of Bessborough, GCMG, PC (d 1956); *b* 2 March 1918; *Educ* privately; *m* 10 Dec 1945, as his 2 w, Sir Denis John Wolko Browne, KCVO, FRCS (d 1967), s of late Sylvester Browne, of Australia; 1 s, 1 da; *Career* SEN 1946; chm Hospitality Ctee Victoria League 1956–62, vice chm Central Cncl Victoria League 1961–65; supt-in-chief St John Ambulance Bde 1970–83 (dep supt-in-chief 1964–70), vice pres Royal Coll of Nursing 1970–85; nat chm Support Gps 1987–93, govr Res into Ageing 1987–; memb of Chapter General Order of St John 1983–; DGStJ 1984 (DSJ 1970, CSJ 1968); hon memb Br Assoc of Paediatric Surgeons; *Recreations* music, fishing, travel; *Clubs* St John House (life memb); *Style*— The Lady Moyra Browne, DBE; ✉ 16 Wilton St, London SW1 7AX (☎ 0171 235 1419)

BROWNE, (James) Nicholas; QC (1995); s of James Christopher Browne, MC (d 1952), of London, and Winifred Jessie, *née* Pirie; *b* 25 April 1947; *Educ* Cheltenham Coll, Univ of Liverpool (LLB); *m* 28 March 1981, Angelica Elizabeth, da of Sir George Mitchell, CB, QC, and Lady Elizabeth Mitchell; 2 da (Emily Elizabeth b 27 Nov 1981, Cassandra Lucy b 10 Dec 1983); *Career* called to the Bar Inner Temple 1971 (Duke of Edinburgh Entrance scholar), criminal practice Midland and Oxford Circuit and SE Circuit, recorder of the Crown Court 1993– (asst recorder 1990–93); memb: Criminal Bar Assoc, Bar Cncl 1992–94; *Recreations* squash, cricket, theatre, spending time with family and friends; *Clubs* Cumberland Lawn Tennis; *Style*— Nicholas Browne, Esq, QC; ✉ 1 Serjeants' Inn, Fleet Street, London EC4Y 1LL (☎ 0171 353 9901)

BROWNE, Percy Basil; DL (Devon 1984); s of Capt W P Browne, MC, of Higher Hougton, Blandford, Dorset (d 1970), and M R Hoare (d 1953); *b* 2 May 1923; *Educ* Eton; *Career* served WWII Italy and NW Europe (cmmnd Royal Dragoons); MP (C) Torrington Div of Devon 1959–64; dir Appledore Shipbuilders Ltd 1965–72 (formerly chm); memb: N Devon Dist Cncl 1973–79 (vice chm 1978–79), SW Regnl Hosp Bd 1967–70; vice chm N Devon Hosp Mgmnt Ctee 1967–74; chm: North Devon Meat Ltd 1982–86, Miny of Agric's SW Regnl Panel 1985–88, Devon & Exeter Steeplechase Ltd 1990–96; dir Western Counties Building Society 1965–85, chm West of England Building Society 1986–89 (vice chm 1985–86), vice chm Regency & West of England Building Society 1989–91; farmer, ret; rode in Grand Nat 1953; High Sheriff of Devon 1978; *Style*— Percy B Browne, Esq, DL; ✉ Ford House, Silverton, Exeter, Devon EX5 4DQ (☎ 01392 881496)

BROWNE, Prof Roger Michael; s of Arthur Leslie Browne (d 1974), of Birmingham, and Phyllis Maud, *née* Baker (d 1942); *b* 19 June 1934; *Educ* Berkhamsted Sch, Univ of Birmingham (BSc, BDS, PhD, DDS); *m* 31 May 1958, Lilah Hilda, da of Issac Harold Manning (d 1960), of Leek; 1 s (Andrew b 1963), 1 da (Nicola b 1960); *Career* Univ of Birmingham: lectr in dental surgery 1960–64, lectr in dental pathology 1964–67, sr lectr in oral pathology 1967–77, prof 1977–, head Dept of Oral Pathology 1979–, dir of Dental Sch 1986–89, postgrad advsr in dentistry 1977–82; visiting prof Univ of Lagos Nigeria 1969; pres: Br Dental Assoc Hosps Gp 1986–87, Br Soc for Oral Pathology 1985–86 and 1990–94, Section of Odontology Birmingham Med Inst 1975–76; Int Assoc of Dental Res Distinguished Scientist Award in Pulp Biology 1991, Charles Tomes Medal RCS London 1995; FDS RCS 1962, FRCPath 1979; *Books* Colour Atlas of Oral Histopathology (with E A Marsland, 1975), A Radiological Atlas of Diseases of the Teeth and Jaws (with H D Edmondson and P G J Rout, 1983), Investigative Pathology of the Odontogenic Cysts (1991), Atlas of Dental and Maxillofacial Radiology and Imaging (jtly, 1994), Self-Assessment Picture Tests: Oral Radiology (with P G J Rout, 1996); *Recreations* walking, tennis, rugby football; *Style*— Prof Roger Browne; ✉ Department of Oral Pathology, Dental School, St Chad's Queensway, Birmingham B4 6NN (☎ 0121 236 8611)

BROWNE, Sheila Jeanne; CB (1977); da of Edward Elliott Browne; *b* 25 Dec 1924; *Educ* Lady Margaret Hall Oxford, Ecole des Chartes Paris; *Career* asst lectr Royal Holloway Coll Univ of London, tutor and fell St Hilda's Coll Oxford and univ lectr in French 1951–61; sr chief inspr DES 1974–83 (formerly staff inspr and chief inspr Secondary Educn, dep sr chief inspr DES 1972–74), princ Newnham Coll Cambridge 1983–92; chm Cncl Selly Oak Colls 1992–; memb: CNAA 1984–93, Marshall Aid Cmmn 1987–, Franco-British Cncl 1987–; hon fell: St Hilda's Coll Oxford 1978, Lady Margaret Hall Oxford 1978; Hon DLitt Warwick 1981; Hon LLD: Exeter 1984, Birmingham 1987; *Style*— Miss Sheila Browne, CB; ✉ Hone House, Sheep Street, Charlbury, Oxon OX7 3RR

BROWNE-CLAYTON, Robert Bruce; s of Lt-Col William Patrick Browne-Clayton (d 1971), of Dublin, and Janet Maitland Bruce, *née* Jardine; *b* 25 April 1940; *Educ* Loretto, RMA Sandhurst, Royal Agric Coll Cirencester; *m* 1 March 1969, Jane Evelyn Reine, da of Eric Peter Butler; 1 s (Benedict John (Ben) b 1970), 1 da (Clare Louise b 1973); *Career* Capt Royal Green Jackets KRRC, served Germany, Borneo and Br Guiana 1960–68; dir and co sec Economy Car Hire Ltd 1968–71, fin conslt 1971–74, desk offr responsible for agric, fisheries, food, forestry and rural affrs Cons Res Dept 1976–84, dir econ and public affrs Building Employers' Confedn 1988–91, fndr and first sec Nat Agric and Countryside Forum, gen sec Chamber of Coal Traders, Coal Merchants Fedn 1993–95, chief exec IFA Promotion Ltd 1995–; cncllr London Borough of Greenwich 1978–82, vice chm Greenwich Cons Assoc 1983–84 and 1987–91; FRSA; *Recreations* shooting, fishing, painting, music, reading, tennis, golf; *Clubs* University and Kildare Street; *Style*— Robert Browne-Clayton, Esq; ✉ 34 Park Vista, Greenwich, London SE10 9LD

BROWNE-WILKINSON, Baron (Life Peer UK 1991), of Camden in the London Borough of Camden; Nicolas Christopher Henry Browne-Wilkinson; kt (1977), PC (1983); s of late Rev Canon Arthur Rupert Browne-Wilkinson, MC, and Mary Theresa Caroline (Molly), *née* Abraham; *b* 30 March 1930; *Educ* Lancing, Magdalen Coll Oxford (BA); *m* 1, 1955, Ursula (d 1987), da of Cedric de Lacy Bacon; 3 s (Hon Simon b 1957, Hon Adam b (twin) 1957, Hon Oliver b 1962), 2 da (Hon Henrietta b 1960, Hon Martha b 1964); m 2, 20 April 1990, Mrs Hilary Isabella Jane Tuckwell, da of Prof James Wilfred Warburton; *Career* QC 1972, judge Ct of Appeal Jersey & Guernsey 1976–77, High Ct judge (Chancery) 1977, Lord Justice of Appeal 1983–85, vice chllr Supreme Ct 1985–91, a Lord of Appeal in Ordinary 1991; *Recreations* gardening, music; *Style*— The Rt Hon Lord Browne-Wilkinson, PC; ✉ House of Lords, London SW1

BROWNING, Angela Frances; MP (C) Tiverton (majority 11,089); da of late Thomas Pearson, and Linda Pearson; *b* 4 Dec 1946; *Educ* Reading Coll of Technol, Bournemouth Coll of Technol; *m* 1968, David Browning; 2 s; *Career* teacher of home economics in adult educn 1968–74, auxiliary nurse 1976–77, freelance conslt to mfrg indust 1977–85, mgmnt conslt specialising in trg, finance and corp communications 1985–92, MP (C) Tiverton 1992–; PPS Dept of Employment 1993–94, Parly sec Min of Agric Fisheries and Food 1994–; dir Small Business Bureau 1985–94, chm Women into Business 1988–92, memb Dept of Employment Advsy Ctee for Women's Employment 1989–92, govt co-chm Women's Nat Cmmn; Parly candidate (C) Crewe and Nantwich 1987, former chm Western Area CPC (and memb CPC Nat Advsy Ctee), official speaker Peace Through NATO; memb: Nat Autistic Soc, Thomas Hardy Soc; FInstSMM; *Style*— Mrs Angela Browning, MP; ✉ House of Commons, London SW1A 0AA

BROWNING, Frank Sacheverel (Chips); s of Frank Sacheverel Browning (d 1993), of Bank Foot, Silver St, Little Dean, Forest of Dean, and Ivy Mary Jean, *née* Spice (d 1967); *b* 28 Oct 1941; *Educ* Dulwich, Univ of St Andrews (MB ChB); *m* 1, 9 July 1966 (m dis 1996), (Carol) Angela, da of George Sutcliffe Seed (d 1958); 1 s (Benjamin Sacheverel b 1968), 2 da (Georgina Mary b 1970, Rebecca Louise b 1973); m 2, 23 Aug 1996, Mollie, da of Joseph Hiley (sometime Cons MP, d 1989); *Career* sr registrar in plastic surgery Leeds and Bradford 1971–80, conslt plastic surgn The Gen Infirmary at Leeds and St James's Univ Hosp 1980–; microsurgery res fell St Vincent's Hosp Melbourne 1975–76; hon surgn and pres Leeds RUFC; med dir Bramham Three Day Event; Freeman City of London; memb: BAPS, BAAPS, Med Equestrian Assoc; FRCS; *Style*— Chips Browning, Esq; ✉ St James's University Hospital, Beckett Street, Leeds LS9 7TF (☎ 0113 243 3144 ext 5721)

BROWNING, (Walter) Geoffrey; s of Lt Walter Samuel Browning (d 1992), and Dorothy Gwendoline, *née* Hill (d 1987); *b* 6 Nov 1938; *Educ* Burnage GS Manchester; *m* 1, 20 June 1964 (m dis 1982), Barbara; 1 s (Matthew b 18 Sept 1967), 2 da (Helen b 11 May 1965, Claire b 22 April 1969), 1 adopted s (Jon b 16 March 1972); m 2, 17 Aug 1983, Pauline Ann, da of William Wilkinson, of Lockgate, West Runcorn, Cheshire; 2 da (Alexandra b 7 June 1984, Danielle b 9 Sept 1985); *Career* CA; asst gp sr Peat Marwick Mitchell and Co 1961–63 (articled clerk 1955–60), div co sec The Steetly Co Ltd 1963–64, fin dir Syd Abrams Ltd 1964–69, jt md Boalloy Ltd 1969–90, dir Marling Industries plc 1990–92; underwriting memb Lloyd's 1980–; FCA; *Recreations* sailing, golf; *Style*— Geoffrey Browning, Esq; ✉ Middlemede, Ballamodha, Ballasalla, Malew, Isle of Man (☎ 01624 825880, fax 01624 825881)

BROWNING, Prof George Gordon; s of George Gordon Browning, of Glasgow, and Janet Smith Ballantyne, *née* Money; *b* 10 Jan 1941; *Educ* Kelvinside Acad, Univ of Glasgow (MB ChB, MD); *m* 1971, Annette Campbell, da of William Mallinson; 2 da (Gillian Gordon b 26 Jan 1973, Jennifer Gordon b 24 Oct 1974), 1 s (Grigor Gordon b 20 Sept 1978); *Career* former appts: resident house surgn and physician then res fell Dept of Surgery Western Infirmary Glasgow, MRC Wernher-Piggott travelling fell Harvard Univ and Massachusetts Eye and Ear Infirmary, sr registrar Glasgow Trg Scheme; sr lectr then titular prof in otorhinolaryngology Univ of Glasgow 1990–; conslt otologist MRC Inst of Hearing Research Glasgow Royal Infirmary 1978–, hon conslt Univ of Glasgow 1978–, hon conslt in charge Dept of Otorhinolaryngology and Scottish Sch of Audiology Glasgow Royal Infirmary 1989–; visiting scholar Sch of Public Health Harvard Univ 1989; memb: Otorhinolaryngological Research Soc (former pres), British Soc of Otolaryngologists, Scottish Otolaryngological Soc; FRCS; *Books* Clinical Audiology and Otology (1986), Updated ENT (3 edn, 1994), Otoscopy - a structured approach (1995); *Recreations* silversmithing, skiing, swimming; *Style*— Prof George Browning; ✉ Department of Otolaryngology and Head and Neck Surgery, Royal Infirmary, Queen Elizabeth Building, 16 Alexandra Parade, Glasgow G31 2ER (☎ 0141 552 3535, fax 0141 304 4896)

BROWNING, Michael Lovelace; s of Harold Louis Browning (d 1963), of Exmouth; *b* 18 March 1937; *Educ* Kelly Coll Tavistock; *m* 1965, Anna Lynne, da of late Lawrence Clifford White, of Sampford Peverell; 3 da (Georgina Alison b 1967, Juliet Sally Lovelace b 1970, Jemma Madeleine b 1974); *Career* Ernst & Whinney CAs 1954–61; HAT Group plc: chief accountant 1961, co sec 1965, gp fin dir 1976; md Lorne Stewart plc 1987–89, fin conslt 1989–; FCA; *Style*— Michael L Browning, Esq; ✉ Elm Tree Farm, Hart's Lane, Hallatrow, Bristol BS18 5EA (☎ and fax 01761 452218)

BROWNING, (David) Peter James; CBE (1984); s of Frank Browning (d 1950), and Lucie Audrey, *née* Hiscock (d 1986); *b* 29 May 1927; *Educ* Christ's Coll Cambridge (MA), Sorbonne, Univ of Strasbourg, Univ of Perugia; *m* 1953, Eleanor Berry, da of John Henry Forshaw, CB, MC (d 1973); 3 s (Paul, Jonathan, Nicholas); *Career* educator; asst dir of educn Cumberland LEA 1962–66, dep chief educn offr Southampton LEA 1966–69; chief educn offr: Southampton 1969–73, Beds 1973–89; memb: Schs Cncl Governing Cncl and 5–13 Steering Ctee 1969–75, Cncl Univ of Southampton 1970–73, C of E Bd of Educn Schs Ctee 1970–75, Cncl Nat Youth Orch 1972–77, Br Educnl Admin Soc (chm 1974–78, fndr memb Cncl of Mgmnt), UGC 1974–79, Taylor Ctee of Enquiry into Mgmnt and Govt of Schs 1975–77, Governing Body Centre for Info on Language Teaching and Res 1975–80, Euro Forum for Educnl Admin (fndr chm 1977–84), Library Advsy Cncl (England) 1978–81, Cambridge Inst of Educn Govrs (vice chm 1980–89), Univ of Cambridge Faculty Bd of Educn 1983–92, Br Sch Technol Cncl of Mgmnt 1984–88; treas Univ of Lancaster 1993– (memb Cncl 1988–); govr: Gordonstoun Sch 1985–92, Lakes Sch Windermere 1988–91, Charlotte Mason Coll of Higher Educn Ambleside 1988–92, Cncl Open Coll of NW 1991–94, Armitt Library Trust 1992– (chm 1994–), Cumbria Arts in Educn Tst (chm 1992–95), Carlisle Diocesan Bd of Educn (chm 1992–), Carlisle Diocesan Advsy Ctee for the Care of Churches (chm 1993–); conslt Miny of Educn: Sudan 1976, Cyprus 1977, Italy 1981; Sir James Matthews Memorial Lecture (Univ of Southampton) 1983; Cavaliere Order of Merit (Italy) 1985, Cdr Order of Palmes Académiques (France) 1989; FRSA 1981–93; *Publications* Julius Caesar for German Students (ed, 1957), Macbeth for German Students (ed, 1959); *Recreations* music, public affairs, travel; *Style*— Peter Browning, Esq, CBE; ✉ Park Fell, Skelwith Bridge, nr Ambleside, Cumbria LA22 9NP (☎ 01539 433978, fax 01539 431552)

BROWNING, Ralph Morgan; s of Lt-Col John Morgan Browning (d 1974), of Coventry, Warwicks, and Anne, *née* Chalker (d 1971); *b* 9 Aug 1925; *Educ* Cheltenham, Queen's Coll Oxford (MA); *m* 6 Dec 1950, Mary Louise, da of Capt Martinell McLachlin (d 1925), of St Thomas, Ontario, Canada; *Career* Lt 1/7 Rajputs IA 1945–47; mktg mangr The Procter and Gamble Co (UK, France, Italy, USA) 1950–66, mktg dir Reynolds Tobacco Co (Europe and ME) 1967–70, dir L'Oréal (UK) 1970–75; Rémy et Associés: jt md 1976–90, chm 1990–91; md Reid Pye and Campbell Ltd 1982–92, chm Eurobrands Ltd 1988–92, dir Rémy Cointreau 1991–; memb Chelsea Cons Assoc; Liveryman Worshipful Co of Distillers 1987; *Recreations* fishing, stalking, tennis; *Clubs* Turf, Hurlingham, United Oxford & Cambridge Univ; *Style*— Ralph M Browning, Esq; ✉ 81 Onslow Square, London SW7 3LT (☎ and fax 0171 584 1443)

BROWNJOHN, Alan Charles; s of Charles Henry Brownjohn (d 1985), of London, and Dorothy, *née* Mulligan (d 1976); *b* 28 July 1931; *Educ* Univ of Oxford (BA); *m* 1, 1960 (m dis 1969), Shirley Toulson; 1 s; m 2, Sandra Willingham; *Career* formerly sch teacher and lectr in Eng; author and poet 1979–; chm Poetry Soc 1982–88; poetry critic: New Statesman 1968–76, Encounter 1977–80, Sunday Times 1990–; reg contrib to TLS and BBC Radio poetry progs; Cholmondeley Award for Poetry 1979, Soc of Authors travelling scholar 1985; memb: Writers' Guild of GB, Soc of Authors; *Books* The Way You Tell Them (1990, Authors' Club prize), Horace (trans, 1996), The Long Shadows (published in Romanian, 1996); poetry: Collected Poems (1988), The Observation Car

(1990), In the Cruel Arcade (1994); anthologies: First I Say This (ed), New Poems 1970–71 (ed with Seamus Heaney and Jon Stallworthy), New Poetry 3 (ed with Maureen Duffy); Torquato Tasso (trans, 1985); *Recreations* walking, travelling, left-wing censoriousness; *Style—* Alan Brownjohn, Esq; ✉ 2 Belsize Park, London NW3 4ET (☎ 0171 794 2479); c/o Rosica Colin Ltd, 1 Clareville Grove Mews, London SW7 5AH (☎ 0171 370 1080)

BROWNJOHN, John Nevil Maxwell; s of Gen Sir Nevil Charles Dowell Brownjohn, GBE, KCB, CMG, MC (d 1973), and Isabelle, *née* White (d 1984); *Educ* Sherborne, Lincoln Coll Oxford (MA); *m* 19 Nov 1968, Jacqueline Sally, da of Geoffrey Byrd (d 1952); 1 s (Jonathan b 1971), 1 da (Emma b 1969); *Career* literary translator, screenwriter; cmmnd Somersetshire LI 1948, served Royal W African Frontier Force 1948–49; chm Exec Ctee Translators' Assoc Soc of Authors 1976; Schlegel-Tieck Special Award 1979, US PEN Goethe-House Prize 1981, Schlegel-Tieck Prize 1993, US Christopher Award 1995; *Books* incl: The Night of the Generals (1963), Memories of Teilhard de Chardin (1964), Klemperer Recollections (1964), Brothers in Arms (1965), Goya (1965), The 20th of July (1965), Rodin (1967), The Interpreter (1967), Alexander the Great (1968), The Wolves (1968), The Poisoned Stream (1969), The Human Animal (1971), Hero in the Tower (1972), The Waters of Aswan (1972), Strength Through Joy (1973), Madam Kitty (1973), A Time for Truth (1974), The Boat (1974), A Direct Flight to Allah (1975), The Manipulation Game (1976), The Night of the Long Knives (1976), The Hittites (1977), Willy Brandt Memoirs (1978), Canaris (1979), Twilight of the Generals (1979), A German Love Story (1980), Life with the Enemy (1982), If This Be Glory (1982), Richard Wagner (1983), The Middle Kingdom (1983), Solo Run (1984), Momo (1985), The Last Spring in Paris (1985), Invisible Walls (1986), Mirror in the Mirror (1986), Assassin (1987), The Battle of Wagram (1988), Daddy (1989), The Marquis of Bolibar (1989), Eunuchs for Heaven (1990), Jaguar (1990), Little Apple (1991), Infanta (1992), Siberian Transfer (1992), Dali (1992), The Swedish Cavalier (1993), Love Letters from Cell 92 (1994), The Survivor (1994), Picasso (1994), Acts: The Autobiography of Wolfgang Wagner (1994), Nostradamus (1995), The Giraffe Has a Long Neck (1995), Claude Monet, Turlupin (1996), Pierre Lalande (1996), Voices in the Dark (1997), Heroes Like Us (1997); *Screen Credits* Tess (in collaboration with Roman Polanski and Gérard Brach, 1980), The Boat (1981), Pirates (1986), The Name of the Rose (1986), The Bear (1989), Bitter Moon (in collaboration with Roman Polanski, 1992); *Recreations* music; *Style—* John Brownjohn, Esq; ✉ The Vine House, Nether Compton, Sherborne, Dorset DT9 4QA (☎ and fax 01935 814553)

BROWNLIE, Alistair Rutherford; OBE (1987); s of James Rutherford Brownlie (d 1966), of Edinburgh, and Muriel, *née* Dickson (d 1971); ancestors were dependants of the Dukes of Hamilton and Brandon; *b* 5 April 1924; *Educ* George Watson's Coll, Univ of Edinburgh (MA, LLB, Dip Admin Law); *m* 20 June 1970, Martha Barron, da of Thomas Mounsey (d 1964); *Career* served WWII as bombardier RA and radio operator with 658 Air OP Sqdn RAF in Europe and India; slr in private practice; memb Lord Merthyr's Ctee (House of Lords) on the Bastardy (Blood Tests) Bill and thereafter of Lord Amulree's Ctee, memb Cncl Law Soc of Scot 1966–78, slr for the poor in High Ct (immediately prior to introduction of Criminal Legal Aid in Scot), served Legal Aid Central Ctee 1970–86; fndr memb, sometime pres and currently hon memb Forensic Sci Soc (Silver medal 1977); memb Scot Legal Aid Bd 1986–90, lectr and author on legal aspects of forensic science, vice chm Scottish Cncl of Law Reporting; elder Morningside Utd Church Edinburgh; sec Soc of Slrs in Supreme Courts of Scot 1970–95; chm Edinburgh Western Diabetes Research Tst; FRSA 1991; *Books* Drink Drugs and Driving (jtly), Mental Health - A Guide to the Law in Scotland (jtly), Crime Investigation (ed), A Scottish Family Firm; *Recreations* the spade, the pen and the saw; *Style—* Alistair R Brownlie, Esq, OBE; ✉ Cherrytrees, 8 Braid Mount, Edinburgh EH10 6JP (☎ 0131 447 4255); 2 Abercromby Place, Edinburgh EH3 6JZ (☎ 0131 556 4116, fax 0131 556 1624)

BROWNLIE, Prof Ian; CBE (1993), QC (1979); s of John Nason Brownlie (d 1952), and Amy Isabella, *née* Atherton (d 1975); *b* 19 Sept 1932; *Educ* Alsop HS Liverpool, Oxford (MA, DPhil, DCL); *m* 1, 1957, Jocelyn Gale; 1 s, 2 da; m 2, 1978, Christine Apperley, LLM; *Career* called to the Bar Gray's Inn 1958, in practice 1967–, bencher Gray's Inn 1988; fell Wadham Coll Oxford 1963–76, prof of int law LSE 1976–80, Chichele prof of public int law Oxford 1980–; sr ed Br Year Book of International Law, dir of studies Int Law Assoc 1982–91; author of various works on public int law; fell All Souls Coll Oxford 1980–; FBA 1979; *Style—* Prof Ian Brownlie, CBE, QC, FBA; ✉ 43 Fairfax Rd, Chiswick, London W4 1EN (☎ 0181 995 3647); 2 Hare Court, Temple London EC4Y 7BM (☎ 0171 583 1770); All Souls College, Oxford (☎ 01865 279342)

BROWNLOW, Air Vice-Marshal Bertrand; CB (1982), OBE (1967), AFC (1962); s of Robert John Brownlow, and Helen Louise Brownlow; *b* 13 Jan 1929; *Educ* Beaufort Lodge Sch; *m* 1958, Kathleen Shannon; 2 s, 1 da; *Career* joined RAF 1947, def and air attaché Stockholm 1969–71, CO Experimental Flying (Royal Aircraft Estab) Farnborough 1971–73, Dir Flying (Research and Devpt) MOD 1974–77, Cmdt Aeroplane and Armament Experimental Estab Boscombe Down 1977–80, RAF Coll Cranwell (AOC 1980–82, Asst Cmdt, Offr and Flying Training 1973–74), Dir-Gen Training RAF 1982–83, ret 1984; dir Marshall of Cambridge Aerospace Ltd 1984–94; memb Bd CAA 1994; awarded Silver medal of the Royal Aero Club for services to gliding; FRAeS; *Style—* Air Vice-Marshal Bertrand Brownlow, CB, OBE, AFC; ✉ Woodside, Abbotsley Rd, Croxton, Huntingdon, Cambridgeshire PE19 4SZ (☎ 01480 880663)

BROWNLOW, 7 Baron (1776 GB), of Belton; Sir Edward John Peregrine Cust; 10 Bt (1677 E); s of 6 Baron Brownlow (d 1978), by his 1 w, Katherine (d 1952), da of Brig-Gen Sir David Kinloch, 11 Bt, CB, MVO; *b* 25 March 1936; *Educ* Eton; *m* 1964, Shirlie, da of late John Yeomans, of The Manor Farm, Hill Croome, Upton-on-Severn; 1 s; *Heir* s, Hon Peregrine Edward Quintin Cust b 9 July 1974; *Career* memb Lloyd's 1961–88; dir Hand-in-Hand Fire and Life Insur Soc (branch of Commercial Union Assurance Co Ltd) 1962–82, chm and md Harris & Dixon (Underwriting Agencies) Ltd 1976–82, dir Ermitage International Ltd; High Sheriff of Lincs 1978–79; *Clubs* White's, Pratt's, United (Jersey); *Style—* The Rt Hon the Lord Brownlow; ✉ La Maison des Prés, St Peter, Jersey JE3 7EL, CI

BROWNLOW, James Hilton; CBE (1984), QPM (1978); s of late Ernest Cuthbert Brownlow, and Beatrice Annie Elizabeth Brownlow; *b* 19 Oct 1925; *Educ* Worksop Central Sch; *m* 1947, Joyce Key; 2 da; *Career* served WWII RAF Flt Sgt 1943–47; slr's clerk 1941–43, police constable Leicester City Police 1947, police constable rising to detective chief supt Kent County Constabulary 1947–69, asst chief constable Hertfordshire Constabulary 1969–75, asst to HM Chief Inspector of Constabulary Home Office 1975–76, dep chief constable Greater Manchester Police 1976–79, chief constable S Yorks Police 1979–82, HM Inspector of Constabulary for NE England 1983–89 (ret), advsr on Safety and Crowd Control to FA 1990–94, memb Parole Bd 1991–94; *Recreations* golf, music, gardening, travel; *Style—* James Brownlow, Esq, CBE, QPM; ✉ 10 Walford Lodge, The Carriages, Booth Road, Altringham, Cheshire WA14 4AF (☎ 0161 928 3548)

BROWNLOW, Jeremy Taylor; *b* 4 Dec 1945; *Educ* Heversham Sch, St Catharine's Coll Cambridge; *m* 1971, Lynden, *née* Snape, 3 s, 1 da; *Career* articled clerk then asst slr Clifford-Turner 1968–73, ptnr Company Dept Clifford Chance 1973–; *Style—* Jeremy Brownlow, Esq; ✉ Clifford Chance, 200 Aldersgate St, London EC1A 4JJ

BROWNLOW, Katharine Charlotte Deirdre (Katie); da of James Nesbitt Brownlow, of Portugal, and Deirdre Maire, *née* Mooney; *b* 16 Aug 1964; *Educ* Princess Gardens Sch, Univ of Southampton, French Inst, London Sch of Sports Massage, Univ of Westminster; *Career* amateur rower (lightweight and openweight); memb Thames Rowing Club 1987–93; nat rep: stroke coxless fours lightweight squad 1988–92 (team capt 1988–91), stroke Olympic eight 1992–; achievements incl: Silver medal Nat Championships (for Thames RC), 4 times champion Lucerne Int Regatta 1988–91, Silver medal lightweight coxless fours Bled Yugoslavia 1989 and Vienna 1991, seventh place open eights Olympic Games Barcelona 1992, over 15 other Gold medals from int regattas, winner fours head 1992; sec Tech Dept BOA 1990–91, currently teaching English as a foreign language Java Indonesia; *Recreations* music, clubbing, reading, running, growing vegetables, talking; *Style—* Ms Katie Brownlow; ✉ c/o 11 Stockhurst Close, Putney, London SW15 1NB

BROWNLOW, Peter; s of Frederick Brownlow, of Leeds, and Margaret Brownlow, *née* Pearce (d 1985); *b* 4 June 1945; *Educ* Rothwell GS; *m* 1971, Judith Margaret, da of Douglas Alton, of Leeds; 2 s (Nicholas Simon b 1975, James Mark b 1978); *Career* Border Television plc: fin dir until 1996, md 1996–; dir Cumberland Building Soc; dir various radio cos; ACMA; *Recreations* hill walking, sailing, the garden; *Clubs* Brampton Sailing; *Style—* Peter Brownlow; ✉ Quarry Bank, Capon Hill, Brampton, Cumbria CA8 1QN; Border Television plc, The Television Centre, Carlisle CA1 3NT (☎ 01228 25101, fax 01228 511193)

BROWNLOW, Col William Stephen; JP (Co Down 1956); er s of Col Guy James Brownlow, DSO, DL (d 1960), of Ballywhite, Portaferry, Co Down, and Elinor Hope Georgina (d 1978), 2 da of Col George John Scott, DSO; descended from a jr branch of Lord Lurgan's family (*see* Burke's Irish Family Records 1976); *b* 9 Oct 1921; *Educ* Eton; *m* 11 Jan 1961, Eveleigh Finola Margaret, o da of Lt-Col George William Panter, MBE (d 1946), of Enniskeen, Newcastle, Co Down; 1 s (James George Christy b 20 Sept 1962), 2 da (Camilla Jane b 29 July 1964, Melissa Anne b 8 May 1968); *Career* Maj RB 1940–54 (wounded, despatches), Staff Coll Camberley 1951, Hon Col 4 Bn Royal Irish Rangers TAVR 1973–78; High Sheriff of Co Down 1959, DL Co Down 1961, Lord Lieut of Co Down 1990–96; Cdr St John's Commandery of Ards 1990–; memb: Irish Nat Hunt Ctee 1956–, Down CC 1969–72, NI Assembly 1973–75, Irish Turf Club 1982–; master E Down Foxhounds 1959–62; chm: Downpatrick Race Club 1960–90, NI Region Br Field Sports Soc 1971–90; *Recreations* field sports; *Clubs* Army and Navy; *Style—* Col William Brownlow, JP; ✉ Ballywhite House, Portaferry, Co Down, N Ireland BT22 1PB (☎ 01247 728325)

BROWNRIGG, Sir Nicholas Gawen; 5 Bt (UK 1816); s of Gawen Egremont Brownrigg (d 1938, 2 s of 4 Bt), and Lucia, *née* Baroness von Borosini; suc gf, Rear Adm Sir Douglas Egremont Robert Brownrigg, 4 Bt, CB, 1939; *b* 22 Dec 1932; *Educ* Midland Sch, Stanford Univ; *m* 1, 1959 (m dis 1965), Linda Louise, da of Jonathan B Lovelace, of Beverly Hills, California, USA; 1 s (Michael Gawen b 1961), 1 da (Sylvia Alderyn b 1964); m 2, 1971, Valerie Ann, da of Julian A Arden, of Livonia, Michigan, USA; *Heir* s, Michael Gawen Brownrigg b 11 Oct 1961; *Style—* Sir Nicholas Brownrigg, Bt; ✉ PO Box 548, Ukiah, Calif 95482, USA

BROWNRIGG, Philip Henry Akerman; CMG (1964), DSO (1945), OBE (1953), TD (1945); s of Charles Edward Brownrigg (d 1942), of Oxford, and Valerie, *née* Akerman (d 1929); *b* 3 June 1911; *Educ* Eton, Magdalen Coll Oxford; *m* 1936, Marguerite Doreen (d 1992), da of Capt C R Ottley (d 1936); 3 da; *Career* served WWII Royal Berks Regt then Reconnaissance Corps (RAC) NW Europe, Lt-Col 1944; journalist 1934–52, ed Sunday Graphic 1952; Anglo American Corp of SA 1953; dir in: Rhodesia 1961–63, Zambia 1964–65; dir Nchanga Consolidated Copper Mines Ltd and Roan Consolidated Mines Ltd 1969–80; pres Zambia Soc 1980–; Insignia of Honour (Zambia) 1981; *Books* Biography of Kenneth Kaunda (1989); *Recreations* golf, sport on TV; *Style—* Philip Brownrigg, Esq, CMG, DSO, OBE, TD; ✉ Wheeler's, Checkendon, nr Reading, Berks (☎ 01491 680328)

BROWSE, Prof Sir Norman Leslie; kt (1994); s of late Reginald Dederic Browse, BEM, and late Margaret Louise, *née* Gillis; *b* 1 Dec 1931; *Educ* East Ham GS, Bart's Med Coll (MB BS), Bristol Univ Med Sch (MD); *m* 6 May 1957, Jeanne Audrey, da of Lt-Col Victor Richard Menage, RE (d 1952); 1 s (Dominic James b 1962), 1 da (Sarah Lesley b 1960); *Career* Capt RAMC 1957–59; lectr in surgery Westminster Hosp 1962–64, res assoc/Harkness Cwlth fell Mayo Clinic 1964–65, prof of surgery St Thomas's Hosp London 1982–96 (conslt surgn and reader in surgery 1965–72, prof of vascular surgery 1972–82); civilian conslt in vascular surgery to: RAF 1982–96, Army 1983–96; pres: Euro Soc for Cardiovascular Surgery 1984–86, Surgical Res Soc 1989–91, Venous Forum RSM 1989–91, Vascular Surgical Soc of GB and Ireland 1991–92, RCS 1992–95; chm: Assoc of Profs of Surgery 1985–88, Specialist Advsy Ctee in Surgery 1985–89, Br Atherosclerosis Discussion Gp 1988–91, UK Jt Consultants Ctee 1994–; cncl memb: Assoc of Surgns of GB & Ireland 1985–88, Royal Coll of Surgns 1986–95, Marlborough Coll 1989–; tstee and chm Lord Brock Meml Tst, tstee RAFT; hon memb: American Soc for Vascular Surgery, Australian Vascular Soc; hon fell: Coll of Med of S Africa 1992, RCPS(Glasgow) 1993, Royal Australasian Coll of Surgns 1994, RCS(I) 1994, American Coll of Surgns 1995, RCS(Ed) 1995; FRCP 1993; *Books* Physiology and Pathology of Bed Rest (1964), Symptoms and Signs of Surgical Disease (1978, 3 edn 1997), Reducing Operations for Lymphoedema (1987), Diseases of the Veins (1988); *Recreations* golf, sailing, marine painting; *Style—* Prof Sir Norman Browse; ✉ Blaye House, 8 Home Farm Close, Esher, Surrey KT10 9HA; Department of Surgery, St Thomas's Hospital, London SE1 (☎ 0171 928 9292 ext 2516)

BRUCE, *see:* Cumming-Bruce, Hovell-Thurlow-Cumming-Bruce

BRUCE, Hon Alastair John Lyndhurst; s and h of 4 Baron Aberdare, KBE, PC; *b* 2 May 1947; *Educ* Eton, Ch Ch Oxford; *m* 1971, Elizabeth Mary Culbert, da of John F Foulkes; 1 s, 1 da; *Career* IBM UK Ltd 1969–91; ptnr Bruce Naughton Wade Public Affairs Research and Counselling 1991–; *Style—* The Hon Alastair Bruce; ✉ 16 Beverley Road, London SW13 0LX

BRUCE, Lord; Charles Edward Bruce; s and h of 11 Earl of Elgin and Kincardine, KT, *qv*; *b* 19 Oct 1961; *Educ* Eton, Univ of St Andrews (MA); *m* in Alaska 29 July 1990, Amanda Leigh, yr da of James Movius, of Fairbanks, Alaska; 2 s (Hon James Andrew Charles Robert, Master of Bruce b 16 Nov 1991, Hon George Benjamin Thomas b 5 July 1993), 1 da (Hon Antonia Jean b 14 Dec 1990); *Career* page of honour to HM Queen Elizabeth The Queen Mother 1975–77; dir Scottish Lime Centre Trust; non-exec dir Michael Kelly Associates 1992–94; *Clubs* Brooks's; *Style—* Lord Bruce; ✉ The Abbey House, Culross, Fife KY12 8JB (☎ 01383 872 344, fax 01383 872 435)

BRUCE, Christopher; s of Alexander Bruce (d 1970), and Ethel, *née* Parker; *b* 2 Oct 1945; *Educ* Rambert Sch; *m* 1967, Marian, da of Frank Meadowcroft, MBE (d 1969); 2 s (Mark Sebastian b 1968, Thomas Benjamin b 1970), 1 da (Molly Ellen b 1975); *Career* choreographer; formerly dancer with London Ballet, Ballet Rambert (roles incl The Poet in Cruel Garden, Prospero in The Tempest, Pierrot in Pierrot Lunaire), English Nat Ballet (roles incl Tchaikovsky/Drosselmeyer in The Nutcracker and title role in Petrouchka), assoc choreographer Ballet Rambert 1979–86 (assoc dir 1975–79), assoc choreographer Eng Nat Ballet 1986–91, resident choreographer Houston Ballet 1989–, dir Rambert Dance Co 1994–; works as choreographer for Ballet Rambert incl: George Frideric (debut, music by Handel) 1969, Ancient Voices of Children 1975, Cruel Garden (with Lindsay Kemp) 1977, Ghost Dances 1981, Requiem 1982, Intimate Pages 1984, Ceremonies 1986; works for Eng Nat Ballet incl: Land 1985, The World Again 1986, The Dream is Over 1987, Symphony in Three Movements 1989; works for Houston Ballet incl: Guatama Buddha 1989, Journey 1990, Nature Dances 1992; works for other companies incl: Unfamiliar Playground (Royal Ballet) 1974, Cantate (Tanz Forum Cologne) 1981, Village Songs (Nederlands Dans Theater) 1981, Silence is the End of our Song (Royal Danish Ballet) 1984, Remembered Dances (Scottish Ballet) 1985, Les Noces (Gulbenkian Ballet Lisbon) 1989, Il Ballo della Ingrate Agrippina and Venus and Adonis (Kent Opera), Rooster (Geneva Ballet) 1991; new ballets created: Kingdom (Geneva) 1993, Moonshine (Nederlands Dans Theater) 1993, Waiting (London Contemporary Dance Theatre) 1993, Crossing (Rambert Dance Co) 1994, Meeting Point (Rambert Dance Co) 1995, Quicksilver (Rambert Dance Co) 1996, Stream (Rambert Dance Co) 1996; subject of BBC documentary 1978, artistic dir Rambert Dance Co 1994; Evening Standard Award for Dance 1974, Prix Italia 1982, International Theatre Inst Award for Dance 1993; *Style*— Christopher Bruce, Esq; ✉ c/o Rambert Dance Co, 94 Chiswick High Road, London W4 1SH

BRUCE, Christopher John; s of Arthur Malcolm Bruce, of Bedale, Yorks, and Evelyn Mary, *née* Holland; *b* 15 Dec 1951; *Educ* Northallerton GS, St Catherine's Coll Cambridge (MA); *m* 28 Sept 1974, Pamela Jane Lynette, *née* Gilchrist; 1 s (Charles John Gilchrist b 26 May 1979), 1 da (Eleanor Charlotte Jane b 17 Sept 1982); *Career* TEFL Italy 1973–76, joined Unilever as UCMDS trainee 1976 (completed Unilever Business Educn Prog at LBS and Bradford Mgmnt Centre 1978); product mangr rising to sr product mangr Birds Eye Walls 1978–81; St Ivel Ltd: joined as mktg mangr 1981, mktg controller Dairy 1987–89 then Non-Dairy 1989–90; mktg dir HP Foods 1990–94, md Greyhound Product Devpt Consultancy 1994–; *Recreations* cricket, landscape painting; *Style*— Christopher Bruce, Esq

BRUCE, David Ian Rehbinder; s of Ian Stuart Rae Bruce, MC (d 1967), and Reinhildt Hilda Henriette Reinholdtsdotter, *née* Baroness Rehbinder; *b* 16 Aug 1946; *Educ* Eton, Oriel Coll Oxford (MA); *m* 4 Dec 1976, Anne Margaret Turquand (Muffyn), da of Col David Frank Turquand Colbeck, OBE (d 1995); 2 s (Edward b 1984, Ian (twin) b 1984); *Career* CA; Peat Marwick Mitchell & Co 1968–72; Cazenove & Co: investmt analyst 1972–79, conslt Ctee to Review the Functioning of Fin Inst 1977–79; Royal Dutch/Shell Gp: asst treas advsr Shell Int Petroleum Co Ltd 1979–80, mangr fin planning Shell Canada Ltd 1980–83, treas & controller Shell UK Ltd 1983–86; exec dir fin and admin The Stock Exchange 1986–90, gp fin dir Guinness Mahon Holdings plc 1990–93, dir of fin Lloyd's of London 1993, dir Crubider 1995–; former memb Hundred Gp, memb Tech Ctee of the Assoc of Corporate Treasurers 1988–; Freeman City of London 1977, Liveryman Worshipful Co of Merchant Taylors 1980; FCA, AIIMR, FCT; *Recreations* music, opera (spectator), shooting, fishing; *Clubs* Pratt's, City of London, White's; *Style*— David Bruce, Esq; ✉ 5 Bolingbroke Grove, London SW11 6ES (☎ 0181 673 1434, fax 0171 787 8144); office: 32 St Mary at Hill, London EC3P 3AJ (☎ 0171 772 7916, fax 0171 772 7267)

BRUCE, (Hon) George John Done; yr s of 11 Baron Balfour of Burleigh (d 1967), and Violet Dorothy Done; does not use courtesy title; *b* 28 March 1930; *Educ* Byam Shaw Sch of Drawing and Painting, educated by sitters; *Career* portrait painter; cmmnd works incl: three portraits of Archbishop Ramsey for the Church of England, Lord Chief Justice Baron Lane for Gray's Inn, Speaker George Thomas for the House of Commons, Baron Butler of Saffron Walden for Trinity Coll Cambridge, Sir Alan Cottrell (vice chllr Univ of Cambridge); RSPP: memb 1959, hon sec 1970–84, vice pres 1984–89, pres 1991–94; memb Soc of Teachers of the Alexander Technique; *Recreations* windsurfing, skiing, hang gliding; *Clubs* Athenaeum; *Style*— George J D Bruce,; ✉ 6 Pembroke Walk, London W8 6PQ (☎ 0171 937 1493)

BRUCE, Maj Sir Hervey James Hugh; 7 Bt (UK 1804), of Downhill, Londonderry; s of Sir Hervey John William Bruce, 6 Bt (d 1971); *b* 3 Sept 1952; *Educ* Eton, Mons Officer Cadet Sch; *m* 1, 1979, Charlotte Sara Jane, da of John Temple Gore (s of late Capt Christopher Gore and Lady Barbara, da of 16 Earl of Eglinton); 1 s (Hervey Hamish Peter b 1986), 1 da (Laura Crista b 1984); m 2, 1992, J M (Anna), yst da of Frank Pope, of Tavistock, Devon; *Heir* s, Hervey Hamish Peter Bruce b 20 Nov 1986; *Career* Maj Grenadier Gds; *Recreations* tapestry, polo; *Clubs* Cavalry and Guards'; *Style*— Major Sir Hervey Bruce, Bt

BRUCE, Ian Cameron; MP (C) Dorset South (majority 13,508); s of Henry Bruce (d 1970), and (Ellen) Flora, *née* Bingham; *b* 14 March 1947; *Educ* Chelmsford Tech HS, Univ of Bradford, Mid-Essex Tech Coll; *m* 6 Sept 1969, Hazel, *née* Roberts; 1 s, 3 da; *Career* apprentice Marconi; work study engr: Sainsbury's, Pye and Marconi; work study mangr Pye; factory mangr: Pye, ESI, Sinclair; md Ian Bruce Associates Ltd, employment and mgmnt conslt, formerly md BOS Recruitment Group; parly advsr: Telecommunication Managers Assoc, Federation of Recruitment and Employment Services, Trevor Gilbert & Assocs; Parly candidate (C) Burnley 1983, Euro Parly candidate (C) Yorkshire West 1984, chm Cons Candidates Assoc 1986–87, MP (C) Dorset S 1987–; memb: Employment Select Ctee 1990–93, Science & Technology Select Ctee 1996–; vice chm Cons Employment Ctee 1992–93 and 1994–, vice chm Cons Social Security Ctee 1992–93 and 1994–, PPS to Social Security Mins 1992–94; *Recreations* badminton, sailing, tennis, wind surfing, scouting, camping; *Style*— Ian C Bruce, Esq, MP; ✉ House of Commons, London SW1A 0AA (☎ 0171 219 5086, fax 0171 219 6151, sec ☎ and fax 01305 833320)

BRUCE, Prof Ian Waugh; s of Thomas Waugh Bruce (d 1980), and Una Nellie, *née* Eagle (d 1987); *b* 21 April 1945; *Educ* King Edward VI Sch Southampton, Central HS Arizona, Univ of Birmingham (BSoc Sc); *m* 19 June 1971, Anthea Christine (Tina), da of Dr P R Rowland, of London; 1 da (Hannah b 20 Dec 1976), 1 s (William Waugh (Tom) b 18 May 1979); *Career* apprentice chem engr Courtaulds 1964–65, mktg trainee then mangr Unilever 1968–70, appeals and PR offr then asst dir Age Concern England 1970–74, dir Volunteer Centre UK 1975–81, controller of secretariat then asst chief exec Borough of Hammersmith and Fulham 1981–83, dir gen RNIB 1983–; chm Coventry Int Centre 1964, memb Arts Cncl of GB Art Panel, Art Film Ctee and New Activities Ctee 1967–71, conslt UN Div of Social Affrs 1970–72; spokesman: Artists Now 1973–77, Nat Good Neighbour Campaign 1977–79; sec Volunteurope Brussels 1979–81, advsr BBC Community Progs Unit 1979–81, co-chm Disability Benefits Consortium 1987–; memb: Exec Ctee Nat Cncl for Voluntary Orgns 1978–81 and 1990–94, Cncl Ret Execs Action Clearing House 1978–83, Advsy Cncl Centre for Policies on Ageing 1979–83, Educn Advsy Cncl IBA 1981–83, Steering Ctee Disability Alliance 1985–92, Exec Ctee Age Concern Eng 1986–92, Nat Advsy Cncl on Employment of Disabled People 1987–, Bd Central London TEC 1990– (dep chm 1996); City Univ Business Sch: visiting prof 1991–, hon dir VOLPROF (Centre for Vol Sector and Not-for-Profit Mgmnt) 1991–; Sir Raymond Priestley Expeditionary Award Univ of Birmingham 1968; hon DSoc Sc Univ of Birmingham 1995; memb ICA, MIMgt 1975, FIMgt 1981, CIMgt 1991, FRSA 1991; *Books* Public Relations and the Social Services (1972), Patronage of the Creative Artist (jtly, 1974, 2 edn 1975), Blind and Partially Sighted Adults in Britain (1991), Managing and Staffing Britain's Largest Charities (jtly, 1992), Management for Tomorrow (jtly, 1993), Meeting Need - Successful Charity Marketing (1994); author of papers on visual handicap, voluntary and community work, old people, contemporary art and marketing; *Recreations* the arts, the countryside; *Style*— Prof Ian Bruce; ✉ 54 Mall Road, London W6 9DG; RNIB, 224 Great Portland Street, London W1N 6AA (☎ 0171 388 1266)

BRUCE, Hon James Michael Edward; CBE (1992), JP (Perthshire 1962); 2 s of 10 Earl of Elgin and 14 of Kincardine (d 1968); *b* 26 Aug 1927; *Educ* Eton, RMC, RAC Cirencester; *m* 1, 1950, Hon (Margaret) Jean Dagbjørt Coats, da of 2 Baron Glentanar, KBE (d 1971); 2 s (and 1 s decd), 1 da; m 2, 1975, Morven-Anne (d 1994), da of Alistair Macdonald; 2 s, 2 da; *Career* served Scots Gds; chm: SWOAC Holdings Ltd, Scottish Woodlands Ltd 1968–93; memb Home Grown Timber Advsy Ctee 1963–94, vice pres Scottish Opera 1988–93; hon fell: Scottish Cncl for Devpt and Industry 1994, The Game Conservancy 1994; FRSA, FInstD; *Clubs* New (Edinburgh), Pratt's; *Style*— The Hon James Bruce, CBE, JP; ✉ Dron House, Balmanno, by Perth PH2 9HG (☎ 01738 812786)

BRUCE, Kenneth Robertson (Ken); s of Peter Smith Bruce (d 1984), and Williamina McKenzie, *née* Dunbar; *b* 2 Feb 1951; *Educ* Hutchesons' Boys' GS Glasgow; *m* 1 (m dis), Fiona Frater; 2 s (Campbell McKenzie b 20 Nov 1979, Douglas Robertson b 23 March 1981); m 2, 16 Feb 1989, Anne Gilchrist; 1 da (Kate Anne b 15 Oct 1992); *Career* broadcaster; BBC staff announcer 1976–80 (progs incl: Good Morning Scotland, SRO Road Show, Ken Bruce's Saturday (BBC Radio Scot), Midday Concert (BBC Radio 3), Music To Remember (BBC Radio 4)); freelance broadcaster 1980–, own daily prog BBC Radio Scot 1980–84; BBC Radio 2: reg dep work 1982–83, own Saturday night show 1984, own daily morning prog 1985–90 and 1991–, presenter daily late night prog 1990; weekly prog BBC World Service 1986–93, presenter Breakaway (BBC Radio 4) 1990–92; main presenter Nat Music Day 1992–95; other progs incl: The 'What If' Show, The ABC Quiz, Pop Score, Comedy Classics (BBC Radio 2), Freewheeling, Pick of the Week (BBC Radio 4); TV progs incl: Swap Shop, Song for Europe, Countdown, Children in Need, Crosswits, A Word in Your Ear; commentaries: Commonwealth Games 1986, Seoul Olympics 1988, Eurovision Song Contest (BBC Radio 2) 1988–; *Recreations* films, reading, music, theatre; *Style*— Ken Bruce, Esq; ✉ c/o Jo Gurnett Personal Management, 2 New Kings Road, London SW6 (☎ 0171 736 7828, fax 0171 736 5455)

BRUCE, Malcolm Gray; MP (Lib Democrat) Gordon (majority 274); s of David Stewart Bruce, of Wirral, and late Kathleen Elmslie, *née* Delf; *b* 17 Nov 1944; *Educ* Wrekin Coll Shropshire, Univs of St Andrews and Strathclyde (MA, MSc); *m* 1969 (m dis 1992), Veronica Jane, da of Henry Coxon Wilson, of West Kirby, Wirral; 1 s (Alexander b 1974), 1 da (Caroline b 1976); *Career* Parly candidate (Lib): North Angus and Mearns Oct 1974, West Aberdeenshire 1979; MP (Lib 1983–88, Lib Dem 1988–) Gordon 1983–, ldr Scot Lib Democrats 1988–92, vice pres Nat Deaf Children's Soc; memb: Scottish Select Ctee 1983–87, Trade and Industry Ctee 1987–89 and 1992–94, Treasy Ctee 1994–; Treasy spokesman 1994–; *Clubs* Nat Lib; *Style*— Malcolm Bruce, Esq, MP; ✉ House of Commons, London SW1A 0AA

BRUCE, Lady Martha Veronica; OBE (1958), TD, DL (Fife 1987); da of late 10 Earl of Elgin and (14 of) Kincardine, KT, CMG, TD, CD, and the late Hon Dame Katherine Cochrane, DBE, da of late 1 Baron Cochrane of Cults, and Lady Gertrude Boyle, OBE, da of 6 Earl of Glasgow; *b* 7 Nov 1921; *Educ* Downham; *Career* Lt-Col WRAC (TA) CWRAC 51 Highland Div (TA); lady-in-waiting to HRH the late Princess Royal Jan to March 1965; govr: Greenock Prison 1969–75 (asst govr 1967–69), HM Instn Cornton Vale 1975–83; memb Jt Prison Chaplaincies Bd 1989–96; *Recreations* gardening, hill walking; *Style*— The Lady Martha Bruce, OBE, TD, DL; ✉ Gardener's Cottage, The Old Orchard, Limekilns, Dunfermline KY11 3HS

BRUCE, Sir (Francis) Michael Ian; 12 Bt (NS 1628), of Stenhouse, Stirlingshire; s of Sir Michael William Selby Bruce, 11 Bt (d 1957); discontinued use of Christian name Francis; *b* 3 April 1926; *m* 1, 1947 (m dis 1957), Barbara Stevens, da of Francis J Lynch; 2 s (Michael Ian Richard b 1950, Robert Dudley b 1952); m 2, 1961 (m dis 1963), Frances Keegan; m 3, 1966 (m dis 1975), Marilyn Anne, da of Carter Mullaly; m 4, 9 Nov 19–, Patricia Gail, da of Frederich Root; m 5, 1994, Alessandro Conforto, MD; *Heir* s, Michael Ian Richard Bruce b 10 Dec 1950; *Career* US Marine Corps 1943–46, memb Sqdn A 7 Regt NY 1948 (ret); ptnr Gossard-Bruce Co 1953–, Master Mariner's Ticket 1968; pres: Newport Sailing Club Inc Calif 1978–, Newport Academy of Sail Inc Calif 1979–, American Maritime Co 1980–; dir Lenders Indemnity Corp 1985–; *Clubs* Balboa Bay (Newport Beach), Vikings of Orange (Newport Beach); *Style*— Sir Michael Bruce, Bt; ✉ 34 Cormorant Circle, Newport Beach, Calif 92663, USA; Newport Sailing Club and Academy of Sail, 3432 Via Oporto, Suite 204, Newport Beach, Calif 92663, USA (☎ 714 675 7100)

BRUCE, Robert Bryson; s of Robert Bruce (d 1952), of Pinnacle, Ancrum, Jedburgh, and Mary Bryson, *née* MacTaggart; *b* 18 June 1930; *Educ* Loretto, Edinburgh Coll of Agriculture (DIP); *m* 19 July 1955, Maureen Rough, da of Dr Andrew Simpson (d 1973), of Hawick, Roxburghshire; 1 s (Robert Simpson b 21 May 1960), 2 da ((Elizabeth) Susan b 17 May 1957, Katrina Mary b 23 Nov 1962); *Career* farmer and landowner; elder Ancrum Church, govr Loretto Sch, chm BFSS Borders Region, former MFH Duke of Buccleuchs Hunt; *Recreations* golf, fishing, shooting, fox hunting; *Clubs* Hon Co of Edinburgh Golfers (Muirfield Gullane), Royal and Ancient Golf (St Andrews); *Style*— Robert Bruce, Esq; ✉ Williamrig, Ancrum, Jedburgh, Roxburghshire TD8 6UP (☎ 01835 830371)

BRUCE, Robert Charles; s of late Maj James Charles, MC (and Bar), of Morpeth, Northumberland, and Enid Lilian, *née* Brown; *b* 5 May 1948; *Educ* Belmont House, Solihull Sch, City of London Coll (BSc); *Career* trainee accountant Edward Moore and Sons 1971–75; Accountancy Age: staff writer and news ed 1976–81, ed 1981–90, assoc ed 1990–93; accountancy columnist The Times 1992–; Accountancy Journalist of the Year 1995; FRSA; *Books* Winners - How Small Businesses Achieve Excellence (1986); *Recreations* cricket, buying books; *Clubs* Surrey CCC; *Style*— Robert Bruce, Esq; ✉ 87 Marylands Rd, London W9 2DS (☎/fax 0171 286 0211); The Times, 1 Pennington Street, London E1 9XN (☎ 0171 782 5000, fax 0171 782 5112)

BRUCE, Steve Roger; s of Joseph Bruce, of Newcastle upon Tyne, and Sheenagh, *née* Creed; *b* 31 Dec 1960; *Educ* Benfield Comp Sch Newcastle upon Tyne; *m* Janet, da of Lesley Smith; 1 s (Alex b 23 Sept 1984), 1 da (Amy b 24 May 1987); *Career* professional footballer (defender); Gillingham 1978–84: league debut 1979, 205 league appearances, 28 goals; Norwich City 1984–87: joined for a fee of £135,000, 141 league appearances, 14 goals; transferred for a fee of £825,000 to Manchester Utd 1987–96 (over 100 appearances), capt 1994–96; transferred to Birmingham City 1996–; England: 8 youth caps, 1 B cap (capt); honours: League Cup 1985, FA Cup 1990, Euro Cup Winners' Cup 1991, Rumbelows Cup 1992, winners inaugural FA Premier League Championship 1992/93, winners League and FA Cup double 1994 and 1996 (setting record), winners Charity Shield 1993 and 1994; *Style*— Steve Bruce, Esq; ✉ c/o Birmingham City FC, St Andrews, Birmingham B9 4NH

BRUCE, Prof Victoria Geraldine (Vicki); da of Charles Frederick Bruce, and Geraldine Cordelia Diane, *née* Giffard; *b* 4 Jan 1953; *Educ* Church HS Newcastle, Newnham Coll Cambridge (MA, Sarah Smithson Studentship, PhD); *m* 1, 1978 (m dis), John Paul Fox; m 2, 1984, Anthony Michael Burton; *Career* demonstrator Dept of Psychology Univ of Newcastle 1977–78; Univ of Nottingham: lectr in psychology 1978–88, reader 1988–90, prof of psychology 1990–92; Univ of Stirling: prof of psychology 1992–, dep principal (research) 1995–; pres Euro Soc for Cognitive Psychology 1996–98 (memb 1987–, memb Ctee 1994–), chm Psychology Panel 1996 Research Assessment Exercise; memb: Neurosciences and Mental Health Bd MRC 1989–92, ESRC 1992–96 (chm Research Programmes Bd 1992–96), SHEFC 1995–; memb Editorial Advsy Bd Psychological Research 1988–; memb Editorial Bd: Euro Jl of Cognitive Psychology 1988–, Visual Cognition 1993–, Applied Cognitive Psychology 1994–95; ed British Jl of Psychology 1995–; consulting ed Jl of Experimental Psychology: Applied 1994–; memb: Experimental Psychology Soc 1980– (memb Ctee 1986–89), Psychonomic Soc 1988–; FBPsS 1989, CPsychol 1989, FRSE 1996; *Publications* Visual Perception: Psychology and Ecology (with P Green, 1985, 2 edn 1990, 3 edn with P

Green and M Georgeson 1996), Recognising Faces (1988), Visual Cognition: computational, experimental and neuropsychological perspectives (with G Humphreys, 1989), Face Recognition (ed, 1991), Processing Images of Faces (ed jtly with M Burton, 1992), Processing the Facial Image (ed jtly, 1992), Object and face recognition (ed jtly with G Humphreys, 1994), Perception and Representation (with I Roth, 1995), Unsolved Mysteries of Mind: tutorial essays in cognition (ed, 1996); also author of numerous articles and papers in learned jls; *Recreations* dogs, walking, games; *Style*— Prof Vicki Bruce, FRSE; ✉ Department of Psychology, University of Stirling, Stirling FK9 4LA

BRUCE-GARDNER, Sir Douglas Bruce; 2 Bt (UK 1945), of Frilford, Co Berks; s of Sir Charles Bruce-Gardner, 1 Bt (d 1960); *b* 27 Jan 1917; *Educ* Uppingham, Trinity Coll Cambridge; *m* 1, 27 July 1940 (m dis 1964), Monica Flumerfelt, o da of late Prof Sir Geoffrey Jefferson, CBE, FRS; 1 s (Robert Henry b 1943), 2 da (Erica Judith (Mrs Paul H Blackburn) b 1941, Sarah Tanis (Mrs Richard W Towse) b 1952); m 2, 18 March 1964, Sheila Jane, da of late Roger Stilliard, of Seer Green, Bucks; 1 s (James Graham b 1969), 1 da (Joanna Margaret b 1966); *Heir* s, Robert Henry Bruce-Gardner, *qv*; *Career* chm: GKN Steel Co Ltd 1965–67, GKN Rolled and Bright Steel Ltd 1968–72, GKN (South Wales) Ltd 1968–72, Miles Druce & Co 1974–77; dep chm GKN Group 1974–77; dir: Guest Keen & Nettlefolds Ltd 1960–82, BHP-GKN Holdings Ltd 1977–78, Iron Trades Employers' Insurance Association 1977–87, Iron Trades Mutual Insurance Co 1977–87; Prime Warden Worshipful Co of Blacksmiths 1983–84; *Style*— Sir Douglas Bruce-Gardner, Bt; ✉ Stocklands, Lewstone, Ganarew, nr Monmouth, Gwent NP5 3SS (☎ 01600 890 216)

BRUCE-GARDNER, Robert Henry; s and h of Sir Douglas Bruce Bruce-Gardner, 2 Bt, *qv*, by his 1 w, Monica Flumerfelt, *née* Jefferson; *b* 10 June 1943; *Educ* Uppingham, Univ of Reading; *m* 1979, Veronica Ann Hand-Oxborrow, da of late Rev W E Hand; 2 s (Thomas Edmund Peter b 28 Jan 1982, Richard Tyndall Jowett b 1983); *Career* dir Dept of Conservation and Technol Courtauld Inst of Art; *Clubs* Travellers'; *Style*— Robert Bruce-Gardner, Esq; ✉ 121 Brackenbury Road, London W6 0BQ (☎ 0181 748 7652); Department of Conservation and Technology, Courtauld Institute of Art, University of London, Somerset House, Strand, London WC2R 0RN

BRUCE-JONES, Tom Allan; s of Tom Bruce-Jones (d 1984), of Blairlogie, Stirlingshire, and Rachel Inglis, *née* Dunlop; *b* 28 Aug 1941; *Educ* Charterhouse, Lincoln Coll Oxford (BA); *m* 1, 1965 (m dis 1980), R Normand; 1 s (Tom b 8 Sept 1968), 1 da (Caroline b 23 Nov 1966); m 2, 6 March 1981, Stina Birgitta, da of Harry Ossian Ahlgren (d 1982), of Helsinki; *Career* dir Price and Pierce (Woodpulp) Ltd 1973–77, vice pres Georgia-Pacific International Inc 1977–79, chm and md James Jones and Sons Ltd 1995– (jt md 1979–87, md 1987); dir: Jones and Campbell (Hldgs) Ltd 1988–, Jones Buckie Shipyard Ltd 1988–95, Highland Sawmillers plc 1988–94, Forestry Committee of Great Britain Ltd 1989–, Highland Timber plc 1990–, Scottish Woodlands Ltd 1990–, Stella-Jones Inc (Montreal) 1993– (chm 1994–), Burt Boulton and Haywood Ltd 1994–, Larbert Timber plc 1995–; consul for Finland Glasgow 1994–; *Recreations* fishing, golf, music; *Clubs* Hon Co of Edinburgh Golfers; *Style*— Tom Bruce-Jones, Esq; ✉ 15 Queen's Gate, Dowanhill St, Glasgow; James Jones & Sons Ltd, Broomage Ave, Larbert, Stirlingshire FK5 4NQ (☎ 01324 562 241, fax 01324 556 642)

BRUCE LOCKHART, Robin Norman; s of Sir Robert Hamilton Bruce Lockhart, KCMG (d 1970), and late Jean Haslewood, *née* Turner; *b* 13 April 1920; *Educ* RNC Dartmouth, Pembroke Coll Cambridge (BEcon); *m* 1, 1941, Margaret Crookdake; 1 da (Sheila Margaret b 1951); m 2, 1955, Ginette de Noyelle (d 1985); m 3, 1987, Eila Owen; *Career* WWII Lt RNVR 1939–46; asst to Br Naval Attaché Paris, Naval Intelligence Admty, Flag Lt to C-in-C China, Flag Lt to C-in-C Eastern Fleet, Ceylon, staff C-in-C Plymouth; foreign mangr Financial Times 1946–53, sr exec Beaverbrook Newspapers 1953–61, dep chm Central Wagon Co Ltd 1965–69; chm: Moorgill Properties Ltd 1967–72, Chasebrook Ltd 1967–72, 37/38 Adelaide Crescent (Hove) Ltd 1983–; memb London Stock Exchange 1962; author; *Books* Reilly Ace of Spies (1967–, TV series 1984–85), Reilly the First Man (1967), Halfway to Heaven (1985); *Recreations* salmon fishing, travel; *Clubs* MCC, Royal Scottish Automobile; *Style*— Robin Bruce Lockhart, Esq; ✉ 37 Adelaide Crescent, Hove, Sussex; Quand Meme, Rue Romain Rolland, Collioure, Pyrénées Orientales, France

BRUCE OF DONINGTON, Baron (Life Peer UK 1974); Donald William Trevor Bruce; s of William Trevor Bruce (d 1934), of Norbury, Surrey; *b* 3 Oct 1912; *Educ* The GS Donington Lincs; *m* 1, 1939 (m dis 1980), Joan Letitia, da of late H C Butcher, of London; 1 s, 2 da (and 1 da decd); m 2, 1981, Cyrena Heard, *née* Shaw; *Career* served WWII UK and France in rank of Maj (despatches); practising CA 1936–; economist and author; MP (Lab) Portsmouth N 1945–50, PPS to Min of Health 1945–50; memb Euro Parl 1975–79; oppn spokesman on: Trade and Industl matters 1983–87, Treasy matters 1979–83 and 1987–90; sits as Lab Peer specialising in EEC matters; FCA; *Recreations* swimming; *Style*— The Rt Hon the Lord Bruce of Donington; ✉ Hobson House, 155 Gower Street, London WC1E 6BH (☎ 0171 387 2888, fax 0171 388 0600)

BRUCE-RADCLIFFE, Godfrey Martin; s of Roy Bruce-Radcliffe (d 1976), of Surrey, and Joyce Evelyn, *née* Shewring (d 1996); *b* 19 June 1945; *Educ* King's Coll Taunton, Guildford Coll of Law; *Career* articled clerk Trower Still & Keeling (now Trowers and Hamlins) 1964, admitted slr 1970, ptnr D J Freeman & Co (now D J Freeman) 1978–94 (joined 1977), ptnr Hobson Audley Hopkins & Wood 1994–; Freeman City of London 1986; memb Law Soc 1970; *Recreations* sailing, walking, gardening, music; *Style*— Godfrey Bruce-Radcliffe, Esq; ✉ Hobson Audley Hopkins & Wood, 7 Pilgrim Street, London EC4V 6DR (☎ 0171 450 4580, fax 0171 248 0672, DX 401 London)

BRUCE-SMYTHE, Simon Carrington; s of Capt Reginald Oliver Bruce-Smythe (d 1969), and Jane Bruce-Smythe (d 1976); *b* 1 Aug 1942; *Educ* Downside; *m* 22 Oct 1966, Caroline Ann, da of Derek Godfrey Leach; 2 s (Charles Oliver b 19 Feb 1971, Peter Carrington b 30 Sept 1976); *Career* Price Waterhouse: joined 1965, ptnr 1977–, various exec appts; ACA 1966; *Recreations* horse racing, shooting, fishing; *Style*— Simon Bruce-Smythe, Esq; ✉ Price Waterhouse, Southwark Towers, London SE1 9SJ (☎ 0171 939 3000)

BRUCK, Steven Mark; s of Herbert Martin Bruck, of London, and Kathe Margot Bruck; *b* 30 Sept 1947; *Educ* Hendon GS, Univ of Southampton (BSc), LSE (MSc); *m* 1 July 1971, Mirela, da of Alexander Izsak; 1 s (Jonathan b 1977), 1 da (Tamara b 1974); *Career* articled clerk Chalmers Impey CAs 1969–72, gp accountant Halma plc 1972–73, special projects accountant Overseas Containers Ltd 1973–75, Pannell Fitzpatrick 1975–78, ptnr Mercers Bryant 1978–84, corp fin ptnr Pannell Kerr Forster 1984–; memb Bd Belsize Square Synagogue; FCA 1972; *Recreations* family, theatre, eating; *Style*— Steven Bruck, Esq; ✉ Pannell Kerr Forster, New Garden House, 78 Hatton Garden, London EC1N 8JI (☎ 0171 831 7393, fax 0171 405 6736)

BRUCKNER, Dr Felix Ernest; s of William Bruckner, of London, and Anna, *née* Hahn; *b* 18 April 1937; *Educ* London Hosp Med Coll, Univ of London (MB BS); *m* 24 June 1967, Rosalind Dorothy, da of George Edward Farley Bailey, of Herts; 2 s (James b 1974, Thomas b 1976), 1 da (Catherine b 1981); *Career* conslt physician and rheumatologist St George's Hosp London 1970–; med advsr Bd of Mgmnt New Victoria Hosp Kingston upon Thames; pres Rheumatology and Rehabilitation Section Royal Soc of Med 1994–95; FRCP; *Publications* numerous chapters and papers on rheumatological subjects; *Recreations* chess, music, reading; *Clubs* Royal Society of Medicine; *Style*— Dr Felix Bruckner; ✉ 12 Southwood Ave, Kingston upon Thames, Surrey KT2 7HD (☎ 0181 949 3955); Parkside Hospital, 53 Parkside, Wimbledon, London SW19 5NX (☎ 0181 946 4202, fax 0181 944 8461)

BRUDENELL, Edmund Crispin Stephen James George; DL (Northants 1977); s of George Brudenell (2 s of Cdr Lord Robert Brudenell-Bruce, RN, 4 s of 3 Marquess of Ailesbury); *b* 24 Oct 1928; *Educ* Harrow, RAC Cirencester; *m* 8 Nov 1955, Hon Marian Cynthia, *née* Manningham-Buller, eldest da of 1 Viscount Dilhorne, PC; 2 s (Robert b 1956, Thomas (twin) b 1956), 1 da (Anna Maria b 1960); *Career* contested (C) Whitehaven 1964; High Sheriff of Leics 1969, High Sheriff of Northants 1987; landowner; Liveryman Worshipful Co of Fishmongers; *Recreations* shooting, deer stalking, travelling; *Clubs* Carlton, Pratt's; *Style*— Edmund Brudenell, Esq, DL; ✉ Deene Park, Corby, Northants (☎ 01780 450223, fax 01780 450282); 18 Laxford House, Ebury St, London SW1W 9JU (☎ 0171 730 8715)

BRUDENELL, (John) Michael; s of Clement Shenstone Brudenell (d 1964), of Ashford, Middx, and Elizabeth Marjery, *née* James; *b* 13 April 1925; *Educ* Hampton Sch, King's Coll London and King's Coll Hosp London (MB BS); *m* 6 April 1957, Mollie, da of Arthur Herbert Rothwell (d 1974), of Audenshaw, Lancs; 4 s (Timothy b 1958, Jeremy b 1960, Marcus b 1962, Edward b 1967); *Career* Capt RAMC 1950–52, Maj AER Field Surgical Team 1953–63; conslt obstetrician and gynaecologist: Bradford Royal Infirmary Yorks 1961–64, King's Coll Hosp London 1964–90; conslt gynaecologist King Edward VIII Hosp London 1980–, sr conslt gynaecologist Queen Victoria Hosp 1964–90; Freeman City of London 1974, Liveryman Worshipful Soc of Apothecaries 1967; hon fell Royal Soc of Med Barcelona 1979; FRCS 1956 (memb Cncl 1985–90), FRCOG 1973 (memb Cncl 1973–89, hon treas 1980–87), FRSM (former pres Section of Obstetrics and Gynaecology); *Recreations* reading, tennis, skiing; *Clubs* Gynaecological Travellers'; *Style*— Michael Brudenell, Esq; ✉ The Barn, Station Rd, Hever, Kent TN8 7ER (☎ 01732 863086); 73 Harley St, London W1N 1DE (☎ 0171 935 5098, fax 0171 224 6853)

BRUDENELL, Thomas Mervyn; s of Edmund Crispin Stephen James George Brudenell, of Deene Park, Corby, Northamptonshire, and Marian Cynthia, *née* Manningham Buller; *b* 12 Aug 1956; *Educ* Eton; *m* 1, 5 May 1984, Venetia Jane (d 1993), da of Maj Robert Patricius Chaworth Musters (d 1992), of Felley Priory, Jacksdale, Nottinghamshire; 2 da (Sophia b 12 April 1985, Victoria b 11 Feb 1987); m 2, 27 June 1996, Mrs Amanda J Skiffington, da of Alick David Yorke Naylor-Leyland, MVO (d 1991), and the Countess of Wilton; *Career* called to the Bar Inner Temple 1977; chm Horserace Betting Levy Appeal Tbnl 1995–; *Recreations* fishing, shooting, stalking, bridge, racing; *Clubs* Pratt's; *Style*— Thomas Brudenell, Esq; ✉ 70 Alderney Street, London SW1 (☎ 0171 976 5277); Queen Elizabeth Building, Temple, London EC4 (☎ 0171 797 7837)

BRUETON, Dr Martin John; s of Neville Frederick William Brueton (d 1981), of Bristol, and Nancy Rushton, *née* Baldwin; *b* 2 Feb 1944; *Educ* Bristol GS, Bart's Med Sch (MB BS, MD, DCH, FRCP), Univ of Birmingham (MSc); *m* May 1967, Patricia Ann, da of Geoffrey Oliphant May (d 1994), and Jean, *née* Hayward (d 1986); 2 da (Nicola Ann b 18 June 1969, Catherine Jane b 16 March 1975), 1 s (Mark Richard b 25 May 1971); *Career* jr registrar Bart's 1970–71 (house physician 1968), sr registrar Ahmadu Bello Univ Zaria Nigeria 1971–73, lectr in paediatrics Univ of Birmingham/Children's Hosp Birmingham 1973–78, sr lectr and hon conslt paediatrician Westminster Children's Hosp 1979–93, hon conslt paediatrician Chelsea and Westminster, Charing Cross and Royal Brompton Hosps London and reader in child health Charing Cross and Westminster Med Sch London 1979–, clinical dir Women and Children's Directorate Chelsea and Westminster Healthcare NHS Trust 1994–95; regularly invited to lecture at overseas univs and to participate in meetings/working gps in the fields of paediatric gastroenterology and nutrition; Wellcome Tst jr research fell 1976; memb: Br Paediatric Assoc, Br Soc of Gastroenterology, Br Soc of Paediatric Gastroenterology and Nutrition, Euro Soc of Paediatric Gastroenterology and Nutrition; FRCP; *Books* Diseases of Children in Subtropics and Tropics (jt ed, 1991), Practical Paediatric Therapeutics (jtly, 1991); *Recreations* tennis, music, theatre; *Clubs* RSM; *Style*— Dr Martin Brueton; ✉ Academic Department of Child Health, Chelsea and Westminster Hospital, 369 Fulham Road, London SW10 9NH (☎ 0181 746 8628, fax 0181 746 8770, e-mail m.brueton@cxwms.ac.uk)

BRUGES, (Charles) James Long; s of Maj (Charles) Eric Lond Bruges (d 1967), of Semington, Trowbridge, Wilts, and Beatrice Rose Campbell, *née* Leighton Stevens; *b* 25 Aug 1933; *Educ* Sheikh Bagh Kashmir, Kelly Coll Devon, Architectural Assoc London (AA Dip); *m* 4 June 1971, Anthea, da of (Oliver) Maldwyn Davies, of Bath; 1 s (Benedict b 1961), 3 da (Clare b 1963, Kate b 1972, Beatrice b 1974); *Career* asst architect Trevor Dannatt Assocs 1958–60, resident architect Khartoum Univ 1960–63, assoc Whicheloe Macfarlane 1963–69, ptnr Towning Hill and Ptnrs 1969–73, princ Bruges Tozer Architects 1973–; fndr memb Concept Planning Gp 1988, advsr on urban design Br Devpt Corp 1989, fndr memb and dir Energy Audit Co, dir Bristol C of C and Initiative; winner Huddersfield Urban Design Competition 1996; memb: Bristol City Docks Gp, Civic Soc, Bristol Visual & Environmental Gp, RIBA; *Recreations* painting, tennis, music; *Style*— James Bruges, Esq; ✉ 23 Sydenham Road, Bristol BS6 5SJ (☎ 0117 942 5834); Bruges Tozer Partnership, 7 Unity St, Bristol BS1 5HH (☎ 0117 927 9797)

BRUGES, Katharine Georgia (Kate); da of Christopher John Farara, of Guildford, Surrey, and Alison Mary, *née* Duguid; *b* 19 Nov 1962; *Educ* Queen Elizabeth II Silver Jubilee Sch, Woking Sixth Form Coll, Newnham Coll Cambridge (MA); *m* 7 Sept 1991, Richard Michael Bruges, s of Maj Michael Bruges; 2 s (Max b 16 June 1993, Harry b 16 June 1995); *Career* J Walter Thompson: joined as graduate trainee 1984, appointed to assoc bd, youngest bd appointment 1989, currently dir of brand communications and trg; *Recreations* riding, playing flute and piano, contemporary literature; *Style*— Mrs Kate Bruges; ✉ J Walter Thompson Co Ltd, 40 Berkeley Square, London W1X 6AD (☎ 0171 499 4040, fax 0171 493 8432/8418)

BRUGHA, Dr Traolach Seán; s of Ruairi Brugha, of Dublin, and Maire, *née* MacSwiney; *b* 6 Jan 1953; *Educ* Gonzaga Coll Dublin, Univ Coll Dublin (MB BCh, MD); *m* 3 April 1976, Máire Nic Eoghain; 3 da (Rossa Eoghain, Lia Patricia, Cillian Traolach); *Career* registrar in psychiatry St Vincent's Hosp Elm Park Dublin 1979–80, registrar then sr registrar Bethlem and Maudsley Hosp London 1980–87, clinical scientist MRC Social Psychiatry Unit London 1982–87, hon lectr in psychiatry Inst of Psychiatry London 1984–87, sr lectr Univ of Leicester 1987–, hon conslt psychiatrist Leicester Health Authy 1987–, seconded as SMO Dept of Health London 1995–97; MRCPsych 1981; *Recreations* photography, cycling, music; *Style*— Dr Traolach Brugha; ✉ Department of Psychiatry, University of Leicester, Leicester (☎ 0116 252 3240, fax 0116 252 3293)

BRUINVELS, Peter Nigel Edward; er s of Capt Stanley Bruinvels, of Dorking, Surrey, and Ninette Maud, *née* Kibblewhite; *b* 30 March 1950; *Educ* St John's Sch Leatherhead, Univ of London (LLB), Cncl of Legal Educn (Bar exams); *m* 20 Sept 1980, Alison Margaret, da of Maj David Gilmore Bacon, of Lymington, Hants; 2 da (Alexandra Caroline Jane b 6 April 1986, Georgina Emma Kate b 20 Oct 1988); *Career* princ Peter Bruinvels Assocs (media mgmnt corporate communications and public affrs conslts) 1986–, managing ed Bruinvels News & Media (press and broadcasting agents) 1993–, political commentator, freelance journalist and author 1987–, special external advsr DTI 1992–, memb Child Support and Social Security Appeals Tbnls 1994–; non-exec dir Cheyney Goulding 1995–; OFSTED Denominational Schs Inspector 1994–; MP (C) Leicester East 1983–87, memb Cons Home Office & NI Ctees 1983–87; jt vice chm: Cons

Urban Affrs and New Towns Ctee 1984–87, Cons Educn Ctee 1985–87; promoter Crossbows Act 1987; campaign co-ordinator gen election Eastbourne 1992, prospective Parly candidate The Wrekin 1995; memb Cons NUEC 1976–81, vice chm SE Area Conservatives 1977–79, pres Dorking Conservatives 1995–; Church Cmmr 1993–; memb: Guildford Diocesan Synod 1979–, Gen Synod C of E 1985–, Bd of Patrons 1985–, Parly Legislative Ctee (C of E) 1991–96, Gen Synod Bd of Educn 1996–; Freeman City of London 1980; FRSA, MJI, MCIM, MIPR, Fell Indust and Parl Tst; *Books* Zoning in on Enterprise (1982), Light up the Roads (1984), Sharing in Britain's Success: A Study in Widening Share Ownership Through Privatisation (1987), Investing in Enterprise: A Comprehensive Guide to Inner City Regeneration and Urban Renewal (1989); *Recreations* politics in the C of E, political campaigning, the media; *Clubs* Carlton, Inner Temple, Corporation of Church House, Jersey Wildlife Preservation; *Style*— Peter Bruinvels, Esq; ✉ 14 High Meadow Close, St Paul's Road West, Dorking, Surrey RH4 2LG (☎ and fax 01306 887082, mobile ☎ 0421 411 688)

BRUMMER, Alexander; s of Michael Brummer, of Brighton, and Hilda, *née* Lyons; *b* 25 May 1949; *Educ* Brighton Hove & Sussex GS, Univ of Southampton (BSc), Univ of Bradford Mgmnt Centre (MBA); *m* 26 Oct 1975, Patricia Lyndsey, da of Saul Leopold Magrill; 2 s (Justin Adam b 29 Sept 1980, Gabriel Joseph b 30 Dec 1981), 1 da (Jessica Rachel b 5 Jan 1978); *Career* journalist; De La Rue Company 1971–72, Haymarket Publishing 1972–73; The Guardian: fin corr 1973–79, Washington corr 1979–85, Washington bureau chief 1985–89, foreign ed 1989, fin ed 1990–; asst ed (business) The Observer 1996–; winner Best Foreign Corr in US (Overseas Press Club) 1989; *Books* American Destiny (jt author, 1985), Hanson: A Biography (1994); *Recreations* reading, antiques; *Style*— Alexander Brummer, Esq; ✉ The Guardian, 119 Farringdon Rd, London EC1 3ER (☎ 0171 239 9886)

BRUMMER, Malcolm Howard; s of David Brummer, of London, and Sylvia, *née* Miller; *b* 21 March 1948; *Educ* Haberdashers' Aske's, Downing Coll Cambridge (MA); *m* 12 March 1980, Yvonne Simy, *née* Labos; 1 s (Richard Joseph b 16 Feb 1982), 1 da (Natasha Nina b 1 Dec 1985); *Career* Berwin Leighton: articled clerk 1970–72, ptnr 1975–, head Property Dept 1983–89, chm Fin Ctee 1987–93, chm 1990–94; memb Law Soc 1972; *Recreations* family, opera, stamps; *Style*— Malcolm Brummer, Esq; ✉ 3 Milton Close, Hampstead Garden Suburb, London N2 OQH (☎ 0181 209 0213); Berwin Leighton Solicitors, Adelaide House, London Bridge, London EC4R 9HA (☎ 0171 623 3144, fax 0171 623 4416)

BRUNDLE, Martin John; s of late Alfred Edward John Brundle, and Alma, *née* Coe; *b* 1 June 1959; *Educ* King Edward VII GS Kings Lynn, Norfolk Coll of Arts and Technol; *m* Elizabeth Mary; 1 da (Charlotte Emily b 9 May 1988), 1 s (Alexander Martin b 7 Aug 1990); *Career* motor racing driver; began racing aged 12, turned professional 1984; Formula One teams driven for: Tyrrell, Zakspeed, Williams, Brabham, Benetton, McLaren, Ligier, Jordan 1996–; drove for Jaguar in World Sportscar Championship 1985–91; achievements incl: runner-up Br Formula 3 1983, fifth place in first ever grand prix 1984, world sportscar champion 1988, winner Le Mans 24–hr Race 1990, runner-up Italian Grand Prix 1992, third place Br, French, Japanese and Australian Grands Prix 1992, third place San Marino Gp 1993, runner-up Monaco Grand Prix 1994, third place Belgian Grand Prix 1995; awards: Grovewood Award for most promising young driver in Cwlth 1982, Seagrave Trophy for exceptional performance on land or sea 1988, Br Racing Drivers' Club Gold Medal 1988; *Recreations* helicopter flying, golf; *Style*— Martin Brundle, Esq; ✉ Fourways Garage, Tottenhill, King's Lynn, Norfolk PE33 0SR

BRUNNER, Adrian John Nelson; QC (1994); s of Cdr Robert Henry Hugh Brunner, DSC, RN (d 1981), and Elizabeth Elliott, *née* Colbé; *b* 18 June 1946; *Educ* Ampleforth, BRNC, Coll of Law; *m* 1970, Christine Anne, da of late Thomas Peter Hughes, of Buntingford; 4 da (Elizabeth b 1971, Kate b 1972, Sarah b 1974, Samantha b 1981), 1 s (David b 1976); *Career* served RN 1963–66 (RNR 1966–74); called to the Bar Inner Temple (Major scholarship) 1968, recorder of the Crown Court 1990–; *Recreations* yachting, shooting; *Clubs* Royal Yacht Squadron, Bar Yacht; *Style*— Adrian Brunner, Esq, QC; ✉ Furneaux Pelham Hall, Buntingford, Hertfordshire SG9 0LB; Holborn Head Farm, Scrabster, Caithness KW14 7UW; Ground Floor, 2 Harcourt Buildings, Middle Temple Lane, Temple, London EC4Y 9DB (☎ 0171 583 9020, fax 0171 583 2686)

BRUNNER, Elizabeth, Lady; (Dorothea) Elizabeth; OBE (1965), JP (Oxon 1946); o da of Henry Brodribb Irving (d 1919), and Dorothea, *née* Baird; gda of Sir Henry Irving, the actor; *m* 1926, Sir Felix Brunner, 3 Bt (d 1982); 3 s (and 2 s decd); *Career* chm: Nat Fedn of Women's Insts 1951–56, Keep Britain Tidy Gp 1958–67 (pres 1967–85), Women's Gp on Public Welfare The Nat Cncl of Social Servs 1960–70; *Style*— Elizabeth, Lady Brunner, OBE, JP; ✉ Greys Court, Henley-on-Thames, Oxon RG9 4PG (☎ 01491 628296)

BRUNNER, Hugo Laurence Joseph; s of Sir Felix John Morgan Brunner, 3 Bt (d 1982), of Greys Court, nr Henley-on-Thames, Oxon, and Elizabeth, Lady Brunner, OBE, *qv*; *b* 17 Aug 1935; *Educ* Eton, Trinity Coll Oxford (MA); *m* 7 Jan 1967, Mary Rose Catherine, da of Arthur Joseph Lawrence Pollen (d 1968), of Harpsden Wood, Henley-on-Thames, Oxon; 5 s (Joseph b 1967, Samuel b 1972, Magnus b 1974, Philip b 1977, Francis b 1982), 1 da (Isabel b 1969); *Career* various appts Oxford Univ Press 1958–65 and 1977–79, dir Chatto and Windus 1967–76 and 1979–85 (md 1979–82, chm 1982–85); dir Caithness Glass 1966– (chm 1985–90), dir Brunner Investment Tst 1987–; Parly candidate (Lib) Torquay 1964 and 1966; chm Oxford Diocesan Advsy Ctee for Care of Churches 1985–; High Sheriff of Oxon 1988–89; Lord-Lieut of Oxon 1996– (DL 1994–96); hon fell Trinity Coll Oxford 1995; *Recreations* hill walking, church crawling; *Clubs* Reform; *Style*— Hugo Brunner, Esq; ✉ 26 Norham Rd, Oxford OX2 6SF (☎ 01865 54821); The Brunner Investment Trust plc, 20 Fenchurch St, London EC3M 3LB (☎ 0171 956 6600)

BRUNNING, His Hon Judge David Wilfrid; s of Wilfred George Brunning (d 1983) of Burton on Trent, and Marion, *née* Humphries; *b* 10 April 1943; *Educ* Burton-upon-Trent GS, Worcester Coll Oxford (BA, DPA); *m* 8 July 1967, Deidre Ann Shotton; 3 s (b 1972, 1974, 1977); *Career* articled clerk Leicester CC 1966–67, called to the Bar Middle Temple 1969, in practice (Midland and Oxford Circuit) 1970–88, circuit judge (Midland and Oxford Circuit) 1988–; chm: Kirk Lodge Probation Hostel Mgmnt Ctee 1973–88, Leicester Anchor Club 1983–89; *Recreations* walking, squash, campanology, music; *Style*— His Honour Judge Brunning; ✉ Nottingham Combined Court Centre, Canal St, Nottingham

BRUNO, Franklin Roy (Frank); MBE (1990); s of Robert Bruno (d 1977), and Lynette, *née* Cambell; *b* 16 Nov 1961; *Educ* Oak Hall Sch Sussex; *m* 5 Feb 1990, Laura Frances, da of Peter James Mooney; 2 da (Nicola Frances b 24 July 1982, Rachel Lynette b 28 Aug 1986), 1 s (Franklin Robert Bruno Jnr b 28 March 1995); *Career* professional boxer; began boxing with Wandsworth Boys' Club 1970, memb Sir Philip Game Amateur Boxing Club 1977–80, turned professional 1982; achievements as amateur: 21 contests, 20 victories, represented Young England 1980, winner nat and London ABA heavyweight titles 1980; achievements as professional: 45 contests, 40 victories (38 inside the distance), Euro heavyweight champion 1985–86 (relinquished title), world heavyweight title challenges v Tim Witherspoon 1986, Mike Tyson 1989 and Lennox Lewis 1993, WBC world heavyweight champion defeating Oliver McCall 1995 (first British heavyweight to win world title on British soil this century), lost title against Mike Tyson 1996, ret from boxing Aug 1996; memb Equity; appeared in pantomime: Dominion Theatre 1989, Nottingham 1990, Bristol 1991; former presenter People (BBC), guest appearances on numerous TV shows; TV Times Sports Personality of the Year 1990, SOS Sports Personality of the Year 1990, runner up BBC Sports Personality of the Year 1995; winner Lifetime Achievement Award BBC Sports Personality of the Year Awards 1996; *Recreations* swimming, training, driving, eating, shopping for good clothes, listening to jazz-funk and soul records, watching old boxing videos; *Style*— Frank Bruno, Esq, MBE; ✉ PO Box 2266, Brentwood, Essex CM15 0AQ (fax 01277 822209)

BRUNSKILL, Prof Ronald William; OBE (1990); s of William Brunskill (d 1986), of Morecambe, Lancs, and Elizabeth Hannah, *née* Gowling (d 1991); *b* 3 Jan 1929; *Educ* Bury HS, Univ of Manchester (BA, MA, PhD); *m* 20 June 1960, Miriam, da of late Joseph Allsopp, of Weirsdale, Florida; 2 da (Lesley (Mrs Glass) b 27 Oct 1961, Robin b 9 Sept 1963); *Career* Nat Serv 1953–55, 2 Lt RE, served in Suez Canal zone; studio asst in architecture Univ of Manchester 1951–53; architectural asst: London CC 1955, Univ of Manchester 1955–56; Cwlth Fund (Harkness) fell and visiting fell MIT Boston 1956–57, architect to Williams Deacon's Bank Manchester 1957–60, reader in architecture Univ of Manchester 1983–89 (lectr 1960–73, sr lectr 1973–83, hon fell 1989–94), prof De Montfort Univ Leicester 1995–; visiting prof: Univ of Florida Gainesville 1969–70, De Montfort Univ Leicester 1994–95; architect in private practice, ptnr Carter Brunskill Assocs 1965–70; vice chm Royal Cmmn on Ancient and Historical Monuments of Wales 1993– (memb 1983–); memb: Historic Bldgs Cncl for Eng 1978–84, Historic Buildings and Monuments Cmmn (Eng Heritage) 1989–95 (chm Historic Bldgs and Ancient Monuments Advsy Ctees 1989–95 (memb 1984–89), chm Cathedrals and Churches Advsy Ctee 1989–95), Cathedrals Advsy Cmmn for Eng 1981–91, Cathedral Fabric Cmmn for England 1991–96, Cathedral Fabric Ctees Manchester and Blackburn 1991–96 and Chester 1991–94, Diocesan Advsy Ctee Manchester 1973–79 and 1987–92; chm Urban Parks Advsy Panel Heritage Lottery Fund 1995–; govr Bolton Inst for Higher Education 1982–89, pres Cumberland and Westmorland Archaeological and Antiquarian Soc 1990–93, vice pres Weald and Downland Museum Tst; chm: Ancient Monuments Soc 1990–, Friends of Friendless Churches 1990–; patron Lancs Heritage Tst 1996–; ARIBA 1951, FSA 1975; *Books* Illustrated Handbook of Vernacular Architecture (1971, 3 edn 1987), Vernacular Architecture of the Lake Counties (1974), Brick Building (with Alec Clifton-Taylor, 1978), Houses (1982), Traditional Buildings of Britain (1981, 2 edn 1992), Traditional Farm Buildings of Britain, (1982, 2 edn 1987), Timber Building in Britain (1985, 2 edn 1994), Brickwork in Britain (1990), Houses and Cottages of Britain (1996); *Recreations* enjoying the countryside; *Clubs* Athenaeum; *Style*— Prof Ronald Brunskill, OBE, FSA; ✉ Three Trees, 8 Overhill Road, Wilmslow SK9 2BE (☎ 01625 522099); Glan Gors, Harlech, Gwynedd

BRUNSON, Michael; *b* 12 Aug 1940; *Educ* Bedford Sch, Queen's Coll Oxford (MA); *m* Susan Margaret, *née*, Brown; 2 s (Jonathan b 1966, Robin b 1969); *Career* journalist; VSO teacher Prince of Wales Sch Sierra Leone 1963–64, scriptwriter, researcher and bdcaster BBC External Servs 1964, reporter South East (BBC Radio) 1964–66, asst prodr 24 Hours (BBC TV) 1966–68; ITN: joined 1968, US corr 1972–77, gen assignment reporter 1977–79, newscaster 1977–81, Euro corr 1979–80, dip ed 1980–86, political ed 1986–; major assignments incl: first Reagan-Gorbachev summit Geneva, various EC summits, overseas visits by PM and foreign sec, gen elections 1979–, Conservative leadership contests 1990 and 1995; regular contributor Week in Westminster feature Westminster House Magazine 1988–90; chm Parly Lobby Journalists 1994; *Recreations* reading (especially Charles Dickens), classical music, gardening; *Style*— Michael Brunson, Esq; ✉ Independent Television News Ltd, 200 Gray's Inn Rd, London WC1X 8XZ (☎ 0171 833 3000)

BRUNT, Prof Peter William; OBE (1994); s of Harry Brunt, of Prestatyn, Clwyd, and Florence Jane Josephine, *née* Airey; *b* 18 Jan 1936; *Educ* Manchester GS, King George V Sch, Univ of Liverpool; *m* 1961, (Marina Evelyn) Anne, da of Rev Reginald Henry Lewis (d 1974), of Liverpool; 3 da (Kristin, Nicola, Coralie); *Career* house surgn and house physician Liverpool Royal Infirmary 1959–60, med registrar hosps in Liverpool region 1960–64, res fell Dept of Med Genetics Johns Hopkins Hosp and Sch of Med Baltimore USA 1965–66, lectr in med Univ of Edinburgh 1967–68, sr registrar in gastroenterology Western Gen Hosp Edinburgh 1968–69, hon lectr in med Univ of London 1969–70, conslt physician and gastroenterologist Aberdeen Royal Infirmary, hon clinical prof in med Univ of Aberdeen, physician to HM The Queen (in Scotland); non stipendiary deacon Scottish Episcopal Church; author of numerous chapters in books and articles mainly on liver and alimentary diseases and alcohol; FRCP, FRCPEd (memb Cncl); *Books* Diseases of Liver and Biliary System (1984), Gastroenterology (1984); *Recreations* mountaineering, music; *Clubs* Association of Physicians; *Style*— Prof Peter Brunt, OBE; ✉ 17 Kingshill Rd, Aberdeen AB2 4JY (☎ 01224 314204); Aberdeen Royal Infirmary, Foresterhill, Aberdeen (☎ 01224 681818 ext 52287, fax 01224 840711)

BRUNTISFIELD, 2 Baron (UK 1942); Sir John Robert Warrender; 9 Bt (GB 1715), OBE (1963), MC (1943), TD (1967), DL (Somerset 1965); s of 1 Baron Bruntisfield, MC (d 1993), and his 1 w, Dorothy Etta, *née* Rawson (d 1975); *b* 7 Feb 1921; *Educ* Eton, RMC Sandhurst; *m* 1, 1948, Ann Moireen (d 1976), 2 da of Lt-Col Sir Walter Fendall Campbell, KCIE; 2 s (Hon Michael John Victor b 1949, Hon Jonathan James b 1954), 2 da (Hon Julian Mary (Hon Mrs Akers-Douglas) b 1950, Hon Sarah Jane (Hon Mrs Bune) b 1952); m 2, 1977, Shirley (d 1981), formerly w of Jonathan J Crawley, and da of Sqdn Ldr Edward Ross, RAF ret; 3 step s; m 3, 1985, Joanna (Jan) K, formerly w of Colin Hugh Campbell Graham, and da of late David Chancellor, of Pencaitland, E Lothian; 2 step s, 1 step da; *Heir* s, Hon Michael John Victor Warrender b 1949; *Career* Col RARO, Brig Queen's Body Guard for Scotland (Royal Co of Archers), ret 1985, late Capt 2 Dragoons, Royal Scots Greys, ADC to Govr of Madras 1946–48 and cmdg N Som Yeo and 44 Royal Tank Regt 1957–62; *Clubs* New (Edinburgh); *Style*— The Rt Hon the Lord Bruntisfield, OBE, MC, TD, DL; ✉ 18 Warriston Crescent, Edinburgh, EH3 5LB (☎ and fax 0131 556 3701)

BRUNTON, Ann Jean; da of Walter Thomas Williams (d 1990), of Gravesend, Kent, and Jeanne Grace, *née* Perkins; *b* 7 Aug 1938; *Educ* Gravesend Tech Sch for Girls; *m* 2 Sept 1963 (m dis 1987), John Malcolm Brunton, s of John Brunton; 2 da (Sophie Wright b 1 Nov 1968, Sadie Wright b 7 Nov 1971); *Career* early career at Bowaters, subsequent experience in publicity dept of maj fashion co 1954–56 and Deane & Phillips show business consultancy 1956–58; Welbeck Golin/Harris Communications (formerly Welbeck Public Relations): joined 1958, various positions rising to md until 1993, chief exec 1993–; MIPR 1965; *Recreations* travel, food, cookery; *Style*— Mrs Ann Brunton; ✉ Welbeck Golin/Harris Communications Ltd, 43 King Street, Covent Garden, London WC2E 8RJ (☎ 0171 836 6677, fax 0171 836 5820)

BRUNTON, Sir Gordon Charles; kt (1985); s of late Charles Arthur Brunton, and Hylda Pritchard; *b* 27 Dec 1921; *Educ* Cranleigh Sch, LSE; *m* 1, 1946 (m dis 1965), Nadine Lucile Paula Sohr; 1 s, 2 da (and 1 s decd); m 2, 1966, Gillian Agnes Kirk; 1 s, 1 da; *Career* cmmnd RA 1942, joined IA 1942, served in India, Assam and Burma 1942–46; joined Tothill Press (appointed to bd 1954), md Tower Press Gp of Cos 1958–61, PA to md Odhams Press Ltd 1961, md Thomson Pubns Ltd 1961, dir Thomson Orgn Ltd 1963, md and chief exec Thomson Orgn 1968; pres Int Thomson Orgn Ltd; md and chief exec Int Thomson Orgn plc, ret 1984; chm: Bemrose Corp plc 1978–91, Sotheby Parke Bennet Group plc 1982–83 (dir 1978–83, currently chm emeritus), Green Field Leisure Gp Ltd, Martin Currie Pacific Tst plc 1985–92, The Racing Post plc 1985–, Euram Consltg Ltd 1985–92, Community Ind Ltd until 1992, Ingersoll Pubns Ltd until

1991, Verity Group plc (formerly Wharfdale plc) 1992–, Phonelink plc 1993–, Racing International Ltd; dir: Cable and Wireless plc 1981–91, Sotheby's Holdings Inc 1983–85; Yattendon Investmt Tst plc; dir Arts Cncl South Bank Bd to 1992, memb Fin Ctee OUP to 1992; fell LSE; pres Cwlth Press Union 1991–94; former pres: Nat Advertising Benevolent Soc, Periodical Publishers Assoc Ltd, Printers' Charitable Corp; patron History of Advertising Tst; *Recreations* breeding horses, books; *Style*— Sir Gordon Brunton; ✉ North Munstead, Godalming, Surrey GU8 4AX

BRUNTON, Dr James Lauder; s and h of Sir (Edward Francis) Lauder Brunton, 3 Bt, *qv*; *b* 24 Sept 1947; *Educ* Selwyn House Sch Montreal, Bishops Coll Sch Lennoxville, McGill Univ (BSc 1968, MDCM 1972); *m* 1, 1 July 1967 (m dis 1983), Susan Elizabeth, da of Charles Hons; 1 s (Douglas Lauder b 1968), 1 da (Jennifer Anne b 1971); m 2, 1984, Beverly Anne Freedman; 1 s (Robert James b 1987); *Career* Univ of Toronto: prof of medicine, head Div of Infectious Diseases Dept of Medicine; microbiologist in chief The Toronto Hosp Toronto; FRCP (Canada); *Style*— Dr James Brunton; ✉ 30 Strathallan Blvd, Toronto, Ontario, Canada M5N 1S7 (☎ 00 1 485 2716); Department of Microbiology, The Toronto Hospital, 200 Elizabeth St, Toronto, Canada M5G 2C4 (☎ 00 1 416 340 3183)

BRUNTON, Sir (Edward Francis) Lauder; 3 Bt (UK 1908), of Stratford Place, St Marylebone; s of Sir (James) Stopford Lauder Brunton, 2 Bt (d 1943); *b* 10 Nov 1916; *Educ* Trinity Coll Sch Port Hope Ontario, Bryanston Sch, McGill Univ (BSc, MD, CM); *m* 1946, Marjorie Grant, only da of David Sclater Lewis, MSc, MD, FRCP (Canada), of Montreal; 1 s (James Lauder b 1947), 1 da (Nancy Elizabeth (Mrs Ian Willson) b 1949); *Heir* s, James Lauder Brunton b 24 Sept 1947; *Career* hon attending physician: Royal Victoria Hosp Montreal, St Martha's Hosp; life govr Nova Scotia Art Gallery; fell: Int Soc of Hematology, American Coll of Physicians; memb American Soc of Hematology; *Style*— Sir Lauder Brunton, Bt; ✉ PO Box 140, Guysborough, Nova Scotia, Canada

BRUTON, Prof Michael John; CBE (1995); s of (Patrick) John Bruton, of Hertford, and Louise Ann, *née* Roberts; *b* 28 March 1938; *Educ* Richard Hale Sch Hertford, Univ Coll London (BA), Imperial Coll London (MSc, DIC), Regent St Poly (Dip TP); *m* 2 March 1963, Sheila Grace, da of Alexander Kyle Harrison; 2 da (Suzy b 1969, Catherine b 1972); *Career* princ planning offr Bucks CC 1966–67 (Lanarkshire CC 1965–66), princ lectr town planning Oxford Poly 1967–72, head school planning and landscape Birmingham Poly 1972–77, prof of town planning Univ of Wales Cardiff (formerly Univ of Wales Coll of Cardiff) 1977–, dep princ and registrar UWIST 1985–88, registrar Univ of Wales Cardiff 1988–95; chief exec Residuary Body for Wales 1995–; govr Centre for Environmental Studies 1978–81, chm CNAA Town Planning Bd 1978–84; memb: Countryside Cmmn for Wales 1981–85, Univ Grants Ctee Social Studies Sub-Ctee 1985–88, ESRC Post Graduate Bd 1985–93; chm Regnl Rivers Advsy Ctee for Wales 1989–93, planning advsr to Univ Funding Cncl 1989–93; FRTPI, FCIT, MIHT; *Books* Introduction to Transportation Planning (3 edn, 1985), Spirit and Purpose of Planning (2 edn, 1984), Local Planning in Practice (1987); *Recreations* watching rugby and cricket, travel; *Clubs* Cardiff and County; *Style*— Prof Michael Bruton, CBE; ✉ The Residuary Body for Wales, Ffynnon-las, Tŷ Glas Avenue, Llanishen, Cardiff CF4 5DZ (☎ 01222 681241, fax 01222 681308)

BRYAN, Sir Arthur; kt (1976); s of William Woodall Bryan, and Isobel Alan, *née* Tweedie; *b* 4 March 1923; *Educ* Longton HS Stoke-on-Trent; *m* 1947, Betty, da of F G Ratford, of Essex; 1 s (Lawrence), 1 da (Linda); *Career* Wedgwood: joined 1947, gen sales mangr 1959, dir 1960, md 1963, chm 1968–86, pres and dir Waterford Wedgwood 1986–88; dir: Friends Provident Life Office 1985–93, UK Fund Inc (USA), Rank Organisation plc until 1994, JCB Inc of America until 1994, Dartington Crystal Group 1995–; HM Lord-Lt Staffs 1968–93; memb Ct Univ of Keele; Hon MUniv Keele 1978, Hon DLitt Univ of Staffordshire 1993; CIMgt, FInstM, CICeram, FRSA 1964; KStJ; *Recreations* walking, tennis, reading; *Style*— Sir Arthur Bryan; ✉ Parkfields Cottage, Tittensor, Stoke-on-Trent, Staffs ST12 9HQ (☎ 01782 372686)

BRYAN, Dora (Mrs William Lawton); OBE (1996); da of Albert Broadbent, and Georgina, *née* Hill; *b* 7 Feb 1923; *Educ* Hathershaw Council Sch; *m* 1954, William Lawton; 2 s (Daniel b 1959, William b 1962), 1 da (Georgina b 1960); *Career* actress; WWII ENSA Italy and England; vice pres Assoc of Lancastrians in London 1991; Hon MA Univ of Manchester; *Theatre* pantomimes: London Hippodrome 1936, Manchester Palace 1937, Alhambra Glasgow 1938, Oldham Rep 1939–44; Chichester Festival Seasons 1971–74, London Palladium Season 1971, London Palladium Pantomime Season 1973–74; other credits incl: Travellers' Joy, Accolade, Lyric Review, Simon and Laura, The Water Gypsies, Gentlemen Prefer Blondes, Six of One, Too True to be Good, Hello Dolly!, They Don't Grow on Trees (Her Majesty's) 1979, The Merry Wives of Windsor (Regents Park) 1984, She Stoops to Conquer (NT) 1985, The Apple Cart (Haymarket) 1986, Charlie Girl (Victoria Palace 1986, Birmingham 1988), Pygmalion (Plymouth, NY) 1987, revival of Hello Dolly (nat tour) 1989, 70 Girls 70 (Chichester and West End) 1991, The Birthday Party (RNT) 1994, School for Scandal and When We are Married (Chichester Festival) 1995 and 1996; *Television* most recently Absolutely Fabulous; *Films* incl: The Fallen Idol 1949, Two A Penny 1968, Apartment Zero 1988; *Awards* Br Acad Best Actress for A Taste of Honey, Variety Club of GB and Manchester Evening News Best Actress for She Stoops to Conquer, Olivier Award for Best Actress in a Supporting Role for The Birthday Party 1995; *Books* According to Dora (autobiography); *Recreations* patchwork quilts, reading, cats, dogs; *Style*— Ms Dora Bryan, OBE; ✉ Clarges, 118 Marine Parade, Brighton, E Sussex (☎ 01273 603235)

BRYAN, Prof Eric Reginald; OBE (1993); s of Reginald Harold Bryan (d 1991), of Kingston upon Thames, and Elizabeth Ellen, *née* Cowlard (d 1980); *b* 20 Dec 1927; *Educ* Tiffin Boys' Sch Kingston upon Thames, Univ of London (MSc, PhD), DSc (Manchester); *m* 31 March 1951, Jean, da of Walter Cyril Wrigley; 2 s (Roger Stephen b 5 March 1952, Julian Simon b 13 July 1958), 1 da (Lydia Catharine b 1 Oct 1953); *Career* Alkali Div ICI 1948–60 (civil engrg designer, construction mangr, design engr); sr lectr Dept of Engrg Univ of Manchester 1965–70 (lectr 1960–65); Dept of Civil Engrg Univ of Salford: prof of structural engrg 1970–85, pro vice chancellor 1979–82, prof of civil engrg and chm of dept 1985–88, res prof of civil engrg 1988–93; former chm Sub Ctees Br and Euro Standards; Sir Arnold Waters Medal Inst of Structural Engrs, Distinguished Serv Medal Euro Convention for Constructional Steelwork; fell Br Constructional Steelwork Assoc, FIStructE 1969, FICE 1970, FEng 1988; *Books* The Stressed Skin Design of Steel Buildings (1973), Manual of Stressed Skin Diaphragm Design (with J M Davies, 1982); *Recreations* travel, historic properties, woodwork; *Style*— Prof Eric Bryan, OBE, FEng; ✉ 5 Churchfields, Bowdon, Altrincham, Cheshire WA14 3PL (☎ 0161 928 4735)

BRYAN, Felicity Anne (Mrs Alexander Duncan); da of Sir Paul Bryan, DSO, MC, *qv*, and Betty Mary, *née* Hoyle (d 1968); *b* 16 Oct 1945; *Educ* Courtauld Inst of Art, Univ of London; *m* 23 Oct 1981, Alexander Duncan, s of Patrick Duncan (d 1967), and Cynthia Duncan; 2 s (Maxim Paul b 1983, Benjamin Patrick b 1987), 1 da (Alice Mary b 1982); *Career* journalist: Financial Times 1968–70, The Economist 1970–72; literary agent and dir Curtis Brown Ltd 1972–88, fndr The Felicity Bryan Agency 1988–; *Books* The Town Gardener's Companion (1982), A Garden for Children (1986), Nursery Style (1989); *Recreations* opera, gardening, travel, entertaining; *Clubs* Groucho; *Style*— Ms Felicity Bryan; ✉ The Felicity Bryan Agency, 2a North Parade, Banbury Rd, Oxford OX2 6PE (☎ 01865 513816, fax 01865 310055)

BRYAN, Gerald Jackson; CMG (1964), CVO (1966), OBE (1960), MC (1941); s of George Bryan, OBE, of Belfast (d 1929), and Ruby Evelyn, *née* Jackson (d 1975); *b* 2 April 1921; *Educ* Wrekin, RMA Woolwich, New Coll Oxford; *m* 1947, Georgiana Wendy Cockburn, da of William Barraud Hull (d 1967), of Mbabane, Swaziland; 1 s (Caesar), 2 da (Diana, Mary); *Career* Maj RE, served with 11 (Scottish) Commando in M East; Colonial Serv 1944–67: Swaziland, Barbados, Mauritius; admin: Virgin Is 1959–62, St Lucia 1962–67, ret 1967; govt sec and head of Civil Serv IOM 1967–69; gen mangr Londonderry Devpt Cmmn 1969–73, Bracknell Devpt Corpn 1973–82, memb Lord Chllr's Panel 1982–91; dir: Lovaux Engrg Co 1982–88, MDSL Estates Ltd 1988–; sec gen Assoc of Contact Lens Mfrs 1983–88; memb (C) Berks CC 1983–85; FIMgt 1969; CStJ 1964, KStJ 1985; *Recreations* swimming; *Style*— Gerald Bryan, Esq, CMG, CVO, OBE, MC; ✉ Whitehouse, Murrell Hill Lane, Binfield, Berks RG42 4BY (☎ 01344 425 447)

BRYAN, (James) Howard; s of (Albert) Marriott Bryan (d 1984), of Leeds, and Theresa Edna Gwendolyn (Gwen); *b* 24 April 1944; *Educ* Silcoates Sch Wakefield, Univ of Leeds (LLB); *m* 18 March 1972, Jacquelyn Sarah, da of Percy Herbert Stanley Pilcher; 1 s (Ross James b 11 Feb 1979), 1 da (Louise Victoria b 5 July 1983); *Career* admitted slr 1968; ptnr Eversheds Leeds (formerly Eversheds Hepworth & Chadwick) 1971–; govr Silcoates Sch 1978; Liveryman Worshipful Co of Wheelwrights; memb: Law Soc, British-German Jurists Assoc, Industl Law Soc; *Recreations* sailing, skiing, tennis; *Clubs* Royal Northern and Clyde Yacht, Royal Ocean Racing, Clyde Cruising, Leeds; *Style*— Howard Bryan, Esq; ✉ Eversheds Cloth Hall Court, Leeds LS1 2JB (☎ 0113 243 0391, fax 0113 245 6188)

BRYAN, Kenneth J; *b* 1939; *Educ* Farnborough GS; *m*; 1 da; *Career* early career as Lloyd's insurance broker, served Army as Maj; HSBC Group: sr mgmnt conslt Hongkong and Shanghai Banking Corp (on secondment from Peat Marwick Mitchell Hong Kong) 1978, joined gp permanently 1979, fin controller domestic banking ops Hong Kong 1981–86, sr mangr banking servs 1986–88, head of gp finances 1988–93, chief financial offr Midland Bank plc (following takeover by HSBC Holdings) 1993–96; memb Central Cncl and Fin & Planning Ctee Chartered Inst of Bankers; CIMA, FCIB; *Recreations* golf, fly-fishing; *Style*— Kenneth Bryan, Esq

BRYAN, Sir Paul Elmore Oliver; kt (1972), DSO (1943), MC (1943); s of Rev John Thomas Ingram Bryan (d 1953), of Milton Ernest, Bedford; *b* 3 Aug 1913; *Educ* St John's Sch Leatherhead, Gonville and Caius Coll Cambridge; *m* 1, 1939, Betty Mary (d 1968), da of James Cars Hoyle; 3 da (Elizabeth, Felicity Bryan, *qv*, Bernadette ((Rev) d 1995); m 2, 1971, Cynthia Duncan, da of late Sir Patrick Ashley Cooper, of Hexton Manor, Herts; *Career* MP (C): Howden 1955–83, Boothferry 1983–87; min of state Dept of Employment 1970–72; dir: Granada Television, Granada Theatres, Greater Manchester Independent Radio Ltd 1972–83, Furness Withy Ltd 1983–89, The Scot Lion Insurance Co Ltd 1984–95, Port of Felixstowe Ltd 1991–95; dep chm Furness Withy Ltd 1984–89, chm United Cable TV (London S) 1985–96; *Style*— Sir Paul Bryan, DSO, MC; ✉ 5 Westminster Gardens, Marsham Street, London SW1 (☎ 0171 834 2050); Park Farm, Sawdon, nr Scarborough, N Yorks YO13 9EB (☎ 01723 859370, fax 01723 859326)

BRYAN, Rex Victor; s of Bertram Henry Bryan (d 1970), of Purley, Surrey, and Annie Ella Margaret, *née* King; *b* 2 Dec 1946; *Educ* Wallington GS, Jesus Coll Oxford (MA); *m* 1, 31 July 1971 (m dis 1981), Catherine, da of Samuel Carbery, of Ballymena, Co Antrim, NI; 1 s (Roland Patrick b 1977); m 2, 9 Aug 1982, Mary Elizabeth, da of Brendan Joseph O'Toole, of Frinton-on-Sea, Essex; 2 s (Adam Francis b 1985, Thomas Edward b 1988), 2 da (Victoria Louise b 1986, Leonora Rose b 1991); *Career* called to the Bar Lincoln's Inn 1971, head of chambers 1986–, recorder of the Crown Court 1994–; *Recreations* carpentry, languages; *Style*— Rex Bryan, Esq; ✉ 5 Pump Ct, Temple, London EC4Y 7AP (☎ 0171 353 2532, fax 0171 353 5321)

BRYAN, Robert Hedley; s of Joseph William Bryan (d 1976), and Gladys, *née* Bacon; *b* 25 Aug 1934; *Educ* Derby GS, Univ of Hull (BSc, DipEd); *m* 1 March 1963, Ann Mollie, da of Alfred Edgar Daly (d 1971); 2 da (Joanna b 1968, Emma b 1970); *Career* theatre and TV lighting designer and theatre lighting conslt; fndr team memb Theatre Projects Lighting Ltd 1960–78; designed lighting for numerous venues incl: Royal Opera House, ENO, Glyndebourne Festival Opera, NT, RSC, Staatsoper Vienna, Paris Opera, Geneva, Nice, Australian Opera Sydney; memb: Soc of Br Theatre Lighting Designers 1970, Soc of TV Lightning Dirs 1980; *Recreations* reading, walking, film and television; *Style*— Robert Bryan, Esq; ✉ 19 Blatchington Hill, Seaford, E Sussex BN25 2AH (☎ 01323 892308)

BRYANS, Dame Anne Margaret; *née* Gilmour; DBE (1957, CBE 1945); da of Col Rt Hon Sir John Gilmour, 2 Bt, GCVO, DSO, MP (d 1940); *b* 29 Oct 1909; *Educ* private; *m* 1932, Lt Cdr John Reginald Bryans, RN (d 1990), s of Rev R du F Bryans (d 1922); 1 s; *Career* HQ Staff 1938; Br Red Cross and St John War Orgn: dep cmmr, Middle East cmmn 1943, cmmr Jan-June 1945, dep chm 1953–64, vice chm 1964–76; memb Exec Ctee BRCS, lay memb Cncl for Professions Supplementary to Med until 1979; memb: Ethical Practices Sub Ctee Royal Free Hosp 1974–, Royal Free Hosp Sch Cncl 1968–83, Bd of Govrs Eastman Dental Hosp 1973–79, Camden and Islington AHA 1974–79; vice pres Open Section RSM 1975 (pres 1980–82), former memb ITA (later IBA); memb: Govt Anglo-Egyptian Resettlement Bd, BBC/ITA Appeals Ctee Med Sch St George's Hosp; special tstee and former chm Royal Free Hosp and Friends of Royal Free Hosp, pres Friends of Royal Free Hosp, former chm Bd of Govrs Royal Free Hosp; memb Cncl Florence Nightingale Hosp, tstee Florence Nightingale Aid in Sickness Tst 1979–, govr Royal Star and Garter Home 1975–87; memb Exec Ctee Royal Soc of Medicine 1982–84, vice pres Royal Coll of Nursing, former govr Westminster Hosp; chm Order of St John of Jerusalem and BRCS Service Hosp Welfare Ctee and VAD Ctee 1960–89, vice chm Jt Ctee and BRCS 1976–81, chm Grants Ctee Nations Fund for Nurses; DStJ; Hon FRSM 1995 (FRSM 1976); *Clubs* Royal Lymington Yacht, New Cavendish; *Style*— Dame Anne Bryans, DBE; ✉ 57 Elm Park House, Elm Park Gardens, London SW10 9QD

BRYANT, Prof Christopher Gordon Alastair; s of Gordon Douglas Clifford Bryant (d 1975), of Bristol, and Edna Mollie, *née* Shrubb; *b* 14 April 1944; *Educ* Kingston GS, Univ of Leicester (BA, MA), Univ of Southampton (PhD); *m* Elizabeth Mary, da of George Thomas Martyn Peters; 2 da (Catherine Elizabeth, Lucy Ann); *Career* tutorial asst Dept of Sociology Univ of Leicester 1965–66, lectr Dept of Sociology and Social Admin Univ of Southampton 1968–76 (asst lectr 1966–68); Dept of Sociology Univ of Salford: sr lectr 1976–82, chm 1982–90, prof 1982–, dir Inst for Social Research 1993–; guest prof Goethe Univ of Frankfurt am Main 1973; visiting fell: Ohio State Univ Columbus 1981, Univ of Utrecht 1986–91, Central European Univ Warsaw 1996; memb: Br Sociological Assoc 1966–, Exec Ctee Br Sociological Assoc 1987–91 (chm Pubns Ctee 1989–91), Ed Bd British Jl of Sociology 1991–; *Books* Sociology in Action (1976), Positivism in Social Theory and Research (1985), What Has Sociology Achieved? (1990), Giddens' Theory of Structuration (1991), The New Great Transformation? (1994), Practical Sociology (1995), Democracy, Civil Society and Pluralism in Comparative Perspective (1995); *Recreations* theatre, concerts, walking, seeing friends; *Style*— Prof Christopher Bryant; ✉ Department of Sociology, University of Salford, Salford M5 4WT (☎ 0161 745 5000, fax 0161 745 5424, telex 668680 SULIB)

BRYANT, David John; CBE (1980, MBE 1969); s of Reginald Samuel Harold Bryant (d 1978), of Avon, and Evelyn Clair, *née* Weaver (d 1987); *b* 27 Oct 1931; *Educ* Weston-super-Mare GS, St Paul's Coll Cheltenham, Redland Coll Bristol; *m* 2 April 1960, Ruth Georgina, da of George Roberts (d 1971), of Avon; 2 da (Jacqueline Anne b 7 May 1962, Carole Jayne b 6 Jan 1965); *Career* schoolmaster 1955–71; dir: Sporting Boutiques 1971–78, Drakelite Ltd (bowls conslts) 1978–; professional bowler 1980–; Cwlth Games Singles Gold Medallist 1962, 1970, 1974 and 1978, Cwlth Games Fours Gold Medallist

1962, World Outdoor Bowls Singles Champion 1966, 1980 and 1988, World Indoor Bowls Singles Champion 1979, 1980 and 1981, World Indoor Pairs Champion 6 times, English Outdoor Singles Champion 6 times, English Indoor Singles Champion 9 times, British Isles Singles Outdoor Champion 4 times, British Isles Singles Indoor Champion 4 times, Int Invitation Masters Singles Champion 9 times; patron Francis Drake Fellowship; *Books* Bryant on Bowls (1966), Bowl with Bryant (1984), The Game of Bowls (1990), Bowl to Win (1994); *Recreations* gardening, angling; *Clubs* Clevedon Bowling, Clevedon Conservative; *Style—* David Bryant, Esq, CBE; ✉ 47 Esmond Grove, Clevedon, N Somerset BS21 7HP (☎ 01275 794015); Drakelite Ltd, 81 High Street, Southwold, Suffolk IP18 6DS (☎ 01502 722002)

BRYANT, His Hon Judge David Michael Arton; s of late Lt-Col Arthur Denis Bryant, and Dorothy Alice, *née* Arton, of W Tanfield, Ripon, N Yorks; *b* 27 Jan 1942; *Educ* Wellington, Oriel Coll Oxford (scholar, BA); *m* (Diana) Caroline, da of Brig Charles Walker Sloan, CBE, of Ripon, North Yorkshire; 2 s (Edward Denis Charles b 1971, William Robert b 1982), 1 da (Lucinda Mary b 1972); *Career* called to the Bar Inner Temple 1964, practised NE Circuit 1965–89, recorder 1985–89, circuit judge (NE Circuit) 1989–; memb Ripon Deanery Synod; *Recreations* gardening, shooting, medieval history; *Clubs* Carlton; *Style—* His Hon Judge Bryant; ✉ Teeside Combined Court Centre, Middlesbrough, Cleveland

BRYANT, Air Vice-Marshal Derek Thomas; CB (1987), OBE (1974); s of (Joseph) Thomas Bryant (d 1957), and (Daisy Elizabeth) Mary, *née* Thurley; *b* 1 Nov 1933; *Educ* Latymer Upper GS Hammersmith; *m* 4 Aug 1956, Patricia, da of William Dodge (d 1977); 1 s (Iain David b 1957), 1 da (Janine b 1960); *Career* fighter pilot 1953, flying instr 1957, Sqdn Cdr 228–OCU and 14 Sqdn 1968–74, Station Cdr RAF Coningsby 1976–78, SASO 38 Gp 1982–84, Dep Cdr RAF Germany 1984–87, Cmdt RAF Staff Coll 1987–88; *Recreations* gardening, golf; *Clubs* RAF; *Style—* Air Vice-Marshal D T Bryant, CB, OBE; ✉ The Old Stables, Lower Swell, Fivehead, Taunton, Somerset TA3 6PH (☎ 01460 281209)

BRYANT, Prof Greyham Frank; s of Ernest Noel Bryant (d 1981), and Florence Ivy, *née* Russell (d 1974); *b* 3 June 1931; *Educ* Univ of Reading (BSc), Imperial Coll London (PhD); *m* 2 July 1955, Iris Sybil, da of Albert Edward Jardine (d 1980); 2 s (Mark Greyham b 2 Jan 1963, David Nicholas b 18 Aug 1966); *Career* sr scientific offr Br Iron and Steel Res 1959–64; Imperial Coll London: res fell 1964–67, reader in industl control 1975–82, prof of control 1982–, dep dir Interdisciplinary Res Centre in Systems Engrg 1989–; chm Broner Conslts 1979–88, chm Greycon Conslts 1985–, dir Circulation Res 1989–94; MIEE, FIMA, FEng 1988; *Books* Automation of Tandem Mills (jtly), Multivariable Control System Design Techniques; *Recreations* music; *Clubs* Athenaeum; *Style—* Prof Greyham Bryant, FEng; ✉ 18 Wimborne Ave, Norwood Green, Middx UB2 4HB (☎ 0181 574 5648); Department of Electrical Engineering, Imperial College, London SW7 2AZ (☎ 0171 589 5111)

BRYANT, Hugh D; *Educ* Oriel Coll Oxford (open exhibitioner, MA); *Career* early positions with Thomas R Miller & Son and GEC Diesels Ltd; admitted slr; formerly with: Hill Dickinson & Co Liverpool (now Hill Dickinson Davis Campbell), Holman Fenwick & Willan, Waltons & Morse (ptnr); former chief underwriter and dir Liverpool and London P & I (protection and indemnity) Management Ltd; former ptnr and head Marine & Aviation Dept Penningtons slrs, Penningtons' team ldr actg for Shetlands Islands Cncl over BRAER oil spill 1993, currently ptnr Williamson & Horrocks slrs; chief legal advsr for the creation and launch of Shoreline Mutual (Bermuda) Ltd; regular speaker and seminar & conf lectr incl: Master Mariners' Soc of Pakistan, 'Managing the Marine Environment - The Shetland Standard' Conf Lerwick, Tanker Legislation '93 Conf Washington DC, Mariners' Club Houston, Coll of Petroleum and Energy Studies Oxford; memb Br Maritime Law Assoc, supporting memb London Maritime Arbitrators' Assoc; *Clubs* Anglo-German (Hamburg), India House (New York); *Style—* Hugh Bryant, Esq; ✉ Williamson & Horrocks, Forum House, 15–18 Lime Street, London EC3M 7AP (☎ 0171 623 4452, fax 0171 626 3591, e-mail bryant@cix.compulink.co.uk, mobile 0374 275069)

BRYANT, Prof John Allen; s of Joseph Samuel Bryant (d 1990), of Croydon, Surrey, and (Beatrice Maud) Patricia, *née* Wallace-Page (d 1990); *b* 14 April 1944; *Educ* Whitgift Sch Croydon, Queens' Coll Cambridge (BA, MA, PhD); *m* 27 July 1968, Marjorie Joan, da of Maj Gerald C G Hatch (d 1983), of Hingham, Norfolk; 2 s (Mark b 1 Jan 1972, Simon b 3 Jan 1974); *Career* res fell Univ of East Anglia 1969–70, lectr Univ of Nottingham 1970–74, reader Univ Coll Cardiff 1982–85 (lectr 1974–77, sr lectr 1977–82), prof of biological sciences Univ of Exeter 1985– (head of biology 1986–91); chm Biotechnology South West; Soc for Experimental Biology: memb Cncl 1981–87 and 1992–, hon sec 1983–87, memb Cell Biology Ctee 1988–97; memb: Plant Sci and Microbiology Ctee SERC 1986–89, Bd of Dirs E African Inst for Scientific Res and Devpt 1991–, Professional and Educn Ctee Biochemical Soc 1994–97; memb Editorial Bd: Jl of Experimental Botony, Molecular Biotechnology, Sci and Christian Belief, Trends in Biotechnology; memb Annals of Botany Company; CBiol 1984, FIBiol 1986 (MIBiol 1970), FRSA 1989; *Recreations* cross-country (formerly at intercounty level) and road running, birdwatching, walking, sailing; *Style—* Prof John Bryant; ✉ Dept of Biological Sciences, University of Exeter, Exeter EX4 4QG (☎ 01392 264672, fax 01392 264668, e-mail J.A.Bryant@exeter.ac.uk)

BRYANT, Judith Marie (Mrs H M Hodkinson); da of John Frederick Bryant (d 1945), and Joan Marian Summerfield (d 1948); *b* 31 Dec 1942; *Educ* City of London Sch for Girls, Hove County GS, Brunel Univ (MPhil), The London Hosp Whitechapel (RGN); *m* 22 Nov 1986, Prof (Henry) Malcolm Hodkinson, *qv*; *Career* staff nurse Paediatric Ward The London Hosp Whitechapel 1964–65, staff nurse and ward sister Intensive Therapy Unit Univ Coll Hosp London 1965–69, nursing offr Intensive Therapy Unit Northwick Park Hosp Harrow 1969–71 (sr nursing offr Personnel Dept 1971–75), divnl nursing offr Community and Geriatrics Harrow Health Dist 1975–78, dist nursing offr Enfield Health Authy 1978–82, chief nursing offr Victoria Health Authy 1982–85, chief nursing offr and dir of quality assurance Riverside Health Authy 1985–86, regnl nursing offr N East Thames Regnl Health Authy 1986–90, fell in clinical servs mgmnt King's Fund Coll 1990–95; Florence Nightingale meml scholar USA and Canada 1970, serv advsr to DHSS Res Liaison Gp for the Elderly 1977–83, memb Royal Coll of Nursing Mgmnt Gp 1980–90, memb S West Hertfordshire Dist Health Authy 1981–87, memb NHS Trg Authy Nursing and Midwives Staff Trg Ctee 1986, vice-chm 1930 Fund for Dist Nurses 1986–, memb Bd Nurseline 1996–; *Recreations* opera, gardening, ceramics; *Style—* Ms Judith Bryant; ✉ 8 Chiswick Square, London W4 2QG (☎ 0181 747 0239)

BRYANT, Julius John Victor; s of Robert John Stanley Bryant, of Caldicot, Gwent, and Dena, *née* Bond; *b* 17 Dec 1957; *Educ* St Albans Sch, UCL (Rudolf Wittkower prize, BA), Courtauld Inst London; *m* 1984, Barbara Ann, *née* Coffey; 1 s (Maximilian Stanley Bond b 10 Sept 1988); *Career* 19th C British paintings cataloguer Sotheby's 1980–81, researcher Walt Disney Productions 1981, museum asst Educn Dept V&A 1982–83; English Heritage: asst curator The Iveagh Bequest Kenwood 1983–88, acting curator Kenwood 1989, head Museums Div English Heritage 1990–93, dir Historic Properties London (Kenwood, Chiswick House, Marble Hill House, The Ranger's House, Westminster Abbey Chapter House, The Jewel Tower Westminster, Eltham Palace, Winchester Palace, London Wall, Coombe Conduits) 1993–95, dir of collections 1995, dir of Museums and Collections 1996–; visiting fell Yale Center for British Art USA 1985, Mayers Fndn fell Huntington Library and Art Gallery Calif 1992; memb London Museums Consultative Ctee; pres Hampstead Heath Decorative and Fine Arts Soc; *Books* The Victoria and Albert Museum Guide (1986), Finest Prospects: Three Historic Houses (1986), Marble Hill House (1988), Mrs Howard: A Woman of Reason (1988), The Iveagh Bequest Kenwood (1990), The Landscape of Kenwood (with C Colson, 1990), Robert Adam, Architect of Genius (1992), London's Country House Collections (1993), The London Historic House Museums Review 1990–92 (ed, 1993), The Trojan War Sculptures by Anthony Caro (with J Spurling, 1994), Turner: Painting the Nation (1996); contrib nine entries on 18th c British sculptors to Macmillan's Dictionary of Art (1996); author of numerous reviews, articles and pamphlets; *Recreations* British sculpture, jogging, family life; *Style—* Julius Bryant; ✉ c/o English Heritage, 429 Oxford Street, London W1R 2HD (☎ 0171 973 3535)

BRYANT, Kenneth Marrable; s of Philip Harry Bryant (d 1979), of Guildford, Surrey, and Hilda Gertrude, *née* Linch (d 1988); *b* 13 June 1927; *Educ* Latymer Upper Sch, King's Coll London, Charing Cross Hosp Med Sch (MB BS); *m* 26 July 1952, Rosemary, da of Thomas Hawkins (d 1962), of Ealing, London; 1 s (Richard b 12 Jan 1962), 2 da (Elizabeth b 9 Aug 1957, Angela b 25 Nov 1959); *Career* Flt Lt 1952–55 RAF Orthopaedic Serv, RAF Hosp Ely; sr registrar Charing Cross and Royal Nat Orthopaedic Hosp; conslt orthopaedic surgn: St James Hosp London 1965–88, Bolingbroke Hosp 1972–92; hon sr lectr St George's Hosp Med Sch 1976–92, hon orthopaedic surgn Cheyne Centre for Spastic Children 1978–88, conslt orthopaedic surgn St George's Hosp 1980–92, conslt orthopaedic surgn Parkside Hosp 1983–; visiting orthopaedic surgn HM Prison Serv 1979–, hon orthopaedic surgn St George's Hosp 1992–; lay chm Ealing Deanery Synod; churchwarden; Freeman City of London 1966, Liveryman Worshipful Soc of Apothecaries 1966; memb Soc of Genealogists; FRSM, sr fell BOA, FRCS, AKC; *Recreations* gardening, fine bookbinding, pottering about in churches; *Style—* Kenneth Bryant, Esq; ✉ Orthopaedic Department, Parkside Hospital, London SW19 5NX (☎ 0181 946 4202); Mitchell Mews, Truro, Cornwall TR1 1JS

BRYANT, Martin Warwick; s of Douglas William Bryant, of Chichester, Sussex, and Elsie Marjorie Sylvia, *née* Simpkins; *b* 30 June 1952; *Educ* Chichester HS, ChCh Oxford (MA), Univ of Leeds (MA), Cranfield Sch of Mgmnt (MBA); *m* 26 May 1979, Hilary May, da of Philip Readhead Southall, of Rednal, Worcs; 1 s (Laurence Michael b 1984), 2 da (Emily Anna b 1981, Madeleine Rose b 1989); *Career* Swaziland ODI 1975–77, business analyst Foster Wheeler Ltd 1978–82, planning mangr BOC Group plc 1983–86; dir of corporate devpt: Charles Barker plc 1986–89, Boots Co plc 1989–95; md Boots Opticians Ltd 1995–; *Recreations* golf, skiing, cycling; *Clubs* Ski Club of GB; *Style—* Martin Bryant, Esq; ✉ Upton Grange, Upton, nr Newark, Notts NG23 5SY (☎ 0636 812901); Boots Opticians Ltd, St Mary's Court, Nottingham NG2 3AA (☎ 0115 949 3710)

BRYANT, Michael Dennis; CBE (1988); s of William Frederick Bryant (d 1954), of London, and Ann Mary Kerrigan, *née* Jackson (d 1965); *b* 5 April 1928; *Educ* Battersea GS; *m* 1, 1958 (m dis 1980), Josephine Martin; 2 s (Kerrigan, Simon), 2 da (Sarah, Josephine); m 2, 1990, Judith Mary Coke; *Career* actor; ordinary seaman MN 1945, 2 Lt 7 Queen's Own Hussars 1947–49; memb Cncl RADA 1982–, tstee Nat Theatre Fndn 1991–; *Theatre* RSC 1964–65: roles incl Victor, The Jew of Malta, Henry VI, The Home Coming, The Return of A J Raffles; Nat Theatre player 1977–: roles incl State of Revolution (Best Actor, SWET Awards), The Voysey Inheritance (Olivier Award Best Supporting Actor), The Threepenny Opera, Dalliance, The American Clock, Hamlet (Olivier Award Best Supporting Actor), King Lear, Trelawny of the "Wells", Racing Demon (Olivier Award Best Supporting Actor), Murmuring Judges, Absence of War, The Wind in the Willows, Duke of York in Richard II 1995, Lord Kintyre in The Prince's Play 1996; *Televison* incl: Roads to Freedom, Colditz, Talking to a Stranger, Anna Lee, Absence of War; *Films* incl: Goodbye Mr Chips, Nicholas and Alexandra, The Ruling Class, Gandhi, Sakharov; *Recreations* walking; *Style—* Michael Bryant, Esq, CBE; ✉ c/o The Royal National Theatre, South Bank, London SE1 9PX

BRYANT, Michael Sydney; s of Sydney Cecil Bryant (d 1977), of Keynsham, Avon, and Lily May, *née* Jefferies; *b* 16 March 1944; *Educ* Bristol GS, Univ of Exeter, City of London Coll; *m* 1 Oct 1994, Sheila Daviron; *Career* Estate Duty Office Inland Revenue 1965–70, assoc dir Bevington Lowndes Ltd 1970–75, marketing dir Rathbone Brothers plc (formerly Comprehensive Financial Services plc) 1975–; contrib: Daily Telegraph, Sunday Times, Money Mktg; memb Cncl FIMBRA 1986–88 and 1990–91, chm Insur and Compensation Ctee FIMBRA, memb Tax Ctee IFAA; IBRC 1977; *Recreations* food, wine, travel; *Clubs* Carlton; *Style—* Michael Bryant, Esq; ✉ Flat 2, 53 Cadogan Square, London SW1X 0HY (☎ 0171 245 9120); Rathbone Brothers plc, University House, Lower Grosvenor Place, London SW1W 0EX (☎ 0171 630 5611, fax 0171 821 1437, telex 262257)

BRYANT, William Wells; s of Frank Wells Bryant, and Helen Muff, *née* Doe; *b* 24 May 1931; *Educ* Bungay GS, Univ of Durham (BSc), Univ of London (MSc); *m* 31 March 1956, Patricia Margaret, da of James Wesley Davison; 2 da (Karen Anne (Mrs Bryant-Mole) b 1957, Rachel Jane (Dr Waugh) b 1959); *Career* Nat Serv RAF 1949–51; dep dir NV Philips Gloeilampenfabrieken 1972–76, tech dir Polygram Record Operations Ltd 1977–87; cncllr Reigate and Banstead Borough Cncl 1986– (chm Fin Ctee 1994–), lay chm Epsom Deanery Synod 1989–96, non-exec dir Mid Surrey DHA 1989–95, vice chm Eastern Surrey Health Cmmn 1995–; memb: Bishop's Cncl 1989–, Gen Synod Church of England 1995–, Bd Heritage Care Ltd 1996–; fell Inst of Statisticians 1959; CStat; *Style—* William Bryant, Esq; ✉ 10 Bolters Lane, Banstead, Surrey SM7 2AR (☎ 01737 357053)

BRYCE, Andrew John; s of John Robert Murray Bryce, of Lymington, Hampshire, and Eileen Josephine, *née* Denham; *b* 31 Aug 1947; *Educ* Thorpe GS Norwich, Univ of Newcastle (LLB), Coll of Law Lancaster Gate; *m* 1, 1972 (m dis 1994), Karalee Frances Lovegrove; 1 s (Alexander Henry b 22 June 1977), 1 da (Lucy Charlotte b 21 May 1980); m 2, 1994, Rosalind Beverley Hardy; 1 s (Matthew Cameron b 2 Oct 1986); *Career* Cameron Markby Hewitt slrs (previously Cameron Kemm Nordon): articled clerk 1969–71, admitted slr 1971, ptnr 1973–94; in own practice specialising in environmental law Andrew Bryce & Co Nov 1994–; UK Environmental Law Assoc: fndr memb 1986, vice chm 1987–88, chm 1988–91, memb Cncl 1986–; memb and former vice chm Planning and Environmental Sub Ctee City of London Law Soc; memb Law Soc 1973 (memb Planning Panel); *Recreations* birdwatching, travel, decorative arts, tennis; *Clubs* BTO, RSPB; *Style—* Andrew Bryce, Esq; ✉ Andrew Bryce & Co, 7 Queen Street, Coggeshall, Colchester, Essex CO6 1UF (☎ 01376 563123, fax 01376 563336)

BRYCE, Sir (William) Gordon; kt (1971), CBE (1963); s of late James Chisholm Bryce, and Emily Susan, *née* Lees; *b* 2 Feb 1913; *Educ* Bromsgrove, Hertford Coll Oxford (MA); *m* 1940, Molly Mary, da of late Arthur Cranch Drake; 2 da; *Career* chief justice of the Bahamas 1970–73 (formerly attorney gen Gibraltar, Aden, Bahamas); *Style—* Sir Gordon Bryce, CBE; ✉ Nevis, Broad Lane, Brancaster, Norfolk

BRYCE, Iain Ross; TD, DL (Co of East Riding of Yorkshire 1977); s of William James Noel Bryce (d 1971), and Jessie (Jerry) Fleming, *née* Ross (d 1972); *b* 19 March 1936; *Educ* Bridlington GS; *m* 13 Jan 1962, Janet Elizabeth, da of Reginald Wilfred Arro; 2 da; *Career* Nat Serv, TA and Vol Reserve 1958–83: 131 Para Engr Regt, cmd 72 Engr Regt (Tynes) 1974–76, Dep Cdr 29 Engr Brigade 1976–79, Col RE, ret; ptnr Ernst & Young and preceding firms 1966–94; memb Eng Advsy Ctee on Telecommunications 1993–; dir: Prospect Industries plc 1994–, Horncastle Group plc 1994–; Prov Grand Master Yorks N & E Ridings 1984–91, Dep Grand Master United Grand Lodge of England 1991–; chm Bridlington RNLI 1990–, memb Ctee of Mgmnt RNLI 1995–; chm

Hull Coll 1993–96, govr Bridlington Sch 1994–; memb: Worshipful Co of Merchant Adventurers of York, Co of Merchants of the Staple of England; FCA; *Recreations* golf, freemasonry; *Clubs* Army & Navy, Ganton Golf (Scarborough), Bridlington Golf, Royal Yorkshire Yacht (Bridlington); *Style*— Iain R Bryce, Esq, TD, DL; ✉ Tighvonie, 76 Cardigan Road, Bridlington, East Yorkshire YO15 3JT (☎ 01262 672312, fax 01262 608073)

BRYCE, Prof Tom G K; s of Thomas Knox Bryce (d 1974), of Glasgow, and Minnie Josephine, *née* Oswald (d 1984); *b* 27 Jan 1946; *Educ* King's Park Secdy Sch Glasgow, Univ of Glasgow (BSc, MEd, PhD); *m* Karen Douglas, *née* Stewart; 1 da (Laura b 24 May 1986), 1 s (Colin b 1 Oct 1988); *Career* teacher of physics Jordanhill Coll Sch 1968–71, princ teacher of physics King's Park Secdy Sch 1971–73, pt/t lectr in psychology Univ of Glasgow 1972–75; Jordanhill Coll of Educn: lectr in psychology 1973–83, head of psychology 1983–87, head Div of Educn and Psychology 1987–94; prof Faculty of Educn Univ of Strathclyde Jordanhill Campus 1993–; dir Techniques for the Assessment of Practical Skills in Sci (TAPS) Projects 1980–90 and co-dir Assessment of Achievement Prog (AAP) Sci Projects 1985– (funded by SO Educn Dept); chm Editorial Bd Scottish Educational Review 1988–; CPsychol 1990; *Publications* author of articles, chapters and texts incl How to Assess Open-ended Practical Investigations in Biology, Chemistry and Physics (jtly, 1991); *Recreations* mountaineering, badminton; *Style*— Prof Tom Bryce; ✉ Department of Educational Studies, Faculty of Education, University of Strathclyde, Jordanhill Campus, Southbrae Drive, Glasgow G13 1PP (☎ 0141 950 3366)

BRYCE-SMITH, Prof Derek; s of Charles Philip Smith (d 1938), of Wanstead, London, and Amelia, *née* Thick (d 1962); *b* 29 April 1926; *Educ* Bancrofts Sch Woodford Wells (Drapers' Co scholar), SW Essex Tech Coll, West Ham Municipal Coll, Bedford Coll London (BSc, PhD, DSc); *m* 1, 5 Sept 1956, Marjorie Mary Anne (d 1966), da of Maj Eric Stewart, MC (d 1937), of London; 2 s (Duncan b 1959, David b 1963), 2 da (Madeleine b 1957, Hazel b 1961); m 2, 21 June 1969, Pamela Joyce Morgan, da of Marius Andreas Thorndahl (d 1942), of Denmark; 2 step da (Pamela b 1948, Diana b 1953); *Career* ICI postdoctoral fell King's Coll London 1951–55 (asst lectr 1955–56); Univ of Reading: lectr 1956–63, reader 1963–65, prof 1965–89, pt/t prof 1989–91, prof emeritus 1991–; sr reporter Royal Soc of Chem; conslt Pharmakopius International 1993–; formerly conslt to: Shell, Esso, EI Du Pont de Nemours (USA), Dutch State Mines; non-exec dir Nature's Own Ltd; endowed lectureship Royal Soc of Chem 1984 (John Jeyes Silver Medal); numerous radio and television broadcasts in UK and abroad largely on environmental chemistry topics; FRSC (chm Photochemistry Subject Gp 1975–93), CChem; *Publications* Lead or Health (with R Stephens, 1980), The Zinc Solution (with L Hodgkinson, 1986), Photochemistry Vols 1–25 (sr reporter); *Recreations* singing, piano playing, gardening, debating; *Style*— Prof Derek Bryce-Smith; ✉ Highland Wood House, Mill Lane, Kidmore End, Reading RG4 9HB (☎ 0118 972 3132)

BRYCESON, Prof Anthony David Malcolm; s of Lt-Col Donald John Bryceson (d 1978), and Muriel Gertrude, *née* Hutton (d 1978); *b* 16 Nov 1934; *Educ* Winchester, Univ of Cambridge (MB BChir, MD), Westminster Hosp Med Sch; *m* 25 Oct 1969, Ulla, da of Axel Skalts; 1 s (William b 16 Aug 1972), 1 da (Maia b 16 Dec 1974); *Career* MO Colombo Plan Laos 1961–63, med registrar Hosp for Tropical Diseases London 1964, asst prof Haile Selassie I Univ Addis Ababa Ehiopia 1965–67, Wellcome res fell 1968, external scientific staff MRC Ahmadu Bello Univ Zaria Nigeria 1970–74, conslt physician Hosp for Tropical Diseases 1974–, prof London Sch of Hygiene and Tropical Med 1996– (sr lectr 1974–96), seconded as WHO conslt Clinical Res Centre Nairobi 1980–82, hon conslt in tropical diseases for the Army 1982–; memb Royal Soc of Tropical Med and Hygiene (hon sec 1984–89); DTM & H (Eng) 1961; FRCP: Edinburgh 1972, London 1984; *Books* Leprosy (with R E Pfaltzgraff, 3 edn 1990); *Recreations* ornithology, photography, travel; *Style*— Prof Anthony Bryceson; ✉ Hospital for Tropical Diseases, 4 St Pancras Way, London NW1 0PE (☎ 0171 387 4411, fax 0171 383 0041)

BRYDEN, William Campbell Rough (Bill); CBE (1993); s of late George Bryden, and Catherine Bryden; *b* 12 April 1942; *Educ* Greenock HS, Univ of Glasgow; *m* 1970, Hon (Monica) Deborah, *née* Morris, da of 3 Baron Killanin, MBE, TD; 1 s (Dillon Michael George b 1976), 1 da (Mary Kate b 1975); *Career* TV and theatre dir; documentary writer Scottish TV 1963–64; asst dir: Belgrade Theatre Coventry 1965–67, Royal Court Theatre London 1967–69; assoc dir: Royal Lyceum Theatre Edinburgh 1971–74, Royal National Theatre 1975; head of drama television BBC Scotland 1984–94; dir: Cottesloe Theatre (Nat Theatre) 1978–80, Royal Opera House Covent Garden (productions include Parsifal 1988 and The Cunning Little Vixen 1990), Bernstein's Mass (Guidhall Sch of Music & Drama) 1987, A Life in the Theatre Haymarket 1989, The Ship Glasgow 1990; exec producer BBC TV: Tutti Frutti (by John Byrne) 1987 (best series BAFTA awards), The Play on One (series) 1989; dir The Shawl (by David Mamet) BBC TV 1989; winner: Dir of the Year (Laurence Olivier Awards) 1985, Best Dir Award (Evening Standard) for The Mysteries Nat Theatre 1985, Assoc and Drama Magazine Awards 1986, Gulliver Award; Hon DUniv Queen Margaret Coll Edinburgh 1989; memb bd Scottish TV 1979–85; plays: Willie Rough (1972), Benny Lynch (1974), Old Movies (1977); *Recreations* music; *Style*— Bill Bryden, Esq, CBE; ✉ c/o William Morris Agency (UK) Ltd, 31/32 Soho Square, London W1V 6DG (☎ 0171 434 2191, fax 0171 437 0238)

BRYDON, Donald Hood; OBE (1993); s of James Hood Brydon (d 1975), of Edinburgh, and Mary Duncanson, *née* Young; *b* 25 May 1945; *Educ* George Watson's Coll Edinburgh, Univ of Edinburgh (BSc); *children* 1 s (Angus b 1977), 1 da (Fiona b 1975); *Career* res asst Dept of Economics Univ of Edinburgh; investmt mangr: Airways Pension Scheme (British Airways), Barclays Bank; dir Barclays Investment Management, chm (formerly chief exec) BZW Investment Management Ltd, dep chief exec BZW 1994–96, chm BZW Private Equity 1994–96, dir Edinburgh Inca Trust plc 1995–; vice chm Nat Assoc of Pension Funds 1988–90, chm Institutional Shareholders Ctee 1989–90, dir London Stock Exchange 1991–, memb Auditing Practices Bd 1991–94; ldr Bracknell DC 1977–80; AIIMR 1972; *Books* Economics of Technical Information Services (jtly, 1972), Pension Fund Investment (jtly, 1988); *Recreations* golf; *Clubs* Caledonian; *Style*— Donald Brydon, Esq, OBE; ✉ c/o The London Stock Exchange, Old Broad Street, London EC2N 1HP (☎ 0171 797 1000)

BRYER, Prof Anthony Applemore Mornington; s of Gp Capt Gerald Mornington Bryer, OBE, AFC (d 1994), and Joan Evelyn, *née* Grigsby (d 1994); *b* 31 Oct 1937; *Educ* Canford, Sorbonne, Balliol Coll Oxford (MA, DPhil); *m* 2 Aug 1961, Elizabeth (d 1995), da of John Milman Lipscomb; 3 da (Theodora Jane b 3 Feb 1965, Anna Caroline b 2 Sept 1966, Sarah Katherine b 19 March 1971); *Career* Nat Serv RAF Adjutant 1956–58; prof of Byzantine studies Univ of Birmingham 1980– (res fell, lectr, sr lectr, reader 1964–80, first dir of Centre for Byzantine Studies 1976–94, public orator 1991–); res fell Univ of Athens 1961–62, Hellenic Travellers Club guest lectr 1967–, five times visiting fell Dumbarton Oaks Harvard Univ 1970–, Loeb lectr Harvard Univ 1980, visiting Byzantinist Medieval Acad of America 1984, visiting fell Merton Coll Oxford 1985, res advsr to Govt of Cyprus 1988; visiting lectr: Finland 1987, Sweden 1988, Aust 1989, Poland 1993; Wiles lectr Belfast 1990; sr research assoc King's Coll London 1996–; chm: Br Nat Ctee of Int Byzantine Assoc, Soc for The Promotion of Byzantine Studies 1989–95; corresponding memb Hellenic Fndn; FSA 1973, FRHistS 1994; *Books* Iconoclasm (1977), The Empire of Trebizond and the Pontos (1980), The Byzantine Monuments and Topography of the Pontos (2 vols, 1985), Continuity and Change in Late Byzantine and Early Ottoman Society (1986), Peoples and Settlement in Anatolia and the Caucasus 800–1900 (1988), From Mantzikert to Lepanto (1991), Mount Athos (1996); *Recreations* travel, fighting Scottish midges; *Clubs* Buckland (Birmingham), Lochaline Social (Morvern), Black Sea (Trebizond); *Style*— Prof Anthony Bryer; ✉ 33 Crosbie Rd, Harborne, Birmingham B17 9BG (☎ 0121 427 1207); Centre for Byzantine, Ottoman and Modern Greek Studies, University of Birmingham, Birmingham B15 2TT (☎ 0121 414 5777)

BRYER, Dr David Ronald William; CMG (1996); s of Ronald Bryer, of Malvern, Worcs, and Betty, *née* Rawlinson; *b* 15 March 1944; *Educ* King's Sch Worcester, Worcester Coll Oxford (MA, DPhil), Univ of Manchester (Dip TEFL); *m* 1980, Margaret Isabel, da of Sir Eric Bowyer, KCB, KBE, and Elizabeth Caine, *née* Nicholls; 1 da (Helen b 1983), 1 s (Nicholas b 1985); *Career* teacher Lebanon and UK 1964–74 and 1979–81; Oxfam: field dir ME 1975–79, coordinator Africa 1981–84, overseas dir 1984–91, dir 1992–; memb Cncl VSO 1990, memb Eurostep (grouping of 22 euro devpt agencies) 1993–, chm Steering Ctee for Humanitarian Response (SCHR) Geneva; *Books* The Origins of the Druze Religion (1975); *Style*— Dr David Bryer, CMG; ✉ 5 First Turn, Upper Wolvercote, Oxford OX2 8AG; Director, Oxfam, 274 Banbury Road, Oxford OX2 7DZ (☎ 01865 311311, fax 01865 312600)

BRYER, (Alastair) Robin Mornington; s of Gp Capt Gerald Mornington Bryer, OBE, AFC (d 1994), and Joan Evelyn, *née* Grigsby (d 1994); *b* 13 May 1944; *Educ* Dauntsey's Sch, King's Coll Durham (BA); *m* 16 Sept 1976, Jennifer Sheridan, da of Lt-Col Richard Sheridan Skelton, OBE; 1 s (William b 1977); *Career* sr planning asst Hampshire CC 1967–73, ptnr Inland and Waterside Planners 1973–77, ind chartered town planner (one of the first in private practice) assisting landowners, developers, MPs, conservation bodies and govt depts 1977–; award winner Tomorow's New Communities Competition 1991; exhibited in architectural section of RA 1980, guest lectr Hellenic Travellers' Club 1980–; chm PEST (Tory pressure gp) 1966–68, memb Consultancy Bd Royal Town Planning Inst 1980–83, chm Old Dauntseians' Assoc 1985–86; Guildsman City Guild of Old Mercers 1988; Freeman City of London 1987; MRTPI 1973; *Books* Jolie Brise, A Tall Ships Tale (1982), Roving Commissions (ed 1983–86); *Recreations* sailing; *Clubs* Royal Cruising, Royal Lymington Yacht; *Style*— Robin Bryer, Esq; ✉ Princes Place, Closworth, Yeovil, Somerset BA22 9RH (☎ 01935 872268)

BRYERS, Brig Richard Hugh Castellain; CBE (1963); s of Rev John Shaw Bryers (d 1945), of Bowers Gifford Rectory, Essex, and Charlotte Susan, *née* Newman (d 1959); *b* 12 Sept 1911; *Educ* Harrow, St John's Coll Cambridge (BA); *m* 1, July 1938, Phyllis (d 1964), da of Major David Lewis Hankin (d 1949), of N Rhodesia; 2 s (Humphrey b and d 1941, John Richard Feneran b 1944), 1 da (Eliane Susan Gray b 1942); m 2, 22 May 1965, Isabella Marjorie, da of Percy Cromwell Clark (d 1928), of Wallington, Surrey; *Career* King's Own Royal Regt 1933–63, served WWII India, Iraq and Burma, Instr Staff Coll 1942–44, Staff Appts War Office 1945–48 and 1957–60, BJSM Washington 1950–52, served Korea 1953–54, cmd 5 Bn Malay Regt Malayan Emergency 1954–56, Cdr Land Forces Persian Gulf 1960–63; dep pres Red Cross Suffolk Branch 1977–89 (memb 1968–89, branch dir 1974–76); *Recreations* shooting, gardening; *Clubs* Army and Navy, Western India; *Style*— Brig Richard Bryers, CBE; ✉ Thorndon Old Rectory, nr Eye, Suffolk IP23 7LX (☎ 0137 971 284)

BRYMER, Jack; OBE (1960); s of Jack Brymer, of South Shields, Co Durham (d 1975), and Mary, *née* Dixon (d 1960); *b* 27 Jan 1915; *Educ* South Shields GS, Goldsmiths' Coll London (DipEd); *m* 21 Oct 1939, Joan, da of Jack Richardson (d 1924), of Lancaster, Lancs; 1 s (Timothy b 1951); *Career* princ clarinet: RPO 1947–63, BBC Symphony Orch 1963–71, LSO 1971–86; prof: Royal Acad 1952–58, Kneller Hall 1963–67, Guildhall Sch of Music 1981–89; dir: Shell LSO Scholarship 1982–, London Wind Soloists; broadcaster: On a Personal Note, Music You Love, At Home J B Presents; has recorded complete wind works of Mozart, Bach, Haydn and Beethoven; presenter Play the Clarinet video; Corbbett Medal Worshipful Co of Musicians 1989; Hon MA Univ of Newcastle; Hon DMus: Univ of Kingston 1992, De Montfort Univ 1995; Hon RAM, Hon FGSM, FGCL 1991; *Books* The Clarinet (Menuhin Guides), From Where I Sit (autobiography), In The Orchestra; *Recreations* golf, gardening; *Clubs* Croham Hurst Golf; *Style*— Jack Brymer, Esq, OBE; ✉ Underwood, Ballards Farm Rd, South Croydon, Surrey CR2 7JA (☎ 0181 657 1698)

BRYNING, Charles Frederick; s of Frederick Bryning (d 1982), of Norbreck, Blackpool, and Dorothy Edith Bryning; *b* 17 July 1946; *Educ* Arnold Sch, Blackpool Lancs; *m* 29 April 1983, Katrina Carol, da of John Carol Boris Ely, of Lytham St Anne's; 1 s (Simon b 1983); *Career* CA; ptnr Jones Harris & Co 1972–, chief exec the Alexander Walker Gp of Cos 1987–91; FCA; *Style*— Charles Bryning, Esq; ✉ 17 St Peters Place, Fleetwood, Lancs FY7 6EB (☎ 01253 874255)

BRYSON, Col (James) Graeme; OBE (1954), TD (1949), JP (Liverpool 1956), DL (1968); s of John Conway Bryson, slr (d 1959), of Liverpool, and Oletta, *née* Olsen; *b* 4 Feb 1913; *Educ* St Edward's Coll Liverpool, Univ of Liverpool (LLM), Open Univ (BSc, 1994); *m* 1938, Jean (d 1981), da of Walter Cook Glendinning, of Liverpool; 2 s (and 1 s decd), 4 da; *Career* cmmnd from Univ of Liverpool OTC to 89 Field Bde RA (TA) 1936, cmdg various units 1939–45, promoted Lt-Col 1944, cmd 470 (3 W Lancs) HAA Regt 1947–52, cmd 626 HAA Regt 1952–55, Bt-Col 1955, Hon Col 33 Signal Regt (V) 1975–81; admitted slr 1935, sr dist registrar High Ct of Justice Liverpool and Admiralty Registrar 1947–78, dep circuit judge 1978–82; memb Lord Chllr's (Payne) Ctee for Enforcement of Debts 1965–69, memb IOM Cmmn for Reform Enforcement Laws 1972–74, chm Med Appeal Tbnl 1978–86; pres City of Liverpool Royal Br Legion 1950– (pres NW England 1979–90), hon life pres West Lancs Co Royal Br Legion 1993–; hon life pres Merseyside Cncl of Ex-Service and Regtl Assocs 1986–; HM Vice Lord-Lt Merseyside 1979–89; Queen's Commendation for Brave Conduct 1961; KHS 1974, KCHS 1990, Knight Hon Soc of Knights of the Round Table 1990, KCSG 1996; FRSA 1989; *Books* Execution in Halsbury's Laws of England (jtly, 3 edn 1976); *Recreations* ex-service interests, local history, boating; *Clubs* Athenaeum (Liverpool, pres 1969); *Style*— Col Graeme Bryson, OBE, TD, JP, DL; ✉ Sunwards, 2 Thirlmere Rd, Hightown, Liverpool L38 3RQ (☎ 0151 929 2652)

BRYSON, Adm Sir Lindsay Sutherland; KCB (1981); s of James McAuslan Bryson (d 1976), and Margaret, *née* Whyte (d 1946); *b* 22 Jan 1925; *Educ* Allan Glen's Sch Glasgow, Univ of London (BSc); *m* 1951, Averil, da of W T Curtis-Willson (d 1957); 1 s, 2 da; *Career* joined RN 1945, dir Naval Guided Weapons 1973, dir Surface Weapons Project (Navy) 1974–77, dir gen Weapons (Naval) 1977–81, Chief Naval Engr Offr 1979–81, controller of the Navy 1981–84; pres IEE 1985–86; chm: Marine Technology Directorate Ltd 1987–92, ERA Technology Ltd 1990– (non-exec dir 1985–); dep chm GEC Marconi Ltd 1987–90; non-exec dir: Molins plc 1988–, Elswick plc 1990–94; pres: Soc of Underwater Technol 1989–91, Sussex SATRO 1990–94, Assoc of Project Managers 1991–95; chm: Cncl Univ of Sussex 1989–95, Brighton Festival Tst 1991–, Bd of Govrs Brighton Coll 1990–, New Sussex Opera 1990–, Brighton W Pier Tst 1995–; Worshipful Co of Cooks: Liveryman 1964, Asst 1980, Warden 1985, Second Master 1986, Master 1987; Lord Lt E Sussex 1989–; hon fell Paisley Coll of Technol 1987; Hon DSc Univ of Strathclyde 1987, Hon DEng Univ of Bristol 1988, Hon LLD Univ of Sussex 1995; FEng 1982, FRSE 1984, FRAeS, FIEE, Hon FIEE 1991, Hon FIMechE 1991; KStJ 1990; *Recreations* sailing, opera; *Clubs* Army and Navy, MCC; *Style*— Adm Sir Lindsay Bryson, KCB, FEng, FRSE; ✉ 74 Dyke Road Ave, Brighton, Sussex BN1 5LE (☎ 01273 553638, fax 01273 562478)

BUBB, Nicholas Henry (Nick); s of John William Edward Bubb, of Orsett, Essex, and Diana Rosemary, *née* Willetts; *b* 24 March 1955; *Educ* Gillingham GS, ChCh Oxford (MA); *m* 10 April 1982, Susan Mary, da of Joan Dare, of Chichester, Sussex; 1 s (Alexander Benjamin Thomas b 1985), 1 da (Amy Louise Harriet b 1988); *Career* retailing analyst: Rowe & Pitman & Co 1977–79, Citicorp Scrimgeour Vickers (formerly Kemp-Gee & Co and Scrimgeour Kemp-Gee) 1979–88 (ptnr 1983), Morgan Stanley 1988–95 (exec dir), Mees Pierson 1996–; memb British Cncl of Shopping Centres; AIIMR, MSI; *Recreations* cricket, travel, golf, reading, films, wine; *Clubs* Oriental, Riverside Sports Chiswick, MCC; *Style—* Nick Bubb, Esq; ✉ 6 Orchard Rise, Richmond, Surrey TW10 5BX

BUBNOV, Vladislav Bubnov; s of Sergei Bubnov, of Moscow, and Valentina, *née* Tishenko (d 1991); *b* 23 Oct 1969; *Educ* Bolshoi Sch Moscow, Bolshoi Acad of Dancing (Teaching Cert); *Career* soloist The Bolshoi Ballet 1987–92, first princ Scottish Ballet 1992–; repertoire incl: Mercutio in Grigorovich's Romeo & Juliet, Jester in Swan Lake, Bronze Idol in La Bayadere, Shepherd in Spartacus, Spanish Harlequin in The Nutcracker, Pan in Lavrovsky's Walpurgisnacht, Barachio in Boccadoro's L'amour pour l'amour, Two Friends in Balanchine's Prodigal Son, princ in Concerto Borocco, princ in Scotch Symphony, soloist in Bournonville's Conservatoire, James in La Sylphide, Combat/Franz in Wright's Coppelia, Prince in Darrell's The Nutcracker and Cinderella, Lysander/Puck in Cohan's Midsummer Night's Dream, Spring in Cohan's Four Seasons, princ in North's Troy Game, Red Couple in Tippet's Bruch Violin Concerto No 1, Vronsky/Levin in Prokovsky's Anna Karenina, soloist in Vespri, Peter in Lustig's Peter Pan, Prince Florimund/Bluebird in Samsova's The Sleeping Beauty, princ in Baldwin's Haydn Pieces and Ae Fond Kiss, Le Corsaire Pas de Deux, Belong Pas de Deux; *Style—* Vladislav Bubnov, Esq; ✉ 8 Belhaven Terrace 2/2, Kirklee, Glasgow G12 0TF (☎ 0141 337 3475); Scottish Ballet, 261 West Princes Street, Glasgow G4 9EE (☎ 0141 331 2931, fax 0141 331 2629)

BUCCLEUCH AND QUEENSBERRY, 9 and 11 Duke of (S 1663 and 1684); Walter Francis John Montagu Douglas Scott; KT (1978), VRD (1959), JP (Roxburgh 1975); also Lord Scott of Buccleuch (S 1606), Lord Scott of Whitchester and Eskdaill, Earl of Buccleuch (both S 1619), Earl of Dalkeith (S 1663), Earl of Doncaster, Baron Scott of Tynedale (both E 1663), Lord Douglas of Kinmont, Middlebie and Dornoch, Viscount of Nith, Thorthorwald and Ross, Earl of Drumlanrig and Sanquhar, and Marquess of Dumfriesshire (all S 1706); s of 8 and 10 Duke of Buccleuch and Queensberry, KT, GCVO, TD, PC (d 1973), and (Vreda Esther) Mary (d 1993), da of Maj William Frank Lascelles (ggs of 2 Earl of Harewood); *b* 28 Sept 1923; *Educ* Eton, Christ Church Oxford; *m* 1953, Jane, da of John McNeill, QC, of Drumavuic, Argyll; 3 s (Earl of Dalkeith (*qv*), Lord (William Henry) John b 1957, Lord Damian Torquil Francis Charles b 1969), 1 da (Lady Charlotte-Anne (Comtesse Bernard de Castellane) b 1966); *Heir* s, Earl of Dalkeith, DL; *Career* served RNVR & RNR 1942–71 Lt Cdr; Hon Capt RNR 1988; memb Roxburgh CC 1958–; MP (C) Edinburgh N 1960–73, PPS to Sec of State for Scotland 1961–64; DL: Selkirk 1955, Midlothian 1960, Roxburgh 1962, Dumfries 1974; Lord-Lt: Roxburghshire 1974–75, Selkirk 1975, Roxburgh, Ettrick and Lauderdale 1975–; chm Assoc of Lord-Lieutenants 1990–; Capt Royal Co of Archers (Queen's Body Guard for Scotland), Chllr Order of the Thistle 1994–; pres: Royal Highland & Agricultural Soc for Scotland 1969, St Andrew's Ambulance Assoc 1973–, Royal Blind Asylum & Sch, E of England Agric Soc 1976, Royal Scot Agric Benevolent Inst, Scot Nat Inst for War Blinded, Royal Assoc for Disability and Rehabilitation 1993– (chm 1973–93), Cwlth Forestry Assoc 1979–, Royal Scottish Forestry Soc 1994–, Moredun Foundation for Animal Health & Welfare 1994–; chm: Buccleuch Heritage Tst 1985–, Living Landscape Tst 1986–; FRAgS 1996; *Recreations* music, painting, field sports, photography, travel; *Clubs* New (Edinburgh); *Style—* His Grace the Duke of Buccleuch and Queensberry, KT, VRD, JP; ✉ Drumlanrig Castle, Thornhill, Dumfriesshire (☎ 01848 30248); Boughton House, Kettering, Northants; Bowhill, Selkirk (☎ 01750 20732)

BUCHAN, Dr Alexander Stewart; s of Samuel Buchan (d 1992), of Carnoustie, and Mary, *née* Stewart (d 1982); *b* 7 Sept 1942; *Educ* Loretto, Univ of Edinburgh (MB ChB); *m* 24 Feb 1968, Henrietta Young, da of William Constable Dalrymple, of Edinburgh; 1 s (Alexander b 1969); *Career* conslt anaesthetist 1975–: Royal Infirmary Edinburgh, Royal Hosp for Sick Children, Princess Margaret Rose Orthopaedic Hosp; admin conslt for obstetric anaesthesia Simpson Memorial Maternity Pavilion 1988–; memb: Scottish Soc of Anaesthetists, Edinburgh and East of Scotland Soc of Anaesthetists; FFARCS 1970; *Books* Handbook of Obstetric Anaesthesia (1991); *Recreations* fishing, sailing, golf; *Style—* Dr Alexander Buchan; ✉ 21 Chalmers Crescent, Edinburgh EH9 1TS (☎ 0131 667 1127); Department of Anaesthetics, Royal Infirmary, Edinburgh (☎ 0131 563 1000)

BUCHAN, District Judge; (James Alexander) Bruce; s of James Welsh Ross Buchan (d 1982), and Phyllis Clare, *née* Buckle (d 1990); *b* 4 May 1947; *Educ* Fulneck Boys Sch, Univ of Birmingham (LLB); *Career* admitted slr; ptnr Dibb Lupton Broomhead 1975–92, district judge 1992–; nat chm Young Slrs' Gp Law Soc 1982–83; govr Fulneck Sch, churchwarden St John the Baptist Leeds; memb Law Soc, hon memb Leeds Law Soc; *Recreations* walking and golf; *Clubs* The Leeds, Headingly Golf (Leeds); *Style—* District Judge Buchan; ✉ Dewsbury County Court, Eightlands Road, Dewsbury, W Yorks WF13 2PE (☎ 01924 465860)

BUCHAN, Dennis Thorne; s of David S Buchan; *b* 25 April 1937; *Educ* Arbroath HS, Dundee Coll of Art (DA); *m* 1965 (m dis 1976), Elizabeth, *née* Watson; 1 da (Wendy), 1 s (John MacGregor); *Career* artist; lectr Duncan of Jordanstone Coll of Art 1965–94; memb Dundee Group Artists Ltd 1975–81; RSA 1991 (ARSA 1975) *Solo Exhibitions* Douglas and Foulis Gall 1965, Saltire Soc (Edinburgh Festival) 1974, Compass Gall 1975, A Span of Shores 1994, Traquair House 1996; *Group Exhibitions* Five Dundee Painters 1961, + - 30 (Hunterian Museum and tour) 1964, Six Coastal Artists (Demarco Gall) 1965, Scottish Contemporary Painting (Aberdeen Art Gall) 1970, Seven Painters in Dundee (Scottish Nat Gall of Modern Art, McManus Gall) 1972, Painters in Parallel (Scottish Arts Cncl Festival Exhbn) 1978, Kindred Spirits (Ancrum Gall) 1990, Compass Contribution (Tramway) 1990, Scottish Contemporary Painting (Flowers East) 1993, Paperworks (Seagate Gall) 1993, Artists in Angus (Meffan Gall) 1993, Five Scottish Artists (Centre d'Art en L'Ile Geneva) 1994; *Collections* Edinburgh Hosp Gp, Dundee Coll of Educn, Kingsway Tech Coll, Univ of Leicester, Scottish Arts Cncl, Dundee Museum and Art Galls, Vincent Price Collection, Aberdeen Royal Infirmary; *Awards* Keith Prize RSA 1962, Latimer Award RSA 1963, Arts Cncl Award 1973, William McCaully Award for most distinguished work in RSA Exhbn 1988, William Gillies Bequest Fund Award RSA 1991; *Style—* Dennis Buchan, Esq, RSA; ✉ 8 Inchcape Road, Arbroath, Tayside DD11 1DF (☎ 01241 873080)

BUCHAN, (Hon) (Charles Walter) Edward Ralph; 2 s of 3 Baron Tweedsmuir, and his 2 wife Barbara Howard, *née* Ensor (d 1969); *b* 5 Aug 1951; *Educ* Magdalen Coll Sch Oxford, Univ of Southampton (BSc); *m* 27 Nov 1982, Fiona Jane, da of Capt E P Carlisle, of Llanigon, Hay-on-Wye; 1 s (William b 1984), 3 da (Annabel b 1986, Laura b 1988, Amilia b 1992); *Career* Hill Samuel Bank Ltd: joined 1977, dir 1985–96, md 1993–96; md Close Brothers Corporate Finance Ltd 1996–; FCA 1976; *Clubs* Travellers; *Style—* Edward Buchan, Esq; ✉ Close Brothers Corporate Finance Ltd, 12 Appold Street, London EC2A 2AA (☎ 0171 426 4375, fax 0171 247 1214)

BUCHAN, Hon James Ernest; 3 s of 3 Baron Tweedsmuir, *qv*, and Barbara Howard, *née* Ensor (d 1969); *b* 11 June 1954; *Educ* Eton, Magdalen Coll Oxford (MA); *m* 1986, Lady Evelyn Rose Phipps, da of 4 Marquess of Normanby, KG, CBE (d 1994); 2 da (Elizabeth Blanche b 1989, Rose Barbara Averil b 1995), 1 s (Nicholas Adam b 1992); *Career* Financial Times: corr Saudi Arabia 1978–80, corr Bonn 1982–84, columnist Lex Column 1984–86, corr NY 1987–90; contrib Independent on Sunday Review 1990–94, chief book critic Spectator 1990–94; Harold Wincott Award for Business Journalism 1986; FRGS, FRAS, fell Zoological Soc of London; *Books* The House of Saud (with Richard Johns and David Holden, 1981), A Parish of Rich Women (1984, Whitbread First Novel Award, Yorkshire Post Award, David Higham Award), Davy Chadwick (1987), Slide (1990), Hearts Journey in Winter (1995, Guardian Fiction Award), High Latitudes (1996); *Style—* The Hon James Buchan; ✉ c/o Caroline Dawnay, Peters Fraser & Dunlop, The Chambers, Chelsea Harbour, London SW10 0XF (☎ 0171 344 1000, fax 0171 321 7356)

BUCHAN, Hon John William Howard de l'Aigle (Toby); s and h of 3 Baron Tweedsmuir and his 2 w, Barbara Howard, *née* Ensor (d 1969); *b* 25 May 1950; *m* 1977, Amanda Jocelyn, 2 da of Sir Gawain Westray Bell, KCMG, CBE, of Hidcote Bartrim Manor, Chipping Campden, Glos: 2 s (John Alasdair Gawain b 20 Nov 1986, Christopher Charles Westray b 1988); *Style—* The Hon Toby Buchan; ✉ c/o Lloyds Bank, Wallingford, Oxon

BUCHAN, 17 Earl of (S 1469); Malcolm Harry Erskine; JP (Westminster 1972); also Lord Auchterhouse (S 1469), Lord Cardross (S 1610), and Baron Erskine (UK 1806); s of 16 Earl of Buchan (d 1984), and Christina, *née* Woolner (d 1994); *b* 4 July 1930; *Educ* Eton; *m* 1957, Hilary Diana Cecil, da of late Sir Ivan McLannahan Cecil Power, 2 Bt; 2 s (Henry Thomas Alexander (Lord Cardross) b 1960, Hon Montagu John b 1966), 2 da (Lady Seraphina Mary b 1961, Lady Arabella Fleur (Lady Arabella Biddle) b 1969); *Heir* s, Lord Cardross; *Career* pres Sane Planning in the SE (SPISE) 1995–, chm The Dogs Home Battersea, memb Rare Breeds Survival Tst; Liveryman Worshipful of Grocers; *Style—* The Rt Hon the Earl of Buchan, JP; ✉ Newnham House, Newnham, Hook, Hants RG27 9AS

BUCHAN-HEPBURN, Capt Sir (John) Alastair Trant Kidd; 7 Bt (UK 1815), of Smeaton Hepburn, Haddingtonshire; s of John Trant Buchan-Hepburn (d 1953), and Edith Margaret (Mitchell), *née* Robb (d 1980); suc cousin, Sir Ninian Buchan-Hepburn of Smeaton-Hepburn, 6 Bt (d 1992); *b* 27 June 1931; *Educ* Charterhouse, Univ of St Andrews, RMA Sandhurst; *m* 1957, Georgina Elizabeth Turner, SRN, Lt Queen Alexandra's Royal Army Nursing Corps, da of Oswald Morris Turner, MC (d 1953), of Armathwaite, Cumberland; 1 s (John Christopher Alastair b 1963), 3 da (Caroline Georgina (Mrs A W P Thomson) b 1958, Sarah Elizabeth (Mrs D A Cox) b 1960, Louise Mary (Mrs A D S Kinnear) b 1966); *Heir* s, (John) Christopher Alastair Buchan-Hepburn, *qv*, b 9 March 1963; *Career* Capt 1st King's Dragoon Gds, ADC to GOC-in-C Malaya Cmd 1956–57, attached to Swiss Army Cavalry, served BAOR and Far East, attached Household Cavalry; brewing sr exec Arthur Guinness & Co Ltd 1958–86, ret; agent Royal Insurance Co; dir: Broughton Brewery Ltd 1987–95, Broughton Ales Ltd 1995–; memb: Inst of Brewing, Burgess and Guild Bros of Glasgow, Incorporation of Maltmen, Baronets' Tst; life memb St Andrew Preservation Tst; Freeman Citizen of Glasgow; *Recreations* gardening, shooting, fishing, walking, old china and glass, golf, tennis, travel in Scottish Islands; *Clubs* Royal and Ancient Golf (St Andrews); *Style—* Capt Sir Alastair Buchan-Hepburn, Bt; ✉ Chagford, 60 Argyle St, St Andrews, Fife KY16 9BU; (☎ 01334 472161); office: Broughton Ales Ltd, Broughton, By Biggar, Lanarkshire ML12 6HQ (☎ 01899 830345)

BUCHAN-HEPBURN, (John) Christopher Alastair; s and hp of Capt Sir (John) Alastair Trant Kidd, 7 Bt, *qv*; *b* 9 March 1963; *Educ* Cheltenham Coll, Hereford Coll of Art, Univ of Portsmouth (BA, post grad Dip in Architecture); *m* 4 Aug 1990, Andrea, twin da of Kenneth Frederick Unwin, of Ryarsh, Kent; 1 s ((John) James Christopher Thomas b 1 Dec 1992); *Career* architect; The Miller Partnership (Glasgow) 1986–87, The Ash Powell Partnership (Romsey) 1988–89, The GMW Partnership (London and Bishop's Waltham) 1989–92, princ offr of performance Dundee City Cncl 1993–; RIBA 1987; *Books* Experiencing Doorways (1988); *Recreations* golf, tennis, fishing, shooting, gardening and garden restoration, biographies, art, conservation, history; *Clubs* New Golf (St Andrews); *Style—* Christopher Buchan-Hepburn, Esq; ✉ Chagford, 60 Argyle Street, St Andrews, Fife KY16 9BU (☎ 01334 472161); Dundee City Council, Housing Department, Dundee DD1 3AH (☎ 01382 434933, fax 01382 434930)

BUCHAN OF AUCHMACOY, Capt David William Sinclair; JP (Aberdeenshire 1959, Westminster 1972); s of Capt Stephen Lloyd Trevor, JP (d 1959), and Lady Olivia, *née* Sinclair, da of 18 Earl of Caithness, CBE (d 1947); suc maternal gf (18 Earl) as Chief of the Name of Buchan and recognised as such by Lord Lyon 1949; *b* 18 Sept 1929; *Educ* Eton, RMA Sandhurst; *m* 1961, Hon (Blanche) Susan Fionodhbar, *née* Scott-Ellis, da and co-heiress of 9 Baron Howard de Walden; 4 s, 1 d; *Heir* s, Charles Buchan of Auchmacoy the younger, *qv*; *Career* cmmnd Gordon Highlanders 1949, served Berlin, BAOR and Malaya, Capt and ADC to GOC-in-C Singapore 1951–53, ret 1955; memb London Stock Exchange, sr ptnr Gow & Parsons 1961–68; memb: Queen's Body Guard for Scotland, The Pilgrims, Friends of Malta GC, Alexandra Rose Day Cncl, Cook's Soc (Australia), Cncl Royal Sch of Needlework 1987, Cons Industl Fund Ctee 1988; govr London Clinic 1988; vice pres: Aberdeenshire CCC 1962, Bucks CCC 1984–; memb Worshipful Co of Broderers (Master 1992), Freeman City of London; KStJ 1987 (OStJ 1981), memb Cncl for London Order of St John; FInstD; *Recreations* cricket, tennis, squash; *Clubs* White's, Turf, City of London, Pratt's, RAC, MCC, Puffins (Edinburgh), Canada, Pitt (London); *Style—* Capt David Buchan of Auchmacoy, JP; ✉ Auchmacoy House, Ellon, Aberdeenshire (☎ 01358 20229); 28 Little Boltons, London SW10 (☎ 0171 373 0654, fax 0171 373 7587); D-310, Puenta Romana, Marbella, Spain

BUCHAN OF AUCHMACOY YR, (John) Charles Augustus David; s and h of Capt David Buchan of Auchmacoy, JP, *qv*, and Hon Susan, *née* Scott-Ellis, da of 9 Baron Howard de Walden, to which Barony he is in remainder through his m; *b* 1 March 1963; *Educ* Ampleforth, RAC Cirencester; *Career* investmt banker; CIBC 1986–89, estate agent Mellersh & Harding 1990–91, currently self employed property developer; Liveryman: Worshipful Co of Shipwrights, Worshipful Co of Borderers; *Recreations* fishing, tennis, shooting, jungle exploration; *Clubs* RAC, Turf; *Style—* Charles Buchan of Auchmacoy Yr

BUCHANAN, *see:* Leith-Buchanan, Macdonald-Buchanan

BUCHANAN, Alistair John; s of John James Buchanan (d 1983), and Phoebe Leonora, *née* Messel (d 1952), of Grosvenor Square, London; *b* 13 Dec 1935; *Educ* Eton, New Coll Oxford; *m* 1, 1959, Louise Parker (d 1961); *m* 2, 1963, Ann Hermione, da of Raymond Alexander Baring (d 1967); 3 da (Katie, Tessa, Helen); *Career* 2 Lt 2 Bn Coldstream Guards 1954–56; Layton-Bennett Billingham & Co 1959–62, Allen Harvey & Ross Ltd 1962–81, A Sarasin & Co Ltd 1980–87, chm Cater Allen Holdings plc 1981–85, md Morgan Grenfell Govt Securities 1985–87, dep chm and md Mees & Hope Securities Holdings Ltd 1987–91; chm: Premium Management Ltd 1989–, Lorne House Trust Ltd 1991–; dir: LIFFE 1981–84, Heritage of London Trust Ltd 1982–, Mannin Industries Ltd, Feathercombe Farm Ltd, Eyecare Products PLC 1994–; FCA, MSI; *Recreations* golf, gardening, shooting, stalking; *Clubs* White's, Swinley Forest Golf, City of London; *Style—* Alistair Buchanan, Esq; ✉ Hillbarn House, Great Bedwyn, Marlborough, Wilts (☎ 01672 870207, fax 01672 871015)

BUCHANAN, Sir Andrew George; 5 Bt (UK 1878), of Dunburgh, Stirlingshire; s of Maj Sir Charles James Buchanan, 4 Bt (d 1984), and Barbara Helen (d 1986), da of Lt-Col

Rt Hon Sir George Frederick Stanley, GCSI, GCIE, CMG; *b* 21 July 1937; *Educ* Eton, Trinity Coll Cambridge, Wye Coll London; *m* 26 April 1966, Belinda Jane Virginia Buchanan, JP, da of Donald Colquhoun Maclean and wid of Gresham N Vaughan (d 1964); 1 s (George Charles Mellish b 1975), 1 da (Laura Evelyn (Mrs James Mayes) b 1967), 1 step s, 1 step da; *Heir* s, George Charles Mellish Buchanan b 27 Jan 1975; *Career* 2 Lt Coldstream Guards 1956–58, Major cmd A Sqdn Sherwood Rangers Yeo (TA) 1971–74, Hon Col B Sqdn (Sherwood Rangers Yeo) Queen's Own Yeomanry 1989–94; farmer, chartered surveyor, land agent; High Sheriff Nottinghamshire 1976–77; chm Bd of Visitors HM Prison Ranby 1983–84; DL Notts 1985; Lord-Lieut of Nottinghamshire 1991–; KStJ 1991; *Recreations* walking, forestry; *Clubs* Boodle's; *Style*— Sir Andrew Buchanan, Bt; ✉ Hodsock Priory, Blyth, Worksop, Notts S81 0TY (☎ 01909 591204, fax 01909 591578)

BUCHANAN, Prof (Robert) Angus; OBE (1993); s of Robert Graham Buchanan (d 1975), of Sheffield, and Bertha Buchanan, MBE, JP, *née* Davis (d 1975); *b* 5 June 1930; *Educ* High Storrs GS Sheffield, St Catharine's Coll Cambridge (BA, MA, PhD); *m* 10 Aug 1955, Brenda June, da of George Henry Wade (d 1955), of Sheffield; 2 s (Andrew Nassau b 1958, Thomas Claridge b 1960); *Career* Nat Serv RAOC 1948–50, GHQ FARELF 1949–50; educn offr Royal Fndn of St Katharine Stepney 1956–60, co-opted memb London CC Educn Ctee 1958–60; Univ of Bath: formerly lectr, sr lectr and reader, prof 1990–95 (emeritus 1995–), dir Centre for the History of Technol Sci & Soc 1964–; royal cmmr Royal Cmmn for Historical Monuments 1979–93, properties ctee memb Nat Tst 1974–; pres: Assoc for Industl Archaeology 1975–77, Newcomen Soc for History of Engrg and Technol 1981–83, Int Ctee for the History of Technol 1993– (sec gen 1981–93); vice-pres Soc of Antiquaries of London 1995–; visiting prof Aust Nat Univ 1981, Jubilee prof Chalmers Univ Sweden 1984, visiting lectr Wuhan People's Republic of China 1983; chm Bath Branch Historical Assoc 1987–90, dir Nat Cataloguing Unit for the Archives of Contemporary Scientists 1987–95; Hon DSc Chalmers Univ Sweden 1986; Leonardo da Vinci medal Soc for the History of Technol 1989; FRHistS 1978, FSA 1990, FRSA 1993; *Books* Technology and Social Progress (1965), Industrial Archaeology in Britain (1972), History and Industrial Civilisation (1979), The Engineers - A History of the Engineering Profession in Britain 1750–1914 (1989), The Power of the Machine (1992); *Recreations* walking, rambling, travelling; *Style*— Prof R Angus Buchanan, OBE, FSA; ✉ Centre for the History of Technology Science and Society, University of Bath, Claverton Down, Bath BA2 7AY (☎ 01225 826826, fax 01225 826381)

BUCHANAN, Cameron Roy Marchand; s of late Maj Alexander Bell Watson Buchanan, MC, TD, of Woking, Surrey, and Katharine Norma, *née* Stiles; *b* 17 Sept 1947; *Educ* St Edward's Sch Oxford, Sorbonne Paris; *m* 11 May 1973, Diana Frances, da of Hugh Wilson Jones (d 1979); 1 s (Alexander Cameron b 4 April 1977), 1 da (Tanya Katharine b 18 Sept 1974); *Career* md Harrisons of Edinburgh Ltd (formerly George Harrison & Co Edinburgh Ltd) 1985–; dir Br Knitting and Clothing Export Cncl (chm Menswear Ctee); Scottish Entrepreneur of the Year 1992; Freeman Worshipful Co of Merchants Edinburgh, Liveryman Worshipful Co of Glovers 1987; hon consul for Iceland in Scotland; *Recreations* skiing, golf, tennis; *Clubs* New (Edinburgh); *Style*— Cameron Buchanan, Esq; ✉ Gateside, Old Church Lane, Duddingston Village, Edinburgh EH15 3PX (☎ 0131 661 1889); Harrisons of Edinburgh Ltd, 24 Jane Street, Edinburgh EH6 5HJ (☎ 0131 555 3532, fax 0131 555 3606)

BUCHANAN, Rt Rev Colin Ogilvie; *see:* Woolwich, Bishop of

BUCHANAN, Prof Dennis Langston; s of Langston Llewellyn Buchanan (d 1954), and Georgina Vera, *née* Wheatley; *b* 15 April 1947; *Educ* Cambridge High, Rhodes Univ (BSc), Univ of Pretoria (MSc), Univ of London (PhD), Imperial Coll London (DIC); *m* 17 Dec 1970, Vaughan Elizabeth, da of Fritz Reitz Hayward, of Port Elizabeth; 1 s (James George), 1 da (Alexandra Claire); *Career* Union Corp Ltd SA 1969–73, res fell Univ of Witwatersrand SA 1978–79 (res asst 1976–77), prof of mining geology Royal Sch of Mines Imperial Coll 1984– (res asst 1976–77, lectr 1980–83); independent consulting minin geologist and dir Altyn-Tas Jt Venture Kazakhstan 1994; vice pres Inst of Mining and Metallurgy; CEng 1976, FGSSA 1986, FIMM 1989; *Books* Platinum Group Element Exploration (1988); *Recreations* jogging; *Clubs* Royal Sch of Mines Assoc, Chaps; *Style*— Prof Dennis Buchanan; ✉ Department of Geology, Imperial College, London SW7 2BP (☎ 0171 594 6440, fax 0171 594 6540)

BUCHANAN, Prof (John) Grant; s of Robert Downie Buchanan (d 1937), of Dumbarton, and Mary Hobson (Molly), *née* Wilson; *b* 26 Sept 1926; *Educ* Dumbarton Acad, Glasgow Acad, Christ's Coll Cambridge (MA, PhD, ScD); *m* 14 July 1956, Sheila Elena (d 1996), da of Reginald Lugg (d 1961), of Highgate, London; 3 s (Andrew b 1959, John b 1962, Neil b 1965); *Career* res fell Univ of California at Berkeley 1951–52, res asst Lister Inst of Preventive Med London 1952–54; Univ of Newcastle upon Tyne: lectr in organic chemistry King's Coll 1955, sr lectr 1962, reader in organic chemistry 1965; Heriot-Watt Univ: prof of organic chemistry 1969–91, head Dept of Chemistry 1987–91, prof emeritus 1991–; professorial fell Univ of Bath 1991–; pres Euro Carbohydrate Orgns 1991–93; FRSC 1981 (memb Cncl 1982–85), FRSE 1972 (memb Cncl 1980–83), CChem 1981; *Publications* over 160 original papers and reviews on organic and bio-organic chemistry; *Recreations* golf; *Clubs* Bath Golf; *Style*— Prof Grant Buchanan, FRSE; ✉ 37 Woodland Grove, Claverton Down, Bath BA2 7AT (☎ 01225 466118); School of Chemistry, University of Bath, Claverton Down, Bath BA2 7AY (☎ 01225 826433, fax 01225 826231)

BUCHANAN, Hugh Charles Stanley; s of Maj Sir Charles Buchanan, 4 Bt (d 1984), and Barbara Helen, *née* Stanley; *b* 26 Aug 1942; *Educ* Eton, McGill University (BA); *m* 10 Dec 1969, Nony Caroline Vatcher, da of Lt-Col John Johnston Dingwall, DSO, of Lyford Grange, Wantage, Oxfordshire; 1 s (James Iain Stanley b 6 March 1974), 2 da (Clarissa Victoria Rosamond b 9 Oct 1972, Arabella Patricia Dingwall b 9 Sept 1981); *Career* admitted slr 1980; currently ptnr: Cole & Cole, Morland & Son; memb Oxon CC 1985–89; *Recreations* gardening, shooting, skiing, reading, photography; *Style*— Hugh Buchanan, Esq; ✉ The Manor House, Little Milton, Oxford OX44 7QB (☎ 01844 279368); Larriberau, Loubersan, Gascony, France; Morland & Son, Bath St, Abingdon OX14 3RL (☎ 01235 520204, fax 01235 532954)

BUCHANAN, James Meredith; s of Donald Geoffrey Buchanan (d 1978), and Violet Hetherington, *née* Bell; *b* 4 March 1943; *Educ* Haberdashers' Aske's, St George's Hosp Med Sch Univ of London (MB BS, AKC); *m* 4 May 1974, Judith, da of James Edward Spence, of Sedgefield, Co Durham; 3 da (Helen, Charlotte, Sarah); *Career* registrar: Norfolk and Norwich Hosp 1972, St Mary's Hosp Portsmouth 1973; sr registrar St George's Hosp London 1974–77 (house offr posts 1967), conslt orthopaedic surgn Sunderland Gp of Hosps 1977–; hon clinical lectr Univ of Newcastle upon Tyne 1979; author of paper in RCS annals; LRCP 1967, FRCS 1972, fell Br Orthopaedic Assoc 1977; *Recreations* marathon running, rugby football; *Clubs* Chester-Le-Street A/C, Blaydon RUFC; *Style*— James Buchanan, Esq; ✉ 8 Grange Terrace, Stockton Rd, Sunderland, Tyne and Wear SR2 7DF (☎ 0191 5100 555)

BUCHANAN, Prof Keith; s of James Deans Buchanan (d 1976), of Thornliebank, Glasgow, and Helen Parker, *née* Watson; *b* 24 July 1934; *Educ* Shawlands Sch, Univ of Glasgow (MB ChB); *m* 21 March 1961, Maureen, da of James Bryans (d 1982); 2 s (Fraser James b 10 July 1965, Neil Bryans b 16 May 1972), 2 da (Carol Elizabeth b 2 Sept 1963, Kirsty Anne b 19 Jan 1970); *Career* sr registrar in med Glasgow Royal Infirmary 1962–68, prof of metabolic med Queens Univ of Belfast 1976– (sr lectr in med 1969–76); over 300 pubns in jls; *Recreations* golf, gardening, swimming; *Style*— Prof Keith Buchanan; ✉ 30 North Circular Rd, Lisburn, Co Antrim, N Ireland BT28 3AH (☎ 01846 601207); Wellcome Research Laboratories, Dept of Medicine, Mulhouse, Grosvenor Rd, Belfast BT12 6BJ (☎ 01232 240503)

BUCHANAN, Nigel James Cubitt; s of Rev Basil Roberts Buchanan (d 1987), of Cambridge, and Elene, *née* Cubitt; *b* 13 Nov 1943; *Educ* Denstone Coll; *m* 6 July 1968, (Katherine) Mary, da of Prof Sir Arthur Llewellyn Armitage (d 1984); 1 s (James Kenyon b 20 Nov 1979), 2 da (Katherine Lucy b 21 Sept 1975, Elizabeth Mary b 15 May 1978); *Career* Price Waterhouse: ptnr 1978–, Euro dir Fin Servs Practice 1988–, vice chm World Financial Services Practice 1989–, memb Bd East European Firm 1994–, sr client ptnr 1994–; FCA; *Books* Accounting for Pensions (jtly), PW/Euromoney Debt Equity Swap Guide (jtly); *Recreations* tennis, golf; *Clubs* Carlton; *Style*— Nigel Buchanan, Esq; ✉ Longwood, 16 Park Avenue South, Harpenden, Herts AL5 2EA (☎ 01582 763076); Price Waterhouse, Southwark Towers, 32 London Bridge St, London SE1 9SY (☎ 0171 939 3000, fax 0171 378 0647)

BUCHANAN-BARROW, Paul M; s of Rev Dr H R Buchanan-Barrow; *b* 23 April 1945; *Educ* Univ of St Andrews (MA); *m* 12 July 1969, Eithne A, da of G W M O'Shea, of Richmond, Surrey; 2 da (Perdita b 1972, Jessica b 1974); *Career* merchant banker and dir County Bank Ltd 1981–86, exec search conslt and md Goddard Kay Rogers & Assocs 1986–92, manging ptnr Korn/Ferry International 1992–, dir Korn/Ferry International Inc; govr Royal Star & Garter Home 1989–; *Recreations* politics, squash, chess; *Clubs* Reform, Honourable Artillery Co, MCC; *Style*— Paul Buchanan-Barrow, Esq; ✉ 127 Queens Rd, Richmond, Surrey; Thyme Cottage, Luxborough, Somerset; Korn/Ferry International Ltd, 252 Regent Street, London W1R 5DA (☎ 0171 312 3100, fax 0171 312 3130)

BUCHANAN-JARDINE, John Christopher Rupert; s and h of Sir (Andrew) Rupert John Buchanan-Jardine, 4 Bt, MC, JP, DL, *qv*; *b* 20 March 1952; *Educ* Harrow, RAC Cirencester; *m* 1975, Pandora Lavinia, yr da of Peter Murray Lee; 1 s (James Rupert b 28 July 1994), 5 da (Tessa Mary b 1979, Katie Luella b 1980, Lorna Jane b 1984, Juliet Marina b 1986, Alice Fiona b 1988); *Style*— John Buchanan-Jardine, Esq

BUCHANAN-JARDINE, Sir (Andrew) Rupert John; 4 Bt (UK 1885), of Castle Milk, Co Dumfries; MC (1945), JP (Dumfriesshire 1957), DL (1978); s of Capt Sir John William Buchanan-Jardine, 3 Bt, JP (d 1969), and his 1 w, Jean (d 1989), da of Lord Ernest Hamilton, sometime MP N Tyrone (7 s of 1 Duke of Abercorn, KG, PC, and Lady Louisa Russell, 2 da of 6 Duke of Bedford, KG); *b* 2 Feb 1923; *Educ* Harrow, RAC Cirencester; *m* 1950 (m dis 1975), Jane Fiona, da of Sir Archibald Charles Edmonstone, 6 Bt, and Gwendolyn, da of Marshall Field, of Chicago; 1 s (John Christopher Rupert b 1952), 1 da (Diana Gwendolyn Jean b 1955); *Heir* s, John Christopher Rupert Buchanan-Jardine b 20 March 1952; *Career* farmer and landowner, formerly Maj RHG; master Dumfriesshire Foxhounds 1950–; KASG; *Recreations* country pursuits; *Clubs* MCC; *Style*— Sir Rupert Buchanan-Jardine, Bt, MC, JP, DL; ✉ Dixons, Lockerbie, Dumfriesshire (☎ 01576 202508)

BUCHANAN-SMITH, Rev the Hon Robin Dunlop; 3 s of Brig Baron Balerno, CBE, TD (Life Peer; d 1984), and Mary Kathleen, *née* Smith (d 1947); *b* 1 Feb 1936; *Educ* Edinburgh Acad, Trinity Coll Glenalmond, Pembroke Coll Cambridge (BA), New Coll Edinburgh, Princeton Theol Seminary USA (ThM); *m* 13 July 1966, Sheena Mary, da of Alexander Edwards (d 1951), of Oban; 2 s (Beppo, Chay); *Career* minister Christ's Church Dunollie Oban 1962–66; chaplain: 8 Bn Argyll and Sutherland Highlanders 1962–66, St Andrews Univ and St Andrews Univ OTC 1966–73, Highland Volunteers 1966–68; chllr's assessor St Andrews Univ 1981–85; dir Scottish Television plc 1982–96, ptnr Isle of Eriska Hotel; chm Scottish Television Staff Tst; tstee: Cross Tst (chm), Carnegie Tst for the Univs of Scotland, Scottish Orthopaedic Research Tst into Trauma; *Recreations* sailing, country; *Clubs* Caledonian, Royal Highland Yacht; *Style*— The Rev the Hon Robin Buchanan-Smith; ✉ Isle of Eriska, Ledaig, Oban, Argyll PA37 1SD (☎ 01631 720371, fax 01631 720531)

BUCK, Sir (Philip) Antony (Fyson); kt (1983), QC (1974); yr s of late A F Buck, of Ely; *b* 19 Dec 1928; *Educ* King's Sch Ely, Trinity Hall Cambridge; *m* 1, 1955 (m dis 1989), Judy Elaine, o da of late Dr C A Grant, of Cottesloe, Perth, W Australia; 1 da; m 2, 22 March 1990 (m dis 1993), Bienvenida Perez-Blanco, da of late Francisco Perez, of Valencia; m 3, June 1994, Mrs Tamara Norashkaryan; *Career* MP (C): Colchester 1961–83, Colchester N 1983–92; min for RN 1972–74, chm Select Ctee on Parly Cmmn for Admin (Ombudsman) 1977–92, chm Cons Pty Def Ctee 1979–88; *Recreations* most sports, reading; *Clubs* Oxford & Cambridge; *Style*— Sir Antony Buck, QC

BUCK, Antony Charles; s of Stephan Frank Buck, of London NW7 and Rosemary, *née* Tyoran; *b* 8 Aug 1963; *Educ* Haberdashers' Aske's, Univ of Warwick (BSc, Hockey and Tennis First teams); *m* 2 July 1989, Jane Amanda, da of Anthony Halperin; *Career* advertising exec; bd account planning dir BMP DDB Needham until 1993 (joined 1985); winner first prize IPA Advertising Effectiveness awards for: Kia-Ora 1988, Clarks Desert Boots 1988, Alliance & Leicester 1990; fndr Calcraft Buck mktg consultancy 1993; *Recreations* antique collecting, big game photography, fishing, tennis, golf; *Style*— Antony Buck, Esq

BUCK, David Shuttleworth; s of Douglas Shuttleworth Buck (d 1960), and Gladys May (Pearl) (d 1988); *b* 8 April 1934; *Educ* Ashville Coll Harrogate N Yorks, Queen Elizabeth GS Gainsborough Lincs, Emmanuel Coll Cambridge (BA); *m* 16 Aug 1958, Jennifer, da of Clifford Kenneth Boundy (d 1992), of Stratford-upon-Avon; 1 s (Stephen b 1963), 3 da (Vanessa b 1961, Katherine b 1964, Margaret b 1969); *Career* Nat Serv FEAF Hong Kong 1952–54, PO RAF Fighter Control; mktg mangr Fibres Div ICI Ltd 1957–76, commercial mangr J Bibby & Sons Henry Cooke 1976–77, assoc ptnr textile analyst Laing & Cruickshank 1978–83, ptnr textile analyst De Zoete and Bevan 1983–86, dir of res Barclays de Zoete Wedd 1986–95, dir Hollas Group plc 1990–; leading city textile analyst 1984–88, fndr own co DB Research 1990; Star Analyst 1986, 1987, and 1988, Top Star Analyst 1987 and 1988; memb Stock Exchange 1982 (now MSI (Dip)); Liveryman Worshipful Co of Framework Knitters; AIIMR 1981, FTI 1985, FCFI 1986; *Recreations* golf, fell walking, travel; *Clubs* Welwyn Garden City Golf; *Style*— David S Buck, Esq; ✉ D B Research, 124 Parkway, Welwyn Garden City, Herts AL8 6HN (☎ 01707 336827, fax 01707 335946)

BUCK, Louisa; da of Sir Antony Buck, QC, MP, and Judy Breakell, *née* Grant; *b* 10 July 1960; *Educ* Queensgate Sch London, Girton Coll Cambridge (BA), Courtauld Inst of Art Univ of London (MA); partner, Tom Dewe Mathews; 1 s (Alfred Benedict b 7 Jan 1992), 1 da (Nancy Eleanor b 23 March 1995); *Career* freelance lectr, bdcaster and journalist; freelance lectr on Twentieth Century Art 1983–84 (Tate Gallery, Sotheby's fine art courses, art courses in London and Europe), Tate Gallery 1984–85 (cataloguer of John Banting and Edward Burra material, curator of exhibition of Bantings graphic work, public lectr), ran Bonhams Modern Pictures Dept 1985; freelance journalist, broadcaster lectr and researcher 1986–; arts correspondent, contrib ed and visual arts columnist GQ magazine; contrib to: Arena Magazine, New Statesman & Society, Mirabella magazine, City Limits, Guardian arts pages, Tatler, Vogue, Marie Claire, The Evening Standard, Sunday Correspondent; radio 1988–90: visual arts critic LBC, currently visual art reviewer Kaleidoscope BBC Radio 4; lectr on Twentieth Century art design and culture: Tate Gallery, RCA, Saatchi Collection, Univ of Reading, ICA; *Books* author of catalogue essays for: A Salute to British Surrealism (Minories Gallery Colchester, 1985), The Surrealist Spirit in Britain (Whitford & Hughes, 1988), Sylvia Ziranek: Ici Villa Moi (Watermans Arts Centre, 1989), Jacqueline Morreau: Paradise Now (Odette Gilbert

Gallery, 1990), Meret Oppenheim retrospective Barcelona, Relative Values or What's Art Worth? (jtly, 1990), Something the Matter: Helen Chadwick, Cathy de Monchaux, Cornelia Parker (Saô Paulo Bienal, 1994); *Recreations* gardening, swimming, travelling; *Style*— Ms Louisa Buck; ✉ 10 Chapter Road, London SE17 3ET (☎ 0171 582 3796, fax 0171 587 0090)

BUCKBY, Anthony Jonathan; MBE (1996); s of Gordon Harry Buckby (d 1985), of Worcs, and Muriel, *née* Darby; *b* 1 Sept 1951; *Educ* King's Sch Worcester (scholar), Univ of Nottingham (BA), Univ of Essex (MA); *m* Giuliana, da of Mario Salvagno; *Career* teacher of English in UK, Germany and Italy 1974–76, reader Univ of Naples 1978–79, asst dir of studies British Council Naples 1979–82 (teacher 1976–78, teacher trainer 1978–79), sch dir British Inst of Florence 1987–90 (acad advsr 1982–86), dir British Council Bologna 1990–96, asst dir (Language Servs) British Council Italy 1996–; sr assessor Univ of Cambridge Local Examinations Syndicate (UCLES), memb British C of C in Italy 1991–, treas Associazione Italiana Scuole di Lingua Inglese 1989–90 (sec 1988–89); Advanced Trg Award British Council 1982; *Books* Variety (jtly, 1985); *Recreations* gardening; *Style*— Anthony Buckby, Esq, MBE; ✉ Via Bellombra 10, Bologna, Italy; Faircroft, Aberedw, Builth Wells, Powys; The British Council, Via Quattro Fontane 20, 00184 Roma, Italy

BUCKERIDGE, Anthony Malcolm; s of Ernest George Buckeridge (ka France 1917), and Gertrwd Alice, *née* Smith (d 1965); *b* 20 June 1912; *Educ* Seaford Coll, UCL; *m* 1, 1936, Sylvia Goulden, da of John Brown; 1 da (Jennifer Sally b 1938), 1 s (Timothy John Guy b 1941); m 2, 1962, Eileen Norah, da of Alexander Sydney Selby, musician; 1 s (Steven Corin b 1964); *Career* Nat Fire Serv 1940–45; teacher St Lawrence Coll Ramsgate to 1950; writer of books, TV and radio plays and musicals 1950–; Jennings plays BBC Children's Hour 1948–64; stories for magazines 1970–74; memb: Soc of Authors, Writers' Guild of GB, British Actors' Equity; *Books* Jennings (25 titles 1950–92), Rex Milligan (4 titles, 1954–60), A Funny Thing Happened (1953); *Recreations* acting, directing plays; *Style*— Anthony Buckeridge, Esq; ✉ East Crink, Barcombe Mills, Lewes, Sussex BN8 5BL (☎ 01273 400383)

BUCKHAVEN, Simon; *b* 30 Sept 1944; *Educ* Lancing (Music scholar), Manitoba Univ, Cncl of Legal Educn; *m* Sept 1971, Charlotte Vanderlip, da of Sir Robertson Crichton; 1 da (Katie b 4 May 1976), 1 s (Robertson b 4 Aug 1977); *Career* called to the Bar Gray's Inn 1970, asst parly boundary cmmr 1993–, head of chambers 1993–; *Recreations* painting, reading; *Clubs* Athenaeum; *Style*— Simon Buckhaven, Esq; ✉ 1 Harcourt Buildings, Temple, London EC4Y 9DA (☎ 0171 353 9421, fax 0171 353 4170)

BUCKINGHAM, Archdeacon of; *see:* Morrison, Ven John Anthony

BUCKINGHAM, Bishop of 1994–; Rt Rev Colin James Bennetts; s of James Thomas Bennetts, of Lymington, Hants, and Winifred Florence, *née* Couldrey; *b* 9 Sept 1940; *Educ* Battersea GS, Jesus Coll Cambridge (open exhibitioner, MA), Ridley Hall Cambridge; *m* Oct 1966, Veronica Jane, da of Norman Leat; 2 s (Duncan James b 1967, Jonathan Mark b 1971), 2 da (Katharine Louise b 1970, Anna Jane b 1973); *Career* ordained (Rochester Cathedral): deacon 1965, priest 1966; asst curate: St Stephen Tonbridge 1965–68, St Aldate Oxford 1969–72 (concurrently chaplain to the Oxford Pastorate); chaplain Jesus Coll Oxford 1975–79 (asst chaplain 1973–75), vicar St Andrew Oxford 1979–90, rural dean of Oxford 1984–89, canon residentiary Chester Cathedral and diocesan dir of ordinands 1990–94, select preacher before the Univ of Oxford 1994; *Recreations* DIY, Mediaeval and Renaissance music, woodcutting; *Style*— The Rt Rev the Bishop of Buckingham; ✉ Sheridan, Grimms Hill, Great Missenden, Bucks HP16 9BD (☎ 01494 862173, fax 01494 890508)

BUCKINGHAM, Prof (Amyand) David; s of Reginald Joslin Buckingham (d 1956), and Florence Grace, *née* Elliot (d 1977); *b* 28 Jan 1930; *Educ* Barker Coll Hornsby NSW, Univ of Sydney (BSc, MSc), Corpus Christi Coll Cambridge (PhD, ScD); *m* 24 July 1965, Jillian, da of Harold Vincent Bowles, OBE (d 1965); 1 s (Mark b 1968), 2 da (Lucy b 1967, Alice b 1971); *Career* jr censor ChCh Oxford 1963–65 (lectr 1955–57, student 1957–65), lectr in inorganic chemistry Univ of Oxford 1958–65, prof of theoretical chemistry Univ of Bristol 1965–69; Univ of Cambridge: prof of chemistry 1969–, fell Pembroke Coll 1970–, pres Cambridge Univ Cricket Club 1992–; pres Faraday Div Royal Soc of Chemistry 1987–89; Docteur (hc) Univ de Nancy 1979, Hon DSc Univ of Sydney 1993; foreign assoc Nat Acad of Scis USA, foreign hon memb American Acad of Arts and Scis, memb Int Acad of Quantum Molecular Sci; FRS (Hughes Medal 1996); *Books* The Laws and Applications of Thermodynamics (1964), Organic Liquids (ed, 1978), Principles of Molecular Recognition (ed, 1993); *Journals* Molecular Physics (ed 1968–72), int reviews in Physical Chemistry (ed 1981–89), Chemical Physics Letters (ed 1978–); *Recreations* cricket, tennis, travel; *Clubs* ESU; *Style*— Prof David Buckingham, FRS; ✉ University Chemical Laboratory, Lensfield Rd, Cambridge CB2 1EW (☎ 01223 336376, fax 01223 336362)

BUCKINGHAM, Ven Hugh Fletcher; s of Rev Christopher Leigh Buckingham (d 1963), of Alciston, Sussex, and Gladys Margaret, *née* Shellabear (d 1984); *b* 13 Sept 1932; *Educ* Lancing, Hertford Coll Oxford (MA), Westcott House Cambridge; *m* 7 Jan 1967, Alison Mary, da of John Heywood Cock, of Norwich; 1 s (William Hugh b 28 Sept 1971), 1 da (Harriet Jane b 10 Dec 1969); *Career* curate: Halliwell St Thomas Bolton 1957–60, St Silas Sheffield 1960–65; incumbent: Hindolveston and Guestwick Norfolk 1965–70, Fakenham Norfolk 1970–88; rural dean Burnham Walsingham Norfolk 1981–87, chm Diocesan Bd for Social Responsibility Diocese of Norwich 1981–88, hon canon Norwich Cathedral 1985–88, archdeacon of East Riding and canon York Minster 1988–; memb Ecclesiastical Law Soc; *Books* How To Be A Christian In Trying Circumstances (1985), Feeling Good (1989); *Recreations* pottery, gardening; *Style*— The Ven the Archdeacon of the East Riding; ✉ Brimley Lodge, Beverley, E Yorkshire HU17 7DX (☎ 01482 881659)

BUCKINGHAM, Prof Julia Clare; da of Jack William Harry Buckingham (d 1991), of Feock, Cornwall, and Barbara Joan, *née* Baker; *b* 18 Oct 1950; *Educ* St Mary's Sch Calne Wilts, Univ of Sheffield (BSc), Univ of London (PhD, DSc); *m* 1974, Simon James Smith, s of Sidney George Smith (1972); *Career* sr lectr in pharmacology Royal Free Hosp Sch of Med 1980–87 (research fell Dept of Pharmacology 1974–80), prof and head Dept of Pharmacology Charing Cross and Westminster Med Sch London 1988–; Gaddum Meml Prize Br Pharmacological Soc 1994, Soc Medal Soc for Endocrinology 1994; memb: Soc for Endocrinology 1975 (treas 1996–), Br Pharmacological Soc 1977, Int Soc for Neuroendocrinology 1980, Physiological Soc 1980, Soc for Meds Research 1980, Brain Research Assoc 1985, Biochemical Soc 1988; *Recreations* music, skiing, sailing; *Clubs* Sloane; *Style*— Prof Julia Buckingham; ✉ Department of Pharmacology, Charing Cross and Westminster Medical School, Fulham Palace Road, London W6 8RF (☎ 0181 846 7279, fax 0181 846 7253)

BUCKINGHAM, Michael Simm; s of Maurice William Buckingham (d 1989), of Aylesbury, Bucks, and Edith Gwendolin, *née* Simm; *b* 6 Feb 1944; *Educ* Berkhamsted Sch, St Bartholomew's Hosp Med Sch (MB BS), Univ of Southampton (DM); *m* 10 Oct 1970, Hazel Diana, da of Thomas William White, of Meranti Lodge, Clifton, Rugby; 1 s (Timothy b 1976), 1 da (Susannah b 1974); *Career* conslt obstetrician and gynaecologist Royal Hampshire Co Hosp 1981–; memb BMA, FRCOG 1987 (MRCOG 1974); *Recreations* fly fishing; *Style*— Michael Buckingham, Esq; ✉ Royal Hampshire County Hospital, Romsey Rd, Winchester, Hants (☎ 01962 863535)

BUCKINGHAMSHIRE, 10 Earl of (GB 1746); Sir (George) Miles Hobart-Hampden; 14 Bt (E 1611); Baron Hobart (GB 1728); s of Cyril Langel Hobart-Hampden (d 1972), ggs of 6 Earl of Buckinghamshire; suc kinsman 1983; *b* 15 Dec 1944; *Educ* Clifton, Univ of Exeter (BA), Univ of London (MA); *m* 1, 1968 (m dis), Susan Jennifer, o da of late Raymond W Adams, of Halesowen, Worcs; m 2, 1975, Alison Wightman (DL Bucks 1995), da of late William Forrest, of Edinburgh; 2 step s; *Heir* kinsman, Sir John Hobart, 3 Bt, *qv*; *Career* Hong Kong and Shanghai Banking Corporation 1963–64, Hudson Bay Co 1968–70, Noble Lowndes & Partners Ltd 1970–81; dir: Scottish Pension Trustees Ltd 1979–81, Anthony Gibbs Pension Services 1981–86, The Angel Trustee Co 1983–86, WISLI Nominees Ltd 1986–91, Wardley Investment Services (Luxembourg) SA 1988–91, Wardley Global Selection 1988–91, WISL Bahamas 1988–91; md Wardley Investment Services International Ltd 1988–91; chm: Wardley Unit Trust Managers Ltd 1988–91, Wardley Fund Managers (Jersey) Ltd 1988–91; (Anthony Gibbs Pension Services and Wardley Cos are memb cos of the HongkongBank Group); dir: Gota Global Selection (Sicav) 1988–95, The Wyatt Co (UK) Ltd 1991–95; partner Watson Wyatt Partners 1995–; memb House of Lords Select Ctee EC Sub Ctee on Fin Trade and External Relations 1990–92 (on Social and Consumer Affairs 1985–90); pres Buckingham Cons Constituency Assoc; patron: Hobart Town (1804) Early Settlers Assoc (Tasmania), John Hampden Soc; FInstD; *Recreations* squash, real tennis, fishing, music, reading, walking, rugby football; *Clubs* Western (Glasgow), West of Scotland Football, Hatfield Tennis Court, Leamington Tennis Court; *Style*— The Rt Hon the Earl of Buckinghamshire; ✉ House of Lords, London SW1A 0PW; Watson Wyatt Partners, P O Box 77, Gate House, Fretherne Road, Welwyn Garden City, Herts AL8 6PP

BUCKLAND, Christopher Robert; s of Claude Buckland (d 1987), of Burnley, Lancs, and Vera, *née* Greenwood (d 1949); *b* 4 Jan 1944; *Educ* Burnley GS, Univ of Birmingham (BSocSc); *Career* reporter Daily Mail Manchester 1964–65 (Belfast 1965–66); Daily Mirror: reporter Dublin 1966–70, bureau chief Belfast 1970–72, home affrs corr London 1972–74, chief political corr 1974–76, corr Washington DC 1976–78, head of US Bureau 1978–81, foreign ed London 1981–82; political ed: Sunday People 1982–85, Today 1985–89; Daily Express: asst ed (political and foreign) 1989–95, assoc ed (politics and foreign) 1995–; *Recreations* classical music, playing the piano, racing, soccer spectating, travel; *Clubs* Wig & Pen, Archway Snooker, Burnley FC; *Style*— Christopher Buckland; ✉ 2 Walden Lodge, 48 Wood Lane, London N6 5UU (☎ 0181 340 4453); Express Newspapers, 245 Blackfriars Rd, London (☎ 0171 922 7222, fax 0171 620 1654)

BUCKLAND, Gerald David; s of Francis G Buckland (d 1994), of Cheshunt, Hertfordshire, and Elizabeth, *née* Hamilton-Allen; *b* 22 March 1948; *Educ* St Ignatius' Coll, E Herts Coll; *m* 27 May 1975, Paula, da of Mark Gandy (d 1989); 1 s (Anthony Francis Gerald b 3 Jan 1988), 2 da (Marianne Paula Elizabeth b 10 Feb 1980, Isabella Louise Geraldine b 9 June 1983); *Career* press offr BP Chemicals Ltd 1977–80, PR coordinator BP Int Ltd 1980–82, PR mangr Marathon Int Petroleum Inc 1982–88, corporate rels dir TVS Entertainment plc 1988–91, md Sunrise Media Communications 1991–94, ptnr The Buckland Consultancy 1994–; memb: RTS, BAFTA; *Recreations* music, travel, languages; *Clubs* Groucho; *Style*— Gerald Buckland, Esq; ✉ 5 Dean Street, London W1V 5RN; home (☎ 0181 882 0499, fax 0181 447 8570)

BUCKLAND, Ross; s of William Arthur Haverfield Buckland, and Elizabeth, *née* Schmitzer; *b* 19 Dec 1942; *Educ* Sydney Boys' HS; *m* 22 Jan 1966, Patricia Ann, da of William Stephen Bubb, of Warriewood, NSW, Aust; 2 s (Sean William b 1968, Mark Charles b 1970); *Career* held various positions in companies engaged in banking, engrg, office equipment and food indust 1958–66; dir fin and admin Elizabeth Arden Pty Ltd 1966–73, md Kellogg (Aust) Pty Ltd 1978 (various positions 1973–77), pres and chief exec offr Kellogg Salads Canada Inc 1979–80, vice pres Kellogg Co USA, chm Kellogg Company of Great Britain Ltd to 1990 (dir European Operations), gp chief exec Unigate plc 1990–; pres Food & Drink Fedn 1987 89; hon fell Inst of Logistics 1996; CIMgt, FICS, FASCPA, FIGD; *Recreations* walking; *Style*— Ross Buckland, Esq; ✉ Unigate plc, Unigate House, Wood Lane, London W12 7RP (☎ 0181 576 6002, fax 0181 576 6003)

BUCKLAND-WRIGHT, Dr (John) Christopher; s of John Buckland-Wright (d 1954), of Dunedin, NZ, and Mary Elizabeth, *née* Anderson (d 1976); *b* 19 Nov 1945; *Educ* Lycée Francais De Londres, King's Coll London (BSc, AKC, PhD), Univ of London (DSc 1995); *m* 11 Nov 1975, Rosalin, da of Charles W G T Kirk, OBE (d 1986), of Hemel Hempstead; 2 da (Helen b 1977, Alexandra b 1978); *Career* asst head Dept of Comparative Osteology Centre of Prehistory and Paleontology Nairobi Kenya 1966–67, teacher Lycée Francais de Londres 1971–72, anatomy lectr St Mary's Hosp Med Sch London 1973–76; Guy's Hosp Med Sch London: lectr 1976–80, sr lectr 1980–89, reader in radiological anatomy 1989–; Guy's Hosp: head Macroradiographic Res Unit Guy's Hosp 1981–88, head Arthrology Unit 1988–96, chm Applied Clinical Anatomy 1996–; memb Int Cmmn on Radiation Units and Measurements 1987–93; pioneered med applications of high definition macroradiography, author of over 150 scientific pubns on microfocal radiography and its application to the study of bone and arthritis; Freeman City of London 1980, Liveryman and Hon Librarian Worshipful Co of Barbers 1980; memb: Anatomy Soc 1974, Br Soc of Rheumatology 1984, Br Inst of Radiology 1992, Osteoarthritis Res Soc 1992; *Books* Cockerel Cavalcade (1988), The Engravings of John Buckland-Wright (1990), Bathers and Dancers (1993), Baigneuses (1995); *Recreations* fine art and antiquarian books, drawing, painting, walking, sailing; *Clubs* City Livery; *Style*— Dr Christopher Buckland-Wright; ✉ 50 Beechwood Avenue, Kew, Richmond, Surrey TW9 4DE (☎ 0181 876 2011); Anatomy Department, United Medical and Dental School of Guy's and St Thomas's Hosp, London SE1 9RT (☎ 0171 955 4364, fax 0171 955 2753, e-mail c.bucklandw@umds.ac.uk)

BUCKLE, Roger Nicholas; s of Leslie Grieves Buckle (d 1981), of Cottingham, Yorks and Kidlington, Oxford, and Rachel Joan, *née* McLaren (d 1987); *b* 19 Oct 1942; *Educ* Rev Gould's Sch Recife Brazil, Pocklington; *m* 9 Sept 1972, Evelyn, da of Leonard Alfred Douglas Fenton (d 1960), of Sydney; *Career* articled clerk Critchley Ward and Pigott Oxford 1961–65, Thomson McLintock & Co (now KPMG) London 1966–72, treasy mangr The Boots Co plc; hon treas The Vale of Belvoir Protection Gp, memb the Georgian Gp; FCA 1976 (ACA 1966); *Recreations* travel, architecture, interior and garden design, country pursuits; *Style*— Roger Buckle, Esq; ✉ The Old Rectory, Denton, Grantham, Lincs NG32 1JT (☎ 01476 870796)

BUCKLEY, Prof Adrian Arthur; s of Arthur Penketh Buckley (d 1977), and Beatrice May Buckley (d 1953); *b* 28 Dec 1938; *Educ* Poole GS, Univ of Sheffield and Open Univ (BA), Univ of Bradford (MSc), Free Univ Amsterdam (PhD); *m* 6 August 1966, Jenny Rosalie Buckley (d 1977); 2 s (Peter James Scott b 24 Dec 1971, David John Scott b 4 April 1974); *Career* Corp Fin Charterhouse Bank 1971–73, gp treas Redland plc 1973–79, prof Cranfield Sch of Mgmnt 1986– (joined 1980); FCA 1963, FCT 1985; *Books* Multinational Finance (1 edn 1986, 2 edn 1992, 3 edn 1996), The Essence of International Money (1 edn 1990, 2nd 1996), International Capital Budgeting (1996); *Recreations* skiing, walking, theatre; *Style*— Prof Adrian Buckley; ✉ Cranfield School of Management, Cranfield University, Cranfield, Bedford MK43 0AL (☎ 01234 754385)

BUCKLEY, Rt Hon Sir Denys Burton; kt (1960), MBE (Mil 1945), PC (1970); 4 s of 1 Baron Wrenbury (d 1935); *b* 6 Feb 1906; *Educ* Eton (OS), Trinity Coll Oxford (BA, MA, hon fell); *m* 1932, Gwendolen Jane (d 1985), yr da of Sir Robert Armstrong-Jones, CBE, JP, DL (d 1943); 3 da (Jane, Catherine, Miranda); *Career* served 1939–45 in RAOC (temp Maj GSOII, Sigs Directorate, War Office); called to the Bar Lincoln's Inn 1928 (bencher 1949, pro-treasurer 1967, treasurer 1969), High Court Judge (Chancery Div) 1960–70, Lord Justice of Appeal 1970–81; memb Ct of Assts Worshipful Co of Merchant Taylors (Master 1972–73); pres: Senate of Inns of Court 1970–72; Treasury jr counsel

(Chancery) 1949–60; hon fell American Coll of Trial Lawyers 1970; CStJ 1966, Medal of Freedom (USA) 1945; *Clubs* Beefsteak; *Style—* Rt Hon Sir Denys Buckley, MBE; ✉ Flat 6, 105 Onslow Square, London SW7 3LU (☎ 0171 584 4735)

BUCKLEY, Ian Michael; s of Frank Leslie Buckley (d 1973), and Edith Mary, *née* Brown; *b* 16 Nov 1950; *Educ* Bradfield Coll, Univ of Southampton (BSc); *m* 20 July 1974, Sarah Ann, da of Arthur William Sale; 2 da (Anna Louise b 11 April 1978, Camilla Alice b 8 Aug 1981); *Career* CA Peat Marwick Mitchell & Co 1972–82 (articled clerk 1972–75); Smith and Williamson: joined 1982, ptnr and dir of securities 1983–86, gp chief exec 1986–95; chief exec Private Bank and Trust Co Ltd 1997– (dir 1995–, also md Asset Mgmnt subsid), dep chm Zotefoams plc; FCA 1975, FCCA 1987; *Clubs* City of London; *Style—* Ian Buckley, Esq; ✉ The Private Bank and Trust Company Ltd, 12 Hay Hill, London W1X 8EE (☎ 0171 872 3700, fax 0171 872 3706)

BUCKLEY, James; s of Harold Buckley (d 1966), and Mabel, *née* Taylor; *b* 5 April 1944; *Educ* Sheffield City GS, Imperial Coll of Sci & Technol (BSc, ARCS); *m* 15 Aug 1972, Valerie (Elizabeth), da of Ivor Powles, of Newport, Gwent; 1 da (Louise b 1976); *Career* scientific offr RAF Coastal Cmd MOD 1965, princ CSD 1971, private sec to Min for Civil Service and Ldr House of Lords (successively Lord Peart, Lord Soames and Baroness Young) 1979–82, private sec to Govr Rhodesia 1979–80, sec Civil Service Coll 1982–85, chief exec BVA 1985–87, dep dir-gen Gen Cncl Br Shipping 1987–91, chief exec The Baltic Exchange; *Recreations* photography, painting, tennis; *Style—* Mr James Buckley; ✉ The Baltic Exchange, St Mary Axe, London EC3A 8BH (☎ 0171 623 5501)

BUCKLEY, Sir John William; kt (1977); s of John William Buckley, and Florence Buckley; *b* 9 Jan 1913; *m* 1, 1935 (m dis 1967), Bertha Bagnall; 2 s; *m* 2, 1967, Molly Neville-Clarke; 1 step s, and 1 step s decd; *Career* gen mangr George Kent 1945–50 (joined 1934); md: Emmco Pty Australia 1950–55, BMC Pty 1955–60; vice chm and dep chm Winget Gloucester Ltd 1961–68, chm Alfred Herbert 1975–79; memb BSC 1978–, pres Anglo-Soviet C of C 1977–83, former dir BOTB; chm: Davy Ltd 1973–82 (md and dep chm 1968–73), Oppenheimer International 1983–87; FRSA, Hon FIChemE, FIEE; *Style—* Sir John Buckley; ✉ 49 Drayton Gardens, London SW10 9RX

BUCKLEY, Maj (William) Kemmis; MBE (1959), DL (Carmarthenshire, latterly Dyfed 1969); o s of Lt-Col William Howell Buckley, DL, of Castell Gorfod, Dyfed, and Karolie Kathleen, *née* Kemmis; *b* 18 Oct 1921; *Educ* Radley, New Coll Oxford; *Career* served WWII, Lt-Col Welsh Gds (despatches) and Suez 1956, mil asst to Vice-CIGS 1958–59; dir: Rhymney Brewery (now Whitbread) 1962, Felinfoel Brewery 1975; pres Buckley's Brewery 1983–86 (chm 1972–83); lay memb Press Cncl 1967–73; High Sheriff Carmarthenshire 1966–67, Vice Lord-Lt Dyfed 1989; KStJ 1983; *Recreations* tapestry, gardening; *Clubs* Brooks's, Cardiff and County; *Style—* Maj Kemmis Buckley, MBE, DL; ✉ Briar Cottage, Ferryside, Dyfed (☎ 01267 267359)

BUCKLEY, Peter Neville; s of Edward Richard Buckley, and Ina Heather, *née* Cayzer; *b* 23 Sept 1942; *Educ* Eton, Manchester Business Sch (Dip); *m* 2 Feb 1969, Mary Barabel, *née* Stewart; 2 da (Arabella Mary b 29 July 1970, Roseanna Neville b 26 Jan 1972); *Career* chartered accountant; articled clerk McClelland Moores & Co (later Ernst & Young); British & Commonwealth Shipping Company (later British & Commonwealth Holdings plc): joined 1968, asst to fin dir, exec dir 1974–87, non-exec dir 1987–88; Caledonia Investments plc: dir 1976–, dep chm and chief exec 1987–94, chm and chief exec 1994–; Amber Industrial Holdings plc: dir 1970–, chm 1988–; Sterling Industries plc: dir 1973–, chm 1988–; non-exec chm: English & Scottish Investors plc 1988–, Bristow Helicopter Group Ltd 1991–; non-exec dir: Provident Mutual Life Assurance Assoc 1980–95, Ralston Investment Trust plc 1988–93, Société Générale de Surveillance 1991–, Daily Telegraph plc 1992–96, Exco plc 1992–, Close Brothers Group plc 1995–; hon treas Feathers Clubs Assoc; memb Ct of Assts Worshipful Co of Shipwrights; *Recreations* gardening, golf, shooting; *Style—* Peter Buckley, Esq; ✉ Caledonia Investments PLC, Cayzer House, 1 Thomas More St, London E1 9AR (☎ 0171 481 4343, fax 0171 488 0896)

BUCKLEY, Lt Cdr Sir (Peter) Richard; KCVO (1982, CVO 1973, MVO 1968); 2 s of Alfred Buckley (d 1952), and Elsie Gwendoline Buckley (d 1987); *b* 31 Jan 1928; *Educ* Wellington; *m* 1958, Theresa Mary, da of Charles Peter Neve, OBE (d 1990); 2 s, 1 da; *Career* joined RN as cadet 1945, invalided 1961, Lt Cdr; private sec to TRH The Duke and Duchess of Kent 1961–89; dir Malcolm McIntyre Consultancy 1989–92; govr Wellington Coll and Eagle House 1989–; *Recreations* sailing, fishing, beekeeping; *Clubs* Army and Navy, Royal Dart Yacht, Royal Yacht Sqdn, All England Lawn Tennis; *Style—* Lt Cdr Sir Richard Buckley, KCVO; ✉ Coppins Cottages, Iver, Bucks (☎ 01753 653004)

BUCKLEY, Prof Richard Anthony; s of late Alfred Buckley, of Southampton, and Dorothy Iris, *née* Neale; *b* 16 April 1947; *Educ* Queen Elizabeth GS Wakefield, Merton Coll Oxford (MA, DPhil); *m* 1993, Alison Mary, *née* Jones; 1 da (Olivia b 26 Nov 1995); *Career* called to the Bar Lincoln's Inn 1969; lectr in law King's Coll London 1970–75, fell and tutor in law Mansfield Coll Oxford 1975–93, prof of Law Univ of Reading 1993–; writer of various articles for legal periodicals, memb Ed Bd Rights of Way Law Review 1993– (ed 1991–93); *Books* The Law of Nuisance (1 edn 1981, 2 edn 1996), The Modern Law of Negligence (1 edn 1988, 2 edn 1993), Salmond and Heuston on Torts (21 edn, with R F V Heuston, 1996); *Recreations* walking, swimming, working; *Style—* Professor Richard Buckley; ✉ Department of Law, Old Whiteknights House, University of Reading, PO Box 217, Whiteknights, Reading RG6 2AH (☎ 0118 987 5123)

BUCKLEY, Roger John; s of Frederick William Buckley, of Mersham, Kent, and Eileen, *née* Street; *b* 11 Jan 1945; *Educ* Plymouth Coll, Exeter Coll Oxford, St Thomas' Hosp Med Sch (MA, BM BCh); *m* 30 Jan 1971, Elizabeth Arnold, da of William Joseph Arnold Sykes (d 1986), of Speldhurst, Kent; 1 s (Adam b 1978), 1 da (Harriet b 1974); *Career* house surgn St Thomas' Hosp London 1970, sr registrar Westminster Hosp 1978, conslt ophthalmologist and dir Contact Lens and Prosthesis Dept Moorfields Eye Hosp 1981 (res surgical offr 1975); memb: Br Standards Instn Contact Lens Ctee 1984–89, Ctee on Dental and Surgical Materials DHSS 1983–94, Gen Optical Cncl 1988–; pres Med Contact Lens Assoc 1989–92, vice pres Int Soc for Contact Lens Research 1993–; hon med advsr: Musicians' Benevolent Fund 1991–, Royal Soc of Musicians 1994–, Br Assoc for Performing Arts Med 1995–; author of a number of papers and chapters on the cornea, contact lenses and ocular allergy; ATCL 1964, FRCS 1978, FRCOphth 1989; *Recreations* music, hill walking; *Clubs* RSM; *Style—* Mr Roger Buckley; ✉ 57A Wimpole Street, London W1M 7DF (☎ 0171 486 8959, fax 0171 935 5429); Moorfields Eye Hospital, City Road, London EC1V 2PD (☎ 0171 253 3411, fax 0171 253 4696, telex 266129)

BUCKLEY, Stephen; s of Leslie Buckley (d 1972), of Leicester and Nancy Throsby (d 1989); *b* 5 April 1944; *Educ* City of Leicester Boys' GS, Univ of Newcastle upon Tyne (BA), Univ of Reading (MFA); *m* 1973, Stephanie James; 1 s (Felix Rupert b 1978), 1 da (Scarlet Matilda b 1973); *Career* artist in residence King's Coll Cambridge 1972–74, ind work 1974–; prof and head Dept of Fine Art Univ of Reading 1994–; over 60 one man shows worldwide to date incl retrospective Museum of Modern Art Oxford 1985 and Yale Center for British Art Newhaven Conn 1986; prizewinner at: John Moores Liverpool Exhbn 1974 and 1985, Chichester Nat Art Exhbn 1975, Tolly Cobbold Exhbn 1977; work in collections of: Arts Cncl GB, British Cncl, Tate Gallery, V & A, Contemporary Arts Soc, Aberdeen Art Gallery, City Art Gallery Bristol, Eastern Arts Assoc, Walker Art Gallery Liverpool, Whitworth Art Gallery Manchester, Southampton City Art Gallery, Metropolitan Museum NY, Museum of Modern Art Caracas, Australian Nat Gallery Canberra, Nat Gallery Wellington NZ, Kettle's Yard Gallery Univ of Cambridge; in collaboration with Rambert Dance Co 1987 and 1989; *Style—* Prof Stephen Buckley, Esq; ✉ Department of Fine Art, University of Reading, 1 Earley Gate, Whiteknights Road, Reading, Berks RG6 6AT

BUCKMASTER, Hon Colin John; s of late 2 Viscount Buckmaster, and his 1 w, Joan, da of Dr Garry Simpson; hp of bro, 3 Viscount Buckmaster, *qv*; *b* 17 April 1923; *Educ* Winchester; *m* 1946, May, da of late Charles Henry Gibbon, of The Lodge, Great Bentley, Essex; 3 s, 2 da; *Career* late Flt-Lt RAF; *Clubs* Brooks's; *Style—* The Hon Colin Buckmaster; ✉ Ryece Hall, Brettenham, Ipswich, Suffolk

BUCKMASTER, 3 Viscount (UK 1933); Martin Stanley Buckmaster; OBE (1979); also Baron Buckmaster (UK 1915); s of 2 Viscount (d 1974), and his 1 w, Joan, da of Dr Garry Simpson; *b* 11 April 1921; *Educ* Stowe; *Heir* bro, Hon Colin Buckmaster, *qv*; *Career* served HM Forces (Capt TA) 1939–46; HM Dip Serv: FO 1946, asst political offr Sharjah 1951–53, political offr Abu Dhabi 1955–58, first sec Libyan Arab Republic (Benghazi and Tripoli) 1958–63, first sec Bahrain 1963–67, FCO 1967–69, first sec Br High Cmmr Kampala 1969–71, Beirut 1971–73, FCO 1973–77, head of chancery Yemen Arab Republic 1977–81, ret; memb Exec Ctee Cncl for the Advancement of Arab-British Understanding; patron: Christian Broadcasting Cncl, Cons Family Campaign; FRGS 1954; *Recreations* music, travelling, walking, Arab and African affairs, religious affairs, railways; *Clubs* Travellers'; *Style—* The Rt Hon The Viscount Buckmaster, OBE; ✉ 90 Cornwall Gardens, London SW7 4AX

BUCKNALL, Dr Clifford Adrian (Cliff); s of Eric Bucknall, of Berkswell, W Midlands, and Elsie Constance, *née* Whittaker; *b* 25 Feb 1956; *Educ* Leamington Coll, King's Coll London, Westminster Med Sch London (MB BS, MD); *m* 30 July 1983 (m dis 1996); 2 s (Sam b 1984, Tom b 1986); *Career* house surgn Warwick 1979–80, house physician Westminster 1980, sr house physician Nottingham 1980–82, registrar Brighton 1984–85, sr registrar in cardiology Guy's Hosp 1987–89 (res fell 1982–84), conslt cardiologist King's Coll Hosp 1989–92 (registrar 1985–86, locum sr registrar 1986–87), conslt cardiologist Dulwich Hosps 1989–92; dir of cardiology and conslt cardiologist: Guy's Hosp 1992–93, Guy's and St Thomas's Hosp 1993–; chief med offr Sun Alliance 1993–; FRSM 1979, LRCP 1979, MRCS 1979, MRCP 1982, FRCP 1994, memb Br Cardiac Soc; *Books* Horizons In Medicine no 1 (contrib, 1989); *Recreations* hockey, tennis, swimming; *Style—* Dr Cliff Bucknall; ✉ Cardiac Department, Guy's Hospital, St Thomas's Street, London SE1 9RT (☎ 0171 403 7503, fax 0171 378 7881)

BUCKNER, Jack Richard; s of Rev Richard Pentland Buckner (d 1992), and Anne Margaret, *née* Ferguson; *b* 22 Sept 1961; *Educ* St Petroc's Sch Bude, Worksop Coll, Loughborough Univ (BSc, MBA); *m* 10 Sept 1983, Kerin, da of Anthony John Wilson; 2 s (Eliot Wilson b 9 Dec 1991, Christian Richard b 15 July 1994); *Career* 5000m runner; Silver medal Cwlth Games 1986, Gold medal Euro Championships 1986, Bronze medal World Championships 1987, Olympic Games Seoul 1988, Olympic Games Barcelona 1992; prog mangr Management Devpt Centre Univ of Loughborough 1991–93; business unit mangr Adidas UK 1993–96, strategic business mangr Adidas International 1996–; *Recreations* reading, theatre, cinema, walking, writing; *Style—* Jack Buckner, Esq

BUCKS, Ven Michael William; QHC (1993); *b* 2 June 1940; *Educ* Rossall Sch, KCL (BD, AKC), St Boniface Coll Warminster; *m* 1972, Mary Currie; 1 s (Roger), 1 da (Jennifer); *Career* ordained deacon 1964, priest 1965; asst curate Workington PC 1964–69; RN chaplain 1969, served HM Ships Eagle, Albion and Fearless and on exchange in the US Navy in Desron Ten, shore appts HM Ships Victory, Raleigh, Neptune and Mauritius, completed Lt's Greenwich Course, subsequently appointed to RNEC Manadon, staff chaplain to Chaplain of the Fleet then chaplain HM Naval Base Portsmouth and staff of C-in-C Naval Home Cmd, chaplain HMS Warrior and staff of C-in-C Fleet, chaplain of the Fleet, archdeacon for the RN and DG Naval Chaplaincy Servs 1993–; *Style—* The Ven M W Bucks, QHC; ✉ Room 203, Victory Building, HM Naval Base, Portsmouth PO1 3LS

BUCKS, Peter; s of Nathan Bucks (d 1959), and Winifred José Beryl, *née* Hooper (d 1959); *b* 30 Sept 1947; *Educ* Sevenoaks Sch, Univ of Southampton (BSc); *m* 1973, Sarah Ann, da of Leslie Bernard Dobson (d 1983); 2 s (Oliver b 1978, Toby b 1982), 1 da (Eleanor b 1980); *Career* merchant banker; dir Hill Samuel Bank Ltd 1987; *Style—* Peter Bucks, Esq; ✉ 104 Addison Gardens, London W14 0DS (☎ 0171 603 9629); 100 Wood St, London EC2P 2AJ (☎ 0171 600 6000)

BUCKS, Simon; s of Nathan Bucks (d 1959), of Oxted, Surrey, and Jose, *née* Hooper (d 1960); *b* 31 July 1952; *Educ* Clifton Coll Bristol; *m* 1, 1976 (m dis), Rita, *née* Goldberg; *m* 2, 1981, Cheryl Armitage *née* Davey; 1 da (Anna), 1 s (Jonathan); *Career* South West News Service Bristol 1972–75, journalist HTV West Bristol 1975–81, sub-ed then chief sub-ed ITN 1981–87, programme ed Weekend News 1987–89, programme ed News At Ten 1989–92, ed Lunchtime News and sr programme ed Independent Television News 1992–94, controller of programmes London News Network 1996– (head of news 1994–96); *Style—* Simon Bucks, Esq; ✉ London News Network, London Television Centre, London SE1 (☎ 0171 827 7702)

BUCKWELL, Prof Allan Edgar; s of George Alfred Donald Buckwell, of Farmborough, Avon, and Jessie Ethel Neave (d 1989); *b* 10 April 1947; *Educ* Gillingham GS, Univ of London (BSc), Univ of Manchester (MA); *m* (m dis 1990); 2 s (Andrew Simon b 1967, Timothy James b 1971); *Career* lectr Univ of Newcastle upon Tyne 1973–84, prof of agric econs Univ of London 1984–; memb Agric Econs Soc, pres Euro Assoc of Agric Economists 1993–96; *Books* Costs of the Common Agricultural Policy (with D R Harley, K Parton and K J Thompson, 1982), Chinese Grain Economy and Policy (with Cheng Liang Yu, 1990); *Style—* Prof Allan Buckwell; ✉ Department of Agricultural Economics, Wye College, University of London, Wye, Ashford, Kent TN25 5AH (☎ 01233 812401, fax 01233 813006)

BUCKWELL, Anthony Basil; s of Maj Basil Adam Buckwell, DSO, MC (d 1996), and Y E S (Betty) Buckwell, *née* Tomlin (d 1996); *b* 23 July 1946; *Educ* Winchester, RAC Cirencester; *m* 27 April 1968, Henrietta Judith, da of Ronald K Watson, WS; 2 da (Tara b 1970, Alexia b 1971); *Career* merchant banker; dir: Absentminders Ltd London 1976–, Kleinwort Benson Ltd London 1985–91, Centro Internationale Handelsbank AG Vienna 1985–91, Capital Trust Ltd London 1991–96, CAIC Ltd; *Recreations* fishing, riding; *Clubs* Brooks's; *Style—* Anthony B Buckwell, Esq; ✉ Craven Keep, Hamstead Marshall, Newbury, Berkshire RG20 0JQ

BUCKWELL, (John) Jeremy Beaumont; s of John Beaumont Buckwell (d 1987), and Margaret Elaine, *née* Lindsay; *b* 12 April 1934; *Educ* Bedford Sch, Trinity Hall Cambridge (MA); *m* 1, 30 March 1964 (m dis 1977), Cynthia Jane, da of William Denis Heymanson (d 1988); 2 s (Oliver Charles Beaumont b 1966, William Dominic Heymanson b 1970), 1 da (Rebecca Geraldine b 1967); *m* 2, 19 Sept 1990, Gilda, da of William Hyde Clarke; *Career* Nat Serv Sub Lt RNVR 1952–54; admitted slr 1960; Gates & Co: ptnr 1961–86, sr ptnr 1986–88; FitzHugh Gates: sr ptnr 1988–95, conslt 1995–; chm: Brighton Round Table 1972–73, Dist Nursing Assoc Tst 1974–85, Somerset Day Centre Brighton 1978–85; pres Brighton & Hove Chamber of Commerce and Trade 1985–86, memb Nat Chamber of Trade Legislation and Taxation Ctee 1984–89; Freeman City of London 1960, Liveryman Worshipful Co of Skinners 1960; sec Nat Young Slrs 1967–69; memb: Law Soc 1960– (memb Planning Ctee 1988–), RTPI 1964– (memb Cncl 1978–94); *Recreations* skiing, sailing, golf; *Clubs* Itchenor Sailing, W Sussex Golf, Dyke Golf, Ski Club of GB; *Style—* Jeremy Buckwell, Esq; ✉ 19 Cornwall Gardens, Brighton BN1 6RH (☎ 01273 552000); FitzHugh Gates, 3 Pavilion Parade, Brighton BN2 1RY (☎ 01273 686811, fax 01273 676837)

BUCZACKI, Prof Stefan Tadeusz; s of Tadeusz Buczacki (d 1978), and Madeleine Mary Cato, *née* Fry; *b* 16 Oct 1945; *Educ* Ecclesbourne Sch Duffield, Univ of Southampton (BSc), Linacre Coll Oxford (DPhil); *m* 1970, Beverley Ann, da of Sidney Charman; 2 s (Julian Nicholas Edward b 10 Nov 1973, Simon James Alexander b 25 March 1977); *Career* princ scientific offr Nat Vegetable Res Station Wellesbourne 1970–84, freelance broadcaster and author 1984–; radio incl: Gardeners' Question Time 1982–94 (chm 1993–94), The Gardening Quiz (originator, writer and presenter) 1988–93, Classic Gardening Forum (presenter) 1994–; TV incl: Gardeners' Direct Line 1983–85, Gardeners' World 1990–91, That's Gardening 1989–92, Chelsea Flower Show 1990–91, Bazaar 1989–93, Good Morning 1992–96, Stefan Buczacki's Gardening Britain 1996; hon prof in plant pathology Liverpool John Moores Univ; tstee: Brogdale Horticultural Tst, Hestercombe Gardens Tst; patron: Parrs Wood Rural Studies Centre, Langdon Gardens Tst, Friends of Hestercombe Garden; memb: Cncl Gardeners' Royal Benevolent Soc, British Mycological Soc (vice pres 1994, Benefactor's Medal 1996); CBiol, FIBiol, FIHort, FLS, ARPS; *Books* Collins Guide to the Pests, Diseases and Disorders of Garden Plants (jt, 1981), Gem Guide to Mushrooms and Toadstools (1982), Collins Shorter Guide to the Pests, Diseases and Disorders of Garden Plants (jt, 1983), Zoosporic Plant Pathogens (ed, 1983), Beat Garden Pests and Diseases (1985), Gardener's Questions Answered (1985), Three Men in a Garden (jt, 1986), Ground Rules for Gardeners (1986), Beginners Guide to Gardening (1988), Creating a Victorian Flower Garden (1988), Garden Warfare (1988), New Generation Guide to the Fungi of Britain and Europe (1989), A Garden for all Seasons (1990), Understanding Your Garden (1990), The Essential Gardener (1991), Dr Stefan Buczacki's Gardening Hints (1992), The Plant Care Manual (1992), The Budget Gardening Year (1993), Mushrooms and Toadstools of Britain and Europe (1993), The Gardeners' Handbook (ed, 1993), Stefan Buczacki's Best Gardening Series: Climbers (1994), Foliage Shrubs (1994), Shade Plants (1994), Soft Fruit (1994), Water Plants (1995), Herbs (1995), Roses (1996), Container Plants (1996), Classic FM Garden Planner (jtly, 1996), Stefan Buczacki's Gardening Britain (1996); numerous contribs to magazines, newspapers and learned jls; *Recreations* gardening, fishing, riding, travel, live theatre, fine music, book collecting, photography, my Jaguar XK120; *Style*— Prof Stefan Buczacki; ✉ c/o Barbara Levy, 64 Greenhill, Hampstead High Street, London NW3 5TZ (☎ 0171 435 9046)

BUDD, Sir Alan Peter; kt (1997); s of Ernest Frank Budd (d 1981), and Elsie Nora, *née* Hambling (d 1985); *b* 16 Nov 1937; *Educ* Oundle, LSE (BSc), Churchill Coll Cambridge (PhD); *m* 18 July 1964, Susan, da of late Prof Norman Millott, of Millport, Isle of Cumbrae; 3 s (Joel b 1973, Nathaniel b 1976, Saul b 1978); *Career* lectr Univ of Southampton 1966–69, Ford visiting prof Carnegie-Mellon Univ of Pittsburgh 1969–70, sr econ advsr HM Treasy 1970–74, high level conslt OECD 1976, prof of economics London Business Sch 1981–88 (sr res fell 1974), Res Bank of Australia res prof Univ of NSW 1983, memb Securities and Investmts Bd 1987–88, econ advsr Barclays Bank 1988–91, chief economic advsr to HM Treasy and head Govt Economic Service 1991–; memb Bloomsbury DHA 1986–88, govr LSE 1994–; *Books* The Politics of Economic Planning (1976); *Recreations* music, gardening; *Clubs* Reform; *Style*— Sir Alan P Budd; ✉ 30 Laurier Rd, London NW5 1SG (☎ 0171 485 3779); HM Treasury, Parliament Street, London SW1P 3AG (☎ 0171 270 5203)

BUDD, Rt Rev (Hugh) Christopher; *see:* Plymouth, Bishop of (RC)

BUDD, Rachel; *b* 1960; *Educ* Univ of Newcastle upon Tyne, Royal Coll of Art; *Career* artist; exhibitions: Painters at the RCA (Gloucestershire Coll of Art and Technol) 1986, Platform (Axiom Gallery Cheltenham) 1986, Contemporary Arts Soc Market (Covent Garden) 1986 and 1987, Groucho Club Soho 1986, Christies Fine Arts Course common room 1987, The London Gp Show (RCA Henry Moore Gallery) 1987, Athena Art Awards (The Barbican Arts Centre) 1987, Art for the City (Lloyds Bldg) 1987, Pomeroy Purdy Gallery 1988 and 1990, Mary Somerville Art Fair (Smiths Gallery Covent Garden) 1988, Bath Art Fair 1988 and 1989, Al Fresco (Royal Acad) 1988, Olympia Art Fair 1989, Whitechapel Open (Eastend Open Studios) 1989, Summer Show (Pomeroy Purdy Gallery) 1989, 3 Ways (Br Cncl RCA Travelling Show, Hungary, Poland, Czechoslovakia) 1990, My Favourite Tree (Financial Times) 1990, Imagination Bldg (Gallery of Design and Communications Bldg) 1990, Moods and Spaces (Young Gallery Salisbury) 1990; work in various public and private collections; *Awards* A W Smiles Travel Scholarship, Northern Arts Purchase Award, Jeffrey Archer Prize GLC Painting Competition, Picker Fellowship Kingston Poly, Henry Moore Prize The London Gp Show RCA, Mark Rothko Meml Tst Fund Travel Bursary for USA; *Style*— Ms Rachel Budd; ✉ Purdy Hicks Gallery, Jacob Street Film Studios, Mill Street, London SE1 2BA (☎ 0171 237 6062)

BUDDS, Alan Roy; s of Leonard Frederick George Budds (d 1994), of Hants, and Olive Miriam, *née* Bone (d 1964); *b* 26 April 1934; *Educ* Luton GS; *m* 28 June 1958, Dorothy Blanche, da of Stephen John Lower, of Luton (d 1980); 2 s (Jonathan Paul b 1963, Richard Mark b 1965), 1 da (Andrea Lorraine b 1960); *Career* admitted slr 1957; ptnr Alan Budds & Co; cmmr for Oaths 1962, dep dist judge Co Ct SE Circuit 1985–91; pres Luton and Dunstable Law Soc 1983, chm British Legal Assoc 1991–93; *Recreations* tennis, ecology, gardening, travel; *Style*— Alan R Budds, Esq; ✉ 6 Salisbury Ave, Harpenden, Herts AL5 2QG; Alan Budds & Co, Solicitors, 29 King St, Luton LU1 2DW (☎ 01582 30544)

BUDGE, Anthony Frederick (Tony); OBE (1985), DL (Notts 1991); s of Frederick Thomas Frank Budge (d 1985), and Charlotte Constance Annie (d 1990), *née* Parker; *b* 9 Aug 1939; *Educ* Boston GS; *m* 1960, Janet, da of Harry Cropley (d 1983); 1 s (Karl), 3 da (Elizabeth, Karen, Lindsay); *Career* UK chm and md A F Budge (Holdings) Ltd and group cos 1962–; FICE, FIHT; *Clubs* Carlton, Turf, Jockey; *Style*— Tony Budge, Esq, OBE, DL; ✉ Osberton Hall, Worksop, Notts S81 0UF; A F Budge (Holdings) Ltd, West Carr Rd, Retford, Notts DN22 7SR (☎ 01777 708100, fax 01777 860122)

BUDGE, David; s of Alistair Budge, of Wick, and Elizabeth, *née* Henderson; *b* 18 Oct 1957; *Educ* Wick HS, Glasgow Coll (SHND, Dip Indust Admin); *m* 5 Aug 1983, Christine Margaret, da of James Deans Rankin (d 1970); 2 da (Alexandra, Catherine), 1 s (Andrew John); *Career* res exec Consensus Res Pty Brisbane 1979–80, press offr Wolf Electric Tools Ltd London 1980–81, dir PR Consultants Scotland 1987–94 (joined 1982), ptnr Budge Newton 1994–; dir Glasgow Cncl on Alcohol; winner IPR Sword of Excellence 1986; MInstD, MIPR; DipCAM; *Recreations* tennis, badminton; *Clubs* Blantyre Sports; *Style*— David Budge, Esq; ✉ 4 Lytham Meadows, Bothwell, Strathclyde G71 8ED (☎ 01698 852900, fax 01698 424000)

BUDGE, Prof Ian; s of John Elder Budge (d 1985), of Edinburgh, and Elizabeth, *née* Barnet (d 1979); *b* 21 Oct 1936; *Educ* Wardie and George Heriot's Schs Edinburgh, Univ of Edinburgh, Univ of Yale; *m* 17 July 1964, Judith Beatrice Ruth, da of Richard Franklin Harrison (d 1973), of Preston, Lancs; 1 s (Gavin b 1965), 1 da (Eileen Elizabeth b 1968); *Career* lectr Univ of Strathclyde 1963–66, prof Univ of Essex 1977– (formerly lectr, sr lectr, reader); visiting prof: Univ of Wisconsin Madison USA 1969–70, Euro Univ Inst Florence 1982–85, Univ of California Irvine 1989, Wissenschaftzentrum Berlin 1990, Universitat Autònoma Barcelona 1991, Netherlands Inst for Advanced Study in the Social Sciences (NIAS) 1995–96; memb Political Studies Assoc of UK, exec dir Euro Consortium for Political Res 1979–83; FRSA; *Books* jtly: Scottish Political Behaviour (1966), Belfast: Approach to Crisis (1973), Voting and Party Competition (1978), Explaining and Predicting Elections (1983), The New British Political System (1988); Parties and Democracy (1990), Party Policy and Coalition Government (1992), Parties, Policies and Democracy (1994); *Recreations* gardening, walking, travel, Italy; *Style*— Prof Ian Budge; ✉ 4 Oxford Rd, Colchester, Essex CO3 3HW (☎ 01206 46622); Department of Government, University of Essex, Colchester CO4 3SQ (☎ 01206 872128, fax 01206 873598)

BUDGE, Keith Joseph; s of William Henry Budge (d 1976), and Megan, *née* Parry; *b* 24 May 1957; *Educ* Rossall Sch, Univ Coll Oxford (MA, PGCE); *m* 1983, Caroline; 2 s (Alastair b 1987, Joseph b 1990), 1 da (Lara b 1991); *Career* asst master: Eastbourne Coll 1980–84 and 1989–91, Marlborough Coll 1984–88; instr in English The Stevenson Sch Pebble Beach California 1988–89, housemaster (Cotton House) Marlborough Coll 1991–95, headmaster Loretto Sch 1995–; memb HMC; *Recreations* walking, fishing, theatre, reading; *Clubs* Vincent's; *Style*— Keith Budge, Esq; ✉ Headmaster, Loretto School, Musselburgh, Mid Lothian EH21 7AF (☎ 0131 665 5003, fax 0131 653 2773)

BUDGEN, Nicholas William; MP (C) Wolverhampton SW (majority 4,966); s of Capt G N Budgen (d 1942), of Lichfield; *b* 3 Nov 1937; *Educ* St Edward's Oxford, Corpus Christi Coll Cambridge; *m* 1964, Madeleine Elizabeth, only da of Col Raymond Kittoe, OBE, by his w Rosalind, *née* Arbuthnot (a distant cousin of the Viscounts of Arbuthnott); 1 s, 1 da; *Career* called to the Bar Gray's Inn 1962, practised Midland and Oxford circuit; MP (C) Wolverhampton SW Feb 1974–, asst govt whip 1981–82, memb Select Ctee on the Treasy and Civil Serv 1983–; *Recreations* farming, hunting; *Style*— Nicholas Budgen, Esq, MP; ✉ Malt House Farm, Colton, nr Rugeley, Staffs (☎ 01889 577059)

BUELLES, *see:* Delroy-Buelles

BUENO, Antonio de Padua Jose Maria; QC (1989); s of Antonio de Padua Bueno (d 1987), and Ana Teresa de Jesus, *née* Zuloaga; *b* 28 June 1942; *Educ* Downside, Salamanca Univ; *m* 22 July 1966, Christine Mary, da of Michael Lees, of Milton Abbas, Dorset; 3 da (Nicola b 20 July 1967, Julia b 3 April 1972, Emily b 28 Dec 1988); *Career* called to the Bar Middle Temple 1964, recorder of the Crown Court 1989– (asst recorder 1984–89), head of chambers; *Books* Atkin's Court Forms: Banking (jt ed, 1976), Byles On Bills of Exchange (asst ed 1979, jt ed 1988), Paget's Law of Banking (asst ed, 1982); *Recreations* fishing, shooting; *Clubs* Flyfishers, East India, MCC; *Style*— Antonio Bueno, Esq, QC; ✉ 5 Paper Buildings, Temple, London EC4Y 7HB (☎ 0171 353 8494, fax 0171 583 1926, car 0836 216634)

BUERK, Michael Duncan; s of Capt Gordon Charles Buerk (d 1974), and Betty Mary Buerk (d 1960); *b* 18 Feb 1946; *Educ* Solihull Sch, Warwickshire; *m* 9 Sept 1968, Christine, da of late Bernard Joseph Lilley, of Hereford; 2 s (Simon, Roland (twins) b 30 Nov 1973); *Career* BBC TV News: joined 1973, energy corr 1976–79, Scotland corr 1979–81, special corr 1981–82, corr and presenter 1982–83, Africa corr 1983–87, presenter 1987–; presenter 999 (BBC 1) 1993–; *Awards* RTS Television Journalist of the Year 1984, RTS Int News Award 1984, George Polk Award (US) Foreign TV Reporting 1984, Nat Headlines Award (US) 1984, Int News/Documentary Award Monte Carlo Festival 1984, BAFTA News & Documentary Award 1985, James Cameron Meml Award 1987, Glaxo Science Writer of the Year Award 1989; *Recreations* oenophily; *Style*— Michael Buerk, Esq; ✉ c/o 9 O'Clock News Desk, Room 6239, BBC TV Centre, Wood Lane, London W12 7RJ (☎ 0181 576 7779)

BUFFHAM, Prof Bryan Austin; s of William Austin Buffham (d 1979), of Ilford, and Florence Ethel Mary, *née* London (d 1957); *b* 2 Nov 1936; *Educ* County HS Ilford, UCL (BSc), Yale (MEng), Loughborough Univ of Technol (PhD), Univ of London (DSc); *m* 12 Nov 1960, Dolores Marie, da of Alfred Lane (d 1986), of Allentown Pa, USA; 1 s (Timothy b 1967), 2 da (Robin b 1961, Christine b 1962); *Career* chemical engr Air Products and Chemicals Inc Allentown Pa USA 1959–64; Loughborough Univ (formerly Loughborough Univ of Technol): res fell 1964–65, lectr 1965–71, sr lectr 1971–81, reader 1982–86, prof 1986–; ed Chemical Engineering Journal 1970–92; FIChemE 1979; *Books* Mixing in Continuous Flow Systems (with E B Nauman, 1983); *Recreations* cycling; *Style*— Prof Bryan Buffham; ✉ 21 Springfield, Kegworth, Derby DE74 2DP (☎ 01509 672938); Department of Chemical Engineering, Loughborough University, Loughborough, Leics LE11 3TU (☎ 01509 222503)

BUFORD, William Holmes (Bill); s of William Holmes Buford, Jr, of Los Angeles, and Helen McCollough Shiel, of W Palm Beach, Florida; *b* 6 Oct 1954; *Educ* Univ of Calif Berkeley (BA), King's Coll Cambridge (Marshall scholar, MA); *m* 6 July 1991, Alicja, *née* Kobiernicka; *Career* ed Granta 1979–95, publisher Granta Books 1989–95, chm Granta Publications Ltd until 1995, literary and fiction ed New Yorker 1995–; *Books* Among the Thugs (1991), The Granta Book of Travel Writing (ed, 1992), The Granta Book of Reportage (1993), The Granta Book of The Family (ed, 1995); *Style*— Bill Buford, Esq; ✉ The New Yorker, 20 W 43rd Street, New York, NY 10036, USA (☎ 00 1 212 536 5800, fax 00 1 212 997 7852); c/o Gillon Aitken, Aitken & Stone, 20 Fernshaw Road, London SW10 0TG (☎ 0171 351 7756, fax 0171 376 3594)

BUGBIRD, Anthony (Tony); s of Capt Thomas Anthony Bugbird, and Laura Gertrude Irene, *née* Fletcher; *b* 12 April 1937; *Educ* Bromsgrove Sch (awarded Millicken-Smith Cup, represented sch at rugby, athletics, cross country, swimming and hockey), London Coll of Printing (CXE Layton student award, Kodak Colour scholarship); *m* 21 Oct 1972, Judith Susannah, da of Leslie David Burbridge; 2 c (Robbie Laura Jane b 30 Oct 1977, Thomas Alexander b 15 Jan 1980); *Career* sapper Royal Engrs 1955–58; head of trg Agfa-Gevaert 1968–74, head of photography trg Printing and Publishing Indust Trg Bd 1974–82, gen mangr Dawson Strange Ltd 1985, owner Merrow Photographers Guildford 1986–; vice pres BIPP 1995–; Advertising Assoc award 1961, certificate of excellence Worlds Fair NY 1963; fell Assoc of Photographic Technicians 1972, fell Master Photographers' Assoc 1973, FBIPP 1974, assoc RPS 1991; *Recreations* swimming, photography, business, family; *Style*— Tony Bugbird, Esq; ✉ Merrow Photographers, The Old School, Compton, Guildford, Surrey GU3 1JF (☎ 01483 860816)

BUGDEN, Paul William; s of Frederick William Bugden, and Rosemary Anne Matilda Winifred Bugden (d 1995); *b* 18 April 1953; *Educ* Merchant Taylors', Univ of Kent (BA); *m* 14 Feb 1984, Nicola Ann, da of Peter Raynes, OBE; 1 s (James William b 22 March 1985), 1 da (Jessica Lucy b 29 Sept 1986); *Career* articled clerk Russell-Cooke Potter & Chapman 1976–77; Clyde & Co: articled clerk 1977–78, admitted slr 1978, based Hong Kong 1981–84, ptnr 1982–; memb: Law Soc, Br Insurance Law Assoc; *Recreations* golf, reading, theatre, running; *Clubs* Bramley Golf; *Style*— Paul Bugden, Esq; ✉ Clyde & Co, Beaufort House, Chertsey Street, Guildford, Surrey GU1 4HA (☎ 01483 31161, fax 01483 67330)

BUGGY, Niall Michael; s of Martin William Buggy (d 1985), of Ireland, and Kathleen Veronica, *née* Bourke; *b* 3 Oct 1948; *Educ* Sandy Mount HS, Brendan Smith Acad, Abbey Theatre Sch; *Career* actor; joined Abbey Sch aged 15, various roles incl Trofimov in The Cherry Orchard, The Seagull; *Theatre incl* Crucible Theatre Sheffield: Stanley in The Birthday Party, Estragon in Waiting for Godot; RNT: Lucius O'Trigger in The Rivals, Scandal in Love for Love, Gal in Rough Crossing; other roles incl: Christie Mahon in Playboy of The Western World (Actor of the Year Award), Seamus Shields in Shadow of A Gunman (Young Vic, nominated for Helen Hayes Award), Memoir (Dublin and London), Spokesong (King's Head, Plays and Players' Award for Best Newcomer 1978), Baron Tusenbach in Three Sisters (Harvey Award), Major General in Pirates of Penzance (Best Supporting Actor Award), Casimir in Aristocrats (winner Clarence Derwent, Time Out and Obie Awards), Bluntshli in Arms and the Man, Player King in Hamlet, Captain Boyle in Juno and the Paycock (TMA Regional Theatre Best Actor Award), Dead Funny (Vaudeville, Olivier Award for Best Comedy Performance 1995), Song at Sunset (one man show, Hampstead 1996, NY 1997); *Television* incl: Once in a

Lifetime, The Gathering Seed, The Citadel, Red Roses for Me, The Promise, The Little Mother, Chinese Whispers, The Full Wax, 99–1, Little Napoleon, Agony Again, Upwardly Mobile; *Films* incl: Zardoz, Portrait of the Artist as a Young Man, Alien 3, Playboys, King David, Close My Eyes, Anna Karenina, The Butcher Boy; *Style*— Niall Buggy, Esq; ✉ c/o Sally Long Innes, ICM Ltd, Oxford House, 76 Oxford Street, London W1N 0AX (☎ 0171 636 6565, fax 0171 323 0101)

BUITER, Prof Willem Hendrik; s of Harm Geert Buiter, of Groningen, Netherlands, and Hendrien, *née* van Schooten; *b* 26 Sept 1949; *Educ* European Sch Brussels, Univ of Amsterdam, Emmanuel Coll Cambridge (BA), Yale Univ (MA, MPhil,PhD); *m* 4 August 1973, Jean, da of Alan Simeon Albert Archer; 1 s (David Michael Alejandro b 22 Feb 1991), 1 da (Elizabeth Lorca b 6 August 1993); *Career* asst prof of public and int affrs Princeton Univ 1975–76 and 1977–79, lectr in economics LSE 1976–77, prof of economics Univ of Bristol 1980–82, Cassel prof of economics with special reference to money and banking LSE 1982–85, Juan T Trippe prof of economics Yale Univ 1990–94 (prof of economics 1985–89), prof of int macroeconomics Univ of Cambridge 1994–; Irving Fisher visiting prof Yale Univ 1983–88, visiting prof Univ of Groningen June-July 1986 and June 1988, visiting prof LSE 1987–88; conslt: AT&T 1976, Oxford Analytica Ltd 1977, IMF 1985, World Bank 1986–, Inter-American Devpt Bank 1992–, EBRD 1994; research assoc Nat Bureau of Economic Research 1979, research fell Centre for Economic Policy Research 1983; specialist advsr House of Commons Select Ctee on the Treasy and Civil Serv 1980; assoc ed: World Politics 1978, Economic Jl 1980–85; jt winner Sanwa Monograph on Int Financial Markets Award 1993, winner Dr Hendrik Muller Prize (Netherlands prize for Social Scis) 1995; corr memb Royal Netherlands Acad of Scis 1989, memb Int Inst of Public Finance 1993; *Books* Temporary and Long-Run Equilibrium (1979), Budgetary Policy, International and Intertemporal Trade in the Global Economy (1989), Macroeconomic Theory and Stabilization Policy (1989), Principles of Budgetary and Financial Policy (1990), International Macroeconomics (1990), Financial Markets and European Monetary Cooperation (with G Corsetti and P Pesent, 1997); author of numerous articles in learned jls and also of book reviews, comments and discussions; *Recreations* tennis, science fiction and phantasy, poetry; *Style*— Prof Willem Buiter; ✉ Faculty of Economics and Politics, University of Cambridge, Austin Robinson Building, Sidgwick Avenue, Cambridge CB3 9DD (☎ 01223 335210, fax 01223 335475)

BUKHT, Michael John; OBE (1996); s of Mirza Jawan Bukht (d 1971), of London, and Lilian Ray, *née* Oaten; *b* 10 Sept 1941; *Educ* Haberdashers' Aske's Sch Hampstead, King's Coll London (BA, winner NUS Drama Award as director); *m* 11 Sept 1964, Jennie Mary, *née* Jones; 3 da (Annabel Kate b 12 Nov 1965, Susannah Jane b 9 May 1971, Lucy Taliesin b 1 Nov 1979), 1 s (Mirza Jonathan William b 16 May 1968); *Career* joined BBC as gen trainee 1963, worked on Tonight and 24 Hours 1964–67, prog controller Jamaica Broadcasting Corporation 1967–69, ed 24 Hours then ed special projects (incl supervising ed Gen Election 1970) BBC 1969–72, prog controller Capital Radio 1972–76, prog controller Radio 604 1979–80, princ Nat Bdcasting Sch 1980–85, md Invicta Radio 1985–88; prog controller: GWR Group 1988–92, Classic FM 1992– (Classic FM awarded National Station of the Year Sony Radio Awards 1993); food journalist (as Michael Barry) Food and Drink Prog (BBC2); chm Kentish Fare, pres Kent branch Chartered Inst of Mktg; author of 18 books; memb ACTT; fell Radio Acad; FRSA; *Recreations* dance, theatre, military history, sailing, cooking, travel; *Clubs* East India, Whitstable Yacht; *Style*— Michael Bukht, Esq, OBE; ✉ Classic FM, Academic House, 24–28 Oval Road, London NW1 7QD (☎ 0171 284 3000, fax 0171 713 3630)

BULFIELD, Prof Grahame John; s of Frederick Robert Bulfield (d 1956), of Cheshire, and Madge, *née* Jones (d 1968); *b* 12 June 1941; *Educ* King's Sch Macclesfield, Univ of Leeds (BSc), Univ of Edinburgh (Dip in Animal Genetics, PhD); *Career* Fulbright fell and NIH postdoctoral fell Dept of Genetics Univ of California 1968–70, res assoc Inst of Animal Genetics Univ of Edinburgh 1971–76 (SRC resettlement fell 1970–71), lectr and convenor of med genetics Dept of Genetics Univ of Leicester 1976–81, head of genetics gp AFRC Poultry Res Centre 1981–86, head of station and assoc dir Edinburgh Res Station Inst of Animal Physiology and Genetic Res 1988–93 (head of gene expression gp 1986–88), dir Roslin Inst 1993–; hon prof Div of Biological Science Univ of Edinburgh 1990– (hon fell Dept of Genetics 1981–90); conslt CEC DG VI Strategic Assessment in Science and Technol Framework Prog-4 1992, assessor Norwegian Agric Biotechnology Prog 1992; memb: Genetical Soc 1971– (memb Ctee 1980–83 and 1986–90), Advsy Ctee on Genetic Modification 1990–96, SDA Working Pty AgBio 2000 1991, Scientific Advsy Bd AFRC Centre for Genome Res 1992–, AFRC Animals Res Grants Bd 1992–94, AFRC Animal Res Ctee 1992–94, BBSRC Planning and Resources Bd 1994–96; chm: Assessment Panel in Developmental Biology and Genome Mapping CEC DG XII Framework Prog-3 BIOTECH 1991, Exec Ctee Edinburgh Centre for Rural Res 1993–96 (memb 1989–); fndr ed Genes and Development 1987–90, memb Editorial Advsy Bd Animal Breeding Abstracts 1990–, memb Advsy Bd Animal Genetics 1993–, author of res papers and book chapters on biochemical and molecular genetics; FRSE 1992, CBiol, FIBiol 1995; *Recreations* fell walking and cricket; *Style*— Prof Grahame Bulfield, FRSE; ✉ Roslin Institute (Edinburgh), Roslin, Midlothian EH25 9PS (☎ 0131 527 4200, fax 0131 448 2613)

BULFIELD, Peter William; s of Wilfred Irving Roden Bulfield (d 1969), of Midhurst, and Doris Margaret, *née* Bedford (d 1974); *b* 14 June 1930; *Educ* Beaumont Coll; *m* 21 June 1958, Pamela June, da of Arthur Henry Frederick Beckett (d 1963), of Buenos Aires; 2 da (Julia Therese b 1960, Marion Louise b 1963); *Career* CA Scotland 1953; dir: Newsphere Trading Co 1963, J Henry Schroder Wagg 1967–86, Darling Holdings Aust 1973–82; vice chm Mitsubishi Trust and Banking Corporation (Europe) SA 1973–84, jt dep chm Schroder Int 1977–86, exec dir Yamaichi Int (Europe) Ltd 1986–88, dep chm Yamaichi Bank (UK) plc 1991–93 (md and chief exec 1988–91), dir London Italian Bank Ltd 1989–91; dep chm Crown Agents for Overseas Govts and Admins 1982–85 (memb 1978–85); memb: Overseas Projects Bd 1983–86, Export Guarantees Advsy Cncl 1986–88, Finances Ctee CAFOD 1993–; *Recreations* music, sailing, painting; *Clubs* Royal Thames Yacht; *Style*— Peter Bulfield, Esq; ✉ The Mill House, Merrieweathers, Mayfield, E Sussex TN20 6RJ (☎ 01435 872177)

BULGIN, Ronald Arthur; s of Wing Cdr Arthur Bulgin, OBE, of Essex; *b* 20 Aug 1935; *Educ* Westminster, Merton Coll Oxford; *m* 1, 1958 (m dis), Margaret Gray; 2 s, 1 da; m 2, 1969, Elaine Harvey; 1 s, 1 da; *Career* chm A F Bulgin & Co plc; *Recreations* riding, golf; *Clubs* Essex Farmers Hunt, Chigwell Golf, RAC; *Style*— Ronald Bulgin, Esq; ✉ A F Bulgin & Co plc, Bypass Road, Barking, Essex IG11 0AZ (☎ 0181 594 5588)

BULKELEY, *see:* Williams-Bulkeley

BULL, Andrew Richard (Andy); s of Richard Abbott Bull (d 1991), of Rainham, Kent, and Audrey May, *née* Shipp; *b* 10 July 1956; *Educ* Rainham Mark GS, Univ of Lancaster (BA); *m* 29 Oct 1983, Elena, *née* Curti; 1 da (Beatrice b 18 Dec 1987), 1 s (Freddie b 23 Nov 1990); *Career* grad trainee Hastings Observer 1977–81, news sub ed S Wales Echo 1981, features ed Bedfordshire Times 1981–83, dep features ed Reading Evening Post 1983–84, asst features ed Daily Mail 1984–86, successively dep features ed, weekend ed and pictures ed The Independent 1986–93; asst ed Mail on Sunday 1996– (features ed 1994–96); highly commended Br Newspaper Awards, Arthur Sandells Award 1990; *Books* Coast to Coast, A Rock Fan's US Tour (1993), Strange Angels (1995); *Recreations* gardening, travel, writing, reading; *Style*— Andy Bull, Esq; ✉ The Mail on Sunday, Associated Newspapers, 2 Derry Street, London W8 5TT (☎ 0171 938 6592)

BULL, Christopher; s of William Albert Bull (d 1984), of Taunton, Somerset, and Norah Bull; *b* 6 Sept 1936; *Educ* Taunton Sch; *m* Patricia Marcelline Barbara, da of Henry John Gardner (d 1983), of Paris; 1 s (James b 1965), 2 da (Helen b 1963, Fiona b 1974); *Career* CA; Goodland Bull & Co Taunton 1957–68, Price Waterhouse Trinidad 1968–71, Price Waterhouse London 1971–95 (ptnr 1974–95); Freeman City of London 1996, Liveryman Worshipful Co of Fishmongers 1996; FCA 1972 (ACA 1962); *Recreations* golf, choral singing; *Clubs* Carlton, North Hants Golf; *Style*— Christopher Bull, Esq; ✉ Kantara, Reading Road North, Fleet, Hampshire GU13 8AQ (☎ 01252 615008, fax 01252 816193)

BULL, Christopher Robert Howard; s of Robert Golden Bull (d 1994), of Settle, N Yorks, and Audrey, *née* Ineson; *b* 14 May 1942; *Educ* Christ's Hosp, Corpus Christi Coll Cambridge (MA); *m* 1 April 1967, Rosemary Anne, da of Frank Coltman (d 1979), of Bromley, Kent; 2 s (Jeremy b 1969, Andrew b 1972), 1 da (Stephanie b 1976); *Career* Whinney Murray & Co 1964–68, Centre for Interfirm Comparison 1968–71, industl gas div controller Air Products Ltd 1971–75, head of gp fin analysis BICC plc 1975–80, fin dir BICC Technologies Ltd 1981–84, corp treas BT 1984–88; fin dir: BTR plc 1988–91, RTZ Corporation plc 1991– (dir CRA Ltd Dec 1995–); FCA 1968; *Recreations* music, sailing; *Style*— Christopher Bull, Esq; ✉ RTZ Corporation plc, 6 St James's Square, London SW1Y 4LD (☎ 0171 753 2121, fax 0171 753 2200, telex 24639)

BULL, David Neill; s of Denis Albert Bull (d 1986), of Grays, Essex, and Doreen Lilian, *née* Durham; *b* 21 June 1951; *Educ* Palmer's Sch for Boys Grays, Univ of Sussex (BA), Univ of Bath (MSc); *m* 1978, Claire, da of Peter Grenger; 1 da (Kate b 1984); *Career* public affrs offr Oxfam 1979–84, exec dir Environment Liaison Centre (Kenya) 1984–87, gen sec World University Service (UK) 1987–90, dir Amnesty International UK 1990–; memb: Bd (vol) The Pesticides Tst, Exec Ctee (vol) Assoc of Chief Execs of Nat Vol Orgns; *Books* A Growing Problem: Pesticides and the Third World Poor (1982), The Poverty of Diplomacy: Kampuchea and the Outside World (1983); *Style*— David Bull, Esq; ✉ Director, Amnesty International UK, 99–119 Rosebery Avenue, London EC1R 4RE (☎ 0171 814 6200, fax 0171 833 1510)

BULL, Deborah Clare; da of Rev (Michael) John Bull, of London, and Doreen Audrey, *née* Plumb; *b* 22 March 1963; *Educ* The Royal Ballet Sch, Academie de Danse Classique de Monte Carlo; *Career* Royal Ballet: joined 1981, soloist 1986, princ 1992; major dance roles incl: Rite of Spring, La Bayadère, Sleeping Beauty, Prince of the Pagodas, Violin Concerto, Agon, Giselle, Song of the Earth, Don Quixote, In the Middle, somewhat Elevated, Swan Lake; created major roles in: Still Life at the Penguin Café, Pursuit, Piano, Fearful Symmetries; memb cast In the Middle, Somewhat Elevated (Laurence Olivier Award 1993), danced in Italy, Canada and N America with Wayne Eagling's Co (Principals of the Royal Ballet), regularly invited to tour with Irek Mukhamedov and Co; organised and performed in An Evening of British Ballet at The Sinatra Festival 1994 and 1995; addressed Oxford Union 1996, delivered Arts Cncl Annual Lectr 1996; winner Prix de Lausanne 1980, voted one of the Dancers of the Year by readers of Dance and Dancers 1991 and 1992; Olivier Award nomination for Outstanding Achievement in Dance (for Steptext at ROH) 1996; *Recreations* literature, Mozart, food, wine and mountain air; *Clubs* Pegs; *Style*— Miss Deborah Bull

BULL, George Anthony; OBE (1990); s of George Thomas Bull (d 1937), and Bridget Philomena, *née* Nugent (d 1983); *b* 23 Aug 1929; *Educ* Wimbledon Coll, Brasenose Coll Oxford (MA); *m* 2 March 1957, Dido Marjorie, *née* Griffin; 2 s (Julian, Simon), 2 da (Catherine, Jennifer); *Career* Nat Serv Royal Fus 1947–49; foreign news ed Financial Times 1956–59, news ed McGraw Hill World News 1959–60, The Director magazine 1960–84 (dep ed, ed in chief), dir Anglo-Japanese Economic Institute 1986–, ed International Minds 1989, publisher and ed Insight Japan 1992–; pres Central Banking Publications Limited, vice pres British-Italian Soc 1994–; govr Westminster Cathedral Choir Sch 1994–; author; hon treas Royal Soc of Literature 1992–, memb Soc of Art Historians; FRSL, FRSA; *Books* incl translations for Penguin Classics and OUP, Inside the Vatican (1982), Michelangelo (biography, 1995); *Style*— George A Bull, Esq, OBE, FRSL; ✉ 19 Hugh St, London SW1V 1QJ; The Anglo-Japanese Economic Institute, Morley House, 314–322 Upper Regent St, London W1R 5AD (☎ 0171 637 7872)

BULL, George Jeffrey; s of Michael Herbert Perkins Bull (d 1965), and Hon Noreen Madeleine Hennessy, da of 1 Baron Windlesham; *b* 16 July 1936; *Educ* Ampleforth; *m* 7 Jan 1960, Jane Fleur Thérèse, da of Patrick Freeland (d 1977); 4 s (Sebastian b 1960, Rupert b 1963, Justin b 1964, Cassian b 1966), 1 da (Tamsin b 1972); *Career* Lt Coldstream Gds 1954–57, served in Germany and UK; joined Dorland Advertising Ltd 1957, joined Twiss Browning & Hallowes wine merchants 1958, md Gilbey Vintners Ltd 1970, md International Distillers & Vintners UK Ltd 1973, md IDV Europe Ltd 1977, dep md IDV Ltd 1982, dir Grand Metropolitan Ltd 1985, chief exec Grand Metropolitan Drinks Sector and IDV Ltd 1987, chm and chief exec IDV Ltd until 1992 (non-exec dir 1992–), chm and chief exec Grand Metropolitan Food Sector 1992–93, gp chm Grand Metropolitan plc 1995– (gp chief exec 1993–95); non-exec dir: The Pillsbury Co 1992–96, United News & Media plc (formerly United Newspapers plc) 1993–; memb: President's Ctee CBI, BACC Advsy Bd; chm MENCAP Jubilee Appeal Ctee 1996–97; dir The Mktg Cncl, vice pres Chartered Inst of Mktg 1995, pres Advtg Assoc (AA) 1996; *Recreations* golf, shooting, photography; *Clubs* Cavalry and Guards', Royal Worlington Golf; *Style*— George Bull, Esq; ✉ The Old Vicarage, Arkesden, Saffron Walden, Essex (☎ 01799 550445); Grand Metropolitan plc, 8 Henrietta Place, London W1M 9AG (☎ 0171 518 5200, fax 0171 518 4641)

BULL, Prof (Roger) John; *b* 31 March 1940; *Educ* Churchers' Coll Petersfield, LSE (BSc); *m* 1964, Margaret Evelyn, *née* Clifton; 1 s, 1 da; *Career* student accountant then systems accountant Ford Motor Co 1958–62, lectr II in accounting NE London Poly 1965–66, res fell Dept of Educn and Science/ICAEW 1966–67, sr lectr in accounting NE London Poly 1967–68, princ lectr in accounting Trent Poly 1968–72, head Sch of Accounting and Applied Economics Leeds Poly 1972–84, dir/vice-chllr and chief exec Univ of Plymouth (formerly Poly of the South West) 1989– (dep dir 1985–89); treas Ctee of Vice-Chllrs and Principals, memb Cncl for Industry and Higher Educn; non-exec dir Plymouth Hosps NHS Tst, chm Open Learning Fndn, cncl memb SW C of C; FCCA 1976 (ACCA 1962); *Publications* incl: Accounting for the Non Specialist (1968), Accounting for Business (1968, 6 edn 1990), Managing Change from the Top of Universities and Colleges (contrib, 1994); *Recreations* tennis, walking, music as performer and listener; *Style*— Prof John Bull; ✉ 3 Westmoor Park, Tavistock, Devon PL19 9AA; University of Plymouth, Drake Circus, Plymouth PL4 8AA (☎ 01752 232000, fax 01752 232011)

BULL, His Hon Judge; John Michael; QC (1983), DL (Surrey 1996); s of John Godfrey Bull (d 1969), and Eleanor, *née* Nicholson (d 1994); *b* 31 Jan 1934; *Educ* Norwich Sch, CCC Cambridge (Parker exhibitioner, MA, LLM); *m* 20 Dec 1959, Sonia Maureen, da of Frank Edward Woodcock, of Norwich; 1 s ((John) Michael Curties b 14 March 1968), 3 da (Caroline Elisabeth b 15 Dec 1961, Rachel Clare b 26 Feb 1963, Francesca Margaret b 23 Nov 1964); *Career* called to the Bar Gray's Inn 1960, dep circuit judge 1972, standing counsel to Inland Revenue Western Circuit 1973–83, recorder Crown Ct 1980–91, circuit judge (SE Circuit) 1991–, dep High Ct judge (Queen's Bench Div) 1991–, additional judge of Employment Appeal Tbnl 1991–, resident judge of the Crown Ct at Guildford 1992–; *Recreations* music and punting; *Style*— His Hon Judge John Bull, QC, DL; ✉ The Crown Court at Guildford, Bedford Road, Guildford, Surrey GU1 4ST

BULL, Sir Simeon George; 4 Bt (UK 1922), of Hammersmith, Co London; s of Sir George Bull, 3 Bt (d 1987), and Gabrielle Muriel, *née* Jackson (d 1989); *b* 1 Aug 1934;

Educ Eton, Innsbruck (Law Faculty), Ecole de Notariat Paris; *m* 17 June 1961, Annick Elisabeth Geneviève Renée, yr da of late Louis Bresson (d 1960), of Château des Masselins, Chandai, Orne, France; 1 s (Stephen Louis b 5 April 1966), 2 da (Jacqueline-Hester b 15 Oct 1964, Sophia Ann b 2 March 1971); *Heir* s, Stephen Louis Bull; *Career* admitted slr 1959; sr ptnr legal firm of Bull & Bull; Cdre London Corinthian Sailing Club 1968–71, fndr hon sec Assoc of Thames Valley Sailing Clubs 1972–78, memb Cncl Royal Yachting Assoc 1977–79; Freeman City of London 1955, Liveryman Worshipful Co of Fishmongers; *Recreations* sailing, foreign travel, gardening, carpentry, reading; *Clubs* Royal Thames Yacht, MCC; *Style*— Sir Simeon Bull, Bt; ✉ Beech Hanger, Beech Rd, Shepherd's Hill, Merstham, Surrey RH1 3AE (☎ 01737 645041); Pen Enez, Tréméoc, Pont l'Abbé, S Finistère, France; Bull & Bull, 199 Piccadilly, London W1V 9LE (☎ 0171 405 7474, fax 0171 734 9107)

BULL, Stephen Howard; s of James Howard Bull (d 1963), and Violet May, *née* Loader; *b* 20 Dec 1943; *Educ* Monmouth Sch, St Catherine's Coll Oxford (BA); *m* 1, 11 Dec 1982; 1 s (Benedict b 31 May 1983); m 2, 16 Jan 1992, Anne Jocelyn Dod Inglis; 1 s (Thomas), 1 da (Victoria b 4 Feb 1995); *Career* experience with various advtg agencies incl Collett Dickenson Pearce 1965–72; self-taught chef; fndr/proprietor: Meadowsweet Restaurant Llanrwst Gwynedd 1973, Lichfield's Restaurant Richmond Surrey 1978 (Michelin Star 1980–87), Stephen Bull Restaurant 1989–, Stephen Bull's Bistro 1992–, Fulham Road Restaurant 1994–96; *Recreations* horseracing (spectator and one time owner); *Style*— Stephen Bull, Esq; ✉ Stephen Bull Restaurants Ltd, 5–7 Blandford Street, London W1H 3AA (☎ 0171 486 9696)

BULL, Tony Raymond; s of Henry Albert Bull (d 1963), and Phyllis Rosalie, *née* Webber; *b* 21 Dec 1934; *Educ* Monkton Combe Sch, London Hosp Med Coll; *m* June 1959, Jill Rosemary Beresford, da of Air Vice-Marshal Albert Frederick Cook, CBE; 1 s (Antony b 1965), 2 da (Amanda b 1960, Karen b 1962); *Career* conslt surgn: Charing Cross Hosp, Royal Nat Throat Nose & Ear Hosp, King Edward VII's Hosp for Officers; Liveryman Worshipful Soc of Apothecaries; FRCS; *Recreations* tennis (Somerset County), hockey (Essex County); *Clubs* MCC, Queen's, Hurlingham; *Style*— Tony Bull, Esq; ✉ 26 Scarsdale Villas, London W8 (☎ 0171 937 3411); 107 Harley Street, London W1 (☎ 0171 935 3171)

BULLARD, Sir Julian Leonard; GCMG (1987, KCMG 1982, CMG 1975); s of Sir Reader Bullard, KCB, KCMG, CIE (d 1976), sometime ambass Teheran, and Miriam (d 1973), da of late A L Smith, sometime Master Balliol Coll Oxford; *b* 8 March 1928; *Educ* Rugby, Magdalen Coll Oxford; *m* 1954, Margaret Stephens; 2 s, 2 da; *Career* served HM Forces 1950–52; FO 1953–88, served: Vienna, Amman, Bonn, Moscow, Dubai; head E Euro and Soviet Dept 1971–75, min Bonn 1975–79, dep under-sec and political dir FCO 1979–82, dep to perm under-sec and political dir 1982–84, ambass Bonn 1984–88; fell All Souls Coll Oxford, hon fell St Antony's Coll Oxford; chm Cncl and pro-chllr Univ of Birmingham 1989–94; *Style*— Sir Julian Bullard, GCMG; ✉ 18 Northmoor Rd, Oxford OX2 6UR

BULLEN, James Edward; s of Albert Edward Bullen (d 1977), and Doris Josephine, *née* McHale (d 1976); *b* 26 March 1943; *Educ* Univ of London (LLB); *m* 1, 1973 (m dis 1984); m 2, 27 Sept 1985, Mary, da of late Patrick Keane; 1 s (William James b 1986); *Career* called to the Bar Gray's Inn 1966, memb Senate of Inns of Ct and Bar 1979–82; *Recreations* music, reading, walking; *Clubs* Garrick, RAC; *Style*— James Bullen, Esq; ✉ 1 Paper Buildings, Temple, London EC4Y 7EP

BULLEN, Air Vice-Marshal Reginald; CB (1975), GM (1945); s of Henry Arthur Bullen (d 1932), of London, and Alice May, *née* Quaife (d 1947); *b* 19 Oct 1920; *Educ* Grocers' Co Sch, Gonville and Caius Coll Cambridge (MA); *m* 12 March 1952, (Doreen) Christiane, da of Eric Kenneth Phillips (d 1958), of Marseilles, France; 1 s (Michael b 1958), 1 da (Danielle b 1953); *Career* 39 Sqdn Malta and 458 Sqdn N Africa 1942–44, Air Miny 1945–50, RAF Coll Cranwell 1952–54, RAF Staff Coll Bracknell 1955, exchange USAF Washington DC 1956–58, DSD RAF Staff Coll 1959–61, admin Staff Coll Henley 1962, PSO to CAS 1962–64, NATO Def Coll Paris 1965, Adj-Gen AAFCE 1965–68, dir of personnel RAF 1968–69, IDC 1970, Dep AOA Maintenance Cmd 1971, AOA RAF Trg Cmd 1972–75; fell and sr bursar Gonville and Caius Coll Cambridge 1975–87, life fell and property devpts conslt Gonville and Caius Coll Cambridge 1987–; chm Huntingdon Health Authy 1981–92; FIMgt 1979 (MIMgt 1971); *Recreations* work, travel; *Clubs* RAF; *Style*— Air Vice-Marshal Reginald Bullen, CB, GM; ✉ Gonville and Caius Coll, Cambridge CB2 1TA (☎ 01223 332437 or 332455, fax 01223 332437)

BULLEY, Philip Marshall; s of Alfred Whishaw Bulley (d 1976), of Carpenters, Udimore, nr Rye, Sussex, and Eileen Mary, *née* Prentice; *b* 1 Aug 1934; *Educ* Radley, CCC Cambridge (MA); *m* 11 Dec 1963, Anne Dione, step da of Samuel Carson Fitzwilliam Allen (d 1984), of Lathbury Park, Newport Pagnell, Bucks; 2 da (Charlotte b 1965, Isabel b 1967); *Career* Nat Serv Intelligence Corps 1953, cmmnd 2 Lt 1954, SMIS served in Malaya 1954–55; dir: J Weiner Ltd 1962–69 (md 1967–69), City Magazines 1963–69, Berrows of Worcester Ltd 1963–69, Bees Ltd 1967–73; admitted slr 1979, ptnr Mergers & Acquisitions, Corp Restructuring & Recovery Theodore Goddard 1987– (articled clerk 1976–78); *Recreations* golf, opera; *Clubs* Rye Golf; *Style*— Philip Bulley, Esq; ✉ Sackville Court, Kennington Park Rd, London SE11 4JS (☎ 0171 735 0503); Theodore Goddard, 150 Aldersgate St, London EC1A 4EJ (☎ 0171 606 8855, fax 0171 606 4390)

BULLIMORE, His Hon Judge; John Wallace MacGregor; s of James Wallace Bullimore (d 1981), of Dewsbury, and Phyllis Violet Emily, *née* Brandt; *b* 4 Dec 1945; *Educ* Queen Elizabeth GS Wakefield, Univ of Bristol (LLB); *m* 20 Dec 1975, Christine Elizabeth, da of late Valentine Sidney Charles Kinch; 2 s (Matthew James b 16 Dec 1977, Andrew Charles b 14 Oct 1981), 1 da decd; *Career* called to the Bar Inner Temple 1968, in practice 1968–91, circuit judge (NE Circuit) 1991–; chllr Diocese of: Derby 1981, Blackburn 1990; memb Gen Synod of the C of E 1970–; *Style*— His Hon Judge Bullimore; ✉ c/o NE Circuit Office, West Riding Street, Albion Street, Leeds LS1 5AA (☎ 0113 244 1841)

BULLMORE, (John) Jeremy David; CBE (1985); s of Francis Edward Bullmore, and Adeline Gabrielle, *née* Roscow; *b* 21 Nov 1929; *Educ* Harrow, ChCh Oxford; *m* 1958, Pamela Audrey Green; 2 s, 1 da; *Career* J Walter Thompson: joined 1954, dir 1964, dep chm 1975, chm 1976–87; dir J Walter Thompson (USA) 1980–87; non-exec dir: WPP Group plc 1988–, Guardian Media Group plc 1988–; chm Advertising Assoc 1981–87, memb Nat Ctee for Electoral Reform 1978–; *Publications* Behind the Scenes in Advertising; *Clubs* Arts; *Style*— Jeremy Bullmore, Esq, CBE; ✉ 20 Embankment Gardens, London SW3 (☎ 0171 351 2197); WPP Group plc, 27 Farm Street, London W1X 7RD (☎ 0171 408 2204)

BULLOCH, Brig Gavin; MBE (1973); s of David Carnie Bulloch (d 1974), and Maud Alice, *née* Knowles (d 1951); *b* 2 Oct 1938; *Educ* King's Coll Taunton; *m* 18 April 1964, Sandra Valerie, step da of Roy Francis Powys Malise Speer (d 1966); 1 s (James b 1965); *Career* cmmnd Middx Regt 1957, transfd Queen's Regt 1967, staff appts in UK and Germany, CO 3 Bn Queen's Regt 1979–81 (Despatches 1979), MOD Central Staff 1984–86, NATO HQ (Strategic Plans) 1987–89, Defence and Military Attaché Athens 1991–93; military author HQ Doctrine and Devpt Directorate Upavon Wilts; *Recreations* country sports, travel, avoiding crowds; *Style*— Brig Gavin Bulloch, MBE

BULLOCK, Baron (Life Peer UK 1976); Sir Alan Louis Charles Bullock; kt (1972); s of Rev Frank Allen Bullock, of Bradford, Yorks; *b* 13 Dec 1914; *Educ* Bradford Sch, Wadham Coll Oxford (MA, DLitt); *m* 1940, Hilda Yates, da of Edwin Handy, of Bradford; 3 s, 2 da; *Career* historian and writer; fell, dean and tutor New Coll Oxford 1945–52, founding master St Catherine's Coll Oxford 1960–80, vice-chllr Oxford Univ 1969–73; chm of tstees Tate Gallery 1973–80; FBA; *Books* Hitler, A Study in Tyranny (1952), The Life and Times of Ernest Bevin (Vol I 1960, Vol II 1967), Ernest Bevin, Foreign Secretary (1983), The Humanist Tradition (1955), Hitler and Stalin, Parallel Lives (1991); *Style*— The Rt Hon The Lord Bullock; ✉ Gable End, 30 Godstow Rd, Oxford OX2 8AJ

BULLOCK, Douglas Keith (Doug); s of Roland Bullock, of Leicester, and Amy Ethel, *née* Waterfield (d 1977); *b* 30 Dec 1946; *Educ* Wyggeston GS Leicester, Univ of Manchester (BSc), INSEAD Fontainebleau France; *m* 19 July 1969, Jennifer Elizabeth, da of Alec Blackburn; 3 s (James Andrew Douglas b 24 March 1972, Peter Edward Mark b 29 Jan 1975, Christopher Alexander b 5 Aug 1987), 1 da (Katherine Elizabeth b 21 March 1984); *Career* Coopers & Lybrand: articled clerk Cooper Brothers & Co 1968–71, ptnr 1979–, Sheffield office 1971–76, Middlesbrough office 1976–84, Newcastle upon Tyne office 1968–71 and 1984–95, Leeds office 1995–, sr tax ptnr Northern Region 1991–, memb Tax Bd 1994–, head of ops UK Private Client and Middle Market Tax Div 1996–; FCA 1971; *Recreations* orchestral music, opera, theatre; *Clubs* Northern Counties (Newcastle upon Tyne); *Style*— Doug Bullock, Esq; ✉ Broomfield, Church Lane, Pannal, Harrogate, North Yorkshire HG3 1NG (☎ 01423 873932); Coopers & Lybrand, Benson House, Wellington Street, Leeds LS1 4JP (☎ 0113 289 4000, car 0831 584588)

BULLOCK, Prof Frederick William; s of Frederick Bullock (d 1936), of Bramshott, Hants, and Elizabeth May, *née* Kent (d 1979); *b* 24 April 1932; *Educ* GS, UCL (BSc, PhD); *m* 1, 1 s (Ross b 7 July 1958); m 2, 30 Oct 1964, Margaret Ann, da of Robert Francis Tully (d 1973), of Dunstable, Beds; 2 s (Iain Robert b 22 Feb 1966, Andrew b 20 May 1967); *Career* UCL: res asst 1958–63, lectr 1963–74, reader in physics 1978–88, dean Faculty of Mathematical and Physical Sciences 1989–92, prof 1988–, vice provost 1992–; memb: Particle Physics Ctee of the SERC 1985–90, Nuclear Physics Bd of the SERC 1986–90; chm Particle Physics Grants Sub-Ctee of the SERC 1986–90; FInstP, CPhys, FRSA; *Recreations* golf, walking, watching Luton Town FC; *Style*— Prof Frederick Bullock; ✉ Vice-Provost's Office, North Cloisters, University College London, Gower St, London WC1E 6BT (☎ 0171 380 7854, fax 0171 380 7043)

BULLOCK, Gareth Richard; s of George Haydn Bullock, of Richmond, Surrey, and Veronica, *née* Jackson; *b* 20 Nov 1953; *Educ* Marling Sch Stroud, St Catharine's Coll Cambridge (MA); *m* 3 Sept 1983, Juliet Lucy Emma, da of Maj Cyril Vivian Eagleson Gordon, MC, of Winterbourne Gunner, Wilts; 3 s (Joshua b 1985, Marcus b 1987, Caspar b 1992); *Career* vice pres Citibank NA London 1984 (joined 1977), exec dir Swiss Bank Corp Investment Banking Ltd 1984–90, dep md UBS Phillips & Drew 1990–92, head of corporate banking Société Générale 1993–96, head of corporate banking NE Asia Standard Chartered Bank 1996–; memb: Ctee St Catharine's Coll Soc, RSPB; *Publications* Euronotes and Euro-Commercial Paper (1987); *Recreations* second-hand book collecting, ornithology; *Style*— Gareth Bullock, Esq; ✉ 47 Kingston Lane, Teddington, Middlesex TW11 9HN; Standard Chartered Bank, 4–4a DVR, Central Hong Kong (☎ 2821 1360)

BULLOCK, Hazel Isabel; *née* MacNaughton-Jones; da of Henry MacNaughton-Jones, MD (d 1950), and Isabel Jessie, *née* Pownceby (d 1929); *b* 12 June 1919; *Educ* Kingsley Sch Hampstead, RADA, St Martin's Sch of Art, Sir John Cass Coll of Art; *m* 1, 8 March 1945 (m dis 1950), Vernon Kelso (d 1959); m 2, 13 Feb 1951, Ernest Edgar Bullock, s of Ernest Peter Bullock (d 1962); *Career* actress and painter (stage name Hazel Lawrence); BBC TV and London Stage 1943–51; exhibitions in London at: Loggia Gallery 1973, Judd St Gallery 1985, Phoenix Gallery 1989; gp exhibitions in London at: Browse and D'Arby, Whitechapel Art Gallery, Nat Soc, RBA, HAC, FPS; memb Free Painters & Sculptors Soc; *Recreations* travel; *Clubs* Arts; *Style*— Mrs Hazel Bullock; ✉ 32 Devonshire Place, London W1N 1PE (☎ 0171 935 6409); Las Cancelas, La Herradura, Granada, Spain

BULLOCK, John; s of Robert Arthur Bullock (d 1960), of London, and Doris Edith Jane, *née* Thomas (d 1992); *b* 12 July 1933; *Educ* Latymer Upper Sch; *m* 3 Sept 1960, Ruth Jennifer, da of Vernon William Bullock (d 1979), of Coulsdon, Surrey; 3 s (Mark b 1965 d 1982, Alastair b 1967, Robert b 1969); *Career* cmmnd RAF 1956–58; Smallfield Fitzhugh Tillett & Co 1949–56 and 1958–61; Robson Morrow: joined 1961, ptnr 1965–70 (Robson Morrow merged with Deloitte Haskins & Sells); ptnr i/c Deloitte Haskins & Sells Management Consultants 1971–79; Deloitte Haskins & Sells: managing ptnr 1979–85, dep sr ptnr 1984–85, sr ptnr 1985–90, vice chm Deloitte Haskins & Sells Int 1985–89, chm Deloitte Europe 1985–89; jt sr ptnr and dep chm Coopers & Lybrand (formerly Coopers & Lybrand Deloitte) and chm Coopers & Lybrand Europe 1990–92, ret; non-exec dir: Kingfisher plc 1992–, Nuclear Electric Ltd 1993–, British Energy plc 1995–, Bright Reasons Ltd; pt/t memb UK Atomic Energy Authy 1981–94, memb Sheehy Inquiry into Police Responsibilities and Rewards 1992–93; Liveryman Worshipful Co of Chartered Accountants 1989; FCA, FCMA, FIMC; *Recreations* opera, theatre, ballet, skiing, tennis; *Style*— John Bullock, Esq; ✉ Braddocks, Oak Avenue, Sevenoaks, Kent TN13 1PR (☎ 01732 459336, fax 01732 740935)

BULLOCK, John Angel (aka Bulloch); s of William Percy George Bullock (d 1938), and Dorothy, *née* Motyer (d 1985); *b* 15 April 1928; *Educ* Penarth Co Sch, HMS Conway; *m* 1, 1951 (m dis 1971), Hazel Maxeen Campbell; 1 s; m 2, 1972 (m dis 1985), Susan Olivia Birkett; 1 s, 1 da; m 3, 1986, Jill Valerie Brown; 1 s (adopted), 1 da (adopted); *Career* served in MN; journalist; worked on local papers in S Wales and NE Eng before joining Press Assoc in 1955; Daily Telegraph: joined 1958, Central Africa corr 1960–69, ME corr 1969–76, memb Dip Staff 1978–86; dip corr BBC World Service 1977; dip ed: The Independent 1988–90 (ME ed 1986–88), The Independent on Sunday 1990–91; *Books* Spy Ring (1961), MI5 (1963), Akin to Treason (1966), Death of a Country (1977), The Making of a War (1979), Final Conflict (1983), The Gulf (1984), The Gulf War (with Harvey Morris, 1989), Saddam's War (with Harvey Morris, 1991), No Friends but the Mountains (1992), Water Wars (with Adel Darwish, 1993); *Recreations* growing vegetables, brewing beer; *Style*— John Bullock, Esq; ✉ 71 Bainton Road, Oxford OX2 7AD (☎ 01865 310587, fax 01865 558096)

BULLOCK, John Charles Ernest; s of Ernest Henry Bullock (d 1957), of Kingston upon Hull, and Emily, *née* Boodie (d 1974); *b* 15 Aug 1942; *Educ* Hymers Coll Hull; *m* 23 May 1969, Dilys Rosalyn Cross, da of Francis Robert Metcalfe (d 1970), of Kirk Ella; 1 s (Richard), 1 da (Amanda); *Career* admitted slr 1969; dir: Derwent Valley Railway Co 1976–86, Derwent Valley Holdings plc 1984–86; underwriting memb Lloyd's 1981–; memb Law Soc 1969; *Recreations* sailing (yacht Zuleika D), golf, walking; *Clubs* Royal Yorkshire Yacht, Royal Cruising, Lloyds Yacht; *Style*— John Bullock, Esq; ✉ Westwood Hall, 63 Westwood Rd, Beverley, Humberside HU17 8EN; Wilston House, Manor St, Kingston Upon Hull HU1 1YX (☎ 01482 23697, fax 01482 585299)

BULLOCK, Hon Matthew Peter Dominic; yst s of Baron Bullock (Life Peer); *b* 9 Sept 1949; *Educ* Magdalen Coll Sch Oxford, Peterhouse Cambridge; *m* 1970, Anna-Lena Margareta, da of Sven Hansson, of Uppsala, Sweden; 1 s, 2 da; *Career* banker; dir of risk mgmnt Banking Div Barclays Bank plc 1993–94 (joined 1974); BZW Ltd: dir of debt capital mkts 1994–96, md Investment Banking Servs 1996–; *Recreations* gardening, reading, walking; *Clubs* United Oxford and Cambridge Univ; *Style*— The Hon Matthew Bullock; ✉ Easby House, High Street, Great Chesterford, Saffron Waldon, Essex CB10 1PL; BZW Ltd, Ebbgate House, 2 Swan Lane, London EC4R 3TS (☎ 0171 623 2323)

BULLOCK, (Hon) Dr (Oliver) Nicholas Alan; eldest s of Baron Bullock (Life Peer); *b* 28 April 1942; *Educ* King's Coll Cambridge (MA, PhD, DipArch); *m* 1, 1967 (m dis);

m 2, 1972 (m dis), Ellen J Blatt; 2 children, 2 step children; m 3, 1984 Sally Todd, da of late Sinclair Holmes, of Bolden; *Career* former vice provost King's Coll Cambridge, lectr Univ of Cambridge; *Style*— Dr Nicholas Bullock; ✉ King's College, University of Cambridge, Cambridge CB2 1ST (☎ 01223 331100)

BULLOCK, Peter Bradley; s of William H Bradley Bullock, of Benson, Oxon; *b* 9 June 1934; *Educ* Dudley GS, QMC London (BSc); *m* 1958, Joyce Frances Muriel, da of Horace Rea (d 1957); 2 da; *Career* md Flymo Ltd (memb of Electrolux Group Sweden), jt md Electrolux Group UK until 1983; chief exec: James Neill Holdings plc 1983–89, Spear & Jackson International plc 1985–89; chm: London & Geneva Securities Ltd (formerly Henley Business Consultants Ltd) 1990–, The Paterson Photax Group Ltd 1992–94, James Dickie plc 1993–; non-exec dir: 600 Group plc 1989–, Syltone plc 1990–, Wetherby Consultants Ltd 1990–96; Queen's Award: for Export 1966 and 1982, for Technol 1979 and 1983; CEng, MInstE, MCIM; *Recreations* sailing; *Clubs* Phyllis Court (memb Cncl), Leander (Henley on Thames); *Style*— Peter Bullock, Esq; ✉ The Cottage, Queenwood, Christmas Common, Watlington, Oxford OX9 5HW (☎ and fax 01491 612406)

BULLOCK, Richard Henry Watson; CB (1971); er s of Sir Christopher Llewellyn Bullock, KCB, CBE (d 1972), of Kensington, London, and Barbara May, *née* Lupton (d 1974); *b* 12 Nov 1920; *Educ* Rugby, Trinity Coll Cambridge; *m* 20 Dec 1946, Beryl, da of Haddan John Markes (d 1950), of Ipoh, Federated Malay States, and Shripney; 1 s (Osmund Haddan Watson b 1951), 1 da (Susan Amaryllis Watson b 1947); *Career* served WWII 1940–46: 102 OCTU RAC 1940–41, cmmnd 2 Co of London Yeo (Westminster Dragoons) 1941, served England, NW Europe, Italy, Germany 1941–45, instr Armd Corps Offr Trg Sch India 1945–46, demob 1947 (Maj); Civil Serv: joined 1947, asst sec Miny of Supply 1956–60 (asst princ 1947–49, princ 1949–56), on loan to WO 1960–61, Miny of Aviation 1961–64 (under sec 1963), Miny of Technol 1964–70 (head of Space Div 1969–70), dep sec DTI 1970–80, ret 1980; DG Electronic Components Indust Fedn 1984–90 (conslt dir 1981–84); dir: Berkeley Seventh Round Ltd 1981–87, Grosvenor Place Amalgamations Ltd 1982–95; conslt Faulkbourn Consultancy Services 1981–; vice pres Westminster Dragoons Assoc 1972– (welfare offr 1950–72, chm 1978–82), dir Rugby Sch Devpt Campaign 1981–86, pres Old Rugbeian Soc 1984–86 (memb Exec Ctee 1950–), vice pres CS Hockey Ctee 1984–90 (pres 1978–84); pres: Rugby Alternatives Hockey Club 1976–, Dulwich Hockey Club 1962–90; *Recreations* watching cricket, playing tennis, fly-fishing; *Clubs* MCC, Hawks (Cambridge), Hurlingham, Cambridge Union, Dulwich Hockey; *Style*— R H W Bullock, Esq, CB; ✉ 12 Peterborough Villas, London SW6 2AT (☎ 0171 736 5132)

BULLOCK, Susan Margaret; da of John Robert Bullock (d 1994), of Cheadle Hulme, Cheshire, and Mair, *née* Jones; *b* 9 Dec 1958; *Educ* Cheadle Hulme Sch, Royal Northern Coll of Music (Jr Sch), Royal Holloway Coll London (BMus), Royal Acad of Music (LRAM), National Opera Studio; *m* Lawrence Archer Wallington, singer, s of Rev Christopher Wallington (d 1988); *Career* soprano; memb Glyndebourne Festival Chorus 1983–84, princ soprano English National Opera 1985–89; has performed with numerous major orchs incl: London Philharmonic, Royal Philharmonic, Royal Liverpool Philharmonic, BBC Nat Orch of Wales, BBC Scottish Symphony, Bournemouth Symphony, London Mozart Players, CBSO, Philharmonia, Hallé, Manchester Camerata, BBC Philharmonic; regularly performs at overseas festivals incl Beaune, Istanbul, Aix-en-Provence, Prague Spring Festival; bdcasts regularly with BBC Concert Orch; ARAM; *Roles* with ENO incl: Pamina in Die Zauberflöte, Gilda in Rigoletto, Tatyana in Eugene Onegin, Ellen Orford in Peter Grimes, title role in Madame Butterfly, Alice Ford in Falstaff, Yum Yum in The Mikado, Micaela in Carmen, Donna Anna in Don Giovanni, title role in Jenufa, Princess Natalie in The Prince of Homburg; others incl: title role in Jenufa (Glyndebourne, New Israeli Opera), title role in Katya Kabanova (Glyndebourne), Hecuba in King Priam (Flanders Opera), Andromache in King Priam (Batignano Festival), Gilda in Rigoletto (Bergen Festival), Marguerite in Faust (New Israeli Opera), Lisa in The Queen of Spades (Glyndebourne), Madame Butterfly (New Israeli Opera and Portland Opera USA); *Recordings* incl: The Mikado (with ENO under Peter Robinson, TER) 1988, Street Scene (with ENO under Carl Davis, TER) 1989, Mahler's 8th Symphony (with London Philharmonic under Klaus Tennstedt, EMI/Virgin) 1990, La Traviata/Acting (BBC TV, directed by Jonathan Miller), The Little Sweep (Thames TV), The Mikado (Thames TV), solo album (Sain label) 1994, Songs (La Nouvelle Musique Consonante) 1995, Hindemith Sancta Susanna and Songs (with BBC Philharmonic under Yan Pascal Tortelier, Chandos) 1997; *Awards* Royal Over-Seas League Singers Award, Decca/Kathleen Ferrier Prize, Worshipful Co of Musicians' Silver Medal; *Recreations* theatre, films, playing the piano, cooking, reading, jazz; *Style*— Ms Susan Bullock; ✉ c/o Harrison Parrott, 12 Penzance Place, London W11 4PA (☎ 0171 229 9166, fax 0171 221 5042)

BULLOUGH, Prof Donald Auberon; s of William Bullough (d 1961), and Edith Shirley, *née* Norman (d 1974); *b* 13 June 1928; *Educ* Newcastle-under-Lyme HS, Univ of Oxford (MA); *m* 1, 12 Dec 1963 (m dis 1994), Belinda Jane, da of John Turland (d 1955); 2 da (Caroline b 1965, Elizabeth b 1968); m 2, 1995, Dr Alice Harting-Correa; 4 step c; *Career* Nat Serv RA 1947, transferred TA, seconded OTC 1956, Maj RA 1961, res list 1967; Fereday res fell St John's Coll Oxford 1952–55, lectr Univ of Edinburgh 1955–66, visiting prof Southern Methodist Univ of Dallas 1965–66, prof Univ of Nottingham 1966–73, prof Univ of St Andrews 1973–91 (dean Faculty of Arts 1984–88, currently emeritus prof); visiting prof: Rutgers Univ New Jersey USA 1991–92 and 1993–94, Inst for Advanced Study Princeton New Jersey USA 1994–95, Univ of Auckland NZ 1996; acting dir Br Sch at Rome 1984; fndr Gunner Heritage Appeal Fndn 1991; Korrespondierende Mitglied (corresponding memb) Monumenta Germaniae Historica 1983; FRHistS 1958, FSA Scot 1959, FSA 1968, FRPSL 1993; *Books* The Age of Charlemagne (1965, new edn 1973), Carolingian Renewal - Sources and Heritage (1991); *Recreations* talk, looking at buildings, postal history, cooking; *Clubs* Athenaeum, Royal Over-Seas League; *Style*— Prof Donald Bullough, FSA; ✉ c/o Murray and Donald, Kinburn Castle, St Andrews, Fife KY16 9DS

BULLOUGH, Prof Ronald; s of Ronald Bullough (d 1953), of The Bungalow, Larkhill, Kearsley, Lancs, and Edna, *née* Morrow (d 1937); *b* 6 April 1931; *Educ* Farnworth GS, Univ of Sheffield (BSc, PhD, DSc); *m* 31 July 1954, Ruth, da of late Joseph Corbett, of Newton le Willows, Merseyside; 4 s (David Andrew, Timothy John, Mark Adrian, Neil Philip); *Career* res scientist Fundamental Res Laboratory Assoc Electrical Industs 1956–63, head Material Devpt Div Harwell Laboratory 1984–87 (gp ldr Theoretical Physics Div 1963–84), dir res and chief scientist AEA 1987–93, conslt with various professorial appointments in UK and USA 1993– (scientific advsr Nat Physical Laboratory 1995–); visiting prof: Rensselaer Poly Inst USA 1968, Univ of Wisconsin USA 1978, Univ of Illinois USA 1964, 1973 and 1979; visiting scientist: Oak Ridge Nat Laboratory 1969 and 1979 (Nat Bureau of Standards 1965), Univ of Florida 1994; memb: Individual Merit Panel Res Cncl, Awards Ctee Royal Soc; author of several books and numerous scientific publications; hon citizen of Tennessee 1967; FInstP 1963, FIM 1964, FRS 1985, FRSA 1986; *Recreations* golf, walking, reading, music; *Style*— Prof Ronald Bullough, FRS; ✉ 4 Long Meadow, Manor Road, Goring, Reading, Berks RG8 9EQ (☎ and fax 01491 873266)

BULMER, (James) Esmond; s of Edward Bulmer, and Margaret, *née* Roberts; *b* 19 May 1935; *Educ* Rugby, King's Coll Cambridge; *m* 1, 1959 (m dis 1990), Morella Kearton; 3 s, 1 da; m 2, 1990, Susan Bower; *Career* cmmnd Scots Gds 1954; H P Bulmer Holdings: dir 1962–, dep chm 1980–82, chm 1982–; dir W Midlands and Wales Regnl Bd National Westminster Bank plc 1982–92, chm Fleming High Income Investment Trust PLC; memb Exec Ctee National Tst 1977–87, chm Herefordshire Health Authy 1987–94; MP (C): Kidderminster Feb 1974–83, Wyre Forest 1983–87; *Clubs* Boodle's; *Style*— Esmond Bulmer, Esq; ✉ H P Bulmer Holdings plc, The Cider Mills, Plough Lane, Hereford HR4 0LE (☎ 01432 352000)

BULMER, Oliver Frederick; s of Robert Harold Bulmer (d 1985), of Hereford, and Pamela Mary Pleasance, *née* Dudding; *b* 29 Oct 1948; *Educ* Hereford Cathedral Sch, Univ of Bristol (BA); *m* 8 Sept 1980, Mary Rose, da of Ian Francis Henry Sconce, OBE, of Westerham, Kent; 3 da (Claire Olivia b 23 July 1981, Felicity Helena b 21 Oct 1982, Alison Rosemary b 2 Aug 1984); *Career* chartered accountant; ptnr Pannell Kerr Forster 1979–; FCA 1974, MBCS; *Recreations* tennis, skiing; *Style*— Oliver Bulmer, Esq; ✉ Pannell Kerr Forster, New Garden House, 78 Hatton Garden, London EC1N 8JA (☎ 0171 831 7393, fax 0171 405 6736)

BULPITT, Dr David Charles Henry; s of Kenneth Charles Bulpitt, of Billericay, Essex, and Patricia Lilian, *née* Gully; *b* 31 Oct 1958; *Educ* Ashford GS, King's Coll London (MB BS), Westminster Med Sch (MRCGP, AFOM); *m* 19 Nov 1983, Patricia Ann; 1 da (Jennifer b 15 April 1987), 1 s (Adam b 13 March 1989); *Career* Southend Vocational Trg Scheme for Gen Practice 1985, gen practice trainee 1986–87, ptnr Aveley Med Centre 1988–; advsr Basildon and Thurrock HA 1990–93; med advsr: Paper Sacks Ltd Northfleet Kent 1988–, United Distillers London 1995–; Cncl rep RCGP 1993– (memb Bd Essex Faculty 1990–), chm SW Essex Gen Practice Exec 1995; memb: BMA, Soc of Occupational Med 1993; *Recreations* cycling, badminton, canoeing; *Clubs* CAMRA; *Style*— Dr David Bulpitt; ✉ Aveley Medical Centre, 22 High Street, Aveley, Essex RM15 4AD (☎ 01708 865461, fax 01708 891658, e-mail dbulpitt@cix.compulink.co.uk)

BULTEEL, Kenneth Michael; s of Gerald Melville Bulteel, of Stansted, and Nancy Georgina Bulteel; *b* 4 Nov 1947; *Educ* Birkenhead Sch, Fitzwilliam Coll Cambridge (MA); *m* 29 Jan 1972, Lynda, da of Frank Milner; 3 s (Simon Courtenay b 2 March 1974, Peter Hillesden b 8 April 1975, Paul Bellenden b 6 Feb 1978); *Career* L Messel & Co Stockbrokers 1969–74, Hill Samuel Group 1974–80, dir of mgmnt servs Noble Lowndes Group 1990–93 (systems dir 1981–90), operations dir Sedgwick Noble Lowndes 1993–94, dir of admin Towers Perrin 1994–; *Clubs* Buxted Park Cricket, Stoics Cricket, East Grinstead Hockey, Piltdown Golf; *Style*— Kenneth Bulteel, Esq; ✉ Philbeech, Pound Green, Buxted, East Sussex TN22 4JW (☎ 01825 732152)

BUNBURY, *see:* Richardson-Bunbury

BUNBURY, Sir Michael William; 13 Bt (E 1681), of Stanney Hall, Cheshire; s of Sir (John) William Napier Bunbury, 12 Bt (d 1985), and Margaret Pamela, *née* Sutton; *b* 29 Dec 1946; *Educ* Eton, Trinity Coll Cambridge (MA); *m* 1976, Caroline Anne, da of Col Anthony Derek Swift Mangnall, OBE, of The Old Vicarage, Little Bedwyn, Marlborough, Wilts; 2 s (Henry Michael Napier b 1980, Edward Peter b 1986), 1 da (Katherine Rosemary b 1978); *Heir* s, Henry Michael Napier Bunbury b 4 March 1980; *Career* farmer and company director; dir Smith and Williamson; landowner (1100 acres); apptd to the Cncl of the Duchy of Lancaster 1993; *Recreations* shooting; *Clubs* Boodle's; *Style*— Sir Michael Bunbury, Bt; ✉ Naunton Hall, Rendlesham, Woodbridge, Suffolk IP12 2RD (☎ 01394 460235); No1, Riding House Street, London W1A 3AS (☎ 0171 637 5377)

BUNCE, Michael John; er s of Roland John Bunce, ARIBA (d 1977), and Dorie, *née* Woods (d 1992); *b* 24 April 1935; *Educ* St Paul's, Kingston Coll; *m* 1 April 1961, Tina, *née* Sims; 2 s (Charles b 1962, Rupert b 1966 d 1990), 2 da (Miranda b 1968, Arabella b 1970); *Career* Nat Serv RAF; joined BBC as engr, subsequently studio mangr; prodr: People and Politics (World Service), A Man Apart - The Murderer 1965, Minorities in Britain, The Younger Generation, Italy and the Italians; dir Gallery; ed: The Money Programme 1968–70, BBC Nationwide 1970–75; BBC chief asst Current Affairs 1976–78 (also ed Tonight), head of Information Servs TV 1978–82, head of Information Div 1982–83, controller Information Services 1983–91; exec dir RTS 1991–; visiting ed in residence Univ of Alabama 1987–92; memb: EBU Working Pty Direct Elections 1978, Francis Ctee 1977, Advsy Bd Centre for Media Performance and Communications Univ Coll Salford; chm Nat Industs PR Offrs 1991–92; Shell International TV award 1969; Marshall Fund fell USA 1975; FRTS 1989; *Recreations* gardening, visiting interesting buildings, fishing; *Clubs* Groucho; *Style*— Michael Bunce, Esq; ✉ Royal Television Society, Holborn Hall, 100 Gray's Inn Road, London WC1X 8AL (☎ 0171 430 1000)

BUNCE, Dr Ross John; s of Ross Frederick Bunce, DFC, of Gerrards Cross, Bucks, and Gwendoline Janet, *née* Fox; *b* 28 March 1948; *Educ* Kingsbury County GS, Univ Coll London (BSc, PhD); *m* 29 Dec 1972, Monique Irene, da of Pierre Roy; 2 s (Philippe Ross b 27 Oct 1978, John Marc Alexander b 26 April 1980); *Career* asst vice pres: Investment Management Bankers Trust Co London 1974–81, Mercury Asset Management 1981– (dep chm 1989); dir: Mercury Asset Management Ltd 1983, Mercury Asset Management Holdings 1987, Mercury Asset Management plc 1987– (vice chm 1991), Mercury Int Investment Tst Ltd 1995; AIIMR; *Recreations* squash, tennis, golf; *Clubs* Southgate Squash, Porters Park Golf, Hadley Wood Tennis, Hadley Wood Golf; *Style*— Dr Ross Bunce; ✉ 31 Beech Hill, Hadley Wood, Hertfordshire; Mercury Asset Management, 33 King William St, London EC4R 9AS (☎ 0171 280 2800)

BUNCH, Anthony William Samson; s of Dennis John Bunch (d 1989), of Ramsgate, Kent, and Francisca, *née* Schwam; *b* 8 Feb 1953; *Educ* Chatham House GS Ramsgate, Univ of Nottingham (BA); *m* June 1980, Alison Jane, da of Ralph Cordell; 2 da (Naomi Leah Rebecca b 21 Sept 1983, Sarah Marie b 25 June 1985), 2 s (Adam Samuel b 29 June 1987, Simon Daniel b 1 Oct 1991); *Career* Masons: articled 1976–78, admitted slr 1978, salaried ptnr 1978, equity ptnr 1982–, admitted slr Hong Kong 1985, sr resident ptnr Hong Kong Office 1985–90, fndr Alternative Dispute Resolution (ADR) Unit 1990, managing ptnr Masons 1991–, also chm Mgmnt Bd and ptnr in Construction Dept; rep various professional bodies in dispute resolution; memb: ADR Ctee Chartered Inst of Arbitrators, Departmental Advsy Ctee on New Arbitration Act, Int Advsy Bd Arbitration Inst of Stockholm C of C; ACIArb; *Publications* National Report on Hong Kong in International Handbook on Commercial Arbitration (co-author); *Recreations* antiques, playing saxophone, theatre and the arts; *Style*— Anthony Bunch, Esq; ✉ The Red House, 14 Loom Lane, Radlett, Herts WD7 8AD (☎ 01923 856704); Masons, 30 Aylesbury Street, London EC1R 0ER (☎ 0171 490 4000, fax 0171 490 2545, direct ☎ 0171 490 6216, direct fax 0171 490 6201)

BUNCH, Sir Austin Wyeth; kt (1983), CBE (1978, MBE 1974); s of Horace William Bunch (d 1953), and Winifred Ada Bunch; *b* 20 March 1918; *Educ* Christ's Hosp; *m* 1944, Joan Mary, *née* Peryer; 4 da; *Career* Lt Essex Regt 1940–44; Deloitte Plender Griffiths 1935–48, Southern Electricity Bd 1949–76 (chm 1974–76); chm: British Electricity International Ltd 1976–81, The Electricity Cncl 1981–83 (dep chm 1976–81); nat pres Br Limbless Ex-Serv Men's Assoc 1983–92 (vice patron 1992–); FCA, companion IEE; *Recreations* sports for the disabled; *Clubs* Victory (Services); *Style*— Sir Austin Bunch, CBE; ✉ Sumner, School Lane, Cookham, Berks SL6 9QJ

BUNDY, Prof Alan Richard; s of Stanley Alfred Bundy (d 1994), and Joan Margaret Bundy; *b* 18 May 1947; *Educ* Heston Secdy Modern, Springgrove GS, Leicester Univ (BSc, PhD); *m* 23 Sept 1967, Josephine, da of John Maule; 1 da (Rachel b 26 Nov 1970); *Career* tutorial asst Univ of Leicester 1970–71; Univ of Edinburgh: research fell 1971–74, lectr 1974–84, reader 1984–87, professorial fell 1987–90, prof 1990–; SPL Insight Award 1986; FRSA 1988, fell American Assoc for Artificial Intelligence 1990, FRSE 1996; *Books* Artificial Intelligence: An Introductory Course (1978), The Computer Modelling of

Mathematical Reasoning (1983), The Catalogue of Artificial Intelligence (1984), Eco-Logic: Logic based approaches to ecological modelling (1991); *Recreations* wine and beer making, valley walking, bridge; *Style—* Prof Alan Bundy, FRSE; ✉ Department of Artificial Intelligence, University of Edinburgh, 80 South Bridge, Edinburgh EH1 1HN (☎ 0131 650 2716, fax 0131 650 6516, e-mail A.BUNDY@ed.ac.uk)

BUNDY, Christopher; *b* 7 Oct 1945; *Educ* Cheshunt GS; *m* 8 Aug 1970, Wendy Constance; 1 s (Dominic b 1973), 2 da (Phillipa b 1975, Prudence b 1979); *Career* CA; fin accountant Caravans Int Ltd, fin dir subsidiary cos Lex Service Group PLC, chm and md E J Arnold and Son, indust advsr; md Nice-Pak International Ltd; currently chm: Waterstone Glassware Ltd, Beaver Holdings Ltd; currently dir: A1 Security & Electrical Ltd, BLP Group PLC; FCA; *Recreations* wine, computers; *Style—* Christopher Bundy, Esq

BUNGEY, Michael; s of William George Bungey, and Irene Edith Bungey; *b* 18 Jan 1940; *Educ* St Clement Danes GS, LSE (BScEcon); *m* 1976, Darleen Penelope Cecilia, *née* Brooks; 1 s, 2 da; *Career* Mktg Research Dept Nestlé 1961–65, assoc dir Crawfords (advtg agency) 1965–69, bd dir S H Benson Company 1969–72, fndr Michael Bungey and Partners 1971 (bought by DFS NY 1983, merged with Dorland Advertising 1984), chm and chief exec offr Bates Dorland (formerly DFS Dorland, then BSB Dorland) 1987–; Bates Worldwide (formerly Backer Spielvogel Bates Worldwide): pres and chief operating offr 1993–, chief exec 1994–, concurrently chm and chief exec offr Bates Americas Region and Bates Inc USA; dir Cordiant plc 1995–; FIPA; *Clubs* Hurlingham; *Style—* Michael Bungey, Esq; ✉ Bates Worldwide Inc, The Chrysler Building, 405 Lexington Avenue, New York, NY 10174, USA (☎ 00 1 212 297 7000)

BUNKER, Dr Christopher Barry; s of Nigel Vincent Delahuntey Bunker, MBE (d 1967), and Joy, *née* Bolsover; *b* 22 Nov 1956; *Educ* Wycliffe Coll Glos (top scholar), St Catharine's Coll Cambridge (Kitchener scholar, MA, MD, Sir Walter Langdon Brown prize), Westminster Med Sch London (Kitchener scholar, MB BS, MRCS, FRCP); *m* 1991, Anna Christina, yst da of Dr J Kurowski, of Hull; 2 da (Minette b 1992, Matilda b 1995); *Career* currently: conslt dermatologist in private practice and at Chelsea and Westminster Hosp, Charing Cross Hosp and St Luke's Hosp for the Clergy, memb Academic Bd and hon sr lectr Charing Cross and Westminster Med Sch; *awards* Sir Jules Thorn res fell 1988–90, overseas scholar (World Congress of Dermatology 1992), Silver award 1990, Gold award 1991 and Bronze award 1992 (American Acad of Dermatology, Historical Poster section); *Publications* author of numerous original papers and articles; *Style—* Dr Christopher Bunker; ✉ 152 Harley Street, London W1N 1HH (☎ 0171 935 0444)

BUNKER, Christopher Jonathan; s of Jonathan William Bunker, and Beryl Kathleen Rose, *née* Wood; *b* 16 Dec 1946; *Educ* Ilford County HS, King's Coll London; *m* 9 Sept 1972, Julia Doris, da of Arthur James Seymour Russell (d 1954); 2 da (Jennifer b 1978, Elizabeth b 1982); *Career* accountant; fin dir Westland Group plc 1987–96, Tarmac plc 1996–; *Style—* Christopher Bunker, Esq; ✉ Tarmac plc, Hilton Hall, Essington, Wolverhampton WV11 2BQ (☎ 01902 307407, fax 01902 307408)

BUNKER, Very Rev Michael; *b* 22 July 1937; *Educ* Benjamin Adlard Sch Gainsborough Lincs, Acton and Brunel Colls London, Oak Hill Theol Coll Southgate; *m*; *Career* asst curate: St James's Alperton Middx 1963–66, St Helens Parish Church St Helens Merseyside (curate-in-charge daughter church St Andrew's) 1966–70; vicar: St Matthew's Muswell Hill London 1970–78, St James's Muswell Hill 1978–92; area dean W Haringey 1985–90, preb St Paul's Cathedral London 1990–92, dean of Peterborough Cathedral 1992–; memb: Edmonton Area Synod 1982–92, Diocesan (London) Synod 1985–91, Area Bishop's Cncl 1985–91, C of E Evangelical Cncl 1991–92, Diocesan (London) Fin Ctee 1992; chm Edmonton Area Evangelical Fellowship 1989–91, chm Diocesan (Peterborough) Cncl for Evangelism 1995–96; chm Peterborough Tourism 1996–; chm Govrs: St James's CE Primary Sch 1978–92, King's Sch Peterborough 1992–; govr St David & St Katharine's C of E Comp Sch 1985–90; memb Ct Nene Coll Northampton 1995–; tstee: Oakham Sch 1992–, Uppingham Sch 1992–; *Publications* The Church on the Hill (St James's Church, 1988), Ten Growing Churches (contrib); *Style—* The Very Rev the Dean of Peterborough; ✉ The Deanery, Peterborough, Cambs PE1 1XS (☎ 01733 62780)

BUNKER, Peter John; OBE (1988); s of Leslie John Daniel Bunker (d 1985), of Hove, and Rosa Amelia, *née* Sands (d 1961); *b* 26 Feb 1928; *Educ* Brighton Hove and Sussex GS, Gonville and Caius Coll Cambridge (MA, LLM); *m* 31 May 1952, Angela Elizabeth, da of David Higham (d 1957), of Brighton; 1 s (John b 1957), 3 da (Elizabeth b 1955, Margaret b 1960, Catherine b 1965); *Career* admitted slr 1954, awarded Law Soc Broderip and Mellersh prizes, in practice Bunkers Solicitors; pres Sussex Law Soc 1979–80, fndr chm (currently vice pres) PACT Community Projects; chm: Frederick Soddy Tst, Appeal Ctee Stanmer House Preservation Tst; former chm of Govrs: Goldstone Junior Sch Hove, Blatchington Mill Comp Sch Hove; fndr chm: Martlet Housing Assoc, E Sussex Cncl on Alcoholism; memb Ct Univ of Sussex; elder Brighthelm United Reform Church; FRGS 1978; *Recreations* gardening, skiing, listening to music; *Style—* Peter Bunker, Esq, OBE; ✉ 38 Shirley Drive, Hove, East Sussex (☎ 01273 503729); Bunkers Solicitors, 7 The Drive, Hove, East Sussex BN3 3JS (☎ 01273 329797, fax 01273 324082)

BUNKER, Richard David Charles; s of Albert Rowland Bunker, CB, and Irene Ruth Ella, *née* Lacey (d 1996); *b* 1 May 1942; *Educ* Ealing GS, St Peter's Coll Oxford (MA), Univ of Nottingham (PGCE); *m* 5 Aug 1967, Jennifer, da of George Calow (d 1986); 2 s (Andrew b 1971, Jonathan b 1973); *Career* English language asst 1963–64, personnel offr Unilever 1965–66; languages teacher: Drayton Manor GS Ealing 1966, Haberdashers' Aske's 1967–70; asst educn offr London Borough of Hillingdon 1970–74, asst educn offr then sr asst educn offr Beds CC 1974–80, dir of educn W Sussex CC 1985– (dep dir 1980–85); hon treas Nat Fndn for Educnl Res, dir Nfer-Nelson Ltd, chm Careers Guidance Trg Cncl; memb: Ct Univ of Sussex, Ct Univ of Southampton; tstee Chichester Festival Theatre; FIMgt 1984, FRSA 1984, FIL 1989; *Recreations* travel, languages; *Clubs* Royal Over-Seas League; *Style—* Richard Bunker, Esq; ✉ 15 Stanton Drive, Chichester, W Sussex PO19 4QN; Education Department, W Sussex County Council, County Hall, West St, Chichester, W Sussex PO19 1RF (☎ 01243 777750, fax 01243 777229)

BUNN, Douglas Henry David; s of George Henry Charles Honeybunn (d 1967), of Selsey, nr Chichester, W Sussex, and Alice Ann, *née* Philpot (d 1986); *b* 1 March 1928; *Educ* Chichester HS, Trinity Coll Cambridge (MA); *m* 1, 26 June 1952 (m dis 1959), Rosemary Heather, da of John Pares Wilson, of Shelford, Cambs; 3 da (Claudia b 27 Sept 1953, Lavinia b 6 June 1956, Theresa b 24 Sept 1958); m 2, 16 March 1960 (m dis 1979), Diana Susan Beverley, da of Archie Dennis-Smith; 2 s (Edward b 22 Jan 1961, John b 18 May 1966), 1 da (Elizabeth b 8 Nov 1963); m 3, 12 March 1979 (sep 1993), Lorna Margaret, da of Joseph Kirk, of Cambridge; 2 s (Douglas b 7 Oct 1981 d 1981, Charles b 30 March 1987), 2 da (Chloe b 3 April 1980, Daisy b 24 Jan 1983); *Career* called to the Bar Lincoln's Inn, practised 1953–59; Br Show Jumping Team 1957–68; founded: White Horse Caravan Co Ltd 1958, All England Jumping Course Hickstead 1960; chm: Southern Aero Club 1968–72, Br Show Jumping Assoc 1969 and 1992–96, Br Show Jumping Selection Ctee 1991; memb Br Equestrian Fedn, jt master Mid Surrey Draghounds 1976; *Recreations* horses, flying, books, wine; *Clubs* Saints & Sinners, Turf; *Style—* Douglas Bunn, Esq; ✉ Hickstead Place, Hickstead, Sussex RH17 5NU (☎ 01273 834666); All England Jumping Course, Hickstead, Sussex RH17 5NU (☎ 01273 834315, fax 01273 834452, car 0831 763166)

BUNNEY, John Herrick; *b* 2 June 1945; *m* 1970, Pamela Anne Simcock; 1 s (b 1973), 1 da (B 1976); *Career* 2 Sec FCO 1971, MECAS 1971, 1 sec Damascus 1974–78, consul Sana'a 1981–83, first sec FCO 1983–87, Tunis 1987–90, first sec FCO 1990–93, cnsllr Riyadh 1993–; *Style—* John Bunney, Esq; ✉ c/o FCO (Riyadh), King Charles Street, London SW1A 2AH

BUNTING, Martin Brian; s of Thomas Brian Bunting (d 1988), of Maidstone, and Renee Conworth, *née* Fish (d 1988); *b* 28 Feb 1934; *Educ* Rugby; *m* 11 July 1959, Veronica Mary, da of Bertam Harold Cope, of Wolverhampton; 2 s (Timothy, Nigel), 1 da (Caroline (Countess of Southesk, see Southesk, Earl of); *Career* 2 Lt 1952–54 8 King's Royal Irish Hussars; md Courage (Central) Ltd 1969–71; Courage Ltd: asst md 1972, gp md 1975; Imperial Group Ltd: joined 1961, dir 1975, dep chm Imperial Brewing & Leisure Ltd, ret 1986; chief exec Clifford Foods plc 1990–93 (non-exec dir 1989–90); chm: Marr Holdings Ltd 1992–96, Marr Taverns Ltd 1992–96, Bluebird Toys plc 1996– (non-exec dir 1991–), Inn Business plc 1996–; non-exec dir: Horndean Hotels Ltd 1984–, George Gale & Co Ltd 1984–, Longman Cartermill Ltd 1985–90, Norcros plc 1986–93, Shepherd Neame Ltd 1986–, NAAFI 1993–, Hobson plc 1994–96; Gen Cmmr of Income Tax 1986–94; memb MMC 1982–88; Freeman Worshipful Co of Brewers; FCA 1960; *Clubs* Travellers'; *Style—* Martin Bunting, Esq; ✉ The Lodge, Riseley, Berks RG7 1QD (☎ 0118 988 3234, fax 0118 988 5414)

BUNTING, Michael Geoffrey; s of late James Norman Bunting, of St Anne's on Sea, Lancs, and Dorothy, *née* Lowndes; *b* 20 May 1947; *Educ* King Edward VII Sch Lytham, Trinity Coll Cambridge (BA, MA), Manchester Business Sch (MBA); *m* 18 Feb 1984, Sheila Carolyn, da of George Herbert Booth, of Cheltenham; 2 s (Adrian b 1986, Richard b 1988), 2 da (Julia b 1984, Caroline b 1992); *Career* gp treas: Tootal Gp plc 1982–84, The Boots Co plc 1984–; *Recreations* mountaineering; *Style—* Michael Bunting, Esq; ✉ 7 Highgrove Gdns, Edwalton, Nottingham, NG12 4DF (☎ 0115 923 1406); The Boots Co plc, Head Office, Nottingham, Notts NG2 3AA (☎ 0115 968 7128)

BUNTON, Christopher John; s of John Bunton, and Marion Helen, *née* Gotobed; *b* 22 Feb 1948; *Educ* Charterhouse, Trinity Coll Cambridge (MA), London Graduate Sch of Business Studies (MSc); *m* 10 May 1975, Jane Melanie, da of Antony J S Cartmell; 2 s (Anthony, Michael); *Career* with Gulf Oil Corpn 1973–1985, gp treas Saatchi & Saatchi plc (now Cordiant plc) 1986–; *Recreations* music; *Clubs* Hawks; *Style—* Christopher Bunton, Esq; ✉ Cordiant plc, 83/89 Whitfield Street, London W1A 4XA (☎ 0171 436 4000)

BUNYAN, Dr Peter John; s of Charles Bunyan (d 1976), and Jenny, *née* Crawley; *b* 13 Jan 1936; *Educ* Raynes Park Co GS, Univ of Durham (BSc, DSc), King's Coll London (PhD); *m* 1961, June, *née* Child; 2 s; *Career* post doctoral fell: King's Coll London 1960–62, UCL 1962–63; MAFF: sr scientific offr Infestation Control Laboratory 1963–69, princ scientific offr Pest Infestation Control Laboratory 1969–73, head of Pest Control Chemistry Dept 1973–80, head of Food Science Div 1980–84, head of Agric Scientific Serv ADAS 1984–87, dir R & D Serv ADAS 1987–90, DG ADAS and MAFF Regnl Orgn 1990–91, chief scientific advsr 1990–95; visiting prof of agriculture De Montfort Univ 1996–; vice chm Br Crop Protection Cncl 1995–; FRSC 1971, FIBiol 1984 (hon sec 1996–), FIFST 1984, FRSA 1989; *Recreations* gardening, jogging; *Clubs* Farmers'; *Style—* Dr Peter Bunyan; ✉ Flushings Meadow, Church Road, Great Bookham, Surrey KT23 3JT (☎ 01372 456798, fax 01372 456798)

BUNYARD, Sir Robert Sidney; kt (1991), CBE (1986), QPM (1978); s of Albert Percy Bunyard, and Nellie Maria, *née* Mount; *b* 20 May 1930; *Educ* Queen Elizabeth GS Faversham, Regent Street Poly Mgmnt Sch (DMS), Open Univ (BA); *m* 1948, Ruth; 2 da (Anne, Christine); *Career* joined Met Police 1952; chief superintendent: Lewisham 1969–71, Greenwich 1971–72; asst chief constable Leics 1972–77; RCDS 1977, chief constable Essex 1978–87 (dep chief constable 1977); chm: ACPO Computer Ctee 1980–82, ACPO Training Ctee 1984–87, No 5 Regional Crime Squad Ctee 1980–87; HM Inspector of Constabulary 1988–93, Cmdt Police Staff Coll 1988–93; memb: Royal Cmmn on Criminal Justice 1991–93, Parole Bd 1994–; regnl chm Royal Assoc in Aid of Deaf People 1994–95; MIPD, CIMgt; *Books* Police Organisation and Command (1978), Police Management Handbook (1979); *Recreations* music, opera, painting; *Style—* Sir Robert Bunyard, CBE, QPM; ✉ Bellmans, Mounthill Avenue, Springfield, Chelmsford, Essex CM2 6DB

BUNZL, Eur Ing Thomas F; s of Dr Max Bunzl; *b* 13 Dec 1934; *Educ* Bembridge Sch IOW, Univ of Glasgow, Univ of California; *m* 1959, Marian, da of Walter Strauss; 2 da; *Career* md Electrautom Ltd 1965–89, chm Robots International Ltd; MIEE, MIEEE, FISM, FIPM, Eur Ing 1989; *Style—* Eur Ing Thomas Bunzl; ✉ 126 West Heath Rd, London NW3 (☎ 0181 458 2691)

BUONAGUIDI, David Mervyn; s of Gianfranco Buonaguidi, of Esher, Surrey, and Karen, *née* Petersen; *b* 13 Aug 1964; *Educ* City of London Freemens' Sch Ashtead Surrey, Epsom Sch of Art and Design Epsom Surrey (DATEC graphics); *Career* advtg art dir: TBWA 1984–85, Wight Collins Rutherford Scott 1985–88, Howell Henry Chaldecott Lury 1988–91, J Walter Thompson 1991–92, Howell Henry Chaldecott Lury 1992–93; jt creative dir St Luke's (formerly Chiat/Day) 1993–; *Style—* David Buonaguidi, Esq; ✉ St Luke's, 22 Duke's Road, London WC1H 9AB (☎ 0171 380 8888, fax 0171 380 8899)

BURBIDGE, Sir Herbert Dudley; 5 Bt (UK 1916), of Littleton Park, Co Middlesex; o s of late Herbert Edward Burbidge, 2 s of 1 Bt; suc kinsman, Sir John Richard Woodman Burbidge, 4 Bt, 1974; *b* 13 Nov 1904; *Educ* University Sch Victoria BC Canada; *m* 1933, Ruby (d 1994), da of Charles Ethelbert Taylor, of Comox, Vancouver 1, BC; 1 s; *Heir* s, Peter Dudley Burbidge, *qv*; *Career* mangr Silverwood Industries (Vancouver) 1931–70; *Style—* Sir Herbert Burbidge, Bt; ✉ 3809 West 24th Avenue, Vancouver, British Columbia, Canada

BURBIDGE, Peter Dudley; o s and h of Sir Herbert Dudley Burbidge, 5 Bt, *qv*; *b* 20 June 1942; *m* 1967, Peggy Marilyn, da of Kenneth Anderson, of Ladner, BC; 1 s (John Peter b 1975), 1 da (Kathleen Jean b 1973); *Style—* Peter Burbidge, Esq; ✉ 3809 West 24th Ave, Vancouver, BC, Canada

BURBRIDGE, Very Rev (John) Paul; s of John Henry Gray Burbridge (d 1980), of Warninglid, Sussex, and Dorothy Vera, *née* Pratt (d 1981); bro of Stephen Nigel Burbridge, CB, *qv*; *b* 21 May 1932; *Educ* King's Sch Canterbury, King's Coll Cambridge (MA), New Coll Oxford (MA), Wells Theol Coll; *m* 7 July 1956, Olive Denise, da of Denis Arthur Grenfell, of Holcombe, Dawlish, S Devon; 4 da (Rachel (Mrs Howgego) b 1960, Deborah (Mrs Johnson) b 1962, Sarah (Mrs Bourne) b 1966, Felicity (Mrs Rinde) b 1969); *Career* Nat Serv cmmnd RA 1957, Asst Adj 80 LAA Regt RA; curate Eastbourne Parish Church 1959–62, chamberlain York Minster 1962–76 (canon residentiary and precentor 1966–76), archdeacon of Richmond 1976–83, dean of Norwich 1983–95 (dean emeritus 1995); FSA; *Style—* The Very Rev Paul Burbridge, FSA; ✉ The School House, High Fremington, Richmond, N Yorkshire DL11 6AS (☎ 01748 884440)

BURBRIDGE, Stephen Nigel; CB (1992); s of John Henry Gray Burbridge (d 1980), and Dorothy Vera, *née* Pratt (d 1981); bro of Very Rev (John) Paul Burbridge, FSA, *qv*; *b* 18 July 1934; *Educ* King's Sch Canterbury, ChCh Oxford (MA); *Career* Nat Serv 2 Lt RA 1953–55; asst princ BOT 1958; first sec: commercial Karachi 1963, econ Rawalpindi 1965; DTI: princ 1967, asst sec 1971, under sec 1980; sec to the MMC 1986–93, ret; *Recreations* books, golf; *Clubs* Reform, Rye Golf, West Sussex Golf; *Style—* Stephen Burbridge, Esq, CB; ✉ Chesil Cottage, Brede Hill, Brede, nr Rye, E Sussex

BURCH, Maj-Gen Keith; CB (1985), CBE (1977, MBE 1965); s of Christopher Burch (d 1994), of Saltdean, Sussex, and Gwendoline Ada, *née* James (d 1991); *b* 31 May 1931;

Educ Bedford Modern Sch, RMA Sandhurst; *m* 12 June 1957, Sara Vivette, da of Reginald Thomas Hales (d 1974); 1 s (Giles St John b 1966), 2 da (Amanda b 1958, Emma b 1960); *Career* cmmnd Essex Regt 1951, dir staff Staff Coll Camberley 1968–69, cmd 3 Bn The Royal Anglian Regt 1969–71, asst sec Chiefs of Staff Ctee MOD 1972–75, Col GS HQ 2 Armoured Div 1975–78, dir Admin Planning (Army) MOD 1978–80, Indian Nat Def Coll New Delhi 1981, dep dir Army Staff Duties MOD 1981–83, asst chief of the Def Staff (personnel and logistics) MOD 1984, dir personnel MOD 1985; chapter clerk York Minster 1985–95; *Recreations* country pursuits, swimming; *Style—* Maj-Gen Keith Burch, CB, CBE; ✉ Mayfield, Sandy Lane, Stockton-on-the-Forest, York YO3 9US (☎ 01904 400305)

BURCHFIELD, Dr Robert William; CBE (1975); s of Frederick Burchfield (d 1979), and Mary Lauder, *née* Blair (d 1974); *b* 27 Jan 1923; *Educ* Wanganui Tech Coll NZ, Victoria Univ Coll Wellington NZ, Magdalen Coll Oxford; *m* 1, 1949 (m dis 1976), Ethel May Yates; 1 s (Jonathan), 2 da (Jennifer, Elizabeth); m 2, 1976, Elizabeth Austen, da of Cedric Hankinson Knight (d 1983); *Career* RNZA 1941–46, NZ and Italy, Sgt 1941–44; lectr in English language ChCh Oxford 1953–57, fell and tutor in English language St Peter's Coll Oxford 1963–79 (sr res fell 1979–90, emeritus fell 1990); ed A Supplement to the Oxford English Dictionary 1957–86; *Books* The Oxford Dictionary of English Etymology (assisted C T Onions and G W S Friedrichsen, 1966), A Supplement to the Oxford English Dictionary Vol 1 A-G (1972), Vol 2 H-N (1976), Vol 3 O-Scz (1982), Vol 4 Se-Z (1986), The Spoken Word (1981), The English Language (1985), The New Zealand Pocket Oxford Dictionary (1986), Studies in Lexicography (1987), Unlocking the English Language (1989), Points of View (1992), Cambridge History of the English Language Vol V (ed, 1994); *Recreations* investigating English grammar, travelling; *Clubs* Athenaeum; *Style—* Dr Robert Burchfield, CBE; ✉ 14 The Green, Sutton Courtenay, Oxfordshire OX14 4AE (☎ 01235 848645); St Peter's College Oxford OX1 2DL

BURD, Keith Francis; OBE (1986); s of Frederick Thomas Burd (d 1984), and Norma Kathleen Burd; *b* 5 Dec 1945; *Educ* Central GS Birmingham, Univ of Sheffield (BA), Univ of Sussex (MA); *m* 1, 1968 (m dis 1985), Stephanie, *née* Perkins; m 2, 1993, Helene Nike Sara, *née* Pickford-Gordon; *Career* British Council: joined 1968, served in Kenya and Nigeria, dir Uganda 1983–87, dep dir Educn and Science Div (UK) 1989–93, dir Bangladesh 1993–96; *Recreations* squash, tennis, soccer; *Style—* Keith Burd, Esq, OBE; ✉ c/o The British Council, 10 Spring Gardens, London SW1A 2BN (☎ 0171 930 8466)

BURDEN, Norman; s of Walter Burden (d 1975), of Sefton Park, Liverpool, and Margaret Jane, *née* Thomas (d 1979); *b* 24 Sept 1934; *Educ* Liverpool Collegiate Sch, Christ's Coll Cambridge (MA); *m* 29 March 1958, Margot Asquith, da of George Lowe Tennant (d 1947); 3 da (Sarah b 1960, Xanthe b 1963, Celia b 1965); *Career* RAF 1956–58, Pilot Offr 1956, Flying Offr 1957; dir gp mktg Compair Ltd 1971–77, int chief exec Burmah Indust Prods Ltd 1979–81, chief exec The Rawlplug Group 1981–85, ptnr Templewood Assocs 1985–, dir Dzus International Ltd 1990–93; chm: Vitalograph Ltd 1990–92, Juliana's Leisure Group Ltd 1992–94, The Timeshare Cncl 1992–96; vice pres European Timeshare Federation 1993–95, nat chm Chartered Inst of Mktg 1985 and 1986 (former vice chm and treas), Br rep Euro Mktg Cncl 1980–86; memb Governing Bd Mktg Quality Assurance 1990–; singing memb The Windsor and Eton Choral Soc; Freeman City of London 1982, Liveryman Worshipful Co of Marketors 1982; FCIM 1974, FRSA 1984, FInstD 1986; *Recreations* choral music, running; *Style—* Norman Burden, Esq; ✉ Penwern, 23 Mayflower Way, Farnham Common, Bucks SL2 3TU (☎ and fax 01753 642325)

BURDEN, Peter Victor; OBE (1996); s of late Paul Burden, and Norah Burden; *Educ* Hove Coll E Sussex; *m* Jennifer June; 1 s (Miles), 1 da (Fiona); *Career* journalist; formerly with: Sussex Express & County Herald, South London Press; chief crime corr: Daily Sketch 1962–71, Daily Mail 1971–95 (crime conslt 1996–); Crime Reporter of the Year 1979, High Court Journalist's prize for medical and legal reporting 1981; pres Crime Reporters' Assoc 1990– (memb Exec 1980–89), memb London Bd of Crime Stoppers 1994–95; *Books* The Burglary Business and You (1980); *Recreations* wine tasting, cooking, travelling; *Style—* Peter Burden, Esq, OBE; ✉ The Daily Mail, Northcliffe House, 2 Derry St, London W8 5TT (☎ 0171 938 6104, fax 0171 937 5287)

BURDEN, Richard; MP (Lab) Birmingham Northfield (majority 630); s of Kenneth Burden, and late Pauline Burden; *b* 1 Sept 1954; *Educ* Wallasey Tech GS, Bramhall Comp Sch, St John's Coll of FE Manchester, Univ of York (BA), Univ of Warwick (MA); *Career* pres York Univ Students' Union 1976–77, dist offr W Midlands Dist NALGO 1981–92 (branch organiser N Yorks branch 1979–81); Parly candidate (Lab) Meriden 1987, MP (Lab) Birmingham Northfield 1992– (TGWU sponsored); fndr memb Bedale Lab Pty 1980, fndr sec Jt Action on Water Services (JAWS) 1985–90, sec Parly All Pty Water Group, sec Parly Lab Pty Trade and Indust Ctee 1996– (vice chm 1995–96), vice chair Lab Middle E Cncl 1995–96, chair Lab Campaign for Electoral Reform 1996–, memb House of Commons Euro Standing Ctee, jt chair Parly Advsy Cncl for Tport Safety, exec memb Cncl for Advancement of Arab/Br Understanding; memb Socialist Environment and Resources Assoc, Fabian Soc, Co-op Pty, CND, War on Want, Greenpeace; sec House of Commons Motor Club; *Recreations* cinema, motor racing, travel, reading, food; *Clubs* Kingshurst Labour, Rover Social, Austin Branch British Legion, 750 Motor; *Style—* Richard Burden, Esq, MP; ✉ House of Commons, London SW1A 0AA (☎ 0171 219 5002, constituency office 0121 475 9295)

BURDEN, Roger Francis; s of Henry Burden (d 1974), of Bristol, and Rosalind, *née* Wiggins (d 1992); *b* 3 June 1946; *Educ* Cheltenham Tech HS; *m* 19 Sept 1970, Julie Ann, da of James Hopkins; 2 s (Stephen Paul b 22 June 1974, Peter David b 19 Jan 1977); *Career* cashier (foreign exchange, securities) Martins Bank Ltd 1963–67; Dowty Rotol Ltd: cashier Accounts Dept 1967–68, computer programmer 1968–69; Cheltenham & Gloucester plc (formerly Cheltenham & Gloucester Building Society): various appts Data Processing Depts 1969–77, data processing mangr 1977–79, asst gen mangr 1979–87, gen mangr 1987–88, dep md 1988–, information systems dir 1989–91, ops dir 1991–; memb Cncl Football Assoc, govr Bournside Comp Sch and Sixth Form Centre; MBCS 1975, FCBSI 1987 (ACBSI 1982), FCIB 1993; *Recreations* football (dep chm Gloucestershire FA, Class 1 Association Football referee); *Clubs* Lilleybrook Golf; *Style—* Roger Burden, Esq; ✉ Cheltenham & Gloucester plc, Barnett Way, Gloucester GL4 7RL (☎ 01452 373449, fax 01452 373970)

BURDETT, Crispin Peter; o s and h of Sir Savile Aylmer Burdett, 11 Bt, *qv*; *b* 8 Feb 1967; *m* Aug 1988, Julia Winifred Gresham, yr da of John Gresham Copeland, of Church Lawton, Cheshire; *Style—* Crispin Burdett, Esq; ✉ 6 Chequers Road, Writtle, Chelmsford, Essex

BURDETT, Noel Henry; OBE (1986); s of Frederick Deane Burdett, of Philippine Islands (bro of Sir Henry Burdett KCB, KCVO, fndr of Nat Pension Fund for Nurses), and Janet Grant, *née* Chavasse (d 1959) (great niece of the writer George Eliot (Mary Ann Evans)); *b* 24 March 1920; *Educ* Christ's Hosp Horsham, Peterhouse Cambridge (BA, MA); *m* 17 May 1941, Rachel Mary (d 1994), da of Capt William Dobson Womersley, of Westwick, Cambs; 1 s (Francis b 1952), 2 da (Christina b 1955, Jane b 1956); *Career* Capt RA 1940–45, served in N Africa and W Euro (despatches); dir of Richard Haworth & Co Ltd 1951–53, md of Cluett Peabody and Co (UK) Ltd 1959–65 (dir of Euro servs 1954–59 and 1965–85), chm Abbeyfield Cambs Soc 1961, vice pres Abbeyfield (Nat) Soc 1985–91 (chm 1977–85, dir 1972); dep chm The Housing Corporation 1983–86 (bd memb 1980), jt chm Abbeyfield International 1988–96; chm: First Stansted Assured Properties plc, Stansted Airport Homes plc; *Recreations* painting, reading, travelling, voluntary housing; *Clubs* Savile, Pitt; *Style—* Noel H Burdett, Esq, OBE; ✉ Westwick Hall, Oakington, Cambridgeshire CB4 5AR (☎ 01223 232477, office ☎ and fax 01223 232240)

BURDETT, Robert Pierpoint; s of Scott Langshaw Burdett, CBE, MC (d 1961), and Frances Eileen Davis, *née* Workman (d 1976); *b* 23 May 1935; *Educ* Marlborough; *m* 11 April 1959, Robina Clare Lindsay, da of Rear Adm Ralph Lindsay Fisher, CB, DSO, OBE, DSC (d 1988); 2 s (John b 1962, James b 1967), 2 da (Clare b 1961, Helen b 1965); *Career* RN 1953–72, ret as Lt Cdr; admitted slr 1975; in private practice 1975–80, ptnr Dyer Burdett & Co 1980–; *Recreations* sailing; *Clubs* Royal Cruising, RN Sailing Assoc; *Style—* Robert P Burdett, Esq; ✉ 64 West St, Havant, Hants PO9 1PA (☎ 01705 492472, fax 01705 492462)

BURDETT, Sir Savile Aylmer; 11 Bt (E 1665), of Burthwaite, Yorkshire; s of Sir Henry Aylmer Burdett, 10 Bt, MC (d 1943); *b* 24 Sept 1931; *Educ* Wellington, Imperial Coll London; *m* 1962, June Elizabeth Campbell, o da of late Dr James Mackay Rutherford, of Knowl Hill, Woking, Surrey; 1 s, 1 da (Felicity Susan b 1963); *Heir* s, Crispin Peter Burdett b 8 Feb 1967; *Career* late temporary Sub-Lt RNVR; md Rapaway Energy Ltd 1977–; *Style—* Sir Savile Burdett, Bt; ✉ Farthings, 35 Park Ave, Solihull, W Midlands B91 3EJ (☎ 0121 711 1454)

BURDETT-COUTTS, William Walter; s of William Ashmead Francis Burdett-Coutts, and Nancy Chevalier, *née* Gervers; *b* 17 Feb 1955; *Educ* St Felix Sch Felixstowe, Radley Coll Oxford, Rhodes Univ S Africa, Univ of Essex; *Career* asst mangr Cockpit Theatre 1978–80, touring stage mangr 1980, artistic dir Assembly Rooms for Edinburgh Festival 1981–, festival dir Mayfest Glasgow 1987–90, head of arts Granada Television 1990–93, dir Riverside Studios 1993–; exec prodr Assembly Film and Television; chm Kiss 102 1993–; *Style—* William Burdett-Coutts, Esq; ✉ Riverside Studios Ltd, Crisp Road, Hammersmith, London W6 9RL (☎ 0181 741 2251, fax 0181 563 0336)

BURDON, (Gerald) Desmond Patrick; s of Dr Joseph Burdon (d 1987), and Kathrine, *née* O'Reilly (d 1986); *b* 12 June 1956; *Educ* Notre Dame Int Sch Rome, Poly of NE London; *Career* formerly photographers' asst, advtg photographer in own studio 1984–; numerous int clients; memb Assoc of Photographers (former chm Awards Ctee and vice chm Cncl); *Awards* Ilford Advtg Photographer of the Yr, Kodak Calender Award; *Style—* Desmond Burdon, Esq; ✉ Studio 4, 38 St Oswalds Place, Vauxhall, London SE11 5JE (☎ 0171 582 0559, fax 0171 582 4528, mobile 0836 575051, e-mail dburdon@dircon.co.uk)

BURDON, Prof Roy Hunter; s of Ian Murray Burdon (d 1956), and Rose Carnegie Burdon (d 1962); *b* 27 April 1938; *Educ* Glasgow Acad, Univ of St Andrews (BSc), Univ of Glasgow (PhD); *m* 4 Sept 1962, Margery Grace; 2 s (Ian J, Keith A); *Career* Univ of Glasgow: asst lectr 1959–63, lectr 1964–68, sr lectr 1968–74, reader in biochemistry 1974–77, titular prof in biochemistry 1977–89; post doctorate and res fell Univ of NY 1963–64, guest prof of microbiology Polytechnical Univ of Denmark Copenhagen 1977–78, prof of molecular biology Univ of Strathclyde 1985– (chm Dept of Bioscience and Biotechnology 1986–88); chm Br Coordinating Ctee Biotechnol 1991–93; The Biochemical Soc: hon meetings sec 1981–85, hon gen sec 1985–89, chm 1989–92; chm Scientific Advsy Ctee Euro Fedn of Biotechnology 1991; govr W of Scotland Coll of Agric; FIBiol 1987, FRSE 1975; *Books* RNA Biosynthesis (1976), Molecular Biology of DNA Methylation (1985), Free Radical Damage and its Control (1994); *Recreations* painting, golf, clarinet/saxophone playing; *Style—* Prof Roy Burdon, FRSE; ✉ 144 Mugdock Rd, Milngavie, Glasgow G62 8NP (☎ 0141 956 1689); Department of Bioscience & Biotechnology, Todd Centre, University of Strathclyde, Glasgow G4 0HR (☎ 0141 552 4400 ext 3536)

BURDON-COOPER, Alan Ruthven; s of Sqdn-Ldr Ruthven Hayne Burdon-Cooper (d 1970), of Radlett, and Anna (Nan) Kathleen Beverley, *née* Farquharson (d 1992); *b* 27 June 1942; *Educ* Oundle, Emmanuel Coll Cambridge (MA, LLB); *m* 2 Sept 1967, Virginia Louise, da of Archibald George Mobsby (d 1989), of Radlett; 1 s (John Ruthven b 1968, d 1993), 1 da (Sarah b 1970); *Career* admitted slr 1968; ptnr Collyer-Bristow (sr ptnr 1985–94); life memb Cambridge Union, govr Rose Bruford Coll 1992–; Liveryman Worshipful Co of Dyers; memb Law Soc 1968; *Recreations* sport, music, gardening, philately; *Style—* Alan Burdon-Cooper, Esq; ✉ Nettleden Farm, Nettleden, Hemel Hempstead, Herts HP1 3DQ (☎ 01442 872072); Collyer-Bristow Solicitors, 4 Bedford Row, London WC1R 4DF (☎ 0171 242 7363, fax 0171 405 0555, telex 21615)

BURDUS, (Julia) Ann; da of Gladstone Beaty (d 1966), of Alnwick, Northumberland, and Julia Wilhamena Charlton, *née* Booth (d 1988); *b* 4 Sept 1933; *Educ* Univ of Durham (BA); *m* 1, 1956 (m dis 1961), William Ramsay Burdus; m 2, 11 June 1981, Ian Buchanan Robertson; *Career* clinical psychologist 1956–60, res exec Mather & Crowther 1961–67, res dir Garland Compton (later Compton Partners) 1967–71, res dir McCann Erickson 1971–75, vice chm McCann UK 1975–77, sr vice pres McCann International 1977–79, chm McCann & Co 1979–81, dir strategic planning Interpublic Group of Cos 1981–83, dir AGB Research plc 1983–89, sr vice pres mktg and communications Olympia & York Canary Wharf Ltd 1989–92, chm The Marketing Triangle Group Ltd 1992–; pt/t dir: Civil Aviation Authy, Dawson International plc, Argyll Group plc 1993–95; dir: Next Plc 1993–, BEM Ltd 1992–95; chm Advertising Assoc 1980–81; memb: NEDC 1984–88, Top Salaries Review Bd 1990–94, Ctee Automobile Association 1995–, Cncl IOD 1995–; *Recreations* home building; *Style—* Miss Ann Burdus; ✉ c/o Next Retail Ltd, Desford Road, Enderby, Leicester, Leics LE9 5AT

BURFORD, Earl of; Charles Francis Topham de Vere Beauclerk; s and h of 14 Duke of St Albans, *qv*; *b* 22 Feb 1965; *Educ* Sherborne, Hertford Coll Oxford; *m* 29 Dec 1994, Louise Ann Beatrice Fiona, eldest da of Col Malcolm Vernon Robey; 1 s (James Malcolm Aubrey Edward de Vere, Lord Vere of Hanworth b 2 Aug 1995); *Career* apptd Brig-Gen of Louisiana by Governor Edwin Edwards 1986; chm and fndr De Vere Soc, tstee Shakespearian Authorship Tst, apptd a vice-chm The Royal Stuart Soc 1989; pres Shakespeare Oxford Soc 1995; Liveryman Worshipful Co of Drapers 1990; *Clubs* Brooks's; *Style—* Earl of Burford; ✉ c/o Viscount Exmouth, Ashwell House, Ugbrooke, nr Chudleigh, Devon TQ13 0AD

BURFORD, His Hon Judge; Jeremy Michael Joseph; QC (1987); s of Major Alexander Joseph Burford, and Constance Grace Arlene, *née* Blakeley; *b* 3 June 1942; *Educ* Rondebosch Boys' HS S Africa, Diocesan Coll S Africa, Univ of Cape Town (BA), Emmanuel Coll Cambridge (MA, LLB, pres of Cambridge Union 1965), Harvard Law Sch (LLM, Kennedy Scholar 1966–67); *Career* called to the Bar Inner Temple 1968, recorder 1991–93, circuit judge (Western Circuit) 1993–; *Style—* His Honour Judge Burford, QC; ✉ Combined Court Centre, London Road, Southampton, Hants

BURFORD, Dr Robert John; s of Robert John Burford, of Welham Green, Herts, and Grace Violet, *née* Piacentini; *b* 29 Jan 1941; *Educ* East Barnet GS, King's Coll London (BSc, PhD); *m* 2 March 1968, (Stephanie) Kaye, da of Ernest James Woodley, of Rugby, Warwicks; 2 s (David b 1970, Paul b 1972), 1 da (Tracey b 1969); *Career* OR analyst NCB 1965–66, conslt GPS Sciences Ltd 1966–71, divnl dir Software Sciences Ltd 1980–82 (princ conslt 1971–80), dir ASYST Systems Consultants Ltd 1982–83, sr mangr Perkin-Elmer Data Systems 1983–85, tech dir Data Logic Ltd 1985–; MBCS 1974, MORS 1968, CEng 1991; *Recreations* American square dancing, travelling; *Style—* Dr Robert J Burford; ✉ 8 Winding Wood Drive, Camberley, Surrey GU15 1ER (☎ 01276 28397); Data Logic Ltd, Cl Tower, High Street, New Malden, Surrey KT3 4HH (☎ 0181 715 9696, fax 0181 715 1771)

BURG, Gisela Elisabeth; Hon CBE (1987); da of Oberstudiendirektor Friedrich Schlüsselburg, of Langen, Germany, and Gerda Schlusselburg; *b* 12 Oct 1939; *Educ* Gymnasium Philippinum Weilburg Germany, Ladies' Coll Wetzlar Germany; *Career* fndr and md Expotus Ltd; chm Fedn of Br Audio 1976–78 (vice-pres 1978–82); memb: NEDO Electronic SWP 1979–82, Br Overseas Trade Bd 1982–87; chm Advsy Ctee on Telecommunications for Small Businesses OFTEL (BACT) 1994–96; non-exec dir The Royal Mint 1993; named Times/Clicquot Businesswoman of the Year 1981; CIEx 1993; *Recreations* golf, horseracing; *Style*— Ms Gisela Burg, CBE; ✉ 82 Kensington Heights, Campden Hill Rd, London W8 7BD; Expotus Ltd, 95 Gray's Inn Rd, London WC1 8TX (☎ 0171 405 9665)

BURGE, Prof Ronald Edgar; s of John Henry Burge, and Edith Beatrice, *née* Thompson; *b* 3 Oct 1932; *Educ* Canton HS Cardiff, King's Coll London (BSc, PhD, FKC), Univ of London (DSc); *m* 1953, Janet Mary, *née* Pitts; 2 s; *Career* King's Coll London: asst lectr in physics 1954–58, lectr in physics 1958–62, reader in biophysics 1962–63, prof of physics and head Dept of Physics 1984–92 (prof of physics and head Dept of Physics Queen Elizabeth Coll 1963–84), dean Faculty of Mathematics and Physical Sci 1985–87, Wheatstone prof of physics 1989–; dir of research in x-ray imaging (Leverhulme Tst grant) Univ of Cambridge 1994–98; life memb Clare Hall Cambridge 1993 (visiting fell 1992); memb: Bd of Mgmnt Univ of London Computer Centre 1968–74, Planning Sub-Ctee and Univ Central Coordinating (Computing) 1968–90, Starlink Ctee SERC 1978–82, Computer Bd for Univs and Res Cncls (invited by Min of State for Educn and Sci) 1978–82, Swinnerton-Dyer Ctee 1979–82, Synchrotron Radiation Ctee SERC 1982–86, Computer Policy Ctee Univ of London (chm Networking Sub-Ctee) 1987–90, Cncl King's Coll (vice princ 1987–91), King's Coll Fin and Gen Purposes Ctee 1987–91; chm: Coll Computing Ctee 1968–93, Computer Users Ctee Univ of London 1968–73, Computer Planning Sub-Ctee Univ of London 1974–78; chm Bd of Examiners for DSc in Physics Univ of London 1990–; author of papers in sci jls on theory of scattering (electrons, x-rays and radar) and devpt in electron microscopy and x-ray microscopy Rodman Medal RPS 1993, Daiwa Award for X-Ray Lasers 1994; CPhys, FInstP, fell Microscopical Soc, memb Br Biophysics Soc (successively meeting sec, sec, chm), MRI 1988; *Style*— Prof Ronald Burge; ✉ 5 Toft Lane, Great Wilbraham, Cambridge CB1 5JH (☎ 01223 881378)

BURGE, Dr (Peter) Sherwood; s of Graham Mowbray Burge (d 1974), of Shiplake, Oxon, and Anne Elizabeth, *née* Batt; *b* 8 July 1944; *Educ* Lancing, Royal Free Hosp Sch of Med, London Sch of Hygiene & Tropical Med (MB BS, MSc, MD); *m* 18 Aug 1968, Dr Anne Willard, da of Canon James Stanley Willard (d 1988), of Holland-on-Sea, Essex; 2 s (Cedd b 1974, Chad b 1977); *Career* lectr in Dept of Clinical Immunology Cardiothoracic Inst London 1976–80, conslt physician Solihull Hosp 1980–93, conslt chest physician Birmingham Heartlands Hosp 1980–, dir Occupational Lung Disease Unit Birmingham 1980–; numerous sci pubns on: occupational lung diseases, indoor air quality and sick building syndrome, asthma and bronchitis; assembly chm and memb Cncl Euro Respiratory Soc, temporary advsr to WHO, NATO and EEC on indoor air quality and occupational lung disease; MRCS 1969, MFOM 1984, FRCP 1985, FFOM 1991; *Recreations* punt racing, skiing, brass rubbing, playing the recorder; *Style*— Dr Sherwood Burge; ✉ Birmingham Heartlands Hospital, Bordesley Green East, Birmingham B9 5ST (☎ 0121 766 6611, fax 0121 772 0292)

BURGE, Stuart; CBE (1974); s of Henry Ormsby Burge (d 1968), and Kathleen, *née* Haig; *b* 15 Jan 1918; *Educ* Felsted; *m* 22 Dec 1949, Josephine, da of Alan Parker (d 1965); 3 s (Stephen, Nicholas, Matthew), 2 da (Lucy, Emma); *Career* artistic dir: Nottingham Playhouse 1968–73, Royal Court 1978–81; assoc Stratford ONT 1964; recent screen work incl: Naming the Names, The Rainbow, Circles of Deceit, House of Bernarda Alba, After the Dance, Maigret, The Wexford Trilogy, The Writing Game; recent theatre incl: The Black Prince, Sunsets and Glories, The Provoked Wife (touring partnership), The Father; memb bd English Stage Co Royal Court; *Style*— Stuart Burge, Esq, CBE; ✉ Harriet Cruickshank, 97 Old South Lambeth Rd, London SW8 1XU (☎ 0181 735 2933)

BURGEN, Sir Arnold Stanley Vincent; kt (1976); s of late Peter Burgen, and Elizabeth, *née* Wolfers; *b* 20 March 1922; *Educ* Christ's Coll Finchley, Univ of London; *m* 1, 1946, Judith (d 1993), da of Frederick Browne; 2 s (Andrew, Stephen), 1 da (Jenny); *m* 2, 5 Dec 1993, Dr Olga Kennard, OBE, FRS, *qv*; *Career* med scientist, dir Nat Inst Med Res 1971–82, master Darwin Coll Cambridge 1982–89; pres Academia Europaea 1988–94; FRS; *Recreations* sculpture, music; *Style*— Sir Arnold Burgen, FRS; ✉ 8A Hills Avenue, Cambridge CB1 4XA (☎ 01223 415381)

BURGESS, Anthony Jack; s of late Edgar Jack Burgess, and late Emma Marie, *née* Shafe; *b* 27 June 1925; *Educ* Lewes Co GS, Hertford Coll Oxford (MA); *m* 24 Sept 1949, Barbara Evelyn, da of late Bertram Tofts; 3 s (Quentin b 1950, Rupert b 1958, Jeremy b 1963), 2 da (Charlotte b 1954, Emma b 1961); *Career* Capt RA 1943–48; Notary Public and sr ptnr Cheeswright Murly & Co 1958, memb Baltic Exchange 1987, cncllr Colchester Borough Cncl 1962–65; awarded Gold Greek Naval Medal 1st Class (for servs to the Hellenic Merchant Marine) 1992; Freeman Worshipful Co of Scriveners 1958 (Master 1969–70); *Publications* The Notary in Opera (1994); *Recreations* reading, history, music, theatre (Shakespeare), wine, golf; *Style*— Anthony Burgess, Esq; ✉ 33 Riverside Court, Nine Elms Lane, London SW8; Henpools House, Lower Littleworth, Stroud, Gloucestershire; Cheeswrights, 10 Philpot Lane, London EC3M 8AA (☎ 0171 623 9477, fax 0171 623 5428, car tel 0860 330481, telex 883 806)

BURGESS, (Dilys) Averil; OBE (1994); da of David Evans, of Berthlwyd, Nantmor, Nantgwynant, Gwynedd, and Dorothy, *née* Owen; *b* 8 July 1938; *Educ* Ashby de la Zouch Girls' GS Leics, Queen Mary Coll London (BA); *m* 5 Dec 1959 (m dis 1973), Clifford Charles Antony Burgess, s of Sidney Burgess, of Boreham Wood, Herts; *Career* Fulham Co Sch 1965–69, head of history and second mistress Wimbledon HS GPDST 1969–74, headmistress South Hampstead HS GPDST 1975–93; pres GS Assoc 1988–89; memb: Cncl For Accreditation of Teacher Educn 1991–93, Nat Cmmn on Educn 1991–93; chm: Ind Schs Jt Cncl Policy Gp, Camden and Islington Family Health Servs Authy 1992–96, Ind Schs' Jt Cncl Accreditation, Review and Consultancy Serv 1993–; tstee GHN Fndn 1992–; govr: Central Sch of Speech and Drama until 1995, The Museum of London 1994–; non-exec memb Camden and Islington HA 1996–98; FRSA 1992; *Recreations* reading, music, meals, mountain walking, cross-country skiing; *Style*— Mrs Averil Burgess, OBE; ✉ 123 North Hill, Highgate, London N6 4DP (☎ and fax 0181 348 7646)

BURGESS, David Charles William; s of Leonard Cecil Burgess (d 1970), and Comfort, *née* Horler; *b* 25 Sept 1947; *Educ* Ermysted GS Skipton Yorks, St Catharine's Coll Cambridge (MA); *m* 4 July 1987, Youdon, *née* Lhamo; 1 s (Tenzin b 21 May 1981), 2 da (Dechen b 21 June 1978, Kusang b 7 Aug 1985); *Career* admitted slr 1972, ptnr Winstanley-Burgess 1975; *Style*— David Burgess; ✉ Winstanley-Burgess, 378 City Rd, London EC1V 2QA (☎ 0171 278 7911, fax 0171 833 2135)

BURGESS, Rev David John; s of Albert Burgess, of the Pinfold, Ailsworth, Cambs, and Mary, *née* Kelsey; *b* 4 Aug 1939; *Educ* The King's Sch Peterborough, Trinity Hall Cambridge (MA), Cuddesdon Theol Coll Oxford, Halki Studentship Istanbul; *m* 17 Feb 1976, Katherine Lousie, da of Lindsay Costeloe (d 1978); 1 s ((Patrick) Rollo Lindsay b 25 May 1978), 1 da (Frances Mary b 26 July 1981); *Career* curate All Saints Maidstone 1965–66; Univ Coll Oxford: asst chaplain 1966, chaplain and fell 1969, domestic bursar 1971; canon Windsor 1978–87, treas Coll of St George, guild vicar St Lawrence Jewry Next Guildhall 1987; Chaplain to HM the Queen 1987; Freeman: City of London, Worshipful Co of Haberdashers; hon chaplain and memb Ct of Assts: Worshipful Co of Loriners, Worshipful Co of Distillers, Worshipful Co of Chartered Surveyors, Worshipful Co of Actuaries; hon fell Inst of Clerks of Works; *Books* Signs of Faith, Hope and Love (contrib, 1988); *Recreations* The Aula, Omar Khayyam; *Style*— The Rev David Burgess; ✉ The Vicarage, St Lawrence Jewry Next Guildhall, London EC2V 5AA (☎ 0171 600 9478)

BURGESS, Gen Sir Edward Arthur; KCB (1982), OBE (1972); s of Edward Burgess, and Alice Burgess; *b* 30 Sept 1927; *Educ* All Saints Sch Bloxham, Lincoln Coll Oxford, RMA Sandhurst; *m* 1954, Jean Angelique Leslie Henderson; 1 s (John), 1 da (Fiona); *Career* cmmnd RA 1948, served BAOR, Far East and M East, GSO 1 Staff Coll 1968–70, CO 25 Light Regt RA 1970–72, Cdr RA 4 Div 1972–74; dir: Army Recruiting 1975–77, Combat Devpt 1977–79; GOC Artillery Div 1979–82, Cdr UK FD Army and Inspr Gen TA 1982–84, Col Cmdt RA 1982–92, Dep Supreme Allied Cdr Europe 1984–87; ADC Gen 1985–87; Gentleman Usher to the Sword of State 1988–; Hon Col: 6/7/Vol Bn The Queen's Regt 1991–92, 6/7 Bn The Princess of Wales's Royal Regt 1993–; pres: Army Football Assoc 1982–88, Royal Br Legion 1987–93; dep grand pres Br Cwlth Ex-Servs League 1996–; hon life memb Returned and Services League of Aust 1991; Freeman City of London, Liveryman Worshipful Co of Glaziers, Hon Liveryman Worshipful Co of Haberdashers; *Recreations* fishing, music, wines; *Clubs* Army & Navy; *Style*— Gen Sir Edward Burgess, KCB, OBE; ✉ c/o Lloyds Bank, Haslemere, Surrey

BURGESS, Rear Adm John; CB (1987), LVO (1975); s of Albert Burgess (d 1957), of Styvechale, Coventry, and Winifred, *née* Evans; *b* 13 July 1929; *Educ* RNEC, RNC Greenwich (advanced engrg); *m* 21 June 1952, Avis, da of William Johnson-Morgan (d 1953), of Coventry; 2 da (Sara b 14 Jan 1958, Jenny (Mrs Andersson) b 6 Aug 1960; *Career* RN Serv 1945–; HMS: Aisne, Maidstone, Theseus, Implacable, Cumberland, Caprice; cmmnd 1952, lectr in Thermodynamics RNEC 1962–65, HMS Victorious, appt Cdr 1968, nuclear design and manufacture Rolls Royce 1968–70, naval staff Washington DC 1970–72, Royal Yacht Britannia 1972–75, head Forward Design Gp Ship Dept 1975–77, appt Capt 1976, naval asst to Controller Navy 1977–79, OC HMS Defiance 1979–81, OC HMS Sultan 1981–83, appt Adm 1983, md HM Docky Rosyth 1984–87; dir: Rolls Royce 1987– (special projects, business devpt), Rolls Royce Nuclear Ltd, Rolls Royce and Associates Ltd; contrib various papers for professional socs and periodicals; chm local cncl; memb: naval charities, local church socs, conservation socs; Hon Freeman New Orleans 1974; CEng, FIMechE, FIMarE; *Recreations* sailing, golf, music, theatre; *Style*— Rear Adm John Burgess, CB, LVO; ✉ Rolls Royce and Associates Ltd, Raynesway, Derby (☎ 01332 661461)

BURGESS, Keith; s of W H (Bert) Burgess, of Bargoed, Rhymney Valley; *b* 1 Sept 1946; *Educ* Lewis Sch for Boys Pengam, Univ of Bristol (BSc, PhD); *m* Dr Pat Burgess; 2 da (b 1972 and 1976); *Career* Andersen Consulting (formerly Arthur Andersen Mgmnt Conslts): joined 1971, managing ptnr UK and Ireland 1989–94, worldwide managing ptnr Business Integration and Competency Practices 1994–, memb Worldwide Mgmnt Ctees; pres Mgmnt Consultancies Assoc 1994; Liveryman Worshipful Co of Info Technologists, memb Ct of Assts Guild of Mgmnt Consultants; chm Corporate Action for the Homeless; patron Univ of Bristol Campaign for Resources; FIMC; *Clubs* Reform; *Style*— Keith Burgess, Esq; ✉ Andersen Consulting, 2 Arundel Street, London WC2R 3DA (☎ 0171 438 5000, fax 0171 831 1133)

BURGESS, Michael John Clement; s of David Clement Burgess (d 1966), and Dr Ethne Nannette Moira Barnwall, *née* Ryan, of Kingston upon Thames; *b* 31 March 1946; *Educ* Beaumont Coll Old Windsor Berks, King's Coll London; *m* 31 July 1971, Catherine Vivian, da of Vivian John Du Veluz Gout, of Mulhausen, W Germany; 1 s (Peter b 1980), 2 da (Alexandra b 1974, Nicola b 1976); *Career* admitted slr 1970, conslt McNamara Ryan Weybridge 1986– (ptnr 1972–86), coroner Surrey 1986– (asst dep coroner 1979–86), dep coroner to the Royal Household 1991–; sec Coroners Soc of England and Wales 1993– (asst sec 1991–93), pres SE England Coroners Soc 1990–91; pres West Surrey Law Soc 1985–86 (hon treas 1979–84), memb Catholic Union 1974–, chm Fin Ctee and memb Parish Cncl St Francis de Sales RC Church Hampton, helper (formerly gp ldr and regnl chm) Handicapped Children's Pilgrimage Tst, advsr to several local charities and trusts; Freeman: City of London, Worshipful Co of Feltmakers 1967; memb: Law Soc 1970, Coroner's Soc; *Recreations* reading, art, music, gardening; *Clubs* Surrey Law; *Style*— Michael Burgess, Esq; ✉ c/o McNamara Ryan, Ashburton House, 3 Monument Green, Weybridge, Surrey KT13 8QR (☎ 01932 846041, fax 01932 857709)

BURGESS, Prof Robert George; s of George Burgess, and Olive, *née* Andrews; *b* 23 April 1947; *Educ* Bede Coll Univ of Durham (CertEd), Univ of Durham (BA), Univ of Warwick (PhD); *m* 1974, Hilary, da of Rev H R Joyce; *Career* Univ of Warwick: lectr 1974–84, sr lectr 1984–88, Dept chair 1985–88, dir Centre for Educnl Devpt Appraisal and Research (CEDAR) 1987–, prof of sociology 1988–, chm Faculty of Social Scis 1988–91, fndr chm Grad Sch 1991–95, pro-vice-chllr 1995–; ESRC: memb Research Resources Bd 1991–96, vice-chm Postgrad Trg Bd 1996– (memb 1989–93), memb Cncl 1996–; fndr chm UK Cncl for Grad Educn 1993–; pres: Br Sociological Assoc 1989–91, Assoc for the Teaching of the Soc Scis 1991–; memb HEFCE review of postgrad educn 1995–96, memb CVCP review of clinical academic careers 1996–; memb BERA; *Books* Experiencing Comprehensive Education (1983), In the Field (1984), Education, Schools and Schooling (1985), Sociology, Education and Schools (1986), Implementing In-Service Education (jtly, 1993), Research Methods (1993); also ed of 20 books on methodology and education; *Recreations* walking, listening to music and some gardening; *Style*— Prof Robert Burgess; ✉ CEDAR/Department of Sociology, University of Warwick, Coventry CV4 7AL (☎ 01203 523806, fax 01203 524472, e-mail ceral@snow.csv.warwick.ac.uk)

BURGESS, Robert Lawie Frederick (Robin); s of Sir John Burgess (d 1987), of Carlisle, and Lady Burgess, *née* Gilleron; *b* 31 Jan 1951; *Educ* Trinity Coll Glenalmond; *m* 20 Sept 1986, Alexandra Rosemary, da of W A Twiston-Davies, of Herefordshire; 1 s (James b 15 July 1994), 3 da (Rose, Catherine, Rachel); *Career* 2 Lt The King's Own Royal Border Regt 1969–72; md C N Group Ltd (formerly Cumbrian Newspapers Group Ltd) 1985–; dir: Cumberland and Westmorland Herald Printing Co Ltd 1985–, Border TV plc 1987–; *Clubs* Garrick, Army and Navy; *Style*— R L F Burgess, Esq; ✉ C N Group Ltd, Dalston Rd, Carlisle, Cumbria CA2 5UA

BURGESS, Sir (Joseph) Stuart; kt (1994), CBE (1984); *b* 20 March 1929; *Educ* Barnsley Holgate GS Yorks, UCL (BSc, PhD); *m* 1955, Valerie Ann, *née* Street; 1 da (Jacqueline Ann b 23 March 1959), 1 s (Timothy Stuart b 6 Oct 1961); *Career* devpt chemist The Radiochemical Centre Ltd 1953–61, planning mangr UKAEA Risley 1961–62; Amersham International plc: mkt res supr 1962–66, asst mktg mangr 1966–69, mktg controller 1972–75, pres Amersham Corp USA 1975–77, gp mktg controller 1977–79, chief exec 1979–89; conslt Immuno International AG Vienna 1990–96, chm Immuno UK Ltd 1993–96, chm Finsbury Worldwide Pharmaceutical Trust PLC 1995–; non-exec dir: Haemonetics Corp USA 1992–, Anagen plc UK 1993–; chm: Oxford RHA 1990–94, Anglia & Oxford RHA 1994–; fell UCL 1994; FRSC 1960, CIMgt 1986; *Recreations* golf, theatre, music, travel; *Clubs* RSM; *Style*— Sir Stuart Burgess, CBE; ✉ Flint Barn, Flint Barn Court, Church Street, Amersham, Bucks HP7 0DB (☎ 01494 431579, fax 01494 721896)

BURGH, 7 Baron (E 1529); Alexander Peter Willoughby Leith; s of 6 Baron (d 1959); *b* 20 March 1935; *Educ* Harrow, Magdalene Coll Cambridge; *m* 29 Aug 1957 (m dis 1982), Anita Lorna, da of Frederick Charles Eldridge (d 1973), of Gillingham, Kent;

2 s (Hon (Alexander) Gregory Disney b 16 March 1958, Hon Patrick Simon Vincent b 26 April 1964), 1 da (Hon Rebecca Moraigh Eveleigh b 17 Dec 1959); *Heir* s, Hon Gregory Leith, *qv*; *Career* formerly RAF Pilot Offr; *Style*— The Rt Hon The Lord Burgh; ✉ c/o House of Lords, London SW1

BURGH, Anita, Lady; Anita Lorna Leith; da of Frederick Clements Eldridge (d 1973), and Alice Milner (d 1989); *b* 9 June 1937; *Educ* Chatham GS; *m* 29 Aug 1957 (m dis 1982), 7 Baron Burgh, *qv*; 2 s, 1 da; *partner* William Westall Jackson; 1 da (Kate Rosalind Scarlett b 25 March 1971); *Career* novelist 1987–; memb: Romantic Novelists' Assoc 1987, Soc of Authors 1990; *Novels* as Anita Burgh: Distinctions of Class (1987), Love the Bright Foreigner (1988), The Azure Bowl (1989), The Golden Butterfly (1990), The Stone Mistress (1991), Advances (1992), Overtures (1993), Avarice (1994), Lottery (1995), Breeders (1996): as Annie Leith: Tales From Sarson Magna: Molly's Flashings (1991), Hector's Hobbies (1994); *Recreations* bulldogs and gossip; *Style*— Anita Burgh; ✉ c/o The Mic Cheetham Agency, 138 Buckingham Palace Road, London SW1W 9SA (☎ 0171 730 3027, fax 0171 730 0037)

BURGH, Sir John Charles; KCMG (1981), CB (1975); *b* 9 Dec 1925; *Educ* Friends' Sch Sibford, LSE; *m* 1957, Ann Sturge; 2 da; *Career* under sec Employment Dept 1968–71 (formerly with BOT, Colonial Office, DEA), dep chm Community Rels Cmmn 1971–72; dep sec: CPRS 1972–74, Prices and Consumer Protection 1974–79, Dept of Trade 1979–80; dir gen Br Cncl 1980–87, pres Trinity Coll Oxford 1987–96; chm: Associated Bd Royal Sch of Music 1987–94, Int Student House 1987–90; sec Opera Ctee Royal Opera House Covent Garden 1972–80, dir English Shakespeare Co 1989–94, chm Nat Opera Coordinating Ctee 1991– (sec 1972–91); exec memb Political and Econ Planning 1970–78; memb Cncl: Policy Studies Inst 1978–85, VSO 1980–87, RSA 1982–86, RIIA (Chatham House) 1993–95; hon fell LSE 1982 (govr 1980–, chm of govrs 1985–87); Hon LLD Bath; FRCM, Hon FRNCM; *Style*— Sir John Burgh, KCMG, CB; ✉ c/o Royal Over-Seas League, Park Place, London SW1A 1LR

BURGHES, Prof David Noel; s of Edmund Noel Burghes (d 1944), and Lilian Mary, *née* Luckhurst; *b* 21 March 1944; *Educ* Christ's Coll Finchley, Univ of Sheffield (BSc, PhD); *m* 21 Sept 1968, Jennifer Jean, da of Dr Donald Harry Smith (d 1971); 4 s (Andrew b 1970, Christopher b 1972, Jamie b 1974, Timothy b 1975); *Career* asst lectr Dept of Applied Mathematics Univ of Sheffield 1970–71 (jr res fell 1968–70), lectr Sch of Mathematics Univ of Newcastle 1972–75, dir Cranfield Centre for Teacher Servs Cranfield Inst of Technol 1980–81 (lectr 1975–79); Univ of Exeter: prof of educn 1981–, dir Centre for Innovation in Mathematics Teaching 1986–, dir Kassel Project (int comparative study in sch mathematics) 1994–, dir Mathematics Enhancement Project 1996–; author and co-author of over twenty books on mathematics and educn mathematics dir Spode Group 1980–; chm Indust and Educn Maths Ctee DTI 1985–88, founding ed jl Teaching Mathematics and its Applications 1985–; FIMA 1970; *Recreations* reading train timetables, travelling; *Style*— Prof David Burghes; ✉ Centre for Innovation in Mathematics Teaching, University of Exeter, Exeter, Devon EX1 2LU (☎ 01392 217113, 01392 264772)

BURGHLEY, Lord; Anthony John Cecil; s and h of 8 Marquess of Exeter; *b* 9 Aug 1970; *Educ* Eton, Oxford Univ; *Style*— Lord Burghley; ✉ 100 Mile House, PO Box 8, Br Columbia V0K 2E0, Canada (☎ 001 604 395 2767)

BURGIN, Adrian Gwyn John; s of Arthur Carver Burgin (d 1985), of Lincs, and Anne Mary, *née* Hassall; *b* 23 Sept 1950; *Educ* St James Sch Peterborough; *m* 8 Sept 1973, Susan Georgina, da of George Falconer McLean (d 1980), of Lincs; 2 s (John b 1979, Thomas b 1982), 1 da (Holly b 1981); *Career* CA; sr ptnr Burgin Kingston (formerly Burgin & Co); treas Stamford Festival Association Ltd 1983; FICA; *Recreations* mountaineering, cricket, literature; *Clubs* Daniel Lamberts, Lyke Wake, Motley Crew Cricket; *Style*— Adrian Burgin, Esq; ✉ The Warden's House, 4 Broad St, Stamford, Lincs (☎ 01780 51315, fax 01780 53352)

BURGIN, Patrick Leslie; s of The Rt Hon Edward Leslie Burgin, MP, the first Min of Supply (d 1945), of South Beds, and Dorothy Theresa, *née* Cooper (d 1975); *b* 28 Nov 1919; *Educ* St George's Sch Harpenden, Le Rosey Rolle Gstaad Switzerland, Gonville & Caius Coll Cambridge; *m* 27 April 1950, Elizabeth Lavender, da of Benjamin John Uren (d 1972), of St Ives, Cornwall; 1 s (Mark b 1954), 2 da (Caroline b 1952, Rosemary b 1957); *Career* WWII joined The Beds & Herts 1940, 2 Lt Northamptonshire Regt 1941, Capt Instructor Intelligence Sch Karachi India 1941–42, GIII(I) Lucknow Dist HQ 1943, Maj Security Intelligence Planning Sect GIII(I) Army HQ New Delhi 1943, Burma E Gp 1944–45 (despatches), repatriated UK, GII(I) Scottish Cmd HQ Edinburgh until June 1946; admitted slr 1948; Denton Hall & Burgin (later Denton Hall Burgin & Warrens, now Denton Hall): ptnr 1948–94, sr ptnr 1978–88, conslt 1994–; chm: Rentokil Gp plc 1969–81 (dir 1953–85), Dentsply Ltd (formerly Amalgamated Dental Co) 1970–85, Val de Travers Asphalte Ltd (alternate dir Iraq, Basrah, Mosul & Qatar Petrol Cos) 1952–; former dir (resigned) Total Oil Holdings Ltd (chm until 1991); dir: Associated British Picture Corp 1964–72, Total Oil Marine plc, Total Oil Great Britain Ltd 1994–; conslt; chm Govrs St George's Sch Harpenden; memb Herts CC 1966–76; Liveryman Worshipful Co of Gold & Silver Wyre Drawers; memb Law Soc 1948; Order of Dannebrog Denmark 1967, Legion d'Honneur France 1988; *Recreations* hunting, gardening, skiing, reading; *Clubs* Oriental, RAC; *Style*— Patrick Burgin, Esq; ✉ 10 Park Ave South, Harpenden, Herts AL5 2EA (☎ 01582 712035); Denton Hall, 5 Chancery Lane, Clifford's Inn, London WC2A 1BU (☎ 0171 242 1212, fax 0171 404 0087, telex 263567

BURGIN, Peter Brinton; s of George Burgin, of Huddersfield; *b* 3 Aug 1934; *Educ* Holme Valley GS Holmfirth; *m* 1960, Jean, da of Donovan Hartshorne, of Tamerton Foliat; 1 s, 1 da; *Career* mktg dir: Crittall Windows 1974–78, Dow-Mac Concrete 1985–88; dir and sec Dow-Mac Concrete 1978–81, md Lion Foundry Co Ltd 1981–85; practice mangr Landscape Design Assocs 1988–; ACMA, MBCS, MCIM; *Recreations* golf, gardening; *Style*— Peter Burgin, Esq; ✉ 4 Briar Walk, Bourne, Lincs PE10 9TG (☎ 01778 425 361); Landscape Design Associates, 17 Minster Precincts, Peterborough PE1 1XX (☎ 01733 310471)

BURGIN, Victor; s of Samuel Burgin (d 1991), of Sheffield, Yorks, and Gwendolyn Ann, *née* Crowther (d 1973); *b* 24 July 1941; *Educ* Firth Park GS for Boys Sheffield, Sheffield Coll of Art (NDD), RCA (ARCA), Yale Univ (MFA); *m* 1, 1964 (m dis), Hazel Patricia, da of Louis Rowbotham; 2 s (Julian Alexander b 1967, Gaius Louis b 1970); m 2, 1988, Francette Marie-Anne, da of Guy Edouard Pacteau; *Career* lectr: Sch of Fine Art Trent Poly 1965–73, Sch of Communication Central London Poly 1973–88, Bd of Studies in Art History Univ of California at Santa Cruz 1988–95, Bd of Studies in History of Consciousness Univ of California at Santa Cruz 1995–; US/UK Bicentennial Arts Exchange fell NY 1976–77, Deutsche Akademische Austausdienst fell Berlin 1978–79; *Books* Work and Commentary (1973), Thinking Photography (1982), Between (1986), The End of Art Theory (1986), Passages (1991), In/Different Spaces (1996), Some Cities (1996); *Style*— Victor Burgin, Esq; ✉ 1223 Diamond St, San Francisco, CA 94131, USA (☎ 00 1 415 821 4384, fax 00 1 415 821 4277); Oakes College, University of California at Santa Cruz, Santa Cruz, CA 95064, USA (☎ 00 1 408 459 4565, fax 00 1 408 459 3535)

BURGNER, Thomas Ulric; s of John Henry Burgner (d 1974), of London, and Doerte, *née* Wolf; *b* 6 March 1932; *Educ* Haberdashers' Aske's, St Catharine's Coll Cambridge (BA, MA); *m* 5 June 1958, Marion; 2 s (David Paul b 1964, Steven Alexander b 1968); *Career* Flying Offr RAF 1953–55; Nat Coal Bd 1955–61, Assoc of Chemical and Allied Employers 1961–64, Dept of Econ Affrs 1965–69, head Gen Aid Div HM Treasy 1974–76 (head Exchange Control 1972–74), sec NEDC 1976–80, head Indust, Agric and Employment Gp 1984–89 (head Public Enterprises Gp 1980–84); sec Ctee of Vice Chllrs and Princs of Univs of UK (CVCP) 1989–95; tstee Anna Freud Centre 1993–, conslt LTW; FRSA 1990; *Style*— Thomas Burgner, Esq; ✉ 12 Kingsley Place, London N6 5EA (0181 340 9759)

BURGON, Geoffrey Alan; s of Alan Wybert Burgon (d 1983), and Ada Vera Isom; Huguenot descent; *b* 15 July 1941; *Educ* Pewley Sch Guildford, Guildhall Sch of Music and Drama; *m* 1, 1963 (m dis), Janice Elizabeth, da of Frank Garwood; 1 s (Matthew b 1967), 1 da (Hannah b 1965); m 2, Jacqueline Louise, da of David Krofchak; 1 s (Daniel Milo b 1994); *Career* composer and conductor; dramatic works include: Joan of Arc 1970, Orpheus 1982, Hard Times 1990; orchestral music includes: Concerto for String Orchestra 1963, Gending 1968, Trumpet Concerto 1993; orchestral music with voices includes Requiem 1976, The World Again 1983, Revelations 1984, Mass 1984, Title Divine 1986, A Vision 1990, City Adventures (world premiere BBC Proms) 1996; ballet music includes: The Golden Fish 1964, Running Figures 1975, Songs Lamentations and Praises 1979, The Trials of Prometheus 1988; choral music includes: Three Elegies 1964, Short Mass 1965, Two Hymns to Mary 1967, Mai Hamama 1970, A Prayer to the Trinity 1972, The Fire of Heaven 1973, Noche Oscura 1974, Dos Coros 1975, This World From 1974, Laudate Dominum 1980, But Have Been Found Again 1983, The Song of the Creatures 1987; chamber music includes: Gloria 1973, Six Studies 1980; chamber music with voices includes: Five Sonnets of John Donne 1967, Worldës Blissë 1971, Lunar Beauty 1986; film and tv scores include: The Changeling 1973, Dr Who and the Terror of the Zygons 1975, Monty Python's Life of Brian 1979, Tinker Tailor Soldier Spy 1979, The Dogs of War 1980, Brideshead Revisited 1981, Turtle Diary 1985, The Death of the Heart 1985, Bleak House 1986, The Chronicles of Narnia 1988, Children of the North 1990, Robin Hood 1991, The Agency 1991, Martin Chuzzlewit 1994; *Recreations* cricket, jazz, wasting money on Bristol cars; *Style*— Geoffrey Burgon, Esq; ✉ c/o Chester Music, 8–9 Frith St, London W1V 5TZ (☎ 0171 434 0066, fax 0171 287 6329)

BURGOYNE, Dr John Henry; CBE (1980); s of Sir John Burgoyne, OBE, JP (d 1969), of Luton, and Florence Emily Burgoyne, *née* Farrow (d 1964); *b* 4 Aug 1913; *Educ* Luton Modern GS, Univ of London (BSc, PhD, DSc); *m* 8 March 1944, Margaret Graves, da of Herbert Beeston Tupholme (d 1963), of Sheffield; 1 s (John b 1944); *Career* lectr in chem engrg Imperial Coll London 1946–64 (latterly sr lectr and reader), ind conslt 1964–68, sr ptnr Dr J H Burgoyne ptnrs 1968–78, conslt Burgoyne Gp 1978–; visiting prof and sr fell City Univ 1972–83, visiting prof Univ of Sheffield 1986–; chm Safety in Mines Res Advsy Bd Miny of Fuel & Power 1970–75, memb Advsy Ctee on Major Hazards Health and Safety Cmmn 1976–83, chm Inquiry into Offshore Safety Dept of Energy 1979–80, pres Assoc of Consulting Scientists 1987–96; Hon DEng Univ of Sheffield 1991; CChem 1948, FEng 1982, FCGI 1984, FRSA 1993; *Recreations* music, photography, travel; *Style*— Dr J H Burgoyne, CBE, FEng; ✉ The Lodge, 2 Silverdale Rd, Sheffield S11 9JL (☎ 0114 235 2600); The Burgoyne Group, 39A Bartholomew Close, London EC1A 7JN (☎ 0171 726 4951, fax 0171 726 8980, telex 884957 BGOYNE G)

BURKE, Adrian Richard; s of Patrick Ernest Burke, of Cheltenham, Glos, and Annie Evelyn, *née* Bryer; *b* 8 May 1961; *Educ* St Gregory's HS Kenton Middx, Pinner Sixth Form Coll Middx, Paddington Coll Paddington Green London (City & Guilds Photography), Salisbury Coll of Art Salisbury Wilts (Higher DATEC Dip in Professional Photography); *Career* photographer; trainee med photographer 1979–82, asst to Robert Golden 1985–86, freelance asst working for various photographers incl Iain McKell, John Brown and Michael Joseph Feb-July 1986, first asst to Andrew Whittuck 1986–88, asst to Jerry Oke Jan-Aug 1988, self-employed advtg photographer 1991–; clients incl: Boddington Beer, Dunhill, Sainsbury's, Ford, Whiskas, Volkeswagen, Halifax Building Society, Clerical Medical, Cow and Gate, Royal Bank of Scotland, British Telecom, British Airports Authority, Sanyo, RSPCA; *Group Exhibitions* Benson & Hedges Awards (Hamilton Gallery 1983, 1984 and 1985, ICA Gallery 1990), Direction magazine Still Life Award (Store Street Galleries 1991); *Awards* incl: Commercial AFAEP Professional Awards 1986, commended Benson & Hedges Awards 1988 (student prize 1983 and 1984), second prize Professional Category Benson & Hedges Awards 1990, nominated Best Young Still Life Photographer Direction magazine 1991, two Commercial Assoc of Photographers Awards 1993; *Style*— Adrian Burke, Esq; ✉ 10–13 Newbury Street, London EC1A 7HU (☎ 0171 600 9119, fax 0171 600 2727)

BURKE, David Christopher; s of William Burke (d 1987), and Norah, *née* Barry; *b* 14 Sept 1962; *Educ* St Aidan's CBS Dublin, Cathal Brugha Street Coll of Catering Dublin (City and Guilds); *m* 25 June 1993, Susie, da of Roy Battam; *Career* chef de partie Ballymaloe House Shanagarry Co Cork, chef de partie Park Lane Hotel London, sous chef Bibendum Restaurant London 1989–91, chef dir/pt owner Le Pont de la Tour and Cantina del Ponte 1991–; contrib: cook books, magazines, newspapers; television and radio appearances incl Master Chef and The Bite Stuff; *Awards* Courvoisier Book of the Best Restaurants 1994, London Docklands Restaurant of the Year 1995, Roy Ackerman Guide Clover Leaf 1995, Michelin Guide Red M 1996; *Books* Gastrodrome Cook Book (contrib, 1995); *Recreations* friends and family, gardening, reading, malt whisky, sport (skiing, horse riding, clay pigeon shooting, memb Chelsea Football Supporters Club); *Style*— David Burke, Esq; ✉ Le Pont de la Tour, 36D Shad Thames, Butlers Wharf, London SE1 2YE (☎ 0171 403 8403, fax 0171 403 0267)

BURKE, Chief Constable David Michael; QPM; s of Desmond Francis Burke (d 1963), of Selby, and Lois Mary, *née* Stephenson; *b* 18 Jan 1939; *Educ* Open Univ (BA), Yorks Coll of Agric (NCA); *m* 18 April 1960, Eleanor Elizabeth (Betty), da of George Leslie Lister (d 1979), of Pickering; 1 s ((John) Stephen b 1961); *Career* Nat Serv RAF 1958–60; constable rising to asst chief constable: N Riding constabulary, York and NE Yorks Police, N Yorks Police 1963–83; dep chief constable Warwickshire 1983–89, chief constable N Yorks 1989–; county pres BHS, vice pres and NE regnl chm RLSS; Queen's Silver Jubilee Medal 1977, Police Long Service Medal 1985, Pro Ecclesia Et Pontifice by The Pope 1983; SBStJ, memb Royal Acad of Arts 1995; *Recreations* riding, carriage driving, shooting, swimming; *Clubs* St John's; *Style*— Chief Constable David Burke, QPM; ✉ Police HQ, Newby Wiske Hall, Northallerton, N Yorks DL7 9HA (☎ 01609 783131)

BURKE, David Patrick; s of Patrick Burke (d 1965), and Mary, *née* Welsh (d 1980); *b* 25 May 1934; *Educ* St Francis Xavier's Coll Liverpool, Corpus Christi Coll Oxford, RADA; *m* 30 March 1971, Anna, da of Arthur Calder-Marshall; 1 s (Tom b 30 June 1981); *Career* actor; *Theatre* RSC 1986–87: Hector in Troilus and Cressida, Bessemenow in Philistines, Melons; NT 1988–91: William Goodchild in The Strangeness of Others, Zeal-of-the-Land Busy in Bartholomew Fair, Ghost and First Gravedigger in Hamlet, Mr Voysey in The Voysey Inheritance, Reverend John Hale in The Crucible, Watch on the Rhine; Birmingham Rep: Measure for Measure, The Devil is an Ass; Hampstead Theatre (and West End): Bodies, Rocket to the Moon; Othello (Young Vic), A Flea in her Ear (Thorndike), Slow Dance on the Killing Ground (Greenwich) 1991, Claudius and Ghost in Hamlet (Riverside Studios) 1992, The Colonel in States of Shock (Salisbury Playhouse) 1993, Simonides in Pericles (RNT) 1994, New England (RSC) 1994, The Woman In Black (Fortune) 1995; *Television* Granada: Dr Watson in The Mysteries of Sherlock Holmes, Ron Fisher in Casualty, James Maybrick in The James Maybrick Case, Crown Court, Holly and Inheritance; BBC: Sir John Crowborough in The House of Eliott, Sir Arthur Stanley in Hickory Dickory Dock, Oedipus in An A-Z of Greek Democracy, Kipling, Two Days in the Love of Michael Reagan, Barlowe at Large, Love School, Fair

Trading on the Dance Ground, Esther Waters, Pope Pius XII, The Murder Machine, The Comedians, A Winter's Tale, Nannie, Henry VI Parts 1 and 2, Richard III, Dreams, Secrets, Beautiful Lies, Run for the Life Boat, Taking Liberties; ATV: The Woodlanders, Hotel in Amsterdam, Hine and Crimes of Passion; Thames: Rooms, Hammer and Sickle, Quiet as a Nun; LWT: The Guardian, Villain; De Vauzesnes in Mesmer (film) 1993; *Recreations* tennis, swimming; *Style*— David Burke; ✉ c/o Jean Clark Management

BURKE, David Thomas (Tom); CBE (1997); s of Jeremiah Vincent Burke, DSM (d 1990), of Nazareth House, Plymouth, Devon, and Mary, *née* Bradley; *b* 5 Jan 1947; *Educ* St Boniface's Coll Plymouth, Univ of Liverpool (BA); *Career* lectr: Carlett Park Coll Cheshire 1970–71, Old Swan Tech Coll 1971–73; Friends of the Earth: local gps co-ordinator 1973–75, exec dir 1975–79, dir special projects 1979–80, vice chm 1980–81; dir The Green Alliance 1982–91 (memb Exec Ctee 1979–82), special advsr to Sec of State for the Environment 1991–; non-exec dir Earth Resources Res 1975–88; memb: Waste Mgmnt Advsy Cncl 1976–80, Packaging Cncl 1978–82, Exec Ctee NCVO (also chm Planning and Environment Gp) 1984–89, UK Nat Ctee Euro Year of the Environment 1986–88, Exec Ctee Euro Environmental Bureau 1988–91 (policy advsr 1978–88), Exec Bd World Energy Cncl Cmmn 1990–93, Co-operative Insur Servs Environment Tst Advsy Ctee 1990–92, Cncl RSA 1990–92 (memb Environment Ctee 1989–); hon visiting fell Manchester Business Sch 1984–86, visiting fell Cranfield Sch of Mgmnt 1990–94; numerous radio and TV bdcasts, scriptwriter Crumbling Britain (BBC Radio 4) 1983; Parly candidate (SDP): Brighton Kemptown 1983, Surbiton 1987; Royal Humane Soc Testimonial on Parchment 1969 (on Vellum 1966); UNEP Global 500 laureate; FRSA 1987; *Books* incl: Europe Environment (1981), Pressure Groups in the Global System (1982), Ecology 2000 (co-author and picture ed, 1984), The Gaia Atlas of Planetary Management (contrib, 1984), The Green Capitalists (with John Elkington, 1987), Green Pages (with John Elkington and Julia Hales, 1988), Ethics, Environment and the Company (with Julie Hill, 1990); *Recreations* birdwatching, landscape photography, military history, walking; *Clubs* Reform; *Style*— Tom Burke, Esq, CBE; ✉ 36 Crewdson Rd, London SW9 OLJ (☎ 0171 735 9019); Department of the Environment, 2 Marsham St, London SW1 (☎ 0171 276 4299, fax 0171 276 3269)

BURKE, Prof Derek Clissold; CBE (1994), DL (Norfolk 1992); s of Harold Burke (d 1973), of Avon, Warwickshire, and Ivy Ruby, *née* Clissold (d 1973); *b* 13 Feb 1930; *Educ* Bishop Vesey's GS Sutton Coldfield, Univ of Birmingham (BSc, PhD); *m* 21 May 1955, Mary Elizabeth, da of Theodore Tiner Dukeshire; 1 s (Stephen Dukeshire b 1962), 3 da (Elizabeth Anne b 1957, Rosemary Margaret b 1962, Virginia Ruth b 1964); *Career* res fell in chemistry Yale 1953–55, scientist Nat Inst for Medical Res London 1955–60, lectr and sr lectr Dept of Biological Chem Univ of Aberdeen 1960–69, prof of biological scis Univ of Warwick 1969–82, Eleanor Roosevelt fell Univ of Colorado USA 1975–76, vice pres and scientific dir Allelix Inc Toronto Canada 1982–87, vice chllr UEA 1987–95; pres Soc of Gen Microbiology 1987–90, chm Advsy Ctee on Novel Foods and Processes 1988–, dir Cancer Res Campaign 1989–, chm Cncl Paterson Inst of Cancer Res 1992–; memb: Advsy Ctee on Genetic Modification 1987–95, Technol Foresight Steering Gp Office of Science and Technol 1993–95, Sci and Engrg Bd and Technol Interaction Bd Biotechnology and Biological Scis Res Cncl 1994–; dir: Inst for Food Research 1994–, Babraham Inst 1995–; specialist advsr to House of Commons Sci and Technol Ctee 1995–; tstee Norfolk and Norwich Festival 1988–96, memb Bd Wingfield Arts Tst 1996–; Hon LLD Univ of Aberdeen 1982, Hon ScD UEA 1995; memb Soc for Gen Microbiology, memb Euro Molecular Biology Orgn; *Books* Creation and Evolution (1985), numerous scientific and popular articles on interferon and viruses; memb Editorial Bd Jl of General Virology 1969–92, ed in chief Jl of General Virology 1978–82; *Recreations* music, opera, walking; *Clubs* Royal Over-Seas League; *Style*— Prof Derek Burke, CBE, DL; ✉ 13 Pretoria Road, Cambridge CB4 1HD (☎ and fax 01223 301159); Sea-Green Cottage, Walberswick, Suffolk IP18 6TU (☎ and fax 01502 723607)

BURKE, Frank Desmond; *b* 23 March 1944; *Educ* Newcastle (MB BS); *m* Linda Margaret; 2 s (Richard b 1972, Timothy b 1979), 1 da (Sarah b 1975); *Career* fell in hand surgery: Louisville Kentucky 1976, Iowa City 1977; conslt hand surgn Derbyshire Royal Infirmary 1981–; visiting prof of hand surgery Med Scis Dept Univ of Derby; sec Br Soc for Surgery of the Hand 1989, pres Br Assoc of Hand Therapists 1989, memb American Soc of Surgery of The Hand 1989; FRCS 1972; *Books* Principles of Hand Surgery (with D A McGrougher and P J Smith, 1990); *Style*— Frank Burke, Esq; ✉ The Hand Unit, Derbyshire Royal Infirmary NHS Trust, London Rd, Derby (☎ 01332 347141 ext 4751)

BURKE, Sir James Stanley Gilbert; 9 Bt (I 1797), of Marble Hill, Galway; s of Sir Thomas Stanley Burke, 8 Bt (d 1989), and Susanne Margaretha, *née* Salvisberg (d 1983); *b* 1 July 1956; *m* 1980, Laura, da of Domingo Branzuela, of Catmon, Cebu, Philippines; 1 s (Martin James b 1980), 1 da (Catherine Elizabeth b 1982); *Heir* s, Martin James Burke b 22 July 1980; *Style*— Sir James Burke, Bt; ✉ Lindenbergstr 231, CH-5618 Bettwil, Switzerland (☎ 00 41 56 6673124)

BURKE, Jeffrey Peter; QC (1984); s of Samuel Burke, of London, and Gertrude Burke; *b* 15 Dec 1941; *Educ* Shrewsbury, Brasenose Coll Oxford (open exhibitioner, BA); *m* Joanna Mary Heal; 1 s (Patrick Samuel b 1996); 2 s and 1 da by previous m (Jason Daniel b 1970, Adam Francis b 1972, Sonya Clare b 1977); *Career* called to the Bar Inner Temple 1964, recorder of the Crown Court 1983–; memb Mental Health Review Tbnl 1993–; *Recreations* soccer, cricket, wine, reading, removing brambles; *Clubs* Economicals AFC, Falconhurst Cricket; *Style*— Jeffrey Burke, Esq, QC; ✉ Devereux Chambers, Devereux Court, London WC2R 3JJ (☎ 0171 353 7534, fax 0171 353 1724)

BURKE, His Hon Judge; John Kenneth; QC (1985); s of Kenneth Burke (d 1960), of Stockport, and Madeline Lorina, *née* Eastwood; *b* 4 Aug 1939; *Educ* Stockport GS; *m* 30 March 1962, Margaret Anne, da of Frank Scattergood, of Nottingham; 3 da (Virginia b 1963, Joanna b 1967, Geraldine b 1969); *Career* Nat Serv with Cheshire Regt in Far E 1958–60, Capt 12/13 Bn The Parachute Regt (TA) 1962–67, Capt/Actg Maj 4 Bn The Parachute Regt (TAVR) 1974; called to the Bar Middle Temple 1965; recorder of the Crown Court 1980–95, bencher Middle Temple 1992, circuit judge (Northern Circuit) 1995–; *Recreations* walking, drawing, painting; *Style*— His Hon Judge Burke, QC; ✉ Manchester Crown Court, Crown Square, Manchester M3 3FL (☎ 0161 954 1800)

BURKE, Michael John; s of Ulick Burke (d 1986), and Dorothy Margaret, *née* Clark; *b* 22 June 1934; *Educ* Westcliff HS, Univ of Nottingham (LLB); *m* 9 Nov 1959, Margaret, da of Harry Charles (d 1987); 1 s (Anthony b 1961), 3 da (Jane b 1962, Henrietta b 1965, Sophia b 1970); *Career* admitted slr 1958; Cameron Markby Hewitt (formerly Cameron Markby, previously Layton & Co): assoc slr 1962–64, ptnr 1967–92, conslt 1992–; sec Assoc of Br Factors and Discounters 1992–; govr Westcliff Girls Sch 1966–93, hon slr Essex Yacht Club 1978–95; memb: City Livery Club Cncl 1976–, City Slrs Co, Livery Consultative Ctee 1981–93; dep clerk Carmen's Co 1974–; clerk: Farriers Co 1962–70, Dowgate Ward 1974–94; Freeman City of London 1962; Liveryman Worshipful Co of: Solicitors 1962, Farriers 1963, Carmen 1984 (hon dep clerk); *Recreations* sailing, golf, walking; *Clubs* Essex Yacht, City Livery; *Style*— Michael Burke, Esq; ✉ 66 Undercliff Gardens, Leigh on Sea, Essex (☎ 01702 79871, fax 01702 72217); Cameron Markby Hewitt, Sceptre Ct, 40 Tower Hill, London EC3N 4BB (☎ 0171 702 2345, fax 0171 702 2303, telex 925779)

BURKE, Prof Philip George; CBE (1993); s of Henry Burke (d 1969), of S Woodford, London, and Frances Mary, *née* Sprague (d 1980); *b* 18 Oct 1932; *Educ* Wanstead Co HS London, Univ Coll Exeter (BSc London), UCL (PhD); *m* 29 Aug 1959, Valerie Mona, da of Harold William Martin (d 1987), of Eastbourne, Sussex; 4 da (Helen Frances b 1961, Susan Valerie b 1963, Pamela Jean b 1964, Alice Charlotte b 1973); *Career* research asst UCL 1956–57, asst lectr Computer Unit Univ of London 1957–59; research assoc Lawrence Radiation Laboratory Univ of California Berkeley: Alvarez Bubble Chamber Gp 1959–61, Theory Gp 1961–62; successively research fell, princ sci offr then sr princ sci offr Theoretical Physics Div UK Atomic Energy Authy Harwell 1962–67, prof of mathematical physics Queen's Univ Belfast NI 1967–, head of Theory and Computational Sci Div Daresbury Lab (jt appt) 1977–82; over 300 pubns in learned jls; memb: Physics Ctee SRC 1967–71, Synchrotron Radiation Research Ctee SRC 1971–75, Atlas Computer Ctee SRC 1973–76, Jt Policy Ctee on Advanced Res Computing 1988–90, Cncl SERC 1989–94, Cncl Royal Soc 1990–92; chm: Synchrotron Radiation Panel SRC 1969–71, Sci Bd Computer Ctee SRC 1976–77 and 1984–86, Computer Bd Computer Conslt Cncl 1983–85, Atomic, Molecular and Optical Physics Div Inst of Physics 1987–90, Allocations and Resources Panel Jt Research Cncls Advanced Research Computing Ctee 1988–89, SERC Scientific Computing Advsy Panel 1989–94, SERC Supercomputing Mgmnt Ctee 1991–94 (memb Advsy Bd for Res Cncls Supercomputing Sub-Ctee 1991–94); Hon DSc Univ of Exeter 1981, Guthrie Medal and Prize Inst of Physics 1994; FInstP 1970, fell American Physical Soc 1970, MRIA 1974, FRS 1978, fell UCL 1986; *Books* Atomic Processes and Applications (1976), Potential Scattering in Atomic Physics (1977), Atoms in Astrophysics (1983), Electron Molecule Scattering and Photoionisation (1988), Atomic and Molecular Processes: An R-Matrix Approach (1993), Theory of Electron-Atom Collisions: Part I - Potential Scattering (1995); *Recreations* swimming, walking, reading, listening to music; *Style*— Prof Philip Burke, CBE, FRS; ✉ 33 Leverogue Rd, Lisburn, N Ireland BT27 5PP (☎ 01232 826416); Brook House, Crowton, nr Northwich, Cheshire CW8 2RR (☎ 01928 788301); Department of Applied Mathematics and Theoretical Physics, Queen's University, Belfast, N Ireland BT7 1NN (☎ 01232 335047, fax 01232 239182, telex 74487)

BURKE, Richard Sylvester; s of David Burke (d 1948), and Elizabeth, *née* Kelly (d 1987); chieftain of Burke, Bourke and de Burgh clan 1990–92 (hon life pres 1992–); *b* 29 March 1932; *Educ* Christian Brothers Sch Thurles and Dublin, Nat Univ of Ireland (BA, MA, HDipEd); *m* 1961, Mary Josephine, da of John J Freeley (d 1934); 3 s (Joseph (d 1962), David Joseph b 1964, Richard Anthony b 1969), 3 da (Mary Carmel b 1963, Audrey Elisabeth b 1966, Avila Therese b 1971); *Career* taught at: Presentation Coll 1953–55, Blackrock Coll 1955–72; govr Univ Coll Dublin 1967–70; memb Dublin CC 1967–73 (chm 1972–73); barr at law King's Inns 1973–; TD 1969–77 and 1981–82, opposition chief whip and spokesman on Posts and Telegraphs 1969–73, Min for Educn 1973–76; memb and vice pres Cmmn of Euro Communities 1977–81 and 1982–85; chm Player and Wills 1981–82; dir: Abbey Life 1981–82, Sedgwick Europe BV 1985–86; special advsr Euro Community Office Ernst and Young 1985–95, pres and chief exec offr Canon Fndn in Europe 1988–; memb Conseil d'Administration FIDEPS UNESCO Paris 1990–, memb Devpt Cncl Eurasia Inst HEC Paris 1990–, memb Academia Scientiarum et Artium Europaea Salzburg 1996–; assoc fell Harvard Univ Centre for Int Affairs 1980–81; Pro Merito Europa medal European Parliament 1980, Order of Leopold II (Grand-Cross) Belgium 1981, Order of Phoenix (Grand-Cross) Greece 1983; *Books* Anthology of Prose (ed, 1967); *Recreations* golf, music, travel; *Clubs* Royal Golf De Belgique (Brussels), Portmarnock Golf (Dublin), Galway Bay Golf, Connemara Golf, Hibernian United Services (Dublin); *Style*— Richard Burke, Esq; ✉ 67 Ailesbury Road, Dublin 4, Ireland (☎ 00 353 1 269 2520); Rijnsbergerweg 3, 2334 BA Leiden, Netherlands (☎ 00 31 71 515 6555, fax 00 31 71 515 7027)

BURKE-GAFFNEY, John Campion; s of late Dr Henry Joseph O'Donnell Burke-Gaffney, tropical medicine expert, and late Constance Mary, *née* Bishop; *b* 27 Feb 1932; *Educ* Douai Sch; *m* 7 July 1956, Margaret Mary Jennifer, da of Lt-Col Humphrey Herbert Stacpoole (d 1971); 2 s (Jonathan b 1959, Rupert b 1962), 2 da (Sarah b 1957, Frances b 1964); *Career* Nat Serv cmmnd RAC 1950–52, TA East Riding Yeo (Lieut-Actg Capt) 1952–56; called to the Bar Gray's Inn 1956; Shell Mex & BP Ltd 1956–75, Shell UK Ltd 1975–77, md Shell & BP Zambia Ltd 1977–81, Shell International Petroleum Co Ltd 1981–85; dir gen Br Red Cross Soc 1985–90; *Style*— John Burke-Gaffney, Esq; ✉ c/o Coutts & Co, Park Lane Branch, 1 Old Park Lane, London W1A 4AL

BURKE-GAFFNEY, Michael Anthony Bowes; QC (1977); s of late Dr Henry Joseph O'Donnell Burke-Gaffney, of Bagshot, Surrey, and late Constance May, *née* Bishop; *b* 1 Aug 1928; *Educ* Douai Sch, RMA Sandhurst, SOAS; *m* 1961, Constance Caroline, da of Lt-Col Alan Murdoch; 2 s (Timothy Henry James b 6 Sept 1966, Giles Peter Anthony b 26 April 1978), 1 da (Constance Emma Mary b 12 Jan 1968); *Career* cmmnd 1948, served 1 Bn RIF Akaba, Gibraltar, Rhine; served 1 Bn Royal Ulster Rifles Korea and Hong Kong 1951–52, Sch of Oriental and African Studies Univ of London 1955–56, Turkish interpreter Istanbul 1956–57, Capt on Staff 44 Inf Div 1957–58, ret; called to the Bar Gray's Inn 1959 (bencher 1988), recorder Crown Court 1986–92; *Recreations* cricket, wine, family, plants; *Clubs* Naval and Military; *Style*— Michael Burke-Gaffney, Esq, QC; ✉ Lamb Chambers, Lamb Building, Temple, London EC4Y 7AS (☎ 0171 797 8300, fax 0171 797 8308, home fax 01672 563323)

BURKETT, John; s of Alfred Burkett, MC (d 1986), of Stoke Bishop, Bristol, and Marjorie, *née* Wingfield (d 1972); *b* 17 Feb 1926; *Educ* Eltham Coll, Jesus Coll Cambridge, Architectural Assoc Sch (AADipl); *m* 1, 24 April 1948, Patricia Ann (d 1988), da of Stanley Walter Mack (d 1985), of Chislehurst, Kent; 2 da (Deborah Jane b 1953, Sarah Louise b 1955); m 2, 1990, Noel Jocelyn Wurr, MBE, da of Charles Dore; *Career* Flt Lt RAFVR 1944–48; lectr Architectural Assoc Sch of Architecture 1955–57; ptnr: D J Mclennan & Ptnrs, John Burkett Assocs, Scarlett Burkett Assoc 1971–78; sr ptnr Scarlett Burkett Griffiths 1979–87; winner: Civic Tst awards 1968 and 1972, Financial Times Indust Architecture award 1971, Heritage Landscape award 1976; memb Cncl Assoc of Conslt Architects, chm Construction Industry Cncl Ctee on Adjudication; FRIBA, FCIArb; *Recreations* gardening, skiing; *Clubs* Architectural Assoc; *Style*— John Burkett, Esq; ✉ 62 Belsize Park Gardens, London NW3 4NE (☎ 0171 586 9004, fax 0171 722 4060)

BURKETT, Mary Elizabeth; OBE (1978); da of Ridley Burkett (d 1965), of France, and Mary Alice Gaussen (d 1965); The Gaussens were a Huguenot family from Lunel, this branch settled at Loughneagh; *b* 7 Oct 1924; *Educ* Musgrave Sch, Univ of Durham (BA); *Career* art teacher Wroxall Abbey 1942–55, art lectr Charlotte Mason Coll Ambleside 1955–62; dir: Abbot Hall Art Gallery and Museums Kendal 1967–86, Border TV 1982–93; memb: N Western Museums and Art Gallery Servs Area Cncl 1975–86, Arts Cncl Art Fin Ctee 1978–80, Nat Tst NW Regional Exec Ctee 1978–85; memb Cumbria CC: Museums Advsy Gp 1975, Museums Offrs' Working Pty 1975–87; judge: Scottish Museum of the Year Award 1977–, English Museum of the Year Award 1986–; memb: Br Tourist Authy Museums Mission to USA 1981, DAC Carlisle 1979–96; tstee: Carlisle Cathedral Appeal 1981–, Armitt Tst 1982–86, Senhouse Tst 1985–; pres: Feltmakers' Assoc 1984, Exec Ctee Lake District Art Gallery Tst 1993–, Carlisle Cathedral Fabric Ctee 1993–, Blencathra Appeal Ctee 1993–95; FRSA, FMA, FRGS; *Publications* The Art of the Feltmaker (1979), Kurt Schwitters (in the Lake District) (1979), William Green of Ambleside (with David Sloss, 1984), Monograph on Christopher Steele (Walpole Society Journal, 1987), Read's Point of View (with David Sloss, 1995); *Recreations* travelling, birdwatching, photography; *Style*— Miss Mary E Burkett, OBE; ✉ Isel Hall, Cockermouth, Cumbria CA13 0QG

BURKHARDT, Prof (George) Hugh; s of Dr (George) Norman Burkhardt (d 1991), of Manchester, and Caroline Mary, *née* Bell; *b* 4 April 1935; *Educ* Manchester GS, Balliol Coll Oxford (BA), Univ of Birmingham (PhD); *m* 21 Dec 1955, Diana Jeanette, da of Stapley Farmer (d 1970); 2 s (Roger b 1960, Ian b 1963), 1 da (Jan b 1962); *Career* res fell: Columbia Univ 1958–59, California Inst of Technol 1959–60; lectr then sr lectr in mathematical physics Univ of Birmingham 1960–76, prof of mathematical educn Univ of Nottingham 1976–92; dir Shell Centre for Mathematical Educn 1976–92; visiting prof: UCLA 1968–69, CERN 1964–66 and 1973–74, UC Berkeley 1992–95; memb: Jt Mathematical Cncl of the UK 1979–85 (treas 1982–85), Nat Curriculum Mathematical Working Gp 1987–88; nat memb Int Cmmn on Mathematics Instruction 1980–88; *Books* Dispersion Relation Dynamics (1969), The Real World and Mathematics (1981), Problem Solving - A World View (1988), Curriculum - towards the Year 2000; *Recreations* oboe, theatre, dance; *Style*— Prof Hugh Burkhardt

BURLAND, James Alan; s of James Glyn Burland, and Elizabeth Beresford, *née* Thompson (d 1978); *b* 25 Sept 1954; *Educ* King Henry VIII Sch Coventry, Univ of Bath (BSc, BArch); *Career* architect; Arup Associates 1978–86, Philip Cox Richardson Taylor and Partners Sydney Australia 1986–90, dir and princ architect Arup Architects 1996– (re-joined 1990); projects incl: Stockley Park Heathrow, Bedford HS Jr Sch, Durham New Coll, Manchester Olympic and National Stadium, Johannesburg Athletics Stadium, Glasgow Nat Arena, Plantation House London; private cmmns The Body Shop Bath, Liverpool and Brighton 1982–83; external tutor Sydney Univ 1987–88; memb: London Docklands Urban Design Advsy Gp, Cardiff Bay Design Advsy Gp, Nat Tst; RIBA 1983; *Recreations* racing bicycles, watercolouring, guitar, theatre; *Clubs* Chelsea Arts; *Style*— James Burland, Esq; ✉ Arup Associates, 37 Fitzroy Square, London W1P 6AA (☎ 0171 465 5555, fax 0171 465 2561)

BURLAND, Prof John Boscawen; s of John Whitmore Burland (d 1994), and Margaret Irene, *née* Boscawen (d 1986); *b* 4 March 1936; *Educ* Parktown Boys' HS Johannesburg, Univ of the Witwatersrand (BSc, MSc, DSc), Emmanuel Coll Cambridge (PhD); *m* 30 March 1963, Gillian Margaret, da of John Kenneth Miller (d 1981); 2 s (David 1965, Timothy 1967), 1 da (Tamsin 1969); *Career* engr Ove Arup and Ptnrs London 1961–63; Building Res Estab: SSO, PSO 1966–72, SPSO head Geotechnics Div 1972–79, asst dir DCSO 1979–80; visiting prof Univ of Strathclyde 1973–82, prof of soil mechanics Imperial Coll of Sci Technol and Med 1980–; memb Cncl Royal Acad of Engrg 1994–; Hon DEng Heriot-Watt Univ 1994; MICE 1969, MIStructE 1976, FEng 1981, FICE 1982; *Recreations* golf, sailing, painting; *Style*— Prof John Burland, FEng; ✉ Department of Civil Engineering, Imperial College of Science, Technology and Medicine, Imperial College Rd, London SW7 2BU (☎ 0171 594 6079, fax 0171 594 6053)

BURLEIGH, Robert Haydon (Robin); s of Thomas Haydon Burleigh, of Kirkgate, Holme, Hunstanton, Norfolk PE36 6LH, and Kathleen Mary Lenthall Eager (d 1992); *b* 16 Aug 1941; *Educ* Dragon Sch Oxford, Repton, Trinity Coll Oxford (MA, Golf blue); *m* 31 May 1969, Ann Elizabeth Lea, da of Cecil George Steddy; 1 s (Edward Thomas Haydon b 5 July 1980), 1 da (Emma Susan Lenthall b 16 Sept 1977); *Career* articled clerk Robert Gray Clegg & Sons Sheffield 1964–66, admitted slr 1966; Clifford-Turner (became Clifford Chance 1988): joined 1968, ptnr 1971, Amsterdam 1972–73, assigned Salah Hejailan Riyadh Saudi Arabia 1978–80; Freeman Worshipful Co of Slrs; memb Law Soc; *Recreations* golf, skiing, fishing, music; *Clubs* City of London, Royal and Ancient, Moles GS, Vincent's; *Style*— Robin Burleigh, Esq; ✉ 33 Burnsall St, London SW3 3SS (☎ 0171 584 5158); Clifford Chance, 200 Aldersgate Street, London EC1A 4JJ (☎ 0171 600 1000, fax 0171 600 5555, direct ☎ 0171 282 6100)

BURLEY, Prof Jeffery; CBE (1991); s of Jack Burley (d 1978), and Eliza Nellie Victoria, *née* Creese (d 1949); *b* 16 Oct 1936; *Educ* Portsmouth GS, Univ of Oxford (BA, MA, Basketball blue), Yale Univ (MF, PhD); *m* 26 Aug 1961, Jean Shirley, da of Douglas MacDonald Palmer (d 1989); 2 s (Jeremy Andrew b 1963, Timothy John b 1966); *Career* Lt Royal Signals short serv cmmn 1954–57; UNESCO expert offr i/c Forest Genetics Res Laboratory Agric Res Cncl of Central Africa 1965–68, sr res offr Cwlth Forestry Inst Oxford 1968–76, lectr in forestry Univ of Oxford 1976–83, head Dept of Forestry and dir Cwlth Forestry Inst 1983–84, dir Oxford Forestry Inst and professorial fell Green Coll 1985–; forty consultancies with int devpt agencies; advsr, sponsor or ctee memb: Earthwatch (UK), Tree Aid, Cwlth Forestry Assoc, Br Cncl, Int Soc of Tropical Foresters; vice pres Int Union of Forestry Research Organisations; *Books* Tropical Trees: variation, breeding and conservation (ed with B T Styles, 1976), A Tree for all Reasons (with P J Wood), Managing Global Genetic Resources: forest trees (jtly); *Style*— Prof Jeffery Burley, CBE; ✉ Woodside, Frilford Heath, Abingdon, Oxon OX13 5QG (☎ 01865 390754); Oxford Forestry Institute, Department of Plant Sciences, University of Oxford, South Parks Road, Oxford OX1 3RB (☎ 01865 275050, fax 01865 275074, e-mail jeff.burley@plants.ox.ac.uk)

BURLEY, (William) John; s of William John Rule Burley, (d 1935), of Falmouth, and Annie, *née* Curnow (d 1956); *b* 1 Aug 1914; *Educ* Cornwall Tech Schs (Keam scholar), Balliol Coll Oxford (BA, Herbertson prize); *m* 10 April 1938, Muriel, da of Edward Wolsey; 2 s (Alan John b 13 June 1940, Nigel Philip b 4 Aug 1943); *Career* writer; student engr in gas engrg 1931–36, asst mangr Truro Gas Undertaking 1936–40, mangr several small gas undertakings South West Gas and Water Corp 1940–50, head of biology Richmond and East Sheen GS 1953–55, head of biology and sixth form tutor Newquay Sch 1955–74; full time writer 1974–; memb: Crime Writers' Assoc, SW Writers, Authors' Licensing and Collecting Soc; *Television* ITV Network series (on Wycliffe) of 6 1994, 8 1995, 1996 and 1997; *Books* A Taste of Power (1966), Three-Toed Pussy (1968), Death in Willow Pattern (1969), To Kill a Cat (1970), Guilt Edged (1971), Death in a Salubrious Place (1973), Death in Stanley Street (1974), Wycliffe and Pea-green Boat (1975), Wycliffe and the Schoolgirls (1976), The Schoolmaster (1977), Wycliffe and the Scapegoat (1978), The Sixth Day (1978), Charles and Elizabeth (1979), Wycliffe in Paul's Court (1980), The House of Care (1981), Wycliffe's Wild Goose Chase (1982), Wycliffe and the Beales (1983), Wycliffe and the Four Jacks (1985), Wycliffe and the Quiet Virgin (1986), Wycliffe and the Winsor Blue (1987), Wycliffe and the Tangled Web (1988), Wycliffe and the Cycle of Death (1990), Wycliffe and the Dead Flautist (1991), Wycliffe and the Last Rites (1992), Wycliffe and the Dunes Mystery (1993), Wycliffe and the House of Fear (1995), Wycliffe and the Redhead (1997); *Recreations* gardening and watercolour painting; *Style*— John Burley, Esq; ✉ St Patrick's, Holywell, Newquay, Cornwall TR8 5PT (☎ 01637 830362); c/o Victor Gollancz, Wellington House, 125 Strand, London WC2R 0BB

BURLEY, Philip George; s of Victor George Burley (d 1990), of Croydon, Surrey, and Blanche Clara, *née* Coleman (d 1962); *b* 31 Dec 1943; *Educ* Whitgift Sch Croydon, London Coll of Printing; *m* 8 June 1974, Christine Elizabeth, da of Istvan Komaromy, of Shirley, Surrey; 3 da (Victoria b 1976, Elisabeth b 1979, Georgina b 1981); *Career* musician 1961–63, md Joint Marketing and Publishing Services Ltd 1970 (graphic designer 1963–69), fndr ptnr Design Counsellors and Incentive Counsellors 1971, fndr ptnr and creative dir The Incentive Group 1972, chm The Quadrant Group 1982, chm and chief exec Excelsior Group Productions Ltd 1989– (pres 1989–91), exec prodr The Darling Buds of May 1990–, exec prodr A Touch of Frost 1992–; composer of music for TV incl: The Language of Music (also writer and presenter) 1980, title music for Database 1985, title music for The Darling Buds of May 1990 (Ivor Novello Award for Best Television Theme Music 1991); work for charities incl: Tadworth Court Children's Hosp, The Variety Club of Great Britain, St Piers Lingfield, Surrey Assoc of Boys' Clubs, Polesden Lacey Open Air Theatre; *Recreations* music, theatre, art, reading, golf; *Clubs* Foxhills Golf and Country; *Style*— Philip Burley, Esq; ✉ Excelsior Group Productions Ltd, Dorking Rd, Walton-on-the-Hill, Tadworth, Surrey KT20 7TJ (☎ 01737 812673, fax 01737 813163)

BURLIN, Prof Terence Eric; s of Eric Jonas Burlin, and Winifred Kate, *née* Thomas; *b* 24 Sept 1931; *Educ* Acton Co Sch, Univ of Southampton (BSc), Univ of London (BSc, PhD, DSc); *m* 23 March 1957, Plessey Pamela, da of John William Carpenter; 1 s (Adrian b 1962), 1 da (Helen b 1965); *Career* physicist Mount Vernon Hosp and Radium Inst 1953–57, sr physicist Hammersmith Hosp 1957–62, pt/t princ physicist St John's Hosp for Diseases of Skin 1960–90; Univ of Westminster (formerly Poly of Central London): sr lectr 1962–69, reader 1969–71, pro dir 1971–74, sr pro rector 1974–82, rector 1982–95; chm Br Ctee on Radiation Units and Measurements 1984–95 (memb 1955–95); govr: Quintin Kynaston Sch 1971–73, Central Sch of Speech and Drama 1980–94; memb: Longfield Sch Managing Body 1973–76, Cncl Inst for Study of Drug Dependence 1974–86, Academic Bd Harrow Coll of Higher Educn 1979–84, Sci Bd SERC 1986–89 (Polys Ctee 1976–78), Paddington Coll Governing Body 1986–90, Br Cncl Ctee for Int Co-operation in Higher Educn 1988–94; hon treas Ctee of Dirs of Polys 1985–93; FInstP 1969, CPhys 1976, FIPSM 1988, FIEE 1976; Hon FCP 1990; *Recreations* tennis, music; *Clubs* Athenaeum; *Style*— Prof Terence Burlin; ✉ Deveron, Mayfield Drive, Pinner, Middx HA5 5QT (☎ 0181 866 2424)

BURLINGTON, Earl of; William Cavendish; s of Marquess of Hartington, *qv*; *b* 6 June 1969; *Clubs* Arsenal FC; *Style*— Earl of Burlington

BURMAN, Sir (John) Charles; kt (1961), JP (Birmingham 1942), DL (Warwicks 1967); s of Sir John Bedford Burman, JP (d 1941), of Tibbington House, Edgbaston, and Elizabeth Vernon, *née* Pugh; *b* 30 Aug 1908; *Educ* Rugby; *m* 1936, Ursula, da of John Herbert Hesketh-Wright, and Millicent Ella, *née* Pickering, of Bournemouth; 2 s, 2 da; *Career* Lord Mayor Birmingham 1947–49; chm: S Staffs Waterworks Co 1959–79, Tarmac Ltd 1961–71; memb: Govt Ctee on Admin Tbnls 1955, Royal Cmmn on Police 1960; chm: Birmingham Cons Assoc 1963–72, Barber Inst of Fine Arts 1979–90 (tstee 1936–90); High Sheriff Warwicks 1958–59; Hon LLD Univ of Birmingham 1986; KStJ 1961; *Recreations* gardening; *Style*— Sir Charles Burman, JP, DL; ✉ Little Bickerscourt, Danzey Green, Tanworth-in-Arden, Warwicks B94 5BL (☎ 01564 742711)

BURMAN, Peter Ashley Thomas Insull; MBE (1991); s of Thomas Bayliss Insull Burman (d 1975), and Eileen Patricia Winifred, *née* King-Morgan; *b* 15 Sept 1944; *Educ* Tudor Grange GS, King's Coll Cambridge (exhibitioner, BA); *Career* successively asst sec, dep sec and sec C of E Cncl for the Care of Churches and Cathedrals Advsy Cmmn for England 1968–; dir Centre for Conservation Studies Inst of Advanced Architectural Studies Univ of York 1990–; memb Fabric Ctee Durham Cathedral; chm: Fabric Advsy Ctees St Paul's and Lincoln Cathedrals, York Art Workers' Assoc, North Yorkshire Moors Building Preservation Tst; *Books* Chapels and Churches: Who Cares (with Marcus Binney, 1977), Change and Decay: The Future of our Churches (1977), St Paul's Cathedral (1989), Treasures on Earth (ed and contrib, 1993), Thomas Gambier Parry Catalogue (contrib, 1993), Economic Aspects of Architectural Conservation (ed and contrib, 1995), Conserving the Railway Heritage (ed and contrib, 1996), Heritage and Renewal: European Cathedrals in the late Twentieth Century (ed and contrib, 1996); *Recreations* playing the piano, mountain biking, travelling; *Style*— Peter Burman, Esq, MBE; ✉ The Petch House, 34 Howe End, Kirkbymoorside, N Yorks YO6 6BD (☎ 01751 431547); Centre for Conservation Studies, University of York, The King's Manor, York YO1 2EP (☎ 01904 433963, fax 01904 433949)

BURN, (Bryan) Adrian Falconer; s of Reginald Falconer Burn (d 1981), and Kathleen Ruth, *née* Davis; *b* 23 May 1945; *Educ* Abingdon Sch; *m* 1968, Jeanette Carol; 4 c (Clare b 1976, Victoria b 1979, Katharine b 1983, James b 1985); *Career* chartered accountant Whinney Murray 1968–72 (articled clerk 1964–68); Binder Hamlyn: joined 1973, ptnr 1977, London Region managing ptnr 1988–94, managing ptnr 1994–; non-exec dir Brent International PLC 1994–; FCA (ACA 1968); *Style*— Adrian Burn, Esq; ✉ Binder Hamlyn, 20 Old Bailey, London EC4M 7BH (☎ 0171 489 9000/6012, fax 0171 489 6280)

BURN, Edward Hector; s of Edward Burn (d 1982), and Bertha Maud, *née* Hector (d 1976); *b* 20 Nov 1922; *Educ* St Edward's Oxford, Wadham Coll Oxford (BCL, MA); *m* 21 Dec 1948, Helen Joyce, da of Maj Merrick Hugh McConnel, RHA (ka 1917); *Career* cmmnd 1 Bucks Bn, Oxford Bucks, Capt GSO 3 1 Airborne Corps, Maj GSO 2 26 Indian Div (despatches Normandy 1944 and Sumatra 1946); called to the Bar Lincoln's Inn 1951; student and tutor in jurisprudence Christ Church Oxford 1954–90, Censor of Christ Church 1959–64, lectr in law Inns of Ct 1965–80, Hon Master of the Bench Lincoln's Inn 1980, prof City Univ 1990– (visiting prof 1983–90), lectr in law St Hugh's Coll Oxford 1990–; cmmr of Inland Revenue 1975– (memb Tst Law Ctee), govr St Edward's Sch Oxford; Hon DCL: City Univ 1990, King's Univ Halifax Nova Scotia (Canada) 1991; *Books* Maudsley and Burn Trusts and Trustees (5 edn, 1996), Maudsley and Burn Land Law (6 edn, 1992), Cheshire and Burn Modern Law of Real Property (15 edn, 1994); *Clubs* Athenaeum, MCC; *Style*— Edward Burn, Esq; ✉ St Hugh's College, University of Oxford, Oxford OX2 6LE (☎ 01865 274900)

BURN, Geoffrey Robert Hale; s of George Robert Burn (d 1974), and Grace, *née* Downs; *b* 19 Nov 1945; *Educ* St Peter's Coll, RMA, Pacific Western Univ (BSc, MBA), Univ of Brighton (postgraduate Dip); *m* 29 Dec 1985, Judith Irene, da of John William Palmieri, of Windsor; 1 s (Hale, decd), 2 da (Sacha b 1987, Vita b 1990); *Career* Lt RA 1967–71; sales exec Prentice Hall 1971–72, managing ed McGraw Hill 1971–72, publishing and mktg dir Methuen Publications 1975–82, pres Butterworth Canada 1982–87, md Butterworth Sci 1987–90; exec dir of publishing BMA 1990–95, chief exec Thomson Science and Professional 1995–; faculty memb publishing courses and prog dir academic and professional publishing Banff Sch of Fine Arts 1986–87; dir: Canadian Book Publishers' Cncl 1977–82, Academic and Professional Gp Publishers' Assoc 1988–90; memb: Canadian Law Info Cncl 1982–87, The Strategic Planning Soc; lay minister Hosp Chaplaincy; Liveryman Worshipful Soc of Apothecaries; FInstD; Order of Polonia Restituta; *Recreations* farming, gardening, reading, skiing; *Clubs* Athenaeum; *Style*— Geoffrey R H Burn, Esq; ✉ Thomson Science and Professional, 2–6 Boundary Row, London SE1 8HN (☎ 0171 865 0066)

BURN, Gordon; s of James Edward Burn, and Joyce, *née* Fisher; *b* 16 Jan 1948; *Educ* Rutherford GS Newcastle upon Tyne, Univ of London (BA); *partner* since 1971, Carol Gorner, painter; *Career* writer; freelance writer and author 1969–, writer Sunday Times 1974–82; reg contrib to The Observer, TLS, London Review of Books, Modern Painters, Independent on Sunday, Esquire; Columnist of the Yr Award Magazine Publishing Awards 1991 (for column in Esquire); Hon DLitt Univ of Plymouth 1993; *Books* Somebody's Husband, Somebody's Son - The Story of the Yorkshire Ripper (1984, shortlist Silver Dagger Award CWA of GB 1984, shortlist Edgar Allen Poe Award CWA of USA 1985), Pocket Money (1986), Alma Cogan (1991, Best First Novel Whitbread Prize 1991), Fullalove (1995); *Recreations* idling in pubs, reading, music, walking, drinking; *Style*— Gordon Burn, Esq; ✉ Aitken & Stone Ltd, 29 Fernshaw Road, London SW10 0TG (☎ 0171 351 7561, fax 0171 376 3594)

BURN, (John) Ian; s of Cecil Walter Burn (d 1983), and Margaret Hannah, *née* Cawthorne (d 1988); *b* 19 Feb 1927; *Educ* Taunton Sch, St Bartholomew's Hosp Med Coll (MB BS, capt athletics team and United Hosps cross country team); *m* 1951, Fiona May, da of late Alexander Allan; 2 s (Alastair James b 1952, Jonathan Mark b 1964), 2 da (Hilary Kathryn (Mrs Stevens) b 1954, Lindsay Margaret (Mrs O'Kelly) b 1958);

Career RAF Med Serv 1952–54; Anatomy Dept Univ of Cambridge 1954–55, training posts in surgery St Bartholomew's Hosp and Hammersmith Hosp 1955–65, cancer res scholarship USA 1961–62; conslt surgn: Hammersmith Hosp 1965–73, Charing Cross Hosp Fulham 1973–87 (hon consulting surgn 1987–), Harley St Clinic 1973–91; visiting conslt surgn King Edward VII Hosp Midhurst 1988– (med dir 1993–95); specialist in malignant disease (surgical oncology); Hunterian prof RCS 1967; pres: Br Assoc of Surgical Oncology 1980–83 (fndr memb 1973), Euro Soc of Surgical Oncology 1987–90 (fndr memb 1983), World Fedn of Surgical Oncology Socs 1992–95 (fndr memb 1992); vice pres RSM 1989–91 (hon sec 1981–87), chm Treatment of Cancer Project Ctee Int Union Against Cancer 1989–94 (Roll of Honour 1996); Freeman City of London 1986, Liveryman Worshipful Co of Barbers of London 1986; hon memb Finnish Surgical Soc 1986, hon assoc memb Belgian Royal Soc for Surgery 1987; FRCS 1956, memb Assoc of Surgeons of GB 1963; *Books* Systematic Surgery (1965), Understanding Cancer (co-ed, 1977), Surgical Oncology (co-ed, 1989), Breast Cancer (co-ed, 1989), Operative Cancer Surgery (co-ed, 1992); author of numerous chapters and articles on cancer; *Recreations* opera, visiting islands, history of medicine; *Clubs* Carlton, MCC, Petworth Park Cricket (vice pres); *Style*— Ian Burn; ✉ King Edward VII Hospital, Midhurst, W Sussex GU29 0BL

BURN, Prof John; s of Henry Burn, of Bishop Auckland, Co Durham, and Margaret, *née* Wilkinson; *b* 6 Feb 1952; *Educ* Barnard Castle GS, Univ of Newcastle upon Tyne (BMedSci, MB BS, MD); *m* 5 Aug 1973, Linda Marjorie, da of Charles Frederick Wilson, of Winston, Darlington, Co Durham; 1 da (Danielle Louise b 17 Aug 1977), 1 s (James Richard David b 20 Sept 1981); *Career* jr med trg Newcastle teaching hosps 1976–80, hon sr registrar in clinical genetics Gt Ormond St Hosp 1981–84, conslt clinical geneticist Royal Victoria Infirmary Newcastle 1984–91; Univ of Newcastle upon Tyne: clinical lectr 1984–91, prof of clinical genetics 1991–, head Div of Human Genetics 1992–; gen sec Clinical Genetics Soc of GB 1989–95, memb: Ctee on Clinical Genetics RCP 1991–93, Bd Euro Soc of Human Genetics 1995–98; MRCP 1978, FRCP 1989; *Recreations* running, snooker; *Style*— Prof John Burn; ✉ Northern Region Genetics Service, 19–20 Claremont Place, Newcastle upon Tyne NE2 4AA (☎ 0191 232 5131)

BURN, Rear Adm Richard Hardy; CB (1992), AFC (1970); s of Douglas Courtney Burn (d 1978), and Margaret Theresa, *née* Hardy (d 1989); *b* 26 May 1938; *Educ* Berkhamsted Sch; *m* 4 Feb 1967, Judith Mary, da of Jack Tigg, of Dorset; 1 s (Joseph b 1969), 1 da (Sasha b 1971), 1 step s (Philip b 1962), 1 step da (Kylie b 1961); *Career* BRNC Dartmouth 1955, HMS Broadsword 1958, qualified as Naval Aviator 1960, HMS Hermes and HMS Ark Royal 1960–62, RNEC Manadon 1962–65, Empire Test Pilot Sch USN exchange 1967, Test Pilot A&AEE Boscombe Down 1968–70, USN Test Pilot Sch Staff Patuxent River 1971–74, NDC Latimer 1975, Sea Harrier Devpt (PE) MOD 1975–78, Ops Offr A&AEE 1978–79, Air Engr Offr RNAS Yeovilton 1980, promoted Capt 1981, RCDS 1985; MOD: Asst Dir of Engrg (Navy) 1981–84, Dir of Aircraft Maintenance and Repair (Navy) 1986–88, Dir of Helicopter Projects (PE) 1988–90, Dir Gen of Aircraft (Navy) 1990–92; CEng 1968, FIMechE 1992, FRAeS 1981, FIMgt 1981; *Recreations* golf, skiing; *Style*— Rear Adm Richard Burn, CB, AFC; ✉ Ministry of Defence (Navy), Whitehall, London SW1

BURNELL, (Andrew) Paul; s of Andrew Keith Burnell, of Reading, and Sheila Elizabeth, *née* Bell; *b* 29 Sept 1965; *Educ* Reading Blue Coat Sch, Leicester Poly; *Career* Rugby Union prop forward; clubs: Marlow, Harlequins, Leicester, London Scottish 1988– (capt 1994–); Scotland: 41 caps (debut v England 1989), memb tour to Zimbabwe, NZ and Argentina; memb: British Lions tour to NZ 1993, World Cup squad 1995; Rugby World Unsung Hero 1990; with London Fiduciary Trust 1987–92, dir Anglo Scottish Finance 1992–; *Recreations* gardening, golf; *Style*— Paul Burnell, Esq; ✉ c/o London Scottish FC, Richmond Athletic Ground, Kew Foot Road, Richmond, Surrey TW9 2SS (☎ 0181 332 2473, fax 0181 332 6775)

BURNET, George Wardlaw; LVO (1981), JP (1991); s of Sheriff John Rudolph Wardlaw Burnet, KC (d 1941), and Lucy Margaret Ord, *née* Wallace (d 1962); *b* 26 Dec 1927; *Educ* Edinburgh Acad, Lincoln Coll Oxford (BA), Univ of Edinburgh (LLB); *m* 26 July 1951, Jane Elena Moncrieff, da of late Malcolm Moncrieff Stuart, CIE, OBE; 2 s (Peter b 1957, Andrew b 1962), 1 da (Sarah b 1955); *Career* Served Black Watch (RHR) TA, ret Capt 1957; WS 1954; sr ptnr Murray Beith & Murray WS (ret 1991); chm: The Life Assoc of Scotland Ltd 1985–93, The Caledonian Res Fndn; dir of various cos; Lord-Lt of Midlothian 1992– (DL 1975), cncllr Midlothian 1967–76, convener Church of Scotland Fin Ctee 1980–83; Brig Royal Company of Archers (HM The Queen's Body Guard for Scotland); legal advsr RIAS 1962–92 (hon fell 1980); KStJ; *Recreations* shooting, gardening, architecture; *Clubs* New (Edinburgh); *Style*— George Burnet, Esq, LVO, JP; ✉ Rose Court, Inveresk, Midlothian EH21 7TD (☎ 0131 665 2689, fax 0131 665 1673)

BURNET, Sir James William Alexander (Alastair); kt (1984); s of late Alexander and Schonaid Burnet, of Edinburgh; *b* 12 July 1928; *Educ* The Leys Sch Cambridge, Worcester Coll Oxford; *m* 1958, Maureen Campbell Sinclair; *Career* editor: The Economist 1965–74, Daily Express 1974–76; news presenter ITN 1976–91, assoc ed News at Ten 1982–91; dir: Times Newspaper Holdings Ltd 1982–94, ITN 1982–90, United Racecourses Holdings Ltd 1985–96; memb Cncl Office of the Banking Ombudsman; *Style*— Sir Alastair Burnet; ✉ 43 Hornton Court, Campden Hill Road, London W8 7RU (☎ 0171 937 7563); 33 Westbourne Gardens, Glasgow G12 9PF (☎ 0141 339 8073)

BURNETT, (Robert) Andrew; s of Wing-Cdr Robert Leslie Burnett (d 1990), AFC, of Barton-on-Sea, and Barbara Noel, *née* Pink; *b* 20 Feb 1942; *Educ* St Lawrence Coll Kent; *m* 8 Feb 1964, Patricia, da of John Holden, of Bournemouth; 2 s (Robert Gwyer b 27 Nov 1966, Richard John b 14 April 1969), 2 da (Sarah Louise b 6 Sept 1965, Ann-Marie Frances b 23 Aug 1970); *Career* served HAC 1960–65; Price Waterhouse: joined 1960, ptnr 1974, former nat dir of Fin and IT, currently Euro fin ptnr; dir American C of C; FCA 1965; *Recreations* computers, skiing, golf, jogging; *Clubs* North Hants Golf (Fleet), Hon Artillery Co; *Style*— Andrew Burnett, Esq; ✉ Sutherland, 75 Elvetham Road, Fleet, Hants GU13 8HL (☎ 01252 621419); Price Waterhouse, Southwark Towers, 32 London Bridge Street London SE1 9GY (☎ 0171 939 2441, fax 0171 939 2784)

BURNETT, Air Chief Marshal Sir Brian Kenyon; GCB (1970, KCB 1965, CB 1961), DFC (1942), AFC (1939); s of Kenneth Burnett (d 1959), of Hurley, Maidenhead, Berks, and Anita Catherine, *née* Evans (d 1964); *b* 10 March 1913; *Educ* Charterhouse, Wadham Coll Oxford (BA); *m* 4 Nov 1944, Valerie Mary, da of Joseph St Ludger (d 1952), of Bromsgrove, Worcs; 2 s; *Career* joined RAF 1934, Non-Stop Long Distance Record Flight 7158 miles Egypt to Australia Nov 1938, served WWII Bomber and Trg Cmds, dir Bomber and Reconnaissance Ops Air Miny 1956–57, IDC 1958, air offr Admin HQ Bomber Cmd 1959–61, AOC No 3 Gp Bomber Cmd 1961–64, vice chief of Air Staff 1964–67, air sec MOD 1967–70, C-in-C Br Forces Far East Cmd Singapore 1970–71, ret 1972; ADC to HM The Queen 1953–57 and Air ADC 1969–72; hon fell Wadham Coll Oxford 1974; pres Squash Racquets Assoc 1972–75; vice pres All England Lawn Tennis Club Wimbledon 1984– (chm 1974–83); *Recreations* lawn tennis, golf, skiing; *Clubs* RAF, Int Lawn Tennis of GB, Vincents' (Oxford); *Style*— Air Chief Marshal Sir Brian Burnett, GCB, DFC, AFC; ✉ Heather Hill, Littleworth Cross, Seale, Farnham, Surrey GU10 1JN (☎ 01252 782165)

BURNETT, (Ronald) Bruce Owen; s of Lt Col Ronald John Burnett, OBE, of Bentworth, Hampshire, and Stella Ruth, *née* Cundy; *b* 17 April 1959; *Educ* Denstone Coll, Univ of London (BA); *m* 2 Nov 1991, Pippa Lesley, da of Sqdn Ldr Leslie Sands; *Career* Rowntree Mackintosh: sales rep 1981–82, nat accounts exec 1982–83, trade devpt exec 1983–84, trade mktg/sales promotion mangr 1984–85, asst nat sales mangr 1985–86, brand mangr 1986–87, sr brand mangr 1987–89, gp mktg mangr 1989–91; Trebor Bassett (subsid of Cadbury Schweppes): mktg mangr 1991–92, mktg gen mangr 1992–93, mktg dir 1993–; *Recreations* horse riding, polo, mountaineering, art and architecture, antiques; *Clubs* Cowdray Park Polo; *Style*— Bruce Burnett, Esq; ✉ Trebor Bassett Ltd, Hertford Place, Denham Way, Maple Cross, Herts WD3 2XB (☎ 01923 896565, fax 01923 897347)

BURNETT, Charles David; s and h of Sir David Burnett, 3 Bt, MBE, TD, *qv*; *b* 18 May 1951; *Educ* Harrow, Lincoln Coll Oxford; *m* 21 Oct 1989, Victoria Joan, er da of James Simpson, of Rye, Sussex; 1 da (Roberta Elizabeth b 24 July 1992); *Career* international insurance broker; *Recreations* wine, fishing, travel; *Clubs* Brooks's, Turf, 106; *Style*— Charles Burnett, Esq

BURNETT, Charles John; s of Charles Alexander Urquhart Burnett (d 1977), of Fraserburgh, Aberdeenshire, and Agnes, *née* Watt; *b* 6 Nov 1940; *Educ* Fraserburgh Acad, Gray's Sch of Art Aberdeen (DA), Aberdeen Coll of Educn, Univ of Edinburgh (MLitt, 1992); *m* 29 April 1967, Aileen Elizabeth, da of Alexander Robb McIntyre (d 1982), of Portsoy, Banffshire; 2 s (Sandy b 1972, John b 1976), 1 da (Sara b 1969); *Career* Advertising Dept House of Fraser 1963–64, Exhibitions Div Central Office of Information 1964–68, asst curator Letchworth Museum and Art Gallery 1968–71, head of design Nat Museum of Antiquities of Scotland 1971–85, curator of fine art Scot United Servs Museum Edinburgh Castle 1985–; heraldic advsr Girl Guide Assoc Scotland 1978–, vice patron Genealogical Soc of Queensland Aust 1986–, vice pres Soc of Antiquaries of Scot 1992–95 (memb Cncl 1986–88), memb Advsy Bd Heraldry Soc of Ireland 1986–, vice pres Heraldry Soc of Scot 1987–, librarian Priory of the Order of St John in Scot 1987–; tstee Bield Retirement Housing Tst 1992–96, numerous pubns on Scottish history and heraldry; HM Offr of Arms: Dingwall Pursuivant 1983, Ross Herald 1988–; hon citizen State of Oklahoma USA 1989; convenor Companions of the Order of Malta 1991–94; FSA Scot 1964, AMA 1972, FHSS 1989; KStJ 1991 (CStJ 1982, OStJ 1974, SBStJ 1972); *Recreations* reading, visiting places of historic interest; *Style*— Charles J Burnett, Esq; ✉ 7 Spottiswoode Road, Marchmont, Edinburgh EH9 1BH (☎ 1031 447 3111); Scottish United Services Museum, Edinburgh Castle EH1 2NG (☎ 0131 225 7534); Court of the Lord Lyon, HM New Register House, Edinburgh EH1 3YT (☎ 0131 556 7255)

BURNETT, David Henry; s of George Dawson Burnett, CBE, TD, of Surrey, and Ferdinanda Anna, *née* van den Brandeler; *b* 16 Dec 1951; *Educ* Tonbridge, Churchill Coll Cambridge (MA); *Career* dir of capital markets HSBC Markets Ltd; *Style*— David H Burnett, Esq; ✉ Faircroft, Vale of Health, London NW3 1AN; HSBC Markets Ltd, 10 Queen Street Place, London EC4R 1BQ

BURNETT, Sir David Humphery; 3 Bt (UK 1913), of Selborne House, Co Borough of Croydon; MBE (1945), TD; s of Col Sir Leslie Trew Burnett, 2 Bt, CBE, TD, DL (d 1955), and Joan, *née* Humphery (d 1994); *b* 27 Jan 1918; *Educ* Harrow, St John's Coll Cambridge (MA); *m* 21 July 1948, Geraldine Elizabeth Mortimer, da of late Sir Godfrey Arthur Fisher, KCMG; 2 s (and 1 s decd); *Heir* s, Charles David Burnett, *qv* b 18 May 1951; *Career* served WWII (despatches) in France, N Africa, Sicily and Italy, temp Lt-Col GSO1 1945; ptnr David Burnett & Son (chartered surveyors) 1947–50; dir: Proprietors of Hay's Wharf Ltd 1950–80 (chm 1964–80), Guardian Royal Exchange Assurance Ltd 1967–88; memb Port of London Authy 1962–75; one of HM Lieuts of City of London 1953; chm: London Wharfingers Assoc 1964–71, S London Botanical Inst 1976–81 (pres 1985); memb Cncl Brighton Coll 1971–92; Master Co of Watermen and Lightermen of the River Thames 1964, memb Ct of Assts Worshipful Co of Girdlers (Master 1970), Liveryman Worshipful Co of Glaziers & Painters of Glass; FRICS, FLS; *Style*— Sir David Burnett, Bt, MBE, TD; ✉ Tandridge Hall, nr Oxted, Surrey RH8 9NJ; Twizel Millhouse, Tillmouth Park, Cornhill-on-Tweed, Northumberland TD12 4UX

BURNETT, David John Stuart; s of John Edward Burnett (d 1989); *b* 6 Feb 1958; *Educ* Oundle, Peterhouse Cambridge; *m* 1988, Anne, da of C J C Humfrey (d 1993); 1 s (Joe Alexander Stuart b 9 Aug 1990), 1 da (Laura Frances Kathleen b 16 June 1992); *Career* stockbroker; formerly: ptnr Rowe & Pitman, dir S G Warburg Securities Ltd (head of Japanese equities 1992–94, head of fixed interest and treasy 1994–95); md SBC Warburg (head of S African Equities 1995–96, global head Primary Equity 1996–); *Style*— David Burnett, Esq; ✉ Hall Farm, Wigsthorpe, Northamptonshire PE8 5SE (☎ 01832 720488, fax 01832 720588); 49 Montagu Mansions, London W1 (☎ 0171 935 1372); SBC Warburg, 1 Finsbury Avenue, London EC2M 2PP (☎ 0171 382 4382)

BURNETT, (Ernest) John; s of Ernest Burnett, MBE (d 1991), of Staplehurst, Kent, and Norah Agnes, *née* Davies (d 1982); *b* 7 Oct 1931; *Educ* Liverpool Collegiate Sch, Colfe's GS; *m* 17 Dec 1955, Anne, da of Walter Hazell (d 1946), of IOW; 2 s (Jonathan b 1959 (d 1992), David b 1963), 1 da (Brigitte b 1956); *Career* CA 1955; ptnr Victor Stewart & Co 1959–69, princ John Burnett & Co (later John Burnett McMahon & Co) 1969–; cncllr Maidstone Borough 1972–84; Freeman City of London, Renter Warden Worshipful Co of Bowyers (sometime memb Ct of Assts); FCA, ATII; *Recreations* philosophy, music, walking; *Style*— John Burnett, Esq; ✉ Chequers, High St, Headcorn, Ashford, Kent TN27 9NE (☎ 01622 890052); John Burnett McMahon & Co, 103 Newgate St, London EC1A 7AP (☎ 0171 606 4861, fax 0171 606 4862)

BURNETT, Prof John; s of Arthur Burnett (d 1971), of Nottingham, and Evelyn, *née* Thornton (d 1961); *b* 20 Dec 1925; *Educ* High Pavement Sch Nottingham, Emmanuel Coll Cambridge (BA, MA, LLB), LSE (PhD); *m* 2 Aug 1951, Denise, da of Frank Brayshaw (d 1973), of Morecambe, Lancs; 1 s (Mark Thornton b 1961); *Career* lectr Guildford Tech Coll 1948–59, head of liberal studies Poly of South Bank 1959–63, head of general studies Brunel Coll 1963–66, pro vice chllr Brunel Univ 1980–83 (reader in social history 1966–72, prof 1972–92, emeritus prof 1992–); Leverhulme emeritus fell 1991–93; chm Social History Soc of the UK 1985–90; author of 9 books and numerous papers, articles and reviews; *Books* incl: A History of the Cost of Living (1969 and 1993), Destiny Obscure (1982 and 1994), Useful Toil (1984 and 1994), A Social History of Housing (1986), Plenty and Want. A Social History of Food (1966 and 1989), The Autobiography of the Working-Class (3 Vols, 1984–89), Idle Hands - The Experience of Unemployment 1790–1990 (1994); *Recreations* writing, architecture, antiques, jazz (clarinet); *Style*— Prof John Burnett; ✉ Dept of Government, Brunel University, Uxbridge, Middx (☎ 01895 274000)

BURNETT, Sir John Harrison; kt (1987); s of Rev T Harrison Burnett, of Paisley; *b* 21 Jan 1922; *Educ* Kingswood Sch Bath, Merton Coll Oxford; *m* 1945, Enid Margaret, er da of Rev Dr Edgar W Bishop; 2 s; *Career* served WWII Lt RNVR (despatches) Atlantic, Channel, Mediterranean; fell Magdalen Coll Oxford 1949–54; prof of botany: Univ of St Andrews 1955–60, Univ of Newcastle 1960–68; Regius prof of botany Univ of Glasgow 1968–70, Sibthorpian prof of rural economy and fellow St John's Oxford 1970–79, princ and vice chllr Univ of Edinburgh 1979–87; exec sec World Cncl for the Biosphere 1987–93; chm: Coordinating Cmmn for Biological Recording 1988–, Int Orgn for Plant Info 1991–96; hon research prof Open Univ 1996–; Hon LLD: Dundee 1982, Strathclyde 1983, Glasgow 1987; Hon DSc: Buckingham 1981, Pennsylvania 1983; Dr hc Edinburgh 1988, Hon FRCS Edinburgh 1983, hon fell Green Coll Oxford 1987–; Commendatore Order of Merit Italian Republic 1990; FRSE 1957, FIBiol 1969; *Books* Vegetation of Scotland (1964), Fundamentals of Mycology (1968, 1976 and 1994), Mycogenetics (1975), Fungal Walls and Hyphal Growth (with A J P Trinci, 1979),

Edinburgh University Portaits II (1985), Speciation in Fungi (1988), Maintenance of the Biosphere (with N Polunin, 1990), Surviving with the Biosphere (with N Polunin, 1993), Biological Recording in the United Kingdom (jtly, 1995); *Recreations* writing, walking, gardening; *Clubs* Athenaeum (London); *Style*— Sir John Burnett; ✉ 13 Field House Drive, Oxford OX2 7NT

BURNETT, Richard Leslie; s of Sir Leslie T Burnett, Bt, CBE (d 1955), of Godstone, Surrey, and Joan, *née* Humphery; *b* 23 June 1932; *Educ* Eton, RCM, King's Coll Cambridge; *m* Katrina Eveline, *née* Hendrey; *Career* concert pianist, specialising in fortepianos (early pianos) 1970–; fndr and dir Finchcocks Museum; *Recordings* incl: Schubert's Die Schöne Müllerin (with Nigel Rogers) and Die Winterreise, Haydn's Sonatas, The Romantic Fortepiano, Clementi's Fortepiano Works, Beethoven's Violin Sonatas and Songs, Hummel's Violin and Piano Works, Mozart Piano Quartets, Mendelssohn's Clarinet Works, Brahms' Clarinet Trio; *Style*— Richard Burnett, Esq; ✉ Finchcocks, Goudhurst, Kent TN17 1HH (☎ 01580 211702, fax 01580 211007)

BURNETT, Dr Rodney Alister; s of Ronald Andrew Burnett (d 1961), of Congleton, Cheshire, and Agnes Shirlaw, *née* McGauchie (d 1988); *b* 6 June 1947; *Educ* Sandbach Sch Cheshire, Univ of St Andrews (MB ChB); *m* 1974, Maureen Elizabeth, da of William Patrick Dunn (d 1982), of Burnside, Glasgow; 2 da (Claire Marie b 15 April 1975, Katharine Victoria b 2 June 1981); *Career* lectr in pathology Univ of Glasgow 1974–79, conslt pathologist and head admin Dept of Pathology Stobhill Hosp Glasgow 1979–85, conslt pathologist with responsibility for diagnostic servs Univ Dept of Pathology Western Infirmary Glasgow 1985–; sec Caledonian Branch ACP 1987–94; FRCPath, FRIPHH 1992 (memb Cncl, chm Bd of Educn and Examination for Anatomical Pathology Technicians), FRCP(Glas) 1994; *Recreations* golf; *Style*— Dr Rodney Burnett; ✉ Department of Pathology, Western Infirmary, Glasgow (☎ 0141 211 2000 ext 2343); Royal Institute of Public Health and Hygiene, 28 Portland Place, London W1

BURNETT, Timothy Adrian John; s of late Lt-Col Maurice John Brownless Burnett, DSO, DL, of Dunsa Manor, Dalton, Richmond, North Yorks, and Crystal Henrietta Deschamps, *née* Chamier; *b* 12 April 1937; *Educ* Eton, Trinity Coll Cambridge (BA); *m* 15 July 1961, (Catherine Barbara) Jean, da of Dr Julius Harald Beilby (d 1978), of Aiskew House, Bedale, North Yorks; 1 s (James b 1964), 1 da (Henrietta b 1962); *Career* 2 Lt Coldstream Gds 1956–58; asst keeper Dept of Manuscripts Br Museum 1961, manuscripts librarian Br Library 1986–; owner Dunsa Manor Estate, tstee Kiplin Hall Tst; *Books* The Rise and Fall of a Regency Dandy, The Life and Times of Scrope Berdmore Davies (1981), Byron, Childe Harold Canto III (1988); *Recreations* architectural history, travel, sailing, shooting, fishing; *Clubs* Beefsteak, Pratt's, Royal Yacht Sqdn; *Style*— Timothy Burnett, Esq; ✉ 11 Highbury Place, London N5 1QZ (☎ 0171 226 6234); Dunsa Manor, Dalton, Richmond, North Yorks DL11 7HE; Department of Manuscripts, British Library, Great Russell Street, London WC1B 3DG (☎ 0171 412 7523)

BURNETT-HALL, Richard Hamilton; s of Basil Burnett-Hall (d 1982), and Kathleen Ruth, *née* Wilson (d 1992); *b* 5 Aug 1935; *Educ* Marlborough, Trinity Hall Cambridge (MA); *m* 25 April 1964, Judith Diana (Judy), da of Robert Newton, CMG (d 1983); 2 s (John b 1967, Graham b 1970), 1 da (Louisa b 1965); *Career* Nat Serv RCS 1954–56, 2 Lt 1955; Carpmaels & Ransford 1960–68, Int Synthetic Rubber Co Ltd 1968–71; McKenna & Co Slrs: joined 1971, admitted slr 1974, ptnr 1974–94; ptnr and head of Environmental Gp Bristows Cooke & Carpmael Slrs 1995–; cncl memb UK Environmental Law Assoc; Freeman Berwick-upon-Tweed 1965; memb Law Soc, FCIPA, FRSA; *Books* Environmental Law (1995); *Recreations* music; *Clubs* United Oxford & Cambridge; *Style*— Richard Burnett-Hall, Esq; ✉ Bristows Cooke & Carpmael, 10 Lincoln's Inn Fields, London WC2A 3BP (☎ 0171 400 8000, fax 0171 400 8050)

BURNETT-HITCHCOCK, (Basil) James; *b* 3 Dec 1943; *Educ* Eton, St Edmund Hall Oxford (BA Jurisprudence); *m* March 1973, Elizabeth Jane, *née* Samuel; 2 da (Gemma b 13 June 1977, Laura b 8 July 1980), 1 s (Tom b 25 Aug 1982); *Career* admitted slr 1971; ptnr: Oswald Hickson Comier & Co 1972–78, Cameron Kenn Nordon 1978–80, Cameron Markby 1980–88, Cameron Markby Hewitt 1988– (head Litigation Dept 1990–96); qualified mediator CEDR/ADR Gp; memb Civil Litigation Ctee Law Soc 1993–98, memb Law Soc Working Party on Lord Woolf's reforms; former pres Land Slrs' Litigation Assoc; memb: Law Soc 1971, City Slrs' Co; *Recreations* sailing, boat-building, music, reading, gardening; *Clubs* Helford River Sailing, Bewl Valley Sailing; *Style*— James Burnett-Hitchcock, Esq; ✉ Cameron Markby Hewitt, Sceptre Court, 40 Tower Hill, London EC3N 4BB (☎ 0171 702 2345, fax 0171 702 2303)

BURNEY, Sir Cecil Denniston; 3 Bt (UK 1921), of Preston House, Preston Candover, Co Southampton; s of Sir Charles Dennistoun Burney, 2 Bt, CMG (d 1968), and Gladys, *née* High (d 1982); *b* 8 Jan 1923; *Educ* Eton, Trinity Coll Cambridge; *m* 5 Sept 1957, Hazel Marguerite, yr da of Thurman Coleman (d 1939), of Weymouth, Dorset, and former w of Trevor de Hamel; 2 s (Nigel Dennistoun b 1959, Philip Julian Gerard b 1961); *Heir* s, Nigel Dennistoun Burney, *qv*; *Career* served WWII Special Branch RNVR, Lt; chm: JMD Group plc 1986–92, Hampton Trust plc 1975–87; memb Legislative Cncl of N Rhodesia 1959–64, MP Zambia 1964–68; chm Public Accounts Ctee Zambia 1964–67; Liveryman Worshipful Co of Gunmakers; *Recreations* tennis, skiing; *Clubs* White's, Turf, Carlton, Buck's, Leander, Harare, Ndola; *Style*— Sir Cecil Burney, Bt; ✉ 5 Lyall St, London SW1X 8DW (☎ 0171 235 4014); Plaza 535, Unit 1.23, King's Road, London SW10 0SZ (☎ 0171 352 4001, fax 0171 376 8966)

BURNEY, Nigel Dennistoun; s and h of Sir Cecil Dennistoun Burney, 3 Bt, *qv*; *b* 6 Sept 1959; *Educ* Eton, Trinity Coll Cambridge; *m* 1992, Lucy Vanessa, yst da of Robert Anthony Brooks, *qv*, of Chelsea; 2 s (Max b 19.., Otto James Cecil b 1 Dec 1995); *Clubs* Turf, Annabel's; *Style*— Nigel Burney, Esq; ✉ 1 Broomwood Road, London SW11 (☎ 0171 738 2017)

BURNHAM, Rev Anthony Gerald; s of Selwyn Burnham (d 1972), of Southport, and Sarah, *née* Rush (d 1973); *b* 2 March 1936; *Educ* Silcoates Sch, Univ of Manchester (BA), Northern Coll Manchester; *m* 1961, Valerie Florence, da of Arthur Cleaver; 2 da (Rachel b 1963, Ruth Joyce b 1965), 1 s (John b 1967); *Career* ordained 1961; min: Brownhill Congregational Church Blackburn 1961–66, Poulton-le-Fylde and Hambleton Congregational Churches 1966–69; lectr Northern Coll Manchester 1969–77, min SW Manchester United Reformed Churches 1973–81, provincial moderator NW Province 1981–92, gen sec The United Reformed Church 1992–; regular broadcaster Thought for the Day (BBC Radio 4); *Books* In the Quietness (1981), Say One for Me (1990); *Recreations* theatre, cinema, jazz; *Style*— The Rev Anthony G Burnham; ✉ The United Reformed Church, 86 Tavistock Place, London WC1H 9RT (☎ 0171 916 2020, fax 0171 916 2022)

BURNHAM, 6 Baron (UK 1903); Sir Hugh John Frederick Lawson; 6 Bt (UK 1892); s of 4 Baron Burnham, CB, DSO, MC (d 1963), and Marie Enid, CBE, *née* Scott Robson (d 1979); suc bro 5 Baron Burnham, JP, DL (d 1993); *b* 15 Aug 1931; *Educ* Eton, Balliol Coll Oxford (MA); *m* 1955, Hilary Margaret, yr da of Alan Hunter, of Huntingtowerfield House, Almondbank, Perthshire; 1 s (Hon Harry Frederick Alan b 1968), 2 da (Hon Charlotte Ann b 1960, Hon Emma Lucia b 1961); *Heir* s, Hon Harry Frederick Alan Lawson b 22 Feb 1968; *Career* Scots Gds 1950–51; dep md Daily Telegraph 1984–86 (joined 1955); DG King George's Fund for Sailors 1988–93; *Clubs* Pratt's, Royal Yacht Sqdn; *Style*— The Rt Hon the Lord Burnham; ✉ Woodlands Farm, Beaconsfield, Bucks

BURNHAM, Peter Michael; s of Frank Burnham (d 1980), of Chislehurst, and Winifred Eileen, *née* Fyson (d 1972); *b* 13 May 1935; *Educ* Eltham Coll, Univ of Bristol (BA); *m* 6 Feb 1963, Jill, da of Cdr Langton Gowlland, RN (ret), of Godalming, Surrey; 2 da (Sarah Jane Reily b 6 June 1964, Emma Elizabeth Reily b 6 April 1965); *Career* Nat Serv Pilot Offr RAF 1959–61 (Sword of Honour 1960); Sturges Fraser Cave & Co 1956–59; Coopers & Lybrand: joined 1961, ptnr 1970–93, dep md consulting practice 1981–88, dir 1993–95, ret; dir Satellite Observing Systems Ltd 1993–95, memb Bd Environment Agency 1995–; memb Advsy Ctee for HM Inspectorate of Pollution 1994–95, memb The Archbishops' Cmmn on Cathedrals 1992–94 (memb Follow Up Gp 1995–), dir and dep chm London E Trg and Enterprise Cncl 1989–93, cmmr Historic Bldgs & Monuments Cmmn 1984–88, dir UK Cncl for Computing Devpt 1984–88; Liveryman Worshipful Co of Information Technologists; FCA 1969 (ACA 1959), FCMA 1963; *Recreations* sailing, travelling, listening to music; *Clubs* Reform, Royal Air Force, Royal Thames Yacht; *Style*— Peter Burnham, Esq; ✉ Church Hill House, Church Hill, Midhurst, West Sussex GU29 9NX (☎ 01730 812841, fax 01730 817142); Casalera, Jardinas de la Bahia 1, La Herradura, Granada, Spain (☎ and fax 00 34 58 827426)

BURNINGHAM, John Mackintosh; *b* 27 April 1936; *Educ* Summerhill Sch Leiston Suffolk, Central Sch of Art Holborn (Dip); *m* 1964; *Career* children's author and illustrator; *Books* Borka (1963, Kate Greenaway medal), Trubloff (1964), Chitty Chitty Bang Bang (1964, illustrator), John Burningham's ABC (1964), Humbert (1965), Cannonball Simp (1966); Wall Friezes: Birdland, Lionland, Storyland (1966), Harquin (1967), The Extraordinary Tug-of-War (1968), Wall Friezes: Jungleland, Wonderland (1968), Seasons (1969), Mr Gumpy's Outing (1970, Kate Greenaway award), Around the World in Eighty Days (1972), Wall Friezes - Around the World (1972), Mr Gumpy's Motor Car (1973); Little Book series: The Baby, The Rabbit, The School, The Snow (1974), The Blanket, The Cupboard, The Dog, The Friend (1975), The Adventures of Humbert, Simp and Harquin (1976), Come Away from the Water, Shirley (1977), Time to Get Out of the Bath, Shirley (1978), Would You Rather (1978), The Shopping Basket (1980), Avocado Baby (1982), The Wind In the Willows (1983, illustrator), First Words (1984), Granpa (1984), Play and Learn Books: abc, 123, Opposites, Colours (1985), Where's Julius? (1986), John Patrick Norman McHennessy - the Boy Who is Always Late (1987); John Burningham's: Alphabet Book, Numbers Book, Colours Book, Opposites Book (1987); Oi! Get Off Our Train (1989), Aldo (1991), England (1992), Harvey Slumfenburger (1993), Courtney (1994), Cloudland (1996); *Style*— John Burningham, Esq

BURNLEY, Bishop of 1994–; Rt Rev Martyn William Jarrett; s of Frederick William Cyril Jarrett, of Bristol, and Ivy Ruth, *née* Marsh (d 1989); *b* 25 Oct 1944; *Educ* Cotham GS, KCL (BD, AKC), Univ of Hull (MPhil); *m* 1968, Betty Mabel, da of Herbert Frank Wallis; 2 da (Mary Ruth b 1970, Judith Miriam b 1973); *Career* asst curate: St George E Bristol 1968–70, Swindon New Town 1970–74; vicar: St Joseph the Worker Northolt W End 1976–81 (priest-in-charge 1974–76), St Andrew Uxbridge 1981–85; sr selection sec ACCM 1989–91 (selection sec 1985–88), vicar Our Lady and All Saints Chesterfield 1991–94; *Recreations* psephology, biographies; *Style*— The Rt Rev the Bishop of Burnley; ✉ Dean House, 449 Padiham Road, Burnley, Lancs BB12 6TE (☎ 01282 423564, fax 01282 835496)

BURNS, (Robert) Andrew; CMG (1992); s of Robert Burns, CB, CMG (d 1971), and Mary, *née* Goodland; *b* 21 July 1943; *Educ* Highgate Sch, Trinity Coll Cambridge (MA); *m* 19 July 1973, Sarah, da of Peter Cadogan (d 1962); 2 s ((Robert) Duncan b 29 May 1975, Thomas Alexander Luckwell b 15 March 1977), 1 step da (Ella Jane Kenion b 23 Nov 1968); *Career* HM Dip Serv: 3 sec UK Mission to UN 1965, 2 sec New Delhi 1967–71, 1 sec FCO and UK del Conf on Security and Co-operation in Europe 1971–75, 1 sec and head of Chancery Bucharest 1976–78, private sec to Perm Under Sec FCO 1979–82, cnsllr (Information) Washington 1983–86, head S Asian Dept FCO 1986–88, head News Dept FCO 1988–90, asst under sec of state (Asia) FCO 1990–92, ambass to Israel 1992–Nov 1995, dep under sec of state (non-Europe and trade) FCO 1995–; fell Center for Int Affairs Harvard Univ 1982–83; *Books* Diplomacy, War and Parliamentary Democracy (1985); *Recreations* music, theatre, country pursuits; *Clubs* Garrick, RAC; *Style*— Andrew Burns, Esq, CMG; ✉ c/o Foreign and Commonwealth Office, King Charles Street, London SW1A 2AH (☎ 0171 270 2156, fax 0171 270 2780)

BURNS, Dr Christopher Robert; s of Harold Charles Burns, and Ruby Burns; *b* 13 Feb 1943; *Educ* BSc, MSc, PhD, London Business Sch (Sloan fell); *m* 1970, Sandy Burns; 3 s (James b 23 April 1975, Edward b 11 March 1978, Oliver b 12 Nov 1981); *Career* graduate apprentice rising to gen mangr Engrg Div Alfred Herberts Ltd 1965–78, plant dir T I Jackson 1978–82; md: Glacier Metals 1978–82, Lucas Aerospace (UK) Ltd 1984–88; dep md Staveley Industries plc 1988–89, dir Aerospace Div Hawker Siddeley plc 1990–91; BTR plc: joined 1991, successively chief exec BTR Aerospace, chief exec Aerospace & Batteries, regnl chief exec (CRB), exec dir 1994–; memb Advsy Cncl Imperial Coll Mgmnt Sch; FIProdE 1968, FRSA 1983, CIMgt 1996; *Recreations* running, swimming, theatre, antiques, history; *Style*— Dr Christopher Burns; ✉ BTR plc, Silvertown House, Vincent Square, London SW1P 2PL (☎ 01372 360230, fax 01372 360340, mobile 0468 255680)

BURNS, David Allan; CMG (1993); s of Lt Col Allan Robert Desmond Burns, GM (d 1968), of New Station House, Bagshot, Surrey, and Gladys Frances, *née* Dine (d 1993); *b* 20 Sept 1937; *Educ* Brentwood Sch, Sch of E Euro and Slavonic Studies Univ of London; *m* 15 June 1971, Inger Ellen, da of Nils Gustav Kristiansson, of Stockholm, Sweden; 1 s (Paul b 1971), 1 da (Anna b 1974); *Career* 2 Lt RCS 1956–58; jr appts FO Belgrade and Bangkok 1959–71, head of chancery Br Embassy Belgrade 1972–75, asst head Arms Control Dept FCO 1976–79, political cnsllr Br Embassy Bangkok 1979–83, HM consul gen Boston 1983–87, head N America Dept FCO 1988–91, head Br Mission to Supreme Nat Cncl of Cambodia 1991–93, ambass to the Kingdom of Cambodia 1993–94, ambass to Finland 1995–; memb Marshall Scholarships Selection Ctee for New Eng 1983–87; Freeman City of Lowell Massachusetts 1987; *Recreations* cinema; *Clubs* Travellers; *Style*— HE Mr David Burns, CMG; ✉ c/o Foreign and Commonwealth Office (Helsinki), King Charles Street, London SW1A 2AH

BURNS, Maj-Gen Sir (Walter Arthur) George; GCVO (1991, KCVO 1962), CB (1961), DSO (1944), OBE (1953), MC (1940); s of Walter Spencer Morgan Burns (d 1929) (whose mother was Mary, sister of J Pierpont Morgan, the American financier), of North Mymms Park, Hatfield, Herts, by his w Ruth (herself 2 da of William Cavendish-Bentinck, MP, who was in his turn ggs of 3 Duke of Portland); *b* 29 Jan 1911; *Educ* Eton, Trinity Coll Cambridge; *Career* served Coldstream Gds from 1932: CO 3 Bn (Italy) 1943–44 and Palestine 1947–50, Bde Maj Household Bde 1945–47, CO 3 Bn 1948–50, DAG London Dist 1950–52, Regtl Lt-Col 1952–55, cdr 4 Gds Bde 1955–59, GOC London Dist and Household Bde 1959–62, Col 1966; Lord-Lieut Herts 1961–86; also served as ADC to Viceroy India 1938–40 and Staff Coll Camberley 1945; steward Jockey Club 1964–67; a lay canon of St Albans Cathedral 1992; *Style*— Major-General Sir George Burns, GCVO, CB, DSO, OBE, MC; (☎ 01707 645117)

BURNS, Gordon; s of James Frederic (Fred) Burns (d 1989), of Belfast, and Jean Burns (d 1992); *b* 10 June 1942; *Educ* Dulwich Coll, Campbell Coll Belfast; *m* Sheelagh; 1 s (Tris b 30 Jan 1966), 1 da (Anna b 29 Sept 1978); *Career* freelance broadcaster; early career in newspapers, with Belfast Telegraph, moved into radio with BBC Sports Unit, joined Ulster Televison 1967 (later presenter UTV Reports, host The Gordon Burns Hour), joined Granada TV 1973, presenter and prodr (covering party political bdcasts and presenting Reports Politics and reporting for World In Action progs); presenter and conslt (from inception) The Krypton Factor 1977–, host Searchline feature on Surprise, Surprise 1987–91, co-devisor and presenter A Word In Your Ear (BBC 1) 1993–94, The Family Channel 1995–; writer and presenter A Way Of Life (BBC 2); also presenter: Situations Vacant (BBC) 1991, Future Perfect (Meridian) 1993, Time Off 1993, Treasure Trail (Action Time for Meridian) 1994, Photofinish (Anglia) 1995, Relatively Speaking (BBC) 1996; numerous guest celebrity appearances on various shows; owner and md Stag Presentations Ltd; *Recreations* squash, golf, running, watching Liverpool FC; *Clubs* Mere Golf and Country; *Style—* Gordon Burns, Esq; ✉ c/o David Warwick, David Anthony Promotions, 649 Knutsford Road, Latchford, Warrington, Cheshire WA4 1JJ (☎ 01925 632496, fax 01925 416589)

BURNS, Graham Gordon; s of Gordon Burns, of Bebington, Merseyside, and Freda, *née* Bayley; *b* 9 Aug 1958; *Educ* King's Sch Chester, Univ of Durham (BA); *Career* admitted slr 1983; ptnr Stephenson Harwood 1988– (articled clerk 1981–83, asst slr 1983–88); Freeman City of London Slrs Co 1989; memb Law Soc 1983; *Books* Shipping Finance (ed, 1991, 2 edn 1995); *Recreations* hockey, skiing, cricket, walking; *Clubs* Wimbledon Hockey; *Style—* Graham Burns, Esq; ✉ 2 North View, Wimbledon, London SW19 4UJ; Stephenson Harwood, One St Paul's Churchyard, London EC4M 8SH (☎ 0171 329 4422, fax 0171 606 0822, telex 886789 SHSPC G)

BURNS, Iain Keatings; *b* 6 April 1948; *Educ* Univ of Glasgow (BSc); *m* Adrienne, *née* Kelly; 2 s, 2 da; *Career* South of Scotland Electricity Bd 1970–73, Collins Publishers 1973–82, fin dir International Thomson Publishing Ltd 1982–85, gp fin dir Octopus Publishing Group PLC 1985–87, chief exec Abaco Investments PLC 1988–90 (gp fin dir 1987–88), dir British-Commonwealth Holdings PLC 1988–90, gp md Macmillan Ltd 1993–95 (non-exec dir 1990–93), gp chief exec Aspen Communications PLC 1996–, non-exec dir The Harvill Press Ltd 1996–; ACMA 1973; *Recreations* music, opera; *Style—* Iain K Burns, Esq; ✉ Aspen Communications PLC, Christ Church, Cosway Street, London NW1 5NJ (☎ 0171 479 8534, fax 0171 479 8535)

BURNS, Ian Morgan; CB (1990); s of Donald George Burns (d 1993), and Margaret Brenda Burns (d 1979); *b* 3 June 1939; *Educ* Bootham Sch York, Univ of London (LLM); *m* Susan; 2 da (Juliet b 1969, Annabel b 1971); *Career* Nat Serv 1957–59; examiner Estate Duty Office Inland Revenue 1960–65, princ Home Office 1969–72 (asst princ 1965–69), asst sec Northern Ireland Office 1974–77 (princ 1972–74), asst sec Home Office 1977–79, asst under sec of state Northern Ireland Office 1979–85; DHSS: under sec 1985–87, gen mangr Disablement Servs 1986–87; dep under sec of state Northern Ireland Office 1987–90, head Police Dept Home Office 1990–95, DG Policy Lord Chllr's Dept 1995–; *Clubs* Commonwealth, Athenaeum; *Style—* I M Burns, Esq, CB; ✉ Lord Chancellor's Department, Selborne House, 54–60 Victoria Street, London SW1E 6QB (☎ 0171 210 8719)

BURNS, Dr James; s of John Burns (d 1971), of Liverpool, and Margaret, *née* Eales (d 1945); *b* 20 May 1937; *Educ* St Francis Xavier's Coll Liverpool, Univ of Liverpool (MB ChB, MD); *m* 28 July 1964, Noreen Susan, da of John Dudley Pauling (d 1988), of Liverpool; 2 s (John b 1966, Michael b 1968), 1 da (Sarah b 1969); *Career* lectr in forensic pathology Univ of Liverpool 1969–73, conslt pathologist St John Gen Hosp New Brunswick Canada and hon lectr Dalhousie Univ of Nova Scotia Canada 1973–78, Home Office pathologist City of Birmingham (1978–81), conslt pathologist Selly Oak Hosp Birmingham 1978–81, Home Office pathologist Merseyside 1981–, sr lectr in forensic pathology Univ of Liverpool 1981–, hon conslt histopathologist Royal Liverpool Univ Hosp 1981–; author of papers on pathology and forensic pathology in various jls; memb Bd of Examiners RCPath, cncl memb Br Assoc in Forensic Med (pres elect 1995), memb Govt Policy Advsy Bd for Forensic Pathology, meetings sec Merseyside Medico-Legal Soc; FRCPath 1980 (MRCPath 1969); *Recreations* golf, music, literature; *Clubs* The Xaverian, Birch House; *Style—* Dr James Burns; ✉ 5 Sinclair Drive, Liverpool L18 0HN (☎ 0151 722 6266); Sub-Department of Forensic Pathology, Duncan Building, Royal Liverpool Hospital, PO Box 147, Liverpool L69 3BX (☎ 0151 706 4300, fax 0151 706 5859, tlx 627095 UNILPL G)

BURNS, Julian Delisle (Jules); *b* 18 Sept 1949; *Career* Granada TV: joined as mangr Regnl Programmes 1976, head Programme Servs 1987–88, dir Business Affrs 1988–93 (also co sec and responsible for Personnel Jan-Dec 1993), dir (Main Bd) Programme and Mgmnt Servs and md Granada Enterprises Dec 1993–94, jt md Granada TV and md Dlvnl Ops 1995–, jt md Granada Productions 1996–; *Style—* Jules Burns, Esq; ✉ Granada Television Ltd, Quay Street, Manchester M60 9EA (direct ☎ 0161 827 2090, fax 0161 953 0282)

BURNS, Keith John; s of Brian Brendan Burns, of Leigh, Lancashire, and Veronica Josephine, *née* Renton; *b* 1 Dec 1962; *Educ* St Aelred's HS Newton Merseyside, Manchester Youth Theatre, Mountview Theatre Sch London (singing scholar); *Career* actor; *Theatre* incl: Narrator in The Threepenny Opera (Sweden) 1984, Riff-Raff in The Rocky Horror Show (Nat tour) 1984–85, Montparnasse in Les Miserables (Barbican) 1985–86, Marius in Les Miserables (Palace) 1986, princ performer in Merrily We Roll Along (The Shaftesbury) 1988, Duncaire in Carmen (Vienna Kammeroper) 1988–89, Thuy in Miss Saigon (Drury Lane) 1989, Judas in Jesus Christ Superstar The Concert (Barbican) 1990 and tour 1992, princ performer in Sondheim Masterclasses (Univ of Oxford) 1990; prodr: Kiss of the Spider Woman, Friday Night Tears (musical) 1988, Man in the Moon; *Television* incl: Royal Variety Performance 1987, Olivier Awards 1987, Stage by Stage 1988, The Heat Is On (The Making of Miss Saigon) 1989; *Recordings* original cast recordings incl: Miss Saigon, Les Miserables (also symphonic recording), Jesus Christ Superstar (The Concert Album); *Recreations* travel, walking, records, tennis, Coronation St, reading (crime); *Clubs* Browns, Great Queen St; *Style—* Keith Burns, Esq; ✉ c/o London Management, 2–4 Noel Street, London W1V 3RB (☎ 0171 287 9000, fax 0171 287 3036)

BURNS, Michael James; s of William James Burns (d 1977), and Belle Evelyn, *née* Harrison (d 1970); *b* 18 June 1925; *Educ* St Paul's, Hertford Coll Oxford (MA); *Career* gen mangr and dir Equity & Law Life Assur Soc 1974–86 (joined 1948); non exec dir: Nat Home Loans 1985–91, Ecclesiastical Insur Office 1987–95; memb Cncl Inst Actuaries 1973–82 (treas 1979–81); hon treas: Nat Fedn Music Socs 1981–88, Insur Benevolent Fund 1987–; Freeman City of London 1979; Liveryman: Worshipful Co of Musicians 1981, Worshipful Co of Actuaries 1984; FIA 1955; *Recreations* music, travel; *Style—* Michael Burns, Esq; ✉ 7 Laverton Mews, London SW5 OPB (☎ 0171 370 4709)

BURNS, Paul; s of Edward Burns, of Hamilton, and Gertrude, *née* Press; *b* 28 May 1947; *Educ* St Aloysius Coll Glasgow, Univ of Glasgow (LLB); *m* 11 Sept 1977, Diana Mary, da of Thomas Taylor (d 1986); 1 da (Madeleine Kirsty b 1985); *Career* Lieut RCT; slr; sr ptnr Hamilton Burns & Moore 1987–; fndr and chm Legal Defence Union 1986–, fndr and ed Glasgow Legal Review, memb Cncl Law Soc; *Recreations* flying, fencing, writing, philosophy, archaeology; *Clubs* RSAC, Royal Cwlth Soc; *Style—* Paul Burns, Esq; ✉ Hamilton Burns & Moore, 13 Bath Street, Glasgow G2 1HY (☎ 0141 353 2121)

BURNS, Sandra Pauline; CB (1989); da of John Burns, and Edith Maud, *née* Manning; *b* 19 June 1938; *Educ* Manchester Central HS for Girls, Somerville Coll Oxford (BA, BCL); *Career* called to the Bar Middle Temple 1964, parliamentary counsel 1980–91; computer software designer 1989–; *Style—* Miss Sandra Burns, CB (business name Sandra Skemp); ✉ 997 Finchley Road, London NW11 7HB (☎ 0181 455 7335, fax/answerphone 0181 458 2164)

BURNS, Simon Hugh McGuigan; MP (C) Chelmsford (majority 18,260); s of late Maj Brian Stanley Burns, MC, of Wilts, and Shelagh Mary Nash; *b* 6 Sept 1952; *Educ* Christ the King Sch Accra Ghana, Stamford Sch, Worcester Coll Oxford (BA); *m* 1982, Emma Mary, da of David Clifford, of London; 1 s (Bobby b 1991), 1 da (Amelia b 1987); *Career* political asst to Rt Hon Mrs Sally Oppenheim MP 1975–81, dir What to Buy Ltd 1981–83, conf organiser IOD 1983–87; MP (C) Chelmsford 1987–; PPS to Tim Eggar MP: as Min of State at the Dept of Employment 1989–90, at the Dept of Education 1990–92, as Min of State DTI 1992–93, PPS to Rt Hon Mrs Gillian Shephard as Min of Agriculture 1993–94, asst govt whip 1994–95, a Lord Cmmr to HM Treasy (govt whip) 1995–96, Parly under-sec of state Dept of Health 1996–; *Recreations* photography, travelling, swimming; *Clubs* Chelmsford Conservatives (patron), Essex; *Style—* Simon Burns, Esq, MP; ✉ House of Commons, London SW1 (☎ 0171 219 3000)

BURNS, Sir Terence; GCB (1995), kt (1983); s of Patrick Owen Burns, and Doris Burns; *b* 13 March 1944; *Educ* Houghton-le-Spring GS, Univ of Manchester (BA), London Business Sch; *m* 1969, Anne Elizabeth Powell; 1 s, 2 da; *Career* chief econ advsr to Treasy and head Govt Econ Serv 1980–91, perm sec to Treasy 1991–; vice pres: Soc of Business Economists 1985–, Royal Economic Soc 1992–; memb Bd of Mgmnt Manchester Business Sch 1993–; fell London Business Sch 1989–, visiting fell Nuffield Coll Oxford 1991–; CIMgt 1992; *Recreations* soccer (spectator), golf, music; *Clubs* Reform; *Style—* Sir Terence Burns, GCB; ✉ HM Treasury, Parliament Street, London SW1P 3AG (☎ 0171 270 4360)

BURNS, Prof (Duncan) Thorburn; s of James Thorburn Burns (d 1953), and Olive Mary Constance, *née* Waugh (d 1987); *b* 30 May 1934; *Educ* Whitcliffe Mount Sch, Univ of Leeds (BSc, PhD); *m* 1, 16 Dec 1961 (m dis 1994), Valerie Mary, *née* Vinten; 1 s (James Fredrick Thorburn b 1979), 2 da (Mary Jane Thorburn b 1963, Susan Jean Thorburn b 1967); *m* 2, 28 May 1994, Celia Mary Thorburn-Burns; *Career* lectr in physical chemistry Medway Coll of Technol 1959–63 (asst lectr 1958–59), sr lectr in analytical chemistry Woolwich Poly 1965–66, reader Loughborough Univ of Technol 1971–75 (sr lectr 1966–71), prof of analytical chemistry Queen's Univ Belfast 1975–; author of numerous papers, books and reviews; chm Cmmn V/I IUPAC 1987–89, pres Analytical Div RSC 1988–90, memb Poisons Bd of NI 1989–; Theophilus Redwood Lecture RSC 1982, Analytical Reactions and Reagents Medal and Award RSC 1984, Boyle-Higgins Gold Medal Inst of Chemistry of Ireland 1990, AnalaR Gold Medal and Lecture BDH/RSC 1990, Erhen Gold Nadel Analytical Inst Tech Univ Vienna 1990, SAC Gold Medal RSC 1993, Pregl Medal Austrian Chem Soc 1993; FRSC 1976, MRIA 1984, FRSE 1984; *Recreations* history of chemistry, walking; *Clubs* Savage, Irish; *Style—* Prof Thorburn Burns, FRSE; ✉ Department of Chemistry, Queen's University, Belfast, Northern Ireland BT9 5AG (☎ 01232 335422, fax 01232 247895, telex QUBADM 74487)

BURNSTOCK, Dr Aviva Ruth; da of Prof Geoffrey Burnstock, of London, and Nomi, *née* Hirschfeld; *b* 1 Sept 1959; *Educ* King Alfred Sch Hampstead, Univ of Sussex (BSc), Courtauld Inst of Art (Dip in Conservation, PhD 1991); *m* 1988, Hugh, s of Dr Stephen Sebag-Montefiore; *Career* paintings conservator Art Gall of NSW Sydney 1984–85, scientist National Gallery London 1986–92, lectr Dept of Conservation and Technol Courtauld Inst of Art 1992–; memb Int Inst of Conservation 1981–; *Style—* Dr Aviva Burnstock; ✉ Department of Conservation, The Courtauld Institute of Art, Somerset House, Strand, London WC2R 0RN (☎ 0171 873 2192)

BURNSTOCK, Prof Geoffrey; s of James Burnstock (d 1947), and Nancy, *née* Green (d 1978); *b* 10 May 1929; *Educ* Greenford Co GS, King's Coll London (BSc), King's Coll and UCL (PhD), Melbourne Univ (DSc); *m* 9 April 1957, Nomi, da of Sigmund Hirschfeld (d 1988); 3 da (Aviva b 1959, Tamara b 1960, Dina b 1964); *Career* Nat Serv 1947–48; Nat Inst for Med Res London 1956–57, Dept of Pharmacology Univ of Oxford 1957–59, Dept of Physiology Univ of Illinois (Rockefeller travelling fellowship) 1959; Univ of Melbourne Aust: sr lectr Dept of Zoology 1959–62, reader in physiological zoology 1962–64, prof of zoology and chm of dept 1964–75, assoc dean of biological sci 1969–72; visiting prof Dept of Pharmacology UCLA 1970; UCL: prof of anatomy and head Dept of Anatomy and Developmental Biology 1975–, convener Centre for Neuroscience 1979–, vice dean Faculty of Med Sci 1980–83; visiting prof RSM Fndn New York 1988; author of over 950 pubns in scientific and med jls and books; chm Scientific Advsy Bd Eisai London Ltd 1990–, vice pres Anatomical Society of Great Britain and Ireland 1990, memb Gt Barrier Reef Ctee, fndr memb Int Cncl for Scientific Devpt and Int Acad of Sci; memb Cncl: The Bayliss and Starling Soc, Royal Postgrad Med Sch; memb: Int Cncl Neurovegetative Res, Bd MRC, MRC Inst for Molecular Cell Biology, Br Physiological Soc, Aust Physiological and Pharmacological Soc, Int Soc for Biochemical Pharmacology, Br Pharmacological Soc, Br Anatomical Soc, Euro Artery Club, Int Brain Res Orgn, Int Soc for Devptal Neuroscience, Euro Neuroscience Assoc, Clinical Autonomic Res Soc, Euro Neuropeptide Club, Neurogastroenterology Soc, Academia Europaea 1992; foreign memb Russian Soc of Neuropathology 1993; Otto Krayer lecture Harvard 1976, Synthelabo lecture Paris 1979, British Physiological Soc Review lecture Birmingham 1979, Cumings Meml lecture 1980, Schueler Distinguished lecture in pharmacology Tulane Inst New Orleans 1982, First Ulf von Euler lecture in physiology Stockholm 1985, First John T Shepherd lecture Mayo Clinic Rochester 1986, Harold Lamport lecture in physiology Seattle 1986, Oliver-Sharpey lecture RCP 1987, Ariëns lecture Utrecht 1987, Heymans memorial lecture Gent 1990, Knight visiting prof lecture Miami 1993, Charnock Bradley lecture Edinburgh 1994, C Ladd Prosser lectr Illinois 1995; ed in chief Journal of the Autonomic Nervous System, series ed The Autonomic Nervous System Vols 1–14 1992–97; memb Editorial Bd of over 30 other Journals incl: Jl of Anatomy, Jl of Vascular Research, Int Jl of Developmental Neuroscience, Jl of Autonomic Nervous System (ed-in-chief); memb int advsy bd NeuroReport, conslt to Euro Jl of Pharmacology; Hon MSc 1962; FAA 1971, FRS 1986, Hon MRCP 1987; *Books* How Cells Work (1972), Adrenergic Neurons: Their Organisation, Function and Development in the Peripheral Nervous System (jtly, 1975); An Atlas of the Fine Structure of Muscle and its Innervation (jtly, 1976), Vascular Neuroeffector Mechanisms (jt ed, 1976), Purinergic Receptors (ed, 1981), Somatic and Autonomic Nerve-Muscle Interactions (jt ed, 1983), Nonadrenergic Innervation of Blood Vessels (jt ed, 1988), Peptides - A Target for New Drug Development (jt ed, 1991), Neural Endothelial Interactions in the Control of Vascular Tone (jt author, 1993); *Recreations* wood sculpture and tennis; *Style—* Prof Geoffrey Burnstock, FRS; ✉ Dept of Anatomy and Developmental Biology, UCL, Gower St, London WC1E 6BT (☎ 0171 380 7053, fax 0171 380 7349)

BURNTON, Stanley Jeffrey; QC (1982); s of Harry Burnton, of London, and Fay, *née* Levy; *b* 25 Oct 1942; *Educ* Hackney Downs GS, St Edmund Hall Oxford (MA); *m* 26 Feb 1971, Gwenyth, da of Frank Castle, of Aust; 1 s (Simon b 1974), 2 da (Abigail b 1972, Rebecca b 1976); *Career* called to the Bar Middle Temple 1965, bencher of the Middle Temple, recorder of the Crown Court; *Recreations* music, theatre, wine, travel, reading; *Style—* Stanley Burnton, Esq, QC; ✉ 9 Kidderpore Ave, London NW3 7SX (☎ 0171 431 2819); 1 Essex Court, Temple, London EC4Y 9AR (☎ 0171 583 2000, fax 0171 583 0118)

BURR, Martin John; s of Bertram John Burr, and Margaret, *née* Mapleson; *b* 19 Feb 1953; *Educ* Berkhamstead Sch, Pembroke Coll Oxford (BA, MA, Dip Comp Phil); *Career* called to the Bar Middle Temple 1978; joined: Lincoln's Inn 1980, Inner Temple 1988; head of chambers 1993– (joint head 1989–93); memb: Sion Coll, Henry Sweet Soc, Int Arthurian Soc, Seldon Soc, Philological Soc, Br Archeological Assoc, Henry Bradshaw Soc, Soc of Trusts and Estates Practitoners, Anglican and Eastern Churches Assoc, Ecclesiastical Law Soc; sec Guild Church Cncl St Dunstan-in-the-West Fleet St; Freeman

City of London; ACIArb 1990 *Oratorios Composed* incl: Vita Sci Bonifati, Vita Sci Justi, Vita Sci Cuthberti, Vita Sci Ceddis, Vita Sci Dunstani, Vita Sci Edwardi, Confessoris et Regis, Vita Sci Bedae, Vita Moysis, Vita Eliae, Vita Sci Iohannis Baptistae, Vita Sci Pirani, Vita Abrahami, Vita Sci Petroci, Vita Isaiae, Vita Sci Brendani, Vita Job, Vita Sci Davidis, Vita Sci Jospehi, Vita Sci Patrici, Vita Adae, Vita Sci Mandeti, Vita Noe, Vita Sci Euci; *Publications* The Law and Health Visitors (1982), Chancery Practice (1991/94); papers incl: Legal Punctuation - Past and Present? (1986), Anglo-Saxon Wills their Beginnings and Continuations but not their Ends (1989), The Taxation of Trusts (1990), The Finance Act 1988 - Points for Practitioners (1990), The Saxons said 'Said' and 'Aforesaid' (1991), CGT and IHT in the Finance Act 1990 (1991), Trusts and the Accountant - Pitfalls and Possibilities (1991), Pitfalls in Trust Drafting - Fiduciary Minefields and Quagmires (1991), At Home or Not At Home? (1992), The Prayer, The Soul and Frankalmoign Tenure in Anglo-Saxon England (1993), Bar Conveyancing Casebook (ed, 12 edn, 1994), Bar Conveyancing Textbook (ed, 15 edn, 1994/95), Bar GPII - 1994 Trinity Examinations Suggested Solutions (Trusts) (1994, 1995 edn, 1995), Bar Practical Conveyancing- 1994 Trinity Examination Suggested Solutions (1994, 1995 edn, 1995), Church and Court in Anglo-Saxon England (1995), A Church in Trust (1995); poems published: The River Dart Devonshire, The River Otter Devonshire, Rougemont Gardens Exeter, Pictures of Suffolk, Epiphany at Winchester, Maundy Mass, Easter Morning, Easter Day, Buckfast Abbey Devonshire, The River Axe, The Land of the Celtic Saints, The Waters of Sherborne, Lyme Regis, Dorset, Silence, A Saxon Church; *Recreations* theology, liturgiology, opera, plainsong, singing, composing music, neumology, philology, writing poetry, railways; *Style—* Martin Burr, Esq; ✉ Chambers of Martin Burr, 4th Floor, Eldon Chambers, 30–32 Fleet Street, London EC4Y 1AA (☎ 0171 353 4636, fax 0171 353 4637)

BURR, His Hon Judge Michael Rodney; s of Frank Edward Burr, of Mayals Rd, Swansea, and Aileen Maud, *née* May; *b* 31 Aug 1941; *Educ* Brecon Boys GS, King Edward VI Sch Chelmsford; *m* 30 March 1963, Rhoda, da of Ernest Rule, of Aberdare, Mid Glamorgan; 4 s (David b 1964, Richard b 1965, Andrew b 1967, Edwin b 1973), 1 da (Elizabeth b 1970); *Career* admitted slr 1964; asst slr Hilliard and Ward Chelmsford 1964–69, sr ptnr Peter Williams and Co Swansea 1972–92, recorder 1988–92 (asst recorder 1983–88), circuit judge (Wales and Chester Circuit) 1992–; sec Inc Law Soc of Swansea and Dist 1980–83; non cncl memb of Law Soc ctees: Professional Purposes Ctee 1985–86, Adjudication Ctee 1986–89; memb Law Soc; *Recreations* flying; *Style—* His Honour Judge Burr

BURRAGE, Kenneth Walter; *b* 27 April 1939; *Educ* Churchers Coll Petersfield, Guildford and Wimbledon Tech Coll (ONC, HNC); *m*; 3 c; *Career* British Railways Bd (now Railtrack PLC): signal engrg student Southern Region 1956–61, Signalling Design Office Southern Region 1961–65, project mgmnt (signalling and telecommunications projects) 1965–71, divnl signal engr SW Div Southern Region 1971–74, princ asst engr Regnl HQ Southern Region 1974–77, regnl signal engr Western Region 1977–81, chief signal and telecommunications engr London Midland Region 1981–88, dir of signal and telecommunications engrg Bd HQ 1989–92 (dep dir 1988–89), dir of engrg standards Bd HQ 1992–94, memb BRT Bd 1993–94, controller Safety Standards Railtrack PLC 1994–95; dir Westinghouse Signals Ltd 1995–; memb Cncl (Senate from 1996) Engrg Cncl 1992– (memb Working Party on Unification of Engrg profession, chm Implementation Panel for Risk Code), memb Cncl IEE 1994–; CEng, FIEE, FIRSE, FCIT; FRSA; *Recreations* music, sport, walking, ornithology, DIY and house alterations; *Style—* Kenneth Burrage, Esq; ✉ Westinghouse Signals Ltd, PO Box 79, Pew Hill, Chippenham, Wilts SN15 1JD (☎ 01249 441441, fax 01249 441901)

BURRELL, Denis James; CBE (1982), DL (Bucks 1995); s of Edwin Charles Merrick Burrell (d 1950); *b* 25 May 1930; *Educ* Rugby, Clare Coll Cambridge (MA); *m* 1977, Susan, da of Eric Alwyn Ingham (d 1978); 1 s (Charles); *Career* chm and md Martin Baker Aircraft Co Ltd 1981– (mfr of ejection seats for use in mil aircraft); winner: Queen's Award for Export 1982 and 1986, Queen's Award for Technol 1993; Liveryman Worshipful Co of Coachmakers & Coach Harness Makers (Master 1991–92, memb Ct of Assts), Freeman Guild of Air Pilots and Air Navigators; FRAeS; *Recreations* tennis, gardens; *Clubs* Boodle's; *Style—* Denis Burrell, Esq, CBE, DL; ✉ Denham Mount, Denham, nr Uxbridge, Middx; Martin-Baker Aircraft Co Ltd, Higher Denham, nr Uxbridge, Middx UB9 5AJ (☎ 01895 836500)

BURRELL, (Francis) Gary; QC (1996); *b* 7 Aug 1953; *Educ* Belfast Boys' Model, Univ of Exeter (LLB); *Career* called to the Bar Inner Temple 1977, recorder of the Crown Ct 1996– (asst recorder 1992), specialist in personal injury and med negligence litigation; memb Bar Cncl, NE Circuit rep Personal Injury Bar Assoc, former pres S Yorks Medico Legal Soc; memb Professional Negligence Bar Assoc; *Publications* author of various articles in periodical Quantum and in Personal Injury Bar Assoc Newsletter; *Recreations* sailing, fishing; *Style—* Gary Burrell, Esq, QC; ✉ Paradise Square Chambers, 12 Paradise Square, Sheffield S1 2DE (☎ 0114 273 8951); Gough Square Chambers, 9 Gough Square, London EC4A 3DE (☎ 0171 353 5371)

BURRELL, Mark William; yr s of Sir Walter Burrell, 8 Bt, CBE, TD, DL (d 1985); *b* 9 April 1937; *Educ* Eton, Pembroke Coll Cambridge (BA); *m* 1966, Margot Rosemary, yr da of Westray Pearce, of Killara, NSW, Aust; 2 s (William, Anthony), 1 da (Sophie); *Career* dir Lazard Bros & Co Ltd 1974–86 (joined corp fin dept 1970), development dir Pearson plc 1986– (non-exec dir 1977–86); non-exec chm Royal Doulton Ltd; *Style—* Mark Burrell, Esq; ✉ Pearson plc, 3 Burlington Gardens, London W1X 1LE (☎ 0171 411 2000, fax 0171 411 2229)

BURRELL, Michael Ian; s of Sydney Burrell, of Haslemere, Surrey, and Mary, *née* Smith; *b* 25 June 1950; *Educ* Godalming Co GS Surrey, St Peter's Coll Oxford (MA); *Career* journalist Durham Advertiser 1971–72, local govt corr Evening Argus Brighton 1972–73, lobby corr Westminster Press 1973–83, Profile PR 1983–86; chm European Strategy 1990–, md Westminster Strategy 1986–, chief exec The Grayling Group 1991–; author of various articles on lobbying Westminster, Whitehall and the European Union; *Recreations* doing nothing in the sunshine; *Style—* Michael Burrell, Esq; ✉ Westminster Strategy, 1 Dean's Yard, London SW1P 3NR (☎ 0171 799 9811, fax 0171 233 0124); European Strategy, 13A avenue de Tervueren, 1040 Brussels, Belgium (☎ 00 32 2 732 7040, fax 00 32 2 732 7176)

BURRELL, Sir (John) Raymond; 9 Bt (GB 1774), of Valentine House, Essex; s of Lt-Col Sir Walter Raymond Burrell, 8 Bt, CBE, TD, DL (d 1985), and Hon Anne Judith, OBE, da of 3 Baron Denman, GCMG, KCVO, PC, JP; *b* 20 Feb 1934; *Educ* Eton; *m* 1, 1959 (m dis 1971), Rowena Frances, da of Michael H Pearce; 1 s; m 2, 1971, Margot Lucy, da of F E Thatcher, of Sydney; 1 s (Andrew John b 1974), 1 da (Catherine Anne Lucy b 1977); *Heir* s, Charles Raymond Burrell b 27 Aug 1962; *Style—* Sir Raymond Burrell, Bt; ✉ Baynton House, Coulston, Westbury, Wiltshire BA13 4NY (☎ 01380 830 273, fax 01380 830 988)

BURRETT, (Frederick) Gordon; CB (1974); s of Frederick Harold John Burrett, of London (d 1957), and Marion, *née* Knowles (d 1956); *b* 31 Oct 1921; *Educ* Emanuel Sch, St Catharine's Coll Cambridge (BA); *m* 17 April 1943, Margaret Joan, da of Edward George Giddins of Petersfield, Hants (d 1969); 1 s (John b 1954), 2 da (Ann b 1948, Jill b 1949); *Career* served in RE, N Africa, Italy, Yugoslavia, Greece 1942–45, Capt (despatches); Dip Serv: joined 1946, 3 sec Budapest 1946–49, FO 1949–51, vice consul NY 1951–54, FO 1954–57, 1 sec Rome 1957–60; HM Treasy 1960–67 (private sec to chief sec to the Treasy 1963–64, asst sec 1964–67), Cabinet Office 1967–68 (sec Review Bodies on Doctors and Dentists' Remuneration and on Pay of Higher Civil Serv 1967–68), Civil Serv Dept 1969–81 (under sec 1969–72, dep sec 1972–81, memb Bd Civil Serv Pay Research Unit 1978–81), ret Civil Serv 1981; conducted Govt scrutiny of V & A and Science Museums 1982; ldr UK Govt reviews of: policies and operations of Cwlth Inst 1987, responsibilities of the dirs of the nat museums and galleries 1987, grading of sr Arts Cncl and Br Film Inst posts 1988; advsr to Govt of Oman on Civil Serv reorganisation 1984, chm Ctee of Inquiry into Civil Serv Pay Hong Kong 1988–89; chm: Churches Conservation Tst (formerly Redundant Churches Fund) 1982–95, Wagner Soc 1984–87; Archbishops' Silver Cross of St Augustine 1995; FSA 1985; *Publications* article on the watercolours of J M Wright (1777–1866) in vol 54 Old Water Colour Society's Club Annual; *Recreations* reading, music, walking; *Clubs* Athenaeum; *Style—* Gordon Burrett, Esq, CB, FSA; ✉ 14 Church Rd, Claygate, Surrey KT10 0JP (☎ 01372 462783)

BURRIDGE, Rev Dr Richard Alan; s of Alan Burridge, of Exmouth, Devon, and Iris Joyce, *née* Coates (d 1994); *b* 11 June 1955; *Educ* Bristol Cathedral Sch (County scholar), Univ Coll Oxford (MA), Univ of Nottingham (CertEd, Dip in Theology, PhD); *m* 1 Sept 1979, Susan Burridge, *née* Morgan; 2 da (Rebecca b 5 Aug 1986, Sarah b 1 March 1988); *Career* classics master and house tutor Sevenoaks Sch 1978–82, curate St Peter and St Paul Bromley Parish Church 1985–87, Lazenby chaplain and pt/t lectr Depts of Theology and Classics and Ancient History Univ of Exeter 1987–94, dean and hon lectr Dept of Theology and Religious Studies KCL 1994–; lecture tour to American Univs and Seminaries 1993, St Matthiastide lecture Bristol 1994, Boundy Memorial lectures Univ of Exeter 1993, preacher Univ Sermon Univ of Oxford 1994, inaugural lecture KCL 1995; memb: Cncl of Mgmnt St John's Coll Nottingham Ltd 1986–, Cncl of Reference Monarch Publications 1992–, Gen Synod Church of England 1994–, Studiorum Novi Testamenti Societas (SNTS) 1995–, Society for the Study of Theology (SST) 1995–; chm Eric Symes Abbot Memorial Fund 1994–, tstee Christian Evidence Soc 1994–, external examiner to South West Ministry Training Course 1995–, chm C of E's Educnl Validation Ctee 1996–; *Publications* Sex Therapy: Some Ethical Considerations (1985), What are the Gospels? A Comparison with Graeco-Roman Biography (1992, paperback reprint 1995), Four Gospels, One Jesus? (1994, USA reprint 1996); *Recreations* golf, swimming, cycling, being with my family; *Style—* The Rev Dr Richard Burridge; ✉ The Dean, King's College London, Strand, London WC2R 2LS (☎ 0171 873 2333, fax 0171 873 2344)

BURRIDGE, Simon St Paul; s of James Dugdale Burridge, of Ab Kettleby, nr Melton Mowbray, Leics, and Anne Henrietta-Maria St Paul, *née* Butler; *b* 20 March 1956; *Educ* Sherborne, Queen's Coll Oxford; *m* 13 Sept 1986, Camilla Rose, da of Bryan Rogerson Barkes; 3 da (Felicity Rose St Paul b 3 May 1989, Laura St Paul b 5 Sept 1991, Katie Victoria St Paul b 12 May 1994); *Career* advertising exec; graduate trainee Ayer Barker Hegemann Feb-July 1979, account exec Minden Luby & Associates 1979–1981; Dewe Rogerson: account exec 1981–82, account dir 1982–84, dir 1984–87; dir: J Walter Thompson 1988–93 (sr assoc dir 1987–88), Abbott Mead Vickers BBDO 1994–96, J Walter Thompson 1996–; *Recreations* horse racing (family owns Desert Orchid), literature; *Style—* Simon Burridge, Esq; ✉ J Walter Thompson Company Ltd, 40 Berkeley Square, London W1X 6AD (☎ 0171 499 4040)

BURRILL, Timothy Peckover; yr s of Lyonel Peckover Burrill, OBE (d 1983), and Marjorie Sybil, *née* Hurlbutt (d 1976); *b* 8 June 1931; *Educ* Eton, Sorbonne; *m* 1, 1959 (m dis 1966), Philippa, o da of Maurice Hare; 1 da (Rebecca Nina b 1961); m 2, 1968 (m dis 1989), Santa, er da of John Raymond; 1 s (Joshua Hal Peckover b 1973), 2 da (Jemima Lucy b 1970, Tabitha Sara b 1974); *Career* served Grenadier Gds 1949–52, 2 Bn 1950–52; jr mgmnt Cayzer Irvine & Co 1952–56; entered film indust 1956, joined Brookfield Productions 1965, md Burrill Productions 1966–, dir World Film Services 1967–69, first prodn admin Nat Film and TV Sch 1972; md: Allied Stars (responsible for Chariots of Fire) 1979–80, Chargeurs Productions Ltd 1994–; dir: Artistry Ltd (responsible for Superman and Supergirl films) 1982, Central Casting 1988–92; conslt: Nat Film Devpt Fund 1980–81, The Really Useful Gp 1989–90; UK film indust rep on Eurimages 1994–; chm: BAFTA 1981–83 (vice chm 1979–81), Film Asset Development plc 1987–94, First Film Fndn 1989–; prodr memb: Cinematograph Films Cncl 1980–83, Gen Cncl ACTT 1975–76, Exec Ctee Br Film and TV Prodrs' Assoc 1981–90; govr: Nat Film and TV Sch 1981–92, Royal Nat Theatre 1982–88; vice chm The Producers' Assoc (PACT) 1993–94 (memb Exec Ctee 1990–), chm Industrial Production Trg Fund 1993–; *Recreations* gardening, theatre; *Style—* Timothy Burrill, Esq; ✉ New Poplars, Hornton, nr Banbury, Oxon OX15 6BW (☎ 01295 678015, fax 01295 678023, mobile 0385 298680)

BURRINGTON, Ernest; s of Harold Burrington (d 1978), of Chadderton, Lancs, and Laura, *née* Slater; *m* 5 Jan 1950, Nancy, da of Fred Crossley (d 1988), of Lees, Oldham; 1 s (Peter), 1 da (Jill); *Career* served Army 1943–47; reporter and sub ed Oldham Chronicle 1947–49 (reporter 1941–43), sub ed Bristol Evening World 1950; Daily Herald: sub ed Manchester 1950, night ed 1955, London night ed 1957; asst ed The Sun (IPC) 1965 (night ed 1964), asst ed and night ed The Sun (News International) 1969; Mirror Group Newspapers: dep night ed Daily Mirror 1970, ed Sunday People 1985–88 and 1989–90 (dep ed 1971, assoc ed 1972), asst publisher and dep chm 1988–91, md 1990–91, chm 1991–92; dep chm Mirror Publishing Co 1988–91; dir: MGN Magazine and Newsday Ltd 1989–91, Sunday Correspondent 1990, Sygma Photo Agency Paris 1990–91, The European Ltd 1990–91, IQ Newsgraphics Ltd 1990–91; chm: Syndication International 1989–92, Sygma Picture Agency Paris 1990–91; dep publisher Globe Communications USA 1993–95 (vice pres publishing 1995); memb: Int Press Inst 1988–92, Foreign Press Assoc, Cncl Newspaper Publishers' Assoc 1988–92; tstee: Int Inst of Child Studies, Youthscan 1988–91; *Recreations* travel, bridge; *Style—* Ernest Burrington, Esq; ✉ South Hall, Dene Park, Shipbourne Road, Tonbridge, Kent TN11 9NS (☎ 01732 368517); 17499 Tiffany Trace Drive, Boca Country Club, Boca Raton, Florida, USA (☎ 00 1 407 995 9897)

BURROUGH, (Anthony) Paul; s of Evan Jerome Ridgway Burrough (d 1986), of Oxford, and Elaine Shelton, *née* Bliss; *b* 14 Dec 1943; *Educ* Beaumont Coll, RAC Cirencester; *m* 1, 7 June 1968, Veronica Ann, da of Lt-Col Reginald Walter (d 1982); 1 s (Daniel b 7 March 1969), 1 da (Kirsty b 19 Feb 1971); m 2, Gillian Olivia Courtenay, da of Alfred Edward Courtenay Snell (d 1985); *Career* fndr Burrough & Co Estate Agents 1979; MICAC; *Recreations* shooting, riding, racing; *Style—* Paul Burrough, Esq; ✉ 1 Manor Farm Cottages, Lower Green, Inkpen, Newbury Berks (☎ 01488 668882); Burrough & Co, Kennet House, High St, Hungerford, Berks (☎ 01488 682349, car 0836 292976)

BURROUGHS, Dr Andrew Kenneth; s of Kenneth Douglas Burroughs, of Pineto, Italy, and Vidia, *née* Sfredda; *b* 26 May 1953; *Educ* Kent Coll Canterbury, Univ of Liverpool (MB ChB, MRCP 1978, FRCP (London) 1991); *m* 1, 19 Aug 1979 (m dis 1991), Rajesvarie, da of Govindarajoloo Kamalason Nulliah, of Lydiate, Liverpool; 1 da (Natasha b 1983); m 2, 27 Nov 1993, Clare, da of James Davey, of Box, Wilts; 1 s (James b 1994), 1 da (Helena b 1996); *Career* registrar in gen med and gastroenterology Royal Free Hosp London 1979–81, hon clinical lectr Royal Free Hosp Sch of Med 1981–83; Royal Free Hosp and Sch of Med: lectr in med and hon sr registrar 1983–87, sr lectr and hon conslt physician 1988–93, conslt physician and hepatologist 1993–; ctee memb Br Assoc for the Study of the Liver, memb Cncl Br Soc of Gastroenterology 1993–96; Cavaliere Ufficiale al Ordine del Merito della Repubblica Italiana 1989; *Recreations* philately, tourism; *Style—* Dr Andrew Burroughs; ✉ Liver Transplantation and

Hepato-biliary Medicine, Royal Free Hospital and School of Medicine, Pond St, Hampstead, London NW3 2QG (☎ 0171 794 0500 ext 3978, fax 0171 794 4688)

BURROUGHS, Andrew St John Wolfe; s of Peter Noel Gore Burroughs, of Sudbury, Suffolk, and Jennifer Wolfe, *née* Potter; *b* 5 April 1958; *Educ* Bedford Sch, St Catharine's Coll Cambridge (exhibitioner, MA), Guildhall Sch of Music and Drama (studied viola, pt/t); *m* 1980 (m dis 1992), Jacqueline Margaret, da of Anthony Wylson; 1 da (Ellen Lora b August 1984), 1 s (Toby Walter Wolfe b Dec 1987); *Career* news trainee Westminster Press 1979, with Far East Broadcasting Seychelles 1982–84; BBC: with BBC World Service 1984–85, BBC Radio 4 1985–86, prodr BBC TV News and Current Affrs 1986–88, religion, arts and community affrs corr Social Affrs Unit BBC TV 1988–94, sometime social affrs corr, currently arts and religion corr Social Affrs Unit; highly commended BP Arts Journalism Award 1991, TV Award Race in the Media 1994; memb Wolfe Society; *Books* BBC Review of the Year 1990 and 1991 (contrib); *Recreations* composer and performer of jazz and blues guitar; *Style*— Andrew Burroughs; ✉ BBC Social Affairs Unit, Room 7083, Television Centre, Wood Lane, London W12 7RJ (☎ 0181 576 7588, fax 0181 749 9016, car 0860 533828)

BURROUGHS, Philip Anthony; s of Anthony John Burroughs, of Holt, Norfolk, and Brenda Mabel, *née* Downing; *b* 2 Oct 1955; *Educ* Hemel Hempstead GS, Univ of Bristol (LLB); *m* 23 July 1977, Katharine Mary, da of Douglas Campbell Doughty, of Tring, Herts; 1 s (Alastair b 1984), 1 da (Rebecca b 1982); *Career* admitted slr 1980; asst slr Freshfields 1980–83, ptnr Lawrence Graham 1985–93 (asst slr 1983–85), ptnr Coudert Brothers 1993–; chm Langleys Round Table 1988–89 (memb 1984); Freeman Worshipful Co of Solicitors; memb: Law Soc, City of London Law Soc, Westminster Law Soc; affiliate: Br Cncl of Shopping Centres, City Property Assoc; *Recreations* reading, wine, gardening; *Style*— Philip Burroughs, Esq; ✉ Messrs Coudert Brothers, 20 Old Bailey, London EC4M 7JP (☎ 0171 248 3000, fax 0171 248 3001)

BURROW, Dr Charles Thomas; s of Richard Burrow, of Lancaster, and Ivy Reta, *née* Coates; *b* 22 Sept 1945; *Educ* Lancaster Royal GS, Univ of Liverpool (MB ChB); *m* Ann Jane, da of William George Frederick Gunstone (d 1977); 1 s (Michael b 1987), 2 da (Katharine b 1976, Lucy b 1977); *Career* lectr Univ of Liverpool 1975–77, conslt pathologist Walton Hosp Liverpool 1978–; FRCPath 1988 (MRCPath 1976); *Style*— Dr Charles Burrow; ✉ Fazakerley Hospital, Lower Lane, Liverpool (☎ 0151 525 5980)

BURROW, John Halcrow; CBE (1993, OBE 1987); *b* 1935; *Educ* Police Staff Coll Bramshill, UCL (Bramshill scholarship, LLB), RCDS; *m* ; 3 c; *Career* Met Police: joined 1958, sgt 1958–63, inspr 1963–71, chief inspr and unit cdr Kingston-upon-Thames 1971–72, supt and sub-divnl cdr Wimbledon 1972–75, chief supt and divnl cdr Central London 1975–77; dep chief constable Merseyside Police 1983–88 (joined as asst chief constable 1977), chief constable Essex Police 1988–; Foreign Office appointed reviewer of Royal Swaziland Police 1981; ACPO: chm Conditions of Serv Ctee, chm ACPO Working Gp on Data Protection; pres ACPO 1992–93; memb Cncl St John Ambulance Essex, pres League of Friends Chelmsford Trg Centre; *Recreations* walking (especially in Cumbria), classical music; *Style*— John Burrow, Esq, CBE; ✉ Essex Police HQ, PO Box No 2, Springfield, Chelmsford, Essex CM2 6DA (☎ 01245 491491, fax 01245 452123)

BURROW, Prof John Wyon; s of Charles Wyon Burrow, of Exeter, and Amy Alice, *née* Vosper; *b* 4 June 1935; *Educ* Exeter Sch, Christ's Coll Cambridge (MA, PhD); *m* 11 Oct 1958, Diane Margaret, da of Harold William Dunnington (d 1983), of Cambridge; 1 s (Laurence b 1961), 1 da (Francesca b 1968); *Career* res fell Christ's Coll Cambridge 1959–62, fell Downing Coll Cambridge 1962–65, lectr UEA 1965–69; prof of intellectual history Univ of Sussex 1982–95 (reader in history 1969–82), prof of European thought Univ of Oxford 1995–; fell Balliol Coll Oxford 1995; Dr in Scienze Politiche (Bologna) 1988; FRHistS, FBA; *Books* Evolution and Society (1966), A Liberal Descent (1981), Gibbon (1985), Whigs and Liberals (1988); *Style*— Prof John Burrow, FBA; ✉ c/o Balliol College, University of Oxford, Oxford OX1 3BJ (☎ 01865 277777)

BURROW, Robert Philip; s of Robert F Burrow, and Rosalind, *née* Hughes; *b* 24 March 1951; *Educ* St George's Coll Weybridge, Fitzwilliam Coll Cambridge (MA); *m* 21 July 1984, Angela Mary, da of Henry Cornelius Bourne Hill; 2 s (Matthew Robert Henry b 5 June 1985, Simon Richard Philip b 20 July 1987), 1 da (Julia Rosamund Mary b 28 June 1991); *Career* admitted slr 1975; slr; Clifford Turner 1975–76 (articled clerk 1973–75), Linklaters & Paines 1976–78; dir RIT Management Ltd 1979; md: J Rothschild & Co 1981–85, Transcontinental Service Group NV 1983–88; non-exec dir: Control Components Ltd 1983, Wickes plc 1989–; ptnr S J Berwin & Co 1985– (currently head Corp Fin); memb Law Soc; *Style*— Robert P Burrow, Esq; ✉ 11 Lambourne Ave, London SW19 7DW; S J Berwin & Co, 222 Grays Inn Road, London WC1X 8HB (☎ 0171 533 2222, fax 0171 533 2000)

BURROWES, Norma Elizabeth (Mrs Emile Belcourt); da of Henry Burrowes (d 1973), of Bangor, Co Down, N Ireland, and Caroline Mathers, *née* Irwin (d 1987); *b* 24 April 1946; *Educ* Sullivan Upper Sch Holywood Co Down, Queen's Univ Belfast (BA), Royal Acad of Music; *m* 23 Dec 1969 (m dis 1979), Steuart John Rudolph Bedford, s of Leslie Herbert Bedford; m 2, 27 Feb 1987, Emile Adrien Belcourt, s of Adrien Joseph Belcourt; 1 s (Sébastien), 1 da (Romilly); *Career* soprano; debuts: Glyndebourne 1970, ENO 1971, Royal Opera House Covent Garden 1970, Salzburg Fesival 1973, Paris Opera 1975, Met Opera New York 1979, La Scala Milan 1982; performed at numerous other venues incl: Berlin, Buenos Aires, Geneva, Lyons; recordings incl: Die Entführing aus dem Serail, Die Schöpfung, Carmina Burana, Fauré Requiem, Semele, Acis and Galatea; Hon DMus Queen's Univ Belfast 1979; FRAM; *Recreations* swimming, needlework; *Style*— Miss Norma Burrowes

BURROWS, Sir Bernard Alexander Brocas; GCMG (1970, KCMG 1955, CMG 1950); s of Edward Henry Burrows (d 1910), and Ione, *née* Macdonald; *b* 3 July 1910; *Educ* Eton, Univ of Oxford (BA); *m* 1944, Ines, da of late John Walter, of Wokingham, Berks; 1 s (Rupert), 1 da (Antonia); *Career* Foreign Serv 1934: ambass to Turkey 1958–62, dep under sec of state FO 1963–66, perm Br rep N Atlantic Cncl 1966–70; DG Fed Tst for Educn and Res 1979–82; *Books* Footnotes in the Sand (1990); *Style*— Sir Bernard Burrows, GCMG; ✉ Rubens West, East Dean, Chichester, W Sussex

BURROWS, Prof Clifford Robert; s of Edward Stephen Burrows (d 1969), and Edith Mable, *née* Aspland; *b* 20 July 1937; *Educ* West Cliff HS for Boys, Univ of Wales (BSc), Univ of London (PhD, DScEng); *m* 8 July 1961, Margaret Evelyn, da of Harry Percy Mathews (d 1983); 3 s (Stephen Peter b 1 Jan 1963, Paul Robert b 8 March 1965, John Alastair b 11 March 1967), 1 da (Rachael Elizabeth b 8 June 1974); *Career* reader Univ of Sussex 1980–82 (lectr 1969), prof of dynamics and control Univ of Strathclyde 1982–87; Univ of Bath: prof of systems engrg and dir of the Fluid Power Centre 1987–, head School of Mechanical Engineering 1990–95, dean (designate) Faculty of Engrg and Design 1996–, dir Engineering Design Centre in Fluid Power Systems 1992–; author of over 120 res papers; memb Cncl and chm Machine Systems Computing and Control Gp Ctee IMechE; Joseph Bramah medal IMechE 1993, 83rd Thomas Hawksley lectr IMechE; non stipendiary priest C of E 1977; FIMechE 1982; *Books* Fluid Power Control (1972); *Recreations* digging potatoes, rugby football; *Style*— Prof Clifford Burrows; ✉ School of Mechanical Engineering, University of Bath, Claverton Down, Bath BA2 7AY (☎ 01225 826935, fax 01225 826928, telex 449097)

BURROWS, Prof Desmond David; *b* 11 July 1930; *Educ* Queen's Univ Belfast (MB BCh, BAO, MD, MRCPEd); *Career* house offr Royal Victoria Infirmary 1953–54, asst lectr Dept of Pathology Queen's Univ Belfast 1954–56, sr registrar in dermatology Royal Victoria Hosp 1958–60 (registrar in dermatology 1956–58), MRC research fell Inst of Dermatology London 1960–61, conslt dermatologist Royal Victoria Hosp 1961– (chm Med Div 1981–83); Queen's Univ Belfast: memb Faculty of Med 1981–, hon lectr in dermatology 1985–, hon prof Clinical Med Sch 1990–; memb: Central Consults and Hosp Specialities Ctee BMA 1980–82, Scientific Advsy Ctee Gen (Internal) Med and Related Specialities DHSS 1986; chm: Med Exec Ctee Royal Gp of Hosps 1984–86, Med Specialties Ctee Postgraduate Cncl NI 1989–; sec: Euro Soc for Contact Dermatitis 1986–90 (memb Cncl 1987), Irish Dermatological Soc 1965–71; pres: Irish Assoc of Dermatologists 1975–77, Br Assoc of Dermatologists 1991–92 (memb Cncl 1975–77 and 1980–86), Euro Soc of Contact Dermatology 1990–92; chm Br Contact Dermatitis Gp 1983–86 (memb Exec Ctee 1981–89); memb Cncl: Ulster Medical/Legal Soc 1976–78, Int League of Dermatological Socs 1981–88, Euro Environmental and Contact Dermatitis Gp 1985–, BMA 1986–87, RCPEd; memb Editorial Bd: Contact Dermatitis - Environmental and Occupational Dermatitis, Jl of the American Acad of Dermatology, Jl of the Euro Acad of Dermatology and Venereology, Bollettino di Dermatologia Allergologia e Professionale; hon memb: Finnish Soc of Dermatology 1986, Swedish Dermatological Soc 1986, American Dermatology Assoc 1987, Academia Espanola de Dermatologia 1988, Norweigian Dermatological Soc (corresponding memb), N American Clinical Dermatology Soc 1993, Br Assoc of Dermatologists 1993; memb: Ulster Med Soc, Dowling Dermatological Soc, St John's Hosp Dermatological Soc; FRCPEd 1969, FRCP Dublin 1982, FRCP 1986, FRSM (memb Dermatological Section); *Books* Chromium: Metabolism and Toxicity (1983); author of various book chapters and numerous published papers; *Clubs* Corrigan; *Style*— Prof Desmond Burrows; ✉ 11 Broomhill Park, Belfast BT9 5JB (☎ 01232 381699, fax 01232 664901)

BURROWS, General Eva Evelyn; AC (1994, AO 1986); da of Robert John Burrows (d 1970), and Ella Maria, *née* Watson (d 1967); *b* 15 Sept 1929; *Educ* Brisbane State HS, Queensland Univ (BA), Univ of London (Cert Ed), Sydney Univ (MEd); *Career* Salvation Army: missionary educator Howard Inst Zimbabwe 1952–67, princ Usher Inst Zimbabwe 1967–69, princ Int Coll for Offrs London 1974–75 (vice princ 1970–73), leader Women's Social Servs in GB and Ireland 1975–77; Territorial Cdr: Sri Lanka 1977–79, Scotland 1979–82, Australia 1982–86; General (Int Leader) The Salvation Army 1986–93; Hon Doctorate of Liberal Arts Ewha Women's Univ Seoul S Korea 1988, Hon LLD Asbury Coll USA 1988, Hon Doctorate of Sacred Theology Houghton Coll USA 1992, Hon DPhil Univ of Queensland 1993, Hon DUniv Griffith Univ 1994, Hon LLD Univ of NSW; *Recreations* classical music, reading, travelling; *Style*— General Eva Burrows, AC; ✉ 102 Domain Park, 193 Domain Road, South Yarra, Victoria 3141, Australia (☎ 00 61 03 9820 9701, fax 00 61 03 9866 5240, e-mail eburrows@werfl.net.au)

BURROWS, Peter Malcolm Grant; s of John Grant Burrows, of Flint, North Wales, and Elizabeth Eleanor, *née* Fright; *b* 14 Dec 1952; *Educ* Holywell GS, Univ of Aberystwyth; *m* 26 Sept 1981, Louise Elizabeth, da of Dr W G Wenley; 1 da (Clare Elizabeth b 1 March 1984); *Career* articled clerk Philip Jones Hillyer & Jackson Chester 1975–77, slr Winter Wilkinson St Neots & St Ives 1977–87; Norton Rose: joined 1987, ptnr 1989–, mangr Commercial Property and Planning Dept 1994–; Freeman: City of London, City of London Slrs' Co 1987; memb Law Soc 1977; *Recreations* cycling, polishing my car; *Style*— Peter Burrows, Esq; ✉ Norton Rose, Kempson House, PO Box 570, Camomile Street, London EC3A 7AN (☎ 0171 283 6000, direct ☎ 0171 444 3714, fax 0171 283 6500)

BURROWS, (Anthony) Richard Brocas; s of Lt-Gen Montagu Brocas Burrows (d 1966), and Molly Rose, *née* Le Bas (d 1996); *b* 27 Jan 1939; *Educ* Eton; *m* 6 Oct 1966, Angela Margaret, da of John Vincent Sheffield; 1 s (Brocas b 1975), 3 da (Carey (Mrs Rupert English) b 1968, Joanna b 1969, Petra b 1972); *Career* chm: Le Bas Investment Trust, Tex Holdings, I S & G Steel Stock Holders; Liveryman Worshipful Co of Grocers; *Recreations* golf, tennis, travel; *Clubs* White's; *Style*— Richard Burrows, Esq; ✉ Le Bas Investment Trust Ltd, Claydon Industrial Park, Gipping Rd, Great Blakenham, Ipswich IP6 0NL (☎ 01473 830055)

BURSELL, His Hon Judge; Rupert David Hingston; QC (1986); s of Rev Henry Bursell (d 1983), and Cicely Mary, *née* Pawson (d 1977); *b* 10 Nov 1942; *Educ* St John's Sch Leatherhead, Univ of Exeter (LLB), St Edmund Hall Oxford (MA, DPhil), St Stephen House Oxford; *m* 1 July 1967, Joanna Ruth, da of Maj Robert Peter Davies Gibb, of Arbutus, 2 The Chestnuts, Winscombe; 2 s (Michael Hingston b 1970, James David Hingston b 1972), 1 da (Polly Joanna Hingston b 1976); *Career* called to the Bar Lincoln's Inn 1968, circuit judge (Western Circuit) 1988–, official referee 1992–; ordained deacon 1968, priest 1969; hon curate: St Marylebone 1968–69, St Mary The Virgin Almondsbury 1969–71, St Francis Bedminster 1971–83, Christ Church, St Stephen Bristol 1983–88, St Mary The Virgin Cheddar 1993–; chllr, vicar gen and official princ: Dio of Durham 1989–, Dio of Bath & Wells 1992–93, Dio of St Albans 1992–; dep chllr Dio of York 1994–; hon chaplain Intelligence and Security Gp (vols) 1996–; *Books* Atkins Court Forms (contrib Ecclesiastical Law), Halsbury's Laws of England: Cremation and Burial and Ecclesiastical Law (contrib), Principles of Dermatitis Legislation (contrib), Crown Court Practice (jtly), Liturgy, Order and the Law; *Recreations* church music, military history, archaeology of Greece, Turkey and the Holy Land; *Clubs* MCC; *Style*— His Hon Judge Bursell, QC; ✉ The Law Courts, Small Street, Bristol BS1 2HL (☎ 0117 976 3030)

BURSTALL, Prof Rodney Martineau; s of Alfred Reginald Burstall, and Annie, *née* Lammie; *b* 11 Nov 1934; *Educ* King George V GS Southport, Univ of Cambridge (BA, MSc), Univ of Birmingham (PhD); *m* Seija-Leena (d 1990), da of Anton Ilmari Ihalainen (d 1975), of Kotka, Finland; 3 da (Kaija b 27 Feb 1961 d 1994, Taru b 5 July 1962, Taina b 6 Nov 1963); *Career* Nat Serv Flying Offr RAF Radar Servicing 1956–58; Univ of Edinburgh: lectr Experimental Programming Unit 1967–70, prof Dept of Artificial Intelligence 1977–79 (reader 1970–77), prof Dept of Computer Sci 1979–; memb: Shambhala Buddhist Soc, Academia Europaea; FRSE; *Books* Computational Category Theory (1988); *Style*— Prof Rodney Burstall; ✉ Department of Computer Science, University of Edinburgh, The King's Buildings, Mayfield Rd, Edinburgh EH9 3JZ (☎ 0131 650 5155, fax 0131 667 7209, telex 727442 UNIVED G)

BURSTEIN, Joan; da of Ashley Harvey Jotner (d 1956), and Mary, *née* Pleeth (d 1956); *b* 21 Feb 1926; *Educ* Henrietta Barnet Sch, Hampstead Garden Suburb; *m* Sidney Burstein, s of Barnet Burstein; 1 s (Simon b 1951), 1 da (Caroline b 1949); *Career* opened Browns on South Molton St 1970, introduced many designers to London, Donna Karan, Giorgio Armani, Ralph Lauren, Calvin Klein, Romeo Gigli; *Style*— Mrs Joan Burstein; ✉ Browns, 27 South Molton St, London W1Y 1DA

BURSTIN, Nicholas Ernest; s of Capt Oswald Burstin, of London, and Lydia, *née* Hammerschmid; *b* 29 April 1957; *Educ* Univ Coll School London, Jesus Coll Cambridge, Harvard Business Sch; *m* 3 Aug 1988, (Sarah) Anne, da of Lt James William Roylance, of Melbourne, Aust; 1 da (Sophie Alexandra), 1 s (Dominic Hugo); *Career* dir J Walter Thompson Co Ltd 1989–; *Recreations* sailing, music; *Style*— Nicholas Burstin, Esq; ✉ J Walter Thompson Co Ltd, 40 Berkeley Square, London W1 (☎ 0171 499 4040, fax 0171 493 8432/8418, car 0836 314944)

BURT, Alistair James Hendrie; MP (C) Bury North (majority 4,764); s of James Hendrie Burt and Mina Christie Robertson; *b* 25 May 1955; *Educ* Bury GS, St John's Coll Oxford, Chester Coll of Law; *m* 1983, Eve Alexandra Twite; 1 s, 1 da; *Career* slr; memb London Borough of Haringey 1982–84; MP (C) Bury North 1983–, PPS to Rt Hon Kenneth Baker MP 1985–90, Parly under-sec of state for Social Security 1992–95, min of state DSS 1995–; sponsor min for Manchester and Salford 1994; former vice pres Tory Reform Gp, patron Lawyers Assoc working for Soviet Jewry; *Recreations* family, modern art, music, sport, church and religious affairs; *Style*— Alistair Burt, Esq, MP; ✉ House of Commons, London SW1A 0AA (☎ 0171 219 3527)

BURT, David Jeffery; OBE (1985); *b* 24 March 1935; *Career* trainee Cadbury, technician Nat Serv; clerk National Provincial Bank, salesman Hellerman Plastics Ltd, sales mangr then dir IMI Plastics Ltd, personnel dir Bowthorpe Holdings, md Deutsch Ltd 1985–; former chm: CBI (Sussex), Dental Rate Study Gp; chm General Optical Cncl 1988–; memb: Advsy Ctee on Conscientious Objectors House of Lords 1991–, Civil Service Arbitration Tbnl 1993–; Liveryman Worshipful Co of Spectacle Makers 1993, Freeman City of London; FIPM, FRSA; *Recreations* sculptor (exhibited at RA Summer Exhbn), Morgan driver, farmer, squash player; *Style*— David Burt, Esq, OBE; ✉ Deutsch Ltd, East Grinstead, Sussex RH18 1RW (☎ 01342 410246)

BURT, Peter Alexander; s of Robert Wallace Burt (d 1970), of Longniddry, E Lothian, and May Henderson, *née* Rodger (d 1991); *b* 6 March 1944; *Educ* Merchiston Castle Sch, Univ of St Andrews (MA), Univ of Pennsylvania (Thouron scholar, MBA); *m* 23 April 1971, Alison Mackintosh, da of John M Turner, OBE (d 1991), of Kilmarnock; 3 s (Michael Wallace b 1975, Hamish Jonathan b 1978, Angus Moncrieff b 1984); *Career* Hewlett Packard Co Palo Alto Calif USA 1968–70, Conversational Software Ltd Edinburgh 1970–74, Edward Bates & Sons Edinburgh 1974; Bank of Scotland: joined 1975, asst gen mangr Int Div 1979–84, divnl gen mangr Int Div 1984–85, jt gen mangr Int Div 1985–88, treas and chief gen mangr 1988–96, main bd dir 1995–, chief exec 1996–; non-exec dir British Linen Bank Group Ltd; FCIB (Scotland); *Recreations* golf, tennis, skiing, reading; *Clubs* Hon Co of Edinburgh Golfers, Gullane Golf; *Style*— Peter Burt, Esq; ✉ Bank of Scotland, The Mound, Edinburgh EH1 1YZ (☎ 0131 243 5400)

BURT, Terence William; s of Terence William Burt, of Walgrave, Northants, and Dorothy Evelyn, *née* Jones; *b* 21 June 1956; *Educ* Pilgrim GS, Univ of Hertfordshire; *m* 20 Sept 1980, Susan, da of John Hudson, of Bedford; 4 s (Michael b 1983, Philip b 1984, Nicholas b 1986, Darren b 1989); *Career* md Star Computers Ltd 1985, sec & gp fin dir Star Computer Gp plc 1985; ret 1988; formed K2 Group plc (sold to 4 Front Group 1994); currently md 4 Front Services Division; ACMA; *Style*— Terence Burt, Esq; ✉ 274 Kimbolton Road, Bedford MK41 8AD (☎ 01234 358919); 4–6 Colonial Business Park, Colonial Way, Watford WD2 4PR (☎ 01923 294500, fax 01923 294605)

BURTCH, Mervyn Arthur; s of Walter James Powell Burtch (d 1956), and Mary Ann, *née* Jones (d 1992); *b* 7 Nov 1929; *Educ* Lewis Sch Pengam, Univ Coll Cardiff; *Career* composer; operas incl: Alice in Wonderland 1981, Canterville Ghost 1984, various smaller operas; other works incl: I Saw a Child for choir and orchestra 1985, 11 String Quartets (number 1 1985, 2 1986, 3 1987, 4 1992, 5, 6 and 7 1994, 9 and 10 1995, 11 1996); large quantity of smaller chamber, vocal and choral works; *Style*— Mervyn Burtch, Esq; ✉ 5 Oakfield St, Ystrad Mynach, Hengoed, Mid Glam CF8 7AF (☎ 01443 812100); Welsh College of Music and Drama, North Rd, Cardiff, S Glam (☎ 01222 342854)

BURTON, Amanda; *b* 10 Oct 1956; *Educ* Derry HS, Manchester Poly Sch of Theatre; *m* Sven Arnstein; 2 da (Phoebe Marie, Brid Irina); *Career* actress; *Theatre* incl: Mother Goose (Playhouse Theatre Lancaster), Shakespeare to Ayckbourne (Octagon Theatre Bolton); *Television* incl: Heather in Brookside (Channel 4), Margaret Daly in Boon (Central), Where There's A Will (TSW), Inspector Morse (Zenith), A Casualty of War, The Greek Myths - Theseus and the Minotaur (Jim Henson Organisation), Van Der Valk (Thames), Stay Lucky (Yorkshire), Lovejoy (WitzEnd for BBC), Minder (Thames), Medics (Granada), Peak Practice (3 series, Central), Silent Witness (BBC), The Precious Blood (Screen 2); *Style*— Ms Amanda Burton; ✉ c/o Paul Lyon-Maris, ICM Ltd, Oxford House, 76 Oxford Street, London W1N 0AX (☎ 0171 636 6565, fax 0171 323 0101)

BURTON, Amanda Jane; da of Michael Charles Pearson Burton, of N Yorks, and Ann Margaret Verity, of W Yorks; *b* 3 Jan 1959; *Educ* Queen Ethelburga's Harrogate, Bradford Girls' GS, Univ of Durham (BA), Coll of Law Guildford; *Career* slr Slaughter and May 1982–86, asst co sec Tiphook PLC 1986–90, co sec Ratners Group PLC 1990–92, co sec Meyer International PLC 1992–; affiliate memb Inst of Risk Mgmnt, memb Law Soc, MIRS, AIRMIC, MIPR; *Recreations* piano, interior design, theatre, swimming; *Clubs* Annabel's, Champney's; *Style*— Miss Amanda Burton; ✉ Meyer International PLC, Aldwych House, 81 Aldwych, London WC2B 4HQ (☎ 0171 400 8888, fax 0171 400 8787)

BURTON, Anthony George Graham; s of Donald Graham Burton (d 1960), and Irene, *née* Trotter (d 1992); *b* 24 Dec 1934; *Educ* King James's GS Knaresborough, Univ of Leeds; *m* 28 March 1959, Pip, da of Walter Sharman (d 1961); 2 s (Jonathan b 1961, Nicholas b 1964), 1 da (Jenny b 1963); *Career* freelance writer and broadcaster; *Books* incl: A Programmed Guide to Office Warfare (1969), The Jones Report (1970), The Canal Builders (1972, 2 edn 1981, 3 edn 1993), The Reluctant Musketeer (1973), Canals in Colour (1974), Remains of a Revolution (1975), The Master Idol (1975), The Navigators (1976), The Miners (1976), Josiah Wedgwood (1976), Canal (with Derek Pratt, 1976), Industrial Archaeological Sites of Britain (1977), A Place to Stand (1977), Back Door Britain (1977), The Green Bag Travellers (with Pip Burton, 1978), The Past at Work (1980), The Past Afloat (1982), The Shell Book of Curious Britain (1982), The Changing River (1982), The Waterways of Britain (1983), The National Trust Guide to Our Industrial Past (1983), The Rise and Fall of King Cotton (1984), Walking the Line (1985), Wilderness Britain (1985), Britain's Light Railways (jtly, 1985), Britain Revisited (1986), The Shell Book of Undiscovered Britain and Ireland (1986), Landscape Detective (jtly, 1986), Opening Time (1987), Steaming Through Britain (1987), Walking Through History (1988), Walk the South Downs (1988), The Yorkshire Dales and York (1989), The Great Days of the Canals (1989), Astonishing Britain (1990), Cityscapes (1990), Slow Roads (1991), The Railway Builders (1992), Canal Mania (1993), The Grand Union Canal Walk (with Neil Curtis, 1993), The Railway Empire (1994), The Rise and Fall of British Shipbuilding (1994), The Dales Way (1995), The Cotswold Way (1995), The West Highland Way (1996), The Southern Upland Way (1997), Wye Valley Walk (1997); *Recreations* steam engines, boats, walking, beer; *Style*— Anthony Burton, Esq; ✉ 25 Cowper Road, Redland, Bristol BS6 6NZ

BURTON, Anthony Philip; s of Frank Burton (d 1975), and Lottie, *née* Lax; *b* 25 Oct 1942; *Educ* The King's Sch Macclesfield, Wadham Coll Oxford (MA, BLitt); *m* 21 Sept 1985, Carol Deborah, da of Adrian Hilary Baker; *Career* asst keeper in the directorate V & A Museum 1979–81 (asst keeper of the library 1968–79), head Bethnal Green Museum of Childhood 1981–97, research fell Research Dept V & A Museum 1997–; *Style*— Anthony Burton, Esq; ✉ 59 Arlington Ave, London N1 7BA (☎ 0171 226 0394); Victoria & Albert Museum, South Kensington, London SW7 2RL (☎ 0171 938 8500)

BURTON, Sir Carlisle Archibald; kt (1979), OBE (1968); *b* 29 July 1921; *Educ* Harrison Coll Barbados, Univ of London (BA), Sch of Librarianship Leeds (ALA), Univ of Pittsburgh (MS); *m* 1946, Hyacinth Marjorie Adelle Barker; *Career* perm sec PM's Office and head of Civil Service Barbados 1972–81; Barbados high cmmr to the Bahamas 1978–93; chm: Public Serv Cmmn Barbados 1981–87, Public Servs Cmmn Turks & Caicos Islands 1988–90; memb Cwlth Observer Gp at gen elections in Southern Rhodesia (Zimbabwe) 1980 and Malaysia 1990; chm Cave Hill Campus Cncl, Univ of the W Indies 1984–94; public admin conslt, co dir; memb Cncl Barbados Museum & Historical Soc 1994–, pres Barbados Assoc of Retired Persons Inc 1995–; Hon LLD Univ of the W Indies 1995; *Style*— Sir Carlisle Burton, OBE; ✉ Caradelle, Mountjoy Avenue, Pine Gardens, St Michael, Barbados, West Indies

BURTON, Caroline M; *Career* joined Guardian Royal Exchange 1973, variously investmt mangr (Stock Exchange Overseas), md Guardian Asset Management Ltd and md Guardian Unit Managers Ltd, gp exec dir (investment) Guardian Royal Exchange plc 1990–; non-exec dir Scottish Metropolitan Property plc, memb Bd London Pension Funds Authy; *Style*— Miss Caroline Burton; ✉ Guardian Royal Exchange plc, Royal Exchange, London EC3V 3LS (☎ 0171 283 7101, fax 0171 621 2599)

BURTON, Charles Philip Henry; s of Sir George Vernon Kennedy Burton, CBE, DL, *qv*, of Hadleigh, Suffolk, and Sarah Katherine, *née* Tcherniavsky; *b* 6 Dec 1952; *Educ* Charterhouse, Univ of Exeter (BA); *m* 2 Nov 1985, Susanna Louise, da of Peter Henry Buller, of Bramley, Surrey; 2 da (Sophie Mary b 7 July 1993, Rose Elizabeth b (twin) 7 July 1993); *Career* economist Beecham Pharmaceuticals Ltd 1974–75; CBI 1975–85: head industl trends and economic forecasting, dep dir Economic Directorate; business devpt mangr Wharton Econometric Forecasting Assocs Ltd 1985–88, chief exec Business Strategies Ltd 1996– (jt md 1988–96); memb Soc of Business Economists (memb Cncl 1996–), memb Econ Advsy Ctee Univ of Strathclyde 1996–; FRSA; *Books* Competition and Markets (1990); *Recreations* music, history, photography; *Clubs* RAC; *Style*— Charles Burton, Esq; ✉ Business Strategies Ltd, 192 Vauxhall Bridge Road, London SW1V 1DX (☎ 0171 630 5959, fax 0171 828 1408)

BURTON, Christopher Michael; *b* 12 Oct 1947; *Educ* Univ of London (BSc(Econ)); *Career* Lloyd's insurance; articled clerk Peat Marwick Mitchell & Co then CA Spicer and Pegler, formerly dir Alexander Howden Underwriting Ltd, currently fin dir Syndicate Group Archer Group Holdings plc; FCA; *Style*— Christopher Burton, Esq; ✉ Archer Group Holdings plc, 2 Minster Court, Mincing Lane, London EC3R 7FL (☎ 0171 369 3000, fax 0171 369 3100)

BURTON, (Anthony) David; CBE (1992); s of Leslie Mitchell Burton (d 1967), and Marion, *née* Marsh (d 1976); *b* 2 April 1937; *Educ* Arnold Sch Blackpool; *m* 30 May 1964, Valerie, da of Harry Swire, of Burnley, Lancs; 1 s (Michael John b 1971), 2 da (Judith Alison b 1966, Anne Louise b 1968); *Career* Nat Serv RAPC 1955–57; chief dealer Bank of America NT & SA 1967–72, exec dir S G Warburg & Co Ltd 1979–92; LIFFE: fndr memb Working Party 1979, dir 1980–94, chm Membership & Rules Ctee 1982–88, dep chm 1985–88, chm 1988–92; chm: S G Warburg Futures & Options Ltd 1988–92, chm Marshalls Finance Ltd (int money brokers) 1989–; fndr memb Assoc of Futures Brokers and Dealers 1986–88; memb: Br Invisible Exports Cncl 1988–90, Euro Ctee Br Invisibles 1990–92; dir: British Invisibles 1992–93, The Securities Inst 1992–93; memb Governing Bd City Res Project 1991–94; Freeman City of London 1984, Liveryman Worshipful Co of Glass Sellers 1984; FCIB, FCT; *Books* collector, lectr and writer on: early English glass c 1600–1800, English blackjacks and leather bottles c 1550–1700, early German Rhenish pottery c 1500–1650; *Recreations* fine wine, gardening, sport, music, opera; *Clubs* MCC; *Style*— David Burton, Esq, CBE; ✉ Marshalls Finance Ltd, Lloyds Chambers, 1 Portsoken Street, London E1 8DF (☎ 0171 488 4588, fax 0171 702 3951, car 0836 279854)

BURTON, David Gowan; s of Reginald Frank Burton (d 1967), of Woodford Green, Essex, and Nellie Erwin, *née* Biggs; *b* 3 April 1943; *Educ* McEntree Tech Sch; *m* 8 Aug 1970, Hilary Kathleen, da of Canon Robert Smith; 2 s (Matthew Edward Gowan b 21 Oct 1972, Simon James Gowan b 19 May 1983), 1 da (Emma Claire b 8 Sept 1975); *Career* articles with Keens Shay Keens & Co 1960–65, Thomson McLintock 1965–73 (latterly sr mangr), sr mangr Neville Russell & Co 1973–75; Touche Ross & Co: sr mangr 1975–79, ptnr 1979–93, seconded from London to IOM 1983–91, estab Green Field office IOM 1985, ptnr Cambridge office 1991–93; estab private consultancy and corp fin practice 1993; memb Advsy Bd Campbell Lutyens & Co Ltd (Corp Fin Boutique), sr conslt Kroll Associates; memb Bd of Management: Springboard Housing Assoc, St Francis Hospice; treas Church Army; govr Chigwell Sch 1992; FCA 1976 (ACA 1965), FRSA 1993; *Recreations* family, golf, walking, gardening, farming; *Clubs* Castletown Golf IOM, Chigwell Golf; *Style*— David Burton, Esq; ✉ 3 The Green, Woodford Green, Essex IG8 0NF (☎ 0181 505 5402)

BURTON, Dr David John Franklin; OBE (1997); s of Jack William Burton, OBE (d 1973), and Jessie Agnes Burton; *b* 9 Dec 1944; *Educ* Surbiton GS for Boys, Univ of London (external BSc, CertEd), Univ of Reading (PhD); *m* Denise, da of Tony Burrell; 2 s (Paul William b 15 Dec 1982, Luke David b 19 April 1984), 1 da (Nicola Barbara b 11 Nov 1986); *Career* asst master Westcliff HS for Boys 1967–68, asst examiner Cambridge Overseas Examinations Syndicate 1968–70; British Council: joined 1971, asst rep Madras 1972–74, science offr New Delhi 1974–77, science offr Madrid 1977–78; asst registrar CNAA 1979–81; British Council: science offr Riyadh 1982–85, dep rep Warsaw 1985–86, head Mgmnt Information Servs and mgmnt accountant London 1986–89, dep dir Cairo 1990–94, dir Jordan 1994–; FZS 1968; *Recreations* golf, fishing, reading; *Clubs* Commonwealth, Royal Over-Seas League; *Style*— Dr David Burton, OBE; ✉ The British Council, Rainbow Street (off First Circle), PO Box 634, Amman 11118, Jordan (☎ 00 962 6 636147, fax 00 962 6 656413)

BURTON, Diane Elizabeth; da of Victor St Clair Yates, of Durban, SA, and Betty, *née* Woolliscroft; *b* 26 July 1954; *Educ* BA, Postgrad CertEd, DipPR; *m* 1979, Andrew Thomas Guy Burton; 1 da (Sarah St Clair b 1980), 1 s (Rupert Thomas b 1982); *Career* prodn mangr Burmeister & Gyoury (TV commercials) Johannesburg SA 1980–82, PRO/advtg mangr Hazard Equipment Johannesburg 1983–85, emmigrated to UK 1985, account mangr The Public Relations Co 1987–88, dir Moss International Ltd 1988–89, ptnr Cicada Consultants 1989–; sr lectr Leeds Business Sch 1992–94, Sch of Media Univ of Leeds 1994–; memb Mktg Standards Lead Body for Dept for Educn and Employment NVQ Devpt; MInstD 1989, MIPD 1994, FIPR 1995; *Publications* The South African Handbook of Public Relations (contrib Film Production section, MacMillan, 1982), Promoting the Product or Service in Financing Growth (for Leeds Poly, 1989), Management and Strategy Module (for CAM Distance Learning Prog, 1994); *Recreations* tennis, horse riding, gardening; *Style*— Mrs Diane Burton; ✉ Cicada Consultants, Elton Villas, Birstwith, Harrogate HG3 2NF (☎ 01423 770256, fax 01423 771712, e-mail d.burton@tasc.ac.uk)

BURTON, Frances Rosemary; da of Maj Richard Francis Heveningham Pughe, DFC, ERD, of Ridlington, Norfolk (d 1990), and Pamela Margaret, *née* Coates (d 1978); *b* 19 June 1941; *Educ* St Mary's Convent Bishops Stortford Herts, Tortington Park Arundel Sussex, Lady Margaret House Cambridge, St Anne's Coll Oxford, Univ of London (LLB), Univ of Leicester (LLM); *m* 1, 26 Oct 1963 (m dis 1973), Robert Scott Alexander (now Lord Alexander of Weedon, QC), s of Samuel James Alexander (d 1965), of Fleet, Hants; 2 s (David Robert James b 1964, William Richard Scott b 1969), 1 da (Mary Frances Anne b 1966); m 2, 28 Nov 1975 (m dis 1991), David Michael Burton, s of Frank Raymond Burton (d 1965), of Wellington, Shropshire; 2 da (Jane Richenda Frances b 1979, Charlotte Alice Octavia b 1981); *Career* called to the Bar Middle Temple 1970 (ad eundem Lincoln's Inn 1972), practised Chancery Bar until 1975, tutor for Bar and Law Soc examinations, lectr and tutor Dept of Law and Faculty of Business City of London Poly 1989–93, dir of Bar courses BPP Law Sch 1992–93 (memb Advsy Bd 1993–), sr lectr in Law London Guildhall Univ 1993–, dep traffic cmmr S Eastern & Metropolitan Eastern and Western Traffic Areas 1996–, memb Ctee Assoc of Women Barristers 1996–; author of legal text books; govr Westminster Coll until 1973; numerous fundraising activities incl: Justice Br Section Int Cmmn of Jurists 1963–, Peckham Settlement 1973–, Jubilee Sailing Tst 1985–, Cancer Res Campaign 1986–, Duke of Edinburgh's Award Scheme 1987; chm Ctee Justice Ball 1983 and 1985, memb Exec

Ctee Big Bang City Ball 1986; memb Soc of Cons Lawyers; *Books* Family Law Textbook (1988, revised edn 1990), Bar Final General Paper Textbook (1990), Family Law - Documents, Forms and Precedents (1992), Newman and Burton's Bar Final Guide (1993), Criminal Litigation (jtly, 1994, 2 edn 1996), Family Law (1996), Guide to the Family Law Act 1996 (1996); *Recreations* opera, history, archaeology; *Clubs* RAF (assoc memb), Utd Oxford and Cambridge Univ; *Style*— Mrs Frances Burton; ✉ Flat 4, 5 Star Yard, London WC2A 2JL (☎ 0171 831 1866); 10 Old Square, Lincoln's Inn, London WC2A 3SU (☎ 0171 405 0758, fax 0171 831 8237)

BURTON, Sir George Vernon Kennedy; kt (1977), CBE (1972, MBE 1945), DL (Suffolk) 1980; s of George Ethelbert Earnshaw Burton, and Francesca, *née* Holden-White; *b* 21 April 1916; *Educ* Charterhouse, Weimar Univ; *m* 1, 1945 (m dis), Sarah Katherine Tcherniavsky; 2 s; m 2, 1975, Priscilla Margaret, da of Cecil Harmsworth King, and formerly w of St John Gore, *qv*; *Career* formerly Capt RA WW II; chm Fisons 1973–86; dir: Barclays Bank International 1976–82, Thomas Tilling 1976–82, Rolls-Royce 1976–83; memb Cncl CBI 1970–84, chm CBI Overseas Ctee 1975–83; memb: BOTB 1972–82, NEDC 1975–79, Assoc Br Sponsorship of the Arts 1978–84; Br Nat Ctee of Int C of C 1979–86, govr Suttons Hosp in Charterhouse 1979–92; Cdr Order of Ouissam Alaouite Morroco 1968, Cdr Order of Leopold II Belgium 1974; FRSA; *Recreations* music; *Clubs* Farmers', Oriental; *Style*— Sir George Burton, CBE, DL; ✉ Aldham Mill, Hadleigh, Suffolk IP7 6LE

BURTON, Gerald; s of Edward Neville Burton (d 1985), of Kelsall, nr Chester, and Mary Elizabeth, *née* Bull (d 1977); *b* 12 Aug 1938; *Educ* Liverpool Collegiate GS; *m* 4 May 1963, Gillian Margaret, da of John Dean Wilson (d 1986), of West Kirby, Cheshire; 3 s (John, James, Andrew), 1 da (Deborah); *Career* Kidsons Impey chartered accountants: joined 1961, ptnr 1965, sr ptnr 1989–92; chief exec WRVS 1992–; non-exec dir: Regent House Properties Ltd 1993–, Bradford and Bingley Building Soc London region 1994–, Bethlem Maudsley NHS Tst 1994–; Freeman City of London 1980, memb Ct and Liveryman Worshipful Co of Basketmakers 1982; FCA; *Recreations* golf, music; *Clubs* City Livery, Wig & Pen; *Style*— Gerald Burton, Esq; ✉ Hilbre, Old Farm Close, Knotty Green, Beaconsfield, Bucks (☎ 01494 671560); Women's Royal Voluntary Service, 234–244 Stockwell Road, London SW9 9SP (☎ 0171 416 0146, fax 0171 416 0148)

BURTON, HE Graham Stuart; CMG (1987); s of Cyril Stanley Richard Burton (d 1982), and Jessie Blythe Burton; *b* 8 April 1941; *Educ* Sir William Borlase's Sch Marlow; *m* 30 Jan 1965, Julia Margaret Lappin; 1 da (b 1966), 1 s (b 1967); *Career* HM Dip Serv: FO 1961, Abu Dhabi 1964, ME Centre for Arabic Studies 1967, Kuwait 1969, FCO 1972, Tunis 1975, UK Mission to UN 1978, cnsllr Tripoli 1981, FCO 1984–87, consul-gen San Francisco 1987–90; HM ambass: UAE (Abu Dhabi) 1990–94, Indonesia (Jakarta) 1994–; *Recreations* golf, watching all sports, opera; *Clubs* MCC; *Style*— HE Mr Graham Burton, CMG; ✉ c/o Foreign and Commonwealth Office (Jakarta), London, SW1A 2AH

BURTON, Humphrey McGuire; s of Harry Philip Burton (d 1980), and Kathleen Alice, *née* Henwood (d 1982); *b* 25 March 1931; *Educ* Long Dene Sch Chiddingstone Kent, The Judd Sch Tonbridge, Univ of Cambridge (BA); *m* 1, 1957 (m dis), Gretel, *née* Davis; 1 s (Matthew), 1 da (Clare); m 2, 1970, Christina, da of Svante Hellstedt; 1 s (Lukas), 1 da (Helena); *Career* head Music and Arts BBC TV 1965–67 and 1975–81; TV presenter: BBC Young Musician of the Year 1978–92, Cardiff Singer of the World 1991; broadcaster Classic FM's: Life of Leonard Bernstein (seventeen progs) 1994, Menuhin - Master Musician (20 progs) 1996; TV dir operas and concerts worldwide, artistic dir The Scandinavian Arts Festival (Barbican Centre) Nov-Dec 1992, artistic advsr Barbican Centre 1990–94; chm TV Music Working Pty EBU 1976–85; columnist Classic FM Magazine, feature writer Evening Standard; Chevalier de l'Ordre des Arts et des Lettres France; *Books* Leonard Bernstein (1994); *Recreations* music, tennis, travel; *Clubs* Vanderbilt, Garrick; *Style*— Humphrey Burton, Esq; ✉ 123 Oakwood Court, London W14 8LA

BURTON, Iris Grace; da of Arthur Robert Burton, of Lewisham, London, and Alice Elizabeth Burton (d 1980); *Educ* Roan Girls' GS, City of London Coll; *m* Joseph Thomas Lucas, s of Elio Lucas (d 1987), of Spain; 1 s (Joseph b 8 Aug 1976), 1 da (Rachel b 12 April 1971); *Career* asst ed TV Times 1978–80; ed: Woman's Own 1980–86, Prima 1986–87, Best magazine 1987–88; ed and dir G & J UK 1988–91; ed-in-chief: Woman's Realm and Woman's Weekly 1991–, Me magazine 1993–94, Eva magazine 1994–; *Recreations* walking, gardening; *Style*— Ms Iris Burton; ✉ IPC Magazines, Kings Reach Tower, Stamford Street, London SE1 9LS (☎ 0171 261 5000)

BURTON, (Sara) Jocelyn Margarita Elissa; da of Wing Cdr Roland Louis Ernest Burton, AFC (ret), of Correze, France, and Sian Joan, *née* Gwilliam Evans (d 1980); *b* 10 Jan 1946; *Educ* St Clare's Sch Devon, Lady Margaret House Cambridge, Sir John Cass Coll Central Sch of Art; *Career* Diamonds Int award 1968, first solo exhibition Archer Gallery Dover St 1971, modern silver collection for Jean Renet Bond St 1970–75; pieces in many public and private collections throughout world; works incl: silver table fountain for Worshipful Co of Fishmongers 1975, Fitzwilliam Cup 1984, centrepiece for Sir Roy Strong V & A; Freeman: City of London 1974, Worshipful Co of Goldsmiths; *Recreations* playing harpsichord, travel, reading; *Clubs* Blacks (Dean Street); *Style*— Miss Jocelyn Burton; ✉ 50C Red Lion Street, Holborn, London WC1R 4PF (☎ 0171 405 3042, fax 0171 405 3042 and 0171 831 9324)

BURTON, Prof John Lloyd; s of Lloyd Burton (d 1986), of Loscoe, Derbyshire, and Dorothy Mary, *née* Pacey; *b* 29 Aug 1938; *Educ* Heanor GS, Univ of Manchester (BSc, MD); *m* 12 Sept 1964, Dr Patricia Anne, da of Walter Crankshaw; 1 s (Ben b 1969), 2 da (Jane b 1967, Helena b 1977); *Career* jr med trg 1964–68 (Manchester, London, Edinburgh), sr registrar and res fell Dept of Dermatology Newcastle upon Tyne 1968–73, conslt dermatologist Bristol Royal Infirmary 1973–, prof of dermatology Univ of Bristol 1993–; ed British Journal of Dermatology 1981–85 (asst ed 1977–81), MRCP examiner RCP, advsr in dermatology to Chief Med Offr Dept of Health 1988–94, pres Dermatology Section RSM 1994, pres Br Assoc of Dermatologists 1995; Dowling orator RSM 1980, Parkes Weber lectr RCP 1988; contrib over 200 articles to med and scientific jls; *Books* Essential Medicine (1976), Aids to Medicine for Nurses (1981), Textbook of Dermatology 4 vols (jt ed, 5 edn, 1992), Aids to Postgraduate Medicine (6 edn, 1994), Aids to Undergraduate Medicine (6 edn, 1997), Essentials of Dermatology (3 edn, 1990); *Recreations* bookbinding, painting; *Style*— Prof John Burton; ✉ Norland House, Canynge Rd, Clifton, Bristol BS8 3LD (☎ 0117 973 3933); Department of Dermatology, Bristol Royal Infirmary, Bristol BS2 8HW (☎ 0117 923 0000 ext 2770)

BURTON, John Malcolm; s of Malcolm Leslie Burton, of Culcheth, Warrington, and Ruby Lorina, *née* Clark; *b* 29 July 1957; *Educ* Culcheth HS, QMC London (LLB), Cncl of Legal Educn; *m* 26 July 1986, Karen (d 28 Nov 1992), da of Kenneth Falkingham; 2 s (James Andrew Clark b 13 July 1988, Charles Kenneth b 20 Sept 20 Sept 1990); *Career* called to the Bar Inner Temple 1979, in common, criminal and gen civil law practice 1979–, head of chambers Mitre Ct Temple 1992–; *Recreations* skiing, reading; *Style*— John Burton, Esq; ✉ Mitre Court Chambers, Temple, London EC4A (☎ 0171 353 9394, fax 0171 353 4188)

BURTON, John Michael; s of Gerald Victor Burton, of Northampton, and Kathleen Blodwyn, *née* Harper; *b* 21 May 1945; *Educ* Oxford Sch of Architecture; *m* 11 Sept 1971, Sally, da of Norman Donaby Bason (d 1987), of Northampton; 1 s (Thomas Donaby b 19 April 1977), 1 da (Amy Victoria b 17 Jan 1975); *Career* architect; conservation of: Wingfield Coll 1972–74, Lavenham Guildhall 1973–94, Holy Trinity Church Long Melford 1974–, Melford Hall 1975–, Flatford Mill for Nat Tst 1979–85, Colchester Castle 1980–90, Newnham Coll Cambridge 1984–, St Mary's Thaxted 1988–, Manor House Bury St Edmunds 1990–94, Hunsdon House Herts 1990–; Surveyor of the Fabric of Canterbury Cathedral 1991–, cmmr on Cathedral Fabric Cmmn for England 1996–; chm: Colchester Arts Centre 1985–90, Redundant Churches Uses Ctee Chelmsford, Cathedral Architects Assoc 1996; memb Diocesan Advsy Ctees: Chelmsford, St Edmundsbury, Ipswich; govr Kent Inst of Art & Design; MRIBA; *Recreations* sail boarding, archaeology; *Clubs* Trinity Rotary; *Style*— John Burton, Esq; ✉ St Mary's Hall, Rawstorn Road, Colchester, Essex CO3 3JH (☎ 01206 549487, car 0850 936294)

BURTON, 3 Baron (UK 1897); Michael Evan Victor Baillie; s of Brig Hon George Evan Michael Baillie, MC, TD (s of Baroness Burton, to whom Barony passed from 1 Baron by special remainder, and her 1 husband, Col James Baillie, MVO, JP, DL, sometime MP Inverness-shire), by his w, Lady Maud, *née* Cavendish, CBE, JP, widow of Capt Angus Mackintosh, RHG, and da of 9 Duke of Devonshire, KG; suc grandmother 1962; *b* 27 June 1924; *Educ* Eton; *m* 1, 1948 (m dis 1977), (Elizabeth) Ursula (d 1993), da of late Capt Anthony Wise; 2 s, 4 da; m 2, 1978, Coralie, da of late Claude Cliffe, of S Africa; *Heir* s, Hon Evan Baillie, *qv*; *Career* sits as Conservative in House of Lords; formerly Lt Lovat Scouts and Scots Gds; landowner; memb: Inverness CC 1948–75, Inverness DC 1984–92; JP 1961–75, DL 1963–65; Grand Master Mason 1993–; *Recreations* stalking, shooting, fishing, hunting; *Clubs* Cavalry and Guards', Pratt's, New (Edinburgh); *Style*— The Rt Hon the Lord Burton; ✉ Dochfour, Inverness IV3 6JY (☎ 0146 386 252, fax 0146 386 366, office 0146 386 218)

BURTON, Michael John; QC (1984); s of Henry Burton, QC (d 1952), and Hilda, *née* Shaffer (d 1986); *b* 12 Nov 1946; *Educ* Eton, Balliol Coll Oxford (MA); *m* 17 Dec 1972, Corinne Ruth (d 1992), da of Dr Jack Cowan, MC, of Putney; 4 da (Josephine b 1977, Isabel b 1979, Genevieve b 1982, Henrietta b 1986); *Career* called to the Bar Gray's Inn 1970, recorder of the Crown Court 1989–, dep judge of the High Ct 1993–, head of Chambers 1991–; bencher Gray's Inn 1993–; memb Bar Cncl Legal Servs Cmmn 1995; lectr in law Balliol Coll Oxford 1970–73; candidate (Lab) Kensington Cncl 1971, Parly candidate (Lab) Stratford-on-Avon 1974, candidate (Social Democrat) GLC Putney 1981; *Recreations* amateur theatricals, lyric writing, singing, bridge, watching Wimbledon FC; *Style*— Michael Burton, Esq, QC; ✉ High Trees, 63 Murray Rd, Wimbledon, London SW19; Littleton Chambers, Temple, London EC4Y 7HR (☎ 0171 797 8600, fax 0171 797 8699)

BURTON, HE Sir Michael St Edmund; KCVO (1992), CMG (1987); s of Brig G W S Burton, DSO (d 1981), and Barbara, *née* Kemmis Betty; *b* 18 Oct 1937; *Educ* Bedford Sch, Magdalen Coll Oxford (MA); *m* 1 April 1967, Henrietta Jindra, da of Joseph Hones, of Nicosia, Cyprus; 1 s (Nicholas b 1969), 2 da (Samantha b 1968 d 1970, Amanda b 1971); *Career* FCO: joined 1960, asst political agent Dubai Trucial States 1962–64; served: Khartoum 1967–69, Paris 1969–72, Amman 1975–77, Kuwait 1977–79; secondment to BP as head of Policy Review Unit 1984–85, Br minister and dep cmdt Berlin 1985–90, head British Embassy Berlin office 1990–92, asst under sec of state (Middle E) FCO 1993–94, ambass Prague 1994– (to retire 1997); *Recreations* tennis, travel, opera; *Clubs* United Oxford and Cambridge Univ, Hurlingham; *Style*— Sir Michael Burton, KCVO, CMG; ✉ c/o Foreign & Commonwealth Office (Prague), King Charles St, London SW1A 2AH

BURTON, Richard St John Vladimir; CBE (1996); s of Percy Basil Harmsworth Burton, and Vera, *née* Poliakoff; *b* 3 Nov 1933; *Educ* Bryanston, AA Sch of Architecture (AADipl); *m* 3 April 1956, Mireille, da of Joseph Dernbach-Mayen; 3 s (Mark b 24 April 1957, David b 25 Oct 1958, Jonathan b 2 Jan 1960), 1 da (Catherine b 7 Jan 1962); *Career* ptnr & dir Ahrends Burton & Koralek Architects 1961–; princ works incl: Chichester Theological Coll Gillett House 1965, Trinity Coll Dublin Library & Arts Building 1967 and 1979, Chalvedon & Northlands Housing Basildon 1968 and 1980, Templeton Coll Oxford 1969–, Nebenzahl House 1972, extensions Keble Coll Oxford 1976, W H Smith Head Office Marketing Swindon 1985, Burton House 1987, British Embassy Moscow 1988–, Hooke Park Coll 1990, Docklands Light Railway Extension 1990–, John Lewis Kingston on Thames 1991, St Mary's Isle of Wight 'Low Energy' Hosp 1991; chm: Percent for Art Steering Gp Arts Cncl of GB 1989, RIBA Steering Gp on Educn 1991, Architecture Advsy Panel Arts Cncl of England 1994–; RIBA 1957, FRSA 1980; *Recreations* building, writing; *Style*— Richard Burton, Esq, CBE; ✉ Ahrends Burton and Koralek, Unit 1, 7 Chalcot Road, London NW1 8LH (☎ 0171 586 3311)

BURTON-CHADWICK, *see:* Chadwick

BURTON-PAGE, Piers John; s of John Garrard Burton-Page, and Audrey Ruth Burton-Page (d 1989); *b* 25 July 1947; *Educ* Harrow, Wadham Coll Oxford (MA), Univ of Sussex (MA); *m* 1976, Patricia Margaret, da of Howard Cornish, OBE; 2 s (Andrew Patrick Bedeir b 1973 (adopted 1981), Thomas Andrew b 1977); *Career* teacher St John's Sch Northwood 1965–66, pt/t tutor Open Univ 1972–73; BBC: studio mangr 1971–75, newsreader and announcer Radio 4 1975–77, prodr Gramophone Dept Radio 3 1977–82, seconded as sr asst Management Unit BBC Secretariat 1981–82, music organiser BBC External Servs 1982–85, presentation ed Radio 3 1985–90, sr prodr and presenter Radio 3 1990–; Ohio State Award for The Elements of Music 1986; *Publications* Philharmonic Concerto - The Life and Music of Sir Malcolm Arnold (1994); *Recreations* theatre, cricket, travel, languages, philosophy, tennis, reading; *Clubs* Bushmen; *Style*— Piers Burton-Page; ✉ BBC, Broadcasting House, London W1A 1AA (☎ 0171 765 4404)

BURTON-RACE, John William; s of Denys Arthur Race, and Shirley, *née* Manning; *b* 1 May 1957; *Educ* St Mary's Coll Southampton, Highbury Tech Coll (City & Guilds 706/1, 706/2), Portsmouth Poly (HCITB Cert of Apprenticeship), Westminster Coll; *m* 1978 (m dis 1996); 1 da (Naomi Lea May b 5 June 1989), 1 s (Maximillian John b 26 Jan 1994); *Career* apprentice Wessex Hotel Winchester 1973–75, commis Quaglino's Hotel Meurice London 1975–76, first commis Chewton Glen Hotel 1976–78, chef Olivers Midhurst 1978–79, chef tournant La Sorbonne Oxford 1979–82, private chef MacKenzie-Hill Property Development International 1982–83, sous chef Les Quat' Saisons Oxford 1983–84, head chef and mangr Le Petit Blanc Oxford 1984–86, chef and md L'Ortolan Shinfield 1986–; memb: Chambre Syndicate de Haute Cuisine Francaise, Restaurateurs' Assoc of GB; *Awards* Mumm prizewinner 1987, Acorn award (Caterer and Hotelkeeper Magazine), Best in Britain award (Ackerman Guide), five stars (AA), three stars (Egon Ronay), Restaurant of the Year (Egon Ronay) 1991, included in Relais Gourmand, five out of five (Good Food Guide) 1990–94, four and a half out of five (Good Food Guide) 1995–96, eighteen out of twenty and three red toques (Gault Millau Guide), two stars (Michelin) 1991–96 (one star 1987–90), Personalité de l'Année (Chef Laureat Paris) 1991, one Silver and two Gold medals Madrid Euro Olympics 1992, Grand Prix de l'Art de la Cuisine (Int Acad of Gastronomy) 1994, Chef of the Year (Caterer and Hotelkeeper Magazine) 1995; *Television* series advsr and consIt to Chef (starring Lenny Henry, BBC1); contrib: Best Fish, Best Game, Best Chocolate series 1987, Master Chefs of Europe 1988, Great British Chefs 1989, Great European Chefs 1990; *Books* Recipes from an English Masterchef (1994); *Recreations* Porsche motor sports, fishing, shooting; *Clubs* 190 Queen's Gate, Acorn Club; *Style*— John Burton-Race, Esq; ✉ L'Ortolan, The Old Vicarage, Church Lane, Shinfield, nr Reading, Berks RG2 9BY (☎ 0118 988 3783 and 0118 988 4498, fax 0118 988 5391)

BURWELL, Prof (Richard) Geoffrey; s of Capt Arthur Reginald Burwell (d 1960), from Leeds, and Mabel Walker, *née* Robinson (d 1988); *b* 1 July 1928; *Educ* Leeds GS, Harrogate GS, Univ of Leeds (BSc, MB ChB, MD); *m* 19 Jan 1963, Helen Mary, *née* Petty, da of Capt Frank Petty (d 1952); 1 s (Matthew b 30 Dec 1963), 1 da (Jane b 8 Dec 1965);

Career Capt RAMC jr surgical specialist Gibraltar Hosps 1955–57; orthopaedic registrar Gen Infirmary Leeds 1957–58 (house surgn 1952), lectr in surgery Univ of Leeds 1963–65 (lectr in anatomy 1958–63), sr registrar in traumatic and orthopaedic surgery Robert Jones and Agnes Hunt Orthopaedic Hosp Oswestry 1965–68; prof of Orthopaedics Univ of London 1968–72, prof of human morphology and experimental orthopaedics Univ of Nottingham 1974–93 (emeritus prof 1993); former hon conslt in orthopaedics Nottingham Health Authy; pres: Br Orthopaedic Res Soc 1982–84, Br Scoliosis Soc 1989–95 (pres 1987–89); FRCS 1955; *Recreations* family, history, travel, archaeology; *Clubs* Old Oswestrians (pres 1989–91); *Style—* Prof Geoffrey Burwell; ✉ 34 Dovedale Road, W Bridgford, Nottingham NG2 6JA (☎ 0115 923 2745, fax 0115 923 2272, e-mail GEOFFREY.BURWELL@NOTTINGHAM.AC.UK); Department of Human Morphology, Queen's Medical Centre, Clifton Boulevard, Nottingham NG7 2UH (☎ 0115 970 9417, fax 0115 970 9732, telex 37346 Uninot G)

BURY, John Edward; DL (1989); s of Col John Bury, OBE (d 1969), of Berden Lodge, Berden, Herts, and Ruth Alice, *née* Le Marchant (d 1982), eld da of Brig Gen Sir E T Le Marchant (4 Bt) KCB, CBE, JP, DL; *b* 26 Sept 1927; *Educ* Prince of Wales Nairobi Kenya, Exeter Coll Oxford (MA); *m* 28 June 1961, Diana Mary, eld da of Lt-Col Godfrey Sturdy Incledon-Webber, TD, DL (d 1986), of Buckland Manor, Braunton; 1 s (Henry b 5 May 1962), 5 da (Mary Helen (Mrs Cumberlege) b 1964, Anne b 1965, Eleanor b 1967, Jane b 1971, Clare b 1972); *Career* London Stock Exchange 1952–80, ptnr Pidgeon de Smitt and predecessor firms; chm: Croyde Bay Holidays Ltd 1986–88 (md 1981–86), Incledon Estates Ltd 1988–89, Lobb Fields Ltd 1991–; NFU: memb Devon Cncl 1983–91, memb Devon Exec Cncl 1992–, memb SW Regnl Cereals Ctee 1993–, chm Barnstaple Branch 1995– (vice chm 1993–94); dir Br Holiday and Home Park Association Ltd 1983–89, vice pres Devon Agric Assoc 1984–, memb Exec Ctee West Country Tourist Bd 1985–88, dep pres Devon Branch BRCS 1985– (Badge of Honour 1991); memb: TAVRA W Wessex 1986–, Agric Land Tbnl SW Area 1987–, Ctee Devon Branch CLA 1987–96, Ctee N Devon C of C and Indust 1996–; pres: Braunton and Dist Museum 1988–, Gt Torrington Hort Soc 1988–; vice chm Grenville Coll Bideford 1995– (govr 1989–); fell Woodard Schs (Western Div) 1991–; Freeman City of London 1964, Liveryman Worshipful Co of Clothworkers 1966; *Recreations* gardening; *Clubs* Army and Navy; *Style—* John Bury, Esq, DL; ✉ Buckland Manor, Braunton, N Devon EX33 1HN (☎ 01271 812016)

BURY, Lady Mairi Elizabeth; *née* Vane-Tempest-Stewart; JP (Co Down); da of 7 Marquess of Londonderry, KG, MVO, TD, PC (d 1949); *b* 25 March 1921; *Educ* privately; *m* 10 Dec 1940 (m dis 1958), Lt-Col Viscount Bury (d 1968), s of 9 Earl of Albemarle; 2 da (Elizabeth, Rose); *Career* farmer and estate owner; patron BRCS N Ireland, former pres and chm of Ards Women's Unionist Assoc N Ireland; Liveryman Guild of Air Pilots and Air Navigators; fell Royal Philatelic Soc London; *Recreations* philately; *Style—* The Lady Mairi Bury, JP; ✉ Mount Stewart, Newtownards, Co Down, NI BT22 2AD (☎ 01247 788217)

BURY, Dr Robert Frederick (Bob); s of William George Bury, and Evelyn Winifred, *née* Liggins; *b* 10 Aug 1948; *Educ* Kettering GS, Univ of London (BSc), Middx Hosp Med Sch (MB BS); *m* 18 Nov 1972, Linda Joyce, da of Samuel Hart; 3 s (Nicholas b 1974, Mathew b 1977, Tom b 1984), 1 da (Kate b 1976); *Career* MO RAF Med Branch 1971–88: med cadetship 1971–73, surgn PMRAF Hosp 1974–79 (55 Field Surgical Team 1976–77), radiologist 1979–88; conslt radiologist nuclear med 1988–; asst ed Clinical Radiology 1990–, ed Royal Coll of Radiologist Newsletter 1992–; FRCS 1978, FRCR 1983; *Books* Radiology: A Practical Guide (1988), Imaging Strategy: A guide for clinicians (with Dr Richard Fowler, 1992); *Recreations* hill walking, fishing, writing; *Style—* Dr Bob Bury; ✉ Department of Nuclear Medicine, Leeds General Infirmary, Great George St, Leeds LS1 3EX (☎ 0113 292 6471)

BURY, Thomas Edmund Oswell (Tom); s of Michael Oswell Bury, of Ingatestone, Essex, and Jean Threlkeld, *née* Wood; *b* 14 May 1958; *Educ* Charterhouse, St Edmund Hall Oxford (BA); *m* 5 Dec 1992, Patricia, *née* Lowe; 1 da (Grace Rebecca b 5 April 1994); *Career* Young & Rubicam Ltd London 1980–85: graduate trainee, account mangr 1982, account supervisor 1983; Ogilvy & Mather: account supervisor 1985, account dir 1985, bd dir 1987, mgmnt supervisor 1988, new business dir 1988, head of client services 1989–93 (responsible for the accounts of Ford UK, Guinness UK, Brooke Bond, Coley Porter Bell, Worldwide Fund for Nature), gp bd dir 1990–, gp md 1993–, int bd dir 1996–; MIPA; *Recreations* cricket, golf, squash, racquets, books; *Clubs* United Oxford and Cambridge Univ, RAC, MCC, Arabs, I Zingari, Old Carthusians; *Style—* Tom Bury, Esq; ✉ Ogilvy and Mather Advertising Ltd, 10 Cabot Square, Canary Wharf, London E14 4QB (☎ 0171 345 3000)

BUSBRIDGE, Raymond John; s of John Charles Busbridge (d 1968), and Marie Ida, *née* Stratton; *b* 11 Dec 1946; *Educ* Woodside Secdy Sch; *m* 1, June 1966 (m dis 1979), Dianne Rosemary, *née* Webster; 1 s (Phillip James b 8 May 1970), 1 da (Claire Nanette b 21 Nov 1974); m 2, 13 March 1982, Mary Claire, da of Paul Fennelly, of Kilkenny, Ireland; *Career* Leslie & Godwin 1963–64, aviation asst underwriter R W Sturge 1964–75; aviation underwriter: Assicurazioni Generali 1975–80, JFC Dugdale (later Octavian Underwriting); fndr A J M Drake (later Busbridge Aviation Syndicate), exec dir Octavian Group Ltd, chm Lloyd's of London Shotgun Club, memb Lloyd's 1985–; *Recreations* shooting, fishing, painting; *Style—* Raymond Busbridge, Esq; ✉ Octavian Group Ltd, 84 Fenchurch St, London EC3M 4BY (☎ 0171 265 0071, fax 0171 626 3281)

BUSBY, (Thomas Samuel) Charles; CBE (1977, OBE 1971), AE (1946), DL (Kent 1981); s of Thomas William Busby (d 1974), and Alice, *née* Feaver (d 1972); *b* 28 July 1919; *Educ* Cranbrook Sch Kent; *m* 1949, Diana Daun, da of William Spence Cruickshank Dalgarno (d 1954), of Aberdeen; *Career* joined 500 Sqdn (Co Kent) RAuxAF 1939, served RAF Sqdns as Flt Lt (demobilised 1946); FSVA incorporated surveyor, auctioneer and estate agent (ret 1984); chm Royal Br Legion Village and Industries 1965–, life vice pres Kent Br Legion 1967– (vice chm 1952, chm 1962–67), vice chm Central Kent Hosp Mgmnt Ctee 1970–72 (memb 1964), chm Preston Hall Hosp Ctee 1970–74, memb Cncl Br Cwlth Ex-Services League 1971–, memb Maidstone and Dist Hosp Mgmnt Ctee 1972–74, memb Kent Family Practitioner Ctee 1974–75, nat vice pres Royal Br Legion 1993 (chm Pensions Disabled and Employment Ctee 1965–72 and 1978–92, nat vice chm 1972–75, nat chm 1975–78), chm Br Membs' Cncl World Veterans Fedn 1977– (lay memb Med Advsy Ctee), memb Maidstone Health Authy 1984–89 (chm Mental Handicapped Ctee), pres SE Area Royal Br Legion 1986–93; *Recreations* gardening, rugby football and cricket; *Clubs* RAF, Royal Over-Seas League; *Style—* Charles Busby, Esq, CBE, AE, DL; ✉ Willow Cottage, Benenden, Cranbrook, Kent TN17 4DB (☎ 01580 240466)

BUSBY, John Philip; s of Eric Alfred Busby, MBE (d 1983), and Margaret Elizabeth, *née* Ware; *b* 2 Feb 1928; *Educ* Ilkley GS, Leeds Coll of Art (NDD), Edinburgh Coll of Art (DA Edin); *m* 18 July 1959, Joan, da of Fred Warriner, of Cleveland; 1 s (Philip b 1960), 2 da (Rachel b 1962, Sarah b 1966); *Career* Nat Serv RAF 1946–48; lectr Edinburgh Coll of Art 1956–88; pres Soc of Scottish Artists 1973–76, fndr memb Soc of Wildlife Artists; memb RSW 1983, ARSA 1987; *Books* The Living Birds of Eric Ennion (1982), Drawing Birds (1986), Birds in Mallorca (1988), John Busby: Nature Drawings (1993); *Recreations* ornithology, travel, music; *Style—* John P Busby, Esq; ✉ Easter Haining, Ormiston Hall, Ormiston, E Lothian EH35 5NJ (☎ 01875 340512)

BUSBY, Richard Anthony; s of Ronald Arthur Busby (d 1991), of Bromley, Kent, and Sheila Annora, *née* Fitzherbert; *b* 4 June 1950; *Educ* St Dunstan's Coll S E London, Univ of Essex (BA); *m* 1, 24 July 1977 (m dis 1983), Karen, da of Ian Barr, of Edinburgh; m 2, 5 July 1985, Kathleen, da of Daniel Henebury (d 1984); 2 step s (Nicholas b 1961, Richard b 1964); *Career* articled clerk Touche Ross 1968–69, asst prodn mangr Hodder & Stoughton 1973–76, mktg mangr Futura Publications 1976–77, md C & C Communications 1977–85, chm and chief exec offr Strategic Sponsorship Ltd 1985–93, chief exec offr BDS Sponsorship Ltd 1993–; memb Variety Club of Great Britain; involved with various environmental and charitable orgns; *Recreations* reading, current affairs, art, theatre, opera, sport, jazz and cinema; *Style—* Richard Busby, Esq; ✉ BDS Sponsorship Ltd, 7A Langley Street, London WC2 (☎ 0171 240 3252, fax 0171 240 3243)

BUSCALL, Robert Edmond; JP (Norfolk 1971), DL (Norfolk 1989); o s of Lt-Col Victor Henley Buscall (d 1979), of Carbrooke Hall, Thetford, Norfolk, and Gwendolene Mary Angela, *née* Mahony (d 1991); *b* 2 April 1935; *Educ* Downside, RAC Cirencester (MRAC); *m* 7 Oct 1961, Livia, da of Sir Stephen Lycett Green, 4 Bt, CBE (d 1996), of Ken Hill, Snettisham, King's Lynn; 2 s (Harry Charles b 1963, Patrick Edward b 1965); *Career* Lt Irish Guards 1953–56; farmer; cncllr Breckland DC 1983–91, gen cmmr of income tax 1983–91; memb: Bd of Visitors Wayland Prison 1984–87, Agric Land Tbnl (E Area) 1983; High Sheriff Norfolk 1993–94; *Recreations* country pursuits, gardening; *Clubs* White's, Allsorts (Norfolk); *Style—* Robert Buscall, Esq, JP, DL; ✉ Carbrooke Hall, Thetford, Norfolk (☎ 01953 881274)

BUSH, Catherine (Kate); *b* 30 July 1958; *Career* singer and songwriter; debut single Wuthering Heights (1978, UK no 1); albums: The Kick Inside (1978, reached UK no 3), Lionheart (1978, UK no 6), Never For Ever (1980, UK no 1), The Dreaming (1982, UK no 3), Hounds of Love (1985, UK no 1), The Whole Story (compilation, 1986, UK no 1), The Sensual World (1989, UK no 2), This Woman's Work (box set, 1990), The Red Shoes (1993); Ivor Novello Award 1978–79, Best British Female Artist BRIT Awards 1987; film The Line, The Cross and The Curve (premiered London Film Festival) Nov 1993; *Style—* Miss Kate Bush; ✉ c/o EMI Records (UK), EMI House, 43 Brook Green, London W6 7EF (☎ 0171 605 5000)

BUSH, Geoffrey Hubert; s of Sidney Arthur Bush, of Bristol, and Dorothy Elizabeth, *née* Rowlands (d 1990); *b* 5 April 1942; *Educ* Cotham GS Bristol; *m* Sylvia Mary, da of Walter Frank Squibb (d 1996); 1 s (Jonathan Mark b 1966), 1 da (Sarah Jane Mary b 1968); *Career* Inland Revenue: tax offr 1959, inspr of taxes 1968, dist inspr 1973, princ inspr 1981, under sec 1988, dep sec and cmmr 1994–; *Recreations* tennis, golf, sailing, country pursuits; *Clubs* Knowle Lawn Tennis, Topsham Sailing; *Style—* Geoffrey Bush, Esq; ✉ Board of Inland Revenue, Somerset House, London WC2R 1LB (☎ 0171 438 6543)

BUSH, (Claude) Harry; *b* 26 Sept 1932; *Educ* BA (Marketing), FCIS; *Career* retired chief exec of a gp of banks; currently non-exec chm Countess of Chester Hosp NHS Tst; former swimmer: English, British, Welsh and Scottish champion, 2 British records (200m breast stroke), Euro Silver (100m breast stroke); *Style—* Harry Bush, Esq; ✉ Countess of Chester Hospital NHS Trust, Liverpool Road, Chester CH2 1UL (☎ 01244 366374)

BUSH, Adm Sir John Fitzroy Duyland; GCB (1970, KCB 1965, CB 1963), DSC (1941, and two bars 1941 and 1944); s of Fitzroy Bush (d 1949), of Beach, Bitton, Glos; *b* 1 Nov 1914; *Educ* Clifton; *m* 1938, Ruth Kennedy, da of Capt Herbert K Horsey, RN, of Fareham, Hants; 3 s, 2 da; *Career* RN; formerly: C-in-C Western Fleet, Allied C-in-C Channel, Allied C-in-C E Atlantic 1967–70, Vice-Adm of UK and Lt of Admiralty 1979–84; Clifton Coll Cncl: memb 1971–87, chm 1978–81, pres 1982–87; *Recreations* fishing, gardening; *Style—* Adm Sir John Bush, GCB, DSC; ✉ Becksteddle House, Colemore, nr Alton, Hants (☎ 01420 588367)

BUSH, Paul Anthony; s of Anthony Clive Bush, and Beatrice Catherine Bush; *b* 11 June 1958; *Educ* South Wigston HS Leics, Gateway Boys' Sch Leicester, Borough Road Coll of Physical Educn Middx, Dunfermline Coll of Physical Educn Edinburgh (Dip in Sports Coaching); *m* 15 April 1989, Katriona Christine, da of late James Edward Bayley; *Career* accounts clerk Gen Accident Life Assurance Co 1978–79, trainee surveyor Dist Valuer's Office Leicester 1979–81, chief coach Leics Amateur Swimming Assoc 1979–81, swimming devpt offr/chief coach City of Bradford Met Cncl 1982–84, chief coach City of Leicester Swimming Club 1984–87, swimming devpt offr Leeds Leisure Servs 1987–92, gen sec Br Swimming Coaches Assoc 1986–92, chm Br Swimming Grand Prix 1987–88 (sec 1987–90), sr team mangr Eng Swimming Team 1989–, gen mangr Eng Swimming Team Cwlth Games Auckland 1990, GB Swimming Team mangr Olympic Games Barcelona 1992, dir of swimming Amateur Swimming Assoc 1992–96, dir of swimming Cwlth Games Victoria Canada 1994, asst head of development Sports Cncl 1996–, dir of swimming Olympic Games Atlanta 1996, sr team mangr English Swimming Team 1996–; European Youth Olympics: dep chef de mission BOA Holland 1993, chef de mission BOA Bath 1995; conslt Gezira Sporting Club Egypt 1982 and 1983, tech dir Euro Jr Swimming and Diving Championships 1989 and 1992; dir of aquatics Universiade Sheffield 1991 (rep FISU Tech Ctee 1991); bd dir World Swimming Coaches Assoc 1994–; memb: Exec Ctee and Swimming Ctee Yorks Amateur Swimming Assoc 1991–, Swimming Ctee North Eastern Counties Amateur Swimming Assoc 1990–92, Swimming Ctee Amateur Swimming Assoc 1991–; event dir Leeds Cycling Events (incl World Cyclo Cross Championships 1992) 1991–92; govr Gateway Boys' Sch 1996–; memb: Br Inst of Sports Coaches 1987–, Inst of Swimming Teachers and Coaches 1980–, Br Swimming Coaches Assoc 1981– (hon life fell 1992), Inst of Leisure and Amenity Mgmnt 1992–; fell Br Inst of Sports Administrators; *Books* Take up Swimming (jtly, 1989), author of numerous articles in Swimming Times; *Recreations* most sports (especially golf, swimming, squash and running), travel, theatre, gardening; *Style—* Paul Bush, Esq; ✉ The Sports Council, 16 Upper Woborn Place, London (☎ 0171 388 127, fax 0171 383 240, e-mail P.Bush@bshsport.demon.co.uk)

BUSH, Prof Stephen Frederick; s of Albert Edward Bush (d 1982), and Winifred May, *née* Maltby (d 1995); *b* 6 May 1939; *Educ* Isleworth GS, Trinity Coll Cambridge (MA, PhD), MIT (MSc); *m* 26 Oct 1963, Gillian Mary, da of Reginald Charles Layton, of Thorpe Bay, Essex; 1 s (James Henry b 1970), 1 da (Jane Elizabeth b 1972); *Career* gp mangr of chem engrg ICI Corporate Laboratory 1969–72, mangr Systems Technol Dept ICI Europa Ltd 1972–79, prof of polymer engrg UMIST 1979–; md Prosyma Research Ltd 1987–, chm and co-fndr N of England Plastic Processors Consortium 1990–; chm Applied Mechanics Ctee SERC 1985–87, vice chm Campaign for Ind Britain 1991–, memb Schs Examination and Assessment Ctee for Technol 1992–94; worldwide patents in polymer composites 1990–96; Sir George Nelson Prize 1960, Moulton Medal 1969, Sir George Beilby Medal and Prize 1979; FIMechE (memb Cncl 1978–81), FIChemE; FPRI (memb Cncl 1985–87), FIM; *Books* Chemical Reaction Engineering (contrib, 1972), Macromolecular Chemistry Reports (contrib, 1980), Polymer Engineering (contrib, 1984), Synthetic and Biological Networks (contrib, 1988); *Recreations* mountain walking, British imperial history, music, tennis; *Clubs* Royal Over-Seas League; *Style—* Prof Stephen Bush; ✉ University of Manchester Institute of Science and Technology, PO Box 88, Manchester M60 1QD (☎ 0161 200 3760, fax 0161 200 3767)

BUSHELL, Garry Llewellyn; s of George Frederick Henry Bushell, BEM, of Greenhill, Kent, and Evelyn May Mary, *née* Barker (d 1987); *b* 13 May 1955; *Educ* Colfe's GS, NE London Poly (BA), London Coll of Printing (NCTJ); *m* 31 July 1976, Carol Ann Cousins, da of Francis Cousins; 2 s (Danny John b 25 Aug 1980, Robert Llewellyn b 1 April 1988), 1 da (Julie Ann b 23 Nov 1978); *Career* TV critic The Sun 1987–; TV and radio broadcaster, presenter Bushell on the Box (Carlton/Central for ITV) 1996–; freelance writer; *Recreations* curry, Quasar, comedy; *Clubs* Charlton Athletic FC; *Style—* Garry

Bushell, Esq; ✉ The Sun, Virginia Street, London E1 9BD (☎ 0171 782 4000, telex 262135)

BUSHELL, John Hudson; s of (Charles) Harold Bushell, OBE, of Reigate, Surrey, and Bessie Mary, *née* Smith; *b* 13 Oct 1941; *Educ* Haileybury; *m* 8 Oct 1966, Marian Elisabeth, da of Eric Percival Marsh, of Woking, Surrey; 1 s (Alistair b 1970), 2 da (Emma b 1968, Heather b 1978); *Career* dir J Henry Schroder Wagg & Co Ltd 1975–85, chm and chief exec London Shop plc 1986–89 (dir 1982–89, exec vice chm 1985–86), non-exec chm Dencora plc 1989–, non-exec dir Woolwich Building Soc 1990–; FCA 1964; *Recreations* golf, cricket, tennis; *Clubs* Tyrrell's Wood Golf, Headley Cricket, Oxshott Cricket; *Style*— John Bushell, Esq; ✉ Dencora plc, Dencora House, Blyburgate, Beccles, Suffolk NR34 9TQ (☎ 01502 712729); Woolwich Building Society, Corporate Headquarters, Watling St, Bexleyheath, Kent DA6 7RR (☎ 0181 298 5000)

BUSK, Maj-Gen Leslie Francis Harry; CB (1989); s of Lt-Col Charles William Francis Busk (d 1959), and Alice Van Bergen; *b* 12 Sept 1937; *Educ* Wellington, RMCS Shrivenham (BSc); *m* 1, 9 Jan 1960, Jennifer Helen Busk (d 1992); 3 s (Jonathan b 1963, Edward b 1966, Crispin b 1974); m 2, 10 Dec 1993, Glennis McElwain; *Career* cmmnd RE 1957, cmdg offr 35 Engr Regt 1977–79, Cdr II Engr Brigade 1981–83, RCDS 1984, dir Army Air Corps 1987–89; DG Br Heart Fndn 1990–, chm Assoc of Med Res Charities 1991–95; *Recreations* tennis, gardening, golf; *Clubs* Army and Navy; *Style*— Maj-Gen Leslie Busk, CB; ✉ Director General, British Heart Foundation, 14 Fitzhardinge Street, London W1H 4DH (☎ 0171 935 0185, fax 0171 486 5820)

BUSS, Nicola Sian (Nicky); da of Dr David Buss, and Heather, *née* Parr; *b* 14 Oct 1967; *Educ* Farnborough Hill Convent Coll, Magdalen Coll Oxford (entrance scholar, Demy scholar, MA Philosophy & Psychology, Alec Varley Psychology Prize); *Career* Booz Allen & Hamilton/OC & C Strategy Consulting 1988–90, bd dir Planning Dept Saatchi & Saatchi Advertising 1991–94 (APG Gold Creative Planning Award for British Airways Club World, first prize AMSO Research Effectiveness Award), vice pres Strategy and Planning MTV Europe 1994–96, strategic planning dir Ammirati Puris Lintas London 1996–; memb: MRS 1991, Account Planning Gp 1991, Media Research Gp 1995; *Publications* AMSO Research Works (1992), Greener Communications (1993), Creative Planning, Outstanding Advertising (1994); *Recreations* sailing, music, fashion; *Clubs* Harbour; *Style*— Miss Nicky Buss; ✉ Ammirati Puris Lintas, 84 Eccleston Square, London SW1V 1PX (☎ 0171 932 8636, fax 0171 932 8679, mobile 0802 847112, e-mail nicky.buss@ammirati-puris-lintas.sprint.com)

BUSS, Robin Caron; s of Kenneth Caron Buss (d 1961), and Lilian May Buss; *b* 10 May 1939; *Educ* Westminster, Univ of Paris (Licence-ès-Lettres, Doctorat de l'Université de Paris-Sorbonne); *m* 1, 1963 (m dis 1991), Patricia Anne Lams; 1 s (Louis Caron b 1963), 1 da (Claudia Caron b 1968); m 2, 1995, Natalia Georgievna Filatova; *Career* film and TV critic; research asst FO 1967–75, lectr in French Woolwich Coll of FE 1976–91; Times Educnl Supplement: film critic 1985–90 and 1994–, TV critic 1985–94; TV previewer Independent on Sunday 1992–; *Publications* The French Through Their Films (1988), Italian Films (1989); French Film Noir (1994); trans: Letters From Russia (Custine, 1991), The Art of Cinema (Cocteau, 1992), The Princesse de Clèves (Mme de Lafayette, 1992), César Birotteau (Balzac, 1994), The Count of Monte Cristo (Dumas, 1995); author of various articles in English and French on cultural topics, cinema, TV and French lit, contrib Encyclopaedia Britannica; *Style*— Robin Buss, Esq; ✉ 6 Park Place House, Park Vista, Greenwich, London SE10 9ND (☎ 0181 858 4978); Independent on Sunday, 1 Canada Square, Canary Wharf, London E14 5AP (☎ 0171 293 2000, fax 0171 293 2435)

BUSSELL, Darcey Andrea; OBE (1995); da of Philip Michael Bussell, and Andrea Pemberton, *née* Williams; *b* 27 April 1969; *Educ* Arts Educnl Sch, Royal Ballet Sch; *Career* ballerina; appeared in 1986 and 1987 Royal Ballet Sch performances, joined Sadler's Wells Royal Ballet (now Birmingham Royal Ballet) 1987; Royal Ballet: joined as soloist 1988, first soloist 1989, princ 1989 (currently Royal Ballet's youngest princ dancer); also international guest performances with various other cos; *Performances* first professional leading role Myrthe in Giselle; classical repertory incl: Odette/Odile in Swan Lake, Princess Aurora in The Sleeping Beauty, Sugar Plum Fairy in The Nutcracker, Nikiya and Gamzatti in La Bayadere, title role in Giselle, Raymonda in Raymonda Act III; Sir Kenneth MacMillan ballets: cr role of Princess Rose in The Prince of the Pagodas, cr role of Masha in Winter Dreams 1991 (Farewell pas de deux created in advance for her and Irek Mukhamedov and performed at the HM the Queen Mother's 90th Birthday Tribute and Royal Opera House 1990, also televised), title role in Manon, Juliet in Romeo and Juliet, leading role in Song of the Earth, leading role in Elite Syncopations, Agnus Dei role in Requiem, Mitzi Caspar in Mayerling; Balanchine ballets incl: appeared in Royal Ballet's first performances of Rubies and Stravinksy Violin Concerto, princ roles in Agon, Symphony in C, Tchaikovsky pas de deux, Duo Concertant and Ballet Imperial, Terpsichore in Apollo, Siren in Prodigal Son; leading roles in other major ballets incl: Sir Frederick Ashton's Cinderella, Monotones II and Illuminations, William Forsythe's In the Middle Somewhat Elevated 1992 and Hermann Schmerman 1993, first Royal Ballet performance of Glen Tetley's La Ronde (role of Prostitute), Dame Ninette de Valois' Checkmate (role of Black Queen), Galanteries, David Bintley's The Spirit of Fugue (cr leading role), Enigma Variations (role of Lady Mary), Ashley Page's Bloodlines (cr leading role), Twyla Tharp's Mr Worldly Wise (cr role of Mistress Truth-on-Toe) 1995, Dances with Death (cr role) 1996, Anastasia (role of Kschessinska) 1996; *Awards* Prix de Lausanne 1986, Dancer of the Year Dance and Dancers magazine 1990, Most Promising Artiste of 1990 Variety Club of GB, Evening Standard Award 1991, Olivier Award (for In the Middle Somewhat Elevated) 1992; *Style*— Miss Darcey Bussell, OBE; ✉ The Royal Ballet, Royal Opera House, Covent Garden, London WC2E 9DD (☎ 0171 240 1200)

BUSTON, Lt-Col Roger; TD (1985); s of Russell Buston (d 1992), of Parkstone, Dorset, and Kathleen, *née* Williams (d 1955); *b* 24 May 1953; *Educ* Colchester RGS, Poole GS, Queen Mary Coll London (LLB); *Career* Univ of London OTC 1971–; 36 Signal Regt (TA): Troop Cmd 1974, Sqdn Cmd 1986–, Regtl Ops Offr 1988–90, Regtl 2 i/c 1990–92, S02 AVN 3 Regt AAC 1993, S01 (D & P) The Royal Sch of Signals 1994–; admitted slr 1977; sole practitioner Asher Prior & Son 1981–, ptnr Asher Prior Bates (Colchester) and Bates Group 1986, managing ptnr Asher Prior Bates (Colchester) 1995–; MIMgt; *Recreations* skiing, sailing; *Style*— Lt-Col Roger Buston, TD; ✉ New House, Wellesley Rd, Colchester CO3 3HF (☎ 01206 45986); Asher Prior Bates (Solicitors), Blackburn House, 32 Crouch St, Colchester, Essex CO3 3HH (☎ 01206 573089, fax 01206 760096, mobile 0370 305977)

BUSUTTIL, Prof Anthony; s of Anthony Busuttil (d 1973), of Malta, and Maria, *née* Vassallo (d 1978); *b* 30 Dec 1945; *Educ* St Aloysius' Coll Malta; *m* 31 Aug 1969, Angela, da of Angelo Bonello (d 1979), of Gozo; 3 s (Godwin b 1970, Christopher b 1973, Joseph b 1978); *Career* lectr in pathology Univ of Glasgow 1971–76, conslt pathologist Lothian Health Bd 1976–87, currently regius prof of forensic med Univ of Edinburgh (sr lectr in pathology 1976–87), contrib to several books on gastroenterology, genitourinary and forensic pathology; chm Euro Cncl for Legal Med; memb: BMA, Assoc of Clinical Pathology; DMJ(Path); fell Br Assoc of Forensic Med, MRCPath, FRCPath, FRCPE, FRCPGlas; *Recreations* classical music, reading; *Clubs* RSM; *Style*— Prof Anthony Busuttil; ✉ 78 Hillpark Ave, Edinburgh EH4 7AL (☎ 0131 336 3241); Forensic Medicine Unit, Medical School, University of Edinburgh, Teviot Place, Edinburgh EH8 9AG (☎ 0131 650 3281, fax 0131 650 6529)

BUTCHARD, Timothy Robin (Tim); s of Capt John Bryan Butchard, RN (ret), of Wylye, Wilts, and Patricia Deidre Broke, *née* Tonks (niece of painter and Slade prof Henry Tonks); *b* 24 Dec 1944; *Educ* Shrewsbury, CCC Cambridge (MA), Univ of Exeter (PGCE); *Career* vol VSO India 1968–69, asst master Fettes Coll Edinburgh 1969–71; British Cncl: VSO field offr Kenya 1971–75, dir Documentary Exhbns London 1975–79, dep dir Thailand 1979–83, first sec (cultural) Br Embassy Beijing 1984–87, dir Courses Dept London 1987–92, head Drama and Dance Dept London 1992–; *Recreations* tennis, travel, the arts, the Orient; *Clubs* Lansdowne, Siam Soc (Bangkok); *Style*— Tim Butchard, Esq; ✉ 4 Dorville Crescent, London W6 0HJ (☎ 0181 741 0836)

BUTCHER, Anthony Edward William Hugh (Tony); s of Humphrey George Herbert Butcher, and Mary Josephine, *née* McCaffrey; *b* 6 Nov 1940; *Educ* Ampleforth; *m* 18 Sept 1965, Sarah, da of Raymond Stuart Harwood; 3 da (Louise b 18 July 1966, Katherine b 14 Feb 1969, Clare b 23 Nov 1974); *Career* CA; articled clerk J S Streets & Co Lincoln 1959–64, Turquand Youngs & Co London 1964–65, Selincourt Group 1965–67, Price Waterhouse 1967–85, ptnr Pannell Kerr Forster 1985– (joined 1985); FCA, MInstD; *Recreations* rugby, board sailing, travel, gardening; *Clubs* Nottingham Rugby Football, Nottingham and Notts United Services; *Style*— Tony Butcher, Esq; ✉ Pannell Kerr Forster, Regent House, PO Box 80, Clinton Avenue, Nottingham NG5 1LJ (☎ 0115 960 8171, fax 0115 962 2229)

BUTCHER, Ian George; s of George Wilfred Robert Butcher, of Winchmore Hill, London, and Joyce Patricia, *née* Payne; *b* 13 April 1950; *Educ* Winchmore Sch, City of London Coll; *m* 15 Sept 1978, Sarah Jane, da of Donald Percy Jeffery, of Aston Hill Farmhouse, Halton, Bucks; 1 s (Harry b 1987), 2 da (Emma b 1981, Kellie b 1984); *Career* Touche Ross & Co (chartered accountants) 1969–74, exec dir County Bank Ltd 1974–84, fin dir Addison Page plc 1984–86, corp devpt dir Addison Conslt Group plc 1986–87, gp fin dir Charles Barker plc 1987–89, chm Lefax Publishing Ltd 1984–88, dir Whitehead Mann Group plc 1989–; FCA; *Recreations* cricket, tennis, music, reading; *Clubs* MCC, RAC; *Style*— Ian G Butcher, Esq; ✉ Aston Hill Farmhouse, Aston Hill, Halton, nr Aylesbury, Bucks HP22 5NQ (☎ 01296 630643); Whitehead Mann Group plc, 11 Hill Street, London W1X 8BB (☎ 0171 290 2000)

BUTCHER, Prof Paul Newman; s of Henry Butcher (d 1970), of Ashford, Kent, and Beatrice Ada, *née* Bridges (d 1968); *b* 11 Aug 1929; *Educ* Ashford GS, Imperial Coll London (BSc, DIC, PhD); *m* 2 Aug 1952, Alfreda (Freda), da of Frederick Stone (d 1929); *Career* scientific civil serv 1951–67, head Theoretical Physics Group RSRE Malvern 1964–67, prof of theoretical physics Univ of Warwick 1967–96 (emeritus prof 1996–); visiting prof: Ohio State Univ 1963–64, Danish Tech Univ Copenhagen 1970; 200 pubns on topics incl: microwave tubes, nonlinear optics and electronics, amorphous and crystalline semiconductors, electronic microstructures; ARCS, FIEE, former fell Physical Soc; *Books* The Principles of Nonlinear Optics (1990); *Recreations* walking, music; *Style*— Prof Paul N Butcher; ✉ c/o Physics Department, University of Warwick, Coventry CV4 7AL (☎ 01203 523989, fax 01203 692016)

BUTCHER, Stephen James; s of Geoffrey Cecil Butcher, and Audrey Ray, *née* Vince (d 1985); *b* 25 Feb 1952; *Educ* Stonyhurst Coll, St John's Coll Oxford (BA); *m* 11 Nov 1989, Jane Mary, da of Dr Toby Thorne; 2 da (Catherine Mary b 18 April 1992, Eleanor Margaret b 16 Dec 1995); *Career* md Academic Div Cassell 1995–; *Style*— Stephen Butcher, Esq; ✉ Cassell, Wellington House, 125 Strand, London WC2R 0BB (☎ 0171 420 5555, fax 0171 240 7261)

BUTE, 7 Marquess of (GB 1796); Sir John Colum Crichton-Stuart; 12 Bt (S 1627); also Lord Crichton (S 1488), Earl of Dumfries, Viscount of Air, Lord Crichton of Sanquhar and Cumnock (S 1633), Earl of Bute, Viscount Kingarth, Lord Mountstuart, Cumra(e) and Inchmarnock (S 1703), Baron Mountstuart of Wortley (GB 1761), Baron Cardiff of Cardiff Castle (GB 1776), Earl of Windsor and Viscount Mountjoy (GB 1796); Hereditary Sheriff and Coroner of Co Bute, Hereditary Keeper of Rothesay Castle; patron of 9 livings (but being a Roman Catholic cannot present); s of 6 Marquess of Bute, KBE (d 1993), and his 1 w, (Beatrice) Nicola Grace, *née* Weld-Forester; *b* 26 April 1958; *m* 1984 (m dis 1993), Carolyn, da of Bryson Waddell (d 1975); 1 s (John Bryson, Lord Mount Stuart b 21 Dec 1989), 2 da (Lady Caroline b 1984, Lady Cathleen b 1986); *Heir* s, Lord Mount Stuart b 21 Dec 1989; *Career* motor racing driver (as Johnny Dumfries) 1980–91; British Formula Three champion 1984, runner-up FIA European Formula Three Championship 1984, contracted to Ferrari Formula One team as test driver 1985, number two driver for John Player Special Team Lotus 1986, works driver for World Champion Sports Prototype Team Silk Cut Jaguar 1988 (jt winner Le Mans 1988), lead driver for Toyota GB World Sports Prototype Championship 1989 and 1990; *Style*— Johnny Dumfries; ✉ Mount Stuart, Rothesay, Isle of Bute PA20 9LR (☎ 01700 502730)

BUTLER, Rt Hon Sir Adam Courtauld; kt (1986), PC (1984), DL (Warwicks 1993); s of Baron Butler of Saffron Walden, KG, CH, PC (d 1982), and his 1 w, Sydney, da of Samuel Courtauld; *b* 11 Oct 1931; *Educ* Eton, Pembroke Coll Cambridge; *m* 1955, Felicity, da of Kemyel Molesworth St Aubyn (s of Sir Hugh Molesworth-St Aubyn, 13 Bt, JP, by his w, Emma, da of Adm Charles Wake, 2 s of Sir Charles Wake, 10 Bt; Adm Charles Wake m Emma, da of Sir Edward St Aubyn, 1 Bt, and sis of 1 Baron St Levan); 2 s, 1 da; *Career* Nat Serv 2 Lt KRRC 1950–51; dir: Kayser Bondor 1966–73, Aristoc Ltd 1966–73, Capital & Counties Property Co Ltd 1973–79, HP Bulmer Holdings 1988–; chm Samuel Courtauld Tst; MP (C) Bosworth 1970–87, Cons whip 1974–75, PPS to Rt Hon Margaret Thatcher 1975–79; min of state: Indust 1979–81, NI 1981–84, Defence 1984–85; chm Airey Neave Tst 1990–, pres Br Horse Soc 1990–92; memb Ct of Assts Worshipful Co of Goldsmiths; farmer; *Recreations* field sports, music, pictures; *Style*— The Rt Hon Sir Adam Butler, DL; ✉ The Old Rectory, Lighthorne, Warwick (☎ 01926 651214)

BUTLER, Alan Edward; s of Albert Frederick Butler (d 1978), of Clacton on Sea, and Lillian Elizabeth, *née* Carlson (d 1969); *b* 6 Dec 1940; *Educ* Raine's Fndn GS, UCL (BSc); *m* 27 Nov 1981, Gail Katharine; 2 s (Richard b 1984, James b 1990); *Career* md: Carl Byoir and Associates Ltd 1975–85 (dir 1970), Communications Strategy Ltd 1985–86, Countrywide Communications Ltd 1987–93; managing ptnr Kudos Communications 1993–, dir YTJ Pacific Singapore 1994–, conslt Kudos Consulting Dubai 1994–; former chm Strangers Gallery NW Surrey House of Commons Dining Club, former chm PRCA; Freeman City of London; Liveryman Worshipful Co of Marketors 1988; memb: Mktg Soc, IABC; MBCS, MIPRA, FIPR, FInstD; *Recreations* most sports; *Clubs* Wig and Pen; *Style*— Alan Butler, Esq; ✉ Kudos Communications, Little Owls, Priest Hill, Old Windsor, Berks SL4 2JN (☎ 01784 430461, fax 01784 473204)

BUTLER, Anthony John (Tony); s of Martin Edward Butler, of Folkestone, Kent, and Freda Alice, *née* Matson; *b* 30 Jan 1945; *Educ* Maidstone GS, Univ Coll Oxford (exhibitioner, MA), Trinity Hall Cambridge and Inst of Criminology Cambridge (Dip in Crimimology), Columbia Univ Law Sch NY; *m* Margaret Ann, da of George Randon; 1 da (Catherine b 19 July 1968), 1 s (James b 21 July 1971); *Career* Home Office 1969–96: successively asst princ Police Dept, private sec to Min of State, princ Sex Discrimination Legislation Unit, Race Relations Legislation Unit and Bdcasting Dept, private sec to Home Sec, asst sec Bdcasting Dept, Fin Dept and Prison Dept, asst under sec of state, seconded as dir Inner Cities DOE, princ fin offr, dir Personnel Fin and Servs HM Prison Serv until 1996; currently dir Oxford Univ Careers Serv; fell Inst of Personnel and Devpt, fell New Coll Oxford; *Recreations* music gardening; *Style*— Tony Butler, Esq; ✉ Oxford University Careers Service, 56 Banbury Road, Oxford OX1 6PA (☎ 01865 274646)

BUTLER, Arthur William; ERD (1964); s of Frederick Butler (d 1975), and Elizina, *née* Bond (d 1992); *b* 20 Jan 1929; *Educ* Wanstead HS, LSE (BSc); *m* 3 May 1958, Evelyn

Mary, da of Thomas Alexander Luetchford (d 1988); 1 da (Caroline b 7 May 1966); *Career* Offr Cadet India Cadet Co 1946, 2 Lt RAOC 1947–48, Capt AER 1957–64 (Lt 1953); trainee Kemsley Newpapers Graduate Trg Course 1951–55, political corr News Chronicle 1956–60, political ed Reynolds News 1960–62, political corr Daily Express 1963–69, political ed Daily Sketch 1969–71, md Partnerplan Public Affrs 1971–74, dir Public Affrs Div John Addey Assocs 1974–77, vice chm Charles Barker Watney and Powell 1987–89 (jt md 1978–87), dir C S M Parliamentary Consultants Limited 1995–; conslt on Parly relations McAvoy Bayley 1989–93; jt ed English edn The Free Romanian Newspaper 1985–94, jt managing ed Science in Parliament 1995–; memb Middlesbrough Trades Cncl 1952–55; sec: Parly All Party Roads Study Gp 1974–86, Roads Campaign Cncl 1974–86, Parly Scientific Ctee 1978–95; govr Sch for Disabled Putney 1975–79, fndr sec Parly Info Technol Ctee 1981–84; Liveryman Worshipful Co of Tobacco Pipe Makers, Freeman City of London 1976; hon life memb Parly and Scientific Ctee 1995–; *Books* No Feet to Drag (with Alfred Morris, MP, 1972), The First Forty Years - A History of the Parliamentary and Scientific Committee (1980), Lobbying in the British Parliament (with Douglas Smith, 1986); *Recreations* walking, gardening, collecting books and militaria, travel; *Clubs* RAC; *Style*— Arthur Butler, Esq, ERD; ✉ 30 Chester Way, Kennington, London SE11 4UR (☎ 0171 587 5170); Science in Parliament, 16 Great College Street, London SW1P 3RX (☎ 0171 222 7085)

BUTLER, Audrey Maude Beman; da of Robert Beman Minchin (d 1972), and Vivien Florence Fraser, *née* Scott (d 1976); *b* 31 May 1936; *Educ* Queenswood Sch Herts, Univ of St Andrews (MA); *m* 1959 (m dis 1981), Anthony Michael Butler, s of Michael John Butler; 2 da (Clare, Siobhan); *Career* geography teacher; head of geography St Michael's Burton Park 1970–73 and 1976–78, housemistress Manor House Lancing Coll 1978–81, headmistress Queenswood Hatfield Herts 1981–; govr: Duncombe Sch 1982–, Aldenham Sch, Tockington Manor 1987– (chm 1995–), Maltman's Green Sch 1988–; memb Girls' Schs' Assoc 1987–, memb and chm Boarding Schs' Assoc 1989–91 (vice chm 1991–92), vice chm Bloxham Project 1992–; FRGS, MInstD 1986; *Recreations* golf, tennis, swimming, walking, theatre; *Style*— Mrs Audrey Butler; ✉ Queenswood, Shepherd's Way, Brookmans Park, Hatfield, Herts AL9 6NS (☎ 01707 652262)

BUTLER, Auriol Lilian Evelyn; da of Alexander Ross Biddle (d 1927), of Temple Hill, East Budleigh, Devon, and Margaret Louise, *née* Allfrey (d 1958); *Educ* Byam Shaw Sch of Art, Slade Sch London; *m* 30 April 1940, Maj Richard S Butler (d 1988), s of Col Charles Walter Butler, OBE (d 1942), of Longham, Cornwood, Devon; 1 s (Patrick James Richard b 1944), 1 da (Penelope Eve); *Career* artist; portraits incl: The Princess Royal, Sir William Scott, Gen Sir Michael Rose; landscapes shown in: Paris Salon, RBA London, Nat Soc, United Soc; assoc Société des Artistes Française, Gold and Silver Medallist Academia Internaziale Rome, Diploma di Distinzione di Premio d'Italia, Slade Certificate of Fine Art, Diploma Academia Internaziale; FRSA, fell Int Inst of Art; *Recreations* archaeology; *Style*— Mrs Auriol Butler; ✉ Glebe Studio, Longham, Cornwood, Ivybridge, Devon PL21 9QZ (☎ 01752 837229)

BUTLER, Basil Richard Ryland; OBE (1976); s of Hugh Montagu Butler (d 1971), of Churchdown, Glos, and Annie Isabel, *née* Wiltshire (d 1969); *b* 1 March 1930; *Educ* Denstone Coll Staffs, St John's Coll Cambridge (MA); *m* 26 June 1954, Lilian Joyce, da of Reginald Merryweather Haswell (d 1989), of Amersham, Bucks; 1 s (Richard b 1957), 2 da (Clare b 1960, Helen b 1964); *Career* 2 Lt 5th Royal Inniskilling Dragoon Gds 1948–50; reservoir engr Trinidad Leaseholds Ltd 1954, petroleum engr to Chief Petroleum Engr and Supt Prodn Planning Div Kuwait Oil Co 1958–68, ops mangr BP (Colombia) 1968, ops mangr and gen mangr BP Alaska Inc 1970, seconded to Kuwait Oil Co as gen mangr ops 1972; mangr: Ninian Developments, BP Petroleum Development Co Ltd (London) 1975, Sullom Voe Terminal Shetland Islands 1976; BP Petroleum Development Ltd: gen mangr exploration and prodn (Aberdeen) 1978, chief exec (London) 1980; international dir BP International Ltd, md and chief exec BP Exploration Co Ltd 1981, md The BP Co plc 1986–91, chm BP Exploration Co Ltd 1986–89, chm BP Solar International 1989–94; chm: Brown and Root Ltd, K S Biomedix Holdings plc, Devonport Management Ltd until 1994; dir Murphy Oil Corp USA, conslt to the World Bank, chm Royal Dockyard Plymouth 1991–94; former pres Inst of Petroleum, chm Euro Cncl of Applied Sci and Engrg (EuroCASE) 1992–; Royal Acad of Engrg: memb Cncl (now Senate) 1985–, int sec 1995–, sr vice pres 1996–; Freeman: City of London, Worshipful Co of Shipwrights 1988; FEng 1985, FIMM 1985, Hon FIChemE 1992; *Recreations* sailing, music; *Clubs* IOD; *Style*— Basil Butler, Esq, OBE, FEng; ✉ Brown and Root Ltd, 150 The Broadway, Wimbledon, London SW19 1RX (☎ 0181 544 6600, fax 0181 544 6950)

BUTLER, Christopher John; s of Dr John Lynn Butler, of Cardiff, and late Eileen Patricia Butler; *b* 12 Aug 1950; *Educ* Cardiff HS, Emmanuel Coll Cambridge (MA); *m* 25 March 1989, Jacqueline Clair, *née* Harper; 1 s (David John Robert b 29 Jan 1994); *Career* market res conslt 1972–77, Cons Res Dept 1977–80, Political Office 10 Downing St 1980–83, special advsr to Sec of State for Wales 1983–85, market res conslt 1985–86, special advsr to Min for Arts 1986–87, MP (C) Warrington S 1987–92; political conslt 1992–; fell Indust and Parly Tst; *Recreations* writing, tennis, collecting books, deltiology; *Style*— Christopher J Butler, Esq; ✉ 15B Connaught House, Clifton Gardens, London W9 1AL (☎ 0171 417 4170)

BUTLER, Sir Clifford Charles; kt (1983); s of C H J Butler, of Earley, Reading; *b* 20 May 1922; *Educ* Reading Sch, Univ of Reading (BSc, PhD); *m* 1947, Kathleen Betty Collins; 2 da; *Career* former physics lectr Univ of Manchester, prof of physics and head Physics Dept Imperial Coll London 1963–70, dean Royal Coll Sci 1966–69, dir Nuffield Fndn 1970–75; vice chllr Loughborough Univ of Technol 1975–85; memb: Schs Cncl 1965–84, Univ Grants Ctee 1966–71, Open Univ Cncl 1971–95, Br Cncl Sci Advsy Ctee 1980–85; chm: Cncl Educn & Trg Health Visitors 1977–83, Advsy Ctee Supply & Educn Teachers 1980–85; Steering Ctee DES Educnl Counselling & Credit Transfer Info Serv Project 1983–89, ABRC/NERC study into Geological Surveying 1985–87; Hon DSc Univ of Reading, Hon DUniv Open Univ, Hon DTech Loughborough Univ of Technol; FRS; *Style*— Sir Clifford Butler, FRS; ✉ Low Woods Farm House, Low Woods Lane, Belton, Loughborough, Leics LE12 9TR (☎ 01530 223125)

BUTLER, Dr David Edgeworth; CBE (1991); s of Prof Harold Edgeworth Butler (d 1951), and Margaret Lucy, *née* Pollard (d 1982); *b* 17 Oct 1924; *Educ* St Paul's, New Coll Oxford, Princeton Univ, Nuffield Coll Oxford (BA, MA, DPhil); *m* 1962, Dr Marilyn Speers Butler, FRSL, *qv*, da of Sir Trevor Evans (d 1981); 3 s (Daniel b 1963, Gareth b 1965, Edmund b 1967); *Career* Lt Staffs Yeo 1943–45; fell Nuffield Coll Oxford 1951–, PA to HM Ambass Washington 1955–56; Hon DUniv: Paris 1978, Essex 1993; Hon DSSc Univ of Belfast 1985; FBA 1994; *Books* British General Election Studies (contrib, 1951–92), Political Change in Britain (1974), British Political Facts 1900–1994 (1994); *Style*— Dr David Butler, CBE, FBA; ✉ Nuffield College, Oxford OX1 1NF (☎ 01865 279644)

BUTLER, David John; s of Sidney James Butler, and Sylvia Joan, *née* Board; *b* 23 Feb 1953; *Educ* Sir John Cass Sch; *m* 8 June 1974, Bernadette Sheila, *née* Teahan; 2 s (Daniel David b 5 Sept 1981, Sean Francis b 18 March 1984); *Career* stockbroker; dealer Spencer Thornton 1972–80, int salesman Fielding Newson Smith 1980–82, head Int Dept Credit Suisse Buckmaster & Moore 1982–87, head of UK and Euro equity sales and exec dir Yamaichi Int 1987–; Freeman City of London; memb Securities Inst; *Style*— David Butler, Esq; ✉ Yamaichi Int, Finsbury Court, 111–117 Finsbury Pavement, London EC2A 1EQ (☎ 0171 638 7947, fax 0171 588 3134)

BUTLER, David John; s of John Carrol Butler (d 1979), of Sunderland, and Doris, *née* Stockdale; *b* 28 Sept 1952; *Educ* Bede Sch Sunderland, Sunderland Coll of Art; *Career* painter, printmaker and community artist 1985; ed: Making Ways 1985, 1987 and 1992, Artists Newsletter 1985–95; devpt dir AN Publications 1995–; freelance writer and ed 1985–; dir 'Round Midnight - an Inquiry into the State of the Visual Arts in the UK 1996; *Books* Live Art (ed with Robert Ayers, 1991), Across Europe (1992); *Style*— David Butler, Esq; ✉ 79 Grosvenor Gardens, Jesmond Vale, Newcastle upon Tyne NE2 1HQ (☎ 0191 281 6557, e-mail David@anpubs.demon.co.uk)

BUTLER, His Hon Judge; Gerald Norman; QC (1975); s of Joshua Butler (d 1978), and Esther, *née* Lampel; *b* 15 Sept 1930; *Educ* County HS Ilford, LSE (LLB), Magdalen Coll Oxford (BCL); *m* 2 April 1959, Stella, da of Harris Isaacs (d 1975); 1 s (Mark b 28 Feb 1963), 2 da (Jane b 26 Oct 1960, Charlotte b 29 April 1967); *Career* 2 Lt RASC 1954–56; called to the Bar Middle Temple 1955, recorder of Crown Ct 1977–82, circuit judge (SE Circuit) 1982–, sr judge of Southwark Crown Court 1984–; *Recreations* opera, rugby, reading; *Clubs* MCC; *Style*— His Honour Judge Butler, QC; ✉ Southwark Crown Court, 1 English Grounds, off Battlebridge Lane, London SE1 2HU

BUTLER, Gwendoline; *Educ* Haberdashers' Aske's, Lady Margaret Hall Oxford (BA); *m* Dr Lionel Butler (decd), historian and author; 1 da (Lucilla b 1955); *Career* crime writer and novelist, lectr and broadcaster; author of over 60 books, series characters detectives John Coffin and Charmian Daniels, also writes under pseudonym Jennie Melville; memb Ctee and chm of judges of Gold Dagger Awards Crime Writers' Assoc; Silver Dagger Award Crime Writers' Assoc (for Coffin for Pandora) 1974, Romantic Novelists' Award (for The Red Staircase) 1981, Ellery Queen Short Story Award; sec Detection Club 1992–95; memb: Crime Writers' Assoc, Mystery Writers of America; FRSA; *Clubs* Reform, Detection; *Style*— Mrs Gwendoline Butler; ✉ 32 Harvest Rd, Englefield Green, Egham, Surrey TW20 0QS (☎ 01784 437864, fax 01784 477696); c/o Vanessa Holt Ltd, 59 Crescent Rd, Leigh-on-Sea, Essex SS9 2PF (☎ 01702 73787, fax 01702 471890)

BUTLER, Ian Geoffrey; CBE; s of Hubert Desramaux Butler, of Cumbria; *b* 12 April 1925; *Educ* Stowe, Trinity Coll Oxford; *m* 1973, Anne, da of James Robertson, of Dunbartonshire; 2 da; *Career* Lt Coldstream Gds 1945–47; ptnr Tansley Witt 1951–55; Cookson Group plc (formerly Lead Industries Group, mfr of specialist industl materials): md 1973–84, chm 1976–June 1990 and Nov 1990–1991, non-exec dir 1991–; non-exec dir Helical Bar plc 1993–; Liveryman Worshipful Co of Fanmakers; FCA; *Recreations* yachting (National Swallow Skua), skiing; *Clubs* Royal Yacht Sqdn, Royal Thames Yacht, Itchenor Sailing; *Style*— Ian Butler, Esq, CBE; ✉ Wyke Hse, Ellanore Lane, W Wittering, West Sussex PO20 8AN (☎ 01243 513269); 105 Abingdon Rd, London W8 6QU (☎ 0171 937 5220)

BUTLER, Ian John; s of Donald Butler, and Eileen, *née* Green; *b* 26 Feb 1954; *Educ* Mexborough GS, Central Sch of Art & Design (BA Sculpture), Univ of Liverpool (BA Architecture), PCL (Dip Arch); *m* 1980, Theresa Mary, da of Patrick Tomlins; 2 s (David George b 1990, Peter John b 1992); *Career* architect; with Powell Moya & Partners 1983, Llewelyn-Davies Weeks 1984–87, RMJM London Ltd 1985–91 (currently assoc), md RMJM Hong Kong Ltd 1991–; project architect several large complex building projects in Kong Kong and London; RIBA 1983; memb: ARCUK 1983, Hong Kong Inst of Architects 1993, Hong Kong Architects Registration Bd 1993; *Recreations* photography; *Style*— Ian Butler, Esq; ✉ RMJM Hong Kong Limited, 21/F Pacific Plaza, 410 Des Voeux Road West, Hong Kong (☎ 00 852 548 1689, fax 00 852 547 6386)

BUTLER, (Percy) James; CBE (1981), DL (1995); s of Percy Ernest Butler (d 1942), of The Hill, Batheaston, Bath, and Phyllis Mary Butler (d 1950); *b* 15 March 1929; *Educ* Marlborough, Clare Coll Cambridge (MA); *m* 26 June 1954, Margaret Prudence, da of Percy Copland (d 1968); 1 s (David James b 1961), 2 da (Elizabeth Anne b 1957, Susan Margaret b 1958); *Career* Nat Serv 1947–49, 2 Lt RA; KPMG Peat Marwick: joined 1952, ptnr 1967, managing ptnr 1980–85, dep sr ptnr 1985, sr ptnr 1986–93, memb Exec Ctee and Cncl KPMG 1987–93, memb Euro Bd KPMG 1989–93, chm KPMG 1991–93; dir: Camelot Plc 1994– (dep chm 1995–), Royal Opera House 1994–, Tomkins Plc 1994, Wadworth & Co Ltd 1994–, Nicholson Graham & Jones Solicitors (non-exec) 1994–; pt/t memb BR Bd 1994–96, chm Euro Passenger Servs 1994–96, chm Union Railways 1995–96; tstee Winchester Cathedral Tst, chm Cncl Marlborough Coll, chm Winchester Cathedral Appeal, memb Indust & Commerce Gp and Cncl Save the Children Fund, dep chm The Royal Opera House Tst (chm 1992–96); dep chm Mersey Docks & Harbour Co (and govt dir) 1972–90, memb Govt Ctee on British Rail Fin, memb Financial Aspects of Corporate Governance Ctee, memb Cncl Prince of Wales Business Leaders Forum; Master Worshipful Co of Cutlers 1995–96 (also memb Ct), memb Worshipful Co of Chartered Accountants; FCA (ACA 1955), FIMgt; *Recreations* farming, bridge, opera, ballet, shooting; *Clubs* Boodles; *Style*— James Butler, Esq, CBE, DL; ✉ Littleton House, Crawley, Winchester, Hants SO21 2QF (☎ 01962 880206); Flat 8, 3 Lennox Gardens, London SW1X 0DA (☎ 0171 581 8759); c/o Camelot Group plc, Head Office, Tolpits Lane, Watford, Herts WD1 8RN

BUTLER, Dr James Morris; s of Frederick Thomas Butler; *b* 15 June 1926; *Educ* Hull GS, Univ of Cambridge; *m* 1950, Freda; 1 s, 2 da; *Career* formerly chm McKechnie plc; currently chm F Atkinson Ltd; formerly: pres Br Non-Ferrous Metals Fedn, chm Int Wrought Copper Cncl; FIM, CEng; *Recreations* golf; *Style*— Dr James Butler; ✉ 2 Byron Court, Upper Longdon, Staffs (☎ 01543 490068)

BUTLER, James Walter; s of Walter Arthur Butler (d 1942), and Rosina Harriet, *née* Kingman (d 1967); *b* 25 July 1931; *Educ* Maidstone GS, Maidstone Sch of Art, St Martin's Sch of Art; *m* 1 (m dis); 1 da (Kate b 12 Dec 1966); m 2, 1975, Angela Elizabeth, da of Col Roger Berry; 4 da (Rosie b 23 Aug 1975, Saskia b 12 April 1977, Candida b 24 April 1979, Aurelia b 11 Aug 1983); *Career* sculptor; tutor of sculpture and drawing City and Guilds London Art Sch 1960–75; works in public places: portrait statue Pres Kenyatta (Nairobi) 1973, Monument to Freedom Fighters of Zambia (Lusaka) 1975, sculpture of Burton Cooper (Staffs) 1977, Meml to King Richard III (Leicester) 1980, portrait statue Field Marshal Earl Alexander of Tunis (Wellington Barracks) 1985, bronze sculpture Skipping Girl (Harrow) 1985, Dolphin Fountain (Dolphin Square, London) 1987, portrait statue Sir John Moore and Figures of Rifleman and Bugler (Sir John Moore Barracks, Winchester) 1986, portrait statue John Wilkes (New Fetter Lane, London) 1988, bronze sculpture The Leicester Seamstress (Leicester) 1990, portrait head Sir Hugh Wontner (Savoy Hotel) 1990, War Memorial to Royal Electrical and Mechanical Engineers (Arborfield) 1992, portrait statue Thomas Cook (Leicester) 1994, bronze sculpture The Stratford Jester (Stratford-on-Avon) 1994, portrait statue James Henry Greathead (Cornhill, London) 1994, meml statue Reg Harris (sprint cycling champion) 1995, portrait statue Billy Wright, CBE (Molineux, Wolverhampton) 1996, D Day Memorial to Green Howard Regt (Crepon, Normandy) 1996; RA 1972 (ARA 1964), RWA, FRBS; *Recreations* golf, astronomy; *Clubs* The Arts; *Style*— James Butler, Esq, RA; ✉ Valley Farm, Radway, Warwickshire CV35 0UJ (☎ 01926 641938, fax 01926 640624)

BUTLER, Hon John Fitzwalter; s and h of 28 Baron Dunboyne; *b* 31 July 1951; *Educ* Winchester College, Trinity College Cambridge (MA), London Business School (Sloan Fellow); *m* 1975, (Diana) Caroline, da of Sir Michael Sanigear Williams, KCMG (d 1984); 1 s (Richard b 1983), 3 da (Genevieve b 1977, Imogen b 1979, Cleone b 1986); *Style*— The Hon John Butler; ✉ Argos Hill House, Rotherfield, E Sussex TN6 3QG

BUTLER, Keith Stephenson; CMG (1977); s of Raymond Renard Butler (d 1972), of St Leonards on Sea, Sussex, and Gertrude, *née* Stephenson (d 1972); *b* 3 Sept 1917; *Educ*

Liverpool Coll, Univ of Oxford (MA), Canadian Nat Def Coll; *m* 1, 1952, Geraldine Marjorie Clark (d 1979); m 2, 1979, Mrs Priscilla Wittels, da of Cdr John Boldero, DSC (and Bar), RN (d 1984), of Bridport, Dorset; *Career* HM Forces 1939–46: Maj RA, N Africa, Greece and Crete, POW in Germany 1941–45 (despatches); foreign corr Sunday Times 1947–50, HM Dip Serv 1950–77 (HM consul gen: Seville 1968–69, Bordeaux 1969–74, Naples 1974–77); appeal dir for various charities 1978–; *Recreations* historical res; *Clubs* Oxford Union Soc; *Style*— Keith Butler, Esq, CMG; ✉ Sheilings, 10 Station Road, Kintbury, Hungerford, Berks RG17 9UP (☎ 01488 658350)

BUTLER, Dr Marilyn Speers; da of Sir Trevor Maldwyn Evans, CBE (d 1981), of Kingston-on-Thames, and Margaret Speers, *née* Gribbin; *b* 11 Feb 1937; *Educ* Wimbledon HS, St Hilda's Coll Oxford (MA, DPhil); *m* 3 March 1962, Dr David Edgeworth Butler, CBE, FBA, *qv*, s of Harold Edgeworth Butler (d 1951); 3 s (Daniel b 1963, Gareth b 1965, Edmund b 1967); *Career* trainee and talks producer BBC 1960–62; Univ of Oxford: res and teaching 1962–70, jr res fell St Hilda's Coll 1970–73, fell and tutor St Hugh's Coll 1973–86; King Edward VII prof of Eng lit Univ of Cambridge 1986–93; fell King's Coll Cambridge 1988–93, rector Exeter Coll Oxford 1994–; FRSL, FRSA; *Books* Maria Edgeworth, a Literary Biography (1972), Jane Austen and the War of Ideas (1975), Peacock Displayed (1979), Romantics Rebels and Reactionaries (1981, 1985), Burke Paine Godwin and the Revolution Controversy (1984), The Works of Mary Wollstonecraft (ed, 1989), Maria Edgeworth - Castle Rackrent and Ennui (ed, 1992), Mary Shelley - Frankenstein (ed, 1993), Jane Austen - Northanger Abbey (ed, 1995); *Style*— Dr Marilyn Butler, FRSL; ✉ Exeter College, Oxford OX1 3DP (☎ 01865 279600, fax 01865 279630)

BUTLER, Sir Michael Dacres; GCMG (1984, KCMG 1979, CMG 1975); s of T D Butler, of Almer, Blandford, Dorset, and Beryl May, *née* Lambert; *b* 27 Feb 1927; *Educ* Winchester, Trinity Coll Oxford; *m* 1951, (Margaret) Ann, da of Rt Hon Lord Clyde (d 1975, MP (C) North Edinburgh 1950–54, Lord Justice-Gen of Scotland 1954–72); 2 s, 2 da; *Career* HM Dip Serv: entered 1950, under sec in charge of EEC affairs FCO 1974–76, dep under sec of state FCO 1976–79, UK perm rep to EC Brussels 1979–85, ret; dep chm Bd of Tstees Victoria & Albert Museum 1985–; dir: Hambros Bank 1986–, Wellcome Fndn 1986–94; chm: European Strategy Bd ICL 1988–, European Unification Bd Hercules Europe 1989–94, Oriental Art Magazine 1988–94, Business Link Dorset 1994–, Pathway Group Ltd 1995–; pro-provost and chm Cncl Royal College of Art 1991–96; *Books* Europe More Than a Continent (1986), Seventeenth Century Chinese Porcelain from the Butler Family Collection (1990); *Recreations* collecting Chinese porcelain, tennis, skiing; *Clubs* Brooks's; *Style*— Sir Michael Butler, GCMG; ✉ 36A Elm Park Rd, London SW3 6AX

BUTLER, Prof Michael Gregory; s of Maurice Gregory Butler (d 1973), and Winifred May, *née* Barker; *b* 1 Nov 1935; *Educ* High Pavement Sch Nottingham, Fitzwilliam Coll Cambridge (MA), Trinity Coll Oxford (DipEd), CNAA (PhD); *m* 31 Dec 1960, Jean Mary, da of William John Griffith (d 1966); 1 s (Julian Michael b 1964), 1 da (Emma Catherine b 1967); *Career* asst master: King's Sch Worcs 1958–61, Reuchlin Gymnasium Pforzheim FRG 1961–62; head of German Ipswich Sch 1962–70; Univ of Birmingham: lectr 1970, sr lectr 1980–86, head Dept of German Studies 1984–, prof of modern German literature 1986–, head Sch of Modern Languages 1988–93; ed Samphire 1968–81; FIL 1967; *Books* The Novels of Max Frisch (1975), Englische Lyrik der Gegenwart (ed, 1981), The Plays of Max Frisch (1985), Frisch - Andorra (1985), Rejection and Emancipation - Writing in German-speaking Switzerland 1945–91 (ed, 1991), The Narrative Fiction of Heinrich Böll (ed, 1994); *Recreations* walking, talking; *Style*— Prof Michael Butler; ✉ 45 Westfields, Catshill, Bromsgrove, Worcs B61 9HJ (☎ 01527 874189); Department of German Studies, University of Birmingham, Edgbaston, Birmingham B15 2TT (☎ 0121 414 6173)

BUTLER, Michael Howard; s of Howard Butler, of Beech Ct, Mapperley, Notts, and Constance Gertrude, *née* King; *b* 13 Feb 1936; *Educ* Nottingham HS; *m* 27 July 1961, Christine Elizabeth, da of Sidney Frank Killer, of West Bridgeford, Notts; 2 s (Ian Michael b 1965, Andrew John b 1967), 1 da (Ruth Elizabeth b 1971); *Career* dir gen of fin NCB 1980 (treas 1978), fin dir Br Coal Corp (formerly NCB) 1985–93 (corp memb 1986–93), non-exec chm CIN Management Ltd 1993–96 (non-exec dir 1986–96); chm British Investment Tst Plc 1993–, chm Mineworkers Pension Fund Tstees 1995–; FCA 1958, CIMgt 1987; *Recreations* tennis, music, gardening assoc, football; *Style*— Michael Butler, Esq; ✉ Mineworkers Pension Scheme, 1 Hussar Court, Hillsborough Barracks, Sheffield, South Yorkshire S6 2LW (☎ 0114 285 4601, fax 0114 285 4605)

BUTLER, Sir (Reginald) Michael Thomas; 3 Bt (UK 1922), of Old Park, Devizes, Wilts; QC (Can 1967); s of Sir (Reginald) Thomas Butler, 2 Bt (d 1959); *b* 22 April 1928; *Educ* Brentwood Coll Victoria BC, Univ of BC (BA), Osgoode Hall Sch of Law Toronto; *m* 1, 1952 (m dis 1967), Marja Margaret Elizabeth, o da of late Ewen H McLean, of Toronto; 3 s ((Reginald) Richard Michael b 1953, Geoffrey MacLean b 1956, Thomas David b 1960); m 2, 1968 (m dis 1974), Mrs Barbara Anne Hogan, da of late Kevin Cahill, of Dublin; 1 step and adopted s (Patrick Colman b 1958); *partner*, Judith Ann, da of late Harold Blackwell, of London, Ontario; *Heir* s, (Reginald) Richard Michael Butler b 3 Oct 1953; *Career* barr and slr Ontario 1954 and BC 1967, ret ptnr Messrs Butler Angus (Victoria, BC); dir Teck Corporation and other companies; *Style*— Sir Michael Butler, Bt, QC; ✉ Old Park Cottage, 634 Avalon Street, Victoria, BC V8V 1N7, Canada

BUTLER, Prof Neville Roy; s of Dr Cuthbert John Butler (d 1937), of Harrow, Middx, and Ida Margaret, *née* Soman (d 1959); *b* 6 July 1920; *Educ* Epsom Coll, Charing Cross Hosp Med Sch (MB BS); *m* 14 May 1954 (m dis 1979), Jean Ogilvie, da of John McCormack (d 1983); 2 da (Claire b 1957, Fiona b 1959); *Career* Capt RAMC; first asst Paediatric Unit UCH 1950, med registrar and pathologist Hosp for Sick Children Gt Ormond St 1953, conslt paediatrician Oxford and Wessex RHB 1957–63, dir Perinatal Mortality Survey (National Birthday Tst Fund 1958), conslt physician Hosp for Sick Children Gt Ormond St and sr lectr Inst of Child Health Univ of London 1963–65, co-dir Nat Child Devpt Study (1958 Cohort) 1965–75, prof of child health Univ of Bristol 1965–85 (emeritus prof 1985–); dir: Child Health and Educn Study (1970 Cohort) 1970–85, Int Centre for Child Studies 1982–, Youthscan UK 1985–90; vice pres: RCM 1972–, HVA 1975–; memb: BPA 1958, Neonatal Soc 1961, Cuban Paediatric Soc 1973, Hungarian Paediatric Soc 1979; FRCP, FRCOG; *Books* jt author: Perinatal Mortality (1963), 11,000 Seven Year Olds (1966), Perinatal Problems (1969), From Birth to Seven (1972), ABO Haemolytic Disease of the Newborn (1972), The Social Life of Britain's Five Year Olds (1984), From Birth to Five (1986); *Recreations* running a charity; *Style*— Prof Neville Butler; ✉ 86 Cumberland Road, Bristol BS16 6UG (☎ 0117 925 0835)

BUTLER, (John) Nicholas (Nick); OBE (1988); s of William Butler (d 1974), of Normanton, Yorks, and Mabel Annie Butler (d 1974); *b* 21 March 1942; *Educ* Sch of Industl Design Leeds Coll of Art (NDD), Dept of Industl Design RCA (DesRCA); *m* 1967, Kari Anne, da of George Morrison; 2 s (Finn b 24 June 1969, Liam b 22 July 1971); *Career* chartered designer; IBM fellowship to USA 1965–66, project ldr GLC Industrialised Building Systems 1966–67, currently chm and md BIB Design Consultants (fndr 1967), chief exec Design Gp and memb Bd BAA plc 1992–; Design Council: memb Awards Judging Panel 1975–, memb Industl Advsy Ctee 1978–, memb Exec Ctee 1990–, shadow design dir 1994–; chm: Br Design Export Group 1980–81, Br Design Awards Scheme (consumer and contract goods) 1988–; memb: Design Bd RSA 1986, Design Cncl 1988; presented two papers at ICSID World Design Conf Washington USA 1985, keynote speaker DTI Design Commitment Conf London 1986, main speaker Int Design Conf World Trade Centre NY 1986, visiting speaker Warren Centre Sydney Univ 1987, design address Aust Govt Canberra 1987, visiting prof Faculty of Design RCA 1987, judge Br Design in Japan competition Tokyo 1987, opened Drawn from Britain (British Designers Work Overseas) exhbn Design Cncl 1988, external assessor Massey Univ NZ 1993–; FCSD 1975 (hon treas 1978–80 and 1980–82), RDI 1981 (Master 1995–97), FRSA 1983; *Style*— Nick Butler, Esq, OBE, RDI; ✉ BIB Design Consultants, The Mill, Whitchurch-on-Thames, Oxon RG8 7DG (☎ 0118 984 3384, fax 0118 984 5111)

BUTLER, Norman John Terence (Terry); CBE (1993); s of Arthur Reginald Butler, and Lucy Mary Butler; *b* 18 Feb 1946; *Educ* Peveril Bilateral Sch Nottingham, Trent Poly Nottingham, Nat Inst of Social Work London, Brunel Univ (MA); *children* 2 da; *Career* mental welfare offr Nottingham 1965–71, sr social worker Nottingham 1971–73, area mangr Haringey 1974–81, asst dir of social services Royal Borough of Kingston-upon-Thames 1981–83, dep dir of social services E Sussex 1983–88, dir of social services Hampshire 1988–, seconded as co-ldr Community Care Support Force Dept of Health 1992–93; memb: Govt's Firth Ctee 1987, Ed Bd Community Care Management and Planning Jl, Home Office Advsy Bd on Restricted Patients, Data Protection Tbnl Bd; vice pres Relatives' Assoc; author of articles in various jls incl Social Work Today, Insight and Community Care; *Recreations* tennis, soccer, entertaining, being entertained; *Clubs* Kingsgate Tennis; *Style*— Terry Butler, Esq, CBE; ✉ 2 Lantern Court, 90 Christchurch Road, St Cross, Winchester, Hants SO23 9JR (☎ 01962 856489); Hampshire County Council, Trafalgar House, The Castle, Winchester, Hants SO23 8UQ (☎ 01962 841841, fax 01962 847159)

BUTLER, Dr Paul; s of Frank William Butler (d 1966), and Elizabeth, *née* Wright (d 1993); *b* 4 June 1952; *Educ* Cotham GS, UCL (BSc), Westminster Med Sch (MB BS); *m* 28 Jan 1978, Janet Ann Butler, da of Percival Jack Barber, of Meadow Way, Sawbridgeworth, Herts; 1 s (David b 20 Oct 1982), 1 da (Claire b 19 Dec 1980); *Career* med registrar rotation Leicester AHA 1979, trainee in radiodiagnosis Manchester RHA 1983, sr registrar neuroradiology Manchester Royal Infirmary, currently consIt neuroradiologist The Royal Hosps Trust; consIt neuroradiologist: London Ind Hosp, London Clinic, Harley St Clinic, BMI Blackheath Clinic; Freeman City of London, Liveryman Worshipful Soc of Apothecaries; memb Br Soc of Neuroradiologists, MRCP 1979, DMRD 1983, FRCR 1983; *Publications* Imaging of the Nervous System (ed, 1990), Multiple Choice Questions FRCR Part 1 (jtly, 1991); *Recreations* classical music, opera; *Style*— Dr Paul Butler; ✉ Department of Neuroradiology, The Royal London Hospital, Whitechapel, London E1 1BB (☎ 0171 377 7165)

BUTLER, (James) Pearse; s of James Butler, of Liverpool, and Nancy, *née* McManus; *b* 27 Jan 1957; *Educ* St Mary's Coll Crosby, Keble Coll Oxford (BA); *m* 11 Aug 1979, Deborah Veronica, *née* Downing; 1 s (Daniel John b 28 July 1985), 1 da (Alison Patricia b 26 Nov 1987); *Career* community worker Liverpool Cncl for Voluntary Serv 1979–80, hosp admin S Birmingham Health Authy 1980–83, dep admin then admin Bolton Gen Hosp 1983–85, mgmnt consIt HAY-MSL Management Consultants 1985–86, gen mangr Obstetric and Gynaecology Serv Liverpool Health Authy 1986–88, dist gen mangr Chester Health Authy 1988–89; chief exec: Royal Liverpool Children's NHS Tst 1989–93, Wirral Health 1993–; EEC Young Hosp Admin Exchange Scheme (Denmark) 1982; *Recreations* sport, family, opera; *Clubs* West Lancs Golf, Campion Lawn Tennis; *Style*— Pearse Butler, Esq; ✉ Wirral Health, St Catherine's Hospital, 1st Floor, Administration Block, Church Road, Tranmere, Birkenhead L42 0LQ (☎ 0151 651 0011)

BUTLER, Peter; MP (C) Milton Keynes North East (majority 14,176); s of late Kenneth Butler, and Barbara Butler; *b* 10 June 1951; *Educ* Adams GS Newport Shropshire, St Edmund Hall Oxford (MA, PGCE); *m* 1 Sept 1973, Peggy Mary, *née* Nott; 3 da; *Career* admitted slr 1978, slr Thames Valley Police 1978–80, ptnr Linnells slrs 1981–92 (conslt 1992–), MP (C) Milton Keynes NE 1992–; PPS: to Min of State Dept of Health 1994–95, to Chllr of the Exchequer 1995–; nat chm Trainee Slrs of England and Wales 1976–77, vice pres Berks Bucks and Oxon Law Soc 1991–92; cncllr Oxfordshire CC 1985–89; ptnr in sch for emotionally and behaviourally disturbed children 1975–91, memb Home Affrs Select Ctee 1992–96, sch govr 1985–92; *Recreations* music, driving vintage cars, family, avoiding organised exercise; *Clubs* Carlton, Vintage Sports Car; *Style*— Peter Butler, Esq, MP; ✉ House of Commons, London SW1A 0AA (☎ 0171 219 6423)

BUTLER, Peter Robert; *b* 17 May 1949; *Educ* Southend HS, Univ of Bristol (BSc Economics and Accounting); *m* Linley; 1 s (Simon b 1980), 1 da (Rachel b 1984); *Career* articled clerk and accountant Touche Ross & Co 1970–75; BOC Group plc: investigations accountant BOC Ltd London 1975–77, fin dir/fin mangr BOC Ltd Far East Singapore 1977–79, fin controller Oilfield Servs 1980, mangr Corp Fin (Welding) 1980–83, gp commercial mangr (Welding) 1983–84; British Sugar plc and Berisford International plc: joined as gp ops controller 1984–86, assoc dir Fin S & W Berisford 1987–88, fin dir British Sugar plc and Bristar Food & Agribusiness Div 1988–90, chief fin offr and exec dir Berisford International plc 1991–93; gp fin dir Hi-Tec Sports plc 1993–95; corp focus exec Hermes Pensions Management Ltd 1996–; MInstD, FCA 1979 (ACA 1973); *Recreations* cricket, football (Southend Utd FC, player/manager Old Southendians FC Veterans XI), France; *Clubs* MCC, Essex CCC; *Style*— Peter Butler, Esq; ✉ Hermes Pensions Management Ltd, Standon House, 21 Mansell Street, London E1 8AA (☎ 0171 702 0888, fax 0171 702 9452)

BUTLER, Hon Piers James Richard; s and h of 17 Viscount Mountgarret; *b* 15 April 1961; *Educ* Eton, Univ of St Andrews; *m* 2 Sept 1995, Laura Brown Gary, da of Mrs Albert Dickens Williams, Jr, of Lake Forest, Illinois, USA; *Clubs* White's, Union (New York); *Style*— The Hon Piers Butler; ✉ 44 Stanmer Street, London SW11 3EG (☎ 01488 658229)

BUTLER, Hon Sir Richard Clive; kt (1981), DL (Essex 1972); s of late Baron Butler of Saffron Walden, KG, CH, PC (Life Peer), by his 1 w, Sydney, da of Samuel Courtauld; *b* 12 Jan 1929; *Educ* Eton, Pembroke Coll Cambridge; *m* 1952, Susan Anne Maud, da of Maj Patrick Walker, MBE (s of Sir James Walker, 3 Bt); 2 s, 1 da; *Career* 2 Lt RHG BAOR 1948–49; farmer; pres NFU 1979–86 (memb cncl 1962–); dir: National Westminster Bank plc 1986–96, Natwest Investment Bank Ltd 1989–92, NatWest Investment Management Ltd 1989–96 (chm), Ferruzzi Trading (UK) Ltd 1986–94 (chm), The National Farmers' Union Mutual Insurance Soc 1985–96, Agroceres & Co Ltd 1994– (chm); tstee The Butler Tst; memb Ct of Assts Worshipful Co of Skinners (Master 1994–95), Sr Warden Worshipful Co of Farmers 1996–97; *Recreations* hunting, shooting, DIY; *Clubs* Farmers'; *Style*— The Hon Sir Richard Butler, DL; ✉ Gladfen Hall, Halstead, Essex CO9 1RN (☎ 01787 472828)

BUTLER, Sir Richard Pierce; 13 Bt (I 1628), of Cloughgrenan, Co Carlow, Ireland; s of Sir Thomas Pierce Butler, 12 Bt, CVO, DSO, OBE (d 1994), and Rosemary Liège Woodgate, *née* Davidson-Houston; *b* 22 July 1940; *Educ* Eton, NY Univ, MBA; *m* 21 Oct 1965, Diana Anne, yr da of Col Stephen John Borg (d 1971), of The Palms, St Julians, Malta; 3 s (Thomas Pierce b 1966, Stephen Patrick b 1968, Rupert Dudley b 1971), 1 da (Anne Virginia b 1973); *Heir* s, Thomas Pierce Butler b 1966; *Career* ptnr Charles Wakeling & Co 1964–66; dir: The First Boston Corp (NY) 1967–78, PaineWebber International Bank 1978–89, Emesco Industrial Equity Company SA 1987–, The Transportation Gp Ltd 1989–94, Ibercapital SA 1990–, Rauscher Pierce & Clark Inc 1993–; memb Cncl Pestalozzi Children's Village Trust 1983–, govr Summer Fields Sch Oxford 1984–; FCA; *Style*— Sir Richard Butler, Bt; ✉ c/o Barclays Bank, 160 Piccadilly, London W1A 2AB

BUTLER, Sir (Frederick Edward) Robin; GCB (1992, KCB 1988), CVO (1986); s of Bernard Daft Butler, and Nora, *née* Jones, of St Annes on Sea, Lancs; *b* 3 Jan 1938; *Educ* Harrow, Univ Coll Oxford (BA); *m* 1962, Gillian Lois, da of Dr Robert Galley, of Teddington, Middlesex; 1 s (Andrew b 1968), 2 da (Sophie b 1964, Nell b 1967); *Career* private sec to: Rt Hon Edward Heath 1972–74, Rt Hon Harold Wilson 1974–75; princ private sec to Rt Hon Margaret Thatcher 1982–85, second perm sec HM Treasy 1985–87, Sec of the Cabinet and Head of the Home Civil Service 1988–; hon memb Worshipful Co of Salters; *Recreations* competitive games, opera; *Clubs* Anglo-Belgian, Athenaeum, Brooks's, United Oxford and Cambridge Univ; *Style*— Sir Robin Butler, GCB, CVO; ✉ Cabinet Office, 70 Whitehall, London SW1A 2AS (☎ 0171 270 0101)

BUTLER, Robin Noel Holman; s of George Noël Butler (d 1969), of Honiton, and Marjorie Blanche, *née* Dunn (d 1993); *b* 26 April 1943; *Educ* Allhallows Sch; *m* 17 Feb 1995 (sep 1996), Wendy, da of Arthur Knott; *Career* schoolmaster 1961–63, family antiques business 1963–, memb Br Antique Dealers' Assoc 1970– (cncl 1984–87); *Books* Arthur Negus Guide to English Furniture (1978), Book of Wine Antiques (1986); *Recreations* photography, cooking, snooker and golf; *Clubs* Clifton; *Style*— Robin Butler, Esq; ✉ The Mews House, 20 Clifton Road, Bristol BS8 1AQ (☎ 0117 973 3017)

BUTLER, Roger John; *b* 19 June 1947; *Educ* Cheltenham GS; *m* 31 Aug 1968, Kathleen Teresa; 1 da (Caroline b 1979); *Career* ptnr Fryer Whitehill & Co 1971–80; Arthur Young: ptnr 1981–89, latterly regnl managing ptnr London; chief exec: Butler Corporate Finance Ltd 1989–95, Newton Investment Management Ltd 1996–; FCA 1969; *Recreations* golf, tennis; *Style*— Roger Butler, Esq; ✉ Far End, Wagon Way, Loudwater, Herts WD3 4JE (☎ 01923 774 110); Newton Investment Management Ltd, 71 Queen Victoria Street, London EC4V 4DR (☎ 0171 332 9000, fax 0171 332 9033)

BUTLER, Rosemary Jane; da of Samuel Laight Medlar (d 1990), and Rosemary Peggy, *née* Bendix; *b* 15 July 1946; *Educ* Maynard Sch Exeter, LSE (BSc(Econ)); *m* Anthony David Butler; *Career* Central Statistical Office 1967–73, Dept of Employment 1973–80 (Unit for Manpower Studies 1973–77), MOD 1980–85, HM Treasy 1985–89, DSS 1989–91, dir of statistics Dept of Health 1991–; FRSS, FRSA 1993; *Recreations* music, theatre, birdwatching; *Style*— Mrs Rosemary Butler; ✉ Director of Statistics, Department of Health, Room 455C, Skipton House, 80 London Road, London SE1 6LW (☎ 0171 972 5362, fax 0171 972 5660)

BUTLER, (Stanley) Roy; s of Harry Butler (d 1950) of Epsom, and Emily, *née* Whiteing (d 1950); *b* 16 Feb 1923; *m* 14 July 1951, Jessie, da of Edward James Fletcher (d 1966), of Brixton; 1 s (Glenn b 1961), 1 da (Deborah b 1958); *Career* departmental head Hawker Aircraft 1940–42, RA Ordnance Corps 1942–47, serv ME 1943–46; sr ptnr Wallis & Wallis The Militaria Arms and Armour auctioneers 1962–, dir Arms Fairs Ltd 1967–; fndr The Military Heritage Museum (Lewes) 1977; TV appearances: Going for a Song 1973, BBC Antiques Roadshow (arms and militaria expert) 1977–96, ITV Heirlooms 1987–88, BBC Heirs and Graces 1988, BBC Going Live 1991–92, BBC Antiques Roadshow The Next Generation 1992–93; conslt ed Miller's Annual Antiques Guide, pres St John Ambulance (Lewes Div) 1981–, benefactor and life memb Soc of Friends of RN Museum, life memb HMS Warrior Assoc, memb Rotary Club of Lewes 1968–; Freeman City of London 1981, memb Worshipful Co of Pipemakers 1979; *Recreations* swimming, snooker, gardening; *Clubs* IOD; *Style*— Roy Butler, Esq; ✉ Wallis & Wallis, West Street, Auction Galleries, Lewes, Sussex BN7 2NJ (☎ 01273 480208, fax 01273 476562)

BUTLER, Prof William Elliott; s of William Elliott Butler (d 1996), of Black Mountain, N Carolina, and Maxine Swan Elmberg; *b* 20 Oct 1939; *Educ* American Univ Washington DC (BA), Johns Hopkins Univ Baltimore (MA), Harvard Law Sch (JD), Johns Hopkins Univ (PhD), Univ of London (LLD); *m* 1, 2 Sept 1961, Darlene Mae Johnson (d 1989); 2 s (William Elliott III, Bradley Newman); m 2, 6 Dec 1991, Maryann Elizabeth Gashi; *Career* research asst Washington Centre of Foreign Policy Research Johns Hopkins Univ 1966–68, research assoc in law Harvard Law Sch and Assoc Russian Research Centre Harvard 1968–70; Univ of London: reader in comparative law 1970–76, prof of comparative law 1976–, dean Faculty of Laws UCL 1977–79, dean Faculty of Laws Univ of London 1988–90; memb Cncl Clifford Chance 1992–94, ptnr White & Case 1994–; visiting scholar: Moscow State Univ 1972 and 1980, USSR Acad of Sci 1976, 1981, 1983, 1984, and 1988, Mongolian State Univ 1979; memb Cncl SSEES 1973–88 and 1989–93 (vice chm 1983–88); prof of int and comparative law and dean Faculty of Law Moscow Sch of Social and Econ Sci 1995–; visiting prof: NY Univ Law Sch 1978, Ritsumeikan Univ 1985, Harvard Law Sch 1986–87; coordinator UCL-USSR Acad of Sci Protocol on Co-operation in Social Sci 1981–, dir The Vinogradoff Inst Univ Coll London 1982–, lectr Hague Acad of Int Law 1985, memb Ctee of Mgmnt Inst of Advanced Legal Studies Univ of London 1985–88, govr City of London Poly 1985–89, visiting fell Research Centre for Int Law Univ of Cambridge 1991–92, Leverhulme Research Grant 1991–92, author of more than 80 books, 800 articles, reviews, and translations on int and comparative law, especially Soviet and Russian Law and other socialist legal systems, bookplates, and bibliography; sec The Bookplate Soc 1978–86 (foreign sec 1988–94), fndr ed The Bookplate Jl 1983–86 (co-ed 1989–92), fndr ed Bookplate International 1994–, VP Fed Int des Sociétés d'Amateurs d'Ex-Libris 1984–86 (exec sec 1988–); memb: Dist of Columbia Bar, Bar of US Ct of Appeals for Dist of Columbia, Bar of US Supreme Ct, Cncl Cole Corette and Abrutyn (London and Moscow) 1989–92, Russian Acad of Nat Sciences (section Russian Encyclopedia) 1992–, EC Jt Task Force for Law Reform in the CIS 1992–93, Acad of Sciences Ukraine 1992–, Russian Court of Int Commercial Arbitration 1995–, Bar of Uzbekistan 1996–; special counsel USSR Cncl of Ministers Cmmn for Econ Reform 1989–91; hon memb: All Union Soc of the Book (USSR) 1989, Soviet Maritime Law Assoc (USSR) 1990, USSR Union of Jurists 1990; memb Associé Int Acad of Comparative Law 1986; awarded F F Martens Prize 1996; FRSA 1986, FSA 1989; *Recreations* book collecting, bookplate collecting; *Clubs* Cosmos, Grolier; *Style*— Prof William Butler, FSA; ✉ 20 Ainger Rd, London NW3 3AS (☎ 0171 586 2454, fax 0171 483 4014); Faculty of Laws, University College London, Bentham House, Endsleigh Gardens, London WC1H OEG (☎ 0171 391 1469, fax 0171 387 9597, telex 28722 UCPHYS G)

BUTLER-SLOSS, Rt Hon Lady Justice; Rt Hon Dame (Ann) Elizabeth Oldfield Butler-Sloss; DBE (1979), PC (1987); da of Hon Mr Justice Cecil Havers (d 1977), High Ct Judge (Queen's Bench Div), and Enid, *née* Snelling (d 1956), and sister of Baron Havers, PC, QC (d 1992); *b* 10 Aug 1933; *Educ* Wycombe Abbey; *m* 1958, Joseph William Alexander Butler-Sloss; 2 s, 1 da; *Career* called to the Bar Inner Temple 1955, registrar Principal Registry, Probate Div (subsequently Family Div) 1970–79, judge of the High Court of Justice (Family Div) 1979–88, a Lord Justice of Appeal 1988–, reader Inner Temple 1997–; Parly candidate (Cons) Lambeth Vauxhall 1959; sometime vice pres Medico-Legal Soc, memb Judicial Studies Bd 1985–89, chm Cleveland Child Abuse Inquiry 1987–88; vice chm Cncl King's Coll London; memb Cncl Wycombe Abbey Sch; hon memb American Law Inst; chllr West of England Univ 1993–; hon fell St Hilda's Coll Oxford, presentation fell King's Coll London 1991; Hon DLitt Univ of Loughborough 1992; Hon LLD: Univ of Hull 1989, Univ of Keele 1991, Univ of Bristol 1991, Univ of Exeter 1992, Brunel Univ 1992, Univ of Manchester 1995; Hon FRCP 1992, Hon FRCPsych 1992, Hon FRCPCH; *Style*— The Rt Hon Lady Justice Butler-Sloss, DBE; ✉ Royal Courts of Justice, Strand, London WC2A 2LL

BUTLIN, Martin Richard Fletcher; CBE (1990); s of Kenneth Rupert Butlin (d 1965), and Helen Mary, *née* Fletcher, MBE; *b* 7 June 1929; *Educ* Rendcomb Coll, Trinity Coll Cambridge (MA), Courtauld Inst of Art Univ of London (DLit); *m* 31 Jan 1969, Frances Caroline, da of Michael Anthony Chodzko, of France; *Career* Nat Serv RAMC; asst keeper Tate Gallery 1955–67, keeper Historic Br Collection Tate Gallery 1967–89, conslt Christie's 1989–; involved in selection and cataloguing of exhibitions on Blake and Turner, author of numerous articles and reviews for magazines; FBA 1984; *Publications* incl: A Catalogue of the Works of William Blake in the Tate Gallery (1957, 2 edn 1971, 3 edn 1990), Samuel Palmer's Sketchbook of 1824 (1962), Turner Watercolours (1962), Turner (with Sir John Rothenstein, 1964), Tate Gallery Catalogues, The Modern British Paintings, Drawings and Sculpture (with Mary Chamot and Dennis Farr, 1964), The Later Works of JMW Turner (1965), William Blake (1966), The Blake-Varley Sketchbook of 1819 (1969), The Paintings of JMW Turner (with Evelyn Joll, 1977, 2 edn 1984), The Paintings and Drawings of William Blake (1981), Aspects of British Painting 1550–1800 from the collection of the Sarah Campbell Blaffer Foundation (1988), William Blake in the collection of the National Gallery of Victoria (with Tedd Gott, 1989), Turner at Petworth (with Mollie Luther and Ian Warrell, 1989); *Recreations* opera, ballet, travel; *Style*— Martin Butlin, Esq, CBE, FBA; ✉ 74C Eccleston Square, London SW1V 1PJ

BUTT, Geoffrey Frank; s of Frank Thomas Woodman Butt (d 1946), of Exeter, and Dorothy Rosamond, *née* Grasemann (d 1968); *b* 5 May 1943; *Educ* Royal Masonic Sch Bushey, Univ of Reading (BA); *m* 8 July 1972, Lee Anne, da of Frederick Arthur Davey, of Exmouth; 2 s (David b 1973, Richard b 1976), 1 da (Anne (twin) b 1976); *Career* princ asst slr Office of the Solicitor for Customs and Excise 1986–93 (joined 1971, qualified slr, sr legal asst 1974, asst slr 1982), princ asst slr Inland Revenue 1993–96; memb Law Soc 1970; *Recreations* family life, gardening, classical music, literature and art; *Style*— Geoffrey Butt, Esq

BUTT, Sir (Alfred) Kenneth Dudley; 2 Bt (UK 1929), of Westminster, Co London; s of Sir Alfred Butt, 1 Bt (d 1962); *b* 7 July 1908; *Educ* Rugby, BNC Oxford; *m* 1, 1938 (m dis 1948), Kathleen Breen, da of E Farmer, of Shanklin, IOW; m 2, 1948, Marie Josephine, da of John Bain, of Wadhurst, and wid of Lt-Col Ivor Watkins Birts; *Heir* none; *Career* bloodstock breeder and farmer; Lloyd's underwriter 1931–74, dir Brook Stud Co 1949 (md and chm 1962–81); chm Thoroughbred Breeders' Assoc 1973; pres Aberdeen Angus Cattle Soc 1967–68; *Recreations* shooting, paintings, racing; *Clubs* Carlton; *Style*— Sir Kenneth Butt, Bt; ✉ Wheat Hill, Sandon, Buntingford, Herts SG9 0RB (☎ 01763 287203)

BUTT, Michael Acton; s of Leslie Acton Kingsford Butt and Mina Gascoigne Butt; *b* 25 May 1942; *Educ* Rugby, Magdalen Coll Oxford, INSEAD France (MBA); *m* 1, 1964 (m dis 1986), Diana Lorraine, *née* Brook; 2 s; m 2, 1986, Zoë Bennett; *Career* joined Bland Welch Group 1964, dir Bland Payne Holdings 1970, chm Sedgwick Ltd 1983–87, dep chm Sedgwick Group plc 1985–87, chm and chief exec Eagle Star Holdings plc 1987–91, dir BAT Industries plc 1987–91, chm and chief exec Eagle Star Insurance Co 1987–91; dir: Marceau Investissements SA (France) 1987–95, Mid Ocean Ltd and Mid Ocean Reinsurance Co Ltd (now pres and Chief exec) 1992–, Phoenix Securities Ltd 1992–95; Liveryman Worshipful Co of Insurers; memb: Bd INSEAD France, Instituto Nazionale delle Assicurazioni (INA) Rome 1994–; *Recreations* tennis, opera, reading, family, the European Movement; *Style*— Michael Butt, Esq; ✉ Harrowby, 9 Cedarberry Drive, Hamilton Parish, CR 04, Bermuda (☎ 00 441 293 1378, fax 00 441 293 8511); Mid Ocean Reinsurance Company Ltd, PO Box HM 1066, Hamilton HM EX, Bermuda (☎ 00 441 292 1358, fax 00 441 292 5226)

BUTT, Richard Bevan; s of Roger William Bevan Butt, of Esher, Surrey, and Jean Mary, *née* Carter; *b* 27 Feb 1943; *Educ* Magdalen Coll Oxford (BA), Univ of Lancaster (MA); *m* 25 July 1976, Amanda Jane, da of late Hon Judge John Finlay; 2 s (Matthew b 1979, Nicholas b 1983); *Career* asst sec HM Treasy 1978–86 (on secondment to Dip Serv as fin cnsllr, UK rep to Euro Community 1981–84), head of conservation English Heritage 1986–89, currently chief exec Rural Devpt Cmmn; CIMgt; *Recreations* ceramics, music, travel, books; *Style*— Richard Butt, Esq; ✉ Dacre House, 19 Dacre Street, London SW1H 0DH

BUTT, Ronald Herbert; CBE (1987); s of Herbert Butt (d 1965), and Elizabeth Clare, *née* Morley (d 1948); *b* 17 Feb 1920; *Educ* St Dunstan's Coll, St Catherine's Coll Oxford (BA, MA); *m* 20 Oct 1956, (Daphne) Margaret Forfar, da of Theodore William Chaundy (d 1966), of Oxford; 2 s (Oliver b 1960, Edmund b 1963), 2 da (Bridget b 1959, Elizabeth b 1966); *Career* served Army Intelligence Corps; The Financial Times 1951–67: leader writer, political corr then political ed; res fell Nuffield Coll Oxford 1964–65, asst ed and political commentator Sunday Times 1967–83; The Times: assoc ed 1983–85, columnist on public affrs 1968–91; freelance contributor to The Times and various other jls 1991–; memb: Butler Ctee on Mentally Abnormal Offenders 1972–75, Cncl Westfield Coll Univ of London 1971–89; *Books* The Power of Parliament (1967), A History of Parliament: The Middle Ages (1989); *Recreations* music, reading, walking, history; *Clubs* Carlton; *Style*— Ronald Butt, Esq, CBE; ✉ 22 Denewood Road, Highgate, London N6 4AJ

BUTTER, Maj Sir David Henry; KCVO (1991), MC (1942); s of Col Charles Adrian James Butter, OBE, JP, DL (d 1944), of Cluniemore, Pitlochry, Perth, and Agnes Marguerite, *née* Clark, of New Jersey, USA (d 1972); *b* 18 March 1920; *Educ* Eton, Oxford; *m* 1946, Myra Alice, CVO (1992), yr da of Maj-Gen Sir Harold Augustus Wernher, 3 Bt, GCVO, of Luton Hoo, Luton, Beds, and Lady Zia Wernher, CBE, da of HIH Grand Duke Michael of Russia and his morganatic wife Countess Torby; 1 s, 4 da; *Career* landowner, farmer, co dir; 2 Lt Scots Gds 1940, served WWII in N Africa, Italy and Sicily, Temp Maj 1946; Ensign Queen's Body Guard for Scotland (Royal Co of Archers); HM Lord Lt: Perthshire 1971–75 (DL 1956, vice Lord Lt 1960), Kinross 1974–75, Perth and Kinross 1975–95; pres Highland TAVR 1979–1984, hon pres Perth Distict Battalion Boys Brigade, patron Perth and Kinross Branch Scottish Branch British Red Cross, co cncllr Perthshire 1955–74; *Clubs* Royal and Ancient St Andrews, Turf; *Style*— Maj Sir David Butter, KCVO, MC; ✉ Cluniemore, Pitlochry, Perthshire (☎ 01796 472006); 64 Rutland Gate, London SW7 (☎ 0171 589 6731)

BUTTER, His Hon Judge; Neil McLaren; QC (1976); s of late Andrew Butter, MD, of London, and late Ena Butter; *b* 10 May 1933; *Educ* The Leys Sch, Queens' Coll Cambridge; *m* 1974, Claire Marianne, da of A Miskin, of Ifield Court Farm, Ifield, Kent; *Career* called to the Bar Inner Temple 1955, asst and dep recorder Bournemouth 1971, recorder Crown Ct 1972–82, circuit judge (SE Circuit) 1982–, judge Bow Co Ct 1986–94, judge Central London Co Ct 1994–, bencher Inner Temple 1994; tstee Kingdon-Ward Speech Therapy Tst 1980–87; *Recreations* holidays, motoring; *Clubs* Royal Over-Seas League; *Style*— His Hon Judge Butter, QC; ✉ c/o 3 Serjeants' Inn, London EC4Y 1BQ

BUTTER, Prof Peter Herbert; s of Capt Archibald Edward Butter, CMG (d 1928), of Newton Hall, Gifford, E Lothian, and Helen Cicely, *née* Kerr (d 1976); *b* 7 April 1921; *Educ* Charterhouse, Balliol Coll Oxford (MA); *m* 30 Aug 1958, Bridget Hope, da of Lt-Col Henry Johnson Younger (d 1940), of Baro, Haddington, E Lothian; 1 s (Archibald b 1962), 2 da (Rachel (Mrs David Clough) b 1965, Helen b 1970); *Career* WWII, RA 1941–46 (Capt 1945); lectr in English Univ of Edinburgh 1948–58, prof of English Queen's Univ Belfast 1958–65, regius prof of English language and lit Univ of Glasgow 1965–86; chm Kilmartin House Tst 1994–; various articles in periodicals; memb Int Assoc Univ Profs of English (sec and treas 1962–70); *Books* Shelley's Idols of the Cave (1954), Francis Thompson (1961), Edwin Muir (1962), Edwin Muir - Man and Poet (1966), Shelley's Alastor and other Poems (ed, 1971), Selected Letters of Edwin Muir (ed, 1974), Selected Poems of William Blake (ed, 1982 and 1993), The Truth of Imagination - Uncollected Prose of Edwin Muir (ed, 1988), Complete Poems of Edwin Muir (ed, 1991), William Blake (ed, 1996); *Recreations* gardening, art collecting, book collecting; *Clubs* New

(Edinburgh); *Style—* Prof Peter Butter; ✉ Ashfield, Prieston Rd, Bridge of Weir, Renfrewshire PA11 3AW (☎ 01505 613139)

BUTTERFIELD, Baron (Life Peer UK 1988), of Stechford in the Co of W Midlands; Sir (William) John Hughes Butterfield; kt (1978), OBE (1953); s of late William Hughes Butterfield, of Hampton-in-Arden, Warwicks, and Mrs Doris North; *b* 28 March 1920; *Educ* Solihull Sch, Exeter Coll Oxford, Johns Hopkins Univ USA, DM, FRCP; *m* 1, 1946, Ann (d 1948), da of late Robert Sanders, of New York, USA; 1 s (Hon Jonathan West Sanders b 23 Oct 1948); m 2, 1950, Isabel-Ann, da of Dr Foster Kennedy (d 1952), neurologist, of New York City; 2 s (Hon Jeremy John Nicholas b 23 Dec 1954, Hon Toby Michael John b 6 Dec 1965), 1 da (Hon Sarah Harriet Ann (Hon Mrs Willetts) b 28 Aug 1953); *Career* Maj RAMC; Regius prof of physic Cambridge 1975–87, master Downing Coll Cambridge 1978–87; vice chllr: Univ of Nottingham 1970–75, Univ of Cambridge 1983–85; chm: E Midlands Econ Devpt Cncl 1973–75, Medicines Cmmn 1976–81, Health Promotion Res Tst 1982–96; memb Bd Prudential Corporation plc 1981–92; memb Cncl St George's House Windsor 1987–92; asst emeritus Worshipful Soc of Apothecaries; *Recreations* real tennis, cricket; *Clubs* Athenaeum, MCC, Vincent's, Hawks (chm); *Style—* The Rt Hon the Lord Butterfield, OBE; ✉ 39 Clarendon St, Cambridge CB1 1JX (☎ 01223 328854)

BUTTERFIELD, Leslie Paul; s of Leslie John Butterfield (d 1983), and Ruth, *née* Andräs; *b* 31 Aug 1952; *Educ* N East London Poly (BA), Univ of Lancaster (MA); *m* 14 May 1988, Judy Mary Tombleson; *Career* advertising exec; account planner and assoc dir Boase Massimi Pollitt Ltd 1975–80, planning dir Abbott Mead Vickers/SMS Ltd 1980–87; Butterfield Day Devito Hockney: planning dir 1987–93, chm 1987–, md 1993–94; IPA 1990– (chm Educn and Trg Ctee and memb Cncl); *awards* IPA Advertising Effectiveness Award 1984; FIPA 1988; *Books* How to Plan Advertising (1987); *Style—* Leslie Butterfield, Esq; ✉ Butterfield Day Devito Hockney, 47 Marylebone Lane, London W1M 5FN (☎ 0171 224 3000, fax 0171 935 9865)

BUTTERFIELD, Hon Sarah Harriet Anne (Hon Mrs Willetts); da of Baron Butterfield, OBE, *qv*, and Isabel Ann Foster, *née* Kennedy; *b* 28 Aug 1953; *Educ* Sherborne Sch for Girls, Univ of Edinburgh (BA), Ruskin Sch of Fine Art and Drawing Oxford Univ, Univ of Bristol (Dip Arch); *m* 19 April 1986, David Lindsay Willetts, MP, *qv*, s of John Roland Willetts, of Birmingham; 1 da, 1 s; *Career* architect 1978–86: California, Bristol, London; illustrator for Experimental Psychology Dept Cambridge Univ 1976–78, art critic Oxford Mail 1978; artist; exhibitions incl: RCA 1978, Mall Galleries 1980, 1984, 1986 and 1988, Young Contemporaries Agnews 1988, Richmond Gallery London 1990, Roy Miles Gallery London 1991 and 1994, one man shows Cadogan Contemporary London 1991 and 1994; Egerton Coghill Landscape award 1976, Windsor & Newton award 1978, finalist Hunting Gp Art Competition 1987, commended Spector Three Cities Competition 1988; paintings on permanent view at: British Airways Terminal 4 Heathrow Airport, Wimbledon Lawn Tennis Museum, The Prudential, Trust House Forte Hotels; ARCUK; *Books* Word Order Comprehension Test (with Dr Gillian Fenn); *Style—* The Hon Sarah Butterfield

BUTTERFIELD, Stewart; *Career* European media dir McCann-Erickson Ltd advtg agency 1989–91 (joined 1974), dir of advtg sales and mktg Channel Four Television 1991–; *Style—* Stewart Butterfield, Esq; ✉ Channel 4 Television Corporation, 124 Horseferry Road, London SW1P 2TX (☎ 0171 396 4444, fax 0171 306 8356)

BUTTERFILL, John Valentine; MP (C) Bournemouth W (majority 12,642); s of George Thomas Butterfill (d 1980), and Elsie Amelia, *née* Watts (d 1974); *b* 14 Feb 1941; *Educ* Caterham Sch, Coll of Estate Mgmnt London; *m* 1965, Pamela Ross, da of Frederick Ross-Symons; 1 s (James b 1975), 3 da (Natasha (Mrs Toby Rougier) b 1969, Samara b 1974, Jemima b 1976); *Career* chartered surveyor; valuer Jones Lang Wootton 1962–64, sr exec Hammerson Gp 1964–69, dir Audley Properties Ltd (Bovis Gp) 1969–71, md St Paul's Securities Gp 1971–76, dir Micro Business Systems Ltd 1977–79, sr ptnr Curchod & Co Chartered Surveyors 1977–92, dir Pavilion Services Group Ltd 1992–94, conslt Curchod & Co 1992–, chm Conservation Investments Group, pres European Properties Associates; contested (C) London S Inner in Euro election 1979, contested Croydon NW by-election 1981, MP (C) Bournemouth W 1983–; vice chm Backbench Tourism Ctee 1985–88 (sec 1983–85), sec Backbench Trade and Indust Ctee 1987–88 and 1990; PPS to: Sec of State for Energy 1988–89, Sec of State for Tport 1989–90, Min of State for NI 1991–92; memb Trade and Indust Select Ctee 1992–; vice chm: Fin Ctee 1992–, Euro Affairs Ctee 1992–; chm All Pty Gp on Occupational Pensions 1992–; dep chm Euro Democrat Forum 1981–87, vice chm Foreign Affairs Forum 1983–92, chm Cons Gp for Europe 1989–92; Parly conslt to BIIBA 1992–, Parly advsr to BVCA 1994–; memb Cncl of Mgmnt PDSA 1990–; memb Ct Univs of Reading, Southampton and Exeter; memb Cncl of Mgmnt People's Dispensary for Sick Animals; FRICS 1974; *Recreations* skiing, tennis, riding, bridge, music; *Clubs* Carlton; *Style—* John Butterfill, Esq, MP; ✉ House of Commons, London SW1A OAA

BUTTERS, Francis Arthur; s of Arthur Butters (d 1968), of Westcliff-on-Sea, Essex, and Elsie Beatrice Annie, *née* Wood (d 1975); *b* 4 March 1920; *Educ* Lindisfarne Coll; *m* 20 July 1946, Heather Margaret Butters, JP, da of Gilbert Harris (d 1969), of Stone, Staffs; 1 s (Richard b 8 Jan 1948), 3 da (Margaret (Mrs Grieve) b 20 Dec 1949, Rosalind (Mrs Southworth) b 9 Aug 1952, Veronica (Mrs Kempton) b 14 Sept 1957); *Career* mobilised RNV (W) (R) telegraphist, served minesweeping trawlers, cmmnd 1940, served armed merchant cruisers coastal forces, ops dir Admty 1941, ADC and private sec (Lt RNVR) to Lord Swinton (resident min) W Africa 1942, Miny of Civil Aviation 1944–45 (memb UK Delegation Int Civil Aviation Confs Chicago 1944, Cape Town 1945), i/c PR private office Civil Aviation Miny 1945, info work HQ Miny Civil Aviation 1945, 1 PR Offr Heathrow Airport 1948; joined firm of PR conslts 1950, fndr own PR cos 1957, ret 1986; Berks CC 1956–89 (former ldr Cncl and vice chm Cncl, former chm Gen Purposes Ctee); chm Educn and Social Servs Thames Valley Police Authy; memb: Ct and Cncl Univ of Reading 1973–89, Industl Tbnls 1976–88, ACC 1962–77 and 1984–89 (former chm Police Ctee); chm PDSA 1987–94 (memb Cncl Mgmnt 1976–) former chm Police Cncl UK, has served on various Home Office Working Parties (incl Miny of Tport); dir Thames Valley Broadcasting, various int radio appearances; FIPR 1969 (MIPR 1949, chm Educn Ctee), memb Soc of Tech Analysts 1988; *Books* The Government Explains (with study gp Royal Inst of Public Admin, 1965); various pubns incl articles and photographs (world exclusive pictures of Prince of Wales Crown); *Recreations* still and video photography, music, information technology, travel; *Style—* Francis Butters, Esq; ✉ 56 Lillibrooke Crescent, Maidenhead, Berks SL6 3XG (☎ 01628 824068)

BUTTERWICK, Antony James; s of (James) Cyril Butterwick (d 1966), and Hon (Agnes) Désirée Butterwick, OBE (d 1986), da of 1 Baron Dickinson, KBE; *b* 27 Sept 1930; *Educ* Eton, Trinity Coll Oxford (BA); *m* 8 Oct 1958, Joanna Vivien, yr da of Col Hugh A G Vanderfelt (d 1982); 2 s (James Hugo b 1962, (Antony) Guy b 1966), 1 da (Henrietta b 1960); *Career* Nat Serv cmmn Rifle Bde; with Grieveson Grant & Co stockbrokers 1953–58, chief passenger mangr Union Castle Line 1958–65, formerly jt md P & O Containers Ltd (previously Overseas Containers Ltd); chm: Inchcape Family Investments Ltd, Inchcape Family Trustees Ltd, Minories Ltd; dir Glenapp Estates Ltd; chm Jt Educnl Tst; memb Advsy Panel Nat Marine Aquarium, chm of Govrs Gresham's Sch Holt; memb Ct of Assts Worshipful Co of Fishmongers (past prime warden); *Recreations* golf, shooting; *Style—* Antony Butterwick, Esq; ✉ Pinkneys House, Pinkneys Green, Berks SL6 6QD (☎ 01628 21726, fax 01628 28176)

BUTTERWICK, John Newton; TD (1961); s of (James) Cyril Butterwick (d 1966), of Old Park, Beaconsfield, and Hon (Agnes) Desirée Butterwick, OBE (d 1986), da of 1 Baron Dickinson, KBE; *b* 3 March 1923; *Educ* Eton, Trinity Coll Oxford; *m* 1956, Marcia, o da of John Scott, of Pittsburgh, USA (d 1969); 3 s (Nicholas Scott b 1959, Christopher Hugh b 1963, William Toby b 1965), 1 da (Sarah b 1958); *Career* Capt KRRC WWII NW Europe 1942–46, TA 1949–62, ret with rank Brevet Col; vice chm Lazard Bros & Co 1981–83 (dir 1972–80); dir: Glyn Mills & Co (later Williams & Glyn's Bank) 1961–72, London Merchant Securities plc 1963–, Lazard Unquoted Companies Fund Ltd 1986–91; chm: FennoScandia Bank Ltd 1983–86, Parrot Corporation Ltd 1984–85, East Anglian Securities Trust Ltd 1983–86, Baker Street Investment Company Ltd 1984–91, Mrs Monro Ltd 1996– (dir 1991–); vice chm NDL International Ltd 1986–90; govr Aldenham Sch 1975–, hon fell Eton Coll 1996–; Liveryman Worshipful Co of Goldsmiths; FRSA; *Recreations* golf, gardening; *Clubs* Sloane, Royal West Norfolk Golf; *Style—* John Butterwick, Esq, TD; ✉ Danyells, Sandon, Buntingford, Herts SG9 0RF (☎ and fax 01763 287312); The Gables, Brancaster, King's Lynn, Norfolk PE31 3AU (☎ 01485 210242)

BUTTERWORTH, Arthur Eckersley; MBE (1995); s of Harold Butterworth (d 1945), and Maria, *née* Nelson (d 1935); *b* 4 Aug 1923; *Educ* N Manchester GS, Royal Manchester Coll of Music; *m* 12 July 1952, Diana, da of Charles Stewart, OBE (d 1967); 2 da (Nicola Diana b 1960, Carolin Ann b 1962); *Career* RE attached 51 Highland Div 1942–47; composer: Symphony No 1 op 15 Cheltenham Festival 1957 and BBC Proms 1958, Symphony No 2 op 25 Bradford 1965, Organ Concerto 1973, Violin Concerto 1978, Symphony No 3 op 52 Manchester 1979, Piano Trio Cheltenham Festival Cmmn 1983, Symphony No 4 op 72 Manchester 1986, Odin Symphony for Brass op 76 National Brass Band Festival London 1989, Northern Light op 88 Leeds 1991, Concerto alla Veneziana op 93 York 1992, Viola Concerto op 82 Manchester 1993, Mancunians op 96 Hallé Orch Cmmn Manchester 1995; conductor Huddersfield Philharmonic Soc 1964–93, various guest conductor appearances 1965–; *Recreations* country-living, animal welfare, oil and water colour painting; *Style—* Arthur Butterworth, Esq, MBE; ✉ Pohjola, Dales Ave, Embsay, Skipton, N Yorks BD23 6PE (☎ 01756 792968)

BUTTERWORTH, Eur Ing David; s of John Butterworth (d 1971), and Annie May, *née* Claughton; *b* 24 Oct 1943; *Educ* Audenshaw GS, UCL (BSc(Eng)); *m* 2 Aug 1966, Pauline Patricia, da of Leonard Morgan; 1 s (Richard David b 9 Feb 1968); *Career* AEA Technology Harwell: res scientist/engr 1965–69, section ldr 1969–76, gp ldr 1977–89, md Heat Transfer and Fluid Flow Serv 1989–95 (business centre mangr 1980–89, sr conslt 1995–); visiting engr MIT 1976–77, visiting industl prof Dept of Mechanical Engrg Univ of Bristol 1993– (fell 1984–93), visiting prof Sch of Mechanical Engrg Cranfield Univ 1995–; D Q Kern Award for industl application of heat transfer technol American Inst of Chem Engrs 1986; chm Heat Transfer Steering Gp Engrg Sciences Data Unit 1986–94, pres UK Heat Transfer Soc 1988–89; memb: Cncl and Engrg Practice Ctee Inst of Chem Engrs 1989–92 (also hon librarian), Scientific Cncl Int Centre for Heat and Mass Transfer 1990–, Int Ctee Royal Acad of Engineering 1993–96; jt ed Heat Exchanger Design Updates Jl 1993–; contrib to many courses and summer schs; CEng 1969, FIChemE 1985, FEng 1991, Eur Ing 1991, FRSA 1993; *Books* Introduction to Heat Transfer (1977), Two Phase Flow and Heat Transfer (jt ed, 1977, 1978 and 1979, also published in Russian 1980), Design and Operation of Heat Exchangers (jt ed, 1992); *Recreations* painting, cooking; *Style—* Eur Ing David Butterworth, FEng; ✉ 29 Clevelands, Abingdon, Oxon OX14 2EQ (☎ 01235 525955, fax 01235 200906, e-mail 101322.302@compuserve.com)

BUTTERWORTH, Prof Ian; CBE (1984); s of Harry Butterworth, and Beatrice, *née* Worsley; *b* 3 Dec 1930; *Educ* Bolton Co GS, Univ of Manchester (BSc, PhD); *m* 9 May 1964, Mary Therese Butterworth; 1 da (Jody); *Career* scientific offr and sr scientific offr UKAEA AERE Harwell 1954–58; Imperial Coll London: lectr 1958, sr lectr 1965, head of High Energy Nuclear Physics Gp 1971, head Dept of Physics 1980, hon fell 1988, sr res fell 1991–; prof of physics Univ of London 1971–91 (prof emeritus 1991), princ QMC (now Queen Mary and Westfield Coll) London 1986–91; visiting physicist Lawrence Berkeley Laboratory Univ of California 1964–65, gp leader Bubble Chamber Res Gp Rutherford Laboratory as sr princ scientific offr 1968–71, visiting prof Univ of California Riverside 1970, res dir CERN 1983–86; author of numerous papers in learned jls; FRS; *Recreations* reading, art history; *Style—* Prof Ian Butterworth, CBE, FRS; ✉ The Blackett Laboratory, Imperial College, Prince Consort Rd, London SW7 2BZ (☎ 0171 594 7851, fax 0171 823 8830, telex 929484 IMPCOLC G)

BUTTERWORTH, Jane Elisabeth; da of Leslie John Moore (d 1979), of London, and Madeleine Ruth, *née* Bloomfield; *b* 10 Feb 1948; *Educ* Brigidine Convent Sch; *m* 1, 1967 (m dis 1973), Roger William Butterworth; m 2, 5 July 1975, Brian Charles Haydn Wright, s of Haydn Charles Wright (d 1984); *Career* editorial asst: Photoplay Magazine 1964–65, BTA Publications 1965–67; book ed AA Publications 1967–69; features writer: TTG Trade Publications 1969–70, Loving Magazine 1970–73; freelance writer of human interest and health features for numerous women's and health magazines 1973–88, health ed Ms London 1988–91, problems page ed/agony aunt News of the World 1994– (asst to problems page ed 1991–94); memb: Medical Journalists' Assoc 1994, Guild of Health Writers; *Books* Spotlight on Sam (1986), Wild in the Country (1987), Born to be Wild (1988), The Rights Stuff (1989), Don't Just Sit There (1989), Thrush (1991), Why am I Afraid to Divorce (1994), Straight Talk (1993), Hysterectomy (1995), Jane Butterworth's Sex Files (1996); *Recreations* walking, reading, fitness training, collecting antiques, socialising; *Style—* Ms Jane Butterworth; ✉ News of the World, News International PLC, 1 Virginia Street, London E1 9XR (☎ 0171 782 4444)

BUTTERWORTH, John; *b* 11 June 1946; *Educ* Blackpool Sch of Art; *Career* freelance journalist: The Sunday Times and The Observer 1973–76, The Sun 1976–79, London Evening News 1979–81, New York Daily News 1981–; art ed The Mail on Sunday 1981–; *Style—* John Butterworth, Esq; ✉ The Mail on Sunday, Northcliffe House, 2 Derry Street, Kensington, London W8 5TS (☎ 0171 937 7090)

BUTTERWORTH, Baron (Life Peer UK 1985), of Warwick, Co Warwick; John Blackstock Butterworth; CBE (1982), JP (Coventry 1963), DL (W Midlands 1974); only s of John William Butterworth, by his wife, Florence, da of John Blackstock, of Dumfries; *b* 13 March 1918; *Educ* Queen Elizabeth's GS Mansfield, Queen's Coll Oxford; *m* 1948, Doris Crawford, da of George Elder, of Edinburgh; 1 s (Hon John William Blackstock b 1952), 2 da (Hon Anna Elizabeth Blackstock (Hon Mrs Walker) b 1951, Hon Laura Blackstock (Hon Mrs Burley) b 1959); *Career* Maj RA 1939–46; called to the Bar Lincoln's Inn 1947, hon bencher 1988; fell New Coll Oxford 1946–63, bursar 1956–63, managing tstee Nuffield Fndn 1964–85 (tstee 1985–); first vice chllr Univ of Warwick 1963–85; govr Royal Shakespeare Theatre 1964–, memb Bd Br Cncl 1981–86; memb: Jarratt Ctee on Univ Efficiency 1986, Croham Ctee on Review of UGC 1987, Fulbright Cmmn 1988–94; chm Fndn for Sci and Technol 1990–; JP City of Oxford 1962, DL Warwicks 1967–74; Hon DCL Sierra Leone 1976, Hon DSc Univ of Aston 1985, Hon LLD Univ of Warwick 1986; *Clubs* Athenaeum; *Style—* The Rt Hon Baron Butterworth, CBE, JP, DL; ✉ The Barn, Barton, Guiting Power, Glos GL54 5US (☎ 01451 850297, fax 01451 850108); London (☎ 0171 581 4838, fax 0171 823 9388)

BUTTON, Roger Martin; s of Frederick Charles Button, of Harrow-on-the-Hill, Middx (d 1970), and Una Florence, *née* Martin; *b* 7 Feb 1931; *Educ* Winchester Coll, Pembroke Coll Cambridge (MA Arch); *m* 2 April 1955, Shirley Gwynfryd, da of Dr Rodney Howell Holt, of Eastbourne, Sussex (d 1970); 2 s (Rupert b 1959, Benjamin b 1962, d 1978), 1 da (Myfanwy b 1969); *Career* Lt RE 1949–51; ptnr: Adie Button & Ptnrs 1963–93, Waterhouse Ripley 1968–93 (conslt 1993–); asst architect to Sir Basil Spence for Coventry Cathedral Reconstruction 1955–62; *Recreations* sailing, swimming, gardening; *Clubs* Royal Ocean Racing, Royal Engineer Yacht, Artworkers' Guild; *Style*— Roger M Button, Esq; ✉ The Old Stores, Ashampstead, Reading, Berkshire RG8 8RT (☎ 01635 578559); Waterhouse Ripley Adie Button Partnership, 109 Bermondsey St, London SE1 3TX (☎ 0171 403 1392)

BUTTRESS, Donald Reeve; LVO (1997); s of Edward Crossley Buttress, of Manchester, and Evelyn Edna, *née* Reeve-Whaley; *b* 27 April 1932; *Educ* Stockport Sch, Univ of Manchester (MA); *m* 15 Dec 1956, Elsa Mary, da of Herbert Bardsley, of Bramhall (d 1964); 2 s (Richard b 1960, John b 1966), 3 da (Helen b 1958, Fiona b 1962, Lucy b 1973); *Career* Flying Offr RAF 1958–61; architect and ecclesiastical surveyor; architect to: Sheffield and Bangor Cathedrals 1978–88, Leeds RC Cathedral 1978–, Llandaff Cathedral 1986–; surveyor of the fabric: Chichester Cathedral 1985–, Westminster Abbey 1988–; RIBA; FSA; *Recreations* walking, countryside conservation, books; *Clubs* RAF; *Style*— Donald Buttress, Esq, LVO, FSA; ✉ 2B Little Cloister, Westminster Abbey, London SW1P 3PA; 31–33 Princess Street, Manchester M2 4BF (☎ 0161 236 3303)

BUTTREY, Prof Theodore Vern; s of Theodore Vern Buttrey (d 1982), and Ruth Jeanette, *née* Scoutt; *b* 29 Dec 1929; *Educ* Phillips Exeter Acad, Princeton Univ USA (BA, Stinnecke prize, PhD); *m* 1954 (m dis 1967), Marisa, *née* Macina; 3 s (James b 1956, Claude b 1959, Samuel b 1961), 1 da (Stephanie b 1955); m 2, 1967 (m dis 1980), Ann Elizabeth, *née* Johnston; *Career* asst prof Dept of Classics Yale Univ 1958–64 (instr 1954–58); Dept of Classics Univ of Michigan: assoc prof 1964–68, prof of Greek and Latin 1968–85, dept chm 1968–71 and 1983–84, prof emeritus 1985–; dir Kelsey Museum of Archaeology 1969–71, keeper Dept of Coins and Medals Fitzwilliam Museum Cambridge 1988–91; chm Regnl Ctee (Europe) Mellon Fellowships in the Humanities 1984–92, life memb Clare Hall Cambridge 1972– (visiting fell 1971–72), pres Royal Numismatic Soc 1989–94 (medal 1983, life fell), hon sec UK Numismatic Tst 1989–; Huntington medal American Numismatic Soc 1996; publisher Pevensey Press 1979–; fndr memb Pica Club, life memb American Philological Assoc, life memb Archaeological Inst of America, corresponding memb Royal Danish Acad of Scis and Letters; FSA; *Publications* numerous articles on Greek literature and ancient and modern numismatics; *Recreations* Ernest Bramah, P G Wodehouse, running the half-marathon; *Style*— Prof Theodore Buttrey, FSA; ✉ 6 de Freville Avenue, Cambridge CB4 1HR (☎ and fax 01223 351156)

BUXTON, Andrew Edward; s of Desmond Gurney Buxton (d 1987), of Hoveton Hall, Norfolk, and Rachel Mary, *née* Morse (d 1994); gggs of Sir Edward Buxton, 2 Bt, MP; *b* 3 March 1935; *Educ* Eton, Magdalene Coll Cambridge (MA); *m* 1967, Barbara, yr da of Capt Cyril Gascoigne Lloyd; 1 s (Harry b 1972), 2 da (Laura (Mrs Charles Erith) b 1968, Nicola b 1971); *Career* exec dir RTZ Corporation plc 1974–92; non-exec dir: Norwich Union Group, Mercury World Mining Trust PLC, TR Far East Income Trust plc; *Recreations* forestry, shooting, tennis; *Clubs* Boodle's; *Style*— Andrew Buxton, Esq; ✉ 36 Burnsall St, London SW3 3SP; Hoveton Hall, Norwich, Norfolk NR12 8RJ

BUXTON, Andrew Robert Fowell; s of Capt Joseph Gurney Fowell Buxton, Grenadier Gds (ka 1943, gggs of Sir Thomas Buxton, 1 Bt), and Elizabeth (da of late Maj Robert Barbour, of Bolesworth Castle, Tattenhall, Chester) who m subsequently Alexander Grant; *b* 5 April 1939; *Educ* Winchester, Pembroke Coll Oxford; *m* 1965, Jane Margery, da of Lt-Col Ian (John Peter) Grant, MBE, of Rothiemurchus, and Lady Katherine Grant; 2 da; *Career* 2 Lt Grenadier Gds; Barclays Bank plc: dir 1984–, gp md 1988–92, vice chm 1988–91, dep chm 1991–92, chief exec 1992–93, chm 1993–; non-exec dir SmithKline Beecham plc 1987–; *Style*— Andrew Buxton, Esq; ✉ Barclays plc, 54 Lombard Street, London EC3P 3AH (☎ 0171 626 1567)

BUXTON, Henry Alexander Fowell; DL (Herts 1993); s of John Fowell Buxton (d 1970), of Wareside, Herts, and Katherine, *née* Bacon; *b* 21 May 1937; *Educ* Maidwell Hall, Eton; *m* 10 Oct 1964, Victoria, da of Ronald Bennett, of Bibury, Glos; 2 s (Nicholas Fowell b 17 March 1966, Anthony John b 3 April 1968), 1 da (Katharine Louise b 27 May 1971); *Career* farmer and landowner; Nat Serv 16th/5th The Queen's Royal Lancers; chm Herts Country Landowners' Assoc 1978–79; dir: Truman Hanbury Buxton 1961–72, Camgrain Ltd; govr: Abingdon Sch, Baesh Almshouses, Mico Coll Kingston Jamaica; High Sheriff Herts 1992; Liveryman Worshipful Co of Mercers; *Recreations* fishing, shooting; *Clubs* Brooks's; *Style*— Henry Buxton, Esq, DL; ✉ Mardocks Mill, Wareside, Ware, Herts SG12 7QN (☎ 01920 463673)

BUXTON, James Anthony Fowell; s of Robert James Buxton (d 1968), of Yeovil, Somerset, and Lilla Mary Alyson, *née* Pumphrey (d 1979); *Educ* Harrow, Trinity Coll Cambridge (MA); *m* 4 Nov 1975, Margaret Elizabeth, da of Adm The Hon Sir Guy Russell, GBE, KCB, DSO; 2 s (Edward b 1978, Charles b 1986), 2 da (Harriet b 1976, Meriel b 1980); *Career* called to the Bar 1971, in Chambers of late Joseph Jackson QC 1972–78, Chambers of Sir David Calcutt QC 1978–82; admitted slr 1984, ptnr Burges Salmon Bristol 1984–; memb Law Soc; *Books* contrib: Law of Agricultural Holdings (1989), Halsburys Laws of England, Butterworths Forms and Precedents Agriculture Volume; *Recreations* shooting, fishing, tennis, walking, skiing; *Clubs* Brooks's, St James's; *Style*— James Buxton, Esq; ✉ Galhampton Manor, Yeovil, Somerset BA22 7AL (☎ 01963 440297); Narrow Quay House, Prince St, Bristol BS1 4AH (☎ 0117 939 2000, telex 44736, fax 0117 929 4705, car 0836 605694)

BUXTON, James Desmond; s of Desmond Gurney Buxton (d 1987), of Hoveton Hall, Norfolk, and Rachel Mary, *née* Morse (d 1994); *b* 20 Aug 1947; *Educ* Eton, Magdalene Coll Cambridge (MA); *m* 1975, Annabella, yst da of Douglas Collins; 2 s (Jasper Francis b 10 April 1979, Oliver Desmond b 10 Sept 1980); *Career* Evening Echo Hemel Hempstead 1969–72; Financial Times: joined 1972, foreign staff ME and N Africa 1973–80, Rome corr 1980–86, Scottish corr 1986–; winner Ischia Prize Italy 1986; *Recreations* travel, reading, music; *Clubs* Norfolk; *Style*— James Buxton, Esq; ✉ Redcroft, 23 Murrayfield Road, Edinburgh EH12 6EP; Financial Times, 80 George St, Edinburgh EH2 3BU (☎ 0131 220 1420, fax 0131 220 1578)

BUXTON, Hon (Aubrey) James Francis; yr s of Baron Buxton of Alsa, *qv*; *b* 20 March 1956; *Educ* Ampleforth, Royal Agricultural Coll Cirencester; *m* 1981, Melinda, da of Peter Henry Samuelson, of Ugley Hall, Essex; 1 s (Henry James Aubrey b 19 May 1988), 2 da (Emma Lucie Maria b 1984, Olivia Louise b 1986); *Career* ptnr Bidwells Chartered Surveyors Cambridge; *Recreations* shooting, painting, vintage cars, music; *Clubs* White's; *Style*— The Hon James Buxton; ✉ Church Farm, Carlton, Newmarket, Suffolk (☎ 01223 290511); Bidwells Chartered Surveyors, Trumpington Road, Cambridge CB2 2LD (☎ 01223 841841)

BUXTON, Sir Jocelyn Charles Roden; 7 Bt (UK 1840), of Belfield, Dorset; VRD; s of Capt Roden Henry Victor Buxton, CBE, RN (d 1970), and his 1 w, Dorothy Alina, *née* St John (d 1956); suc kinsman, Sir Thomas Fowell Victor Buxton, 6 Bt (d 1996); *b* 8 Aug 1924; *m* 1960, Ann Frances, da of Frank Smitherman, MBE; 3 da (Frances Dorothy (Mrs Henry Jones-Davies) b 1960, Harriet Lucy (Hon Mrs Michael Dalrymple) b 1962, Caroline Sarah (Mrs Nicholas Jarrett) b 1964); *Heir* bro, Gerard St John Roden Buxton b 1927; *Career* WWII (despatches) Korea Lt Cdr RNVR; *Style*— Sir Jocelyn Buxton, Bt, VRD; ✉ Rodwell House, Loddon, Norwich, Norfolk

BUXTON, Prof John Noel; s of John William Buxton (d 1971), and Laura Frances, *née* Whitehead; *b* 25 Dec 1933; *Educ* Bradford GS, Trinity Coll Cambridge (MA); *m* 8 Feb 1958, Moira Jean, da of William E C O'Brien (d 1972); 2 s (Nigel b 1961, Patrick b 1965), 2 da (Jocelyn b 1959, Delia b 1963); *Career* flight trials engr de Havilland Propellers 1955–59, ops res scientist Br Iron & Steel Res Assoc 1959–60, Applied Sci Dept IBM UK 1960–62, lectr Inst of Computer Sci Univ of London 1962–66, chief software conslt SCICON (formerly CEIR) 1966–68, prof of computer sci Univ of Warwick 1968–84, prof of info technol King's Coll London 1984–94, chm Room Underwriting Systems Ltd 1994–; visiting scholar Harvard Univ 1979–80; UNDP project mangr Int Computer Educn Centre Budapest 1975–77, dir systems engrg DTI 1989–91, memb various SERC Ctees 1987–; FBCS 1968, CEng 1990; *Books* Simulation Programming Languages (ed, 1968), Proceedings of NATO Software Engineering Conf (jt ed, 1970), The Craft of Software Engineering (jtly, 1987); *Recreations* mountaineering, music, restoration of medieval homes; *Clubs* Lansdowne, Climbers; *Style*— Prof John Buxton; ✉ Bull's Hall, Yaxley, Eye, Suffolk IP23 8BZ; Room 643, Lloyd's, 1 Lime Street, London EC3M 7HA

BUXTON, Hon Lucinda Catherine; 2 da of Baron Buxton of Alsa, and Pamela Mary, *née* Birkin; *b* 21 Aug 1950; *Educ* New Hall Sch Chelmsford; *Career* wildlife cinematographer/dir; has made 18 TV films for Survival Wildlife series and 2 TV films for Partridge Films Ltd; tstee Falkland Islands Appeal; vice pres: Falkland Islands Fndn, United Kingdom Falkland Islands Ctee; Media Award 1982, The Cherry Kearton Award (RGS) 1983; FRGS; *Books* Survival in the Wild (1980), Survival - South Atlantic (1983); *Recreations* tennis, flying, diving; *Style*— The Hon Lucinda Buxton; ✉ 1800 Hoyt Street, Lakewood, Colorado 80215, USA (☎ and fax 303 283 9197)

BUXTON, Hon Mrs (Margaret Evelyn); *née* Bridges; da of 1 Baron Bridges, KG, GCB, GCVO, MC (d 1969), and Hon Katharine, da of 2 Baron Farrer (d 1986); *b* 9 Oct 1932; *Educ* Downe House Newbury, Lady Margaret Hall Oxford (MA, DPhil); *m* 1, 1954 (m dis 1969), Trevor Aston; m 2, 1971, as his 2 w, Paul William Jex Buxton, s of Denis Alfred Jex Buxton (d 1964), and gggs of Sir Thomas Buxton, 1 Bt; 2 da; *Career* lectr St Anne's Coll Oxford 1956–59, res fell Newnham Coll Cambridge 1961–66, hon sr res fell Queen's Univ Belfast 1984–85; FRHistS, FBA, FSA; *Books* (under name of Margaret Aston) Thomas Arundel (1967), The Fifteenth Century (1968), Lollards and Reformers (1984), England's Iconoclasts vol 1 (1988), Faith and Fire (1993), The King's Bedpost (1994), The Panorama of the Renaissance (ed, 1996); *Style*— The Hon Mrs Buxton, FBA, FSA; ✉ Castle House, Chipping Ongar, Essex CM5 9JJ (☎ 01277 362642)

BUXTON, Dr Paul Kenneth; s of Kenneth Buxton, of Swallowfield Park, Reading, Berks, and Agnes, *née* Bragg; *b* 28 Feb 1936; *Educ* Trinity Coll Cambridge, St Thomas's Hosp London; *m* 22 Dec 1962, Heather Clive, da of Lt-Col J C Edlmann; 1 s (Jonathan Charles Fowell b 30 June 1965), 1 da (Joanna Rachel (Mrs Francis Hobbs) b 12 April 1967); *Career* staff Royal Jubilee Hosp Victoria 1971–81, conslt dermatologist Royal Infirmary Edinburgh and Fife Health Bd 1981–; pres Fife Branch BMA 1986–87; FRSM, FRCPEd 1985; *Books* ABC Dermatology (1988); *Recreations* seafaring, books, farming; *Clubs* New (Edinburgh); *Style*— Dr Paul Buxton; ✉ Old Inzievar House, By Dunfermline, Fife KY12 8HA (☎ 01383 880297); University Department of Dermatology, Royal Infirmary, Edinburgh EH3 9YW (☎ 0131 536 2042)

BUXTON, Hon Simon Campden; 2 s of 2 Baron Noel-Buxton (d 1980); *b* 9 April 1943; *Educ* Bryanston, Balliol Coll Oxford; *m* 1981, Alison, da of S J Liddle, of Budleigh, Salterton; 1 s (Christopher John Noel b 11 June 1988), 1 da (Katherine Helen b 1983); *Career* editor social action programmes Thames Television 1987–93, fndr Buxton Productions 1993; tstee: Noel-Buxton Tst, Sir James Colyer-Fergusson Tst; govr Kingsway Coll 1990–94, memb Arts Access Ctee, dir The Quest Tst 1994–; *Recreations* music, cricket, wine; *Clubs* MCC; *Style*— The Hon Simon Buxton; ✉ The Orchard, Bathford, Bath BA1 7TG

BUXTON OF ALSA, Baron (Life Peer UK 1978), of Stiffkey, Co Norfolk; Aubrey Leland Oakes Buxton; MC (1943), DL (Essex 1975); s of late Leland William Wilberforce Buxton, s of Sir Thomas Fowell Buxton, 3 Bt, GCMG, JP, DL; *b* 15 July 1918; *Educ* Ampleforth, Trinity Coll Cambridge; *m* 1946, Pamela Mary (d 1983), da of Sir Henry Ralph Stanley Birkin, 3 Bt, and widow of Maj Samuel Luckyn Buxton, MC, 17/21 Lancers; 2 s, 4 da; m 2, 16 July 1988, Mrs Kathleen Peterson, of Maine, USA; *Career* Maj Supplementary Reserves; chief exec Anglia TV Group (dir 1955–88, chm 1986–88), chm ITN 1981–86; pres Royal TV Soc 1973–77, treas London Zoological Soc 1977–83, chm Survival Anglia 1986–92; memb: Countryside Cmmn, Royal Cmmn on Pollution, Nature Conservancy Cncl 1988–90; prodr of television and wildlife films; vice pres Wildfowl & Wetlands Tst; Queen's award for Industry 1974; Extra Equerry to HRH The Duke of Edinburgh 1964–, High Sheriff of Essex 1972; *Style*— The Rt Hon the Lord Buxton, KCVO, MC, DL; ✉ Old Hall Farm, Stiffkey, Wells-next-the-Sea, Norfolk NR23 1QJ (☎ 0132 875 347)

BUZZARD, Sir Anthony Farquhar; 3 Bt (UK 1929), of Munstead Grange, Godalming, Surrey; s of Rear Adm Sir Anthony Wass Buzzard, 2 Bt, CB, DSO, OBE (d 1972), and Margaret (d 1989), da of Sir Arthur Knapp, KCIE, CSI, CBE; *b* 28 June 1935; *Educ* Charterhouse, Ch Ch Oxford (MA), Ambassador Coll Pasadena Calif (BA), Bethany Theological Coll (MA Th); *m* 1970, Barbara Jean, da of Gordon Arnold, of Michigan; 3 da (Sarah Jane b 1971, Claire Judith b 1974, Heather Elizabeth b 1988); *Heir* bro, Timothy Macdonnell Buzzard b 28 Jan 1939; *Career* modern languages teacher at American School in London 1974–81, lectr in theology Atlanta Bible Coll Morrow Georgia (formerly Oregon Bible Coll Illinois) 1982–; articles on Christology & Eschatology in various theological journals, fndr of Restoration Fellowship; *Books* The Coming Kingdom of the Messiah: A Solution to the Riddle of the New Testament (1987), The Doctrine of the Trinity: Christianity's Self-Inflicted Wound (1994), Our Fathers Who Aren't in Heaven: The Forgotten Christianity of Jesus the Jew (1995); *Recreations* music, tennis; *Style*— Sir Anthony Buzzard, Bt; ✉ 185 Summerville Drive, Brooks, GA 30205, USA (☎ 00 1 770 719 7694)

BUZZARD, Timothy Macdonnell; s of Rear Adm Sir Anthony Wass Buzzard, 2 Bt, CB, DSO, OBE (d 1972); hp of bro, Sir Anthony Buzzard, 3 Bt; *b* 28 Jan 1939; *Educ* Royal Acad of Music; *m* 1970, Jennifer Mary, da of Peter Patching (d 1971); 1 s (Jonathan Mark b 1977), 1 da (Rachel Mary b 1974); *Career* freelance musician; LRAM, GRSM; *Style*— Timothy Buzzard, Esq; ✉ Kennel Cottage, East Mascalls, Lindfield, West Sussex (☎ 01444 483420)

BYAM SHAW, Nicholas Glencairn; s of Lt Cdr David Byam Shaw, OBE, RN (ka 1941), and (Clarita) Pamela Clarke (who m 2, Louis G Zinnecker, and d 1995); gs of John Byam Liston Shaw (d 1919), painter and fndr Byam Shaw Sch of Art; *b* 28 March 1934; *Educ* RNC Dartmouth; *m* 1, 1956, Joan, da of Maj Hedley Edmund Dennis Elliott (d 1958), of Roundabout, West Chiltington, Sussex; 2 s (Justin b 1960, Matthew b 1963), 1 da (Clare b 1957); m 2, 1987, Constance, da of Rev Serson Clarke (d 1979), of Ottawa, Canada; *Career* Lt RN (cmmnd 1953), promoted 1956; publisher; md Macmillan Publishers Ltd 1969–93; chm: Pan Books Ltd 1986–, Macmillan Ltd 1990– (md 1983–93); dir St Martin's Press NY and other Macmillan cos, also dir Verlagsgruppe Georg von Holtzbrinck; *Recreations* gardening, music, theatre; *Style*— Nicholas Byam Shaw, Esq; ✉ Macmillan Ltd, 25 Eccleston Place, London SW1W 9NF (☎ 0171 881 8000)

BYATT, Antonia Susan; CBE (1990); da of His Hon Judge John Frederick Drabble, QC (d 1983), of Martlesham, Suffolk, and Kathleen Marie Bloor (d 1984); *b* 24 Aug 1936; *m* 1959 (m dis 1969), I C R Byatt; 1 s (Charles b 1961, d 1972), 1 da (Antonia b 1960); m 2, 1969, Peter John Duffy; 2 da (Isabel b 1970, Miranda b 1973); *Career* teacher: Westminster Tutors 1962–65, Extra-mural Dept Univ of London 1962–71; pt/t lectr Dept of Lib Studies Central Sch of Art and Design 1965–69, lectr Dept of Eng UCL 1972–81, tutor for admissions Dept of Eng UCL 1980–82 (asst tutor 1977–80), sr lectr Dept of Eng UCL 1981–83; full-time writer 1983–; regular reviewer: various newspapers, The Times Literary Supplement, BBC Kaleidoscope; external assessor in lit Central Sch of Art and Design, external examiner UEA; judge Booker Prize 1974; memb: Panel of Judges Hawthornden Prize, Communications and Cultural Studies Bd CNAA 1978–83, Creative and Performing Arts Bd 1984–87, BBC's Social Effects of TV Advsy Gp 1974–77, Kingman Ctee on Eng Language 1987–88, Lit Advsy Panel Br Cncl 1990–, London Library Ctee 1990–, Advsy Bd Harold Hyam Wingate Fellowship 1988–, Bd British Cncl 1993–; assoc Newnham Coll Cambridge 1977–82, chm Ctee of Mgmnt Soc of Authors 1986–88 (dep chm 1985–); Hon DLitt: Bradford 1987, Durham 1991, York 1991, Nottingham 1992, Liverpool 1993, Portsmouth 1994, Univ of London 1995; FRSL; *Books* Shadow of the Sun (1964, reissued 1991), Degrees of Freedom (1965, reissued 1994), The Game (1967), Wordsworth and Coleridge in their Time (1970, reissued as Unruly Times 1989), The Virgin in the Garden (1978), Still Life (1985), Sugar and Other Stories (1987), Possession: A Romance (Booker Prize, Irish Times/Aer Lingus Int Fiction Prize, 1990), George Eliot The Mill on the Floss (Penguin, ed), George Eliot Selected Essays and Other Writings (Penguin, ed, 1990), Passions of The Mind (essays, 1991), Angels and Insects (1992), The Matisse Stories (1994), The Djinn and the Nightingale's Eye: Five Fairy Stories (1995), Babel Tower (1996), Imagining Characters (with Ignês Sodré); author of varied literary criticism, articles, prefaces, reviews and broadcasts; *Style*— Mrs A S Byatt, CBE, FRSL; ✉ 37 Rusholme Rd, London SW15 3LF

BYATT, Sir Hugh Campbell; KCVO (1985), CMG (1979); s of Sir Horace Archer Byatt, GCMG (d 1933), and Lady Byatt, MBE, *née* Olga Margaret Campbell (d 1943); *b* 27 Aug 1927; *Educ* Gordonstoun, New Coll Oxford (MA); *m* 1954, Fiona Mary Mckenzie, da of Ian Pountney Coats, DL; 2 s (Andrew Lorne Campbell b 1955, Duncan Ian Arthur Campbell b 1962), 1 da (Dr Lucinda Margaret Granozio b 1957); *Career* Nat Serv RN 1945–48 (Sub Lieut RNVR); Nigerian Political Serv 1952–57, CRO, India and Cabinet Office 1957–67, head of chancery Lisbon 1967, asst head South Asia Dept FCO 1970, consul gen Mozambique 1971–73, inspr HM Dip Serv 1973–75, RCDS 1976, dep high cmmr Kenya 1977–78, first ambass to Angola 1978–81, Portugal 1981–86; chm of governors Centre for Info of Language Teaching and Res (CILT) 1986–90, advsr RTZ plc 1986–96, dir Japan Trust Plc (Edinburgh Fund Managers); chm: Dragon Trust plc, Java Trust plc (Edinburgh Fund Managers), Malcolm Sargent Cancer Fund for Children Ctee for Scotland 1991–96; memb Parole Bd for Scotland 1991 and 1992; hon sheriff Campbeltown Argyll; Kt GCMO of Christ (Portugal 1985); FSA (Scot); *Recreations* sailing, fishing, gardening, watercolouring; *Clubs* New (Edinburgh), Royal Ocean Racing, Royal Highland Yacht (Oban); *Style*— Sir Hugh Campbell Byatt, KCVO, CMG; ✉ c/o Adam & Co, 22 Charlotte Square, Edinburgh EH2 4DF

BYATT, Ian Charles Rayner; s of Charles Rayner Byatt (d 1944), and Enid Marjorie Annie, *née* Howat (d 1977); *b* 11 March 1932; *Educ* Kirkham GS, St Edmund Hall Oxford, Nuffield Coll Oxford (BA, DPhil), Harvard Univ; *m* 4 July 1959 (m dis 1969), Antonia Susan, da of His Hon Judge J F Drabble, QC (d 1982); 1 s (Charles Nicholas John b 1961, d 1972), 1 da ((Helen) Antonia b 1960); *Career* serv RAF 1950–52; lectr in econs Univ of Durham 1958–62, econ conslt HM Treasy 1962–64, lectr LSE 1964–67, sr econ advsr DES 1967–69, dir of econs and statistics Miny of Housing (later DOE) 1969–72, dep chief econ advsr HM Treasy 1978–89 (head of public sector 1972–78), DG of Water Servs 1989–; vice pres Strategic Planning Soc; Freeman City of London; Hon DUniv Brunel, Hon FIWEM; memb: Holy Cross Church, Holy Cross Centre Tst, Royal Econ Soc; CIMgt; *Books* British Electrical Industry 1875–1914 (1979); *Recreations* painting; *Clubs* Oxford and Cambridge; *Style*— Ian Byatt, Esq; ✉ Office of Water Services, 13–15 Floor, Centre City Tower, 7 Hill St, Birmingham B5 4UA (☎ 0121 625 1350, fax 0121 625 1348)

BYATT, Ronald Archer Campbell (Robin); CMG (1980); s of Sir Horace Archer Byatt, GCMG (d 1933), of Meesdon Hall, Buntingford, Herts, and Olga Margaret Byatt, MBE, *née* Campbell (d 1943); *b* 14 Nov 1930; *Educ* Gordonstoun, New Coll Oxford (BA), King's Coll Cambridge; *m* 10 July 1954, Ann Brereton (Jilly), da of C B Sharpe (d 1993), of Field Cottage, Terrington, N Yorks; 1 s (Andrew b 1959), 1 da (Ann b 1957); *Career* Nat Serv RNVR 1949–50; admin offr HMOCS Nyasaland 1954–59; HM Dip Serv: Foreign Office 1959–61, Havana 1961–63, Foreign Office 1963–66, head of chancery UK Mission to UN NY 1966–70, Kampala 1970–71, cnsllr to Head of Rhodesia Dept FCO 1972–75, memb UK Delgn to Rhodesian Constitutional Conf Geneva 1976, head of chancery UK Mission to UN NY 1977–79, asst under sec of state FCO 1979–80, high cmmr to Zimbabwe 1980–83, memb directing staff RCDS London 1983–84, ambass to Morocco 1985–87, high cmmr to NZ and Western Samoa 1987–90, govr of Pitcairn Islands 1987–90; visiting fell Univ of Glasgow 1975–76; tstee: Beit Tst 1987–, Antarctic Heritage Tst 1993–; panel chm Civil Serv Selection Bd 1992–95; memb Home-Grown-Timber Advsy Ctee 1993–, chm Environment Sub-Ctee Forestry Cmmn 1993–; Order of the Throne Morocco 1987; *Recreations* sailing, bird watching, gardening; *Clubs* United Oxford and Cambridge Univ; *Style*— Robin Byatt, Esq, CMG; ✉ Drim Na Vullin, Lochgilphead, Argyll PA31 8LE

BYERS, Hon Charles William; o s of Baron Byers, OBE, PC, DL (Life Peer, d 1984), and Baroness Byers; *b* 24 March 1949; *Educ* Westminster, Ch Ch Oxford; *m* 8 July 1972, Suzan Mary, o da of Aubrey Kefford Stone (d 1980); 2 s (Jonathan Charles b 11 April 1975, George William b 19 Nov 1977); *Career* called to the Bar Gray's Inn 1977, recorder of the Crown Court 1993–; *Style*— The Hon Charles Byers; ✉ 36 Essex Street, 3rd Floor, London WC2R 3AS (☎ 0171 413 0353, fax 0171 413 0374)

BYERS, Eric; s of Sidney Byers (d 1993), of Cockermouth, Cumbria, and Mary, *née* Watson (d 1981); *b* 17 Sept 1935; *Educ* Cockermouth GS, Univ of Manchester (BA History); *m* 1980, Diana Elizabeth; *Career* product devpt dir Cussons Group 1965–70, dir of product servs Borg Textiles UK Ltd 1971–75, dep area admin Kent AHA 1975–80, dist admin Tunbridge Wells DHA 1980–85, chief exec Bethlem and Maudsley NHS Tst 1985–; Allan Brooking travel fellowship 1983, King's Fund travel bursary 1987; memb Round Table; MIMgt 1962 (former chm Kent Branch, fndr chm W Kent Branch); *Recreations* wine, theatre, reading, travel; *Style*— Eric Byers, Esq; ✉ 18 Park Road, Southborough, Kent TN4 0NX (☎ 01892 523536); Bethlem & Maudsley NHS Trust, Monks Orchard Road, Beckenham, Kent BR3 3BX (☎ 0181 776 4762, fax 0181 777 6039)

BYERS, Sir Maurice Hearne; kt (1982), CBE (1978), QC (1960); s of Arthur Tolhurst Byers (d 1950), and Mabel Florence, *née* Hearne (d 1950); *b* 10 Nov 1917; *Educ* St Aloysius Coll Sydney, Sydney Univ (LLB); *m* 1949, Patricia Therese, da of Charles Henry Davis (d 1947); 2 s, 1 da; *Career* barr, slr-gen of Aust 1973–83, ldr Aust Delgn to UN Cmmn on Int Trade Law 1974, 1976–81; chm: Police Bd of NSW 1984–88, Aust Constitutional Cmmn 1985–88; *Style*— Sir Maurice Byers, CBE, QC; ✉ 14 Morella Rd, Clifton Gdns, Sydney, NSW 2088, Australia (☎ 00 61 2 969 8257)

BYERS, Stephen John; MP (Lab) Wallsend (majority 19,470); s of late Robert Byers; *b* 13 April 1953; *Educ* Chester City GS, Chester Coll of FE, Liverpool Poly (LLB); *Career* sr lectr in law Newcastle Poly 1977–92; Parly candidate (Lab) Hexham 1983, MP (Lab, UNISON sponsored) Wallsend 1992–; chm Ctee Parliamentary Labour Party Home Affairs 1992–94, oppn whip 1994–95, oppn spokesman on Educn and Employment 1995–; N Tyneside MBC: cncllr 1980–92, chm Educn Ctee 1982–85, dep ldr 1985–92; chm Educn Ctee Assoc of Met Authorities 1990–92, ldr Cncl of Local Educn Authorities 1990–92, chm Nat Employers' Orgn for Teachers 1990–92, ldr Mgmnt Panel Nat Jt Cncl for FE 1990–92; memb: NATFHE 1975–84, NUPE 1984–; FRSA; *Recreations* cinema, travel, theatre, walking; *Style*— Stephen Byers, Esq, MP; ✉ House of Commons, London SW1A 0AA (☎ 0171 219 4085)

BYFIELD, Trevor Mills; s of Col Charles William Byfield, and Kathleen Florence, *née* Duggins; *b* 20 Oct 1943; *Educ* Preston GS; *m* 5 March 1966, Janet Yvonne, da of Richard Douglas Offor; 2 s (Dean Trevor b 20 March 1967, Adam Trevor b 12 June 1970); *Career* actor; mktg conslt for Neways; *Theatre* incl: Hair (West End), Jesus Christ Superstar, Mother Earth (Round House), The Rocky Horror Show; *Television* incl: Cats Eyes, Minder, The Professionals, The Gentle Touch, Dempsey and Makepeace, Metal Mickey, New Scotland Yard, The Lotus Eaters, Bust, The Manageress, The Bill, El CID, A Wanted Man, Birds of a Feather, The Chief, Lovejoy, Inspector Morse, Only Fools and Horses, Chancer, Rides, One Foot in the Grave, So Haunt Me, Fool's Gold, Bermuda Grace, Boon, Between the Lines, Casualty, Pale Horse, Crocodile Shoes, Thieftakers, The Knock, Taggart; *Films* incl: Who Dares Wins, Shock Treatment, Riding High, Slayground, Crime in the City, Wolves of Willoughby Chase, Pleasure, Goldeneye; *Albums* incl: Running, Yesterday's Dreams; composer Virgin Warrior; *Recreations* gardening, cooking, raising the awareness and credibility of the network marketing industry; *Style*— Trevor Byfield, Esq; ✉ c/o Caroline Dawson Associates, Apartment 9, 47 Courtfield Road, London SW7 4DB (☎ 0171 370 0708, fax 0171 835 1403)

BYFORD, Sir Lawrence; kt (1984), CBE (1979), QPM (1974), DL (1987); s of George Byford (d 1949), of Normanton, Yorks, and Monica Irene Byford; *b* 10 Aug 1925; *Educ* Univ of Leeds; *m* 1950, Muriel Campbell Massey; 2 s (one of whom Mark Byford, *qv*), 1 da; *Career* barr; joined W Riding Police 1947, divnl cdr Huddersfield 1966–68, chief constable Lincs 1973–77 (asst chief constable 1968–70, dep chief constable 1970–73), HM Inspr of Constabulary for SE Region 1977–78, for NE Region 1978–83, HM Chief Inspr of Constabulary 1983–87; Hon LLD Univ of Leeds 1987; now engaged as mgmnt and security conslt; *Clubs* MCC, Royal Over-Seas League (chm 1989–92, vice pres), Yorkshire CCC (pres and chm 1991–); *Style*— Sir Lawrence Byford, CBE, QPM, DL; ✉ c/o Royal Over-Seas League, Park Place, St James's St, London SW1A 1LR

BYFORD, Mark; s of Sir Lawrence Byford, CBE, QPM, DL, *qv*, and Muriel, *née* Massey; *b* 13 June 1958; *Educ* Lincoln Christ's Hosp Sch, Univ of Leeds (LLB), Wharton Business Sch Univ of Pennsylvania; *m* Hilary Bleiker; 2 s (Sam b 1986, Harry b 1994), 3 da (Molly b 1988, Flora b 1992, Lily b 1996); *Career* regnl journalist BBC North 1979–82, asst news ed BBC South 1982–87, news ed BBC West 1987–88, home news ed BBC News and Current Affrs 1988–89, head of centre Leeds BBC North 1989–90; BBC Regnl Broadcasting: asst controller 1990–91, controller 1991–94, dep md 1994–96, dir of regnl broadcasting BBC Broadcast 1996–; memb RTS; *Recreations* family life, entertaining close friends, the seaside (esp Scarborough and the Solent), football (esp Leeds Utd FC and Southampton FC), cricket (esp Yorks CCC), tennis, swimming, fell walking, rock music, cinema, theatre, visiting cathedrals, exploring Winchester and the New Forest; *Clubs* Yorkshire Co Cricket; *Style*— Mark Byford, Esq; ✉ Bolberry House, 1 Clifton Hill, Winchester SO22 5BL (☎ 01962 860197, fax 01962 860944); BBC Regional Broadcasting, Room 702, Henry Wood House, London W1A 1AA (☎ 0171 765 4260, fax 0171 765 2812)

BYGRAVE, Clifford; s of Fred Bygrave (d 1993), of Caddington, nr Luton, and Beatrice Rose Bygrave; *b* 24 May 1934; *Educ* Luton GS; *m* 15 July 1961, Jean Elizabeth, da of Edward Neale (d 1986); 3 da (Angela Joy b 1964, Paula Jane b 1968, Heather Alison b 1972); *Career* RNVR 1955–59; CA; ptnr: Hillier Hills Frary & Co 1962–81, Arthur Young (now Ernst & Young) 1981–96; memb: Mgmnt Ctee Beds, Bucks and Herts Soc of CAs 1971– (pres 1975–76 and 1993–94), Cncl ICAEW 1980–; non-exec dir Beds HA; vice chm Ashton Schs Fndn Dunstable, tstee and treas Friends of Luton Parish Church, vice pres Luton Town FC; Clerk Worshipful Co of Chartered Accountants, Freeman City of London; FCA 1958, ATII 1964; *Recreations* golf, soccer; *Clubs* Farmers', Dunstable Downs Rotary, Ashridge Golf; *Style*— Clifford Bygrave, Esq; ✉ The Rustlings, Valley Close, Studham, Dunstable, Beds (☎ 01582 872070)

BYGRAVES, Max Walter William; OBE (1983); s of Henry Walter Bygraves (d 1974), and Lilian Mary Bygraves (d 1985); *b* 16 Oct 1922; *Educ* St Joseph's London; *m* 1942, Blossom Mary; 1 s (Anthony b 1947), 2 da (Christine b 1943, Maxine b 1953); *Career* fitter RAF 1940–45; performed as entertainer in shows for troops; turned professional 1946, has appeared all over world; 19 Royal Command Performances; 31 Gold Disc recordings; former host Family Fortunes TV show; *Books* I Wanna Tell You a Story (1976), The Milkman's On His Way (1977), After Thoughts (1988), I Wanna Tell You a Funny Story (1992); *Recreations* golf, travel, short story writing; *Clubs* St James's, East India, RAC; *Style*— Max Bygraves, Esq, OBE; ✉ 2 Stafford Mansions Place, London SW1E 6NL (☎ 0171 828 4595, fax 0171 976 5882)

BYLES, David Warner; s of Charles Humphrey Gilbert Byles (d 1970), of Kemsing, Kent, and Pamela Beatrice Byles; *b* 6 April 1954; *Educ* Sevenoaks Sch, Univ of Kent (BA); *m* 1981, Susan Jane, da of Edward Fowles; 1 s (Thomas Edward b 1988), 1 da (Jennifer Mary b 1985); *Career* advtg exec; asst to Co Sec HP Drewry (Shipping Consultants) Ltd 1976–77; Benton & Bowles: graduate trainee 1977–78, media exec 1978–79, media gp head 1979–81; J Walter Thompson: dep media gp mangr 1981–82, media gp mangr 1982–83, asst media dir 1983–87, bd dir media 1987–89, media dir 1989–95, media dir Latin America (Mexico) and worldwide media dir working on Kellogg's account 1995–; accounts handled for JWT incl: Nestlé Rowntree, NatWest, Thomson Holidays, St Ivel, Kellogg; RAF Special Flying award 1970–71; memb RSPB 1985, MIPA 1988; *Recreations* ornithology, motorcycling, scuba diving; *Clubs* RAC; *Style*— David Byles, Esq; ✉ J Walter Thompson Co Ltd, Ave Ejercito National No 519, Colonia Granada, 11520 Mexico, DF

BYLLAM-BARNES, Joseph Charles Felix Byllam; s of Cyril Charles Byllam-Barnes (d 1976), of Boothby House, Ashtead, Surrey, and Barbara Isabel Mary, *née* Walls; *b* 30 Aug 1928; *Educ* The Modern Sch Streatham, Shaftesbury, City of London Freemen's Sch; *m* 1 April 1978, Maureen Margaret Mary, da of Maj Claude Montague Castle, MC (d 1940), of Hampstead, London; *Career* RAMC 1946–49, i/c Mil and Public Health Servs Eritrea 1948–49; with Barclays Bank plc 1945–92 (Head Office inspr 1976–92); banking law conslt 1992–; pres Farringdon Ward Club 1990–91; vice pres and hon sec Royal Soc of St George City of London Branch (chm 1994–95); memb: Cncl City Livery Club, Governing Body United Wards Club of the City of London, Castle Baynards Ward Club, Guild of Freemen of the City of London (Ct of Assts 1990), Hon Artillery Co, Royal United Servs Inst for Defence Studies; hon sec Ward of Cheap Club; Oblate Quarr Abbey 1963; Freeman: City of London 1983, Worshipful Co of Upholders 1984 (treas 1985, memb Ct of Assts 1986, Master 1993–94); Liveryman Worshipful Co of Fletchers 1995; FCIB, FFA, FRSA; *Recreations* music, opera, walking, study of law and theology; *Clubs* Carlton, Guards' Polo, City Livery Yacht (ctee memb), Surrey CCC; *Style*— Joseph Byllam-Barnes, Esq; ✉ Walsingham House, Oldfield Gardens, Ashtead, Surrey KT21 2NA (☎ 01372 277667, fax 01372 271533)

BYNG, Julian Michael Edmund; assumed surname of Byng by Deed Poll 1952 in lieu of his patronymic, and was granted Royal Licence to bear the arms of Byng 1969 in accordance with the will of his grandfather the 6th Earl of Stafford; s of Capt Michael William Millicent Lafone (d 1966), of Lusaka Turf Club, N Rhodesia, by his first w, Lady (Florence) Elizabeth Alice Byng (resumed her maiden surname by Deed Poll 1952, in accordance with her father's will and d 1987), elder da of 6 Earl of Strafford; descended from Adm Sir George Byng (1 Viscount Torrington), Hon Robert Byng (Govr of Barbados), and FM Sir John Byng (1 Earl of Strafford, Col of Coldstream Gds and Cdr of Gds Bde at Waterloo); *b* 20 Oct 1928; *Educ* Eton, Lausanne Univ, King's Coll Cambridge; *m* 28 Oct 1960, Eve Finola, da of Captain Michael St Maur Wellesley-Wesley (d 1982), of Doon, Tahilla, Co Kerry; 3 s (Robert b 1962, Patrick b 1965, Thomas b 1970), 1 da (Georgiana (Mrs Piers Monckton) b 1964); *Career* called to the Bar Inner Temple 1954; farmer, thoroughbred breeder, landowner (in excess of 1000 acres); chm Herts branch Country Landowners' Assoc 1970–73; *Recreations* shooting, skiing, flying, racing; *Clubs* Brooks's, Pratt's, Jockey (Paris), Cercle de Deauville; *Style*— Julian Byng, Esq; ✉ 15A Chemin Rieu, Geneva 1208, Switzerland (☎ 00 41 22 789 0038, fax 00 41 22 789 0845)

BYRD, (Joseph) Alton; s of Oscar Byrd (d 1974), of San Francisco, and Clarine, *née* Bradford; *b* 3 Nov 1957; *Educ* St Dominic's GS San Francisco, Riordan HS San Francisco, Columbia Univ NY; *m* 3 Dec 1983, Joni, da of Roy Williams; 1 da (Alana Theresa b 18 Aug 1985), 1 s (Miles David b 13 May 1990); *Career* basketball player: clubs: Crystal Palace 1979–82, Murray International Edinburgh 1982–87, Manchester Utd 1987–88 (capt 1987–88), Kingston 1988–92, Guildford Kings 1992–94, Crystal Palace 1994–; honours incl: Nat League Player of the Year 1980 and 1981, Most Valuable Player Nat Cup and Wembley Play off 1980, 1981 and 1982, Scot League Player of the Year 1982–87, Carlsberg Player of the Year 1991 and 1992, quarter-finalist Euro Cup 1982, 1988 and 1991, Cwlth Gold medallist 1992; rep: England 1990–, GB at Olympic Games 1992; fndr and owner Alton Byrd Associates; *Style*— J Alton Byrd, Esq; ✉ Alton Byrd Associates, Wimbledon Village Business Centre, Thornton House, Thornton Rd, London SW19 4NG (☎ 0181 944 6688, fax 0181 677 5210)

BYRD, Andy John; s of Peter George Byrd, of Beckford, nr Tewkesbury, Glos, and Doreen Hilda, *née* Harding; *b* 1 Sept 1951; *Educ* Univ of Bristol (BA, Postgrad Dip in Mktg and Advtg); *m* 12 July 1986, Claire, da of late Ken Mollart; 2 s (George Peter b 2 Sept 1989, Charles Andrew b 16 Dec 1991), 1 da (Annabel Lucy b 21 July 1995); *Career* Van Den Burghs & Jurgens 1974–77; DMB&B advtg: joined 1977, bd dir 1985–86, client servs dir 1986–91, memb Mgmnt Team 1986–, dep md 1990–; *Recreations* rugby, windsurfing, golf; *Clubs* RAC, Royal Wimbledon Golf, St Enodoc Golf; *Style*— Andy Byrd, Esq; ✉ D'Arcy Masius Benton & Bowles, 123 Buckingham Palace Road, London SW1W 9DZ (☎ 0171 630 0000, fax 0171 630 0033)

BYRNE, Anthony John; s of Benjamin James Byrne, of Dublin, and Ruby Anne, *née* O'Brien (d 1975); *b* 9 Aug 1947; *Educ* Oakham Sch Rutland, Univ of Lancaster, Univ of Colorado, Sidney Sussex Coll Cambridge; *m* 5 Sept 1971, Kathy, da of Carl Strain, of Denver, Colorado; 2 da (Rachel, Jenny); *Career* PA to gen mangr Central Lancs Devpt Corpn 1973–77, Inst of Advanced Architectural Studies Univ of York 1977–78, dir Bicentenary of the Iron Bridge Ironbridge Gorge Museum Tst 1978, project dir Watershed Media Centre Bristol 1980–83, dir Bristol Mktg Bd 1983–87, dir BAFTA 1987–94, dir of devpt Corpus Christi Coll Cambridge 1994–; chm Sci-Tech Film and TV Festivals 1987 and 1989; tstee: Brunel Tst Temple Meads Bristol, Vivat Tst, Wildscreen Tst; Parly candidate (Lab) Rutland and Stamford 1972–74; *Style*— Anthony Byrne, Esq; ✉ The Development Office, Corpus Christi College, Cambridge CB2 1RH (☎ 01223 338048)

BYRNE, John Edward Thomas; s of John Byrne (d 1979), and Violet Mary, *née* Harris; *b* 16 Feb 1935; *Educ* Kilkenny Coll, Mountjoy Sch Dublin, Trinity Coll Dublin (BA, MB BCh, BAO); *m* 23 Nov 1963, Margaret Elizabeth Ross, da of William Albert Wilson (d 1975); 2 da (Katharine b 1969, Johanna b 1971); *Career* house surgn and house physician Dr Steeven's Hosp Dublin 1961–62, fell in otology Wayne State Univ Detroit 1973, conslt in otolaryngology Belfast City Hosp 1974–; pres Irish Otolaryngological Soc 1994 (hon ed Proceedings 1974–93); external examiner to constituent colls Nat Univ of Ireland, examiner RCSI (otolaryngology), author of various pubns on blast injury to ears; memb: ORS, Irish Otolaryngological Soc, Ulster Med Soc, Br Cochlear Implant Gp, TCD Assoc; FRCSI 1970; *Books* Scott/Brown's Otolaryngology (contrib, 1987); *Recreations* sailing, maritime history, gardening, theatre; *Clubs* Strangford Lough Yacht; *Style*— John Byrne, Esq; ✉ Mulroy Lodge, Ballymenoch Park, Holywood, N Ireland BT18 0LP (☎ 01232 423374); Belfast City Hospital, Belfast BT9 7AB (☎ 01232 329241, fax 01232 313249)

BYRNE, John Napier; s of Christopher Thomas Byrne (d 1973), and Christian McDougall, *née* Napier; *b* 28 Aug 1953; *Educ* Bangor GS, Gonville and Caius Coll Cambridge (MA); *m* 16 May 1981, (Birgit) Marita, da of Arne Gotthard Westberg; 1 s (Daniel b 1986); *Career* admitted slr 1978; ptnr Freshfields 1985 (joined 1978); Freeman City of London Slrs Co; *Clubs* Lansdowne; *Style*— John Byrne, Esq; ✉ Fortuny 6–3, Madrid 28010, Spain

BYRNE, Patrick Philip; *Educ* O'Connell Sch Dublin; *Career* Ford Motor Co: various appts in the UK, Ireland and mainland Europe 1963–87, chm and md Ford Portugal 1977–81, md and vice chm Ford Spain 1981–87, rejoined gp 1991, dir Eastern Europe and export ops Ford of Europe Inc 1991–93, dir of sales Ford of Britain 1993–; with Waterford Wedgwood Group 1987–90: chm Waterford Wedgwood UK plc 1987–90, chief operating offr for Ireland and UK Waterford Wedgwood Group Jan-April 1989, gp chief exec Waterford Wedgwood plc 1989–90, chm and chief exec Wedgwood cos 1988–89, dir Waterford Wedgwood cos in Australia, USA, Japan and Singapore 1987–90; FIMI, CIMgt 1988; *Recreations* music, literature, golf; *Style*— Patrick P Byrne, Esq; ✉ Ford Motor Co Ltd, Eagle Way, Warley, Essex CM13 3BW (☎ 01277 253000, fax 01277 253349)

BYROM, Peter John; s of John Byrom (d 1988), and Mary, *née* Hinch; *b* 23 June 1944; *Educ* Perse Sch, Univ of Southampton (BSc); *m* 2 June 1987, Melanie Signe, da of John Palmer; 3 da (Nicola b 20 June 1987, Olivia b 31 March 1989, Serena Melanie b 1 Oct 1993); *Career* Arthur Andersen & Co 1966–72; dir: N M Rothschild & Sons Ltd 1972–, Adwest Group plc 1989–94, Peter Black Holdings plc 1984–; dep chm: T&N plc 1989–96, Domino Printing Sciences plc 1996–; chm Leeds Life Assurance Ltd 1994–96, dir China Investment Trust plc 1995–; govr Res into Ageing; Freeman City of London 1989, Liveryman Goldsmiths' Co 1993; FCA; *Clubs* Royal Lymington Yacht, Kandahar Ski; *Style*— Peter Byrom, Esq; ✉ Chalton Priory, Chalton, Hampshire PO8 0BG (☎ 01705 595181, fax 01705 596591)

BYROM, Richard John; JP (1973); s of Richard Byrom (d 1961), of Bury, and Bessie, *née* Jardin; *b* 12 Oct 1939; *Educ* Denstone Coll, Univ of Manchester (BA, MPhil); *m* 4 April 1964, Susan Hope, da of Richard Clegg (d 1984), of Gwydir; 2 s (Peter b 1965, David b 1967), 1 da (Joy b 1968); *Career* ptnr in private architectural practice 1964–, dir Byrom Clark Roberts Architects Surveyors and Consulting Engrs Manchester 1989–; practising arbitrator; ISVA: chm Building Surveying Ctee 1986–90, chm Manchester and Dist Branch 1995–; reader Hawkshaw Parish Church 1964–; memb: Manchester Soc of Architects, Soc of Construction Law; RIBA 1965, FCIArb 1977, FSVA 1976; *Recreations* industrial archaeology, antiquarian books; *Clubs* St James's (Manchester); *Style*— Richard J Byrom, Esq, JP; ✉ 3 Hawkshaw Lane, Bury, Lancs BL8 4JZ (☎ 0120 488 3110); Byrom Clark Roberts Ltd, The Building Centre, 117 Portland St, Manchester M1 6EH (☎ 0161 236 9601, fax 0161 236 8675)

BYRON, 13 Baron (E 1643); Robert James Byron; 2 (but only surviving) s of 12 Baron Byron (d 1989), and his 2 w, Dorigen Margaret, *née* Esdaile (d 1985); *b* 5 April 1950; *Educ* Wellington Coll, Trinity Coll Cambridge; *m* 1979, Robyn Margaret, da of John McLean, of Hamilton, NZ; 1 s (Hon Charles Richard Gordon b 1990), 3 da (Hon Caroline b 1981, Hon Emily b 1984, Hon Sophie b 1986); *Heir* s, Hon Charles Richard Gordon Byron b 28 July 1990; *Career* barr 1974; admitted slr 1978; ptnr Holman Fenwick & Willan 1984–; *Style*— The Rt Hon the Lord Byron; ✉ Holman Fenwick & Willan, Marlow House, Lloyds Avenue, London EC3N 3AL

BYRT, His Hon Judge (Henry) John; QC (1976); s of Albert Henry Byrt, CBE (d 1966), and Dorothy Muriel Thorne (d 1972); *b* 5 March 1929; *Educ* Charterhouse, Merton Coll Oxford; *m* 1957, Eve Hermione, da of Lt-Col Gordon McLaurin Bartlett (d 1964); 1 s (Charles b 1966), 2 da (Frances b 1962, Hermione b 1964); *Career* called to the Bar 1953, in practice SE Circuit, circuit judge (SE Circuit) 1983–; vice princ The Working Men's Coll 1978–82 (princ 1982–87, memb Corp 1978–); memb Cncl Queen's Coll Harley St 1981–; pres Social Security Appeal Tbnls and Med Appeal Tbnls 1983–90; *Clubs* Leander; *Style*— His Hon Judge John Byrt, QC; ✉ 65 Gloucester Crescent, London NW1 7EG (☎ 0171 485 0341); The Mayors and City of London Court, 32 Threadneedle Street, London EC2

BYSTRAM, Charles Anthony; s of Baron Cyprian Bystram, Col in Polish Army (d 1961), of London, and Sophia, *née* Smolicz (d 1978); *b* 23 Dec 1929; *Educ* Douai Sch, Univ of Cambridge (BA); *m* 11 Jan 1958, Jean Denise, da of Col Ian Hardie, DSO, RA (d 1977); 1 s (Michael b 1967), 2 da (Nicola b 1960, Antonia b 1963); *Career* Plant Protection Ltd (ICI plc): mgmnt trainee 1951–53, area export mangr 1953–57; gen mangr subsids Rank Organisation plc 1958–60, sr conslt McKinsey & Co 1960–65; United Biscuits (Holdings) plc: divnl md 1965–71, gp corp planning dir 1971–74, dir 1972–85, md Ortiz SA (subsid) 1974–76 (chm 1976–85), md United Biscuits International 1977–85, dir gp corp devpt 1980–83, dir gp res and devpt 1981–82, dir external affrs 1983–85; dir: Lu-Brun SA 1974–75, Lewmar plc 1985–87, Stakis plc 1987–93 (dep chm 1989–90); chm: Geest plc 1986–90, Spikes Cavell & Co 1992–96, ADAS 1992–96; memb Overseas Ctee CBI 1983–92, dep chm Liverpool Victoria Friendly Soc (Liverpool Victoria Insurance) 1992–; CIMgt 1987; *Recreations* travel, good food and wine, various sports; *Style*— Charles Bystram, Esq

C

CABLE, Sir James Eric; KCVO (1976), CMG (1967); s of Eric Grant Cable, CMG (d 1970), and Nellie Margaret, *née* Skelton; *b* 15 Nov 1920; *Educ* Stowe, CCC Cambridge; *m* 1954, Viveca, da of Dr Ragnar Hollmerus, of Helsinki; 1 s; *Career* served WWII Army 1941–46; HM Dip Serv: entered FO 1947, asst under sec of state FCO 1972–75, ambass to Finland 1975–80, ret; writer on int rels and naval affrs; *Style*— Sir James Cable, KCVO, CMG; ✉ 8 Essex Close, Cambridge CB4 2DW

CABLE-ALEXANDER, Lt-Col Sir Patrick Desmond William; 8 Bt (UK 1809), of the City of Dublin; s of Sir Desmond William Lionel Cable-Alexander, 7 Bt (d 1988), and his 1 w Mary Jane, *née* O'Brien; *b* 19 April 1936; *Educ* Downside, RMA Sandhurst; *m* 1, 1961 (m dis 1976), Diana Frances, eldest da of late Col Paul Heberden Rogers, of Bushey, Herts; 2 da (Melanie Jane b 1963, Louise Fenella b 1967); m 2, 1976, Jane Mary, da of Dr Anthony Arthur Gough Lewis, MD, of Benson, Oxon; 1 s (Fergus William Antony b 1981); *Heir* s, Fergus William Antony Cable-Alexander b 19 June 1981; *Career* former Lt-Col Royal Scots Dragoon Guards (Carabiniers and Greys), cmmnd 1956, serv BAOR, UK and Aden, Army Staff Coll 1967, asst mil attaché Saigon 1968–70, BAOR, MOD, Nat Def Coll 1975–76, cmd Duke of Lancaster's Own Yeo 1978–80, COS HQ NW Dist 1981–83, ret 1984; bursar and clerk Cncl Lancing Coll 1984–; *Recreations* the arts, painting, gardening, cricket, reading; *Style*— Lt-Col Sir Patrick Cable-Alexander, Bt; ✉ Windrush House, Hoe Court, Lancing, W Sussex BN15 0QX

CABORN, Richard George; MP (Lab) Sheffield Central (majority 17,294); s of George and Mary Caborn; *b* 6 Oct 1943; *Educ* Hurlfield Comprehensive Sch, Granville Coll of Further Education, Sheffield Polytechnic; *m* 1966, Margaret; 1 s, 1 da; *Career* engineer; convenor of shop stewards Firth Brown Ltd 1967–79; MP (Lab) Sheffield Central 1983–, MEP (Lab) Sheffield 1979–84; *Style*— Richard Caborn, Esq, MP; ✉ 29 Quarry Vale Rd, Sheffield (☎ 0114 239 3802); office: Barkers Pool House, Burgess Street, Sheffield S1 2HF (☎ 0114 273 7947)

CACOYANNIS, Michael; s of Sir Panayotis Cacoyannis (d 1980), and Angeliki, *née* Efthyvoulou (d 1982); *b* 11 June 1922; *Educ* Greek Gymnasium Limassol Cyprus, Central Sch of Dramatic Art; *Career* director stage and screen; called to the Bar Gray's Inn 1943, actor on English stage 1946–51; Order of Golden Phoenix (Greece) 1965, Commandeur Des Arts Et Des Lettres (France) 1986; Hon Doctorate Columbia Coll Chicago 1975, hon citizen Limassol Cyprus 1976; *Theatre* plays NY: The Trojan Women 1964, Things that go Bump in the Night 1965, The Devils 1966, Iphigenia in Aulis 1968, Lysistrata 1972, The Bacchae 1980, Zorba (musical) 1985; dir Oedipus Rex (Abbey Theatre Dublin); dir plays Paris: The Trojan Women 1965, Romeo and Juliet 1968, 7 + 7 1970, The Bacchae 1977; dir plays Greece incl: Miss Margarita 1975, The Glass Menagerie 1977, Antony and Cleopatra 1979, The Three Sisters 1981, Electra 1983, Naked 1989, Henceforward 1990, The Trojan Women 1995; dir opera: Mourning Becomes Electra (Met Opera NY) 1967, La Bohème (Juilliard NY) 1972, Clemenza di Tito (Aix-en-Provence, Strasbourg, Orleans 1988–89), La Traviata (Greece) 1983, Iphigenia in Aulis and Iphigenia in Tauris (Frankfurt State Opera) 1987, Medea (Greece) 1995; choreographed full length ballet to Theodorakis music (Greece) 1969; *Films* incl: Windfall in Athens 1954, Stella 1955, A Girl in Black 1956 (Golden Globe Award, Silver Bear Award), A Matter of Dignity 1958, Our Last Spring 1960, The Wastrel 1961, Electra 1962 (Cannes Grand Prix du Jury), Zorba the Greek 1964 (3 Oscars, Golden Globes), The Day The Fish Came Out 1967, The Trojan Women 1972, Attila '74 1975, Iphigenia 1977, Sweet Country 1986, Up Down and Sideways 1991; *Publications* translations into Greek incl: Antony and Cleopatra, Hamlet, Coriolanus; translation into English of Euripides' The Bacchae; *Recreations* swimming, painting; *Style*— Michael Cacoyannis, Esq; ✉ 15 Mouson St, Athens, 117–41, Greece (☎ 00 30 1 922 2054, fax 00 1 301 921 6483); 96 BD Montparnasse, Paris 75014, France (☎ 00 33 1 43 35 45 33)

CADBURY, Sir (George) Adrian Hayhurst; kt (1977); s of Laurence John Cadbury, OBE (d 1982), of Birmingham, and Joyce, *née* Mathews, OBE; *b* 15 April 1929; *Educ* Eton, King's Coll Cambridge (MA); *m* 1, 1956, Gillian Mary (d 1992), da of Edmund Drane Skepper (d 1962), of Neuilly-sur-Seine, France; 2 s (Benedict, Matthew), 1 da (Caroline); m 2, 1994, Susan Jacqueline, da of David Bowie Sinclair (d 1945); *Career* chm: Cadbury Group 1965–69, Cadbury Schweppes plc 1975–89 (dep chm and md 1969–74); dir: Bank of England 1970–94, IBM (UK) Ltd 1975–94; chm: W Mids Econ Planning Ctee 1967–70, CBI Econ and Financial Policy Ctee 1974–80, Food and Drink Industs Cncl 1981–83, PRO NED (orgn for promotion of non-exec dirs) 1984–95, Ctee on Financial Aspects of Corporate Governance (Cadbury Ctee) 1991–95; memb Covent Garden Market Authy 1974–89, chllr Aston Univ 1979–, pres Birmingham Chamber of Indust and Commerce 1988–89; Freeman City of Birmingham 1982; Hon DSc: Aston Univ 1973, Cranfield Inst 1985; Hon LLD: Univ of Bristol 1986, Univ of Birmingham 1989, Univ of Lancaster 1993, Univ of Cambridge 1994; Liveryman Worshipful Co of Grocers; CIMgt, FIPM, Hon FInstM; *Clubs* Athenaeum, Boodle's, Hawks' (Cambridge), Leander; *Style*— Sir Adrian Cadbury; ✉ Rising Sun House, Baker's Lane, Knowle, Solihull, W Midlands B93 8PT (fax 01564 771130)

CADBURY, Peter Egbert; s of Sir Egbert Cadbury, DSC, DFC, JP, DL (d 1967), and Mary Forbes, *née* Phillips (d 1968); gs of George Cadbury, founder of Cadbury Bros, Bournville; *b* 6 Feb 1918; *Educ* Leighton Park Sch, Trinity Coll Cambridge (MA); *m* 1, 13 Dec 1947 (m dis 1968), (Eugenie) Benedicta, da of late Maj Ewen Cameron Bruce, DSO, MC, of Montpelier Gardens, Cheltenham, and former w of St John Donn-Byrne; 1 s (Justin Peter b 13 April 1951), 1 da ((Eugenie Mary) Felicity (Mrs John Loudon) b 14 Dec 1948); m 2, 1970 (m dis 1976), Jennifer Victoria (now Mrs Jennifer d'Abo, *qv*), da of Maj Michael William Vernon Hammond-Maude, of Amerdale House, Arncliffe, Yorks, and former w of Capt David Gwyn Morgan-Jones, The Life Guards; 1 s (Joel Michael b 28 July 1971); m 3, 1976, Angela Jane, *née* Thoyts, former w of Humphrey Mead, of Moyaux, Normandy; 2 s (George, James); *Career* experimental test pilot 1941–45; Parly candidate (Lib) Stroud 1945; called to the Bar Inner Temple 1946, in practice until 1954; exec chm of various cos: Keith Prowse Ltd, Ashton & Mitchell, Alfred Hays 1954–71, Westward TV 1960–80, Air Westward 1976–78, Prowest Ltd, Preston Estates, George Cadbury Trust 1979– (chm), Westward Travel Ltd 1981–84, Educational Video Index Ltd 1982–85, Testworth Ltd (t/a Spycatcher, ProwlaWatch (CCTV) and VASCON (Video & Audio Surveillance Control)); Freeman City of London 1946, Liveryman Worshipful Co of Curriers 1946; *Recreations* flying (Cessna 340 'G-Pete', Helicopter (Squirrell 'G-Jany'), sailing (express 55' motor cruiser 'Colinette V'), golf, tennis, shooting, travelling, owner of racehorses (Cool Million, Egbert, Westward Lad, Westward Ho); *Clubs* MCC (hon life memb), Buck's, Royal Motor Yacht, RAF Yacht, Island Sailing, Royal Thames Yacht, The Academy, Special Forces, Hawks (Cambridge), Lord's Taverners'; *Style*— Peter Cadbury, Esq; ✉ Upton Grey Lodge, Upton Grey, nr Basingstoke, Hampshire RG25 2RE (☎ 01256 862374, fax 01256 862988, car 0836 220214)

CADBURY, Peter Hugh George; 3 s of (John) Christopher Cadbury, of Beaconwood, Rednal, nr Birmingham, by his 1 w, Honor Mary, *née* Milward (d 1957); *b* 8 June 1943; *Educ* Rugby; *m* 1969, Sally, er da of Peter Frederick Strouvelle, of Cape Town, S Africa; 1 s (Simon b 1975), 1 da (Eleanor b 1973); *Career* admitted slr; dep chm Deutsche Morgan Grenfell & Co Ltd, chm TR Smaller Companies Investment Trust plc; non-exec dir Lincoln National (UK) plc; dir and memb Exec Ctee UK-S Africa Business Assoc; FRSA; *Clubs* City of London; *Style*— Peter Cadbury, Esq; ✉ Deutsche Morgan Grenfell & Co Ltd, 23 Great Winchester St, London EC2N 2JA (☎ 0171 545 8000, fax 0171 545 6180)

CADDICK, Andrew Richard (Andy); *b* 21 Nov 1968; *Educ* Papanui HS Christchurch NZ; *m* 27 Jan 1995, Sarah; *Career* professional cricketer; rep NZ Youth World Cup 1987–88; Somerset CCC: debut 1991, awarded county cap 1992; England: debut 1992, A Team to Aust 1992–93, memb team v Australia 1993, touring W Indies 1993/94; 9 tests, 5 one day ints; Rapid Cricketline Player of the Year 1991; *Style*— Andy Caddick, Esq; ✉ c/o Somerset CCC, The County Ground, Taunton, Somerset TA1 1JT (☎ 01823 272946)

CADDY, David Henry Arnold Courtenay; s of Colonel John Caddy, of Highgate Village, London, and Elizabeth, *née* Day; *b* 22 June 1944; *Educ* Eton; *m* 24 July 1971, Valerie Elizabeth Margaret, da of Dr Kelly Swanston, of Helmsley, N Yorks; 1 s (Julian b 1972), 1 da (Henrietta b 1978); *Career* articled to Layton Bennett Billingham and Co London 1962–68, CA 1968; Coopers & Lybrand: joined 1968, ptnr Liberia 1974, managing ptnr Liberia 1974–77, ptnr UK 1977–, regnl ptnr i/c UK South and East 1993–; memb Ctee: London Soc of CAs 1980, Cncl of Partners Coopers & Lybrand 1989–, Bd of Coopers & Lybrand 1994–, ICAEW 1968–, ICA (Ghana) 1983–, ICA (Nigeria) 1983–; *Recreations* horse racing (owner), art, golf, swimming, walking, reading, theatre; *Clubs* Boodle's, Leander; *Style*— David Caddy, Esq; ✉ Ivy House, Highgate Hill, London N6 5HD (☎ 0181 340 9067); Coopers and Lybrand, Harman House, 1 George St, Uxbridge, Middx UB8 1QQ (☎ 01895 273305, fax 01895 256413, car 0820 913664)

CADE, David Patrick Gordon; s of Richard William Poole Cade, of Lyme Regis, Devon, and Mabel, *née* Lamb; *b* 17 Nov 1942; *Educ* The Leys Sch, Queens' Coll Cambridge (MA); *m* 18 June 1966, Julia Christine, *née* Cooper; 2 da (Heather b 1969, Angela b 1973); *Career* consult Arthur Andersen chartered accountants (ptnr 1976); FCA 1967; *Recreations* sailing, music; *Clubs* RAC, Sea View Yacht; *Style*— David Cade, Esq; ✉ Arthur Andersen, 1 Surrey Street, London WC2R 2PS (☎ 0171 438 3000)

CADELL, Vice Adm Sir John Frederick; KBE (1983); s of Henry Dunlop Mallock Cadell (d 1936), of York, and Elizabeth, *née* Vandyke (d 1989), of Faversham; *b* 6 Dec 1929; *Educ* BRNC Dartmouth, RNC Greenwich; *m* 15 Feb 1958, Jaquetta Bridget, da of Paterick Gould Nolan (d 1968); 1 s (Charles Henry b 1965), 2 da (Caroline Elizabeth b 1959, Alexandra Jane b 1961); *Career* Capt 3 Frigate Sqdn 1975, DG Naval Personal Servs 1980, COS to Cdr Naval Forces South 1982; dist and gen mangr Canterbury & Thanet Health Authy 1986–94; *Recreations* skiing, tennis, chess; *Style*— Vice Adm Sir John Cadell, KBE; ✉ Great Mongeham House, nr Deal, Kent CT14 0HD (☎ 01304 373658)

CADELL, Patrick Moubray; s of Henry Moubray Cadell (d 1967), and Christina Rose, *née* Nimmo; *b* 17 March 1941; *Educ* Merchiston Castle Sch, Trinity Coll Cambridge (BA), Toulouse Univ (Dip); *m* 3 August 1968, Sarah Margaret Florence, da of The Rev William Melville King; 1 da (Sophia Margaret (b 27 August 1970), 2 s (Alexander Moubray b 19 Nov 1973, William Melville b 19 May 1978); *Career* English language asst Ministère de l'Éducation Nationale France 1962–64, asst keeper Dept of Manuscripts British Museum 1966–68 (Information Serv 1964–66), keeper of manuscripts Nat Library of Scotland 1983–90 (asst keeper Dept of Manuscripts 1968–83), Keeper of the Records of Scotland 1991–; memb Soc of Archivists 1979–, pres Round Table of Int Cncl on Archives; FSAS 1980, FRHistS 1993; *Books* The Iron Mills at Cramond (1973), Sudden Slaughter - The Murder of the Regent Moray (pamphlet, 1975), Royal Visits to Scotland (1977), The Abbey Court and the High Constables of Holyrood (1983), The Eye of the Mind - The Scot and His Books exhbn catalogue (ed and main contrib, 1983), The Water of Leith (contrib, 1984), A Sense of Place (contrib, 1988), For the Encouragement of Learning - Scotland's National Library (ed and contrib, 1989), The County of West Lothian Vol XXI of The Third Statistical Account (ed and contrib, 1992); *Recreations* walking and the French language; *Style*— Patrick Cadell, Esq; ✉ Scottish Record Office, HM General Register House, Edinburgh EH1 3YY (☎ 0131 535 1312, fax 0131 535 1360)

CADELL OF GRANGE, William Archibald; DL (W Lothian 1982); s of Col Henry Moubray Cadell (d 1967), and Christina Rose Nimmo; descended from William Cadell, burgess of Haddington, b 1668, sr rep of the family of Cadell of Grange and Banton; *b* 9 March 1933; *Educ* Merchiston, Trinity Coll Cambridge (MA), London Poly (DipArch); *m* 1960, Mary-Jean Carmichael; 3 s (John b 1963, Patrick b 1965, Benjamin b 1972); *Career* architect in private practice (ret 1995); Nat Tst for Scot: memb Exec Ctee 1991–95, Curatorial Ctee 1991–, Buildings Ctee 1995–; cmmr the Royal Fine Art Cmmn for Scot 1992–; RIBA, FRIAS; *Style*— William Cadell of Grange, DL; ✉ Grange, Linlithgow, W Lothian EH49 7RH (☎ 01506 842946)

CADMAN, 3 Baron (1937 UK); John Anthony Cadman; s of 2 Baron Cadman (d 1966); *b* 3 July 1938; *Educ* Harrow, Selwyn Coll Cambridge, RAC Cirencester; *m* 1975, Janet, da of Arthur Hayes, of Morecambe; 2 s (Hon Nicholas, Hon Giles Oliver Richard b 5 Feb 1979); *Heir* s, Hon Nicholas Anthony James Cadman b 18 Nov 1977; *Career* farmer and restaurateur; *Style*— The Lord Cadman; ✉ c/o The House of Lords, London SW1A 0PW

CADOGAN, 7 Earl (1800 GB) William Gerald Charles Cadogan; MC (1943), DL (County of London 1958); also Baron Cadogan of Oakley (GB 1718), Viscount Chelsea (GB 1800), and Baron Oakley of Caversham (UK 1831); s of 6 Earl (d 1933), and Lilian, *née* Coxon (d 1973), who m 2, 1941, Lt-Col H E Hambro; the name Cadogan, of Welsh origin, was spelt Cadwgan to *c* 1600; *b* 13 Feb 1914; *Educ* Eton, Sandhurst; *m* 1, 1936 (m dis 1959), Hon Primrose Yarde-Buller, da of 3 Baron Churston and sis of Viscountess Camrose, Denise Lady Ebury (ex-w of 5 Baron) and Lydia, Duchess of Bedford (ex-w of 13 Duke); 1 s, 3 da; m 2, 1961, Cecilia, da of Lt-Col Henry K Hamilton-Wedderburn, OBE; *Heir* s, Viscount Chelsea; *Career* Capt Coldstream Guards (ret), Lt Col Royal Wiltshire Yeomanry (TA); patron of four livings; Mayor of Chelsea 1964, Pro Grand Master United Grand Lodge of Freemasons 1969–82; landowner; chm Cadogan Estates Ltd and subsidiaries 1935–92; *Style*— The Rt Hon the Earl Cadogan, MC, DL; ✉ 18 Cadogan Gardens, London SW3 2RP (☎ 0171 730 4567); Snaigow, Dunkeld, Perthshire PH8 0RD (☎ 01738 710223)

CAFFYN, Robert James Morris; s of Sir Sydney Morris Caffyn, CBE (d 1976), and Annie, *née* Dawson (d 1989); *b* 1 June 1935; *Educ* Eastbourne Coll, Peterhouse Cambridge (MA); *m* 1961, Gillian Mabel Ann, *née* Bailey; 1 s, 2 da; *Career* jt md Caffyns plc 1972–; hon treas: Free Church Federal Cncl 1976–82, Br Cncl of Churches 1982–90, Churches Together in England 1990–; FCA; *Style*— Robert Caffyn, Esq; ✉ Field House, Old Willingdon Rd, Friston, nr Eastbourne, E Sussex BN20 0AT (☎ 01323 423100)

CAHILL, Teresa Mary; da of Henry Daniel Cahill, of Rotherhithe (d 1948), and Florence, *née* Dallimore (d 1964); *b* 30 July 1944; *Educ* Notre Dame HS Southwark, Guildhall Sch of Music & Drama, London Opera Centre; *m* 1971 (m dis 1978), John Anthony Kiernander; *Career* opera and concert singer; Glyndebourne debut 1969, Covent Garden debut 1970, La Scala Milan 1976, Philadelphia Opera 1981, Liceo Barcelona 1991, specialising in Mozart & Strauss; concerts: all the London orchestras, Boston Symphony Orch, Chicago Symphony Orch, Vienna Festival 1983, Berlin Festival 1987, Rotterdam Philharmonic 1984, Hamburg Philharmonic 1985, West Deutscher Rundfunk Cologne 1985; promenade concerts BBC Radio & TV; recordings incl Elgar, Mozart, Strauss and Mahler for all major cos; recitals and concerts throughout Europe, USA and the Far East; examiner and vocal adjudicator Masterclasses, external examiner Univ of Reading 1992–, vocal conslt Univ of York 1994–; prof of singing: Royal Northern Coll of Music, Trinity Coll of Music, Guildhall Sch of Music and Drama; Silver medal Worshipful Co of Musicians, John Christie award 1970; AGSM, LRAM; *Recreations* cinema, theatre, travel, reading, collecting antique furniture; *Clubs* Royal Over-Seas League; *Style*— Miss Teresa Cahill; ✉ 65 Leyland Rd, London SE12 8DW

CAHN, Sir Albert Jonas; 2 Bt (UK 1934), of Stanford-upon-Soar, Co Nottingham; s of Sir Julien Cahn, 1 Bt (d 1944); *b* 27 June 1924; *Educ* Harrow; *m* 1948, Malka, da of Reuben Bluestone (d 1961); 2 s (Julien Michael b 1951, Edward John b 1959), 2 da (Madeleine Jane (Mrs Smith) b 1949, Valerie Janet (Mrs Perry Crosthwaite) b 1954); *Heir* s, Julien Michael Cahn, *qv*; *Career* former clinical dir The Elm Therapy Centre New Malden Surrey; *Style*— Sir Albert Cahn, Bt; ✉ 10 Edgecoombe Close, Warren Rd, Kingston upon Thames, Surrey (☎ 0181 942 6956)

CAHN, Andrew Thomas; s of Robert Wolfgang Cahn, of Cambridge, and Patricia Lois, *née* Hanson; *b* 1 April 1951; *Educ* Bedales, Trinity Coll Cambridge (BA); *m* 1976, Virginia, da of David Fordyce Beardshaw; 1 da (Jessica b 1983), 2 s (Thomas b 1986, Laurence b 1994); *Career* civil servant; MAFF 1973–76, FCO 1976–77, MAFF 1977–81 (private sec to Perm Sec 1977–78), first sec perm rep to EC (FCO) 1982–84, Cabinet of Lord Cockfield (as Vice-Pres of EC) 1985–88, MAFF 1988–92; princ private sec: to Chllr of Duchy of Lancaster 1992–94, to Min for Agric Fisheries and Food 1994–95; under sec Cabinet Office 1995–; non-exec dir Cadbury Ltd 1990–92; govr Bedales Sch 1993–; FRSA 1979; *Recreations* family, mountains, squash, reading; *Clubs* Royal Automobile; *Style*— Andrew Cahn, Esq; ✉ European Secretariat, Cabinet Office, 70 Whitehall, London SW1A 2AS (☎ 0171 270 0177, fax 0171 270 0122)

CAHN, Julien Michael; s and h of Sir Albert Jonas Cahn, 2 Bt, *qv*; *b* 15 Jan 1951; *Educ* Harrow; *m* 1987, Marilynne Janelle, da of Frank Owen Blyth; 1 s (Benjamin Albert b 28 Feb 1988), 1 da (Jessie Laura b 1976); *Style*— Julien Cahn, Esq; ✉ 1 Court Hope Villas, Wimbledon, London SW19

CAILLARD, Air Vice-Marshal (Hugh) Anthony; CB (1981); s of Col Felix Caillard, MC (d 1955), and Monica Yoland (d 1991), yr da of Count Riccardi-Cubitt; *b* 16 April 1927; *Educ* Downside, Oriel Coll Oxford, RAF Coll Cranwell; *m* 20 Aug 1957, Margaret Ann, da of late Kenneth Malcolm Crawford, of Palm Beach, NSW, Australia; 4 s (Richard b 1958, Andrew b 1959, David b 1961, John b 1963); *Career* RAF 1945–82, ret as dir of Ops Central Region Air Forces NATO; dir gen Br Australia Soc 1982–89; air advsr House of Commons Defence Ctee 1985–92; chm: Ex-Servs Fellowship Centres 1987–93, Ex-Servs Mental Welfare Soc 1990–93; memb Grants and Appeals Ctee RAF Benevolent Fund 1988–93; *Recreations* yachting; *Clubs* RAF, Union (Sydney); *Style*— Air Vice-Marshal Anthony Caillard, CB; ✉ 58 Hilltop Road, Clareville 2107, New South Wales, Australia

CAIN, John Clifford; s of William John Cain (d 1940), and Florence Jessie, *née* Wood (d 1975); *b* 2 April 1924; *Educ* Emanuel Sch, Univ of London (BSc, MSc), Open Univ (BA, PhD 1996); *m* 1954, Shirley Jean, da of Edward Arthur Roberts, of Brierley Hill, W Midlands; 2 da (Charlotte, Susannah); *Career* RAF Aircrew Flt Sgt 1943–47; mathematics and sci teacher 1950–59, sci museum lectr 1959–61, asst head Sch of Bdcasting Assoc Rediffusion 1961–63, prodr and sr prodr BBC 1963–71, asst head Further Educn Television BBC 1971–72 (head 1972–77), asst controller Educnl Broadcasting 1977–80, controller Public Affrs BBC 1981–84, res historian BBC 1984–92; Bdcasting Support Servs: chm 1980–85, tstee 1980–89, hon vice pres 1989–; memb Health Educn Cncl 1978–83, dir Bdcasters Audience Res Bd 1982–84; memb: Royal Television Soc; FRSA; *Books* Talking Machines (1961), Mathematics Miscellany (jtly, 1966), Culture, Education and the State (contrib, 1988), The BBC - 70 Years of Broadcasting (1992), In a Class of Its Own - BBC Education 1924–94 (co-author, 1994), numerous articles, obits and reviews; *Recreations* reading, music, gardening, theatre, research; *Style*— John Cain, Esq; ✉ 63 Park Rd, London W4 3EY (☎ 0181 994 2712)

CAIN, (Thomas) William; QC (1989); s of James Arthur Cain (d 1956), of IOM, and Mary Edith Cunningham Robertson, *née* Lamb (d 1965); *b* 1 June 1935; *Educ* Marlborough, Worcester Coll Oxford (BA, MA); *m* 25 Nov 1961, Felicity Jane, da of Rev Arthur Stephen Gregory (d 1989); 2 s (Patrick Arthur b 18 June 1964, Simon Thomas Hugh b 10 July 1966), 1 da (Joanna Penelope b 14 Jan 1963); *Career* Nat Serv RAC 1953–55, cmmnd 2 Lt 1954, served Middle East 1954–55; called to the Bar Gray's Inn 1959, advocate Manx Bar with TW Cain & Sons Douglas IOM 1961–79, HM Attorney Gen IOM 1980–93, second deemster IOM 1993–; pres IOM Law Soc 1985–89, chm Manx Nature Conservation Tst 1973–, pres Friends of Manx Youth Orchestra; *Recreations* sailing; *Clubs* Ellan Vannin; *Style*— William Cain, Esq, QC; ✉ Ivie Cottage, Kirk Michael, IOM IM6 1AU (☎ 01624 878266); General Registry, Finch Road, Douglas, IOM (☎ 01624 685242)

CAINE, Sir Michael Harris; kt (1988); o s of Sir Sydney Caine, KCMG (d 1991), and his 1 w, Muriel Ann, *née* Harris (d 1962); *b* 17 June 1927; *Educ* Bedales Sch, Lincoln Coll Oxford (BA), George Washington Univ Washington DC; *m* 1, 30 Aug 1952 (m dis 1987), Janice Denise, *née* Mercer; 1 s (Richard Jonathan Harris b 24 Nov 1955), 1 da (Amanda b 7 Feb 1954); m 2, 9 May 1987, Emma Harriet Nicholson, MP, *qv*, da of Sir Godfrey Nicholson, 1 Bt (d 1991); *Career* RNAS 1945–47; chm Booker plc 1979–93 (joined 1952, dir 1964, chief exec 1975–84); non-exec dir Booker Tate 1993–; dep chm The Cwlth Equity Fund 1990–94, chm Africa Emerging Markets Fund 1993–, dir International Pepsi-Cola Bottlers Investments Ltd 1996–; chm: Mgmnt Ctee Booker Prize for Fiction 1972–95, Cncl for Tech Educn and Trg for Overseas Countries (TETOC) 1973–75, UK Cncl for Overseas Student Affrs 1979–93, Royal African Soc 1984–96 (pres 1996–), Cwlth Scholarship Cmmn in UK 1987–96, The One World Bdcasting Tst 1987–96, FiveTV 1991–, Africa '95 1993–, Africa Centre 1996–; dep chm: Cwlth Devpt Corp 1989–94 (dir 1985–94), Artisan Tst 1992–; memb: Governing Body Inst of Devpt Studies Sussex 1975, Nat Inst of Econ and Social Res 1979–, Queen Elizabeth House Oxford 1983–95, IBA 1984–89; govr Cwlth Inst 1993–; CIMgt, FRSA; *Recreations* reading, gardening; *Clubs* Reform; *Style*— Sir Michael Caine; ✉ Booker plc, Portland House, Stag Place, London SW1E 5AY (☎ 0171 411 5500, fax 0171 411 5555)

CAINE, Michael (né Maurice Joseph Micklewhite); CBE (1992); s of late Maurice Micklewhite, and Ellen Frances Marie Micklewhite; *b* 14 March 1933; *Educ* Wilson's GS Peckham; *m* 1, 1955 (m dis), Patricia Haines; 1 da; m 2, 1973, Shakira Baksh; 1 da; *Career* actor; served Army Berlin and Korea 1951–53; asst stage mangr Westminster Repertory Horsham Sussex 1953, actor Lowestoft Repertory 1953–55, Theatre Workshop London 1955, numerous TV appearances 1957–63; *Films* incl: A Hill in Korea 1956, How to Murder a Rich Uncle 1958, Zulu 1964, The Ipcress File 1965, Alfie 1966, The Wrong Box 1966, Gambit 1966, Hurry Sundown 1967, Woman Times Seven 1967, Deadfall 1967, The Magus 1968, Battle of Britain 1968, Play Dirty 1968, The Italian Job 1969, Too Late the Hero 1970, The Last Valley 1971, Get Carter 1971, Zee & Co 1972, Kidnapped 1972, Pulp 1972, Sleuth 1973, The Black Windmill 1974, Marseilles Contract 1974, The Wilby Conspiracy 1974, Fat Chance 1975, The Romantic Englishwoman 1975, The Man who would be King 1975, Harry and Walter Go to New York 1975, The Eagle Has Landed 1976, A Bridge Too Far 1976, Silver Bears 1976, The Swarm 1977, California Suite 1978, Ashanti 1979, Beyond The Poseidon Adventure 1979, The Island 1979, Dressed to Kill 1979, Escape to Victory 1980, Death Trap 1981, Jigsaw Man 1982, Educating Rita 1982, The Honorary Consul 1982, Blame it on Rio 1984, Water 1985, The Holcroft Covenant 1985, Mona Lisa 1986, The Fourth Protocol 1987, The Whistle Blower 1987, Surrender 1987, Jaws The Revenge 1987, Without a Clue 1988, Dirty Rotten Scoundrels 1988, Bullseye 1989, Mr Destiny 1990, A Shock to the System 1990, Noises Off 1992, Blue Ice 1992, The Muppets Christmas Carol 1992, On Deadly Ground 1994, Bullet to Beijing 1994, Blood and Wine 1995, 20,000 Leagues under the Sea 1996; films for TV: Jack The Ripper 1988, Jekyll and Hyde 1989, Then There Were Giants 1993, World War II: When Lions Roared 1994, One Man One Vote 1996; *Books* Not Many People Know That (1985), Not Many People Know This Either (1986), Moving Picture Show (1988), Acting In Film (1990), What's It All About? (autobiography, 1992); *Recreations* cinema, theatre, travel, gardening; *Style*— Michael Caine, Esq, CBE; ✉ c/o Dennis Sellinger, ICM Ltd, Oxford House, 76 Oxford Street, London W1N 0AX (☎ 0171 636 6565, fax 0171 323 0101)

CAIRD, Rt Rev Donald Arthur Richard; s of George Robert Caird (d 1966), and Emily Florence, *née* Dreaper (d 1961); *b* 11 Dec 1925, Dublin; *Educ* privately, Wesley Coll Dublin, Trinity Coll Dublin (sr exhibitioner, scholar of the house, MA, DD, HDipEd, Semitic Languages prize, Kyle prize, Mental and Moral Sci prize, Lilian Mary Luce prize for Berkelian Philosophy); *m* 12 Jan 1963, Nancy Ballantyne, o da of Prof William Sharpe, MD, and Gwendoline Wolfe, of NY; 2 da (Dr Ann Ballantyne Caird b 18 Feb 1967, Helen Charlotte b 24 Jan 1972), 1 s (Dr John Dudley Dreaper Caird b 18 Feb 1967); *Career* ordained: deacon 1950, priest 1951, bishop 1970; curate St Mark's Church Belfast 1950–53, asst master and chaplain Portora Royal Sch Enniskillen 1953–57, lectr in philosophy St David's UC Lampeter Wales 1957, rector Rathmichael PC Dublin 1960, asst master St Columba's Coll Dublin 1960–67, lectr in philosophy of religion Theol Coll Dublin 1962–63, asst lectr in philosophy Trinity Coll Dublin 1962–63, dean of Ossory 1969–70, bishop of Limerick, Ardfert and Aghadoe 1970–76, bishop of Meath and Kildare 1976–85, archbishop of Dublin, bishop of Glendalough and primate of Ireland and Metropolitan 1985–96; chm: Mgmnt Ctee Church of Ireland Theol Coll, Clergy Daughters' Sch Tst, Cmmn for the Care of the Elderly, Bd of Tstees and Govrs Marsh's Library, Church of Ireland Youth Cncl 1971–81, Cncl Alexandra Coll, Bd Church of Ireland Coll of Educn; patron: Nat Fedn of Youth Clubs, Moun Temple Comp Sch, E Glendalough Sch, Newpark Comp Sch; memb Bd: Thomond Coll Limerick, Siamsa Tire (The Irish Nat Theatre), na Gaeilge (Govt Bd for Promotion of Irish Language), St Patrick's Hosp Dublin, Rotunda Hosp, Kings' Hosp Sch, Wilson's Hosp Sch; mangr Colaiste Moibhi (Irish Speaking Coll); memb RTE Review Ctee 1971–74; fell Columba's Coll Dublin 1972; Hon DD Trinity Coll Dublin 1988; Hon LLD: Nat Cncl for Educn Awards 1993, Nat Univ of Ireland 1995; *Books* Directions (1970); *Recreations* reading, walking, swimming, cycling, painting; *Clubs* Kildare Street and University; *Style*— The Rt Rev D A R Caird; ✉ c/o Dublin and Glendalough Diocesan Office, Church of Ireland House, Church Avenue, Rathmines, Dublin 6, Ireland (00 353 1 4966981)

CAIRD, George; s of George Bradford Caird (d 1984), and Viola Mary, *née* Newport; *b* 30 Aug 1950; *Educ* Magdalen Coll Sch Oxford, RAM (LRAM, ARCM), Nordwestdeutsche Musikakademie Detmold, Peterhouse Cambridge (BA, MA); *m* 1974, Sarah Verney; 3 s (Adam Benjamin b 23 April 1977, Oliver Ralph b 22 June 1978, Edmund George b 4 July 1989), 1 da (Iona Katharine Mary b 10 July 1991); *Career* freelance oboist 1972–, memb Albion Ensemble 1976–, memb Acad of St Martin-in-the-Fields 1984–92; RAM: prof 1984–93, head Woodwind 1987–93, head Instrumental Studies 1990–93; princ Birmingham Conservatoire Univ of Central England 1993–; memb: Exec Incorporated Soc 1994, Royal Soc of Musicians 1996; tstee The Rivendell Tst 1976–, memb Ctee Br Double Reed Soc, memb Nat Youth Orch; FRAM 1989 (ARAM 1985), FRSA 1993; *Recordings* incl: Mozart and Beethoven Quintets (Albion Ensemble) 1981, Kenneth Leighton Veris Gratia 1986, Mozart Serenade K361 (Albion Ensemble) 1989; *Recreations* reading, theatre, languages, travel, sport, children; *Style*— Professor George Caird; ✉ Birmingham Conservatoire, Paradise Place, Birmingham B3 3HG (☎ 0121 331 5910, fax 0121 331 5906, e-mail georgecaird@uce.ac.uk)

CAIRD, John Newport; s of late Rev George Bradford Caird and Viola Mary, *née* Newport; *b* 22 Sept 1948; *Educ* Selwyn House Sch Montreal, Magdalen Coll Sch Oxford, Bristol Old Vic Theatre Sch; *m* 1, 1972 (m dis 1982), Helen Frances Brammer; m 2, 1982 (m dis 1990), Ann Dorzynski; 2 s, 1 da; m 3, 1990, Frances Ruffelle; 1 s, 1 da; *Career* theatre director; hon assoc dir RSC 1990–, chm Facing the Music (6th Birmingham Theatre Conference at Univ of Birmingham) 1995, fell Welsh Coll of Music and Drama; *Theatre* assoc dir Contact Theatre Manchester 1974–76: Look Back in Anger, Downright Hooligan, Krapp's Last Tape, Twelfth Night; resident dir RSC 1977–82: Dance of Death 1977, Savage Amusement 1978, Look Out Here Comes Trouble 1978, Caucasian Chalk Circle 1979, Nicholas Nickleby (co-dir with Trevor Nunn in London, NY and LA) 1980, 1982 and 1986, Naked Robots 1981, Twin Rivals 1981, Our Friends in the North 1982, Peter Pan (co-dir with Trevor Nunn) 1982–84; assoc dir RSC 1982–90: Twelfth Night 1983, Romeo and Juliet 1983, The Merchant of Venice 1984, Red Star 1984, Philistines 1985, Les Miserables (co-dir with Trevor Nunn in London, Washington, NY, Boston, Oslo, LA, Tokyo, Sydney and Paris) 1985–92, Every Man in His Humour 1986, Misalliance 1986, A Question of Geography 1987, The New Inn 1987, As You Like it 1989, A Midsummer Night's Dream 1989, The Beggar's Opera 1992, Columbus and the Discovery of Japan 1992, Antony and Cleopatra 1992; dir: Song and Dance (London) 1982, As You Like It (Stockholm, for TV 1985) 1984, Siegfried & Roy Show (Las Vegas) 1989, Zaïde 1991, The Beggar's Opera (RSC, Barbican) 1993, Trelawny of the Wells (RNT) 1993, Life Sentences (Second Stage Theatre NY) 1993, The Seagull (RNT) 1994, Watch your Step (Her Majesty's Theatre fundraiser) 1995, Henry IV (also adaptor for BBC) 1995, The Millionairess (UK tour) 1995, Stanley (RNT) 1996, Jane Eyre (Toronto) 1996; script writer: Beethoven, The Kingdom of the Spirit (a concert for a actor and string quartet) 1986; writer and dir Children of Eden (with music and lyrics by Stephen Schwartz) 1991, *Awards* SWET Award 1980, Tony Award for Best Dir 1982 (both for Nicholas Nickleby); Tony Award for Best Dir 1986 and 1987 (for Les Miserables); *Style—* John Caird, Esq; ✉ Church House, 10 South Grove, Highgate, London N6 6BS (☎ 0181 348 1996, fax 0181 340 5030)

CAIRD, Richard Francis; s of Prof Francis Irvine Caird, of Oxford, and Angela Margaret Alsop (d 1983); *b* 20 Jan 1958; *Educ* Glasgow Acad, New Coll Oxford (BA Jurisprudence), Coll of Law Guildford; *m* 1985, Helen Vanessa, da of Anthony Simpson; 1 da (Julia Margaret b 1 July 1989), 1 s (James Francis b 27 Jan 1992); *Career* articled clerk Radcliffes & Co 1980–82; Wilde Sapte: asst slr 1983–87, ptnr 1987–, head Litigation Dept 1994–; memb Law Soc; *Recreations* sport, theatre, reading; *Style—* Richard Caird, Esq; ✉ Wilde Sapte, 1 Fleet Place, London EC4M 7WS (☎ 0171 246 7000, fax 0171 246 7777)

CAIRNCROSS, Sir Alexander Kirkland (Alec); KCMG (1967, CMG 1950); 3 s of Alexander Kirkland Cairncross (d 1948), of Lesmahagow, Lanark, and Elizabeth Andrew Cairncross; *b* 11 Feb 1911; *Educ* Hamilton Acad, Univ of Glasgow, Univ of Cambridge (PhD); *m* 1943, Mary Frances, da of Maj Edward Francis Glynn, TD (d 1948), of Ilkley; 3 s, 2 da; *Career* univ lectr 1935–39, civil servant 1940–46, memb of staff of The Economist 1946, econ advsr to: BoT 1946–49, Organisation for European Econ Cooperation 1949–50; prof of applied economics Univ of Glasgow 1951–61, dir of Econ Development Inst Washington DC 1955–56, econ advsr to HM Govt 1961–64, head Govt Econ Serv 1964–69; master St Peter's Coll Oxford 1969–78, pres GPDST 1972–92, chllr Univ of Glasgow 1972–96; pres: Royal Economic Soc 1968–70, Br Assoc for the Advancement of Sci 1971; hon memb American Acad of Arts and Sci, Hon FRSE; FBA 1961; *Books include* Introduction to Economics (1944, 6th edn 1982), Home and Foreign Investment 1870–1913 (1953), Monetary Policy in a Mixed Economy (1960), Factors in Economic Development (1962), Snatches (1980), Years of Recovery (1985), The Price of War (1986), Economics and Economic Policy (1986), A Country to Play With (1987), Planning In Wartime (1991), The British Economy since 1945 (1992, 2 edn 1995), Austin Robinson: the life of an economic adviser (1993), Economic Ideas and Government Policy (1995), Managing the British Economy in the 1960's (1996), The Wilson Years (1996); *Recreations* travelling, writing; *Style—* Sir Alec Cairncross, KCMG, FBA; ✉ 14 Staverton Rd, Oxford (☎ 01865 552358)

CAIRNCROSS, Frances Anne; *see:* McRae, Frances Anne

CAIRNCROSS, Neil Francis; CB (1971); s of James Cairncross (d 1964), and Olive Hunter, *née* Amner (d 1969); *b* 29 July 1920; *Educ* Charterhouse, Oriel Coll Oxford (MA); *m* 26 July 1947, Eleanor Elizabeth, da of Herbert Walter Leisten (d 1927); 2 s (Ian b 1950, David b 1951), 1 da (Julia (Mrs Wallace) b 1948); *Career* serv in Royal Sussex Regt 1940–45; called to the Bar Lincoln's Inn 1948; joined Home Office 1948, a private sec to Prime Minister 1955–58, sec Royal Cmmn on the Press 1961–62, dep sec Cabinet Office 1970–72, dep sec NI Office 1972, dep under sec of state Home Office 1972–80; memb: Parole Bd 1982–85, Home Grown Timber Advsy Ctee 1981–90, Avon Probation Ctee (co-opted) 1983–89; *Recreations* painting; *Clubs* Utd Oxford and Cambridge Univ; *Style—* Neil Cairncross, Esq, CB; ✉ Little Grange, The Green, Olveston, Bristol BS12 3EJ (☎ 01454 613060)

CAIRNES, (Simon) Paul Steven; s of Edward Michael Hornby Cairnes, and Audrey Mary, *née* Stevens; *b* 19 Dec 1957; *Educ* Christ Coll Brecon, UCW Aberystwyth (LLB); *Career* called to the Bar Gray's Inn 1980 (NSW Aust 1989); memb Barrs Euro Gp 1989–; *Recreations* sailing, skiing, music, travelling; *Style—* Paul Cairnes, Esq; ✉ 3 Paper Buildings, Temple, London EC4Y 7EU (☎ 0171 353 8192, fax 0171 353 6271)

CAIRNS, Hon (Hugh) Andrew David; yr s of 5 Earl Cairns, GCVO, CB (d 1989); *b* 27 Aug 1942; *Educ* Wellington, Trinity Coll Dublin (BA); *m* 1966, (Cella) Elizabeth Mary, da of Lt-Col Francis Cecil Leonard Bell, DSO, MC, TD, of Cross Glades, Chiddingfold, Surrey; 1 s, 1 da; *Career* banker; regnl dir Barclays Bank PLC; dir United Services Tstee; chm Tay Salmon Fisheries Company Limited; Liveryman Worshipful Co of Fishmongers; *Recreations* shooting, fishing, golf; *Clubs* Pratt's, Royal St George's Golf; *Style—* The Hon Andrew Cairns; ✉ Knowle Hill Farm, Ulcombe, nr Maidstone, Kent (☎ 01622 850240); Barclays Bank PLC, North London & Luton Regional Office, Eagle Point, 1 Capability Green, Luton LU1 3LQ

CAIRNS, Christine Wilson; da of late Thomas Cairns, of Saltcoats, Scotland, and late Christine Dawson Galloway, *née* Wilson; *b* 11 Feb 1959; *Educ* Ardrossan Acad, RSAMD; *m* 13 July 1991, John David Peter Lubbock, *qv*, s of Michael Ronald Lubbock; 2 s (Adam Thomas b 28 Nov 1991, Alexander Michael b 30 June 1993); *Career* mezzo-soprano; performed with orchs incl: LA Philharmonic, London Philharmonic, Royal Philharmonic, LSO, Vienna Philharmonic, BBC Scottish, Cleveland and Philadelphia Orchs, Euro Community Youth Orch; worked with conductors incl: Sir Colin Davis, André Previn, Vladimir Ashkenazy, Yuri Temirkanov, Simon Rattle, Christoph von Dohnányi, John Lubbock; *Recordings* incl: Mendelssohn's Midsummer Night's Dream (with André Previn and the Vienna Philharmonic) 1986, Prokofiev's Alexander Nevsky (with André Previn and the LA Philharmonic) 1986, Mendelssohn's Die Erste Walpurgisnacht (with Christoph von Dohnányi and the Cleveland Orch) 1988; *Style—* Ms Christine Cairns; ✉ c/o Harrison/Parrott Ltd, 12 Penzance Place, London W11 4PA (☎ 0171 229 9166, fax 0171 221 5042)

CAIRNS, David Howard; OBE (1995); s of David Lauder Cairns, of Birmingham, and Edith, *née* Rose; *b* 4 June 1946; *Educ* Cheadle Hulme Sch, LSE (MSc); *m* 1 May 1980, Stella Jane, da of Stanley Cecil Askew, DSO, DFC (d 1996); *Career* CA; Pannell Kerr Forster 1964–71, Carlsberg Brewery Ltd 1971–72, Black & Decker Ltd 1972–75, PD Leake fell LSE 1973–75, ptnr Stoy Hayward 1975–85, sec gen Int Accounting Standards Ctee 1985–94, dir Int Fin Reporting Gp 1995–; ed Financial Times World Accounting Report 1997–; visiting fell LSE 1995–; memb: Bd of Govrs Int Capital Markets Gp 1993–94, Advsy Bd Centre for Int Accounting Res Univ of Hull 1993–; pres Thames Valley Soc of CAs 1979–80; FCA 1974 (ACA), FIMgt 1982, FRSA 1996; *Books* Current Cost Accounting after Sandilands (1976), Financial Times Survey of 100 Major European Companies Reports and Accounts (1979), Financial Times World Survey of Annual Reports (1980), Survey of Accounts and Accountants (1983–84), A Guide to Applying International Accounting Standards (1995); *Recreations* cricket, collecting contemporary British paintings, music; *Clubs* RAC; *Style—* David Cairns, Esq, OBE; ✉ Bramblewood, Turville Heath, Henley-on-Thames, Oxon RG9 6JY (☎ and fax 01491 638296)

CAIRNS, The Hon Mrs Andrew Cairns; (Cecilia) Elizabeth Mary; da of Lt-Col Francis Cecil Leonard Bell, DSO, MC, TD, of Cross Glades, Chiddingfold, Surrey, and Mary Wynne, *née* Jacob; *b* 14 Sept 1943; *Educ* Priors Field Godalming Surrey, Trinity Coll Dublin (BA, LLB); *m* 22 Oct 1966, Hon (Hugh) Andrew David, s of Rear Adm The Earl Cairns, GCVO, CB (d 1989); 1 s (Bertie b 28 Jan 1972), 1 da (Katherine b 27 June 1974); *Career* Charity Commission 1972–78; ptnr Jaques and Lewis 1984–90; specialist in charity law; *Books* Charities: Law and Practice (1988), Fundraising for Charity (1996); *Recreations* gardening, fishing; *Style—* The Hon Mrs Andrew Cairns; ✉ Knowle Hill Farm, Ulcombe, Maidstone, Kent ME17 1ES (☎ 01622 850240)

CAIRNS, Air Vice-Marshal Geoffrey Crerar; CBE (1970), AFC (1960); s of James William Cairns (d 1949), and Marion, *née* Crerar (d 1993); *b* 21 May 1926; *Educ* Loretto, Gonville and Caius Coll Cambridge; *m* 1948, Carol (d 1985), da of Ivan Evernden (d 1979); 4 da (Madeline b 1949, Claudia b 1952, Catherine b 1960, Eliza b 1964); *Career* RAF 1944–80 (AVM), Cmdt A & AEE Boscombe Down 1971–74, Asst Chief of Air Staff (Operational Requirements) 1975–76, Cmdt Southern Maritime Air Region 1976–77, Chief of Staff 18 Gp 1978–80; def conslt Marconi Avionics Ltd 1980–81; dir: Trago Aircraft Ltd 1982–88, ORCA Aircraft Ltd 1988–89; conslt FLS Aerospace (Lovaux Ltd) 1991–; FRAeS 1979, FBIM; *Recreations* golf, music, railways; *Clubs* RAF; *Style—* Air Vice-Marshal Geoffrey Cairns, CBE, AFC

CAIRNS, Prof John Harper (Jack); s of John Cairns (d 1984), of Colwyn Bay, and Edith, *née* Harper (d 1962); *b* 20 Jan 1932; *Educ* William Hulme's Sch Manchester, Univ of Manchester (BSc, MSc, PhD); *m* 17 Aug 1957, Monica Mary, da of Lawrence Lonnon (d 1976), of Zeals, Wiltshire; 1 s (Ian b 1963), 2 da (Rosemary b 1958, Stephanie b 1961); *Career* asst lectr then lectr in metallurgy UMIST 1956–60, co tech exec Yorkshire Imperial Metals Ltd 1964–71 (former head of res 1960–64), md Anson Cast Products Ltd 1971–79; Univ of Bradford: prof of industl technol 1979–85 and 1991–93, emeritus prof 1993, pro-vice- chllr 1985–88, dep vice-chllr 1988–90; FIM 1967, CEng 1977; *Books* Technology of Heavy Non Ferrous Metals (1967); *Recreations* sailing, fell walking; *Style—* Prof Jack Cairns; ✉ Crest Hill House, Shadwell Ring Rd, Leeds LS17 8NJ (☎ 0113 265 0684); University of Bradford, Bradford, West Yorks BD7 1DP (☎ 01274 733466, fax 01274 305340, telex 51309 UNIBFDG)

CAIRNS, Joyce Winifred; da of Lt-Col Robert William Cairns, MBE, TD, (d 1972) of Peebles, and Marjorie Helen, *née* Dickson (d 1983); *b* 21 March 1947; *Educ* Mary Erskine Sch for Girls Edinburgh, Gray Sch of Art Aberdeen (dip and post dip), RCA (MA), Goldsmiths' Coll London (ATC); *m* 1, 1975, Christopher George Dowland; m 2, 1980, Arthur James Watson; m 3, 1989, Capt Robert Kemp Hamilton Cunningham; *Career* artist and lectr; lectr Grays Sch of Art Aberdeen 1976–; visiting lectr: Glasgow Sch of Art, Duncan of Jordanston Coll of Art Dundee; fell Glos Coll of Art & Design; Scottish Arts Cncl: memb Art Ctee 1986–89, memb Awards Panel 1981–83 and 1987–90; memb: Aberdeen Artists Soc 1978 (first woman pres), Royal Scottish Soc of Painters in Watercolours 1979; ARSA 1985; *Solo Exhibitions* Compass Gallery Glasgow 1980, ESU Edinburgh 1981, Peacock Printmakers Aberdeen 1981, Art Space Galleries Aberdeen 1984, Perth Museum and Art Gallery 1986, 369 Gallery Edinburgh 1986, The Third Eye Gallery Glasgow 1987, Talbot Rice Gallery Univ of Edinburgh 1991, Peacock Gallery Aberdeen 1991, Odette Gilbert Gallery London 1991, Kirkcaldy Art Gallery & Museum 1992, An Lanntair Stornoway 1992, Lamont Gallery 1993, Elektra Fine Art Toronto, Roger Billcliffe Gallery Glasgow 1995; *Work in Public Collections* Aberdeen Art Gallery, Scottish Arts Cncl, Univ of Aberdeen, Fife Regnl Cncl, Graves Art Gallery & Museum Sheffield, Edinburgh City Arts Centre, Lanarkshire CC, Univ of Strathclyde, The Contemporary Arts Soc, BBC, Glasgow Art Gallery & Museum, Perth City Art Gallery and Museums, Glasgow Museum of Modern Art; *Awards* incl: Carnegie Travelling Scholarship, First Prize Arbroath Art Competition, ESU Scholarship to USA, Latimer Award RSA, bursary Scottish Arts Cncl, First Prize Morrison Portrait Competition 1989, May Marshall Brown Award RSW, W P J Burness Award RSA, First Prize Shell Expro; *Recreations* eating and carousing; *Style—* Ms Joyce Cairns; ✉ 5 New Pier Road, Footdee, Aberdeen AB2 1DR (☎ 01224 575331); Grays School of Art, Robert Gordon's University, Garthdee Road, Aberdeen AB9 2QD (01224 262000)

CAIRNS, Peter Granville; er s of Maj Hugh William Cairns, MC (gs of 1 Earl Cairns), and Diana, *née* Soames; *b* 3 Sept 1940; *Educ* Eton; *m* 10 May 1991, Mrs Ann Camilla Carlton, da of late J B Leworthy, of Beacon Hill, Westerham, Kent; *Career* Lt Royal Scots Greys, ret; banker; dir: Cater Ryder 1976–81, Cater Allen 1981–; *Recreations* fox-hunting; *Clubs* Turf, White's; *Style—* Peter Cairns, Esq; ✉ Cater Allen, 20 Birchin Lane, London EC3V 9DJ (☎ 0171 623 2070)

CAIRNS, Dr Roger John Russell; s of Arthur John Cairns (d 1982), and Edith Ann, *née* Russell (d 1979); *b* 8 March 1943; *Educ* Ranelagh Sch Berks, Univ of Durham (BSc), Univ of Bristol (MSc, PhD); *m* 20 July 1966, Zara Corry, da of Herbert Bolton (d 1970); 2 s (Nigel b 1969, Alistair b 1973), 1 da (Kirsten b 1975); *Career* oilfield water mgmnt BP 1978–81, planner Qatar General Petroleum Corp 1981–83; md: Trafalgar House Oil and Gas Ltd (tech and commercial dir 1983–89), Hardy Oil and Gas plc 1989–; memb: SPE, IOD; FRSC, EurChem, CChem, FInstPet; *Recreations* theatre and music, wine making, tennis, reading, chess; *Style—* Dr Roger Cairns; ✉ High Larch, Lewis Lane, Chalfont Heights, Gerrard's Cross, Bucks SL9 9TS; Hardy Oil and Gas plc, 10 Great George Street, London SW1P 3AE (☎ 0171 470 2200)

CAIRNS, 6 Earl (UK 1878); Simon Dallas Cairns; CBE (1992); also Baron Cairns (UK 1867) and Viscount Garmoyle (UK 1878); s of 5 Earl Cairns, GCVO, CB (d 1989); *b* 27 May 1939; *Educ* Eton, Trinity Coll Cambridge; *m* 4 Feb 1964, Amanda Mary, o da of late Maj Edgar Fitzgerald Heathcoat-Amory, RA; 3 s (Viscount Garmoyle, Hon (David) Patrick b 1967, Hon Alistair Benedict b 1969); *Heir* s, Viscount Garmoyle b 26 March 1965; *Career* formerly with J A Scrimgeour; S G Warburg Group plc: jt vice chm 1987, chief exec and dep chm S G Warburg Group plc, resigned 1995; chm: BAT Industries plc 1996– (dir 1990–), Voluntary Serv Overseas (VSO) 1981–92, Commonwealth Development 1995–, Overseas Development Inst; Receiver Gen Duchy of Cornwall 1990–; memb Ct of Assts Worshipful Co of Fishmongers; *Clubs* Turf; *Style—* The Rt Hon the Earl Cairns, CBE; ✉ Bolehyde Manor, Allington, Chippenham, Wilts (☎ 01249 652105)

CAITHNESS, 20 Earl of (S 1455); Malcolm Ian Sinclair; 15 Bt (S 1631), PC (1990); also Lord Berriedale (S 1592); s of 19 Earl of Caithness (d 1965), and his 2 w Madeleine Gabrielle, *née* de Pury (d 1990); *b* 3 Nov 1948; *Educ* Marlborough, RAC Cirencester; *m* 1975, Diana Caroline (d 1994), da of Maj Richard Coke, DSO, MC, DL (gs of 2 Earl of Leicester); 1 s, 1 da (Lady Iona b 1978); *Heir* s, Lord Berriedale; *Career* Savills 1972–78, Brown and Mumford 1978–80, dir of various companies 1980–84; a Lord in Waiting and Government Whip 1984–85, under sec for transport 1985–86, Minister of State Home Office 1986–88, Minister of State Dept of the Environment 1988–89, Paymaster Gen and Min of State HM Treasy 1989–90; Minister of State: FCO 1990–92, Min of Transport 1992–94; conslt to and non-exec dir of various companies 1994–; FRICS; *Style—* The Rt Hon the Earl of Caithness, PC; ✉ c/o House of Lords, London SW1A OPW

CALAM, Dr Derek Harold; OBE (1997); s of Richard Hellyer Calam (d 1993), of Northwood, and Winifred Ella, *née* Nortier (d 1986); *b* 11 May 1936; *Educ* Christ's Hosp, Wadham Coll Oxford (MA, DPhil); *m* 15 Sept 1965, Claudia, da of Gerald Marcus Summers (d 1967); 2 s (Duncan b 1969, Douglas b 1973), 1 da (Josephine b 1971); *Career* Nat Serv 2 Lt RA 1954–56; Nat Inst for Med Res 1962–66 and 1969–72, Rothamsted Experimental Station 1966–69, Euro co-ordinator Nat Inst for Biological Standards and Control 1994– (joined 1972, head Chemistry Div 1975–94), author of numerous pubns in jls; vice chm Br Pharmacopoeia Cmmn 1995– (memb 1982–), first vice chm Euro Pharmacopoeia Cmmn 1995– (memb 1988–); expert advsr WHO 1984–; CChem, FRSC 1977, Hon MRPharmS 1992; *Recreations* walking, travel; *Style—* Dr Derek Calam, OBE; ✉ National Institute for Biological Standards and Control, Blanche Lane, South Mimms, Potters Bar, Herts EN6 3QG (☎ 01707 654753, fax 01707 646730, telex 21911)

CALAM, Dr John; s of Christopher Towers Calam, of Alderley Edge, Cheshire, and Irene May Calam; *b* 17 Feb 1948; *Educ* The King's Sch Macclesfield, Univ of Liverpool Med Sch (MD); *m* 18 Aug 1973, Joyce Elizabeth, da of Harold Cecil Rooney, of Nuneaton, Warwickshire; 1 s (Jeffrey), 2 da (Amy, Molly); *Career* reader and conslt physician Royal Postgraduate Med Sch and Hammersmith Hosp 1983–, first to demonstrate a causal link between gastric helicobacter bacteria and excessive acid secretion in patients with duodenal ulcers, reported in the Lancet and The Sunday Times 1989; FRCP 1988;

Recreations sailing; *Clubs* The Physiological Soc of London; *Style*— Dr John Calam; ✉ 16 Cranbourne Drive, Pinner, Middx HA5 1BZ (☎ 0181 868 8263); Department of Medicine, Royal Postgrad Medical School, Hammersmith Hospital, Du Cane Road, London W12 0NN (☎ 0181 383 3266, fax 0181 749 3436)

CALCUTT, Sir David Charles; kt (1991), QC (1972); s of Henry Calcutt (d 1972); *b* 2 Nov 1930; *Educ* Cranleigh, King's Coll Cambridge (MA, LLB, MusB); *m* 1969, Barbara Ann, da of Vivian Walker (d 1965); *Career* called to the Bar Middle Temple 1955, bencher 1981; dep chm Somerset QS 1970–71, recorder 1972–89, Dept of Trade inspr Cornhill Consolidated 1974–77, judge Courts of Appeal of Jersey and Guernsey 1978–; chm: Civil Serv Arbitration Tbnl 1979–94, Inst of Actuaries' Appeal Bd 1985–94, Falklands Islands Cmmn of Enquiry 1984, Cyprus Servicemen Inquiry 1985–86, Panel on Takeovers and Mergers 1989–; master Magdalene Coll Cambridge 1986–94 (hon fell 1994–); pres Lloyd's of London Appeal Tribunal 1987– (dep pres 1983–87); chllr dioceses of Exeter and Bristol 1971– and Europe 1983–; chm Cncl Cranleigh and Bramley Schs 1987–; dir Edington Music Festival 1956–64, dep chm RCM 1988–90; memb: Criminal Injuries Compensation Bd 1977–, Cncl on Tbnls 1980–86, Gen Cncl of the Bar 1968–72, Senate of the Inns of Court and the Bar 1979–85 (chm of the Senate 1984–85, chm of the Bar 1984–85), UK Delgn Consultative Ctee Bars and Law Socs EEC 1979–83, Colliery Ind Review Body 1985–88, Interception of Communications Tribunal 1986–; arbitrator Int Centre for the Settlement of Investment Disputes Washington DC 1986–, ind memb Diplomatic Service Appeal Bd 1986–93; ind assessor of compensation for miscarriages of justice: for Home Office 1989–, for MOD 1994–; chm Ctee on Privacy and Related Matters 1989–90, review of Press Self-Regulation 1992–93; fell Winchester Coll 1992–; hon memb: American Bar Assoc 1985–, Canadian Bar Assoc 1985–; Hon LLD Univ of Exeter 1996; fell Int Acad of Trial Lawyers (NY), FRCM 1988; *Recreations* hill farming on Exmoor; *Clubs* Athenaeum, New (Edinburgh), Hawks (Cambridge); *Style*— Sir David Calcutt, QC; ✉ 35 Essex Street, Temple, London WC2A 3AR

CALDECOTE, 2 Viscount (UK 1939) Robert Andrew Inskip (Robin); KBE (1987), DSC (1941), DL (1991); s of 1 Viscount Caldecote (Rt Hon Sir Thomas Walker Hobart Inskip, CBE, d 1947), and Lady Augusta Orr Ewing (d 1967), wid of Charles Orr Ewing, MP, and er da of 7 Earl of Glasgow; *b* 8 Oct 1917; *Educ* Eton, King's Coll Cambridge (MA), RNC Greenwich; *m* 22 July 1942, Jean Hamilla, da of Rear Adm Hugh Dundas Hamilton (d 1963); 1 s, 2 da; *Heir* s, Hon Piers James Hampden Inskip; *Career* served RNVR 1939–45; asst mangr Vickers Armstrong Naval Yard 1947–48, lectr in engrg Engrg Dept Univ of Cambridge 1948–54 (fell King's Coll 1948–55); dir: English Electric Co 1953–69, British Aircraft Corporation 1960–69 (dep md 1961–67), Delta plc 1969–82 (chm 1972–82), Consolidated Gold Fields 1969–78, Lloyds Bank 1975–88, W S Atkins Ltd 1982–92; chm: Legal and General Group 1977–80, Investors in Industry Group plc 1980–87, Industry Ventures Ltd 1989–93; pres: Soc of British Aerospace Cos 1965–66, Int Assoc of Aeronautical and Space Equipment Mfrs 1966–68, Parly and Scientific Ctee 1966–69, Metals Soc 1975–76, Fellowship of Engrg 1981–86, Royal Inst of Naval Architects 1987–90; chm: EDC Movement of Exports 1965–72, Export Cncl for Europe 1970–71, Design Cncl 1972–80, BBC Gen Advsy Cncl 1982–85, Mary Rose Tst 1983–92, Crown Appointments Cmmn 1990; memb: Church Assembly 1950–55, Review Bd for Govt Contracts 1969–76, Inflation Accounting Ctee 1974–75, Engrg Industs Cncl 1975–82, BR Bd 1979–85, Advsy Cncl for Applied Research and Devpt 1981–84, Engrg Cncl 1982–85; tstee: Prince's Youth Business Tst 1986–90, Church Urban Fund 1987–90; fell Eton Coll 1953–72, pres Dean Close Sch 1960–90, pro chllr Cranfield Inst of Technol 1976–84; Liveryman Worshipful Co of Coachmakers & Coach Harness Makers, Liveryman Worshipful Co of Engineers; Hon DSc: Cranfield, Aston, Bristol, City; Hon LLD: London, Cambridge; FEng 1977, Hon FIEE, Hon FICE, Hon FIMechE, FRINA, Hon FSIAD 1976; *Recreations* sailing (yacht 'Citara III'), shooting, golf; *Clubs* Pratt's, Royal Yacht Sqdn, Royal Ocean Racing, Royal Cruising, Athenaeum; *Style*— The Rt Hon the Viscount Caldecote, KBE, DSC, DL, FEng; ✉ Orchard Cottage, South Harting, Petersfield, Hants GU31 5NR (☎ 01730 825529, fax 01730 825763)

CALDECOTT, Andrew Hilary; QC (1994); s of Andrew Caldecott, CBE (d 1990), and Zita, *née* Belloc; *b* 22 June 1952; *Educ* Eton, New Coll Oxford (BA); *m* 1977, Rosamond Ashton, *née* Shuttleworth; 2 s (Harry b 1981, Edmund b 1985), 2 da (Zita b 1983, Xanthe 1991); *Career* called to the Bar Inner Temple 1975; *Style*— Andrew Caldecott, Esq, QC; ✉ 1 Brick Court, Temple, London EC4Y 8BY (☎ 0171 353 8845)

CALDER, Dr Angus Lindsay Ritchie; s of Ritchie Calder (d 1982), and Mabel Jane Forbes, *née* McKail of Edinburgh; *b* 5 Feb 1942; *Educ* Wallington Co GS for Boys, Kings Coll Cambridge (MA), Univ of Sussex (DPhil); *m* 1, 1 Oct 1963, Jennifer Rachel, da of David Daiches; 2 da (Rachel b 21 Aug 1965, Gowan b 29 May 1967), 1 s (Gideon b 10 April 1971); m 2, 19 Dec 1987, Catherine Janet Kyle, da of William Young; 1 s (Douglas b 28 May 1989); *Career* writer; lectr in literature Univ of Nairobi 1968–71, visiting lectr Univ of Malawi Zomba 1978, staff tutor in arts and reader in cultural studies Open Univ in Scotland 1979–93, visiting prof of English Univ of Zimbabwe Harare 1992; co-ed Jl of Commonwealth Literature 1981–87; founding convener Scottish Poetry Library 1982–88, convener Cwlth Writers Conf Edinburgh 1986, convener Writing Together Glasgow 1989–90; chair Artistic Policy Review Sub-Ctee and bd memb Royal Lyceum Theatre Edinburgh 1984–96, bd memb Fruitmarket Gallery Edinburgh 1984–92, bd memb 7:84 Theatre Co 1986–92, memb panel of judges Saltire Soc Scottish Book of the Year Award 1983–, judge Eurasian Section Cwlth Writers Prize 1996; Eric Gregory Award 1967, John Llewellyn Rhys Meml Prize 1970, Scottish Arts Cncl Book Awards 1981 and 1994; *Books* The People's War - Britain 1939–45 (1969), Russia Discovered (1976) Revolutionary Empire - The Rise of the English Speaking Empires from the 15th Century to the 1780's (1981), T S Eliot (1987), Byron (1987), The Myth of the Blitz (1991), Revolving Culture (1994), Waking in Waskato (poems, 1997); ed and co-ed of numerous books; contrib reviews and articles to jls and newspapers; *Recreations* curling, cooking, cricket, listening to music; *Clubs* 37 Curling; *Style*— Dr Angus Calder; ✉ 15 Spittal Street, Edinburgh EH3 9DY (☎ and fax 0131 229 8196)

CALDER, Brig Anthony John Kennion; OBE (1985); s of William John Calder, of Melbourn, Royston, Herts, and Louise Forbes, *née* Morton; *b* 22 Oct 1943; *Educ* Millfield, RMA Sandhurst; *m* 1 July 1967, Caroline Melesina, da of Lt-Col Anthony Richard Reeve, MBE, TD, of Netherhampton, Salisbury, Wilts; 3 s (Charles b 26 Sept 1968, Jason b 23 Oct 1969, Nicholas b 7 Sept 1973), 1 da (Melesina b 5 May 1982); *Career* cmmnd IE Anglian Regt 1963 (later R Anglian Regt), cmd IR Anglian 1982–85, promoted Col 1986, Brig 1992, ret 1995; conslt HQ 2 Airmobile; *Recreations* cricket, sailing, skiing, shooting; *Style*— Brig Anthony Calder, OBE; ✉ HQ 24 Airmobile, Colchester, Essex (☎ 01206 782102)

CALDER, Finlay; OBE (1990); s of Robin Calder, of Haddington, East Lothian, and Elizabeth Guthrie, *née* Hamilton; *b* 20 Aug 1957; *Educ* Daniel Stewarts and Melville Coll Edinburgh; *m* 22 July 1978, Elizabeth Agnes, da of Alexander George Lyal; 1 s (David Alexander Finlay b 4 Oct 1983), 1 da (Hazel Elizabeth Spottiswoode b 5 Aug 1985); *Career* Rugby Union flanker Stewart's Melville FP RFC and Scotland (34 caps); clubs: Melrose RFC 1975–80 (135 appearances), Stewart's Melville FP 1981–92, Edinburgh 1982–90 (43 appearances); Scottish Schs 1974 (3 caps); for Scotland: Aust tour (5 appearances) 1982, Romania tour (1 appearance) 1984, debut v France Murrayfield 1986, World Cup squad 1987, capt 1989, Championship Winners 1990, NZ tour 1990; capt British Lions Aust tour (3 test appearances, won series 2–1) 1989; memb: Scotland Seven Aust tour 1988, Barbarians Seven HK 1989; winner Middx Sevens 1982; with Ceres (UK) Ltd 1985–94, Glencore Grain UK Ltd 1994–; *Style*— Finlay Calder, Esq, OBE

CALDER, Dr John Forbes; s of Alexander Beattie Calder, of Glasgow, and Annie Scott, *née* Milne; *b* 13 May 1942; *Educ* The HS of Glasgow, Univ of Glasgow (MB ChB); *m* 28 March 1967, Marion, da of John Anderson Miller (d 1964), of Kirkintilloch; 1 s (Nicholas b 1972), 1 da (Lorna b 1975); *Career* govt MO Malawi 1968–70, sr registrar in radiology Glasgow 1973–76 (registrar in radiology 1971–73); sr lectr in radiology: Univ of Nairobi 1976–80, Univ of Aberdeen 1980–86; conslt radiologist Victoria Infirmary Glasgow 1986–; elder Church of Scotland, memb Scottish Radiological Soc; FRCR (memb RCR 1975), memb RCPSG 1993, FRCP 1995 (MRCP 1993); *Books* An Atlas of Radiological Interpretation The Bones (1988); *Recreations* music, hill walking, soccer; *Clubs* Cwlth; *Style*— Dr John Calder; ✉ 145 Clober Rd, Milngavie, Glasgow, G62 7LS (☎ 0141 956 3535); Department of Radiology, Victoria Infirmary, Glasgow G42 9TY (☎ 0141 201 6000)

CALDER, John Mackenzie; s of James Calder, of Ardargie, Forgandenny, Perthshire, and Lucianne Wilson; *b* 25 Jan 1927; *Educ* McGill Univ, Sir George Williams Coll, Univ of Zürich; *m* 1, 1949, Mary Ann Simmonds; 1 da; m 2, 1960 (m dis 1975), Bettina Jonic; 1 da; *Career* publisher, ed, author; fndr and md: John Calder (Publishers) Ltd 1950–91, Calder Publications Ltd 1991–; dir of other associated publishing cos; co-fndr Def of Lit and the Arts Soc, chm Fedn of Scot Theatres 1972–74; contested (Lib): Kinross and W Perthshire 1970, Hamilton 1974, Central Scot (Euro election) 1979; Chev des Arts et des Lettres, Chev Ordre de Mérite Nat; FRSA; *Books* The Garden of Eros (1989), The Defence of Literature (1994), The Philosophy of Samuel Beckett (1995); ed: A Samuel Beckett Reader, Beckett at 60, The Nouveau Roman Reader, Gambit International Drama Review, William Burroughs Reader, Henry Miller Reader, As No Other Dare Fail - For Samuel Beckett on his 80th Birthday; author of fiction and plays; *Clubs* Caledonian, Scottish Arts; *Style*— John Calder, Esq; ✉ Calder Publications Ltd, 179 King's Cross Road, London WC1X 9BZ

CALDER, Michael John; s of Geoffrey Charles Calder (d 1974), of Dulwich, and Mary Patricia Calder (d 1982); *b* 28 Nov 1931; *Educ* Dulwich, ChCh Oxford (MA); *m* 10 June 1965, Sheila, da of Herbert Maughan (d 1962), of Sunderland; 2 s (James b 1966, Andrew b 1968); *Career* Lt RA 1950–56; Shell 1956–57; CA 1959–; conslt Calder & Co (gs of fndr, former sr ptnr); FCA; *Recreations* music, travel, cricket; *Clubs* Travellers; *Style*— Michael Calder, Esq; ✉ 42 Carson Rd, Dulwich, London SE21 8HU (☎ 0181 670 6207); Calder & Co, 1 Regent Street, London SW1Y 4NW (☎ 0171 839 6655, fax 0171 839 6016)

CALDER, (Hon) Nigel David Ritchie; eldest s of Baron Ritchie-Calder, CBE (Life Peer, d 1982); *b* 2 Dec 1931; *Educ* Merchant Taylors', Sidney Sussex Coll Cambridge (MA); *m* 1954, Elisabeth, da of Alfred James Palmer; 2 s, 3 da; *Career* writer New Scientist 1956–66 (ed 1962–66); freelance author and TV scriptwriter; fell American Assoc for the Advancement of Science, FRAS, FRGS; author of over 20 books; *Books* incl: Einstein's Universe (1979), Nuclear Nightmares (1979), The Comet is Coming (1980), Timescale (1983), The English Channel (1986), Spaceship Earth (1991), Giotto to the Comets (1992), The Manic Sun (1997); *Recreations* sailing; *Clubs* Cruising Assoc; *Style*— Nigel Calder, Esq; ✉ 26 Boundary Road, Northgate, Crawley, Sussex RH10 2BT (☎ 01293 549969, fax 01293 547083)

CALDERWOOD, James William; s of Rev James W Calderwood (d 1971), of Bready, Strabane, Co Tyrone, and Kathleen Calderwood; *b* 3 Dec 1936; *Educ* Foyle Coll Londonderry, Queen's Univ Belfast (MB BCh, BAO); *m* 29 Aug 1967, Dr (Catherine) Lesley Crozier, da of George Crozier, of Enniskillen (d 1963); 2 da (Catherine, Claire); *Career* consIt orthopaedic surgn Belfast City and Musgrave Park Hosp 1975, Royal Victoria Hosp 1977; examiner of RCSEd 1986–; memb: Br Soc for Surgery of the Hand 1980, Ulster Surgeons Travelling Club 1990–; fell Br Orthopaedic Assoc (memb Cncl 1995–); FRCS 1970, FRSM 1986; *Recreations* skiing, jogging, golf; *Style*— James Calderwood, Esq; ✉ 8 Broomhill Park, Belfast BT9 5JB (☎ 01232 666940); Belfast City Hospital, Lisburn Rd, Belfast (☎ 01232 329241)

CALDERWOOD, Sir Robert; kt (1990); s of Robert Calderwood (d 1952), and Jessie Reid, *née* Marshall (d 1990); *b* 1 March 1932; *Educ* Darvel HG Sch, William Hulme's Sch Manchester, Univ of Manchester (LLB); *m* 6 Sept 1958, Meryl Anne, da of David Walter Fleming (d 1977); 3 s (Robert b 1959, David b 1965, Iain b 1968), 1 da (Lyn b 1962); *Career* slr Supreme Ct of Judicature 1956; town clerk and chief exec: Salford 1966–69, Bolton 1969–73, Manchester 1973–79; chief exec Strathclyde Regnl Cncl 1980–92, non-exec dir and chm Strathclyde Buses Ltd 1989–93, chm Greater Glasgow Health Bd 1993–; dir: Glasgow Garden Festival 1988 Ltd, European Summer Special Olympic Games 1990 (Strathclyde) Ltd, GEC Scotland Ltd 1991–; dep chm Scottish Opera 1992– (dir 1991–); dep pres NUS 1954; memb: UN Assocs, Discharged Pensioners Aid Orgns, Parole Bd England 1971–73, advsy ctees on community rels and crime prevention for Sec of State for Scot, Glasgow Trades House, Industl Soc 1981–93; govr Glasgow Caledonian Univ 1994–96; hon fell Institution of Water and Environmental Mgmnt 1992; CIMgt 1981; *Recreations* UN activities, walking, swimming, garden, reading, theatre; *Style*— Sir Robert Calderwood; ✉ 6 Mosspark Avenue, Milngavie, Glasgow G62 8NL (☎ and fax 0141 956 4585)

CALDERWOOD, Robert; *b* 11 Oct 1953; *Educ* Camphill Sr Secdy Sch, Glasgow Coll of Technol (HNC and HND in Business Studies), Inst of Health Serv Mangrs (DipHSM), Univ of Aberdeen (Cert in Health Economics); *m*; 1 s; *Career* admin trainee Western Regnl Hosp Bd 1971–74; Argyll and Clyde Health Bd 1974–85: various admin posts 1974–78, actg princ admin asst to Dist Gen Admin Inverclyde Dist 1979–81, admin (Acute Servs) Inverclyde Dist 1981–84, dep unit admin (Acute Servs) Renfrew Dist 1984–85; Greater Glasgow Health Bd 1985–93: hosp admin Unit West 1 Western Infirmary 1985–87, unit admin Gartnavel Hosp Unit 1987–88, dir of property and strategic planning 1988–91, unit gen mangr Southern Gen Hosp Unit 1991–93; chief exec Southern Gen Hosp NHS Tst 1993–; chm Scottish Tst Chief Execs Gp 1995–97 (vice chm 1994–95); variously memb Jt Working Gps of Scottish Office, currently memb Bd Nat Centre for Trg and Educn in Prosthetics and Orthotics Univ of Strathclyde; MHSM; *Recreations* golf, formerly youth coaching and development with Clyde Football Club; *Style*— Robert Calderwood, Esq; ✉ Management Office, Southern General Hospital NHS Trust, 1345 Govan Road, Glasgow G51 4TF (☎ 0141 201 1207, fax 0141 201 2999)

CALDICOTT, Dame Fiona; DBE (1996); da of Joseph Maurice Soesan, of Coventry, and Elizabeth Jane, *née* Ransley; *b* 12 Jan 1941; *Educ* City of London Sch for Girls, St Hilda's Coll Oxford (MA, BM BCh); *m* 5 June 1965, Robert Gordon Woodruff Caldicott, s of Capt Gordon Ezra Woodruff (d 1941), of Louisville, Kentucky; 1 s (Richard Woodruff b 1971, d 1990), 1 da (Lucy Woodruff b 1968); *Career* conslt psychiatrist Univ of Warwick 1979–85, conslt psychiatrist Uffculme Clinic 1979–96, sr clinical lectr in psychotherapy Univ of Birmingham 1982–96, unit gen mangr Mental Health Unit Central Birmingham Health Authy 1989–91, dir Adult Psychiatric and Psychotherapy Services S Birmingham Health Authy 1991–94, med dir S Birmingham Mental Health NHS Tst 1994–96; princ Somerville Coll Oxford autumn 1996–; chm Conf (now Acad) of Med Royal Colls and their faculties in UK 1995–96; memb: Central Manpower Ctee BMA 1977–89 and 1996–, Med Workforce Advsy Ctee 1991–, Nat Advsy Ctee on Mentally Disordered Offenders 1993–96, Standing Ctee on Postgrad Med Educn 1993–; conslt advsr to Commissioners for High Security Psychiatric Care; RCPsych: chm

Manpower Ctee 1981–89, sub dean 1987–90, dean 1990–93, pres 1993–96; memb Czech Psychiatric Soc 1994; FRCPsych 1985, FRSM 1990, fell Acad of Med Singapore 1994, FRCP 1995, FRCPI 1996; *Clubs* Reform; *Style*— Dame Fiona Caldicott, DBE; ✉ Somerville College, Oxford OX2 6HD (☎ 01865 270630, fax 01865 270606)

CALDWELL, Edward George; CB (1990); s of Prof A F Caldwell (d 1990), of Herts, and Olive Gertrude, *née* Riddle; *b* 21 Aug 1941; *Educ* St Andrew's Singapore, Clifton, Worcester Coll Oxford; *m* 1, 1965 (m dis 1992), Bronwen Anne, *née* Crockett; 2 da (Bronwen Lucy b 1968, Sophie b 1971); m 2, 1992, Helen, da of Mrs M D Burtenshaw, *née* Rose; *Career* slr Fisher Dowson & Wasbrough 1966, Law Cmmn 1967, 1974–76 and 1987–88, Parly counsel 1981– (joined Office of Parly Counsel 1969); sec Cwlth Assoc of Legislative Counsel; *Style*— Edward Caldwell, Esq, CB; ✉ Office of the Parliamentary Counsel, 36 Whitehall, London SW1A 2AY (☎ 0171 210 6617)

CALDWELL, Prof John Bernard; OBE (1979); s of Dr John Revie Caldwell (d 1968), of Barkbooth, Winster, Cumbria, and Doris, *née* Bolland (d 1929); *b* 26 Sept 1926; *Educ* Bootham Sch York, Univ of Liverpool (BEng), Univ of Bristol (PhD); *m* 12 Aug 1955, Jean Muriel Frances, da of Leonard Francis Duddridge (d 1993); 2 s (Philip b 1959, Michael b 1961); *Career* shipbuilding apprentice Vickers-Armstrong 1943–48, res fell in naval architecture Univ of Bristol 1953–55, sr sci offr then princ sci offr RN Scientific Serv 1955–60, asst prof of applied mechanics RNC Greenwich 1960–66, visiting prof MIT 1962–63; Univ of Newcastle Upon Tyne: prof of naval architecture 1966–91, head of dept 1966–83, dean Faculty of Engrg 1983–86, head Sch of Marine Technol 1975–80 and 1986–88, prof emeritus 1991–; visiting lectr: Norway 1969, Singapore 1970, Brazil 1973, SA 1974, Hong Kong 1975, Canada 1976, Egypt 1979, China 1980, Malaysia 1981, Yugoslavia 1985, Aust 1986, USA, Holland, Italy, Poland, Indonesia, Japan; visiting prof Univ of Br Columbia Canada 1989; David Taylor medal from the American Soc of Naval Architects and Marine Engrs 1987; memb Tyne Port Authy 1973–75; non-exec dir: Nat Maritime Institute Ltd 1983–85, Marine Design Consultants Ltd 1985–89, Newcastle Technol Centre 1985–90, Marine Technol Directorate Ltd 1986–90; memb Engrg Cncl 1988–94, chm Bd for Engrs Registration 1990–92, chm Standing Ctee on Engrg Profession 1992–94; author of numerous papers and articles on marine matters; Hon DSc Tech Univ of Gdansk Poland 1985; FRINA 1966 (Froude medal 1984, pres 1984–87), MIStructE 1966–91, FEng (fndr memb) 1976, FNECInst 1977 (Gold medal 1973, pres 1976–78), hon memb Soc of Naval Architects and Marine Engrs Singapore 1978, FRSA; *Recreations* reading, listening, seeing, thinking; *Style*— Prof John Caldwell, OBE, FEng; ✉ Barkbooth, Winster, Windermere, Cumbria LA23 3NZ (☎ 015395 68222)

CALDWELL, Dr Neil Edward; s of Robert Aldridge Caldwell, of Alfreton, Derbs, and Kathleen Constance, *née* Barnard; *b* 17 April 1952; *Educ* Dr Challoner's GS Amersham, UCW Aberystwyth (BSc), Poly of Wales (PhD); *m* 1977, Betsan Charles, *née* Jones; 1 da (Catrin Lowri Iorwerth b 1978), 1 s (Owain Rhys Iorwerth b 1980); *Career* vice pres Aberystwyth Guild of Students 1973–74, pres NUS Wales 1975–77, res student Poly of Wales 1977–82; National Trust warden: for Llŷn 1982–85, for Gower 1985–88; dir Campaign for the Protection of Rural Wales 1988–94; dir: Prince of Wales' Ctee 1994–96, The Prince's Trust - Bro 1996–; former ed Rural Wales Magazine; memb: European Environmental Bureau, Welsh Language Bd; vice chair Wales Wildlife and Countryside Link; FRSA; *Books* Environment of Wales (contrib, 1993); *Recreations* walking, cycling, reading, travelling; *Style*— Dr Neil Caldwell; ✉ The Prince's Trust - Bro, 4th Floor, Empire House, Mount Street Square, Cardiff CF1 6DN (☎ 01222 471121, fax 01222 482086)

CALDWELL, Wilfrid Moores (Bill); s of Col Wilfrid Caldwell (d 1935), and Mabel Gertrude, *née* Moores; *b* 14 Oct 1935; *Educ* Marlborough, Magdalene Coll Cambridge (MA); *m* 8 April 1972, Linda Louise, da of Robert Ian Hamish Sievwright (d 1978); 2 s (William b 1978, James b 1981), 1 da (Fiona b 1976); *Career* Nat Serv 2 Lt RA 1954–56, Lt (TA) 1956–59; CA, ptnr Price Waterhouse 1970–92 (joined 1959); non-exec chm H Young Holdings plc 1993–; dir: China Investment Tst plc 1993–, Ronson plc 1993–, Powersceen International plc 1994–, Korea Liberalisation Fund Ltd 1995–; chm of govrs: Redcliffe Sch Fulham 1979–89, Arundale Sch Pulborough 1985–95; FCA 1963; *Recreations* golf, skiing, bridge, philately; *Clubs* Carlton; *Style*— Bill Caldwell, Esq; ✉ The Grange, Hesworth Lane, Fittleworth, Pulborough, W Sussex RH20 1EW (☎ 01798 865384)

CALEDON, 7 Earl of (I 1800); Nicholas James Alexander; JP; Baron Caledon (I 1790), Viscount (I 1797); s of 6 Earl of Caledon (d 1980), by his 2 w, Baroness Anne (d 1963), da of Baron Nicolai de Graevenitz (Grand Duchy of Mecklenburg-Schwerin 1847, Russia (Tsar Nicholas I) 1851); *b* 6 May 1955; *Educ* Gordonstoun; *m* 1, 1979 (m dis 1985), Wendy Catherine, da of Spiro Nicholas Coumantaros, of Athens; m 2, 19 Dec 1989, Henrietta Mary Alison, er da of John Newman, of Compton Park, Compton Chamberlayne, Wilts; 1 s (Frederick James, Viscount Alexander b 15 Oct 1990), 1 da (Lady Leonora Jane b 26 May 1993); *Heir* s, Viscount Alexander b 15 Oct 1990; *Career* HM Lord Lieutenant for Co Armagh 1989–; chm Caledon Estates; *Recreations* travel, skiing, flying; *Clubs* Corviglia Ski, Helicopter Club of Ireland; *Style*— The Rt Hon the Earl of Caledon, JP; ✉ Caledon Castle, Caledon, Co Tyrone, NI (☎ 01232 568232)

CALIGARI, Prof Peter Douglas Savaria; s of Flt Lt Kenneth Vane Savaria Caligari, DFM, ret, of Worcester, and Mary Annetta, *née* Rock; *b* 10 Nov 1949; *Educ* Hereford Cathedral Sch, Univ of Birmingham (BSc, PhD, DSc); *m* 23 June 1973, Patricia Ann, da of John Feeley (d 1988); 2 da (Louise b 13 Jan 1978, Helena b 26 Sept 1980); *Career* res fell Univ of Birmingham 1974–81 (res asst 1971–74), princ scientific offr Scottish Crop Res Inst 1984–86 (sr scientific offr 1981–84), prof of agric botany Univ of Reading 1986– (head Dept of Agric Botany 1987–); md BioHybrids International Ltd; author of numerous scientific articles and reports; sr ed Int Jl of Heredity 1988–91 (jr ed 1985–88), memb Editorial Bd Euphytica 1991–, chm Pubns Ctee XVIIth Int Genetics Congress (1993) 1991–93; memb Governing Body Plant Science Research Ltd 1991–94, memb Governing Cncl John Innes Centre 1994–; memb Conf of Agric Profs 1986–, hon res assoc Welsh Plant Breeding Station Inst for Grassland and Environmental Res 1987–; memb: Assoc of Applied Biologists, EUCARPIA (Euro Assoc for Res in Plant Breeding), Euro Assoc for Potato Res, Genetical Soc of GB (ex officio ctee memb 1985–91), Int Assoc for Plant Tissue Culture (IAPTC), The Potato Assoc of America, Int Lupin Assoc, La Asociación para la Cooperación en Investigaciones Bananeras en el Caribe y en América Tropical (ACORBAT); FRSA 1990; *Books* Selection Methods in Plant Breeding (with I Bos, 1995), Compositae Vol II Biology and Utilisation (ed with N Hind); *Style*— Prof Peter Caligari; ✉ Department of Agricultural Botany, School of Plant Sciences, University of Reading, Whiteknights, PO Box 221, Reading RG6 6AS (☎ 0118 931 8091, fax 0118 931 6577, telex 847813 RULIBG)

CALLADINE, Prof Christopher Reuben; s of Reuben Calladine (d 1968), of Stapleford, Nottingham, and Mabel, *née* Boam (d 1963); *b* 19 Jan 1935; *Educ* Nottingham HS, Peterhouse Cambridge (BA), MIT (SM), Univ of Cambridge (ScD); *m* 4 Jan 1964, Mary Ruth Howard, da of Alan Howard Webb (d 1990), of Bengeo, Hertford, and Constance, *née* Askham (d 1978); 2 s (Robert James b 1964, Daniel Edward b 1967), 1 da (Rachel Margaret b 1966); *Career* devpt engr English Electric Co 1958–60; Univ of Cambridge: univ demonstrator 1960–63, univ lectr 1963–78, reader in structural mechanics 1978–86, prof of structural mechanics 1986–; sr fell Peterhouse 1992– (fell 1960–); memb Gen Bd Univ of Cambridge 1984–88; former fndn govr Cherry Hinton Infants Sch, former govr Richard Hale Sch Hertford, FRS 1984, FICE 1992, FEng 1994; *Style*— Prof Christopher Calladine, FRS, FEng; ✉ Peterhouse, Cambridge CB2 1RD (☎ 01223 338200, fax 01223 337578)

CALLAGHAN, Rev Brendan Alphonsus; SJ; s of Dr Alphonsus Callaghan (d 1975), and Dr Kathleen Callaghan, *née* Kavanagh; *b* 29 July 1948; *Educ* Stonyhurst, Heythrop Coll Oxon, Campion Hall Oxford (MA), Univ of Glasgow (MPhil), Heythrop Coll London (MTh); *Career* voluntary serv teacher Zimbabwe 1966–67; Soc of Jesus: joined 1967, ordained priest 1978, memb Formation Cmmn 1990–; superior Brixton Jesuit Community 1993–94; clinical psychologist: Glasgow Southern Gen Hosp 1974–76, Middx Hosp 1976–79; conslt various orders and dioceses 1975–, conslt Catholic Marriage Advsy Cncl 1981–; Heythrop Coll London: lectr in psychology 1980– (also Allen Hall Chelsea 1981–87), memb Academic Bd 1982–97, memb Governing Body 1982–97, princ 1985–97; Univ of London: chm Bd of Examiners Theology and Religious Studies 1987–89, memb Schs Examination Bd 1987–97, memb Collegiate Cncl and Senate 1989–94, memb Cncl 1994–97; memb Governing Body: Inst of Med Ethics 1989– (hon asst then assoc dir 1976–89), Syon House Angmering 1985–97, Campion Hall Univ of Oxford 1985–95; memb: Academic Advsy Ctee Jews Coll, Ctee for People in Higher Educn RC Bishop's Conf of Eng and Wales 1985–, Centre for the Study of Communication and Culture St Louis Univ (chm) 1990–, Inst of St Anselm (chm) 1991–, Family Res Tst 1991–; dep chm Research Ethics Ctee St Thomas' Hospital 1989–; visiting lectr St Joseph's Inst of Theology Kwazolo-Natal 1987 and 1997, visiting prof Fordham Univ NY 1990, visiting scholar Weston Sch of Theology Cambridge Mass 1992; memb: Br Psychological Soc (assoc fell), Royal African Soc, American Psychological Assoc (int affiliate) Catholic Inst for Int Rels, CND, Amnesty Int, Greenpeace, Centre for the Study of Theology Univ of Essex, Br and Irish Assoc for Practical Theology, Br Assoc for the Study of Religions; Hon FCP; FRSM, AFBPsS, CPsychol; *Publications* Life Before Birth (co-author, 1986); author of various articles, book reviews and poetry in jls; *Recreations* photography, long distance walking, poetry; *Style*— The Rev Brendan Callaghan, SJ; ✉ c/o Heythrop College, Kensington Square, London W8 5HQ (☎ 0171 795 6600, fax 0171 795 4200)

CALLAGHAN, James; MP (Lab) Heywood and Middleton (majority 8,074); s of James Callaghan; *b* 28 Jan 1927; *Career* lectr St John's Coll Manchester 1959–74; former borough councillor Middleton; MP (Lab): Middleton and Prestwich 1974–1983, Heywood and Middleton 1983–; oppn front bench spokesman on: Euro and Community Affairs 1983–87, Tport 1987–92, National Heritage 1992–; *Style*— James Callaghan, Esq, MP; ✉ 17 Towncroft Ave, Middleton, Manchester M24 3LA (☎ 0161 643 8108)

CALLAGHAN, Hon Michael James; s of Baron Callaghan of Cardiff, KG, PC (Life Peer), *qv*; b 1945; *Educ* Dulwich, Univ of Wales Cardiff, Manchester Business Sch; *m* 1968, Jennifer Mary, *née* Morris; 1 s (Joseph Edwin James b 1981), 2 da (Kate Elizabeth b 1970, Sarah Jane b 1972); *Career* dir of public and govt affrs Ford Motor Co Ltd 1994–; *Style*— The Hon Michael Callaghan; ✉ Ingrave Lodge, Brentwood Rd, Ingrave, Brentwood, Essex CM13 3QZ; Ford Motor Company, Eagle Way, Brentwood, Essex CM13 3BW (☎ 01277 253000)

CALLAGHAN, Dr (Thomas) Stanley; s of Thomas Callaghan, of Wyncroft, Killane Rd, Limavady, NI, and Marion, *née* Whyte; *b* 11 Feb 1948; *Educ* Limavady GS NI, The Queen's Univ Belfast (MB BCh, MD), Univ of Abertay Dundee (MSc(HRM)); *m* 12 July 1973, Irene Helen, da of R Bowie, of Stenhouse, Edinburgh; 1 s (Gavin b 29 March 1979), 1 da (Rhona b 29 Jan 1975); *Career* resident Royal Victoria Hosp Belfast 1972–73, registrar in med, cardiology and metabolic med, sr registrar in med and cardiology Royal Victoria Hosp Belfast and Belfast City Hosp, conslt physician in gen med and cardiology Angus NHS Tst 1982–; memb: MRS, Br Hyperlipidaemia Soc; fell Ulster Soc of Internal Med; memb: Aberdeen Medico-Chirological Soc, Scottish Soc Physicians, Forfarshire Med Soc, Scottish Cardiac Soc, Br Cardiac Soc; MRCP, FRCPEd; *Recreations* walking, shooting, photography, music; *Clubs* Edinburgh Angus; *Style*— Dr Stanley Callaghan; ✉ Department of Medicine, Stracathro Hospital, Brechin, Angus DD9 7QA (☎ 01356 647291)

CALLAGHAN OF CARDIFF, Baron (Life Peer UK 1987), of the City of Cardiff, Co S Glamorgan; Sir (Leonard) James Callaghan; KG (1987), PC (1964); s of James Callaghan, Chief Petty Offr RN, of Portsmouth; *b* 27 March 1912; *Educ* Portsmouth Northern Secondary Sch; *m* 1938, Audrey Elizabeth, da of Frank Moulton, of Loose, Kent; 1 s (Hon Michael James Callaghan, *qv*), 2 da; *Career* joined Civil Service 1929, asst sec Inland Revenue Staff Fedn 1936–47; MP (Lab) South Cardiff 1945–50, South East Cardiff 1950–83, Cardiff South and Penarth 1983–87; Parly sec Min of Transport 1947–50, Parly and fin sec Admiralty 1950–51, Chllr of the Exchequer 1964–67, home sec 1967–70, sec of state for Foreign and Cwlth Affairs 1974–76, min of Overseas Devpt 1975–76, Prime Minister and first Lord of the Treasury 1976–79, leader of Oppn 1979–80, father of the House of Commons 1983–87; fndr, chm then pres Advsy Ctee on Protection of the Sea 1953–; pres and hon fell Univ of Wales Swansea 1985–95, hon fell Univ of Portsmouth, hon fell Univ of Wales Cardiff, hon life fell Nuffield Coll Oxford, hon bencher Inner Temple; Hon LLD Univs of: Wales, Birmingham, Sussex, Sardar Patel (India), Meisei (Tokyo), Univ of Westminster, Open Univ and Univ of Liverpool; Hon Freeman: City of Cardiff, City of Sheffield, City of Portsmouth, City of Swansea; *Books* A House Divided: The Dilemma of Northern Ireland (1973), Time and Chance (memoirs, 1987); *Style*— The Rt Hon Lord Callaghan of Cardiff, KG, PC; ✉ House of Lords, London SW1A 0PW

CALLAHAN, J Loughlin; s of John G P Callahan, Lt-Col US Air Force (d 1992), of Dayton, Ohio, USA, and Marie, *née* Loughlin (d 1995); *b* 18 Jan 1948; *Educ* Holy Cross Coll Worcester Massachusetts (BA), Harvard Law Sch Cambridge Massachusetts (Juris Dr, cum laude); *m* 5 May 1973, Mary, da of Vincent Reilly (d 1969), of Tinton Falls, New Jersey, USA; 1 s (Christopher b 1974), 1 da (Denise b 1976 d 1996); *Career* law Davis Polk & Wardwell New York 1972–80; investment banking dir: S G Warburg & Co Ltd 1983–86, S G Warburg Securities 1986–92; investment mgmnt dir Mercury Asset Management plc 1992–; dir: International Primary Market Association 1986–91 (vice chm 1988–91), Euroclear Clearance System Société Cooperative 1991–93; *Recreations* art, music, theatre and tennis; *Style*— J L Callahan, Esq; ✉ 7 Spencer Hill, London SW19 4PA (☎ 0181 947 7726, fax 0181 947 1772); Mercury Asset Management plc, 33 King William Street, London EC4R 9AS (☎ 0171 280 2977, fax 0171 280 2066)

CALLAN, Maj-Gen Michael; CB (1979); s of Maj John Callan, and Elsie Dorothy, *née* Fordham; *b* 27 Nov 1925; *Educ* Farnborough GS, Army Staff Coll, JSSC, RCDS; *m* 1948, Marie Evelyn, *née* Farthing; 2 s; *Career* 1 Gurkhas IA 1944–47, RAOC 1948–80, DDOS 1972–73, commanded Rhine Area BAOR 1975–76, DG Ordnance Servs (MOD) 1976–80, Col Cmdt RAOC 1981–89 (Rep Col Cmdt 1982, 1985, 1988), Hon Col SW London ACF 1982–89; pres and chm Bd of Tstees RAOC Charitable Trust 1993–96; *Recreations* jogging, sailing, gardening, DIY; *Style*— Maj-Gen Michael Callan, CB; ✉ c/o Royal Bank of Scotland (Drummonds Branch), 49 Charing Cross, London SW1A 2DX

CALLARD, Sir Eric John (Jack); kt (1974); s of Frank Callard (d 1951), of Torquay; *b* 15 March 1913; *Educ* Queen's Coll Taunton, St John's Coll Cambridge (MA); *m* 1938, Pauline Mary, da of Rev Charles Pengelly (d 1941); 3 da; *Career* chartered mechanical engr; chm: ICI Ltd 1971–75, British Home Stores 1976–82; dir: Midland Bank 1971–87, Commercial Union Assurance 1975–83, Ferguson Industrial Holdings 1975–86, Equity Capital for Industry 1976–84; Hon DSc Cranfield Inst of Technol; FEng 1976 (fndr fell), Hon FIMechE; *Recreations* fly fishing, gardening; *Clubs* Flyfishers'; *Style*— Sir Jack Callard, FEng; ✉ Crookwath Cottage, High Row, Dockray, nr Penrith, Cumbria CA11 0LG

CALLARD, Jonathan Edwards Brooks; s of John Brooks Callard, of Bridgnorth, Shropshire, and Averil, *née* Hiles; *b* 1 Jan 1966; *Educ* Bassaleg Comp Newport, St Paul's and St Mary's Coll Cheltenham; *m* 28 May 1992, Gail, da of David Crowther; *Career* Rugby Union full back; 120 appearances Newport RFC 1985–89, Bath RFC 1989–; honours with Bath: Courage League Champions 1996, winners Pilkington Cup 1996; England: debut v NZ 1993, 5 caps; PE teacher Downside Sch 1989–; *Recreations* golf and most sports; *Style*— Jonathan Callard, Esq; ✉ c/o Bath RFC, Recreation Ground, Bath

CALLAWAY-FITTALL, Betty Daphne; *née* Roberts; MBE (1984); da of William Arthur Roberts (d 1965), and Elizabeth Theobald, *née* Hayward (d 1972); *b* 22 March 1928; *Educ* St Paul's Convent, Graycoat Sch London; *m* 1, 1949, E Roy Callaway; m 2, 1978, late Capt William Percival Fittall; *Career* ice skating trainer; nat trainer W Germany 1969–72; pupils include: Angelika and Erich Buck (Euro Champions and second in World Championships 1972), Chrisztina Regoczy and Andras Sally (Hungarian and World Champions and Olympic Silver medallists 1980), Jayne Torvill and Christopher Dean (World and Euro Champions 1981, 1982, 1983–84, Olympic Champions 1984, Olympic Bronze medallists 1994); hon citizen Ravensburg Germany 1972, Gold medal Nat Skating Assoc 1955, Hungarian Olympic medal 1980, now skating dir International Ice Dance Acad Slough; Coach of the Year Nat Coaching Fndn 1995; *Recreations* water skiing, music, gardening; *Style*— Betty Callaway-Fittall, MBE; ✉ 35 Long Grove, Seer Green, Beaconsfield, Bucks (☎ 01494 67 6370)

CALLCUTT, John; s of Roy Cyril Callcutt, of Englefield Green, Surrey, and Winifred Elizabeth, formerly Newton; *b* 15 Jan 1947; *Educ* Salesian Coll Chertsey Surrey, Brooklands Tech Coll, Coll of Law Guildford; *m* 3 June 1973, Claudie Jeanette, da of Bernard Le Coursonnois; 1 s (Marc Roy b 16 Nov 1979), 1 da (Nadine Elizabeth b 18 Sept 1982); *Career* articled clerk Lovegrove & Durant slrs Windsor, legal asst Stephenson Harwood & Tatham slrs until 1974; Crest Homes plc: legal asst 1974–77 (admitted slr 1977), regnl chief exec Westerham Kent 1977–79, company slr 1979, legal dir 1980–82, md 1982; Crest Nicholson plc (parent co of Crest Homes): main bd dir 1985–, chm subsids Crest Homes plc and Pearce Construction plc 1988, md ops 1989–91, chief exec 1991–; memb Law Soc 1977, FRSA; *Recreations* reading fiction, cooking, music, art; *Style*— John Callcutt, Esq; ✉ Crest Nicholson plc, 39 Thames Street, Weybridge, Surrey KT13 8JL (☎ 01932 847272, fax 01932 840150)

CALLERY, Simon Laurence Christopher; s of Christopher Thomas Callery, and Shirley Fay, *née* Tennant; *Educ* Bloxham Sch Oxon, Campion Sch Athens, Berkshire Coll of Art & Design, S Glamorgan Inst of Higher Educn (BA Fine Art Sculpture); *Career* artist; artist in residence Camden Art Centre London 1992; *Solo Exhibitions* E14 SE10 (Free Trade Wharf London) 1991, Simon Callery (Anderson O'Day Gallery London) 1993, Anderson O'Day Gallery 1994, Muri Galleria Christian Stein Turin 1994–95, Anthony Wilkinson Fine Art London 1996; *Group Exhibitions* incl: New Contemporaries (ICA London) 1983, Young Cardiff Artists (Nat Museum of Wales) 1984, National Eisteddfod (S Wales) 1986, Arts Cncl touring exhbn (Chapter Arts Centre Cardiff and Arts Cncl Gallery Belfast) 1987, The Forming Image (Raab Gallery London) 1987, Whitechapel Open (Whitechapel Gallery London) 1988, 1990 and 1992, Landscape (Raab Gallery Berlin) 1990, Strictly Painting (Cubitt St Gallery London) 1993, John Moores 18 (Walker Art Gallery Liverpool, prizewinner) 1993, Young British Artists III (Saatchi Gallery) 1994, Landescapes (Ex-Lanificio Bona Torino) 1994, Equinozio D'Autunno (Castello Di Rivara Italy) 1994, About Vision (Museum of Modern Art Oxford) 1996–97; *Awards* Arts Cncl Young Artists grant 1983 and 1984, Gold Medal Nat Eisteddfod S Wales; *Style*— Simon Callery, Esq; ✉ Ishild, Fishery Road, Bray, Berks SL6 1UN (☎ 01628 23647)

CALLIL, Carmen Thérèe; da of late Frederick Alfred Louis Callil, and Lorraine Clare, *née* Allen; *b* 15 July 1938; *Educ* Star of the Sea Convent Gardenvale Melbourne, Loreto Convent Mandeville Hall Melbourne, Melbourne Univ (BA); *Career* editorial asst: Hutchinson Publishing Co 1965–66, B T Batsford 1966–67; publicity mangr: Panther Books then also Granada Publishing Ltd 1967–70, André Deutsch Ltd 1972; publicity for Ink Newspaper 1972, md and chm Carmen Callil Ltd (book publishing co) 1972–76; Virago Press: fndr 1972, md 1972–82, chm 1972–95; md Chatto & Windus and The Hogarth Press 1982–93; publisher-at-large Random House UK and Australia 1993–94, ed at large Alfred A Knopf NY and Pantheon & Vintage USA 1993–94; memb Bd Channel 4 1985–91; chm of judges Booker Prize for Fiction 1996 (memb Ctee 1979–84), fndr dir Groucho Club London 1984–94; winner Distinguished Service Award Int Women's Writing Guild; Hon DLitt: Univ of Sheffield 1994, Univ of York 1995, Oxford Brookes Univ 1995, Open Univ 1997; *Recreations* books, gardening, houses, France, travelling, animals, politics, TV; *Style*— Ms Carmen Callil

CALLMAN, His Hon Judge; Clive Vernon Callman; o s of Felix Callman, and Edith Callman; *b* 21 June 1927; *Educ* Ottershaw Coll, St George's Coll Weybridge, LSE (BSc); *m* 1967, Judith Helen, o da of Gus Hines, OBE, JP, of Adelaide, S Aust; 1 s, 1 da; *Career* called to the Bar Middle Temple 1951, in practice London and Norwich 1951–73, dep circuit judge in Civil and Criminal Jurisdiction 1971–73, circuit judge (SE Circuit) and dep High Ct judge 1973–; sitting: Royal Cts of Justice, Family Div, Mayor's and City of London Ct, Crown Cts; memb: Standing Ctee of Convocation 1958–79, Cncl Anglo-Jewish Assoc 1956–, Careers Advsy Bd 1979–, Advsy Ctee for Magistrates Courses 1979–, Statute 32 Ctee 1994–; memb Editorial Bd: Media Law and Practice, Professional Negligence, Jl of Child Law, Child and Family Law Quarterly; Univ of London: memb Senate 1978–94, memb Governing Cncl 1994–; govr: Birbeck Coll London, LSE, Hebrew Univ of Jerusalem, Ct City Univ; *Recreations* the arts, travel, reading; *Clubs* Bar Yacht; *Style*— His Hon Judge Callman; ✉ 11 Constable Close, London NW11 6UA (☎ 0181 458 3010)

CALLOW, Simon; *b* 15 June 1949; *Career* actor, director and writer; *Theatre* roles incl: The Resistable Rise of Arturo Ui (Half Moon) 1978, Titus in Titus Andronicus (Bristol Old Vic), Mary Barnes (Royal Court) 1978, Plumbers Progress (Prince of Wales), Orlando in As You Like It (NT) 1979, title role in Amadeus (NT) 1979, Sisterly Feelings (NT), Verlaine in Total Eclipse (Lyric Hammersmith), Lord Are in Restoration (Royal Court) 1981, Beastly Beatitudes (Duke of York's) 1981, Lord Foppington in The Relapse (Lyric Hammersmith) 1983, Perelli in On The Spot (Watford and West End) 1984, Melancholy Jacques (Traverse and Bush), Kiss of the Spiderwoman (Bush) 1985, Faust (Lyric Hammersmith) 1988, Single Spies (NT and Queens' Theatre) 1988 and 1989, The Destiny of Me (also dir, Haymarket Leicester) 1993, Face in The Alchemist (Birmingham and RNT) 1996; as director incl: Loving Reno (Bush) 1984, The Passport (Offstage) 1985, Amadeus (Clwyd) 1986, The Infernal Machine (Lyric Hammersmith) 1986, Cosi fan Tutte (Luzern, Switzerland) 1987, Shirley Valentine (West End/Broadway) 1988, Carmen Jones (Old Vic) 1991, Shades (West End) 1992, My Fair Lady (nat tour) 1992, Il Trittico (Broomhill) 1995, La Calisto, Glimmerglass (NY) 1996, Les Enfant du Paradis (RSC) 1996; *Television* BBC incl: Instant Enlightenment Inc VAT, Napoleon in Man of Destiny, Juvenalia, poet in La Ronde, Molière in All the World's a Stage, Hugo in Deadhead, Mr Micawber in David Copperfield (serial) 1986, Cariani and the Courtesan 1987, Quass in Old Flames 1989, Patriot Witness, John Mortimer in Trials of Oz, vicar in Femmes Fatale, Mr Prosecutor in Crime and Punishment; other credits incl: Wings of Song (Granada), Bye Bye Columbus (Greenpoint), lead role in Chance in a Million (Thames) 1983 and 1985–86, Scarecrow and Mrs King (Warner Bros), title role in Handel (film, Channel 4), Jacob in The Christmas Tree (YTV), guest lead in Inspector Morse (Central); *Radio* incl documentaries on: Charles Laughton (1987), Michéal MacLiammóir (1992); *Film* Shikaneder in Amadeus 1983, Rev Beebe in A Room with a View 1986, Varda in The Good Father 1986, Mr Ducie in Maurice 1987, Manifesto 1988, Mr and Mrs Bridges 1991, Crucifer of Blood, Postcards from the Edge 1991, Eddie Cheese in Soft Top Hard Shoulder 1992, Four Weddings and a Funeral 1994, Jefferson in Paris 1995, Le Passanger Clandestin 1995, When Nature Calls 1995, England My England 1995, Victory 1995; also director: The Ballad of the Sad Café 1991; *Books* Being an Actor (1984), A Difficult Actor: Charles Laughton (1987), Shooting the Actor (1990), Acting in Restoration Comedy (1991), Orson Wells: The Road to Xanadu (1995); *Audio* incl: Shooting the Actor (1992), Fairy Tales (by Oscar Wilde, 1995), Handful of Dust (1995), Dance to the Music of Time (1995); *Style*— Simon Callow, Esq; ✉ c/o Marina Martin Associates, 12–13 Poland Street, London W1V 3DE (☎ 0171 734 4818, fax 0171 734 4832)

CALMAN, Prof Sir Kenneth Charles; KCB (1996); s of Arthur MacIntosh Calman (d 1951), and Grace Douglas, *née* Don; *b* 25 Dec 1941; *Educ* Allan Glens Sch Glasgow, Univ of Glasgow (BSc, MB ChB, PhD, MD); *m* 8 July 1967, Ann, *née* Wilkie; 1 s (Andrew John b 5 Feb 1970), 2 da (Lynn Ann b 16 Nov 1971, Susan Grace b 6 Nov 1974); *Career* lectr in surgery Univ of Glasgow 1968–74, res fell Chester Beatty Inst London 1972–74, prof of oncology Univ of Glasgow 1974–84, dean of postgrad med 1984–89, chief med offr England (Scotland 1989–91) Dept of Health 1991–; Hon DUniv Stirling 1991, Hon DSc Univ of Strathclyde 1993; Hon MD: Univ of Nottingham 1994, Univ of Birmingham 1996; Hon DSc Univ of Glasgow 1996; FRCS, FRCP, FRCGP, FRCPATH, FRCR, FFPHM, FRSE 1979; *Books* Healthy Respect (with RS Downie, 2 edn 1994); *Recreations* gardening, golf, cartoons; *Clubs* Reform, New (Edinburgh); *Style*— Prof Sir Kenneth Calman, KCB, FRSE; ✉ Department of Health, Richmond House, 79 Whitehall, London SW1A 2NS (☎ 0171 210 5150, fax 0171 210 5407)

CALNE, Prof Sir Roy Yorke; kt (1986); s of Joseph Robert Calne (d 1984), and Eileen Calne (d 1989); *b* 30 Dec 1930; *Educ* Lancing, Guy's Hosp Med Sch; *m* 2 March 1956, Patricia Doreen; 2 s (Russell b 1964, Richard b 1970), 4 da (Jane b 1958, Sarah b 1959, Deborah b 1962, Suzanne b 1963); *Career* Nat Serv RAMC BMH Singapore RMO to KEO 2 Gurkhas 1954–56; conslt and sr lectr (surgery) Westminster Hosp London 1962–65, prof of surgery Univ of Cambridge 1965–, conslt surgn Cambridge Health Authy 1965–; pres Transplantation Soc 1992–94; fell Trinity Hall Cambridge 1965; Hon FRCSE 1993, hon fell UMDS 1995; hon fell Royal Coll of Surgns of Thailand 1992; *Books* Renal Transplantation (1963), Lecture Notes in Surgery (with H Ellis, 1965), A Gift of Life (1970), Clinical Organ Transplantation (ed 1971), Organ Grafts (1974), Liver Transplantation (ed & contrib 1983), A Colour Atlas of Transplantation (Renal (1984), Pancreas (1985), Liver (1985)), Transplant Immunology (ed & contrib 1984), Living Surgical Anatomy of the Abdomen (1988), Operative Surgery (ed with S Pollard, 1991), Too Many People (1994), Art, Surgery and Transplantation (1996); *Recreations* squash, tennis, painting; *Style*— Prof Sir Roy Calne; ✉ 22 Barrow Road, Cambridge (☎ 01223 359831); Department of Surgery, Addenbrooke's Hospital, Hills Road, Cambridge CB2 2QQ (☎ 01223 242708, fax 01223 410772)

CALNE AND CALSTONE, Viscount; Simon Henry George Petty-Fitzmaurice; s and h of Earl of Shelburne and gs of 8 Marquess of Lansdowne, PC; *b* 24 Nov 1970; *Educ* Eton, Univ of Cambridge (MA); *Style*— Viscount Calne and Calstone

CALTHORPE, *see:* Anstruther-Gough-Calthorpe

CALTHORPE, 10 Baron (GB 1796); Sir Peter Waldo Somerset Gough-Calthorpe; 11 Bt (1728); s of Hon Frederick Gough-Calthorpe (d 1935), and Dorothy, *née* Vernon-Harcourt (d 1985); suc bro, 9 Baron, 1945; *b* 13 July 1927; *Educ* Stowe; *m* 1, June 1956 (m dis 1971), Saranne Frances (d 1984), o da of James Harold Alexander, of Dublin; m 2, 1979, Elizabeth, da of James Young, of Guildford, Surrey; *Career* late Lt Welsh Gds Palestine; airline pilot (freelance, later for Aer Lingus, then Jersey Airlines) 1951–59; md Mercury Airlines 1960–65; author of two novels published under pseudonym Peter Somerset 1966–67; gp investment mangr 1970–81; *Recreations* theatre, paintings (not modern); *Style*— The Rt Hon the Lord Calthorpe; ✉ c/o IOM Bank Ltd, 2 Athol St, Douglas, Isle of Man

CALVERLEY, 3 Baron (UK 1945) Charles Rodney Muff; s of 2 Baron Calverley (d 1971); *b* 2 Oct 1946; *Educ* Moravian Boys' Sch Fulneck; *m* 1972, Barbara Ann, da of Jonathan Brown, of Colne, Lancs; 2 s (Hon Jonathan Edward b 1975, Hon Andrew Raymond b 1978); *Heir* s, Hon Jonathan Edward Muff b 16 April 1975; *Career* memb W Yorkshire Police; formerly with City of Bradford Police; *Style*— The Rt Hon the Lord Calverley; ✉ 110 Buttershaw Lane, Wibsey, Bradford, W Yorkshire BD6 2DA (tel 01274 676414)

CALVERLEY, Prof Peter Martin Anthony; s of Peter Calverley, and Jennifer, *née* Taylor; *b* 27 Nov 1949; *Educ* Queen Elizabeth GS Blackburn, Univ of Edinburgh (MB ChB); *m* 28 June 1973, Margaret Elizabeth, da of William Tatam, of Grantham, Lincs; 4 s (Adam Richard b 1977, James Iain (twin) b 1977, Robert Andrew b 1979, Thomas Peter b 1981); *Career* house offr Edinburgh 1973–74, sr house offr Dept of Med Leicester 1975–76, clinical fell MRC 1977–79, sr registrar Dept of Med Univ of Edinburgh 1979–85, MRC (Can) travelling fell McGill Univ Montreal 1982–83; currently: hon conslt physician Aintree Hosps Liverpool, prof of med (pulmonary rehabilitation) Univ of Liverpool; assoc ed Thorax; memb Br Thoracic Soc (chm Scientific Ctee), sec NW Thoracic Soc, chm Grants Ctee Br Lung Fndn; memb: American Thoracic Soc, Assoc of Physicians of GB and Ireland; FRCP, FRCPE, FCCP; *Recreations* travel, skiing and talking; *Style*— Prof Peter Calverley; ✉ Aintree Chest Centre, Fazakerley Hospital, Longmoor Lane, Liverpool L9 7AL (☎ 0151 525 5980, fax 0151 529 3762)

CALVERT, (Louis Victor) Denis; CB (1985); s of late Louis Victor Calvert, of Belfast, and Gertrude Cherry, *née* Hobson (d 1985); *b* 20 April 1924; *Educ* Belfast Royal Acad, Queen's Univ Belfast (BSc), Administative Staff Coll Henley-on-Thames; *m* 24 Aug 1949, Vivien Millicent, da of George Albert Lawson (d 1958); 2 s (David b 1951, Steven b 1952), 1 da (Jacqueline b 1961); *Career* RAF 1943–47, FO navigator (UK, Europe, S Africa); NI Civil Serv 1947–80: Miny of Agriculture 1947–56 (dep princ 1951), princ Miny of Finance 1956–63, Miny of Health and Local Govt 1963–65 (asst sec 1964), Miny of Devpt 1965–73 (sr asst sec 1970, dep sec 1971), Miny of Housing Local Govt and Planning 1973–76, DOE for NI 1976–80, comptroller and auditor gen for NI 1980–89; *Recreations* gardening, golf, reading, television; *Style*— Denis Calvert, Esq, CB; ✉ c/o Northern Ireland Audit Office, 106 University Street, Belfast BT7 1EU

CALVERT, Prof (Alan) Hilary; *b* 18 Feb 1947; *Educ* Univ of Cambridge (BA), UCH London (MB BChir, MRCP), Chelsea Coll London (MSc), MD; *m*; 3 c; *Career* house physician St Charles' Hosp London 1972–73, house surgn Northwick Park Hosp Harrow Middx 1973, SHO Renal Unit Royal Free Hosp London 1973–74, SHO in med Royal Marsden Hosp London 1974, locum registrar Renal Unit Royal Free Hosp Oct-Dec 1974; Royal Marsden Hosp: research fell 1975–77, hon sr registrar 1977–80, hon conslt in med Div of Med 1980–85, hon conslt Div of Med 1985–89; Inst of Cancer Research: lectr 1977–80, sr lectr 1980–85, reader in clinical pharmacology and team leader Clinical Pharmacology Team Drug Devpt Section 1985–89; Univ of Newcastle upon Tyne: prof of clinical oncology and dir Cancer Research Unit 1989–, head Div of Oncology 1990–; formerly memb: SW Thames Head and Neck Co-operative Gp, MRC Bladder Cancer Chemotherapy Sub-gp, Advsy Panel Beatson Laboratories, Scientific Ctee Leukaemia Research Fund; currently memb: Phase I Clinical Trials Ctee Cancer Research Campaign, Drug Devpt Ctee and Pharmacokinetics and Metabolism Gp Euro Orgn for Research on Treatment of Cancer (memb Advsy Panel 1979); memb: Int Agency for Research on

Cancer Working Gp on the Evaluation of the Carcinogenic Risk of Chemicals to Humans 1980, EORTC/Nat Cancer Inst (USA) Liaison Ctee 1988, EORTC/NCI/CRC Coordinating Ctee; author of numerous pubns and abstracts in learned jls; ed-in-chief Cancer Chemotherapy and Pharmacology, assoc ed Cancer Surveys; memb Editorial Bd: Anticancer Drug Design, Cancer Topics, Biochemical Pharmacology; numerous invited lectures in Europe, USA, Canada and NZ; memb: Br Assoc for Cancer Research, American Assoc for Cancer Research, Assoc of Cancer Physicians, American Soc of Clinical Oncology, Euro Soc of Med Oncology (invited memb), NY Acad of Scis (invited memb); FRCP 1988 (accreditation in med oncology 1987); *Style*— Prof Hilary Calvert; ✉ Division of Oncology, Newcastle General Hospital, Westgate Road, Newcastle upon Tyne NE4 6BE (☎ 0191 273 8811 ext 22617, fax 0191 273 4867, e-mail hilary.calvert@newcastle.ac.uk)

CALVERT, Margaret Ada Tomsett; JP; da of Donald Arthur Hodge, of Seaford, Sussex, and Ada Constance Janette, *née* Tomsett (d 1973); *b* 8 Jan 1924; *Educ* Haberdashers' Aske's, UCL (BA); *m* 4 July 1953, Dr Jack Maxwell Calvert, s of Albert Henry Calvert (d 1978), of Selby, Yorks; 4 s (David b 1955, Ian b 1956, Jonathan b 1958, Alastair b 1967); *Career* WWII WRNS 1942–46; CA; princ accountant (first woman) Univ of Oxford 1952–53, in public practice as int tax specialist 1954–; lectr in comparative taxation Univ of Manchester 1958–88, memb Taxation Advsy Panel ICEAW 1984–89; memb and one time divnl pres Cheshire Branch Br Red Cross, cmmr and memb Cncl Girl Guides Assoc, pres Br Fedn of Univ Women 1987–90, treas Br Fedn of Women Graduates 1992–95; former treas: Int Fedn Univ Women, World Assoc of Girl Guides and Girl Scouts; memb: VAT Tbnls 1972–, Nat Insur Tbnl, Community Health Cncl, Women's Nat Cmmn 1990–93, Consumer Panel Personal Investment Authy 1993–; FCA 1959; *Recreations* travel, photography; *Style*— Mrs Margaret Calvert, JP; ✉ 3 Chyngton Place, Seaford, E Sussex BN25 4HQ (☎ and fax 01323 490685)

CALVERT, Michael John; MBE (1995), JP (1972), DL (Surrey 1974); s of John Charles Calvert (d 1974); *b* 15 Sept 1930; *Educ* Eton, RMA Sandhurst; *m* 1963, Sally Noel, da of Noel Victor Sharpe Cannon (d 1958); 3 da (Clare, Nicola, Celia); *Career* KRRC 1949–62, Adjt Queen's Royal Rifles 1962–64; farmer and market gardener 1964–; memb Dorking & Horley RDC 1970–74, gen cmmr of income tax 1978–; chm: Surrey TAVRA 1980–87, Surrey Community Devpt Tst 1982–95, Bd Royal Alexandra and Albert Sch 1991–; High Sheriff of Surrey 1979–80; non-exec dir Seeboard 1985–90; Exec Cncl Magistrates Assoc 1996– (memb 1991–); *Recreations* shooting, fishing, golf; *Clubs* Farmers'; *Style*— Michael J Calvert, Esq, MBE, JP, DL; ✉ Ockley Court, Ockley, nr Dorking, Surrey RH5 5LS (☎ 01306 711160, fax 01306 711321)

CALVERT, Paul Thornton; s of John Thornton Calvert, CBE (d 1987), of London, and Barbara Adamson Calvert, QC, *née* Parker; *b* 17 March 1949; *Educ* Rugby, Univ of Cambridge (MA, MB BChir); *m* 20 July 1972, Deborah Deidre Anne, da of late Hon Alison Merivale- Austin; 1 s (Dominic b 1979), 1 da (Natasha b 1976); *Career* conslt orthopaedic and traumatic surgn: Hinchingbrooke Hosp Huntingdon 1985–86, St George's Hospital 1986–, Royal National Orthopaedic Hosp 1993–; author of scientific papers related to shoulder injury and children's orthopaedics; FRCS 1977, FRSM 1983, fell Br Orthopaedic Assoc 1985; *Recreations* squash, tennis; *Clubs* Hawks'; *Style*— Paul Calvert, Esq; ✉ Consultant Orthopaedic Surgeon, St George's Hospital, Blackshaw Rd, London SW17 0QT (☎ 0181 672 1255)

CALVERT, Prof Peter Anthony Richard; s of Raymond Calvert (d 1959), of Helen's Bay, Co Down, NI, and Irene Calvert, MP, *née* Earls; *b* 19 Nov 1936; *Educ* Campbell Coll Belfast, Queens' Coll Cambridge (MA, PhD), Univ of Michigan USA (AM); *m* 1, 1962 (m dis 1987); 2 c; m 2, 8 May 1987, Susan Ann, da of Leonard John Milbank, of Slough, Berkshire; 2 s; *Career* Regular Army (NI Enlistment) 1955–57; teaching fell Univ of Michigan 1960–61; Univ of Southampton: lectr 1964–71, sr lectr 1971–74, reader in politics 1974–83, prof of comparative and international politics 1984–; visiting lectr Univ of California Santa Barbara 1966, res fell Charles Warren Centre for Studies in American History Harvard Univ 1969–70, visiting prof Dept of Politics and Sociology Birkbeck Coll London 1984–85; memb Cambridge City Cncl 1962–64, co-opted memb Dorset Educn Ctee 1984–89; FRHistS 1972; *Books* The Mexican Revolution 1910–1914: The Diplomacy of Anglo American Conflict (1968), Latin America: Internal Conflict and International Peace (1969), A Study of Revolution (1970), Revolution (Key Concepts in Political Science) (1970), Mexico (1973), The Mexicans: How They Live and Work (1975), The Concept of Class (1982), The Falklands Crisis: The Rights and the Wrongs (1982), Politics Power and Revolution: An Introduction to Comparative Politics (1983), Revolution and International Politics (1984, 2 edn 1996), Guatemala, A Nation in Turmoil (1985), The Foreign Policy of New States (1986), The Process of Political Succession (ed, 1987), The Central American Security System: North-South or East-West? (ed, 1988), Argentina: Political Culture and Instability (jtly, 1989), Latin America in the Twentieth Century (jtly, 1990, 2 edn 1993), Revolution and Counter-Revolution (1990), Political and Economic Encyclopaedia of South America and the Caribbean (ed, 1991), Sociology Today (jtly, 1992), An Introduction to Comparative Politics (1993), The International Politics of Latin America (1994), Politics and Society in the Third World (jtly, 1995); *Recreations* running, walking; *Style*— Prof Peter Calvert; ✉ 87 Bassett Green Close, Bassett, Southampton SO16 3QX (☎ 01703 320490); Department of Politics, University of Southampton, Highfield, Southampton SO17 1BJ (☎ 01703 592577, fax 01703 593276, e-mail pcpol@socsci.soton.ac.uk)

CALVERT, Phyllis (Mrs Murray Hill); da of Frederick Bickle (d 1964), and Annie Williams (d 1957); *b* 18 Feb 1915; *Educ* French Lycee, Margaret Morris Sch Dancing and Acting; *m* 1941, Peter Auriol Murray Hill (d 1957), s of George Murray Hill (d 1941); 1 s (Piers), 1 da (Auriol); *Career* actress; *Theatre* incl: A Woman's Privilege (Kingsway Theatre) 1939, Punch without Judy (Embassy) 1939, Flare Path (Apollo) 1942, Escapade (St James's) 1953, It's Never Too Late (Strand) 1954, River Breeze (Phoenix) 1956, The Complaisant Lover (Globe) 1959, The Rehearsal (Globe) 1961, Ménage à Trois (Lyric) 1963, Portrait of Murder (Savoy and Vauderville) 1963, A Scent of Flowers (Duke of York's) 1964, Present Laughter (Queen's) 1965, A Woman of No Importance (Vauderville) 1967, Blithe Spirit (Globe) 1970, Crown Matrimonial (Haymarket) 1973, Dear Daddy (Ambassadors) 1976, Mrs Warren's Profession (Worcester) 1977, She Stoops to Conquer (Old World Exeter) 1978, Suite in Two Keys (tour) 1978, Before the Party (Queen's) 1980, The Heiress (Chichester Festival) 1989; *Television* incl: Kate 1970, Lady Killers 1981, Month in the Country 1984, PD James' Cover Her Face 1984, Death of the Heart (Granada) 1985, Boon (Central) 1986, Capsticks Law (Granada) 1987, Across the Lake (BBC) 1987, Victoria Wood (BBC) 1989, Jute City (BBC) 1991, After Henry 1990, Woof 1991, The House of Elliot (BBC) 1993, Sherlock Holmes (Granada) 1993, Bed (BBC) 1994, Casualty (BBC) 1996; *Films* 1939–; Kipps, The Young Mr Pitt, Man in Grey, Fanny by Gaslight, Madonna of the Seven Moons, They were Sisters, Time out of Mind, Broken Journey, My Own True Love, The Golden Madonna, A Woman with No Name, Mr Denning Drives North, Mandy, The Net, It's Never too Late, Child in the House, Indiscreet, The Young and The Guilty, Oscar Wilde, Twisted Nerve, Oh! What a Lovely War, The Walking Stick, Mrs Dalloway; *Style*— Phyllis Calvert; ✉ 1 Sandringham Court, Westleigh Avenue, London SW15 6RE (☎ 0181 789 7868); c/o agent, Jeremy Conway, 18–21 Jermyn Street, London SW1Y 6HP (☎ 0171 287 0077)

CALVERT, (William) Roger Spencer; s of Charles Gilbert Calvert (d 1983), of Hale, Cheshire, and Eva, *née* Rathbone; *b* 18 May 1938; *Educ* Liverpool Coll, Rossall Sch, Selwyn Coll Cambridge (MA, LLM); *m* 11 Jan 1973, Evelyn Moira, da of Kenneth Harland Wilson (d 1967); 1 s (Simon Harland Spencer b 5 April 1974), 1 da (Nicola Eve b 7 June 1977); *Career* cmmnd Nat Serv (active serv Aden and Kenya) 1958–59; admitted slr 1966; asst slr: Slaughter & May 1966–69, North Kirk & Co Liverpool 1969–71; ptnr Cuff Roberts (formerly North Kirk & Co then Cuff Roberts North Kirk) 1971–; sec Pool Promoters' Assoc 1983–; memb Law Soc 1966; *Recreations* golf, rugby (watching now!), music, gardening; *Clubs* Liverpool Racquet, Waterloo RFC, Northern Cricket, Formby Golf; *Style*— Roger Calvert, Esq; ✉ Messrs Cuff Roberts Solicitors, 100 Old Hall, Liverpool L3 9TD (☎ 0151 227 4181, fax 0151 227 2584)

CALVERT-SMITH, David; s of Arthur Eustace Calvert-Smith, of Bury, W Sussex, and Stella Margaret, *née* Tilling (d 1995); *b* 6 April 1945; *Educ* Eton, Kings Coll Cambridge (MA); *m* 4 Dec 1971, Marianthe; 1 s (Richard b 1972), 1 da (Stella b 1975); *Career* called to the Bar 1969, recorder of the Crown Court 1986–, first sr Treasy Counsel 1995– (counsel 1986–91, sr Treasy counsel 1991–95); *Style*— David Calvert-Smith; ✉ Queen Elizabeth Building, Temple, London EC4Y 9BS (☎ 0171 583 5766, fax 0171 353 0339)

CALVIN, Michael; s of Charles Calvin, of Watford, and Margaret, *née* Platts; *b* 3 Aug 1957; *Educ* Watford GS; *m* Lynn-Marie, da of Oliver Frank Goss; 3 s (Nicholas b 17 April 1987, Aaron b 15 April 1989, William b 20 Jan 1995); *Career* Watford Observer 1974–77, Hayters Sports Agency 1977–79, chief sports writer Westminster Press Newspapers 1979–83, sports reporter Thames TV 1983–84; sports columnist Daily Telegraph 1996– (gen sports feature writer 1984–86, chief sports feature writer 1986–96), md Calvin Communications (sports consultancy) 1996–; memb winning British team Camel Trophy off-road rally around Amazon basin 1989, finished third on yacht Hofbrau Lager in British Steel Challenge round the world yacht race 1992–93; winner Seagrave Medal for Outstanding Achievement 1990; ldr Daily Telegraph sports writing team Newspaper of the Year in Sport for Disabled Media Awards 1991, 1992, 1993 and 1994; Sports Reporter of the Year 1992, Sports Journalist of the Year 1992, special award for services to yachting journalism 1994; memb Sport Writers Assoc; *Books* Cricket Captaincy (1978); *Recreations* innocent adventure; *Clubs* Cape Horners', Royal Ocean Racing; *Style*— Michael Calvin, Esq; ✉ Broomwood, Higher Rads End, Eversholt, Beds MK17 9ED (☎ 01525 280300, fax 01525 280182); The Daily Telegraph, 1 Canada Square, Canary Wharf, London E14 5DT (☎ 0171 538 6785, fax 0171 513 2507)

CALVIN-THOMAS, Joseph Wyndham (known as Wyn Calvin); MBE (1989); s of John Calvin-Thomas (d 1959), and Ethel Mary, *née* Griffiths (d 1974); *b* 28 Aug 1927; *Educ* Canton HS Cardiff; *m* 1975, Carole Tarvin-Jones; *Career* served RASC 1944–45; non-stop theatre and broadcasting 1945–; memb Ctee Entertainment Artistes Benevolent Fund 1960–, chm Wales Ctee Variety Club of GB 1980–82, 1984–86 and 1993–, vice pres Cor Meibion de Cymru (Massed Male Choir of S Wales), London-Welsh Male Choir, vice chm SOS (Soc of Stars); hon prodr Wales Festival of Remembrance (Royal Br Legion); barker Variety Club of GB 1963–, "King" Grand Order of Water Rats 1990–91, Freeman City of London 1992; fell Univ of Wales Coll of Music and Drama 1994; *Recreations* writing, reading, world-wandering; *Style*— Wyn Calvin, Esq, MBE; ✉ 121 Cathedral Rd, Cardiff CF1 9PH (☎ 01222 232777)

CALVOCORESSI, Maj Ion Melville; MBE (1945), MC (1942); s of Matthew John Calvocoressi, and Agnes Hermione, da of late Judge Robert Melville, of Sussex and Salop; *b* 12 April 1919; *Educ* Eton, Magdalen Coll Oxford (MA); *m* 1947, Katherine, da of Capt Edward Coverley Kennedy, RN (ka 1939, ggs of Hon Robert Kennedy, bro of 1 Marquess of Ailsa and 3 s of 11 Earl of Cassillis), and Rosalind, da of Sir Ludovic Grant, 11 Bt; 3 s, 1 da; *Career* Scots Gds 1939–46: Middle East, Sicily, Italy, SE Asia 1941–45, ADC, GOC 8 Army 1944, Mil Asst; CGS ALFSEA 1945; memb London Stock Exchange 1949–92; High Sheriff of Kent 1978–79; *Recreations* cricket, gardening; *Clubs* Cavalry & Guards', Pratt's, MCC, Kent CCC; *Style*— Maj Ion Calvocoressi, MBE, MC; ✉ Court Lodge, Westerham, Kent TN16 2DH (☎ 01959 563358)

CALVOCORESSI, Peter John Ambrose; s of Pandia John Calvocoressi (d 1965), of 31 Albion Gate, London W2, and Irene, *née* Ralli; *b* 17 Nov 1912, Karachi; *Educ* Eton, Balliol Coll Oxford; *m* 1938, Hon Barbara Dorothy Eden, da of late 6 Baron Henley; 2 s; *Career* serv WWII Wing Cdr RAFVR (Air Intelligence); called to the Bar Inner Temple 1935; contested (Lib) Warwicks (Nuneaton Div) 1945; author; dir Chatto & Windus Ltd and The Hogarth Press Ltd 1954–65; reader in Int Relations Univ of Sussex 1966–71, editorial dir and chief exec Penguin Books 1972–76; chm: The Africa Bureau 1963–72, The London Library 1966–72, Open Univ Educnl Enterprises 1979–89; memb UN Sub-Ctee on Discrimination and Minorities 1962–71; memb Cncl: Royal Inst of Int Affairs, Inst of Strategic Studies; *Books* Nuremberg - The Facts, the Law and the Consequences (1947), Surveys of International Affairs Vols 1–5 (1947–54), Middle East Crisis (with Guy Wint, 1957), South Africa and World Opinion (1961), World Order and New States (1962), World Politics Since 1965 (1968, 6 edn 1991), Total War (with Guy Wint, 1972, 2 edn 1989), The British Experience 1945–75 (1978), Top Secret Ultra (1980), Independent Africa and the World (1985), A Time for Peace (1987), Who's Who in the Bible (1987), Resilient Europe 1870–2000 (1991), Threading my Way (1994); *Clubs* Garrick; *Style*— Peter Calvocoressi, Esq; ✉ 1 Queen's Parade, Bath BA1 2NJ

CAMBER, Richard Monash; s of Maurice Camber (d 1991), of Glasgow, and Libby Camber (d 1981); *b* 22 July 1944; *Educ* Glasgow HS, Univ of Edinburgh (MA), Univ of Paris, Univ of London; *m* 26 Oct 1970, The Hon Angela Felicity, da of Baroness Birk (Life Peer), by her husband Ellis Birk; 1 s (Thomas b 1980), 2 da (Alice b 1974, Chloe b 1980); *Career* asst keeper Dept of Medieval and Later Antiquities Br Museum 1970–78; dir: Sotheby's London 1983–87, Sotheby's, Sotheby's International; conslt Euro Works of Art 1988–; FSA; *Recreations* reading, listening to music (particularly opera); *Style*— Richard Camber, Esq, FSA

CAMDEN, 6 Marquess (UK 1812); David George Edward Henry Pratt; also Baron Camden (GB 1765), Earl Camden and Viscount Bayham (GB 1786), and Earl of Brecknock (UK 1812); s of 5 Marquess Camden, JP, DL (d 1983), and his 1 w, Marjorie Minna, DBE (d 1989), da of late Col Atherton Edward Jenkins; *b* 13 Aug 1930; *Educ* Eton; *m* 1961 (m dis 1985), Virginia Ann, only da of late Francis Harry Hume Finlaison, of Windsor; 2 s (1 decd), 1 da; *Heir* s, Earl of Brecknock, *qv*; *Career* late 2 Lt Scots Gds; *Style*— The Most Hon the Marquess Camden; ✉ Wherwell House, Andover, Hants SP11 7JP (☎ 01264 860020, fax 01264 860123)

CAMERON, (John) Alastair; *see:* Abernethy, Hon Lord

CAMERON, Maj Allan John; MBE (1988), JP (Ross and Cromarty 1960), DL; s of Col Sir Donald Cameron of Lochiel, KT, CMG (d 1951), and Lady Hermione Graham (d 1978), da of 5 Duke of Montrose; *b* 25 March 1917; *Educ* Harrow, RMC Sandhurst; *m* 1945, (Mary) Elizabeth, da of Col Arthur Vaughan-Lee, MVO (d 1933), of Dillington, Somerset; 2 s (and 1 s decd), 2 da; *Career* Regular Offr Queen's Own Cameron Highlanders 1936, served WWII Maj (POW 1942), ret 1948; landowner and farmer; served on: BBC Cncl for Scot, Countryside Cmmn of Scot, Red Deer Cmmn, Ross-shire CC (chm County Educn Ctee 1962–75); convener Ross-Cromarty DC 1991–96; pres Royal Caledonian Curling Club 1963–64, Vice Lord-Lieut Ross and Cromarty Highland Region 1977–92; *Recreations* shooting, fishing, curling, golf, gardening; *Clubs* Naval and Military; *Style*— Maj Allan Cameron, MBE, JP, DL; ✉ Allangrange, Munlochy, Ross and Cromarty IV8 8NZ (☎ 0146 381 1249)

CAMERON, Prof Averil Millicent; *b* 8 Feb 1940; *Educ* Westwood Hall Girls' HS Leek Staffs, Somerville Coll Oxford (exhibitioner, Passmore Edwards scholar, Rosa Hovey scholar, state student, MA), UCL (PhD); *m* 1962 (m dis 1980), Alan Douglas Edward Cameron; 1 s, 1 da; *Career* KCL: asst lectr in classics 1965–68, lectr in classics 1968–70, reader in ancient history 1970–78, prof of ancient history 1978–89, memb Cncl 1982–85, head Dept of Classics 1985–89, fell 1987–, prof of late antique and Byzantine studies 1989–94, dir Centre for Hellenic Studies 1989–94, chair Humanities Res Centres 1992–94; warden Keble Coll Oxford 1994–; chair: British Nat Byzantine Ctee 1983–89, Roman Soc Schs Ctee 1986–88, Classics Sub-Ctee Univ of London Arts Review 1987, Univ of London Byzantine Library Subject Sub-Ctee 1990–94; pres London Assoc of Classical Teachers schs 1988–90; memb: Cncl British Acad 1983–86, JACT Ancient History Ctee 1985–89, Ctee of Mgmnt and Fin Ctee Warburg Inst 1986–93; business mangr Dialogos Hellenic Studies Review 1994, memb Bd of Mgmnt Inst of Classical Studies 1990–94; ed Jl of Roman Studies 1985–90; visiting asst prof Columbia Univ NYC 1967–68, visiting memb Inst of Advanced Study Princeton New Jersey 1977–78, Sather prof of classical literature Univ of Calif Berkeley 1986, visiting prof Collège de France 1987, distinguished visitor Inst of Advanced Study Princeton 1992, Landsdowne lectr Univ of Victoria 1992; memb Ctee of the Prosopography of the Byzantine Empire, co-dir Late Antiquity and Early Islam Project, pres Soc for the Promotion of Roman Studies 1995–; Hon DLitt Univ of Warwick 1996; FBA 1981, FSA 1981; *Books* Procopius (abridged trans, 1967), Agathias (1970), Corippus In Laudem Iustini minoris libri quattuor (1976), Continuity and Change in Sixth-Century Byzantium (collected articles, 1981), Images of Women in Antiquity (ed with Amelie Kuhrt, 1983, revd 1993), Constantinople in the Eighth Century: the Parastaseis Syntomoi Chronikai (ed with Judith Herrin et al, 1984), Procopius and the Sixth Century (1985), The Greek Renaissance in the Roman Empire (ed with Susan Walker, 1989), History as Text (ed, 1989), Christianity and the Rhetoric of Empire (Sather lectr, 1991), The Byzantine and Early Islamic Near East I: Problems in the Literary Sources (ed with Lawrence I Conrad, 1992), Storia dell'età tardoantica/L'antiquité tardive (1992), The Later Roman Empire: Fontana History of the Ancient World (1993), The Mediterranean World in Late Antiquity AD 395–600: Routledge History of Classical Civilization (1993), The Byzantine and Early Islamic Near East II: Land Use and Settlement Patterns (ed with Geoffrey King, 1994), The Byzantine and Early Islamic Near East III: States, Resources and Armies (ed, 1995), Changing Cultures in Early Byzantium (1996); author of many articles in jls; *Style—* Prof Averil Cameron, FBA, FSA; ✉ Keble College, Oxford OX1 3PG (☎ 01865 272700, fax 01865 272785)

CAMERON, Rt Rev (Andrew) Bruce; *see:* Aberdeen and Orkney, Bishop of

CAMERON, David Roderick Simpson; s of J Roderick Cameron, and Dorothy M Pearson; *b* 2 June 1941; *Educ* Angusfield, George Watson's Coll, Edinburgh Coll of Art, Univ of Newcastle; *m* 28 July 1973, Filitsa, *née* Boulton; 1 s (James), 2 da (Helena, Katrina); *Career* urban design conslt; formerly architect with Rowand Anderson, Kininmonth & Paul, conservation offr Edinburgh Corp/DC, dep dir planning City of Edinburgh 1983–96; project mangr Euro Union ECOS Project for revival of the Kazimierz area of Krakow Poland 1993–95; convener: Steering Ctee for the Historic Burghs Assoc of Scotland 1993–, Charles Cameron Campaign Ctee (18th C architect to Ct of Russia St Petersburg) 1994–, Saltire Planning and Environment Ctee 1995–, Scottish Environment and Amenity Link 1996–; chm: The Saltire Soc 1990–95, Sir Patrick Geddes Meml Tst 1991–; memb: Exec Ctee Scottish Soc of Directors of Planning 1988–96, Cncl Nat Trust for Scotland 1994–, Scottish Homes Advsy Gp on Physical Quality 1996–, Grants Cncl Caledonian Fndn 1996–; vice pres Clan Cameron Assoc 1995–; hon sec Edinburgh Architectural Assoc 1972–75 (ed Review 1980–84); memb Int Soc of City and Regnl Planners 1987; RIBA, ARIAS, MRTPI, FSA (Scot); *Recreations* art, angling, Scottish and Greek history; *Style—* David Cameron, Esq; ✉ Chambers Design, 4 Dovecot Road, Corstorphine, Edinburgh EH12 7LE (☎ and fax 0131 539 2745)

CAMERON, Dr Douglas; s of Dr Robert Cameron (d 1949), of Cambridge, and Louise Patricia, *née* Smith (d 1991); *b* 2 Aug 1943; *Educ* The Leys Sch Cambridge, Univ of Glasgow (BSc, MD); *m* 5 July 1969, Catherine Love, da of William Leslie Bews (d 1971), of Glasgow; 2 da (Esther b 1970, Sarah b 1972); *Career* conslt psychiatrist specialising in alcohol problems Leicestershire Health Authy 1976–91, sr lectr in substance misuse Univ of Leicester 1991–; fndr Leicestershire Community Alcohol and Drugs Servs 1978, interim then full exec memb Alcohol Concern 1983–87; fndr memb New Directions in the Study of Alcohol Gp 1976– (chair 1990–92); inaugural chair The Addictions Forum 1992–95; FRCPsych 1988 (MRCPsych 1974); *Publications* papers incl: Lessons from an Out-Patient Controlled Drinking Group (Journal of Alcoholism, with M T Spence, 1976), Teenage Drinking in South West Scotland (British Journal of Addiction, with R J McKechnie, I A Cameron and J Drewery, 1977), Rate of Onset of Drunkenness (Journal of Studies on Alcohol, with M T Spence and J Drewery, 1978); contrib: Alcoholism - A Multidisciplinary Approach (1977), The Misuse of Alcohol - Crucial Issues in Dependence, Treatment and Prevention (ed, N Heather, I Robertson and P Davies, 1985), Alcohol and The Public Health (1991); Liberating Solutions to Alcohol Problems (1995); assoc ed Addiction Research 1992–; *Recreations* participant observation of public house culture!; *Style—* Dr Douglas Cameron; ✉ Drury House, 50 Leicester Rd, Narborough, Leicestershire LE9 5DF (☎ 0116 286 3267, fax 0116 275 2840)

CAMERON, Rt Rev Douglas MacLean; *see:* Argyll and The Isles, Bishop of

CAMERON, Prof Dugald; s of Andrew Cameron, and May Irene, *née* Jamieson; *b* 4 Oct 1939; *Educ* HS of Glasgow, Glasgow Sch of Art (DA, Post Grad Dip); *m* Aug 1972, Nancy Cowan, da of late George and late Jean Inglis; *Career* freelance industrial designer and aviation artist 1962–; Glasgow Sch of Art: visiting lectr 1963–70, sr lectr in product design 1970–, chm of furniture/interior/product design 1975–, govr 1976–82, head of design 1982–, dir (princ) 1991–; memb: Engrg Advsy Ctee Scottish Ctee Cncl of Industrial Design 1966–, Industrial Design (Engrg) Panel CNAA 1978–, 3D Design Bd CNAA 1978–, Scottish Ctee on Higher Educn Design Cncl 1985–; fndr Squadron Prints Ltd 1977; hon prof Univ of Glasgow 1993; chm Skelmorlie Community Cncl 1987; memb Master Ct Incorporation of Weavers 1987; FCSD 1974, CRAeS 1996; *Books* Glasgow's Own - A History of 602 Sqdn Royal Aux Air Force (1987), Glasgow's Airport (1989), Eagles in the Sky - A Celebration of the RAF on its 75th Birthday (jtly, 1993); author of numerous articles on design and aviation; *Recreations* flying, railways, drawing; *Clubs* Glasgow Art; *Style—* Prof Dugald Cameron, Esq; ✉ Glasgow School of Art, 167 Renfrew Street, Glasgow G3 6RQ (☎ 0141 353 4521, fax 0141 353 4528)

CAMERON, Ewen James Hanning; DL (Somerset 1989); s of Maj Allan Cameron, MBE, JP, DL, *qv*, of Allangrange, Munlochy, Ross-shire, and Mary Elisabeth, *née* Vaughan-Lee; *b* 24 Nov 1949; *Educ* Harrow, Univ of Oxford (MA); *m* 1975, Caroline Anne, da of H D Ripley (d 1967), sometime chm of Willis Faber & Dumas insurance brokers; 3 s (Ewen Allan Hanning b 10 July 1977, James Alexander Hanning 14 May 1979, Angus Derek Hanning b 19 March 1983), 1 da (Flora Elisabeth Patricia b 13 Oct 1986); *Career* owner and mangr Dillington Estate Somerset; fndr and chm Orchard FM independent radio station; pres Somerset Fedn of Young Farmers' Clubs 1990–91, nat pres CLA 1995–; High Sheriff of Somerset 1986–87; FRICS 1992 (ARICS 1979), FRAgS 1996, FRSA 1996; *Recreations* shooting, skiing, tennis, windsurfing; *Style—* Ewen Cameron, Esq, DL; ✉ Dillington Estate, Ilminster, Somerset TA19 9EQ (☎ 01460 54614)

CAMERON, Prof Iain Thomas; s of Maj James David Cameron (d 1993), of Preston, and Stella, *née* Turner; *b* 21 Feb 1956; *Educ* Hutton GS, Univ of Edinburgh (BSc, MB ChB, MD), Univ of Cambridge (MA), MRCOG, MRACOG; *m* 1, 1983 (m dis), Sally, *née* Herries; 2 da (Sarah b 22 Aug 1985, Fiona b 6 Jan 1988); m 2, 1992, Heidi, da of Alan Francis Wade (d 1995); 1 s (James b 7 April 1993), 1 da (Mhairi b 13 July 1995); *Career* house offr: Western Infirmary Glasgow, Royal Infirmary Edinburgh; SHO Simpson Meml Maternity Pavilion Edinburgh 1980–82, lectr and registrar Dept of Obstetrics and Gynaecology Univ of Edinburgh 1984–86 (res fell 1982–84), lectr Monash Univ 1987–88 (clinical res fell 1986–88), sr registrar Royal Women's Hosp Melbourne 1988–89; Univ of Cambridge: lectr 1989–92, sr registrar 1989–91, conslt 1991–92; regius prof of obstetrics and gynaecology Univ of Glasgow 1993–; memb: Soc for the Study of Fertility 1983, Blair Bell Research Soc 1985, Fertility Soc of Aust 1986, British Fertility Soc 1991, American Fertility Soc 1992, Endocrine Soc 1992, Soc for the Study of Reproduction 1992, American Assoc for the Advancement of Science 1993, Glasgow Obstetrical and Gynaecological Soc 1993, Gynaecological Visiting Soc 1993; *Style—* Prof Iain T Cameron; ✉ University of Glasgow, Department of Obstetrics & Gynaecology, The Queen Mother's Hospital, Yorkhill, Glasgow G3 8SJ (☎ 0141 201 0567, fax 0141 357 3610)

CAMERON, Prof Ian Rennell; s of James Cameron (d 1985), of London, and Frances Mary, *née* Little (d 1959); *b* 20 May 1936; *Educ* Westminster, CCC Oxford (MA), St Thomas's Hosp Med Sch (BM BCh, DM); *m* 1, 1 Feb 1964, Jayne Heather, da of Lt-Col Frank Bustard, OBE (d 1974), of Haslemere, Surrey; 1 s (Hugh Nicholas b 1968), 1 da (Lucinda Emma b 1970); m 2, 24 Dec 1980, Jennifer Jane, da of George Stewart Cowin (d 1978), of IOM; *Career* St Thomas's Hosp Med Sch: med registrar and lectr 1963–68, sr lectr 1969–75, reader in med 1975–79, prof of med 1979–94, dean 1986–89; res fell Cedars - Sinai Med Center LA, asst prof Dept of Physiology Univ of California LA 1968–69; provost and vice-chllr Univ of Wales Coll of Med 1994–; princ UMDS 1989–92, dir R & D SE Thames RHA 1993–94; chm Mgmnt Team W Lambeth DHA 1982–83, memb Medway Health Authy 1981–86, memb Cncl KCL 1993–; Freeman City of London 1984, Liveryman Worshipful Soc of Apothecaries 1985 (Yeoman 1976); memb: CVCP 1994–, GMC 1994–; FRCP 1976; *Books* Respiratory Disorders (with N T Bateman, 1983); *Recreations* collecting books, china, paintings; *Clubs* Athenaeum; *Style—* Prof Ian Cameron; ✉ Provost and Vice-Chancellor, University of Wales College of Medicine, Heath Park, Cardiff CF4 4XN (☎ 01222 742071, fax 01222 745306)

CAMERON, Ivy; *b* 25 Jan 1948; *Educ* Rolle Coll of Educn Exmouth Devon (CertEd), LSE (Dip in Industrial Relations and Trade Union Studies); *Career* English teacher Bristol LEA and TEFL Lerida Spain 1969–72; Banking Insurance and Finance Union: area organiser W Midlands, negotiating offr Int Banks, asst sec, nat negotiator 1972–90; ptnr Cameron Woods Assocs 1990–93; memb: Trade Union Congress Women's Ctee, EEC's IRIS Training Network; England rep to European Women's Lobby; German Marshall Fund fell Cornel Univ NY 1980, visiting fell Industrial Relations Pembroke Coll Univ of Oxford 1989; FRSA 1993; author of numerous articles in a variety of nat newspapers and int TU and mgmnt magazines; *Recreations* singing, dancing, reading, walking, cross-country skiing; *Style—* Ms Ivy Cameron; ✉ Cameron Woods Associates, Prospect House, 5 Hill Road, Clevedon BS21 7NE (☎ 01275 342660, fax 01275 342661)

CAMERON, John Bell; CBE; s of Capt John Archibald, MC (d 1960), and Margaret (d 1974); *b* 14 June 1939; *Educ* Dollar Acad; *m* 24 July 1964, Margaret, da of James Clapperton, OBE (d 1977); *Career* pres NFU of Scotland 1979–84 (first long term pres); chm: EEC Sheepmeat Ctee 1983–90, World Meats Gp 1983–, UK Sheep Consultative Ctee 1984–86, BR (Scotland) Bd 1988–95, United Auctions Ltd 1988–92; memb BR Bd 1988–95; memb Bd: SW Trains 1995–, Island Line 1995–; chm Bd of Govrs Dollar Acad; FRAgS; *Recreations* flying, shooting, swimming; *Style—* John Cameron, Esq, CBE; ✉ Balbuthie Farm, Leven, Fife, Scotland (☎ 01333 730210)

CAMERON, Prof John Robinson (Robin); s of Rev Dr George Gordon Cameron (d 1981), of Edinburgh, and Mary Levering, *née* Robinson (d 1989); *b* 24 June 1936; *Educ* Dundee HS, Univ of St Andrews (MA, BPhil); *m* 1, 19 Aug 1959, Mary Elizabeth (d 1984), da of Rev Dr Charles Wesley Ranson (d 1988), of Lakeville, USA; 1 s (Ian b 1967), 2 da (Margaret b 1962, Catherine b 1965); m 2, 25 June 1987, Barbara Elizabeth, da of James Moncur (d 1967), of Newport-on-Tay; *Career* lectr in philosophy Queen's Coll Dundee 1963–67 (asst lectr 1962–63), sr lectr Univ of Dundee 1973–78 (lectr 1967–72); regius prof of logic Univ of Aberdeen 1979–; elder Church of Scotland; *Recreations* bricolage; *Style—* Prof Robin Cameron; ✉ Department of Philosophy, University of Aberdeen, King's College, Old Aberdeen AB9 2UB (☎ 01224 272365)

CAMERON, Sir John Watson; kt (1981), OBE (1960); s of Capt Watson Cameron and Isabel Mann; *b* 16 Nov 1901; *Educ* Lancing; *m* Lilian Florence, *née* Sanderson; 1 s, 2 da; *Career* cmmd Durham RGA 1920; J W Cameron & Co Brewery: joined 1922, md 1940, chm 1943–75, pres 1977–; memb Northern Area Econ League 1950–80 (chm 1964–67), chm Northern Area Cons Pty (treas 1967–72); Hartlepool Cons Pty: chm 1942–45, pres 1945–76, patron 1976–78, pres and patron 1978–; *Style—* Sir John Cameron

CAMERON, Prof Keith Colwyn; s of Leonard George Cameron (d 1969), of Cwmbran, Gwent, and Ethel Cameron; *b* 1 April 1939; *Educ* Jones' West Monmouth Sch, Univ of Exeter (BA), Univ of Cambridge (Cert Ed), Université de Rennes (LèsL, Doct de l'univ); *m* 4 Aug 1962, Marie-Edith Françoise, da of Francis Marie-Joseph Briens (d 1978), of I et V, France; 3 da (Anne b 1963, Cécilia, b 1964, Virginia b 1968); *Career* asst lectr Univ of Aberdeen 1964–66; Univ of Exeter: lectr 1966–76, sr lectr 1976–88, reader 1988–94, dean Faculty of Arts 1991–94, prof of French and Renaissance studies 1994–; gen ed: Exeter Textes littéraires 1970–, CALL 1989–, European Studies 1993, Europa 1994; dir: Exeter Tapes 1972–, Elm Bank Pubns 1972–; chm Euro Movement Devon Branch; *Books* Montaigne et l'humour (1966), Agrippa d'Aubigné (1977), Henri III - a Maligned or Malignant King? (1978), Montaigne and his Age (1981), René Maran (1985), B Palissy, Recepte véritable (1988), Concordance de Du Bellay (1988), Computer Assisted Language Learning (1989), From Valois to Bourbon (1989), Louise Labé: Renaissance Poet and Feminist (1990), Humour and History (1993), The Nation Myth or Reality (1994), The Literary Portrayal of Passion through the Ages: An Interdisciplinary View (1996); *Recreations* theatre, walking, travel; *Style—* Prof Keith Cameron; ✉ Department of French, Queen's Building, The Queen's Drive, The University, Exeter EX4 4QH (☎ 01392 264221, fax 01392 264222, telex 42894 EXUNI)

CAMERON, Prof Kenneth; CBE (1987); s of Angus Whittaker Cameron (d 1948), of Habergham, Burnley, Lancs, and Elizabeth Alice, *née* Hargreaves (d 1989); *b* 21 May 1922; *Educ* Burnley GS, Univ of Leeds (BA), Univ of Sheffield (PhD); *m* 8 Dec 1948, Kathleen (d 1977), da of Frank Ewart Heap, of Burnley, Lancs; 1 s (Iain b 1955), 1 da (Susan (Mrs Cole) b 1949); *Career* WWII Flt Lt RAF 1941–45; asst lectr Univ of Sheffield 1947–50; Univ of Nottingham: sr lectr 1959–62, reader 1962–63, prof of Eng language 1963–87, head Dept of Eng Studies 1984–87, prof emeritus 1988; external prof Univ of Loughborough 1990–93; Sr Israel Gollancz Meml prize Br Acad 1969, Sahlgren prize Royal Gustav Adolfs Acad 1990; hon dir English Place Name Soc 1967–93; Hon Fil Dr Univ of Uppsala 1977, Hon DLitt Univ of Sheffield 1991; FBA 1976, FRHS 1970, FSA 1984; *Books* The Place-Names of Derbyshire (3 vols 1959), English Place-Names (1961, revised 1996), The Place-Names of Lincolnshire (4 vols, 1985, 1991, 1992 and 1996), Studies in Honour of Kenneth Cameron (1987), Place-Name Evidence for the Anglo-Saxon Invasion and Scandinavian Settlements (1975); *Recreations* sports (supporting); *Style—* Prof Kenneth Cameron, CBE, FBA; ✉ 16 The Cloisters, Salthouse Lane, Beeston, Nottingham NG9 2FR (☎ 0115 925 4503); The University of Nottingham, Nottingham NG5 2RD (☎ 0115 951 5151 ext 2892)

CAMERON, Sheriff Lewis; s of James Cameron (d 1946), of Glasgow, and Marie Isobel, *née* McKenzie (d 1992), of Glasgow; *b* 12 Aug 1935; *Educ* St Aloysius Coll Glasgow, Blairs Coll Aberdeen, St Sulpice Paris, Univ of Glasgow (MA, LLB); *m* Sheila Colette, da of Hugh Gallacher, OBE; 2 da (Julie Colette b 26 Nov 1963, Madeleine Jane b 29 May

1966), 2 s (Neville Stuart b 12 April 1970, Lewis James b 16 Aug 1975); *Career* Nat Serv RAF 1954–56; admitted slr 1962; sheriff of S Strathclyde, Dumfries & Galloway: at Dumfries 1988–94, at Hamilton 1994–; tutor Univ of Strathclyde 1981–88; Legal Aid sec Airdrie 1978–87, dean Airdrie Soc of Slrs 1984–85; chm: Social Security Appeals Tbnl 1983–88, Dumfries & Galloway Family Conciliation Serv 1988–92, Dumfries & Galloway Scottish Assoc for the Study of Delinquency 1989–92, PHEW (respite care for parents of mentally handicapped) 1994–; memb: Law Soc of Scotland 1962–, Legal Aid Central Ctee 1970–80, Scotland Ctee NCH - Action for Children (formerly Nat Children's Homes) 1991–94; treas Monklands Victim Support Scheme 1983–88, tstee Oscar Marzaroli Tst 1990–92; *Recreations* cinema, theatre, travel, tennis; *Clubs* New (St Andrews), Ross Priory (Gartocharn Loch Lomond), Royal Scottish Automobile; *Style—* Sheriff Lewis Cameron; ✉ Sheriff Court Hamilton, 4 Beckford Street, Hamilton, Strathclyde ML3 6AA (☎ 01698 282957, fax 01698 284403)

CAMERON, Malcolm Maben; s of Charles Cameron, of Waikanae, NZ, and Margaret Isabella Jean, *née* Brash (d 1976); *b* 10 July 1941; *Educ* Rongotai Coll Wellington NZ, Victoria Univ Wellington NZ (BSc), Otago Med Sch NZ (MB ChB); *m* 12 Dec 1987, Cecily Anne, da of John Honeyford; 1 s (Jody Brent Alexander b 3 Aug 1981); *Career* Capt TA NZ 1967–72; sr registrar neurosurgery Salford 1976–, conslt neurosurgn Wakefield 1979–; author of 23 articles on neurosurgical lit 1974–89; surgical assessor Int Soc of Paediatriconcology, chm Local Div Surgery, memb Cncl N of England Neurological Assoc; memb: SIOP, SBNS, NENA; FRCS (Ed) 1973; *Books* Complications of Paediatric Surgery (contrib, 1982), Complications In Spinal Surgery (jtly, 1989), Spinal Surgery-Science and Practice (jtly, 1989); *Recreations* swimming, shooting, reading, writing; *Style—* Malcolm Cameron, Esq; ✉ Liley Beck, Clough Lane, Upper Hopton, Mirfield, W Yorks WF14 8EQ (☎ 01924 480588); Department of Neurosurgery, Pinderfields General Hospital, Wakefield, W Yorks WF1 4DG (☎ 01924 201688)

CAMERON, Peter John; MBE; s of John Gordon Cameron (d 1945), of Cheadle Hulme, and Beatrice, *née* Ward (d 1955); *b* 28 Sept 1926; *Educ* Xaverian Coll Manchester, Univ of Manchester Inst of Sci and Technol (BSc); *m* 1957, Helen Cecilia, da of Daniel Whealing; 2 s (John Gordon b 1958, Adrian Peter b 1960), 3 da (Ann Elizabeth b 1959, Margaret Bernadette b 1962, Catherine Cecilia b 1964); *Career* served Army rising to the rank of Capt REME 1946–48; jr engr Steam Turbine Dept Metropolitan Vickers 1951–54 (coll apprentice 1949–51); NNC Ltd (formerly AEI John Thompson Nuclear Energy Company): engr 1955–60, gp head Projects 1961–69, chief engr Heysham II and Torness Power Stations 1981–87, projects gen mangr Gas Reactor Construction 1987–89; conslt for Nuclear Safety and Station Decommissioning Scottish Nuclear Ltd 1989–; FIMechE 1970, CEng 1970, FEng 1990; *Recreations* walking, swimming, reading; *Style—* Peter Cameron, Esq, MBE, FEng; ✉ 42 Edenbridge Road, Cheadle Hulme, Cheadle, Cheshire SK8 5PX (☎ 0161 485 1408)

CAMERON, Prof Robert Andrew Duncan; s of late George Duncan Cameron, of Chichester, W Sussex, and Margaret Mary, *née* Walker; *b* 7 April 1943; *Educ* Marlborough, St John's Coll Oxford (BA), Univ of Manchester (PhD); *m* 12 April 1969, Margaret, da of Romilly Ingram Redfern, of Ipswich; 1 s (Alexander b 1974), 1 da (Harriet b 1976); *Career* res fell and lectr Portsmouth Poly 1967–73; Univ of Birmingham: lectr in zoology 1973–80, sr lectr 1980–86, dep head of the Sch of Continuing Studies 1984–94, reader in ecological genetics 1986–89, prof of evolutionary biology 1989–94; dir Div of Adult Continuing Educn Univ of Sheffield 1994–; memb: Lib Dems, Br Ecological Soc, Malacological Soc of London, The Conchological Soc of GB and Ireland; FLS 1969, FIBiol, CBiol; *Books* British Land Snails (with M Redfern, 1976), A Field Guide to the Land Snails of Britain and NW Europe (with M P Kerney, 1979); *Recreations* reading, photography, politics; *Style—* Prof Robert Cameron; ✉ Division of Adult Continuing Education, University of Sheffield, 196–198 West Street, Sheffield S1 4ET (☎ 0114 282 5400)

CAMERON, Sheila Morag Clark; QC (1983); da of Sir James Clark Cameron, CBE, TD (d 1991), and Lady Irene Maud, *née* Ferguson (d 1986); *b* 22 March 1934; *Educ* Commonweal Lodge Sch Purley Surrey, St Hugh's Coll Oxford (MA); *m* 3 Dec 1960, Gerard Charles Ryan; 2 s (Andrew b 21 Aug 1965, Nicholas b 6 Dec 1967); *Career* called to the Bar Middle Temple 1957, Harmsworth law scholar 1958, pt/t lectr in law Univ of Southampton 1960–64, pt/t tutor Cncl of Legal Educn, recorder of the Crown Court 1985–, bencher Middle Temple 1988; memb: Bar Cncl 1967–70, Cncl on Tbnls 1986–90, Boundary Cmmn for England 1989–; chllr: Diocese of Chelmsford 1969–, Diocese of London 1992–; memb: Cncl Wycombe Abbey Sch 1972–86, Legal Advsy Cmmn Gen Synod of C of E 1975; Vicar Gen Province of Canterbury 1983–; *Clubs* Caledonian; *Style—* Miss Sheila Cameron, QC; ✉ 2 Harcourt Buildings, Temple, London EC4Y 9DB (☎ 0171 353 8415, fax 0171 353 7622)

CAMERON, Thomas Anthony (Tony); s of late Thomas Alexander Cameron, and late Olive Cameron; *b* 3 Feb 1947; *Educ* Stranraer HS; *m* Elizabeth Christine, *née* Sutherland; 2 s (Andrew, Iain); *Career* Dept of Agric and Fisheries for Scotland 1966–72; Scottish Office: private sec to dep under sec of state 1972–73, private sec to perm under sec of state 1973–74; Dept of Agric and Fisheries for Scotland: higher exec offr 1974–77, princ 1977–82, asst sec 1982–87; Scottish Office: Fin Div 1987–92, under sec (agriculture) 1992–; memb Duke of Edinburgh's Sixth Commonwealth Study Conf 1986, Aust and Scottish coordinator and memb of Programme and Study Tours Ctee Duke of Edinburgh's Seventh Commonwealth Study Conf UK 1992; *Recreations* reading, mountaineering, cycling; *Style—* Tony Cameron, Esq; ✉ Scottish Office, Agriculture and Fisheries Department, Pentland House, 47 Robb's Loan, Edinburgh EH14 1TW (☎ 0131 244 6032, fax 0131 244 6511)

CAMERON-HAYES, Col John; MVO; s of Hugh Cameron-Hayes (d 1967), and Mabel Henrietta, *née* Jones (d 1971); *b* 30 July 1925; *Educ* Clifton; *m* 11 Aug 1951, Patricia Mary, da of Lt-Col Geoffrey Hartley Yates, OBE (d 1983); 1 s (Jonathan b 1953), 1 da (Nicola b 1957); *Career* active serv ME and Far E The King's Troop RHA, i/c gun carriage funeral HM King George VI, first army offr instr Britannia RNC 1964–66, cmd Regt BAOR 1966–68, RAF Staff Coll Bracknell 1969, asst dir def policy MOD 1970–72, ret 1972; amateur rider nat hunt steeplechases, hurdle and flat races, competitor Badminton, Prince of Wales Cup winner Earl's Court (showjumping); chief exec Racecourse Assoc 1972–89, conslt worldwide to firms building racecourses and polo grounds; county branch sec SSAFA/FHS; *Recreations* racing, polo, three day events; *Style—* Col John Cameron-Hayes, MVO; ✉ Stable Cottage, New Hayward, Hungerford, Berks RG17 0PZ (☎ 01488 681314)

CAMERON OF LOCHBROOM, Baron (Life Peer UK 1984), of Lochbroom, in the District of Ross and Cromarty; Kenneth John Cameron; PC (1984), QC (1972); s of Hon Lord (John) Cameron, KT, DSC (d 1996), and his 1 w, Eileen Dorothea, *née* Burrell (d 1943); *b* 11 June 1931; *Educ* Edinburgh Acad, Univ of Oxford (MA), Univ of Edinburgh (LLB); *m* 1964, Jean Pamela, da of late Col Granville Murray; 2 da (Hon Victoria Christian (Hon Mrs Fraser) b 1965, Hon Camilla Louise b 1967); *Career* served RN 1950–52; advocate 1958, chm Industl Tbnls Scotland 1966–81, pres Pensions Appeal Tbnl Scotland 1976–84 (chm 1975), chm Ctee for Investigation in Scotland of Agric Mktg Schemes 1980–84, Lord Advocate of Scotland 1984–89, senator Coll of Justice 1989–; chm Royal Fine Art Cmmn for Scotland 1995–; Hon FRIAS 1994, FRSE 1990; *Clubs* Scottish Arts, New (Edinburgh), Beefsteak; *Style—* The Rt Hon the Lord Cameron of Lochbroom, PC, QC, FRSE; ✉ Court of Session, Parliament House, Parliament Square, Edinburgh EH1 1RF (☎ 0131 225 2595)

CAMERON OF LOCHIEL, Col Sir Donald Hamish; KT (1973), CVO (1970), TD (1944), JP; 26 Chief of the Clan Cameron; s of Col Sir Donald Walter Cameron of Lochiel, KT, CMG, 25 Chief of the Clan Cameron (d 1951), and Lady Hermione Graham (d 1978), da of 5 Duke of Montrose; *b* 12 Sept 1910; *Educ* Harrow, Balliol Coll Oxford; *m* 1939, Margaret, da of Lt-Col Hon Nigel Gathorne-Hardy, DSO; 2 s, 2 da; *Heir* s, Donald Angus Cameron yr of Lochiel b 1946; *Career* dir: Royal Bank of Scotland 1954–80 (vice chm 1969–80), Scottish Widows Fund 1955–81 (chm 1964–67), Save & Prosper Securities 1968–85; Lt-Col cmdg Lovat Scouts 1945; Hon Col: 4/5 Bn Queen's Own Cameron Highlanders 1958–69, 2 Bn 51 Highland Volunteers 1970–75; Scottish Railways Bd 1964–72 (chm Scottish Area Bd 1959–64); pt/t memb BR Bd 1962–64; Crown Estate cmmr 1957–69, govr Harrow Sch 1967–77, pres Royal Highland Agric Soc of Scotland 1971, 1979 and 1987; chm Scottish Ctee Malcolm Sargent Cancer Fund for Children 1971–91; Lord-Lt of County of Inverness 1971–85 (formerly Vice-Lt); FCA; *Clubs* New (Edinburgh), Pratt's; *Style—* Sir Donald Cameron; ✉ Achnacarry, Spean Bridge, Inverness-shire (☎ 01397 712708)

CAMERON OF LOCHIEL, yr, Donald Angus; DL (Lochaber, Inverness and Badenoch and Strathspey, 1986); s and h of Col Sir Donald Cameron of Lochiel, KT, CVO, TD, *qv*, Chief of Clan, and Margaret, *née* Gathorne-Hardy; *b* 2 Aug 1946; *Educ* Harrow, ChCh Oxford (MA); *m* 1 June 1974, Lady Cecil Nennella Therese Kerr, da of 12 Marquess of Lothian, KCVO, *qv*; 1 s (Donald Andrew John b 26 Nov 1976), 3 da (Catherine Mary b 1 March 1975, a bridesmaid to HRH The Princess of Wales, Lucy Margot Therese b 5 July 1980, Emily Frances b 18 Jan 1986); *Career* 2 Lt 4/5 Queen's Own Cameron Highlanders (TA) 1966–68; dir J Henry Schroder & Co Ltd 1984–; pres Highland Soc of London 1994–; FCA 1971; *Clubs* Pratt's, New (Edinburgh); *Style—* Donald Cameron of Lochiel, yr, DL; ✉ 26 The Little Boltons, London SW10 (☎ 0171 373 0999); c/o J Henry Schroder & Co Ltd, 120 Cheapside, London EC2 (☎ 0171 382 6000)

CAMERON WATT, Prof Donald; s of Robert Cameron Watt (d 1982), and Barbara, *née* Bidwell (d 1977); *b* 17 May 1928; *Educ* Rugby, Oriel Coll Oxford (MA, DLitt); *m* 1, 1951, Marianne Ruth, *née* Grau (d 1962); 1 s (Ewen Cameron Watt, *qv* b 24 June 1956); m 2, 29 Dec 1962, Felicia Cobb Stanley, *née* Cobb; 1 step da (Cathy); *Career* Nat Serv Sgt BTA 1946–48; FO Res Dept 1951–54, Rockefeller res fell Washington Centre for Policy Res 1960–61; LSE: asst lectr 1954–56, lectr 1956–62, sr lectr 1962–65, reader 1966–71, titular prof of int history 1972–82, Stevenson prof of int history 1982–93 (emeritus 1993); official historian Cabinet Office 1977–93; sec and chm Assoc of Contemporary Historians 1966–85, chm Greenwich Forum 1974–84, sec and treas Int Cmmn for the History of Int Rels 1982–95; memb Editorial Bd: Political Quarterly, Review International Studies, Intelligence and National Security, Modern History Review; FBA, FRHistS; *Books* Britain and the Suez Canal (1956), Britain Looks to Germany (1965), Personalities and Policies (1965), Survey of International Affairs 1961–63 (ed, 1965–71), A History of the World in the Twentieth Century Part 1 (1967), Contemporary History in Europe (ed, 1969), Hitler's Mein Kampf (ed, 1969, 1992), Current British Foreign Policy (annual vols, 1970–72), Too Serious a Business (1975, 1991), Succeeding John Bull - America in Britain's Place 1900–1975 (1984), How War Came (1989), Argentina Between the Powers (ed, 1991); *Recreations* exploring London, cats; *Clubs* Players Theatre; *Style—* Prof Donald Cameron Watt; ✉ c/o London School of Economics, London WC2A 2AE (☎ 0171 405 7686, fax 0171 955 6800, telex 24655 B)

CAMERON WATT, Ewen; s of Prof Donald Cameron Watt, *qv*, and Marianne Ruth Grau; *b* 24 June 1956; *Educ* St Paul's, Oriel Coll Oxford (BA); *m* 8 Jan 1983, Penelope Ann Cameron Watt, *qv*, da of Robert Henry Weldon, of Stone, Bucks; 2 da (Heather Frances b 31 Dec 1991, Flora Imogen b 4 Sept 1995); *Career* ptnr E B Savory Milln 1979–85, divnl dir SG Warburg Securities (formerly Rowe & Pitman) 1986–90, dir SG Warburg Securities 1990–; *Recreations* walking, travel, Scottish watercolours; *Clubs* Vincent's (Oxford); *Style—* Ewen Cameron Watt, Esq; ✉ House 12, Redhill Park, 12 Pak Pat Shan Road, Tai Tam, Hong Kong; SG Warburg Securities Far East Ltd, 25th Floor, Alexander House, 16–20 Chater Rd, Central Hong Kong (☎ 01852 5246113, fax 01852 8452075)

CAMERON WATT, Penelope Ann; *née* Weldon; da of Robert Henry Weldon, and Brenda Marianne, *née* Jones; *b* 10 May 1959; *Educ* Clifton HS Bristol, St Hugh's Coll Oxford (BA); *m* 8 Jan 1983, Ewen Cameron Watt, *qv*, s of Prof Donald Cameron Watt, *qv*, of London; 2 da (Heather Frances b 31 Dec 1991, Flora Imogen b 4 Sept 1995); *Career* EB Savory Milln 1980–82, Wico Galloway and Pearson 1982–84, Kleinwort Benson 1984–87, investmt mangr Robert Fleming 1987, dir Indosuez Asia Investment Services 1990–; *Recreations* travel, walking, Japanese language; *Style—* Mrs Ewen Cameron Watt; ✉ House 12, Redhill Park, 12 Pak Pat Shan Road, Tai Tam, Hong Kong; Indosuez Asia Investment Services, Suite 2606/2608, One Exchange Square, Central Hong Kong (☎ 00 852 5214231, fax 00 852 8681447)

CAMI, Aziz; s of Viktor Cami, of Vienna, and Francesca Cami; *b* 1 Nov 1950; *Educ* Ravenswood Sch for Boys, Camberwell Sch of Art, London Coll of Printing; *m* 15 June 1991, Jean, *née* Hedley; *Career* graphic designer; asst: Moura George Briggs 1973, Ken Briggs and Associates 1974; dir PIC Design 1976; fndr: C S & S Design 1978, The Partners 1983; award winning work for 48 clients incl: Citibank, Freshfields, Hewlett-Packard, IBM, NatWest Group, Rexam, Warner Brothers, Wedgwood; 4 Silver D&AD Awards and 7 Silver nominations; pres D&AD 1992–93; memb Exec Cncl Design Business Assoc 1992–93; FCSD, FRSA; *Recreations* music, art, photography; *Clubs* Mosimann's; *Style—* Aziz Cami, Esq; ✉ The Partners, Albion Courtyard, Greenhill Rents, Smithfield, London EC1M 6BN (☎ 0171 608 0051, fax 0171 250 0473/3917, e-mail ac@partnersdesign.co.uk)

CAMM, Prof (Alan) John; s of John Donald Camm, and Joan Camm; *b* 11 Jan 1947; *Educ* Guy's Hosp Medical Sch Univ of London (BSc, MB BS, MD); *m* 1987, Joy-Maria, *née* Frappell; 1 s, 1 da; *Career* Guy's Hosp: house surgeon 1971, house physician 1971–72, jr registrar 1972, jr lectr in medicine 1972–73, registrar in cardiology 1973–74; clinical fell in cardiology Univ of Vermont 1974–75; St Bartholomew's Hosp: Br Heart Fndn res registrar 1975–76, sr registrar 1977–79, Wellcome sr lectr and hon conslt cardiologist 1979–83, Sir Ronald Bodley Scott prof of cardiovascular med 1983–86; Prudential prof of clinical cardiology St George's Hosp Medical Sch Univ of London 1986– (head Div of Cardiology); memb Cncl: RCP, Br Cardiac Soc; Freeman City of London, Liveryman Worshipful Soc of Apothecaries; CStJ 1990; LRCP, MRCS 1971, FACC 1981, FRCP 1984, FESC 1988; *Books* First Aid - Step by Step (1978), Pacing for Tachycardia Control (1983), Heart Disease in the Elderly (1984 and 1994), Clinical Electrophysiology of the Heart (1987), Heart Disease in Old Age (1988, 1990), Clinical Aspects of Arrythmias (1988), Diseases of the Heart (1989); approx 350 papers in major jls; *Recreations* collector of prints, watercolours and antiques, model railway enthusiast; *Clubs* Athenaeum; *Style—* Prof A John Camm; ✉ St George's Hospital Medical School, Cranmer Terrace, Tooting, London SW17 0RE

CAMOYS, 7 Baron (E 1264; called out of abeyance 1839); (Ralph) Thomas Campion George Sherman Stonor; DL (Oxon 1994); s of 6 Baron Camoys (d 1976), and Mary Jeanne, *née* Stourton (d 1987); the Stonors inherited the Barony through a Mary Biddulph who m Thomas Stonor 1732, descended from an earlier Thomas Stonor and Jeanne, da of John de la Pole, Duke of Suffolk, thus descending from Geoffrey Chaucer, the poet; *b* 16 April 1940; *Educ* Balliol Coll Oxford; *m* 11 June 1966, Elisabeth Mary Hyde, o da of Sir William Hyde Parker, 11 Bt; 1 s, 3 da (Hon Alina (Hon Mrs

Barrowcliff) b 1967, Hon Emily b 1969, Hon Sophia b 1971); *Heir* s, Hon (Ralph) William Robert Thomas Stonor b 10 Sept 1974; *Career* lord in waiting to HM The Queen 1992; chm: Robert Jackson & Co Ltd 1968–85, Amex Bank 1977–78 (md 1975–77); dir: Barclays de Zoete Wedd Limited 1978– (chief exec 1986–88, dep chm 1987–), Barclays Bank PLC 1979–94, National Provident Institution 1982– (dep chm 1992–), Barclays PLC 1984–94, The Administrative Staff College 1989–, 3i Group plc 1991–, Perpetual PLC 1994–, Cary's; vice chm Barclays Merchant Bank Ltd 1985–86 (md 1978–85); dep chm Sotheby's 1993–; cmmr Eng Heritage 1984–87, memb Royal Cmmn on Historical MSS 1987–94; consultor Extraordinary Section of the Administration of the Patrimony of the Holy See 1991; memb Court of Assts Fishmongers' Co (Prime Warden 1992–93); 1 class Order of Gorkha Dakshina Bahu (Nepal) 1980; *Recreations* the arts, shooting; *Clubs* Boodle's, Pratt's, Leander; *Style*— The Rt Hon the Lord Camoys, DL; ✉ Stonor Park, Henley-on-Thames, Oxon RG9 6HF (☎ 01491 638644); Barclays de Zoete Wedd Ltd, Ebbgate House, Swan Lane, London (☎ 0171 623 2323); Sotheby's Auctioneers, 34 New Bond Street, London W1 (☎ 0171 408 5370)

CAMP, Anthony John; s of Henry Victor Camp (d 1954), of Walkern Lodge, Herts, and Alice Emma, *née* Doidge (d 1973); *Educ* Alleyne's Sch Stevenage, UCL (BA); *m* 24 Aug 1976 (m dis 1978), Deborah Mary, da of Joseph Donald Jeavons, of Bristol; 1 s (Gavin b 1977); *Career* Soc of Genealogists: res asst 1957, librarian 1959, dir of res 1962, dir 1979, hon fell 1982; lectr: English Genealogical Confs 1975–, Nat Genealogical Confs USA (yearly) 1981–, Australasian Congress Canberra 1986, Sesquicentennial Conf Auckland 1990, First Irish Genealogical Congress 1991, Sesquicentennial Conf Boston 1995; contrib Daily Diary Family Tree Magazine 1984–; award of merit Nat Genealogical Soc 1984, fell Utah Genealogical Assoc 1989; hon genealogical advsr Assoc to Combat Huntington's Chorea 1974–93; Assoc of Genealogists and Record Agents: fndr memb 1968, memb Cncl 1968–75, chm 1973–75, vice pres 1980–; memb Cncl: Br Record Soc 1967–71 and 1983–, Br Archaeology 1973–, English Genealogical Congress 1975–90 (pres 1991–92), Br Records Assoc (Records Preservation Section) 1980–83 and 1985–88, Friends of Public Record Office 1988–94, Fed of Family History Socs 1992–; pres Herts Family History and Population Soc 1982–; Freeman City of London 1984; *Books* Genealogists Handbook (1964), Tracing Your Ancestors (1964), Wills and Their Whereabouts (2 edn, 1974), Everyone Has Roots (1978), Index to Wills Proved in Prerogative Court of Canterbury 1750–1800 (1976–92), My Ancestor was a Migrant (1987), My Ancestors came with the Conqueror (1988); *Style*— Anthony Camp, Esq; ✉ 65 Fursecroft, George St, London W1H 5LG (☎ 0171 723 3758); 14 Charterhouse Buildings, Goswell Rd, London EC1M 7BA (☎ 0171 251 8799)

CAMP, Clarence Victor (Larry); s of George Victor Camp (d 1955), of Colless Rd, London, and Marjorie, *née* Salmon (d 1977); *b* 7 May 1920; *Educ* Down Lane Sch London; *m* 17 Nov 1945, Kathleen, da of Walter Moody (d 1948), of Shouldham St, London; 2 s (Stuart Roger b 26 March 1949, Stephen Geoffrey b 8 Feb 1954); *Career* RAOC 1940–46: 8 Army 1941–44, served Malta 1944–45, NI 1946; with Brown Shipley Merchant Bank 1946–47; Bank of England 1947–80: Econ Intelligence Dept 1952–63, mangr Mgmnt Servs Dept 1963–74, memb Decimalisation Delgn to Aust and NZ 1967, princ Job Evaluation Div 1974–80; City of London Magistrates: JP 1974–90, dep chm 1981–90, memb Cts Ctee 1978–87 (vice chm 1984–87), chm Licensing Ctee 1978–82, chm Probation Ctee 1980–82, chm Ct User Gp 1986–90; memb Ctee Ashtead Residents' Assoc 1990–96; Freeman City of London 1957, Liveryman Worshipful Co of Carmen 1976; *Books* Bankers Management Handbook (contrib, 1976); *Recreations* reading, theatre, gardening, walking; *Clubs* Bread Street Ward, Probus; *Style*— C V Camp, Esq, JP; ✉ Headley Cottage, 19 Grays Lane, Ashtead, Surrey KT21 1BZ (☎ 01372 274000)

CAMP, Jeffery Bruce; s of George and Caroline Camp; *b* 17 April 1923; *Educ* Lowestoft and Ipswich Art Schs, Edinburgh Coll of Art; *m* 1963, Laetitia, *née* Yhap; *Career* artist; pt/t lectr Slade Sch of Fine Art Univ of London; public collections incl: Arts Cncl of GB, City Art Gallery Bradford, Br Cncl, Contemporary Arts Soc, DOE, Fermoy Art Gallery King's Lynn, Univ of London, Manchester Educn Dept, Norwich Castle Museum, The Nuffield Orgn, Tate Gallery, Towner Art Gallery Eastbourne, Harris Museum and Art Gallery Preston, RA; *Solo Exhibitions* Edinburgh Festival 1950, Galerie de Seine London 1958, Beaux Arts Gallery London 1959, 1961 and 1963, New Art Centre London 1968, Fermoy Art Gallery King's Lynn 1970, South London Art Gallery (Retrospective) 1973, Royal Shakespeare Theatre Stratford 1974, Serpentine Gallery (Arts Cncl) 1978, Bradford City Art Gallery 1979, Browse and Darby 1984, The 29 Aldeburgh Festival in assoc with the Arts Cncl of GB 1986, Nigel Greenwood Gallery 1986–87 and 1990, The Library Gallery Univ of Surrey 1988, Royal Albert Museum Exeter (Retrospective) 1988, Royal Acad of Arts London 1988, Manchester City Art Gallery 1988, Laing Art Gallery Newcastle 1988, Browse & Darby 1993; *Gp Exhibitions* incl: Aldeburgh Festival 1958, 1961 and 1963, Cafe Royal Centenary 1965, Marlborough Gallery London 1968, Br Painting 1974, Hayward Gallery London 1974, Br Painting 1952–77, Royal Acad Drawings at Burlington House 1977, Drawing and Watercolours for China (Edinburgh, Br Cncl Touring) 1982, Br Cncl Exhibition Delhi and Bombay 1985, Proud and Prejudiced Twining Gallery NY 1985, The Self Portrait A Modern View Artsite Gallery Bath and tour 1987, Small is Beautiful Angela Flowers Gallery London 1988, Picturing People - Figurative Painting from Britain 1945–89 (Br exhib, Kuala Lumpar) 1988–89, Salute to Turner (Thos Agnew & Sons) London 1989, Images of Paradise Harewood House 1989, Nine Contemporary Painters Bristol Art Gallery 1990, For a Wider World (Br Cncl), RA Summer Exhbn 1990, Coastlines (Br Cncl) 1993, Nat Tst Exhbn Christies 1994; RA 1984 (ARA 1974); *Style*— Jeffery Camp, Esq, RA

CAMPBELL, Sir Alan Hugh; GCMG (1979, KCMG 1976, CMG 1964); s of late Hugh Elphinstone Campbell, of Bantham, S Devon, and Ethel, *née* Warren; *b* 1 July 1919; *Educ* Sherborne, Gonville and Caius Coll Cambridge; *m* 1947, Margaret Jean, da of Gilbert Taylor, of Sydney, NSW; 3 da; *Career* Dip Serv 1946–79: ambass to Ethiopia 1969–72, dep under sec of state FO 1973–76, ambass to Italy 1976–79, ret; *Books* Colleagues and Friends (1988); *Clubs* Beefsteak, Brooks's; *Style*— Sir Alan Campbell, GCMG; ✉ 45 Carlisle Mansions, Carlisle Place, London SW1

CAMPBELL, Hon Alastair Colin Leckie; s (by 1 m) and h of 3 Baron Colgrain; *b* 16 Sept 1951; *Educ* Eton, Trinity Coll Cambridge; *m* 1979, Annabel Rose, da of Hon Robin Hugh Warrender (s of 1 Baron Bruntisfield, MC); 2 s (Thomas Colin Donald b 9 Feb 1984, Nicholas Robin b 12 Dec 1986); *Style*— The Hon Alastair Campbell; ✉ The Stables, Everlands, Sevenoaks, Kent

CAMPBELL, Lt-Col the Hon Alastair James Calthrop; yr s of Baron Campbell of Croy, MC, PC (Life Peer); *b* 6 Jan 1952; *Educ* Eton, Oxford (MA); *m* 18 Sept 1993, Primrose F, er da of William Palmer, of Nun Monkton, York; 2 s (Ferdinand James Marc b 29 April 1994, Edward Henry Brunel b 31 Aug 1996), 1 da (Leonora Mary Felicia b 19 June 1995); *Career* cmmnd Queen's Own Highlanders 1973, Capt 1976, Maj 1984, Lt-Col 1991–; memb Royal Co of Archers (Queen's Body Guard for Scotland); FRGS; *Recreations* bagpipes, squash, skiing; *Clubs* Brooks's; *Style*— Lt-Col the Hon Alastair Campbell; ✉ Holme Rose, Cawdor, Nairn

CAMPBELL, Alastair John; s of Donald Campbell, of Embsay, Yorks, and Elizabeth Howie, *née* Caldwell; *b* 25 May 1957; *Educ* City of Leicester Boys' Sch, Gonville and Caius Coll Cambridge (MA); *partner* Fiona Millar; 2 s (Rory b 23 Oct 1987, Calum b 29 July 1989), 1 da (Grace b 30 April 1994); *Career* trainee reporter Tavistock Times and Sunday Independent Truro Mirror Group Training Scheme 1980–82, freelance reporter London 1982–83, reporter Daily Mirror 1983–85, news ed Sunday Today 1985–86, reporter Daily Mirror 1986; Sunday Mirror: political corr 1986–87, political ed 1987–89, columnist 1989–92; Daily Mirror: political ed 1989–93, columnist 1992–93; asst ed (politics) and columnist Today 1993–94, columnist Tribune 1993–, political commentator LBC 1993–94; press sec to Tony Blair as Ldr Lab Pty 1994–; presenter Week in Westminster (BBC) 1992–94; *Recreations* children, bagpipes, Burnley Football Club; *Style*— Alastair Campbell, Esq; ✉ c/o House of Commons, London SW1A 0AA

CAMPBELL, Prof Alexander George Macpherson (Alex); s of Alexander McCorkindale Campbell, DSO, OBE, TD, of Islay, Argyllshire, and Isabel Catherine, *née* Macpherson (d 1990); *b* 3 Feb 1931; *Educ* Dollar Acad, Univ of Glasgow (MB ChB); *m* 19 Sept 1959, Sheila Mary, da of Sir Peter George Macdonald (d 1983), of Edinburgh; 1 s (Andrew Alexander Macdonald b 1965), 2 da (Fiona Ann b 1960, Patricia Mary b 1963); *Career* Nat Serv Parachute Field Ambulance 16 Ind Parachute Bde 1956–58; registrar paediatrics Royal Hosp for Sick Children Edinburgh 1959–61, res house offr Gt Ormond St Hosp 1961–62, asst chief res physician Children's Hosp of Philadelphia USA 1962–63; fell: paediatric cardiology Hosp for Sick Children Toronto Canada 1963–64, perinatal physiology Nuffield Inst for Med Res Oxford 1964–66; lectr in child health Univ of St Andrews 1966–67, asst (later assoc prof) paediatrics Yale Univ Sch of Med Connecticut USA 1967–73, prof of child health Univ of Aberdeen 1973–92; chm Jt Ctee for Vaccination and Immunisation Dept Health 1989–96; FRCPE; *Style*— Prof Alex Campbell; ✉ 34 Woodburn Crescent, Aberdeen (☎ 01224 319152, fax 01224 312187)

CAMPBELL, District Judge Ann Rosemary; da of Sqdn Ldr Richard Henry Beeching, and Gladys Maud, *née* Trussler; *b* 13 Dec 1948; *Educ* Lady Eleanor Holles Sch, New Hall Cambridge (MA); *m* His Hon Judge (John) Quentin Campbell, *qv*; 1 da (Arabella b 27 June 1977), 1 s (Frederick b 28 June 1982); *Career* slr in private practice 1972–92, formerly ptnr Henmans Oxford, district judge 1992–, asst recorder 1995–; *Style*— District Judge Campbell; ✉ Oxford Combined Court Centre, St Aldates, Oxford

CAMPBELL, Anne; MP (Lab) Cambridge (majority 580); da of late Frank Lucas, and late Susan Lucas; *b* 6 April 1940; *Educ* Penistone GS, Newnham Coll Cambridge (MA); *m* 10 Aug 1963, Dr Archie Campbell; 1 s, 2 da; *Career* various teaching posts 1962–70, lectr then sr lectr in statistics Cambridgeshire Coll of Arts and Technol 1970–83, head of statistics and data processing Nat Inst of Agric Botany Cambridge 1983–92; MP (Lab) Cambridge 1992–; cncllr Cambridgeshire CC 1985–89; fell Inst of Statisticians 1987, fell Royal Statistical Soc 1987, FRSA 1993; *Recreations* gardening, jogging, tennis, mountain walking; *Style*— Mrs Anne Campbell, MP; ✉ House of Commons, London SW1A 0AA (☎ 0171 219 5089)

CAMPBELL, The Hon Mr Justice; Hon Sir (William) Anthony; kt (1988); s of Harold Ernest Campbell, CBE (d 1980), of Rockmore, Newcastle, Co Down, and Marion Fordyce, *née* Wheeler (d 1996); *b* 30 Oct 1936; *Educ* Campbell Coll Belfast, Queens' Coll Cambridge (BA); *m* 8 July 1960, (Isobel Rosemary) Gail, da of Frederick Malcolm McKibbin, JP, of Holywood, Co Down; 3 da (Fiona (Mrs Chamberlain) b 1961, Nicola (Mrs Vernon-Powell) b 1963, Susan (Mrs Haig) b 1964); *Career* called to the Bar Gray's Inn 1960, hon bencher 1995; Inn of Court NI 1960, bencher 1983; QC 1974, sr crown counsel NI 1984–88, judge of the High Court of Justice NI 1988–; chm Cncl of Legal Educn NI, chm Judicial Studies Bd for NI; memb Cncl St Leonards Sch St Andrews 1985–94, govr Campbell Coll Belfast; *Recreations* hill walking, sailing; *Clubs* Royal Ulster Yacht, New (Edinburgh); *Style*— The Hon Mr Justice Campbell; ✉ Royal Courts of Justice, Belfast BT1 3JY (☎ 01232 235111)

CAMPBELL, Archibald Grieg (Archie); s of William Greig Campbell (d 1986), and Isabel Hamilton, *née* Gordon (d 1961); *b* 17 March 1934; *Educ* Kelvinside Acad (capped for Scotland in rugby), Univ of Glasgow; *m* 1, 1960 (m dis 1986), Madge Eileen, da of John Iain Baillie; 3 da (Deborah Elaine b 1963, Angela Gillian b 1965, Claire Patricia b 1967); m 2, 1986, Teresa Lois, *née* Kingsbury; *Career* Touche Ross (now Deloitte & Touche): joined 1958, regnl ptnr Asia Pacific Region Singapore 1975–78, dir Int Servs New York 1978–81, regnl ptnr Europe 1981–90, dep regnl dir Special Projects Europe 1990–92, dep chief exec offr 1992–; MICAS 1958, ACA 1977, ICA Hong Kong 1978, ICA Malasyia 1978, ICA Singapore 1978; *Recreations* golf, tennis; *Style*— Archie Campbell, Esq; ✉ Water's Edge, Loddon Drive, Wargrave, Berks RG10 8HN; Deloitte & Touche, Hill House, 1 Little New Street, London EC4A 3TR (☎ 0171 936 3000, fax 0171 353 8648)

CAMPBELL, (Mary Lorimer) Beatrix; da of James William Barnes, of Carlisle, Cumbria, and Catharina Johana, *née* Lorier; *b* 3 Feb 1947; *Educ* Harraby Secdy Mod Sch, Carlisle HS, AA; *m* 28 Oct 1968 (m dis 1978), Bobby Campbell; *Career* journalist: Morning Star 1967–76, Time Out 1979, City Limits 1981–87; freelance reporter: New Statesman, Guardian, The Observer, Marxism Today; columnist The Independent 1993–95; columnist The Guardian 1995–; broadcaster: I Shot My Husband and No One Asked Me Why (documentary, Channel 4 TV), Listening to the Children (documentary, Channel 4 TV), Vice and Virtue (Radio 4); memb Women's Liberation Movement; *Books* Sweet Freedom (with Anna Coote, 1981), Wigan Pier Revisited (1984, winner of Cheltenham Literary Festival), The Iron Ladies - Why Women Vote Tory (1987, winner of Fawcett Prize), Unofficial Secrets - The Cleveland Child Sex Abuse Case (1988), Goliath - Britain's Dangerous Places (1993); *Style*— Ms Beatrix Campbell; ✉ The Guardian, 119 Farringdon Road, London EC1R 3ER (☎ 0171 278 2332, fax 0171 837 2114)

CAMPBELL, Col (George) Bryan; OBE (1977, MBE 1968); s of Capt Ian Bryan Campbell, OBE (d 1951), and Anne Baron, *née* Black (d 1949); *b* 22 Dec 1935; *Educ* The Edinburgh Acad, Royal Military Acad Sandhurst; *m* 22 Dec 1959, (Loyola Megan) Tui, da of Frederick Godrey Vaughan-Morgan (d 1972); 1 s (Maj Nicholas Bryan Vaughan Campbell, RHF); *Career* cmmnd 1955; served: Malaya, Cyprus, Aden, Malta, Singapore, NI, Italy; cmd 1 Bn The Royal Highland Fusiliers 1974–77 (despatches 1978), Dep Cdr 39 Infantry Bde 1983–85, Col Gen Staff AFSE 1985–89 (despatches 1986), regnl controller Defence Housing Executive Scotland 1995; *Recreations* gardening, shooting; *Style*— Col Bryan Campbell, OBE; ✉ Oaklea, Athelstaneford, North Berwick, East Lothian EH39 5BE (☎ 01620 880280, 0131 310 5324)

CAMPBELL, Bryn; s of Brinley Campbell (d 1990), and Dorothy Irene, *née* Hughes; *b* 20 May 1933; *Educ* Mountain Ash GS (awarded Viscount Hall travel scholarship), Univ of Manchester; *m* 1960, Audrey Campbell, da of late Thomas Idris Berryman; *Career* Nat Serv photographer RAF 1951–53, industl photographer London 1956–57, agency photographer Fleet St 1957–58, asst ed Practical Photography and Photo News Weekly 1959–60, ed Cameras 1960–61, assoc ed British Journal of Photography 1962–63, redesigned and picture edited BJ Annual 1964, picture ed The Observer (helped to launch The Observer Colour Magazine) 1964–66, freelance photographer (retained by The Observer) 1966–72, official photographer Br Headless Valley Expedition (which carried out first ever N-S transnavigation of Canada by water) 1972, nominee photographer Magnum Photos 1972–73, external examiner in photography to eight polys and art colls 1974–80, first foreign photographer to lecture to Guild of Finnish Photographers Univ of Vaasa Finland 1974, hon assoc lectr PCL 1974–77, photographed final stages of Vietnam War 1975, travelled widely on assignment for maj magazines 1975–77, writer and presenter BBC TV series and book Exploring Photography 1978, official photographer Transglobe Expedition (which carried out first ever transnavigation of the world's surface on its polar axis) 1979–82, ed World Photography (UK, USA and Japan) 1981; conslt picture ed: Sunday Express Magazine 1984–85, The Illustrated London News 1985–87 and 1989–93, Daily Telegraph Magazine 1987–88;

occasional appearances Saturday Review BBC TV 1985–86; memb: Photography Bd CNAA 1977–78, Arts Panel Arts Cncl of GB 1980–83 (memb Photography Ctee 1978–80); chm Sports Pictures of the Year Judging Panel 1984–88; Br judge: World Press Photo competition 1985, Int Center for Photography annual awards NY 1989; editorial conslt Photographers International magazine 1995–; tstee The Photographers' Gallery London 1974–84; solo exhibitions incl: Reports and Rumours (The Photographers' Gallery London and tour) 1973, Village School (Chichester 900 festival Sussex and tour) 1975, Caring and Concern (Kodak Gallery London) 1976, Sports View (Watford and tour) 1977, retrospective (Salzburg Coll Austria) 1978, Antarctic Expedition (Olympus Gallery London) 1980, colour retrospective (The Photographers' Gallery London then tour) 1981; gp exhibitions incl: The Camera and the Craftsman (Crafts Centre London) 1975, Personal View (Br Cncl London and tour) 1977, European Colour Photography (The Photographers' Gallery London) 1978, Kindness: The Keflex Collection (Hamiltons Gallery London) 1982, The Other Britain (Nat Theatre London) 1983; author of numerous books on photography; FBIPP 1969, Hon FRPS 1996 (FRPS 1971); *Awards* 1st Prize (News) Br Press Pictures of the Year 1969, Kodak Bursary 1973; *Books* Village School (1995), The Imprecise Image (1995, both books of own photographs); *Style*— Bryn Campbell, Esq; ✉ Stonehaven, Charterhouse Road, Godalming, Surrey GU7 2AT (☎ 01483 424915, fax 01483 417719)

CAMPBELL, Christopher James; CBE (1993); s of Dr David Heggie Campbell (d 1979), and Nettie Phyllis, *née* Burgess (d 1944); *b* 2 Jan 1936; *Educ* Epsom Coll Surrey; *Career* Nat Serv 2 Lt RAPC 1959–61, Capt Paymaster HAC Inf Bn 1960–63; dir: Harvey Nichols Ltd 1973–78, Lotus Ltd 1973–78; md Hardy Amies Ltd 1978–79; dir: Debenhams Fashion Div 1980–84, Debenhams Dept Store Bd 1984–86, Debenhams Finance Ltd 1984–86; exec memb National Bus Co 1986–88 (non-exec memb 1988–91), fin dir Nat Rivers Authy Advsy Ctee 1988–89, chm British Shipbuilders 1989–, dir Harrods Bank Ltd 1991–, dir Riverside Mental Health Tst 1992–96, dir British Railways Bd 1996– (vice chm 1994–96); govr Gen Cncl United World Coll of the Atlantic 1992–; FCA 1959; *Recreations* reading, visual arts, listening to music, entertaining, indifferent bridge; *Clubs* Brooks's; *Style*— Christopher Campbell, Esq, CBE; ✉ 19 Morpeth Mansions, Morpeth Terrace, London SW1P 1ER (☎ 0171 630 7527)

CAMPBELL, Christopher Robert James (Chris); s of late Kenneth James Campbell, and Barbara Muir Kirkness Campbell; *b* 1 Dec 1958; *Educ* Daniel Stewart's and Melville Coll Edinburgh, Univ of Edinburgh (LLB Hons); *m* 10 Sept 1983, Katharine Mairi, da of Archibald Macdonald; 1 s (Andrew Archibald Kenneth b 16 Nov 1988), 1 da (Victoria Barbara Dorothy b 8 April 1991); *Career* Dundas & Wilson CS: apprentice 1980–82, asst 1982–87, ptnr 1987–, ptnr i/c Glasgow office 1991–96, dep managing ptnr 1995–96, managing ptnr 1996–; *Recreations* golf, cycling, football, photography; *Clubs* Murrayfield Golf (Edinburgh), Royal Scottish Automobile; *Style*— Chris Campbell, Esq; ✉ Dundas & Wilson, Saltire Court, 20 Castle Terrace, Edinburgh EH1 2EN (☎ 0131 228 8000, fax 0131 228 8888, car 0860 333011)

CAMPBELL, Colin John Bruce; s of Capt Richard Galbraith Campbell (d 1975), and Margaret Kathleen, *née* Spoor (d 1970); *b* 6 April 1939; *Educ* Gordonstoun, Royal Marines; *m* 15 Aug 1964, Angela Rosemary, da of the late Lt-Col Colin Gordon Irving-Bell; 2 da (Shuna Catherine Islay b 1965, Ffyona Jane Alison b 1967); *Career* Nat Serv cmmnd RM 1959–61, regular cmmn 1961, Troop Cdr 45 commando Aden 42 Commando Borneo 1962–63, flying trg RAF Linton on Ouse and RNAS Culdrose 1964–65, Fleet Air Arm Helicopter Pilot 845 NACS HMS Bulwark 1965–67, qualified Helicopter Flying Instr 1967, Flying Instr RNAS Culdrose 1967–69, exchange appt USMC New River N Carolina 1969–71, display pilot 1971–72, Helicopter Standards instr RAE Farnborough 1972–74, VIP Pilot RNAS Lee-on-Solent 1974–76; capt Br Airways Helicopters 1976–89, hotelier 1989–91, Capt Jersey Euro Airways 1991–; *Recreations* sailing, hill walking, skiing; *Clubs* Argyllshire Gathering; *Style*— Capt Colin J B Campbell; ✉ 5 Mount Boone, Dartmouth, Devon (☎ 01803 833438)

CAMPBELL, Sir Colin Moffat; 8 Bt (NS *ca* 1668), of Aberuchill, Perthshire; MC (1945); s of Sir John Alexander Coldstream Campbell, 7 Bt (d 1960); *b* 4 Aug 1925; *Educ* Stowe; *m* 1952, Mary Anne Chichester, da of Brig George Alexander Bain, OBE (d 1982); 2 s (James Alexander Moffat Bain b 1956, John Alistair Chichester b 1960), 1 da (Janet Mary Bain (Mrs Nicholas Muir) b 1953 d 1978); *Heir* s, James Alexander Moffat Bain b 23 Sept 1956; *Career* James Finlay and Co Ltd: Calcutta 1948–58, Nairobi 1958–71, dir 1971–92, dep chm 1973–75; chm James Finlay and associated cos 1975–90; pres Fedn of Kenya Employers 1962–70; chm: Tea Bd of Kenya 1961–71, E African Tea Trade Assoc 1960–61, 1962–63 and 1966–67; memb: Scottish Cncl CBI 1979–85, Cncl CBI 1981–92, Commonwealth Devpt Corpn 1981–89 (dep chm 1983–89); *Recreations* gardening, racing, travel, cards; *Clubs* Boodle's, Western (Glasgow), Royal Calcutta Turf, Tollygunge (Calcutta), Nairobi (Kenya); *Style*— Sir Colin Campbell, Bt, MC; ✉ Kilbryde Castle, Dunblane, Perthshire (☎ 01786 823104)

CAMPBELL, Prof Sir Colin Murray; kt (1994), DL (Notts 1996); s of Donald and Isobel Campbell; *b* 26 Dec 1944; *Educ* Robert Gordon's Coll Aberdeen, Univ of Aberdeen (LLB); *m* 15 Aug 1974, Elaine, da of Roger Carlisle; 1 s (Andrew William Roger b 1983), 1 da (Victoria Louise b 1979); *Career* lectr: Faculty of Law Univ of Dundee 1967–69, Dept of Public Law Univ of Edinburgh; Queen's Univ of Belfast: prof of jurisprudence 1974–88, dean Faculty of Law 1977–80, pro vice chllr 1983–87; vice chllr Univ of Nottingham 1988–; chm: Qubis Ltd 1983–88, Lacemarket Development Co 1989–; memb: Cncl Soc for Computers and Law 1973–88, Standing Advsy Cmmn on Human Rights for NI 1977–80, Legal Aid Advsy Ctee NI 1978–82, Mental Health Legislation Review Ctee NI 1978–82, UGC 1987–88, Nottingham Devpt Enterprise 1988–91, UFC Scottish Ctee 1989–92; chm: Ind Advice Gp on Consumer Protection in NI 1984, NI Econ Cncl 1987–94, Human Fertilization and Embryology Authy 1990–94, Med Workforce Standing Advsy Ctee 1991–, Food Advsy Ctee 1994–; memb: HEFCE 1992–, Inquiry into Police Responsibilty and Rewards 1992–93, Trent RHA 1994–96; vice chm CVCP 1992–93; *Books* Law & Society (co-ed, 1979), Do We Need a Bill of Rights? (ed, 1980), Data Processing and the Law (ed, 1984); contrib numerous articles in books and periodicals; *Recreations* sport, walking, music, reading; *Style*— Prof Sir Colin Campbell, DL; ✉ University of Nottingham, University Park, Nottingham NG7 2RD (☎ 0115 951 3001, fax 0115 951 3005, telex 37346 Uninot G)

CAMPBELL, Hon David Anthony; o s and h of 6 Baron Stratheden and Campbell, *qv*; *b* 13 Feb 1963; *m* 14 Aug 1993, Jennifer Margaret, *née* Owens; 1 da (Rebecca Hilary b 25 Feb 1995); *Career* memb Master Plumbers' Assoc; *Clubs* Harley (Victoria); *Style*— The Hon David Campbell; ✉ 71 Magpie Lane, Cooroy, Queensland 4563, Australia

CAMPBELL, David Lachlan; *b* 4 Sept 1959, Glasgow; *Educ* Washington Univ St Louis USA (AB, MBA); *m*; *Career* General Mills US until 1982, Pepsi-Cola NY and London 1982–86, joined Virgin Entertainment Group 1986, i/c Virgin's Euro TV post prodn cos until 1992, chief exec Virgin Radio 1993– (dir 1992–); featured in: 40 Under 40 (Business Age magazine) 1995, 20 Most Influential People in the Music Business (Vox magazine) 1995; Freeman City of Glasgow, memb Guild of Hammermen of Glasgow; memb: Mktg Soc 1984, Radio Acad 1992; *Recreations* flying (licensed helicopter pilot), travelling and live music; *Style*— David Campbell, Esq; ✉ Virgin Radio, 1 Golden Square, London W1R 4DJ (☎ 0171 434 1215, fax 0171 434 1515, e-mail rockin@vradio.co.uk)

CAMPBELL, Prof Sir Donald; kt (1994), CBE (1987); s of Archibald Peter Campbell, DSM (d 1949), of Glasgow, and Mary Campbell (d 1947); *b* 8 March 1930; *Educ* Pitlochry HS, Hutchesons' Boys' GS, Univ of Glasgow; *m* 1, Nancy Rebecca (d 1974); 1 s (Alistair Mackintosh b 18 May 1954), 1 da (Kirsteen Mary b 26 Aug 1956); m 2, 29 Nov 1975, Catherine Conway, da of George Bradburn, of Glasgow; 2 da (Barbara Jane b 1 Sept 1976, Pamela Margaret b 13 April 1978); *Career* conslt anaesthetist Glasgow Royal Infirmary 1961–76, prof of anaesthesia Univ of Glasgow 1976–92 (dean Faculty of Med 1987–91); dean Faculty of Anaesthetists RCS 1982–85 (vice dean 1981–82), vice pres RCS 1985–87, pres RCPSGlas 1992–94 (visitor 1990–92); chm Scot Cncl for Postgrad Med Educn 1985–90, chm Steering Ctee Nat Enquiry into Postoperative Deaths 1988–92; hon fell: RACP 1993, American Coll of Physicians 1993, RCPE 1993, RCSEd 1993, RCGP 1993; hon memb Assoc of Anaesthetists 1993, FFARCS (Ireland) 1979, FRCPGlas 1983, FRCS (Eng) 1985; *Books* A Nurse's Guide to Anaesthetics, Resuscitation and Intensive Care (jtly, 7 edn 1983), Anaesthetics, Resuscitation and Intensive Care (jtly, 9 edn 1996); *Recreations* curling, angling, game-shooting; *Style*— Prof Sir Donald Campbell, CBE; ✉ Novar, 27 Tannoch Drive, Milngavie, Glasgow G62 8AR

CAMPBELL, Donald Angus; s of William Alexander Campbell, of Elgin, Moray, and Williamina Scott, *née* Allan; *b* 10 April 1948; *Educ* Elgin Acad, Univ of Edinburgh (BSc, MB ChB); *m* 9 Sept 1972, Görrel Anna Kristina, da of (Stig Ture) Olof Sahlberg, of Sweden; 1 s (Alasdair Olof b 7 Oct 1981); *Career* neurosurgn: Karolinska Sjukhuset 1972, Royal Infirmary of Edinburgh 1972–73 and 1978–78; surgn: Köpings Lasarett 1973–76, King's Coll London 1976–77, Royal Marsden Hosp 1977–78; neurosurgn Walton Hosp Liverpool 1981–84, conslt neurosurgn to W Midlands RHA 1984–; med supt Svenska Londondoktorer 15 Harley Street; res papers on: chronic pain, epilepsy, head injury, meningiomas, stereotactic surgery; hon pres Headway Staffs; FRCS 1977, FRCSE 1977, FRSM 1977; *Recreations* model aircraft engineering, parachuting, private pilot, photography; *Clubs* Soc of Model Aeronautical Engrs; *Style*— Donald Campbell, Esq; ✉ 32 Willowbank, Robertsbridge, Kent TN32 5NH (☎ 01580 881087); 15 Harley Street, London W1N 1DA (☎ 0171 636 7780); Sussex Nuffield Hospital, Woodingdean, East Sussex BN2 6DX (☎ 01273 624488); South Cheshire Private Hospital, Leighton, Crewe CW1 4QP (☎ 01270 500411)

CAMPBELL, Elizabeth, Lady; Elizabeth; *née* Wills-Webber; *b* 30 Jan 1926; *Educ* Hemdean House, Queen Anne's Caversham; *m* 1 (m dis), D H Parker; m 2, 17 Aug 1956, Col Sir Guy Theophilus Halswell Campbell, 5 Bt, OBE, MC (d 1993); 2 s (Sir Lachlan Philip Kemeys, 6 Bt, *qv* b 1958, Rory Charles FitzGerald b 1961); *Career* stage name Lizbeth Webb; studied drama and singing with Julian Kimbell and Prof Georges Cunelli, first engagement BBC with Albert Sandler Trio, singer of ballads and opera with Jack Payne's concert orchestra (frequent broadcasts and Sunday concerts); freelancer BBC concerts incl: Louis Levey's Orchestra, BBC Concert Orchestra, Tom Jenkins, Max Jaffa, Villem Tauski; frequent bdcaster in German propaganda progs during War years, leading part Charles B Cochrane's production Big Ben 1945, Sir Alan Herbert and Vivian Ellis cmmnd by Cochrane to write Bless the Bride for her 1947, singer for army of occupation Austria and Germany, appeared in Ivor Novello's last production Gay's the Word, entertainer Br troops Korea 1953, played Sarah Brown in Guys and Dolls 1953, Royal Variety Performance 1953, over next few years appeared in many TV progs and concerts, played the lead in The Merry Widow (Cambridge Theatre), currently restorer of period costumes and textiles for museums and exhibitions worldwide at antique shop Fumbles Great Missenden (with ptnr Mrs Michael Holden); portrait painted by Sir William Russell Flint RA (wearing Bless the Bride costume designed by Tanya Moisevitch) 1949 (exhibited RA); *Recreations* writing, making period doll's clothes, collecting records of past opera singers; *Style*— Elizabeth, Lady Campbell; ✉ 18 Lansdown Terrace, Malvern Road, Cheltenham, Glos GL50 2JT (☎ 01242 243320)

CAMPBELL, Gordon Arden; s of Hugh Eric Campbell (d 1991), and Jessie, *née* Arden; *b* 16 Oct 1946; *Educ* Oldershaw GS, Churchill Coll Cambridge (MA); *m* Jennifer, *née* Vaughan; 2 da (Shona Alison b 1978, Claire Eleanor b 1983); *Career* Courtaulds PLC: joined Courtaulds res 1968, jr prodn mangr Courtaulds Acetate 1970–71, yarn salesman 1972, mgmnt acct 1973–74, gen mangr Rocel Ltd 1974–76, prodn dir Courtaulds Acetate 1976–80, dep md Courtaulds Acetate 1980–81, chief exec Courtaulds Acetate 1982–85, main bd dir 1987–, chief exec July 1996– (dep chief exec until 1996); md Saiccor (Pty) Ltd 1985; dir Usutu 1987; pres Comité International de Rayonne et Fibres Synthetiques; vice pres Inst of Chemical Engrg, non-exec memb UKAEA; CIMgt, FEng 1992; *Recreations* golf, rugby, skiing; *Style*— Gordon Campbell, Esq, FEng; ✉ Courtaulds plc, 50 George Street, London W1A 2BB (☎ 0171 612 1143, fax 0171 612 1520)

CAMPBELL, Graham Gordon; CB (1984); s of late Lt-Col P H Campbell; *b* 12 Dec 1924; *Educ* Cheltenham, Gonville and Caius Coll Cambridge (BA); *m* 1955, Margaret Rosamond Busby; 1 da; *Career* WWII, RA 1943–46; Miny of Fuel and Power: asst princ 1949, private sec to Parly Sec 1953–54, princ 1954; asst sec Miny of Power 1965, under sec DTI 1973, under sec Dept of Energy 1974–84; *Style*— Graham Campbell, Esq, CB; ✉ 3 Clovelly Ave, Warlingham, Surrey CR6 9HZ (☎ 01883 624671)

CAMPBELL, Hugh Hall; QC (Scot 1983); s of William Wright Campbell (d 1992), of Cambuslang, Lanarkshire, and Marianne Doris Stewart, *née* Hutchison (d 1988); *b* 18 Feb 1944; *Educ* Glasgow Acad, Glenalmond Coll, Exeter Coll Oxford (BA), Univ of Edinburgh (LLB); *m* 1969, Eleanor Jane, da of Sydney Charles Hare (d 1990), of Stoke Poges; 3 s (Benjamin b 1972, Timothy b 1975, Thomas b 1978); *Career* advocate Scottish Bar 1969, standing jr counsel to Admty 1976; FCIArb 1986; *Recreations* music, golf; *Clubs* Hon Co of Edinburgh Golfers; *Style*— H H Campbell, Esq, QC; ✉ 12 Ainslie Place, Edinburgh EH3 6AS (☎ 0131 225 2067)

CAMPBELL, Hugh James Foster; s of Archibald Dunlop Campbell (d 1988), of Troon, Ayrshire, and Margaret, *née* Foster (d 1988); *b* 16 April 1932; *Educ* Marr Coll Troon, Univ of Glasgow (MA); *m* 1, 1957, Yvonne Elizabeth, *née* Russell (d 1972); 1 s (Iain Russell b 1961), 1 da (Judith b 1960); m 2, 1987, Lindsay Raymonde Clifford, da of Keith Stainton; *Career* publisher; William Collins Sons & Co Ltd Glasgow: mgmnt trainee 1955–57, dep publishing dir for reference books, classics etc 1957–61; Longman Group London & Harlow: dep to prodn dir 1961–66, prodn dir 1966–68; Hamlyn Publishing Group: prodn dir 1968–70, publishing dir 1970–72, chief exec 1972–83, chm 1977–83, dir of International Publishing Corp 1973–83, chm Dean & Son Ltd 1973–83, chm A & W Publishing Group NYC 1975–80; md British Museum Publications Ltd 1984–94; dir BAS Printers 1994–; publishing conslt RHS 1994–; dep chm Book Devpt Cncl 1977–80, cncl memb Publishers Assoc 1982–88 (chm Working Party on Teleordering 1983), bd memb Book Trade Benevolent Soc and chm Bookrest Fundraising Ctee 1985–92; *Recreations* cooking, golf, music; *Clubs* Garrick, Berkshire Golf, Royal Cinque Ports Golf; *Style*— Hugh Campbell, Esq; ✉ 2 Mansfield Street, London W1M 9FE (☎ 0171 580 2591)

CAMPBELL, Iain; s of Joeseph Love Campbell, of Belfast, and Helen Mae, *née* Lyons; *b* 9 Nov 1953; *Educ* Sullivan Upper GS Holywood Co Down, Univ of Edinburgh (BSc); *m* 14 May 1977, Linda Jeanne, da of James Walter Stanley Fenwick; 1 s (Jamie Ross Euan b 8 Dec 1988), 2 da (Nicola Jane b 10 Nov 1980, Donna Melanie b 6 June 1984); *Career* Fairhurst and Partners 1976–78, Balfour Beatty Construction (Scotland) Ltd 1979–81, Freeman Fox Ltd 1981–87 (projects incl Musselburgh and Tranent Bypasses, redevelopment of RNAD Coulport Dumbartonshire), civil and structural engr ptnr Building Design Partnership 1988–; MICE 1982, MIStructE 1984, MConsE 1993, MIEI 1994; *Style*— Iain Campbell, Esq; ✉ 12 Maralin Avenue, Bangor, N Ireland BT20 4RQ (☎ 01247 455673); Building Design Partnership, 2 Bruce St, Belfast BT2 7JD (☎ 01232 243394, fax 01232 329337)

CAMPBELL, Ian James; s of James Patrick Campbell (d 1983), of Hythe, Kent, and Phyllis Eileen, *née* Hammond (d 1993); *b* 27 Aug 1947; *Educ* Ashford GS, Univ of Newcastle (BA); *m* 4 April 1970, Janette Elizabeth, da of Wilfred Johnston Bradley; 2 s (Christian James b 2 Oct 1976, Simon John b 13 Oct 1978); *Career* graduate trainee then relief station mangr British Overseas Airways Corporation 1969–73; Berol Corporation: export exec 1973–74, export mangr 1974–75, regnl mangr Africa/ME 1975–77; Caffrey Saunders Group of Companies: sales and mktg dir and latterly dep md Caffrey Saunders & Co Ltd 1977–84, md Caffrey Saunders & Co Ltd 1984–88, md Caffrey Saunders Services Ltd 1988–91; DG and sec Inst of Export 1992–; chm British Exporters' Assoc 1987–90, memb Advsy Ctee BOTB Export Clubs 1992–; regular contrib to nat and int seminars and confs on trade related issues, author of numerous articles and commentaries on int trade in professional jls; Int Export Assoc Award for Services to Export 1975; Freeman Worshipful Co of World Traders 1996 (memb 1992); MInstD, MIMgt 1981, FRSA 1992, FIEx 1995 (MIEx 1981); *Recreations* sailing, coaching junior rugby, theatre, food and wine; *Clubs* Caledonian, Royal Yachting Assoc; *Style*— Ian Campbell, Esq; ✉ Institute of Export, Export House, 64 Clifton Street, London EC2A 4HB (☎ 0171 247 9812, fax 0171 377 5343, e-mail institute@export.co.uk)

CAMPBELL, Ian Matthew; s of John Strange Campbell (d 1978), and Mary Brown, *née* Wright; *b* 4 April 1952; *Educ* Coatbridge HS, Univ of Glasgow (BSc Hons); *m* 1975, Carolyn Jean, da of Robin Dalziel Vanstone, of Coatbridge; 2 s (Andrew b 1978, Jamie b 1985), 1 da (Deborah b 1980); *Career* actuary (life assurance, pensions and investmt); FS Assurance Ltd 1974–89, Sedgwick Noble Lowndes 1989–; dir: FS Investment Services Ltd 1987–89, FS Investment Managers 1984–89, FS Assurance Tstees Ltd 1986–89, Northern Mortgage Corp 1986–89, Sedgwick Actuarial Services Ltd 1990–; FFA; *Recreations* golf, gardening; *Clubs* Coloquhoun, Scottish Actuaries, Lenzie Golf; *Style*— Ian M Campbell, Esq; ✉ 6 Grove Park, Lenzie, Glasgow G66 5AH (☎ 0141 775 0481); Sedgwick Noble Lowndes Ltd, 26 Blythswood Square, Glasgow G2 4BP (☎ 0141 248 4222, fax 0141 221 4615)

CAMPBELL, Air Vice-Marshal Ian Robert; CB (1976), CBE (1964), AFC (1948); s of late Maj Duncan Elidor Campbell, DSO (gs of 2 Earl Cawdor) and Hon Florence Evelyn, *née* Willey, da of 1 Baron Barnby; *b* 5 Oct 1920; *Educ* Eton, RAF Coll Cranwell; *m* 1, 1953, Beryl Evelyn (d 1982), da of Brig Thomas Kennedy Newbigging, MC (d 1968), of Thaxted, Essex; 1 s; m 2, 1984, Elisabeth Lingard-Guthrie; *Career* joined RAF 1939, air attaché Bonn 1968–70, DMSI MOD 1970–72, Air Cdre 1965, Air Vice-Marshal 1970, Chief of Staff No 18 (Maritime) Gp 1973–75; *Clubs* Boodle's, Royal Air Force; *Style*— Air Vice-Marshal Ian Campbell, CB, CBE, AFC; ✉ Pike Farm, Fossebridge, Cheltenham, Glos GL54 3JR (☎ 01285 720537)

CAMPBELL, Cdr Sir Ian Tofts; kt (1988), CBE (1984), VRD (1961), JP (1987); s of Capt John Walter Campbell (d 1982), and Mary Hardie, *née* Scott (d 1982); *b* 3 Feb 1923; *Educ* Daniel Stewart's Coll Edinburgh; *m* 7 March 1961, Marion, da of William Shiel (d 1943); *Career* RN 1942–46, Cdr RNR 1946–65; md MacGregor Wallcoverings Ltd 1966–78, dep chm Heath (Scotland) Ltd 1987–95, dir Travel Systems Ltd 1987–89, chm Select Assured Properties plc 1988–95, dir Hermiston Securities 1990; fin dir Cons Bd of Fin 1977–90, cncllr City of Edinburgh Dist Cncl 1984–88; Freeman City of Glasgow 1992; memb Inst Sales Mgmnt 1954, FInstD 1960; OStJ 1987; *Recreations* golf, water colour painting, vintage cars; *Clubs* New (Edinburgh), Caledonian (Edinburgh); *Style*— Cdr Sir Ian Campbell, CBE, VRD, JP; ✉ Merleton, Boswall Rd, Edinburgh EH5 3RH (☎ 0131 552 4825)

CAMPBELL, James Alexander Moffat Bain; s and h of Sir Colin Moffat Campbell, 8 Bt, MC, *qv*; *b* 23 Sept 1956; *Educ* Stowe; *m* 6 Feb 1993, Carola Jane, yr da of George Denman, of Stratton House, Stoney Stratton, Somerset: 2 da (b 10 Nov 1994 and 16 May 1996); *Career* Capt Scots Gds ret 1983, Capt London Scottish 1/51 Highlanders 1984–87; insurance broker 1983–; *Recreations* motorcycling, trees; *Clubs* Perth; *Style*— James Campbell, Esq; ✉ Kilbryde Castle, Dunblane, Perthshire (☎ 01786 824897)

CAMPBELL, Prof John; OBE (1993); s of Clarence Preston Campbell (d 1979), and Catherine Mary, *née* Crossley; *b* 2 Dec 1938; *Educ* Gateway Sch Leicester, Fitzwilliam Coll Cambridge (MA), Univ of Sheffield (MMet), Univ of Birmingham (PhD, DEng); *m* 1, Jacqueline Pamela, *née* Harrison; 1 da (Zoe Elizabeth); m 2, Sheila Margaret, *née* Taylor; *Career* graduate trainee Tube Investments Ltd 1963–64, British Iron and Steel Research Assoc 1967–70, Fulmer Research Inst 1970–78; UNIDO: Cairo 1973, Lahore 1976, tech dir Cosworth R & D Ltd 1978–85, tech dir Cosworth Castings Ltd 1984–85; Triplex Alloys Ltd: tech dir 1985–89, R&D dir 1989–91; dir Triplex Zeus Ltd 1989–91, dir Campbell Technology 1988–; non-exec dir: Cast Metals Development Ltd 1992–96, Alfer Ltd 1994–95, Alloy Technologies Ltd 1996–; Univ of Birmingham: visiting prof 1989–92, Baxi prof of casting technology 1992–; chm VK Educnl Foundry Trust 1989–; ACTA Metallurgica lectr 1992–94; editorial bd: Cast Metals jl 1988–, Materials Science & Technology jl 1991–; hon dir Light Metals Founders Assoc R & D Ltd 1987–94; fell: Inst of Materials 1985, Inst of British Foundrymen 1985; memb American Foundrymens Soc 1990; Liveryman Worshipful Co of Founders; Sir Jonathan North Gold Metal 1957–58, Wilkinson Medal Staffs Iron and Steel Inst 1990; FEng 1991; *Books* Castings (1991); *Recreations* music, walking, writing; *Style*— Prof John Campbell, OBE, FEng; ✉ Rosedale, Park Road, West Malvern WR14 4BJ (☎ 01684 573915, fax 01684 893303); IRC in Materials, The University of Birmingham, Birmingham B15 2TT (☎ 0121 414 5246/5215, fax 0121 414 3441)

CAMPBELL, John; *see:* Hughes, George

CAMPBELL, John Davies; CVO (1980), CBE (1981, MBE 1957), MC and Bar (1945); s of late Maj William Hastings Campbell, and Hon Eugenie Anne Westenra, *née* Plunkett, da of 14 Baron Louth; *b* 11 Nov 1921; *Educ* Cheltenham, Univ of St Andrews; *m* 1959, Shirley Bouch; 1 s, 2 da; *Career* serv WWII 1940–46, Argyll and Sutherland Highlanders and No 1 Demolition Sqdn (Popski's Private Army); HM Colonial Service 1949–61 (despatches 1957); joined HM Dip Serv 1961 (formerly with Col Serv), cncllr Ottawa 1972–77, consul gen Naples 1977–81; Commendatore dell'Ordine al Merito della Repubblica Italiana 1980; *Clubs* Special Forces, Victory Services; *Style*— John Campbell, Esq, CVO, CBE, MC; ✉ Townsend House, Luston, Leominster, Herefordshire HR6 0DZ (☎ and fax 01568 612446)

CAMPBELL, John Donington; s of Maj John Donington Campbell, of Heathfield, Sussex, and Edith Jean, *née* Crick; *b* 23 April 1959; *Educ* Harrow, RMA Sandhurst; *m* 4 June 1988, Catriona Helen Cecelia, da of John Spence Swan, of Letham, Fife; 1 da (Iona Helen b 18 Feb 1996); *Career* cmmnd Royal Scots Dragoon Guards 1979, ADC to General Offr Cmd Scot 1985–87; Phoenix Burners Ltd 1977–79, Ivory and Sime plc 1987–89; md: Instate plc 1989–91, Framlington Pensions Management 1991–93, Latchly Management Ltd 1996–; dir: Cursitor Management Ltd 1993–, Cursitor Alliance Management Ltd 1996–; memb Exec Ctee Christian Assoc of Business Ethics and The Inst of Business Ethics 1995–; *Recreations* country pursuits, tobogganing, tennis; *Clubs* Cavalry and Guards, St Moritz Tobogganing; *Style*— John Campbell, Esq; ✉ Currburn, Yetholm, Roxburghshire; Cursitor Alliance Management Ltd, 53 Stratton Street, London W1X 6JJ (☎ 0171 470 1540, fax 0171 470 0112)

CAMPBELL, Dr John Malcolm; s of Malcolm Rider Campbell (d 1991), of London, and latterly Wiltshire, and Sheila Stuart, *née* Robertson (d 1979); *b* 2 Sept 1947; *Educ* Charterhouse, Univ of Edinburgh (MA, PhD); *m* 1972, Alison Elizabeth, da of Thomas Archibald McCracken, and Olive Minnie, *née* Blackman, of Hawkhurst, Kent; 1 da (Robin Alexandra b 1981), 1 s (Patrick McCracken b 1983); *Career* freelance historian/biographer; memb Soc of Authors; author of book reviews for The Times, TLS, New Statesman etc; FRHistS; *Books* Lloyd George: The Goat in the Wilderness (second prize Yorkshire Post Award for Best First Book, 1977), F E Smith, First Earl of Birkenhead (1983), Roy Jenkins: A Biography (1983), Nye Bevan and the Mirage of British Socialism (1987), The Experience of World War II (ed, 1989), Makers of the Twentieth Century (series ed, 1990–91), Edward Heath: A Biography (1993, winner NCR Award for Non-Fiction 1994); *Recreations* tennis, golf, theatre, music, amateur dramatics/directing; *Style*— Dr John Campbell; ✉ 35 Ladbroke Square, London W11 3NB (☎ and fax 0171 727 1920)

CAMPBELL, (Alastair) John Wilson; s of Wilson William Campbell (d 1975), of Warkworth, Northumberland, and Pearl Gray, *née* Ackrill; *b* 18 Feb 1947; *Educ* King's Sch Canterbury, Sidney Sussex Coll Cambridge (MA); *m* 25 Feb 1972, Sarah Jane, da of Patrick Philip Shellard (d 1982); 2 s (Milo b 1974, Rollo b 1978), 1 da (Coco b 1976); *Career* exec NM Rothschild & Sons Ltd 1969–72, dir Noble Grossart Ltd 1973–88, md McLeod Russel 1979–82, dir Campbell Lutyens & Co Ltd 1988–; *Clubs* Reform, New (Edinburgh); *Style*— John Campbell, Esq; ✉ 25 Lansdowne Rd, London W11 3AG (☎ 0171 229 6768); Campbell Lutyens & Co Ltd, 5 Clifford St, London W1X 1RB (☎ 0171 439 7191, fax 0171 437 0153)

CAMPBELL, Joseph; s of John James Campbell (d 1983), and Helen, *née* Mitchell; *b* 16 Aug 1939; *Educ* Kirkcudbright Acad; *m* 6 Dec 1969, Sheila Margaret, da of Dr Alexander Craig; 1 s (John Alexander b 15 Jan 1971), 2 da (Susan Jean b 8 June 1972, Fiona Sheila b 1 Oct 1975); *Career* with Dumfries and Galloway Constabulary 1958–63; md: Tarff Valley Ltd 1964–69 (dir 1963–64), United Farmers Ltd 1969–77, Kintyre Farmers Ltd 1977–83, West Sound plc 1983–, Beechgrove Homes Ltd 1985–, South West Sound Ltd 1990–; fndr chm Ayrshire Nursing Homes Fedn 1987–, vice chm Opera West Ltd 1987–90, fndr dir Ayrshire Local Enterprise Co 1989–; dir: Scottish Agricultural Organisation Society Ltd 1980–83, Ayr C of C 1987–, Scottish Irish Radio Sales 1988–; chm ASA Security Ltd; hon pres Burns Federation 1995–; Royal Humane Soc Award 1963; *Recreations* music, painting, golf, reading; *Clubs* Farmers', London & Southerness Golf, Royal Troon Golf; *Style*— Joseph Campbell, Esq; ✉ West Sound Radio Ltd, Radio House, Holmston Road, Ayr KA7 3BE (☎ 01292 283662, fax 01292 283665); South West Sound FM, Campbell House, Bankend Road, Dumfries DG1 4TH (☎ 01387 250999, fax 01387 265629)

CAMPBELL, Juliet Jeanne d'Auvergne; CMG (1988); da of Maj-Gen W d'Auvergne Collings, CB, CBE (d 1984), of St Peter Port, Guernsey, and Harriet Nancy Draper, *née* Bishop (d 1983); *b* 23 May 1935; *Educ* Lady Margaret Hall Oxford (MA); *m* 28 July 1983, Alexander Elmslie (Alec) Campbell; *Career* FCO: joined 1957, Brussels Conf 1961–63, Bangkok 1964–66, News Dept 1967–70, The Hague 1971–74, Euro Integration Dept 1974–77, press cnsllr Paris 1977–80, RCDS 1981, cnsllr Jakarta 1982–83, head Trg Dept 1984–88, ambass Luxembourg 1988–91; mistress Girton Coll Cambridge 1992–, dep vice chllr Univ of Cambridge 1993– (memb Cncl of the Senate 1993–); govr Queen's Coll 1993–, tstee Changing Faces 1992–; hon fell Lady Margaret Hall 1992; *Style*— Mrs Juliet Campbell, CMG; ✉ Girton College, Cambridge CB3 0JG (☎ 01223 338951)

CAMPBELL, Ken; s of late Antony Colin Campbell, and Elsie, *née* Handley; *b* 10 Dec 1941; *Educ* Gearies Sch Barkingside, Chigwell Sch Chigwell, RADA; *m* 1978, Prunella, *née* Gee; 1 da (Daisy Eris 1978); *Career* actor, director and writer; Ken Campbell's Roadshow 1969, fndr and dir Science Fiction Theatre of Liverpool 1976, artistic dir Everyman Theatre Liverpool 1980, presenter Reality on the Rocks (Channel 4); *Plays* Old King Cole, Skungpoomery, Jack Sheppard, School for Clowns, You See the Thing is This, One Night I Danced with Mr Dalton, Clowns on a School Outing, Madness Museum, Bendigo, Walking Like Geoffrey, The Recollections of a Furtive Nudist, Pigspurt (Time Out Award for One Man Show 1992), Jamais Vu (Evening Standard Best Comedy Award 1993, Best Entertainment and Best Comedy Performance Olivier Awards 1994), Mystery Bruises, Knocked Sideways, Violin Time; *Recreations* pursuit of the weird; *Style*— Ken Campbell, Esq; ✉ c/o Peters, Fraser & Dunlop, 503/4 The Chambers, Chelsea Harbour, London SW10 0XF (☎ 0171 344 1000, fax 0171 352 7356)

CAMPBELL, Sir Lachlan Philip Kemeys; 6 Bt (UK 1815); er s of Col Sir Guy Theophilus Halswell Campbell, 5 Bt, OBE, MC (d 1993), and Elizabeth (stage name Lizbeth Webb), da of Alfred Rich Wills-Webber (d 1958) (*see* Campbell, Elizabeth, Lady); *b* 9 Oct 1958; *Educ* Lycée Français, Temple Grove, Eton, RMA Sandhurst; *m* 1986, Harriet Jane Sarah, o da of Frank Edward Jex Girling, of W Malvern, Worcs; 1 s (Archibald Edward FitzGerald b 13 June 1990), 1 da (Georgia Charlotte Clementine b 10 May 1995); *Heir* s, Archibald Edward FitzGerald Campbell b 13 June 1990; *Career* The Royal Green Jackets, served in N Ireland (short service cmmn), Queen Victoria's Rifles (TA); *Recreations* painting, rugby, cricket, golf; *Clubs* Army & Navy, MCC, London Scottish; *Style*— Sir Lachlan Campbell, Bt

CAMPBELL, Louis Auchinbreck; s and h of Sir Robin Auchinbreck Campbell, 15 Bt, *qv*; *b* 17 Jan 1953; *m* 1976, Fiona Mary St Clair, da of Gordon King, of Middlehill, Marlborough, NZ; 2 da (Lucinda Louise b 1982, Charlotte Virginia b 1985); *Style*— Louis Campbell, Esq

CAMPBELL, Lucy B; *née* Barnett; da of James Allen Barnett, of Portland, Oregan, and Jane, *née* Dodge (d 1952); *b* 26 Jan 1940; *Educ* Nightingale Bamford Sch NYC, The Garland Coll Boston Mass; *m* 1, 1959 (m dis 1963), Clifford Smith, Jr, s of Clifford Smith (d 1961), of Rockport, Maine; 2 s (Clifford Allen b 24 Aug 1960, Grafton Dodge b 3 Dec 1961); m 2, 1965 (m dis 1981), Colin Guy Napier Campbell, s of Archibald Campbell (d 1975), of London; 2 da (Georgina Dorothy b 24 Jan 1969, Tessa Sylvia b 3 April 1971); *Career* art dealer in antiquarian prints and pictures; proprietor Lucy B Campbell Gallery London (founded 1984) and Lucy B Campbell Ltd New York; exhibitions: The Fine Art and Antiques Fair Olympia Feb 1995, The British Antique Dealers' Fair Duke of York's HQ London May 1995, The Fine Art and Antiques Fair Olympia 1995 and 1996; memb British Antique Dealers' Assoc; *Style*— Mrs Lucy B Campbell; ✉ 21 Eaton Square, London SW1W 9DE; Lucy B Campbell Gallery, 123 Kensington Church St, London W8 7LP (☎ 0171 727 2205, fax 0171 229 4252)

CAMPBELL, Maggie; *b* 11 Nov 1950; *Educ* Haverstock Sch Chalk Farm London; *m* 3 Nov 1984, Joseph Washington Morton Campbell III; 1 da (Melissa Poppy b 7 Oct 1986); *Career* TV prodr/assoc dir Boase Massimi Pollitt Advertising 1973–88, sr prodr/assoc dir J Walter Thompson Advertising 1988–91, head of TV/dir Publicis Advertising 1991–94; memb D&AD, MIPA; *Recreations* cooking (qualified London Cordon Bleu School); *Clubs* East Sussex National Golf; *Style*— Mrs Maggie Campbell; ✉ Town House Farm, Sloop Lane, Scaynes Hill, W Sussex RH17 7NP

CAMPBELL, Malcolm; s of Malcolm Brown Campbell (d 1940), and Helen Munro, *née* Carruthers (d 1992); *b* 3 Jan 1934; *Educ* Glenalmond Coll; *m* 1, 25 Sept 1960 (m dis 1977), Fiona, *née* McLaren; 3 s (Colin b 30 Sept 1961, David b 19 April 1963, Graham b 6 March 1967); m 2, 18 Feb 1983, Susan Elizabeth Patten, da of Sydney David (d 1965), of Mid Glamorgan; 1 s (James b 29 June 1984), 1 step da (Elizabeth b 7 Oct 1975); *Career* Nat Serv RA 1953–55; chm Malcolm Campbell Ltd 1969– (joined 1955, sales mangr 1959, sales dir 1961, md 1966); dir and pres Glasgow C of C 1995, memb Cncl Br Chambers of Commerce 1995–96; winner Scottish Special Free Enterprise Award by Aims of Indust 1988; memb: Bd of Govrs Queen's Coll Glasgow 1989–93, Court Glasgow Caledonian Univ 1993– (chm 1996–); Freeman City of London 1978, Liveryman Worshipful Co of Fruiterers 1978; *Recreations* golf (Western Gailes capt 1974), sailing; *Clubs* Royal and Ancient (St Andrews), Prestwick, Western; *Style*— Malcolm Campbell,

Esq; ✉ Malcolm Campbell Ltd, 24 George Square, Glasgow G2 1EG (☎ 0141 204 4455, fax 0141 204 4360)

CAMPBELL, Malcolm Godfrey Wilson; s of Wilson William Campbell (d 1975), of Northumberland, and Pearl Gray, *née* Ackrill; *b* 30 July 1945; *Educ* The King's Sch Canterbury, Jesus Coll Oxford (MA); *Career* Oxford Univ Air Sqdn 1963–66; slr, ptnr Linklaters & Paines 1977–; memb Law Soc 1970; *Recreations* sport, flying, travel, photography; *Style*— Malcolm Campbell, Esq; ✉ Linklaters & Paines, Barrington House, 59–67 Gresham St, London EC2V 7JA (☎ 0171 606 7080, fax 0171 606 5113, telex 884349)

CAMPBELL, Prof Malcolm Murray; *b* 22 Aug 1943; *Educ* Bellahouston Acad Glasgow, Univ of Glasgow (BSc, PhD, DSc); *Career* postdoctoral res Univ of Madison 1968–69; lectr then sr lectr Heriot-Watt Univ 1969–79; sabbatical conslt Pfizer Inc Conn USA 1979–80; prof Univ of Bath 1980– (head of sch 1984–87 and 1990–93); consult: Organon AKZO 1974–, Pfizer Inc 1978–83, Hoechst 1983–88, Oxford Chemicals 1987–88, ICI Agrochemicals (occasional), Open Univ 3rd level course team 1988– (2nd level course team 1974–76), Bird and Bird (patent agents) 1992–, Ciba Pharmaceuticals 1994–; chm Organizing Ctee: 4th Medicinal Chemistry Conf Cambridge 1986, Ctee RSC Fine Chemicals and Medicinals Gp Conf for Schoolteachers 1988; memb: Fine Chemicals and Medicinals Gp Ctee RSC Industl Div 1984–, Organizing Ctee for 5th Medicinal Chemistry Conf Cambridge 1989, Organizing Ctee for Int Molecular Recognition Conf Exeter 1989, Euro Fedn for Medicinal Chemistry Ctee 1989–, Heads of Univ Chemistry Depts Ctee 1983–87 and 1990–93, Perkin Cncl RSC 1993– (Conf Ctee and Standing Ctee 1993–), Bd of Govrs Bristol Poly 1986–89; memb Univ of Bath: Long Term Planning Ctee 1984–87, Senate (elected) 1987–89 and 1989–91 (ex officio 1983–87), Policy Bd 1990–93; CChem, FRSC, FRSE 1983; *Publications* author of over 100 papers, text chapters and reviews; *Style*— Prof Malcolm Campbell, FRSE; ✉ Department of Chemistry, University of Bath, Claverton Down, Bath, Somerset BA2 7AY (☎ 01225 826130)

CAMPBELL, Margaret Jane (Mrs Margaret Bain); da of Dr Colin Campbell, of Waddesdon, Aylesbury, Bucks, and Daphne E M, *née* Robbins; *b* 15 June 1957; *Educ* Aylesbury HS, RCM; *m* 22 Dec 1990, Christopher Bain; 3 s; *Career* princ flute: City of Birmingham Symphony Orchestra 1977–86, Orchestra of the Royal Opera House Covent Garden 1986; winner Nat Fedn of Music Socs award for young concert artists 1981; ARCM; *Style*— Ms Margaret Campbell; ✉ 90 Haven Lane, Ealing, London W5 2HY (☎ 0181 998 6246)

CAMPBELL, Sir Matthew; KBE (1963), CB (1959); s of Matthew Campbell (d 1952), of High Blantyre, Lanarkshire; *b* 23 May 1907; *Educ* Hamilton Acad, Univ of Glasgow; *m* 1939, Isabella, da of late John Wilson, of St Conans, Rutherglen, Lanarkshire; 2 s (Colin, John); *Career* HM Civil Serv: joined 1928, sec Dept of Agric and Fisheries 1958–68 (under-sec 1953–58); dep chm White Fish Authy 1968–78; FRSE 1961; *Style*— Sir Matthew Campbell, KBE, CB, FRSE; ✉ 10 Craigleith View, Edinburgh (☎ 0131 337 5168)

CAMPBELL, (Walter) Menzies; CBE (1987), QC (Scot 1982), MP (Lib Dem) Fife NE (majority 3,808); s of George Alexander Campbell, and Elizabeth Jean Adam, *née* Phillips; *b* 22 May 1941; *Educ* Hillhead HS Glasgow, Univ of Glasgow (MA, LLB), Stanford Univ California; *m* 1970, Elspeth Mary Grant-Suttie, da of Maj-Gen R E Urquhart, CB, DSO; *Career* admitted advocate 1968, advocate depute 1977–80, standing jr counsel to the Army 1980–82; pt/t chm: VAT Tbnl 1984–87, Med Appeal Tbnl 1985–87; memb: Legal Aid Central Ctee 1983–86, Scottish Legal Aid Bd 1986–87, Broadcasting Cncl for Scotland 1984–87; Parly candidate (Lib): Greenock and Port Glasgow 1974 (both Gen Elections), E Fife 1979, NE Fife 1983; MP (Lib 1987–88, Lib Dem 1988–) Fife NE 1987–; Lib then Lib Dem spokesman on sport 1987–, Lib Dem spokesman on defence 1988–95, Lib Dem spokesman on foreign affairs and defence 1995–; memb Defence Select Ctee House of Commons 1992– (Trade and Indust Select Ctee 1990–92); capt UK athletics team 1965 and 1966, competed in Olympic Games 1964 and Cwlth Games 1966, UK 100 metres record holder 1967–74; *Clubs* Reform; *Style*— Menzies Campbell, Esq, CBE, QC, MP; ✉ House of Commons, London SW1A 0AA (☎ 0171 219 3000)

CAMPBELL, Michael David Colin Craven; DL (Hampshire 1994); s of Bruce Colin Campbell (d 1980), and Doris, *née* Craven-Ellis; *b* 12 Dec 1942; *Educ* Radley; *m* 6 April 1967, Linda Frances, da of Charles Brownrigg (d 1982); 1 s (Jamie Loudoun Craven b 1970), 2 da (Alexandra Jane (Mrs James Andrew) b 1968, Laura Grace b 1977); *Career* Ellis Campbell Group: md 1977–, chm 1987–; patron Small Business Bureau 1983–; memb Hampshire CC 1983–87; chm, govr and tstee The Treloar Tst 1993–; tstee: Hants Building Preservation Tst 1984–, Hants Garden Tst 1986–; chm Whitchurch Silk Mill Tst 1986–; *Recreations* shooting, sailing, cars, escaping to Scotland; *Clubs* Boodle's, Royal Yacht Squadron, Highland Society of London; *Style*— Michael Campbell, Esq, DL; ✉ The Steading, Shalden Park, Shalden, Alton, Hants GU34 4DS (☎ 01256 381821, fax 01256 381921)

CAMPBELL, Lady Moyra Kathleen; *née* Hamilton; CVO (1963); only da of 4 Duke of Abercorn (d 1979); *b* 22 July 1930; *m* 1966, Cdr Peter Colin Drummond Campbell, LVO, OBE, DL, *qv*, s of Maj-Gen Sir Douglas Campbell, KBE, CB, DSO, MC (d 1980); 2 s; *Career* a train bearer to HM The Queen at Coronation 1953, lady-in-waiting (temp) to HRH Princess Alexandra of Kent 1954–64, a lady-in-waiting 1964–66, and an extra lady-in-waiting 1966–69; *Style*— The Lady Moyra Campbell, CVO; ✉ Hollybrook House, Randalstown, Co Antrim, N Ireland BT41 2PB (☎ 0184 94 72224)

CAMPBELL, Sir Niall Alexander Hamilton; 8 Bt (UK 1831), of Barcaldine and Glenure, Argyllshire; 15 Chieftain, Hereditary Keeper of Barcaldine Castle; s of Sir Ian Vincent Hamilton Campbell, 7 Bt, CB (d 1978), and Madeline Lowe Reid, *née* Whitelocke (d 1929); *b* 7 Jan 1925; *Educ* Cheltenham, CCC Oxford; *m* 1, 1949 (m dis 1956), Patricia Mary, da of R Turner; m 2, 1957, Norma Joyce, da of W N Wiggin, of Albrighton, Shropshire; 2 s (Roderick Duncan Hamilton b 1961, Angus Charles Dundas b 1967), 2 da (Fiona Madeline Hamilton b 1958, Lucy Catriona Margaret b (twin) 1967); *Heir* s, Roderick Duncan Hamilton Campbell b 24 Feb 1961; *Career* Lt RM 1943–46; called to the Bar Inner Temple 1951, hospital administrator 1953–70, dep chief clerk Inner London Magistrates' Courts 1970–76, clerk to Justices of Barnstaple, Bideford and Great Torrington and S Molton (N Devon Divs) 1976–; *Style*— Sir Niall Campbell, Bt; ✉ The Old Mill, Milltown, Muddiford, Barnstaple, Devon EX31 1DX (☎ 01271 341); The Law Courts, Civic Centre, Barnstaple, Devon (☎ 01271 72511); Barcaldine Castle, Benderloch via Connel, Argyllshire

CAMPBELL, (Henrietta) Nina Sylvia; da of John Archibald Campbell (d 1974), and Elizabeth, *née* Pearth (d 1996); *b* 9 May 1945; *Educ* Heathfield Sch Ascot Berks; *m* 1 (m dis 1978), Andrew Guy Louis De Chappuis Konig; 1 da (Henrietta Lucy Elizabeth b July 1973), 1 s (Maximillian John b Nov 1976); m 2 (m dis 1991), John Henry Deen; 1 da (Alice Nina b 6 Aug 1982); *Career* interior decorator; apprenticeship with John Fowler of Colefax & Fowler; own interior decoration business and shop 1974–; cmmns for many private residences in UK and abroad incl: Sunninghill Park (for Duke and Duchess of York), new sales rooms Christies London, Hotel de Vigny Paris, Mark's Club London, Hotel Balzac Paris, Parc Victor Hugo Paris; tstee V&A, govr Heathfield Sch; Women Who Most Influenced Style Internationally award Night of Stars 1990 (Fashion Gp Int); *Books* Elsie de Wolfe - A Decorative Life (1992), Nina Campbell on Decoration (1996); *Style*— Miss Nina Campbell; ✉ Nina Campbell Ltd, 9 Walton Street, London SW3 2JD (☎ 0171 225 1011, fax 0171 225 0644)

CAMPBELL, Paddy (Patricia Ann); da of Tom Webster (Daily Mail cartoonist, d 1963), and Ida Shelley, *née* Michael (d 1991); *b* 10 July 1940; *Educ* La Sainte Union des Sacrées Coeurs Highgate, RADA; *m* 1 Jan 1965, John Charles Middleton Campbell, s of Lord Campbell of Eskan; 3 da; *Career* fashion designer; began career as actress, entered fashion indust 1974, estab own business and opened first shop St Christopher's Place 1979, opened second shop Beauchamp Place 1984, signed licensing deal with Japanese co 1985, wholesaling since 1990; vice pres The Women of the Year Lunch (raising money for Gtr London Fund for the Blind, former chm); *Style*— Mrs Paddy Campbell; ✉ 8 Gees Court, St Christopher's Place, London W1M 5HQ (☎ 0171 493 5646)

CAMPBELL, Maj-Gen (Charles) Peter; CBE (1977); s of Charles Alfred Campbell (d 1975), and Blanche, *née* Appleton (d 1983); *b* 25 Aug 1926; *Educ* Gillingham GS, Emmanuel Coll Cambridge; *m* 1, 11 May 1949, Lucy (d 1986), da of William David Kitching (d 1960); 2 s (Murray b 2 July 1951, Colin b 16 May 1954); m 2, 22 Nov 1986, Elizabeth Barbara, da of Maj William Barington Tristram (ka 1942); *Career* cmmnd RE 1945; army staff course 1957; OC 11 Ind Field Sqdn RE in Far East 1960–62, Jt Servs Staff Course 1963, Co Cdr RMA Sandhurst 1965–67, CRE 1 Div BAOR 1967–70, GSO1 Plans MOD 1970–71, CRE 3 Div UK 1971, cmd 12 Engrg Bde UK 1972–73, RCDS 1974, COS in HQ UK 1975–77, Engr-in-Chief (Army) 1977–80; Col Cmdt RE 1981–86; Hon Col 101 (London) Engr Regt (EOD)(V) 1986–91; chm RE Assoc 1983–89, dir Quicks Gp plc 1982–91, conslt Terex Equipment 1983–89, govr Gordon's Sch 1993– (memb fndn 1991–); FBIM 1971; *Recreations* painting, collecting militaria; *Clubs* Naval and Military; *Style*— Maj-Gen Peter Campbell, CBE; ✉ c/o Lloyds Bank, 32 High Street, Shaftesbury, Dorset SP7 8JJ

CAMPBELL, Cdr Peter Colin Drummond; LVO (1960), OBE (1996), DL (Antrim 1984); s of Maj-Gen Sir (Alexander) Douglas Campbell, KBE, CB, DSO, MC (d 1980), and Patience Loveday, *née* Carlyon (d 1996); *b* 24 Oct 1927; *Educ* Cheltenham, RNC Dartmouth; *m* 1966, Lady Moyra Kathleen Campbell, CVO, *qv*, da of 4 Duke of Abercorn (d 1979); 2 s; *Career* late Cdr RN; equerry to HM the Queen 1957–60; farmer; Ireland rep Irish Soc 1974–96; dir Bann System Ltd; life vice pres RN Assoc 1979–; High Sheriff Co Antrim 1985; Freeman City of London 1975; *Recreations* field sports, boating; *Clubs* Army & Navy; *Style*— Cdr Peter Campbell, LVO, OBE, DL; ✉ Hollybrook House, Randalstown, Co Antrim, NI BT41 2PB (☎ 01849 472224, fax 01849 479486); Rathlin Island, Co Antrim (☎ 01265 763911)

CAMPBELL, Peter James Atkinson; s of Richard Douglas Campbell (d 1957), of Torphins, Aberdeenshire, and Elizabeth Hendrie, *née* Atkinson; *b* 22 July 1948; *Educ* Ardvreck Sch Crieff, Fettes Coll Edinburgh; *m* 1970, Janet, da of Duncan Stuart MacGillivray (d 1968); 3 s (Duncan Craig b 1972, Kevin Andrew b 1974, Malcolm James b 1978); *Career* apprentice AG Murray & Co 1966–71, Touche Ross & Co (Edinburgh) 1971–72, CA 1972, Ochtertyre Theatre & Estate 1972–74, fin dir Graeme Dawson Design Ltd 1974–76; Pannell Kerr Forster: audit supervisor (Gambia) 1976–78, sr gp audit mangr (Kenya) 1978–80, ptnr (Aberdeen) 1980–, princ auditor (Falkland Islands, S Georgia and British Antarctica) 1985–; CPA (K) 1979; Grampian ambass 1993; *Recreations* fishing, windsurfing; *Clubs* Aboyne Rugby, Nairobi, Royal Northern & University; *Style*— Peter Campbell, Esq; ✉ Pannell Kerr Forster, 38 Albyn Place, Aberdeen, Scotland AB9 1US (☎ 01224 589195, fax 01224 581529)

CAMPBELL, Eur Ing Peter Leonard; JP (1976); s of Edgar Lionel Campbell, and Nancy Bertha, *née* Parmenter; *b* 29 Jan 1932; *Educ* Purley GS, Brixton Sch of Building (South Bank Univ), Imperial Coll of Sci Tech & Medicine (FCGI, DIC); *m* Dec 1953, Pam, *née* Harding; 1 s (Kevin Peter b 1966), 2 da (Corinne Gay b 1956, Julia Mary b 1959); *Career* Ove Arup & Partners 1951–62, fndr Campbell Reith Hill 1962 (conslt 1992–); memb Univ Academic Advsy Bd at: Surrey, Kingston, Imperial Coll; memb Cncl: Inst of Structural Engrs 1979–93 (pres 1988–89), Assoc of Consltg Engrs 1989–93 (chm 1991–92); chm: MERGE (Multidiscipline Engrg Resources Group Europe), Construction Disputes Resolution Gp 1991–, CONSTRUCT (The Concrete Structures Gp) 1993–96 (life pres 1996), Euro Concrete Building Project Implimentation Ctee 1994; vice pres Register of Engrs for Disaster Relief 1992; UK rep Exec Ctee Federation Internationale des Ingenieurs Conseils (FIDIC) 1993–; fndr and hon curator Museum of Concrete Amberley W Sussex, memb Bd of Tstees Southern Industl History Museum Amberley 1993–; Liveryman Worshipful Co of Paviors 1982, Freeman City of London; MInstD; FIStructE 1971 (MIStructE 1957), FRSA 1976, FIMarE 1983, FIHT 1984, FICE 1985, FEng 1990; *Books* Structural Engineering - Two Centuries of British Achievement (jtly, 1984), Ove Arup 1895–1995 (jtly, 1995); author of numerous published articles, book reviews and lectures; *Recreations* gardens, equestrian activities, bridge, golf; *Style*— Eur Ing Peter Campbell, JP, FEng; ✉ Earlymist, The Bridle Path, Leazes Avenue, Chaldon, Caterham, Surrey CR3 5AG (☎ and fax 01883 343204); Campbell Reith Hill, Tudor House, 26 Upper Teddington Road, Kingston-upon-Thames, Surrey KT1 4DY (☎ 0181 943 2211, fax 0181 943 1622)

CAMPBELL, Prof Peter Walter; s of Walter Clement Howard Campbell (d 1958), of Bournemouth, and Lillian Muriel, *née* Locke (d 1979); *b* 17 June 1926; *Educ* Bournemouth Sch, New Coll Oxford (MA), Nuffield Coll Oxford; *Career* lectr in govt Univ of Manchester 1949–60; Univ of Reading: prof of political economy 1960–64, prof of politics 1964–91, emeritus prof 1991, dean of Faculty of Letters and Social Scis 1966–69, chm Graduate Sch of Contemporary Euro Studies 1971–73; vice chm Social Serv Reading DC 1966–71, chm Reading Romilly Assoc 1965–69, Berks Electoral Reform Gp 1979–80, Reading Campaign for Homosexual Equality 1979–80, sec and treas Political Studies Assoc of UK 1955–58, chm Inst of Electoral Res 1958–65, memb Cncl Hansard Soc for Parliamentary Govt 1962–77, ed Political Studies 1963–69; memb: Cwlth Scholarship Cmmn's Advsy Panel 1964–73, Political Sci Ctee SSRC 1968–72, various bds and panels CNAA 1969–78, Soc Studies Sub-Ctee UGC 1973–83, Cncl of Mgmnt Albany Soc 1988–91; vice pres Electoral Reform Soc 1973–; chm: Cons Gp for Homosexual Equality 1982–88 (vice pres 1988–), Soc for Individual Freedom 1992–93; tstee Civic Educational and Research Tst 1993–95; treas Conservative Action for Electoral Reform 1990–94; patron Univ of Buckingham 1984–; *Books* Encyclopaedia of World Politics (with W Theimer, 1950), French Electoral Systems and Elections 1789–1957 (1958), The Constitution of the Fifth Republic (1958); *Recreations* idling, ambling; *Clubs* Athenaeum, Oxford and Cambridge; *Style*— Prof Peter Campbell; ✉ 6 Treyarnon Court, 37 Eastern Avenue, Reading, Berks RG1 5RX (☎ 0118 966 1888)

CAMPBELL, His Hon Judge (John) Quentin; s of John McKnight Campbell, OBE, MC (d 1949), and Katherine Margaret, *née* Grant (d 1983); *b* 5 March 1939; *Educ* Loretto, Wadham Coll Oxford (MA); *m* 1, 1960, Penelope Jane Redman; 3 s (James Alistair b 1962, John Marcus b 1964, Matthew b 1967), 1 da (Jessica Louise b 1970); m 2, 1977, Ann Rosemary (Dist Judge Campbell), *qv*, da of Sqdn Ldr Richard Henry Beeching (ret); 1 da (Arabella b 27 June 1977), 1 s (Frederick b 28 June 1982); *Career* admitted slr 1965, met stipendiary magistrate 1981–96, recorder of the Crown Court 1989–96, circuit judge (SE Circuit) 1996–; chm of Govrs Bessels Leigh Sch Oxford 1977–96; *Clubs* Travellers', Frewen (Oxford); *Style*— His Hon Judge Quentin Campbell; ✉ 12 Park Town, Oxford OX2 6SH; The Crown Court, Inner London Sessions House, Newington Causeway, London SE1 6AZ

CAMPBELL, Robert; s of Robert Stewart Campbell (d 1966), of Coughton, Warwickshire, and Isobella Frances, *née* Nettleton (d 1957); *b* 18 May 1929; *Educ* Loughborough Univ (DLC, MSc); *m* 1950, Edna Maud, da of Thomas Henry Evans (d 1949); *Career* chartered engr 1954–69, various appts in water industry, miny inspr

1969–74, asst dir Anglian Water 1974–77; chief exec Epping Forest Dist Cncl 1977–79, md Thomas Telford Ltd, chm REM Campbell International Management Consultants 1982–; sec Inst of Civil Engrs (tstee Benevolent Fund 1979–82), dir Watt Ctee Energy Ltd; FICE; *Recreations* music, gardening, watching cricket; *Clubs* MCC; *Style*— Robert Campbell, Esq; ✉ Bronafon, Llechryd, Cardigan SA43 2NR; Jubilee House, Weston Favell, Northampton NH3 4HW (☎ 01604 414500, fax 411192)

CAMPBELL, (Alistair) Robert Macbrair; s of Dr Bruce Campbell, OBE, and Margaret Campbell; *b* 9 May 1946; *Educ* Marlborough, Univ of Aberdeen (BSc); *m* 7 Sept 1968, Frances Rosemary, *née* Kirkwood; 1 s (Tomas b 11 Aug 1971), 2 da (Chloe b 5 July 1973, Nancy b 15 May 1977); *Career* md Blackwell Science Ltd 1987–; chm: Blackwell Science Inc (USA) 1988–, Arnette (France) 1989–, Blackwell Wissenschafts (Germany) 1989–; *Books* A Guide to the Birds of the Coast (1976), Microform Publishing (1979), Journal Publishing (1987, 2 edn 1996), Journal Production (1992); *Recreations* fly-fishing, writing, wine; *Style*— Robert Campbell, Esq; ✉ Blackwell Science Ltd, Osney Mead, Oxford OX2 0EL (☎ 01865 206206, fax 01865 791542)

CAMPBELL, Robin Alexander; s of Robert Campbell (d 1986), of Sway, Hants, and Marion Steele, *née* Davidson; *Educ* Aldenham, Wadham Coll Oxford (MA); *m* 1968, Heather-Ann, da of Gordon Henderson Munro, TD (d 1980), of Inverness; 1 s (Alexander b 1972), 1 da (Fiona b 1974); *Career* Nat Serv 2 Lt: Gordon Highlanders, 4 King's African Rifles (Kenya and Uganda); dist offr HM Overseas Civil Serv N Rhodesia 1961–64, magistrate Zambia 1964–65, called to the Bar Middle Temple 1967, asst cmmr Parly Boundary Cmmn 1992, legal assoc RTPI 1995–; *Books* Seneca: Letters from a Stoic (translation, 1969), Lumley's Public Health Acts (jt ed, 1970–72); *Recreations* mountain walking, sea canoeing, drawing and watercolours, wildlife; *Style*— Robin Campbell, Esq; ✉ 5 Arlington Square, London N1 7DS (☎ 0171 359 2334); Pollanaich, Nedd, Drumbeg by Lairg, Sutherland IV27 4NN (☎ 01571 833292); 4–5 Gray's Inn Square, Gray's Inn, London WC1R 5AY (☎ 0171 404 5252, fax 0171 831 0202)

CAMPBELL, Sir Robin Auchinbreck; 15 Bt (NS 1628), of Auchinbreck; s of Sir Louis Hamilton Campbell, 14 Bt (d 1970), and Margaret Elizabeth Patricia (d 1985), da of Patrick Campbell; *b* 7 June 1922; *Educ* Eton; *m* 1, 1948, Rosemary (Sally) (d 1978), da of Ashley Dean, of Christchurch, New Zealand; 1 s (Louis Auchinbreck b 1953), 2 da (Rosemary Fiona b 1955, Sophia Louise b 1960); m 2, 1978, Elizabeth Mary, da of Sir Arthur Colegate, MP, and formerly w of Richard Wellesley Gunston; *Heir* s, Louis Auchinbreck Campbell, *qv*; *Career* formerly Lt (A) RNVR; sheep farmer; *Clubs* Bembridge Sailing, Christchurch; *Style*— Sir Robin Campbell, Bt; ✉ 287A Waikawa Road, Picton, New Zealand

CAMPBELL, Roderick Duncan Hamilton; yr of Barcaldine and Glenure; s and h of Sir Niall Campbell, 8 Bt, *qv*; *b* 24 Feb 1961; *m* 15 April 1989, Jean Caroline, da of Laurence Bicknell, of Tom's Hill, Lobb, Braunton, N Devon; 2 da (Kate Emily Dennistoun b 25 Feb 1990, Anna Iona Hamilton b 10 July 1993); *Style*— Roderick Campbell, Esq; ✉ Barcaldine Castle, Ledaig, By Oban, Argyll PA37 1SA

CAMPBELL, Prof Ronald William Fearnley; s of Robert Walter Campbell, of Falkirk, Stirlingshire, and Mary Campbell Dawson, *née* Jack; *b* 11 Oct 1946; *Educ* Dollar Acad Scotland, Univ of Edinburgh (MB ChB); *m* 18 July 1969, Agnes Margaret, da of Charles Struth, of Grangemouth, Stirlingshire; 1 da (Xanthe b 3 Nov 1974); *Career* med positions Edinburgh Teaching Gp Hosps 1969–75, Sir Henry Wellcome fellowship (MRC) Duke Univ Durham N Carolina USA 1975–76, sr lectr in academic cardiology Newcastle Gp Hosps 1976–86, Br Heart Fndn prof of cardiology Univ of Newcastle and hon conslt cardiologist Freeman Hosp Newcastle 1986–, UCCA selector Univ of Newcastle, med advsr Northumbria Ambulance Serv; chm Arrhythmia Gp Euro Soc of Cardiology 1994; memb: Ctees Br Heart Fndn, Ball Ctee Newcastle Annual Heart Ball, Br Cardiac Soc 1979 (hon treas 1992, pres elect 1995, pres 1997); FRCPE 1981, FRCP 1984, fell Euro Soc of Cardiology; *Books* Dynamic Electrocardiography (1985), Paediatric Cardiac Arrhythmias (1996); *Recreations* skiing, fell walking, videography; *Style*— Prof Ronald Campbell; ✉ Academic Cardiology, Freeman Hospital, Newcastle upon Tyne NE7 7DN (☎ 0191 223 1073, fax 0191 213 0498)

CAMPBELL, Ronnie; MP (Lab) Blyth Valley (majority 8,044); s of Ronald Campbell, and Edna, *née* Howes; *b* 14 Aug 1943; *Educ* Ridley HS; *m* 17 July 1967, Deirdre, da of Edward McHale (d 1976); 5 s (Edward b 1968, Barry b 1971, Shaun b 1973, Brendan b 1973, Aiden b 1977), 1 da (Sharon b 1969); *Career* former miner, chm Bates NUM; MP (Lab) Blyth Valley 1987–; cncllr: Blyth Borough Cncl 1969–74, Blyth Valley DC 1974–88; *Style*— Ronnie Campbell, MP; ✉ House of Commons, London SW1A OAA

CAMPBELL, Steven MacMillan; s of George Campbell, of Rutherglen, Glasgow, and Martha Dallas McKenzie, *née* MacMillan; *b* 19 March 1953; *Educ* Rutherglen Acad, Glasgow Sch of Art (BA), Pratt Inst NY; *m* 4 July 1975, Carol Ann, da of Andrew Crossan Thompson, of Glasgow, Scotland; 1 s (Rory Thompson b 6 June 1988), 2 da (Lauren Holly b 22 May 1984, Greer Caitlin b 25 Feb 1987); *Career* artist; solo exhibitions incl: Barbara Toll Fine Arts NY 1983, John Webber Gallery NY 1983, Dart Gallery Chicago 1983, Rona Hoffman Gallery Chicago 1984, Galerie Six Freidrich Munich Germany 1984, Riverside Studios London 1984, Fruitmarket Gallery Edinburgh 1985, Barbara Toll Fine Arts NY 1985, Walker Art Center Minneapolis 1985, Middendorf Gallery Washington DC 1985, Galerie Pierre Huber Geneva 1986, John Berggruen Gallery San Francisco 1986, Marlborough Fine Art London 1987, Marlborough Fine Art NY 1988, Riva Yares Gallery Scotsdale Arizona 1989, The Third Eye Centre Glasgow 1990, Rex Irwin Gallery Sydney Australia 1990, Marlborough Fine Art Tokyo 1990, Oriel Mostyn Llandudno Wales 1990, Aberdeen Art Gallery 1990, Whitworth Art Gallery Manchester 1990, Southampton City Art Gallery 1991, Talbot Rice Gallery Edinburgh 1993, Marlborough Fine Art New York 1994; public collections incl: Arts Cncl of GB, Art Inst of Chicago, City Art Gallery Southampton, Glasgow Art Gallery and Museum, Contemporary Art Soc London, Tamayo Museum Mexico City, Walker Arts Center Minneapolis, Aberdeen Art Gallery and Museum, Danheiser Fndn NY, Metropolitan Museum NY, Leeds City Art Gallery, Tate Gallery London, Tate Gallery Liverpool, Br Cncl, Scottish Arts Cncl, Phoenix Art Museum, Hirshorn Museum Washington DC, Chase Manhattan Bank NY, Southampton Gallery, High Museum of Art Atlanta Georgia; awarded Fulbright scholarship 1982–83; *Recreations* angling, reading, mathematics, detective novels; *Style*— Steven Campbell, Esq; ✉ Rennies Loan, The Cross, Kippen, Stirlingshire FK8 3DX (☎ 01786 870370); Marlborough Fine Art (UK) Ltd, 6 Albemarle St, London W1X 4BY (☎ 0171 629 5161, fax 0171 629 6338)

CAMPBELL, Sulzeer (Sol); *b* 18 Sept 1974; *Career* professional footballer (defender); joined Tottenham Hotspur FC 1992; England: former memb under 21 team, 3 full caps (as at Jan 1997), memb squad Euro 96; *Style*— Sol Campbell, Esq; ✉ c/o Tottenham Hotspur FC, 748 High Road, Tottenham, London N17 0AP (☎ 0181 808 6666)

CAMPBELL, Vivian; *Career* guitarist with Def Leppard 1992–; formerly with DIO, Whitesnake, River Dogs, Lou Gramm; albums with Def Leppard: Adrenalize (1992), Retro-Active (1993), Slang (1996); *Style*— Vivian Campbell, Esq; ✉ c/o Bludgeon Riffola, Mercury, Chancellors House, 72 Chancellors Road, London W6 9QB (☎ 0181 910 5678, fax 0181 910 5896)

CAMPBELL, William; s of Donald Russell Campbell (d 1977), and Elizabeth, *née* Houliston (d 1989); *b* 22 Feb 1936; *Educ* St Paul's, New Coll Oxford (BA), Univ of Leeds (Dip in TEFL); *m* 9 Jan 1962, Maria Angeles, da of Jose-Maria Alvargonzalez; 2 da (Isabel Angela Anne b 24 Oct 1962, Helen Josephine Mercedes b 21 Oct 1963), 2 s (Edward William Russell b 18 Dec 1966, Alexander Donald Henry b 29 Jan 1971); *Career* Nat Serv Royal Corps of Signals 1954–56; British Council: trainee 1960–61, lectr Istanbul 1961–62, Jakarta 1963–64 and Tehran 1964–66, dir Tabriz 1967–71, asst dir Students Centre 1971–73, dir of studies Ankara 1973–77, English language offr Chile 1977–79 and Sudan 1979–82, dir Lahore 1982–86, Chile 1986–91 and Colombia 1991–95, ret; *Recreations* book collecting, stamp collecting, Islamic and Hispanic culture, hill walking; *Style*— William Campbell, Esq; ✉ 9 Ewell Bypass, Ewell, Epsom, Surrey; c/o La Parata, Apartado de Correos 75, Garrucha, Almeria, Spain

CAMPBELL, Maj-Gen William Tait; CBE (1945, OBE 1944); s of late Dr Robert B Campbell, MD, FRCPE, of Edinburgh; *b* 8 Oct 1912; *Educ* Fettes Coll, RMC Sandhurst; *m* 1942, Rhoda Alice, da of late Adm Algernon Walker-Heneage-Vivian, CB, MVO; 2 da; *Career* 2 Lt The Royal Scots (Royal Regt) 1933, served 1 Airborne Div 1941–44, 1 Allied Airborne Army 1944–45, Lt-Col cmdg 1 Bn The Royal Scots 1954–57 (despatches), Brig i/c admin Malaya 1962, Maj-Gen 1964, DQMG MOD (Army Dept) 1964–67, ret 1967; Col The Royal Scots 1964–74; dir Fairbridge Soc 1969–78; *Style*— Maj-Gen William T Campbell, CBE; ✉ Ashwood, Boarhills, St Andrews, Fife KY16 8PR

CAMPBELL GARRATT, Jane Louise; da of Thomas Tertius Campbell Garratt (d 1973), and Patricia Marjorie, *née* Cobb, of Stoke d'Abernon, Surrey; *b* 6 July 1948; *Educ* Brooklands Sch, Claremont; *m* 25 June 1988, Patrick Antony Stuart Rucker; *Career* account exec S H Benson advtg 1970–71 (joined 1966); Ogilvy & Mather: joined 1971, bd dir 1986–, mgmnt supervisor 1989–90, dir of recruitment and trg 1990–93, vice chm 1993–97; recipient Francis Ogilvy award; memb Women's Advertising Club of London; *Recreations* gardening, antiques, 18th Century literature; *Clubs* Reform, 2 Brydges Place; *Style*— Jane Campbell Garratt

CAMPBELL GOLDING, (Frederick) Keith; s of Dr Frederick Campbell Golding (d 1984), of The Barn, Hursley, Winchester, Hants, and Barbara, *née* Hubbard; *b* 17 May 1947; *Educ* Mill Hill Sch; *children* 1 s (Angus b 1987), 3 da (Amy b 1981, Tania b 1981, Juliette b 1984); *Career* md Campbell Golding Associates Ltd 1977–84, exec dir EBC AMRO Bank Ltd 1986–89, md EBC AMRO Asset Management Ltd 1986–91, first vice pres BSI-Banca della Svizzera Italiana 1991–94, md The Golding Guides Ltd 1995–; *Recreations* field sports, family; *Clubs* Buck's; *Style*— Keith Campbell Golding, Esq; ✉ Queen's Court, Tockenham, Wootton Bassett, Wilts SN4 7PH (☎ 01793 853186); The Golding Guides Limited, The Barn House, Queen's Court, Tockenham, Wootton Bassett, Wilts SN4 7PJ (☎ 01793 854500, fax 01793 854501)

CAMPBELL-GRAY, Hon Andrew Godfrey Diarmid Stuart; *see:* Gray, Master of

CAMPBELL-HARRIS, Alastair Neil; s of Maj Arthur Edward Campbell-Harris, MC, of London (d 1970), and Doris Marie, *née* Robson (d 1964); *b* 9 Feb 1926; *Educ* Sunningdale Sch, RNC Dartmouth; *m* 9 Jan 1962, Zara Carolyn, da of William Herbert Harrison, of Staffs (d 1975); 1 s (James Neil b 1966), 2 da (Clare Louise b 1963, Lucinda Zara b 1968); *Career* joined RN 1943, midshipman in Atlantic and East Indies 1943, Sub Lt in Med 1945, Lt Far East 1947–50, home waters 1950–52, ADC to Govr Gen of NZ 1952–55, ret as Lt 1955; fin PR conslt; dep chm Streets Financial Strategy Ltd 1986 (dir Streets Financial Ltd 1975–86), chm Citigate Communications Group Ltd 1987–; *Recreations* fishing, golf, gardening; *Style*— Alastair Campbell-Harris, Esq; ✉ Gattendon Lodge, Goring-on-Thames, nr Reading, Berks RG8 9LU (☎ 01491 872292); Citigate Communications Group Ltd, 26 Finsbury Square, London EC2A 1DS (☎ 0171 282 8000)

CAMPBELL-JOHNSON, Alan; CIE (1947), OBE (1946); s of Lt-Col James Alexander Campbell-Johnson (ka 1918), of S Aust, and Gladys Susanna, *née* Geering (d 1976); *b* 16 July 1913; *Educ* Westminster, ChCh Oxford (BA, MA); *m* 8 Oct 1938, (Imogen) Fay de la Tour, da of Ernest Alexander Dunlap (d 1923), of Jacksonville, Illinois, USA; 1 s (Keith b 1945 d 1970), 1 da (Virginia b 1942); *Career* Nat Serv RAFVR 1941–46, Combined Operations HQ 1942–43, HQ Supreme Allied Cdr SE Asia (Wing Cdr i/c Inter Allied Records Section) 1943–46; political sec to Rt Hon Sir Archibald Sinclair as Ldr of the Lib Pty 1937–39, Parly candidate (Lib) Salisbury and S Wilts 1945 and 1950; press attaché to Viceroy and Govr Gen of India 1947–48; PR conslt; fndr and chm Campbell-Johnson Ltd 1953–78, dir Hill and Knowlton (UK) Ltd 1978–85; former pres Inst of PR; US Legion of Merit 1947; Hon DLitt Univ of Southampton; FIPR 1954 (MIPR 1948), Hon FIPR 1988, MRI 1956, FRSA 1957; *Books* Growing Opinions (ed, 1935), Peace Offering (1936), Anthony Eden - A Biography (1938, revised 1955), Viscount Halifax - A Biography (1941), Mission with Mountbatten (1951, republished 1971 and 1985); *Recreations* watching cricket, listening to music; *Clubs* Brooks's, Nat Lib, MCC; *Style*— Alan Campbell-Johnson, Esq, CIE, OBE; ✉ 21 Ashley Gardens, Ambrosden Avenue, London SW1P 1QD (☎ 0171 834 1532, office 0171 630 1653, fax 0171 828 6633)

CAMPBELL OF AIRDS, Alastair Lorne; er s of Brig Lorne Campbell of Airds, VC, DSO, OBE, TD (d 1991), and (Amy) Muriel Jordan, *née* Campbell (d 1950); *b* 11 July 1937; *Educ* Eton, Sandhurst; *m* 1960, Mary Ann, da of Lt-Col (George) Patrick Campbell-Preston, MBE; 4 c; *Career* md Waverley Vintners Ltd 1977–83; chm Christopher and Co Ltd 1975–83, chief exec Clan Campbell 1984–, dir Beinn Bhuidhe Holdings Ltd 1983–; HM Unicorn Pursuivant of Arms, memb Ct of the Lord Lyon 1987–, memb The Queen's Body Guard for Scotland (Royal Co of Archers); *Style*— Alastair Campbell of Airds

CAMPBELL OF AIRDS BAY, Maj Michael McNeil; yr twin s of Rear Adm Keith McNeil Campbell-Walter, CB (d 1976), and Frances Henriette, eldest da of Sir Edward Campbell of Airds Bay, 1 Bt, MP (d 1945); *b* 3 March 1941; *Educ* Wellington, RMA Sandhurst; *m* 1963, Anne Catriona, da of late Capt Ian Andrew Tait, Queen's Own Cameron Highlanders; 1 s, 2 da; *Career* 2 Lt Scots Gds 1961, Adjt 1 Bn 1967–69, Maj 1970, ret 1971; recognized by Lord Lyon 1954 as representor of family of Campbells of Airds Bay and matriculated as successor and representor to his uncle Sir Duncan Campbell of Airds Bay, 2 and last Bt (d 1954); memb Queen's Body Guard for Scotland (Royal Co of Archers); Hon ADC to Lt-Govr of Jersey 1973–80; sec-gen Confedn of Jersey Indust 1976–85; *Style*— Major Michael Campbell; ✉ La Valette, Parcq de Cadoret, Ruette Pinel, St Helier, Jersey JE2 3HF (☎ 01534 865810)

CAMPBELL OF ALLOWAY, Baron (Life Peer UK 1981), of Ayr, in the District of Kyle and Carrick; Alan Robertson Campbell; ERD, QC (1965); s of late John Kenneth Campbell; *b* 24 May 1917; *Educ* Aldenham, Trinity Hall Cambridge, Ecole des Sciences Politiques Paris; *m* 1957, Vivien, yr da of late Cdr A H de Kantzow, DSO, RN; *Career* sits as Cons Peer in House of Lords; cmmnd 2 Lt RA supp reserve 1939, served in BEF France and Belgium 1939–40 (POW 1940–45); called to the Bar Inner Temple 1939, bencher 1972, Western Circuit, recorder Crown Ct 1976–89, head of chambers; conslt to Sub-Ctee of Legal Ctee of Cncl of Europe on Industl Espionage 1965–74, chm Legal Res Ctee Soc of Cons Lawyers 1968–80; memb: Law Advsy Ctee Br Cncl 1974–80, Mgmnt Ctee Assoc for European Law 1975–90, Old Carlton Club Political Ctee 1967–79; co-patron Inns of Court Conservative Soc 1996–; memb House of Lords Select Ctee on: Murder and Life Imprisonment 1988–89, Privileges 1982–, Personal Bills 1987–; *Clubs* Carlton, Pratt's, Beefsteak; *Style*— The Rt Hon Lord Campbell of Alloway, ERD, QC; ✉ 2 King's Bench Walk, Temple, London EC4 7DE (☎ 0171 353 9276, fax 0171 353 9949)

CAMPBELL OF CROY, Baron (Life Peer UK 1974), of Croy, Co Nairn; Gordon Thomas Calthrop Campbell; PC (1970), MC (1944 and Bar 1945); s of Maj-Gen James Alexander Campbell, DSO (d 1964), and Violet Constance Madeline Calthrop (d 1978); *b* 8 June 1921; *Educ* Wellington; *m* 1949, Nicola Elizabeth Gina, da of Capt Geoffrey

Spencer Madan, and Marjorie, er da of Sir Saxton Noble, 3 Bt; 2 s, 1 da; *Career* regular army 1939–46, Major 1942 (wounded and disabled); HM Dip Serv 1946–57: served variously FO, UN NY, private sec to Cabinet Sec 1954–56, Br Embassy Vienna; MP (C) Moray and Nairn 1959–74, asst govt whip 1961–62, a Lord Cmmr of the Treasury (Govt whip) 1962–63, parly under-sec of state for Scotland 1963–64, oppn spokesman on Defence and Scottish Affairs 1966–70, sec of state for Scotland 1970–74; dir Alliance and Leicester Building Society (formerly Alliance Building Society) 1983–91 (chm Scottish Bd 1976–94); ptnr Holme Rose Farms and Estate; conslt Chevron Cos; chm: Scottish Cncl of Independent Schs 1974–78, Stoic Insurance Services 1979–93, Advsy Ctee on Pollution of the Sea 1979–81 and 1987–89; tstee Thomson Fndn 1978–; chm Int Year of Disabled People in Scotland 1981; pres Anglo-Austrian Soc 1991–; first fell Nuffield Provincial Hosp Tst, Queen Elizabeth the Queen Mother fellowship 1981; DL Nairnshire 1985; Vice Lieut Nairnshire 1988; *Books* Disablement: Problems and Prospects in the United Kingdom; *Style*— The Rt Hon the Lord Campbell of Croy, PC, MC; ✉ Holme Rose, Cawdor, Nairnshire

CAMPBELL OF DUNSTAFFNAGE, Michael John Alexander; 22 Hereditary Capt and Maor of Dunstaffnage; s of Michael Eadon Campbell of Dunstaffnage, and Kathleen Weddall, *née* Lundon; *b* 22 Nov 1953; *Educ* Stowe; *m* 1 (m dis); 1 s (Angus Arthur Eadon b 1983), 1 da (Claire Ingrid b 1981); m 2, 1989 Elizabeth, da of Capt David MacCall; 1 da (Stephanie Melissa b 1991), 1 s (Sean Michael Alexander b 1994); *Career* yacht Capt 1973–77; chm Bencamp Ltd, dir Halfway House Enterprises Ltd, proprietor Dunstaffnage Marine Services; *Recreations* sailing, shooting; *Style*— The Captain of Dunstaffnage; ✉ Dunstaffnage, Connel, Argyll, Scotland

CAMPBELL OF STRACHUR, (Ian) Niall Macarthur; 24 Chief of the Macarthur Campbells of Strachur and Representor of Baronial House of Campbell of Strachur, who held their Barony of Strachur direct from the Crown, for galley service; s of Lt-Col Kenneth John Campbell of Strachur (d 1965); *b* 23 Nov 1916; *Educ* Beaumont Coll; *m* 1947, Diana Susan, da of of Ernest Albert Sursham, JP, Lord of the Manor of Markyate, Herts; 1 s, 1 da; *Career* 2 Lt Black Watch 1939–45, Maj 1945; GRA Property Trust 1951–64; hon sec Br Field Sports Soc (Roxburghshire) 1980–; memb Scot Ctee 1984–, sponsorship steward The Argyllshire Gathering 1983–93; *Recreations* fishing, shooting, skiing; *Clubs* Puffin's (Edinburgh); *Style*— Niall Campbell of Strachur; ✉ Newtonlees, Kelso, Roxburghshire (☎ 01573 470229)

CAMPBELL OF STRACHUR yr, David Niall MacArthur; s of (Ian) Niall MacArthur Campbell of Strachur, and Diana, *née* Sursham; *b* 15 April 1948; *Educ* Eton, Exeter Coll Oxford; *m* 1974, Alexandra Wiggin, Marquesa de Muros, da of Sir Charles Wiggin, KCMG, Marques de Muros (d 1977); 1 s (Charles Alexander b 26 May 1977), 1 da (Iona Margot b 15 Jan 1979); *Career* int publishing dir of Hachette (Paris) 1983–90, publisher Everyman's Library 1990–; *Clubs* White's; *Style*— David Campbell of Strachur yr; ✉ 51 Northumberland Place, London W2; Barbreck House, By Lochgilphead, Argyll PA31 8QW (☎ 01852 500293)

CAMPBELL OF SUCCOTH, Sir Ilay Mark; 7 Bt (UK 1808), of Succoth, Dunbartonshire; s of Capt Sir George Ilay Campbell, 6 Bt, JP, DL (d 1967), and Clematis Elizabeth Denys, *née* Waring (d 1986); *b* 29 May 1927; *Educ* Eton, ChCh Oxford (MA); *m* 22 July 1961, (Margaret Minette) Rohais, da of (James) Alasdair Anderson of Tullichewan (d 1982); 2 da (Cecilia Margaret Lucy (Mrs MacGregor, younger of MacGregor) b 1963, Candida Harriett Rohais (Mrs Gerard J Rafferty) b 1964); *Heir* none; *Career* Christies: Scottish agent 1968, jt Scottish agent 1973–92, chm Scotland 1978–96; pres Assoc for the Protection of Rural Scotland 1978–90, convener Church of Scotland Ctee for Artistic Matters 1987–91, hon vice pres Scotland's Garden Scheme 1983–, Scottish rep Nat Art Collections Fund 1972–83; dir High Craigton Farming Co; tstee Tree Register of the British Isles 1988–; memb: Historic Buildings Cncl for Scotland 1989–, Gardens Ctee Nat Tst for Scotland 1994–; chm Church Building Renewal Tst (Glasgow) 1995–; FRSA 1986; *Recreations* heraldry, family history, collecting heraldic bookplates; *Clubs* Turf; *Style*— Sir Ilay Campbell of Succoth, Bt; ✉ Crarae Lodge, Inveraray, Argyll PA32 8YA (☎ 01546 86274, fax 01546 86262)

CAMPBELL-ORDE, Sir John Alexander; 6 Bt (GB 1790), of Morpeth, Northumberland; s of Maj Sir Simon Arthur Campbell-Orde, 5 Bt, TD (d 1969), and Eleanor Hyde, *née* Watts (d 1996); *b* 11 May 1943; *Educ* Gordonstoun; *m* 1973 (m dis 1991), Lacy Rals, o da of T Grady Gallant, of Nashville, Tennessee, USA; 1 s (John Simon Arthur b 1981), 3 da (Alexandra Louise b 1974, Alice Theodora b 1976, Octavia Maie b 1978); *Heir* s, John Simon Arthur Campbell-Orde, b 15 Aug 1981; *Career* art dealer; *Clubs* Caledonian, Lansdowne; *Style*— Sir John Campbell-Orde, Bt; ✉ PO Box 22974, Nashville, TN 37202, USA

CAMPBELL REGAN, (Maurice David) Brian; s of Flt Lt Maurice O'Regan, RAFMS (d 1991), and Margaret, *née* McElearney; *b* 7 Nov 1936; *Educ* Ampleforth, Sorbonne Paris; *m* 1 Aug 1970, Jasmine, da of Ivor Elystan Campbell-Davys, JP (d 1965), of Neuaddfawr, Llandovery, Dyfed, and Askomel, Campbelltown, Argyll; 1 s (Justin), 2 da (Ciaran, Alice); *Career* FCA; ptnr Buzzacott; govr St Mary's Sch Ascot; *Recreations* fishing, shooting, reading, painting; *Clubs* Reform; *Style*— Brian Campbell Regan, Esq; ✉ Beauchamps, Wyddial, Buntingford, Herts SG9 0EP (☎ 01763 71382); Buzzacott, 4 Wood St, London EC2V 4JJ (☎ 0171 600 0336)

CAMPBELL-SAVOURS, Dale Norman; MP (Lab) Workington (majority 10,449); s of John Lawrence, and Cynthia Lorraine Campbell-Savours; *b* 23 Aug 1943; *Educ* Keswick Sch, Sorbonne Paris; *m* 1970, Gudrun Kristin Runolfsdottir; 3 s; *Career* formerly co dir; Parly candidate (Lab) Darwen Feb and Oct 1974, MP (Lab) Workington 1979– (also contested by-election 1976); front bench spokesman: overseas devpt 1991–92, agriculture 1992–94; memb: Public Accounts Ctee 1980–91, Procedure Ctee 1983–91, Member's Interests Select Ctee 1983–92, Agriculture Select Ctee 1994–96, standards and Privileges Ctee 1996–; memb TGWU and UNISON 1970–; *Publications* The case for the Supplementary Vote (1990), The case for the University of the Lakes (1995); *Style*— Dale Campbell-Savours, Esq, MP; ✉ House of Commons, London SW1A 0AA

CAMPBELL-WALTER, Richard Keith; s of Rear Adm Keith McNiel Campbell-Walter, CB (d 1976), of London SW7, and Frances Henriette, da of Sir Edward Taswell Campbell, 1 Bt, MP (d 1945); *b* 3 March 1941; *Educ* Milton Abbey, RAC Cirencester; *m* 1, 1963 (m dis), Marion Clare, o da of F G Minter, MBE; 2 da (Lavinia b 1964, Petrina b 1967); m 2, Dorothy Ann, yst da of late T W Oliver; 1 s (Jamie Oliver b 1972); *Career* 2 Lt Argyll and Sutherland Highlanders 1958–1964 TA; Simpsons of Piccadilly Ltd: dir 1982–, retail dir 1990–92, PR and advertising dir 1992–; *Style*— Richard K Campbell-Walter, Esq; ✉ 98 Battersea High Street, London SW11 (☎ 0171 223 2601); Simpsons of Piccadilly Ltd, 203 Piccadilly, London W1 (☎ 0171 734 2002)

CAMPDEN, Viscount; Anthony Baptist Noel; s and h of 5 Earl of Gainsborough, *qv*; *b* 16 Jan 1950; *Educ* Ampleforth, RAC Cirencester; *m* 1972, Sarah Rose, LVO (1996), er da of Col Thomas Foley Churchill Winnington, MBE, *qv*; 1 s; *Heir* s, Hon Henry Robert Anthony Noel b 1 July 1977; *Clubs* White's, Pratt's; *Style*— Viscount Campden; ✉ 105 Earls Court Rd, London W8 (☎ 0171 370 5650); Exton Park, Oakham, Rutland, Leics LE15 8AN (☎ 01572 812209)

CAMPION, David Bardsley (Barry); s of Norman Campion (d 1987), of Southport, Lancs, and Enid Mary, *née* Bardsley; *b* 20 March 1938; *Educ* Shrewsbury; *m* 1, 1962 (m dis 1972), Victoria Wild; 1 s (Mark), 1 da (Sarah); m 2, 1979, Sally, da of Frank Walter Manning Arkle; *Career* dir Wheatsheaf Distribution and Trading 1968–78, dir Linfood Holdings 1978–81, chm Food Div CWS Ltd 1982–87, chief exec Monarchy Foods Ltd 1987–90: chm: BAF Securities Ltd (dir 1972–), Meridian Foods Ltd 1990–, Wilsons of Holyhead 1991–, Burgess Supafoods 1996–; dep chm Gold Crown Foods Ltd 1993–94; dir: Bensons Crisps plc 1990–, West Trust plc 1991–93, Sutton Hoo Produce Ltd 1995–, Gott Foods Ltd 1996–; FIGD 1983; *Recreations* golf, cricket, sailing; *Clubs* MCC, Delamere Forest Golf, Royal Birkdale Golf, Holyhead Golf, Trearddur Bay Sailing; *Style*— Barry Campion, Esq; ✉ Monarchy Hall Farm, Utkinton, Tarporley, Cheshire CW6 0JZ (☎ 01829 752064, fax 01829 752075)

CAMPION, Prof Peter David; s of John Neville Campion, and Dorothy Mabel, *née* Shave (d 1968); *b* 14 April 1946; *Educ* Southend HS for Boys, Pembroke Coll Oxford (open exhibitioner, BA), London Hosp Med Coll (BM BCh, MRCP, MRCGP), DCCH (Edinburgh); *m* Jan 1971, Janet Elizabeth, *née* Davison; 4 c; *Career* house surgn (gen surgery and ENT) then house physician London Hosp 1971, jr lectr in morbid anatomy London Hosp Med Coll 1972, SHO in paediatrics Queen Elizabeth Hosp for Children 1973, princ in Gen Practice Brentwood Essex 1974–80, lectr in gen practice Univ of Dundee and memb Med Sch Teaching Practice 1980–85, sr lectr in gen practice Univ of Liverpool 1985–96 (head Dept of Primary Care 1991–96), prof of primary care med Univ of Hull 1996–, ptnr Drs Jary, Rawcliffe, Kapur, Greene and Campion 1996–; memb Course Coordinating Ctee Faculty of Med 1988–92, jt chair Core Curriculum Working Gp 1992–94; external examiner Sultan Qaboos Univ Oman 1993–96; RCGP: memb Panel of Examiners 1988–, memb Working Pty on the Use of Video as a Clinical Assessment 1992–, memb MRCGP Critical Reading Paper Nuclear Gp 1992–; memb Examination Bd DCH (RCP) 1992–95; referee Br Med Jl and Br Jl of Gen Practice 1985–, memb Editorial Bd Jl of Educn for Gen Practice; ordained elder Church of Scotland Dundee, deacon and latterly sec Baptist Church in Liverpool; FRCGP 1990; *Videos incl* Problems in Doctor-patient encounters (series, RSM, 1986), Turning from alcohol and Reflections on alcohol (both Univ of Liverpool TV Serv, 1991); *Books* Teaching General Practice to Undergraduates (with Prof M Roland and Prof C Whitehouse, 1995); also author of numerous refereed and review articles; *Recreations* playing the organ and piano, my family; *Style*— Prof Peter Campion; ✉ 8 North View, Little Weighton, Cottingham, E Yorks HU20 3UL (☎ 01482 842035, work ☎ 01482 466036, fax 01482 466040)

CAMPION-SMITH, (William) Nigel; s of H R A Campion-Smith, of Gerrards Cross, Bucks, and Moyra, *née* Campion; *b* 10 July 1954; *Educ* King George V Sch Southport, Royal GS High Wycombe, St John's Coll Cambridge (MA); *m* 31 July 1976, Andrea Jean, da of Edward Willacy, of Hale Barns, Cheshire; 2 s (Jonathan b 1985, Timothy b 1990), 1 da (Joanna b 1983); *Career* admitted slr 1978; ptnr Travers Smith Braithwaite 1982–; memb Law Soc 1978; *Style*— Nigel Campion-Smith, Esq; ✉ Travers Smith Braithwaite, 10 Snow Hill, London EC1A 2AL (☎ 0171 248 9133, fax 0171 236 3728)

CAMPLIN, Jamie Robert; *b* 27 April 1947; *Educ* Bishop's Stortford Coll, Corpus Christi Coll Cambridge (BA, MA); *Career* editorial dir Thames & Hudson 1979–; *Books* The Rise of the Plutocrats - Wealth and Power in Edwardian England (London 1978, NY 1979); *Style*— Jamie Camplin, Esq; ✉ 10 Church Lane, London SW19 3PD (☎ 0181 542 7015); Thames & Hudson Ltd, 30–34 Bloomsbury Street, London WC1B 3QP (☎ 0171 636 5488, fax 0171 636 4799)

CAMPLING, The Very Rev Christopher Russell; s of Rev Canon William Charles Campling (d 1972), and Phyllis Russell, *née* Webb; *b* 4 July 1925; *Educ* Lancing, St Edmund Hall Oxford (MA); *m* 1953, Juliet Marian, *née* Hughes; 1 s, 2 da; *Career* temp Sub Lt (special cypher) RNVR 1943–47; curate Basingstoke 1951–55; chaplain: King's Sch Ely and minor canon Ely 1955–60, Lancing Coll 1960–67; vicar Pershore 1968–76, rural dean Pershore 1970–76, hon canon Worcs Cathedral 1974–84, archdeacon Dudley 1976–84, priest i/c St Augustine's Church Dodderhill and dir religious educn Worcs Dio 1976–84, dean Ripon 1984–95, ret; memb Gen Synod 1970–94, chm Cncl for Care of Churches 1988–94; *Books* The Way, the Truth and the Life (6 volumes: a series for schools), Words for Worship, The Fourth Lesson (ed), The Food of Love: Reflections on Music and Faith (1997); *Recreations* music, golf, theatre; *Clubs* Naval; *Style*— The Very Rev Christopher Campling

CAMPLING, Dr Graham Ewart George; s of Reginald Ewart Campling, of Lindfield, Sussex, and Elsie Clara, *née* Wodhams; *b* 27 Aug 1938; *Educ* evening study Birkbeck and Imperial Colls Univ of London (BSc, PhD); *m* 1 April 1961, Zena Margaret, da of George William Birkbeck (d 1969); 2 s (Noel b 1963, Jeremy b 1969); *Career* Lt TA 1959–62; Bank of England 1956–63, Selfridges Ltd 1963–65; lectr and sr lectr in computing Brighton Univ 1965–69, head of Dept of Mgmnt S Bank Univ 1969–72, vice princ Kilburn Poly 1973–77, princ Dacorum Coll Hemel Hempstead 1978–89; gp trg mangr BAA plc 1989–92; memb: Cuckfield UDC 1968–74 (chm Ctee 1969–73, vice chm Cncl 1971–72), Mid Sussex DC 1974–76; chm of govrs: Lindfield Primary Sch's 1971–79, Oathall Comp Sch 1972–81; pres Assoc of Princ's of Colls 1989 (hon sec 1985–88, vice pres 1988–89), chm Educn Ctee Inst of Admin Mgmnt 1973–81 (Inst medal 1982); gen cmmr of Income Tax 1993–; Freeman City of London 1967; vice pres Sussex E District United Reformed Church 1996; MBCS 1970, FIMgt 1980, CEng 1990, MCIT 1992; *Books* Can You Manage Statistics? (1968); *Recreations* transport organisation, music, film-making; *Style*— Dr Graham Campling; ✉ 46 Hickmans Lane, Lindfield, Haywards Heath, West Sussex RH16 2BY (☎ 01444 483539)

CAMROUX-OLIVER, Timothy Patrick; s of Wing Cdr George Leonard, DFC, AFC (d 1984), and Patricia Rosamund, *née* Douglas; *b* 2 March 1944; *Educ* Christ's Hosp; *m* 18 July 1966, Susan Elizabeth, da of Maj Frederick Wilson Hanham, of Bucks; 2 s (James Richard b Sept 1967, Charles Guy b 1 April 1970), 1 da (Alexa Kate Louise b 25 Dec 1974); *Career* asst gen mangr IGI (SA) 1969–71; dir: Manson Byng Group 1971–, Hampden Russell plc 1987–; chm: Hampden Insurance Holdings Ltd 1973–, Market Run-Off Services Plc 1984–; memb Lloyd's 1977; Freeman City of London 1966, memb Worshipful Co of Ironmongers 1966; FRGS 1963, FInstD; *Style*— Timothy Camroux-Oliver, Esq; ✉ Hampden House, Great Hampden, Bucks HP16 9RD (☎ 01494 488888); Hampden Russell plc, Gallery Ten, Lloyd's of London, 1 Lime St, London EC3M 7DQ (☎ 0171 626 3036, fax 0171 929 0044, telex 83688 Market G, car tel 0860 515552)

CAMSEY, Granville Thomas Bateman; s of Thomas Camsey (d 1970), and May, *née* Bradley (d 1966); *b* 1 March 1936; *Educ* Univ of Salford, Univ of Birmingham (MSc), Manchester Business Sch; *m* Maureen; 1 s (Jonathan Bickerstaff b 22 March 1964), 1 da (Megan Elizabeth b 10 April 1967); *Career* CEGB: joined as trainee N Western Region 1952, subsequently various appts at Trawsfynydd and Oldbury Nuclear Power Stations, dep station mangr Heysham 1 AGR nuclear station 1972–76, station mangr Rugeley A and B power stations 1976–80, various managerial posts London becoming dir of prodn S Eastern Region until 1987; md designate China Light and Power Co Hong Kong 1987–88, rejoined CEGB as chief exec designate Nat Power Div (Thermal) 1988, exec dir National Power plc 1990–96, md Gp Technol National Power plc 1993–96; non-exec dir Stone & Webster Engineering Ltd 1996–, professional assoc Gemini Consulting Ltd 1996–; memb Cncl (now Senate) Engrg Cncl (re-elected 1995); memb Cncl Royal Acad of Engrg; Freeman City of London, Liveryman Worshipful Co of Engrs; CIMgt, FInstD, FInstE, FIMechE, FEng 1992; *Recreations* golf, wood-carving; *Style*— Granville T B Camsey, FEng; ✉ c/o Engineering Council, 10 Maltravers Street, London WC2R 3ER (☎ 0171 240 7891)

CANADY, Diane Elizabeth; da of late Jimmy Roger Canady, of High Wycombe, Bucks, and Kathleen Ann, *née* Knight; *b* 22 May 1954; *Educ* USAF Central HS USA, High Wycombe Tech Coll, Univ of Essex (BA, MA); *m* 2 Dec 1977, Brian Armistead, s of Douglas Armistead; 1 s (Benjamin James b 25 May 1981); *Career* grad trainee McCann

Erickson advtg 1977–81, account supr Royds Advertising 1981–82, account dir NCK Advertising 1982–83, gp product mangr Levi Strauss 1983–84, bd dir Geers Gross 1984–91, client servs dir and exec bd dir Publicis (following merger with Geers Gross) 1991–; lectr in advtg for CAM course Coll of Distributive Trades; memb Cosmetic Exec Women; *Recreations* music, interior decorating, reading, cooking; *Style—* Ms Diane Canady; ✉ Publicis, 82 Baker Street, London W1M 2AE (☎ 0171 935 4426, fax 0171 487 5351, mobile 0860 702140)

CANAVAN, Dennis Andrew; MP (Lab) Falkirk West (majority 9,812); s of Thomas Canavan (d 1974), of Cowdenbeath, and Agnes Canavan; *b* 8 Aug 1942; *Educ* St Columba's HS Cowdenbeath, Edinburgh Univ (BSc(Hons), DipEd); *Career* princ teacher of Maths Dept St Modan's HS Stirling 1970–74, asst head Holy Rood HS Edinburgh 1974; cncllr Stirling DC 1973–74 (Lab Gp leader 1974); MP (Lab): West Stirlingshire 1974–83, Falkirk W 1983–; special interests: foreign affrs, campaigning for a Scottish parliament, health service, education, Br-Irish relations, disarmament, sport; Scottish Parly Lab Gp: chm 1980–81, chm PLP NI Ctee 1989–; memb Foreign Affrs Select Ctee 1982–, Parly spokesperson for Scottish Ctee on Mobility for the Disabled 1976–, memb British-Irish Inter-Parly Body 1992–; fndr and convener All-Party Parly Scottish Sports Gp 1987–; *Recreations* hill climbing, swimming, running, angling, football spectating (former Scottish Univs' football internationalist); *Clubs* Camelon Labour, Bannockburn Miners' Welfare; *Style—* Dennis Canavan, Esq, MP; ✉ Constituency Office, 37 Church Walk, Denny, Stirlingshire FK6 6DF (☎ 01324 825922); House of Commons, London SW1A 0AA (☎ 0171 219 4127)

CANBY, Guy Richard; JP (Rotherham 1990); s of Arthur John Canby (d 1985), of Cottingham, Humberside, and Ivy Gladys, *née* Hutton; *b* 13 April 1950; *Educ* Hymers Coll Hull, RAC; *m* 19 July 1975, Diana Mary, da of Capt John Buckingham Segrott, of E Lothian; 2 s (Michael John b 1978, James Guy b 1981), 1 da (Charlotte Mary b 1984); *Career* asst factor Lothian Estates 1973–83; resident land agent: Thonock and Somerby Estates 1983–86, Fitzwilliam (Wentworth) Estates 1986–; FRICS, MRAC; *Recreations* shooting, fishing, squash, tennis, golf; *Style—* Guy Canby, Esq, JP; ✉ Cortworth House, Wentworth, Rotherham, S Yorks (☎ 01226 742288); Estate Office, Clayfields Lane, Wentworth, Rotherham, S Yorks (☎ 01226 742041)

CANBY, Michael William; s of Clarence Canby, and Mary Frances, *née* Drake; *b* 11 Jan 1955; *Educ* Buckhurst Hill County HS, Univ of Cambridge (MA, LLB); *m* 6 Sept 1980, Sarah, da of John Houghton Masters (d 1965); 1 s (Philip Charles Houghton b 1988), 1 da (Harriet Georgina Mary b 1991); *Career* admitted slr 1980; Linklaters & Paines: New York office 1982–84, ptnr 1986–, Paris office 1989–95; memb Law Soc; *Style—* Michael Canby, Esq; ✉ c/o Linklaters & Paines, Barrington House, 59/67 Gresham Street, London EC2V 7JA

CANDY, Prof David Charles Alexander; s of Arthur Edward Candy, of Hove, and Gwen May, *née* Chatfield; *b* 5 Dec 1947; *Educ* Pulteney GS Adelaide S Aust, Univ of Adelaide (MB BS), Univ of London (MSc), Univ of Birmingham (MD); *m* 16 Aug 1979, Christine Elizabeth, da of Charles Walter Stannett, of Cowes, IOW; 1 s (Rupert b 5 Oct 1980), 1 da (Felicity b 22 June 1987); *Career* Wellcome sr lectr Dept of Child Health Univ of Birmingham 1984–88; hon consIt paediatrician 1984–88: The Children's Hosp Birmingham, Dept of Communicable and Tropical Diseases E Birmingham Hosp; prof Dept of Child Health King's Coll Sch of Med and Dentistry 1988–; FRCP 1989, MCPCH 1996; *Books* Manual of Paediatric Gastroenterology and Nutrition (with J H Tripp, 1985, 2 edn 1992); *Recreations* my family, dining out; *Style—* Prof David C A Candy; ✉ 81 Lauderdale Tower, Barbican, London EC2Y 8BY; Department of Child Health, King's College School of Medicine and Dentistry, Bessemer Road, London SE5 8RX (☎ 0171 346 3563, fax 0171 346 3564)

CANDY, Thomas Frank; s of Frank Patrick Candy, and Jacqueline Honoreen, *née* Vroome; *b* 18 Dec 1955; *Educ* Eastbourne Coll, Univ of Surrey; *m* Emma, *née* Bishop; 1 s (Peter b 12 April 1990), 1 da (Isabel b 20 March 1992); *Career* banker; exec dir Eurobond Dept Hambros Bank Ltd; *Recreations* tennis, squash, windsurfing, skiing, golf; *Clubs* Queen's, Wilderness; *Style—* Thomas Candy, Esq; ✉ Hambros Bank Ltd, 41 Tower Hill, London EC3N 4DU (☎ 0171 480 5000)

CANE, Alison; da of Ronald Cane, of Hutton Mount, Essex, and Jeanne, *née* Snow; *b* 18 Aug 1960; *Educ* Ongar Comp Sch Essex, Loughton Coll of Further Educn Essex, St Martin's Sch of Art; *Career* freelance designer 1982, designer Michael Peters plc 1982–86, asst creative dir Coley Porter Bell 1986–93, currently sr design dir Landor Associates; clients incl: Prestige, Corgi Toys, Marks and Spencer, Jacksons of Picadilly, Bryant & May, Terrys of York, A&P-USA, Cadburys, Sainsburys, Reuters, Philips, Yardley of London; various D&AD and Clio nominations, winner Design Effectiveness Award (food packaging) 1990, Clio winner (best packaging dairy) 1991, highly commended Int Design Annual Awards 1990, winner Best of Show (for Masterpiece Range) Int Brand Packaging Awards 1993; *Style—* Ms Alison Cane; ✉ Landor Associates, Klamath House, 18 Clerkenwell Green, London EC1R 0DP (☎ 0171 880 8346, fax 0171 880 8538)

CANETTY-CLARKE, Neil; *b* 12 July 1962; *Career* gp fin dir: LWT (Holdings) plc 1993–94, Guardian Media Group plc 1995–; *Style—* Neil Canetty-Clarke, Esq; ✉ Guardian Media Group plc, 75 Farringdon Road, London EC1M 3JY (☎ 0171 713 4453)

CANN, (John William) Anthony; s of Dr John Cann (d 1991), and Enid Grace, *née* Long; *b* 21 July 1947; *Educ* Old Malthouse Sch Swanage, Shrewsbury, Univ of Southampton (LLB); *m* 6 Jan 1973, Anne, da of Harold Thorswald Clausen (d 1994), of Johannesburg; 2 s (John Harold b 25 Nov 1973, Robert Charles b 13 Aug 1984), 1 da (Sally Elizabeth b 10 Jan 1978); *Career* admitted slr 1972; Linklaters & Paines: joined 1970, asst slr 1972–78, New York office 1975–82, ptnr 1978–, head Corp Dept 1995–; memb Advsy Ctee CAB Battersea 1973–75; Freeman City of London Slrs Co 1978; memb Law Soc; *Books* Mergers & Acquisitions Handbook (Part D), Mergers and Acquisitions in Europe (United Kingdom); *Recreations* photography, sports; *Clubs* MCC, Wimbledon, Wimbledon Squash and Badminton, Trojans; *Style—* Anthony Cann, Esq; ✉ Langrick, 13 Murray Rd, Wimbledon, London SW19 4PD (☎ 0181 946 6731); Linklaters & Paines, Barrington House, 59–67 Gresham St, London EC2V 7JA (☎ 0171 606 7080, fax 0171 606 5113, telex 884349, 888167)

CANN, James (Jamie); MP (Lab) Ipswich (majority 265); s of Charles Cann, and Brenda Cann; *b* 28 June 1946; *Educ* Barton on Humber GS, Kesteven Coll of Educ; *m* 26 May 1970, Rosemary, *née* Lovitt; 2 s; *Career* teacher rising to dep head Handford Hall Primary Sch Ipswich 1967–92; Ipswich BC: cncllr 1973–92, ldr Lab Gp 1976–91, ldr of the Cncl 1979–91; MP (Lab) Ipswich 1992–; non-exec dir Ipswich Port Authy 1986–92, memb NUT; *Style—* Jamie Cann, Esq, MP; ✉ House of Commons, London SW1A 0AA

CANN, Prof Johnson Robin (Joe); s of late Johnson Ralph Cann, and Ethel Mary, *née* Northmore; *b* 18 Oct 1937; *Educ* St Alban's Sch, St John's Coll Cambridge (BA, MA, PhD, ScD); *m* 10 Aug 1963, Janet Mary Teresa (d 1994), da of Prof Charles John Hamson (d 1987), of Trinity Coll Cambridge; 2 s (John b 1964, David b 1966); *Career* res fell St John's Coll Cambridge 1962–65, post doctoral res Cambridge 1962–66, Br Museum (Natural History) 1966–68, lectr then reader Sch of Environmental Sciences UEA 1968–77, J B Simpson prof of geology Univ of Newcastle upon Tyne 1977–89, adjunct scientist Woods Hole Oceanographic Instn 1987–91, prof of earth sciences Univ of Leeds 1989–; chm UK Ocean Drilling Program Grants Ctee 1987–; memb Bridge Coordinating Ctee 1988–; Murchison Medal Geological Soc London 1990; FGS, FRS 1995; *Style—* Prof Joe Cann; ✉ Department of Earth Sciences, University of Leeds, Leeds LS2 9JT (☎ 0113 233 5200, fax 0113 233 5259, e-mail j.cann@earth.leeds.ac.uk)

CANNING, Alison Mary; da of Dr William Carbis Canning, of Knowle, W Mids, and Bertha Sheila, *née* McGill; *b* 15 April 1959; *Educ* Marlborough, Poly of Central London (BA), City Univ Business Sch (MBA); *m* 23 Sept 1994, Richard Albert Moore; *Career* Burson-Marsteller PR: graduate trainee rising to account exec London 1983–85, account supr rising to vice pres/client servs mangr NY 1986–88, bd dir London 1988–89; sr vice pres/md Cohn & Wolfe PR London 1989–94 (Best New Consultancy 1990 and 1991, numerous other UK and int awards), chief exec offr Burson-Marsteller UK 1994–96; memb: Forum UK, Amnesty Int Br Business Gp, Mktg Soc; MInstD; *Recreations* skiing, sailing, opera, music; *Style—* Ms Alison Canning

CANNING, Prof Elizabeth Ursula; da of Maj Miles Howell Canning MC, TD (d 1950), and Winifred, *née* Jenkins (d 1980); *b* 29 Sept 1928; *Educ* Truro HS, Imperial Coll London (BSc, DSc), London Sch of Hygiene and Tropical Med (PhD); *m* 15 Aug 1953, Christopher Maynard Wilson, s of George Henry Cyril Wilson (d 1973); 1 s (Miles Richard Guy b 29 April 1966), 2 da (Victoria Jane (Mrs M J Harvey) b 16 March 1958, Catherine Alexandra (Mrs J P Williams) b 3 March 1960); *Career* Imperial Coll London: lectr 1951–70, sr lectr 1970–71, reader 1971–81, prof of protozoology 1981–93, sr research fell 1993–95, sr research investigator 1995–; former pres, vice pres and sec Br Section Soc of Protozoologists, former vice pres Int Soc of Protozoologists (hon life memb 1993), memb Royal Soc of Tropical Med and Hygiene; ARCS, FIBiol; *Books* The Microsporidia of Vertebrates (1986); *Recreations* golf, crossword puzzles, bridge; *Style—* Prof Elizabeth Canning; ✉ Tiles Cottage, Forest Rd, Winkfield Row, nr Bracknell, Berks RG42 6NR; Imperial College at Silwood Park, Garden Wood Laboratories (West), Ascot, Berks SL5 7PY (☎ 01344 294244, fax 01344 294339)

CANNING, Hugh Donaldson; s of David Donaldson Canning, of Whissendine, nr Oakham, Leics, and Olga Mary, *née* Simms; *b* 28 May 1954; *Educ* Oakham Sch, Pembroke Coll Oxford (BA), Univ Coll Cardiff (Dip Theatre Studies); *Career* regular contrib The Western Mail 1977–82, freelance writer 1979 (Music & Musicians, Opera, Times Higher Educn Supplement), freelance contrib on music The Guardian 1983–87, music critic London Daily News 1987, music critic and feature writer (contract) The Guardian 1987–89, music critic (contract) Sunday Times 1989–; memb Editorial Bd Opera 1987–; opera critic The Listener (until closure); contrib: Opera, The Gramophone; Critic of the Yr 1994 (Br Press Awards) 1995; memb Critics' Circle; *Recreations* theatre, music, eating out, watching tennis, gossip; *Style—* Hugh Canning, Esq; ✉ Music Critic, The Sunday Times, 1 Pennington Street, London E1 9XN

CANNINGS-BUSHELL, David John; s of Thomas Meredith Cannings-Bushell, of Cirencester, Glos, and Julia Dorothy, *née* Dawe; *b* 8 April 1949; *Educ* Cirencester GS; *m* 31 July 1971 (m dis 1990), Jennifer Ann, da of Meurig Jones, of Meifod, Powys; 2 da (Catherine Sarah b 5 Feb 1974, Louisa Frances 24 Nov 1976); m 2, 29 Dec 1990, Monica Anne Goddard, *née* Trinder; *Career* lighting dir TV drama Pebble Mill BBC 1983 (engr 1968, lectr 1978); maj prodns: Deadhead 1985, Lizzies Pictures 1986, Vanity Fair 1987, Franchise Affair 1988, Shalom, Salaam 1989, Debut on Two, Bingo 1990, The Fallout Guy, Specials 1991, Roots 1992, Olly's Prison 1993; BAFTA nomination for Video Lighting 1987; memb Soc of TV Lighting Dirs 1981; *Recreations* choral singing, photography, painting, walking; *Style—* David Cannings-Bushell, Esq; ✉ 6 Broadway Close, Fladbury, Pershore, Worcs WR10 2QQ (☎ 01386 860 922); BBC, Pebble Mill, Birmingham (☎ 0121 414 8418, fax 0121 414 8834)

CANNON, Prof John Ashton; CBE (1985); s of George Ashton Cannon, and Gladys Violet Cannon; *b* 8 Oct 1926; *Educ* Hertford GS, Peterhouse Cambridge (BA, MA), Univ of Bristol (PhD); *m* 1, 1948 (m dis 1953), Audrey Elizabeth, da of G R Caple, of Bristol; 1 s (Marcus b 1948), 1 da (Hilary b 1952); m 2, 1953, Minna Sofie, da of Frederick Pedersen, of Denmark; 1 s (Martin b 1966), 2 da (Susan b 1955, Annelise b 1962); *Career* RAF Flt Lt 1947–49 and 1952–55; reader Univ of Bristol 1970–75 (lectr 1961–67, sr lectr 1967–69), pro vice chllr Univ of Newcastle upon Tyne 1983–86 (prof of modern history 1976–92, dean Faculty of Arts 1979–82), chm Radio Bristol 1970–74; memb Univ Grants Ctee 1983–89 (vice chm 1986–89, chm Arts Sub Ctee 1983–89); FRHistS, FRSA; *Books* The Fox-North Coalition (1970), Parliamentary Reform (1973), The Letters of Junius (ed 1978), The Historian at Work (1980), The Whig Ascendancy (1981), Aristocratic Century (1984), Dictionary of Historians (ed 1988), Oxford Illustrated History of The Monarchy (with R Griffiths, 1988), Samuel Johnson and the politics of Hanoverian England (1994); *Recreations* music, sailing, tennis; *Style—* Prof John Cannon, CBE; ✉ 35 Osborne Road, Jesmond, Newcastle upon Tyne NE2 2AH (☎ 0191 281 4096); Alma House, Grosmont, Gwent; Department of History, University of Newcastle upon Tyne (☎ 0191 232 8511, ext 6694)

CANNON, Nicholas Charles; s of Dr Ronald Cannon, of W Sussex, and Anita, *née* Foux; *b* 21 April 1951; *Educ* Northease Manor Lewes Sussex, Davies's Tutors Hove Sussex, King's Coll London (LLB), Inns of Court Sch of Law; *Career* called to the Bar Gray's Inn 1973, lectr Inns of Court Sch of Law 1974–77, barr in the Chamber of R A K Wright QC 1977–78, legal advsr Br Bankers' Assoc 1978–80; author of various articles on int fin law; memb Legal Ctee EEC Banking Cmmn, legal advsr Scandinavian Bank Group plc 1980–89 (gp legal advsr and exec dir 1987), consIt Canadian Inst 1990–91, consIt (banking law) Int Business Communications Ltd London 1991–93, ptnr The Bolt Partnership (prodr of business films etc), fndr and md Stratton Publications 1993; memb Inst of Strategic Studies London; *Recreations* opera, art history, international politics and relations, tennis, travel; *Style—* Nicholas C Cannon, Esq

CANNON, (Jack) Philip; s of William George Cannon (d 1973), of Perranporth, Cornwall, and Charlotte Loraine, *née* Renoir (d 1984); *b* 21 Dec 1929; *Educ* Falmouth GS, Dartington Hall, RCM; *m* 15 July 1950, Jacqueline Playfair Laidlaw (d 1984), da of Hugh Alexander Lyon Laidlaw; 1 da (Virginia Shona Playfair b 29 June 1953); *Career* composer; dep prof RCM 1953–59, lectr in music Univ of Sydney 1959–60, prof of composition RCM 1960–, author of many articles for music jls; compositions incl: Morvoren (opera) 1964, String Quartet (winner of Grand Prix and Prix de la Critique Paris) 1965, Oraison Funèbre de L'Ame Humaine (symphony cmmnd by ORTF) 1971, Lacrimae Mundi (cmmnd by Gulbenkian Fndn for Music Gp of London) 1972, Son of Man (symphony cmmnd by BBC to mark Britain's entry to the Euro Community) 1973, The Temple (cmmnd by The Three Choirs Festival) 1974, Te Deum (cmmnd by HM Queen for St George's Day) 1975, Logos (clarinet quintet cmmnd by BBC for Silver Jubilee) 1977, Lord of Light Requiem (cmmnd by The Three Choirs Festival) 1980, Cinq Supplications sur une Bénédiction (cmmnd by RF) 1983, Dr Jekyll and Mr Hyde (cmmnd by BBC TV), A Ralegh Triptych (cmmnd by The Three Choirs Festival) 1992, Septain (in memoriam John Ogdon) 1993, Piano Quintet (for John Lill and the Medici String Quartet) 1994, Symphony (for BBC Philharmonic) 1996; memb Royal Philharmonic Soc, FRCM 1971; memb: ISM, Composers' Guild of GB; *Recreations* exploring comparative philosophies, travel; *Clubs* Savile, Chelsea Arts; *Style—* Philip Cannon, Esq; ✉ 25 Ansdell Street, Kensington Square, London W8 5BN (☎ 0171 937 6768)

CANNON, Prof Thomas; s of Albert Edward Cannon (d 1986), and Bridget, *née* Ryan; *b* 20 Nov 1945; *Educ* St Francis Xavier's GS, South Bank Poly; *m* Frances, da of Bernard Constable; 1 da (Rowan), 1 s (Robin); *Career* res assoc Univ of Warwick 1968–71, lectr Enfield Coll of Technol 1971–72, brand mangr Imperial Group 1973–76, lectr Univ of Durham 1973–81, prof Univ of Stirling 1981–89, dir Manchester Business Sch 1989–92, chief exec Mgmnt Charter Initiative 1995–; visiting prof of business admin Kingston

Univ; chief exec MDE Services, dir Stirling Group plc; pres N Cheshire Branch and memb Educn Ctee IM; fell: Inst of Physical Distribution Mgmnt, Inst of Export; CIMgt, FInstM, FRSA; *Books* Advertising Research (1972), Distribution Research (1973), Advertising: The Economic Implications (1975), How to Win Profitable Business (1984), How to Win Business Overseas (1985), Small Business Development (1987), Enterprise (1991), Basic Marketing (1991, 5 edn 1996), The World of Business (1991), Women as Entrepreneurs (1991), Corporate Responsibility (1992), How to get Ahead in Business (1994), Guinness Book of Business Records (1996); *Recreations* supporting Everton, computing; *Style*— Prof Thomas Cannon; ✉ The Management Charter Initiative, Russell Square House, 10–12 Russell Square, London WC1 (☎ 0171 872 9000, fax 0171 872 9099)

CANNON-BROOKES, Dr Peter; s of Victor (Joe) Montgomery Cannon Brookes, and Nancy Margaret, *née* Markham Carter (d 1994); *b* 23 Aug 1938; *Educ* Bryanston, Trinity Hall Cambridge (MA), Courtauld Inst of Art Univ of London (PhD); *m* 13 April 1966, Caroline Aylmer, da of Lt Col John Aylmer Christie-Miller, CBE, TD, DL, of Manor House, Bourton-on-the-Hill, Glos; 1 s (Stephen William Aylmer b 1966), 1 da (Emma Wilbraham Montgomery b 1968); *Career* keeper Dept of Art: City Museum and Art Gallery Birmingham 1965–78, Nat Museum of Wales 1978–86; ed International Journal of Museum Management and Curatorship 1981–, dir museum servs Stipple Database Services Ltd 1986–89, consit curator The Tabley House Collection 1988–, int museum consit 1990–; Int Cncl of Museums: memb Exec Bd UK Ctee 1973–81, pres Int Art Exhibitions Ctee 1977–79 (Exec Bd 1975–81), vice pres Conservation Ctee 1978–81 (Exec Bd 1975–81); memb Art Ctee Welsh Arts Cncl 1979–84, memb Craft Ctee 1983–87, memb Projects and Orgns Ctee Crafts Cncl 1985–87, pres Welsh Fedn of Museums 1980–82, pres S Wales Art Soc 1980–87; memb: Town Twinning Ctee Birmingham Int Cncl 1968–78, Birmingham Dio Synod 1970–78, Birmingham Dio ADU Ctee for Care of Churches 1972–78, Edgbaston Deanery Synod 1970–78 (lay jt chm 1975–78); JP: Birmingham 1973–78, Cardiff 1978–82; Liveryman Worshipful Co of Goldsmiths 1974 (Freeman 1969); FMA, FIIC, FRSA; *Books* European Sculpture (with H D Molesworth, 1964), Baroque Churches (with C A Cannon-Brookes, 1969), Lombard Painting (1974), After Gulbenkian (1976), The Cornbury Park Bellini (1977), Michael Ayrton (1978), Emile Antoine Bourdelle (1983), Ivor Roberts-Jones (1983), Czech Sculpture 1800–1938 (1983), Paintings from Tabley (1989), The Painted Word (1991); *Recreations* cooking, growing vegetables, photography; *Clubs* Athenaeum; *Style*— Dr Peter Cannon-Brookes; ✉ Thrupp House, Abingdon, Oxon OX14 3NE (☎ 01235 520595, fax 01235 534817)

CANOSA MONTORO, Francisco Octavio (Frank); s of Dr Francisco Canosa Lorenzo, and Elisa, *née* Montoro de la Torre; *b* 28 May 1951; *Educ* Columbia Univ NY (BA), Fordham Univ NY (JD); *m* 1, Dec 1972 (m dis 1975), Gloria de Aragón; m 2, 15 Sept 1979, Belinda Mary, da of Lt-Col Charles Reginald Clayton Albrecht, OBE, TA, of Pulborough, Sussex; 2 da (Alexandra Elisa b 12 Jan 1983, Isabel Christina b 20 June 1985); *Career* asst to pres Bank of America NY 1975, asst vice pres Manufacturers Hanover Trust Co NY 1978; Bank of America International Ltd London: vice pres 1980, exec dir 1985, head corporate fin UK and Europe 1987–89; vice pres and sr mktg offr Bankers Trust Co 1989–92, first vice pres and head of private banking Banca della Svizzera Italiana 1992–95, sr vice pres and head of private banking Bank Julius Baer & Co Ltd 1995–; *Clubs* RAC, Nuevo Club, Madrid; *Style*— Frank Canosa Montoro, Esq; ✉ 38 St Mary's Grove, London W4 3LN (☎ 0181 994 6827); Bank Julius Baer & Co Ltd, Bevis Marks House, Bevis Marks, London EC3A 7NE (☎ 0171 623 4211, fax 0171 283 6146, telex 887272)

CANTACUZINO, Sherban; CBE (1988); s of Prince Georges Matei Cantacuzino (d 1960), and Princess Alexandra, *née* Princess Stirbey (d 1992); *b* 6 Sept 1928; *Educ* Winchester, Magdalene Coll Cambridge (MA); *m* 29 Jan 1954, Anne Mary, da of Maj Cecil Edward Trafford, MC (d 1948); 1 s (Sherban d 1978), 2 da (Ilinca, Marina); *Career* ptnr Steane Shipman & Cantacuzino Chartered Architects 1956–65, in private practice as Sherban Cantacuzino Assocs 1965–73, exec ed Architectural Review 1973–79 (asst ed 1967–73), sr lectr Dept of Architecture Coll of Art Canterbury 1967–70; sec Royal Fine Art Cmmn 1979–94; tstee: Thomas Cubitt Tst 1978–, Design Museum (Conran Fndn) 1981–; memb: Arts Panel Arts Cncl 1977–80, Steering Ctee Aga Khan Award for Architecture 1980–83 (memb of Master Jury 1980), Cncl RSA 1980–85, Design Ctee London Tport 1981–82, Advsy Panel Railway Heritage Tst 1986–, Fabric Ctee Canterbury Cathedral 1987–, Getty Grant Program Architectural Conservation Grants Advsy Ctee 1992–, Landscape Fndn 1995–; memb Exec Ctee and pres UK Ctee Int Cncl of Monuments and Sites (ICOMOS); chm Princess Margarita of Romania Tst 1995– (tstee 1992–); Hon DUniv York 1996; Freeman City of London 1988, Liveryman Worshipful Co of Chartered Architects 1990; FRIBA 1969 (ARIBA 1956); *Books* Modern Houses of the World (1964, 3 edn 1966), Great Modern Architecture (1966, 2 edn 1968), European Domestic Architecture (1969), New Uses for Old Buildings (1975), Architectural Conservation in Europe (ed, 1975), Wells Coates, a monograph (1978), Saving Old Buildings (with Susan Brandt, 1980), The Architecture of Howell, Killick, Partridge and Amis (1981), Charles Correa (1984), Architecture in Continuity: building in the Islamic world today (ed, 1985), Re/Architecture: old buildings, new uses (1989), What Makes a Good Building? (1994); articles in Architectural Review; *Clubs* Garrick; *Style*— Sherban Cantacuzino, Esq, CBE; ✉ 140 Iffley Rd, London W6 0PE (☎ 0181 748 0415)

CANTER, Prof David Victor; s of Chaim Yizchak (Harry) Canter (d 1959), and Coralie Lilian, *née* Hyam (d 1970); *b* 5 Jan 1944; *Educ* Liverpool Collegiate GS, Univ of Liverpool (BA, PhD); *m* 10 Nov 1967, Sandra Lorraine, da of late Alfred Smith; 1 s (Daniel b 1972), 2 da (Hana b 1970, Lily Rebecca b 1979); *Career* visiting lectr Birmingham Sch of Architecture 1967–70, visiting res fell Tokyo Univ 1970–71, lectr Univ of Strathclyde 1970–71 (res fell Building Performance Res Unit 1965–70); Univ of Surrey: lectr 1972–78, reader 1978–83, personal chair in applied psychology 1983–87, chair of psychology 1987–94, head of dept 1987–91, academic head of dept 1991–94; prof of psychology Univ of Liverpool 1994–; managing ed Journal of Environmental Psychology 1981–, series ed Ethnoscopes: Current Challenges in the Environmental Social Sciences 1988–; numerous contribs to jls, TV and radio; chm Psychologists for Peace 1985–88; memb: Res Cncl for Complementary Med, London Advsy Bd Salvation Army, CND; Golden Dagger Award for non-fiction 1994; Freeman City of Quito 1985; Hon MD 1987, hon memb Japanese Inst of Architects 1970; FBPsS 1975, FAPA 1985, FIMgt 1985, CPsychol 1988; *Books* Architectural Psychology (1970), Psychology for Architects (1974), Psychology and the Built Environment (1974), Environmental Interaction (1975), The Psychology of Place (1977), Designing for Therapeutic Environments (1979), Fires and Human Behaviour (1980, revised 1990), Psychology in Practice (with S Canter, 1982), Facet Theory: Approaches to Social Research (1985), The Research Interview: Uses and Approaches (1985), Environmental Social Psychology (1986), Environmental Perspectives (1988), Environmental Policy Assessment and Communication (1988), New Directions in Environmental Participation (1988), Periballontike Psychologia (in Greek, 1988), Football In Its Place (with M Comber and D Uzzell, 1989), Empirical Approaches to Social Representations (with G Breakwell, 1993), Criminal Shadows (1994), The Faces of Homelessness (1995), Psychology in Action (1996); *Recreations* clarinet, collage, horse riding; *Style*— Prof David Canter; ✉ Department of Psychology, The University of Liverpool, PO Box 147, Liverpool L69 3BX (☎ 0151 794 3910, fax 0151 794 3938)

CANTERBURY, Archdeacon of; *see:* Pritchard, Ven John Lawrence

CANTERBURY, Dean of; *see:* Simpson, Very Rev John Arthur

CANTERBURY, 103 Archbishop of 1991–; Most Rev the Rt Hon Dr George Leonard Carey; PC (1991); s of George Thomas Carey, and Ruby Catherine, *née* Gurney; *b* 13 Nov 1935; *Educ* Bifrons Secdy Modern Sch, London Coll of Divinity, King's Coll London (ALCD, BD, MTh, PhD); *m* 25 June 1960, Eileen Harmsworth, da of Douglas Cunningham Hood; 2 s (Mark Jonathan b 28 Feb 1965, Andrew Stephen b 18 Feb 1966), 2 da (Rachel Helen b 30 May 1963, Elizabeth Ruth b 26 Oct 1971); *Career* Nat Serv 1954–56, served Egypt, Shaibah Iraq; curate St Mary's Islington 1962–66; lectr: Oakhill Theol Coll London 1966–70, St John's Theol Coll Notts 1970–75; vicar St Nicholas's Church Durham 1975–82, princ Trinity Coll Bristol 1982–87; bishop of Bath and Wells 1987–91; memb Cncl Bath Int Art Festival, patron and pres of many organizations; Freeman of the City of Wells 1990; *Books* I Believe in Man (1976), God Incarnate (1977), The Church in The Market Place (1982), The Great Acquittal (1983), The Gate of Glory (1985, updated and reissued 1992), The Meeting of The Waters (1986), The Message of the Bible (1988), The Great God Robbery (1989), I Believe (1991), Sharing a Vision (1993), Spiritual Journey (1994); *Recreations* walking, reading, music, family life; *Style*— Most Rev and Rt Hon Archbishop of Canterbury; ✉ Lambeth Palace, London SE1 7JU; The Old Palace, Canterbury, Kent

CANTLAY, Charles Peter Thrale; s of Peter Allen Cantlay, and Elizabeth Ann Cantlay; *b* 4 Feb 1954; *Educ* Radley Coll, Oriel Coll Oxford (BA); *m* 1985, Sandra Jane; *Career* Alexander Howden Reinsurance Brokers Ltd: joined 1976, dir Marine Div 1983–86, md Marine Div 1986–92, chief exec offr 1992–; Liveryman Worshipful Co of Haberdashers; *Recreations* golf, hockey, skiing; *Clubs* Tandridge Golf, Oxted Hockey; *Style*— Charles P T Cantlay, Esq; ✉ Alexander Howden Reinsurance Brokers Ltd, 8 Devonshire Square, London EC2M 4PL (☎ 0171 623 5500, fax 0171 621 1511, telex 882171)

CANTOR, Prof Brian; *b* 11 Jan 1948; *Educ* Manchester GS, Christ's Coll Cambridge (MA, PhD), Univ of Oxford (MA 1981); *m* 1, 1967 (m dis 1979), m 2, 1981 (widowed 1993); 2 s; *Career* research fell/lectr in materials science Sch of Engrg Univ of Sussex 1972–81; Dept of Materials Univ of Oxford: lectr in metallurgy 1981–91, reader in materials processing 1991–95, Cookson prof of materials and head Dept 1995–; lectr then sr research fell Jesus Coll Oxford 1985–95, professorial fell St Catherine's Coll Oxford 1995–; univ visiting fell Dept of Mechanical Engrg Northeastern Univ Boston USA 1976, Br Cncl fell Dept of Metallurgy Banaras Hindu Univ India 1980, industl fell GEC Research Labs Schenectady USA 1982, hon prof Northeastern Univ Shenyang PRC 1996–; dir Oxford Centre for Advanced Materials and Composites Univ of Oxford 1990–95; conslt: Alcan Int Research Labs 1986–94, Rolls-Royce plc 1996–; ed advsr/series ed Materials Science Publications (Adam Hilger/Inst of Physics Press) 1983–; Rosenhain Medal Inst of Materials 1993; Assoc memb Inst of Physics 1975, memb American Inst of Mining and Metallurgical Engrs 1980; CEng 1979, FIM 1989 (MIM 1970), FRMS 1993; *Books* Rapidly Quenched Metals III (ed, 1978), A Tribute to J W Christian (ed jtly, 1992), Thermal Analysis of Advanced Materials (ed jtly, 1994), Stability of Microstructure in Metals and Alloys (jtly, 2 edn, 1996); also author of numerous articles in learned jls; *Style*— Prof Brian Cantor; ✉ Department of Materials, University of Oxford, Parks Road, Oxford OX1 3PH (☎ 01865 273737, fax 01865 273738, e-mail head.department@materials.oxford.ac.uk)

CANTY, Brian George John; CBE (1993, OBE 1988); s of George Robert Canty (d 1971), of Chingford, London, and Phoebe Charlotte, *née* Cobb (d 1984); *b* 23 Oct 1931; *Educ* S W Essex Tech Coll, Univ of London (external); *m* 4 Sept 1954, Maureen Kathleen (Kenny), da of William George Kenny (d 1982), of IOW; 1 s (Nigel b 1959), 1 da (Elaine b 1957); *Career* RN 1950–57; Civil Serv: Air Miny 1957, Fin Advsr's Office Cyprus 1960, Air Force Dept MOD 1963, RAF Staff Coll Bracknell 1970; Dip Serv: entered 1971, Br Embassy Oslo 1973, Br High Cmmn Kingston 1977, consul Vienna 1979, FCO London 1984, dep govr Bermuda 1986, govr Anguilla 1989–92, ret 1992; dir A S Trust Bank Ltd 1994–; JP Bermuda 1986; *Recreations* sailing, skiing, DIY; *Clubs* RAC; *Style*— Mr Brian Canty, CBE, JP; ✉ c/o NatWest Bank, PO Box 3038, 57 Victoria Street, London SW1H 0HN

CAPELLINO, Ally (aka Alison Lloyd); *b* 1956; *Educ* Middx Poly (BA fashion and textiles); *Career* fashion designer; Courtaulds Central Design Studio 1978–79, estab Ally Capellino 'Little Hat' (initially selling accessories) 1979, developed clothing and participated in individual clothes show 1979, developed and sold Ally Capellino label internationally (Italy, USA, Japan) 1980–86, introduced menswear collection 1986, first showed London (mens and womenswear) 1986, signed 5 year contract with Japanese clothing co GCO 1987, opened flagship store Soho 1988, launched diffusion sportswear collection 'Hearts of Oak' 1990, design conslt to Coats Viyella for Marks & Spencer 1990 (developed range of jersey sportswear 1992), signed promotional licensing agreement with Coats Viyella plc, renewed licensing deal with GCO Japan; *Style*— Ms Alison Lloyd; ✉ Ally Capellino, N1R, Metropolitan Wharf, Wapping Wall, London E1 9SS (☎ 0171 488 9777, fax 0171 488 9852)

CAPES, Geoffrey Lewis (Geoff); s of George William Capes, of Holbeach, Spalding, Lincs, and Eileen Nelie, *née* Newham; *b* 23 Aug 1949; *Educ* George Farmer Comp Sch; *partner* Kashmiro Davy Bhatti; 1 s (Lewis Leonard), 1 da (Emma Jane); *Career* GB shot put international 1967–80: 17 nat titles, twice Cwlth champion, 2 Gold, 2 Silver and 1 Bronze medal Euro Indoor Championships, Bronze medal Euro Championships, 3 times Euro Cup champion, 3 times Olympian; turned professional Highland Games and strong man competitor 1980; 6 times World Highland Games champion, twice World's Strongest Man, 3 times Br Strongest Man, 3 times Euro Strongest Man; physical training instructor Police Force 1969–80, dir Geoff Capes Promotions 1980–; record of 67 int caps for male UK athlete, record of 35 wins; Churchill scholar 1974, Queen's Jubilee medal 1977; *Books* Big Shot (autobiography); *Recreations* fishing, gardening, breeding budgerigars; *Clubs* Enfield Harriers; *Style*— Geoff Capes, Esq; ✉ c/o Bagnall Harvey, 141–143 Drury Lane, London WC2B 5TB (☎ 0171 379 4625)

CAPIE, Prof Forrest Hunter; s of Daniel Forrest Capie (d 1975), and Isabella Ferguson, *née* Doughty (d 1996); *b* 1 Dec 1940; *Educ* Nelson Coll NZ, Univ of Auckland NZ (BA), LSE (MSc, PhD); *m* 11 Feb 1967, Dianna Dix, da of William John Harvey, of Auckland, NZ; *Career* economics tutor LSE 1970–72; lectr: Dept of Economics Univ of Warwick 1972–74, Sch of Economics Univ of Leeds 1974–79; Centre for Banking and Int Fin City Univ London: lectr 1979–82, sr lectr 1982–83, reader 1983–86, prof of econ history 1986–, head of dept 1988–; ed Economic History Review 1993–; memb: Econ History Soc 1970 (memb Cncl 1986–), Cliometric Soc 1986; FRSA; *Books* The British Economy Between the Wars (with M Collins, 1983), Depression and Protectionism, Britain Between the Wars (1983), Monetary History of the United Kingdom 1870–1970: Data Sources and Methods (with A Webber, 1985), Financial Crises and the World Banking System (ed with G E Wood, 1986), Monetary Economics in the 1980s: Some Themes from Henry Thornton (ed with G E Wood, 1988), A Directory of Economic Institutions (ed, 1990), Major Inflations in History (ed, 1991), Have the Banks Failed British Industry? (1992), Protectionism in World Economy (1992), Monetary Regimes in Transition (1993); *Recreations* golf, watching sport, classical music, opera, theatre; *Clubs* Travellers', Political Economy, Hampstead Golf, Middx Cricket; *Style*— Prof Forrest Capie; ✉ 2 Fitzroy Road, Primrose Hill, London NW1 8TZ (☎ 0171 722 7456); Department of Banking and Finance, City University Business School, Frobisher Crescent, Barbican, London EC2 (☎ 0171 477 8736)

CAPLAN, Harold; s of Samuel Caplan (d 1981), and Gertrude Caplan (d 1972); *b* 13 March 1927; *Educ* Queen Elizabeth's Hosp Bristol, The Coll of Aeronautics Cranfield (MSc); *m* 22 Nov 1968, Isabel, da of Stephen Randall (d 1978); *Career* chartered insurance practitioner; called to the Bar Middle Temple 1955; head Legal Dept The British Aviation Insurance Co Ltd 1960–69 (chief tech offr 1955), md International Insurance Services Ltd 1981–94 (jt gen mangr 1970–81), dir Airclaims Insurance Services Ltd 1987–92, gp legal dir Airclaims Group 1992–94; legal advsr Int Union of Aviation Insurers 1985–94 (conslt 1994–), fndr memb Air Law Gp Royal Aeronautical Soc, memb Bar Assoc for Commerce Finance and Indust; CEng, FRAeS, FCIArb, MIMechE; *Recreations* iconoclasm; *Clubs* Athenaeum, City of London; *Style—* Harold Caplan, Esq; ✉ 3 The Pennards, Sunbury on Thames, Middx TW16 5JZ (☎ 01932 781200, fax 01932 779694)

CAPLAN, Jonathan Michael; QC (1991); s of Malcolm Denis Caplan, and Jean Hilary, *née* Winroope (d 1984); *b* 11 Jan 1951; *Educ* St Paul's, Downing Coll Cambridge (Harris open scholar, law tripos); *m* Selena Anne, *née* Peskin; 2 s, 1 da; *Career* called to the Bar Gray's Inn 1973 (Holker scholar), recorder of the Crown Ct 1995– (asst recorder 1990–95); chm Bar Cncl Ctee on Televising the Courts 1989, chm Public Affrs Ctee Bar Cncl 1990–92; memb Editorial Bd Jl of Criminal Law; FRSA 1991; *Books* The Confait Confessions (1977), The Bar on Trial (1978), Disabling Professions (1979); *Recreations* tennis, Thai and Khmer art, collecting manuscripts and historical newspapers, reading, writing, music; *Clubs* Queen's; *Style—* Jonathan Caplan, Esq, QC; ✉ 1st Floor, 5 Paper Buildings, Temple, London EC4Y 7HB (☎ 0171 583 6117, fax 0171 353 0075)

CAPLAN, The Hon Lord; Philip Isaac Caplan; QC (Scot 1970); s of Hyman Caplan (d 1962), of Glasgow, and Rosalena Silverstone (d 1985); *b* 24 Feb 1929; *Educ* Eastwood Secdy Sch, Univ of Glasgow (MA, LLB); *m* 1, 1953, Elaine Marcia, da of Abraham Gelfer, of Glasgow; 2 s, 1 da; m 2, 1974, Joyce Ethel, da of Walter Stone, of London; 1 da; *Career* admitted Faculty of Advocates 1957, former standing jr counsel to the Accountant of Ct, former chm Plant and Seeds Tbnl (Scot); Sheriff of Lothian and Borders at Edinburgh 1979–83, Sheriff Princ of N Strathclyde 1983–88, Sheriff Ct Rules Cncl 1984–88, senator Coll of Justice 1989–; cmmr Northern Lighthouse Bd 1983–88; chm: Scottish Assoc for the Study of Deliquency 1985–89 (hon vice pres 1989), The James Powell UK Tst 1992–; hon pres Family Mediation Scotland 1994; Hon LLD Glasgow 1996; FRPS, AFIAP; *Recreations* photography, music, reading; *Clubs* New (Edinburgh); *Style—* The Hon Lord Caplan; ✉ Court of Session, Parliament Square, Edinburgh (☎ 0131 225 2595)

CAPLAN, Simon Anthony; s of Malcolm Denis Caplan and Jean Hilary, *née* Winroope (d 1984); *b* 13 Dec 1946; *Educ* Carmel Coll Wallingford; *m* 6 Sept 1970, Yolande Anne, da of Simon Albert (d 1978); 1 s (Benjamin b 1974), 1 da (Amanda b 1971); *Career* Touche Ross 1970; jt fndr Fin Advice Panels (within CAB); fndr Caplan Montagu Assoc, chief exec CMP (The Creative Management Management Partnership) Ltd, chm and md of Stagestruck Gp of Cos; Barker of the Variety Club of GB; memb: BAFTA, Royal TV Soc; JP 1986 (ret); Gen Cmmr of Income Tax 1988; Freeman City of London 1980; FTII, FAPA; *Recreations* art and antique collecting, theatre; *Clubs* Reform, Savage, Rugby; *Style—* Simon A Caplan, Esq; ✉ Stowe March, Barnet Lane, Elstree, Borehamwood, Herts WD6 3RQ

CAPNER, Gareth Roger John; s of John Hammond Capner (d 1973), and Clarice May, *née* Gibbins (d 1971); *b* 14 May 1947; *Educ* Taunton Sch Somerset, Univ of Sheffield (BA, MA); *m* 2 Jan 1971, Susan Mary, da of Arthur Snell, of S Humberside (d 1994); *Career* princ planning offr Berkshire CC 1973–79; Barton Willmore Planning Partnership: assoc 1979–81, ptnr 1981–85, sr ptnr 1985–; MIMgt 1978; FRTPI 1983 (MRTPI 1974); *Recreations* sailing, skiing, shooting and gourmet dining; *Style—* Gareth Capner, Esq; ✉ Shepherds Hill House, Boxford, Newbury, Berks RG20 8DX; The Old Mill, Mill Lane, Lymington, Hants SO41 9AZ; The Barton Willmore Planning Partnership, Beansheaf Farmhouse, Calcot, Reading, Berks RG31 7BW (☎ 01189 425577, fax 01189 418410, car 0850 491320)

CAPON, Timothy Wills Hugh; s of Rev Martin Gedge Capon, of Exmouth, Devon, and Mary Wills Hamlyn (d 1978); *b* 26 Oct 1940; *Educ* Prince of Wales Sch Nairobi Kenya, Magdalene Coll Cambridge (BA, LLB); *m* 3 Sept 1966, Elizabeth Fleming, da of Henry Campbell McAusland, OBE; 1 s (Oliver Fleming b 1 Aug 1970), 2 da (Sarah Elizabeth b 19 March 1969 d 1995, Lucy Jane b 10 July 1972); *Career* admitted slr 1965; res ptnr NY office Linklaters and Paines 1974–77 (ptnr 1970), exec dir The Diamond Trading Co (Pty) Ltd 1977–; dir: Bank Leumi UK plc, De Beers Consolidated Mines Ltd, De Beers Centenary AG; *Clubs* Hurlingham; *Style—* Timothy Capon, Esq; ✉ 17 Charterhouse Street, London EC1N 6RA (☎ 0171 404 4444, fax 0171 430 1507)

CAPPIN, John Michael; s of Louis Cappin, of London, and Yetta Cappin; *b* 7 Dec 1938; *Educ* Mercers' Sch, Univ of Cambridge (MA, MB BChir, DO); *m* 2 April 1967, Marion Kay, da of Ernest Clifford Stammers (d 1967), of Tunbridge Wells; 2 s (Simon James b 7 July 1969, Matthew Jonathen b 25 Nov 1978), 1 da (Melissa Catherine b 1 Nov 1972); *Career* conslt ophthalmic surgn Leicester Health Authy 1975–; FRCS, FRCOphth 1989; *Recreations* pianist, choral conductor, tennis; *Style—* John Cappin, Esq; ✉ Leicester Clinic, Scraptoft Lane, Leicester (☎ 0116 276 9502)

CAPRON, (George) Christopher; s of Lt-Col George Theodore Herbert Capron (d 1970), of Southwick Hall, Peterborough, and Hon Edith Christian Hepburne-Scott, 3 da of 9 Baron Polwarth (d 1989); *b* 17 Dec 1935; *Educ* Wellington, Trinity Hall Cambridge (BA); *m* 1958, Edna Naomi, da of Chanania Goldrei (d 1973); 1 s (David), 1 da (Naomi); *Career* 2 Lt 12 Royal Lancers (POW) 1954–56; BBC TV 1959–87: ed Tonight 1976–77, Panorama 1977–79, asst head current affrs programmes 1979–81 (head 1981–85), head of Parly bdcasting 1985–87; ind TV prodr Capron Prodns Ltd 1987–; memb BAFTA, FRTS 1996; *Recreations* tennis, village cricket; *Clubs* Northamptonshire CCC, Hurlingham; *Style—* Christopher Capron, Esq; ✉ 32 Amerland Rd, London SW18 (☎ 0181 874 4829)

CAPSTICK, His Hon Judge; Brian Eric; QC (1973); o s of late (Norman) Eric Capstick, and Betty Capstick; *b* 12 Feb 1927; *Educ* Sedbergh, Queen's Coll Oxford (MA); *m* 1960, Margaret Elizabeth Harrison; 1 s, 1 da; *Career* called to the Bar Lincoln's Inn 1952, bencher 1980, recorder 1980–85, circuit judge (SE Circuit) 1985–; dep chm Northern Agric Tribunal 1976–, asst boundary cmmr 1978–85, appeal steward Br Bd of Boxing Control 1985–, memb Parole Bd 1996–; *Recreations* shooting, reading, cooking; *Clubs* Garrick; *Style—* His Hon Judge Capstick, QC; ✉ c/o Central Criminal Court, Old Bailey, London EC4M 7EH

CAPSTICK, Charles William; CB (1992), CMG (1972); s of late William Capstick, and Janet Frankland; *b* 18 Dec 1934; *Educ* King's Coll Durham (BSc), Univ of Kentucky (MS); *m* 1962, Joyce Alma, da of late William Dodsworth; 2 s; *Career* MAFF: asst agric economist 1961, princ agric economist 1966, sr princ agric economist 1968, asst sec Milk and Milk Products Div 1977, under sec and dir of economics and statistics 1977–89, dep sec Food Safety Directorate 1989–94; *Style—* Charles Capstick, Esq, CB, CMG

CARBERRY, Deborah Claire (Debbie); da of Robert John Stephens, of Horsham, Sussex, and Sylvia Marie, *née* Mogford; *b* 11 Aug 1960; *Educ* Holy Trinity C of E Sch Sussex, Crawley Coll of Further Educn; *Career* PR exec; sec Int Mktg Div EMI Music Ltd 1978–79, PR asst Constructors John Brown Ltd 1979–80, jr then sr account exec Max Redlich Ltd 1980–81; account mangr: Imprimatur (PR) Ltd 1981–82, Peter Walker Associates 1982–83; sr account dir Genesis (acquired by Daniel J Edelman Ltd 1985) 1983–85, assoc dir then main bd dir Daniel J Edelman Ltd 1985–87, dir Biss Lancaster plc 1988–91, md Carberry Communications 1992–94, sr dir Hill & Knowlton (UK) Ltd 1995–; *Recreations* fitness training, gardening, wine appreciation, reading; *Style—* Ms Debbie Carberry; ✉ Hill & Knowlton (UK) Ltd, 5–11 Theobalds Road, London WC1X 8SH (☎ 0171 413 3214, fax 0171 413 3222)

CARBERY, 11 Baron (I 1715); Sir Peter Ralfe Harrington Evans-Freke; 7 Bt (I 1768); s of Maj the Hon Ralfe Evans-Freke, MBE (d 1969), 2 s of 9 Baron; suc unc, 10 Baron, 1970; *b* 20 March 1920; *Educ* Downside; *m* 1941, Joyzelle Mary, o da of late Herbert Binnie, of Sydney, NSW; 3 s (Hon Michael Peter b 11 Oct 1942, Hon John Anthony b 9 May 1949, Hon Stephen Ralfe b 2 March 1952), 2 da (Hon Maura Clare (Hon Mrs Fanshawe) b 1946, Hon Angela Mary (Hon Mrs Tomlins) b 1954); *Heir* Hon Michael Evans-Freke, *qv*; *Career* served WWII 1939–45 as Capt RE in India and Burma; former memb London Stock Exchange; author of novels, plays and poetry; MICE; *Style—* The Rt Hon the Lord Carbery; ✉ 2 Hayes Court, Sunnyside, Wimbledon, London SW19 4SH (☎ 0181 946 6615)

CARBUTT, Billy (Francis); s of George H Carbutt (d 1956), and Ann, *née* de Montmorency (now Mrs E W Swanton); *b* 16 July 1936; *Educ* Eton Coll; *m* 19 July 1958, Sally Fenella, da of James C Harris (d 1996), of Ampfield, Hants; 1 s (George Henry de Montmorency b 1963), 1 da (Emma Louise (Mrs Alexander Swinton) b 1961); *Career* Nat Serv Lt Rifle Bde 1954–56; CA; ptnr Ernst & Young 1967–94 (joined 1956); chm Parity plc; chm: Ct of the Mary Rose 1987–94, City of London Club 1991–94, Distressed Gentlefolk Aid Assoc 1994–; memb Cncl Alexandra Rose Day Tst 1994–; govr Oundle Sch 1984–; memb: City Livery Ctee 1991–95, Ct Worshipful Co of Grocers 1984 (Master 1990/91); Chevalier Ordre des Coteaux de Champagne; FCA 1961; *Recreations* swimming, photography, gardening, all kinds of music; *Clubs* Boodle's, City of London, MCC; *Style—* Billy Carbutt, Esq; ✉ The White House, Langham, Colchester, Essex CO4 5PY (business ☎ and fax 01206 322982, home ☎ 01206 323182)

CARDALE, David Michael; s of Brig W J Cardale, OBE (d 1986), of Bury St Edmunds, Suffolk, and Audrey Vere, *née* Parry-Crooke (d 1996); *b* 26 Dec 1947; *Educ* Eton, Univ of Essex (BA), INSEAD (MBA); *m* 31 Aug 1985, Fionna, *née* MacCormick; 1 s (Hugo William b 7 March 1989), 2 da (Natasha Lucy Vere b 19 Dec 1990, Alicia Daisy Catherine b 11 May 1993); *Career* County Bank: exec 1972–78, asst dir 1978–81, N American rep 1981–83, dir 1983–87; exec dir County NatWest 1987–90, dir NatWest Ventures 1990–95; co-fndr and managing ptnr MBO Advisory Partners 1995–; non-exec dir: Sphere Investment Trust Plc 1988–, The Emerging Markets Country Investment Trust Plc 1994–; dir Toolex Alpha Vorvaltnings AB (Sweden) 1995–; *Recreations* hunting, tennis, windsurfing; *Style—* David Cardale, Esq; ✉ MBO Advisory Partners, 12 Upper Grosvenor Street, London W1X 9PA (☎ 0171 208 0880, fax 0171 208 0886)

CARDALE, William Tyndale; s of Brig W J Cardale, OBE, ADC (d 1986), and Vere Audrey, *née* Parry-Crooke (d 1996); *b* 10 Dec 1945; *Educ* Eton; *m* 13 Aug 1988, Lynn Meriel, da of Alan Thomas Brown, CBE, DL, *qv*; 1 s (Thomas William b 24 Feb 1990); *Career* CA; UK dir of trust and accounting servs Price Waterhouse 1994– (chm Trust Liaison Gp); lectr in taxation Univ of Birmingham (on secondment from Price Waterhouse) and at various accountancy bodies' courses; memb team revising Tolley's Estate Planning Guide; FCA, ATII, assoc memb Securities Inst (co-opted memb Birmingham Branch Ctee) 1995; *Recreations* riding (hunter trials and events), tennis; *Style—* William T Cardale, Esq; ✉ West Lodge, Bradfield St George, Bury St Edmunds, Suffolk; 71 Ravenhurst Rd, Harborne, Birmingham B17 9TB (☎ 0121 427 1271)

CARDEN, Sir John Craven; 7 Bt (I 1787), of Templemore, Tipperary; s of Capt Sir John Valentine Carden, 6 Bt, MBE (d 1935), and his 2 w, Dorothy Mary, *née* McKinnon; *b* 11 March 1926; *Educ* Eton; *m* 1947, Isabel Georgette, yst da of late Robert de Hart; 1 da (Isabel Mary b 1952); *Heir* kinsman, Derrick Charles Carden, CMG, b 21 Oct 1921; *Style—* Sir John Carden, Bt; ✉ PO Box N-3718, Nassau, Bahamas

CARDEW, Anthony John; s of Lt-Col Martin Philip Cardew, of Rookley Manor, Rookley, IOW, and Anne Elizabeth, *née* Foster; *b* 8 Sept 1949; *Educ* Bishop Wordsworth's Sch Salisbury, Marlborough Coll; *m* 10 Dec 1971, Janice Frances, da of Alec Anthony Smallwood (d 1985); 1 s (James), 1 da (Sarah); *Career* chief reporter Surrey Mirror 1968–70, news reporter UPI 1970–71, fin corr Reuters 1972–74, dir then head of fin PR Charles Barker Ltd 1974–83, chm Grandfield Rork Collins 1985–91 (dir 1983–91), chm Cardew & Co Ltd 1991–; *Recreations* book collecting, walking, shooting; *Clubs* Reform, Thunderers; *Style—* Anthony Cardew, Esq; ✉ Cardew & Co Ltd, 12 Suffolk St, London SW1Y 4HQ (☎ 0171 930 0777, fax 0171 925 0647)

CARDIFF, Archbishop of (RC) 1983–; Most Rev John Aloysius Ward; s of Eugene Ward and Hannah, *née* Cheetham; *b* 24 Jan 1929; *Educ* Prior Park Coll Bath; *Career* OFMCap 1945–, ordained priest 1953, guardian and parish priest Peckham 1960–66, provincial definitor 1963–69, minister provincial 1969–70, gen definitor Rome 1970–80, Bishop Coadjutor of Menevia 1980–81, Bishop of Menevia 1981–83; *Style—* His Grace the Archbishop of Cardiff, OFMCap; ✉ Archbishop's House, 41–43 Cathedral Road, Cardiff CF1 9HD (☎ 01222 220411)

CARDIGAN, Earl of; David Michael James Brudenell-Bruce; s and h of 8 Marquess of Ailesbury; *b* 12 Nov 1952; *Educ* Eton, Rannoch, Royal Agric Coll Cirencester; *m* 1980, Rosamond Jane, er da of Capt W R M Winkley, of Bruton, Somerset, and Mrs Jane Winkley, of Pewsey, Wilts; 1 s (Hon Thomas b 1982), 1 da (Lady Catherine b 1984); *Heir* s, Viscount Savernake; *Career* 31st Hereditary Warden of Savernake Forest (position created in 1067) 1987–, owner mangr Savernake Forest; sec Marlborough Conservatives; memb exec Devizes Constituency Conservative Assoc; *Style—* Earl of Cardigan; ✉ Savernake Lodge, Savernake Forest, Marlborough, Wilts (☎ 01672 512161, fax 01672 512105)

CARDOZO, Prof Linda Dolores; da of Felix Elia Cardozo (d 1971), of London, and Olga Annette, *née* Watts (d 1992); *b* 15 Sept 1950; *Educ* Haberdashers' Aske's, Acton Tech Coll, Univ of Liverpool (MB ChB, MD); *m* 13 July 1974, Stuart Ian Hutcheson, s of Ian Steen Hutcheson (d 1994); 1 s (Marius b 27 July 1990), 2 da (Melissa b 27 Feb 1989, Juliet (twin) b 27 July 1990); *Career* house offr and sr house offr in obstetrics and gynaecology Liverpool, res registrar in urodynamics St George's Hosp London 1976–78, conslt obstetrician and gynaecologist specialising in female urinary incontinence King's Coll Hosp 1985– (registrar then sr registrar 1979–85), prof of urogynaecology KCL 1994–; memb: RSM, BMA, Int Urogynaecology Assoc, Int Continence Soc; FRCOG 1991 (MRCOG 1980); *Books* Basic Urogynaecology (1993), Urogynaecology (1996); *Recreations* theatre, bridge, gardening, scuba diving, skiing, water skiing; *Style—* Prof Linda Cardozo; ✉ The Sloes, Potter St Hill, Pinner, Middlesex HA5 3YH (☎ 0181 866 0291, fax 0181 866 0129); King's College Hospital, Denmark Hill, London SE5 9RS; 8 Devonshire Place, London W1N 1PB (☎ 0171 935 2357, fax 0171 224 2797)

CARDROSS, Lord; Henry Thomas Alexander Erskine; s and h of 17 Earl of Buchan, JP, *qv*; *b* 31 May 1960; *Educ* Eton, Central Sch of Art and Design; *m* 28 Feb 1987, Charlotte Catherine Lucinda, da of Hon Matthew Beaumont; 2 s (Alexander Henry David John b 26 April 1990, Frederick Alastair b 22 April 1992); *Career* product designer and stained glass artist; *Recreations* cars, motor cycles, photography, video, travel, history; *Style—* Lord Cardross

CARDWELL, Jennifer Lesley Winter; *b* 14 Feb 1943; *Educ* Tottenham Co Sch, Nevilles Cross Coll Durham; *m* 7 April 1966, Benjamin Jon Cardwell; 1 s (Angus Blair b 18 Dec 1975), 1 da (Joanna Emily b 2 Jan 1973); *Career* hockey coach and mangr; player: Ipswich Ladies Hockey Club 1968–82, counties second XI 1962–68 (Durham, Essex, Sussex), Suffolk first XI 1968–82, East territory 1968–72, 1973–75, 1976–80, 30 caps England 1970–72 and 1973–74 (England B 1970); coach: East Srs 1985–91 (jrs 1982), Ealing Ladies Hockey Club 1987–89, Essex Ladies 1985–90; mangr: England Sr Women's team 1989–93 (coach 1983–86), Euro champions 1991, GB Women's team 1993–96; achievements as coach: East Srs champions 3 times, Ealing nat champions 3 times, Essex territorial champions 3 times, England fourth place Euro Cup 1983 and fifth place World Cup 1986 (fourth 1990 as mangr), England fourth place Olympic Games Atlanta 1996; pt/t PE teacher Ashford Sch for Girls 1992–; *Recreations* golf (two holes-in-one), keeping fit, learning to relax; *Style*— Mrs Jennifer Cardwell; ✉ Little Dene, 13 Manor Rise, Bearsted, Maidstone, Kent ME14 4DB (☎ and fax 01622 737736); c/o Liz Howard, 42 Woolacombe Lodge Road, Selly Oak, Birmingham B29 6PX (☎ and fax 0121 472 3458)

CARDWELL, Paul; s of Charles Alexander Cardwell, and Irene Julia-Ann, *née* Moodie; *b* 10 June 1952; *m* May 1984, Christina Hughes, da of Fergus Hughes Boyter; 2 da (Rebecca Caterina Madelaine Macdonald b 15 March 1986, Amelia Iona Francis b 29 Aug 1988); *Career* with advtg agencies: Foote Cone & Belding 1978–79, Young & Rubicam 1979–85, Publicis 1985–87; bd dir Leo Burnett 1987–89, joint chm and creative dir GGK London 1993–95 (creative dir 1989–93), creative dir Doner Cardwell Hawkins 1995–; contrib Horizon (BBC) and Channel 4 as freelance documentary writer through Brand X Ltd; winner (1991): Gold Medal The One Show NY, Lion D'Or Cannes Advtg Festival, Gold Award Art Dirs' Club of Europe, ITV Award, Gold and Silver Br TV Advtg Awards, Silver D&AD Award; memb: D&AD 1979, Royal Photographic Soc 1990, The Photographers Gallery 1991; *Books* The Race Against Time - The Story of Sport Aid (1988); *Recreations* theatre, travel, reading, photography; *Style*— Paul Cardwell, Esq; ✉ 2 Spenser Road, Strawberry Hill, Middx; The Lytchgate, Painswick, Glos; Doner Cardwell Hawkins, 76 Dean Street, London W1V 5AB (☎ 0171 734 0511)

CARDWELL, Prof Richard Andrew; s of Lt Cdr Albert Cardwell RN (d 1995), of Marlborough, Hillcrest, Helston, Cornwall, and Mary Margarethe, *née* Knight; *b* 16 July 1938; *Educ* Helston GS, Univ of Southampton (BA, DipEd), Univ of Nottingham (PhD); *m* 29 July 1961, Oithona Shaguine (Bunty), da of Edgar Treadwell (d 1968); *Career* lectr UCW Aberystwyth 1965–67 (asst lectr 1964–65); Univ of Nottingham: lectr 1967–74, sr lectr 1974–78, reader 1978–83, prof of modern Spanish lit and head Dept of Hispanic Studies 1983–; visiting prof Johns Hopkins Univ 1992; author of numerous articles; memb: Assoc of Br Hispanists, Anglo-Catalan Soc, Assoc of Teachers of Spanish and Portuguese, Real Academia Sevillana de Buenas Letras Seville Spain; Boy Scouts' Assoc Silver Cross for Gallantry and Royal Humane Soc Testimonial on Vellum for Gallantry 1958; *Books* Blasco Ibanez's La Barraca (1972), Juan Ramòn Jimenez: The Modernist Apprenticeship (1977), Espronceda (1981), Gabriel Garcia Marquez: New Readings (1987), Virgil: Essays for the Bimillenium (1987), Literature and Language (1989); Espronceda: Student of Salamanca (1990), Qué es el Modernismo? (1992), Zorrilla: Centennial Readings (1994); *Recreations* gardening, garden design, walking, conversation with intelligent women; *Style*— Prof Richard A Cardwell; ✉ The Yews, 6 Town St, Sandiacre, Nottingham NG10 5DP (☎ 0115 939 7316); Department of Hispanic Studies, University of Nottingham, University Park, Nottingham NG7 2RD (☎ 0115 951 5800, fax 0115 951 5814)

CARDY, Peter John Stubbings; s of Gordon Douglas Stubbings, of Gosport, Hants, and Eva, *née* Walker; assumed the surname of Cardy by deed 1987; *b* 4 April 1947; *Educ* Price's Sch, Univ Coll Durham (BA), Cranfield Inst of Technol (MSc); *m* 5 Sept 1987, Christine Mary, da of Ronald Edward Francis Doyle, of Manchester; *Career* dist sec WEA N of Scotland 1971–77, dep dir Volunteer Centre UK 1977–87, dir Motor Neurone Disease Assoc 1987–94, chief exec MS Soc of GB and NI 1994–; memb: Carnegy Ctee Community Educn in Scotland 1976–77, Conseil de Rédaction Aménagement et Nature Paris 1979–84; visiting lectr Australian Red Cross Soc 1981, treas Volonteurope 1981–84, Socio de Honor Assoc Geriatrica Valenciana Spain 1983, res assoc Policy Studies Inst London 1984, chm Ctee Local Devpt Agencies Fund 1985–89, memb Bdcasting Support Servs 1985–90, memb Morrison Ctee Broadcasting and Voluntary Action 1986–87, chm Nat Assoc Volunteer Bureaux 1988–91; panellist Charities Effectiveness Review Tst 1990–94; admin tstee Fund For People in Need 1991–93, adver Migraine Tst 1991–92, sec gen Int Alliance of ACS/MND Assocs 1992–94, non-exec dir Northampton Healthcare NHS Tst 1993–; *Recreations* sailing, conversation, travel; *Clubs* Reform; *Style*— Peter Cardy, Esq; ✉ MS Society of Great Britain and Northern Ireland, 25 Effie Road, Fulham, London SW6 1EE (☎ 0171 610 7171, fax 0171 736 9861)

CARE, Prof Anthony Deuchar; s of Clarence Deuchar Care (d 1984), and Florence Edith, *née* Wills (d 1987); *b* 28 Sept 1928; *Educ* Ilkley GS, Downing Coll Cambridge (MA), Univ of Leeds (PhD, DSc), Univ of Edinburgh (BVMS); *m* 12 July 1958, Grizel Rosemary Frances, da of Sir John Taylor, KBE, CMG (d 1973); 1 s (Ian Colin Deuchar b 1 May 1960), 2 da (Fiona b 19 Feb 1962, Ailsa b 29 May 1966); *Career* princ scientific offr ARC Inst of Animal Physiology Babraham Cambridge 1961, sr princ scientific offr Rowett Res Inst Bucksburn Aberdeen 1968, prof and head of Dept of Animal Physiology and Nutrition Univ of Leeds 1971–90, hon prof in biochemistry University Coll Wales 1990–; MRCVS 1959; *Recreations* farming, cliff walking, gardening; *Style*— Prof Anthony Care; ✉ Mill Farm, Manorowen, Fishguard, Dyfed SA65 9PT; Institute of Biological Sciences, University College Wales, Aberystwyth SY23 3DD (☎ 01970 828 236, fax 01970 617 172, telex 35181 ABYUCW G)

CAREW, 7 Baron (I 1834 and UK 1838); Patrick Thomas Conolly-Carew; s of 6 Baron Carew, CBE (d 1994), and Lady Sylvia Gwendoline Eva Maitland (d 1991), da of 15 Earl of Lauderdale; *b* 6 March 1938; *Educ* Harrow, RMA Sandhurst; *m* 30 April 1962, Celia Mary, da of Col Hon (Charles) Guy Cubitt, CBE, DSO, TD; 1 s (Hon William Patrick b 1973), 3 da (Hon Virginia Mary (Hon Mrs McGrath) b 1965, Hon Nicola Rosamond b 1966, Hon Camilla Sylvia b 1969); *Heir* s, Hon William Patrick Conolly-Carew b 27 March 1973; *Career* late Capt RHG, former int show jumping rider; memb Irish Olympic Three Day Event team: Mexico 1968, Munich 1972, Montreal 1976; pres Equestrian Fedn of Ireland 1979–84, chm Three Day Event Ctee Federation Equestre Internationale (memb Bureau) 1989; *Recreations* all equestrian sports, shooting, cricket, bridge; *Clubs* Kildare St and Univ (Dublin); *Style*— The Rt Hon the Lord Carew; ✉ Donadea House, Naas, Co Kildare, Ireland (☎ 00 353 458 68204, fax 00 353 458 61105)

CAREW, Sir Rivers Verain; 11 Bt (E 1661), of Haccombe, Devon; s of Sir Thomas Palk Carew, 10 Bt (d 1976), and his 2 wife, Phyllis Evelyn, *née* Mayman; *b* 17 Oct 1935; *Educ* St Columba's Coll Co Dublin, Univ of Dublin (MA, BAgrSc Hort); *m* 1, 1968 (m dis 1991), Susan Babington, yr da of late Harold Babington Hill, of London; 1 s (and 1 s decd), 3 da (Marcella Tamsin b 1970, Marina Lys b 1972, Miranda Rose b 1973); m 2, 1992, Siobhán, da of late Criostóir Seán Mac Cárthaigh, of Cork; *Heir* s, Gerald de Redvers Carew b 24 May 1975; *Career* ed, journalist and author; asst ed Ireland of The Welcomes (Irish Tourist Bd magazine) 1964–67, jt ed The Dublin Magazine 1964–69, journalist Irish TV 1967–, BBC World Serv 1987–93; *Books* Figures out of Mist (poems with T Brownlow, 1966); *Recreations* reading, music, reflection; *Style*— Sir Rivers Carew, Bt; ✉ Cherry Bounds, Hicks Lane, Girton, Cambridge CB3 0JS (☎ 01223 277155)

CAREW POLE, Sir (John) Richard Walter Reginald; 13 Bt (E 1628), of Shute House, Devonshire; s of Col Sir John Gawen Carew Pole, 12 Bt, DSO, TD (d 1993), and Cynthia Mary Burns, OBE (d 1977); *b* 2 Dec 1938; *Educ* Eton, RAC Cirencester; *Heir* s, Tremayne John Carew Pole b 22 Feb 1974; *Career* late Coldstream Gds; memb Devon and Cornwall Ctee Nat Tst 1978–83, pres Surf Life Saving Assoc of GB 1978–87; High Sheriff of Cornwall 1979; pt/t dir SW Electricity Bd 1981–90, regnl dir Portman Building Society 1989–91; pres Royal Cornwall Agric Show 1981, chm Devon and Cornwall Police Authy 1985–87; govr: Seale Hayne Agric Coll 1979–89, Plymouth Coll 1981–96; dir Theatre Royal Plymouth 1985–; Cornwall CC: cncllr 1973–93, chm Planning and Employment Ctee 1980–84, chm Finance Cmmn 1985–89, chm Property Ctee 1989–93; tstee: Nat Heritage Memorial Fund 1991–, Tate Gallery 1993–; memb Countryside Cmmn 1991–96; Liveryman Worshipful Co of Fishmongers (memb Ct 1993–); ARICS 1969; *Recreations* walking, travelling, contemporary pictures, gardening; *Clubs* Pratt's; *Style*— Sir Richard Carew Pole, Bt; ✉ Antony House, Torpoint, Cornwall PL11 2QA (☎ 01752 814914)

CAREY, Conan Jerome; s of Dr James J Carey (d 1982), and Marion, *née* O'Sullivan (d 1979); *b* 8 Aug 1936; *Educ* Belvedere Coll Dublin, RMA Sandhurst; *m* 27 May 1966, (Elizabeth) Gay, da of Col L R Docker, OBE, MC, TD (d 1980), and Cynthia, *née* Washington; 1 s (James b 1970), 2 da (Verna b 1967, Philippa b 1981); *Career* cmmnd RASC 1956: Army Air Corps 1960–65, RCT 1965, RMCS 1967, Staff Coll Camberley 1968, CO 155 RCT (TA) 1976–78, Def Staff Br Embassy Washington DC USA 1979–82, Col 1982, Brig 1985, Dep DG Tport and Movements 1985–88; DG Home Farm Tst 1988–; MInstD; FCIT, FIPD, FIMgt, FRSA; *Recreations* golf; *Clubs* Army and Navy, Tracy Park Golf (Bath); *Style*— Conan Carey, Esq; ✉ The Home Farm Trust Ltd, Bristol BS1 4RW (☎ 0117 927 3746, fax 0117 922 5938)

CAREY, de Vic Graham; s of Michael Carey (d 1964), of Guernsey, and Jean, *née* Bullen (d 1975); *b* 15 June 1940; *Educ* Cheam Sch, Bryanston, Trinity Hall Cambridge (BA, MA), Caen Univ; *m* 22 June 1968, Bridget, da of Maj John Lindsay Smith (ka 1943); 2 s (Perrin b 1971, Julius b 1980), 2 da (Jenette b 1974, Henrietta b 1979); *Career* slr Supreme Ct of Judicature 1965, advocate Royal Ct of Guernsey 1966, in private practice 1966–76; Guernsey: HM Slr-Gen 1977–82, HM Attorney-Gen 1982–92, HM Receiver-Gen 1985–92; QC 1989, dep bailiff of Guernsey 1992–; people's dep States of Guernsey April-Dec 1976, memb Gen Synod C of E 1982–, chm House of Laity Winchester Diocesan Synod 1993–; *Style*— de Vic Graham Carey, Esq; ✉ Les Padins, St Saviours, Guernsey, Channel Islands GY7 9JJ (☎ 01481 64587, fax 01481 63687); The Bailiff's Chambers, Royal Court House, Guernsey, Channel Islands (☎ 01481 726161)

CAREY, George Leonard; *see:* Canterbury, Archbishop of

CAREY, Godfrey Mohun Cecil; QC (1991); s of Dr Godfrey Fraser Carey, MVO (d 1972), of Connaught Sq, London, and Prudence Loveday, *née* Webb (d 1977); *b* 31 Oct 1941; *Educ* Eton; *m* 1, 1965 (m dis 1975), Caroline Jane, *née* Riggall; 2 s (Sebastian Fraser b 1969, d 1971, Hugo b 1972), 1 da (Miranda b 1967); m 2, 1978 (m dis 1985), Dorothy; 1 da (Lucy b 1978); *Career* legal asst Rolls Royce 1966–70; called to the Bar Inner Temple 1969, recorder of the Crown Court 1986–; *Recreations* tennis, jazz, Woodruff, Aztec culture; *Clubs* Lansdowne; *Style*— Godfrey Carey, Esq, QC; ✉ 40 Walton Street, London SW3 1RD (☎ 0171 584 0160); 5 Paper Buildings, Temple, London EC4Y 7HB (☎ 0171 583 6117)

CAREY, Prof John; s of Charles William Carey (d 1965), of Barnes, London, and Winifred Ethel, *née* Cook (d 1967); *b* 5 April 1934; *Educ* Richmond and E Sheen County GS, St John's Coll Oxford (MA, DPhil); *m* 1960, Gillian Mary Florence, da of Reginald Booth (d 1968), of Wilmslow, Cheshire; 2 s (Leo b 1974, Thomas b 1977); *Career* 2 Lt E Surrey Regt 1953–54; Harmsworth sr scholar Merton Coll Oxford 1957–58, lectr ChCh Oxford 1958–59, Andrew Bradley jr res fell Balliol Oxford 1959–60; tutorial fell: Keble Coll Oxford 1960–64, St John's Coll Oxford 1964–75; Merton prof of English literature Univ of Oxford 1975–; princ book reviewer Sunday Times 1977–, author of articles in Modern Language Review, Review of English Studies etc; chm judges Booker Prize 1982; hon fell: St John's Coll Oxford 1991, Balliol Coll Oxford 1992; FRSL, FBA 1996; *Books* The Poems of John Milton (ed with Alastair Fowler, 1968), Milton (1969), The Private Memoirs and Confessions of a Justified Sinner (ed, 1970), The Violent Effigy: a Study of Dickens' Imagination (1973, 2 edn 1991), Thackeray: Prodigal Genius (1977), John Donne: Life, Mind and Art (1981, 2 edn 1990), Original Copy: Selected Reviews and Journalism 1969–1986 (1987), The Faber Book of Reportage (ed, 1987), The Intellectuals and the Masses (1992), The Faber Book of Science (ed, 1995); *Recreations* swimming, gardening, beekeeping; *Style*— Prof John Carey, FBA; ✉ Brasenose Cottage, Lyneham, Oxon; 57 Stapleton Rd, Headington, Oxford (☎ 01865 64304); Merton Coll, Oxford (☎ 01865 276389)

CAREY, Peter John; s of Percival William (d 1974), and Mollie, *née* Griffin; *b* 17 Aug 1946; *Educ* Haverstock Hill Hampstead, Univ of Westminster (Dip in Photography); *m* 1967, Lena Margaret, da of Ernest Sailor; 1 s (Timothy Patrick b 15 Jan 1975), 1 da (Catherine Blossom b 24 July 1972); *Career* freelance photographer 1965–66, sr photographer Summit Studios London 1966–68, estab studio (with Stephen Ward) Carey Ward Ltd Camden London 1968–76 (specialising in advtg photography for maj clients), visiting lectr Univ of Westminster (formerly PCL) 1970–, freelance photographer 1976–, specialist in digital imaging and networking; fndr Photography Summer Sch Swansea 1989–; winner D&AD Poster award Simple as Blinking Kodak; chm RPS Distinctions Panel (Applied), acting chm Admissions and Qualifications Panel (Sector 4) BIPP, memb Educn and Trg Ctee BIPP; ABIPP 1967, FBIPP 1972, FRPS 1984; *Recreations* liaising with industry and students on work experience to facilitate new blood, volunteer advisor on drug abuse help, collecting artefacts and ephemera on writing equipment in preparation for a history of the subject; *Style*— Peter Carey, Esq; ✉ Instantaneous Photographist, 157 Junction Rd, Islington, London N19 5PZ (☎ 0171 272 6516)

CAREY, Peter Philip; s of Percival Stanley Carey (d 1984), and Helen Jean Carey (d 1991); *b* 7 May 1943; *Educ* Geelong GS Australia; *m* 1 (m dis), Leigh Weetman; m 2, 16 March 1985, Alison Margaret, da of Stanley Newnham Summers (d 1987); 2 s (Sam Summers Carey b 1986, Charley Carey Summers b 1990); *Career* writer; teacher Princeton and NY Univs; Hon DLitt Univ of Queensland 1989; FRSL; *Awards* NSW Premier Award for Lit 1979 and 1980, Miles Franklin Award 1980 and 1989, Nat Book Cncl Award 1980 and 1985, Victorian Premier Award 1985, Age Book of the Year Award 1985, Booker Prize 1988; *Books* The Fat Man in History (1979), Bliss (1980), Illywhacker (1985), Oscar and Lucinda (1988), The Tax Inspector (1991), The Unusual Life of Tristan Smith (1994); *Recreations* swimming; *Style*— Peter Carey, Esq

CAREY, Sir Peter Willoughby; GCB (1982, KCB 1976, CB 1972); s of Jack Delves Carey, of Portsmouth, Hants, and Sophie Carey; *b* 26 July 1923; *Educ* Portsmouth GS, Oriel Coll Oxford; *m* 1946, Thelma, da of John Brigham Young, of Portsmouth; 3 da; *Career* dep sec Cabinet Office 1971; DTI: second perm sec 1973–76, perm sec 1976–83; chm Dalgety 1986–92; sr advsr Morgan Grenfell Group plc 1989–96 (chm 1987–89); Hon Doctorate: Birmingham, Cranfield, City Univ; *Clubs* United Oxford and Cambridge Univ; *Style*— Sir Peter Carey, GCB; ✉ 5 Rushmere Place, Marryat Road, Wimbledon, London SW19 5RP (☎ 0181 947 5222)

CAREY-EVANS, David Lloyd; OBE (1983), JP (Portmadoc 1969), DL (Gwynedd 1988); s of Sir Thomas John Carey-Evans MC, FRCS (d 1947), and Lady Olwen Elizabeth, DBE, *née* Lloyd George (d 1990), da of 1 Earl Lloyd George of Dwyfor; *b* 14 Aug 1925; *Educ* Oundle, Univ of Wales Bangor (BSc); *m* 14 Nov 1959, Annwen, da of William Williams, of Craig, Llanerchymedd, Anglesey; 3 s (Thomas Robert b 1961, William Lloyd b 1962, Richard Huw b 1968), 1 da (Davina b 1964); *Career* Sub Lt RNVR 1943–46; farmer 1947–; chm: Welsh Cncl NFU 1978–81, Cncl WAOS 1987–; pres RWAS 1996; *Clubs* Sloane; *Style*— D L Carey-Evans, Esq, OBE, JP, DL; ✉ Eisteddfa, Criccieth, Gwynedd LL52 0PT

CAREY-JONES, Norman Stewart; CMG (1965); s of Samuel Carey-Jones (d 1963), of Swansea, and Jessie Isabella Stewart; *b* 11 Dec 1911; *Educ* Monmouth Sch, Merton Coll Oxford (MA); *m* 1946, Stella (d 1990), da of Maj Claud Myles (d 1961), of Cape Town, SA; 2 s (David, Owen); *Career* Colonial Audit Serv 1934–54, Colonial Admin Serv 1954–65, perm sec Miny of Lands and Settlement Kenya 1962–65, dir in devpt admin Univ of Leeds 1965–77; *Books* The Pattern of a Dependent Economy, The Anatomy of Uhuru, Politics Public Enterprise and the Industrial Development Agency; *Clubs* Royal Cwlth Soc; *Style*— Norman Carey-Jones, Esq, CMG; ✉ Mawingo, Welsh St Donats, nr Cowbridge, S Glamorgan CF7 7SS (☎ 01446 772841)

CARGILL, Kenneth George; s of George Reid Cargill, of Arbroath, Angus, Scotland, and Florence Jean, *née* Mitchell; *b* 17 Feb 1947; *Educ* Arbroath HS, Univ of Edinburgh (MA, LLB); *m* 17 Feb 1988, Una Gallacher; *Career* BBC Scotland: researcher 1972–73, TV reporter Current Account 1973–78, film dir current affrs 1978–79, prodr 1979–84, dep ed TV news and current affrs 1984–88, ed Scotland 2000 1986–87, ed TV news and current affrs 1988–90, head TV news, current affrs and sport 1990–94, head news & current affrs and TV sport 1994–; *Books* Scotland 2000 (ed, 1987); *Recreations* fine cigars, malt whisky and observational gardening (preferably simultaneously), books; *Style*— Kenneth Cargill; ✉ BBC Scotland, Broadcasting House, Queen Margaret Drive, Glasgow G12 8DG (☎ 0141 338 2250, fax 0141 338 2789, e-mail ken.cargill@bbc.co.uk)

CARINE, Rear Adm James; s of Amos Carine (d 1953), of Castletown, IOM, and Kathleen Prudence, *née* Kelly (d 1986); *b* 14 Sept 1934; *Educ* Victoria Rd Sch Castletown IOM, King William's Coll IOM; *m* 26 Aug 1961, (Carolyn) Sally, da of Surgn Capt Wilfred Bertram Taylor (d 1990), of Alverstoke, Hants; 5 s (Andrew b 1963, Patrick b and d 1964, David (twin) b and d 1964, Malcolm b 1965, Gregory b 1984), 1 da (Catriona b 1970); *Career* joined RN 1951, sec Second Sea Lord 1979–82, Capt 1980, SACLANT HQ Norfolk VA 1982–85, Naval Home Cmd 1985–88, Cdre 1988, in cmd HMS Drake 1988–89, Rear Adm 1989, COS to C in C Naval Home Cmd, ret 1991; dir The United Services Trustee 1995–; registrar and general mangr to the Arab Horse Soc; pres Royal Naval Assoc (IOM) 1992–; memb Ctee London Campaign for Multiple Sclerosis 1993–, memb Mgmnt Ctee Ex-Services Mental Welfare Soc 1997–; Freeman City of London 1988, Sr Warden Worshipful Co of Chartered Secs and Admins; FCIS 1971; Kt of the Order of St Gregory the Great (Civil Div) Rome 1983; *Recreations* dinghy sailing, horse racing; *Style*— Rear Adm James Carine; ✉ 1 Chiseldon Court, Chiseldon, Wilts SN4 0NE

CARINGTON, Hon Rupert Francis John; s and h of 6 Baron Carrington; *b* 2 Dec 1948; *Educ* Eton, Univ of Bristol; *m* 12 Sept 1989, Daniela, da of Flavio Diotallevi; 1 s (Robert b 7 Dec 1990), 2 da (Francesca b 24 July 1993, Isabella Iona b 19 May 1995); *Career* dir: Morgan Grenfell International 1983–87, Hartwell plc 1990–, The Fleming Smaller Companies Investment Trust plc 1990–, The Flemings Natural Resources Investment Trust PLC 1994–; chm: Korea Asia Fund Limited 1990–, Schroder Asia Pacific Fund plc 1995–, Schroder Emerging Countries Fund plc 1996–; *Clubs* White's; *Style*— The Hon Rupert Carington; ✉ 16 Mallord St, London SW3 6DU (☎ 0171 376 5626)

CARLESS, Hugh Michael; CMG (1976); s of Henry Alfred Carless, CIE (d 1975), and Gwendolen Mary, *née* Pattullo (d 1989); *b* 22 April 1925; *Educ* Sherborne, SOAS, Trinity Hall Cambridge; *m* 1957, Rosa Maria, da of Martino Frontini, of São Paulo; 2 s; *Career* Dip Serv 1950–85; served: Kabul, Rio de Janeiro, Tehran, Budapest, Luanda, Bonn; head of Latin America Dept FCO 1973–77, chargé d'affaires Buenos Aires 1977–80, seconded to Northern Engineering Industries International 1980–82, ambass to Caracas 1982–85; currently int conslt; exec vice pres Hinduja Fndn 1987–, dep chm S Atlantic Cncl 1987–, a vice pres Cncl Royal Soc of Asian Affairs 1992–95, tstee Cwlth Health Tst 1994–, chm Br Ctee for Argentine Br Confs 1994–; *Recreations* golf; *Clubs* Travellers', Royal Mid Surrey; *Style*— Hugh Carless, Esq, CMG; ✉ 15 Bryanston Square, London W1H 7FF

CARLETON-SMITH, Maj-Gen Michael Edward; CBE (1979, MBE 1966), DL (Leics 1992); s of Lt-Col Dudley Lancelot Guy Carleton-Smith (d 1984), and Barbara Leticia Camilla, *née* Popham (d 1980); *b* 5 May 1931; *Educ* Radley, RMA Sandhurst (psc, jssc, ndc, rcds); *m* 1963, (Helga) Katja (d 1993), da of Josef Stoss (d 1973); 3 s (Mark, Andreas, Sebastian); *Career* cmmnd Rifle Bde 1951; Cdr Gurkha Field Force Hong Kong 1977–79, dep dir staff duties MOD 1981–82, Maj-Gen def advsr and mil advsr Canberra Aust and mil advsr Wellington NZ 1982–85; DG Marie Curie Cancer Care 1985–96; *Recreations* riding, gardening; *Style*— Maj-Gen Michael Carleton-Smith, CBE, DL; ✉ Plough Cottage, Drayton, Market Harborough, Leics LE1 8SD

CARLIER, Maj-Gen (Anthony) Neil; CB (1992), OBE (1982); s of Geoffrey Anthony George Carlier (d 1966), and Sylvia Maude, *née* Emerson; *b* 11 Jan 1937; *Educ* Highgate Sch, RMA Sandhurst, RMCS (BSc), RCDS; *m* 18 May 1974, Daphne Kathleen, da of Capt Langley Humphreys, of Church View, Coombe Cross, Bovey Tracey, S Devon; 1 s (Christopher b 18 May 1975), 1 da (Donna b 27 June 1980); *Career* cmmnd RE 1957, RMCS 1958–61, Troop Cdr RE 1961–63, GS03 1964–65, instr RMA Sandhurst 1966–69, RNC and Army Staff Coll Shrivenham 1970–71, GS02 RN 1972–73, Sqdn Cdr 50 Field Sqdn 1974–75, 2 i/c 2 Armd Div Engr Regt 1976–77, CO 39 Engr Regt 1978–79, MA to Army Bd Memb (MGO) 1980–82, Col ASD 2 MOD 1982–83, Cdr 11 Engr Gp 1984–85, RCDS 1986, Cdr Br Forces Falkland Islands 1987–88, Chief Jt Servs Liaison Orgn Bonn 1989–90, head Logistic Support Review 1991, ret Army 1992; dir Douglas Haig Meml Homes 1992–; pres: Officers' Christian Union, Mission to Mil Garrisons; capt Army Team Round the World Yacht Race 1977–78, Flag Offr Army Sailing Assoc 1978–87, Cdre Royal Engrs Yacht Club 1984–87; tstee: Cornelius Tst, Royal Engrs' Yacht Club; MIRE 1958; *Recreations* offshore sailing, fly-fishing, DIY, gardening; *Clubs* Int Soc of Cape Horners, RHS; *Style*— Maj-Gen Neil Carlier, CB, OBE; ✉ Ewshot, Farnham, Surrey

CARLILE, Alexander Charles (Alex); QC, MP (Lib Dem) Montgomery (majority 5,209); s of Erwin Falik, MD, and Sabina Falik; *b* 12 Feb 1948; *Educ* Epsom Coll Surrey, King's Coll London (LLB, AKC), Inns of Court Sch of Law; *m* 1968, Frances, da of Michael Soley; 3 da; *Career* Parly candidate (Lib) Flintshire E Feb 1974 and 1979, chm Welsh Lib Pty 1980–82, MP (Lib then Lib Dem) Montgomery 1983–, ldr Welsh Lib Dems and spokesman on Welsh Affrs, Justice and Home Affairs; a recorder of the Crown Court, hon recorder of the City of Hereford, bencher Gray's Inn, lay memb GMC, fell and tstee Indust and Parliament Tst; *Style*— Alex Carlile, Esq, QC, MP; ✉ House of Commons, London SW1A 0AA

CARLILL, Rear Adm John Hildred; OBE (1969), DL (Surrey); s of Dr Hildred Bertram Carlill (d 1942), and Mildred Constance, *née* Godfrey (d 1984); *b* 24 Oct 1925; *Educ* RNC Dartmouth; *m* 1955, (Elizabeth) Ann, da of Lt-Col Willis Southern (d 1968), of Guildford, Surrey; 3 da (Jennifer, Gale, Joanne); *Career* RN 1939–82; serv WWII: HMS Mauritius 1943–45, Med, Normandy, N Atlantic, Arctic; psc 1961, jssc 1967, Capt 1972, sec to Flag Offr Naval Air Cmd, dir Naval Manning and Trg (S) MOD, sec to Second Sea Lord MOD, pres Admty Interview Bd, Cdre HMS Drake, Rear Adm 1980, Adm Pres RN Coll Greenwich; sec The Engrg Cncl 1983–87, chm Guildford Sea Cadet Ctee 1987–95; currently: pres Guildford Branch RN Assoc, chm ABTA Appeal Bd; *Recreations* walking, DIY, gardening, water colour painting; *Style*— Rear Adm John Carlill, OBE, DL; ✉ Crownpits Barn, Crownpits Lane, Godalming, Surrey GU7 1NY (☎ 01483 415022)

CARLINE, Gordon David; s of David Smith Carline (d 1961), and Helen Louise, *née* Carpenter (d 1941); *b* 25 June 1933; *Educ* BEC GS, Westminster Tech Coll London; *m* 14 Aug 1954, Doreen Margaret, da of Albert Edward Brown (d 1941); 1 s (David Stuart b 1961), 1 da (Denise Elizabeth b 1959); *Career* trainee draughtsman Laidlaw Smith 1949–51, draughtsman/designer Johnson Ireton 1951–54, draughtsman/designer Moore and Tucker 1954–55, engr John F Farquharson and Ptnrs 1955–61; Andrews Kent and Stone: engr 1961–65, assoc 1965–72, ptnr 1972–93, dir (following incorporation as ltd co) 1993–; FIStructE 1959, FICE 1966, FCIOB 1979, FASI 1963 (pres 1986–87), FRSA 1987, FIHEEM 1972; *Recreations* reading; *Clubs* Clarendon (Oxford); *Style*— Gordon Carline, Esq; ✉ Chaumont, 55 Clifden Rd, Worminghall, nr Aylesbury, Bucks HP18 9JR (☎ 01844 339209); Andrews Kent & Stone Ltd, Seacourt Tower, West Way, Botley, Oxford OX2 0JJ (☎ 01865 240071, fax 01865 248 006, car 0860 531586)

CARLING, William David Charles (Will); OBE (1992); yr s of Lt-Col W D J Carling; *b* 12 Dec 1965; *Educ* Sedbergh, Univ of Durham; *m* 18 June 1994 (m dis 1996), Julia C E, only da of H B Smith; *Career* rugby union centre three quarter; clubs: formerly Durham Univ RFC, currently Harlequins FC; England: debut v France 1988, capt 1988–96 (resigned after Five Nations' Championship), tour Aust and Fiji (3 test appearances) 1988–89, tour Argentina 1990 and Aust 1991, Grand Slam winners 1991, 1992 and 1995, runners-up World Cup 1991, tour to S Africa 1994, 4th place World Cup S Africa 1995, 65 caps (58 as capt); most capped English capt of all time, world record holder for victories as capt (43 in 58 matches); memb British Lions' team touring NZ 1993; Player of the Year Whitbread/Rugby World Awards 1992; proprietor Insights Ltd (mgmnt trg co); *Books* Captain's Diary 1989–91 (1991), The Way to Win (1995); *Recreations* painting, sketching; *Clubs* Groucho; *Style*— Will Carling, Esq, OBE; ✉ Harlequin FC, Stoop Memorial Ground, Craneford Way, Twickenham, Middlesex (☎ 0181 892 0822)

CARLISLE, Anthony Edwin Charles Glen; s of George Geddes Glen Carlisle (d 1980), and Dorothy Louise, *née* Pickering; *b* 10 March 1947; *Educ* Charterhouse, Univ of Sussex (BA); *m* Nancy Susan, *née* Hayward; *Career* Lintas Advertising 1968–70; Dewe Rogerson Ltd: joined 1970, chief exec and dep chm 1986–95, exec chm 1995–; Freeman City of London, Liveryman Worshipful Co of Glovers; MIPA, memb PRCA; *Recreations* travel, books, music, wine; *Style*— Anthony Carlisle, Esq; ✉ Dewe Rogerson Ltd, 3 1/2 London Wall Building, London Wall, London EC2M 5SY (☎ 0171 638 9571)

CARLISLE, Archdeacon of; *see:* Turnbull, Ven David Charles

CARLISLE, Esmé, Countess of; Esmé Mary Shrubb Howard; da of Charles Edward Iredell; *b* 7 Feb 1914; *Educ* St Paul's Girls Sch, Univ of London; *m* 1947, as his 2 w, 11 Earl of Carlisle (d 1963); 1 da (Lady Susan Ankaret de Meyer); *Career* special duties Civil Service (London, Aden, Athens, Cairo, Algiers and Rome) 1936–44, Western Dept Foreign Office 1944–46, conslt and sec to Working Parties Museums and Galleries Cmmn 1971–86 (actg sec to Cmmn Feb-July 1976); *Style*— The Rt Hon Esmé, Countess of Carlisle; ✉ Duns Tew Manor, Oxfordshire OX6 4JP (☎ 01869 340721)

CARLISLE, 13 Earl of (E 1661); George William Beaumont Howard; Master of Ruthven; also Viscount Howard of Morpeth, Baron Dacre of Gillesland (both E 1661) and 13 Lord Ruthven of Freeland (S 1651); s of 12 Earl of Carlisle, MC, DL (d 1994), and Hon Ela Hilda Aline Beaumont, da of 2 Viscount Allendale, KG, CB, CBE, MC; *b* 15 Feb 1949; *Educ* Eton, Balliol Coll Oxford (MA); *Heir* bro, Hon Philip Charles Wentworth Howard b 1963; *Career* joined 9/12 Royal Lancers 1967, Lt 1970, Capt 1974, Maj (Prince of Wales, Royal Armoured Corps) 1981–87, Parly candidate (Lib) Easington Co Durham 1987; *Clubs* Beefsteak; *Style*— The Rt Hon the Earl of Carlisle; ✉ Naworth Castle, Brampton, Cumbria (☎ 06977 2621)

CARLISLE, Hugh Bernard Harwood; QC (1978); s of William Harwood Carlisle (d 1979), and Joyce Carlisle; *b* 14 March 1937; *Educ* Oundle, Downing Coll Cambridge (MA); *m* 1964, Veronica Marjorie, da of George Arthur Worth, MBE, DL, of Manton, Rutland; 1 s, 1 da; *Career* Nat Serv 2 Lt RA; called to the Bar Middle Temple 1961, head of chambers, jr treasy counsel (personal injuries cases) 1975–78, inspr Dept of Trade Inquiry into Bryanston Finance Ltd 1978–87, memb Criminal Injuries Bd 1982–, recorder of the Crown Court 1983–, inspr Dept of Trade Inquiry into Milbury plc 1985–87; *Recreations* fishing, croquet; *Clubs* Garrick, Hurlingham (chm 1982–85); *Style*— Hugh Carlisle Esq, QC; ✉ 1 Temple Gardens, London EC4Y 9BB (☎ 0171 583 1315)

CARLISLE, John Russell; MP (C) Luton North (majority 13,095); s of Andrew Russell Carlisle (d 1967), and Edith Carlisle (d 1964); *b* 28 Aug 1942; *Educ* Bedford Sch, St Lawrence Coll Ramsgate, Univ of London; *m* 1964, Anthea Jane Lindsay, da of Cedric May (d 1995); 2 da; *Career* MP (C): Luton W 1979–83, Luton N 1983–; memb Select Ctee on Agric 1986–88; former vice chm Parly All Party Football Ctee, chm Cons Back Bench Sports Ctee 1981–94, former treas Br Gibraltar Gp, former chm Br South Africa Gp; non-exec dir BMG Charles Sidney plc; pres: Luton 100 Club, Luton Band, Beds CCC; memb: London Corn Exchange 1970–94, Baltic Exchange 1991–; *Recreations* watching sport, shooting; *Clubs* Farmers', Rugby, MCC, XL; *Style*— John Carlisle, Esq, MP; ✉ House of Commons, London SW1A 0AA (☎ 0171 219 4571, fax 0171 219 5961)

CARLISLE, Sir Kenneth Melville; kt (1994), MP (C) Lincoln (majority 2,049); s of Maj Kenneth Ralph Malcolm (Peter) Carlisle, TD (d 1983), and Hon Elizabeth Mary McLaren (d 1991), er da of 2 Baron Aberconway, CBE; *b* 25 March 1941; *Educ* Harrow, Magdalen Coll Oxford; *m* July 1986, Carla, da of A W Heffner, of Maryland USA; 1 s (Sam Fenimore Cooper b 28 Jan 1989); *Career* called to the Bar 1965; with Brooke Bond Liebig 1966–74, farmer; MP (C) Lincoln 1979–, an asst Govt whip 1987–88, a Lord Cmmr of the Treasy (Govt whip) 1988–90; Parly under sec: Miny of Defence 1990–92, Miny of Transport 1992–93; memb Public Accounts Ctee 1995; memb Lloyd's; *Style*— Sir Kenneth Carlisle, MP; ✉ House of Commons, London SW1A 0AA

CARLISLE, Sir (John) Michael; kt (1985), DL (S Yorkshire 1996); s of John Hugh Carlisle (d 1958), and Lilian Amy, *née* Smith (d 1990); *b* 16 Dec 1929; *Educ* King Edward VII Sch Sheffield, Univ of Sheffield (BEng); *m* 1957, Mary Scott, da of Robert Magnus Young (d 1972); 1 s (Andrew b 1962), 1 da (Janet b 1960); *Career* non-exec dir: Fenchurch (Midlands) 1985–94, Norhomes plc 1989–, Welpac plc 1991–95, York Science Park Ltd 1992–, York Science Park (Innovation Centre) Ltd 1994–; chm: Residences at York plc 1992–, Headrow Northern plc 1992–, Headrow Western plc 1993–; former dir: Diesel Marine International (and gp subsid cos in Norway, Holland, Greece, Singapore and Hong Kong), Eric Woodward (Electrical) Ltd, Lockwood and Carlisle Ltd, Torday and Carlisle plc; chm: Sheffield Productivity Assoc 1970, N Sheffield Univ Hosp Mgmnt Ctee 1971–74 (memb 1969–71), Sheffield Area Health Authy (teaching) 1974–82, Sheffield Health Authy 1982, Trent RHA 1982–94, Community Health Sheffield NHS Trust 1994–, NHS Policy Bd 1993–94; memb: Cncl Sheffield C of C 1967–79 (pres Sheffield Jr C of C 1967–68), Cncl Prodn Engrg Res Assoc 1968–73, Bd of Govrs Utd Sheffield Hosps 1972–74, Sheffield Univ Careers Advsy Bd 1973–82, Cncl Med Res Cncl 1991–95; memb Ct: Univ of Sheffield, Univ of Nottingham 1982–94, Univ of York 1990– (also memb Cncl) govr: Sheffield City Poly 1979–82 (hon fell 1977), Sheffield HS 1980–87; Hon LLD: Univ of Sheffield 1988, Univ of Nottingham 1992; Freeman Co of Cutlers of Hallamshire, Freeman City of London 1989; FRSA, FIMechE, FIMarE, CIMgt; *Recreations* golf, walking in N Yorkshire, watercolour painting; *Clubs* Royal Society of Medicine, Sickleholme Golf, Kirbymoorside Golf; *Style*— Sir Michael Carlisle, DL; ✉ 7 Rushley Ave, Dore, Sheffield S17 3EP (☎ and fax 0114 236 5988); St Ovins, Lastingham, N Yorks YO6 6TL (☎ 01751 417341)

CARLISLE OF BUCKLOW, Baron (Life Peer UK 1987), of Mobberley, Co Cheshire; Mark Carlisle; PC (1979), QC (1971), DL (Cheshire 1983); 2 s of late Philip Edmund Carlisle, of Alderley Edge, Cheshire, and Mary Carlisle; *b* 7 July 1929; *Educ*

Radley, Univ of Manchester (LLB); *m* 1959, Sandra Joyce, da of John Hamilton Des Voeux (d 1963), of St Ives, Cornwall; 1 da (Hon (Vanessa) Lucy (Hon Mrs von Schoenberg)); *Career* called to the Bar Gray's Inn 1954, bencher 1980; recorder of the Crown Court 1976–79 and 1981–; Parly under sec of state Home Office 1970–72, min of state Home Office 1972–74, sec of state for educn and science 1979–81; chm Criminal Injuries Compensation Bd 1989–, chm Review Ctee on the Parole System in England and Wales 1988; a judge of the Courts of Appeal Jersey and Guernsey 1990–; *Recreations* golf; *Clubs* Garrick, St James's (Manchester); *Style*— The Rt Hon Lord Carlisle of Bucklow, PC, QC, DL; ✉ Queen Elizabeth Building, Temple, London EC4 (☎ 0171 583 5766); 3 Holt Gardens, Mobberley, Cheshire (☎ 0156 587 2275)

CARLOW, Viscount; Charles George Yuill Seymour Dawson-Damer; eldest s and h of 7 Earl of Portarlington; *b* 6 Oct 1965; *Educ* Eton, Univ of Edinburgh (MA); *Career* page of honour to HM The Queen 1979–81; *Style*— Viscount Carlow; ✉ c/o Yuills Ltd, Bride House, 18–20 Bride Lane, London EC4Y 8DX; c/o John Swire & Sons Ltd, GPO Box 1, Hong Kong

CARLOWE, Melvyn Ian; s of Harold Carlowe (d 1975), and Ann, *née* Brenner; *b* 13 April 1941; *Educ* Hackney Downs GS, Univ of Birmingham (BSoc Sci); *m* 15 Dec 1963, Jacqueline, da of Jacob Pressman; 2 da (Michaela Sally b 1965, Joanna Laura b 1968); *Career* schoolteacher Hockley Birmingham 1963–64; Jewish Welfare Bd: social worker 1964–67, chief social worker 1967–71, exec dir 1971–89; chief exec Jewish Care 1990–; hon sec Central Cncl for Jewish Social Servs 1972–; *Recreations* swimming, travel; *Style*— Melvyn Carlowe, Esq; ✉ Chief Executive, Jewish Care, Stuart Young House, 221 Golders Green Road, London NW11 9DQ (☎ 0181 458 3282, fax 0181 455 7185)

CARLTON, Vivienne Margaret; da of John Carlton, and Phyllis Florence Kaye, *née* Minchin; *b* 28 Sept 1947; *Educ* Herts & Essex HS Bishop's Stortford, Trent Park Coll, Univ of London; *m* 1985, Julian Charles Bray, *qv*; 1 s (William Charles b 18 Aug 1989); *Career* account dir: Biss Lancaster plc 1980–82, Opus PR Ltd 1982–84; dir: Osca plc 1985–86, Leadenhall Associates Ltd 1986–91, NTN Television News Ltd 1988–, Alpha Strategy Management Ltd 1991–94, sr conslt Chelgate Ltd 1994–; MIPR, MInstD, MIMgt; *Recreations* theatre, interior design; *Style*— Ms Vivienne Carlton

CARLTON-PORTER, Robert William; s of Francis William Porter, of Derbyshire, and Cyrilla, *née* Carlton; *b* 29 Nov 1944; *Educ* St Helens Derby; *m* 9 Oct 1987, Angela, da of William Jenkins, of Ledbury, Herefordshire; 1 s (Alexander William b 8 Aug 1988); *Career* fin dir Hoechst UK Ltd 1973–83, fin dir English China Clays plc 1983–92, chm Queensbury International Ltd and subsid; non-exec dir: Newport Holdings plc (chm), EBC Group plc (chm); tstee Treasure Tag Fndn; former chm Assoc of Corp Treasurers, former memb Stock Exchange Pre-emption Ctee; ACIB 1968, MCInstM 1973, FIMgt 1976, FCT 1979 (fndn fell); *Recreations* antiques, philately, gardening, charity work; *Style*— Robert Carlton-Porter, Esq; ✉ Church Farm, Church Road, Bitton, South Gloucestershire BS15 6LJ (☎ 0117 932 9939)

CARLUCCIO, Antonio Mario Gaetano; s of Giovanni Carluccio (d 1978), and Maria, *née* Trivellone (d 1992); *b* 19 April 1937, Vietri Sul Mare, Italy; *Educ* Roland Matura Schule Vienna; *m* 22 Dec 1981, Priscilla Marion, da of Gerard Rupert Conran; *Career* former corr Gazzetta del Popolo and La Stampa Turin, resident in Germany 1963–75, wine merchant England 1975–81; restaurateur Neal Street Restaurant 1981– (proprietor 1989–), jt proprietor (with wife) Carluccio's food retailers 1992–; numerous TV appearances incl: regular contribs to Food and Drink (BBC 2) 1986– (on Italy, Turkey, Egypt, Morocco, Spain, Czechoslovakia, and Hungary), Hot Chefs (BBC 2) 1991, Antonio Carluccio's Italian Feasts (six part series, BBC 2) 1996; author of numerous articles on food for The Times and other pubns; memb Guild of Food Writers; *Books* An Invitation to Italian Cooking (1986, Bejam Best Cook Book of the Year UK), A Passion for Mushrooms (1989), A Passion for Pasta (1993), Antonio Carluccio's Italian Feasts (book of TV series, 1996); *Style*— Antonio Carluccio, Esq; ✉ The Neal Street Restaurant, 26 Neal Street, London WC2H 9PS (☎ 0171 836 8368); Carluccio's Italian Food Shop, 28a Neal Street, London WC2H 9PS (☎ 0171 240 1487, fax 0171 497 1361)

CARLYLE, Nigel Stewart; s of Thomas Edward Carlyle (d 1982), of Scothern, Lincoln, and Gertrude Ellen, *née* Strutt; *b* 14 July 1938; *Educ* Queen Elizabeth Boys' GS Mansfield, Univ of Leeds (LLB); *m* 22 Sept 1962, Susan Margaret, da of Capt John Hugh Storey (d 1975), of Harrogate; 2 s (Nicholas Stuart b 1963, Jonathan Stuart b 1967), 2 da (Helen Margaret b 1965, Kathryn Margaret b 1970); *Career* slr; John Barran Ltd 1968–69, mangr of fin analysis Rolls Royce Motors Ltd 1971–73, sr ptnr Hodgson Carlyle and Co Slrs 1979–89, ptnr Epton & Co Slrs 1990–; memb Cncl Lincolnshire Law Soc 1985–89, chm Lincoln Ramblers Assoc, memb Scothern CC, chm Lincoln Branch Gideons Int 1987–90; FCA; *Recreations* rambling, badminton, classical music; *Style*— Nigel S Carlyle, Esq; ✉ Churchside House, Scothern, Lincoln LN2 2UA (☎ 01673 862412); Epton & Co, Slrs, 2 Bank St, Lincoln LN2 1DR

CARMAN, George Alfred; QC (1971); o s of Alfred George Carman, of Blackpool, and late Evelyn Carman; *b* 6 Oct 1929; *Educ* St Joseph's Coll Blackpool, Balliol Coll Oxford (BA); *m* 1, 1960 (m dis 1976), Cecilia Sparrow; 1 s; m 2, 1976 (m dis 1984), Frances Elizabeth (now Frances Atkins, *qv*), da of Thomas Venning, MBE, of Ilkley, N Yorks; *Career* acting Capt RAEC 1948–49; called to the Bar Lincoln's Inn 1953, recorder of the Crown Court 1972–, bencher Lincoln's Inn 1978, head of chambers; *Clubs* Garrick; *Style*— George Carman, Esq, QC; ✉ chambers: New Court Chambers, 5 Verulam Buildings, Gray's Inn, London WC1R 5LY (☎ 0171 831 9500, fax 0171 269 5700)

CARMICHAEL, *see:* Gibson-Craig-Carmichael

CARMICHAEL, Andrew James; s of James Horsfall Elliott Carmichael, MD, FRCR, DMRD, of Liverpool, and Maureen Catherine Carmichael, JP, *née* McGowan; *b* 8 Aug 1957; *Educ* St Edward's Coll Liverpool, Downing Coll Cambridge (MA); *Career* Linklaters & Paines: articled clerk 1979–81, slr 1981, ptnr 1987–; special min of St Thomas More Catholic Church; *Recreations* art, theatre; *Style*— Andrew Carmichael, Esq; ✉ Flat 29A, Tower 2, Clovelly Court, 12 May Road, Hong Kong (☎ 00 852 2842 4875); Linklaters & Paines, Barrington House, 59–67 Gresham St, London EC2V 7JA; Linklaters & Paines, 14th Floor, Alexandra House, Chater Road, Central Hong Kong

CARMICHAEL, Ian Gillett; s of Arthur Denholm Carmichael (d 1958), of North Ferriby, N Humberside, and Kate, *née* Gillett (d 1962); *b* 18 June 1920; *Educ* Scarborough Coll, Bromsgrove Sch, RADA; *m* 1, 6 Oct 1943, Jean Pyman (d 1983), da of Donald Pyman MacLean (d 1970), of Sleights, N Yorks; 2 da (Carol Lee (Mrs West) b 2 April 1946, Sally Maclean (Mrs Hennen) b 9 Sept 1949); m 2, 9 July 1992, Kathryn Ann, da of Ray Fenton (d 1985), of Marple, Cheshire; *Career* theatre, film, television and radio actor; WWII served 22 Dragoons, Maj NW Europe (despatches); most recently Sir Peter Teazle in The School for Scandal (Chichester Festival Theatre) 1995; TV performances incl: The World of Wooster, Lord Peter Wimsey, Strathblair; Hon DLitt Univ of Hull 1987; *Books* Will the Real Ian Carmichael...(autobiography, 1979); *Recreations* gardening, walking, reading; *Clubs* MCC; *Style*— Ian Carmichael, Esq; ✉ c/o London Management, 2–4 Noel Street, London W1V 3RB (☎ 0171 287 9000, fax 0171 287 3036)

CARMICHAEL, Keith Stanley; CBE (1981); s of Stanley Carmichael (d 1949), of Bristol, and Ruby Dorothy, *née* Fox (d 1980); *b* 5 Oct 1929; *Educ* Charlton House Sch, Bristol GS; *m* 1958, Cynthia Mary, da of John David Robert Jones (d 1971); 1 s (Richard John Carmichael b 1968); *Career* qualified CA 1951, ptnr Wilson Bigg and Co 1957–69; dir: H Foulks Lynch & Co Ltd 1957–69, Radio Rentals Ltd 1967–69; sole practitioner 1968–81 and 1990–, managing partner Longcrofts 1981–90; memb Monopolies and Mergers Cmmn 1983–92, Lloyd's underwriter 1979–90; pres Hertsmere Cons Assoc; chm Bd of Govrs and Tstees of Rickmansworth Masonic Sch; memb Editorial Bd Simons Taxes 1970–82; memb Ct of Assts Worshipful Co of Chartered Accountants until 1996; FCA, FInstD, FTII, TEP; *Books* Spicer and Peglers Income Tax (1965), Ranking Spicer and Peglers Executorship Law and Accounts (ed, 1965–87), Corporation Tax (1966), Capital Gains Tax (1966), Taxation of Lloyd's Underwriters (with P Wolstenholme, 1988), Strategic Tax Planning (contrib, 1991); *Recreations* gardening, reading, golf; *Clubs* Carlton, MCC, Lord's Taverners'; *Style*— Keith Carmichael, Esq, CBE; ✉ 117 Newberries Ave, Radlett, Herts WD7 7EN (☎ 01923 855098, fax 01923 855654); Flat 1, Princess Court, Bryanston Place, London W1H 7FP (☎ and fax 0171 258 1577)

CARMICHAEL, Dr Peter; CBE (1981); s of Robert Carmichael (d 1986), of Perthshire, and Elizabeth Paterson (d 1987); *b* 26 March 1933; *Educ* Univ of Glasgow (BSc); *m* 1 (m dis); 2 s (Colin David b 1957, Angus Robert b 1961), 4 da (Sheena Elizabeth b 1956, Fiona Helen b 1959, Morag Isobel b 1964, Heather Jane b 1967); m 2, 1980, June, da of Ronald D Philip, of Perthshire; *Career* design engr Ferranti Ltd 1958–65; Hewlett-Packard: project ldr 1965–68 (i/c instrument design which won Queen's Award to Indust 1967), prodn engrg mangr 1968–69, quality assur mangr 1969–72, R&D mangr 1972–74, mfrg mangr 1974–75, gen mangr 1975–78, jt md 1978–81; dir of small business and electronics Scottish Devpt Agency 1981–87, exec dir for E of Scotland Scottish Devpt Agency 1987–89; non-exec chm: Hillhouse Holdings 1989–92, Strathclyde Fabricators 1989–93; chm: Wolfson Microelectronics 1990–93, Esmée Fairbairn Res Centre Heriot-Watt Univ 1990–95; specialist in antique clocks and barometers 1989–; Hon DSc Heriot-Watt Univ 1984; *Recreations* music, gardening, antique clock restoration; *Style*— Dr Peter Carmichael, CBE; ✉ 86 Craiglea Drive, Edinburgh EH10 5PH (☎ 0131 447 6334); Marchbank Cottage, Ballantrae, South Ayrshire (☎ 01465 831355)

CARMICHAEL OF KELVINGROVE, Baron (Life Peer UK 1983), of Camlachie in the Dist of the City of Glasgow; Neil George Carmichael; s of James Carmichael (d 1966, former MP Glasgow Bridgeton); *b* 1921; *Educ* Eastbank Acad Glasgow, Royal Coll of Science and Technology Glasgow; *m* 1948, Catherine McIntosh, da of John Dawson Rankin, of Glasgow; 1 da (Hon Sheena M Carmichael); *Career* memb Glasgow Corp 1962; MP (Lab): Glasgow Woodside 1962–74, Glasgow Kelvingrove 1974–83; PPS to Min of Technol 1966–67; Parly sec to Min of Technol and Power 1969–70; Parly under-sec of state: Miny of Tport 1967–69, DOE 1974–75, DOI 1975–76; memb Select Ctee on Tport 1980–83; *Style*— The Rt Hon the Lord Carmichael of Kelvingrove; ✉ 53 Partick Hill Rd, Glasgow G11 5AB (☎ 0141 334 1718); House of Lords, London SW1A 0PW

CARNAC, *see:* Rivett-Carnac

CARNARVON, 7 Earl of (GB 1793); Henry George Reginald Molyneux Herbert; KCVO (1982), KBE (1976), DL (Hants 1965); also Baron Porchester (GB 1780); o s of 6 Earl (d 1987) and his 1 w Anne Catherine Tredick, *née* Wendell; *b* 19 Jan 1924; *Educ* Eton, RAC Cirencester (DipAg); *m* 7 Jan 1956, Jean Margaret, er da of Hon Oliver Malcolm Wallop (s of 8 Earl of Portsmouth); 2 s (Lord Porchester, Hon Henry Malcolm b 1959), 1 da (Lady Carolyn Penelope b 1962); *Heir* s, Lord Porchester, *qv*; *Career* late Lt Royal Horse Gds, Hon Col 115 (Hants Fortress) Engineer Regt (TA) 1963–67; appointed racing mangr to HM The Queen 1969; pres Thoroughbred Breeders' Assoc 1969–74 and 1986–91 (chm 1964–66), chm Agric Res Cncl 1978–82, vice pres Game Res Assoc 1967 (chm and fndr memb 1960–67), memb and vice pres Game Conservancy 1967–, chm Stallion Advsy Ctee to Betting Levy Bd 1974–86, pres Royal Agric Soc 1980–81; Hants CC: cncllr 1954, Alderman 1965–74, vice chm 1971–74, chm 1973–77; vice chm Assoc of CCs 1972–74; chm House of Lords All-Pty London Gp 1993–; chm: Sports Cncl Planning Ctee 1965–70, S E Econ Planning Cncl 1971–79, Standing Conf on Countryside Sports 1978–, Basingstoke and N Hants Med Tst 1981–, Newbury Racecourse plc 1985–, Equine Virology Res Fndn 1986–, Standing Conf on London and SE Regnl Planning Authorities 1989–; pres: Amateur Riders' Assoc 1970–76, Hants Assoc for the Care of the Blind 1975–, Basingstoke Sports Tst 1983–86 (chm 1970–82), Hants and IOW Naturalist Tst 1987–94; memb: Nature Conservancy Cncl 1953–66, Forestry Cmmn 1967–70, Jockey Club 1964– (chm Race Planning Ctee 1967–84); Verderer of the New Forest 1961–65, High Steward of Winchester 1977–; hon fell Portsmouth Poly 1976; Hon DSc Univ of Reading 1980; *Clubs* White's, Portland, Hampshire CCC (pres 1966–68), S Wales Hunts Cricket (hon memb 1994); *Style*— The Rt Hon the Earl of Carnarvon, KCVO, KBE, DL; ✉ Milford Lake House, Burghclere, Newbury, Berks RG20 9EL (☎ 01635 253387, fax 01635 253984)

CARNE, Dr Christopher Alan; s of Colin Ewing Carne, of London, and Philippa, *née* Trouton; *b* 31 Oct 1953; *Educ* Bryanston, Middx Hosp Med Sch (MB BS), Univ of London (MD, FRCP), Univ of Cambridge (MA); *m* 1992, Julia Warnes; 1 s (Daniel b 1993); *Career* lectr genito-urinary med Middx Hosp Medical Sch 1984–87, conslt genito-urinary med Addenbrooke's Hosp Cambridge 1987–, assoc lectr Faculty Clinical Med Cambridge 1988–; asst ed Genito-Urinary Medicine; sec British Clinical Cooperative Gp 1993–; memb: STD Advsy Gp HEA 1990–92, Working Pty on HIV/AIDS Funding Dept of Health 1991, HIV and AIDS Clinical Trials Working Pty MRC 1991–, memb Cncl MSSVD 1992–, Working Pty on Koerner Coding in Genitourinary Med Dept of Health 1994, Steering Gp UK Register of HIV Seroconverters 1994–; memb BMA 1978, MSSVD 1983; *Books* Aids (1987, 3 edn 1989); *Recreations* tennis, cycling; *Style*— Dr Christopher Carne; ✉ Genitomedical Clinic, Addenbrooke's Hospital, Hills Road, Cambridge CB2 2QQ (☎ 01223 217774)

CARNE, Dr Stuart John; CBE (1986, OBE 1977); s of late Bernard Carne, and Millicent, *née* Chaikin; *b* 19 June 1926; *Educ* Willesden County GS, Middx Hosp Med Sch (MB BS, MRCS, LRCP, DCH); *m* 16 Dec 1951, Yolande Judith, da of Michael Cooper; 2 s (Simon b 1956, Charles b 1962), 2 da (Victoria b 1954, Emma b 1964); *Career* RAF Flt Lt Med Branch 1952–54, civil conslt in gen practice to RAF 1974–91 (hon civil conslt 1991–); house surgn Middlesex Hosp 1950–51; Queen Elizabeth Hosp for Children 1951–52: house physician, house surgeon, casualty offr; in gen practice London 1954–, sr ptnr Grove Health Centre 1967–91, sr tutor in gen practice Royal Postgrad Med Sch 1970–91, conslt in primary care NE Thames RHA 1992–93; DHSS: memb Central Health Servs Cncl 1976–79, memb Personal Social Servs Cncl 1976–80, memb Children's Ctee 1978–81, chm Standing Med Advsy Ctee 1982–86 (memb 1974–86), chm Jt Ctee on Contraception 1983–86 (memb 1975–86); RCGP: memb 1958, memb Cncl 1961–91, hon treas 1964–81, fell 1970, pres 1988–91; pres World Orgn of Nat Colls and Acads of Gen Practice and Family Med 1976–78 (memb Cncl 1970–80), memb Exec Cncl Br Diabetic Assoc 1981–87, pres Inst of Med Illustration 1990–91; hon med offr Queen's Park Rangers FC 1960–90 (vice pres 1991–); examiner in medicine Soc of Apothecaries 1980–88 (currently Liveryman); chm St Mary Abbots Court Ltd 1981–; Freeman City of London 1984; memb Irish Coll of Gen Practitioners, hon memb BPA 1982; FRSM, Hon FCPCH 1996, fell Royal NZ Coll of GPs 1990, fell Coll of GPs (Pakistan) 1991; *Publications* Paediatric Care (1976), DHSS Handbook on Contraceptive Practice (jtly, 4 edn, 1988); contribs to Lancet, British Medical Journal and other learned jls; *Recreations* music, photography, philately; *Clubs* Royal Air Force; *Style*— Dr Stuart Carne, CBE; ✉ 5 St Mary Abbots Court, Warwick Gardens, London W14 8RA (☎ 0171 602 1970)

CARNEGIE, Lt-Gen Sir Robin Macdonald; KCB (1979), OBE (1968), DL (1990); yr s of Sir Francis Carnegie, CBE (d 1946), and Theodora, *née* Matthews; *b* 22 June 1926; *Educ* Rugby; *m* 1955, Iona, da of Maj-Gen Sir John Sinclair, KCMG, CB, OBE (d 1977); 1 s, 2 da; *Career* cmmnd 7 Hussars 1946, cmd QOH 1967–69, cmd 11 Armd Bde 1971–72, student RCDS 1973, GOC 3 Div (Maj-Gen) 1974–76, COS HQ BAOR 1976–78, mil sec 1978–80, DG Army Trg MOD 1981–82, Col QOH 1981–87, non-service memb Home Office Selection Bd 1987–96; *Style*— Lt-Gen Sir Robin Carnegie, KCB, OBE, DL

CARNEGY, Christopher Roy; s of Julian Roy Carnegy, of New Malden, Surrey, and Vivien, *née* Kay-Menzies; *b* 9 Dec 1961; *Educ* Kingston GS, Univ of Southampton (BA, controller Southampton Univ Radio Glen); *Career* presenter Radio Victory Portsmouth 1984–86, prog controller Ocean Sound Southampton 1986–92, md Spire FM Salisbury 1992–96, md The Local Radio Co 1996–; sometime freelance bdcaster LBC, IRN and TVS; nominated for Best Local Radio Prog Sony Radio Awards 1986, winner Sony Radio Award Best Local Radio Station 1994; *Recreations* eating, drinking, arguing; *Style*— Christopher Carnegy, Esq; ✉ The Local Radio Company, 29 Hulse Road, Salisbury, Wiltshire SP1 3LU (☎ 01722 415188, fax 01722 339220)

CARNEGY, Colin David; s of Canon Patrick Charles Alexander Carnegy (d 1969), and Joyce Eleanor, *née* Townsley (d 1995); bro of Patrick Charles Carnegy, *qv*; *b* 16 Aug 1942; *Educ* Rugby, Jesus Coll Oxford (MA); *m* 1 Sept 1973, Rosemary Frances Deschamps, da of Saunders Edward Chamier, MC (d 1990), of Wadhurst, Sussex; 3 s (Charles b 15 Aug 1975, Edward b 3 Oct 1977, Francis b 10 Oct 1981), 1 da (Henrietta b 18 Oct 1983); *Career* admitted slr 1968, ptnr Parker Bullen Salisbury 1974–; NP; pres Salisbury Slrs Assoc 1990; chm Govrs Berwick St James First Sch Salisbury 1988–92; memb: Law Soc; *Recreations* music and skiing; *Style*— Colin Carnegy, Esq; ✉ The Parsonage, Stapleford, Salisbury, Wilts SP3 4LJ (☎ 01722 790334); Parker Bullen, 45 Castle St, Salisbury, Wilts SP1 3SS (☎ 01722 412000, fax 01722 411822)

CARNEGY, Patrick Charles; s of Canon Patrick Charles Alexander Carnegy (d 1969), and Joyce Eleanor, *née* Townsley (d 1995); bro of Colin David Carnegy, *qv*; *b* 23 Sept 1940; *Educ* Trinity Hall Cambridge (MA); *Career* writer, lectr, broadcaster on music, theatre and lit; journalist TES 1964–69, asst ed TLS 1969–78, ed music books Faber and Faber Ltd 1978–88, dir Faber Music Ltd 1979–88, dramaturg Royal Opera House 1988–92, Leverhulme research fell 1994–96; broadcasting incl contribs to BBC Radio 4's arts magazine Kaleidoscope; documentaries on: Kafka, Thomas Mann, Wagner's Ring; founding memb Bayreuth Int Arts Centre; memb: BBC Central Music Advsy Ctee 1986–89, BBC Gen Advsy Cncl 1990–; *Books* Faust as Musician: A Study of Thomas Mann's novel 'Doctor Faustus' (1973), Christianity Revalued (ed, 1974); *Recreations* mountains, wine; *Style*— Patrick Carnegy, Esq; ✉ 5 The Causeway, Elsworth, Cambs CB3 8HT

CARNEGY-ARBUTHNOTT, Bt-Col David; TD (1969), DL (Co of City of Dundee 1973–89, Co of Angus 1989–); s of Lt-Col Wilmot Boys Carnegy-Arbuthnott (d 1973), and Enid Carnegy-Arbuthnott (d 1986), thirteenth of Balnamoon and thirteenth of Findowrie; Alexander Carnegy, 5 of Balnamoon, took part in 1715 rebellion, captured, imprisoned, pardoned 1721, estates forfeited, repurchased 1728. James Carnegy, subsequently 6 of Balnamoon, took part in 1745 rebellion, captured, tried but not convicted, because of misnomer - he had married Margaret Arbuthnott who became 5 of Findowrie and added her name to his; *b* 17 July 1925; *Educ* Stowe; *m* 1949, Helen Adamson, da of Capt David Collier Lyell, MC (d 1970); 2 s (James, Hugh), 2 da (Sarah, Bridget); *Career* emergency cmmn Black Watch 1944–47, TA 1955–69, Bt-Col 1969, Hon Col First Bn 51 Highland Volunteers (TA) 1980–89; CA 1953, in practice Dundee 1956–89; landowner through family cos (3500 acres); pres Dundee C of C 1971–72, memb Ct Univ of Dundee 1977–85, govr Dundee Coll of Educn 1985–87 and Northern Coll of Educn 1987–91, convener Standing Ctee of the Scottish Episcopal Church 1987–92, tstee Scottish Episcopal Church 1992–; memb Queen's Bodyguard for Scotland (Royal Co of Archers) 1959–; Hon LLD Univ of Dundee 1982; *Recreations* shooting, country pursuits; *Clubs* New (Edinburgh), Army and Navy, Puffins (Edinburgh); *Style*— Bt-Col David Carnegy-Arbuthnott of Balnamoon, TD, DL; ✉ Balnamoon, Brechin, Angus DD9 7RH (☎ 01356 660208)

CARNEGY OF LOUR, Baroness (Life Peer UK 1982), of Lour in the District of Angus; Elizabeth Patricia Carnegy of Lour; DL (Angus 1988); eld da of Lt-Col Ughtred Elliott Carnegy of Lour, 12 of Lour, DSO, MC, JP, DL (d 1973), and Violet, MBE, *née* Henderson (d 1965); *b* 28 April 1925; *Educ* Downham Sch Essex; *Career* worked in Cavendish Laboratory Cambridge 1943–46; Girl Guide Assoc: joined 1947, co cmmr Angus 1956–63, trg advsr Scotland 1958–62, trg advsr Cwlth HQ 1963–65, pres Angus 1971–84, pres Scotland 1979–89; co-opted onto Angus CC Educn Ctee 1967–75; chm: Working Pty on Professional Trg for Community Educn in Scotland 1975–77, Scottish Cncl Community Educn 1981–88 (memb 1978–88), MSC for Scotland 1981–83, Tayside Ctee on Med Res Ethics 1990–93; memb: Cncl Tertiary Educn Scotland 1979–83, MSC 1979–82, Scottish Econ Cncl 1981–93, Cncl Open Univ 1984–96, Admin Cncl Royal Jubilee Tsts 1984–88, Ct Univ of St Andrews 1991–96; cncllr Tayside Regnl Cncl 1974–82 (convener Recreation and Tourism 1974–76 and Educn Ctee 1977–81); Hon Sheriff 1969–84; hon pres Scottish Library Assoc 1989–92; Hon LLD Univ of Dundee 1991; Hon Fell Scottish Cncl for Community Education; FRSA; *Clubs* Lansdowne; *Style*— The Rt Hon the Lady Carnegy of Lour, DL; ✉ Lour, Forfar, Angus DD8 2LR (☎ 01307 820237); House of Lords, Westminster SW1A 0PW

CARNEY, Dr Michael William Patrick; s of Major Patrick Leo Carney, Croix de Guerre (d 1984), of Staines, Middx, and Gladys Louise Carney; *b* 8 Jan 1931; *Educ* St Joseph's Acad Blackheath London, Univ Coll Dublin (MB BCh, BAO, MD, DPM); *m* 19 Sept 1963, Dr (Margaret) Meg Carney, da of Dr Andrew Bell Hamilton Irvine of Morpeth, Northumberland; 3 s (John Niall b 25 Sept 1964, Andrew Patrick b 30 April 1966, Peter Michael b 21 March 1969); *Career* med offr RAMC 1956–60 (trainee in psychiatry 1956–58, MELF 1959–60), house physician St Vincent's Hosp Dublin 1954, sr registrar to Sir Martin Roth Royal Victoria Infirmary Newcastle upon Tyne 1960–63; conslt psychiatrist: Blackpool and Fylde Hosps 1963–74, Northwick Park Hosp and Clinical Res Centre Harrow 1974–90, Clementine Churchill Hosp Harrow; visiting conslt: Priory Hosp Roehampton, Bowden House Clinic Harrow on the Hill, Royal Masonic Hosp London, Grovelands Priory Hosp Southgate, Bishopswood Private Hosp Northwood 1990–94; 154 published papers in med and scientific jls, contrib to med text books, author of med book reviews, referee of original papers for British Journal of Psychiatry; former assessor and examiner: GMC Health Ctee NW Thames Region, Gen Dental Cncl Health Ctee NW Thames Region; Gen Nursing Cncl Health Ctee examiner for nurses midwives and health visitors; memb Nat Counselling and Welfare Serv for Sick Drs; FRCPI 1971, FRCPsych 1974; *Recreations* archaeology, walking, jogging, swimming, reading, and amateur antiquary; *Clubs* 71 Club, Northwick Park Hospital; *Style*— Dr Michael Carney

CARNOCK, 4 Baron (UK 1916); Sir David Henry Arthur Nicolson; 14 Bt (NS 1637), of Carnock, Co Stirling; recognised by Lord Lyon 1984 as holder of the Baronetcy of Lasswade (NS 1629) and as chief of the Clan Nicolson and Nicolson of that Ilk; s of Captain 3 Baron Carnock, DSO, JP, RN (d 1982), by his w, Hon Katharine Lopes (d 1968), da of 1 Baron Roborough; *b* 10 July 1920; *Educ* Winchester, Balliol Coll Oxford; *Heir* 1 cous, Nigel Nicolson, MBE; *Career* served 1940–46 Royal Devon Yeo Staff, DAQMG HQ Land Forces Hong Kong, Maj 1945; admitted slr 1949, ptnr Clifford-Turner Slrs 1955–86; Liveryman Worshipful Co of Scriveners; *Recreations* shooting, fishing, gardening, foreign travel; *Clubs* Travellers', Beefsteak; *Style*— The Rt Hon the Lord Carnock; ✉ 90 Whitehall Court, London SW1A 2EL (☎ 0171 839 5544); Ermewood House, Harford, Ivybridge, Devon PL21 0JE (☎ 01752 892519)

CARNWATH, Francis Anthony Armstrong; s of Sir Andrew Hunter Carnwath, KCVO, DL (d 1995), and Kathleen Marianne, *née* Armstrong (d 1968); bro of The Hon Mr Justice Carnwath, CVO, *qv*; *b* 26 May 1940; *Educ* Eton (Oppidan scholar), Trinity Coll Cambridge; *m* 1 March 1975, Penelope Clare, da of Sir Charles Henry Rose, 3 Bt (d 1965), of Hardwick House, Whitchurch-on-Thames, Oxon; 1 s (Alexander Patrick b 1980), 2 da (Flora Helen b 1976, Catriona Rose b 1978 d 1985); *Career* dir Baring Bros and Co Ltd 1979–89, chm Ravensbourne Registration Services Ltd 1981–89, dep dir The Tate Gallery 1990–94, advsr National Heritage Memorial Fund 1995– (actg dir 1995); dir Foreign Anglican Church and Educational Association Ltd 1973– (co sec 1973–85), tstee and treas Shelter Nat Campaign for the Homeless 1968–76 (dep chm 1973–76), treas VSO 1979–84, tstee Phillimore Estates 1982–, chm Spitalfields Historic Bldg Tst 1984–, chm Henley Soc (Civic Amenity Tst Soc) 1984–88, treas Friends of Tate Gallery 1985–90, memb London Advsy Ctee English Heritage 1990–, tstee Whitechapel Art Gallery 1994–; Master Worshipful Co of Musicians 1995–96; *Recreations* music, gardening, walking; *Clubs* Garrick, Naval and Military; *Style*— Francis Carnwath, Esq; ✉ Southernhay, Nettlebed, Henley-on-Thames, Oxon RG9 5BD (☎ 01491 641357); 2 John Islip Street, London SW1P 4PX (☎ 0171 821 0377)

CARNWATH, Hon Mr Justice; Hon Sir Robert John Anderson; kt (1994), CVO (1995); s of Sir Andrew Hunter Carnwath, KCVO, DL (d 1995), and Kathleen Marianne, *née* Armstrong (d 1968); bro of Francis Carnwath, *qv*; *b* 15 March 1945; *Educ* Eton, Trinity Coll Cambridge (MA, LLB); *m* 18 May 1974, Bambina, da of G D'Adda, of Bergamo, Italy; *Career* called to the Bar 1969; jr counsel to Revenue 1980–85, QC 1985–94, attorney-gen to Prince of Wales 1988–94, judge of the High Court of Justice (Chancery Div) 1994–; author of various legal pubns; memb Governing Body RAM; tstee Britten - Pears Fndn 1996–; Freeman Worshipful Co of Musicians; Hon FRAM 1994; *Recreations* violin, singing, tennis, golf; *Style*— The Hon Mr Justice Carnwath, CVO; ✉ Royal Courts of Justice, Strand, London WC2

CARO, Sir Anthony Alfred; kt (1987), CBE (1969); s of late Alfred Caro and Mary Rose Edith Caro (d 1995, aged 100); *b* 8 March 1924; *Educ* Charterhouse, Christ's Coll Cambridge, Regent St Poly, Royal Acad Schs (one bronze and two silver medals); *m* 1949, Sheila May Girling, the painter; 2 s (Timothy b 1951, Paul b 1958); *Career* sculptor; Fleet Air Arm RN 1944–46; pt/t asst to Henry Moore 1951–53, pt/t teacher St Martin's Sch of Art 1953–79, teacher of sculpture Bennington Coll Vermont USA 1963–65; teacher Triangle Artist's Workshop in: US 1982–90 (fndr), Maastricht Holland 1985, Barcelona Spain 1987, Obama Japan 1990; visiting artist: Emma Lake summer workshop Univ of Saskatchewan 1977, workshop in Berlin 1987, Univ of Alberta Canada 1989, Red Deer Coll Alberta 1989; memb Cncl Royal Coll of Art 1981–83, tstee Tate Gallery 1982–89, memb Cncl Slade Sch of Art London 1982–89; hon fell: Christ's Coll Cambridge 1981, RCA 1986; hon memb American Acad of Arts and Sciences 1979; Freeman City of NY 1976, Liveryman Worshipful Co of Horners; Hon DLitt: York Univ Toronto 1979, UEA 1979, Brandeis Univ Mass 1981; Hon LittD Cambridge 1985, Hon DUniv Surrey 1987; Hon DFA: Yale Univ Conn 1989, Univ of Alberta 1990; Hon Doctorate RCA 1994; *Solo Exhibitions* incl: Galleria del Naviglio Milan 1956, Gimpel Fils Gallery London 1957, Whitechapel Gallery 1963, Andre Emmerich Gallery NYC 1964 (and subseq every two years), Kasmin Gallery London 1965 (and subseq every two years), retrospective exhbn Rijksmuseum Kroller-Muller Otterlo 1967, retrospective exhbn Hayward Gallery 1969, Norfolk and Norwich Triennial Festival 1973, retrospective exhbn Museum of Modern Art NYC and touring 1975, int touring exhbn of table sculptures 1977, Serpentine Gallery and touring 1984, Walker Hill Art Center Seoul 1989, Sculpture Toward Architecture Tate Gallery 1991, retrospective exhbn Trajan Markets Rome 1992; *Group Exhibitions* incl: New Painters and Painters-Sculptors (ICA) 1955, New London Situation (Marlborough New London Gallery) 1961, British Sculpture in the Sixties (Tate Gallery) 1965, Five Young British Artists (Venice Biennale) 1966, Noland, Louis and Caro (Metropolitan Museum of Art NYC) 1968, Tenth Sao Paulo Biennale (prizewinner) 1969, Tower of Discovery at Expo' 92 Seville 1992; *Work in Public Collections* incl: Arts Cncl of GB, Bostom Museum of Fine Arts, Guggenheim Museum NYC, Hirshhorn Museum Washington DC, Israel Museum Jerusalem, Los Angeles Museum of Art, Metroploitan Museum NYC, Museum of Modern Art NYC, Joan Miro Fndn Spain, Nat Gallery Washington DC, Scottish Nat Gallery of Modern Art, Tate Gallery, Yale Univ Art Gallery, Smithsonian Inst Washington DC; *Awards* Paris Biennale 1959, Ford Fndn-ESU grant 1959, David E Bright Fndn prize Venice Biennale 1966, 7th Henry Moore Grand Prize and Nobutaka Shikanai Prize 1991 (The Moroccans), Praemium Imperiale for Sculpture Japan Art Assoc 1992; *Recreations* listening to music; *Style*— Sir Anthony Caro, CBE; ✉ 111 Frognal, London NW3 6XR

CAROE, Martin Bragg; s of Alban Douglas Rendall Caroe, OBE (d 1991), of London, and Gwendolen Mary, *née* Bragg (d 1984); *b* 15 Nov 1933; *Educ* Winchester, Trinity Coll Cambridge (BA), Kingston upon Thames Sch of Architecture (DipArch); *m* 15 Sept 1962, Mary Elizabeth, da of Capt Stephen Wentworth Roskill, CBE, DSC, RN (d 1982), of Cambridge; 2 s (William b 1967, d 1974, Oliver b 1968), 3 da (Rebecca b 1965, Ruth b 1972, Emily b 1976); *Career* Lance Corpl KRRC 1952, 2 Lt 1 Royal Fus 1952–53, Capt 8 Royal Fus 1954–62; ptnr Caroe and Partners 1962; third generation conservation architect specialising in care of historic bldgs; work incl: St David's Cathedral 1966, Wells Cathedral West Front Sculpture Conservation 1981–86, repair on accession to Nat Tst Kingston Lacy 1982–84, surveyor Rochester Cathedral 1982–, conslt architect Tower of London 1991–; Civic Tst Award Wells Vicars Close 1984; pres EASA (Ecclesiastical Architects' & Surveyors' Assoc) 1978–79; memb: Faculty Jurisdiction Cmmn 1980–84, Exec Ctee Cncl for the Care of Churches 1986–92, cmmn English Heritage 1989–92, cmmn on Faculties Church in Wales 1991–93, cmmn Cathedrals and Churches (Wales) 1994–; memb Ct of Assts Worshipful Co of Plumbers (Master 1986); ARIBA 1960, FSA 1988; UN Medal Korea; *Recreations* care and showing of Jekyll garden, punting; *Style*— Martin Caroe, Esq, FSA; ✉ 1 Greenland Place, London NW1 0AP (☎ 0171 267 9348, fax 0171 267 9344)

CAROLIN, Dr Brian; s of Lawrence Carolin, of Ellington, Northumberland, and Hazel, *née* Charlton; *b* 2 July 1956; *Educ* Ashington GS, Univ of Newcastle (BA Politics and Economics), LSE (PhD Industl Rels); *m* 20 Sept 1975, Diane; 1 da (Sarah Carolin b 8 June 1987); *Career* graduate trainee Ford Motor Co Ltd 1980–84; Nissan 1984–: various positions incl personnel mangr, gen mangr Product Control and gen mangr Purchasing Nissan Motor Manufacturing (UK) Ltd Sunderland 1984–92, various positions incl gen mangr Corp Support and gen mangr Product Mktg Nissan Europe NV Holland 1992–95, mktg dir Nissan Motor (GB) Ltd 1996–; *Recreations* cycling, reading; *Style*— Dr Brian Carolin; ✉ Nissan Motor (GB) Ltd, The Rivers Office Park, Denham Way, Maple Cross, Rickmansworth, Herts WD3 2YS (☎ 01923 899022, fax 01923 899911)

CARPANINI, Prof David Lawrence; s of Lorenzo Carpanini, of Abergwynfi, W Glam, and Gwenllian, *née* Thomas (d 1990); *b* 22 Oct 1946; *Educ* Glan Afan GS Port Talbot, Gloucestershire Coll of Art & Design (DipAD), RCA (MA), Univ of Reading (Art Teacher's Cert); *m* 1972, Jane Carpanini, *qv*; 1 s (Noel Dominic b 22 Aug 1977); *Career* artist and teacher; dir of art Kingham Hill Sch Oxon 1972–79, dir of art Oundle Sch 1979–86, sr lectr in art and design W Midlands Coll of HE 1986–89, head Dept of Art and Design Sch of Educn Univ of Wolverhampton (formerly Wolverhampton Poly) 1989–, prof of art Univ of Wolverhampton 1992–; pres Royal Soc of Painter-Printmakers 1995, vice pres Royal Soc of Br Artists 1982–86; subject of documentaries Every One a Special Kind of Artist (Channel 4) 1984 and David Carpanini (HTV) 1987; de Lazlo

Medal RBA 1980; Hon RWS 1996; RBA 1976, RWA 1977, RE 1979, NEAC 1983, RCA 1992; *Solo Exhibitions* incl: Paintings, Etchings, Drawings (John Hansard Gallery Univ of Southampton) 1972, Paintings and Drawings at the John Nevill Gallery 1973, Paintings (Bristol Arts Centre) 1975, Etchings (The Arts Club London) 1982, Paintings and Drawings (Tegfryn Gallery) 1982, Etchings (Park Gallery Cheltenham) 1982, Paintings and Etchings (Ceri Richards Gallery Taliesin Art Centre Univ Coll Swansea) 1983, Paintings and Etchings (Business Art Galleries at the Royal Acad) 1984, permanent display of combined GLC and ASTMS (now MSF) collection of David Carpanini works at MSF HQ London and mgmnt coll Bishops Stortford 1984–, Paintings and Etchings (East Gate Gallery Warwick) 1986, Paintings and Etchings (Mostyn Gallery Llandudno) 1988, Paintings and Etchings (Rhondda Heritage Park) 1989, Paintings 1968–88 (Walsall Museum and Art Gallery) 1989, David Carpanini Paintings and Prints (Attic Gallery Swansea) 1994; *Two Person Exhibitions* with Jane Carpanini: Yarrow Gallery Oundle 1979, David and Jane Carpanini Paintings 1968–80 (Welsh Arts Council Exhbn) 1980, Paintings, Etchings and Watercolours (Queen Elizabeth Theatre Gallery Oakham) 1987, Paintings, Etchings and Drawings (Albany Gallery Cardiff) 1991, Rhondda Heritage Park Gallery 1994; also Paintings and Etchings with Richard Bawden RE (Royal Exchange Theatre Gallery Manchester) 1993; *Group Exhibitions* incl: Royal Acad Summer Exhbn 1973–, Royal W of England Acad Annual Exhbn 1973–, Royal Soc of Br Artists Annual Exhbn 1975–, Industl Soc exhbn London 1974, The Artist in Society (Whitechapel Gallery London and Ulster Museum Belfast) 1978, Twelve Regular RA Exhibitors (Patricia Wells Gallery) 1979, Royal Soc of Painter-Etchers and Engravers Annual Exhbn 1979–, Six Welsh Artists: A View of Wales (Ceri Richards Gallery Swansea as part of National Eisteddfod) 1982, NEAC Annual Exhbn 1983–, Tradition and Innovation in Printmaking Today (national touring) 1985–86, Int Contemporary Art Fair (Olympia and Bath, with Bankside Gallery) 1985–, Contemporary Printmakers (Cadogan Fine Arts London) 1986–, Glynn Vivian Art Gallery Swansea 1986, Reflections of Summer (Bankside Gallery London) 1987, Contemporary Art Soc for Wales Collection (National Museum of Wales Cardiff) 1987, The Face of Wales (seven artists, tour of Wales) 1987–88, 20th Century Br Art Fair (with Fosse Gallery) 1988, Bristol Open Printmaking Exhbn (Royal W of England Acad) 1988, various exhbns of gallery artists Fosse Gallery (John Lindsey Fine Art) 1988–, British Printmaking Today (Br Cncl touring former Soviet Union) 1989–91, Wales Art Fair (Cardiff, with Albany Gallery) 1990 and (also with Attic Gallery) 1991, Art 90 Fair (Olympia, with Fosse Gallery) 1990, Albany Gallery 25th Anniversary Exhbn of Gallery Artists 1990, Past and Present RAs and RA Exhibitors (John Noott 20th Century Broadway) 1991, Welsh Coalmining - The End of an Era (New Gallery Swansea as part of Swansea Festival) 1991, Invited Members of the RE and RWS (Gorstella Gallery Chester) 1991, The NEAC in Wales (Albany Gallery Cardiff) 1992, Invited Members of the RE (Shell International London) 1992, RWS Open Exhbn (Bankside Gallery) 1993, Invited Members and Guests Royal Cambrian Acad 1993, Fedn of Br Artists National Print Exhbn (Mall Galleries) 1994, 1995 and 1996, Paintings, Drawings and Prints by Invited Artists (Gorstella Gallery Chester) 1994; *Work in Collections* incl: Ashmolean Museum Oxford, Fitzwilliam Museum Cambridge, Nat Museum of Wales, Nat Library of Wales, Newport Museum and Art Gallery, Glynn Vivian Art Gallery Swansea, Contemporary Art Soc for Wales, Univ Coll Swansea, Coleg Harlech, National Coal Board, British Steel plc, Rank Xerox, Redpath Mining Corp Ontario, ASTMS (now MSF), Dept of the Environment, Royal Coll of Art, GLC, numerous private collections in Europe, N America, Australia and Saudi Arabia; *Awards* Royal Instn Annual Scholarship for Engraving 1969, Catto Gallery Award RWS Open Exhbn 1993, first prize Daler Rowney Award RWS Open Exhbn 1995; *Recreations* opera, ballroom dancing, cycling; *Clubs* Arts; *Style*— Prof David Carpanini; ✉ Fernlea, 145 Rugby Road, Milverton, Leamington Spa, Warwickshire CV32 6DJ (☎ 01926 430658); c/o The Bankside Gallery, 48 Hopton Street, Blackfriars, London SE1 9JH (☎ 0171 928 7521, fax 0171 928 2820)

CARPANINI, Jane; da of Derrick Stanley Allen, of Streatley, Beds, and Joan, *née* Collins; *b* 13 Oct 1949; *Educ* The High Sch Bedford, Luton Coll of Technol Sch of Art, Faculty of Art & Design Brighton Poly (DipAD), Sch of Education Univ of Reading (Art Teacher's Cert); *m* 1972, Prof David Lawrence Carpanini, *qv*, s of Lorenzo Carpanini; 1 s (Noel Dominic b 22 Aug 1977); *Career* artist; art teacher: The High Sch Bedford 1972–73, Bishops Cleeve Comp 1973–76, Oundle Sch 1980–86 (pt/t); head of art and design King's HS for Girls Warwick 1987–; vice pres Royal Watercolour Soc 1992–93 (hon treas 1983–86); RWA 1977, RWS 1978, RBA 1978, RCA 1992; *Solo exhibitions* Watercolours and Drawings (Bristol Art Centre) 1975, Watercolours (Patricia Wells Gallery Thornbury Bristol) 1976, Watercolours and Drawings (Tegfryn Gallery) 1982, Watercolours (Ceri Richards Gallery Univ Coll Swansea) 1983, Watercolours of Wales (Nat Museum of Wales) 1984, Watercolours by Jane Carpanini (Warwick Museum) 1990, Watercolours (Albany Gallery Cardiff) 1991; *Exhibitions with David Carpanini* David and Jane Carpanini Paintings 1968–80 (Welsh Arts Council Exhbn) 1980, Yarrow Gallery Oundle 1979, Rhondda Heritage Park Gallery 1994; *Group exhibitions* incl: Royal W of England Acad Summer Exhbn annually 1973–, RA Summer Exhbn 1974–80, Royal Soc of Br Artists Exhbn annually 1975–, Royal Soc of Painters in Watercolours annual London and tourning exhbns 1978–, Twelve Regular RA Exhibitors (Patricia Wells Gallery Thornbury) 1979, The Native Land (Welsh Arts Cncl Exhbn Mostyn Gallery Llandudno) 1980, Mason Watts Fine Art Warwick 1990 and 1993, Royal Cambrian Academy Annual Exhbn 1993, invited members of the RWS exhbn Gorstella Gallery Chester 1994; *Work in collections* incl: Nat Library of Wales, Nat Museum of Wales, Br Nat Oil Museum, Dixons Photographic, Diploma Collection of RWS, Burnley Building Society, Coleg Harlech, numerous private collections; *Awards* Hunting Group Prize for watercolour of the year by a Br artist 1983; *Recreations* opera, travel, ballroom dancing; *Style*— Mrs Jane Carpanini; ✉ Fernlea, 145 Rugby Road, Milverton, Leamington Spa, Warwickshire CV32 6DJ (☎ 01926 430658); c/o The Bankside Gallery, 48 Hopton Street, Blackfriars, London SE1 9JH (☎ 0171 928 7521, fax 0171 928 2820)

CARPENTER, David Iain; RD (1994); s of Jeffrey Frank Carpenter, of Epsom, Surrey, and Joyce Cumming, *née* Mitchell; *b* 14 Oct 1951; *Educ* Sutton GS, Kingston upon Thames Sch of Architecture, BRNC Dartmouth, Heriot-Watt Sch of Architecture Edinburgh (DipArch); *m* 20 Jan 1979, Anne Richmond, da of Dr Norman John McQueen, of Appin, Argyll; 4 s (Angus b 1980, Edward b 1981, Alexander b and d 1983, Simon b 1984); *Career* supply and secretariat offr RN 1974–78, RNR 1979– (head Public Affrs Branch since 1996 (memb 1992–) incl serv in former Yugoslavia 1993–); architect J & F Johnston & Partners 1982–88 (assoc dir 1987), in own practice David Carpenter Architect Edinburgh 1988–; memb (as architect) Relocation Team to move the Minor War Vessel Flotilla from Rosyth to new base ports 1994–96; architect Norwegian devpt team 1996–; *Recreations* sailing, sketching, reading; *Style*— David Carpenter, Esq; ✉ David Carpenter Architect, 3 Argyle Park Terrace, Edinburgh EH9 1JY (☎ and fax 0131 229 1383)

CARPENTER, Harry Leonard; OBE (1991); s of Harry Carpenter (d 1974), and Adelaide May, *née* Lascelles (d 1991); *b* 17 Oct 1925; *Educ* Ashburton Sch Shirley Surrey, Selhurst GS Croydon Surrey; *m* 22 Sept 1950, Phyllis Barbara, da of William Matthews; 1 s (Clive Harry b 20 Sept 1954); *Career* sports commentator; journalist: Greyhound Express 1941–43, Greyhound Owner 1946–48, Speedway Gazette 1949–50, Sporting Record 1950–54, Daily Mail 1954–62; sports commentator: BBC TV 1949–94, BBC radio 1951–94; DAVI award Best Sports Prog on Video 1983, TRIC award Sports Personality of the Year 1989, American Sportscasters' Assoc award Int Sportscaster of the Year 1989; *Books* Masters of Boxing (1964), History of Boxing (1975), The Hardest Game (1981), Where's Harry? (1992); *Recreations* golf; *Clubs* Royal & Ancient Golf (Scotland), Royal St George's Golf (Kent), Dulwich and Sydenham Hill Golf (London); *Style*—Harry Carpenter, Esq, OBE; ✉ Sommerfield Ltd, 35 Old Queen Street, London SW1H 9JD (☎ 0171 222 9070)

CARPENTER, Humphrey William Bouverie; s of Rt Rev Harry James Carpenter, Bishop of Oxford (d 1993), and Urith, *née* Trevelyan; *b* 29 April 1946; *Educ* Dragon Sch Oxford, Marlborough, Keble Coll Oxford (MA, DipEd); *m* 1973, Mari Christina, da of Caradog Prichard (d 1980); 2 da; *Career* author, broadcaster, musician; BBC gen trainee 1968–70, staff prodr BBC Radio Oxford 1970–74, freelance writer and broadcaster 1975–; fndr of band Vile Bodies (1920s and 1930s jazz and dance music), resident Ritz Hotel London 1986–; FRSL 1983; *Awards* Somerset Maugham Award 1978, E M Forster Award American Acad of Arts and Letters 1984, Duff Cooper Meml Prize 1988; *Books* A Thames Companion (with Mari Prichard, 1975), J R R Tolkien - A Biography (1977), The Inklings (1978), Jesus (1980), The Letters of J R R Tolkien (jt ed with Christopher Tolkien, 1981), W H Auden - A Biography (1981), The Oxford Companion to Children's Literature (with Mari Pritchard, 1984), OUDS - A Centenary History of the Oxford University Dramatic Society (1985), Secret Gardens - The Golden Age of Children's Literature (1985), Geniuses Together - American Writers in Paris (1987), A Serious Character - The Life of Ezra Pound (1988), The Brideshead Generation - Evelyn Waugh and his Friends (1989), Benjamimn Britten - A Biography (1992); *Children's Books* The Joshers (1977), The Captain Hook Affair (1979), Mr Majeika (1984), Mr Majeika and the Music Teacher (1986), Mr Majeika and the Haunted Hotel (1987), The Television Adventures of Mr Majeika (1987), More Television Adventures of Mr Majeika (1988), Mr Majeika and the Dinner Lady (1989), Further Television Adventures of Mr Majeika (1990), Mr Majeika and the School Play (1991), Mr Majeika and his School Book Week (1992); Mr Majeika books serialized on television 1988–90; *Recreations* sleep; *Style*— Humphrey Carpenter, Esq

CARPENTER, Dr (George) Iain; s of George Anthony Carpenter (d 1967), of Horsmonden, Kent, and Dr Annie Pack MacKinnon; *b* 2 June 1950; *Educ* Christ's Hospital Horsham Sussex, Univ of Edinburgh (BSc, MD); *m* 1, 22 Feb 1970 (m dis 1982), (Marie) Catrine, da of Gaston Bauer, of Le Verger, Route de Lamonly, Anglet, Bayonne, France; 1 s (Edward b 24 May 1979), 1 da (Violaine b 1 May 1976); m 2, 11 June 1983, Bridget Mary, da of Robert Charles Combley, of Headington, Oxford; 1 s (James b 30 Jan 1986), 1 da (Annie b 18 Aug 1984); *Career* sr registrar in geriatric med: Brighton Gen Hosp 1978–80, Bolingbroke 1980–81, St George's Hosp 1980–81; conslt geriatrician 1981–95 and conslt in rehabilitation medicine 1990–95: Royal Hampshire Co Hosp, St Paul's Hosp Winchester; regnl med advsr and dir of screening Beaumont Med Serv 1986–89, dir ICS Med Ltd 1989–91, sr lectr in health care of the elderly King's Coll Sch of Med and Dentistry 1995–; memb: Br Geriatric Soc, BMA; FRCP 1993, FRCPEd 1994; *Books* All Of Us - Strategies for Health Promotion for Old People (jtly, 1989), Housing, Care and Frailty (jtly, 1990), Assessment in Continuing Care Homes: Towards a National Standard Instrument (jtly, 1996); *Recreations* walking, swimming, scuba diving, windsurfing, radio controlled model aircraft; *Style*— Dr Iain Carpenter; ✉ Glebe Cottage, St Stephen's Green, Canterbury, Kent CT2 7JU; Centre for Health Service Studies, George Allen Wing, The University of Kent at Canterbury, Kent CT2 7NF (☎ 01227 827760)

CARPENTER, Maj-Gen (Victor Harry) John; CB (1975), MBE (1945); s of Harry Carpenter, and Amelia Carpenter; *b* 21 June 1921; *m* 1946, Theresa McCulloch; 1 s, 1 da; *Career* 2 Lt RASC 1939, Maj-Gen 1971; tport offr in chief MOD 1971–73, dir of movements (Army) MOD 1973–75, ret; chm Traffic Cmmrs Yorks Traffic Area 1975–85, traffic cmmr Western Traffic Area Bristol 1985–89 (sr traffic cmmr 1989–91), ret 1991; nat pres 1940 Dunkirk Veterans' Assoc, pres Artificers Royal Artillery Assoc; Cdr Order of Leopold II; FCIT, Hon FIRTE; *Style*— Maj-Gen John Carpenter, CB, MBE

CARPENTER, Leslie Arthur; s of William and Rose Carpenter; *b* 26 June 1927; *Educ* Hackney Tech Coll; *m* 1, 1952, Stella Louise Bozza; 1 da; m 2, 1989, Louise Botting, *qv*; *Career* dir: Country Life 1965, George Newnes 1966; md Odhams Press Ltd 1968, dir International Publishing Corporation 1972, chm and chief exec IPC Ltd 1974; Reed International plc: dir 1974–, chief exec 1982–86, chm 1985–87; non-exec dir Watmough (Holdings) plc 1988–; *Recreations* racing, gardening; *Style*— Leslie Carpenter, Esq

CARPENTER, Dr Percival Benjamin; s of Harold Percival Carpenter, of Walsall, West Midlands, and Ida, *née* Baker; *b* 4 Aug 1932; *Educ* Queen Mary's GS Walsall, Univ of Birmingham (MB ChB); *m* 8 Sept 1956, Janet Elizabeth, da of Arthur James Bourne; 2 s (David Bryan b 15 Jan 1958, Michael Anthony b 7 Sept 1960), 2 da (Gillian b 1 Oct 1962, Petra Jane b 12 Jan 1969); *Career* Nat Serv Capt RAMC 1958–60; house offr St Chad's Hosp Birmingham 1957–58, sr registrar in radiology United Birmingham and other Birmingham Hosps 1963–65 (registrar 1960–63); conslt radiologist: West Birmingham Hosps 1966–85, Walsall Hosps 1975–; unit gen mangr Acute Services Walsall Hosp 1985–90 (chm Med Exec Ctee 1982–85), med dir Walsall Hosps NHS Trust 1990–; FRCR 1965; *Recreations* model engineering, DIY, music; *Style*— Dr Percival Carpenter; ✉ 6 Sandra Close, Aldridge, West Midlands (☎ 01922 53214); Manor Hospital, Moat Rd, Walsall, West Midlands

CARPENTER, Robert David Evans; s of Ernest Henry Carpenter (d 1973), of Reading, and Muriel Carpenter; *b* 22 Jan 1940; *Educ* Mill Hill; *m* 16 Sept 1967, Gloria Faith Davies Clarke, da of Gordon Stuart Clarke (d 1980); 1 s (James Nicholas b 9 June 1970), 1 da (Caroline Claire b 18 Dec 1972); *Career* Montagu Loebl Stanley & Co 1968–85 (ptnr 1979–85), dir of investmt res Kitcat & Aitken 1985–90, asst dir Kleinwort Benson Securities 1991–; AIB 1962; *Recreations* squash, country walking, bridge; *Style*— Robert Carpenter, Esq; ✉ Kleinwort Benson Securities Ltd, 20 Fenchurch Street, London EC3P 3DB (☎ 0171 623 8000, fax 0171 929 5997)

CARR, *see:* Baker-Carr

CARR, Bryan; *Career* ptnr B & JC Carr & Son (Preston); non-exec dir: Glasson Grain Ltd, Glasson Fertilisers Ltd, Glasson Estates Ltd; non-exec chm: AF plc, Blackpool Victoria Hosp NHS Tst; *Style*— Bryan Carr, Esq; ✉ Blackpool Victoria Hospital NHS Trust HQ, Whinney Heys Road, Blackpool, Lancs FY3 8NR (☎ 01253 306857, fax 01253 306873)

CARR, Francis Christopher (Fred); s of Allan Eric John Carr, of San Francisco, and Elizabeth Constance, *née* Hope-Jones (d 1989); *b* 6 March 1945; *Educ* Eton, Keble Coll Oxford (BA); *m* 7 May 1983, Corinna Elizabeth, da of Lt Cdr Cedric Wake-Walker, of Rogate, Hants; 2 da (Polly b 1985, Matilda b 1987); *Career* memb London Stock Exchange 1971, ptnr Smith Rice and Hill 1973, dir Capel-Cure Myers 1979–89; chief exec: W I Carr (Investments) Ltd 1991–93, Carr Sheppards 1993–; dir The Smaller Companies Investment Trust plc 1993–; chm The City of Oxford Investment Tst 1985– (dir 1973–); *Recreations* fishing, shooting, aquatics, cooking; *Clubs* White's, Pratt's, Chelsea Arts, Leander, Vincents; *Style*— Fred Carr, Esq; ✉ 49 Moore Park Rd, London SW6 2HP (☎ 0171 731 2724); Carr Sheppards Ltd, 122 Leadenhall Street, London EC3V 4SS (☎ 0171 303 1234)

CARR, Henry James; s of Malcolm Lester Carr (d 1984), of Liverpool, and Dr Sara Carr, *née* Leigh; *b* 31 March 1958; *Educ* King David Sch Liverpool, Hertford Coll Oxford (BA), Univ of British Columbia (LLM); *m* 22 Sept 1988, Jan Mary, da of Maj Richard Alfred Dawson, of Harrogate; 3 s (Oliver b 1989, Harry b 1991, Charlie b 1994); *Career* called to the Bar Gray's Inn 1982; *Books* Protection of Computer Software in the United

Kingdom (1986, co-author 2 edn with R Arnold, 1992); *Recreations* tennis, swimming, skiing; *Clubs* RAC, Harbour, Hurlingham; *Style*— Henry Carr, Esq; ✉ 11 South Square, Gray's Inn, London WC1R 5EU (☎ 0171 405 1222, fax 0171 242 4282)

CARR, Ian Cufaude; DL (Cumbria 1988); s of Laurence Carr (d 1938), and Beryl, *née* Cufaude (d 1979); *b* 12 Aug 1928; *Educ* Rugby; *m* 1, 24 May 1952 (m dis 1975), Doreen, *née* Hindle; 2 s (Jonathan Michael Ian b 12 April 1954, Dominic David b 11 Oct 1966), 2 da (Melanie Elizabeth b 3 Nov 1956, Stephanie Clare b 31 May 1960); m 2, 1976, Mrs Rilla Cameron Diggle, *née* Carr; 1 step s (Peter), 1 step da (Alison); *Career* chm Carr's Milling Industries plc 1964–; chm: E Cumbria Health Authy 1986–94, N Cumbria Health Authy 1994–; chm: Penrith and Border Conservative Assoc 1970–75, Solway Rural Initiative 1992–94; High Sheriff of Cumbria 1991–92; *Recreations* shooting, golf; *Clubs* Royal and Ancient Golf, Silloth Golf, Southerness Golf, Border and County (Carlisle); *Style*— Ian Carr, Esq, DL; ✉ Brown Hill, Walton, Brampton, Cumbria CA8 2JW (☎ 016977 2540); Carr's Milling Industries plc, Stanwix, Carlisle CA3 9BA (☎ 01228 28291)

CARR, Ian Henry Randell; s of Thomas Randell Carr (d 1979), of Gosforth, Newcastle upon Tyne, and Phyllis Harriet Carr (d 1985); *b* 21 April 1933; *Educ* Barnard Castle Sch, King's Coll Newcastle Upon Tyne (BA, DipEd); *m* 1, 28 June 1963, Margaret Blackburn (d 1967), da of John Lowery Bell (missing presumed dead 1943), of Annfield Plain, Co Durham; 1 da (Selina b 29 July 1967); m 2, 9 Dec 1972 (m dis 1989), Sandra Louise, *née* Major; *Career* Nat Serv 2 Lt Royal Northumberland Fusiliers 1956–58, served NI and W Germany; performer: Emcee Five Quintet 1960–62, Rendell-Carr Quintet 1963–69, Ian Carr's Nucleus 1969–89, The United Jazz and Rock Ensemble 1975– (worldwide tours); composed: Solar Plexus 1970, Labyrinth 1973, Will's Birthday Suite (for the Globe Theatre Tst) 1974, Out of the Long Dark 1978, Northumbrian Sketches 1988; assoc prof Guildhall Sch of Music and Drama; many presentations BBC Radio 3; memb Greater London Arts Assoc 1975–80; patron: Live Theatre Co Newcastle upon Tyne 1985–, Art at the Whittington Hosp Appeal Islington; PRS 1970; memb: Royal Soc of Musicians of GB 1982, Assoc of Professional Composers 1983, Central Music Advsy Ctee BBC Radio and TV 1987–89; Italian Calabria award 1982; *Books* Music Outside (1973), Miles Davis: A Critical Biography (1982), Keith Jarrett: The Man and his Music (1991), Rough Guide to Jazz (jtly, 1995); *Recreations* music, the visual arts, world literature, travel; *Style*— Ian Carr, Esq; ✉ 34 Brailsford Rd, London SW2 2TE (☎ 0181 671 7195)

CARR, Marian Jane; da of David Fitzroy Ashmore (d 1974), and Marigold Vaugham, *née* Wilkes (d 1964); *b* 13 Dec 1946; *Educ* Wycombe Abbey; *m* 22 March 1975 (m dis 1987), Kenneth; *Career* Midland Ladies golf champion 1979, admin sec Ladies Golf Union 1986–87, sec Eng Ladies Golf Assoc 1987–; *Recreations* golf; *Clubs* Edgbaston Golf, Royal St David's Golf (Harlech); *Style*— Mrs Marian Carr; ✉ Coal Cottage, 87 Northfield Road, Harborne, Birmingham B17 0ST (☎ 0121 681 1774), English Ladies Golf Association, Edgbaston Golf Club, Church Rd, Birmingham B15 3TB (☎ 0121 456 2088)

CARR, Peter Derek; CBE (1989); s of George William (d 1972), of Mexborough, Yorkshire, and Marjorie, *née* Tailby; *b* 12 July 1930; *Educ* Fircroft Coll Birmingham, Ruskin Coll Oxford, Garnett Coll London; *m* 12 April 1958, Geraldine Pamela, da of Alexander Quarrier Ward, of Babbacombe; 1 s (Steven John b 1959), 1 da (Alyce b 1963); *Career* Nat Serv Mountain Rescue Serv RAF 1951–53; site mangr Construction Indust 1944–60, sr lectr in mgmnt Thurrock Coll Essex 1964–69, advsr Nat Bd for Prices and Incomes 1967–69, dir Cmmn on Industl Rels 1969–74, section dir ACAS 1974–78, dip serv cnsllr Br Embassy Washington DC 1978–83, regnl dir DOE Northern and ldr Govt City Action Team 1983–89; chm: Northern Regnl Health Authy 1990–94, Co Durham Devpt Co 1990–, Northern Screen Cmmn, NHS Supra Regnl Services Advsy Gp 1993–94, Durham County Waste Management Co 1993–, Occupational Pensions Bd 1994–; sr ptnr Peter D Carr and Assocs, visiting fell Univ of Durham 1990–; *Books* Worker Participation and Collective Bargaining in Europe, Industrial Relations in the National Newspaper Industry; *Recreations* cabinet making, cycling, cooking; *Style*— Peter D Carr, Esq, CBE; ✉ Corchester Towers, Corbridge, Northumberland NE45 5NR (☎ 01434 632841, fax 01434 633726)

CARR, Sir (Albert) Raymond Maillard; kt (1987); s of Reginald Maillard Carr, of Bath; *b* 11 April 1919; *Educ* Brockenhurst Sch, Christ Church Oxford; *m* 1950, Sara, da of Algernon Strickland, of Apperley, Glos; 3 s, 1 da; *Career* former fell of All Souls' and New Coll Oxford, prof of Latin American history Univ of Oxford 1967–68, warden of St Antony's Coll Oxford 1968–87; author; DLitt Univ of Oxford; FBA; *Recreations* foxhunting; *Style*— Sir Raymond Carr, FBA; ✉ Burch, North Molton, South Molton, Devon EX36 3JU (☎ 01769 550267)

CARR, Rodney Paul (Rod); s of Capt George Paul Carr, of Whatton-in-the-Vale, Nottingham, and Alma, *née* Walker (d 1960); *b* 10 March 1950; *Educ* Carlton Le Willows GS Nottingham, Univ of Birmingham (BSc); *m* 21 July 1971, Lynne Alison, da of Charles Wilfred Ashwell; 1 s (David b 15 Feb 1982), 1 da (Joanne b 17 Oct 1979); *Career* yachtsman; instr London Borough of Haringey 1972–75, chief instr and dep dir Nat Sailing Centre Cowes IOW 1979–81 (instr 1975–79), memb winning Br Admirals Cup team 1981, chief racing coach (yachting) Royal Yachting Assoc 1984– (olympic coach 1981–92), olympic team mangr 1992–; coach to: J Richards and P Allan Flying Dutchman Class Bronze medal Olympics 1984, M McIntyre and B Vaile Star Class Gold medal Olympics 1988; mangr of: Ben Ainstie, John Merricks and Ian Walker (Olympic Silver Medallists 1996); *Recreations* sailing, music; *Style*— Rod Carr, Esq; ✉ 14 Spring Way, Alresford, Hampshire S024 9LN (☎ 01962 734148); Royal Yachting Association, RYA House, Romsey Rd, Eastleigh, Hants (☎ 01703 629962, fax 01703 629924)

CARR, Roger Martyn; *b* 22 Dec 1946; *Educ* Nottingham HS, Nottingham Poly; *m* Stephanie; 1 da; *Career* various appts Honeywell, gen mgmnt appts various engrg cos until 1982; Williams Holdings PLC: joined 1982, gp md 1988–94, chief exec 1994–; non-exec dir Thames Water plc; memb Econ Affairs Ctee CBI, dir Landau Forte City Technology Coll; *Style*— Roger Carr, Esq; ✉ Williams Holdings PLC, Pentagon House, Sir Frank Whittle Road, Derby DE21 4XA (☎ 01332 202020, fax 01332 384402)

CARR, Dr Stephen Paul; s of Denis Carr, and Muriel Betty, *née* Jamieson; *b* 1 May 1955; *Educ* Marple Hall GS, Univ of Warwick (BA), Univ of Oxford (DPhil); *m* 9 July 1977, Pamela Susan, da of Prof Harold Leslie Rosenthal; 2 s (Jonathan Gilbert b 1989, David Gerald b 1991); *Career* food mfrg analyst Rowe and Pitman 1979–89; Warburg Securities: divnl dir 1986–89, head of UK res and dir Warburg Securities Ltd 1989–93, head of Group Equity Research 1993–95; md and head of Global Research SBC Warburg 1995–; *Style*— Dr Stephen Carr; ✉ Lower Woodside Farm, Woodside Lane, Lower Farringdon, Alton, Hants GU3X 3EX (☎ 01420 587384); SBC Warburg, 1 Finsbury Ave, London EC2M 2PA (☎ 0171 606 1066)

CARR, Dr Thomas Ernest Ashdown (Tommy); CB (1977); s of Laurence Hudson Ashdown Carr (d 1959), and Norah E V, *née* Taylor; *b* 21 June 1915; *Educ* Co HS for Boys Altrincham, Victoria Univ Manchester (BSc, MB ChB); *m* 1940, Mary Sybil, da of Percy Harold Enoch Dunkey (d 1979); 1 s, 2 da; *Career* served WWII Maj RAMC NW Europe; RCGP: provost SE England Faculty 1962–64, memb Cncl 1964–66; princ med offr DHSS 1966, sr princ med offr GP and Regnl Med Serv 1967–79, pt/t med referee 1979–87; chm: QUIT (Nat Soc of Non-Smokers) 1982–86 (vice pres 1986–93), Guildford Div BMA 1988–89; memb: Guildford Philharmonic Soc 1963–89, Yvonne Arnaud Theatre Club 1964–89, Guildford Soc 1968–89, Richmond Concert Soc 1987–91, Putney Music 1987–, Putney Soc 1989–, Barnes and Castlenau Music Soc 1991–95; DObstRCOG, FRCGP, FFCM; *Recreations* music, photography; *Clubs* Civil Service, RSM; *Style*— Dr Tommy Carr, CB; ✉ 17 Westpoint, Putney Hill, London SW15 6RU (☎ 0181 788 9969)

CARR, Thomas James (Tom); OBE (1992); s of Thomas James Carr (d 1956), and late Mary, *née* Workman; *b* 21 Sept 1909; *Educ* Oundle, Slade Sch of Art London; *m* 1935, Stella Francesca, da of late Harold Robbins; 3 da (Ann Francesca b 1935, Veronica Mary b 1941, Stella Jemmima (Jemma) b 1949); *Career* artist; numerous exhibitions in London in early 1930s (associated with Euston Rd Gp), returned to Ireland 1939; work in public collections incl: Arts Cncl, Queens Univ Belfast, The Tate Gallery, Haverty Tst, Southampton Art Gallery, Bristol Art Gallery, V & A Museum, Ulster Museum; private collections incl HM Queen Elizabeth the Queen Mother; Hon DLitt Queens Univ Belfast 1992; memb Royal Ulster Acad, hon memb RHA, NEAC; *Style*— Tom Carr, Esq, OBE; ✉ Manor House, Wolterton Road, Itteringham, Norwich NR11 7AF

CARR, Very Rev Dr (Arthur) Wesley; s of Arthur Eugene Carr, and Irene Alice, *née* Cummins; *b* 26 July 1941; *Educ* Dulwich, Jesus Coll Oxford (MA), Jesus Coll Cambridge (MA), Ridley Hall Cambridge, Sch of Ecumenical Studies Geneva, Univ of Sheffield (PhD); *m* 20 April 1967, Natalie Gay, da of Norman Robert Gill; 1 da (Helga b 1973); *Career* curate Luton Parish Church 1967–71, tutor Ridley Hall 1970–71 (chaplain 1971–72), Sir Henry Stephenson fell in biblical studies Univ of Sheffield 1972–74, hon curate Ranmoor Parish Church Sheffield 1972–74, chaplain Chelmsford Cathedral 1974–78 (canon residentiary 1978–87), dep dir and programme dir Chelmsford Cathedral Centre for Research and Trg 1974–82, Bishop of Chelmsford's dir of trg 1976–84, examining chaplain to Bishop of Chelmsford 1976–86, dean of Bristol 1987–97, dean of Westminster Feb 1997–; hon fell Dept of Christian Ethics and Applied Theology New Coll Edinburgh 1986–94; *Books* Angels and Principalities (1981), 'Angels' and 'The Devil' in A Dictionary of Christian Spirituality (1983), The Priestlike Task (1985), Brief Encounters, Pastoral Ministry through the Occasional Offices (1985), The Pastor as Theologian (1989), Lost in Familiar Places (with E R Shapiro, 1991), Manifold Wisdom (1991), A Handbook of Pastoral Studies (1997); articles in various jls; *Recreations* reading, writing, music, gardening; *Style*— The Very Rev Dr Wesley Carr; ✉ The Deanery, Deans Yard, Westminster Abbey, London SW1P 3PA (☎ 0171 222 2953)

CARR-ELLISON, Col Sir Ralph Harry; kt (1973), TD (1962), ED (TAVR 1974); s of Maj John Campbell Carr-Ellison (d 1956), of Hedgeley Hall, and his 1 wife, Daphne Hermione Indica, *née* Cradock (m dis 1946, d 1984); *b* 8 Dec 1925; *Educ* Eton; *m* 1951, Mary Clare McMorrough (d 1996), da of Maj Arthur Thomas McMorrough Kavanagh, MC (d 1953), of Borris House, Co Carlow; 3 s, 1 da; *Career* served: RGH CMF 1945–46, The Royal Dragoons BAOR 1946–49, TA and TAVR 1949–73; Lt-Col cmdg Northumberland Hussars 1966–69, Territorial Col (TAVR) 1969–73, Hon Col Northumbrian Univs OTC 1982–86, Northumberland Hussar Sqdns 1986–88, Queen's Own Yeo 1988–90, Col Cmdt The Yeomanry 1990–94, ADC (TAVR) to HM The Queen 1970–75; dir: Newcastle and Gateshead Water Co 1964–73, Trident Television 1972–81 (dep chm 1976–81); chm: Northumbrian Water Authy 1973–82, Tyne Tees Television Ltd 1974– (dir 1966–); dir Yorkshire-Tyne Tees Holdings plc 1992– (dep chm 1992–93); chm: N Tyne Area Manpower Bd MSC 1983–84, N of England Territorial Assoc 1976–80 (pres 1987–90, vice pres 1990–), Univ of Newcastle Devpt Tst 1979–81 (tstee 1992–); pres The Automobile Association 1995– (vice chm 1985–86, chm 1986–95); memb Ct Univ of Newcastle 1979–, vice chm Nat Union of Cons and Unionist Assoc 1969–71, govr Swinton Cons Coll 1967–81, pres Northern Area Cons Cncl 1974–78 (treas 1961–66, chm 1966–69), memb Cncl Scout Assoc 1982– (co cmmr Northumberland 1958–68, pres 1989–); former JP Northumberland, High Sheriff 1972, DL 1981–85, Vice Lord Lt Northumberland 1984, Lord Lt for County of Tyne and Wear 1984–; Hon DCL Univ of Newcastle upon Tyne 1989; FRSA 1983; KStJ 1984; *Recreations* jt master West Percy Foxhounds 1950–90; *Clubs* Cavalry and Guards', Pratt's, White's, Northern Counties (Newcastle); *Style*— Col Sir Ralph Carr-Ellison, TD, ED; ✉ Beanley Hall, Beanley, Alnwick, Northumberland NE66 2DX (☎ 01665 578273, fax 01665 578080); Newcastle upon Tyne (☎ 0191 261 0181)

CARR-LOCKE, Prof David Leslie; s of Dennis Charlton Carr-Locke, of Melksham, Wilts, and Ruby Marjorie, *née* Gibbs; *b* 19 Aug 1948; *Educ* Hardenhuish GS Chippenham, Gonville and Caius Coll Cambridge (MA, MB BChir); *m* Sandra Anne Cialfi; 1 s (Alexander Charles Scott b 26 Nov 1974), 1 da (Antonia Louise Papworth b 26 Nov 1974); *Career* med and surgical house offr Kettering Gen Hosp 1972–73; sr house offr: obstetrics and gynaecology Orsett Hosp Essex 1973–74, med specialities Leicester Gp of Hosps 1974–75; lectr in med (gastroenterology) Univ of Leicester 1975–83, res fell in gastroenterology New England and Baptist Hosp Boston USA 1978–79, conslt physician in gastroenterology Royal Infirmary 1983–89, dir of endoscopy and dir of clinical gastroenterology Brigham and Women's Hosp 1989–, assoc prof of med Harvard Med Sch 1989–; pres Int Hepato-Pancreato-Biliary Assoc 1994–96; FRCP 1988; *Books* Endoscopy (1990); *Recreations* music, tennis, skiing, travel; *Clubs* Harvard (Boston USA); *Style*— Prof David Carr-Locke; ✉ Division of Gastroenterology, Brigham and Women's Hospital, 75 Francis St, Boston, MA 02115, USA (☎ 00 1 617 732 7414, fax 00 1 617 732 7407)

CARR OF HADLEY, Baron (Life Peer UK 1975), of Hadley in Greater London; (Leonard) Robert Carr; PC (1963); s of late Ralph Edward Carr, and Katie Elizabeth Carr, of Totteridge, Herts; *b* 11 Nov 1916; *Educ* Westminster, Gonville and Caius Coll Cambridge; *m* 1943, Joan Kathleen, da of Dr E W Twining, of Cheadle, Cheshire; 1 s (decd), 2 da (Hon Susan Elizabeth (Hon Mrs Rhodri Bradley-Jones), Hon Virginia Sarah (Hon Mrs Michael Fox)); *Career* MP (C) Mitcham 1950–74, Sutton (Carshalton) 1974–75; former PPS to Sir Anthony Eden; Parly sec to Min of Lab and Nat Serv 1955–59, sec for Tech Co-operation 1963–64, sec of state for Employment 1970–72, Lord Pres of the Cncl and ldr of the House of Commons 1972, sec of state for Home Affairs 1972–74; former dir: Prudential Corporation plc (chm 1980–85), Prudential Assurance Co Ltd (chm 1980–85), Securicor Ltd 1961–63, 1965–70 and 1974–85, SGB Group Ltd 1974–86, Cadbury Schweppes Group plc 1979–87; former govr and dep chm of governing body Imperial Coll of Science and Technol (fell 1985), chm Business in the Community 1984–87; *Recreations* tennis, music, gardening; *Clubs* Brooks's, Surrey County Cricket (pres 1985–86), All England Lawn Tennis and Croquet (vice pres 1990–); *Style*— The Rt Hon the Lord Carr of Hadley, PC; ✉ 14 North Court, Great Peter St, London SW1

CARR-SMITH, Maj Gen Stephen R; *b* 3 Dec 1941; *Educ* RMA Sandhurst, Open Univ (BA 1992); *m*; 2 s, 1 da; *Career* cmmnd Royal Corps of Signals 1962, various staff and regtl appts UK, Germany, Aden and Libya, RMCS 1971, psc 1972, sometime instr RMA Sandhurst; instr Army Staff Coll Camberley (as Lt Col) 1982–84, promoted Col 1984, chief exec Tech Trg Coll Harrogate 1984–86, head of Private Office to Chief Exec Equipment Procurement (Army) MOD London 1986–88, promoted Brig 1988, Dir Communications and Info Systems Plans and Policy Branch SHAPE 1988–91, promoted Maj Gen 1991, Dep DG NATO Communications and Info Systems Agency (NACISA) Brussels 1992–95; currently: dir of special devpts Defence Systems Ltd, sr mil advsr CORDA and BAeSEMA, Hon Col Women's Tport Serv (FANY), Col Cmdt Royal Signals; former pres and chm Army and Combined Servs Cricket and Hockey Assocs; FIMgt 1990; *Recreations* politics and international affairs, bridge, golf, theatre, most sports; *Style*— Maj Gen S R Carr-Smith; ✉ c/o Cox's and King's, 7 Pall Mall, London SW1Y 5NA

CARRAGHER, Patrick Matthew; s of Thomas A Carragher (d 1977), and Eileen M Carragher; *b* 21 Sept 1957; *Educ* St Catharine's Coll Cambridge (BA); *m* 1990, Alexandra;

2 da (Charlotte Maeve and Maria); *Career* gen sec Br Assoc of Colliery Mgmnt 1996– (full time offr 1981–); involved in a number of coal industry orgns incl Coal Soc, Coal Industry Social Welfare Orgn among others; *Recreations* hockey, squash, cinema, music; *Style*— Patrick Carragher, Esq; ✉ British Association of Colliery Management, 17 South Parade, Doncaster, S Yorks DN1 2DR (☎ 01302 815551, fax 01302 815552)

CARRATU, Nicholas Francis Ralph; s of L Mario Carratu, and L Anna, *née* Abate (d 1971); *b* 9 Jan 1937; *Educ* St Lawrence Coll Ramsgate; *m* 12 July 1964, Judith Anne, da of G Talbot-Spence; 2 s (Matthew b 2 March 1966, Benedict b 9 Aug 1969), 1 da (Charlotte b 27 Dec 1967); *Career* articled clerk Mann Judd & Co 1959–64; McLintock & Whinney Murray: joined 1965, conslt, ptnr 1971–76; Ernst & Young (and predecessor firms) 1976–91: ptnr, ptnr i/c fin mgmnt consultancy; ind conslt 1991–; FCA (ACA 1964), FIMC; *Recreations* sailing, mountaineering, sculpture; *Clubs* Little Ship; *Style*— Nicholas Carratu, Esq; ✉ Park House, 5 Weybridge Park, Weybridge, Surrey KT13 8SJ (☎ and fax 01932 853080)

CARRELL, Prof Robin Wayne; s of Ruane George Carrell, of Christchurch, NZ, and Constance Gwendoline, *née* Rowe; *b* 5 April 1936; *Educ* Christchurch Boys' HS NZ, Univ of Otago (MB ChB), Univ of Canterbury (BSc), Univ of Cambridge (MA, PhD); *m* 27 Jan 1962, Susan Wyatt, da of John Leonard Rogers (d 1975), Christchurch, NZ; 2 s (Thomas Wyatt George b 1968, Edward Robin William b 1970), 2 da (Sarah Anne b 1963, Rebecca Susan b 1964); *Career* MRC Abnormal Haemoglobin Unit Cambridge 1965–68, dir clinical Biochemistry Christchurch NZ 1968–75, lectr and conslt Addenbrooke's Hosp and Univ of Cambridge 1976–78, prof of pathology Christchurch Clinical Sch Univ of Otago 1978–86, prof of haematology Univ of Cambridge 1986–; Cwlth fell St John's Coll Cambridge 1985–86, fell Trinity Coll Cambridge 1987–; memb Gen Bd Univ of Cambridge 1989–92; FRACP 1973, FRCPath 1976, FRCP 1990, FRSNZ 1980; *Recreations* gardening, walking; *Style*— Prof Robin Carrell; ✉ 19 Madingley Road, Cambridge CB3 0EG (☎ 01223 312970); Haematology Department, University of Cambridge, MRC Centre, Hills Road, Cambridge CB2 2QH (☎ 01223 336788, fax 01223 336827)

CARRICK, 10 Earl of (I 1748); David James Theobald Somerset Butler; also Viscount Ikerrin (I 1629) and (sits as) Baron Butler of Mount Juliet (UK 1912); s of 9 Earl of Carrick (d 1992), and his 1 w, (Mary) Belinda (d 1993), da of Maj David Constable-Maxwell, TD; *b* 9 Jan 1953; *Educ* Downside; *m* 1975, Philippa Janice Victoria, da of Wing Cdr Leonard Victor Craxton, RAF (ret), of Lydgate One, West Road, Milford on Sea, Lymington, Hants; 3 s ((Arion) Thomas Piers Hamilton, Viscount Ikerrin b 1975, Hon Piers Edmund Theobald Lismalyn b 1979, Hon Lindsay Simon Turville Somerset b (twin) 1979); *Heir* s, Viscount Ikerrin b 1 Sept 1975; *Style*— The Earl of Carrick; ✉ Pant yr Eos, Moelfre, Llansilin, Oswestry, Shropshire SY10 7QR

CARRICK, HE Sir Roger John; KCMG (1995, CMG 1983), LVO (1972); s of John Horwood Carrick, of Whitchurch, Hants, and Florence May, *née* Pudner; *b* 13 Oct 1937; *Educ* Isleworth GS, London Univ Sch of Slavonic and East Euro Studies; *m* 1962, Hilary Elizabeth, da of Terence Verdun and Truda Blinman; 2 s (John, Charles); *Career* RN 1956–58; HM Dip Serv: FO 1958–61, Br Legation Sofia 1962–65, FO 1965–67, Br Embassy Paris 1967–71, Head of Chancery Br High Cmmn Singapore 1971–73, FCO 1973, cnsllr and dep head Personnel Ops Dept 1976, visiting fell Inst of Int Studies Univ of California Berkeley 1977–78, cnsllr Br Embassy Washington 1978–82, head Overseas Estate Dept FCO 1982–85, HM consul gen Chicago 1985–88, asst under sec of state (economic) FCO 1988–90, ambassador to Republic of Indonesia 1990–94, high cmmr to Cwlth of Australia 1994– (to retire 1997); Churchill fell (life) Westminster Coll Fulton Missouri 1987; *Books* East-West Technology Transfer in Perspective (1978); *Recreations* sailing, music, reading, avoiding gardening; *Clubs* Royal Over-Seas League, Melbourne, Australian (Sydney), Lord's Taverners, Canberra, Cook Society, Pilgrims; *Style*— HE Sir Roger Carrick, KCMG, LVO; ✉ c/o FCO (Canberra), King Charles Street, London SW1A 2AH

CARRINGTON, Prof Alan; s of Albert Carrington (d 1971), of Chandler's Ford, Hants, and Constance, *née* Nelson; *b* 6 Jan 1934; *Educ* Colfes GS, Univ of Southampton (BSc, PhD); *m* 7 Nov 1959, (Noreen) Hilary, da of Patrick Ferraby Taylor (d 1981); 1 s (Simon Francis b 1966), 2 da (Sarah Elizabeth b 1962, Rebecca Anne b 1964); *Career* res fell Univ of Minnesota 1957–58, asst dir res and official fell Downing Coll Cambridge 1963–67 (GEC res fell 1959–60, asst res and res fell Downing Coll 1960–63), Royal Soc res prof Univ of Southampton 1979–84 and 1987– (prof of chemistry 1967–76, SERC sr res fell 1976–79), Royal Soc res prof and professorial fell Jesus Coll Oxford 1984–87; awards: Harrison Meml Medal and Prize Chem Soc 1962, Meldola Medal Royal Inst of Chemistry 1963, Marlow Medal Faraday Soc 1966, Corday-Morgan Medal and Prize Chem Soc 1967, Award and Medal for Structural Chemistry Chem Soc 1970, Tilden Medal and lectureship Chem Soc 1972, Faraday Medal Royal Soc of Chemistry 1985, Davy Medal Royal Soc 1992; Hon DSc Univ of Southampton 1985; foreign hon memb American Acad of Arts and Scis 1987, foreign assoc US Nat Acad of Scis 1994; FRS 1971 (memb Ctees), FRSC 1989, CChem 1989, FInstP, CPhys 1993; *Books* Introduction to Magnetic Resonance (with A D McLachlan, 1967), Microwave Spectroscopy of Free Radicals (1974); *Recreations* music; *Style*— Prof Alan Carrington, FRS; ✉ 46 Lakewood Rd, Chandler's Ford, Hants SO53 1EX (☎ 01703 265092); Department of Chemistry, Univ of Southampton, Hants SO17 1BJ (☎ 01703 593431, telex 37661)

CARRINGTON, Maj-Gen Colin Edward George; CB (1991), CBE (1983); s of Edgar John Carrington (d 1988), and Ruth, *née* West (d 1990); *b* 19 Jan 1936; *Educ* Royal Liberty Sch, RMA Sandhurst, Army Staff Coll, Nat Def Coll, RCDS; *m* 5 Aug 1967, Joy, da of Albert Louis Bracknell (d 1987); 1 s (Damian Edward Colin b 21 Oct 1970), 1 da (Hannah Jane b 17 April 1974); *Career* Troop Cdr BAOR 1956–59, Air Despatch duties 1960–64, instr RMA Sandhurst 1964–68, Sqdn Cdr BAOR 1972–74, Directing Staff Staff Coll 1976–78, CO 1 Armd Div Tport Regt 1978–80, Dep COS 1 Armd Div 1980–82, dir Manning Policy (Army) 1984–86, Cdr Tport 1 (BR) Corps 1986–88, dir gen Tport and Movements (Army) 1988–91, Cdr Army Security Vetting Unit 1991–, Col Comdt The Royal Logistic Corps, Hon Col 152 (Ulster) Amb Regt RLC (TA); tstee Army Benevolent Fund; Freeman City of London, Liveryman Worshipful Co of Carmen; FCIT 1988, FILDM 1989; *Recreations* gardening, golf, reading; *Style*— Maj-Gen Colin Carrington, CB, CBE; ✉ ASVU, RMA Woolwich, Woolwich, London (☎ 0181 854 2242 ext 5640)

CARRINGTON, Hon Mrs (Jennifer Michelle); *née* Souter; da and co-hp of 25 Baron Audley, *qv*; *b* 23 May 1948; *m* 1978, Michael William Carrington; 2 s (Jesse Michael b 1978, Jonah David b 1980), 1 da (Holly Rosina b 1975); *Style*— The Hon Mrs Carrington; ✉ 620 Vista Del Mar, Aptos, California 95003, USA

CARRINGTON, Matthew Hadrian Marshall; MP (C) Fulham (majority 6,579); s of Walter Hadrian Marshall Carrington, of London, and Dilys Mary Gwyneth Carrington; *b* 19 Oct 1947; *Educ* French Lycée London, Imperial Coll London (BSc), London Business Sch (MSc); *m* 29 March 1975, Mary Lou, da of Robert Darrow, of Columbus, Ohio, USA; 1 da (Victoria b 11 June 1981); *Career* prodn foreman GKN Sankey 1969–72; banker: First National Bank of Chicago 1974–78, Saudi International Bank 1978–87; MP (C) Fulham 1987–, PPS to Rt Hon John Patten MP as Sec of State for Educn 1992–94, memb Treasy and Civil Serv Select Ctee 1994–; *Recreations* cooking, political history; *Style*— Matthew Carrington, Esq, MP; ✉ House of Commons, London SW1A 0AA (☎ 0171 219 6855)

CARRINGTON, Nigel Martyn; s of Thomas Ronald Carrington, and Vera, *née* Yeoman; *b* 1 May 1956; *Educ* Brighton Coll, St John's Coll Oxford (BA, pres Oxford Univ Law Soc 1977); *m* 2 Jan 1988, Elisabeth Buchanan; 1 s (Leo b 10 May 1990), 2 da (Olivia b 2 Sept 1993, Isabella b 12 Oct 1996); *Career* Baker & McKenzie: articled clerk 1979–81, assoc 1981–87, ptnr 1987–, managing ptnr 1994–; memb City of London Slrs' Co; *Books* Acquiring Companies and Businesses in Europe (1994); *Recreations* swimming, music, wine; *Clubs* Royal Automobile; *Style*— Nigel Carrington, Esq; ✉ Managing Partner, Baker & McKenzie, 100 New Bridge Street, London EC4V 7JA (☎ 0171 919 1000, fax 0171 919 1999)

CARRINGTON, 6 Baron (I 1796, GB 1797); Peter Alexander Rupert Carington; KG (1985), GCMG (1988, KCMG 1958), CH (1983), MC (1945), PC (1959); s of 5 Baron Carington, JP, DL (d 1938, n of 3 Baron, KG, GCMG, PC, JP, DL, sometime MP High Wycombe, and also 1 and last Marquess of Lincolnshire, govr of New South Wales, Lord Great Chamberlain of England and Lord Privy Seal) by his w, Hon Sybil, da of 2 Viscount Colville of Culross; *b* 6 June 1919; *Educ* Eton, RMC Sandhurst; *m* 1942, Iona, yr da of Sir Francis Kennedy McClean, AFC (d 1955); 1 s, 2 da (Hon Mrs de Bunsen, Hon Virginia); *Heir* s, Hon Rupert Carington; *Career* served as Maj Gren Gds NW Europe; Parly sec Miny of Agric and Fisheries 1951–54, MOD 1954–56, high cmmr Australia 1956–59, First Lord of Admiralty 1959–63, min without portfolio and ldr of House of Lords 1963–64, ldr of oppn House of Lords 1964–70 and 1974–79; sec of state: for defence 1970–74, Dept of Energy 1974; min of aviation supply 1971–74; sec of state for foreign and Cwlth affrs and min of overseas devpt 1979–82; chm Cons Party 1972–74, sec gen NATO 1984–88, chm EC Peace Conf on Yugoslavia 1991–92; JP Bucks 1948, DL 1951; chm GEC 1983–84 (dir 1982–84); dir: Christies International Ltd 1988– (chm 1988–93), The Telegraph plc 1990–, M C European Capital Holdings SA; non-exec dir Chime Communications 1993–; fell Eton 1966–81, hon fell St Antony's Coll Oxford 1982–; memb Int Bd United World Colls 1982–84, chm Bd of Tstees V&A Museum 1983–88; chllr: Order of St Michael and St George 1984–94, Univ of Reading 1992–, Order of the Garter 1994–; pres: Pilgrims 1983–, VSO 1993–; Hon Bencher Middle Temple 1983, Hon Elder Brother Trinity House 1984; Hon LLD Univs of: Leeds 1981, Cambridge 1981, Philippines 1982, S Carolina 1983, Aberdeen 1985, Harvard 1986, Sussex 1989, Reading 1989, Buckingham 1989, Nottingham 1993, Birmingham 1993; Hon DSc Cranfield 1983, Hon DUniv Essex; Liveryman Worshipful Co of Clothworkers; *Books* Reflect on Things Past - The Memoirs of Lord Carrington (1988); *Clubs* Pratt's, White's; *Style*— The Rt Hon the Lord Carrington, KG, GCMG, CH, MC, PC; ✉ 32A Ovington Square, London SW3 1LR (☎ 0171 584 1476); The Manor House, Bledlow, Princes Risborough, Bucks HP27 9PB (☎ 01844 343499)

CARRINGTON, Robert George (Bob); s of Jack Day Carrington, of Wigan, and Florence Mary, *née* Swift; *b* 1 June 1946; *Educ* Bolton Sch, Univ of E Anglia (BA), Univ of Leeds (Dip in TESL, MA); *m* (m dis); 2 da (Anita Garcia b 26 June 1975, Marina Garcia b 21 May 1982), 1 s (Michael Garcia b 22 March 1978); *Career* EFL teacher Bell Sch of Languages 1969–70, teacher/dep supt of teacher trg Anglo-Brazilian Cultural Soc São Paulo 1970–74, lectr in TEFL/TESL St John's Coll of FE Manchester 1975–76, supt Campinas branch Anglo-Brazilian Cultural Soc 1976–79, dir of studies Linguarama do Brasil 1979–80, asst dir of studies Anglo-Brazilian Cultural Soc São Paulo 1981–83, exec dir Anglo-Brazilian Cultural Soc Curitiba 1983–89, assoc dir Phil Young's English Sch Curitiba 1989, ptnr and md Euro-American Language Center Curitiba 1990; British Council: asst dir of studies Lisbon 1991–92, dir Coimbra 1992–93, dir Porto 1993–; examiner in TEFL and TESL RSA 1975–; fndr pres BRAZ-TESOL/IATEFL 1986–89 (life memb 1991–), memb ESU; *Recreations* sports, amateur dramatics, reading, travel; *Clubs* Oporto Cricket and Lawn Tennis; *Style*— Bob Carrington; ✉ The British Council, Rua do Breyner 155, 4050 Oporto, Portugal (☎ 00 351 207 3060, fax 00 351 207 3068)

CARRINGTON, Simon Robert; s of Robert Carrington, of Suffolk, and Jean, *née* Hill, of Wilts; *b* 23 Oct 1942; *Educ* ChCh Cathedral Choir Sch Oxford, The King's Sch Canterbury, King's Coll Cambridge, New Coll Oxford; *m* 2 Aug 1969, Hilary Elizabeth, da of Leslie Stott (d 1964); 1 s (Jamie b 1973), 1 da (Rebecca b 1971); *Career* dir The King's Singers 1968–93; freelance Double Bass player, teacher and adjudicator; dir Choral Summer Sch Marlborough Coll Wilts and Berwang Austria; with The King's Singers: 40 LPs for EMI, tours worldwide, concerts, workshops and master classes; regular TV appearances worldwide incl: Live at the Boston Pops 1983, BBC TV Series The King's Singers Madrigal History Tour 1984, ABC TV (USA) The Sound of Christmas from Salzburgh 1987, 8 appearances on the Johnny Carson Tonight Show (NBC TV, USA) 1983–90; festival dir Barbican Summer in the City Festivals 1988–89, 20 Anniversary Concerts Worldwide 1988, Grammy nomination USA 1986; prof, dir of choral activities and artist in residence Univ of Kansas 1994–; choral conductor, clinician and memb int juries: German Nat Music Competition 1994 and 1996, Florilège Vocal de Tours, Int Choral Festival Arnhem Holland; FRSA; *Books* The King's Singers - a Self Portrait (1981); choral arrangements for publication; *Recreations* vintage cars, inland waterways, gardens, trees, walking, jogging; *Clubs* Royal Soc of Musicians, Inc Soc of Musicians; *Style*— Simon Carrington, Esq; ✉ 1325 Strong Avenue, Lawrence, Kansas 66044, USA (☎ 00 1 913 832 2408); Department of Music and Dance, School of Fine Arts, 452 Murphy Hall, Lawrence, Kansas 66045–2279, USA (☎ 00 1 913 864 3248, fax 00 1 913 864 5387); Puy Calvel, 46249 Lamothe Cassel, France (☎ 00 33 65 36 81 25)

CARROL, Charles Gordon; s of Charles Muir Carrol (d 1974), of Edinburgh, and Catherine Gray, *née* Napier; *b* 21 March 1935; *Educ* Melville Coll Edinburgh, Univ of Edinburgh (MA, DipEd); *m* 1970, Frances Anne, da of John A Sinclair, of Edinburgh; 3 s (Simon b 1971, Christopher b 1974, David b 1979); *Career* educn offr: Govt of Northern Nigeria 1959–65, Cwlth Inst Scotland 1965–71; dir Cwlth Inst Scotland 1971–; lay memb Press Cncl 1978–83; *Recreations* hill walking, angling; *Clubs* Edinburgh Univ Staff; *Style*— Charles Carrol, Esq; ✉ 11 Dukehaugh, Peebles, EH45 9DN (☎ 01721 21296); Commonwealth Institute Scotland, 8 Rutland Square, Edinburgh EH1 2AS (☎ 0131 229 6668)

CARROLL, Ben; s of Joseph Carroll, of Harrow, Middx, and Margaret, *née* O'Carroll; *b* 5 May 1945; *Educ* London Oratory; *m* 13 May 1967, Rosemary-Anne, da of Morris Tucker; *Career* Scottish Widows Fund & Life Assurance Soc 1964–66, Keith Shipton (Life & Pensions) Ltd 1966–68; Noble Lowndes & Partners Ltd 1968–93: md Noble Lowndes International Ltd 1986, md Employee Benefits 1988, md Personal Fin Servs 1990–93 (author of papers on behalf of firm); chief exec Bain Hogg Financial Services Ltd 1994, chm Bain Hogg Asset Management Ltd 1994, md Towry Law Financial Planning Ltd 1995, dir Towry Law plc; dir IFA Promotion Ltd 1993–96, dir IFA Assoc Ltd 1994; dir Soc of Fin Advsrs 1992– (chm 1992–95); memb Memb Ctee PIA 1994–; FPMI (pres 1987–89), FCII, MSFA; *Recreations* golf, travel, opera, theatre, modern films, art; *Clubs* RAC, Croham Hurst Golf; *Style*— Ben Carroll, Esq; ✉ Springhurst Close, Shirley, Surrey CR0 5AT

CARROLL, Dina; *Career* singer; debut album So Close (1993, UK no 2); Best Br Female Solo Artist BRIT Awards 1994; *Style*— Ms Dina Carroll

CARROLL, Gerald John Howard; s of John Robert Carroll, and Catherine Florence, *née* Howard; lineal descendant of ancient Sept O'Carroll, Princes of Ely, Barons of Ely O'Carroll, Co Offaly, Ireland; *b* 9 Oct 1951; *Educ* Herrington House, Ipswich Sch; *Career* tstee Carroll Foundation 1972–, chm The Carroll Corporation and associated worldwide cos 1972–, chief exec Farnborough Aerospace Group Ltd 1985–; dir: Solid State Securities Ltd 1973–, Dukes Park Industrial Estates Ltd 1974–75, Culver Developments 1980–, Automated Machine Industries Ltd 1980–, Strategic R & D Corporation Ltd 1985–, Carroll Aircraft Corporation Ltd 1985–, The Manchester Canal and Business Park Development Corporation Ltd 1986–, Anglo Soviet Development Corporation Ltd 1988–,

Carroll Anglo American Corporation 1989–, Carroll Australia Corporation Pty Ltd 1989–, Carroll Global Corporation plc 1989–, PYBT Development Fund (Northern) Ltd 1989–, Imperial Trading Corporation 1992–, Carroll Estate Corporation 1992–; tstee: Carroll Institute, Carroll Art Collection 1990–; memb: Br Helicopter Advsy Bd 1985–, Royal United Servs Inst 1988–, Chllr's Court of Benefactors Univ of Oxford 1990–, Capitol Historical Soc Washington DC; hon benefactor The Armoury Museum Kremlin Moscow; *Recreations* racing, sailing, shooting; *Clubs* Royal Thames Yacht, Old Ipswichian, Cavalry and Guards' (hon memb); *Style*— Gerald Carroll, Esq; ✉ 29 Eaton Square, Belgravia, London SW1W 9DF; Warren Park, Newmarket, Suffolk CB8 8QL; Carroll Group of Companies, 2–6 Catherine Place, Westminster, London SW1E 6HF (☎ 0171 828 6842)

CARROLL, John; s of Sean Carroll, of Bentley, nr Doncaster, and Norah, *née* Coombes; *b* 15 April 1964; *Educ* St Peter's HS Doncaster; *m* 17 Nov 1989, Tracy, da of John Hunter; 2 da (Danielle b 29 Oct 1990, Lauren b 4 Jan 1994); *Career* flat race jockey 1981–, best season 94 winners 1993; achievements: winner of Molecomb Stakes Group Three Goodwood 1988, winner of Cocked Hat of the North 1991, runner up Heinz 57 Group One Phoenix Park, winner Flying Childers Stakes Group Two on Paris House 1991, winner Newbury Sales Super Sprint Trophy on Paris House 1991, winner King George V Handicap on Learmont (Royal Ascot) 1993; winner Palace House Stakes Group Three: on Paris House 1993, on Mind Games 1995; winner Temple Stakes Group Two: on Paris House 1993, on Mind Games 1995; winner Norfolk Stakes Group Three on Mind Games; two winners inaugural Dubai World Cup Meeting 1996; *Recreations* shooting, fishing, playing football, golf; *Style*— John Carroll, Esq; ✉ The Paddocks, 279 Park Lane, Preesall, nr Blackpool, Lancs FY6 0LT (☎ 01253 812299, mobile 0589 860797); c/o Mr R Hale (☎ 01768 892291, mobile 0374 161202)

CARROLL, Prof John Edward; s of Sidney Wentworth Carroll (d 1959), and May Doris, *née* Brand; *b* 15 Feb 1934; *Educ* Oundle, Queens' Coll Cambridge (BA, MA, PhD, ScD); *m* Vera Mary, *née* Jordan; *Career* princ scientific offr Servs Electronic Res Laboratory 1961–67; Univ of Cambridge Engrg Dept: lectr 1967–76, reader 1976–83, prof 1983–, head of Electrical Div 1992–; chm Cncl School of Technology Univ of Cambridge 1996; fell Queens' Coll Cambridge 1961–; FIEE 1965, FEng 1985; *Books* Hot Electron Microwave Generators (1970), Semiconductor Devices (1974), Rate Equations in Semiconductor Electronics (1985); *Recreations* carpentry, walking, reading; *Style*— Prof John Carroll, FEng; ✉ Department of Engineering, University of Cambridge, Trumpington Street, Cambridge CB2 1PZ (☎ 01223 332675, fax 01223 332616)

CARROLL, His Hon Judge; Michael John; s of Matthew Carroll, of Holbrook, Suffolk, and Gladys, *née* Hensman; *b* 26 Dec 1948; *Educ* Shebbear Coll N Devon, City of London Coll Business Sch (BA Business Law), Cncl of Legal Educn (Bar finals); *m* 24 Aug 1974, Stella, da of Thomas Reilly; 3 da (Lisa b 27 July 1971, Erin b 8 Aug 1979, Joanna b 30 June 1986 (decd)), 2 s (Matthew b 4 May 1985, Padraig b 25 Jan 1989); *Career* called to the Bar Gray's Inn 1973, recorder 1994–96 (asst recorder 1990), circuit judge (SE Circuit) 1996–; *Recreations* antiques, reading, football; *Style*— His Hon Judge Carroll; ✉ 2 Paper Buildings, Temple, London EC4Y 7ET (☎ 0171 936 2613, fax 0171 353 9439)

CARRUTHERS, Dr (George) Barry; s of George Harry Carruthers, CBE (d 1979), and Mary, *née* Barry (d 1990); *b* 22 Dec 1924; *Educ* St Paul's, The Middx Hosp London (MD, MB BS); *m* 1; 4 s (Graeme David Barry b 2 June 1956, Stephen Robert b 3 Jan 1958, Richard Barry b 7 Jan 1965, Simon b 13 May 1967), 1 da (Nicola Jane Mary b 8 April 1971); m 2, 9 June 1990, Lesley Ann Connolly; *Career* med offr RAF 1949–57; med offr: Bank of England Printing Works 1956–71, Nat Heart Hosp 1960–, Royal Northern Hosp 1966–83; conslt in male infertility and dir of laboratories Royal Northern Hosp 1968–83, hon conslt Dept of Urology St Thomas' Hosp 1971–, med dir Wimpole St Med Centre 1981–; memb RSM 1971; *Books* Virility Diet (1973), Infertility (1981), Love Me, Love My Dog (1994); *Recreations* antiquarian books and prints, golf, bridge; *Clubs* Reform; *Style*— Dr Barry Carruthers; ✉ 55 Wimpole St, London W1M 7DF (☎ 0171 486 4646)

CARRUTHERS, Philip Anthony (Tony); s of Donald Carruthers (d 1983), of Torquay, Devon, and Beatrice Ada, *née* Tremain (d 1987); *b* 29 Nov 1934; *Educ* Homelands Tech HS Torquay, S Devon Tech Coll Torquay; *m* 4 April 1964, Sheila Mary, da of Rowdon Atkins (d 1956), and Kathleen Atkins, *née* Mooney (d 1971), of St Marychurch, Torquay, Devon; 1 da (Anne-Marie Carole (Mrs Andrew Adams, JP) b 1966); *Career* RN 1951–54, RNR 1954–59; dir: Charles Moxham & Co Ltd 1960–68 (joined 1954), Moxhams of Torquay Ltd (Barlow Group) 1968–72, Thos Barlow Motors Ltd 1970–72, Barlow Handling Ltd 1972–94 (co sec 1975–94), Barlow Handling (Properties) Ltd 1973–94, Barlow Handling Group Ltd 1975–94, Thos Barlow (Holdings) Ltd (Materials Handling Div of J Bibby & Sons plc) 1985–94, Barlow Pension Trust Ltd 1986–, DD Lamson plc 1990–94; voluntary advsr Occupational Pension Advsy Serv (OPAS) London 1994–; memb Employers' Panel Industl Tbnls Eng and Wales 1992–; memb: Henley Royal Regatta, Henley Festival of Music and Art; FInstD 1968; *Recreations* home computers, gardening, theatre, looking after two Bedlington terriers, music, opera, Probus, eating out, wine, enjoying retirement; *Clubs* Leander (asst hon sec), Phyllis Court (Henley), IOD; *Style*— Tony Carruthers, Esq; ✉ St Marymead, Wargrave, Berks (☎ 0118 940 2693); Moongates, Torquay, Devon

CARRUTHERS, Rutherford; s of William Arthur Carruthers (d 1989), of Pitlochry, and Annie Laing, *née* Stephen (d 1988); *b* 24 Jan 1934; *Educ* Pitlochry HS, Dundee Coll of Technol, Dundee Coll of Commerce (HNC); *m* 1964, Marianne Helen, da of John Hutcheson Thomson; 2 s (Stephen Ford b 4 Oct 1965, Andrew David b 12 Jan 1971), 1 da (Judith Marieanne (Mrs Judith Dingwall) b 16 March 1968); *Career* apprentice TV engr R W Bell (Electrical) Pitlochry Ltd 1949–55, electronic technician UK Atomic Energy Cmmn 1955–56, rejoined R W Bell as service engr 1956–59, mangr Retail Div Lowdon Bros & Co Engineers Ltd 1967–72 (branch mangr Arbroath 1959–67); chm: R W Bell (Electrical) Pitlochry Ltd 1972–, R Carruthers (Electrical) Ltd 1972–87, Expert UK Ltd mktg conslts 1978–81, Expert International GmbH Switzerland 1978–85, Novafon Ltd direct mktg 1986–, Highland Perthshire Development Co Ltd Enterprise Tst 1988–90, Heartland FM local radio 1990–96; small business cnsllr Scottish Devpt Agency 1985–87; pres Electrical Contractors' Assoc of Scotland 1991–93; memb: Scottish Cncl Royal Cwlth Soc for the Blind 1988–96, Bd Perth Coll of FE; MCIM, MIMgt; *Recreations* golf, music, theatre, community radio; *Clubs* Pitlochry Rotary (past pres), Pitlochry Golf (past capt); *Style*— Rutherford Carruthers, Esq; ✉ Gayfields, 1 Duff Avenue, Moulin, Pitlochry, Perthshire PH16 5EN; R W Bell (Electrical) Pitlochry Ltd, 3 Atholl Rd, Pitlochry, Perthshire PH16 (☎ 01796 472735, fax 01796 473479)

CARSBERG, Sir Bryan Victor; kt (1989); s of Alfred Victor Carsberg, of Chesham Bois, Bucks, and Maryllia Cicely, *née* Collins (d 1996); *b* 3 Jan 1939; *Educ* Berkhamsted, LSE (MSc), Univ of Manchester (MA); *m* 1960, Margaret Linda, da of Capt Neil McKenzie Graham (d 1966); 2 da (Debbie, Sarah); *Career* in sole practice as CA 1962–64, lectr in accounting LSE 1964–68, visiting lectr Graduate Sch of Business Univ of Chicago 1968–69, prof of accounting Univ of Manchester 1969–81 (dean Faculty of Econ and Social Studies 1977–78), visiting prof of business admin Univ of California Berkeley 1974, asst dir of res and technical activities Financial Accounting Standards Bd USA 1978–81, Arthur Andersen prof of accounting LSE 1981–87, dir of research (pt/t) ICAEW 1981–87, visiting prof of accounting LSE 1987–89; dir gen of telecommunications OFTEL 1984–92, dir gen Office of Fair Trading 1992–95, sec gen International Accounting Standards Ctee 1995–, pt/t prof of accounting London Business Sch 1995–; memb Cncl ICAEW 1975–79, dep chm Accounting Standards Bd 1990–92 (memb 1990–94); dir: Economists Advsy Gp 1976–84, Economist Bookshop 1981–91, Philip Allan Publishers 1981–92 and 1995–, Nynex CableComms 1996–; memb: Bd Radiocommunications Agency 1990–92, Cncl Univ of Surrey 1990–92; CAs Founding Society's Centenary award 1988; hon fell LSE 1990; Hon ScD Univ of E Anglia 1992, Hon DLitt Loughborough Univ 1994, Hon DUniv Essex 1995, Hon DLaws Univ of Bath 1996; FCA 1970; *Books* An Introduction to Mathematical Programming for Accountants (1969), Modern Financial Management (with H C Edey, 1969), Analysis for Investment Decisions (1974), Indexation and Inflation (with E V Morgan and M Parkin, 1975), Economics of Business Decisions (1975), Investment Decisions under Inflation (with A Hope, 1976), Current Issues in Accountancy (with A Hope, 1977), Topics in Management Accounting (with J Arnold and R Scapens, 1980), Current Cost Acccounting (with M Page, 1983), Small Company Financial Reporting (with M Page and others, 1985); *Recreations* road running, theatre, opera, music; *Style*— Sir Bryan Carsberg; ✉ International Accounting Standards Committee, 167 Fleet Street, London EC4A 2ES (☎ 0171 353 0565, fax 0171 353 0562)

CARSLAKE, Hugh Bampfield; s of John Carslake, DL (d 1991), and Dorothea Jeanne, *née* Nesbitt; *b* 15 Nov 1946; *Educ* West House Sch Birmingham, Rugby, Trinity Coll Dublin (BA, LLB), Coll of Law; *m* 10 Oct 1970, June Helen, da of George Pratt McVitty; 6 c; *Career* slr; articled clerk Freshfields 1970–72, ptnr Martineau Johnson (formerly Ryland Martineau) Birmingham 1974–, NP 1981; cncl memb Birmingham & Midland Inst 1974–, tstee Worcester Cathedral Appeal 1988–, chm The Barber Inst of Fine Arts Univ of Birmingham 1989–, memb Cncl Univ of Birmingham 1991–; registrar Dio of Birmingham 1992–; memb Law Soc; *Recreations* music and family; *Style*— Hugh Carslake, Esq; ✉ Martineau Johnson, St Philips House, St Philips Place, Birmingham B3 2PP (☎ 0121 200 3300, fax 0121 625 3330)

CARSLEY, (Robert) Clive; s of Robert Alfred Carsley (d 1975), and Phylis, *née* Evans (d 1973); *b* 17 July 1944; *Educ* Warwick Sch, Jesus Coll Oxford (MA); *m* 1966, Carol Madeleine, da of Paul Emmanuel Shields, OBE; 1 s (Michael Robert b 14 Aug 1969), 2 da (Joanna Jane b 18 Aug 1971, Natasha Emma b 10 Jan 1980); *Career* called to the Bar Middle Temple 1966, in practice as barr 1966–68, with Brown & Polson Ltd 1968–70, Dick & Goldschmidt Ltd 1970–72, commercial dir Humphrys & Glasgow Ltd 1972–86, dep sec Babcock International plc 1986–87, gp sec Carless plc 1987–89; Thames Water plc: gp co sec 1989–95, gp legal dir 1995–; *Recreations* sailing, the countryside; *Clubs* RAC, Royal Motor Yacht; *Style*— Clive Carsley, Esq; ✉ Boulders, Beckenham Place Park, Beckenham, Kent BR3 2BP (☎ 0181 658 8181); Thames Water plc, Nugent House plc, Vastern Road, Reading, Berks RG1 8DB (☎ 0118 959 3227, fax 0118 956 7526)

CARSON, Ciaran Gerard; s of William Carson, of Belfast, and Mary Ellen, *née* Maginn; *b* 9 Oct 1948; *Educ* St Mary's Christian Brothers' Sch, Queen's Univ Belfast (BA); *m* 16 Oct 1982, Deirdre, da of Patrick Shannon; 2 s (Manus b 5 April 1986, Gerard 29 Oct 1987), 1 da (Mary Ellen b 3 Oct 1990); *Career* poet; traditional arts offr Arts Cncl of NI 1975–; Gregory Award 1976, Alice Hunt Bartlett Award 1988, Irish Times/Aer Lingus Award 1990, T S Eliot Poetry Prize 1993; *Books* poetry: The New Estate (1976), The Irish for No (1987), Belfast Confetti (1989), First Language (1993), Opera Et Cetera (1996); non-fiction: The Pocket Guide to Irish Traditional Music (1986), Last Night's Fun (1996); *Recreations* playing traditional music; *Style*— Ciaran Carson, Esq; ✉ Arts Council of Northern Ireland, 181A Stranmillis Rd, Belfast BT9 5DU (☎ 01232 381591)

CARSON, (Thomas) Richard; s of Johnston Carson (d 1961), of Co Fermanagh, and Rebecca, *née* Farrell (d 1958); *Educ* Portora Royal Sch (Seale open scholar), Queen's Univ Belfast (Sullivan open scholar, BSc, PhD); *m* 1971, Ursula Margaret Mary, *née* Davies; 1 s (David Richard b 1973); *Career* theoretical physicist/astrophysicist; lectr Dept of Natural Philosophy Univ of Glasgow, sr scientific offr AWRE Aldermaston, currently reader (formerly sr lectr) in astrophysics Univ of St Andrews; sometime: conslt Atomic Weapons Research Establishment Aldermaston, visiting fell and prof Univ of Colorado, sr res assoc NASA Inst for Space Studies NY, visiting staff memb Los Alamos Nat Laboratory Univ of California, visiting prof Australian Nat Univ Canberra; memb: Int Astronomical Union 1966, American Astronomical Soc 1968, NY Acad of Sciences 1989; fndr memb Euro Astronomical Soc 1991; FRAS 1959; former: jr and sr 1 mile champion ATC (NI Cmd), co-holder NI and All Ireland 4 x 440 yards relay record; *Books* Atoms and Molecules in Astrophysics (ed with M J Roberts, 1972), also author of numerous research papers, reviews and articles in scientific literature; *Recreations* skiing, tennis, swimming, reading French prose and German verse, listening to *Lieder* and classical music; *Style*— Richard Carson, Esq; ✉ 7 Cairnsden Gardens, St Andrews, Fife KY16 8SQ; School of Physics and Astronomy, University of St Andrews, North Haugh, St Andrews KY16 9SS

CARSON, (Edward) Rory; s of The Hon Edward Carson, MP (d 1987), of Hastings, Sussex, and Hon Mrs Heather Carson, *née* Sclater; *b* 25 May 1949; *Educ* Ludgrove and Radley Coll; *m* 19 April 1975, Araminta, da of Sir John Horlick, Bt, of Scotland; 4 s (Toby b 1977, Jonathen b 1979, Oliver b 1982, Bartholomew b 1988); *Career* dir: Swift 103 Ltd 1984–, London Motorentals Ltd 1984–91, Corporate Rental Services 1991–; *Recreations* tennis, walking, exotic pets; *Clubs* Raffles; *Style*— Rory Carson, Esq; ✉ Perseverance Cottage, Harpsden, Henley-on-Thames, Oxon R59 4AS (01491 573206); c/o Messrs Coutts and Co, 15 Lombard Street, London EC3; Kensington Close Hotel, Wrights Lane, Kensington, London W8 (☎ 0171 938 4700, fax 0171 938 1836)

CARSON, William Hunter Fisher (Willie); OBE (1983); s of Thomas Whelan Carson, and Mary Hay; *b* 16 Nov 1942; *Educ* Riverside Sch Sterling; *m* 1, 1963 (m dis 1979), Carole Jane Sutton; 3 s (Antony Thomas, Neil John, Ross William); m 2, 5 May 1982, Elaine, da of John B Williams; *Career* racehorse jockey; apprentice to: Capt G Armstrong 1957–63 (first winner Catterick 1962), Fred Armstrong 1963–66; first jockey to: Lord Derby 1967, Dick Hern 1977–; appointed Royal jockey 1977; major races won: 2000 Guineas 4 times (High Top 1972, Known Fact 1980, Don't Forget Me 1987, Nashwan 1989), Oaks 4 times (Dunfermline 1977 for HM The Queen, Bireme 1980, Sun Princess 1983, Salsabil 1990), Derby 4 times (Troy 1979, Henbit 1980, Nashwan 1989, Erhaab 1994), King George VI and Queen Elizabeth Diamond Stakes 4 times (Troy 1979, Ela-Mana-Mou 1980, Petoski 1985, Nashwan 1989), St Leger 3 times (Dunfermline 1977 for HM The Queen, Sun Princess 1983, Minster Son 1988), the Eclipse twice (Nashwan 1989, Elmaamul 1990), Ascot Gold Cup 1983 (Little Wolf), 1000 Guineas 1990 (Salsabil); champion jockey 1972, 1973, 1978, 1980, 1983; has ridden over 100 winners every season since 1972 (except 1984 when injured), became third most successful Br jockey with 3,112 wins Aug 1990 (incl over 100 group one races), jt record holder with six wins at one meeting Newcastle 1990, only jockey to ride and breed Classic winner (Minster Son, St Leger 1988); *Recreations* hunting; *Style*— Willie Carson, Esq, OBE; ✉ Minster House, Barnsley, Cirencester, Gloucestershire

CARSTAIRS, Ian Andrew; s of Alexander Gordon Carstairs, of Leics, and Dorothy Mary, *née* Carr; *b* 13 Feb 1951; *Educ* Hinckley GS (now John Cleveland Coll), St John's Coll Cambridge (MA); *m* 1973, Kay, da of Keith Reginald Muggleton, of Leics; 3 s (Thomas Andrew b 1979, Benjamin James b 1980, Joseph William b 1983); *Career* Sun Life Assurance Society Ltd 1972–80, J Rothschild Investment Management Ltd 1980–84, Target Investment Management Ltd 1984–89, Mercury Asset Management Ltd 1989–92, INVESCO Asset Management 1992–; *Recreations* tennis, squash, swimming, food and wine, crosswords; *Style*— Ian Carstairs, Esq; ✉ INVESCO Asset Management Ltd, 11 Devonshire Square, London EC2 (☎ 0171 626 3434)

CARSWELL, John Patrick; CB (1977); s of Donald Carswell (d 1940), and Catherine Roxburgh Macfarlane (d 1946); *b* 30 May 1918; *Educ* Merchant Taylors', St John's Coll Oxford (MA); *m* 1945, Ianthe, da of Capt Eric Bramley Elstob, RN (d 1946); 2 da; *Career* serv WWII 1940–46, Inf Maj India and E Bengal; Civil Serv 1946–77, Miny of Pensions Nat Insur 1946–60, HM Treasy 1960–64, under sec DES 1964–74, sec UGC 1974–77; sec Br Acad 1978–83; author; FRSL; *Recreations* writing, war on a small scale; *Clubs* Garrick; *Style—* John Carswell, Esq, CB, FRSL; ✉ 5 Prince Arthur Rd, London NW3 6AX (☎ 0171 794 6527); Berins Hill, Ipsden, Oxfordshire

CARSWELL, Rt Hon Lord Chief Justice; Rt Hon Sir Robert Douglas; kt (1988), PC (1993); s of Alan Edward Carswell (d 1972), of Belfast, and Nance Eileen, *née* Corlett; *b* 28 June 1934; *Educ* Royal Belfast Academical Inst, Pembroke Coll Oxford (MA), Univ of Chicago Law Sch; *m* 1961, Romayne Winifred, da of James Ferris, JP, of Co Down; 2 da (Catherine, Patricia); *Career* called to the Bar NI 1957, English Bar (Gray's Inn) 1972, counsel to Attorney Gen for NI 1970–71, QC 1971, sr Crown counsel in NI 1979–84, judge of the High Court of NI 1984–93, Lord Justice of Appeal NI 1993–97, Lord Chief Justice of NI Jan 1997–; bencher Inn of Ct of NI 1979, hon bencher Gray's Inn 1993; chm Law Reform Advsy Ctee NI 1989; pro-chllr and chm Cncl Univ of Ulster 1984–94, chllr Dioceses of Armagh and of Down and Dromore 1990; *Recreations* golf; *Clubs* Ulster Reform (Belfast); *Style—* The Rt Hon Sir Robert Carswell; ✉ c/o Royal Courts of Justice, Belfast BT1 3JF (☎ 01232 235111)

CARTE, Brian Addison; TD (1976); s of late James Carte; *b* 7 Aug 1943; *Educ* St Lawrence Coll Ramsgate, Wharton Business Sch Univ of Pennsylvania; *m* 1969, Shirley Anne, da of Lt-Col W H Brinkley; 2 da; *Career* Co Cdr Queen's Regt TA, Maj GSO II HQ London Dist, asst project offr DTA and C, RARO 1987; dir County Bank Ltd 1976–85, md National Westminster Insurance Services Ltd 1985–89, chief exec Lombard North Central plc 1989–96 (dir 1996–); chm Motability Finance Ltd 1992–95; non-exec dir: Cuffyns plc 1996–, PPP Ltd 1996–; former pres Assoc of Corp Treasurers; govr St Lawrence Coll, memb Cncl Order of St John Surrey; Freeman and Liveryman Worshipful Co of Scriveners; FCIB, FCT, FRSA; *Recreations* golf, shooting, opera; *Clubs* New Zealand Golf, RAC; *Style—* Brian Carte, Esq, TD; ✉ Fairfield Lodge, Hardwick Close, Knott Park, Oxshott, Surrey KT22 0HZ; Private Patients Plan Ltd, PPP House, Vale Road, Tunbridge Wells, Kent TN11 1BJ (☎ 01892 512345)

CARTER, Alan Owen; s of Arthur Henry Carter (d 1958), of Cardiff, and Lily May, *née* Jones (d 1983); *b* 28 July 1932; *Educ* Penarth GS, Univ of Wales Cardiff (BA, Hockey colours); *m* July 1962, Wendy Barbara, da of Sidney Clifford Page; 1 s (Matthew Christian Alan b June 1967), 1 da (Emma Siân b Aug 1971); *Career* cmmnd educn offr RAF 1955–58; Stanwell Sch Penarth 1959–91 (head of history, head of careers, head of sixth form, govr); pres: Welsh Hockey Assoc 1986–91, Welsh Hockey Umpires' Assoc 1985–95, Univ of Wales Cardiff Hockey Club 1990–, Penarth Hockey Club 1991–; life memb Welsh Hockey Assoc 1991–; vice chm Welsh Hockey Union 1995–97; memb: Euro Hockey Fedn 1988, Euro Club Championship Ctee (Hockey) 1988–92, Int Hockey Fedn (umpire) 1979–85; Welsh nat umpire (outdoor and indoor) 1979–83; Euro hockey official at tournaments in: Russia 1987, Finland 1988, Sardinia 1989 and 1996, Sweden 1990, Gibraltar 1991 and 1994, Denmark 1991, Holland 1992, France 1993; member S Glamorgan Young Enterprise Bd 1991–94; *Recreations* reading, theatre, art, music, cricket; *Style—* A O Carter, Esq; ✉ 48 Minehead Avenue, Sully, Penarth, Vale of Glamorgan CF64 5TJ (☎ 01222 530561)

CARTER, Andrew; CMG (1995); s of Eric Harry Carter (d 1988), and Margaret Elizabeth, *née* Maycock; *b* 4 Dec 1943; *Educ* Latymer Upper Sch, Jesus Coll Cambridge (MA), RCM; *m* 1, 1973 (m dis 1986), Anne Caroline Morgan; 1 da (Catherine b 1978); m 2, 21 May 1988, Catherine Mary, da of Peter Haswell Tyler, of Frogmore, S Devon; 1 s (Benjamin b 1993), 1 da (Alice b 1989); *Career* asst master Marlborough 1965–70; HM Diplomatic Service 1971–; Warsaw 1972–74, Geneva 1975, Bonn 1975–78, FCO 1978–86, UK delegation to NATO Brussels 1986–90, dep govr of Gibraltar 1990–95, min Moscow 1995–; FRCO 1979, ARCM 1962, LRAM 1979; *Recreations* music; *Style—* Andrew Carter, Esq, CMG; ✉ c/o Foreign and Commonwealth Office (Moscow), King Charles St, London SW1A 2AH

CARTER, Bernard Thomas; s of Cecil Carter (d 1962), and Ethel, *née* Darby (d 1961); *b* 6 April 1920; *Educ* Haberdashers' Aske's, Goldsmiths' Coll of Art London (NDD, ATD); *m* 1952, Eugenie Mary (d 1993), da of Capt David William Alexander, RD, RNR (d 1952); 1 s (John); *Career* RAF 1939–46; art lectr 1952–68; Nat Maritime Museum: asst keeper of prints and drawings 1968, dep keeper and head Picture Dept 1970, keeper and head Dept of Pictures and Conservation 1972–77; full time artist 1977–; one man exhibitions: Arthur Jeffress Gallery 1955, twelve one man exhibitions Portal Gallery Grafton St W1; pictures in many public collections in UK and abroad; memb Advsy Cncl on Export of Works of Art 1970–77; Hon RE; *Recreations* music, theatre, restaurants, gardening, travel, reading, TV; *Style—* Bernard Carter, Esq; ✉ 56 King George St, Greenwich, London SE10 8QD (☎ 0181 858 4281)

CARTER, His Hon Judge (Frederick) Brian; QC (1980); s of late Arthur Carter, and late Minnie Carter; *b* 11 May 1933; *Educ* Stretford GS, King's Coll London (LLB); *m* 1960, Elizabeth Hughes, JP, da of late W B Hughes; 1 s (and 1 s decd), 3 da; *Career* called to the Bar Gray's Inn 1955; practised Northern Circuit 1957–85, prosecuting counsel for Inland Revenue Northern Circuit 1973–80, recorder of the Crown Court 1978–85, circuit judge (Northern Circuit) 1985–; *Recreations* golf, travel; *Clubs* Chorlton-cum-Hardy Golf, Big Four (Manchester); *Style—* His Hon Judge Carter, QC

CARTER, Sir Charles Frederick; kt (1978); yst s of Frederick William Carter, FRS (d 1950), of Rugby; *b* 15 Aug 1919; *Educ* Rugby, St John's Coll Cambridge (MA); *m* 1944, Janet, da of Edward Shea (d 1923), of Newcastle; 1 s, 2 da; *Career* lectr in statistics Univ of Cambridge 1947–51, fell Emmanuel Coll Cambridge 1947–51 (now hon fell); prof of economics: Queen's Univ Belfast 1950–59, Univ of Manchester 1959–63; vice chllr Univ of Lancaster 1963–79, jt pres Policy Studies Inst 1989–97; vice chm Joseph Rowntree Foundation 1981–94 (tstee 1966–94); chm: Sir Halley Stewart Tst 1986–97, N Ireland Econ Cncl 1977–87, Cncl Goldsmiths' Coll Univ of London 1988–94; formerly: jt ed Economic Journal and Journal of Industrial Economics, pres Manchester Statistical Soc, pres Br Assoc for Advancement of Sci; formerly chm: Schools' Broadcasting Cncl, NW Econ Planning Cncl, Centre for Studies in Social Policy; Hon DSc: Univ of Lancaster, Queen's Univ Belfast, New Univ Ulster; Hon LLD: Univ of Liverpool, Trinity Coll Dublin; Hon DEconSc National Univ Ireland; FBA; *Recreations* gardening; *Style—* Sir Charles Carter, FBA; ✉ 1 Gosforth Rd, Seascale, Cumbria CA20 1PU (☎ 019467 28359)

CARTER, Dr Christopher John (Chris); s of Archibald Raymond Carter (d 1978), and Isobel Louisa, *née* Toogood; *b* 5 Feb 1941; *Educ* Ottershaw Sch Chertsey, Univ of Birmingham (BA, William Cadbury prize), Univ of Glasgow (scholar, PhD); *m* 20 Sept 1969, Ann Fisher, da of Jack Fisher Prince (d 1993); 1 s (Colin Andrew b 31 Oct 1975), 1 da (Vanessa Caroline b 1978); *Career* surveyor Highways Dept Ontario 1959–60, planning asst Cumbernauld New Town 1963–64 and 1967–68, visiting lectr in geography Brock Univ Ontario 1968–69, sr lectr in planning Glasgow Sch of Art 1969–76, princ lectr in planning Coventry Poly 1976–78; Duncan of Jordanstone Coll of Art Univ of Dundee: sr lectr and head Sch of Town and Regnl Planning 1978–81, vice princ 1981–93, princ 1993–94, dir Duncan of Jordanstone Coll and dep princ Univ of Dundee 1994–; memb: CNAA Ctee on Institutional Reviews 1983–87, Scottish Ctee Universities Funding Cncl 1988–92, Bd of Govrs Dundee Inst of Technol 1989–91, Scottish Higher Educn Funding Cncl 1992–94, Bd of Govrs Northern Coll of Educn 1994–95; RTPI Prize 1970, Faculty Enrichment Award Canadian High Cmmn 1981; MRTPI 1972, FIMgt 1981, FRSA 1982; *Recreations* skiing, running, hill walking, photography; *Clubs* Scottish Ski; *Style—* Dr Chris Carter; ✉ Duncan of Jordanstone College, University of Dundee, Perth Road, Dundee DD1 4HT (☎ 01382 223261, fax 01382 227304)

CARTER, Clive; s of Eric Carter (d 1965), of London, and Jacqueline, *née* Digby; *b* 12 Jan 1953; *Educ* Sir William Collins Sch London, LAMDA; *m* 5 Oct 1975, Anita Helen, da of Lt-Col Harry Beresford Richards (ret); 1 s (Richard Nigel Beresford b 7 Sept 1985), 1 da (Louise Erica Beresford b 21 Sept 1987); *Career* actor; repertory work in cities incl: York, Leicester, Exeter, Nottingham, Cambridge; has performed in many concerts and one-off charity shows; *Theatre* incl: Julius Caesar (Mermaid), Othello (Mermaid), Marilyn (Adelphi), Wild Wild Woman (Astoria), Sister Mary Ignatius Explains It All For You (Ambassadors), Two Into One (Shaftesbury), Les Miserables (Barbican, Palace Theatre), Someone Like You (Strand), Into the Woods (Phoenix, nominated Olivier Award), Phantom of the Opera (Sydmonton Festival and Her Majesty's), Rocky Horror Show (Euro tour), Manchurian Candidate (Lyric Hammersmith), Harvey (Shaftesbury), Revue (Jermyn Street Theatre); New Shakespeare Co: A Midsummer Night's Dream, O'Flaherty VC, Tranio in Taming of the Shrew 1993, Martin in Connecticut Yankee (London and tour) 1993; *Television* incl: The Bill, Mitch, Never the Twain, Robin's Nest, Rep, Wogan; *Films* incl: Death on the Nile, Officer; *Recordings* incl: Les Miserables (orginal cast album), Into the Woods (London cast album), Wuthering Heights (concept album), Andrew Lloyd Webber Essentials (collection), Oscar; *Recreations* keep fit, running, swimming, modern and classical music, reading, collecting vintage ports, antique clocks; *Clubs* Arts, Metropolitan; *Style—* Clive Carter, Esq; ✉ c/o London Management, 2–4 Noel Street, London W1V 3RB (☎ 0171 287 9000, fax 0171 287 3036)

CARTER, (William) David Antony; s of William Henry Newton Carter, CBE (d 1981) and Joan Stuart Carter (d 1983); *b* 21 Feb 1938; *Educ* Oundle, Oriel Coll Oxford (MA); *m* 27 April 1963, Angela Mary, *née* Peel; 2 s (Justin Mark b 1964, Dominic William b 1967), 3 da (Catherine Sarah (Kate) b 1965, Emma Rachel b 1971, (Mary) Jessica b 1975); *Career* 2 Lt RA 1956–58; ptnr KPMG 1975–95: head of corp fin serv 1986–90, mgmnt buyout specialist 1981–91, head of forensic accounting 1992–94; memb Govrs' Advsy Body Ampleforth Abbey; FCA 1974 (ACA 1964); *Recreations* opera, cricket, redundant Devon farmhouse; *Clubs* Oxford & Cambridge; *Style—* David Carter, Esq; ✉ 7 Bois Ave, Amersham, Bucks HP6 5NS (☎ 01494 727 109)

CARTER, Prof Sir David Craig; kt (1996); s of Horace Ramsay Carter, and Mary Florence, *née* Lister; *b* 1 Sept 1940; *Educ* Univ of St Andrews (MB ChB), Univ of Dundee (MD); *m* 23 Sept 1967, Ilske Ursula, da of Wolfgang August Luth (d 1945), of Riga, Latvia; 2 s (Adrian b 5 Jan 1969, Ben b 3 Nov 1970); *Career* St Mungo prof of surgery Univ of Glasgow 1979–88, regius prof of clinical surgery Univ of Edinburgh 1988–; surgn to HM The Queen in Scotland 1993–, CMO for Scotland 1996–; former memb: Biomedical Res Ctee Scottish Home and Health Dept, Br Broadcasting Cncl Scotland, Cncl RCSEd, Int Surgical Gp; chm: Scottish Fndn for Surgery in Nepal 1987–, Scottish Cncl for Postgrad Med Educn 1990–96; pres: Int Hepato-Biliary and Pancreatic Assoc 1988–89, Surgical Research Soc 1996–; pres Assoc of Surgns of GB and I 1996–97; hon sec: Br Jl of Surgery 1991–95, hon sec James IV Assoc of Surgns; Hon FRCSI, Hon FACS; FRCSEd, FRCPEd, FRCSGlas, FRCS (Eng), FRSE; *Books* Peptic Ulcer (1983), Principles and Practice of Surgery (1985), Atlas of General Surgery (1986), British Journal of Surgery (co-ed, 1986–91), Perioperative Care (1988), Pancreatitis (1989), Surgery of the Pancreas (1993), Rob & Smith's Operative Surgery series (co-ed); *Recreations* golf, music; *Clubs* Royal and Ancient (St Andrews), New (Edinburgh), Luffness New; *Style—* Prof Sir David Carter, FRSE; ✉ 19 Buckingham Terrace, Edinburgh EH4 3AD (☎ 0131 332 5554); University Department of Surgery, Royal Infirmary, Edinburgh EH3 9YW (☎ 0131 229 2477 ext 2266, fax 0131 228 2661, telex 727442 UNIVED G)

CARTER, Baron (Life Peer UK 1987), of Devizes, Co Wilts; Denis Victor Carter; s of Albert William Carter (d 1973), of Sussex, and Annie Julia, *née* Tynan (d 1972); *b* 17 Jan 1932; *Educ* Xaverian Coll Brighton, East Sussex Coll of Agric, Essex Coll of Agric (Nat Dip in Agric), Worcester Coll Oxford (BLitt); *m* 1957, Teresa Mary, da of Cecil William Walter Greengoe (d 1972), of Sussex; 1 s (Andrew Peter b 1963 d 1982), 1 da (Hon Catherine Mary b 1959); *Career* audit clerk; Sgt Army, Suez Canal zone; farmer and agricultural conslt; dir: AKC Ltd (Agricultural Accounting and Mgmnt) 1957– (and fndr), United Oilseeds Ltd 1968–, Cave Holdings/WE and DT Cave Ltd 1976–; oppn spokesman on agric 1988–, oppn spokesman on social security agric and health 1989–, oppn dep chief whip 1990–92; dir TV prodn co 1988–; pres: Br Inst of Agric Conslts 1991–, Guild of Agricultural Journalists 1994–; chm United Kingdom Cooperative Cncl 1993–; cncl memb Royal Agric Soc 1994–; tstee: Rural Housing Tst 1993–, John Arlott Memorial Tst 1994–; fell Inst of Agricultural Mgmnt 1992–; *Recreations* reading, walking, supporting Southampton FC; *Clubs* Farmers, Turners, Grasshoppers; *Style—* The Rt Hon Lord Carter; ✉ c/o House of Lords, London SW1A 0PW

CARTER, Sir Derrick Hunton; kt (1975), TD (1952); s of Dr Arthur Hunton Carter (d 1961), of Sedbergh, and Winifred, *née* MacMeikan (d 1947); *b* 7 April 1906; *Educ* Haileybury, St John's Coll Cambridge (MA); *m* 1, 1933, Phyllis, da of Denis Best, of Worcester; 1 s, 1 da; m 2, 1948, Madeline (d 1992), da of Col Denis Moriarty O'Callaghan, CMG, DSO; 1 da; *Career* served WWII RA Lt-Col 1942; civil engr Dominion Bridge Co (Canada) 1927–28, res engr ICI 1928–33 (sales mangr 1933–39, md 1953); chm: Gen Chem Div ICI 1961, Mond Div ICI Ltd 1963–67, Remploy Ltd 1972–76; Freeman City of London 1973, Liveryman Worshipful Co of Coachmakers & Coach Harness Makers; *Recreations* gardening, woodworking; *Style—* Sir Derrick Carter, TD; ✉ Withington House, Withington, Cheltenham, Glos GL54 4BB (☎ 01242 89286)

CARTER, Elliot Cook; *b* 11 Dec 1908; *Educ* Harvard (MA), Longy Sch of Music, Ecole Normale de Musique Paris; *Career* composer; studied under: Gustav Holst 1930–32, Nadia Boulanger 1932–35; music dir George Balanchine's Ballet Caravan 1937–39, prof Yale Univ 1960, Ford Fndn composer-in-residence Berlin 1964, composer-in-residence American Acad Rome 1968; subject of several int retrospectives and television documentaries (incl LWT); compositions incl: Pocahontas (ballet) 1939, Symphony No 1 1942, Holiday Overture 1944, Piano Sonata 1946, The Minotaur (1947), Cello Sonata 1948, Eight Etudes and a Fantasy for woodwind quartet 1949, String Quartet No 1 (first prize Concours Internationale de Quatuors a Cordes 1953) 1951, Sonata for Harpsichord, Flute, Oboe and Cello (Naumburg Prize) 1952, Variations for Orchestra 1955, String Quartet No 2 (Pulitzer Prize 1960) 1959, Double Concerto 1961, Piano Concerto 1967, Concerto for Orchestra 1969, String Quartet No 3 (Pulitzer Prize 1973) 1973, Duo for Violin and Piano 1974, A Mirror on Which to Dwell 1976, A Symphony of Three Orchestras 1976, Syringa 1978, Night Fantasies 1980, In Sleep, In Thunder 1982, Triple Duo 1983, Penthode 1985, String Quartet No 4 1986, Oboe Concerto 1988, Three Occasions for orchestra 1986–89, Violin Concerto 1990, Quintet for piano and winds 1991, Scrivo in Vento for solo flute 1991, Trilogy for harp and oboe 1992, Partita for orch 1994, Of Challenge and Of Love for soprano and piano 1994, Adagio Tenebroso for orch (cmmnd BBC, world premiere BBC Proms 1995) 1995, Esprit Rude/Esprit Doux II for flute clarinet and marimba 1995, String Quartet No 5 1995; Prix de Rome 1953, Gold Medal for Eminence in Music Nat Inst of Arts & Letters 1971, Ernst Von Siemens Music Prize 1985, Nat Medal of Arts (awarded by Pres of USA) 1985, Commandeur dans l'Order des Arts et des Lettres 1987, Commendatore Order of Merit of Italy 1991; Hon PhD: Princeton Univ 1967, Harvard Univ 1970, Yale Univ 1970, Univ of Cambridge 1983; *Recordings* incl: Night Fantasies, Variations for Orchestra, Cello Sonata, A Mirror on Which to Dwell, Four String Quartets (winner Grammy Award and Grand Prix du Disque), Syringa, In Sleep In Thunder, Triple Duo; *Style*— Elliot Carter, Esq; ✉ c/o Boosey & Hawkes Music Publishing Ltd, 295 Regent Street, London W1R 8JH (☎ 0171 580 3060, fax 0171 436 5815/3490)

CARTER, Eric Stephen; CBE (1986); s of Albert Harry Carter, MBE (Dep Chief Constable of Glos, d 1973), and Doris Margaret, *née* Mann (d 1983); *b* 23 June 1923; *Educ* Lydney GS Glos, Univ of Reading (BSc); *m* 23 Oct 1948, Audrey, da of Joseph Windsor (d 1970), of Bream, Glos; 1 s (Michael b 1958); *Career* dist agric offr Nat Agric Advsy Serv Glos 1946–57, sr dist agric advsr Lincs 1957–63, co agric offr Lincs 1963–69, dep regnl dir Yorks/Lancs Region and regnl agric offr 1969–74, chief regnl offr MAFF 1974–75, dep dir-gen Agric Devpt and Advsy Serv MAFF 1975–81; nat advsr Farming and Wildlife Advsy Gp 1981–88 (fndr memb 1969); memb: Royal Agric Soc of England 1976– (ed of jl 1985–94), Governing Body Grassland Res Inst 1976–87, Selection Ctee Nuffield Farming Scholarship Tst 1981–92, Long Ashton Res Station Agric Ctee 1984–90, Cncl Assoc of Agric 1985–92, Welsh Plant Breeding Station Advsy Ctee 1987–91, Governing Body Inst for Grassland & Environmental Res 1989–91; convener Standing Conference on Country Sports 1988–; visiting lectr Univ of Nottingham 1984–96; hon fell RASE 1988, hon Nuffield scholar 1992; FIBiol 1974 (vice pres 1993–96), FRAgS 1985; *Books* Modern Farming and the Countryside (with M H R Soper, OBE 1985, 2 edn 1991), British Farming - Changing Policies and Production Systems (with J M Stansfield, 1994); *Recreations* gardening, travel, reading, music; *Clubs* Farmers'; *Style*— Eric Carter, Esq, CBE; ✉ 15 Farrs Lane, East Hyde, Luton, Beds LU2 9PY (☎ 01582 760504)

CARTER, Geoffrey Henry; s of Henry Richard Thomas Carter, of Ashford, Kent, and Alice Florance, *née* Stubbs; *b* 25 April 1937; *Educ* Brixton Sch of Bldg; *m* Margaret Ann Carter; 2 s (Andrew Henry Rosam b 18 Nov 1964, Timothy Ian b 16 Oct 1967); *Career* architect: YRM 1960–61, Middx CC 1961–64, David Landan & Partners 1964–70, Chu & Carter 1970–74, PSA 1974–79; asst chief architect PO 1979–85, chief architect and design advsr PO Counters Ltd 1985–93, in own practice 1993–; projects incl: Norwich Telephone Exchange 1978, Guernsey PO HQ (Civic Tst award) 1984, corp design for PO Counters 1987; memb Design Mgmnt Gp Ctee and Membership Gp CSD; ARIBA 1963, FCSD 1990; *Style*— Geoffrey Carter, Esq; ✉ Carter Associates, 9 Redgrave Road, Putney, London SW15 1PX (☎ and fax 0181 788 3943)

CARTER, (William) George Key; CBE, DL; s of Lt-Col William Tom Carter, OBE, JP (d 1956), and Georgina Margaret, *née* Key (d 1986); *b* 29 Jan 1934; *Educ* Warwick Sch; *m* 30 June 1965, Anne Rosalie Mary, da of Trevor Acheson-Williams Flanagan (d 1987); 1 s (Alexander Corfield Key b 1971), 1 da (Louisa Mary-Anne b 1968); *Career* 2 Lt 16/5 The Queen's Royal Lancers 1958–60 (asst Adj 1959); qualified CA 1957; Price Waterhouse: joined 1956, mangr 1963, ptnr 1966, sr ptnr (W Midlands) 1982–94; chm: W Midlands Devpt Agency 1989–95, Black Country Development Corporation 1994–; pres Birmingham Chamber of Commerce and Indust 1993–94; memb: Cncl W Midlands CBI 1988–, N Worcs Health Authy 1994–96; vice chm Birmingham Marketing Partnership 1993–95, dir Birmingham Ecomonic Devpt Partnership 1991–95, memb Advsy Bd Univ of Birmingham Business Sch 1993–; memb: Ferrous Foundry Indust Advsy Ctee 1974–80, Pharmacist Review Bd 1980–, Cncl Aston Univ 1995–; feoffee and govr Old Swinford Hosp Sch 1986–; chm: Cncl Order of St John W Midlands 1994–, Lunar Soc 1996–; FCA 1957, FRSA 1993; *Books* The Work of the Investigating Accountant; *Recreations* golf, shooting, sailing, gardening; *Clubs* Cavalry and Guards'; *Style*— George Carter, Esq, CBE, DL; ✉ The Old Rectory, Elmley Lovett, Droitwich, Worcs WR9 OPS (01299 851251, fax 01299 851458, e-mail 100433,1623@compuserve.com, car 0836 245455); 28 Westmorland Terrace, London SW1 (☎ 0171 630 0597)

CARTER, Godfrey James; CBE (1984); s of Capt James Shuckburgh Carter, Grenadier Gds (ka 1918), and Diana Violet Gladys, *née* Cavendish (d 1962); *b* 1 June 1919; *Educ* Eton, Magdalene Coll Cambridge (MA, LLM); *m* 15 June 1946, Cynthia, da of Eric Strickland Mason, of Iden, Rye, Sussex; 3 s (James b 1948, Simon b 1953, Hugh b 1960); *Career* WWII Capt Rifle Bde 1940–45, served 8 Army ME (twice wounded); called to the Bar Inner Temple 1946; Parly Counsel Office 1949–56 and 1964–79 (ret); Commercial Depts Bristol Aeroplane Co and Bristol Siddeley Engines 1956–64; draftsman of: Companies Act 1985, Insolvency Act 1986, Insolvency Rules 1986; *Clubs* Travellers'; *Style*— Godfrey Carter, Esq, CBE; ✉ Old Bournstream House, Wotton-under-Edge, Glos GL12 7PA (☎ 01453 843246)

CARTER, John; s of Eric Gordon Carter (d 1991), and Mercia Gertrude, *née* Edmonds; *b* 3 March 1942; *Educ* Twickenham Sch of Art, Kingston Sch of Art, British Sch in Rome; *m* 11 July 1986, Belinda Juliet, da of Alan Cadbury; *Career* artist; *Solo Exhibitions* incl: Redfern Gall 1968, 1971, 1974 and 1977, Univ of Reading 1979, Nicola Jacobs Gall 1980, 1983, 1987 and 1990, Retrospective 1965–83 1983, Warwick Arts Tst 1983, Moris Gall Tokyo 1987 and 1989, Gall Yamaguchi Osaka, Sumi Gall Okayama 1989, Galerie Hoffmann Friedberg 1990, Galerie Wack Kaiserlautern 1991, Knoedler Gall London 1991, Museum Moderner Kunst Landkreis Cuxhaven 1994, Belloc Lowndes Fine Art Chicago 1995, Gudrun Spielvogel Galerie Munich 1995, Ecole Superiere des Arts Visuels de la Cambre Brussels 1995, Francis Graham-Dixon Gall London 1996; *Group Exhibitions* incl: New Generation Whitechapel Gall 1966, New British Painting and Sculpture UCLA Art Galleries Los Angeles and touring USA, British Painting Hayward Gall 1974, British Art Show Mappin Art Gall Sheffield and touring 1979, The British Cncl Collection Serpentine Gall 1980, British Art 1940–80 The Arts Cncl Collection Hayward Gall 1981, British Art Show Birmingham Museum and touring 1984, New Works on Paper Br Cncl and World tour 1984, Die Ecke Galerie Hoffmann Friedberg 1986, Britannica - 30 ans de Sculpture Musée André Malraux Le Havre 1988, The Presence of Painting Aspects of British Abstraction 1957–88 Mappin Art Gall and touring 1988, Britse Sculptuur 1960–88 Mus van Hedendaagse Kunst Antwerp 1989, Arte Constructivo y Sistematico Centro Cultural de la Villa Madrid 1989, 1000 Kubikzentimeter Geom Minituren Wilhem Hack Mus Ludwigshafen 1990, Universal Progression Manege Moscow 1990, Konstruktive Tendenzen Messer Ladwig Galerie Berlin 1990, Piccolo Formato Arte Struktura Milan 1990, Geometrisk Abstraktion X Konstruktiv Tendens Stockholm 1991, Aspects de la Mouvance Construite Internationale Musée des Beaux Arts Verviers 1993, Skulptur und Architektur: Ein Diskurs T H Lichtwiese Darmstadt 1993, Interférences Musée des Beaux-Arts Mons, Blick über den Armelkanal Pfalzgalerie Kaiserslautern 1994, Kunstmuseum Thun 1996; *Awards* Leverhulme travelling scholarship to Italy 1963, Peter Stuyvesant Fndn travel bursary to USA 1966, Arts Cncl awards 1977 and 1979; *Style*— John Carter, Esq; ✉ 71A Westbourne Park Road, London W2 5QH (☎ 0171 229 3242, fax 0171 792 4836); Edition & Galerie Hoffmann, Görbel Heimer Mühle, D-61169 Friedberg, Germany (☎ 00 49 761 31 24 43); Francis Graham-Dixon Gallery, 17/18 Great Sutton Street, London EC1V 0DN (☎ 0171 250 1962)

CARTER, John G T; *Career* Commercial Union plc: i/c UK ops 1984–87, dir 1987–, chief exec 1994–, chm Commercial Union Assurance Company plc (princ operating subsid) 1994–; Liveryman Worshipful Co of Insurers; *Style*— John Carter, Esq; ✉ Commercial Union plc, St Helen's, 1 Undershaft, London EC3P 3DQ (☎ 0171 283 7500)

CARTER, Dr John Timothy (Tim); *b* 12 Feb 1944; *Educ* Dulwich Coll, CCC Cambridge (MA, BA, BChir), UCH, London Sch of Hygiene and Tropical Med (MSc); *Career* lectr London Sch of Hygiene 1974–75, med advsr BP 1975–83; Health & Safety Exec: dir med servs 1983–, dir health policy 1989–92, dir field ops 1992–; FRCP, FFOM; *Style*— Dr Tim Carter; ✉ 41 Clarence Road, St Albans AL1 4NP

CARTER, (Thomas) Mark; JP (1971), DL (Staffs 1983); s of William Edward Carter, JP (d 1965), of Eccleshall Castle, Staffs, and Rose Margaret Eleanor, *née* Morris-Eyton (d 1982); *b* 20 May 1936; *Educ* Harrow, RAC Cirencester; *m* 3 July 1965, Cecilia Catherine, da of Maj Henry Cecil Wenger, of Staffs; 2 da (Melissa Margaret b 1966, Catherine Elizabeth b 1973); *Career* Lt Grenadier Gds Suez Canal Zone and Kenya 1954–56; chartered surveyor, then farmer and landowner; High Sheriff Staffs 1974–75; hunt sec and master N Staffs Hunt 1963–76, gen cmmr Inland Revenue; memb: Agric Lands Tbnl, Bd of Mgmnt Heart of England Tourist Bd 1985–88, Cncl Historic Houses Assoc 1986–95; engaged in opening Eccleshall Castle to the public; Knight SMO (Malta); *Recreations* bridge, horticulture; *Clubs* Cavalry and Guards', MCC; *Style*— Mark Carter, Esq, JP, DL; ✉ Eccleshall Castle, Stafford ST21 6LS (☎ 01785 850151); Estates Office, Eccleshall Castle, Stafford ST21 6LS (☎ 01785 850151)

CARTER, Dr Mary Elizabeth; *Educ* St Mary's Hosp Med Sch Univ of London (women's entrance scholar, MB BS, MD, MRCPEd, FRCPEd); *Career* house physician Med Unit and Dept of Psychiatry St Mary's Hosp London then house surgn in gen and orthopaedic surgery Paddington Gen Hosp London 1954, house physician in gen med, cardiology and neurology King Edward Meml Hosp Ealing 1955, house physician St Mary's Hosp London 1956; MRC Rheumatism Research Unit Canadian Red Cross Meml Hosp Taplow: registrar 1957–59 and 1960–62, Empire Rheumatism Cncl research fell 1959–60; sr registrar in gen med St Mary's Hosp London 1963–65, hon research rheumatologist St Mary's Hosp 1965–70, med advsr to Medicovision (closed circuit colour TV progs for int postgrad centres) 1970–71, hon clinical sr lectr and conslt physician in rheumatology and rehabilitation St Mary's Hosp (first woman conslt clinician and fndr first Dept of Rheumatology and Rehabilitation) 1971–91, sr research fell in clinical rheumatology Centre for Biological and Med Systems Imperial Coll and hon consulting physician St Mary's Hosp 1991–; pres Paddington Branch Arthritis Care 1974–94; chm: Disability Action Westminster 1985–, Ctee for Employment of Disabled People NE London 1986–91; memb: Exec Ctee Gtr London Assoc for Disabled People 1986–91, Cncl and Distribution Ctee Metropolitan Hosp Sunday Fund 1989–; RCPEd: regnl advsr for Gtr London and NW Thames 1982–, rep Central Conslts and Specialists Ctee 1983–, memb Cncl 1994–, rep Lister Inst of Preventive Med 1994–; advsy memb Social and Community Agencies Standing Ctee Euro League Against Rheumatism 1975–, memb Exec Ctee Br Soc for Rehabilitation Med 1987–90; memb: Br Soc for Rheumatology (formerly Heberden Soc) 1958, Soc for Back Pain Research 1987; FRSM 1960; *Publications* author of various book chapters and numerous scientific and socio-medical papers; fndr chief ed Excerpta Medica: Rheumatology Abstracts; *Recreations* opera, theatre, stage and costume design, fine art, music, gardening, travel; *Clubs* RSM; *Style*— Dr Mary Carter; ✉ Imperial College of Science, Technology and Medicine, Centre for Biological and Medical Systems, Sir Leon Bagrit Centre, Exhibition Road, London SW7 2BX (☎ 0171 594 5185/5176, fax 0171 584 6897)

CARTER, Michael James Frederick; CBE (1987); s of Dr David Michael Frederick Carter (Surgn Lt RN, d 1975), and Alice, *née* McNally (d 1981); *b* 23 March 1941; *Educ* Downside; *m* 29 April 1967, Camilla Gillian Carter, JP, da of Arthur Gordon Taylor; 2 s (James Gordon Frederick b 15 Nov 1968, David John b 29 Dec 1971), 1 da (Rachel Jane b 16 April 1970); *Career* dir: Olives Holdings plc, Altsprung Furniture Group plc; chm E Somerset NHS Hosp Tst; memb: Somerset Health Authy 1978–90, Nat Union of Cons and Unionist Assocs 1979–, Royal Bath and West Show Arts Ctee; High Sheriff of Somerset 1987–88; *Books* Modern British Painters 1900–40 (1978); *Recreations* gardening; *Style*— Michael Carter, Esq, CBE

CARTER, Peers Lee; CMG (1965); s of Peers Owen Carter (d 1971), and Edith, *née* Lee (d 1982), of Bolton, Lancs; *b* 5 Dec 1916; *Educ* Radley, ChCh Oxford (MA); *m* 1940, Joan Eleanor, da of Capt Alfred Victor Robertson Lovegrove, DSO, RD, RNR, of Vancouver; 1 s; *Career* serv WWII Fezzan and N Africa, Southern Europe, Maj; HM Foreign Serv: entered 1939, vice-consul Amsterdam 1939–40, second then first sec Baghdad 1945–49, first sec Cmmr Gen's Office Singapore 1951–54, cnsllr Washington 1958–61, head Perm Delgn to UN Geneva 1961–63, inspr then chief inspr HM Dip Serv 1963–68, ambass Afghanistan 1968–72, asst under sec of state and ministerial interpreter FCO 1973–76, ret; memb Int Assoc of Conf Interpreters 1976–87, former chm Afghanaid 1987–92; Sardar-e A'ala 1971; *Recreations* bee keeping, photography; *Clubs* Special Forces; *Style*— Peers Carter, Esq, CMG; ✉ Dean Land Shaw, by Jobes, Balcombe, Haywards Heath, W Sussex RH17 6HZ (☎ 01444 811205)

CARTER, Peter; *b* 1945; *Educ* Manchester GS, St Catharine's Coll Cambridge; *m*; 5 c; *Career* HM Dip Serv 1967–78: served Lebanon, Jordan and Denmark, latterly dealing with EC fisheries policy FCO; Dept of Energy 1978–93: initially dealing with int energy matters, subsequently responsible for energy conservation policy, the coal indust then UK gas supply and demand issues, dir for research and devpt Offshore Supplies Office Glasgow 1987–93; dep dir gen Office of Electricity Regulation (OFFER) Oct 1993– (dep dir gen Scotland until Oct 1993); *Style*— Peter Carter, Esq; ✉ Office of Electricity Regulation, Hagley House, Hagley Road, Birmingham B16 8QG (☎ 0121 456 2100, fax 0121 456 6365)

CARTER, Peter; QC (1995); s of Tom and Winifred Carter, of Huddersfield; *b* 8 Aug 1952; *Educ* King James' GS Huddersfield, UCL (LLB); *m* 1973, Caroline Ann, da of Leslie Hugh Adams; 1 s (Jonathan Edwin b 3 Nov 1988); *Career* called to the Bar Gray's Inn 1974; sec Criminal Bar Assoc 1985–89; govr Br Inst of Human Rights, memb Cncl Deathwatch, memb Legal Section Amnesty; *Books* Offences of Violence; *Recreations* poetry, sport, walking; *Style*— Peter Carter, Esq, QC; ✉ 5 King's Bench Walk, Temple, London EC4Y 7DN (☎ 0171 797 7600, 0171 797 7468)

CARTER, Peter Basil; QC (1990); s of Albert George Carter (d 1961), and Amy Kathleen FitzGerald Carter (d 1973); *b* 10 April 1921; *Educ* Loughborough GS, Oriel Coll Oxford (BCL, MA, Vinerian scholar); *m* 1, 1960, Elizabeth Maxwell Ely (decd); m 2, 1982, Lorna Jean Sinclair; *Career* served WWII, Capt; called to the Bar Middle Temple 1947, hon bencher Middle Temple 1981; jt ed Int and Comparative Law Quarterly 1961–; fell Wadham Coll Oxford 1949–88 (emeritus fell 1988–), former visiting prof various Canadian, Aust and United States univs; chm Univ Life Assurance Soc 1980–91 (dir 1969–91); chm East Oxfordshire Div Gen Cmmrs for Income Tax Appeals 1991–95 (cmmr 1965–95); JP 1959–88; Croix de Guerre 1944; FInstD 1984; *Recreations* criticising bad architecture; *Clubs* United Oxford and Cambridge University; *Style*— P B Carter, Esq, QC; ✉ Wadham College, Oxford OX1 3PN (☎ 01865 277900, fax 01865 277937)

CARTER, Sir Philip David; kt (1991), CBE (1981); s of Percival Carter and Isobell, *née* Stirrup; *b* 8 May 1927; *Educ* Waterloo GS Liverpool; *m* 1946, Harriet Rita, *née* Evans; *Career* Fleet Air Arm 1945; Littlewoods Orgn 1944–83 (chief exec 1976–83), ret; chm: Mail Order Traders of GB 1979–83, Man Made Fibre Working Pty 1980, Empire Trust 1986–, Merseyside Tourism Bd 1986–92, Liverpool Cons Assoc 1985–; pres: Euro Mail Order Traders Assoc 1983, Football League 1986–88, dir Everton FC (chm 1977–91); memb: Jt Textile Ctee NEDO 1979, Distributive Trades EDC 1980, Merseyside Devpt Corp 1981– (chm 1987–91), Manchester Olympic Bid Ctee 1989; chm John Moores Univ Trust 1993– (dep chm of govrs 1994–), pro-chllr John Moores Univ Liverpool 1994–;

Recreations private flying, music, theatre, football; *Style*— Sir Philip Carter, CBE; ✉ Oak Cottage, Noctorum Rd, Noctorum, Wirral, Merseyside L43 9UQ

CARTER, Philip Mark (Phil); s of Brian Carter, of Norwich, Norfolk, and Barbara Mary, *née* Herod; *b* 26 Sept 1955; *Educ* Thorpe GS Norwich, Great Yarmouth Coll of Art, Norwich Sch of Art (BA), Royal Coll of Art (MA); *m* 1984, Deborah, da of David Catford; 1 s (Joseph b 1985), 1 da (Caitlin b 1989); *Career* designer Minale Tattersfield & Partners 1980–83, fndr ptnr/creative dir Carter Wong & Partners 1984–; work featured in various pubns incl: D&AD Annual 1983, 1985, 1988, 1989, 1990, 1994 and 1995, Graphis Annual 1996; D&AD Silver Award (Heal's Corp Identity) 1983, Media Natura Award (Marine Conservation Identity) 1988; external assessor: Bath Coll of Higher Educn 1991–96, Kingston Univ 1994–97; memb: Exec Ctee D&AD 1992–94, DBA; *Recreations* swimming, cycling, rugby, tennis; *Clubs* London Polytechnic; *Style*— Phil Carter; ✉ Carter Wong & Partners Ltd, 29 Brook Mews North, London W2 3BW (☎ 0171 224 9139, fax 0171 402 4122, e-mail cwpart@mail.bogo.co.uk)

CARTER, Prof Robert Lewis; OBE (1991); s of Edwin Christopher Carter (d 1964); *b* 23 Aug 1932; *Educ* Univ of London (BScEcon), Univ of Sussex (DPhil); *m* 1954, Pearl Rita Carter; 1 s, 2 da; *Career* emeritus prof of insurance studies Univ of Nottingham; govt nominee to Insur Brokers Registration Cncl 1979–82 and 1986–92, memb Cncl Insur Ombudsman Bureau 1981–93, fndr govr Inst of Risk Mgmnt 1986–90; visiting prof of insur American Graduate Sch of Int Mgmnt 1982–83; FCII, FIRM, FRSA; *Recreations* reading, pottering in the garden, travelling, walking; *Style*— Prof Robert Carter, OBE; ✉ 4 Bramcote Lane, Beeston, Nottingham NG9 5EN; School of Management and Finance, University of Nottingham, Nottingham NG7 2RD (☎ and fax 0115 951 5269)

CARTER, Stephen Andrew; s of Mr and Mrs G R Carter, of Pitlochry, Scotland; *b* 12 Feb 1964; *Educ* Univ of Aberdeen (LLB); *m* Anna Maria, da of Kevin Gorman; 1 s (Max Gorman Alexander b 11 Oct 1996); *Career* J Walter Thompson Co Ltd: grad trainee 1987–89, assoc dir 1989–91, bd dir 1991–93, dep md 1993–95, md 1995–; *Style*— S A Carter, Esq; ✉ J Walter Thompson Co Ltd, 40 Berkeley Square, London W1X 6AD (☎ 0171 631 7519, fax 0171 493 0109, mobile 0468 421481, e-mail Stephen.Carter@JWT.co.uk)

CARTER, Air Vice-Marshal Wilfred; CB (1963), DFC (1943); s of Samuel Carter (d 1943), of Nottingham; *b* 5 Nov 1912; *Educ* Witney GS; *m* 1950, Margaret Enid, da of Herbert Jones Bray, of Gainsborough, Lincs; 1 s (decd), 1 da; *Career* joined RAF 1929, Air Cdre 1960, AOA Bomber Command 1965–67, Air Vice-Marshal 1965, ret 1967; dir Australian Counter Disaster Coll 1969–78, int disaster conslt 1978–; Officer of Order of Cedars of Lebanon (1954); *Books* Disaster Preparedness and Response, Disaster Management; *Recreations* swimming, walking; *Style*— Air Vice-Marshal Wilfred Carter, CB, DFC; ✉ Blue Range, Macedon, Vic 3440, Australia

CARTER, Will; *b* 30 Nov 1956, Madras, India; *Educ* Malvern, Jesus Coll Oxford (BA); *m*; 1 c; *Career* United Biscuits (UK) Ltd 1979–: mktg trainee/asst product mangr 1979–81, product mangr/sr product mangr 1981–84, brand gp mangr/sr brand gp mangr 1984–86, mktg controller McVities 1986–89, mktg dir Terry's Group 1989–93 (business devpt dir April-Oct 1989), UK mktg dir KP Foods Group 1993–96 (mktg devpt dir July-Oct 1993), dir of Snacks 1996–; *Recreations* family, motorcycles, skiing, hill walking; *Style*— Will Carter, Esq; ✉ KP Foods Group, Heathgate House, 57 Colne Road, Twickenham, Middx TW2 6QA (☎ 0181 894 5600, fax 0181 894 6715)

CARTER, Sir William Oscar; kt (1972); s of Oscar Carter (d 1952), of Norwich, and Alice Carter; *b* 12 Jan 1905; *Educ* Swaffham GS, City of Norwich Sch; *m* 1934, Winifred Rose, da of Sidney Charles Thompson (d 1952), of Wymondham, Norfolk; *Career* served WWII Wing Cdr RAF; slr 1931; conslt Eversheds, Daynes Hill and Perks (Slrs) Norwich, memb Cncl Law Soc 1954–75 (vice pres 1970, pres 1971–72); pres: East Anglian Law Soc 1952–80, Norfolk and Norwich Inc Law Soc 1959, Int Legal Aid Assoc 1974–80; life memb Cncl Int Bar Assoc (first vice pres 1976–78); memb: Co Ct Rules Ctee 1956–60, Supreme Ct Rules Ctee 1960–75, Criminal Injuries Compensation Bd 1967–82 (dep chm 1977–82); hon memb The Fellows of the American Bar Fndn; Liveryman Worshipful Co of Glaziers (Master 1985); *Recreations* swimming, foreign travel; *Clubs* Army and Navy, Norfolk (Norwich); *Style*— Sir William Carter

CARTER-PEGG, Hallam; s of Carter Pegg (d 1970), of S Croydon, Surrey, and Helen Elise, *née* Johnson (d 1975); f played cricket for the London Counties with W G Grace; *b* 7 May 1932; *Educ* Whitgift Sch Croydon; *m* 16 April 1960, Margaret Edith, da of Norman Dale Mant (d 1957), of S Croydon; 2 s (Nicholas Hallam b 1964, Christopher Norman b 1973), 1 da (Karen Margaret b 1967); *Career* sr ptnr Pegg Robertson CAs 1970–; chm: Peckham Building Society 1980–90 (dir 1968–80), South London Investment and Mortgage Corporation Ltd 1988–90, Slim Systems Ltd 1988–94; dir Lizzard & Co Ltd 1991–95; Medal of Merit and Silver Acorn awards for serv to scouting; FCA; *Recreations* scouting, gardening, shooting; *Style*— Hallam Carter-Pegg, Esq; ✉ Whyteacre, 16 Manor Way, South Croydon, Surrey CR2 7BR; Pegg Robertson, Wandle House, 47 Wandle Rd, Croydon, Surrey CR0 1DF (☎ 0181 686 8011, fax 0181 681 8993, car 0860 516793)

CARTER-RUCK, Peter Frederick; s of Frederick Henry Carter-Ruck (d 1968), of Gerrards Cross, Bucks, and Nell Mabel, *née* Allen; *b* 1914; *Educ* St Edward's Oxford; *m* 6 July 1940, Pamela Ann, only da of Gp Capt Reginald Stuart Maxwell, MC, DFC, AFC (d 1960), of Thorney Island, Emsworth; 1 s (Brian b 1943 d 1973), 1 da (Julie b 1941); *Career* served RA 1939–44, Capt Instr in Gunnery; admitted slr 1937; sr ptnr: Oswald Hickson Collier & Co 1945–81, Peter Carter-Ruck and Partners 1981–; specialist memb Cncl Law Soc 1971–84; pres: City of Westminster Law Soc 1976, Media Soc 1981–82 and 1984–86; chm: Law Reform Ctee Law Soc 1980–83, Media Ctee Int Bar Assoc 1983–85; memb: Cncl of Justice, Intellectual Property Ctee Law Soc; hon conslt slr: Chartered Inst of Journalists, Media Soc; Lloyd's underwriter; govr St Edward's Sch Oxford 1950–78, past chm and fndr govr Shiplake Coll Henley 1960–73; memb City of London Solicitors' Co 1949; *Books* Libel and Slander (4 edn, 1992), The Cyclist and the Law (with Ian Mackrill, 1953), Copyright: Modern Law and Practice (with Edmund Skone James, 1965), Memoirs of a Libel Lawyer (1990); *Recreations* writing, cinematography, wood-turning, ocean racing and cruising; *Clubs* Garrick, Press, Royal Yacht Sqdn, Law Soc Yacht (past Cdre), Royal Ocean Racing, Ocean Cruising (past Cdre); *Style*— Peter Carter-Ruck, Esq; ✉ Latchmore Cottage, Great Hallingbury, Bishop's Stortford, Herts CM22 7PJ (☎ 01279 654357, fax 01279 504921); Eilagadale, N Ardnamurchan, Argyll PH36 4LG (☎ 01925 10267); Peter Carter-Ruck and Partners, 75 Shoe Lane, London EC4A 3BQ (☎ 0171 353 5005, fax 0171 353 5553)

CARTLAND, Dame Barbara Hamilton; DBE (1991); o da of Maj Bertram Cartland, Worcs Regt (ka 1918), of Littlewood House, Polbrook, nr Malvern, Worcs, and late Polly Cartland; *b* 9 July 1901; *m* 1, 23 April 1927 (m dis 1932), as his 1 w, Alexander George McCorquodale (d 1964), of Cound Hall, Shropshire, s of Alexander Cowan McCorquodale, JP (d 1941), of Cound Hall; 1 da (Comtesse Jean-François de Chambrun, *qv*); m 2, 28 Dec 1936, Hugh McCorquodale, MC (d 1963), 2 son of Harold McCorquodale, JP, DL (d 1943), of Forest Hall, Ongar, Essex, and 1 cousin of her 1 husband; 2 s (Ian Hamilton McCorquodale, *qv*, Glen b 1939); *Career* best selling authoress in the world (Guinness Book of Records 1992), has written more books than any other British author, has also published plays, poems, biography and autobiography; former chm St John Ambulance Exhibition Ctee, fndr Barbara Cartland Onslow Romany Gypsy Fund, fndr pres Nat Assoc for Health 1966; awarded Woman of Achievement by Nat Home Fashions League 1981, received Bishop Wright Air Ind award for the development of aviation 1984; past pres St John Cncl for Herts (first woman on Chapter General for 1000 yrs); La Medaille de Vermeil de la Ville de Paris 1988; DStJ 1972; FRSA; *Books* 645 (5 made into films); *Style*— Dame Barbara Cartland, DBE; ✉ Camfield Place, nr Hatfield, Herts AL9 6JE (☎ 01707 642612/642657, fax 01707 642640)

CARTLAND, John Barrington; s of Sir George Barrington Cartland, CMG, of Sandy Bay, Hobart, Tasmania, and Dorothy, *née* Rayton (d 1993); *b* 4 March 1941; *Educ* Rossall Sch, Balliol Coll Oxford (MA); *m* 11 March 1967, Gillian Margaret Campbell, da of Alastair Robert Campbell Cunningham (d 1994); 2 da (Claire Louise b 4 April 1968, Nicola Janet b 5 Jan 1972); *Career* CA 1966; KPMG Peat Marwick (formerly Peat Marwick Mitchell & Co): articled clerk 1963–66, ptnr 1969–73 (Peat Marwick Mitchell & Co Uganda, Lawrie Prophet & Co, E H Shelton & Co), sr mangr i/c trg and recruitment Birmingham 1976, sr mangr in charge of computer devpt 1983, ptnr 1984–93; memb BSES expedition to arctic Sweden 1959; treas and memb Cncl Outward Bound Tst of Uganda 1967–73; pres Birmingham and W Midlands Soc of CAs 1992–93, hon treas Royal Soc for the Prevention of Accidents 1993–; FCA; *Style*— John Cartland, Esq; ✉ Broomhall Grange, Norton Road, Worcester WR5 2PD (☎ 01905 356111, fax 01905 355157)

CARTLEDGE, Sir Bryan George; KCMG (1985, CMG 1980); s of Eric Montague George Cartledge, and Phyllis, *née* Shaw; *b* 10 June 1931; *Educ* Hurstpierpoint Coll, St John's Coll Cambridge, St Antony's Coll Oxford; *m* 1, 1960, Ruth Hylton, da of John Gass; 1 s, 1 da; m 2, 11 June 1994, Dr Freda Gladys Newcombe; *Career* Lt Queen's Royal Regt 1950–52; Dip Serv 1960–88: private sec overseas affrs to PM 1977–79, ambass to Hungary 1980–83, asst under sec of state Def 1983–84, dep sec of the Cabinet 1984–85, ambass to Soviet Union 1985–88; princ Linacre Coll Oxford 1988–96; hon fell: St John's Coll Cambridge 1985, St Antony's Coll Oxford 1987, Linacre Coll Oxford 1996; *Publications* Monitoring the Environment (ed, 1992), Energy and the Environment (ed, 1993), Health and the Environment (ed, 1994), Population and the Environment (ed, 1995), Transport and the Environment (ed, 1996), Mind, Brain and Environment (ed, 1997); *Style*— Sir Bryan Cartledge, KCMG; ✉ Jasmine House, Holton, Oxford OX33 1PU

CARTTISS, Michael Reginald Harry; MP (C) Great Yarmouth (majority 5,309); s of Reginald Carttiss and Doris Culling; *b* 11 March 1938; *Educ* Great Yarmouth Tech HS, Goldsmiths' Coll Univ of London, LSE; *Career* teacher 1961–69, Cons constituency agent for Gt Yarmouth 1969–82, MP (C) Great Yarmouth 1983–; cncllr: Norfolk CC 1966–85, Gt Yarmouth Borough Cncl 1973–82 (ldr 1980–82); *Style*— Michael Carttiss, Esq, MP; ✉ House of Commons, London SW1A 0AA

CARTWRIGHT, Christopher Egerton; s of Herbert Edward Cartwright (d 1978), and Ruth, *née* Collins; *b* 19 Oct 1944; *Educ* Kings Sch Worcester, Univ of Bristol; *m* 30 Dec 1967, Susan Lois, da of Antony John Mindham, of Brighton, Sussex; 1 s (James Egerton b 1971), 1 da (Sarah Elizabeth b 1974); *Career* formerly ptnr and dir Wood MacKenzie & Co and head of equities Paribas Capital Markets; chm City Executive Consultants Ltd; MSI, memb Inst of Investment Mgmnt and Res, FCA 1969; *Recreations* gardening, microcomputing, angling, guitar; *Style*— Christopher Cartwright, Esq; ✉ Hostye Farm, Cudham Lane North, Cudham, Kent TN14 7QT (☎ 01959 573163); City Executive Consultants Ltd, 69 King William Stret, London EC4N 7HR (☎ 0171 929 6900, fax 0171 929 6901, mobile 0831 687035)

CARTWRIGHT, Harry; CBE (1979, MBE Mil 1946); s of Edwin Harry Cartwright, and Agnes Alice, *née* Gillibrand; *b* 16 Sept 1919; *Educ* William Hulme's GS, St John's Coll Cambridge; *m* 1950, Catharine Margaret Carson Bradbury; 2 s; *Career* Dept of Atomic Energy: joined 1949, chief engr 1955, dir Industl Power 1960–64, dir Water Reactors 1964–70, dir Fast Reactor Systems 1970–73; dir Atomic Energy Estab Winfrith 1973–83; pres Euro Nuclear Soc 1983–85; *Style*— Harry Cartwright, Esq, CBE; ✉ Tabbit's Hill House, Corfe Castle, Wareham, Dorset (☎ 01929 480582)

CARTWRIGHT, Ian David; s of Cyril Cartwright, of Pistyll, Gwynedd, and Doreen Cartwright; *b* 28 March 1952; *Educ* The County GS Hyde Cheshire, Ashton-under-Lyne Coll of Further Educn, Leeds Poly (BA); *m* 1976, Christine May, da of William Robertson Lennie; 1 s (Lewis Edward b 15 April 1983); *Career* asst photographer Technical Public Relations and Graham Powell Studios 1975–78; photographer: Woburn Studios 1978–82, Montage 1982–87; photographer and md Avalon 1987–; memb Assoc of Photographers; FBIPP 1989; *Recreations* skiing, tai chi, painting, drawing; *Clubs* The Ski Club of Manchester (chm 1990–92), The Ski Club of GB; *Style*— Ian D Cartwright, Esq; ✉ Avalon Photography Limited, 5 Pittbrook St, Ardwick, Manchester M12 6LR (☎ 0161 274 3313, fax 0161 272 7277)

CARTWRIGHT, Jim; s of Jim Cartwright, of Farnworth, Lancs, and Edna, *née* Main; *b* 27 June 1958; *Educ* Harper Green Secdy Sch Farnworth; *m* Angela Louise, da of Samuel Jones; 1 s (James Lewis b 22 Oct 1984), 1 da (Georgina Lucy b 12 June 1996); *Career* writer; *Plays* Road (performed Royal Court Theatre 1986–87, adapted for BBC TV 1987), Baths (radio, 1987), Vroom (film, 1988), Bed (NT 1989), TO (Octagon Bolton and Young Vic London 1989–90), Eight Miles High (Octagon Bolton 1991, retitled Stone Free, Bristol Old Vic 1994 and 1995), June (BBC TV 1990), Wedded (BBC TV 1990), The Rise and Fall of Little Voice (NT then Aldwych 1992); *Awards* for Road: Drama Magazine award, George Devine award, jt winner Plays and Players Best New Play and Samuel Beckett Award; Golden Nymph award for Best Film at Monte Carlo TV and Film Festival; for TO: Manchester Evening News Theatre award for Best New Play; for The Rise and Fall of Little Voice: Best Comedy Evening Standard Drama Awards 1992, Best Comedy Laurence Olivier Awards 1993; *Style*— Jim Cartwright, Esq; ✉ Judy Daish Associates, 2 St Charles Place, London W10 6EG (☎ 0181 964 8811, fax 0181 964 8966)

CARTWRIGHT, John Cameron; JP (1970); s of late Aubrey John Randolph Cartwright, and Ivy Adeline Billie Cartwright; *b* 29 Nov 1933; *Educ* Woking Co GS; *m* 1959, Iris June Tant; 1 s, 1 da; *Career* exec civil servant 1952–55, Lab Pty agent 1955–67, dir Royal Arsenal Co-op Society Ltd 1972–74 (political sec 1967–72); MP (Lab until 1981, SDP 1981–90, Social Democrat 1990–92): Greenwich Woolwich E 1974–83, Woolwich 1983–92; PPS to Sec of State for Educn and Sci 1976–77, fndr memb SDP March 1981, Parly spokesman on housing, local govt and the environment, SDP whip 1983–92, SDP spokesman on defence 1983–92, memb Defence Select Ctee 1979–82 and 1986–92, pres SDP 1988–90 (vice pres 1987–88), sec Parly Retail Indust Gp 1991–92; former tstee Nat Maritime Museum, dep chm Police Complaints Authy 1993– (memb 1992–); *Books* Cruise, Pershing and SS20 (jtly, 1985), View from the House (jtly, 1986); *Style*— John Cartwright, Esq, JP; ✉ 17 Commonwealth Way, London SE2 0JZ (☎ 0181 311 4394)

CARTWRIGHT, John Wallace; s of Reginald Cartwright (d 1982), of Cambridge, and Iris Marion, *née* Dear (d 1992); *b* 10 March 1946; *Educ* Bedford Sch, Cranfield Mgmnt Sch (MBA); *m* 1973, Christine Elise, da of Jack Whitaker, of Newbury; 1 s (Timothy b 1975), 2 da (Genevieve b 1978, Bethany b 1980); *Career* merchant banker; dir: emerging mkts fund mgmnt ANZ Banking Group Ltd 1989– (formerly dir risk placement and syndication), ANZ Grindlays 3i Investment Services Ltd 1989, Second Indian Investment Fund Ltd 1990; FCIB; *Recreations* gardening, golf; *Style*— John Cartwright, Esq; ✉ 16 Millfield, Berkhamsted HP4 2PB (☎ 01442 864984); ANZ Banking Group Ltd, Minerva House, Montague Close, London SE1 9DH (☎ 0171 378 2864, fax 0171 378 2900)

CARTWRIGHT, Dr Keith Anthony Vincent; s of Albert George Frank Cartwright (d 1983), and Jean Cartwright (d 1994); *b* 21 Sept 1946; *Educ* Mill Hill Sch, Univ of Oxford (MA, BM BCh); *m* 13 Sept 1969, Prudence Lilian, da of John Edward Serby, CB, CBE, of Farnham, Surrey; 1 s (Julian b 1975), 2 da (Katharine b 1973, Victoria b 1976); *Career* conslt microbiologist Western Gen Hosp Edinburgh 1978–80, dir Gloucester Public Health Laboratory Gloucester 1981–95, gp dir Public Health Laboratory Serv SW 1995–; res advsr Meningitis Tst; FRCPath 1988 (MRCPath 1978); *Recreations* mountaineering, rock climbing; *Clubs* Oxford Alpine, Climbers; *Style*— Dr Keith Cartwright; ✉ Public Health Laboratory, Gloucestershire Royal Hospital, Great Western Road, Gloucester GL1 3NN (☎ 01452 305334)

CARTWRIGHT, Dame Mary Lucy; DBE (1969); da of Rev William Digby Cartwright (d c1926), sometime Rector of Aynho, and Lucy Harriette Maud, *née* Bury (d 1950); *b* 17 Dec 1900; *Educ* Godolphin Sch Salisbury, St Hugh's Coll Oxford (MA, DPhil), (ScD Cantab); *Career* Univ of Cambridge: univ lectr in mathematics 1935–59, reader in the theory of functions 1959–68, emeritus reader 1968–, mistress Girton Coll 1949–68 (former res staff fell, life fell 1968); cmdt Br Red Cross Detachment Cambs 112 1940–44; conslt on US Navy mathematical research projects at Stanford and Princeton Univs 1949; visiting prof: Brown Univ Providence Rhode Island 1968–69, Claremont Graduate Sch Calif 1969–70, Case Western Reserve 1970 and 1971, Polish Acad of Sciences 1970, Univ of Wales 1971; Hon LLD Univ of Edinburgh 1953; Hon DSc: Univ of Leeds 1958, Univ of Hull 1959, Univ of Wales 1962, Univ of Oxford 1966, Brown USA 1969; Cdr Order of the Dannebrog 1961; FRS, hon FRSE; *Style*— Dame Mary Cartwright, DBE; ✉ c/o Nigel Cartwright, Trotton Place, Midhurst, Sussex GU31 5EN

CARTWRIGHT, Prof Nancy Delaney; *b* 24 June 1944; *Educ* Univ of Pittsburgh (BS), Univ of Illinois (Carnegie fell, Danforth fell, Woodrow Wilson fell, PhD); *Career* asst prof of philosophy Univ of Maryland 1971–73; Stanford University: asst prof of philosophy 1973–77, assoc prof 1977–83, prof 1983–91, chair Philosophy Dept 1988–90; LSE: prof of philosophy, logic and scientific method 1991–, dir Centre for Philosophy of Natural and Social Science 1993–; visiting lectr Univ of Cambridge 1974, visiting asst prof UCLA 1976, visiting assoc prof Princeton Univ 1978, visiting prof Univ of Pittsburgh 1984, short term visiting prof Univ of Oslo 1993 and 1994, short term visiting prof Univ of California San Diego 1995; fell: Center for Interdisciplinary Research (ZiF) Bielefield Germany 1976–77 (memb Advsy Bd 1993–), Philosophy of Science Center Univ of Pittsburgh 1982–83 and 1984, Inst for Advanced Study Wissenschaftskolleg Berlin 1987–88 (memb Advsy Bd 1991–96); pres Soc for Exact Philosophy 1985, pres American Assoc of Univ Profs Stanford Chapter 1986–87; memb Nat Sci Fndn: Award Panel History & Philosophy of Sci 1985–87, Oversight Ctee for History and Philosophy of Sci 1989–90; memb: US Nat Ctee Int Union of History and Philosophy of Sci 1989–90, Advsy Bd Centre for History and Economics Cambridge 1991–, MIND Exec Ctee 1992–97; memb Editorial Bd: Int Studies in the Philosophy of Sci, Jl of Economic Methodology, Studies in History and Philosophy of Modern Physics, Erkenntnis, Synthese, Pacific Philosophical Quarterly, Philosophical Perspectives, Philosophy and Economics, Philosophy of Science; MacArthur Fndn Award 1993; Old Dominion fell Princeton Univ 1996; FBA 1996; *Books* How the Laws of Physics Lie (1983), Nature's Capacities and their Measurement (1989), Otto Neurath: Philosophy between Science and Politics (jtly, 1995); also author of numerous book reviews and articles in learned jls; *Style*— Prof Nancy Cartwright, FBA; ✉ Department of Philosophy, Logic, and Scientific Method, London School of Economics and Political Science, Houghton Street, London WC2A 2AE (☎ 0171 955 7341/7901, fax 0171 955 6845)

CARTWRIGHT, Rt Rev Richard Fox; s of Rev George Frederick Cartwright (vicar of Plumstead, d 1938), and Constance Margaret, *née* Clark (d 1975); *b* 10 Nov 1913; *Educ* The King's Sch Canterbury, Pembroke Coll Cambridge (BA, MA), Cuddesdon Theol Coll; *m* 6 Sept 1947, Rosemary Magdalen, da of Francis Evelyn Bray (d 1973), of Woodham Grange, Surrey; 1 s (Andrew Martin b 1948), 3 da (Rosemary Jane (Mrs Turner) b 1951, Mary Katharine (Mrs Bradley) b 1953, Susan Margaret (Mrs Meikle) b 1958); *Career* curate St Anselm Kennington Cross 1936–40, princ Lower Kingswood 1940–45; vicar: St Andrew Surbiton 1945–52, St Mary Redcliffe Bristol (with Temple 1956– and St John Bedminster 1965–) 1952–72; hon canon Bristol 1960–72, suffragan bishop of Plymouth 1972–81; asst bishop: Diocese of Truro 1982–91, Diocese of Exeter 1988–; proctor in convocation 1950–52, memb Gen Synod 1976–80; chm Govrs Kelly Coll Tavistock 1973–88, govr Summerfields Sch Oxford 1964–88; dir: Ecclesiastical Insurance Gp 1964–85, All Churches Tst 1985–91; Grand Chaplain Utd Grand Lodge of England 1973–75; Hon DD Univ of the South Tennessee 1969; OStJ 1957; *Recreations* fly fishing, gardening, water colour painting; *Clubs* Army and Navy; *Style*— The Rt Rev Richard Cartwright; ✉ 5 Old Vicarage Close, Ide, nr Exeter, Devon EX2 9RT (☎ 01392 211270)

CARTWRIGHT, Sally Amanda; da of Dennis Cartwright (d 1990), and Eileen Sergeant Cartwright (d 1979); *b* 8 May 1944; *Educ* Merton House Sch Keymer Sussex; *m* 1, 23 Feb 1973, John William Robinson; m 2, 29 Feb 1980, John Brian Hutchings; *Career* secretary 1961–69; IPC Magazines: merchandising exec 1970, promotions exec 1971–76, publicity mangr 1976–79, asst publisher 1979–82, publisher (responsible for Woman's Journal and Ideal Home Magazines) 1983–86; md: Capital Magazine 1987, Harmsworth Publications (pt of Assoc Newspapers) 1988–90; publishing dir Hello! magazine 1990–; pres Women's Advtg Club of London 1992–93, assoc Women of the Year Luncheon, dir PPA (chm Environmental Working Gp); *Recreations* reading, embroidery, skiing, swimming, opera, theatre; *Clubs* Ski Club of GB (memb Cncl); *Style*— Ms Sally Cartwright; ✉ Hello Limited, Wellington House, 69/71 Upper Ground, London SE1 9PQ (☎ 0171 334 7404, fax 0171 334 7411)

CARTY, Dr Austin Timothy; s of Dr Thomas James Augustine (Gus) Carty (d 1975), of Glasnevin, Dublin, and Dr Catherine Anne Carty, *née* Quinn (d 1981); *b* 22 June 1941; *Educ* Belvedere Coll Dublin, University College Dublin (MB BCh, BAO); *m* 23 Sept 1967, Prof Helen Carty, *qv*, da of Roland Moloney (d 1971), of Dun Laoghaire, Co Dublin and Dungarvan, Co Waterford; 1 s (Timothy b 1968), 2 da (Jennifer b 1970, Sarah b 1973); *Career* conslt radiologist Liverpool Health Authy 1974–, clinical sub-dean Univ of Liverpool at Royal Liverpool Hosp 1987–90, chm Dist Med Advsy Ctee Liverpool Health Authy 1989–90, med dir Royal Liverpool Univ Hosp NHS Tst 1991–; Liverpool Med Inst: pres 1990–91, ed Transactions 1991–, hon librarian 1995–; FRCR, FRCPI, FFR RCSI; *Recreations* dinghy sailing, opera, wine; *Clubs* Twenty (Liverpool) (pres 1990–91), Innominate (Liverpool), Artists (Liverpool); *Style*— Dr Austin Carty; ✉ 6 Grosvenor Rd, Cressington Park, Liverpool L19 0PL (☎ 0151 427 6727); X-Ray Department, Royal Liverpool Hospital, Prescot St, Liverpool L7 8XP (☎ 0151 706 2751, fax 0151 706 5824)

CARTY, Prof Helen; da of Roland Moloney (d 1971), of Dublin, and Honor, *née* Frame (d 1981); *b* 12 May 1944; *Educ* St Mary's Arklow Co Wicklow Eire, Univ Coll Dublin (MB BCh, BAO); *m* 23 Sept 1967, Dr Austin Carty, *qv*, s of Dr Thomas J A Carty (d 1975), of Dublin; 1 s (Timothy Mark b 13 Oct 1968), 2 da (Jennifer Ann b 29 Aug 1970, Sarah Lucy b 7 Feb 1973); *Career* house offr and med registrar Mater Hosp Dublin 1967–71, registrar in radiology St Thomas' Hosp London 1971–74, sr registrar Broadgreen Hosp Liverpool 1974–75, clinical dir radiology Alder Hey Hosp Liverpool 1977– (conslt radiologist 1975–); prof of paediatric radiology Univ of Liverpool 1996–; chm Intercollegiate Standing Ctee on Nuclear Med London 1989–95; pres Liverpool Med Instn 1993–94; RCR: sometime memb Bd of Faculty, Cncl and Educn Bd, examiner Final Fellowship 1988–91; memb Steering Ctee Dept of Health for monitoring Nat Breast Screening Prog; *Books* Imaging Children: A Textbook of Paediatric Radiology (jt ed and author of several chapters, 1994); *Recreations* birdwatching, theatre, cooking; *Style*— Prof Helen Carty; ✉ 6 Grosvenor Road, Cressington Park, Liverpool L19 0PL (☎ 0151 427 6727); Department of Radiology, Royal Liverpool Children's Hospital, Alder Hey, Eaton Road, Liverpool L12 2AP (☎ 0151 252 5432, fax 0151 252 5533)

CARTY, Hilary; da of Solomon Carty, of London, and Catherine, *née* Bailey; *b* 26 May 1962; *Educ* Waverley Girls Sch, Leicester Poly (BA), Cultural Trg Centre Jamaica (Cert in Dance Educn), Univ of Westminster (MBA); *Career* community arts devpt offr Leicester Expressive Arts 1984–86, dance and mime offr E Midlands Arts 1986–90, gen mangr Adzido 1990–94, dir of dance Arts Cncl of England 1994–; FRSA 1996; *Books* Folk Dances of Jamaica (1988); *Style*— Miss Hilary Carty; ✉ Arts Council of England, 14 Great Peter Street, London SW1P 3NQ (☎ 0171 973 6489, fax 0171 973 6590, e-mail HILARY.CARTY.ACE@ARTSFB.ORG.UK)

CARTY, James Patrick; s of James Patrick Carty (d 1958), and Phyllis Elizabeth Carty; *b* 3 March 1937; *Educ* Cotton Coll, Univ of London (BSc), Univ of Lancaster (MA); *Career* Price Waterhouse 1965–72 (articled clerk, asst mangr), lectr in accounting and fin Univ of Lancaster 1972–74, sec Accounting Standards Ctee 1974–81, accountant in public practice James Carty & Co 1981–87, ptnr Robson Rhodes 1987–; memb Urgent Issues Task Force 1995–; FCA 1975, FCCA 1983; *Books* Practical Financial Management (ed 1984); *Style*— James Carty, Esq; ✉ Robson Rhodes, 186 City Rd, London EC1V 2NU (☎ 0171 251 1644, fax 0171 250 0801)

CARUS, Louis Revell; s of Lt-Col Martin MacDowall Carus-Wilson, RAEC (d 1969), and Enid Madeleine Thaxter, *née* Revell (d 1973); *b* 22 Oct 1927; *Educ* Rugby, Brussels Conservatoire of Music, Peabody Conservatory of Music (USA); *m* 11 July 1951, Nancy Reade, da of Percival Edward Noell (d 1981), of Durham, N Carolina, USA; 2 s (Kenneth Edward b 20 Feb 1953, Colin Martin b 4 Sept 1956), 1 da (Alison Noell (Mrs L J Du Cane) b 29 May 1955); *Career* violinist, teacher and administrator; memb Scot Nat Orch 1950–55, head of strings Royal Scot Acad of Music and Drama 1955–75, dean of Faculty Birmingham Sch of Music (now Birmingham Conservatoire) 1975–87, artistic dir Int String Quartet Week 1985–, conslt Benslow Tst Musical Instrument Loan Scheme 1987–; former pres ISM, former chm Euro String Teachers' Assoc (Br Branch); FRCM, FRSAMD, FBSM, Hon RAM, hon fell Univ of Central England; *Recreations* gardening, walking, painting; *Style*— Louis Carus, Esq; ✉ 15 King's End Rd, Powick, Worcs WR2 4RA (☎ 01905 831715)

CARUTH, David Alexander; s of Maj Robert Alexander Caruth (d 1939), and Ruby Duncan, *née* Hodgson (d 1980); *b* 31 July 1931; *Educ* Wellington Coll, Univ of Southampton; *m* 1, 1963; 3 da (Sophie b 1964, Melissa b 1966, Julia Jill b 1968); m 2, 1987, Ann Thomas, da of Col Alan Clarence Langford; *Career* admitted slr 1956, advocate Kenya 1958; Linklaters & Paines until 1990: joined 1960, corp ptnr 1966, ptnr i/c New York 1983–86; dir and gp legal advsr J Henry Schroder & Co Ltd 1990–96; non-exec dir: Bradbury Wilkinson & Co Ltd 1972–83, Matthew Hall & Co Ltd 1978–83, Allstate Insurance Ltd 1979–83, Diagonal plc 1996–; memb Oxfordshire CC 1977–81, inspr DTI 1988–89; govr: Wallingford Sch 1977–81, St Mary's Sch Calne 1978–83; memb: Law Soc 1956, Lowtonian Soc 1972 (hon memb 1996), New York Bar Assoc 1983; Liveryman City of London Solicitors' Co; *Recreations* racing, swimming, gardening; *Clubs* Boodle's, The 1900, The 65; *Style*— David Caruth, Esq; ✉ 37 Lennox Gardens, London SW1X 0DF (☎ 0171 581 0402, fax 0171 581 0461)

CARVELL, John Edward; s of Robert Charles Carvell (d 1984), of Perth, Scotland, and Ivy, *née* Dutch (d 1987); *b* 30 May 1946; *Educ* Perth Acad, Univ of St Andrews (MB ChB), Univ of Dundee (MMSc); *m* 22 July 1972, Carol, da of Gilbert D Ritchie, of Broughty Ferry, Dundee; 1 s (Robin b 1979), 1 da (Claire b 1976); *Career* registrar in orthopaedics Royal Utd Hosps Bath 1976–77, sr registrar in orthopaedics Nuffield Orthopaedic Centre Oxford and John Radcliffe Hosp Oxford 1978–83, conslt orthopaedic and trauma surgn Salisbury Odstock District Hosp 1983–; regnl and dist pres Arthritis and Rheumatism Cncl; memb Int Soc of Arthroscopy Knee Surgery and Orthopaedic Sports Med; FRCSE 1976, fell Br Orthopaedic Assoc 1983, fell Br Scoliosis Soc 1988; *Recreations* music, gardening, squash, tennis; *Clubs* Moonrakers (Salisbury), Salisbury Lawn Tennis; *Style*— John Carvell, Esq; ✉ Newstead, 143 Bouverie Avenue South, Salisbury, Wilts SP2 8EB (☎ 01722 330519); New Hall Hospital, The Lodge, Bodenham, Salisbury (☎ 01722 331021)

CARVER, (James) John; s of James Carver, and Jean Mary, *née* Kerry; *b* 28 Sept 1957; *Educ* Dulwich, Canterbury Coll of Art; *m* Jan 1987, Susan Jane, *née* Silvester; *Career* md designate J Carver & Co 1977–79, account exec International Marketing & Promotions (pt of the Masius Gp) 1979–81, creative exec Promotional Marketing Limited (pt of O & M) 1981–82, freelance art dir and writer 1982–85, creative dir and fndr ptnr The Leisure Process 1985–; winner various advtg prizes and awards from the music indust and mktg/advtg sector 1985–91; memb: ITV Assoc Zoo Check; *Books* Duran Duran (1985), Michael Jackson (1985); *Recreations* marlin fishing, hot air ballooning, historic car racing, classic car collecting, angling, aerobics, Thai boxing, travel; *Clubs* Fred's, Mercedes-Benz, Maserati Club of GB; *Style*— John Carver, Esq; ✉ The Leisure Process Ltd, 126 Great Portland St, London W1N 5PH (☎ 0171 631 0666, fax 0171 631 3753, car 0836 768422)

CARVER, Prof Martin Oswald Hugh; s of Lt-Col John Hobart Carver, of Exmoor Gate, Odiham, Hants, and Jocelyn Louisa Grace, *née* Tweedie; *b* 8 July 1941; *Educ* Wellington, RMA Sandhurst, RMC of Science Shrivenham (BSc), Univ of Durham; *m* 1, 5 April 1964 (m dis), Carolyn Rose, da of John Wolsely Haig; 1 s (Justin John), 1 da (Emma Rose); m 2, 2 April 1981, Madeleine Rose Hummler; 3 s (Frédéric Hugh, Jacques Francis, Louis Alexandre), 1 da (Geneviève Louise); *Career* adj 4 RTR 1968–70 (cmmnd RTR 1960), ret as Capt 1972; freelance archaeologist 1972–78, dir Field Archaeology Unit Univ of Birmingham 1978–86, prof and head Dept of Archaeology Univ of York 1986–; presenter and scriptwriter on Sutton Hoo BBC Films 1984, 1986, and 1988; dir Sutton Hoo Res Project 1983–, dir Tarbzt Discovery Prog 1994–; FSA, FSAS, MIFA; *Books* Medieval Worcester (1980), Underneath English Towns (1987), The Age of Sutton Hoo (1992), Arguments in Stone (1993); *Style*— Prof Martin Carver, FSA; ✉ Department of Archaeology, University of York, King's Manor, York YO1 1JZ (☎ 01904 433901, fax 01904 433902)

CARVER, Baron (Life Peer 1977), of Shackleford, Co Surrey; Field Marshal Sir (Richard) Michael Power Carver; GCB (1970, KCB 1966, CB 1957), CBE (1945), DSO (1943) and Bar (1943), MC (1941); 2 s of late Harold Power Carver, of Ticklerton, Salop, and Winifred Anne Gabrielle, *née* Wellesley; *b* 24 April 1915; *Educ* Winchester, RMA Sandhurst; *m* 1947, Edith, da of Lt-Col Sir Henry Lowry-Corry, MC (gs of 3 Earl Belmore); 2 s (Hon Andrew Richard b 1950, Hon John Antony b 1961), 2 da (Hon Susanna Mary b 1948, Hon Alice Elizabeth (Hon Mrs Walters) b 1954); *Career* sits as Ind peer in House of Lords; 2 Lt RTC 1935, cmd 4 Armd Bde 1944–47, Lt-Col 1942, Brig 1944; GOC 3 Div (Maj-Gen) 1962–64, Dep Cdr UN Force in Cyprus 1964, DSD MOD 1964–66, C-in-C Far East 1967–69, GOCIC Southern Cmd 1969–71, CGS 1971–73, Field-Marshal 1973, CDS 1973–76; Col Cmdt: REME 1966–76, RAC 1973–77; British Resident Cmmr (Designate) in Rhodesia 1977–78; Hon DLitt Univ of Southampton 1991; *Books* El Alamein (1962), Tobruk (1964), The War Lords (ed, 1976), Harding of Petherton (1978), The Apostles of Mobility (1979), War Since 1945 (1980), A Policy for Peace (1982), The Seven Ages of The British Army (1984), Dilemmas of the Desert War (1986), Twentieth Century Warriors (1987), Out of Step (1989), Tightrope Walking (1992);

Recreations sailing, tennis, gardening; *Clubs* Anglo-Belgian, Cavalry and Guards'; *Style—* Field Marshal The Rt Hon Lord Carver, GCB, CBE, DSO, MC; ✉ Wood End House, Wickham, Fareham, Hants PO17 6JZ (☎ 01329 832143)

CARVER, Peter William John; JP (1973), DL (Humberside 1983); 23 patron of North Cave living; s of Maj John Henton Carver, JP, TD (d 1968), and Juliet (d 1969), er da of Col T C Clitherow, DSO (d 1963), of Hotham Hall, York; *b* 18 June 1938; *Educ* Uppingham; *m* 1963, Jacqueline Sarah, da of James Boyce, of Fornham All Saints, Suffolk (d 1984); 1 s (Christian Henton James); *Career* Nat Serv 2 Lt DCLI; staff broadcaster with: Br Forces Network Germany 1959–62, Radio Luxembourg 1962–64; dir: Hull City AFC 1981, Viking Radio; underwriting memb of Lloyd's 1971–; cncllr E Riding Yorks CC 1971–74, contested (C) Hull Central/North 1974 (twice), pres Humberside Euro Constituency 1983–88 (chm 1978–83); pres Humberside Scout Assoc 1991– (chm 1978–83, co cmmr 1983–90), memb Ctee of the Cncl Scout Assoc 1986–90; memb Yorks Regnl Ctee Nat Tst 1985–90, dep chm S Hunsley Magistrates, co cmmr St John Ambulance Bde (Humberside) 1991–95, cmmr-in-chief St John Ambulance Bde 1995–; farmer and landowner; High Sheriff of The East Riding of Yorkshire 1997–98; KStJ; *Style—* Peter Carver, Esq, JP, DL; ✉ The Croft, North Cave, East Yorks (☎ 01430 422203); Hotham Estate Farms, North Cave, East Yorks HU15 2NG; The Croft, North Cave, East Yorks HU15 2NG

CARVER, Wyndham Houssemayne; s of Capt Edmund Squarey Carver, DSC, RN, and Freda Wilmot Houssemayne, *née* Du Boulay (d 1970); *b* 4 May 1943; *Educ* Malvern Coll, Harvard Business Sch (PMD); *m* 11 May 1974 (m dis 1984), Jocelyn Mary Anne, da of Graham Rogers, of Hungerford House, Hyde, Fordingbridge, Hants; m 2, Shona Leslie, da of Maj Ian McKillop, of Ladys Walk, East Cholderton, nr Andover, Hants; 1 da (Tamsin b 7 Sept 1985); *Career* with International Distillers & Vintners (subsid of Grand Metropolitan) 1965–, seconded to DTI 1995–; *Recreations* squash, tennis, golf, forestry, travel; *Clubs* Boodle's, Lansdowne; *Style—* Wyndham Carver, Esq; ✉ Rondle Wood House, Nr Milland, Liphook, Hants GU30 7LA (☎ 01730 821397, home ☎/fax 01730 821136)

CARY, Nicolas Robert Hugh; s and h of Sir Roger Hugh Cary, 2 Bt, *qv*; *b* 17 April 1955; *Educ* St Paul's, Univ of London (BA); *m* 1, 1979 (m dis 1991), Pauline Jean, da of Dr Thomas Ian Boyd, of Grays, Essex; 3 s (Alexander Robert b 1981, Nathaniel Ian b 1983, Peter b 1988); m 2, 1994, Lesley Anne, da of John Henry Gilham, of Kelvedon Common, Essex; *Career* with Sotheby's 1977–82 (production asst Catalogue Dept 1979–82); city print rep Westerham Press 1982–85, mktg dir Financial Statements Ltd (now Holmes & Marchant Corporate Design) 1985–86, dir Shandwick Advertising Ltd 1987, fndr md Fairfax Consultancy Ltd (formerly Shandwick Design Ltd) 1987– (chm and md 1993–), md Ashdown Press Ltd 1993–; *Recreations* book collecting, creative writing, travel and exploration, rock climbing, cookery; *Style—* Nicolas Cary Esq; ✉ 27 Seaforth Lodge, Barnes High St, London SW13 9LE

CARY, Sir Roger Hugh; 2 Bt (UK 1955); s of Sir Robert Archibald Cary, 1 Bt (d 1979), sometime MP for Eccles and Manchester (Withington), PPS to Capt Harry Crookshank 1951–55; *b* 8 Jan 1926; *Educ* Ludgrove, Eton, New Coll Oxford (BA); *m* 1, 1948 (m dis 1951), Marilda (d 1996), da of Maj Philip Pearson-Gregory, MC; 1 da (Marcia Susan (Hon Mrs Robin Gibson-Watt) b 1949); m 2, 1953, Ann Helen Katharine, eldest da of Hugh Blair Brenan, OBE; 2 s (Nicolas Robert Hugh b 1955, Dr (Roger) Nathaniel Blair b 1957), 1 da (Charlotte Rhoda Rosamond (Mrs David Mayou) b 1960); *Heir* s, Nicolas Robert Hugh Cary, *qv*; *Career* served Grenadier Gds 1944–47 (Signals Offr Gds' Trg Bn 1946–47); former sub ed and leader writer The Times and dep ed The Listener, sr asst then special asst (public affairs) BBC 1972–77, special asst to md BBC TV 1977–82, chief asst to dir of programming BBC TV 1983–86, conslt to Dir Gen BBC 1986–; tstee Kedleston 1989–; *Recreations* looking at pictures; *Clubs* Pratt's, First Guards'; *Style—* Sir Roger Cary, Bt; ✉ 23 Bath Rd, London W4 1LJ; BBC, Broadcasting House, London W1A 1AA (☎ 0171 580 4468 ext 3838)

CARY-ELWES, Charles Gervase Rundle; s of Lt-Col Oswald Aloysius Joseph Cary-Elwes (d 1994), and (Elisabeth) Pamela Rundle, *née* Brendon (d 1996); *b* 8 Nov 1939; *Educ* Ampleforth, Sorbonne, Trinity Coll Oxford (MA); *m* 2 April 1972, Angela Jean, da of Maj Eric Rowland, TD, TA (d 1960); 1 s (James b 1976), 1 da (Lucy b 1974); *Career* stockjobber Durlacher Oldham Mordaunt Godson 1962–65, in film prodn 1965–74, Peat Marwick Mitchell & Co CAs 1975–79, corporate fin exec Grieveson Grant & Co 1980–83, Exco International plc 1983–85; dir: British & Commonwealth Holdings plc 1986–89, Leopold Joseph & Sons Ltd 1991–93, Woolton Elwes Ltd 1993–, Orion Publishing Group Ltd 1994–; FCA, ATII; *Recreations* golf, music, theatre, travel; *Clubs* Dulwich and Sydenham Hill Golf; *Style—* Charles Cary-Elwes, Esq

CASE, Anthea Fiendley; da of Thomas Fiendley Stones, OBE, of London, and Bessie Mackie (d 1985); *b* 7 Feb 1945; *Educ* Christ's Hosp, St Anne's Coll Oxford (BA); *m* David Charles Case, *qv*, s of Charles Kendall Case (d 1993); 2 da (Melissa b 1977, Laura b 1983); *Career* HM Treasy: various posts 1967–70, private sec to Fin Sec 1970–71, princ 1971–80, asst sec 1980–88, under sec Home Educn Gp 1988–90, under sec Pay and Industl Rels Gp 1990–92, under sec Fiscal Policy Gp 1992–95, dep dir Budget and Public Finances 1995; dir Nat Heritage Meml Fund 1995–; *Style—* Mrs Anthea Case; ✉ The National Heritage Memorial Fund, 10 St James Street, London SW1A 1EF (☎ 0171 930 0963)

CASE, David Charles; s of Charles Kendal Case (d 1993), and Grace Tennent, *née* Smith; *b* 18 Oct 1943; *Educ* Oakham Sch, Univ of Oxford (MA); *m* 3 June 1967, Anthea Fiendley Case, *qv*, da of Thomas Fiendley Stones, OBE; 2 da (Melissa Katherine b 1977, Laura Alexandra b 1983); *Career* ICI 1967–68, export mangr British Sidac 1968–72, dir CCA Galleries plc (formerly Christie's Contemporary Art) 1972–89, dir Marlborough Fine Art Ltd; fell Royal Soc of Painter-Printmakers; *Style—* David Case Esq; ✉ Marlborough Fine Art Ltd, 6 Albemarle Street, London W1 (☎ 0171 629 5161)

CASE, David Winston; s of Stanley Herbert George Case, of Broadstairs, Kent, and Doreen, *née* Jeans; *b* 10 June 1952; *Educ* Dane Court GS, St Martin's Sch of Art (BA); *m* 1, 1987; 1 s (James Alexander b 9 Sept 1986), 1 da (Rachael Mary Louise b 2 July 1988); m 2, 1 July 1995, Kiki, da of Khim Chandaria; *Career* graphic artist: The Sunday Times 1975–78, TV Times magazine 1978–79; head of graphics Now! magazine 1979–81, asst art ed The Mail on Sunday 1981–84, art ed Which? magazine (Consumer Association) 1984–86, design dir Financial Times 1986–; awards: Best Design award Daily Nat Newspaper (Financial Times) 1990, Best Design award Sunday Nat Newspaper (The Sunday Correspondent) 1990, awards for illustration by Soc for News Design USA 1990, Best Design Feature Pages Nat Newspaper (with Andrew Chappin) 1991; fndr memb and vice pres Euro Soc for News Design; FCSD 1994; *Style—* David Case, Esq; ✉ Financial Times, Number One, Southwark Bridge, London SE1 9HL (☎ 0171 873 3000, fax 0171 407 5700)

CASE, Janet Ruth; da of James Anthony Simpson, of Exeter, and Cathleen, *née* King; *b* 29 June 1943; *Educ* Bishop Blackall Sch Exeter, Univ of Durham (LLB); *m* 1965 (m dis 1982), Jeremy David Michael Case, s of Glyn Pryce (d 1980), of Gunley; 1 s (Edwin b 1969), 1 da (Charlotte b 1966); *Career* called to the Bar Inner Temple 1975, Wales and Chester Circuit 1975; chm Med Appeals Tbnl 1988, recorder of the Crown Court 1995–; *Recreations* gardening, opera; *Clubs* Lansdowne; *Style—* Mrs Janet Case; ✉ Croeswylan, Oswestry, Shropshire (☎ 01691 653726); 40 King St, Chester (☎ 01244 323886)

CASE, Prof (Richard) Maynard; s of John (Jack) Case (d 1985), of Stockport, Cheshire, and Joycelyn Mary, *née* Ashcroft; *b* 23 July 1943; *Educ* Stockport GS Cheshire, King's Coll Durham (BSc), Univ of Newcastle (MRC scholar, PhD); *m* 22 Dec 1967, Gillian Mary, da of John Guy; *Career* Dept of Physiology Univ of Newcastle: lectr 1967–75, sr lectr 1975–76, reader 1976–79; Univ of Manchester: prof of physiology 1979–, head Dept of Physiology 1980–86, head Dept of Physiological Scis 1986–90, dean Sch of Biological Scis 1990–94; lectr Inst of Physiology Aarhus Univ Denmark 1970–71, Northern regnl tutor Open Univ 1973–75, lectr Dept of Physiology Sydney Univ 1976–77; res leave fell Wellcome Tst 1994–; memb: Animal Scis and Psychology Sub-Ctee Biological Scis Ctee SERC 1981–84, Res and Med Advsy Ctee Cystic Fibrosis Res Tst 1982–87, Grants Ctee A Cell Bd MRC 1983–87, Scientific and Res Awards Ctee Br Digestive Fndn 1989–93, Biochemistry and Cell Biology Ctee BBSRC 1994–96; managing ed Cell Calcium 1978–; memb ed bd: Gut 1984–87, Yonsei Med Jl 1986–, Pancreas 1986–92; Br Soc of Gastroenterology: Res Medal 1981, chm Basic Scis Section 1986–88, memb Res Ctee 1991–93; chm Gastrointestinal Cmmn Int Union of Physiological Scis 1993–; Daiwa Prize Daiwa Anglo-Japanese Fndn 1994; memb: Physiological Soc (memb Ctee 1996–), Biochemical Soc, Soc for Experimental Biology, Br Biophysical Soc, Br Soc for Cell Biology, Euro Pancreatic Club (memb Cncl 1983–85 and 1992–95, pres 1985); *Books* Stimulus-Secretion Coupling in the Gastrointestinal Tract (co-ed, 1976), Electrolyte and Water Transport across Gastrointestinal Epithelia (co-ed, 1982), Secretion: Mechanisms and Control (co-ed, 1984), Variations in Human Physiology (ed, 1985), EPC - European Pancreatic Club Extracts (ed, 1985), The Exocrine Pancreas (ed, 1990), Human Physiology: Age, Stress and the Environment (2 edn of Variations in Human Physiology, co-ed, 1994); author of over 130 articles in learned scientific journals; *Recreations* Italy, gardening; *Style—* Prof Maynard Case; ✉ University of Manchester, School of Biological Sciences, G 38 Stopford Building, Oxford Road, Manchester M13 9PT (☎ 0161 275 5406, fax 0161 275 5600, e-mail rmcase@man.ac.uk)

CASE, Richard Ian; *b* 14 June 1945; *Educ* Cranfield Inst of Technol (MSc); *m*; 2 c; *Career* Westland Helicopters Ltd: joined as apprentice 1961, various positions 1969–78, tech mangr Arab British Helicopters (Egypt) 1978, chief designer 1982, divnl dir (engrg) and chief designer 1985, engrg dir 1985, EH101 project dir and engrg dir 1988, md Westland Helicopters Ltd 1992–; dir: Westland Group plc 1993–, EH Industries, Aerosystems International; MIMechE 1973, FRAeS 1985 (MRAeS 1982), FEng 1993; *Recreations* opera, theatre, golf, travel; *Style—* Richard Case, Esq, FEng; ✉ Westland Helicopters Ltd, Lysander Road, Yeovil, Somerset BA20 2YB (☎ 01935 702505, fax 01935 702012)

CASEWELL, Prof Mark William; s of William John Ivor Casewell (d 1951), of Hants, and Phyllis Rebecca, *née* Raymond (d 1976); *b* 17 Aug 1940; *Educ* Royal Masonic Sch, Univ of London (BSc, MB BS, MD); *m* 1, 8 July 1967 (m dis 1972), Carolle Anne, da of Richard Eaton, of Portsmouth, Hants; m 2, 9 Dec 1995, Rosa Coello, of Madrid, Spain; *Career* house physician St Bartholomew's Hosp 1965–66, asst pathologist Univ of Cambridge 1967–70, sr lectr in microbiology (former lectr) St Thomas' Hosp 1971–81, reader and hon conslt in microbiology The London Hosp 1982–84, prof and head of Dulwich Public Health Laboratory and Med Microbiology King's Coll Sch of Med and Dentistry 1984–; memb: AIDS Advsy Gp King's Healthcare, Editorial Bds of Jl of Hosp Infection and Jl of Antimicrobial Chemotherapy; chm Hosp Infection Soc 1987–91 (fndr memb 1979); MRCS 1965, LRCP 1965, FRCPath 1986 (MRCPath 1975), Hon MRCP 1994; *Books* numerous contribs incl: British Medical Students' Association Annual Educational Report (1963), Journal of Clinical Pathology (1973), Journal of Hospital Infection (1980), Skin Microbiology: Relevance to Clinical Infection (1981), Recent Advances in Infection (1982), Journal of Antimicrobial Chemotherapy (1984), Methicillin-Resistant Staphylococcus Aureus: Clinical Management and Laboratory Aspects (1992), Hospital Infection Control: Policies & Practical Procedures (jtly, 1995); *Recreations* cooking, southern Europe, very fast cars; *Clubs* Wig & Pen, Porsche GB, Fountain (Barts); *Style—* Prof Mark Casewell; ✉ 43 Primrose Gardens, London NW3 4UL; Dulwich Public Health Laboratory and Medical Microbiology, King's College School of Medicine and Dentistry, Bessemer Rd, London SE5 9PJ (☎ 0171 346 3213, fax 0171 346 3404)

CASEY, Gavin Frank; *b* 18 Oct 1946; *Career* CA Harmood Banner & Co 1965–69, Cooper Brothers & Co 1970–71, various appts rising to dep chief exec County Natwest Ltd 1972–89, with Smith New Court plc 1989–95, chief admin offr international equities Merrill Lynch International Ltd (following takeover of Smith New Court) 1995–96, chief exec London Stock Exchange 1996–; Freeman City of London, memb Worshipful Co of Chartered Accountants in England and Wales; FCA 1970; *Recreations* horse racing, shooting, theatre; *Clubs* City of London; *Style—* Gavin Casey, Esq; ✉ The London Stock Exchange, Old Broad Street, London EC2N 1HP (☎ 0171 797 1000)

CASEY, Kevin Lawrence; s of James Casey, of Hillingdon, and Theresa, *née* Daly; *b* 2 Oct 1949; *Educ* Gunnersbury GS; *m* 5 Aug 1972, Theresa Margaret, da of Patrick Rooney, of Galway, Eire; 2 da (Emma b 1977, Claire b 1979); *Career* serv 10 Bn (V) Para Regt 1970–74; qualified ACA 1973; Price Waterhouse: ptnr 1984–, ptnr i/c UK Customs and VAT 1985, chm World Customs Specialists 1988, ptnr i/c Euro VAT Servs 1989; fndr VAT Practitioners Gp 1982; former memb: London Soc of CAs VAT Ctee, ICAEW VAT Ctee; FCA; *Recreations* music, reading, marathon running, cooking; *Style—* Kevin Casey, Esq; ✉ Price Waterhouse, Place St Lambert 14, B-1200, Brussels, Belgium (☎ 00 32 2 773 4972)

CASEY, Michael Vince; OBE; s of Charles John Casey (d 1966), and May Louise, *née* Yeulett (d 1981); *b* 25 May 1927; *Educ* Glossop GS, Univ of London (BSc); *m* 1954, Elinor Jane (d 1987), da of Alfred George Harris (d 1982), of Purton, Wilts; 2 s (William, Edward), 2 da (Annabel, Angela); *Career* various engrg posts with BR 1944–78, engrg dir BR Engineering Ltd 1978–82, dir of mech and electrical engrg BR 1982–87, project dir BREL Privatisation 1987–89; chief engr Channel Tunnel Rail Link Gp 1989–90; ret; FEng 1985, FIMechE; *Recreations* gardening, philately; *Style—* M V Casey, Esq, OBE, FEng; ✉ Anakiwa, Wards Road, Chipping Norton, Oxon (☎ 01608 642644)

CASEY, Prof Patricia Rosarie; da of James Casey (d 1991), of Co Cork, and Margaret Casey; *b* 27 Oct 1952; *Educ* Presentation Convent Fermoy Co Cork, Univ Coll Cork (MD); *m* John McGuiggan, barr-at-law; 2 s (James b 29 Nob 1987, Gavan b 19 Aug 1991); *Career* MRC research fell MRC Unit for Epidemiological Studies in Psychiatry Royal Edinburgh Hosp 1982–84, statuatory lectr in psychiatry Regnl Hosp Cork 1984–91, prof of psychiatry Univ Coll Dublin/Mater Hosp Dublin 1991–; elected memb: Irish Med Cncl 1994–, Cncl Royal Coll of Psychiatrists 1995–; FRCP, FRCPsych, fell Irish Coll of Physicians; *Publications* A Guide to Psychiatry in Primary Care (1990, 2 edn 1996), Social Function: the hidden axis of psychiatric diagnosis (1990); contrib to 20 books; *Recreations* listening to classical music, cooking, writing for newspapers; *Style—* Prof Patricia Casey; ✉ Department of Psychiatry, Mater Hospital, Eccles Street, Dublin 7, Ireland (☎ and fax 00 353 1 830 9323)

CASEY, William; s of Air Cdre Bernard Casey (d 1979), and Margaret, *née* Jones (d 1965); *b* 2 Dec 1949; *Educ* Downside, Brasenose Coll Oxford (open exhibition, MA); *Career* sr mangr Peat Marwick (London, Rio de Janeiro, São Paulo) 1971–80, fin controller Herman Miller UK 1980–83, managing conslt Coopers & Lybrand Associates London 1983–86, Binder Hamlyn Fry 1986– (currently md), ptnr Andersen Worldwide 1996–; FCA 1979 (ACA 1974), MIMC 1990, MIQA 1993; *Recreations* hill-walking, skiing, wine, early medieval history; *Style—* William Casey; ✉ Binder Hamlyn Fry, 20 Old Bailey, London EC4M 7BH (☎ 0171 489 9000)

CASH, Prof John David; s of John Henry Cash (d 1982), and May Annie, *née* Taylor (d 1986); *b* 3 April 1936; *Educ* Ashville Coll, Univ of Edinburgh (BSc, PhD, MB ChB);

m 22 Sept 1962, Angela Mary, da of Robert David Thomson (d 1980); 1 s (Michael Peter b 1965), 1 da (Julie Suzanna b 1967); *Career* dir Regnl Blood Transfusion Serv Edinburgh and S E Scotland 1974–79, nat med dir Scot Nat Blood Transfusion Serv 1979–90, nat med and science dir Scottish Nat Blood Transfusion Serv 1990–; pres Royal Coll of Physicians of Edinburgh; hon prof Univ of Edinburgh 1986; FRCPE, FRCPath, FRCP (Glasgow), FRCSEd; *Recreations* fishing, gardening; *Style*— Prof John Cash; ✉ Scottish Nat Blood Transfusion Serv, Headquarters' Unit, Ellen's Glen Rd, Edinburgh EH17 7QT (☎ 0131 664 2317, fax 0131 658 1639)

CASH, William Nigel Paul (Bill); MP (C) Stafford (majority 10,900); s of Capt Paul Trevor Cash, MC (ka Normandy 1944), and Moyra Margaret Elizabeth, *née* Morrison; *b* 10 May 1940; *Educ* Stonyhurst, Lincoln Coll Oxford (MA); *m* 1965, Bridget Mary, da of James Rupert Lee; 2 s (William, Samuel), 1 da (Laetitia); *Career* slr William Cash and Co; MP (C) Stafford 1984–, vice chm Cons Constitutional Ctee 1986, chm Cons Backbench Ctee Euro Affrs 1989–91; chm All Pty Parly Ctee: on E Africa 1988–, on Complementary and Alternative Medicine 1991–; memb Select Ctee on Euro Legislation; fndr and chm European Foundation; *Books* Against a Federal Europe - The Battle for Britain (1991), Europe - The Crunch (1992), Are We Really Winning on Europe? (1995), Response to Chancellor Kohl (1996), The Blue Paper (1996); monthly editorials Euro Jl 1993–; *Recreations* cricket, tennis, jazz, heritage, cutting lawns, cutting red tape; *Clubs* Beefsteak, Carlton, Vincent's (Oxford); *Style*— Bill Cash, Esq, MP; ✉ Upton Cressett Hall, nr Bridgnorth, Shropshire (☎ 01746 714307); European Foundation, 61 Pall Mall, London SW1Y 5HZ (☎ 0171 930 7319, fax 0171 930 9706); House of Commons, London SW1A 0AA (☎ 0171 219 6330)

CASHEL AND OSSORY, Bishop of (901) 1980–; Rt Rev Noel Vincent Willoughby; 58 Bp of Cashel (901), 89 Bp of Ossory (441), 63 Bp of Waterford (1096), 70 Bp of Lismore (631); s of George Willoughby, and Mary Jane Willoughby; *b* 15 Dec 1926; *Educ* Tate Sch Wexford, Trinity Coll Dublin; *m* 1959, Valerie Moore, of Dungannon, Tyrone; 2 s, 1 da; *Career* deacon 1950, priest Armagh Cathedral 1951; curate: Drumglass Parish 1950–53, St Catherine's Dublin 1953–55, Bray Parish 1955–59; rector: Delgany Parish 1959–69, Glenageary Parish 1969–80; hon sec General Synod 1976–80, treas St Patrick's Cathedral Dublin 1976–80, archdeacon of Dublin 1979–80; *Books* What We Believe (1985); *Style*— The Rt Rev the Bishop of Cashel and Ossory; ✉ The Palace, Kilkenny, Ireland (☎ 00 353 56 21560)

CASHMAN, Michael Maurice; s of John Cashman, of London, and Mary Alvena, *née* Clayton; *b* 17 Dec 1950; *Educ* Cardinal Griffin Secdy Modern, Gladys Dare's Sch; *Career* actor in theatre, musical theatre, TV, films and radio; first role in Oliver 1963, formerly Colin in EastEnders (BBC), Horst in RNT prodn of Bent, Noises Off (Mobil Touring Theatre) 1995; patron: London Lighthouse, London Friend, Family Welfare Assoc, Space, Survivors (Leeds); chm Stonewall Grp 1988–96, chm Stonewall Lobbying Gp, memb Lab Pty, cncllr and hon treas Br Actors' Equity 1994–; special serv award from American Assoc of Physicians for Human Rights; fell RSA 1996; *Recreations* travel, photography; *Style*— Michael Cashman, Esq; ✉ Guild House, Upper St Martin's Lane, London WC2

CASHMORE, Prof Roger John; s of Cyril John Charles Cashmore, of Dudley, Worcs, and Elsie May, *née* Jones; *b* 22 Aug 1944; *Educ* Dudley GS, St John's Coll Cambridge (MA), Balliol Coll and Univ Coll Oxford (DPhil, Weir jr res fell, 1851 res fell); *m* 6 Aug 1971, Elizabeth Ann, da of Rev S J C Lindsay; 1 s (Christopher John Hrothgar Lindsay-Cashmore b 1976); *Career* res assoc Stanford Linear Accelerator Centre Calif 1969–74; Univ of Oxford: res offr 1974–78, lectr Christ Church 1976–78, sr res fell Merton Coll 1977–79, tutorial fell Balliol Coll and univ lectr in physics 1979–90, reader in experimental physics 1990–91, prof of experimental physics 1991–; SERC sr res fell 1982–87, guest scientist Fermilab Chicago 1986–87, visiting prof Vrije Univ Brussels 1982; CV Boys Prize Inst of Physics 1983, Alexander Von Humbold Fndn Humboldt Research Award 1995–96; memb Academia Europa 1992; FInstP, FRSA 1996; *Recreations* sports, wine; *Style*— Prof Roger Cashmore; ✉ Balliol College, Oxford OX1 3BJ; Department of Particle and Nuclear Physics, Oxford University, Keble Road, Oxford OX1 3RH (☎ 01865 273323, fax 01865 273418, e-mail CASHMORE@UK.AC.OX.PH)

CASKEN, Prof John; *b* 15 July 1949; *Educ* Barnsley & District Holgate GS, Univ of Birmingham (BMus, MA), Univ of Durham (DMus), Acad of Music Warsaw; *Career* lectr in music Univ of Birmingham 1973–79, fell in composition Huddersfield Poly 1980–81, lectr in music Univ of Durham 1981–92, prof of music Univ of Manchester 1992–; currently composer in assoc Northern Sinfonia; compositions incl: Kagura 1972–73, Music for the Crabbing Sun 1974, Thymehaze 1976, Tableaux des Trois Ages for orch 1976–77, Amarantos 1977–78, Ia Orana, Gauguin 1978, Firewhirl 1979–80, String Quartet No 1 1981–82, Masque 1982, Erin 1982–83, To Fields We Do Not Know 1983–84, Piper's Linn 1983–84, Orion Over Farne 1984, Vaganza 1985, Salamandra 1986, Golem (chamber opera) 1986–88, Maharal Dreaming 1989, Piano Quartet 1989–90, Cello Concerto 1990–91, Still Mine 1991–92 (premiered BBC Proms 1992), Darting the Skiff 1992–93, String Quartet No 2 1993, Infanta Marina 1993–94, Violin Concerto 1994–95 (premiered BBC Proms 1995), Sortilège 1996; recordings on: Collins Classics, Merlin Records, Wergo, Virgin Classics; *Awards* first Britten Award for Golem 1990, Northern Electric Performing Arts Award 1990, Gramophone Award for Golem (recording) 1991, Fondation Prince Pierre de Monaco Prize for Still Mine 1993; *Style*— Prof John Casken; ✉ c/o Sally Groves, Schott & Co Ltd, 48 Great Marlborough Street, London W1V 2BN (☎ 0171 494 1487, fax 0171 287 1529)

CASS, Alain Jules; s of Edouard Catzeflis (d 1985), and Irene Lempicka (d 1986); *b* 6 Oct 1944; *Educ* Victoria Coll Alexandria Egypt, Athens Coll Greece, Bradfield Coll Berkshire; *m* 1, 8 March 1968 (m dis 1978), Susan Jean Freeman; 1 s (Julian b 7 Feb 1976), 1 da (Claudia b 18 Nov 1972); m 2, 18 Dec 1985 (m dis 1992); m 3, 21 Oct 1994, Victoria Horton; *Career* feature writer then foreign corr Daily Express 1967–74 (assignments incl NI 1969–71 and Oct Middle East War 1973); Financial Times: Middle East specialist 1974–76, foreign news ed 1976–82, Asia ed and asst foreign ed 1982–86, asst ed of the Financial Times and ed International Edition 1986–89, asst ed (news) 1989–94; conslt Kaleidoscope Project Kingston upon Thames 1995–; *Recreations* music, travel, painting, scuba-diving; *Style*— Alain Cass, Esq; (☎ 0171 736 9993, fax 0171 731 5277)

CASS, Sir Geoffrey Arthur; kt (1992); s of Arthur Cass (d 1982), of Darlington and Oxford, and Jessie, *née* Simpson (d 1967); *b* 11 Aug 1932; *Educ* Queen Elizabeth GS Darlington, Jesus Coll Oxford (BA, MA), Dept of Social and Administrative Studies Oxford, Nuffield Coll Oxford, Jesus Coll Cambridge (MA), Clare Hall Cambridge; *m* 1957, Olwen Mary, JP, da of late William Leslie Richards, of Brecon; 4 da (Fiona (Mrs Patrick Allen), Karen, Miranda (Mrs John Hosking), Fleur); *Career* cmmnd PO RAFVR (Oxford Univ Air Sqdn) 1954, Nat Serv PO 1958, Flying Offr 1960, Air Min Directorate Work Study RAF 1958–60; conslt PA Mgmnt Conslts 1960–65; private mgmnt conslt: British Communications Corporation, Controls and Communications Ltd 1965; md George Allen & Unwin 1967–71 (dir 1965–67); dir: Controls and Communications Ltd 1966–69, Chicago Univ Press (UK) Ltd 1971–86; chief exec Cambridge Univ Press 1972–92 (sec the Press Syndicate 1974–92, University Printer 1982–83 and 1991–92); dir Weidenfeld Publishers Ltd 1972–74; dir: Newcastle Theatre Royal Tst 1984–89, American Friends Royal Shakespeare Theatre 1985–, Cambridge Theatre Co 1986–95, Theatres Tst 1991–; tstee and guardian Shakespeare Birthplace Tst 1982–94 (life tstee 1994); chm: Royal Shakespeare Company 1985– (govr 1975–), Royal Shakespeare Theatre Tst 1983– (fndr dir 1967–); Lawn Tennis Assoc of GB: memb Cncl 1976–, memb Mgmnt Bd 1985–90 and 1993–, chm Nat Ranking Ctee 1990–, memb Int Events Ctee 1991–93, memb Nat Trg and Int Match Ctee 1982–90 and 1992–93 (chm 1985–90), memb Reorganisation Working Pty 1984–85 and 1994– (chm), dep pres 1993–96, pres 1996–; Wimbledon Championships: memb Ctee of Mgmnt 1990–, memb Jt Fin Ctee 1993– (Jt Fin Bd 1989–93); govr Perse Sch for Girls Cambridge 1977– (chm Bd of Govrs 1978–88); memb: Governing Syndicate Fitzwilliam Museum Cambridge 1977–78, Univ of Cambridge Ctee and Exec Sub Ctee of Mgmnt of Fenners 1976–, Exec Ctee Univ of Cambridge Careers Service Syndicate 1982– (memb 1977–); Oxford tennis blue 1953, 1954 and 1955 (sec 1955), Oxford badminton blue 1951 and 1952 (Capt 1952); chm Cambridge Univ Lawn Tennis Club 1977–, pres Cambridgeshire Lawn Tennis Assoc 1980–82; played Wimbledon Championships: 1954, 1955, 1956, 1959; played in inter-county lawn tennis championships for Durham Co (singles champion 1951) then for Cambridgeshire (singles champion 1975) 1952–82, represented RAF 1958–59; Br Veterans Singles (45 and over) champion Wimbledon 1978; memb Br Veterans Int Championships Dubler Cup Team: Barcelona 1978, Milano Marittima 1979 (Capt); hon Cambridge tennis blue 1980; fell Clare Hall Cambridge 1979; FInstD 1968, FIWM 1979, FIIM 1979, CIMgt 1980, FRSA 1991; Chevalier de L'Ordre des Arts et des Lettres France 1982; *Recreations* lawn tennis, theatre; *Clubs* All England Lawn Tennis and Croquet, Hurlingham, Hawks', IOD, Int Lawn Tennis of GB, The 45, Cambridge Univ Lawn Tennis, Veterans Lawn Tennis GB; *Style*— Sir Geoffrey Cass; ✉ Middlefield, Huntingdon Rd, Cambridge CB3 0LH; Royal Shakespeare Theatre, Stratford-upon-Avon CV37 6BB (☎ 01789 412609)

CASS, Richard Martin; s of Edward Charles Cass, of Cheshire, and Hazel Rosemary; *b* 25 May 1946; *Educ* High Wycombe GS, Sheffield Univ (BArch, MA); *m* 1977, Judith Claire, da of Dr Linton Morris Snaith, of Newcastle upon Tyne; 2 s (Simon b 1983, Alexander b 1986); *Career* architect and landscape architect; dir Brian Clouston and Ptnrs 1979–82, princ Cass Assocs 1982–; *Recreations* music, theatre, gardening, sailing, reading; *Style*— Richard M Cass, Esq; ✉ Osborne House, Fulwood Park, Liverpool (☎ 0151 727 7614); Cass Associates, Albion House, 30 James St, Liverpool (☎ 0151 236 9074, fax 0151 236 1582)

CASSAR, Dr Joseph; s of Charles George Cassar, and Sabina, *née* Debono; *b* 22 Sept 1940; *Educ* Royal Univ of Malta (MD), Imperial Coll of Science and Technol (DIC), Univ of London (PhD); *m* 21 Feb 1976, Carol Anne, da of William Richmond Wilson; 1 s (Christopher b 8 June 1979), 1 da (Claire b 19 Nov 1977); *Career* rotating intern: Middlesex Meml Hosp Middletown Connecticut USA 1966, sr house offr Westminster Med Sch 1966–67, Cwlth scholar 1967–70; registrar: KCH 1970–71, Royal Free Hosp 1971–73; sr registrar Royal Postgrad Med Sch 1973–79, conslt physician W Middlesex Univ Hosp 1979–; author of papers on diabetes endocrinology and gen med; memb: BDA, BMA, RSM; MRCP, FRCP; *Recreations* tennis, sail boarding, walking, chess, reading; *Style*— Dr Joseph Cassar; ✉ 16 Queens Gardens, Ealing, London W5 1SF (☎ 0181 998 2576); W Middlesex University Hospital, Isleworth, London TW7 6AF (☎ 0181 565 5390); 22 Harley St, London W1 (☎ 0181 637 0491)

CASSEL, His Hon Sir Harold Felix; 3 Bt (1920 UK), of Lincoln's Inn, City of London, TD (1975), QC (1970); s of Sir Felix Cassel, 1 Bt, PC, QC (d 1953); suc bro, Sir Francis Edward Cassel, 2 Bt 1969; *b* 8 Nov 1916; *Educ* Stowe, CCC Oxford; *m* 1, 1940 (m dis 1963), Ione Jean, da of late Capt Evelyn Hugh Barclay; 3 s (Timothy Felix Harold b 1942, Jeremy James b 1950, Evelyn Martin b 1952), 1 da (Miranda Phyllis (Mrs Ronald Ryer) b 1946); m 2, 1963, Mrs Eileen Elfrida Smedley, da of James Rider Faulkner; *Heir* s, Timothy Felix Harold Cassel, QC, *qv*, b 30 April 1942; *Career* called to the Bar 1946, dep chm Herts QS 1959–62, recorder Great Yarmouth 1968–71, recorder Crown Court 1972–76, circuit judge 1976–88; memb Cncl BCEL 1988–; JP Herts 1959–62; *Style*— His Hon Sir Harold Cassel, Bt, TD, QC; ✉ 49 Lennox Gardens, London SW1X 0DF (☎ 0171 584 2721)

CASSEL, Jeremy James; s of His Hon Sir Harold Cassel, Bt, TD, QC, *qv*, of London, and Ione Jean, *née* Barclay; *b* 7 June 1950; *Educ* Eton, Sorbonne; *m* 7 June 1982, Vivien Helen, da of David John Hayter, of Adbury Court, Newtown, Newbury, Berks; 2 s (Hugo b 1982, Felix b 1988), 1 da (Sieglinde b 1984); *Career* trained Savoy Hotel Gp 1970, gen mangr Compleat Angler Marlow 1978, hotels and restaurants conslt 1982, md Cassel Hotels and Restaurants plc 1989; tstee King Edward VII Br-German Fndn; *Recreations* racing; *Style*— Jeremy Cassel, Esq; ✉ c/o The Grange Hotel, Clifton, York YO3 6AA (☎ 01904 644744)

CASSEL, Timothy Felix Harold; QC (1988); s and h of His Hon Sir Harold Cassel, 3 Bt, TD, QC, *qv*; *b* 30 April 1942; *Educ* Eton; *m* 1, 1971 (m dis 1975), Mrs Jenifer Samuel, da of Kenneth Bridge Puckle; 1 s (Alexander James Felix b 25 May 1974), 1 da (Natalia Hermione b 1972); m 2, 1979, Ann, cr a Life Peer 1991 (*see* Baroness Mallalieu), only da of Sir William Mallalieu; 2 da (Hon Bathsheba Anna b 1981, Hon Cosima b 1984); *Career* called to the Bar Lincoln's Inn 1965; jr prosecutor for the Crown of the Central Criminal Ct 1978, asst boundary cmmr 1979, sr prosecutor for the Crown 1986, Bencher Lincoln's Inn 1994; *Recreations* country sports, opera, skiing; *Clubs* Garrick; *Style*— Timothy Cassel, Esq, QC; ✉ 5 Paper Buildings, Temple, London EC4

CASSELS, Sir John Seton; kt (1988), CB (1978); s of Alastair Macdonald Cassels, and Ada White, *née* Scott; *b* 10 Oct 1928; *Educ* Sedbergh Sch Yorks, Trinity Coll Cambridge; *m* 1956, Mary Whittington; 2 s, 2 da; *Career* Miny of Labour 1954, under sec Nat Bd for Prices and Incomes 1968–71, chief exec Training Services Agency 1972–75, dir Manpower Services Cmmn 1975–81, 2 perm sec MPO 1981–83, dir gen NEDO 1983–88, dir Nat Cmmn on Educn 1991–; Policy Studies Inst: memb Cncl 1983–88, distinguished visiting fell 1989, sr fell 1990–; memb Cncl Inst of Manpower Studies 1982– (pres 1989–); former memb Cncl: Industl Soc, CRAC; former dir Consumer Association Ltd; assoc fell Templeton Coll Oxford 1988; CIMgt, FIPM, hon CGIA 1989; *Books* Britain's Real Skill Shortage (1990); *Clubs* Reform; *Style*— Sir John Cassels, CB

CASSIDI, Adm Sir (Arthur) Desmond; GCB (1982, KCB 1978); s of Cdr Robert Alexander Cassidi, RN (d 1966), and his 1 wife Clare Florinda, *née* Alexander (d 1925); *b* 26 Jan 1925; *Educ* RNC Dartmouth; *m* 1, 1950, (Dorothy) Sheelagh Marie Scott (d 1974), da of Rev Canon Robert Francis Scott, of Garvagh, Co Derry; 1 s, 2 da; m 2, 1982, Deborah Marion, *née* Bliss, widow of Dr Anthony M Pollock, of Omagh, Co Tyrone; *Career* serv Midshipman and Sub Lt 1942–45, CO HMS Ark Royal 1972–73, Flag Offr Carriers and Amphibious Ships 1974–75, dir gen Naval Manpower Trg 1975–77, Flag Offr Naval Air Cmd 1978–79, Chief of Naval Personnel and Second Sea Lord 1979–82, C-in-C Naval Home Command 1982–85; Flag ADC to HM The Queen 1982–85; pres: FAA Museum Yeovilton, Royal Naval Assoc until 1995; dep grand pres Br Cwlth Ex Services League 1986–96; Liveryman Worshipful Co of Shipwrights; *Recreations* country pursuits; *Style*— Adm Sir Desmond Cassidi, GCB; ✉ c/o Barclays Bank, 2 Victoria Street, London, SW1H 0ND

CASSIDY, Bryan Michael Deece; MEP (C) Dorset and East Devon (majority 2,264); s of William Francis Deece Cassidy (d 1986), and Kathleen Selina Patricia, *née* Geraghty (d 1989); *b* 17 Feb 1934; *Educ* Ratcliffe Coll Leicester, Sidney Sussex Coll Cambridge (MA); *m* 27 Aug 1960, Gillian Mary, da of Austen Patrick Bohane (d 1988); 1 s (Dominic b 1964), 2 da (Katherine b 1961, Siobhan b 1962); *Career* cmmnd RA 1955–57 (Malta and Libya), HAC 1957–62; with Ever Ready, Beechams and Reed Int; memb Cncl CBI 1981–84, dir gen Cosmetic Toiletry and Perfumery Assoc 1981–84; Parly candidate Wandsworth Central 1966, memb GLC (Hendon North) 1977–85 (oppn spokesman on indust and employment 1983–84), MEP (C): Dorset East and Hampshire West 1984–94,

Dorset and East Devon 1994–; *Recreations* country pursuits; *Clubs* Carlton; *Style—* Bryan Cassidy, Esq, MEP; ✉ 11 Esmond Court, Thackeray St, London W8 5HB; Constituency HQ, 135 Hankinson Road, Bournemouth, Dorset BH9 1HR

CASSIDY, Denis Patrick; *b* 2 Feb 1933; *Career* chm: The Boddington Group plc until 1 June 1995, Ferguson International Holdings plc 1988–, The Oliver Group plc 1992–, Kingsbury Group Plc until 1996, Liberty PLC 1995–; non-exec dir: Seeboard plc 1994–96, Compass Group plc 1994–; *Style—* Denis Cassidy, Esq; ✉ c/o Ferguson International Holdings plc, 75 Baker Street, London W1M 1AH (☎ 0171 487 3464, fax 0171 224 3072)

CASSIDY, Ven George Henry; s of Joseph Abram Cassidy (d 1979), and Ethel, *née* McDonald (d 1973); *b* 17 Oct 1942; *Educ* Belfast HS, Queen's Univ Belfast (BSc), UCL (MPhil), Oak Hill Theol Coll; *m* 17 Dec 1966, Jane Barling, da of Rev Frank Hayman Stevens; 2 da (Sarah, Gael); *Career* civil servant: NI 1967–68, Govt of Kenya 1968–70; curate Christ Church Clifton Bristol 1972–75; vicar: St Edyth's Sea Mills Bristol 1975–82, St Paul's Portman Sq W1 1982–87; archdeacon of London and canon residentiary of St Paul's Cathedral 1987–; sub dean Most Excellent Order of the Br Empire 1996–; Freedom of the City of London 1988, Liveryman Worshipful Co of Tylers and Bricklayers 1988, Hon Chaplain Worshipful Co of CAs 1989, Hon Freeman Worshipful Co of Founders 1994; *Recreations* rugby football, art, chamber music, walking in Quantocks; *Clubs* National; *Style—* The Ven the Archdeacon of London; ✉ 2 Amen Court, Warwick Lane, London EC4M 7BU (☎ 0171 248 3312, fax 0171 489 8579)

CASSIDY, Very Rev Herbert; s of Herbert Cassidy (d 1985), of Cork, and Frederica Jane, *née* Summerville; *b* 25 July 1935; *Educ* Cork GS, Trinity Coll Dublin (BA, MA, Carson, Kyle, Downes and Moncrieff-Cox Divinity Sch prizes); *m* 4 April 1961, Elizabeth Ann, da of Rev H F O Egerton; 2 da (Nicola Jane (Mrs Heatley) b 1 Feb 1962, Joanne Patricia (Mrs Bates) b 4 March 1968), 1 s (Ian Richard b 31 May 1964); *Career* curate asst: Holy Trinity Belfast 1958–60, Christ Church Londonderry 1960–62; rector: Aghavilly and Derrynoose 1962–65, St Columba's Portadown 1965–85; dean of Kilmore 1985–89, dean of Armagh and keeper of the library 1989–; *Recreations* gardening, travelling, music; *Clubs* Armagh Rotary; *Style—* The Very Rev Herbert Cassidy, Dean of Armagh; ✉ The Deanery, Library House, Abbey Street, Armagh BT61 7DY (☎ 01861 523142, fax 01861 524177)

CASSIDY, John Joseph; s of John Bernard Cassidy, of Leeds, and Julie Theresa, *née* Vaughan; *b* 31 Jan 1963; *Educ* Cardinal Heenan HS, UC Oxford (BA), Harvard Univ (visiting student), Grad Sch of Journalism Columbia Univ NY (MA); *m* 12 Aug 1989, Patricia Emily, *née* Mollach, of Syracuse, NY; *Career* Harkness fell USA 1984–86, intern The Financial Times 1985; The Sunday Times: fin reporter 1986–87, NY corr 1987–88, Washington corr 1988–91, business ed 1992–; contrib: East Village Eye, Mirabella magazine, The Sunday Times Magazine, Management Today, Investors' Chronicle, The Times; commendation Br Press Awards 1987; *Recreations* travel, reading, golf, pop culture, America; *Style—* John Cassidy, Esq; ✉ The Sunday Times, 1 Pennington Street, London E1 9XW

CASSIDY, Michael John; s of Francis Cassidy, and Vera Rosina, *née* Valler; *b* 14 Jan 1947; *Educ* Downing Coll Cambridge (BA), City Univ Business Sch (MBA); *m* 7 Sept 1974 (m dis 1988), Amanda, da of Richard George Fitzgerald (d 1981); 1 s (Thomas b 1981), 2 da (Kate b 1977, Annabel b 1979); *Career* sr ptnr Maxwell Batley Slrs 1991– (ptnr 1971–); former dir: Cannon Assurance Ltd, Conrad Ritblat Residential Properties Ltd, Baker Harris Saunders plc, London American Growth Trust plc; currently dir: British Land plc, London First; Corp of London: memb Cncl 1980–, chm Planning and Communications Ctee 1986–89, chm Policy and Resources Ctee 1992–97 (dep chm 1991–92); memb Court of Assts: Worshipful Co of Slrs, Worshipful Co of Fletchers; Hon Degree: City Univ 1996, South Bank Univ 1996; hon fell London Business Sch, Hon FRIBA; memb Law Soc 1971, FRSA; *Recreations* boating; *Style—* Michael Cassidy, Esq; ✉ 202 Cromwell Tower, Barbican, London EC2 8AB (☎ 0171 628 5687); Maxwell Batley, 27 Chancery Lane, London WC2A 1PA (☎ 0171 405 7888, fax 0171 242 7133, car 0836 288467)

CASSIDY, Michael Warren Arkinstall; s of George Edward Cassidy, of Kew, Richmond, Surrey, and Kathleen Mary, *née* Roberts; *b* 22 March 1939; *Educ* Latymer Upper Sch Hammersmith, UCL (BA Arch), Univ of California (Harkness fell 1968, MCP); *m* 1, 5 Jan 1963 (m dis), Mary Madeline, da of Joseph Burnhill; m 2, 13 Nov 1981, Marianthi, da of Constantino P Constantinu (d 1969); 1 da (Melina b 1982); *Career* architect and town planner; head planner Environmental Studies Group GLC 1970–75, ptnr Cassidy Taggart Ptnrship 1987–94; work includes until 1983: Univ of Warwick, John Radcliffe Hosp, teaching hosp Enugu Nigeria, med coll Basrah Univ Iraq (large commissions Bahrain, Hong Kong, Jordan); work includes 1983–: residences for heads of state, Govt Conf Centre Kuwait, BRIT Sch for the Performing Arts London, Abdulla Al-Ahmad Street Devpt Project Kuwait (project dir), maj ind commercial and planning projects UK, Middle and Far East; visiting prof (arch) Washington Univ St Louis, lectr Univ Coll London; RIBA, MRTPI; *Publications* frequent tech papers in architectural jls; *Recreations* painting, walking, travelling; *Style—* Michael Cassidy, Esq; ✉ c/o Al-Marzouk and Abi-Hanna, PO Box 1913, Safat 13020, Kuwait (☎ 00 965 5312830/9, fax 00 965 5330634)

CASSIDY, Nigel Peter; s of Rev Albert Cassidy (d 1970), and Hilda May, *née* Newport (d 1996); *b* 26 Dec 1954; *Educ* Thames Valley GS, Univ of Portsmouth, London Coll of Printing; *m* Ann, da of Donald Clark (d 1995); 2 da (Ruth, Claire); *Career* trainee Dimbleby Newspapers 1972–74; BBC: Radio Sussex 1974–77, Radio London 1978–86, Lime Grove TV 1986–87, Radio News 1987–88, Parly Unit 1988–89, business presenter and reporter 1989–, business correspondent Today programme 1995–; chair: (deviser and co-writer) The Board Game 1992–, Newstalk 1993–, Workplace 1994, Shelf Lives 1994–; *Awards* Conorco Motoring Award (for Rush Hour), New York Radio Festival Award (for The Board Game); *Recreations* cutting things out of newspapers, children, theatre, food, gardening; *Style—* Nigel Cassidy, Esq; ✉ BBC Radio News and Current Affairs, Broadcasting House, London W1A 1AA (☎ 0171 927 5566)

CASSIDY, Dr Sheila Anne; da of Air Vice Marshal John Reginald Cassidy, CBE (d 1974), and Barbara Margaret, *née* Drew; *b* 18 Aug 1937; *Educ* Our Lady of Mercy Coll Parramatta NSW Australia, Univ of Sydney, Univ of Oxford (BM BCh, MA); *Career* Radcliffe Infirmary 1963–68, Leicester Royal Infirmary 1968–71, went to Santiago Chile to work in Assistencia Publica in emergency hosp and church clinic 1971, detained for 2 months for treating wounded revolutionary, tortured and expelled 1975, writer and human rights worker 1975–77, student Ampleforth Abbey York 1977–78, novice St Bernards Convent Slough 1978–80, sr house offr Dept of Radiotherapy Plymouth Gen Hosp 1980–82, med dir St Lukes Hospice Plymouth 1982–93, palliative care specialist Plymouth Gen Hosp 1993–; regular writer, bdcaster and preacher, lectr on med and religious issues throughout UK and abroad; Valiant for Truth media award Order of Christian Unity; Hon DSc Univ of Exeter 1991, Hon DLitt Cheltenham and Glos Coll of HE (via CNNA); memb: Br Psychosocial Oncology Gp, Assoc of Palliative Med; *Books* Audacity to Believe (1977), Prayer for Pilgrims (1979), Sharing the Darkness (1989), Good Friday People (1991, special award Collins Religious Book Award), Light from The Dark Valley (1994), The Loneliest Journey (1995), The Creation Story (1996); *Recreations* writing, sewing, painting, entertaining, TV; *Style—* Dr Sheila Cassidy; ✉ Department of Palliative Care, Freedom Fields Hospital, Plymouth PL6 8DH (☎ 01752 834472, fax 01752 661273)

CASSIDY, (Michael) Stuart; s of John Michael Cassidy, of Tunbridge Wells, Kent, and Jacqueline Eleanor, *née* Allison; *b* 26 Sept 1968; *Educ* White Lodge, Royal Ballet Sch; *Career* principal dancer; Royal Ballet: Siegfried in Swan Lake, Romeo in Romeo and Juliet, Prince in Sleeping Beauty, Prince of The Pagodas, Nutcracker and Cinderella, Solor in La Bayadere, Lescaut in Manon, Basilio in Don Quixote, Colas in La Fille Mal Gardee, Jean de Brienne in Raymonda, Gloria, Song of the Earth, Galantries, Persuit, Pas de Six, Elite Syncopations; cr roles in David Bintley's Spirit of Fugue and Ashley Page's Piano; Ashton's Pas de Deux in the opera Die Fledermaus (BBC2) 1990; Nora Roche award 1984, Prix de Lausanne professional prize 1987; *Recreations* classic cars, music (all types), computers, pasta, cakes; *Style—* Stuart Cassidy, Esq; ✉ c/o The Royal Ballet, Royal Opera House, Covent Garden, London WC2E 9DD (☎ 0171 240 1200)

CASSIDY, Thomas Daniel; s of Joseph Cassidy (d 1963), and Mary, *née* Gilligan (d 1974); *b* 3 May 1920; *Educ* St Dunstan's RC Elementary Sch Manchester; *m* 16 Sept 1944, Bridget Mary (Bridie), da of the late Joseph Donnelly, of Belfast, NI; 2 s (Paul b 1945, Timothy b 1958), 4 da (Bernadette b 1949, Patsy b 1951, Frances b 1961, Michelle b 1963); *Career* fndr Cassidy Brothers 1946 (USM listed 1989, currently chm); former memb Lions Club and Rotary Club; former chm and vice pres Br Toy and Hobby Assoc, former sr master Vale of Lune Harriers; current memb: Catenian Assoc (past pres), Blackpool and Fylde Soc for the Blind; *Recreations* hunting, shooting, fishing, photography; *Style—* Thomas Cassidy, Esq; ✉ Calder House, Garstang, nr Preston, Lancs PR3 1ZE (☎ 01995 603345); Cassidy Brothers plc, Mitcham Road, Blackpool, Lancs FY4 4QW (☎ 01253 766411, fax 01253 691486)

CASSON, Sir Hugh Maxwell; CH (1985), KCVO (1978), kt (1952); s of late Randal Casson, and late May Caroline, *née* Man; *b* 23 May 1910; *Educ* Eastbourne Coll, St John's Coll Cambridge; *m* 1938, Margaret MacDonald, da of Dr James MacDonald Troup, of Pretoria; 3 da; *Career* architect; dir of architecture Festival of Britain 1948–51, prof RCA 1953–75, memb Royal Fine Art Cmmn 1960–83, pres Royal Acad 1976–84, architectural advsr to Commons Servs Ctee 1983–; Hon Liveryman Worshipful Co of Furniture Makers; hon fell UCL 1983; RDI 1951; *Books* Hugh Casson's Diary (1980), Hugh Casson's London (1983), Hugh Casson's Oxford (1987), Hugh Casson's Cambridge (1992), Tower of London - An Artist's Portrait (1993); *Style—* Sir Hugh Casson, CH, KCVO; ✉ 6 Hereford Mansions, Hereford Road, London W2 5BA (☎ 0171 221 7774)

CASSON, Prof Mark Christopher; s of Rev Stanley Christopher Casson (d 1988), and Dorothy Nowell, *née* Barlow (d 1974); *b* 17 Dec 1945; *Educ* Manchester GS, Univ of Bristol, Churchill Coll Cambridge; *m* 26 July 1975, Janet Penelope, da of William Louis Close (d 1961); 1 da (Catherine Mary b 1984); *Career* Dept of Economics Univ of Reading: lectr 1969–77, reader 1977–81, prof 1981–, head of dept 1987–94; memb Cncl Royal Economic Soc 1985–90; fell Acad of Int Business 1993, FRSA 1996; *Books* Introduction to Mathematical Economics (1973), The Future of the Multinational Enterprise (1976), Alternatives to the Multinational Enterprise (1979), Youth Unemployment (1979), The Entrepreneur: An Economic Theory (1982), Unemployment: A Disequilibrium Approach (1981), Economics of Unemployment: An Historical Perspective (1983), Growth of International Business (1983), Economic Theory of the Multinational Enterprise: Selected Papers (1985), Multinationals and World Trade (1986), The Firm and the Market: Studies in Multinational Enterprise and the Scope of the Firm (1987), Enterprise and Competitiveness: A Systems View of International Business (1990), Multinational Corporations (1990), Entrepreneurship (1990), Economics of Business Culture: Game Theory, Transaction Costs and Economic Performance (1991), Global Research Strategy and International Competitiveness (1991), International Business and Global Integration (1992), Multinational Enterprises in the World Economy (1992), Industrial Concentration and Economic Inequality (1993), Entrepreneurship and Business Culture (1995), The Organization of International Business (1995), Theory of the Firm (1996), Informartion and Organization: A New Perspective on the Theory of the Firm (1997); *Recreations* book collecting; *Style—* Prof Mark Casson; ✉ 6 Wayside Green, Woodcote, Reading RG8 0QJ (☎ 01491 681483); Department of Economics, University of Reading, Box 218, Reading RG6 2AA (☎ 0118 931 8227, fax 0118 975 0236, telex 847813)

CASSON, (Frederick) Michael; OBE (1983); s of William Casson (d 1953), of London, and Dorothy, *née* Miller; *b* 2 April 1925; *Educ* Tollington GS, Hornsey Coll of Art (NDD, ATD); *m* 2 April 1955, Sheila, *née* Wilmot; 1 s (Ben b 1960), 2 da (Clare b 1958, Lucy b 1960); *Career* potter; pt/t teacher 1952–73; Harrow Sch of Art: jt fndr (with Victor Magrie) Studio Pottery Course 1963, head Ceramics Dept 1971–73; awarded Craft Cncl bursary to develop own work 1973, presenter The Crafts of the Potter (BBC) 1975; pt/t teacher history of ceramics Cardiff Coll of Art 1983, visiting lectr Banff Centre Canada 1986, presenter workshops and lectures USA 1984–, speaker Aust Bicentennial Ceramics 88 Conference Sydney 1988, artist in residence Chisholm Melbourne May-June 1988; solo exhibitions incl: Heals London 1959, 10 Years at Wobage Farm 1988, Oxford Gallery and Craftman Potters' Assoc London 1990–91; advsr: Holburne Museum Bath, Museum of Wales Cardiff; winner Gold medal Int Acad of Ceramics Prague 1964; Craftsman Potters' Assoc: fndr memb 1958, memb Cncl 1958–70, chm 1963–66; vice chm Br Crafts Cncl 1985–88; *Books* Pottery in Britain Today (1967), The Craft of the Potter (1976); *Recreations* historical research especially ceramic; *Style—* Michael Casson, Esq, OBE; ✉ Wobage Farm, Upton Bishop, nr Ross-on-Wye, Herefordshire HR9 7QP (☎ 01989 780233)

CASSTLES, Col David Stewart; TD, DL (Essex 1983); s of Joseph Cecil Casstles (d 1956); *b* 5 March 1936; *Educ* Brentwood Sch, Univ of Cambridge; *m* 1964, Lynne Frances, *née* Alexandre; 1 s (Andrew b 1969), 1 da (Amanda b 1966); *Career* Courtaulds 1961–69, P E International 1969–79, investment banker Midland Montagu/HSBC Investment Bank 1979–96; TA 1957–87: cmdg Essex Yeo 1972–80, 71 (Yeo) Signal Regt 1981–83, TA Col 1983–86, ADC 1985; *Recreations* opera-going, dining, sailing, shooting; *Clubs* Army and Navy; *Style—* Col David Casstles, TD, DL; ✉ Sandylay House, Great Leighs, Essex CM3 1PS (☎ 01245 361258)

CASTALDI, Dr Peter; s of Francis Castaldi (d 1986), and Sarah Jane Castaldi; *b* 13 Jan 1942; *Educ* Neath GS for Boys, Welsh Nat Sch of Med (MB BCH); *m* 15 July 1967, Joan, da of James Sherratt (d 1966); 1 da (Amanda Jayne b 21 Feb 1969), 1 s (Ian Francis b 14 Jan 1972); *Career* house surgn Llandudno General Hosp 1966–67, house physician Royal Alexandra Hosp 1967; sr house offr in obstetrics and gynaecology St David's Hosp 1967–75, sr house offr in paediatrics Royal Alexandra Hosp 1975–78, princ in gen practice 1979–89 (locum 1978, asst 1978–79); DSS: joined 1979, med offr 1982–84, sr med offr 1984–86, princ med offr Fylde War Pensions and Benefits Directorate 1986–92, chief med advsr 1992–96, ret; dir of medical servs Benefits Agency 1992–96, ret; CStJ 1993; FRSM 1995, FRSA 1995; *Recreations* squash, swimming, bird watching, rugby critic (armchair variety only); *Clubs* St Anne's Lawn Tennis and Squash, Fylde Rugby Football; *Style—* Dr Peter Castaldi

CASTENSKIOLD, Holger; OBE (1993); s of Ludvig Helmuth Frederik Holger Castenskiold (d 1957), of Gyllingnaes, Denmark, and Gudrun, *née* Thorsen; *b* 5 April 1931; *Educ* Oester Borgerdyd Copenhagen, Commercial HS Copenhagen, City of London Coll; *m* 27 Oct 1962, Gurli Bering, da of Capt Arthur Hermann Franz Pittelkow (d 1964), of Copenhagen; 1 s (Erik b 1 Feb 1967), 1 da (Birgitte b 14 Dec 1963); *Career* Royal Danish Navy 1951–52; The East Asiatic Co Ltd (Copenhagen, London, Manila, Singapore) 1949–72; dir Andrew Weir & Company Limited 1987–92, chm and md United Baltic Corporation Limited 1972–92; chm The London Steamship Owners Mutual Insurance Assoc 1985–92; chm Anglo-Danish Soc 1995– (vice chm 1990–95); *Recreations* golf, gardening, travels, fly fishing; *Clubs* MCC, Moor Park Golf, Wig and Pen; *Style*— Holger Castenskiold, Esq, OBE; ✉ 1 The Broad Walk, Northwood, Middlesex HA6 2XF (☎ 01923 822875)

CASTLE, Andrew Nicholas; s of Frank James Castle (d 1985), and Lyn Mathers, *née* Pollock; *b* 15 Nov 1963; *Educ* Huish's GS Taunton, Millfield, Wichita State Univ USA (BA); *m* 18 May 1991, Sophia Anna Stuart Runham; 2 da (Georgina b 11 Dec 1992, Claudia b 30 July 1994); *Career* former tennis player; memb: GB Davis Cup team 1986–91, Euro Cup team 1986–90, GB Olympic team Seoul 1988 and Barcelona 1992; nat singles champion 1987, 1989 and 1991, nat doubles champion 1987 and 1989–91, reached third round US Open (lost to Boris Becker) 1987, finalist Korean Open Grand Prix 1988, winner Dunlop Masters of Japan 1988; doubles champion: Rye Brook (NY), Madeira, Cherbourg, Singapore, Nagoya, Adelaide, Korea, Malaysian Open; presenter Skysports: basketball, PGA European Tour, tennis; commentator ATP Tour Highlights Show (TWI); contrib: Sunday Times, The Observer, The Guardian; *Clubs* International Club of GB, All-England Lawn Tennis and Croquet; *Style*— Andrew Castle, Esq; ✉ Sky Sports, Centaurs Business Park, Grant Way, Isleworth, Middlesex TW7 5QD

CASTLE, Enid; OBE (1997), JP; da of Bertram Castle, and late Alice, *née* Sykes; *b* 28 Jan 1936; *Educ* Hulme GS for Girls Oldham, Royal Holloway Coll London (BA), Univ of London; *Career* teacher Colne Valley HS Linthwaite Huddersfield 1958–62, head of History Dept Kenya HS Nairobi 1962–65, head of History Dept and sr mistress Queens Coll Nassau Bahamas 1965–68, dep head Roundhill HS Thurmaston Leicester 1969–72; headmistress: HS for Girls Denmark Rd Gloucester 1973–81, The Red Maids' Sch Bristol 1982–87; princ The Cheltenham Ladies Coll 1987–96; memb: Girls' Schs' Assoc (pres 1990–91), Secdy Heads' Assoc (former pres Area 7), Boarding Schs' Assoc; govr: Godstowe Sch, Beaudesert Sch, Crypt Sch; former chm: Gloucester Careers Advsy Ctee, Conf of Gloucestershire Secdy Heads 1977–80; pres Gloucester Soroptimist Club 1979–80; *Recreations* tennis, squash, bridge, choral music, travel; *Clubs* Univ Women's; *Style*— Miss Enid Castle, OBE, JP

CASTLE, Geoffrey Ellis Trevor; s of Richard Basil Trevor Castle, OBE (d 1986), of Cuckfield, West Sussex, and Geraldine Therese, *née* Ellis; *b* 12 Aug 1936; *Educ* Uppingham, Coll of Estate Mgmnt; *m* 5 Oct 1963, Sarah Margaret Sherwin, da of Francis (Frank) Neville (d 1986), of Cookham, Berks; 2 da (Frances b 1966, Helen b 1968); *Career* asst surveyor Jones Lang Wootton 1961–69, ptnr B A James and Co 1970–72, dir Herring Daw 1972–76, ptnr Dron and Wright 1976– (sr ptnr 1984–); Freeman City of London, memb Worshipful Co of Chartered Surveyors 1984, FRICS 1973 (ARICS 1961), MBAE 1993; *Recreations* gardening, arts; *Clubs* Arts Club; *Style*— Geoffrey Castle, Esq; ✉ Dron and Wright, St George's House, 12a St George St, London W1 (☎ 0171 491 7332)

CASTLE OF BLACKBURN, Baroness (Life Peer UK 1990), of Ibstone in the County of Buckinghamshire; Barbara Anne Castle; PC (1964); Baroness Castle; da of Frank Betts (d 1945), and Annie Rebecca Betts; *b* 6 Oct 1910; *Educ* Bradford Girls' GS, St Hugh's Coll Oxford; *m* 1944, Edward Cyril (Ted) Castle (d 1979), cr Baron Castle (Life Peer) 1974; *Career* ed Town and County Councillor 1936–40, admin offr Miny of Food 1941–44, housing corr and affairs advsr Daily Mirror 1944–45; memb St Pancras BC 1937, memb Metropolitan Water Bd 1940–43; Labour Party: MP Blackburn 1945–79, memb Nat Exec Ctee 1950–79, vice chm 1957–58 (chm 1958–59); min for overseas devpt 1964–65, min of tport 1965–68, first sec of state for employment and productivity 1968–70, sec of state for social services, vice chm Socialist Gp in Europe; MEP Greater Manchester West 1984–89 (Greater Manchester North 1979–84); hon fell: St Hugh's Coll Oxford 1966, Bradford and Ilkley Community Coll 1985, UMIST 1991; Hon DTech: Bradford Univ 1968, Loughborough Univ 1969; Hon LLD: Lancaster Univ 1991, Univ of Manchester 1993; hon fell: Humberside Poly 1991, Univ of York 1992; Cross of Order of Merit of the Federal Republic of Germany 1990; *Books* The Castle Diaries 1974–76 (1980), The Castle Diaries 1964–70 (1984), Sylvia and Christabel Pankhurst (1987), The Castle Diaries 1964–76 (1990), Fighting All the Way (1993); *Style*— The Rt Hon Baroness Castle of Blackburn, PC; ✉ House of Lords, London SW1A OPW

CASTLE STEWART, 8 Earl (I 1800) Arthur Patrick Avondale Stuart; 15 Bt (S 1628); also Baron Castle Stuart (I 1619), and Viscount Castle Stuart (I 1793); s of 7 Earl Castle Stewart, MC (d 1961), and Eleanor May (d 1992), da of Solomon R Guggenheim, of New York; *b* 18 Aug 1928; *Educ* Eton, Trinity Coll Cambridge; *m* 1952, Edna, da of William Edward Fowler; 1 s, 1 da; *Heir* s, Viscount Stuart; *Career* late Lt Scots Gds; farmer; FIMgt; *Clubs* Carlton; *Style*— The Rt Hon the Earl Castle Stewart; ✉ Manor Farm, Babcary, Somerton, Somerset TA11 7DT (☎ 01458 223040); Stuart Hall, Stewartstown, Co Tyrone (☎ 0186 8738208)

CASTLEDEN, Prof (Christopher) Mark; s of Dr Leslie Ivan Mark Castleden (d 1984), and Joan, *née* Plumbe; *b* 22 July 1944; *Educ* UCS, Bart's and Univ of London (MB BS, MD); *m*; 3 da (Emily Jayne b 1972, Lorraine b 1974, Caroline b 1975); *Career* RCP: memb 1972, memb Geriatrics Ctee 1979–85, fell 1984, prof 1987; chm: Advsy Sub Ctee Geriatrics Med Tst 1981, Regl Educn Ctee on Geriatric Medicine 1994–; memb: Ctee Safety of Meds 1984–86, Advsy Ctee on NHS Drugs 1991–, Br Geriatrics Soc (chm Scientific Ctee 1994–); *Recreations* sailing, gardening, antiques, reading; *Style*— Prof Mark Castleden; ✉ Leicester General Hosp, Division of Medicine for the Elderly, Gwendolen Rd, Leicester LE5 4PW (☎ 0116 249 0490, fax 0116 258 4666)

CASTLEMAINE, 8 Baron (I 1812); Roland Thomas John Handcock; MBE; s of late 7 Baron (1973); *b* 22 April 1943; *Educ* Campbell Coll Belfast; *m* 1988, Lynne Christine, eldest da of Maj J M Gurney, RAEC; 1 s; *Heir* s, Hon Ronan Michael Edward Handcock b 27 March 1989; *Career* Lt-Col Army Air Corps, ret; aviation conslt; *Style*— The Rt Hon the Lord Castlemaine; ✉ Keeper's Cottage, Winterbourne Stoke, Salisbury, Wilts

CASTLEMAN, Christopher Norman Anthony; s of S Phillips (d 1969), and Mrs Joan Pyper; *b* 23 June 1941; *Educ* Harrow, Clare Coll Cambridge (MA); *m* 1, 1967, Sarah Victoria (d 1979), da of Judge Frank Alleyne Stockdale (d 1989); 1 s (Jonathan b 1971), 1 da (Amanda b 1967); *m* 2, 1980, Caroline Clare, da of Thomas Norman Westcott, of S Africa; 2 da (Alexandra b 1982, Georgia b 1984); m 3, 1990, Susan Mary, da of Geoffrey Michael Twycross, of S Africa; 1 s (Nicholas b 2 Dec 1993), 1 da (Sasha Leila b 10 March 1995); *Career* corp fin dept Hill Samuel & Co Ltd (formerly M Samuel & Co Ltd) 1965–69, gen mangr Hill Samuel Australia Ltd 1970–72, corporate fin dir Hill Samuel & Co Ltd 1973–75, md Hill Samuel International Ltd 1976–77; chief exec: Hill Samuel Group (SA) Ltd 1978–80, Hill Samuel Group plc 1980 (resigned 1987), Manpower plc 1987 (resigned 1988); fin advsr Christopher Castleman & Co 1988–91, dir Standard Chartered plc 1991–; non-exec chm Johnson Fry Holdings PLC until 1995; *Recreations* travel, sports; *Clubs* MCC (assoc); *Style*— Christopher Castleman, Esq; ✉ Tofte Manor, Souldrop Road, Sharnbrook, Bedford MK44 1HH (☎ 01234 781425)

CASTRO, Dr John Edward; s of Edward George Castro, of Norfolk, and Ivy Leuze Castro; *b* 10 Aug 1940; *Educ* Barnet GS, UCL (scholar, BSc, Suckling Prize for Anatomy), UCH Med Sch (Fanny Magrath scholar in surgery, MRCS, LRCP, MB BS, MS, PhD, Sir Frances Walshe prize in neurology, Erichson prize for practical surgery); *m* 1 (m dis), Sylvia Rosemary Barber; 1 s (Ashley John b 1967), 2 da (Naomi Jane b 1970, Rebecca Elizabeth b 1973); m 2, Pamela Elizabeth, da of Rev Preb John Clifford Dale; *Career* house surgn UCH July-Dec 1965 (house physician Jan-June 1965), GP 1966; sr house surgn: Accident Service Luton and Dunstable Hosp Jan-June 1967, Hammersmith Hosp July-Dec 1967; res fell and hon urological registrar RPMS 1968–69, rotating surgical registrar Norfolk and Norwich Hosp 1969–71, scientific worker 1971–73 (Nat Inst for Med Res Mill Hill and Clinical Res Centre Harrow), res grant Cancer Res Campaign 1975, Arris-Gale lectr RCS 1975, hon conslt urologist Hammersmith Hosp 1975–79 (sr surgical registrar urology 1973–75), sr lectr in urology RPMS 1975–79 (tutor in surgery and lectr in immunology 1973–75), conslt urologist and transplant surgn 1979–; Patey Prize Surgical Res Soc 1973 and 1975, Univ Medal Univ of Hiroshima 1975, Ethicon Travel fellowship 1977; memb: Int Transplant Soc, BMA, Br Assoc of Urological Surgeons, European Dialysis and Transplantation Assoc, Euro Assoc of Urology; fndr memb Br Transplantation Soc, FRSM, FRCS (Edinburgh) 1968, FRCS (Eng) 1970; *Books* Treatment of Benign Prostate Hypertrophy and Neoplasia (1974), Immunology for Surgeons (1976), Immunological Aspects of Cancer (1978), Treatment of Renal Failure (1980); *Recreations* gardening, cooking, collecting card cases; *Clubs* Chelsea Clinical Soc; *Style*— Dr John Castro; ✉ 9 Lammas Park Gardens, Ealing, London W5 5HZ (☎ 0181 587 0578); Suite 8, 103 Harley Street, London W1N 1HD (☎ 0171 487 4899, fax 0171 224 3975, car 0860 319194)

CATCHPOLE, Prof David Ridley; s of Rev Cyril Walter John Catchpole (d 1973), and Winifred Patricia Mary, *née* Critchell; *b* 1 May 1938; *Educ* Cheltenham GS, Queen's Coll Oxford (MA), Pembroke Coll Cambridge (PhD); *m* 21 Aug 1963, Dorothy Ann, da of Lt-Col Charles Alexander Scott (d 1960); 2 da (Helen Margaret b 1966, Catherine Ailsa b 1970); *Career* tutor Clifton Theol Coll Bristol 1966–69, lectr and sr lectr Dept of Religious Studies Univ of Lancaster 1969–84, prof of theological studies Univ of Exeter 1984–; sec Soc for New Testament Study 1983–88, memb Gen Synod C of E 1970–75 (reader C of E 1970–); *Books* The Trial of Jesus (1971), The Quest for Q (1993); *Recreations* gardening, cricket, croquet, theatre; *Style*— Prof David Catchpole; ✉ 9 Uplowman Rd, Tiverton, Devon EX16 4LU (☎ 01884 252100); Department of Theology, University of Exeter, Queen's Building, The Queen's Drive, Exeter EX4 4QH (☎ 01392 264242)

CATCHPOLE, Nancy Mona; OBE (1987); da of George William Page (d 1980), of New Eltham, and Mona Dorothy, *née* Cowin (d 1979); *b* 6 Aug 1929; *Educ* Haberdashers' Aske's Hatchman Girls' Sch, Bedford Coll London (BA); *m* 1959, Geoffrey David Arthur Catchpole; 1 s, 1 da; *Career* pres Br Fedn of Univ Women 1981–84, jt sec Women's Nat Cmmn 1985–88 (co chm 1983–85), conslt RSA Women's Trg Roadshow Prog, RSA Women's Working Gp (now Women's Advsy Gp) 1989–94 (vice chm 1985–94), chm BFWG Charitable Fndn 1995– (vice chm 1992–95), chm Bath Branch Historical Assoc 1993–96; memb of Wessex Regnl Health Authy 1986–90, lay assoc memb Avon FSHA 1990–; FRSA 1986; *Style*— Nancy Catchpole, OBE; ✉ 66 Leighton Rd, Weston, Bath BA1 4NG (☎ 01225 423338); BFWG Charitable Foundation, 28 Great James Street, London WC1N 3ES (☎ 0171 404 6447)

CATER, Sir Jack; KBE (1979, CBE 1973, MBE 1956); yr s of Alfred Francis Cater and Pamela Elizabeth Dukes; *b* 21 Feb 1922; *Educ* Sir George Monoux GS Walthamstow, Queen's Coll Oxford, Imperial Def Coll; *m* 1950, Peggy Gwenda Richards; 1 s, 2 da; *Career* served WWII Sqdn Ldr RAFVR; Mil Govt Hong Kong 1945–46: Colonial Admin Service 1946, memb Exec Cncl and Legislative Cncl at various times 1970–81, dir of commerce and indust 1970–72, sec for info 1972 and home affrs 1973, founding cmmr Ind Cmmn Against Corruption 1974–78, chief sec (actg govr and dep govr on various occasions) 1978–81, Hong Kong cmmr in London 1982–84; dep gen mangr Guangdong Nuclear Power Joint Venture Company China 1985–86 (dir 1987–89), md Hong Kong Nuclear Investment Co Ltd 1987–89 (conslt 1990–); dir: Hong Kong Cable Communications 1990–92, The Scottish Asian Investment Co Ltd 1990–, TVB 1992–, TVE (H) 1992–96, Springfield Bank and Trust Ltd 1994–, Dao Heng Bank Group Ltd 1996–; chm: HG Asia Securities Ltd 1992–95 (dir and conslt 1990–), The Oriental Development Co Ltd 1992–; conslt: Philips China & Hong Kong Group 1990–92, International Bechtel Inc 1990–, Shaw Brothers (Hong Kong) Ltd 1990–, Hutchison Whampoa Ltd 1991–94; pres Agency for Volunteer Serv Hong Kong 1982–, memb Int Bd Utd World Colls UK 1981–92, dir Li Po Chun Utd World Coll of Hong Kong 1989–; memb Ct: Univ of Hong Kong, Hong Kong Baptist Univ 1995– (formerly Baptist Coll of Hong Kong (govr 1990–95)); Hon DSSc Univ of Hong Kong 1982, Hon LLD Univ of Bath 1995; *Clubs* Hong Kong, Royal Hong Kong Jockey; *Style*— Sir Jack Cater, KBE, JP; ✉ 36 St George's Court, 85 Kadoorie Avenue, Kowloon, Hong Kong (☎ 00 852 2 715 4004)

CATER, Sir John Robert (Robin); kt (1984); s of Sir John James Cater (d 1962), of Edinburgh, and Jessie Sheila MacDonald, *née* Moodie (d 1948); *b* 25 April 1919; *Educ* George Watson's Coll Edinburgh, Jesus Coll Cambridge (MA); *m* 1945, Isobel Calder Ritchie; 1 da; *Career* chm: The Distillers Co 1976–83, The Scotch Whisky Assoc 1976–83; *Style*— Sir Robin Cater; ✉ Avernish, Elie, Fife, Scotland KY9 1DA (☎ 01333 330 667)

CATES, Armel Conyers; s of Conyers Seely Cates (d 1965), of Guildford, and Jacqueline Maude, *née* Geoffroy (d 1988); *b* 3 May 1943; *Educ* Charterhouse, Univ of Southampton (LLB); *m* 8 July 1967, Pamela Susan, da of Colin Huson Walker, of Barrington, Cambs; 2 s (Tom b 1974, Sam b 1978), 1 da (Ilaria b 1980); *Career* articled to Theodore Goddard (London) and Vinters (Cambridge) 1967–69, admitted slr 1969; asst slr Coward Chance 1970–72, Clifford-Turner 1972–76, ptnr Clifford Chance 1976–; former editorial advsr International Financial Law Review; tstee Charterhouse Mission in Southwark; memb: Law Soc 1969, Int Bar Assoc; Liveryman Worshipful Co of Slrs; *Recreations* golf, tennis, photography; *Style*— Armel Cates, Esq; ✉ Graves Farm, Catmere End, Saffron Walden, Essex CB11 4XG; Clifford Chance, 200 Aldersgate Street, London EC1A 4JJ (☎ 0171 600 1000, fax 0171 600 5555)

CATFORD, Gordon Vivian; s of Harry George Bascombe (d 1984), of Weston-super-Mare, and Gladys Annie, *née* Horton (d 1951); *b* 23 Nov 1927; *Educ* Clifton, Univ of Bristol (MB ChB); *m* 10 June 1955, June Crichton, da of Robert Baxter (d 1983), of Edinburgh; 2 s (Gordon Baxter b 1958, Paul Nicholas b 1961); *Career* Nat Serv, Sqdn Ldr RAF Med Br CME 1954–56; house appts: Bristol Infirmary 1951–52, Bristol Eye Hosp 1952–54; chief clinical asst Moorfields Eye Hosp 1960–64 (house appt 1958–60); conslt ophthalmic surgn: St George's Hosp London 1963–88 (first asst 1961–63), Royal London Homoeopathic Hosp 1969–88, Royal Masonic Hosp London 1973–, St Luke's Hosp for the Clergy 1988–; ophthalmologist: Linden Lodge Sch for the Blind 1978–89, Greenmead Sch for Multiple Handicapped 1978–89, John Aird Sch 1978–93; memb Med Appeals Tbnl London South 1988–, advsr Br Orthoptic Soc; govr: Linden Lodge Sch 1978–89, Clifton Coll 1982– (memb Cncl 1982–93); hon fell of orthoptics Br Orthoptic Soc 1988; Freeman City of London 1963, Liveryman Worshipful Soc of Apothecaries 1963; memb BMA 1952, FRSM 1961, FRCS 1961, FRCOphth 1988 (hon archivist); *Recreations* gardening; *Style*— Gordon Catford, Esq; ✉ 9 St Johns Wood Park, London NW8 6QP; 11 Devonshire Place, London W1N 1PB (☎ 0171 935 9523)

CATFORD, Sir (John) Robin; KCVO (1993), CBE (1990); er s of Adrian Leslie Catford (d 1979), and Ethel Augusta, *née* Rolfe (d 1988); *b* 11 Jan 1923; *Educ* Hampton GS, Univ of St Andrews (BSc), St John's Coll Cambridge (Dip Agric); *m* 21 Aug 1948, Daphne Georgina, da of Col John Francis Darby, CBE, TD (d 1951); 3 s (John Charles b 1949, Simon Leslie b 1956, Francis James Robin b 1959), 1 da (Lucy Georgina b 1952); *Career* Sudan CS Dept of Agric and Forests 1946–55; commercial appts in UK 1955–66; MAFF 1966–82 (princ 1966, asst sec 1972, under sec 1979); transferred to PM's office 1982, sec for appts to PM and ecclesiastical sec to Lord Chllr 1982–93; crafts advsr Radcliffe Tst 1993–; *Recreations* sailing, travel, theatre, arts; *Clubs* United Oxford and Cambridge Univ; *Style*— Sir Robin Catford, KCVO, CBE; ✉ Priory Cottage, Priory Road, Chichester, W Sussex PO19 1NS (☎ 01243 783197)

CATHCART, 6 Earl (UK 1814); Alan Cathcart; CB (1973), DSO (1945), MC (1944); also 15 Lord Cathcart (S *circa* 1447), Baron Greenock and Viscount Cathcart (both UK 1807); s of 5 Earl Cathcart (d 1927), and Vera Estelle, *née* Fraser (d 1993); *b* 22 Aug 1919; *Educ* Eton, Magdalene Coll Cambridge; *m* 1, 1946, Rosemary Clare Marie Gabrielle (d 1980), da of late Air-Cdre Sir Henry Smyth-Osborne, CMG, CBE; 1 s, 2 da; m 2, 1984, Marie Isobel, da of late Hon William Joseph French (3 s of 4 Baron de Freyne), and widow of Sir Thomas Brian Weldon, 8 Bt; *Heir* s, Lord Greenock (*qv*); *Career* sits as Cons in House of Lords; 2 Lt Scots Gds 1939, Brig Ops Div SHAPE 1967–69, Maj-Gen 1969, GOC Yorks Dist 1969–70, GOC Berlin (Br Sector) 1970–73, ret; dep speaker House of Lords 1976–89; pres ROSPA 1982–86; Brig Queen's Body Guard for Scotland (Royal Co of Archers), Commodore Royal Yacht Sqdn 1974–80; dep grand pres Br Cwlth Ex-Services League 1975–86, pres Army Cadet Force Assoc 1976–82; Lord Prior Order of St John of Jerusalem 1985–88; *Clubs* Brooks's, Royal Yacht Squadron; *Style—* The Rt Hon the Earl Cathcart, CB, DSO, MC; ✉ Moor Hatches, West Amesbury, Salisbury, Wilts SP4 7BH (☎ 01980 623839)

CATHCART, Brian John; s of (Hektor) Rex Cathcart (d 1994), of Coleraine, N Ireland, and Hazel Jane, *née* Storey (d 1988); *b* 26 Oct 1956; *Educ* Sandford Park Sch Dublin, Campbell Coll Belfast, Trinity Coll Dublin (BA); *m* 1 Nov 1985, Ruth, da of Thomas William Griffiths; 2 s (Thomas William b 25 June 1989, Patrick Richard b 31 Jan 1992); *Career* Reuters News Agency: trainee journalist 1978–81, corr Paris 1981–85, diplomatic corr London 1985–86, corr Netherlands 1986; The Independent: sub ed (foreign) 1986–88, asst foreign ed 1988–89; The Independent on Sunday: foreign ed 1989–92, asst ed 1992–95, dep ed 1995–; *Style—* Brian Cathcart, Esq; ✉ The Independent on Sunday, 1 Canada Square, Canary Wharf, London E14 5AP (☎ 0171 293 2000, fax 0171 293 2043)

CATHERWOOD, Sir (Henry) Frederick Ross (Fred); kt (1971); s of late Harold Matthew Stuart, and late Jean Catherwood, of Co Londonderry; *b* 30 Jan 1925; *Educ* Shrewsbury, Clare Coll Cambridge; *m* 1954, Elizabeth, er da of Rev Dr D Martyn Lloyd-Jones, of Westminster Chapel, London; 2 s (Christopher b 1955, Jonathan b 1961), 1 da (Bethan b 1958); *Career* articled clerk Price Waterhouse, qualified CA 1951; sec Laws Stores Ltd Gateshead 1952–54, chief exec Richard Costain Ltd 1955–60 (sec and controller 1954–55), md British Aluminium Co 1962–64 (asst md 1960–62), chief industl advsr DEA 1964–66, dir gen NEDC 1966–71 (memb Cncl 1964–71), md and chief exec John Laing & Son Ltd 1972–74; chm Br Overseas Trade Bd 1975–79; MEP (EDG) Cambridge and North Bedfordshire 1979–94; Euro Parl: chm Ctee on External Economic Relations 1979–84, a vice pres 1989–92, vice pres Foreign Rels Ctee 1992–94; Br Inst of Mgmnt: memb Cncl 1961–66 and 1969–79, vice chm 1972, chm 1974–76, vice pres 1976–; pres: Fellowship of Ind Evangelical Churches 1977 (vice pres 1976), Univs and Colls Christian Fellowship 1983–84 (chm Cncl 1971–77), Evangelical Alliance 1992–; vice pres Int Fellowship of Evangelical Students 1995– (treasurer 1979–91); memb Central Religious Advsy Ctee to BBC and IBA 1975–79; Hon DSc Aston Univ 1972, Hon DSc (Econ) Queen's Univ of Belfast 1973, Hon DUniv Surrey 1979; *Books* The Christian in Industrial Society (1964), Britain with the Brakes Off (1966), The Christian Citizen (1969), A Better Way (1976), First Things First (1979), God's Time God's Money (1987), Pro Europe? (1991), David - Poet, Warrior, King (1993), At the Cutting Edge (1995), Neighbours in Need (1997); *Recreations* music, gardening, reading; *Clubs* United Oxford and Cambridge University; *Style—* Sir Frederick Catherwood; ✉ Sutton Hall, Balsham, Cambridgeshire CB1 6DX (fax 01223 894032)

CATHIE, Kyle Anne Bewley (Mrs Charles ap Simon); yst da of Dr Ian Aysgarth Bewley Cathie, DL (d 1989), of Moreton-in-Marsh, Glos, and Dr Marian Josephine Cunning (d 1982); *b* 10 Oct 1948; *Educ* Chipping Norton GS, Cheltenham; *m* 21 April 1973, (David) Charles ap Simon; 2 s (Thomas b 1978, Nicholas b 1980), 1 da (Josephine b 1985); *Career* sr ed Pan Books 1983, editorial dir Elm Tree Books 1983–86, Papermac publisher and editorial dir Macmillan London Ltd 1986–89, md and publisher Kyle Cathie Ltd 1989–; *Books* Complete Calorie Counter (1978 and 1990), Complete Carbohydrate Counter (1980), The Corgi Calorie Counter (1989 and 1993); *Recreations* beekeeping, opera, theatre; *Style—* Ms Kyle Cathie; ✉ 3 Vincent Square, London SW1P 2LX (☎ 0171 973 9710)

CATLIN, Angela; da of Courtney Catlin, of London, and Rose-Margaret Catlin; *b* 11 Aug 1961; *Educ* St Thomas Aquinas Edinburgh, CBP Glasgow (higher dip in photography); *Career* freelance photographer, staff photographer The Herald 1988–; *Awards* winner Portrait Section Essex Int Show of Photography 1979; Scottish Press Photography Awards: Scottish Press Photographer of the Year 1990 and 1995 (commended 1989), winner Sequence Section 1995 (runner-up 1988), winner Features Section 1995; highly commended British Press Photographer of the Year Awards 1989, highly commended UK Press Gazette Press Awards 1989; Features Section Fuji European Press Awards: winner 1992, Cert of Merit 1993; *Books* Natural Light - Portraits of Scottish Writers (1985); *Recreations* travel, food, wine, ardent Sheffield Wednesday fan; *Style—* Ms Angela Catlin; ✉ c/o Picture Desk, The Herald, 195 Albion Street, Glasgow G1 1QP (☎ 0141 552 6255)

CATLIN, John Anthony; s of John Vincent Catlin (d 1961), and Kathleen Glover Brand (d 1982); *b* 25 Nov 1947; *Educ* Ampleforth, Univ of Birmingham (LLB); *m* 25 Aug 1974, Caroline Jane, *née* Goodman; 1 s, 2 da; *Career* Gregory Rowcliffe & Co: articled clerk 1970–72, admitted slr 1972, asst slr 1972–75; Civil Serv: joined as legal asst Treasy Slrs' Dept 1975 (sr legal asst 1978), transferred to Dept of Environment as asst slr 1984–89, appointed dep slr (under sec (legal)) Dept of Environment 1989, currently on secondment to DSS; memb Law Soc 1972; *Recreations* music, history, computers; *Style—* John Catlin, Esq; ✉ Office of the Solicitor, Department of Social Security, Room 436, New Court, Covey Street, London WC2A 2LS (☎ 0171 412 1465)

CATLING, Brian David; s of Leonard Frederick Catling, of London, and Lilian Alice Catling; *b* 23 Oct 1948; *Educ* N East London Poly, RCA London; *m* 1; 1 s (Jack Ishmael b 19 Dec 1983); m 2, Clare Carswell; 1 s (Finn Bell b 23 Nov 1990), 1 da (Florence Pike b 13 April 1989); *Career* artist; visiting lectr: Jan Van Eyck Akademie Maastricht Netherlands 1980–84, Chelsea Sch of Art, Royal Acad, Vestlandets Kunsteakademi Bergen Norway, Kunsteakademi Trondheim Norway; Henry Moore fell in sculpture Norwich Sch of Art 1982–85, tutor in sculpture RCA 1983–90, princ lectr in sculpture Brighton Poly, head of sculpture Ruskin Sch of Drawing and Fine Art 1991–, fell Linacre Coll Oxford 1991; also poet; FRCA; *Solo Exhibitions* incl: Air Gallery 1977, Camden Arts Centre 1979, Arnolfini Gallery 1980, Norwich Sch of Art Gallery 1982–84, Atlantis Gallery 1984, South Hill Park Gallery 1984, Liefsgade 22 Copenhagen 1986, Hordaland Kunstnercentrum Bergen Norway 1987, Matts Gallery 1987, Neuw Gallerie (Sammlung Ludwig Aachen) 1988, Museum of Modern Art Oxford 1989, At the Lighthouse (Matts Gallery London) 1991, Gallerie Satellite Paris 1993, TEN Gallery Fukuoka Japan 1993, The Blindings (Serpentine Gallery), A Conceptual Telescope for Bergen (cmmnd public sculptures over five sites) 1994, Window (installed sculpture for Br Embassy Dublin) 1995; *Group Exhibitions* incl: Sculptors Attitude to Drawing 1974, Albion Island Vortex (Whitechapel Gallery) 1974, Imagination is the Venom (Ikon Gallery) 1981, Art and the Sea (Arnolfini and ICA) 1982, Nordic Winter Symposium (Geilo Norway) 1982, Licence and Device (Herbert Read Gallery) 1985, Edel Smeldelgroep (Valkenberg & Stolberg) 1987, Bookworks (V & A Museum) 1988, Torben Grondael Gallery Copenhagen 1989, MOBSHOP IV (Viborg and Malmo Kunsthaller Sweden) 1989, Upturned Art (Pitt Rivers Museum Oxford) 1990, Nylistasfnid (The Living Art Museum Iceland) 1990, Belluard Festival Fribourg Switzerland, Gianozzo Festival Berlin 1992, 3 Artists from Oxford (St Catherine's Coll, Kobe Japan) 1993, Cyclops (Galerie Satellite Paris) 1995; *Performance Works* incl: Miltonian Ghost Dance (Whitechapel Gallery) 1980, Spogelsemasse (Leifscade 22 Copenhagen) 1986, Readings from the Gamble Room (Bookworks project, V & A Museum) 1987, 5 performances cmmnd by Museum of Modern Art Oxford 1989, Two Works for Trondheim (Trondelac Arts Centre Trondheim Norway) 1990, Faint Object (Centrum Sztuki Wspotczesnej Zamek Ujazdowski Warsaw Poland) 1993, Refined White (Tate Gallery London) 1993, Augenlied (Schloss Plüschow Art Centre Mecklenburg Germany) 1993, Peformance (Kitakyushu Municipal Museum of Art Japan) 1993, Performance (Solaria Plaza Fukuoka Japan) 1993, Sunflint (Artifact Gallery Tel Aviv Israel) 1993, Reading Room Bookworks, The Oxford Mound, British Library Reading Room, King's Library, Revenge of the Reforgotten (Royal Albert Hall) 1995, Hidden Cities (bus tour, Laboratory Gallery Oxford) 1995, Konsum Projekt (Baitz, Land Brandenburg Germany) 1995, Clepsydra (S London Gallery) 1996, Freiwild Festival (Halle Germany) 1996; *Publications* The First Electron Heresy (1977), Vorticegargen (1979), Pleides in Nine (1981), Vox Humana (1984), Das Kranke Tier (1984), The Tulpa Index (1986), Lair (1987), Boschlog (1988), Boschlog (1989), The Stumbling Block (1990), Future Exiles (1991), The First London Halo (1994), Thyhand (1994), The Bindings (1995); *Style—* Brian Catling, Esq; ✉ Ruskin School of Drawing & Fine Art, 74 High Street, Oxford OX1 (☎ 01865 276940)

CATO, Michael John; s of William Henry Cato (d 1978), and Gladys Annie Hayes; *b* 13 Dec 1933; *Educ* Mercers' Sch London; *m* 1, 1959, Rosemary (d 1978), da of Thomas Topping (d 1991); 2 s (Timothy b 1961, Alastair b 1963), 2 da (Jane Rosalind b 1960, Catherine b 1966); m 2, 1985, Helen Peeples, da of Col Leonard Frederick Butler, OBE, MC (d 1968); 1 step s (Benson b 1977), 2 step da (Lesley b 1976, Emily b 1979); *Career* chm and md William Cato and Sons Ltd 1971–91 (dir 1961); chm and dir Br Hardware Fedn Merchandising Co 1981–85, memb Nat Ctee Br Hardware Fedn 1974–92 (memb Bd of Mgmnt 1976–85 and 1990–92, chm Marketing Gp 1981–85); memb Royal Metal Trades Bd of Mgmnt 1982–87; churchwarden Benefice of Farnham Royal St Mary's Hedgerley 1974–84, Burnham Deanery Synod 1970–84; Freeman City of London; Guildman Civic Guild of Old Mercers 1989–94, fell Nat Inst of Hardware; *Recreations* cricket, sailing, association football; *Clubs* MCC, Old Mercers' (pres 1988–89); *Style—* Michael Cato, Esq; ✉ 230 Moraine Street, Marshfield, Mass 02050, USA (☎ 00 1 617 834 1622)

CATOR, Albemarle John; s of John Cator, of Woodbastwick, Norfolk, and Elizabeth Jane, *née* Kerrison; *b* 23 Aug 1953; *Educ* Harrow; *m* 1, 29 Nov 1980 (m dis 1992), Fiona Mary, da of Robert Edgar Atheling Drummond; 2 s (John b 1983, Robert Henry b 1985); m 2, 17 May 1995, Victoria Katherine, da of Maj-Gen David Pank, CB, *qv*; 1 s (Christian David b 22 Sept 1996); *Career* Lt Scots Guards 1971–74; with Samuel Montagu 1975–84; exec dir: Chemical Bank International Ltd 1984–88, Chemical Securities Ltd 1988–91; vice pres Chemical Bank 1988–91; md NatWest Capital Markets Ltd 1995– (exec dir 1991–95); *Recreations* sailing, shooting, skiing; *Clubs* RYS, Pratt's; *Style—* Albemarle Cator, Esq; ✉ Whitehouse Farm, Woodbastwick, Norwich, Norfolk; NatWest Capital Markets Ltd, 135 Bishopsgate, London EC2M 3UR (☎ 0171 334 1000)

CATT, Michael John (Mike); s of James Ernest Catt, of Port Elizabeth, S Africa, and Anne Gillian, *née* Crowther; *b* 17 Sept 1971; *Educ* Grey HS Port Elizabeth; *Career* rugby union back; club Bath 1993–; honours with Bath: Courage League Champions 1996, winners Pilkington Cup 1996; England: U21, A v New Zealand 1993, Emerging Players v New Zealand 1993, first full cap v Wales 1994, World Cup team S Africa (6 matches) 1995 (4th place), 18 caps; represented South West Div v New Zealand 1993; Bath Player of the Year 1994, Most Promising Player of the Year Award 1995; *Recreations* socialising, golf; *Style—* Mike Catt, Esq; ✉ c/o Masters International, Hurst Grove, Sandford Lane, Hurst, Berkshire RG10 0SQ (☎ 0118 934 4111, fax 0118 934 2778)

CATTANACH, Bruce Macintosh; s of James Cattanach (d 1970), and Margaretta May, *née* Fyfe (d 1970); *b* 5 Nov 1932; *Educ* Heaton GS Newcastle upon Tyne, King's Coll Durham (BSc), Inst of Animal Genetics Univ of Edinburgh (PhD, DSc); *m* 17 Sept 1966, Margaret Bouchier (d 1996), da of Percival Bouchier Crewe (d 1972); 2 da (Jean Margaret b 3 June 1967, Susan Elizabeth b 4 Jan 1969); *Career* scientific staff MRC Induced Mutagenesis Unit Edinburgh 1959–62, NIH post doctoral res fell Biology Div Oak Ridge Nat Laboratory Tennessee USA 1962–64, sr scientist City of Hope Med Centre Duarte Calif 1966–69; MRC Radiology Unit Chilton Oxfordshire: scientific staff 1969–, head Genetics Div 1987–95; acting dir MRC Mammalian Genetics Unit Chilton Oxon 1995–; FRS 1987; *Recreations* constant activity; *Style—* Dr Bruce Cattanach, FRS; ✉ Down's Edge, Reading Road, Harwell, Oxon OX11 0JJ (☎ 01235 835410); Genetics Division, MRC Radiobiology Unit, Chilton, Didcot, Oxfordshire OX11 0RD (☎ 01235 834393, fax 01235 835691)

CATTERALL, Anthony; s of Robert Christopher Fielden Catterall (d 1992), of Headley, Epsom, and Phyllis Joyce Margery, *née* Sykes; *b* 27 Jan 1936; *Educ* Winchester, Trinity Coll Cambridge (BA), UCHMS (MB BChir), Univ of Cambridge (MChir); *m* Jan 1961, Jillian Susan, s of Dr J C Gregory; 1 da (Amanda 12 May 1965), 2 s (Peter b 16 Nov 1968, Andrew b 12 Aug 1971); *Career* pre-registration appts UCH, postgrad trg in gen surgery UCH, orthopaedic trg Royal Nat Orthopaedic Hosp London; conslt to Charing Cross Hosp London 1970–91 (resigned), Royal Nat Orthopaedic Hosp 1971–; Br Orthopaedic Assoc: sec 1977–81, treas 1992–, vice pres elect 1994, pres 1995–96; pres Br Soc of Children's Orthopaedic Surgery 1994–96 (sec 1984–93); memb: RSM, Br Orthopaedic Assoc; FRCS 1963; *Books* Recent Advances in Orthopaedics (ed, Vol 5 1987, Vol 6 1992); *Recreations* sailing; *Style—* Anthony Catterall, Esq; ✉ Royal National Orthopaedic Hospital, 51–54 Bolsover St, London W1 (☎ 0171 387 5070, fax 0181 954 2300)

CATTERALL, John Stewart; s of John Bernard Catterall (d 1965), and Eliza, *née* Whitiker; *b* 13 Jan 1939; *Educ* Blackpool Tech Coll Sch of Art; *m* 18 Sept 1965, (Ann) Beryl, da of Edgar Watkin Hughes; 2 s (Andrew b 4 Aug 1969, Stewart b 3 Feb 1971); *Career* Nat Serv band memb 12 Royal Lancers 1958–60; dep auditor Preston CBC 1966–68, sr accountant Derby CBC 1968–70, mgmnt and chief accountant Cambs and Isle of Ely CC 1970–73, asst co treas Cambs CC 1973–76, dist treas Southampton & SW Hants Health Authy 1976–78, area treas Hants AHA 1978–82, regnl treas NE Thames RHA 1982–85; dep dir fin mgmnt Dept of Health and head Health Serv 1985–88, dir consultancy for health 1988–89; md and chief exec C International Ltd 1989–92, dir Healthcare Consultancy Capita plc 1992–93, md E & T Ltd 1993–; memb CIPFA; *Recreations* golf, tennis; *Style—* John Catterall, Esq; ✉ Birkdale, Green Lane, Chilworth, Southampton SO1 7JW (☎ 01703 769402)

CATTO, Hon Alexander Gordon; 2 s (by 1 m) of 2 Baron Catto; *b* 22 June 1952; *Educ* Westminster, Trinity Coll Cambridge; *m* 1981, Elizabeth Scott, da of the late Maj T P Boyes, MC, of Brookvale Cottage, Whitford, Devon; 2 s (Thomas Innes Gordon b 1983, Alastair Gordon b 1986), 1 da (Charlotte Gordon b 1988); *Career* vice pres Morgan Guaranty Trust Co of New York 1980–85; dir: Yule Catto & Co plc 1981–, Morgan Grenfell & Co Ltd 1986–88; md: Lazard Bros & Co 1988–94, CairnSea Investments Ltd and other private and public cos; *Style—* The Hon Alexander Catto; ✉ Yule Catto & Co plc, Temple Fields, Harlow, Essex CM20 2BH (☎ 01279 442791)

CATTO, Prof Graeme Robertson Dawson; s of Dr William Dawson Catto, of Aberdeen, and Dora Elizabeth, *née* Spiby (d 1978); *b* 24 April 1945; *Educ* Robert Gordon's Coll Aberdeen, Univ of Aberdeen (MB ChB, MD, DSc), Harvard Univ; *m* 14 July 1967, Joan, da of James Alexander Sievewright (d 1958), of Aberdeen; 1 s (Simon b 1972), 1 da (Sarah b 1970); *Career* house offr Aberdeen Royal Infirmary 1969–70, Harkness fell in med Harvard Med Sch USA 1975–77; Univ of Aberdeen: lectr in med 1970–75, sr lectr in med 1977–88, prof of med and therapeutics 1988–, dean Faculty of Clinical Med 1992–, vice-princ 1995–; co-ordinator of clinical services Acute Services Unit Grampian Health Board 1988–92, chm Robert Gordon's Coll Aberdeen, vice chm Aberdeen Royal Hosps NHS Tst 1992–; hon conslt physician and nephrologist Grampian Health Board 1977–; memb: Assoc of Physicians of GB and I, Rotary Club of Aberdeen; Burgess of Guild City of Aberdeen; FRCP, FRCPEd, FRCPGlas, FRSE 1996; *Books* Clinical Nephrology (1988), Transplant Immunology (1993); *Recreations* hill walking, curling; *Clubs* Royal Northern and University; *Style*— Prof Graeme Catto, FRSE; ✉ 4 Woodend Avenue, Aberdeen AB2 6YL (☎ 01224 310509); Department of Medicine and Therapeutics, University of Aberdeen, Foresterhill, Aberdeen AB9 2ZD (☎ 01224 681818, fax 01224 699884)

CATTO, Hon Innes Gordon; s (by 1 m) and h of 2 Baron Catto, *qv*; *b* 7 Aug 1950; *Educ* Grenville Coll, Shuttleworth Agric Coll; *Career* dir Caledonian Opera Co; *Style*— The Hon Innes Catto; ✉ Flat 17, Centre Point Flats, St Giles High Street, London WC2

CATTO, 2 Baron (UK 1936); Sir Stephen Gordon Catto; 2 Bt (UK 1921); s of 1 Baron Catto, CBE, PC (d 1959), and Gladys Forbes, *née* Gordon (d 1980); *b* 14 Jan 1923; *Educ* Eton, Trinity Coll Cambridge; *m* 1, 28 July 1948 (m dis 1965), Josephine Innes, er da of late George Herbert Packer, of Alexandria, Egypt; 2 s (Hon Innes Gordon b 1950, Hon Alexander Gordon b 1952), 2 da (Hon Christian Victoria Gordon (Hon Mrs Menzies-Wilson) b 1955, Hon Ariane Madeleine Gordon b 1960); m 2, 27 Jan 1966, Margaret, da of James Stuart Forrest, of Dilston, Tasmania; 1 s (Hon James Stuart Gordon b 1966), 1 da (Hon Georgina Lucinda Gordon (Hon Mrs Newman) b 21 May 1969); *Heir* s, Hon Innes G Catto; *Career* served RAFVR 1943–47; chm: Yule Catto & Co 1971–, Australian Mutual Provident Society (UK Branch) 1973–91, Pearl Group plc 1989–91; Morgan Grenfell & Co Ltd 1948–79 (dir 1957, chm 1973–79), pres Deutsche Morgan Grenfell Group plc 1987– (chm 1980–87); dir: GEC plc 1959–93, News International plc 1969–, The News Corporation Ltd 1979–89, Times Newspapers Holdings Ltd 1981–; memb: Advsy Cncl ECGD 1959–65, London Transport Bd (pt/t) 1962–68, London Advsy Ctee Hong Kong and Shanghai Banking Corporation 1966–80; chm Cncl RAF Benevolent Fund 1978–91, tstee and chm Exec Ctee Westminster Abbey Tst 1973–; FCIB, Hon FRCPath; *Recreations* music, gardening; *Clubs* Oriental, Melbourne (Australia); *Style*— The Rt Hon the Lord Catto; ✉ 41 William Mews, Lowndes Square, London SW1X 9HQ; Deutsche Morgan Grenfell Group plc, 23 Great Winchester St, London EC2P 2AX (☎ 0171 545 8000, fax 0171 826 6557, telex 8953511 MG LDNG)

CATTRALL, Peter Jeremy; s of Ralph W Cattrall, of Margate, Kent, and Sally, *née* Lunn; *b* 8 Jan 1947; *Educ* King's Sch Canterbury, Trinity Coll Oxford (MA); *m* 26 April 1975, Amanda Jane Maria, da of Maj Gen W N J Withall, CB, of Wiltshire; 1 s (Charles David b 1 March 1980), 1 da (Sarah Louise b 21 Sept 1982); *Career* sch master Holmewood House Kent; admitted slr 1974, asst slr Knocker and Foskett Kent 1974–77, slr to Esso UK plc (formerly Esso Petroleum Co Ltd) 1977–96, on assignment to Esso Exploration and Production UK Ltd; memb: Kent Co Squash Side 1970–78; memb: Oxford Union, Law Soc, IBA; *Recreations* golf, swimming, watching sport, reading, music, current affairs; *Clubs* United Oxford and Cambridge University, MCC, Rye Golf, Free Foresters, I Zingari, Arabs, Jesters, Band of Brothers, Harlequins, Vincent's, Beckenham Cricket; *Style*— Peter Cattrall, Esq; ✉ 21 Whitmore Road, Beckenham, Kent (home ☎ 0181 658 7265, office 0171 245 3661, fax 0171 245 3617)

CAULCOTT, Thomas Holt; s of late Louis William Caulcott, and late Doris Poynton Caulcott; *b* 7 June 1927; *Educ* Solihull Sch, Emmanuel Coll Cambridge; *m* 1, 1954 (m dis 1987); 1 s (Stephen b 1959, d 1978), 1 da (Celia b 1957); m 2, 8 Jan 1988, Jane Marguerite, da of Denis Thomas Allsopp, of Harborne, Birmingham; *Career* Central Land Bd and War Damage Cmmn 1950–53; HM Treasy: private sec to Economic Sec to Treasy 1965, princ HM Treasy 1956–60, private sec to Chllr of the Exchequer 1960–64; princ private sec to First Sec of State (DEA) 1964–65, asst sec Treasy 1965–67, asst sec Miny of Housing and Local Govt 1967–69, Civil Serv Dept 1969–70, under sec Machinery of Govt Gp 1970–73, princ fin offr local govt fin policy Dept of Environment 1973–76, sec Assoc of Metropolitan Authys 1976–82, chief exec City of Birmingham 1982–88, mgmnt conslt 1988–; memb South Shropshire District Cncl 1991–95; memb Ctee of Mgmnt Hanover Housing Assoc 1989–94, memb Bd W Midlands Arts 1995–; Harkness fell Harvard and Brookings Inst USA 1961, hon fell Inst of Local Govt Studies Univ of Birmingham 1987–, hon fell Univ of Central England (formerly Birmingham Poly) 1990–; *Books* Articles in Public Administration: Control of Public Expenditure (1962), Government Organisation in Sweden (1972); *Recreations* music, gardening, walking; *Style*— Thomas Caulcott, Esq; ✉ 37 Lower Broad St, Ludlow, Shropshire SY8 1PH (☎ and fax 01584 875154)

CAUSLEY, Charles Stanley; CBE (1986); s of Charles Causley, and Laura, *née* Bartlett; *b* 24 Aug 1917; *Educ* Launceston Nat Sch, Horwell GS, Launceston Coll, Peterborough Trg Coll; *Career* poet; served WWII RN; hon visiting fell in poetry Univ of Exeter; former literary ed Signature and Apollo BBC W Region Radio; Queen's Gold Medal for Poetry 1967, Cholmondeley Award 1971, Signal Poetry Award 1986, Kurt Maschler Award 1987, Ingersoll TS Eliot Award (USA) 1990; has contributed to numerous anthologies of verse UK and USA; Hon DLitt Univ of Exeter, Hon MA Open Univ; FRSL; *Books* Hands to Dance (1951), Union Street (1957), Underneath the Water (1968), The Puffin Book of Magic Verse (ed, 1974), Collected Poems 1951–75 (1975), The Last King of Cornwall (1978), The Puffin Book of Salt-Sea Verse (ed, 1978), 25 Poems by Hamdija Demirovic (trans, 1980), The Ballad of Aucassin and Nicolette (1981), The Sun, Dancing (ed, 1982), Secret Destinations (1984), 21 Poems (1986), Kings' Children (trans, 1986), Early in the Morning (1986), Jack the Treacle Eater (1987), A Field of Vision (1988), Figgie Hobbin (poetry collection, 1990), The Young Man of Cury (1991), Collected Poems 1951–92 (1992), Collected Poems for Children (1996); *Recreations* travel, piano, the re-discovery of native town; *Style*— Charles Causley, Esq, CBE; ✉ 2 Cyprus Well, Launceston, Cornwall (☎ 01566 772731)

CAUTE, (John) David; JP (1993); *b* 16 Dec 1936; *Educ* Edinburgh Acad, Wellington, Wadham Coll Oxford; *m* 1, 1961 (m dis 1970), Catherine Shuckburgh; 2 s; m 2, 1973, Martha Bates; 2 da; *Career* served Army Gold Coast 1955–56; novelist and historian; Henry fell Harvard Univ 1960–61, fell All Souls Oxford 1959–65, visiting prof NY and Colombia Univs 1966–67, reader in social and political theory Brunel Univ 1967–70, Regent's lectr Univ of California 1974, visiting prof Univ of Bristol 1985; literary ed New Statesman 1979–80, co-chm Writers' Guild 1981–82; *Novels* At Fever Pitch (1959, winner of Authors' Club Award and John Llewelyn Rhys Prize), Comrade Jacob (1961), The Decline of the West (1966), The Occupation (1971), The Baby-Sitters (as John Salisbury, 1978), Moscow Gold (as John Salisbury, 1980), The K-Factor(1983), News From Nowhere (1986), Veronica or the Two Nations (1988), The Women's Hour (1991), Dr Orwell and Mr Blair (1994); *Plays* Songs for an Autumn Rifle (1961), The Demonstration (1969), The Fourth World (1973); *Radio Plays* Fallout (1972), The Zimbabwe Tapes (1983), Henry and the Dogs (1986), Sanctions (1988), Animal Fun Park (1995); *Non-Fiction* Communism and the French Intellectuals 1914–1960 (1964), The Left in Europe Since 1789 (1966), Essential Writings of Karl Marx (ed, 1967), Fanon (1970), The Illusion (1971), The Fellow-Travellers (1973, revised edn 1988), Cuba, Yes ? (1974), Collisions - Essays and Reviews (1974), The Great Fear - The Anti-Communist Purge under Truman and Eisenhower (1978), Under the Skin - The Death of White Rhodesia (1983), The Espionage of the Saints (1986), Sixty-Eight - The Year of the Barricades (1988), Joseph Losey: A Revenge on Life (1994); *Style*— David Caute, Esq, JP; ✉ 41 Westcroft Sq, London W6 OTA

CAVALIER, David John; s of John Richard Cavalier, of Bloxwich, Birmingham, and Jackie Ormma, *née* Wheatley; *b* 12 Feb 1962; *Educ* Mandeville County Secdy Sch, Aylesbury Coll of Further Educn (City and Guilds Certs, Cert of Royal Inst of Health and Hygiene), Ealing Coll of Higher Educn (City and Guilds Cert); *m* 2 Feb 1985, Susan Caroline, da of Ronald Dorsett; 2 da (Jennifer b 22 Oct 1988, Alexandra b 24 Oct 1995); *Career* commis chef Royal Garden Hotel 1979–81, first commis chef Grosvenor House Hotel 1981–82, chef de partie Dorchester Hotel 1982–84, sous chef Auberge du Mail France 1984, first sous chef Berkeley Hotel 1984–85; chef and proprietor: Pebbles Restaurant 1985–87, Cavalier's Restaurant 1987–; head chef: The Bell Inn Aston Clinton 1992–93, L'Escargot 1993–95; jt proprietor Chapter One 1996–, proprietor Memo restaurant 1996–; winner: Gold medal (potato work) Hotel Olympia, Gold medal for best exhibit in jr class, finalist Young Chef of the Year competition 1987; awarded: 1 rosette AA Guide, 1 star Michelin Guide, black clover Ackerman Guide, 1 star Egon Ronay; memb Restaurant Assoc GB 1985; *Recreations* classic cars, fishing; *Style*— David Cavalier, Esq; ✉ 11 Rochelle Close, London SW11 2UR

CAVALIER, Stephen Ronald (Steve); s of Ronald Ernest Cavalier, of Romford, Essex, and Jean, *née* Chinery; *b* 25 June 1952; *Educ* Harold Hill GS Essex, Colchester Sch of Art; *m* 1 Sept 1979, Christine, da of William Alfred Guerrier; 1 s (James William b 11 Feb 1985), 1 da (Clare Jean b 31 Aug 1982); *Career* photographer; asst with advertising photographers London 1971–77, fndr Steve Cavalier Studios 1977– (Central London then moving to St John's Wood); Gold and Silver Awards Design and Art Directors' Assoc, Gold and Silver Campaign Press Awards, Gold Award The One Show NY, commendation Benson & Hedges Gold Award 1990, Silver Award Campaign Poster Awards 1995; memb: Assoc of Photographers (formerly Assoc of Fashion, Advertising and Editorial Photographers), Design and Art Directors Assoc; *Style*— Steve Cavalier, Esq; ✉ Steve Cavalier Studios, 25 Woronzow Rd, St John's Wood, London NW8 6AY (☎ 0171 586 7418, fax 0171 586 7419)

CAVALIERO, Roderick; s of Eric Cavaliero (d 1961), and Valerie de Vesci, *née* Logan (d 1975); *b* 21 March 1928; *Educ* Tonbridge, Hertford Coll Oxford (BA); *m* 31 Aug 1957, Mary, da of John McDonnell (d 1981); 1 s (Rohan b 1963), 4 da (Louisa b 1958, Annamaria b 1960, Rosalind b 1967, Juliana b 1969); *Career* Br Cncl offr 1958–88: rep Brazil 1967–70, controller personnel and staff recruitment 1970–75, rep Italy 1975–77, asst DG 1977–82, dep DG 1982–88; chm Educn and Trg Export Ctee 1979–88, pres Br Educnl Equipment Assoc 1988–92; tstee: Charles Wallace India Tst 1982–, St George's Eng Sch Rome 1982–; memb Cncl: Br Sch at Rome (chm Mgmnt Ctee) 1989–96, Keats-Shelley Meml Assoc 1988–; *Books* Olympia and the Angel (1958), The Last of the Crusaders (1960), The Independence of Brazil (1993), Admiral Satan, the Life and Campaigns of the Bailli de Suffren (1994); *Recreations* gardening, reading, writing; *Style*— Roderick Cavaliero, Esq; ✉ 10 Lansdowne Rd, Tunbridge Wells, Kent TN1 2NJ (☎ 01892 533452, fax 01892 519142)

CAVAN, 13 Earl of (I 1647); Roger Cavan Lambart; has not yet established claim; also Viscount Kilcoursie (I 1647) and Lord Lambart, Baron of Cavan (I 1617); o s of Frederick Cavan Lambart (d 1963; o s of Maj Charles Edward Kilcoursie Lambart, 4 s of Maj Frederick Richard Henry Lambart, 2 s of Cdr Hon Oliver Matthew Lambart, RN, 2 s of 7 Earl of Cavan), and Audrey May, *née* Dunham; s kinsman, 12 Earl of Cavan, TD 1988; *b* 1 Sept 1944; *Educ* Wilson's Sch Wallington Surrey, King's Coll London, St Clare's Oxford; *Heir* kinsman, Cavan Cyril Ernest Lambart b 27 March 1957 (presumed heir); *Style*— The Rt Hon the Earl of Cavan; ✉ 34 Woodleigh Gdns, London SW16

CAVANAGH, Charles Terrence Stephen; s of Arthur Lawrence Cavanagh (d 1963), of USA, and Coleen, *née* Ludrick; *b* 29 July 1949; *Educ* Univ of Oklahoma (BLitt), Univ of Cambridge (BA, MA), Univ of Oxford (Cert in Theol); *Career* Hedderwick Stirling Grumbar & Co 1978–81, SG Warburg & Co 1981–91, Mercury Asset Management plc 1981–91 (dir 1984–91); dir: Kleinwort Benson Investment Management Ltd 1991–96 (head UK Institutional Investment and chm Kleinwort Benson Pension and Charities Div), First Debenture Finance PLC, Kleinwort Endowment Policy Trust PLC, Langbourn Property Investment Services Ltd, Kleinwort European Privatisation Investment Trust PLC, Kleinwort Second Endowment Policy Trust PLC; C of E priest 1980–92; hon curate: St Peter's Clapham 1980–84, St Peter's Streatham 1985–92; dir and treas Extemporary Dance Theatre Ltd 1985–91 (actg chm 1989–90); tstee: The Buttle Trust 1991–95, The Newton Charitable Trust 1990–96; memb Bd of Govrs British Liver Tst 1992–95; *Recreations* modern dance, contemporary art, cooking, wine; *Clubs* Athenaeum; *Style*— Charles Cavanagh, Esq; ✉ Via Degli Ibernesi 20, 00184 Rome, Italy

CAVANAGH, John Eric; s of Charles Cavanagh, and Jean Burns Cavanagh; *b* 27 Dec 1964; *Career* broadcaster; presenter: Earshot (BBC Radio 5) 1990–93, evening and weekend shows for BBC Radio Scotland 1990–, Mission Moon (BBC Radio 1) 1994, The Music Machine (BBC Radio 3) 1994, Radio One Rock Show 1995–96; other radio experience incl: presentation and continuity announcer BBC Radio and TV, contrib to Saturday Sequence (BBC Radio 1), Educn Progs (BBC 2), also contrib to BBC Radio 2, 3, 4, 5 Live, World Service and Radio International, music presenter Radio Clyde; launched new record label Boa Records 1996; *Recreations* collecting mechanical music: phonographs, gramophones, musical boxes, vintage recordings; *Clubs* BBC, Pastelism; *Style*— John Cavanagh, Esq; ✉ BBC Radio One, Glasgow G12 8DG (fax 0141 637 4343, e-mail JOHN.CAVANAGH@BBC.CO.UK)

CAVE, *see:* Haddon-Cave

CAVE, Sir Charles Edward Coleridge; 4 Bt (UK 1896), of Cleve Hill, Mangotsfield, Co Gloucester, Sidbury Manor, Sidbury, Co Devon, and Stoneleigh House, Clifton, Bristol; JP (Devon 1972), DL (1977); o s of Sir Edward Charles Cave, 3 Bt (d 1946), and Betty Christabel, da of Maj Rennell Coleridge, ggn of S T Coleridge, the poet, and 3 cous of 2 Baron Coleridge; *b* 28 Feb 1927; *Educ* Eton; *m* 1957, Mary Elizabeth, da of John Francis Gore, CVO, TD (d 1983, 3 s of Sir Francis Gore, KCB, who was nephew of 4 Earl of Arran), and Lady Janet Campbell, er da of 4 Earl Cawdor; 4 s (John Charles b 1958, Nicholas Stephen b 1961, Thomas Henry b 1964, Richard Hugh b 1967); *Heir* s, John Charles Cave b 8 Sept 1958; *Career* formerly Lt Devonshire Regt; ADC to Govr Punjab 1947; High Sheriff of Devon 1969; FRICS; *Style*— Sir Charles Cave, Bt, JP, DL; ✉ Sidbury Manor, Sidmouth, Devon EX10 0QE (☎ 01395 597207)

CAVE, Francis Joseph (Frank); ERD (1968); s of Joseph Cave (d 1950), of Leicester, and Emily, *née* Potter (d 1938); *b* 11 June 1912; *Educ* Mill Hill Boys' Sch Leicester, Leicester Coll of Art and Technol, Northampton Poly London, Univ of Liverpool, Univ of London (BSc); *m* 14 Nov 1939, (Sophia) Joan, da of Tom Herrick (d 1947), of Leicester; 1 s (Anthony b 13 Oct 1946), 1 da (Frances b 9 Sept 1942); *Career* Res Cmmn RE 1936, 105 Corps FD Park Co Liverpool 1937–39, WWII active serv, FD Co RE Dunkirk 1940, Maj 62 FD Co RE, Maj 58 Mech Equipment Co RE (serv India, Assam, Burma) returned from Rangoon 1945; trainee and articled civil engr 1928–33, asst engr (Willesden, Birkenhead, Oxford) 1933–39, chief asst engr Willesden 1946–48, dep borough engr West Ham 1948–52, borough engr Northampton 1952–58, borough surveyor Hendon Middx 1958–65, city engr Westminster 1965–74, md Halcrow Caribbean Ltd WI 1975–78, conslt engr and surveyor 1978–; memb and chm Tech and Advsy Ctees: RICS, Inst Municipal Engrs, Method of Measurement (Inst Civil Engrs); Br Standards Inst:

memb Cncl Codes of Practice for Bldg and Codes of Practice for Mechanical Engrs, memb Drafting Ctees; memb: Examination Panel London Dist Surveyors, Bd Govrs Westminster Tech Coll; chm Cncl Royal Soc of Health 1969, pres Rotary Club Westminster West 1973; hon memb: American Public Health Assoc 1969, Inst Public Health 1971; Freeman City of London, Liveryman Worshipful Co of Paviors 1966; FRSH 1948 (memb 1935), FIMunE 1952 (memb 1936), FICE 1955 (memb 1938), FRICS 1955 (memb 1948), FRTPI 1958 (memb 1949), FRSA 1972; *Recreations* travelling, art, DIY; *Clubs* RAC; *Style*— Frank Cave, Esq, ERD; ✉ 8 Borodale, Kirkwick Ave, Harpenden, Herts AL5 2QW (☎ 01582 712666)

CAVE, Hugh Walford Melville; s of Alexander Melville Cave (d 1964), and Mary Elizabeth, *née* Bennett (d 1987); *b* 10 July 1932; *Educ* Shrewsbury; *m* 14 Oct 1961, Diana Patricia, da of Brig Edward Antrobus James, OBE, TD, DL (d 1976); 2 s (Timothy b 1962, Andrew b 1964), 1 da (Victoria b 1966); *Career* Nat Serv RA, Lt TA; chartered surveyor; sr ptnr Chesshire Gibson chartered surveyors Birmingham, London and LA 1982–88 (ptnr 1961–88); dir DTZ Debenham Thorpe 1988–94, chm Debenham Tewson Chesshire 1988–93; memb Bd Birmingham Heartlands Devpt Corp 1995–; chm: Rhodes Almshouse Tst, Old Salopian Club 1978–79; pres Midland Club Cricket League 1992–93; Freeman City of London; *Recreations* golf; *Clubs* Army and Navy, Birmingham, Little Aston Golf; *Style*— Hugh W M Cave, Esq; ✉ 2 Heather Court Gardens, Four Oaks, Sutton Coldfield, W Midlands (☎ 0121 308 2004)

CAVE, John Charles; eldest s and h of Sir Charles Edward Coleridge Cave, 4 Bt, *qv*; *b* 8 Sept 1958; *Educ* Eton; *m* 1984, Carey Diana, er da of John Lloyd, of Coombeland, Cadeleigh, Tiverton, Devon; 2 s (George Charles b 8 Sept 1987, William Alexander b 7 May 1992), 1 da (Alice Elizabeth b 28 June 1989); *Style*— John Cave, Esq; ✉ Buckley, Sidbury, Sidmouth, Devon (☎ 01395 597212)

CAVE, Prof Terence Christopher; s of Alfred Cyril Cave (d 1979), and Sylvia Norah, *née* Norman (d 1989); *b* 1 Dec 1938; *Educ* Winchester, Gonville and Caius Coll Cambridge (BA, MA, DPhil); *m* 31 July 1965 (m dis 1990), Helen Elizabeth; 1 s (Christopher b 1969), 1 da (Hilary b 1970); *Career* lectr Univ of St Andrews 1963–65 (asst lectr 1962–63), sr lectr Univ of Warwick 1970–72 (lectr 1965–70), prof of French literature Univ of Oxford 1989– (fell and tutor St John's Coll 1972–); visiting posts: Cornell Univ 1967–68, Univ of California Santa Barbara 1976, Univ of Virginia 1979, Princeton Univ 1984, Univ of Alberta Edmonton 1992, Univ of Paris 7 1995; visiting fell All Souls Coll Oxford 1971; memb Academia Europaea 1990, hon sr res fell Inst of Romance Studies London; FBA 1991; *Books* Devotional Poetry in France (1969), The Cornucopian Text (1979), Recognitions (1988); *Style*— Prof Terence Cave, FBA; ✉ St John's Coll, Oxford OX1 3JP (☎ 01865 277345, fax 01865 277435)

CAVE-BROWNE-CAVE, Myles Alfred; s of Bryan William Cave-Browne-Cave, OBE (d 1980), of Birket Houses, Winster, Windermere, and Margaret Royston, *née* Cooke, MBE (d 1978); *b* 26 Aug 1949; *Educ* Rugby, St Edmund Hall Oxford (MA); *m* 24 Oct 1986, Sally Jayne Hill; 1 s (Sam b 10 Jan 1990); *Career* admitted slr 1974; ptnr Denton Hall; *Style*— Myles Cave-Browne-Cave; ✉ Denton Hall, Five Chancery Lane, Clifford's Inn, London EC4 (☎ 0171 242 1212)

CAVE-BROWNE-CAVE, Sir Robert; 16 Bt (E 1641), of Stanford, Northamptonshire; s of Sir Clement Charles Cave-Browne-Cave, 15 Bt (d 1945), and Dorothea Plewman, *née* Dwen; *b* 8 June 1929; *Educ* St George's Sch Vancouver, Univ Sch Victoria, British Columbia Univ; *m* 1, 1954 (m dis 1975), Lois Shirley, da of John Chalmers Huggard, of Winnipeg, Canada; 1 s (John Robert Charles b 1957), 1 da (Lise Irène b 1955); *m* 2, 1977, Joan Shirley, da of Dr Kenneth Ashe Peacock, of W Vancouver, BC; *Heir* s, John Robert Charles Cave-Brown-Cave b 22 June 1957; *Career* pres Cave and Co Ltd, Seabord Chemicals Ltd; *Style*— Sir Robert Cave-Browne-Cave, Bt; ✉ 20901–83 Avenue, RR11, Langley, British Columbia V3A 6Y3, Canada

CAVE-WOOD, Geoffrey Peter; s of John Frederick Cave-Wood (d 1986), and Norah Margaret Brisley, *née* Veal (d 1994); *b* 25 June 1938; *Educ* Dover Coll; *m* 8 June 1968, Rosalind Mary, da of Richard Clippingdale (d 1977); 2 da (Philippa b 21 Aug 1969, Anna b 28 Oct 1972); *Career* co-fndr and chm Cave Wood Transport Ltd 1962–93, fndr and md Kudos Logistics Development Ltd; chm Festival of Languages; MCIT, FIFF; *Recreations* sport, gardening, travel, European history; *Style*— Geoffrey Cave-Wood, Esq; ✉ The Manor House, Hull Place, Sholden, nr Deal, Kent; Kudos Logistics Development Ltd, Dover, Kent CT16 2HU (☎ 01304 828822, fax 01304 828833, car 0836 536653)

CAVELL, Rt Rev John Kingsmill; o s of William H G Cavell, of Deal, Kent, and Edith May, *née* Warner; *b* 4 Nov 1916; *Educ* Sir Roger Manwood's GS Kent, Queens' Coll Cambridge (MA), Wycliffe Hall Oxford; *m* 1942, Mary Grossett, da of Christopher Penman, of Devizes, Wilts; 1 da (Margaret); *Career* ordained 1940; vicar Christ Church Cheltenham 1952–62, St Andrew's Plymouth 1962–72 (formerly prebendary of Exeter Cathedral and rural dean of Plymouth); bishop of: Southampton 1972–84, HM Prisons 1975–85; asst bishop of Salisbury and hon canon of Salisbury Cathedral 1988–; vice pres Soc of Genealogists; *Recreations* genealogy, local history; *Style*— The Rt Rev John Cavell; ✉ 5 Constable Way, West Harnham, Salisbury SP2 8LN (☎ 01722 334782)

CAVENAGH-MAINWARING, Charles Rafe Gordon; s of Capt Maurice Kildare Cavenagh-Mainwaring, DSO, RN, and Iris Mary, *née* Denaro; *Educ* Downside; *m* 20 Oct 1973, Rosemary Lee, da of Capt Thomas Lee Reay Hardy (d 1982), of London; 1 s (Rupert William b 1976); *Career* Lt RM Reserve 1964–67, Lt HAC (RHA) 1967–73, transferred to RARO 1974; dir Hinton Hill Underwriting Agents Ltd 1987–89, conslt Allied Dunbar 1990–96, fin advsr Eggar Forrester 1996–; govr Salesian Coll; Knight of Honour and Devotion Sovereign Mil Order of Malta, Knight of Justice of the Sacred Mil Order of Constantine of St George; MCII; *Recreations* shooting, skiing, watching rugby union football, tennis; *Clubs* Hurlingham; *Style*— Charles Cavenagh-Mainwaring, Esq; ✉ 3 Bridge Lane, London SW11 3AD

CAVENDISH, Lady Elizabeth Georgiana Alice; CVO (1997, LVO 1976), JP (London 1961); da of late 10 Duke of Devonshire, KG, MBE, TD; *b* 24 April 1926; *Educ* privately; *Career* appointed an extra lady-in-waiting to HRH The Princess Margaret 1951–; chm: of N Westminster PSD 1980–83, Inner London Juvenile Courts 1983–86, Bd of Visitors Wandsworth Prison 1970–73; memb Advertising Standards Authy 1981–91; lay memb: the Senate of the Inns of Court Professional Conduct Ctee (Bar Council) 1983– (memb Senate's Disciplinary Ctee Tbnl 1983–), Cncl St Christopher's Hospice Sydenham 1991–96; chm Cancer Research Campaign 1981–96; memb: Marre Ctee on the Future of Legal Profession 1986–89, Press Complaints Cmmn 1991–96; *Style*— The Lady Elizabeth Cavendish, CVO, JP; ✉ 19 Radnor Walk, London SW3 4BP (☎ 0171 352 0774); Moor View, Edensor, Bakewell, Derbyshire DE45 1PH (☎ 01246 582204)

CAVENDISH, Michael Edward; s of Morton Edward Cavendish (d 1940), and Agnes Emily, *née* Pattison (d 1976); *b* 5 Aug 1936; *Educ* Victoria Coll Jersey, St Clement Dane's GS, Guy's Hosp Med Sch London (BSc, MB BS), Univ of Liverpool (MCh Orth); *m* 6 July 1963, Jean Ann, da of Edward Willis (d 1987); 5 s (Andrew Morton b 1964, Paul b 1965, Michael James b 1968, John Richard b 1972, James Edward b 1980), 1 da (Fiona Jane b 1966); *Career* orthopaedic house surgn Guy's Hosp 1961–68, orthopaedic registrar and sr registrar United Liverpool Hosps 1968–72, conslt orthopaedic surgn St Helens and Knowsley Hosp Trust 1972–; author of papers on joint replacement and related basic res (in particular joint replacement of elbow); chm Fund Raising Ctee St Helens YMCA 1989, pres St Helens Med Soc 1985, past pres and sec Liverpool Orthopaedic Circle; chm community service Rotary District 1280; memb: Liverpool Med Inst, SECEC 1987, Br Elbow and Shoulder Soc 1989; chm Newton Hosp Welfare Assoc; FRCS 1967, FBOA 1969; *Recreations* sailing; *Style*— Michael Cavendish, Esq; ✉ 88 Rodney Street, Liverpool L1 9AR (☎ 0151 708 6070)

CAVENDISH, Maj-Gen Peter Boucher; CB (1981), OBE (1969), DL (1989); s of Brig Ronald Valentine Cecil Cavendish, OBE, MC (ka 1943, gs of Lt-Col William Cavendish, Groom-in-Waiting to Queen Victoria, and Lady Emily Lambton, da of 1 Earl of Durham. William was gs of 1 Earl of Burlington of the 1831 creation and 1 cous of 7 Duke of Devonshire), and Helen, *née* Boucher; *b* 26 Aug 1925; *Educ* Abberley Hall Worcester, Winchester, New Coll Oxford; *m* 1952, Marion Loudon, 2 da of Robert Constantine, TD, JP, and Marie, *née* van Haaren (descended from William the Silent, Prince of Orange); 3 s (Ronald b 1954, Mark b 1955, Rupert b 1962); *Career* enlisted 1943, cmmnd Royal Dragoons 1945, 3 King's Own Hussars 1946 and Queen's Own Hussars 1958, 14/20 Hussars 1965 (CO 1966–69 and Hon Col 1976–81), Cmdt RAC Centre 1971–74, sec to Mil Ctee Int Mil Staff HQ NATO 1975–78, dir Armaments Standardisation and Interoperability Div 1978–81; chm: Mil Agency for Standardisation NATO HQ 1978–81, Royal British Legion (Derbyshire) 1981–94, Derbyshire FLAG 1992–; chm and vice pres SSAFA (Derbyshire) 1986–, Hon Col Queen's Own Mercian Yeo TAVR 1982–87, Col Cmdt the Yeomanry 1986–90, High Sheriff of Derbyshire 1986; Peak Park Planning Bd 1982–91 (vice chm 1987–91); *Style*— Maj-Gen Peter Cavendish, CB, OBE, DL; ✉ The Rock Cottage, Middleton-by-Youlgrave, Bakewell, Derby DE45 1LS (☎ 01629 636225, fax 01629 636325)

CAVENDISH, Hon Roderick Alexander; s and h of 7 Baron Waterpark, *qv*; *b* 10 Oct 1959; *m* 2 Sept 1989, Anne, da of Hon Luke Asquith (d 1994); 1 s (Luke Frederick b 17 Sept 1990); *Style*— The Hon Roderick Cavendish; ✉ 25 Archel Road, London W14 9QJ

CAWDOR, 7 Earl (UK 1827); Colin Robert Vaughan Campbell; also Baron Cawdor of Castlemartin (GB 1796) and Viscount Emlyn (UK 1827); the full designation of the Earldom in its patent of 1827 was Earl Cawdor of Castlemartin; s of 6 Earl Cawdor (d 1993), and his 1 w, Cathryn, *née* Hinde; *b* 30 June 1962; *Educ* Eton, St Peter's Coll Oxford; *m* 21 Oct 1994, Lady Isabella Rachel Stanhope, da of 11 Earl of Harrington; *Heir* bro, Hon Frederick William Campbell b 1965; *Style*— The Rt Hon the Earl Cawdor; ✉ Cawdor Castle, Nairn, Scotland; Cawdor Estate Office, Nairn IV12 5RD

CAWDRON, Peter Edward Blackburn; *Career* with Peat Marwick Mitchell 1961–70, S G Warburg & Co Ltd 1970–77, D'Arcy MacManus & Masius (advtg agency) 1977–83; Grand Metropolitan plc: joined 1983, gp planning dir 1983–87, gp strategy development dir 1987–, main bd dir 1993–; non-exec dir Compass Group plc; *Style*— Peter Cawdron, Esq; ✉ Grand Metropolitan plc, 8 Henrietta Place, London W1M 9AG (☎ 0171 518 5200, fax 0171 518 4641)

CAWLEY, Sir Charles Mills; kt (1965), CBE (1957, OBE 1946); s of John Cawley (d 1938), of Gillingham, Kent, and Emily Cawley; *b* 17 May 1907; *Educ* Sir Joseph Williamson's Mathematical Sch Rochester, Imperial Coll of Sci and Technol (DIC, MSc, PhD, DSc); *m* 1934, Florence (Sally) Mary Ellaline (d 1996), da of James Shepherd (d 1925), of York, and Ada Shepherd; 1 da; *Career* Capt Army Special Serv 1945; temporarily employed with the rank of Col by the Control Cmmn for Germany 1946–47, IDC 1949; employed Fuel Res Station DSIR 1929–53 (seconded to the Petroleum Warfare Dept 1939–45), dir DSIR HQ 1953–59, chief scientist Miny of Power 1959–67, cmmr Civil Serv 1967–69, ret; fell Imperial Coll of Sci and Technol; ARCS, CChem, FRSC, SFInstE, FRSA; *Publications* author of articles in various tech jls; *Style*— Sir Charles Cawley, CBE; ✉ 8 Glen Gardens, Ferring-by-Sea, Worthing, West Sussex BN12 5HG (☎ 01903 501850)

CAWLEY, 3 Baron (1918 UK); Sir Frederick Lee Cawley; 3 Bt (UK 1906); s of 2 Baron Cawley (d 1954), and Vivienne (d 1978, aged 100), da of Harold Lee, of Manchester and sis of Sir Kenneth Lee, 1 and last Bt; *b* 27 July 1913; *Educ* Eton, New Coll Oxford (MA); *m* 1944, Rosemary Joan, da of Reginald Edward Marsden, former bursar of Eton, and Hon Vere Dillon (d 1990, sis of 18 and 19 Viscounts Dillon), and whose twin sis Iris m Lord Cawley's yr bro, Hon Stephen Cawley; 6 s, 1 da; *Heir* s, Hon John Francis Cawley; *Career* served WWII Capt RA Leics Yeo (wounded) NW Europe; called to the Bar Lincoln's Inn 1938, practised at the Patent Bar 1946–73; dep chm Ctees House of Lords 1958–67, chm of many private bill select ctees; *Style*— The Rt Hon Lord Cawley; ✉ Bircher Hall, Leominster, Herefordshire HR6 0AX (☎ 01568 780218)

CAWLEY, Hon John Francis; s and h of 3 Baron Cawley, *qv*; *b* 28 Sept 1946; *Educ* Eton; *m* 1979, Regina Sarabia, da of late Marquès de Hazas (cr of 1873 by King Amadeo I), of Madrid; 3 s (William Robert Harold b 2 July 1981, Thomas Frederick José-Luis b 1982, Andrew David b 1988), 1 da (Susan Mary b 1980); *Style*— The Hon John Cawley; ✉ Castle Ground, Ashton, Leominster, Herefordshire HR6 0DN (☎ 01584 711209)

CAWLEY, Dr Michael Ian David; RD; s of late William Miller Seddon Cawley, CBE, of Bexhill, E Sussex, and Edith Mary, *née* Setchell; *b* 14 Oct 1935; *Educ* Caterham Sch Surrey, Bart's Med Coll Univ of London (MB BS, MD, MRCP); *Career* Nat Serv Lt and Capt RAMC 1960–62, surgn Lt Cdr RNR 1970–90; house offr 1959–60: Norwich, Bournemouth, Bart's; med registrar 1962–68: Bart's, Lewisham Hosp London; Aylwen res fell Bart's 1965–66, sr registrar and tutor in med Bristol Royal Hosp 1968–70, ARC visiting res fell Univ of Texas at Dallas 1971–72, lectr in rheumatology Univ of Manchester 1970–73; conslt physician rheumatology: Wrightington Hosp Lancs 1973–74, Southampton Univ Hosps 1974– (clinical tutor 1979–82, hon sr lectr 1990–); civilian conslt to RN 1989–; author of papers and chapters on rheumatic diseases; memb: Ctee on Rheumatology RCP 1983–89 (dist tutor 1987–93), Cncl Br Soc of Rheumatology 1986–88, Central Conslts and Specialists Ctee BMA 1986–93; Heberden roundsman Br Soc for Rheumatology 1992; pres S Wales S West and Wessex Rheumatology Club 1986–89; memb: American Coll of Rheumatology, Br Soc for Rheumatology, Br Soc for Immunology, Bone and Tooth Soc; Liveryman Worshipful Soc of Apothecaries 1990 (Freeman 1982); FRCP 1979; *Recreations* classical music, sailing, skiing; *Clubs* Royal Lymington Yacht, Royal Navy Sailing Association, Royal Southampton Yacht, Ski Club of Great Britain; *Style*— Dr Michael Cawley; ✉ 4 Pond Cottages, Braishfield, Romsey, Hants SO51 0PR (☎ 01794 368584); Southampton General Hospital, Shirley, Southampton SO9 4XY (☎ 01703 796770)

CAWS, Genevra Fiona Penelope Victoria (Mrs James Curtis); QC (1991); da of Richard Byron Caws, CBE, *qv*, of London, and Fiona Muriel Ruth Elton, *née* Darling; *b* 21 Feb 1949; *Educ* Notting Hill and Ealing HS, Lady Margaret Hall Oxford (scholar, MA, Gibbs prize for law); *m* 27 July 1985, James William Ockford Curtis, *qv*, s of Eric William Curtis, MC, of Bedford; 1 da (Polly Joanna Sarah Clare b 26 Nov 1987); *Career* called to the Bar Inner Temple 1970 (Inn scholar); *Recreations* fishing, skiing, sheep breeding; *Style*— Ms Genevra Caws, QC; ✉ 4/5 Gray's Inn Square, London WC1R 5AY (☎ 0171 404 5252)

CAWS, Richard Byron; CVO (1997), CBE (1984); s of Maxwell Caws, of London (d 1976), and Edith Caws (d 1979); *b* 9 March 1927; *m* 28 May 1948, Fiona Muriel Ruth Elton, da of Lt-Col Edwin Darling, MC, RA (d 1949); 2 s (Eian b 1950, Andrew b 1952, decd), 2 da (Genevra Fiona Penelope Victoria Caws, QC, *qv* b 1949, Alexandra b 1953); *Career* ptnr: Nightingale Page and Bennett Chartered Surveyors Kingston upon Thames 1944–60, Debenham Tewson and Chinnocks Chartered Surveyors London 1961–87; chm Caws & Morris Chartered Surveyors London 1987–, sr advsr Barclays de Zoete Wedd Property Advsy Gp 1993–, sr conslt (Real Estate) Goldman Sachs International Corp London 1987–93; non-exec dir Allied London Properties Plc 1995–; chm Jr Orgn RICS

1959–60, dep chm CNT Land 1994–96 (memb 1976–96), chm Property Ctee 1978–94); Crown Estates Cmmr 1971–96; memb: Dobry Ctee on Review of the Devpt Control System 1973–75, DOE Advsy Gp on Commercial Property Devpt 1973–77; dep chm DoE Property Advsy Gp 1978–88, memb Cncl Queen's Coll Harley Street, govr Royal Agricultural Coll Cirencester 1985–88, dir Br and Int Sailors' Soc; Hon Asst Worshipful Co of Chartered Surveyors (Master 1982–83); *Recreations* sailing, travel; *Clubs* Boodle's, Royal Thames Yacht, Little Ship; *Style*— Richard Caws, Esq, CVO, CBE; ✉ 36 Mount Park Rd, Ealing, London W5 2RS (☎ 0181 997 7739); Caws & Morris, Chancery House, 53/64 Chancery Lane, London WC2A 1QU (☎ 0171 404 4303, fax 0171 831 0390)

CAWTHRA, David Wilkinson; CBE (1997); s of Jack Cawthra (d 1974), and Dorothy, *née* Wilkinson; *b* 5 March 1943; *Educ* Heath GS Halifax, Univ of Birmingham (BSc); *m* Maureen Mabel, da of late Eric Arthur Williamson; 1 s (Richard Giles b 18 Oct 1969), 1 da (Caroline Eleanor b 30 Jan 1974); *Career* Mitchell Construction Co Ltd: jr engr 1964, site agent 1967, contracts mangr 1970; divnl dir Tarmac Construction Ltd 1976–79 (contracts mangr 1973–76), gen mangr Balfour Beatty Ltd 1981 (divnl dir 1979); md: Balfour Beatty Construction Ltd 1985, Balfour Beatty Ltd 1988; chief exec: Balfour Beatty Ltd 1990–91, Miller Group Ltd 1991–94; mgmnt conslt Cawthra & Co 1995–; Freeman City of London, memb Worshipful Co of Engineers; FICE 1980, CIMgt 1989, FEng 1990; *Recreations* hillwalking, golf, American history; *Clubs* RAC, Pall Mall; *Style*— David Cawthra, Esq, CBE, FEng; ✉ Redhurst, 68 Ravelston Dykes, Edinburgh EH12 6HF (☎ 0131 337 2155, fax 0131 346 1131)

CAYLEY, Dr (Arthur) Charles Digby; s of Dr Forde Everard de Wend Cayley, MBE, of Hove, Sussex, and Eileen Lillian, *née* Dalton; *b* 8 Nov 1946; *Educ* Middx Hosp Med Sch Univ of London (MB BS); *m* 1 Nov 1969, Jeanette Ann, da of George Richard Avery (d 1968), of Plymouth; 3 s (George b 1971, Adam b 1975, Seth b 1980); *Career* sr registrar in geriatric medicine and hon lectr Middx Hosp 1974–76, conslt physician in medicine of the elderly Parkside Health Tst and Central Middx Hosp Tst 1976–, clinical dir Care of the Elderly 1988–, recognised teacher of the Univ of London, hon clinical sr lectr St Mary's Hosp Med Sch Univ of London; contrib: Lancet, Br Med Jl, Res and Clinical Forums, Post Grad Med Jl, Br Jl of Hosp Med, Care of the Elderly; memb: Br Geriatric Soc (former chm of NW Thames region), BMA; memb Ctee of the Brent Triangle; FRCP 1989 (memb 1973); *Books* Hospital Geriatric Medicine (1987); *Recreations* walking, listening to classical music; *Style*— Dr Charles Cayley; ✉ Department of Medicine for the Elderly, Central Middlesex Hospital, Acton Lane, London NW10 7NS (☎ 0181 453 2184, fax 0181 961 1827)

CAYLEY, Sir Digby William David; 11 Bt (E 1661), of Brompton, Yorkshire; o s of William Arthur Seton Cayley (d 1964; ggs of 7 Bt), and Natalie Maud, *née* Grey (d 1994); suc his kinsman Maj Sir Kenelm Henry Ernest Cayley, 10 Bt, 1967; *b* 3 June 1944; *Educ* Malvern, Downing Coll Cambridge (MA); *m* 1, 19 July 1969 (m dis 1987), Christine Mary, o da of late Derek Francis Gaunt, of Ilkley; 2 da (Emma Jane b 1974, Catherine Mary b 1975); m 2, 1993, Cathryn M, elder da of Brian Russell, of Gosport, Hants; *Heir* kinsman, George Paul Cayley, *qv*; *Career* asst classics master: Portsmouth GS 1968–73, Stonyhurst Coll 1973–81; mangr C P Stockbridge Ltd Cambs 1982–83; antique dealer 1981–89; asst classics master: Marlborough Coll 1989–90, Abingdon Sch 1990–; *Style*— Sir Digby Cayley, Bt; ✉ Heylyns, 70A Bath Street, Abingdon, Oxon OX14 1EB

CAYLEY, George Paul; s of Capt Charles Paul Cuthbert Cayley, RE (d 1945; ggs of 7 Bt), and Cassandra Rosamond Elaine, *née* Legard; hp of kinsman, Sir Digby William David Cayley, 11 Bt, *qv*; *b* 23 May 1940; *Educ* Felsted; *m* 1967, Shirley Southwell, da of Frank Woodward Petford, of Kirby Cane, Norfolk; 2 s (Paul Alistair b 1971, Kevin George b 1974); *Style*— George Cayley, Esq; ✉ Applegarth, Brewers Green, Roydon, Diss, Norfolk IP22 3SD

CAYLEY, Michael Forde; s of Forde Everard De Wend Cayley, of Hove, Sussex, and Eileen Lilian, *née* Dalton; *b* 26 Feb 1950; *Educ* Brighton Coll, St John's Coll Oxford (MA); *m* 1987, Jennifer Athalie Jeffcoate, *née* Lytle; *Career* Inland Revenue: admin trainee 1971–73, private sec to Chm of the Price Cmmn 1973–75, princ Capital Tax Policy 1975–78, princ Co-ordinating Recruitment and Manpower Control 1978–81, princ Co Tax Policy 1981–82, asst sec Int Tax Policy 1982–86, asst sec Policy on Taxation of Capital Gains 1986–91, dir Capital and Valuation Div 1991–95, dir Fin Instns Div 1994–, dir Co Tax Div 1995–; *Books* Moorings (poems, 1971), Selected Poems of Richard Crashaw (ed, 1972), The Spider's Touch (poems, 1973); *Recreations* reading, piano-playing, walking, crosswords; *Style*— Michael Cayley, Esq; ✉ Board of Inland Revenue, Somerset House, Strand, London WC2R 1LB (☎ 0171 438 7739, fax 0171 438 7170)

CAYZER, Hon Charles William; s of 2 Baron Rotherwick (d 1996); *b* 26 April 1957; *Educ* Harrow; *m* 1985, Amanda Cosbie Sara, 2 da of John Squire, of Marbella, Spain; 1 s ((Charles) William b 14 July 1991), 1 da (Victoria Amanda b 22 June 1989); *Career* late The Life Guards; dir: Caledonia Investments PLC, Abacus Self Storage Ltd, The Cayzer Trust Company Ltd, The Sloane Club Group Ltd; *Style*— The Hon Charles Cayzer; ✉ Finstock Manor, Finstock, Oxon OX7 3DG

CAYZER, Sir James Arthur; 5 Bt (UK 1904), of Gartmore, Co Perth; s of Sir Charles William Cayzer, 3 Bt, MP (d 1940), and Eileen (Lady Cayzer, OBE) (d 1981), da of James Meakin (d 1912), and Emma Beatrice (d 1935), later wife of 3 Earl Sondes; suc his bro, Sir Nigel John Cayzer, 4 Bt, 1943; *b* 15 Nov 1931; *Educ* Eton; *Heir* kinsman, Lord Cayzer, *qv*; *Career* dir: Caledonia Investments 1958–88, Cayzer Trust Co 1988–; Liveryman Worshipful Co of Clockmakers; *Clubs* Carlton; *Style*— Sir James Cayzer, Bt; ✉ Kinpurnie Castle, Newtyle, Angus PH12 8TW (☎ 01828 650207)

CAYZER, Baron (Life Peer UK 1981), of St Mary Axe in the City of London; Sir (William) Nicholas Cayzer; 2 Bt (UK 1921), of Roffey Park, Horsham, Co Sussex; er s of Sir August Cayzer, 1 Bt, JP (d 1943, himself 3 s of Sir Charles Cayzer, 1 Bt, of Gartmore), and Ina, da of William Stancomb, JP; hp of 1 cous once removed, Sir James Cayzer, 5 Bt, of Gartmore, *qv*; *b* 21 Jan 1910; *Educ* Eton, CCC Cambridge; *m* 1935, Elizabeth Catherine (d 1995), da of late Owain Williams; 2 da (Hon Nichola (Hon Mrs Colvin) b 1937, Hon Elizabeth (Hon Mrs Gilmour) b 1946); *Heir* (to Btcy only) none; *Career* chm: British and Commonwealth Shipping Co Ltd 1958–87, Clan Line Steamers 1958–87 (dir 1938–87), Cayzer Irvine & Co Ltd 1958–87 (dir 1939–87), Union Castle Mail Steamship Co Ltd 1958–87 (dir 1956–87); pres Caledonia Investment plc 1994– (chm 1958–94); *Clubs* Brooks's; *Style*— The Rt Hon the Lord Cayzer; ✉ 95 Eaton Square, London SW1 (☎ 0171 235 5551); The Grove, Walsham-le-Willows, Suffolk (☎ 01359 259263)

CAYZER, Nigel Kenneth; s of Anthony Galliers-Pratt, of Mawley Hall, Worcs, and Angela, da of late Sir Charles Cayzer, 3 Bt; bro of Rupert Galliers-Pratt, *qv*; *b* 30 April 1954; *Educ* Eton; *m* 1986, Henrietta, da of Sir Richard Sykes, 7 Bt (d 1978); 2 s (Arthur James Richard b 24 March 1988, another b 30 Oct 1996), 2 da (Virginia Angela b 17 Jan 1990, Angelica Eileen Rose b 11 Sept 1992); *Career* chm Oriel Group plc; *Clubs* Turf, White's; *Style*— Nigel Cayzer, Esq; ✉ Thriepley House, Lundie, Dundee DD2 5PA (☎ 01382 581268)

CAZALET, Hon Lady (Camilla Jane); *née* Gage; da of 6 Viscount Gage, KCVO, by his 1 w, Hon Imogen Grenfell; *b* 12 July 1937; *Educ* Benenden; *m* 24 April 1965, Hon Sir Edward Stephen Cazalet (Hon Mr Justice Cazalet), *qv*; 2 s, 1 da; *Career* dir Lumley Cazalet 1967–; tstee Glyndebourne Arts Tst 1978–; memb Royal National Theatre Bd 1991–; *Recreations* theatre, opera, music, tennis; *Style*— The Hon Lady Cazalet; ✉ Shaw Farm, Plumpton Green, Lewes, Sussex BN7 3DG (☎ 01273 890 207); 58 Seymour Walk, London SW10 9NF (☎ 0171 352 0401)

CAZALET, Hon Mr Justice; Hon Sir Edward Stephen; kt (1988), DL (E Sussex 1989); s of Peter Victor Ferdinand Cazalet, JP, DL (d 1973), the race horse trainer, and his 1 w, Leonora, *née* Rowley, step da of Sir P G Wodehouse; *b* 26 April 1936; *Educ* Eton, ChCh Oxford; *m* 24 April 1965, Hon Camilla Jane, da of 7 Viscount Gage, KCVO (d 1982); 2 s (David b 1967, Hal b 1969), 1 da (Lara b 1973); *Career* subaltern Welsh Guards 1954–56; called to the Bar Inner Temple 1960 (bencher 1985), QC 1980, recorder of the Crown Court 1985–88, judge of the High Court of Justice (Family Div) 1988–; chm: Horse Race Betting Levy Appeal Tbnl 1979–88, CAB Royal Courts of Justice 1993–; fell Eton Coll 1989; *Recreations* riding, ball games, chess; *Clubs* Garrick, White's; *Style*— The Hon Mr Justice Cazalet, DL; ✉ Royal Courts of Justice, Strand, London WC2A 2LL

CAZALET, (Charles) Julian; s of Vice Adm Sir Peter Grenville Lyon Cazalet, KBE, CB, DSO, DSC (d 1982), of Newick, E Sussex, and Lady Beatrice Elise, *née* Winterbotham; *b* 29 Nov 1947; *Educ* Uppingham, Magdalene Coll Cambridge (MA); *m* 29 Nov 1986, Jennifer Clare, da of Maurice Nelson Little (d 1985), of Laverton, Glos; 1 s (Charles b 1987), 1 da (Fleur b 1989); *Career* ptnr Cazenove and Co Stockbrokers 1978–; FCA 1977; *Recreations* sailing, skiing; *Clubs* City Univ (chm 1994–); *Style*— Julian Cazalet, Esq; ✉ 38 Norland Sq, London W11 4PZ (☎ 0171 727 1756); Cazenove and Co, 12 Tokenhouse Yard, London EC2R 7AN (☎ 0171 588 2828, fax 0171 606 9205)

CAZALET, Sir Peter Grenville; kt (1989); s of Vice Adm Sir Peter Grenville Lyon Cazalet, KBE, CB, DSO, DSC (d 1982), of Newick, E Sussex, and Lady Beatrice Elise Cazalet; *b* 26 Feb 1929; *Educ* Uppingham, Magdalene Coll Cambridge (MA); *m* 1957, Jane Jennifer, yr da of Charles Harry Rew (d 1972), of Guernsey; 3 s (Peter Charles b 1959, Andrew b 1960, William b 1968); *Career* dep chm BP Petroleum Co plc 1986–89 (md 1981–89); dir: P and O Steam Navigation Co Ltd 1980–, De la Rue plc 1983–95; chm APV plc 1989–96, non-exec dep chm GKN plc 1989–96; chm Armed Forces Pay Review Body 1989–93, memb Top Salaries Pay Review Body 1989–94; govr The Wellcome Tst 1992–96 (tstee 1989–92); memb Ct of Assts Worshipful Co of Tallow Chandlers (Master 1991–92), Liveryman Worshipful Co of Shipwrights; *Recreations* theatre, travel; *Clubs* Brooks's, Royal Wimbledon Golf, MCC; *Style*— Sir Peter Cazalet; ✉ 22 Hill Street, London W1X 7FU (☎ 0171 496 4423, fax 0171 496 4436)

CAZENOVE, Bernard Michael de Lerisson; TD; s of late David Michael de Lerisson Cazenove, and Euphemia, *née* Maclean; *b* 14 June 1947; *Educ* Radley, RMA Sandhurst; *m* 19 Dec 1971, Caroline June, da of Richard Moore (d 1963), of Wellington, NZ; 2 s (Richard b 1974, George b 1977), 1 da (Edwina b 1984); *Career* cmmnd Coldstream Guards 1967, ADC to HE Governor General of New Zealand 1970, transferred Parachute Regt (TA) 1973; ptnr Cazenove & Co (stockbrokers) 1982– (joined 1973); *Clubs* White's, Pratt's, Rock Sailing; *Style*— Bernard Cazenove, Esq, TD; ✉ Brocas, Ellisfield, Basingstoke, Hampshire RG22 2QS; Cazenove & Co, 12 Tokenhouse Yard, London EC2R 7AN (☎ 0171 588 2828)

CAZENOVE, Christopher de Lerisson; s of Brig Arnold de Lerisson Cazenove, CBE, DSO, MVO (d 1969; descended from Arnaud de Cazenove, Seigneur de Lerisson, of Guienne, France who m 1, 1578, Anne de Bruil, and m 2, 1596, Marie de Laumond), and Elizabeth Laura (d 1994), 3 da of late Sir Eustace Gurney, JP, of Walsingham Abbey, Norfolk; *b* 17 Dec 1943; *Educ* Eton, Bristol Old Vic Theatre Sch; *m* 12 Sept 1973 (m dis 1993), Angharad Mary Rees, *qv*, the actress, da of Prof Linford Rees, CBE, FRCP, FRCPsych, *qv*; 2 s (Linford b 20 July 1974, Rhys William b 12 Dec 1976); *Career* actor; *Theatre* West End incl: The Lionel Touch 1969, My Darling Daisy 1970, The Winslow Boy 1970, Joking Apart 1979, The Sound of Music 1992; Broadway incl: Goodbye Fidel 1980; Aust incl: Peter Pan 1996; *Television* incl: The Regiment 1971–72, The British Hero, The Pathfinders, K is for Killer 1973, The Duchess of Duke Street 1976–77, Jenny's War, Lace II, Dynasty 1986–87, Ticket to Ride 1988–89, To Be the Best 1990, The Way to Dusty Death 1994; *Films* incl: Royal Flash 1975, East of Elephant Rock 1976, Zulu Dawn 1979, Eye of the Needle 1980, From A Far Country 1980, Heat and Dust 1982, Until September 1984, The Fantasist 1985, Souvenir 1987, Tears in the Rain 1987, Hold my Hand I'm Dying 1988, Three Men And a Little Lady 1990, Aces 1991, The Proprietor 1995; *Style*— Christopher Cazenove, Esq; ✉ Peters Fraser & Dunlop Ltd, 503 The Chambers, Chelsea Harbour, Lots Road, London SW10 0XF (☎ 0171 352 4446, fax 0171 352 7356)

CECIL, Hon Anthony Robert; s and h of 3 Baron Rockley, *qv*, and Lady Sarah Primrose Beatrix, da of 7 Earl Cadogan, MC; *b* 29 July 1961; *Educ* Eton, Cambridge; *m* 9 Jan 1988, Katherine Jane, da of G A Whalley, of Chipperfield, Herts; 1 s (William Evelyn b 7 July 1996), 2 da (Emily Sarah b 15 Nov 1991, Lydia Elizabeth b 3 Jan 1994); *Recreations* rugby, squash, tennis; *Style*— The Hon Anthony Cecil; ✉ Lytchett Heath, Poole, Dorset (☎ 01202 622228)

CECIL, Henry Richard Amherst; 4 s (twin) of Hon Henry Kerr Auchmuty Cecil (ka 1942), and Elizabeth Rohays Mary, *née* Burnett of Leys (later Lady Boyd-Rochfort); *b* 11 Jan 1943; *Educ* Canford, RAC Cirencester; *m* 1, 18 Oct 1966 (m dis), Julia, da of Sir (Charles Francis) Noel Murless (d 1987); 1 s (Noel b 3 Feb 1973), 1 da (Katrina b 17 June 1971); m 2, 15 Feb 1992, Natalie, da of Richard Payne; 1 s (Jake Henry Richard Amherst b 22 Feb 1994); *Career* champion racehorse trainer on the flat (10 times); trained three Derby winners, three Oaks winners, two 2000 Guineas winners, four 1000 Guineas winners, and four St Leger winners; *Books* On The Level; *Recreations* gardening, shooting; *Style*— Henry Cecil, Esq; ✉ Warren Place, Newmarket, Suffolk CB8 8QQ (☎ 01638 662387); office ☎ 01638 662192, fax 01638 669005)

CECIL, Jonathan Hugh; s of Lord Edward Christian David Gascoyne Cecil, CH (d 1986), of Cranbourne, and Rachel Mary Veronica, *née* MacCarthy (d 1982); *b* 22 Feb 1939; *Educ* Eton, New Coll Oxford (BA), LAMDA; *m* 1, 1963, Vivien Sarah Frances, da of David Granville Heilbron (d 1993), of Glasgow; m 2, 3 Nov 1976, Anna Sharkey, *qv*; *Career* actor and writer; contrib to: The Independent, The Spectator, TLS; regular book reviewer for The Evening Standard; memb Exec Ctee Actor's Church Union 1993; Earphones Award 1996; *Theatre* incl: A Heritage and its History 1965, Halfway Up the Tree 1967, The Ruling Class 1969, Lulu 1971, Cowardy Custard 1972, The Bed Before Yesterday 1976, The Orchestra 1981, Good Morning Bill 1987, Uncle Vanya 1988, Poor Nanny 1989, The Dressmaker 1990, The Family Reunion 1992, Twelfth Night 1992, The Taming of the Shrew 1993, The Incomparable Max (one man show) 1994, 1995 and 1996, The Seagull 1995, The Importance of Being Ernest 1995, Pride and Prejudice 1996; *Television* incl: Maggie 1964, Love's Labours Lost 1975, Gulliver in Lilliput 1981, The Puppet Man 1984, 13 at Dinner 1985, Murder in 3 Acts 1987, The Sign of Command 1989, F.L.I.P. 1991, Beethoven Is Not Dead 1992, The Rector's Wife 1993, Late Flowering Lust 1993, Murder Most Horrid 1993, Madawiad Arthur 1994, Just William 1994, The Entertainers 1995; has also starred in numerous comedy series; *Films* incl: The Great St Trinian's Train Robbery 1965, Otley 1968, Catch Me a Spy 1971, Barry Lyndon 1973, Joseph Andrews 1976, History of the World Part 1 1980, E la Nave Va (Fellini) 1983, The Fool 1990, Tchin Tchin 1990, Kleptophilia 1992, As You Like It 1992; *Audio* recorded twelve Jeeves novels and others for Chivers Audio Books 1984–95; *Recreations* writing, reading, history of theatre and music hall; *Clubs* Garrick; *Style*— Jonathan Cecil, Esq; ✉ c/o Kate Feast Management, 10 Primrose Hill Studios, Fitzroy Road, London NW1 8TR (☎ 0171 586 5502, fax 0171 586 9817)

CECIL, Rear Adm Sir (Oswald) Nigel Amherst; KBE (1979), CB (1978); s of Cdr the Hon Henry Cecil, OBE, RN (d 1962; himself 4 s of Baroness Amherst of Hackney by her husb Lord William Cecil, CVO, 3 s of 3 Marquess of Exeter), and Hon Yvonne Cornwallis (d 1983; 3 da of 1 Baron Cornwallis); *b* 11 Nov 1925; *Educ* Ludgrove, RNC

Dartmouth; *m* 1961, Annette (CStJ 1980), er da of Maj Robert Barclay, TD, of Bury Hill, Dorking, Surrey; 1 s (Robert Barclay Amherst b 1965); *Career* joined Navy 1939, Flag Lt to Adm Br Jt Services Mission Washington DC 1948–50, Cdr 1959, Chief Staff Officer London Division RNR 1959–61; cmd: HMS Corunna 1961–63, HMS Royal Arthur 1963–66, Capt 1966; Central Defence Staff 1966–69, Capt (D) Dartmouth Trg Sqdn and in cmd HM Ships Tenby and Scarborough 1969–71, Cdre Sr Br Naval Offr S Africa, naval attaché Cape Town and in cmd HMS Afrikander 1971–73, dir Naval Operational Requirements 1974–75, Naval ADC to HM The Queen 1975, Rear Adm 1975, Cdr Br Forces Malta and flag offr Malta 1975–79, Cdr NATO S Eastern Mediterranean 1975–77, ret 1979; Lt-Govr IOM and pres of Tynwald 1980–85; pres: St John Cncl IOM 1980–85, St John Ambulance IOW 1991–96, St John Cncl IOW 1996–; vice pres Royal UK Beneficent Assoc 1991–, vice patron Naval Offrs Assoc of Southern Africa 1973–; KStJ 1980 (OStJ 1971); FIMgt 1980; *Clubs* White's, Lansdowne, MCC; *Style*— Rear Adm Sir Nigel Cecil, KBE, CB; ✉ The Old Rectory, Shorwell, Isle of Wight PO30 3JL

CECILLON, Jean-Francois; *b* 24 Sept 1958; *Educ* Institut Superieur De Gestion Paris (MBA); *m* 22 May 1982, Catherine Belougne; 1 da (Jessica Flore b 20 Aug 1991), 1 s (Johan Laurent b 4 April 1995); *Career* professional mangr A & R Chappell Intersong France 1983–85, mktg mangr EMI France 1986–87 (product mangr 1985–86), mktg dir Polygram France 1987–90, vice pres Mktg EMI Int UK 1990–92, md EMI UK 1992–95, pres and chief exec offr EMI Record Group UK 1995–; dir BPI 1995–; *Clubs* Queen's, Mosiman's; *Style*— Jean-Francois Cecillon, Esq; ✉ EMI Records Group UK and Ireland, EMI House, 43 Brook Green, London W6 7EF (☎ 0171 605 5151, fax 0171 605 5062)

CELESTIN, Dr (Louis) Roger; s of Louis Abel Celestin, CBE, MC (d 1966), of Mauritius, and Marie Marcelle, *née* Legris (d 1962); *b* 19 Oct 1925; *Educ* Royal Coll of Mauritius (Gold medal in Sci), UCL (MB BS); *m* 1, 6 Aug 1954 (m dis 1967), Patricia Irene, da of Herbert Bernard Thomas; 2 da (Claire b 1957, Michele b 1958); m 2, 4 July 1968, Shirley June, da of Harry Gledhill; *Career* surgn and gastroenterologist; registrar Royal Postgrad Med Sch Hammersmith Hosp, sr registrar Bristol Royal Infirmary, conslt surgn Frenchay Hosp 1968–90, clinical lectr Univ of Bristol 1968–90; author of chapters in numerous maj textbooks, inventor of oesophageal prosthesis and oesophageal dilators; winner Br Soc of Endoscopy prize 1980; pres: Anglo-French Med Soc 1985–93, Cossham Med Soc 1989–90; past pres Ileostomy Assoc, ARRIS and Gale lectr RCS 1973; FRCS, FRCSEd; memb: Br Soc of Endoscopy, Br Soc of Gastroenterology; *Books* Disorders of the Oesophagus (with Watson, 1984), The Surgery and Management of Intestinal Stomas (1987); *Recreations* travelling, numismatics, opera; *Style*— Dr Roger Celestin; ✉ Sutton House, Clifton Down, The Promenade, Clifton, Bristol BS8 3HT (☎ 0117 973 7360)

CELLAN-JONES, (Alan) James Gwynne; s of Cecil John Cellan-Jones, OBE (Lt-Col RAMC, d 1968), of Swansea, and Lavinia Alicia Sophia, *née* Johnson-Dailey, MBE (d 1963); *b* 13 July 1931; *Educ* Dragon Sch Oxford, Lycée Jaccard Lausanne, Charterhouse, St John's Coll Cambridge (BA, MA); *m* 2 April 1957, Margaret Shirley, da of Ernest William Eavis (d 1972), of Burnham on Sea; 3 s (Rory b 1958, *qv*, Simon b 1962, Deiniol b 1965), 1 da (Lavinia b 1967); *Career* director; Nat Serv cmmnd RE 1953, Troop Cdr Korea later Airborne; BBC 1963 (joined as callboy 1954); W D Thomas meml lectr Univ Coll Swansea 1992; memb: Cncl DGGB (vice chm 1989, chm 1991–94), BAFTA (chm 1983–85, vice chm 1995–); FRSA 1992; *Productions* as freelance dir: Forsyte Saga, Portrait of a Lady, Jennie (with Lee Remick), Caesar and Cleopatra (with Alec Guinness), The Kingfisher (with Rex Harrison), Bequest to the Nation (with Peter Finch and Glenda Jackson), Much Ado About Nothing (Royal Lyceum Edinburgh), The Adams Chronicles NY 1976; head of plays BBC TV 1976–79; also dir School Play, The Day Christ Died, A Fine Romance, Oxbridge Blues, Comedy of Errors, Fortunes of War, A Perfect Hero, The Gravy Train Goes East, Maigret, Harnessing Peacocks, Chouchou (France), The Vacillations of Poppy Carew; *Awards* DGA Award 1976, Br Critics' Award 1983 and 1987, US Cable Award 1985, Golden Nymph Award for Best Film (Monte Carlo Festival) 1994; *Recreations* scuba diving, wine making; *Clubs* Garrick; *Style*— James Cellan-Jones, Esq; ✉ 19 Cumberland Rd, Kew, Surrey (☎ 0181 940 8742); Worthy Cottage, Pilton, nr Shepton Mallet, Somerset; c/o Jane Annakin, William Morris Agency (UK) Ltd, 20th Century House, 31 Soho Square, London W1V 6DG (☎ 0171 434 2191, fax 0171 437 0238)

CELLAN-JONES, (Nicholas) Rory; s of James Cellan-Jones, *qv*, of Kew, Surrey, and Sylvia, *née* Parish; *b* 17 Jan 1958; *Educ* Dulwich, Jesus Coll Cambridge (BA); *m* 7 April 1990, Diane Coyle; 1 s (Adam Joseph b 13 Sept 1990); *Career* BBC TV: researcher Look North BBC Leeds 1981–83, 1983–85 (sub ed TV News London, asst prodr Newsnight, prodr TV News Special Projects), reporter BBC Wales Cardiff 1986–88, reporter Breakfast Time 1988, business reporter TV News and Money Programme 1989–, business corr BBC TV business progs 1994–; *Style*— Rory Cellan-Jones, Esq; ✉ BBC TV, Wood Lane, London W12 (☎ 0181 576 7486, e-mail r.cellan-jones@bbcnc.org.uk)

CELLIER, Peter François; s of Frank Cellier (d 1948), and Phyllis Maud, *née* Shannaw; *b* 12 July 1928; *Educ* Harrow, Brighton Sch of Music; *m* 12 June 1950, Nonie, da of Cecil Lawrence Pashley; 1 da (Jeannine b 1952); *Career* actor; *Theatre* Stratford-upon-Avon: Hamlet, Merchant of Venice, Othello, Loves' Labour Lost, Measure for Measure, Toad of Toad Hall, As You Like It, King John, Julius Caesar, Cymbeline; Old Vic: Twelfth Night, Hamlet, Henry V; Chichester Festival Theatre: The Work House Donkey, St Joan, The Royal Hunt of the Sun; NT at the Old Vic (fndr memb): Hamlet, The Royal Hunt of the Sun, Edward II, Andorra, The Master Builder, Mother Courage, The Crucible, Philoctetes, A Flea in her Ear, Juno and the Paycock, Love for Love, The Recruiting Officer, Volpone, Rosencrantz and Guildenstern are Dead; West End: The Winslow Boy, A Private Matter, The Case in Question, Me and My Girl, Body and Soul, Ross, An Absolute Turkey; Theatre Royal Windsor: The Bad Soldier Smith, Up and Running, Mind Millie for Me; *Television* incl: The Scarlet Pimpernel, Softly Softly, A Matter of Honour, The New Avengers, The Saint, Rumpole of the Bailey, Crown Court, It Ain't 'Arf 'Ot Mum, Shelley, Code Name Icarus, Tales of the Unexpected, Tandoori Nights, Sorry, Pygmalion, The Assassin, Callan, Country Matters, Mansfield Park, Upstairs, Downstairs, Special Branch, A Most Public Affair, The Professionals, Armchair Thriller, Yes Minister, The Gentle Touch, Doctor Who, Up the Elephant and Round the Castle, Yes Prime Minister, Brush Strokes, Small World, KYTV, Chancer, Paradise Postponed, Don't Wait Up, Password, Bergerac, Keeping up Appearances, Never the Twain, Europe on the Brink; *Films* incl: A Suitable Case for Treatment, Sink the Bismark, Luther, Young Winston, Holocaust 2000, Jabberwocky, Man Friday, The Prince and the Pauper, Man About the House, Passage to India, A Room with a View, Clockwise, Personal Services, Shadow under the Sun, Chariots of Fire, The Last Days of Pompeii, Howard's End, The Red Fox, Andrew and Fergie, The Remains of the Day, The Luck of Barry Lindon, I'll Take Manhattan, E la Nave Va, One Against the Wind, Bahji on the Beach, How to Speak Japanese, Stanley's Dragon, Mrs Dalloway, Ain't Misbehavin; *Recreations* shooting, photography, restoration of old house, music; *Style*— Peter Cellier, Esq; ✉ c/o Peters Fraser & Dunlop, 503 The Chambers, Chelsea Harbour, Lots Road, London SW10 0XF (☎ 0171 352 4446, fax 0171 352 8135)

CHACKSFIELD, Air Vice-Marshal Sir Bernard Albert; KBE (1968, OBE 1945), CB (1961); s of Edgar Chacksfield (d 1919), of Ilford, Essex; *b* 13 April 1913; *Educ* County HS, RAF Halton, RAF Cranwell; *m* 1, 1937, Myrtle Elsa Alexena (d 1984), da of Walter Matthews (d 1947), of Rickmansworth, Herts; 2 s, 2 da; m 2, 1985, Elizabeth Beatrice, da of James Meek (d 1969), and wid of Frederick Ody (d 1982); *Career* joined RAF 1928, Gp Capt 1951, Air Cdre 1956 (Fighter Cmd), Actg Air Vice-Marshal SASO Tech Trg Cmd 1960, Air Vice-Marshal AOC No 22 Group 1960–62, Cmdt-Gen RAF Regt and Inspr Ground Defence 1963–68, ret 1968; chief cmmr Scouts for England 1968–80, pres: Soc Model Aeronautical Engrs (now Br Model Flying Assoc) 1969–, Bourne End Community Assoc 1995–; chm: Burma Star Assoc 1979–, Bd Royal Masonic Hosp 1989–92; CEng, FRAeS; *Recreations* travelling, youth work, flying, sailing, music, drama; *Clubs* RAF; *Style*— Air Vice-Marshal Sir Bernard Chacksfield, KBE, CB; ✉ No 8 Rowan House, Bourne End, Bucks SL8 5TG (☎ 01628 520829)

CHADD, David Francis Lanfear; s of Joseph Chadd (d 1976), and Hilda Birica Lanfear (d 1983); *b* 10 Sept 1943; *Educ* Keble Coll Oxford (MA); *m* 23 Sept 1983, Julia Mary Martin, da of Dr Alan John Rowe, OBE, of Haughley Grange, Stowmarket, Suffolk; 2 s (Alexander b 1984, Tobias b 1988), 1 da (Helena b 1986); *Career* asst lectr Univ of Durham 1966–67; UEA: lectr 1967–79, sr lectr 1979, dean Sch of Art History and Music 1987–90; sec Henry Bradshaw Soc 1985–, memb Int Advsy Editorial Bd Plainsong and Medieval Music 1989–; memb Ctee Norfolk Gardens Tst 1991–95; numerous articles in learned jls and collections; *Recreations* gardening, mountaineering, visual arts, repairing old houses; *Style*— David Chadd, Esq; ✉ Thornage Old Rectory, Holt, North Norfolk (☎ 01263 861096)

CHADDER, Roger Vivyan James; s of William James Chadder (d 1967), of Cheam, Surrey, and Winifred Hepworth (d 1973); *b* 9 Nov 1937; *Educ* Dulwich, Clare Coll Cambridge (MA); *m* 1961, Rosemary, da of Thomas Gibson; 1 s (Philip Thomas James b 1966), 2 da (Clare Mary b 1964, Kate Frances b 1969); *Career* Peat Marwick Mitchell & Co (now KPMG): articled to Sir Ronald Leach 1959, qualified 1962, ptnr 1973, gen ptnr 1980, conslt 1993–; hon treas Royal Philanthropic Soc 1993–; FCA 1972; *Books* Leasing Finance (contrib, 1990); *Recreations* music, golf; *Clubs* RAC, Royal Wimbledon Golf; *Style*— Roger Chadder, Esq; ✉ 64 Church Road, Wimbledon, London SW19 5AA (☎ and fax 0181 944 5926); KPMG, 1 Puddle Dock, Blackfriars, London EC4V 3PD (☎ 0171 311 8320, fax 0171 311 8718)

CHADERTON-MATOS, HE Roy; s of Roydel Y Chaderton-Farrier, and Elena, *née* Matos; *b* 17 Aug 1942, Caracas, Venezuela; *Educ* Central Univ of Venezuela (law); *Career* Venezuelan diplomat; second sec Poland 1969–72, first sec FRG 1973, first sec Miny of Foreign Affrs 1973–75, first sec Canada 1975–77, cnsllr Belgium 1977–78, cnsllr Perm Mission of Venezuela to UN NY 1978–79, cnsllr Miny of Foreign Affrs 1979, min consllr Miny of Foreign Affrs 1979–82, ambass-alternate Perm Rep of Venezuela to UN NY 1982–83, ambass at large Miny of Foreign Affrs 1983–85, ambass to Gabon 1985–87, ambass to Norway 1987–90, DG of Foreign Policy Miny of Foreign Affrs 1990–93, ambass to Canada 1993–94, ambass to Ct of St James's 1995–; *Decorations* Bernardo O'Higgins (Chile), Knight of Madara (Bulgaria), Francisco de Miranda (Venezuela), Mayo (Argentina), Cruzeiro do Sul (Brazil), Saint Olav (Norway); *Recreations* sport (tennis and jogging); *Style*— HE Mr Roy Chaderton-Matos; ✉ Venezuelan Embassy, 1 Cromwell Road, London SW7 (☎ 0171 584 4206, fax 0171 589 8887)

CHADLINGTON, Baron (Life Peer UK 1996), of Dean in the County of Oxfordshire; Peter Selwyn Gummer; s of Rev Canon Selwyn Gummer, and (Margaret) Sybille Vera, *née* Mason (d 1993); bro of Rt Hon John Selwyn Gummer, MP, *qv*; *b* 24 Aug 1942; *Educ* King's Sch Rochester, Selwyn Coll Cambridge (BA, MA); *m* 23 Oct 1982, Lucy Rachel, da of Antony Ponsonby Dudley-Hill (d 1969), of Sandle Manor, Fordingbridge, Hants; 1 s (Hon James b 4 Aug 1990), 3 da (Hon Naomi b 10 Jan 1984, Hon Chloe b 17 Nov 1985, Hon Eleanor b 5 Aug 1988); *Career* Portsmouth and Sunderland Newspaper Group 1964–65, Viyella International 1965–66, Hodgkinson & Partners 1966–67, Industrial & Commercial Finance Corporation (later 3i Group) 1967–74, chm Shandwick International plc 1974–; non-exec dir: CIA Group PLC 1990–94, Halifax Building Society 1994– (non-exec dir London Bd 1990–94); non-exec memb: NHS Policy Bd 1991–95, Arts Cncl of GB 1991–94, Arts Cncl of England 1994–96 (chm Arts Cncl Lottery Bd until 1996); chm: Understanding Industry Tst 1991–95, Royal Opera House 1996–; FRSA, FInstD, FIPR, fell Inst of Mktg; *Recreations* opera, cricket, rugby; *Clubs* Garrick, MCC, Hurlingham, Carlton; *Style*— The Rt Hon Lord Chadlington; ✉ Shandwick International plc, 61 Grosvenor Street, London W1X 9DA (☎ 0171 408 2232, fax 0171 493 3048)

CHADWICK, Charles McKenzie; CBE (1992, OBE 1985); s of Trevor McKenzie Chadwick (d 1976), and Marjorie Charlotte Louisa Elton, *née* Freeman; *b* 31 July 1932; *Educ* Charterhouse, Trinity Coll Univ of Toronto (BA); *m* 23 Jan 1965, Evelyn Ingeborg, da of Rheinhold Ihlenfeldt (d 1988); 1 s (James b 16 Oct 1966); *Career* 2 Lt Glos and Royal Leics Regt 1950–52; dist offr HMOCS Northern Rhodesia 1958–64, head of admin trg Staff Trg Coll Lusaka 1965–67 (lectr 1964), Mgmnt Servs Dept Br Cncl 1968–70, dep rep Kenya 1970–73, dep rep Nigeria 1973–75, regnl dir Sao Paulo Brazil 1975–76, dir Specialist Tours Dept 1976–80, provincial election supervisor Zimbabwe 1980, admin Tech Educn and Trg Overseas 1981, rep Canada 1981–88, rep (then dir) Poland 1989–92; memb Cwlth Observer Team: Ghanaian presidential elections 1992, Pakistan Nat Assembly elections 1993; regnl co-ordinator Kwazulu-Natal Euro Union Election Unit SA 1994, FCO observer Uganda parly elections 1996, OSCE supr Bosnia elections 1996; govr Hampstead Sch 1993–; *Style*— Charles Chadwick, Esq, CBE; ✉ 25a Denning Rd, London NW3 1ST (☎ 0171 794 2866)

CHADWICK, Prof David William; s of Harold Chadwick (d 1979), of Rochdale, and Elsie, *née* Mills (d 1983); *b* 14 Dec 1946; *Educ* Bolton Sch, St Catherine's Coll Oxford (MA, DM); *m* 30 July 1969, Vivienne Ruth, da of Richard Jones (d 1979), of St Helens; 1 s (Benjamin b 1975), 1 da (Ellen b 1977); *Career* lectr in neurology Univ Dept of Neurology Inst of Psychiatry London 1974–76, first asst in neurology Univ of Newcastle-upon-Tyne 1978–79, conslt neurologist Mersey RHA 1979–92, prof of neurology Univ of Liverpool 1993–; sec Br Branch Int League Against Epilepsy 1984–88; FRCP 1984; *Books* Living With Epilepsy (1987), Medical Neurology (1989); *Style*— Prof David Chadwick; ✉ Department of Medicine and Surgical Neurology, Walton Hospital, Rice Lane, Liverpool L9 1AE (☎ 0151 525 3611 ext 4348)

CHADWICK, Dr Derek James; s of Dennis Edmund Chadwick (d 1955), and Ida Chadwick (d 1979); *b* 9 Feb 1948; *Educ* St Joseph's Coll Blackpool, Keble Coll Oxford (Pfizer industl scholar, Open scholar, sr scholar, BA, BSc, MA, DPhil); *m* 20 Dec 1980, Susan, da of Dr (Hugh) Alastair Reid, OBE (d 1983); 2 s (Andrew John b 1984, (Frederick) Mark b 1986); *Career* ICI fell Univ of Cambridge 1972–73, Prize fell Magdalen Coll Oxford 1973–77, Royal Soc Euro exchange fell ETH-Zürich (Switzerland) 1975–77, lectr, sr lectr then reader Univ of Liverpool 1977–88, dir The Ciba Fndn London 1988–; Emilio Noelting visiting prof Ecole Nationale Supérieur Mulhouse France 1988, visiting prof Univ of Trondheim Norway 1995–; vice chm Assoc of Medical Research Charities 1994–96; memb: Scientific Ctee Louis Jeantet Fndn Geneva 1989–, Steering Ctee Media Resource Serv Scientists' Inst for Public Information NY 1989–; sec Hague Club of Directors of Euro Fndns 1993–; Liveryman Worshipful Soc of Apothecaries 1990; FRSC 1982; *Books* contrib to: Aromatic & Heteroaromatic Chemistry (1979), Comprehensive Heterocyclic Chemistry (1984), The Research and Academic Users' Guide to the IBMPC (1988), Physical and Theoretical Aspects of 1H-Pyrroles (1990); author of over 100 pubns incl papers in learned jls, book chapters and computer progs; *Recreations* gardening, music, skiing; *Style*— Dr Derek Chadwick; ✉ 4 Bromley Ave, Bromley, Kent BR1 4BQ (☎ 0181 460 3332); The Ciba Foundation, 41 Portland Place, London W1N 4BN (☎ 0171 636 9456, fax 0171 436 2840)

CHADWICK, Fiona Jane; da of William Max Barrowclough Chadwick (d 1989), and Anne, *née* Whitehead; *b* 13 May 1960; *Educ* Royal Ballet Sch; *m* 1, 17 March 1990 (m dis), Antony Peter Dowson, *qv*, s of John Robert Dowson; 1 da (Emily b 23 April 1991); m 2, 3 Aug 1996, Robert Cave, s of Sir Richard Cave; *Career* ballerina; Royal Ballet Co: joined 1978, soloist 1981, princ 1984; danced leading roles incl: Swan Lake, Sleeping Beauty, Giselle, The Nutcracker Suite, Romeo and Juliet, Prince of the Pagodas, La Fille Mal Gardée, Cinderella, Ride of Spring, Apollo, Bayadere, Scenes of Ballet, Firebird, Daiser de la Fee, Gloria, Galanteries Pursuit; guest appearance AMP Swan Lake; currently ballet administrator Royal Ballet Sch White Lodge; *Style—* Miss Fiona Chadwick; ✉ Royal Opera House, Covent Garden, London WC2 (☎ 0171 240 1200)

CHADWICK, Prof (Sir) Henry; KBE (1989); s of John Chadwick (d 1931), of Bromley, Kent, and Edith, *née* Horrocks; bro of Sir John Chadwick (d 1987) and Prof (William) Owen Chadwick, *qv*; *b* 23 June 1920; *Educ* Eton, Magdalene Coll Cambridge (DD); *m* 1945, Margaret Elizabeth, da of late W Pemell Brownrigg, of Moorhill, Co Kildare; *Career* formerly regius prof of divinity and canon of Ch Ch Oxford (dean 1969–79), del Oxford Univ Press 1960–79, regius prof of divinity Univ of Cambridge 1979–82, master of Peterhouse Cambridge 1987–93; fell Magdalene Coll Cambridge 1979–86; German Order Pour le Mérite 1993; FBA; *Books* Boethius (1981), Augustine (1986), Augustine's Confessions (1991); *Recreations* music; *Clubs* Royal Commonwealth, Cambridge Univ Wanderers (hockey); *Style—* Prof Henry Chadwick, KBE; ✉ 46 St John Street, Oxford OX1 2LH (☎ 01865 512814)

CHADWICK, Dr John; s of late Fred Chadwick, ISO, and late Margaret Pamela, *née* Bray; *b* 21 May 1920; *Educ* St Paul's, Corpus Christi Coll Cambridge (MA, LittD); *m* 10 July 1947, Joan Isobel, da of Thomas Edgar Hill, MBE (d 1963); 1 s (Anthony b 1954); *Career* WWII, Lt RNVSR 1940–45; editorial asst Oxford Latin Dictionary 1946–52, P M Laurence reader in classics Univ of Cambridge 1966–84 (asst lectr 1952–54, lectr 1954–66), hon fell Downing Coll Cambridge 1984– (Collins fell 1960–84); hon degrees: Univ of Athens 1958, Université Libre de Bruxelles 1969, Trinity Coll Dublin 1971, Univ of the Basque Country 1985, Univ of Salzburg 1990; corr memb: Deutsches Archäologisches Institut zu Berlin 1957, Oesterreichische Akademie der Wissenschaften 1974, Académie des Inscriptions et Belles Lettres Institut de France 1975 (Associé étranger 1985); foreign fell Accademia Nazionale dei Lincei (Rome) 1992, hon fell Athens Archaeological Soc 1974 (hon cncllr 1987), pres Swedenborg Soc London 1987; Cdr Order of the Phoenix Repub of Greece 1984, Ehrenzeichen für Wissenschaft und Kunst Repub of Austria 1992; FBA; *Books* The Medical Works of Hippocrates (with W N Mann, 1950), Documents in Mycenaean Greek (with M Ventris, 1956), The Decipherment of Linear B (1958), The Mycenaean World (1976), Corpus of Mycenaean Inscriptions from Knossos Vol 1 (ed-in-chief, 1986, Vol 2 1991), Linear B and Related Scripts (1987), Lexicographica Graeca (1996); E Swedenborg - The True Christian Religion (translator, 1988), E Swedenborg - Conjugial Love (translator, 1996); *Recreations* travel; *Style—* Dr John Chadwick, FBA; ✉ 75 Gough Way, Cambridge CB3 9LN

CHADWICK, Hon Mr Justice; Hon Sir John Murray Chadwick; kt (1991), ED (1979); s of Capt Hector George Chadwick, (ka 1942), and Margaret Corry, *née* Laing (d 1977); *b* 20 Jan 1941; *Educ* Rugby, Magdalene Coll Cambridge (MA); *m* 5 Dec 1975, Diana Mary, da of Charles Marshall Blunt, DL (d 1986), of March, Cambs; 2 da (Jane b 1976, Elizabeth b 1978); *Career* called to the Bar Inner Temple 1966 (bencher 1986), jr counsel Dept of Trade 1974–80, QC 1980, judge of the Courts of Appeal of Guernsey and Jersey 1986–91, recorder of the Crown Court 1990–91, judge of the High Court of Justice (Chancery Division) 1991–, Chancery supervising judge Birmingham, Bristol and Cardiff 1995–; Maj (TAVR) 4 Bn Royal Green Jackets 1973–76; memb Wine Standards Bd of Vintners' Co 1983–90, memb Gen Cncl of the Bar 1989–91; *Recreations* sailing; *Clubs* Atheneaum, Beefsteak, Royal Yacht Squadron; *Style—* The Hon Mr Justice Chadwick; ✉ Royal Courts of Justice, Strand, London WC2A 2LL

CHADWICK, Sir Joshua Kenneth Burton; 3 Bt (UK 1935), of Bidston, Co Palatine of Chester; s of Sir Robert Burton-Chadwick, 2 Bt (d 1983), and his 2 w (Beryl) Joan, *née* Brailsford; *b* 1 Feb 1954; *Heir* none; *Style—* Sir Joshua Burton-Chadwick, Bt; ✉ 3/1933 Gold Coast, Highway, Burleigh Heads, Queensland 4220, Australia

CHADWICK, Julian William Mark; s of Douglas Herbert Chadwick, of Beaconsfield, Bucks, and Elizabeth Mary, *née* Evans (d 1994); *b* 3 Jan 1957; *Educ* RGS High Wycombe, ChCh Oxford (MA); *Career* admitted slr 1982; ptnr: Gamlens 1985–90, Penningtons 1990– (managing ptnr Newbury Office); memb PCC St John's Church Newbury; former: jt master West Welsh Foot Beagles, sr master Christ Church and Farley Hill Beagles; memb: Law Soc, Assoc of Masters of Beagles and Harriers; *Recreations* field sports; *Clubs* Oxford & Cambridge; *Style—* Julian Chadwick, Esq; ✉ Penningtons, Phoenix House, 9 London Road, Newbury, Berks RG13 1JL (☎ 01635 523344); Bryntawel, Drefach, Llanbydder, Dyfed (☎ 01570 480267)

CHADWICK, (Bernard) Keith; s of Sydney Bernard Chadwick (d 1957), of Blackpool, and Ethel Chadwick; *b* 21 Jan 1941; *Educ* Baines GS Poulton-le-Fylde Lancs, Univ of Birmingham; *m* 1959 (m dis 1984); 3 s (Philip Keith b 16 May 1960, Christopher Alan b 24 Jan 1962, Anthony Simon b 9 March 1968); *Career* lectr in maths Univ of Libya 1963–68, insur, mortgage and finance broker 1969–81, co-fndr Independent British Healthcare PLC 1981– (currently chief exec); *Style—* Keith Chadwick, Esq; ✉ Independent British Healthcare PLC, Prudential House, Topping Street, Blackpool FY1 3AX (☎ 01253 23901, fax 01253 22153, car 0831 141433)

CHADWICK, Lynn Russell; CBE (1964); s of Verner Russell Chadwick (d 1957), and Margery Brown, *née* Lynn (d 1936); *b* 24 Nov 1914; *Educ* Merchant Taylors'; *m* 1, (m dis), Charlotte Ann Secord; 1 s (Simon David b 8 May 1942); m 2, Frances Mary Jamieson (d 1964); 2 da (Sarah Russell b 25 Nov 1958, Sophie Russell b 20 May 1960); m 3, 4 June 1965, Eva Yvonne, da of Gabriel Etien Reiner (d 1942), of Hungary; 1 s (Daniel Sebastian b 25 May 1965); *Career* Lt (A) Fleet Air Arm RNVR 1941–44; sculptor; numerous exhibitions UK and abroad; recent exhbns incl: retrospective (Yorkshire Sculpture Park) 1991, Bronzes (Cheltenham Museum and Art Gallery) 1993; work in public collections: Tate, Br Cncl, Arts Cncl of GB, V&A, Pembroke Coll Oxford, City Art Gallery (Bristol), Art Gallery (Brighton), Whitworth Art Gallery (Univ of Manchester), Musée National D'Art Moderne (Paris), Boymans van Beuningen Museum (Rotterdam), Staaliche Graphische Sammlung (Munich), Art Gallery (Gothenburg), Musées Royaux des Beaux-Arts de Belgique (Brussels), Galleria D'Arte Moderna (Rome), Museo Civico (Turin), Nat Gallery of SA (Adelaide), Nat Gallery of Canada (Ottawa), Museum of Fine Arts (Montreal), Museum of Modern Art (NY), Carnegie Inst (Pittsburgh), Albright Art Gallery (Buffalo), Art Inst (Chicago), Inst de Artes Contemporáneas (Lima); Cdr Ordre des Arts et Lettres (France) 1992 (Officier 1986), Order of Andres Bello First Class (Venezuela); hon fell Cheltenham & Gloucester Coll of HE 1995, assoc Academie Royale de Belgique 1995; *Style—* Lynn Chadwick, Esq, CBE; ✉ Lypiatt Park, Stroud, Gloucestershire GL6 7LL (☎ 01452 770210, fax 01452 770777)

CHADWICK, Prof (Sir) (William) Owen; OM (1983), KBE (1982); s of John Chadwick (d 1931), of Bromley, Kent; er bro of Prof (Sir) Henry Chadwick, KBE, *qv*, yr bro of Sir John Chadwick (d 1987), and also bro of Lady McNicoll (d 1993) (w of Vice Adm Sir Alan McNicoll (d 1987), former Australian ambass to Turkey); *b* 20 May 1916; *Educ* Tonbridge, St John's Coll Cambridge; *m* 1949, Ruth Romaine, eldest da of Bertrand Leslie Hallward, formerly Vice-Chllr of Univ of Nottingham; 2 s, 2 da; *Career* former dean and fellow of Trinity Hall Cambridge, sometime chm tstees Univ Coll later Wolfson Coll Cambridge, hon fell 1977, regius prof of mod history Univ of Cambridge 1968–83, vice chllr 1969–71, master of Selwyn Coll 1956–83; memb Royal Cmmn on Historical Manuscripts 1984–91, chllr Univ of East Anglia 1985–94, chm Nat Portrait Gallery 1988–94 (tstee 1978); Hon DD: St Andrews, Oxford, Wales; Hon DLitt: Kent, Bristol, London, E Anglia, Leeds, Cambridge; Hon DLett Columbia USA, Hon LLD Aberdeen; FBA 1962 (pres 1981–85); *Style—* Prof Owen Chadwick; ✉ 67 Grantchester St, Cambridge

CHADWICK, Peter; s of Kenneth Fred Chadwick (d 1985), and Grace Jean, *née* Holden (d 1991); *b* 19 Aug 1946; *Educ* St Paul's, Churchill Coll Cambridge (BA, MA); *m* 27 Oct 1971, Diana Kathryn Lillian, da of Frank Richard Stanford Kellett; 1 da (Lindsey Nicola b 1974); *Career* princ Dept of Indust 1977–79; KPMG: ptnr 1982–, managing ptnr Kent 1983–91; FCA 1979 (ACA 1970); *Recreations* art, travel; *Clubs* Arts; *Style—* Peter Chadwick, Esq; ✉ The Old Rectory, Little Chart, Ashford, Kent TN27 0QH; 21 Rosebery, Charles Street, Mayfair, London W1X 7HB; KPMG, 1 Puddle Dock, London EC4V 3PD (☎ 0171 311 1000, fax 0171 311 6811)

CHADWICK, Prof Peter; s of Jack Chadwick (d 1991), of Huddersfield, and Marjorie, *née* Castle (d 1982); *b* 23 March 1931; *Educ* Huddersfield Coll, Univ of Manchester (BSc), Univ of Cambridge (PhD, ScD); *m* 2 April 1956, Sheila (Gladys), da of Clarence Frederick Slater (d 1939), of Colchester; 2 da (Janice b 1958, Susan b 1970); *Career* sr scientific offr AWRE Aldermaston 1957–59 (scientific offr 1955–57), sr lectr in applied mathematics Univ of Sheffield 1964–65 (lectr 1959–64); UEA: prof of mathematics 1965–91, emeritus prof 1991–, dean Sch of Maths and Physics 1979–82, Leverhulme emeritus fell 1991–93; visiting prof Univ of Queensland 1972; Hon DSc Glasgow; FRS; *Books* Continuum Mechanics - Concise Theory and Problems (1976); *Recreations* walking, music; *Style—* Prof Peter Chadwick, FRS; ✉ 8 Stratford Crescent, Cringleford, Norwich NR4 7SF (☎ 01603 451655); School of Mathematics, University of East Anglia, University Plain, Norwich NR4 7TJ (☎ 01603 456161, fax 01603 458553, e-mail p.chadwick @ uea.ac.uk)

CHADWICK, Peter Douglas; s of Douglas Herbert Chadwick, of Beaconsfield, Bucks and Bryntawel, Llanwenog, Dyfed, and Elizabeth Mary (Nan), *née* Evans (d 1994); *b* 27 Jan 1947; *Educ* Royal GS High Wycombe, UCL (BA); *Career* memb staff Church Cmmrs for England 1970–87 (seconded to Gen Synod C of E 1978–82), sec Church Urban Fund 1987–; *Recreations* East European and Oriental studies, cycling; *Style—* Peter Chadwick, Esq; ✉ Church Urban Fund, 2 Great Peter St, London SW1P 3LX (☎ 0171 222 7010, fax 0171 799 1828)

CHADWICK, Peter Robert Procter; s of Robert Everard Chadwick, and Audrey Monica, *née* Procter; *b* 26 June 1951; *Educ* Oundle, Univ of Newcastle upon Tyne (LLB); *m* 1973, Ann Louise, *née* Sellick; 2 s (Thomas b 1986, Edmund b 1988), 1 da (Esther b 1984); *Career* admitted slr 1975; ptnr Eversheds (formerly Hepworth & Chadwick) 1978–, dir Next plc 1981–86; tstee Selby Abbey and Leeds Parish Church Appeal Funds; memb Law Soc; *Recreations* mountaineering, fishing, music; *Clubs* Leeds, Yorkshire Ramblers', Yorkshire Flyfishers'; *Style—* Peter Chadwick, Esq; ✉ Newlaithes Manor, Newlaithes Rd, Horsforth, Leeds LS18 4LG; Eversheds, Cloth Hall Court, Infirmary St, Leeds LS1 2JB (☎ 0113 243 0391)

CHADWICK, Robert; s of Jack Chadwick, of Pitcoudie, Glenrothes, Fife, and Margaret, *née* Lyons (d 1991); *b* 18 Aug 1949; *Educ* Montrose Acad; *m* 9 May 1988, Eileen Joan, da of Leo Hubert Skelton (d 1938), and Florence (d 1981); *Career* RA 22 Battery Sch of Artillery Larkhill 1966–70; Meteorological Office: joined 1970, Prestwick Airport 1970–83, forecaster 1984, Glasgow Weather Centre 1984–88, higher forecaster 1988, RAF Honington 1988–92, environment mangr Met Office HQ 1992–94, dep chief forecaster HQ RAF Strike Command 1994–; Flt Lt RAFVR 1990–; memb: Trollope Soc, Br Field Sports Soc, BASC, R S Surtees Soc, Game Conservancy, CGA, CLA, Inst of Mathematics and its Applications 1989, Inst of Physics 1990; FRMetS 1987; FRGS 1990; *Recreations* shooting, fishing, reading; *Clubs* Civil Service, RAF; *Style—* Robert Chadwick, Esq; ✉ Oakacre, Fen Street, Hopton, Diss, Norfolk

CHADWICK, Timothy John Mackenzie; s of Arthur John Mackenzie Chadwick, of Gstaad, Switzerland, and Patricia Cambell, *née* Hiller; *b* 19 Aug 1946; *Educ* Le Rosey Sch Switzerland, Amherst Coll USA, Trinity Coll Oxford; *m* 26 June 1980, Jacqueline Brewster, *née* Johnson; 1 s (William Hiller Mackenzie b 26 Oct 1982); *Career* md: Associated Business Programmes Ltd 1975–78, Aurum Press Ltd 1978–89; dir: Benecia Industries Inc California USA 1987–, Hamleys of Regent St Ltd 1989–, Tunesure Ltd 1990–; chm: All Children's Co Ltd 1989–, ABC 1991–, TMT Ltd 1993–; *Recreations* skiing, tennis, reading, leaning on fences; *Clubs* Knickerbocker (USA), Queen's, Vincent's, White's; *Style—* Timothy Chadwick, Esq; ✉ ABC, 33 Museum St, London WC1A 1LD (☎ 0171 436 6300)

CHADWYCK-HEALEY, Sir Charles Edward; 5 Bt (UK 1919), of Wyphurst, Cranleigh, Co Surrey, and New Place, Luccombe, Somerset; s of Sir Charles Arthur Chadwyck-Healey, 4 Bt, OBE, TD (d 1986), and Viola, *née* Lubbock (d 1995); *b* 13 May 1940; *Educ* Eton, Trinity Coll Oxford (MA); *m* 16 Sept 1967, Angela Mary, eldest da of late John Metson, of Little Dunmow, Essex; 1 s (Edward Alexander b 1972), 2 da (Catherine b 1970, Faith b 1977); *Heir* s, Edward Alexander Chadwyck-Healey b 2 June 1972; *Career* publisher; chm: Chadwyck-Healey Ltd 1973–, Chadwyck-Healey Inc 1974–; pres Chadwyck-Healey France SA 1985–; cmmr: Marshall Aid Commemoration Cmmn, Library and Info Cmmn; pres Euro Info Assoc; Liveryman: Worshipful Co of Fishmongers, Stationers & Newspaper Makers; FRGS; *Clubs* Brooks's; *Style—* Sir Charles Chadwyck-Healey, Bt; ✉ Manor Farm, Bassingbourn, Cambs SG8 5NX (☎ 01763 242447)

CHAITOW, Christopher John Adam; s of Boris Reuben Chaitow (d 1995), and of Elizabeth, *née* Rice (d 1980); *b* 19 Jan 1943; *Educ* Worthing HS; *m* 18 May 1974, Susan Patricia, da of George Joseph Foley, of Keystone Rd, Cardiff; 1 s (Daniel b 1984), 1 da (Ella b 1983); *Career* research/institutional sales Northcote & Co 1968–70 (trainee 1964–68), ptnr Beamish & Co 1970–75, returned to institutional sales Northcote & Co 1975–79; technical analyst: Simon & Coates 1979–86, Chase Manhattan Securities 1986, Morgan Grenfell Securities 1986–88; dir Value and Momentum Research and Chartroom UK 1989–92; technical analyst Credit Lyonnais Laing 1992–94, dir and head of technical analysis Robert Fleming Securities 1995–; *Recreations* music, golf; *Style—* Christopher Chaitow, Esq; ✉ Caroline House, 29–30 Alwyne Rd, London N1 (☎ 0171 226 4471); Robert Fleming Securities, 25 Copthall Avenue, London EC2R 7DR (☎ 0171 638 5858)

CHAKRABORTI, Dr Debabrata; s of Nagendra Nath Chakraborti (d 1966), of Bally, Howrah, India, and Suniti Majumder; *b* 1 Jan 1937; *Educ* Univ of Calcutta (MB BS, DPM), Conjoint Bd Eng (DPM), FRCPsych; *m* 10 July 1966, Monika, da of Kumud Ranjan Chowdhury (d 1987); 1 s (Saptarshi b 14 June 1968), 1 da (Debika b 11 Dec 1973); *Career* conslt psychiatrist in mental handicap NW Anglia Health Care Tst 1976–, regnl tutor in mental handicap; Br Med Jl: book reviews, TV reviews, contraception and the mentally handicapped (jtly, 1984), sterilisation and the mentally handicapped; asst devpt NHS facilities for mentally handicapped W Norfolk; memb BMA; *Recreations* writing, listening to Indian music, reading biographies; *Style—* Dr Debabrata Chakraborti; ✉ 4 Binham Road, Priory Park, South Wootton, King's Lynn, Norfolk PE30 3TB (☎ 01553 671869); Park View Resource Centre, Birch Tree Close, London Road, King's Lynn, Norfolk PE30 5QD (☎ 01553 766266 ext 5512)

CHALDECOTT, Axel James; s of John James Chaldecott, of Beltinge, Kent, and Alix Mathilde, *née* Von Kauffmann; *b* 11 Dec 1954; *Educ* Charterhouse, Canterbury Coll of

Art (BA); *m* 14 Feb 1987, Claire, da of Kenneth Evans; *Career* art dir: Ogilvy & Mather 1977–80, Crawfords 1980–81, Gold Greenlees Trott 1981–85; creative gp head Wight Collins Rutherford Scott 1985–87, creative ptnr HHCL and Partners 1987–; *Style*— Axel Chaldecott, Esq; ✉ HHCL and Partners, Kent House, 14–17 Market Place, Great Titchfield St, London W1N 7AJ (☎ 0171 436 3333, fax 0171 436 2677)

CHALFONT, Baron (Life Peer UK 1964); Alun Arthur Gwynne Jones; OBE (1961), MC (1957), PC (1964); s of Arthur Gwynne Jones (d 1982), and Eliza Alice, *née* Hardman (d 1975); *b* 5 Dec 1919; *Educ* West Monmouth Sch, Sch of Slavonic Studies Univ of London; *m* 1948, Mona, da of late Harry Douglas Mitchell, of Grimsby; 1 c decd; *Career* sits as Independent in House of Lords, pres Lords All-Party Defence Gp; Col (ret) S Wales Borderers (Reg Army Offr 1940–61, served Burma, Ethiopia, Malaya, Cyprus, Egypt); former defence and mil correspondent The Times; min of state FO 1964–70, Br perm rep to WEU 1969–70; foreign ed New Statesman 1970–71; dir: IBM UK Holdings Ltd, IBM UK Ltd 1973–90; non-exec dir: Lazard Bros 1981–90, Shandwick plc, The Television Corporation 1996–; pres Nottingham Building Soc 1983–90; chm: The Radio Authy 1990–95, VSEL plc until 1996, Euro Atlantic Gp, Exec Ctee Pilgrims Soc; pres Royal Nat Inst for Deaf until 1990; Liveryman Worshipful Co of Paviors; *Books* The Sword and the Spirit (1963), The Great Commanders (1973), Montgomery of Alamein (1976), Waterloo - Story of Three Armies (1979), Star Wars - Suicide or Survival (1985), By God's Will - a portrait of the Sultan of Brunei (1989); *Recreations* music, theatre; *Clubs* Garrick, MCC; *Style*— The Rt Hon the Lord Chalfont, OBE, MC, PC; ✉ House of Lords, London SW1A 0PW

CHALK, Clive Andrew; s of Herbert Chalk (d 1981), of Chelsfield, Kent, and Gertrude Edith, *née* Taylor (d 1992); *b* 2 Nov 1946; *Educ* St Dunstan's Coll, Univ of Exeter (LLB), Harvard Business Sch (AMP); *m* 1, 7 March 1970 (m dis), Judith Rosamond, da of Dr Samuel Dudley Sawyer; 2 da (Harriet Rosamond Louise b 17 Oct 1975, Olivia Emma Jane b 8 March 1977); m 2, 20 Dec 1985, Iris Marita, da of Lars Hjelt; 2 s (Nicholas Gyles Edward b 24 Sept 1986, Jonathan Clive Alexander b 20 Jan 1989); *Career* Coopers & Lybrand 1968–73, Williams & Glyn's Bank 1973–77, dir Samuel Montagu & Co Ltd 1982–96 (joined 1977), dir of corp fin HSBC Samuel Montagu 1996–; FCA 1972; *Recreations* sailing, skiing, golf, cricket, rugby, bridge, opera, ballet; *Clubs* Royal Thames Yacht, Harvard Business Sch of London; *Style*— Clive Chalk, Esq; ✉ HSBC Samuel Montagu, Vintners Place, 68 Upper Thames Street, London EC4V 3BJ (☎ 0171 336 9000, fax 0171 336 9500)

CHALK, Gilbert John; s of Ronald Arthur Chalk (d 1993), of Chorleywood, Herts, and Elizabeth, *née* Talbot; *b* 21 Sept 1947; *Educ* Lancing, Univ of Southampton (BSc), Univ of Lancaster (MA), Columbia Univ New York (MBA); *m* 9 June 1975, Gillian Frances Audrey, da of Sir Gervase Blois, 10 Bt (d 1967); 2 s (Alexander John Gervase b 1976, Christopher Harry Gilbert b 1985), 1 da (Nicola Elizabeth b 1978); *Career* dir: Centaur Communications Ltd 1981–, Hambros Bank Ltd 1984–94, Hambro Group Investments 1988–94; md Hambro European Ventures Ltd 1987–94; sr advsr: ECI Ventures Ltd 1994–95, ABSA Bank Ltd 1995–; *Recreations* tennis, riding, skiing; *Clubs* Queen's, Turf, Berkshire Golf; *Style*— Gilbert Chalk, Esq; ✉ 103 Elgin Crescent, London W11 2JF (☎ 0171 727 1981); Foxcote Grange, Andoversford, Glos (☎ 01242 820322)

CHALK, Kenneth Stephen; s of Montague Frederick Chalk, and Jean Patricia, *née* Craig (d 1983); *b* 27 Dec 1947; *Educ* St Nicholas GS Northwood Middx; *children* 1 s (James b 4 April 1975), 3 da (Zoe b 6 Dec 1972, Naomi b 26 Sept 1979, Olivia b 30 April 1995); *Career* CA; articled Mann Judd & Co London 1966–71, Hendry Rae & Court Perth WA 1971–73, ptnr Tansley Witt & Co Bristol 1975 (joined London office 1973, merger with Arthur Andersen 1979), ptnr Arthur Andersen Bristol 1979–87, ptnr Spicer & Oppenheim Manchester 1987–90; Touche Ross (now Deloitte & Touche): ptnr i/c Corp Special Servs Div Touche Ross Manchester 1990–93 (following merger with Spicer & Oppenheim), corp recovery ptnr Thames Valley Office 1993–; memb: Soc of Practitioners in Insolvency, Inst of Credit Mgmnt; licensed insolvency practitioner, FCA 1979 (ACA 1970); *Recreations* travel, music, theatre, walking; *Style*— Kenneth Chalk, Esq; ✉ Deloitte & Touche, Columbia Centre, Market Street, Bracknell, Berks RG12 1PA (☎ 01344 54445, fax 01344 422681)

CHALK, Philip Alexander Forbes; s of Charles Philip Chalk, of Much Hadham, Herts (d 1964), and Ann, *née* Forbes (d 1974); *b* 1 May 1930; *Educ* Selwyn Coll Univ of Cambridge, The London Hosp Med Coll (MA, MB BChir); *m* 17 May 1958, Jean Graham, da of Bertram Doughty (d 1978), of Gt Dunmow, Essex; 1 s (David b 1959), 2 da (Alison b 1961, Hilary b 1963); *Career* resident accoucheur The London Hosp 1958, registrar then sr registrar The Middlesex Hosp 1964–69, conslt obstetrician and gynaecologist The Royal Free Hosp London 1969–91; govr Queen Mary Coll London 1982–91, memb Cncl St Luke's Hosp for the Clergy 1991–; memb Ct of Assts Worshipful Co of Drapers (Master 1992); FRCS, FRCOG; *Recreations* fishing, shooting, campanology; *Clubs* Royal Soc of Med, Flyfishers'; *Style*— Philip Chalk, Esq; ✉ The Barn House, Hurstbourne Priors, Whitchurch, Hants RG28 7SB (☎ 01256 893133)

CHALKER OF WALLASEY, Baroness (Life Peer UK 1992), of Leigh-on-Sea in the County of Essex; Lynda Chalker; PC (1987); da of late Sidney Henry James Bates, and late Marjorie Kathleen Randell; *b* 29 April 1942; *Educ* Roedean, Univ of Heidelberg, Westfield Coll London, Central London Poly; *m* 1, 1967 (m dis 1973), Eric Robert Chalker (chm Greater London Young Conservatives 1966–67); m 2, 1981, Clive Landa (chm Tory Reform Gp 1979–82 and chm Young Cons 1972–74); *Career* statistician Research Bureau Ltd (Unilever subsid) 1963–69, market researcher Shell Mex & BP Ltd 1969–72, chief exec Int Div Louis Harris International 1972–74; chm Gtr London Young Cons 1969–70, nat vice chm Young Cons 1970–71; MP (C) Wallasey 1974–92; memb BBC Gen Advsy Ctee 1975–79, oppn spokesman for Social Servs 1976–79; Parly under sec of state: DHSS 1979–82, Tport 1982–83; min of state: Tport 1983–86, FCO 1986–; min for Overseas Devpt 1989–; hon fell: John Moores Univ, Inst of Highways and Transportation, Market Res Soc, Royal Statistical Soc; Hon Dr: Univ of Westminster, Cranfield Univ, Univ of Bradford, Univ of Warwick; *Recreations* theatre, driving; *Style*— The Rt Hon Baroness Chalker of Wallasey, PC; ✉ Minister of State (for Africa, Commonwealth and Overseas Development), Foreign and Commonwealth Office, King Charles St, London SW1P 2AH (☎ 0171 917 0410, fax 0171 917 0634)

CHALLACOMBE, Dr David Nicholas; s of Harold Bruce Challacombe (d 1985), of Lulworth, Dorset, and Nancy Llinos, *née* Williams; *b* 22 June 1936; *Educ* Truro Sch Cornwall, Harrisons Coll Barbados, KCH (MD), Univ of London; *m* 19 Jan 1963, Janice Stewart, da of Alfred Henry Siemon (d 1986), of Perth, W Australia; 1 s (Andrew Nicholas b 1965), 1 da (Emma Jane b 1967); *Career* house offr KCH 1960–61, sr house offr Hosp for Sick Children Gt Ormond St 1963, registrar St Mary's Hosp London 1965–68, sr registrar Bristol Royal Hosp for Sick Children 1968–70, lectr Univ of Birmingham 1970–73, conslt paediatrician Somerset Health Authy 1973–, fndr and dir Somerset Children's Res Unit 1973–, dir of research Taunton and Somerset NHS Tst 1994–; hon med offr and ctee memb Somerset CCC 1974–85; pres SW Paediatric Club 1994–; chm: SW Regnl Paediatric Advsy Ctee 1985–90, W Somerset Ethics Ctee 1985–; memb: SW Regnl Res Ctee, Euro Soc for Paediatric Gastroenterology and Nutrition, British Paediatric Assoc, Br Soc of Gastroenterology, hon memb British Dietetic Assoc; MRCS, FRCP (regnl lectr 1995); *Publications* Food Allergy (1985); author of numerous publications on paediatric and adult gastroenterological res topics; *Recreations* watching and playing cricket, eighteenth century English porcelain; *Style*— Dr David Challacombe; ✉ The Somerset Children's Research Unit, Musgrove Park Hospital, Taunton, Somerset TA1 5DA (☎ 01823 333444); 2 Mount Terrace, Mount St, Taunton, Somerset TA1 3QG (☎ 01823 337164)

CHALLIS, Dr Christine Joyce; da of Bernard Arthur Black (d 1995), of Nottingham, and Nora Alice, *née* Willoughby (d 1985); *b* 24 Feb 1940; *Educ* Queen Ethelburga's Sch Harrogate, Nottingham HS for Girls, Bedford Coll London (BA), Queen Mary Coll London (PhD); *m* 4 Jan 1967, Christopher Edgar Challis, *qv*, s of Edgar Challis; *Career* pt/t tutor in history Univ of London, public relations offr Castlefield Textiles 1964–69; Univ of Leeds: admin asst 1969–72, asst sec 1972–74, dep sec 1974–83; pt/t CVCP admin trg offr for UK univs 1980–83, sec LSE 1983–; dir: Enterprise LSE, LSE LETS, VELSE, Univs Superannuation Scheme Ltd, Southern Universities Management Services; chm Organising Gp UK/Swedish Univ Registrars and Secretaries Seminars; memb: Audit Ctee South Bank Univ, Trg Mgmnt Bd and Careers Advsy Bd Univ of London, SAUL Negotiating Ctee Frank Knox Fellowship Selection Panel; contrib to historical and univ jls and publications; memb Advsy Cncl Civil Serv Coll 1986–89; govr Fulneck Girls' Sch Pudsey W Yorks 1973–83; FRSA; *Recreations* music, vernacular architecture; *Style*— Dr Christine Challis; ✉ London School of Economics and Political Science, Houghton Street, London WC2A 2AE (☎ 0171 955 7009, fax 0171 404 5510)

CHALLIS, Dr Christopher Edgar; s of Edgar Challis (d 1957), of Leeds, and Hilda May, *née* Elsworth (d 1989); *b* 5 Feb 1939; *Educ* Cockburn HS Leeds, Univ of Bristol (BA, Cert Ed, PhD); *m* 4 Jan 1967, Christine Joyce Challis, *qv*, da of Bernard Arthur Black, of Nottingham; *Career* Univ of Leeds: asst lectr 1964–67, lectr 1967–78, sr lectr 1978–82, reader 1982–, chm of the sch 1988–91; ed British Numismatic Journal 1980–89; vice pres Br Numismatic Soc 1995– (pres 1988–93), tstee UK Numismatic Tst 1988–, memb Royal Mint Advsy Ctee on the Design of Coins, Medals, Seals and Decorations 1991–; awarded John Sanford Saltus Gold Medal of Br Numismatic Soc 1992; FRHistS 1970, FSA 1987, FRSA 1991; *Books* The Tudor Coinage (1978), A New History of the Royal Mint (ed, 1992); *Recreations* walking, horse-riding; *Style*— Dr Christopher Challis, FSA; ✉ School of History, University of Leeds, Leeds LS2 9JT (☎ 0113 243 1751)

CHALLIS, George Hubert; CBE (1991); s of Hubert William Challis (d 1969); *b* 26 May 1921; *Educ* King Edward VI Sch Stourbridge; *m* 1946, Margaret Beatrice, da of Reginald Percy Bonner (d 1965); 1 s, 1 da; *Career* served 1940–46 1/9 Gurkha Rifles (despatches twice); banker and co dir; with Lloyds Bank plc 1938–81 (head of Premises Div 1974–81); dir: Lloyds Bank Property Co 1974–81, Towco Group Ltd 1982–84, Westminster Property Group plc 1983–84; memb: Ct of Common Cncl (City of London) 1978–, Cncl London Chamber of Commerce and Indust 1979–89, Thames Water Authy 1982–83; dep govr The Hon Irish Soc 1983–84; chm: City Lands and Bridge House Estates Ctee 1990 and 1991, Port and City of London Health and Social Servs Ctee 1988–90; Master Worshipful Co of Tobacco Pipe Makers and Tobacco Blenders 1992–93, Hon Liveryman Worshipful Co of Chartered Secretaries and Administrators (Hon Clerk 1984–94); Cdr of the Order of Merit (Federal Republic of Germany) 1986, Commendatore Order of Merit (Republic of Italy) 1990; *Recreations* travel, reading, music; *Clubs* RAC, MCC, Guildhall, City Livery; *Style*— George Challis, Esq, CBE; ✉ 77 West Hill Ave, Epsom, Surrey KT19 8JX (☎ 01372 721705)

CHALMERS, Craig Minto; s of Robert Brian Chalmers, and Georgina Byers, *née* Minto; *b* 15 Oct 1968; *Educ* Melrose GS, Earlston HS; *m* 24 July 1993, Lucy Chalmers; 2 s (Sam Robert Minto b 1994, Ben Bryden b; *Career* rugby union fly-half; clubs: Melrose RFC, Barbarians RFC; rep: Scotland U15, Scotland U18, Scotland U19, Scotland U21, Scotland B (debut 1988, youngest rep player); Scotland: debut v Wales 1989, Grand Slam winners 1990, tour NZ (2 tests) 1990, memb World Cup squad 1991 and 1995, 47 caps; memb British Lions tour Aust (1 test) 1989; scorer of 120 points for Scotland (5 tries, 8 drop goals, 7 conversions, 24 penalties); PR Scottish Power; *Recreations* golf, snooker, tennis, football; *Clubs* Melrose Golf; *Style*— Craig Chalmers, Esq; ✉ Marchmont, Newlyn Road, Melrose, Roxburghshire TD6 9QX; c/o Melrose RFC, The Greenyards, Melrose, Roxburghshire TD6 9SA (☎ 01896 822993)

CHALMERS, Harvey Paxton; s of William Harvey Chalmers (d 1985), and Elizabeth, *née* Davidson; *b* 18 Feb 1947; *Educ* Univ of Glasgow (LLB), Magdalene Coll Cambridge (PhD); *Career* admitted slr 1978; articled clerk Shepherd & Wedderburn WS 1972–74, slr Linklaters & Paines 1974–85, ptnr Simmons & Simmons 1986– (slr 1985–86); avocat à la cour de Paris 1994; memb: Law Soc, Law Soc of Scotland; *Style*— H P Chalmers, Esq; ✉ 2 avenue Bugeaud, 75116 Paris, France (☎ 00 33 1 45 01 67 67, fax 00 33 1 45 01 22 32)

CHALMERS, Ian Pender; CMG (1993), OBE (1980); s of John William Pender Chalmers (d 1976), and Beatrice Miriam, *née* Emery (d 1973); *b* 30 Jan 1939; *Educ* Harrow, Trinity Coll Dublin; *m* 1962, Lisa Christine, da of Prof John D Hay; 2 s (James William Pender b 27 July 1964, Nicholas John Pender b 4 May 1971), 3 da (Sara Pender b 8 Sept 1965 (decd), Lisa Francesca Pender b 1 Oct 1968, Charlotte Anne Pender b 8 March 1976); *Career* entered HM Dip Serv 1963, second sec Beirut 1966–68, FCO 1968–70, first sec Warsaw 1970–72, FCO 1972–76, first sec Paris 1976–80, FCO 1980–84, cnsllr UK Mission to UN Geneva 1984–87, cnsllr FCO 1987–; *Recreations* golf, reading, walking, skiing; *Clubs* Huntercombe Golf, Frilford Heath Golf; *Style*— Ian Chalmers, Esq, CMG, OBE; ✉ c/o Foreign & Commonwealth Office, King Charles Street, London SW1A 2AH

CHALMERS, Judith; OBE (1994); da of David Norman Chalmers (d 1953), and Millie Locke, *née* Broadhurst; *b* 10 Oct 1937; *Educ* Withington Girls' Sch Manchester, LAMDA; *m* 3 Jan 1964, Neil Durden-Smith, OBE, s of Anthony James Durden-Smith, FRCS (d 1963); 1 s (Mark b 1 Oct 1968), 1 da (Emma b 4 March 1967); *Career* began broadcasting in Manchester BBC Children's Hour at age of 13 (while still at school); interviewer/presenter many radio and TV programmes in north and then London from 1960 with BBC; joined Thames TV with own afternoon programme 1972; first series of travel programme Wish You Were Here 1973...? (current series is 23nd); developed own idea for home interest programme Hot Property since 1987; joined Radio 2 to host own daily programme 1990; commentator for many royal and state occasions; travel ed Woman's Realm; past memb Nat Consumer Cncl; memb Peacock Ctee on Broadcasting; Freeman City of London; pres Lady Taverners, vice chm Holiday Care Service; memb: British Guild of Travel Writers, British Assoc of Travel Editors; *Books* Wish You Were Here ...?: 50 of the Best Holidays (1987); *Recreations* walking, bird watching, photography; *Clubs* Wig and Pen, Mossiman's Rugby; *Style*— Miss Judith Chalmers, OBE; ✉ c/o Julie Ivelaw-Chapman, The Ship, 74 Vicarage Road, Pitstone, Beds LU7 9EY (☎ 01296 662441)

CHALMERS, Dr Neil Robert; s of William King Chalmers, and Irene Margaret, *née* Pemberton; *b* 19 June 1942; *Educ* King's Coll Sch Wimbledon, Magdalen Coll Oxford (BA), St John's Coll Cambridge (PhD); *m* 28 Feb 1970, Monica Elizabeth, *née* Byanjeru; 2 da (Emily Anne Nsemere b 5 Dec 1970, Louise Jane Kobuyenje b 11 Oct 1978); *Career* lectr in zoology Makerere Univ Coll Kampala Uganda 1966–69, scientific dir Nat Primate Res Centre Nairobi Kenya 1969–70, dean of sci Open Univ 1985–88 (lectr, sr lectr then reader in biology 1970–85), dir Natural History Museum 1988–; pres Assoc for the Study of Animal Behaviour 1989–92; FZS, FLS, FIBiol, FRSA 1988; *Books* Social Behaviour in Primates (1979), contrib numerous papers on animal behaviour to various jls; *Recreations* music, squash; *Style*— Dr Neil Chalmers; ✉ Natural History Museum, Cromwell Road, London SW7 5BD (☎ 0171 938 9123, fax 0171 938 8799)

CHALMERS, Norman Ashley; s of Reginald Chalmers (d 1984), of Berkhamsted, and Francis, *née* Flynn (d 1980); *b* 19 June 1933; *Educ* Berkhamsted Sch, RMA Sandhurst; *m* 12 July 1958, Susan, da of Leslie Bradford Harvey (d 1984), of Nantwich, Cheshire; 2

da (Caroline b 3 March 1964, Sarah b 23 Oct 1966); *Career* The Black Watch Royal Highland Regt 1951–58, cmmnd 1953; sr ptnr Arthur Andersen & Co CAs; chm: Nat Mutual Life Assur Soc 1992– (dep chm 1980–92), Silver Estates Group 1980–; dir Stoke Poges Golf Club; dir Families at Risk 1987–, dir World Family of Foster Parents Plan 1983–, memb Ct of Assts and Past Master Worshipful Co of Gardeners, Freeman City of London; FCA; *Recreations* golf, shooting, fishing; *Clubs* Wentworth, Stoke Poges, City Livery, United Wards; *Style*— Norman Chalmers, Esq; ✉ Brook House, Templewood Lane, Farnham Common, Bucks SL2 3HW; Arthur Andersen & Co, 1 Surrey St, London WC2R 2PS (☎ 0171 438 3743)

CHALMERS, Dr Robert James Guille; s of James Alexander Chalmers, of Oxford, and Lois Guille, *née* Taudevin (d 1980); *b* 18 Nov 1950; *Educ* St Edward's Sch Oxford, Middx Hosp Med Sch (MB BS); *m* 1 Oct 1988, Elizabeth Joyce, da of Leonard Cater (d 1980), of Bal West, Penzance; *Career* conslt dermatologist 1983–: Salford Royal Hospitals NHS Trust, Bolton Hospitals NHS Trust, Manchester Royal Infirmary; FRCP; *Recreations* travelling, playing the bassoon; *Clubs* Royal Society of Medicine; *Style*— Dr Robert Chalmers; ✉ The Dermatology Centre, Hope Hospital, Stott Lane, Eccles, Lancs M6 8HD (☎ 0161 787 1025)

CHALONER, John Seymour; s of Ernest Joseph Chaloner (d 1954), and Lenore Maud Chaloner, MBE, *née* Barling (d 1974); *b* 5 Nov 1924; *Educ* Beltane Sch Wimbledon, Carleton Coll Ottawa Canada; *m* 1, 1952; 2 s (Nicholas b 1956, Ben b 1960); m 2, 1978, Patricia Ann; *Career* served as Maj Westminster Dragoons in NW Europe 1944–45; founded post war German newspapers incl Der Spiegel 1946; fndr and chm Seymour Press Group London 1948–76, awarded Officers Cross of the Order of Merit of the Federal Republic of Germany (1990); memb Wandsworth Borough Cncl 1961–68; govr St George's Hosp London 1961–68; chm Publishing Div Inst of Dirs 1984–89; *Books* Three for The Road, To Europe with Love, To The Manner Born, Bottom Line, Occupational Hazard, 9 illustrated children's titles; *Recreations* shooting, sailing, skiing; *Style*— John Chaloner, Esq; ✉ 4 Warwick Square, London SW1 (☎ 0171 834 9871)

CHALONER, Hon Thomas Peregrine Long (Perry); s and h of 3 Baron Gisborough; *b* 17 Jan 1961; *Educ* Eton, Univ of Buckingham (LLB); *m* 28 March 1992, Karen E, only da of Alan Thomas; *Career* barrister-at-law (Inner Temple); commercial pilot 1986–92; md Gisborough Farms (South Africa) Pty Ltd 1992–; *Recreations* diving, windsurfing, waterskiing, mountainbiking, flying; *Style*— The Hon Perry Chaloner; ✉ Falcons Nest, PO 1274, Stellenbosch 7599, South Africa

CHALSTREY, Sir (Leonard) John; kt (1996); s of Leonard Chalstrey (d 1991), of Tipton, Staffordshire, and Frances Mary, *née* Lakin (d 1996); *b* 17 March 1931; *Educ* Dudley Sch, Queens' Coll Cambridge, St Bartholomew's Hosp Med Coll (MA, MD, BChir, DSc, FRCS); *m* 6 Sept 1958, Aileen Beatrice, da of Harold Bayes (d 1984); 1 s (Jonathan b 1962), 1 da (Susan b 1959); *Career* sr lectr in surgery Bart's Med Coll 1969–, conslt surgn Bart's and Homerton Hosps 1969–94, conslt surgn Royal Hospitals NHS Tst 1994–96; examiner in surgery: Univ of London 1976–95, Univ of Cambridge 1988–93; memb City and Hackney Health Authy 1992–93; hon conslt surgn St Luke's Hosp for the Clergy 1975–93; Alderman (Ward of Vintry) Corporation City of London 1984– (memb Common Cncl 1981–), Aldermanic Sheriff City of London 1993–94, Lord Mayor of London 1995–96, memb HM Lieutenancy for City of London; memb Cncl City Univ (chllr 1995–96); memb Ct of Assts: Worshipful Soc of Apothecaries (Master 1994–95), Worshipful Co of Barbers (Middle Warden 1993–94); memb: Cncl City Livery Club (patron 1995–96), Guild of Freemen City of London, Br Soc of Gastroenterology, Assoc of Surgns of GB and Ireland; vice pres City of London Section BRCS 1993, surgn in chief and co-chm Med Bd St John Ambulance 1993–; Maj RAMC (V), ret 1986; KStJ 1995 (OStJ 1992), FRSM, FRSH (hon), FRSA; *Books* Gastro-Intestinal Disorders (1986); contributor: numerous papers on surgical subjects to medical press GB and USA, Maingot's Abdominal Operations (7 edn 1980, 8 edn 1985), Cancer in the Elderly (1990); *Recreations* painting in oils; *Clubs* United Oxford and Cambridge Univ, The City Livery; *Style*— Sir John Chalstrey; ✉ Danebury, 113 The Chine, London N21 2EG (☎ 0181 360 8921); 116 Harley Street, London W1N 1AG (☎ 0171 935 7413)

CHALTON, Simon Nicholas Ley; s of Thomas Ley Chalton (d 1978), of Leeds, and Constance Mary, *née* Whittle (d 1946); *b* 7 June 1932; *Educ* Stowe; *m* 2 May 1959, Linda Mary, da of Donald Frank Chown; 1 s (Giles Edward Ley b 12 Nov 1960), 2 da (Nicola Jane b 23 Sept 1963, Caroline Mary b 5 April 1966); *Career* admitted slr 1958; formerly ptnr Dibb Lupton & Co, currently practising slr and conslt to Bird and Bird in computer law; current directorships incl: Yorkshire Post Newspapers Ltd, The West of England Trust Ltd, Jordan Limited; former chm: Intellectual Property Ctee BCS, Legal Gp Nat Computing Centre; chm Standing Ctee Int Bar Assoc; fell Coll of Law Practice Mgmnt USA; memb: Law Soc, BCS; FCIArb; *Books* Data Protection Law (with Shelagh Gaskill, 1988), Encyclopaedia of Data Protection (with Shelagh Gaskill and J A L Sterling, 1988–); *Recreations* gardening, theatre, music, walking; *Clubs* The Leeds; *Style*— Simon Chalton, Esq; ✉ Beech House, High Kilburn, York YO6 4AJ (☎ 01347 868641, fax 01347 868689)

CHAMBERLAIN, Arthur; s of Lt-Col Arthur Chamberlain, MC, TD (d 1986), of Edgbaston, Birmingham, and Elizabeth Susan, *née* Edwards (d 1986); *b* 20 Feb 1952; *Educ* Milton Abbey Sch, Oxford Brookes Univ; *m* 18 June 1988 (m dis 1993), Dominique Jane Patricia, da of Robert Rossborough, of Geneva; 1 da (b 17 Oct 1991); *Career* Bank of London and S America Ecuador 1975–76, Bank of London and Montreal Guatemala 1976–77, Lloyds Bank International London 1977–79, dir Banco La Guaira International Venezuela 1979–82, md Lloyds Bank Nigeria Ltd 1982–84, sr corp mangr Lloyds Bank Plc London 1984–; Liveryman Worshipful Co of Gunmakers, Freeman Woshipful Co of Corwainers, Freeman City of London; *Recreations* shooting, fishing, travel, photography; *Clubs* East India, Shikar; *Style*— Arthur Chamberlain, Esq; ✉ Lloyds Bank Plc, Corporate Banking Division, 6–8 Eastcheap, London EC3 (☎ 0171 418 3621)

CHAMBERLAIN, Dr Douglas Anthony; CBE (1988); *b* 4 April 1931; *Educ* Ratcliffe Coll Leicester, Queens' Coll Cambridge, Bart's Med Coll London (MB BChir, MD (Cantab)); *m* 1958, Jennifer Ann; 2 da (Mary Ann b 5 April 1960, Frances Jane b 25 April 1961), 2 s (Antony Peter b 27 Feb 1963, Christopher David b 2 Oct 1964); *Career* house appts Barts 1956–57, SHO in med Royal Utd Hosp Bath 1957–58, resident MO Nat Heart Hosp Country Branch Maids Moreton 1958; Nat Serv jr med specialist i/c Med Div Br Mil Hosp Hostert BAOR 1959–61; med registrar Brompton Hosp 1961; Bart's: res fell Dept of Cardiology 1962–64, registrar in gen med 1964–65, sr registrar 1966–67 and 1969–70; res asst Harvard Med Sch in the Cardiac Catheterisation Unit Mass Gen Hosp Boston 1968, conslt cardiologist and physician Brighton Health Care 1970–96; concurrently: conslt cardiologist to CAA, hon sr visiting res fell Univ of Sussex Brighton, hon clinical teacher Dept of Pharmacy Univ of Brighton; former: pres Br Cardiac Soc, memb Cncl Br Heart Fndn, chm Cardiology Ctee RCP London, chm Cardiology Speciality Sub-ctee SE Thames RHA (and ex-officio memb Regnl Med Ctee), memb Cncl Coronary Prevention Gp; currently: pres Assoc of Aviation Med Examiners, advsr to Br Nat Formulary, memb Resuscitation Cncl UK, fndr memb Jt Colleges Ambulance Liaison Ctee, fndr memb and offr Euro Resuscitation Cncl, co-chm Int Liaison Ctee/Euro Resuscitation Cncl/American Heart Assoc/ECC Ctee, memb Editorial Bds Euro Heart Jl; former ed-in-chief Resuscitation, former chm of govrs Cardinal Newman Sch Hove, former chm St Thomas' Fund for the Homeless; currently: pres Brighton Orpheus Choir; Asmund S Laerdal Award (Br Assoc of Immediate Care) 1987, Paul Harris fell (Rotary Fndn of Rotary Int) 1989, Hon DSc Sussex 1989; KSG 1987, OStJ 1989; hon memb Assoc of Anaesthetists 1992; FRCP (London) 1974, FESC 1988, FACC 1992, FRCA (by special election) 1994; *Publications* author or co-author of over 140 major pubns in nat and int jls; *Style*— Dr Douglas Chamberlain, CBE; ✉ 25 Woodland Drive, Hove, E Sussex BN3 6DH (☎ 01273 882084, fax 01273 566526); Department of Cardiology, Royal Sussex County Hospital, Eastern Road, Brighton, E Sussex BN2 5BE (☎ 01273 696955, fax 01273 684554, e-mail chambda@pavilion.co.uk)

CHAMBERLAIN, Prof Geoffrey Victor Price; RD (1974); s of Albert Victor Chamberlain, MBE (d 1978), of Penylan, Cardiff, and Irene May Chamberlain, MBE, *née* Price (d 1996, aged 102); *b* 21 April 1930; *Educ* Llandaff Cathedral Sch, Cowbridge GS, UCL, University Coll Hosp Med Sch (MB BS, MD); *m* 23 June 1956, Prof Jocelyn Olivia Peter Chamberlain, da of Sir Peter Kerley, KCVO (d 1979), of Putney, London; 3 s (Christopher b 1957, Mark b 1959, Patrick b 1962), 2 da (Hilary b 1961, Virginia (Mrs James F Puzy) b 1966); *Career* RNVR 1955–57, RNR 1957–74, Surgn Lt 1955–61, Surgn Lt Cmdr 1961, Surgn Cdr 1970–74; demonstrator in anatomy Royal Univ of Malta 1956–57, resident Royal Postgraduate Med Sch, Hosp for Sick Children Great Ormond Street, and others 1958–62, registrar then sr registrar King's Coll Hosp 1962–69, visiting res fell George Washington Univ USA 1966–67, conslt obstetrician & gynaecologist Queen Charlotte's Hosp for Women 1970–82, prof and head Dept of Obstetrics & Gynaecology St George's Hosp Med Sch 1982–95, conslt obstetrician Singleton Hosp Swansea 1995–; pres RCOG 1993–94; ed-in-chief Br Jl of Obstetrics and Gynaecology 1992–94; visiting prof: USA 1984, Hong Kong 1985, Brisbane 1987, S Africa 1988, Peshwar 1993, Chicago 1995; med examiner: Univ of London 1972–, Univ of Liverpool 1973–75 and 1991–94, Univ of Manchester 1979–83, Univ of Birmingham 1979–82, Univ of Cambridge 1981–86, Univ of Glasgow 1985–87, Univ of Kuala Lumpur 1986–87, Univ of Nottingham 1987–90, Univ of Wales 1988–90, Univ of Malta 1988–91, Univ of Columbo Sri Lanka 1993–94; examiner RCOG 1972–, chm Scientific Ctee Nat Birthday Tst, chm Assoc of Profs in Obstetrics and Gynaecology; pres: Blair Bell Res Soc (former chm), Birthright Charity 1993–95, Victor Bourne Soc 1993–95; hon gynaecologist Br Airways, fell UCL, treas RSM, inspr of Nullity; Freeman of the City of London 1982, Liveryman Worshipful Soc of Apothecaries; FRCS 1960, MRCOG 1963, FRCOG 1978, FACOG (Hon) 1992, Hon FSLCOG (Sri Lankan Coll of Obstetrics & Gynaecology) 1993, Hon FFFP (Faculty of Family Planning RCOG) 1996; *Books* Lecture Notes in Obstetrics (1984, 1992, 1996), Practice of Obstetrics and Gynaecology (1985, 1990), Pregnancy Survival Manual (1986), Birthplace (1987), Lecture Notes in Gynaecology (1988, 1989, 1995), Manual of Obstetrics (1988), Obstetrics (1989), Ten Teachers in Obstetrics and Gynaecology (1990 and 1995); Preparing for Parenthood (1990), Illustrated Textbook of Obsetrics (1991), ABC of Antenatal Care (1992, 1994, 1996), Pregnacy Care in the 1990s (1992), Pain and its Relief in Childbirth (1993), Homebirths (1996), Clinical Physiology in Obstetrics (1997); *Recreations* opera, gardening, writing, travel; *Clubs* Perinatal, Blair Bell Soc, McDonald; *Style*— Prof Geoffrey Chamberlain; ✉ Sycamores, Llanmadoc, Gower, Swansea SA3 1DB (☎ 01792 386325, fax 01792 356400)

CHAMBERLAIN, Kevin John; CMG (1992); s of Arthur James Chamberlain, of Purley, Surrey, and Gladys Mary, *née* Harris; *b* 31 Jan 1942; *Educ* Wimbledon Coll, King's Coll London (LLB); *m* 23 Sept 1967, Pia Rosita, da of Jean Frauenlob, of Geneva, Switzerland; 1 da (Georgina b 26 Aug 1975); *Career* called to the Bar Inner Temple 1965; FCO: asst legal advsr 1965–73, legal advsr Br Mil Govt Berlin 1973–76, first sec (legal advsr) HM Embassy Bonn 1976–78, legal cnsllr 1979–83, cnsllr (legal advsr) Office of the UK Perm Rep to the EC 1983–87 (legal cnsllr 1987–90, dep legal advsr 1990–); *Recreations* opera, sailing, tennis, skiing; *Style*— Kevin Chamberlain, Esq, CMG; ✉ Foreign and Commonwealth Office, London SW1 2AH (☎ 0171 270 3084)

CHAMBERLAIN, The Rev (George Ford) Leo; OSB; s of late Brig Noel Chamberlain, CBE, and late Sally, *née* Ford; *b* 13 Aug 1940; *Educ* Ampleforth, Univ Coll Oxford (open scholar, MA); *Career* Ampleforth Abbey: novitiate 1961, solemn profession 1964, ordained priest 1968; Ampleforth Coll: history, politics and religious studies teacher 1968–, housemaster St Dunstan's House 1972–92, sr history master 1975–92, acting headmaster 1992–93, headmaster Jan 1993–; memb: HMC, Cncl of Mgmnt Keston Inst, Catholic Bishops' Advsy Ctee on Europe, Catholic Independent Schs Conference Ctee; *Recreations* engaged in the support of Eastern European Christians since 1970; *Clubs* East India; *Style*— The Rev Leo Chamberlain, OSB; ✉ Ampleforth College, York YO6 4ER (☎ 01439 766800, fax 01439 788330)

CHAMBERLAIN, (Leslie) Neville; CBE (1990); s of Leslie Chamberlain (d 1970), and Doris Anne, *née* Thompson; *b* 3 Oct 1939; *Educ* King James GS Bishop Auckland, King's Coll Univ of Durham; *m* 13 April 1971, Joy Rachel, da of Capt William Wellings (d 1979); 1 s (Andrew b 1984), 3 da (Louise b 1972, Elizabeth b 1974, Christina b 1981); *Career* UKAEA: mgmnt trainee 1962–64, health physicist Springfields 1964–67, res scientist Capenhurst 1967–71; mangr URENCO 1971–77; BNFL: works mangr Springfields 1977–81, enrichment business mangr Risley 1981–84, dir Enrichment Div Risley 1984–86; chief exec British Nuclear Fuels plc Risley 1986–96 (dep chm 1995–); chm Euro Nuclear Cncl 1996, Euro vice chm Int Nuclear Energy Acad; FInstM, CIMgt, FInstPh; *Recreations* racing, swimming, music; *Style*— Neville Chamberlain, Esq, CBE; ✉ Oaklands, 2 The Paddock, Hinderton Road, Neston, South Wirral, Cheshire L64 9PH (☎ 0151 353 1980); British Nuclear Fuels plc, Risley, Warrington, Cheshire (☎ 01925 835006, fax 01925 820313, telex 627581)

CHAMBERLAIN, Peter Edwin; s of Dr Eric Alfred Charles Chamberlain, OBE, and Susan Winifred Louise, *née* Bone; *b* 25 July 1939; *Educ* Royal HS, Univ of Edinburgh (BSc), RNC Manadon, RNC Greenwich, RCDS; *m* 27 July 1963, Irene May, *née* Frew; 2 s (Mark b 1964, Paul b 1965), 1 da (Louise b 1970); *Career* MOD 1963–92: asst constructor ship and submarine design ME and Bath 1963–68, constructor 1968–69, submarine construction Birkenhead 1969–72, ship structures R&D Dunfermline 1972–74, mgmnt of Postgrad Progs of Naval Architecture UCL 1974–77, Ship Design Bath 1977–78, chief constructor and head of Secretariat to DG Ships 1978–80, Surface Ship Forward Design Bath 1980–82, asst sec head of Secretariat to MGO London 1984–85, under sec dir gen Future Material Programmes 1985–87, dep controller Warship Equipment 1987–88, chief Underwater Systems Exec 1988–89, head Def Res Agency Implementation Team 1989–92; engrg dir British Aerospace Defence Ltd 1992–; memb Int Cncl on Systems Engrg (INCOSE) 1994; RCNC 1960, FRINA 1986, FEng 1988; *Recreations* jogging, music, visual arts, poetry, computing; *Style*— Peter Chamberlain, Esq, FEng; ✉ Engineering Director, British Aerospace Defence Ltd, Systems and Services Division, Warton Aerodrome, nr Preston, Lancs PR4 1AX

CHAMBERLAIN, (Richard) Sebastian Endicott; s of Lawrence Endicott Chamberlain, of Tonerspuddle, Dorchester, and Anne Zacyntha, *née* Eastwood (d 1969); *b* 13 April 1942; *Educ* Radley; *m* 1 Oct 1966, Lady Catherine Laura Chetwynd-Talbot, da of late 21 Earl of Shrewsbury and Waterford; 1 s (Tom b 1973), 2 da (Sophie b 1968, Amy b 1971); *Career* London Div RNR 1961–70, demobbed as Lt; Maguire Roy Marshall (formerly Maguire Kingsmill): joined 1960, ptnr 1974; W Greenwell & Co 1986; dir: Greenwell Montagu Stockbrokers 1987–92, Allied Provincial Securities 1993–95; div dir Brewin Dolphin Bell Lawrie 1995–; memb New Forest Dist Cncl 1973–79; Freeman: City of London 1963, Worshipful Co of Cordwainers 1963; memb Int Stock Exchange 1964; MSI; *Recreations* sailing; *Clubs* Royal Lymington Yacht; *Style*— Sebastian Chamberlain, Esq; ✉ Stocks Farm, Burley Street, Ringwood, Hampshire (☎ 01425 33313); 98 High Street, Lymington, Hampshire (☎ 01590 674288)

CHAMBERLAIN, William Richard Frank; DL (1991); s of Lt Cdr Richard Chamberlain (d 1967), and Elizabeth, *née* Robson (d 1965); *b* 13 April 1925; *Educ*

Uppingham; *m* 1960, Gillian Diarmid, da of Laurence Malcolm Trevor Castle; 1 s, 1 da; *Career* chm Stead & Simpson PLC 1983–89, regnl dir Eastern Regn National Westminster Bank PLC 1983–90; pres Northants CCC; chm: Test and County Cricket Bd 1990–94, Cricket Cncl; High Sheriff of Northamptonshire 1990–91; hon memb Worshipful Co of Pattenmakers (past Master); *Recreations* shooting, cricket; *Clubs* Naval and Military, MCC, East India; *Style—* William Chamberlain, Esq, DL; ✉ Manor House, Swineshead, Bedford MK44 2AF (☎ 01234 708283)

CHAMBERLAYNE, Michael Thomas; *b* 14 Aug 1943; *Educ* Wellington Coll; *Career* Baring Brothers: joined 1968, mangr 1977–79, asst dir 1979–85, dir 1985–86; chm: Baring Brothers Private Asset Management Ltd, Baring Brothers Trust Co Ltd, Baring Private Investment Management Ltd, Baring Managed Funds Service Ltd, Hearn Nominees Ltd; dir: Baring Asset Management Ltd, Baring Stratton Investment Trust plc, Banque Baring Brothers (Suisse) Ltd, Baring Brothers (Guernsey) Ltd; chm Bicton Park Trust Co, memb RNLI Fin Ctee; FCA (ACA 1967); *Clubs* Royal Yacht Squadron, Royal Thames Yacht, City of London; *Style—* Michael Chamberlayne, Esq; ✉ Baring Asset Management Ltd, 155 Bishopsgate, London EC2M 3XY (☎ 0171 628 6000, fax 0171 214 1657)

CHAMBERLAYNE-MACDONALD, Major Nigel Donald Peter; LVO (1960), OBE (1980), DL (1975); s of Sir Geoffrey Bosville Macdonald of the Isles, 15 Bt, MBE (d 1951), and Hon Rachael Audrey, *née* Campbell (d 1978); *b* 10 June 1927; *Educ* Radley; *m* 15 April 1958, Penelope Mary Alexandra, da of Tankerville Chamberlayne; 2 s (Alexander Nigel Bosville b 1959, Thomas Somerled b 1969), 2 da (Diana Mary (Countess of Lindsay) b 1961, Frances Penelope b 1965 d 1985); *Career* cmmnd Scots Gds 1946, served Italy 1946–47 and Malaya 1950–51, Canal Zone 1952–53; equerry to HRH The Duke of Gloucester 1954–55, asst private sec 1958–60; High Sheriff Hampshire 1974–75; a Gentleman Usher to HM The Queen 1979; memb The Queen's Body Guard for Scotland (Royal Co of Archers); chm Hants Assoc of Boys' Clubs 1967–82, a vice chm Nat Assoc of Boys' Clubs 1969–90; pres: The Coaching Club 1982–90, Eastleigh and Chandlers Ford Boy Scouts Assoc; OStJ 1958; *Recreations* coaching, shooting, stalking; *Clubs* White's, Brooks's, Pratt's, Royal Yacht Squadron; *Style—* Major Nigel Chamberlayne-Macdonald, LVO, OBE, DL; ✉ Cranbury Park, Winchester, Hants SO21 2HL (☎ 01703 252617); Glaschoille House, Knoydart, Mallaig (☎ 01687 462244); 17 William Mews, London SW1 (☎ 0171 235 5867)

CHAMBERLEN, Capt Christopher John Tankerville; LVO (1972); s of Leonard Saunders Chamberlen (d 1987), and Lillian Margaret, *née* Webley (d 1996); *b* 3 Sept 1933; *Educ* RNC Dartmouth; *m* 6 Aug 1967, Eila Margaret, da of Maj George Danielsen, MBE (d 1943); 3 da (Venetia b 1968, Annabel b 1969, Jessica b 1972); *Career* RN Capt, QHM Portsmouth 1984–87, ret 1988; chm: Victorian Cruise Line Ltd 1988–, MC Resources Ltd 1995– (dir 1992–); dir Bright Green Shipping plc 1996–; memb: Br Maritime Charitable Fndn, Hampshire Sculpture Tst, Waterman and Lighterman Coy; Freeman City of London; *Recreations* painting, shooting, racing; *Clubs* RYS, Boodle's, Farmers'; *Style—* Capt Christopher Chamberlen, LVO, RN; ✉ Home Farm Cottage, Longparish, nr Andover, Hampshire SP11 6QQ (☎ 01264 720691, fax 01264 720788)

CHAMBERLEN, Nicholas Hugh; s of Rev Leonard Saunders Chamberlen, MC (d 1987), of Heathfield, Sussex, and Lillian Margaret, *née* Webley (d 1996); *b* 18 April 1939; *Educ* Sherborne, Lincoln Coll Oxford (BA); *m* 18 Sept 1962, Jane Mary, da of Paul Lindo (d 1970); 3 s (Julian b 1964, Mark b 1965, Alexander b 1970), 1 da (Camilla b 1967); *Career* Nat Serv RN 1957–59, Lt RNR, with NCR 1962–67; Clive Discount Co Ltd 1967– (dir 1969, chm 1977–93); chm: London Discount Market Assoc 1985–87, European Corporate Finance Prudential-Bache Securities (UK) Inc 1990–92, dir Imperial Group Pension Trust Ltd 1993–; *Recreations* shooting, golf, cricket; *Clubs* Turf, R & A; *Style—* Nicholas Chamberlen, Esq; ✉ Church Farmhouse, Berwick, Polegate, East Sussex BN26 6SB

CHAMBERLIN, Peter Guy; s of Guy Ronald Chamberlin (d 1991), and his 1 w, Geraldine Mary, *née* Payne Cook (d 1963); *b* 23 June 1942; *Educ* Eton, Aix-en-Provence Univ, RMA Sandhurst (Sword of Honour); *m* 30 Nov 1968, Marion Jacqueline, da of Lt-Col John Alan Burns (d 1987); 1 s (Edward b 1974), 2 da (Lucinda b 1970, Vanessa b 1977); *Career* Army Offr; cmmnd Green Jackets 1963; served Far East, Berlin, W Germany, NI, Canada, Hong Kong, Lt-Col CO Light Div Depot Winchester, SHAPE MA D/Saceur, UKLO Heeresamt, Cologne, ret 1989; assoc dir Christies Fine Arts Auctioneers 1993– (joined 1989); HM Bodyguard Hon Corps of Gentlemen at Arms 1993–; FIMgt; *Recreations* cricket, golf, tennis and racquets, military history; *Clubs* Army & Navy, MCC, I Zingari; *Style—* Peter Chamberlin, Esq; ✉ Drove House, Coombe Bissett, Salisbury, Wilts; Christie, Manson & Woods Ltd, 8 King Street, London SW1Y 6QT (☎ 0171 839 9060)

CHAMBERLIN, Richard Alexander; s of John Alexander Chamberlin, MC, of Lenham, Kent, and Kathleen Mary, *née* Fraser (d 1990); *b* 1 July 1951; *Educ* The King's Sch Canterbury, Jesus Coll Cambridge (BA); *m* 1977, Mary-Angela, da of Norman William Stoakes Franks, of Folkestone, Kent; 2 da (Zoe b 1977, Naomi b 1979); *Career* articled Clerk Wedlake Bell 1973–75, admitted slr 1975, ptnr Freshfields 1981– (joined 1976); memb Worshipful Co of Solicitors; memb Law Soc; *Recreations* archaeology, sailing; *Clubs* Leander, Kent Archaeological Soc, Cambridge Soc (Kent Branch); *Style—* Richard Chamberlin, Esq; ✉ Freshfields, Whitefriars, 65 Fleet St, London EC4Y 1HT (☎ 0171 936 4000)

CHAMBERS, Andrew David; s of (Lewis) Harold Chambers (d 1963), of Brundall, Norfolk, and Florence Lilian, *née* Barton (d 1979); *b* 7 April 1943; *Educ* St Albans Sch, Hatfield Coll Durham (BA); *m* 1, 1969 (m dis 1984), Mary Elizabeth Ann Kilbey; 2 s (Gregory b 1976, Thomas b 1979); m 2, 2 Oct 1987, Celia Barrington, da of Rev Hugh Pruen, of Ashleigh, Old Bolingbroke, Lincs; 2 s (Theo b 1990, Cosmo b 1992), 2 da (Chloë b 1988, Phoebe b 1992), 1 step s (Henry b 1985); *Career* audit sr Arthur Andersen & Co 1965–69, admin exec Barker & Dobson 1969–70, systems gp mangr fin United Biscuits 1970–71; City University Business School: lectr computer applications in accountancy 1971–74, Leverhulme sr res fell internal auditing 1974–78, sr lectr audit and mgmnt control 1978–83, prof of internal auditing 1983–93, admin sub-dean 1983–86, dean 1986–91 (acting dean 1985–86); prof of audit and control Univ of Hull 1994–; visiting prof in computer auditing Univ of Leuven Belgium 1980–81 and 1991–92; warden Northampton Hall City Univ 1983–86 (dep warden 1972–76); memb: Cncl BCS 1979–82, Educn Training & Technol Transfer Ctee Br Malaysian Soc 1987–91; dir: National Home Loans plc, National Mortgage Bank 1991–92, Management Audit Ltd 1991–; govr Islington Green Sch 1989–91; CEng, FBCS, FCCA, FCA, FIIA, FRSA; *Books* Keeping Computers Under Control (with O J Hanson, 1975), Internal Auditing (1981), Computer Auditing (1981), Effective Internal Audits (1992), Auditing the IT Environment (with G Rand, 1994), Auditing Contracts (with G Rand, 1994), Internal Auditing (ed, 1996); *Recreations* family, conservation; *Clubs* Reform, Travellers'; *Style—* Andrew Chambers; ✉ Management Audit Ltd, Watermill, Moat Lane, Old Bolingbroke, Spilsby, Lincs PE23 4EU (☎ 01790 763350, fax 01790 763253)

CHAMBERS, Antony Craven; s of Brig Samuel Craven Chambers, CBE, of 45 Hillhead Rd, Fareham, and Mary Agnes, *née* McAllister; *b* 8 Dec 1943; *Educ* Ampleforth, St Catherine's Coll Oxford (MA), Manchester Business Sch (MBA); *m* 24 July 1965, Rosemary Isabel, da of Wing Cdr Gerald Constable Maxwell, MC, DFC, AFC, AEM (d 1959), of Alresford House, Alresford, Hants; 3 s (Dominic b 1966, Sebastian b 1967, Mungo b 1977), 2 da (Antonia b 1974, Alexandra b 1979); *Career* joined Gren Gds 1966, served Cyprus, Trucial States and Northern Ireland; with Hill Samuel & Co Ltd 1970–71; First Chicago 1972: project fin 1972–74, business devpt UK 1975–77, gp head banking and mktg 1978–83, head strategic planning Europe 1984; Robert Fleming & Co Ltd: dir responsible for commercial banking 1984–, head of Gp Treasy, Stocklending and Custody Ops 1994; dir Robert Fleming Holdings Ltd 1991–, chm Flemings Offshore 1995 and memb Gp Exec Ctee 1996–; memb Exec Ctee and Control Bd Army Benevolent Fndn 1979, vice chm Army Cadet Force Assoc 1993; *Recreations* sailing; *Style—* Antony Chambers, Esq; ✉ Robert Fleming & Co Limited, 25 Copthall Avenue, London EC2R 7DR (☎ 0171 638 5858, fax 0171 382 8185, telex 297451)

CHAMBERS, David Phillip; s of Joseph Christopher Chambers (d 1994), and Bernadette Mary, *née* Costello (d 1978); *b* 2 Aug 1953; *Educ* Beaufoy Sch Lambeth, Slough Coll of Further Educn (City and Guilds basic cookery), Ealing Coll of Further Educn (City and Guilds Chefs Dip), Westminster Coll of Further Educn; *m* 7 March 1987, Helena, da of Branko Nikola Jovicich; 2 da (Zoe Anne b 17 April 1975, Amy Louise b 21 Aug 1978), 1 s (Liam Christie b 12 Nov 1992); *Career* apprentice chef: Piccadilly Hotel 1969–70, St Ermins Hotel 1970–71; chef tournant St Ermins Hotel 1971–72, chef saucier East Indian Sports and Public Schools Club 1972, Claridges Hotel 1973–74 (commis poissonier, commis saucier), chef gardemanger St Ermins Hotel 1974; sous chef: Mullard House 1974–75, Army and Navy Club 1975–76, Carlton Tower Hotel 1976–78; executive chef Portman Intercontinental 1980–81 (sous chef rising to first sous chef 1978–80), exec chef Le Restaurant Dolphin Square 1981, first sous chef Hyatt Carlton Tower 1981–82, chef de cuisine Dukes Hotel 1982–85; exec head chef: Le Meridien Piccadilly 1985–94, London Hilton on Park Lane 1994–; various tv appearances; awards for the Oak Room Restaurant: one Michelin Star, three AA rosettes, one Star Egon Ronay, 4/5 Good Food Guide, 17/20 and three Toques Gault Millau; awards for Windows Roof Restaurant: three AA rosettes, 3/5 Good Food Guide, 16/20 and two Toques Gault Millau; memb: Academie Culinaire de France, Conseil Culinaire Français (Palmes Culinaires), Guilde des Fromagers Compagnon de Saint-Uguzon; *Recreations* cooking, reading; *Style—* David Chambers, Esq; ✉ London Hilton on Park Lane, 22 Park Lane, London W1Y 4BE (☎ 0171 493 8000, fax 493 4957)

CHAMBERS, Dr Douglas Robert (Bob); s of Douglas Henry Chambers, of East Sheen (d 1979), and Elizabeth Chambers, *née* Paterson, of Richmond (d 1987); *b* 2 Nov 1929; *Educ* Sheen GS, King's Coll London (AKC, MB BS), Univ of London (external LLB), Univ Coll Swansea (MA), FInstBiol; *m* 8 Jan 1955, Barbara (June), *née* Rowe; 1 s (Robert Mark b 1958), 2 da (Barbara Lynn b 1955, Judith Elizabeth b 1961); *Career* Flt Lt RAF Med Branch 1955–58 (served Jordan 1956–57); called to the Bar Lincoln's Inn 1965; divnl dir (medical) Hoechst Pharmaceuticals 1965–70; HM Coroner: Inner N London 1970–94, City of London 1994–; hon lectr in legal med: City Univ, Royal Free Hosps; chm Animal Welfare in Res and Educn Inst of Biology 1992–95; awarded Baron C ver Heyden de Lancey Law/Medicine prize by RSM 1990; *Recreations* history of coroners, scouting; *Clubs* Auriol-Kensington Rowing; *Style—* Dr Bob Chambers; ✉ 4 Ormond Ave, Richmond, Surrey TW10 6TN (☎ 0181 940 7745); Coroners Court, Milton Court, Moor Lane, London EC2Y 9BL (☎ 0171 332 1598, fax 0171 260 1119)

CHAMBERS, Lt Col John Craven; s of Ernest Chambers (d 1996), of Seaton, Devon, and Margaret Joyce, *née* Batty; *b* 17 March 1947; *Educ* Latymer Upper, RMA Sandhurst (Agar Meml Prize), RMCS (BSc), Cranfield Univ (MSc), Army Staff Course (Div 1), RAF Advanced Staff Course; *m* 4 Sept 1971, Sandra, da of Herbert William Raby (d 1996); 1 da (Kathryn Jay b 11 August 1973), 1 s (Daniel John b 1 March 1975); *Career* cmmnd Royal Corps of Signals 1967, served various staff and field appts MOD and res estabs in Germany, Cyprus and the Falkland Islands until 1993; sec/chief exec Masonic Tst for Girls and Boys 1993–; Freeman City of London 1994; *Recreations* music (organ playing and singing), golf, bridge, Freemasonry; *Clubs* Naval and Military; *Style—* Lt Col John Chambers; ✉ Rustlings, Castle Road, Horsell, Surrey GU21 4ET (☎ and fax 01483 723543); Secretary, Masonic Trust for Girls and Boys, 31 Great Queen Street, London WC2B 5AG (☎ 0171 405 2644, fax 0171 831 4094)

CHAMBERS, Lucinda Anne; da of Michael and Anne Chambers; *b* 17 Dec 1959; *Educ* Convent of the Sacred Heart Woldingham; *children* 1 s (Toby Knott b 23 Feb 1988); *m* June 1991, Simon Crow; *Career* sr fashion ed Elle Magazine UK 1986–88, fashion dir Vogue Magazine 1992– (former exec fashion ed); *Style—* Miss Lucinda Chambers; ✉ Vogue, Vogue House, Hanover Square, London W1R 0AD (☎ 0171 499 9080)

CHAMBERS, Nicholas Mordaunt; QC (1985); s of Marcus Mordaunt Bertrand Chambers, and Lona Margit, *née* Gross (d 1987); *b* 25 Feb 1944; *Educ* King's Sch Worcester, Hertford Coll Oxford; *m* 1966, Sarah Elizabeth, da of Thomas Herbert Fothergill Banks; 2 s, 1 da; *Career* called to the Bar Gray's Inn 1966 (bencher 1994), recorder of the Crown Court 1987–, dep High Ct judge 1994–; *Recreations* sketching; *Clubs* Garrick, Lansdowne; *Style—* Nicholas Chambers, Esq, QC; ✉ Brick Court Chambers, 15–19 Devereux Court, London WC2R 3JJ (☎ 0171 583 0777)

CHAMBERS, Prof Richard Dickinson; *b* 16 March 1935; *Educ* Stanley GS, Univ of Durham (PhD, DSc); *m* 17 Aug 1959, Anne, *née* Boyd; 1 s (Mark b 1963), 1 da (Louise b 1965); *Career* res fell Univ of BC Canada 1959–60, visiting lectr Fulbright fell Case Western Reserve Univ Cleveland Ohio 1966–67, fndn fell Univ of Durham 1988–89 (lectr 1960, reader 1968, prof 1976–, head of dept 1983–86); memb: Royal Soc of Chem, American Chem Soc; *Books* Fluorine in Organic Chemistry (1973); *Recreations* opera, soccer, jogging; *Style—* Prof Richard Chambers; ✉ 5 Aykley Green, Whitesmocks, Durham DH1 4LN (☎ 0191 386 5791); Department of Chemistry, University Science Laboratories, South Rd, Durham DH1 3LE (☎ 0191 374 3120, fax 0191 374 3741, e-mail R.D.CHAMBERS@durham.ac.uk)

CHAMBERS, His Hon Judge; Richard Rodney (Dick); QC (1965); s of John Hilliard Chambers (d 1976), and Maud Mary, *née* Jamison (d 1973); *b* 15 Aug 1927; *Educ* Royal Belfast Academical Inst, Queen's Univ Belfast (LLB, Rugby Blue); *m* 15 Sept 1953, Brenda Elizabeth, da of William Cox; 3 da ((Elizabeth) Jane b 24 March 1955, (Barbara) Jill b 8 Jan 1957, Karen Caroline b 28 July 1967), 1 s ((Richard) Alan b 26 May 1959); *Career* called to the Bar NI 1950, counsel to Speakers of NI Parl 1967, chm Mental Health Review Tbnl 1971–73, co court judge (assigned to Tyrone & Fermanagh, Armagh and North Antrim) 1973–, chief social security cmmr NI 1985–; Bencher Inn of Court NI; played rugby for Ireland 1951 and 1952; *Recreations* gardening, golf; *Style—* His Hon Judge Chambers, QC; ✉ Beira-Mar, 692 Shore Road, Jordanstown, Newtownabbey, Co Antrim BT37 0PS

CHAMBERS, Robert George; s of Peter Bertram Chambers, of Thetford, Norfolk, and Wendy, *née* Randall; *b* 30 May 1954; *Educ* Oundle, Univ of Hull (BSc); *m* 16 May 1987, (Christine) Belinda, da of Roy Johnson, of Littlington, Hertfordshire; 2 s (Nicholas b 6 Dec 1989, Charles Robert b 10 Aug 1993), 1 da (Serena b 13 Dec 1990); *Career* ptnr Wedd Durlacher Mordaunt and Co 1985–86; dir: Barclays de Zoete Wedd 1986–89, ABN AMRO Hoare Govett Securities 1989–; memb London Stock Exchange 1980; *Recreations* shooting, fishing, cricket, golf; *Clubs* MCC, Royal Worlington Golf; *Style—* Robert Chambers, Esq; ✉ ABN AMRO Hoare Govett, 4 Broadgate, London EC2 (☎ 0171 601 0101)

CHAMBERS, Prof Robert John Haylock; OBE (1995); *b* 1 May 1932; *m* Jennifer; 3 c; *Career* fell IDS Univ of Sussex 1972–; memb Admin Staff Coll Hyderabad India 1989–91; varied experience incl rural field res India, Kenya and Sri Lanka and participatory rural appraisal devpt and trg; formerly: evaluation offr UNHCR Geneva, lectr Univ of Glasgow, prog offr Ford Fndn New Delhi, memb Band Aid/Live Aid Project Ctee; tstee

Action Aid 1993–; sometime conslt: Aga Khan Fndn, Br Cncl, FAO, Ford Fndn, Consultative Gp for Int Agric Res, House of Commons, Int Inst for Environment and Devpt, ILO, INTRAC, League of Red Cross and Res Crescent Socs, Swedish Int Devpt Agency, Swiss Devpt Cooperation, ODA, World Bank; *Books* incl: Settlement Schemes in Tropical Africa (1969), Managing Rural Development - Ideas and Experience from East Africa (1974), Seasonal Dimensions to Rural Poverty (jt ed, 1981), Rural Development - Putting the Last First (1983), Managing Canal Irrigation - Practical Analysis from South Asia (1988), To the Hands of the Poor - Water and Trees (jtly, 1989), Farmer First - Farmer Innovation and Agricultural Research (jt ed, 1989), Challenging the Professions: frontiers for rural development (1993), Whose Reality Counts? Putting the first last (1996); over 100 articles in jls and chapters in books; *Recreations* rock climbing, mountaineering; *Style*— Prof Robert J H Chambers, OBE; ✉ Institute of Development Studies, University of Sussex, Brighton BN1 9RE (☎ 01273 606261, fax 01273 621202/691647)

CHAMBERS, Timothy Lachlan; JP (Bristol 1993); adopted s of Victor Lachlan Chambers (d 1970), of Purley, Surrey, and Elsie Ruth, *née* Reynolds; *b* 11 Feb 1946; *Educ* Wallington Co GS, King's Coll London and King's Coll Hosp Univ of London (MB BS); *m* 9 Oct 1971, (Elizabeth) Joanna, da of John Carrington Ward (d 1989), of Barnstone, Notts; 1 s (Oliver Lachlan Dorrington b 1978), 2 da (Catherine Louise b 1973, Rachel Elizabeth b 1976); *Career* physician: Derbyshire Children's Hosp and Children's Depts of Nottingham Hosps 1976–79, Royal Hosp for Sick Children Bristol, Dept of Paediatrics Southmead Hosp and Weston-super-Mare General Hospital 1979–; Univ of Bristol: clinical lectr in child health 1979–, a clinical dean 1983–90; conslt in paediatrics to Miny of Defence 1985–, civilian conslt in paediatrics to RN 1993–; Major RAMC (V); dep med dir Southmead Health Servs NHS Tst 1994–96; pres: Union of Nat Euro Paediatric Socs and Assocs 1990–92 and 1992–94, Paediatric Section RSM 1994–95, Bristol Medico-Chirurgical Soc 1996–97; censor RCP 1993–94 (pro-censor 1992–93); memb: Cncl RCP 1979–80, 1981–82 and 1990–92, Paediatric Bd RCP 1991–94, Ctee Bristol Medico-Legal Soc 1990–94; regional advsr (SW England) RCPEd 1996–; memb Governing Bd: Inst of Child Health Univ of Bristol 1987–, Hosps for Sick Children (London) Special Health Authy 1994–94; present and past examiner to: Univs of Bristol and Colombo, Royal Colls of Physicians of London, Edinburgh and Ireland, Soc of Apothecaries, Conjoint Bd, Royal Coll of Midwives; patron Lifeline charity, memb and chm numerous local, national and international professional advsy ctees; reader and Eucharistic min Cathedral Church of SS Peter and Paul Clifton; memb: Coll of Paediatrics and Child Health (formerly Br Paediatric Assoc) 1976– (hon sec 1984–89), Euro Soc for Paediatric Nephrology 1978–, Philosophical Soc Oxford 1990–; membre correspondant de la Société Française de Pédiatrie 1994; Liveryman Worshipful Soc of Apothecaries 1982, Freeman City of London 1983; FRSM 1979 (memb Cncl Paediatrics 1995–, memb Nephrology and Utd Servs Sections), FRCP 1983, FRCPEd 1985, FRCPI 1995; *Books* Fluid Therapy in Childhood (1987), Clinical Paediatric Nephrology (chapter, 1986 and 1994), author of many contribs to scientific and lay literature; *Clubs* Athenaeum, Army and Navy, Clifton (Bristol); *Style*— Dr Timothy Chambers; ✉ 4 Clyde Park, Bristol BS6 6RR (☎ 0117 974 2814); (rooms) 2 Clifton Park, Bristol BS8 3BS (☎ 0117 973 0622)

CHAMBRUN, Comtesse Jean-François de; Raine; da of Alexander McCorquodale (1 cous of 1 Baron McCorquodale of Newton, PC) by his 1 w Dame Barbara Cartland, DBE, *qv*; *b* 9 Sept 1929; *m* 1, 1948 (m dis 1976), as his 1 w, 9 Earl of Dartmouth; 3 s (Viscount Lewisham, Hon Rupert Legge, Hon Henry Legge), 1 da (Lady Charlotte Legge (Duchesa di Carcaci)); m 2, 1976, as his 2 w, 8 Earl Spencer, LVO, DL (d 1992); m 3, 8 July 1993 (m dis 1996), as his 2 w, Comte Jean-François Pineton de Chambrun, 3 s of Marquis de Chambrun; *Career* formerly a LCC Voluntary Care Ctee worker in Wandsworth and Vauxhall, and actively involved in the welfare of the elderly in other areas; memb Lewisham W LCC 1958–65; memb: GLC (Richmond) 1967–73, GLC Gen Purposes Ctee 1971–73; former memb BBC Nat Agric Advsy Ctee, chm Govt Working Pty on the Human Habitat for UN Conference on the Environment (which produced The Dartmouth Report, How Do You Want To Live?), and a UK delegate at the Conf in Stockholm 1972; chm: GLC Historic Bldgs Bd 1968–71, Covent Gdn Devpt Ctee 1971–75, UK Exec Ctee of European Architectural Heritage Year 1975; memb: English Tourist Bd 1971–75, BTA Infrastructure Ctee 1972–, Advsy Cncl V & A 1980–, BTA 1982–93, Ctee Prestige Tourism for City of Nice, Special Jury for the Improvement of the Promenade des Anglais Nice; chm: BTA Spas Ctee 1981–83, BTA Hotels and Restaurants Ctee 1983–87, BTA Accommodation Ctee 1987–93, BTA Commendation Schemes Panel 1982–89, BTA Devpt Ctee 1987–93, BTA Come to Britain Awards 1990–93, BTA Britain Welcomes Japan Ctee of Honour and Exec Ctee 1989, Ctee for Business Sponsorship of the Arts; awarded a Gold medal for public speaking, and a former guest speaker at Oxford Univ and Cambridge Univ debates; lectr at: Holloway, Maidstone and Wandsworth Prisons; *Books* The Spencers on Spas (with photographs by Earl Spencer); *Style*— Comtesse Raine de Chambrun; ✉ 24 Farm Street, London W1X 7RE (☎ 0171 495 4525, fax 0171 495 4524)

CHAMPION, Dr Audrey Elizabeth; da of Robert George Champion, of Alveston, N Avon, and Muriel Madge, *née* Matthews; *b* 13 July 1951; *Educ* Thornbury GS, Univ of Sheffield (MB ChB); *m* 8 Oct 1977, John Robert Glover Rogerson, s of Benjamin Rogerson, of Morley, Leeds (d 1955); 1 s (Alastair b 1989), 1 da (Kathryn b 1987); *Career* dir (designate) North Wales Cancer Centre 1997–; visiting conslt: Doncaster Health Authy 1984–92, Rotherham Health Authy 1992–97; conslt in clinical oncology Weston Park Hosp NHS Tst Sheffield 1984–97; dir CME Royal Coll of Radiologists 1996–; memb: BMA, Br Oncological Assoc; FRCR 1981, FRCP 1996 (MRCP 1977); *Style*— Dr Audrey Champion; ✉ Glan Clwyd District General Hospital, Rhyl, Denbighshire LL18 5UJ (☎ 01745 583910, fax 01745 583143)

CHAMPION, Jonathan Martin (Jon); s of David Yeo Champion, of York, and Maureen Ray, *née* Wilby; *b* 23 May 1965; *Educ* Archbishop Holgate's GS York, Trinity and All Saints' Coll Leeds (BA); *m* 1 Oct 1994, Anna Clare, *née* Clarke; 1 da (Emily Susannah b 6 July 1995); *Career* sports broadcaster; sports reporter BBC Radio Leeds 1988–89, presenter BBC Night Network 1989, presenter/commentator BBC Radio Sport 1990–96 (incl: occasional presenter Sports Report, presenter Champion Sport Radio 5, worked at World Cups 1990 and 1994 and Olympic Games 1992 and 1996); football commentator Match of the Day BBC TV 1995–; *Recreations* music (piano and violin player), fell walking, cycling, cricket; *Clubs* York CC; *Style*— Jon Champion, Esq; ✉ BBC TV Sport, Television Centre, Wood Lane, London W12 7RT (☎ 0181 743 8000)

CHAMPION, Robert (Bob); MBE; s of Bob Champion (d 1987), and Phyllis Doreen Champion, of Newmarket, Suffolk; *b* 4 June 1948; *Educ* Earl Haig Sch Guisborough Yorks; *m* 1, Oct 1982 (m dis 1985), Jo; 1 s (Michael Robert b 1983); m 2, Oct 1987, Denise Frances (Dee), da of Frank Leonard Taylor (d 1972), of Hatfield Heath, Bishops Stortford; 1 da (Henrietta Camilla b 1988); *Career* jockey and racehorse trainer; one of the four top jockeys of the 1970s, recovered from cancer to win 1981 Grand National on Aldaniti (portrayed by John Hurt in film Champions 1984); fndr Bob Champion Cancer Tst; *Books* Champion Story; *Recreations* riding; *Style*— Bob Champion, Esq, MBE

CHAMPNESS, John Ashley; *b* 17 April 1938; *m* Sandra; 2 da (Joanna Louise, Charlotte Helen); *Career* chm: Lowndes Lambert Marine Ltd, Lowndes Lambert Aviation Ltd; dir: Lowndes Lambert Group Ltd, Lowndes Lambert Group (Holdings) Ltd, Lambert Brothers (Hong Kong) Ltd, Lowndes Lambert Marine Holdings Ltd, Jeffreys Coates and Associates Ltd, Ramon International Ltd; *Style*— John Champness, Esq; ✉ Stoneraise, Plummers Plain, Horsham, W Sussex; Lowndes Lambert Group Ltd, Friary Court, Crutched Friars London EC3N 2NP (☎ 0171 560 3000)

CHANCE, Alan Derek; s of Derek Arthur Chance, of Funtington, Chichester, and Kay, *née* Renshaw (d 1988); *b* 12 April 1951; *Educ* Eton, Merton Coll Oxford (BA); *m* 30 May 1981, Sarah Elizabeth, da of (William) Dennis Delany, of Chelwood, West Broyle Dr, nr Chichester; 2 s (Benjamin b 1984, Thomas b 1987); *Career* dir Streets Financial Ltd 1979–83, chm Chance Plastics Ltd 1978–87; md: Money Marketing Ltd 1983–86, The Moorgate Group plc 1988–89 (dir 1986), ptnr Chance Jarosz 1990–93, dir Allison Mitchell Ltd 1992–; *Recreations* skiing, backgammon, croquet; *Clubs* Hurlingham; *Style*— Alan Chance, Esq; ✉ Allison Mitchell Ltd, 54 Artillery Lane, London E1 7LS (☎ 0171 247 7893)

CHANCE, Sir (George) Jeremy ffolliott; 4 Bt (UK 1900), of Grand Avenue, Hove, Co Sussex; s of Sir Roger James Ferguson Chance, 3 Bt, MC (d 1987), and Mary Georgina, *née* Rowney (d 1984); *b* 24 Feb 1926; *Educ* Gordonstoun, Ch Ch Oxford (MA); *m* 4 March 1950, his cousin, Cecilia Mary Elizabeth, 2 da of Sir (William) Hugh Stobart Chance, CBE (d 1981); 2 s ((John) Sebastian b 1954, Roger William Tobias (Toby) b 1960), 2 da (Victoria Katharine Elizabeth b 1952, Helena Mary ffolliott (Mrs Beaufoy) b 1957); *Heir* s, (John) Sebastian Chance b 2 Oct 1954; *Career* late Lt RNVR, former dir Massey-Ferguson Ltd Coventry; *Recreations* making lakes, planting trees, choral singing, painting; *Style*— Sir Jeremy Chance, Bt; ✉ Rhosgyll Fawr, Chwilog, Pwllheli, Gwynedd (☎ 01766 810584)

CHANCE, Michael Edward Ferguson; s of John Wybergh Chance (d 1984), of London, and Wendy Muriel Chance (d 1970); *b* 7 March 1955; *Educ* Eton, King's Coll Cambridge (MA); *Career* opera and concert singer; BBC Promenade Concerts 1985–, Lincoln Centre NY 1985, La Scala Milan 1985, Lyon Opera 1985 Andronico in Tamerlano, Paris Opera 1988 Ptolomeo in Giulio Cesare, princ singer Kent Opera 1984–88, debut Glyndebourne Festival 1989 Oberon in A Midsummer Night's Dream, Netherlands Opera 1990 Anfinomo in Il Ritorno D'Ulisse, Sao Carlo Lisbon 1991 Gofredo in Rinaldo; debuts: Royal Opera House Covent Garden 1992 Apollo in Death in Venice, ENO 1992 Anfinomo in Return of Ulysses, Scottish Opera 1992 title role in Julius Caesar, Australian Opera Sydney 1993 Oberon in A Midsummer Night's Dream; made over 50 recordings; *Style*— Michael Chance, Esq; ✉ c/o Philip Cole, IMG Artists Europe, Media House, 3 Burlington Lane, London W4 2TH (☎ 0181 747 9977)

CHANCE, Michael Spencer; s of Ernest Horace Chance (d 1980), of Church Stretton, Shropshire, and Florence, *née* Kitson (d 1992); *b* 14 May 1938; *Educ* Rossall; *m* 9 June 1962, Enid Mabel, da of Harry Carter (d 1958), of West Hagley, Worcs; 3 da (Karen b 1963, Helen b 1965, Susan b 1965); *Career* slr; asst DPP 1981–85, chief crown prosecutor for N London 1986–87, dep dir Serious Fraud Office 1987–90, exec counsel Accountants' Joint Disciplinary Scheme 1993–; *Style*— Michael Chance, Esq; ✉ Box Tree Cottage, Arkesden, Saffron Walden, Essex CB11 4EX (☎ 01799 550800)

CHANCELLOR, Alexander Surtees; s of Sir Christopher John Chancellor, CMG (d 1989), and Sylvia Mary, OBE (d 1996), eld da of Sir Richard Paget, 2 Bt, and his 1 w, Lady Muriel Finch-Hatton, CBE, only da of 12 Earl of Winchilsea and Nottingham; *b* 4 Jan 1940; *Educ* Eton, Trinity Hall Cambridge; *m* 1964, Susanna, da of Martin Debenham, JP (3 s of Sir Ernest Debenham, 1 Bt, JP, and Cecily, niece of Rt Hon Joseph Chamberlain); 2 da; *Career* Reuters News Agency 1964–74, ed The Spectator 1975–84, asst ed The Sunday Telegraph 1984–86; dep ed The Sunday Telegraph 1986, US ed The Independent 1986–88, ed The Independent Magazine 1988–92, writer The New Yorker 1992–93, assoc ed The Sunday Telegraph 1994–95, ed The Sunday Telegraph Magazine 1995, currently freelance and weekly columnist Saturday Guardian; *Style*— Alexander Chancellor, Esq

CHANDLER, Charles Henry; s of late Charles Chandler; *b* 6 March 1940; *Educ* Highgate; *m* 1965, Christine Elizabeth, *née* Dunn; 1 s (Stephen), 1 da (Dani); *Career* chm Walthamstow Stadium Ltd 1976–; dir: Greyhound Racing Association Ltd 1965–, British Greyhound Racing Board 1992–, British Greyhound Racing Fund 1993–; chm NGRC Racecourse Promoters Ltd 1992–; *Style*— Charles Chandler, Esq; ✉ Mymfield, Kentish Lane, Brookmans Park, Hatfield, Herts AL9 6NQ (☎ 01707 652478, fax 01707 653414); office (☎ and fax 0181 903 2775)

CHANDLER, Sir Colin Michael; kt (1988); s of Henry John Chandler, and Mary Martha, *née* Bowles; *b* 7 Oct 1939; *Educ* St Joseph's Acad Blackheath, Hatfield Poly; *m* 8 Aug 1964, Jennifer Mary Crawford; 1 s (Jamie), 1 da (Pippa); *Career* commercial apprentice de Havilland Aircraft Co 1956–61, contracts offr Hawker Siddeley Aviation Hatfield 1962–66; Hawker Siddeley Aviation Kingston: commercial mangr 1967–72, commercial dir 1973–76, dir and gen mangr 1977; gp mktg dir British Aerospace 1983–85 (divnl md Kingston-Brough Div 1978–82), seconded to MoD as Head of Defence Export Servs 1985–89; chief exec Vickers PLC 1992– (md 1990–92); non-exec dir: TI Group plc 1992–, Guardian Royal Exchange plc 1995–; vice pres Engrg Employers' Fedn, ctee memb DTI Priority Japan Campaign; memb: Nat Defence Industries Cncl, DTI Overseas Project Bd Healthcare Sector Gp, Devpt Bd Royal Inst of Int Affairs; Cdr Order of the Lion of Finland 1982; FRAeS; *Recreations* tennis, jogging, gardening, theatre; *Clubs* Reform, Mark's; *Style*— Sir Colin Chandler; ✉ Vickers PLC, Millbank Tower, Millbank, London SW1P 4RA (☎ 0171 828 7777, fax 0171 828 6585)

CHANDLER, Sir Geoffrey; kt (1983), CBE (1976); s of Dr Frederick George Chandler (d 1942), and Marjorie, *née* Raimes (d 1988), of Newdigate, Surrey; *b* 15 Nov 1922; *Educ* Sherborne, Trinity Coll Cambridge (MA); *m* 1955, Lucy Bertha, da of Prof Patrick Buxton, CMG (d 1956); 4 da; *Career* BBC 1949–51, Financial Times 1951–56; Royal Dutch/Shell Group 1956–78 (chm and md Shell Trinidad Ltd 1964–69; dir: Shell International, Shell Petroleum, Shell Petroleum NV); dir gen NEDO 1978–83, dir Indust Year 1986 1984–86, ldr Indust Matters 1987–89, indust advsr to Royal Soc of Arts 1987–92, chm Nat Cncl for Voluntary Orgns 1989–96, chm Amnesty Int UK Business Gp 1992–; hon fell: Sheffield Hallam Univ, Girton Coll Cambridge; Hon DSc: CNAA, Univ of Bradford, Aston Univ; *Recreations* gardening, music; *Style*— Sir Geoffrey Chandler, CBE; ✉ 46 Hyde Vale, Greenwich, London SE10 8HP (☎ 0181 692 5304)

CHANDLER, Godfrey John; *b* 4 July 1925; *Educ* Clarks Coll London; *m* 1948, Audrey Haydee, *née* Pilon; 3 s (Timothy b 1952, Graham b 1953, Henry b 1960), 1 da (Susan b 1949); *Career* ptnr Cazenove & Co 1957–85; dir: Globe Investment Trust plc 1980–90, Strata Investment Trust plc 1985–90, Stratton Investment Trust plc 1986–90, Lloyds Development Capital Ltd 1986–90, Halifax Building Soc (London Bd 1981–87); dep chm W H Smith Group 1982–88; govr Jawarharlal Nehru Meml Tst 1986–95; hon fell Darwin Coll Cambridge; *Recreations* gardening, chess; *Clubs* City of London; *Style*— Godfrey Chandler, Esq; ✉ Stormont Court, Godden Green, Sevenoaks, Kent TN15 OJS (☎ 01732 761505)

CHANDLER, Dr (William) John; s of Harold Grant Chandler (d 1985); *b* 31 May 1932; *Educ* Welwyn Garden City GS, Jesus Coll Cambridge (MA), Brunel Univ (PhD); *m* 1956, Margaret Rosa, da of Herbert B Thomas (d 1977); 3 c; *Career* called to the Bar Middle Temple; International Publishing Corp: co sec 1963, admin dir 1970; exec and planning dir Reed Int 1975, strategic mgmnt conslt 1988; chm: Chandlers, Prospektus Ltd; former prof Dept of Cybernetics Brunel Univ; ASCA, FCybS; *Books* Techniques of Scenario Planning (with Paul Cockle), Science of History (1984), Practical Business Planning (1987); *Recreations* yachting, music, history; *Style*— Dr John Chandler; ✉ 3 Willow Grove, Welwyn Garden City, Herts (☎ 01707 324600, fax 01707 376003)

CHANDLER, Prof Tony John; s of Harold William Chandler (d 1975), and Florence Ellen, *née* Moore (d 1970); *b* 7 Nov 1928; *Educ* Alderman Newton GS Leicester, King's Coll London (BSc, DipEd, MSc, PhD, MA); *m* 4 Sept 1954, Margaret Joyce; 1 s (Adrian Mark b 1960), 1 da (Kathryn Anne (Mrs Peneycad) b 1957); *Career* Nat Serv 1 Lt RAF 1950–52; prof: UCL 1969–73 (lectr 1956–65, reader 1965–69), Univ of Manchester 1973–77; master of Birkbeck Coll London 1977–79 (lectr 1952–56); author of numerous articles in meteorological and geographical jls; vice pres RMS 1973–75 (sec 1969–73); memb: NERC, Ctee of Experts on Major Hazards Health and Safety Exec, Royal Cmmn on Environmental Pollution 1973–77, Royal Soc Study Gp on Pollution in the Atmosphere 1974–77, Standing Ctee on Energy and the Environment 1978; *Books* The Climate of London (1965), Modern Meteorology and Climatology (1972 and 1981); *Recreations* clock making and collecting, reading, travel, music; *Style—* Prof Tony Chandler; ✉ Charnwood, 44 Knoll Rise, Orpington, Kent BR6 0EL (☎ 01689 832880)

CHANDOS, 3 Viscount (1954 UK); Thomas Orlando Lyttelton; s of 2 Viscount Chandos (d 1980, himself ggs of 4 Baron Cobham) and Caroline (da of Sir Alan Lascelles, who was in his turn gs of 4 Earl of Harewood); *b* 12 Feb 1953; *Educ* Eton, Worcester Coll Oxford; *m* 19 Oct 1985, Arabella Sarah Lucy, da of Adrian Bailey, by his 1 wife Mary Katherine (now Lady Mary Russell), o da of 12 Earl of Haddington, KT; 2 s (Hon Oliver, Hon Benedict b 30 April 1988), 1 da (Hon Rosanna Mary b 19 March 1990); *Heir* s, Hon Oliver Antony Lyttelton b 21 Feb 1986; *Career* corp fin dir Kleinwort Benson 1985–93, exec dir Botts & Co 1994–; non-exec dir: Capital and Regional Properties plc 1993–, Lopex 1993–, Chrysalis Group plc 1994–96; *Style—* The Rt Hon the Viscount Chandos; ✉ 149 Gloucester Avenue, London NW1 8LA (☎ 0171 722 8329); Botts & Company Ltd, Lintas House, 15–19 New Fetter Lane, London EC4A 1BA (☎ 0171 379 5040, fax 0171 379 3101)

CHANG, Jung; *née* Er-Hong; da of Shou-Yu Chang (d 1975), of Yibin, China, and De-Hong Xia, *née* Bao-Qin Xue; *b* 25 March 1952; *Educ* No 4 Middle Sch Chengdu (oldest state sch in China, founded 141 BC), Sichuan Univ (BA), Ealing Coll of Higher Educn, Univ of York (PhD, first person from Communist China to receive PhD from British inst); *m* 26 July 1991, Jon Arthur George Halliday; *Career* author; Hon DLit Buckingham Univ 1996; *Books* Wild Swans - Three Daughters of China (1992, NCR Book Award 1992, Writers' Guild of GB Best Non-Fiction Award 1992, Fawcett Soc Book Award 1992, Book of the Year 1993, Humo's Gouden Bladw'jzer Belgium 1993 and 1994, Bjørnsonrdenen Den Norske Orden for Lit Norway 1995; *Recreations* reading, travelling, swimming, gardening, tennis; *Style—* Ms Jung Chang

CHANG, Sarah; *b* 1982; *Career* violinist; orchs worked with incl: l'Orchestre National de France, UN concert with Leipzig Gewandhaus Orchestra, Cleveland Orch, Toronto Symphony Orch, Hong Kong Philharmonic Orch, Los Angeles Philharmonic Hollywood Bowl, LSO with Sir Colin Davies 1994, Berlin Philharmonic with Zubin Mehta, NY Philharmonic with Kurt Masur, San Francisco Symphony Orch under Daniel Barenboim, Israel Philharmonic with Andrew Litton, Oslo Philharmonic with Valery Gergiev, Deutsches Symphonie Orchester Berlin 1995, Met Orch under James Levine Carnegie Hall 1996, LSO with Andre Previn 1996, City of Birmingham Symphony Orch with Sir Simon Rattle, Helsinki Philharmonic, BBC Symphony Orch under Andrew Davis (BBC Proms) 1996; other performances incl: Ravinia Festival (with James Levine and Chicago Symphony Orch), Presidential Gala Concert Seoul S Korea 1990, Concert for Planet Earth Rio de Janeiro Earth Summit 1992, debut Carnegie Hall (with Montreal Symphony Orch and Charles Dutoit) 1994, New World Symphony under Michael Tilson Thomas Monte Carlo 1995, debut Tanglewood Festival (with Boston Symphony Orch) 1995; *Recordings* incl: Debut 1992, Tchaikovsky Concerto (with LSO and Sir Colin Davis), Paganini Concerto No 1, Vaughan Williams A Lark Ascending (with LPO and Bernard Haitink), works by Saint-Saens (with Wolfgang Sawallisch and Philadelphia Orch); *Awards* Gramophone Magazine Young Artist of the Year 1993, Echo Schallplattenpreis 1993, Debut Award Royal Philharmonic Soc 1993, Newcomer of the Year Int Classical Music Awards 1994, Nan Pa Award S Korea; *Style—* Ms Sarah Chang; ✉ c/o ICM Artists (London) Ltd, Oxford House, 76 Oxford Street, London W1R 1RB (☎ 0171 323 3223, fax 0171 636 3528)

CHANG, Yat Sen; *Educ* Cuba Nat Ballet Sch; *Career* ballet dancer; Nat Ballet of Cuba (under Alicia Alonso) 1989–92, touring in Brazil, Colombia, Argentina, Mexico, Peru and Bulgaria; took part in Int Dance Festival of La Baule France 1992, 1993 and 1996; Jeune Ballet de France 1992–93 performing in Poland, Mongolia, China, Vietnam, The Philippines, Singapore, Hong Kong and Thailand; princ English National Ballet 1993–; roles incl: Bluebird in The Sleeping Beauty, Gopak in The Nutcracker, Paquita, Dances from Napoli, Franz in Hynd's Coppelia, Mercutio in Nureyev's Romeo and Juliet, Mauro Bigonzetti's X N Tricities, White Rabbit in Alice in Wonderland; *Awards* Best Partner Varna 1990, Gold Medal Chicloyo Peru, reached finals Contemporary Dance Competition Paris 1993; *Style—* Yat Sen Chang, Esq; ✉ English National Ballet, Markova House, 39 Jay Mews, London SW7 2ES (☎ 0171 581 1245, fax 0171 225 0827)

CHANNON, Prof Derek French; s of John French Channon; *b* 4 March 1939; *Educ* Eastbourne GS, Univ Coll London (BSc), Univ of Manchester (MBA), Harvard Grad Sch of Business Admin (DBA); *m* 1963, Ann Lesley (m dis 1987); 1 s, 1 da; *Career* formerly with Royal Dutch Shell Gp, md Evode Hldgs 1976–77, prof of marketing Manchester Business Sch 1978–90; prof of strategic mgmnt and mktg Imperial Coll London 1990–; assoc dir Manchester Business Sch 1986–87; dir: Royal Bank of Scotland 1988–95, Royal Bank of Scotland Group 1990–95, Istel Ltd 1982–87, Bray Technologies plc 1983–92; pres Strategic Mgmnt Soc 1986–88 (memb Bd 1983–), memb Supervisory Bd Minihouses NV 1983–86; FCIM; *Books* Strategy and Structure of British Enterprise (1973), The Service Industries (1976), British Banking Strategy (1977), Multinational Strategic Planning (1979), Bank Strategic Management and Marketing (1986), Global Banking Strategy (1988); *Style—* Prof Derek Channon; ✉ Imperial College of Science, Technology and Medicine, South Kensington, London SW7 2AZ (☎ 0171 589 5111, fax 0171 584 7596)

CHANNON, Gordon Anthony; s of Walter Henry Channon (d 1953), of St Thomas, Exeter, and Rose, *née* Kelly (d 1968); *b* 2 July 1926; *Educ* The John Stocker Sch Exeter, Univ of Exeter (MA); *m* 3 Sept 1966, Christine, da of Willie Doughty; 1 da (Helen Louise b 30 June 1967), 1 s (Alistair John b 14 Feb 1969, d 26 Jan 1975); *Career* Yeo & Co: articled clerk 1952–57, qualified chartered accountant 1957, ptnr 1959–69; tax ptnr Simpkins Edwards 1969–91, tax conslt 1991–; p/t lectr Dept of Economics Univ of Exeter 1975–; chm: S W Soc of CAs Tax Ctee 1980–, Exeter & Dist Soc of CAs 1985–86; pres: S W Branch Inst of Taxation 1984–87, S W Eng Branch Chartered Assoc of Certified Accountants 1985–86, S W Soc of CAs 1990–91 (EC rep 1989–); FCA 1967 (ACA 1957), MIMgt 1975, FTII 1980, FCCA 1980; *Books* Inheritance Tax (with J Coombes, 1988), Economics of Taxation Work Book (jtly, 1978–); *Recreations* wine, food, drama; *Style—* Gordon Channon, Esq; ✉ 12 Cricket Field Court, Cricket Field Lane, Budleigh Salterton, Devon EX9 6JB (☎ 01395 442927, fax 01395 445931); Simpkins Edwards, Chartered Accountants, Michael House, Castle St, Exeter, Devon EX4 3LQ (☎ 01392 211233, fax 01392 413173)

CHANNON, Rt Hon (Henry) Paul Guinness; PC (1980), MP (C) Southend W (majority 11,902); s of late Sir Henry ('Chips') Channon, MP (d 1958), of Kelvedon Hall, Brentwood, Essex, and Lady Honor Svejdar, *née* Guinness, da of 2 Earl of Iveagh; *b* 9 Oct 1935; *Educ* Eton, Ch Ch Oxford; *m* 1963, Ingrid, formerly w of Hon Jonathan Guinness, and da of Maj Guy Wyndham, MC (gs of Hon Percy Wyndham, 2 s of 1 Baron Leconfield), by his 2 w Grethe, da of G Wulfsberg, of Bergen, Norway; 1 s (Henry b 1970), 2 da (Olivia d 1986, Georgia b 1966); *Career* served RHG 1954–56; MP (C) Southend W 1959–; Miny of Power 1959–60; PPS to: Home Sec 1960–62, Foreign Sec 1963–64; oppn spokesman on arts and amenities 1967–70, Parly sec Miny of Housing and Local Govt 1970, Parly under sec DOE 1970–72, min of state for N Ireland 1972, min Housing and Construction Environment Dept 1972–74, oppn spokesman on prices and consumer protection 1974, oppn spokesman on environmental affairs 1974–75, min of state CSD 1979–81, min for the arts 1981–83, min for trade 1983–86, sec of state for trade and indust 1986–87, sec of state for tport 1987–July 1989; Liveryman Worshipful Co of Goldsmiths; *Style—* The Rt Hon Paul Channon, MP; ✉ House of Commons, London SW1A 0AA

CHANON, Charles; s of Ben Shimon Shimon (d 1974), and Behar Zelda (d 1989); *b* 16 May 1934; *Educ* École Alliance Française Baghdad, Shamash Sch Baghdad, Technion Israel Inst of Technol Haifa (BSc); *m* 22 July 1964 (m dis 1986), Nepomiachty Marina, da of Leonid (d 1962); 1 s (Robert b 7 Oct 1965), 2 da (Sophie b 23 May 1967, Nathalie b 6 May 1975); *Career* design engr Schwartz Hautmont Paris 1957–60 (chief engr Paris 1960–64), chief engr London 1964–69, assoc ptnr Lowe Rodin and OTH 1969–71, md OTH UK London 1971–73, pres Charles Chanon & Partners London 1973–, main bd dir Finotel plc London 1984–, cnsllr French C of C London 1991, contrib numerous articles to professional jls; MInstM 1972, FIMgt (MIMgt 1973), CEng 1975, MICE 1975, Eur Ing 1995, FInstD 1996; *Books* Construction in the Common Market (1974), The Business of Building in France (jtly, 1993); *Recreations* swimming, shooting, music; *Clubs* Champney's; *Style—* Charles Chanon, Esq; ✉ 12 Admiral Court, Chelsea Harbour, London SW10 0XD (☎ 0171 823 3159); Charles Chanon & Partners, 9 Belgrave Rd, London SW1V 1QB (☎ 0171 828 7570/5470, fax 0171 233 6024)

CHANT, Anthony; s of Percival James Chant, and Ethel Eleanor, *née* Quick (d 1987); *b* 21 Feb 1938; *Educ* Hitchin GS, Univ of London (BSc, MB BS, MS); *m* 21 March 1959, Ann Nadia, da of Edwin Venning (d 1940); 3 s (Ben b 1963, Harvey b 1964, Thomas b 1966); *Career* conslt vascular surgn and sr lectr: Wessex Med Sch, Southampton Univ Hosps Trust; author of works on vascular physiology, vascular and gen surgery, med mgmnt and ethics; FRCS; *Recreations* fishing; *Style—* Anthony Chant, Esq; ✉ Royal South Hants Hospital, Southampton (☎ 01703 634288 ext 2405/2654)

CHANTER, Rev Canon Anthony R; s of Charles Harry Chanter (d 1989), of Jersey, CI, and Eva Marjorie, *née* Le Cornu (d 1966); *b* 24 Oct 1937; *Educ* Hautlieu Sch Jersey, Salisbury Theol Coll, Open Univ (BA), Univ of London (MA); *m* 10 Sept 1966, Yvonne, da of Flt Lt William Reid (ka 1944); 2 da (Fiona b 31 May 1968, Alison b 15 May 1975); *Career* priest vicar Lincoln Cathedral 1970–73; headmaster: Bishop King Sch Lincoln 1970–73, Grey Court Sch Ham Richmond-upon-Thames 1973–77, Bishop Reindorp Sch Guildford 1977–84; dir of educn Dio of Guildford 1984–, hon canon Guildford Cathedral 1984–; memb Educn Ctee Surrey CC 1984–, dir Guildford Diocesan Bd of Fin; memb Nat Assoc of Headteachers; *Books* Student Profiling (co-author 1980); *Recreations* golf, cricket, country skiing, windsurfing, music, opera; *Clubs* Sion Coll, Worplesdon Golf; *Style—* The Rev Canon Anthony Chanter; ✉ Grasshoppers, Woodland Ave, Cranleigh, Surrey GU6 7HU (☎ 01483 273833); Diocesan Education Centre, Stag Hill, Guildford, Surrey (☎ 01483 450423)

CHANTER, Lady Emma Mary Helena; *née* French; 3 da of 3 Earl of Ypres by his 1 w Maureen Helena, da of late Maj H J P Kelly (US Army); *b* 8 Dec 1958; *Educ* private tutor; *m* 1, 11 Jan 1980 (m dis 1989), Charles Geoffrey Humfrey, s of Charles Michael Humfrey, of Alderney; 1 s (Charles Hamish Lowndes French b 17 Feb 1986); m 2, 5 Oct 1991, Christopher Francis Wolferstan Chanter, s of David Wolferstan Chanter, of Abbott's Leigh, Somerset; 1 s (Thomas Fulco French Wolferstan b 21 Aug 1992); *Career* dir Masterplan Marketing; *Recreations* wine, pigs; *Style—* The Lady Emma Chanter

CHANTLER, Prof Sir Cyril; kt (1996); s of Fred Chantler (d 1957), of Blackpool, and Marjorie, *née* Clark; *b* 12 May 1939; *Educ* Wrekin Coll Shropshire, St Catharine's Coll Cambridge (BA), Guy's Hosp Med Sch London (MB BChir), Univ of Cambridge (MD); *m* 1963, Shireen M Saleh; 2 s (Paul Frederick b 29 July 1965, Jonathan Mark b 22 June 1967), 1 da (Nariane Emma b 24 May 1970); *Career* Guy's Hosp: sr lectr in paediatrics and conslt paediatrician 1971, chm Mgmnt Bd and unit gen mangr 1985–88; prof of paediatric nephrology Guy's Hosp Med Sch 1980, princ United Med and Dental Schs of Guy's and St Thomas' Hosp 1992– (clinical dean 1989–92); MRC: memb external staff 1967, clinical research fell 1967–69, travelling fell Univ of Calif 1971; memb: Registration Ctee Euro Dialysis and Transplant Assoc 1975–80, Cncl Euro Soc for Paediatric Nephrology 1978–81, Academic Bd Br Paediatric Assoc 1983–86, NHS Policy Bd 1989–95, Cncl Renal Assoc 1981, Grants Cncl Br Kidney Patients' Assoc 1985–, GMC 1994–; chm Scientific Advsy Ctee Fndn for the Study of Infant Deaths 1987–90, med advsr Children Nationwide Med Res Fund 1986–; examiner in paediatrics: Univ of Hong Kong 1985, Univ of Birmingham 1985–87, Conjoint Bd 1979–85, RCP 1985–, Univ of Kebangsaan 1988, Royal Coll of Surgery of Ireland 1990; RCP: lectr 1987, pro-censor 1989, censor 1990; pres Br Assoc of Med Mangrs 1991; co-ed Paediatric Nephrology 1986–; *Publications* jt author of reports for Br Assoc of Paediatric Nephrology: Future Care of Children with Renal Failure (1975), Siting of Units to Care for Children with Chronic Renal Failure (1980); contrib to scientific literature on paediatrics, kidney disease and management in the NHS; *Recreations* squash, golf, walking, reading, opera; *Style—* Prof Sir Cyril Chantler; ✉ 60 Herne Hill, London SE24 9QP (☎ 0171 274 6061); Dean's Office, United Medical and Dental Schools, Guy's Hospital, London SE1 9RT (☎ 0171 955 4222, fax 0171 407 0082)

CHANTLER, Paul Anthony; s of Peter Victor Chantler, of Tunbridge Wells, Kent, and Joy Edith, *née* Austin; *b* 12 Oct 1959; *Educ* Skinners' Sch Tunbridge Wells Kent; *Career* trainee reporter Kent & Sussex Courier 1978–82, reporter Kent Messenger 1982–83, sr reporter Kent Evening Post 1983–84, journalist and presenter Invicta Radio 1984–88, news ed Southern Sound 1988–89, breakfast show presenter BBC Wiltshire Sound 1989; Chiltern Radio Network: head of news 1989–90, prog controller 1990–92, gp prog dir 1992–95; md Network News 1991–95, chief exec Galaxy Radio 1994–96, prog dir Essex Radio 1996–; *Books* Local Radio Journalism (1991); *Recreations* pop music, cinema, videos, reading, nightclubs; *Clubs* Rotary Club, Radio Academy; *Style—* Paul Chantler, Esq; ✉ Essex Radio, Radio House, 19–21 Clifftown Road, Southend-on-Sea, Essex SS1 1SX (☎ 01702 333711, fax 01702 333916)

CHANTRY, Dr George William; s of George William Chantry (d 1979), of Wallasey, Merseyside, and Sophia Veronica, *née* Johnson (d 1973); *b* 13 April 1933; *Educ* St Francis Xavier's Coll Liverpool, ChCh Oxford (MA, DPhil); *m* Diana Margaret Rhodes, da of William Rhodes Martin (d 1969), of Littlehampton, Sussex; 2 s (Richard b 1959, Paul b 1967), 1 da (Catherine b 1961); *Career* res assoc Cornell Univ 1958–60; NPL Teddington: sr res fell 1960–62, sr sci offr 1962–67, princ sci offr 1967–73, sr princ sci offr 1973–82; cnsllr (sci and technol) HM Embassy Bonn 1982–85, asst dir (indust) SDIPO/MOD 1985–90, sr vice pres (Europe) Carnahan & Assocs and conslt on SDI Technology Transfer to the MOD 1990–; FInstP 1973, FIEE 1976, CEng 1976, CPhys 1985; *Books incl* Long-Wave Optics (1982); *Recreations* music, philately, bridge, gardening; *Style—* Dr George Chantry; ✉ 42 Cranwell Grove, Shepperton, Middx TW17 0JR (☎ 01932 560524); Business (☎ 01932 569951, fax 01932 570513)

CHAPLIN, John Cyril; CBE (1988); s of Ernest Stanley Chaplin (d 1966), of Keswick, Cumbria, and Isobel, *née* Mackereth (d 1944); *b* 13 Aug 1926; *Educ* Keswick Sch Cumbria; *m* 17 Sept 1949, Ruth Marianne, da of Raymond Livingstone (d 1961), of

Owslebury, Winchester, Hants; 2 s (Peter b 1951, Alistair b 1965), 2 da (Rosalind b 1954, Sarah b 1958); *Career* aeronautical engr; CAA: DG Airworthiness 1979–83, gp dir Safety Regulation 1983–88, memb Bd 1983–88, memb Ops Advsy Ctee 1994–; FEng 1987; *Recreations* sailing, photography; *Clubs* Cruising Assoc (vice pres 1995–); *Style—* John Chaplin, Esq, CBE, FEng; ✉ Norman Croft, Vicarage Lane, Mattingley, Hook, Hampshire RG27 8LF (☎ 0118 932 6207)

CHAPMAN, Angela Mary; da of Frank Dyson Rowe, of Cleveland, and Mary, *née* Almond; *b* 2 Jan 1940; *Educ* Queen Victoria HS Stockton-on-Tees, Sorbonne (Diplôme de Civilisation Française), Univ of Bristol (scholarship, BA); *m* 20 June 1959, Ian Michael Chapman, s of Oswald Percy Chapman (d 1973); 2 s (Jonathan Ashley b 23 July 1960, Callum Michael b 23 Oct 1963); *Career* teacher of French Bede Sch Sunderland 1970–80, dep head Newcastle-upon-Tyne Church HS 1980–84, headteacher Central Newcastle HS GPDST 1984–; FRSA; *Recreations* walking, tennis, military history; *Style—* Mrs Angela Chapman, FRSA; ✉ 14 Alpine Way, Humbledon Hill, Sunderland, Tyne & Wear SR3 1TN (office ☎ 0191 281 1768)

CHAPMAN, Prof Antony John; s of Arthur Charles Chapman, of Canterbury, and Joan Muriel Chapman; *b* 21 April 1947; *Educ* Milford Haven GS, Bexley GS, Univ of Leicester (BSc, PhD); *m* 1 June 1985, Siriol Sophia Jones, da of Cledan David, of Llanddowror, Dyfed; 2 s (David Charles Luke b 1987, Luke Christopher David b 1989), 2 da (Harriet Emily Siriol b 1991, Madeleine Sophie Elizabeth b 1993); *Career* sr lectr UWIST Cardiff 1978–83 (lectr 1971–78); Univ of Leeds: prof 1983–, dir Centre for Applied Psychological Studies Univ of Leeds 1987–90, dean of science 1992–94, pro vice-chllr 1994–; co-ed 16 books 1976–, ed British Journal of Psychology 1989–95, co-ed Current Psychology 1984–; pres: Br Psychological Soc 1988–89, Psychology Section Br Assoc for the Advancement of Science 1993–94, Assoc Learned Socs in the Social Sciences 1995–; FBPsS, CPsychol; *Style—* Prof Antony Chapman; ✉ Department of Psychology, University of Leeds, Leeds LS2 9JT (☎ 0113 233 5717, fax 0113 284 1221)

CHAPMAN, Prof Christine Muriel; CBE (1991, OBE 1984); da of Richard D F Chapman (d 1978), and Doris M, *née* Hulbert (d 1994); *b* 15 Oct 1927; *Educ* King's Norton GS, Goldsmiths' Coll London (BSc, MPhil); *Career* Gen Hosp Birmingham 1951–52 (registered nurse and staff nurse 1949–50, night sister 1950–51); nurse tutor: Royal Salop Infirmary Shrewsbury 1957–59 (ward sister 1952–55), The Middx Hosp London 1959–60; lectr in health serv mgmnt Univ of York, dean of nursing studies Univ of Wales Coll of Med 1987– (dir 1972, prof 1984, ret 1989, emeritus prof 1989–); dir St Loye's Fndn for Training Disabled, chm Ctee St Loye's Occupational Therapy Sch 1991–; chm: RCN Bd of Educn 1976–89, Welsh Nat Bd for Nursing Midwifery Health Visiting 1986–90; lay memb GMC 1987–; FRCN (1977 MRCN 1949), FRSM 1988; *Books* Sociology for Nurses (3 edn, 1986), Theory of Nursing (1987), Professional and Ethical Issues in Nursing (with P Burnard, 1988, 2 edn 1993), Nursing Education; The Way Ahead (with P Burnard, 1989); *Recreations* music, gardening, embroidery; *Style—* Prof Christine Chapman, CBE; ✉ Pedlars, Pound Lane, Woodbury, Devon EX5 1JE

CHAPMAN, Christopher Henry George (Kit); MBE (1989); s of Peter Francis Chapman, of Taunton, and Georgette (Etty), *née* Rosi; *b* 10 March 1947; *Educ* Taunton Sch, Univ of Surrey (BSc, pres Food and Wine Soc); *m* 1971, (Marie) Louise Anne, da of Peter Edward Guiver; 2 s (Dominic Alexander Pierre b 1973, Nicholas Mark Christopher b 1975); *Career* in advertising 1969–76 (latterly with Benton and Bowles Ltd); md The Castle Hotel Taunton 1980–; chm Prestige Hotels 1985–87, dir Orchard Media Ltd 1992–; columnist Caterer and Hotelkeeper 1983–88; writer and presenter: Simply the Best: A Celebration of British Food (12 films for ITV and Channel 4) 1991 and 1993, Of Madeleines and Other Masterpieces (arts prog, BBC Radio 2) 1994; W Country Tourist Bd: memb Exec Ctee 1977–, chm Commercial Membs' Gp 1980–86, vice pres 1986–; ministerial appointee Exmoor Nat Park Ctee 1979–81; memb: Leisure Industs Econ Devpt Ctee NEDC 1987–89, Bd Somerset Training and Enterprise Cncl (TEC) 1989–94; Freeman City of London 1984; Master Innholder, memb Guild of Food Writers; *Awards* Caterer and Hotelkeeper Awards (CATEYS) Tourism Award 1987, Ward Cavendish Trophy for the Small Business Award 1980 and 1981, British Airways and BTA Award for Overseas Mktg 1981, Good Hotel Guide César Award for Best Town Hotel 1987, CATEYS Function Menu of the Year Award 1989, Guild of Food Writers Michael Smith Award 1996; *Books* Great British Chefs (1989, shortlisted André Simon Book Award 1990), Great British Chefs 2 (1995); *Recreations* good food and wine, walking the Quantocks with the dogs, reading, keeping a journal; *Clubs* Garrick; *Style—* Kit Chapman, Esq, MBE; ✉ The Castle Hotel, Taunton, Somerset TA1 1NF (☎ 01823 272671, fax 01823 336066, e-mail kit_chapman@the_castle_hotel.com)

CHAPMAN, Prof Christopher Hugh; s of John Harold Chapman, of Milton under Wychwood, Oxford, and Margaret Joan, *née* Weeks; *b* 5 May 1945; *Educ* Latymer Upper Sch, Christ's Coll Cambridge (BA, MA, PhD); *m* 1 June 1974, Lillian, da of Michael Tarapaski, of Redwater, Alberta, Canada; 1 s (Timothy b 26 May 1978), 1 da (Heather b 24 June 1981); *Career* asst prof Dept of Geology and Geophysics Univ California Berkeley 1972–73, assoc prof Dept of Physics Univ of Alberta Canada 1973–74 (asst prof 1969–72), Green scholar Univ of California San Diego 1978–79, prof Dept of Physics Univ of Toronto Canada 1980–84 and 1988–90 (assoc prof 1974–80), prof of geophysics Dept of Earth Sciences Cambridge 1984–88, scientific advsr Schlumberger Cambridge Research 1991–; memb: SEG, SSA, FRAS, FAGU; *Recreations* sailing, photography; *Style—* Prof Christopher Chapman; ✉ 7 Spinney Drive, Great Shelford, Cambridge CB2 5LY (☎ 01223 845007); Schlumberger Cambridge Research, High Cross, Madingley Road, Cambridge CB3 0EL (☎ 01223 315576)

CHAPMAN, David John; s of John and Anthea Chapman, of Woodhouse, Sheffield; *b* 29 April 1936; *Educ* Eckington GS, Sheffield Coll of Technol (Nat Cert in Electrical Engrg), Sheffield Poly (Dip in Mgmnt Studies, Acheson Prize), Sheffield City Poly (MSc); *m* 1, 1967 (m dis 1988), Margaret, *née* Adams; m 2, 1994, Dr Maria Angyalova, da of late Jozef Andal, of Slovakia; *Career* Safety in Mines Research Estab 1954–59, Computer and Instrumentation Dept United Steels Company Ltd 1959–61, Chilton Electric Products Ltd 1961–65, Davy Instruments Ltd 1965–69, gen mangr Nuclear Equipment Div Savage Industries Ltd 1969–74, Sheffield Poly 1974–75, sr conslt INCA 1975–82, md TFL Mantegna Ltd 1982–83; Sheffield Business Sch 1983–: dir Regnl Mgmnt Centre for Yorkshire and Humberside 1986–90, head of business centres and assoc head of sch 1990–93, assoc head and mangr Exec Progs 1993–96, mangr of int business devpt 1996–; visiting prof Masaryk Inst of Advanced Studies Czech Tech Univ Prague 1992–; dir: Adams Chapman Consultants Ltd 1982–, PIQA Ltd 1989–, CIM Holdings Ltd 1992–, Libanus Press Ltd 1990–; CIM: chm Sheffield Branch 1992–93, memb Nat Exec Ctee 1992–, nat vice chm 1994–, nat treas 1995–96, sr vice chm 1996–; Pres's Award CIM 1993; Freeman City of London 1996, Liveryman Worshipful Co of Marketors 1996; FCIM 1988 (MCIM 1972); *Books* contrib: Make Ready for Success (1982), Measures for Success (1985), Profit from Marketing (1986), Pricing for Profit (1987), The Power of Value Added (with Barrie Hill, 1993), Gower Handbook of Marketing (contrib 4 edn, 1995); *Recreations* specialist car restoration, electronic design, travel; *Clubs* Abbeydale Sports; *Style—* Mr David Chapman; ✉ Sheffield Business School, Totley Campus, Sheffield S17 4AB (☎ 0114 253 2808, fax 0114 253 2980, e-mail d.j.chapman@shu.ac.uk)

CHAPMAN, Sir David Robert Macgowan; 3 Bt (UK 1958), of Cleadon, Co Durham; s of Col Sir Robert (Robin) Chapman, 2 Bt, CBE, TD, JP, DL (d 1987), and Barbara May, *née* Tonks; *b* 16 Dec 1941; *Educ* Marlborough, Grenoble Univ, McGill Univ Montreal (BCom); *m* 19 June 1965, Maria Elizabeth de Gosztonyi-Zsolnay, da of Dr Nicholas de Mattyasovszky-Zsolnay, of Montreal, Canada; 1 s (Michael Nicholas b 1969), 1 da (Christina Elisabeth b 1970); *Heir* s, Michael Nicholas Chapman, b 21 May 1969; *Career* stockbroker; chm Stock Exchange NE Region Advsy Gp; dir: Wise Speke Ltd 1987– (ptnr Wise Speke & Co 1971–87), Northern Rock Building Society 1994– (formerly dir North of England Building Society (before merger) 1974–94), Breathe North Ltd 1988–95, British Lung Fndn 1989–94, Team General Partner (chm) 1993–, Montfort Press Ltd 1994–95, Gordon Durham & Co Ltd 1994–, Sunderland City Radio Ltd 1995–; memb Cncl The Stock Exchange 1979–88; memb: The Greenbury Ctee 1995, Northern Regnl Cncl CBI 1996–; govr St Aidan's Coll Univ of Durham; chm Northumbria Coalition against Crime 1995–; High Sheriff Tyne and Wear 1993–94; *Recreations* travel, tennis, reading; *Clubs* Northern Counties (Newcastle); *Style—* Sir David Chapman, Bt; ✉ Westmount, 14 West Park Rd, Cleadon, Sunderland, Tyne and Wear SR6 7RR (☎ 0191 536 7887); Wise Speke Ltd, Commercial Union House; 39 Pilgrim St, Newcastle upon Tyne NE1 6RQ (☎ 0191 201 3800)

CHAPMAN, Denis Henry Clarke; s of Alderman R F Chapman, JP (d 1963), of Scarborough, and Henrietta, *née* Stothard (d 1985); *b* 26 May 1934; *Educ* Scarborough Coll; *m* 4 April 1959, Mavis Lee, da of Robert Duncanson (d 1961); 1 s (Robert b 1971), 2 da (Fiona Henrietta Clarke (Mrs James Fergus Chance) b 1966 d 1994, Lisa b 1968); *Career* RAF 1952–54; chartered surveyor; chief exec H C Chapman & Son; memb Gen Cncl RICS 1984–94; FRICS; *Recreations* farming, shooting, gardening, walking; *Clubs* Farmers'; *Style—* Denis H C Chapman, Esq; ✉ H C Chapman & Son, The Auction Mart, North St, Scarborough YO11 1DL (☎ 01723 372 424, fax 01723 500 697)

CHAPMAN, Prof Dennis; s of George Henry Chapman, and Katherine Hannah Beckwith, *née* Magnus; *b* 6 May 1927; *Educ* Univ of London (BSc, DSc), Univ of Liverpool (PhD); *m* 1, 1948, Elsie Margaret (d 1989), da of Capt William Stephenson; 2 s (Michael, Paul), 1 da (Alison); m 2, 1993, Françoise Nioukleen; *Career* Comyns Berkeley fell Caius Coll Cambridge 1960–63, head Gen Res Div Unilever Ltd 1963–69, assoc prof Univ of Sheffield 1968–76, sr Wellcome Tst fell 1976–77; Royal Free Hosp Sch of Med: prof of biophysical chem, head Dept of Protein and Molecular Biology 1977–94, head Div of Basic Med Sciences 1988–89, vice dean 1990–93, chm Educn Ctee 1990–93, assoc dir IRC Centre in Biomedical Materials 1991–96; fndr and non-exec dir Biocompatibles Ltd 1984; visiting prof Univs of: California, Catania, Bologna, Memorial, Penn State; Langmuir lectr USA 1992; author of over 450 scientific pubns; Royal Free Hosp Sch of Med Medal 1987, Harden Medal 1995; Hon DSc: Utrecht Univ, Memorial Univ Canada, Pais Vasco Univ Spain, Cluj Univ Romania; Hon MRCP, FRSC (Interdisciplinary Award 1993), FRS; *Books* Biological Membranes Vols I-V; *Recreations* golf, Spanish; *Clubs* Athenaeum; *Style—* Prof Dennis Chapman, FRS; ✉ 10 One Tree Lane, Beaconsfield, Bucks, HP9 2BU (☎ 01494 675818, fax 01494 677718); Royal Free Hospital School of Medicine, IRC Centre in Biomedical Materials, Surgery Department, Rowland Hill St, London, NW3 2PF (☎ 0171 794 0500 ext 3246, fax 017 830 2260)

CHAPMAN, Derek James; s of Eric James Chapman (d 1980), of Southampton, and Phyllis Edith, *née* Cook; *b* 1 Oct 1940; *Educ* King Edward VI Sch Southampton; *m* 2 s (Adam Geoffrey b 19 Aug 1972, Stephen Alistair b 4 Oct 1973); *Career* CA 1968 (Taxation prize ICAEW); Touche Ross (now Deloitte & Touche): joined 1967, tax ptnr 1972–83, ptnr i/c Southern Region Tax Function 1983–92, nat dir of tax 1992–; FCA (ACA 1968), ATII 1968; *Recreations* golf; *Clubs* Hindhead and Sonning Golf; *Style—* Derek Chapman, Esq; ✉ Deloitte & Touche, Hill House, 1 Little New St, London EC4A 3TR (☎ 0171 936 3000, fax 0171 583 8517)

CHAPMAN, Ernest; s of Arthur Leslie Chapman (d 1983), of 7 Gainford Road, Moorends, Doncaster, S Yorkshire, and Alice, *née* Lucas (d 1978); *b* 2 Dec 1933; *Educ* Thorne GS Nr Doncaster, St John's Coll Oxford (MA); *m* 4 Aug 1956, Dorothy, da of Alfred Sutton (d 1978), of Hall Green, Wakefield; 3 s (Michael b 1958, Neil b 1960, Alexander b 1963), 1 da (Sarah b 1965); *Career* Nat Serv Sgt RAEC 1952–54; admitted slr 1961; sr ptnr Dixon Coles and Gill Wakefield 1979–93, currently in private practice; Registrar Wakefield Dio 1979–93 (dep registrar 1965–79), dep coroner 1990–93 (dep asst coroner 1984–90), dep dist judge and High Ct registrar 1989–; memb Wakefield Festival Chorus; vice pres Wakefield Amateur Operatic Soc, pres Stanley Falcon Cricket Club, Yorks Cricket Cncl 1982–84; *Recreations* cricket, singing, languages, reading, gardening and sport in general; *Style—* Ernest Chapman, Esq; ✉ 1 Pennine View, Darton, Barnsley, S Yorkshire S75 5AT (☎ 01226 382 796)

CHAPMAN, His Hon Judge Frank Arthur; s of Dennis Arthur Chapman, of Culcheth, Warrington, Cheshire, and Joan, *née* Dickinson; *b* 28 May 1946; *Educ* Newton-le-Willows GS, Univ Coll London (LLB, LLM, Brigid Coker prizewinner 1994); *m* 27 July 1968, Mary Kathleen, da of late Edwin Keith Jones, and Marion Jones, of Pontypool, Gwent; 1 da (Rachel Lynn b 21 March 1971), 1 s (Thomas William Lawson b 21 Oct 1973); *Career* called to the Bar 1968, practiced Midland & Oxford Circuit 1969–91, asst recorder 1982–86, recorder 1986–92, circuit judge (Midland and Oxford Circuit) 1992–; memb Bar Cncl 1989–91; *Recreations* mountaineering, angling, travel; *Style—* His Hon Judge Chapman; ✉ Midland and Oxford Circuit, 2 Newton Street, Birmingham B4 7LU

CHAPMAN, Frank Watson; s of Thomas Chapman (d 1965), of Bournemouth, and Beatrice, *née* Padgett (d 1976); *b* 7 Nov 1929; *Educ* Swindon Coll, Marine Sch of South Shields; *m* 18 March 1955, Wendy Joanna, da of Roger Philip Holly (d 1972), of Switzerland; 1 s (Thomas b 1963), 1 da (Susie b 1956); *Career* cadet MN 1946; deck offr: Union Steamship Co NZ 1951–54, Royal Mail Lines 1954–58, Cunard Steamship Co 1958–62; salesman Telephone Rentals 1962; fndr and md 1964: Bahamas Properties Ltd, Sovereign Travel Ltd; purchased Loch Rannoch and Forest Hills Hotels Scotland 1974, fndr Multi-Ownership & Hotels Ltd 1975 (thereby becoming fndr of Timeshare in UK), 2 devpts in Wales 1978, 3 devpts Forest Hills Hotel 1980, sold co to Barratt Developments plc 1982 (md until 1988); fndr and chm Sovereign Travel & Leisure Group plc 1988–, dir Biocure Holdings plc 1989–, md Clowance Holdings Ltd 1991–; chm The Timeshare Cncl 1995–; *Recreations* travel, gardening, reading, swimming; *Style—* Frank Chapman, Esq; ✉ Norbury Park, Mickleham, Surrey RH5 6DN (☎ 01372 372633); Sovereign Travel & Leisure Group plc, 2 Chertsey St, Guildford, Surrey GU1 4HD (fax 01483 726217)

CHAPMAN, Geoffrey Richard; s of Frank Chapman (d 1950), of Eversden, Cambs, and Mabel Emma, *née* Winwood (d 1972); *b* 14 Feb 1944; *Educ* Hilderthorp Sch Bridlington, Impington Sch Cambridge, Coll of Electrical and Mech Engrg Borden Hants; *m* 1, 1967 (m dis 1980), Elizabeth, *née* Peacock; 1 s (Mark John Winwood b 1972), 1 da (Joanna Clare b 1975); m 2, 1980, Jennifer Mary Westoby, da of Peter N Johnson; 1 da (Quinta Frederica b 1990); *Career* instr electrical systems REME 1962–67 (trainee 1960–62), zone mangr Sun Corporation Chicago USA 1967–70, systems sales exec Philips Business Systems Ltd Cambridge 1970–72, chm Barkway Electronics Ltd 1972–87, md Multi Media Communications Consultants Ltd 1987–; dir: Allison & Busby publishers, Sunhill Day Nursery Group, Bd of Mgmnt PRCA; MCIM 1977; *Recreations* flying (PPL), skiing, the Arts; *Style—* Geoffrey Chapman, Esq; ✉ Multi Media Communications Consultants Ltd, 179 King's Cross Road, London WC1 (☎ 0171 833 9111)

CHAPMAN, (Francis) Ian; CBE (1988); s of Rev Peter Chapman (d 1962), of Glasgow, and Frances Maud, *née* Burdett; *b* 26 Oct 1925; *Educ* Shawlands Acad Glasgow, Ommer Sch of Music Glasgow; *m* 1953, Marjory Stewart, *née* Swinton; 1 s, 1 da; *Career* aircrew cadet RAF 1943–44, Nat Serv coal mines 1945–47; William Collins Sons & Co Ltd:

joined as mgmnt trainee 1947, NY Branch 1950–51, gen sales mangr London 1955, gp sales dir 1959; jt md William Collins (Holdings) Ltd 1967 (dep chm 1976); dir: Hatchards Ltd 1961, Pan Books Ltd 1962–84, Ancient House Bookshop (Ipswich) Ltd 1972–89, Scottish Opera Theatre Royal Ltd 1974–79, Book Tokens Ltd 1981–95, IRN Ltd 1983–85, Stanley Botes Ltd 1985–89, United Distillers plc 1987–91; chm: Scottish Radio Holdings plc 1972–96 (pres 1996–), Hatchards Ltd 1976–89, Harvill Press Ltd 1976–89, William Collins Publishers Ltd 1979, The Listener Publications 1988–93; chm and gp chief exec William Collins plc 1981–89, non-exec dir Guinness plc 1986–91, jt chm Harper and Row NY 1987–89, chm and md Chapmans Publishers 1989–94, chm Guinness Publishing 1992–, gp dep chm The Orion Publishing Group 1993–94; The Publishers' Assoc: memb Cncl 1962–77, vice pres 1978 and 1981, pres 1979, tstee 1992–; memb Bd Book Devpt Cncl 1967–73, tstee Book Trade Benevolent Soc 1982–, memb Governing Cncl SCOTBIC 1983, chm Advsy Bd Univ of Strathclyde Business School 1985–88; Scot Free Enterprise Award 1985; Hon DLitt Univ of Strathclyde 1990; CIMgt 1982, FRSA 1985; *Recreations* music, golf, reading, grandchildren; *Clubs* Garrick, Groucho, Royal Wimbledon Golf, MCC, Prestwick Golf, Walton Heath Golf; *Style*— Ian Chapman, Esq, CBE; ✉ Kenmore, 46 The Avenue, Cheam, Sutton, Surrey SM2 7QE (☎ 0181 642 1820, fax 0181 770 0225)

CHAPMAN, Ian Stewart; s of Francis Ian Chapman, of Kenmore, Cheam, Surrey, and Marjory Stewart, *née* Swinton; *b* 15 Jan 1955; *Educ* Cranleigh Sch Surrey, Univ of Durham (BA, 1 XI Cricket); *m* Maria, da of late Daniel Samper; 1 s (Gabriel Ian Daniel b 22 July 1983), 2 da (Sabrina Stewart Burdett b 11 Nov 1986, Natalya Alexa Campbell b 5 Nov 1990); *Career* publisher; asst on shop floor W H Smiths Paris 1974–75; trainee: Doubleday & Co Inc NY 1980–81, Berkley Publishers The Putnam Group NY May-Nov 1981; editorial asst William Morrow & Co Inc NY 1981–82, ed rising to editorial dir Hodder & Stoughton Ltd London 1983–87, publishing dir Pan Books Ltd rising to gp publisher Pan Macmillan Ltd 1987–, md Macmillan General Books 1994–; *Recreations* cricket, golf, cycling, squash, walking; *Clubs* Garrick, Chelsea Arts; *Style*— Ian Chapman, Esq; ✉ Benedict House, Staple Cross Road, Northiam, E Sussex TN31 6JJ (☎ 01580 830222, fax 01580 830027); Macmillan General Books, 25 Eccleston Place, London SW1W 9NF (☎ 0171 881 8000, fax 0171 881 8001)

CHAPMAN, James Keith (Ben); s of John Hartley Chapman (d 1983), of Kirkby Stephen, Cumbria, and Elsie Vera, *née* Bousfield (d 1978); *b* 8 July 1940; *Educ* Appleby GS Cumbria; *m* 1970 (m dis 1984), Jane Deirdre, da of Norman Roffe, of Morecambe, Lancs; 3 da (Bridget b 1971, Charlotte b 1973, Clare b 1975); *Career* PO RAFVR (T) 1959–61; Miny of Pensions and Nat Insur 1958–62, Miny of Aviation/BAA 1962–67, Rochdale Ctee of Inquiry into Shipping 1967–70, BOT 1970–74, first sec (commercial) Dar es Salaam 1974–78, first sec (econ) Accra 1978–81, asst sec DTI 1981–87, commercial cnsllr Br Embassy Beijing 1987–90, DTI dep regnl dir NW and DTI dir Merseyside 1991–93, DTI regnl dir NW 1993–94, dir Trade and Industry in the Government Office for the NW 1994–95; fndr Ben Chapman Associates 1995–; ptnr The Pacific Practice 1996–; chm Advsy Bd: China Gateway North West (at UMIST) 1996–, China Technology Link (at UMIST) 1996–; dir: Wirral C of C 1996–, Heswall Soc 1996–; memb Cncl Lake District Summer Music, Int Friend of the Wirral 1995–; former memb: Chemicals EDC (chm Forward Assessment Gp), Tyre EDC, Plastics Processing EDC; Int Natural Rubber Agreement: former chm UNCTAD Econ Ctee, former chm Buffer Stock; former DG Int Wool Study Gp; former chm Int Cotton Advsy Conf; chm Rural Challenge Cumbria; former vice pres Int Students Advsy Cncl for Merseyside; memb 48 Group Club 1994–; former memb: Business Link Implementation Strategy Gp, Advsy Cncl Liverpool Business Sch, Business Devpt Panel BBC Philharmonic Orchestra; FIMgt; *Recreations* opera, theatre, music, walking; *Clubs* St James's (Manchester), Portico Library (Manchester); *Style*— Ben Chapman, Esq; ✉ Ben Chapman Associates, Anvil Cottage, Village Road, Lower Heswall, Wirral L60 0DZ (☎ 0151 342 7293)

CHAPMAN, Jennifer Mary; da of Peter Norman Johnson, of Royston, Herts, and Agnes Mabel, *née* Taylor (d 1989); *b* 19 Feb 1950; *Educ* St Albans HS Herts; *m* 1, 1971 (m dis 1979), Paul Robin Moncrieff Westoby; 2 da (Frances b 1974, Anna b 1976); m 2, 1980, Geoffrey Richard Chapman; 1 da (Quinta b 1990); *Career* NCTJ apprenticeship Westminster Press 1968–72, Heart of England Newspapers 1972–73, Coventry Evening Telegraph 1974, Mid-Anglia Newspapers 1976–80, fndr Multi Media PR consultancy 1980–; co-fndr Media House Literary Agents 1995–; Midlands Journalist of the Yr 1974; memb: Soc of Authors 1982, English PEN (hon treas) 1993; MIPR 1986; *Books* The Geneva Touch (thriller, as Lydia Hitchcock, 1982), The Long Weekend (novel, 1984), Mysterious Ways (novel, 1985), Not Playing the Game (novel, 1986), Regretting It (novel, 1987), The Last Bastion - the case for and against women priests (1989), Barnardo's Today (foreword by HRH the Princess of Wales, 1991), Made in Heaven (1993); *Clubs* Groucho; *Style*— Mrs Jennifer Chapman; ✉ Multi Media, The Mount, Sun Hill, Royston, Herts SG8 9AT (☎ 01763 247474)

CHAPMAN, John Anthony; s of Wilfrid Norman Chapman, of Leicester, and Joan Marjory, *née* Cockayne; *b* 23 May 1940; *Educ* The Beauchamp GS Leics, St Edmund Hall Oxford (MA), Dept of Educn Univ of Oxford (dip of educn), Univ of Bradford (MSc educnl res); *m* 22 August 1964, Elizabeth, da of Peter Hobden Shipp (d 1985); 2 da (Annick Elizabeth b 23 May 1967, Fiona Jane Margaret b 2 April 1973), 1 s (Robin John Christopher b 27 June 1975); *Career* head of history Woodhouse Grove Sch Bradford 1966–69 (asst 1963–66), research officer Bloxham Project Research Unit Oxford 1969–73, pt/t tutor in educn Dept of Educnl Studies Univ of Oxford 1970–73, headmaster The Bishop of Hereford's Bluecoat Sch Hereford 1978–86 (dep head 1973–78), headmaster Leighton Park Sch Reading 1986–96; chm Bloxham Project 1991–96; govr: Hereford Cathedral Sch, Waverley Sch, St Thomas Cantilupe Sch; memb HMC; fell Coll of St Mary and St Paul Cheltenham 1979–; *Books* Free for All (with Robin Richardson, 1971), Images of Life (with Robin Richardson, 1973), Launchings (ed, with Christopher Herbert, 1977); *Recreations* golf, walking, opera, European travel, football; *Clubs* East India; *Style*— John Chapman, Esq; ✉ The Threshing Barn, Kingstone, Hereford HR2 9HU (☎ 01981 251303)

CHAPMAN, Dr John Clifford; s of James Clifford Crossley Chapman (d 1983), and Marion, *née* Harrison (d 1992); *b* 21 Feb 1923; *Educ* Ilford HS, Imperial Coll London (BSc, PhD); *m* 18 Oct 1947, Roberta Blanche, da of Robert Broughton Gingell; 1 s (Andrew b 1958), 1 da (Sarah b 1953); *Career* Capt RE 1942–46; res fell and reader in structural engrg Imperial Coll 1950–71, dir Constructional Steel R & D Orgn 1971–73, gp tech dir George Wimpey plc 1973–81, dir Chapman Associates (formerly Chapman Dowling Associates Ltd) consulting engrs 1981–, visiting prof Imperial Coll of Science Technol and Med London 1991–; FEng 1979, FCGI 1987, FICE, FRINA, FIStructE, MConsE; *Publications* many papers on structural engrg in professional jls; *Recreations* tennis, squash, mountain walking, music; *Clubs* Athenaeum; *Style*— Dr John C Chapman, FEng; ✉ Chapman Associates, 41 Oathall Rd, Haywards Heath, West Sussex RH16 3EG

CHAPMAN, Kenneth James; s of Kenneth Roland Chapman, of Lincoln, and Marie Louise, *née* Robinson; *b* 14 Sept 1950; *Educ* Hornchurch GS, The Sweyne Sch Rayleigh Essex, Univ of Wales (BSc, DipTP); *m* 31 Aug 1970, Pamela Margaret, da of Alan Henry Sertin, of Midsomer Norton, Bath, Avon; 2 s (Mark b 1974, Daniel b 1979), 1 da (Kelly b and d 1977); *Career* Glamorgan CC 1972–73, Mid Glamorgan CC 1974–75, Monmouth Borough Cncl 1975–79, Edwin H Bradley & Sons Ltd 1979–81, managing ptnr Chapman Warren 1981–; chm Swindon Town FC 1990–91; memb Cncl Swindon Chamber of Commerce and Indust; MRTPI 1978, MIMgt 1979; *Recreations* hockey, power boats, junior soccer; *Style*— Kenneth Chapman, Esq; ✉ Brynards Hill Farm, Wootton Bassett, Wiltshire SN4 7ER (☎ 01793 850015); Chapman Warren, Town Planning & Development Consultants, Fairwater House, 1 High Street, Wroughton, Swindon, Wiltshire (☎ 01793 814800, fax 01793 814818, car 0836 251321)

CHAPMAN, Mark Fenger; CVO (1979); s of late Geoffrey Walter Chapman, of Dyfed, and Esther Marie Hauch, *née* Fenger; *b* 12 Sept 1934; *Educ* Cranbrook Sch, St Catharine's Coll Cambridge (BA), SOAS; *m* 28 July 1959, Patricia Mary, da of late Henry Nelson Long, of Norfolk; 4 s (Giles b 1960, Jeremy b 1962 d 1983, Julian b 1965, Adrian b 1971); *Career* Nat Serv 1953–55 Royal Sussex Regt, Nigeria Regt, Lt 1955; HM Dip Serv 1958–89: third (later second) sec Bangkok 1959–63, second (later first) sec FO 1963–67, head Chancery Maseru 1967–71, asst head dept FCO 1971–74, head Chancery Vienna 1975–76, dep high cmmr Lusaka 1976–79, Dip Serv inspr 1979–82, cnsllr The Hague 1982–86, ambass Reykjavik 1986–89; memb Police Complaints Authy 1991–95; *Clubs* Royal Cwlth Soc; *Style*— Mark Chapman, Esq, CVO; ✉ Half Moon House, Briston, Melton Constable, Norfolk NR24 2LG

CHAPMAN, Michael Christopher; s of George Thomas Lisle Chapman, and Kathleen, *née* Pallister; *b* 12 June 1950; *Educ* Friends' Sch Cumberland; *m* 18 Sept 1976, Sheena Mary, da of Alan Christopher Craig, of Wark, Northumberland; 1 da (Helen b 1980); *Career* Deloitte Haskins & Sells 1968–78, gp fin controller and co sec Barratt Developments plc 1978–85, fin dir Bryant Group plc 1985–; govr Sharmans Cross Jr Sch Solihull W Midlands; FCA; *Recreations* mountaineering, hill walking; *Clubs* Wanneys Climbing; *Style*— Michael Chapman, Esq; ✉ Bryant Group plc, Cranmore House, Cranmore Boulevard, Solihull, West Midlands B90 4SD (☎ 0121 711 1212, fax 0121 711 2610)

CHAPMAN, Ven Michael Robin; s of Robert Frankland Chapman (d 1962), and Kathleen, *née* Surtees (d 1948); *b* 29 Sept 1939; *Educ* Lichfield Cathedral Sch, Ellesmere Coll, Univ of Leeds (BA), Coll of The Resurrection Mirfield; *m* 28 April 1973, Mary Bernadette, da of late Charles Taylor; 1 s (Paul Michael b 23 March 1974), 1 da (Kathleen Mary b 5 May 1975); *Career* ordained (Durham Cathedral): deacon 1963, priest 1964; curate St Columba Sunderland 1963–68, chaplain RN 1968–84, vicar of Hale Surrey 1984–91, rural dean of Farnham 1988–91, archdeacon of Northampton 1991–; *Recreations* walking, gardening, wine making; *Style*— The Ven the Archdeacon of Northampton; ✉ Westbrook, 11 The Drive, Northampton NN1 4RZ (☎ 01604 714015, fax 01604 792016)

CHAPMAN, Nigel Peter; s of Lt Col Sidney Rex Chapman, MC, of Lincolnshire, and Joan Mary, *née* Bates; *b* 31 Jan 1950; *Educ* Kimbolton Sch; *m* 26 Sept 1981, Heather Elizabeth, da of James Lindsay, of London; 2 s (Nicolas b 1982, Daniel b 1984), 2 da (Jennifer b 1987, Clare b 1990); *Career* CA; sr ptnr Chapman Wong CAs until 1991 (joined firm 1975), md Luxury Family Hotels plc 1991–; *Recreations* tennis, cricket; *Clubs* Reform, RAC, Lansdowne; *Style*— Nigel P Chapman, Esq; ✉ Woolley Grange, Bradford on Avon, Wiltshire BA15 1TX (☎ 01225 864705, fax 01225 864059)

CHAPMAN, Peter Richard; s of Lt Ernest Richard Chapman, RNVR (d 1974) and Edith Winifred, *née* Softly; *b* 1 April 1942; *Educ* St Paul's Cathedral Choir Sch, St John's Sch Leatherhead; *m* 1 June 1974, Stephanie Daynel, da of Kenneth Paul Alexander Watson; 2 s (Richard b 1975, Philip b 1978); *Career* CA 1964; Ogden Parsons & Co: joined 1959, ptnr 1970–71; ptnr: Harmood Banner & Co 1972–73, Deloitte Haskins & Sells 1974–90, Coopers & Lybrand 1990– (chm Int Banking Indust Gp); chm: DH&S Banking Indust Gp 1983–89, Inst of Chartered Accountants Banking Ctee; memb: ICAEW Business Law Ctee, Ctee Bankers' Club, Sch Cncl St Paul's Cathedral Choir Sch, Church Urban Fund 1988–94, Ct of Advsrs St Paul's Cathedral, Tadworth Church Choir; tstee Monteverdi Choir and Orchestra; FCA, CMI; *Recreations* music, golf; *Clubs* Walton Heath, RAC, Bankers; *Style*— Peter Chapman, Esq; ✉ Coopers & Lybrand, 1 Embankment Place, London WC2N 6NN (☎ 0171 583 5000, fax 0171 212 3293)

CHAPMAN, Hon Mrs (Rhiannon Elizabeth); *née* Philipps; da (by 1 m) of 2 Viscount St Davids (d 1991); *b* 21 Sept 1946; *Educ* Tormead Sch, King's Coll London (LLB, AKC); *m* 1974 (m dis 1991), Donald Hudson Chapman, s of late Francis Robert Chapman; 2 step s; *Career* dir of personnel London Stock Exchange 1980–90; dir: The Industrial Society 1991–93, Plaudit 1994–, Welsh Devpt Agency 1994–, S R Gent plc 1994–, National Australia Group CIF Trustee Ltd 1994–; memb: Policy Studies Inst, Employment Appeals Tbnl; FIPM, FRSA, CIMgt; *Recreations* opera and theatre, travel, handcrafts, keeping fit; *Clubs* Espree; *Style*— The Hon Mrs Chapman; ✉ 39 Spice Court, Asher Way, London E1 9JD (☎ 0171 709 0226)

CHAPMAN, Dr Roger William Gibson; s of Lt-Col Roy Chapman, OBE, of Pantmawr, Whitchurch, S Wales, and Margaret Gibson, *née* Abraham; *b* 16 Feb 1949; *Educ* Whitchurch GS Cardiff, St Bartholomew's Med Sch (BSc, MD, MB BS, MRCP); *m* 24 Apr 1972, Gillian Patricia, da of Dr James C Prestwich (d 1969), of Portsmouth; 3 s (James b 1977, Andrew b 1979, George b 1983), 1 da (Emily b 1987); *Career* house physician Bart's 1974–76, med registrar Southampton 1976–78, med lectr Liver Unit Royal Free Hosp 1978–81, conslt physician John Radcliff Hosp Oxford 1987– (sr registrar 1981–87); sec Br Assoc for the Study of the Liver 1990–; *Books* Topics in Gastroenterology (co-ed and written with Dr D P Jewell, 1985); *Recreations* tennis, golf, skiing, cinema; *Style*— Dr Roger Chapman; ✉ Department of Gastroenterology, John Radcliffe Hospital, Headington, Oxford OX3 9DU (☎ 01865 220618)

CHAPMAN, Roy de Courcy; s of (Edward Frederic) Gilbert Chapman, and Aline de Courcy Ireland; *b* 1 Oct 1936; *Educ* Univ of St Andrews, Moray House Coll of Educn Edinburgh; *m* 1959, Valerie Rosemary Small; 2 s, 1 da; *Career* head of modern languages Marlborough Coll 1968–75, rector Glasgow Acad 1975–82, headmaster Malvern Coll 1983–96; chm Common Entrance Bd 1988–93, chm HMC 1994; *Books* Le Français Contemporain (1972), Le Français Contemporain - Passages for Comprehension and Translation (with D Whiting, 1975); *Style*— Roy de Courcy Chapman, Esq; ✉ c/o Malvern College, Malvern, Worcs

CHAPMAN, Roy John; s of William George Chapman (d 1978), of Kettering, and Frances Harriet, *née* Yeomans (d 1981); *b* 30 Nov 1936; *Educ* Kettering GS, St Catharine's Coll Cambridge (Athletics blue, MA); *m* 23 Sept 1961, Janet Gibbeson, da of Roy Gibbeson Taylor (d 1955), of Worthing, Sussex, and Vera Constance Taylor (d 1993); 2 s (William b 1962, Henry b 1972), 1 da (Lucy b 1964); *Career* CA; Arthur Andersen: joined 1958, ptnr 1970–93, managing ptnr London 1984–89, sr ptnr UK 1989–93; non-exec dir: Halifax Building Soc 1994–, Eurotunnel plc 1995–; chm Post Office Pension Fund 1995–; memb: Advsy Cncl London Enterprise Agency 1985–88, Governing Body SOAS Univ of London 1990–, Cncl Business in the Community 1991–93; pres St Catharine's Coll Cambridge Soc 1994–95; Liveryman Worshipful Co of Farriers 1992–; FCA, CIMgt, FIMC, FBPICS, FRSA; *Recreations* cricket, walking, reading, travel; *Clubs* United Oxford and Cambridge Univ, Hawks' (Cambridge), MCC; *Style*— Roy Chapman, Esq; ✉ 9 Chislehurst Road, Bickley, Kent BR1 2NN (☎ 0181 467 3749)

CHAPMAN, Sir Sydney Brookes; MP (C) Chipping Barnet (majority 13,951); s of W Dobson Chapman (d 1965), of Prestbury, Cheshire, and Edith Laura, *née* Wadge (d 1978); *b* 17 Oct 1935; *Educ* Rugby, Univ of Manchester; *m* 1976 (m dis 1987), Claire Lesley, *née* Davies; 2 s, 1 da; *Career* memb Exec Ctee Nat Union of Cons and Unionist Assocs 1961–70, nat chm Young Cons 1964–66, contested (C) Stalybridge and Hyde 1964; MP (C): Birmingham Handsworth 1970–74, Chipping Barnet 1979–; PPS: to Sec of State for Tport 1979–81, to Sec of State for Social Servs 1981–83; memb Select Ctees on:

Environment 1983–87, House of Commons Services 1983–87; asst Govt whip 1988–90, a Lord Cmmr of the Treasy (Govt whip) 1990–92, Vice Chamberlain of HM Household 1992–95; non-practising chartered architect and chartered town and country planner; vice pres Cncl RIBA 1974–76 (memb 1972–76); instigator Nat Tree Planting Year 1973, vice pres Tree Cncl; pres: Arboricultural Assoc 1983–89, London Green Belt Cncl 1986–89; Queen's Silver Jubilee medal 1977; RIBA, FRTPI, Hon ALI, Hon FIAAS, Hon FFB, FRSA; *Clubs* United and Cecil (vice chm); *Style*— Sir Sydney Chapman, MP; ✉ House of Commons, London SW1A 0AA

CHAPPELL, Helen Diane; da of George Chappell, and Olivia Patricia, *née* Spellman; *Educ* Pasir Panjang Sch Singapore, The Downer Sch Middx, New Hall Cambridge (BA, MA); *Career* journalist and broadcaster (radio and TV); feature writer New Society magazine 1981–84, winner Catherine Pakenham Award 1980, contrib and Third Person columnist The Guardian 1984–89, commendation British Soc of Magazine Eds Awards 1985; current contrib to: The Independent, New Statesman and Society magazine, Midweek magazine, Ideal Home, Sunday Review, The Independent on Sunday; memb: New Hall Soc, Soc of Authors, Women Writers' Network; *Books* The Other Britain (contrib, 1982), The Bedside Guardian (contrib, 1990); *Style*— Ms Helen Chappell; ✉ c/o Independent on Sunday, 1 Canada Square, Canary Wharf, London E14 5AP (☎ 0171 293 2000, fax 0171 293 2435)

CHAPPIN, Andrew Darryl; s of Dennis John Chappin, and Margaret Violet, *née* Howell; *b* 9 July 1954; *Educ* St Albans Sch, Brighton Poly Faculty of Art & Design (BA); *Career* designer Granada Publishing 1977–78, asst art ed New Scientist 1978–79, sr designer Now! magazine 1979–81, art ed Eagle Moss Publications April-Nov 1981, designer The Times 1981–82, art ed Sunday Express Magazine 1982–86, art dir London Daily News 1986–87, art ed Financial Times 1987–; Soc of Newspaper Design USA: award of excellence 1988, 1990, 1991 and 1993, Silver award 1990; NDA/Linotype Awards (with David Case): Best Designed Newspaper 1990, Best News Pages 1990; memb: D&AD Assoc 1988, Soc of Newspaper Design USA 1987, Typographic Circle 1994; jt fndr (former chm) Euro Soc for News Design; *Recreations* playing rugby, skiing, scuba diving and golf, watching football, cinema, reading; *Clubs* Old Albanian; *Style*— Andrew Chappin, Esq; ✉ Financial Times, Number One, Southwark Bridge, London SE1 9HL (☎ 0171 873 3328, fax 0171 407 5700)

CHAPPLE, Brian John; s of Capt John Ernest Chapple (d 1977), and Mildred, *née* Fairbrother (d 1988); *b* 24 March 1945; *Educ* Highgate Sch, RAM (GRSM, LRAM); *m* 20 Dec 1973, Janet Mary, *née* Whittaker-Coldron; 1 da (Rosalind Bailey); *Career* composer; compositions incl: Trees Revisited 1970, Hallelujahs 1971, Scherzos 1970 (premiered Proms Royal Albert Hall 1976), 5 Blake Songs, Praeludiana 1973 (premiered Royal Festival Hall), Green and Pleasant 1973 (BBC Monarchy 1000 Prize), Veni Sancte Spiritus 1974, In Ecclesiis 1976, Piano Concerto 1977, Cantica 1978 (cmmnd Highgate Choral Soc), Venus Fly Trap 1979 (cmmnd London Sinfonietta), Little Symphony 1982 (cmmnd Haydn Society), Lamentations of Jeremiah 1984, Piano Sonata 1986 (cmmnd Dartington Int Summer Sch), Magnificat 1987 (cmmnd Highgate Choral Soc), Confitebor 1989, In Memoriam 1989, Tribute I and II 1989 and 1990, Requies 1991, Missa Brevis 1991 (cmmnd St Paul's Cathedral), Three Motets 1992, Songs of Innocence 1993 (cmmnd Finchley Children's Music Gp), Holy Communion Sevice in E 1993 (cmmnd St John the Baptist, Chipping Barnet), Ebony and Ivory 1994, A Bit of a Blow 1996, anthems and canticles for New Coll Oxford, Canterbury Cathedral and St Paul's Cathedral, children's songs, piano and instrumental music; PRS, MCPS, memb Assoc of Professional Composers; *Style*— Brian Chapple, Esq; ✉ c/o Chester Music, 8/9 Frith St, London W1V 5TZ

CHAPPLE, Baron (Life Peer UK 1985), of Hoxton, Greater London; Francis Joseph Chapple (Frank); s of Frank Chapple, of Shoreditch, and his w, Emily, da of Joseph Rook, of Hoxton; *b* 8 Aug 1920, Aug; *Educ* Elementary Sch; *m* 1944, Joan Jeanette (d 1994), da of James Nicholls; 2 s (Hon Roger Francis b 1947, Hon Barry Joseph b 1951); *Career* former electrician; gen sec Electrical, Electronic, Telecommunication and Plumbing Union 1966–84; memb TUC Gen Council 1971–83, chm TUC 1982–83, memb NEDC 1979–83; dir: National Nuclear Corpn 1980–86, Southern Water Authority 1983–89, Inner City Enterprises 1983–88, N G Bailey Organisation 1989–; *Style*— The Rt Hon Lord Chapple; ✉ House of Lords, London SW1A 0PW

CHAPPLE, Glen; *b* 23 Jan 1974; *Career* professional cricketer; debut Lancashire CCC 1992; England: memb U18 team to Canada 1991, U19 tour to NZ 1991, Pakistan 1992 and India 1993, A tour to India 1995; *Recreations* golf, football (Liverpool supporter); *Style*— Glen Chapple, Esq; ✉ c/o Lancashire CCC, Old Trafford, Manchester M16 0PX (☎ 0161 848 7021)

CHAPPLE, Field Marshal Sir John Lyon; GCB, CBE, DL (Greater London 1996); s of Charles Chapple (d 1970), and Dr Elsie Chapple, *née* Lyon (d 1989); *b* 27 May 1931; *Educ* Haileybury and Imperial Serv Coll, Trinity Coll Cambridge (MA); *m* 31 March 1959, Annabel, da of John Hill; 1 s (David b 1962), 3 da (Rachel Lucy b 5 Dec 1960, Kate (Mrs Edward Temple-Morris) b 29 April 1963, Sasha (Mrs John Holt) b 15 Oct 1964); *Career* Nat Serv joined KRRC 1949, cmmnd RA 1950; joined 2nd KEO Goorkhas 1954; served: Malaya, Borneo Hong Kong; Staff Coll 1962, jssc 1969, cmd 1 Bn 2 Goorkhas 1970–72, DS Staff Coll 1972–73, Bde Cdr 48 Gurkha Inf Bde 1976, Gurkha Field Force 1977–78, PSO to CDS 1978–79, Cdr Br Forces Hong Kong and Maj-Gen Bde of Gurkhas 1980–82, Dir Mil Ops 1982–84, Dep CDS (progs and personnel) 1985–87, Col 2nd Goorkhas 1986–94, C in C UKLF 1987–88, ADC Gen to HM The Queen 1987–92, CGS 1988–92; Govr and C-in-C Gibraltar 1993–95; pres Zoological Soc of London 1992–94, tstee WWF UK 1985–93, chm King Mahendra UK Tst for Nature Conservation 1992– (memb 1986–); memb: Conservation Fndn, RSPB, ICBP, Norfolk Naturalist Tst, Flora and Fauna Preservation Soc; pres Army Ornithological Soc; Freeman City of London 1990; pres: Mil History Soc 1992, Soc for Army History Res 1993; dep chm Cncl Nat Army Museum 1987–93, cmmr Royal Hosp Chelsea 1990–; FZS 1948, FRGS 1950, FLS 1988; *Clubs* Beefsteak; *Style*— Field Marshal Sir John Chapple, GCB, CBE, DL

CHAPPLE, Prof (Alfred) John Victor; s of Alfred Edward Chapple (d 1942), and Frances Lilian, *née* Taylor (d 1972); *b* 25 April 1928; *Educ* St Boniface's Coll Plymouth, UCL (BA, MA); *m* 6 Aug 1955, Kathleen, da of James Sheridan Bolton (d 1979); 4 s (Andrew b 1958, John b 1960, James b 1964, Christopher b 1967), 1 da (Clare b 1962); *Career* Nat Serv RA 1946–49: 2 Lt 1947, short serv cmmn as Lt; res asst Yale Univ 1955–58, asst Univ of Aberdeen 1958–59, asst lectr, lectr then sr lectr Univ of Manchester 1959–71, prof of English Univ of Hull 1971–92 (dean of Arts 1980–82, pro vice chllr 1985–88), visiting fell Corpus Christi Coll Cambridge 1992; memb Int Assoc of Profs of English 1986–, chm Gaskell Soc 1990–; *Books* The Letters of Mrs Gaskell (ed with Arthur Pollard, 1966), Documentary and Imaginative Literature 1880–1920 (1970), Elizabeth Gaskell: A Portrait In Letters (1980), Science and Literature in the Nineteenth Century (1986), Private Voices: the Diaries of Elizabeth Gaskell and Sophia Holland (ed with Anita Wilson, 1996); *Recreations* music, wine, gardening, calligraphy; *Style*— Prof John Chapple; ✉ 173 Newland Park, Hull HU5 2DX (☎ 01482 343406)

CHAPPLE-HYAM, Peter William; s of William Henry Chapple-Hyam, of Itchington, Warwicks, and Mary Constance, *née* Mann; *b* 2 April 1963; *Educ* Princethorpe Coll; *m* 24 June 1990, Jane Fiona, da of Andrew Sharpe Peacock; *Career* racehorse trainer; Young Trainer of the Year 1991 and 1992; trainer winner of: The Derby, 2,000 Guineas and Irish 2000 Guineas (all 1992), Italian Derby 1993, Irish 2000 Guineas 1994 and 1995; *Recreations* soccer, cricket, tennis; *Style*— Peter Chapple-Hyam, Esq; ✉ Stone Cottage, Manton House Estate, Manton, Marlborough, Wiltshire SN8 1PN (☎ 01672 514901)

CHAPUT DE SAINTONGE, Dr (David) Mark; s of Lt-Col Rolland Alfred Aime, CMG (d 1989), and Barbara, *née* Watts; *b* 1 Oct 1942; *Educ* Whitgift Sch Croydon, London Hosp Med Coll (BSc, PhD, MB BS); *m* 15 Dec 1973, Gail Nicola, da of Norman Mason (d 1985); 3 s (Luke b 1976, Daniel b 1978, Edward b 1980); *Career* sr house offr Med Unit Nottingham Gen Hosp 1968–69, sr lectr in clinical pharmacology and therapeutics London Hosp Med Coll 1973– (lectr 1969); conslt physician in gen med: Bethnal Green Hosp 1976–79, London Hosp 1976–; sr lectr in clinical pharmacology Bart's 1981–; assoc Center Res on Judgement Policy at Inst Cognitive Sci Univ of Colorado 1984–, memb Editorial Bd Br Jl of Clinical Pharmacology 1983–89, assoc ed Drug and Therapeutics Bulletin 1986–90; elder Pembury Free Church; FRCP 1986; *Books* Current Problems in Clinical Trials (with Prof D W Vere, 1984), numerous scientific papers on clinical trials and med judgement; *Recreations* pottery, shooting; *Style*— Dr Mark Chaput de Saintonge; ✉ c/o St Bartholomew's Hospital Medical College, West Smithfield, London EC1A 7BE

CHARAP, Prof John Michael; s of Samuel Lewis Charap (d 1995), and Irene, *née* Shaw (d 1984); *b* 1 Jan 1935; *Educ* City of London Sch, Trinity Coll Cambridge (MA, PhD); *m* 11 June 1961, Ellen Elfrieda, da of Eric Kuhn (d 1986); 1 s (David b 1965); *Career* res assoc: Univ of Chicago 1959–60, Univ of California (Berkeley) 1960–62; memb Inst for Advanced Study Princeton NJ 1962–63, lectr in physics Imperial Coll London 1964–65 (sr scientific offr 1963–64); Queen Mary Coll (since 1989 Queen Mary and Westfield Coll) London: reader in theoretical physics 1965–78, prof of theoretical physics 1978–, head Dept of Physics 1980–85, dean Faculty of Sci 1982–85, pro princ 1987–89, vice princ 1989–90; Univ of London: chm Bd of Studies in Physics 1976–80, memb Senate 1981–94, memb Ct 1989–94, memb Cncl 1994–; memb: American Physical Soc 1960, European Physical Soc 1980; FInstP 1979, CPhys 1988; *Recreations* walking, talking; *Style*— Prof John Charap; ✉ 67 South Hill Park, London NW3 2SS (☎ 0171 975 5039, fax 0181 981 7517, telex 893750)

CHARD, Phillip; *b* 23 Feb 1963; *Educ* Pentrehafod Swansea, stage mgmnt and design course; *Career* various appts asst/dep/stage/prodn mangr for theatre/TV 1984–88; theatrical agents asst Sheila Bourne Management 1989, jr theatrical agent Hatton and Baker 1989–90, head London office The Brunskill Management Co 1990–94, currently md Macfarlane Chard Assocs; *Style*— Phillip Chard, Esq; ✉ Macfarlane Chard Associates, 7/8 Little Turnstile, London WC1V 7DX (☎ 0171 404 2332, fax 0171 404 7456)

CHARD, Prof Tim; s of Dr Henry Francis Chard (d 1983), of London, and Dorothea Elaine, *née* Marsh; *b* 4 June 1937; *Educ* Merchant Taylors', St Thomas's Hosp Med Sch Univ of London (MB, MD); *m* 1, 1965 (m dis 1978), Marty Jane, *née* Batten; 2 s (Declan Tarn b 1970, Jiri Alexander b 1972); *m* 2, 1978, Linda Kay, *née* Elmore; *Career* jr hosp posts 1960–65, fell MRC 1965–68, currently prof of obstetrics, gynaecology and reproductive physiology and dir i/c Academic Unit St Bartholomew's Hosp (lectr then sr lectr 1968–73); author of numerous scientific papers; memb various public and private sector ctees; FRCOG 1975; medal of the Univ of Helsinki; *Books* Radioimmunoassay (1986), Computing for Clinicians (1988), Basic Sciences for Obstetrics (1990); *Recreations* fine arts, venture capital; *Style*— Prof Tim Chard; ✉ Reproductive Physiology, St Bartholomew's Hosp, London EC1A 7BE (☎ 0171 601 8250, 0171 601 8251, 0171 600 1439)

CHARING, Rabbi Douglas Stephen; *b* 1945, London; *Educ* Leo Baeck Coll London; *m* Oct 1972, Eve; 1 s (Benjamin); *Career* ordained rabbi 1970; former: rabbi to progressive synagogues in N and W London and Leeds, visiting rabbi Bristol & The West Progressive Synagogue, pt/t dir Jewish Information Serv, pt/t lectr Theol and Religious Studies Dept Univ of Leeds and Gtr Manchester Police Coll, specialist advsr Theol and Religious Studies Bd CNAA, memb Planning Ctee Centre for the Study of Judaism and Jewish/Christian Rels, pt/t dir Concord Multi-Faith Resources Centre, visiting rabbi Sha'arei Shalom Synagogue Manchester; currently: dir Jewish Educn Bureau (fndr), tutor Greenwich Univ, conslt Int Consultancy on Religion, Educn and Culture, specialist assessor Higher Educn Funding Cncl for Wales; memb: Inter-European Cmmn on Church and Sch, Cncl of Christians and Jews, World Congress of Faiths, Inter-Faith Network, Cncl of Reform and Liberal Rabbis, Advsy Ctee Nat Community Folktale Centre, Christian-Jewish Consultation of the United Reformed Church, Bd of Dirs Anne Frank Educnl Tst UK, Exec Cncl for Religious Educn, Professional Cncl for Religious Educn, Assoc of Religious Educn Insprs, Advsr & Consltts (AREIAC); *Publications incl* Comparative Religions (jtly, 1982, reprinted 1984 and 1991), The Jewish World (1983, reprinted 1985, 1992 and 1995), Visiting a Synagogue (1984, reprinted 1988), The Torah (1993), Religion in Leeds (contrib, 1994), Renewing the Vision (contrib, 1996); writer of Rabbinic stories for children on BBC TV; *Style*— Rabbi Douglas Charing; ✉ 8 Westcombe Avenue, Leeds LS8 2BS (☎ 0113 293 3523, fax 0113 293 3533)

CHARING CROSS, Archdeacon of; *see:* Jacob, Ven Dr William Mungo

CHARKHAM, Jonathan Philip; s of Louis Charkham (d 1962), of London, and Phoebe Beatrice, *née* Miller; *b* 17 Oct 1930; *Educ* St Paul's, Jesus Coll Cambridge (MA); *m* 3 Nov 1954, Moira Elizabeth Frances, da of Barnett Alfred Salmon (d 1965), of London; 2 s (Graham b 1959, Rupert (twin) b 1959), 1 da (Fiona Shackleton, *qv*, b 1956); *Career* called to the Bar Inner Temple 1953; md Morris Charkham Ltd 1953–63, divnl dir Rest Assured 1963–68; Civil Serv 1969–82; Bank of England: on secondment as dir PRO NED 1982–85, chief advsr 1985–88, advsr to the Govrs 1988–93; dir: The Great Universal Stores plc 1993–, Crestacare plc 1993–, CLM plc 1993–, Leopold Joseph Holdings plc 1994–, Home Medicine Ltd 1996–; memb: Advsy Bd David Hume Inst Steering Ctee of Corporate Takeovers Inquiry 1989–90, Columbia Univ Center for Law & Economic Studies Institutional Investor Project NY 1986–93, US President's Sub-Cncl on Corp Governance & Fin Markets (part of Competitive Policy Cncl) 1990–92, Sir Adrian Cadbury's Ctee on Fin Aspects of Corp Governance 1990–92, Ctee Knightsbridge Assoc 1985–, Steering Ctee on Corp Governance in the NHS 1993–94, Panel Jt Disciplinary Scheme of the Accountancy Profession 1994–; Sheriff City of London 1994–95; Freeman City of London, memb Ct of Assts Worshipful Co of Upholders (Master 1979–80 and 1980–81); CIMgt 1988, FRSA; *Books* Effective Boards (1985), Non-Executive Directors: A Practical Guide (1987), Corporate Governance and the Market for Control of Companies (1989), Corporate Governance and the Market for Companies: Aspects of the Shareholders Role (1989), Keeping Good Company: A Study of Corporate Governance in 5 Countries (1994); Bank of England papers: Discussion Paper 44 (Corp governance aspects of the shareholders role), Panel Paper 25 (Corp governance and market for control of companies); *Recreations* golf, music, shooting, wine; *Clubs* Athenaeum, City Livery, MCC; *Style*— Jonathan Charkham Esq; ✉ The Yellow House, 22 Montpelier Place, Knightsbridge, London SW7 1HL (☎ 0171 589 9879, fax 0171 581 8520)

CHARKHAM, Stephen Julian; s of Louis Charkham (d 1963), of Kensington, and Phoebe Beatrice, *née* Miller; *b* 19 Nov 1934; *Educ* St Paul's; *m* 6 Jan 1959, Ann Fredricka Snell Johnson, da of Coll H H Johnson (d 1956); 3 da (Abigail Sarah b 1966, Miranda Jane b 1967, Louise Clare b 1971); *Career* Nat Serv as Lt Somerset Light Inf 1953–55; jt dir Morris Charkham Ltd (family firm, furniture manufacturers) 1955–64, dir Seak Ltd (footwear manufacturers) 1964–73; Hosp Conslts and Specialists Assoc: press offr and ed jl The Consultant 1974–88, chief exec 1988–; cncllr Berks CC 1981–85; FRSM

1988; *Recreations* golf, garden, touring Europe, eating; *Clubs* Berkshire Golf (captain 1987), Royal and Ancient; *Style—* Stephen Charkham, Esq; ✉ Holly Cottage, Chapel Street, North Waltham, nr Basingstoke, Hants RG25 2BZ (☎ 01256 397442); Hospital Consultants and Specialists Association, Number One, Kingsclere Road, Overton, nr Basingstoke, Hampshire RG25 3JA (☎ 01256 771777)

CHARKIN, Richard Denis Paul; s of Frank Charkin (d 1963), and Mabel Doreen, *née* Rosen; *b* 17 June 1949; *Educ* Haileybury and ISC, Trinity Coll Cambridge (MA); *m* 7 Aug 1972, Susan Mary, da of Sidney William Poole; 1 s (Toby b 1975), 2 da (Emily b 1973, Boo b 1977); *Career* Oxford University Press: med ed 1974–76, head of Sci and Med Div 1976–80, head of Reference Div 1980–84, md Academic Div 1984–88; exec dir Octopus Publishing Group 1988–, chief exec Reed Consumer Books 1990–94, chief exec Reed International Books 1994–95, currently with Reed Elsevier (UK) Ltd; *Recreations* cricket, music; *Style—* Richard Charkin, Esq; ✉ Reed Elsevier (UK) Ltd, 6 Chesterfield Gardens, London W1A 1EJ (☎ 0171 491 8346, fax 0171 491 8345)

CHARLEMONT, 14 Viscount (I 1665); John Day Caulfeild; also Lord Caulfeild, Baron of Charlemont (I 1620); s of Eric St George Caulfeild (d 1975), and Edith Evelyn, da of Frederick William Day, of Ottawa; suc unc, 13 Viscount (d 1985); *b* 19 March 1934; *m* 1, 1964, Judith Ann (d 1971), da of James Dodd, of Ontario; 1 s (Hon John Dodd Caulfeild b 1966), 1 da (Hon Janis Ann b 1968); m 2, 1972, Janet Evelyn, da of Orville Nancekivell, of Ontario; *Heir* s, Hon John Dodd Caulfeild b 15 May 1966; *Style—* The Rt Hon the Viscount Charlemont; ✉ 39 Rossburn Drive, Etobicoke, Ontario M9C 2P9, Canada

CHARLES, His Hon Judge; Bernard Leopold (Leo); QC (1980); s of Chaskiel Charles (d 1960), of Grosvenor Square, London, and Mary, *née* Harris (d 1980); *b* 16 May 1929; *Educ* Kings Coll Taunton; *m* 1, 13 Aug 1958, Margaret Daphne, da of Arthur Lawrence Abel (d 1978), of Harley St, London; 1 s (Edward Duncan b 1963), 2 da (Margaret Lucy b 1966, (Katriona Mary) Katy b 1968); m 2, 16 Sept 1994, Mrs Judith Lynda Orus; *Career* Nat Serv 1948–50, Capt RAEC 1949; called to the Bar Gray's Inn 1955, circuit judge (SE Circuit) 1990– (recorder 1985–90); *Recreations* music, gardening; *Style—* His Hon Judge Charles, QC; ✉ Knightsbridge Crown Court, 1 Pocock Street, London SE1 0BT; Lamb Building, Temple, London EC4 (☎ 0171 797 8300, fax 0171 353 4686, telex 261511 JURIST G)

CHARLES, Caroline (Mrs Malcolm Valentine); *b* 18 May 1942; *Educ* Sacred Heart Convent Woldingham Surrey, Swindon Coll of Art Wilts; *m* 8 Jan 1966, Malcolm Valentine; 2 c (Kate, Alex); *Career* fashion designer; apprentice to Michael Sherard British Couture Curzon St London 1960, worked for Mary Quant London 1961, estab Caroline Charles London 1963; exhibitor V & A Museum Summer Exhbn 1989; *Awards* Yardley Young Designer award NY 1964, Evening Standard Design Award 1978; *Books* Weekend Wardrobe; *Recreations* travel, theatre, tennis; *Clubs* British Colour & Textile Group; *Style—* Ms Caroline Charles; ✉ 56–57 Beauchamp Place, London SW3 1NY (☎ 0171 225 3197, fax 0171 584 2521)

CHARLES, Jacqueline Fay; JP (Barnet 1968); da of Henry Burton, QC (d 1952), and Hilda, *née* Shaffer (d 1986); *b* 26 Aug 1934; *Educ* Roedean, King's Coll London (LLB, JELF medal); *m* 14 July 1957, Eric Charles, s of Joseph John Charles (d 1951); 2 s (John b 1959, Henry b 1961), 1 da (Susan b 1964); *Career* called to the Bar Gray's Inn 1956; asst to town clerk Southwark Borough Cncl 1956, law reporter 1964–78; chm: Rent Assessment Ctee 1978–, Social Security Tbnl 1985–; memb CAB 1966–70; *Recreations* reading, travel, music; *Style—* Mrs Jacqueline Charles, JP; ✉ 38 Chester Close North, Regents Park, London NW1 4JE (☎ 0171 935 6968)

CHARLES, Jonathan; s of Henry Simon Charles, of Nottingham, and Diane Betty, *née* Lewis; *b* 9 July 1964; *Educ* Nottingham Boys' HS, Oriel Coll Oxford; *Career* editorial trainee ITN 1986–87; BBC: joined as reporter 1987, New York corr 1989, Europe reporter Paris 1989–90, Europe business corr Brussels 1990–; *Recreations* reading, music (classical and popular), golf; *Style—* Jonathan Charles, Esq; ✉ BBC TV News, Boite 59, IPC 1, Boulevard Charlemagne, Brussels 1040, Belgium (☎ 00 322 2 230 2120)

CHARLES, Kate (real name Carol Ann Chase); da of Elmer C Fosher, of Bloomington, Illinois, USA, and Kathryn Lucile, *née* Fancher; *b* 13 July 1950; *Educ* Bloomington HS, Illinois State Univ (BA), Indiana Univ (MLS); *m* 14 July 1973, Rory Lee Chase, s of late Leroy F Chase; *Career* writer; speaker: Cambridge Book Assoc 1992, World Mystery Convention 1992, 1994 and 1995, Oxford Mystery Conf 1994 and 1995, Dept for Continuing Educn Univ of Oxford 1995, The Dorothy L Sayers Lecture 1996, Herts Litfest 1996; Crime Writers' Assoc: memb 1991–, vice chm 1995–96, chm 1996–; memb: Soc of Authors 1992–, Sisters in Crime 1992–, PEN 1993–, Exec Ctee Barbara Pym Soc 1994–; *Books* A Drink of Deadly Wine (1991), The Snares of Death (1992), Appointed to Die (1993), A Dead Man Out of Mind (1994), Evil Angels Among Them (1995); contrib Oxford Companion to Crime and Mystery Writing; *Recreations* visiting churches, travelling, music/singing, cooking/entertaining; *Style—* Mrs Carol Chase; ✉ Greene & Heaton Ltd Literary Agency, 37 Goldhawk Road, London W12 8QQ (☎ 0181 749 0315, fax 0181 749 0318)

CHARLES, Susan Jane; da of Alfred Norman Harris, of Solihull, and Esme Joyce, *née* Skey; *b* 2 Jan 1959; *Educ* Tudor Grange Girls' GS, Solihull Sixth Form Coll, St Catherine's Coll Oxford (BA Biochemistry, MA, Swimming half blue), Cranfield Sch of Management (MBA, PR Week scholar), Chartered Inst of Marketing (DipM); *m* 1 Sept 1992, Ian George Charles; *Career* pre-doctoral res asst Univ of Leicester 1981–84 (res demonstrator 1984–85); Kempsters Communication Group: tech conslt 1984–85, PR tech writer 1985, PR account exec 1985–87, PR dir 1987–89, gp business dir 1989–91; princ conslt Charles Consultants 1991–, jt md De Facto Consultants Ltd 1991–, dir BioScape Ltd 1994–; non-exec chm Bang Communications Ltd 1991–, non-exec dir Genus Communications Ltd 1994–; memb: Cranfield Mgmnt Assoc, Oxford Union Soc, Assoc of MBAs; MCIM, MIPR; *Style—* Mrs Susan Charles; ✉ De Facto Consultants, Network House, Basing View, Basingstoke, Hants RG21 4HG (☎ 01256 842274, fax 01256 469308, e-mail s.charles@defacto.co.uk)

CHARLES, (Arthur) William Hessin; s of Arthur Attwood Sinclair Charles, and Dr May Davies Charles, *née* Westerman, of Frith Common, Nr Tenbury Wells, Worcs; *b* 25 March 1948; *Educ* Malvern Coll, Christ's Coll Cambridge (MA); *m* 22 June 1974, Lydia Margaret, da of John Barlow Ainscow, of Gale Rigg, Ambleside, Cumbria; 1 s (Simon b 1980), 1 da (Florence b 1983); *Career* called to the Bar Lincoln's Inn 1971, jr counsel to the Crown Chancery 1986–89, first jr counsel to the Treasy in chancery matters 1989; *Recreations* golf and tennis; *Clubs* Hawks' (Cambridge), Denham Golf; *Style—* William Charles, Esq; ✉ 13 Old Square, Lincoln's Inn, London WC2A 3UA (☎ 0171 404 4800, fax 0171 405 4267, telex 22487 INNLAW G)

CHARLESWORTH, Allan Christopher (Chris); s of James Henry Charlesworth, of Skipton, N Yorkshire, and Betty, *née* Brotherton (d 1969); *b* 16 May 1947; *Educ* St Peter's Sch York; *m* Lisa Anne, da of Joseph Pettibone; 1 da (Olivia Anne b 1992), 1 S (Sam Joseph b 1995); *Career* reporter: Craven Herald & Pioneer Skipton 1964–67, Telegraph & Argus Bradford 1967–68, Slough Evening Mail 1968–70; successively feature writer, news ed, American ed (based in NY) Melody Maker 1970–77, head of press and publicity RCA Records London 1978–80, freelance author 1980–83, ed-in-chief Omnibus Press 1983–; prodr The Who - 30 Years of Maximum R & B (a 4 CD career retrospective of the music of The Who); co-prodr The Who CD re-issues: Live At Leeds, A Quick One, The Who Sell Out and Who's Next 1995, Tommy, Quadrophenia, The Who By Numbers and Who Are You 1996; contrib numerous: articles to magazines and newspapers in UK and USA, liner notes to LP records; *Books* incl: David Bowie Profile (1981), The Who (1982), Pete Townshend - A Biography (1983); *Recreations* watching cricket, listening to and playing music, cryptic crossword puzzles; *Style—* Chris Charlesworth, Esq; ✉ Omnibus Press, 8–9 Frith Street, London W1V 5TZ (☎ 0171 434 0066, fax 0171 734 2246)

CHARLESWORTH, David Anthony; s of David Harold Charlesworth, MBE (d 1970), and Jessie Vilma, *née* Waldron (d 1970); *b* 19 July 1936; *Educ* Haileybury & ISC; *m* 1970 (m dis 1975), Carol Ann, *née* Green; *Career* Capt RAPC; dir and sec: Sika Contracts Group of Cos 1965–76, Surban Trading Co Ltd 1968–; dir: SGB Group 1973–76, Johnson and Avon Ltd 1977–82, Michael Ashby Fine Art Ltd 1978–84, NHM Agency Holdings Ltd 1982–91, Michael Watson (Management) Ltd 1983–87, P J Dewey (Agencies) Co 1983–91, Shaftesbury Mews Co Ltd 1984–, Nelson Hurst & Marsh Agencies Ltd 1985–90, Jardine (Lloyd's Agencies) 1990–91, Rimmer Properties Limited 1990–92, Glenrand Marsh Ltd 1992–95, Andrew Wallas & Marsh Ltd 1994–; underwriting memb of Lloyd's 1975–; *Recreations* bridge, listening to Mozart, motorcycling, reading biographies; *Clubs* IOD; *Style—* David Charlesworth, Esq; ✉ 1 Shaftesbury Mews, Stratford Rd, London W8 6QR (☎ 0171 937 3550); 41 Seawest Boulevard De La Plage, Le Touquet, 62520, France (☎ 00 33 21 05 68 44)

CHARLESWORTH, Paul Lane; s of Harold Charlesworth (d 1987), and Mary, *née* Tomlinson (d 1993); *b* 1 Oct 1932; *Educ* Wheelwright GS, Univ of Manchester (BSc); *m* 12 Oct 1962, Shirley Margaret, da of Edward Sykes, of Huddersfield; 1 s (Andrew b 1964), 1 da (Helen b 1965); *Career* BOC Group plc: gen mangr mktg BOC Gases Div 1972–75, non-exec dir Irish Industrial Gases Ltd 1974–80, md BOC Cryoplants Ltd 1975–89, non-exec dir Daisan-BOC Japan 1980–85, md BOC Cryoplants (USA) 1983–89, pres BOC AG Switzerland 1986–90, pres Cryostar (France) SA 1986–90 (non-exec dir 1990–96), chm Sturtevant Engineering Co Ltd 1988–92, non-exec dir Firth Rixon plc (formerly Johnson & Firth Brown plc) 1989–, dir The BOC Fndn for the Environment 1990–; FIChemE 1966, FEng 1986 (memb Cncl until 1993); author of numerous articles on cryogenic engrg; *Recreations* golf, photography; *Style—* Paul Charlesworth, Esq, FEng; ✉ Shenstone, 70 Shenfield Road, Shenfield, Brentwood, Essex CM15 8EW (☎ 01277 226807)

CHARLESWORTH, His Hon Judge; Peter James; s of Joseph William Charlesworth (d 1969), of East Yorkshire, and Florence Mary, *née* Fisher (d 1991); *b* 24 Aug 1944; *Educ* Hull GS, Univ of Leeds (LLB, LLM); *m* 12 Aug 1967, Elizabeth Mary, da of Ronald Herbert Postill (d 1945), of East Yorkshire; 1 s (Robin b 1972), 1 da (Caroline b 1975); *Career* called to the Bar Inner Temple 1966, recorder 1982–89, circuit judge (NE Circuit) 1989–; *Recreations* tennis, rugby league (spectating), walking in the Yorkshire Dales, reading, travel; *Clubs* Hull Rugby League FC (vice pres), Leeds YMCA (tennis); *Style—* His Hon Judge Charlesworth; ✉ Daleswood, Creskeld Gardens, Bramhope, Leeds LS16 9EN; 53 Piecefields, Threshfield, nr Skipton BD23 5MR

CHARLTON, Clive Arthur Cyril; s of Harold Arthur Charlton (d 1965), of Bexhill, Sussex, and Hilda Gertrude, *née* White (d 1968); *b* 30 Sept 1932; *Educ* King's Coll Taunton, Univ of London, Bart's (MB BS, MS); *m* 9 July 1960, Sheelagh Jennifer, da of Gordon Edward Price (d 1986), of London; 3 s (Simon b 1961, Jason b 1968, Harry b 1970), 1 da (Clare b 1963); *Career* research fell Dept of Surgery Univ of Kentucky Med Sch USA 1965–66, sr registrar St Paul's Hosp and Inst of Urology London 1967–68; conslt urological surgn: Bart's 1968–72, Royal Utd Hosp Bath 1972–94; memb Cncl: Section of Urology RSM 1973–76, Br Assoc of Urological Surgns 1979–82 and 1984–87; memb Editorial Ctee Br Jl of Surgery 1979–86, asst ed Br Jl of Urology 1981–90, hon sr clinical lectr Inst of Urology 1984–94, memb Ct of Examiners RCS 1988–94, memb Bath DHA 1982–84, med memb Pensions Appeal Tbl 1993–; Freeman City of London 1973, Yeoman Worshipful Soc of Apothecaries 1971; FRSM 1968, FRCS 1963; *Books* The Urological System (2 edn, 1984); contrib: Textbook of Genito-Urinary Surgery (1986), Calculus Disease (1988), New Trends in Urinary Tract Infections (1988), Operative Surgery and Management (1994); *Recreations* golf, theatre, biographies, medical history; *Style—* Clive Charlton, Esq; ✉ Radford Villa, Timsbury, nr Bath (☎ 01761 470658)

CHARLTON, David; s of Robert Charlton (d 1968), of Kenilworth, and Alice Jane Stephenson, *née* Pescod; *b* 17 Oct 1936; *Educ* Dame Allan's Sch Newcastle upon Tyne, Univ of Durham Law Sch; *m* 4 Aug 1976, Doreen, da of Joseph Woodward, of Kenilworth; 1 s (Angus b 1964); *Career* admitted slr 1959; arbitrator; co slr Euro Ferries plc 1962–66, sr ptnr Angel and Co Coventry and Kenilworth 1966–90; adjudicator for nat savings 1993–95; memb Panel Chartered Inst of Arbitrators 1979–95, arbitrations conslt to Law Soc 1991–95, chm Ind Tbnl Service 1995–; chm Talisman Theatre Kenilworth 1982–95; memb Kenilworth UDC 1970–74; Liveryman Worshipful Co of Arbitrators; FCIArb; *Recreations* performing arts, golf; *Clubs* Royal Over-Seas League; *Style—* David Charlton, Esq; ✉ 4 Ferndale Drive, Kenilworth, Warwickshire CV8 2PF (☎ 01926 54453)

CHARLTON, (Richard Wingate) Edward; s of Col Wingate Charlton, OBE, DL, of Great Canfield Park, Takeley, Essex, and Angela Margot, *née* Windle; *b* 3 May 1948; *Educ* Eton, Univ of Neuchatel; *m* 1 Feb 1979, Claudine Marie Germaine, da of Maître Hubert Maringe (d 1988), of Champlin, Premery, Nievre, France; 1 s (Andrew b 9 Nov 1981), 2 da (Emma b 29 Sept 1985, Jessica b 28 April 1989); *Career* Frere Cholmeley & Co Slrs 1968–73, Swales & Co Slrs 1974–76, Hambros Bank 1977–81, exec dir Banque Paribas London 1981–88, md Banque Internationale à Luxembourg London 1988–; various co directorships; slr of the Supreme Ct 1976; Freeman City of London, memb Ct Worshipful Co of Merchant Taylors; MInstD; *Recreations* various active sports, cinema and family pursuits; *Clubs* White's, Turf, City of London; *Style—* Edward Charlton, Esq; ✉ Banque Internationale a Luxembourg, Shackleton House, Hay's Galleria, 4 Battle Bridge Lane, London SE1 2GZ (☎ 0171 556 3000, fax 0171 556 3055, telex 884032)

CHARLTON, (William Wingate) Hugo; s of Lt Col D R W G Collins-Charlton, MBE, DL, and Angela Margot, *née* Windle; *b* 23 Sept 1951; *Educ* Eton, Univ of York (BA); *m* 1, 21 Oct 1978 (m dis 1984); m 2, 21 July 1994, Jane Louise, da of Donald Frank Sidnell; *Career* called to the Bar Gray's Inn 1978; Distillers Company 1977–84, in practice as barrister 1986–; Inns of Court and City Yeomanry 1987–94; the law offr Green Party 1991–; Freeman: City of London, Worshipful Co of Merchant Taylors; *Recreations* riding, skiing, scuba; *Style—* Hugo Charlton, Esq; ✉ 5 Pump Court, Temple, London EC4 (☎ 0171 5837133)

CHARLTON, Jack (John); OBE (1974); s of Robert Charlton (d 1985), and Elizabeth (Cissie), *née* Milburn (d 1996); *b* 8 May 1935; *Educ* Hirst Park Sch Ashington; *m* 1958, Patricia; 2 s, 1 da; *Career* former professional football player and manager; player Leeds Utd 1952–73, 35 full England caps 1965–70; mangr: Middlesbrough 1973–77, Sheffield Wednesday 1977–83, Newcastle Utd 1984–85, Republic of Ireland 1986– Dec 1995; honours as player: League Championship 1969, FA Cup winners 1972 (runners up 1965 and 1970), League Cup 1968, Fairs Cup 1968 and 1971 (runners up 1967), World Cup winners England v W Germany 1966; honours as mangr: Div 2 Championship Middlesbrough 1974, promotion to Div 2 Sheffield Wednesday 1980, Republic of Ireland qualified for Euro Championships W Germany 1988, World Cup Italy 1990 and USA 1994; regular TV and radio appearances on various football programmes; *Style—* Jack Charlton, Esq, OBE; ✉ c/o Football Association of Ireland, 8 Merrion Square, Dublin 2, Ireland

CHARLTON, John Fraser; s of late Dr Paul Henry Charlton, of Cardigan, Dyfed, and Margaret, *née* Smith; *b* 23 April 1940; *Educ* Winchester, Magdalene Coll Cambridge (BA); *m* 1966, Susan Ann, da of late Walter Herbert Allan, of Esher, Surrey; 1 s (David b 1969), 2 da (Anna b 1967, Lisa b 1971); *Career* publisher; dir: Chatto and Windus 1967–93, The Hogarth Press 1970–93, Chatto Bodley Head and Jonathan Cape Ltd 1977–89 (co name changed to Random House UK Ltd 1988); chm: Great Gardens of England Investments Ltd 1973–, Chatto and Windus Ltd 1985–93; *Recreations* sport; *Clubs* Garrick, Groucho; *Style*— John Charlton, Esq; ✉ 4 Selwood Place, London SW7 3QQ (☎ 0171 370 1711); The Garden Centre, Syon Park, Brentford, Middx TW8 8JG (☎ 0181 560 0884)

CHARLTON, Prof Kenneth; s of late George Charlton, and Lottie, *née* Little (d 1976); *b* 11 July 1925; *Educ* Chester GS, Univ of Glasgow (MA, MEd), Jordanhill Coll of Educn Glasgow; *m* 2 April 1953, Maud Tulloch, da of Peter Renwick Brown, MBE (d 1955); 1 s (Peter b 3 Feb 1957), 1 da (Shelagh b 3 June 1955); *Career* Sub Lt RNVR 1943–46; history master Dalziel HS Motherwell 1950, sr history master Uddingston GS Lanarkshire 1950–54, sr lectr in educn Univ of Keele 1964–66 (lectr 1954–64), prof of history and philosophy of educn Univ of Birmingham 1966–72, prof of history of educn and dean Faculty of Educn King's Coll London 1972–83, emeritus prof of history of educn Univ of London 1983–, Leverhulme Tst emeritus res fellowship 1984–86, visiting scholar Rockefeller Fndn Centre Bellagio Italy Feb-March 1989, Br Cncl distinguished visiting fell Japan 1990; *Books* Education in Renaissance England (1955); *Recreations* gardening, listening to music; *Style*— Prof Kenneth Charlton; ✉ 128 Ridge Langley, Sanderstead, Croydon, Surrey CR2 OAS (☎ 0181 651 1488)

CHARLTON, Louise; da of John Charlton, and Patricia Mary Crawford, *née* Hulme; *b* 25 May 1960; *m* 1985, Andrew, s of David Durant; 2 s (Sam b 10 Sept 1991, Jack b 14 Feb 1996), 1 da (Olivia b 16 Aug 1993); *Career* Broadstreet Associates 1984–87, dir Brunswick Public Relations 1987–; *Recreations* family, swimming; *Style*— Ms Louise Charlton; ✉ Brunswick Public Relations Ltd, 16 Lincoln's Inn Fields, London WC2A 3ED (☎ 0171 404 5959, fax 0171 831 2823)

CHARLTON, Prof (Thomas) Malcolm; s of William Charlton (d 1974), of Great Wyrley, Staffs, and Emily May, *née* Wallbank (d 1950); *b* 1 Sept 1923; *Educ* Doncaster GS, Univ Coll Nottingham (BSc), Univ of Cambridge (MA); *m* 18 Sept 1950, Valerie, da of Dr Colin McCulloch (d 1947), of Hexham; 3 s (Richard b 1951, William b and d 1956, Edward b 1958); *Career* jr sci offr Miny of Aircraft Prodn TRE Malvern 1943–46, asst engr Merz and McLellan 1946–54, lectr in engrg Univ of Cambridge 1954–63 (fell and tutor Sidney Sussex Coll 1959–63), prof of civil engrg Queen's Univ Belfast 1963–70 (dean Faculty of Applied Sci 1967–70), Jackson prof of engrg Univ of Aberdeen 1970–79 (professor emeritus 1979), historian of engrg sci 1979–; memb: Advsy Cncl UDR 1969–71, Bd of Fin Diocese of Hereford 1980; hon foreign memb Finnish Acad of Tech Sciences 1967, FRSE 1973, Personal Symposium Turin Politecnico 1989, contrib Rendiconti Lincei Rome 1991; *Books* Model Analysis of Structures (1954, 1966), Hydro-electric Engineering Practice (contrib, 1958), Energy Principles in Applied Statics (1959), Analysis of Statically-Indeterminate Frameworks (1961), Principles of Structural Analysis (1969, 1977, Arabic translation 1984), Energy Principles in Theory of Structures (1973), The Works of Isambard Kingdom Brunel (contrib, 1976), A History of Theory of Structures in the Nineteenth Century (1982), Professor Emeritus (1991); *Recreations* walking, ecclesiastical history; *Clubs* Royal Northern and University (Aberdeen); *Style*— Prof Malcolm Charlton, FRSE; ✉ The Old School House, 72 North Street, Burwell, Cambridge CB5 OBB (☎ 01638 741351)

CHARLTON, Mervyn; s of Rowland Charlton (d 1986), of Warwick, and Madge Louise, *née* Eaton; *b* 2 July 1945; *Educ* Loughton Coll of FE (Art Fndn Course), Nottingham Art Coll; *m* 1982, Ann, da of John James Hewitson; 1 s (Conrad Alexander b 1 March 1986); *Career* artist-in-residence: Holly Spring Jr Sch (South Hill Park Artist in Schs Project) 1981, Guildford House 1983, Hammond Middle Sch Surrey (in conjunction with SE Arts) 1994; *Solo Exhibitions* Moira Kelly Fine Art 1981 and 1982, Festival Gallery Bath 1983, Sally Hunter/Patrick Seale Fine Art 1985, Anne Berthoud Gallery 1988, Sally Hunter Fine Art 1989, South Hill Park Arts Centre Bracknell 1991, Boundary Art Gallery London 1992, The Economist London 1994, The Yehudi Menuhin Sch Surrey 1994; *Group Exhibitions* incl: Metro Show (Docklands Art Gallery) 1980, London Summer Show (Whitechapel Art Gallery) 1980, Third and Fourth Nat Exhibition Tours (Tolly Cobbald) 1981 and 1983, Subjective Eye Midland Gp (Nottingham and tour) 1981–82, Leicestershire Schs Exhibition 1982, Whitechapel Open (Whitechapel Gallery) 1982, 1983 and 1984, The London Gp (Camden Arts Centre and tour) 1982, Eight in the Eighties (NY) 1983, Touring Exhibition of Hosps (City Gallery Milton Keynes, funded by Arts Cncl) 1983–84, Art for Schs (Gainsborough's House 1983 and Sackhouse Gallery Norwich 1984), Royal Academy Summer Exhibition 1984, Guildford House Summer Show Guildford 1984, London Group Show (RCA) 1984, Bath Festival Show 1984 and 1987, Curwen Gallery 1984, Open House (City Gallery Arts Tst Milton Keynes) 1984, Quintin Green Gallery London 1985, Side By Side (Nat Art Gallery Kuala Lumpur and Br Cncl tour) 1985, Vorpal Gallery (NY) 1987, Mixed Summer Show (Thumb Gallery) 1987–90, The Circus Comes to Town (Northern Centre for Contemporary Art Sutherland and tour) 1988, CAS Art Market (Smith's Gallery) 1990–91 and 1992, Boxes and Totems (England & Co) 1990, Ikon Gallery Group Touring Exhibition 1991, Leleco Art Gallery London 1991, 1st Reading Arts Festival 1992, Touch of Red (Boundary Gallery London) 1992, Art for Sale (Whiteleys, in conjunction with The Guardian) 1992–93, Contemporary Art Fair London 1993, Royal Acad Summer Exhibition London 1993, The New Ashgate Gallery 1993, Interiors (Open Show Towner Art Gallery Eastbourne) 1993, Christmas Show (Boundary Gallery) 1993, East West Gallery London 1993, New Collectables (Stormont Studio Rye) 1994, CAS Festival Hall London 1994, FARA Romanian Appeal Bonhams London 1994, The Colour Blue Boundary Gallery London 1995, ojects of obsession (Boundary Gallery) 1996, Strange Encounters (Sally Hunter Fine Art London) 1996; *Work in Collections* incl: BP, Unilever, Euro Parl Luxembourg, Leics Schs, Blond Fine Art, Guildford House, Nat Art Gallery Kuala Lumpur, South East Arts, Halton Roy Productions/Howard Guard Productions, England & Co Art Gallery, Electra Management Trust Ltd, Lady Antonia Fraser, Lady Patricia Gibberd, Tim Sayer, Nancy Balfour, Coopers & Lybrand, Boundary Gallery, The Economist Building London; Gulbenkian Printmaker award 1983; *Recreations* interest in non-western belief systems and their religious expressions and in exotic art in general, walking, travel, reading; *Style*— Mervyn Charlton, Esq; ✉ 17 Church St, Cobham, Surrey KT11 3EG (☎ 01932 860107)

CHARLTON, Philip; OBE (1987); s of late George Charlton, of Chester, and Lottie, *née* Little (d 1976); *b* 31 July 1930; *Educ* City GS Chester; *m* 27 June 1953, Jessie, da of Joseph Boulton (d 1966), of Chester; 1 s (Philip John b 1962), 1 da (Margaret b 1959); *Career* Nat Serv RN 1947–49; gen mangr: Chester Savings Bank 1966–75, TSB Wales and Border Counties 1975–81; chief gen mangr Central Bd Trustee Savings Bank 1982–83 (dep chief gen mangr 1981–82); dir: TSB Computer Services (Wythenshawe) Ltd 1976–81, TSB Trust Co Ltd 1979–82, TSB Holdings Ltd 1982–86, TSB Group Computer Services Ltd 1981–84, Central Trustee Savings Bank 1982–86; chief gen mangr TSB England and Wales 1983–85, dir TSB England and Wales 1985–87, gp chief exec TSB Group plc 1986–89 (non-exec dep chm 1990–91), chm Philip Charlton Associates Ltd 1991–96; vice pres The Inst of Bankers 1991– (memb Cncl 1982–, dep chm 1988–89, pres 1990–91); memb Bd of Admin: Int Savings Banks Inst Geneva 1985–91 (vice pres 1985–91), Euro Savings Bank Gp Brussels 1989–91; FCIB, CIMgt, FRSA; *Clubs* Chester City, RAC; *Style*— Philip Charlton, Esq, OBE; ✉ 62 Quinta Drive, Arkley, Herts EN5 3BE (☎ 0181 440 4477)

CHARMLEY, John Denis; s of John Charmley (d 1977), of Birkenhead, and Doris, *née* Halliwell (d 1990); *b* 9 Nov 1955; *Educ* Rock Ferry HS, Pembroke Coll Oxford (open scholar, MA, A M P Read scholar, DPhil); *m* 1, 1977 (m dis 1992), Ann Dorothea; 3 s (Gervase Nicholas Edward b 8 Jan 1980, Gerard Timothy John (twin) b 8 Jan 1980, Christian Francis Robin (Kit) b 14 June 1989); m 2, 1992, Lorraine, da of K G Charles, MBE; *Career* reader in English history UEA 1996– (lectr 1979–93, sr lectr 1993–96); visiting fell Churchill Coll Cambridge 1985, Fulbright prof Westminster Coll Fulton MO 1992–93; FRHistS 1986; scriptwriter Peace In Our Time (Channel 4) 1989; *Books* Duff Cooper (1986, Yorkshire Post best First Book prize 1986), Lord Lloyd and the Decline of the British Empire (1987), Chamberlain and the Lost Peace (1989), Churchill - The End of Glory (1993), Churchill's Grand Alliance (1995), A History of Conservative Politics 1900–1996 (1996); *Recreations* reading, writing letters, dining out; *Clubs* Savile; *Style*— John Charmley, Esq; ✉ The Retreat, The Street, East Tuddenham, Dereham, Norfolk NR20 3LT (☎ and fax 01603 880877); c/o Felicity Bryan, 2A North Parade, Oxford OX2 6PE (☎ 01865 513816)

CHARNLEY, Sir (William) John; kt (1981), CB (1973); s of George Edward Charnley (d 1983), and Catherine Charnley; *b* 4 Sept 1922; *Educ* Oulton HS Liverpool, Univ of Liverpool (MEng); *m* 1945, Mary, da of Richard Paden (d 1933); 1 s, 1 da; *Career* aeronautical engr; chief scientist RAF 1973–77, controller R & D Estabs and Res MOD 1977–82 (controller guided weapons and electronics 1972–73), tech conslt 1982–; conslt: NATS (Nat Air Traffic Servs), Kidde International; pres Royal Inst of Navigation 1987–90, pres Euro Orgn for Civil Aviation Equipment 1993–; tstee Richard Ormonde Shuttleworth Remembrance Tst 1987–; Hon FRAeS 1992 (Silver medal 1973, Gold medal 1980), FRIN 1963 (Bronze medal 1960), FEng 1982, Cumberbatch Trophy (Guild of Air Pilots, Air Navigators) 1964; Hon DEng Univ of Liverpool 1988; *Recreations* sport, hill walking, chess; *Clubs* RAF; *Style*— Sir John Charnley, CB, FEng; ✉ Kirkstones, 29 Brackendale Close, Camberley, Surrey GU15 1HP (☎ and fax 01276 22547)

CHARNLEY, William Francis; s of Louis and Pauline Mary Charnley; *b* 21 Aug 1960; *Educ* Rivington and Blackrod GS, Bolton Inst of Technol (HND), Sheffield City Poly (Postgrad Dip in Co Admin), Univ of Lancaster (LLB), Manchester Poly (Law Soc Finals); *Career* articled clerk Slater Heelis 1985–87, corp fin ptnr Booth & Co Leeds 1989–94 (slr 1987–89), corp fin ptnr Corp Dept Simmons & Simmons 1994–; tstee Children's Heart Surgery Fund (charity); memb Assoc of Lancastrians in London; memb Inst of Chartered Secs and Administrators, memb Law Soc 1987; *Recreations* Impressionist and modern British art, keeping fit, country pursuits, classic motor cars, music, food, wine; *Style*— William Charnley, Esq; ✉ Simmons & Simmons, 21 Wilson Street, London EC2M 2TX (☎ 0171 628 2020, fax 0171 628 2070)

CHARNOCK, (Frederick) Mark Luckhoff; s of Frederick Niven Charnock, of Cape Town, SA, and Alta Anna, *née* Luckhoff; *b* 20 June 1945; *Educ* Diocesan Coll Cape Town SA, Univ of Cape Town (MB ChB) FRCS (Eng), FRCS(Ed), FRCOG; *m* 8 April 1970, Margaret Isobel, da of Frances Neale Murray, of Cape Town, South Africa; 1 s (Alasdair b 1984), 1 da (Annabel b 1982); *Career* house offr: Queen Charlotte's Hosp 1971, Samaritan Hosp 1975–76; registrar and sr registrar Bart's 1977–80; currently: conslt obstetrician and gynaecologist Radcliffe and Churchill Hosp Oxford, hon sr lectr Univ of Oxford; examiner: RCOGS, RCS, Univs of Oxford, Cambridge, and London; memb and cncllr: RCOG 1983–89, RCS; sec Section O & G RSM 1989–90; Liveryman Worshipful Soc of Apothecaries 1989, Freeman City of London 1985; *Recreations* tennis, skiing, reading, opera, art; *Style*— Mark Charnock, Esq; ✉ Manor Farm House, Bletchingdon, Oxon OX5 3DP (☎ 01869 350149); 23 Banbury Road, Oxford OX2 6NX (☎ 01865 512729, fax 01865 310342)

CHARTERIS, Lt-Col John Anthony; MBE (1996), MC (1972); s of Lt-Col John Douglas Archibald Charteris (d 1977), of Cullivait, Locharbriggs, Dumfries, and Joan Winifred, *née* Hobson; *b* 4 Sept 1940; *Educ* Wellington, RMA Sandhurst; *m* 5 Aug 1967, Antoinette Daphne Margaret, da of late Lt-Col Reginald Higginson Lowe, of Southview, Bradninch, Devon; 1 s (John Nicholas Robert Dunbar b 21 Oct 1977), 2 da (Camilla Antoinette 10 Sept 1968, Annabel Claire b 27 July 1970); *Career* cmmnd Royal Scots 1961; served: Libya, Aden, Borneo, Hong Kong, Malaysia, NI, Falkland Islands; Cdr Recruiting and Liaison Staff Scotland 1987–90, MOD Defence Public Relations 1990–91, Commandant Otterburn Army Field Trg Centre 1991–95, ret; memb The Queen's Body Guard for Scotland (The Royal Company of Archers); *Recreations* hunting, shooting, fishing, stalking, skiing; *Clubs* New (Edinburgh), Royal Scots, Whistle; *Style*— Lt-Col John Charteris, MBE, MC; ✉ Cullivait, Locharbriggs, Dumfries DG1 1QX (☎ 01387 710352)

CHARTERIS OF AMISFIELD, Baron (Life Peer UK 1977), of Amisfield, E Lothian; Hon Martin Michael Charles Charteris; GCB (1977, KCB 1972, CB 1958), GCVO (1976, KCVO 1962, MVO 1953), QSO (1978), OBE (1946), PC (1972); s of late Capt (Hugo Francis Charteris) Lord Elcho (d 1916), and bro of 12 Earl of Wemyss and March; *b* 7 Sept 1913; *Educ* Eton, Sandhurst; *m* 16 Dec 1944, Hon (Mary) Gay Hobart Margesson, da of 1 Viscount Margesson; 2 s (Hon Andrew Martin b 1947, Hon Harold Francis b 1950), 1 da (Hon Francesca Mary b 1945); *Career* Lt KRRC 1936, serv WWII Middle E, Palestine, Lt-Col 1944; private sec to HRH The Princess Elizabeth 1950–52, asst private sec to HM The Queen 1952–72, private sec to HM The Queen and keeper of HM's Archives 1972–77, a permanent lord in waiting to HM The Queen 1978–; dir: De La Rue Co 1978–85, Rio Tinto Zinc Corporation 1978–84, Connaught Hotel (former dir Claridge's Hotel); provost of Eton 1978–91; tstee Br Museum 1979–89, chm tstees Nat Heritage Meml Fund 1980–92, pres Prayer Book Soc; Hon DCL (Oxon) 1978, Hon LLD (London) 1981; invested with Royal Victorian Chain 1992; *Recreations* sculpting; *Clubs* White's; *Style*— The Rt Hon the Lord Charteris of Amisfield, GCB, GCVO, QSO, OBE, PC; ✉ 11 Kylestrome House, Cundy Street, London SW1W 9JT (☎ 0171 730 2959); Wood Stanway House, Wood Stanway, Cheltenham, Glos GL54 5PG (☎ 01386 584480)

CHARTRES, Rt Rev Richard John Carew; *see:* London, Bishop of

CHASE, Carol; *see:* Charles, Kate

CHASE, Lorraine; *b* 16 July 1951; *Career* actress; *Theatre* debut The Undertaking (with Annette Crosbie and Kenneth Williams, later transferred to West End); other credits work incl: Eliza in Pygmalion (Young Vic), Audrey in Little Shop of Horrors (nat tour), Harriet in Key for Two, Sally in Me and My Girl (West End), Run for Your Wife (West End); *Television* Campari advertising campaign, The Other 'Arf (with John Standing), Lame Ducks (with Brian Murphy and John Duttine), presenter for Holiday 90, commentator for the wedding of the Prince and Princess of Wales; *Film* credits incl Love and Bullets Charlie (with Charles Bronson); *Recreations* tennis, gym; *Clubs* Hurlingham, Ritz, Holmes Place; *Style*— Ms Lorraine Chase; ✉ c/o Peter Charlesworth Ltd, 2nd Floor, 68 Old Brompton Road, London SW7 3LQ (☎ 0171 581 2478, fax 0171 589 2922)

CHASE, Robert Henry Armitage; s of Philip Martin Chase (d 1987), of Foxley, Norfolk, and Jean Alison, *née* Barr (d 1976); *b* 10 March 1945; *Educ* Ipswich Sch; *m* 1972, Moya, da of Dr William Jones (d 1985), of Shotley Bridge, Co Durham; 2 s (Patrick William Armitage b 1975, Thomas Martin b 1986), 1 da (Ella Kathleen b 1977); *Career* CA; Voluntary Serv Nigeria 1963; articled clerk Lovewell Blake & Co Norwich 1964–69, with Cooper Brothers London and Kenya 1969–76, fin dir Mackenzie (Kenya) Ltd 1976, asst md GEC Hong Kong 1982–86 (fin dir 1981–82), chief fin offr Orient Overseas

(Holdings) Ltd 1986–87, dir Furness Withy & Co Ltd 1987–90, gp md and ctee memb The Automobile Association 1990–96, non-exec dir London Transport 1996–; chm International Association of Financial Executives Insts 1995; Liveryman Worshipful Co of Information Technologists 1990, Freeman City of London 1991; FCA 1969, MCT 1984; *Recreations* golf, skiing, vintage automobiles; *Clubs* Carlton, Hong Kong; *Style—* Robert Chase, Esq; ✉ Turrill House, Southington, Overton, Hants RG25 3DA (☎ 01256 770227, fax 01256 771539, e-mail 100113.3016@compuserve.com)

CHASE, Rodney F; *m* Diana; 2 s; *Career* The British Petroleum Co plc: joined 1964, various appts with BP Shipping, Refining & Marketing, Distribution, Oil Trading, Gas, Finance and Strategic Planning, chief exec BP Finance and gp treas (incl t/o of Standard Oil and Britoil), chief exec Western Hemisphere BP Exploration Inc and exec vice pres/chief financial offr BP America Inc until 1992, an md The BP Co plc 1992– (i/c Western Hemisphere region and chief exec BP Exploration/Production); non-exec dir BOC Group plc 1995–; chm World Industry Cncl on the Environment, memb UK Advsy Ctee on Business and the Environment; FCT; *Recreations* golf, downhill skiing; *Style—* Rodney Chase, Esq; ✉ The British Petroleum Co plc, 1 Finsbury Circus, London EC2M 7BA (☎ 0171 496 4000)

CHASSELS, (James) David Simpson; s of Robert Brown Chassels, and Frances Amelia, *née* Simpson; *b* 2 April 1947; *Educ* Rannoch Sch; *m* 21 May 1976, Angela Elizabeth, da of James Nicol Martin Bulloch; 2 s (Ross b 30 Nov 1977, Scott b 29 March 1980), 1 da (Nicola b 28 Feb 1983); *Career* articled clerk then chartered accountant French & Cowan Glasgow 1965–70, Arthur Young Edinburgh 1970–74, investmt exec 3i (formerly ICFC) Glasgow & Edinburgh 1974–81, dir 3i Corporate Finance 1981–93, ptnr BDO Binder Hamlyn CAs Glasgow 1993–95; dir: Buchanan Holdings Ltd 1993–, Datacore Ltd 1994–; memb Cncl Inst of CAs of Scotland 1993–; govr Rannoch Sch 1972–, memb Polmont Borstal Visiting Ctee 1978–83; former Deacon Incorporaton of Barbers Trades House of Glasgow 1985–86; MICAS 1973; *Recreations* sailing, skiing; *Clubs* RSAC, CCC (hon treas 1993–); *Style—* David Chassels, Esq; ✉ 10 Duart Drive, Newton Mearns, Glasgow G77 5DS (☎ 0141 639 3914)

CHASTNEY, John Garner; s of Alec Richardson Chastney (d 1981), and Constance May, *née* Edwards (d 1983); *b* 5 Jan 1947; *Educ* Henry Mellish GS Nottingham, Univ of Lancaster (MA); *m* 4 Aug 1973, Susan Thirza, da of Norman Dunkerley; 2 s (Martin Richard b 1980, David Paul b 1982), 1 da (Catherine Jane b 1978); *Career* CA; princ lectr Sheffield Hallamshire Univ 1974–79, curenty ptnr Neville Russell (sr nat trg mangr 1979–83, devpt ptnr 1983–88, head Consultancy Div 1990–94), on secondment as under sec DTI/dir Indust Devpt Unit 1988–90; prize essayist; FCA 1973; *Books* True and Fair View (1974), European Financial Reporting: The Netherlands (with J H Beeny, 1976); *Clubs* Square Mile, National; *Style—* John Chastney, Esq; ✉ Neville Russell, 24 Bevis Marks, London EC3A 7NR (☎ 0171 377 1000, fax 0171 377 8931)

CHATAWAY, Rt Hon Sir Christopher John; kt (1995), PC (1970); s of James Denys Percival Chataway, OBE (d 1953), and Margaret Pritchard, *née* Smith (d 1988); *b* 31 Jan 1931; *Educ* Sherborne, Magdalen Coll Oxford; *m* 1, 1959 (m dis 1975), Anna Maria, da of H Lett; 2 s, 1 da; m 2, 1976, Carola Cecil Walker, da of Maj Charles Ashton, DSO; 2 s; *Career* athletics rep GB Olympic Games 1952 and 1956, world record holder 5,000m 1954; jr exec Arthur Guinness Son & Co 1953–55, news reporter ITN 1955–56, current affrs commentator BBC TV 1956–59; MP (Cons): Lewisham N 1959–66, Chichester 1969–74; parly under sec of state Dept of Educn and Sci 1962–64; min for: Posts and Telecommunications 1970–72, Industrial Devpt 1972–74; chm Civil Aviation Authy 1991–96; md Orion Royal Bank 1974–88, dir BET plc 1974–96; leader ILEA 1967–69; tstee: Action Aid 1985– (hon treas 1975–85, chm 1985–92), Fndn for Sports and the Arts; chm: Groundwork 1985–89, Alcohol Educn and Res Cncl 1991–94, Chartered Inst of Tport 1994–96; Hon DLitt Loughborough Univ 1985, Hon DSc Cranfield Univ 1994; *Books* War Without Weapons (with Philip Goodhart, 1968); *Style—* The Rt Hon Sir Christopher Chataway; ✉ c/o Garrick Club, 15 Garrick Street, London WC2E 9AY

CHATAWAY, Mark Denys; s of The Rt Hon Sir Christopher Chataway, *qv*, and Anna Maria, *née* Lett; *b* 21 March 1960; *Educ* Troy State Univ Alabama (BSc), NY Univ (MSc); *Career* programme dir WRNG Atlanta USA 1980–82, exec prodr WMCA NY 1982–83, dir of communications GMHC (the AIDS Serv and Educn Fndn USA) 1983–84, vice pres heading Med Info Div Van Vechten and Associates NY 1984–87; Hill and Knowlton (UK): dir Special Servs Div 1987–89, md Mktg Communications Div 1990, md Eurosciences Communications Div 1991–93; princ Interscience Communications 1993–; former freelance TV journalist for Turner Broadcasting/CNN (US) and TV-AM, former freelance radio assignments for BBC, Ind Radio News (UK), CBS and Capital Radio (S Africa); author of feature or news articles for various UK and US publications; Govt of Botswana del to UN Conf on Environment and Devpt (Earth Summit) 1992; memb: Bd of Dirs Crusaid (nat AIDS fundraising charity), Bloomsbury Central Baptist Church; MIPR, memb Chartered Inst of Journalists; *Recreations* physical fitness, languages, running, church activities; *Style—* Mark Chataway, Esq; ✉ Interscience Communications, Africa House, 64 Kingsway, London WC2B 6AH (☎ 0171 331 0331, fax 0171 331 0333)

CHATE, (Frederick) Ian; s of Frederick John Chate (d 1992), and Edith Sybil, *née* Newman; *b* 12 May 1945; *Educ* Reed's Sch Cobham Surrey, Univ of Bristol (LLB), Sydney Univ (postgrad course in industl law); *m* 5 Aug 1978, Anne Alexandra, da of Dr Eric Greenwood Jenner; 1 da (Alexandra Clare b 8 Nov 1979), 1 s (Adam Ian b 24 April 1982); *Career* articled A T Elliot & Co Bristol, admitted slr 1970, asst slr Stephen Jaques & Stephen (Sydney) 1970–72, asst slr Linklaters & Paines 1972–75, head of Legal Dept Gulf Oil GB Ltd 1975–77, legal advsr Gulf Oil International 1977–84, gen counsel Texas Estern Corp 1984–89; Ocean Group plc: head of Legal Dept Ocean Transport & Trading plc (now Ocean Group) 1989–92, gp legal advsr and co sec 1993–; memb: Law Soc (ctee memb Commerce and Industry Gp 1992–), Int Bar Assoc; *Recreations* golf, swimming, theatre, travel, family, collecting antiquarian books and first editions; *Clubs* RAC, Lensbury; *Style—* Ian Chate, Esq; ✉ Ocean Group plc, Ocean House, The Ring, Bracknell, Berkshire RG12 1AN (☎ 01344 302000, fax 01344 710031)

CHATER, Geoffrey (aka Geoffrey Chater Robinson); s of Lawrence Chater Robinson (d 1978), of Broadstairs, Kent, and Gwendoline Dorcas, *née* Gwynn; *b* 23 March 1921; *Educ* Marlborough, Chillon Coll Glion-sur-Montreux Switzerland; *m* 22 June 1949, Jennifer Robin Fergus, da of Francis James Hill, of Fiveacres, Wormley, Surrey; 2 s (Simon, Piers), 1 da (Annabel); *Career* actor; WWII serv 1940–45, cmmnd Royal Fus 1941, serv UK and N Ireland 1942, Leics Regt Karachi 1943, N Staffs Regt Arakan Burma and Dinapore India 1943–44, Capt 1944, reinforced Royal Worcs Regt Burma 1945; devised and performed revue for battalion in Pyinmana 1945; early theatre work incl: Theatre Royal Windsor 1946–47, Alexandra Theatre Birmingham 1948–49, Shakespeare Season Old Vic Theatre 1954–55; *Theatre* London roles incl: Duke of Florence in Women Beware Women (RSC) 1962, Yslaev in A Month in the Country (with Ingrid Bergman and Michael Redgrave, Cambridge Theatre) 1965, Dr Bradman in Blithe Spirit (NT) 1976–77, Henry Craxton in Cousin Vladimir (RSC) 1978, Polonius in Hamlet (Royal Court) 1980, The Doctor in Three Sisters (Albery) 1987; *Television* numerous appearances incl: Dusty Miller in The Last Reunion 1956, Stanley Leibowitz in The Scotsboro Case 1972, Control in The Specialist 1979, Guy Liddell in Blunt 1987, Rafe Hollingsworth in Chelworth 1988, Fabian in Rumpole of the Bailey 1990, The Bishop in The Rector's Wife 1993, Frobisher in The Detectives 1994; *Films* incl: If, 10 Rillington Place, Barry Lyndon, Ghandi; *Recreations* golf, swimming, crocquet, watching cricket; *Clubs* MCC, Rye Golf; *Style—* Geoffrey Chater, Esq; ✉ c/o Bernard Hunter Associates, 13 Spencer Gardens, London SW14 7AH (☎ 0181 878 6308, fax 0181 392 9334)

CHATER, Stephen Paul; s of John Charles Chater, of Northallerton, N Yorks, and Patricia Norby, *née* Oakes; *b* 2 March 1956; *Educ* Hartlepool GS, ChCh Oxford (MA); *m* 10 Sept 1988, Susan Frances Margaret, da of late Charles Harborne Stuart, of Combe, Oxford; 1 s (Anthony Charles Thomas b 10 Aug 1996); *Career* slr; ptnr Allen & Overy 1989– (articled 1979–81, asst slr 1981–88); Freeman Worshipful Co of Slrs 1989; memb: Law Soc, Soc of Genealogists, Durham CCC; *Recreations* music, genealogy, cricket; *Style—* Stephen Chater, Esq; ✉ Allen & Overy, One New Change, London EC4M 9QQ (☎ 0171 330 3000, fax 0171 330 9999)

CHATFIELD, 2 Baron (1937 UK); Ernle David Lewis Chatfield; s of 1 Baron Chatfield, GCB, OM, KCMG, CVO, PC (Admiral of the Fleet, d 1967); *b* 2 Jan 1917; *Educ* Dartmouth, Trinity Coll Cambridge; *m* 16 May 1969, (Felicia Mary) Elizabeth, da of late Dr John Roderick Bulman, of Hereford; *Career* ADC to Govr-Gen of Canada 1940–44; *Style—* The Rt Hon the Lord Chatfield; ✉ 535 Island Road, Victoria, BC V8S 2T7, Canada

CHATFIELD, Sir John Freeman; kt (1993), CBE (1982), DL (E Sussex 1986); s of Cecil Freeman Chatfield (d 1974), of Eastbourne, and Florence Dorothy, *née* Greed (d 1985); *b* 28 Oct 1929; *Educ* Southdown Coll Eastbourne, Roborough Sch Eastbourne, Lawrence Sheriff Sch Rugby, Lewes GS, Sch of Law London; *m* 18 Sept 1954, Barbara Elizabeth, da of Frank Hubert Trickett (d 1969), of Montford, nr Shrewsbury, Shropshire; *Career* sr ptnr Hart Reade & Co slrs Eastbourne 1976–89 (ptnr 1956–76), conslt slr 1989–95; dep registrar County Ct 1965–78; East Sussex CC: cncllr 1972–93, ldr 1981–85, chm 1985–87, vice chm 1987–89; chm: Sussex Police Authy, Police Ctee ACC, Official Side Police Negotiating Bd UK 1982–85; pres Eastbourne Cons Assoc 1975–94 (chm 1971–75), vice chm Exec Cncl ACC (ldr Cons Gp) 1986–89; chm: Exec Cncl ACC 1989–92, UK Local Govt Int Bureau 1989–92, Consultative Cncl of Local and Regnl Authys in Europe with the Euro Cmmn 1990–94, Int Cncl for Local Environment Initiatives 1990–94; vice-pres British Section Int Union of Local Authys and Cncl of European Municipalities and Regions 1992–; memb: Advsy Cncl ICLEI 1993–95, Ct and Cncl Univ of Sussex 1981–85 and 1991– (vice chm Univ Cncl 1996–), Police Advsy Bd England and Wales 1980–85, Cons Nat Local Govt Advsy Ctee 1982–93 (vice chm 1989–92), Nat Union of Cons and Unionist Assocs Nat Exec Ctee 1982–92, Cncl Pestalozzi Tst 1987–91; pres Eastbourne Law Soc 1972–73; Freeman City of London 1994, Liveryman Worshipful Co of Basketmakers; *Recreations* music, theatre; *Style—* Sir John Chatfield, CBE, DL; ✉ Underhill House, Went Way, East Dean, Eastbourne, E Sussex BN20 0DB; 306 Nell Gwynn House, Sloane Ave, London SW3 3AX

CHATMAN, William C; s of Edgar T Chatman (d 1939), and Gertrude, *née* Hewett (d 1977); *b* 20 Nov 1930; *Educ* Drexel Univ (BSc); *m* 6 Sept 1952, Helen S, da of August Siefert (d 1981); 3 da (Linda (Mrs Thomsen) b 1954, Sandra (Mrs Loether) b 1957, Susan (Mrs Webb) b 1960); *Career* engr; dir of ops Société Foster Wheeler Francaise 1983–86, chm and chief exec Foster Wheeler Ltd 1986–96, ret; vice pres IChemE, vice pres and dir American C of C (UK), chm British Chemical Engineering Contractors' Assoc (BCECA); CEng, FICHE, CIMgt; *Recreations* singing (London Philharmonic Choir), skiing; *Style—* William C Chatman, Esq; ✉ 43 N Main Street, Essex, CT 06426, USA

CHATTERJEE, Mira; da of Dr Haradlan Chatterjee (Capt IMS/IAMC SEAC, Burma Star), of Chigwell, Essex, and Kamala, *née* Banerjee; *b* 19 April 1948; *Educ* City of London Sch for Girls; *m* 19 April 1980, Dr Gautam Chaudhuri, s of Dr Punendu Chandhuri, of Calcutta; 1 da (Sandra b 28 Jan 1981); *Career* called to the Bar Middle Temple 1973, in practice SE circuit; FRSA; *Recreations* reading, philosophy; *Clubs* Wig and Pen; *Style—* Miss Mira Chatterjee; ✉ 4 Brick Court, Middle Temple, London EC4Y 9AD (☎ 0171 797 8910, fax 0171 797 8929)

CHATTERJEE, Dr Satya Saran; OBE (1971); s of Basanta Kumar Chatterjee (d 1956), of Patna, India, and Saabani Chatterjee (d 1924); *b* 16 July 1922; *Educ* Patna Univ; *m* 1948, Enid May, da of Joseph Adlington (d 1965), of Birmingham; 1 s (Nigel), 2 da (Camille, Petula); *Career* Capt Indian Army 1944; conslt chest physician i/c Dept of Respiratory Physiology Wythenshawe Hosp Manchester 1959–87; pres Overseas Doctors' Assoc; memb North Western RHA 1976–86; chm: Ed Bd ODA News Review 1985–, Manchester Ctee on Ethnic Minority Health 1993–; memb: Standing Advsy Cncl on Race Relations 1977–86, GMC 1979–92; vice pres Manchester Cncl for Community Relations 1974–; author of various res papers on various projects related to cardio/pulmonary disorders; FRCP, FRCPEd; *Recreations* gardening, bridge; *Clubs* Manchester Bridge, Rotary (Wythenshawe); *Style—* Dr Satya Chatterjee, OBE

CHATTERJI, Dr Debajyoti; *Career* various R&D appts General Electric Co US 1973–83; The BOC Group plc: joined 1983, vice pres tech activities 1983–90, chief exec tech activities March-Oct 1990, md technol 1990–, also dir BOC Fndn; bd memb Industl Research Inst, govr Imperial Coll London 1993–; *Style—* Dr Debajyoti Chatterji; ✉ The BOC Group plc, Chertsey Road, Windlesham, Surrey GU20 6HJ (☎ 01276 477222)

CHATTINGTON, Barry John; s of John William Chattington (d 1967), of Kent, and Rose Amelia, *née* Darlington; *b* 24 April 1947; *Educ* Dartford Tech High Sch; *Career* film ed 1963–66, film dir 1972–; md: Goldcrest Facilities Ltd 1988, Elstree Studios, Roger Cherrill Ltd, Cherry Video Ltd 1991; currently chm Renaissance Productions Ltd; works incl: numerous long and short films for Paul McCartney, Pink Floyd and others, drama series for US TV, major documentary for Kuwait TV, charity films with the Prince of Wales and the Princess Royal; awards: 4 Golden Halos from S Calif Motion Picture Cncl, Silver award NY Int Film and TV Festival 1982, numerous D&AD commendations; memb Br Kinematograph Sound & TV Soc 1963; chm: Directors' Guild of GB 1985–86, Producers' and Directors' Section ACTT 1985–86; Br delegate on Federation Européene des Industries Techniques de l'Image et du Son; *Clubs* Groucho, Variety, Reform, Chelsea Arts; *Style—* Barry Chattington, Esq; ✉ Renaissance Productions Ltd, 2B South Hill Park, Hampstead Heath, London NW3 2SB (☎ 0171 431 7414, fax 0171 431 7415)

CHATTO, Beth; da of late William George Little, and late Bessie Beatrice, *née* Styles; *b* 27 June 1923; *m* Andrew Edward Chatto, s of Andrew Chatto; 2 da (Diana Peacock b 17 March 1946, Mary Elizabeth Marshall 7 Sept 1948); *Career* proprietor Unusal Plants 1967–89, currently md The Beth Chatto Gardens Ltd (fndr 1989); lectr various venues professionally and for charity 1967–; memb RHS (Victoria medal of Honour 1988, Lawrence Memorial medal 1988); Hon DUniv Essex 1988; *Books* The Dry Garden (1978), The Damp Garden (1982), Plant Portraits (1985), Beth Chatto's Garden Notebook (1988), The Green Tapestry (1989); *Recreations* gardening, music, reading, cooking, family; *Style—* Mrs Beth Chatto; ✉ The Beth Chatto Gardens, Elmstead Market, Colchester, Essex CO7 7DB (☎ 01206 822007, fax 01206 825933)

CHATTO, Lady Sarah Frances Elizabeth; *née* Armstrong-Jones; *see:* HRH Princess Margaret, Countess of Snowdon in *Royal Family Section*

CHAUDHURI, Amit Prakash; s of Nages Chandra Chaudhuri, and Bijoya, *née* Nandi Majumdar; *b* 15 May 1962; *Educ* Cathedral and John Connon Sch Bombay, UCL (BA), Balliol Coll Oxford (Dervorguilla scholar, DPhil); *m* 12 Dec 1991, Rosinka Shubhasree, da of Shiva Ranjan Khastgir; *Career* writer; Harper-Wood studentship for English poetry and literature St John's Coll Cambridge 1992–93, Creative Arts fell Wolfson Coll Oxford 1992–95; bursary Kathleen Blundell Trust; Arts Cncl Writers Award 1994; fiction and poetry have appeared in London Review of Books, Observer, London

Magazine and Oxford Poetry; contrib articles and reviews to TLS, London Review of Books, Guardian, Observer, Spectator, Vogue and other jls; trained singer N Indian classical trad (released albums on HMV, 1992 and 1994); *Books* A Strange and Sublime Address (1991, Betty Trask Award Soc of Authors, runner-up Guardian Fiction Award, Cwlth Writer's Prize for Best First Book (Eurasia)), Afternoon Raag (1993, Encore Award Soc of Authors 1994, Southern Arts Lit Prize 1994, runner-up Guardian Fiction Award 1993), Noon in Calcutta (contrib, anthology), New Writing 2 (contrib, British Cncl anthology, eds Malcolm Bradbury and Andrew Motion); *Style—* Amit Chaudhuri, Esq; ✉ 6 Sunny Park, Flat 10, 8th Floor, Calcutta 700 019, India

CHAVASSE, Christopher Patrick Grant; s of Alban Ludovick Grant Chavasse (d 1953), of Colne House, Rickmansworth, and Maureen Shingler, *née* Whalley; *b* 14 March 1928; *Educ* Bedford, Clare Coll Cambridge (MA); *m* 1955, Audrey Mary, da of the late Hugh Robert Leonard, of Ladywalk, Heronsgate; 2 s (Maj Nicholas Robert Grant Chavasse, MBE, Royal Green Jackets b 1956, Timothy James Grant b 1960), 1 da (Kathryn Margaret Grant (Mrs D M Tobey) b 1957); *Career* cmmnd RB 1947, served Palestine (despatches) 1948, RAFVR 1949; admitted slr 1955; ptnr: Jacobs and Greenwood 1960, Woodham Smith 1970; pres Holborn Law Soc 1977–78, vice pres Nat Assoc of Decorative and Fine Art Socs 1986–, chm NADFAS Tours Ltd 1986–91; vice pres: Chiltern DFAS 1986–, Totnes DFAS 1996–; hon steward Westminster Abbey 1950–, treas St Mary le Bow Church 1981–88, sec Governing Body of Oundle and Laxton Schs 1981–88; Clerk Worshipful Co of Grocers 1981–88 (Hon Liveryman), memb Ct Corp of Sons of the Clergy 1985–, Liveryman City of London Solicitors' Co; *Publications* Conveyancing Costs (1971), Non Contentious Costs (1975), The Discretionary Items in Contentious Costs (1980); articles in: Law Soc Gazette, New Law Journal and Slrs Journal; *Recreations* boating and shooting; *Style—* Christopher Chavasse, Esq; ✉ Duncannon House, Stoke Gabriel, Totnes, Devon TQ9 6QY (☎ 01803 782291)

CHAWLA, Dr Shanti Lal; s of Puran Chand Chawla, of Delhi, and Indra Wati Chawla; *b* 26 Oct 1936; *Educ* Univ of Delhi (BSc), Punjab Univ India (LSMF, MB BS), Univ of London (DMRT), Dublin (FFRRCSI); *m* 12 May 1967, Mrs Kamlesh, da of Chuni Lal Monga, of New Delhi; 2 da (Sangita b 21 Feb 1971, Rita b 26 May 1972); *Career* house surgn Dayanand Med Hosp India 1963–64, asst surgn Govt Dispensary Gurgoan India 1964, res MO in med and surgery Tirath Ram Hosp Delhi 1966–67, asst surgn Govt Dispensary Delhi 1967–69, registrar in radiotherapy Cookridge Hosp Leeds 1971–72 (sr house offr 1969–71), sr registrar Catterbridge Hosp Cheshire 1974–80 (registrar in radiotherapy 1972–74); S Cleveland Hosp: conslt in radiotherapy and oncology 1980–, head of dept 1980–91, clinical dir 1991–94; hon clinical lectr in radiotherapy Univ of Newcastle upon Tyne 1980–; Gold Award Northern Regnl Health Authy Newcastle 1990, Bronze Medallion ABI Medical Community Award Newcastle upon Tyne 1991; numerous pubns in jls; pres: Indian Assoc of Cleveland 1991 (pres 1987–89, vice pres 1990), Indian Doctors of Cleveland 1993– (treas 1985–91); chm Local Negotiating Ctee SCH 1996–; treas Hindu Cultural Soc 1990– (sec 1985–89), memb various orgns of Middlesbrough Cncl; memb BMA (accredited memb LNC), MRCR; *Style—* Dr Shanti Chawla; ✉ South Cleveland Hospital, Marton Rd, Middlesbrough, Cleveland (☎ 01642 850850)

CHAYTOR, Sir George Reginald; 8 Bt (UK 1831), of Croft, Yorkshire, and Witton Castle, Durham; s of William Richard Carter Chaytor (d 1973), gs of 2 Bt, and Anna Laura, *née* Fawcett (d 1947); suc kinsman, Sir William Chaytor, 7 Bt, 1976; *b* 28 Oct 1912; *m* 1970, Mrs Elsie Magdeline Rogers; *Heir* cousin, (Herbert) Gordon Chaytor; *Career* patron (alternatively) of Witton-le-Wear Vicarage; *Style—* Sir George Chaytor, Bt; ✉ 103–9372 Fletcher Avenue, Chilliwack, Bc, Canada

CHAZAL, *see:* de Chazal

CHAZAN, Dr Bernard Isaac; s of Rev Philip Chazan (d 1961), of Glasgow, and Millicent, *née* Levine (d 1980); *b* 1 June 1931; *Educ* Queen's Park Secdy Sch Glasgow, Univ of Glasgow (MB ChB, MD); *m* 1, 29 Dec 1959 (m dis 1975), Valerie, da of S C Levy, of Mill Hill, London; 2 s (Yigal b 20 Nov 1961, Guy b 20 Sept 1965), 1 da (Sharon b 12 May 1963, d 12 Oct 1987); m 2, 23 Oct 1977, Irene Anne, da of Max Silberg, of Leeds; *Career* Nat Serv RAMC: Lt 1956–57, Capt 1957–58; asst physician Hadassah Med Sch Jerusalem 1961–65, sr asst physician Meir Hosp Kfar Saba Israel 1965–67, res assoc med Joslin Res Lab Boston 1967–69, sr resident Joslin Clinic 1969, conslt physician Sunderland Dist Gen Hosp 1969– (physician i/c Diabetic Service 1973–96, physician i/c Endocrine Unit 1976–96); memb: BMA, Br Diabetic Assoc, AJEX, IMA, Br Endocrine Soc; MRCP 1958, FRCP 1976; *Books* Treatment of Diabetic Retinopathy (1969), Systematic Endocrine Investigation (1986 and 1992), Treatment Guidelines for Sunderland City Hospitals (ed, 1991 and 1994); *Recreations* walking, piano playing, Hebrew literature; *Style—* Dr Bernard Chazan; ✉ Department of Medicine, District General Hospital, Sunderland SR4 7TP (☎ 0191 565 6256)

CHECKETTS, Sir David John; KCVO (1979, CVO 1969, MVO 1966); 3 s of late Reginald Ernest George Checketts, and late Frances Mary Checketts; *b* 23 Aug 1930; *m* 1958, Rachel Leila Warren Herrick; 1 s, 3 da; *Career* RATG Rhodesia 1948–49, 14 Sqdn Germany 1950–54, FWS Leconfield 1954–57, Air ADC AFMED Malta 1957–59, 3 Sqdn Germany 1960–61, ret Sqdn-Ldr 1967; equerry to HRH The Duke of Edinburgh 1961–66, equerry to HRH The Prince of Wales 1967–70 and extra equerry 1979–, private sec 1970–78; chm Rainbow Boats Trust, tstee The Wilderness Tst; FInstD, memb RUSI; *Style—* Sir David Checketts, KCVO; ✉ Church Cottage, Winkfield, Windsor, Berks

CHECKLAND, Sir Michael; kt (1992); s of Leslie Checkland, and Ivy Florence, *née* Bernand; *b* 13 March 1936; *Educ* King Edward's GS Fiveways Birmingham, Wadham Coll Oxford; *m* 1, 25 March 1960 (m dis 1983), Shirley Frances Corbett; 2 s (Philip Michael b 1962, Richard Bruce b 1965), 1 da (Helen Julia b 1968); m 2, 23 Oct 1987, Susan, da of Ernest Harold Walker, ISO; *Career* auditor Parkinson Cowan Ltd 1959–62, accountant Thorn Electronics 1962–64; BBC: sr cost accountant 1964–67, head of Central Finance Unit 1969–71, chief accountant Central Finance Services 1969, chief accountant TV 1971, fin controller 1976, controller planning and resource mgmnt TV 1977, dir of resources TV 1982, chm BBC Enterprises 1986–87 (dir 1979–92), dep DG 1985, DG 1987–92; dir: Visnews 1980–85, National Youth Music Theatre 1992–, Nynex Cable Communications Ltd 1995–; fell and vice pres RTS, pres Cwlth Broadcasting Assoc 1987–88; chm: NCH Action for Children 1991–, Brighton Festival 1993–, CBSO 1995– (dir 1993–95); govr: Westminster Coll Oxford 1993–, Birbeck Coll London 1993–; tstee Reuters 1994–; hon fell Wadham Coll Oxford 1989; FCMA; *Recreations* music, theatre, travel; *Style—* Sir Michael Checkland; ✉ Orchard Cottage, Park Lane, Maplehurst, West Sussex RH13 6LL

CHECKLAND, Prof Peter Bernard; s of Norman Checkland (d 1983), and Doris, *née* Hiscox (d 1976); *b* 18 Dec 1930; *Educ* George Dixons GS Birmingham, St John's Coll Oxford (BSc); *m* 29 July 1955, Glenys Margaret (d 1990), da of Leonard George Partridge (d 1936); 2 da (Kristina b 13 May 1959, Katherine b 22 July 1961); *Career* Nat Serv RAF Sgt-instr 1948–49; tech offr, section ldr, assoc res mangr ICI Fibres Ltd 1955–69, prof of systems Univ of Lancaster 1969–, hon conslt prof Northwestern Poly Univ Xi'an China 1987–, visiting prof Univ of New England Aust 1990–; former memb: UK Nat Ctee for Int Inst for Applied Systems Analysis, DTI Ctee for Terotechnol; memb: Operational Res Soc, Int Soc for the Systems Sciences (pres 1986–87); Hon DSc City Univ 1991, Hon Doctorate Open Univ 1996; Most Distinguished and Outstanding Contributor Award Br Computer Soc 1994; *Books* Systems Thinking, Systems Practice (1981), Soft Systems Methodology in Action (with J Scholes, 1990); *Recreations* rock climbing, studying the evolution of the jazz idiom; *Style—* Prof Peter Checkland; ✉ Department of Management Science, University of Lancaster, Bailrigg, Lancaster LA1 4YX (☎ 01524 65201, fax 01524 844885, telex 65111 Lancul G)

CHECKLAND, Sarah Jane (Mrs Gervase Webb); da of Prof Sydney George Checkland (d 1986), of Cambridge, and Edith Olive, *née* Anthony; *b* 14 June 1954; *Educ* The Mount York, UEA (BA); *m* 16 May 1992, Gervase Webb; *Career* former tour guide, singer Zanzibar Club, dep ed Homes and Jobs magazine 1979, press offr Nat Gallery 1979–83, sub ed arts and focus page Sunday Times 1983–85, art critic Sunday Today March-Nov 1986, freelance galleries corr The Times 1984–86, freelance art sales writer The Sunday Times 1984–86, art critic and corr London Daily News 1986–87, art market corr The Times 1987–, currently freelance art market corr The Guardian and Sunday Telegraph; *Recreations* making music; *Clubs* Groucho; *Style—* Ms Sarah Jane Checkland

CHECKLEY, Dr Stuart Arthur; s of Arthur William George Checkley, of Eastbridge, Suffolk, and Hilda Dorothy, *née* Chapman; *b* 15 Dec 1945; *Educ* St Albans Sch, Brasenose Coll Oxford (BA, BM, BCh); *m* 1 Aug 1970, Marilyn Jane, da of Dr Percy Cyril Connick Evans, of Hampton, Middx; 1 s (Andrew John b 15 March 1977), 1 da (Anna Mary b 2 July 1974); *Career* conslt psychiatrist Maudsley Hosp, prof of psychoneuroendocrinology and dean Inst of Psychiatry; numerous articles in jls on depression; FRCPsych, FRCP; *Recreations* bird watching; *Style—* Prof Stuart Checkley; ✉ Institute of Psychiatry, De Crespigny Park, London SE5 8AF (☎ 0171 703 5411, fax 0171 703 5796)

CHEDLOW, Barry William; QC (1969); *b* 8 Oct 1921; *Educ* Burnage HS, Univ of Manchester; *m* 1944, Anne Sheldon; 1 s, 1 da; *Career* Flt Lt RAF 1943; called to the Bar Middle Temple 1947, recorder of the Crown Ct 1974–94; memb Criminal Injuries Compensation Bd 1976; *Recreations* helicopter and fixed wing pilot; *Style—* Barry Chedlow, Esq, QC; ✉ 12 King's Bench Walk, Temple, London EC4 7EL (☎ 0171 583 0811)

CHEESEMAN, Prof Ian Clifford; s of Richard Charles Cheeseman (d 1962), and Emily Ethel, *née* Clifford (d 1962); *b* 12 June 1926; *Educ* Andover GS, Imperial Coll London (BSc, PhD); *m* 27 July 1957, Margaret Edith, da of Christopher Allen Pither (d 1970); 1 s (Richard Iain b 16 July 1960), 2 da (Angela Rachel (Mrs Degallaix) b 8 July 1958, Jeannette Sarah (Mrs Sax) b 17 March 1962); *Career* aeroelastician Vickers Supermarine 1951–53, head of helicopter res A&AEE Boscombe Down 1953–56, theoretical physicist on weapon effects AWRE 1956–58, head of Powered Lift and Noise Div Nat Gas Turbine Establishment Pyestock 1958–70; Univ of Southampton: Westland prof of helicopter engrg 1970–83, head Dept of Aeronautics and Astronautics 1978–83, visiting and emeritus prof 1983–92; res dir Stewart Hughes Ltd 1983–88, ind conslt 1988–89; memb and past pres Airship Assoc; ARCS, FRAS 1966, CEng 1966; *Books* 40 Years of the Spitfire (with R A East); *Recreations* gardening, dog breeding, concert going; *Style—* Prof Ian Cheeseman; ✉ Abbey View, Tarrant Keynston, Blandford Forum, Dorset DT11 9JE (☎ 01258 456877)

CHEESMAN, Anthony David (Tony); s of Leslie Charles Cheesman, of Shoreham-by-Sea (d 1968), and Eileen, *née* Griggs (d 1994); *b* 14 Nov 1939; *Educ* Steyning GS, Charing Cross Hosp Medical Sch, Univ of London (BSc, MB BS); *m* 24 Sept 1966, Janet, da of Eric James Bristow, of Haywards Heath, Sussex; 2 s (David b 1969, James b 1972), 1 da (Katherine b 1974); *Career* conslt surgn; ENT surgn Univ Hosp of W Indies Jamaica 1972–74; otolaryngologist head and neck surgn: Charing Cross Hosp, Royal Nat Throat Nose and Ear Hosp; Hunterian professorship RCS 1994–95; memb: RSM (pres Section of Laryngology & Rhinology 1994–95), Ct of Examiners RCS; FRCS; *Books* numerous papers and chapters on otolaryngology; *Recreations* yachting, skiing, flying, avoiding correspondence; *Clubs* Sussex Yacht, Politzer Soc, Little Ship; *Style—* Mr A D Cheesman; ✉ Charing Cross Hospital, Fulham Palace Road, London W6 8RF (☎ 0181 846 7798)

CHEETHAM, Anthony John Valerian; s of Sir Nicolas John Alexander Cheetham, KCMG, *qv*, of 50 Cadogan Square, London, and Jean Evison, *née* Corfe; *b* 12 April 1943; *Educ* Eton, Balliol Coll Oxford (BA); *m* 1, 1969 (m dis), Julia Rollason; 2 s (Nicolas b 1971, Oliver b 1973), 1 da (Flavia b 1976); m 2, 1979 (m dis 1996), Rosemary de Courcy; 2 da (Emma b 1981, Rebecca b 1983); *Career* editorial dir Sphere Books 1968; md: Futura Publications 1973, Macdonald Futura 1979, Century Hutchinson 1985–89; fndr and chm Century Publishing 1982–85, chm and chief exec Random Century Group 1989–91, fndr Orion Publishing Group 1991–; *Books* Richard III (1972); *Recreations* walking, tennis, gardening; *Style—* Anthony Cheetham, Esq; ✉ 20 Grove Park, Camberwell, London SE5 8LH; Paxford Manor, Paxford, nr Chipping Campden, Glos GL55 6XP

CHEETHAM, Christopher Geoffrey; s of Geoffrey Cheetham, of Southport, and Irene, *née* Turner; *b* 3 Jan 1951; *Educ* St Philip's Christ Church, Blackpool Coll of Art (BA); *m* 1993, Michele, *née* Griffiths; *Career* advtg photographer; asst 1972–78, estab Chelsea studio 1979; awards: Assoc of Photographers 1985, 1986, 1989, 1992 and 1993, D&AD 1982 and 1992; memb Assoc of Photographers (formerly AFAEP); *Recreations* swimming; *Clubs* Chelsea Arts; *Style—* Christopher Cheetham, Esq; (☎ 0171 352 1500, fax 0171 376 8088)

CHEETHAM, Prof Juliet; OBE (1995); da of Col Harold Neville Blair (d 1989), of London, and Isabel, *née* Sanders (d 1988); *b* 12 Oct 1939; *Educ* Univ of St Andrews (MA), Univ of Oxford; *m* 26 April 1965, (Christopher) Paul Cheetam, s of Robert Cheetham, of Wallasey; 1 s (Matthew b 1969), 2 da (Rebecca b 1972, Sophie b 1983); *Career* probation offr 1959–65, lectr in applied social studies and fell Green Coll Oxford 1965–85, prof and dir Social Work Res Centre Univ of Stirling 1986–95 (prof emeritus 1995–); co-ordinator Scottish Higher Educn Funding Cncl 1996–; memb: Ctee of Enquiry into the Working of the Abortion Act 1971–74, Cmmn for Racial Equality 1977–84, Social Security Advsy Ctee 1983–84; BASW; *Books* Social Work with Immigrants (1972), Unwanted Pregnancy and Counselling (1977), Social Work and Ethnicity (1982), Social Work with Black Children and their Families (1986), Evaluating Social Work Effectiveness (1992); *Recreations* canal boats; *Style—* Prof Juliet Cheetham, OBE; ✉ Peffermill House, 91 Peffermill Road, Edinburgh EH16 5UX (☎ and fax 0131 661 0948); Social Work Research Centre, Department of Applied Social Science, University of Stirling, Stirling FK9 4LA (☎ 01786 67724, fax 01786 467689)

CHEETHAM, Sir Nicolas John Alexander; KCMG (1964, CMG 1953); s of late Sir Milne Cheetham, KCMG (d 1938) and his 1 wife (m dis 1923) Anastasia Cheetham, CBE, DStJ (later Mrs Nigel Law) (d 1976), *née* Mouravieff; *b* 8 Oct 1910; *Educ* Eton, Ch Ch Oxford; *m* 1, 1937 (m dis 1960), Jean Evison, da of Col Arthur Cecil Corfe, DSO (d 1949); 2 s; m 2, 1960, Lady Mabel Kathleen (d 1985), da of 8 Earl of Roden and formerly w of Sir Richard Neville Brooke, Bt, *qv*; *Career* joined HM Dip Serv 1934, min to Hungary 1959–61, asst under sec FO 1961–64, ambass to Mexico 1964–68; *Books* A History of Mexico, New Spain, Medieval Greece, Keepers of the Keys; *Style—* Sir Nicolas Cheetham, KCMG; ✉ 50 Cadogan Square, London SW1

CHEEVERS, Anthony William; s of Thomas Joseph Cheevers (d 1984), and Jessie, *née* Strahan; *b* 1 May 1956; *Educ* Finchley GS, Royal Holloway Coll, Univ of London (BMus); *Career* joined BBC 1978; Music Dept BBC Radio 3: prodr 1984–90, ed Speech and Music 1991–93, ed Music Talks and Documentaries 1993–95; head of features Mentorn Radio 1995–; *Style—* Anthony Cheevers, Esq; ✉ Head of Features, Mentorn Radio, 140 Wardour Street, London W1V 4LJ (☎ 0171 292 1029, fax 0171 287 4267)

CHELMER, Baron (Life Peer UK 1963), of Margaretting, Co Essex; Eric Cyril Boyd Edwards; kt (1954), MC (1944), TD, DL (1971); s of Col Cyril Ernest Edwards, DSO, MC, TD, JP, DL (d 1953), of Bullwood Hall, Hockley, Essex, and Jessie, *née* Boyd;

b 9 Oct 1914; *Educ* Felsted, Univ of London (LLB); *m* 2 June 1939, Enid, da of Frank W Harvey, of Leigh-on-Sea, Essex; 1 s (Hon Robin Ernest b 1940); *Career* served WWII Lt-Col Essex Yeo; admitted slr 1937; memb Conservative Party Policy Advsy Ctee 1954–82; chm National Union of Conservative Assocs 1957–64, treas Conservative Party 1965–77; chm Provident Financial Group 1977–83, dir NEM Group of Cos 1977–; chm Greycoats Estates Ltd; former JP Essex; memb Ct of Assts Worshipful Co of Tin Plate Workers; *Recreations* 'improving'; *Clubs* Carlton, Royal Ocean Racing; *Style—* The Rt Hon the Lord Chelmer, MC, TD, DL; ✉ Peacocks, Margaretting, Essex CM4 9HY (☎ 01277 353181)

CHELMSFORD, 3 Viscount (UK 1921); Frederic Jan Thesiger; also Baron Chelmsford (UK 1858); s of 2 Viscount (d 1970), and Gilian Lubbock (great niece of 1 Baron Avebury); 1 cous once removed of Sir Wilfred Thesiger, *qv*, the Arabist and traveller; *b* 7 March 1931; *m* 16 Aug 1958, Clare Rendle, da of Dr George Rendle Rolston, of Haslemere, Surrey; 1 s (Hon Frederic b 6 March 1962), 1 da (Hon Tiffany b 23 April 1968); *Heir* Hon Frederic Thesiger, *qv*; *Career* late Lt Inns of Ct Regt; Lloyd's insur broker Willis Corroon plc 1951–91; dir Euro Informatics Mkt; pres: Intelligent Tport Systems, Inst for the Mgmnt of Info Systems; memb: Cncl Parly IT Ctee, Ctee UK Confedn of EDI Standards, Ctee Electronic Commerce Assoc, All Party Gp on Parly Insurance & Fin Services; tstee Lloyd's Support Fund; *Style—* The Rt Hon the Viscount Chelmsford; ✉ 26 Ormonde Gate, London SW3 4EX (☎ 0171 352 5636)

CHELMSFORD, Bishop of 1996–; Rt Rev John Freeman Perry; s of Richard Henry Perry (d 1990), and Elsie Agnes, *née* Freeman (d 1992); *b* 15 June 1935; *Educ* Mill Hill, London Coll of Divinity (ALCD, LTh), Westminster Coll Oxford (MPhil); *m* 8 Aug 1959, Gay Valerie, da of Henry Cornelius Brown; 2 da (Karen Jane b 19 July 1961, Susanni Rachel b 1 Jan 1967); 3 s (Andrew Nicholas b 23 Dec 1962, Timothy Richard b 30 July 1964, Jonathan Freeman b 7 Jan 1969); *Career* Nat Serv RCS 1953–55; ordained: deacon 1959, priest 1960; curate Christ Church Woking (Guildford Dio) 1959–62, vicar St Andrew's Chorleywood (St Albans Dio) 1962–77 (curate in charge 1962), rural dean Rickmansworth 1972–77, warden Lee Abbey (Exeter Dio) 1977–89, rural dean Shirwell 1980–84, bishop of Southampton 1989–96, hon canon Winchester Catheral 1989–96; *Books* Effective Christian Leadership (1983); *Recreations* a large family, jogging (completed London Marathon 1990), golf, tennis, walking, travel; *Style—* The Rt Rev the Bishop of Chelmsford; ✉ Bishopscourt, Margaretting, Ingatestone, Essex CM4 0HD (☎ 01277 352001, fax 01277 355374)

CHELSEA, Viscount; Charles Gerald John Cadogan; DL (Greater London 1996); s and h of 7 Earl Cadogan; *b* 24 March 1937; *Educ* Eton; *m* 1, 6 June 1963, Lady Philippa Dorothy Bluett Wallop (d 1984), 2 da of 9 Earl of Portsmouth (d 1984); 2 s (Hon Edward b 1966, Hon William b 1973), 1 da (Hon Anna-Karina b 1964); m 2, 1989 (m dis 1994), Jennifer Jane Greig, da of (J E) Keith Rae, and Mrs S Z de Ferranti; m 3, 25 July 1994, Dorothy Ann, MVO, yr da of late Dr W E Shipsey; *Heir* s, Hon Edward Charles Cadogan b 10 May 1966; *Career* dir Cadogan Estates and Group of Cos; chm Leukaemia Research Fund; Liveryman Guild of Air Pilots and Air Navigators; *Style—* Viscount Chelsea, DL; ✉ 7 Smith St, London SW3 4EE (☎ 0171 730 2465); Marndhill, Ardington, Wantage, Oxon (☎ 01235 833273)

CHELSOM, Peter Anthony; s of Maj Reginald James Chelsom (d 1970), and Catherine, *née* Rodan (d 1977); *b* 20 April 1956; *Educ* Wrekin Coll, Central Sch of Speech & Drama; *Career* actor; leading roles: Royal Shakespeare Co, Nat Theatre, Royal Court; TV incl: Sorrell and Son, Woman of Substance, Christmas Present; writer and dir of films incl: Treacle (BAFTA nomination), Hear My Song 1992, Funny Bones (The Peter Sellers Award for Comedy (1995 Evening Standard Awards)) 1994; dir of commercials; memb: Equity, ACTT; *Clubs* RAC; *Style—* Peter Chelsom, Esq; ✉ Taylor McMillan Films, 60 Poland Street, London W1V 3DF (☎ 0171 287 3039)

CHELTENHAM, Archdeacon of; *see:* Lewis, Ven John Arthur

CHELTON, Capt Lewis William Leonard; s of Lewis Walter Chelton (d 1959), and Doris May, *née* Gamblin (d 1961); *b* 19 Dec 1934; *Educ* RNC Dartmouth; *m* 11 May 1957, Daphne Joan, da of Lt-Col R P Landon, MC, RA (d 1936); 3 s (Simon Roger Lewis b 1958, Roderick Charles Dominic b 1960, Hugo Rupert Philip b 1966); *Career* RN: Naval Cadet 1951, Midshipman 1953, Sub Lt 1955, Lt 1956, staff of Flag Offr Flying Trg 1956–57; serv in: HMS Torquay, HMS Scarborough (5 Frigate Sqdn) 1958–59; staff of C in C Med 1960–61, HMS Caprice (8 Destroyer Sqdn) 1962–64, Lt Cdr 1964, legal trg 1964–66, called to the Bar Inner Temple 1966, sec to Cdr Naval Forces Gulf (Sr Naval Offr Persian Gulf) 1967–69, asst sec to Flag Offr Scotland and NI 1970–71, serv HMS Hampshire 1972, Cdr 1972, sec to Flag Offr Carriers and Amphibious Ships 1973–74, NDC Latimer 1975, HMS Fearless 1976–77, naval admin plans MOD 1978–79, Fleet Supply Offr 1979–81, Capt 1981, Chief Naval Judge Advocate 1982–84, dep dir Naval Serv Conditions, ret 1987; sec the Engrg Cncl 1987–, memb Ctee Strand Aldwych Assoc, tstee R S Surtees Soc; *Recreations* shooting, gardening, country pursuits; *Clubs* Farmers'; *Style—* Capt Lewis Chelton, RN; ✉ Palmers Green House, Hatch Beauchamp, Nr Taunton, Somerset (☎ 01823 480221); 51 Badminton Rd, London SW12; The Secretary of the Engineering Council, 10 Maltravers Street, London WC2 (☎ 0171 240 7891, fax 0171 240 7517)

CHENERY, Peter James; s of Dudley James Chenery, and Brenda Dorothy, *née* Redford; *b* 24 Oct 1946; *Educ* Forest Sch, Christ Church Oxford (MA, hon sec ChCh Boat Club, chm OU Tory Reform Gp), SOAS (cert in Arabic); *m* 1979, (Alice) Blanche, *née* Faulder; 3 da (Athena b 1980, Elizabeth b 1983, Victoria b 1987); *Career* teacher Ghana Teaching Serv 1967–70; British Cncl: joined 1970, Amman 1971–73, Middle East Dept 1973–77, Freetown Sierra Leone 1978–80, dir Jedda Saudi Arabia 1981–84, dir Sana'a Yemen 1984–88, dir Munich 1988–90, sec of the Cncl and head of public affairs 1990–; Bronze medals of Univs of Sana'a and Ulm; FRSA; *Recreations* books, pubs, gardening, early English coins; *Clubs* Leander (Henley); *Style—* Peter Chenery, Esq; ✉ The British Council, 10 Spring Gardens, London SW1A 2BN (☎ 0171 389 4345, fax 0171 389 4984)

CHENEY, Donald Harvey; s of Arthur Stanley Cheney (d 1975), and Jessie Cheney (d 1986); *b* 16 Jan 1931; *Educ* Eggars GS Alton Hants, Harrow Weald Co GS Middx, Regent St Poly Sch of Architecture (DipArch); *m* 13 Feb 1956, Gillian Evelyn Florence Frances Cheney, JP, da of Guy Holman Tatum (d 1969); 3 da (Frances b 1956, Fiona (Mrs Ford) b 1960, Claire b 1968); *Career* qualified as architect 1955, in practice NZ 1956–62, in practice S Coast of England 1963–96, ptnr Cheney & Thorpe architects (joined 1970), ret; cncl memb RIBA 1983, external examiner Canterbury Sch of Architecture 1982–87, memb Franco-Br Union of Architects 1977–; Freeman City of London 1983; Liveryman Worshipful Co of Arbitrators 1983; RIBA 1956, assoc memb NZ Inst of Architects 1956, FCIArb 1981 (ACIArb 1976); *Recreations* sailing, photography; *Clubs* Royal Cinque Ports Yacht, St John House; *Style—* Donald Cheney, Esq; ✉ Crosstrees, North Rd, Hythe, Kent (☎ 01303 268720); La Lande Du Burgos, Guehenno 56, France

CHERKAS, Christopher John; s of John Charles Cherkas, and Marian, *née* Chilcott; *b* 14 Oct 1950; *Educ* Headlands GS Swindon, West Bromwich Coll of Commerce (HND); *m* 7 June 1975, Anna Maria; 2 s (Alexander Robert b 1979, Nicholas Charles b 1982); *Career* manpower offr The Plessey Company 1971–73 (mgmnt trainee 1967–71), industl rels offr Rubery Owen 1973; personnel mangr: The Plessey Co 1974–78, Stone Platt Industries 1978–80; divnl personnel mangr Honeywell Information Systems 1980–83, dir of manpower Whittaker Life Sciences 1983–84, personnel dir Data General Corporation 1984–90, human resources dir Unisys UK 1990–93, vice pres human resources Unisys Computor Systems Europe, Middle East Africa 1993–; FIPM; *Recreations* classic cars, watching motor racing; *Style—* Christopher Cherkas, Esq; ✉ Unisys Europe Middle East Africa, Zuercherstrasse 59–61, 8800 Thalwil, Switzerland (☎ 41 1 723 3827)

CHERNOV, Vladimir; *Educ* Moscow State Conservatory, Accademia della Scala; *m* Olga; 1 s (Vladimir); *Career* baritone; soloist Kirov Opera Co 1981; *Roles* incl: Figaro in The Barber of Seville (Kirov Opera, Covent Garden debut 1990, Vienna Staatsoper 1991, new prodn Théâtre de la Monnaie Brussels 1992), Germont in La Traviata (Kirov Opera, Met Opera 1991), title role in Eugene Onegin (Kirov), Dr Malatesta in Don Pasquale (Kirov), Valentin in Faust (Kirov), Marquis of Posa in Don Carlos (Los Angeles Opera 1989, Met Opera NY 1992, Arena di Verona 1992, La Scala Milan 1992), Prince Andrei in War and Peace (Seattle 1989, also filmed), Don Carlo in La Forza del Destino (Scottish Opera 1990, San Francisco 1992), Miller in Luisa Miller (Rome Opera 1989, Met Opera debut 1991), Nottingham in Roberto Devereux (Carnegie Hall and Mexico City) 1990, Ezio in Attila (Covent Garden and San Francisco) 1991, Marcello in La Boheme (Boston Opera (US debut) 1989, Stuttgart 1991, Arena di Verona 1992), Yeletsky in La Pique Dame (Kirov, new prodn Vienna Staatsoper 1992), Capt Anckarstroem in Un Ballo in Maschera (Chicago Lyric Opera 1992, Met Opera tour of Japan 1992–93), Count of Luna in Il Trovatore (Met Opera) 1992; *Recordings* incl: Il Trovatore (with Met Opera Co under James Levine, Sony 1991), Luisa Miller (with Met Opera Co under James Levine, Sony 1991), Don Carlos (with Met Opera Co under James Levine, Sony 1992), Rigoletto (with Met Opera Co under James Levine, Deutsche Grammophon 1993), various video recordings; *Awards* second prize and Special Jury Prize Glink Competition USSR 1981, bronze medal Tchaikovsky Competition Moscow 1982, second prize Voci Verdiane competition Busseto Italy 1983, Carlo Galetti Prize 1983, first prize and Tito Gobbin Prize Miriam Helin Vocal Competition Helsinki 1984; *Style—* Vladimir Chernov, Esq; ✉ c/o Columbia Artists Management Inc, 165 West 57th Street, New York, New York 10019–2276, USA (☎ 001 212 841 9500, fax 001 212 841 9557)

CHERNS, Penelope Ann (Penny); da of Albert Bernard Cherns (d 1987), of Sussex, and Barbara Simone, *née* Brotman; *b* 21 May 1948; *Educ* North London Collegiate Sch, Univ of Kent (BA), Drama Centre London (Dip in Directing); *Career* director; numerous teaching appts incl: LAMDA, RADA Drama Centre, WSCAD, RCM, Trent Poly, Univ of Loughborough, Oslo, Univ of Iowa, Juillard Sch NY, Guildhall Sch of Drama, Nat Film Sch, Cultura Inglesa Sao Paolo Brazil, Anglo Inst Montevideo Uruguay, Amsterdam Int Theatre Workshop, Institut del Teatr Barcelona, Brandeis Univ USA; script conslt: Channel 4 1987, Warner Sisters (Hothouse Warner Sisters 1989); *Theatre* Hallo and Goodbye Pal Joey 1974, Stop The World 1975, My Fair Lady 1975, West Side Story 1976 (all Northcott Theatre Exeter), Smile for Jesus (ICA and Sheffield Crucible Studio) 1976, A Winter's Tale 1977, Guys and Dolls 1977, Cabaret 1977 (all Gateway Theatre Chester), Queen Christina (RSC) 1977, School for Clowns (Haymarket Leicester) 1977, Dusa, Fish, Stas and Vi (Bristol Old Vic) 1977, Wreckers (7:84) 1977, Prodigal Father (Soho Poly) 1978, Kiss Me Kate 1978, Beaux Stratagem 1978, Alice 1978 (all Nottingham Playhouse), You Never Can Tell 1978, Side By Side By Sondheim 1979 (both Palace Theatre Watford), Julius Caesar 1979, Teeth 'n' Smiles 1979 (both Nottingham Playhouse), Trees in the Wind (7:84) 1979, Statements (Bristol Old Vic) 1980, Heroes 1979, Letters Home 1980, Strangers 1981 (all New End), Chicago 1981, Pinocchio 1981 (both Newcastle Playhouse), The Boyfriend (Churchill Theatre Bromley) 1982, Duet for One (Br Cncl India Tour) 1983, A Day In The Death of Joe Egg (Haymarket Leicester) 1984, Vigilantes (Asian Co-op Theatre) 1985, Mourning Pictures (Monstrous Regiment) 1981, Alarms (Monstrous Regiment 1986, Riverside Studios 1987) Panorama (The King's Head) 1988, The Millionairess (Greenwich) 1988, Iranian Nights (Royal Court) 1989, Revelations (Traverse Edinburgh) 1992, Tant Per Tant Shakespeare (Barcelona) 1995; *Television and Films* for Channel Four: Letters Home 1982, The Inner Eye (asst prodr only) 1986, Iranian Nights 1989, Bite the Ball 1989, Mixing It 1990; for BBC: Prisoners of Incest (Horizon) 1983, Battered Baby (Horizon) 1985, Home Front 1988, And The Cow Jumped Over The Moon 1990; other credits incl: Clients and Professionals and Managing Change (Melrose Film Productions) 1990; *Recreations* travel, languages, swimming; *Style—* Ms Penny Cherns

CHERRY, Alan Herbert; MBE (1985); *Career* chm Countryside Properties PLC, dep chm London Industrial PLC; House Builders' Fedn: past nat pres, former memb New Homes Environmental Study Gp, currently chm Housing Policy Panel; memb: Duke of Edinburgh's Inquiry into Br Housing 1985–90, Inner City Cmmn 1987, Bd Teesside Devpt Corp, Joseph Rowntree Fndn Inquiry into Planning for Housing; chm CBI Eastern Region; former chm New Homes Mktg Bd; former memb Advsy Bd Nat Westminster Bank plc; govr Anglia Poly Univ; Freeman City of London, memb Worshipful Co of Blacksmiths; FRICS, FSVA; Hon MRTPI; *Style—* Alan Cherry, Esq, MBE; ✉ Countryside Properties plc, Countryside House, The Drive, Brentwood, Essex CM13 3AT (☎ 01277 260000, fax 01277 690690)

CHERRY, Colin; s of Reginald Cherry (d 1970), of Hull, and Dorothy, *née* Brooks (d 1939); *b* 20 Nov 1931; *Educ* Hymers Coll; *m* 2 Aug 1958, Marjorie Rose, da of Thomas Harman, of Holderness; 2 da (Nicola (Mrs Gatt) b 1962, Jacqueline b 1965); *Career* Nat Serv RAEC 1950–52, Lt TA E Yorks Regt 1952–58; Inland Revenue 1952, HM Inspr of Taxes 1958–85, under sec/dir of ops Inland Revenue 1985–90; chm Civil Serv Retirement Fellowship 1992–94, tax advsr IMF 1994–; *Clubs* Reform; *Style—* Colin Cherry, Esq; ✉ 13 Wathen Rd, Dorking, Surrey RH4 1JZ (☎ 01306 885921)

CHERRY, David Norman; *b* 29 April 1937; *Educ* Univ of London; *m*; 3 c; *Career* Nat Serv RAF; chartered surveyor; Frank Durrant Westmore & Reeves London 1962–65, City of Oxford 1966–69; Donaldsons: joined 1969, Bradford and Leeds Offices 1969–86, head Edinburgh Office specialising mainly in shopping centre mgmnt & devpt 1978–86, dep sr ptnr Head Office Jermyn St London 1987–89, sr ptnr 1989–; sec Bradford Area Devpt Assoc 1970s; chm Yorks Divnl Branch RICS, Yorks rep on Gen Practice Divnl Ctee RICS HQ; Liveryman Worshipful Co of Glovers; *Recreations* various sports incl sailing, choral singing; *Style—* David Cherry, Esq; ✉ Donaldsons, 70 Jermyn Street, London SW1Y 6PE (☎ 0171 930 1090, fax 0171 839 2743)

CHERRY, John Mitchell; QC (1988); s of John William (Jack) Cherry (d 1967), of Cheshunt, Herts, and Dorothy Mary, *née* Maybury (d 1975); *b* 10 Sept 1937; *Educ* Cheshunt GS; *m* 7 Oct 1972, Eunice Ann; 2 s (Troy Alexander b 10 July 1968 d 1995, Matthew John b 13 April 1971), 2 da (Suzanne Marie b 3 Jan 1970, Katherine Ann (twin) b 3 Jan 1970); *Career* called to the Bar Gray's Inn 1961, recorder of the Crown Court 1987– (asst recorder 1984–87); memb Criminal Injuries Compensation Bd 1989–; *Recreations* cricket, rugby, food, wine; *Style—* John Cherry, Esq, QC; ✉ Winterton, Turkey St, Enfield, Middlesex EN1 4RJ (☎ 01992 719018); 8 Stone Buildings, Lincoln's Inn, London WC2A 3TA (☎ 0171 831 9881, fax 0171 831 9392)

CHERRY, Richard John; s of John Cherry, and Rosina Florence, *née* Walker; *b* 3 Feb 1944; *Educ* Enfield GS, London Hosp Med Coll (MB BS); *m* 18 May 1968, Pamela Joan, da of Roy Percival Stanley Bevin; 1 s (David b 1971), 1 da (Elizabeth b 1972); *Career* sr lectr in orthopaedic surgery Univ of Warwick 1995–; memb: Christian Med Fellowship, BMA; FRCS 1972, FIMgt 1980; *Recreations* music, photography, sailing, skiing; *Clubs* Naughton Dunn, Olton Mere, Birmingham Medico-Legal Soc; *Style—* Richard Cherry, Esq; ✉ 95 Kineton Green Road, Olton, Solihull B92 7DT (☎ 0121 706 8842, e-mail 100031.1734@compuserve.com); Coventry and Warwickshire Hospital, Stoney Stanton Road, Coventry (☎ 01203 224055)

CHERRY, Prof Richard John; s of Leslie George Cherry (d 1970), and Dorothy Emily, *née* Tasker (d 1969); *b* 3 Jan 1939; *Educ* Hitchin Boys GS, St John's Coll Oxford (BA),

Univ of Sheffield (PhD); *m* 23 June 1962, Georgine Mary, da of George Walter Ansell; 2 s (Simon Richard b 1965, Matthew James b 1972); *Career* scientific offr SERL 1960–64, scientist Unilever Res 1964–70, res fell Dept of Chemistry Univ of Sheffield 1970–73, privat dozent Dept of Biochemistry ETH Zürich 1973–82, prof of biological chemistry Univ of Essex 1982–; memb Editorial Bd: Biochemical Journal 1984–91, European Journal of Biophysics 1984–91, Progress in Lipid Research 1990–; SERC Membranes Initiative co-ordinator 1989–93; memb Molecular and Cell Panel Wellcome Tst 1988–91, memb Biochemistry and Cell Biology Ctee BBSRC 1994–; Ruzicka prize for chem Switzerland 1981; memb: Biochemical Soc 1971, Biophysical Soc 1973; *Books* Techniques for the Analysis of Membrane Proteins (with C I Ragan, 1986), New Techniques of Optical Microscopy and Microspectroscopy (1991), Structural and Dynamic Properties of Lipids and Membranes (with P J Quinn, 1992); *Recreations* photography, gardening, music; *Style—* Prof Richard Cherry; ✉ Department of Biological and Chemical Sciences, University of Essex, Colchester CO4 3SQ (☎ 01206 872244, fax 01206 873598)

CHERRYMAN, John Richard; QC (1982); s of Albert James Cherryman (d 1963), and Mabel, *née* Faggetter; *b* 7 Dec 1932; *Educ* Farnham GS, LSE (LLB), Harvard Law Sch; *m* 18 Sept 1963, Anna, da of Edward Greenleaf Collis; 3 s (Oliver b 1964, Nicholas b 1966, Rupert b 1968), 1 da (Louise b 1971); *Career* called to the Bar Gray's Inn 1955, recorder of the Crown Court; bencher 1989–; *Recreations* restoring property in France, gardening; *Style—* John Cherryman, Esq, QC; ✉ 4 Bream's Buildings, Lincoln's Way, London EC4A 1AQ (☎ 0171 353 5835)

CHESHAM, 6 Baron (UK 1858); Nicholas Charles Cavendish; er s of 5 Baron Chesham, PC, TD (d 1989); *b* 7 Nov 1941; *Educ* Eton; *m* 1, 4 Nov 1965 (m dis 1969), Susan Donne, eldest da of late Frederick Guy Beauchamp, of London; m 2, 1973, Suzanne Adrienne, eldest da of late Alan Gray Byrne, of Sydney; 2 s (Hon Charles Gray Compton, Hon William George Gray b 13 April 1980); *Heir* s, Hon Charles Gray Compton Cavendish b 11 Nov 1974; *Career* chartered accountant; investment advsr; Capt of the Queen's Body Guard of the Yeoman of the Guard (dep chief whip House of Lords) 1995–; *Recreations* tennis, skiing, shooting; *Clubs* Pratt's, Australian (Sydney), Royal Sydney Golf; *Style—* The Rt Hon the Lord Chesham; ✉ Manor Farm, Preston Candover, nr Basingstoke, Hants RG25 2EN

CHESHIRE, Lt-Col Colin Charles Chance; OBE (1993); s of Air Chief Marshal Sir Walter Graemes Cheshire, GBE, KCB, ADC (d 1978), and Mary Cheshire, DL (d 1992); *b* 23 Aug 1941; *Educ* Worksop; *m* 1, 8 Aug 1968, Cherida Evelyn, da of Air Chief Marshal Sir Wallace Kyle, GCB, KCVO, CBE, DSO, DFC; 1 s (Christopher b 1971), 1 da (Philippa b 1969); m 2, 2 Oct 1976, Angela Mary, da of D Fulcher, of Bury St Edmunds, Suffolk; 2 step da (Sarah Linnington b 1968, Emma McMillen b 1970); *Career* Lt-Col RTR (ret 1981); served: Aden, Borneo, Singapore, Malaysia, BAOR, NI, UK, Armour Sch Bovington Camp 1968 (tt), RMC of Sci 1972–73 and Staff Coll Camberley 1974 (psc); sales and marketing mangr: def equipment Vickers Instruments Ltd York 1981–83, army systems Ferranti Computer Systems Ltd Cwmbran 1983–85; gp sales and mktg dir Wallop Group (md Walloptronics Ltd) Andover 1985–87; bursar Oundle Sch 1987–95, memb Exec Ctee Ind Schools' Bursar Assoc 1992–95; National Rifle Assoc: vice chm Exec Ctee 1990–92, memb Cncl 1990–95, vice chm 1992–95, chief exec 1995–; chm GB Target Shooting Fedn 1994–; rifle shooting (int full bore); rep: England 1970–, GB 1970– (vice capt 1982 and 1989, adj 1988, capt 1992, 1994 and 1995), Army 1967–81, Yorks, Hereford Worcs and Hants (capt 1987–89); cmdt Br Cadet Athelings Rifle Team 1990; FIMgt; *Recreations* full bore target rifle shooting, golf; *Clubs* HAC; *Style—* Lt-Col Colin Cheshire, OBE; ✉ The Barn, Queen Victoria Way, Bisley Camp, Brookwood, Woking, Surrey GU24 0NY; National Rifle Association, Bisley Camp, Brookwood, Woking, Surrey GU24 0PB (☎ 01483 797777, fax 01483 797285)

CHESHIRE, Dr (Christopher) Michael; s of Gordon Sydney (d 1983), of Birmingham, and Vera, *née* Hepburn; *b* 18 July 1946; *Educ* West Bromwich GS, Univ of Manchester (BSc, MB ChB); *m* 1 Aug 1970, Jane Mary, da of Claude Cordle, of Norwich; 1 s (Jonathan Christopher b 5 Nov 1980), 1 da (Amy Tamsin b 1 April 1977); *Career* house offr Manchester Royal Infirmary and Hope Hosp Salford 1976–77 (pharmacist 1969–71), SHO Central and S Manchester Hosps 1976–79, lectr in geriatric med Univ of Manchester 1979–83, conslt physician in geriatric med Manchester Royal Infirmary and Barnes Hosp 1983, dean of clinical studies Manchester Med Sch 1991–93, med dir Central Manchester Health Care Tst 1993–; memb: Br Geriatrics Soc, British Assoc of Medical Managers; FRCP 1990; *Recreations* gardening, running; *Style—* Dr Michael Cheshire; ✉ 38 The Crescent, Davenport, Stockport, Cheshire SK3 8SN (☎ 0161 483 2972); Barnes Hospital, Cheadle, Cheshire; The Royal Infirmary, Oxford Road, Manchester (☎ 0161 491 2300, 0161 276 4840)

CHESSHYRE, (David) Hubert Boothby; LVO (1988); s of Col Hubert Layard Chesshyre, of Whatmer Hall, Sturry, Canterbury (d 1981), and (Katharine) Anne, *née* Boothby (d 1995); *b* 22 June 1940; *Educ* King's Sch Canterbury, Trinity Coll Cambridge (MA), ChCh Oxford (DipEd); *Career* former vintner and language teacher; green staff offr at Investiture of Prince of Wales 1969, Rouge Croix Pursuivant 1970–78, on staff of Sir Anthony Wagner as Garter King of Arms 1971–78, Chester Herald of Arms 1978–95, Norroy and Ulster King of Arms 1995–; Registrar Coll of Arms 1992–; lay clerk Southwark Cathedral, lectr for NADFAS and Foyles, Westminster Abbey Architectural Advsy Panel 1985–; hon genealogist Royal Victorian Order 1987, sec of the Order of the Garter 1988; Freeman City of London, Liveryman Worshipful Co of Musicians 1995 (Freeman 1994); memb: Hon Artillery Co 1964–65, Bach Choir 1979–93, Madrigal Soc, Soc of Genealogists; fell Heraldry Soc 1990 (memb Cncl 1973–85), FSA; *Books* Heraldry of the World (ed, 1973), The Identification of Coats of Arms on British Silver (1978), The Green, A History of the Heart of Bethnal Green (with A J Robinson, 1978), Heralds of Today (with Adrian Ailes, 1986), Dictionary of British Arms Medieval Ordinary Vol I (jt ed, 1992); *Recreations* singing, gardening, motorcycling; *Style—* Hubert Chesshyre, Esq, LVO, FSA, Norroy and Ulster King of Arms; ✉ Hawthorn Cottage, 1 Flamborough Walk, London E14 7LS; College of Arms, Queen Victoria St, London EC4V 4BT (☎ and fax 0171 248 1137)

CHESTER, Archdeacon of; *see:* Hewetson, Ven Christopher

CHESTER, Bishop of 1996–; Rt Rev Peter Robert Forster; s of Thomas Forster (d 1991), of Birmingham, and Edna, *née* Russell; *b* 16 March 1950; *Educ* Tudor Grange GS for Boys Solihull, Merton Coll Oxford (MA Chemistry), Univ of Edinburgh (BD, PhD), Edinburgh Theol Coll; *m* 1978, Elisabeth Anne, da of Rev Dr Eric Stevenson; 2 da (Inge b 1979, Helen b 1985), 2 s (Thomas b 1981, Douglas b 1993); *Career* curate Mossley Hill Parish Church Liverpool 1980–82, sr tutor St John's Coll Durham 1983–91, vicar Beverley Minster 1991–96; *Recreations* tennis, woodwork, family life, gardening; *Style—* The Rt Rev the Bishop of Chester; ✉ Bishop's House, Abbey Square, Chester CH1 2JD (☎ 01244 350864, fax 01244 314187)

CHESTER, Richard Waugh; s of Cyril Waugh Chester, of Great Broughton, Yorkshire, and Margaret, *née* Dally; *b* 19 April 1943; *Educ* Friends' Sch Great Ayton, Huddersfield Coll of Technol (ARCM), Royal Acad of Music (ARAM, GRSM); *m* 12 Dec 1970, Sarah, da of Thomas Arthur Leopold Chapman-Mortimer (d 1979); 1 s (Matthew b 1973), 2 da (Lucy b 1976, Emily b 1979); *Career* flautist; fndr memb Nash Ensemble 1964; BBC NI 1965–67; princ flautist and soloist with performances of works by: Mozart, Nielson, Chaminade, Martin; Scottish Nat Orchestra 1967–87; fndr memb and solo flautist Cantilena 1971, dir Nat Youth Orchestra of Scotland 1987–; fndr memb Euro Fedn of Nat Youth Orchestras; chm Glasgow Festival Strings, fndr ctee memb World Youth Orchestra Conference; govr St Mary's Music Sch Edinburgh, conductor and examiner; FRSA; *Recreations* squash, walking, tennis, reading; *Style—* Richard Chester, Esq; ✉ Milton of Cardross, Port of Menteith, Stirling, Scotland (☎ 01877 385634); 13 Somerset Place, Glasgow (☎ 0141 332 8311, fax 0141 332 3915)

CHESTERFIELD, Archdeacon of; *see:* Garnett, Ven David Christopher

CHESTERMAN, (Henry) David; s of Sir Clement Chesterman (d 1983), and Winifred, *née* Spear (d 1981); *b* 17 April 1920; *Educ* Monkton Combe Sch Bath; *m* 5 Sept 1945, Jean, da of Sir Harold Kenward (d 1947); 2 s (Andrew b 1946, Daniel b 1954), 1 da (Clare b 1949); *Career* served army 1940–45; Dunlop Rubber Co Ltd 1945–66, PA to Sir Robert Mayer chm of Youth and Music, mangr Ernest Read Music Assoc 1971–76, dir Br Cncl for Prevention of Blindness 1976–94; *Recreations* music, tennis, walking, theatre, getting to know 8 grandchildren; *Style—* David Chesterman, Esq; ✉ 15 Shire Lane, Chorleywood, Herts WD3 5NQ

CHESTERMAN, Sir Ross; kt (1970); s of Dudley Edmund Chesterman (d 1950), of Bexhill, Sussex, and Ettie Esther, *née* Thorington; *b* 27 April 1909; *Educ* Hastings GS, Imperial Coll London (BSc, MSc, PhD, Acland Eng Essay Prizeman); *m* 1, 1938, Audrey Mary (d 1982), da of Rev Arthur Herbert Horlick (d 1950), of Portishead; 1 s (John), 1 da (Jane); m 2, 1985, Patricia, da of Frederic Burns Bell; *Career* sci master in various grammar schs, former headmaster Meols Cop Secdy Sch Southport, chemistry lectr Woolwich Poly, sch inspr and chief county schs inspr Worcs 1948–53, warden Goldsmiths' Coll Univ of London 1953–74 (hon fell 1980), dean Coll of Craft Educn 1958–60 (hon fell 1958), Ford Foundation Travel Award to American Univ 1966, educnl conslt to numerous overseas countries 1966–73, master Coll of Craft Design and Technol 1982–; author of scientific papers in chemical jls and jls of natural history and articles in educnl periodicals; chm: Nat Cncl for Supply and Trg of Teachers Overseas 1971, Advsy Ctee for Teacher Trg Overseas FCO (ODA) 1972–74; Freeman and Liveryman Worshipful Co of Goldsmiths; *Books* Teacher Training in Some American Universities (1967), Science in Schools (chapter, 1958), Golden Sunrise (1996); *Recreations* writing, music, painting, natural history, travel; *Style—* Sir Ross Chesterman; ✉ The Garden House, 6 High St, Lancaster LA1 1LA (☎ 01524 65687)

CHESTERS, Prof Graham; s of Thomas Leslie Chesters (d 1972), and Nellie, *née* Tortington (d 1995); *b* 10 Oct 1944; *Educ* Crewe Co GS, Univ Coll of Swansea (BA, MA); *m* 26 Oct 1968, Veronica Anne; 1 s (Tim b 1976), 1 da (Anna b 1982); *Career* lectr in French Queen's Univ Belfast 1970–72; Univ of Hull: lectr in French 1972–80, sr lectr 1980–88, prof 1988; pro-vice-chllr Sch of Euro Languages and Cultures 1991–96 (dean 1988–91); dir Computers in Teaching Initiative Centre for Modern Languages 1989–; *Books* Some Functions of Sound-Repetition (1975), Anthology of Modern French Poetry (1976), The Appreciation of Modern French Poetry (1976), Baudelaire and the Poetics of Craft (1988); *Recreations* chess; *Style—* Prof Graham Chesters; ✉ School of European Languages and Cultures, University of Hull, Hull (☎ 01482 465625, fax 01482 465877)

CHESTERTON, Fiona Mary; da of Clarence Herbert Chesterton (d 1977), of Leicester, and Mary Biddulph; *b* 19 May 1952; *Educ* Wyggeston Girls' GS Leicester, Lady Margaret Hall Oxford (BA); *m* 1 Jan 1980, Howard Anderson; 2 da (Sarah Elizabeth b 26 June 1984, Rachel Clare b 22 April 1987); *Career* BBC: news trainee 1975–77, TV news scriptwriter 1977–79, prodr TV current affairs esp Nationwide 1979–87, ed London Plus 1987–89, ed Newsroom South East 1989–91, ed Bi-Media South East 1991–92; commissioning ed Daytime Ch4 TV 1996– (dep commissioning ed news & current affrs 1992–96); *Recreations* swimming, gardening, tennis; *Style—* Ms Fiona Chesterton; ✉ Huntingdon, Cambs; Channel Four Television, 124 Horseferry Road, London SW1P 2TX (☎ 0171 396 4444, fax 0171 306 8359)

CHESTERTON, (John Sydney) Keith; s of Maj Hugh Chesteron, MBE (d 1962), of Sussex, and Phyllis Mary, *née* Harries (d 1986); *b* 26 April 1927; *Educ* Sherborne, Corpus Christi Coll Cambridge; *m* 1, 29 March 1953 (m dis), Penelope Ann; 1 s (Christopher b 1957), 1 da (Venetia b 1955); m 2, 19 Aug 1964, Diana Margaret; *Career* Lt RN 1945–56; admitted slr 1961; HM Coroner IOW 1980–94; *Recreations* sailing, gardening; *Clubs* Royal Naval Sailing Assoc, Royal Victoria Yacht, Seaview Yacht; *Style—* Keith Chesterton, Esq; ✉ Shirleys Yard, Yafford, Shorwell, Newport, Isle of Wight PO30 3LH

CHESTERTON, Sir Oliver Sidney; kt (1969), MC (1943); s of Frank Sidney Chesterton, and Nora Chesterton; *b* 28 Jan 1913; *Educ* Rugby; *m* 1944, Violet Ethel, yst da of Henry Robert Jameson, of Dublin; 2 s (Michael, Sam), 1 da (Jane); *Career* served WWII Irish Gds; Crown Estate cmmr 1969–83; qualified as chartered surveyor 1934, sr ptnr Chesterton and Sons, chm Woolwich Equitable Building Society 1976–84 (formerly vice chm); dir: Property Growth Assurance 1972–85, London Life Association 1975–84, Estates Property Investment Company 1979–88; govr Rugby Sch 1972–89; Hon Asst Worshipful Co of Curriers, Hon Asst Worshipful Co of Chartered Surveyors; FRICS (hon sec 1972–74, past pres); *Clubs* New Zealand Golf; *Style—* Sir Oliver Chesterton, MC; ✉ Hookfield House, Abinger Common, Dorking, Surrey

CHESWORTH, John; s of Frank Chesworth (d 1970), and Florence Lilian, *née* Battye; *b* 8 June 1937; *Educ* Burnage GS; *m* 1, 24 June 1961 (m dis 1972), Wendy Ann Smith; 3 da (Debra b 1 May 1962, Sandra b 8 June 1967, Diane b 1 March 1969); m 2, 17 March 1973, (Elizabeth) Ann, da of Frank Noel Martin, of Stockport, Cheshire; 2 s (James b 21 Oct 1974, Robert b 28 June 1977); *Career* articled clerk Burne Phillips & Co 1958–63, chartered accountant Deloitte & Co 1964–67, fin accountant Kellogg Co of GB Ltd 1967–68, gp accountant Nemo Heat Treatments Ltd 1968–71, chief exec Bodycote Group 1972–, md Bodycote (UK) International plc 1980–; dir: HIP Ltd, Metallurgical Testing Services International, Industrial Materials Technology Inc (USA and Europe); non-exec dir Danish Paper Packaging (UK) Ltd, non-exec chm Zinc Alloy Ltd 1980–, chm Capital and Counties Developments Ltd 1989–; memb ICAEW; *Books* The Economics of Heat Treatment (Iron & Steel, 1971), Heat Treatment 50 Years On (Metallurgia, 1985), The Changing Role of Sub Contract Heat Treatment (Foundry trade jl, 1987), Leading With Quality (Quality in Action, 1988), Achieving Total Quality in Heat Treatment Partnerships (Materials World, 1993); *Recreations* sailing, golf, swimming, soccer; *Clubs* Tytherington, Royal Yacht; *Style—* John Chesworth, Esq; ✉ Bodycote International plc, 140 Kingsway, Manchester 19 (☎ 0161 257 2345)

CHETWODE, 2 Baron (UK 1945); Sir Philip Chetwode; 8 Bt (E 1700); s (by 1 m) of Capt Hon Roger Charles George Chetwode (d 1940, s of 1 Baron), and Hon (Molly) Patricia, *née* Berry (d 1995), da of 1 Viscount Camrose; suc grandfather 1950; *b* 26 March 1937; *Educ* Eton; *m* 1, 10 Aug 1967 (m dis 1979), Susan Janet, da of Capt Voltelin James Howard Van der Byl, DSC, RN (ret), and formerly wife of Alwyn Richard Dudley Smith; 2 s (Hon Roger b 1968, Hon Alexander b 1969), 1 da (Hon Miranda b 1974); m 2, 12 July 1990, Mrs Fiona Holt, da of late Christos Tsintsaris, of 15 Alexandrou Mihailidi, Thessaloniki, Greece; *Heir* s, Hon Roger Chetwode b 29 May 1968; *Career* Capt (ret) Royal Horse Guards; dir NCL Investments 1986–95; *Clubs* White's; *Style—* The Rt Hon the Lord Chetwode; ✉ The Mill House, Chilton Foliat, Hungerford, Berks; 72 Eaton Place, London SW1

CHETWOOD, Sir Clifford Jack; kt (1987); s of Stanley Jack Chetwood, and Doris May Palmer; *b* 2 Nov 1928; *m* 1953, Pamela Phyllis Sherlock; 1 s, 3 da; *Career* chm George Wimpey 1984–92 (md and chief exec 1982–90); chm Chetwood Associates Ltd (architects); chm Broadgate Properties plc; tstee Victoria and Albert Museum; chm Devpt Tst ICE 1989–, pres Building Employers' Confedn 1989–92, chm Construction Indust Trg Bd 1990–; pres Building Industry Youth Tst; memb Cncl Imperial Soc of Knights Bachelor 1988–95, pres The Royal Ct Club Hampton Ct Palace 1989–; vice pres City &

Guilds Inst 1992; Prince Philip Medal for Exceptional Service to Industry 1987 (City and Guilds Inst); Master Guild of Freemen of the City of London 1993–94, Liveryman Worshipful Co of Basketmakers; Hon FICE, Hon FCGI; FCIOB, FRSA, FRSH; *Style*— Sir Clifford Chetwood; ✉ Construction Industry Training Board, 8th Floor, Hillgate House, 26 Old Bailey, London EC4M 7QA (☎ 0171 489 1662)

CHETWYN, Robert; s of Frederick Reuben Suckling (d 1963), and Eleanor Lavinia, *née* Boffee; *b* 7 Sept 1933; *Educ* Rutlish Sch Merton, Central Sch of Drama; *Career* director; actor with Dundee Repertory Co 1952; in repertory at: Hull, Alexandra Theatre Birmingham 1954, Birmingham Rep Theatre 1954–56; various TV plays 1956–59, first prodn Five Finger Exercise (Salisbury Playhouse) 1960, dir of prodns Opera House Harrogate 1961–62, artistic dir Ipswich Arts 1962–64, assoc dir Mermaid Theatre 1966; *Theatre* The Beaver Coat (3 one-act plays by Shaw), There's A Girl in my Soup (Globe) 1966, Music Box (NY) 1967, A Present For The Past (Edinburgh Festival) 1966, The Flip Side (Apollo) 1967, The Importance of Being Earnest (Haymarket) 1968, What the Butler Saw (Queens) 1968, The Country Wife (Chichester Festival) 1968, The Band-Waggon (Mermaid 1968, Sydney 1970), Cannibal Crackers (Hampstead) 1969, When We Are Married (Strand) 1970, Hamlet (Rome, Zurich, Vienna, Antwerp, Cologne, Cambridge) 1971, The Sandboy (Greenwich), Parents Day (Globe) 1972, Restez Donc Jusq'au Petit Dejeuner (Belgium) 1973, Who's Who (Fortune) 1973, At The End Of The Day (Savoy) 1973, Chez Nous (Globe) 1974, Qui Est Qui (Belgium) 1974, The Doctors Dilemma (Mermaid) 1976, Getting Away with Murder (Comedy) 1976, A Murder is Announced (Vaudeville) 1977, Arms and the Man (Greenwich) 1978, Bent (Royal Ct, transferred to Criterion) 1979, Pygmalion (Nat Theatre of Belgium), Moving (Queens) 1981, Beethoven's Tenth (Vaudeville, Los Angeles and NY) 1983, Number One (Queens) 1984, Why Me? (Strand) 1985, Selling the Sizzle (Hampstead); *Television* Private Shultz 1980–81, The Irish RM 1982, Tropical Moon Over Dorking 1984, That Uncertain Feeling 1985, Born in the Gardens 1985–86, Small World 1987–88, The Case of the Late Pig 1989, Westbeach 1992; *Recreations* sport, gardening; *Style*— Robert Chetwyn, Esq; ✉ c/o Casarotto Ramsay Ltd, National House, 4th Floor, 60–66 Wardour Street, London W1V 3HP (☎ 0171 287 4450, fax 0171 287 9128)

CHETWYND, 10 Viscount (I 1717); Adam Richard John Casson; also Baron Rathdown (I 1717); s of 9 Viscount (d 1965); *b* 2 Feb 1935; *Educ* Eton; *m* 1, 19 Feb 1966 (m dis 1974), Celia Grace, er da of Cdr Alexander Robert Ramsay, DSC, RNVR; 2 s (Hon Adam, Hon Robert Duncan b (twin) 26 Feb 1969), 1 da (Hon Emma Grace b 5 May 1967); m 2, 1975, Angela May, o da of Jack Payne McCarthy (d 1982), of Nottingham; *Heir* s, Hon Adam Douglas Chetwynd b 26 Feb 1969; *Career* Lt Queen's Own Cameron Highlanders; life assurance agent Prudential Assurance Co of SA Ltd 1978–; fellow Inst of Life and Pension Advsrs; Freeman Guild of Air Pilots and Air Navigators; *Recreations* squash, travel, flying; *Clubs* Rand; *Style*— The Rt Hon the Viscount Chetwynd; ✉ c/o J G Ouvry, Lee Bolton and Lee, 1 The Sanctuary, Westminster, London SW1P 3JT; Prudential Assurance Co of SA Ltd, Sandton Branch, Johannesburg, South Africa (☎ 00 27 11 783 7125)

CHETWYND, Sir Arthur Ralph Talbot; 8 Bt (GB 1795), of Brocton Hall, Staffordshire; s of Hon (William) Ralph Chetwynd, MLA, MC (d 1957), bro of 7 Bt; and Frances Mary, *née* Jupe (d 1986); suc unc 1972; *b* 28 Oct 1913, Walhachin, BC; *Educ* Provincial Normal Sch BC; *m* 26 Aug 1940, Marjory May MacDonald, da of Robert Bruce Lang (d 1940), of Vancouver; 2 s (Robin John Talbot b 1941, William Richard Talbot b 1946); *Heir* s, Robin John Talbot Chetwynd, b 21 Aug 1941; *Career* served RCAF 1943–45; rancher in Br Columbia 1928–36, teacher 1937–39, physical rehabilitation 1939–42, chief instr in med reconditioning RCAF, assoc in physical and health educn Univ of Toronto 1946–52, pres and gen mangr Chetwynd Films Ltd (Toronto) 1950–78; chm: Chetwynd Productions Inc 1986, Brocton Hall Communications (Toronto) 1989– (pres 1978–88); served in Red Cross Soc and many other orgns; chm Nat Cncl Royal Cwlth Soc of Canada 1993–96; memb: Monarchist League, Heraldry Soc, Standing Cncl of the Baronetage; Voluntary Serv and Victory Medals 1945, Queen's Jubilee Medal 1977, Order of Barbados (Silver Crown of Merit) 1984; Freedom City of London 1989; *Recreations* swimming, travel; *Clubs* Albany (Toronto), Empire (Canada, past pres), Royal Cwlth Soc (Toronto (chm 1982–87), and London); *Style*— Sir Arthur Chetwynd, Bt; ✉ 117 King St East, Apt 3, Coburg, Ontario K9A 1L2, Canada (☎ 00 1 416 372 8323); The Carib, Holetown, St James, Barbados, West Indies (☎ 00 1 809 432 1583)

CHEUNG, William (Will); s of Wah Cheung, of Colchester, and King Duen Tsang; *b* 9 Aug 1957; *Educ* Sir Charles Lucas Sch Colchester; *Career* warehouse asst Colchester Photographic Wholesale 1976–77, civilian clerk Essex Police 1978–79, warehouse mangr Colchester Photographic Wholesale 1979–84; Practical Photography magazine: tech writer Jan-Nov 1985, tech ed 1985–88, asst ed (tech) 1988–89; ed Video Answers 1989–90; returned to Practical Photography as dep ed 1990–91 (ed 1991–); one-man exhbn 1980, personal monograph published by Royal Photographic Soc 1989; FRPS 1983 (ARPS 1982); *Books* Bronica Manual, Collins Practical Photography Diary; *Recreations* photography, keeping fit; *Style*— Will Cheung, Esq; ✉ Practical Photography, EMAP Apex Publications, Apex House, Oundle Road, Peterborough PE2 9NP (☎ 01733 898100, fax 01733 894472)

CHEVALLIER, Andrew Bretland; s of Lt Cdr John Bretland Chevallier, RN (d 1995), of Barnston, Wirral, Merseyside, and Rosemary Catherine, *née* Wylie; *b* 20 Feb 1953; *Educ* Tonbridge, Univ of Warwick (BA), NE London Poly (postgrad cert in educn), Sch of Phytotherapy Hailsham Sussex (cert of herbal med); *m* 1985, Maria Mercedes, *née* Uribe; 1 s by prev m (Leon b 26 Aug 1978), 1 step da (Tamara Davidson-Uribe b 6 Aug 1980); *Career* in private practice as conslt med herbalist 1985–, tutor and examiner in pharmacology Sch of Phytotherapy 1987–93 (tutor and supervisor Sch Trg Clinic 1988–93), lectr in herbal med Middlesex Univ 1994–95, sr lectr in herbal med and prog ldr BSc in herbal med Middx Univ 1995–; med herbalist memb Multi Disciplinary Complementary Health Practice St Leonard's Hosp London 1990–95; Nat Inst of Med Herbalists: memb 1985–, a dir and student liaison offr 1989–91, vice pres and dir of educn 1991–, pres 1994–96, chm Nat Inst of Med Herbalists Educnl Fndn 1996–; memb Cncl Natural Med Soc 1993–96, chm Cncl for Complementary and Alternative Med 1996– (memb 1991–); *Publications* Herbal First Aid (1993), Herbal Teas: A Guide for Home Use (1994), Encyclopaedia of Medicinal Plants (1996); *Style*— Andrew Chevallier, Esq; ✉ 154 Stoke Newington Church Street, London N16 0JU (☎ 0171 249 2990)

CHEVALLIER GUILD, John Marjoribanks; s of Cyril Harrower Guild (d 1978), and Perronelle Mary, *née* Chevallier; *b* 23 Aug 1933; *Educ* RN Coll Dartmouth; *m* 18 Dec 1965, Jennifer Isobel, da of Col Brian Sherlock Gooch, DSO, TD, DL, JP; 2 s (John Barrington b 1967, Henry b 1968); *Career* Lt Cdr RN serv at sea 1951–63, HM Yacht Britannia 1959, Staff Coll Camberley 1964, cmd HM Ships Badminton, Upton, Bronington 1965–67, served BRNC Dartmouth 1967–69; ret RN to take over family owned cyder, apple juice and cyder vinegar business Aspall Cyder (estab 1728); *Recreations* gardening, travel, good food; *Clubs* Army & Navy; *Style*— John Chevallier Guild, Esq; ✉ Aspall Hall, Stowmarket, Suffolk IP14 6PD (☎ 01728 860492); Aspall Cyder, Aspall Hall, Stowmarket, Suffolk IP14 6PD (☎ 01728 860510, fax 01728 861031)

CHEVILLARD, Pierre Marie; s of Etienne Chevillard, of Regny, France, and Thérese, *née* Becouze; *b* 15 Aug 1958; *Educ* local schs Regny France; *m* 5 June 1982, Alison Jane, da of Leonard Simpson Beamish; 1 s (Jacques Leonard b 5 July 1986), 1 da (Lauren Marie b 11 Dec 1984); *Career* chef; apprentice Les Favieres L'Hopital sur Rhins 1973–76, commis Troisgros Roanne 1976–79; Chewton Glen Hotel: chef garde mangr 1980, sous chef 1981, head chef 1982–; memb Academie Culinaire de France UK, awarded Michelin Rosette; *Recreations* jogging, tennis; *Style*— Pierre Chevillard, Esq; ✉ Chewton Glen Hotel, New Milton, Hants BH25 6QS (☎ 01425 275341)

CHEVRE, Eric Hubert Jean; s of Marcel Chevre, and Colette, *née* Thyebaut; *b* 21 May 1957; *Educ* Ecole des Hautes Etudes Commerciales (MBA); *m*; 2 c; *Career* commercial attaché French Embassy Saudi Arabia 1980–81; Banque Indosuez (Paris): area mangr International Dept 1981–85, sr account exec Domestic Corp Banking Dept 1985–88, vice pres and head of origination International Primary Equity Market (France Asia, Northern Europe) 1988–92, chief exec Indosuez Capital Securities (UK) Ltd (formerly Carr Kitkat & Aitken Ltd) 1992–; *Style*— Eric Chèvre, Esq; ✉ Indosuez Capital Securities (UK) Ltd, 122 Leadenhall Street, London EC3V 4QH (☎ 0171 303 1010, fax 0171 303 1007)

CHEVSKA, Maria Elizabeth; da of Klemens Skwarczewski (d 1985), and Susan Tovell; *b* 30 Oct 1948; *Educ* Our Lady's Convent Abingdon Oxon, Oxford Poly, Byam Shaw Sch of Art London; *Career* artist; head of painting Ruskin Sch of Fine Art Univ of Oxford (fell BNC); *Solo Exhibitions* incl: Air Gallery London 1982, Midland Group Nottingham 1985, Mario Flecha Gallery London 1986, Chapter Gallery Cardiff 1986, Bernard Jacobson Gallery London 1987, Anderson O'Day Gallery London 1989, 1990, 1992 and 1994, Brasenose Coll Oxford 1990, Warehouse Gallery Amsterdam 1993, Angel Row Gallery Nottingham 1994; *Group Exhibitions* incl: Art and the Sea (John Hansard Gallery Univ of Southampton, ICA London) 1981, British Drawing (Hayward Annual London) 1982, Whitechapel Open (Whitechapel Gallery London) 1983–92, Gulbenkian Fndn Award Winners' Prints (touring GB and Ireland) 1983, New Blood on Paper (MOMA Oxford) 1983, Landscape Memory and Desire (Serpentine Gallery London) 1984, Air Gallery Retrospective (London) 1985, Four Selected Painters (Guildhall London) 1986, XXII Int Festival of Painting (Chateau Musée Music Grimaldi France) 1990, Crossover (Anderson O'Day Gallery) 1993, British Painting (Arts Cncl Collection, Royal Festival Hall) 1993, Museo Pigorini Rome 1994, New Painting (touring Darlington, Newcastle and Norwich) 1994, Permission to Speak (Worcester City Museum and Art Gallery, touring Derby and Peterborough); *Work in Public Collections* Arts Cncl of GB, Bolton City Art Gallery, Gulbenkian Fndn, Br Cncl, World Bank, Contemporary Art Soc, New Hall Coll Cambridge; *Awards* Arts Cncl of GB Award 1977, Gtr London Arts Assoc Award 1979 and 1984, Gulbenkian Fndn Printmakers' Award 1982, Austin Abbey Award British Sch Rome 1994; *Style*— Ms Maria Chevska; ✉ Anderson O'Day Gallery, 5 St Quintin Avenue, London W11 (☎ 0181 969 8085, fax 0181 960 3641)

CHEW, (Gaik) Khuan; *b* 10 Oct 1956; *Educ* Roedean Sch, Bath HS GPDST, Univ of London (BMus), RAM, Trinity Coll of Music, London Coll of Furniture, Inchbald Sch of Design (Dip in Interior Design); *Career* interior designer (construction and bldg indust); design dir David Hicks International plc 1986–88, in practice Khuan Chew and Associates (London, Tokyo, Riyadh, Kuala Lumpur, Nicosia) 1988–; int projects incl: Stultan of Brunei's Palace and Parly bldgs, Conf Centre Kuwait, Hotel Okura Tokyo and Kobe, International Tourist Hotel Dubai, Hilton International Hotels Jeddah, Madinah, and Durban (South Africa), Hotel Esplanade Marienbad; FCSD; *Style*— Miss Khuan Chew; ✉ Khuan Chew & Associates International, 101 Westminster Business Square, Durham Street, London SE11 5JE (☎ 0171 582 8898, fax 0171 582 8860)

CHEYNE, David Watson; s of Brig William Watson Cheyne, DSO, OBE (d 1970), and Laurel Audrey, *née* Hutchison; *b* 30 Dec 1948; *Educ* Stowe, Trinity Coll Cambridge (BA); *m* 22 April 1978, (Judith) Gay McAuslane, da of David Anstruther Passey, of The Barn, Bullocks Mills, Herefordshire; 3 s (Alexander William David b 25 Nov 1980, Rory Alistair Watson b 22 Aug 1984, Rupert Valentine Hutchison b 20 Feb 1989); *Career* ptnr Linklaters & Paines 1980– (articled clerk 1972–74, asst slr 1974–80); memb: City of London Slrs' Co 1980, Law Soc; *Recreations* shooting, fishing, collecting antiques; *Style*— David Cheyne, Esq; ✉ 19 Ladbroke Gardens, London W11 2PT (☎ 0171 229 0096); Linklaters & Paines, 59–67 Gresham St, London EC2V 7JA (☎ 0171 606 7080, fax 0171 606 5113, telex 884349,888167)

CHEYNE, Sir Joseph Lister Watson; 3 Bt (UK 1908), of Leagarth, Fetlar, and North Yell, Co Zetland; OBE (1976); s of Col Sir Joseph Cheyne, 2 Bt, MC (d 1957); *b* 10 Oct 1914; *Educ* Stowe, CCC Cambridge; *m* 1, 14 Jan 1938 (m dis 1955), Mary Mort (d 29 Oct 1959), er da of Vice Adm John Derwent Allen, CB (d 1958); 1 s (Patrick John Lister b 1941), 1 da (Ann Caroline Lister (Mrs Ronald E C Adam) b 1939); m 2, 6 Aug 1955, Cicely, da of Thomas Metcalfe, of Padiham, Lancs; 2 s (John Joseph Peter b 1956, James Andrew Watson b 1957), 1 da (Helen Margaret Watson (Mrs Rinaldo G M Rinaldi) b 1959); *Heir* s, Patrick John Lister Cheyne, *qv*; *Career* served WWII North Africa and Italy, Maj; former first sec Br Embassy Rome; curator Keats-Shelley Meml House Rome 1976–90; *Clubs* Circolo della Caccia (Rome); *Style*— Sir Joseph Cheyne, Bt, OBE; ✉ The Haa, Gloup, Cullivoe, Yell, Shetland ZE2 9DD (☎ 01957 744204)

CHEYNE, Patrick John Lister; s (by 1 m) and h of Sir Joseph Lister Watson Cheyne, 3 Bt, OBE, *qv*; *b* 2 July 1941; *Educ* Lancing; *m* 8 June 1968, Helen Louise Trevor, yr da of Louis Smith, of Marine Lodge, 25 Driftwood Gardens, Southsea, Hants; 1 s (Louis Richard Patrick Lister b 25 March 1971), 3 da (Elizabeth Henrietta Louise b 1969, Mary Catherine Fleur b 1974, Caroline Victoria Alice b 1979); *Career* short serv cmmn Lt RN; fine art valuer and auctioneer; FSVA; *Recreations* squash, photography, gardening; *Style*— Patrick Cheyne, Esq; ✉ 37 Chapel Lane, Hale Barns, Cheshire WA15 0AG (☎ 0161 980 3094/941 4879)

CHIANDETTI, Gian Battista (Tito); s of Giovanni Battista Chiandetti (d 1942), and Pauline, *née* Caron (d 1980); *b* 17 March 1935; *Educ* Douai Sch Woolhampton Berks, Harvard Business Sch; *m* 18 March 1968, Maria-Elisa, da of Mario Bulferi-Bulferetti, of Lugano, Switzerland; 1 s (Marco Paolo Angelo b 25 Aug 1973), 1 da (Corinna Elena Paola b 13 Nov 1970); *Career* Trusthouse Forte (now Forte plc): md prods 1973–75, main bd dir 1975–96, with Trusthouse Forte Catering Ltd 1977–84 (md 1979–84), dep chief exec 1984–96, ret; Cavaliere Ufficiale al Merito della Repubblica Italiana; FHCIMA; *Recreations* mountain walking, swimming, rock collecting; *Style*— Tito Chiandetti, Esq; ✉ Daneswood, Monks Walk, South Ascot, Berks SL5 9AZ (☎ 01344 26036)

CHICHESTER, Archdeacon of; *see:* Brotherton, Ven (John) Michael

CHICHESTER, Dermot Michael Claud; s of Lord Desmond Chichester, MC, of Hitchin, Herts, and Felicity Stella, *née* Harrison; *b* 22 Nov 1953; *Educ* Harrow; *m* 1, 26 April 1975 (m dis 1979), Frances Jane Berners, da of Michael Edward Ranulph Allsopp, of Faringdon, Oxon; m 2, 14 July 1982, Shan, da of Alastair Ros McIndoe (d 1984); 1 s (Rory b 1985), 2 da (Ottilie b 1988, Sapphira b 1990); *Career* joined Christie's Fine Art Auctioneers 1974, md Christie Manson and Woods Ltd 1990–93; chm: Christie's South Kensington Ltd 1994– (md 1987–90), Christie's Scotland Ltd 1996– (md 1982–87); *Recreations* cricket, golf, shooting, tennis, skiing; *Clubs* White's; *Style*— Dermot Chichester, Esq; ✉ Lowick House, Lowick, Kettering, Northamptonshire NN14 3BL (☎ 01832 734993); Christie's, 8 King St, London SW1Y 6QT (☎ 0171 839 9060, fax 0171 839 1611, car 0374 271797)

CHICHESTER, 99 Bishop of 1974–; Rt Rev Eric Waldram Kemp; Bishopric founded in Isle of Selsey by Wilfrid, 2 Archbishop of York, removed to Chichester by Stigand after 1075; patron of 96 livings and 9 alternately, the Archdeaconries of Chichester, Lewes and Hastings, and Horsham, and the Prebends (including the three residentiaries) in the Cathedral; s of Tom Kemp, and Florence Lilian, *née* Waldram, of Grove House, Waltham, Grimsby, Lincs; *b* 27 April 1915; *Educ* Brigg GS Lincs, Exeter

Coll Oxford, St Stephen's House Oxford; *m* 1953, Leslie Patricia, 3 da of late Rt Rev Kenneth Escott Kirk, former Bishop of Oxford (d 1954); 1 s, 4 da; *Career* deacon 1939, fell and chaplain Exeter Coll Oxford 1946–69, dean of Worcester 1969–74; author; Hon DD Berne Univ 1987, Hon DLitt Univ of Sussex, DD Oxon; *Clubs* Nat Liberal (pres 1993–); *Style*— The Rt Rev the Lord Bishop of Chichester; ✉ The Palace, Chichester, Sussex (☎ 01243 782161, fax 01243 531332)

CHICHESTER, Giles; MEP (Cons) Devon and E Plymouth (majority 700); s of Sir Francis Charles Chichester KBE (d 1972), and Sheila Mary, *née* Craven (d 1989); *b* 29 July 1946; *Educ* Westminster, Christ Church Coll Oxford (MA); *m* 1979, Virginia; 2 s (George b 1981, Charles b 1990), 1 da (Jessica b 1984); *Career* trainee Univ of London Press and Hodder & Stoughton 1968–69, mangr family business Francis Chichester Ltd 1969–; contested: ILEA election Fulham Parly constituency 1986, Hammersmith and Fulham BC election 1986; PA to Chm Cons Pty Orgn (Lord Tebbit) gen election campaign 1987; campaign asst to Sir Gerard Vaughan MP 1992; MEP (C) Devon and E Plymouth 1994–; chm: St James's Ward Ctee Westminster 1982–84 (memb 1975–88 and 1989–), Hammersmith Cons Assoc 1984–87, London W Euro Constituency Cncl 1987–88, Political Ctee Carlton Club 1992–95 (hon sec 1988–92), Foreign Affairs Forum 1987–90 (hon treas 1985–87), Westminster branch Small Business Bureau (fndr) 1983–88, Dr Edwards' and Bishop King's Estate Charity 1990–93, St James's Place Assoc (conservation/environment) 1980–; memb: Exec Ctee Cons Nat Union 1988–90, Advsy Ctee Gtr London CPC 1984–91 (GP Ctee 1989–91), Nat Advsy Ctee CPC (co-opted) 1987–90 and 1994–, Gen Cncl Cons Gp for Euro 1991–95, Exec Cncl Parly Gp for Energy Studies 1994–; vice pres Euro Energy Fndn 1995–; tstee: Hammersmith United Charities (caring for the elderly) 1985–95, United Charities of St James's Church Piccadilly 1977–, 6s & 7s Club 1980–; primary sch govr: Tower Hamlets 1983–86, Hammersmith 1983–; memb Cncl Air League 1995–; MRIN, FRGS 1972; *sporting career* rowed for sch, coll and England VIIIs (jr trials medal in VIIIs for Oxford), capt and navigator across N Atlantic 1978, 1979 and 1981, and S Indian Ocean 1979; *Recreations* rowing, sailing, snooker, vegetarian cooking; *Clubs* Carlton, London Rowing, Pratts, Royal Western Yacht of England, Royal Yacht Sqdn, United & Cecil; *Style*— Giles Chichester, Esq, MEP; ✉ Longridge, West Hill, Ottery St Mary, Devon EX11 1UX; Francis Chichester Ltd, 9 St James's Place, London SW1A 1PE (☎ 0171 493 0931, fax 0171 409 1830); constituency office: 48 Queen Street, Exeter EX4 3SR (☎ 01392 491815, fax 01392 491588)

CHICHESTER, James Henry Edward; s and h of Sir (Edward) John Chichester, 11 Bt, *qv*; *b* 15 Oct 1951; *Educ* Eton; *m* 10 Feb 1990, (Margaret) Anne, o da of Maj John Walkelyne Chandos-Pole, JP, DL (d 1994), of Radburne Hall, Derbyshire; 2 s (Edward John Chandos-Pole b 27 July 1991, Charles James b 24 Oct 1992); *Career* fndr Chichester Trees and Shrubs Ltd; *Recreations* shooting, fishing, big game hunting and dendrology; *Style*— James Chichester, Esq; ✉ The Mill Studio, Beaulieu, Brockenhurst, Hants SO42 7YG (☎ 01590 612198, fax 01590 612194)

CHICHESTER, Sir (Edward) John; 11 Bt (E 1641), of Raleigh, Devonshire; s of Cdr Sir Edward Chichester, 10 Bt, RN (d 1940); *b* 14 April 1916; *Educ* Radley, RMC Sandhurst; *m* 23 Sept 1950, Hon Anne Rachel Pearl Douglas-Scott-Montagu, da of 2 Baron Montagu of Beaulieu, and widow of Maj Howel Joseph Moore-Gwyn, Welsh Guards; 2 s (James Henry Edward b 1951, Julian John Raleigh b 1963), 3 da (Coral Anne (Mrs Christopher A McEwen) b 1954, Georgina Caroline (Mrs Christopher J Leyland) b 1955, Mary Rose (Mrs Greville P C Howard) b 1957 d 1980); *Heir* s, James Henry Edward Chichester, *qv*; *Career* serv WWII former Capt Royal Scots Fusiliers, Lt RNVR, King's Foreign Service Messenger 1947–50, ICI Ltd 1950–60; patron of one living; *Style*— Sir John Chichester, Bt; ✉ Battramsley Lodge, Boldre, Lymington, Hants SO41 8PT

CHICHESTER, 9 Earl of (UK 1801); Sir John Nicholas Pelham; 14 Bt (E 1611); also Baron Pelham of Stanmer (GB 1762); s of 8 Earl of Chichester (ka 1944), and Ursula (d 1989), da of Walter de Pannwitz, of Benebroek, Holland; *b* 14 April 1944, (posthumously); *Educ* Stanbridge Earls Sch, Mozarteum Salzburg; *m* 1975, Mrs June Marijke Hall, da of Gp-Capt E D Wells, DSO, DFC, of Marbella; 1 da (Lady Eliza b 12 May 1983); *Heir* kinsman, Richard Pelham; *Career* farmer; chm Viva! Health & Leisure Clubs Ltd; *Recreations* music, theatre; *Style*— The Rt Hon the Earl of Chichester; ✉ 53 Shawfield St, London SW3 (☎ 0171 352 1516); Little Durnford Manor, Salisbury, Wilts SP4 6AH

CHICHESTER, Julian Edward; o s of Cdr Michael Guy Chichester, RN, and Eleanor Sarah, *née* Riddell-Blount; *b* 16 Oct 1949; *Educ* Bedales, Univ of Sussex; *Career* called to the Bar Inner Temple 1977, practising barrister 1979–; *Recreations* photography, modelmaking, skiing, scuba diving, travel; *Style*— Julian Chichester, Esq; ✉ 4/5 Gray's Inn Square, Gray's Inn, London WC1R 5AY (☎ 0171 404 5252, fax 0171 242 7803)

CHICHESTER-CLARK, Sir Robert (Robin); kt (1974); s of Capt James Jackson Lenox-Conyngham Chichester-Clark, DSO (and Bar), DL, MP, and Marion Caroline Dehra, *née* Chichester (later Mrs Charles Edward Brackenbury); bro of Baron Moyola, PC, DL (Life Peer), *qv*; *b* 10 Jan 1928; *Educ* Magdalene Coll Cambridge (BA); *m* 1, 6 Nov 1953 (m dis 1972), Jane Helen, o da of Air Marshal Sir (Robert) Victor Goddard, KCB; 1 s, 2 da; *m* 2, 1974, Caroline, o child of Col Anthony Bull, CBE, RE, of London; 2 s; *Career* MP (UU) for Londonderry City and Co 1955–74, Lord Cmmr of the Treasy 1960–61, comptroller of HM Household 1961–64; chief oppn spokesman on: NI 1964–70, Public Bldg and Works 1965–70 and The Arts 1965–68; min of state Dept of Employment 1972–74; mgmnt conslt; dir: Alfred Booth and Co 1975–86, Welbeck Group Ltd; chm: Restoration of Appearance and Function Tst 1988–, Devpt Ctee Arvon Fndn 1995–; tstee RPO Development Tst 1993–Dec 1995; Hon FIWM, FIPM; *Clubs* Brooks's; *Style*— Sir Robin Chichester-Clark

CHICK, Dr Jonathan Dale; s of Cdr William E Chick, DSC, of Darlington, and Vonda Hope, *née* Dale; *b* 23 April 1945; *Educ* Queen Elizabeth GS Darlington, Corpus Christi Coll Cambridge (MA), Univ of Edinburgh (MB ChB, MPhil); *m* 8 March 1969, Josephine Anna; 2 s (Gregory b 8 Sept 1976, Aylwin b 24 Nov 1978); *Career* med posts Edinburgh teaching hosps 1971–76, memb scientific staff MRC 1976–79, conslt psychiatrist and pt/t sr lectr in psychiatry Univ of Edinburgh 1979–, over 50 contribs to scientific books and jls; fndr memb Plinius Maior Soc 1994, advsr WHO, hon memb Minister of Tport Med Advsy Ctee On Driving and Alcohol and Substance Abuse; MRCP 1973, FRCPsych 1988, FRCPE 1990; *Books* Drinking Problems (1984, 2 edn 1992), Seminars in Alcohol and Drug Misuse (1994); *Style*— Dr Jonathan Chick; ✉ Royal Edinburgh Hospital, Edinburgh EH10 5DF (☎ 0131 537 6442, fax 0131 447 3317, e-mail 106036.411@compuserve.com)

CHIDEYA, HE Dr Ngoni Togarepi; s of Abel Mupfumira Chideya, of Mhondoro, Zimbabwe, and Mary, *née* Mutimusakwa; *b* 14 Nov 1944; *Educ* State Univ of NY Buffalo (BA, EdM, PhD); *m* 11 March 1972, Florence Zano, *née* Manjengwa; 1 s (Simukai Bassopo b 26 Oct 1972), 1 da (Paidamoyo Chiwoneso b 20 July 1979); *Career* Zimbabwean diplomat; asst to the Vice Chllr Univ of Zimbabwe 1982–90, dep sec Miny of Foreign Affrs July-Oct 1990, ambass to Sweden, Norway, Denmark and Finland Oct 1990–93, high cmmr to the Ct of St James's 1993–, concurrently ambass to Ireland 1994–; *Books* The Role of the University and its Future in Zimbabwe (co-ed, 1982); *Recreations* music, reading; *Style*— HE Dr Ngoni Togarepi Chideya; ✉ High Commission for the Republic of Zimbabwe, Zimbabwe House, 429 Strand, London WC2R 0SA (☎ 0171 836 7755)

CHIDGEY, David William George; MP (Lib Dem) Eastleigh (majority 9,239); s of Cyril Cecil Chidgey, of Bruton, Somerset, and Winifred Hilda Doris, *née* Weston; *b* 9 July 1942; *Educ* Brune Park Sch, Royal Naval Coll Portsmouth, Portsmouth Poly (Dip in Civil Engrg); *m* 1964, April Carolyn, da of Glyn Idris-Jones; 1 s (David Ryan b 1965), 2 da (Joanna Louise b 1969, Caitlin Victoria b 1971); *Career* grad mech and aeronautical engr The Admiralty 1958–64, sr highways and civil engr motorway design and construction Hants CC 1965–72; Brian Colquhoun and Partners Consltg Engrs 1973–94: princ engr traffic mgmnt studies 1973–78, dir Ireland and chief tech advsr Dept of Tport and Dublin Tport Authy integrated tport planning 1978–88, assoc ptnr (projects totalling over £200m) Repub of Guinea W Africa 1979–83, assoc ptnr and dir responsible for Central and Southern England (incl facilities mgmnt of 13 military bases for MOD) 1988–94; MP (LD) Eastleigh 1994–; parly spokesman: Employment and Training 1995, Transport 1995–; memb Assoc of Consulting Engrs of Ireland 1993, fell Inst of Engrs of Ireland 1990; CEng 1971, MCIT 1983, FIHT 1990, FICE 1993; *Recreations* golf, reading; *Clubs* National Liberal; *Style*— David Chidgey, Esq, MP; ✉ House of Commons, London SW1A OAA (☎ 0171 219 6944)

CHIENE, John; *b* 27 Jan 1937; *Educ* Rugby, Queens' Coll Cambridge (BA); *m* 1; 1 s, 1 da; *m* 2; 1 da; *Career* memb Stock Exchange 1964; Wood Mackenzie and Co stockbrokers: ptnr 1964, managing ptnr 1971, sr ptnr 1974, chm 1984; dir Hill Samuel Group plc 1984, jt chief exec and head of investmt banking Hill Samuel & Co 1986–87, chm County NatWest Wood Mackenzie 1989–90 (chm and chief exec 1988–89), dep chm County NatWest Ltd 1989–90, dir NatWest Investment Bank 1989–90; CIMgt 1984; *Recreations* opera, golf, skiing; *Clubs* Cavalry and Guards', City, New (Edinburgh); *Style*— John Chiene, Esq; ✉ 7 St Leonards Terrace, London SW3 4QB (☎ 0171 730 8979)

CHIGNELL, Anthony Hugh; s of Thomas Hugh Chignell (d 1965), and Phyllis Una, *née* Green; *b* 14 April 1939; *Educ* Downside, St Thomas' Hosp London (MB BS, DO); *m* 16 June 1962, Phillippa Price, da of Rear Adm F B P Brayne-Nicholls, CB, DSC, RN, of London; 1 s (Christopher Damien b 1965), 2 da (Caroline Paula b 1963, Georgina Natalie b 1966); *Career* conslt ophthalmic surgn St Thomas' Hosp 1973–, civilian conslt in ophthalmology to Army 1983–, conslt surgn King Edward VII Hosp for Offrs 1985–, advsr in ophthalmology to Met Police 1987–; author of numerous papers on retinal detachment surgery; govr Royal Nat Coll for the Blind 1987–, memb Cncl Guide Dogs for the Blind 1989–; memb: Oxford Ophthalmology, Club Jules Gonin; OstJ; memb Ct Worshipful Co Spectacle Makers 1987; FRCS 1968; *Books* Retinal Detachment Surgery (2 edns); *Recreations* fly-fishing, golf, the country; *Clubs* Flyfishers', Anglo-Belgian; *Style*— Anthony Chignell, Esq; ✉ 44 Wimpole St, London W1M 7DG (☎ 0171 935 7022, fax 0171 224 3722)

CHILCOTT, Gareth James; s of Dai Chilcott, of Bedminster, Bristol, and Doreen Chilcott; *b* 20 Nov 1956; *Educ* Park Comprehensive; *m* Ann, da of Idris Walters; *Career* rugby union prop forward; clubs: Old Redcliffians RFC, Bath RFC 1976 (over 400 appearances, incl 7 Cup Final victories); rep: Somerset Colts, Somerset RFU, South and Southwest Counties RFU; England: debut v Aust 1984, Five Nations debut v Ireland 1985, memb World Cup squad Aust 1987, tour Aust and Fiji 1988; Br Lions tour Aust 1989; TV pundit (ITV) Rugby World Cup 1991 and 1995; french polisher, lumberjack, mangr security company, md travel co, sports promoter; appeared in Cinderella (Bath Theatre Royal) 1992 and 1994 (Southampton 1993); *Books* Cooch, Mr Chilcott to You (1990); *Recreations* golf, boxing, any sports, spending time with wife, children and friends; *Style*— Gareth Chilcott, Esq; ✉ c/o MP Associates, 156 Sutherland Avenue, London W9 1HP (☎ 0171 286 1793, fax 0171 289 1989)

CHILD, Dr David Francis; s of Canon William Thomas Child (d 1978), and Mary Minwel, *née* Price (d 1990); *b* 4 Feb 1944; *Educ* Abersychan GS, Univ of Birmingham (MB ChB); *m* 6 Dec 1975, Sheila Margaret, da of Rev Robert Edwards McLean (d 1972); 1 s (John Robert b 8 July 1984); *Career* RMO Hammersmith Hosp 1972–75, lectr in med Univ of Manchester 1975–79, conslt physician Wrexham Maelor Hosp 1979–; author of res papers on endocrinology and diabetes; FRCP 1988; *Recreations* photography, model railways; *Style*— Dr David Child; ✉ Whitegate Farm, Gyfelia, Wrexham LL13 0YH; Wrexham Maelor Hospital, Wrexham LL13 7TD (☎ 01978 291100, fax 01978 290951)

CHILD, Denis Marsden; CBE (1987); s of Percival Snowden (d 1964), and Alice (d 1963); *b* 1 Nov 1926; *Educ* Woodhouse Grove Sch; *m* 2, 1973, Patricia, da of Arthur Charlton (d 1979); 2 s (Nicholas b 1958, Richard b 1961), 1 da (Elizabeth b 1956); *Career* chm: International Commodities Clearing House Ltd 1990–93, Lombard North Central plc 1991–96; dir: Coutts and Co 1983–, Nat Westminster Bank plc 1982–96 (dep gp chief exec until 1986), IBM UK Pensions Trust Ltd 1984– (chm 1993–), Eurotunnel plc; memb: Accounting Standards Ctee 1985–90, Securities and Investmts Bd 1986–92; chm: Exec Ctee Br Bankers' Assoc 1986–87, Investors Compensation Scheme 1990–92; Liveryman Worshipful Co of Chartered Secretaries & Administrators; FCIS, FIB, FCT; *Recreations* golf, gardening; *Clubs* Stoke Poges Golf; *Style*— Denis Child, Esq, CBE; ✉ Fairways, Park Road, Farnham Royal, Bucks SL2 3BQ; c/o Coutts & Co, 440 Strand, London WC2R 0QS (☎ 0171 753 1000, fax 0171 753 1066)

CHILD, Prof Dennis; OBE (1997); s of Ronald Wren Child (d 1986), and Elsie May, *née* Dennis; *b* 10 July 1932; *Educ* Blackburn Technical HS and Coll, Univ of London (BSc), Univ of Leeds (MEd), Univ of Bradford (PhD); *m* 10 July 1954, Eveline, da of Thomas Barton (d 1979); 1 s (Paul b 1962), 1 da (Louise (Mrs Greaves) b 1964); *Career* navigator and pilot offr RAF 1951–54; asst teacher in gen sci Easingwold Comprehensive Sch York 1957–59, asst teacher in physics and chemistry Bootham Sch York 1959–62, sr lectr in educn City of Leeds Coll of Educn 1962–67, sr lectr in psychology of educn Univ of Bradford 1973–76 (lectr 1967–73), visiting res prof Psychology Dept Univ of Illinois 1972–73 (visiting prof to Educnl Psychology Dept 1973), prof and head of educn Univ of Newcastle upon Tyne 1976–81; Univ of Leeds: prof of educnl psychology 1981–92, emeritus prof 1992, head Sch of Educn 1984–87; examining posts incl: educnl examiner for Hull, Nottingham, Exeter and Leeds, educnl psychology examiner Sheffield 1974–77, chief external examiner in educnl psychology Univ of Bristol 1975–80, external examiner in educn Leeds 1976–80, chief external examiner in education psychology Sunderland Poly 1978–82, examiner in physiotherapy London 1982–86, chief external examiner in educnl psychology Cambridge 1983–86, examiner for MEd Univs of Cambridge, Hong Kong and Hull 1988–93, examiner for radiography South Bank Univ (formerly South Bank Poly) 1990–94; advsr: Canadian Jl of Behavioural Science, Jl of Multivariate Experimental Personality and Clinical Psychology, Durham and Newcastle Res Review; ed Br Jl of Educational Psychology 1976–84; memb: Scientific Ctee Euro Review of Applied Psychology, Educn Ctee CNAA, Educnl Res Bd SSRC, sub ctees for allocation to insts and for microcomputers in schs, Exec Ctee UCET, Bd of Studies Coll of Radiographers, Advsy Panel Univ of London, Br Psychological Soc Pubns Ctee, Electors' Panel for Profs of Educn Univ of Cambridge, Educn Advsy Panel Yorkshire Arts, Bd of Govrs Northern Sch of Contemporary Dance, Bd of Govrs UC Ripon and York St John; chm: Academic and Registration Bd Coll of Speech Therapists (memb Ethics Ctee), Educn Advsy Panel London Festival Ballet (memb Bd of Govrs), Cncl for the Advancement of Communication with Deaf People; advsr Br Cncl; FBPsS, FCST, CPsychol; *Books* incl: The Essentials of Factor Analysis (1970, 2 edn 1990), Initiating Research in Colleges of Education (jtly, 1968), Motivation and Dynamic Structure (with Prof R B Cattell, 1975), Psychology and the Teacher (1973, 6 edn 1997), Taking the DC Test: A Guide for Candidates, Applications of Psychology for the Teacher (1986), Nurse

Selection - Helping Applicants and Selectors Make Decisions (1988), Theory and Practice of Education (gen ed), Painters in the Northern Counties of England and Wales (1994); contribs incl: British Journal of Educational Psychology, Education (1965), British Journal of Social and Clinical Psychology (1966), Educational Research (1970), Physiotherapy (1974), British Journal of Guidance and Counselling (1976), Vocational Aspect (1979), Personality, Cognition and Values (1985), The Analysis of Personality in Research and Assessment: A Tribute to Raymond B Cattell (1988); *Recreations* walking, travel, memb Bradford Festival Choral Soc, watching ballet, North of England artists; *Style—* Prof Dennis Child, OBE; ✉ School of Education, University of Leeds, Leeds LS2 9JT (☎ 0113 233 4672, fax 0113 244 5260)

CHILD, Graham Derek; s of Albert Edward Child, of Broadstone, Dorset (d 1992), and Phyllis, *née* Wooldridge (d 1973); *b* 24 June 1943; *Educ* Bedford Sch, Worcester Coll Oxford (MA); *Career* Slaughter and May: asst slr 1968–75, ptnr 1976–95, resident ptnr Frankfurt 1993–95, Slaughter and May visiting fell in Euro law and regulation Lincoln Coll Oxford 1995–; memb Law Soc; *Books* Common Market Law of Competition (with C W Bellamy QC, 1978); *Recreations* outdoor activities, European languages; *Clubs* Hurlingham, Highgate Golf, Woking Golf; *Style—* Graham Child, Esq; ✉ Lincoln College, Oxford OX1 3DR (☎ 01865 279800)

CHILD, Sir (Coles John) Jeremy; 3 Bt (UK 1919), of Bromley Palace, Bromley, Kent; s of Sir (Coles) John Child, 2 Bt (d 1971), and Sheila, *née* Mathewson (d 1964); *b* 20 Sept 1944; *Educ* Eton, Poitiers Univ (Dip); *m* 1, 1971 (m dis 1976), Deborah Jane, da of Henry Percival Snelling; 1 da ((Honor) Melissa b 1973); m 2, 1978 (m dis 1987), Jan Todd, yst da of Bernard Todd, of Kingston-upon-Thames; 1 s ((Coles John) Alexander b 10 May 1982), 1 da (Leonora b 25 July 1980); m 3, 1987, Elizabeth, yst da of Rev Grenville Morgan, of Canterbury, Kent; 1 s (Patrick Grenville b 3 Jan 1991), 1 da (Eliza Caroline b 29 Jan 1989); *Heir* s, (Coles John) Alexander Child b 10 May 1982; *Career* actor; trained Brisol Old Vic Theatre Sch, subsequently in rep Windsor, Guildford, Bromley and Colchester; *Theatre* 3 plays Royal Court, Misalliance (Mermaid), Scenes from an Execution (with Glenda Jackson, Almeida), Dr Richard Warren in The Madness of George III (RNT); West End: Conduct Unbecoming (Queen's), Donkey's Years (Globe), Oh Kay and An Ideal Husband (Westminster); Out of Order (Far East tour) 1995 *Television incl* Father, dear Father, Wings, Glittering Prizes, Edward and Mrs Simpson, The Jewel in the Crown, Edge of Darkness, Fairly Secret Army, First Among Equals, Game Set and Match, The Gravy Train Goes East, Fools Gold, Harnessing Peacocks, Headhunters, Demob, Sharpe's Enemy, Frank Stubbs; *Films incl* High Road to China 1982, Give My Regards to Broad St 1982/83, A Fish Called Wanda 1987, Taffin 1987, The Madness of George III 1994; *Recreations* travel, cooking, gardening; *Clubs* Garrick; *Style—* Sir Jeremy Child, Bt; ✉ c/o Joyce Edwards Representation, 275 Kennington Road, London SE11 6BY (☎ 0171 735 5736, fax 0171 820 1845)

CHILD, Prof John; s of Clifton Child (d 1994), and Hilde, *née* Hurwitz; *b* 10 Nov 1940; *Educ* Purley GS (state scholar), St John's Coll Cambridge (scholar, MA, PhD, ScD); *m* 1965, Dr Elizabeth Anne Mitchiner, da of Geoffrey Mitchiner; 1 s (Martin Edmund b 12 Jan 1970), 1 da (Caroline Marianne b 10 April 1973); *Career* personnel offr and systems analyst Rolls Royce Ltd 1965–66, research fell Aston Univ 1966–68, sr research offr London Business Sch 1968–73, prof of organizational behaviour Aston Univ 1973–91, dean Aston Business Sch 1986–89, Guinness prof of mgmnt studies Univ of Cambridge 1991–; fell St John's Coll Cambridge 1991–; visiting prof Euro Inst for Advanced Studies in Mgmnt 1971–75; dean and dir China-Euro Community Mgmnt Inst Beijing China 1989–90, dir Judge Inst of Mgmnt Studies Univ of Cambridge 1992–93, dir Centre for Int Business and Mgmnt 1995–, dir Strategic Partnerships International Ltd 1996–; ed-in-chief Organization Studies 1992–96; fndr memb Br Acad of Mgmnt 1987; memb Mgmnt and Industl Relations Ctee SSRC 1978–82; memb: Br Sociological Assoc 1962, Inst of Mgmnt (formerly Br Inst of Mgmnt) 1973, Acad of Mgmnt 1977, Acad of Int Business 1993; distinguished lectr Acad of Mgmnt 1980 and 1991; Hon Dr Helsinki Sch of Economics 1996; *Publications* author of 14 books incl: Management in China (1994), Management Issues in China (with Y Lu, 1996); also author of numerous articles; *Recreations* dinghy sailing, mountain walking, bridge; *Clubs* Earlswood Lakes Sailing; *Style—* Prof John Child; ✉ St John's College, Cambridge CB2 1TP (☎ 01223 339616, fax 01223 339617, e-mail JC160@hermes.cam.ac.uk)

CHILD, John Frederick; s of Frederick George Child (d 1980), and Doris Frances, *née* Henley; *b* 18 April 1942; *Educ* King Edward's Sch Bath, Univ of Southampton (BA), Sidney Sussex Coll Cambridge (scholar, LLB), Univ of Columbia Leiden (Dip American Law); *m* 2 Sept 1972, Dr Jean Alexander, da of Dr Albert Alexander Cunningham, of Glenone, Haymeads Drive, Esher; 2 s (Andrew b 25 May 1974, Jeremy b 11 May 1977); *Career* called to the Bar Lincoln's Inn 1966, Droop Scholar and Tancred Common Law Student; Chancery barr; memb Hon Soc of Lincoln's Inn, supervisor in law Sidney Sussex Coll Cambridge 1966–78; memb: Chancery Bar Assoc, Revenue Bar Assoc; *Books* main contrib Vol 19 (Sale of Land) Encyclopaedia of Forms and Precedents (4 edn), Accumulation and Maintenance Settlements, Encyclopaedia of Forms and Precedents (4 edn); *Recreations* tennis, badminton; *Style—* John Child, Esq; ✉ 17 Old Buildings, Lincolns Inn, London, WC2A 3UP (☎ 0171 405 9653, fax 0171 404 8089)

CHILD, Prof Mark Sheard; *b* 17 Aug 1937; *Educ* Pocklington Sch Yorks, Clare Coll Cambridge (BA, PhD); *m*; 3 c; *Career* lectr in theoretical chemistry Univ of Glasgow 1963–66; Univ of Oxford: lectr in theoretical chemistry 1966–89, Aldrichian praelector in chemistry 1989–92, prof of chemical dynamics 1992–94, Coulson prof of theoretical chemistry 1994–; professorial fell University Coll Oxford 1994–, emeritus fell St Edmund Hall Oxford 1994– (tutorial fell 1966–94); FRS 1989; *Style—* Prof Mark Child, FRS; ✉ Physical and Theoretical Chemistry Laboratory, South Parks Road, Oxford OX1 3QZ

CHILDERLEY, Stuart Michael; s of Michael Childerley, of Willoughby-on-the Wolds, Notts, and Ann, *née* Baker; *b* 17 Feb 1966; *Educ* Burleigh Community Coll; *Career* yachtsman; World and Euro youth champion 1984, Finn Dinghy Class Euro champion 1987, fourth place Finn Class Olympic Games 1988 and 1992, Euro champion Finn Class 1992, Soling Class World Matchrace champion 1995; first tactician Br team Admiral's Cup winners (Indulgence) 1989, skipper Br Admiral's Cup team 1993; coach Royal Yachting Assoc Youth Prog; *Recreations* golf, squash, swimming; *Clubs* Staunton Harold Sailing; *Style—* Stuart Childerley, Esq

CHILDS, Edward Samuel (Ted); OBE (1997); s of Samuel Walter Childs (d 1980), of London, and Helena Elizabeth, *née* Flynn; *b* 26 Dec 1934; *Educ* St Bonaventure's Sch London E7, Univ of Nottingham (BA); *m* 1963, Kathleen Anne, da of Denis Houlihan; 2 da (Anne-Marie b 28 Aug 1965, Madeleine b 21 June 1968); *Career* Nat Serv cmmnd Pilot Offr RAF 1958, Flying Offr 1959; ABC Television Ltd: joined as trainee prog dir 1960, documentary prodr 1967–73 (progs incl This Week and The World at War); television drama prodr Euston Films Ltd 1973–78 (progs incl The Sweeney, Van Der Valk and Quatermass), freelance writer, prodr and dir 1978–84; Central Independent Television plc: head of drama 1984–87, md Central Films 1987–95, exec prodr various series incl Inspector Morse, Cadfael, Soldier Soldier, Peak Practice and Kavanagh QC; chm BAFTA 1993/94; Cyril Bennett Award RTS 1995, RTS Baird Medal 1995; FRTS 1991; *Recreations* sailing, walking, theatre, cinema; *Clubs* RAC, Royal Harwich Yacht; *Style—* Ted Childs, Esq, OBE; ✉ c/o Carlton UK Television Ltd, 35–38 Portman Square, London W1H 0NU (☎ 0171 612 7395)

CHILDS, Norman; s of late Rev Leonard Arthur Childs, of Melton Mowbray, Leicestershire and Dorothy May, *née* Taylor; *b* 14 Nov 1944; *Educ* The Winifred Portland Sch, Nottingham Coll of Art, Central London Poly, Harrow Coll of Technol; *m* 16 April 1966, Judith, da of Alfred Lidster; 1 s (Nigel Christopher b 9 Feb 1974), 1 da (Helen Ruth b 10 July 1971); *Career* asst med photographer Inst of Obstetrics and Gynaecology Chelsea Hosp for Women 1963–64, photographer Chester Beatty Res Inst, Inst of Cancer Res 1964–67, head Photographic Unit Colt International Ltd Havant Hants 1967–77, M T Walters & Assocs Mexborough S Yorks 1977–81 (assignments ME and Sudan), set up Norman Childs Photography 1981; Br Inst of Professional Photography: memb Industl Ctee 1977–82, memb Cncl 1979–82; memb Admissions and Qualifications Bd 1986–; CSD assessor of external examinations in photography Blackpool Coll of Technol 1983–86, memb Industl Liaison Ctee Wednesbury Coll of Technol 1984; *Awards* best black and white photograph Financial Times 1972, BIPP Wessex and Yorkshire Region award 1975 and 1978, 3M Professional Photographic Products award 1980, BIPP Central Region awards 1984, 1985 and 1987, Silver award World Cncl of Professional Photographers 1988–89, 2 Silver awards BIPP Nat Exhibition 1991, 1 Bronze award BIPP Nat Exhibition 1992 and 1993, two Bronze awards 1994; FBIPP 1977, FCSD 1980; *Recreations* land yachting; *Clubs* Anglia Land Yacht (chm); *Style—* Norman Childs, Esq

CHILLINGWORTH, John Henry; *b* 18 Jan 1928; *Career* trainee Hulton Press Ltd 1944–46; served RE as field engr instr and photographer 1946–49; photo journalist Picture Post 1949–56, freelance photojournalist 1956–68; ptnr, exec dir and dir of various advertising and mktg agencies 1968–79; mangr gp publicity Celcon Group 1979–85, ptnr JHC Communication (mktg advertising and creative consultancy) 1985–; writer on photography, lectr on photographic journalism; BIPP Presidential Award 1988; Soc of Authors; FBIPP (ret); *Style—* John Chillingworth, Esq; ✉ 5 Thames Close, Warminster, Wilts BA12 9QB (☎ 01985 846928, fax 01985 212526)

CHILSTON, 4 Viscount (UK 1911); Alastair George Akers-Douglas; s of late Capt Ian Stanley Akers-Douglas (gs of 1 Viscount Chilston), by his 2 w, Phyllis Rosemary; suc kinsman, 3 Viscount Chilston, 1982; *b* 5 Sept 1946; *Educ* Ashdown House, Eton; *m* 1971, Juliet Anne, da of late Lt-Col Nigel Lovett, of The Old Rectory, Inwardleigh, Okehampton, Devon; 3 s (Hon Oliver, Hon Alexander Hugh b 1975, Hon Dominic b 1979); *Heir* s, Hon Oliver Ian Akers-Douglas b 17 Oct 1973; *Career* film producer; *Style—* The Rt Hon the Viscount Chilston; ✉ The Old Rectory, Twyford, nr Winchester, Hants (☎ 01962 712300)

CHILTON, John James; s of Thomas William Chilton (d 1943), and Eileen Florence, *née* Burke (d 1967); *b* 16 July 1932; *m* 1963, Teresa, da of Thomas McDonald; 1 da (Jennifer b 1963), 2 s (Martin b 1964, Barnaby b 1971); *Career* jazz musician, writer, composer; worked in advertising agency then nat newspaper; professional jazz trumpeter 1957–; ldr own band 1958, memb Bruce Turner's Jump Band 1958–63, memb various big bands led by Mike Daniels and Alex Welsh 1960s, ldr own band and backing musician for Buck Clayton, Ben Webster, Bill Coleman, Charlie Shavers, Roy Eldridge 1963–69, ldr Feetwarmers 1972– (jt ldr with Wally Fawkes 1969–72), musical dir for George Melly 1972–; *Awards* Grammy for best album notes 1983, ARSC Award USA for best researched jazz and blues book 1992; *Books* Who's Who of Jazz (1970), Billie's Blues (1974), McKinney's Music (1978), Teach Yourself Jazz (1979), A Jazz Nursery (1980), Stomp Off Let's Go (1983), Sidney Bechet - The Wizard of Jazz (1987), The Song of the Hawk (1990), Let The Good Times Roll (1992), Who's Who of British Jazz (1996); *Style—* John Chilton, Esq

CHILTON, (Frederick) Paul; s of Charles Frederick Chilton, of Rochester, Kent, and Elizabeth, *née* Docherty; *b* 28 July 1946; *Educ* St Stephens Roman Catholic Sch, NW Kent Coll of Technol; *m* 1991, Moira, *née* Seaward; *Career* dir Alexander Group Howden Ltd; memb UK Int Insur Brokers Ctee; *Recreations* shooting, fishing, equestrian sports; *Style—* Paul Chilton, Esq; ✉ Alexander Howden Group Ltd, 8 Devonshire Sq, London EC2M 4PL (☎ 0171 623 5500, fax 0171 216 3760)

CHILVER, Brian Outram; s of Flt Lt Bertram Montagu Chilver (d 1990), and Edith Gwendoline, *née* Adams (d 1984); *b* 17 June 1933; *Educ* Univ Coll Sch; *m* 23 June 1956, Erica Mary, da of Lawrence Trewhella Howell (d 1993), of Goring on Sea, Sussex; 2 s (Andrew b 1961, David b 1963), 2 da (Hazel b 1957, Heather b 1959); *Career* Flying Offr RAF 1955–57; trainee CA Temple Gothard and Co 1949–55 (qualified 1954), Barton Mayhew 1957–59, sr ptnr Temple Gothard 1974–85 (re-joined 1959, ptnr 1960), conslt Touche Ross and Co 1985–87; chm: Laing Properties plc 1987–90 (non-exec dir 1982, dep chm 1986), Seafield plc 1990–96, Eskmuir Properties plc 1990–, TEAR Fund 1990–, Forward Technology Industries plc 1991–, Hildenborough Evangelistic Trust Ltd 1982–; dir: Premier Livestock Auctions Ltd (formerly Yeovil Livestock Auctioneers Ltd) 1965–, John Laing plc (non-exec) 1988–, London Christian Housing plc 1991–, International Christian Films Ltd 1991–; FCA, ACWA; *Recreations* walking, swimming, reading, travel, Christian charitable activity in UK and overseas; *Style—* Brian Chilver, Esq; ✉ Bretaye, Limbourne Lane, Fittleworth, W Sussex RH20 1HR (☎ 01798 865366); Eskmuir Properties plc, 8 Queen Anne St, London W1M 9LD (☎ 0171 436 2339, fax 0171 436 2307)

CHILVER, Baron (Life Peer UK 1987), of Cranfield, Beds; Sir (Amos) Henry Chilver; kt (1978); e s of Amos Henry Chilver, of Southend-on-Sea, and A E Chilver, *née* Mack; *b* 30 Oct 1926; *Educ* Southend HS, Univ of Bristol; *m* 1959, Claudia Mary Beverley, o da of Sir Wilfrid Vernon Grigson, CSI (d 1948), of Pelynt, Cornwall; 3 s (Hon John b 1964, Hon Mark b 1965, Hon Paul b 1967), 2 da (Hon Helen (Hon Mrs Prentice) b 1960, Hon Sarah (Hon Mrs Vaughan) b 1962); *Career* prof of civil engrg Univ of London 1961–69, vice chllr Cranfield Inst of Technol 1970–89; chm: English China Clays plc 1989–95, Milton Keynes Development Corporation 1983–92, RJB Mining plc 1992–, Chiroscience plc 1995–, Plymouth Devpt Corp 1996–; dir: ICI plc 1990–93, Zeneca plc 1993–95; pres: Inst of Mgmnt Servs 1982–, Inst of Logistics 1993–95; Hon DSc: Leeds 1982, Bristol 1983, Salford 1983, Strathclyde 1986, Bath 1986, Cranfield 1989, Buckingham 1990, Compiegne (France) 1990; hon fell CCC Cambridge 1981; FRS 1982, FEng 1977, CIMgt; *Clubs* Athenaeum, United Oxford and Cambridge; *Style—* The Rt Hon Lord Chilver, FRS, FEng; ✉ Lanlawren House, Trenewen, Looe, Cornwall PL13 2PZ

CHIN, Dr Lincoln Li-Jen; s of Pun-Jian Chin, and Grace Chin, *née* Sun; *b* 2 Nov 1942; *Educ* Christ's Coll Cambridge, MIT USA (ScD); *m* 21 Jan 1971, Lillian Chen Ming, da of Wen Hsiung Chu; 1 s (Nicholas b 1973), 1 da (Tamara b 1975); *Career* dep chm Chindwell Co Ltd; memb Forest Stewardship Cncl; *Recreations* walking, swimming, travelling, music; *Clubs* Utd Oxford and Cambridge; *Style—* Dr Lincoln Chin; ✉ Chindwell Co Ltd, Hyde House, The Hyde, London NW9 6JT (☎ 0181 205 6171, fax 0181 205 8800)

CHINN, James (Jimmie); s of Edith Chinn (d 1985); *b* 30 March 1940; *Educ* Durnford Street Secdy Modern Middleton Manchester, RADA, Whitelands Coll Putney; *Career* teacher in Southall Middx, full time playwright 1984–; memb Writers' Guild of GB; *Radio* From Here to the Library, Too Long An Autumn, A Woman Who Does, In Room Five Hundred and Four, A Different Way Home, Where Evening Gathers; *Stage* Our Linda, Our Carol and Freda 1986, To The Island 1986, Albert Make Us Laugh 1987, After September 1989, Straight and Narrow 1992 (nominated Writers' Guild Macallan Award for Best West End Play 1992), Sylvia's Wedding, Whatever Happened to Kathy Kirby?, Home Before Dark, Finishing Touches; *TV* writer on Emmerdale (Yorks TV) 1988–, A Different Way Home; *Screenplay* In By The Half; *Work Published* From Here to the Library, A Respectable Funeral, Take Away the Lady, Too Long An Autumn, In Room Five Hundred and Four, But Yesterday, Pity About Kitty, Interior Designs,

Straight and Narrow, In By the Half, After September, Home Before Dark; *Recreations* reading, walking, listening to radio; *Style*— Jimmie Chinn, Esq; ✉ Richard Hatton Ltd, 29 Roehampton Gate, London SW15 5JR (☎ 0181 876 6699, fax 0181 876 8278)

CHINN, Sir Trevor Edwin; kt (1990), CVO; s of Rosser Chinn, and Sarah, *née* Feitelson; *b* 24 July 1935; *Educ* Clifton, King's Coll Cambridge; *m* 1965, Susan Avril, da of Louis Speelman; 2 s (David b 1966, Simon b 1969); *Career* Lex Service PLC: joined 1955, joined bd 1959, md 1968, chm and chief exec 1973–96, chm 1996–; tstee: Duke of Edinburgh's Award Scheme 1978–88, Royal Acad Tst (dep chm 1996–); dir Hampstead Theatre; chief barker Variety Club of GB 1977 and 1978, vice chm Great Ormond St Hosp Redevpt Appeal, pres Jt Israel Appeal of GB, chm Br/Israel Public Affrs Centre; Freeman: City of London, Worshipful Co of Painter-Stainers; *Recreations* fishing; *Clubs* RAC; *Style*— Sir Trevor Chinn, CVO; ✉ Lex Service PLC, Lex House, 17 Connaught Place, London W2 2EL (☎ 0171 705 1212, telex 23668 LEXGRP G, fax 0171 723 5501)

CHINUBHAI, Sir Udayan; 3 Bt (UK 1913), of Shahpur, Ahmedabad, India; original name of baronetcy Runchorelal; s of Sir Chinubhai Madhowlal Runchorelal, 2 Bt (d 1990), and Tanumati Zaverilal (d 1970), da of Zaverilal Bulakhiram Mehta, of Ahmedabad; *b* 25 July 1929; *m* 1953, Muneera Khodadad, da of Khodadad Mancherjee Fozdar, of Bombay; 1 s, 3 da; *Heir* s, Prashant Chinubhai b 15 Dec 1955; *Career* nat pres India Jr Chamber 1961–62, currently a Jaycee senator; represented Gujarat in Ranji Trophy in Cricket and played the combined Univ XI against Pakistan; represented India in int events in target shooting on 4 occasions; awarded Arjun award for target shooting 1972–73; *Recreations* cricket, target shooting; *Style*— Sir Udayan Chinubhai, Bt

CHIODINI, Dr Peter Leslie; s of Leslie Chiodini (d 1990), of London, and Catherine Beatrice, *née* Coleman; *b* 27 Oct 1948; *Educ* Dunstable GS, King's Coll Hosp Med Sch (BSc, PhD, MRCS, LRCP, MB BS, MRCP); *m* 5 Sept 1981, Jane Heather, da of Alan Edgar Bennett; 2 s (James Peter b 13 Jan 1986, Jonathan Peter b 19 Aug 1988); *Career* house physician KCH 1978, house surgn Royal Sussex Co Hosp 1979, SHO: St James's Hosp 1979–80, Royal Marsden Hosp 1980; med registrar: St George's Hosp 1981, Broadgreen Hosp 1981–82; sr registrar East Birmingham Hosp 1982–85, conslt parasitologist Hosp for Tropical Diseases 1985–; hon sr lectr LSHTM; Stephen Whittaker prize West Midlands Physicians' Assoc 1984, Medicine-Gillilland travelling fell 1985; FRSTM&H 1970 (memb Cncl 1987–90), FRCP 1992, FRCPath 1996; *Recreations* cathedrals, running, angling; *Style*— Dr Peter Chiodini; ✉ 9 Lavenham Drive, Biddenham, Bedford MK40 4QR; Department of Clinical Parasitology, Hospital for Tropical Diseases, 4 St Pancras Way, London NW1 0PE (☎ 0171 387 4411, fax 0171 383 0041)

CHIPPERFIELD, David Alan; s of Alan John Chipperfield, and Peggy, *née* Singleton; *b* 18 Dec 1953; *Educ* Wellington, Architectural Association (AADipl); *partner*, Dr Evelyn Stern; 3 s (Chester, Gabriel, Raphael), 1 da (Celeste); *Career* architect; princ David Chipperfield Architects, visiting lectr Harvard Univ 1986–87; visiting prof: Univ of Naples 1991, Univ of Graz 1992, Ecole Polytechnique Fédérale de Lausanne 1993; prof of Staatliche Akademie de Bildenden Künste in Stuttgart 1995; projects incl: shops for Issey Miyake London and Japan 1986–87, Arnolfini Gallery Bristol 1987, private museum Tokyo 1989, River and Rowing Museum Henley-on-Thames 1994; fndr and dir 9H Gallery London; winner Premio Palladio 1993; tstee Architectural Fndn London; RIBA; *Books* Theoretical Practice (1994); *Style*— David Chipperfield, Esq; ✉ 28 Cleveland Square, London W2 6DD (☎ 0171 262 3422); David Chipperfield Architects, 1a Cobham Mews, Agar Grove, London NW1 9SB (☎ 0171 267 9422, fax 0171 267 9347)

CHIPPINDALE, Christopher Ralph; s of Keith Chippindale, and Ruth Chippindale; *b* 13 Oct 1951; *Educ* Sedbergh, St John's Coll Cambridge (BA), Girton Coll Cambridge (PhD); *m* 1976, Anne, *née* Lowe; 2 s, 2 da; *Career* ed: Penguin Books, Hutchinson Publishing Group 1974–82, Antiquity 1987–; res fell in archaeology Girton Coll Cambridge 1985–87, asst curator Cambridge Univ Museum of Archaeology and Anthropology 1987–; *Books* Stonehenge Complete (1983 and 1994), Who Owns Stonehenge? (1990); *Recreations* archaeology, worrying; *Style*— Christopher Chippindale, Esq; ✉ 85 Hills Rd, Cambridge

CHISHOLM, Prof Alexander William John (Alec); s of Thomas Alexander Chisholm (d 1948), of Bryn yr Efail Cwm y Glo Gwynedd, and Maude Mary, *née* Robinson (d 1972); *b* 18 April 1922; *Educ* Brentwood Sch Essex, Northampton Poly, Manchester Coll of Sci and Technol, Royal Tech Coll Salford, Univ of London (BSc Eng); *m* 29 March 1945, Aline Mary (d 1995), da of Roy Eastwood (d 1995); 1 s (Roger b 21 Oct 1951), 1 da (Diana b 4 June 1955); *Career* Nat Fire Serv WWII; gp head Res Dept Metropolitan Vickers Electrical Co Ltd 1944–49, sr scientific offr (later princ scientific offr) Nat Engrg Laboratory 1949–57, UK Scientific Mission Br Embassy USA 1952–54, head Dept of Mechanical Engrg (later prof) Royal Coll of Advanced Technol Salford 1957–67, prof of mechanical engrg Univ of Salford 1967–82, res prof (later professorial fell) Univ of Salford 1982–94, emeritus prof Univ of Salford 1994–; visitor Engrg Dept Univ of Cambridge, visiting fell Wolfson Coll Cambridge 1973–74, chm Univ of Salford Industrial Centre Ltd 1976–82 (incorporated 1976); chm: Indust Admin Gp IMechE 1960–62, Mechanical/Prodn Engrg Ctee Nat Cncl for Technol Awards (vice chm Bd of Studies Engrg, govr 1960–65), Engrg Profs Conf 1976–80; pres CIRP 1983–84 (hon life memb 1987); memb Technol Ctee UGC 1969–74, memb Ct Cranfield Inst of Technol 1974–90; author of numerous papers in tech and professional literature; FIMechE 1959, FIEE 1963; *Recreations* hill walking, sailing, tree planting; *Clubs* Athenaeum; *Style*— Prof Alec Chisholm; ✉ 12 Legh Road, Prestbury, Macclesfield, Cheshire SK10 4HX (☎ and fax 01625 829412); University of Salford, Room S016 Statham Building, Salford M5 4WT (☎ 0161 745 5000, fax 0161 745 5999)

CHISHOLM, John A R; *b* 27 Aug 1946; *Educ* Univ of Cambridge (BA); m, 2 c; *Career* apprentice Vauxhall Motors Luton 1964–69; Scicon Ltd: analyst and programmer London 1969–74, managing conslt and fndr memb Milton Keynes Branch 1974–76, gp mangr 1976–79; CAP Scientific: fndr 1979–81, md 1981–86, memb Bd 1986–88, md UK 1988–91; chief exec Defence Evaluation and Res Agency 1991–; memb Cncl CSA; CEng, FIEE, FEng 1996; *Style*— John Chisholm, Esq, FEng; ✉ Defence Evaluation and Research Agency (DERA), Farnborough, Hants GU14 6TD (☎ 01252 394500, fax 01252 370753)

CHISHOLM, Malcolm; MP (Lab) Edinburgh Leith (majority 4,985); *b* 7 March 1949; *Educ* Univ of Edinburgh (MA, DipEd); *m*; 3 c; *Career* former teacher of English Castlebrae HS and Broughton HS; MP (Lab) Edinburgh Leith 1992–; memb Educnl Inst of Scotland; *Style*— Malcolm Chisholm, Esq, MP; ✉ House of Commons, London SW1A 0AA

CHISHOLM, Prof Michael Donald Inglis; s of Samuel Martin Chisholm (d 1985), of London, and Alice Winifred, *née* Lee; *b* 10 June 1931; *Educ* St Christopher Sch Letchworth Herts, St Catharine's Coll Cambridge (MA, ScD); *m* 1, 12 Sept 1959 (m dis 1981), Edith Gretchen Emma, da of Adolf Hoof (d 1984); 1 s (Andrew b 1966), 2 da (Annabel b 1960, Julia b 1962); m 2, 13 Dec 1987, Judith Carola, da of Henry Murray (d 1960); *Career* Nat Serv 1950–51, cmmnd 2 Lt 1950; dept demonstrator Inst for Agric Econs (formerly Inst for Res in Agric Econs) 1954–59, lectr in geography Bedford Coll London 1962–64 (asst lectr 1960–62), visiting sr lectr in geography Univ of Ibadan Nigeria 1964–65, prof of econ and social geography Univ of Bristol 1972–76 (lectr in geography 1965–67, reader in econ geography 1967–72), prof of geography Univ of Cambridge 1976–96 (emeritus prof 1996), head Dept of Geography Univ of Cambridge 1976–84; memb: SSRC 1967–72, Local Govt Boundary Cmmn for Eng 1971–78, Rural Devpt Cmmn 1981–90, Eng Advsy Ctee on Telecommunications 1990–92, Local Govt Cmmn for Eng 1992–95; conservator for the River Cam 1979– (chm 1991–); memb Inst of Br Geographers 1954, FRGS 1954; *Books* Rural Settlement and Land Use (1962), Freight Flows and Spatial Aspects of the British Economy (jtly, 1973), The Changing Pattern of Employment (jtly, 1973), Inner City Waste Land (jtly, 1987), Regional Forecasting (jt ed, 1971), Spatial Policy Problems of the British Economy (jt ed, 1971), Modern World Development (1982), Regions in Recession and Resurgence (1990), Shared Space: Divided Space (jt ed, 1990), Britain on the Edge of Europe (1995); *Style*— Prof Michael Chisholm; ✉ University of Cambridge, Department of Geography, Downing Place, Cambridge CB2 3EN (☎ 01223 333399, fax 01223 333392)

CHISHOLM, Dr (Diana) Morag; da of Prof Erik Chisholm (d 1965), and Diana Brodie Chisholm (d 1984); *b* 11 June 1933; *Educ* Univ of Capetown (MB ChB, MD); *m* 12 Dec 1952, Professor Ralph Wright (d 1990); 5 da (Dr Teresa Lyn Wright b 9 Feb 1954, Dr Deirdre Jane Wright b 4 Jan 1957, Jennifer Gail b 3 Feb 1959, Dr Fiona Alison Wright b 4 March 1963, Erika Morag b 15 Dec 1965); *Career* res asst Dept of Haematology and Med Radcliffe Infirmary Oxford 1962–71, res fell Dept of Haematology Yale Univ Med Sch 1968–69, lectr in haematology Univ of Southampton 1974–75, conslt haematologist and sr lectr in haematology Univ of Southampton Gp of Hosps; memb: BMA, Br Soc for Haematology; FRCPath 1986; *Style*— Dr Morag Chisholm; ✉ St Cross Lodge, St Cross Road, Winchester SO23 9RX (☎ 01962 866499); Department of Haematology, Southampton General Hospital, Tremona Rd, Southampton SO9 4XY (☎ 01703 796267, fax 01703 794134)

CHISM, Nigel William Michael Goddard; s of His Hon Judge Michael William McGladdery Chism, of London, and May Elizabeth Collins, *née* Goddard (d 1993); *b* 2 July 1954; *Educ* The John Lyon Sch Harrow, Poly of Central London; *m* Christine Pamela, da of Eric Leonard Brown, of Berks; 1 s (William b 23 July 1982); *Career* TA 4 V Bn Royal Green Jackets 1972–75; CA; Arthur Young (formerly Josolyne Layton Bennett and Co, now Ernst & Young) 1974–82, asst govt auditor Bermuda 1982–83, jt md Kingsway Rowland Ltd 1988–90 (joined 1983), md College Hill Associates Ltd 1991–; hon treas Family Welfare Assoc; Freeman City of London, Liveryman Worshipful Company of Wheelwrights; FCA 1989 (ACA 1979); *Recreations* motoring and car restoration, travel, shooting, reading; *Style*— Nigel Chism, Esq; ✉ 2 Abingdon Court, Abingdon Villas, London W8 6BS (☎ 0171 376 0103)

CHITNIS, Baron (Life Peer UK 1977), of Ryedale, Co N Yorks; Pratap Chidamber Chitnis; s of late Chidamber N Chitnis, and Lucia Mallik; *b* 1 May 1936; *Educ* Penryn Sch, Stonyhurst, Univ of Birmingham, Univ of Kansas; *m* 1964, Anne, da of Frank Mansell Brand; 1 s (decd); *Career* sits as ind peer in House of Lords, head of Liberal Pty Orgn 1966–69; chief exec Rowntree Social Serv Tst 1974 (dir 1975–88); memb Community Relations Cmmn 1970–77; chm Br Refugee Cncl 1986–; author of ind reports on the elections in Zimbabwe 1979 and 1980, Guyana 1980, El Salvador 1982, 1984 and 1988 and Nicaragua 1984; *Style*— The Lord Chitnis; ✉ House of Lords, London SW1A 0PW

CHITTOCK, John Dudley; OBE (1982); s of James Hiram Chittock (d 1973), of Leytonstone, and Phyllis Lucy Milner (d 1985); *b* 29 May 1928; *Educ* Oxford and Elson House, Forestdene, SW Essex Tech Coll; *m* 1947, Joyce Kate, da of Roy Ayrton Winter (d 1969), of Kent; *Career* writer, film prodr, publisher; exec ed Focal Press 1954–58, sr ptnr Films of Indust 1958–61, video and film columnist The Financial Times 1963–87, chm Screen Digest 1974–96 (fndr 1971); dir National Video Corporation Ltd 1981–86, non-exec chm NVC Cable Ltd 1983–86; chm: Br Fedn of Film Socs 1969–78 (vice pres 1978–), The Grierson Meml Tst 1989– (fndr 1974), Kraszna-Krausz Fndn (media book prize and grants) 1996– (tstee 1985–); dep chm Br Screen Advsy Cncl 1986–90; conslt ed Royal TV Soc Journal 1978–82; chm of various film and TV indust ctees and numerous media confs, prodr and dir of over 30 documenatry films, author of numerous articles, papers and books on film, TV and video; Hood Medal Royal Photographic Soc 1973, Queen's Silver Jubilee Medal 1977, Presidential Award Incorporated Inst of Photographers 1983, Video Writer of the Year Award 1983; FRPS, FRTS, FBKS; *Recreations* the human condition, period home and antiques, cooking, gardening, work, the arts; *Clubs* RAC; *Style*— John Chittock, Esq, OBE; ✉ The Old Vicarage, Wickhambrook, Suffolk; Screen Digest, 37 Gower St, London WC1E 6HH (☎ 0171 580 1502, fax 0171 580 1504)

CHITTY, Alison Jill; da of Ernest Hedley Chitty, and Irene Joan Waldron; *b* 16 Oct 1948; *Educ* King Alfred Sch London, St Martin's Sch of Art, Central Sch of Art and Design, Arts Cncl scholar; *Career* theatre designer; co-dir Motley Theatre Design course; Victoria Theatre Stoke-on-Trent 1970–79 (designed over 40 prodns, head of design 4 years); *Theatre* RNT (as resident designer) incl: A Month in the Country, Don Juan, Much Ado About Nothing, The Prince of Homburg, Danton's Death, Major Barbara, Kick for Touch, Tales from Hollywood, Antigone, Martine, Venice Preserv'd, Fool for Love, Neaptide, Antony and Cleopatra, The Tempest, The Winter's Tale, Cymbeline; RSC incl: Tartuffe, Volpone, Breaking the Silence, Romeo and Juliet, Orpheus Descending (Haymarket), The Rose Tattoo (Playhouse); other prodns incl: Old King Cole (Theatre Royal Stratford East), Ecstasy and Uncle Vanya (Hampstead Theatre Club), Measure for Measure and Julius Caesar (Riverside Studios), The Way South (Bush), Carmen Jones and Lennon (Crucible Sheffield); *Opera* The Marriage of Figaro (Opera North), New Year (Huston Grand Opera), BowDown/Down by the Green Wood Side (Southbank), The Siege of Calais (Wexford), The Vanishing Bridegroom (St Louis Opera Theatre), Gawain (Royal Opera House), Falstaff (Gottenburg Music Theatre), Jenufa (Dallas Opera) 1994, Billy Budd (Grand Theatre Geneva) 1994, Blond Eckbert (Santa Fé Opera) 1994, Khovanshchina (ENO) 1994, Billy Budd (ROH) 1995, Modern Painters (Santa Fé Opera) 1995, Arianna (ROH) 1995, Billy Budd (Opera Bastille Paris) 1996, The Mask of Orpheus (Royal Festival Hall) 1996, Die Meistersinger von Nürnberg (Danish Royal Opera Copenhagen) 1996; *Films* Blue Jean, Aria, Life is Sweet, Black Poppies (BBC), Naked 1993, Secrets and Lies (Palm D'Or Cannes) 1996; *Style*— Ms Alison Chitty; ✉ c/o Curtis Brown Group Ltd, 28–29 Haymarket, London SW1Y 4SP (☎ 0171 396 6600, fax 0171 396 0110)

CHITTY, Andrew Edward Willes; s and h of Sir Thomas Willes Chitty, 3 Bt, *qv*; *b* 20 Nov 1953; *Style*— Andrew Chitty Esq

CHITTY, Dr Anthony; s of Ashley George Chitty (d 1980), of Surrey, and Doris Ellen Mary Buck; *b* 29 May 1931; *Educ* The Glyn GS Epsom, Imperial Coll London (BSc, PhD, DIC, CEng); *m* 1956, Audrey, da Edward Charles Munro (d 1965); 2 s (Martin b 1958, David b 1962), 1 da (Claire b 1960); *Career* GEC Res Labs 1953–55; head Creep of Steels Lab ERA 1959–63, GEC Power Group 1963–66, chief metallurgist CA Parsons 1966–73; dir: Advanced Technol Div Clarke Chapman-John Thompson 1973–78, Int Res and Devpt Co 1978–79; gen mangr engrg prods NEI Parsons 1979–84; regnl industl advsr DTI NE Region 1984–88, dir Corporate Engrg Northern Engineering Industries 1989–94, conslt Rolls-Royce Industrial Power Group (formerly Northern Engineering Industries) 1994–; visiting prof Aston Univ 1977–84; *Style*— Dr Anthony Chitty; ✉ 1 Willow Way, Darras Hall, Ponteland, Newcastle Upon Tyne

CHITTY, Susan Elspeth (Lady Chitty); da of Rudolph Glossop (d 1993), and Antonia White, FRSL (d 1980); *b* 18 Aug 1929; *Educ* Godolphin Sch Salisbury, Somerville Coll Oxford (scholar); *m* 23 Aug 1951, Sir Thomas Willes Chitty, Bt, *qv*, s of Sir (Thomas) Henry Willes Chitty, 2 Bt (d 1955); 1 s (Andrew Edward Willes, *qv*, b 20 Nov 1953), 3 da (Cordelia Anne b 1955, Miranda Jane b 1967, Jessica Susan b 1971); *Career* writer;

journalist for: Vogue London (winner Vogue Talent Contest 1952), Punch, Harpers & Queen, Observer, The Sunday Telegraph, The Daily Telegraph, Times Literary Supplement and Quest; broadcaster for BBC incl: Any Questions, Woman's Hour, What's in the Picture?, Book Programme; subject of two films Southern Television; shortlisted for Silver Pen Award PEN; memb Author's Soc; *Books* novels: The Diary of a Fashion Model (1958), White Huntress (1963), My Life and Horses (1966); biographies: The Woman who wrote Black Beauty (1971), The Beast and the Monk (1975), Charles Kingsley and North Devon (1976), Gwen John, A Biography (1981), Now to My Mother, Biography of Antonia White (1985), Edward Lear, A Biography (1988), Diaries of Antonia White (ed, 1991, 1992); misc: The Intelligent Woman's Guide to Good Taste (ed, 1958), The Puffin Book of Horses (ed, 1975), On Next to Nothing (with Thomas Hinde, *qv*, 1976), The Great Donkey Walk (with Thomas Hinde, 1977); *Recreations* country pursuits; *Clubs* Academy; *Style*— Susan Chitty; ✉ Bow Cottage, West Hoathly, Sussex RH19 4QF (☎ 01342 810269); c/o Mike Shaw, Curtis Brown Group Ltd, 162 Regent Street, London W1R 5FE (☎ 0171 872 0331, fax 0171 872 0332)

CHITTY, Sir Thomas Willes; 3 Bt (UK 1924), of The Temple; s of Sir (Thomas) Henry Willes Chitty, 2 Bt (d 1955); *b* 2 March 1926; *Educ* Winchester, Univ Coll Oxford; *m* 23 Aug 1951, Susan Chitty, *qv*), da of Rudolph Glossop (d 1993), and Antonia White, FRSL (d 1980); 1 s (Andrew Edward Willes Chitty, *qv* b 1953), 3 da (Cordelia Anne b 1955, Miranda Jane b 1967, Jessica Susan b 1971); *Heir* s, Andrew Edward Willes Chitty b 20 Nov 1953; *Career* served RN 1944–47; Granada Arts fell Univ of York 1964–65, visiting prof Boston Univ 1969–70; novelist, biographer (pen name: Thomas Hinde); *Style*— Sir Thomas Chitty, Bt; ✉ Bow Cottage, West Hoathly, Sussex RH19 4QF

CHIVERS, Christopher John Adrian (Kit); s of Reginald Chivers, of Cardiff, and Dorothy Nicholson, *née* Jenkins; *b* 8 March 1945; *Educ* Bradford GS, Solihull Sch, Glasgow HS, Univ of Glasgow (MA), Trinity Coll Oxford (MA); *m* 22 July 1969, Geertje Bouwes; 1 da (Guinevere Beatrice Joanna b 24 Nov 1972), 1 s (Gregory Richard Reginald b 30 March 1976); *Career* HM Treasy: asst princ Expenditure and Taxation Divs 1968–71, asst private sec to Chancellor of the Exchequer 1971–73, princ Overseas Fin Gp 1973–76; first sec (fin) Br Embassy Washington 1976–78; HM Treasy: princ Defence Div 1978–81, asst sec and head Treasy Expenditure Div 1981–84; DOE Jan - June 1984, grade 5 Efficiency Unit PM's Office 1984–86; HM Treasy: head Pay Div 1986–90, head Specialist Support Gp 1990–93, head privatisation of Forward Civil Service Catering (sub-dept of HM Treasy) 1993–94, Fundamental Expenditure Review of Treasy March - Nov 1994; Dept of Nat Savings: dir of resources 1994–95, acting dir of savings 1995– (dep dir 1994–95); hon sec Brixton Cncl of Churches, treas Brixton Methodist Circuit; *Recreations* cycling, swimming, golf; *Style*— Kit Chivers, Esq; ✉ 6 Thornton Road, Clapham Park, London SW12 0JU (☎ 0181 674 7913, fax 0181 674 7913); Department for National Savings, Charles House, 375 Kensington High Street, London W14 8SD (☎ 0171 605 9462, fax 0171 605 9481, mobile 0378 966335, e-mail kchivers.dns.ch@gtnet.gov.uk)

CHLEBIK, Jan Stefan; s of Marian Wladyslaw Chlebik, and Maria Barbara, *née* Niedziolka; *b* 24 April 1958; *Educ* Leeds Poly (BA); *m* 1982, Zofia Anna, da of Aleksander Lozinski (d 1978), and Izabella, *née* Podobinska; 1 s (Josef Alexander b 30 July 1993); *Career* freelance photographer 1984–; merit (personal landscape) Eleventh Awards Assoc of Photographers; memb Assoc of Photographers; *Style*— Jan Chlebik

CHOAT, Jonathan Martin Cameron; *b* 8 Jan 1940; *Educ* BA; *Career* mktg: Lever Bros, Texaco, J Lyons, Burmah Oil; fndr and md Cameron Choat and Partners (PR consultancy); Hon Asst Worshipful Co of Fruiterers; FRSA; *Style*— Jonathan Choat, Esq; ✉ The Rookery, Walsham Le Willows, Bury St Edmunds, Suffolk IP31 3BD; Cameron Choat & Partners, Bury House, 126–128 Cromwell Rd, London SW7 4ET (☎ 0171 373 4537)

CHODEL, Peter; s of Stanislaw Chodel (d 1978), of Mirfield, W Yorks, and Helena, *née* Naczenko; *b* 15 April 1956; *Educ* Mirfield Secdy Mod, Batley Art Sch, Central Sch of Art and Design (BA); *m* 1 Aug 1981, Vanessa, da of James Fredrick Lowery King, OBE; 1 s (Fredrick Stanislaw b 9 Feb 1988), 1 da (Molly Irena b 15 Feb 1990); *Career* freelance designer Mitchell Beazley Books 1979; designer: Observer Magazine 1979 (summer vacation placement 1978), Stadden Hughes Ltd 1980–84; design dir Michael Peters Group plc (Annual Reports Ltd, Right Angle, Michael Peters Corporate Literature, Michael Peters Literature) 1984–91, jt creative dir Addison Design Company Ltd 1991–; judge D&AD Awards 1994; *Awards* D&AD award (for Yorkshire TV Good Companions Brochure 1981), MEAD Annual Report Show awards (for Michael Peters Group 1984 annual report 1985 and for Prestwich Holdings plc 1986 annual report 1987), Business Magazine/Price Waterhouse Annual Report of the Yr award (for Tesco plc 1990); *Recreations* home and family, things Medieval; *Style*— Peter Chodel, Esq; ✉ 20 Finsen Road, Camberwell, London SE5 9AX (☎ 0171 274 3848); Addison Design Company Ltd, 2 Cathedral Street, London SE1 9DE (☎ 0171 403 7444, fax 0171 403 1243)

CHOLERTON, (Frederick) Arthur; CBE (1978); s of Frederick Arthur Cholerton (d 1968), of Stoke-on-Trent, and Charlotte, *née* Wagstaff (d 1968); *b* 15 April 1917; *Educ* Penkhull Sr Sch Stoke-on-Trent; *m* 25 Feb 1939, Ethel, da of late Albert Jackson, of Stoke-on-Trent; 1 s (Frederick Arthur b 1939, d 1940); *Career* footplate London Midland and Scot Railway 1934, ret as engine driver from BR 1977; memb North Staffs Postal Users Advsy Ctee; chm: N Staffs Hosp Bldg Tst, The Bldg Blocks Appeal, N Staffs Bereavement Centre; Staffs CC: memb 1973–89, vice chm 1973–77, oppn ldr 1977–81, chm 1981–89; vice pres: Staffs Community Cncl, Staffs Sports Tst for Disabled; chm Poplars Resource Management Co Ltd; Lord Mayor Stoke-on-Trent 1971–72 (cncl memb 1951–87); Freeman City of Stoke-on-Trent 1989, Hon MUniv of Keele 1988; *Recreations* gardening, serv with voluntary charitable organisations; *Style*— Arthur Cholerton, Esq, CBE; ✉ 12 Werburgh Drive, Trentham, Stoke-on-Trent, Staffs ST4 8JP (☎ 01782 657457)

CHOLMELEY, Sir Montague John; 6 Bt (UK 1806), of Easton, Lincolnshire; s of Lt-Col Sir Hugh John Francis Sibthorp Cholmeley, 5 Bt, CB, DSO (d 1964), and Cecilia, *née* Ellice (d 1980); *b* 27 March 1935; *Educ* Eton; *m* 18 Oct 1960, Juliet Auriol Sally, yr da of Maj-Gen Sir (Eustace) John Blois Nelson, KCVO, CB, DSO, OBE, MC (d 1993); 1 s, 2 da (Camilla (Mrs William Murdoch) b 1962, Davina (Mrs N Morgan) b 1964); *Heir* s, (Hugh John) Frederick Sebastian Cholmeley b 3 Jan 1968 (m 31 July 1993, Ursula Ann, eldest da of Hugh Peter Derwyn Bennett, QC); *Career* Capt Grenadier Gds 1954–64; *Style*— Sir Montague Cholmeley, Bt; ✉ Church Farm, Burton le Coggles, Grantham, Lincs (☎ 01476 550329); Easton Hall, Grantham

CHOLMONDELEY, 7 Marquess of (UK 1815); David George Philip Cholmondeley; also Viscount Cholmondeley of Kells (I 1661), Baron Cholmondeley of Namptwich (E 1689), Viscount Malpas and Earl of Cholmondeley (GB 1706), Baron Newborough (I 1715), Baron Newburgh (GB 1716), and Earl of Rocksavage (UK 1815); o s of 6 Marquess of Cholmondeley, GCVO, MC (d 1990); *b* 27 June 1960; *Educ* Eton, La Sorbonne Paris; *Heir* cousin, Charles George Cholmondeley b 18 March 1959; *Career* a page of honour to HM The Queen 1974–76; jt Hereditary Lord Great Chamberlain of England 1990–; *Style*— The Most Hon the Marquess of Cholmondeley; ✉ Cholmondeley Castle, Malpas, Cheshire (☎ 01829 22202); Houghton Hall, King's Lynn, Norfolk

CHOLMONDELEY, Marchioness of; Lavinia Margaret; *née* Leslie; DL; o da of late Lt-Col John Leslie, DSO, MC, of Appletree Cottage, Brancaster, Norfolk, and Margaret Nanette Helen, *née* Gilliat; *b* 9 Sept 1921; *m* 14 June 1947, 6 Marquess of Cholmondeley, GCVO, MC (d 1990); 1 s, 3 da; *Style*— The Most Hon the Marchioness of Cholmondeley, DL; ✉ Cholmondeley Castle, Malpas, Cheshire (☎ 01829 720202)

CHOLMONDELEY CLARKE, Marshal Butler; s of Maj Cecil Cholmondeley Clarke (d 1924), of Holycross, Co Tipperary, and late Fanny Ethel Carter; *b* 14 July 1919; *Educ* Aldenham; *m* 1947, Joan Roberta, da of late John Kyle Stephens, JP, of Holywood, Co Down; 2 s (Edward, Robert); *Career* slr 1943, ptnr Burton Yeates and Hart slrs 1946–72; pres City of Westminster Law Soc 1971–72, memb Cncl of Law Soc 1966–72; chm: Family Law Ctee 1970–72, Legal Aid Ctee 1972, Chancery Procedure Ctee 1968–72; master of the Supreme Ct of Judicature (Chancery Div) 1973–92; ed of The Supreme Ct Practice 1987–92; *Books* Sweet & Maxwell's High Court Litigation Manual (conslt ed); *Recreations* reading, genealogy; *Clubs* Turf; *Style*— Marshal Cholmondeley Clarke, Esq; ✉ 16 Cheyne Ct, Flood St, London SW3 5TP

CHOMÉ WILSON, Prof Maryse Ingrid; da of Eric Edouard Percy Chomé (d 1979), of Bergerac, France, and Winsome, *née* Coe (d 1995); *Educ* Ecole des Jeunes Filles Bergerac, Bournemouth Sch for Girls, Royal Acad of Music, Conservatoire de Musique Paris; *m* 23 Aug 1958, Frank Ernest Wilson, s of Frank Harvey Wilson (d 1984); 2 s (Douglas Eric Frank b 1959, Nicholas Clyde b 1960); *Career* violoncellist, performer and teacher; princ cello: Walter Gore Ballet Co Orch 1954, Alexandra Chamber Orch (and soloist) 1955, Festival Ballet Orch 1955–57, Royal Ballet Orch 1957–58, Jose Limon American Dance Co Orch 1958; memb: BBC Concert Orch 1958–59, Grissell Piano Quartet 1963, Chomé Piano Trio 1993–; prof of jr exhibitors RAM 1964, lectr and examiner in and prof of violoncello Trinity Coll of Music London 1965–91, dep govr American Biographical Inst Res Assoc 1990–; regular performer with ENO until 1980s; hon fell Trinity Coll of Music London; LRAM, ARCM; *Recreations* genealogy, gardening, art; *Clubs* RAM; *Style*— Prof Maryse Chomé Wilson

CHOO, Jimmy; s of Kee-Yin Choo, of Penang, Malaysia, and Ah-Yin Moo Choo, of Penang, Malaysia; *b* 15 Nov 1952; *Educ* Cordwainer Coll; *Career* shoe designer; started own label 1988; conslt and featured on fashion prog MBC TV; Best Accessories Award (Bridal Awards) 1989, nominated 6 times for Best Accessories (Br Fashion Awards) 1989–94; has designed for the Royal Shakespeare Co and for the films Goldeneye (featuring character James Bond) and French Kiss; *Style*— Jimmy Choo, Esq; ✉ Studio 50, The Metropolitan Workshop, Enfield Rd, London N1 5AZ (☎ 0171 249 2082)

CHOPE, Christopher Robert; OBE (1983); s of His Hon Judge Robert Charles Chope (d 1988), and Pamela, *née* Durell; *b* 19 May 1947; *Educ* Marlborough, Univ of St Andrews (LLB); *m* Christine, *née* Hutchinson; 1 s (Philip Robert b 1992), 1 da (Antonia); *Career* called to the Bar 1972; ldr Wandsworth Borough Cncl 1979–83 (memb 1974–83); MP (C) Southampton Itchen 1983–92; Parly under sec of state: DOE 1986–90, Dept of Transport 1990–92; conslt Ernst & Young 1992–; memb: Health and Safety Cmmn 1993–, Local Govt Cmmn 1994–95; *Style*— Christopher Chope, Esq, OBE; ✉ 63 Roupell Street, Waterloo, London SE1 8SS (☎ 0171 633 9129)

CHOPE, Dr John Norman; JP (Devon); s of William Pearse Chope, and Kathleen Mary, *née* Calvert (d 1955); *b* 27 June 1948; *Educ* Waverley GS Birmingham, Dartmouth RNC (Reserved Cadetship), Univ of Bristol (scholar, BSc, BDS, MRC Award, L E Attenborough Medal, George Fawn Prize), LDS RCS England, DGDP (UK) RCS England; *m* 1970, Susan Mary, da of Clinton Le Page; 1 da (Jenny Kathleen b 28 Sept 1976); *Career* neurophysiologist USA and subsequently Sudan (helped found Khartoum Dental Sch) 1969–73, SHO (oral surgery) United Bristol Hosps 1973; assoc dental surgn: Backwell Somerset 1973, Stockwood Bristol and Shepton Mallet Somerset 1973–74; princ dental surgn and dental practice owner: Holsworthy Devon 1974–, Hartland Devon 1975–, Bude Cornwall 1981–90, Okehampton Devon 1983–; hypnotherapist 1977–; former memb N Devon Dist and SW Regnl Dental Advsy Ctees, former chm N Devon BDA 199, currently memb N Devon Dental Postgrad Ctee, fndr memb, treas and memb Divnl Bd SW Div Faculty of Gen Dental Practice Royal Coll of Surgns of England, chm Nat Cncl Confedn of Dental Employers, fndr memb and memb Ctee N Devon Independent Dental Practitioners' Gp; memb GDC 1996–; memb numerous professional socs incl: BDA, RSM, GDPA, CODE, FGDP (UK), RCS England, BMDHS, FDI, AOG; farmer/landowner 1976–, proprietor small specialist bldg co 1979–, chm Speke Valley Services Ltd (t/a Firmadenta) dental wholesale and mktg co 1993–; memb: CLA, Cwlth Judges' and Magistrates' Assoc; *Recreations* architecture and building structural design, gardening, swimming, walking, recreational skiing and theatre; *Style*— Dr John Chope, JP; ✉ Delivery 1, Hartland, Devon EX39 6DZ

CHORARIA, (Bhim) Raj; s of Shri Panna Lal Choraria (d 1956), of Panna Estate, Nagaur, and Shrimati Naini Devi, *née* Sancheti (d 1975); *b* 16 Nov 1936; *Educ* Presidency Coll Calcutta, The Med Coll Calcutta (MB BS), Gujrat Univ (MD), Univ of Aberdeen (DMRD), FFR RCSI; *m* 1 July 1963, Vimala, da of Shri K M Jain (d 1960), of Jodhpur, India; 1 s (Sumeet b 1972), 2 da (Roopali b 1966, Sonali b 1971); *Career* NCC India 1955–60; personal physician to Mr J K Birla Delhi 1964–66, chief radiologist SDM Hosp cum Med Res Inst Jaipur 1972–76, sr registrar Glasgow Royal Infirmary 1981–85, conslt radiologist Tameside Gen Hosp 1985–; memb: ODA, BMA; MRCR; *Recreations* yoga, swimming, ballroom dancing, Indian music; *Clubs* Forum Ballroom Dancing; *Style*— Raj Choraria, Esq; ✉ Tameside General Hospital, Fountain St, Ashton-under-Lyne, Lancs (☎ 0161 331 6000 ext 6556)

CHORLEY, Prof Richard John; s of Walter Joseph Chorley (d 1952), of Bridgwater, Somerset, and Ellen Mary, *née* Ketnor (d 1965); *b* 4 Sept 1927; *Educ* Minehead GS, Univ of Oxford (MA), Univ of Cambridge (ScD); *m* 11 Sept 1965, Rosemary Joan Macdonald, da of David George More (d 1986), of Cambridge; 1 s (Richard b 1966), 1 da (Eleanor b 1968); *Career* Nat Serv Lt RE 1946–48; instr: in geography Columbia Univ NY 1952–54, in geology Brown Univ USA 1954–57; Univ of Cambridge: demonstrator in geography 1958, lectr 1963, reader in geography 1970, appointed Ad Hominen chair in geography 1974, emeritus 1994, head Dept of Geography 1984–89, vice-master Sidney Sussex Coll Cambridge 1990–93; former pres Cambridge branch Geographical Assoc, corresponding memb Italian Geographical Soc; Patron's Medal RGS 1987, Hon DSc Univ of Bristol; *Books* incl: The History of the Study of Landforms (jtly, 1964–91), Frontiers in Geographical Teaching (ed jtly, 1965), Models in Geography (ed jtly, 1967), Atmosphere, Weather and Climate (jtly, 1968–92), Network Analysis in Geography (jtly, 1969), Physical Geography (jtly, 1971), Spatial Analysis in Geography (ed jtly, 1971), Directions in Geography (ed jtly, 1973), Environmental Systems, Philosophy, Analysis and Control (jtly, 1978), Geomorphology (jtly, 1984); *Recreations* genealogy, grave renovation; *Style*— Prof Richard Chorley; ✉ 76 Grantchester Meadows, Cambridge CB3 9JL; Department of Geography, University of Cambridge, Downing Place, Cambridge CB2 3EN (☎ 01223 333399)

CHORLEY, 2 Baron (UK 1945); Roger Richard Edward Chorley; s of 1 Baron Chorley, QC (d 1978); *b* 14 Aug 1930; *Educ* Stowe, Gonville and Caius Coll Cambridge (BA); *m* 31 Oct 1964, Ann Elizabeth, yr da of late Archibald Scott Debenham, of Ingatestone, Essex; 2 s (Hon Nicholas Rupert, Hon Christopher Robert Hopkinson b 1968); *Heir* s, Hon Nicholas Rupert Chorley b 15 July 1966; *Career* memb: Royal Cmmn on the Press 1975–78, Ordnance Survey Advsy Bd 1982–85, Bd British Cncl 1981– (vice chm 1991–), Bd Nat Theatre 1980–90, NERC 1988–94; ptnr Coopers & Lybrand (CA) 1967–89; hon vice pres Royal Geographical Soc 1993– (pres 1987–90), chm Nat Tst 1991–96; Hon DSc: Reading 1990, Kingston 1992; Hon LLB Lancaster 1995; FCA; *Style*— The Rt Hon the Lord Chorley; ✉ House of Lords, London SW1

CHOVIL, (Edward) Roger Clive; s of Clive Newey Chovil (d 1980), and Marjorie Mary, *née* Coffey; *b* 29 Sept 1945; *Educ* Shrewsbury; *m* Elizabeth Alison Mary, da of Alison Petitpierre; 3 c (Lucy Elizabeth Patricia b 1976, Tania Kate Marie b 1978, Charles Roger Michael b 1980); *Career* ptnr Coopers & Lybrand 1978– (joined 1965); Freeman City of London; FCA; *Clubs* RAC; *Style—* Roger Chovil, Esq; ✉ Coopers & Lybrand, No 1 Embankment Place, London WC2N 6NN

CHOWN, Christopher Richard; s of Dr Charles Stanley Malcolm Chown, of Betws-y-Coed, Gwynedd, and Elisabeth Annan, *née* Dickson (d 1978); *b* 29 June 1957; *m* 25 June 1988, Gunna, da of Heine á Trødni (d 1987), of Grønlandsfekagid, Faroe Islands; 1 step s (Peder b 7 June 1970), 1 step da (Tania b 29 May 1966); *Career* audit jr Peat Marwick Mitchell 1980–81, rebuilt and converted derelict house in Clapham 1982–83, kitchen asst teacher La Petite Cuisine Sch of Cookery Richmond 1983–84, commis chef Terrace Restaurant Dorchester 1984, sous chef Restaurant Riesbächli Zürich Switzerland 1984–85; converted and opened Plas Bodegroes 1986, bought and refurbished The Hole in the Wall Restaurant 1994; *Awards* Good Food Guide Gwynedd Newcomer of the Year 1988, Michelin Red M 1989, Taste of Wales Restaurant of the Year 1990, Good Food Guide Highest Rated Restaurant in Wales 1990–96, 1995, AA Guide Rosette for Cooking 1991 (three rosettes 1992, 1993, 1994 and 1995), Michelin Star 1991, 1992, 1993, 1994 and 1995 (the only one in Wales), Good Hotel Guide César Award 1992; memb N Wales Tourism Mktg Bureau 1986–, treas Llyn Peninsula Tourist Assoc 1986–88, memb Taste of Wales 1989–, memb Dwyfor Business Forum Ctee 1992; *Recreations* photography, architecture, gardening, music and opera; *Style—* Christopher Chown, Esq; ✉ Plas Bodegroes Ltd, Pwllheli, Gwynedd LL53 5TH (☎ 01758 612363, fax 01758 701247); The Hole in the Wall Restaurant, 16 George Street, Bath BA1 2EH (☎ 01225 425242)

CHOYCE, Prof (David) Peter; s of Prof Charles Coley Choyce, CMG, CBE (d 1937), and Gwendolen Alice, *née* Dobbing (d 1957); *b* 1 March 1919; *Educ* Stowe, UCL (BSc, MB BS), UCH (MS), Moorfields Eye Hosp and Inst of Ophthalmology London; *m* 3 Sept 1949, Diana, da of Thomas Nadin (d 1978), of Leigh on Sea; 3 s (Jonathan b 1951, David Gregory b 1955, Matthew Quentin b 1963); *Career* med offr HM Tports 1942–46; served N and S Atlantic, Caribbean, Med, Indian Ocean; conslt in ophthalmology: Southend on Sea Gp of Hosps 1953–84, Hosp for Tropical Diseases 1953–88; world authority on: intraocular lenses and implants, refractive surgery, tropical ophthalmology; overseas conslt Dept of Ophthalmology Henry Ford Hosp Detroit; Hunterian prof RCS; author of over 100 scientific papers; hon memb: Int Intraocular Implant Club, American, UK, Japanese, S African and Yugoslav Implant Socs; Palealogus Award Kerato Refractive Soc 1986, Innovators lecture American Soc of Cataract and Refractive Surgery 1993; Liveryman Worshipful Soc of Apothecaries; FRSM 1942, FRCS 1947, FRCOphth 1988, MAE; *Books* Intra-Ocular Lenses and Implants (1964); *Recreations* golf, history, food and wine, the opposite sex; *Clubs* Rochford Hundred Golf, Moor Park Golf, Variety Club of GB; *Style—* Prof Peter Choyce; ✉ 9 Drake Road, Westcliff on Sea, Essex SS0 8LR (☎ 01702 343 810, fax 01702 342 611); 45 Wimpole St, London WIM 7DG (☎ 0171 935 3411); Vila Colunata, Praia da Luz, Algarve, Portugal

CHRISFIELD, Lawrence John (Larry); s of Sydney George Chrisfield (d 1977), and Minnie, *née* Underwood; *b* 31 March 1938; *Educ* St Olave's and St Saviors GS; *m* Patricia Maureen, *née* Scoble; 4 c (Cindy Jane b 1961, Susan Melinda b 1962, Carol Ann b 1964, David Alexander b 1967); *Career* Merrett Son and Street 1955–63 (articled clerk, accountant), Arthur Young McClelland Moores & Co 1963–72 (tax sr, mangr), UK tax mangr Unilever plc 1972–74, ptnr Arthur Young (now Ernst & Young) 1975– (mangr 1974–75); dir: British Film Cmmn, Independent Production Trg Fund, PACT Finance Ctee; chm LFVDA; FCA 1963, ATII 1963; *Recreations* amateur dramatics, photography; *Style—* Larry Chrisfield, Esq; ✉ 121 King George St, Greenwich, London SE10 8PX (☎ 0181 858 5147); Ernst & Young, Becket House, 1 Lambeth Palace Rd, London SE1 7EU (☎ 0171 928 2000, fax 0171 401 2136)

CHRISTIAN, Nigel Robin Gladwyn; s of Geoffrey Gladwyn Christian (d 1960), of London, and Patricia Wynne Cavendish, *née* Shelly (d 1988); *b* 4 Aug 1942; *Educ* Harcourt Sch, Cranleigh; *m* 22 July 1972, Susan Anne Leila, da of Col Robert de Lisle King, CBE (d 1996), of Smarden, nr Ashford, Kent; 2 s (Alexander b 1974, Edward b 1981), 1 da (Annabel b 1977); *Career* Price Forbes 1960–61, Lambert Bros 1962–64; dir: Leslie & Godwin Ltd 1987–92 (joined 1964, asst dir 1972), Leslie & Godwin Aviation Ltd 1980; dep chm Leslie and Godwin Aviation Ltd 1989–92, dir Leslie & Godwin International Ltd 1990–92; exec dir C T Bowring Aviation Ltd 1992–; a managing dir Marsh & McLennan Inc 1993–; *Recreations* gardening, golf, tennis, sailing, skiing; *Clubs* Rye Golf; *Style—* N R G Christian, Esq; ✉ C T Bowring Aviation Ltd, The Bowring Building, Tower Place, London EC3P 3BE

CHRISTIAN, Prof Reginald Frank; of Herbert Alexander Christian (d 1965), of Liverpool, and Jessie Gower, *née* Scott (d 1969); *b* 9 Aug 1924; *Educ* Liverpool Inst, Queen's Coll Oxford (MA); *m* 29 March 1952, Rosalind Iris, da of Capt Malcolm Napier (d 1973), of Brockenhurst, Hants; 1 s (Giles Nicholas b 1955), 1 da (Jessica Ilott b 1953); *Career* WWII Flying Offr 231 Sqdn and Atlantic Ferry Unit RAF 1943–46; FO Br Embassy Moscow 1949–50, lectr in Russian Univ of Liverpool 1951–55, prof of Russian and head of dept Univ of Birmingham 1955–66 (former sr lectr), assoc dir Centre for Russian and E European Studies 1963–66, visiting prof McGill Univ Montreal 1961–62, visiting prof Moscow 1964–65, prof of Russian and head of dept Univ of St Andrews 1966–92 (dean faculty of arts, hon prof 1992–), memb Int Ctee of Slavists; vice pres Assoc of Teachers of Russian 1959–, pres Br Univs Assoc of Slavists 1975–78; *Books* Korolenko's Siberia (1954), Russian Syntax (1959), Tolstoy's War and Peace (1961), Russian Prose Composition (1962), Tolstoy - A Critical Introduction (1969), Tolstoy's Letters (ed and trans, 1978), Tolstoy's Diaries (ed and trans, 1985, revised and abridged edn, 1994); *Recreations* violin, hill-walking; *Style—* Prof Reginald Christian; ✉ University of St Andrews, Fife (☎ 01334 476161); Culgrianach, 48 Lade Braes, St Andrews, Fife KY16 9DA (☎ 01334 474407); Scioncroft, Knockard Rd, Pitlochry, Perthshire PH16 5HJ (☎ 01796 472993)

CHRISTIANS, Sharon Jane; da of John Hlywka (d 1982), and Rose Theresa, *née* Yastremski (d 1990); *b* 6 Oct 1951; *Educ* Notre Dame Coll Sch Canada, Carleton Univ of Ottawa Canada (BA); *m* 18 Aug 1988, Ian Douglas Christians, s of Douglas Tamplin Christians, of Swansea, Wales; *Career* researcher and speech writer House of Commons Ottawa Canada 1972–75, dir Ontario Youth Secretariat 1975–76, fed affrs analyst Canadian Inst of CA 1976–78; dir of public affrs: Northern Pipeline Agency Alaska Highway Gas Pipeline Project Canada 1978–80, Ontario Energy Corporation 1980–82; mangr International Communications General Electric USA 1982–88; dir of corporate affrs: THORN EMI plc 1988–90, Stanhope Properties plc 1990–91; dir of corporate affrs and sec to the Bd Amersham International plc 1991–93, dir of corp affrs EMI Group plc (formerly THORN EMI) 1994–; non-exec dir Ashford Hosp NHS Tst Middx 1992–94; FRSA 1990; *Recreations* Russian studies, tennis, languages; *Style—* Mrs Sharon Christians; ✉ EMI Group plc, 4 Tenterden Street, Hanover Square, London W1A 2AY (☎ 0171 355 4848, telex 264855 THORN G)

CHRISTIE, (Forrest) Brian; s of Lt-Col George Hewitt Christie (d 1951), of Eastbourne, and Audrey Maude, *née* Forrest (d 1959); *b* 10 Jan 1934; *Educ* Tonbridge, Univ of London (BDS FDS, DOrth); *m* 28 July 1962, Jennifer Anne, da of Gp Capt John Gilbert Wigley (d 1979), of Epsom, Surrey; 1 s (Rawdon b 1967), 1 da (Nicola (Mrs Miller) b 1966); *Career* conslt orthodontist 1972–75: Glasgow Dental Hosp, Royal Hosp for Sick Children Glasgow, Plastic Surgery Unit Canniesburn Glasgow; conslt orthodontist: Stoke Mandeville Hosp 1975–97, Wycombe Gen Hosp 1975–96; chm Paisley and Aylesbury Sections BDA; memb: Br Soc for the Study of Orthodontics, Craniofacial Soc, Euro Orthodontic Soc, RSM; ctee memb several amateur operatic societies; *Books* contrib: Surgery in Infancy and Childhood (ed W H Dennison, 1971), Plastic Surgery in Infancy and Childhood (ed J C Mustarde and I T Jackson); *Recreations* music, fell walking, golf; *Clubs* 250, Studley Wood Golf; *Style—* Brian Christie, Esq; ✉ c/o Department of Oral Surgery and Orthodontics, Stoke Mandeville Hospital, Aylesbury, Bucks (☎ 01296 315692)

CHRISTIE, Dr Campbell; s of Thomas Christie (d 1944), and Johnina, *née* Rolling (d 1965); *b* 23 Aug 1937; *Educ* Albert Senior Secdy Sch Glasgow, Langside Coll Glasgow, Woolwich Poly London; *m* 2 Feb 1963, Elizabeth Brown, da of Alexander Cameron (d 1968); 2 s (Andrew Cameron b 1963, Douglas Campbell b 1965); *Career* RN 1956–58; Civil Serv: Admiralty 1954–59, DHSS 1959–72; Soc of Civil and Public Servants 1972–85 (dep gen sec 1975–85), gen sec Scottish TUC 1986–, visiting prof Glasgow Caledonian Univ and Univ of Glasgow; non-exec dir Falkirk Royal Infirmary NHS Tst; memb Bd: Wildcat Theatre Co, Scottish Coal Co, Theatre Royal Glasgow, Edinburgh Festival Theatre Tst, Glasgow Devpt Agency; memb: EEC Economic and Social Ctee, Scottish Economic Cncl; Hon DLit Napier Univ; FScotvec; *Recreations* golf; *Clubs* Glenbervie Golf; *Style—* Dr Campbell Christie; ✉ 31 Dumyat Drive, Falkirk FK1 5PA (☎ 01324 624555); 16 Woodlands Terrace, Glasgow G5 (☎ 0141 332 4946, fax 0141 332 4649)

CHRISTIE, David; s of William Christie (d 1971), and Jean Dempsey, *née* McDowall (d 1996); *b* 22 Feb 1942; *Educ* Dollar Acad, Univ of Strathclyde (BA), Univ of London (BSc(Econ)), Univ of Glasgow (Dip Ed); *m* 1969, Elsa Margaret, da of Dr Ernest James Mollison Shearer; 1 s (James Alexander b 20 April 1975), 2 da (Alison Jean b 23 Nov 1972, Catriona Helen b 2 Oct 1982); *Career* lektor Br Centre Folkuniversity of Sweden 1966, asst master George Watson's Coll Edinburgh 1966–72, lectr in economics Moray House Coll of Educn Edinburgh and research assoc The Esmee Fairbairn Res Centre Heriot-Watt Univ 1972–77, teacher Euro Sch Luxembourg 1977–83, Faculty memb Euro Centre Miami Univ 1980–83, head of economics Winchester Coll 1983–88, warden St Edward's Sch Oxford 1988–; ed educn section Economics 1971–78, memb then chm Economics and Business Studies Panel Scottish Examination Bd 1973–78, memb IBA Ctee for Scotland 1973–77, dep chm HMC Working Party on Inspection 1994–, chm Oxford Conf on Educn 1996–; FRSA 1994; *Books* Curriculum Development in Economics (contrib, 1973), Teaching Economics (contrib, 1976), Economics in Action (with Prof A Scott, 1976), Golfer's Handbook (contrib, 1988), Cambridge Guide to Literature in English (contrib, 1988); also author of numerous book reviews and articles in journals; *Recreations* golf, book collecting, hill walking, skiing; *Clubs* Royal & Ancient Golf, East India; *Style—* David Christie, Esq; ✉ Warden's House, St Edward's School, Woodstock Road, Oxford OX2 7NN (☎ 01865 319323, fax 01865 319242)

CHRISTIE, Sir George William Langham; kt (1984), DL (E Sussex 1983); s of John Christie, CH, MC (d 1962), and Audrey, *née* Mildmay (d 1953); *b* 31 Dec 1934; *Educ* Eton, Trinity Coll Cambridge; *m* 8 Aug 1958, (Patricia) Mary, da of late Ivor Percy Nicholson, and step da of Cdr Alan McGaw; 3 s (Hector b 1961, Augustus b 1963, Ptolemy (Tolly) b 1971), 1 da (Louise b 1966); *Career* exec chm Glyndebourne Productions Ltd 1956–, fndr chm London Sinfonietta 1968–88; memb Arts Cncl of GB and chm Music Panel 1987–92; Cavaliere al Merito della Repubblica Italiana 1977; Hon Dr: Univ of Sussex 1990, Univ of Keele 1993, Univ of Exeter 1994; hon FRCM 1986, hon FRNCM 1986; hon memb Guildhall Sch of Music and Drama 1991; *Style—* Sir George Christie, DL; ✉ Glyndebourne, Lewes, E Sussex BN8 5U8 (☎ 01273 812321, fax 01273 812783)

CHRISTIE, John Ireland; s of John Ireland Christie, of Clepington Street, Dundee, and Catherine Duke, *née* McDonald; *b* 8 May 1962; *Educ* Menziehill HS, Kingsway Tech Coll, Univ of Abertay; *m* 24 June 1989, Angela, da of William McGoldrick, of Frederick Street, Dundee; 2 s (Barry John Ireland b 16 Jan 1983, Jordan James Doyle b 18 May 1990), 1 da (Lisa Victoria b 24 Sept 1984); *Career* hockey player; 77 Scot caps; Silver medal Under 21 Euro Championships, top goalscorer indoor hockey in Scotland 1985–92, most goals scored in one game indoor (21), most goals scored in season (265 in 63 games), Bronze medal Euro Championships Birmingham 1991; memb Menzieshill Hockey Club: Midlands League winners 1978–95, Glenfiddich winners 1985, 1988 and 1991, League winners 1988, 1990, 1991, 1992, 1994 and 1995, Scottish Cup winners 1984, 1985, 1988, 1990, 1991, 1992, and 1994; European B Div Gold medal winners; Scottish nat coach sr men's indoor squad; *Style—* John Christie, Esq; ✉ Ardminish Place, Balumbie, Dundee; Tayside House, Dundee (☎ 01382 461173)

CHRISTIE, Linford; MBE (1990); *b* 2 April 1960; *Career* athlete; full UK int 1980– (over 50 appearances); achievements at 100m: UK champion 1985, 1987, 1990, 1991, 1992 and 1993, AAA champion 1986, 1988, 1989, 1991, 1992 and 1993, Gold medal Euro Championships 1986, 1990 and 1994, Gold medal Cwlth Games 1990 and 1994 (Silver medal 1986), Gold medal Dinner Europa Cup 1987, 1989, 1991 and 1993, Gold medal World Cup 1989 and 1992, Gold medal Olympic Games 1992 (Silver 1988), Gold medal World Championships 1993 (Silver medal 1991), Gold medal World Cup 1994; achievements at 200m: AAA indoor champion 1981, 1982, 1987, 1988, 1989 and 1991, UK champion 1985 and 1988, AAA champion 1988, Gold medal Euro Indoor Championships 1986 (Bronze 1988), winner Europa Cup 1987, Bronze medal Euro Championships 1990, Silver medal World Cup 1992; achievements at 60m: Gold medal Euro Indoor Championships 1988 and 1990, AAA indoor champion 1989, 1990 and 1991; also winner various 4 x 100m relay medals; record holder: UK, Euro and Cwlth 60m and 100m, UK and Cwlth 4 x 100m relay; only person to win both 60m and 200m at AAA Indoor Championships (twice, 1989 and 1991); Male Athlete of the Year - Br Athletics Writers' Assoc 1988 and 1992, Panasonic Sports Personality of the Year 1992, BBC Sports Personality of the Year 1993; involved with various charities incl: Westminster Drugs Project, Sportability, Br Assoc of Sport for Disabled; Freeman Borough of Hammersmith and Fulham 1988; *Books* Linford Christie - An Autobiography (1989); *Style—* Linford Christie, MBE; ✉ c/o Susan Barrett, Nuff Respect, The Coach House, 107 Sherland Road, Twickenham, Middx; Fan Club with Colin Jackson MBE:- LCJ Club, PO Box 295, Twickenham, Middx TW1 4XJ

CHRISTIE, Nan Stevenson; da of James Cowan Christie, of Ayr, and Henrietta, *née* Rock (d 1988); *b* 6 March 1948; *Educ* Ayr Acad, RSAMD, London Opera Centre; *m* 16 June 1972, Andrew S Hendrie, s of William Hendrie; 1 s (Ross b 2 July 1983); *Career* soprano; operatic debut as Fiametta in The Gondoliers (Scottish Opera), Covent Garden debut as First Esquire in Parsifal; toured in Switzerland, Portugal, Germany, Poland and Japan, princ guest artist Frankfurt Opera; worked with conductors incl: Claudio Abbado, André Previn, Sir John Pritchard, Bernard Haitink, Sir Simon Rattle, Sir Alexander Gibson, John Mauceri, Michael Gielen; awarded James Caird travelling scholarship, Peter Stuyvesant scholarship, study prize Hertogen Bosch Singing Competition; *Roles* incl: Pamina in The Magic Flute (Eng Music Theatre, Opera de Nancy), Sophie in Tom Jones (Eng Music Theatre), Xenia in Boris Godunov (Scot Opera), Flora in The Turn of the Screw (Scot Opera), Galla in The Cataline Conspiracy (Scot Opera), Tytania in A Midsummer Night's Dream (Scot Opera, Opera North), Susanna in The Marriage of Figaro (Scot Opera, Frankfurt Opera), Despina in Cosi fan Tutte (Scot Opera, Netherlands Opera, Glyndebourne), Frasquita in Carmen (Edinburgh Festival, Earls Court, Japan), Oscar in Un Ballo in Maschera (Frankfurt Opera), Marie in Die Soldaten (Frankfurt Opera), Euridice in Orpheus in the Underworld (ENO),

Countess Adele in Count Ory (ENO), Adele in Die Fledermaus (ENO), Queen of Night in The Magic Flute (Scot Opera, Marseille, ENO), Arbace in Idomeneo (La Fenice Venice, Italian debut) 1991; *Recordings* audio incl: La Vita Nuova (with the Nash Ensemble and Nicholas Maw), Anthology of Italian Opera, Gli Orazie ed i Curiazi, Melancholia (by Dusapin, with Orchestra de Lyon); video incl: various Gilbert and Sullivan, Gianetta in The Gondoliers, Aline in The Sorcerer, title role in Princess Ida; *Recreations* painting, reading, gardening; *Style*— Ms Nan Christie

CHRISTIE, Philippa; *see:* Pearce, (Ann) Philippa

CHRISTIE, Stuart; s of Samuel Albert Christie (d 1977), and Alice Duncan, *née* Fellows; *b* 26 Nov 1934; *Educ* Liverpool Inst HS, Univ of Liverpool (LLB); *m* 1972, Her Hon Judge Elizabeth Mary Steel, DL, *qv*, da of late His Hon Edward Steel; 2 c (Elspeth Victoria b 19 Nov 1976, Iain Duncan b 17 Feb 1978); *Career* Nat Serv RA 1959–61; Alsop Stevens & Co (now Alsop Wilkinson): articled clerk 1954–58, asst slr 1958–59 and 1961–63, ptnr 1963–91, conslt 1992–; memb City of London Slrs' Co, Freeman City of London (by purchase); memb: The Liverpool Law Soc, The Notaries Soc; hon German consul for Merseyside; *Recreations* choral singing (Royal Liverpool Philharmonic Choir); *Clubs* Athenaeum (Liverpool, pres 1992–93); *Style*— Stuart Christie, Esq; ✉ 70 Knowsley Rd, Cressington Park, Liverpool L19 OPG (☎ 0151 427 3760); Alsop Wilkinson, India Buildings, Water St, Liverpool L2 0NH (☎ 0151 227 3060)

CHRISTIE, Sir William; kt (1975), MBE (1970), JP (Belfast 1951), DL (Belfast 1977); s of Richard and Ellen Christie, of Belfast; *b* 1 June 1913; *Educ* Ward Sch Bangor N Ireland; *m* 1935, Selina, *née* Pattison; 1 s (and 1 s decd), 2 da; *Career* High Sheriff Belfast 1964–65, Lord Mayor 1972–75 (Dep Mayor 1969), Alderman 1973–77; co dir; *Style*— Sir William Christie, MBE, JP, DL

CHRISTIE, (Eric) William Hunter; s of Harold Alfred Hunter Christie, QC, TD, treas Lincoln's Inn (d 1960), and Norah Agnes Veronica, *née* Brooks (d 1965); gs of Sir William Christie, FRS, Astronomer Royal (by his w Violette, 3 da of Sir Alfred Hickman, 1 Bt, MP), ggs of Prof Samuel Hunter Christie, FRS, and gggs of James Christie (b 1739), of Leicester Sq (collateral of Christie of Durie); *b* 18 Aug 1922; *Educ* Marlborough, RMA Sandhurst (OCTU); *m* 20 May 1950, Dorothy Ursula Merle, da of Roderick Macleod, of Angmering, Sussex (d 1947); 2 s (Robert b 1951, Nial b 1960), 2 da (Fiona b 1956, Catriona b 1968); *Career* Lt Coldstream Gds 1941–43 (wounded); FO: S American Dept 1944–46, 3 sec Br Embassy Buenos Aires 1946–48; Scott Polar Res Inst Cambridge 1948–50; called to the Bar Lincoln's Inn 1952 (bencher 1989), head of chambers; memb: Cncl Inland Waterways Assoc 1950–52 (hon life memb 1968), Chelsea Met Borough Cncl 1956–65 (chm Ctees of Cncl); hon sec UK Falkland Island Ctee 1968–76, chm Falkland Island Res and Devpt Assoc Ltd (Falkland Island Office) 1976–83; chm: S Atlantic Fisheries Ctee 1977–82, Falkland Island Assoc 1983–85; Freedom of Stanley Falkland Islands 1993; memb Ct Worshipful Co of Clockmakers 1968 (Master 1979), pres Br Horological Inst 1979, pres Nat Clock and Watchmakers Benevolent Soc 1979; FBHI; *Books* The Antarctic Problem: An Historical and Political Study (1950), Portrait of Trent in Collection Portraits of Rivers (1953); contributor to legal and specialist publications; *Recreations* country life; *Clubs* Flyfishers'; *Style*— William Christie, Esq; ✉ 13 Old Square, Lincoln's Inn, London WC2A 3UA (☎ 0171 404 4800, fax Gps 2 and 3 071 405 4267, telex 22487 INNLAW G)

CHRISTIE-BROWN, Jeremy Robin Warrington; s of Robson Christie-Brown (d 1971), and Mildred, *née* Warrington (d 1970); *b* 15 July 1936; *Educ* Harrow, Univ of Oxford (MA, BM BCh), Univ Coll Hosp Med Sch, FRCP, FRCPsych, DPM; *m* 3 Nov 1962, Margaret Elizabeth, da of Frederick Stafford (d 1979); 2 s (Dominic b 9 Oct 1963, Jonathan b 15 Nov 1964), 1 da (Sarah b 3 May 1968); *Career* conslt psychiatrist UCH and Friern Hosp 1971–76, conslt psychiatrist The Maudsley Hosp 1976–1995 (conslt emeritus 1995); *Style*— Dr Jeremy Christie-Brown; ✉ 130 Harley Street, London W1N 1AH

CHRISTIE-MILLER, Andrew William Michael; DL (Wilts 1993); o s of Maj Samuel Vandeleur Christie-Miller, CBE (d 1968), of Clarendon Park, Salisbury, and Esmée Antoinette Fraser, *née* Hutcheson; *see* Burke's Landed Gentry, 18 edn, vol II, 1969; *b* 22 Sept 1950; *Educ* Eton, RAC Cirencester (Dip Rural Estate Mgmnt, Dip Advanced Farm Mgmnt); *m* 6 Feb 1976, Barbara, da of Maj Charles Alexander Neil (d 1959), of London; 1 s (Alexander William Henry b 1982), 2 da (Rebecca Claire b 1976, Victoria Phoebe b 1978); *Career* Spicer & Pegler 1970–73, Savills 1978–82; chm SCATS Ltd; memb Wilts CC 1985–93; chm Forestry Indust Cncl of GB, vice chm Game Conservancy; High Sheriff of Wiltshire 1996–97; ARICS 1979; *Recreations* shooting, travel, bicycling, conservation; *Clubs* White's, New (Edinburgh); *Style*— Andrew Christie-Miller, Esq, DL; ✉ Clarendon Park, Salisbury, Wilts SP5 3EP (☎ 01722 710217, fax 01722 710845); Estate Office, Clarendon Park, Salisbury, Wilts SP5 3EW (☎ 01722 710233, car 0836 740220)

CHRISTMAS, Colin Adrian; s of R F Christmas, and M Haskey; *b* 11 Dec 1938; *Educ* Forest Sch, architectural Colls Essex and London; *m* 31 March 1962, Elisa Curling, da of H H Curling Hope; 1 s (Paul b 7 Feb 1968), 1 da (Laura b 14 Oct 1966); *Career* with Sir Giles Gilbert Scott Son and Partner 1959–63; work on: Liverpool Cathedral, Bankside Power Station; Fitzroy Robinson Partnership: designer/planner 1963, ptnr 1987–92, conslt 1992–; designs for: shopping, office, residential and industl complexes in UK and abroad; responsible for design and implementation of extension and refurbishment of Royal Exchange London 1983–91, Pinners Hall City of London; Civic Tst commendation for Watling Court, Design award Chancery House Sutton, Stone Fedn commendation and City Heritage award winner for Royal Exchange; *Books* The Caliphs Design (conslt, ed by Paul Edwards, 1986); *Recreations* east coast sailing, music, travel, art; *Style*— Colin Christmas, Esq; ✉ 33 The Drive, North Chingford, London E4 7AJ (☎ and fax 0181 529 0925); The Fitzroy Robinson Partnership, 77 Portland Place, London W1 (☎ 0171 636 8033)

CHRISTMAS, Dr David; s of Henry Christmas, of Shrewsbury, Shropshire, and Irene Elsie, *née* Teece; *b* 27 April 1953; *Educ* Priory Sch for Boys Shrewsbury, Univ of Birmingham (MB ChB); *m* 12 April 1980, Amanda Victoria Anne, da of Roy Griffiths, of Shrewsbury, Shropshire; 1 s (Matthew b 1982), 1 da (Kate b 1985); *Career* house offr: gen surgery 1976, gen med 1977; conslt in anaesthetics and intensive care Telford Gen Hosp 1989– (sr offr 1977–79, registrar 1979–81, sr registrar 1981–83, conslt in anaesthetics 1984–89); memb: Royal Soc for Nature Conservation, Wildfowl Tst, fell RSPB; fell Coll of Anaesthetists 1980, memb Intensive Care Soc 1983; *Recreations* ornithology; *Style*— Dr David Christmas; ✉ Hilston Mount, Grove Lane, Rodington, Shropshire SY4 4QP (☎ 01952 770730); Dept of Anaesthetics, Princess Royal Hospital, Apley Castle, Telford, Shropshire TF6 6TF (☎ 01952 641222)

CHRISTMAS, Timothy John; s of Leslie George Christmas, of Poole, Dorset, and Lydia Valerie, *née* Brown; *b* 2 Feb 1956; *Educ* Bournemouth, Middx Hosp Med Sch London (Simmonds' scholar, MB BS, MD, Univ of London laurels 1979); *Career* house surgn Middx Hosp 1980, demonstrator in anatomy Univ of Cambridge 1981, SHO rotation Addenbrooke's Hosp Cambridge 1982–83, SHO/registrar surgical rotation Univ Hosps Nottingham 1983–85; surgical registrar: Addenbrooke's Hosp 1985, Royal London Hosp 1985–87; research fell UC and Middx Sch of Med 1987–90, sr registrar Bart's 1990–92, research fell Norris Cancer Hosp Univ of Southern Calif LA 1992, RCS Ethicon travelling scholar 1992, Shackman travelling scholar 1992, William Cook scholar 1996, conslt urological and transplant surgn Charing Cross and Chelsea and Westminster Hosps 1992–; memb: Br Assoc of Urological Surgns 1992, Br Assoc of Surgical Oncology 1995; FRCS 1984, FRCS(Urol) 1991, FEBU 1992, FRSM 1990; *Books* Urodynamics Made Easy (jtly, 1989), Benign Prostatic Hyperplasia (jtly, 1993), Benign Prostatic Hyperplasia: a colour guide (jtly, 1994), Prostate Cancer (jtly, 1995); *Recreations* travel, ornithology, photography, skiing, warm-hearted abuse; *Style*— Timothy Christmas, Esq; ✉ Private Patients Wing, 15th Floor, Charing Cross Hospital, Fulham Palace Road, London W6 8RF (☎ 0181 846 1146, fax 0181 846 7696)

CHRISTOPHER, (Phyllis) Ann; da of William Christopher (d 1986), of Rickmansworth, Herts, and Phyllis, *née* Vennal; *b* 4 Dec 1947; *Educ* Watford Girls GS, Harrow Sch of Art, W of Eng Coll of Art (Dip AD); *m* 19 July 1969, Kenneth Harold Cook, s of Harold Gilbert Cook, of Oldland Common, nr Bristol; *Career* sculptor; numerous gp and solo exhibitions 1969–; works in public collections incl: Bristol City Art Gallery, Univ of Bristol, Glynn Vivian Art Gallery Swansea, Royal W of Eng Acad, Chantrey Bequest Royal Acad, Harrison Weir Collection London; RWA 1983 (assoc 1972), RA 1989 (assoc 1980), FRBS 1992; *Recreations* cinema, travel, architecture, gardens; *Style*— Miss Ann Christopher, RA

CHRISTOPHER, Anthony Martin Grosvenor (Tony); CBE (1984); s of George Russell Christopher (d 1951), and Helen Kathleen Milford, *née* Rowley (d 1971); *b* 25 April 1925; *Educ* Cheltenham GS, Westminster Coll of Commerce; *m* 1962, Adela Joy Thompson; *Career* chm Trades Union Unit Trust Mangrs Ltd 1983; Inland Revenue Staff Fedn: asst sec 1957–60, asst gen sec 1960–74, jt gen sec 1975, gen sec 1976–88; dir Civil Serv Bldg Soc 1958–87, pres TUC Gen Cncl 1988–89 (memb 1976–89); memb: Bd Civil Serv Housing Assoc 1958–96 (vice chm 1988–96), Cncl of Nat Assoc for Care and Resettlement of Offenders 1956 (chm 1973), Home Sec's Advsy Cncl for Probation and After-Care Ctee 1966–79, Home Sec's Working Party on Treatment of Habitual Drunken Offenders 1969–71, Cncl of Policy Studies Inst, Cncl Inst of Manpower Studies, Econ Social Res Cncl 1985–88, TUC Gen Cncl 1976–89, TUC Econ Ctee 1977–89, TUC Educn Ctee 1977–85, TUC Employment Policy and Orgn Ctee 1979–89, TUC Int Ctee 1982–89, TUC Media Working Group 1979–89 (chm 1985–89), TUC Fin Gen Purposes Ctee 1984–89, TUC Educn and Trg Ctee 1985–86, Tax Consultative Ctee 1974–88, Royal Cmmn on Distribution of Income and Wealth 1979–80, IBA 1978–83, Bdcasting Complaints Cmmn 1989–96, Audit Cmmn 1989–95, Gen Med Cncl 1989–94, Ind Inquiry into Rover Cowley Works Closure Proposals 1990; tstee Inst for Public Policy Res (treas 1991–94); chm: NEDO Tyre Ind Econ Devpt Ctee 1983–84, Alcoholics Recovery Project 1970–76; FRSA 1989; *Books* Policy for Poverty (1970), The Wealth Report (jtly, 1979); *Recreations* gardening, reading, music; *Clubs* Beefstead, Wig and Pen; *Style*— Tony Christopher, Esq, CBE; ✉ c/o T J Fund Managers Ltd, Congress House, Great Russell Street, London WC1B 3LQ

CHRISTOPHER, John; *see:* Youd, Sam

CHRISTOPHERS, Richard Henry Tudor (Harry); s of Richard Henry Christophers (d 1991), of Canterbury, Kent, and Constance Clavering, *née* Thorp (d 1987); *b* 26 Dec 1953; *Educ* Canterbury Cathedral Choir Sch, King's Sch Canterbury, Magdalen Coll Oxford; *m* 2 June 1979, Veronica Mary, da of Francis Vincent Hayward; 2 s (Dominic James b 18 March 1987, Sebastian John b 14 April 1989), 2 da (Antonia Lucy Mary b 30 Nov 1984, Cecilia Mary b 1 March 1991); *Career* conductor; South Bank debut 1983, Salzburg Festival debut 1989, Proms debut 1990, Opera debut (Lisbon Opera) 1994, conductor and fndr The Sixteen Choir and Orch; orchs conducted incl: Tapiola Sinfonietta, Avanti!, Scot Chamber Orch, RTE Concert Orch, BBC Singers, Deutsche Kammerphilharmonie, Royal Concertgebouw Chamber Orch, Lahti Symphony Orch, City of London Sinfonia, BBC Nat Orch of Wales, English Chamber Orch; *Recordings* numerous recordings with The Sixteen Choir and Orch incl: Taverner's Festival Masses Vols I-VI (1984–93) and Missa Gloria Tibi Trinitas (1989, Grand Prix du Disque), Monteverdi's Masses (1987) and Vespers (1988), Handel's Messiah (1989, Grand Prix du Disque), Byrd's Mass à 5 (1989) and Mass à 4 (1990), Poulenc's Figure Humaine (1990), Bach's St John Passion (1990), Palestrina's Missa Papae Marcelli (1990), 20 Century Christmas Collection (1990), Eton Choirbook Vols 1–5 (1991–95, Vol 1 winner Gramophone Award 1992), Handel's Alexander's Feast (1991, Deutschen Schallplatten, 1992), Purcell's Fairy Queen (1991), Sheppard's Sacred Music Vols 1–4 (1990–92), 20 Century American Collection (1991), Britten's Choral Music Vols 1–3 (1992–93, Vol 2 Deutschen Schauplatten, 1993), Bach's Christmas Oratorio (1993), Handel's Israel in Egypt (1993), Bach's B Minor Mass (1994), Stravinsky's Symphony of Psalms (1995, Diapason d'Or 1995), Handel's Esther (1996), Messiaen's Cinq Rechants (1996); video Handel's Messiah in Dublin (1992); *Recreations* cooking, Kent CCC, Arsenal FC; *Style*— Harry Christophers, Esq; ✉ c/o The Sixteen Ltd, First Floor, Enslow House, Station Road, Enslow, Kidlington, Oxon OX5 3AX (☎ 01869 331711, fax 01869 331011)

CHRISTOPHERSON, Sir Derman Guy; kt (1969), OBE (1946); s of Rev Derman Christopherson (d 1945), of Blackheath, and Edith Frances Christopherson; *b* 6 Sept 1915; *Educ* Sherborne Sch, Univ Coll Oxford (BA, DPhil), Harvard Univ (SM); *m* 1940, Frances Edith (d 1988), da of James Tearle (d 1940); 3 s (Oliver, James, Peter), 1 adopted da (Ann); *Career* engaged on scientific res in connection with the War effort 1939–45; prof of mechanical engrg Univ of Leeds 1949–55, prof of applied science with reference to engrg Imperial Coll of Sci and Technol 1955–60, vice chllr Durham Univ 1961–78, master of Magdalene Coll Cambridge 1979–85 (former fell and bursar); chm Royal Fine Art Cmmn 1979–85; FRS 1960, FEng 1976 (fndr fell), MICE, MIMechE; *Recreations* university life in all its aspects; *Clubs* United Oxford and Cambridge University; *Style*— Sir Derman Christopherson, OBE, FRS, FEng; ✉ c/o 10 Hallam Road, Mapperley, Nottingham NG3 6HA

CHRISTOPHERSON, Romola Carol Andrea; da of Albert Edward Christopherson, and Kathleen, *née* Marfitt; *b* 10 Jan 1939; *Educ* Collegiate Sch for Girls Leicester, St Hugh's Coll Oxford (BA); *Career* DSIR Miny of Technol 1962–70, Dept of Environment 1970–78, MAFF 1978–81, N Ireland Office 1981–83, dep press sec to PM 1983–84, head of info Dept of Energy 1984–86, dir of info Dept of Health (formerly DHSS) 1986–; *Recreations* amateur dramatics, antiques; *Style*— Ms Romola Christopherson; ✉ Department of Health, Richmond House, Whitehall, London SW1A 2NS

CHRUSZCZ, Charles Francis; QC (1992); s of Janik Francis Chruszcz, of Cheadle, Cheshire, and Kathleen Whitehurst; *b* 19 Nov 1950; *Educ* Brookway HS, Queen Mary Coll London (LLB); *m* Margaret Olivia, da of John Chapman; 3 s (Alexander John b 30 Aug 1977, Edward Charles b 26 Mar 1979, Thomas Robert b 20 May 1981); *Career* called to the Bar Middle Temple 1971, entered chambers at Peters St Manchester 1973, recorder of the Crown Court 1991– (asst recorder 1986–91); *Recreations* keen interest in lacrosse, rugby, reading, music, politics and the outdoors; *Style*— Charles Chruszcz, Esq, QC; ✉ 28 St John Street, Manchester M3 4DJ (☎ 0161 834 8418)

CHRYSTAL, Prof (Kenneth) Alexander (Alec); s of Kenneth Hugh Chrystal (d 1945), and Dorothy Belle, *née* Anderson; *b* 21 Jan 1946; *Educ* Oldershaw GS Wallasey, Univ of Exeter (BA), Univ of Essex (MA, PhD); *m* 1,4 April 1972 (m dis 1978); 1 s (Mark Kenneth James b 1972); m 2, 29 July 1995, Alison Anne Wigley; *Career* lectr: Univ of Manchester 1971–72, Civil Serv Coll 1972–75; econ advsr HM Treasy 1975–76, lectr Univ of Essex 1976–84, visiting prof Univ of California at Davis 1979–80, visiting scholar Federal Reserve Bank of St Louis 1983–84, prof of economics Univ of Sheffield 1984–88, prof of monetary economics City Univ Business Sch 1988– (head Dept of Banking Fin 1996–); FSS 1967, FRSA 1995; *Books* Controversies in Macroeconomics (1979), Political Economics (with J Alt, 1983), Exchange Rates and the Open Economy (ed with R Sedgwick, 1987), Introduction to Positive Economics (with R G Lipsey, 1995); *Recreations* squash, tennis, economics; *Style*— Prof Alec Chrystal; ✉ 30 Owlstone Road,

Cambridge CB3 9JH (☎ 01223 358435); Department of Banking and Finance, City University Business School, Barbican Centre, London EC2Y 8HB (☎ 0171 477 8734, fax 0171 477 8880, e-mail sg393@city.ac.uk)

CHU, Dr Anthony Christopher; s of Yu-Chang Chu, of Bexley, Kent, and Frances Nelly Chu; *b* 13 May 1951; *Educ* Alleyn's Sch Dulwich, Guy's Hosp Med Sch (BSc, MB BS); *m* 11 March 1978 (m dis 1987), Sian Meryl, da of John Daniel Griffths, of Hailey Manor, Hailey, Oxon; 2 da (Jessica Louise b 1979, Alexandra Mary b 1980); m 2, 30 Dec 1989, Jenny Frances, da of Robert Morris, of Shrub Farm, Haughley Green, Suffolk; *Career* various posts NHS 1975–80, sr staff assoc coll of physicians and surgns Columbia Presbyterian Hosp New York 1980–81, sr registrar St John's Hosp for Skin Diseases 1981–82; sr lectr (also conslt dermatologist and Wellcome sr res fell): Royal Post Grad Med Sch Hammersmith Hosp, St John's Hosp for Skin Diseases 1982–89; sr lectr and conslt dermatologist: Royal Postgrad Med Sch Hammersmith Hosp, Ealing Hosp 1989–; memb and sec: Int Histiocyte Soc, Br Assoc of Univ Teachers of Dermatology; chm Acne Support Gp; Freeman City of London 1991, Liveryman Worshipful Soc of Apothecaries 1989; FRCP 1993 (MRCP 1978); *Recreations* horticulture, painting; *Style—* Dr Anthony Chu; ✉ Unit of Dermatology, Royal Postgraduate Medical School, Hammersmith Hospital, Du Cane Rd, London W12 0NN (☎ 0181 740 3264)

CHUBB, Hon (George) William Michael; s and h of 3 Baron Hayter, KCVO, CBE; *b* 9 Oct 1943; *Educ* Marlborough, Univ of Nottingham (BSc); *m* 8 Jan 1983, Waltraud, yr da of J Flackl, of Sydney, Aust; 1 s (Thomas Frederik b 1986); *Career* md Uniqey Security Ltd mfrs of electronic hotel locks; dir William Chubb Associates 1991–96; memb Ct of Assts Worshipful Co of Weavers; *Style—* The Hon William Chubb; ✉ Mapledurwell House, Mapledurwell, nr Basingstoke, Hants RG25 2LT

CHUNN, Louise; da of Jeremiah Alfred Chunn, of 469 Parnell Rd, Auckland 1, NZ, and Yvonne Chunn; *b* 24 July 1956; *Educ* St Joseph's Convent Otahuhu NZ, Baradene Coll Remuera NZ, Univ of Aukland NZ (BA); *m* 15 Aug 1981 (m dis), Dominic Anthony Free; 1 s (Charlie b 11 March 1986), 1 da (Alice b 23 June 1988); *Career* ed Just Seventeen 1985–86, dep ed Elle 1986–89; The Guardian: ed Women's Page 1989–94, ed Madame Figaro 1993–95, assoc features ed 1994–95; Vogue: assoc ed 1995–, features ed 1996–; fndr memb Women in Journalism; *Style—* Ms Louise Chunn; ✉ Vogue, Vogue House, Hanover Square, London W1 (☎ 0171 499 9080, fax 0171 408 0559)

CHURCH, Ian Berkeley; s of late Leslie Humphreys Church, DSO, TD, of Church Brampton, Northants, and Leila Grace, *née* Berkeley; *b* 23 Jan 1927; *Educ* Stowe; *m* 14 Feb 1956, Elizabeth Anne Linley, da of Lt-Col Linley Francis Messel, TD (d 1980); 1 s, 1 da; *Career* Church and Co plc (mfrs and retailers of shoes): bd memb 1975–, chm until 1991, non-exec dir 1991–95; *Clubs* Buck's; *Style—* Ian Church, Esq; ✉ 12 Cranley Mews, London SW7 (☎ 0171 373 8278)

CHURCH, Ian David; s of John Jasper (d 1980), of London, and Violet Kathleen, *née* Treacher; *Educ* Roan Sch; *m* 3 Oct 1964, Christine Mabel, da of Arthur Frank Stevenson, of Newick, East Sussex; 1 da (Nicola b 1970); *Career* journalist: Dundee Courier & Advertiser 1959–64, Press Assoc 1964–66, The Scotsman 1966–68, The Times 1968–72; Official Report (Hansard): reporter 1972–88, dep ed 1988, ed 1989–; *Recreations* photography, writing fiction; *Style—* Ian Church, Esq; ✉ Official Report (Hansard), House of Commons, London SW1A OAA (☎ 0171 219 3388, fax 0171 219 6323)

CHURCH, Judith; MP (Lab) Dagenham (majority 13,344); da of Edmund Church (d 1977), and Helen, *née* Anderson; *b* 19 Sept 1953; *Educ* St Bernard's Sch Slough, Univ of Leeds (BA), Huddersfield Poly (PGCE Tech), Aston Univ (postgrad Dip in Occupational Health and Safety), Thames Valley Coll (postgrad Dip in Management Studies); *children* 2 s (Matthew b 22 June 1988, Edward b 8 April 1991); *Career* teacher VSO W Africa 1975–77, tech offr GAF UK 1978–79, process research Mars UK 1979–80, HM inspr of factories HSE 1980–86, nat health and safety offr MSF (formerly ASTMS) 1986–94, MP (Lab) Dagenham 1994– (contested (Lab) Stevenage 1992); memb NEC Lab Pty 1992–94 and jt chair Econ Policy Cmmn, memb Bd and tstee Inst for Public Policy Research 1992–95; fndr dir New Century Magazine 1993–96; MIOSH; *Recreations* keeping fit; *Style—* Ms Judith Church, MP; ✉ House of Commons, London SW1A 0AA (☎ 0171 219 6000, fax 0171 219 0076)

CHURCH, Prof Roy Anthony; s of William Alfred Church (d 1973), of Kettering, and Lillian Gertrude Church (d 1990); *b* 21 Feb 1935; *Educ* Kettering GS, Univ of Nottingham (BA, PhD); *m* 10 Oct 1959, Gwenllian Elizabeth, da of James Whyte Martin (d 1984), of Kettering; 3 s (Benjamin b 1964, Joseph b 1969, Thomas b 1970), 1 da (Naomi b 1980); *Career* econ historian; BBC 1958–60, Purdue Univ Indiana USA 1960–61, Univ of Washington Seattle USA 1961–62, Univ of Br Columbia Vancouver Canada 1962–63, Univ of Birmingham 1963–72, UEA 1972– (pro-vice chllr 1986–89); pres Assoc of Business Historians; memb: Cncl of Econ History Soc, Social Sci Res Cncl, Business Archives Cncl, Econ and Social Res Cncl; govr History of Advertising Trust; FRHistS 1972; ed Economic History Review 1982–90; *Books* Economic and Social Change in a Midland Town 1815–1900: Victorian Nottingham (1966), Kenricks in Hardware: A Family Business, 1790–1965 (1969), The Great Victorian Boom (1975), Herbert Austin: The British Motor Car Industry to 1941 (1979), The Dynamics of Victorian Business (ed, 1980), The History of the British Coal Industry, Volume 3: 1830–1913, Victorian Pre-eminence (1986, Wadsworth Prize), The Rise and Decline of the British Motor Industry (1994); *Recreations* tennis, badminton, fell walking, theatre; *Style—* Prof Roy Church; ✉ School of Economic and Social Studies, University of East Anglia, Norwich (☎ 01603 456161)

CHURCH, William Henry; s of Henry Albion Church (d 1981), and Iris Edith, *née* Duddy (d 1986); *b* 23 July 1946; *Educ* St Joseph's Coll Ipswich, King's Coll, Univ of London (MB BS); *m* 6 Jan 1973, Jane Ann, da of Hugh Parry, of Aberdaron, Gwynedd; 3 s (Edward b 1974, James b 1976, Martin b 1977), 1 da (Sarah b 1981); *Career* sr registrar in ophthalmology Royal Victoria Infirmary Newcastle upon Tyne 1984–88, conslt ophthalmologist Aberdeen Royal Infirmary 1988–; mountaineering achievements: first solo ascent N Face Mount Kenya 1969, first ascent N face Koh-i-Mondi Afghanistan with P Boardman, M Wragg and C Fitzhugh 1972, first ascent Chong Kumdan I (7,071m) E Karakoram India with D Wilkinson, N McAdie and J Porter 1992; MRCP 1975, FRCS 1983, FRCOphth 1991; *Recreations* mountaineering, rock climbing, skiing; *Clubs* Alpine; *Style—* William Church, Esq; ✉ Aberdeen Royal Infirmary, Foresthill, Aberdeen AB9 2ZB (☎ 01224 681818)

CHURCHER, Neville John (Nev); MBE (1996); s of Nigel Churcher, of Gosport, and Eileen Helen, *née* Ryman; *b* 22 May 1945; *Educ* Portsmouth GS, Portsmouth Sch of Architecture (Dip Arch (with Distinction)); *m* 1970, Marilyn Jean, da of Anthony John Stapleton; 2 c (Joe b 1972, Eppie b 1976); *Career* architect; Miny of Public Buildings & Works 1970–71, W H Saunders & Son (architects and town planners) 1971–72, Dept of Architecture and Design Portsmouth City Council 1972–78, with Architects' Dept Hampshire CC 1978–; work incl educnl, fire and social services projects, restoration and devpt of historic buildings and private house cmmns; pt/t educator and lectr; RIBA 1980, FCSD 1996, FRSA 1996; *Awards* incl: Brick Devpt Assoc Award for Jamaica Cottage (own house) 1977, for Woodlea Primary Sch Bordon: The Educn Award 1992, Regnl and Nat Award and President's Building of the Year Award (RIBA) 1993, Architecture and Environment Award and Designer of the Year Award (BBC Design Awards) 1994; *Recreations* gliding, restoring vintage gliders, playing and listening to music (classical and jazz/improvised), photography; *Clubs* VGC, VSCC; *Style—* Nev Churcher, Esq, MBE; ✉ Jamaica Cottage, Jamaica Place, Gosport, Hampshire PO12 1LX (☎ 01705 527202); Hampshire County Council Architects' Department, Three Minsters' House, High Street, Winchester, Hants (☎ 01962 847909)

CHURCHHOUSE, Prof Robert Francis; CBE (1982); s of Robert Francis Churchhouse (d 1995), of Manchester, and Agnes, *née* Howard (d 1985); *b* 30 Dec 1927; *Educ* St Bede's Coll Manchester, Univ of Manchester (BSc), Univ of Cambridge (PhD); *m* 7 Aug 1954, Julia Gertrude, da of John McCarthy (d 1929), of Irlam, Lancs; 3 s (Gerard b 1955, Robert b 1956, John b 1960); *Career* sci serv RN 1952–63; head of programming Atlas Computer Laboratory 1963–71, prof of computing maths Univ of Wales Coll of Cardiff 1971–95; chm Computer Bd 1979–83, pres Inst of Maths and its Applications 1986–88, memb Univs Funding Cncl 1989 (memb UFC Welsh Ctee 1989–92); Hon DSc South Bank 1993; FRAS 1962, FIMA 1964, FBCS 1967; KSG 1988; *Books* Computers in Mathematical Research (with J C Herz, 1968), The Computer in Literary and Linguistic Studies (with A Jones, 1976), Numerical Analysis (1978), Handbook of Applicable Mathematics Vol III (1981); *Recreations* cricket, astronomy; *Style—* Prof Robert Churchhouse, CBE; ✉ 15 Holly Grove, Lisvane, Cardiff CF4 5UJ (☎ 01222 750250)

CHURCHILL, Caryl Lesley; da of Robert Churchill, and Jan, *née* Brown; *b* 3 Sept 1938; *Educ* Trafalgar Montreal Canada, LMH Oxford; *m* David Richard Harter; 3 s (Joe b 1963, Paul b 1964, Rick b 1969); *Career* playwright; wrote: one-act play Downstairs (produced by Oriel Coll Oxford) 1958, Having A Wonderful Time (Questors Theatre) 1960, Easy Death (Oxford Playhouse) 1962; BBC radio plays incl: The Ants (Third Prog) 1962, Lovesick 1967, Indentical Twins 1968, Abortive 1971, Not..Not..Not..Not Enough Oxygen 1971, Schreber's Nervous Illness 1972 (subsequently adapted for stage, King's Head Theatre Islington), Henry's Past 1972, Perfect Happiness 1973; BBC TV plays incl: The Judge's Wife 1972, Turkish Delight 1974, The After Dinner Joke 1978, Crimes 1982; other stage plays incl: Owners (Theatre Upstairs, Royal Court) 1972, Objections To Sex And Violence (Royal Court) 1975, Light Shining in Buckinghamshire (Joint Stock UK tour, Theatre Upstairs, Royal Court), Vinegar Tom (Monstrous Regt UK tour, ICA Theatre) 1976, Traps (Theatre Upstairs, Royal Court) 1977, Cloud 9 (Joint Stock UK tour, Royal Court 1978 and 1980, 2 years Off-Broadway), Three More Sleepless Nights (Soho Poly and Theatre Upstairs, Royal Court) 1980, Top Girls (Royal Court, New York Shakespeare Festival Theatre) 1982–83, Fen (Joint Stock UK tour, Almeida Theatre, New York Shakespeare Festival Theatre) 1983–84, Softcops (RSC, The Barbican) 1984, A Mouthful of Birds (with David Lan, Joint Stock UK tour, Royal Court) 1986, Serious Money (Royal Court, Wyndhams Theatre, New York Shakespeare Festival then Broadway) 1987–88, Ice Cream (Royal Court) 1989, Ice Cream with Hot Fudge (Public Theatre) 1989, Mad Forest (Central Sch of Speech and Drama London, Nat Theatre Bucharest, Royal Court) 1990, Lives of the Great Poisoners (with Orlando Gough and Ian Spink, Second Strike UK tour, Riverside Studios) 1991, The Skriker (RNT) 1994, Thyestes (trans, Royal Court Theatre Upstairs) 1994; *Awards* incl: Obie for Cloud 9 1982, Obie for Top Girls 1983, Hollywood Dramalogue Critics Award for Cloud 9, Susan Blackburn Award 1984 and 1987, Best Play Olivier Award, Best Comedy Evening Standard Award and the Plays and Players Award all for Serious Money 1987; *Style—* Ms Caryl Churchill; ✉ Casarotto Ramsay Ltd, National House, 60–66 Wardour Street, London W1V 3HP (☎ 0171 287 4450, fax 0171 287 9128)

CHURCHILL, Dr Kenneth Geoffrey; OBE (1995); s of Edward John Churchill (d 1976), and Florence Ruby, *née* Adams; *b* 28 June 1947; *Educ* Weymouth GS, Judd Sch Tonbridge, Clare Coll Cambridge (MA, PhD); *m* 15 Jan 1972, Paulette Marie, *née* Leveque; 1 da (Caroline Sarah b 15 Jan 1975), 1 s (Andrew Edward Paul b 13 Jan 1976); *Career* British Council: asst dir Madras 1973–75, asst dir Rome 1975–77, Literature Dept 1977–80, dep dir Accra 1980–83, Literature Dept 1983–85, dep dir Cologne 1985, dep dir Paris 1985–89, dir Dublin 1989–94, dir Belgium and Luxembourg 1994–; *Books* Italy and English Literature (1980); *Recreations* travel, reading; *Style—* Dr Kenneth Churchill, OBE; ✉ The British Council, 15 rue de la Charité, 1210 Brussels, Belgium

CHURCHILL, 3 Viscount (UK 1902); Victor George Spencer; also Baron Churchill (UK 1815); s of 1 Viscount Churchill, GCVO (d 1934), by his 2 w Christine Sinclair (Lady Oliphant); suc half-bro 1973; *b* 31 July 1934; *Educ* Eton, New Coll Oxford (MA); *Heir* (to Barony only) kinsman, Richard Spencer; *Career* Lt Scots Gds 1953–55; Morgan Grenfell and Co Ltd 1958–74, investmt mangr The Central Bd of the Church of England and the Charities Official Investmt Fund 1974–; dir: Local Authorities' Mutual Investmt Tst 1978–, CCLA Investment Management Ltd 1987–, Kleinwort Charter Investment Tst plc 1992–, Schroder Split Fund plc 1993–, Foreign & Colonial Income Growth Investment Trust plc 1994–; *Style—* The Viscount Churchill; ✉ 6 Cumberland Mansions, George St, London W1H 5TE (☎ 0171 262 6223)

CHURCHILL, Winston Spencer; MP (C) Davyhulme (majority 4,426); s of Hon Randolph Frederick Edward Spencer Churchill, MBE (d 1968), (s of Sir Winston Churchill, KG, OM, CH, FRS) by his 1 w, Hon Pamela Harriman, *qv*, da of 11 Baron Digby, KG, DSO, MC, TD; *b* 10 Oct 1940; *Educ* Eton, ChCh Oxford (MA); *m* 15 July 1964 (sep), Mary Caroline (Minnie), da of late Sir Gerard d'Erlanger, CBE; 2 s, 2 da; *Career* circumnavigated Africa in single-engined aircraft 1962–63; author, journalist and war corr 1962–70 (incl Vietnam 1966 and Middle E 1967), BBC presenter 1964–65, roving foreign corr The Times 1969–70; Parly candidate (C) Manchester Gorton 1967, MP (C) Stretford 1970–83, MP (C) Davyhulme 1987–; PPS: to Min of Housing and Construction 1970–72, to Min of State FCO 1972–73; Cons spokesman on defence 1976–78, vice chm Cons Pty Defence Ctee 1979–83, memb Exec 1922 Ctee 1979–83, treas 1922 Ctee 1987–88, Cons Party coordinator for Defence and Disarmament and chm Campaign for Defence and Multilateral Disarmament 1982–84; memb Select Ctee on Defence 1984–; sponsored: Motor Vehicles (Passenger Insurance) Act 1972, Crown Proceedings (Armed Forces) Act 1987; pres Trafford Park Industl Cncl (TRAFIC) 1971–; tstee: Winston Churchill Meml Tst 1968–, Nat Benevolent Fund for the Aged 1974– (chm 1995–), Sandy Gall's Afghanistan Appeal 1995–; govr English Speaking Union 1975–80; memb Cncl: The Air League 1982–96, Consumers' Assoc 1990–93, Br Kidney Patients' Assoc 1990–; memb and vol pilot St John's Ambulance Air Wing 1975–93; hon fell: Churchill Coll Cambridge 1969, Soc of Engrs 1988; Hon LLD Westminster Coll Fulton Missouri 1972; Commercial Pilot's Licence (UK) 1982, Airline Tport Pilot's Licence (USA) 1982; *Books* First Journey (1964), The Six Day War (1967), Defending the West (1980), Memories and Adventures (1989), His Father's Son (1996); *Clubs* Buck's, White's, Press, Air Sqdn, St Moritz Tobogganing; *Style—* Winston S Churchill, Esq, MP; ✉ House of Commons, London SW1A 0AA (☎ 0171 219 3405)

CHURCHMAN, Michael Anthony; s of Richard John Churchman (d 1978), of Islington, London, and Mary, *née* Bradley; *b* 6 Feb 1952; *Educ* St Ignatius Coll London, Worcester Coll Oxford (MA); *m* 1974, Christine Elizabeth, da of Bryan Bernard George Dyer, of Cotmer Rd, Lowestoft, Suffolk; 3 s (Anthony Laurence b 4 Aug 1979, Christopher Michael b 28 July 1981, Alexander Richard b 19 Nov 1986); *Career* account exec Young and Rubicam 1973–75, account mangr Benton and Bowles 1975–77, account supervisor Lintas 1977–79, account dir Wasey Campbell Ewald 1979–83; bd dir: AAP Ketchum 1983–87, Grey Ltd 1987–89; md PML Creative Strategy 1990–91, fndr Churchmans Marketing Communications Ltd 1991–; memb: Advertising Advsy Ctee ITC, Cncl of Nat Advertising Benevolent Soc 1975–, FIPA 1989 (MIPA 1982), FInstD (dip in co mgnt 1988); *Recreations* family activities, running, reading, classical music, theatre going; *Clubs* United Oxford and Cambridge Univ, IOD; *Style—* Michael Churchman, Esq; ✉ 20 Rutland Place, Maidenhead, Berkshire SL6 4JA (☎ 01628 39404, fax 01628 418677)

CHURSTON, 5 Baron (UK 1858), of Churston Ferrers and Lupton, Devon; Sir John Francis Yarde-Buller; 6 Bt (GB 1790); o s of 4 Baron Churston, VRD (d 1991), and his 1 w, Elizabeth Mary, *née* Du Pre (d 1951); *b* 29 Dec 1934; *Educ* Eton; *m* 1973, Alexandra Joanna, o da of Anthony Contomichalos; 1 s (Hon Benjamin Francis Anthony b 1974), 2 da (Hon Katherine Marina b 1975, Hon Francesca Elizabeth b 1980); *Heir* s, Hon Benjamin Anthony Francis Yarde-Buller b 13 Sept 1974; *Career* late 2 Lt RHG; *Clubs* Buck's, White's; *Style*— The Rt Hon the Lord Churston; ✉ Yowlestone House, Puddington, Tiverton, S Devon

CHUTE, Robin Vere; Lord of the Manor of Sherborne St John; s of Anthony Vere Chute (d 1987), of Suffolk, and Daphne Gore, *née* Darley (d 1992); family descends from Alexander Chute, living 1268; Philip Chute was standard bearer to Henry VIII, and Chaloner Chute (1595–1659) speaker of the House of Commons, and first Chute of The Vyne, Basingstoke (*see* Burke's Landed Gentry, 1937 edn); *b* 24 May 1947; *Educ* Winchester, RAC Cirencester; *m* 30 Sept 1978, Julia Mary Susan, da of John Perkins, of Chippenham, Wilts; 1 s (Charles John Vere b 1981), 1 da (Arabella Julia Handasyd b 1984); *Career* estates bursar Winchester Coll 1981–; FRICS 1982; *Recreations* shooting, fishing, cricket, rackets; *Clubs* MCC, Flyfishers', T & R Assoc; *Style*— R V Chute, Esq; ✉ 15 Kingsgate Street, Winchester, Hants; Winchester College, Winchester, Hants (☎ 01962 864242)

CHYNOWETH, David Boyd; s of Ernest Chynoweth (d 1982), and Blodwen, *née* Griffiths; *b* 26 Dec 1940; *Educ* Simon Langton Sch Canterbury, Univ of Nottingham (BA); *m* 15 June 1968, Margaret, da of Thomas Slater, of Edensor, Derbyshire; 1 s (Richard b 1981), 2 da (Susan b 1971, Claire b 1974); *Career* dep co treas W Suffolk CC 1969–73, co treas S Yorks CC 1973–85, dir of fin Lothian Regnl Cncl 1985–94, chief exec Universities Superannuation Scheme Ltd 1994–; pres CIPFA 1992–93 (vice pres 1991–92); *Recreations* sailing, photography; *Clubs* Royal Over-Seas League; *Style*— David Chynoweth, Esq; ✉ Ardvulin, 37 Clifford Rd, N Berwick, E Lothian EH39 4PP (☎ 01620 893652); Universities Superannuation Scheme Ltd, Royal Liver Building, Liverpool L3 1PY (☎ 0151 227 4711, fax 0151 236 3173)

ČIČIN-ŠAIN, HE Dr Ante; s of Jerko Čičin-Šain (d 1976), and Anka, *née* Jerkovič; *b* 29 Sept 1935; *Educ* Odenwaldschule Heppenheim Hessen, Univ of Hamburg, Univ of Turin, Univ of Heidelberg (BA, PhD), Univ of Oxford; *m* 8 July 1967, Vesna, da of Dr Nikola Fiolič; 2 da (Ana b 18 Jan 1968, Jelena b 6 Nov 1977), 1 s (Jerko b 5 April 1970); *Career* Croatian diplomat; economic affrs offr UN Economic Cmmn for Europe 1960–61, tutor/asst prof Univ of Heidelberg 1961–63, res fell Inst of Economics Zagreb 1964–72, visiting post-grad fell Cornell Univ Ithaca 1970–72, res fell Vienna Inst for Int Economic Comparisons 1972, prof of int economics Univ of Zagreb 1972–74, head of Res Dept Central Bank of Croatia 1974–82, UNDP conslt on monetary cooperation W Africa 1982–86, sr res fell/prof of int economics Inst of Economics Univ of Zagreb 1986–90, govr Central Bank of Croatia 1990–92; Croatian ambass: to the Euro Community Brussels 1992–94, to the Ct of St James's 1994–, to Ireland 1995–; patron Irish-Croatian Friendship Soc 1995–; pres Croatian Cncl of The Euro Movement 1992–94; frequent guest lectr to several Euro and American univs, memb various governmental or parly gps working on int economic rels, foreign exchange regulation and foreign investment since 1965, memb Fed Cncl on the Reform of Yugoslav Economic System; *Publications* author of over 180 articles in professional jls and newspapers in ex-Yugoslavia and in several Euro countries relating to int economic integration, banking and finance; *Recreations* sailing, hiking, tennis, skiing; *Style*— HE Dr Ante Čičin-Šain; ✉ Embassy of the Republic of Croatia, 21 Conway Street, London W1P 5HL (☎ 0171 387 2022, fax 0171 387 0310, car 0836 521307)

CICLITIRA, Prof Paul Jonathan; s of Dennis J Ciclitira, and Grace, *née* Cooksley; *b* 7 July 1948; *Educ* Wycliffe Coll, Bart's Med Sch (MB BS, MRCP), Univ of Cambridge (MD, PhD); *m* Dr Diane Watson; 1 da (Katherine Anne b 1989), 1 s (James Alexander b 1992); *Career* SHO in gen med: Rochford Hosp 1972–73 (house offr 1971), Bart's 1973–74 (house offr in gen surgery 1971), Royal Marsden Hosp 1975; hon sr registrar Addenbrooke's Hosps 1977–80 (med registrar 1975–77), trg fell MRC Lab of Molecular Biology Cambridge 1980–83 (Drummond nutrition fell 1977–80), hon sr registrar Guy's Hosp 1980–83; UMDS Guy's and St Thomas' Hosp Tst: sr res fell Wellcome Tst 1983–89, sr lectr and hon conslt physician 1983–, prof of gastroenterology 1994–, head of Research Unit The Rayne Inst; memb: Darwin Coll Cambridge, Editorial Bd Clinical and Experimental Immunology; Br Soc of Gastroenterology Res Medal 1986, Br and Eire Socs of Gastroenterology and Lilly Res Award 1988, Euro Soc of Gastroenterology and Lilly Res Award 1989; memb: Assoc of Physicians of the UK, Biochemical Soc, Br Soc of Gastroenterology (memb Nutrition Ctee), Br Soc of Immunology, Euro Soc of Clinical Investigation, Med Res Soc of GB, Soc of Cell Biology; FRSM, FRCP 1991; *Publications* author of various pubns in learned jls particularly on coeliac disease; *Recreations* squash, swimming, theatre, cooking, wine tasting; *Clubs* Athenaeum, Chelsea Arts, Groucho; *Style*— Prof Paul J Ciclitira; ✉ Gastroenterology Unit, UMDS, The Rayne Institute, St Thomas' Hospital, London SE1 7EH (☎ 0171 928 9292 ext 3063, fax 0171 620 2597)

CIECHANOWIECKI, Count Andrew Stanislaus; s of Count George Ciechanowiecki (d 1930), Polish diplomat and landowner, and Matylda, *née* Countess Osiecimska-Hutten-Czapska (d 1991), Dame of Honour and Devotion SMOM, Dame Grand Cross of Justice Constantinian Order of St George, Dame Cdr Order of SS Mauritius and Lazarus; *b* 28 Sept 1924, Warsaw; *Educ* Lycée S Batory Warsaw, Higher Sch of Economic Studies Kraków (BA), Jagiellonian Univ Kraków (MA), Karl Eberhard Univ Tübingen (PhD); *Career* anti Nazi resistance in Poland 1941–45 (Lt Home Army, Polish war decorations); cnsllr Polish FO in Govt of National Unity and chef de protocole Miny of Foreign Trade 1945–46; political prisoner 1950–56; former lectr Jagiellonian Univ Kraków, sometime museum curator in Poland; md: Mallett at Bourdon House (London) 1961–65, Heim Gallery (London) Ltd 1965–86, Old Masters Gallery (London) Ltd 1986–93; fndr Ciechanowiecki Family Fndn Royal Castle Warsaw 1986; memb Presidential Advsy Bd for Culture in Poland, tstee various Polish charities in Poland and elsewhere abroad; memb and hon memb numerous learned Polish and foreign bodies; hon prof Acad of Fine Arts Warsaw; Hon PhD: Univ of Warsaw, Univ of Minsk, Univ of New Mexico; various other academic awards; FSA; Knight Grand Cross Order of Polonia Restituta, Knight Grand Cross Order of St Gregory the Great (Holy See), Knight Cdr Order of Merit (Italy), Cdr Grosses Silbernes Ehrenzeichen (Austria), Cdr Order of Merit (Senegal), Cdr Order of the Polar Star (Sweden), Bundesverdienstkreuz First Class (Germany), Chevalier Légion d'Honneur (France), Order of F Skaryna (Belorus), Knight Grand Cross of Honour and Devotion and Knight Grand Cross of Merit SMOM, vice pres Polish Assoc of SMOM (chm of its fndns in Britain and Poland), Knight Order of St Januarius, Bailiff Grand Cross of Justice Constantinian Order of St George (decorated with the Collar), Royal House of Naples (and memb Deputation), Knight Grand Cross Orders of SS Andrew, Alexander and Anne of Russia (dynastic), Knight Cdr Order of SS Mauritius and Lazarus, Knight Grand Cross Order of Civil Merit of Savoy, Gentleman of His Holiness The Pope, Offr of the Doorward Guard of the Lord High Constable of Scotland; Merentibus Medal Jagiellonian Univ Kraków, hon citizen towns of Ciechanowiec and Zastaw; *Books* author of several books and numerous articles in the field of art and history of culture; *Recreations* reading, genealogy, travelling; *Clubs* Brooks's, Polish Hearth; *Style*— Count Andrew Ciechanowiecki, FSA; ✉ Flat 2, 92 Mount Street, London W1Y 5HG (☎ 0171 491 1967, fax 0171 629 9774)

CIERACH, Lindka Rosalind Wanda; da of Edek (Edward) Cierach, MBE (d 1992), of Starydom, St Just-in-Roseland, Truro, Cornwall, and Diana Rosemary, *née* Wilson; f mapped large tracts of Africa, decorated for Battle of Monte Cassino with highest Order of Virtuti Military, Kirzyz Walecznych, Star medal 1939–44, Star Italian Campaign, Star of Monte Cassino, Star Defense MBE; *b* 8 June 1952; *Educ* Uganda, Convent of the Holy Child Jesus Mayfield Sussex; *Career* fashion designer; designed wedding dress for Duchess of York's marriage on 23 July 1986; Designer of the Year Award 1987; *Recreations* travelling, photography, arts, music, opera; *Style*— Lindka Cierach; ✉ 1c Clareville Grove, London SW7 3AU (☎ 0171 373 3131, fax 0171 373 1675)

CIESINSKI, Kristine Frances; *b* 5 July 1952, Wilmington, Delaware, USA; *Educ* Temple Univ, Univ of Delaware, Boston Univ (BA); *m* 1985, Norman Bailey, CBE, *qv*; *Career* soprano; New York concert debut (solist) Handel's Messiah 1977, with Salzburg Landestheater 1979–81 (Euro operatic debut as Baroness Freimann in Der Wildschutz 1979), memb Bremen State Opera 1985–88; guest appearances: Cincinnati Opera, Florentine Opera Milwaukee 1983 and 1987, Cleveland Opera 1985, Scottish Opera 1985 and 1989, Canadian Opera 1986, Opera North Leeds 1986 and 1988, Augsburg Opera 1986, Mexico City 1986, Welsh National Opera 1987 and 1989, Bregenz Festival 1987, Zagreb National Opera 1988, Wexford Festival 1988, English National Opera 1989–96, Munich State Opera 1989–95, Baltimore Opera 1989, Winnipeg Opera 1989 and 1991, Frankfurt State Opera 1990–97, Bolshoi Opera 1990, Kirov Opera 1990, Basel Opera 1991, Paris-Bastille Opera 1992, New Orleans Opera 1992, Leipzig Opera 1992–95, La Scala Milan 1992, Dresden-Semperoper 1994, Spoleto Festival 1994, Teatro Colon Buenos Aires 1995, Glyndebourne Festival 1995 and 1997, Dallas Opera 1995, Dusseldorf 1996–97; roles incl: Medea, La Wally, Eva, Senta, Donna Anna in Don Giovanni, Tosca, Aida, Ariadne, Salome, Lady Macbeth in Verdi's Macbeth, title role in Shostakovich's Lady Macbeth of Mtsensk, Schönberg's Erwartung, Judith from Bartok's Bluebeard, Marie in Berg's Wozzeck, Leonora in Beethoven's Fidelio, Tatiana in Tchaikovsky's Eugene Onegin, Emilia Marty in Janáček's Makropulous Case, title role in Katya Kabanova, also many conert engagements in a repertory ranging from traditional works to contemporary scores; has made several recordings; films incl: Secret Life of Alban Berg (BBC) 1993, Abfallprodukte der Liebe by Werner Schroeter 1996; honours: Gold medal Geneva Int Competition 1977, first prize Salzburg Int Competition 1977; *Style*— Ms Kristine Ciesinski; ✉ c/o William Guerri, Columbia Artists Management Inc, Arbib Division, 165 West 57 St, NYC, NY 10019–2276, USA (☎ 00 1 212 841 9546, fax 00 1 212 841 9516)

CINA, Colin; s of Louis Cina of Glasgow, and Ettie, *née* Barkofsky; *b* 24 April 1943; *Educ* Glasgow Sch of Art, Central Sch of Art (DipAD); *m* 1962, Gill, *née* Nicholas; 2 da (Jane b 1972, Chloe b 1976); *Career* artist and fine art teacher; visiting fell in fine art Univ of Newcastle upon Tyne 1971–72; pt/t teaching: Manchester Sch of Art (fine art) 1967–71, Central Sch of Art 1968–75; princ lectr in charge of painting Wimbledon Sch of Art 1975–80 (acting head of fine art 1975–76), head of fine art Chelsea Sch of Art 1988 (head of Painting Dept 1980), dean Sch of Art Chelsea Coll of Art and Design 1989–; fine art and fndn external examiner for various colls and univs, author of various articles and catalogues; govr London Inst 1986–89 (memb of various Ctees); coll govr: Canterbury Coll of Art 1982–86, Duncan of Jordanstone Sch of Art Univ of Dundee 1989; CNAA Fine Art Panel: specialist advsr 1982–, memb of Panel 1985–87, specialist register 1987–; memb CNAA Ctee for Art and Design 1989–91; memb Architects and Artists Action Gp 1983–84, chm Nat Assoc for Fine Art Educn 1989–90 (vice chm 1988–89); ELIA (The European League of Insts of the Arts): memb Founding Ctee 1989–90, elected memb Bd 1996–98; conslt for various orgns incl: BBC, Dept of Tport, Kent Inst of Art and Design, RNIB, European Union, Ontario Coll of Art; *Solo Exhibitions* incl: Serpentine Gallery 1980, Library Gallery Univ of Surrey 1983, Angela Flowers London 1984; recent *Group Exhibitions* incl: Redhill Street Open Studios London 1987, 21st Anniversary Exhibition of Richard Demarco Gallery (Smiths Gallery) London 1988, Scottish Art Since 1900 (Gallery of Modern Art Edinburgh Festival 1989–90), Barbican Art Gallery London 1989/90, Master Class (London Inst Gallery) 1991, Small is Beautiful (Flowers East Gallery) 1992; *Public Collections* incl: Arts Cncl of GB, City Art Gallery Bristol, Contemporary Arts Soc, CNAA, National Gallery Budapest Hungary, Scot Arts Cncl, Scot Nat Gallery of Modern Art Edinburgh, Nat Gallery of Iceland, V & A, Allende Museum Chile; *Style*— Colin Cina, Esq; ✉ Flowers East Gallery, 199/205 Richmond Rd, London E8 (☎ 0181 985 3333)

CINNAMOND, Prof Michael James; s of James Herbert Cinnamond (d 1977), and Mary Elizabeth, *née* Stewart; *b* 16 Sept 1943; *Educ* The Methodist Coll Belfast, The Queen's Univ Belfast (MB BCh, BAO); *m* 18 Dec 1965, Judith Patricia, da of William Edmund Guthrie, of Newcastle, Co Down; 2 s (Michael b 8 Nov 1966, Neill b 31 March 1971), 1 da (Adrienne b 7 Nov 1972); *Career* conslt otolaryngologist 1976–79: Royal Belfast Hosp for Sick Children, Royal Victoria Hosp, Belfast City Hosp; sr lectr otorhinolaryngology Queen's Univ Belfast 1979–81; conslt paediatric otolaryngologist 1979–81 and 1981–: Royal Belfast Hosp for Sick Children, Belfast City Hosp; prof of otorhinolaryngology Queen's Univ Belfast 1981–; memb: Industl Injuries Advsy Cncl, Speciality Advsy Ctee in Otolaryngology to Jt Ctee Higher Surgical Trg; FRCS Ed 1974, FRCSI ad eundem 1987; *Books* Scott-Brown's Otolaryngology (5 edn, contrib, 1987), Accident and Emergency Medicine (2 edn, contrib, 1989); *Style*— Prof Michael Cinnamond; ✉ Department of Otorhinolaryngology, University Floor, Tower Block, Belfast City Hospital, Belfast BT9 7AB (☎ 01232 329241 ext 2356)

CIPOLLA, Joseph Angelo; s of Anthony Joseph Cipolla, of Buffalo, New York, USA, and Joanna, *née* D'anna; *b* 16 Nov 1959; *Educ* Saint Joseph's Collegiate Inst, American Acad of Ballet, Buffalo State Coll; *m* 30 July 1983, Julie Patrica, da of Patrick Felix; 2 da (Joanna Leanne b 22 May 1987, Natalie Rose b 2 Sept 1990); *Career* ballet dancer; with Dance Theatre of Harlem 1979–86; performances incl: Swan Lake, Giselle, The Four Temperaments, Square Dance, Agon, Serenade, Voluntaries, Fete Noir, Equus, Fall River Legend, A Streetcar Named Desire, Firebird, Paquita, Graduation Ball, Mirage, Troy Game; princ dancer The Birmingham Royal Ballet (formerly Sadler's Wells Royal Ballet) 1986–; performances incl: Prince Siegfried in Swan Lake, Franz in Coppelia, Colas in La Fille Mal Gardee, Albrecht in Giselle, Prince Florimund in The Sleeping Beauty, Captain Belaye in Pineapple Poll, Fred Beenstock in Hobson's Choice, Romeo in Sir Kenneth Macmillan's Romeo and Juliet; other appearances: A Street Car Named Desire for PBS TV shown on C4, the White House 1980, closing ceremony Olympic Games in LA 1984, opening of The Fonteyn Centre 1990, Margot Fonteyn's Magic of Dance; created roles in: Michael Corda's Gloriana, Jennifer Jackson's One by Nine, Susan Crow's Private City, Graham Lustig's The Edge of Silence, Vincent Redmon's Meridian of Youth, Oliver Hindle's Sacred Symphony and Dark Horizans, Mathew Hart's Street, William Tuckett's Lisence My Roving Hands and Game; nominated Olivier Award for Outstanding Achievement in Dance (for performance of Kurt Joos's The Green Table, Sadler's Wells Theatre) 1993; *Recreations* movies (cinema), wine; *Style*— Joseph Cipolla, Esq; ✉ Birmingham Royal Ballet, Birmingham Hippodrome, Hurst St, Birmingham

CITRINE, 2 Baron (UK 1946), of Wembley, Co Middlesex; Dr the Rt Hon Norman Arthur Citrine; s of 1 Baron Citrine, GBE, PC (d 1983, former chm Central Electricity Authority, pres World Fedn of Trade Unions, chm World Anti-Nazi Cncl, gen sec TUC), and Doris Helen (d 1973), da of Edgar Slade; *b* 27 Sept 1914; *Educ* Univ Coll Sch, Law Soc London (LLB 1938); *m* 4 Jan 1939, Kathleen Alice, da of late George Thomas Chilvers, of Saxmundham, Suffolk; 1 da; *Heir* bro, Dr the Hon Ronald Eric

Citrine; *Career* Lt RNVR 1940–46; slr 1937, general practitioner 1937–39, 1951–84, author of numerous legal and technical works, lectr, legal adviser to TUC 1946–51; pres Devon and Exeter Law Soc 1971–72; emigrated NZ 1985; LLD London 1993; *Recreations* writing, yachting, camping, painting, rambling, music, literature, art, numerous constructional crafts; *Style*— Dr the Rt Hon the Lord Citrine; ✉ Casa Katrina, The Mount, Opua, Bay of Islands, New Zealand

CLAGUE, Andrew Charlesworth; s of John Charlesworth Clague, of Canterbury, and Margaret Elsie, *née* Musgrave; *b* 15 May 1951; *Educ* St Edmunds Sch Canterbury, Kent Inst of Design (DipArch); *m* 1, 23 June 1973 (m dis 1991), Alison Francesca; 2 s (James Charlesworth, Nicholas Charlesworth), 2 da (Anna Genevieve, Isabel Lucy); m 2, 24 Dec 1992, Kim Wilkinson, da of Alfred Leggatt, MBE; *Career* sr ptnr Clague (architects, town planners and landscape architects) Canterbury (HQ) and Ashford Kent, ptnr The Old Rectory (care home) Ickham, fndr and dir Countryman Properties Ltd 1986–; RIBA: chm Canterbury and Dist 1989–91 memb Cncl 1995–, chm SE Region 1996–; memb Rotary Club (Canterbury), chm Round Table (Canterbury and Dist) 1990–91; memb St Edmunds Soc (St Edmunds Sch old pupils); *Recreations* sailing, music; *Clubs* Kent and Canterbury, Inst of Dirs; *Style*— Andrew Clague, Esq; ✉ The Old Rectory Cottage, Ickham, Canterbury CT3 1QN (☎ 01227 721400); Clague, 62 Burgate, Canterbury, Kent CT1 2HJ (☎ 01227 762060, fax 01227 762149, car 0585 771055)

CLAGUE, Dr Roy Bridson; s of William Alan Clague, of Douglas, IOM, and Doris, *née* Bridson; *b* 16 Jan 1948; *Educ* Douglas HS for Boys IOM, Univ of Newcastle upon Tyne (MB BS, MD); *m* 16 Jan 1971, Helen da of John de Legh, of Manchester; 3 da (Bethany b 1971, Emma b 1973, Joanna b 1978); *Career* registrar in gen med 1973–76, sr registrar in rheumatology 1976–80, trg fell MRC 1976–79, conslt rheumatologist Withington Hosp Manchester and Devonshire Royal Hosp Derbyshire 1980–91, conslt rheumatologist Noble's Hosp Douglas IOM 1991–; memb Rheumatology Cmmn RP 1988–93, pres local branch Arthritis and Rheumatism Cncl IOM; FRCP 1989 (MRCP 1974); *Recreations* golf, previously dinghy sailing; *Style*— Dr Roy Clague; ✉ Noble's Hospital, Douglas, Isle of Man IM1 4QA (☎ 01624 642642)

CLAMP, Hugh John Derek Mence; OBE (Mil, 1973), VRD (1963, Clasp 1973); s of John William Clamp (d 1955), of Woodford, and Mary Florence, *née* Mence (d 1986); *b* 3 Oct 1927; *Educ* Chigwell Sch, Reading Blue Coat Sch, Barlett Sch of Architecture UCL (BA), Landscape Sch Thames Poly (Dip Landscape Architecture); *m* 19 Feb 1955, (Isobel) Barbara, da of John Galbraith Quiros Worledge (d 1985), of Sydney, Aust; 1 s (John b 6 April 1959), 1 da (Felicity b 25 April 1956); *Career* Nat Serv RNVR 1949–51, Sub Lt 1950, London Div RNR 1951–76, Cdr 1968; architect and landscape conslt; asst: Sir Frederick Gibberd & Ptnrs 1951–52, Elie Mayorcas 1952–53, Farmer and Dark 1953–54; in private practice 1955–, fndr ptnr Manning Clamp & Ptnrs 1956; dir: Manning Clamp 1990–92, Broadway Malyan Landscape 1991–93; projects incl: Carnatic Halls of Residence Univ of Liverpool, Portland Terrace Richmond Green, Enid Haupt Conservatory Bronx Botanical Gardens NYC, Sir Joseph Banks Centre Royal Botanic Gardens Kew, alterations at Hampton Court, Buckingham Palace, Rochester and Windsor Castle; Nat Joint Consultative Ctee for Building: memb Good Practice Panel 1968–78 (chm 1978), memb Main Ctee 1970–78 (chm 1979); RIBA: memb Contract Ctee 1968– (chm 1984–91), memb Practice Ctee 1980–94 (chm 1991–93), memb Cncl 1989–95, memb Arbitration Ctee 1990–, vice pres 1991–93, chm Disciplinary Ctee 1994–; Landscape Inst: memb Tech Ctee 1976–89 (chm 1985–89), chm Internal Affrs Ctee 1989–91, memb Cncl 1985–95, vice pres 1989–91, pres 1991–93; RIBA memb Joint Contracts Tbnl 1968–81 and 1989–94, RIBA memb Tree Cncl 1989–94, chm RIBA SE Soc of Architects 1991–93, Landscape Inst memb Joint Cncl for Landscape Industries 1978–94, memb DoE Construction Industry Liaison Gp 1987–94, RIBA memb Architects Registration Cncl UK 1995–, memb Professional Purposes Ctee 1995– (chm 1996); pt/t lectr Thames Poly 1976–82; 29 RIBA, DoE and Civic Tst awards and commendations; Royal Botanic Gardens Kew Gold medal 1980; memb Manchester Olympic 2000 Design Advsy Panel 1992–93; Centenary Fell Thames Poly 1990; *Publications* NJCC Clients Guide (with Ian Bampton, 1973), Building Maintenance and Preservation (contrib, 1980), The Shorter Forms of Building Contract (1984, 3 edn 1993), Spons Landscape Contract Manual (1986, 2 edn 1995), Landscape Professional Practice (1988 and 1989), Which Contract (with Stanley Cox, 1989); *Recreations* opera, music, theatre, sketching, foreign travel and things hellenic, the English countryside, growing vegetables, geriatric skiing; *Clubs* Army and Navy; *Style*— Hugh Clamp, Esq, OBE, VRD; ✉ Mill Farm, Mill Lane, Yetminster, nr Sherborne, Dorset

CLANCARTY, 9 Earl of (I 1803); Nicholas Power Richard Le Poer Trench; also (sits as) Viscount Clancarty (UK 1823), Baron Kilconnel (I 1797), Viscount Dunlo (I 1801), Baron Trench (UK 1815), Marquis of Heusden in the Kingdom of the Netherlands (1818); s of Hon Power Edward Ford Le Poer Trench (yst s of 5 Earl; d 1975), and Jocelyn Louise, *née* Courtney (d 1962); suc uncle, 8 Earl of Clancarty 1995; *b* 1 May 1952; *Educ* Ashford GS, Plymouth Polytechnic, Univ of Colorado; *Career* artist and film-maker; *Style*— The Rt Hon the Earl of Clancarty; ✉ c/o House of Lords, London SW1A OPW

CLANCY, Laurence Joseph; s of Joseph Alfred Clancy (d 1983), of Clayton, Bradford, and Agnes, *née* Hunter (d 1965); *b* 15 March 1929; *Educ* English Sch Cairo, Univ of Liverpool (Gibson-Sinclair entrance scholar, BSc, Derby research student), Coll of Aeronautics Cranfield (DCAe), Univ of Bradford (MSc); *m* 1, 1952 (m dis 1971), Barbara, da of late Edward Consterdine; 1 s (Peter Joseph b 1953), 3 da (Helen Judith b 1956, Caroline Mary b 1959, Jillian Barbara b 1961); m 2, 1971 (m dis 1988), Eileen Gladys Tyne, da of Sidney Smith; m 3, 1992, Dorothy Jane Bingham, da of Leonard Levy; *Career* perm cmmn RAF Educn Branch 1951–67: maths tutor RAF Coll Cranwell 1951–56, Flt Lt 1953, seconded for postgraduate studies Cranfield 1956–58, lectr in maths RAF Tech Coll Henlow 1958–60, lectr then sr lectr in aerodynamics RAF Coll Cranwell 1960–67 (head of dept 1964–67), Sqdn Ldr 1961; warden Havelock Hall and lectr in engrg maths Univ of Newcastle upon Tyne 1967–70; Univ of Bradford 1970–: lectr in engrg maths 1970–82, dep chm of industl technol 1982–88, head Dept of Industrial Technol 1988–93, dean of engrg 1993–96, currently advsr to the Vice-Chllr; Sword of Honour RAF Offr Cadet Trg Unit 1951; assoc fell (subsequently memb) RAeS 1960, CEng 1966, FIMA 1965; *Books* Aerodynamics (1975); *Recreations* opera, theatre, literature, hockey and cricket when younger (memb univ 1st XI teams), squash; *Style*— Laurence Clancy, Esq; ✉ 13 Calder Bank, Queensbury, Bradford, W Yorks BD13 1BY (☎ 01274 882028); Office of the Vice-Chancellor, University of Bradford, Richmond Road, Bradford, W Yorks BD7 1DP (☎ 01274 384241, fax 01274 391333)

CLANDERMOND, Countess of; Iris Elizabeth Andrew; da and co-heiress of John Kirk Brodie (d 1960), of Inverkip; cous of Ninian Brodie of Brodie, *qv*, Chief of his Name; *b* 1926; *Educ* privately; *m* 1952, John Spence Gibson Davison (d 1979), Baron of Kilcoe, s and h of Walter Scott Corry Davison, Count of Clandermond (d 1953); 1 s (The Count of Clandermond, *qv*), 1 da (Elizabeth (Mrs Paul Lorimer)); *Career* Hon Lady-in-Waiting to HM Queen Susan of the Albanians, Niadh Nask, Dame Cdr Order of Polonia Restituta; *Style*— The Countess of Clandermond

CLANDERMOND, Count of (Kingdom of Munster ca 1250 by King Donal II; confirmed Kingdom of France 1756 by King Louis XV); John Andrew Brodie Davison; also Lord of Clandermond, Baron of Kilcoe and Baron of Cloghan; head of the House of Davison of Broughshane; Chamberlain to The MacCarthy Mór, *qv*, Prince of Desmond; hereditary Constable of Mashanaglass Castle, Co Cork; o s of John Spence Gibson Davison (d 1979), Count of Clandermond, Silver Cross Mil Order of Virtuti Militari (cous of the Rt Hon the Baron Broughshane), and Iris Elizabeth Andrew Brodie (descended from the ancient Scottish Chiefly House of Brodie of Brodie, of Brodie Castle, Moray) hon lady-in-waiting to HM Queen Susan of the Albanians; *b* 1954; *Educ* privately; *Career* author of heraldic, genealogical and historical articles and books; admin Royal Eoghanacht Soc, hon ed The Stag Trippant, sec-gen The Niadh Nask; fell: Royal Cwlth Soc, Winston Churchill Memorial Tst, Royal Soc of Antiquaries of Ireland, Royal Eoghanacht Soc; memb: Royal Celtic Soc of Edinburgh, Nat Art Collection Fund, Clan Davidson Assoc (memb Cncl); co-patron The Davison Soc; descendant memb (from the Earl of Stafford, KG, temp Edward III) Soc of the Friends of St George's, Windsor Castle; offr and memb of several orders incl: hereditary Niadh Nask, Knight Sacred Military Constantinian Order of St George of Naples, Knight Offr Royal Italian Order of St Maurice and St Lazarus, Knight Cdr Polonia Restituta; Hon Col State of Alabama 1994; *Clubs* Royal Commonwealth Soc; *Style*— The Count of Clandermond

CLANFIELD, Viscount; Ashton Robert Gerard Peel; s and h of 3 Earl Peel, *qv*; *b* 16 Sept 1976; *Style*— Viscount Clanfield

CLANMORRIS, 8 Baron (I 1800) Simon John Ward Bingham; s of 7 Baron Clanmorris (d 1988), and Madeleine Mary, da of Clement Ebel; *b* 25 Oct 1937; *Educ* Downside, Queens' Coll Cambridge (MA); *m* 1971, Gizella Maria, da of Sandor Zverko, of Budapest (d 1979); 1 da (Lucy Katherine Gizella); *Heir* kinsman, John Temple Bingham b 1923; *Career* 13/18 Royal Hussars (QMO) 1956–58; chm: Telnet Int Group, Real Leisure plc; FCA 1975; *Recreations* skiing, sailing; *Style*— The Lord Clanmorris; ✉ c/o Child & Co, 1 Fleet Street, London EC4Y 1BD

CLANRANALD, The Capt of (c 1380); Ranald Alexander Macdonald of Clanranald; 24 Chief of Clanranald; s of Capt Kenneth Macdonald, DSO (d 1938), of Inchkenneth and Gribune; suc kinsman Angus Macdonald, Capt of Clanranald 1944; *b* 27 March 1934; *Educ* Christ's Hosp; *m* 1961, Jane, da of Ivar Campbell-Davys, of Llandovery; 2 s (Ranald b 1963, Andrew b 1965), 1 da (Catriona b 1972); *Heir* s, Ranald (Og Angus) Macdonald, yr of Clanranald, b 17 Sept 1963; *Career* fndr, chm and md Tektura Wallcoverings, chm Br Contract Furnishing Assoc 1975–76; memb Standing Cncl Scot Chiefs 1957–, pres Highland Soc London 1988–91 (dir 1959–80), exec chm Clan Donald Lands Tst 1978–80, chm Museum of Isles 1980–89, founding exec tstee Lord of the Isles Gally Tst 1991–; *Recreations* off-shore sailing, fishing; *Clubs* White's, Pratt's, Beefsteak, Puffins, New (Edinburgh); *Style*— The Captain of Clanranald; ✉ 15 Eccleston Street, London SW1W 9LX (☎ 0171 823 6587); Grooms Bell, The Haining, Selkirk, Scotland TD7 5LR (☎ 01750 23209)

CLANWILLIAM, 7 Earl of (I 1776); Sir John Herbert Meade; 9 Bt (I 1703); also (sits as) Baron Clanwilliam (UK 1828), Viscount Clanwilliam and Baron Gillford (I 1766); yr s of Adm the Hon Sir Herbert Meade-Fetherstonhaugh, GCVO, CB, DSO, s of 4 Earl of Clanwilliam; suc his cousin, 6 Earl of Clanwilliam, 1989; *b* 27 Sept 1919; *Educ* RNC Dartmouth; *m* 1956, Maxine, o da of late James Adrian Hayden Scott, and former w of Michael John Willson Levien; 1 s (Lord Gillford), 2 da (Lady Rowena Katherine (Lady Rowena Crichton-Stewart) b 1957, Lady Tania Frances (Lady Tania Compton) b 1963); *Heir* s, Lord Gillford, *qv*; *Clubs* Turf; *Style*— The Rt Hon the Earl of Clanwilliam; ✉ House of Lords, London SW1

CLAPHAM, Adam John; s of Sir Michael John Sinclair Clapham, KBE, *qv*, and Hon Elisabeth Russell Rea (d 1994), yr da of 1 Baron Rea of Eskdale, PC; *b* 8 April 1940; *Educ* Bryanston, Univ of Grenoble; *Career* Anglia TV 1960–63, scriptwriter ABC TV 1963; BBC TV: prodr Man Alive 1965–69, ed Braden's Week 1969–71, ed Man Alive 1972–75, exec prodr documentary features 1975–82; chief exec Griffin Productions 1982–; dir British Pathé News Ltd 1991–92; Imperial Relations Tst Bursary 1971, Leverhulme fell Sri Lanka 1979; Freeman City of London 1976, Liveryman Worshipful Co of Bowyers 1976; *Books* As Nature Intended (1982); *Clubs* Oriental; *Style*— Adam Clapham, Esq; ✉ 254 Alexandra Park Rd, London N22 4BG (☎ 0181 889 9035); Griffin Productions, 15 Bloomsbury Square, London WC1A 2LJ (☎ 0171 312 3700, fax 0171 312 3708)

CLAPHAM, Prof Christopher S; s of Anthony Clapham (d 1973), and Veronica Mary, *née* Lake; *b* 20 March 1941; *Educ* Bryanston, Keble Coll Oxford (MA, DPhil); *m* 1 Nov 1975, Caroline Margaret, da of Brig John J S Tutton, CBE, of Awre, Glos; 1 s (Thomas b 1979), 1 da (Phoebe b 1977); *Career* lectr in law Univ of Addis Ababa 1966–67, res fell Univ of Manchester 1968–71, prof of politics and int rels Univ of Lancaster 1989– (lectr 1971–74, sr lectr 1974–89); memb Cncl: Br Tst for Ornithology 1976–79, African Studies Assoc of the UK 1981–84 and 1989–94 (pres 1992–94); Liveryman Worshipful Co of Ironmongers 1968; *Books* Haile-Selassie's Government (1969), Liberia and Sierra Leone (1976), Third World Politics (1985), Transformation and Continuity in Revolutionary Ethiopia (1988), Africa and the International System (1996); *Recreations* ornithology; *Style*— Prof Christopher Clapham; ✉ Department of Politics and International Relations, University of Lancaster, Lancaster LA1 4YL (☎ 01524 594264)

CLAPHAM, David J; *Career* J Sainsbury plc: joined 1964, area dir 1982–87, departmental dir branch ops 1987–89, md Savacentre 1989–92, dir produce, delicatessen, bakery, specialist businesses and scientific services 1992–96, bd dir trading 1996–; *Style*— David Clapham, Esq; ✉ J Sainsbury plc, Stamford House, Stamford Street, London SE1 9LL (☎ 0171 921 6000)

CLAPHAM, Michael; MP (Lab) Barnsley West and Penistone (majority 14,504); *b* 15 May 1943; *Educ* Barnsley Tech Coll, Leeds Poly (BSc), Univ of Leeds (PGCE), Univ of Bradford (MPhil); *m*; 1 s, 1 da; *Career* miner 1958–70, lectr 1975–77, dep head Compensation Dept NUM 1977–83, head Industl Relations Dept NUM 1983–92, MP (Lab, NUM sponsored) Barnsley W and Penistone 1992–, memb Select Ctee Trade and Industry 1992; vice chm back bench Trade and Industry Ctee 1995–96, chm All Pty Group on Occupational Safety and Health 1996; memb: Lab Pty 1979–, Co-operative Pty, NUM, GMB/APEX, Greenpeace; *Style*— Michael Clapham, Esq, MP; ✉ House of Commons, London SW1A 0AA; constituency office: 18 Regent Street, Barnsley S70 2HG (☎ 01226 731244, fax 01226 779429)

CLAPHAM, Sir Michael John Sinclair; KBE (1973); s of Prof Sir John Clapham, CBE, LittD, FBA (d 1946), of Storey's End, Cambridge, and Mary Margaret, *née* Green (d 1965); *b* 17 Jan 1912; *Educ* Marlborough, King's Coll Cambridge (BA, MA); *m* 18 May 1935, Hon Elisabeth Russell Rea (d 1994), da of 1st Baron Rea of Eskdale; 3 s (Adam, *qv*, Marcus, Giles d 1990), 1 da (Antonia); *Career* dep chm: ICI plc 1968–74 (dir 1961–74), Lloyds Bank plc 1974–81 (dir 1971–82); pres CBI 1972–74; chm: IMI plc 1974–81, BPM Holdings plc 1974–81; non-exec dir: Grindlays Bank Ltd 1975–84, Heytesbury (UK) Ltd 1988–90, Stoll Moss Theatres Ltd 1986–90; Hon DSc Aston (1973), Hon LLD CNAA (1978), Hon LLD London (1984); *Recreations* sailing, cooking; *Clubs* Royal Yacht Sqdn; *Style*— Sir Michael Clapham, KBE; ✉ 26 Hill St, London W1X 7FU (☎ 0171 499 1240)

CLAPHAM, Dr Peter Brian; CB (1996); *b* 3 Nov 1940; *Educ* Ashville Coll Harrogate, UCL (BSc), PhD (London, external); *m* Jean; 2 s (Andrew, Matthew); *Career* Scientific Civil Service: joined 1960, R & D in vacuum deposited optical thin films, infra-red sources and diffraction grating technology at National Physical Laboratory (NPL) 1960–70, sec Advsy Ctee on Res on Measurement and Standards 1971–72, mangr section concerned with vacuum and pressure metrology (with personal res on laser interferometry) 1973–78, head of mktg and publicity in Directorate 1978–80, head of engrg metrology work 1980–81, transferred to Res and Technol Policy Div Dept of Indust HQ 1981–82, supt Div of Mechanical and Optical Metrology NPL 1982–84, dir

Nat Weights and Measures Laboratory 1984–90; dir and chief exec NPL 1990–95, dir and chief exec National Engineering Laboratory 1995–96, conslt 1996–; memb Int Ctee of Weights and Measures 1991, chm Consultative Ctee on the Definition of the Metre 1991; vice pres Inst of Trading Standards Admin 1992; fell UCL 1996, Hon DSc Kingston Univ 1993; FInstP 1980, CEng 1989; *Recreations* walking, travel, arts and crafts; *Style—* Dr Peter Clapham, CB; ✉ 2 Darnley Park, Weybridge, Surrey KT13 8EY (☎ 01932 856765)

CLAPP, Peter Michael; s of Percival Dennis Clapp (d 1994), of Exmouth, Devon, and Lily, *née* Duck (d 1988); *b* 12 March 1943; *Educ* Exeter Sch, Dept of Architecture Hammersmith Coll of Art and Building (DipArch, RIBA Sir Bannister Fletcher silver medal); *m* 26 Sept 1964, Ann; 2 s (Giles Benedict b 25 Dec 1966, Adam Julian b 10 Oct 1968); *Career* architect and designer; own practice and RIBA res award 1964–67, assoc ptnr in various practices incl Whinney McKay Lewis and Louis de Soissons 1968–74, Architect's Dept London Borough of Camden 1975–80; W H Smith: responsible for Do-it-All building prog 1981–82, dep chief architect 1983–86, design mangr 1987–92 (with overall responsibility for all design, architecture, advtg, art purchasing and corp identity); chief architect The Sports Cncl 1996– (princ architect 1992–96) (responsible for multi-disciplinary team advising on buildings for sport and the Nat Cycling Centre Manchester); 2 Civic Tst awards 1981, DoE good design in housing award 1982; Civic Tst assessor 1982–; visiting lectr: London Business Sch, RCA, Templeton Coll Oxford; ARIBA 1966 (memb Cncl 1972–75), FCSD 1991; *Recreations* landscape photography, theatre, music, walking; *Style—* Peter Clapp, Esq; ✉ The Laggar, Laggar Lane, South Woodchester, Stroud, Glos GL5 5EJ (☎ 01453 872544); The Sports Council, 16 Upper Woburn Place, London WC1H 0QP (☎ 0171 388 1277)

CLAPPERTON, Prof Chalmers Moyes; s of Thomas Ballantyne Clapperton (d 1988), of Hawick, and Eleanor Stirling, *née* Chalmers (d 1986); *b* 9 Aug 1938; *Educ* Hawick HS, Univ of Edinburgh (MA, PhD); *m* 1962, Elizabeth Morag, da of James Thomson; 2 s (James Chalmers b 11 April 1968, Andrew Chalmers 27 Oct 1971); *Career* Univ of Aberdeen: asst lectr 1962–63, lectr 1963–72, sr lectr 1972–87, reader 1987–92, prof of geography 1992–; visiting prof: Univ of Washington 1984, Panamerican Geographical Inst of Ecuador 1986; external examiner: Univ of Strathclyde 1979–81, Univ of Edinburgh 1984–86, Univ of Glasgow 1988–91, Univ of St Andrews 1992–; President's prize Royal Scottish Geographical Soc 1991; memb: Quaternary Research Assoc 1968, American Quaternary Assoc 1984; FRSE 1992; *Books* Scotland: A New Study (ed, 1983), Quaternary Glaciations of the Southern Hemisphere (ed, 1990), Quaternary Geology and Geomorphology of South America (1993); *Recreations* golf, tennis, running, gardening; *Clubs* Banchory Golf, Banchory Squash, Banchory Tennis, Aboyne Rugby; *Style—* Prof Chalmers Clapperton, FRSE; ✉ Department of Geography, University of Aberdeen, Elphinstone Road, Aberdeen AB9 2UF (☎ 01224 272346, fax 01224 272331)

CLAPPERTON, (Alexander) Wallace Ford; s of Alexander Clapperton (d 1943), of Edinburgh, and Kathleen Nora, *née* Ford (d 1991); *b* 22 July 1934; *Educ* Charterhouse; *m* 27 March 1965, Catherine Anne, da of Sir Henry Horsman, MC (d 1966), of Bermuda; 1 s (Graeme Alexander Ford b 1969), 1 da (Alison Nicola b 1967); *Career* Nat Serv RCS 1957–59; ptnr de Zoete and Bevan stockbrokers (formerly de Zoete and Gorton) 1963–86, dir Barclays de Zoete Wedd Securities Ltd 1986–92; non-exec chm Scantronic Holdings 1992–95, non-exec dir TR Pacific Investment Trust 1992–; MICAS; *Recreations* golf, skiing; *Clubs* Hon Co of Edinburgh Golfers, Denham Golf, Woburn Golf, City of London; *Style—* Wallace Clapperton, Esq; ✉ Broomfield House, Broomfield Hill, Great Missenden, Bucks HP16 9HT (☎ 01494 862559, fax 01494 890732)

CLAPPISON, James; MP (C) Hertsmere (majority 18,735); s of late Leonard Clappison, and Dorothy Clappison; *b* 14 Sept 1956; *Educ* St Peter's Sch York, Queen's Coll Oxford (scholar); *m* 6 July 1984, Helen Margherita, *née* Carter; 1 s, 2 da; *Career* called to the Bar 1981; Parly candidate (C): Barnsley E 1987, Bootle May and Nov 1990 (by-elections); Euro Parly candidate Yorks S 1989; MP (C) Hertsmere 1992–; PPS to Min of State Home Office (Lady Blatch) 1994–95, parly under-sec of state Dept of the Environment 1995–; *Clubs* United Oxford and Cambridge University, Carlton; *Style—* James Clappison, Esq, MP; ✉ House of Commons, London SW1A 0AA

CLAPTON, Eric Patrick; OBE (1995); *b* 30 March 1945; *Educ* St Bede's Sch Surrey, Kingston Coll of Art; *m* 1979 (m dis 1988), Patti Harrison; 1 s by subseq ptnr (Conor b 1987, d 1991); *Career* guitarist and singer; has worked with Howlin' Wolf, Steve Winwood, The Beatles, The Rolling Stones, Pete Townshend, Elton John, Phil Collins and others; joined Yardbirds as lead guitarist 1963, recorded album Five Little Yardbirds (live, 1964), joined John Mayall's Bluesbreakers 1965; albums with John Mayall: Lonely Years (1965), Blues Breakers (1966, reached UK no 6); formed Cream 1966; albums with Cream: Fresh Cream (1967, UK no 6), Disraeli Gears (1967, UK no 5), Wheels Of Fire (1968, UK no 3), Goodbye (1969, UK no 1), The Best Of Cream (compilation, 1969, UK no 6), Live Cream (live, 1970, UK no 4), Live Cream - Vol 2 (live, 1972, UK no 15); formed Blind Faith 1969, recorded album Blind Faith (1969, UK no 1); started solo career 1970, formed Derek & The Dominoes 1970, recorded albums Layla And Other Love Songs (1970, US no 16), Derek & The Dominoes In Concert (live, 1973, UK no 36); solo albums: Eric Clapton (1970, UK no 17), History Of Eric Clapton (1972, UK no 20), Eric Clapton's Rainbow Concert (live, 1973, UK no 19), 461 Ocean Boulevard (1974, UK no 3), There's One In Every Crowd (1975, UK no 15), E C Was Here (live, 1975, UK no 14), No Reason To Cry (1976, UK no 8), Slowhand (1977, UK no 23), Backless (1978, UK no 18), Just One Night (1980, UK no 3), Another Ticket (1981, UK no 18), Time Pieces - The Best Of Eric Clapton (1982, UK no 20), Money And Cigarettes (1983, UK no 13), Backtrackin' (compilation, 1984, UK no 29), Behind The Sun (1985, UK no 8), August (1986, UK no 3), The Cream Of Eric Clapton (compilation, UK no 3), Crossroads (box set, 1988), Journeyman (1989, UK no 2), 24 Nights (live, 1992), Unplugged (1992, UK no 3); has worked on numerous film soundtracks incl: Tommy, The Colour Of Money, Lethal Weapon, Rush; awards incl Variety Club Best Recording Artist of 1992, six Grammy awards 1993; *Style—* Eric Clapton, Esq, OBE; ✉ Roger Forrester Management, 18 Harley House, Regents Park, London NW1 5HE (☎ 0171 486 8056, fax 0171 487 5663)

CLARE, Prof Anthony Ward; s of Bernard J Clare (d 1995), of Ranelagh, Dublin 6, and Mary Agnes, *née* Dunne (d 1993); *b* 24 Dec 1942; *Educ* Gonzaga Coll Dublin, Univ Coll Dublin (MB BCh, BAO, MD), London Univ (MPhil); *m* 4 Oct 1966, Jane Carmel, da of Gabriel Sarsfield Hogan (d 1989), of Shelbourne Rd, Dublin 4; 3 s (Simon John b 1970, Peter Tobias b 1975, Sebastian Patrick b 1985), 4 da (Rachel Judith b 1967, Eleanor Ruth b 1971, Sophie Carolyn b 1978, Justine Chiara b 1982); *Career* intern St Joseph Hosp Syracuse NY 1966–67; registrar: St Patrick's Hosp Dublin 1967–69, Bethlem Royal and Maudsley Hosps London 1970–72; dep dir Gen Practice Res Unit Inst of Psychiatry 1979–82 (sr registrar and res worker 1973–78), prof and head Dept of Psychological Med St Bartholomew's Hosp Med Coll 1982–88, med dir St Patrick's Hosp Dublin and prof of clinical psychiatry Trinity Coll Dublin 1989–95; chm The Prince of Wales Advsy Gp on Disability; numerous broadcasts incl: Let's Talk About Me, In The Psychiatrist's Chair (BBC 1982–), Stop The Week; FRCPI 1983, FRCPsych 1986 (vice pres); *Books* Psychiatry in Dissent (1976, 2 edn 1980), Let's Talk About Me (1981), In the Psychiatrist's Chair (1984), Lovelaw (1986), In the Psychiatrist's Chair (1992), Depression and How to Survive It (with Spike Milligan, 1993), In the Psychiatrist's Chair II (1995); *Recreations* tennis, opera, family life; *Clubs* Garrick; *Style—* Prof Anthony W Clare; ✉ 87 Coper's Cope Road, Beckenham, Kent BR3 1NR (☎ 0181 650 1784); Delville, Lucan, Co Dublin, Republic of Ireland; St Patrick's Hospital, James's St, Dublin 8, Republic of Ireland (☎ 01001 775423)

CLARE, (Adrian) George Howe; s of late Ernest Vivian Clare, and Betty Kennedy, *née* Hester; *b* 27 Sept 1937; *Educ* Bickley Park Sch, Radley; *m* Helen Aline, da of late Edgar Frederick Shannon, of Wimbledon, Surrey; 3 da (Rosamund b 1964, Alison b 1966, Belinda b 1967); *Career* Nat Serv Royal Ulster Rifles 1957–58, TA London Irish Rifles 1958–63; sec gen Euro Actuarial Consultancy Servs, princ Barnett Waddingham & Co; sec: Effingham Housing Assoc, Horsley Choral Soc; past Master Worshipful Co of Joiners & Ceilers 1987–88; FPMI, ACII, MIMgt; *Recreations* singing, travel, politics; *Clubs* RAC; *Style—* George Clare, Esq; ✉ Old Vicarage, Church Street, Effingham, Leatherhead, Surrey KT24 2LX (☎ 01372 458435); Barnett Waddingham & Co, Bread Street, London EC4

CLARE, Jonathan; s of John Clare, and Sheila, *née* Crush; *b* 25 July 1954; *Educ* Windsor GS, Univ of Lancaster (BA History); *partner* Celeste Warner; *Career* business and fin journalist 1975–86 (Morgan Grampian, Investors Chronicle, Birmingham Post, The Times, Daily Mail), Streets Financial 1986–88, fndr and dep md Citigate Communications Group 1988–; memb: Int Spinal Research Tst, Cruising Assoc, RNLI, RHS, RYA; MIPR; *Recreations* mountain walking, sailing, skiing, reading; *Style—* Jonathan Clare, Esq; ✉ Citigate Communications Group Ltd, 26 Finsbury Square, London EC2A 1DS (☎ 0171 282 8000, fax 0171 282 8060)

CLARE, Chief Constable Pauline; QPM (1996); *b* 26 July 1947; *Educ* Open Univ (BA Psychology); *m*; 2 step da; *Career* joined Lancs Constabulary 1966, various positions Southport and Kirkby until 1974, Police Staff Coll Bramshill 1974, inspr Merseyside Police 1974–83, Jr Cmd Course Police Staff Coll 1983, chief inspr Liverpool City Centre and Community Affrs Dept 1983–87, sub-divnl cdr Southport 1988–89, Intermediate Cmd Course 1989, chief supt 1991, Sr Cmd Course 1991, divnl cdr Bootle 1991–92; Merseyside Police: chief constable (Crime) 1992–94, asst chief constable (Ops) 1994; dep chief constable Cheshire Constabulary 1994–95, chief constable Lancs Constabulary 1995–; Hon Col Lancs ACF (Queen's Lancs Regt), pres Lancs Assoc of Boys' Clubs, chm St John Ambulance Assoc Southport; hon fell Univ of Central Lancs 1994; SSStJ 1995; CIMgt 1996; *Awards* Lancashire Woman of the Year 1993, North West Woman of the Year 1995; *Recreations* gardening, preparing and hosting dinner parties, horse riding, reading, attending the theatre; *Style—* Mrs P A Clare, QPM; ✉ Chief Constable, Lancashire Constabulary HQ, PO Box 77, Hutton, Preston PR4 5SB (☎ 01772 614444)

CLARENDON, 7 Earl of (GB 1776); George Frederick Laurence Hyde Villiers; also Baron Hyde (GB 1756); s of late Lord Hyde and late Hon Marion, *née* Glyn, da of 4 Baron Wolverton; suc gf 1955; *b* 2 Feb 1933; *Educ* Eton, Univ of Madrid; *m* 1974, Jane Diana, da of Edward William Dawson (d 1979), of Idmiston, Salisbury, Wilts; 1 s (George Edward Laurence, Lord Hyde b 12 Feb 1976), 1 da (Lady Sarah Katherine Jane Villiers b 1977); *Heir* s, Lord Hyde; *Career* page of honour to HM King George VI 1948–49; Lt RHG 1951–53; Glyn Mills and Co 1955–60, Seccombe Marshall and Campion 1960–93 (md 1962, chm 1985–93); memb Ct of Assts Worshipful Co of Fishmongers; *Style—* The Rt Hon the Earl of Clarendon; ✉ Holywell House, Swanmore, Hants SO32 2QE (☎ 01489 896090, fax 01489 892353)

CLARIDGE, Prof Michael Frederick; s of Frederick William Claridge (d 1965), of Rugby, Warwickshire, and Eva Alice, *née* Jeffery (d 1969); *b* 2 June 1934; *Educ* Lawrence Sheriff Sch Rugby, Keble Coll Oxford (MA, DPhil); *m* 30 Sept 1967, (Lindsey) Clare, da of Gilbert Hellings (d 1973), of Shipton under Wychwood, Oxon; 2 s (John, Robert), 1 da (Elin); *Career* Univ Coll Cardiff: lectr in zoology 1959–76, reader in entomology 1977–83, personal chair in entomology 1983–89, acting head of zoology 1987 88; prof of entomology Univ of Wales Cardiff 1989– (head Sch of Pure and Applied Biology 1989–94); pres Linnean Soc of London 1988–91 (memb Cncl 1984–91); memb: Cncl Royal Entomological Soc 1971–74, British Ecological Soc (memb Cncl 1976–79); pres Systematics Assoc 1991–94 (memb Cncl 1984–87); FLS, FRES, FIBiol; *Books* The Leafhoppers and Planthoppers (contrib, 1985), The Organization of Communities, Past and Present (contrib, 1987), Prospects in Systematics (contrib, 1988), Handbook for the Identification of Leafhoppers and Planthoppers of Rice (jtly, 1991), Evolutionary Patterns and Processes (contrib, 1993), Planthoppers: Their Ecology and Management (contrib, 1993), Species the Units of Biodiversity (ed and contrib, 1997); *Recreations* cricket, music, natural history; *Style—* Prof Michael Claridge; ✉ 84 The Hollies, Quakers Yard, Treharris, Mid Glamorgan CF46 5PP (☎ 01443 410734); School of Pure and Applied Biology, University of Wales, Cardiff CF1 3TL (☎ 01222 874147)

CLARK, *see also:* Chichester-Clark, Stewart-Clark

CLARK, Rt Rev Alan Charles Anthony; s of William Thomas Durham Clark (d 1977), and Ellen Mary Clark, *née* Compton (d 1950); *b* 9 Aug 1919; *Educ* Westminster Choir Sch, Junior Seminary for Southwark Diocese at Mark Cross, Ven English Coll Rome (scholar), Gregorian Univ Rome (STD); *Career* ordained Parish of St Joseph's Bromley 1945, vice rector Ven English Coll Rome 1954–64, consecrated titular bishop of Elmham and auxiliary of Northampton 1969, bishop (RC) of East Anglia 1976–95, ret; peritus (expert advsr) Second Vatican Cncl 1960–65, co-chm Anglican and Roman Catholic Int Cmmn 1969; chm Dept of Mission and Unity Roman Catholic Episcopal Conf of England and Wales 1984 (pres Nat Cmmn for Ecumenism 1970), co-chm Jt Working Gp of World Cncl of Churches and the Holy See (Vatican) 1985; Freeman City of London 1968; Knight Cdr Equestrian Order of Holy Sepulchre; *Publications* Dialogue in Faith (Publication of Address to Gen Synod of C of E, 1974); *Recreations* music, literature; *Style—* The Rt Rev A C A Clark

CLARK, Rt Hon Alan Kenneth McKenzie; PC (1991); s of Baron Clark, OM, CH, KCB (Life Peer, d 1983) and his 1 w Elizabeth, *née* Martin (d 1976); *b* 13 April 1928; *Educ* Eton, ChCh Oxford; *m* 1958, Caroline Jane, da of Col Leslie Brindley Bream Beuttler (and ggda of Hon George Ogilvie-Grant, 6 s of 6 Earl of Seafield); 2 s (James, Andrew); *Career* served in Household Cavalry Trg Regt 1946 and RAuxAF 1952–54; called to the Bar Inner Temple; military historian, memb Inst for Strategic Studies and Royal United Services Inst for Def Studies; MP (C) Plymouth Sutton Feb 1974–92, vice chm Parly Def Ctee, memb Parly Home Affrs Ctee; under sec of state for employment (responsibilities incl legislation on trade unions' political levy) 1983–86, min of state for trade 1986–89, min of state for defence procurement 1989–92; chm EC Trade Ministers' Cncl 1986–87; *Books* The Donkeys: A History of the BEF in 1915, Barbarosa - Soviet German Conflict 1941, Diaries (1993); *Clubs* Brooks's, Pratt's; *Style—* The Rt Hon Alan Clark; ✉ Saltwood Castle, Kent CT21 4QU (☎ 01303 269300)

CLARK, Alan Richard; s of George Edward Clark, of Ramsgate, Kent, and late Norah Ivy Maria, *née* Hope; *b* 4 Sept 1939; *Educ* Chatham House GS Ramsgate; *m* 5 Aug 1961, Ann Rosemary, da of late George Hosford, of Westgate-on-Sea, Kent; 1 s (Nicholas James b 1976); *Career* Nat Serv RAF 1960–62; HM Dip Serv 1958–: vice consul Tehran 1964–66, admin offr Jedda 1966–68, 2 then 1 sec Paris 1969–71, dep head of mission Freetown 1976–80, dep head W African Dept FCO 1981–84, seconded with rank of cnsllr to Vickers Shipbuilding and Engineering Ltd 1984–86, dep head of mission Bucharest 1986–89, consul-gen Montreal 1990–93, cnsllr FCO 1994–; *Recreations* swimming, walking, reading; *Clubs* Cwlth Tst; *Style—* A R Clark, Esq; ✉ c/o Foreign and Commonwealth Office, King Charles Street, London SW1A 2AH (☎ 0171 210 6702, fax 0171 210 6685)

CLARK, Brig Alastair John McDougall; s of late John Wesley Clark, and late Alice, *née* McDougall; *b* 17 Nov 1938; *Educ* Bishop Vesey's GS, RMA Sandhurst, Defence

Language Sch (Russian interpreter); *m* 19 Dec 1964, Margaret Mary, *née* Froud; 1 s (Stephen b 1967), 1 da (Alexandra b 1969); *Career* 2 Lt RA 1958, Staff Coll 1970–71, staff offr Brixmis Berlin 1972–74, Battery Cdr 176 Battery 1974–76, CO 39 Regt 1978–80, Dep Cdr Artillery Div 1983–85, Cmdt Royal Sch of Artillery 1987–90, Cdr RA Trg Bde and Regtl Brig 1990–93, ret Army 1993; Hon Regtl Col 39 Regt; Admin Offr House of Lords 1993–; FIMgt, MInstD; *Recreations* theatre, languages, watching rugby, walking, computers; *Clubs* Pall Mall; *Style*— Brig Alastair Clark; ✉ 103 Hawkins House, Dolphin Square, London SW1V 3NS (☎ 0171 798 5579); Black Rod's Office, House of Lords, London SW1A 0PW (☎ 0171 219 3100, fax 0171 219 2500, e-mail ajmc@dial.pipex.com)

CLARK, His Hon Albert William; s of William Clark (d 1927), and Cissy, *née* Annis (d 1983); *b* 23 Sept 1922; *Educ* Christ's Coll Finchley; *m* 1951, Frances Philippa, da of Dr Samuel Lavington-Hart, of Cambridge and Tientsin, China; 1 s (Adrian), 1 da (Susan, m 1979 Roderick Banks, *qv*); *Career* served WWII Patrol Serv N Atlantic 1941–45; called to the Bar 1949, met magistrate 1970, acting dep chm London Sessions 1971, dep circuit judge 1972, circuit judge Inner London Crown Court, Middx Crown Ct and Central Criminal Ct 1981–95, ret; *Recreations* fishing, walking, boating; *Clubs* Royal Over-Seas League; *Style*— His Hon Albert Clark; ✉ Pelham, 45 West Parade, Worthing, West Sussex BN11 5EF (☎ 01903 247472)

CLARK, Alistair Campbell; WS (1991); s of Peter Campbell Clark (served Argyll & Sutherland Highlanders, d 1960), of Barnhill, Dundee, Angus, and Janet Mitchell, *née* Scott; *b* 4 March 1933; *Educ* Grove Acad Broughty Ferry, Univ of St Andrews (MA, LLB, pres Law Soc); *m* 30 Nov 1960, Evelyn Macdonald, da of John Bell Johnston (d 1954), of Osborne House, Turriff, Aberdeenshire; 3 s (Johnston Peter b 29 Oct 1962, Alistair Struan b 11 Oct 1964, Campbell John Scott b 2 Oct 1971); *Career* admitted slr 1957, ptnr then sr Blackadder Reid Johnston (formerly Reid Johnston Bell & Henderson) Solicitors Dundee 1961–95 (conslt 1995–); Hon Sheriff Tayside Central and Fife 1986–, memb and latterly chm Angus Legal Aid Ctee 1968–82, memb Tayside Children's Panel Advsy Ctee 1980–82, hon life memb Faculty of Procurators and Slrs Dundee 1991– (dean 1979–81), fndr chm Broughty Ferry & Dist Round Table, fndr pres Claverhouse Rotary Club Dundee, pres Law Soc of Scotland 1989–90 (memb Cncl 1982–91); chm: Dovetail Enterprises 1993–, Scottish Conveyancing and Executry Servs Bd 1996–; *Recreations* golf, travel and family life; *Clubs* New (Edinburgh), Royal and Ancient (St Andrews), Panmure, Barry, Angus; *Style*— Alistair C Clark, Esq, WS; ✉ Blythehill, 16 Balmyle Rd, West Ferry, Dundee (☎ 01382 477989); 30/34 Reform St, Dundee (☎ 01382 229222, fax 01382 201132)

CLARK, (Charles) Anthony; CB (1994); s of Stephen Clark (d 1965), and Winifred Clark (d 1971); *b* 13 June 1940; *Educ* King's Coll Sch Wimbledon, Pembroke Coll Oxford (MA); *m* 1968, Penelope Margaret, da of A John Brett (d 1979); 1 s (Jonathan b 1977), 2 da (Philippa b 1969, Joanna b 1971); *Career* dir Higher Educn Dept for Educn and Employment 1989–; chm Effingham Residents' and Ratepayers' Assoc; *Recreations* running, golf, sailing, reading; *Clubs* Effingham Golf, Epsom and Ewell Harriers (formerly chm); *Style*— Anthony Clark, Esq, CB; ✉ The Paddock, Guildford Rd, Effingham, Surrey (☎ 01372 452337); Department for Education and Employment, London SW1 3BT (☎ 0171 925 5192)

CLARK, Anthony Richard; s of Noel Edmund Clark, and Marianne Edith, *née* Sayres; *b* 4 April 1958; *Educ* Downside Sch Somerset, Univ of Manchester (BA Drama, Dip Playwriting); *m* 1984, Delia Mary, da of John Goddard; 4 c (Anna Magdalene, Gabriel James, Eleanor Pearl, Crispin Lee); *Career* director and writer; dir Orange Tree Theatre Richmond 1981–83, artistic dir Contact Theatre Manchester 1984–1989, assoc dir Birmingham Rep Theatre Co 1990–; dir: Tara Arts (Brit Asian Theatre), Stagecoach (New Playrights Orgn); *Theatre* Contact Theatre prodns incl: Face Value, Two Wheel Tricycle, McAlpine's Fusiliers, Green, Homeland, Mother Courage and her Children, Blood Wedding, A Midsummer Night's Dream, The Duchess of Malfi, To Kill a Mockingbird (European Premiere), Oedipus Rex; Birmingham Rep incl: The Seagull, Of Mice and Men, Saturday Sunday Monday, Cider with Rosie (nat tour), The Threepenny Opera, The Pied Piper, My Mother Said I Never Should, The Grapes of Wrath, The Atheist's Tragedy, The Playboy of the Western World, Peter Pan, Pygmalion, The Red Balloon, The Entertainer, Gentlemen Prefer Blonds; new plays incl: Rough, Playing by the Rules, Nervous Women, Syme (co-prodn with RNT studio); freelance dir incl: Dr Faustus (Young Vic), To Kill a Mockingbird (Greenwich), The Snowman (Leicester Haymarket), The Red Balloon (Bristol Old Vic and RNT), The Day After Tomorrow (RNT), Mother Courage and her Children (RNT); as writer plays incl: Hand it to Them, Wake, The Power of Darkness (Orange Tree), Tidemark (RSC Thoughtcrimes Festival), A Matter of Life and Death (RNT), Green; as writer musical adapts incl: The Snowman, The Little Prince, The Red Balloon, (all Contact Theatre Manchester), The Pied Piper (Birmingham Rep), Starjar (Bolton Octagon Theatre Co); *Awards* RSC Buzz Award 1979, Manchester Evening News Best Prodn Award (for To Kill a Mockingbird) 1984, TMA/Martini Award for Best Dir (for The Atheist's Tragedy) 1994, TMA/Martina Award for Best Show for Children and Young People (for The Red Balloon) 1995, Mentorn First Night Prodn Award (for Playing by the Rules); *Publications* The Power of Darkness (trans Tolstoy, 1987), The Red Balloon (1997); *Style*— Anthony Clark, Esq; ✉ c/o Hamilton Asper Management, Ground Floor, 24 Hanway Street, London W1P 9DD (☎ 0171 636 1221, fax 0171 636 1226)

CLARK, Brian Robert; *b* 3 June 1932; *Career* playwright; *TV* credits incl: Achilles Heel, Operation Magic Carpet, Parole, Easy Go, The Saturday Party, The Country Party, There's No Place, Happy Returns, Telford's Change (10 part series, BBC) 1979, Late Starter (BBC) 1985; *Theatre* Post Mortem, Campion's Interview (Soho Poly Theatre), Whose Life is it Anyway? (Mermaid, Savoy and Broadway) 1978–80 (film 1982), Can You Hear Me at the Back? (Piccadilly Theatre) 1979, Kipling (Mermaid) 1984 (later televised Channel 4), The Petition (Broadway, National Theatre and West End) 1986–87, Hopping to Byzantium (co-wrote with Kathy Levin, premiered Osnabruck West Germany) 1990; *Awards* for Whose Life is it Anyway?: Best Play Society of West End Theatre Awards 1978, Most Promising Playwright Evening Standard Drama Awards 1978, Best Play Plays and Players Award 1978; BAFTA Shell International TV Award (for Telford's Change) 1979; *Style*— Brian Clark, Esq, FRSL; ✉ Judy Daish Associates Ltd, 83 Eastbourne Mews, London W2 6LQ (☎ 0171 262 1101, fax 0171 706 1027)

CLARK, Brian Stephen; s of Stephen Wilfred Clark (d 1974), and Florence Sybil Elizabeth, *née* Webb; *b* 11 Aug 1936; *Educ* Willesden Co GS, LSE (LLB); *m* 17 Feb 1962, Rita, *née* Jones; 2 s (Stephen Nicholas b 2 Oct 1963, Andrew Simon b 26 July 1966); *Career* admitted slr 1961; Goodman Derrick & Co 1958–69 (articled clerk, asst slr, ptnr), exec International Management Group London 1969–71, sr corp ptnr Nabarro Nathanson 1988–93 (ptnr 1971–93), dir of European legal affrs International Management Group 1993–; memb Law Soc; *Recreations* golf, photography, opera; *Style*— Brian Clark, Esq; ✉ International Management Group, Pier House, Strand on the Green, Chiswick, London W4 3NN (☎ 0181 233 5000, fax 0181 233 5001)

CLARK, (Henry) Bruce Greer; s of Henry Wallace Stuart Clark, MBE, DL, of Upperlands, Co Derry, and June Elisabeth Lester, *née* Deane; *b* 30 Sept 1958; *Educ* Shrewsbury (top open scholar), St John's Coll Cambridge (exhibitioner, BA, univ debating prize), Athens Univ (Dip in Modern Greek); *Career* Reuters: graduate trainee 1979, jr corr Paris office 1980–81, corr Athens 1982–86, fin reporter London 1986–87; Euro news ed Financial Times 1987–89, Moscow corr Sunday Correspondent 1989–90, Moscow corr The Times 1990–93, diplomatic corr Financial Times 1994–; *Books* An Empire's New Clothes - The End of Russia's Liberal Dream (1995, updated 1996); *Recreations* entertaining, travel, riding; *Style*— Bruce Clark, Esq; ✉ c/o The Financial Times, 1 Southwark Bridge Road, London SE1 9HL (☎ 0171 873 3000, fax 0171 873 3193)

CLARK, Prof Charles Victor; s of Dennis Clark, and Margaret, *née* Slowther; *b* 11 Aug 1956; *Educ* George Heriot's Sch Edinburgh, Univ of Edinburgh (BSc, MB ChB, MD, ChM, DSc); *m* 15 Dec 1983, Maureen, da of James Corr (d 1978); *Career* sr surgical registrar Moorfields Eye Hosp London 1986–88, conslt ophthalmic surgn Royal Infirmary of Edinburgh and sr lectr in ophthalmology Univ of Edinburgh 1988–91, prof of ophthalmology and dir Glaucoma Servs Univ of Queensland 1991–94, prof of educn Griffith Univ Queensland 1995–; specialist in glaucoma and diabetic eye disease; author of over 60 scientific papers; memb: Assoc for Eye Res, Oxford Ophthalmological Congress, Clinical Autonomic Res Soc; fell RMS 1979, FRCSEd 1985, FRCOphth 1988, CBiol, FIBiol 1991, fell Royal Aust Coll of Ophthalmologists 1991, fell Royal Aust Coll of Surgns 1992, fell American Acad of Opthalmology 1992, fell Aust Coll of Biology 1994; *Recreations* photography, music, theatre, rugby football; *Style*— Prof Charles Clark; ✉ 5th Floor, St Andrew's Place, 33 North Street, Spring Hill, Brisbane, Queensland, Australia 4000

CLARK, Christopher Harvey; QC (1989); s of Harvey Frederick Beckford Clark, of Calmore, Southampton, and Winifred Julia, *née* Caesar; *b* 20 Dec 1946; *Educ* Taunton's Sch Southampton, The Queen's Coll Oxford (MA); *m* 25 March 1972, Gillian Elizabeth Ann, da of Anthony Mullen, of Andover, Hants; 1 s (Patrick Harvey b 1974), 2 da (Melanie Julia b 1976, Lucy Elizabeth b 1980); *Career* called to the Bar 1969; memb Western Circuit 1970–, asst recorder 1982–86, recorder of the Crown Court 1986–; memb Wine Ctee Western Circuit 1985–90, chm Fees and Legal Aid Ctee Western Circuit 1989, chllr Diocese of Winchester 1993–, dep chllr Diocese of Portsmouth 1994–, dep chllr diocese of Chichester 1995–; hon legal advsr to the Hampshire Assoc of Parish and Town Cncls 1996–; chm Stockbridge Dramatic Soc 1977–, memb Longstock Parish Cncl 1979–, youth club organiser (The Longstock Tadpoles) 1981–90; *Recreations* amateur dramatics, golf, cricket, swimming, gardening, walking, skiing, reading; *Style*— C H Clark, Esq, QC; ✉ 3 Pump Court, Temple, London EC4Y 7AJ (☎ 0171 353 0711, fax 0171 353 3319); 31 Southgate St, Winchester, Hampshire (☎ 01962 868161, fax 01962 67645)

CLARK, Christopher John; s of Ronald George Clark (d 1983), and Irene Mary, *née* Moore; *b* 24 May 1961; *Educ* Kingsbury HS, Univ of Southampton (BSc Chemistry); *Career* Kodak 1982–84, Levi-Strauss 1984–87, Lintas Advertising 1987–89, Saatchi & Saatchi 1989–96, md Bates Dorland 1996–; memb Educn and Trg Ctee IPA; FIPA; *Recreations* mountaineering, scuba diving, rugby, horse riding; *Style*— Christopher Clark, Esq; ✉ Bates Dorland Ltd, 121–141 Westbourne Terrace, London W2 6JR (☎ 0171 262 5077, fax 0171 706 3440, mobile 0802 580068)

CLARK, Clive Henry; s of Henry Stephen Clark, and Helena Cissie, *née* Hosegood; *b* 24 Aug 1941; *Educ* King Edward VI GS Chelmsford; *m* 6 July 1968, Gillian Moira, da of Oswald John Casey (d 1977); 3 da (Sharon, Melissa, Nicole); *Career* CA; ptnr Allfields 1973, dep managing ptnr Finnie Ross Allfields, exec ptnr Finnie & Co (Stoy Hayward following merger 1992) 1983; Stoy Hayward (now BDO Stoy Hayward): managing ptnr Chelmsford 1992–95, gp ptnr London 1995–; FCA 1963; *Recreations* gardening, travel; *Style*— Clive Clark, Esq; ✉ BDO Stoy Hayward, 8 Baker Street, London W1M 1DA (☎ 0171 486 5888)

CLARK, Dr David Findlay; OBE (1990), DL (Banffshire 1992); s of Rev Dr David Findlay Clark (d 1966), and Annie, *née* McKenzie (d 1963); *b* 30 May 1930; *Educ* Banff Acad, Univ of Aberdeen (MA, PhD); *m* 9 Oct 1954, Janet Anne, da of Gavin M Stephen, of Brechin, Angus; 2 da (Morag Anne (Mrs Baptie) b 1955, Linda Jane (Mrs Wimble) b 1958); *Career* Flying Offr RAF 1951–53, RAFVR 1953–57; psychologist Leicester Industl Rehabilitation Unit 1953–56, princ clinical psychologist Leicester Area Clinical Psychology Serv 1960–66 (sr clinical psychologist 1956–60), dir and top grade clinical psychologist Grampian Health Bd 1966–90, clinical sr lectr Dept of Mental Health Univ of Aberdeen 1966–, conslt clinical psychologist in private practice 1990–; former: chm Div of Clinical Psychology Br Psychological Soc (memb Cncl), memb Health Serv Planning Cncl, town and co cncllr Banff and Banffshire; Hon Sheriff Grampian and Highlands and Island at Banff 1979–, Safeguarder (under terms of SWK Scotland Act) 1985–; Fell Br Psychological Soc 1969, ARPS 1991; *Books* Help, Hospitals and the Handicapped (1984), contrib to major textbooks and author of numerous jl articles; *Recreations* sailing, golf, photography, painting, guitar, piano, travel, writing; *Clubs* Duff House Royal Golf, Banff Rotary (past pres), Banff Sailing (past cdre); *Style*— Dr David Clark, OBE, DL; ✉ Glendeveron, 8 Deveron Terrace, Banff AB45 1BB Scotland (☎ 01261 812624)

CLARK, Dr David George; MP (Lab) South Shields (majority 13,477); s of George Clark, and Janet, of Askham, Cumbria; *b* 19 Oct 1939; *Educ* Windermere GS, Univ of Manchester (BA, MSc), Univ of Sheffield (PhD); *m* 1970, Christine, da of Ronald Kirkby, of Grasmere; 1 da; *Career* former forester, laboratory asst, student teacher, univ lectr; Parly candidate (Lab) Manchester Withington 1966; MP (Lab): Colne Valley 1970–74 (also contested Oct 1974), South Shields 1979–; oppn spokesman on agric and food 1973–74, oppn spokesman on defence 1980–81, oppn front bench spokesman on the environment 1981–87, memb Shadow Cabinet 1986–; chief oppn spokesman on: agric and rural affairs 1987–92, defence, disarmament and arms control 1992–; *Books* Industrial Manager (1966), Radicalism to Socialism (1981), Victor Grayson (1985), We Do Not Want the Earth (1992); *Style*— Dr David Clark, MP; ✉ House of Commons, London SW1A 0AA

CLARK, David John; *b* 20 Sept 1947; *Educ* Univ of Kent (MA); *m* 1970, Caroline, *née* Russell; 2 s, 3 da; *Career* Dept of Health (formerly DHSS): asst princ 1969–73, princ 1973–83, asst sec 1983–90, under sec 1990–; *Style*— David Clark; ✉ Department of Health, Richmond House, 79 Whitehall, London SW1A 2NS (☎ 0171 210 5834)

CLARK, His Hon Judge; Denis; s of John Clark, of Tranmere, Birkenhead, and Mary Elizabeth, *née* Kenna; *b* 2 Aug 1943; *Educ* St Anselm's Coll Birkenhead, Univ of Sheffield (LLB); *m* 7 Jan 1967; 4 da (Rebecca b 19 Aug 1967, Rachel 25 Jan 1969, Catherine b 7 Jan 1971, Judith b 28 Jan 1972); *Career* called to the Bar Inner Temple 1966, in practice Northern Circuit 1966–88, recorder 1984–88, circuit judge (Northern Circuit) 1988–; *Recreations* Medieval history, theatre, cricket; *Style*— His Hon Judge Clark; ✉ Liverpool Crown Court

CLARK, Dingle Charles; s of Dr Charles Clark (d 1995), of Eltham, London, and Marcelle Pamela, *née* Marrable; *b* 7 June 1959; *Educ* Eltham Coll London, Univ of Southampton (BSc); *m* 15 April 1989, Caroline, da of John Patrick Hough, of Blackheath; 1 da (Charlotte Annabel Felicity b 18 Jan 1991), 2 s (Angus Lorne b 27 March 1993, Hugo Charles Alexander b 24 Sept 1995); *Career* called to the Bar Middle Temple 1981, asst dep coroner (Essex) 1993–; pt/t lectr Cncl of Legal Educn 1987–; cncllr London Borough of Greenwich 1982–90 (Cons chief whip 1985–90); dir Original Holloway Friendly Soc Gloucester 1991–94; govr Woolwich Coll 1990–92; *Recreations* golf, football; *Clubs* Royal Blackheath Golf, Frinton Golf; *Style*— Dingle Clark, Esq; ✉ 1 Dr Johnston's Building, Temple, London EC4Y 7AX (☎ 0171 353 9328, fax 0171 353 4410)

CLARK, Eric; s of Horace Ernest Clark (d 1978), of Weston-super-Mare, Somerset, and Hilda Dorothy, *née* Mitchley (d 1996); *b* 29 July 1937; *Educ* Handsworth GS; *m* 12 April 1972, Marcelle, da of Jacob Bernstein (d 1956), of Manchester; 1 s (Daniel b 1980), 2 da

(Rachael b 1975, Charlotte b 1978); *Career* staff reporter The Daily Mail 1962–64, staff writer The Guardian 1964–66, various appts The Observer 1966–72; articles published in foreign newspapers incl Melbourne Age and Washington Post; writer of fiction and non fiction 1972–; memb: Soc of Authors, Crime Writers Assoc, Mystery Writers of America; Fell Eng Centre Int PEN; *Books* Corps Diplomatique (1973), Black Gambit (1978), The Sleeper (1979), Send in The Lions (1981), Chinese Burn (1984), The Want Makers: The World of Advertising, How They Make You Buy (1988), Hide and Seek (1994); *Recreations* cinema, opera, jazz; *Clubs* Savile; *Style*— Eric Clark, Esq; ✉ Child & Co, 1 Fleet Street, London EC4Y 1BD

CLARK, Felicity Jane; da of Brig F G Clark, CBE (d 1986), and Florence Joy, *née* McHardy; *b* 24 Feb 1938; *Educ* Downe House; *Career* Crawfords Public Relations 1959–64, exec asst to Ed-in-Chief Vogue USA 1964–69, beauty ed Vogue UK 1969–89; dir: Royal Opera House Trust 1990–95, Friends of the Kirov; memb: Devpt Mgmnt Ctee Royal Coll of Music, Main Ctee Women of the Year Lunch (in aid of the Gtr London Fund for the Blind); *Books* Vogue Guides to Skincare, Haircare and Make-Up (1981); *Recreations* music, gardening, cooking, skiing, walking; *Style*— Miss Felicity Clark; ✉ 36 Prothero Road, London SW6 7LZ (☎ 0171 381 4872, fax 0171 610 3167)

CLARK, Sir Francis Drake; 5 Bt (UK 1886), of Melville Crescent, Edinburgh; s of Sir Thomas Clark, 3 Bt (d 1977); suc bro, Sir John Douglas Clark, 4 Bt 1991; *b* 16 July 1924; *Educ* Edinburgh Acad; *m* 14 Aug 1958, Mary, yr da of late John Alban Andrews, MC, FRCS; 1 s (Edward Drake b 27 April 1966); *Heir* s, Edward Drake Clark b 27 April 1966; *Career* RN 1943–46; dir Clark Travel Service Ltd 1948–78; *Style*— Sir Francis Clark, Bt; ✉ Woodend Cottages, Burgh-next-Aylsham, Norfolk NR11 6TS

CLARK, Prof Frank; CBE (1991); *b* 17 Oct 1946; *m*; 2 da; *Career* clerical trainee Bd of Mgmnt Royal Cornhill and Associated Hosps 1965–67, higher clerical offr Kingseat Hosp 1967–69, hosp sec Canniesburn and Schaw Hosps 1970–71 (dep hosp sec 1969–70), admin Glasgow Royal Infirmary 1974–77 (dep hosp sec GRI and Sub-Gp 1971–74), dist gen admin Gtr Glasgow Health Bd Eastern Dist 1981–83 (asst dist admin 1977–81); Lanarkshire Health Bd: dist admin Hamilton and E Kilbride Unit 1983–84, dir of admin servs Hamilton and E Kilbride Unit June-Sept 1984, sec to the Bd 1984–85, gen mangr 1985–96; dir Strathcarrow Hospice 1996–; gen mangr Lothian Health Bd May-Dec 1990; visiting prof Faculty of Health Glasgow Caledonian Univ 1993–; dir Appeal Ctee West of Scotland Postgrad Dental Educn Centre 1981–83; memb: Working Pty on the Introduction of General Mgmnt at Unit Level 1984–85, Advsy Gp on New Devpts in Health Care 1984–90, Nat Specialist Servs Advsy Ctee (NSSAC) 1985–90, Scottish Health Mgmnt Efficiency Gp 1985–91, Univ Grants Ctee (Scottish Sub-ctee) 1987–89, Working Pty on Community Med in Scotland (The Robertson Report) 1988–89, Working Pty on the Future of Dental Educn in Scotland (The McCallum Report) 1988–89 (Sec of State appt to 3 Memb Working Pty), Univs Funding Cncl (Scottish Ctee) 1989–91, Chief Scientists Health Serv Res Ctee 1989–93, Scottish Health Serv Advsy Cncl (Sec of State appt) 1990–93, Scottish Health Bd Gen Managers Gp 1990– (vice chm 1990–93 and 1995, chm 1993–95) Advsy Gp on Acute Serv (successor body to NSSAC) 1990–93, Nat Nursing Strategy Gp 1990–93, West of Scotland Dental Educnl Tst Distance Learning Unit Appeal Ctee 1992–93, Scottish Overseas Health Support Policy Bd 1990–96, Jt Working Gp on Purchasing 1992–96, Bd New Lanarkshire Ltd 1992–, Scottish Implementation Gp Jr Doctors' and Dentists' Hours of Work 1992–96, Scottish Cncl for Postgraduate Med and Dental Educn 1993–96, Editorial Advsy Bd Health Bulletin 1993–96, Scottish Health Services Mgmnt Centre Implementation Gp 1993–95, Judging Panel in Health Care Award 1994–95, Strategy Gp R & D Strategy for NHS in Scotland 1994–96; chm: Working Pty on Introduction of Hay Grading System to the NHS in Scotland 1989–90, Jt Mgmnt Exec/Gen Mangrs Manpower Gp 1990–93, West of Scotland Health Service Res Network 1990–95, Lanarkshire Drugs Action Team 1995–96; vice chm of govrs Queen's Coll Glasgow 1988–93; memb Glasgow Dental Alumnus Assoc 1983; MHSM (DipHSM) 1974; *Clubs* Rotary of Cumbernauld; *Style*— Prof Frank Clark, CBE; ✉ Strathcarrow Hospice, Randolph Hill, Denny, Stirlingshire FK6 5HJ (☎ 01324 826222, fax 01324 824576)

CLARK, Dr Frederick; s of Capt Frederick Clark (d 1964), and Edith Andison Clark, *née* Waggot (d 1987); *b* 5 Aug 1931; *Educ* Barnard Castle Sch Co Durham, Cathedral HS Bombay India, Univ of Durham (MB BS); *m* 1, Ada (m dis 1964); *m* 2, Elke Renate (m dis 1980); 1 s (Frederick Gene (Ricky) b 1970), 1 da (Deirdre Ann (Dee) b 1967); *Career* Nat Serv RAMC MO and Capt served Aden 1956–58; conslt physician Newcastle Health Authy and sr lectr in med Univ of Newcastle 1967–; former memb Newcastle Health Authy; memb Assoc of Physicians of GB and Ireland, FRCP 1973; *Recreations* angling, gardening; *Style*— Dr Frederick Clark; ✉ 38a Leazes Terrace, Newcastle upon Tyne NE1 4LZ (☎ 0191 2610 930); Ward 15 Office, Department of Medicine, Freeman Hospital, Newcastle upon Tyne NE7 7DN (☎ 0191 284 3111, fax 0191 213 1968)

CLARK, Gerald Edmondson; CMG (1989); s of Edward John Clark, and Irene Elizabeth Ada, *née* Edmondson; *b* 26 Dec 1935; *Educ* Johnston GS Durham, New Coll Oxford (MA); *m* 1967, Mary Rose Organ; 2 da; *Career* joined FO 1960, Hong Kong 1961, Peking 1962–63, FO 1964–68, Moscow 1968–70, FCO 1970–73, head of Chancery Lisbon 1973–77, asst sec Cabinet Office 1977–79, seconded to Barclays Bank International 1979–81, commercial cnsllr Peking 1981–83, FCO 1984–87, UK ambass to IAEA and other international orgns in Vienna 1987–92, sr directing staff (Civilian) RCDS 1993, sec-gen Uranium Inst 1994–; *Recreations* architecture, economics and politics; *Clubs* Athenaeum, Commonwealth Trust; *Style*— Gerald Clark, Esq, CMG; ✉ Secretary-General, Uranium Institute, Bowater House, 114 Knightsbridge, London SW1X 7LJ (☎ 0171 225 0303, fax 0171 225 0308, e-mail ui@uilondon.org)

CLARK, Gillian Margaret; MBE (1996); da of John Francis Foulger Clark, of Chart Sutton, Maidstone, Kent, and Patricia Moira, *née* Rodger; *b* 2 Sept 1961; *Educ* Ashford Sch for Girls; *Career* badminton player, TV presenter and commentator; Euro jr champion ladies doubles 1979; Cwlth Games: team Gold medal 1982, 1986, 1990 and 1994, ladies doubles Gold medal 1986, ladies doubles Silver medal 1982, 1990 and 1994, singles Bronze medal 1982 and 1986, mixed doubles Bronze medal 1990, mixed doubles Gold medal 1994; World Cup mixed doubles Silver medal 1986 and 1987; World Championships: ladies doubles Bronze medal 1983, mixed doubles Bronze medal 1993; Euro Championships: ladies doubles champion 1982, 1984 and 1986 (Silver 1988, Bronze 1990 and 1994), mixed doubles champion 1988 (Bronze 1984); nat ladies doubles champion 1985, 1987, 1988, 1989, 1990, 1992 and 1993, nat mixed doubles champion 1982 and 1993; winner of 33 World Grand Prix ladies/mixed titles incl: Taiwan Open (four times), Japan Open (three times), Swedish Open (twice), Finland Open, Malaysian Open (twice), Indonesian Open (twice), Singapore Open, Canadian Open, Dutch Open (four times), Victor Cup, German Open, Danish Open, Scottish Open (three times), Poona Open, Carlton Intersport Cup, Swiss Open, Indian Open; 145 England caps (most capped player); winner Distinguished Service Award Int Badminton Fedn 1995; appeared in over 100 Open Tournament finals; rep GB at badminton's first Olympic Games 1992 (ladies doubles quarter finalist); chm: Int Badminton Players' Fedn 1990–95, English Badminton Players' Assoc 1990–93, Wimbledon Squash and Badminton Club 1993–94; memb Competitors' Cncl BOA 1990–95; *Clubs* All England Badminton, Wimbledon Squash & Badminton; *Style*— Miss Gillian Clark, MBE

CLARK, Gillian Margaret Rose; da of Cyril Geoffrey Gunning Lockwood (d 1981), and Vera Irene Lockwood, *née* Marchant (d 1991); *b* 15 Jan 1949; *Educ* Varndean GS for Girls; *m* 16 Oct 1982, Philip Stephen Clark; 1 da (Juliette Annabelle b 11 March 1984); *Career* chartered insurer 1989; Eagle Star: joined as accident underwriting clerk 1968, head clerk Chatham branch 1972–74, accident underwriting superintendent Maidstone 1974–81, underwriting superintendent UK 1981–82, asst planning mangr 1982–83, asst mktg mangr 1983–86, mktg servs mangr 1986–88, mktg mangr UK Gen Div 1988–90, business devpt mangr 1990–91, divnl dir 1991–; FCII 1974, AIPM 1979, DipMktg, MInstM, MCIM 1986, memb Soc of Fellows London 1987; *Recreations* golf, riding; *Clubs* Sherdons Golf; *Style*— Mrs Gillian Clark; ✉ Hill Barn, Cowley, Glos GL53 9NJ (☎ 01242 870555); Eagle Star Insurance Co Ltd, The Grange, Bishop's Cleeve, Cheltenham, Glos GL52 4XX (☎ 01242 221311 ext 33900, fax 01242 678000)

CLARK, Prof Gordon Leslie; *b* 10 Sept 1950; *Educ* Monash Univ Melbourne Aust (BEcon, MA), McMaster Univ Hamilton Canada (Benefactors Scholar, PhD), Univ of Oxford (MA 1995); *Career* Ford fell in urban studies McMaster Univ 1976–78, asst prof John F Kennedy Sch of Govt and Dept of City and Regnl Planning Graduate Sch of Design Harvard Univ 1978–83, assoc prof Dept of Geography Center for Urban Studies and Center for Organisation Studies Univ of Chicago 1983–85, prof Heinz Sch of Public Policy and Management Center for Labor Studies and Center for Economic Devpt Carnegie Mellon Univ Pittsburgh 1985–91; Monash Univ Melbourne Australia 1989–95: prof and head Dept of Geography and Environmental Science and Graduate Sch of Environmental Science, dir Inst of Ethics and Public Policy Graduate Sch of Government, head Faculty of Arts 1993, memb Advsy Bd Nat Key Center in Industl Relations Graduate Sch of Management; Halford Mackinder prof of Geography Univ of Oxford 1995–; fell St Peter's Coll Oxford 1995–; fell Lincoln Land Inst Cambridge Mass 1981–82, Andrew Mellon fell Nat Acad of Scis 1981–82, fell Acad of Soc Scis Australia 1993–; Conference Medal Royal Australian Inst of Planners 1988; *Books* Interregional Migration, National Policy and Social Justice (1983), State Apparatus: Structures and Language of Legitimacy (jtly, 1984), Judges and the Cities: Interpreting Local Autonomy (1985), Regional Dynamics: Studies in Adjustment Theory (jtly, 1986), Unions and Communities Under Siege: American Communities and the Crisis of Organized Labor (1989), Multiculturalism, Difference and Postmodernism: Image and Representation in Australia (co-ed, 1993), Pensions and Corporate Restructuring in American Industry: A Crisis of Regulation (1993), Management Ethics: Theories, Cases and Materials (co-ed, 1995), Asian Newly Industrialized Economies in the Global Economy: Corporate Strategy and Industrial Restructuring in the 1990s (jtly, 1995); also author of numerous papers and articles in learned jls; *Style*— Prof Gordon Clark; ✉ School of Geography, University of Oxford, Mansfield Road, Oxford OX1 3TB (e-mail gordon.clark@geography.oxford.ac.uk)

CLARK, Graeme; *b* 15 April 1966; *Career* bassist with Wet Wet Wet; 14 top twenty singles incl 3 no 1's (With A Little Help From My Friends 1988 (raised over £600,000 for Childline), Goodnight Girl 1992, Love Is All Around 1994); albums with Wet Wet Wet: Popped In Souled Out (1987, UK no 1), The Memphis Sessions (1988, UK no 3), Holding Back The River (1989, UK no 2), High On The Happy Side (1992, UK no 1), End Of Part One (compilation, 1994, UK no 1), Picture This (1995); participated in: Prince's Trust Rock Gala 1988, 1989 and 1990, concert for Nelson Mandela's 70th birthday 1988, John Lennon Tribute concert 1990; *Style*— Graeme Clark, Esq; ✉ c/o Wet TM Ltd, 14/16 Speirs Wharf, Port Dundas, Glasgow G4 9TB (☎ 0141 353 1515, fax 0141 353 3852)

CLARK, Graham Ronald; s of Ronald Edward Clark, of Preston, Lancs, and Annie, *née* Eckersley (d 1984); *b* 10 Nov 1941; *Educ* Kirkham GS Lancs, Loughborough Coll of Educn (DLC), Univ of Loughborough (MSc); *m* 1, 9 April 1966 (m dis 1975), Susan, da of late Walter George Fenn, of Oxford; m 2, 31 March 1979, Joan Barbara, da of Albert Frederick Lawrence (d 1954), of Dunstable, Beds; 1 step da (Sarah Elisabeth b 8 Oct 1965); *Career* tenor; teacher and dir of PE 1964–69; sr regnl offr The Sports Cncl 1971–75; princ Scottish Opera 1975–77, debut London Bomarzo (Ginastera) 1976, princ ENO 1978–85; 17 leading roles in British, Italian, German, Russian and Czech repertoire; freelance 1985–; int venues 1976– incl: Bayreuther Festspiele Germany (over 100 performances as David in Die Meistersinger, Steuermann in Der Fliegende Holländer, Mime and Loge in The Ring) 1981–92, The Met NY (Herodes in Salome, Steva in Jenufa, Vere in Billy Budd, Bégearss in the Ghosts of Versailles, Hauptmann in Wozzeck, Gregor in Makropulos Case, Loge and Mime in The Ring) 1985–96, Royal Opera House Covent Garden, Vienna, Munich, Zurich, Hamburg, Salzburg, Berlin, Paris, Barcelona, Madrid, Amsterdam, Chicago, San Francisco, Turin, Rome, Toronto, Vancouver, Stockholm, Nice, Toulouse, Bonn, Matsumoto, WNO; festivals incl: Proms, Edinburgh, Paris, Tel Aviv, Brussels, Antwerp, Lucerne, Copenhagen; recordings and videos with: Decca, Philips, Erato, EMI, BBC, Teldec, BMG, Euroarts, The Met; Laurence Olivier Award 1986; *Recreations* sports; *Clubs* Garrick; *Style*— Graham Clark, Esq; ✉ c/o Ingpen & Williams Ltd, 14 Kensington Court, London W8 5DN

CLARK, Gregor Munro; s of Ian Munro Clark (d 1995), of Keills, Isle of Jura, Argyllshire, and Norah Isobel, *née* Joss; *b* 18 April 1946; *Educ* Queen's Park Sr Secdy Sch Glasgow, Univ of St Andrews (LLB); *m* 30 March 1974, Jane Maralyn, da of Leslie John Palmer (d 1972); 1 s (Aidan Benedikt b 1979), 2 da (Flora Daisy Louise b 1982, Madeleine Alexandra Rose b 1984); *Career* called to the Bar Scotland 1972, in practice 1972–74; Lord Advocate's Dept: joined 1974, asst parly draftsman then dep parly draftsman 1974–79, Scottish parly counsel and asst legal sec 1979–, counsel to the Scottish Law Cmmn 1995–; memb Faculty of Advocates 1972; *Recreations* music, Scandinavian languages and literature; *Style*— Gregor Clark, Esq; ✉ 64 Panton Street, Cambridge CB2 1HS (☎ 01223 350201); Lord Advocate's Chambers, 2 Carlton Gardens, London SW1Y 5AA (☎ 0171 210 1046)

CLARK, Guy Wyndham Nial Hamilton; JP (1981), DL (Renfrewshire 1987); s of Capt George Hubert Wyndham Clark (d 1978), and Lavinia Maraquita Smith, *née* Shaw Stewart (d 1971); *b* 28 March 1944; *Educ* Eton, Mons OCS; *m* 28 Jan 1968, Brighid Lovell, da of Maj Lovell Greene, of SA; 2 s (Charles Guy Lovell Wyndham, Thomas Houston Marcus Wyndham), 1 da (Nicola Fiona Vivienne); *Career* cmmnd Coldstream Gds 1962–67; investmt mangr Murray Johnstone Ltd Glasgow 1973–77, ptnr RC Greig & Co (stockbrokers) Glasgow 1977–86, dir Greig Middleton & Co Ltd (stockbrokers) 1986–; memb Exec Ctee Erskine Hosp for Disabled Servicemen Renfrewshire, vice chm JP Advsy Ctee for Inverclyde 1990–; memb Int Stock Exchange 1983, MSI 1992; *Recreations* shooting, hunting, racing, fishing; *Clubs* Turf, Western, MCC; *Style*— Guy Clark, Esq, JP, DL; ✉ Braeton House, Inverkip, Renfrewshire, PA16 ODU (☎ 01475 520619); Greig Middleton & Co Ltd, 155 St Vincent Street, Glasgow G2 5NN (☎ 0141 240 4000, fax 0141 204 4281)

CLARK, Henry Percival Bolton; *b* 4 Oct 1944; *Educ* The Dragon Sch Oxford, Harrow; *m* 2 Dec 1978, Gill; 1 s (Austen b 1980), 1 da (Celia b 1982); *Career* managing ptnr Nottingham office Ernst & Young; treas Harby PCC; CA; *Recreations* avoiding all sport; *Style*— Henry Clark, Esq; ✉ Ernst & Young, Citygate, Toll House Hill, Nottingham NG1 5FY (☎ 0115 958 8000, fax 0115 959 6666)

CLARK, Hugh Victor; s of Lt Cdr Philip Neville Clark, VRD, RNR, of Gorsley, Hereford, and Worcestershire and Winifred Betty, *née* Kiddle; *b* 18 May 1948; *Educ* Brewood GS Staffs; *m* 5 Dec 1970, Rosemary Anne, da of Kenneth Walter Solloway, of Wolverhampton; 1 s (Richard Ian b 1974), 1 da (Michelle Emma b 1977); *Career* Westminster Bank Ltd 1965–67, Canadian Imperial Bank of Commerce 1967–70, Nat Westminster Bank Ltd 1970–77; Tarmac plc: treas accountant 1978–83, asst gp treas 1983–87, gp treas 1987–; ACIB 1975, FCT 1982; *Recreations* photography, motor racing;

Style— Hugh Clark, Esq; ✉ Tarmac plc, Hilton Hall, Essington, Wolverhampton WV11 2BQ (☎ 01902 307407, fax 01902 303122, telex 338544)

CLARK, Ian Robertson; CBE (1979); s of Alexander Clark, and Annie Dundas, *née* Watson; *b* 18 Jan 1939; *Educ* Dalziel HS Motherwell; *m* 1961, Jean Scott Waddell, *née* Lang; 1 s, 1 da; *Career* chm: Ventures Div Costain Group 1986–93, Sigma Resources plc 1986–88, Clark & Associates Ltd 1994–, C & M (Hydraulics) Ltd 1994–; jt md Britoil 1982–85; md Tilbury Douglas Partnerships 1995–; memb Bd British National Oil Corp 1976–82; former co treas Zetland CC; chief exec Shetlands Islands Cncl 1974–76; Hon LLB Univ of Glasgow 1979; memb IPFA; FCCA; *Books* Reservoir of Power (1979); *Recreations* reading, writing, walking; *Style—* Ian Clark, Esq, CBE; ✉ Highwood, Fir Drive, Camberley, Surrey GU17 9BU

CLARK, (Luther) John; s of Eno Treverton Clark, and Mary Opal, *née* Johnson; *b* 27 Aug 1941; *Educ* Wharton Sch Univ of Pennsylvania (BS, MBA); *m* 1965, Judith Anne, *née* Dooley; 1 da (Sandra Faraday b 15 Jan 1971), 1 s (James Treverton b 31 Aug 1972); *Career* corp vice pres and chief of ops staff Singer Sewing and Consumer Durables Gp 1978–81, corp vice pres and chief exec offr Singer Europe, Africa and Middle E 1981–86, exec vice pres VF Corporation 1986–88, chm and chief exec Core-Mark International Inc 1988–91, chief exec and md BET plc 1991–96; non-exec dir Rolls-Royce plc 1993–96, chm Steamboat Capital Group; memb Bd of Overseers and Euro Advsy Bd Wharton Sch Univ of Pennsylvania, tstee Univ of Pennsylvania 1996–; memb London First, memb CBI, FInstD, CIMgt; *Recreations* jogging, golf; *Style—* John Clark, Esq

CLARK, John; s of Gordon Clark, of Newcastle-under-Lyme, and Aileen, *née* Hall; *b* 15 July 1961; *Educ* Newcastle-under-Lyme HS, St Edmund Hall Oxford (open exhibitioner, BA jurisprudence, MA, golf blue, water polo half blue), Coll of Law Guildford; *Career* articled clerk Theodore Goddard 1984–86, paralegal Mallesons Perth Australia 1986; Theodore Goddard: staff slr 1987–90, assoc 1990–92, ptnr 1992–, head Corp Fin 1994–; *Recreations* golf, water polo, tennis, dining, fine wine; *Clubs* Oxford & Cambridge Golf, Worplesdon Golf, Broadgate; *Style—* John Clark, Esq; ✉ Theodore Goddard, 150 Aldersgate Street, London EC1A 4EJ (☎ 0171 606 8855, fax 0171 606 4390)

CLARK, Sir John Allen; kt (1971); eld s of Sir Allen Clark (d 1962), and Jocelyn, *née* Culverhouse; bro of Michael William Clark, *qv*; *b* 14 Feb 1926; *Educ* Harrow, Trinity Coll Cambridge; *m* 1, 1952 (m dis 1962), Deirdre Kathleen, da of Samuel Herbert Waterhouse; 1 s, 1 da; m 2, 1970, Olivia, da of H Pratt; 2 s (twins), 1 da; *Career* served WWII RNVR (Sub-Lt); received early industl trg with Met Vickers and Ford Motor Co; spent year in USA studying electronics indust; asst to gen mangr Plessey International Ltd 1949, dir and gen mangr Plessey (Ireland) and Wireless Telephone Co 1950; The Plessey Co Ltd: dir 1953, md 1962–70, dep chm 1967–70, chm and chief exec 1970–89; dir: International Computers Ltd 1968–79, Banque Nationale de Paris Ltd 1976–89; pres Telecommunications Engrg and Mfrg Assoc 1964–66 and 1971–73; chm Wavertree Technol Park 1983–88; vice pres: Inst of Works Mangrs, Engrg Employers' Fedn; memb: Nat Defence Industs Cncl, Engrg Industs Cncl 1975–89; govr Harrow Sch 1982–; Order of Henry the Navigator (Portugal) 1973; *Recreations* shooting, riding, golf; *Clubs* Boodle's; *Style—* Sir John Clark; ✉ Redenham Park, Redenham, Nr Andover, Hants (☎ 01264 772511, fax 01264 772616)

CLARK, John Edward; OBE (1995); s of Albert Edward Clark (d 1973), of London, and Edith, *née* Brown (d 1984); *b* 18 Oct 1932; *Educ* Clitheroe Royal GS, Keble Coll Oxford (MA, BCL); *m* 1969, Judith Rosemary, da of Dr Arnold Marklew Lester; 1 s (Roy), 1 da (Katherine (decd)); *Career* called to the Bar 1957; dep sec Nat Assoc of Parish Cncls 1961–78, sec Nat Assoc of Local Cncls 1978–95; *Recreations* board games, collecting detective fiction, visiting fortifications, home wine-making; *Style—* John Clark Esq, OBE; ✉ 113 Turney Road, London SE21 7JB

CLARK, Sir Jonathan George; 5 Bt (UK 1917), of Dunlambert, City of Belfast; s of Sir Colin Douglas Clark, 4 Bt, MC (d 1995), and Margaret Coleman, *née* Spinks; *b* 9 Oct 1947; *Educ* Eton; *m* 1971, Susan Joy, da of Brig Thomas Ian Gordon Gray; 1 s (George Simon Gray b 1975), 2 da (Polly Caroline b 1973, Tessa Louise b 1978); *Heir* s, George Simon Gray Clark b 3 Oct 1975; *Career* late Capt Royal Green Jackets, md Paragon Homes Ltd (nursing home and healthcare gp); dir Br Horse Trials Assoc Ltd; *Recreations* horse trials; *Style—* Sir Jonathan Clark, Bt; ✉ Somerset House, Threapwood, Malpas, Cheshire (☎ 01948 770205, fax 01948 770305, office 01270 626060)

CLARK, Keith; s of Douglas William Clark (d 1967), of Chichester, Sussex, and Evelyn Lucy, *née* Longlands; *b* 25 Oct 1944; *Educ* Chichester HS for Boys, St Catherine's Coll Oxford (MA, BA); *m* 2 Nov 1976, Linda Sue, da of Eric Woodger, Ringwood, Hants; 1 s (Nicholas Howard Douglas b 1980), 1 da (Katherine Sara Amy b 1984); *Career* slr; Clifford Chance: joined 1971, ptnr 1977–, sr ptnr 1993–, various mgmnt appts; memb: Law Soc 1971, Slrs' Benevolent Soc, Int Bar Assoc; *Recreations* hiking, family, drama; *Style—* Keith Clark, Esq; ✉ Clifford Chance, 200 Aldersgate Street, London EC1A 4JJ (☎ 0171 600 1000, fax 0171 600 5555, telex 887847)

CLARK, His Hon (Francis) Leo; QC (1972); s of Sydney John Clark (d 1969), of Oxford, and Florence Lilian, *née* Huxtable; *b* 15 Dec 1920; *Educ* Bablake Sch, St Peter's Coll Oxford; *m* 1, 1957, Denise Jacqueline, da of Raymond Rambaud, of Paris; 1 s; m 2, 1967, Dr Daphne Margaret Clark, da of David Humphreys, of Hitchin; *Career* called to the Bar 1947, recorder of the Crown Court 1972–76, circuit judge 1976–93; hon recorder of Oxford 1979–; *Style—* His Hon Leo Clark, QC; ✉ The Ivy House, Charlbury, Oxfordshire OX7 3PX

CLARK, Prof Leslie Arthur; s of Arthur George Clark, of Chadwell Heath, Essex, and Lilian Rosina, *née* Procter; *b* 3 May 1944; *Educ* Ilford Co HS for Boys, Univ of Sheffield (Cicely Courtauld scholar, BEng, PhD, Mappin medal); *m* 29 Dec 1973, Helen Rose, da of William Ireson Tripp; 2 da (Laura Jane b 18 March 1977, Georgina Ann b 2 Dec 1980); *Career* res engr in design Cement and Concrete Assoc 1968–78; Sch of Civil Engrg Univ of Birmingham: lectr 1978–86, sr lectr 1986–91, prof of structural engrg 1991–; FICE 1995 (MICE 1973), FIStructE 1986 (MIStructE 1975), FEng 1994; *Books* Concrete Bridge Design (1983), Concrete Slabs: Analysis and Design (1984); *Recreations* cricket, football, jazz music; *Clubs* MCC; *Style—* Prof Leslie Clark, FEng; ✉ School of Civil Engineering, University of Birmingham, Edgbaston, Birmingham B15 2TT (☎ 0121 414 5083, fax 0121 414 3675)

CLARK, Lynda Margaret; QC (Scot 1989); *Educ* Univ of St Andrews (LLB), Univ of Edinburgh (PhD); *Career* lectr in law Univ of Dundee 1973–76, called to the Scottish Bar 1977, called to the Bar Inner Temple 1990; Bd Memb Scottish Legal Aid Bd 1990–93; Parly candidate (Lab) NE Fife 1992; memb Ct Univ of Edinburgh 1995–; *Style—* Ms Lynda Clark, QC; ✉ Faculty of Advocates, Parliament Square, Edinburgh EH1 1RF (☎ 0131 226 2881)

CLARK, Dr Michael; MP (C) Rochford (majority 26,036); s of late Mervyn Clark, and Sybilla Norma, *née* Winscott; *b* 8 Aug 1935; *Educ* King Edward VI GS Retford, King's Coll London, St John's Coll Cambridge, Univ of Minnesota; *m* 1958, Valerie Ethel, da of C S Harbord; 1 s, 1 da; *Career* mgmnt conslt and industl chemist; with ICI 1960–66, Smiths Industs 1966–69, PA Consulting Gp 1969–93; chm Cambridgeshire Cons Assoc 1980–83 (treas 1975–78, vice chm 1978–80); Parly candidate (C) Ilkeston 1979, MP (C) Rochford 1983–; hon sec: Parly and Scientific Ctee 1985–90, Anglo-Nepalese All Pty Gp 1985–90, All Pty Gp for the Chem Indust 1985–90 (vice chm 1990–94, chm 1994–); hon treas: Br-Malawi All Pty Gp 1987–, Exec Ctee Inter Pty Union 1987 (chm 1990–93), All Pty Space Ctee 1988–90; chm: All Pty Gp for Energy Studies 1992–, Parliamentary Office of Science and Technol 1993–, Br-Russia All Pty Gp 1993–, Br-Venezuela All Pty Gp 1995–; memb: House of Commons Select Ctee for Energy 1983–92 (chm 1989–92), Trade and Indust Select Ctee 1992–; FKC 1987; FRSC 1988; *Recreations* golf, gardening, DIY; *Clubs* Rochford Cons; *Style—* Dr Michael Clark, MP; ✉ House of Commons, London SW1A 0AA

CLARK, Dr Michael Llewellyn; *b* 17 June 1935; *Educ* W Monmouth GS Pontypool Monmouthshire, King's Coll London, St George's Hosp Med Sch Univ of London (LRCP, MRCS, MB BS, MRCP, MD); *m* 2 c; *Career* house physician: Neurological Unit Atkinson Morley's Hosp London 1959–60, Brompton Hosp London 1960; jr med specialist HM Forces QAMH Millbank London 1960–63; St George's Hosp London: house physician 1958, house surgn Surgical Unit 1958–59, med registrar 1963–66, clinical res registrar Med Unit 1964–66, sr registrar in med 1968; fell in gastronenterology Philadelphia Gen Hosp Univ of Pennsylvania 1966–68, conslt physician St Leonards Hosp 1970–84, hon conslt gastroenterologist Royal Marsden Hosp Sutton Surrey 1983–, conslt physician Hackney Hosp 1984–85; Bart's London: clinical res asst and hon lectr in med 1969–70, sr lectr in med Bart's Med Coll 1970–93, postgrad sub-dean Bart's Med Coll 1974–80, head Gastroenterology Dept 1986–91; City & Hackney Health Dist: conslt physician 1970–93, unit gen mangr Hackney Unit 1985–88, unit gen mangr City Unit 1988–90, dir of res and clinical devpt 1990–92; postgrad educnl co-ordinator Royal Hosps Tst 1994–, reg teacher for MRCP examination; FRCP 1975; *Books* Clinical Medicine (jtly, 1987, 1990 and 1994); author of numerous published articles in learned jls; *Style—* Dr Michael Clark; ✉ 7 Sherwood Park Rd, Sutton, Surrey SM1 2SQ (☎ 0181 642 5993); St Bartholomew's Hospital, London EC1A 7BE (☎ 0171 601 8888)

CLARK, Michael William; CBE (1977), DL (1988); s of Sir Allen Clark (d 1962), of Braxted Park, Witham, Essex, and Jocelyn Anina Marie Louise, *née* Culverhouse (d 1964); *b* 7 May 1927; *Educ* Harrow; *m* 1, 1955, Shirley, *née* Macphadzen (d 1974); 1 s (Duncan), 2 da (Marion b 1957 d 1988, Miranda (Mrs Carew-Jones)), 1 step s (Matthew Harragin b 1953); m 2, 6 April 1985, Virginia Ann, Marchioness Camden, da of Francis Harry Hume Finlaison (d 1968); *Career* Subaltern Grenadier Guards 1945–48; Plessey Co: joined 1950, fndr chm Plessey Electronic Systems, former dep chm and dep chief exec, ret 1987; memb: Electronics EDC 1975–80, Cncl IOD, Nat Electronics Cncl, Ct Univ of Essex; pres Essex Branch: SSAFA, Grenadier Gds Assoc; High Sheriff of Essex 1991; CIEE, CompIERE; *Recreations* shooting, fishing, forestry; *Clubs* Boodle's, Pratt's; *Style—* Michael Clark, Esq, CBE, DL; ✉ 16 Ranelagh House, Chelsea, London SW3 3EL; Braxted Park, Witham, Essex CM8 3EN

CLARK, Oswald William Hugh; CBE (1978); s of Rev Hugh Miller Allison Clark (d 1962), of Raynes Park, London SW20, and Mabel Bessie Clark (d 1969); *b* 26 Nov 1917; *Educ* Rutlish Sch Merton, Univ of London (BA, BD), Univ of Wales (LLM); *m* 23 July 1966, Diana Mary, da of William Alfred Hine, of New Milton, Hants; 1 da (Alison Mary Cynthia b 1967); *Career* WWII Maj 2 Derbyshire Yeomanry 8 Army ME NW Europe; asst dir gen GLC 1973–79 (formerly London Co Cncl, joined 1937); C of E: memb Gen Synod (formerly Church Assembly) 1948–90, memb Standing and Legislative Ctees 1950–90, memb Standing Orders Ctee 1950–90, church cmmr 1958–88, chm House of Laity 1979–85 (vice chm 1970–79), vice pres Corp of Church House 1981–, memb Crown Appts Cmmn 1987–90; life fell Guild of Guide Lectrs 1982–, princ Soc of the Faith 1987–92; parish clerk St Andrew by the Wardrobe London; memb Worshipful Co of Parish Clerks; *Recreations* history of London, Goss china, heraldry; *Clubs* Cavalry and Guards, Pratt's; *Style—* O W H Clark, Esq, CBE; ✉ 8 Courtlands Ave, Hampton, Middx TW12 3NT (☎ 0181 979 1081)

CLARK, Paul Evans; s of Harry Frederick Clark, of Derby, and Joyce Evelyn, *née* Margetts; *b* 18 March 1946; *Educ* Bemrose GS Derby, Univ of Manchester (LLB); *m* 25 July 1970, Jane Mary, da of Edmund Patrick Flowers; 2 s (Guy Edmund b 22 Feb 1977, Ben Thomas b 28 July 1980), 2 da (Nina Jane b 13 Dec 1972, Lucy Anna b 25 March 1975); *Career* admitted slr 1970; asst slr: Rubinstein Nash & Co 1970–72 (articled clerk 1968–70), Property Dept Linklaters & Paines 1972–83; head of Property Dept D J Freeman 1990– (joined 1984, ptnr 1985–); memb Law Soc 1970; *Recreations* pianist, music, church membership, reading; *Style—* Paul Clark, Esq; ✉ D J Freeman, 43 Fetter Lane, London EC4A 1NA (☎ 0171 583 4055, fax 0171 353 7377)

CLARK, His Hon Judge Paul Nicholas Rowntree; s of Henry Rowntree Clark (d 1975), and Gwendoline Victoria Clark (d 1992); *b* 17 Aug 1940; *Educ* Bristol GS, New Coll Oxford (MA); *m* 1967; 2 s (Oliver b 1972, Edward b 1977), 1 da (Harriet b 1970); *Career* called to the Bar Middle Temple (Harmsworth scholar) 1966, bencher 1982, barr practising on Oxford Circuit, later Midland and Oxford Circuit 1966–85, recorder 1981–85, circuit judge (Midland and Oxford Circuit) 1985–; *Clubs* Garrick; *Style—* His Hon Judge Paul Clark; ✉ c/o Midland and Oxford Circuit Office, The Priory Courts, 33 Bull Street, Birmingham B4 6DW (☎ 0121 627 1700)

CLARK, Dr Peter John Alleguen; OBE (1993); s of Dr Kenneth Clark (d 1971), and Kitty Matilda, *née* Ruffle (d 1990); *b* 17 May 1939; *Educ* Loughborough GS, Southend HS for Boys, Univ of Keele (BA), Downing Coll Cambridge, Univ of Leicester (PhD); *m* 1, 1968 (m dis 1980), Isobel, *née* Rankin; 1 s (John Paul Jeremy b 1972); m 2, 1980, Theresa Mary Philomena Brown, *née* Alleguen; 1 step da (Kate Philomena b 1968), 2 s (Gabriel Edwin Alleguen b 1981, Nathaniel Luke Alleguen b 1983); *Career* mathematics teacher Ankara Coll and teacher of English British Council 1962–63, tutorial asst Dept of History Univ of Leicester 1964–66, lectr in general studies Duncan of Jordanstone Coll of Art 1966–67; British Council: trg 1967–68, Jordan 1968–70, MECAS 1970–71, Sudan 1971–77, London 1977–80, Yemen 1980–84, Tunisia 1984–88, UAE 1988–92, dir Syria 1992–; memb Middle East Studies Assoc 1993; FRGS 1982, FIL 1993; *Books* Three Sudanese Battles (1977), Henry Hallam (1980), Karari (trans, 1980), Marmaduke Pickthall British Muslim (1986), Dubai Tales (trans, 1991), Thesiger's Return (1992), A Balcony Over Fakihani (trans, 1993), Sabriya (trans, 1995); *Recreations* youth hostelling, translating Arabic, walking in hills; *Clubs* Travellers'; *Style—* Dr Peter Clark, OBE; ✉ British Council, PO Box 33105, Al Jalla, Damascus, Syria (fax 00 963 11 331 0630)

CLARK, Raymond Vincent; s of Peter Clark, of Broxbourne, Herts, and Eileen, *née* Rothery; *b* 26 Feb 1946; *Educ* Tottenham Boys' Sch, NE London Poly (Dip Arch); *m* 16 Aug 1969, Gillian Elizabeth, da of Henry Cook, of Frinton, Essex; 2 s (Simon b 15 May 1978, Iain b 22 July 1982); *Career* ptnr CHQ Partnership 1982– (co-fndr); RIBA 1976, memb ARCUK 1976; *Style—* Raymond Clark, Esq; ✉ Knot's Foss, 73 Hall Lane, Gt Chishill, Royston, Herts (☎ 01763 838 785); CHQ Partnership, The Maltings, 44 Whitehorse St, Baldock, Hertfordshire (☎ 01462 895 110, fax 01462 895 099)

CLARK, Richard David; s of David Clark (d 1975), of Luton, and Enid Beatrice, *née* Harton (d 1988); *b* 2 Sept 1934; *Educ* Univ of Keele (BA, DipEd), Université de Paris (Sorbonne); *m* 12 April 1958, Pamela Mary, da of Frederick Burgess (d 1978), of Luton; 2 da (Sara b 1962, Helen b 1964); *Career* teacher Woodberry Down Comprehensive Sch 1957–61, educn admin Herts CC 1961–69, asst educn offr Lancs CC 1969–71, second dep county educn offr Hants CC 1972–76, chief educn offr Glos CC 1976–83, county educn offr Hants CC 1983–88, chief exec Devon CC 1989–95; clerk to the Lieutenancy 1989–95, clerk to Devon & Cornwall Police Authy 1994–96 (assoc clerk 1989–94); dir Devon & Cornwall Trg and Enterprise Cncl 1989–95; FRSA 1977; *Recreations* books, gardening, croquet; *Clubs* The Sidmouth; *Style—* Richard Clark, Esq; ✉ Bickwell Brook, Bickwell Valley, Sidmouth, Devon EX10 8SQ (☎ 01395 514937)

CLARK, Richard James; s of Hubert Clark, of Sunderland, and Shelagh Mary, *née* Whittaker; *b* 2 April 1965; *Educ* Farringdon Comp, Bournemouth and Poole Coll of Art and Design (HND); *Career* photographer; asst to various photographers incl Christopher

Joyce 1989–92, in own studio specialising in advtg and design orientated photography 1992–; memb Assoc of Photographers (Silver Award 1994 and 1995); *Recreations* fine wines and food, cinema, cycling; *Style*— Richard Clark, Esq; ✉ Richard Clark Photography, 2nd Floor, 1–6 Falconberg Court, London W1V 5FG (☎ 0171 494 0744, fax 0171 287 6118, mobile 0973 326092)

CLARK, Sir Robert Anthony; kt (1976), DSC (1944); yr s of John Clark, and Gladys, *née* Dyer; *b* 6 Jan 1924; *Educ* Highgate, King's Coll Cambridge; *m* 1949, Andolyn Marjorie Beynon Lewis; 2 s, 1 da; *Career* ptnr Slaughter and May slrs 1953–61; dir: Alfred McAlpine plc 1957–96, Hill Samuel Bank Ltd 1961–91 (chm 1974–87), Bank of England 1976–85, Eagle Star Holdings Ltd 1976–87, Rover Group plc 1977–88, Shell Transport and Trading Co plc 1982–94, Vodafone Group plc 1988–; chm: Hill Samuel Group plc 1980–88 (chief exec 1976–80), IMI plc 1981–89, Marley plc 1985–89, Mirror Group plc 1991–, Rauscher Pierce & Clark 1992–, Lowndes Lambert Group Ltd 1995– (dep chm 1992–95); vice chm SmithKline Beecham plc 1987–95, dep chm TSB Group plc 1989–91 (dir 1987–91); chm: Doctors' and Dentists' Review Body 1979–86, Charing Cross and Westminster Hosp Med Sch 1981–95; Hon DSc Cranfield Inst of Technol 1982; *Recreations* reading, music, collecting antiquarian books; *Clubs* Pratt's; *Style*— Sir Robert Clark, DSC; ✉ Munstead Wood, Godalming, Surrey (☎ 01483 417867); Rauscher Pierce & Clark, 56 Green Street, Mayfair, London W1Y 3RH (☎ 0171 491 2434)

CLARK, Prof Robert Bernard; s of Joseph Laurence Clark (d 1980), of London and Burrowbridge, Somerset, and Dorothy, *née* Halden (d 1988); *b* 13 Oct 1923; *Educ* St Marylebone GS, Univ of London (BSc), Univ of Exeter (BSc), Univ of Glasgow (PhD), Univ of London (DSc); *m* 1, 19 July 1956 (m dis 1969), Mary Eleanor, da of Walter Lawrence (d 1969), of San Francisco, USA; m 2, 30 Dec 1970, Susan Diana, da of Lt-Col Leonard Smith (d 1971), of Haslemere, Surrey; 1 s (Stephen Robert Leonard b 1975), 1 da (Juliet Louise b 1972); *Career* asst in zoology Univ of Glasgow 1950–53, asst prof of zoology Univ of Calif at Berkeley USA 1953–55, lectr in zoology Univ of Bristol 1956–65, prof of zoology and dir The Dove Marine Laboratory Univ of Newcastle upon Tyne 1965–89; memb: NERC 1971–77 and 1982–85, Royal Cmmn on Environmental Pollution 1978–82, Advsy Ctee on Pesticides 1985–90; FIBiol 1966, FLS 1969, FRSE 1970; *Books* Dynamics in Metazoan Evolution (1964), Invertebrate Panorama (1971), Marine Pollution (1986), Marine Pollution Bulletin (ed); *Style*— Prof Robert Clark, FRSE; ✉ Highbury House, Highbury, Newcastle upon Tyne NE2 3LN (☎ 0191 281 4672); Department of Marine Sciences, The University, Newcastle upon Tyne NE1 7RU (☎ 0191 222 6661)

CLARK, Robin Douglas; *b* 15 Nov 1956; *Educ* Eastbourne Coll, Univ of Southampton, Harvard Business Sch; *m* 25 April 1981, Sonia Margaret, *née* Glover; 1 s (Christopher b 24 March 1985), 2 da (Stephanie b 23 May 1988, Jennifer b 10 July 1991); *Career* chartered accountant Deloitte Haskins & Sells 1982–83 (articled clerk 1979–82), exec positions ICAEW and Accounting Standards Ctee 1983–85, Lloyd's of London 1986; Investment Mgmnt Regulatory Orgn (IMRO): mangr membership 1987–89, asst dir investigations 1990, dir monitoring 1991–95, dir regulatory relations 1995–; ACA 1982; *Style*— Robin Clark, Esq; ✉ Investment Management Regulatory Organisation, Lloyds Chambers, 1 Portsoken Street, London E1 8BT (☎ 0171 390 5000, fax 0171 480 5905)

CLARK, Prof Robin Jon Hawes; s of Reginald Hawes Clark, JP, of Blenheim, NZ, and Marjorie Alice, *née* Thomas; *b* 16 Feb 1935; *Educ* Christ's Coll Christchurch NZ, Canterbury Univ Coll Univ of NZ (BSc, MSc), UCL (PhD, DSc); *m* 30 May 1964, Beatrice Rawdin Clark, JP, da of Ellis Rawdin Brown (d 1978); 1 s (Matthew b 14 Dec 1971), 1 da (Victoria b 23 June 1967); *Career* UCL: asst lectr 1962, lectr 1963–71, reader 1972–81, prof 1982–88, dean of sci 1988–89, Sir William Ramsay prof and head Dept of Chem 1989–, memb Cncl 1991–94, fell 1993; senator Univ of London 1988–93; chm: 11th Int Conf on Raman Spectroscopy London 1988, Advsy Ctee Ramsay Meml Fellowships Tst 1989–, Steering Ctee Int Confs on Raman Spectroscopy 1990–92; tstee Ramsay Meml Fellowships Tst 1994–; visiting prof: Columbia Univ 1965, Padua 1967, Western Ontario 1968, Texas A and M 1978, Bern 1979, Fribourg 1979, Amsterdam 1979, Auckland 1981, Odense 1982, Sydney 1985, Bordeaux 1988, Pretoria 1991; Royal Soc of Chemistry lectr: Tilden 1983–84, Nyholm 1989–90, Thomas Graham 1991, Harry Hallam 1993; Hon FRSNZ 1989, FRSC 1969, FRS 1990, memb Academia Europaea 1990, FRSA 1992; *Books* The Chemistry of Titanium and Vanadium (1968), The Chemistry of Titanium Zirconium and Hafnium (1973), The Chemistry of Vanadium Niobium and Tantalum (1973), Advances in Spectroscopy Vols 1–25 (co ed, 1975–96), Raman Spectroscopy (co ed, 1988); also author of over 350 scientific papers; *Recreations* golf, swimming, skiing, bridge, music, theatre; *Clubs* Athenaeum, Porters Park; *Style*— Prof Robin Clark, FRS; ✉ 3a Loom Lane, Radlett, Herts WD7 8AA (☎ 01923 857899); Christopher Ingold Laboratories, University College London, 20 Gordon St, London WC1H 0AJ (☎ 0171 380 7457, fax 0171 380 7463)

CLARK, Rodney; *b* 7 Sept 1944; *Educ* Andover GS, UCL; *married*; *Career* mangr family furniture removals business 1965–67, gen asst Welfare Dept Hampshire CC 1967–68, Israeli Kibbutz 1968–69, admin asst Welfare Dept London Borough of Camden 1969–71; London Borough of Islington then Camden and Islington AHA: administrator Personal Health Servs 1971–72, opened and managed Highbury Grange Health Centre 1972–74, sr administrator Islington Sch Health Serv 1974–77, capital projects mangr Islington Health Dist 1977–78; projects administrator RNID 1978–81; chief exec Sense (Nat Deafblind and Rubella Assoc) 1981–; chm SIGN (Anastasia Soc), sec and treas Deafblind International (formerly Int Assoc for the Educn of the Deaf-Blind), treas European Deafblind Network; mgmnt speaker at seminars and confs for voluntary organisations; govr Whitefields Sch; *Recreations* choral singing, tennis, swimming, walking, riding; *Style*— Rodney Clark, Esq; ✉ 2 Herrick Road, Highbury, London N5 2JX (☎ 0171 354 3169); Chief Executive, Sense, 11–13 Clifton Terrace, Finsbury Park, London N4 3SR (☎ 0171 272 7774, fax 0171 272 6012)

CLARK, Prof Ronald George; s of George Clark (d 1968), of Loanhead, Cairnie, Aberdeenshire, and Gladys, *née* Taylor (d 1987); *b* 9 Aug 1928; *Educ* Aberdeen Acad, Univ of Aberdeen (MB ChB); *m* 10 Sept 1960, Tamar Welsh, da of Walter Erskine Harvie (d 1961), of Duntocher, Dunbartonshire; 2 da (Tamar Taylor b 1962, Deborah Harvie b 1964); *Career* lectr Univ of Glasgow 1961–65, surgical res fell Harvard Univ 1960–61; Univ of Sheffield: sr lectr in surgery 1966–71, prof of surgery 1971–93, dean Faculty of Med and Dentistry 1982–85, pro vice chllr 1988–93; memb: Gen Med Cncl 1982–93, Gen Dental Cncl 1989–93, Hon MD; sci govr Br Nutrition Fndn 1983–, memb Cncl Nutrition Soc 1981–84, exec chm Euro Soc of Parental and Enteral Nutrition 1982–87 (pres 1993–94); FRCS, FRCS (Edinburgh); memb: Assoc of Surgns 1969, RSM 1979; *Recreations* golf, walking; *Clubs* RSM, Cwlth Soc; *Style*— Prof Ronald Clark; ✉ 2 Chesterwood Drive, Sheffield S10 5DU (☎ 0114 266 3601)

CLARK, Prof Stephen Richard Lyster; s of David Allen Richard Clark (d 1986), and Mary Kathleen, *née* Finney (d 1992); *b* 30 Oct 1945; *Educ* Nottingham HS, Balliol and All Souls Colls Oxford (MA, DPhil); *m* 1 July 1972 (Edith) Gillian, da of Prof John Callan James Metford, of Bristol; 1 s (Samuel b 1974), 2 da (Alexandra b 1976, Verity b 1985); *Career* fell All Souls Coll Oxford 1968–74, lectr in moral philosophy Univ of Glasgow 1974–83 (Gifford lectr 1982); Univ of Liverpool: prof of philosophy 1984–, dean Faculty of Arts 1995–; ed Jl of Applied Philosophy, Stanton lectr Univ of Cambridge 1987–89, Wilde lectr Univ of Oxford 1990, Scott Holland lectr 1992, Read Tuckwell lectr Univ of Bristol 1994; *Books* Aristotle's Man (1975), The Moral Status of Animals (1977), The Nature of the Beast (1982), From Athens to Jerusalem (1984), The Mysteries of Religion (1986), La Naturaleza De La Bestia (1987), Money, Obedience and Affection (ed, 1989), Civil Peace and Sacred Order (1989), A Parliament of Souls (1990), God's World and the Great Awakening (1991), How to Think about the Earth (1993), How to Live Forever (1995), Animals and their Moral Standing (1996); *Recreations* science fiction, computers; *Style*— Prof Stephen Clark; ✉ 1 Arnside Rd, Oxton, Birkenhead, Merseyside L43 2JU (☎ 0151 653 4908); Department of Philosophy, University of Liverpool, PO Box 147, Liverpool L69 3BX (☎ 0151 794 2788, fax 0151 794 2789)

CLARK, Sir Terence Joseph; KBE (1990), CMG (1985), CVO (1978); s of Joseph Henry Clark (d 1971), of London, and Mary Ann Matilda Clark; *b* 19 June 1934; *Educ* Parmiter's Foundation Sch London, Univ of Grenoble, Univ of Cambridge, Univ of London, Univ of Freiburg; *m* 1960, Lieselotte Rosa Marie, da of Lt Cdr Erich Ernst Müller, of Kiel; 2 s (Adrian, Martin), 1 da (Sonja); *Career* Pilot Offr RAF VR 1955, entered HM Foreign Serv 1955, ME Centre of Arab Studies Lebanon 1956–57; third sec Political Residency Bahrain 1957–58, Br Embassy Amman Jordan 1958–60, vice consul Br Consulate Gen Casablanca 1960–62, FO 1962–65, asst political agent Dubai Trucial States 1965–68, first sec (Info) Belgrade 1969–71, head of Chancery and Consul Muscat Oman 1972–73, asst head ME Dept FCO 1974–75, cnsllr (Info) Bonn 1976–79, cnsllr Belgrade 1979–82, dep ldr of UK Delgn to Conf on Security and Cooperation in Europe (Madrid) 1982–83, head of Info Dept FCO 1983–85, ambass Rep of Iraq 1985–89, ambass Sultanate of Oman 1990–94, ret; hon vice pres Br Archaeological Expedition to Iraq 1985–89; sr conslt Middle East Consultants 1995–, dir Int Crisis Gp Bosnia Project Sarajevo 1996; memb Cncl Soc of Arabian Studies 1994–, chm Anglo-Omani Soc 1995–; *Books* The Saluqi: Coursing hound of the East (maj contrib, 1995); *Recreations* salukis, walking; *Clubs* Hurlingham, Royal Cwlth Soc; *Style*— Sir Terence Clark, KBE, CMG, CVO; ✉ 29 Westleigh Avenue, London SW15 6RQ

CLARK, Terrence Michael; s of Douglas Gordon Clark, of Littlehampton, Sussex, and Doris, *née* Landymore; *b* 5 May 1946; *m* 29 May 1976, Sally-Marie, da of Ronald Strange, of Ripley, Surrey; 2 s (Paul b 1967, Tobias b 1989), 1 da (Rebecca b 1983); *Career* artist craftsman in metals; ed British Blacksmith Magazine 1980–84; vice chm Br Artist Blacksmiths' Assoc 1992–94; organiser and chm The Int Blacksmithing Conf 1985; first artsmith to have a gate accepted by the Royal Acad ctee under sculpture 1986; fell Worshipful Co of Blacksmiths (Silver Medal) 1995; *Exhibitions* incl: Towards a New Iron Age V&A 1982, New York Craft Centre 1982, Br Artist Blacksmiths' Assoc Exhibitions 1983–92, Int Metalwork and Sculpture Exhibition Friedrichshafen W Germany 1987, Fe - an exploration of iron through the senses; won Addy Taylor Cup awarded by Worshipful Co of Blacksmiths 1983; *Commissions* H H Sheik Mohammed Bin Rashid Al Maktoum 1984–95, Guildford Cathedral 1985, public sculpture Horsham Cncl W Sussex 1994, 50m by 4m public cmmn High St Godalming Surrey 1995, external and internal work Grace Barrand Studio Nutfield Surrey 1995; *Books* Towards a New Iron Age (1982), Schmeidearbeiten von Heute (1986), Art From The Fire (1986), Art for Architecture (1987), Metal-Handwerk & Technik (1987); *Recreations* holder of pilot's licence, competition shooting, skiing; *Style*— Terrence Clark, Esq; ✉ Wildfields Farm, Woodstreet Village, Nr Guildford, Surrey GU3 3DT (☎ 01483 235244, fax 01483 236456)

CLARK, Prof Timothy John Hayes; *b* 18 Oct 1935; *Educ* Christ's Hosp Horsham, Guy's Hosp Med Sch London (BSc, MRCS, LRCP, MB BS, MD); *m*; 4 c; *Career* house offr: Guy's Hosp 1961, Brompton Hosp 1961–62, Hammersmith Hosp 1962–63, Nat Hosp for Nervous Diseases London 1963; fell in med Johns Hopkins Hosp Baltimore Maryland USA 1963–64, registrar Hammersmith Hosp 1964–66; Guy's Hosp: sr lectr Depts of Med and Physiology 1966–68, hon sr registrar 1966–68, conslt physician 1968–90, prof of thoracic med Utd Dental and Med Schs of Guy's and St Thomas' Hosps 1977–90; specialist advsr to Social Servs Ctee House of Commons 1980–81 and 1984–85, conslt in thoracic med to the CMO Dept of Health 1985–90; Royal Brompton Hosp: conslt physician 1990– (pt/t 1970–90), prof of pulmonary med Nat Heart and Lung Inst 1990–; dean: Guy's Campus 1984–86, Utd Dental and Med Schs 1986–89 (govr 1982–90), Nat Heart and Lung Inst 1990–; pro-rector (med) Imperial Coll; special tstee Guy's Hosp 1982–89, pro vice chllr for med and dentistry Univ of London 1987–89; pres Br Thoracic Soc 1990–91; memb: Lambeth Southwark and Lewisham AHA 1978–82, Lewisham and N Southwark HA 1982–85, SE Thames RHA 1985–87, Systems Bd MRC 1985–88, Royal Brompton Hospital NHS Tst 1993–; hon prof Xian Med Coll Xian China 1986–; FRCP 1973; *Publications* author of over 200 textbooks, articles and papers on respiratory, pulmonary and thoracic medicine; *Style*— Prof Timothy Clark; ✉ National Heart and Lung Institute, Imperial College School of Medicine, Dovehouse Street, London SW3 6LY (☎ 0171 351 8175, fax 0171 351 3120)

CLARK, (Alastair) Trevor; CBE (1976), LVO (1974); s of Dr William George Clark, CBE, KHP (d 1957), and Gladys Catherine, *née* Harrison (d 1969); *b* 10 June 1923; *Educ* Glasgow and Edinburgh Acads, Magdalen Coll Oxford (MA), Inns of Court, Ashridge Management Coll; *m* 1 May 1965, Hilary Agnes, da of Dr John Binnie Mackenzie Anderson (d 1944); *Career* WWII, cmmnd Queen's Own Cameron Highlanders second RWAFF (temp Maj), served Nigeria, India, Burma 1942–46; served Admin Branch HM Colonial Serv (later HMOCS): Nigeria (sec to Exec Cncl N Region, sr dist offr) 1949–59, Hong Kong (clerk of Cncls, princ asst Colonial Sec, dir social welfare, dep and actg dir Urban Servs, acting chm Urban Cncl) 1960–72, W Pacific (chief sec High Cmmn, dep and acting govr Solomon Islands) 1972–77, ret 1977; called to the Bar Middle Temple 1963; USA State Dept Country Ldr Fellowship 1972, UN Conf on Human Environment Stockholm 1972; memb: Scot Museums Cncl 1980–90 (chm 1981–84 and 1987–90), Cncl Nat Tst for Scotland 1981–84 and 1987–, Cncl Edinburgh Int Festival 1980–86 and 1991–94, Cncl Museums Assoc 1982–86 and 1990–94 (memb Inst Conslt Ctee 1989–95, Public Affrs Ctee 1990–94, Ethics Ctee 1991–94), Sec of State Scotland's Museum Advsy Bd 1983–85, Race Relations Panel (Scot Sheriff Cts) 1983–, Ctee Area Museum Cncls 1981–84 and 1987–90 (vice chm 1983–84), Cons Advsy Ctee on Arts and Heritage 1988–, Scot Cons and Unionist Arts and Heritage Policy Ctee 1995–; tstee: Bd of Nat Museums of Scotland 1985–87, Nat Museums of Scotland Charitable Tst 1987–, Almond Valley Heritage Tst 1990– (vice chm), Bo'ness Heritage Tst 1990–, Stirling Smith Art Gallery & Museum Jt Ctee 1993–; jt fndr Hong Kong Outward Bound Sch 1966; govr Edinburgh Filmhouse 1980–84 and 1987–, dir Edinburgh Acad 1979–84; Leverhulme Tst Grant 1979–81 (biographer of Sir Abubakar Tafawa Balewa, late PM of Nigeria); memb: City of Edinburgh DC 1980–88, Lothian Health Bd 1981–89; FSA (Scot) 1988; *Books* A Right Honourable Gentleman: Abubakar From The Black Rock (1991); *Recreations* listening to music and opera, books, theatre, netsuke, cartophily; *Clubs* Athenaeum, New (Edinburgh); *Style*— Trevor Clark, Esq, CBE, LVO; ✉ 11 Ramsay Garden, Edinburgh EH1 2NA (☎ 0131 225 8070)

CLARK, Cdr Victor Cecil Froggatt; DSC (1940, and Bar 1942); s of Rev Charles Clark (d 1940), of The Valley House, Glassmill Lane, Bromley, Kent, and Amy, *née* Froggatt (d 1966); *b* 24 May 1908; *Educ* Haileybury; *m* 10 May 1975, Danae Heather, da of Frederick James Stileman (d 1982), of Dunster, Somerset; 2 da (Jessica b 1976, Rosalind b 1980); *Career* RN: cadet 1926, Midshipman Med Fleet (HMS Valiant, HMS Wren, HMS Warspite, HMS Courageous) 1927–29, Sub Lt courses Portsmouth and Greenwich 1930, Med Fleet HMS Anthony 1931–32, Home Fleet HMS Watchman 1932–34, Boys Trg Estab HMS Ganges 1935–37, HMS Wild Swan Jubilee Review 1937, Med Fleet HMS Warspite 1937–38, Home Fleet HMS Punjabi active serv Battle Narvik 1938–40, i/c HMS Anthony 1940–41, HMS Repulse (sunk in action off Singapore), organised commando raids (W Coast Raiders) during Malayan Campaign 1941–42, carried out secret evacuation of 2000 troops from behind Japanese lines, sunk in action with superior

Japanese forces, wounded one and a half days in water with broken arm, 6 weeks in Sumatran jungle, betrayed to Japanese 1942, POW Sumatra and Singapore 1942–45, i/c HMS Loch Tralaig and HMS Loch Dunvegan 1946–47, Trg Offr Sea Cadet HQ London 1947–53, ret as Cdr 1953; circumnavigation (48000 miles) yacht Solace 1953–59, lecture tours 1960–61, sail trg i/c schooners Prince Louis and Capt Scott 1962–74; Freeman City of London 1930, Liveryman Worshipful Co of Grocers 1935; *Books* On The Wind of a Dream (1960), Triumph and Disaster (1984); *Recreations* walking, tennis (previously riding); *Clubs* Royal Cwlth Soc, Ocean Cruising, RN; *Style*— Cdr Victor Clark, DSC, RN

CLARK, Victoria Ann; da of Noel E P Clark, of London, Marianne Edith, *née* Sayres; *b* 25 Aug 1961; *Educ* St Mary's Convent Dorset, Convent of the Sacred Heart HS, Univ of York (BA); *Career* teacher Eng as a foreign language: Barcelona 1983–85, Budapest 1985–87; updating Fodor travel guides 1988; journalist The Observer: Bucharest 1989–91, Yugoslavia 1991–93, Russia 1993–96, Home News 1996–; winner David Blundy Prize British Press Awards 1991; *Style*— Ms Victoria Clark; ✉ The Observer, 119 Farringdon Road, London EC1R 3ER (☎ 0171 713 4324)

CLARK, William James; s of William Clark, of Glencarse, Scotland, and Elizabeth Shanks Clark; *b* 3 May 1950; *Educ* Dundee HS, Univ of Edinburgh (BSc), Univ of W Ontario Canada (MBA); *m* 28 Aug 1981, Karen Neergaard, da of HE Jorgen Holm; 2 da; *Career* Chemical Bank: mktg offr 1974–79, regnl mktg mangr Singapore 1979–80, gen mangr Singapore 1980–83, regnl mangr (energy and minerals) London 1984–87, regnl mangr (origination and corp fin) London 1987–91; chief operating offr Pricoa Capital Group Ltd 1995– (dir 1991–), dir Mithras Investment Trust plc 1994–; represented GB at athletics 1973–75, UK triple jump champion 1974, Scot triple jump champion 1975 and 1977–78; *Recreations* sport, farming; *Clubs* RAC; *Style*— William J Clark, Esq; ✉ Pricoa Capital Group Ltd, Cutlers Court, 115 Houndsditch, London EC3A 7BU (☎ 0171 283 8122)

CLARK OF KEMPSTON, Baron (Life Peer UK 1992), of Kempston in the County of Bedfordshire; Sir William Gibson Clark; kt (1980), PC (1990); s of Hugh Clark, of Cautley Ave, London; *b* 18 Oct 1917; *Educ* London; *m* 1944, Irene Dorothy Dawson, da of Edward Francis Rands, of Grimsby, Lincs; 3 s (Hon Richard Anthony b 1947, Hon David William Francis b 1948, Hon Charles Edward Hugh b 1959), 1 da (Hon Angela Margaret Grayson (Hon Mrs Labey)); *Career* served WWII UK and India; contested (C) Northampton 1955; MP (C): Nottingham S 1959–66, E Surrey 1970–74, Croydon S 1974–92; oppn front bench spokesman Econs 1964–66, jt dep chm Cons Pty Orgn 1975–77 (jt treas 1974–75), chm Cons Fin Ctee 1979–92; chm Anglo Austrian Soc 1983; Freeman City of London; ACA; Austrian Grand Gold Cross Austria 1989, Grand Decoration of Honour in Gold with Star (Austria) 1994; *Clubs* Buck's, Carlton; *Style*— The Rt Hon Lord Clark of Kempston, PC; ✉ 3 Barton St, London SW1 (☎ 0171 222 5759); The Clock House, Box End, Bedford (☎ 01234 852361)

CLARKE, Alison Jane; da of Leonard William Clarke, of Cheltenham, Glos, and Florence, *née* Pitt; *b* 17 Oct 1960; *Educ* Pate's GS for Girls, Bulmershe Coll of HE (BA); *m* 6 May 1995, Nigel Andrew Mogridge, s of Ralph John Mogridge; *Career* graduate trainee Pedigree Petfoods; Welbeck Golin/Harris Communications: account exec 1985–90, bd dir 1990–, dep md 1993–96, md 1996–; MIPR 1989; *Recreations* theatre, opera; *Style*— Ms Alison Clarke; ✉ Welbeck Golin/Harris Communications, 43 King Street, Covent Garden, London WC2E 8RJ (☎ 0171 836 6677, fax 0171 836 5820)

CLARKE, Hon Mr Justice; Sir Anthony Peter; kt (1993); s of Harry Alston Clarke (d 1979), and Isobel, *née* Kay; *b* 13 May 1943; *Educ* Oakham Sch, King's Coll Cambridge; *m* 7 Sept 1968, Rosemary, da of K W Adam, of Barnham, Sussex; 2 s (Ben b 7 Jan 1972, Thomas b 20 June 1973), 1 da (Sally b 3 June 1977); *Career* called to the Bar Middle Temple 1965, QC 1979, recorder of the Crown Court 1985–92, bencher 1987, judge of the High Ct 1993–; arbitrator Lloyd's and ICC, wreck cmmr; memb Chambre Arbitrale Maritime until 1992; *Recreations* tennis, golf, holidays; *Style*— Sir Anthony Clarke; ✉ Royal Courts of Justice, Strand, London WC2A 2LL

CLARKE, Arthur C(harles); CBE (1989); s of Charles Wright Clarke, and Nora Mary, *née* Willis; *b* 16 Dec 1917, Minehead, Somerset; *Educ* Huish's GS Taunton, King's Coll London (BSc); *m* 1953 (m dis 1964), Marilyn Mayfield; *Career* science and science fiction writer; auditor HM Exchequer and Audit Dept 1936–41; Royal Air Force: cmmnd Flt Lt 1941, instr No 9 Radio Sch Yatesbury, i/c prototype Ground Controlled Approach (GCA) Radar MIT Radiation Lab until 1946, developed theory of communication satellite 1945; undergraduate King's Coll London 1946–48, asst ed Physics Abstracts IEE 1948–50, chm Br Interplanetary Soc 1946–47 and 1950–53, underwater explorer Great Barrier Reef 1954, emigrated Sri Lanka 1956, lectr in US 1957–70 (also covered Apollo Space Missions for CBS TV), now full-time writer; writer and presenter of Yorkshire Television series: Arthur C Clarke's Mysterious World 1980, Arthur C Clarke's World of Strange Powers 1984, Arthur C Clarke's Mysterious Universe 1994; Vikram Sarabhai prof Physical Research Labs Ahmedabad India 1980, Nehru Meml Lecture New Delhi 1986, Alistair Cooke Lecture 1992; chllr Univ of Moratuwa Sri Lanka 1979–, chllr Int Space Univ, master Richard Huish Coll Taunton; hon chm Soc of Satellite Professionals, pres Br Science Fiction Assoc, hon vice pres H G Wells Soc, hon life pres UN Assoc of Sri Lanka, life memb Assoc of Br Science Writers, cncl memb Soc of Authors, tstee Inst of Integral Educn; patron: Arthur Clarke Centre for Modern Technols Sri Lanka, Sri Lanka Assoc for the Advancement of Studies, Sri Lanka Astronomical Assoc, Sri Lanka Animal Welfare Assoc, Science Fiction Fndn, Br Sub-Aqua Club, Nat Inst for Paraplegics Sri Lanka; memb Advsy Cncl: Int Science Policy Fndn, Fauna International Sri Lanka, Earth Tst; bd memb: Nat Space Soc USA, Space Generation Fndn USA, IAU (SETI) Cmmn 51, Planetary Soc USA, Lindbergh Award Nominations Ctee USA; dir: Rocket Publishing Co UK, Underwater Safaris Sri Lanka; hon fell: Br Interplanetary Soc, American Astronautical Assoc, Int Acad of Astronautics, AIAA, Instn of Engrs Sri Lanka 1983, Ceylon Coll of Physicians 1991; fell: Franklin Inst 1971, King's Coll London 1977, Inst of Robotics Carnegie-Mellon Univ 1981, Int Aerospace Hall of Fame San Diego CA 1989, Int Space Hall of Fame Alamagordo New Mexico 1989; academician World Acad of Art and Science, foreign assoc Nat Acad of Engrg USA 1986, assoc fell Third World Acad of Sciences 1987; memb: Royal Asiatic Soc, Br Astronomical Assoc, Science Fiction Writers of America, Astronomical Soc of the Pacific; Hon DSc Beaver Coll Pennsylvania 1971, Hon DSc Univ of Moratuwa 1979, Hon DLitt Univ of Bath 1988; Freeman Town of Minehead 1992; FRAS, FRSA; *Awards* non-literary awards: Stuart Ballantine Gold Medal Franklin Inst 1963, Aerospace Communications Award AIAA 1974, Bradford Washburn Award Boston Museum of Science 1977, Engrg Award Acad of TV Arts and Sciences 1981, Marconi International Fellowship 1982, Centennial Medal IEEE 1984, Vidya Jyothi Medal (Sri Lankan Presidential Science Award) 1986, Charles A Lindbergh Award 1987, Hall of Fame Soc of Satellite Professionals 1987, Special Achievement Award Space Explorers' Assoc Riyadh 1989, Robert A Heinlein Meml Award Nat Space Soc USA 1990, Int Science Policy Fndn Medal 1992, Lord Perry Award 1992, nominated for Nobel Peace Prize 1994, Hon DLitt Univ of Liverpool (via satellite) 1995, von Karman Award Int Acad of Astronautics 1996; literary awards: International Fantasy Award 1952, Hugo award World Science Fiction Convention 1956, 1974 and 1980, Nebula award SF Writers of America 1973, 1974 and 1979, Kalinga Prize UNESCO 1961, Robert Ball Award Aviation/Space Writers' Assoc 1965, Westinghouse Science Writing Prize AAAS 1969, Playboy Editorial Award 1971 and 1982, John W Campbell Award 1974, Galaxy Award 1979, E M Emme Astronautical Literature Award AAS 1984, Grand Master SF Writers of America 1986; *Books* author of around 80 books, 500 articles and numerous short stories; non-fiction incl: Arthur C Clarke's Mysterious World (with Simon Welfare and John Fairley, 1980), Arthur C Clarke's World of Strange Powers (with Simon Welfare and John Fairley, 1984), Ascent to Orbit (1984), How the World Was One (1992), The Snows of Olympus: A Garden on Mars (1994); fiction incl: Childhood's End (1953), 2001 - A Space Odyssey (1968, also co-author of screenplay with Stanley Kubrick, Oscar nominated for best screenplay), 2010 - Odyssey II (1982, filmed 1984), The Songs of Distant Earth (1986), 2061 - Odyssey III, The Ghost from the Grand Banks (1990), 3001: The Final Odyssey (1997); *Recreations* table tennis, computers, observing Equatorial skies through telescope; *Style*— Arthur C Clarke, Esq, CBE; ✉ Leslie's House, 25 Barnes Place, Colombo 7, Sri Lanka (☎ 00 94 1 694255/699757, fax 00 94 1 698730); Rocket Publishing Co, Dene Court, Bishops Lydeard, Somerset TA4 3LT (☎ 01823 432671); c/o David Higham Associates, 5–8 Lower John St, Golden Square, London W1R 4HA

CLARKE, Barry Michael; s of Ronald Leslie Clarke (d 1981), and Violet Ann, *née* Johnson, of Shoeburyness, Essex; *b* 18 April 1941; *Educ* Southend HS for Boys, Coll of Estate Mgmnt; *m* 1964, Valerie Brenda, da of Norman Henry Staines; 2 s (Jeremy Ian b 30 Nov 1967, Benjamin David b 3 Dec 1969); *Career* articled pupil to Chief Estates Offr Basildon Devpt Corp 1957–61, tech offr Office of the Receiver Metropolitan Police District 1961–63, dep real estate mangr FW Woolworth & Co Ltd 1963–67, dep estates offr South Eastern Gas 1967–77; dir of property resources British Shipbuilders 1977–86, dir Stewart Newiss (London) Ltd and Stewart Newiss (Newcastle) Ltd 1986–92, seconded as gp property controller to Rover Group plc 1987–89, gp md Colliers Stewart Newiss 1990–92; dir: Edward Erdman 1992–93, Erdman Lewis 1993–95; conslt DTZ Debenham Thorpe 1996–; FRICS 1975 (ARICS 1964); *Recreations* golf, skiing, snooker; *Clubs* Holtye Golf (pres, former capt); *Style*— Barry Clarke, Esq; ✉ Stream Cottage, Stream Park, Felbridge, East Grinstead, West Sussex RH19 1QN (☎ 01342 322954); DTZ Debenham Thorpe, 44 Brook Street, London W1A 4AG (☎ 0171 408 1161, fax 0171 491 4593)

CLARKE, Benjamin Bevan (Ben); *b* 15 April 1968; *Educ* Bishop's Stortford Coll, Royal Agricultural Coll Cirencester (Dip in Farm Mgmnt and Advanced Farm Mgmnt); *Career* Rugby Union No 8; clubs: Hertfordshire County Colts, Saracens 1989–91, Bath 1991–96 (winners Courage League Div 1 1993, 1994 and 1996, winners Pilkington Cup 1994, 1995 and 1996), Richmond 1996–; England: B Team v Spain 1990, first full cap v S Africa 1992, Grand Slam winners 1992 and 1995, tour to NZ 1992 and S Africa 1994, World Cup squad S Africa (4th place) 1995, over 28 caps; memb Br Lions team to NZ 1993; South West Sportsman of the Year BBC 1993, Rugby Writers' Player of the Year 1993, Whitbread Player of the Year Award 1994; rugby columnist The Sunday Times; formerly apprentice farmer Somerset, currently employed in sales promotions and mktg National Power; *Books* Ben Rugby Skills (1995); *Recreations* swimming, skiing, golf; *Style*— Ben Clarke, Esq; ✉ c/o Advantage International Ltd, The Limes, 123 Mortlake High Street, London SW14 8SN

CLARKE, Brian; s of Edward Ord Clarke, (d 1979), and Lilian, *née* Whitehead; *b* 2 July 1953; *Educ* Clarksfield Sch Oldham, Oldham Sch of Arts and Crafts (jr scholarship), Burnley Sch of Art, The North Devon Coll of Art and Design (dip in art and design); *m* Elizabeth Cecila, da of Rev John Finch; 1 s (Daniel John Finch b 11 Feb 1989); *Career* artist; major exhibitions: Glass/Light Exhibition (Festival of the City of London with John Piper and Marc Chagall) 1979, New Paintings Constructions and Prints (RIBA) 1981, Paintings (Robert Fraser Gallery Cork St) 1983, 1976–86 Seibu Museum of Art Tokyo 1987, Malerei und Farbfenster 1977–88 (Hessisches Landesmuseum) 1988, Der Architektur der Synagoge (Deutsches Architekturmuseum Frankfurt) 1980, Intimations of Mortality (Galerie Karsten Greve Koln Germany), Paintings (Indar Pasricha Gallery New Delhi) 1989, Into and Out of Architecture (Mayor Gallery London) 1990, Architecture and Stained Glass (Sezon Museum of Art Tokyo) 1990, Architecture and Light (Ingolstadt Germany, in assoc with Future Systems) 1992, Designs on Architecture (Oldham Art Gallery) 1993, New Paintings (The Mayor Gallery London) 1993, Paintings and Stained Glass Works in Architecture (The Tony Shafrazi Gallery NY); major works: St Gabriel's Church Blackburn 1976, All Saints Church Habergham 1976, Queen's Med Centre Nottingham 1978, Laver's & Barraud Building London 1981, Olympus Optical Europa GmbH Headquarters Building Hamburg 1981, King Kahled Int Airport Riyadh Saudi Arabia 1982, The Buxton Thermal Baths Derbyshire 1987, The Lake Sagami Country Club Yamanishi Japan (in assoc with Arata Isozaki) 1988, The New Synagogue Darmstadt Germany 1988, Victoria Quarter Leeds 1989, Cibreo Restaurant Tokyo 1990, Glaxo Pharmaceuticals Stockley Park Uxbridge 1990, Stansted Airport Essex (in assoc with Sir Norman Foster) 1991, The Spindles Shopping Centre Oldham 1991–93, Espana Telefonica Barcelona 1991, Number One America Square London 1991, 35–38 Chancery Lane London 1991, The Carmelite London 1992, 100 New Bridge St London 1992, stage designs for Paul McCartney World Tour 1990, facade of Hotel de Ville des Bouches-du-Rhones Marseille (with Will Alsop) 1992–94, The Glass Dune - Hamburg (with Future Systems) 1992, EAM Building Kassel Germany 1992–93, design of stage sets for Paul McCartney New World Tour 1993, design of stage sets for The Ruins of Time (a ballet in tribute to Rudolph Nureyev by the Dutch National Ballet) 1993, The New Synagogue Heidelberg 1993, Hammersmith Hosp London (design) 1993, W H Smith & Sons Abingdon 1994, SMS Lowe The Grace Building NY 1994, Crossrail Paddington London (design) 1994, Cliveden Hotel 1994, Schadow Arkaden Dusseldorf 1994, Q206 Berlin (design) 1994, Frankfurter Alle Plaza Berlin (design) 1994, The New Synagogue Aachen (design) 1994, Norte Shopping Rio de Janeiro 1995, Rye Hosp Sussex (with Linda McCartney) 1995; Churchill fellowship in architectural art 1974, Art and Work award special commendation 1989, Europa Nostra award 1990, The Leeds Award for Architecture Special Award for Stained Glass 1990; memb Cncl Winston Churchill Meml Tst 1985–, tstee and memb Ctee Robert Fraser Fndn 1990–; subject of six books; judge: The BBC Design Awards 1990, Royal Fine Art Cmmn and Sunday Times Architecture Award 1991; visiting prof of architectural art UCL 1993; FRSA 1988, Hon FRIBA 1993; *Recreations* reading, hoarding; *Clubs* Chelsea Arts; *Style*— Brian Clarke, Esq; ✉ Peel Cottage, 80 Peel St, London W8 7PF; The Tony Shafrazi Gallery, 119 Wooster Street, New York, NY 10012, USA (☎ 00 1 212 274 9300, fax 00 1 212 334 9499)

CLARKE, Prof Bryan Campbell; s of Robert Campbell Clarke (d 1941), of Sywell, Northants, and Gladys Mary, *née* Carter (d 1987); *b* 24 June 1932; *Educ* Fay Sch Southborough Mass, Magdalen Coll Sch Oxford, Magdalen Coll Oxford (MA, DPhil); *m* 20 Aug 1960, Dr Ann Gillian, da of Prof John Jewkes, CBE (d 1988), of Boar's Hill, Oxford; 1 s (Peter b 1971), 1 da (Alexandra b 1975); *Career* PO RAF 1951–52; Univ of Edinburgh: asst in zoology 1959–63, lectr in zoology, reader in zoology 1969–71; Univ of Nottingham: prof of genetics 1971–, vice dean of sci 1986–89, research prof 1994–; SERC sr res fell 1976–81; vice pres: Genetical Soc 1981, Linnean Soc 1983–85, Soc for the Study of Evolution (USA) 1990; scientific expeditions to: Morocco 1955, Polynesia 1962, 1967, 1968, 1980, 1982, 1986, 1991 and 1994; chm: Terrestrial Life Sciences Ctee NERC 1983–86, Biological Sciences Panel HEFCE 1992–, Cncl Royal Soc 1994–96; memb Biological Sciences Ctee SERC 1990–93; hon res fell Nat History Museum 1993–; ed: Heredity 1977–84, Proceedings of the Royal Soc Series B 1989–93; FRS 1982; *Books* Berber Village (1959), The Evolution of DNA Sequences (ed, 1986), Frequency-Dependent Selection (ed, 1988); *Recreations* painting, archaeology; *Clubs* RAF; *Style*— Prof Bryan Clarke, FRS; ✉ Linden Cottage, School Lane, Colston Bassett, Nottingham NG12 3FD (☎ 01949 81243); Department of Genetics, Queen's Medical Centre, Clifton Boulevard, Nottingham NG7 2UH (☎ 0115 970 9397)

CLARKE, Charles Nigel; CBE (1987); s of Charles Cyril Clarke (d 1968), of Gatcombe Court, Flax Bourton, and Olga Helena, *née* Robinson (d 1971); *b* 3 Aug 1926; *Educ* Radley; *m* 21 Jun 1952, Stella Rosemary Clarke, JP, DL, *qv*, da of John Herbert King (d 1973), of Somerlea, Langford, Somerset; 4 s (Giles b 1953, Nigel b 1957, Henry b 1959, Matthew b 1963), 1 da (Bridget b 1955); *Career* Lt Welsh Gds 1944–48, served Germany; admitted slr 1951, Notary Public 1953, sr ptnr Osborne Clarke slrs Bristol, London, Brussels and Copenhagen 1985–91 (ptnr 1952); memb and chm various Health Bds and Authys 1952–86; memb Cncl Nat Assoc of Health Authys 1982–86, tstee Bristol Municipal Charities 1962–87 (chm 1976–87), special tstee United Bristol Hosp 1974–93 (chm 1974–82 and 1986–92); memb Cncl Univ of Bristol 1969–86; maitre commanderie de Bordeaux Bristol 1980–; memb Exec Cncl Historic Houses Assoc 1992– (chm Wessex region 1995–); Lord of the Manor of Gatcombe and patron of the living of Wanstrow and Cloford; memb Soc of Merchant Venturers (master 1967); Hon DLitt Univ of Bristol, Hon LLD Univ of Bath; *Recreations* wine, military history, roses, travel; *Clubs* Army and Navy; *Style*— Charles Clarke, Esq, CBE; ✉ Gatcombe Court, Flax Bourton, Bristol BS19 1PX (☎ 01275 393141, fax 01275 394274)

CLARKE, Dr Charles Richard Astley; s of Prof Sir Cyril Astley Clarke, KBE, FRS, *qv*, and Frieda Margaret Mary, *née* Hart; *b* 12 Feb 1944; *Educ* Rugby, Gonville and Caius Coll Cambridge (BA); *m* 23 March 1971, Dr Ruth Seifert, *qv*, da of Sigmund Seifert (d 1978), of London; 2 da (Rebecca Astley b 1973, Naomi Astley b 1976); *Career* conslt neurologist: Bart's 1979–96, Whipps Cross Hosp London 1983–, Nat Hosp for Neurology & Neurosurgery 1996–; chm Dept of Neurology and Neurosurgery London Bridge Hosp 1989–95, clinical dir Dept of Clinical Neurosciences Bart's 1990–94; hon med offr Br Mountaineering Cncl 1981–89, chm Mount Everest Fndn 1990–92, vice pres Alpine Club 1990–92; dir The Second Step Mountaineering Bookshop Islington London; winner The Robert Atkins prize for Contribution to Sports Med 1991; Freeman: Worshipful Soc of Apothecaries, City of London 1984; FRCP; *Books* Everest - The Unclimbed Ridge (with Sir Chris Bonington, *qv*, 1983); *Recreations* mountaineering, model flying, sailing; *Clubs* Alpine, Royal Geographical Soc; *Style*— Dr Charles Clarke; ✉ 152 Harley Street, London W1 1HH (☎ 0171 935 0444, fax 01713 359 6412)

CLARKE, Christopher David (Chris); s of Frank Clarke, of Mellor, nr Blackburn, and Barbara, *née* Holgate; *b* 4 July 1971; *Educ* Queen Elizabeth's GS Blackburn, Univ of Essex (BA); *Career* croquet player; Southport 1988–89, capt Colchester 1990–, represented GB 1990, 1991, 1992, 1993, 1994 and 95 (Sonoma-Cutrer World Invitational Championships); achievements incl: runner-up Northern Championships 1987, nat jr champion 1988, Eastern champion 1988 and 1990, winner Presidents Cup 1988, 1991 and 1995, winner Western Championships 1992 and 1993, semi-finalist Br Open Championship 1988, 1993 and 1995 (runner-up 1991 and 1994), runner-up World Doubles Championship 1989 (with R Fulford), winner Nat Inter-Club Competition 1990, 1991 and 1992, winner Br Open Doubles Championship 1990, 1991, 1992 and 1993 (with R Fulford, runner-up 1988, 1989, 1994 and 1995), world champion 1995 (semi-finalist World Championships 1991 (runner-up 1994)); youngest winner President's Cup Hurlingham aged 17, voted best under 21 player in the world 1988, currently ranked no 3 in the world; currently working Turners Ltd Fordham; *Recreations* ten-pin bowling, bridge, golf, most sports; *Style*— Chris Clarke, Esq; ✉ 50 Chagny Close, Letchworth, Herts SG6 4BY (☎ 01462 482768)

CLARKE, Christopher George; s of Philip George Clarke (d 1991), and José Margaret Clarke (d 1979); *b* 18 Sept 1944; *Educ* Radley; *m* 1 June 1968, Jane, *née* Ellis; 2 da (Natasha Jane b 12 June 1970, Vanessa Clare b 5 April 1973); *Career* articled clerk Hodgson Morris & Co Chartered Accountants 1963–67 (qualified 1967), investmt mangr Wm Brandts 1968–72, investmt mangr JH Vavasseur London 1972–74; Henderson Administration Group: joined 1974, dir Henderson Administration Ltd 1976–, dir Henderson Administration Group plc 1983–; md Witan Investment Co plc (of which Henderson Administration Group an assoc co) 1993–, dir English National Investment Co plc; memb Investmt Advsy Ctee of Charities Aid Fndn, tstee Sir Robert Menzies Meml Tst, memb Cncl Radley Coll, govr Tudor Hall Sch Banbury; *Style*— Christopher Clarke, Esq; ✉ Henderson Administration Group plc, 3 Finsbury Avenue, London EC2M 2PA (☎ 0171 638 5757, fax 0171 377 5742, telex 88461 GFRIARG)

CLARKE, Christopher John David; s of Maj John Herbert Thomson Clarke (d 1983), and Hazel, *née* Chapman (d 1988); *b* 21 March 1950; *Educ* Fettes, Coll of Law London; *m* 4 April 1992, Catherine, *née* Shuttlewood; 1 da (Lucy b 9 Dec 1992), 1 s (Rory b 22 Feb 1994); *Career* admitted slr England and Hong Kong 1974; Denton Hall: ptnr Hong Kong 1978–84, ptnr London 1984–92, sr ptnr Asia 1992–; memb: Int Bar Assoc, Law Assoc; *Recreations* travel, food; *Clubs* Oriental (London), Hong Kong, China; *Style*— Christopher J D Clarke, Esq; ✉ Denton Hall, 1001 Hutchison House, 10 Harcourt Road, Hong Kong (☎ 00 852 2820 6272, fax 00 852 2810 6434)

CLARKE, Christopher Simon Courtenay Stephenson; QC (1984); yr s of Rev John Stephenson Clarke (d 1982), and Enid Courtenay, *née* Manico; *b* 14 March 1947; *Educ* Marlborough, Gonville and Caius Coll Cambridge (MA); *m* 14 Sept 1974, Caroline Anne, da of Prof Charles Montague Fletcher, CBE; 2 da (Henrietta b 16 Aug 1977, Louisa b 21 June 1979), 1 s (Edward b 31 May 1981); *Career* called to the Bar Middle Temple 1969; advocate of the Supreme Ct of the Turks and Caicos Is 1975, chm Ctee of Inquiry of States of Guernsey into Barnett Christie (Fin) Ltd 1985–87, cncllr Int Bar Assoc 1987–91, recorder of the Crown Court 1990–, bencher Middle Temple 1991–, dep High Ct judge 1993–, currently head of chambers; chm Commercial Law Bar Assoc 1993–95, memb Bar Cncl 1993–; FRSA 1994; *Clubs* Brooks's, Hurlingham; *Style*— Christopher Clarke Esq, QC; ✉ 42 The Chase, London SW4 0NH (☎ 0171 622 0765); Brick Court Chambers, 15/19 Devereux Court, London WC2R 3JJ (☎ 0171 583 0777, fax 0171 583 0941)

CLARKE, Prof Sir Cyril Astley; KBE (1974, CBE 1969); s of Astley Vavasour Clarke, MD, JP, DL, and Ethel Mary, *née* Gee (d 1965); *b* 22 Aug 1907; *Educ* Oundle, Gonville and Caius Coll Cambridge (MD, ScD), Guy's Hosp London; *m* 1935, Frieda (Féo) Margaret Mary, da of Alexander John Campbell Hart; 3 s; *Career* prof of med Univ of Liverpool and dir Nuffield Unit of Med Genetics 1965–72 (now emeritus prof and hon fell), chm Cncl Br Heart Fndn 1982–87, dir Res Unit RCP 1983–88; hon conslt physician: Royal Infirmary, Broadgreen Hosp, Utd Liverpool Hosps; chm Br Soc for Res on Ageing 1987–92; hon fell RSM 1982; pres: RCP 1972–77, Royal Entomological Soc of London 1991–92, Assoc of Physicians 1992; Buchanan Medal Royal Soc 1990; Hon DSc Univs of: Edinburgh, Leicester, E Anglia, Birmingham, Liverpool, Sussex, Hull, Wales, London, Coll of William & Mary Williamsburg Virginia 1992; hon fell UMDS Guy's and St Thomas's 1992, hon memb Br Blood Transfusion Soc 1993; FRS 1970; *Books* Genetics for the Clinician, Selected Topics in Medical Genetics, Rhesus Haemolytic Disease, selected papers and extracts, Human Genetics and Medicine (1970, 1972, 1987), Prevention of Rhesus Haemolytic Diseases (with R B McConnell, 1972); *Recreations* sailing, butterfly genetics; *Clubs* Athenaeum, Oxford and Cambridge Sailing Soc, West Kirby Sailing; *Style*— Prof Sir Cyril Clarke, KBE, FRS; ✉ 43 Caldy Rd, W Kirby, Wirral, Merseyside L48 2HF (☎ 0151 625 8811); Department of Genetics & Microbiology, University of Liverpool, PO Box 147, Liverpool L69 3BX (☎ 0151 794 3622)

CLARKE, David Andrew; s of Douglas Clarke, and Jean, *née* Law; *b* 26 Aug 1949; *m* 26 Oct 1974, Pamela; 2 da (Emily b 19 Nov 1977, Penny b 12 March 1980); *Career* gen mangr Caledonian Hotel Edinburgh 1990–95, dir and gen mangr The Beardmore Hotel Glasgow 1995–; fndr memb Connoisseurs Scotland; Freeman City of London, Liveryman Worshipful Co of Innholders; MInstD, FHCIMA; *Recreations* golf; *Clubs* Dalmahoy Golf; *Style*— David Clarke, Esq; ✉ The Beardmore Hotel, Beardmore Street, Clydebank, Glasgow G81 4SA (☎ 0141 951 6001, fax 0141 951 6018, e-mail david.clarke@hci.co.uk)

CLARKE, His Hon Judge; David Clive; QC (1983); s of Philip George Clarke (d 1991), and José Margaret, *née* Fletcher (d 1979); *b* 16 July 1942; *Educ* Winchester, Magdalene Coll Cambridge (MA); *m* 2 Aug 1969, Alison Claire, da of Rt Rev (Percy) James Brazier (d 1989); 3 s (Andrew b 1970 d 1993, Jonathan b 1972, Edward b 1975); *Career* called to the Bar Inner Temple 1965, in practice Northern Circuit until 1993 (treas 1988–92), recorder of the Crown Ct 1981–93, circuit judge (Northern Circuit) 1993–; *Recreations* canals, sailing, swimming; *Style*— His Hon Judge Clarke, QC; ✉ Queen Elizabeth II Law Courts, Derby Square, Liverpool L2 1XA (☎ 0151 473 7373)

CLARKE, David Edwin; s of Ernest Wilfred Clarke (d 1972), and Irene Elisabeth, *née* Bennett (d 1974); *b* 7 March 1953; *Educ* Solihull Sch Warwickshire, Abington Pa USA; *m* 10 Sept 1977, Nicola Jayne, da of John Frank Cordwell; 2 da (Hannah Jayne b 10 Jan 1982, Caroline May b 18 Aug 1984); *Career* reporter Birmingham Post & Mail Group 1974–78, PRO Midlands Electricity Bd 1978–79, exec Priority PR 1979–80; md: Graham Rote & Co Ltd 1983–86 (dir 1981–83), David Clarke Associates Ltd 1986–; chm Edelman Public Relations Network (UK) 1994–; nat hon treas IPR 1986–89; dir Birmingham Settlement 1992–, memb Birmingham City 2000 1991–, chm Birmingham Business Breakfast Club 1994–; FIPR 1991 (MIPR 1973); *Recreations* walking, travel, keep fit, eating out; *Style*— David Clarke, Esq; ✉ Pinley Cottage, Pinley, Claverdon, Warwickshire CV35 8NA (☎ 01926 84 2266); David Clarke Associates Ltd, Centre Court, 1301 Stratford Road, Birmingham B28 9AP (☎ 0121 702 2525, fax 0121 702 2085)

CLARKE, David H; *Career* Hanson plc: joined 1973, dir 1989–, dep chm and chief exec offr Hanson Industries 1992–95, vice chm Hanson plc 1993–95; chm and chief exec offr US Industries Inc 1995–; *Style*— David H Clarke; ✉ US Industries Inc, 101 Wood Avenue South, Iselin, NJ 08830, USA (00 1 908 767 0700, fax 00 1 908 767 2222)

CLARKE, David Hilton; s of Hilton Swift Clarke, CBE (d 1995), of Cooden, nr Bexhill, Sussex, and Sibyl Muriel, *née* Salter (d 1975); *b* 9 Jan 1938; *Educ* Hurstpierpoint Coll Sussex; *m* 27 Feb 1965, Leonora Virginia, da of Capt Campbell Marshall (d 1970); 2 s (Edward Hilton b 23 Feb 1966, Campbell David Hilton b 10 Aug 1967); *Career* Nat Serv RN 1956–58, RNR 1967–72; Anthony Gibbs and Sons Ltd 1958–67, dir Gerrard and National Holdings plc 1974–90 (joined 1967); advsr to Postgrad Dean Northeast Thames Regnl Health Authy 1991–95; hon treas The Almshouse Assoc 1992–; memb: Bd Middlesex Hosp Med Sch 1984–89, Fin Ctee UCL; special tstee Middlesex Hosp 1990–; sec Coaching Club 1980; Freeman City of London 1984, Liveryman Worshipful Co of Coachmakers & Coach Harness Makers; *Recreations* sailing, skiing; *Clubs* Royal Ocean Racing, Royal Cornwall Yacht; *Style*— David H Clarke, Esq; ✉ West Compton House, West Compton, Somerset BA4 4PD (☎ 01749 890633)

CLARKE, Douglas Hewitt; s of Reginald Douglas Clarke (d 1979), of Liverpool, and Mabel Hewitt, *née* Drew (d 1958); *b* 17 July 1934; *Educ* Liverpool Inst HS for Boys, Birkenhead Tech Coll, King's Coll Univ of Durham; *m* 1, 24 April 1963 (m dis 1968), Eileen Elizabeth Hilton; m 2, 21 May 1977, Christine Mary Jacobs; 1 s (Alexander Douglas b 19 March 1987), 1 da (Karen Mary b 11 April 1978); *Career* asst naval architect Cammell Laird & Co Ltd 1968–71, ship surveyor Lloyd's Register of Shipping 1971–78; dir: Bestgrange Ltd 1978–, Ship System Engrg Gp (SSEG) 1986–87; pres UK Assoc of Professional Engrs 1974–76; Inst of Mechanical and Gen Technician Engrs: chm 1976–78, pres 1978–80, hon treas 1985–88; advsr to HM Princ Sec of State for Trade & Indust (Efficient Ship Programme) 1987–, memb IEC TC80 Working Gp on Digital Interfaces for Navigation Equipment 1987, memb Computers & Communications and IT Working Gps Nautical Inst, memb and hon treas London Branch Royal Inst of Naval Architects, memb Surrey ECRO and Engrg Cncl Assembly; author of numerous articles in journals and magazines and for nat institutions (Institution Gold Medal 'Powering of Ships' 1963, Institution Silver Medal 'Some Notes on Escalators and their Use in Ships' 1959); Freeman City of London 1983, Liveryman Worshipful Co of Shipwrights 1983; CEng, FRINA 1983, FIMarE 1987, CNI 1988, FIMechE; *Recreations* water colour painting; *Style*— Douglas Clarke, Esq; ✉ 10 Treadwell Rd, Epsom, Surrey KT18 5JW (☎ 01372 729 910)

CLARKE, Eric; MP (Lab) Midlothian (majority 10,334); s of late Ernest Clarke, and late Annie Clarke; *b* 9 April 1933; *Educ* Holy Cross Acad, W M Ramsey Tech Coll Edinburgh, Esk Valley Coll Dalkeith; *m* 10 Sept 1955, June, *née* Hewat; 2 s, 1 da; *Career* oncost Roslin Colliery 1949, faceman Lingerwood Colliery 1952, trainee supervisor Bilston Glen Colliery 1967, gen sec Scottish Area NUM 1977–89 (memb 1949–), MP (Lab, NUM sponsored) Midlothian 1992–; Scottish opposition whip 1995–; cncllr: Midlothian CC 1962–75, Lothian Regnl Cncl 1974–78; former memb: Lab Pty NEC, Scottish Cncl for Devpt and Indust, South and West of Scotland Forestry Advsy Ctee; JP Midlothian 1963–78; *Recreations* trout fishing, carpentry, gardening, football; *Clubs* Mayfield Labour, Morris Workingmen's, Danderhall Miners' Welfare; *Style*— Eric Clarke, Esq, MP; ✉ House of Commons, London SW1A 0AA (☎ 0171 219 6373); PO Box 11, 34 Buccleuch Sreet, Dalkeith, Midlothian EH22 1HL (☎ 0131 654 1585, fax 0131 654 1586)

CLARKE, Geoffrey; s of John Moulding Clarke, and Janet, *née* Petts; *b* 28 Nov 1924; *Educ* RCA; *m* 2 s; *Career* artist and sculptor; *Exhibitions* Gimpel Fils Gallery 1952 and 1955, Redfern Gallery 1965, Taranman Gallery 1975, 1976 and 1982; cmmnd work incl: iron sculpture Time Life Building New Bond Street London, cast aluminium relief sculpture Castrol House Marylebone Road London, mosaics Univ of Liverpool Physics Block and Basildon New Town, stained glass windows Treasury Lincoln Cathedral, bronze sculpture Thorn Electric Building Upper St Martin's Lane London, relief sculpture on Canberra and Oriana, three stained glass windows, high altar, cross and candlesticks and the flying cross and crown of thorns Coventry Cathedral, screens in Royal Military Chapel Birdcage Walk, Yorkshire Sculpture Park 1994, Friends Room RA 1994, Christchurch Mansion Ipswich (retrospective, tour) 1994; *Works in Public Collections* V&A Museum, Tate Gallery, Arts Cncl, Museum of Modern Art NY; prizes for engraving: Triennial 1951, London 1953, Tokyo 1957; RA 1976; *Style*— Geoffrey Clarke, Esq, RA; ✉ Stowe Hill, Hartest, Bury St Edmunds, Suffolk IP29 4EQ (☎ 01284 830 319)

CLARKE, Gillian; da of John Penri Williams (d 1957), and Ceinwen, *née* Evans; *b* 8 June 1937; *Educ* Univ Coll Cardiff (BA); *m* 2, David Thomas; 3 c from previous m: 1 da (Catrin b 1961), 2 s (Owain b 1963, Dylan b 1966); *Career* writer, lectr and bdcaster; res asst News Information Dept BBC London 1958–60, pt/t lectr in English and liberal studies Reardon Smith Nautical Coll Cardiff 1965–75, pt/t lectr and poet-in-residence Dept of Art History and Cultural Studies Newport Coll of Art Gwent 1975–84, Welsh Arts Cncl creative writing fell St David's Univ Coll Lampeter 1984–85, Lampeter Writers Workshop Dept of Extra-Mural Studies Univ of Wales Aberystwyth 1984–, tutor MA in creative writing Univ of Glamorgan 1993–; ed The Anglo-Welsh Review 1976–84 (reviews ed 1971–76); chm: English Language Section Academi Gymreig 1988–93, Ty Newydd 1990–93 (life pres); memb: Literature Ctee Welsh Arts Cncl 1976–82 and 1987–93, Gen Advsy Cnl BBC 1992–95, Bd ARTS 2000 Yr of Literature 1992–96; hon fell Univ Coll Cardiff 1985, hon fell Univ of Wales Swansea 1995; *Books* One Moonlight Night (stories for children, trans from Welsh, 1991); *Poems* Snow on the Mountain (1971), The Sundial (1978), Letter from a Far Country (1982), Selected Poems (1985), Letting in the Rumour (1989, Poetry Book Soc recommendation), The King of Britain's Daughter

(1993, Poetry Book Soc recommendation); *Radio* Talking in the Dark (1978), Letter from a Far Country (1981); *TV* Imagine This (BBC 2, 1991); *Anthologies* The Poetry Society Anthology (ed, 1987–88), Welsh Women Poets (co-ed), I Can Move The Sea: Poems by Children (ed, 1995), The Whispering Room: Anthology of Spooky Poems for Children (ed, 1996); *Drama* The Time of the Wolf (for Theatr Powys, 1996); *Recreations* gardening, farming and conserving 17 acres of hills woodland; *Style*— Ms Gillian Clarke; ✉ Blaen Cwrt, Talgarreg, Llandysul, Ceredigion, Cymru SA44 4EU (☎ 01545 590311)

CLARKE, Graham Neil; s of Henry Charles Owen Clarke, MVO, and Doris May, *née* Morgan; *b* 23 July 1956; *Educ* Rutherford Sch London, Sch of Horticulture Wisley; *m* 2 Feb 1980, Denise Carole, da of Robert Fraser Anderson; 2 da (Rebecca Sarah b 1990, Helena Charlotte b 1994); *Career* gardener: Buckingham Palace 1975–76, Royal Parks Nursery 1976; Amateur Gardening: sub-ed 1976–79, chief sub-ed 1979–81, dep ed 1981–86; ed: Home Plus Magazine 1985, Amateur Gardening 1986–; ed IPC Gardening Magazines (gp ed 1993–95): Amateur Gardening, Your Garden, The Gardener, special projects ed 1995–; memb Exec Ctee RHS Garden Club 1975–82, prodr and presenter Hosp Radio London and Bournemouth 1976–89; FLS, MIHort; *Books* Step-By-Step Pruning (1984), A-Z of Garden Plants (1985), Autumn/Winter Colour in the Garden (1986), Your Gardening Questions Answered (1987), The Complete Book of Plant Propagation (1990); *Recreations* gardening, radio, philately; *Style*— Graham Clarke, Esq; ✉ Amateur Gardening, Westover House, West Quay Rd, Poole, Dorset BH15 1JG (☎ 01202 680586, fax 01202 674335)

CLARKE, Graham Steward; TD (1971); s of Douglas Steward Clarke (d 1949), and Beatrice, *née* Auld (d 1988); *b* 16 March 1937; *Educ* St Bees Sch Cumberland, Emmanuel Coll Cambridge (MA); *m* 1964, Rita Elisabeth Karoline, da of Oskar Becker (d 1961); 1 da (Tessa b 1965), 1 s (Douglas b 1968); *Career* Maj RA, Euro theatre; gp fin dir: Telex Computers Ltd 1972–75, Coles Cranes Ltd 1976–81, Fairey Holdings Ltd 1981–86; md Energy and Military Engrg Div Fairey Holdings Ltd 1984–86; chm: Fairey Engineering Ltd 1984–86, Elequip Ltd 1984–86; dir: Fairey Holdings Ltd 1981–86, Fairey Construction Ltd 1984–86, Mathews and Yates Ltd 1984–86, Fairey Nuclear Ltd 1984–86, Fairey Developments Ltd 1981–86, Begley Engineering Ltd 1984–91, Nightingale Secretariat plc 1991–; chm Bourn Management Consultants Ltd 1985–, chm and md Bourn Developments 1986–, proprietor Bourn Estates 1980–; chm Fedn of Oxshott Residents and Associations, involved with town planning, community, environment and green belt issues in Surrey 1993–; FCA, FRSA; *Recreations* bridge, travel, business management; *Clubs* RAC, IOD; *Style*— Graham S Clarke Esq, TD; ✉ Bourn Management Consultants Ltd, Bourn Reach, 9 Montrose Gardens, Oxshott, Surrey KT22 OUU (☎ 01372 843445, fax 01372 842216)

CLARKE, Henry Benwell; s of Stephen Lampard Clarke (d 1984), of Hastings, and Elinor Wade, *née* Benwell (d 1974); *b* 30 Jan 1950; *Educ* St John's Sch Leatherhead Surrey, South Bank Poly (BSc), Imperial Coll London (MSc, DIC, British Airways prize for MSc); *m* 18 Aug 1973, Verena Angela, da of late Dennis Howard Lodge; 4 s (Samuel John b 1977, Timothy Michael b 1980, Philip Andrew b 1982, Jonathan Peter b 1992), 1 da (Jessamy Anne b 1976); *Career* British Rail Property Bd: S Region 1972–78, NW Region 1978–82, E Region 1982–85, regnl estate surveyor and mangr Midland Region 1985–86, chief estate surveyor HQ 1986–87, nat devpt mangr 1987–88; The Crown Estate Cmmn: dep chief exec 1988–, actg chief exec and accounting offr 1989; jt md People and Places International 1993–, md People and Places Property Consultants Ltd 1993–; conslt: Anthony Green and Spencer, Byrom Clarke Roberts, Parkmon Property Management; memb: Cncl Christian Union for Estate Profession 1983–88, Gen Cncl Br Property Fedn 1989–92, Bd Youth With a Mission (Eng) 1990–, Bd Mercy Ships UK, Bd World of Sport International, Br Cncl of Shopping Centres 1990–92, British Urban Regeneration Assoc 1992–, Urban Village Group 1992–; MIMgt 1975, ACIArb 1979, FRICS 1986 (ARICS 1973), MInstD 1993; *Publications* author of various articles in periodicals; *Recreations* reading, walking, architecture, church; *Clubs* The National; *Style*— Henry Clarke, Esq; ✉ 42 Wordsworth Road, Harpenden, Herts AL5 4AF (☎ 01582 460892); People and Places International, 17 Queen Anne's Gate, London SW1H 9BU (☎ and fax 0171 799 2986)

CLARKE, James Samuel; MC (1943, and bar 1944); s of James Henry Clarke (d 1951), of Horley, Surrey, and Deborah Florence, *née* Moliver (d 1984); *b* 19 Jan 1921; *Educ* Reigate GS, St Catharine's Coll Cambridge (MA); *m* 1949, Ilse, da of Herman-Max Cohen, of Iserlohn, Westphalia; 2 da (Jane, Susan); *Career* cmmnd Royal Irish Fus 1941–45, served 1 Bn N Africa and Italy, demobbed Maj 1945; called to the Bar Middle Temple 1946, entered legal serv 1953, under sec and princ asst slr Inland Revenue 1970–81, ret; md Bishop and Clarke Ltd 1981–96; *Recreations* gardening; *Clubs* Nat Lib, RAC; *Style*— James Clarke, Esq, MC; ✉ Dormers, The Downs, Givons Grove, Leatherhead, Surrey (☎ 01372 378254)

CLARKE, Jane; da of Michael David Hilborne-Clarke, and Margaret, *née* Lythell; *b* 14 Oct 1951; *Educ* Norwich HS for Girls, UCL (Campbell Clarke Scholarship Sessional Prize, BA), Slade Film Unit Slade Sch of Fine Art (postgrad research); *children* 1 da (Amelia Frances Clarke Trevette b 6 Sept 1986); *Career* journalist Time Out magazine and freelance and lectr RCA Sch of Film and TV 1978–80, film programmer BFI 1980–82, freelance film programmer Barbican Arts Centre Cinema 1982; TV-am 1982–88: ed Henry Kelly's Saturday Show 1984–85, features ed Good Morning Britain 1985–86, ed After Nine 1987–88; series ed Children First Granada Television 1989, prodr The Other Side of Christmas Thames Television 1989, series ed New Living and dep ed Living Now New Era Television Ltd 1990, controller features Westcountry Television 1991–95, dep dir British Film Inst 1995–; memb: Women in Film and TV; *Books* Move Over Misconceptions - Doris Day Re-appraised (BFI Dossier, with Diana Simmonds, 1980); *Recreations* cinema, literature, current affairs, psychology, scuba diving; *Style*— Miss Jane Clarke; ✉ British Film Institute, 21 Stephen Street, London W1P 2LN (☎ 0171 957 8902, fax 0171 436 0437)

CLARKE, Jane Mary; *b* 2 Aug 1959; *Educ* Holy Trinity Convent Bromley Kent; *m* 16 July 1988, Andrew Sizer; 1 da (Mary Natasha b 28 Feb 1991), 1 s (William James b 5 Feb 1996); *Career* tax asst Smith & Williamson CAs 1977–80, advertisement asst Daily Mail 1981–82, sr account exec (sponsorship) Charles Barker Lyons 1982–87, account gp head Karen Earl Ltd 1987–89, account dir Spero Communications 1989–90, client servs dir Strategic Sponsorship Ltd 1990–93, sabbatical Boston Mass 1993–94, commercial dir CSD 1994–; *Recreations* aerobics, running, cycling, cooking; *Clubs* Barbican; *Style*— Ms Jane Clarke; ✉ Chartered Society of Designers, 32–38 Saffron Hill, London EC1N 8FH (☎ 0171 831 9777, fax 0171 831 6277)

CLARKE, Prof John; s of Victor Patrick Clarke (d 1995), of Cambridge, and Ethel May, *née* Blowers (d 1978); *b* 10 Feb 1942; *Educ* Perse Sch for Boys Cambridge, Univ of Cambridge (BA, MA, PhD); *m* 15 Sept 1979, Grethe, da of Hartwig Fog Pedersen (d 1990), of Copenhagen; 1 da (Elizabeth Jane b 1980); *Career* postdoctoral fell Univ of California 1968–69, princ investigator Materials Sciences Div Lawrence Berkeley Laboratory 1969–; Univ of California Berkeley: asst prof 1969–71, assoc prof 1971–73, prof of physics 1973–, Luis W Alvarez mem chair for experimental physics 1994–; visiting appts: Cavendish Laboratory Cambridge 1972 and 1979, HC Orsted Inst Copenhagen 1972, 1979 and 1985, Univ of Karlsruhe Germany 1978, CEN Saclay France 1986, visiting fell Clare Hall Cambridge 1989; Alfred P Sloan Fndn Fellowship 1970–72, Adolph C and Mary Sprague Miller Res Professorship 1975–76 and 1994–95, John Simon Guggenheim Fellowship 1977–78; Charles Vernon Boys Prize Br Inst Physics 1977, Soc of Exploration Geophysics Award for best paper in Geophysics (with T D Gamble and W M Goubau) 1979, Technology Magazine Technology 100 Award (with Gamble and Goubau) 1981, Distinguished Teaching Award Univ of California Berkeley 1983, Award for Sustained Outstanding Res in Solid State Physics in Dept of Energy's 1986 Materials Sciences Res Competition, California Scientist of the Year 1987, Fritz London Meml Award for Low Temperature Physics 1987, Federal Laboratory Consortium Award for Excellence in Technol Transfer 1992, Dept of Energy Div of Materials Sciences Award for Solid State Physics - Significant Implications for DOE Related Technols 1992, Electrotechnology Transfer Award Inst of Electrical and Electronic Engrs Activities Bd 1995; fell: AAAS 1982, American Physical Society 1985; FRS 1986; *Style*— Prof John Clarke, FRS; ✉ Department of Physics, University of California, Berkeley, CA 94720, USA (☎ 00 1 510 642 3069, fax 00 1 510 642 1304)

CLARKE, Dr John Charles; s of Percy Charles Clarke, of Brackley, Northants, and Gladys May, *née* Gibbard (d 1967); *b* 18 Jan 1947; *Educ* Magdalen Coll Sch Brackley, Wadham Coll Oxford (minor scholar, BA, MA, DPhil); *m* 1976, Celia Imogen, da of Cecil Ralph Wathen (d 1976); *Career* fell All Souls Coll Oxford 1967–1976, 1979–86, 1995–, sr lectr in history Univ Coll at Buckingham 1976–84, lectr in history Wadham Coll Oxford 1979–86, dean of humanities Univ of Buckingham 1994– (reader in history 1984–); *Books* George III (1972), The Age of Cobbett (1976), The Book of Buckingham (1984), British Diplomacy and Foreign Policy (1989), The Book of Brackley (1987), Yesterday's Brackley (1990); *Recreations* railways; *Style*— Dr John Clarke; ✉ Dean Faculty of Humanities, University of Buckingham, Yeomanry House, Hunter Street, Buckingham, Bucks MK18 1EG (☎ 01280 820294)

CLARKE, Prof John Frederick; s of Frederick William Clarke (d 1974), and Clara Auguste Antonie, *née* Nauen (d 1975); *b* 1 May 1927; *Educ* Warwick Sch, QMC (BSc, PhD); *m* 19 Dec 1953, Jean Ruth, da of Joseph Alfred Hector Roberts Gentle (d 1960), 2 da (Jenny b 1956, Julie b 1957); *Career* pupil pilot Naval Aviation RN 1946–48; aerodynamicist English Electric Co Ltd 1956–57, lectr Coll of Aeronautics Cranfield 1958–65, Fulbright scholar and visiting assoc prof of Stanford Univ Calif 1961–62, reader Cranfield Inst of Technol 1965–72 (prof theoretical gas dynamics 1972–91, emeritus 1992–), visiting prof at various UK, Euro, Aust and US univs, memb various ctees for sci, author of various contribs to learned jls; first G C Steward visiting fell Gonville & Caius Coll Cambridge 1992, fell Queen Mary and Westfield Coll Univ of London 1993–; FIMA 1965, FRAeS 1969, FRSA 1986, FRS 1987; *Books* The Dynamics of Real Gases (with M McChesney, 1964), Dynamics of Relaxing Gases (with M McChesney, 1976); *Recreations* Sunday painter; *Style*— Prof John F Clarke, FRS; ✉ Field House, Green Lane, Aspley Guise, Milton Keynes MK17 8EN (☎ 01908 582234)

CLARKE, Prof John Innes; DL (Co Durham 1990); s of late Bernard Griffith Clarke, of Bournemouth, and Edith Louie, *née* Mott; *b* 7 Jan 1929; *Educ* Bournemouth Sch, Univ of Aberdeen (MA, PhD), Univ of Paris; *m* 2 April 1955, Dorothy Anne, da of late George May Watkinson, of Ashbourne, Derbyshire; 3 da (Gemma b 1956, Anna b 1959, Lucy b 1969); *Career* Nat Serv FO RAF 1952–54; asst lectr in geography Univ of Aberdeen 1954–55, lectr in geography Univ of Durham 1955–63; prof of geography: Univ Coll of Sierra Leone 1963–65, Univ of Durham 1968–90 (reader 1965–68); Univ of Durham: pro vice chllr and sub warden 1984–90, Leverhulme emeritus fell 1990–92, emeritus prof 1990–; chm: Exec Ctee HESIN 1987–89, Durham Health Authy 1990–92, N Durham Health Authy 1992–96; non-exec memb County Durham Fndn; FRSA, FRGS (Victoria Medal 1991, vice pres 1991–95); *Books* Population Geography (1965), Population Geography and Developing Countries (1971); ed: An Advanced Geography of Africa (1975), Geography and Population (1984); co-ed: Population & Development Projects in Africa (1985), Population & Disaster (1989), Mountain Population Pressure (1990), Environment and Population Change (1994); *Recreations* hill walking, family history, travel; *Style*— Prof John Clarke, DL; ✉ Tower Cottage, The Avenue, Durham DH1 4EB (☎ 0191 384 8350)

CLARKE, Rear Adm John Patrick; CB (1996), LVO, MBE; s of Frank Clarke (d 1965), and Christine Margaret, *née* Sendell; *b* 12 Dec 1944; *Educ* Epsom Coll, BRNC Dartmouth; *m* 1969 (sep 1995), Ann, da of Bishop A G Parham; 1 s (b 1971), 2 da (b 1973 and 1977); *Career* Capt HMS Oberon 1977–79, Capt HMS Dreadnought 1979–81, Qualifying Course 1981–83, cmdg offr Submarine COs 1983–85, Exec Offr HMY Britannia 1985–86, Capt Submarine Sea Trg 1986–89, Capt 7th Frigate Sqdn and HMS Argonaut 1989–90, Asst Dir Naval Staff Duties 1990–91, Dir Naval Warfare 1992, Dir Naval Mgmnt and CIS 1993–94, Flag Offr Trg and Recruiting 1994–96, Hydrographer of the Navy 1996–; *Recreations* golf, sailing, bee keeping, reading history; *Clubs* Lansdowne, Yeovil Golf; *Style*— Rear Adm John Clarke, CB, LVO, MBE; ✉ Hydrographic Office, Ministry of Defence, Taunton, Somerset TA1 2DN (☎ 01823 337900, fax 01823 325522)

CLARKE, His Hon Sir Jonathan Dennis; kt (1981); eldest s of Dennis Robert Clarke (Master of the Supreme Court, d 1967) and Caroline Alice, *née* Hill; *b* 19 Jan 1930; *Educ* Kidstones Sch, Univ Coll London; *m* 1956, Susan Margaret Elizabeth Ashworth; 1 s, 3 da; *Career* recorder Crown Court 1972–82, circuit judge (Western) 1982–93, ret; memb Criminal Injuries Compensation Bd, pres Law Soc 1980–81; ptnr Townsends 1959–82; *Style*— His Hon Sir Jonathan Clarke; ✉ c/o Midland Bank, The Forum, Marlborough Road, Swindon, Wilts

CLARKE, Keith Edward; *b* 1940; *Educ* Alleyne's GS, Univ of Bradford (BEng), Imperial Coll London (Dip in Computing Sci, MPhil); *m* 1965, Barbara; 1 s, 1 da; *Career* sr exec engr: Miny of Technol (now CCTA) 1969–70, Post Office Research Dept 1970–72; BT Laboratories: head Viewdata Div and Section 1972–79, head Speech Technol Research Div 1983, dep dir Info Technol Products Dept 1985–89, dir Applications and Servs Devpt 1989–92; sr vice-pres Engrg BT North America 1992–93, dir Engrg Collaboration BT 1995– (dir Gp Systems Engrg 1992–95); dir: Cellnet 1989–92, BT (CBP) Ltd 1989–95, Br Approvals Bd for Telecommunications 1992–; memb various IEE ctees incl Standards Policy Ctee 1992–93; memb: Editorial Advsy Bd Telematics and Informatics Jl, DTI Advsy Ctee on Flat Screen Displays technol 1985–87, Parly Gp for Engrg Devpt 1996–; author of numerous articles in professional jls, sometime lectr various educnl estabs, occasional broadcaster; winner Charles Babbage Premium Instn of Electronic and Radio Engrs 1983; Freeman: City of London, Worshipful Co of Info Technologists; FIEE, FBCS, FIMgt, FEng 1995; *Recreations* inland waterways cruising, photography, theatre-going, literature; *Clubs* Ronnie Scott's, Naval and Military, Real Time, Windsor Yacht; *Style*— Keith Clarke, Esq, FEng; ✉ BT Networks and Systems, 120 Holborn, London EC1N 2TE

CLARKE, Rt Hon Kenneth Harry; PC (1984), QC (1980), MP (C) Rushcliffe (majority 19,766); s of Kenneth Clarke, of Nottingham; *b* 2 July 1940; *Educ* Nottingham HS, Gonville and Caius Coll Cambridge (pres Union); *m* 1963, Gillian Mary, da of Bruce Edwards, of Sidcup, Kent; 1 s, 1 da; *Career* called to the Bar Gray's Inn 1963, bencher 1989; MP (C) Rushcliffe 1970–; oppn spokesman: on social servs 1974–76, on indust 1976–79; Parly under sec Dept of Tport 1979–82, min of state (health) DHSS 1982–85, HM paymaster gen and min for employment 1985–87, chllr of the Duchy of Lancaster and min for trade and indust 1987–88, sec of state for health July 1988–Nov 1990, sec of state for education and science Nov 1990–92, home secretary 1992–93, chllr of the Exchequer 1993–; *Recreations* modern jazz, bird watching, watching football, cricket and motor racing; *Style*— The Rt Hon Kenneth Clarke, QC, MP; ✉ HM Treasury, Parliament Street, London SW1P 3AG (☎ 0171 270 5678)

CLARKE, (Samuel) Laurence Harrison; CBE (1988); s of Samuel Harrison Clarke, CBE (d 1994), of Stevenage, and Frances Mary, *née* Blowers (d 1976); *b* 16 Dec 1929; *Educ* Westminster, Trinity Coll Cambridge (BA); *m* 10 June 1952, Ruth Joan, da of Oscar William Godwin, OBE, of Old Colwyn (d 1958); 1 s (Christopher b 1958), 3 da (Susan b 1953, Mary b 1956, Janet b 1960); *Career* asst tech dir GEC plc 1981–91; dir: Alvey Programme 1987 (dep dir 1983–87), Filtronic Components Ltd 1989–93, SIRA Ltd 1989–95 (chm 1994–95); visiting prof UCL 1983–91; FIEE; *Recreations* skiing, Scottish dancing; *Style*— Laurence Clarke, Esq, CBE; ✉ Sarum End, Salisbury Road, Southwold, Suffolk IP18 6LG (☎ 01502 725116)

CLARKE, (Victor) Lindsay; s of Victor Metcalfe Clarke (d 1972), of Halifax, W Yorkshire, and Clara, *née* Bell; *b* 14 Aug 1939; *Educ* Heath GS Halifax, King's Coll Cambridge (BA); *m* 1, 1961 (m dis 1972), Carolyn Pattinson; 1 da (Madeleine Sara b 1966); m 2, 1980, Phoebe Clare Mackmin, *née* Harris; *Career* novelist; sr master ODA Secdy Sch Ghana 1962–65, lectr Gt Yarmouth Coll of Further Educn 1965–67, coordinator of Liberal Studies Norwich City Coll 1967–70, co-dir Euro Centre Friends World Coll 1970–79, writer in residence Univ of Wales 1995; memb PEN Int 1989; *Books* Sunday Whiteman (1987), The Chymical Wedding (Whitbread award for fiction, 1989), Alice's Masque (1994); Cathal of the Woods (radio drama, 1994), A Stone from Heaven (radio drama, 1995); *Recreations* life drawing, divination, shooting pool; *Style*— Lindsay Clarke, Esq; ✉ Peters Fraser & Dunlop, The Chambers, Chelsea Harbour, London SW10 0XF (☎ 0171 376 7676, fax 0171 352 7356)

CLARKE, Martin Courtenay; s of Douglas Archibald Clarke (d 1992), of London, and Marjorie, *née* Blinkhorn (d 1987); *b* 7 Jan 1941; *Educ* Winchester, Trinity Coll Cambridge (MA); *m* 5 Sept 1974, Esmee Frances, da of Col J F Cottrell, OBE, MC (d 1972), of Exmouth; *Career* Deloitte & Touche: ptnr 1973–96, nat dir of res devpt 1982–87, nat dir of mktg 1987–90, ptnr i/c corp fin 1988–95, nat dir of corp fin 1993–95; chm: Haymills Contractors Holdings Ltd 1996–, Specialised Fixings Ltd 1996–; dir Haymills Property Investments Ltd; memb Auditing Practices Ctee Consultative Ctee of Accounting Bodies 1982–88; churchwarden St Lawrence Jewry next Guildhall; Freeman City of London; Liveryman: Worshipful Co of Merchant Taylors 1970 (memb Ct of Assts 1991, Second Upper Warden 1994), Worshipful Co of Loriners 1983; FCA 1973; *Recreations* sailing, gardening, skiing, opera, reading; *Clubs* City of London, Royal Yacht Sqdn, Royal Southampton Yacht; *Style*— Martin Clarke, Esq; ✉ 91 Bedford Gardens, Kensington, London W8 7EQ

CLARKE, Mary; da of late Frederick Clarke, and Ethel Kate, *née* Reynolds (d 1984); *b* 23 Aug 1923; *Educ* Mary Datchelor Girls' Sch; *Career* ed The Dancing Times London 1963–, ballet critic The Guardian 1977–94; author; memb Grand Cncl The Royal Acad of Dancing; Queen Elizabeth II Coronation Award Royal Acad of Dancing 1990, Nijinsky Medal Poland 1995; Knight of the Order of Dannebrog 1992; *Books* The Sadler's Wells Ballet: A History and an Appreciation (1955), Dancers of Mercury: the Story of Ballet Rambert (1962), Design for Ballet (with Clement Crisp, 1978), The History of Dance (with Clement Crisp, 1981), Ballet: an Illustrated History (with Clement Crisp, new edn 1992); contrib to Encyclopedia Britannica (1974); *Recreations* watching dancing, travel, reading; *Clubs* Gautier; *Style*— Miss Mary Clarke; ✉ 54 Ripplevale Grove, Islington, London N1 1HT; The Dancing Times, 45–47 Clerkenwell Green, London EC1R 0EB (☎ 0171 250 3006, fax 0171 253 6679)

CLARKE, Matthew Gerard; QC (Scot 1989); s of Thomas Clarke (d 1978), and Ann, *née* Duddy (d 1984); *Educ* Holy Cross HS Hamilton, Univ of Glasgow (Francis Hunter scholar, Chartered Inst of Secretaries scholar, Cunninghame bursar, LLB, MA); *Career* admitted slr Scotland 1972, admitted memb Faculty of Advocates 1978; lectr Faculty of Law Univ of Edinburgh 1972, standing jr counsel Scot Home and Health Dept 1983–89; pt/t chm Industl Tbnls 1987–; judge Court of Appeals Jersey and Guernsey 1996–; memb: Consumer Credit Licensing Appeal Tbnl 1976–, Estate Agents Tbnls 1980–, UK Delgn Cncl of Euro Bars and Law Socs 1989– (ldr 1993–96), Trademarks Appeal Tbnl 1996; hon fell Faculty of Law Univ of Edinburgh 1995–; *Books* The Unfair Contract Terms Act 1977 (1978), Sweet & Maxwell Encyclopaedia of Consumer Law (Scottish ed, 1978–85), Company Law: The European Dimension (contrib, 1991), EC Legal Systems (contrib, 1992), Green's Guide to European Law in Scotland (contrib, 1996); *Recreations* travel, opera, chamber music, the music of Schubert; *Clubs* Scottish Arts; *Style*— Matthew Clarke, Esq, QC; ✉ 12 Strathearn Place, Edinburgh EH9 2AL (☎ 0131 447 6074); Advocates' Library, Parliament House, Edinburgh (☎ 0131 226 5071, fax 0131 225 3642, telex 727856 FACADI G)

CLARKE, (Christopher) Michael; s of Patrick Reginald Rudland Clarke, of Helmsley, N Yorks, and Margaret Catherine, *née* Waugh; *b* 29 Aug 1952; *Educ* Felsted, Univ of Manchester (BA); *m* 1 July 1978, Deborah Clare, da of Paul Wilfred Cowling; 2 s (Oliver Paul b 29 June 1984, Alexander Patrick b 19 April 1986), 1 da (Emily Louisa b 15 Sept 1992); *Career* art asst York Art Gallery 1973–76, res asst Br Museum 1976–78, asst keeper i/c prints Whitworth Art Gallery Univ of Manchester 1978–84, keeper Nat Gallery of Scotland 1987– (asst keeper 1984–87); visiting fell Paul Mellon Center for Studies in Br Art Yale Univ 1985; FRSA 1996; *Books* The Tempting Prospect: A Social History of English Watercolours (1981), The Arrogant Connoisseur: Richard Payne Knight (co ed with Nicholas Penny, 1982), The Draughtsman's Art: Master Drawings in the Whitworth Art Gallery (1982), Lighting Up The Landscape: French Impressionism And Its Origins (1986), Corot And The Art Of Landscape (1991), Eyewitness Art: Watercolour (1993); *Recreations* golf, badminton, music; *Style*— Michael Clarke, Esq; ✉ 9A Summerside St, Trinity, Edinburgh EH6 4NT (☎ 0131 554 7167); National Gallery of Scotland, The Mound, Edinburgh EH2 2EL (☎ 0131 556 8921, fax 0131 220 0917)

CLARKE, Prof Michael Gilbert; s of Canon Reginald Gilbert (Rex) Clarke (d 1993), of Kirkby Lonsdale, Cumbria, and Marjorie Kathleen, *née* Haslegrave (d 1991); *b* 21 May 1944; *Educ* Queen Elizabeth GS Wakefield, Univ of Sussex (BA, MA); *m* 1 July 1967, Angela Mary, da of John Bowen Cook (d 1988), of Easingwold, N Yorks; 1 s (Thomas John Kempe b 1980), 2 da (Joanna Mary (Mrs Gavin Hill) b 1970, Lucy Elizabeth b 1972); *Career* teaching asst Univ of Essex 1967–78, lectr and dir of studies in politics Univ of Edinburgh 1969–75, dep dir policy planning Lothian Regnl Cncl 1977–81 (asst dir 1975–77), dir Local Govt Training Bd 1981–90, chief exec The Local Govt Mgmnt Bd 1990–93, prof and head Sch of Public Policy Univ of Birmingham 1993–; chm RIPA 1990–92; memb: Gen Synod of C of E 1990–93 and 1995–, Cncl Inst of Citizenship Studies 1991–, Local Govt Cmmn for England 1995–; chm Worcester Civic Soc 1995–; govr Queens Coll Birmingham 1996–; FIPD 1987, FRSA 1992; *Publications* Getting the Balance Right (with Prof J D Stewart, 1990), Choices for Local Government (with Prof J D Stewart, 1991), Renewing Public Management (1996); numerous contribs on local and nat govt to press and academic jls; *Recreations* gardening, reading, history; *Clubs* Reform; *Style*— Prof Michael Clarke; ✉ Millington House, 15 Lansdowne Crescent, Worcester WR3 8JE (☎ 01905 617634); School of Public Policy, University of Birmingham, J G Smith Building, Birmingham B15 2TT (☎ 0121 414 4959, fax 0121 414 4989)

CLARKE, (John) Neil; s of George Philip Clarke (d 1969); *b* 7 Aug 1934; *Educ* Rugby, King's Coll London (LLB); *m* 1958, Sonia Heather, *née* Beckett; 3 s; *Career* dep chm Charter Consolidated plc 1982–88 (chief exec 1980–88); chm: Johnson Matthey plc 1984–89, Molins plc 1989–91, Genchem Holdings Ltd 1989–, British Coal Corporation 1991–; dir Travis Perkins plc 1990–; FCA; *Clubs* MCC, Royal W Norfolk Golf, Addington Golf; *Style*— J Neil Clarke, Esq; ✉ High Willows, 18 Park Ave, Farnborough Park, Orpington, Kent BR6 8LL (☎ 01689 851651); Willow Cottage, Hall Lane, Thornham, Norfolk; British Coal Corporation, Charles House, 5–11 Lower Regenet Street, London SW1Y 4LR (☎ 0171 766 4000, fax 0171 766 4009)

CLARKE, Nicholas Campbell (Nick); s of John Campbell Clarke (d 1966), and Ruth Wilda, *née* McNeile (d 1990); *b* 9 June 1948; *Educ* Bradfield, Fitzwilliam Coll Cambridge (BA); *m* 1991, Barbara Want; 3 c by prev m (Thomas b 1976, Alison b 1976, Peter b 1980); *Career* trainee Yorks Evening Post 1970–72, BBC TV Manchester 1973–79 (northern industl corr 1976–79), BBC Money Programme 1980–85, BBC Newsnight 1986–89; presenter BBC Radio 1989–: The World This Weekend 1989–94, The World at One 1994–, Any Questions, News Quiz and others; *Recreations* cricket, cooking, music; *Style*— Nick Clarke, Esq; ✉ c/o BBC Radio, Broadcasting House, London W1A 1AA (☎ 0171 765 4100)

CLARKE, Olive; OBE (1994, MBE 1978), JP (1960), DL (Cumbria 1993); da of George Teasdale (d 1984), of Milnthorpe, Cumbria, and Sarah, *née* Fawcett (d 1981); *b* 19 May 1922; *Educ* Kendal HS; *m* 10 April 1947, Arthur (d 1995), s of James Anthony Clarke (d 1968), of Carnforth, Lancs; 2 da (Gwendaline Olive (Mrs Cleverly) b 20 Oct 1949, Alison Sarah (Mrs Boxford) b 10 Oct 1951); *Career* in farming partnership 1947–, chm Transport Users Consultative Ctee for N Western England (by appt DTI) 1979–90; chm Womens' Insts 1968–78, memb Bd of Visitors to Durham Prison (Home Office appt) 1971–92, life vice pres Fedn of Young Farmers Clubs 1974, chm S Cumbria Magistrates' Assoc 1981–88, chm then pres Westmoreland and Furness Country Landowners' Assoc 1984–88, chm Gen Commissioners of Income Tax S Westmoreland Division 1992–, tstee Frieda Scott Tst; *Recreations* gardening, travel, use of the English language; *Clubs* Farmers'; *Style*— Mrs Olive Clarke, OBE, JP, DL; ✉ Kaker Mill, Preston Patrick, Milnthorpe, Cumbria LA7 7NZ (☎ 015395 67239)

CLARKE, Oz; *Educ* Canterbury Choir Sch, Kings Sch Canterbury, Pembroke Coll Oxford (MA); *Career* wine writer and broadcaster; co-presenter Food & Drink BBC TV; drinks correspondent The Daily Telegraph; *Books* Oz Clarke's Wine Guide, Oz Clarke's New Classic Wines, Oz Clarke's Wine Atlas, Microsoft Wine Guide; *Recreations* any sport, virtually any music; *Style*— Oz Clarke, Esq; ✉ c/o Limelight, 54 Marshall Street, London W1V 1LR (☎ 0171 734 1218, fax 0171 287 1998)

CLARKE, Maj Sir Peter Cecil; KCVO (1992, CVO 1969, MVO 1964), JP (Hants 1971); s of Capt Edward Denman Clarke, CBE, MC (d 1966), of Crossways, Binstead, IOW, and Audrey, *née* Rant; *b* 9 Aug 1927; *Educ* Eton, RMA Sandhurst; *m* 1950, Rosemary Virginia Margaret Harmsworth, da of late T C Durham, of Appomattox, Virginia, USA; 1 s, 2 da; *Career* Maj (ret) 3rd The King's Own Hussars and 14/20 King's Hussars 1945–64, Adjt 3rd Hussars, GSO2 2 Inf Div, psc 1959; asst priv sec then comptroller to HRH Princess Marina, Duchess of Kent 1961–68, currently extra equerry to HRH Princess Alexandra, the Hon Lady Ogilvy, GCVO (comptroller and extra equerry 1964–69), chief clerk Duchy of Lancaster 1969–92, memb Ct Corp of Sons of the Clergy 1987–; *Style*— Maj Sir Peter Clarke, KCVO, JP; ✉ 6 Gordon Place, W8 4JD (☎ 0171 937 0356)

CLARKE, Prof Peter Frederick; s of John William Clarke (d 1987), and Winifred, *née* Hadfield; *b* 21 July 1942; *Educ* Eastbourne GS, St John's Coll Cambridge (BA, MA, PhD, LittD); *m* 1, 29 March 1969 (m dis 1990), Dillon, *née* Cheetham; 2 da (Emily Jane b 4 July 1974, Liberty Lucy (twin) b 4 July 1974); m 2, 20 July 1991, Dr Maria Tippett, FRS (Canada), of Vancouver, BC; *Career* reader in modern history UCL 1978–80 (asst lectr then lectr in history 1966–78); Univ of Cambridge: lectr in history 1980–87, fell St John's Coll 1980–, tutor St John's Coll 1982–87, reader in modern history 1987–91, prof of modern British history 1991–; chm: Cambs Area Pty of SDP 1981–82, Editorial Bd Twentieth Century British History; FBA 1989; *Books* Lancashire and the New Liberalism (1971), Liberals and Social Democrats (1978), The Keynesian Revolution in the Making (1988), A Question of Leadership: from Gladstone to Thatcher (1991), Hope and Glory: Britain 1900–1990 (1996); *Style*— Prof Peter Clarke, FBA; ✉ St John's College, Cambridge CB2 1TP (☎ and fax 01223 338726)

CLARKE, Peter James; CBE (1993); s of Capt Stanley Ernest Clarke, ISO (d 1985), of Enfield, Middx, and Elsie May, *née* Scales (d 1993); *b* 16 Jan 1934; *Educ* Enfield GS, St John's Coll Cambridge (BA, MA); *m* 16 April 1966, Roberta Anne, da of Robert Browne (d 1942), of New Malden, Surrey; 1 s (Matthew Robert b 1969), 1 da (Elizabeth Ann b 1967); *Career* War Office: exec offr 1952–62 (at univ 1957–60), higher exec offr 1962–67; The Forestry Commission: sr exec offr 1967–72, princ 1972–75; princ Dept of Energy 1975–76; sec Forestry Commissioners 1976–94; *Recreations* gardening, travelling; *Style*— Peter Clarke, Esq, CBE; ✉ 5 Murrayfield Gardens, Edinburgh EH12 6DG

CLARKE, Peter Lovat; JP (1970); s of Harold Clarke (d 1945), of Warrington, and Alice Taylor (d 1992); *Educ* Ellesmere; *m* 1956, Audrey Christine, da of Walter Jonathan Elston, of Cheshire; 3 s (John b 1956, Simon and Timothy b 1964 (twins), 1 da (Denise b 1959); *Career* dir: The Greenalls Group plc (chm Drinks and Leisure Div), The Greenalls Group Pension Trustees Ltd; non-exec dir: Jarvis Porter plc, Winerite Ltd, Halewood Vintners Ltd, Alfred Jones Ltd; former chm North & Mid-Cheshire TEC Ltd, dir Warrington Community Health Care (NHS) Tst until 1996; Liveryman Worshipful Co of Distillers 1979; *Recreations* golf, music, reading, swimming; *Clubs* Warrington Golf, Wine and Spirit Over 40 Club, Old Codgers, Majority, Walton Investment; *Style*— Peter Clarke, Esq, JP; ✉ Brook House, Cann Lane, Appleton, nr Warrington, Cheshire (☎ 01925 261660)

CLARKE, Richard Allen; s of Allen Lee Clarke, of London, and Anne Clarke; *b* 19 Aug 1942; *Educ* Aldenham, The Architectural Assoc Sch (AADipl); *m* 11 May 1968, Mary Mildred Irene, da of Dr James Francis Hanratty, OBE, of London; 2 s (Jason b 1970, Dominic b 1979), 2 da (Antonia b 1973, Louisa b 1976); *Career* architect; sr ptnr Clifford Tee & Gale 1977–; Freeman City of London 1964; RIBA; *Recreations* shooting, gardening; *Style*— Richard Clarke, Esq; ✉ Clifford Tee & Gale, 5 Eccleston Street, London SW1W 9LY (☎ 0171 730 9633, fax 0171 730 0965, car 0860 222632)

CLARKE, Robert Charles; s of John Edward Kenyon Clarke (d 1980), and Elsie Mary, *née* Rand (d 1990); *b* 15 April 1943; *Educ* John Lyon Sch, Harrow; *m* 11 April 1970, Christine Marjorie, da of Ronald Charles Gardner, of Knowle, W Midlands; 2 s (Jonathan b 1970, Laurence b 1972), 2 da (Eleanor b 1974, Georgina b 1977); *Career* CA; Barton Mayhew 1961–70, Peat Marwick Mitchell 1970–72, Viney Merretts 1972–80, Binder Hamlyn 1980–; Freeman: City of London 1976, Worshipful Co of Chartered Accountants 1976; FCA 1971; *Recreations* golf; *Clubs* MCC; *Style*— Robert Clarke, Esq; ✉ Hudnall Farm, Little Gaddesden, Berkhamsted, Herts HP4 1QN (☎ 01442 843214); Binder Hamlyn, 20 Old Bailey, London EC4M 7BH (☎ 0171 489 9000, fax 0171 489 6060)

CLARKE, Sir Robert Cyril; kt (1993); s of Robert Henry Clarke (d 1964), and Rose Lilian, *née* Bratton (d 1952); *b* 28 March 1929; *Educ* Dulwich, Pembroke Coll Oxford (MA); *m* 12 July 1952, Evelyn Mary (Lynne), da of Cyrus Harper (d 1959); 3 s (Tristan, Jonathan (twins) b 26 May 1956, Ben b 13 July 1966), 1 da (Anna b 19 May 1969); *Career* served Royal West Kent Regt 1947–49; Cadbury: trainee Cadbury Bros Ltd 1952–54, gen mangr John Forrest Ltd 1954–57, marketing dir Cadbury Confectionery 1957–62, md Cadbury Cakes Ltd 1962–69, chm Cadbury Cakes and dir Cadbury Schweppes Foods Ltd 1969–71, md McVitie & Cadbury Cakes Ltd 1971–74; United Biscuits (Holdings) plc: joined group 1974, md UB Biscuits 1977–84, chm and United Biscuits (UK) Ltd 1984–95 (dir 1974–95), dir United Biscuits (Holdings) plc 1984–95, gp chief exec 1986–90, chm 1990–95; chm Thames Water plc 1994– (non-exec dir 1988–); non-exec dir and chm special tstees Great Ormond Street Hosp for Children NHS Trust;

hon fell Pembroke Coll Oxford 1993; fell Inst of Grocery Distribution, CIMgt; *Recreations* reading, walking, renovating old buildings, planting trees; *Style*— Sir Robert Clarke; ✉ Thames Water plc, 14 Cavendish Place, London W1M 0NU (☎ 0171 636 8686, fax 0171 833 6134)

CLARKE, Robert Sandifer; s of Robert Arthur Clarke (d 1988), of Abinger Manor, Abinger Common, Surrey, and Agnes Joyce, *née* Coventry (d 1987); *b* 9 May 1934; *Educ* Westminster, ChCh Oxford (MA), College of Law; *m* 12 Sept 1964, Cherry June Leslie, da of William Attwood Waudby, of Mombasa, Kenya; 1 s (Damian Rupert b 4 Jan 1968), 2 da (Vanessa-Jane b 4 Sept 1965, Georgina Ann b 25 Aug 1973); *Career* Nat Serv RN 1952; cmmnd RNVR: Midshipman 1952, Sub Lt 1953, Lt 1955, ret 1960; slr 1962, sr ptnr Wood Nash Kimber (formerly ptnr), UK ed Droit Et Affaires France 1968–75; chm: Fedn Field Sports Assocs (UK) of EEC 1978–83, Br Delgn to Int Cncl of Hunting and Conservation of Game UK 1983–90; vice pres and fell Game Conservancy Fordingbridge; Freeman City of London 1975, Liveryman Worshipful Co of Gunmakers 1975; memb Law Soc 1962; *Recreations* sailing, shooting, skiing, tennis, travel; *Clubs* Turf, Oxford & Cambridge, Shikar, RNSA; *Style*— Robert Clarke, Esq; ✉ Abinger Manor, Abinger Common, Surrey; 2 Cheyne Mews, Cheyne Walk, Chelsea, London SW3 (☎ 0171 242 7322); Wood Nash Kimber, 6 Raymond Buildings, Gray's Inn, London WC1R 5DA (☎ 0171 242 7322, fax 0171 831 9041)

CLARKE, Roger Eric; s of Frederick Cuérel Clarke, of Petts Wood, Kent, and Hilda Josephine, *née* Holbrook (d 1980); *b* 13 June 1939; *Educ* UCS Hampstead, CCC Cambridge (MA); *m* 8 Oct 1983, Elizabeth Jane, da of Gordon William Pingstone, of Beckenham, Kent; 1 da (Rebecca b 1986); *Career* positions held: Civil Aviation Divs of Miny of Aviation, BOT and Depts of Trade and Tport 1961–72 and 1980–85; air traffic rights advsr to Govt Fiji 1972–74; asst sec Insur and Overseas Trade Divs Dept of Trade 1975–80; under sec Dept of Tport: Civil Aviation Policy Directorate 1985, Public Tport Directorate 1989, Shipping Policy 1991, dir of shipping 1996–; *Recreations* family, friends, church, walking, theatre, music, philately, languages, travel; *Clubs* Reform; *Style*— Roger Clarke, Esq; ✉ Department of Transport, Zone 4/14, Great Minster House, 76 Marsham Street, London SW1P 4DR (☎ 0171 271 3933, fax 0171 271 3939)

CLARKE, Prof Roger Howard; *b* 22 Aug 1943; *Educ* King Edward VI Sch Stourbridge, Univ of Birmingham (BSc, MSc), Univ of Westminster (PhD); *m* 15 Oct 1966, Sandra Ann; 1 s, 1 da; *Career* res offr CEGB 1965–77; National Radiological Protection Board: head of nuclear power assessments 1978–82, Bd sec 1983–87, dir 1987–; visiting prof Centre for Analytical Research in the Environment Imperial Coll of Science Technol and Medicine Univ of London, visiting prof in radiation and environmental protection Dept of Physics Univ of Surrey; chm Int Cmmn on Radiological Protection; memb: CEC Gp of Experts in Basic Safety Standards for Radiation Protection, UK Radioactive Waste Mgmnt Advsy Ctee, UK Advsy Ctee on the Safety of Nuclear Installations, Ionising Radiations Advsy Ctee; UK delegate to UN Sci Ctee on Effects of Atomic Radiation; hon fell: Royal Coll of Radiologists, Soc of Radiological Protection; *Publications* Carcinogenesis and Radiation Risk: A Biomathematical Reconnaissance (with W V Mayneord, 1977), author of numerous papers in the scientific literature; *Recreations* theatre, gardening, travel; *Style*— Prof Roger Clarke; ✉ Corner Cottage, Woolton Hill, Newbury, Berks RG20 9XJ (☎ 01635 253957); National Radiological Protection Board, Chilton, Didcot, Oxon OX11 0RQ (☎ 01235 822632, fax 01235 822619, telex 837124 RADPRO G)

CLARKE, Roy; *b* 28 Jan 1930; *m* 1953, Enid, *née* Kitching; 1 s (Stephen b 1955), 1 da (Julia b 1958); *Career* writer; formerly soldier, salesman, policeman and teacher; full time writer 1965–; TV situation comedy series: The Misfits 1970, Last of The Summer Wine 1972–, Open All Hours 1975, Keeping Up Appearances 1990, Ain't Misbehavin' 1994; Writers' Guild Best Series Award 1970, Pye Television Award 1982, Dennis Potter Award 1996; Hon DLitt Univ of Bradford; *Recreations* reading, watching nature; *Style*— Roy Clarke, Esq; ✉ c/o Sheila Lemon, Lemon, Unna & Durbridge, 24 Pottery Lane, Holland Park, London W11 4LZ (☎ 0171 727 1346, fax 0171 727 9037)

CLARKE, Rupert Grant Alexander; s and h of Maj Sir Rupert Clarke, 3 Bt, MBE, *qv*; *b* 12 Dec 1947; *Educ* Melbourne Univ (LLB); *m* 1978, Susannah, da of Sir (Richard) Robert Law-Smith; 1 s (Rupert Robert William b 24 June 1981), 2 da (Samantha Kathleen b 1980, Joanna Georgina b 1983); *Career* hon consul for Principality of Monaco in Melbourne 1986–; *Style*— Rupert Clarke, Esq

CLARKE, Maj Sir Rupert William John; 3 Bt (UK 1882), of Rupertswood, Colony of Victoria; MBE (1943); s of Sir Rupert Turner Havelock Clarke, 2 Bt (d 1926); *b* 5 Nov 1919; *Educ* Eton, Magdalen Coll Oxford (MA); *m* 21 Jan 1947, Kathleen Grant, da of Peter Grant Hay (d 1961), of Melbourne; 2 s (and 1 s decd), 1 da; *Heir* s, Rupert Grant Alexander Clarke, *qv*; *Career* served WWII, Maj Irish Gds (despatches); former chm Cadbury Schweppes Australia Ltd, former dir Cadbury Schweppes plc; chm: P and O Australia Ltd, National Australia Bank Ltd until 1992; dir: Morganite Australia Pty Ltd until 1992, Custom Credit Holdings Ltd until 1992, Howard Florey Inst Melbourne; consul gen for Monaco 1975–; hon fell Trinity Coll Melbourne; pres Royal Humane Soc of Aust, memb Bd Howard Florey Inst Melbourne; Order of Grimaldi 1975, Légion d'Honneur (France) 1979, Officier de L'Ordre de Leopold (Belgium) 1989; FAIM; *Recreations* racing, swimming; *Clubs* Melbourne, Australian, Athenaeum (Melbourne), Union (Sydney), Victoria Amateur Turf, Victoria Racing, Cavalry and Guards' (London); *Style*— Maj Sir Rupert Clarke, Bt, MBE; ✉ Richmond House, 56 Avoca Street, South Yarra, Victoria 3141 (fax 013 670 2629); office: 500 Bourke Street, Melbourne 3000

CLARKE, Sally Vanessa; da of Brian Trent Clarke, of Surrey, and Sheila Margaret, *née* Coomber; *b* 6 Jan 1954; *Educ* Guildford HS, Croydon Tech Coll (Dip in Hotel and Catering Ops); *Career* studied and worked in Paris (Cordon Bleu Advanced Cert) 1974–75, asst cook Leiths Good Food Catering Co 1976–77, head teacher and demonstrator Leiths Sch of Food and Wine 1977–79, moved to Los Angeles to work with Michael McCarty and helped set up Michaels Santa Monica 1979, asst cook and asst night mangr Michaels Santa Monica Calif and West Beach Cafe Venice Calif 1980–83; opened: Clarke's in London 1984, & Clarke's 1988, & Clarke's Bread 1989; *Recreations* cooking, eating, drinking good wine, opera; *Style*— Miss Sally Clarke; ✉ Clarke's, 124 Kensington Church St, London W8 4BH (☎ 0171 221 9225, fax 0171 229 4564)

CLARKE, Stella Rosemary; CBE (1997), JP (Bristol 1968), DL (Avon 1982); da of John Herbert King (d 1973), of Somerlea, Langford, Somerset, and Mollie Isobel Bruce, *née* Riches (d 1983); *b* 16 Feb 1932; *Educ* Cheltenham Ladies Coll, Trinity Coll Dublin; *m* 21 June 1952, Charles Nigel Clarke, *qv*, s of Charles Cyril Clarke (d 1968); 4 s (Giles b 1953, Nigel b 1957, Henry b 1959, Matthew b 1963), 1 da (Bridget b 1955); *Career* chm Long Ashton RDC 1972–74 (memb 1955–74), memb Woodspring DC 1974–77; chm Bristol City Magistrates Bench 1991–; formed Zenzele self-build housing gp in St Paul's Bristol 1981, involved with other housing projects, vice chm Knightstone Housing Assoc 1985– (memb 1980); govr BBC 1974–81, chm of Cncl Univ of Bristol 1987– (memb 1982–); memb: Bristol Urban Devpt Corp 1988–96, Housing Corp 1988–95, National Lottery Charities Bd 1995–; Hon LLD Univ of Bristol; *Recreations* family, diversity of life, poetry, jigsaw puzzles, needlepoint; *Style*— Mrs Stella Clarke, CBE, JP, DL; ✉ Gatcombe Court, Flax Bourton, Bristol BS19 1PX (☎ 01275 393141, fax 01275 394274)

CLARKE, His Hon Judge Stephen Patrick; s of Leslie Clarke, of Weaverham, Northwich, Cheshire, and Anne Mary, *née* Jones (d 1981); *b* 23 March 1948; *Educ* Rostrevor Coll Adelaide S Australia, Univ of Hull (LLB); *m* 6 July 1974, Margaret Roberta, da of Robert Millar, of Buckna, Co Antrim, N Ireland; 2 s (Christopher James b 1975, Andrew Paul b 1977); *Career* called to the Bar Inner Temple 1971; memb Wales and Chester Circuit (jr 1988–89), recorder of the Crown Court 1992–95 (asst recorder 1988–92), circuit judge (Wales & Chester Circuit) 1995–; asst Parly boundary cmmr for Wales; *Recreations* golf, cricket, theatre; *Clubs* Upton-by-Chester Golf; *Style*— His Hon Judge Stephen Clarke; ✉ Seven Gables, 26a Linksway, Upton, Chester CH2 1EA (☎ 01244 380293); The Crown Court, The Castle, Chester CH1 2AN (☎ 01244 317606)

CLARKE, Dr Stewart William; s of Albert Edward Clarke (d 1975), and Elsie Jane, *née* Parker; *b* 12 March 1936; *Educ* Nottingham HS, Univ of Birmingham (MB ChB, MD); *m* 9 June 1962, Gillian Mary, da of Harry Douglas Acres, of Kingswood, Surrey; 2 s (Jonathon b 29 Nov 1968, Andrew b 15 Dec 1971); *Career* asst prof of med Univ of California San Francisco 1969–70, lectr in med Queen Elizabeth Hosp Birmingham 1970–71, conslt physician in gen and thoracic med The Royal Free and Brompton 1971–, conslt physician The King Edward VII Hosp for Officers 1976–; author of numerous papers and chapters on lung disease; sec of The Thoracic Soc 1975–81, chm Med Advsy Ctee of King Edward VII Hosp Midhurst, fell American Coll of Chest Physicians 1984–, censor RCP 1987–89, pres Euro Respiratory Soc 1990; FRCP 1974, Assoc of Physicians of GB and Ireland, memb RSM; *Books* Aerosols and the Lung (1984), Fibreoptic Bronchoscopy (1987); *Recreations* sports fanatic, rugby, squash, golf; *Clubs* Saracens Football, Salcombe Yacht, Hadley Wood Golf; *Style*— Dr Stewart Clarke; ✉ Oak House, 13 Hadley Grove, Hadley Green, Barnet, Herts EN5 4PH (☎ 0181 449 2416); 148 Harley Street, London W1N 1AH (☎ 0171 487 5020)

CLARKE, Thomas Sydney (Tom); s of Thomas William Clarke (d 1991), and Evelyn Elizabeth, *née* Hodge (d 1962); *b* 29 April 1939; *Educ* Isleworth GS; *m* 12 Sept 1961, Margaret Jean, da of Archibald Morgan (d 1953); 1 s (Morgan b 1968), 2 da (Heather b 1964, Donna b 1966); *Career* journalist: Hayes Chronicle, Herts Advertiser St Albans, The Chronicle Bulawayo Southern Rhodesia, Daily and Sunday Nation Nairobi Kenya, Daily Express London, Queen Magazine, Evening Standard; sports ed: Evening Standard 1972–74, Daily Mail 1975–86, The Times 1986–93; ed The Sporting Life 1993–; memb: Press Complaints Cmmn, Sports Aid Fndn; *Recreations* watching sport (particularly racing), playing golf, touring France; *Clubs* Thorndon Park Golf, Hardelot Golf, Reform, Sloane, Lord's Taverners; *Style*— Tom Clarke, Esq; ✉ The Coach House, Horseman Side, Navestock Side, Brentwood, Essex CM14 5ST (☎ 01277 375386, fax 01277 375387); The Sporting Life, 1 Canada Square, Canary Wharf, London E14 5AB (☎ 0171 293 3471, fax 0171 293 3904)

CLARKE, Thomas (Tom); CBE (1980), JP (Lanark 1972), MP (Lab) Monklands West (majority 17,065); s of James Clarke, and Mary, *née* Gordon; *b* 10 Jan 1941; *Educ* Columba HS, Coatbridge and Scottish Coll of Commerce; *Career* former asst dir Scottish Film Cncl; memb Coatbridge Cncl 1964–74, provost Monklands DC 1974–82, pres Convention of Scottish Local Authorities 1978–80 (vice pres 1976–78); MP (Lab): Coatbridge and Airdrie 1982–83, Monklands W 1983–; sponsor Disabled Persons' Act 1986, memb Shadow Cabinet 1992–; chief oppn spokesman: on Scottish affrs 1992–93, on devpt and co-operation 1993–94, on disabled people's rights 1994–; govr BFI; *Books* Managing Third World Debt (co-author); *Style*— Tom Clarke, Esq, CBE, JP, MP; ✉ House of Commons, London SW1A 0AA

CLARKE, (George) Timothy Horace De Courquetaine; s of Denis Horace Hilary Clarke, of Little Witley, Worcs, and Louise Marie, *née* Schlincker; *b* 20 April 1949; *Educ* Oundle, St John's Coll Cambridge (MA); *m* 2 Sept 1989, Henrietta Barbara, da of Alexander Neilson Strachan Walker, CMG (d 1980); 1 s (Matthew Alexander Henry b 24 April 1994), 1 da (Veronica Julia b 31 July 1996); *Career* admitted slr 1974; ptnr Linklaters & Paines 1982–; *Recreations* gardening, reading, France; *Style*— Timothy Clarke, Esq; ✉ Linklaters & Paines, Barrington House, 59–67 Gresham St, London EC2V 7JA (☎ 0171 606 7080, fax 0171 606 5113)

CLARKE, Sir (Charles Mansfield) Tobias; 6 Bt (UK 1831), of Dunham Lodge, Norfolk; adopted name Tobias 1962; s of Sir Humphrey Orme Clarke, 5 Bt (d 1973), and Elisabeth, *née* Cook (d 1967); *b* 8 Sept 1939; *Educ* Eton, ChCh Oxford (MA), The Sorbonne, New York Univ Graduate Business Sch; *m* 1, 1971 (m dis 1979), Charlotte, da of Roderick Walter; m 2, 1984, Teresa Lorraine Aphrodite, da of Somerset Struben de Chair, of St Osyth's Priory, Essex; 1 s ((Charles) Lawrence Somerset b 1990), 2 da (Theodora Roosevelt b 4 Aug 1985, Augusta Elfrida b 25 April 1987); *Heir* s, (Charles) Lawrence Somerset Clarke b 12 March 1990; *Career* vice pres London Branch of Bankers' Tst Co New York 1974–80; assoc dir Swiss Bank Corp London 1992–94; memb Standing Cncl of the Baronetage 1980– (hon treas 1980–92, vice chm 1990–92, chm 1993–96); ed and originator The Baronets' Journal 1987–; tstee Baronets' Tst 1989–95 (chm 1996–); Lord of the Manor of Bibury; *Recreations* hunting, gardening, photography, stimulating conversation; *Clubs* Boodle's, White's, Pratt's, Beefsteak, Pilgrims', Jockey (Paris), The Brook, Racquet and Tennis (NY); *Style*— Sir Tobias Clarke, Bt; ✉ South Lodge, 80 Campden Hill Road, London W8 7AA (☎ 0171 937 3932); The Church House, Bibury, Cirencester, Glos GL7 5NR (☎ 01285 740225)

CLARKE, William Malpas; CBE (1976); s of Ernest Clarke (d 1963), and Florence, *née* Wright (d 1973); *b* 5 June 1922; *Educ* Audenshaw GS, Univ of Manchester (BA); *m* 1, 1946, Margaret Braithwaite; 2 da (Deborah, Pamela); m 2, 1973, Faith Elizabeth, da of Lionel Dawson (d 1987), of Bucks; *Career* journalist; Manchester Guardian: editorial staff 1948–56, asst fin ed 1955–56; The Times: editorial staff 1956–66, dep city ed 1956–57, city ed 1957–62, fin and indust ed 1962–66; conslt The Banker 1967–76 (ed 1966), dir of Studies Ctee on Invisible Exports 1966–67, dir Perm Ctee on Invisible Exports 1968–76 (Ctee became Br Invisible Exports Cncl 1983), fndr dir Euromoney 1969–84, chm City Telecommunications Ctee 1972–87, dir gen and dep chm Br Invisible Exports Cncl 1976–87, dep chm City Communications Centre 1976–87; dir: Grindlays Bank 1966–85 and 1987–89, ANZ Holdings 1985–87, ANZ Grindlays Bank 1989–92, Swiss Re-Insurance (UK) 1977–93; chm: Grindlays Bank (Jersey) 1976–92, ANZ Merchant Bank 1987–91, Central Banking Publications 1990–; govr: Gt Ormond St Hosp for Sick Children 1982–90, Greenwich Theatre 1984–87; chm Appeal Tstees Gt Ormond St Hosp 1984–94; cncl memb RIIA 1970–83, tstee Harold Wincott Fndn 1970–, chm Harold Wincott Financial Journalist of the Year Award Panel 1971–92; Hon DLitt London Guildhall Univ 1992; *Books* The City's Invisible Earnings (1958), Private Enterprise in Developing Countries (1966), The City in the World Economy (1965 and 1967), Britain's Invisible Earnings (for the Ctee on Invisible Exports, 1967), The World's Money (1970, US edn 1972), Money Markets of the World (1971), Inside the City (1979, paperback 1983), How the City of London Works (1986, 1988, 1991 and 1995), The Secret Life of Wilkie Collins (1988, paperback 1989 and 1996, US and Spanish edn 1991), Planning for Europe: 1992 (1989), The Lost Fortune of the Tsars (1994, paperback 1995 and 1996, US and German edns 1995); *Recreations* books, theatre; *Clubs* Reform; *Style*— William Clarke, Esq, CBE; ✉ 37 Park Vista, Greenwich, London SE10 (☎ 0181 858 0979, fax 0181 293 3747)

CLARKE, William Oliver; s of Charles Frederick Orme (Toby) Clarke, of Switzerland, and Silvia Vera, *née* Kaelin; *b* 17 Aug 1943; *Educ* Gordonstoun, Trinity Coll Dublin (MA), Camberwell Sch of Art (Cert in Archive Preservation); *m* 1981, Elizabeth, da of John William Linnell Ivimy; 3 s (Frederick William Michael b 9 July 1982, Percival John Theodore b 29 Oct 1983, Maximilian Tobias Irving b 13 Oct 1986); *Career* Morgan Grenfell & Co Ltd 1968–71, asst conservation offr Oriental Antiquities Dept Br Museum 1974–76, paper conservator Area Museum for SE Eng (AMSEE) Fitzwilliam Museum

1976–78, conservator Courtauld Inst of Art 1978–; memb: Projects Ctee NACF 1978–92, Pembridge Assoc 1988– (chm 1990–95), Cncl Queen Alexandra's House 1997–; govr Bute House Girls' Prep Sch 1990–; memb Worshipful Co of Mercers (Master 1995–96); memb Inst of Paper Conservation 1976; *Publications* A Pragmatic Approach to Environmental Improvements in the Courtauld Institute Galleries in Somerset House (paper for ICOM, jtly with M Cassar, 1993); *Recreations* tennis, country pursuits, painting in watercolours; *Clubs* Boodle's, Hurlingham, Chelsea Arts; *Style*— W O Clarke, Esq; ✉ 13 Pembridge Gardens, London W2 4EA (☎ 0171 229 8518); Courtauld Gallery, Somerset House, Strand, London WC2R 0RN (☎ 0171 873 2567, fax 0171 873 2589)

CLARKSON, Ven Alan Geoffrey; s of Geoffrey Archibald Clarkson, OBE (d 1980), of Lyndhurst, and Essie Isabel Bruce, *née* Bruce-Porter (d 1981); *b* 14 Feb 1934; *Educ* Sherborne, Christ's Coll Cambridge (MA), Wycliffe Hall Oxford; *m* 10 Sept 1959, Monica Ruth, da of Rev Harcourt Robert Henry Lightburne (d 1949), of Upchurch, Kent; 2 s (John b 1961, Michael b 1964), 1 da (Anne b 1960); *Career* Nat Serv 1952–54, cmmnd Lt; ordained deacon 1959, priest 1960; curate: Penn Wolverhampton 1959–60, St Oswald's Oswestry 1960–63, Wrington with Redhill 1963–65; incumbent vicar Chewton Mendip with Emborough 1965–74; vicar: St John's Glastonbury with Godney 1974–84, W Pennard 1981–84, Meare 1981–84, St Benedict Glastonbury 1982–84, Burley 1984–; archdeacon of Winchester and hon canon Winchester Cathedral 1984–; diocesan ecumenical offr 1965–75, proctor in convocation 1970–75, memb Gen Synod 1990–95; *Recreations* gardening, photography, DIY, wood turning, music (bassoon and singing); *Style*— The Ven the Archdeacon of Winchester; ✉ The Vicarage, Church Corner, Burley, Ringwood, Hants BH24 4AP (☎ 01425 402303, fax 01425 403753)

CLARKSON, Alan Malcolm; *b* 12 Sept 1936; *Educ* Nunthorpe GS York; *m* Pauline Rita, *née* Musgrove; 1 s (Kevin Mark b 10 Feb 1964), 1 da (Karen Dawn b 26 April 1967); *Career* swimming administrator; former int swimmer, competed in Cwlth Games 1958, represented GB 1959–62; hon treas: Amateur Swimming Assoc 1986– (pres 1997), Amateur Swimming Fedn of GB 1986–; pres: Yorkshire Amateur Swimming Assoc, N Eastern Counties Amateur Swimming Assoc; memb: Open Water Tech Swimming Ctee Fédèration Internationale de Natation Amateur, Euro Swimming Ctee LEN Bureau, Cwlth Games Cncl for England Ctee, Nat Olympic Ctee; qualified CA; sr ptnr Plummer Clarkson & Lester; FCA; *Clubs* York City Baths; *Style*— Alan Clarkson, Esq; ✉ Amateur Swimming Association, Finance Office, 37 Monkgate, York (☎ 01904 647199, fax 01904 622195)

CLARKSON, Prof Brian Leonard; s of Leonard Coleman Clarkson, of Driffield, E Yorks, and Gertrude Irene, *née* Shouler; *b* 28 July 1930; *Educ* Beverley GS E Yorks, Univ of Leeds (BSc, PhD); *m* 5 Sept 1953, Margaret Elaine, da of Frank Bancroft Wilby (d 1976), of Hedge End, Southampton; 3 s (Stephen Anthony b 1955, John Michael b 1957, Paul Richard b 1965), 1 da (Carol Margaret b 1960); *Career* structural engr de Havilland Aircraft Co 1953–57; Univ of Southampton: Sir Alan Cobham res fell 1957–58, lectr Dept of Aeronautics 1958–63, lectr and sr lectr Inst of Sound Vibration Res 1963–66, prof of vibration studies 1966–82, dir Inst of Sound Vibration Res 1967–78, dean of engrg 1978–80, dep vice chllr 1980–82; sr res assoc NASA USA 1970–71; Univ of Wales Swansea: princ 1982–94, research prof 1994–, hon fell 1996; vice chllr Univ of Wales 1987–89; sec Int Cmmn on Acoustics 1975–81, pres Inst of Acoustics 1980–82, pres Fedn of Acoustical Socs of Europe 1982–84, chm Assoc of Cwlth Univs 1992–93, memb SERC 1984–88; Hon DSc: Univ of Leeds 1984, Univ of Southampton 1987, Univ of Sains Malaysia 1990; Hon LLD Univ of Wales 1996; FEng 1986, hon fell Inst of Acoustics, FRAeS; *Recreations* walking, gardening, golf; *Clubs* Athenaeum; *Style*— Prof Brian Clarkson, FEng; ✉ Highmead, 17 Southgate Road, Southgate, Swansea SA3 2BT (☎ and fax 01792 233216)

CLARKSON, His Hon Derek Joshua; QC (1969); s of Albert Clarkson (d 1955), of Pudsey, W Yorks, and Winifred Charlotte, *née* James (d 1979); *b* 10 Dec 1929; *Educ* Pudsey GS, King's Coll London, (LLB); *m* 1960, Peternella Marie-Luise Ilse, da of R Canenbley, of Leer, Germany; 1 s, 1 da; *Career* Nat Serv RAF 1952–54; called to the Bar 1951; recorder: Rotherham 1967–72, Huddersfield 1972, Crown Ct 1972–77; circuit judge (SE Circuit) 1977–95, Middx liaison judge 1985–95; *Recreations* walking, theatre, book collecting; *Style*— His Hon Derek Clarkson, QC; ✉ 24 John Islip St, London SW1P 4LG; 72A Cornwall Rd, Harrogate, N Yorks HG1 2NE

CLARKSON, Dr Euan Neilson Kerr; s of Dr Alexander Clarkson (d 1946), of Newcastle upon Tyne, and Helen, *née* Griffin (d 1977); *b* 9 May 1937; *Educ* Shrewsbury, Univ of Cambridge (MA, PhD), Univ of Edinburgh (DSc); *m* 31 Aug 1962, Cynthia Margaret, da of Eric Cowie (d 1979), of Kirkby Moorside, Yorks; 4 s (John Alexander Joseph b 21 Nov 1965, Peter Bruce Mark b 21 Jan 1967, Thomas Hamish Martin b 29 Jan 1971, Matthew Dougal Charles b 10 March 1973); *Career* Nat Serv 1955–57; Univ of Edinburgh: asst lectr 1963–65, lectr 1965–78, dir of studies 1967–73, assoc dean Sci Faculty 1978–81, sr lectr 1978–81, reader in geology and geophysics 1981–; author of 78 sci articles in learned jls; memb Edinburgh Geological Soc (pres 1985–87), tstee Natural History Museum 1987–92; FRSE 1984; *Books* Invertebrate Palaeontology and Evolution (1979, 2 edn, 1986, 3 edn 1992); *Recreations* classical music, fell-walking, story-writing, history, travel; *Style*— Dr Euan Clarkson, FRSE; ✉ 4 Cluny Place, Edinburgh, Scotland EH10 4RL (☎ 0131 447 2248); Department of Geology and Geophysics, University of Edinburgh, King's Buildings, West Mains Rd, Edinburgh, Scotland EH9 3JW (☎ 0131 650 1000 ext 8514)

CLARKSON, Gerald Dawson; CBE (1990), QFSM (1983); s of Alexander Dickie Clarkson (d 1986), of St Mary Cray, Kent, and Agnes Tierney, *née* Price (d 1991); *b* 4 June 1939; *Educ* Westminster Tech Coll, Poly of Central London (BA); *m* 21 March 1959, Rose Lilian, da of Thomas Montague Hodgson (d 1971), of Clapham; 1 s (Nicholas b 1963), 1 da (Penelope b 1965); *Career* Nat Serv RE 1959–61; London Fire Brigade: joined 1961, station offr 1969, asst divnl offr 1972, divnl offr 1974, dep asst chief offr 1979, asst chief offr 1980, awarded Fire Serv Long Serv and Good Conduct Medal 1981, dep chief offr 1983, chief offr and chief exec 1987–91; pres Cwlth and Overseas Fire Serv Assoc 1990, memb Fedn of Br Fire Orgns 1989, dir NFPA USA 1987–90, memb Kent Police Authy 1995; Freeman City of London 1983, fndr Master of the Guild of Firefighters; FIMgt 1978, FIMS 1979, FRSH 1987, hon fell IFE 1989, OBStJ 1989; *Recreations* music, sailing, fishing; *Clubs* The East India; *Style*— Gerald Clarkson, Esq, CBE, QFSM

CLARKSON, Jeremy Charles Robert; s of Edward Grenville Clarkson, of Doncaster, and Shirley Gabrielle, *née* Ward; *b* 11 April 1960; *Educ* Repton; *m* Frances Catherine, da of Maj Robert H Cain, VC; 1 s (Finlo Robert Edward b 14 March 1996), 1 da (Emily Harriet b 21 July 1993); *Career* trainee journalist Rotherham Advertiser 1978–83, fndr Motoring Press Agency 1983, presenter Top Gear (BBC) 1989–, fndr BBC Top Gear Magazine 1993, presenter Jeremy Clarkson's Motorworld (BBC) 1995–; currently columnist: The Sun, The Sunday Times, Top Gear Magazine; *Recreations* smoking; *Style*— Jeremy Clarkson, Esq

CLARKSON, Patrick Robert James; QC (1991); s of Cdr Robert Anthony Clarkson, LVO, of Crudwell House, Wiltshire, and Sheelagh Clarissa, *née* Neale; *b* 1 Aug 1949; *Educ* Winchester; *m* 26 July 1975, Bridget Cecilia Doyne, da of Col Robert Harry Doyne (d 1965), of Barrow Court, Galhampton, Somerset; 2 s (Benjamin Robin b 1978, William Patrick b 1985), 1 da (Georgia Emily b 1980); *Career* called to the Bar Lincoln's Inn 1972, recorder of the Crown Court 1996; memb Hon Soc of Lincoln's Inn and Inner Temple; *Recreations* cricket, motor racing, country, reading; *Style*— Patrick Clarkson, Esq, QC; ✉ 1 Serjeants' Inn, Temple, London EC4Y 1NH (☎ 0171 583 1355)

CLARKSON, Dr Peter David; s of Maurice Roland Clarkson (d 1992), and Jessie *née* Baker; *b* 19 June 1945; *Educ* Epsom Coll, Univ of Durham (BSc), Univ of Birmingham (PhD); *m* 1974, Rita Margaret, *née* Skinner; 1 da; *Career* geologist with British Antarctic Survey 1967–89: wintered in Halley Bay Antarctica 1968 and 1969, base cdr 1969, Antarctic field seasons in Shackleton Range (ldr 3 times) 1968–78, in S Shetland Islands 1974–75, ldr in Antarctic Peninsula 1985–86; exec sec Scientific Ctee on Antarctic Research 1989–; articles on Antarctic geology; UK advsr to PROANTAR Brazil 1982; hon sec Trans-Antarctic Assoc 1980–95, Polar Medal 1976, FGS 1980; *Recreations* walking, woodworking, photography, music, all matters Antarctic; *Clubs* Antarctic; *Style*— Dr Peter Clarkson; ✉ Scientific Committee on Antarctic Research, Scott Polar Research Institute, Lensfield Road, Cambridge CB2 1ER (☎ 01223 362061, fax 01223 336549)

CLARRICOATS, Prof Peter John Bell; CBE (1996); s of John Clarricoats, OBE (d 1969), of London, and Alice Cecilia, *née* Bell (d 1982); *b* 6 April 1932; *Educ* Minchenden GS, Imperial Coll London (BSc, PhD, DSc); *m* 1, 6 Aug 1955 (m dis 1963), (Mary) Gillian Stephenson, da of George Gerald Hall (d 1971), of Leeds; 1 s (Michael b 1960), 1 da (Alison b 1962); *m* 2, 19 Oct 1968, Phyllis Joan, da of Reginald Blackburn Lloyd (d 1989), of Newton Abbot; 2 da (Angela b 1969, Caroline b 1969); *Career* scientific staff GEC 1953–59; lectr: Queens Univ of Belfast 1959–62, Univ of Sheffield 1962–63; prof Univ of Leeds 1963–67; QMC London 1968–: prof of engrg 1968–, dean of engrg 1977–80, head of electronic engrg 1979–96, govr 1976–79 and 1987–90; Coopers Hill Meml Prize (IEE) 1964, Measurement Prize (IEE) 1989, JJ Thomson Medal (IEE) 1989, Euro Microwave Prize 1989; chm: IEE Electronics Div 1979, Br Nat Ctee for Radio Sci 1985–89, and numerous conferences on microwaves and antenna; apptd Distinguished lectr IEEE Antenna and Propagation Soc 1986–88; Hon DSc: Univ of Kent 1993, Aston Univ 1995; vice pres: IEE 1989 (hon fell 1993), International Union of Radio Science 1993; FInstP 1964, FIEE 1968, FIEEE 1968, FCGI 1980, FEng 1983, FRS 1990; *Books* Microwave Ferrites (1960), Corrugated Horns for Microwave Antennas (1984), Microwave Horns and Feeds (1994); *Recreations* formerly mountaineering and squash, classical music and photography; *Style*— Prof Peter Clarricoats, CBE, FRS, FEng; ✉ The Red House, Grange Meadows, Elmswell, Suffolk IP30 9GE (☎ 01359 240585); Department of Electronic Engineering, Queen Mary and Westfield College, University of London, Mile End Road, London E1 4NS (☎ 0171 975 5330, fax 0181 981 0259)

CLARY, Julian Peter McDonald; s of Peter John Clary, and Brenda, *née* McDonald; *b* 25 May 1959; *Educ* St Benedict's Sch Ealing, Goldsmiths' Coll London (BA); *Career* comedian and entertainer; *Theatre* Bravo in Splendid's (Lyric) 1995; numerous tours and live shows; *Television* shows/appearances for LWT incl: Saturday Night Live, Friday Live, Aspel & Company, Cilla Says Goodbye to 88, Trick or Treat, Not The Royal Variety, Sunday Sunday; for Channel Four incl: Last Resort, Clive Anderson Talks Back, Sticky Moments with Julian Clary, Sticky Moments on Tour with Julian Clary, Desperately Seeking Roger, One Hour with Jonathan Ross, Terry & Julian, Brace Yourself Sydney; for BBC incl: Wogan, Open Air, Paramount City, All Rise for Julian Clary, Brassen Hussies (Screen Two); Tonight Live with Steve Vizard (Aust TV); *Radio* Steve Wright in the Afternoon (BBC Radio 1), Hey Radio (BBC Radio 1), Big Fun Show (BBC Radio 4), Brian Hayes Show (LBC), John Sachs Show (Capital Radio), Janice Long Show (GLR), Intimate Contact with Julian Clary (BBC Radio 1); *Film* Carry on Columbus 1992; *Recordings* Leader of the Pack (10 Records/Virgin) 1988, Wandrin' Star (Wonderdog Records Ltd) 1990; *Video* Julian Clary aka The Joan Collins Fan Club - The Mincing Machine 1989, The Best of Sticky Moments, My Glittering Passage 1993; *Books* My Life with Fanny the Wonder Dog, How to be a Real Man (1992); *Recreations* housework; *Style*— Julian Clary, Esq; ✉ c/o International Artistes Drama, Mezzanine Floor, 235 Regent Street, London W1R 8AX (☎ 0171 439 8401, fax 0171 409 2070)

CLASPER, Michael; CBE (1995); s of Douglas Clasper (d 1992), and Hilda Clasper; *b* 21 April 1953; *Educ* Bede Sch Sunderland, St John's Coll Cambridge (MA); *m* 6 Sept 1975, Susan Rosemary; 1 da (Jacqueline Sarah b 21 July 1983), 2 s (Matthew Dennis Owen b 16 Jan 1986, Christopher Duncan b 28 Feb 1989); *Career* BR 1974–78; Procter and Gamble Ltd: joined as brand asst 1978, subsequently various posts in advtg then advtg dir 1985–88, gen mangr Holland 1988–91, md UK 1991, md and vice pres Europe 1991–95, regnl vice pres Europe 1995–; memb Advsy Bd Judge Inst Univ of Cambridge; memb Advsy Ctee on Business and the Environment (ACBE); CIMgt; *Recreations* swimming, cycling, skiing, tennis, golf; *Style*— Michael Clasper, Esq, CBE; ✉ Procter & Gamble European Technical Centre, Temselaan 100, B-1853 Strombeek-Bever, Belgium (☎ 00 32 2 456 22 28, fax 00 32 2 456 2973)

CLATWORTHY, Robert Ernest; s of Ernest William Clatworthy (d 1985), of Bridgwater, Somerset, and Gladys, *née* Tugela; *b* 31 Jan 1928; *Educ* Dr Morgan's GS Bridgwater, W of England Coll of Art, Chelsea Sch of Art, Slade Sch of Fine Art; *m* 1954 (m dis 1966), Pamela, *née* Gordon; 2 s (Benn b 1955, Thomas b 1959), 1 da (Sarah Alexandra b 1957); *Career* Nat Serv head Fine Art Wing E Formation Coll 1949; lectr W of Eng Coll of Art 1967–71, visiting tutor RCA 1960–72, memb Fine Art Panel Nat Cncl for Dips in Art and Design 1961–72, govr St Martin's Sch of Art 1970–71, head Dept of Fine Art Central Sch of Art and Design 1971–75; *Exhibitions* Hanover Gallery, Waddington Galleries, Holland Park Open Air Sculpture, Battersea Park Open Air Sculpture, Br Sculpture in the Sixties Tate Gallery, Br Sculptors Burlington House 1972, Basil Jacobs Fine Art Ltd, Diploma Galleries Burlington House, Photographer's Gallery, Quinton Green Gallery, Austin/Desmond Fine Art, Keith Chapman 1991, Keith Chapman Gallery 1990, 1992, 1994 and 1996; works in the collections of: Arts Cncl, Contemporary Art Soc, Tate Gallery, V & A, GLC, Nat Portrait Gallery, Monumental Horse and Rider; RA 1973 (ARA 1968); *Recreations* music; *Clubs* Chelsea Arts; *Style*— Robert Clatworthy, Esq, RA; ✉ Moelfre, Cynghordy, Llandovery, Dyfed SA20 0UW (☎ 01550 720201)

CLAUSON, Oliver Drake Husey; s of Sir Gerard Leslie Makins Clauson, KCMG, OBE (d 1974), and Honor Emily Mary, *née* Husey (d 1978); *b* 23 April 1927; *Educ* Eton, CCC Oxford (MA); *m* 14 Jan 1955, Barbara Susan, da of Major De Symons Harry Lewis-Barned (d 1964), of Maidstone; 3 s (Richard b 1956, Julian b 1960, Francis b 1964), 1 da (Antonia b 1958); *Career* insur clerk Lloyd's 1952–64, underwriting memb Lloyd's 1956–, claims adjudicator leading Personal Accident and Travel Syndicate 1965–90, dir CCGH Agency Ltd 1989–96; hon treas St Peter's and St Paul's Church Marlborough Tst, dir Theatre in the Downs; Liveryman Worshipful Co of Merchant Taylors 1950; *Recreations* amateur acting, producing, stage hand; *Clubs* Army and Navy, Lansdowne; *Style*— Oliver D H Clauson, Esq; ✉ Applegarth, Ogbourne St George, Marlborough, Wilts SN8 1SU (☎ 01672 841219)

CLAVERING, Col John Muir; OBE (1983), MC (1972); s of Alan Douglas Clavering (d 1982), of Tullochard Lairg, and Agnes Evelyn Muir, *née* Stewart (d 1985); *b* 20 March 1938; *Educ* Fettes; *m* 31 March 1965, Jennifer Mary, da of Patrick Wood Sim (d 1952); 3 da (Philippa b 1967, Rosanna b 1968, Henrietta b 1970); *Career* cmmnd Scots Gds 1960, CO 2 Bn 1979–81, cmd Cwlth Mil Training Team Uganda 1982–83, head Jt Mil Intelligence Staff Sultanate of Oman 1983–85, Lt-Col cmdg Scots Gds 1985–87; vice pres Reg Cmmns Bd 1987–88; memb: Queen's Bodyguard for Scotland (Royal Co of Archers), Highland Soc of London; *Recreations* fishing, stalking, shooting, gardening; *Clubs* Perth, Shikar; *Style*— Col John Clavering, OBE, MC

CLAXTON, David John; LVO (1985), TD (1973); s of Rt Rev Charles Robert Claxton (d 1992), former Bishop of Blackburn, and Jane, *née* Stevenson; *b* 15 July 1933; *Educ* Haileybury, Queens' Coll Cambridge (BA, MA); *m* 1, 30 Sept 1967 (m dis 1985), Elizabeth Anne, da of Maj Thomas Henry Baker Cresswell, DL, of Chathill, Northumberland; 3 s (Charles b 1968, Piers b 1970, Christopher b 1971), 1 da (Tassagrie b 1975); m 2, 27 Sept 1986 (m dis 1996), Pamela, da of Charles Mycock (d 1989), of Harpur Hill, Buxton, Derbys; 1 step da (Sharon b 1967); *Career* Duke of Lancaster's Own Yeo 1960–78: Offr Cadet 1960–61, cmmnd 2 Lt 1961, Co Lt-Col 1974–78; asst farm mangr 1952–54, ptnr Joshua Bury Earle & Co Manchester (chartered surveyors and land agents) 1957–73, surveyor of lands Crewe Survey of the Duchy of Lancaster 1973–89, currently chartered surveyor and land agent Prestbury Cheshire; formerly: hon sec Bow Gp (NW), chm Lancs Cheshire and IOM branch Land Agency and Agric Div RICS, pres Cheshire Agric Valuers Assoc; churchwarden Barthomley, Cheshire Co rep Marie Curie Meml Fndn 1989–, tstee Boys' and Girls' Welfare Soc of Cheadle 1989–; FRICS 1963, FAAV 1971; *Recreations* skiing, sailing, mountaineering; *Style—* David Claxton, Esq, LVO, TD; ✉ 14 Bollin Mews, Prestbury, Cheshire SK10 4DP (☎ 01625 829348, mobile 0402 067378)

CLAXTON, Geoffrey Dudley; s of George Philip Claxton (d 1975), and May, *née* Tyrell (d 1981); *b* 29 Nov 1937; *Educ* N Walsham Secdy Mod, Norwich Tech Coll, Lowestoft Tech, Llandaff Tech; *m* 20 April 1963, Edna Christine, da of Cecil Kittle (d 1983); *Career* apprentice engr 1954–60, engr 1960–62, sr engr 1962–63; BBC: laboratory technician Design Dept 1963–64, broadcast engr 1964–66, supt Electronic Workshop 1966–; memb Inst of Radio Electronic Engrg, CEng, MIERE, MIEE; *Recreations* private pilot, builder of a 2 seat aircraft; *Clubs* Glamorgan Flying; *Style—* Geoffrey Claxton, Esq; ✉ BBC, Broadcasting House, Llantrisant Road, Llandaff, Cardiff, South Glamorgan CF5 2YQ (☎ 01222 572888, fax 01222 552973)

CLAXTON, Maj-Gen Patrick Fisher; CB (1972), OBE (1946); s of late Rear Adm Ernest William Claxton, and Kathleen O'Callaghan, *née* Fisher; *b* 13 March 1915; *Educ* Sutton Valence Sch, St John's Coll Cambridge; *m* 1941, Jóna Gudrún Gunnarsdóttir (d 1980), da of Gunnar Gunnarsson, of Reykjavik, Iceland; 2 da; *Career* Cmdt Sch of Transport and ADC to HM the Queen 1966–68, Transport Offr-in-Chief (Army) 1969–71, ret; gen mangr Regular Forces Employment Assoc 1971–81, pres Hindhead Branch Royal Br Legion 1972–; *Style—* Maj-Gen Patrick Claxton, CB, OBE; ✉ The Lodge, Beacon Hill Park, Hindhead, Surrey GU26 6HU (☎ 01428 604437)

CLAY, David Nicholas; s of John Clay, and late Edith Mary Clay; *b* 18 Jan 1944; *Educ* Ellesmere Coll Shropshire, King's Coll London (LLB); *Career* slr; sr ptnr Dodds Ashcroft Liverpool 1986 (articled clerk 1966), merged with Davies Wallis Foyster 1988; *Style—* David Clay, Esq; ✉ Davies Wallis Foyster, 5 Castle Street, Liverpool, L2 4XE (☎ 0151 236 6226, fax 0151 236 3088)

CLAY, HE Edward; CMG; *b* 21 July 1945; *m* 1969, Anne, *née* Stroud; 3 da; *Career* HM Dip Serv 1968–: desk offr N and E African Dept FCO 1968–70, third later second sec (Chancery) Nairobi 1970–72, second later first sec (Chancery) Sofia 1973–75, desk offr Defence Dept FCO 1975–78, first sec (Commercial) Budapest 1979–82, area offr later asst Personnel Ops Dept FCO 1982–85, dep high cmmr Nicosia 1985–89, head Personnel Ops Dept subsequently Personnel Mgmnt Dept 1989–93, high cmmr Uganda 1993–97 (non-resident ambass to Republic of Rwanda 1994–95 and to Republic of Burundi 1994–96); *Style—* HE Mr Edward Clay, CMG; ✉ c/o Foreign & Commonwealth Office (Kampala), King Charles Street, London SW1A 2AH

CLAY, Jennifer Mary Ellen; *née* Coutts; da of Dr William Ernest Coutts (d 1992), of Aberdeenshire, and Nora Margaret Jane, *née* Grassick (d 1995); *Educ* Howell's Sch Llandaff, Univ Coll Cardiff, Univ of Wales (BA, MA), Cornell Univ NY; *m* 1972, John Peter Clay, *qv*, s of Harold Peter Clay (d 1970); 3 da (Teresa, Lalage, Xanthe); *Career* Fulbright scholar; British Airways: sales trg mangr 1974–79, mangr Western USA 1979–82, mangr Scot 1982–84, controller corporate identity 1984–86; gen mangr product design and devpt Pan American World Airways 1986–89, conslt Eastern Airlines and General Aviation 1990–; LTCL, MCIT; *Recreations* music, travel, royal tennis; *Clubs* IOD, The Queen's, The Wings (New York), The Tuxedo (New York), Cornell; *Style—* Ms Jennifer Clay; ✉ 114 East 30th Street, New York, NY 10016, USA (☎ 00 1 212 447 7680, fax 00 1 212 447 7678)

CLAY, His Hon John Lionel; TD (1961); s of Capt Lionel Pilleau Clay (ka 1918), of Rastrick House, Yorks, and Mary Winifred Muriel, da of Ralph Walker; *b* 31 Jan 1918; *Educ* Harrow, CCC Oxford (MA); *m* 30 Aug 1952, Elizabeth, 2 da of Rev Canon Maurice George Jesser Ponsonby, MC, gs of 2 Baron de Mauley (d 1943), and the Lady Phyllis Sydney Buxton, OBE (d 1942), eld da of 1 Earl Buxton; 1 s (Andrew b 1962), 3 da (Fiona b 1954, Catriona b 1955, Joanna b 1958); *Career* served WWII 8 Army (despatches) Rifle Bde, served TA London Rifle Bde Rangers and SAS; barr 1947, recorder 1975–77, circuit judge 1977–88; Freeman City of London 1980, Liveryman Worshipful Co of Gardeners; *Recreations* gardening, fishing; *Style—* His Hon John Clay, TD; ✉ Newtimber Place, Hassocks, Sussex BN6 9BU (☎ 01273 833104)

CLAY, John Martin; s of Sir Henry Clay (d 1954), and his 1 wife Gladys, *née* Priestman; *b* 20 Aug 1927; *Educ* Eton, Magdalen Coll Oxford; *m* 1952, Susan Jennifer, da of Lt-Gen Sir Euan Miller, KCB, KBE, DSO, MC (d 1985); 4 s; *Career* former chm Johnson and Firth Brown Ltd; former dir: Bank of England, C E Heath plc, Trade Indemnity plc; currently dir: Hambros PLC, Guardian Media Group; *Recreations* sailing; *Clubs* Medway Yacht; *Style—* John Clay, Esq; ✉ Hambros PLC, 41 Tower Hill, London EC3N 4HA (☎ 0171 480 5000, telex 883851)

CLAY, John Peter; s of Harold Peter Clay (d 1970), and Mary Dansie Clay (d 1974); *b* 26 June 1934; *Educ* St Paul's, Queen's Coll Oxford (MA); *m* 1972, Jennifer Mary Ellen Clay, *qv*, da of Dr William Ernest Coutts (d 1992), of Wiltshire; 3 da (Teresa, Lalage, Xanthe); *Career* investmt mangr; Vickers da Costa Ltd: joined 1957, dep chm 1976–81; chm Clay Finlay Ltd 1981–; memb Cncl Stock Exchange 1974–77; *Recreations* real tennis, flying; *Clubs* City, Queen's, Tuxedo, Sky (New York); *Style—* John Clay, Esq; ✉ 114 East 30th Street, New York, NY 10016 (☎ 00 1 212 447 7680, fax 00 1 212 447 7678); Maison de la Voûte, Place de l'Amour, La Garde-Freinet, 83680 Var, France (☎ 00 334 94 43 68 71)

CLAY, Nicholas Anthony Philip; s of William Charles Clay, of London, and Rose, *née* Usher; *b* 18 Sept 1946; *Educ* Upbury Manor Gillingham Kent, RADA; *m* 15 Nov 1980, Lorna Elizabeth, da of David Granville Heilbron; 2 da (Ella b 31 March 1983, Madge b 17 July 1986); *Career* actor, teacher, producer and writer; assoc memb RADA, patron Medway Little Theatre, assoc memb Shakespeare & Co Lennox Mass; *Theatre* RNT: Aumerle in Richard II, Giovanni in 'Tis Pity She's A Whore, Nugget/Horseman in Equus, Jumper in Jumpers, Rocca in Saturday Sunday Monday, Young Seward in Macbeth, Acaste in The Misanthrope; Nottingham Playhouse: Leslie Williams in The Hostage, Young Inna in Arturo Ui, King Lear; other roles incl: Hastings in She Stoops to Conquer (world tour), Dick in The Confederacy, Belinga in A Month in the Country (both Chichester Festival Theatre), Maurice in Flint (Criterion), Acaste in The Misanthrope (St James Theatre, New York), Trigorin in The Seagull (Cambridge Theatre Co), Lars in Cerceau (Orange Tree), Ernest in Design for Living (Donmar Warehouse, Gielgud Theatre, dir Sean Mathias, *qv*); *Television* films incl: Russian Night (Screen on Two), Saturday Sunday Monday (Granada), The Unknown Soldier (Screen on Two), Poor Little Rich Girl (CBS); series incl: Shakespeare (ATV), Gentlemen and Players (STV), Virtual Murder (BBC), Berlin Break (Columbia/RTL), Picture of Dorian Grey (BBC), Love Story (Thames), In a Glass Darkly (Thames), Three Musketeers (Goodman Rosan Prodn), Sherlock Holmes (Granada), Shine on Harvey Moon (Alomo Prodn), Bobby Russell in Hotel Shanghai; *Films* incl: Billy in The Night Digger, Darwin in The Darwin Adventure, Lt Raw in Zulu Dawn, Tristan in Tristan and Iseult, Alexander in Alexander The Great, Sir Hugo in Hound of the Baskervilles, Cesare Augustus in Martyrdom of St Sebastian, Lancelot in Excalibur, Patrick Redfern in Evil Under the Sun, Prince in Sleeping Beauty, Lionel in Lionheart, Mellors in Lady Chatterley's Lover; *Recreations* theatre, golf, cycling, reading, food, cricket; *Clubs* John Muir Society, RSPB, World Runners; *Style—* Nicholas Clay, Esq; ✉ c/o Peters Fraser & Dunlop Ltd, 503 The Chambers, Chelsea Harbour, Lots Road, London SW10 0XF (☎ 0171 352 4446, fax 0171 352 8135)

CLAY, Sir Richard Henry; 7 Bt (UK 1841), of Fulwell Lodge, Middlesex; s of Sir Henry Felix Clay, 6 Bt (d 1985), and Phyllis Mary, *née* Paramore (Dowager Lady Clay); *b* 2 June 1940; *Educ* Eton; *m* 14 Sept 1963, Alison Mary, o da of Dr James Gordon Fife, of Summerhill, Aldeburgh, Suffolk; 3 s (Charles Richard, Thomas Henry b 28 July 1967, James Felix b 13 April 1969), 2 da (Virginia Rachel (Mrs Robin P Taylor) b 9 July 1964, Catherine Victoria b 9 June 1971); *Heir* s, Charles Richard Clay b 18 Dec 1965; *Career* FCA 1966; *Recreations* sailing; *Clubs* Aldeburgh Yacht; *Style—* Sir Richard Clay, Bt; ✉ The Copse, Shiplate Rd, Bleadon BS24 ONX (☎ 01934 815203)

CLAYDEN, Dr Graham Stuart; s of Colin Stewart Clayden (d 1985), of Bournemouth, and Amy Joyce, *née* Burrough; *b* 8 Jan 1947; *Educ* Bournemouth Sch, Univ of London (MD); *m* 15 Aug 1970, Christine, da of Reginald Thomas Steele (d 1980); 1 s (Jonathan Stuart b 1972), 1 da (Anna Francesca b 1974); *Career* sr registrar in paediatrics Hosp for Sick Children Gt Ormond St 1977, sr lectr and hon conslt in paediatrics St Thomas' Hosp 1977–89, reader in paediatrics and hon conslt UMDS 1989–; procensor RCP, memb Exec Ctee Royal Coll of Paediatrics and Child Health; founding govr Br Paediatric Computer and Info Gp; MRCP 1972, FRCP 1984; *Books* Treatment and Prognosis in Paediatrics (1988), Catechism in Paediatrics (1987), Constipation in Childhood (1991), Illustrated Paediatrics (1996); *Recreations* choral singing, bassoon; *Style—* Dr Graham Clayden; ✉ Paediatric Unit, United Medical and Dental Schools of Guy's and St Thomas's Hospitals, Lambeth Palace Rd, London SE1 7EH (☎ 0171 928 9292, ext 3046)

CLAYDEN, Phillippa; da of Alan John Clayden, of Truro, Cornwall, and Pauline Vivien, *née* Dye; *b* 4 Aug 1955; *Educ* Creighton Comp, Hackney Stoke Newington Coll of Further Educn, Central Sch of Art & Design (BA), RA (post grad dipl); *Career* artist; study of drawing with Cecil Collins 1977–83, freelance teaching in univs, art centres and community orgns around UK 1982–, visual arts coordinator IAF 1989–; *Exhibitions* incl: New Contemporaries 1977, Whitechapel Open 1977 and 1978, solo show Camden Art Centre 1978, four man show Hackney Art Gallery 1979, Premiums Show RA Dipl Gallery 1981 and 1982 (winner Landseer prize 1981), Islington Arts Factory Gallery 1981, 1982, 1983, 1984, 1985 and 1986, RA Summer Exhbn 1982, 1984, 1985, 1986, 1987, 1989 and 1990, Christie's Pick of the Graduates 1982, Royal Over-Seas League 1982, Camden Arts Centre 1986 (twice), Group Three Boundary Gallery 1989, Discerning Eye ICA 1991, solo show Boundary Gallery 1993; *Recreations* walking, swimming, gardening; *Style—* Ms Phillippa Clayden; ✉ 68 Woodland Rise, Muswell Hill, London N10 3UJ (☎ 0181 883 7985); Islington Studio Arts Factory, 2 Parkhurst Road, Holloway N7 0SF (☎ 0171 607 0561); Agi Katz Boundary Gallery, 98 Boundary Road, London NW8

CLAYDON, David Anthony; s of Victor Edwin Claydon (d 1975), of Southampton, and Muriel Mary, *née* Davis; *b* 13 Sept 1935; *Educ* King Edward VI Sch Southampton, St John's Coll Cambridge (MA); *m* 4 April 1959, Gaynor, da of Harold Herbert Childs; 1 s (David Christopher b 20 April 1973), 3 da (Joanna Jane b 4 Nov 1962, Amanda Mary b 9 Oct 1964, Katharine Sarah b 29 Jan 1969); *Career* works mangr BP Chemicals Ltd Salt End Works Hull 1969–73, div mangr Supply Dept BP International Ltd London 1973–76, commercial vice pres BP N America NY USA 1976–79, dir BP Chemicals Ltd London 1981–82 (gen mangr Engrg Dept 1979–81), gen mangr BP Engrg Dept London 1982, chief exec BP Engrg and Tech Centre London 1983–85, chief exec BP Gas Ltd London 1985–88, chm and chief exec BP Canada Inc 1991–93 (pres and chief exec 1988–91), non-exec dir Chesham Building Soc 1994–; CEng, FIChemE, FEng 1985; *Recreations* woodwork and joinery, tennis, DIY; *Style—* David Claydon, Esq, FEng; ✉ Greenacre, Hollybush Hill, Stoke Poges, Bucks SL2 4QN (☎ and fax 01753 662032)

CLAYDON, Geoffrey Bernard; CB (1990); s of Bernard Claydon (d 1978), and Edith Mary, *née* Lucas (d 1991); *b* 14 Sept 1930; *Educ* Leeds Modern, King Edward's Birmingham, Univ of Birmingham (LLB); *Career* articled clerk Pinsent & Co Birmingham 1950, slr of the Supreme Court 1954, sr legal asst Treasy Slr's Dept 1965 (legal asst 1959), asst slr DTI 1973, asst Treasy slr 1974, princ asst Treasy slr and legal advsr Dept of Energy 1980–90, review of private legislative procedures Dept of Tport 1990–95; vice chm Nat Tramway Museum 1969– (sec 1958–84), vice pres Light Rail Transit Assoc 1968– (chm 1963–68); Tramway & Light Railway Soc: chm 1967–93, vice pres 1993–96, pres 1996–; chm Consultative Panel for the Preservation of Br Tport Relics 1982–, memb: Inst of Tport Admin 1972–, Editorial Bd Jl of Energy and Natural Resources Law 1983–90, Fixed Track Section Confederation of Passenger Transport UK 1995–; *Recreations* rail transport, travel; *Clubs* Royal Automobile; *Style—* Geoffrey Claydon, Esq, CB; ✉ 23 Baron's Keep, London W14 9AT (☎ 0171 603 6400)

CLAYTON, Adam; s of Brian and Josephine (Joe) Clayton; *b* 13 March 1960; *Educ* Castle Park Sch Dalkey, St Columba's Coll Rathfarnham; *Career* bass guitarist and fndr memb U2 1978– (with Bono, *qv*, The Edge, *qv* and Larry Mullen, Jr, *qv*); first U2 release U23 (EP) 1979; *Albums* Boy 1980, October 1981, War 1983 (entered UK chart at no 1), Under A Blood Red Sky (live album) 1983, The Unforgettable Fire 1984 (entered UK charts at no 1), The Joshua Tree 1987 (entered UK charts at no 1, fastest selling album ever in UK), Rattle & Hum 1988 (entered UK charts at No 1), Achtung Baby 1991, Zooropa 1993 (No 1 in 18 countries); *Singles* incl: Fire 1981, New Year's Day (first UK Top Ten hit) 1983, Pride (In the Name of Love) 1984, Unforgettable Fire 1985, With or Without You 1987, I Still Haven't Found What I'm Looking For 1987, Where The Streets Have No Name 1987, Desire (first UK no 1 single) 1988, Angel of Harlem 1988, When Love Comes to Town 1989, All I Want Is You 1989, Night & Day (for AIDS benefit LP Red Hot & Blue) 1990, The Fly (entered UK charts at no 1) 1991, Stay 1993; *Film* Rattle & Hum 1988; *Tours* incl: UK, US, Belgium and Holland 1980, UK, US, Ireland and Europe 1981–83, Aust, NZ and Europe 1984, A Conspiracy of Hope (Amnesty International Tour) 1986, world Joshua Tree tour 1987, Rattle & Hum tour 1988, Zoo TV world tour (played to 5m people) 1992–93; also appeared at: Live Aid 1985 (Best Live Aid Performance Rolling Stone Readers' Poll 1986), Self Aid Dublin, Smile Jamaica (Dominion Theatre, in aid of hurricane disaster relief) 1988, New Year's Eve concert Dublin (broadcast live to Europe and USSR) 1989; performed at venues incl: Wembley Stadium, Madison Square Garden NY, Longest Day Festival Milton Keynes Bowl, Croke Park Dublin, Sun Devil Stadium Arizona; *Awards* Grammy awards: Album of the Year (The Joshua Tree) 1987, Best Rock Performance (Joshua Tree tour) 1987, Best Rock Performance (Desire) 1989, Best Video (Where The Streets Have No Name) 1989, Best Alternative Album (Zooropa) 1993; others incl: Best Band Rolling Stone Readers' Poll 1986 (also jt winner Critics' Poll), Band of the Year Rolling Stone Writers' Poll 1984, Best International Act BPI Awards 1989 and 1990, Best Live Act BPI Awards 1993; *Style—* Adam Clayton, Esq; ✉ c/o Regine Moylett Publicity, First Floor, 145a Ladbroke Grove, London W10 6HJ (☎ 0171 221 0554, fax 0171 221 8532)

CLAYTON, Charles; s of late Charles Harry Clayton, of Overstrand, Norfolk, and Elizabeth, *née* Appleyard-Entwistle; *b* 27 Jan 1947; *Educ* The Royal Sch Armagh, Queen Elizabeth GS Middleton Lancs, Moseley Hall GS Cheadle Cheshire, Loughborough Univ (BSc), Westminster Theological Seminary Philadelphia (MA); *m* 17 Oct 1970, (Christine) Anne, da of late Frank Wharton; 2 da (Rachel Fiona b 2 March 1973, Victoria Elizabeth b 9 Oct 1975); *Career* civil engr City Engineers' Dept Glasgow 1970–72, Scottish area dir The Navigators 1980–84 (area rep 1972–80), sabbatical study USA 1984–86, southern regnl leader The Navigators 1986–89, exec dir World Vision UK 1989–; memb Inst of Mgmnt 1993, memb American Mgmt Assoc Int 1994, MinstD 1995, FRSA 1995; *Recreations* walking, sailing, church activities; *Style*— Charles Clayton, Esq; ✉ Executive Director, World Vision UK, World Vision House, 599 Avebury Boulevard, Milton Keynes MK9 3PG (☎ 01908 841000, fax 01908 841001)

CLAYTON, Sir David Robert; 12 Bt (GB 1732), of Marden Park, Surrey; s of Sir Arthur Harold Clayton, 11 Bt, DSC (d 1985), and his 2 w, Alexandra, *née* Andreevsky; *b* 12 Dec 1936; *Educ* HMS Conway, Sir John Cass Coll London; *m* 1971, Julia Louise, da of Charles Henry Redfearn (d 1969); 2 s (Robert Philip b 1975, John Richard b 1978); *Heir* s, Robert Philip Clayton, b 8 July 1975; *Career* Capt Merchant Navy; *Recreations* shooting, sailing; *Clubs* Royal Dart Yacht, Penarth Yacht (hon memb); *Style*— Sir David Clayton, Bt; ✉ Rock House, Kingswear, Dartmouth, Devon TQ6 0BX

CLAYTON, (Francis) Howard; s of Rev Arthur Clayton (d 1960), of Lichfield, and Frances Ella, *née* Warren (d 1974); *b* 20 May 1918; *Educ* St John's Sch Leatherhead, Univ of Birmingham (BCom); *m* 29 July 1942, Helen Margaret (d 1988), da of Dr Henry Doig, of Lennoxtown, Stirlingshire; 1 s (John b 1950), 2 da (Elizabeth b 1943, Margaret b 1948); *Career* WWII 1939–46: cmmnd RA 1942, S Staffs Regt 1944 (wounded in action Holland 1944, leg amputated); asst sec Manor Hosp Walsall 1949–56; lectr: Wednesbury Coll of Commerce 1957–61, Tamworth Coll of Further Educn 1961–67; freelance writer 1967–, dir Lichfield Cathedral Arts Ltd 1980–91, ptnr Abbotsford Publishing Lichfield 1992–; memb Lichfield DC 1976–87 (chm 1983–84); Sheriff of Lichfield 1978–79, Mayor of Lichfield 1987–88; *Books* The Atmospheric Railways (1966), The Duffield Bank and Eaton Railways (1967), Atlantic Bridgehead (1968), Coaching City (1970), Cathedral City (1976), The Great Swinfen Case (1980), Loyal and Ancient City (1986), Lomax's Lichfield (1991), A History of Lichfield Operatic Society (jtly with Kathleen Simmons, 1993), Lichfield in Old Photographs (jtly with Kathleen Simmons, 1994), The Lilley-White Swann (with Kathleen Simmons, 1996); *Recreations* historic res, music, reading; *Style*— Howard Clayton, Esq; ✉ 2A Brownsfield Road, Lichfield, Staffs WS13 6BT (☎ 01543 255749)

CLAYTON, John Reginald William; *b* 3 Dec 1950; *Educ* King Edward VI Camp Hill Sch, Downing Coll Cambridge (MA Law, Rugby blue); *Career* co sec and dir Legal Secretariat Guardian Royal Exchange plc; admitted slr 1976; *Style*— John Clayton, Esq; ✉ Guardian Royal Exchange plc, Royal Exchange, London EC3V 3LS (☎ 0171 621 2468, fax 0171 696 5301)

CLAYTON, John Robert; CBE (1987); s of late John Clayton; *b* 29 March 1922; *Educ* Highgate, LSE; *m* 1, 1943 (m dis 1956), Doris Louise, *née* Usherwood; m 2, 1958, Aileen Bowen, *née* Morris (d 1981); m 3, 1984, Dr Jean Olive Boyton (d 1994), da of Ernest Marks (d 1978); 1 s; *Career* serv WWII, Capt RCS; industl advsr Fed Govt of Nigeria 1951–61; ptnr John Tyzack and Partners Ltd 1961–69, gp md Pauls and Whites plc (maltsters and animal feed gp) 1970–82; dir: Nat West Bank (SE Regnl Bd) 1974–89, Richard Clay and Co plc 1977–86, Dewe Rogerson Group Ltd 1981–95, IPSENTA Ltd 1982–89 (chm 1982–85); chm: Thurlow Nunn Holdings Ltd 1983–89, Agric Trg Bd 1983–89; memb Suffolk CC 1982–89 (vice chm Educn Ctee 1985–89); gen cmmr of Income Tax 1976–97; memb Ct: Cranfield Inst of Technol 1981–92, Univ of Essex 1987–90; jr memb Ct of Assts Worshipful Co of Glovers; MInstD, CIMgt; *Clubs* Oriental; *Style*— John R Clayton, Esq, CBE; ✉ Erie House, Hadleigh, Suffolk IP7 5AG (☎ 01473 823316)

CLAYTON, Prof Keith Martin; CBE; s of Edgar Francis Clayton (d 1978), and Constance Annie, *née* Clark (d 1985); *b* 25 Sept 1928; *Educ* Bedales Sch, Univ of Sheffield (BSc, MSc), Univ of London (PhD); *m* 1, 1950 (m dis 1976); m 2, 29 Dec 1976, Jennifer Nan; 3 s, 1 da; *Career* Nat Serv 2 Lt RE 1951–53; LSE 1953–67: asst lectr, lectr, reader; UEA Norwich: prof of environmental sciences 1967–93 (emeritus 1993), dean 1967–71, pro vice chllr 1971–73, dean 1987–93; Hon DSc Univ of Lancaster 1995; memb: Cncl NERC 1971–74, Univ Grants Ctee 1974–84, Ministerial Advsy Gp on Environment MOD 1989–, COMARE 1985–; patron's medal RGS 1989; *Recreations* gardening; *Style*— Prof Keith Clayton, CBE; ✉ Well Close, Pound Lane, Norwich NR7 OUA (☎ 01603 433780)

CLAYTON, Michael Aylwin; s of Aylwin Goff Clayton, of Bournemouth, Dorset, and Norah Kathleen Joan, *née* Banfield (d 1978); *b* 20 Nov 1934; *Educ* Bournemouth GS; *m* 1, Mary; 1 s (Marcus b 1967), 1 da (Maxine (Mrs Butler-Gallie) b 1965); m 2, 1979, Barbara J Ryman; m 3, 28 Oct 1988, Marilyn Crowhurst, da of Ernest George John Orrin; *Career* journalist, author, broadcaster; news corr BBC radio and TV 1965–73, ed Horse and Hound 1973–94; ed-in-chief 1994–: Horse and Hound, Country Life, Shooting Times, The Field, Eventing; main bd dir IPC Magazines plc 1994–; *Recreations* fox hunting; *Style*— Michael Clayton, Esq; ✉ IPC Magazines, King's Reach Tower, Stamford Street, London SE1 9LS

CLAYTON, Richard Anthony; s of Dennis Lloyd Clayton (d 1969), of London, and Patricia Estelle, *née* Morris; *b* 25 May 1954; *Educ* Westminster, New Coll Oxford; *m* 1 (m dis 1987); 2 s (Benjamin Daniel, Jack James); m 2, 27 April 1994, Anne Bernadette Burns; *Career* called to the Bar Middle Temple 1977; S Islington Law Centre 1980–82, Osler Hoskin & Harcourt Toronto Canada 1983; memb Ctee Legal Action Gp 1985–; *Books* Practise and Procedure at Industrial Tribunals (1986), Civil Actions Against the Police (2 edn, 1992), A Judicial Review Procedure (2 edn, 1996), Police Actions; a practical guide (2 edn, 1996); *Recreations* reading, theatre, cinema, travel; *Style*— Richard Clayton, Esq; ✉ Devereux Chambers, Temple, London WC2R 3JJ (☎ 0171 353 7534, fax 0171 353 1724)

CLAYTON, Robert; s of Colin Clayton, and Rose Ann Clayton; *b* 23 July 1970; *Educ* Wintringham Sch Grimsby, Grimsby Coll of Technol (BTEC); *partner* Victoria McTernan; *Career* commis chef Menage à Trois Restaurant 1988–89, demi chef Heath Lodge Hotel 1989–90, demi chef Chez Nico 1990–91, head chef Hunstrete House Hotel 1991–; *Awards* finalist Chef of the Year 1994 and 1995, second place Roux Scholarship 1996 (finalist 1994), AA 3 Rosettes 1995 and 1996, Michelin Star 1996; *Recreations* jogging, fly fishing; *Style*— Robert Clayton, Esq; ✉ Hunstrete House Hotel, Hunstrete, Chelwood BS18 4NS (☎ 01761 490490, fax 01761 490732)

CLAYTON-SMITH, David Charles; s of John Anthony Clayton-Smith, of Wall, Lichfield, Staffs, and Winifred Mary, *née* Elvy; *b* 5 Nov 1953; *Educ* St Chad's Cathedral Prep Sch, Malvern, Kingston Poly (BA), Dip in Accounting & Fin; *m* 7 Nov 1987, Katharine Clare, da of Dr Owen Jones; 2 da (Philippa Clare b 11 July 1989, Eleanor Jane b 23 Dec 1990); *Career* Courage Ltd: joined as grad trainee 1977, brand mangr Mktg Dept 1980–83, mktg ops mangr Mktg Dept 1983–85, dir of mktg (Take Home Trade) 1985–87, md (Take Home Trade) 1987–88, regnl sales dir E Region 1988–89, exec dir Sales & Mktg 1989–91, exec dir and gen mangr E Trading Region 1991–92, gp exec dir Mktg 1992–93; mktg and merchandise dir Do it All Ltd 1993–; memb: CBI Mktg Forum 1989–93, Exec Ctee Advtg Assoc 1989–90, Retail Ctee Brewers' Soc 1989–90; chm Ctee of Advtg Practice ASA 1996–; UK rep Supplies Ctee Int Confedn of Chain Store Ops; Freeman: Worshipful Co of Brewers 1990, City of London 1992; memb Mktg Soc 1985, FInstD 1991; *Recreations* family, gardening, motor racing; *Style*— David Clayton-Smith, Esq; ✉ Do it All Ltd, Falcon House, The Minories, Dudley, W Midlands DY2 8PG (☎ 01384 456456)

CLAYTON-WELCH, Anthony Roy; s of Flt Lt Roy Hector Welch, AFC, AE, of Flamstead, Herts, and Barbara Joan, *née* Clayton; *b* 5 Sept 1942; *Educ* St Albans Abbey Sch, Poly of Central London (DipArch), Carpenters Sch (scholarship); *m* 4 Feb 1967, Kathleen Margaret, da of Henry Samuel Norman, of Wembley Park, Middx; 1 s (Bruno b 20 Oct 1975), 1 da (Sophie b 27 Sept 1977); *Career* architect; TA Offr Trg Corps 1962–64; architectural conslt to Camus (GB) Ltd 1967–70, London ptnr Melich & Welch Florida USA 1970–74, fndn ptnr Renton Welch Partnership 1974–; adjudicator and ctee memb Royal Jubilee Tst and Prince's Tst; awards incl: Carpenters Award 1965, Civic Design Award 1987, Educational Award 1988, Environment and Access Awards 1991; educnl advsr: DfEE, DOW; vice chm Local Bd Sch Govrs St John's Sch Stanmore, appointed church architect Diocesan Advsy Cncl (DAC) 1996–; RIBA 1966, FInstD 1995; *Books* 3–D Structural Model Analysis of Space Frames (1967), Rationalised Constructions (1970), Herts CC Educational Building - An Appraisal 1942–70 (1986); *Recreations* tennis, chess, swimming, modelling, voice-overs; *Clubs* The Arts, Morton's, RAF, St Stephens; *Style*— Anthony Clayton-Welch, Esq; ✉ Brousings, The Grove, Stanmore Common, Middlesex HA7 4LD (☎ 0181 954 4625); Renton Welch Partnership, 12 Stucley Place, Camden Town, London NW1 8NS (☎ 0171 482 1418, fax 0171 482 1071)

CLEAL, Adam Anthony; s of Anthony Frederick Graham Cleal (d 1982), of Chelsea, and Yvonne Dallas, *née* Eskell; *b* 10 March 1956; *Educ* Allhallows Sch, Univ of Leeds (LLB); *m* 11 Aug 1984, Noreen, da of George Monger; 2 s (Charles Anthony b 16 Aug 1986, George Hugo b 22 Aug 1992), 1 da (Harriet Catherine b 14 March 1989); *Career* articled clerk 1979–81, slr 1982–91, ptnr Allen & Overy 1991–; Freeman City of London; memb: City of London Slrs' Co, Law Soc; *Recreations* scuba diving, cycling; *Clubs* Reform; *Style*— Adam Cleal, Esq; ✉ Allen & Overy, One New Change, London EC4M 9QQ (☎ 0171 330 3000, fax 0171 330 9999)

CLEARY, (Owen) Alistair; s of Bernard Cleary (d 1968), and Mary Weir, *née* Hamilton (d 1985); *b* 20 June 1931; *Educ* Leith Acad, Royal HS of Edinburgh, Univ of Edinburgh (MA, LLB); *m* 6 Aug 1960, (Elsie) Dylena, da of Adriaan Hendricus Stander Fourie (d 1960), and Susan Jessie, *née* Oosthuizen; 1 step da (Mrs Arlene Dawn Shuttleworth b 1951), 1 step s (Adrian James Cook b 1953), 1 da (Susan-Mary Hamilton Goldstone b 1966); *Career* slr and Notary Public; former dean of Faculty of Procurators of Caithness, former depute procurator fiscal of Caithness; currently clerk to Gen Cmmrs of Income Tax (Caithness Div); memb: Law Soc Scotland, Scottish Congregational Church, SNP, Christian Aid, Mission Without Borders, Release International, The Cliftonhill Soc; first Caithness Sportsman of the Year 1983; *Recreations* running (marathons 1981–86: Dublin, Loch Rannoch, Boston, Paris and Wild Coast (Natal SA), 4th (M 55–59) BVAF marathon, 2nd Over 60 Aberdeen half-marathon 1991, 1992 and 1993, Silver medals (200m, 400m and 1500m) Scottish Veteran Track and Field Championships 1986–92, watching rugby, athletics and Gaelic football, supporting Hibernian FC, East Fife FC, Albion Rovers FC, Boston Red Sox and Jed-Forest RFC, photography, writing poetry, political and religious articles and letters, reading, gardening, growing oak trees, classical music (Mahler, Vaughan-Williams, Nielsen), history and politics of Scotland, South Africa and USA, travel; *Clubs* Royal High Sch, Wick Academy FC, Caithness Harriers, WAGAC; *Style*— Alistair Cleary, Esq; ✉ Elangeni, 5 Upper Dunbar Street, Wick, Caithness KW1 5AN (☎ 01955 602447)

CLEASBY, John Victor; s of Thomas Victor Cleasby (d 1957), of Leeds, Yorkshire, and Grace, *née* Buckle (d 1974); *b* 4 Oct 1932; *Educ* Ludlow GS, Royal Sch of Mines, Univ of London (BSc, ARSM); *m* Sheila Ann, da of John Spencer Williams; 2 da (Tanya Deirdre b 22 Jan 1963, Julia Vikki b 9 Dec 1969); *Career* Nat Serv cmmnd RE 1955–57; gen underground experience Roan Antelope Copper Mines Ltd 1953–57, graduate trainee rising to underground mangr Vaal Reefs Gold Mining Co SA 1959–64, underground mangr rising to asst mangr Western Deep Levels Gold Mining Co S Africa 1964–68, project mangr for design and construction of Cleveland Potash Mine UK 1969–73, gen mangr De Beers Consolidated Mines Ltd S Africa 1973–76; 1976–89: consltg engr Anglo American Corp, consltg engr and head of Tech Dept and alternate dir Charter Consolidated plc, consltg engr Sierra Leone diamond mining ops De Beers, dir several mining and industl cos; private conslt 1989– (work for DTI, Cleveland Potash Ltd and several cos in the Far East); memb Cncl Inst of Mining and Metallurgy (chm Scholarships Ctee), tstee Mining Assoc, govr Camborne Sch of Mines; Consolidated Goldfields Gold Medal Inst of Mining and Metallurgy 1974, Metallurgy Silver Medal for best paper 1975; Freeman City of London 1990, Liveryman Worshipful Co of Engrs 1991; FEng 1984, FIMM; *Publications* papers: Shaft Sinking at Boulby Mine, Environmental Aspects of Boulby Mine, Availability of Strategic Minerals, Mining Practice in the Kimberley Division of De Beers Consolidated Mines Ltd; *Recreations* jogging; *Style*— John Cleasby, Esq, FEng; ✉ Moat Cottage, Pleshey, Essex CM3 1HG (☎ 01245 237202)

CLEAVE, Brian Elseley; CB (1994); s of Walter Edward Cleave (d 1986), and Hilda Lillian, *née* Newman (d 1974); *b* 3 Sept 1939; *Educ* Eastbourne Coll (Duke of Devonshire's scholar), Univ of Exeter (LLB, Lloyd Parry prize, Bracton prize), Kansas Univ, Univ of Manchester; *m* 10 Feb 1979, Celia Valentine, da of Maurice Lovel Burton Williams, MBE, and Patricia Williams; *Career* articled clerk Wilkinson, Howlett & Moorhouse 1963–66, student Coll of Law 1965–66, admitted slr 1966, asst slr Wilkinson, Howlett & Durham 1966–67; Solicitor's Office Inland Revenue: legal asst 1967–72, sr legal asst 1972–78, asst slr 1978–86, princ asst slr 1986–90, slr of Inland Revenue 1990–; FRSA 1995; *Recreations* travel, music, photography, theatre; *Style*— Brian Cleave, Esq, CB; ✉ Solicitor's Office, Inland Revenue, Somerset House, London WC2R 1LB (☎ 0171 438 6645, fax 0171 438 6653)

CLEAVER, Sir Anthony Brian; kt (1992); s of William Brian Cleaver (d 1969), and Dorothea Early Cleaver (d 1989); *b* 10 April 1938; *Educ* Berkhamsted Sch, Trinity Coll Oxford (MA); *m* 1962, Mary Teresa, *née* Cotter; 1 s (Paul Anthony b 31 Aug 1972), 1 da (Caroline b 14 Nov 1977); *Career* IBM United Kingdom Ltd: trainee instr 1962, conslt systems engr 1968, branch mangr 1969; asst to Vice Pres (Devpt) IBM World Trade Corporation USA 1973–74; IBM UK: dist mangr 1974–76, sales dir 1976–77, div dir 1977–80; IBM Europe: gp dir 1980, vice pres (Mktg and Servs) 1981–82; IBM UK: gen mangr 1982–86, chief exec 1986–92, chm 1990–94; chm: UK Atomic Energy Authy 1993–95, AEA Technology plc 1996–, General Cable 1995– (non-exec dir 1994–95); non-exec dir: General Accident Fire and Life Assurance Corporation plc 1988–, Smith & Nephew plc 1993–, Lockheed Martin Tactical Systems UK Ltd 1995–, The Cable Corporation 1995–; dir Nat Computing Centre 1977–80; memb Cncl: Templeton Coll Oxford 1982–93, Policy Studies Inst 1985–89, RIPA 1986–89; memb Bd: Centre for Econ & Environmental Devpt 1985– (dep chm 1989–), Assoc for Business Sponsorship of the Arts 1986–, ENO 1988–, American C of C 1987–90; chm Business In The Environment 1989–, dep chm Business in the Community 1992– (memb Pres's Ctee 1986–92); memb: Presidents' Ctee CBI 1988–92, BOTB 1988–91, Nat Trg Task Force 1989–92, ACBE 1991–93, NACETT 1994–; chm: RSA Inquiry into Tomorrow's Company 1992–95, Industl Devpt Advsy Bd 1993–, Independent Assessors of TECs 1994–; pres Classical Assoc 1995–96; chm of Govrs Birkbeck Coll Univ of London 1989–; UN Environment Prog Global 500 Roll of Honour 1989; Hon LLD: Univ of Nottingham 1991, Univ of

Portsmouth 1996; Hon DSc Cranfield Univ 1995; hon fell Trinity Coll Oxford 1989; FBCS 1976, FCIM (currently vice pres), Hon FCIPS 1996; *Recreations* music, opera, cricket, golf, skiing, reading; *Clubs* RAC, MCC, Lords Taverners; *Style*— Sir Anthony Cleaver; ✉ AEA Technology plc, 15 Lower Regent Street, London SW1Y 4LR (☎ 0171 389 6553, fax 0171 389 6570)

CLEAVER, Air Vice-Marshal Peter Charles; CB (1971), OBE (1945); s of William Henry Cleaver (d 1966), of Warwick; *b* 6 July 1919; *Educ* Warwick Sch, Coll of Aeronautics (MSc), Staff Coll Haifa, IDC; *m* 1948, Jean, da of John Edward Birkett Fairclough (d 1948), of Ledbury; 2 s; *Career* Offr cmdg RAF Swanton Morley 1962–63; AOEng: Flying Trg Cmd 1963–65, HQ FEAF 1967–69, Air Support Cmd 1969–72, ret; sec Cranfield Inst of Technol 1973–78; *Recreations* gardening, walking; *Clubs* RAF; *Style*— Air Vice-Marshal Peter Cleaver, CB, OBE; ✉ Willow House, Watling St, Little Brickhill, Milton Keynes, Bucks MK17 9LS

CLEAVER, William Benjamin; s of David John Cleaver (d 1963), of Rhondda, and Blodwen, *née* Miles (d 1948); *b* 15 Sept 1921; *Educ* Pentre GS Rhondda, Univ of Wales (BSc); *m* 1943, Mary Watkin, da of Watkin James (d 1951), of Dyfed; 1 s (John), 2 da (Pamela, Patricia); *Career* former mining engr; NCB: area gen mangr 1958–67, dep dir (mining) 1967–83, ret 1983; sec Contemporary Art Soc for Wales 1973–91, memb Cncl Nat Museum of Wales 1977–, vice chm Welsh Arts Cncl 1977–83, memb Arts Cncl of GB 1980–83, chm Cncl of Museums in Wales 1986–; Welsh Rugby Int 1947–50 (14 caps, Br Lion NZ and Aust 1950), fndr chm Welsh Youth Rugby Union 1949–57; FIMinE, OStJ; *Recreations* rugby football, fine arts, wine appreciation; *Clubs* Cardiff and County; *Style*— William Cleaver, Esq; ✉ 29 Lon-y-Deri, Rhiwbina, Cardiff CF4 6JN (☎ 01222 693242)

CLEDWYN OF PENRHOS, Baron (Life Peer UK 1979), of Holyhead in the Isle of Anglesey; Cledwyn Hughes; PC (1966), CH (1977); s of late Rev Henry David Hughes, of Frondeg, Holyhead, and Emily Hughes; *b* 14 Sept 1916; *Educ* Holyhead GS, Univ Coll of Wales Aberystwyth; *m* 1949, Jean Beatrice, JP, da of Capt Jesse Hughes, of Holyhead; 1 s (Hon Harri Cledwyn b 1955), 1 da (Hon Emily Ann (Hon Mrs Wright) b 1950); *Career* served RAFVR WWII; memb Anglesey CC 1946–52; admitted slr 1940; MP (Lab) Anglesey 1951–79 (also candidate 1945 and 1950), min of state for the Cwlth 1964–66, sec of state for Wales 1966–68, min of agric, fisheries and food 1968–70, oppn spokesman on agric, fisheries and food 1970–72, cmmr of House of Commons 1979, chm House of Lords Select Ctee on Agric and Food 1980–83, ldr of the Oppn in Lords 1982–92 (dep ldr 1981–82), oppn spokesman (Lords) on Civil Serv, foreign affrs and Welsh affrs 1983–92; chm PLP 1974–79; dir: Shell UK Ltd 1980–83, Anglesey Aluminium Ltd 1980–, Holyhead Towing Ltd 1980–; regnl advsr Midland Bank (with responsibilities for Wales) 1979–94; pro chllr Univ of Wales 1985–95; Alderman Anglesey CC 1973, memb Assoc of County Cncls 1980–, memb Political Honour Ctee 1992–; pres: Housing and Town Planning Cncl 1980–91, Age Concern Wales 1980–88, Soc of Welsh People Overseas 1980–89, UCW Aberystwyth 1976–85, Univ of Wales Bangor 1995–; Hon Freedom Beaumaris 1972, Freeman Borough of Anglesey 1976; Hon LLD: Univ of Wales 1970, Univ of Sheffield 1992, Univ of Glamorgan 1996; *Style*— The Rt Hon the Lord Cledwyn of Penrhos, PC, CH; ✉ Penmorfa, Trearddur, Holyhead, Gwynedd (☎ 01407 860544)

CLEERE, Dr Henry Forester; OBE (1992); s of Christopher Henry John Cleere (d 1981), of London, and Frances Eleanor, *née* King (d 1970); *b* 2 Dec 1926; *Educ* Beckenham GS, UCL (BA), Univ of London Inst of Archaeology (PhD); *m* 1, 1950 (m dis), Dorothy Percy; 1 s (Christopher), 1 da (Elizabeth); m 2, 1974, Pamela Joan, da of Stanley Vertue (d 1979), of Tadley, Hants; 2 da (Josephine, Catherine); *Career* archaeological heritage conslt; dep sec Iron and Steel Inst London 1952–71, industl devpt offr UN Industl Devpt Orgn Vienna 1972–73; archaeologist; dir Cncl Br Archaeology 1974–91 (hon vice pres 1994); memb Exec Ctee Int Cncl on Monuments and Sites (ICOMOS) 1981–90 (world heritage coordinator 1992–); pres: Wealden Iron Res Gp 1985–92, Sussex Archaeological Soc 1987–92 (vice pres 1994), Euro Forum of Heritage Assocs 1990–93; ed Antiquity 1992; hon visiting fell Univ of York 1988–, res fell Univ of Paris (Sorbonne) 1989, sec Euro Assoc of Archaeologists 1992–96; hon memb Inst of Field Archaeologists, fell UCL 1992, Hon DLitt Univ of Sussex 1993; FSA, FRSA, FIMgt; *Clubs* Athenaeum; *Style*— Dr Henry Cleere, OBE, FSA; ✉ Acres Rise, Lower Platts, Ticehurst, Wadhurst, E Sussex TN5 7DD (☎ and fax 01580 200752); 11 Rue Chapon, 75003 Paris, France (☎ 00 33 1 42719719)

CLEESE, John Marwood; s of Reginald Cleese (né Cheese), and Muriel Cleese; *b* 27 Oct 1939; *Educ* Downing Coll Cambridge (MA); *m* 1, 1968 (m dis 1978), Connie Booth; 1 da (Cynthia); m 2, 1981 (m dis 1990), Barbara Trentham; 1 da (Camilla); m 3, 1992, Alyce Faye Eichelberger, *qv*, formerly w of David Eichelberger; 2 step s; *Career* comedian, writer and actor; started making jokes professionally 1963, started on British TV 1966; fndr and former dir Video Arts Ltd; Hon LLD Univ of St Andrews; *Television* series incl: The Frost Report, At Last the 1948 Show, Monty Python's Flying Circus, Fawlty Towers, Look at the State We're In! (BBC) 1995; *Films* incl: Interlude, The Magic Christian, And Now For Something Completely Different, Monty Python and the Holy Grail, Romance with a Double Bass, Life of Brian, Privates on Parade, The Meaning of Life, Silverado, Clockwise, A Fish Called Wanda 1987, Erik the Viking, Frankenstein 1993, Jungle Book 1994, Fierce Creatures 1995; *Books* Families and How to Survive Them (with Dr Robin Skynner, *qv*, 1983), The Golden Skits of Wing Commander Muriel Volestrangler FRHS and Bar (1984), The Complete Fawlty Towers (with Connie Booth, 1989), Life and How to Survive It (with Dr Robin Skynner, *qv*, 1993); *Recreations* gluttony and sloth; *Style*— John Cleese, Esq; ✉ c/o David Wilkinson Associates, 115 Hazlebury Road, London SW6 2LX (☎ 0171 371 5188, fax 0171 731 5161)

CLEGG, Prof Arthur Bradbury; s of Frederick Bradbury Clegg (d 1970), and Beatrice, *née* Andrew (d 1980); *b* 15 March 1929; *Educ* Birkenhead Sch, King's Coll Cambridge (BA, PhD, MA); *m* 23 Oct 1956, Marguerite, da of Arthur G Davis (d 1958); 1 s (Peter David b 30 March 1962), 1 da (Karen Marguerite (Mrs Coumbe) b 21 April 1960); *Career* res fell California Inst of Technol 1955–58, sr res offr Dept of Nuclear Physics Univ of Oxford 1958–66, sr res fell Jesus Coll Oxford 1964–66, prof of nuclear physics Univ of Lancaster 1966–96; writer numerous res papers; memb: Nuclear Physics Bd Sci Res Cncl 1969–73, Particle Physics Ctee Sci and Engrg Res Cncl 1986–89; FInstP 1966; *Books* High Energy Nuclear Reactions (1964); *Recreations* fell walking; *Style*— Prof Arthur Clegg; ✉ Strawberry Bank, Westbourne Rd, Lancaster, Lancs LA1 5EF (☎ 01524 69797); University of Lancaster, Department of Physics, Lancaster, Lancs LA1 4YB (☎ 01524 593614, fax 01524 844037, e-mail a.clegg@lancaster.ac.uk)

CLEGG, Jeremy Paul Jermyn; s of Maj Benjamin Beattie Clegg, MC (d 1993), of The Lawn, Ridgeway, nr Sheffield, and Rosemary Anne, *née* Coles (d 1955); *b* 11 July 1948; *Educ* St Anselms Bakewell, Fettes, Univ of Sussex (BSc); *m* 24 March 1973, Marilyn Anne, da of Edward Towndrow, of Barnet, Herts; 1 s (Oliver b 14 Feb 1980), 1 da (Anna-Louise b 6 March 1978); *Career* Commercial Union 1970–74, Leslie & Godwin 1974–82, MPA Ltd 1982–86; dir: Baring Investment Management (Baring Brothers & Co) 1986–90, Henderson Pension Fund Management (Henderson Administration plc) 1990–95; a vice pres J P Morgan Investment Management Inc 1995–; *Recreations* golf, tennis, photography; *Style*— Jeremy Clegg, Esq; ✉ The Moorings, Bowling Alley, Crondall, Farnham, Surrey GU10 5RN (☎ and fax 01252 850229); J P Morgan Investment Management Inc, 28 King Street, London SW1Y 6XA (☎ 0171 451 8131, fax 0171 451 8033, e-mail clegg_jeremy@jpmorgan.com)

CLEGG, John Fawcett; s of Lt Henry Fawcett Clegg (d 1960), and Vera Mary, *née* Fricker; *b* 24 May 1939; *Educ* Rugby, St John's Coll Cambridge (MA, MB BChir); *m* 18 Oct 1969, Hilary Mary, da of Philip Crabtree; 3 da (Alison Margaret b 9 July 1970, Fiona Louise b 26 April 1973, Charlotte Elizabeth b 15 March 1975); *Career* William Clarke meml fell Hammersmith Hosp London 1965–67, registrar in surgery Davyhulme Park Hosp Manchester 1968, sr registrar Manchester Royal Infirmary 1969–72, conslt surgn Leighton Hosp 1973–, examiner in surgery RCSE; memb: Cncl Assoc Surgns GB and Ireland, Manchester Med Soc, Liverpool and NW Surgical Soc (pres); memb Manchester Med Soc; memb RSM, FRCS, FRCSEd, memb Société Int de Chirurgie; *Recreations* golf, historical literature; *Clubs* Sandway Golf; *Style*— John Clegg, Esq; ✉ Leighton Hospital, Crewe, Cheshire (☎ 01270 255141, car 0860 631113)

CLEGG, Nicholas Peter; s of Dr Hugh Anthony Clegg, CBE (d 1983); *b* 24 May 1936; *Educ* Bryanston, Trinity Coll Cambridge (BA); *m* 1959, Hermance, da of Herman van den Wall Bake; 3 s, 1 da; *Career* banker; with Royal Netherlands Blast Furnaces and Steelworks 1960–62, Proctor and Gamble Brussels 1962–64; dir Hill Samuel and Co Ltd 1970–86; currently advsr Daiwa Europe Ltd (joined as an md 1986, subsquently chm), chm Daiwa Europe Bank 1993–; *Recreations* gardening, skiing, listening to music; *Style*— Nicholas P Clegg, Esq; ✉ Daiwa Europe Ltd, 5 King William St, London EC4N 7AX (☎ 0171 548 8004, fax 0171 929 5717)

CLEGG, His Hon Judge; Philip Charles; s of Charles Ward, and Patricia Doreen, Clegg, of Thornton-Cleveleys, Lancashire; *b* 17 Oct 1942; *Educ* Rossall Sch Fleetwood Lancs, Univ of Bristol (LLB, memb Vintage Austin Trans-Africa Expdn 1963); *m* 11 Sept 1965 (m dis 1996), Caroline Frances, da of Oscar Madley Peall; 2 da (Olivia Doreen b 31 March 1967, Madeleine Flora b 28 July 1973), 1 s (Francis Philip Henry Peall b 22 April 1970); *Career* called to the Bar Middle Temple 1966, practiced in Manchester on Northern Circuit 1966–87, recorder 1980–87, circuit judge (Northern Circuit) 1987–90, circuit judge (SE Circuit) 1990–; *Recreations* vintage cars and sailing; *Style*— His Hon Judge Clegg; ✉ Basildon Combined Court, The Gore, Basildon, Essex SS14 2EU

CLEGG, Richard Ninian Barwick; QC (1979); o s of Sir Cuthbert Barwick Clegg, TD, JP (d 1986), and Helen Margaret, *née* Jefferson (d 1987); *b* 28 June 1938; *Educ* Charterhouse, Trinity Coll Oxford (MA); *m* 3 Aug 1963, Katherine Veronica, da of Andrew Archibald Henry Douglas, of Ashley, Shalbourne, Wilts; 2 s (Aidan b 1966, Sebastian b 1969), 1 da (Flavia b 1968); *Career* called to the Bar Inner Temple 1960; bencher 1985, recorder of the Crown Court 1978–83; chm NW Section Bow Gp 1964–66, vice chm Bow Gp 1965–66, chm Winston Circle 1965–66, pres Heywood and Royton Cons Assoc 1965–68; capt Oxford Pentathlon Team 1959; *Recreations* hunting, shooting, fishing, skiing, travel, music, books; *Clubs* Lansdowne; *Style*— Richard Clegg, Esq, QC; ✉ The Old Rectory, Brereton, via Sandbach, Cheshire (☎ 01477 532358)

CLEGG, William; QC (1991); s of Peter Hepworth Clegg, and Sheila, *née* Needham; *b* 5 Sept 1949; *Educ* St Thomas Moore HS for Boys, Univ of Bristol (LLB); *m* 5 Oct 1974, Wendy Doreen, da of George Chard; 1 s (Peter William Christopher), 1 da (Joanna Sheila); *Career* called to the Bar Gray's Inn 1972, in practice SE Circuit, memb SE Circuit Ctee 1990–, recorder of the Crown Court 1992–; *Recreations* squash, cricket; *Clubs* Sudbury Racquets; *Style*— William Clegg, Esq, QC; ✉ 3 Hare Court, Temple, London EC4Y 7BJ (☎ 0171 353 7561, fax 0171 353 7741)

CLEGG-HILL, Peter David Raymond Charles; s of Maj Hon Frederic Raymond Clegg-Hill (ka 1945), 2 s of 6 Viscount Hill, and Hon Mrs Frederic Clegg-Hill; hp to Viscountcy of cous, 8 Viscount Hill, *qv*; *b* 17 Oct 1945, (posthumously); *Educ* Tabley House Sch; *m* 1973, Sharon Ruth Deane, of NZ; 2 s (Paul Andrew Raymond b 1979, Michael Charles David b 1988), 5 da (Catherine b 1974, Jennifer b 1976, Susan b 1980, Rachel b 1984, Melissa b 1986); *Career* farmer; *Style*— Peter Clegg-Hill, Esq; ✉ The Old Forge, Stone-in-Oxney, Tenterden, Kent

CLELLAND, David Gordon; MP (Lab) Tyne Bridge (majority 15,210); s of Archibald (Clem) Clelland, of 157 Avenue Rd, Gateshead, and Ellen, *née* Butchart; *b* 27 June 1943; *Educ* Kelvin Grove Boys Sch Gateshead, Gateshead and Hebburn Tech Coll; *m* 31 March 1965, Maureen, da of William Potts; 2 da (Jillian, Vicki); *Career* apprentice electrical fitter 1959–64, electrical tester 1964–81; shop steward AEU 1965–79, memb Works Ctee, sec Combine Ctee, sec Health and Safety Ctee; memb Lab Party 1970–, Parly candidate Gateshead West 1983, MP (Lab) Tyne Bridge 1985–; memb Gateshead Cncl 1972–86 (chm Parks and Recreation Ctee 1976–84, leader 1984–86); nat sec Assoc of Cncllrs 1981–86; *Recreations* golf, music, reading; *Style*— David Clelland, Esq, MP; ✉ House of Commons, Westminster, London SW1A OAA

CLEMENCE, John Alistair; CBE (1996), TD (1972); s of L A Clemence (d 1978), of Bexhill on Sea, and Helen, *née* Gillies (d 1982); *b* 17 May 1937; *Educ* Tonbridge, Cutlers' Co Capt Boot scholar; *m* 8 April 1967, Heather May Kerr, da of Canon C J Offer (d 1964), of Ightham, Kent; 3 s (William b 1969, James b 1970, Jonathan b 1973); *Career* Nat Serv Seaforth Highlanders 1956–58, 2 Lt 1957; London Scottish Regt TA 1959–67, Lt 1959, Capt 1963, Regtl Col 1989–95; 51 Highland Volunteers 1967–72, Maj 1970, Dep Hon Col 1 Bn 1989–93, Dep Hon Col The London Regt 1993–95; CA; ptnr BDO Stoy Hayward (and predecessor firms) 1966–; Liveryman Worshipful Co of Skinners 1969; FCA, FInstD, FIMgt, fndr memb Soc of Business Valuers, TEP; *Recreations* gardening; *Clubs* Army and Navy; *Style*— J A Clemence, Esq, CBE, TD; ✉ Bassetts, Mill Lane, Hildenborough, Kent TN11 9LX; BDO Stoy Hayward, 8 Baker Street, London W1M 1DA (☎ 0171 486 5888)

CLEMENCE, Raymond Neal (Ray); MBE; s of William Percy Clemence, and Muriel May, *née* Scott; *b* 5 Aug 1948; *Educ* Lumley Secdy Modern Skegness; *m* Veronica Mary, da of Donald Gillespie; 2 da (Sarah Jayne b 19 Nov 1973, Julie Maria b 17 Dec 1974), 1 s (Stephen Neal b 31 March 1978); *Career* former professional footballer (goalkeeper), football mangr and currently coach; player: Scunthorpe Utd 1965–67, Liverpool FC 1967–81, Tottenham Hotspur FC 1981–88; over 1200 first team appearances in total; hons with Liverpool: 5 League Championships, 3 European Cups, 2 UEFA Cups, 1 FA Cup, 1 League Cup; hons with Tottenham Hotspur: 1 FA Cup, 1 UEFA Cup; 61 full caps (4 under-23 caps); first team coach Tottenham Hotspur until 1993, mangr Barnet FC 1994–96, memb England coaching staff (goalkeeping) 1996–; *Recreations* golf, badminton; *Style*— Ray Clemence, Esq, MBE; ✉ The Football Association, 16 Lancaster Gate, London W2 3LW

CLEMENS, Brian Horace; s of Albert George Clemens (d 1987), of Ampthill, Beds, and Susannah, *née* O'Grady; *b* 30 July 1931; *m* 1, (m dis 1964), Brenda, *née* Prior; m 2, 23 Nov 1979, Janet Elizabeth, da of Filory Loveday East (d 1985), of Bushey Heath, Herts; 2 s (Samuel Joshua Twain b 16 Aug 1980, George Barnaby Langhorne b 14 Dec 1982); *Career* Nat Serv RAOC 1949–51; TV series: prodr and writer The Avengers 1964–70, prodr and writer The New Avengers 1976–78, creator My Wife Next Door 1975 (BAFTA Award), creator prodr and writer The Professionals 1978–82, creator and writer Blueblood 1988–89, series conslt Bugs (BBC) 1995; feature films: writer Blind Terror/See No Evil 1973 (Edgar Alan Poe Award), prodr and writer Dr Jekyll and Sister Hyde 1973 (Cinema Fantastique Award), writer prodr and dir Captain Kronos 1973, writer Golden Voyage of Sinbad 1974 (Fantasy Film Award); writer teleplay Scene of the Crime 1968 (Edgar Alan Poe Award; writer stage plays: Shock 1969, Edge of Darkness 1974, Sting in the Tale 1984, Inside Job 1988; co-prodr The Wicked Stage (amateur prodns to aid nominated charities); memb Writers Guilds of GB and America; *Books* Rabbit Pie (1990); *Recreations* writing, walking, wine, Ferrari cars; *Style*— Brian Clemens, Esq; ✉ Park Farm Cottage, Ampthill, Beds (☎ 01525 402215, fax 01525

402954); Flat 6, 5 Talbot Square, London W2; El Cortijo Viejo, Jesus Pobre, Denia, Alicante, Spain

CLEMENT, Anthony; s of Malcolm David Clement, of Birchgrove, Swansea, and Dorothy May, *née* Mann; *b* 8 Feb 1967; *Educ* Llansamlet Jr Comp Sch, Morriston Sr Comp Sch, Neath Tertiary Coll; *m* 14 July 1990, Debra, da of Byron Griffiths; *Career* rugby union player (mainly full-back); former rep: Swansea schs under 13, 14 and 15, Morriston youth under 19; over 250 appearances Swansea 1985–; Wales: former youth, under 20 (capt), under 21 and B player, full debut v America 1987 (centre), Five Nations debut v England 1988 (full-back), World Cup squad 1995, 37 full caps; other teams: 4 appearances Barbarians, 2 appearances World XV 1989, memb British Lions' team touring Australia 1989 and NZ 1993; awards: Man of the Match Welsh Schweppes Final 1987, Welsh Supporters Back of the Year 1991–92, Swansea Player of the Year 1991–92, Best Int Back BBC Rugby Special Wales 1991–92; contract hire conslt; *Recreations* football, gardening, reading; *Style*— Anthony Clement, Esq; ✉ Swansea Cricket and Football Club, St Helen's Ground, Brynmill Rd, Swansea, W Glamorgan (☎ 01792 466593)

CLEMENT, Barrie John; s of William George Clement (d 1983), and Amy Enid, *née* Parry (d 1986); *b* 21 Sept 1947; *Educ* Neath GS S Wales, Univ of Aston Birmingham (BSc), UC Cardiff (Post Grad Dip in Journalism); *m* Dec 1973, Susan Margaret, da of Alexander James Lane; 3 s (Matthew b 16 Nov 1977, Gareth b 8 Jan 1980, Jonathan b 18 Aug 1984); *Career* Kent Messenger Group 1972–75: gen news reporter then sub-ed Kent Messenger, gen news reporter then sub-ed Kent Evening Post; chief City sub-ed and feature writer Sunday Telegraph 1975–82; The Times 1982–86: dep busines features ed, City reporter, labour reporter; freelance journalist Jan-July 1986; The Independent Aug 1986–: labour reporter, labour corr, currently labour ed; memb NUJ; *Recreations* children, classical music and jazz, rugby, eating hot curries; *Style*— Barrie Clement, Esq; ✉ The Independent, 1 Canada Square, Canary Wharf, London E14 5DL (☎ 0171 293 2000, fax 0171 293 2435)

CLEMENT, John; s of Frederick Clement, and Alice Eleanor Clement; *b* 18 May 1932; *Educ* Bishop's Stortford Coll; *m* 1956, Elisabeth Anne, *née* Emery; 2 s (John Emery b 6 April 1959, Richard Frederick b 10 Dec 1965), 1 da (Anne Catherine Bloomfield b 4 June 1957); *Career* Howard Dairies Westcliff on Sea 1949–64, United Dairies London Ltd 1964–69, asst md Rank Leisure Services Ltd 1969–73, chm and chief exec Unigate plc 1976–91; chm: NV Verenigde Bedrijven Nutricia 1981–92, The Littlewoods Organisation plc 1982–90, Culpho Consultants 1991–, Tuddenham Hall Foods 1991–, Anglo American Insurance Co Ltd 1993–94 (dir 1991–94), Ransomes plc 1993–, Nat Car Auctions Group Ltd 1995–; dir: Eagle Star Holdings 1981–84, Jarvis Hotels Ltd 1993–, Kleinwort Second Endowment Policy Trust plc 1994–; memb Securities & Investments Bd 1986–89; chm: Children's Liver Disease Fndn 1982–95, Br Liver Tst 1992–, King's Coll Cambridge I, II, III and IV (business expansion scheme) 1993–; *Recreations* shooting, sailing, bridge, rugby, tennis, farming; *Clubs* Farmers', London Welsh RFC, Cumberland Lawn Tennis, Royal Harwich Yacht; *Style*— John Clement, Esq; ✉ Tuddenham Hall, Tuddenham, Ipswich, Suffolk IP6 9DD (☎ 01473 785217, fax 01473 785405)

CLEMENT, Dr Michele Ingrid; da of Maj Joseph Cyril Clement (d 1984), and Joyce Mona Clement; *b* 18 Sept 1951; *Educ* Queenswood Sch, UCL (BSc), UCH (MB BS); *m* 30 May 1981, Timothy Henry Corn, s of Harold Henry Corn (d 1985); 2 s (Edward Harry b 1983, Charles Joseph b 1985); *Career* med qualifications and house post UCH; jr med posts: King's Coll Hosp 1977–78, UCH 1978–79; dermatology trg: St John's Hosp 1980, King's Coll Hosp 1980–87; conslt dermatologist Bromley Hosps NHS Tst 1987–; FRCP 1994 (MRCP 1978); *Books* Topical Steroids for Skin Disorders (1987); *Style*— Dr Michele Clement; ✉ Dermatology Department, Orpington Hospital, Sevenoaks Road, Orpington, Kent BR6 9JU (☎ 01689 815261)

CLEMENT-JONES, Timothy Francis; CBE (1988); s of Maurice Llewelyn Clement-Jones (d 1988), of Haywards Heath, Sussex, and Margaret Jean, *née* Hudson; *b* 26 Oct 1949; *Educ* Haileybury, Trinity Coll Cambridge (MA); *m* 1, 14 June 1973, Dr Vicky Veronica Clement-Jones (d 1987), fndr of Br Assoc of Cancer Utd Patients, da of Teddy Yip, of Hong Kong; m 2, 15 July 1994, Jean Roberta Whiteside; *Career* slr; articled clerk Coward Chance 1972–74, assoc Joynson-Hicks & Co 1974–76, corp lawyer Letraset Int Ltd 1976–80, asst head (later head) Legal Servs LWT Ltd 1980–83, legal dir retailing div Grand Met plc 1984–86, gp co sec and legal advsr Kingfisher plc (formerly Woolworth Hldgs plc) 1986–95; vice pres Eurocommerce (Euro Retail Fedn) 1992–95; chm: Assoc of Lib Lawyers 1982–86, Lib Pty 1986–88; Liberal Democrats: chm Fed Fin Ctee 1991–, dir Euro Election Campaign 1992–94, dep chm Gen Election Group 1994–; tstee Br Assoc of Cancer Utd Patients, chm Crime Concern Advsy Bd 1981–95; memb Law Soc; *Recreations* walking, skiing, riding, travelling, reading, eating, talking; *Clubs* National Liberal, RAC; *Style*— Timothy Clement-Jones, Esq, CBE; ✉ 10 Northbourne Rd, London SW4 7DJ (☎ 0171 622 4205, fax 0171 627 0556)

CLEMENTI, David Cecil; s of Air Vice-Marshal Cresswell Montagu Clementi, CB, CBE, and Susan, da of late Sir (Edward) Henry Pelham, KCB; gs of Sir Cecil Clementi, GCMG (d 1947); *b* 25 Feb 1949; *Educ* Winchester, Univ of Oxford (MA), Harvard Business Sch (MBA); *m* 23 Sept 1972, Sarah Louise (Sally), da of Dr Anthony Beach Cowley; 1 s (Tom b 17 April 1979), 1 da (Anna b 26 Nov 1976); *Career* with Arthur Andersen & Co 1970–73; qualified as CA 1973; Kleinwort Benson Ltd: joined 1975, dir 1981–, chief exec 1994–; non-exec dir Thames Water plc 1997–; memb Worshipful Co of Mercers; FCA; *Recreations* sailing; *Style*— David C Clementi, Esq; ✉ Kleinwort Benson Ltd, 20 Fenchurch St, London EC3P 3DB (☎ 0171 623 8000)

CLEMENTS, Alan William; CBE (1990); *b* 1928; *Educ* Culford Sch Bury St Edmunds, Univ of Oxford (BA); *Career* inspr of taxes Inland Revenue 1952–56; ICI 1956–90: memb Treasy Dept rising to gp fin dir 1979 then overseer Investor Rels and Acquisitions Team; non-exec chm: David S Smith (Holdings) PLC 1991–, Cementone plc; non-exec dep chm Mirror Group PLC; former dir: Trafalgar House PLC, Cable & Wireless PLC, Guinness Mahon Holdings PLC, Brent Walker Group PLC, Granada Group PLC; FCT (fndr pres); *Style*— Alan Clements, Esq, CBE; ✉ David S Smith (Holdings) plc, 16 Great Peter Street, London SW1P 2BX (☎ 0171 222 8855, fax 0171 222 8856)

CLEMENTS, Judi; *b* 27 June 1953; *Educ* Nelson Tomlinson Sch Wigton Cumberland, Univ of Birmingham (LLB), Brunel Univ (MA), Dip Inst of Housing, London Business Sch (Exec Programme Cert), Civil Serv/Cabinet Office (Top Mgmnt Programme); *Career* London Borough of Camden: estate mangr 1974–76, sr estate mangr 1976–78, sabbatical (Masters Degree, sponsored) 1978–79, tenancy servs offr and actg dep dist housing offr 1979–81, business systems analyst 1981–82, asst dir of housing (Estate Mgmnt) 1982–87; dep borough housing mangr Brighton Borough Cncl 1987–91, head of mgmnt practice Local Govt Mgmnt Bd 1991–92, chief exec/nat dir Mind (Nat Assoc for Mental Health) 1992–; fndr memb Women in Local Govt Network 1987, memb London Business Sch Alumni (and LBS Women in Business Gp), memb Narwal Inst City Univ; *Style*— Ms Judi Clements; ✉ 43 Sutton Square, Urswick Road, Hackney, London E9 6EQ (☎ 0181 533 4161); National Director, Mind, Granta House, 15–19 Broadway, Stratford, London E15 4BQ (☎ 0181 519 2122, fax 0181 522 1725)

CLEMENTS, Nicholas David Beckwith (Nick); s of Desmond Lyle Clements, of West Park Cottage, Gulval, Cornwall, and Rosemary Jill, *née* Beckwith; *b* 11 Nov 1958; *Educ* Rossall Sch Lancs, John Moores Univ Liverpool; *Career* Euro retail buyer Transocean Group 1979–81, media planner/buyer rising to account mangr Tony Rowse Media 1981–85, sr account mangr Foote Cone and Belding 1985–87, client servs dir/int business dir S P Lintas 1987–95, int bd account dir Bates Dorland 1995–; MIPA 1993, memb D&AD 1993; tstee CRISIS; *Recreations* cricket, riding; *Style*— Nick Clements, Esq; ✉ Bates Dorland Ltd, 121–141 Westbourne Terrace, London W2 6JR (☎ 0171 262 5077)

CLEMENTS, Paul Michael; s of Stanley Clements, and Edna, *née* Garber; *b* 29 April 1953; *Educ* Haberdashers' Aske's, Univ of Birmingham (LLB); *m* 1, 4 June 1983 (m dis 1995), Pamela Anne, da of Robert David Poulton Hughes; 1 s (Simon Lewis b 11 June 1985); m 2, 1 June 1996, Melinda, da of John Pinfold; *Career* admitted slr 1977; litigation asst Bird & Bird 1977–79; Radcliffes Crossman Block (Crossman Block & Keith until 1988, Withers Crossman Block 1988–89, Crossman Block 1989–95): litigation asst 1979–80, salaried ptnr 1980–84, equity ptnr 1985–, head Litigation Dept 1988–89 and 1991–, managing ptnr 1989–91; asst recorder of the Crown Ct 1992–; memb: City of Westminster Law Soc, London Solicitors' Litigation Assoc; memb Law Soc; *Recreations* amateur drama participant, rugby, opera, classical music; *Style*— Paul M Clements, Esq; ✉ Radcliffes Crossman Block Solicitors, 5 Great College Street, Westminster, London SW1P 3SJ (☎ 0171 222 7040, fax 0171 222 6208)

CLEMENTS, Philip Alexander; s of Ronald Alexander Clements, of Canterbury, Kent, and Phyllis Clements; *b* 27 July 1958; *Educ* Simon Langton GS Canterbury, Canterbury Coll of Art (BA); *m* Maria Anne, da of Derek Herring; 2 s (Thomas Alexander b 2 Oct 1988, Jack Alexander b 9 June 1991); *Career* jr designer J Sainsbury plc 1980–82, packaging designer Allied International Designers 1982–88, assoc creative dir Design Bridge Ltd 1988–92; clients incl: Sharwoods, Unilever, Brooke Bond, Oxo, Terrys, Reed International; fndr Clements & Co design consultancy 1992–; *Style*— Philip Clements, Esq

CLEMENTS, Roger Varley; s of Harold William Clements (d 1993), of Harpole, Northampton, and Rose Maud, *née* Smith (d 1978); *b* 26 Feb 1936; *Educ* St Lawrence Coll Ramsgate, CCC Oxford (BA, MA, BM BCh), UCH London; *m* 1, 10 Sept 1959 (m dis 1967), Clemency Mary Holme, da of Thomas Fox; m 2, 1971, Charlotte Susan, da of Maj Charles Robins (d 1995), of Leasowe, Wirral; 1 s (Charles Maxwell b 29 March 1974), 1 da ((Esther) Lucy b 27 Feb 1976); *Career* conslt obstetrician and gynaecologist N Middx Hosp London 1973–94 (clinical dir 1988–91), hon gynaecologist Hammersmith Hosp London and hon lectr in obstetrics and gynaecology Royal Free Hosp Sch of Med London 1990–94, chm Dist Med Advsy Ctee Haringey Health Authy 1988–91, med exec dir N Middx NHS Tst 1991–94; clinical risk mgmnt conslt QRM Health Care Ltd 1994–, ed-in-chief Clinical Risk 1994–; asst prof UK Faculty St George's Med Sch Grenada W Indies; author of papers on central venous pressure monitoring in obstetrics, infertility, high risk pregnancy, osteomalacia in pregnancy, medical negligence and risk mgmnt; examiner: Central Midwives Bd, Conjoint Bd, RCOG, Univ of London (Royal Free), Univ of Ibadan Nigeria, W African Coll of Surgns, Post Grad Coll of Nigeria; Freeman City of London 1984; Liveryman: Worshipful Soc of Apothecaries London 1983, Worshipful Co of Barbers London 1986; memb BMA; FRSM, FRCSEd, FRCOG, FAE; *Books* First Baby After 30 (1985), Safe Practice in Obstetrics and Gynaecology: A Medico-Legal Handbook (1994); *Recreations* cricket, opera; *Clubs* MCC, Savile; *Style*— Roger V Clements, Esq; ✉ 111 Harley St, London W1N 1DG (☎ 0171 486 1781, 0171 637 0701, fax 0171 224 3852, car 0860 499 349)

CLEMENTS, Col William Holliwell; s of Henry Clements (d 1993), and Gladys Nellie, *née* Atkinson; *b* 9 March 1937; *Educ* Campbell Coll Belfast, The Queen's Univ of Belfast (LLB); *m* 16 Dec 1961, Elizabeth, da of Cochrane Morrison (d 1991); 2 s (Nicholas William Simon b 13 Aug 1963, Andrew Timothy Michael b 27 March 1968), 1 da (Jessica Jane b 28 April 1966); *Career* cmmnd Royal Ulster Rifles 1960, Aust Staff Coll 1969, instr RMC Duntroon Aust 1974–76, Co 1 Bn Royal Irish Rangers 1976–78, asst mil sec MOD 1978–81, instr Nigerian Armed Forces Staff Coll 1981–83; def mil and air attaché Br Embassy: Peking 1985–88, Rangoon 1990–92; md Sino-Myanmar Consultants 1992–; dir Abercorn Trading Ltd; sec The Dorneywood Tst; memb: RSAA, China-Br Centre; *Recreations* travel, history, shooting, Chinese snuff bottles; *Style*— Col William Clements; ✉ 6 Lanark Place, London W9 1BS

CLEMINSON, Sir James Arnold Stacey; KBE (1990), kt (1982), MC (1945), DL (Norfolk 1983); s of late Arnold Russel Cleminson, JP, himself sometime chm Reckitt and Colman, and Florence, da of James Stacey, of New Zealand; *b* 31 Aug 1921; *Educ* Rugby; *m* 1950, Helen Juliet Measor; 1 s, 2 da; *Career* served WWII Para Regt; Reckitt and Colman Ltd: joined 1946, dir overseas co 1957, chief exec 1973–80, chm 1977–86; chm Jeyes Hygiene plc 1985–89; vice chm: Norwich Union Life Insurance Society Ltd 1983–92 (dir 1979–92), Norwich Union Fire Insurance Society Ltd, Scottish Union & National Insurance Co (subsids of Norwich Union Life Insurance); non-exec dir: United Biscuits (Holdings) plc 1982–89, Eastern Counties Newspaper Group 1986–93, Fenners plc 1989–97 (dep chm 1993–97), Riggs National Corp 1991–93, Riggs AP Bank Ltd 1985– (non-exec chm 1986–91); pres: Food Mfrs Fedn 1980–82, Endeavour Trg 1984–; chm: Food and Drink Industs Cncl 1983–84, BOTB 1986–90, Nurses Pay Bd 1986–90; memb CBI Cncl 1978– (pres 1984–86); pro-chllr Univ of Hull 1985–94, chm Theatre Royal Norwich Tst 1991–; pres Norfolk Branch SSAFA 1994–; hon fell RCGP, Hon LLD Univ of Hull 1985; *Recreations* field sports, golf; *Clubs* Boodle's, Sloane; *Style*— Sir James Cleminson, KBE, MC, DL; ✉ Loddon Hall, Hales, Norfolk (☎ 01508 520717, fax 01508 528557)

CLEOBURY, Nicholas Randall; s of Dr John Frank Cleobury, of Lower Hardes, Canterbury, Kent, and Brenda Julie, *née* Randall; *b* 23 June 1950; *Educ* King's Sch Worcester, Worcester Coll Oxford (MA); *m* 4 Nov 1978, Heather Noelle, da of Noel Kay (d 1981), of Upper Poppleton, York; 1 s (Simon Randall b 23 Oct 1979), 1 da (Sophie Noelle b 12 Dec 1981); *Career* asst organist: Chichester Cathedral 1971–72, Christ Church Oxford 1972–76; chorus master Glyndebourne Opera 1977–79, asst dir BBC Singers 1978–80, princ conductor of opera RAM 1981–87, dir Aquarius 1983–92, artistic dir Cambridge Festival 1992, music dir Broomhill 1990–94; 1980–: int conductor working throughout UK, Europe, Scandinavia, USA and Australia, regular TV and BBC Radio and Prom appearances, numerous commercial recordings; princ guest conductor Gävle Orch (Sweden) 1989–91, princ conductor Britten Sinfonia 1991–, guest conductor Zurich Opera House; FRCO 1968; hon RAM 1985; *Recreations* cricket, reading, walking, food, wine; *Clubs* Savage, Lord's Taverners; *Style*— Nicholas Cleobury, Esq; ✉ China Cottage, Church Lane, Petham, Canterbury, Kent CT4 5RD (☎ 01227 700584, fax 01227 700827)

CLEOBURY, Stephen John; s of Dr John Frank Cleobury, of Croft House, Street End, Lower Hardres, Canterbury, and Brenda Julie, *née* Randall; *b* 31 Dec 1948; *Educ* King's Sch Worcester, St John's Coll Cambridge (MA, MusB); *m* 3 July 1971, Penelope Jane, da of William Francis Holloway (d 1984); 2 da (Suzannah Helen b 1973, Laura Elizabeth b 1976); *Career* organist St Matthew's Church Northampton, dir of Music Northampton GS 1971–74, sub-organist Westminster Abbey 1974–78, master of music Westminster Cathedral 1979–82, fell, organist and dir of music King's Coll Cambridge 1982–, conductor Cambridge Univ Musical Soc 1983–, chief conductor BBC Singers 1995–; also works in Europe, America and Australasia, regular TV and radio performances; recordings with EMI and Decca Records, Columns Classics and Collins Classics; pres: Inc Assoc of Organists 1985–87, Cathedral Organists' Assoc 1988–90, Royal Coll of Organists 1990–92 (hon sec 1981–90); memb Cncl Royal Sch of Church Music 1981–; memb ISM, FRCO 1968, FRCM; *Recreations* reading; *Style*— Stephen Cleobury, Esq; ✉ 85 Gough Way, Newnham, Cambridge CB3 9LN (☎ 01223 359461); King's College, Cambridge CB2 1ST (☎ 01223 331224, fax 01223 331890)

CLEREHUGH, Gerald; OBE (1989); s of James William Clerehugh, of Dewsbury, W Yorks, and Ann, *née* Wigfield; *b* 6 Jan 1933; *Educ* Wheelwright GS Dewsbury, Univ of Durham (BSc, Final Year Mathematical prize); *m* Joan Margaret, da of Reginald Ramsden; 1 s (Paul Simon b 31 March 1962), 1 da (Jane Elizabeth b 30 Aug 1964); *Career* Tech Dept Fairey Aviation Ltd 1954–58; Brough Div Hawker Siddeley Aviation (formerly Blackburn Aircraft Ltd): chief dynamics engr 1958–62, asst head of structures 1962–65, head of aerodynamics 1965–67; British Gas plc (formerly Gas Cncl then British Gas Corp): mangr of transmission engrg Engrg Res Station Newcastle upon Tyne 1967–74, asst dir Engrg Res Station 1974–78, dir On-Line Inspection Centre Cramlington 1978–83, dir of res 1983–88, dir of technol 1988–95; McRobert award Fellowship of Engrg 1989; Freeman: City of London 1984, Worshipful Co of Engrs 1984 (Master 1993–94); MRAeS 1965, FEng 1979 (process sec 1994–), FInstGasE 1979, FInstE 1990; *Recreations* golf, ornithology, music; *Clubs* RAC; *Style—* Gerald Clerehugh, Esq, OBE, FEng

CLEREY, (Christopher) Kevin Nelson; s of Colin Charlton Clerey, of Guernsey, CI, and Margaret Elizabeth, *née* Nelson (ggda of Sir Amos Nelson of Nelson); *b* 2 Feb 1957; *Educ* Sedbergh, Bristol Poly; *m* 3 Oct 1981, Amanda Jean, da of Ronald Charles Houslip; 2 s (Duncan Christopher Houslip b 18 May 1983, David Alasdair b 16 Sept 1985), 1 da (Helen Jean Alice b 19 July 1990); *Career* Coopers & Lybrand 1976–77, EDG (Europe) Ltd 1977–78; Credit Suisse Fides Trust Ltd (Guernsey Office): joined 1981, dir 1985–, md 1990–94; dir: Credit Suisse Trustees (IOM) Ltd 1988–, Credit Suisse Fund Administration 1988–, Credit Suisse Fides Trust Ltd (Gibraltar Office) 1991–, Credit Suisse Trustee Holdings Ltd 1995–, Inreska Insurance 1992–; md Bank Hofmann Trustees Ltd 1993–96; memb Exec Bd Credit Suisse Fides Trust AG Zurich 1994–; co sec Guernsey Colour Laboratories 1981–; sec: Guernsey Branch Inst of Chartered Secs 1981–85, CI Branch Old Sedberghians Club 1992–95; FCIS 1983, MInstD 1991; *Recreations* fell walking, skiing, golf, the outdoors; *Clubs* Old Sedberghians; *Style—* Kevin Clerey, Esq; ✉ Chalenstrasse 13, CH-8123 Etmatingen, Zurich, Switzerland (☎ and fax 00 41 1 980 46 14); Credit Suisse Fides Trust AG, Dept CKNC, Bleicherweg 33, CH-8027 Zurich, Switzerland (☎ 00 41 1 249 21 21, fax 00 41 1 249 30 08)

CLERK, Robert Maxwell; OBE (1995), DL (1995); s and h of Sir John Dutton Clerk, 10 Bt, CBE, VRD, and Evelyn Elizabeth, *née* Robertson; *b* 3 April 1945; *Educ* Winchester, Univ of London (BSc); *m* 1970, Felicity Faye, yr da of George Collins, of Bampton, Oxford; 2 s (George Napier b 1975, Edward James b 1986), 1 da (Julia Elizabeth b 1973); *Career* ptnr Smiths Gore chartered surveyors; vice pres Assoc of Scottish Dist Salmon Fishery Bds; memb Royal Co of Archers (Queen's Bodyguard for Scotland); FRICS; *Recreations* field sports, gardening; *Clubs* New (Edinburgh); *Style—* Robert Clerk, Esq, OBE, DL; ✉ Penicuik House, Penicuik, Midlothian EH26 9LA

CLERK OF PENICUIK, Sir John Dutton; 10 Bt (NS 1679), of Penicuik, Edinburgh, CBE (1966), VRD, JP; s of Sir George Clerk, 9 Bt (d 1943); *b* 30 Jan 1917; *Educ* Stowe; *m* 10 June 1944, Evelyn Elizabeth, er da of late William Robertson; 2 s, 2 da; *Heir* s, Robert Maxwell Clerk, *qv*; *Career* Cdre RNR ret; Lieut Queen's Body Guard for Scotland (Royal Co of Archers); Lord-Lt Midlothian 1972–92 (formerly Vice-Lt, DL 1956); FRSE 1977; *Style—* Sir John Clerk, Bt, CBE, VRD, JP, FRSE; ✉ Penicuik House, Penicuik, Midlothian EH26 9LA (☎ 01968 674318)

CLERKE, Francis Ludlow Longueville; s and h of Sir John Edward Longueville Clerke, 12 Bt, *qv*; *b* 25 Jan 1953; *Educ* Diocesan Coll Cape Town, Stellenbosch Univ (BA), Witwatersrand Univ (LLB); *m* 1982, Vanessa Anne, only da of Charles Cosman Citron (d 1974), of Mouille Point, Cape Town, S Africa; 1 s (William Francis Talbot b 1987), 1 da (Camilla Frances b 1984); *Career* solicitor (South Africa); *Recreations* windsurfing, squash; *Clubs* Western Province Sports (Cape Town); *Style—* Francis Clerke, Esq

CLERKE, Sir John Edward Longueville; 12 Bt (E 1660), of Hitcham, Buckinghamshire; s of Francis William Talbot Clerke (ka 1916), s of 11 Bt; suc gf, Sir William Francis Clerke, 11 Bt, 1930; *b* 29 Oct 1913; *Educ* Eton, Magdalene Coll Cambridge (MA); *m* 1948 (m dis 1986), Mary, da of Lt-Col Ivor Reginald Beviss Bond, OBE, MC (d 1967); 1 s (Francis Ludlow Longueville b 1953), 2 da (Albinia Jennifer b 1949, Teresa Mary (Mrs M C Waller-Bridge) b 1951); *Heir* s, Francis Ludlow Longueville Clerke, *qv*; *Career* Capt Royal Wilts Yeo (TA); FCA 1948, ret; *Recreations* lawn tennis, shooting, fishing; *Clubs* Lansdowne; *Style—* Sir John Clerke, Bt; ✉ 48 Savernake Avenue, Melksham, Wilts SN12 7HD (☎ 01225 703994)

CLEVELAND, Archdeacon of; *see:* Hawthorn, Ven Christopher John

CLEVERDON, Julia Charity; CBE (1996); (Mrs John Garnett); da of Douglas Cleverdon (d 1987), of London, and Eleanor Nest Lewis; *b* 19 April 1950; *Educ* Camden Sch for Girls, Newnham Coll Cambridge (BA); *m* 1, 30 June 1973 (m dis), Martin Ollard; *m* 2, 3 April 1985, (William) John Poulton Maxwell Garnett, CBE, *qv*, s of Maxwell Garnett, of Horestone Point (d 1960); 2 da (Charity b 1982, Victoria b 1985); *Career* dir of educn The Industl Soc 1981–87, chief exec Business in the Community 1992– (md 1988–); chm: Economic Awareness Ctee, Nat Curriculum Cncl; tstee 300 Gp, fndn govr Camden Sch for Girls, assoc Newnham Coll Roll; *Recreations* gardening, cooking, junk shops; *Style—* Ms Julia C Cleverdon, CBE; ✉ 8 Alwyne Rd, London N1 2HH; Business in the Community, 44 Baker Street, London W1M 1DH

CLEWS, Michael Graham; s of Reginald Alan Frederick Clews, of Bristol, and Alwine Annie, *née* Adams; *b* 11 Oct 1944; *Educ* Kingswood GS, Oxford Sch of Architecture (DipArch); *m* 24 July 1971, Heather Jane, da of Douglas Charles Sharratt, of Coventry; 2 s (Charles b 1978, Jonathan b 1983, d 1984), 2 da (Camilla b 1976, Helena b 1985); *Career* architect; fndr ptnr Clews Architectural Partnership 1972–; works incl historic buildings: Compton Verney, Croome Court, Boscobel House; conslt to PSA on historic buildings 1984–87 (historic buildings survey Oxfordshire, Warwickshire and Northamptonshire for DOE); pilot project for computerisation of historic building records for English Heritage; Surveyor Oxford diocesian; ARIBA; *Recreations* sailing, golf, squash; *Clubs* Tadmarton Heath Golf, Beauchamp Squash; *Style—* Michael Clews, Esq; ✉ Clews Architects Partnership, The Coach House, Great Bourton, Banbury, Oxon (☎ 01295 758101)

CLIBBORN, John Donovan Nelson dalla Rosa; CMG (1997); s of Donovan Harold Clibborn, CMG (d 1996), of Barcelona, Spain, and his 1 w Margaret Mercedes Edwige, *née* Nelson (d 1966); *b* 24 Nov 1941; *Educ* Downside, Oriel Coll Oxford (MA); *m* 11 May 1968, Juliet Elizabeth, da of John Brian Dermer Pagden (d 1980); 2 da (Imogen Margaret Eliabeth b 14 April 1969, Araminta Joan b 29 Jan 1981), 1 s (Benedict John Nelson dalla Rosa b 17 Aug 1971); *Career* HM Dip Serv: FCO 1965–67, third later second sec (devpt aid) Nicosia 1967–69, FCO 1969–72, first sec (economics) Bonn 1972–75, first sec (scientific) UK Rep to Cmmn of EEC Brussels 1975–78, on secondment to Jt Res Centre EEC 1978–81, FCO 1981–88, cnsllr Washington 1988–91, FCO 1991–92, cnsllr Washington 1992–95, FCO 1995–; memb: Soc for the Promotion of Roman Studies 1966, Soc for the Promotion of Hellenic Studies 1967; *Recreations* classical literature and history; *Clubs* Athenaeum; *Style—* John Clibborn, Esq, CMG; ✉ c/o Foreign and Commonwealth Office, King Charles Street, London SW1

CLIFF, Dr Andrew David; s of Alfred Cliff (d 1965), and Annabel, *née* McQuade (d 1975); *b* 26 Oct 1943; *Educ* Grimsby Wintringham Boys' GS, King's Coll London (state scholar, BA), Northwestern Univ Illinois (MA), Univ of Bristol (PhD, DSc 1982); *m* 1964, Margaret, da of Arthur Blyton; 3 s (Ross Andrew b 6 Sept 1966, Michael Peter b 28 July 1968, Timothy Edward b 12 April 1972); *Career* Northwestern Univ: Fulbright scholar, teaching asst in geography 1964–65, head teaching asst in geography 1965–66; lectr in geography Univ of Bristol 1969–72 (research assoc 1968–69), reader in theoretical geography Univ of Cambridge 1991– (univ lectr in geography 1973–91, MA 1973); Christ's Coll Cambridge: dir of studies and Coll lectr 1973–, fell 1974–; visiting scholar: WHO 1989, 1990, 1994 and 1995, Epidemiology Program Office US Centres for Disease Control and Prevention Atlanta Georgia 1990, 1991 and 1993; FSS 1968, FBA 1996; *Books* Spatial Autocorrelation (with J K Ord, 1973), Elements of Spatial Structure: A Quantitative Approach (jtly, 1975), Locational Analysis in Human Geography (with P Haggett and A E Frey, Locational Models and Locational Methods both form pts I and II of this book, 1977), Spatial Processes: Models and Applications (with J K Ord, 1981), Spatial Diffusion: An Historical Geography of Epidemics in an Island Community (jtly, 1981), Spatial Components in the Transmission of Epidemic Waves through Island Communities: the spread of Measles in Fiji and the Pacific (with P Haggett, 1985), Spatial Aspects of Influenza Epidemics (with P Haggett and J K Ord, 1986), Atlas of Disease Distributions: Analytic Approaches to Epidemiological Data (with P Haggett, 1988, 2 edn, 1992), London International Atlas of AIDS (with M R Smallman-Raynor and P Haggett, 1992), Measles: an Historical Geography of a Major Human Viral Disease from Global Expansion to Local Retreat, 1840–1990 (with P Haggett and M R Smallman-Raynor, 1993), Diffusing Geography (ed jtly, 1995); also author of numerous related papers; *Recreations* watching Grimsby Town FC, old roses, theatre; *Style—* Dr Andrew Cliff, FBA; ✉ Department of Geography, University of Cambridge, Downing Place, Cambridge CB2 3EN (☎ 01223 333381, fax 01223 333392)

CLIFFORD, Brian David; s of Lt W D Clifford (d 1978), and Doris Septima, *née* Magnay; *b* 15 July 1942; *Educ* Downhills Central Sch London; *m* 1, 5 Nov 1965 (m dis), Jenny Margaret, da of Morgan Goronwy Rees (d 1980); 2 s (Samuel William b 29 May 1966, Benjamin Luke b 24 Oct 1968); *m* 2, 22 Oct 1977, Linda Mary, *née* Stearns; *Career* picture ed Woman's Mirror Magazine 1961–62, dep picture ed Sunday Mirror 1962–65, exec picture ed The Sun 1965–66, night picture ed Daily Mail 1966–67, prodr Yorkshire TV 1968; BBC TV: script writer TV news 1969, stills mangr 1969–73, sales mangr photographs 1973–79, ed picture publicity 1979–86, chief asst Info Div 1986–87, dep head Info Div 1987–88, head of info servs 1988–92, head of corporate promotions 1992–94; account dir Creative Audio Visual 1994, md Creative Corporate Communications 1995–; Tottenham Schoolboys footballer 1956–57, head chorister St Philip's Church 1955–57; rugby coach Cranbrook RFC 1979–, memb Mgmnt Ctee Biddenden CC 1980; memb: NUJ, Royal Television Soc, Television and Radio Industs Club; FRSA; *Recreations* horse racing, watching Tottenham Hotspur, directing charity stage shows; *Style—* Brian Clifford, Esq; ✉ Mount House, Sissinghurst Castle, Cranbrook, Kent TN17 2AB (☎ 01580 713668)

CLIFFORD, David Robert; s of Mark Clifford, of Puriton, Somerset, and Dorothy Emily, *née* Lee; *b* 14 Sept 1952; *Educ* Dr Morgan's GS Bridgwater Somerset, Univ of Wales Inst of Science and Technol (BSc); *m* 13 Sept 1975, Audrey Elizabeth, *née* Potter; 1 s (John David b 14 May 1980), 1 da (Rachel Elizabeth b 23 Dec 1983); *Career* vice pres compensation and benefits Bank of America NT & SA 1978–86, personnel dir Citicorp Scrimgeour Vickers Ltd 1986–88, personnel dir Citicorp Investment Bank Ltd 1988–92, ptnr KPMG Management Consulting 1992–; memb Inst of Personnel Mgmnt; *Recreations* skiing, family activities; *Style—* David Clifford, Esq; ✉ Chatwin, Wilderness Road, Chislehurst, Kent BR7 5EZ (☎ 0181 468 7230); KPMG Management Consulting, 8 Salisbury Square, London EC4Y 8BB (☎ 0171 311 1000)

CLIFFORD, Max; s of Frank and Lilian Clifford, of London; *b* 1943; *m* Elizabeth; 1 da (Louise); *Career* PR consultant; left school aged 15; successively: on staff local department store (until sacked), jr reporter covering sport Merton and Morden News, Press Office staff EMI (promoting then unknown Liverpool band The Beatles), asst to Syd Gillingham (ex-chief press officer EMI) in new PR company promoting pop stars incl Tom Jones, Jimi Hendrix, the Bee Gees and Cream; fndr proprietor Max Clifford Associates Press and Public Relations Consultants ca 1968–; official/unofficial private clients have included Frank Sinatra, Mohammed Ali, Diana Ross, David Copperfield and OJ Simpson, corp clients incl Laing Homes; subject of various TV and radio progs incl documentary for BBC TV, Is This Your Life? (Channel 4) and Sixty Minutes (American TV), subject of numerous newspaper and magazine articles worldwide; speaker at univs throughout Britain incl Univs of Oxford and Cambridge; *Style—* Max Clifford, Esq; ✉ Max Clifford Associates Ltd, 109 New Bond Street, London W1Y 9AA (☎ 0171 408 2350, fax 0171 409 2294)

CLIFFORD, Nigel Richard; s of John Clifford (d 1995), of Emsworth, Hants, and Barbara Dorothy Clifford; *b* 22 June 1959; *Educ* Downing Coll Cambridge (MA), Univ of Strathclyde (MBA), DipM, DipCAM; *m* 1989, Jeanette, *née* Floyd; 2 s (Aidan b 1990, Brendan b 1992), 1 da (Caitlin b 1995); *Career* British Telecommunications plc 1981–92: commercial mangr 1981–84, product mangr 1984–85, gp product mangr 1985–87, gen mangr BT International Operator Servs 1987–90, sr strategist 1990, head of business strategy BT Mobile 1990–92; chief exec Glasgow Royal Infirmary Univ NHS Tst 1992–; fndr tstee Herald Fndn for Women's Health; FIMgt, FRSA; *Recreations* running, walking; *Clubs* Morpeth Comrades Club and Institute Union; *Style—* Nigel Clifford, Esq; ✉ Glasgow Royal Infirmary University NHS Trust, Glasgow Royal Infirmary, 84 Castle Street, Glasgow G4 0SF (☎ 0141 211 4924, fax 0141 211 4927)

CLIFFORD, Peter; *b* 30 March 1926; *Career* products mangr Johnson & Johnson GB Ltd 1948–55; mktg mangr: William Pearson Ltd 1955–63, Holt Products Ltd 1964–67; gp market res mangr Westminster Press Ltd 1967–86, md Marketing & Media Research Ltd 1986–; hon public offr London Central Branch SSAFA; MCIM 1956, MIAMA 1968, memb MRS; *Books* Test Marketing; *Recreations* church organist; *Clubs* The Organ; *Style—* Peter Clifford, Esq; ✉ 3 Grove Road, Thornton Heath, Surrey CR7 6HN (☎ 0181 684 2965); Marketing & Media Research Ltd, 3 Grove Road, Thornton Heath, Surrey CR7 6HN (☎ and fax 0181 684 2965)

CLIFFORD, Sir Roger Joseph Gerrard; 7 Bt (UK 1887), of Flaxbourne, Marlborough, New Zealand; s (twin, by 1 m) of Sir Roger Charles Joseph Clifford, 6 Bt (d 1982); *b* 5 June 1936; *Educ* Beaumont Coll; *m* 19 April 1968, Joanna Theresa, da of Cyril James Ward, of Christchurch, New Zealand, and gda of Sir Cyril Rupert Joseph Ward, 2 Bt; 2 da (Angela Mary Jane b 1971, Annabel Mary Louise b 1973); *Heir* bro, Charles Joseph Clifford; *Career* vice pres Stonyhurst Centenaries Appeal; *Clubs* Christchurch, Christchurch Golf (capt); *Style—* Sir Roger Clifford, Bt; ✉ 135 Totara Street, Christchurch 4, New Zealand (☎ 00 64 3 348 5958)

CLIFFORD, Timothy Peter Plint; s of Derek Plint Clifford, of Sittingbourne, Kent, and Ann, *née* Pierson (d 1984); *b* 26 Jan 1946; *Educ* Sherborne Dorset, Courtauld Inst, Univ of London (BA), Museums Assoc (Dip Fine Art); *m* 1968, Jane Olivia, yr da of Sir George Paterson, QC, OBE (d 1996), of Sherborne, Dorset; 1 da (Pandora b 1973); *Career* asst keeper: Dept of Paintings Manchester City Art Galleries 1968–72 (acting keeper 1972), Dept of Ceramics V&A Museum London 1972–76, Dept of Prints and Drawings British Museum London 1976–78; dir: Manchester City Art Galleries 1978–84, Nat Galleries of Scotland 1984–; pres NADFAS 1996– (vice pres 1990–96); tstee Abbot Hall Art Gallery; Freeman City of London, Freeman Worshipful Co of Goldsmiths; AMA, FRSA, FSA (Scotland); BIM Special Award 1991; Hon LLD Univ of St Andrews 1996; Cavaliere al Ordine nel Merito della Repubblica Italiana; *Recreations* shooting, birdwatching; *Clubs* Turf, Beefsteak, New (Edinburgh); *Style—* Timothy Clifford, Esq; ✉ National Galleries of Scotland, The Mound, Edinburgh EH2 2EL (☎ 0131 556 8921, fax 0131 220 2753)

CLIFFORD OF CHUDLEIGH, 14 Baron (E 1672) Thomas Hugh Clifford; Count of the Holy Roman Empire; s of 13 Baron Clifford of Chudleigh (d 1988), and Katharine, Lady Clifford of Chudleigh; *b* 17 March 1948; *Educ* Downside; *m* 1, 15 Dec 1980 (m dis 1993), (Muriel) Suzanne, yr da of Maj Campbell Austin; 2 s (Hon Alexander Thomas Hugh b 24 Sept 1985, Hon Edward George Hugh b 1988), 1 da (Hon Georgina Apollonia b 1983); m 2, 21 Nov 1994, Clarissa Anne, da of His Honour Anthony Charles Goodall, MC, DL, *qv*, of Moretonhampstead, Devon; *Heir* s, Hon Alexander Thomas Hugh Clifford b 24 Sept 1985; *Career* late Capt Coldstream Gds, served Norway, Turkey, Berlin, Ireland, British Honduras (Belize); mangr: The Clifford Estate Co, Ugbrooke Enterprises, Ugbrooke Reception Enterprise; KSOM; *Style*— Capt the Rt Hon the Lord Clifford of Chudleigh; ✉ Ugbrooke Park, Chudleigh, S Devon TQ13 OAD (☎ 01626 852179)

CLIFT, Richard Dennis; CMG (1984); s of late Dennis Victor Clift, and Helen Wilmot, *née* Evans; *b* 18 May 1933; *Educ* St Edward's Sch Oxford, Pembroke Coll Cambridge (BA), London Coll of Furniture (HND); *m* 1, 1957 (m dis 1982), Barbara Mary Travis; 3 da; m 2, 1982, Jane Rosamund Barker, *née* Homfray; *Career* HM Dip Serv: FO 1956–57, office of Br Chargé D'Affaires Peking 1958–60, Br Embassy Berne 1961–62, UK delgn to NATO Paris 1962–64, FO 1964–68, head of Chancery Br High Cmmn Kuala Lumpur 1969–71, FCO 1971–73, cnsllr (commercial) Peking 1974–76, Canadian Nat Def Coll 1976–77, seconded to NI Office 1977–79, head of Hong Kong and Gen Dept FCO 1979–84, Br high cmmr Freetown 1984–86, political advsr Hong Kong 1987–89, ret 1989; furniture restorer Richard Clift Restoration 1991–; *Recreations* sailing, walking, woodwork; *Style*— Richard Clift, Esq, CMG; ✉ 18 Langwood Chase, Teddington, Middx

CLIFT, Prof Roland; OBE (1994); s of Leslie William Clift, of Wallington, Surrey, and Ivy Florence Gertrude, *née* Wheeler; *b* 19 Nov 1942; *Educ* Trinity Sch of John Whitgift Croydon, Trinity Coll Cambridge, McGill Univ Montreal; *m* 1, 1968, Rosena Valory, da of Robert Bruce Davison; 1 da (Vanessa b 14 July 1972); m 2, 1979, Diana Helen, da of William Reginald Dermot Manning; 2 s (Julian William Dermot b 2 Oct 1979, Adrian Manning b 3 July 1982); *Career* tech offr and chem engr ICI Ltd 1964–67; McGill Univ: lectr 1967–70, asst prof 1970–72, assoc prof 1972–75; visiting prof Universitá di Napoli 1973–74, lectr in chem engrg Imperial Coll London 1975–76; Univ of Cambridge: lectr in chem engrg 1976–81, fell of Trinity Coll 1978–81, praelector 1980–81; Univ of Surrey: prof of chem engrg 1981–92, head Dept of Chem and Process Engrg 1981–91, prof of environmental technology and dir Centre for Environmental Strategy 1992–; ed-in-chief Powder Technology 1987–95; chm: Process Engrg Ctee SERC 1989–90, Clean Technol Unit SERC and AFRC 1990–94, Engrg Research Bd AFRC 1992–94; memb BBSRC 1994–96; dir: Clifmar Associates Ltd 1986–, Particle Consultants Ltd 1988–; memb: UK Ecolabelling Bd 1992–, Comité des Sages on LCA and Ecolabelling Euro Cmmn 1993–, Tech Opportunities Panel EPSRC 1994–, Royal Cmmn on Environmental Pollution 1996–; Henry Marion Howe Medal American Soc for Metals 1976, Moulton Medal Inst of Chem Engrs 1979; hon citizen Augusta Georgia 1987; FIChemE 1984 (MIChemE 1979), FEng 1986; *Books* Bubbles, Drops and Particles (with J R Grace & M E Weber, 1978), Fluidization (ed with J F Davidson & D Harrison, 1985), Slurry Transport using Centrifugal Pumps (with K C Wilson and G R Addie, 1992), Gas Cleaning at High Temperatures (ed with J P K Seville, 1993); *Recreations* music, arguing; *Style*— Prof Roland Clift, OBE, FEng; ✉ 93 Peperharow Rd, Godalming, Surrey GU7 2PN (☎ 01483 417922); Centre for Environmental Strategy, University of Surrey, Guildford, Surrey GU2 2XH (☎ 01483 259271, fax 01483 259394)

CLIFTON, His Hon Judge; Gerald Michael; s of Frederick Maurice Clifton (d 1988), of Rainford, Lancs, and Jane, *née* Hayes (d 1986); *b* 3 July 1947; *Educ* Liverpool Coll, Brasenose Coll Oxford (open classical scholar, MA); *m* 21 July 1973, Rosemary Anne Vera, da of Reginald Edward Jackson, of Birkdale, Southport; 2 s (Gerald Rupert Edward b 1977, Giles Michael Charles b 1980); *Career* called to the Bar Middle Temple 1970, memb Manx Bar 1992; asst recorder of the Crown Ct 1982–88, recorder Northern Circuit 1988–92, circuit judge (Northern Circuit) 1992–; life govr Liverpool Coll; *Recreations* sailing, tennis, walking, philately; *Clubs* Bar Yacht, Heswall LTC; *Style*— His Honour Judge Clifton; ✉ c/o The Crown Court, QEII Building, Derby Square, Liverpool

CLIFTON, (John) Ian Ernest; MBE; s of John Clifton (d 1973), of Edinburgh, and Daisy, *née* Deacon (d 1993); *b* 26 Aug 1932; *Educ* Boroughmuir HS Edinburgh, Skerry's Coll Edinburgh, Open Univ (BA); *m* 1957, Margaret Govenlock Hepburn; 1 s (Neil Ian b 5 Feb 1959), 1 da (Fiona Anne b 2 March 1965); *Career* athletics administrator; competitive career: Edinburgh Southern Harriers 1949–50 and 1957–65, Lincoln Wellington 1950–57; achievements: Edinburgh Southern Harriers youth champion 1950, Scot Boys' Brigade cross country champion 1950, E Counties cross country champion 1954–55, Lincs Co mile winner 1954–55, Manchester-Blackpool relay medal 1955; athletics admin 1966–; Edinburgh Southern Harriers: memb Ctee 1966–, vice pres 1968–70 and 1977–78, pres 1970–71 and 1979–80; Scot Cross Country Union: memb Ctee 1974–92, chm Organising Ctee World Cross Country Championships 1976–78, vice pres 1977–78, pres 1978–79, gen sec 1982–93; sec: UK Cross Country Cmmn 1989–92 (sr UK team mangr World Cross Country Championships 1990), Scottish Road Running and Cross Country Cmmn 1992–95; Scot Amateur Athletics Assoc: memb Ctee 1979–88, vice pres 1985, pres 1986, immediate past pres 1987–88; memb: Scot Cwlth Games Cncl 1982–88, UK Civil Serv Athletic Assoc 1971–85, Ctee Scot Civil Serv Athletic Assoc 1972–85 (fndr sec 1972), Scot Civil Serv Sports Cncl 1971–85; Edinburgh Area Civil Serv Sports Assoc: memb 1971–85, chm 1982–85, life memb 1985; Civil Serv: clerical offr BT 1950–55, offr then higher exec offr Customs & Excise 1955–85, sr exec offr Customs & Excise 1985–92; *Recreations* reading, hill walking, athletics and cross country; *Style*— Ian Clifton, Esq, MBE; ✉ 2 Doune Park, Dalgety Bay, Fife KY11 5LX

CLIFTON, Bishop (RC) of 1974–; Rt Rev Mervyn Alban Alexander; s of William Paul Alexander (d 1968), of Salisbury, Wilts, and Grace Evelyn, *née* Newman (1973); *b* 29 June 1925; *Educ* Bishop Wordsworth Sch Salisbury, Prior Park Coll Bath, Gregorian Univ Rome (DD); *Career* curate Clifton Pro-Cathedral Bristol 1951–64, RC chaplain Univ of Bristol 1953–67, parish priest Our Lady of Lourdes Weston-super-Mare 1967–72, aux bishop of Clifton 1972–74; *Style*— The Rt Rev the Bishop of Clifton; ✉ St Ambrose, North Road, Leigh Woods, Bristol BS8 3PW (☎ 0117 973 3072)

CLIFTON, Nigel John; s of Henry Clifton, of Helensburgh, Dunbartonshire, and Pamela, *née* Damment; *b* 19 Nov 1951; *Educ* Wellingborough Sch, Univ of St Andrews (MA); *m* 1974, Elizabeth, *née* Dacre; 1 s (Andrew James b 1977); *Career* dep hosp admin Northern General Hosp Sheffield 1976–81, admin W Fife Hosps 1981–83; gen mangr: Community and Acute Servs Chesterfield Royal Hosp 1983–87, Univ Hosp Queens Med Centre Nottingham 1987–90; chief exec Salisbury Health Authy 1990–92, chief exec N Nottinghamshire Health Authy 1992–; memb Inst Health Servs Mgmnt 1979; *Recreations* watching cricket, archery, cooking; *Style*— Nigel Clifton, Esq; ✉ North Nottinghamshire Health, Ransom Hall, Southwell Road West, Rainsworth, Notts NG21 0ER (☎ 01623 672200, fax 01623 653527)

CLIFTON, Rita Ann; da of Arthur Leonard Clifton (d 1970), of Marlow, Bucks, and Iris Mona, *née* Hill; *b* 30 Jan 1958; *Educ* High Wycombe HS, Newnham Coll Cambridge (MA); *partner* Brian Martin Astley; 2 da; *Career* graduate trainee rising to account exec D'Arcy MacManus & Masius advtg agency 1979–81, account supervisor Saatchi & Saatchi 1981–82, account dir J Walter Thompson 1983–86; Saatchi & Saatchi: sr account planner 1986–89, bd dir 1989, gp planning dir 1990–92, dir of strategic planning 1992–95, a vice chm 1995–; memb: IPA, MRS, Account Planning Gp; vice pres Women's Advertising Club of London 1996–97; *Recreations* news, dance, country, riding, environmental affairs; *Style*— Ms Rita Clifton; ✉ Saatchi & Saatchi, 80 Charlotte Street, London W1A 1AQ (☎ 0171 636 5060, fax 0171 637 8489)

CLIFTON-BROWN, Geoffrey; MP (C) Cirencester and Tewkesbury (majority 16,058); s of Robert Clifton-Brown, and Elizabeth Clifton-Brown; *b* 23 March 1953; *Educ* Eton, RAC Cirencester; *m*; 1 s, 1 da; *Career* chartered surveyor PSA Dorchester 1975, investmt surveyor Jones Lang Wootton 1975–79, md own farming business Norfolk 1979–; MP (C) Cirencester and Tewkesbury 1992–; memb Environment Select Ctee 1992, chm All Pty Gp on Population, Devpt and Reproductive Health, PPS to Rt Hon Douglas Hogg as Min for Agric, Fisheries and Food 1995–, chm All Pty Gp on Population, Devpt and Reproductive Health 1995–; chm N Norfolk Constituency Cons Assoc 1986–91, memb Exec Ctee and Agric Ctee Eastern Area Cons Assoc 1986–91; vice chm: Charities Property Assoc 1993–, Small Business Bureau 1995–, Euro Atlantic Gp 1996; Freeman City of London, Liveryman Worshipful Co of Farmers; ARICS; *Recreations* fishing, rural pursuits; *Clubs* Carlton, Farmers; *Style*— Geoffrey Clifton-Brown, Esq, MP; ✉ House of Commons, London SW1A 0AA

CLIFTON OF RATHMORE, Lord; Ivo Donald Stuart Bligh; s and h of 11 Earl of Darnley; *b* 17 April 1968; *Style*— Lord Clifton of Rathmore

CLIFTON-SAMUEL, Anthony David; s of David Clifton-Samuel (d 1960), of London, and Sarah Vera, *née* Cohen; *b* 25 June 1932; *Educ* Emscote Lawns Sch Warwickshire, Merchant Taylors', Univ Tutorial Coll, The Royal Dental Hosp of London, Sch of Dental Surgery (BDS, LDS, RCS, The Parris prize, Robert Woodhouse prize); *m* 26 March 1961, Andrée Josephine, da of Alfred Falcke Fredericks; 1 s (Jason Ian b 1 April 1967), 1 da (Ruth Charlotte b 27 March 1965); *Career* Nat Serv Royal Army Dental Corps 1956–58 (Lt 1956, Capt 1957); OC Army Dental Centre Limassol 1956–57, Derna Cyrennaica 1957–58; in private practice 1958–60, own practice Kensington 1960–81 (Harley St 1965–); memb Kensington Chelsea & Westminster Local Dental Ctee 1964–, rep London Local Dental Ctee (later Fedn) 1966–88, former dental rep St Charles Hosp Med Soc; Gen Dental Practitioners Assoc: joined 1962, chm Southern Branch 1970–85, vice chm Assoc 1978–79 and 1981–82, pres 1979–81 and 1993–May 1996, vice pres 1987–92; memb BDA until 1970 (served on Rep Bd); *Recreations* motor boating, mechanical engineering, electronics, photography, DIY, reading; *Clubs* Kensington Rotary, Royal Yachting Assoc; *Style*— Mr Anthony D Clifton-Samuel; ✉ 42 Harley St, London W1N 1AB (☎ 0171 636 9789)

CLINCH, David John (Joe); s of Thomas Charles Clinch (d 1995), of Surrey, and Madge Isobel, *née* Saker (d 1984); *b* 14 Feb 1937; *Educ* Nautical Coll Pangbourne, Univ of Durham (BA), Indiana Univ USA (MBA); *m* 1963, Hilary, da of John Herbert Jacques (d 1984), of Claxby, Lincs; 1 s (John), 1 da (Helen); *Career* Nat Serv 1955–57, RN Acting Sub-Lt; admin Univ of Sussex 1963–69, sec Open Univ 1981– (dep sec and registrar 1969–80); *Recreations* music, walking; *Style*— Joe Clinch, Esq; ✉ 39 Tudor Gardens, Stony Stratford, Milton Keynes MK11 1HX (☎ 01908 562475); The Open University, Walton Hall, Milton Keynes MK7 6AA (☎ 01908 653213)

CLINTON, (Robert) Alan; s of John (d 1972), of Birmingham, and Leah Millington (d 1986); *b* 12 July 1931; *Educ* George Dixon GS Birmingham, Manchester Business Sch; *m* 1956, Valerie Joy, da of Herbert Allan Falconer (d 1981), of Birmingham; *Career* joined PO 1948, asst dir (personnel) PO HQ 1975, asst dir (operations) 1976, regional dir Eastern Postal Region 1978, dir Postal Operations (UK) 1979, memb PO Bd London 1981–85, resigned 1985; gp md Picton House Ltd 1986; dir until 1994: Picton House (Leicester) Ltd, Picton House Properties Ltd, Picton Homes Ltd, Picton Homes (Wales) Ltd 1986, Picton Homes (Gwent) Ltd, Picton House (W London) Ltd, Picton House Investments Ltd, Picton House Ltd, Picton House (East Anglia) Ltd, Pembroke Services Ltd 1988, Picton House (Holdings) Ltd 1991; pres Clacton and NE Essex Arts and Literary Soc 1992, memb Mgmnt Ctee for Essex Royal Assoc in Aid of Deaf People 1994; chm St Osyth Almshouse Charity 1995; Freeman City of London 1979, Liveryman Worshipful Co of Carmen 1981; FCIT 1982; *Recreations* music, cooking, walking, sailing; *Clubs* City of London; *Style*— Alan Clinton, Esq; ✉ Summer Cottage, The Quay, St Osyth, Clacton-on-Sea, Essex CO16 8EW (☎ 01255 820368)

CLINTON, 22 Baron (E 1299); Gerard Neville Mark Fane Trefusis; JP (Bideford 1963), DL (Devon 1977); s of Capt Charles Fane (ka 1940), s of Hon Harriet Trefusis, herself da of 21 Baron Clinton (d 1957); assumed additional surname Trefusis by Deed Poll 1958 and suc to Barony 1965 on termination of abeyance; *b* 7 Oct 1934; *Educ* Gordonstoun; *m* 1959, Nicola Harriette, da of Maj Charles Robert Purdon Coote (d 1954); 1 s (Hon Charles Patrick Rolle b 21 March 1962), 2 da (Hon Caroline Harriet b 23 May 1960, Hon Henrietta Jane b 31 Jan 1964); *Heir* s, Hon Charles; *Career* memb Prince of Wales's Councils 1968–79; landowner; *Style*— The Rt Hon the Lord Clinton, DL; ✉ Heanton Satchville, nr Okehampton, N Devon

CLINTON-DAVIS, Baron (Life Peer UK 1990), of Hackney in the London Borough of Hackney; Stanley Clinton Clinton-Davis; s of Sidney Davis; assumed the surname of Clinton-Davis by Deed Poll 1990; *b* 6 Dec 1928; *Educ* Hackney Downs Sch, Mercers Sch, King's Coll London; *m* 1954, Frances Jane, *née* Lucas; 1 s, 3 da; *Career* Parly candidate: Portsmouth Langstone 1955, Yarmouth 1959 & 1964; cncllr (Hackney) 1959–71, Mayor Hackney 1968–69; MP (Lab) Hackney Central 1970–83, Parly under sec Trade 1974–79; oppn frontbench spokesman on: Trade 1979–81, Foreign and Cwlth Affrs 1981–83; memb Cmmn of Euro Communities (responsible for tport, environment and nuclear safety) 1985–89, princ spokesperson for the oppn on Tport in the House of Lords and supporting spokesman on trade and indust and on foreign affrs 1990–; slr 1953–; conslt on Euro and environmental law and affrs with S J Berwin & Co slrs 1989–; conslt: Euro Cockpit Assoc 1990–, Soc of Lab Lawyers 1990–; vice pres: Soc of Lab Lawyers 1987–, Chartered Inst of Environmental Health; hon memb Exec Cncl of Justice, exec memb Inst of Jewish Affairs 1993–; memb UN Selection Ctee UNEP-Sasakawa Environment Award 1989–; chm: Refugee Cncl 1989–, Advsy Ctee on pollution of the sea 1989–, Packaging Standards Cncl; memb: GMBH, Advsy Panel CIS Environ Tst; pres: Br Multiple Sclerosis Soc (Hackney Branch), UK Pilots Assoc (Marine), Assoc of Municipal Authorities, Inst of Travel Mgmnt, Br Airline Pilots Assoc, Aviation Environment Federation; tstee: Int Shakespeare Globe Centre, Bernt Carlsson Tst; Grand Cross Order of Leopold II (Belgium) for servs to the EC 1990; Hon Doctorate Poly Univ of Bucharest; fell Queen Mary and Westfield Coll London; Fell Chartered Institution of Water and Environmental Management; *Books* Report of a British Parliamentary Delegation to Chile (jtly, 1982); contrib to books and jls on environment issues; *Recreations* reading political biographies, golf, watching assoc football; *Clubs* Reform; *Style*— The Rt Hon Lord Clinton-Davis

CLITHEROE, 2 Baron (UK 1955), also 3 Bt (UK 1945); Ralph John Assheton; DL (Lancs); s of 1 Baron Clitheroe, KCVO, PC (d 1984), and Hon Sylvia Benita Frances, *née* Hotham (d 1991), er da of 6 Baron Hotham; *b* 3 Nov 1929; *Educ* Eton, ChCh Oxford (MA); *m* 2 May 1961, Juliet, o da of Lt-Col Christopher Lionel Hanbury, MBE, TD; 2 s (Ralph Christopher, John Hotham), 1 da (Elizabeth Jane); *Heir* s, Hon Ralph Christopher Assheton, *qv*; *Career* late Life Guards; former dir: RTZ Corporation plc, First Interstate Bank of California, American Mining Congress; former chm RTZ Borax, currently chm The Yorkshire Bank PLC and dir Halliburton Company; vice lord lieut Lancs; Liveryman Worshipful Co of Skinners; FCIB; *Clubs* Boodle's, Pratt's, RAC; *Style*— The Rt Hon Lord Clitheroe, DL; ✉ Downham Hall, Clitheroe, Lancashire BB7 4DN (☎ 01200 441210)

CLIVE, Eric McCredie; s of Robert M Clive (d 1971), and Mary, *née* McCredie (d 1976); *b* 24 July 1938; *Educ* Stranraer Acad, Stranraer HS, Univ of Edinburgh (MA, LLB), Univ of Michigan (LLM), Univ of Virginia (SJD); *m* 6 Sept 1962, Kay, da of Rev Alastair McLeman (d 1940); 4 c (Gael b 6 Sept 1963 d 1996, Alastair M M b 19 March 1965, Sally b 22 March 1968, Rachel b 9 Sept 1969); *Career* slr; Univ of Edinburgh: lectr 1962–69, sr lectr 1969–75, reader 1975–77, prof of Scots law 1977–81; memb Scottish Law Commission 1981–; *Books* Law of Husband and Wife in Scotland (1974, 3 edn 1992), Scots Law for Journalists (jtly 1965, 5 edn 1988); *Recreations* hill walking; *Style*— Eric Clive, Esq; ✉ Scottish Law Commission, 140 Causewayside, Edinburgh (☎ 0131 668 2131)

CLOAKE, John Cecil; CMG (1977); s of late Dr Cecil Stedman Cloake, of Wimbledon, and Maude Osborne, *née* Newling; *b* 2 Dec 1924; *Educ* KCS Wimbledon, Peterhouse Cambridge; *m* 1956, Margaret Thomure Morris, of Washington DC, USA; 1 s; *Career* Army 1943–46; HM Dip Serv: entered 1948, cnsllr (commercial) Tehran 1968–72, head Trade Relations and Exports Dept FCO 1973–76, ambass to Bulgaria 1976–80, ret 1981; hon treas Br Inst of Persian Studies 1982–90; chm: Richmond Local History Soc 1985–90 (pres 1990–), Museum of Richmond 1986–95; *Books* Templer, Tiger of Malaya (1985), Richmond Past (1991), Royal Bounty (1992), Palaces and Parks of Richmond and Kew (vol 1 1995, vol 2 1996); *Style*— John Cloake, Esq, CMG; ✉ 4 The Terrace, 140 Richmond Hill, Richmond, Surrey TW10 6RN

CLODE, Michael Leslie Hailey; s of Capt Roger Leslie Clode, RN, of Kynance, Lee-on-Solent, Hants, and Patricia Mary, *née* Kyd; *b* 5 Oct 1943; *Educ* St Edward Sch Oxford; *m* 4 April 1970, Isobel McLeod (d 1992), da of Henry Watson Carrick (d 1976); 4 da (Fiona b 1972, Alison b 1974, Jennifer b 1977, Camilla b 1982); *Career* slr; ptnr Freshfields 1974–, memb Cncl St Leonard's Sch St Andrews Fife; Freeman: City of London, Worshipful Co of Solicitors; memb Law Soc; *Recreations* skiing, walking, golf; *Style*— Michael Clode, Esq; ✉ 56 Brompton Square, London SW3 2AG; Chesters, Orchard Way, Esher, Surrey KT10 9DY; Freshfields, Whitefriars, 65 Fleet St, London EC4Y 1HT (☎ 0171 936 4000, fax 0171 832 7397, telex 889292)

CLOGHER, Bishop of 1986–; Rt Rev Brian Desmond Anthony Hannon; s of the Ven (Arthur) Gordon Hannon (d 1978), and Hilda Catherine Stewart-Moore, *née* Denny; *b* 5 Oct 1936; *Educ* St Columba's Coll Dublin, Trinity Coll Dublin (BA, MA); *m* 10 Sept 1964, Maeve Geraldine Audley, *née* Butler, da of Capt Edward Walter Charles Butler (d 1988); 3 s (Desmond b 1965, Brendan b 1968, Neil b 1970); *Career* ordained Church of Ireland: deacon 1961, priest 1962; Diocese of Derry: curate All Saints Clooney 1961–64, rector Desertmartin 1964–69, rector Christ Church Londonderry 1969–82, rural dean Londonderry 1977–82; Diocese of Clogher: rector St Macartin's Cath Enniskillen 1982–86, canon Clogher Cath 1982, dean 1985, bishop 1986; memb House of Bishops (Church of Ireland); pres Church Missionary Soc (Ireland) 1990–, memb Central Ctee World Cncl of Churches 1983–92, chm Western Educn and Library Bd NI 1985–87 and 1989–91; Athletics: capt Dublin Univ 1958, All Ireland 440 Hurdles Champion 1959, Trinity Pink; *Recreations* walking, travel, photography, music; *Clubs* Friendly Brothers of St Patrick (Dublin), Knights of Campanile (Dublin); *Style*— The Rt Rev Brian D A Hannon; ✉ The See House, Fivemiletown, Co Tyrone, N Ireland BT75 0QP (☎ and fax 013655 21265)

CLOGHER, Bishop (RC) of 1979–; Most Rev Joseph Augustine Duffy; s of Edward Duffy (d 1956), and Brigid MacEntee (d 1963); *b* 3 Feb 1934; *Educ* Maynooth (BD), Nat Univ of Ireland (MA, HDipEd); *Books* Patrick In His Own Words (1985), Lough Derg Guide (1978), Monaghan Cathedral (1992); *Recreations* history, travel; *Style*— The Most Rev the Bishop of Clogher; ✉ Tigh an Easpaig, Monaghan, Ireland (☎ 00 353 47 81019, fax 00 353 47 84773)

CLOKE, Anthony John (Tony); s of Maj John Nicholas Cloke (d 1985), of Walsall, and May Eddy, *née* Craghill; *b* 10 Jan 1943; *Educ* Queen Mary's GS Walsall, Clare Coll Cambridge (MA); *m* 7 June 1969, Ann Gwendoline, da of Bertie Cordy (d 1981), of Usk; 2 s (John b 1970, Richard b 1972), 1 da (Caroline b 1974); *Career* admitted slr 1970; ptnr Peter Peter and Wright (and its predecessors) 1973–; slr of the Supreme Ct 1970, Tst and Estate practitioner; widespread involvement in local orgns and activities; *Recreations* farming, golf; *Style*— Tony Cloke, Esq; ✉ Peter, Peter and Wright, 1 West Street, Okehampton, Devon (☎ 01837 52379, fax 01837 53604)

CLOKE, Richard Owen; s of late Owen William Cloke, MBE, of 25 Priests Lane, Brentwood, Essex, and Barbara Ethel Beatrice *née* Abbott; *b* 3 May 1944; *Educ* Reading Sch; *m* 26 June 1969, Carol Ann, da of Frank Wadsworth; 2 s (Ian, Andrew), 1 da (Jackie); *Career* branch mangr Barclays Bank PLC 1979–83 (joined 1960, asst district mangr 1976–79), asst dir Barclays Merchant Bank Ltd 1983–85, dir Barclays de Zoete Wedd Ltd 1986–; *Recreations* tennis, badminton, golf; *Style*— Richard Cloke, Esq; ✉ Barclays De Zoete Wedd Ltd, Ebbgate House, 2 Swan Lane, London EC4R 3TS (☎ 0171 956 3132, fax 0171 956 4591)

CLORE, Melanie Sarah Jane; da of Martin Clore, of London, and Cynthia Clore; *b* 28 Jan 1960; *Educ* Channing Sch Highgate, Univ of Manchester (BA); *m* 22 July 1994, Yaron Meshoulam; 1 s (Theo Felix Clore b 18 May 1996); *Career* Sotheby's: graduate trainee 1981, jr cataloguer in Impressionist and Modern Art Dept 1982, auctioneer 1985–, dep dir 1986–88, dir 1988–91, sr dir 1991–, head of Impressionist and Modern Art Dept 1992–, bd memb Sotheby's Europe 1994–; fndn tstee Whitechapel Art Gallery 1988–; *Recreations* travel, cinema; *Clubs* Groucho; *Style*— Ms Melanie Clore; ✉ Impressionist and Modern Art Department, Sotheby's, 34–35 New Bond St, London W1A 2AA (☎ 0171 408 5394, fax 0171 408 5932)

CLOSE, Anthony Stephen; s of Stephen John Henry Close (d 1972), and Marion Lily, *née* Matthews (d 1989); *b* 9 Aug 1931; *Educ* Colston Sch Bristol, Queen's Coll Oxford (scholar, MA), Birkbeck Coll Univ of London (MSc); *m* 1961, Josephine, da of Oliver G Oakey; 1 da (Alice Ann b 1968); *Career* trainee Shell Int Petroleum, mangr Selection Services BOAC, gp educn and trg offr Beecham Group Ltd, co personnel dir Thomas De Le Rue, sector personnel dir Grand Metropolitan, gp personnel dir Trusthouse Forte; chm Health Educn Authy 1994– (memb 1989–); IOD: memb Cncl 1985–, memb Policy and Exec Ctee, chm Employment Ctee; memb Educn Trg Affairs Ctee CBI, memb Further Educn Funding Cncl 1992–95; author various articles in jls for human resource and mgmnt; AFBPsS (chartered psychologist), FIMgt, FIPD; *Recreations* walking, singing, opera, cooking; *Clubs* Saville; *Style*— Anthony Close, Esq; ✉ Danes, Cox Green Lane, Maidenhead, Berkshire SL6 3EY (☎ 01628 22910); Glebe Cottage, Shipton Oliffe, Gloucestershire; Health Education Authority, Hamilton House, Mabledon Place, London WC1H 9TX (☎ 0171 413 1965, fax 0171 413 2618)

CLOSE, Richard Charles; s of Lt-Col Richard Alwen Close, and Marjorie Anne, *née* Bartlett; *b* 3 Sept 1949; *Educ* Canford, Sidney Sussex Coll Cambridge (MA); *m* 4 Aug 1973, (Elizabeth) Janet Beatrice, da of Gavin Leggat Brown; 1 s (Thomas b 20 Jan 1986), 1 da (Lisa b 16 May 1982); *Career* audit mangr Arthur Young Milan 1974–81, Euro treas Sperry Corp 1984–86 (regnl dir internal audit 1981–84), fin dir Unisys Ltd 1986–87, bd memb for corp fin and planning The Post Office 1989– (dir corp fin 1987–89); chm Chartered Accountants in Business Bd and memb Cncl ICAEW 1994–; FCT 1985, FCA 1979 (ACA 1974); *Recreations* tennis, fishing, walking; *Style*— Richard Close, Esq; ✉ The Post Office, 148 Old Street, London EC1V 9HQ (☎ 0171 250 2052, fax 0171 250 2100)

CLOSE-BROOKS, Jonathan Roger; s of Roger Close-Brooks, DSO (d 1980), and Marian, *née* Beesly (d 1991); *b* 26 Dec 1943; *Educ* Radley, Oriel Coll Oxford (MA); *m* 24 July 1971, Carolyn Elizabeth Rosemary, da of Brig Gilbert Coghlan Wells, CBE, MC; 2 s (Oliver Charles Roger b 14 May 1978, Henry Roland Gilbert b 13 May 1984), 1 da (Camilla Margaret Jane b 12 July 1985); *Career* articled clerk Jackson Pixley (accountants) 1966–69; ptnr: S R Scott Stratten & Co (stockbrokers) 1971–74 (trainee clerk 1969–71), Seymour Pierce and Co (incorporating SR Scott Stratten and Co) 1976–87 (assoc 1974–76); dir: Seymour Pierce & Co Ltd 1987, Seymour Pierce Butterfield Ltd 1987–95, Henry Cooke, Lumsden PLC 1994–; memb Int Stock Exchange 1971, MSI; *Recreations* gardening, skiing, sailing, rowing, punting; *Clubs* Leander, Oriel Tortoise Boat, Aldeburgh Yacht; *Style*— J R Close-Brooks, Esq; ✉ 71 Blenheim Crescent, London W11 2EG (☎ 0171 229 0545); Henry Cooke, Lumsden PLC, 7–9 Copthall Avenue, London EC2R 7EH (☎ 0171 256 2332, fax 0171 256 2333)

CLOTHIER, Sir Cecil Montacute; KCB (1982), QC (1965); s of Hugh Montacute Clothier (d 1961), of Blundellsands, Liverpool; *b* 28 Aug 1919; *Educ* Stonyhurst, Lincoln Coll Oxford (BCL, MA); *m* 1, 1943, Mary Elizabeth (d 1984), da of Ernest Glover Bush (d 1962), of Aughton, Lancs; 1 s, 2 da; *m* 2, 7 Aug 1992, Mrs Diana Stevenson, da of Louis Durrant, lately of Richmond, Surrey; *Career* served WWII 51 Highland Div, Army Staff Washington DC, Hon Lt-Col Royal Signals; called to the Bar Inner Temple 1950, bencher 1972, recorder Blackpool 1965–72, recorder of the Crown Ct 1972–78, judge of Appeal IOM 1972–78, legal assessor to Gen Medical and Gen Dental Cncls 1972–78; memb Royal Cmmn on NHS 1976–78, Parly cmmr Administration and Health Service cmmr for England Wales and Scotland 1979–84; vice pres Interception of Communications Tbnl 1986–96; chm: Police Complaints Authy 1985–89, Cncl on Tbnls 1989–92; conslt SSRB 1995– (memb 1989–95); Rock Carling fell 1988; Hon LLD Univ of Hull 1983; hon fell Lincoln Coll Oxford 1984, hon memb Assoc of Anaesthetists 1987, Hon FRPharmS 1990; *Clubs* Leander; *Style*— Sir Cecil Clothier, KCB, QC; ✉ 1 Temple Gardens, Temple, London EC4Y 9BB (☎ 0171 353 3400)

CLOTHIER, Richard John; s of John Neil Clothier, of Montacute, Somerset, and Barbara Evelyn, *née* Rothwell; *b* 4 July 1945; *Educ* Peterhouse Sch Zimbabwe, Univ of Natal (BSc (Agric)), Harvard Univ (Advanced Mgmnt Prog); *m* 1, 1972, Ingrid Hafner (d 1994); 2 s (Ben Raoul b 21 November 1972, William Neil b 11 March 1976); m 2, 1995, Sarah Riley; *Career* Milk Mktg Bd 1971–77; Dalgety PLC: with Dalgety Agriculture 1977–88, chief exec Pig Improvement Co 1988–92, exec main bd dir 1992–, chief exec 1993–; non-exec dir Granada PLC 1996–; *Recreations* competitive yachting; *Clubs* Royal Thames Yacht; *Style*— Richard Clothier, Esq; ✉ Dalgety PLC, 100 George Street, London W1H 5RH (☎ 0171 486 0200, fax 0171 935 3120, telex 23874)

CLOUDSLEY-THOMPSON, Prof John Leonard; s of Dr Ashley George Gyton Thompson (d 1983), and Muriel Elaine, *née* Griffiths; *b* 23 May 1921; *Educ* Marlborough, Pembroke Coll Cambridge (BA, MA, PhD), Univ of London (DSc 1960); *m* 1944, (Jessie) Anne, da of Capt John Leslie Cloudsley (d 1968); 3 s (Hugh b 1944, Timothy b 1948, Peter b 1952); *Career* cmmnd 4 QOH 1941, transferred 4 Co London Yeo (Sharpshooters), served N Africa 1941–42 (Op Crusader, Knightsbridge tank battle, severely wounded), instr Sandhurst (Capt) 1943, rejoined Regt for D Day (escaped from Villers Bocage), served Caen offensive (Op Goodwood) 1944, hon rank of Capt on resignation; lectr in zoology King's Coll Univ of London 1950–60, prof of zoology Univ of Khartoum and keeper Sudan Natural History Museum 1960–71, prof of zoology (now emeritus prof) Birkbeck Coll Univ of London 1972–86, Leverhulme emeritus fell UCL 1986–89; Nat Sci Fndn sr res fell Univ of New Mexico Albuquerque 1969; visiting prof: Univ of Kuwait 1978 and 1983, Univ of Nigeria 1981, Univ of Qatar 1986, Sultan Qaboos Univ Muscat 1988; visiting res fell: ANU 1987, Desert Ecological Res Unit of Namibia 1989; chm: Br Naturalists Assoc 1974–83 (vice pres 1985), Biological Cncl 1977–82 (Medal 1985); pres: Br Arachnological Soc 1982–85 (vice pres 1985–86), Br Soc for Chronobiology 1985–87; vice pres: Linnean Soc 1975–76 and 1977–78, first World Congress of Herpetology 1989; hon memb: Royal African Soc 1969 (Medal 1969), Br Herpetological Soc 1983 (pres 1991–96), Centre International de Documentation Arachnologique Paris 1995; KSS Charter Award Inst of Biology 1981, JH Grundy Meml Medal RAMC 1987, Peter Scott Meml Award 1993; ed-in-chief Journal of Arid Environments 1978–97; Freeman City of London 1945, Liveryman Worshipful Co of Skinners 1952; Hon DSc and Gold Medal Univ of Khartoum 1981; FIBiol 1962, CBiol, FWAAS 1962, FRES, FLS, FZS; *Books* over 50 incl: Spiders, Scorpions, Centipedes and Mites (1958), Zoology of Tropical Africa (1969), The Temperature and Water Relations of Reptiles (1971), Insects and History (1976), Why the Dinosaurs Became Extinct (1978), Tooth and Claw (1980), Evolution and Adaptation of Terrestrial Arthropods (1988), Ecophysiology of Desert Arthropods and Reptiles (1991), The Nile Quest (novel, 1994), Biotic Interactions in Arid Lands (1996); *Recreations* music (especially opera), photography, travel; *Style*— Prof John Cloudsley-Thompson; ✉ 10 Battishill St, London N1 1TE

CLOUGH, (John) Alan; CBE (1972), MC (1945); s of John Clough (d 1982), and Yvonne, *née* Dollfus; *b* 20 March 1924; *Educ* Marlborough, Univ of Leeds; *m* 1, 1949 (m dis 1961), Margaret Joy, da of A Catton, of Kirkby Overblow; 1 s, 2 da; m 2, 1961, Mary Cowan, da of Harold Mathew Stuart Catherwood; 1 s, 1 da; *Career* Capt, serv N Africa and Italy 1942–47, Maj TA Yorks Hussars 1947–55; chm: Wool Industs Res Assoc 1967–69, Wool Textile Delgn 1969–72; pres: Br Textile Confedn 1974–77, Comitextil-Brussels (co-ordinating Ctee for Textile Industries in EEC) 1975–77, Textile Inst 1979–81 (companion 1975), Confedn of Br Wool Textiles 1982–84; chm: Br Mohair Spinners Ltd to 1984, Textile Res Cncl 1984–89, Instant Muscle 1989–94; Hon DSc Univ of Bradford 1987; Past Mayor Co of Merchants of the Staple of England; *Recreations* travelling, gardening, fishing; *Clubs* Boodle's; *Style*— Alan Clough, Esq, CBE, MC; ✉ The Hays, Monks Eleigh, Suffolk IP7 7AE

CLOUGH, Prunella; da of Eric Clough Taylor, and Thora Clough Taylor; *Educ* Chelsea Sch of Art; *Career* painter; clerical and draughtsman's wartime jobs 1940–45, former teacher Chelsea Sch of Art, teacher Wimbledon Sch of Art; solo exhibitions: Leger Gallery 1947, Roland Browse and Delbanco 1949, Leicester Galleries London 1953, Whitechapel Gallery 1960, Grosvenor Gallery 1964 and 1967, Graves Art Gallery Sheffield 1972, New Art Centre 1973, 1975, 1976, 1979, 1982, Serpentine Gallery 1976, Nat Gallery of Modern Art Edinburgh 1976, Artspace Galleries Aberdeen 1981, Fitzwilliam Museum Cambridge 1982, Warwick Arts Trust 1982, Annely Juda Fine Art 1989, 1992, 1993, Camden Art Centre (retrospective) 1996; gp exhibitions incl: Pittsburgh Int (Carnegie Inst) 1950, Vision and Reality (Wakefield City Art Gallery) 1956, Museum of Modern Art Oxford 1966, Desborough Gallery Perth Western Australia 1974, British Art 1952–1977 (Royal Acad) 1977, Studio ODD Hiroshima 1984, Albermarle Gallery 1988; work in collections incl: Clare Coll Cambridge, Art Gallery of NSW, Tate Gallery, V & A, Nuffield Fndn, DES; City of London Midsummer prize 1977; *Style*— Ms Prunella Clough

CLOVER, Charles Robert Harold; s of Harold Percy Clover (d 1973), and Diana Patricia, *née* Hutchinson Smith (d 1975); *b* 22 Aug 1958; *Educ* Westminster, Univ of York (BA); *m* Pamela Anne, da of Leonard C Roberts; 2 s (Duncan Harold Cairns, Thaddeus John Charles); *Career* asst ed The Spectator 1979; Daily Telegraph: reporter Peterborough Column 1982, rock critic 1983–86, TV critic and feature writer 1986–87, environment corr 1987–89, environment ed 1989–; nat journalist Media Nature's Br environment and media awards 1989 and 1994; *Books* Highgrove (with HRH The Prince of Wales, 1993); *Recreations* fly fishing; *Style*— Charles Clover, Esq; ✉ Daily Telegraph, 1 Canada Square, Canary Wharf, London E14 5DT (☎ 0171 538 6409, fax 0171 538 7842)

CLOWES, Alfred William; s of Alfred Clowes (d 1973), of Stoke on Trent, and Mary Ann, *née* Cain (d 1974); *b* 17 Dec 1931; *Educ* Hanley County GS Stoke on Trent; *m* 31 March 1956, Joan, da of Thomas Colclough (d 1978), of Cheddleton, nr Leek, Staffs; 2 da (Angela b 1957, Julie b 1960); *Career* gen sec Ceramic and Allied Trades Union 1980–95 (asst gen sec 1975–80); *Recreations* golf; *Clubs* Westwood Golf (Staffs); *Style*— Alfred Clowes, Esq; ✉ Ceramic and Allied Trades Union, Hillcrest House, Garth St, Hanley, Stoke on Trent, Staffs ST1 2AB (☎ 01782 272755, fax 01782 284902)

CLUCAS, Sir Kenneth Henry; KCB (1976, CB 1969); o s of Rev J H Clucas (d 1963); *b* 18 Nov 1921; *Educ* Kingswood Sch, Emmanuel Coll Cambridge; *m* 1960, Barbara (d 1993), da of late Rear Adm R P Hunter, USN, of Washington DC, USA; 2 da (Jill, Susan); *Career* served WWII RCS (despatches); Civil Serv: second sec lab HM Embassy Cairo 1950, under sec Miny of Lab 1966–68, sec Nat Bd Prices and Incomes 1968–71, dep sec CSD and first CS cmmr 1971–73, dep sec DTI 1974; perm sec: Dept of Prices and Consumer Protection 1974–79, Dept of Trade 1979–82, ret; memb Cncl on Tbnls 1983–89; chm Nat Assoc of CABx 1984–89, chm Nuffield Fndn Ctee of Inquiry into Pharmacy 1983–86, members' ombudsman Lloyd's of London 1988–94, chm FIMBRA 1993– (memb Cncl 1986–); Hon FRPharmS 1989, FRSA 1991; *Style*— Sir Kenneth Clucas, KCB; ✉ Cariad, Knoll Rd, Godalming, Surrey (☎ 01483 416430)

CLUETT, Shelagh; da of Edwin Geoffrey Cluett (d 1986), and Majorie Mary, *née* Gatehouse (d 1978); *b* 17 Dec 1947; *Educ* Brockenhurst, St Martins Sch of Art, Hornsey Coll of Art (BA), Chelsea Sch of Art (higher postgrad dip); *Career* princ lectr MA course in sculpture Chelsea Sch of Art 1980–; visiting artist: Central Sch of Art, Wolverhampton Poly, Sheffield Poly, NE London Poly, Bath Acad, Canterbury Coll of Art, Univ of Syracuse, RCA, Royal Acad of Art, Slade Sch, Edinburgh Coll of Art, Univ of Ulster, Duncan of Jordanstown, S Glamorgan Inst, Manchester Poly, N Staffordshire Poly, Newcastle Poly, Brighton Poly, Portsmouth Poly, Winchester Sch of Art, Gloucestershire Coll of the Arts, Ecole des Beaux Arts Macon (Erasmus project in collaboration with Brera Acad Milan); CNAA external examiner for BA (hons), MA and MPhil progs at various insts incl: Middlesex Poly, Glasgow Sch of Art, Newcastle Poly; study visits: Burma, Thailand, Malaysia and Sumatra 1988, Laos and Vietnam 1990; memb: Fine Art Bd Panel CNAA 1983–88, Ctee Art Accord, Sculpture Panel Br Sch at Rome; exhibition selector: New Contempories (ICA), Midland View (Midland Gp Nottingham), Camden Open (Camden Inst); *Exhibitions* incl: 7+4 (Richard Demarco Gallery Edinburgh) 1974, Cleveland Int Drawing Biennale 1977, 12 sculptors (WSCAD Gallery) 1978, The First Exhibition (Nicola Jacobs Gallery) 1979, New Sculpture (Ikon Gallery Birmingham) 1979, 55 Wapping Artists (London) 1979, Kunst Idag 1 (Ordropgaard Copenhagen) 1980, Eight Women Artists (Acme Gallery) 1980, 30 ex-ILEA (Whitechapel Art Gallery) 1981, One Person Show (Nicola Jacobs Gallery, Paris Biennale) 1982, Musee des Beaux Arts (Tourcoing France) 1982, Dienst Beelende Kunst (Kruithuis Den Bosch Holland) 1983, Nocturn (Siegal Contemporary Art NY), One Person Show (Nicola Jacobs Gallery) 1984, One Person Show (Herbert Art Gallery Coventry) 1985, The Last Wapping Show 1985, The National Garden Festival (Stoke on Trent) 1986, Nicola Jacobs Gallery 1986, Metal and Motion (Brighton Museum and touring) 1987, Recent Acquisitions of CAS (Mayor Gallery) 1988, Royal Academy Summer Exhibition 1989, Gardner Centre Univ of Sussex 1991, CAC Centenary Portfolio 1991, Sculpture Exhibition (CAC) 1993, The Boat Show (Cafe Gallery) 1993, Selected Works (London Inst Gallery) 1994; *Recreations* travel; *Clubs* Chelsea Arts; *Style*— Ms Shelagh Cluett; ✉ Chelsea College of Art & Design, Manresa Rd, London SW3 6LS (☎ 0171 514 7750, fax 0171 514 7777)

CLUFF, John Gordon (Algy); s of Harold Cluff (d 1989), and Freda Cluff; *b* 19 April 1940; *Educ* Stowe; *m* 1993, Blondel, *née* Hodge; 2 s (Harry b 30 Dec 1993, Philip Randolph Macartney 4 July 1996); *Career* Mil Serv: Lt Gren Gds 1959–62, Capt Gds Parachute Co 1962–64, serv W Africa, Cyprus, Malaysia; chm and chief exec Cluff Mining Ltd, chm The Spectator; Parly candidate (C) Ardwick Manchester 1966; tstee Anglo-Hong Kong Tst, a dir The Centre for Policy Studies, a govr The Commonwealth Inst; *Clubs* White's, Pratt's, Beefsteak, Boodle's, The Brook (New York); *Style*— J G Cluff, Esq; ✉ Cluff Mining Limited, 29 St James's Place, London SW1 (☎ 0171 493 2050)

CLUGSTON, John Westland Antony; s of Leonard Gordon Clugston, OBE, DL (d 1984), and Sybil Mary Bacon (d 1981); *b* 16 May 1938; *Educ* Sandroyd, Gordonstoun; *m* 1, 6 June 1969, Patricia, da of Gordon Columba Harvey (d 1994); 2 s (Alistair b 1970, David b 1972), 2 da (Linda b 1973, Christina b 1976); m 2, Jane Elizabeth Ann, da of Charles Burtt Marfleet (d 1967), of Wykeham Hall, Ludford, Lincs; *Career* Lt Sherwood Rangers Yeo (TA); apprentice: at Huttenwerk Rheinhausen A G Iron and Steel Works (Germany) 1958–60, Lorraine Escaut Iron and Steel Works at Mont-St-Martin and Senelle (France) 1960–61; dir: Clugston Holdings Ltd 1964, Roadstone Div Activities 1965–68 (dir for all subsidiary co's 1970), E Bacon & Co 1985; chm: Roadstone Div 1969, Reclamation Div and St Vincent Plant Ltd 1980; gp chm: Colvilles Clugston Shanks (Holdings) Ltd, Colvilles Clugston Shanks Ltd 1984, Clydesdale Excavating and Construction Co Ltd 1987–; dir: Appleby Group Ltd 1983, Market Rasen Racecourse Ltd 1995–; chm and md: Clugston Holdings Ltd 1984 (gp vice chm and md 1978), Clugston Group Ltd 1991–; dir Yorks and Humberside Assoc of Enterprise Agencies; past pres Humberside branch Br Inst of Mgmnt, pres Lincolnshire Iron and Steel Inst 1989–90, former memb Cncl British Aggregates Construction Materials Industry, chm S Humberside Business Advice Centre, exec chm Humberside Scout Cncl, chm of govrs Brigg Prep Sch; High Sheriff of Humberside 1992–93; Freeman City of London, Upper Warden Worshipful Co of Paviors 1995 (Liveryman 1965, memb Ct of Assts 1986); assoc Inst of Quarrying, MInstD, FIHT 1984; *Recreations* shooting, fishing, tennis, music; *Style*— J W A Clugston, Esq; ✉ The Old Vicarage, Scawby, Brigg, Lincs DN20 9LX (☎ 01652 657100); Clugston Group Ltd, St Vincent Hse, Normanby Rd, Scunthorpe, N Lincs DN15 8QT (☎ 01724 843491, fax 01724 281714)

CLUNIES-ROSS, Prof Anthony Ian; s of Sir Ian Clunies-Ross, CMG (d 1959), and Janet Leslie, *née* Carter (d 1986); *b* 9 March 1932; *Educ* Knox GS Sydney, Scotch Coll Melbourne, Univ of Melbourne (BA), Pembroke Coll Cambridge (MA); *m* 1 July 1961, Morag Fraser, da of James Faulds McVey (d 1975); 2 s (James b 1962 d 1985, David b 1964), 2 da (Sarah b 1965, Brigit b 1972); *Career* lectr then sr lectr in economics Monash Univ 1961–67, sr lectr then prof of economics Univ of Papua New Guinea 1967–74, lectr, sr lectr then prof of economics Univ of Strathclyde 1975–93, prof emeritus 1993; *Books* One Per Cent: The Case for Greater Australian Foreign Aid (jtly, 1963), Australia and Nuclear Weapons (jtly, 1966) Alternative Strategies for Papua New Guinea (jtly, 1973), Taxation of Mineral Rent (jtly, 1983), Migrants From Fifty Villages (1984), Economic Stabilization for Developing Countries (1991); *Recreations* swimming, gardening; *Style*— Mr Anthony Clunies-Ross; ✉ Railway Cottage, Kinbuck, Dunblane, Perthshire, Scotland FK15 0NL (☎ 01786 822684)

CLUTTERBUCK, Dr David; *b* 4 June 1947; *Educ* Christ's Coll Finchley, Westfield Coll London (BA); *m*; 4 s; *Career* Dept of Immigration Home Office 1968–69, ed Journal of the British Nuclear Energy Society (ICE) 1969–70, news ed (technol) New Scientist 1970–73, assoc ed rising to managing ed/ed-in-chief International Management 1973–83; fndr ed: Issues magazine 1984–90, Strategic Direction and Technology Strategies 1985–89, Marketing Business 1988–90; Euro ed On Achieving Excellence 1989–92; chm ITEM Group Plc (communications project mgmnt co) 1982–, sr ptnr Clutterbuck Associates (editorial mgmnt consultancy) 1983–; dir: The European Mentoring Centre 1991–, Mentoring Directors Ltd, Boardroom Effectiveness Ltd 1995–; public sector clients incl: Benefits Agency, NHS, Dept of Employment, Inland Revenue, DTI, DSS, BR Systems, Cabinet Office; private sector clients incl: ASDA, British American Tobacco, Andersen Consulting, Brooke Bond Foods, Shell, British Aerospace, Coates Viyella, District Audit; also leader various in-house research programmes; assoc prof Int Mgmnt Centres (IMC); visiting fell: Sheffield Business Sch, Putteridge Bury; tstee Children's Aid Direct; Hon DLitt and industrial fell IMC; memb: Assoc of Mgmnt Educn and Devpt, Inst of Journalists; MInstD, MIPD, MIMgt; *Publications* incl: How to be a Good Corporate Citizen (1981), The Tales of Gribble the Goblin (1983), New Patterns of Work (1985), Everyone Needs a Mentor (1985), Clore: The Man and his Millions (1986), Businesswoman (1987), Turnaround (1988), The Makers of Management (1990), Making Customers Count (1991), Inspired Customer Service (1993), The Independent Board Director (with Peter Waine, *qv*, 1993), The Power of Empowerment (1994), Charity as a Business (1995), Mentoring in Action (1995); also author of numerous articles and papers in International Management, The Director, Management Today, The Times and others; *Videos* Beyond the Winning Streak (1989), The Service Dimension (1991), Creating Tomorrow's Company Today (1993), The Mentor Dimension (1994); *Style*— Dr David Clutterbuck; ✉ Clutterbuck Associates, Burnham House, High Street, Burnham, Bucks SL1 7JZ (☎ 01628 604882, fax 01628 667155)

CLUTTERBUCK, Vice Adm Sir David Granville; KBE (1968), CB (1965); s of Charles Granville Clutterbuck (d 1958); *b* 25 Jan 1913; *Educ* HMS Conway; *m* 1937, Rose Mere, da of Hubert Earle Vaile, of Auckland, NZ; 2 da; *Career* joined RN 1929, Rear Adm 1963, Vice Adm 1966, Dep Supreme Allied Cdr Atlantic 1966–68, ret; admin dir Business Graduates Assoc Ltd 1969–83; *Style*— Vice Adm Sir David Clutterbuck, KBE, CB; ✉ Burrard Cottage, Walhampton, Lymington, Hampshire SO41 5SA

CLUTTERBUCK, Jasper Meadows; s of late Hugh Meadows Clutterbuck; *b* 5 Feb 1935; *Educ* Eton; *m* 1958, Marguerite Susan, *née* Birnie; 1 s, 1 da; *Career* Lt Coldstream Gds 1953–56; dir Whitbread & Co 1975–88, chm Morland & Co plc 1993–96; *Style*— Jasper Clutterbuck, Esq; ✉ Mottisfont House, Mottisfont, nr Romsey, Hants SO51 0LN

CLUTTERBUCK, Maj-Gen Richard Lewis; CB (1971), OBE (1958); s of Col Lewis St John Rawlinson Clutterbuck, OBE, late RA (d 1965), and Isabella Jessie, *née* Jocelyn (d 1968), ggda of 2 Earl of Roden; *b* 22 Nov 1917; *Educ* Radley, Pembroke Coll Cambridge (MA), Univ of London (PhD); *m* 1948, Angela Muriel, da of Col Bernard Cole Barford, RA, of Bishop's Waltham; 3 s (Peter, Robin, Julian); *Career* 2 Lt RE 1937, Maj-Gen 1968, chief instr (Army) Royal Coll of Def Studies 1971–72, Col Cmdt RE 1972–77; reader in political conflict Univ of Exeter 1972–83, non-exec dir Control Risks Ltd 1977–87; author; memb BBC Gen Advsy Cncl 1975–81; *Books* The Media and Political Violence (1983), Industrial Conflict and Democracy (1984), Conflict and Violence in Singapore and Malaysia (1985), The Future of Political Violence (1986), Kidnap, Hijack and Extortion (1987), Terrorism and Guerrilla Warfare (1990), Terrorism Drugs and Crime in Europe after 1992 (1990), International Crisis and Conflict (1993), Terrorism in an Unstable World (1994), Drugs, Crime and Corruption (1995), Public Safety and Civil Liberties (1997); *Clubs* Army and Navy, Royal Cwlth Soc; *Style*— Maj-Gen Richard Clutterbuck, CB, OBE; ✉ c/o Dept of Politics, Amory Building, University of Exeter EX4 4RJ

CLUTTON, (Bernard Geoffrey) Owen; s of Maj Arthur Henry Clutton, MC (d 1979), and Joyce, *née* Worthington; *b* 3 March 1951; *Educ* St Aidans Coll Grahamstown, Univ of Witwatersrand (BA, LLB), Univ of Oxford (BCL); *m* 12 Oct 1979, Rosemary Elizabeth, da of Geoffrey Thomas Skett; 1 s (William Edward Henry b 28 March 1988), 1 da (Alice Elizabeth Katherine b 5 Aug 1990); *Career* admitted slr 1980; ptnr Macfarlanes 1984–; President's Certificate Nat Playing Fields Assoc; Liveryman Worshipful Co of Slrs; memb Law Soc, ATII; *Style*— Owen Clutton, Esq; ✉ Macfarlanes, 10 Norwich St, London EC4A 1BD (☎ 0171 831 9222, fax 0171 831 9607, telex 296381)

CLUTTON, Rafe Henry; CBE (1992); s of Robin John Clutton (d 1978), and Rosalie Muriel, *née* Birch (d 1978); *b* 13 June 1929; *Educ* Tonbridge; *m* 1954, Jill Olwyn, da of John Albert Evans, of Haywards Heath, Sussex; 4 s (Owen b 1958, Gareth b 1960, Jonathan b 1962, Niall b 1964), 1 da (Helen b 1968); *Career* chartered surveyor; ptnr Cluttons 1955–92 (conslt 1992–); dir: Legal and General Group Ltd 1972–93, Rodamco (UK) BV 1990–95; memb: Bd Royal Nat Theatre 1976–93, Advsy Bd Salvation Army Housing Assoc 1987–95, Royal Cmmn for Exhbn of 1851 1988–; govr Royal Fndn of Greycoat Hosp 1967– (chm 1981–); FRICS; *Recreations* grandchildren, books, and admiring the view; *Clubs* Royal Thames Yacht; *Style*— Rafe Clutton, Esq, CBE; ✉ 25 St Alban's Gardens, Ventnor, Isle of Wight PO38 1DF (☎ 01983 855373) 45 Berkeley Square, London W1X 5DB (☎ 0171 408 1010, telex 23620)

CLUTTON, Lady Sarah Margaret; *née* Fitzalan-Howard; DL (W Sussex 1993); da of 16 Duke of Norfolk, KG, GCVO, GBE, TD, PC (d 1975); *b* 28 Sept 1941; *m* 25 March 1988, Nigel Clutton, s of Robin John Clutton (d 1978), and bro of Rafe Henry Clutton, *qv*; *Career* awarded Pro Ecclesia et Pontifice (highest papal award for ladies) 1983; *Style*— The Lady Sarah Clutton, DL; ✉ The Dover House, Poling, Arundel, West Sussex BN18 9PX

CLUTTON-BROCK, Prof Timothy Hugh (Tim); *b* 13 Aug 1946; *Educ* Rugby, Magdalene Coll Cambridge (MA, PhD, ScD); *Career* Game Dept Zambia 1964–65, researcher Sub-Dept of Animal Behaviour Madingley Cambridge (and field work in Tanzania and Uganda) 1969–70, NERC res fell Animal Behaviour Res Gp Univ of Oxford 1972–73, lectr in biology Sch of Biological Scis Univ of Sussex 1973–76, sr res fell in behavioural ecology Res Centre King's Coll Cambridge 1976–80; Dept of Zoology Univ of Cambridge: fndr Large Animal Res Gp 1980, SERC advanced res fell 1981–83, Royal Soc res fell in biology 1983–88, univ lectr 1987–91, reader in animal ecology 1991–, prof of animal ecology 1994–; co-fndr and dir Wildlife Consultants Ltd 1976–86, chm Deer Specialist Gp IUCN 1980–91; res projects incl: primate ecology, the evolution of mammalian breeding systems, natural and sexual selection, the evolution of sexual care, population regulation in ungulates, management of deer populations; memb Editorial Bd: Jl of Animal Ecology, Behavioural Ecology, Behavioural Ecology and Sociobiology; jt ed Princeton Univ Press Monograph series in behavioural ecology; contrib to various radio and TV progs (incl script for BBC Horizon prog on Rhum); Scientific Medal Zoological Soc of London 1984, C Hart Merriam award American Soc of Mammalogists 1991; FRS 1993; *Publications* Primate Ecology (ed, 1977), Current Problems in Sociobiology (ed, 1982), Red Deer - Behaviour and Ecology of Two Sexes (jtly, 1982, Wildlife Soc of America best book award), Rhum - the Natural History of an Island (ed jtly, 1987), Reproductive Success - Studies of Individual Variation in Contrasting Breeding Systems (ed, 1988), Red Deer in the Highlands (jtly, 1989), The Evolution of Parental Care (1991); author of around 100 articles in learned jls; popular articles in New Scientist, Nat Geographic, Natural History and The Field; *Style*— Prof Tim Clutton-Brock, FRS; ✉ Large Animal Research Group, Department of Zoology, Downing St, Cambridge CB2 3EJ (☎ 01223 336618)

CLWYD, Ann; MP (Lab) Cynon Valley (majority 21,364); da of Gwilym Henri Lewis, and Elizabeth Ann Lewis; *b* 21 March 1937; *Educ* Holywell GS, The Queen's Sch Chester, Univ Coll Bangor; *m* 1963, Owen Dryhurst Roberts; *Career* former journalist The Guardian and The Observer, reporter BBC; Parly candidate (Lab) Denbigh 1970 and Gloucester Oct 1974, MEP (Lab) Mid and W Wales 1979–84, MP (Lab) Cynon Valley 1984–; oppn front spokesperson on educn and women's affrs 1987–88, memb Shadow Cabinet 1989–93, shadow sec on overseas devpt 1989–92, shadow Welsh sec 1992, shadow Nat Heritage sec 1992–93, oppn front bench spokesperson on employment

1993–94, oppn front bench spokesperson on foreign affrs 1994–95, dep to John Prescott 1994–95; vice chm Welsh Arts Cncl 1975–79; memb: Royal Cmmn on NHS 1977–79, Lab NEC 1983–84; *Style*— Ann Clwyd, MP; ✉ 6 Deans Court, Dean Street, Aberdare, Mid Glamorgan; House of Commons, London SW1A 0AA (☎ 0171 219 3000)

CLYDE, Baron (Life Peer UK 1996), of Briglands in Perthshire and Kinross; James John Clyde; PC (1996); s of Rt Hon Lord Clyde (d 1975), and Margaret Letitia Dubuisson (d 1974); *b* 29 Jan 1932; *Educ* The Edinburgh Acad, Univ of Oxford (BA), Univ of Edinburgh (LLB); *m* 1963, Ann Clunie, da of Donald Robert Armstrong Hoblyn (d 1975); 2 s (Hon James b 1969, Hon Timothy b 1973); *Career* advocate Scotland 1959, QC (Scot) 1971, advocate depute 1973–74, chllr to Bishop of Argyll and the Isles 1972–85, memb Scottish Valuation Advsy Cncl 1972–96 (vice-chm 1980–87, chm 1987–96), ldr UK Delgn to the CCBE 1981–84, chm Medical Appeal Tribunals 1974–85, judge in the Cts of Appeal for Jersey and Guernsey 1979–85, senator Coll of Justice 1985–96, a Lord of Appeal in Ordinary 1996–; tstee St Mary's Music Sch 1978–93, dir Edinburgh Acad 1979–88, vice pres The Royal Blind Asylum and Sch 1987–, pres Scottish Young Lawyers' Assoc 1988–, chm Cncl St George's Sch for Girls 1989–, govr Napier Univ (formerly Napier Poly) 1989–93; Univ of Edinburgh: assessor to Chllr 1989–, vice chm of Ct 1993–; pres Scottish Univs Law Inst 1991–; tstee Nat Library of Scotland 1977–94; Hon DUniv Heriot-Watt 1991, Hon DLitt Napier Univ 1995; hon bencher Middle Temple 1996, hon fell Corpus Christi Coll Oxford 1996; *Recreations* music, gardening; *Clubs* New (Edinburgh); *Style*— The Rt Hon Lord Clyde, PC; ✉ 9 Heriot Row, Edinburgh EH3 6HU (☎ 0131 556 7114)

CLYDESMUIR, 3 Baron (UK 1948); David Ronald Colville; s 2 Baron Clydesmuir, KT, CB, MBE, TD (d 1996), and Joan Marguerita, *née* Booth; *b* 8 April 1949; *Educ* Charterhouse; *m* 1978, Aline Frances, da of Peter Merriam, of Holton Lodge, Holton St Mary, Suffolk; 2 s (Hon Richard b 1980, Hon Hamish b 1989), 2 da (Hon Rachel b 1983, Hon Harriet b 1985); *Heir* s, Hon Richard Colville b 21 Oct 1980; *Style*— The Rt Hon the Lord Clydesmuir; ✉ Langlees House, Biggar, Lanarkshire

COAD, Jonathan George; *b* 2 Feb 1945; *Educ* Lancing, Keble Coll Oxford (BA); *m* 16 April 1976, Vivienne Jaques; 2 da (Jennifer b 1982, Felicity b 1986); *Career* historian, archaeologist; inspr of ancient monuments and historic bldgs; head Historic Branch Historic Properties SE English Heritage; hon sec Royal Archaeological Inst; vice pres Soc for Nautical Res; FSA; *Books* Historic Architecture of The Royal Navy (1983), The Royal Dockyards 1690–1850, Architecture and Engineering Works of the Sailing Navy (1989), Dover Castle (1995); *Recreations* reading, travel, woodworking; *Clubs* Eclectic; *Style*— Jonathan G Coad, Esq, FSA; ✉ Baileys Reed, Salehurst, Sussex TN32 5SP

COAKHAM, Prof Hugh Beresford; s of William Coakham (d 1973), and Evelyn Grace, *née* Cale; *b* 17 Sept 1944; *Educ* Windsor GS, UCL (BSc), UCH (MB BS, MRCP); *m* 1, 15 May 1972, Elspeth Margaret, da of Harold Macfarlane; 2 s (Alexander b 22 Dec 1978, Jonathan b 24 April 1982), 1 da (Simone b 29 May 1977); m 2, 11 Sept 1992, Janet James, da of George McKie; *Career* conslt neurosurgeon Frenchay Hosp and Bristol Royal Infirmary 1980–, dir Brain Tumour Res Laboratory 1980–, clinical dir Imperial Cancer Res Fund Paediatric and Neuro-Oncology Group 1990–, prof of neurosurgery Univ of Bristol 1992–; memb: Soc of Br Neurological Surgns, Br Neuropathalogical Assoc, Br Neuro-Oncology Gp, Euro Assoc of Neurosurgical Soc, Editorial Bd Br Jl of Neurosurgery 1991, Editorial Bd Clinical Neurosurgery 1992; author of numerous published papers in int jls of neurosurgery and cancer research; Heart of Gold Award BBC TV 1988 (for NHS fundraising), ABI Medical Award 1991, Hunterian prof Royal Coll of Surgns 1993; FRCS 1974, FRCP 1991; *Books* Recent Advances in Neuropathology (contrib, 1985), Tumours of the Brain (contrib, 1986), Biology of Brain Tumours (contrib, 1986), Medulloblastoma: Clinical and Biological Aspects (contrib, 1986), Progress in Surgery - Vol 2 (contrib, 1987), Progress in Paediatric Surgery - Vol 22 (contrib, 1989); *Recreations* jazz saxophone; *Style*— Prof Hugh Coakham; ✉ Mansion House Stables, Litfield Rd, Clifton, Bristol BS8 3LL (☎ 0117 973 4963); Dept of Neurological Surgery, Frenchay Hospital, Bristol BS16 1LE (☎ 0117 970 1212, fax 0117 970 1508)

COALES, Prof John Flavell; CBE (1974, OBE 1945); s of John Dennis Coales, DSc (d 1942), of Cobham, and Marion Beatrix, *née* Flavell, ARCM (d 1962); *b* 14 Sept 1907; *Educ* Berkhamsted Sch, Sidney Sussex Coll Cambridge (BA, MA, ScD); *m* 1 Aug 1936, (Mary) Dorothea Violet, da of Rev Henry Lewis Guthrie Alison (d 1958), vicar of Kintbury, Berks; 2 s (Edward b 16 May 1939, Martin b 16 March 1943), 2 da (Susan b 17 May 1937, Alison b 7 Jan 1942); *Career* Admiralty Dept of Sci Res and Experiment: jr sci offr 1929–32, sci offr 1933–39, sr sci offr 1940–43, princ 1944–46 (temp Cdr RNVR); res dir Elliott Bros (London) 1946–52; Univ of Cambridge: asst dir res 1952–55, lectr 1956–57, reader 1958–64, prof of engrg 1965–74, emeritus prof 1974, emeritus fell Clare Hall 1974– (fell 1966–74); chm: UK Automation Cncl 1963–66, Cncl of Engrg Insts 1975–76, Cwlth Bd for Engrg Educn and Trg 1975–79; pres: Int Fedn of Automatic Control 1963–66, IEE 1971–72; Freeman City of London, Liveryman Worshipful Co of Engineers; Hon DSc City Univ 1971, Hon DTech Loughborough Univ 1977, Hon DEng Univ of Sheffield 1978, hon fell Univ of Hertfordshire (formerly Hatfield Poly) 1971; FIEE 1943, FInstP 1946, FICE 1973, FIEEE 1968, FRS 1970, Hon FIEE 1985, Hon FInstMC 1971, FIAgrE 1975–80, FEng 1976 (fndr fell); foreign memb Serbian Acadamy of Sciences; Harold Hartley medal 1971, Giorgio Quazza medal 1981, Honda prize 1982; *Books* Automatic and Remote Control (ed, 1967); many papers in tech jls on electrical engrg, systems engrg and educn; *Clubs* Alpine; *Style*— Prof John Coales, CBE, FRS, FEng; ✉ Cambridge University Engineering Dept, Trumpington St, Cambridge CB2 1PZ

COATES, *see:* Milnes Coates

COATES, Anne Voase (Mrs Anne Hickox); da of Maj Laurence Calvert Coates (d 1968), and Kathleen Voase, *née* Rank (d 1977); *b* 12 Dec 1925; *Educ* High Trees Sch Horley, Bartrum Gables Broadstairs; *m* 24 April 1958 (m dis), Douglas Arthur Hickox (d 1988), s of Horace Robert Hickox (d 1987); 2 s (Anthony Laurence Voase b 30 Jan 1959, James Douglas Rank b 20 June 1965), 1 da (Emma Elizabeth b 11 April 1964); *Career* film editor; memb: Acad of Motion Picture Arts and Scis, BAFTA; work incl: Lawrence of Arabia 1961–62, Becket 1963, Tunes of Glory 1960, Murder on the Orient Express 1975, The Elephant Man 1980, Greystoke Lord of the Apes 1983, Ragtime 1984, I Love You to Death 1989–90, Chaplin 1991–92, In the Line of Fire 1992/93, Pontiac Moon 1993–94, Congo 1994–95, Striptease 1995–96; prodr The Medusa Touch 1977; three BAFTA nominations 1975, 1981 and 1993, Academy Award USA 1962 (also nominated 1964 and 1981), three ACE nominations USA 1962, 1964 and 1993; *Style*— Ms Anne Coates; ✉ 8455 Fountain Avenue (Apt 621), Los Angeles, California 90069, USA (☎ 213 654 7282)

COATES, Clive; s of John Alfred Henry Coates (d 1963), and Sonja, *née* van Blaaderen; *b* 21 Oct 1941; *Educ* St Paul's Sch London, Westminster Hotel Sch (Student of the Year 1964); *m* 1, 1965 (m dis 1983), Rosalind, *née* Cohen; 1 da (Emma Jane b 1966), 1 s (Ben Jonathan b 1968); m 2, 1984 (m dis 1994), Juliet Trestini, eld da of David Burns, MW; *Career* promotions mangr IEC Wine Soc of Stevenage Herts 1967–73, dir Genevieve Wine Cellars 1973–75, exec dir Wines Div British Transport Hotels 1975–81, dir Les Amis du Vin (UK) 1981–84, fndr ed The Vine (monthly fine wine magazine) 1985– (special commendation Wine Guild of GB 1992), concurrently ind writer on wine, lectr and conslt; Glenfiddich Trophy for Trade Wine Writer of the Year 1980, Ruffino/Cyril Ray Meml Prize for writing on Italian wine 1994, Rame D'Or for Services to French wine 1994; MW 1971 (chm Educn Ctee 1985, memb Cncl 1976–82 and 1990–93); Chevalier de l'Ordre du Merité Agricole 1994; *Books* Claret (1982), The Wines of France (1990), Grands Vins, The Finest Châteaux of Bordeaux (1994), Côte D'Or - A Celebration of the Great Wines of Burgandy (1997), The Wine Lover's Companion to Burgandy (1997); *Recreations* music, cooking, visiting old churches, watching athletics and cricket, lying by a pool in the south of France with a good book; *Style*— Clive Coates, Esq; ✉ 76 Woodstock Road, London W4 1EQ (☎ 0181 995 8962, fax 0181 995 8943)

COATES, Sir David Charlton Frederick; 3 Bt (UK 1921), of Haypark, City of Belfast; s of Brig Sir Frederick Gregory Lindsay Coates, 2 Bt (d 1994), and Joan Nugent, *née* Spinks; *b* 16 Feb 1948; *Educ* Millfield; *m* 1973, Christine Helen, da of Lewis F Marshall, of Ely, Cambs; 2 s (James Gregory David b 12 March 1977, Robert Lewis Edward b 22 July 1980); *Heir* s, James Gregory David Coates b 12 March 1977; *Style*— Sir David Coates, Bt; ✉ 30 Hauxton Rd, Little Shelford, Cambridge CB2 5HJ

COATES, David Randall; *b* 22 March 1942; *Educ* Leeds GS, Queen's Coll Oxford (BA), LSE (MScEcon); *Career* research asst Univ of Manchester 1966–68, econ advsr Miny of Technol and DTI 1968–74; DTI: sr econ advsr 1974–82, asst sec 1982–89, grade 3 1989–, chief econ advsr 1990–; *Recreations* family, gardening, music; *Style*— David Coates, Esq; ✉ Economics and Statistics Directorate, DTI, 1 Victoria Street, London SW1E 0ET (☎ 0171 215 6059, fax 0171 215 6910)

COATES, Dudley James; s of Edward James Coates, and late Margot Coates; *b* 15 Sept 1946; *Educ* Westcliff HS for Boys, Univ of Sussex (BA); *m* 6 Sept 1969, Rev Dr Jean Margaret Walsingham; 2 da (Mary Ann Walsingham b 1977, Hannah Elizabeth Walsingham b 1981); *Career* HM Civil Serv: asst princ MAFF 1968–70, 2 sec UK Delgn to the Euro Communities 1970–72, princ MAFF 1973–78, lectr Civil Serv Coll 1978–81, head Animal Welfare Div (Grade 5) MAFF 1981–83, head Fin Mgmnt Team MAFF 1983–87, dir gen of corp servs (Grade 4) Intervention Bd for Agric Produce 1987–89, dir of regnl servs (Grade 3) MAFF 1989–96, head of environment gp 1996–; methodist local preacher 1970–, memb Methodist Conf, chair Methodist Publishing House 1996–; *Books* Policies into Practice (contrib); *Recreations* Christian activities, singing, cycling; *Style*— Dudley Coates, Esq; ✉ Ministry of Agriculture, Fisheries and Food, 17 Smith Square, London SW1P 3JR (☎ 0171 238 5684, fax 0171 238 5686)

COATES, (Kenneth) Ian Tod; s of Thomas Coates, of Suffolk, and Mabel, *née* Medcalf; *b* 26 July 1940; *Educ* Oundle, Univ of Manchester, Manchester Tech Coll; *m* 1966, Cynthia, da of Thomas Coop; 2 s (Tod b 1971, James b 1981); *Career* engrg scholarship and apprenticeship Metropolitan Vickers (now AEI) 1958–60, jr asst to Mangr Studio Alexander Manchester 1962–64, fndr Camera 7 Ltd (incl Ian Coates Studios) 1964–; fndr lectr Fuji Sch of Professional Photography 1987–, chm and tutor Acad of Professional Photography and lectr worldwide, memb Admissions and Qualifications Panel BIPP; FBIPP 1974 (MIBP 1959); *Books* Fuji Book of Professional Photography (contrib, 1991); reg author of magazine features; *Recreations* plant breeding, photography of the rich; *Style*— Ian Coates, Esq; ✉ Ian Coates Studios, Parsonage Green, Wilmslow, Cheshire SK9 1HT (☎ 01625 527877, fax 01625 549045)

COATES, James Richard; CB (1992); s of William Richard Coates (d 1974), and Doris Coral, *née* Richmond (d 1992); *b* 18 Oct 1935; *Educ* Nottingham HS, Clare Coll Cambridge (major scholar, MA); *m* 22 March 1969, (Helen) Rosamund, da of John William Rimington, MBE (d 1996); 1 s (Nicholas Benjamin b 14 Nov 1972), 1 da (Beatrice Emma b 28 May 1975); *Career* Miny of Tport: asst princ 1959–63, princ Road Safety and Channel Tunnel Divs 1963–69, private sec to Min 1969–71; DOE: asst sec 1972–77, Urban Tport Policy Div 1972–75, Directorate of Civil Accommodation (PSA) 1975–77, under sec 1977–83, dir of civil accommodation 1977–79, dir London Region (PSA) 1979–83; Dept of Tport: under sec 1983–, Highways Policy and Prog Directorate 1983–85, Railways Directorate 1985–91, Urban and Gen Directorate 1991–94, Urban and Local Tport Directorate 1994–95; independent conslt 1995–; FCIT 1996; *Recreations* reading, listening to music, looking at buildings; *Style*— James Coates, Esq, CB; ✉ 10 Alwyne Road, London N1 2HH (☎ 0171 359 7827)

COATES, Prof John Henry; s of James Henry Coates (d 1970), of Australia, and Beryl Lilian, *née* Lee (d 1952); *b* 26 Jan 1945; *Educ* Australian Nat Univ (BSc), Ecole Normale Superieure Paris, Univ of Cambridge; *m* 8 Jan 1966, Julie Mildred, da of Henry Basil Turner (d 1988); 3 s (David b 3 Jan 1970, Stephen b 7 Nov 1971, Philip b 22 June 1973); *Career* asst prof Harvard Univ 1969–72, assoc prof Stanford Univ 1972–75, lectr Univ of Cambridge 1975–77; prof: Australian Nat Univ 1977–78, Université de Paris XI (Orsay) 1978–85; prof and dir of mathematics Ecolé Normale Superieure Paris 1985–86; Univ of Cambridge: fell Emmanuel Coll 1975–77 and 1986–, Sadleirian prof of mathematics 1986–, head Dept of Pure Mathematics and Mathematical Statistics 1991–; pres London Mathematical Soc 1988–90, vice pres Int Mathematical Union 1991–95; FRS 1985; *Style*— Prof John Coates, FRS; ✉ 104 Mawson Rd, Cambridge CB1 2EA (☎ 01223 360884); Department of Pure Mathematics and Mathematical Statistics, University of Cambridge, 16 Mill Lane, Cambridge CB2 1SB (☎ 01223 337995, fax 01223 337920)

COATES, Prof Kenneth Sydney (Ken); MEP (Lab) Nottinghamshire North and Chesterfield (majority 76,260); s of Eric Arthur Coates, and Mary Coates; *b* 16 Sept 1930; *Educ* Univ of Nottingham (BA); *m* 1969, Tamara Tura; 3 s, 3 da, (1 da decd); *Career* miner Notts Coalfield 1948–56 (various underground jobs, ripper at coal face 1950–56), Adult Education Univ of Nottingham 1960–89 (asst tutor, tutor, sr tutor, reader 1980–89); MEP (Lab): Nottingham 1989–94, Notts N and Chesterfield 1994–; chm Human Rights Sub-Ctee Euro Parliament 1989–94, rapporteur Temp Ctee on Employment 1994–95; jt fndr Movement for Euro Nuclear Disarmament 1980 (jt sec Liaison Ctee 1981–89), memb Bertrand Russell Peace Fndn 1965–, ed Spokesman pubns, launched European Lab Forum journal 1990; special prof Adult Education Univ of Nottingham 1989–; *Books* Poverty: the Forgotten Englishmen (with Bill Silburn, 1970, 4 edn 1983), Industrial Democracy in Great Britain (with Tony Topham, 1967, 3 edn 1976), The New Unionism (with Tony Topham, 1972, 2 edn 1974), Trade Unions in Britain (with Tony Topham, 1980, 3 edn 1988), Heresies (1982), The Most Dangerous Decade (1984), Think Globally, act Locally (1988), The Making of the Transport and General Workers' Union Vol 1 Parts I and II (with Tony Topham, 1991), The Right Work (1995), Full Employment for Europe (with Stuart Holland, 1995), Dear Commissioner (1996); *Recreations* walking, reading; *Style*— Prof Ken Coates, MEP; ✉ 8 Regent Street, Mansfield, Notts NG18 1SS (☎ 01623 427622)

COATES, Marten Frank; s of Frank Herbert Coates, of Henley-in-Arden, Warwicks, and Violet, *née* Livermore; *b* 26 March 1947; *Educ* Pockington Sch Yorks, Univ of Durham (BA); *m* 17 Feb 1973, Susan, da of Dr Derek Anton-Stephens, of Leighton Powys; 3 da (Laura Jane b 17 March 1977, Anna Louise b 10 Oct 1978, Mary Elizabeth (twin) b 10 Oct 1978); *Career* called to the Bar Inner Temple 1972, practising barr, recorder of the Crown Court 1993; *Recreations* genealogy, gardening, walking, wine, cooking; *Style*— Marten Coates, Esq; ✉ 3 Fountain Ct, Steelhouse Lane, Birmingham B4 6DR (☎ 0121 236 5854, fax 0121 236 7008)

COATES, Michael Arthur; s of Joseph Michael Smith Coates, OBE (d 1984), of Wylam, Northumberland, and Lilian Warren, *née* Murray (d 1973); *b* 12 May 1924; *Educ* Uppingham; *m* 1, 1952 (m dis 1970), Audrey Hampton, da of Arthur William Thorne, of Wimborne, Dorset; 1 s (Simon Michael b 1 July 1959), 2 da (Amanda Dorothy b 23 March 1954, Catherine Lilian Mary b 28 March 1962); m 2, 1971 (m dis 1980), Hazel Ruth (Sally) Rogers, *née* Thorne; *Career* served WWII Med 1942–47; Price Waterhouse: Newcastle 1947–54, London 1954–59, ptnr 1959–88, sr ptnr UK 1975–82; chm Price

Waterhouse World Firm 1982–88; memb Tbnl under Banking Act 1979; Freeman City of London, Liveryman Worshipful Co of Chartered Accountants; *Recreations* horticulture, antiques, reading, railways, photography; *Style*— Michael Coates, Esq; ✉ 20 Wilton Crescent, London SW1X 8SA (☎ 0171 235 4423); Cantray House, Croy, Inverness-shire IV1 2PW (☎ 01667 493204); Price Waterhouse World Firm Ltd, Southwark Towers, 32 London Bridge Street, London SE1 9SY (☎ 0171 939 3000, fax 0171 378 0647, telex 884657)

COATES, Michael Odiarne; s of Gordon Lionel Coates (d 1990), of Oxted, Surrey, and Dorothy Madeleine, *née* Nelson; *b* 4 July 1938; *Educ* Haileybury ISC; *m* 20 April 1963, Frances Ann, da of Harold P S Paish; 2 da (Annabel Frances b 29 March 1965, Rebecca Jane b 21 Jan 1967); *Career* qualified chartered quantity surveyor 1962, sr ptnr Gardiner of Theobald 1979– (ptnr 1966–); memb Cncl Benenden Sch 1982–; Past Master Worshipful Co of Chartered Surveyors, memb Worshipful Co of Masons; FRICS 1971; *Recreations* wife and family, farming and viticulture, sports; *Clubs* Boodle's; *Style*— Michael Coates, Esq; ✉ Great Shoesmiths Farm, White Gates Lane, Wadhurst, East Sussex TN5 6QG (☎ 01892 782156); Gardiner & Theobald, 32 Bedford Square, London WC1B 3EG (☎ 0171 209 3000, fax 0171 209 1841)

COATES, Prof Nigel; s of Douglas Coates, of Great Malvern, Worcs, and Margaret Trigg, of Lavenham, Suffolk; *b* 2 March 1949; *Educ* Hanley Castle GS Malvern, Univ of Nottingham (BArch), Architectural Assoc London (AADipl, year prize, Italian Govt scholarship to Univ of Rome); *Career* architect and designer; unit master Architectural Assoc 1979–89, fndr memb Narrative Architecture Today (NATO) 1979–89, course master Bennington Coll Vermont USA 1980–81; fndr ptnr: Branson Coates Architecture (with Doug Branson) 1985–, Omniate (with Anne Brooks) 1987–; work exhibited in London, Milan, NY, Paris and Tokyo and in the collection of V&A London; TV features incl: Building Sites (BBC 2) 1989, Omnibus (BBC 1) 1992; work featured in numerous int pubns and jls; lectr worldwide; prof of architectural design RCA 1995–; external examiner Bartlett Sch of Architecture and Architectural Assoc 1993–94; memb Advsy Bd ICA 1987–89; *Projects* (with Branson Coates): Arca di Noe Japan 1988, Katharine Hamnett Shop London 1988, Hotel Otaru Marittimo Japan 1989, Nishi Azabu Wall Tokyo 1990, Taxim Nightclub Istanbul 1991, Art Silo Building Tokyo 1993, La Fôret and Nautilus Restaurants Schiphol Airport Amsterdam 1993, shops for Jigsaw women and men's fashion in UK, Ireland and Japan, new depts for Liberty store Regent's Street; *Design Commissions* Metropole and Jazz furniture collections (for Rockstone) 1986, Noah collection (for SCP) 1988, Female, He-man and She-woman mannequins (for Omniate) 1988, Tongue chair (for SCP) 1989, carpet collection (for V'soske Joyce) 1990, Slipper chair (for Hitch Mylius) 1994, collection of mannequins (for Stockman London) 1994, David collection (for Liberty) 1995; *Awards* Inter-Design Award for contrib to Japanese cities through architectural work 1990; with Branson Coates: winner limited competition for new gallery Geffrye Museum 1990, finalist invited competition for Museum of the Word Swansea 1994, finalist BBC Design Awards 1994, finalist invited competition for luxury highrise apartments Beirut 1995, invited competition for Millennium Markers Richmond 1995, winner invited competition for new bar Glasgow 1995, winner invited competition for Nat Centre for Popular Music Sheffield 1995; *Monograph* The City in Motion, Rick Poyner (Fourth Estate, 1989); *Recreations* contemporary art, video making, motorcycling; *Clubs* Groucho; *Style*— Prof Nigel Coates; ✉ Branson Coates Architecture, 23 Old Street, London SW1V 9HL (☎ 0181 490 0343, fax 0171 490 0320)

COATES, Prof Philip David; s of Frank Coates (d 1983), of Leeds, and Elsie, *née* Tyreman; *b* 20 Sept 1948; *Educ* Cockburn HS Leeds, Imperial Coll London (BSc), Univ of Leeds (MSc, PhD); *m* 3 July 1971, Jane Margaret, da of Robert (Sandy) McNab (d 1994); 3 da (Emma Caroline b 8 March 1975, Charlotte Ruth b 14 Nov 1977, Laura Jane b 2 Sept 1984), 1 s (John Philip b 6 Aug 1986); *Career* post doctoral res fell in physics Univ of Leeds 1976–78; Univ of Bradford: lectr in manufacturing systems engrg 1978–81, lectr in mechanical engrg 1981–84, sr lectr in mechanical engrg 1984–89, reader 1989–90, prof of polymer engrg Dept of Mechanical and Manufacturing Engrg/IRC in Polymer Sci and Technol Univ of Bradford 1990–, assoc dir IRC in Polymer Sci and Technol 1996–; conslt various cos 1979–, tech assessor DTI 1993–; memb: Plymers and Composites Ctee SERC 1989–92, Structural Composites Ctee DTI/SERC Link 1989–; chm Polymer Processing and Engrg Ctee Inst of Materials 1989–; organiser of seven int confs in polymer field; FIM 1987, FIMechE 1990, FEng 1995; *Awards* Competitive Res Fellowship Sci Research Cncl 1976–78, Silver Medal Plastics and Rubber Inst 1982 and 1987, Personal Res Award Wolfson Fndn 1988; *Publications* Concise Encyclopedia of Polymer Processing (contrib, 1992), Encyclopedia of Advanced Materials (contrib, 1994), Reactive Processing of Polymers (contrib, 1994); author of over 160 scientific pubns; *Recreations* family, playing various musical instruments, computers; *Style*— Prof Philip Coates, FEng; ✉ IRC in Polymer Science & Technology, Department of Mechanical and Manufacturing Engineering, University of Bradford, Bradford BD7 1DP (☎ 01274 384540, fax 01274 384505, e-mail p.d.coates@bradford.ac.uk)

COATES, William Muir Nelson; s of Victor Airth Coates, of Belfast, and Margaret Winifred, *née* Stewart (d 1975); *b* 18 June 1934; *Educ* Fettes, Univ of Edinburgh (BSc); *m* 26 March 1959, Christine, da of Keneth McLeod; 1 s (Iain Roderick b 1968), 1 da (Audrey Diana b 1960); *Career* Flt Lt RAF 1960–63; md Currall Lewis & Martin Ltd 1979; chm Fedn of Civil Engrg Contractors (Midlands) 1989; CEng, MICE; *Style*— William Coates, Esq; ✉ Boxmoor, Meer End, Kenilworth, Warwickshire CV8 1PW (☎ 01676 532038); Currall, Lewis & Martin Ltd, 11 Booth St, Birmingham B21 01BL (☎ 0121 554 6531, fax 0121 554 2423)

COATS, Sir Alastair Francis Stuart; 4 Bt (UK 1905), of Auchendrane, Maybole, Co Ayr; s of Lt-Col Sir James Stuart Coats, 3 Bt, MC (d 1966); *b* 18 Nov 1921; *Educ* Eton; *m* 6 Feb 1947, Lukyn, da of Capt Charles Gordon; 1 s (Alexander James b 1951), 1 da (Sarah Mary (Mrs Archibald D S Lloyd) b 1948); *Heir* s, Alexander James Coats, *qv*, b 6 July 1951; *Career* Capt Coldstream Gds 1939–45; *Style*— Sir Alastair Coats, Bt; ✉ Birchwood House, Durford Wood, Petersfield, Hants GU31 5AW (☎ 01730 892254)

COATS, Alexander James; s and h of Sir Alastair Coats, 4 Bt, *qv*; *b* 6 July 1951; *Educ* Eton; *Style*— Alexander Coats, Esq; ✉ 5 Bina Gardens, London SW5 0LD

COATS, Dr David Jervis; CBE (1984); s of The Rev William Holms Coats, DD (d 1954), of Glasgow, and Muriel Gwendoline, *née* Fowler (d 1984); *b* 25 Jan 1924; *Educ* HS of Glasgow, Univ of Glasgow (BSc); *m* 24 March 1955, Hazel Bell, da of John Livingstone (d 1979), of Glasgow: 1 s (Michael b 1960), 2 da (Gillian b 1956, Pamela b 1958); *Career* REME 1943–47, Major cmdg Mobile Workshop Company in India 1947; Babtie Shaw and Morton: engr in design office and on sites 1947–61, ptnr 1962–78, sr ptnr 1979–87, sr conslt 1988–93; appointed memb all reservoirs panel of engrs under Reservoirs Act 1975 and its predecessors 1968–2000; chm Assoc Consulting Engrs 1979–80; vice pres: Int Cmmn on Large Dams 1983–86 (chm Br Section 1980–83), Inst of Civil Engrs 1987–89; convenor Glasgow Univ Business Ctee of General Cncl 1982–85; chm: Glasgow Univ Tst 1985–92, Scot Construction Indust Gp 1986–92; Hon DSc Univ of Glasgow 1984; FICE, FEng 1982, FRSE 1986, FRSA; *Recreations* walking, swimming; *Clubs* RSAC (Glasgow); *Style*— Dr David Coats, CBE, FEng, FRSE; ✉ 7 Kilmardinny Cres, Bearsden, Glasgow G61 3NP (☎ 0141 942 2593)

COATS, Percy Murray; s of Percy Murray Coats (d 1968), and Lizzie Burroughs Blance (d 1980); *b* 8 Jan 1941; *Educ* Highgate, Bishop Vesey's GS Warwicks, Univ of London, St George's Hosp (MB BS, DCH); *m* 20 Sept 1975, Margaret Elisabeth Joan, da of Donald Clarence Ashley; 1 s (Edward b 1980), 3 da (Louise b 1976, Caroline b 1978, Maria b 1981); *Career* Surgn Lt RN 1966–72; Queen Charlotte's and Chelsea Hosp for Women 1973–74, King's Coll Hosp 1974–80, conslt obstetrician and gynaecologist SW Surrey Health Dist 1980–, dist tutor in obstetrics and gynaecology SW Surrey, med dir Surrey County Hosp NHS Tst 1995– (dir Obstetrics and Gynaecology Dept 1990–95), special professional interest ultrasound and subfertility; author of specialist medical papers; Liveryman Worshipful Soc of Apothecaries; memb: BMA, Euro Assoc of Gynaecologists and Obstetricians, London Obstetrics and Gynaecological Soc; MRCP, FRCS 1974, FRCOG 1988; *Publications* specialist medical papers; *Recreations* fly fishing; *Clubs* Royal Soc of Med, Carlton; *Style*— Percy M Coats, Esq; ✉ Fairacre, Horsham Rd, Bramley, Surrey GU5 0AW; Private Consulting Rooms, 8 Waterden Rd, Guildford, Surrey (☎ 01483 68286)

COATS, Sir William David; kt (1985), DL (Ayr and Arran 1986); s of Thomas Heywood Coats (d 1958), of Nitshall, Glasgow (nephew of 1 Baron Glentamar), and Olivia Violet, *née* Pitman; *b* 25 July 1924; *Educ* Eton; *m* 8 Feb 1950, Hon Elizabeth Lilian Graham, da of 1 Baron MacAndrew, PC, TD; 2 s, 1 da; *Career* chm Coats Paton plc 1981–86 (dep chm 1979–81); dir: Clydesdale Bank 1962–93 (dep chm 1985–93), South of Scotland Electricity Board 1972–81, Murray Caledonian Investment Trust 1961–81, Weir Group 1970–83; Hon LLD Univ of Strathclyde 1977; *Recreations* shooting, golf; *Clubs* Western (Glasgow); *Style*— Sir William Coats, DL; ✉ The Cottage, Symington, Ayrshire KA1 5QG

COBB, Henry Stephen (Harry); CBE (1991); yst s of Ernest Cobb (d 1945), of Wallasey, and Violet Kate, *née* Sleath (d 1975); *b* 17 Nov 1926; *Educ* Birkenhead Sch, LSE (BA, MA), Univ of Liverpool (Archive Dip); *m* 5 April 1969, Eileen Margaret, da of Alfred John Downer (d 1964), of London; *Career* archivist Church Missionary Soc 1951–53, House of Lords: asst archivist 1953–59, asst Clerk of the Records 1959–73, dep Clerk of the Records 1973–81, Clerk of the Records 1981–91; pres Soc of Archivists 1992–96 (chm 1982–84); FSA 1967, FRHistS 1970; *Books* The Local Port Book of Southampton 1439–40 (1961), The Overseas Trade of London 1480–81 - Exchequer Customs Accounts (1990); *Recreations* music, historical research; *Style*— Harry Cobb, Esq, CBE, FSA; ✉ 1 Childs Way, Hampstead Garden Suburb, London NW11 6XU (☎ 0181 458 3688)

COBB, John Martin; s of Richard Martin Cobb (d 1966), of Rochester, Kent, and Ursula Joan, *née* Abell (d 1990); *b* 28 Sept 1931; *Educ* Canford; *m* 25 July 1959, Susan Mary Cochrane, yst da of Roderick Watson (d 1975), of London; 1 s (James b 1964), 2 da (Mary b 1960, Philippa b 1962); *Career* seaman offr RN 1949–69; served Far East, Aust, Med, W Indies and the Persian Gulf, cmd landing ship and anti-submarine frigate; def policy staff MOD 1966–69, ret as Cdr (RN) 1969; Private Clients Dept Sheppards Stockbrokers 1969–91 (ptnr and dir i/c 1982–89), memb London Advsy Bd Bank Julius Baer 1994–; chm Assoc of Private Client Investment Managers and Stockbrokers (APCIMS) 1990–; vice chm Temple Grove Prep Sch Uckfield Sussex; MSI; *Recreations* skiing, riding, gardening, music; *Style*— J M Cobb, Esq; ✉ APCIMS, 112 Middlesex Street, London E1 7HY (☎ 0171 247 7080, fax 0171 377 0939)

COBBAN, Sir James (Macdonald); kt (1982), CBE (1971), TD (1950), JP (Berks 1950, Oxon 1974, does not normally use style of JP), DL (Berks 1966, Oxon 1974); s of Alexander Macdonald Cobban (d 1956), of Scunthorpe; *b* 14 Sept 1910; *Educ* Pocklington Sch, Jesus Coll Cambridge (MA), Univ of Vienna, Pembroke Coll Oxford (MA); *m* 1942, Lorna Mary (d 1961), da of George Stanley Withers Marlow, of Sydenham; 4 da (Mary b 1943, Diana b 1947, Hilary b 1950, Helena b 1952), 1 s decd; *Career* asst master King Edward VI Sch Southampton 1933–36, classical sixth form master Dulwich Coll 1936–40 and 1946–47; 2 Lt TA (Gen List) 1937, Intelligence Corps 1941, GSO3 Directorate of Mil Intelligence 1941, Staff Coll 1943, DAQMG Combined Ops HQ 1943, Staff Offr CCG 1944, Lt-Col 1945; headmaster Abingdon Sch 1947–70; former chm Abingdon County Bench; dep chm Governing Bodies Assoc 1976–82 (hon life memb 1981); former govr: Stowe, Wellington, Campion Sch (Athens), St Helen's Sch, St Stephen's House; former memb Gen Synod Church of England; *Recreations* grandchildren; *Clubs* East India & Public Schools; *Style*— Sir James Cobban, CBE, TD, DL; ✉ 10 Coverdale Court, Preston Road, Yeovil BA21 3AQ (☎ 01935 77835)

COBBE, Stuart Malcolm; s of Brian Morton Cobbe, OBE (d 1991), of Brighton, and Catherine Mary, *née* Caddy (d 1985); *b* 2 May 1948; *Educ* Royal GS Guildford, Univ of Cambridge (MA, MD), St Thomas's Hosp Med Sch (MB BChir); *m* 11 Dec 1970, Patricia Frances, da of George Bertram Barrett, of London; 3 da (Lindsay Ann b 21 Aug 1974, Heather Jane (twin) b 21 Aug 1974, Sarah Caroline b 9 May 1977); *Career* gen med trg in Nottingham, Birmingham, Worthing and St Thomas's Hosp London 1972–76, registrar in cardiology Nat Heart Hosp London 1976–77, res fell in cardiology Cardiothoracic Inst London 1977–79, sr registrar in cardiology John Radcliffe Hosp London 1979–81, res fell Univ of Heidelberg W Germany 1981–82, clinical reader John Radcliffe Hosp Oxford 1982–85, Walton prof of med cardiology Univ of Glasgow 1985–; author of over 100 scientific papers on cardiac metabolism, cardiac arrhythmias, coronary prevention and other cardiac topics; memb: Br Cardiac Soc, Assoc of Physicians of GB and I; FRCP, FRCPG; *Recreations* walking; *Style*— Prof Stuart Cobbe; ✉ Dept of Medical Cardiology, Royal Infirmary, 10 Alexandra Parade, Glasgow G31 2ER (☎ 0141 211 4722, fax 0141 552 4683)

COBBOLD, Anthony Alan Russell; s of Rowland Hope Cobbold, of Bristol (d 1986), and Mary Selby, *née* Parkin; descended from Robert Cobbold, of Tostock, Suffolk (d 1603), founder of the brewing family; ggs of Sir Harry Parkes, GCMG, KCB (d 1885), envoy extraordinaire and min plen in Japan and China; n of Vice-Adm Sir Charles Hughes Hallett, KCB, CBE (d 1985); *b* 15 March 1935; *Educ* Marlborough, Gonville and Caius Coll Cambridge (BA); *m* 1, 15 Aug 1959, Margaret Elizabeth, da of Prof J W Cecil Turner (d 1968), of Cambridge; 3 s (Timothy b 1962, Humphrey b 1964, Jeremy b 1969); m 2, 25 April 1974, Jillianne Bridget (d 1994), formerly wife of Capt Martin J Minter-Kemp, and da of Lt-Col Denis Lucius Alban Gibbs, DSO (d 1984), of Tavistock, Devon; 1 step s (Robin b 1963), 3 step da (Sarah (Mrs Redfern), Emma b 1960, Claire (Mrs Dickins) b (twin) 1963); *Career* Lt Duke of Edinburgh's Royal Regt 1953–55; W & T Avery Ltd 1958–66, W D and H O Wills 1966–71, Evode Group plc 1971–87 and 1990–93, chief exec Regnl Building Centres Ltd 1988–89; dir: Evode Roofing Ltd 1973–87, Evode Joint Sealing 1973–87, Evode Group plc 1980–87, Tekurat Insulations Ltd 1980–87, Building Centre Group Ltd 1985–88, British Roof Mart Ltd 1986–87, First Run Ltd 1993–96, Keeper's Collection Ltd 1993–; *Recreations* genealogy, travel; *Clubs* IOD; *Style*— Anthony Cobbold, Esq; ✉ 32 Fedden Village, Nore Road, Portishead, Bristol BS20 8DN (☎ 01275 817617, fax 01275 817339)

COBBOLD, 2 Baron (UK 1960), of Knebworth, Co Hertford; David Antony Fromanteel Lytton Cobbold; DL (Hertfordshire, 1993–); er s of 1 Baron Cobbold, KG, GCVO, PC (d 1987); assumed by Deed Poll 1960 the additional surname of Lytton before his patronymic; *b* 14 July 1937; *Educ* Eton, Trinity Coll Cambridge (BA); *m* 7 Jan 1961, Christine Elizabeth, 3 da of Maj Sir Dennis Frederick Bankes Stucley, 5 Bt (d 1983); 3 s (Hon Henry Fromanteel, Hon Peter Guy Fromanteel b 1964, Hon Richard Stucley Fromanteel b 1968, a Page of Honour to HM The Queen 1980–82), 1 da (Hon Rosina Kim b 1971); *Heir* s, Hon Henry Fromanteel Lytton Cobbold, b 12 May 1962; *Career* served in RAF 1955–57; Bank of London and S America 1962–72, Finance for Industry 1974–79, BP 1979–87, TSB England and Wales plc 1987–88; dir: Hill Samuel Bank Ltd 1988–89, 39 Production Co Ltd 1987–, Close Brothers Group plc 1993–, Micell Ltd 1994–; md Gaiacorp UK Ltd 1989–94; chm: Lytton Enterprises Ltd 1970–, Forex

Professionals Ltd 1994–; chm Stevenage Community Tst 1990–; hon treas Historic Houses Assoc 1988–, govr Union of Euro Historic Houses Assocs 1993–; pres Devpt Ctee Univ of Herts 1992– (memb Bd of Govrs 1993–); tstee Pilgrim Tst 1993–; fell ACT 1983–; *Style*— The Lord Cobbold, DL; ✉ Knebworth House, Knebworth, Herts SG3 6PY (☎ 01438 812661, fax 01438 811908); 2d Park Place Villas, London W2 1SP (☎ 0171 724 6222)

COBBOLD, Hon Rowland John Fromanteel; yr s of 1 Baron Cobbold, KG, GCVO, PC; *b* 20 June 1944; *Educ* Eton, Trinity Coll Cambridge (MA); *m* 3 June 1969, Sophia Augusta, da of the late B N White-Spunner; 1 s, 1 da; *Career* Lt Kent and Co of London Yeo (TA); with BOAC/Br Airways 1966–80, Swire Group 1980–94, dir Cathay Pacific Airways 1987–94, regnl dir (Europe) Hong Kong Tourist Assoc 1994–, dir Air London plc 1996–; *Clubs* Brooks's, RAC, Hong Kong, Shek-O; *Style*— The Hon Rowland Cobbold; ✉ Hallam House, Ogbourne St George, Marlborough, Wilts SN8 1SG (☎ 01672 841212)

COBDEN, Dr Irving; s of Manuel Cobden, of Newcastle upon Tyne, and Fay, *née* Alexander; *b* 18 May 1950; *Educ* Royal GS Newcastle, Univ of Newcastle Med Sch (MB BS, MD); *m* 1, 1972 (m dis 1991), Jennifer Deborah, da of Mark Gilbert; 3 da (Sarah b 1975, Gemma b 1977, Laura b 1982); m 2, 1992, Carolyn Michelle, da of Kenneth Collett; 1 da (Imogen b 1994); *Career* conslt physician N Tyneside Health Centre 1985–, conslt gastroenterologist Freeman Hosp 1985–, clinical tutor in postgrad med 1986–92, clinical lectr in med Univ of Newcastle upon Tyne 1992–, clinical dir of med Freeman Hosp 1994–; Wyeth USA travelling fell 1988; contrib many pubns on gastroenterology; hon fell Société Royale Belge de Gastro Enterologie; MRCP 1976, FRCP 1991; *Recreations* bridge, angling, travel, golf; *Style*— Dr Irving Cobden; ✉ North Tyneside Hospital, North Shields, Tyne & Wear NE29 8NH; Freeman Hosp, Freeman Rd, Newcastle upon Tyne NE7 7DN (☎ 0191 259 6660)

COBHAM, 11 Viscount (GB 1718); Sir John William Leonard Lyttelton; 14 Bt (E 1618); also Baron Cobham (GB 1718), Lord Lyttelton, Baron of Frankley (1756, renewed 1794), and Baron Westcote of Ballymore (I 1776); s of 10 Viscount, KG, PC, GCMG, GCVO, TD (d 1977); *b* 5 June 1943; *Educ* Eton, Christ's Coll New Zealand, RAC Cirencester; *m* 1974 (m dis 1995), Penelope Ann, eldest da of late Roy Cooper, of Moss Farm, Ollerton, nr Knutsford, Cheshire; *Heir* bro, Hon Christopher Lyttelton; *Style*— The Rt Hon the Viscount Cobham; ✉ Hagley Hall, Stourbridge, W Midlands DY9 9LG (☎ 01562 885823); 20 Kylestrome House, Cundy St, Ebury St, London SW1 (☎ 0171 730 5756)

COBHAM, Sir Michael John; kt (1995), CBE (1981); s of Sir Alan John Cobham, KBE, AFC (d 1973), and Gladys Marie, *née* Lloyd (d 1961); *b* 22 Feb 1927; *Educ* Malvern, Trinity Coll Cambridge (BA, MA); *m* 1, 1954 (m dis 1972), June Oakes; m 2, 1973, Nadine Felicity, da of William Abbott, of Wimborne, Dorset; 1 da; *Career* called to the Bar 1952; non-exec dir (formerly chm) Cobham plc (formerly FR Group plc); Liveryman: Worshipful Co of Coachmakers & Coach Harness Makers, Guild of Air Pilots and Air Navigators; FRAeS, CIMgt; *Recreations* sailing and skiing; *Clubs* Royal Thames Yacht, Royal Southern Yacht, Naval and Military; *Style*— Sir Michael Cobham, CBE; ✉ c/o Cobham plc, Brook Road, Wimborne, Dorset BH21 2BJ (☎ 01202 882020, fax 01202 840523)

COBURN, Alfred Henry (Mick); CBE (1979); s of Alfred George Coburn (d 1977); *b* 12 Feb 1922; *Educ* Sidcup GS; *m* 1, 1944, Betty Winifred (d 1981), da of Flt Lt Percy Robinson (d 1960); 2 da; m 2, 1984, Mary Vera, da of Harold Thomas Read; *Career* chm: Britfish 1959–69, Findus UK Ltd (parent co) to 1983; md: Findus Ltd 1965–83, Chambourcy Food Products Ltd 1973–83; dir: The Nestle Co (UK) Ltd (parent co) until 1983, B G Foods Ltd 1984–, Devon Desserts Ltd 1989–, Next Control Systems Ltd 1992–, Whitworth's Foods Group Ltd 1992–; former pres UK Assoc of Frozen Food Prodrs; FRSA, FIGD; *Recreations* golf, horse racing, travel; *Style*— Mick Coburn, Esq, CBE; ✉ Goodwood, Burnhams Rd, Bookham, Surrey KT23 3BB (☎ 01372 452970)

COCHAND, Charles Maclean (Chas); s of Louis Emile Cochand, DFC, Croix De Guerre, and Morna Aldous, *née* Maclean; *b* 2 May 1951; *Educ* Aiglon Coll Chesieres Villars, Univ of Western Ontario (BA); *m* 6 July 1982, Judith Ann, da of John David Harrison, MBE; 3 s (Nicholas John b 1984, Matthew Charles b 1986, Alexander Maclean b 1989); *Career* called to the Bar Middle Temple 1978, in criminal law practice Western Circuit; *Recreations* sailing, skiing, scouting; *Clubs* Eagle Ski (Gstaad); *Style*— Chas M Cochand, Esq; ✉ Brook Farm, Blissford, nr Fordingbridge, Hants SP6 2JQ; De Grassi Pt, nr Lefroy, Ontario, Canada LOL 1WO; 18 Carlton Crescent, Southampton SO15 2XR (☎ 01703 639001, fax 01703 339625)

COCHRANE, (Alexander John) Cameron; MBE (1987); s of late Dr Alexander Younger Cochrane (d 1988), of Edinburgh, and Jenny Johnstone, *née* Morris; *b* 19 July 1933; *Educ* Edinburgh Acad, Univ Coll Oxford (MA); *m* 14 Aug 1958, Rosemary Aline, da of Robert Alexander Ogg (d 1974), of Glasgow; 2 da (Fiona (Mrs Pearce) b 1961, Sandra (Mrs Gamba) b 1964), 1 s (David Alexander Cameron b 1968); *Career* Nat Serv 2 Lt RA 1952–54; Maj CCF St Edward's Sch 1957–66, Maj ACF Cumberland and Westmorland 1966–69; asst master St Edward's Sch Oxford 1957–66, warden Brathay Hall Ambleside Cumbria 1966–70, asst dir of educn City of Edinburgh 1970–74; headmaster: Arnold Sch Blackpool 1974–79, Fettes Coll Edinburgh 1979–88; princ: Prince Willem-Alexander Coll The Netherlands 1988–91, British International Sch Cairo 1992–95; hon fell Dept of Educational Studies Univ of Edinburgh 1973–74, co-opted memb Lancs Educn Ctee 1976–79; chm of govrs: Ullswater Outward Bound 1979–84, Loch Eil Outward Bound 1984–88; vice pres Lothian Fedn of Boys' Clubs 1987– (chm 1981–84), chm HMC Servs Sub Ctee Inter-Service Ctee 1982–88; cmdt XIII Cwlth Games Athletes' Village Edinburgh 1986; memb: Outward Bound Tst Cncl 1979–88, Advsy Ctee Duke of Edinburgh's award 1982–87; elder Church of Scotland 1972–; MIMgt 1987; *Recreations* games, high lands, beaches, music, family and friends; *Clubs* Public Schools, New (Edinburgh), MCC, Vincent's (Oxford); *Style*— Cameron Cochrane, Esq, MBE; ✉ Fersit House, Roy Bridge, Inverness-shire PH31 4HE (☎ 01397 732208)

COCHRANE, David; s of James Douglas Cochrane, of Edinburgh, and Margaret, *née* Milne (d 1943); *b* 18 July 1943; *Educ* Edinburgh Acad, Edinburgh Coll of Art (DipArch, DipTP); *m* 29 June 1970, Jacqueline, da of George Edward Buller (d 1980); 2 s (John b 1 Nov 1971, Peter b 3 March 1973); *Career* assoc Reiach and Hall Architects Edinburgh 1975; ptnr: Reiach Hall Blyth Iran 1977, Reiach & Hall and Reiach Hall Blyth Edinburgh 1980, Cochrane McGregor Architects and Planners Edinburgh 1982; exec dir Cochrane McGregor Group Ltd (architecture planning design mgmnt conslts) Edinburgh and London 1992–; RIBA 1972, ARIAS 1974, MRTPI 1980; *Recreations* golf, gardening; *Clubs* North Berwick Golf; *Style*— David Cochrane; ✉ Cochrane McGregor Group Ltd, Architecture Planning Design Management Consultants, 45 Timber Bush, Leith, Edinburgh EH6 6QH (☎ 0131 555 6688, fax 0131 555 2666)

COCHRANE, Dr Gordon McLellan (Mac); s of Robert Brown Cochrane, of Cheltenham, and Ivy, *née* Elvidge; *b* 24 Feb 1945; *Educ* Tudor Grange GS Solihull, Univ of London (BSc, MB BS); *m* 3 Sept 1966, Jill Lesley, da of Lt Sidney Herbert Castleton, of Solihull; 1 s (James b 15 April 1974), 1 da (Katie b 12 March 1979); *Career* sr house offr and registrar Brompton Hosp 1971–73, conslt physician Guy's 1977– (houseman 1969–70, lectr and registrar 1973–79), hon sr lectr in physicology UMDS, chm of confidential inquiry into the death of Ms S Bull for Greenwich Health Authy, SE Thames RHA and DHSS 1985–86; educnl film Understanding Asthma won BMA film competition Gold Award 1984, BLAT trophy 1985; Univ of London rep to Greenwich Health Authy 1983–, memb Editorial Bd Thorax 1984–, cncl memb and chm of Manpower Ctee Br Thoracic Soc 1989, memb Int Bd of Soc of Euro Pneumologists; FRCP 1985 (MRCP 1972), FRSM 1986; *Books* Bronchodilator Therapy (ed, 1984), Colour Atlas of Asthma (jtly, 1989); articles: Asthma Mortality (jtly Thorax, 1975), Management of Asthma in General Practice (jtly Respiratory Medicine, 1989), Compliance with Therapy in Asthmatics (European Respiratory Jl, 1993); *Recreations* skiing, walking, wine tasting, photography; *Style*— Dr Mac Cochrane; ✉ Dept of Thoracic Medicine, Guy's Hospital, London Bridge, London SE1 9RT (☎ 0171 955 4148)

COCHRANE, Ian Andrew; s of Lt-Col W A Cochrane (d 1989), of Haxby, York, and Rebecca, *née* Segal (d 1989); *b* 8 Feb 1951; *Educ* Archbishop Holgate's GS York, Univ of Manchester (BSc); *m* 3 Aug 1974, Jennifer Wilna, da of Donald Edward Crisp (d 1983); 3 s (Mark b 1980, James b 1982, Adam b 1984); *Career* CA; Arthur Andersen 1973–78, chief exec Fitch-RS plc 1979–90, dir Landor Associates PLC 1991–92; chm Ticegroup Ltd 1993–; FCA 1976; *Recreations* classic cars, tennis, gardening; *Clubs* Groucho's; *Style*— Ian Cochrane, Esq

COCHRANE, James; *Educ* Marlborough, Univ of Cambridge (MA), London Business Sch (MSc); *Career* E R Squibb & Sons Inc: joined 1971, gen mangr Portugal 1975, gen mangr Benelux 1978, gen mangr UK 1980, pres Northern Europe Bristol-Myers Squibb Co 1988–90; main bd dir European ops Wellcome plc 1990–95, exec dir commercial devpt and memb Bd Glaxo Wellcome plc 1995–; non-exec dir Spirax-Sarco Engineering plc; *Style*— James Cochrane, Esq; ✉ Glaxo Wellcome plc, Lansdowne House, Berkeley Square, London W1X 6BQ (☎ 0171 493 4060, fax 0171 408 0228)

COCHRANE, John Patrick Stuart; s of Herbert Lees Cochrane (d 1991), of Hythe, Kent, and Sheila, *née* Haslop; *b* 5 July 1944; *Educ* St Paul's, Middx Hosp Med Sch (MB BS, MS); *m* 22 June 1968, Caroline Louisa, da of Capt Charles Henry Potten (d 1962); 1 s (Richard b 1974), 1 da (Joanna b 1975); *Career* conslt surgn; training posts 1967–81, Whittington Hosp and Royal Northern Hosps 1981–, undergraduate subdean Univ Coll Middlesex Sch of Med 1982–86, hon conslt surgn Hosp of St John and St Elisabeth London; hon sr clinical lectr: Univ Coll, Middlesex Sch of Med; Penrose May tutor RCS 1990–, Univ of London external examiner MB BS, recognised teacher Univ of London, postgrad dean Whittington Hosp, dir of Academic Centre 1987–90; FRSM, FRCS, Fell Assoc of Surgns of GB and Ireland; *Books* The Breast Book (1989), Complete Guide to Breast Health, Clinical Surgery in General (1993), author of contribs to various med pubns; *Style*— John Cochrane, Esq; ✉ 22 Woodside Avenue, Highgate, London N6 4SS (☎ 0181 444 9180); 19 Wimpole St, London W1M 7AD (☎ 0171 637 9755)

COCHRANE, Sir (Henry) Marc Sursock; 4 Bt (UK 1903), of Woodbrook, Old Connaught, Bray, Co Wicklow, Lisgar Castle, Bailieborough, Co Cavan, and Kildare Street, City of Dublin; s of Sir Desmond Oriel Alastair George Weston Cochrane, 3 Bt (d 1979), and Yvonne, *née* Sursock; *b* 23 Oct 1946; *Educ* Eton, Trinity Coll Dublin (BBS, MA); *m* 28 June 1969, Hala, 2 da of Fouad Mahmoud Bey es-Said, of Beirut; 2 s (Alexander Desmond Sursock b 1973, Patrick Talal b 1976), 1 da (Faiza Maria Rosebud b 1971); *Heir* s, Alexander Desmond Sursock Cochrane b 7 May 1973; *Career* hon consul gen for Ireland in Lebanon 1979–84; dir: Hambros Bank Ltd 1979–85, GT Management plc 1985–; tstee Chester Beatty Library and Gallery of Oriental Art Dublin; *Recreations* electronics, skiing, shooting; *Clubs* Annabel's, Ham & Petersham Rifle and pistol; *Style*— Sir Marc Cochrane, Bt; ✉ Woodbrook, Bray, Co Wicklow, Eire (☎ 00 353 2821421); Palais Sursock, Beirut, Lebanon

COCHRANE, Prof Peter; s of Colin Cochrane, of Sutton-in-Ashfield, Notts, and Gladys, *née* Keeton; *b* 11 July 1946; *Educ* Trent Poly (BSc, IEE Prize of the Year), Univ of Essex (MSc, PhD, DSc); *m* 2 May 1971, Brenda; 2 da (Catherine b 24 Sept 1973, Sarah b 16 Dec 1974), 2 s (Richard b 27 Nov 1981, Paul b 25 Aug 1987); *Career* student engr British PO 1969–73 (technician system maintenance 1962–69), head of gp British PO Research Labs 1979–83 (exec engr 1973–79); British Telecom: head of section BTRL 1983–87, divnl mangr Optical Networks BTRL 1987–91, divnl mangr systems research BT Labs 1991–93, gen mangr BT Research Labs 1993–94, head of BT Labs Advanced Research 1994–; pt/t lectr People's Coll of Further Educn Nottingham 1972, visiting prof CNET Lannion Univ France 1978, visiting industl prof Poly of East London 1980–90, scientific collaborator Univ of Liege 1981–91, industl visiting fell UNCW at Bangor 1985–; visiting prof: Univ of Essex 1988–, Opto-electronics Research Centre Univ of Southampton 1991–, Telecommunications & IT Systems Centre UCL 1994–; hon prof of communication & electronics and memb Ct Univ of Kent 1991–; external examiner: CNAA MSc in Info Systems Robert Gordon's Inst of Technol 1990–93, CNAA BSc in Electrical Engrg Nottingham Poly 1991–94; memb Computer Science Corporation Advsy Bd 1996–; occasional lectr and presenter on telecommunication matters worldwide; author of over 250 scientific papers, patents, articles, edited books and chapters; Hon DUniv Essex 1996, Hon DTech Stafford 1996; FIEE 1987 (MIEE 1977), FIEEE 1992 (MIEEE 1983, sr memb 1987), FEng 1994 (CEng 1977), memb NY Acad of Scis 1995; *Recreations* swimming, running, walking, music, reading, playing with my children, skate-boarding; *Style*— Prof Peter Cochrane, FEng; ✉ BT Laboratories, Admin 3, Martlesham Heath, Ipswich, Suffolk IP5 7RE (☎ 01473 644712, fax 01473 647431, car 0860 378778)

COCHRANE OF CULTS, 4 Baron (UK 1919); (Ralph Henry) Vere Cochrane; DL (Fife, 1976); s of 2 Baron Cochrane of Cults, DSO (d 1968), and his 1 w, Hon Elin, *née* Douglas-Pennant (d 1934), yst da of 2 Baron Penrhyn; suc bro, 3 Baron 1990; *b* 20 Sept 1926; *Educ* Eton, King's Coll Cambridge (MA); *m* 18 Dec 1956, (Janet) Mary (Watson), da of Dr William Hunter Watson Cheyne (d 1957); 2 s (Hon Thomas Hunter Vere b 7 Sept 1957, Lt Cdr Hon Michael Charles Nicholas, RN b 1959); *Heir* Hon Thomas Hunter Vere Cochrane; *Career* Lt RE 1945–48; farmer 1951–; underwriting memb Lloyds 1965–, tstee and vice chm Cupar and Fife TSB 1960–73, Tayside and Central TSB (Fife Area Bd) 1973–83, dir and chm Craigtoun Meadows Ltd 1972–; gen cmmr for Income Tax; cmmr Scout Assoc (incl serv at Scottish HQ) 1952–73; memb Queen's Body Guard for Scot (Royal Co of Archers) 1962–; *Recreations* travel, industrial archaeology; *Clubs* New (Edinburgh); *Style*— The Rt Hon Lord Cochrane of Cults; ✉ House of Lords, Westminster, London SW1A 0PW

COCKBURN, (John) Alasdair Murray; s of James Ronald Murray Cockburn (d 1994), of Kilmacolm, Renfrewshire, and Evelyn Marguerite, *née* Mathieson; *b* 10 July 1946; *Educ* Glenalmond Coll, Univ of Aberdeen (LLB); *m* 19 April 1976, Carole Agnes, da of Karl Godfrey Mohr (d 1972), of Bramhall, Cheshire; 1 s (Iain b 1980), 1 da (Gail b 1977); *Career* qualified CA 1972; Coopers & Lybrand: ptnr i/c Aberdeen 1979–88, in London 1988–; exec ptnr audit and accounting Coopers & Lybrand International 1996–; MICAS, FRSA; *Recreations* golf, sailing; *Clubs* Caledonian, Hankley Common Golf, Prestwick Golf; *Style*— Alasdair Cockburn, Esq; ✉ Catherston, 5 Pine Ridge Drive, Lower Bourne, Farnham, Surrey GU10 3JW (☎ 01252 715529); Coopers & Lybrand, 1 Embankment Place, London WC2N 6NN (☎ 0171 583 5000)

COCKBURN, Charles Christopher; s and h of Sir John Elliot Cockburn, 12 Bt, *qv*, and Glory Patricia, *née* Mullings; *b* 19 Nov 1950; *Educ* Emanuel Sch, City of London Poly (BA), Garnett Coll (CertEd); *m* 1, 1978, Beverly J, o da of B Stangroom, of Richmond, Surrey; m 2, 1985, Margaret Ruth, da of Samuel Esmond Bell, of 18 Portland Drive, Bury Green, Cheshunt, Herts; 1 s (Christopher Samuel Alexander b 24 March 1986), 1 da (Charlotte Elspeth Catherine b (twin) 1986); *Career* lectr; conslt in govt relations, ed Financial Regulation Review, chief exec Portcullis Research (govt relations conslts); MIPR, assoc memb IOD; *Recreations* rowing, cycling, song writing, travelling; *Clubs* Twickenham Rowing; *Style*— Charles Cockburn, Esq; ✉ 4 Connaught Rd, Teddington,

Middlesex TW11 0PS; Portcullis Research, 3/19 Holmbush Rd, Putney, London SW15 3LE (☎ 0181 789 2798)

COCKBURN, Prof Forrester; s of Forrester Cockburn, and Violet Elizabeth, *née* Bunce; *b* 13 Oct 1934; *Educ* Leith Acad, Univ of Edinburgh (MB ChB, MD); *m* 15 Jan 1960, Alison Fisher, da of Roger Allison Grieve; 2 s (David, John); *Career* Huntington - Hartford res fell Univ of Boston USA 1963–65, Nuffield sr res fell Univ of Oxford 1965–66, Wellcome sr res fell Univ of Edinburgh 1966–71, sr lectr Dept of Child Life and Health Univ of Edinburgh 1971–77, Samson Gemmell prof of child health Royal Hosp for Sick Children Glasgow 1977–96, prof emeritus 1996–; FRCPGlas (memb Cncl); *Books* Neonatal Medicine (with Drillien, 1974), Practical Paediatric Problems (with Hutchison, 6 edn, 1986), Craig's Care of the Newly Born Infant (with Turner and Douglas, 1988 Fetal and Neonatal Growth (1988), Diseases of the Fetus and Newborn (jtly, 1995), Children's Medicine and Surgery (jtly, 1995); *Recreations* sailing; *Style—* Prof Forrester Cockburn, CBE; ✉ 53 Hamilton Drive, Glasgow G12 8DP (☎ 0141 339 2973); Department of Child Health, Royal Hosp for Sick Children, Yorkhill, Glasgow G3 8SJ (☎ 0141 201 0236, fax 0141 201 0837)

COCKBURN, James Joseph; s of Dr Joseph Cockburn (d 1957), of Dublin, and Jessey Lovell, *née* Purdy (d 1949); *b* 28 June 1932; *Educ* Rydal Sch, Trinity Coll Dublin (MA, MB BCh, BAO); *m* 5 July 1958, Ellen Margaret Constance, da of late Hugh Pritchard-Jones, of Sutton; 1 s (David b 1963), 3 da (Ann b 1959, Jean b 1962, Kathryn b 1967); *Career* asst lectr in physiology Trinity Coll Univ of Dublin 1956–57, med offr St Patricks Hosp Dublin 1958–59, sr house offr and registrar Bethlem Royal and Maudsley Hosps 1959–62; sr registrar 1963–64: London Hosp, St Clements Hosp, Claybury Hosp; conslt psychiatrist Long Grove Hosp and Kingston Gen Hosp 1964–; chm Southern Div RCPsych, former memb Kingston and Richmond AHA, former chm SW Thames Regnl Ctee for Hosp Med Servs; FRCPI, FRCPsych; *Recreations* hill walking; *Style—* James Cockburn, Esq; ✉ Long Grove Hospital, Epsom, Surrey; Kingston General Hospital, Wolverton Rd, Kingston upon Thames

COCKBURN, Sir John Elliot; 12 Bt of that Ilk (NS 1671); s of Lt-Col Sir John Brydges Cockburn, 11 Bt, DSO (d 1949), and Isabel Hunter, *née* McQueen (d 1978); *b* 7 Dec 1925; *Educ* RNC Dartmouth, RAC Cirencester; *m* 7 Sept 1949, Glory Patricia, er da of late Nigel Tudway Mullings, of Dollar Street, Cirencester, Glos; 3 s (Charles Christopher b 1950, James Chandos b 1952, Jonathan McQueen b 1956), 2 da (Julia Georgina b 1954, Catherine Isabel (Mrs Stephen E Keal) b (twin) 1956); *Heir* s, Charles Christopher Cockburn, *qv*; *Career* served RAFVR 1944–48; wine broker; *Clubs* Naval and Military; *Style—* Sir John Cockburn, Bt; ✉ 48 Frewin Rd, London SW18 3LP

COCKBURN, William; CBE (1989), TD (1980); s of Edward Cockburn (d 1986), of Edinburgh, and Alice, *née* Brennan (d 1983); *b* 28 Feb 1943; *Educ* Holy Cross Acad Edinburgh (Dip); *m* 25 Jul 1970, Susan Elisabeth, da of Maj William Phillpots, MBE; 2 da (Rachel b 1974, Rebecca b 1977); *Career* TA Royal Logistic Corps Postal and Courier Serv 1968, Hon Col 1990; PO: Glasgow 1961, PA to Chm 1971–73, asst dir of fin and planning 1973–77, dir of central planning 1977–78, dir postal fin 1978–79, dir London Postal Region 1979–82, memb PO Bd 1981, memb for Fin Counter Servs and Planning 1982–84, memb for Royal Mail Ops 1984–86; md Royal Mail 1986–92, chief exec The Post Office 1992–95, chm International Postal Corporation 1994–95; chief exec W H Smith Group plc 1996– (dir 1995–); non-exec dir: VAT Watkins Holdings Ltd 1985–93, Lex Service plc 1993–, Whitbread plc 1995 (resigned Nov); non-exec memb Bd Business in the Community 1990–, memb Cncl The Industl Soc 1992–, govr Euro Fndn for Quality Mgmnt 1992–95; Freeman City of London 1980; FCIT 1991, FRSA 1992; *Style—* William Cockburn, Esq, CBE, TD; ✉ W H Smith Group plc, Audrey House, Ely Place, London EC1N 6SN (☎ 0171 404 4242, fax 0171 269 2631)

COCKBURN-CAMPBELL, Alexander Thomas; s and h of Sir Thomas Cockburn-Campbell, 6 Bt, *qv*; *b* 16 March 1945; *m* 1969, Kerry Anne, eldest da of late Sgt K Johnson, of Mount Hawthorne, Western Australia; 1 s (Thomas Justin b 10 Feb 1974), 1 da (Felicity Ann b 9 June 1981); *Style—* Alexander Cockburn-Campbell, Esq; ✉ 11 Templetonia Retreat, Livingston Estate, Canning Vale, Western Australia 6155

COCKBURN-CAMPBELL, Sir Thomas; 6 Bt (UK 1821), of Gartsford, Ross-shire; s of Sir Alexander Thomas Cockburn-Campbell, 5 Bt (d 1935), and Maude Frances Lorenzo, *née* Giles (d 1926); *b* 9 Dec 1918; *Educ* Church of England GS Melbourne Aust; *m* 1, 24 June 1944 (m dis 1981), (Josephine) Zoi, eldest da of Harold Douglas Forward, of Cunjardine, W Australia; 1 s (Alexander); m 2, 19 June 1982 (m dis 1990), Janice Laraine, yst da of William John Pascoe, of Bundoora, Australia; *Heir* s, Alexander Thomas Cockburn-Campbell, *qv*, b 16 March 1945; *Career* pastoralist, publican, nursery owner, now ret; *Books* Land of Lots of Time; *Recreations* antique collecting, reading, writing (Autobiography); *Style—* Sir Thomas Cockburn-Campbell, Bt; ✉ Gartsford Cottage, 14 Lincoln St, York, Western Australia 6302

COCKCROFT, Maj (Jon) Barnaby Briggs; s of Maj Eric Briggs Cockcroft (d 1977), of Bryn Dinarth, Colwyn Bay, and Olive Mary, *née* Brown (d 1991); *b* 27 Aug 1936; *Educ* Sherborne, RMA Sandhurst, Staff Coll Camberley; *m* 4 Oct 1960, Audrey Mary, da of Lt-Col Robert Charles Henry Kidd, OBE (d 1970), of Moat House, Fincham, Norfolk; 1 s (Rupert b 1963), 1 da (Laura b 1967); *Career* Maj Welsh Gds: represented Army at Rugby Football, served Aden 1965–66, NI 1973, Hong Kong 1979–81, ret 1983; sec City of London TAVRA 1985–; memb HM Body Guard Hon Corps of Gentlemen-At-Arms 1987–, memb HM Cmmn of Lieutenancy for the City of London; Freeman City of London; *Recreations* gardening, shooting; *Clubs* Lansdowne; *Style—* Maj Barnaby Cockcroft; ✉ Holt End House, Ashford Hill, Newbury, Berks (☎ 0118 981 3727); Duke of Yorks HQ, Chelsea, London SW3 4RY (☎ 0171 414 5515)

COCKCROFT, Dr John Anthony Eric; s of Eric William Cockcroft, OBE (d 1979), of Todmorden, Yorks, and Haidee Greenlees, *née* Sutcliffe (d 1980); *b* 9 Aug 1934; *Educ* Todmorden GS, Univ of Cambridge (tech state scholarship, BA, MA), Univ of Aberdeen (MLitt), Univ of Manchester (PhD); *m* 5 Sept 1965, Victoria Mary, da of Frank Lawrence Hartley, of Castleford, W Yorks; 2 s (John b 1972, Alexander b 1974), 1 da (Vicki b 1967); *Career* RTR Germany Nat Serv cmmn 1954–55 (Sword of Honour), TA cmmn Duke of Lancasters Own Yeomanry Manchester 1959–65; Ford Motor Co 1959, UK private indust 1960–64, OECD Paris sci and devpt fell Miny of Economic Coordination Athens 1965–67, UK private industry 1968–69, FCO and ODA advsr Inter Ministerial Investment Advsy Ctee Kabul 1970–72, UN expert Miny of Nat Economy Amman 1973, md Anglo W German Manufacturing Co 1974–78, fell NATO Brussels 1979–80, UN conslt Dar es Salaam 1980, fell Centre for Def Studies Univ of Aberdeen 1980, prof of economics and mgmnt Nigeria 1982, Killam fell centre for foreign policy studies Dalhousie Univ Canada 1982–84, leader Int Mgmnt Consultancy Team World Bank and Price Waterhouse Dhaka 1985, md Manchester UK 1986–89, Allied Textiles plc 1990–91, conslt Sekers International-Stoddard Sekers plc 1991–94, leader USAID Adis Ababa 1994; author of private papers for govts and int orgns incl: Science and Development, The Pilot Teams Greece (OECD, jtly), Proposals for Industrial Development Order Kabul (ODA), Export Promotion Investment Attraction Amman (UN), Alliance Economic Co-operation & Military Assistance in South-East Flank (NATO), The Textile Sector Jordan (UN), The Textile Sector Afghanistan (ODA), Contemporary Soviet Strategy & Space Weapons (thesis, Univ of Manchester), Cotton Sector Assessment Ethiopia (USAID), Cereal Seeds Bangladesh (EC); FInstD 1975, CText 1978; memb: RUSI 1979, IISS 1980, RIIA 1980; FTI 1986, MCSD 1990 (MSIAD 1975); *Recreations* music, pictures and prints, tennis, supporting Leeds Utd and Manchester Utd, horse and motor racing; *Clubs* Cavalry & Guards; *Style—* Dr John Cockcroft; ✉ The Old Vicarage, Ledsham, Milford, Leeds LS25 5LT (☎ 01977 683326, fax 01977 685476)

COCKCROFT, John Hoyle; s of late Lionel Fielden Cockcroft, of Todmorden, Yorks, and Jenny, *née* Hoyle; nephew of Sir John Cockcroft (d 1967), who was winner of Nobel prize for physics 1951 and first master of Churchill Coll Cambridge 1959; *Educ* Oundle, St John's Coll Cambridge (sr maj scholar, MA); *m* 1971, Tessa Fay, da of Dr William Shepley (d 1968); 3 da (Lucia b 1972, Gemma b 1974, Eloise b 1978); *Career* Nat Serv 2 Lt RA 1953–55; electronics economist; feature writer Financial Times 1959–61, economist GKN 1962–67 (re-acquisitions 1962–65), seconded to Treasy Public Enterprises Div 1965–66, econ leader writer Daily Telegraph 1967–74; MP (C) Nantwich 1974–79; memb Select Ctee on: Nationalised Industs (tport) 1975–79, Co Secretaries Bill (private members) 1978–79; conslt: GKN 1971–76, Br Field Sports Soc 1975–76, Edman Group 1976–77, Mail Users' Assoc 1976–79, Inst of Chartered Secs 1977–79, Cray Electronics 1982–84, Wedgwood 1983–84, Crystalate Holdings 1983–86, Dowty Group 1983–86, Commed Ltd (telecommunications co) 1983–, Laurence Prust (stockbrokers) 1986–90, Camden Associates (political PR) 1984–88, Cambridge Corporate Consultants 1989–, Raitt Orr (govt relations) 1992–, MAP Securities (corp fin) 1992–, Railway Devpt Soc 1993–, Heathmere (UK) Ltd 1996–; advsr NEI History Archives 1980–85; memb Bd BR (Eastern Region) 1984–89; dir Inst of Pre-Emptive Mil Studies 1996–; memb Cncl: European Movement 1973–74 and 1983–84, Cons Gp for Europe 1980–87; memb Ctee: Assoc of Youth Clubs 1970–74, Cons Computer Forum 1983–90, PITCOM 1985–90; memb Epping Cons Supper Club Ctee 1984–90; treas Cambridge Univ Cons Assoc 1958, pres Cambridge Union 1958; tstee Sanderson Tst (Oundle) 1992–; *Publications* Reforming the Constitution (jtly, 1968), Belgium Quarterly Review (EIU, 1969–71), Self-Help Reborn (jtly, 1969), Why England Sleeps (1971), Internal History of Guest Keen and Nettlefolds (jtly, 1976), Microtechnology in Banking (1984), Microelectronics (booklet, 1979 and 1982); contrib reviews, interviews and articles to Jl of Contemporary British History, The Scotsman, The European and Daily and Sunday Telegraphs 1979–; also columnist and contrib: Microscope 1982–85, Banking World 1984–87, Westminster Watch, Electronics Times 1985–90; *Recreations* reading, writing, walking, entertaining; *Style—* John Cockcroft, Esq; ✉ c/o Institute of Directors, 116 Pall Mall, London SW1Y 5ED

COCKCROFT, Sir Wilfred Halliday; kt (1982); s of Wilfred Cockcroft (d 1958), of Keighley, Yorks, and Bessie, *née* Halliday (d 1967); *b* 7 June 1923; *Educ* Keighley Boys' GS, Balliol Coll Oxford (MA, DPhil); *m* 1, 1949, Barbara Rhona Huggan (d 1982); 2 s; m 2, 1982, Vivien, da of David Lloyd, of Warmington; *Career* prof of pure mathematics Univ of Hull 1961–73, vice chllr New Univ of Ulster 1976–82, chm Secdy Examination Cncl 1983–89, chm Educn Project Resources; FIMA; *Clubs* Athenaeum; *Style—* Sir Wilfred Cockcroft; ✉ The Old Rectory, Warmington OX17 1BU

COCKEL, Dr Roy; s of Harold Victor Ernest Cockel (d 1988), of Northolt, Middx, and Eliza Louisa, *née* Wright (d 1986); *b* 11 Jan 1937; *Educ* Latymer Upper Sch London, Gonville and Caius Coll Cambridge (MA), St Thomas' Hosp (MB BChir); *m* 20 July 1963, Ann Janette, da of Walter Kidman (d 1980), of Melbourn, Cambs; 1 s (Christopher b 1 Aug 1967), 1 da (Susan b 9 March 1966); *Career* conslt physician and gastroenterologist Selly Oak Hosp 1970–, hon conslt gastroenterologist Queen Elizabeth Hosp Birmingham 1974–, sr clinical lectr in med Univ of Birmingham 1975–, dep dean of postgrad med and dental educn Univ of Birmingham and W Midlands RHA 1991–96; hon sec Br Soc for Digestive Endoscopy 1977–80, cncl memb Br Soc of Gastroenterology 1981–84 (endoscopy sec 1980), chm SAC in Gastroenterology JCHMT 1989–93, pres Midland Gastroenterological Soc 1992–93 (sec 1977–82), co chm The Moseley Soc 1993–; FRCP 1978; *Books* A Colour Atlas of Gastrointestinal Endoscopy (with K F R Schiller and R H Hunt, 1986); *Recreations* gardening, DIY, photography, music (classic and jazz); *Style—* Dr Roy Cockel; ✉ 78 Park Hill, Moseley, Birmingham B13 8DS (☎ 0121 449 0197); Selly Oak Hospital, Raddlebarn Rd, Selly Oak, Birmingham B29 6JD

COCKELL, Michael Henry; s of Charles Seaton (d 1966), and Elise Seaton Mandeville (d 1973); *b* 30 Aug 1933; *m* 15 July 1961, (Elizabeth) Janet, da of Dr Gilbert Jamieson Meikle (d 1975); 1 s (Charles Seaton b 21 May 1967), 3 da (Nicola Ann b 13 July 1963, Susan Louise b 28 Dec 1964, Lucinda Jane (twin) b 21 May 1967); *Career* Nat Serv 1952–54, HAC 1954–60; underwriter GN Rouse & others (Syndicate 570) 1968–89, dir Willis Faber & Dumas (UA) Ltd 1969–85; chm: MH Cockell & Co Ltd 1978–87, Harris & Dixon (UA) Ltd 1982–86; chm Lloyds's Non-Marine Assoc 1983 (dep chm 1982), former dep chm Lloyd's 1986 (memb Cncl 1984–87, 1990–93 and 1995–96), sr ptnr MH Cockell & Partners 1986–; *Recreations* sport (especially cricket), music, ornithology, gardening, fishing and the countryside; *Clubs* MCC, I Zingari, HAC, City of London; *Style—* Michael Cockell, Esq; ✉ MH Cockell & Partners, Lloyds Building, 1 Lime Street, London EC3

COCKER, Doug; *b* 23 March 1945; *Educ* Duncan of Jordanstone Coll of Art Dundee; *Career* artist; lectr in sculpture: Nene Coll Northampton 1972–82, Grays Sch of Art Aberdeen 1982–90; *Solo Exhibitions* New 57 Gallery Edinburgh 1969, Northampton Art Gallery 1975, Fruitmarket Gallery Edinburgh 1977, Air Gallery London 1978, Scottish Sculpture Workshop Huntly 1981, Spectro Newcastle 1982, Compass Gallery Glasgow 1982, Artspace Aberdeen 1984, Third Eye Centre Glasgow 1986, Aberdeen Art Gallery 1987 and 1990, Talbot Rice Centre Univ of Edinburgh 1987, Artsite Bath 1989, Crawford Art Centre Univ of St Andrews 1989, Woodlands Gallery Blackheath 1990, Peacock Printmakers Aberdeen 1992, Chelmsford Art Festival 1992, Essex Fine Art Fellowship work touring Essex 1992–93, Talbot Rice Gallery Univ of Edinburgh touring 1995, Perth Festival 1995; *Gp Exhibitions* Scottish Sculpture Open (Kildrummy Castle) 1981–85, Serpentine Gallery London 1984, Glasgow Garden Festival 1988, Scottish Art Since 1900 (Nat Gallery of Modern Art and Barbican) 1989, Virtue and Vision (RSA Edinburgh) 1991, Artists Abroad (RSA Edinburgh) 1992 and others; *Public Collections* Arts Cncl, Scottish Arts Cncl, Glasgow Art Gallery and Museum, Hunterian Art Gallery Glasgow, Worcs Coll of Educn, King Alfred's Coll Winchester, Perthshire Educn Authy, Fife Educn Authy, Peterborough Art Gallery, Essex CC, Greenshields Fndn Montreal, Perth Art Gallery 1995, Scottish Office Edinburgh; *Awards* RSA Andrew Carnegie Travelling Scholarship 1967, RSA Benno Schotz Prize 1967, Greenshields Fndn Fellship, RSA Latimer Award 1970, Arts Cncl Award 1977, E Midlands Arts Award 1979, Scottish Arts Cncl bursary 1989, Wingate Fellship 1990, Essex Fine Art Fellship 1991; ARSA 1984; *Style—* Doug Cocker, Esq; ✉ Lundie Mill, Lundie, Angus DD2 5NW

COCKERAM, Eric Paul; s of John Winter Cockeram (d 1976), of Birkenhead, Cheshire, and Mildred Edith, *née* O'Neill (d 1977); *b* 4 July 1924; *Educ* The Leys Sch Cambridge; *m* 2 July 1949, Frances Gertrude, da of Herbert Irving (d 1979), of Birkenhead; 2 s (Howard b 1950, James b 1955), 2 da (Susan b 1952, Julia (twin) b 1955); *Career* Capt Gloucestershire Regt 1942–46, D-Day landings (wounded twice); MP (C): Bebington 1970–Feb 1974, Ludlow 1979–87; former PPS to: Chllr of the Exchequer, Min for Industry, Min for Posts and Telecommunications; chm: Watson Prickard Ltd, Northern Property Two Ltd; dir: TSB (NW) Ltd, Midshires Bldg Soc, Muller Gp (UK) Ltd; memb Lloyd's; Liveryman (and memb Ct) Worshipful Co of Glovers; Freeman: City of London, City of Springfield Illinois USA; JP Liverpool 1960; *Recreations* shooting, golf, bridge; *Clubs* Carlton; *Style—* Eric Cockeram, Esq; ✉ Fairway Lodge, Caldy, Wirral L48 1NB (☎ 0151 625 1100); Watson Prickard Ltd, North John Street, Liverpool L2 4SH (☎ 0151 236 8841)

COCKERELL, Sir Christopher Sydney; kt (1969), CBE (1966); s of Sir Sydney Cockerell, LittD (d 1962), and Florence Kate, *née* Kingsford (d 1949); *b* 4 June 1910; *Educ*

Gresham's, Peterhouse Cambridge (MA); *m* 1937, Margaret Elinor (d 1996), da of John Horace Belsham (d 1947); 2 da (Anne, Frances); *Career* inventor of the hovercraft; pupil W H Allen's 1931–33, in charge of the design and devpt of aircraft navigational and communications equipment Marconi 1935–51 (filed 36 patents); during WWII responsible for: the design of the communication and navigational equipment for bombers, the design of the display unit of the Navy's long range radar, 'Bagfull' fitted to bombers which enabled all enemy radar stations around the northern coasts of Europe to be located accurately and to be destroyed before D-Day; estab boat-building business Ripplecraft Ltd on Norfolk Broads 1950 (chm 1950–79), commenced work on hovercraft 1953, experimental craft crossed English Channel 1959 (filed 56 patents), former dir and conslt Hovercraft Development Ltd, commenced work on extraction of power from sea waves 1972 (filed 3 patents), formed Wavepower Ltd 1974 (chm 1974–82); tstee Nat Portrait Gallery 1967–79; Albert medal RSA 1966, Royal medal Royal Soc 1966, Inst of Mech Engrs James Watt Int Gold medal 1983; Hon Doctorate RCA 1968; Hon DSc: Univ of Leicester 1967, Heriot-Watt Univ 1971, Univ of London 1975; hon fell Downing Coll and Peterhouse Cambridge; FRS 1967, RDI 1987; *Recreations* fishing, gardening, the visual arts; *Style*— Sir Christopher Cockerell, CBE, FRS; ✉ 16 Prospect Place, Hythe, Hants SO45 6AU (☎ 01703 842931)

COCKERILL, Geoffrey Fairfax; CB (1980); s of Walter Baden Cockerill (d 1981), and Mary Winifred, *née* Buffery (d 1990); *b* 14 May 1922; *Educ* Humberstone Fndn Sch Cleethorpes, Univ Coll Nottingham (BA); *m* 23 Dec 1959, Janet Agnes Cockerill, JP, da of Archibald J Walters, MBE (d 1978); 2 s ((Giles) Martin b 1960, (Timothy) Hugh b 1963); *Career* Miny of Educn (DES 1964–) 1952–82: private sec to last Min of Educn and successive Sec of State for Educn and Sci 1963–65, asst sec 1964, sec Public Schs Cmmn 1966–68, jt sec Schs Cncl 1970–72, under sec 1972–77, dep sec 1978–82, sec Univ Grants Ctee; chm Kingston upon Thames CAB 1985–88; responsible for mgmnt reviews for Govt and Ctee of Vice Chllrs and Princs 1982–85, hon sr res fell King's Coll London 1982–86, hon conslt to Royal Coll of Nursing 1984–85; memb UGC Univ of S Pacific 1984–87; *Recreations* gardening, photography; *Clubs* Athenaeum, Nat Lib, Cwlth Tst; *Style*— Geoffrey Cockerill, Esq, CB; ✉ 29 Lovelace Road, Surbiton, Surrey KT6 6NS (☎ 0181 399 0125)

COCKING, Prof Edward Charles Daniel; s of Charles Edward Cocking (d 1965), and Mary, *née* Murray (d 1994); *b* 26 Sept 1931; *Educ* Buckhurst Hill County HS Essex, Univ of Bristol (BSc, PhD, DSc); *m* 6 Aug 1960, Bernadette, da of Frank Keane (d 1948); 1 s (Sean Daniel b 1961), 1 da (Sarah Anne b 1966); *Career* Civil Serv Cmmn res fell 1956–59; Univ of Nottingham: lectr in plant physiology 1959–66, reader in botany 1966–69, prof of botany 1969–, head Dept of Botany 1969–91; memb: Bd of Tstees Royal Botanical Gardens Kew 1983–93, Cncl Royal Society 1986–88, Governing Body Rothamsted Experimental Station 1991– (memb Lawes Agric Tst Ctee 1987–91); Royal Soc assessor AFRC 1988–90, memb Cncl AFRC 1990–94 (chm Plants & Environment Res Ctee); Leverhulme Tst research fell 1995–; FRS 1983, memb Academia Europaea 1993, hon memb Hungarian Acad of Scis 1995; *Books* Introduction to the Principles of Plant Physiology (with W Stiles, 1969); *Recreations* walking, travelling by train, gothic architecture (A W N Pugin), occassional chess; *Style*— Prof Edward Cocking, FRS; ✉ Plant Genetic Manipulation Group, Department of Life Science, University of Nottingham, Nottingham NG7 2RD

COCKING, Maurice Douglas; s of Cecil Maurice Cocking (d 1967) of Hastings, and Amelia *née* Shorter (d 1972); *b* 28 Oct 1930; *Educ* Beckenham GS, Univ of Exeter (BA), Univ of London (BSc); *m* 11 Sept 1954, Patricia, da of James Charles Fowler (d 1966), of Sevenoaks; 2 s (Crispian b 1961, Kester b 1962); *Career* Nat Serv BAOR 1949–51; fin journalist 1955; city ed: Empire News 1958, Daily Sketch 1964; fin journalist Sunday Times and Daily Express; fndr and chm: FABUS Fin and Business PR Ltd 1967, MDC City Ltd 1994; Liveryman Worshipful Co: of Basketmakers (steward), of Tallow Chandlers; *Recreations* verse, oenology, equestrianism; *Clubs* City Livery, Farringdon, Cheap and Utd Wards, City Pickwick; *Style*— Maurice D Cocking, Esq; ✉ Bardown Cottage, Stonegate, East Sussex TN5 7EL (☎ 01580 200756)

COCKRAM, Sir John; kt (1964); s of Alfred John Cockram (d 1956), of Highgate, and Beatrice Elizabeth Cockram; *b* 10 July 1908; *Educ* St Aloysius Coll Highgate; *m* 1937, Phyllis Eleanor (d 1994), o da of Albert Henning, of Loughton, Essex; 1 s (John), 2 da (Tina, Tandy); *Career* dir Colne Valley Water Co 1952–79 (gen mangr 1941–73), chm Rickmansworth Water Co 1971–86 (dir 1970–86); memb Thames Conservancy 1954–74, pres Br Waterworks Assoc 1957–58 (memb 1948–74), memb Central Advsy Water Ctee 1955–74, chm Water Companies Assoc 1950–79 (life memb); memb Hertfordshire CC 1949–74 (chm 1961–65), life govr Haileybury; FCA; *Style*— Sir John Cockram; ✉ Rebels' Corner, The Common, Chorleywood, Rickmansworth, Herts WD3 5LT

COCKRILL, Maurice Edwin; s of William Edwin Cockrill (d 1970), of Wrexham, Clwyd, and Edith, *née* Godfrey (d 1966); *b* 8 Oct 1936; *Educ* Grove Park GS Wrexham, Wrexham Sch of Art, Univ of Reading; 2 s (Steven Paul b 1958, Joel b 1964); *ptnr* Helen Moslin; 1 s (William Alexander b 1989); *Career* artist; lectr Faculty of Art Liverpool Poly 1967–80; visiting tutor: Winchester Sch of Art 1984–85, Central Sch of Art 1985–88, RCA 1988, Slade Sch of Art 1990, St Martin's Sch of Art 1984–90; *Solo Exhibitions* incl: Peterloo Gallery Manchester 1971, Serpentine Gallery London 1971, Bluecoat Gallery Liverpool 1974, 1979, 1980 and 1982, Liverpool Acad Gallery 1976, Municipal Art Gallery Bootle Liverpool 1978, St Paul's Gallery Leeds 1979, Seven in Two (Lime Street Station Liverpool) 1979–80, February Festival Cmmn Milton Keynes 1981, Univ of Nottingham 1983, Edward Totah Gallery London 1984 and 1985, Kunstmuseum Düsseldorf 1985, Udo Bugdahn Gallery Düsseldorf 1986, Bernard Jacobson Gallery London 1987 and 1990 (NY 1988); *Gp Exhibitions* incl: Art in a City (ICA London) 1967, Spectrum North (Arts Cncl Tour) 1971, John Moores Liverpool Exhibition 9 (prizewinner) 1974, The Face of Merseyside (Walker Art Gallery Liverpool) 1976, Arts Cncl Collection 1976–77 (Hayward Gallery London) 1977, Cleveland Int Drawing Biennale 1981, British Drawing (Hayward Annual London) 1982, Royal Acad Summer Exhibition London 1984, Hommage aux Femmes (ICC Berlin, Leverkusen Cologne) 1985, Athena Art Awards Barbican 1987, John Moores Exhibition 14 1987, Mother and Child (Lefevre Gallery London) 1988, Recent Paintings (Bernard Jacobson Gallery) 1989; work in several public and private collections: *Awards* prizewinner Arts Cncl Flags and other Projects Royal Festival Hall 1977, maj award Arts Cncl of GB 1977–78, project at Lime St Station Liverpool, Arts Cncl Work of Art in Public Spaces 1978–79; *Clubs* Chelsea Arts; *Style*— Maurice Cockrill, Esq; ✉ Bernard Jacobson Gallery, 14A Clifford St, London W1X 1RF (☎ 0171 495 8575, fax 0171 495 6210)

COCKROFT, His Hon Judge (Peter) John; s of Walter Philip Barron Cockroft, of Birstwith, nr Harrogate, and Nora, *née* Collett; *b* 24 Sept 1947; *Educ* Queen Elizabeth I GS Darlington, Queens' Coll Cambridge (BA, LLB); *m* 3 April 1975, Maria Eugenia, *née* Coromina, 2nd da of Carlos Coromina Margui, and Teresa Perandones Moreto; 2 da (Anna Maria b 9 Nov 1979, Isabel Maria b 6 April 1982), 1 s (Thomas Philip Carlos b 25 June 1986); *Career* called to the Bar Middle Temple 1970 (Astbury scholar), tenant at Pearl Chambers 22 E Parade Leeds 1971–93 (memb NE Circuit), recorder 1989–93 (asst recorder 1985–89), circuit judge assigned to Bradford and Leeds area (NE Circuit) 1993–; *Recreations* gardening, visiting Spain; *Clubs* Yorkshire CCC, Yorkshire RUFC; *Style*— His Hon Judge Cockroft

COCKROFT, Richard Robert; s of Albert Hainsworth Cockroft, of Devon, and Jocelyn Courtney Cockroft, OBE, *née* Dart; *b* 7 March 1939; *Educ* Exeter Sch, Trinity Coll Cambridge (MA); *m* 1962, Judith Prunella, da of Cecil Victor Alexander Wearn (d 1964); 1 s (Timothy b 1967), 1 da (Georgina b 1965); *Career* dir Towry Law and Co Ltd 1966–84, md Towry Law (Holdings) Ltd 1971–84, dir M & G Group plc 1984–88, md M & G Assurance Group Ltd 1984–88, chm Independent Market Assistance Group Ltd 1987–88; dir of practice FIMBRA 1988–94, dir Policy Div Personal Investment Authority 1994–; FCII, FRSA; *Recreations* golf, real tennis; *Clubs* MCC, East Berks Golf; *Style*— Richard R Cockroft, Esq; ✉ Arborfield House, Arborfield, nr Reading, Berkshire RG2 9JB; The Personal Investment Authority, 3–4 Royal Exchange Buildings, London EC3V 3NL (☎ 0171 929 0072, fax 0171 929 0693)

COCKS, David John; QC (1982); *Educ* Univ of Oxford (MA); *Career* called to the Bar Linclon's Inn 1961, head of chambers 5 King's Bench Walk, recorder of the Crown Court; *Style*— David Cocks, Esq, QC; ✉ 5 King's Bench Walk, Temple, London EC4Y 7DN (☎ 0171 797 7600)

COCKS, Dr Leonard Robert Morrison (Robin); TD (1979); s of Ralph Morrison Cocks (d 1970), and Lucille Mary, *née* Blackler (d 1996); *b* 17 June 1938; *Educ* Felsted, Hertford Coll Oxford (BA, MA, DPhil, DSc); *m* 31 Aug 1962, Elaine Margaret, da of Canon J B Sturdy; 1 s (Mark b 1964), 2 da (Zoe b 1967, Julia b 1970); *Career* 2 Lt RA 1957–59, active serv Malaya; scientist Nat History Museum 1965, Keeper of Palaeontology 1986–, cmmr Int Cmmn on Zoological Nomenclature 1980–; sec Geological Soc 1985–89; pres: Palaeontological Assoc 1986–88, Palaeontographical Soc 1994–; FGS; *Books* The Evolving Earth (1981), contrib to over 100 articles in sci jls on geology and palaeontology; *Style*— Dr Robin Cocks, TD; ✉ 12 Winchester Park, Bromley BR2 0PY; The Natural History Museum, Cromwell Rd, London SW7 5BD (☎ 0171 938 8845, fax 0171 938 9277)

COCKS OF HARTCLIFFE, Baron (Life Peer UK 1987), of Chinnor, Co Oxfordshire; Michael Francis Lovell Cocks; PC (1976); s of late Rev Harry F Lovell Cocks, of Amersham; *b* 19 Aug 1929; *Educ* Univ of Bristol; *m* 1, 1954, Janet Macfarlane; 2 s, 2 da; m 2, 1979, Valerie Davis; *Career* MP (Lab) Bristol South 1970–87; asst govt whip 1974–76, Parly sec to Treasury and govt chief whip 1976–79, opposition chief whip 1979–85; vice chm Bd of Govrs BBC 1993–; *Style*— The Rt Hon Lord Cocks of Hartcliffe, PC; ✉ c/o House of Lords, London SW1

COCKSHAW, Sir Alan; kt (1992); s of John Cockshaw (d 1986), and Maud, *née* Simpson (d 1996); *b* 14 July 1937; *Educ* Farnworth GS; *m* 17 Dec 1960, Brenda, da of Fred Payne; 1 s (John Nigel b 1964), 3 da (Elizabeth Ann b 1967, Sally Louise b 1970, Catherine Helen b 1979); *Career* formerly chief exec: Fairclough Civil Engineering Ltd 1978–85, Fairclough-Parkinson Mining Ltd 1982–85, AMEC plc 1984–88; chm AMEC plc 1988–; non-exec dep chm NORWEB plc 1992–95; memb British Overseas Trade Bd 1992–95; chm: Overseas Projects Bd 1992–95, Oil & Gas Projects & Supplies Office 1994–, Manchester Millennium Ltd 1996–; sr vice pres ICE 1996–97; hon degree in civil engrg Univ of Leeds; FEng 1986; *Recreations* rugby (both codes), cricket, walking, gardening; *Style*— Sir Alan Cockshaw, FEng; ✉ AMEC plc, Sandiway House, Northwich, Cheshire CW8 2YA (☎ 01606 883885, telex 669708, fax 01606 883996)

CODARIN, Judith; da of William Ernest Walker (d 1971), of Thornham, N Norfolk, and Mary Eileen Jacob; *b* 8 July 1946; *Educ* Kings Lynn HS for Girls, Norwich Sch of Art, Birmingham Coll of Art; *m* Armando Codarin, s of Venceslao Codarin; 1 s (Pierre Daniel b 28 April 1980), 1 da (Melanie Maria b 8 Dec 1973); *Career* design conslt; architectural asst Casson Conder & Partners 1968–72; freelance res and commercial illustrating, designing and concept presentation and development for cos incl: Conran Design Group, Fitch, McColl, Ryman, Rottenberg Associates 1972–76; working with: Franco Nadali Ltd 1973–84, Baker Sayer 1984–88; practises as Judith Codarin Chartered Interior Designers & Design Management for nat and int clients 1988–; lectr in art and design SE Essex Coll (former govr for design indust); author of numerous published articles, developed and ran own restaurant with husband 1978–86; former fndn govr St Bernards Convent HS Westcliff; CSD: memb Cncl 1988, past chm Interiors Gp; *Recreations* walking, swimming, looking at buildings, holidaying with the children; *Style*— Mrs Judith Codarin; ✉ Judith Codarin Chartered Interior Designers & Design Management, 14 Riviera Drive, Southend on Sea, Essex SS1 2RB (☎ 01702 469140, fax 01702 463343)

CODD, (Ronald) Geoffrey; s of Thomas Reuben Codd (d 1976), and Betty Leyster Justice, *née* Sturt; *b* 20 Aug 1932; *Educ* Cathedral Sch Llandaff, The College Llandovery, Presentation Coll Cobh Co Cork; *m* 2 April 1960, Christine Ellen Leone, da of Flt Lt Reginald Arthur John Robertson, of Endways, The Tye, Barking, Needham Market, Suffolk; 1 s (Justin b 27 Oct 1968), 2 da (Louise b 11 May 1962, Emma b 19 July 1966); *Career* RAF Tport Command 1952–57; Rolls-Royce 1957–58, International Computers 1958–61, Marconi Co 1961–70, J Bibby and Sons 1970–74, Weir Group 1974–80, Brooke Bond Group 1981–86, under sec and dir of Info and Risk Management ECGD 1986–90, managing ptnr InterChange Associates 1990–; dir Randolph Enterprise and RE-APM; memb Nat Teleworking Advsy Cncl, non-exec advsr Bd of Customs and Excise; Liveryman Worshipful Co of Info Technologists, Freeman City of London; CEng, FBCS, FIMgt, FInstD; *Publications* contrib to various business pubns; *Recreations* sailing, theatre, practical pastimes; *Clubs* Royal Northern and Clyde Yacht, City Livery, Devonshire House Management; *Style*— Geoffrey Codd, Esq; ✉ Chesterton, Three Gates Lane, Haslemere, Surrey GU27 2LD (☎ 01428 642163, fax 01428 661908)

CODD, (Robin Hugh Ian Anthony) Patrick; TD (1978, 2 Bars); s of Lionel Hugh Codd (d 1979), of Oakford, N Devon, and Isabel Elma, *née* Berry (d 1985); *b* 11 Nov 1937; *Educ* Belmont Coll; *m* 1, Patricia, *née* Grant; 1 da (Antoinette Elizabeth Gallies b May 1964); m 2, Susan Ann, *née* Turner; 1 da (Devona Holly Chelsea Elma b 16 Jan 1987); *Career* journalist/reporter: North Devon Journal Herald, Western Evening Herald, The Sun, Daily Mail, Daily Express; Daily Star: helped launch as feature writer Oct 1978, show business and TV news ed 1981, show business ed 1987–; cncllr (Cons) Royal Borough of Kingston Upon Thames 1994–; *Recreations* military clubs, cinema, Camra recommended pubs, Golden Age American comics; *Style*— Patrick Codd, Esq, TD; ✉ 2 Fairlawn Close, Kingston Hill, Kingston upon Thames, Surrey KT2 7JW (☎ 0181 549 5760); Daily Star, Express Newspapers plc, Ludgate House, 245 Blackfriars Rd, London SE1 9UX (☎ 0171 922 7446, fax 0171 922 7962)

CODRINGTON, Christopher George Wayne; s (by 2 m) and h of Sir Simon Codrington, 3 Bt, *qv*; *b* 20 Feb 1960; *Educ* Hawtreys, Millfield Coll, Royal Agric Coll Cirencester; *m* 25 Oct 1991, Noelle Lynn, da of Dale Wilford Leverson, of Texas, USA; 1 s (Alexander Edward Kristoffer b 9 Nov 1993), 1 da (b 12 Aug 1996); *Career* md and chief exec Internet Music Shop Ltd, pres Codrington Oil & Gas Inc; dir: Codrington Corporation, Conservatives Abroad (Texas); *Style*— Christopher G W Codrington, Esq; ✉ The Old Hundred, Tormarton, Badminton

CODRINGTON, Giles Peter; s of late Lt-Cdr Sir William Codrington, 7 Bt and hp of bro, Sir William Alexander Codrington, 8 Bt, *qv*; *b* 28 Oct 1943; *m* 1989, Shirley Linda Duke; 2 s (Christopher Harry b 1988, Daniel Peter b 1992), 1 da (Michele Anne b 1990); *Recreations* sailing; *Clubs* Antigua Yacht; *Style*— Giles Codrington, Esq; ✉ Villa Félipa, Villefranche-sur-Mer, France

CODRINGTON, Ian Charles; s of Charles Leonard Winterforde Codrington (d 1972), of Bedford, and Enid Mary, *née* Harley (d 1988); *b* 11 Feb 1938; *Educ* Bedford Sch, Fitzwilliam Coll Cambridge (MA); *m* 1, 1962 (m dis 1988), Alice Jennifer Katharine, *née* Laborde; 1 s (Charles b 1967), 2 da (Alice b 1963, Sarah b 1965); m 2, 1993, Karen Jane, *née* Wieland; *Career* admitted slr 1962; currently sr ptnr Sharman & Trethewy, NP; memb Ctee Billy Goat Soc, pres Bedford Rowing Club, memb Ctee Leander Club

Henley-on-Thames, sec Bedford Regatta and Bedford Head of River, former pres Bedford Castle Rotary Club, involved with Paines Plough Ltd (theatre Co); memb Law Soc; Liveryman Worshipful Co of Loriners; FIMgt; *Recreations* rowing; *Clubs* Bedford, The 1900, Carlton; *Style—* Ian Codrington, Esq; ✉ Sharman & Trethewy, 1 Harpur St, Bedford MK40 IPF (☎ 01234 341171, fax 01234 352114)

CODRINGTON, Sir Simon Francis Bethell; 3 Bt (UK 1876), of Dodington, Gloucestershire; s of Sir Christopher William Gerald Henry Codrington, 2 Bt (d 1979), and his 1 wife Joan Mary, *née* Hague-Cook (d 1961); *b* 14 Aug 1923; *Educ* Eton; *m* 1, 3 May 1947 (m dis 1959) Joanne, da of John William Molineaux, of Rock Castle, Kilmacsimon, Co Cork, and widow of William Humphrey Austin Thompson; m 2, 1959 (m dis 1979), Pamela Joy Halliday, da of Maj George Walter Bentley Wise, MBE; 3 s (Christopher George Wayne b 1960, Bethell b 1961, Hugo John b 1964); m 3, 1980 (m dis 1988), Mrs Sarah (Sally) Gwynne Gaze, *née* Pennell; m 4, 28 July 1989, Shirley Ann, da of Percival Lionel Davis; *Heir* s, Christopher George Wayne Codrington b 20 Feb 1960; *Career* formerly Maj Coldstream Gds, served WW II Italy; *Style—* Sir Simon Codrington, Bt; ✉ Sands Court, Dodington, Chipping Sodbury, S Glos BS17 6SE

CODRINGTON, Sir William Alexander; 8 Bt (GB 1721), of Dodington, Gloucestershire; s of Lt Cdr Sir William Richard Codrington, 7 Bt (d 1961), and Joan Kathleen Birelli, *née* Nicholas; *b* 5 July 1934; *Educ* St Andrew Coll S Africa, S African Nautical Coll; *Heir* bro, Giles Peter Codrington, *qv*; *Career* Merchant Navy 1952; currently dir Worldwide Shipping Agency Hong Kong; memb Hon Co of Master Mariners, FNI; *Style—* Sir William Codrington, Bt; (☎ 00 852 842 3820, fax 00 852 810 0617)

CODRON, Michael Victor; CBE (1989, s of I A Codron (d 1981), and Lily, *née* Morgenstern (d 1981); *b* 8 June 1930; *Educ* St Paul's, Worcester Coll Oxford (BA); *Career* theatrical producer and manager, owner Vaudeville Theatre; dir: Royal National Theatre, Hampstead Theatre, Aldwych Theatre, Theatre Mutual Insurance Co; Cameron Mackintosh Visiting Prof of Contemporary Theatre at Oxford Univ 1992–93; *Theatre* prodns incl: Share My Lettuce, Breath of Spring 1957, The Caretaker 1960, Loot 1965, The Killing of Sister George 1968, The Boyfriend (revival) 1967, Absurd Person Singular 1973, Funny Peculiar 1976, The Unvarnished Truth 1978, The Dresser 1980, Noises Off 1982, A View from A Bridge 1987, Uncle Vanya 1988, Henceforward 1988, Hapgood Re:Joyce! 1988, The Cherry Orchard 1989, Man of the Moment 1990, Hidden Laughter 1990, The Rise and Fall of Little Voice 1992, Time of My Life 1993, Dead Funny 1994, Arcadia 1994, The Sisters Rosensweig 1994; *Films* Clockwise 1986; *Recreations* collecting Carolinia (of Brunswick) memorabilia; *Clubs* Garrick; *Style—* Michael Codron, Esq, CBE; ✉ Aldwych Theatre Offices, Aldwych, London WC2B 4DF (☎ 0171 240 8291, fax 0171 240 8467)

CODY, Sebastian; s of Stephen Cody (d 1990), and Maria Schenker-Angerer; *b* 6 Oct 1956; *Educ* King Alfred Sch Hampstead, Univ of Vienna, Univ of York (BA), Nat Film Sch (trained as dir); *Career* researcher BBC TV 1979–81; prodr and dir: Why Do I Believe You...1983, Before His Very Eyes 1984; staff prodr Royal Opera House Covent Garden 1985, ed After Dark (Channel 4) 1987–96; freelance writer and journalist 1979–; exec prodr for Open Media 1987– (progs: The Secret Cabaret 1990–92, James Randi - Psychic Investigator 1991, Opinions 1993–94, Brave New World 1994, Is This Your Life? 1995–96, The Mediator 1995, Natural Causes 1996); *Clubs* Garrick, Magic Circle, London Library; *Style—* Sebastian Cody, Esq; ✉ 9 Leamington Road Villas, London W11 1HS (☎ 0171 221 3658)

COE, Albert Henry (Harry); *b* 28 May 1944; *m*; 2 children; *Career* fin dir Granada Television 1981–88, dep chm Airtours plc 1996– (fin dir 1988–96); *Recreations* cricket, tennis, golf, skiing; *Clubs* Alderley Edge Cricket, Wilmslow Golf, Manchester Ski; *Style—* Harry Coe, Esq; ✉ 48 Broad Walk, Wilmslow, Cheshire SK9 5PL (☎ 01625 522 315); Airtours plc, Parkway Three, Parkway Business Centre, 300 Princess Road, Manchester M14 7QU (☎ 0161 232 6508)

COE, Chief Constable Anthony Thomas; QPM (1990); *b* 1 Dec 1941; *Educ* Nottingham HS, Univ of Nottingham (BA Sociology); *m* Diane; 2 s, 1 da; *Career* served MN as Offr Cadet, constable Derbyshire Constabulary 1962–65, sgt rising to chief inspr Notts Constabulary 1968–77 (Special Course Police Staff Coll), supt Suffolk Constabulary 1977–80 (chief supt Ipswich Div 1980–83), asst chief constable (Ops) then asst chief constable (Admin) Kent Constabulary 1983–86, dep chief constable Leics Constabulary 1986–89, chief constable Suffolk Constabulary 1989–; pres Ipswich Sea Cadet Corps; vice pres: St Elizabeth Hospice, Suffolk Outward Bound Assoc, Suffolk Branch Royal Lifesaving Soc, Disability Care Enterprise; memb: Cncl Order of St John Suffolk, Governing Body E Anglian Sailing Centre for the Disabled; ex-officio memb Suffolk Assoc of Boys Clubs; memb ACPO 1983; *Recreations* boating; *Style—* Chief Constable Anthony Coe, QPM; ✉ Suffolk Constabulary HQ, Martlesham Heath, Ipswich IP5 7QS (☎ 01473 613501, fax 01473 610873)

COË, Peter John Tudor; s of John Robert Tudor Coë (d 1983), and Kathleen Eleanor, *née* Grant (d 1992); *b* 19 May 1959; *Educ* Clifton, Univ of York (BA); *m* Julie Walters; 1 s (Charles John Tudor (Charlie) b 23 Nov 1994); *Career* freelance journalist 1981–85, including UPI Washington and London, UPITN (WTN) London; TV-am: staff reporter 1985–87, financial and economics correspondent 1987–92, presenter Money Matters 1987–89, newsreader 1990–92, presenter First Report 1991–92; co-presenter European Business Today (NHK/FNN/BSB) 1990, business corr and presenter Sky News 1992–93, exec prodr Umbrella Productions 1993–, presenter BBC World (WSTV) 1993–; contrib: The Times, The Daily Telegraph; memb NUJ; *Recreations* swimming, scuba diving, films, theatre; *Clubs* Savile; *Style—* Peter Coë, Esq; ✉ Umbrella Productions, 69A Union Road, Clapham, London SW4 6JF (☎ 0171 720 7157, tel/fax 0171 498 4688)

COE, Sebastian Newbold; OBE (1990, MBE 1981), MP (C) Falmouth and Camborne (majority 3,267); s of Peter Coe, and Angela, *née* Lall; *b* 29 Sept 1956; *Educ* Tapton Sch Sheffield, Univ of Loughborough (BSc); *m* 23 Aug 1990, Nicola McIrvine; 1 s (Harry Sebastian Newbold b 29 Sept 1994), 1 da (Madeleine Rose b 8 July 1992); *Career* former athlete; broke 12 world records incl 800m (current holder), 1500m and 1 mile, Gold medal 1500m Olympic Games 1980 and 1984, Silver medal 800m Olympic Games 1980 and 1984, Gold medal 800m World Cup 1981, Gold medal 800m Euro Championships 1986, ret 1990; MP (C) Falmouth and Camborne 1992–; PPS to Roger Freeman: as Min of State for Defence 1994–95, as Chllr of the Duchy of Lancaster 1995–96; PPS to Michael Hesaltine as Dep PM 1995–96, jr Govt whip 1996–; memb Sports Cncl of GB 1983– (vice chm 1986), chm Sports Cncls Olympic Review 1985–86; memb: Health Educn Authy (formerly Health Educn Cncl) 1986–, Athletes Cmmn, Med Cmmn Int Olympic Ctee 1987–; assoc memb Academie Des Sports France 1982–; steward Br Boxing Bd of Control 1994–; Kiphuth fell Yale Univ 1982, Hon DTech Loughborough Univ 1985, Hon DSc Univ of Hull 1988; *Books* Running Free, Running for Fitness with Peter Coe (1983), The Olympians (1984); *Clubs* East India and Sportsman's; *Style—* Sebastian Coe, Esq, OBE, MP; ✉ House of Commons, London SW1A 0AA

COE, Stephen; s of Richard Gerald Coe, of Brentwood (d 1964), and Mary, *née* Fox (d 1961); *b* 6 Feb 1943, Khartoum; *Educ* Brentwood Sch, London Coll of Printing; *m* 1965 (m dis 1975); 1 s (Simon b 1966), 1 da (Elinor b 1976); *Career* photographer; freelance for Picture Agency until 1963, own studio 1963–93, freelance fine art photographer 1993–; features incl: various cmmns in Vogue 1961–63, American 6 Fleet in Mediterranean, Cassius Clay (Muhammad Ali), covers for Queen and About Town magazines, posters of African landscapes for Athena; advtg campaigns incl: Heinz soup posters 1963–66, Tern Shirts, Remington, Volkswagen, Rolls Royce, Microsoft, COI, Samaritans, Red Cross; exhbns incl: Little Squares of Hampstead 1987, NW3 and Beyond (London, Africa & Scandinavia) 1988, Spirit of Hampstead (Burgh House London) 1994; work in private collections in London, Paris, Melbourne, Nairobi and throughout USA; initial memb Advtg Film and Video Prodrs Assoc (formerly Advtg Film Prodrs Assoc) 1967, initial memb Assoc of Photographers (formerly AFAEP) 1969 (vice chm 1973–74); memb Pilgrims to Willoughby Res Assoc Heath & Old Hampstead; *Awards* Master Photographers Assoc Shield, Layton Award (for Heinz campaign) 1963, various D&AD awards 1965–76, One Show Award (USA) 1966, Communication Art Award (USA) 1966, Venice Film Festival Award (for Diploma) 1968, D&AD Silver Award, Creative Circle Award, Brit Press Award and two Grand Slam Awards for COI campaign Put Your Fingers over Headlights 1976; Publications: Africa Adorned (with Angela Fisher, 1983), Lazy Afternoon (fine art print); articles in Br Jl of Photography; *Recreations* cinema, music, lighting design, memb local initiatives on restoration of Victorian street lighting, conservation and tree mgmnt etc, architectural woodwork, lyric songwriting, hill walking, tennis, skips, creative recycling, browsing, antiquarian books; *Clubs* White Elephant on the River, Club Rollei (Jersey); *Style—* Stephen Coe, Esq; ✉ Denning Hall, 38 Denning Road, London NW3 1SU (☎ 0171 431 1044)

COFFEY, Ann; MP (Lab) Stockport (majority 1,422); da of late John Brown, MBE, and Marie Brown; *b* 31 Aug 1946; *Educ* Nairn Acad, Bodmin GS, Bushey GS, South Bank Poly, Walsall Coll of Educn, Univ of Manchester (BSc, MSc); *m* (m dis); 1 da; *Career* social worker: Birmingham 1972–73, Gwynedd 1973–74, Wolverhampton 1974–75, Stockport 1977–82, Cheshire 1982–88; team ldr (fostering) Oldham Social Servs 1988–92; cncllr Stockport DC 1984–92 (ldr Lab gp 1988–92); Parly candidate (Lab) Cheadle 1987, MP (Lab) Stockport 1992–; memb Select Ctee Trade and Industry, oppn whip 1995–, oppn front bench spokesperson on Health (community care and social servs) 1996–; memb USDAW; *Recreations* photography, drawing, cinema, swimming, reading; *Style—* Ms Ann Coffey, MP; ✉ House of Commons, London SW1A 0AA

COFFEY, Dr Michael; s of James Coffey (d 1968), of Leyland, Lancs, and Rose Lydia, *née* Swain (d 1975); *b* 30 May 1926; *Educ* Preston Catholic Coll, Univ of Manchester (BA), St John's Coll Cambridge (BA, MA, PhD); *m* 28 July 1962, Brigitte, da of Rudolf Stadelmann (d 1949); 2 da (Margaret b 1964, Monica b 1966); *Career* Dept of Latin UCL: asst lectr 1951–54, lectr 1954–67, sr lectr 1967–76, acting head of dept 1977–78, reader 1977–91, hon res fell 1991–; *Books* Roman Satire (2 edn 1989), Seneca Phaedra (with Roland Mayer, 1990); *Recreations* music; *Style—* Dr Michael Coffey; ✉ 61 Laurel Way, Totteridge, London N20 8HT (☎ 0181 445 6059)

COFFIN, Dr Brian John; s of John Francis Charles Coffin (d 1975), of Bournemouth, Dorset, and Marjorie Gwendoline, *née* Henson; *b* 24 Aug 1937; *Educ* Canford, King's Coll (BSc, PhD); *m* 22 Oct 1960, Paula Patricia Coffin, JP, da of Robert Thomas Ingham, of Normandy, nr Guildford, Surrey; 1 da (Linda-Jane b 24 Oct 1961); *Career* sr lectr in chemistry South Bank Univ (formerly South Bank Poly) 1968–96, ret; govr: Royal GS 1977–89, Charterhouse Sch 1981–89, Tomlinscote Sch Frimley 1988–96, Guildford Coll of Technol 1989–93, NE Surrey Coll of Technol 1989–93, Cncl Kingston Mgmnt Centre 1989–93 (hon govr 1994–), Kingston GS 1991–95; cncllr Heatherside and Parkside Div Surrey CC 1970–, memb Exec Cncl Assoc of CCs 1981–89; chm: London and SE Region Library Cncl 1975–92, Surrey Educn Ctee 1981–85, Surrey Fire Bde Ctee 1985–89; memb: NW Surrey Cons Assoc, Surrey Cons and Unionist Club; *Books* Chemistry of Organic Compounds (contrib 1976, 1983 and 1991); *Recreations* travel, gardening; *Style—* Dr Brian Coffin; ✉ 37 High Beeches, Frimley, Camberley, Surrey GU16 5UG (☎ 01276 24390)

COGDELL, Prof Richard John; s of Harry William Frank Cogdell (d 1991), and Evelyn, *née* Passmore; *b* 4 Feb 1949; *Educ* Royal GS Guildford, Univ of Bristol (BSc, PhD); *m*; 2 c; *Career* postdoctoral res Cornell Univ 1973–74, sr fell Dept of Biochemistry Univ of Washington 1974–75; Dept of Botany Univ of Glasgow: lectr in biochemistry 1975–86, sr lectr 1986, head of dept 1987–93, titular prof 1988, Hooker chair of botany 1993–; EMBO fell Univ of Gottingen 1977; visiting res fell: Univ of California 1979, Univ of Illinois 1980; visiting prof: Univ of Munich 1983, Univ of California 1986; memb: Biochemical Soc, Br Photobiology Soc, American Photobiology Soc, Scottish and Newcastle Bioenergetics Gp, Biochemistry and Cell Biology Ctee BBSRC; Alexander von Humboldt Research Prize 1996; FRSE 1991; author of numerous scientific pubns; *Style—* Prof Richard Cogdell, FRSE; ✉ Division of Biochemistry and Molecular Biology, Institute of Biochemical and Life Sciences, University of Glasgow, Glasgow G12 8QQ (☎ 0141 339 8855, fax 0141 330 4447)

COGGAN, Baron (Life Peer UK 1980), of Canterbury and Sissinghurst, Co Kent; Rt Rev the Rt Hon (Frederick) Donald Coggan; PC (1961); s of late Cornish Arthur Coggan, of London, and Fannie Sarah Coggan; *b* 9 Oct 1909; *Educ* Merchant Taylors', St John's Coll Cambridge (MA), Wycliffe Hall Oxford, DD Lambeth 1957; *m* 17 Oct 1935, Jean Braithwaite, da of Dr William Loudon Strain, of Wimbledon; 2 da; *Career* asst lectr in Semitic languages and literatures Manchester Univ 1931–34, ordained 1934, curate St Mary Islington 1934–37, prof of New Testament Wycliffe Coll Toronto 1937–44 (BD, DD hc), princ London Coll of Divinity 1944–56; bishop of Bradford 1956–61; archbishop of York 1961–74 and Canterbury 1974–80; prelate of the Ven Order of St John of Jerusalem 1967–90; chm Liturgical Cmmn 1960–64; pro-chllr: York Univ 1962–74, Hull Univ 1968–74; pres Soc for Old Testament Studies 1967–68, hon pres Int Cncl of Christians and Jews; Hon Freeman City of Canterbury 1976; Hon DD: Cambridge, Leeds, Aberdeen, Tokyo, Saskatoon, Huron, Hull, Manchester, Moravian Theol Seminary, Virginia Theol Seminary; Hon LLD Liverpool, Hon HHD Westminster Choir Coll Princeton, Hon DLitt Lancaster, STD (hc) Gen Theol Seminary NY, Hon DCL Kent, Hon DUniv York; Hon Freeman Worshipful Co of Merchant Taylors; FKC; *Books include* The Heart of the Christian Faith (1978), The Name above all Names (1981), Sure Foundation (1981), Mission to the World (1982), Paul: Portrait of a Revolutionary (1984), The Sacrament of the Word (1987), Cuthbert Bardsley: Bishop, Evangelist, Pastor (1989), God of Hope (1991), Voice from the Cross (1993), The Servant-Son: Jesus Then and Now (1995), A New Way for Preaching (1996); *Recreations* gardening, motoring, music; *Clubs* Athenaeum; *Style—* The Rt Rev the Rt Hon Lord Coggan, PC; ✉ 28 Lions Hall, St Swithun St, Winchester SO23 9HW (☎ 01962 864289)

COGHILL, Sir Egerton James Nevill Tobias (Toby); 8 Bt (GB 1778), of Coghill, Yorkshire; s of Sir Joscelyn Ambrose Cramer Coghill, 7 Bt (d 1983) and his 1 w Elizabeth Gwendoline, *née* Atkins (d 1980); *b* 26 March 1930; *Educ* Gordonstoun, Pembroke Coll Cambridge (MA); *m* 12 April 1958, Gabrielle Nancy, da of Maj Dudley Claud Douglas Ryder, of Rempstone, Corfe Castle, Dorset; 1 s, 1 da (Elizabeth Louisa Gay b 1962); *Heir* s, Patrick Kendal Farley Coghill b 3 Nov 1960; *Career* architect 1952–56, industl devpt conslt 1956–59, mgmnt conslt 1959–61, teacher 1961–64, headmaster Aberlour House 1964–89, educnl conslt, quality assurance advsr 1992–; chm: Inc Assoc of Prep Schs (Scotland) 1984–87, ISIS (Scotland) 1982–89, dir Gordonstoun Fndn 1989–, chm Bd of Govrs Aiglon Coll Switzerland 1991–, Mgmnt Ctee Elgin Museum 1991–95; pres The Moray Soc 1991–95, tstee Scottish Dyslexia Tst 1992–96; md Wallcoatings Scotland Ltd 1996–; *Recreations* country pursuits; *Clubs* Royal Ocean Racing; *Style—* Sir Toby Coghill, Bt

COGHILL, Patrick Kendal Farley; s and h of Sir Toby Coghill, 8 Bt, *qv*; *b* 3 Nov 1960; *Career* consumer electronics installations conslt; *Recreations* skiing, windsurfing, paragliding; *Style—* Patrick Coghill, Esq; ✉ 26 Gowrie Road, London SW11 5NR (☎ 0171 350 1355)

COGHLAN, Gerard Anthony Dillon; CBE (1993, OBE 1982); s of Herbert George Coghlan (d 1943), and Norah Elizabeth, *née* Dillon (d 1976); *b* 6 Nov 1920; *Educ* St Philip's GS Birmingham, Univ of Birmingham (BSc); *m* 13 Sept 1947, Mary Teresa, da of Ernest Arthur Eden (d 1956), of Birmingham; 2 s (Michael b 5 Nov 1951, Simon b 30 Oct 1959), 1 da (Louise b 21 July 1949); *Career* 2 Lt RAOC, 2 Lt and Lt REME 1942, Capt (EME 3 Class) 1943, EME (RA) Gds Div until 1946; asst chief engr Kenrick & Jefferson 1947–48, head of work study (head of corp planning, chief engr, works mangr) Richard Haworth & Co Ltd Manchester 1948–56, mgmnt conslt Tube Investmt Gp Servs 1956–58, exec Wrights Ropes 1958–60, mgmnt conslt Neville Industl Consults Ltd 1960–63, dir and gen mangr Midland Industl Issues Ltd 1963–67; Duport Ltd 1967–81: head of gp mgmnt servs, dir of personnel and industl rels, dep chm Duport Computer Servs, dir Duport Servs Ltd; memb Industl Tbnls 1979–89; memb Birmingham Area Health Authy 1974–81, chm W Birmingham Health Authy 1981–94, memb Police Complaints Bd 1983–85; treas Knutsford Cons Assoc 1956, pres Harborne Ward Cons Assoc 1971–93 (chm 1960–71), guardian The Birm Proof House 1971–90, Cncl memb Univ of Birmingham 1975–95 (life govr 1978–); chm: Cncl for School/Work Links 1979–89, St Paul's Sch for Girls' 1966–, Newman Coll 1972–; gen cmmr of taxes; JP Birmingham 1961; Freeman City of London, Liveryman Worshipful Co of Glovers 1978; Hon LLD Univ of Birmingham 1995; CEng, FIEE, MIMechE, FRSA; Knight of the Most Noble and Equestrian Order of St Gregory (Papal Award) 1980, Knight of the Holy Sepulchre 1995; *Recreations* golf; *Clubs* Naval & Military, The Birmingham, St Paul's, Edgbaston Golf; *Style—* Dr Gerard Coghlan, CBE, JP; ✉ 10 Hamilton Ave, Harborne, Birmingham B17 8AJ (☎ 0121 429 1613)

COGHLAN, Terence Augustine; QC (1993); s of Austin Coghlan (d 1981), of Horsted Keynes, Sussex, and Ruby, *née* Comrie; *b* 17 Aug 1945; *Educ* Downside, Univ of Perugia, Univ of Oxford (MA); *m* 11 Aug 1973, Angela, da of Rev F E Westmacott (d 1987), of Barsham, Suffolk; 1 s (Thomas Alexander b 1975), 2 da (Candida Mary b 1978, Anna Frances b 1988); *Career* RAFVR (Oxford Univ Air Sqdn) 1964–67; film extra 1967–68; called to the Bar Inner Temple (scholar) 1968; in practice 1968–, recorder of the Crown Court 1989– (asst recorder 1985–89); dir City of London Sinfonia; memb Inner Temple; *Recreations* music, birdwatching, cooking, skiing, wines (drinking & making); *Clubs* Omar Khayyam; *Style—* Terence Coghlan, Esq, QC; ✉ 1 Crown Office Row, Temple, London EC4Y 7HH (☎ 0171 797 7500, fax 0171 797 7550)

COGHLAN, Timothy Boyle Lake; s of Patrick Boyle Lake Coghlan (d 1993); *b* 29 March 1939; *Educ* Rugby, Pembroke Coll Cambridge; *m* 1966, Elisabeth, da of Fredrik (d 1996), and Mary af Petersens (d 1995); 1 s (Henry), 1 da (Melindy); *Career* partner de Zoete and Bevan, dir Barclays de Zoete Wedd Securities Ltd; *Style—* Timothy Coghlan, Esq; ✉ Barclays de Zoete Wedd, Ebbgate House, 2 Swan Lane, London EC4R 3TS (☎ 0171 775 1784, fax 0171 956 4612)

COGILL, Julie Antoinette; da of Arthur Harold Berry (d 1971), of Blackburn, and Mary Margaret, *née* Driscoll (d 1991); *b* 25 Aug 1945; *Educ* Notre Dame GS Blackburn, Univ of Liverpool (BSc), King's Coll London (MA); *m* 1967, Stephen Richard Cogill, s of Joseph Cogill (d 1981), of Scarborough; 3 children (Adelene Mary b 1968, Eleanor Ruth b 1969, Geoffrey Owen b 1971); *Career* sr teacher and head of mathematics Tolworth Girl's Sch 1980–87, chief educn offr BBC 1991– (educn offr 1987–88); memb: Mathematical Assoc, Assoc of Teachers of Mathematics, Royal Television Soc; *Recreations* walking, sailing, skiing; *Style—* Mrs Julie Cogill; ✉ BBC Education, 2302 BBC White City, 201 Wood Lane, London W12 7TS (☎ 0181 752 5611/12)

COGSWELL, Dr Jeremy John; s of Dr Alan Philip Lloyd Cogswell (d 1973), and Audrey Sylvia, *née* Jackson; *b* 10 Sept 1937; *Educ* Radley Coll, St John's Coll Cambridge (MA, MB BChir, MD); *m* 22 April 1972, Saranna Leigh, da of Bryan Leigh Heseltine, of Bath; 1 s (Oliver b 1974), 1 da (Katherine b 1975); *Career* paediatrician; formerly Paediatric res fell Univ of Colorado Med Center, respiratory research fell Hosp for Sick Children Gt Ormond Street, sr registrar Dept of Paediatrics Guys Hosp, cnslt paediatrician E Dorset Health Dist; author of papers on paediatric respiratory medicine; FRCP; *Recreations* skiing, viticulture; *Style—* Dr Jeremy J Cogswell; ✉ Warmwell Farm, Flowers Drove, Lytchett Matravers, Poole, Dorset BH16 6BX (☎ 01258 857115); Poole Hospital (☎ 01202 665511)

COHAN, Robert Paul; Hon CBE (1988); s of Walter Cohan, and Billie Cohan; *b* 27 March 1925; *Educ* Martha Graham Sch NY; *Career* joined Martha Graham Co 1946 (ptnr 1950, co-dir 1966); fndr artistic dir Contemporary Dance Trust Ltd 1967, fndr artistic dir and prime choreographer London Contemporary Dance 1969–89, artistic advsr Batsheva Co Israel 1980–89; dir: Univ of York, Toronto Choreographic Summer Sch 1977, Gulbenkian Choreographic Summer Sch Univ of Surrey 1978, 1979, 1982 and 1989, Banff Sch of Fine Arts Choreographic Seminar Canada 1980, choreographic seminar NZ 1982 and Simon Frazer Univ Vancouver 1985 and 1991; with London Contemporary Dance Theatre (LCDT) has toured over 50 countries throughout Europe and the Americas; works incl: Cell 1969 (BBC TV 1982), Stages 1971, Waterless Method of Swimming Instruction 1974 (BBC TV), Class 1975, Stabat Mater 1975 (BBC TV), Masque of Separation 1975, Khamsin 1976, Nympheas 1976 (BBC TV 1983), Forest 1977 (BBC TV), Eos 1978, Songs Lamentations and Praises 1979, Dances of Love and Death 1981, Agora 1984 (with music by Geoffrey Burgon), A Mass for Man broadcast Nov 1985, Ceremony 1986, Interrogations 1986, Video Life 1986; LCDT was only Br dance co invited to Olympic Arts Festival LA 1984 and Seoul 1988, performed at Karmiel Dance Festival Israel 1988; choreographed: A Midsummer Night's Dream for Scottish Ballet 1993 and for Gothenburg Ballet 1995, Vivaldi's Four Seasons for Scottish Ballet 1996; Evening Standard award for Most Outstanding Achievement in Ballet 1975, SWET 1978; ed Chores and Dance Int Jl, ed-in-chief Choreography and Dance Jl; govr Contemporary Dance Tst, chm Robin Howard Fndn; Hon DLit Essex 1993, Hon DUniv Middx 1994, Hon DLitt Univ of Kent 1996; *Books* Contemporary Dance Workshop (1986); *Style—* Robert Cohan, Esq, CBE; ✉ The Place, 17 Dukes Rd, London WC1H 9AB

COHEN, *see:* Waley-Cohen

COHEN, Andrew Timothy; s of John Alan Cohen, of Leeds, and Audrey Pamela Cohen (d 1974); *b* 11 July 1952; *Educ* Leeds GS, Leeds Med Sch (MB ChB); *m* 1977 (m dis 1991); *Career* lectr in anaesthesia Univ of Manchester 1980–83, instr anaesthesiology Univ of Michigan USA 1982–83; St James's Hosp NHS Tst Leeds: conslt anaesthetist, clinical dir Intensive Care Unit 1983–96, div dir Cinical Support Servs 1996–; hon sr lectr Univ of Leeds; memb: BMA, Intensive Care Soc, American Soc of Anaesthesiologists, Med Protection Soc, Assoc Anaesthetists, Euro Soc of Intensive Care Medicine; examiner Royal Coll of Anaesthetists 1996–; DRCOG 1977, FFARCS 1979; *Recreations* wine, skiing, scuba diving, microcomputing, electronics; *Style—* Andrew Cohen, Esq; ✉ 6 Tudor Lawns, Wetherby Rd, Leeds, W Yorks LS8 2JR (☎ 0113 265 7300); St James's Hospital, Beckett St, Leeds LS9 7TF (☎ 0113 243 3144)

COHEN, Arnaldo; s of Eliazar Cohen (d 1985), of Brazil, and Rachel, *née* Ainbinder; *b* 22 April 1948; *Educ* Colegio Pedro II Rio de Janeiro, Sch of Music Federal Univ of Rio de Janeiro; *m* Ann Louise Strickland Cohen, da of William Strickland; 1 s (Gabriel b 12 Oct 1976), 2 step s (Bruno Strickland b 11 Oct 1976, Rodrigo Strickland b 24 Feb 1978), 1 step da (Luiza Strickland b 30 Nov 1979); *Career* pianist, former memb Amadeus Piano Trio; performed with orchs incl: Royal Philharmonic, Philharmonia, Bavarian Radio, Santa Cecilia, Suisse-Romande, City of Birmingham Symphony, Rotterdam Philharmonic, English Chamber Orch; worked with conductors incl: Kurt Masur, Kurt Sanderling, Yehudi Menuhin, Klaus Tennstedt; taught at Sch of Music Federal Univ of Rio de Janeiro and RNCM Manchester, given masterclasses in Italy, Switzerland, Brazil, USA, England and others; appeared at venues incl: Royal Festival Hall, La Scala Milan, Champs-Elysées Paris, Concertgebouw Amsterdam, Musikverein Vienna; jury memb various int competitions incl: Busoni Competition, Liszt Competition; 1st prize: Beethoven Competition 1970, Busoni Competition 1972; *Recordings* incl: Chopin works (1978), Liszt works (1991); *Style—* Arnaldo Cohen, Esq; ✉ Robert Gilder & Co, Enterprise House, 59–65 Upper Ground, London SE1 9PQ (☎ 0171 928 9008, fax 0171 928 9755)

COHEN, Arnold Judah; s of Samuel Cohen (d 1982), of London, and Leah, *née* Sperling; *b* 17 Dec 1936; *Educ* Grocers' Co Sch, Gateshead Talmudical Coll; *m* 1, Ruth (d 1977), da of Leo Kremer, of Zurich; *m* 2, 1978, Sara, da of S D Kaminski, of Brussels; 4 s (Daniel b 25 May 1965, Joseph b 30 July 1968, Moshe Broner b 11 Oct 1970, Avigdor Broner b 13 Sept 1971), 1 da (Yudit Broner b 7 Dec 1974); *Career* Cohen Arnold & Co CAs: articled clerk 1958–62, ptnr 1962–75, sr ptnr 1975–; lectr in economics and accounting Westminster Coll 1968–72, lectr in Talmudics Hillel House 1968, lectr in Jewish civil law Hasmonean HS 1981–86; currently pres Fedn of Synagogues (treas 1986–89); FCA 1967 (ACA 1962), ATII 1967, MInstD 1978–91; *Books* An Introduction to Jewish Civil Law (1990); *Recreations* research into Jewish Civil Law, boating; *Style—* Arnold Cohen, Esq; ✉ 807 Finchley Road, London NW11 8DP (☎ 0181 458 2720); Cohen Arnold & Co, 13/17 New Burlington Place, London W1X 2JP (☎ 0171 734 1362, fax 0171 437 0061)

COHEN, Dr (Stanley) Bernard; s of Dr A Cohen, of Liverpool, and Sophia, *née* Newman; *b* 8 Nov 1938; *Educ* Liverpool Coll, Univ of Liverpool (MB ChB, MD); *m* 9 April 1972, Alison Margot, da of Maj Alan Glass, of Hale, Cheshire; 3 s (Graeme, Stuart, Richard); *Career* conslt physician 1975–, sr res fell Johns Hopkins Univ Baltimore 1974–75; FRCP 1980 (MRCP 1967); *Recreations* music, bridge, theatre; *Style—* Dr Bernard Cohen; ✉ Walton and Fazakerley Hospitals, Liverpool L9 1AE (☎ 0151 525 3611)

COHEN, Dr (Johnson) David; s of John Solomon Cohen (d 1974), and Golda, *née* Brenner (d 1968); *b* 6 Jan 1930; *Educ* Christ's Coll Finchley, Lincoln Coll Oxford (MA), Brandeis Univ USA, King's Coll London, Westminster Hosp Med Sch (MB BS); *m* 28 Aug 1962, Veronica, da of Felix Addison Salmon (d 1969), of London; 2 da (Imogen b 1964, Olivia b 1966); *Career* gen practitioner; memb: Camden and Islington AHA 1973–78, Hampstead DHA 1983–87; govr Hosps for Sick Children Great Ormond St 1974–79, special tstee Royal Free Hosp 1984–88; chm: Camden and Islington Family Practitioner Ctee 1982–87, Camden and Islington Local Medical Ctee 1983–86, chm John S Cohen Fndn 1974– (tstee 1965–), David Cohen Family Charitable Tst 1981–; govr Royal Ballet Schs 1978–93; memb: Int Bd of Govrs Hebrew Univ of Jerusalem 1975–91 (now hon govr), Exec Ctee Prison Reform Tst 1985–88, Bd Opera Factory 1986–, Ballet Bd Royal Opera House Covent Garden 1987–93, Bd ENO 1988–, Cncl London Sinfonietta 1989–; vice pres London Int String Quartet Competition 1989–, chm English Touring Opera (formerly Opera 80) 1987–; memb: Cncl of Friends ENO 1990–95, Cncl of Friends Courtauld Inst 1990–, Bd International Musicians Seminar 1991–94, Chllr's Ct of Benefactors Univ of Oxford 1994–, Cncl of Friends Royal Opera House Covent Garden 1995–; tstee: ENO Benevolent Fund 1990–, ENO Tst 1993–, Royal Philharmonic Orchestra Tst 1995–; hon fell Lincoln Coll Oxford 1986; fell Royal Free Hosp Sch of Medicine 1994; Freeman City of London 1982; Hon GSM 1996; FRCGP, MRCS, LRCP; *Recreations* music, theatre, the arts; *Style—* Dr David Cohen; ✉ 9 Chester Place, London NW1 4NB (☎ 0171 486 1175, fax 0171 486 1952)

COHEN, Prof Gerald Allan; s of Morrie Cohen (d 1985), of Montreal, and Bella, *née* Lipkin (d 1972); *b* 14 April 1941; *Educ* Strathcona Acad Montreal, McGill Univ (BA), Univ of Oxford (BPhil); *m* 24 July 1965, Margaret Florence, da of Henry Aubrey Pearce, of Whitstable, Kent; 1 s (Gideon Patrick Edward b 22 Oct 1966), 2 da (Miriam Florence Laura b 20 Dec 1970, Sarah Judith Tamara b 6 Aug 1975); *Career* reader in philosophy UCL 1978–85 (lectr 1963–78), visiting asst prof McGill Univ 1965, visiting assoc prof Princeton Univ 1975, Chichele prof of social and political theory and fell All Souls Coll Oxford 1995–; FBA; *Books* Karl Marx's Theory of History (1978), History Labour and Freedom (1988), Self-Ownership, Freedom, and Equality (1995); *Recreations* Guardian crossword puzzles, looking at and reading about art and architecture, the politics of India; *Style—* Prof Gerald Cohen; ✉ All Souls Coll, Oxford OX1 4AL (☎ 01865 279339, fax 01865 279299)

COHEN, Harry Michael; MP (Lab) Leyton (majority 11,484); *b* 10 Dec 1949; *m* 1978, Ellen, *née* Hussain; 1 step s, 1 step da, 1 foster s; *Career* accountant; MP (Lab) Leyton 1983–, chm Lab Backbench Def Ctee House of Commons 1987–92, chm Sub Ctee for Econ Co-operation and Convergence with Eastern and Central Europe N Atlantic Assembly Econ Ctee 1994–; cncllr Waltham Forest BC 1972–83 (chm Planning Ctee, sec Lab Gp); master of science, politics and admin Birkbeck Coll London 1994; memb UNISON, former memb CIPFA; *Style—* Harry Cohen, MP; ✉ House of Commons, London SW1A OAA (☎ 0171 219 6376)

COHEN, Sir Ivor Harold; kt (1992), CBE (1985), TD (1968); s of Jack Cohen (d 1987), of London, and Anne, *née* Victor (d 1980); *b* 28 April 1931; *Educ* Central Fndn Sch London, UCL (BA); *m* 4 Jan 1963, Betty Edith, da of Reginald George Appleby (d 1974); 1 da (Elisabeth b 1966); *Career* Nat Serv Royal Signals 1952–54, 2 Lt 1953, TA 1954–69, Maj 1964; Arthur Lyon & Co (Engrs) Ltd 1954–55, Sturtevant Engrg Co Ltd 1955–57, md Mullard Ltd 1979–87 (joined 1957, divnl dir 1973–77); dir: Philips Lighting 1977–79, Philips Electronics Ltd 1984–87; chm Remploy Ltd 1987–93; advsr: Apax Partners & Co Ventures Ltd (formerly Alan Patricof Assocs Ltd) 1987–93, Comet Group plc 1987–90; dir: AB Electronic Products Group plc 1987–93, Oce (UK) Ltd 1988–, Redifon Holdings Ltd 1989–94 (dep chm 1991–94), Redifon Ltd 1989–91, PA Holdings Ltd 1989–, Magnetic Material Group plc March-Sept 1992, Deltron Electronics Ltd 1995–, Electron Technologies Ltd 1994–, Russell Partnership Ltd 1995–; memb: Steering Bd Radiocommunication Agency 1990–, Advsy Ctee Mitsubishi Electric (UK) Ltd 1991–; dir Radio Industs Cncl (RIC) 1980–87; chm Measurement Advsy Ctee DTI 1994–, chm Optima Group Ltd 1995–96; memb: Teletext & Viewdata Steering Gp 1980–84, Cncl Electronic Components Indust Fedn (ECIF) 1980–87, Info Technol Advsy Panel (ITAP) 1981–86, Cncl of Mgmnt Br Schs Technol 1984–87 (tstee dir 1987–89), Computer Software and Communications Requirements Bd DTI 1984–88, Cncl Euro Electronic Components Assoc 1985–87, DTI Steering Gp on Telecommunications Infrastructure 1987–88, Schs Examination & Assessment Cncl 1988–90, Action Japan Ctee BOTB 1994–; NEDO: memb Electronic Components EDC 1980–87, chm Electronic Industs EDC 1990–92 (memb 1982–86 and 1988–92), chm Electronic Applications Sector Group 1988–90; memb: Mgmnt Advsy Gp IT Res Inst Brighton Poly 1987–90, Editorial Bd Nat Electronics Review 1988–90; chm Japan Electronics Business Assoc 1991–; hon memb CGLI 1989; Freeman City of London; Liveryman Worshipful Co of Scientific Instrument Makers (sr warden 1996); fell UCL 1987; FRSA 1981, CIEE 1988, FInstD 1988; Hon FEng 1992; *Recreations* reading, opera, sculpting (occasionally), walking in towns; *Clubs* East India; *Style—* Sir Ivor Cohen, CBE, TD, Hon FEng; ✉ 24 Selborne Rd, Croydon, Surrey CR0 5JQ

COHEN, Janet; da of George Edric Neel (d 1952), of London, and Mary Isabel, *née* Budge; *b* 4 July 1940; *Educ* South Hampstead HS, Newnham Coll Cambridge (BA); *m* 1

(m dis); m 2, 18 Dec 1971, James Lionel Cohen, s of Dr Richard Henry Lionel Cohen, CB, of Cambridge; 2 s (Henry b 1973, Richard b 1975), 1 da (Isobel b 1979); *Career* articled clerk Frere Cholmeley 1963–65, admitted slr 1965, ABT Assoc Cambridge Mass USA 1965–67, John Laing Construction 1967–69, princ (later asst sec) DTI 1969–82; dir: Cafe Pelican Ltd 1983–90, Charterhouse Bank Ltd 1987– (joined 1982); memb Bd of Govrs BBC 1994–; non-exec dir and vice chair Yorkshire Building Soc 1991–; non-exec dir: BPP Holdings plc 1994–, John Waddington plc 1994–; memb Bd Sheffield Development Corp 1993–; writer; *Books* Deaths Bright Angel (as Janet Neel, 1988, John Creasey Award for Best First Crime Novel), Death on Site (1989), Death of a Partner (1991), The Highest Bidder (as Janet Cohen, 1992), Death Among the Dons (1993), Children of a Harsh Winter (as Janet Cohen, 1994), A Timely Death (1996); *Recreations* writing, theatre, restaurants; *Style*— Mrs Janet Cohen; ✉ c/o Charterhouse Bank Ltd, 1 Paternoster Row, St Pauls, London EC4M 7DH (☎ 0171 248 4000, fax 0171 248 1998)

COHEN, Dr (Laurence) Jonathan; s of Israel Cohen (d 1961), of London, and Theresa Cohen (d 1983); *b* 7 May 1923; *Educ* St Paul's, Balliol Coll Oxford (BA, MA, DLitt); *m* 1 July 1953, Gillian Mary, da of Albert Slee (d 1975), of Guildford; 3 s (Stephen Benedict b 4 July 1956, Daniel Charles b 26 October 1957, Robin John b 16 March 1960), 1 da (Juliet Rose b 8 April 1961); *Career* Lt sp RNVR 1945 (Naval Intelligence 1942–45); asst Dept of Logic and Metaphysics Univ of Edinburgh 1947–50, lectr in philosophy Univ of St Andrews at Dundee 1950–57, visiting lectr Hebrew Univ of Jerusalem 1952, Cwlth Fund fell Princeton and Harvard Univs 1952–53, fell and praelector in philosophy The Queen's Coll Oxford 1957–90 (sr tutor 1985–90, emeritus fell 1990–); visiting prof: Columbia Univ USA 1967–68, Yale Univ USA 1972–73; visiting fell Res Sch of Social Sci Aust Nat Univ 1980, hon prof NW Univ Xian China 1987, visiting prof NW Univ USA 1988; general ed Clarendon Library of Logic and Philosophy 1973–; pres Br Soc for Philosophy of Sci 1977–79, chm Br Nat Ctee for Logic Methodology and Philosophy of Sci 1986–90, co-pres Int Union for History and Philosophy of Sci 1987–91, vice pres Oxfordshire Branch Cncl for Protection of Rural England 1988–; govr: Bartholomew Sch Eynsham 1990–93, Wood Green Sch Witney 1992–93; sec gen Int Cncl of Scientific Unions 1993–; FBA 1973; *Books* The Principles of World Citizenship (1954), The Diversity of Meaning (1962), The Implications of Induction (1970), The Probable and the Provable (1977), The Dialogue of Reason (1986), An Introduction to the Philosophy of Induction and Probability (1989), An Essay on Belief and Acceptance (1992); *Recreations* gardening, walking; *Style*— Dr Jonathan Cohen, FBA; ✉ The Queen's College, Oxford OX1 4AW (☎ 01993 881250)

COHEN, Prof Jonathan; s of Dr Norman A Cohen, of London, and Ruth N, *née* Kimche; *b* 11 Oct 1949; *Educ* William Ellis GS, Univ of London (BSc, MB BS, MSc), FRCP, FRCPath; *m* 6 Jan 1974, Dr Noemi Cohen, da of Richard Weingarten (d 1968), of India; 1 s (Richard b 1981), 1 da (Joanna b 1979); *Career* prof and head Dept of Infectious Diseases and hon conslt physician Hammersmith Hosp Royal Postgrad Med Sch London; author of scientific papers and contribs to books on infection and infectious disease; *Recreations* skiing, photography; *Style*— Prof Jonathan Cohen; ✉ Department of Infectious Diseases, Hammersmith Hospital, Royal Postgraduate Medical School, Du Cane Rd, London W12 0NN (☎ 0181 383 3243, fax 0181 383 3394)

COHEN, Lawrence Francis Richard; QC (1993); s of Harris Cohen of Willesden, and Sarah *née* Rich; *b* 4 Nov 1951; *Educ* Preston Manor Sch, Birmingham Univ (LLB), Inns of Court Sch of Law; *m* 24 May 1986, Alison Jane, da of Dr Rowland Patrick Bradshaw of Cobham, Surrey; 1 da (Sophie 1987), 1 s (Leo b 1989); *Career* called to the Bar Gray's Inn 1974; ACIA 1986; *Recreations* reading, cycling; *Style*— Lawrence F R Cohen, Esq, QC; ✉ 24 Old Buildings, Lincoln's Inn, London, WC2A 3UJ (☎ 0171 404 0946, fax 0171 405 1360)

COHEN, Hon Leonard Harold Lionel; OBE (1995); er s of Baron Cohen (Life Peer, d 1973); *b* 1 Jan 1922; *Educ* Eton, New Coll Oxford (BA, MA); *m* 14 July 1949, Eleanor Lucy, da of late Philip Quixano Henriques; 2 s, 1 da; *Career* Rifle Bde 1939–45; barr 1948, bencher Lincoln's Inn 1989; former dir Hill Samuel and Co; former md S Hoffnung and Co Ltd; chm United Service Trustees 1976–81; DG Accepting Houses Ctee 1976–82; chm: Ariel UK Ltd 1982–88, Secure Retirement plc 1987–92, Royal Free Hosp Med Sch Cncl 1982–92, Community Tst for Berkshire 1988–93; Hon Colonel 39th City of London Signal Regt 1973–78; memb Ct of Assts Worshipful Co of Skinners (Master 1971–72); High Sheriff of Berkshire 1987–88; *Recreations* gardening, reading, shooting; *Clubs* White's, Swinley Forest Golf; *Style*— The Hon Leonard Cohen, OBE; ✉ Dovecote House, Swallowfield Park, Reading, Berks RG7 1TG (☎ 0118 988 4775)

COHEN, Michael Alan; s of Harris Cohen, of London, and Cissie, *née* Rich; *b* 30 July 1933; *Educ* Ilford Co HS, UCL (LLB); *m* 3 July 1955, Ann Cohen; 1 s (Julian Andrew b 1967), 1 da (Nicola Amanda b 1970); *Career* Flt Lt RAF 1955–58; called to the Bar; formerly: registered insur broker and independent fin advsr, md Avery Rich Assocs Ltd, ptnr ARA Financial Services, dir ARA Life Assurance Services, dir ADR Centre London; currently: practising arbitrator, mediator, dispute resolver and conslt, ptnr Michael Cohen Associates, dir ARA Conference Services; vice pres Br Insur Law Assoc, chm Acad of Experts; memb: Disciplinary Tbnl Inst of Actuaries, Cncl Int Fedn of Commercial Arbitration Centre, various ctees Chartered Inst of Arbitrators; Freeman City of London; Liveryman Worshipful Cos of: Spectacle Makers, Insurers and Arbitrators; QDR, FCIArb, FInstBA, FAE, FRSA, memb Hon Soc of Gray's Inn and of Lincoln's Inn; *Recreations* sailing, swimming, driving, collecting, yoga; *Clubs* Athenaeum, Royal Southern Yacht, City Livery, Bar Yacht; *Style*— Michael Cohen, Esq; ✉ 2 South Square, Gray's Inn, London WC1R 5HP (☎ 0171 637 0333, fax 0171 637 1893)

COHEN, Michael Antony; s of Gerald Cohen, of Liverpool, and Beatrice, *née* Tarlo; *b* 18 April 1940; *Educ* Quarry Bank GS Liverpool, Univ of Liverpool (BA); *m* 1 March 1967, Jennifer Audrey, da of Charles George Thimbleby Price (d 1964), of St Leonards on Sea, Sussex; 1 s (Thomas Price b 1972), 2 da (Deborah b 1968, Gillian Price b 1970); *Career* planning mangr Bank of London and S America 1965–72, seconded McKinsey and Co 1972, various posts in US and Europe banking Lloyds Bank 1973–78, project fin mangr Lloyds Merchant Bank 1978–82, regnl dir The Housing Corporation 1982–87, chief exec The Guinness Trust 1987–; chm: St Mungo Assoc, Barnet Housing Aid Centre; memb Ctee: Richmond Churches Housing Tst, Cheshire Fndn Housing Assoc; cncllr London Borough of Barnet 1972–78; dir: Phoenix Cinema Tst, Hulme Regeneration; FCA 1970, MIH 1987; *Recreations* walking, eating, reading, cinema, wine, France; *Style*— Michael Cohen, Esq; ✉ 6 Talbot Avenue, East Finchley, London N2 0LS (☎ 0181 883 9433); 17 Mendy Street, High Wycombe, Bucks HP11 2NZ (☎ 01494 535823, fax 01494 459502, car 0850 737846)

COHEN, Lt-Col Mordaunt; TD (1954), DL (Tyne and Wear 1986); s of Israel Ellis Cohen (d 1946), and Sophie, *née* Cohen (d 1991); *b* 6 Aug 1916; *m* 1953, Her Hon Myrella Cohen, QC, *qv*, da of Samuel Cohen (d 1948); 1 s (Jeffrey), 1 da (Sheila); *Career* admitted slr 1938; RA 1940–46, seconded RWAFF (despatches), served TA 1947–55, CO 463 (M) HAA Regt, RA (TA) 1954–55; Alderman Sunderland CBC 1967–74 (ldr 1971–72), chm Mental Health Review Tbnl 1967–76; chm: Sunderland Educn Ctee 1970–72, NE Cncl of Educn Ctees 1971; cncllr Tyne and Wear CC 1973–74, dep chm Northern Traffic Cmmrs 1973–74, regnl chm of Industl Tbnls 1976–89 (chm 1974–76), nat chm Assoc of Jewish Ex-Servicemen and Women 1993–95 (vice pres 1995–); tstee Ajex Charitable Tst, life pres Sunderland Br Ajex 1970; hon life pres Sunderland Hebrew Congregation 1988, memb Bd of Deputies of Br Jews 1964– (chm Provincial Ctee 1985–91, dir Central Enquiry Desk 1990–), former memb Chief Rabbinate Cncl; memb Ct Univ of Newcastle upon Tyne 1968–72, chm Sunderland Poly 1969–72, chm Edgware Sch 1991–96; pres Sunderland Law Soc 1970; *Recreations* watching sport, playing bowls, communal service, promoting inter-faith understanding; *Style*— Lt-Col Mordaunt Cohen, TD, DL; ✉ Flat 1 Peters Lodge, 2 Stonegrove, Edgware, Middlesex HA8 7TY

COHEN, Her Hon Myrella; QC (1970); da of Samuel Cohen (d 1948), of Manchester, and Sarah Cohen (d 1978); *b* 16 Dec 1927; *Educ* Manchester HS for Girls, Colwyn Bay GS, Univ of Manchester (LLB); *m* 1953, Lt-Col Mordaunt Cohen, TD, DL, *qv*; 1 s (Jeffrey), 1 da (Sheila (Mrs Taylor)); *Career* called to the Bar Gray's Inn 1950, recorder Kingston upon Hull 1971–72, circuit judge (SE Circuit) 1972–95 (also sat as judge of Family Div), ret; memb Parole Bd 1983–86; dep pres Int Assoc of Jewish Lawyers and Jurists and chm UK branch; patron: Suzy Lamplugh Tst, Sunderland Cncl for the Disabled; life memb Cncl League of Jewish Women, vice pres NE Cncl for Cancer Research, hon memb Soroptimist International; Hon LLD Univ of Sunderland; FRSA; *Style*— Her Hon Myrella Cohen, QC; ✉ c/o The Crown Court, Harrow, Middx HA1 4TU

COHEN, Prof Philip; s of Jacob D Cohen, of London, and Fanny, *née* Bragman; *b* 22 July 1945; *Educ* Hendon Co GS, UCL (BSc, PhD); *m* 17 Feb 1969, Patricia Townsend, da of Charles H T Wade, of Greenmount, Lancs; 1 s (Simon Daniel b 1977), 1 da ((Suzanne) Emma b 1974); *Career* SRC/NATO fell Univ of Washington Seattle 1969–71; Univ of Dundee: lectr in biochemistry 1971–78, reader in biochemistry 1978–81, prof of enzymology 1981–84, Royal Soc research prof 1984–, dir MRC Protein Phosphorylation Unit 1990–; dir Wellcome Sciences Inst 1995–; author of over 300 articles in learned jls; FRS 1984, FRSE 1984; *Awards* Colworth Medal Br Biochemical Soc 1977, Anniversary Prize Fedn of Euro Biochemical Socs 1977, CIBA Medal Br Biochemical Soc 1991, Prix van Gysel Belgian Royal Acads of Med 1992, Bruce Preller Prize Royal Soc of Edinburgh 1993, Dundee City of Discovery Rosebowl Award 1993; *Books* Control of Enzyme Activity (1976, 2 edn 1983, trans into German, Italian, Russian and Malay), Molecular Aspects of Cellular Regulation (series ed); *Style*— Prof Philip Cohen, FRS, FRSE; ✉ Inverbay II, Invergowrie, Dundee DD2 5DQ (☎ 01382 562 328); Department of Biochemistry, University of Dundee, Dundee, Scotland (☎ 01382 307238, fax 01382 223778)

COHEN, Robert; s of Raymond Cohen, and Anthya, *née* Rael; *b* 15 June 1959; *Educ* Purcell Sch, Guildhall Sch (Cert of Advanced Solo Studies); *m* 1 Aug 1987, Rachel, *née* Smith; 3 s (Joshua b 4 Sept 1992, Isaac b 13 May 1994, Joseph b 15 May 1996); *Career* concert cellist; concerto debut Royal Festival Hall 1971; recital debuts: Wigmore Hall 1976, NY 1979, LA 1979, Washington DC 1979; many TV and radio appearances incl subject of documentary (Thames TV) 1979; gives master classes in: USA, Finland, Norway, France, Turkey, Czechoslavakia, UK, Germany, NZ, Israel; visiting prof RAM 1996–97; patron Beauchamp Music Club, dir Charleston Manor Festival 1989–, fell Purcell Sch for Young Musicians; memb Inc Soc of Musicians; *Performances* major concerto tours since 1980: USA, Europe, Eastern Europe, Scandinavia, Israel, UK, NZ, Aust and Japan; orchs: all major Br orchs, Detroit Symphony, Minnesota Orch, Swiss Romande, Rotterdam Philharmonic, Helsinki Philharmonic, Leipzig Gewandhaus, Netherlands Philharmonic, Oslo Philharmonic, ECYO, Sydney Symphony, etc; chamber ptnrs: Amadeus Quartet, Peter Donohoe, Alan Gravill, Elizabeth Burley, Cohen Trio; *Recordings* Elgar Cello Concerto (silver disc), Dvorak Cello Concerto, Tchaikovsky Rococo Variations, Grieg Sonata/Franck Sonata, Rodrigo Concierto En Modo Galante; virtuoso cello music: Locatelli Sonata, Chopin Intro and Polonaise Brillante, Dvorak Rondo, Popper 3 pieces, Beethoven Triple Concerto (with F P Zimmerman and W Manz), Dvorak Complete Piano Trios (with Cohen Trio), Schubert String Quintet (with Amadeus Quartet), Bach 6 Solo Suites, Howard Blake Diversions 1991, Elgar Concerto 1993, Bliss Concerto 1994, Walton Concerto 1995, Britten 3 Solo Suites 1996, Morton Feldman Concerto 1996, Britten Cello Symphony 1997; recording contract (7 yrs) with Decca/Argo 1992–; *Awards* Suggia prize 1967–71, Martin Tst award 1973–75, winner Young Concert Artists Int Competition NY 1978, Piatigorsky prize USA 1978, winner UNESCO Int Competition Czechoslovakia 1980; *Recreations* photography, driving; *Clubs* Inst of Advanced Motorists; *Style*— Robert Cohen, Esq; ✉ Intermusica Artists Management, 16 Duncan Terrace, London N1 8BZ (☎ 0171 278 5455, fax 0171 278 8434, telex 9312102058)

COHEN, Prof Robert Donald; *b* 11 Oct 1933; *Educ* Clifton, Trinity Coll Cambridge (MA, MD); *m* 14 Feb 1961, Barbara Joan, *née* Boucher; 1 s (Martin b 1966), 1 da (Susan b 1963); *Career* The London Hosp Med Coll Univ of London: prof of metabolic med 1974–82, prof of med 1982–; chm Editorial Bd Clinical Science 1973–75; chm: DHSS Computer R & D Ctee 1976–80, Special Advsy Ctee in Gen Internal Med of Jt Ctee on Higher Med Trg 1985–90, Br Diabetic Assoc Review Body 1990–95, Cncl Imperial Cancer Research Fund 1994– (memb 1989–, vice chm 1991–94); memb: GMC 1988–96 (memb Educn Ctee 1988–89 and 1990–95), Cncl Nat Kidney Res Fund 1992–, Physiological Systems Bd MRC 1990–92, Physiological Med and Infections Bd MRC 1992–94 (dep chm), Health Servs Res Ctee MRC 1990–92, Health Servs and Public Health Bd MRC 1992–94; first vice pres and sr censor RCP London 1991–93; FRCP 1971; *Books* Clinical and Biochemical Aspects of Lactic Acidosis (with H F Woods, 1976), The Metabolic and Molecular Basis of Acquired Disease (ed with B Lewis, K G M M Alberti and A M Denman, 1990); *Recreations* watercolour painting, walking; *Clubs* Athenaeum; *Style*— Prof Robert Cohen; ✉ Medical Unit, The Royal London Hospital, Whitechapel Rd, London E1 1BB (☎ 0171 377 7110, fax 0171 377 7636)

COHEN, Ronald Mourad; s of Michael Mourad Cohen, of Cadogan Gardens, London, and Sonia Sophie, *née* Douek; *b* 1 Aug 1945; *Educ* Orange Hill GS London, Exeter Coll Oxford (BA), Harvard Business Sch (MBA); *m* 1, Dec 1972 (m dis 1975), Carol Marylene, da of Gérard Belmont, of Geneva; m 2, Dec 1983 (m dis 1986), Claire Whitmore, da of Thomas Enders, of New York; m 3, 5 March 1987, Sharon Ruth, da of Joseph Harel, of New York and Tel Aviv; 1 s (Jonathan Michael Harel-Cohen b 3 June 1991), 1 da (Tamara Jennifer Harel-Cohen b 7 Oct 1987); *Career* conslt McKinsey & Co (UK and Italy) 1969–71, chargé de mission Institut de Développement Industriel France 1971–72, fndr chm Apax Partners & Co Ltd (formerly The MMG Patricof Group plc) 1972–; chm Sterling Publishing Group plc until 1993; fndr dir: British Venture Capital Assoc (former chm), Euro Venture Capital Assoc; dir: Spear & Jackson plc, City Group of Smaller Companies (CISCO); vice chm EASDAQ SA; memb: CBI City Advsy Gp (former memb CBI Wider Share Ownership Ctee), Stock Exchange Working Party on Smaller Cos, Exec Ctee Centre for Economic Policy and Research, Franco-British Cncl; advsr Inter-Action Group (charity); former pres Oxford Union Soc; Lib candidate Kensington North Gen Election 1974 and London West for Euro Parl 1979; *Recreations* music, art, tennis, travel; *Clubs* RAC, RIIA, Queens; *Style*— Ronald Cohen, Esq; ✉ 3 Stanley Crescent, London W11 2NB; Apax Partners & Co Ltd, 15 Portland Place, London W1N 3AA (☎ 0171 872 6300, fax 0171 872 8999)

COHN, Prof Paul Moritz; s of late James Cohn, and late Julia Mathilde, *née* Cohen; *b* 8 Jan 1924; *Educ* Trinity Coll Cambridge (BA, MA, PhD); *m* 27 March 1958, Deirdre Sonia Sharon, da of Arthur David Finkle (d 1968), of London; 2 da (Juliet, Ursula); *Career* Chargé de Recherches (CNRS) Univ of Nancy France 1951–52, lectr Univ of Manchester 1952–62, reader QMC London 1962–67, prof and head Dept of Maths Bedford Coll London 1967–84, prof UCL 1984–86 (Astor prof 1986–89, prof emeritus and hon research fell 1989); visiting prof: Yale Univ, Univ of California at Berkeley, Univ of Chicago, SUNY Stonybrook, Rutgers Univ, Univ of Paris, Tulane Univ, Indian Inst of Technol

Delhi, Univ of Alberta, Carleton Univ, Haifa Technion, Univ of Iowa, Univ of Bielefeld, Univ of Frankfurt, Univ of Hamburg (Wilhelm-Blaschke prof), Bar Ilan Univ, Univ d'Etat Mons; author and editor; ctee memb SRC Maths 1977–79, chm Nat Ctee for Maths 1988–89, pres London Math Soc 1982–84 (memb 1957); L R Ford award Math Assoc of America 1972, Berwick prize London Math Soc 1974; FRS 1980 (cncl memb 1985–87); *Books* incl: Lie Groups (1957), Universal Algebra (1965, 1981), Free Rings and Their Relations (1971, 1985), Algebra I (1974, 1982), Algebra II (1977, 1989), Algebra III (1990), Algebraic Numbers and Algebraic Functions (1991), Elements of Linear Algebra (1994), Skew Fields, Theory of General Division Rings (in Encyclopedia of Mathematics and its Applications, vol 57) (1995); translations into Spanish, Italian, Russian and Chinese; *Recreations* language in all its forms; *Style*— Prof P M Cohn, FRS; ✉ Department of Mathematics, University College London, Gower St, London WC1E 6BT (☎ 0171 387 7050, fax 0171 383 5519, e-mail pmc@math.ucl.ac.uk)

COHN-SHERBOK, Rabbi Prof Daniel Mark (Dan); s of Bernard Cohn-Sherbok, of Denver, Colorado, and Ruth Cohn-Sherbok; *b* 1 Feb 1945; *Educ* E Denver HS, Williams Coll Mass (BA), Hebrew Union Coll Cincinnati Ohio (MA, DD), Wolfson Coll Cambridge (MLitt, PhD); *m* 19 Dec 1976, Lavinia Charlotte, da of late Graham Douglas Heath; *Career* ordained rabbi 1971; lectr in theology Univ of Kent 1975– (dir Centre for the Study of Religion and Society 1982–90); visiting prof: Univ of Essex 1993–94, Univ of Middx 1994–, Univ of Wales Lampeter 1994–; fell Hebrew Union Coll 1972, corresponding fell Acad of Jewish Philosophy 1978, visiting fell Wolfson Coll Cambridge 1991; visiting scholar: Mansfield Coll Oxford 1994, Oxford Centre for Postgrad Hebrew Studies 1994; memb: Soc for the Study of Theology 1975, American Acad of Religion 1975, London Soc for the Study of Religion 1981; *Books* On Earth As It Is In Heaven (1987), The Jewish Heritage (1988), Holocaust Theology (1989), A Dictionary of Christianity and Judaism (1990), Rabbinic Perspectives on the New Testament (1990), Blackwell's Dictionary of Judaica (1991), Israel (1992), The Crucified Jew (1992), Atlas of Jewish History (1993), The Jewish Faith (1993), The American Jew (1994), Judaism and Other Faiths (1994), The Future of Judaism (1994), Jewish and Christian Mysticism (1994), Jewish Mysticism: An Anthology (1995), Modern Judaism (1996), The Hebrew Bible (1996), Biblical Hebrew For Beginners (1996), Mediaeval Jewish Philosophy (1996), Fifty Key Jewish Thinkers (1996); *Recreations* keeping cats, walking; *Clubs* Athenaeum, Williams (NY); *Style*— Rabbi Prof Dan Cohn-Sherbok; ✉ Darwin College, University of Kent, Canterbury CT2 7NX (☎ 01227 764000 ext 3409, fax 01227 764026)

COID, Dr Donald Routledge; s of Charles Routledge Coid, of Wheathampstead, Herts, and Marjory Macdonald, *née* Keay; *b* 13 June 1953; *Educ* Bromley GS for Boys, Harrow Co Sch for Boys, Univ of Nottingham (BMedSci, BM BS), London Sch of Hygiene and Tropical Med (MSc), Univ of New South Wales; *m* 1985, Susan Kathleen Ramus, da of Clifford Roy Crocker; 1 da (Joanna Fleur Julia b 6 Dec 1987), 2 adopted da (Amber Ramus b 4 Feb 1976, Holly Ramus b 21 Sept 1978); *Career* house physician Univ Dept of Therapeutics Nottingham July 1976–77, house surgn Univ Dept of Surgery Nottingham 1977, SHO in gen med Brook Hosp London 1977–78, locum med offr Medic International Ltd London 1978–79, research asst (clinical epidemiology) Dept of Community Med Middx Hosp Med Sch 1979, field MO Eastern Goldfields Section Royal Flying Doctor Serv of Aust 1980, MO Community and Child Health Servs Kalgoorlie Western Aust 1981–82, regional dir of public health Eastern Goldfields Western Aust 1982–85 (med superintendent Kalgoorlie Regional Hosp 1984–85); Fife Health Bd: community med specialist 1985–89, conslt in public health 1990–92, asst gen mangr 1992–Dec 1993; chief admin med offr, dir of public health and exec dir Tayside Health Bd 1994–; hon sr lectr Univ of Dundee; author of pubns on various public health topics in learned jls; memb: BMA 1976, Royal Coll of Physicians (Edinburgh and London), Royal Aust Coll of Med Admins 1985; fell Aust Faculty of Public Health Med Royal Australasian Coll of Physicians (FAFPHM) 1991, FFPHM 1996 (MFPHM 1989); memb Br Schools' Exploring Soc; *Recreations* golf, cricket, piano and singing; *Clubs* Royal & Ancient Golf (St Andrews), New Golf (St Andrews); *Style*— Dr Donald R Coid; ✉ 90 Hepburn Gardens, St Andrews, Fife KY16 9LN (☎ 01334 472710); Tayside Health Board, PO Box 75, Vernonholme, Riverside Drive, Dundee DD1 9NL (☎ 01382 645151, fax 01382 669632)

COKE, Edward Peter; s of Lt Cdr John Hodson Coke, RN, of Tone Lodge, Birtley, Hexham, Northumberland, and Kathleen Mary, *née* Pennington; *b* 12 Oct 1948; *Educ* St John's Coll Southsea, Univ of Warwick (LLB); *m* 6 July 1968 (m dis 1994), Josephine Linette, da of Frederick Francis Kennard (d 1987); 1 s (Dominic Francis), 2 da (Sarah Marie, Jessica Mary); *Career* trainee mangr W Woolworth 1966–69, postman PO 1969–71, sr advsy offr Consumer Protection Dept W Midlands CC; called to the Bar Inner Temple 1976, tenant St Ives Chambers 1977– (head of Chambers 1990–), ctee memb Legal Aid Ctee Legal Aid Bd Area No 6; memb: Midland and Oxford Circuit, Birmingham Medico Legal Soc; *Recreations* dry fly fishing, walking, theatre, collecting Royal Navy memorabilia; *Style*— Edward Coke, Esq; ✉ St Ive's Chambers, 9 Fountain Court, Steelhouse Lane, Birmingham B4 6DR (☎ 0121 236 0863/0929/8952, fax 0121 236 6961)

COKE, Viscount; Thomas Edward (Tom) Coke; er s and h of 7 Earl of Leicester, *qv*; *b* 6 July 1965; *Educ* Eton, Univ of Manchester (BA); *m* 21 Dec 1996, Polly M, yst da of (Thomas) David Whately, MC, of Dorset; *Career* page of honour to HM The Queen until 1981, equerry to HRH the Duke of Kent, KG 1991–93; *Style*— Viscount Coke

COKER, Peter Godfrey; *b* 27 July 1926; *Educ* St Martin's Sch of Art, RCA; *m* 1951, Vera Joyce Crook; 1 s (decd); *Career* Fleet Air Army 1943–46; artist; *one-man exhibitions* Zwemmer Gallery 1956, 1957, 1959, 1964, 1967, Magdalane Street Gallery Cambridge 1968, Stone Gallery Newcastle 1969, Thackeray Gallery London 1970, 1972, 1974, 1975, 1976, 1978, Gallery 10 London 1980, 1982, 1984, 1986, 1988, 1989; *retrospective exhibitions* Colchester, Bath, London, Sheffield 1972–73, Chelmsford and Essex Museum 1978, RA 1979, Fitzwilliam Museum Cambridge 1989, Kendal, Royal Acad, Carlisle and Ipswich 1992–93; *gp exhibitions incl* Young Contemporaries 1950 and 1957, Contemporary Art Soc, Tate Gallery 1958, English Artists (Jorden Galleries Toronto) 1958, Recent Acquisitions Contemporary Art Soc 1959, Towards Art (RCA) 1952–62, Bicentenary exhibition (1768–1968) RA 1968, Painting 1950–57 (Scot Arts Cncl Glasgow) 1969, British Painting 1952–77 (Royal Acad London) 1977, Acquisitions since 1980 (Tate Gallery) 1982, The Forgotten Fifties (touring exhbn) 1984, New 20th Century Acquisitions (Nat Portrait Gallery) 1986, Exhibition Road - Painters at the Royal College of Art 1988, This Land is Our Land (Aspects of Agriculture in English Art) 1989, The Kitchen Sink Painters (Mayor Gallery) 1991, New Displays (Tate Gallery) 1992; *selected public collections* Birmingham City Museums and Art Gallery, Br Museum, Nat Portrait Gallery, RA, RCA, Tate Gallery, V&A Museum, City Art Gallery Manchester, Stedelijk Museum Ostend, Salford Museum & Art Gallery, Abbot Hall Art Gallery Kendal; RA 1972 (ARA 1965), ARCA 1953; *Books* Etching Techniques (1976); *Style*— Peter Coker, Esq, RA; ✉ The Red House, Mistley, Manningtree, Essex

COLBOURNE, Christopher Richard Leslie (Chris); s of Robert Henry Colbourne, of Chichester, and Jane Freda, *née* Gardner; *b* 19 Nov 1947; *Educ* Lexington HS Massachusetts, Boston Univ (BA), Architectural Assoc (AADip); *m* 1977, Anne Louise, da of James McElhatton; 1 s (Tom Robert b 25 Jan 1980), 1 da (Clare Rosina b 22 April 1987); *Career* Llewelyn-Davies Weeks: architect planner 1974–78, assoc 1977; ptnr then dir Tibbalds Monro (formerly Tibbalds Colbourne Partnership) 1978–96; *Projects* masterplan for Shahestan Pahlavi Tehran (award winner) Nat Housing Policy Bahrain, environmental impact study for Yanbu Saudi Arabia, Western expansion of Swindon, research parks (for Welsh Devpt Agency, Univ of Surrey, BICC), Direct Line Insurance Headquarters, Croydon Town Hall and Library Complex, Hackney Civic Centre, Prince's Dock Liverpool, Imperial Wharf London, planning Univs of Kingston and Brunel, Nat Univ of Science and Technol Bulawayo; teacher Brunel Univ; external examiner: Kingston Univ, Bartlett Sch of Architecture UCL; memb: London Energy Gp, RIBA Educn Ctee Visiting Bd; memb Cncl Cities of London and Westminster Soc of Architects; Freeman City of London, Liveryman Worshipful Co of Chartered Architects; memb Cncl RIBA (chm London Region 1992–93, vice pres Public Affairs 1994–) 1976; *Recreations* sailing, skiing; *Style*— Chris Colbourne, Esq; ✉ c/o RIBA, 66 Portland Place, London W1N 4AD (☎ 0171 580 5533)

COLCHESTER, Dr Alan Charles Francis; s of John Sparrow Colchester (d 1981), of East Chiltington, Sussex, and Norah Diana Taylor, *née* Pengelley; *b* 4 Oct 1947; *Educ* Haileybury, BNC Oxford (BA), UCH London (BM BCh), Univ of London (PhD); *m* 17 Aug 1974, Nicola Jane, da of Edward Rocksborough Smith (d 1989), of Briantspuddle, Dorset; 1 s (Rupert b 1984), 2 da (Nancy b 1979, Emily b 1981); *Career* research MO RAF Inst of Aviation Med Farnborough 1978–81, registrar in neurology The London Hosp 1982–83, sr registrar in neurology Atkinson Morley's and St George's Hosps 1983–87, sr lectr UMDS 1987–96, conslt neurologist Guy's Hosp London and S Kent Hosps Tst 1987–; reader Kent Inst of Med and Health Scis Univ of Kent at Canterbury 1996–; researcher into computer vision and med image analysis, strobe and image guided surgery and Creutzfeld Jakob disease; chm and ed of proceedings of XIIth Int Conf on Info Processing in Med Imaging 1991; FRSM 1983, FRCP 1993; *Style*— Dr Alan Colchester; ✉ The Old Rectory, Stowting, nr Ashford, Kent TN25 6BE (☎ 01303 862474); KIMHS, Electronic Engineering Laboratories, University of Kent, Canterbury CT2 7NT (☎ 01227 827200)

COLCHESTER, Archdeacon of; *see:* Stroud, The Ven Ernest Charles Frederick

COLCHESTER, Charles Meredith Hastings; s of Rev Halsey Sparrowe Colchester, CMG, OBE (d 1995), of Southrop House, Hook Norton, Oxon, and Rozanne Felicity Hastings, *née* Medhurst; *b* 12 Jan 1950; *Educ* The Dragon Sch, Radley, Magdalen Coll Oxford (BA); *m* 3 July 1976, Dr Serena Laura Peabody, da of Hon John M W North (d 1987), of Wickhambreaux, Kent; 3 s (Alexander North Peabody b 1981, Benjamin Medhurst Pawson b 1983, Zachary Wheatland Maynard b 1988), 3 da (Tamara Sarah Sparrowe b 1985, Chloë Talitha Jacob b 1991, Zoë Francesca Tatiana b 1995); *Career* dir: The Well Tst 1978, The Initiative Project Tst 1980; Christian Action Res and Educn (CARE): chm of campaigns 1982, gen dir 1987–; dir Tear Fund 1989–94, chm of tstees Dolphin Sch Tst 1988–, church warden Holy Trinity Church Brompton 1978–93, dir Well Marine Reinsurance Advisors Ltd 1986–; *Recreations* wife and children, water colouring, travel, reading; *Clubs* Travellers'; *Style*— Charles Colchester, Esq; ✉ CARE, 53 Romney Street, London SW1P 3RF (☎ 0171 233 0455, fax 0171 233 0983)

COLCHESTER, Bishop of 1995–; Rt Rev Edward Holland; *b* 28 June 1936; *Educ* New Coll Sch Oxford, Dauntsey's Sch Wilts, KCL (AKC); *Career* Nat Serv Worcestershire Regt 1955–57; importers co 1957–61, KCL 1961–65; ordained (Rochester): deacon 1965, priest 1966; curate: Holy Trinity Dartford 1965–69, John Keble Mill Hill 1969–72; precentor Gibraltar Cathedral and missioner for Seamen 1972–74, chaplain at Naples Italy 1974–79, vicar of St Mark's Bromley 1979–86, suffragan bishop of Gibraltar in Europe 1986–95; *Style*— The Rt Rev the Bishop of Colchester; ✉ 1 Fitzwalter Road, Lexden, Colchester, Essex CO3 3SS (☎ 01206 576648)

COLCHESTER, Dr Marcus Edward Medhurst; s of Rev Capt Halsey Sparrowe Colchester, CMG, OBE, and Rozanne Felicity Hastings, *née* Medhurst; *b* 15 May 1953; *Educ* Dragon Sch Oxford, Radley, Magdalen Coll Oxford (MA, Dip Ethnology, DPhil); *m* 25 Feb 1984, Jillian Rowena, da of Arthur David Miles, of Nova Scotia, Canada; 2 s (Kito b 1985, Meredith b 1988); *Career* conslt anthropologist Venezuela 1982, regnl coordinator indigenous census Venezuela 1983, Survival Int 1983–89, World Rainforest Movement 1990; Conservation scholar Pew Fndn 1994–96; *Books* The Health and Survival of the Venezuelan Yanoama (1985), Pirates, Squatters and Poachers: The Dispossession of the Native Peoples of Sarawak (1989), Rainforest: Land Use Options in Amazonia (jtly 1989), The Tropical Forestry Action Plan: What Progress? (jtly 1990), Vanishing Amazon (jtly 1991), The Struggle for Land and the Fate of the Forests (jtly, 1993), Slave and Enclave: The Political Ecology of Equatorial Africa (1994), Forest Politics in Suriname (1995); *Style*— Dr Marcus Colchester

COLCLOUGH, Rt Rev Michael John; *see:* Kensington, Bishop of

COLDSTREAM, Sir George Phillips; KCB (1955, CB 1949), KCVO (1968), QC (1960); s of Francis Menzies Coldstream (d 1958), of East Blatchington, Seaford, E Sussex, and Carlotta Mary, *née* Young (d 1940); *b* 20 Dec 1907; *Educ* Bilton Grange, Rugby, Oriel Coll Oxford (MA); *m* 1, 29 Sept 1934 (m dis 1948), (Mary) Morna, da of Maj Alastair Drummond Carmichael (d 1967), of Balendoch, Meigle, Perthshire; 2 da (Grizelda Morna b 1938 d 1945, Rosamund Charlotte b 1939); m 2, 1949, Sheila Hope, da of Lt-Col George Patrick Grant, DSO (d 1955), of Grove House, Woodbridge, Suffolk, and wid of Lt-Col John Henry Whitty, DSO, MC; *Career* called to the Bar Lincoln's Inn 1930; practised at Chancery Bar 1931–34, asst to Parly Counsel HM Treasy 1934–39, legal asst Lord Chllr's Office House of Lords 1939–44, memb Br War Crimes Exec 1942–46, Dep Clerk of the Crown in Chancery 1944–54, Clerk of the Crown in Chancery and Perm Sec Lord Chllr's Office House of Lords 1954–68; memb Royal Cmmn on Assizes and Quarter Sessions 1967–70, special conslt American Inst of Judicial Admin 1968–72, chm Cncl of Legal Educn 1970–73, memb Top Salaries Review Body 1971–83; Hon LLD Columbia Univ USA 1966; hon memb American Bar Assoc, hon memb American Coll of Trial Lawyers; *Recreations* sailing, golf; *Clubs* Athenaeum, Royal Cruising, Sussex, Vincents' (Oxford); *Style*— Sir George Coldstream, KCB, KCVO, QC; ✉ The Gate House, East Blatchington, Seaford, E Sussex BN25 2AH (☎ 01323 892801)

COLDSTREAM, John Richard Francis; s of Gerald Coldstream, and Marian, *née* Gatehouse; *b* 19 Dec 1947; *Educ* Bradfield Coll, Univ of Nice, Univ of Sussex; *m* 1977, Susan Elizabeth, *née* Pealing; *Career* journalist Evening Echo 1971–74, Peterborough Column Daily Telegraph 1974–84; dep literary ed: Daily Telegraph 1984–91, Sunday Telegraph 1989–91; literary ed Daily Telegraph 1991–; *Books* The Daily Telegraph Book of Contemporary Short Stories (ed, 1995); *Clubs* Garrick; *Style*— John Coldstream, Esq; ✉ The Daily Telegraph, 1 Canada Square, Canary Wharf, London E14 5DT (☎ 0171 538 5000)

COLDWELL, Terry; *Career* rapper and dancer; memb East 17, with Brian Harvey, *qv*, Anthony Mortimer, *qv* and John Hendy, *qv*; 14 top twenty singles; singles incl: House Of Love 1992, Gold, Slow It Down, Deep 1993, West End Girls 1993, It's Alright 1993, Around the World 1994, Steam 1994, Stay Another Day (UK no 1) 1994, Let It Rain 1995, Hold My Body Tight 1995, Thunder 1995, Do U Still 1996, Someone to Love 1996, Hey Child 1997; albums: Walthamstow (1992, UK no 1, platinum disc), Steam (UK no 4, 1994), Up All Night (UK no 7, 1995); *Style*— Terry Coldwell, Esq; ✉ c/o London Records 90 Ltd, PO Box 1442, Chancellor's House, Chancellor's Road, London W6 9RS (☎ 0181 910 5111, fax 0181 741 2600)

COLDWELLS, Rev Canon Alan Alfred; s of Alfred Carpenter Coldwells (d 1962), and Leila Philis Eugenie, *née* Livings; *b* 15 Jan 1930; *Educ* Haileybury and ISC, Univ Coll Oxford (BA, MA), Wells Theol Coll; *m* 5 Jan 1963, (Mary) Patricia, da of Arthur Leonard Hemsley, of Rugby; 1 s (Adam b 1969), 2 da (Katie b 1963, Lotti b 1966); *Career* Nat Serv 2 Lt RASC 1948–50; deacon 1955, priest 1956, curate Rugby St Andrew Dio of Coventry 1955–62, curate i/c St George Rugby 1956–62, perpetual curate Sprowston Norwich 1962–73, rector Beeston St Andrew Norwich 1962–73; rural dean: Norwich North 1970–72, Rugby 1973–78; rector Rugby St Andrew 1973–87, hon canon Coventry Cathedral 1983–87 (canon emeritus 1987–), canon of Windsor 1987–95; dir Norwich Samaritans 1970–72; Freeman City of London 1954, chaplain Worshipful Co of Vintners 1992– (Liveryman 1954); *Books* The Story of St Andrew's Rugby (1979); *Recreations* art, painting, local history; *Style*— The Rev Canon Alan Coldwells; ✉ 26 King Street, Slough, Berks SL1 2QS (☎ 01753 538589)

COLE, Dr Anthony Paul; JP (1996); s of Bernard Joseph Cole, ISO (d 1948), and Mary Veronica, *née* Ryden (d 1987); *b* 23 Jan 1939; *Educ* St Boniface Coll, Univ of Bristol (MB ChB); *m* 24 July 1970, Elizabeth Mary, da of Leonard Vaughan-Shaw (d 1957); 2 s (Nicholas b 7 June 1973, Matthew b 24 Oct 1976), 2 da (Sarah b 27 July 1971, Alice b 11 May 1979); *Career* conslt paediatrician Worcester Royal Infirmary 1974, sr clinical lectr Univ of Birmingham 1986; contrib to many scientific pubns incl: Lancet, Acta Paediat Scand, BMJ; govr: Linacre Centre, St Richard Hospice; fndr pres Worcestershire Medico Legal Soc; memb Br Paediatric Assoc 1974; Master Guild of Catholic Doctors 1994; FRCP 1983; Knight of the Holy Sepulchre of Jerusalem (KHS) 1991; *Recreations* music, sailing, golf; *Clubs* Catenians, Royal Commonwealth Soc; *Style*— Dr Anthony Cole, JP; ✉ Downside, Battenhall Road, Worcester WR5 2BT (☎ 01905 352967); Worcester Royal Infirmary, Castle St, Worcester WR1 3AS

COLE, Barry M; s of Theodore Cole (d 1975), and Marjorie Ray, *née* Leewarden; *b* 24 Oct 1944; *Educ* Rugby, Hotel Sch Lausanne Switzerland; *m* 6 April 1971, Jill Valerie, *née* Minton; 1 da (Sara-Louise), 1 s (Benjamin); *Career* Grand Metropolitan Hotels 1967–73: reception Washington Hotel, cashier Mayfair Hotel, asst mangr Rubens Hotel then Rembrandt Hotel, area mangr County Div George Hotel Edinburgh; worked 1970–73: International Basle, Chateau Louis XIII Cannes, Savoy, Claridges, Sacher Hotel Vienna; 1973–79: dir The Fernley Bath and The Grange Keynsham, dir and ptnr The Cathedral Salisbury; proprietor 1979–85: The Three Cocks Hotel nr Hay-on-Wye, The Old Barn Inn, The Wellington Brecon; md: The Osborne Hotel and Luxury Timeshare Torquay 1985–95, Riviera Centre Ltd; dir: Leisure Partnerships Ltd, Leisure Partnerships Consultants Ltd; govr S Devon Coll, Freeman City of London 1983; Master Innholder 1983 (chm 1994–96), FTS 1980, FHCIMA, FInstSMM 1987; *Recreations* hunting, watersports; *Style*— Barry Cole, Esq; ✉ 46 Barnfield Road, Torquay, Devon TQ2 6TA (☎ 01803 690376)

COLE, Cherry Elizabeth; da of Brian William Cole (d 1978), of Solihull, and Patricia Anne, *née* Smith; *b* 14 Oct 1949; *Educ* Newport HS, Solihull HS; *m* 17 April 1971, Richard Brian Fawkes, s of Stanley Victor Fawkes (d 1949), of Camberley; 2 s (Harry Richard b 20 March 1984, Leo Sebastian b 5 June 1986), 1 da (Caitlin Siân b 31 May 1991); *Career* BBC TV 1967–82: PA then researcher then asst prodr Outside Broadcasts, prodr Presentation; head of presentation Channel 4 TV 1988–96 (presentation ed 1982–88), dir of broadcasting Granada Sky Broadcasting 1996–; memb: BAFTA, RTS; *Recreations* sleeping, swimming, skiing; *Style*— Miss Cherry Cole; ✉ Granada Sky Broadcasting, Franciscan Court, 16 Hatfields, London SE1 8DJ (☎ 0171 578 4040)

COLE, Christopher Andrew; s of Clifford Percival Cole (d 1948), of Clevedon, Avon, and Nellie, *née* Pople (d 1983); *b* 30 Sept 1940; *Educ* Sidcot Sch Winscombe, Hotel and Trg Dept S Devon Tech Coll Torquay (Dip in Hotel Mgmnt), Ashridge Mgmnt Coll; *m* 1968, Angela Christine Elizabeth, da of Marcus Spaull; 2 da (Anna-Louise Miranda b 11 Feb 1972, Jocelyn Emma Elizabeth b 19 Dec 1974); *Career* hotelier; hotel trg Dorchester Hotel Park Lane 1961–62, various positions at hotels throughout country 1962–73, mangr (also opened) The Selfridge Hotel London 1973–81, gen mangr Kensington Palace Hotel 1981–83, devpt dir Thistle Hotels 1983 87 (devpt mangr 1982–83), md Lucknam Park Colerne Wilts (opened 1988, four AA red stars, hotel of the year 1991, Michelin Star) 1987–95, chm and chief exec offr Theobalds Park Hotel & Health Spa Ltd 1995; chm Computer Ctee of Corporation, Ptnrs and Membs of the Exec Cncl Steigenberger Hotels Corp Frankfurt 1979–84, chm Bd Prestige Hotels/Small Luxury Hotels of the World 1990–91 (dir 1988–92); Freeman City of London 1991; MHCIMA, MI 1991; *Recreations* gliding, sailing; *Style*— Christopher A Cole, Esq; ✉ 14 Beech Walk, Mill Hill, London NW7 3PH (☎ 0181 959 4317, fax 0181 931 2154)

COLE, Col Sir (Alexander) Colin; KCB (1992), KCVO (1983, CVO 1979, MVO 1977), TD (1972); s of Capt Edward Harold Cole (d 1963), of Croham Hurst, Surrey, and Blanche Ruby Lavinia, *née* Wallis (d 1984); *b* 16 May 1922; *Educ* Dulwich, BNC Oxford (MA, BCL); *m* 5 June 1944, Valerie, o da of late Capt Stanley Walter Card; 4 s (Giles b 1949, Nicholas b 1951, Alexander b 1953, Christopher b 1955), 3 da (Frances b 1956, Mary b 1960, Jane b 1965); *Career* served WWII Capt Coldstream Gds; Maj Inf Bn HAC 1963, Maj 1967, Bt Lt-Col (later Hon Col) 6/7 Vol Bn The Queen's Regt 1981–86, Col RARO 1986–; called to the Bar Inner Temple 1949, hon bencher 1988; Fitzalan Pursuivant of Arms Extraordinary 1953, Portcullis Pursuivant of Arms 1957, Windsor Herald of Arms 1966, Garter Principal King of Arms 1978–92 (registrar and librarian Coll of Arms 1967–74); govr and chm of Bd of Govrs Alleyn's Coll of God's Gift Dulwich 1987–; pres Royal Soc of St George 1982–; fell Heraldry Soc; Knight Principal Imperial Soc of Knights Bachelor 1983–94; Sheriff City of London 1976–77; memb Ct Common Cncl City of London Ward of Castle Baynard 1964–; OStJ; memb Ct of Assts HAC 1962–89; Freeman, Liveryman and memb Ct Worshipful Cos of: Basketmakers, Scriveners, Painter Stainers; Cruz Distinguida San Raimundo de Penafort; *Clubs* Cavalry and Guards', City Livery; *Style*— Col Sir Colin Cole, KCB, KCVO, TD; ✉ Holly House, Burstow, Surrey

COLE, Sir David Lee; KCMG (1975, CMG 1965), MC (1944); s of late Brig David Henry Cole, CBE (d 1957), and Charlotte Louisa Ryles, *née* Wedgwood; *b* 31 Aug 1920; *Educ* Cheltenham, Sidney Sussex Coll Cambridge; *m* 1945, Dorothy, *née* Patton; 1 s (David b 1950); *Career* Royal Inniskilling Fusiliers 1940–45 (serv in Sicily and Italy); Dominions Office 1947; HM Dip Serv: private sec to Rt Hon the Earl of Home 1957–60, high cmmr Malawi 1964–67, min (political) New Delhi 1967–70, asst under sec of state FCO 1970–73, ambass to Thailand 1973–78, ret; *Books* Rough Road to Rome (1983); *Recreations* watercolour painting; *Style*— Sir David Cole, KCMG, MC; ✉ 19 Burghley House, Somerset Rd, Wimbledon, London SW19 5JB

COLE, George; OBE (1992); *b* 22 April 1925; *Educ* Surrey County Cncl Secdy Sch Morden; *m* 1, 1954 (m dis 1966), Eileen Moore; 1 s, 1 da; m 2, 1967, Penelope Morrell; 1 s, 1 da; *Career* actor; serv RAF 1943–47; *Theatre* incl: first stage appearance 1939, Cottage to Let (Birmingham, West End and tour) 1940–41, Goodnight Children (New) 1942, Mr Bolfry (Playhouse) 1943, Dr Angelus (Phoenix) 1947, The Anatomist (Westminster) 1948, Mr Gillie (Garrick) 1950, A Phoenix too Frequent and Thor with Angels (Lyric Hammersmith) 1951, Misery Me (Duchess) 1955, Mr Bolfry (Aldwych) 1956, Brass Butterfly (Strand) 1958, The Bargain (St Martin's) 1961, The Sponge Room and Squat Betty (Royal Court) 1962, Meet Me on the Fence (tour) 1963, Hedda Gabler (St Martin's) 1964, A Public Mischief (St Martin's) 1965, Too True to be Good (Strand) 1965, The Waiting Game (Arts) 1966, The Three Sisters (Royal Court) 1967, Doubtful Haunts (Hampstead) 1968, The Passionate Husband 1969, The Philanthropist (Mayfair) 1971, Country Life (Hampstead) 1973, Déjà Revue (New) 1974, Motive (tour) 1976, Banana Ridge (Savoy) 1976, The Case of the Oily Levantine (Guildford) 1977, Something Afoot (Hong Kong) 1978, Brimstone and Treacle (Open Space) 1979, Liberty Hall (Greenwich) 1980, The Pirates of Penzance (Drury Lane) 1982, A Month of Sundays (Duchess) 1986, A Piece of My Mind (Apollo) 1987, Peter Pan (Cambridge) 1987, Natural Causes (tour) 1992, Theft (tour) 1995, Lock up your Daughters 1996; *Television* incl: Life of Bliss (also radio), A Man of Our Times, Don't Forget to Write, Minder (9 series), The Bounder (2 series), Blott on the Landscape (BBC), Comrade Dad, Natural Causes (YTV), Henry Root (Central), Root into Europe (Central), My Good Friend (Hartswood Films for Anglia TV) 1995–96, An Independent Man 1996; *Films* incl: Cottage to Let 1941, Morning Departure 1949, Laughter in Paradise, Scrooge, Top Secret 1951, Will Any Gentleman? 1952, The Intruder 1952, Happy Ever After 1953, Our Girl Friday 1953, The Belles of St Trinian's 1954, Quentin Durward 1955, The Weapon 1956, It's a Wonderful World 1956, The Green Man 1956, Blue Murder at St Trinian's 1957, Too Many Crooks, Don't Panic Chaps, The Bridal Path 1959, The Pure Hell of St Trinian's 1961, Cleopatra, Dr Syn 1962, One Way Pendulum 1964, The Legend of Dick Turpin 1964, The Great St Trinian's Train Robbery 1965, The Green Shoes 1969, Vampire Lovers 1970, Girl in the Dark 1971, The Blue Bird 1975, Minder on the Orient Express 1985, Mary Reilly 1996; *Style*— George Cole, Esq, OBE; ✉ c/o Joy Jameson Ltd, 219 The Plaza, 535 King's Road, London SW10 0SZ (☎ 0171 351 3971, fax 0171 352 1744)

COLE, Prof George Herbert Avery; s of George Avery Cole (d 1963), of London, and Florence Avelin (d 1986); *b* 12 Jan 1928; *Educ* UCL (BSc), QMC London (PhD), Univ of London (DSc); *m* 6 Sept 1954, Ernestine (Tina) Ann, da of Lt Ernest Wilkinson (d 1934), of Whitney, Oxon; (1 s David George John 1958), 1 da (Annette Clare (Mrs Brindle) b 10 March 1961); *Career* Nat Serv sci offr Admiralty Res Laboratory RN Sci Serv 1952–54; ICI res fell UCL 1954–57, asst prof of physics UCLA 1957–58, sr exec Clark Chapman & Co Ltd Gateshead Co Durham 1958–64; Univ of Hull: prof of theoretical physics 1964–86, prof of engrg physics 1986–; visiting scientist: Euro Space Tech Centre Nordwijk Nd 1965, Euro Space Res Inst Frascati Italy 1968–72; memb Cncl St Williams Fndn York, chm Liaison Ctee Yorks Univ Air Sqdn, former chief regnl sci advsr No 2 Home Def Reg; Freeman City of London; Liveryman: Worshipful Co of Fan Makers, Worshipful Co of Engrs; FIMechE, FRAS 1956, FIP 1965, CEng 1988; *Books* An Introduction to the Statistical Theory of Classical Simple Dense Fluids (1967), Mathematical Techniques and Physical Applications (1971), Solutions Manual: Mathematical Techniques and Physical Applications (1971), The Structure of Planets (1978), Physics of Planetary Interiors (1984), Inside a Planet (1986), Thermal Power Cycles (1991); *Recreations* water colour painting, piano music; *Clubs* Athenaeum; *Style*— Prof George Cole; ✉ Department of Engineering Design and Manufacture, University of Hull, Hull, Humberside HU6 7RX (☎ 01482 465346, fax 01482 466205, telex 592592)

COLE, Graham; *b* 26 Aug 1946; *Educ* Hardye's Sch Dorchester, Univ of Exeter (BA); *Children* 1 s (Simon b 6 Sept 1972), 1 da (Juliet (twin)); *Career* ptnr Deloitte Haskins & Sells 1979–95, dir corp fin Beeson Gregory (stockbrokers) 1995–; non-exec dir Northamber PLC 1995–; chm CISCO Ctee on Corp Governance; Freeman City of London; fell BR Assoc of Hotel Accountants, FCA, MSI; *Recreations* shooting, collecting antiquarian maps; *Clubs* Marks, Harry's Bar, Annabel's, Les Ambassadeurs; *Style*— Graham Cole, Esq; ✉ Beeson Gregory, The Registry, Royal Mint Court, London EC3N 4EY (☎ 0171 488 4040, fax 0171 481 3762)

COLE, John Morrison; s of George Cole, and Alice Jane Cole; *b* 23 Nov 1927; *Educ* Belfast Royal Acad, Univ of London (BA); *m* 1956, Margaret Isobel, da of John S Williamson, of Belfast; 4 s; *Career* Belfast Telegraph 1945–56 (reporter, industl corr, municipal corr, political corr); The Guardian: reporter 1956–57, labour corr 1957–63, news ed 1963–69, dep ed 1969–75; dep ed The Observer 1976–81 (asst ed 1975), political ed BBC 1981–92, currently freelance broadcaster and journalist; work incl: BBC, New Statesman, Daily Telegraph, Sunday Times; RTS Television Journalist of the Year 1991, BAFTA Richard Dimbleby Award 1993; Hon DSSc Queen's Univ Belfast 1992; Hon Dr: The Open Univ 1992, Univ of Ulster 1992, Univ of St Andrews 1993; *Books* The Poor of the Earth (1976), The Thatcher Years - A Decade of Revolution in British Politics (1987), As it Seemed to Me: political memoirs (1995), contrib to various books on British and Irish politics; *Recreations* reading, travel; *Clubs* Athenaeum; *Style*— John Cole; ✉ c/o BBC Office, House of Commons, Westminster, London SW1A 0AA (☎ 0171 219 4765)

COLE, Jonathan Richard; s of John Sydney Richard Cole, QC (d 1989), and Doreen, *née* Matthews (d 1966); *b* 13 Oct 1933; *Educ* Portora Royal Sch NI, Univ of Dublin (BA), Univ of Cambridge, Inns of Court Sch of Law; *m* 12 Feb 1972, Julia Peta; 1 da (Charlotte Louise b 28 Feb 1973), 1 s (Alliott David Richard b 21 July 1978); *Career* called to the Bar Gray's Inn 1964, recorder of the Crown Court 1986–, head of chambers; legal assessor to Gen Medical Cncl and Gen Dental Cncl 1990–; FCIArb 1992; *Recreations* music, reading, gardening, bridge; *Clubs* The Athenaeum, The Kildare St and University (Dublin); *Style*— Jonathan Cole, Esq; ✉ Lamb Chambers, Lamb Building, Temple, London EC4Y 7AS

COLE, Lorna; *Educ* Allerton HS Leeds, Univ of Leeds (LLB); *Career* called to the Bar Lincoln's Inn 1950, currently head of chambers; memb Lord Chancellor's Ctee for Family Servs; chair Friends of the Ferens Art Gallery Hull; *Recreations* walking, music, theatre, art; *Style*— Miss Lorna Cole; ✉ Wilberforce Chambers, 171 High Street, Hull, Humberside HU1 1NE (☎ 01482 323264)

COLE, Maggie; da of Robert Lawrence Cole, of NY, and Cyrella, *née* Golden (d 1972); *b* 30 March 1952; *Educ* Nyack HS NY, Juilliard Sch, Lawrence Univ, Geneva Conservatory of Music; *m* 21 March 1982, Richard Paul Macphail, s of Maj David Lamont Macphail, of Chichester; *Career* harpsichordist; recordings made of Bach, Scarlatti and other seventeenth and eighteenth century composers for Hyperion, Amon Ra and Virgin; performed at a series of Bach concerts at the Wigmore Hall 1985, numerous recordings for BBC Radio 3 and concerts throughout Europe, USA, Poland and Russia; active in organising music in local primary schs in Notting Hill, fund raiser through charity concerts for London Lighthouse (the first hospice for AIDS sufferers in the UK); *Recreations* swimming, walking, reading, looking at paintings; *Style*— Miss Maggie Cole; ✉ c/o Robert White Artist Management, 182 Moselle Ave, London N22 6EX (☎ 0171 221 4681)

COLE, Nicholas Stephen Edward; s of Col Sir Colin Cole, KCVO, TD, BCL, MA, FSA, *qv*, Garter Principal King of Arms, of Burstow, Horley, Surrey, and Valerie, *née* Card; *b* 23 Aug 1951; *Educ* Hurstpierpoint Coll, Central Sch of Art & Design London (BA); *m* 30 Oct 1976 (m dis 1991), Suzanne Maryanne, da of John Duncan Rae; 2 s (Edward b 7 Sept 1979, Frederick b 14 Oct 1981), 1 da (Stephanie b 13 Aug 1977); m 2 (m dis 1995), 18 July 1992, Sybil Angela, da of Barry and Audrey Warmisham; *Career* assoc Jack Howe & Associates 1975–76, art dir PD Design Co Ltd 1979–82; fndr and sr ptnr The Cole Design Consultancy (creative and strategic mktg servs); Freeman City of London, Liveryman Worshipful Co of Scriveners 1975; MCSD 1974; *Style*— Nicholas Cole, Esq; ✉ The Cole Design Consultancy, Link House, 2 Norfolk Square, Brighton East Sussex BN1 2PB (☎ 01273 730072, fax 01273 730002, e-mail coledesign@linkhouse.dial.iql.co.uk)

COLE, Paul Frederick Irvine; s of Maj H W Cole, and Agnes, *née* Irvine; *b* 11 Sept 1942; *Educ* King's Coll Taunton; *m* 13 Feb 1976, Vanessa, da of Capt Edward Dorian Dudley-Ryder; 3 s (Alexander b 10 Nov 1977, Oliver b 18 Oct 1979, Mark b 1 Feb 1987); *Career* racehorse trainer; champion flat trainer 1991; horses trained incl: Culture Vulture, Snurge, Zoman, Dilum, Magic Ring, Generous, Ibn Bey; *Recreations* tennis; *Style*— Paul Cole, Esq; ✉ Whatcombe, nr Wantage, Oxfordshire OX12 9NW (☎ 01488 638433, fax 01488 638609, car 0836 221559)

COLE, Peter George; s of John Cole, of Knutsford, Cheshire, and Louise Helena, *née* Twine; *b* 13 Aug 1942; *Educ* Colyton GS, Univ Coll London (LLB), Tulane Univ New Orleans (LLM); *m* 16 Sept 1995, Barbara Maria; *Career* Alexander Tatham: articled clerk 1964–66, asst slr 1966–68, ptnr 1968–93, managing ptnr 1991–93; nat managing ptnr Eversheds 1993–; memb Law Soc; *Recreations* supporting Chelsea FC, farming, foreign travel; *Style*— Peter Cole, Esq; ✉ National Managing Partner, Eversheds, Senator House, 85 Queen Victoria Street, London EC4V 4JL (☎ 0171 919 4500, fax 0171 919 4919, car 0831 520258)

COLE, Dr Simon Michael; *b* 26 Nov 1944; *Educ* Lincoln Coll Oxford, American Univ of Beirut, St John's Coll Cambridge (BA, MA, PhD); *m* 1970, Oda Irene Katarine von Lichtenau dictus Bludau; 2 s (b 1972 and 1974), 1 da (b 1977); *Career* teacher and dir of studies Int Language Centre Beirut 1966–70, dir Int Language Centre Athens 1970–72, head of English The New Sch Rome 1972–74; British Cncl: asst rep Iraq 1975–76, asst rep Netherlands 1976–81, asst rep I Islamabad Pakistan 1981–85, head Orgn and Methods Mgmnt Servs Dept 1985–86, head India Unit America, Pacific and E Asia Div 1986–89, dir NE Brazil 1989–93, dir Berlin 1993–; *Style*— Dr Simon M Cole; ✉ The British Council, Hardenbergstrasse 20, 10623 Berlin, Germany

COLE, Stephanie; *Educ* Bristol Old Vic Theatre Sch; *m* (m dis 1988), Henry Marshall; 1 da (Emma); *Career* actress; debut Bristol Old Vic; regnl theatre incl: Manchester Royal Exchange, Birmingham Repertory, Liverpool Everyman, Salisbury, Richmond Orange Tree; *Theatre* performances incl: The Relapse (Old Vic), The Tinker (Comedy), Rose (Duke of York), Noises Off (Savoy), Steel Magnolias (Lyric), A Passionate Woman (Comedy Theatre) 1995; *Television* incl: Tenko, Open All Hours, A Bit of a Do, Soldiering On (BBC Talking Heads monologue by Alan Bennett), Return of the Antelope, Going Gently, Amy, Tears in the Rain, Waiting for God (BBC); *Awards* Comedy Actress of the Year 1992; *Recreations* playing the guitar, ukelele and recorder; *Style*— Ms Stephanie Cole; ✉ c/o Michael Ladkin Personal Management, Suite One, Ground Floor, 1 Duchess Street, London W1N 3DE (☎ 0171 436 4626, fax 0171 436 4627)

COLE, Dr William Charles; LVO (1966); s of Frederick George Cole, and Maria, *née* Fry; *b* 9 Oct 1909; *Educ* St Olave's GS, RAM; *m* 1, Elizabeth Brown Caw (d 1942); 3 da (Elspeth, Jennifer, Olivia); m 2, Winifred Grace Mitchell (d 1991); 1 s (Nicholas); *Career* former prof and lectr RAM and former lectr Royal Acad of Dancing, Master of the Music HM The Queen's Chapel of the Savoy 1954–94, hon sec Royal Philharmonic Soc 1969–81, past pres and hon treas Cncl Royal Coll of Organists (memb 1960–), chm Central Music Library 1972–83; Liveryman Worshipful Co of Glaziers & Painters of Glass Co; FRAM, FRCM, FRCO, FSA; *Books* The Form of Music (1969), A Catalogue of Netherlandish and North European Roundels in Britain (1993); articles on stained glass in learned jls; *Recreations* stained glass; *Clubs* Garrick; *Style*— Dr William Cole, LVO, FSA; ✉ Barnacre, Wood Rd, Hindhead, Surrey (☎ 01428 604917)

COLE, William Charles; s of Albert William Cole (d 1989), of West Wickham, Kent, and Rosina, *née* Garratt; *b* 13 Jan 1946; *Educ* St Joseph's Coll; *m* 9 Sept 1972, Sally Freda, da of Frederick James Still (d 1988), of Croydon, Surrey; 2 da (Emma b 6 Dec 1974, Hannah b 27 Dec 1977); *Career* CA 1970–73, stockjobber Stocken and Lazarus 1973–87, merged with Akroyd and Smithers Ltd 1977 and Warburg Securities 1986, fin and admin dir Olliff & Partners plc 1987–92; fin dir 1993–: Loyalward Ltd, Cedrus Ltd, County Partners Ltd, Topgift Ltd; memb: The Stock Exchange 1981, The Securities Assoc (now Securities and Futures Authy) 1988, MSI 1993; FCA 1970; *Recreations* golf, tennis, swimming; *Clubs* RAC, Les Ambassadeurs; *Style*— William C Cole, Esq; ✉ The Timbos, Birchmead, Farnborough Park, Orpington, Kent BR6 8LT (01689 851833)

COLE-HAMILTON, Prof David John; s of Lt Cdr Anthony Mervyn Cole-Hamilton, of Stevenage, Herts, and Monica Mary, *née* Cartwright (d 1954); *b* 22 May 1948; *Educ* Haileybury, Univ of Edinburgh (BSc, PhD); *m* 25 Aug 1973, Elizabeth Ann, da of Bruce Lloyd Brown, of Victoria, BC; 2 s (Alexander Geoffrey b 22 July 1977, Nicholas Anthony Michael b 23 May 1986), 2 da (Rose Monica Elizabeth b 17 June 1979, (Sian) Fiona Non b 23 May 1986 (twin)); *Career* temp lectr Imperial Coll London 1975–78 (post doctoral fell 1974–75), sr lectr Univ of Liverpool 1983–85 (lectr 1978–83), Irvine prof of chemistry Univ of St Andrews 1985–; Royal Soc of Chemistry: Corday Morgan medallist 1983, Sir Edward Frankland fell 1984–85; runner-up Museums and Galleries Cmmn Award for Innovation in Conservation 1995; chm: Chemistry Sectional Ctee Royal Soc of Edinburgh 1994–, Chemistry Section Br Assoc for the Advancement of Science 1995–; 190 pubns on organometallic chemistry and homogeneous catalysis; FRSE 1988, FRSC; *Books* Reactions of Organometallic Compounds with Surfaces (ed, 1989); *Style*— Prof David Cole-Hamilton, FRSE; ✉ School of Chemistry, University of St Andrews, St Andrews, Fife KY16 9ST (☎ 01334 463805, fax 01334 463808)

COLE-HAMILTON, (Arthur) Richard; CBE (1993); s of John Cole-Hamilton, CBE, DL, of Kilwinning, Ayrshire, and Gladys, *née* Cowie; *b* 8 May 1935; *Educ* Ardrossan Acad, Loretto, Univ of Cambridge (BA); *m* 16 Feb 1963, Prudence Ann, da of Dr Lindsay Lamb, of Edinburgh; 1 s (John Liston b 11 March 1971), 2 da (Patricia Joy b 17 Feb 1964, Sara Louise b 21 June 1967); *Career* Nat Serv, 2 Lt Argyll & Sutherland Highlanders; CA; ptnr Brechin Cole-Hamilton CA's 1962–67; Clydesdale Bank plc: asst mangr 1967, head office mangr 1976, chief gen mangr 1982, dir and chief exec 1987, ret 1992; chm Stakis plc 1995– (non-exec dir 1992–, dep chm 1994); non-exec dir: Caledonian Publishing Co plc 1992–95, Securities Trust of Scotland plc 1992–95; memb: Cncl Inst of CAs of Scotland 1981–85, Bd of Tstees Nat Galleries of Scotland 1986–96, Exec Ctee Erskine Hosp; dep chm Ctee Scottish Clearing Bankers 1989–91 (chm 1985–87 and 1991–92); pres: Inst of Bankers (Scotland) 1988–90, Ayrshire C of C and Industry 1991–95; vice pres Scottish Cncl Devpt and Indust 1992–95 (chm 1992); tstee and treas Princess Royal Tst for Carers; *Recreations* golf; *Clubs* Royal & Ancient (chm General Ctee 1994), Prestwick Golf (capt 1987–88), Western Highland Bde; *Style*— Richard Cole-Hamilton, Esq, CBE; ✉ 26 Lady Margaret Drive, Troon, Ayrshire KA10 7AL

COLE-MORGAN, John Anthony; s of Ensor James Henry Cole-Morgan (d 1970), of Swansea, and Kathleen, *née* Thomas; *b* 10 May 1937; *Educ* Swansea GS, Univ of Reading (BSc, Miller Mutal award), DipCAM; *m* 2 May 1964, Maria Tereza da Cunha, da of late Mateus Cardoso Peres; 2 da (Alexandra b 9 May 1965, Anna Marie b 21 Sept 1973), 2 s (Lawrence Ensor b 25 Dec 1966, Dominic Matthew b 15 Aug 1970); *Career* asst farm mangr Nickerson Farms 1960–61, asst PRO Spillers Ltd 1961–63, press and tech offr Agricultural Engineers Assoc 1963–65, account mangr Astral Public Relations 1965–67, PRO Fertilizer Div Fisons 1967–71, head of information ARC 1971–75, head of publicity BOTB 1975–79, dep head of information Dept of Trade 1979–81, dir of PR British Council 1981–84, PR conslt 1984–; memb Salisbury DC 1991, memb Guild of Agric Journalists; FIPR 1980; *Books* Visiting Craft Workshops in the English Countryside (ed, 1992); contrib to several pubns on PR; *Recreations* sailing and the arts; *Style*— John Cole-Morgan, Esq; ✉ Greenstone Byre, Charlton, Shaftesbury, Dorset SP7 0EN (☎ 01747 828840)

COLEBROOK, Miles William Merrill; s of Peter Merrill Colebrook, MC, JP, of Princes Gate, Ascot, and Joyce Hay, *née* Ruthven (d 1969); *b* 14 Jan 1948; *Educ* Shrewsbury, Ann Arbor Univ Michigan; *m* 1 Sept 1973 (m dis); 2 s (Thomas b 1978, George b 1987) 1 da (Lucy b 1977); *Career* J Walter Thompson: media exec 1966–70, account exec 1970–78, bd dir 1978–85, md 1985–88, pres and chief exec Europe 1988–96, int gp pres JWT Worldwide 1996–; FIPA 1990; *Recreations* shooting, skiing, cooking; *Style*— Miles Colebrook, Esq; ✉ c/o J Walter Thompson, 40 Berkeley Square, London W1X 6AD (☎ 0171 499 4040)

COLEBY, Anthony Laurie; s of Dr Leslie James Moger Coleby (d 1971), and Laurie, *née* Shuttleworth; *b* 27 April 1935; *Educ* Winchester, CCC Cambridge; *m* 1966, Rosemary Melian Elisabeth, da of Sir (Isham) Peter Garran, KCMG (d 1991); 1 s, 2 da; *Career* PA to md IMF 1964–67; Bank of England: dep chief cashier 1973–80, asst dir 1980–86, chief monetary advsr to Govr 1986–90, exec dir 1990–94; non-exec dir: Halifax Building Society 1994–, Anglo Irish Bank Corporation 1994–, Italian International Bank 1994–; *Recreations* choral singing, railways, transport; *Style*— Anthony Coleby, Esq; ✉ Halifax Building Society, Trinity Road, Halifax, W Yorks HX1 2RG (☎ 01422 333333)

COLECLOUGH, Stephen Donald; s of Donald Derek Coleclough, of Tamworth, Staffs, and Vera Rosemary Coleclough; *b* 6 April 1962; *Educ* King Edward VI Sch Lichfield, Univ of Sheffield (LLB), Coll of Law Chester (Willis Mills Prize); *Career* slr Graham & Rosen Hull Sept - Dec 1986 (articled clerk 1984–86); Simmons & Simmons: slr Corp Tax Dept 1987–91, ptnr 1991–96, head Corp and Indirect Taxes Gp 1995–96; dir of VAT Coopers & Lybrand 1997–; conslt HM Customs & Excise Trg Bd 1996–; memb: VAT Sub-ctee Revenue Law Ctee Law Soc, Indirect Taxation Sub-ctee Int Bar Assoc, Tech Ctee Chartered Inst of Taxation (chm Indirect Taxes Sub-ctee), VAT Sub-ctee Br Property Fedn; regular speaker at confs UK and overseas; memb Mensa; Freeman City of London, Liveryman City of London Slrs' Co; memb: Law Soc 1986, Int Bar Assoc 1993; ATII 1987, FRSA; *Publications* Butterworths Company Law Service (tax conslt), Butterworths Encyclopaedia of Forms and Precedents (contrib), Longman's Knight on Private Company Acquisitions (contrib 4 and 5 edns); also author of numerous articles in various professional jls; *Recreations* golf, heavy metal music and guitar playing, making preserves; *Clubs* Ruislip Golf, Archway Snooker; *Style*— Stephen Coleclough, Esq; ✉ Coopers & Lybrand, Temple Court, 35 Bull Street, Birmingham B4 6JT (☎ 0121 265 5000, fax 0121 265 5050, mobile 0860 104888)

COLEGATE, Isabel Diana (Mrs Michael Briggs); da of Sir Arthur Colegate, sometime MP (d 1956), and Winifred Mary (d 1955), da of late Sir William Henry Arthington Worsley, 3 Bt; *b* 10 Sept 1931; *Educ* Runton Hill Sch; *m* 12 Sept 1953, Michael Briggs, s of Denis Briggs, CBE; 2 s (Barnaby b 1964, Joshua b 1967), 1 da (Emily (see Jonathan Azis, *qv*) b 1956); *Career* novelist; literary agent Anthony Blond (London) Ltd 1952–57; Hon MA Univ of Bath 1988; FRSL 1981; *Books* The Blackmailer (1958), A Man of Power (1960), The Great Occasion (1962), Statues in a Garden (1964), Orlando King (1968), Orlando at the Brazen Threshold (1971), Agatha (1973), News from the City of the Sun (1979), The Shooting Party (1980, W H Smith literary award, filmed 1985), A Glimpse of Sion's Glory (1985), Deceits of Time (1988), The Summer of the Royal Visit (1991), Winter Journey (1995); *Style*— Isabel Colegate; ✉ Midford Castle, Bath BA2 7BU

COLEGATE, Raymond; CBE (1982); s of Ernest William Colegate, of Gravesend, Kent, and Violet Mary Dubettier Colegate; *b* 31 Aug 1927; *Educ* Co Sch for Boys Gravesend, LSE (BA); *m* 6 April 1961, Cecilia Mary (Sally), da of James Healy (d 1970); 1 s (John b 1965), 1 da (Joanne b 1968); *Career* BOT 1949, Central Statistical Office 1952–53, asst private sec to pres BOT 1955–56, Treasy 1957–59, EFTA Secretariat Geneva and Brussels 1960–64, CRE Dept BOT 1964–67, Aviation Dept BOT and DTI 1967–72; CAA: head Econ Policy and Licensing Dept 1972–75, head Econ Dept 1975–77, gp dir econ regulation 1977–89, non-exec dir 1989–90, air tport conslt 1990–; md (Europe) Global Aviation Associates Ltd 1991–95, dir FTO Trust Fund Ltd 1994–; FCIT; *Recreations* travel, music, reflection; *Style*— Raymond Colegate, Esq, CBE; ✉ 40 Lebanon Park, Twickenham, Middx TW1 3DG

COLEMAN, Professor Alice Mary; da of Bertie Coleman, DCM (d 1970), and Elizabeth Mary, *née* White (d 1959); *b* 8 June 1923; *Educ* Clarendon House Sch Ramsgate, Furzedown Coll (teacher's cert), Birkbeck Coll London (BA), King's Coll London (MA); *Career* teacher i/c geography Northfleet Central Sch Kent 1943–48; King's Coll London 1948–: memb academic staff 1948, asst lectr, sr lectr, reader, prof, fell 1980, emeritus prof 1988–; sabbaticals: Johns Hopkins Univ Baltimore USA 1957–58, Canadian Federal Dept of Energy Mines and Resources 1965, Univ of Western Ontario (first holder of visiting professorship for Distinguished Women Social Scientists) 1976, Hokkaido Univ of Educn Asahikawa Japan 1985; dir: Second Land Utilisation Survey of Britain 1960s, Land Use Research Unit 1977–, DICE, PACE Graphology; res contract DOE DICE Project for Design Improvement of Problem Estates 1988–94; ed: The Graphologist, The Graphological Magazine; Gill Memorial award RGS 1963, Times/Veuve Clicquot award 1974, Busk Gold medal RGS 1987; hon memb British Urban Regeneration Assoc 1995; pres Isle of Thanet Geographical Assoc; memb RGS 1948; *Books* The Planning Challenge of the Ottawa Area (1969), Canadian Settlement and Environmental Planning (1976), Utopia on Trial (1985); *Recreations* reading, graphology; *Style*— Prof Alice Coleman; ✉ King's College, Strand, London WC2R 2LS (☎ 0171 873 2610, fax 0171 873 2287); or (☎ 0181 244 6733)

COLEMAN, Brenda Anne (Mrs Tarquin Gorst); da of Gordon Barton Coleman, and Moira, *née* Vogt; *b* 28 Sept 1959; *Educ* Harrow Co GS, King's Coll London (LLB, intermediate scholar in Law, AKC), Coll of Law Lancaster Gate; *m* 7 Sept 1991, Tarquin Harold Gorst, s of Sir John Gorst, MP, *qv*; 3 s (Thomas Barton b 18 Aug 1992, Charles William Eldon b 23 Feb 1994, Rupert Edward Lowndes b 17 July 1995); *Career* slr Slaughter and May 1984–89 (articles 1982–84), ptnr Herbert Smith (Co Dept Tax Section) 1991– (slr specialising in corporate tax 1989–); author various articles in jls; memb: City of London Slrs' Co, Law Soc; *Recreations* squash, swimming, dance (Ceroc), reading; *Style*— Ms Brenda Coleman; ✉ Herbert Smith (Solicitors), Exchange House, Primrose Street, London EC2A 2HS (☎ 0171 374 8000)

COLEMAN, Charlotte Ninon; da of Francis Coleman, and Ann, *née* Beach; *b* 3 April 1968; *Educ* Camden Sch for Girls, Dartington Hall Sch; *Career* actress; *Theatre* incl: Lorna in Our Own Kind 1993 (Bush Theatre, nominated London Fringe Award for Best Actress); *Television* roles incl: Marmalade in Educating Marmalade (Thames) 1982, Helen in Inappropriate Behaviour (BBC) 1984, Jess in Oranges are not the Only Fruit (BBC, nominated BAFTA Best Actress Award 1988) 1987, Freddi in Freddi & Max (Thames) 1989, Barb in Giving Tong (BBC) 1995; *Films* incl: Scarlett in Four Weddings and a Funeral 1994 (Working Tital Films, nominated BAFTA Best Supporting Actress 1995), Whinni in Young Poisoners' Handbook (Mapp Films) 1994; *Awards* Special Performance Award RTS 1990; *Recreations* travel; *Style*— Ms Charlotte Coleman; ✉ c/o Peters Fraser & Dunlop Ltd, 503 The Chambers, Chelsea Harbour, Lots Road, London SW10 0XF (☎ 0171 344 1010, fax 0171 352 8135)

COLEMAN, David; *see:* Firth, David

COLEMAN, Francis Arthur; s of Bernard James Coleman (d 1939), of Montreal, and Blanche Marie, *née* Prenleloup (d 1952); *b* 12 Jan 1924; *Educ* McGill Univ Montreal, Conservatorium of Music, Conservatoire de Musique et d'Art Dramatique de la Province de Quebec (diploma), Rochester Univ NY, Eastman Sch of Music; *m* 1, 1956 (m dis 1963) Christina McDonald; m 2, 30 July 1966, Ann, da of Claude Ripley Beach (d 1968), of Eastbourne; 2 da (Charlotte b 3 April 1968, Lisa b 10 July 1970); *Career* RCAF Sqdn 406 Westmount Montreal; TV prodr and dir then prog controller CBMT Montreal (CBC radio Canada) 1952–58; prodr and dir: Granada TV 1958–59, ATV 1959–64; exec prodr: LWT 1971–76, Thames TV 1977–83; former exec prodr i/c prodn CTVC Bushey, course dir London Int Film Sch 1985–; visiting lectr City Univ The Barbican 1987; chm Liberal Working Party on the Media, fndr memb Liberal Arts Panel, fndr ITV Arts Panel, fndr memb Euro Bdcasting Union Music Experts Gp; memb ACTT 1958, fell IBA; Chevalier Ordre des Arts (French Miny of Culture); *Awards* Best Canadian Variety 1957,

Coronation Medal (for CBC London TV prodn of the Coronation) 1952, Leonard Brett Award (for best TV prodn 'On the Braden Beat' and 'Ici La France') 1965, Japan Prize (first British award for London Weekend adult series 'On Reflection') 1974, Golden Prague (first British award as writer of new version of Mozart's 'The Impresario' BBC TV) 1975, Prix Italia (first British music prize for Britten's Cantata at St Nicolas) 1982; *Books* Exploring TV (1970), Great Britain (McDonalds Countries series, 1971), Building a Record Library (1971), Bluffer's Guide to Opera (1973), Bluff Your Way in Ballet (1974); *Recreations* music, food, drink; *Clubs* Seven Dials Fox House; *Style*— Francis Coleman, Esq; ✉ 24 Shelton St, Covent Garden, London WC2H 9HP (☎ 0181 883 6111, fax 0171 497 3718)

COLEMAN, John; s of Peter Coleman, of Sawbridgeworth, Herts, and Katherine Jane Drummond Bailey Napier; *b* 17 June 1952; *Educ* Hyndland Sr Secdy Sch, Univ of Glasgow (Bachelor of Accountancy, Authur Young Medal); *m* 5 Oct 1974, Maureen Sheila Helen, da of David Venters (d 1989); 2 s (Euan Stuart b 24 Jan 1986, Neil Scott b 17 Aug 1988); *Career* various fin appts Procter & Gamble Ltd 1974–79, various fin appts Oil Tools International Ltd 1979–83; The Burton Group plc: dep fin dir 1983–86, md Top Shop Retail Ltd 1986–90, md Top Shop/Top Man 1990–91, md Dorothy Perkins Retail Ltd 1991–93; chief exec Texas Homecare 1993–95, main bd dir Ladbroke Group plc (parent co of Texas until 1995) 1993–95, chief exec House of Fraser plc 1996–; CIMA 1977; *Style*— John Coleman, Esq; ✉ House of Fraser plc, 1 Howick Place, London SW1P 1BH (☎ 0171 963 2000, fax 0171 828 8885)

COLEMAN, John Ennis; CB (1990); s of Donald Stafford Coleman (d 1968), Eastbourne, Sussex, and Dorothy Jean Balieff, *née* Ennis (d 1980); *b* 12 Nov 1930; *Educ* Dean Close Sch Cheltenham, Dulwich Coll, Univ of Oxford (MA); *m* 29 March 1958, Doreen Gwendoline, da of Percy Hellinger (d 1970), of Wimbledon; 1 s (David b 1968), 1 da (Kathryn b 1964); *Career* admitted slr 1957; Treasy Slrs Dept: legal asst 1958–64, sr legal asst 1964–71, asst slr 1971–80; legal under sec Depts of Indust and Trade 1980–83, legal advsr Dept for Educn 1983–90, conslt Dept for Educn and Employment 1990–96; currently jt ed Butterworth's The Law of Education; *Style*— John Coleman, Esq, CB

COLEMAN, (Elisabeth) Kay; OBE (1994); da of Harvey Wild, of Prestbury, Cheshire, and Ann, *née* Sutcliffe (d 1977); *b* 28 Dec 1945; *Educ* Brentwood Girls' Sch; *m* 1, 1971 (m dis 1985); 1 s (Julian Graham b 1973), 1 da (Lisa-Kay b 1975); m 2, 1993, Rodney Michael Graves, *qv*, s of Brian William Graves; *Career* mgmnt trainee Harveys & Co (Clothing) Ltd 1962–68, flight stewardess BOAC (Br Airways) 1968–73, former dir Galerie Unique Ltd (retail furniture), currently chief exec Harveys & Co (Clothing) Ltd; memb: Forum UK, Armed Forces Pay Review Body, Sec of States for Educn and Employment's Advsy Gp on Women's Issues, Bd of Govrs Manchester Metropolitan Univ, NW Industl Cncl; various appearances on TV and radio on women's issues, employment and politics; FRSA; *Recreations* bridge, tennis, theatre, horse racing; *Clubs* Carlton; *Style*— Mrs Kay Coleman, OBE; ✉ Tudor Lodge, Hale, Cheshire WA15 9PS; Flat 27, 25 Cheyne Place, London SW3 4HJ; Harveys & Co (Clothing) Limited, Glodwick Road, Oldham OL4 1YU (☎ 0161 624 9535, fax 0161 627 2028)

COLEMAN, Nick; s of Ivan Mark Coleman, of West Hampstead, London NW6, and Loretta, *née* Franks; *b* 2 Dec 1961; *Educ* West HS for Boys Essex, Southend Tech Coll, Kingston Poly, St Martin's Sch of Art (BA); *Career* fashion designer; menswear designer Burberrys July-Dec 1984, estab own label Nick Coleman 1985, Diffusion Line "Shield" 1992; first collection Dustbowl '86 shown London 1985; subsequent collections incl: Shadow of the Spirit 1986–87, Legion of the Lost 1987, Teeth of the Hydra 1987–88, V 1988, Deus ex Machina 1989, Mondo Nuovo Man/Woman 1989–90; menswear designer and conslt Corneliani 1989–90, jt fndr (with Katherine Hamnett) Nick Coleman Ltd 1989–, first collection Kimota Returns 1990–91, first major catwalk show London 1990, opened first retail outlet March 1992; subsequent collections: X 1991 (accompanied by catwalk show, appearances on BBC Clothes Show), Modern European Explorers 1991–92; fndr: Solaris (house music club) 1989–90, Kimota Nightclub 1989–90; memb London Fashion Cncl 1989; *Recreations* music, collecting African art, reading, work; *Style*— Nick Coleman, Esq; ✉ Nick Coleman Shop, 66 Neal Street, London WC2H 9PA (☎ 0171 379 4958, fax 0171 240 4286)

COLEMAN, Rt Rev Peter Everard; s of Pilot Offr Geoffrey Everard Coleman (RAF, d 1942), of Ware, Herts, and Lilian Bessie, *née* Cook (d 1982); *b* 28 Aug 1928; *Educ* Haileybury, Univ of London (LLB), Univ of Bristol (MLitt); *m* 14 May 1960, HSH Princess Elisabeth Donata Regina Emma Clementine, yst da of HSH Prince Heinrich XXXIX Reuss (d 1946); 2 s (Basil b 1963, Benedict b 1965), 2 da (Antonia b 1961, Elena b 1969); *Career* Mil Serv RHG and RA, 2 Lt 1947–49; called to the Bar Middle Temple 1965; ordained Bristol 1955, chaplain and lectr King's Coll London 1960–66, vicar St Paul's Clifton, chaplain Univ of Bristol 1966–71, canon residentiary and dir of trg Bristol 1971–81, archdeacon of Worcester 1981–84, bishop of Crediton 1984–96, ret; clerical memb Ct of Arches 1980–91, memb Gen Synod (House of Bishops) 1990–95, jt ed Theology 1982–91, provost Woodard Corporation (Western Div) 1992–; OStJ; *Books* Experiments with Prayer (1961), A Christian Approach to Television (1968), Christian Attitudes to Homosexuality (1980), Gay Christians - A Moral Dilemma (1989), Ordination of Women (1990); *Recreations* film making, fishing; *Style*— The Rt Rev Peter Coleman

COLEMAN, Peter John; *b* 1954; *Educ* Sch of Arch Brighton Poly (BA, DipArch, Crown Prize for Schs of Arch); *Career* architect; formerly with: Phippen Randall and Parks, Chamberlain Powell and Bon, Manning and Clamp; assoc ptnr Building Design Partnership 1989– (joined 1981); *Projects* current/recent projects incl: diplomatic and residential centre Kensington, mixed devpt Southampton City Centre, mixed devpt Oporto Santa Catarina, residential extension Mormon Temple E Grinstead, upgrading and extending Brent Cross Shopping Centre, new office HQ RAF admin Wyton Huntingdon; masterplan and design proposals (as winner of int competitons) for: mixed devpt on River Seine Paris, urban regeneration of Bugis Junction Singapore (in conjunction with DP Architects); involvement in various retail devpt schemes incl Lancer Square Kensington Church Street, experience of housing design incl housing for sale as part of mixed-use devpt schemes and free-standing residential devpt for private and public sector use; *Exhibitions* 21 New Architects (Design Centre) 1984; memb Br Cncl of Shopping Centres, RIBA; *Style*— Peter Coleman, Esq; ✉ BDP, PO Box 4WD, 16 Gresse Street, London W1A 4WD (☎ 0171 631 4733, fax 0171 631 0393)

COLEMAN, Prof Robert George Gilbert; s of Thomas Lichfield Danks and Sheila Carr Bush, adopted 1934 by George Gilbert Coleman (d 1953), and Rosina Emily Warner (d 1964); *b* 2 Oct 1929, Wellington, NZ; *Educ* St Mark's Sch, Rongotai Coll, Wellington Coll, Victoria Univ of Wellington (MA), Emmanuel Coll Cambridge (MA); *m* 1, 1958 (m dis 1992), Dorothy, *née* Gabe; 1 s; m 2, 1992, Anne Thompson; 2 s; *Career* lectr in humanity King's Coll Aberdeen 1955–60; Emmanuel Coll Cambridge: fell 1960, tutor 1963–71, librarian 1980–85, univ lectr in classics 1960–85, prof of comparative philology 1985–; *Books* The Eclogues of Vergil (ed with intro and commentary, 1977), New Studies in Latin Linguistics (ed, 1991); *Recreations* music, conversation, exploring strange towns; *Style*— Prof Robert Coleman; ✉ 7 Linton Rd, Balsham, Cambridge CB1 6HA; Emmanuel College, Cambridge CB2 3AP (☎ 01223 33 4200)

COLEMAN, Robert John; s of Lt Cdr Frederick Coleman, RN; *b* 8 Sept 1943; *Educ* Devonport HS for Boys Plymouth, Jesus Coll Oxford (MA), Univ of Chicago Law Sch (JD); *m* 23 Sept 1966, Malinda Tigay, da of Preston Skidmore Cutler; 2 da (Emily Ann b 1975, Laura Elizabeth b 1979); *Career* lectr in law Univ of Birmingham 1967–70, fndr memb Legal Aid and Advice Centre Birmingham Settlement 1968–70, called to the Bar 1969, barr at law in civil practice London 1970–73, memb Home Office Legal Advsrs Branch 1973; Euro Cmmn: admin later princ admin 1974–82, dep head of Div (Safeguard Measures and Removal of Non-Tariff Barriers) 1983, head of Div (Intellectual Property and Unfair Competition) 1984–87, dir (Public Procurement) 1987–90, dir (Approximation of Laws, Freedom of Establishment and Freedom to Provide Services, the Professions) 1990–91, dir gen (Transport) 1991–; *Publications* author of various articles on community law and policy; *Recreations* fitness training, music; *Style*— Robert Coleman, Esq; ✉ Commission of the European Communities, 200 Rue La Loi (Beaulieu 33), 1049 Bruxelles, Belgium (☎ 00 32 2 968245, fax 00 32 2 968355, telex 21877 COMEU B)

COLEMAN, Roger; s of Ronald Coleman, of Finchingfield, Essex, and Grace, *née* Thomas (d 1994); *b* 20 March 1943; *Educ* Ealing GS, Univ of Edinburgh (MA), Edinburgh Sch of Art (Andrew Grant scholar, Dip in Art); *m* 1, 1964 (m dis), Alison Fell, *qv*; 1 s (Ivan b 1967); m 2, 1995, Sally Reilly; *Career* visiting lectr Dept of Liberal Studies Bradford Regional Coll of Art 1967–68, lectr Dept of Liberal Studies Leeds Sch of Art and Design 1967–70, sr lectr Dept of Humanities St Martin's Sch of Art and Design 1970–72; fndr memb: Community Press London (printing and publishing co-op) 1972–73, Pitsmoor Builders Sheffield (bldg/design co-op) 1973–75; joiner and wood-machinist John Brignell & Co Ltd Cambridge (specialist joinery and restoration) 1975–76, ptnr Coleman & Hollis Cambridge (furniture and joinery design) 1976–82, conslt and freelance designer 1982–85, dir and project mangr Community Construction & Design Ltd 1984–91, co-dir London Innovation Ltd (R&D co with expertise in design and devpt of socially and environmentally desirable products) 1985–, sr research fell and dir DesignAge prog and co-ordinator Euro Design for Ageing Network RCA 1991–; numerous invited conf papers and lectures at home and abroad, contrib academic and professional jls; featured in Designers: Making Money or Making Sense (through work of London Innovation) BBC 2 1987, co-fndr, advsr and memb Bd Welfare State International 1968–, memb Jury RSA Student Design Awards 1992–; FRCA 1996; *Books* The Art of Work 1988, Designing for our Future Selves (ed, 1993); *Style*— Roger Coleman, Esq; ✉ DesignAge, Royal College of Art, Kensington Gore, London SW7 2EU (☎ 0171 584 5020 ext 329, fax 0171 584 8217)

COLEMAN, Sylvia May; da of Capt Gordon Barton Coleman, of Harrow, Middx, and Marie Jessie Therese, *née* Vogt; *b* 10 Dec 1957; *Educ* Harrow Co GS for Girls, Univ of Birmingham (LLB), Coll of Law Lancaster Gate; *Career* admitted slr 1982; Stephenson Harwood 1980–85, co lawyer Gallaher Ltd 1985–86, dir of corp business affrs and co sec Sony Music Entertainment (UK) Ltd (formerly CBS Records) 1987–95, vice-pres business affrs Sony Music Entertainment Europe 1995–; dir Renaissance Films Ltd 1995–; jt UK promoter Ceroc Dance, jt md Ceroc Enterprises Ltd 1992; chm of tstees Chicken Shed Theatre Co; memb: Action Aid, Law Soc 1980; *Recreations* dance, music; *Clubs* The Kensington Close; *Style*— Miss Sylvia Coleman; ✉ 20 Courtfield Gardens, London SW5 OPD (☎ 0171 370 5161); Sony Music Entertainment, 10/12 Great Malborough Street, London W1 (☎ 0171 911 8305)

COLEMAN, Terence Francis Frank (Terry); s of Jack Coleman (d 1978), of Poole, Dorset, and Doreen, *née* Grose; *b* 13 Feb 1931; *Educ* Univ of London (LLB); *m* 27 June 1981, Vivien Rosemary Lumsdaine Wallace, *qv*; 1 s (Jack b 1984), 1 da (Eliza b 1983); *Career* journalist: Poole Herald, Savoir Faire (ed), Sunday Mercury, Birmingham Post; The Guardian: reporter, arts corr, chief feature writer 1961–74; special writer Daily Mail 1974–76; The Guardian: chief feature writer 1976–78, New York corr 1981, special corr 1982–89; assoc ed The Independent 1989–91; *Awards* Feature Writer of the Year Br Press Awards 1983, Journalist of the Year Granada Awards 1987; *Books* The Railway Navvies (Yorkshire Post Prize for the Best Book of the Year, 1965), A Girl for the Afternoons (1965), Providence and Mr Hardy (with Lois Deacon, 1966), The Only True History (collected journalism, 1969), Passage to America (1972), The Liners (1976), An Indiscretion in the Life of an Heiress (ed 1976), The Scented Brawl (collected journalism, 1978), Southern Cross (1979), Thanksgiving (1981), Movers and Shakers (collected interviews, 1987), Thatcher's Britain (1987), Empire (1994); *Recreations* cricket, opera, circumnavigation; *Clubs* MCC; *Style*— Terry Coleman, Esq; ✉ 18 North Side, London SW4 0RQ

COLEMAN-SMITH, Brian Francis; s of Derek Gordon Coleman-Smith of Putney, London, and Patricia Edwina Cronin (d 1972); *b* 26 Oct 1944; *Educ* Emanuel Sch; *m* 19 Oct 1984, Frances Mary, da of John Alexander Gladstone; 2 step s (Douglas Croxford b 22 Jan 1973, Bruce Croxford b 21 Sept 1979), 1 step da (Alison Croxford b 13 June 1970); *Career* northern fin advertisement mangr The Guardian 1976–79, advertisement dir Financial Weekly 1979–81, fin sales dir The Guardian 1981–85; dir: Burson-Marsteller Financial 1985–91, Burson-Marsteller Ltd 1989–91; fndr md Smith Franklin Ltd 1991–94, jt md Binns & Co Public Relations Ltd 1994–; *Recreations* sport, theatre, cinema, classical music; *Style*— Brian Coleman-Smith, Esq; ✉ Binns & Co Public Relations Ltd, 16 St Helens Place, London EC3A 6DE (☎ 0171 786 9600)

COLENSO, Michael Chudleigh; s of Herbert Stanley Colenso (d 1952), of Johannesburg, and Olive, *née* Hirst (d 1967); *b* 16 Feb 1939; *Educ* Highlands North Sch Johannesburg, Univ of Witwatersrand Johannesburg (BA); *m* 25 Sept 1965, Joan, *née* Burnhope; 1 s (Peter John b 30 Jan 1971), 1 da (Jane b 12 March 1968); *Career* dir: John Wiley & Sons Ltd publishers 1960–72, Cassell & Collier Macmillan Ltd 1972–77, Times Mirror International Ltd 1977–84, Advanced Learning Systems; md: Year Book Mosby publishers 1977–84, Wilson Learning Ltd 1984–89, Wilson Learning SA Paris 1984–89, Wilson Learning GmbH Stuttgart 1984–89, The Open Coll 1989–; assoc Europe Japan Centre; *Books* High Performing Teams (1997); *Style*— Michael Colenso, Esq; ✉ Timbertop, Ruxley Crescent, Claygate, Surrey KT10 0TX (☎ 01372 462601)

COLENSO-JONES, Maj (Gilmore) Mervyn Boyce; s of Dr Gilmore Leonard Colenso Colenso-Jones (d 1990), of London, and Kathleen Edwina, *née* Macartney (d 1939); *b* 4 Sept 1930; *Educ* Rugby; *m* 24 Aug 1968, Rosamond Anne, da of Thomas Iorwerth Bowen (d 1975), of Carmarthen, W Wales; *Career* cmmnd Royal Welch Fusiliers 1950–72, served home and abroad, incl appt as Br Exchange Offr US Continental Army Cmd Virginia 1969–70, attended Jt Servs Staff Coll Latimer, regtl sec Royal Welch Fusiliers Caernarfon 1972–81, priory sec Order of St John Priory for Wales 1981–84, memb HM Bodyguard of the Hon Corps of Gentleman at Arms 1982–; memb S Glamorgan Health Authy 1981–84; CStJ 1981; *Recreations* normal country pursuits, watercolour painting; *Clubs* Army and Navy; *Style*— Maj Mervyn Colenso-Jones; ✉ Savernake Cottage, The Green, East Grafton, Marlborough, Wilts SN8 3DB (☎ 01672 810868)

COLERAINE, 2 Baron (UK 1954); (James) Martin Bonar Law; s of 1 Baron, PC (d 1980, himself s of Andrew Bonar Law, Prime Minister 1922–23); *b* 8 Aug 1931; *Educ* Eton, Trinity Coll Oxford; *m* 1, 30 April 1958 (m dis 1966), Emma Elizabeth, o da of late Nigel Richards; 2 da; m 2, 31 Aug 1966, (Anne) Patricia (d 1993), yr da of late Maj-Gen Ralph Henry Farrant, CB, of King's Acre, Wareham, Dorset; 1 s, 2 da (1 decd); *Heir* s, Hon (James) Peter Bonar Law b 23 Feb 1975; *Style*— The Rt Hon the Lord Coleraine; ✉ 3/5 Kensington Pk Gdns, London W11 (☎ 0171 221 4148)

COLERIDGE, David Ean; s of late Guy Cecil Richard Coleridge, MC, and Katherine Cicely Stewart Smith; *b* 7 June 1932; *Educ* Eton; *m* 1955, Susan, *née* Senior; 3 s (incl Nicholas Coleridge, *qv*); *Career* Lloyd's underwriter; non-exec dir Ockham Holdings PLC (chm 1994–96); chm Lloyd's 1991–92 (dep chm 1985, 1988 and 1989); Liveryman Worshipful Co of Grocers; *Recreations* racing, golf, early English watercolours, family; *Style*— David Coleridge, Esq; ✉ 37 Egerton Terrace, London SW3 2BU (☎ 0171 581

1756, fax 0171 591 0637); Spring Pond House, Wispers, nr Midhurst, W Sussex GU29 0QH (☎ 01730 813277); Ockham Holdings plc, 9 Devonshire Square, London EC2M 4YL (☎ 0171 617 2000)

COLERIDGE, Lady (Marguerite) Georgina Christine; *née* Hay; 2 da of 11 Marquess of Tweeddale (d 1967), and his 1 wife Marguerite Christine, *née* Ralli (d 1944); *b* 19 March 1916; *m* 20 Sept 1941, Capt Arthur Nicholas Coleridge, late Irish Gds (d 1987), s of John Duke Coleridge, FRIBA (d 1934), of Darby Green House, Blackwater, Hants; 1 da (Mrs Neil Smith); *Career* National Magazine Co Ltd 1937–39, with Country Life 1945, ed Homes and Gardens 1949–63; dir: Country Life Ltd 1962–74, George Newnes Ltd 1963–69; publisher: Homes and Gardens, Woman's Journal 1969–71, Ideal Home 1970–71; dir of special projects IPC Women's Magazines 1971–74 (conslt 1974–82); dir Public Relations Counsel Ltd 1974–82; chm: London Dist Inst of Journalists 1954 (fell 1970), Women's Press Club 1959 (pres 1965–67); memb Int Assoc of Women and Home Page Journalists 1968–74, assoc Women in Public Relations 1972–, assoc memb Ladies' Jockey Assoc of GB, fndr memb Media Soc Ltd (Inst of Journalists Fndn) 1973–76, fndr vice pres Woman of the Year Luncheon, vice pres Greater London Fund for the Blind 1981, pres Friends of Moorfields 1981–91, conslt Elderly Accommodation Ctee 1989–; Freeman Worshipful Co of Stationers and Newspaper Makers 1973; *Publications* Grand Smashional Pointers (cartoons, 1934), I Know What I Like (1959), That's Racing (1978), and many articles; *Recreations* racing, writing, cooking, nothing highbrow; *Style—* The Lady Georgina Coleridge; ✉ 33 Peel St, London W8 7PA (☎ 0171 727 7732)

COLERIDGE, Nicholas David; s of David Ean Coleridge, *qv*, and Susan, *née* Senior; *b* 4 March 1957; *Educ* Eton, Trinity Coll Cambridge; *m* 22 July 1989, Georgia, eldest da of George Metcalfe and Mrs John Ungley; 2 s (Alexander James b 22 May 1991, Frederick Timothy b 14 Jan 1993), 1 da (Sophie Cicely b 14 March 1996); *Career* assoc ed Tatler 1980–82, columnist Evening Standard 1982–84, assoc ed Harpers and Queen 1984–86 (ed 1986–89), currently md Condé Nast Publications (editorial dir 1989); Young Journalist of the Year 1984; *Books* Tunnel Vision (collected journalism, 1982), Shooting Stars (1984), Around the World in 78 Days (1984), The Fashion Conspiracy (1988), How I Met My Wife and Other Stories (1991), Paper Tigers (1993), With Friends Like These (1997); *Recreations* travel, shuttlecock; *Clubs* Harry's Bar, Mark's, Annabel's; *Style—* Nicholas Coleridge, Esq; ✉ 39 Kensington Park Gardens, London W11 (☎ 0171 221 4293); Condé Nast, Vogue House, Hanover Square, London W1R 0AD (☎ 0171 499 9080)

COLERIDGE, Paul James Duke; QC (1993); s of James Bernard Coleridge (d 1991), and Jane Evelina, *née* Giffard; *b* 30 May 1949; *Educ* Cranleigh, Coll of Law London; *m* 6 Jan 1973, Judith Elizabeth, da of Hugh Trenchard Rossiter; 1 da (Alice b 19 Sept 1974), 2 s (William b 7 July 1976, Edward b 22 Oct 1980); *Career* called to the Bar Middle Temple 1970, in practice at Queen Elizabeth Bldg 1970–85 and 1989–, int legal advsr Baron Hans Heinnrich Thyssen-Bornemisza Lugano Switzerland 1985–89; *Recreations* Dorset, gardening, motorbikes; *Clubs* MCC; *Style—* Paul Coleridge, Esq, QC; ✉ Queen Elizabeth Building, Temple, London EC4Y 9BS (☎ 0171 797 7837, fax 0171 353 5422)

COLERIDGE, Col the Hon Samuel John Taylor; yr s of 4 Baron Coleridge, KBE, DL (Capt RN, d 1984), and (Cecilia) Rosamund, *née* Fisher (d 1991, er da of Adm Sir William Wordsworth Fisher, GCB, GCVO); *b* 5 Feb 1942, Washington DC; *Educ* Winchester Coll, Trinity Coll Oxford and Trinity Hall Cambridge (MPhil); *m* 1973, Patricia Susan, yr da of John Basil Edwards, CBE (d 1996), of Worcester; 2 da (Jessica Alice Seymour b 1974, Clara Emily Taylor b 1976); *Career* ret Col Grenadier Gds (joined 1962); attached Army Air Corps 1964–68, SO Hong Kong 1975–78, Ecole Supérieure de Guerre Paris 1980–82, Mil Staff NATO HQ Brussels 1982–84, Mil Attaché Algiers and Tunis 1985–88, Sr Br Liaison Offr to French Forces in Germany 1988–91, Brig Defence and Mil Attaché Ankara 1992–95; inspr of physical and adventurous trg for Army 1996–; *Style—* Col the Hon Samuel Coleridge; ✉ The Chanter's House, Ottery St Mary, Devon EX11 1DQ; (London ☎ 0171 384 3296)

COLERIDGE, 5 Baron (UK 1873); William Duke Coleridge; er s of 4 Baron Coleridge, KBE, DL (d 1984; ggs of 1 Baron who was gn Samuel Taylor Coleridge, the poet), and (Cecilia) Rosamund, *née* Fisher (d 1991); *b* 18 June 1937; *Educ* Eton, RMA Sandhurst; *m* 1, 17 Feb 1962 (m dis 1977), Everild Tania, da of Lt-Col Beauchamp Hambrough, OBE; 1 s, 2 da (Hon Tania Rosamund b 1966, Hon Sophia Tamsin b 1970); m 2, 1977, Pamela, da of George William Baker, CBE (d 1996); 2 da (Hon Vanessa Layla b 1978, Hon Katharine Suzannah b 1981); *Heir* s, Hon James Duke Coleridge b 5 June 1967; *Career* served King's African Rifles (pre Kenyan Independence) and Kenyan Army; Maj Coldstream Gds (ret 1977), commanded Guards Independent Parachute Co 1970–72; resident dir Abercrombie & Kent Riyadh 1977–83; dir 1984–90: Abercrombie & Kent, European Leisure Estates PLC, Universal Energy Ltd; dir National Marine Aquarium 1990–, advsr Kroll Associates UK Ltd 1991–; govr Royal West of England Sch for Deaf, patron Colway Theatre Tst; *Recreations* golf, tennis, water-skiing; *Style—* The Rt Hon the Lord Coleridge; ✉ The Chanter's House, Ottery St Mary, S Devon (☎ 0140 481 2417)

COLES, Adrian Michael; s of Kenneth Ernest Coles, and Constance Mary, *née* Sykes; *b* 19 April 1954; *Educ* Holly Lodge Smethwick, Univ of Nottingham (BA), Univ of Sheffield (MA); *m* 23 May 1981, Marion Alma, da of Joseph Henry Hoare; 1 s (David), 1 da (Verity); *Career* economist Electricity Cncl 1976–79; Building Societies Association: economist 1979–81, head of Economics and Statistics Dept 1981–86, head of External Relations Dept 1986–93, dir gen BSA and Cncl of Mortgage Lenders 1993–; examiner econ affrs CBSI 1984–87; dir Housing Securities Ltd; tstee Money Advice Tst; sch govr (chm of Govrs 1991–93), memb Ctee Housing Assoc (chm 1990–93); regular contrib: Mortgage Fin Gazette, Housing Fin Int, Bldg Soc Yearbook; MInstD; *Recreations* family, swimming; *Style—* Adrian Coles, Esq; ✉ The Building Societies Association, 3 Savile Row, London W1X 1AF (☎ 0171 437 0655, fax 0171 734 6416)

COLES, Prof Bryan Randell; s of Charles Frederick Coles (d 1974), of Cardiff, Wales, and Olive Irene, *née* Randell (d 1975); *b* 9 June 1926; *Educ* Canton HS Cardiff, Univ of Wales Cardiff (BSc), Jesus Coll Oxford (DPhil); *m* 27 July 1955, Merivan, da of W Ace Robinson (d 1935), of Minneapolis; 2 s (Matthew b 1965, Jonathan b 1967); *Career* Physics Dept Imperial Coll London: lectr 1950–60, reader 1960–65, prof 1965–91, pro rector 1986–91, sr research fell 1991–; visiting prof: Univ of California 1969, Univ of Minnesota 1983; dean RCS 1984–86; chm: Physics Ctee SRC 1973–77, Neutron Beam Ctee SERC 1984–88; chm Bd Taylor & Francis Ltd scientific publishers 1976–96; FInstP 1968, FRS 1991; *Books* Atomic Theory for Students of Metallurgy (with W Hume-Rothery 1969), Electronic Structures of Solids (with A D Caplin, 1976); *Recreations* music, theatre, natural history; *Style—* Prof Bryan Coles, FRS; ✉ 61 Courtfield Gardens, London SW5 0NQ (☎ 0171 373 3539); Shoe Cottage, Vines Cross, Horam, E Sussex TN21 9EN; Imperial College of Science, Technology and Medicine, South Kensington, London SW7 2AZ (☎ 0171 594 7581)

COLES, His Hon Judge Gerald James Kay; QC (1976); s of James William Coles (d 1977), of Redcar, Yorkshire, and Jane Elizabeth Kay (d 1981); *b* 6 May 1933; *Educ* Coatham Sch, Sir William Turner's Sch Redcar, BNC Oxford (BA, BCL), Harvard Law Sch (LLM); *m* 22 Feb 1958, Kathleen Yolande, da of Alfred John Hobson (d 1970); 3 s (Andrew James Kay b 1961, Christopher John Kay b 1963, Matthew Henry Kay b 1970); *Career* called to the Bar Middle Temple 1957, practised London and NE Circuit 1957–85, prosecuting counsel to the Inland Revenue 1971–76, recorder 1972–85, circuit judge (NE Circuit) 1985–, resident judge Bradford Crown Ct 1992–; memb Mental Health Review Tbnl 1985; *Recreations* music, theatre, photography, opera, Freemasonry (Provincial Grand Master and Grand Superintendant Province of Yorkshire, North and East Ridings 1995); *Clubs* Utd Oxford and Cambridge Univ; *Style—* His Hon Judge Coles, QC; ✉ Redwood, Dean Lane, Hawksworth, Guiseley, Leeds LS20 8NY (☎ and fax 01943 872688)

COLES, Ian Ronald; s of Ronald Frederick Coles, of Mexborough, South Yorks, and Rosena, *née* Haigh; *b* 12 Sept 1956; *Educ* Mexborough GS, Univ of Cambridge (BA), Univ of Harvard (LLM); *m* 27 March 1988, Bethann, da of Bernard Firestone (d 1989); 1 s (Benjamin Charles Frederick b 16 Oct 1992), 1 da (Katharine Emma Mary b 15 Aug 1990); *Career* called to the Bar Lincoln's Inn 1979, attorney NY State Bar 1983; lectr in law City of London Poly 1978–80; Mayer Brown and Platt: assoc NY and London 1981–86, ptnr London 1986–; memb: Bar Assoc for Commerce Fin and Indust 1979, NY State Bar Assoc 1983, Int Bar Assoc 1992; *Recreations* music, wine, books, skiing; *Clubs* Raffles, Capital; *Style—* Ian Coles, Esq; ✉ Mayer Brown & Platt, 162 Queen Victoria St, London EC4V 4BD (☎ 0171 248 1465, telex 8811095, fax 0171 329 4465)

COLES, Jeremy Richard (Dick); s of Hilary Martin Coles (d 1993), of Ipswich, Suffolk, and Matilda Margaret, *née* Carey; *b* 10 April 1945; *Educ* Kingston Coll of Art (DipAD), Ashridge Mgmnt Coll; *m* 1 (m dis); 1 s (Paul Steven Sammons), 1 da (Polly Jane); m 2, 28 March 1987, Susan Joan; *Career* chartered designer ret; former design mangr BBC TV Prodn Design (joined 1978); early assignments incl: Dr Who, It Ain't Half Hot Mum, Z Cars, Dixon of Dock Green, Black and White Minstrel Show; credits incl: Wuthering Heights (drama serial) 1978, Shadows on our Skin (film play) 1979, Shaping Up (studio play) 1980, The Man Who Almost Knew Eamon Andrews (studio play) 1980, Bryon - A Personal Tour (film drama/documentary) 1980, United Kingdom (two part film drama, BAFTA nomination) 1981, Gulliver in Lilliput (four part studio fantasy, BAFTA nomination, RTS Award) 1981, Graham Gaskin (film drama-documentary) 1982, Another Flip for Dominick (play, BAFTA nomination) 1982, Across the Water (play) 1982, Dr Who - Terminus 1982, The Falklands Factor (studio play) 1983, Coriolanus (studio drama) 1983, Martin Luther - Heretic (film) 1983, Knockback (two part film drama, BAFTA nomination) 1984, More Lives than One (play) 1984, Maybe Baby (studio play) 1985, Russian Soldier (location play) 1985, Breaking Up (film drama series, BAFTA nomination) 1986, Star Cops (serial) 1986, Jumping the Queue (two part film drama) 1987, Theatre Night - Strife (studio play) 1987, Through the Looking Glass (history of costume) 1988, Campion - Flowers for the Judge/Dancers in Mourning (both drama series) 1989, Children of the North (four-part drama series) 1990, After the Dance (studio prodn) 1991; memb: FCSD, FRSA; former memb: BAFTA, RTS; *Recreations* trying, but usually failing, to relax, renovating a period fermette in Burgundy; *Style—* Dick Coles, Esq; ✉ Sanverne, 71220 Marizy, Saône-et-Loire, France (☎ 00 33 85 24 50 76)

COLES, Joanna Louise; da of Michael Edward Coles, and Margaret Coles; *b* 20 April 1962; *Educ* Prince Henry's Comprehensive Sch Otley W Yorks, UEA (BA); *Career* dep literary ed The Spectator 1986–89 (graduate trainee 1984–86), news/feature writer Daily Telegraph 1989–; The Guardian: news/feature writer until 1991, arts corr 1991–93, columnist 1993–, weekly Guardian interview 1996–; broadcaster 1993–, launch presenter Radio 4 mediumwave 1993–95; *Style—* Ms Joanna Coles; ✉ The Guardian, 119 Farringdon Rd, London EC1 2ER (☎ 0171 278 2332)

COLES, Sir (Arthur) John; GCMG (1997, KCMG 1989, CMG 1984); s of Arthur Strixton Coles, and Doris Gwendoline Coles; *b* 13 Nov 1937; *Educ* Magdalen Coll Sch Brackley, Magdalen Coll Oxford (BA); *m* 1965, Anne Mary Sutherland (MA, PhD), da of Christopher Graham, of Lymington, Hants; 2 s, 1 da; *Career* served HM Forces 1955–57; HM Dip Serv 1960–: Middle Eastern Centre for Arabic Studies Lebanon 1960–62, third sec Khartoum 1962–64, FO 1964–68, asst political agent Trucial States (Dubai) 1968–71, FCO 1971–75, head of Chancery Cairo 1975–77, cnsllr (Developing Countries) UK Perm Mission to EEC 1977–80, head of S Asian Dept FCO 1980–81, private sec to the PM 1981–84, ambass to Jordan 1984–88, high cmmr Aust 1988–91, dep under sec of state (Asia and the Americas) FCO 1991–93, perm under sec of state for foreign and cwlth affrs and head Dip Serv 1994–; *Style—* Sir John Coles, GCMG; ✉ Foreign & Commonwealth Office, King Charles Street, London SW1A 2AH

COLES, Prof John Morton; s of John Langdon Coles (d 1986), and Alice Margaret, *née* Brown (d 1980); *b* 25 March 1930, Ontario; *Educ* Univ of Toronto (BA, tennis blue), Univ of Cambridge (MA, ScD), Univ of Edinburgh (PhD); *m* 1, 1958 (m dis 1985), Mona McLellan, *née* Shiach; 2 da (Joanne Campbell, Alison Reid), 2 s (Steven Langdon, Ian Dalgleish); m 2, 1985, Bryony Jean Orme; *Career* Univ of Cambridge: univ asst lectr, lectr, reader 1976–80, prof of European prehistory 1980–86, chm Faculty of Archaeology & Anthropology 1982–84; chm: The Fenland Project 1981–, Inst of Field Archaeologists 1985 (Hon MIFA 1991–), NW Wetlands Survey 1989–94, Humber Wetlands Project 1992–; pres The Prehistoric Soc 1978–82; co-dir Somerset Levels Project 1973–89; vice-pres: Cncl for Br Archaeology 1985–88, Somerset Archaeological and Natural History Soc 1976– (pres 1975), Glastonbury Antiquarian Soc 1988–; memb: Academia Europaea 1989–, President's Cncl Victoria Univ in Univ of Toronto 1988–93, Royal Cmmn on the Ancient and Historical Monuments of Scotland 1992–; corresponding memb Deutsches Archäologisches Institut; ed: Proceedings of the Prehistoric Soc 1970–79, Somerset Levels Papers 1975–89, NewsWARP 1986–; res fell Univ of Edinburgh 1959–60, res fell Univ of Exeter 1986–88, prof 1993–, scholar Carnegie Tst 1959–60, visiting Br Acad fell Royal Swedish Acad of Letters, History and Antiquities 1990, visiting fell Japan Assoc for the Promotion of Science 1994–95, visiting prof Centre for Maritime Archaeology Nat Museum of Denmark 1994; fell Fitzwilliam Coll Cambridge 1963– (life fell 1986–, hon fell 1987–), fell McDonald Inst for Archaeological Res Univ of Cambridge 1991–95; FSA 1963 (vice pres 1982–86), FRSA, FBA 1978 (Grahame Clark Medal for Prehistory 1995); *Books* The Archaeology of Early Man (with E S Higgs, 1969), Field Archaeology in Britain (1972), Archaeology by Experiment (1973), The Bronze Age in Europe (with A F Harding, 1979), Experimental Archaeology (1979), Prehistory of the Somerset Levels (with B J Orme, 1980), The Archaeology of Wetlands (1984), Sweet Track to Glastonbury (with B J Coles, 1986, Br Archaeological book award), Meare Village East (1987), People of the Wetlands (with B J Coles, 1989), Images of the Past (1990), From the Waters of Oblivion (1991), Arthur Bulleid and the Glastonbury Lake Village 1892–1992 (with A Goodall and S Minnitt, 1992), Fenland Survey (with D Hall, 1994), Rock Carvings of Uppland (1994), Industrious and fairly civilized: the Glastonbury Lake Village (with S Minnitt, 1995), Enlarging the Past: the contribution of wetland archaeology (with B Coles, 1996), The Lake Villages of Somerset (with S Minnitt, 1996); ed of numerous books and author of approx 250 papers on European prehistory, wetland archaeology, experimental archaeology, rock art and conservation; *Recreations* music, woodlands, wetlands; *Style—* Prof John Coles, FSA, FBA; ✉ Fursdon Mill Cottage, Thorverton, Devon EX5 5JS (☎ 01392 860125, fax 01392 861095)

COLES, Ronald John; s of late Reginald Herbert Coles, and Mary McAlpine McLeish, *née* Leslie; *b* 18 July 1944; *Educ* Wellingborough GS, Sunderland Coll of Educn, Univ of Leeds; *m* 22 Nov 1969, Stefanie, da of late Richard Ewart Smith; 1 s (Toby b 4 Aug 1975), 1 da (Melanie b 11 June 1973); *Career* BBC Radio: prodr local and network radio 1969–75, trg instr radio prodn techniques 1975–76, prog organiser Nottingham 1976–78, mangr Sheffield 1978–80; md: Radio Trent Ltd 1980–89, Midlands Radio plc 1989–92; radio conslt 1992–; Assoc of Ind Radio Contractors: chm Labour Relations Ctee 1982–83, elected to Cncl 1982–92 (chm 1986–87), chm of finance 1988–92; chm Radio Academy 1995– (memb Cncl 1989–, vice chm 1994–95); memb: Rare Breeds Survival Tst, Notts Beekeepers Assoc; ed The Beekeepers' Annual; *Recreations* beekeeping, goats, bearded collie dogs, winemaking, photography; *Style*— Ronald Coles, Esq; ✉ Manor Farm, Main Street, Upton, Nr Newark, Notts NG23 5ST (☎ 01636 812289)

COLFOX, Sir (William) John; 2 Bt (UK 1939), of Symondsbury, Co Dorset, JP (Dorset 1962); s of Sir (William) Philip Colfox, 1 Bt, MC, DL (d 1966), and Mary Frances, *née* Symes-Bullen (d 1973); *b* 25 April 1924; *Educ* Eton; *m* 13 Jan 1962, Frederica Loveday, da of Adm Sir Victor Alexander Charles Crutchley, VC, KCB, DSC, DL, of Mappercombe Manor, Bridport, Dorset; 2 s (Philip John b 1962, Edward Timothy b 1969), 3 da (Victoria Mary b 1964, Charlotte Ismay Joan (Mrs James W H Daniel) b 1966, Constance Ruth b 1971); *Heir* s, Philip John Colfox; *Career* Lt RNVR 1939–45; land agent 1950, chm land Settlement Assoc 1979–81, vice chm Television South West 1981–92; High Sheriff of Dorset 1969; *Style*— Sir John Colfox, Bt, JP, DL; ✉ Symondsbury Hse, Bridport, Dorset (☎ 01308 422956)

COLGAN, (George) Rainey; s of Henry George Colgan (d 1990), and Jane Swan, *née* Hezlett; *b* 29 April 1948; *Educ* Foyle Coll, Trinity Coll Dublin (MA), Univ of London (DipTEFL), Univ of Reading (MA); *m* 1976, Montserrat, da of Jose Perera; 1 s (George Perera Hezlett b 20 Oct 1985); *Career* VSO Sri Lanka 1970–71, student Univ of London 1972–73, teacher Paphos Gymnasium 1973–74, lectr Barcelona Univ 1974–75; British Council: asst rep Oman 1976–78, advsr 1979–81, vice consul Istanbul 1981–83, asst rep S Africa 1984–88, vice consul and dir Br Cncl Valencia 1988–94, int arts offr and dir Br Cncl Glasgow 1994–; *Recreations* theatre, collecting pictures, music and ballet; *Style*— Rainey Colgan, Esq; ✉ The British Council, 6 Belmont Crescent, Glasgow G12 8ES (☎ 0141 339 8651, fax 0141 337 2271)

COLGAN, His Hon Judge; Samuel Hezlett; s of Henry George Colgan (d 1989),of Coleraine, Co Londonderry, and Jane Swan, *née* Hezlett; *b* 10 June 1945; *Educ* Foyle Coll Londonderry, Trinity Coll Dublin (MA, LLB); *Career* called to the Bar Middle Temple 1969, practised on SE Circuit 1969–90, recorder 1987–90, circuit judge (SE Circuit) 1990–; *Recreations* travelling, the arts; *Style*— His Hon Judge Colgan; ✉ Isleworth Crown Court, 36 Ridgeway Road, Isleworth, Middlesex TW7 5LP

COLGRAIN, 3 Baron (UK 1946); David Colin Campbell; s of 2 Baron Colgrain, MC (d 1973), and Margaret Emily (Madge), *née* Carver (d 1989); *b* 24 April 1920; *Educ* Eton, Trinity Coll Cambridge; *m* 1, 20 June 1945 (m dis 1964), Veronica Margaret, da of late Lt-Col William Leckie Webster, RAMC; 1 s, 1 da; m 2, 1973, Mrs Sheila McLeod Hudson; *Heir* s, Hon Alastair Campbell; *Career* served WWII, Lt 9 Lancers, UK and ME (wounded Alamein 1942); exec Grindlays Bank: India and Pakistan 1945–48, London 1949; Antony Gibbs & Sons Ltd and successive cos 1949–83 (dir 1954–83, ret 1983); *Recreations* music, farming, forestry; *Clubs* Cavalry and Guards'; *Style*— The Rt Hon the Lord Colgrain; ✉ Bushes Farm, Weald, Sevenoaks, Kent (☎ 01732 463279)

COLHOUN, Prof John; s of James Colhoun (d 1935), of Castlederg, Co Tyrone, and Rebecca, *née* Lecky (d 1963); *b* 15 May 1913; *Educ* Edwards Sch Castlederg Co Tyrone, The Queen's Univ Belfast (BSc, BAgr, MAgr), Imperial Coll of Sci London (DIC), Univ of London (PhD, DSc); *m* 29 July 1949, Margaret Waterhouse, da of Prof Gilbert Waterhouse, of Belfast; 3 da (Lucy (Mrs Loerzer) b 1950, Georgiana (Mrs Golub) b 1956, Jacqueline (Mrs Chaddock) b 1959); *Career* Miny of Agric for NI: res asst 1939–46, sr sci offr 1946–50, princ sci offr 1951–60; Queen's Univ of Belfast: asst lectr in agric botany 1940–42, asst lectr 1942–45, jr lectr 1945–46, lectr 1946–54, reader in mycology and plant pathology 1954–60; Univ of Manchester: Barker prof of cryptogamic botany 1960–80, dean Faculty of Sci 1974 and 1975, pro vice chllr 1977–80, prof emeritus 1980; jt ed-in-chief Jl of Phytopathology (Phytopathologische Zeitschrift) 1973–91; pres: The Queen's Univ Assoc 1960–61, Br Mycological Soc 1963, The Queen's Univ Club London 1983–85; chm: Fedn of Br Plant Pathologists 1968, Int Ctee of Fusarium Workers 1968–73, Ctee of Euro Discussion Gps in Plant Pathology 1968–75, Sub Ctee on Res on Cereals ARC 1973–78; memb: governing body Glasshouse Crops Res Inst Littlehampton 1967–77, Plants and Soils Ctee ARC 1968–78, Univ of Manchester Cncl and Ct 1973–76 and 1977–80; visiting prof State Univ of Washington USA 1969; govr: Hulme Hall Tst Fndn 1964–93, Manchester HS for Girls 1961–85, City of Manchester Coll of Higher Educn 1978–83; chm: Bd for Awards in Affiliated Colls Univ of Manchester 1977–80; Ctee Ashburne Hall Manchester 1970–80 (memb 1961–70), Ctee The Manchester Museum 1974–80 (memb 1960–94); président d'honneur Third Euro Congress of Mycology 1963, hon memb Br Soc for Plant Pathology 1989; ex-officio MSc Univ of Manchester 1964; FLS 1955, FIBiol 1963; *Books* Diseases of The Flax Plant (1947), Clubroot Disease of Crucifers Caused by Plasmodiophora brassicae Woron (1958); author of numerous papers in: Annals of Applied Biology, Annals of Botany, Trans British Mycological Soc, Nature, Phytopathologische Zeitschrift, Annales Academie Scientiarum Fenniae, Annales Agriculturae Fenniae, Seed Science and Technology, Annual Review of Phytopathology; *Clubs* Athenaeum; *Style*— Prof John Colhoun; ✉ 12 Southdown Cres, Cheadle Hulme, Cheshire SK8 6EQ (☎ 0161 485 2084)

COLIN, John Fitzmaurice; s of Bishop Gerald Fitzmaurice Colin (d 1995), of Louth, Lincs, and Iris Susan Stuart, *née* Weir; *b* 8 March 1942; *Educ* King's Coll London (MB BS), Westminster Med Sch Univ of London (MS); *m* 20 July 1974, Christel Elizabeth, da of Franciskus Kern (d 1981), of Ziegenhain, W Germany; 3 da (Katharine b 1976, Alexandra b 1979, Anna b 1981); *Career* Westminster Hosp: house physician 1965–66, sr registrar 1975–79; conslt surgn United Norwich Hosps 1979–, tutor RCS 1983–89; memb Cncl Assoc of Surgns of GB and I, memb Vascular Surgical Soc; FRSM, LRCP, FRCS; *Recreations* fishing, tennis; *Clubs* Strangers (Elm Hill Norwich); *Style*— John Colin, Esq; ✉ 419 Unthank Road, Norwich, Norfolk NR4 7QB (☎ 01603 259925); Norfolk & Norwich Hospital, BUPA Hospital Norwich

COLIN-JONES, Prof Duncan Gadsby; s of Dr Colin Edgar Colin-Jones, of Hove, Sussex, and Beatrice, *née* Gadsby; *b* 13 April 1939; *Educ* Brighton Coll, St Bartholomew's Hosp London (MB BS, MD); *m* 25 May 1963, Carol, *née* Ditchburn; 1 s (David Duncan b 1966), 1 da (Susan Mary b 1964); *Career* conslt physician and gastroenterologist Queen Alexandra Hosp Portsmouth 1975–, prof of gastroenterology Univ of Southampton (personal chair), clinical dir (med specialties) Portsmouth Hosps NHS Tst 1994–; memb Advsy Ctee on Drugs Dept of Health 1985–91, vice pres of endoscopy and memb Bd of Govrs Euro Endoscopy Assoc 1989–94; Br Soc of Gastroenterology: former chm Endoscopy Ctee and vice pres of endoscopy 1984–85, treas 1987–92, chm Clinical Servs and Standards Ctee 1996–; RCP: regnl advsr 1982–84, chm Regnl Devpt and Evaluation Ctee 1990–; author of articles on peptic ulcers and endoscopy; FRCP 1977; *Clubs* Wessex Physicians (pres); *Style*— Prof Duncan Colin-Jones; ✉ Downland, Station Road, Soberton, Hants SO32 3QU (☎ 01489 877237)

COLKER, Richard Frank; s of Frank Colker (d 1986), of Grosse Pointe Woods, Michigan, USA, and Marjorie, *née* Humphrys (d 1993); *b* 5 Oct 1945; *Educ* Univ of Michigan State, E Lansing USA (BA); *m* 24 Nov 1979, Marie-Claude, da of Jean-Louis Fouché, of Carquefou, France; 3 da (Emilie b 1980, Jennifer b 1982, Stephanie b 1985); *Career* served US Army until 1968; Wells Fargo Bank San Francisco US 1969–72 (London 1973–75), vice pres corp fin Banque de la Société Financière Européenne Paris 1976–83, md investmt banking Kidder Peabody Int London 1983–90, managing ptnr Colker Gelardin & Co 1990–; *Recreations* golf, classical music, European history; *Clubs* Royal St George's Golf (Kent), White's (London), Sunningdale Golf (Berks), Union (New York); *Style*— Richard Colker, Esq; ✉ 6 Pelham Place, London SW7 (☎ 0171 581 5631); 39 South St, Mayfair, London W1Y 5PD (☎ 0171 409 2324, fax 0171 495 1499)

COLLACOTT, Peter Barrie; s of Dr Ralph Albert Collacott, of Great Glen, Leicester, and Ruby Hilda, *née* Nash; *b* 19 June 1944; *Educ* King's Sch Rochester; *m* 4 Sept 1971, Frances Rosamond, da of Lt Cdr Hibbard (d 1983), of Rochester, Kent; 2 s (Nicholas b 1973, Piers b 1978), 2 da (Esther b 1976, Hannah b 1985); *Career* CA; articled clerk Jackson Pixley 1963–68, audit sr Price Waterhouse 1968–71; accountant: Keyser Ullman Ltd 1971–75, N M Rothschild & Sons Ltd 1976–79; accountant/sec MOD 1977–79, auditor gen Govt of Tonga 1979–80, fin controller 1980–85; md fin and admin: Rothschild Asset Management Ltd, Rothschild Fund Management Ltd; non-exec dir: S Rothschild Asset Management (CI) Ltd, International Biotechnology Trust plc; FICA; *Recreations* cricket, squash, tennis; *Style*— Peter B Collacott, Esq; ✉ Rothschild Asset Management Ltd, Five Arrows House, St Swithins Lane, London, EC4N 8NR (☎ 0171 280 5000, fax 0171 929 1643, telex 888031)

COLLCUTT, Michael Francis; s of Edgar Hugh Collcutt, OBE (d 1967), of Robartes, Falmouth Rd, Truro, Cornwall, and Dorothy Marie, *née* Smith (d 1978); *b* 28 July 1928; *Educ* Truro Cathedral Sch, Pembroke Coll Cambridge (BA); *m* 6 March 1954, Iris Audrey, da of George Sowry, of Eastbourne; 1 s (Christopher b 1961), 1 da (Catherine b 1958); *Career* Mil Serv 2 Lt RA 1947–49; admitted slr 1955; formerly: sr ptnr Toller Hales and Collcutt, HM Coroner Northamptonshire; dir numerous private cos, underwriting memb Lloyd's; High Sheriff of Northamptonshire 1996–97; *Recreations* golf, fishing, shooting; *Clubs* IOD, Northampton County Golf, Kettering Golf (past pres), Hawks; *Style*— Michael F Collcutt, Esq; ✉ Isebrook Cottage, Finedon, Wellingborough, Northants; Toller Hales and Collcutt, 55 Headlands, Kettering, Northants NN15 7EY (☎ 01536 315615, fax 01536 315600)

COLLEDGE, Prof Malcolm Andrew Richard; s of Alan Douglas Colledge, and Edith Mary, *née* Sadler; *b* 12 Oct 1939; *Educ* Dulwich, St John's Coll Cambridge (BA, MA, PhD); *m* 1, 22 Aug 1962 (m dis 1974), Margaret, da of David Williams (d 1992), of Croydon, Surrey; 1 s (Alexander b 5 Aug 1967); m 2, 9 Feb 1976, Maria-Jesus Margarita Gomez Cristobal, da of Faustino Gomez Martin (d 1978), of Burgos, Spain; 1 adopted step-da (Caroline b 30 June 1970); *Career* asst lectr in classics Univ Coll Swansea 1964–66, prof of classics Westfield Coll Univ of London 1984–89 (lectr 1967–75, reader 1975–84), prof of classics Queen Mary and Westfield Coll Univ of London 1989–; memb: Soc for the Promotion of Roman Studies (memb Cncl 1971–74), Soc for The Promotion of Hellenic Studies (memb Cncl 1974–77), Br Inst of Archaeology at Amman (memb Cncl 1982–86); contrib to: Classics: An Outline for the Intending Student (1970), XI Classical Archaeology Congress London 1979, The Atlas of Archaeology (1982), The MacMillan Dictionary of Archaeology (1982), Mesopotamia (1987), Hellenism in the East (1987), Roman Art (1988), Empires Ascendant (1988), XII Classical Archaeology Congress Athens 1988, I Australian Classical Archaeology Congress Sydney 1990, Etudes et Travaux Warsaw 1991; FSA 1990; *Books* The Parthians (1967), The Art of Palmyra (1976), Parthian Art (1977), How to Recognise Roman Art (1979), The Parthian Period (1986), IV Greco-Roman Mosaic Congress (1994); *Recreations* pursuit of art, architecture, literature, music and archaeology, travel, cycling; *Style*— Prof Malcolm Colledge, FSA; ✉ Faculty of Arts, Queen Mary and Westfield College, Mile End Road, London E1 4NS (☎ 0171 975 5555)

COLLEE, Prof (John) Gerald; CBE (1991); s of John Gerald Collee, JP (d 1983), of Blenheim, Bo'ness, and Mary Hay Wilson Kirsopp, *née* Cassels; *b* 10 May 1929; *Educ* Bo'ness Acad, Edinburgh Acad, Univ of Edinburgh (MB ChB, MD); *m* 1, 1 April 1952 (m dis 1995), Isobel McNay, da of George Beaumont Galbraith, of Upper Kinneil, Bo'ness; 2 s (John b 1956, George b 1959), 1 da (Carol b 1953); m 2, 16 Feb 1995, Anne Ferguson, da of John Glen, of Cathcart, Glasgow; *Career* Nat Serv Capt RAMC 1952–54: RMO 5 Royal Northumberland Fusiliers, OC Medical Reception Station Newcastle-upon-Tyne; house physician Roodlands Hosp Haddington 1951, asst Gp Shifnal 1954–55; Univ of Edinburgh Med Sch: lectr in bacteriology 1955–64, sr lectr and hon conslt 1964–70, reader 1970–74, personal prof 1974–79; prof of bacteriology, head of Dept of Medical Microbiology and chief bacteriologist Edinburgh Royal Infirmary 1979–91, conslt advsr in microbiology Scottish Home and Health Dept; FRCPath 1975 (MRCPath 1964), FRCPEd 1979 (MRCPEd 1977), FRSE 1993; *Books* Practical Medical Microbiology (author and ed), author, contrib, ed numerous textbooks, numerous papers in learned jls; *Recreations* woodwork, light mechanics, music, painting, poetry, fishing; *Clubs* New (Edinburgh), Scottish Arts, RAMC (Millbank); *Style*— Prof Gerald Collee, CBE, FRSE; ✉ 204 Newhaven Rd, Edinburgh EH6 4QE

COLLEN, Phil; *b* 8 Dec 1957; *Career* guitarist; formerly with Girl, joined Def Leppard 1982; Def Leppard tours: Pyromania 1982, Hysteria 1987, Adrenalize 1992; 1 UK top ten single (Animal 1987), 3 US top ten singles (Hysteria 1988, Pour Some Sugar On Me 1988, Armageddon 1989); albums with Def Leppard: Pyromania (1983, UK no 18, US no 2), Hysteria (1987, UK and US no 1), Adrenalize (1992), Retro-Active (1993), Slang (1996); Awards incl: Favourite Heavy Metal Artist, Favourite Heavy Metal Album (for Hysteria) American Music Awards 1989; *Style*— Phil Collen, Esq; ✉ c/o Bludgeon Riffola, Mercury Records, Chancellors House, 72 Chancellors Road, London W6 9QB (☎ 0181 910 5678, fax 0181 910 5896)

COLLENDER, Andrew Robert; QC (1991); s of John Talbot Collender (d 1966), and Kathleen Collender; *b* 11 Aug 1946; *Educ* Mount Pleasant Boys' HS Salisbury Rhodesia, Univ of Bristol (LLB); *m* 26 Oct 1974, Titia, da of Reinier Tybout, of Holland; 2 s (Guy b 1979, Paul b 1981); *Career* called to the Bar Lincoln's Inn 1969, recorder of the Crown Court 1993–; *Recreations* violin, riding, sailing; *Style*— Andrew Collender, Esq, QC; ✉ 2 Temple Gardens, Temple, London EC4Y 1AY (☎ 0171 583 6041, fax 0171 583 2094)

COLLENS, Geoffrey Alan; s of John Collens (d 1976), and Emily Charlotte, *née* Gomm (d 1975); *b* 11 Jan 1934; *Educ* Leeds Sch of Architecture (DipArch), Univ of Pa (MLA); *Career* architect; asst office of Sir Basil Spence 1957–60, land planner Doxiadis Assoc Philadelphia 1960–62; Derek Lovejoy Partnership: assoc 1962–69, sr assoc 1969–83, ptnr 1983–90 (specialist as landscape professional witness), chm 1990–94, conslt 1994–; chm Landscape Design Tst 1990–, former memb Cncl Nat Tst; RIBA 1957, ARCUK 1958, ALI 1962; *Books* Techniques of Landscape Architecture (contrib), Oxford Companion of Gardens (contrib), Spon's Landscape Handbook (ed); *Recreations* opera, travel, reading, photography; *Style*— Geoffrey Collens, Esq; ✉ Derek Lovejoy Partnership, 8–11 Denbigh Mews, Denbigh St, Pimlico, London SW1V 2HQ (☎ 0171 828 6392, fax 0171 630 6958)

COLLET, Robert Thomson (Robin); s of Robert Alan Collet (d 1979), of Epsom, and Jean Edith Isobel, *née* Thomson (d 1993); *b* 26 Nov 1939; *Educ* Malvern, Pembroke Coll Cambridge (MA); *m* 6 May 1972, Olivia Diana Mary, da of Leonard Clough-Taylor; 1 s (Henry b 1977), 1 da (Eloise b 1974); *Career* CA; dir Tilhill Forestry Ltd 1979–92, gp fin dir Addis Ltd 1992–; Freeman City of London 1964, memb Worshipful Co of Coopers 1964; FCA 1966, FInstD 1993, FRSA 1996; *Recreations* golf, skiing, walking; *Style*— Robin Collet, Esq; ✉ The School House, Wimble Hill, Crondall, Farnham, Surrey GU10 5KL (☎ 01252 850824); Addis Ltd, Princess Mary House, 4 Bluecoats Avenue, Hertford, Herts SG14 1PB (☎ 01992 584221, fax 01992 553050)

COLLETT, Sir Christopher; GBE (1988), JP (City of London 1979); 2 s of Sir Henry Seymour Collett, 2 Bt (d 1971), and Ruth Mildred, *née* Hatch (d 1994); *b* 10 June 1931; *Educ* Harrow, Emmanuel Coll Cambridge (MA); *m* 1959, Christine Anne, da of Oswald Hardy Griffiths, of Nunthorpe, Yorks; 2 s, 1 da; *Career* Capt RA (TA); former ptnr Ernst

& Young Chartered Accountants London; govr: Bridewell Royal Hosp 1982–, Haberdashers' Aske's Schools Elstree 1982–94, King Edward's Sch Witley 1987–94; memb Court of Common Cncl Broad Street Ward City of London 1973–79 (Alderman 1979–), pres Broad Street Ward Club 1979–, Sheriff City of London 1985–86, Lord Mayor 1988–89; Master Worshipful Co of Glovers 1981 (hon memb of Ct); Liveryman Worshipful Co of Chartered Accountants in England and Wales, hon memb Ct Worshipful Co of Haberdashers; chm The Eskdale Fndn 1996–; Hon DSc City Univ 1988; KStJ 1988; Cdr Order of Merit Federal Republic of Germany 1986, Order of Merit (Class II) State of Qatar 1985, Order of Civil Merit (Class II) Spain 1986, Cdr Order of the Niger (Class I) Nigeria 1989, Order of Independence (Class II) UAE; *Recreations* gardening, fishing; *Style—* Sir Christopher Collett, GBE

COLLETT, Sir Ian Seymour; 3 Bt (UK 1934), of Bridge Ward in the City of London; s of David Seymour Collett (d 1962), by his w, now Lady Miskin (w of His Honour Judge Sir James Miskin, QC); suc gf, Sir Henry Seymour Collett, 2 Bt, 1971; *b* 5 Oct 1953; *Educ* Lancing; *m* 18 Sept 1982, Philippa, da of James R I Hawkins, of Preston St Mary, Suffolk; 1 s (Anthony Seymour b 1984), 1 da (Georgina b 1986); *Heir* s, Anthony Seymour Collett, b 1984; *Career* govr Felixstowe Coll 1986–; Notary Public; memb Law Soc 1979–95; *Recreations* fishing, shooting, cricket; *Clubs* MCC, Aldeburgh Golf, Aldeburgh Yacht; *Style—* Sir Ian Collett, Bt

COLLEY, Maj-Gen David Bryan Hall; CB (1988), CBE (1982, OBE 1977, MBE 1968); s of Lawson Colley (d 1970), of Sutton Coldfield, and Alice, *née* Hall (d 1989); *b* 5 June 1934; *Educ* King Edward's Sch Birmingham, RMA Sandhurst; *m* 30 Sept 1957, Marie Therese, da of Louis Auguste Prefontaine (d 1966), of Edmonton, Alberta, Canada; 1 s (John b 1961), 1 da (Michele b 1959); *Career* cmmnd: RASC 1954, RCT 1965; regtl appts in Germany, Belgium, UK, Hong Kong and Singapore; Student Staff Coll Camberley 1964, JSSC Latimer 1970, CO Gurkha Tport Regt & 31 Regt RCT 1971–74, Staff HQ 1 (Br) Corps 1974–77, Cmd Logistic Support Gp 1977–80, Col AQ (Ops and Plans) and dir Admin Planning MOD (Army) 1980–82, Cmd Tport 1 (Br) Corps 1983–86, dir gen Tport and Movements (Army) 1986–88, Col Cmdt RCT 1988–93, Col Cmdt Royal Logistic Corps 1993–; dir gen Road Haulage Assoc 1988–; Freeman City of London 1986, Hon Liveryman Worshipful Co of Carmen 1986; FCIT; *Recreations* travel, information technology, walking; *Clubs* Army & Navy; *Style—* Maj-Gen D B H Colley, CB, CBE; ✉ c/o Midland Bank plc, Church Green West, Redditch, Worcs B97 4EA

COLLEY, Surgn Rear Adm Ian Harris; OBE (1963); s of Aubrey James Colley, and Violet Fulford Colley; *b* 14 Oct 1922; *Educ* Hanley Castle GS, King's Coll London, King's Coll Hosp (MB BS); *m* 1952, Joy Kathleen, *née* Goodacre; *Career* RN Med Serv 1948–80; MO HMS Cardigan Bay and HMS Consort 1949–52, serv with Fleet Air Arm 1955–78, PMO HMS Centaur, MO i/c Air Med Sch, pres Central Air Med Bd, cmd MO to Flag Offr Naval Air Cmd, Surgn Rear Adm (ships and establishments) 1978–80, ret; QHP 1978–80, conslt in aviation med, former examiner to Conjoint Bd RCS and RCP for dip aviation med, vice pres RNLI 1989 (former hon conslt in occupational med, chm Med Survival Ctee); author of papers on aviation med; CStJ 1980; *Style—* Surgn Rear Adm I H Colley, OBE; ✉ c/o Royal Bank of Scotland, Inveraray, Argyll PA32 8TY

COLLEY, Veronica Georgina; da of George William Morgan, and Ernestine Morgan; *b* 25 April 1943; *m* 17 Oct 1970, Christopher Colley; 2 da (Emma Victoria b 15 March 1972, Lucie Elisabeth b 5 July 1976); *Career* trainee then SRN Queen Elizabeth Hosp Birmingham 1961–64, Taplow Memorial Hosp Maidenhead 1965, SCM Bristol Maternity Hosp 1965–67, mid-wife then theatre sister Geneva 1967–71, chef/proprietor St Matthews Hotel Northampton 1971–80, chef/proprietor Little Barwick House Yeovil 1980–; incl in The Women Chefs of Britain (1990); memb Freewheelers (charity); *Awards* Logis Best SW Chef 1994, AA Red Star Award 1994–, Good Food Guide Somerset Restaurant of the Year 1995; *Recreations* golf; *Clubs* Yeovil Golf (ladies capt 1995–96, bronze champion 1995); *Style—* Mrs Veronica Colley; ✉ Little Barwick House, Barwick, Yeovil, Somerset BA22 9TD (☎ 01935 23902, fax 01935 20908)

COLLIER, Andrew John; CBE (1995); s of Francis George Collier (d 1976), and Margaret Nancy, *née* Nockles; *b* 29 Oct 1939; *Educ* Univ Coll Sch, St Johns Coll Cambridge (MA); *m* 25 July 1964, Gillian Ann, da of George Thomas Ernest Churchill (ka 1945); 2 da (Susan b 1965, Sarah b 1968); *Career* asst master Winchester Coll 1962–68, Hants CC Educn Dept 1968–71, sr asst educn offr Bucks 1971–77, chief educn offr Lancs 1980–96 (dep chief offr 1977–79), gen sec Soc of Educn Offrs 1996–; memb: Cncl Univ of Lancaster 1981–86, 1988–93 and 1996–, Visiting Ctee Open Univ 1982–88, Cncl for Accreditation of Teacher Educn 1984–89, Nat Trg Task Force 1989–92, General Synod Bd of Educn 1993–, Educn Ctee Royal Soc 1996–; advsr: Assoc of CC's, Cncl of LEAs; govr Myerscough Coll 1996–; pres: Lancs Young Farmers Clubs 1985–88, Soc of Educn Offrs 1990; Liveryman Worshipful Co of Wheelwrights 1972; FRSA; *Recreations* opera, walking, the greenhouse; *Clubs* Athenaeum, Leander; *Style—* Andrew Collier, Esq, CBE; ✉ Whinfield, Whitechapel, Preston, Lancashire PR3 2EP (☎ 01995 640275)

COLLIER, Anthony; s of Anthony Collier (d 1983); *b* 4 Jan 1947; *Educ* St Mary's GS, Middlesbrough, Leics Poly (Dip Arch); *m* 23 Sept 1973, Judith Ann, da of Henry Reginald Page, of Northants; 1 s (Stephen Benedict b 1977), 1 da (Louise Helen b 1979); *Career* architect and interior designer; DoE medal Good Design in Housing Awards 1979, commended Civic Tst 1978 and 1992, commended Royal Fine Arts Cmmn/Sunday Times Building of the Year Awards 1992, commended Northern Architect's Assoc Hadrian Awards 1993; has designed and supervised many projects for new buildings and refurbishment of existing or derelict buildings, especially in areas to be revitalised; RIBA; *Recreations* travel, golf, tennis, art, music; *Style—* Anthony Collier, Esq; ✉ South Quay Studios, 2–3 South Quay, Maryport, Cumbria CA15 8AB (☎ 01900 814271, fax 01900 818506)

COLLIER, Catrin; *see:* John, Katherine

COLLIER, John Spencer; s of James Bradburn Collier, of Bramhall, Cheshire, and Phyllis Mary Collier (d 1953); *b* 4 March 1945; *Educ* Cheadle Hulme Sch, Trinity Coll Cambridge (BA); *m* 25 March 1972, Theresa Mary, da of Charles John Peers; 2 s (Barnaby James b 26 March 1973, Edward John b 19 Dec 1977), 1 da (Amy Louise b 16 Feb 1975); *Career* tutor in geography King's Coll London 1967–69; Price Waterhouse: student, mangr then sr mangr London and Aust 1969–81, ptnr Aberdeen 1981–84, ptnr Newcastle upon Tyne 1984–92; chief exec The Newcastle Initiative 1992–95, dir Collier Environmental Associates 1992–; pres Northern Soc of CAs 1989–90; ICAEW: memb Cncl 1991–, chm Practice Regulation Directorate 1993–; chm Dance City 1995–, govr Newcastle Coll 1996–; FCA (ACA 1972), MICAS 1981; *Recreations* running, skiing, climbing, community affairs; *Clubs* Northern Counties (Newcastle); *Style—* John S Collier, Esq; ✉ 32 Graham Park Rd, Gosforth, Newcastle upon Tyne NE3 4BH (☎ 0191 285 3651, mobile 0850 215252)

COLLIER, Peter Neville; QC (1992); s of Arthur Neville Collier (d 1990), of Hull, and Joan Audrey, *née* Brewer; *b* 1 June 1948; *Educ* Hymers Coll Hull, Selwyn Coll Cambridge (MA); *m* 1972, Susan Margaret, da of John Williamson; 2 s (Andrew James Neville b 6 Sept 1975, Richard John Stephen b 13 Sept 1978); *Career* called to the Bar Inner Temple 1970, practised NE Circuit 1973–, recorder of the Crown Court 1988–; chllr Diocese of Wakefield 1992–; *Recreations* walking, reading, music; *Style—* Peter Collier, Esq, QC; ✉ 30 Park Square, Leeds LS1 2PF (☎ 0113 243 6388, fax 0113 242 3510)

COLLIN, Lady Clarissa; *née* Duncombe; JP; da of 3 Earl of Feversham (d 1963, when the Earldom became extinct, but the Barony of Feversham passed to a kinsman), and Lady Anne Dorothy Wood, OBE (d 1995), da of 1 Earl of Halifax; *b* 11 Oct 1938; *Educ* Heathfield, Paris France; *m* 14 Dec 1966, Nicholas Spencer Compton Collin, s of late Maj and Mrs Francis Spencer Collin; 1 s (Frederick Slingsby b 30 Oct 1967), 1 da (Laura Anne b 25 Aug 1969); *Career* landowner and farmer; *Recreations* gardening, country activities; *Style—* The Lady Clarissa Collin, JP; ✉ Wytherstone House, Pockley, York YO6 5TE (☎ 01439 770398, fax 01439 770468)

COLLIN, Maj-Gen Geoffrey de Egglesfield; CB (1975), MC (1944), DL (N Yorks 1977); s of late Charles de Egglesfield Collin (d 1960), of Ripon, and Catherine Mary, *née* Smith (d 1972); *b* 18 July 1921; *Educ* Wellington; *m* 1949, Angela Stella, da of Lt-Col Noel Charles Secombe Young (d 1966), and Audrey Harriet, *née* Lawless (d 1990); 1 s, 3 da; *Career* 2 Lt RA 1941, Maj-Gen RA HQ BAOR 1971–73, GOC NE Dist York 1973–76, ret, Col Cmdt RA 1976–83; hon dir Gt Yorks Show 1976–87, pt/t chm Civil Serv Selection Panel 1978–91, pres Yorks Agric Soc 1988; *Recreations* fishing, ornithology, photography; *Clubs* Army and Navy; *Style—* Maj-Gen Geoffrey Collin, CB, MC, DL

COLLIN, Jack; s of John Collin, and Amy Maud, *née* Burton; *b* 23 April 1945; *Educ* Consett GS, Univ of Newcastle (MB BS, MD), Mayo Clinic USA, Univ of Oxford (MA); *m* 17 July 1971, Christine Frances, da of Albert Proud (d 1973), of Durham; 3 s (Neil b 1976, Graham b 1980, Ivan b 1985), 1 da (Beth b 1974); *Career* registrar in surgery Newcastle 1971–80, res fell Mayo Clinic USA 1977, Arris and Gale lectr RCS 1976, Euro fell Surgical Res Soc 1979, Moynihan travelling fell Assoc of Surgeons 1980, reader in surgery Oxon 1980–, conslt surgn John Radcliffe Hosp, professorial fell Trinity Coll Oxford, Hunterian Prof RCS 1988–89; non-exec dir Nuffield Orthopaedic Centre NHS Tst 1990–93; David Dickson Research Prize 1973, Jacksonian prizewinner RCS 1979, Jobst Prize Vascular Surgical Soc 1990, James IV travelling fell 1993; memb: Dist Res Ctee, Regnl Med Advsy Ctee, Bd of Faculty Clinical Medicine (chm 1990–92); examiner: in surgery Univ of Oxford, in anatomy RCS; memb: Governing Body and Bursarial Ctee Trinity Coll, Gen Purposes Ctee Faculty of Clinical Med; memb: Vascular Surgical Soc 1982 (memb Cncl 1992–94), Euro Vascular Surgical Soc 1988, Int Soc of Surgeons 1994, Euro Surgical Assoc 1994; FRCS 1972; *Recreations* food, family, gardening; *Style—* Mr Jack Collin; ✉ Nuffield Department of Surgery, John Radcliffe Hospital, Oxford, OX3 9DU (☎ 01865 221 284/286, fax 01865 68876, telex 83147 VIAORGATT: NDS)

COLLIN, (John) Richard Olaf; s of Dr John Olaf Collin, MB, BChir, of Broom Cottage, Ashdown Rd, Forest Row, E Sussex, and Ellen Vera, *née* Knudsen; *b* 1 May 1943; *Educ* Charterhouse, Univ of Cambridge (MA, MB); *Career* ophthalmic surgeon with conslt appts to Moorfields Eye Hosp and Hosp for Sick Children, Great Ormond Street 1981 and King Edward VII Hosp for Offrs 1993; special interest in eyelid surgery; Liveryman: Worshipful Soc of Apothecaries, Worshipful Co of Coachmakers & Coach Harness Makers; FRCS, DO; *Books* publications on ophthalmic plastic surgery incl: A Manual of Systematic Eyelid Surgery (1983, 2 edn 1989); *Recreations* sailing, shooting, tennis, hunting, opera; *Clubs* Royal Ocean Racing, Hurlingham; *Style—* Richard Collin, Esq; ✉ 67 Harley Street, London W1N 1DE (☎ 0171 486 2699)

COLLING, Rev Canon James Oliver; MBE (1995); s of Leonard Colling (d 1978), of Leigh, Lancs, and Dorothy, *née* Atherton (d 1979); *b* 3 Jan 1930; *Educ* Leigh GS, Univ of Manchester (BA), Cuddesdon Theol Coll Oxford; *m* 31 July 1957, Jean, da of Edward Wright (d 1973), of Leigh, Lancs; 2 s (Oliver Edward b 27 Feb 1967, Guy Leonard (twin) b 27 Feb 1967 d 1970), 1 da (Dorothy Sarah (Mrs Timothy James Allen) b 5 Oct 1962); *Career* Nat Serv cmmnd RAF 1950–52; ordained: deacon 1954, priest 1955; asst curate Wigan Parish Church 1954–59, vicar of Padgate 1959–71, rector 1971–73, rural dean of Warrington 1970–82 and 1987–89, rector of Warrington 1973–, canon diocesan of Liverpool Cathedral 1976–, area dean of Warrington 1989–95, chaplain to HM The Queen 1990–; chm: Warrington C of E Educnl Tst 1973–, Warrington and Dist Soc for the Deaf 1974–93, Warrington Community Health Cncl 1974–82, Warrington Community Cncl 1974–87; vice chm Warrington Health Authy 1982–89; chm: Bd of Govrs Sir Thomas Boteler HS Warrington 1988–, Warrington Charities Tst 1989–91, Boteler Educational Tst 1995–; memb Cheshire Family Health Servs Authy 1990–94; *Recreations* looking at buildings and places, local history; *Style—* The Rev Canon James Colling, MBE; ✉ The Rectory, Warrington, Cheshire WA1 2TL (☎ 01925 635020)

COLLINGE, HE John Gregory; *b* Hastings, NZ; *Educ* Auckland Univ (sr scholar in law, JP Campbell bursary, LLB, capt NZ Univs Cricket XI), Univ of Oxford (Shell scholar, BLitt, Univ Cricket XI and Greyhounds Rugby XV); *children* Miriam, Hilary; *Career* barr and slr High Cts of NZ and Australia; New Zealand high cmmr to Ct of St James's (concurrently non-resident high cmmr to Nigeria and ambass to Ireland) 1994–; chm: New Zealand Pelagic Fisheries Ltd 1975–81, United Distillers (NZ) Ltd 1991; dir: Nelson Fisheries Ltd 1974–80, United Distillers (NZ) Ltd 1986–91, Directus International (NZ) Ltd 1983–86, Interim Auckland Airport Board 1987; pres NZ Nat Pty 1989–94; chm: Commerce Cmmn 1984–89, Alcohol Advsy Cncl of NZ 1991–94, Nat Civil Def Energy Planning Ctee 1992–94; pres Electrical Devpt Assoc of NZ 1991–94 (memb Bd 1990–91), memb Cncl Electricity Supply Assoc of NZ 1991–92; vice patron NZ Soc London 1994–; patron: British/NZ Trade Cncl (Inc) 1994–, NZ Wine Guild 1994–, Capt Cook Birthplace Tst 1994–, Shakespeare Globe Tst 1994–, NZ Univs Graduates' Assoc 1994–; tstee Waitangi Fndn 1994–, memb Bd of Govrs Cwlth Inst 1994–, alternate govr EBRD 1994–, cmmr Cwlth War Graves Cmmn 1994–; recipient NZ 1990 Commemoration Medal; *Major Publications* Restrictive Trade Practices and Monopolies in New Zealand (1982), Tutorials in Contract (1989), The Law of Marketing in Australia and New Zealand (1990); NZ Legal Res Fndn Best Pubn 1983; *Recreations* NZ history, restoring colonial houses and colonial antiques, rugby, cricket; *Clubs* Royal Over-Seas League (vice pres 1994–), Wellington (NZ), Vincents (Oxford); *Style—* HE Mr John G Collinge; ✉ New Zealand High Commission, New Zealand House, Haymarket, London SW1Y 4TQ (☎ 0171 930 8422, fax 0171 839 4580)

COLLINGE, (Richard) Paul; s of Graham Collinge (d 1965), and Winifred Mary, *née* Farley (d 1969); *b* 26 June 1946; *Educ* (Architectural) Thames Poly (ATP); *m* (m dis 1991); 2 s (Jake b 2 May 1974, Luke b 14 Sept 1976), 1 da (Emma b 23 Oct 1972); *Career* princ Aldington Craig & Collinge 1986– (ptnr from 1979); external examiner N London Poly Sch of Architecture 1986–89, assessor RIBA awards 1988; selected in 1985 as one of the 40 under 40 young architects; design awards received: RIBA 1978 (commendation), 1987, two in 1991, and one in 1995, DoE Good Housing award 1978, Civic Tst awards 1978, 1987 and 1988 (commendation 1992), Brick Devpt Assoc Biennial award 1979 and 1991 (also commendation 1991); RIBA 1972, MCSD 1984 (Malcom Dean Award 1996); *Recreations* wine, good food, cricket, golf; *Clubs* Dinton Cricket; *Style—* Paul Collinge, Esq; ✉ Aldington Craig & Collinge, The White House, Moreton Road, Moreton Thame, Oxon OX9 2HH (☎ 01844 260040)

COLLINGE, Roger Arnold; s of Arnold Roy Collinge (d 1971), of Burnley, and Elsie, *née* Loftus (d 1989); *b* 18 Dec 1942; *Educ* Sedbergh; *m* 15 Oct 1966, Alison May, da of Squire Dent; 1 s (David Roger), 1 da (Jane Elizabeth); *Career* articled clerk J H Lord & Co CAs Bacup 1961–66, financial planner Black & Decker then asst to fin dir Reliant Engineering until 1972; ptnr: J H Lord & Co 1972–82, BDO Binder Hamlyn 1982–94, BDO Stoy Hayward 1994–; pres NW Soc of CAs 1990–91; FCA 1971 (ACA 1966); *Recreations* gardening, classic cars, walking, reading; *Clubs* British Over-Seas League; *Style—* Roger Collinge, Esq; ✉ BDO Stoy Hayward, 7–9 Irwell Terrace, Bacup, Lancashire OL13 9AJ (☎ 01706 873213, fax 01706 874211)

COLLINGHAM, Christopher Eric; s of Harold Eric Collingham, of Carlton-in-Lindrick, Notts, and Olive, *née* Radcliffe; *b* 4 Aug 1952; *Educ* Henry Harland Sch Worksop,

Granville Coll Sheffield; *m* 5 July 1975, Michele Kathleen, da of Eric Keep, of Carlton in Lindrick, Notts; *Career* BBC: communications engr 1971–78, mangr special projects 1978–82; chief engr TV-am plc 1983–89 (joined 1982), md Broadcast Projects Ltd 1989–, tech dir Channel S TV 1990–93, controller Engrg and Ops Channel 5 Broadcasting Ltd 1996–; memb RTS; *Recreations* gliding, power flying; *Style—* Christopher Collingham, Esq; ✉ 2 Longdean Park, Hemel Hempstead, Herts HP3 8BS

COLLINGS, Dr Anthony Denis; s of Cyril John Collings, of Westcliff-on-Sea, Essex, and Mary Honora, *née* Fitzgerald; *b* 26 Dec 1946; *Educ* Westcliff HS for Boys, Univ of Newcastle upon Tyne (MB BS); *m* 6 Dec 1975 (m dis 1986), Melanie, da of Walter Robson (d 1979), of Colwell, Northumbria; 1 s (Simon b 1978), 1 da (Catherine b 1977); *Career* former cmmnd Capt RAMC (V) 1985, conslt physician to Army with rank of Actg Maj; conslt physician Southend Health Dist 1981– (specialising in med of old age, gastroenterology and neurology); acts as med expert witness for both crown and def in Crown and High Courts; former sec local branch BMA, chm local branch Physicians Ctee, former chm regnl advsy ctee on geriatric med; FRCP; memb: BMA, Br Geriatrics Soc, RSM, BATS Soc Newcastle upon Tyne; *Style—* Dr Anthony Collings; ✉ Southend General Hospital, Prittlewell Chase, Southend-on-Sea, Essex (☎ 01702 435555)

COLLINGS, Peter Glydon; s of Alfred James Collings, of Poole, Dorset, and Margot Lavinia, *née* Harper; *b* 4 Nov 1942; *Educ* Worksop Coll; *m* 1 Sept 1967, Rosemary Anne, da of Henry William Wesley-Harkcom (d 1966); 2 da (Sarah Jane b 1968, Emma Louise b 1970); *Career* asst regnl mangr Old Broad St Securities Ltd Birmingham 1970–75, regnl mangr Grindlays Industrial Finance Ltd Birmingham 1976–82, jt chief exec W Midlands Enterprise Board Ltd 1982–; dir: Aston Manor Brewery Co Ltd 1986–, Fairne Textile Holdings Ltd 1986–, Tangye Ltd 1986–87, Raydyot Ltd 1987–, E R Hammersley & Co Ltd 1989–91, Jeenay plc 1990–, D H Haden plc 1991–, Airfield Estates Ltd 1992–, G R Smithson & Co Ltd 1992–, Somers Handling plc 1992–96, Butler Group plc 1994–, Excalibur Manufacturing Jewellers Ltd 1995–, Clamas Holdings Ltd 1995–, Barker Ellis Silver Company Ltd 1996–, Payton Pepper Ltd 1996–; memb: Main Ctee Birmingham and West Midlands Soc of CAs 1995–, OFFER Midlands Regn Electricity Consumers Ctee 1996–, Old Worksopian Soc Ctee 1996–; FCA 1966; *Recreations* rugby football, cricket, theatre, opera, jazz; *Clubs* Sutton Coldfield RFC (vice pres), Warwickshire CCC; *Style—* Peter Collings, Esq; ✉ Squirrels Leap, 15 Oaklands Rd, Four Oaks, Sutton Coldfield, W Midlands B74 2TB (☎ 0121 308 5434); Wellington House, 31/34 Waterloo St, Birmingham B2 5TJ (☎ 0121 236 8855, fax 0121 233 3942)

COLLINGWOOD, Charles Henry; s of Henry Ernest (Jack) Collingwood (d 1994), of Charlton, Hants, and Evelyn Mary (Molly), *née* Atherton; *b* 30 May 1943; *Educ* Sherborne, RADA; *m* 13 Nov 1976, Judy Bennett; 1 da (Jane Molly b 4 June 1979), 2 step s (Toby Daniel Scott-Hughes b 20 March 1967, Barnaby William Scott-Hughes b 23 Jan 1969); *Career* radio and television actor; *Theatre* extensive repertory work in Guildford, Canterbury, Derby, Liverpool and Harrogate; roles incl: William Featherstone in How The Other Half Loves (Greenwich) 1973, Cocklebury-Smythe in Dirty Linen (Arts) 1979–80, Philip in Relatively Speaking (Globe Theatre Co: Hong Kong, Singapore, Bangkok) 1996; *Television* numerous shows incl: Undermanning (co-host with Bernard Manning), The Bretts, Hannay, Inspector Morse, For The Greater Good, Chief, Tonight at 8:30, Up The Garden Path, The Upper Hand, Hot Metal, Trouble in Mind, 10%ers, Telly Addicts; over 20 years continual work for BBC Sch TV as presenter, actor and commentator: 3 series of Castles Corner (with Roy Castle), 3 series with Harry Worth, 2 series with Jack Smethurst, 4 series of Stilgoes Around (with Richard Stilgoe); *Radio* numerous leading roles in BBC Radio Drama notably Brian Aldridge in The Archers 1975–; *Books* The Book of the Archers (co-author, 1994); *Recreations* cricket, golf, fishing and gardening; *Clubs* MCC, Stage Cricket, Cryptics Cricket, Stage Golf Soc, Cross Arrows Cricket; *Style—* Charles Collingwood, Esq; ✉ c/o David Daly Associates, Personal Management, 68 Old Brompton Road, London SW7 3LQ (☎ 0171 581 0121, fax 0171 589 2922)

COLLINS, Adrian John Reginald; s of John Reginald Maulden Collins, MBE, and Jennifer Anne, *née* Wasey; *b* 29 May 1954; *Educ* Leys Sch Cambridge; *m* 1, 6 Aug 1984 (m dis); 1 s (Mark John Ford), 1 da (Seil Charlotte); m 2, 28 July 1994, Susan Margaret, *née* Greenwood; 2 s (Robert Jonathan Mauldon b 20 Nov 1994, Theodore Oliver Mauldon b 1 Nov 1996); *Career* chief exec: Gartmore Investment 1974–84, Royal Trust Asset Management Ltd 1985–90, Fincorp International Ltd 1984, Lazard Investors Ltd 1994–96; currently with Buccanan Capital Managament Ltd; *Clubs* City of London; *Style—* Adrian Collins, Esq; ✉ 4 Campden Hill Square, London W8 7LB (☎ 0171 229 5100, fax 0171 221 7157); Buccanan Capital Management Ltd, Buccanan House, 3 St James's Square, London SW1 (☎ 0171 973 8070, fax 0171 973 8082)

COLLINS, Aletta Rachel; da of Michael John Collins, of Lower Street, Cavendish, Suffolk, and Sonja Anne, *née* O'Hanlon; *b* 12 April 1967; *Educ* LCDT; *Career* choreographer; memb 4D Performance Group 1987–88, cmmnd Place Portfolio choreographer 1988, choreographer Phoenix Dance Co Leeds (Digital Dance award) 1988, res choreographer Place Theatre 1988–89, dancer LCDT 1990–; freelance choreography incl: Stand By Your Man (LCDT), Samson and Dalila (Bregenz Festival) 1988 and 1989, Carmen (Earls Court, Tokyo, Aust), The Aletta Collins Collection (Place Theatre), Beatrice and Benedict (ENO), Sunday in the Park with George (NT), It's Gonna Rain (LDCT), Gang of Five (Bonnie Bird award, Phoenix Dance Co) 1990, assoc dir and choreographer King Priam (Opera North) 1991, co-dir and choreographer La Bohème (Stuttgart Opera) 1991, co-dir and choreographer Don Giovanni (Scottsh Opera) 1992, Shoes (London Contemporary Dance Theatre) 1993, Alistair Fish (BBC2/Arts Cncl short, dance film) 1993; *Awards* incl: first prize 2 Concorso Internazionale Di Citta Cagliari Italy 1987, major prize for Dance Theatre Twentieth Int Choreographic Meeting Bagnolet France 1990; *Style—* Ms Aletta Collins; ✉ c/o Harriet Cruickshank, 97 Old South Lambeth Road, London SW8 1XU (☎ 0171 735 2933, fax 0171 820 1081)

COLLINS, Andrew John; s of John William Collins, and Christine, *née* Ward; *b* 4 March 1965; *Educ* Weston Favell Upper Sch Northampton, Nene Coll Northampton, Chelsea Sch of Art; *m* 3 Sept 1994, Julie, *née* Quirke; *Career* freelance illustrator 1987–88, features ed New Musical Express 1991–92 (asst art ed 1988–89, staff writer 1990–91), staff writer Vox magazine 1990–91; features ed: Select magazine Jan-Sept 1993, Q magazine Oct 1993–95; ed: Empire 1995, Q magazine 1995–; BBC: co-writer and performer Fantastic Voyage Radio 5 1993, weekly series Collins and Maconie's Hit Parade (with Stuart Maconie, Radio 1) 1994–, presented (with Stuart Maconie) Mercury Music Prize and Brit Awards (Radio 1) 1994, 1995 and 1996, regular appearances on the Mark Radcliffe show (Radio 1); appeared in own weekly satire slot (with Stuart Maconie) for Naked City (C4) 1994; winner: Thames TV bursary 1986, Sony Radio Award for Collins & Maconie's Hit Parade 1995; nominated Writers' Guild of GB Award 1993; *Recreations* cats, music, film, video collecting, decent fiction, poetry, wine, cooking, showbiz autobiographies, TV detective series, modern art, the British countryside, computer games, trivia; *Style—* Andrew Collins, Esq; ✉ Q magazine, EMAP Metro, Mappin House, 4 Winsley Street, London W1N 7AR (☎ 0171 436 1515, fax 0171 312 8247)

COLLINS, Andrew Seymour; TD (1977); s of Seymour John Collins, JP (d 1970), and Nancye Westray, *née* Yarwood; *b* 2 Nov 1944; *Educ* Radley, Coll of Law; *m* 1, 17 July 1971 (m dis 1985), Susan Lucretia, da of Cdr John Weston Chase, RN (d 1989); 3 s (Charles b 1972, James b 1975 d 1993, Giles b 1977), 1 da (Amelia b 1974); m 2, 26 Nov 1986, Virginia Mary Crisp, da of John Richard Craik-White, MC (d 1988); *Career* TA/TAVR 1964–87, memb Ctee TA&VRA 1981–85; admitted slr 1969; ptnr: Walker Martineau 1986–94, Laytons 1995–; Gen Cmmr of Taxes 1983; memb Cncl London C of C and Trade; chm Multilaw Eastern and Central Euro Gp 1992–94; Liveryman: Worshipful Co of Fanmakers 1970 (Master 1996–97), Worshipful Co of Slrs, Worshipful Co of Info Technologists; memb: Law Soc, Holborn Law Soc (memb Ctee 1990–94), City of London Law Soc, Br Hungarian Law Assoc (memb Ctee 1994), British Czech Law Assoc, British Hungarian Soc; *Recreations* sailing, hunting, shooting, tennis; *Clubs* Royal Thames Yacht, HAC; *Style—* Andrew Collins, Esq, TD; ✉ Central Farm, Canons Ashby, Daventry, Northants NN11 3SD (☎ 01327 361553, mobile 0468 611587)

COLLINS, Sir Arthur James Robert; KCVO (1980, CVO 1963), ERD; s of Col William Fellowes Collins, DSO, JP, DL, of Cundall Manor, York, Lord of the Manor of Cundall and Patron of the livings of Cundall and Farnham, and Lady Evelyn Innes-Ker, OBE (4 da of 7 Duke of Roxburghe); *b* 10 July 1911; *Educ* Eton, Ch Ch Oxford (MA); *m* 1965, Elizabeth, da of Rear Adm Sir Arthur Bromley, 8 Bt, KCMG, KCVO, and widow of 6 Baron Sudeley (killed on active serv 1941); *Career* Maj RHG, Adj 2 Household Cavalry Regt (despatches) 1941–45; slr, ptnr Withers and Co 1937, sr ptnr 1962–82; conslt 1982; Liveryman Worshipful Co of Gunmakers; *Clubs* Turf, White's; *Style—* Sir Arthur Collins, KCVO, ERD; ✉ Kirkman Bank, Knaresborough, N Yorks HG5 9BT (☎ 01423 863136); 38 Clarence Terrace, London NW1 (☎ 0171 723 4198)

COLLINS, Basil Eugene Sinclair; CBE (1983); s of Albert Collins (d 1971), and Pauline Alicia, *née* Wright; *b* 21 Dec 1923; *Educ* Great Yarmouth GS; *m* 1942, Doris, da of Harry Meyer Slott (d 1944); 2 da; *Career* dep chm and chief exec Cadbury Schweppes plc 1980–83 (md 1974–80), chm Nabisco Group Ltd 1984–89; dir: Thomas Cook Group 1980–85, British Airways 1982–88, Royal Mint 1984–88; life vice pres Royal Coll of Nursing (hon treas, chm of Fin Ctee 1970–86), hon fell UEA 1995 (memb Cncl 1987–94), tstee and dir Inst of Econ Affrs 1987–92; FZS, FRSA; *Recreations* music, languages, English countryside; *Style—* Basil Collins, Esq, CBE; ✉ Wyddial Parva, Buntingford, Herts SG9 0EL

COLLINS, Bryan; OBE (1996); s of Leslie George Thomas Collins (d 1981), and Ivy Clara, *née* Biggs; *b* 21 April 1936; *Educ* Cambridge Central GS; *m* 1 March 1958, Mary Josephine, da of Walter George Cole (d 1970), of Cambridge; 1 s (Timothy Howard b 1961), 1 da (Louise Mary b 1963); *Career* md and chief exec Bristow Helicopter Group Ltd 1979–96; chm Bromley Family Health Serv Authy 1985–92, memb Bromley Health Authy 1992–93, chm Bromley Hosps NHS Tst 1993–; FSCA, FRAeS; *Recreations* golf, tennis, shooting; *Clubs* IOD, Sloane, Royal Soc of Medicine; *Style—* Bryan Collins, Esq, OBE; ✉ Wymondley, Hookwood Park, Limpsfield, Surrey RH8 0SG (☎ and fax 01883 723281)

COLLINS, Bryan Thomas Alfred; OBE (1989), QFSM (1983); *b* 4 June 1933; *Educ* Queen Mary's Sch (Cooper Jordan Co scholar); *m* 1959, Terry; 1 da, 1 s; *Career* served RAF 1951–53; Fire Service: joined 1954, station cdr Stafford 1961–64, div cdr Central Div Staffs 1966–70 (dep div cdr 1964–66), asst chief offr Co Fire Service W Riding 1970–73, dep chief offr Bucks 1973–79, chief fire offr Humberside 1979–89, HM inspr of fire servs Northern Area 1989–93, HM inspr of fire servs Midlands & Wales 1993–94, HM chief inspr of fire servs 1994–; lectr on local govt fin Brigade Command Course Fire Service Coll 1987–89; Inst of Fire Engrs: sec Midland Branch 1966–70, memb Nat Examination Marking Panel 1966–81, chm S Midland Branch 1975–77 (vice chm 1973–75); nat chm Assoc for Petroleum and Explosives Admin (memb Nat Cncl 1978–79); Chief and Asst Chief Fire Offrs Assoc (CACFOA): chm NE District 1984– (vice chm 1979–84), chm Fire Prevention Working Party 1979–84, chm Fire Prevention Tech Ctee 1981–89 (vice chm 1980–81), CACFOA rep on various BSI ctees; Fire Services Nat Benevolent Fund: chm Bucks Branch 1977–79, chm Humberside Branch 1979–89, memb No 6 Gp Cncl 1976–78, memb No 2 Gp Cncl 1979–89; pres Humberside Branch Nat Assoc of Fire Brigade Pensioners 1979–89; ACC 1984–89: princ advsr to Fire and Emergency Planning Ctee, rep on various jt ctees Central Fire Brigades' Advsy Cncl, memb Local Govt Fin Grants Working Gp, memb Br Approvals for Fire Equipment 1986–87; DOE: memb Building Regulations Advsy Ctee 1987–88, memb Building Regulations Fire Advsy Panel 1987–89; memb: Access Ctee for England Centre on Environment for the Handicapped 1984–89, St John Cncl Humberside 1979–89; CIMgt, FIFireE; *Style—* Bryan Collins, Esq, OBE, QFSM; ✉ HM Fire Service Inspectorate, Horseferry House, Dean Ryle Street, London SW1P 2AW (☎ 0171 217 8599)

COLLINS, Charles Douglas; s of Prof Douglas Henry Collins, OBE (d 1964), of Sheffield, and Jean, *née* Wright; *b* 18 March 1939; *Educ* St Edward's Sch Oxford, Queens' Coll Cambridge (MA, MB BChir), Univ of Sheffield (MB ChM); *m* 5 June 1965, Jhoann Temlett, da of Jack Marke (d 1977), of Huish Champflower, Somerset; 2 s (James b 8 Dec 1969, William b 15 July 1974), 1 da (Victoria b 11 Feb 1971); *Career* conslt surgn in Taunton 1973–, med dir Taunton and Somerset NHS Tst 1991–95; regnl advsr RCS 1990–, med advsr WPA 1994–; memb: BMA 1963–, Cncl RCS (Eng) 1995–; FRCS 1967; *Style—* Charles Collins, Esq; ✉ Crowcombe House, Crowcombe, Taunton, Somerset TA4 4AE (☎ 01984 618266); Taunton and Somerset Hosp, Musgrove Park, Taunton, Somerset (☎ 01823 342100)

COLLINS, David Stuart; s of James Henry Collins, of Dalkeith, Midlothian, Scotland, and Hilda, *née* Oldfield (d 1977); *b* 24 Feb 1945; *Educ* Fazakerley Comprehensive Liverpool, Liverpool Coll of Commerce; *m* 14 Oct 1967, Penelope Noël, da of Herbert Lancelot Charters, of Maghull, Liverpool; 1 s (Mark Stuart b 1977), 1 da (Nicola Caroline b 1980); *Career* Granada Publishing Ltd: mangr S Africa 1974–77, area sales mangr N Africa, M East, India and Pakistan 1977–81, trade mangr 1981–83; export sales mangr Harrap Ltd 1983–84 (sales dir 1984–91), Columbus Books Ltd 1986–91, md Verulam Publishing Ltd 1992–; *Recreations* travel, walking, reading, swimming, good conversation; *Style—* David Stuart Collins, Esq; ✉ Home and Office: 152A Park Street Lane, Park St, St Albans AL2 2AU (☎ 01727 872770, fax 01727 873866)

COLLINS, Mrs Michael; (Lesley) Elizabeth; *see:* Appleby, (Lesley) Elizabeth

COLLINS, Hannah; da of Clifford Collins, of Horsham, Sussex, and Christine Collins; *b* 10 Aug 1956; *Educ* Lady Eleanor Holles Sch, Slade Sch of Fine Art UCL (Dip in Fine Art) Fulbright-Hays scholar to USA; partner, John Egan; 1 s (Echo Collins Egan b 29 Feb 1988); *Career* artist and photographer; lectr in fine art Chelsea Sch of Fine Art London; *Solo Exhibitions* Films Stills (Matt's Gallery, London) 1986, New Works (ICA) 1988, Viewpoints (Walker Art Centre, Minneapolis) 1989, Xavier Hufbens Gallery Brussels 1989, Galerie Tanit Cologne Germany 1990; *Gp Exhibitions* Antidotes to Madness (Riverside Studios, London) 1986, The British Edge (ICA Boston USA) 1987, The Big Picture - The New Photography (John and Mable Ringling Museum, Florida) 1987, Australian Biennale Sydney and Melbourne 1988, Aperto '88 (Venice Biennale Italy) 1988, A British View (Museum für Gestaltung Zürich) 1988, Another Objectivity (ICA) 1988, Matter of Facts (Musée des Beaux Arts, Nantes) 1988, Une Autre Objectivité (Centre Nationale Des Arts Plastiques, Paris) 1989, Portraits (Contemporary Art Fndn) 1989, Shifting Focus (Arnolfini Gallery, Bristol) 1989, Polaroid Works (V & A Museum) 1989, Stuart Regen Gallery LA 1990, British Artists in Russia (Kiev and Moscow) 1990, Art and Photography (Modern Art Museum Kyoto and Museum of Modern Art Tokyo) 1990, Turner Prize Exhibition (Tate Gallery, shortlisted) 1993; *Work in Public Collections* Eastern Arts Assoc England, Polaroid Int, Arts Cncl of GB, Br Cncl, Walker Art Center Minneapolis, V & A Museum London, FRAC Rhone Alpes France, FRAC Lyon France, FRAC Bretagne France, FNAC France; *Style—* Ms Hannah Collins; ✉ Baixada de Viladecols, 08002 Barcelona, Spain; c/o Matts Gallery (☎ 0181 983 1771)

COLLINS, Prof Jeffrey Hamilton; *b* 22 April 1930; *Educ* Univ of London (BSc, MSc, DSc); *Career* laboratory technician Physics Dept Guy's Hosp Med Sch 1946–48, scientific staff memb GEC Hirst Res Centre 1951–56, pt/t lectr Mathematics Dept Sir John Cass Coll London 1955–56, sr staff engr Ferranti Ltd Edinburgh 1956–57, lectr then sr lectr Dept of Electrical Engineering Univ of Glasgow 1959–66, res engr Stanford Univ 1966–68, dir Physical Sci Dept Electronics Div Rockwell International and res dir autonetics Rockwell International Science Center 1968–70, prof of Industl Electronics Dept of Electrical Engrg Univ of Edinburgh 1973–77 (res prof 1970–73), visiting prof of electrical engrg The Univ of Texas at Arlington 1976–77; Univ of Edinburgh: prof of electical engrg and head Dept of Electrical Engrg 1977–84, emeritus prof of electrical engrg 1984–, fell The Centre for Speech Technol Res 1984–87; dir: Scottish Engineering Training Scheme Ltd 1981–83, Integrated Microapplications Ltd 1981–84, Racal Group Services Ltd 1981, Racal-MESL Ltd 1970–81 (formerly MESL Ltd), Filtronic Components Ltd 1981–85, Advent Technology 1981–86, Scottish Electronics Technology Group 1983–86, Burr-Brown Ltd 1984–86, Lattice-Logic Ltd 1986, Automation and Robotics Res Inst Univ of Texas at Arlington 1987–90, Riverbend Bank Fort Worth 1987–90; sr tech specialist Lothian Regnl Cncl Edinburgh 1991–93, prof and specialist advsr to Vice-Chllr Napier Univ 1994–; 195 pubns in sci and engrg jls; IEE 1985–86 (chm Electronics Div UK, memb Cncl, memb Learned Soc Bd); memb: Information Engrg Ctee SERC 1983–86, Computer Bd for Univs and Res Cncls Dept of Educn and Sci 1984–86, Advanced Devices and Materials Ctee DTI 1984–86, Cncl Royal Acad of Engrg 1984–86, Info Systems Ctee UFC 1992–93, Jt Information Systems Ctee Higher Educn Funding Cncls 1993–94; chm Edinburgh Parallel Computing Centre 1990–94; hon fell Univ of Edinburgh 1990–96, CPhys, FEng 1981, FIEE, FInstP, FIEEE, FRSE 1983; *Style—* Prof Jeffrey Collins, FRSE, FEng; ✉ 28 Muirfield Park, Gullane, East Lothian EH31 2DY (☎ 01620 843006)

COLLINS, Joan Henrietta; OBE (1997); da of Joseph William Collins (d 1988), and his 1 w, Elsa, *née* Bessant (d 1962); *b* 23 May 1933; *Educ* Francis Holland Sch, St Margaret's Middx, RADA; *m* 1, 23 May 1954 (m dis 1957), Maxwell Reed, actor (d 1974); m 2, May 1963 (m dis), Anthony Newley, actor; 1 s (Alexander b 8 Sept 1965), 1 da (Tara b 12 Oct 1963); m 3, Feb 1972 (m dis 1983), Ron Kass, film prodr; 1 da (Katyana b 20 June 1972); m 4, 6 Nov 1985 (m dis 1987), Peter Holm; *Career* film and television actress since 1951; guest ed Christmas edn Marie Claire 1993; *Theatre* incl Last of Mrs Cheyne 1980, Private Lives (Aldwych Theatre and US tour/Broadway) 1990; *Television* Br TV incl: Tales of the Unexpected, The Persuaders; US TV incl: Star Trek 1975, Batman 1975, The Moneychangers 1976, Mission Impossible 1976, Police Woman 1976, Starsky and Hutch 1978, Space 1999 1979, Fantasy Island 1981, The Making of a Male Model 1983, My Life as a Man 1984, Dynasty 1981–89, Sins 1985, Monte Carlo 1986, Rosanne 1991, Mamas Back 1992, Annie - A Royal Adventure 1995, Hart to Hart (TV film) 1995; *Films* Br films incl: The Road to Hong Kong 1962, Can Hieronymus Merkin Ever Forget Mercy Humppe and Find True Happiness 1969, Tales From the Crypt 1972, The Big Sleep 1977, The Stud 1978, The Bitch 1979, Decadence 1993, In the Bleak Mid-Winter 1995; US films incl: Land of the Pharaohs 1954, The Virgin Queen 1955, The Opposite Sex 1956, Rally Round the Flag, Boys 1958, Esther and the King 1960; *Awards* Hollywood Women's Press Club Golden Apple Award 1982, Golden Globe Best Actress in a TV Drama Award (Alexis in Dynasty) 1983, People's Choice Most Popular Actress Award 1983 and 1984; *Books* Past Imperfect (1978), Joan Collins' Beauty Book (1982), Katy - A Fight for Life (1983), Prime Time (1988), Love and Desire and Hate (1990), My Secrets (1994), Too Damn Famous (1995), Second Act (1996); *Recreations* travelling, collecting 18 century antiques, writing; *Style—* Miss Joan Collins, OBE; ✉ 16 Bulbecks Walk, South Woodham Ferrers, Essex CM3 5ZN; c/o Stella Wilson Publicity, 130 Calabria Road, Highbury, London N5 1HT (☎ 0171 354 5672, fax 0171 354 2242)

COLLINS, Sir John Alexander; kt (1993); s of Maj John Constantine Collins, of Bodmin, Cornwall, and Nancy Isobel, *née* Mitchell; *b* 10 Dec 1941; *Educ* Campbell Coll Belfast, Univ of Reading (BSc); *m* 24 April 1965, Susan Mary, da of Robert Reid Hooper, of Wimbourne, Dorset; 1 s (Robert b 18 May 1970), 1 da (Helen b 18 June 1968); *Career* Shell Group: joined Shell International Chemicals 1964, various appts in Shell Kenya, Nigeria and Colombia until 1984, md Shell Chemicals UK Ltd and Shell UK Ltd 1984, supply and mktg coordinator and dir Shell International Petroleum Company and dir Shell UK (Holdings) 1989, chm and chief exec Shell UK Ltd 1990–93; chief exec Vestey Group plc 1993–; memb PM's Advsy Ctee for Queen's Awards for Export, Technological and Environmental Achievement; chm Advsy Ctee on Business and the Environment 1991–93; non-exec dir: British Sky Broadcasting Group plc 1994–, NM Rothschild & Sons Ltd 1995–; non-exec chm Cantab Pharmaceuticals 1996–; govr Wellington Coll; memb: Advsy Cncl London Symphony Orchestra, Action on Addiction, Fundraising Ctee Ocean Youth Club; CIMgt; *Recreations* opera, theatre, sailing, golf, tennis, a love of the New Forest; *Style—* Sir John Collins; ✉ Vestey Group plc, 16 St John's Lane, London EC1M 4AF (☎ 0171 248 1212, fax 0171 490 2170); Vestey Group plc, 16 St John's Lane, London EC1M 4AF

COLLINS, John Frederick Norman; OBE; s of Harry Norman Collins (d 1973), of Chester, and Doris Emily Collins (d 1972); *b* 15 Sept 1924; *Educ* King Edward's Sch Birmingham, Birmingham Sch of Architecture (Dip Arch), Sch of Planning and Res for Regnl Devpt London (SP Dip); *m* 1, 27 July 1955, Angela Mary (Jill) (d 1973), da of Donald Hutton Cox (d 1973); 3 s (Timothy John b 12 Feb 1959, Dr Matthew James b 12 May 1960, Richard Studholme b 26 April 1971), 3 da (Emma Louise (Mrs M Hawkins) b 26 April 1962, Katharine Lucy (Mrs V Persson) b 8 June 1965, Joanna Mary (Mrs P Rozsich) b 11 Aug 1968); m 2, 14 May 1976, Mary Muriel; *Career* RAF 1944–47, served Africa and Aden; project architect local authy housing Birmingham 1953–55, architect and town planner gp ldr Coventry 1955–59, project architect works abroad (Cyprus) then sr architect R & D WO Works Directorate 1959–63, sr assoc Graeme Shankland Assocs Liverpool 1963–67, co planner Cheshire CC 1969–88 (2 dep co planning offr 1967–69), sr ptnr Long Collins Partnership Chester 1988–96; conslt Lawson-Price 1996–; chief physical planner Montserrat West Indies 1990–93; pres: Chester Soc of Architects 1983–85, RTPI 1980–82 (memb Cncl 1970–89); chm NW Regnl Cncl RIBA; ARIBA 1951, FRTPI 1955; *Recreations* theatre, golf, sailing, travel; *Style—* John Collins, Esq, OBE; ✉ Greenlooms House, Martins Lane, Hargrave, Chester, Cheshire CH3 7RX (☎ 01829 741070); Glan Yr Aig, Borth, Ceredigion, Dyfed; Lawson-Price, Richmond Place, 125 Boughton, Chester, Cheshire CH3 5BJ (☎ 01244 312387, fax 01244 314538)

COLLINS, John Joseph; s of Patrick Collins (d 1982), of Killiney, Dublin, Ireland, and Mary Josephine, *née* O'Brien (d 1954); *b* 23 May 1944; *m* 25 Jan 1970, (Eline) Mary, da of James Cullen (d 1978); 2 s (Patrick James b 1971, Paul Ivor b 1976), 1 da (Aisling Mary b 1972); *Career* called to the Bar King's Inns Ireland 1967, in practice 1967–71, called to the Bar Middle Temple 1971; fndr chambers at 11 South Square Gray's Inn 1980; fndr and head of chambers in: Lewes 1987, Pinner 1992, Hastings and Chichester 1996; called to the Aust Bar in Supreme Ct of NSW 1989; memb Ctee Int Bar Assoc 1990–, chm Int Assoc of Irish Lawyers 1992–; *Recreations* reading, walking, swimming; *Style—* John Collins, Esq; ✉ Hazeldene, 703 Pinner Road, Pinner, Middlesex HA5 5QZ (☎ 0181 868 4106); Westgate Chambers, 144 High Street, Lewes, E Sussex BN7 1XT (☎ 01273 480510, fax 01273 483179)

COLLINS, John Morris; s of Emmanuel Cohen, MBE (d 1980), of Leeds, and Ruby Cohen (d 1988); *b* 25 June 1931; *Educ* Leeds GS, Queen's Coll Oxford (MA); *m* 19 March 1968, Sheila, da of David Brummer, of Hendon, London; 1 da (Simone Natalie b 1974); *Career* called to the Bar Middle Temple 1956, head of chambers 1966–, dep co ct judge 1970–71, asst recorder of the Crown Ct 1971, dep circuit judge 1972–80, recorder of the Crown Court 1980–; *Recreations* walking, communal work; *Style—* John M Collins, Esq; ✉ 14 Sandhill Oval, Leeds LS17 8EA (☎ 0113 268 6008); 9 Woodhouse Square, Leeds LS3 1AD (☎ 0113 245 1986, fax 0113 244 8623)

COLLINS, Dr John Vincent; s of Thomas Ernest Collins (d 1987), of Denham, Bucks, and Zillah Phoebe, *née* Jessop; *b* 16 July 1938; *Educ* Univ of London (BDS, MB BS, MD, MRCP), Guy's Hosp, St Mary's Hosp, Westminster Hosp; *m* 1963, Helen Eluned, da of William Alan Cash; 1 s (Jonathan James b March 1972), 1 da (Philippa Helen b Sept 1977); *Career* house physician Guy's Hosp 1966–67, house surgn 1966–67, sr house offr in neurology St Mary's Hosp 1967, med registrar 1968–70, sr med registrar Westminster and Brompton Hosp 1970–72, sr lectr in med and conslt physician Bart's Med Coll 1973–76; conslt physician: Royal Brompton and National Heart Hosps 1976–, Riverside Health Authy 1979–; med dir and dir Chest Dept Chelsea and Westminster Hosp, dir Fibreoptic Bronchoscopy Unit Royal Brompton Hosp, hon sr lectr Cardiothoracic Inst; FRCP 1981; memb: Br Thoracic Soc, BMA, American Thoracic Soc; *Recreations* tennis, drawing, painting; *Style—* Dr John Collins; ✉ Royal Brompton National Heart & Lung Hospitals, Sydney St, London SW3 6NP

COLLINS, Julian Peter; s of Edward Arthur Burnette Collins, and Dorothy, *née* Wragg (d 1989); *b* 15 Nov 1942; *Educ* Nottingham HS, Gonville and Caius Coll Cambridge (MA, LLM); *Career* admitted slr 1967, head of Industl Branch Legal Dept NCB 1973, legal advsr and slr Br Coal Corpn 1988, slr British Coal Pension Schemes 1993; memb Cncl JUSTICE; memb: Law Soc (chm Commerce and Indust Gp 1993–94); *Recreations* theatre, travel; *Style—* Julian Collins, Esq; ✉ 59 Gilpin Avenue, E Sheen, London SW14 8QX (☎ and fax 0181 876 6347); 33 Cavendish Square, London W1A 2NE (☎ 0171 396 7152, fax 0171 396 7239)

COLLINS, Kenneth Darlingston; MEP (Lab) Strathclyde E (majority 52,340); s of late Nicholas Collins and Ellen Williamson; *b* 12 Aug 1939; *Educ* St John's GS, Hamilton Acad, Univ of Glasgow (BSc Hons), Univ of Strathclyde (MSc); *m* 1966, Georgina Frances, *née* Pollard; 1 s, 1 da; *Career* steelworks apprentice 1956–59, planning offr 1965–66, tutor-organiser WEA 1966–67; social geographer; lectr Glasgow Coll of Bldg 1967–69, lectr Paisley Coll of Technol 1969–79; dep ldr Labour Gp Euro Parl 1979–84, chm Environment Public Health and Consumer Protection Ctee 1979–84 and 1989– (vice chm 1984–87); MEP (Lab) Strathclyde East 1979–, Euro Parl socialist spokesman on environment, public health, and consumer protection 1984–89; memb: E Kilbride Town and DC 1973–79, Lanark CC 1973–75, E Kilbride Devpt Corp 1976–79, Socialist Int Environment Ctee, Fabian Soc, Amnesty Int, Labour Movement in Europe, Scot Educn and Action for Devpt, Friends of the Earth (Scotland); hon vice pres: Socialist Environment and Resources Assoc, Royal Environmental Health Inst of Scot, Int Fedn on Environmental Health, Town and Country Planning Assoc, Nat Soc for Clean Air, Inst of Trading Standards Admin; hon sr res fell Dept of Geography Lancaster Univ, memb Advsy Ctee Euro Public Policy Inst Univ of Warwick, dir Inst for Euro Environmental Policy London; Euro advsr: BECTU, AEEU, UNISON; fell Indust and Parl Tst, FRSGS; *Recreations* Labour Party, music, boxer dogs, cycling; *Style—* Kenneth Collins Esq, MEP; ✉ 11 Stuarton Park, East Kilbride, Lanarkshire G74 4LA (☎ 01355 237282, fax 01355 249670)

COLLINS, Lewis; *b* 27 May 1946; *Educ* LAMDA; *m*; 2 c; *Career* actor; lectr and conducted workshops UCLA; memb Actors' Equity; *Theatre* incl: full repertory season Chesterfield Theatre 1970, major classical roles (The Citizen's Theatre Glasgow, Edinburgh Festival) 1971–73, The Farm (dir Lyndsey Anderson, Royal Court, transferred Mayfair W End) 1973–74, Dialogue Between Friends (Open Space) 1974, Blues White and Reds 1974, City Sugar (UK tour Prospect Theatre Co) 1976, Christmas pantomimes (His Majesty's Theatre, Theatre Royal, Hanley Trent Theatre Stockport) 1981–85, Death Trap (Aust tour) 1986; dir: Double Double (Actors Maximus Arena, co-author with James Saunders) 1973, The Real Inspector Hound (Actors Maximus Arena) 1973, Rita Joe (Univ of Vancouver) 1973; *Television* incl: The Real Inspector Hound 1973, The Cuckoo Waltz 1974–76, The New Avengers 1977, The Professionals 1977–81, A Night on the Town 1983, Jack the Ripper 1988, The Man Who Knew Too Little 1988, A Ghost in Monte Carlo 1989; *Films* Who Dares Wins 1982, Codename Wildgeese 1984, Commando Leopard 1985, The Commander 1987; *Recreations* flying (PPL holder), skydiving; *Style—* Lewis Collins, Esq; ✉ c/o Susan James Personal Management, 22 Westbere Road, London NW2 3SR (☎ 0171 794 1286, fax 0171 794 8620)

COLLINS, Lydia; da of Joel Collins (d 1962), and Pamela, *née* Btesh; *Educ* Howell's Sch Llandaff, UCL (LLB); *m* 30 Dec 1974, Morris L Bierbrier, *qv*; *Career* res asst Soc of Genealogists 1979–88, sec Royal Asiatic Soc 1988–; Assoc of Genealogists and Record Agents: memb 1981–, memb Cncl 1983–87 and 1989–93; *Books* Marriage Licences in the Library of the Society of Genealogists (1981), Monumental Inscriptions in the Library of the Society of Genealogists (1984–87); *Recreations* genealogy; *Style—* Miss Lydia Collins; ✉ Royal Asiatic Society, 60 Queen's Gardens, London W2 3AF

COLLINS, (John) Martin; QC (1972); s of John Lissant Collins (d 1962), of Grange-over-Sands, Lancs, and Marjorie Mary, *née* Jefferson (d 1982); *b* 24 Jan 1929; *Educ* Uppingham, Univ of Manchester (Dauntsey prize int law); *m* Daphne Mary, da of George Swindells (d 1960), of Prestbury; 2 s (Benedict George, Toby Francis), 1 da (Arabella Jane); *Career* called to the Bar: Gray's Inn 1952 (bencher 1981), Gibraltar 1990; dep chm Cumberland Quarter Sessions 1964–72, recorder of the Crown Court 1972–88, judge Ct of Appeal Jersey and Guernsey 1984–; memb: Senate of Inns of Court and Bar 1981–84, Gen Cncl of the Bar 1991; Liveryman Worshipful Co of Makers of Playing Cards 1982; *Clubs* Carlton; *Style—* Martin Collins, Esq, QC; ✉ 12 Gray's Inn Square, Gray's Inn, London WC1R 5JP (☎ 0171 404 6299); 10 Essex St, Outer Temple, London WC2 (☎ 0171 240 6981, fax 0171 240 7722)

COLLINS, Michael Geoffrey; QC (1988); s of (Francis) Geoffrey Collins (d 1982), of Scottburgh, Natal, SA, and Margaret Isabelle, *née* Harper-Gow (d 1989); *b* 4 March 1948; *Educ* Peterhouse Marandellas Rhodesia, Univ of Exeter (LLB); *m* 13 April 1985, Bonnie Gayle, da of John Wilbur Bird (d 1988), and Frances Ratliff Bird (d 1995), of New Albany, Indiana; *Career* called to the Bar Gray's Inn 1971; *Books* Private International Litigation (contrib, 1988); *Recreations* golf, tennis, watercolour painting, amateur dramatics; *Clubs* Woking Golf, Liphook Golf; *Style—* Michael Collins, Esq, QC; ✉ 9809 E Bexhill Drive, Kensington, Maryland 20895, USA; Essex Court Chambers, 24 Lincoln's Inn Fields, London WC2A 3ED (☎ 0171 813 8000, fax 0171 813 8080)

COLLINS, Prof Michael John; s of Frederick Allenby Collins, and Gwendoline Violet, *née* Hersey-Walker; *b* 27 Jan 1962; *Educ* RCM (ARCM Hons); *Career* clarinetist; with Nash Ensemble 1982–88; principal clarinet: London Sinfonietta 1982–, Philharmonia Orch 1988–; prof RCM 1985–; soloist with Russian Nat Orch BBC Proms 1996; winner: BBC TV Young Musician of the Year 1978, Leeds Nat Competition for Musicians 1980, Int Rostrum of Young Performers UNESCO 1985, Worshipful Co of Musicians Medal 1980, Tagore Gold Medal RCM; *Recreations* record collecting; *Style—* Prof Michael Collins; ✉ c/o Clarion/Seven Muses, 47 Whitehall Park, London N19 3TW (☎ 0171 272 4413, fax 0171 281 9687)

COLLINS, Dr Michael Lawrence; s of Sidney Collins, of 4 Birkdale Walk, Leeds, and Essie, *née* Gross; *b* 26 May 1943; *Educ* Roundhay Sch Leeds, Univ of Leeds Sch of Med (MB ChB); *m* 27 June 1971, Jackie, da of Theodore Hall, of 3 Garmont Rd, Leeds; 1 s

(Spencer b 1974), 1 da (Antonia b 1977); *Career* house surgn and sr house offr United Leeds Hosps 1969–72, teaching fell Univ of BC 1972–73, registrar Leeds Maternity Hosp and Hosp for Women 1973–76 (house surgn, sr house offr 1969–72), specialist in gynaecological endocrinology and infertility McMaster Univ Med Centre Ontario Canada 1977–79, princ gen practice Middx 1980–84, specialist practice in gynaecological endocrinology 1980–, med advsr Well Woman Clinics 1980–, clinical dir Lynbrook Hosp 1992–94, lectr in medical gynaecology; tstee Deafax Charity Reading Univ; memb: Hillingdon FPC 1980–84, Hillingdon Local Med Ctee 1980–84, Hillingdon Brunel Univ Liaison Ctee; MDU; memb: BMA, RSM; *Recreations* art, photography, writing, antiquarian books, croquet; *Clubs* Phyllis Court, Henley; *Style*— Dr Michael Collins; ✉ 57 Harley Street, London W1N 1DD, The London Welbeck Hospital, Welbeck Street, London W1M 7PG; (☎ 01334 28383); Harley Clinic, Boca Raton, Florida, USA

COLLINS, Neil Adam; s of Clive Dinant Collins, and Joan Collins; *Educ* Uppingham, Selwyn Coll Cambridge; *m* 1981 (m dis 1994), Vivien Goldsmith; 1 da (Alice Laura b 30 July 1982); *Career* journalist: Daily Mail 1974–79; city ed: Evening Standard 1979–84, The Sunday Times 1984–86, The Daily Telegraph 1986–; *Style*— Neil Collins, Esq; ✉ c/o Jackie Wiblin, The Daily Telegraph, Salters' Hall, 4 Fore Street, London EC2Y 5DT (direct ☎ 0171 538 6900)

COLLINS, Patrick Michael; s of Patrick John Collins (d 1990), of London, and Julia Ann, *née* Canty (d 1988); *b* 23 Nov 1943; *Educ* St Joseph's Acad Blackheath London; *m* 1969, Julie Kathleen, da of Leslie Gordon Grundon; 3 s (Michael Patrick b 19 Sept 1970, Daniel Timothy b 7 Feb 1972, Patrick Joseph Gerard b 13 Jan 1983), 1 da (Mary Julie b 31 Dec 1974); *Career* sports writer; cub reporter Kentish Mercury 1962–65; sports writer: Sunday Citizen 1965–67, News of the World 1967–78; sports columnist: London Evening News 1978–80, London Evening Standard 1980–82; chief sports writer Mail on Sunday 1982–, sports columnist Punch 1990–92; Br Sports Journalist of the Year 1989 and 1990; commendations: Br Press Awards 1978, 1987, 1988 and 1991, Sports Cncl Awards 1979, 1981, 1986, 1988 and 1992, Br Magazine Columnist of the Year 1990, Sports Feature Writer of the Year Br Sports Journalism Award 1993; former sports rep: Kent rugby union XV, London schs athletics team; *Books* The Sportswriter (1996); *Recreations* golf, lunch; *Clubs* Shooters Hill Golf; *Style*— Patrick Collins, Esq; ✉ Mail on Sunday, Northcliffe House, 2 Derry St, London W8 5TS (☎ 0171 938 6000)

COLLINS, His Hon Judge Paul Howard; s of Michael Collins, and Madie Collins; *b* 31 Jan 1944; *Educ* Orange Hill GS Edgware, St Catherine's Coll Oxford (MA); *m* 24 Oct 1987, Susan; 1 stepson (Daniel Fallows b 14 Nov 1973); *Career* called to the Bar 1966, asst recorder 1985–89, recorder 1989–92, circuit judge (SE Circuit) 1992–; *Recreations* theatre, cycling, the Internet; *Clubs* The Questors; *Style*— His Hon Judge Paul Collins; ✉ 1 Garden Court, Temple, London EC4 (☎ 0171 797 7900)

COLLINS, Dr Peter Donald Bruce; s of Douglas Collins (d 1982), and Marjorie, *née* Reynolds; *b* 3 Jan 1939; *Educ* William Hulme's GS Manchester, Univ of Bristol (lacrosse colours, BSc, PhD); *m* 1970, Margaret, *née* Purnell; 2 s (Andrew Richard Purnell b 1974, Nigel Antony Lawrence b 1976); *Career* research fell Univ of California at Berkeley 1963–65; Univ of Durham: lectr in theoretical physics 1965–73, sr lectr 1973–83, reader 1983–, dean Faculty of Science 1988–91, pro-vice-chllr 1991–, sub warden 1994–; chm Higher Edcn Support for Industry in the North (HESIN) 1993–; dir: Regnl Technol Centre (North) 1990–, County Durham Development Co 1994–, Northern Infomatics Applications Agency 1995–; memb American Physical Soc 1964–; FRSA 1991, FInstP 1992; *Books* Regge Poles in Particle Physics (with E J Squires, 1967), Regge Theory and High Energy Physics (1976), Hadron Interactions (with A D Martin, 1984), Particle Physics and Cosmology (with A D Martin and E J Squires, 1989); *Recreations* cricket, gardening, house restoration, railway modelling; *Clubs* Durham County Cricket; *Style*— Dr Peter Collins; ✉ Pro Vice Chancellor, University of Durham, Old Shire Hall, Old Elvet, Durham DH1 3HP (☎ 0191 374 2945)

COLLINS, Air Vice-Marshal Peter Spencer; CB (1985), AFC (1961); s of Sqdn-Ldr Frederick Wildbore Collins, OBE (d 1962), of Essex, and Mary, *née* Spencer (d 1939); *b* 19 March 1930; *Educ* Royal GS High Wycombe, Univ of Birmingham (BA); *m* 25 June 1953, Sheila Mary, da of Sidney John Perks (d 1985), of Wolverhampton; 3 s (Timothy b 1955, Paul b 1960, Christopher b 1963), 1 da (Fiona b 1957); *Career* RAF 1951–85; cmd: No 111 Sqdn 1970–72, RAF Gutersloh 1974–76; Dir of Forward Policy (RAF) 1978–81; Sr Air Staff Offr No 11 Gp 1981–83; Dir Gen of Communications, Info Systems and Orgn 1983–85; non exec dir Marconi Radar Systems Ltd 1985–91 (conslt 1991–95), conslt GEC-Marconi Research Centre 1989–95; *Recreations* golf, music; *Clubs* RAF; *Style*— Air Vice-Marshal Peter Collins, CB, AFC; ✉ Babylon, Church Road, Boreham, Essex CM3 3EJ

COLLINS, Prof Philip Arthur William; s of Arthur Henry Collins (d 1963), of Little Burstead, Essex, and Winifred Nellie, *née* Bowmaker (d 1968); *b* 28 May 1923; *Educ* Brentwood Sch, Emmanuel Coll Cambridge (MA); *m* 1, 1952 (m dis 1963) Mildred, *née* Lowe; m 2, 18 Aug 1965, Joyce, da of James Wilfred Dickins; 2 s (Simon Charles Oliver, Marcus James Arthur), 1 da (Rosamund Patricia); *Career* Sgt RAOC 1942–44, Lt Royal Norfolk Regt 1944–45; Univ of Leicester 1947–: warden of Vaughan Coll 1954–62, prof of Eng 1964–82, public orator 1976–78 and 1980–82, emeritus prof 1982–; visiting prof: Univ of California 1967, Univ of Columbia 1969, Univ of Victoria NZ 1974; scripted and appeared on BBC TV and Radio progs, co author The Canker and the Rose (Mermaid Theatre London) 1964; sec Leicester Theatre Tst 1962–87; memb: Arts Cncl Drama Panel 1970–75, Nat Theatre Bd of Dirs 1976–82; govr Br American Drama Acad 1983–, chm Tennyson Soc 1983–, pres Dickens Fellowship 1984–86; *Books* Dickens and Crime (1962), Dickens - The Critical Heritage (1971), Thackeray - Interviews and Recollections (1983); *Recreations* theatre, music; *Style*— Prof Philip Collins; ✉ 26 Knighton Drive, Leicester LE2 3HB (☎ 0116 270 6026)

COLLINS, Prof Roy; s of Reginald George Collins (ka 1940), and Bertha Mary, *née* Smith; *b* 4 March 1937; *Educ* Southfield Sch Oxford, Univ of Bristol (Hele-Shaw Prize, Albert Fry Prize, BSc), Univ of London (PhD); *m* 1962, Elissa Kedward, da of Edwin John Parry; 2 s (Loel b 8 Oct 1965, Matthew b 20 Aug 1969); *Career* AERE Harwell 1959–61; UCL: lectr 1961–73, sr lectr 1973–85, reader 1985–92, prof of mechanical engrg 1992–, dean Faculty of Engrg 1995–; MIMechE; CEng 1972; *Publications* author of numerous papers in scientific jls incl: Proceedings of The Royal Society, Jl of Fluid Mechanics, Chemical Engineering Science; *Recreations* music, piano, cabinet making and joinery; *Style*— Prof Roy Collins; ✉ 131 Whiteknights Road, Reading, Berks RG6 7BB; Department of Mechanical Engineering, University College London, Torrington Place, London WC1E 7JE (☎ 0171 380 7184, fax 0171 383 0831, e-mail r_collins@meng.ucl.ac.uk)

COLLINS, Roy William; s of Charles Albert Collins (d 1987), and Lilian Maud, *née* Williamson (d 1960); *b* 17 July 1948; *Educ* South East Essex County Tech HS; *m* 1, 1971 (m dis 1975), Barbara Anne, *née* Askew; m 2, 1987, Sheila Anne Love, da of Leslie Arthur Love; 1 da (Lucy Elizabeth b 3 Jan 1987); *Career* general reporter Barking Advertiser 1967, sports ed Express & Independent Walthamstow 1967–68, sports writer Essex & East London Newspapers 1968–69, sports columnist Evening Echo Southend 1969–74, freelance sports and news features journalist Fleet Street 1974–79, gen sports writer then columnist Sunday People 1979–83, freelance sports and gen journalist 1983–86, chief sports writer and columnist Today 1986–95 (following paper's closure), sports columnist The People 1996–; memb: SWA, Football Writers' Assoc; *Recreations* tennis, running, chess, pubs, horse racing; *Clubs* Nothing Writers' Overseas Dining (treas), Coolhurst Tennis; *Style*— Roy Collins, Esq; ✉ 48 Rosebery Road, Muswell Hill, London N10 2LJ (☎ 0181 883 6706)

COLLINS, Terence Bernard; s of late George Bernard Collins, and Helen Teresa, *née* Goodfellow; *b* 3 March 1927; *Educ* Marist Coll Hull, Univ of St Andrews (MA); *m* 1956, Barbara, *née* Lowday; 2 s, 2 da; *Career* dir: Hoechst UK plc 1979–86, A G Stanley Holdings plc 1979–86, Hoechst Australia Investments Pty 1980–86, Mayborn Group plc 1986–92, Cranfield Precision Engineering Ltd 1990–95; chm: Berger Jenson Nicholson plc 1984–86 (vice chm and md 1975–86), Phoenix Developments Ltd 1987–93 and 1995–, Cranfield Conference Services Ltd 1986–93, Mgmnt Ctee Kingline Consultancy Ltd 1989–90, Interact Ltd 1994–; dir CIT Holdings Ltd 1989–93, chm Cranfield Ventures Ltd 1989–93, chm Interact Design & Print Ltd 1995–; memb Int Fellowship Ctee Duke of Edinburgh's Award 1987–89 (memb Int 1978–86), memb Court Cranfield Univ (formerly Cranfield Inst of Technol) 1981– (memb Cncl 1982–93), tstee Atlas Fndn 1986–93, vice chm Cncl Buckingham Univ 1987–95 (chm Fin and Gen Purposes Ctee 1987–94); Hon Dr Univ of Buckingham 1994; *Recreations* music, golf, gardening; *Clubs* Directors', Aldeburgh Golf; *Style*— Terence Collins, Esq; ✉ Aldehurst, Church Walk, Aldeburgh, Suffolk IP15 5DX

COLLINS, Thomas Brendan; s of Stephen Paul Collins, of Lurgan, Co Armargh, N Ireland, and Mary Ethna, *née* Breen; *b* 12 Aug 1959; *Educ* St Colman's Coll Co Down, New Univ of Ulster, City Univ London (BA); *m* Mary Christina, da of late James Dugan; *Career* ed Carrickfergus Advertiser and E Antrim Gazette 1984–85 (reporter 1983–84), chief sub ed The Ulster News Letter 1988–90 (dep chief sub ed 1985–88), ed The Irish News 1993– (dep ed 1990–93); memb Guild of Editors 1994–; regnl newspaper ed of the year 1995; dir: Ulster Orch, Contemporary Music Centre Dublin, N Belfast Employment Centre; memb NI Regnl Ctee Malcolm Sargent Cancer Fund for Children; *Recreations* classical music, opera; *Style*— Thomas B Collins, Esq; ✉ The Irish News, 113–117 Donegall Street, Belfast BT1 2GE (☎ 01232 322226, fax 01232 337505)

COLLINS, Lt-Col William John Neilson; s of William John Collins (d 1986), of Dunfermline, Fife, and Ann French Moncur, *née* Neilson (d 1980); *b* 25 March 1940; *Educ* Univ of St Andrews (BDS), Univ of London (MSc), RCPS (FDS); *m* 16 Oct 1963, Vanda, da of Guido Corrieri (d 1987), of Dunfermline, Fife; 1 s (Simon b 27 June 1969), 2 da (Lesley b 11 Aug 1964, Anneli b 19 May 1968); *Career* Army 1962–79 serv in Hong Kong, Borneo, Germany, UK, ret from army with rank of Lt-Col, conslt Dental surgn and 2 i/c TA 205 Gen Hosp RAMC (V) 1979–95; dir Sch of Dental Hygiene Glasgow Dental Hosp 1979–90, hon lectr Univ of Glasgow 1979–90, chief dental offr for NI 1990–; examiner: Nat Exam Bd for Dental Surgery Assts, Royal Soc of Health, RCPS Glasgow, Gen Dental Cncl; author of numerous lectureships; numerous papers in jls; chm W Lothian Children's Panel Advsy Ctee 1987–90, sec W Lothian Branch of Soldiers' Sailors' Airmen's Families' Assoc; RCPS; *Books* Handbook for Dental Hygienists (with J Forrest and T Walsh, 1978), Guide to Periodontics (with W Jenkins and C Allan, 1984), Dental Hygienist Self-Assessment Book (1984); *Recreations* music; *Clubs* Bathgate Golf; *Style*— Lt-Col William Collins; ✉ Brucefield, Marjoribanks St, Bathgate, West Lothian EH48 1AH (☎ 01506 632658); Chief Dental Officer, DHSS, Castle Buildings, Stormont, Belfast BT4 3RA

COLLINSON, Alicia Hester; da of His Hon Judge Richard Jeffreys Hampton Collinson (d 1983), and Gwendolen Hester, *née* Ward; *b* 12 Aug 1956; *Educ* Birkenhead HS, St Hugh's Coll Oxford (MA, MPhil); *m* 23 April 1988, Damian Howard Green, *qv*, s of Howard Green, KSG; 2 da (Felicity Charlotte Hester Green b 20 March 1990, Verity Mary Sophie Green b 10 Nov 1993); *Career* called to the Bar Middle Temple 1982 (Harmsworth scholar), in practice Midlands and Oxford circuit; memb Bar Cncl 1990–93; memb PCC St Dunstan with St Thomas Church Acton; memb Ct of Common Cncl Corporation of London 1991–; Freeman City of London; *Clubs* Oxford Union; *Style*— Miss Alicia Collinson; ✉ 2 Harcourt Buildings, Temple, London EC4 9DB (☎ 0171 353 6961, fax 0171 353 6968); Harcourt Chambers, Churchill House, St Aldates Courtyard, 38 St Aldates, Oxford OX1 1BN (☎ 01865 791559, fax 01865 791585)

COLLINSON, Anthony Raymond; s of Jack Collinson, of IOM, and Irene Collinson; *b* 9 April 1949; *m* 1 March 1975, Carol Ann (d 1991), da of David Horsfall, of Poole House, Arkholme, Carnforth (s of Sir Donald Horsfall, 2 Bt), 1 s (Jack b 4 Aug 1980), 1 da (Poppy b 9 Aug 1983); *Career* slr; sr ptnr Whiteside & Knowles Morecambe 1983– (ptnr 1975–); dir Westfield War Meml Village Lancaster, memb Cncl Blackburn Branch Prayer Book Soc, tstee St John's Hospice Lancaster; *Recreations* country pursuits, reading, local history; *Style*— Anthony Collinson, Esq; ✉ 5/7 Skipton St, Morecambe, Lancashire LA4 4AW (☎ 01524 416315, fax 01524 831008)

COLLINSON, Leonard; s of Sidney Lupton Collinson (d 1987), and Jane, *née* Crooks, of Immingham; *b* 30 March 1934; *Educ* Humberstone Fndn Sch Cleethorpes, Univ of Nottingham (Dip); *m* 17 Sept 1955, Shirley Grace, da of Ernest Frederick Funnell (d 1962); 2 s (Christopher b 1956, Andrew b 1962); *Career* Nat Serv RAF 1952–54; dep nat mangr Co-operative Wholesale Soc Baking Group 1958–66, dir of Manpower Plessey Telecommunications and Office Systems 1966–71, exec chm Collinson Grant Group Ltd 1971–96; chm: European Consortium of Management Consultants 1991–, Granville North West Venture Fund 1993–, Grosvenor Career Services; dir: United Gas Industries 1975–82, Wormald International Holdings 1979–83, Newsco Publications 1994–; CBI: memb Smaller Firms Cncl 1980–86, memb NW Regnl Cncl 1987–93, memb Nat Cncl 1995–; dir: Manchester TEC 1989–92, Universities Superannuation Scheme 1989–, Forum of Private Business 1994–; memb Ct Univ of Manchester 1994–, chm Manchester Diocesan Cncl for Church in the Economy 1994–; tstee Nat Museum of Labour History; MCIM 1967, FIPD 1970, FIMC 1980 (CMC), CIMgt 1985, FRSA 1990; *Books* Employment Law Keynotes (with C M Hodkinson, 1985), Manual for Small Business (1983), The Line Manager's Employment Law (16 edns since 1978); *Recreations* Wales, stamps, the business; *Clubs* RAC, Portico; *Style*— Leonard Collinson, Esq; ✉ Whimbrel, Kirklake Rd, Formby, Merseyside L37 2DA (☎ 01704 876928); Collinson Grant Group Ltd, Colgran House, 20 Worsley Rd, Swinton, Manchester M27 5WW (☎ 0161 793 9028, fax 0161 794 0012)

COLLINSON, Prof Patrick; CBE (1993); s of William Cecil Collinson (d 1952), and Belle Hay, *née* Patrick (d 1972); *b* 10 Aug 1929; *Educ* King's Sch Ely, Pembroke Coll Cambridge (MA, College prize), Univ of London (PhD); *m* Dec 1960, Elizabeth Albinia Susan, da of Geoffrey Selwyn (d 1934); 2 da (Helen Hay b 1962, Sarah Christina b 1965), 2 s (Andrew Cecil b 1963, Stephen Selwyn b 1968); *Career* Univ of London: postgrad student Royal Holloway Coll 1952–54, res fell Inst of Hist Res 1954–55, res asst UCL 1955–56; lectr in history Univ of Khartoum 1956–61, lectr in ecclesiastical history King's Coll London 1962–69 (asst lectr 1961–62); prof of history: Univ of Sydney 1969–75, Univ of Kent at Canterbury 1976–84; prof of modern history Univ of Sheffield 1984–88, fell Trinity Coll and regius prof of modern history Univ of Cambridge 1988–96; visiting fell All Souls Coll Oxford 1981, Andrew W Mellon fell Huntingdon Library Calif 1984, chm Advsy Editorial Bd Jl of Ecclesiastical History 1982–93; pres Ecclesiastical History Soc 1985–86, memb Cncl Br Acad 1986–89, memb Academia Europaea 1989, corresponding memb Mass Hist Soc 1990; Hon DUniv York 1988; Hon DLitt: Kent at Canterbury 1989, Trinity Coll Dublin 1992, Sheffield 1995; FRHistS 1967 (memb Cncl 1977–81, vice pres 1983–87 and 1994–), FBA 1982; *Books* The Elizabethan Puritan Movement (1967, USA 1967, reprinted 1982), Archbishop Grindal 1519–1583 - The Struggle for a Reformed Church (1979, USA 1979), The Religion of Protestants - The Church in English Society 1559–1625 (Ford Lectures Univ of Oxford 1979 and 1982), Godly People - Essays on

English Protestantism and Puritanism (1983), English Puritanism (1983), The Birthpangs of Protestant England - Religious and Cultural Change in the 16th and 17th Centuries (1988), Elizabethan Essays (1994), A History of Canterbury Cathedral (ed with N Ramsay and M Sparks, 1995); articles and reviews in Bull Inst of Historical Res, Eng History Review, Jl of Ecclesiastical History, Studies in Church History, TLS; *Recreations* hill walking, music, playing keyboard instruments, gardening; *Style*— Prof Patrick Collinson, CBE, FBA; ✉ The Winnats, Cannon Fields, Hathersage, Sheffield S30 1AG (☎ 0114 265 0333); Trinity College, Cambridge CB2 1TQ (☎ 01223 338400)

COLLIS, Pamela Caroline Neild; da of Michael Neild Collis, of Beds, and Ann, *née* Strong; *b* 9 March 1957; *Educ* Rosemead Sch for Girls Littlehampton Sussex, Univ of Bristol (LLB), Guildford Coll of Law; *m* 22 Dec 1987, Joseph Sinyor, s of Samuel Joseph Sinyor; 2 s (Joshua Samuel b 17 Nov 1988, Benjamin Jonathon b 30 June 1990); 1 da (Jessica Claire Rachael b 1 Jan 1994); *Career* asst slr Herbert Smith 1981–82 (articled clerk 1979–81); Kingsley Napley: joined 1982, ptnr 1985–, head Family Law Dept 1989–; memb City of London Slrs' Co 1994; memb: Law Soc, Slrs' Family Law Assoc, Justice; fell Acad of Int Matrimonial Lawyers; *Recreations* windsurfing, cycling, reading; *Style*— Ms Pamela Collis; ✉ Kingsley Napley, Knights Quarter, 14 St John's Lane, London EC1M 4AJ (☎ 0171 814 1200, fax 0171 490 2288)

COLLIS, Terrence Ivor; *b* 1 Feb 1954; *Educ* Laxton GS Oundle, Univ of Durham (BSc); *m* 21 Oct 1989, Sarah Lilian, da of Derek Anderson; 1 s (Benjamin Ivor b 7 May 1991), 1 da (Sophie Helena b 14 April 1993); *Career* press serv exec Nicholas Mendes & Associates 1975–76, press and PRO Barlow Handling Ltd 1976–78, press offr Lucas Group 1978–81, sr PR exec Hawker Siddeley Group 1981–85; Vickers plc: media rels mangr 1985–87, dep dir of public affrs 1988, dir of public affrs 1988–92; md Lowe Bell Financial 1992–97, dir of corp affrs and memb Exec Mgmnt Ctee National Westminster Bank plc 1997–; MIPR 1988, FRSA 1993; *Recreations* wicket-keeping, astronomy; *Clubs* Pimlico Interplanetary, Mortlake Casuals Cricket; *Style*— Terrence Collis, Esq; ✉ Director of Corporate Affairs, National Westminster Bank plc, 41 Lothbury, London EC2P 2BP (☎ 0171 726 1000, fax 0171 726 1920)

COLLISCHON, (Robert) David; s of Robert Frederick Collischon (d 1969), and Vera May, *née* Pilbeam; *Educ* Chigwell Sch; *m* 3 April 1965, Lesley Elizabeth, *née* Chard; 1 s (Adrian Robert b 1975), 2 da (Lois Anne b 1970, Hayley Claire b 1971); *Career* mktg mangr Fontana Books 1962–64, sales dir Studio Vista Ltd 1964–69, Crowell Collier MacMillian 1969–72, md Gower Press Ltd 1976 (mktg dir 1972–73), chm Bowker Publishing Co Ltd 1982–85 (md 1977–81), chm and md Norman & Hill Ltd 1980–87, chm Filofax Group plc 1987– (chief exec 1987–90); chm: Govrs and Tstees Davenant Fndn Sch 1992– (govr and tstee 1988–, chm Fin Ctee 1988–92), Chelmsford Diocesan Bd of Finance 1991–; Liveryman and memb Ct of Assts Worshipful Co of Marketors; *Books* Furniture Making (1967); *Recreations* sailing, badminton, bridge, music, gardening; *Clubs* IOD, RYA; *Style*— David Collischon, Esq; ✉ Filofax Group plc, Waverley House, 7–12 Noel St, London W1V 4BA (☎ 0171 432 3000, fax 0171 437 3594)

COLLIVER, David John; s of John Arthur Colliver (d 1963), of Penzance, and Evoline Gwendoline, *née* Padfield (d 1969); *b* 4 March 1939; *Educ* Humphry Davy GS Penzance, City Univ (BSc (Eng)); *m* 1964, Judith Carole, da of Peter Kelk Feather; 2 s (Timothy Jackson b 1966, Steven Peter b 1968), 1 da (Helen Janette b 1968); *Career* RSRE Malvern: project mangr Radar Systems 1973–81, divnl mangr Microwave Semiconductor Div 1981–85; tech mangr STC Semiconductors 1985–86, asst dir Directorate for Components, Valves and Devices MOD London 1986–89, tech dir (Electronics) Defence Research Agency 1996– (mangr Electronics Research Dept 1989–96); former conservator Malvern Hills, chm Falmouth Seagoing Trg Ship; played rugby for Blackheath, Hants and Cornwall; FIEE 1986 (MIEE 1968), FEng 1996; *Publications* Compound Semiconductor Technology (1976), Radar Hostile Fire Location (1980), Advanced Millimeter Wave Technology (1983); *Recreations* walking, cycling, water colour painting; *Clubs* Malvern Art; *Style*— David Colliver, Esq, FEng; ✉ 11 Stocks Lane, Newland, Malvern, Worcestershire WR13 5AZ (☎ 01886 832743); Defence Research Agency, St Andrew's Road, Malvern, Worcestershire WR14 3PS (☎ 01684 895049, fax 01684 895774, e-mail djcolliver@dra.hmg.gb)

COLLIVER, Douglas John; s of Douglas John Colliver (d 1983), of Farnborough, Hants, and Alice Emily, *née* White; *b* 22 March 1947; *Educ* The GS Farnborough, Univ of Bristol (LLB); *m* 27 Feb 1971, Lulu, da of Henry William Hayes (d 1983), of Camberley, Surrey; 3 s (Toby b 1972, Jasper b 1979, Giles b 1981), 1 da (Sophy b 1974); *Career* slr; articled clerk Durrant Cooper and Hambling 1969–71, ptnr Norton Rose Botterell and Roche (now Norton Rose) 1978– (joined 1973); memb: Int Bar Assoc, Law Soc, City of London Slrs' Co; *Recreations* reading, guitar, walking; *Style*— Douglas Colliver, Esq; ✉ Norton Rose, Kempson House, Camomile St, London EC3A 7AN (☎ 0171 283 6000, fax 0171 283 6500, telex 883652)

COLLS, Alan Howard Crawfurd; s of Maj Derek Archibald Colls, MBE (d 1991), of London, and Amy, *née* Christie-Crawfurd (d 1982); *b* 15 Dec 1941; *Educ* Harrow; *m* 20 March 1969, Janet Mary, da of Capt Michael Gillespie (d 1986); 1 s (Toby b 19 Dec 1970), 1 da (Nina b 15 Jan 1970); *Career* dir Stewart Wrightson Holdings plc 1981–87; chm: Stewart Wrightson Aviation Ltd 1975–86, Stewart Wrightson International Group 1981–85, Stewart Wrightson Ltd 1986–87, Nicholson Chamberlain Colls Ltd 1988–94, Nicholson Leslie Ltd 1994–; dep chm Lloyd's Insurance Brokers' Ctee 1986–87 and 1989–90 (chm 1991–92), memb Lloyd's Market Bd 1992–94; *Recreations* tennis, golf, travel; *Clubs* Annabel's; *Style*— Alan Colls, Esq; ✉ 23 Victoria Road, London W8 5RF (☎ 0171 937 7226); Nicholson Leslie Ltd, PO Box 615, Beaufort House, 15 St Botolph St, London EC3A 7QQ (☎ 0171 247 4466, ext 2001, fax 0171 375 1760, telex 929464)

COLLUM, Hugh Robert; s of Robert Archibald Hugh Collum (d 1976), and Marie Vivien, *née* Skinner (d 1978); *b* 29 June 1940; *Educ* Eton; *m* 24 July 1965, Elizabeth Noel, da of Gordon Stewart (d 1990), of Pontefract, Yorks; 2 da (Lucinda Elizabeth b 1967, Melissa Jane b 1969); *Career* Coopers and Lybrand 1959–64, dir Plymouth Breweries Ltd and Courage Western Ltd 1965–72; fin dir: Courage Ltd 1973–81, Cadbury Schweppes plc 1981–86, Beecham Group plc 1987–89, SmithKline Beecham plc 1989–; non-exec dir: Imperial Tobacco Ltd 1978–81, Ladbroke Courage Holidays Ltd 1976–81, Cncl of Brewers' Soc 1978–81, Sedgwick Group plc 1987–92, M & G Group plc 1992–, Ladbroke Group plc 1994–96; chm The Hundred Group of Fin Dirs 1990–92, memb Cadbury Ctee on Financial Aspects of Corp Governance 1991–95; Liveryman Worshipful Co of Wax Chandlers, memb Ct of Assts Worshipful Co of Chartered Accountants; FCA; *Recreations* sport, opera, shooting, travel; *Clubs* Boodle's, MCC; *Style*— Hugh R Collum, Esq; ✉ Clinton Lodge, Fletching, E Sussex TN22 3ST (☎ 01825 722952); SmithKline Beecham plc, One New Horizons Court, Brentford, Middlesex TW8 9EP (☎ 0181 975 2028, fax 0181 975 2040)

COLLYEAR, Sir John Gowen; kt (1986); s of John Robert Collyear (d 1968), and Amy Elizabeth, *née* Gowen (d 1995); *b* 19 Feb 1927; *Educ* Watford GS, Univ of Manchester, Univ of Leeds (BSc); *m* 1953, Catherine Barbara, da of William James Newman; 1 s (John), 2 da (Elizabeth, Kathryn); *Career* Lt RE; engr; chm: Glacier Metal Co Ltd 1972–76, AE plc (formerly Assoc Engrg) 1981–86 (gp md 1975–81), MK Electric Group plc 1987–88, USM Texon Ltd 1987–95; memb Senate Engrg Cncl 1996; pres: MIRA 1988–, Inst of Materials 1992–94; Liveryman Worshipful Co of Coachmakers & Coach Harness Makers; FEng 1979, Hon FIMechE, FIEE, FIM, FRSA, CIMgt; *Books* Management Precepts (1975), The Practice of First Level Management (1976); *Recreations* golf, bridge, music; *Clubs* Athenaeum; *Style*— Sir John Collyear, FEng; ✉ Walnut Tree House, Nether Westcote, Oxon OX7 6SD (☎ 01993 831247, fax/☎ 01993 830794)

COLLYMORE, Peter Keith; s of Eric Claude Collymore (d 1965), and Evelyn Marjorie, *née* Keith (d 1986); *b* 20 April 1929; *Educ* Marlborough, Univ of Cambridge (MA), Architectural Assoc Sch (Dip); *Career* Nat Serv 2 Lt 1947–49; architect; asst architect: Skidmore Owings and Merrill NY 1956, Robert Mathew and Johnson Marshall London 1957–59; architect in private practice 1959–; some 300 projects incl: library and rehearsal room for Benjamin Britten Aldeburgh, studies and house at Lancing Coll Sussex, many private houses and small shops nationally; former: assessor for Civic Tst, memb Professional Literature Ctee RIBA; *Books* House Conversion and Renewal (1974), The Architecture of Ralph Erskine (1982, revised 1994); *Recreations* cricket, painting; *Clubs* MCC; *Style*— Peter Collymore, Esq; ✉ Barrington Cottage, Byworth, Petworth, W Sussex GU28 0HJ (☎ and fax 01798 342978); Peter Collymore & Associates Architects, 80 Lamble St, London NW5 4AB (☎ 0171 267 7567, fax 0171 284 0860)

COLMAN, Hon Mr Justice; Hon Sir Anthony Colman; kt (1992); s of Solomon Colman (d 1991), and Helen, *née* Weiss (d 1987); *b* 27 May 1938; *Educ* Harrogate GS, Trinity Hall Cambridge (BA, MA); *m* 23 Aug 1964, Angela Barbara, da of Hyman Glynn (d 1984), of London; 2 da (Deborah b 1967, Rosalind b 1971); *Career* Nat Serv Instr RAEC 1957–59; called to the Bar Gray's Inn 1962; in commercial practice 1963 (specialising in shipping, int trade and insur), QC 1977, chm ctees of enquiry and disciplinary ctees at Lloyd's 1982–84, recorder of the Crown Court 1985, bencher Gray's Inn 1986, dep High Court judge 1987, judge of the High Court of Justice (Queen's Bench Div) 1992–, judge i/c Commercial List 1996–; memb Bar Cncl 1989–92; chm: Commercial Bar Assoc 1991–92 (treas 1989–91), The British-Bulgarian Law Assoc 1993–96; FCIArb 1978; *Books* Mathew's Practice of the Commercial Court (2 edn 1965), The Practice and Procedure of the Commercial Court (1983, 2 edn 1986, 4 edn 1995), The Encyclopaedia of International Commercial Litigation (gen ed and contrib, 1 edn 1991); *Recreations* cricket, tennis, gardening, painting; *Style*— The Hon Mr Justice Colman; ✉ Royal Courts of Justice, Strand, London WC2A 2LL (☎ 0171 936 7132, fax 0171 936 7421)

COLMAN, Prof David Robert; s of Colin Robert Colman, of London, and Jessica Ada, *née* Gregson (d 1972); *b* 14 May 1940; *Educ* Bury GS, Latymer Upper Sch, Wye Coll Univ of London (BSc), Univ of Illinois (MS), Univ of Manchester (PhD); *m* 9 Aug 1969, Susan, da of William Blundell (d 1952); 2 da (Lucy b 1974, Sophie b 1976); *Career* res asst Univ of Illinois 1963–65, tech advsr Govt of Malawi 1972–73, visiting prof Cornell Univ 1978–79; Univ of Manchester: lectr 1965–74, sr lectr 1974–79, prof 1979–, head Sch of Economic Studies 1994–; chm Exec Agric Economics Soc 1980–83 and 1989–91 (pres 1994–95); memb: AES 1965, IAEA 1974 (AAEA 1968); *Books* The United Kingdom Cereals Market (1972), Principles of Agricultural Economics (1989), Economics of Change in Less-Developed Countries (3 edn, 1994); *Recreations* badminton, fishing, philately, theatre, food and drink; *Style*— Prof David Colman; ✉ 11 Brooklyn Crescent, Cheadle, Cheshire SK8 1DX; School of Economic Studies, University of Manchester, Manchester M13 9PL (☎ 0161 275 4793, fax 0161 275 4929)

COLMAN, Jeremiah Michael Powlett (Jamie); s and h of Sir Michael Colman, 3 Bt; *b* 23 Jan 1958; *Educ* Eton, Univ of Leicester (LLB); *m* 10 Oct 1981, Susan Elizabeth, da of John Henry Britland, of York; 3 s (Joseph Jeremiah b 31 Nov 1988, Nathaniel James b 19 July 1990, Jacob Robert John b 4 June 1996), 1 da (Eleanor Mary b 1985); *Career* slr, ptnr Williams Davies Meltzer; *Recreations* forestry, shooting, golf; *Style*— Jamie Colman, Esq; ✉ 20 Henderson Road, London SW18 3RR

COLMAN, Jeremy Gye; s of Philip Colman, and Georgina Maude, *née* Gye; *b* 9 April 1948; *Educ* John Lyon Sch Harrow, Peterhouse Cambridge (MA), Imperial Coll London (MSc, DIC); *m* 20 Oct 1978 (m dis 1996), Patricia Ann, da of William Walter Stewart; *Career* CS offr 1971–75, princ HM Treasy 1975–78, CS Dept 1978–81, private sec to Head of Home Civil Service 1980–81, princ HM Treasy 1981–84, private sec to Permanent Sec and Jt Head of Home Civil Service 1981–82, asst sec HM Treasy 1984–87; dir County NatWest Ltd 1988–90, ptnr Price Waterhouse 1991–93, dir National Audit Office 1993–; *Recreations* cookery, opera, wine; *Clubs* United Oxford and Cambridge Univ, Ski Club of Great Britain; *Style*— J G Colman, Esq; ✉ 204 Clive Road, London SE21 8BS; Flat G, 10 Highbury Crescent, London N5 1RN (☎ 0181 761 8542); National Audit Office, 157–197 Buckingham Palace Road, London SW1W 9SP (☎ 0171 798 7000, fax 0171 828 3774)

COLMAN, Lady Mary Cecilia; *née* Bowes Lyon; da (twin) of Hon Michael Claude Hamilton Bowes Lyon (d 1953), 5 s of 14 Earl of Strathmore; sis of 17 Earl; raised to the rank of an Earl's da 1974; *b* 30 Jan 1932; *m* 10 Nov 1951, Timothy James Alan Colman, *qv*; 2 s, 3 da; *Career* an extra lady-in-waiting to HRH Princess Alexandra, the Hon Lady Ogilvy 1970–; *Style*— Lady Mary Colman; ✉ Bixley Manor, Norwich, Norfolk NR14 8SJ

COLMAN, Sir Michael Jeremiah; 3 Bt (UK 1907), of Gatton Park, Gatton, Surrey; s of Sir Jeremiah Colman, 2 Bt (d 1961); *b* 7 July 1928; *Educ* Eton; *m* 29 Oct 1955, Judith Jean Wallop, da of late Vice Adm Sir Peveril Barton Reibey William-Powlett, KCB, KCMG, CBE, DSO; 2 s (Jeremiah Michael Powlett b 1958, John Powlett b 1962), 3 da (Olivia Helena Judith (Mrs Patrick J Whitworth) b 1956, Victoria Rose (Mrs Matthew S Persson) b 1960, Alice Mary (Mrs Timothy A C Page) b 1965); *Heir* s, Jeremiah Michael Powlett Colman b 23 Jan 1958; *Career* chm Reckitt and Colman plc 1986–95; first church estates cmmr Church Commissioners 1993–; dir: Foreign & Colonial Ventures Advisors Ltd 1988–, UK Centre for Economic and Environmental Devpt 1985– (chm 1996–); memb Cncl: Royal Warrant Holders 1977– (pres 1984), Chemical Industries' Assoc 1983–84; assoc Trinity House 1984–93, memb Lighthouse Bd 1984–93, Younger Brother 1994–; memb Gen Cncl and Finance Ctee King Edward's Hosp Fund for London 1978–, special tstee for St Mary's Hosp 1988–, tstee The Royal Fndn Grey Coat Hosp 1989–; memb Cncl The Scouts' Assoc 1985–, memb Cncl of Mgmnt The Urban Fndn (London); memb Ct of Assts of Worshipful Co of Skinners 1985– (Master 1991); tstee Allchurches Tst Ltd 1994–; FRSA; *Recreations* farming, forestry, golf, shooting; *Clubs* Cavalry and Guards'; *Style*— Sir Michael Colman, Bt; ✉ Malshanger, Basingstoke, Hants RG23 7EY (☎ 01256 780252); Tarvie, Bridge of Cally, Blairgowrie, Perthshire PH10 7PJ (☎ 0125 0881 264); Church Commissioners, 1 Millbank, London SW1P 3JZ (☎ 0171 222 7010)

COLMAN, Dr Richard Douglas; s of Jack Douglas Colman, of Huby, York, and Muriel, *née* Longden; *b* 5 March 1949; *Educ* Ansdell County Secdy Mod Lytham St Annes, King Edward VII Lytham St Annes, Magdalene Coll Cambridge (MA, MB BChir), Bart's Med Coll, DipRCOG, MRCGP, Cert Moral Philosophy (Hull); *m* 17 March 1979, Mary Janet van der Westhuizen, da of Dr Fiona Waugh; 3 da (Rose Mary Fiona b 10 Sept 1983, Bethany Ellen b 19 May 1985, Shannon Elizabeth b 31 May 1992), 2 s (Jack Pieter Dale b 24 Feb 1987, Rowan Richard Grant b 27 June 1989); *Career* vocational trg in gen practice, ind med practice 1985– (challenged UK law on restrictions on advtg, lost High Ct judgement but appealed to Euro Ct of Human Rights, subsequently accepted friendly settlement with Govt following GMC's removal of restrictions at insistance of DTI 1993), current interest occupational med and the concept of stress (exercised individually in practice and at corp level); memb GMC 1994–; *Recreations* outdoor activities, practical self sufficiency; *Clubs* Hawks; *Style*— Dr Richard Colman; ✉ Cowl House, Bransdale, Fadmoor, York YO6 6JW (☎ 01751 432342); Holistic Counselling and Therapy Practice, 156 Fulford Road, York YO1 4DA (☎ 01904 620091)

COLMAN, Sir Timothy James Alan; KG (1996); s of Capt Geoffrey Russell Rees Colman (d 1935), of Framingham Chase, Norwich; *b* 19 Sept 1929; *Educ* RNC Dartmouth and Greenwich; *m* 1951, Lady Mary Cecelia Bowes Lyon (*see* Lady Mary Cecelia Colman); 2 s, 3 da; *Career* RN 1943–53, Lt 1950; chm Eastern Counties Newspapers Group Ltd 1969–96; dir: Reckitt & Colman plc 1978–89, Whitbread & Co plc 1980–86, Anglia Television Group Ltd 1987–94; JP Norfolk 1958, High Sheriff Norfolk 1970, Lord Lieut Norfolk 1978 (DL Norfolk 1968), pro-chllr Univ of East Anglia 1974– (chm Cncl 1974–85), tstee Carnegie UK Tst (chm 1982–87), chm Royal Norfolk Agric Assoc 1984– (pres 1982), chm of Tstees Norfolk and Norwich Festival; memb: Eastern Regnl Ctee Nat Tst 1967–71, Countryside Cmmn 1971–76, Advsy Ctee England Nature Conservancy Cncl 1974–80, Water Space Amenity Cmmn 1973–76; chm Norfolk Naturalists Tst 1962–74; Hon DCL Univ of E Anglia 1973; KStJ 1979; FRSA; *Clubs* Turf, Pratt's, Norfolk, Royal Yacht Squadron; *Style*— Sir Timothy Colman, KG; ✉ Bixley Manor, Norwich, Norfolk NR14 8SJ (☎ 01603 625298)

COLQUHOUN, Andrew John; s of Maj Kenneth James Colquhoun, MC (d 1990), and Christine Mary, *née* Morris; *b* 21 Sept 1949; *Educ* Tiffin Sch, Univ of Nottingham (BSc), Univ of Glasgow (PhD), City Univ (MBA); *m* 22 Feb 1975, Patricia, da of John Beardall; 1 s (Simon James b 1976), 1 da (Helen Elizabeth b 1978); *Career* FCO: joined 1974, served London and ME, seconded to Cabinet Office 1981–83, Planning Staff 1983–84; Shandwick Consultants 1984–86 (seconded to ICAEW), sec and chief exec ICAEW 1990– (dir of educn and trg 1987–90); sec Consultative Ctee of Accountancy Bodies 1990–; author of various articles on accountancy, educn and recruitment; *Recreations* bird watching, reading, walking, country life; *Clubs* Reform; *Style*— Andrew Colquhoun, Esq; ✉ Radford, Haywards Heath Road, Balcombe, West Sussex RH17 6NJ (☎ 01444 811367); ICAEW, PO Box 433, Moorgate Place, London EC2P 2BJ (☎ 0171 920 8100, fax 0171 920 8467, telex 884443)

COLQUHOUN, Prof David; *b* 19 July 1936; *Educ* Univ of Leeds (BSc), Univ of Edinburgh (PhD); *m* April 1976, Margaret Anne, *née* Boultwood; 1 s (Andrew Stuart b 24 Dec 1984); *Career* asst lectr Dept of Pharmacology Univ of Edinburgh 1962–64, visiting asst then assoc prof Dept of Pharmacology Yale Univ Sch of Med 1964–72, sr lectr Dept of Physiology and Biochemistry Univ of Southampton 1972–75 (acting head of dept 1974–75), sr lectr in pharmacology St George's Hosp Med Sch 1976–79; UCL: reader of pharmacology 1979–83, prof 1983–, chair 1985–, dir Wellcome Laboratory for Molecular Pharmacology 1993–; visiting scientist Dept of Physiology and Biophysics Univ of Washington 1974, visiting prof Max Planck Institut für Medizinische 1990–91; memb: Editorial Bd Jl of Physiology 1974–81, Sir Ronald Fisher Meml Ctee 1975– (tstee Meml Fund), Sectional Ctee Royal Soc 1988–91 (chm 1990), Editorial Bd Royal Soc Pubns 1989, Academia Europaea 1992; J C Krantz prize lectr Univ of Maryland 1987, Alexander von Humboldt prize 1990; FRS 1985; *Style*— Prof David Colquhoun, FRS; ✉ UCL, Gower Street, London WC1E 6BT

COLQUHOUN, (Ernest) Patrick; s of Wing-Cdr Edgar Edmund Colquhoun, MBE (d 1953), and Elizabeth Colquhoun (d 1986); *b* 5 Jan 1937; *Educ* Shrewsbury, Univ of Cambridge; *m* 16 Jan 1964, Patricia Susan Alexandra, da of Baron and Baroness Frederick von Versen (d 1953); 3 s (James b 1966, Henry b 1969, Frederick b 1980); *Career* Lt Scots Gds 1955–57; banker; md Henderson Administration Ltd 1969–76, vice pres Swiss Bank Corp 1983–88; dir: Electra Group Services Ltd 1978–79, Cavendish Partners Ltd 1990–; memb: Advsy Cncl Brazilian Investments SA 1975–, Trading Ctee Royal Sch of Needlework 1988–89, Int Advsy Ctee Befrienders Int 1990–94; *Recreations* shooting, cricket, music, ballet, fine art; *Clubs* Boodle's, Pratt's, MCC; *Style*— Patrick Colquhoun, Esq; ✉ 40 Markham Street, London SW3 3NR (☎ 0171 352 2737); Cavendish Partners Ltd, 36 Queen Anne Street, London W1M 9LB (☎ 0171 436 4770)

COLQUHOUN-DENVERS, Nicholas John Arthur; s of HE John Dalrymple Colquhoun-Denvers, Australian Consul-Gen, of Bombay, India, and Winifred May, *née* Mitchell; *b* 5 Jan 1949; *Educ* Christ Church Coll, Perth; *m* 20 May 1978, Anne Patricia, da of Maj Charles Walter Douglas Wellesley Alexander (d 1983), late of 3 Carabiniers and Royal Scots Dragoon Gds; *Career* offr RA served BAOR, Hong Kong, N Ireland Capt 1969–77, ret; sec to Chm Australian Public Service Bd Canberra 1966–69, with Adnan Khashoggi's Triad Corporation 1977–85; md: CLC 1985–87, Hurlingham (Management) Ltd 1987–, Fal Energy (UK) Ltd; Gen Service Medal 1971; *Recreations* polo, shooting, skiing; *Clubs* Carlton, Guards Polo, Ham Polo (chm); *Style*— Nicholas Colquhoun-Denvers, Esq; ✉ Dorchester Court, 77 Sloane Street, London SW1X 9SE (☎ 0171 259 5654/6808), 7 Wimpole Mews, London W1N 7TE (☎ 0171 486 2600, car 0860 366544)

COLQUHOUN OF LUSS, Capt Sir Ivar Iain; 8 Bt (GB 1786), of Luss, Dumbarton, JP (Dunbartonshire 1951), DL (1952); Chief of the Clan Colquhoun; s of Lt-Col Sir Iain Colquhoun, 7 Bt, KT, DSO, LLD (d 1948); *b* 4 Jan 1916; *Educ* Eton; *m* 17 April 1943, Kathleen, 2 da of late Walter Atholl Duncan, of 53 Cadogan Square, SW1; 1 s (and 1 s decd), 1 da (Iona Mary (Duchess of Argyll) b 1945); *Heir* s, Malcolm Rory Colquhoun b 20 Dec 1947; *Career* Capt Grenadier Gds; Hon Sheriff (former Hon Sheriff substitute); *Clubs* White's, Puffin's, Royal Ocean Racing; *Style*— Capt Sir Ivar Colquhoun of Luss, Bt, JP, DL; ✉ Camstraddan, Luss, Argyllshire G83 8NX (☎ 0143 686245)

COLQUHOUN, YR OF LUSS, Malcolm Rory; s and h of Capt Sir Ivar Colquhoun of Luss, 8 Bt; *b* 20 Dec 1947; *Educ* Eton, London Univ; *m* 1, 1978, Susan, da of Stewart W Timmerman, of Harrisburg, Penn, USA; 1 s (Patrick John b 17 Dec 1980); m 2, 6 Oct 1989, Katharine A H, eldest da of A C Mears, of Canberra, Australia; 1 s (Fergus Alexander Mears b 15 May 1991), 1 da (Georgina Iona Helena b 4 Feb 1993); *Clubs* White's, Turf; *Style*— Malcolm Colquhoun, yr of Luss; ✉ 74 Nightingale Lane, London SW12 8NR

COLSTON, His Hon Judge; Colin Charles; QC; yr s of Eric Lawrence Colston, JP (d 1975), of Buckinghamshire, and Catherine Colston; *b* 2 Oct 1937; *Educ* Rugby, Trinity Hall Cambridge (MA); *m* 23 March 1963, Edith Helga, da of Dr Wilhelm Hille (d 1993), of Austria; 2 s (Martin b 1965, Dominic b 1968), 1 da (Helen-Jane b 1970); *Career* Nat Serv 1956–58, cmmnd RNR 1957–64, Lt RNR; called to the Bar Gray's Inn 1962; in practice Midland and Oxford Circuit (recorder Midland Circuit 1968–69); memb of the Senate of the Inns of Court and Bar 1977–80, recorder Crown Court 1978–83, circuit judge (SE Circuit) 1983–, resident judge of Crown Court at St Albans 1989–; lay judge Court of Arches for Province of Canterbury 1992–; memb Criminal Ctee Judicial Studies Bd 1989–92, chm St Albans Diocesan Bd of Patronage 1989–; *Recreations* shooting, fishing; *Style*— His Hon Judge Colston, QC; ✉ The Crown Court, Bricket Road, St Albans, Herts AL1 3HY

COLT, Sir Edward William Dutton; 10 Bt (E 1694), of St James's-in-the-Fields Liberty of Westminster, Middlesex; s of Major John Rochfort Colt, N Staffs Regt (d 1944), half-bro of 9 Bt; suc unc Sir Henry Archer Colt, 9 Bt, DSO, MC (d 1951); *b* 22 Sept 1936; *Educ* Stoke House Seaford, Douai Sch, Univ Coll London (MB, FRCP); *m* 1, 20 Aug 1966 (m dis 1972), Jane Caroline, da of James Histed Lewis; m 2, 1979, Suzanne Nelson, *née* Knickerbocker; 1 s (Tristan Charles Edward b 1983, d 19 May 1992), 1 da (Angela Cecily b 1979); *Heir* none; *Career* assoc attending physician St Luke's Hosp New York, assoc clinical prof of med Columbia Univ; FACP; *Style*— Sir Edward Colt, Bt; ✉ 12 East 88 St, New York, NY 10128, USA

COLTART, Dr (Douglas) John; s of Frank Joseph John Coltart (d 1974), of Blandford, Dorset, and Hilda Kate, *née* Moore; *b* 7 Oct 1943; *Educ* Hardye's Sch Dorchester, St Bartholomew's Med Sch Univ of London (MD); *m* 7 May 1977, Linda Maitland, da of Stuart Douglas Luxon, of Maidensgrove, Riversdale, Bourne End, Bucks; 1 s (Rupert b 4 July 1978), 3 da (Cordelia b 7 Feb 1980, Clementine b 23 Sept 1982, Christianna b 19 June 1991); *Career* conslt physician and cardiologist Royal Masonic Hosp London 1974, conslt physician to St Luke's Hosp for The Clergy 1975 and St Dunstan's Hosp for the Blind 1980, currently conslt physician and cardiologist Guy's and St Thomas' Hosp London, conslt physician to the Met Police; visiting prof: univs in Middle East and Far East, Stanford Univ USA; author of chapters in textbooks of med and over 200 scientific pubns; sec Br Cardiac Soc, vice pres Postgrad Fedn, memb Exec Bds Br Heart Fndn Coronary Prevention Gp; memb: Br Cardiac Soc, Med Defence Union; Buckston Browne Prize of the Harveian Soc; Liveryman Worshipful Soc of Apothecaries, Freeman City of London; FRCP, FACC, FESC; *Books* Cardio-vascular Pharmacology (textbook); *Recreations* athletics, tennis, keep fit; *Style*— Dr John Coltart; ✉ 15 Upper Wimpole Street, London WIM 2TD (☎ 0171 4865787, fax 0171 486 5470, car 0860 735242)

COLTART, His Hon Judge; Simon Stewart; s of Gilbert McCallum Coltart, of Lindfield, Sussex, and Mary Louise, *née* Kemp; *b* 3 Sept 1946; *Educ* Epsom Coll, Univ of Leeds (LLB); *m* 8 March 1973, Sarah Victoria, da of John Claude Birts; 3 s (Mark Cresswell b 23 Nov 1974, Edward John (twin) b 23 Nov 1974, William James 3 June 1978); *Career* Called to the Bar Lincoln's Inn (Eastham Sch) 1969, jr SE Circuit Bar Mess 1970–71, jr Sussex Bar Mess 1973–86, recorder SE Circuit Bar Mess 1987–90, recorder 1987–91, circuit judge (SE Circuit) 1991–; memb Ct of Assts Worshipful Co of Grocers 1991 (Freeman 1975, Liveryman 1984); *Recreations* sailing, golf; *Clubs* Bar Yacht, Rye Golf; *Style*— His Hon Judge Coltart; ✉ Lewes Combined Court, High Street, Lewes, East Sussex BN7 1YB

COLTHURST, Charles St John; s and h of Sir Richard La Touche Colthurst, 9 Bt, *qv*; *b* 21 May 1955; *Educ* Eton, Magdalene Coll Cambridge (MA), Univ Coll Dublin; *m* 31 Oct 1987, Nora Mary, da of Mortimer Kelleher, of Dooniskey, Lissarda, Co Cork; 1 s (John Conway La Touche b 13 Oct 1988), 2 da (Charlotte Louisa Margaret b 31 May 1990, Isabel Janet Denys b 14 Nov 1991); *Career* slr (memb Law Soc of Ireland); farmer; *Recreations* tennis, watersports, golf, skiing, reading; *Clubs* MCC, Royal Irish Automobile, Royal Dublin Soc; *Style*— Charles Colthurst, Esq

COLTHURST, (George Silver) Oliver Annesley; yr s of Sir Richard St John Jefferyes Colthurst, 8 Bt (d 1955), of Blarney Castle, Co Cork, and Denys Maida Hanmer, *née* West (d 1965); *b* 1 March 1931; *Educ* Harrow, Trinity Coll Cambridge (MA); *m* 1, 10 Oct 1959 (m dis 1966), Hon Elizabeth Sophia Sidney, eld da of 1 Viscount De L'Isle, VC, KG, GCMG, GCVO, PC; 1 da (Shaunagh Anne Henrietta (Hon Mrs Crispin Money-Coutts) b 1961); m 2, 22 May 1968, Caroline Romaine, 2 da of late Cdr Anthony Boyce Combe, RN (d 1990), of South Creake, Fakenham, Norfolk; 2 da (Romaine Louisa b 1969, Rowena Barbara b 1971); *Career* Nat Serv 2 Lt LG; former memb London Stock Exchange; ptnr: de Zoete & Gorton 1961–76, de Zoete & Bevan 1976–81; conslt Tilney & Co until 1995, ret; memb Ct of Common Cncl (Broad Street Ward) 1976–80; Liveryman Worshipful Co of Goldsmiths; *Recreations* tennis, shooting, dendrology; *Clubs* Turf, Pratt's, MCC, I Zingari; *Style*— Oliver Colthurst, Esq; ✉ Le Bourg, 16450 Beaulieu-sur-Sonnette, St Claud, Charente, France (☎ 00 33 45 85 73 13, fax 00 33 45 85 73 29)

COLTHURST, Sir Richard La Touche; 9 Bt (I 1744), of Ardrum, Inniscarra, Co Cork; er s of Sir Richard St John Jefferyes Colthurst, 8 Bt (d 1955), and Denys Maida Hanmer, *née* West (d 1965); *b* 14 Aug 1928; *Educ* Harrow, Peterhouse Cambridge (MA); *m* 24 Oct 1953, Janet Georgina, da of Leonard Almroth Wilson-Wright (d 1971), of Coolcarrigan, Co Kildare; 3 s (Charles St John b 21 May 1955, James Richard b 1957, Henry Nicholas Almroth b 1959), 1 da (Georgina Margaret b 1961); *Heir* s, Charles St John Colthurst, *qv*; *Career* J & P Coats Ltd 1953–55, Lloyd's 1955–92; memb Dendrology Soc; Freeman of City of London, Liveryman Worshipful Co of Grocers; *Recreations* Blarney Castle International Horse Trials, cricket, gardening, forestry; *Clubs* MCC; *Style*— Sir Richard La Touche Colthurst, Bt; ✉ Blarney Castle, Co Cork, Republic of Ireland

COLTMAN, (Arthur) Leycester Scott; CMG (1993); s of Arthur Cranfield Coltman (d 1982), and Vera, *née* Vaid (d 1971); *b* 24 May 1938; *Educ* Rugby, Magdalene Coll Cambridge; *m* 21 March 1969, (Maria) Piedad Josefina, *née* Cantos Aberasturi, da of Excmo Sr Antonio Cantos Guerrero, of Gen Moscardo 20, Madrid 20, Spain; 2 s (Roland b 1974, Stephen b 1978), 1 da (Beatrice b 1971); *Career* FCO: joined 1961, third sec Copenhagen 1963–64; second sec: Cairo 1964–66, Madrid 1966–69; Manchester Business Sch 1969–70 (sabbatical year), FCO 1970–74, first sec Brasilia 1974–77, FCO 1977–79; cnsllr and head of chancery: Mexico City 1979–83, Brussels 1983–87; head Mexico and Central American Dept FCO 1987–90, head Latin America Dept FCO 1990–91; HM ambass: Cuba 1991–94, Colombia 1994–; *Recreations* squash, chess, books, music; *Style*— HE Mr Leycester Coltman, CMG; ✉ c/o Foreign & Commonwealth Office (Bogota), King Charles St, London SW1A 2AH

COLTON, Prof Christopher Lewis; s of Lewis Henry Colton (d 1983), of Northfield, Nottingham, and Florence Clarke, *née* Haynes (d 1992); *b* 9 Sept 1937; *Educ* Worksop Coll, St Thomas's Hosp Med Sch (MB BS); *m* 1, 16 Feb 1960 (m dis 1980), Verena Hilary, da of Anthony David Hunt (d 1980), of Chichester; 3 s (Mark Anthony b 1 Aug 1960, Carl Andrew b 5 July 1962, Douglas John b 14 Sept 1963), 1 da (Samantha Mary b 15 Dec 1964); m 2, 2 Dec 1980, Josephine Mary, da of Joseph Peacock, of Barnsley, S Yorks; *Career* Hon Lt-Col Nigerian Armed Forces Med Servs 1968; lectr in orthopaedic surgery Inst of Orthopaedics Univ of London 1970–73, sr surgical offr Royal Nat Orthopaedic Hosp London 1970–73, prof of trauma and orthopaedic surgery Nottingham Univ Hosp 1973–; pres Br Orthopaedic Assoc; FRCS 1963, LRCP, FBOA 1973, FRCSEd 1979; *Books* Orthopaedics (with Hughes and Benson, 1987), Frontiers in Fracture Management (with Bunker and Webb, 1988), Atlas of Orthopaedic Surgical Approaches (with Hall, 1991), AO/ASIF Instrumentation - A Technical Handbook (with Texhammer, 1993); *Recreations* running, skiing, computer graphics, public speaking; *Style*— Prof Christopher Colton; ✉ Queen's Medical Centre, Nottingham NG7 2UH (☎ 0115 924 9924)

COLTON, Mary Winifred; da of James Colton (d 1952), and Winifred Alice, *née* Smith; *b* 2 Jan 1933; *Educ* Kingsbury Co Sch, Univ of London (LLB); *Career* called to the Bar Middle Temple 1955, SE Circuit, recorder of the Crown Court 1989–; *Style*— Miss Mary Colton; ✉ 4 Brick Court, The Temple, London EC4Y 9AD (☎ 0171 583 8455, fax 0171 353 1699)

COLTRANE, Robbie (formerly McMillan); s of Dr Ian Baxter McMillan (d 1969), of Rutherglen, Glasgow, and Jean Ross, *née* Howie; *b* 31 March 1950; *Educ* Trinity Coll Glenalmond, Glasgow Sch of Art (Dip Drawing and Painting); *Career* actor; BAFTA Best Actor nomination for Tutti Frutti 1987, Evening Standard Peter Sellers Award for contribution to Br film comedy 1990; involved with: Lab Pty, Amnesty, Greenpeace, Friends of the Earth, CND, Freeze; hon pres Herriot-Watt Univ; *Theatre* toured univs with the San Quentin Theatre Workshop 1974–75, John Byrne's Slab Boys and Threads (Traverse Theatre Edinburgh) 1975–79, Snobs and Yobs (Edinburgh Festival) 1980, Your Obedient Servant (one man show on Dr Samuel Johnson, Lyric Hammersmith) 1987, Mistero Buffo 1990; *Television* incl: Alfresco (2 series), A Kick Up the Eighties, The Lenny Henry Show, The Comic Strip Presents (various programmes), Laugh I Nearly Paid My Licence Fee, The Young Ones (several guest roles), Saturday Night Live, Girls on Top, Tutti Frutti (lead role), Blackadder III (guest role) and Blackadder Xmas Special, Emma Thompson Show, Arena, Robbie Coltrane Special, GLC and S Atlantic Raiders (Comic Strip Presents), Mistero Buffo 1990, The Bogie Man, Alive and Kicking 1991; co-writer (with Morag Fullarton) and dir Jealousy (short film for BBC2), Coltrane in a Cadillac (ITV) 1993, Cracker (Granada 1993–95, winner Broadcast Press Guild Best Actor Award 1994, BAFTA Best TV Actor Award 1994, 1995 and 1996,

RTS Best Male Performance Award 1994, Cable Ace (USA) Award for Best Actor 1995), Silver Nymph (Best Performance TV Series, Monte Carlo 1994, FIPA Award for Best Actor Nice 1994); *Films* incl: Scrubbers 1982, The Supergrass (Comic Strip feature film) 1984, Defence of the Realm 1985, Caravaggio 1985, Absolute Beginners 1985, Mona Lisa 1985, Eat the Rich 1987, The Fruit Machine 1987, Slipstream 1988, Danny Champion of the World 1988, Henry V (as Falstaff) 1988, Let It Ride 1988, Nuns on the Run 1989, Perfectly Normal 1989, The Pope Must Die 1990, Oh What a Night 1991, Huck Finn 1992, Goldeneye 1995; *Recreations* vintage cars, painting, sailing, clubs, playing piano; *Clubs* Groucho, Colony Room, Moscow, Glasgow Arts; *Style*— Robbie Coltrane, Esq; ✉ c/o CDA, 47 Courtfield Rd, London SW3 (☎ 0171 370 0708, fax 0171 835 1403)

COLVILL, Robert; *Career* Marks and Spencer plc: md Marks and Spencer Financial Services 1985, dir financial activities 1990, fin dir 1993–; non-exec dir Witan Investment Company 1994–; chm Money Advice Tst 1995–; *Style*— Robert Colvill, Esq; ✉ Marks and Spencer plc, Michael House, Baker Street, London W1A 1DN (☎ 0171 935 4422)

COLVILLE, Hon Angus Richmond; yst s of Cdr 3 Viscount Colville of Culross, RN (k on active service 1945), and Kathleen Myrtle, Viscountess Colville of Culross, OBE, *née* Gale (d 1986); *b* 29 April 1939; *Educ* Rugby; *Career* Lt Grenadier Gds (Reserve); chartered surveyor; ptnr Colvilles Tavistock; FRICS; *Style*— The Hon Angus Colville; ✉ 1 Bedford Place, Tavistock, Devon PL19 8AZ (☎ 01822 614206, office 01822 614507, fax 01822 617577)

COLVILLE, Master of; Hon Charles Mark Townshend Colville; s and h of 4 Viscount Colville of Culross, *qv*; *b* 5 Sept 1959; *Educ* Rugby, Univ of Durham (BA); *Style*— The Master of Colville

COLVILLE, John; s of James Colville, and Mary Jane, *née* Orr; *b* 28 June 1930; *Educ* Royal Belfast Acad Inst, Queen's Univ Belfast; *m* 11 October 1956, Edith Naomi, da of T J Johnston; 2 s (James Jay b 1958, John Colin b 1960); *Career* conslt plastic surgn; pres Br Soc for Surgery of the Hand 1988, pres Br Assoc of Plastic Surgns 1990; FRCSEd, FRCSI; *Recreations* sailing, model engineering; *Style*— John Colville, Esq; ✉ Belmore, Ballylesson, Belfast BT8; 7 Derryvolgie Ave, Belfast BT9 (☎ 01232 381530)

COLVILLE, Lady Margaret; *née* Egerton; CVO (1994); da of 4 Earl of Ellesmere; *b* 20 July 1918; *m* 20 Oct 1948, Sir John Rupert Colville, CB, CVO (d 1987); 2 s (Alexander George b 1955, Rupert Charles b 1960), 1 da ((Elizabeth) Harriet (Mrs David Bowes-Lyon) b 1952); *Career* ATS (Jr Subaltern) 1939–45; lady-in-waiting to HRH Princess Elizabeth 1946–49, extra lady-in-waiting to HM Queen Elizabeth The Queen Mother; pres Friendly Almshouses; *Style*— The Lady Margaret Colville, CVO; ✉ The Close, Broughton, nr Stockbridge, Hants (☎ 01794 301331)

COLVILLE, Dr Robert Lawson Kellock; s of William Innes Colville (d 1974), of Glasgow, and Lille, *née* Lawson (d 1955); *b* 13 Feb 1928; *Educ* Hutchesons Boys' GS, Univ of Glasgow (MB ChB); *m* 12 Aug 1954, Jean Murray, da of William Angus McKenzie (d 1981), of Glasgow; 2 s (Douglas (Dr) b 1956, Graeme b 1959); *Career* Lt RA 1946–48; hon clinical lectr Univ of Glasgow (assoc advsr in gen practice 1975); non-exec dir Victoria Infirmary NHS Tst Glasgow 1993–; RCGP: chm W of Scot Faculty 1981–85, vice chm UK Cncl 1985–86, chm Educn Div 1986–89; chm Open Learning Unit Scot Cncl for Postgrad Med Educn; DRCOG 1954, FRCGP 1978, AFOM 1981; *Recreations* golf; *Clubs* Prestwick Golf, Western Gailes Golf, Pollock Golf, Royal Scot Automobile; *Style*— Dr Robert Colville; ✉ 34 Fairfield Drive, Clarkston, Glasgow G76 7YH (☎ 0141 644 1664); 43 Los Altos de Marbella, Marbella, Costa del Sol, Spain

COLVILLE OF CULROSS, 4 Viscount (UK 1902); John Mark Alexander Colville; QC (1978); also 14 Lord Colville of Culross (S precedency 1609) and 4 Baron Colville of Culross (UK 1885); s of 3 Viscount (k on active service 1945); 1 cous of Lord Carrington and 1 cous once removed of late Sir John Colville; *b* 19 July 1933; *Educ* Rugby, New Coll Oxford; *m* 1, 4 Oct 1958 (m dis 1973), Mary Elizabeth, da of Col Mostyn Hird Wheeler Webb-Bowen, RM; 4 s; m 2, 1974, Margaret Birgitta, LLB, JP (Inner London), barr 1985, da of Maj-Gen Cyril Henry Norton, CB, CBE, DSO, and former w of 2 Viscount Davidson; 1 s (Hon Edmund Carleton b 1978); *Heir* s, Master of Colville, *qv*; *Career* sits as cross-bench Peer in Lords; Lt Gren Gds (Reserve); called to the Bar Lincoln's Inn, bencher Lincoln's Inn 1986, recorder 1990–93, circuit judge (SE Circuit) 1993–; min of state Home Office 1972–74, UK rep UN Human Rights Cmmn 1980–83, special rapporteur on Guatemala 1983–87, memb UN Human Rights Ctee 1996–; exec dir Br Electric Traction Co 1981–84 (and cos in gp 1968–84), dir Securities and Future Authy until 1993; chm: Mental Health Act Cmmn 1983–1987, Alcohol Educn and Res Cncl 1984–90, Parole Bd for England and Wales 1988–92; memb Royal Co of Archers (Queen's Body Gd for Scotland); *Style*— His Hon Judge The Viscount Colville of Culross, QC; ✉ Worlingham Hall, Beccles, Suffolk NR34 7RA (☎ 01502 713191); Harrow Crown Court, Hailsham Drive, off Headstone Drive, Harrow HA1 4TU

COLVIN, Andrew James; s of Gilbert Russell Colvin, OBE, and Dr Beatrice Colvin; *b* 28 April 1947; *Educ* LLM; *m* 1971, Helen Mary, *née* Ryan; 3 da (Clare b June 1975, Fiona b March 1979, Sarah b March 1982), 1 s (Simon b May 1977); *Career* admitted as slr 1975, articled clerk then asst town clerk London Borough of Ealing 1971–82, dep town clerk and borough slr Royal Borough of Kensington and Chelsea 1982–89, the Comptroller and City Slr The Corp of London 1989–; Vice Chamberlain of London; pres City of London Arizona Educnl Tst Inc; advsr: LBA 1985, AMA 1990, ALG 1996; govr: St Gregory's RC Sch 1989–92, Cardinal Wiseman RC Sch 1992–; Freeman City of London 1989; *Recreations* sailing, cycling, music; *Style*— Andrew Colvin, Esq; ✉ The Comptroller and City Solicitor, The Corporation of London, PO Box 270, Guildhall, London EC2P 2EJ (☎ 0171 606 3030 ext 1660)

COLVIN, Dr Brian Trevor; s of Clifford James Leslie Colvin (d 1990), of Sevenoaks, and Ivy Emmeline, *née* Goodchild (d 1996); *b* 17 Jan 1946; *Educ* Sevenoaks Sch, Clare Coll Cambridge (MA, MB BChir), London Hosp Med Coll; *m* 21 Aug 1971, Kathryn Frances, da of Ernest Osborne (d 1966); *Career* sr lectr in haematology and conslt haematologist: St Peter's Hosp Gp and Inst of Urology 1977–86, St Bartholomew's & the Royal London Hosp Sch of Med and Royal Hosps Tst; med postgrad sub dean London Hosp Med Coll 1987–96, dir of postgrad med and dental educn Royal Hosps Tst 1996–; memb: Standing Ctee of Membs RCP 1973–77, Ctee Br Soc for Haematology 1983–86, Med Advsy Ctee The Haemophilia Soc 1993–; chm: Haemostasis and Thrombosis Sub-Ctee BCSH 1991–94, Steering Ctee UK Nat External Quality Assurance Scheme (NEQAS) in Blood Coagulation 1992–96, UK Haemophilia Centre Dirs Orgn 1993–96, Panel of Examiners in Haematology RCPath 1994–, Nat Quality Assurance Advsy Panel in Haematology 1996–; pres Cncl Pathology Section RSM 1996–; Liveryman Worshipful Soc of Apothecaries; memb BMA; FRCPath 1988 (MRCPath 1976), FRCP 1990 (MRCP 1972), FRSM 1989; *Publications* author of various papers, articles and contrib to books incl Haematology Pocket Consultant (with A C Newland, 1988); *Recreations* foreign travel, opera, cricket; *Clubs* MCC; *Style*— Dr Brian Colvin; ✉ Department of Haematology, Royal London Hospital, Whitechapel Rd, London E1 1BB (☎ 0171 377 7455, fax 0171 377 7016)

COLVIN, HE David Hugh; CMG (1993); s of Maj Leslie Hubert Boyd Colvin, MC (d 1996), of Great Baddow, Essex, and Edna Mary, *née* Parrott; *b* 23 Jan 1941; *Educ* Lincoln Sch, Trinity Coll Oxford (MA); *m* 15 May 1971, Diana Caroline Carew, da of Gordon MacPherson Lang Smith, of London; 1 s (Thomas b 1983), 1 da (Charlotte b 1991); *Career* asst princ Bd of Trade 1966; HM Foreign Serv: Central Dept FO 1967, second sec Bangkok 1968–71, Euro Integration Dept FCO 1971–75, first sec Paris 1975–77, first sec (press and info) UK Perm Representation to the Euro Community Brussels 1977–82, cnsllr on loan to the Cabinet office 1982–85, cnsllr and head of Chancery Budapest 1985–88, head SE Asian Dept FCO 1988–92, min Br Embassy Rome 1992–96, HM ambass Brussels 1996–; *Recreations* shooting, tennis, military history, rallying antique cars; *Clubs* Travellers'; *Style*— HE Mr David Colvin, CMG; ✉ c/o FCO (Brussels), King Charles St, London, SW1A 2AH

COLVIN, John Horace Ragnar; CMG (1967); s of Adm Sir Ragnar Colvin, KBE, CB (d 1953), and Frances Sibyl, *née* Kays (d 1985); *b* 18 June 1922; *Educ* RNC Dartmouth, Univ of London; *m* 1, Nov 1948 (m dis 1961), (Elizabeth) Anne, da of Walford Manifold, MC (d 1960), of Mortlake, Victoria, Aust; 1 s (Mark b 1953), 1 da (Zoe b 1955); m 2, 11 Nov 1967, Moranna Sibyl de Lerisson, da of David de Lerisson Cazenove (d 1989), of Woodham Mortimer Lodge, Essex; 1 s (David b 1970), 1 da (Joanna b 1968); *Career* RN 1935–51; HM Dip Serv 1951–80; Oslo, Vienna, Kuala Lumpur, Hanoi (HM consul-gen), Ulan Bator (HM ambass), Washington; vice pres and dir international relations Chase Manhattan Bank 1980–86, dir Robert Fraser & Ptnrs 1986–92; dir Weighbridge Trust; *Publications* Twice Around The World, Not Ordinary Men, Volcano under Snow, Lions of Judah; *Clubs* Beefsteak, Brooks's; *Style*— John Colvin, Esq, CMG; ✉ 12A Evelyn Mansions, Carlisle Place, London SW1 (☎ 0171 834 6514)

COLVIN, Michael Keith Beale; MP (C) Romsey and Waterside (majority 15,304); s of Capt Ivan Beale Colvin, RN, and Joy Frances, OBE, *née* Arbuthnot (*see* Burke's Landed Gentry, 18 edn, Vol I, 1965); *b* 27 Sept 1932; *Educ* Eton, RMA Sandhurst, RAC Cirencester; *m* 1956, Hon Nichola, da of Baron Cayzer (Life Peer), *qv*; 1 s (James b 1965), 2 da (Amanda b 1957, Arabella b 1960); *Career* served Grenadier Guards 1950–57: Queen's Co 1954–55, BAOR Berlin 1954–55, Suez Campaign, Cyprus 1956–57; with J Walter Thompson Co Ltd 1958–63, Andover RDC 1965–72, vice chm Test Valley BC 1972–74 (fndr pres); MP (C): Bristol NW 1979–83, Romsey and Waterside 1983–; PPS: to Baroness Young Dep Foreign Sec 1983–85, to Rt Hon Richard Luce FCO and Min of the Arts and Civil Serv 1983–87; memb Select Ctee for: Employment 1981–83, Energy 1990–92, Defence 1992– (chm 1995–); Cons Foreign Affrs Ctee: sec 1987–91, vice chm 1991–92, chm 1992–; memb Post Office Stamp Advsy Ctee 1981–84; chm: Cons Aviation Ctee 1982–83 and 1987–92, West Country MPs 1982–83, Br Gibraltar Gp, Br Lithuania Gp, Cncl for Country Sports 1987–, Test Valley Arts Fndn 1988–, Cons Abroad 1992–; vice chm Cons Smaller Business Ctee 1980–83; dep chm Winchester Cons Assoc 1973–76; farmer and landowner; fndr pres Council for the Protection of Rural England (CPRE), pres Hampshire Young Farmers' Clubs 1973–75, vice chm Br Field Sports Soc 1987–94, memb Cncl and Exec Ctee CLA; dir: Royal British Legion Training Company, Ludgate Laud Ltd 1993–95; govr Enham Tst 1965–; Parly advsr: Royal British Legion, Nat Licenced Victuallers' Assoc 1983–88; memb Lloyd's; *Books* Britain, a View from Westminster (jtly); *Recreations* painting, field sports; *Clubs* Turf, Pratt's, Kennel; *Style*— Michael Colvin, Esq, MP; ✉ Tangley House, Andover, Hants SP11 0SH (☎ 01264 730215); c/o The House of Commons, London SW1A 0AA (☎ 0171 219 4208)

COLWYN, 3 Baron (UK 1917); Sir (Ian) Anthony Hamilton-Smith; 3 Bt (UK 1912), CBE (1989); s of 2 Baron Colwyn (d 1966); *b* 1 Jan 1942; *Educ* Cheltenham Coll, Univ of London (BDS, LDS, RCS); *m* 1, 30 May 1964 (m dis 1977), Sonia Jane, er da of Peter Henry Geoffrey Morgan; 1 s, 1 da (Hon Jacqueline b 5 March 1967); m 2, 1977, Nicola Jeanne, da of Arthur Tyers; 2 da (Hon Kirsten b 17 Jan 1981, Hon Tanya b 14 Jan 1983); *Heir* s, Hon Craig Peter Hamilton-Smith b 13 Oct 1968; *Career* dental surgeon 1966–, chm Dental Protection Ltd 1995–; non-exec dir Cortecs International; sits as Conservative in House of Lords, jt pres Parly All Pty Gp on Alternative and Complementary Medicine 1989; memb Cncl Medical Protection Soc; pres: Natural Medicines Soc 1988, Arterial Health Fndn 1993, Soc for Advancement of Anaesthesia in Dentistry, Huntington's Disease Assoc; patron: Blackie Fndn, Res Cncl for Complementary Medicine, Eastman Research Inst; musician, leader of own dance band and orchestra; *Style*— The Rt Hon the Lord Colwyn, CBE; ✉ 53 Wimpole St, London W1M 7DF (☎ 0171 935 6809)

COLWYN-THOMAS, Anthony (Tony); s of Bertie Colwyn-Thomas, of Bridgend, and Brenda, *née* Kendrick; *b* 5 Oct 1956; *Educ* Ogmore GS, Univ of Southampton (BSc); *m* 1982, Janet, da of James Harries; 2 s (Owain b 19 Dec 1986, Trystan b 1 July 1988); *Career* qualified as chartered accountant KPMG 1978–82, internal auditor and fin accountant Bass plc 1982–85, gp fin accountant Forte plc 1985–87, co accountant Hamells (subsid of C & A) 1987–88, fin controller/co sec ACL (subsid of Standard Chartered Bank plc) 1988–93, mangr Business Planning and Risk Mgmnt Halifax Mortgage Services Ltd 1993–; memb Cncl ICAEW; memb Ctee S Wales Dist Soc of Chartered Accountants, former memb Br Jr Chamber Cardiff; FCA 1991 (ACA 1981); *Recreations* local history, football, gardening, bringing up two very active young sons; *Style*— Tony Colwyn-Thomas, Esq; ✉ Halifax Mortgage Services Ltd, Trinity Court, 21–27 Newport Road, Cardiff CF2 1AA (☎ 01222 783932, fax 01222 783898)

COLYER, His Hon Judge; John Stuart; QC (1976); s of Stanley Herbert Colyer, MBE (d 1986), of Worthing, Sussex and Sevenoaks, Kent, and Louisa, *née* Randle (d 1976); *b* 25 April 1935; *Educ* Dudley GS, Shrewsbury, Worcester Coll Oxford (open scholar); *m* 24 June 1961, Emily Warner, da of the late Stanley Leyland Dutrow, of Blue Ridge Summit, Pennsylvania, USA; 2 da (Dr Elizabeth Emily Stuart b 13 April 1964, Mary Susan Stuart b 2 July 1969); *Career* Nat Serv 1953–55, 2 Lt RA, serv BAOR with T Battery (Shah Sujah's Troop) RA at Celle; called to the Bar Middle Temple 1959 (bencher 1983); instr Univ of Pennsylvania Law Sch Philadelphia USA 1959–60 (asst prof 1960–61); memb Midland and Oxford (formerly Oxford) Circuit 1962–91, in practice London; recorder of the Crown Ct 1985–91, circuit judge (SE Circuit) 1991–; Inns of Court Sch of Law: lectr in law of landlord and tenant 1970–89, hon reader 1982–; memb Cncl of Legal Educn 1983–92, vice pres Lawyers' Christian Fellowship 1990– (chm 1981–89); *Books* Modern View Law of Torts (1966), Encyclopaedia Forms and Precedents (Landlord and Tenant) (ed jtly, 4 edn, vols 11 and 12), Megarry's Rent Acts (gen ed, 11 edn, 1988), Halsbury's Laws (Landlord & Tenant) (4 edn 1981, re-issued 1994); *Recreations* travel, gardening (especially collecting & growing Lithops & cacti), opera; *Style*— His Hon Judge Colyer, QC; ✉ c/o Law Courts, Barker Road, Maidstone, Kent ME16 8EQ

COLYER-FERGUSSON, Sir James Herbert Hamilton; 4 Bt (UK 1866), of Spitalhaugh, Peeblesshire; s of Capt Max Christian Hamilton Colyer-Fergusson, RASC (ka 1940, s of 3 Bt); suc gf Sir Thomas Colyer Colyer-Fergusson, 3 Bt, 1951; *b* 10 Jan 1917; *Educ* Harrow, Balliol Coll Oxford (BA, MA); *Heir* none; *Career* formerly Capt The Buffs; offr British Railways, ret; *Style*— Sir James Colyer-Fergusson, Bt; ✉ Flat 8, 61 Onslow Square, London SW7 3LS

COMBERMERE, 5 Viscount (UK 1826); Sir Michael Wellington Stapleton-Cotton; 10 Bt (E 1677); Baron Combermere (UK 1814); s of 4 Viscount Combermere (d 1969); *b* 8 Aug 1929; *Educ* Eton, King's Coll London (BD, MTh); *m* 4 Feb 1961, Pamela Elizabeth, da of Rev Robert Gustavus Coulson, of The Old Vicarage, Moulsford, nr Wallingford, Oxon; 1 s, 2 da; *Heir* s, Hon Thomas Robert Wellington Stapleton-Cotton b 30 Aug 1969; *Career* short serv cmmn pilot RAF 1950–58, ret as Flt Lt; lectr in biblical and religious studies Birkbeck Coll Centre for Extra Mural Studies Univ of London 1972–94 (sr lectr 1988–94); chm World Congress of Faiths 1983–88; *Clubs* RAC; *Style*— The Rt Hon the Viscount Combermere; ✉ Vanners, Bucklebury, nr Reading, Berkshire (☎ 0118 971 3336)

COMFORT, Dr Alexander; s of late Alexander Charles Comfort, and Daisy Elizabeth Comfort; *b* 10 Feb 1920; *Educ* Highgate Sch, Trinity Coll Cambridge (Robert Styring scholar, sr scholar, MB BCh, MA), London Hosp (scholar, DCH, PhD, DSc); *m* 1, 1943 (m dis 1973), Ruth Muriel Harris; 1 s; m 2, 1973, Jane Tristram Henderson (d 1991); *Career* physician, poet, novelist; lectr in physiology London Hosp Med Coll 1948–51, hon res assoc Dept of Zoology UCL 1951–73, dir res gerontology UCL 1966–73, prof Dept of Pathology Univ of California Sch of Med 1976–78, conslt psychiatrist Brentwood VA Hosp LA 1978–81, clinical lectr Dept of Psychiatry Stanford Univ 1979–83, adjunct prof Neuropsychiatric Inst Univ of California 1980–91, conslt Ventura Co Hosp (Medical Educn) 1981–91; pres Br Soc for Res on Ageing 1967; memb RSM; *Publications* The Silver River (1937), No Such Liberty (novel, 1941), Into Egypt (play, 1942), A Wreath for the Living (poems, 1943), The Almond Tree (novel, 1943), The Powerhouse (novel, 1944), Letters From an Outpost (stories, 1947), Art & Social Responsibility (essays, 1974), The Signal to Engage (poems, 1974), On This Side Nothing (novel, 1948), Barbarism and Sexual Freedom (essays, 1948), Authority and Delinquency in the Modern State (social psychology, 1950), Come Out to Play (novel, 1961), The Koka Shastra (translation, 1964), The Process of Ageing (science, 1965), The Joy of Sex (counselling, 1973), More Joy of Sex (counselling, 1974), The Facts of Love (with Jane T Comfort, 1979), A Practice of Geriatric Psychiatry (1979), Tetrarch (trilogy of novels, 1980), Reality and Empathy (1983), What about Alcohol? (with Jane T Comfort, textbook, 1983), The Patient (novel, 1987), The Philosophers (novel, 1989), The New Joy of Sex (Mitchell Beazley, 1992), Mikrokosmos (poems, 1994); *Style—* Dr Alexander Comfort; ✉ 2 Fitzwarren House, Hornsey Lane, London N6 5LX

COMINS, Peter Crawford Melhuish; s of late Capt Dennis Comins, MC; *b* 25 Nov 1930; *Educ* Ampleforth, Lincoln Coll Oxford; *m* 1963, Dinah, *née* Collins; 3 s; *Career* dir: Borax Consolidated Ltd, Borax Holdings Ltd 1969–90; chm Lowestoft Enterprise Tst 1990– (dir 1987–); *Recreations* shooting, skiing; *Style—* Peter Comins, Esq; ✉ Hornpie House, Wiveton, Holt, Norfolk (☎ 01263 740311)

COMNINOS, Michael; s of John Michael Comninos (d 1976), of Holland Park, London, and Elsie Rose, *née* Turner (d 1990); *b* 25 July 1931; *Educ* Malvern; *m* 14 Jan 1956, Ann, da of Stanley Graves (d 1985); 1 s (Charles b 1956), 1 da (Sarah Helen b 1962); *Career* Lt RTR 1950–52; ptnr N M Rothschild & Sons 1965–70; dir: N M Rothschild & Sons Ltd 1970–91, Old Court International Reserves Ltd 1980–94, Old Court Currency Fund Ltd 1991–94; non-exec dir: First National Finance Corporation plc 1991–95, Tyndall & Co Ltd 1991–94; FCIB, FCIS, FCT, AIIMR; *Recreations* collecting antiquities, skiing; *Clubs* Brooks's, Bankers; *Style—* Michael Comninos, Esq; ✉ Staithe House, Chiswick Mall, London W4 2PR (☎ 0181 995 8026)

COMPSTON, Prof (David) Alastair Standish; s of Dr Nigel Dean Compston, CBE, MD, FRCP (d 1986), and Diana Mary, *née* Standish; *b* 23 Jan 1948; *Educ* Rugby, Middx Hosp Med Sch London (MB BS, FRCP, PhD); *m* 21 July 1973, Juliet Elizabeth, da of Sir Denys Page (d 1978); 1 da (Polly Clare b 5 Nov 1981); *Career* various hosp appts 1971–82, conslt neurologist Univ Hosp of Wales Cardiff 1982–85; prof of neurology: Univ of Wales Coll of Med Cardiff 1987–88, Univ of Cambridge 1989–; professorial fell Jesus Coll Cambridge 1990–, hon conslt neurologist Addenbrooke's Hosp Cambridge 1989–; chm MRC Cambridge Centre for Brain Repair 1990–; ed Journal of Neurology 1989–; memb Neurological Assoc 1991–; FRCP 1986; *Publications* author of articles in periodicals on human and experimental demyelinating disease; *Recreations* being outside, antiquarian books; *Clubs* Garrick; *Style—* Prof Alastair Compston; ✉ Pembroke House, Mill Lane, Linton, Cambridge CB1 6JY (☎ 01223 893414); University of Cambridge Neurology Unit, Level 5, Addenbrooke's Hospital, Hills Rd, Cambridge CB2 2QQ (☎ 01223 217091, fax 01223 336941)

COMPSTON, His Hon Judge; Christopher Dean; s of Vice Adm Sir Peter Maxwell Compston, KCB, *qv* and Valerie Marjorie, *née* Bocquet; *b* 5 May 1940; *Educ* Epsom Coll, Magdalen Coll Oxford (MA); *m* 1, Bronwen, da of Martin Henniker Gotley, of Derwenlas, Machynlleth, Wales; 2 s (Harry b 1969 (decd), Joshua Richard b 1970, d 1996), 1 da (Emily b 1972); m 2, Caroline Philippa, da of Paul Odgers, of Haddenham, Bucks; 2 s (Rupert b 1987, Benjamin b 1992), 1 da (Harriet b 1985); *Career* called to the Bar Middle Temple 1965, recorder of the Crown Court 1982–86, memb Senate Inns of Court 1983–86, circuit judge (SE Circuit) 1986–; *Recreations* the arts, writing; *Clubs* Seaview Yacht; *Style—* His Honour Judge Compston; ✉ Wandsworth County Court, 76–78 Upper Richmond Road, London SW15 2SU

COMPSTON, David; s of Denis Compston, of Sandside, Cumbria, and Nancy Morley; *b* 21 Oct 1938; *Educ* Mill Hill Sch London, Manchester Coll of Science and Technol; *m* 1962, Helga Ann, da of Richard Postlethwaite; 1 s (James Richard b 4 June 1965); *Career* chm: Allott & Lomax (Holdings) Ltd 1989–, INKOPLAN GmbH 1990–, Allott & Lomax (Hong Kong) Ltd, Fairbairn Services Ltd, Ceramic Industrial Projects Ltd, Allott Projects Ltd; chm Manchester TEC 1992– (estab Business Link Manchester 1994); dir: Trafford Park Mfrg Inst, Marketing Manchester; memb Construction Indust Sector Gp NEDO 1990–93, memb Personnel Standards Vocational Qualifications Lead Body (and its Advsy Forum) 1993–94, memb Nat Cncl TEC 1996–; tstee Westmorland Soc MENCAP; FICE 1973, FEng 1996; *Publications* Design and Construction of Buried Thin Walled Pipes (1978), Rihand Power Station Civil Works - An Indo-British Solution (1986); *Recreations* fly fishing, hill walking; *Clubs* Royal Over-Seas League, St James's (Manchester); *Style—* David Compston, Esq, FEng; ✉ Allott & Lomax Group, Fairbairn House, Sale, Manchester M33 6WP (☎ 0161 962 1214, fax 0161 969 5131)

COMPSTON, Vice Adm Sir Peter Maxwell; KCB (1970, CB 1967); s of Dr George Dean Compston, of Halton, Yorks; *b* 12 Sept 1915; *Educ* Epsom Coll; *m* 1, 1939 (m dis), Valerie M Bocquet; 1 s, 1 da; m 2, 1954, Angela (d 1994), da of late Harry Brickwood, of Bembridge, IOW; *Career* RN 1937, Rear Adm 1965, Chief of Br Naval Staff and NA Washington 1965–67, flag offr Flotillas W Fleet 1967–68, Dep SACLANT (Vice Adm) 1968–70, ret; *Style—* Vice Admiral Sir Peter Compston, KCB; ✉ 10 Berehurst, Borovere Lane, Alton, Hants GU34 1PA (☎ 01420 542443)

COMPTON, Earl; Daniel Bingham Compton; s and h of 7 Marquess of Northampton; *b* 16 Jan 1973; *Style—* Earl Compton; ✉ Compton Wynyates, Tysoe, Warwicks CV35 0UD

COMPTON, Ivor; s of Samuel Harry Cohen (d 1940), and Jane Anne, *née* Kanovich (d 1964); *b* 12 Aug 1933; *Educ* Hackney Downs GS; *m* 3 July 1955, Lorna Frances, da of Lewis Greene (d 1984); 1 s (Stanford Harvey b 1957), 1 da (Michèle Alison b 1959); *Career* RAF 1951–53; chm and md: Hall of Cards Ltd 1968–94 (ret), I C Associates Ltd, Domino Group Ltd, Factory Price Shops Ltd, Wag Marketing Ltd; chm Lorimist Ltd; Liveryman Worshipful Co of Makers of Playing Cards; *Recreations* golf, theatre, family and charitable works; *Clubs* Potters Bar Golf, MCC, IOD; *Style—* Ivor Compton, Esq; ✉ Brookside, Mimms Lane, Ridge, nr Potters Bar, Herts EN6 3LY (☎ 01707 654321); Domino Group Ltd (t/a Berryhurst, and Showtours), Keltan House, 1 Sail Street, London SE11 6NQ (☎ 0171 582 0244); I C Associates Ltd, I C G House, Oldfield Lane North, Greenford, Middlesex UB6 0AL (☎ 0181 813 2973)

COMPTON, Robert Edward John (Robin); DL (N Yorks 1981); s of Maj Edward Robert Francis Compton, JP, DL (d 1977; s of Lord Alwyne Compton, DSO, DL, 3 s of 4 Marquess of Northampton), and his 1 w, Sylvia, *née* Farquharson (d 1950); *b* 11 July 1922; *Educ* Eton, Magdalen Coll Oxford; *m* 5 July 1951, (Ursula) Jane, 2 da of Maj Rodolph Kenyon-Slaney, JP, DL, and formerly w of (i) Lt-Col Peter Lindsay, DSO (d 1971), (ii) Sir Max Aitken, 2 Bt, DSO, DFC (d 1985), by whom she had 2 das; 2 s (James Alwyne b 30 May 1953, Richard Clephane b 16 April 1957); *Career* served WWII with Coldstream Guards 1941–46 (wounded), military asst to British Ambass Vienna 1945–46 with rank of Maj; sr account exec W S Crawford Ltd advtg agency 1951–54; Time Life International: joined 1954, dir Time Life International Ltd 1958– (chm 1979–90, md 1985–87), advtg dir Time UK 1958–62, public affairs dir Time Life International Europe 1965–70; chm: Newby Hall Estate Co Ltd 1965–69, CXL UK Ltd 1971–73; bd dir Extel Corporation Chicago 1973–80, dir Transtel Communications Ltd 1974–83, pres Highline Financial Services SA 1985–94; Nat Tst: vice chm Yorkshire Ctee 1970–85, memb Gardens Panel, former memb Properties Ctee; former pres: Ripon Tourist Assoc, N of England Horticultural Soc 1984–86, Northern Horticultural Soc 1985–96, Yorkshire Agric Soc 1995–96; pres Nat Cncl for Conservation of Plants and Gardens 1994– (chm 1988–94), vice pres RHS 1995 (VMH 1993); High Sheriff North Yorkshire 1977; FInstD 1951–91; *Recreations* gardening, music, golf, shooting; *Clubs* White's, Swinley Forest Golf; *Style—* Robin Compton, Esq, DL; ✉ 17 Brompton Square, London SW3 2AD; Newby Hall, Ripon, N Yorkshire HG4 5AE (☎ 01423 323315)

COMRIE, Rear Adm Alexander Peter; CB (1982); s of late Robert Duncan Comrie (d 1957), and Phyllis Dorothy, *née* Jubb; *b* 27 March 1924; *Educ* Sutton Valence, RCDS; *m* 1945, Madeleine Irene (d 1983), da of Leslie Bullock (d 1956); 1 s, 1 da; *Career* RN 1945, Capt HMS Daedalus 1974–75, dir Weapons Co-ordination and Acceptance (Naval) 1975–77, dep controller Aircraft MOD (PE) 1978–81, dir gen Aircraft (Naval) 1981–83, ret; co dir and chm 1983–, def conslt 1984–, chm Exec Gp Ctee 3 of the Engrg Cncl 1986–94, vice pres Inst Electrical Engrs 1988–91 (memb Cncl 1981–84); CEng, FIEE, FRAeS, Eur Ing; *Recreations* sailing, gardening; *Clubs* Royal Cwlth Soc, Hayling Island Sailing; *Style—* Rear Adm A P Comrie, CB

COMYN, The Hon Sir James Peter; kt (1978); o s of late James Comyn, QC, of Dublin, and late Mary Comyn; *b* 8 March 1921; *Educ* The Oratory, New Coll Oxford (MA); *m* 1967, Anne, da of late Philip Chaundler, MC, of Biggleswade, Beds; 1 s, 1 da; *Career* former pres Oxford Union; called to the Bar England 1942 (Ireland 1947); recorder Crown Court 1972–77; judge: High Court Family Div 1978–79, Queen's Bench Div 1979–85; chm Bar Council 1973–74, vice chm Parole Board 1980–85; *Recreations* farming, writing, planting trees; *Style—* The Hon Sir James Comyn; ✉ Belvin, Tara, Co Meath, Ireland

COMYNS, Jacqueline Roberta; da of late Jack Fisher, and late Belle, *née* Offenbach (d 1994); *b* 27 April 1943; *Educ* Hendon Co GS, LSE (LLB); *m* 29 Aug 1963, Dr Malcolm John Comyns, s of Louis Comyns (d 1962); 1 s (David b 13 Aug 1975); *Career* called to the Bar Inner Temple 1969, in practice SE Circuit, metropolitan stipendiary magistrate 1982–, recorder of the Crown Court 1991–; *Recreations* travel, theatre, swimming, tennis; *Style—* Mrs Jacqueline Comyns; ✉ Tower Bridge Magistrates Court, Tooley Street, London SE1 2JY (☎ 0171 407 4232)

CONAN DOYLE, Air Cmdt Dame Jean Lena Annette (Lady Bromet); DBE (1963, OBE 1948), AE; da of late Sir Arthur Conan Doyle, and Jean Elizabeth, *née* Leckie; *b* 21 Dec 1912; *Educ* Granville House Eastbourne; *m* 1965, Air Vice-Marshal Sir Geoffrey Bromet (d 1983, lieut-govr Isle of Man 1945–52); *Career* No 46 (Co of Sussex) ATS RAF Co 1938, cmmnd WAAF and RAF 1940, dep dir WRAF 1952–54 and 1960–62, inspector of the WRAF 1954–56 and 1959–60, CO RAF Hawkinge 1956–59, Air Cmdt 1963, dir WRAF 1963–66, Hon ADC to HM The Queen 1963–66, ret 1966; a pres Not Forgotten Assoc 1981–91, a govr Royal Star and Garter Home 1968–82; holder of father's USA copyright; *Clubs* RAF, Naval and Military; *Style—* Air Cmdt Dame Jean Conan Doyle, DBE, AE; ✉ Flat 6, 72 Cadogan Square, London SW1X 0EA

CONANT, (Simon) Edward Christopher; s and h of Sir John Ernest Michael Conant, 2 Bt, *qv*, and Periwinkle Elizabeth, *née* Thorp (d 1985); *b* 13 Oct 1958; *Educ* Eton, RAC Cirencester; *Career* chartered surveyor; underwriting memb Lloyd's 1984; ARICS 1986; *Style—* Edward Conant, Esq; ✉ The Estate Office, Lyndon Hall, Oakham, Rutland LE15 8TU (☎ 0157 737 786)

CONANT, Guy Timothy Geoffrey; DL (Northants 1972), JP (Northants 1960); s of Sir Roger Conant, 1 Bt (d 1973), and Daphne Lorraine, *née* Learoyd (d 1979); *b* 7 Oct 1924; *Educ* Stowe; *m* 1, 27 June 1953 (m dis), Elizabeth, da of Alfred Trevor Handley, of IOW; 1 s (Rupert b 1964), 3 da (Sheena b 1954, Jane b 1955, Diana b 1960); m 2, 31 Jan 1981, Davina Huntley, da of Sir Guy Holland, 3 Bt; 1 da (Melissa b 1984); *Career* Flt Lt RAF; High Sheriff of Northants 1969; landowner and farmer; *Recreations* shooting, fishing; *Clubs* Boodle's; *Style—* Guy T G Conant, Esq, DL, JP; ✉ Bulwick Park, Corby, Northants NN17 3DZ (☎ 01780 450245)

CONANT, Sir John Ernest Michael; 2 Bt (UK 1954), of Lyndon, Co Leics; s of Sir Roger John Edward Conant, 1 Bt, CVO (d 1973); *b* 24 April 1923; *Educ* Eton, Corpus Christi Coll Cambridge; *m* 1, 16 Sept 1950, Periwinkle Elizabeth (d 1985), er da of late Dudley Thorp, of Brothers House, Kimbolton, Hunts; 2 s ((Simon) Edward Christopher b 1958, William John Nathaniel b 1970) (and 1 s decd), 2 da (Fiona Elizabeth (Mrs Jonathan P N Driver) b 1955, Melanie Lucinda (Mrs Richard A Firmston-Williams) b 1961); m 2, 11 July 1992, Mrs (Mary) Clare Attwater, yr da of William E Madden, of Petersfield, Hants; *Heir* s, (Simon) Edward Christopher Conant, *qv*; *Career* farmer, High Sheriff Rutland 1960; *Style—* Sir John Conant, Bt; ✉ Periwinkle Cottage, Lyndon, Oakham, Rutland, LE15 8TU (☎ 01572 737275)

CONCANNON, Rt Hon John Dennis (Don); PC (1978); s of James Concannon, formerly of Rossington, Doncaster, subsequently of Somercotes, Derby; *b* 16 May 1930; *Educ* Rossington Secdy Sch, WEA; *m* 1953, Iris May, da of Charles Wilson, of Mansfield; 2 s, 2 da; *Career* served Coldstream Gds 1947–53; memb NUM 1953–66, memb Mansfield Borough Cncl 1963–, MP (Lab) Mansfield 1966–87, asst govt whip 1968–70, oppn whip 1970–74, vice chamberlain HM Household 1974, min of state NI Office 1976–79 (Parly under sec of state 1974–76); oppn spokesman: Defence 1979–81, NI 1981–83; memb: Select Ctee for Energy 1983–87, Cwlth War Graves Cmmn 1986–93; *Style—* The Rt Hon Don Concannon; ✉ 69 Skegby Lane, Mansfield, Notts (☎ 01623 27235)

CONCANON, (Brian) Anthony Ross; s of Austin Brian Concanon (d 1965), of Plymouth, and Joyce Ruth, *née* Chadderton; *b* 2 March 1943; *Educ* Downside; *m* 1 (m dis); 2 s (Lee b 1966, Jonathan b 1977), 3 da (Tracey b 1961, Nina b 1964, Juliet b 1974); m 2, 31 May 1986, Annabell; *Career* Deloitte Haskins & Sells 1961–71, Norton Rose 1971–76; admitted slr 1976; UK tax attorney Texaco (UK) Ltd 1976–78; corporate tax ptnr McKenna & Co 1981– (joined 1978); ICEAW 1967, memb Law Soc 1976; CA 1967; *Recreations* English cartography; *Clubs* Royal Automobile; *Style—* Anthony Concanon, Esq; ✉ McKenna & Co, Mitre House, 160 Aldersgate St, London EC1A 4DD (☎ 0171 606 9000)

CONDER, (Hugh) Neville; CBE (1986); s of John Reynolds Conder (d 1959), and Edna Frances, *née* Benson (d 1938); *b* 30 April 1922; *Educ* Charterhouse, Architectural Assoc (Holloway and Henry Florence scholar, SADG medallist, dip); *m* 1, 1946 (m dis 1967), Jean, *née* MacArthur; 1 s (Simon Charles b 1947), 1 da (Lucy Frances Caroline b 1950); m 2, 1970, Susan Ruth, *née* Heller; 1 s (Gabriel Benson b 1971), 1 da (Alexandra Frances Claire b 1974); *Career* architect and painter; consulting architect to Bd of Trade 1950–53, section designer Festival of Britain 1951, fndr (with Sir Hugh Casson) Casson Conder Partnership 1956, sr ptnr 1987–93, conslt 1993–; work incl: various buildings Cambridge and Birmingham Univs, George VI Memorial Hostel, Elephant House London Zoo, General Dental Cncl Building, Swindon Civic Centre, Wyvern Theatre, Civic Halls Derby, Ismaili Centre London, Queen Elizabeth Country Park Butser, Civic Offices Basingstoke, Sidgwick Ave Site Univ of Cambridge, various designs for Tayco Boiler and street furniture; landscape design incl: Millfield Sch, New Pulteney Weir Bath, Univ of Birmingham, Savill Garden Windsor; memb Cncl: Architectural Assoc 1951–59, Design Cncl Award Panel 1960–61, Street Furniture Panel 1962–88; FRIBA 1956 (ARIBA 1947, hon sec 1973–75, vice pres 1976), FCSD 1952–89; *Awards* winner Open Competition for Telephone Kiosk Eire 1948, winner Competition for Post Office Telephone Kiosk 1958; *Books* An Introduction to Modern Architecture (1948); *Recreations* gardening; *Style—* Neville Conder, Esq, CBE; ✉ 49 Thurloe Square, London SW7 2SX (☎ 0171 584 2214)

CONDON, Sir Paul; kt (1994), QPM (1989); *Educ* St Peter's Coll Oxford (MA Jur); *m*; 1 da, 2 s; *Career* Metropolitan Police: joined 1967, served various stations in East End 1967–72, St Peter's Coll Oxford 1972–75, uniformed Inspr West End 1975–78, Chief Inspr Community Relations Branch 1978–81, Supt Bethnal Green 1981–82, staff offr to Sir David McNee as Cmmr 1982–84, Sr Cmd Course Police Staff Coll 1984; Asst Chief Constable Kent Constabulary 1984–87, Dep Asst Cmmr i/c W London then Asst Cmmr i/c personnel and trg Metropolitan Police 1987–89, Chief Constable Kent 1989–93, Cmmr Metropolitan Police 1993–; hon fell St Peter's Coll Oxford; CIMgt 1992, FRSA 1992; *Recreations* swimming, horse riding, reading; *Style—* Sir Paul Condon, QPM; ✉ Metropolitan Police Commissioner, New Scotland Yard, London SW1H 0BG (☎ 0171 230 1212)

CONGDON, David; MP (C) Croydon North East (majority 7,473); s of Archibald Congdon, and late Marjorie Congdon; *b* 16 Oct 1949; *Educ* Alleyns Sch Dulwich, Thames Poly (BSc(Econ)); *m* 21 Oct 1972, Teresa, da of late Thomas Hill and late Norah, *née* Hogan; (1 da); *Career* trainee systems analyst ICL 1970, Philips Electronics 1973–92, computer conslt; MP (C) Croydon NE 1992–; memb Select Ctee on Health, PPS to Min for Disabled; sec Greater London MPs; London Borough of Croydon: cncllr 1976–92, vice chm Highways Ctee 1978–79, vice chm Educn Ctee 1979–83, chm Social Services Ctee 1983–86 and 1991–92, dep ldr 1986–92; chm: Dulwich Young Conservatives 1971–72, Group 5 Div Greater London Young Conservatives 1971–72; govr Croydon Coll 1979–92; *Recreations* tennis, badminton, theatre, reading history and biography; *Style—* David Congdon, Esq, MP; ✉ House of Commons, London SW1A 0AA

CONGDON, Prof Timothy George (Tim); s of Douglas George Congdon, of Colchester, and Olive Emma, *née* Good; *b* 28 April 1951; *Educ* Colchester Royal Grammar Sch, St John's Coll Oxford (open scholar, BA), Nuffield Coll Oxford; *m* 18 June 1988, Dorianne, da of Percy Preston-Lowe; 1 da (Venetia Andrea Dorianne b 30 July 1991); *Career* economics staff The Times 1973–76, chief economist L Messel & Co 1976–87 (ptnr 1980–86), chief UK economist Shearson Lehman 1987–88, econ advsr Gerrard & National Holdings plc 1989–, md Lombard Street Research 1989–; memb HM Treasy Independent Panel of Economic Forecasting Advisers 1992–; non-exec dir: INVESCO Recovery Trust 1991–, High Income Tst 1993–; non-exec chm SBW Insurance Research 1994–; hon prof Cardiff Business Sch 1990–; MSI, FRSA 1990; *Books* Monetarism - Essay in Definition (1978), Monetary Control in Britain (1982), The Debt Threat (1988), Monetarism Lost (1989), Reflections on Monetarism (1992); *Recreations* opera, walking and other country pursuits, chess, reading; *Clubs* RAC; *Style—* Prof Tim Congdon; ✉ Lombard Street Research, Cannon Bridge, 25 Dowgate Hill, London EC4R 2GN (☎ 0171 337 2975, fax 0171 337 2999)

CONGLETON, 8 Baron (UK 1841); Sir Christopher Patrick Parnell; 11 Bt (I 1766); s of 6 Baron Congleton (d 1932), and Hon Edith Mary Palmer Howard, MBE, da of late Baroness Strathcona and Mount Royal (in her own right) and R J B Howard; suc bro 1967; *b* 11 March 1930; *Educ* Eton, New Coll Oxford (MA); *m* 19 Nov 1955, Anna Hedvig, er da of Gustav Adolf Sommerfelt, of Oslo; 2 s, 3 da; *Heir* s, Hon John Parnell; *Career* Salisbury and Wilton RDC 1964–74 (chm 1971), chm Salisbury and S Wilts Museum 1972–77, memb Advsy Bd for Redundant Churches 1981–87; pres Br Ski Fedn 1976–81, pres Ski Club of GB 1991–; tstee: Sandroyd Sch Tst 1972–92 (chm 1980–84), Wessex Med Tst 1984–90, Univ of Southampton Devpt Tst 1986–; Hon LLD Univ of Southampton 1990; *Recreations* music, fishing, skiing; *Style—* The Rt Hon the Lord Congleton; ✉ West End Farm, Ebbesbourne Wake, Salisbury, Wilts SP5 5JW

CONI, Dr Nicholas Keith; s of Edward Keith Coni (d 1962), and Kathleen Mary, *née* Griffin; *b* 29 May 1935; *Educ* Harrow, Trinity Coll Cambridge (MA, MB BChir); *m* 17 Nov 1962, (Sarah) Sally Theresa, da of Flt Lt John Arthur Lawrence Taylor (ka 1943); 3 s (Keith b 1965, Hugh b 1967, Miles b 1970); *Career* SSC RAMC Capt 1965, Maj 1968–70; house offr Hammersmith Hosp 1963–64, med registrar Westminster Hosp 1964–65 (house offr 1961–62), sr specialist in med BMH Singapore 1968–70, conslt physician in geriatric med Addenbrooke's Hosp Cambridge 1971–, assoc lectr Faculty of Clinical Med Univ of Cambridge 1971–, chief examiner (written) for Dip in Geriatric Med Royal Coll of Physicians 1994–; co-fndr and tstee Univ of The Third Age Cambridge; former chm Cambridge Branch Cruse; former memb: Cambridge Health Authy, Advsy Cncl Centre for Policy on Ageing; memb Exec Bd Addenbrooke's Hosp 1989–; FRCP (Canada) 1968, FRCP 1984; *Books* Ageing - The Facts (1984, 2 edn 1992), The Geriatric Prescriber (1986), Lecture Notes on Geriatrics (4 edn, 1993), Anatomy of a Hospital (as Julian Ashley, 1988), Bodyclock (contrib, 1989), Life Span Extension (contrib, 1991); *Recreations* holidaying and watersports in Menorca; *Style—* Dr Nicholas Coni; ✉ 29 Barrow Rd, Cambridge CB2 2AP (☎ 01223 361614); Addenbrooke's Hospital, Hills Rd, Cambridge CB2 2QQ (☎ 01223 217784/5/6)

CONINGSBY, His Hon Judge; Thomas Arthur Charles; QC (1986); s of Francis Charles Coningsby, of Chipstead, Surrey, and Eilleen Rowena, *née* Monson; *b* 21 April 1933; *Educ* Epsom Coll, Queens' Coll Cambridge (MA); *m* 8 Aug 1959, Elaine Mary, da of Edwin Stanley Treacher (d 1983), of Sussex; 2 s (Andrew b 1960, James b 1964), 3 da (Sara b 1962, Elizabeth b 1963, Katharine (twin) b 1963); *Career* Nat Serv RA 1951–53, Capt City of London Field Regt (TA) and Aerial Photographic Interpretation (Intelligence Corps) 1953–67; called to the Bar Gray's Inn 1957, recorder of the Crown Ct 1986–92, dep High Ct judge (Family Div) 1989–, circuit judge (SE Circuit) 1992–, head of Barristers' Chambers 3 Dr Johnson's Bldgs Temple 1988–92; chllr Diocese of York 1977–, vicar gen Province of York 1980–, chllr Diocese of Peterborough 1989–; memb: Gen Synod of C of E 1970–, Legal Advsy Cmmn of Gen Synod 1976–; chm Chipstead Village Preservation Soc 1983–88, memb Matrimonial Causes Rule Ctee 1985–89, chm Family Law Bar Assoc 1988–90 (sec 1986–88); memb: Gen Cncl of the Bar 1988–90, Supreme Ct Procedure Ctee 1988–92; hon treas Bar Lawn Tennis Soc 1969–92, pres Chipstead Tennis Club 1985– (chm 1981–85); *Recreations* lawn tennis; *Clubs* Athenaeum; *Style—* His Honour Judge Coningsby, QC; ✉ Leyfields, Elmore Rd, Chipstead, Surrey (☎ 01737 553304); Croydon Combined Court Centre, The Law Courts, Altyre Road, Croydon CR9 5AB (☎ 0181 681 2533)

CONLAN, John Oliver; s of Eugene J Conlan, of Dublin, Ireland, and Bridgid, *née* Hayes; *b* 13 July 1942; *Educ* Thurles Christian Brothers Sch Ireland; *m* 19 March 1968, Carolyn Sylvia, da of Raymond Ingram, of Luton, Beds; 3 da (Tara Louise b 1972, Amanda Carolyn b 1973, Alison Theresa b 1980); *Career* md: EMI Leisure 1980–81, Trust House Forte Leisure 1981–83; chief exec First Leisure Corporation plc 1988– (md 1983–88); gen cmmr for taxes London 1986–; *Recreations* golf; *Style—* John Conlan, Esq; ✉ First Leisure Corporation, 7 Soho St, London W1V 5FA (☎ 0171 437 9727, car tel 0836 231396)

CONLEY, Sandra (Mrs Grater); da of Ronald Conley (d 1960), of Hatfield, Herts, and Sophia Emily, *née* Ward (d 1980); *b* 24 Oct 1943; *Educ* Royal Ballet Upper Sch; *m* 28 Dec 1968, Adrian Michael Grater, s of Montague Lewis Grater (d 1980), of Crawley Down, Sussex; 1 da (Abigail b Dec 1974); *Career* ballerina: Sadler's Wells Royal Ballet 1962–70 (soloist 1968), Royal Ballet 1970– (princ 1978, princ character artist 1989); appearances: Swan Lake, Giselle, A Month in the Country, Mayerling, Isadora, Sleeping Beauty; *Recreations* reading, theatre; *Style—* Miss Sandra Conley; ✉ c/o The Royal Opera House, Covent Garden, London WC2E 9DD (☎ 0171 240 1200)

CONLIN, Geoffrey David; s of Geoffrey Charles Conlin (d 1943), and Mary Agnes Conlin; *b* 17 Dec 1938; *Educ* RMA Sandhurst; *m* 23 Sept 1972, Caroline Margaret, da of Capt Melville Stuart Jameson (d 1971), of Easter Logie, Blairgowrie, Perthshire; 3 s (Nicholas b 1974, Geoffrey b 1976, James b 1984), 1 da (Elizabeth b 1975); *Career* joined Army 1956, cmmnd Royal Irish Fusiliers 1958, resigned 1970; called to the Bar Inner Temple 1973, recorder of the Crown Court 1991–; chm Res Ctee Soc of Cons Lawyers 1980–83; *Recreations* shooting; *Clubs* Boodle's, Pratt's; *Style—* Geoffrey D Conlin, Esq; ✉ 3 Serjeant's Inn, London EC4Y 1BQ (☎ 0171 353 5537, fax 0171 353 0425, telex 264093)

CONLON, James; *b* 1950, New York City; *Educ* Juilliard Sch; *Career* conductor; music dir Cincinnati May Festival 1979–, music dir Rotterdam Philharmonic 1983–91, chief conductor Cologne Opera 1989–, music dir Gurzenich Orchestra Cologne 1990–, currently gen music dir City of Cologne; Met Opera NY debut 1976, Royal Opera House Covent Garden debut 1979; worked with orchs incl: Chicago Symphony, Boston Symphony, Philadelphia Orch, Cleveland Orch, Nat Symphony, Berlin Philharmonic, Staatskapelle Dresden, London Philharmonic, LSO, BBC Symphony, Orchestre de Paris, Orchestre National de France, Munich Philharmonic, RSO-Berlin, Orchestre de la Suisse Romande, Orchestra di Santa Cecilia, European Community Youth Orch; operatic works conducted incl: Die Zauberflöte (Met Opera debut 1976 over 200 performances), Don Carlos (Covent Garden debut 1976), Il Tabarro and Il Pagliacci (Opèra de Paris debut 1982), La Forza del Destino (Chicago Lyric Opera debut 1988), La Scala (Milano debut 1992 with Oberon), Der Fliegende Hollander, Pelleas et Melisande, Lady Macbeth of Mtsensk, Die Entfuhrung aus dem Serail, Semiramide, Don Giovanni, Cosi fan Tutte, Die Zauberflöte, The Marriage of Figaro, Lohengrin, Aida, La Bohème, Boris Godunov, Carmen, Jenufa, Khovanrina, Salome, Tosca, La Traviata, Il Trovatore, Peter Grimes, Macbeth; *Style—* James Conlon, Esq; ✉ c/o Harold Holt Ltd, 31 Sinclair Road, London W14 ONS (☎ 0171 603 4600, fax 0171 603 0019, telex 22339 HUNTER)

CONLONG, George Francis; s of George Conlong (d 1966), of Manchester, and Amelia, *née* Carr; *b* 14 April 1935; *Educ* Xaverian Coll Manchester; *m* 1961, Patricia Mary, da of Charles Everett Kirk; 1 s (Philip John b 16 July 1962), 2 da (Jane Elizabeth b 19 July 1963, Ursula Patricia b 23 Sept 1964); *Career* articled clerk J Frith & Co CAs Manchester 1951–55, qualified 1956; Nat Serv HM Forces 1957–59, RAPC Sgt, served BAOR Germany, attached RE; Jones Crewdson Youatt CAs Manchester 1959–60, Deloitte Plender Griffiths CAs Manchester 1960–63, cost accountant Mirlees National Ltd Manchester (Hawker Siddeley Group) 1963–65, mgmnt accountant Shell Chemicals UK Ltd and refinery accountant Shell Oil Ltd 1965–68, gp fin accountant and divnl fin controller Wedgwood Group 1969–73, in own practice Conlong & Co CAs Staffordshire 1973–; pres: N Staffs Soc of CAs 1991–92, Stoke on Trent Catenian Assoc; FCA 1967 (ACA 1957); *Recreations* music (including choral singing), golf, game fishing, fell walking; *Style—* George F Conlong, Esq; ✉ Conlong & Co, 162A London Road, Chesterton, Newcastle-under-Lyme, Staffs (☎ 01782 566156)

CONNAGHAN, John Gerard; s of John Connaghan (d 1984), of Glasgow, and Mary, *née* Hendry; *b* 2 Sept 1954; *Educ* St Mungo's Acad, Glasgow Coll of Technol (BA), Univ of Strathclyde (DMS, MBA); *m* 1 Oct 1983, Evelyn Joyce, da of J W B Steven, of Flode, Dornoch; 3 s (Christopher b Oct 1986, James b Dec 1988, Paul b March 1990), 1 da (Ruth b 6 Feb 1994); *Career* mgmnt trainee then quality controller Wm Collins & Sons Ltd 1977–79; Charles Letts (Scotland) Ltd Edinburgh: quality control mangr 1979–81, planning mangr 1981–82, gen mangr 1982–87; unit gen mangr Greater Glasgow Health Bd 1987–93; chief exec: Victoria Infirmary NHS Tst 1993–94, Western General Hospitals NHS Tst 1994–; FIMgt, MHSM; *Recreations* hillwalking, cycling, fine wines, reading; *Style—* John Connaghan, Esq; ✉ Western General Hospitals NHS Trust, Western General Hospital, Crewe Road South, Edinburgh EH4 2XU (☎ 0131 537 1000, fax 0131 537 1001)

CONNARTY, Michael; MP (Lab) Falkirk East (majority 7,969); s of late Patrick Connarty, and Elizabeth, *née* Plunkett; *b* 3 Sept 1947; *Educ* St Patrick's HS Coatbridge, Univ of Stirling (BA(Econ)), Jordanhill Coll of Educn, Univ of Glasgow (DCE); *m* 9 Aug 1969, Margaret, *née* Doran; 1 s, 1 da; *Career* teacher of children with special needs 1976–92, ldr Stirling DC 1980–90 (cncllr 1977–90), memb Lab Pty Scottish Exec Ctee 1981–92; MP (Lab) Falkirk E 1992–; memb: Euro Directives Ctee A (Agriculture, Environment, Health and Safety) 1992–, Select Ctee on the Parliamentary Cmmr for Administration; sec PLP Science and Technol Ctee 1992–; memb Standing Ctees on: Bankruptcy (Scotland) Act 1993, Prisoners and Criminal Proceedings Act 1993, Local Govt Etc (Scotland) Act 1994, Children (Scotland) Bill 1995, Crime and Punishment (Scotland) Bill 1996; Scottish PLP Gp: exec memb, chm Economy, Industry & Energy Ctee; task force leader on skills and training in Scotland and Youth & Students Scottish co-ordinator Labour Crime & Drugs Campaign; chm: Lab Pty Scottish Local Govt Ctee 1989–91, Stirlingshire Co-operative Pty 1990–92; vice chm Lab Gp COSLA 1988–90; *Recreations* family, reading, music, hill walking, Falkirk FC, Bo'ness United FC; *Style—* Michael Connarty, Esq, MP; ✉ House of Commons, London SW1A 0AA (☎ 0171 219 3000)

CONNAUGHTON, Col Richard Michael; s of Thomas Connaughton (d 1981), of Huntingdon, and Joan Florence, *née* Lisher (d 1979); *b* 20 Jan 1942; *Educ* Duke of York's Royal Military Sch Dover, MPhil (Cantab); *m* 12 June 1971, (Annis Rosemary) Georgina, da of Capt George Frederic Matthew Best, OBE, RN (d 1994), and Rosemary Elizabeth, *née* Brooks, of Dorset; 1 s (Michael b 1972), 1 da (Emma b 1974); *Career* RMA Sandhurst 1960–61, III Co RASC (Guided Weapons) W Germany 1962–64, 28 Co Gurkha Army Serv Corps Hong Kong 1965–67, Jr Ldrs' RCT Taunton 1967–69, 28 Sqdn Gurkha Tport Regt Hong Kong 1969–71 (Adj 1971–73), student Army Staff Coll Camberley 1974, GSO 2 Co-ord MVEE Chertsey 1975–76, cmd 2 Sqdn RCT W Germany 1977–79, 2 i/c Logistic Support Gp Regt Aldershot 1979–81, cmd 1 Armd Div Tport Regt RCT W Germany 1982–84, memb Directing Staff Army Staff Coll Camberley and Australian Army Cmd and Staff Coll Fort Queenscliff Victoria 1984–86, Col Tport HQ BAOR W Germany 1987–89; def fellowship St John's Coll Cambridge 1989–90, Colonel Defence Studies 1990–92, exec dir National & International Consultancy 1992–; hon research fell Centre for Defence and Int Security Studies Lancaster Univ; FIMgt 1981, FCIT 1989; *Books* The War of The Rising Sun and Tumbling Bear (1989), The Republic of the Ushakovka (1990), Military Intervention in the 1990s - a New Logic of War (1992), To Loose the Bands of Wickedness (contrib, ed Nigel Rodley, 1992), The Changing Face of Armed Conflict - Today and Tomorrow (1994), Shrouded Secrets - Australia's Mainland War with Japan 1942–44 (1994), The Nature of Future Conflict (1995), The Battle for Manila 1945 (with Drs Anderson and Pimlott, 1995), Celebration of Victory (1995), Descent into Chaos (1996), Just Wars and Genocide (1997); *Recreations* writing, family tennis; *Clubs* Army and Navy; *Style—* Col Richard Connaughton; ✉ Wallhayes, Nettlecombe, Bridport, Dorset DT6 3SX (☎ 01308 485002, fax 01308 485446)

CONNAUGHTON, Shane; s of Brian Connaughton (d 1983), and Elizabeth, *née* Moylett (d 1979); *b* 4 April 1951; *Educ* St Tiarnachs Clones, Bristol Old Vic Theatre Sch; *m* Ann-Marie, da of Paul Hammersley-Fenton; 1 da (Tara b 17 March 1974), 1 s (Tom b 10 March 1979); *Career* writer; actor in repertoire and Nat Theatre London and Abbey

Theatre Dublin; Hennessy Award for Irish Fiction 1985, The Irish Post Award 1987; *Novels* A Border Station (1989, shortlist GPA Literary Award), The Run of the Country (1991); *Plays* Sir Is Winning (1977, NT), Weston Coyney Cowboy (1975, Stoke-on-Trent), George Davis is Innocent OK (1976, Half Moon), Divisions (1981, Dublin Theatre Festival), Lily (1984, The Irish Co); *Screenplays* Every Picture Tells A Story (Channel 4), Dollar Bottom (1981, Paramount, Oscar Best Short Film), My Left Foot (1990, Oscar nomination Best Adapted Screenplay), The Playboys (Samuel Goldwyn Co, 1992), various others for BBC and ITV; *Recreations* smelling flowers, my wife; *Style—* Shane Connaughton, Esq; ✉ William Morris Agency, El Camino Drive, Beverley Hills, CA 90212 (☎ 310 859 4435, fax 310 859 4462)

CONNELL, (Frances) Elizabeth; da of (Gordon) Raymond Connell (d 1968), and (Maud) Elizabeth, *née* Scott (d 1994); *b* 22 Oct 1946; *Educ* Springs Convent S Africa, Univ of Witwatersrand, Johannesburg Coll of Educn, London Opera Centre; *Career* opera singer; debut: Wexford Festival 1972, Aust Opera 1973–75, ENO 1975–80, Covent Garden 1976, Bayreuth 1980, La Scala 1981, Salzburg 1983, Glyndebourne 1985, Metropolitan Opera 1985, Paris 1987; has sung with major orchs, opera houses, festivals and maestri throughout the world; recordings incl: duets with Sutherland and Pavarotti, I Due Foscari, Suor Angelica, Guglielmo Tell, Poliuto, Mahler No 8, Mendelssohn No 2, Schubert Lieder recital, Vaughan Williams Serenade to Music, Schoenberg Gurrelieder, Lohengrin, Verdi Requiem Mass, Schreker Die Gezeichneten; awarded Maggie Teyte prize 1972; *Style—* Ms Elizabeth Connell; ✉ c/o IMG Artists, Media House, 3 Burlington Lane, Chiswick, London W4 2TH (☎ 0181 233 5800, fax 0181 233 5801)

CONNELL, John William; s of William J Connell (d 1947), and Maud Emily Edge (d 1983); *b* 4 Feb 1933; *Educ* St Edward's Coll Liverpool; *m* 28 Sept 1957, Joan, da of Walter Bromley (d 1978); 3 da (Gillian b 1962, Janet b 1964, Elizabeth b 1965); *Career* chief exec: Bibby Group of Factors Lt 1995–, Maddox Factoring (UK) Ltd 1993–, Bibby Financial Services Ltd 1981–, Bibby Factors Ltd 1990–, other factoring gp cos; currently chm: Liverpool and London Steamship Protection and Indemnity Assoc Ltd, The Association of Invoice Factors Ltd; also dir of numerous other cos incl: Bibby Line Ltd 1989–, Liverpool and London P & I Management Ltd, Grayhill Insurance Co (Bermuda) Ltd, Grayhill Insurance (Cayman) Ltd; *Style—* John W Connell, Esq; ✉ 105 Duke Street, Liverpool L1 5JQ (☎ 0151 708 8000, fax 0151 794 1002)

CONNELL, Hon Mr Justice; Hon Sir Michael Bryan; kt (1991); s of Larry Connell (d 1995), and Joan Connell (d 1969); *b* 6 Aug 1939; *Educ* Harrow, Brasenose Coll Oxford (MA); *m* 17 Dec 1965, Anne Joan, da of late E P Pulham; 3 s (Sean James b 7 Sept 1967, Jonathan Edward b 26 Aug 1968, Simon Michael b 16 Aug 1979), 1 da (Lisa Anne (Mrs Adrian Gregory) b 16 Nov 1970); *Career* called to the Bar Inner Temple 1962, recorder of the Crown Court 1980, QC 1981, bencher 1988, judge of the High Court of Justice (Family Div) 1991–; led inquiry into voided Grand National 1993; govr Harrow Sch; Liveryman Worshipful Co of Farriers; *Recreations* steeplechasing, fox hunting; *Clubs* Buck's, MCC, Jockey; *Style—* The Hon Mr Justice Connell; ✉ Royal Courts of Justice, Strand, London WC2A 2LL

CONNELL, Dr Philip Henry; CBE (1986); s of George Henry Connell (d 1928), of Selby, Yorks, and Evelyn Hilda Sykes (d 1969); *b* 6 July 1921; *Educ* St Paul's, St Bartholomew's Hosp Med Sch London (MB BS, MRCS, LRCP, DPM, MD); *m* 1, April 1948 (m dis 1973), (Marjorie) Helen, da of John Gilham, of Ashford, Kent; 2 s (Michael Charles b 25 Jan 1953, David Nicholas b 19 Aug 1955); m 2, Cecily Mary (Celia), da of Edward Russell Harper, MC (d 1959); *Career* house physician St Stephen's Hosp London 1951–53, registrar and sr registrar Inst of Psychiatry Bethlem Royal Hosp and Maudsley Hosp 1953–57, conslt psychiatrist and physician i/c Child Psychiatry Unit Newcastle Gen Hosp in assoc with King's Coll Univ of Durham 1957–63, physician Bethlem Royal Hosp and Maudsley Hosp 1963–86 (emeritus physician 1986–), over 90 contribs to professional jls and pubns, memb editorial bd various med jls; extensive nat and int work on drug addiction and dependence for: WHO, Cncl of Europe, CENTO and on maladjusted and psychiatrically ill children and adolescents; memb: Standing Mental Health Advsy Ctee DHSS 1966–72 (vice chm 1967–72), Standing Advsy Ctee on Drug Dependence (Wayne Ctee 1966– and Sub Ctees), Wootton Ctees on cannabis and LSD and on amphetamines and barbiturates; conslt advsr (addiction) DHSS 1966–71 and 1981–86, pres Soc for Study of Addiction 1973–76, vice pres Int Cncl on Alcohol and Addictions 1982 (chm Scientific and Prof Advsy Bd 1971–79); chm: Inst for Study of Drug Dependence 1975–90, Advsy Cncl on Misuse of Drugs 1982–88 (statutory body set up under the Misuse of Drugs Act 1977), Sec of State for Tport's Advsy Panel on Alcohol Abuse 1988–95; memb Cncl: Royal Medico-Psychological Assoc 1962–67, Royal Coll of Psychiatrists 1971–81 (vice pres 1979–81); memb: Bd of Govrs Bethlem Royal Hosp and Maudsley Hosp 1966–73 (chm Med Ctee 1969–72), Mgmnt Ctee Inst of Psychiatry 1968–74, Trethowan Ctee DHSS (the role of psychologists in Health Serv) 1968–72, Gen Med Cncl 1979–91; preliminary screener for health 1982–91; Dent meml lectr King's Coll and Soc for Study of Addiction 1985; memb Bd of Govrs Mowden Hall Sch Northumberland and 1976–82; FRCP 1976, Hon FRCPsych 1992 (FRCPysch 1971); *Books* Amphetamine Psychosis (1958), Cannabis and Man (jt ed, 1975); *Recreations* bridge, music; *Clubs* Athenaeum, Roehampton; *Style—* Dr P H Connell, CBE; ✉ 25 Oxford Rd, Putney, London SW15 2LG (☎ 0181 788 1416)

CONNELL, Stephanie Lee; da of George Saul (d 1982), of Yorks, and Tena, *née* Wheater (d 1987); *b* 21 Aug 1945; *Educ* Univ of London (DipEd), Univ of Leeds (DipEFL), Univ of Bristol, NE London Poly (MA); *m* 30 Oct 1971 (m dis 1980); *Career* sr lectr Univ of E London 1972–94 (course tutor and staff devpt offr (Enterprise Unit) 1992–), educn advsr and conslt writer Thames TV plc 1975, literary conslt and contributor Anabas Productions 1986–, freelance writer of children's educnl and literary works, television progs; dir Bd and fell ABI; *Recreations* appreciating Louis Roederer Cristal, travelling, sailing; *Style—* Miss Stephanie Connell; ✉ Thorndon Hall, Apt 46, Ingrave, Brentwood, Essex (☎ 01277 811780); Rafol 14, Calpe, Alicante, Spain (☎ 00 34 6 5833826)

CONNELLY, Jennifer Emily; da of Samuel Henry Smith, and Cecelia Beryl Smith; *b* 20 Jan 1947; *Educ* Notre Dame GS Southport, Loreto GS Nottingham, El Colegio de la Virgen Maria Vizcaya Spain, L'Alliance Française Paris, Sorbonne Paris, Lanchester Poly Coventry (BA, CNNA), Univ of Manchester (Post Grad Cert of Advanced French); *m* 1974, John Joseph Connelly; *Career* teacher Ruffwood Comp Sch Kirkby 1971–72, teacher Ashmead Boys' Sch Reading 1972–74, head of French Smithmills Moor GS Bolton 1974–82, head Dept of Modern Languages Sharples Sch Bolton 1982–87, dep head Westhoughton HS Bolton 1987–90, headteacher Sale GS Cheshire 1990–; *Recreations* theatre, music, reading, travel; *Clubs* Old Salians RUFC (pres); *Style—* Mrs Jennifer Connelly; ✉ Sale Grammer School, Marsland Road, Sale, Cheshire

CONNER, Angela Mary (Mrs Conner Bulmer); da of late Judge Cyril Conner, of Midhurst, Sussex, and Mary Stephanie, *née* Douglass; *Educ* spent much of childhood travelling; *m* John Frederick Bulmer; 1 da (Georgia Sophia McCullough Bulmer); *Career* sculptor; worked for Dame Barbara Hepworth UK then full-time painter and sculptor, work incl 350 paintings of East River from one window of the UN Building; *Solo Exhibitions* incl: Browse & Darby London, Istanbul Biennale, Lincoln Centre NY, UN, Jewish Art Museum NY, Lincoln Center NYC; *Group Exhibitions* incl: Chicago Arts Fair, Gimpel Fils NY, Carnegie Museum Pittsburgh, Nat Portrait Gallery London, Washington Museum, Royal Acad; researched and developed use of water, sun and wind for abstract mobile sculptures in contemporary art and contrib to field of environmental art and bronze portraits; *Important Public Works* incl: three works for Lincoln Center NY, Great Tipper, Germany, large centrepiece for Horsham, Victims of Yalta Meml (Brompton Rd London), Quartet (water sculpture and co-designed Plaza (Heinz Hall Pittsburgh USA)), bigger than life size portrait de Gaulle (Carlton Gardens) London, water sculptures for King Fahid, 20ft water mobile Aston Univ, 30ft water mobile Economist Plaza (St James) London, steel sculpture for St Andrews Cuffley St Albans, sculptured arch for Warwickshire Educn Ctee, numerous private cmmns for Duke of Devonshire Collection, Gunter Sachs; *Portraits* incl: HRH Prince of Wales, Lord Sainsbury, Drue Heinz, Duke of Devonshire, Churchill, Harold MacMillan (Earl of Stockton), Sir John Betjeman, Lord Goodman, Lucien Freud, Rab Butler (Central Hall House of Commons), Dame Lis Frink, Paul Mellon; *Awards* incl: Honor Award of American Inst of Architects, winner Lexington Airport Int Competition, Best Br Equestrian Sculpture Award of Br Sporting Art Tst; winner: Hereford City Nat Competition, W Midlands Arts Nat Competition for Aston Univ (18 foot Centre Piece), De Gaulle Competition; fell Soc of Equestrian Artists, fell Royal Soc of Br Sculptors; *Recreations* breeding and showing Morgan horses and co-founded the breed in Britain; *Style—* Angela Conner; ✉ George and Dragon Hall, Mary Place, London W11 4PL (☎ 0171 221 4510, fax 0171 243 1167)

CONNER, Rt Rev David John; *see:* Lynn, Bishop of

CONNERADE, Prof Jean-Patrick; s of George Auguste Joseph Louis Connerade, and Marguerite Marie, *née* David; *b* 6 May 1943; *Educ* Lycée Français Charles De Gaulle, Imperial Coll London (BSc, PhD, DIC, DSc); *m* 19 Dec 1970, Jocelyne Charlette, da of Eugene Dubois, of Mareil-Marly, France (d 1988); 1 s (Florent b 1971), 1 da (Laetita b 1973); *Career* ESRO fell 1968–70, scientist Euro Space Res Inst Italy 1970–73, visiting prof Ecole Normale Supèrieure Paris 1979–80, prof of atomic and molecular physics Imperial Coll London 1985– (lectr 1973–79, reader 1980–85); guest researcher Physikalisches Institut Univ of Bonn 1969–; hon ed of jl Physics B, hon treas Save Br Sci Soc, memb Ampboard of Euro Physical Soc; FInstP; *Books* Atomic and Molecular Physics in High Field (co-ed, 1982), Giant Resonances in Atoms Molecules and Solids (1986); *Recreations* painting; *Style—* Prof Jean-Patrick Connerade; ✉ Blackett Laboratory, Imperial College of Science Technology and Medicine, Prince Consort Rd, London SW7 2BZ (☎ 0171 225 8860, fax 0171 589 9463, telex 929484 IMPCOLG)

CONNERY, Jason; s of Sean Connery, *qv*, and Diane, *née* Cilento (now Mrs Anthony Shaffer); *b* 1963, London; *Career* actor; *Theatre* incl: Stanhope in Journey's End (Whitehall), D'Artagnan in The Three Musketeers (Bristol Old Vic), Christian in Cyrano De Bergerac (Greenwich), Arthur Gower in Trelawny of the Wells, Petruchio in The Taming of the Shrew (Nuffield); *Television* incl: lead in Robin of Sherwood, Serenade for Dead Lovers, The Train (with Ben Kingsley), Mountain of Diamonds, The Other Side of Paradise; *Films* incl: Lords of Discipline, The First Olympics, The Boy Who Had Everything, La Veneziana, Puss in Boots, Bye Bye Baby, Casablanca Express, Spymaker (known as The Secret Life of Ian Fleming in America), The Sheltering Desert, True Love, Bullet to Beijing 1994, Midnight in St Petersburg (with Michael Caine) 1994, The Successors 1995; *Style—* Jason Connery, Esq; ✉ c/o Joy Jameson Limited, 2–19 The Plaza, 535 Kings Road, London SW10 0SZ (☎ 0171 351 3971, fax 0171 352 1744)

CONNERY, Sean Thomas; s of Joseph Connery, and Euphamia Connery; *b* 25 Aug 1930; *m* 1, 29 Nov 1962 (m dis 1974), Diane (who m 3, 1985, Anthony Shaffer, playwright), da of Sir Raphael West Cilento (d 1985), and former w of Andrea Volpt; 1 s (Jason Connery, *qv*, b 1963); m 2, Jan 1975, Micheline Roquebrune; *Career* actor, fell Royal Scottish Academy of Music and Drama; Freeman City of Edinburgh 1991; Hon DLitt Heriot-Watt Univ 1981; Golden Globe Cecil B De Mille Lifetime Achievement Award 1996; films incl: Tarzan's Greatest Adventure 1959, The Longest Day 1962, Dr No 1963, From Russia With Love 1964, Goldfinger 1965, Thunderball 1966, A Fine Madness 1966, You Only Live Twice 1967, Shalako 1968, Diamonds are Forever 1971, Murder on the Orient Express 1974, The Man Who Would be King 1975, Outland 1981, Never Say Never Again 1983, Highlander 1986, The Name of the Rose 1986, The Untouchables 1987, The Presidio 1988, Indiana Jones - The Last Crusade 1989, The Hunt For Red October 1990, Family Business 1990, Highlander II 1991, Robin Hood Prince of Thieves 1991, The Russia House 1991, The Medicine Man 1992, Just Cause 1995, King Arthur in First Knight 1995, The Rock 1996, the voice of Draco in Dragonheart 1996; *Style—* Sean Connery Esq; ✉ Creative Artists Agency Inc, 9830 Wilshire Boulevard, Beverly Hills 90212, Los Angeles, California, USA

CONNICK, Harold Ivor; s of Aaron Connick, of London (d 1963), and Raie, *née* Winner (d 1972); *b* 25 Jan 1927; *Educ* Ealing GS, LSE (LLB); *m* 16 Oct 1955, Claire Grace, da of John William Benson, of London; 2 s (David b 1956, Jeremy b 1963), 1 da (Lesley b 1956); *Career* attached Army War Crimes Singapore 1946–48; admitted slr 1952; sr ptnr Thornton Lynne and Lawson 1959–91; dir: UDS Group plc 1975–83 (dep chm 1983), Land Securities plc 1987–, A Beckman plc 1991–; exec conslt Finers 1991–94; vice pres Br ORT 1989– (chm 1984–89), chm Central Bd World ORT Union; *Recreations* golf, theatre, cricket; *Clubs* MCC, Roehampton, IOD; *Style—* H I Connick, Esq; ✉ 54 Fairacres, Roehampton Lane, London SW15 5LY (☎ 0181 876 7188, fax 0181 878 6198)

CONNOCK, Stephen Leslie; s of Leslie Thomas Connock, of Peterborough, Cambs, and Gladys Edna, *née* Chappell; *b* 16 Nov 1949; *Educ* Univ of Sheffield (BA), LSE (MPhil); *m* 18 Aug 1973, Margaret Anne, da of Richard Bolger, of Palmers Green, London; 2 s (Adrian b 1981, Mark b 1985); *Career* Philips Electronics: mgmnt devpt mangr 1985–87, industl relations mangr 1979–85; gen mangr human resources Pearl Assurance plc 1987–92, customer and corp affrs dir Eastern Group plc (formerly Eastern Electricity plc) 1992–; MIPD 1973; *Books* Industrial Relations Training for Managers (1981), Cost Effective Strategies in Industral Relations (1985), H R Vision - Managing a Quality Workforce (1991), Ethical Leadership (1995); *Recreations* music (chm Ralph Vaughan Williams Soc), writing; *Clubs* Reform, Athenaeum; *Style—* Stephen Connock, Esq; ✉ Eastern Group plc, Wherstead Park, Wherstead, Ipswich, Suffolk IP9 2AQ (☎ 01473 553001)

CONNOLLY, Billy; *b* 24 Nov 1942; *m* 1990, Pamela Stephenson; 3 da (Daisy, Amy, Scarlett); *Career* comedian, actor, playwright and presenter; started work as apprentice welder, began show business career with Gerry Rafferty and The Humblebums; as playwright The Red Runner (Edinburgh Fringe) 1979; *Theatre* The Great Northern Welly Boot Show (Palladium), The Beastly Beatitudes of Balthazar B (West End) 1982; *Television* Androcles and the Lion 1984, Return to Nose and Beak (Comic Relief), HBO special (with Whoopi Goldberg) 1990, South Bank Show Special (25th Anniversary commemoration) 1992, Down Among the Big Boys (BBC) 1993, Head of the Class, Billy, Billy Connolly's World Tour of Scotland (6 part documentary) 1994, The Big Picture (BBC) 1995, Billy Connolly's World Tour of Australia 1996; *Films* incl: Absolution (with Richard Burton) 1979, Bullshot 1984, Water (with Michael Caine) 1984, The Big Man (with Liam Neeson) 1989, Pocahontas 1995 (animation), Billy Big Bones in Treasure Island (Muppet Movie) 1996, William Brodie in Deacon Brodie (BBC Film) 1996; *Videos* numerous releases incl: Bite your Bum 1981 (Music Week and Record Business Award 1982), 25 BC, Billy and Albert, An Audience with Billy Connolly, Billy Connolly Live, Hand-Picked by Billy Connolly 1982, Live at Hammersmith 1991, Live' 94; *Albums* numerous releases incl: The Great Northern Welly Boot Show (incl no 1 hit DIVORCE), Pick of Billy Connolly (gold disc) 1982; *Books* Gullible's Travels (1982); *Style—* Billy Connolly, Esq; ✉ c/o Tickety-boo Limited, 160 Munster Road, Fulham, London SW6 5RA (☎ 0171 610 9464, fax 0171 610 9465)

CONNOLLY, Denys E; OBE; *Career* with Peat Marwick Mitchell & Co CAs 1955–85 (sr ptnr Hong Kong 1978–85); non-exec dir: HSBC Holdings plc 1990–, HongkongBank

1985–, Kowloon-Canton Railway Corp 1990–; FCA; *Style*— Denys Connolly, Esq, OBE, JP; ✉ 17 Sheko, Hong Kong (☎ 00 852 809 4476)

CONNOLLY, Prof John Henry; s of John Henry Connolly (d 1953), of Bangor, Co Down, and Catherine Anne, *née* Campbell (d 1973); *b* 4 Sept 1930; *Educ* Bangor GS, the Queen's Univ of Belfast (MB BCh, MD); *m* 11 April 1963, Patricia Wilhelmina Robinson, da of Thomas Dennison Corbett (d 1982), of Bangor, Co Down; 1 s (Paul b 1964); *Career* res fell Nat Fund for Poliomyelitis Res 1956–57, visiting asst prof Johns Hopkins Univ Baltimore USA 1959–60, conslt virologist Royal Victoria Hosp Belfast 1968–93, hon prof Sch of Clinical Medicine Queen's Univ Belfast 1991–95 (hon lectr 1960–91); memb Jt Advsy Ctee on Dangerous Pathogens of Health and Agric Mins and Health and Safety Cmmn London 1983–87, govr Bangor GS; MRCPI 1964, FRCPI 1975, MRCPath 1966, FRCPath 1978; *Publications* numerous papers on polio vaccines, Q fever and measles virus in subacute sclerosing panencephalitis; *Recreations* golf; *Clubs* Bangor Golf (Co Down); *Style*— Prof John Connolly; ✉ 50 Broadway, Bangor, Co Down BT20 4RG (☎ 01247 460020)

CONNOLLY, Joseph Edward; s of Patrick Joseph Connolly (d 1985), and Kathryn Mary, *née* Mcnaney; *b* 15 June 1950; *Educ* Cornell Univ (AB), Harvard Univ (MBA); *Career* second vice pres Continental Bank London 1975–81, gp head Bank of Boston London 1981–83, sr analyst Moody's Investors NY 1984–86, dir Euro Ratings Ltd London 1986–88, vice pres and gp head Citibank London 1988–; memb Irish Club of Eaton Square London; *Books* The International Data Communications Market; *Recreations* racing, looking at pictures, squash; *Style*— Joseph Connolly, Esq; ✉ 52A Eaton Place, London SW1 (☎ 0171 245 1223); 83 Montvale Ave, Woburn, Massachusetts; Citibank NA, 335 Strand, London WC1 (☎ 0171 438 0437)

CONNOLLY, Dr (Charles) Kevin; TD (1981); s of Dr Charles Vincent Connolly (d 1961), of Rothwell, Kettering, Northamptonshire, and Frances Elliott, *née* Turner; *b* 26 Sept 1936; *Educ* Ampleforth, Gonville and Caius Coll Cambridge, Middx Hosp Med Sch (MA, MB BChir); *m* 24 Oct 1970, Rachel Bronwen, da of Lewis Philip Jameson Evans (d 1972), of Bromsgrove, Worcs; 3 da (Kate b 1971, Celia b 1973, Clare b 1975); *Career* house physician Middx Hosp 1961, resident med offr Brompton Hosp 1963, sr med registrar St George's Hosp 1967, conslt physician Darlington and Northallerton Hosp 1970–, clinical tutor Northallerton Health Dist 1974–82, examiner Temporary Registration and Provisional Licence Assessment Bd 1975–, hon clinical lectr Dept of Med Univ of Newcastle upon Tyne 1988–; vice pres Nat Assoc of Clinical Tutors 1981–83, past and present memb various ctees RCP and Br Thoracic Soc; pres: Northallerton Div Br Med Assoc 1974–76, Yorks Thoracic Soc 1982–84, Northern Thoracic Soc 1991–92; memb: Darlington Health Authy 1981–90, Thoracic Soc, Med Res Soc, Exec Ctee Breathe North; Liveryman Worshipful Co of Apothecaries 1964; MRCP 1964, FRCP 1977; *Recreations* tennis, skiing; *Style*— Dr C K Connolly, TD; ✉ Aldbrough House, Aldbrough St John, Richmond, N Yorks DL11 7TP (☎ 01325 374244); 30 St Cuthberts Consulting Rooms, Darlington, Co Durham DL1 1GB (☎ 01325 364624)

CONNOLLY, Kevin; s of John Connolly, of Worcester, and Jo, *née* Donovan; *b* 6 Feb 1961; *Educ* Sacred Heart Coll Droitwich, Brasenose Coll Oxford; *m* 1989, Irene, *née* Kirkpatrick; 1 s (Christopher Patrick b 11 June 1989); *Career* reporter Reading Evening Post 1982–83, City reporter Thomson Newspapers 1983–84; BBC Radio: reporter Northern Ireland 1986–87, Dublin corr 1987–88, Eastern Europe corr (based Warsaw) 1988–89, Moscow corr 1990–94, Paris corr 1994–; awarded: Daily Star Gold Medal for Courage 1992, New York Radio Festival Int Reporting Prize 1993; *Recreations* eating, tennis, going to funfairs with my son; *Style*— Kevin Connolly, Esq; ✉ home: Belfast; office: c/o BBC Paris Bureau, 155 rue du Faubourg St Honoré, Paris 75366, France (☎ 00 33 1 45 63 15 88, fax 00 33 1 45 63 67 12); c/o Foreign Affairs Unit, BBC Radio News and Current Affairs, Broadcasting House, London W1A 1AA

CONNOR, (Jill) Alexandra; da of John Connor, and Ella Crossley, *née* Worthington; *b* 23 April 1959; *m* (m dis); *Career* writer and artist; one woman exhibitions: Marina Henderson Gallery, Richmond Gallery; work cmmnd by RSC and Aspreys; former presenter Past Masters on This Morning (Granada), featured in documentary 40 Minutes (BBC); subject of many articles in national newspapers and magazines, numerous appearances on TV, regular radio slots; *Books* non-fiction: The Wrong Side of the Canvas (1989), Rembrandt's Monkey (1991); fiction: The Witch Mark (1986), Thomas (1987), The Hour of the Angel (1989), The Mask of Fortune (1990), The Well of Dreams (1992), The Green Bay Tree (1993), Winter Women: Midsummer Men (1994); as Alexandra Hampton: The Experience Buyer (1994), The Deaf House (1995), The Moon is My Witness (1997); *Recreations* breeding birds, collecting masks and rare art books; *Style*— Ms Alexandra Connor; ✉ David Grossman Literary Agency, 118b Holland Park Avenue, London W11 4UA (☎ 0171 221 2770, fax 0171 221 1445)

CONNOR, Howard Arthur; s of Arthur Albert William Connor (d 1969, Sgt RAF), of Chingford, London, and Winifred Edith, *née* Rugg (d 1983); *b* 31 Jan 1938; *Educ* Richmond House Sch Chingford, Chingford Co HS; *m* 23 July 1960, Dorothy Myrtle, da of Frederick Hobbs (d 1981), of Chingford, London; 2 da (Alison b 1964, Melinda b 1966); *Career* CA; princ G H Attenborough and Co, md The Business and Financial Advisory Co Ltd; life vice pres Hoddesdon and Broxbourne C of C, memb and former chm Broxbourne Parliamentary Cons Assoc Business Gp; FCA, ATII; *Recreations* horse riding, skiing, badminton; *Clubs* Rotary of Hoddesdon (former pres); *Style*— Howard Connor, Esq; ✉ Spinney House, The Spinney, Broxbourne, Hertfordshire (☎ 01992 468071); 34 Fawkon Walk, Hoddesdon, Herts (☎ 01992 460016)

CONNOR, His Hon Judge; Jeremy George; s of Joseph Connor (d 1975), and Mabel Emmeline, *née* Adams (d 1985); *b* 14 Dec 1938; *Educ* Beaumont, UCL (LLB, DRS); *Career* called to the Bar Middle Temple 1961; circuit judge (SE Circuit) 1996–; appointed to Treasy List Central Criminal Ct 1973, met stipendiary magistrate 1979–96, chm Inner London Youth Courts 1980–96, chm Inner London Family Courts, memb Central Cncl of Probation Exec Ctee 1981, chm Inner London Probation Ctee 1989–96, memb Judicial Studies Bd 1989–94, pres Br Acad of Forensic Sciences 1990 (chm Exec Cncl 1983), chm Inst for Study and Treatment Delinquency 1992–93, referee Mental Health Fndn 1993–, memb Lord Chllr's Advsy Ctee for Legal Educn and Conduct 1996–; tstee: Grubb Inst, Stapleford Tst for Addiction, Assoc of Blind Catholics; Freeman City of London 1980, memb Ct of Assistants Worshipful Co of Fanmakers 1995– (memb Livery Ctee 1987–90); *Publications* chapter (Jury) in Archbold, Criminal Pleading, Evidence and Practice (38 and 39 edns); *Recreations* travel, theatre, occasional broadcasting; *Clubs* Garrick, RSM; *Style*— His Hon Judge Connor

CONNOR, Leslie John; s of William John Connor (d 1980), of Lancs, and Doris Eliza, *née* Neild; *b* 23 April 1932; *Educ* St Mary's Coll Crosby, Univ of Liverpool (BA), California Univ of Advanced Studies (MBA); *m* 1951, Jean Margaret, da of Roger Pendleton, of Lancashire; 2 da (Christine Lesley b 1964, Hilary Elaine b 1968); *Career* exec trainee C & A Modes 1956–58, Great Universal Stores 1958–63, Connor Finance Corporation Ltd 1963–, md Leisure and General Holdings Ltd 1970–73, fndr and chm First Castle Electronics plc 1973–86; dir: Connor Finance Corporation Ltd, W J Connor Properties Ltd, Southern Litho Supplies Ltd, Wavetown Ltd 1994; Br Show Pony Soc (BSPS): memb Cncl 1978–83, treas 1979–83, show pres 1994–; tstee Monks Ferry Trg Tst 1988–91; *Books* The Managed Growth of a Quoted British Public Company, The Working Hunter Pony (jtly); *Recreations* showing horses, farming, antiques, porcelain and painting, walking, writing, golf; *Clubs* Farmers'; *Style*— Leslie Connor, Esq; ✉ Greenacres, Bowker's Green Farm, Bowker's Green, Aughton, Lancs L39 6TA; Connor Finance Corporation Ltd, Bowker's Green Court, Bowker's Green Aughton, Lancashire L39 6TA (☎ 01695 424200, fax 01695 424109)

CONNOR, Martin; *Educ* Portsmouth Tech HS, Rose Bruford Coll; *Career* actor and director; dir Actors' Co 1979–81, fndr and co-administrator London Comedy Co 1982–93, dir Vivian Ellis Workshop from its inception in 1985; hon memb Guildhall Sch of Music and Drama; *Theatre* incl: Lovewell in The Clandestine Marriage (West End debut, Savoy Theatre), appeared in Tomfoolery (Criterion), created role of Edward Bristow in Ray Cooney's Two Into One (Shaftesbury), played Pooh Bah in Ned Sherrin's The Metropolitan Mikado (Festival Hall), Shakespeare Revue (RSC, Vaudeville); dir numerous prodns; recent credits: Babes in Toyland (Houston Grand Opera USA), Cinderella (Tokyo, Japan), Sugar (W Yorks Playhouse), Madame Sherry (Goodspeed Opera House Conn, USA), Oh Kay! (Goodspeed Opera House and tour to Detroit), Mr Cinders (Goodspeed Opera House), Wonderful Town (starring Maureen Lipman, Queens Theatre), Stepping Out (Strand), Maddie (Vaudeville), HMS Pinafore (nat Aust tour), You Can't Take it With You (King's Head), Rough Crossing (King's Head); productions for Guildhall Sch Barbican incl: My Favourite Year, Do I Hear a Waltz?, On The Twentieth Century, Lady Be Good, Girl Crazy, Out of this World, You Never Can Tell; dir Royal Masque (Drapers' Hall); other credits incl: Royal Gala with Victoria Wood (Sadler's Wells), Work (Orange Tree), Noises Off (Salisbury), The Jealous Husband (Arts Theatre), Old King Cole (Actors' Co), Happiest Days Of Your Life (Webber Douglas), Pippin (Webber Douglas); *Style*— Martin Connor, Esq; ✉ c/o Marmont Management Ltd, Langham House, 308 Regent Street, London W1R 5AL (☎ 0171 637 3183)

CONNOR, Prof (James) Michael; s of James Connor (d 1981), of Grappenhall, Cheshire, and Mona, *née* Hall; *b* 18 June 1951; *Educ* Lymm GS, Univ of Liverpool (BSc, MB ChB, MD, DSc); *m* 6 Jan 1979, Rachel Alyson Clare, da of Donald Brooks, of Woodbridge, Suffolk; 2 da (Emily b 1986, Katherine b 1987); *Career* res fell Univ of Liverpool 1977–79, resident in internal med and instr in med genetics Johns Hopkins Univ Baltimore USA 1979–82, Wellcome Tst sr lectr Univ of Glasgow 1984–87, prof of med genetics, dir of the W of Scotland Regnl Genetics Serv and hon conslt Univ of Glasgow 1987–; memb: Assoc of Physicians, Br Soc of Human Genetics, American Soc of Human Genetics; FRCP Glasgow, FRCPEd; *Books* Essential Medical Genetics (5 edn, 1997), Prenatal Diagnosis in Obstetric Practice (2 edn, 1995), Emery and Rimoin's Principles and Practice of Medical Genetics (3 edn, 1996); *Recreations* windsurfing, farming; *Clubs* Arlington Baths; *Style*— Prof Michael Connor; ✉ East Collarie Farm, Waterside, by Fenwick, Ayrshire KA3 6JJ (☎ 01560 600790); Institute of Medical Genetics, Yorkhill, Glasgow G3 8SJ (☎ 0141 201 0365, fax 0141 357 4277)

CONNOR, Michael Henry; s of Henry Connor (d 1982), and Agnes Cecilia, *née* Lindsey; *b* 5 Aug 1942; *Educ* St John's Coll Portsmouth; *m* 1964, Valerie Jannita, da of Robert Cunningham; 3 s (Benjamin b 31 Jan 1971, Matthew b 14 May 1972, Jonathan b 7 Nov 1975); *Career* HM Dip Serv: joined FCO 1964, attaché Cairo 1968–70, commercial offr Vienna 1970–73, second sec (commercial/aid) Kathmandu 1973–76, FCO 1976–81 (first sec 1979), first sec (commercial) and consul Havana 1981–82, first sec and head of Chancery Havana 1982–83, head of Chancery Ottawa 1983–88, FCO 1988–91, ambass and consul-gen El Salvador 1991–95, dir of Trade Promotion for Spain and commercial cnsllr Madrid 1995–; *Recreations* swimming, walking, photography, theatre; *Style*— Michael Connor, Esq; ✉ c/o Foreign & Commonwealth Office (Madrid), King Charles Street, London SW1A 2AH

CONNOR, His Hon Judge Roger David; s of Thomas Bernard Connor (d 1962), of Aisby, Lincolns, and Susie Violet, *née* Spittlehouse (d 1964); *b* 8 June 1939; *Educ* Merchant Taylors', Brunel Coll of Advanced Sci and Technol; *m* 25 March 1967, Sandra, da of Eldred Rolef Holmes, of Bicester, Oxon; 2 s (Hugh b 1969, Rupert b 1970); *Career* admitted slr 1968; ptnr Messrs Hodders 1970–83, met stipendiary magistrate 1983, recorder of the Crown Court 1987, circuit judge (SE Circuit) 1991–; *Recreations* music, gardening, golf; *Style*— His Hon Judge Roger Connor; ✉ Watford County Court, Cassiobury House, 11/19 Station Road, Watford, Herts WD1 1EZ

CONOLEY, Mary Patricia; da of Sir Jack Rampton (d 1994), of Tonbridge, Kent, and Lady Rampton, *née* Eileen Hart; *b* 7 Sept 1951; *Educ* Walthamstow Hall Kent, Univ of Birmingham (BA); *m* 1972, (m dis 1980), Christopher Conoley; *Career* PR offr (UK) The Dredging & Construction Co Ltd 1973–77, PR consultant UK and Aust 1977–81, sr public affairs offr Woodside Offshore Petroleum Pty Ltd 1981–84, gp PR exec The Littlewoods Organisation 1985–88, dir Shandwick Communications Ltd 1989–91, jt md Shandwick PR 1991, dir corp affrs Hawker Siddeley Group 1991, head of corp communications National Power plc 1992–96; FRGS 1984; *Recreations* skiing, diving, cooking, gardening; *Style*— Mrs Mary Conoley; ✉ Stone Well Place, Edgeworth, Stroud, Glos GL6 7JQ

CONQUEST, Dr (George) Robert Acworth; CMG (1996), OBE (1955); s of Robert Folger Westcott Conquest (d 1959), of Vence, Alpes Maritimes, and Rosamund Alys, *née* Acworth (d 1973); *b* 15 July 1917; *Educ* Winchester, Univ of Grenoble, Magdalen Coll Oxford (MA, DLitt); *m* 1, 1942 (m dis 1948), Joan, *née* Watkins; 2 s (John b 1943, Richard b 1945); m 2, 1948 (m dis 1962), Tatiana, *née* Mikhailova; m 3, 1964 (m dis 1978), Caroleen, *née* Macfarlane; m 4, 1979, Elizabeth, da of late Col Richard D Neece, USAF; *Career* writer; Capt Oxfordshire and Bucks LI 1939–46; HM Foreign Serv 1946–56: second sec Sofia, first sec UK Delgn to the UN, princ FO; fell LSE 1956–58, visiting poet Univ of Buffalo 1959–60, literary ed The Spectator 1962–63, sr fell Columbia Univ 1964–65, fell The Woodrow Wilson Int Center 1976–77, sr res fell The Hoover Inst Stanford Univ 1977–79 and 1981–, visiting scholar The Heritage Fndn 1980–81, research assoc Harvard Univ 1983–; memb Soc for the Promotion of Roman Studies; FBIS 1968, FRSL 1972, FBA 1994; *Books* incl: Poems (1955), Power and Policy in the USSR (1961), Between Mars and Venus (1963), The Great Terror (1968), Lenin (1972), The Abomination of Moab (1979), Present Danger (1979), Forays (1979), The Harvest of Sorrow (1986), New and Collected Poems (1988), Stalin (1991); *Clubs* Travellers'; *Style*— Dr Robert Conquest, CMG, OBE, FBA, FRSL; ✉ 52 Peter Coutts Circle, Stanford, California 94305, USA; Hoover Institution, Stanford, California 94305, USA (☎ 00 1 415 723 1647)

CONRAN, Elizabeth Margaret; *née* Johnston; OBE (1994); da of James Johnston (d 1954), and Elizabeth Russell, *née* Wilson (d 1987); *b* 5 May 1939; *Educ* Falkirk HS, Univ of Glasgow (MA); *m* 26 Nov 1970, (George) Loraine Conran (d 1986), s of Col George Hay Montgomery Conran (d 1940); 1 da (Violet b 1972); *Career* res asst Univ of Glasgow 1959–60, asst curator The Iveagh Bequest Kenwood House London 1960–63, keeper of paintings City Art Gallery Manchester 1963–74, arts advsr Greater Manchester Cncl 1974–79, curator The Bowes Museum Barnard Castle Co Durham 1979–; tstee Teesdale Bldgs Preservation Tst; FMA 1969, FRSA 1987; *Recreations* dance, gardens; *Style*— Mrs Elizabeth Conran, OBE; ✉ 31 Thorngate, Barnard Castle, Co Durham DL12 8QB (☎ 01833 631055); The Bowes Museum, Barnard Castle, Co Durham DL12 8NP (☎ 01833 690606, fax 01833 637163)

CONRAN, Jasper Alexander; s of Sir Terence Conran, *qv*, and Shirley Ida Conran, *née* Pearce, *qv*; *b* 12 Dec 1959; *Educ* Bryanston, Parsons Sch of Design NY; *Career* md and designer Jasper Conran Ltd; Fil d'Or (Int Linen award) 1982 and 1983, British Fashion Cncl Designer of the Year award 1986–87, Fashion Gp of America award 1987, Laurence Olivier Costume Designer of the Year award 1991 for Jean Anouilh's The Rehearsal (Almeida Theatre 1990, Garrick Theatre 1990–91), British Collections award

British Fashion Awards 1991; *Style—* Jasper Conran Esq; ✉ Jasper Conran Ltd, 6 Burnsall Street, London SW3 (☎ 0171 352 3572)

CONRAN, Shirley Ida; da of W Thirlby Pearce, and Ida Pearce; *b* 21 Sept 1932; *Educ* St Paul's Girls' Sch; *m* 1955 (m dis 1962), as his 2 w, Terence Orby Conran (now Sir Terence), *qv*; 2 s (Sebastian Conran, Jasper Conran, *qv*); *Career* designer/writer; co fndr Conran Fabrics Ltd 1957, memb Selection Ctee Design Centre 1961, first woman ed Observer Colour Magazine 1964–69, woman ed Daily Mail 1968; *Books* Superwoman (1974), Superwoman Year Book (1975), Superwoman in Action (1977), Futures (with E Sidney), Lace (1982), The Magic Garden (1983), Lace 2 (1984), Savages (1987), The Amazing Umbrella Shop (1990), Down with Superwoman (Penguin, 1990), Crimson (1992), Tiger Eyes (1994); *Style—* Ms Shirley Conran; ✉ Monaco

CONRAN, Sir Terence Orby; kt (1983); *b* 4 Oct 1931; *Educ* Bryanston; *m* 2, 1955 (m dis 1962), Shirley Ida Pearce (Shirley Conran, *qv*); 2 s (Jasper Conran, *qv*, Sebastian Conran); m 3, 1963 (m dis 1996), Caroline Herbert (the cookery writer Caroline Conran); 2 s, 1 da; *Career* currently chm: The Conran Shop Ltd (shops in London, Paris and Tokyo) 1976–, Jasper Conran Ltd 1982–, Benchmark Ltd 1989–, Blue Print Cafe Ltd 1989–, Terence Conran Ltd 1990–, Conran Shop Holdings 1990–, Le Pont de la Tour Ltd 1991–, Quaglino's Restaurant Ltd 1991–, The Butlers Wharf Chop-house Ltd 1992–, CD Partnership 1993–, Conran Holdings Ltd 1993–, Mezzo Ltd 1993–, The Bluebird Store Ltd 1994–; currently dir: Conran Ink Ltd 1969–, Conran Roche Ltd 1980–, Conran Octopus Ltd 1983–, Bibendum Restaurant Ltd 1986–, Michelin House Investment Co Ltd 1989–; jt chm Ryman Conran Ltd 1968–71; Habitat/Storehouse group: fndr 1971, chm Habitat Group Ltd 1971–88, chm Habitat France SA 1973–88, chm J Hepworth and Son Ltd 1981–83 (dir 1979–83), chm Habitat Mothercare plc (following merger) 1982–88, chm Richard Shops Ltd 1983–87, chm Heal and Son Ltd 1983–87, chm and chief exec Storehouse plc (following merger of Habitat/Mothercare with British Home Stores) 1986–88 (chm only 1988–90, non-exec dir 1990), dir BhS plc 1986–88; also formerly dir: RSCG Conran Design (formerly Conran Design Group/Conran Associates) 1971–92, The Neal Street Restaurant 1972–89, Conran Stores Inc 1977–88, Electra Risk Capital Group plc 1981–84, Savacentre Ltd 1986–88; memb: Royal Cmmn on Environmental Pollution 1973–76, Cncl RCA 1978–81 and 1986–, Advsy Cncl V & A 1979–83, Bd of Tstees V & A 1984–90, Assoc for Business Sponsorship of the Arts; estab Conran Fndn for Design Educn and Res 1981; chm Design Museum 1992– (tstee 1989–), vice pres FNAC 1985–89, pres D&AD Awards 1989; Cdr de l'Ordre des Arts et des Lettres (France) 1991; Hon FRIBA 1984, FSIAD; *Awards* Daily Telegraph/Assoc for Business Sponsorship of the Arts Award to Habitat Mothercare 1982, SIAD Medal 1982, RSA Bicentenary Medal 1984, RSA Presidential Medal for Design Mgmnt to Conran Gp, RSA Presidential Award for Design Mgmnt to Habitat Designs 1975, Hon Doctorate RCA 1996; *Books* The House Book (1974), The Kitchen Book (1977), The Bedroom and Bathroom Book (1978), The Cook Book (with Caroline Conran, 1980), Terence Conran's New House Book (1985), Conran Directory of Design (1985), Plants at Home (1986), The Soft Furnishings Book (1986), Terence Conran's France (1987), Terence Conran's DIY By Design (1989), Terence Conran's Garden DIY (1991), Toys and Children's Furniture (1992), Terence Conran's Kitchen Book (1993), The Essential House Book (1994), Terence Conran on Design (1996); *Recreations* gardening, cooking; *Style—* Sir Terence Conran; ✉ Terence Conran Ltd, 22 Shad Thames, London SE1 2YU (☎ 0171 378 1161, fax 0171 403 4309)

CONROY, Harry; *b* 6 April 1943; *m* Margaret; 3 children (Lynn, Stuart and Ewan); *Career* trainee laboratory technician Southern Gen Hosp 1961–62, night messenger (copy boy) Scottish Daily Express 1962–63, reporter Scottish Daily Mail 1966–67, fin corr Daily Record 1969–85 (reporter 1964–66 and 1967–69); NUJ: memb 1963–, memb Nat Exec Cncl 1976–85, vice pres 1980–81, pres 1981–82, gen sec 1985–90; campaign dir Scottish Constitutional Convention 1990–92; business writer, author and PR conslt 1992–; TUC delegate 1981, 1982 and 1983; STUC delegate 1981–85; assoc memb Gen and Municipal Boilermakers' Union 1984–85; *Books* Guilty by Suspicion (with James Allison, 1995), The Long March of the Market Men (with Allan Stewart, MP, 1996); *Recreations* stamp collecting, hillwalking, supporting Glasgow Celtic FC; *Style—* Harry Conroy, Esq; ✉ 24 Eskdale Drive, Rutherglen, Glasgow G73 3JS (business ☎ 0141 418 0002, fax 0141 418 0003, home ☎ 0141 643 0837)

CONROY, Stephen Alexander; s of Stephen James Conroy, of Renton, Dunbartonshire, and Elizabeth Ann, *née* Walker; *b* 2 March 1964; *Educ* St Patrick's HS Dunbarton, Glasgow Sch of Art (BA, Harry McLean Bequest, Jock McFie award, postgrad award); *Career* artist; solo exhibitions: Marlborough Fine Art London 1989 (and tour 1989), Glasgow Art Gallery & Museum 1989, Whitworth Art Gallery Manchester 1989, Marlborough Fine Art London 1992; gp exhibitions incl: The Vigorous Imagination - New Scottish Art (Scottish Nat Gallery of Modern Art, Edinburgh) 1987, The New British Painting tour USA 1988, Scottish Art Since 1990 (Scottish Nat Gallery of Modern Art Edinburgh and The Barbican London) 1989, Glasgow's Great British Art Exhibition 1990; work in the collections of: Aberdeen Art Gallery, The British Cncl, Birmingham Art Gallery, Contemporary Art Soc, Metropolitan Museum of Art NY, RCS, Robert Fleming Holdings Ltd, Scottish Nat Gallery of Modern Art, Scottish Nat Portrait Gallery; *Style—* Stephen Conroy, Esq; ✉ Marlborough Fine Art, 6 Albemarle St, London W1X 4BY (☎ 0171 629 5161, fax 0171 629 6338)

CONRY, Martin John; s of Kevin John Conry (d 1969), of Wombwell, Yorks, and Joan Mary Conry; *b* 18 Feb 1954; *Educ* St Mary's Sch Nairobi Kenya, Hodder Place, St Mary's Coll, Stonyhurst, Univ of Lancaster (BA, Cricket Colts, Rugby 2nd XV, Tennis 1st VI (colours)); *m* 7 Aug 1975, Christine Anne, da of Ronald Webster; 3 s (Paul John b 13 Aug 1979, Richard Andrew b 7 May 1982, Michael Joseph b 3 July 1985); *Career* grad trainee IPC Magazines 1975–77; Northern ad mangr: British European Associated Publishers 1977–79, Cavenham Communications 1979–81; TMD Carat (Manchester) Ltd (predecessors: TMD (Manchester) Ltd, formerly All Media Services North, TMD Manchester): joined 1981, bd dir 1985–91, dep md 1991–92, md 1992–; *Recreations* sport, flying; *Style—* Martin Conry, Esq; ✉ TMD Carat (Manchester) Ltd, 12th Floor, Portland Tower, Portland Street, Manchester M1 3LS (☎ 0161 834 9793, fax 0161 835 1363)

CONSTABLE, Prof (Charles) John; s of Charles Constable, of Bedford, and Gladys May, *née* Morris; *b* 20 Jan 1936; *Educ* Durham Sch, Univ of Cambridge (MA), Univ of London (BSc), Harvard (DBA); *m* 9 April 1960, Elisabeth Mary, da of Ronald Light (d 1981); 3 s (Charles b 1962, Giles b 1965, Piers b 1971), 1 da (Harriet b 1961); *Career* mgmnt educator and conslt; visiting prof Cranfield Sch of Mgmnt and Durham Univ Business Sch; dir Cranfield Sch of Mgmnt 1982–85 (prof of mgmnt 1971–82); dir gen Br Inst of Mgmnt 1985–86; non-exec dir: Lodge Ceramics Ltd and SIMAC Ltd 1982–90, International Military Services Ltd 1984–91, Lloyds Abbey Life Plc 1987–, Sage Group plc 1996–; govr Harpur Tst 1979– (chm 1994–); memb: NEDO Heavy Electrical Machinery EDC 1977–87, N Beds DHA 1987–90; chm Bright Tech Developments Ltd 1989–; *Books* Group Assessment Programmes (with D A Smith, 1966), Text and Cases in Operations Management (with C C New, 1976), Cases in Strategic Management (with J Stopford and D Channon, 1980), The Making of British Managers (with R McCormick, 1987); *Recreations* family, golf; *Clubs* Bedfordshire Golf, Minehead and W Somerset Golf; *Style—* Prof John Constable; ✉ 20 Kimbolton Rd, Bedford MK40 2NR (☎ 01234 212576); Gore Point, Porlock Weir, Minehead, Somerset

CONSTABLE, Gp Capt John Hurn; s of Prof F H Constable (d 1975), and Sance Helena Catherock, *née* Robson (d 1981); *b* 19 Aug 1934; *Educ* Hitchin GS, RAF Coll, RAF Staff Coll, Nat Def Coll, Univ of London, Open Univ (BA); *m* 12 Aug 1961, Karin, da of Karsten Emmanuel Amundsen, of Oslo, Norway; 1 s (Harald John Catherock b 6 June 1962), 1 da (Helen Katrine (Dr Lindley) b 19 Nov 1964); *Career* cmmnd RAF (Sec Branch) 1956 (Sword of Honour), various appts Norway, MOD, Germany then RAF Wyton 1976–78, Directing Staff Nat Def Coll 1978–80, Dep Dir RAF Ground Trg MOD 1980–83, Cmd Accountant RAF Support Cmd 1983–87, ret 1987; Secondary of London and Under Sheriff, High Bailiff of Southwark 1987–; hon sec City of London Sheriffs' Soc 1987–; memb Ctee: Sheriff's and Recorder's Fund 1987–, Assoc of Under Sheriffs of England and Wales 1996–; dep vice chm (Air) Gtr London TAVRA 1992–, memb European Atlantic Gp 1993–; hon sec St Boniface PCC 1970–73, hon treas St Mary's PCC 1983–85, vol St Botolph's Crypt Project 1993–, tstee Cambs Historic Churches Tst 1996–; ed jls: RAF Coll, RAF Staff Coll, Nat Def Coll; Freeman City of London 1982, Jr Warden Worshipful Co Chartered Secs and Admins 1996; SBOStJ 1996; FRGS 1975, FRSA 1977, FCIS 1977, FInstAM 1977, FIMgt 1980; *Recreations* fell walking, travel, classical music and fine art, history; *Clubs* RAF; *Style—* Gp Capt John Constable; ✉ Central Criminal Court, Warwick Square, Warwick Lane, London EC4M 7BS (☎ 0171 248 3277, fax 0171 489 8451)

CONSTABLE, Paule; da of Wing Cdr Paul Constable, RAF, AFC, of Saudi Arabia, and Evelyn Rose Hadley; *b* 9 Nov 1966; *Educ* Goldsmiths' Coll; *Partner* Ian Richards; 1 da (Morgan Jezebel Richards b 14 May 1996); *Career* lighting designer; appts as lighting electrician incl: Midnight Design Ltd 1988–1990, Opera 80 (dep) 1990, Edinburgh Int Theatre (chief for Churchill Theatre 1990, dep chief for Playhouse Theatre 1991), English Shakespeare Co (chief) 1990–91, Rose English's The Double Wedding (prodn, LIFT) 1991, Shared Experiences's UK tour of Anna Karenina (prodn) 1991, Rosie Lee (prodn) 1992, Mayfest (chief) 1992; appts as prodn mangr incl: International Workshop Festival 1990, Theatre de Complicite's The Winters Tale (UK tour) 1992, Theatre de Complicite's The Street of Crocodiles (World tour) 1993–94; tstee Cmmn to Promote Ribald Discourse Amongst Lighting Designers; memb Assoc of Lighting Designers; *Theatre* prodns incl: The Resistable Rise of Arturo Ui (7:84 Scotland) 1991, Scotland Matters (7:84 Scotland) 1992, The Street of Crocodiles (Theatre de Complicite/RNT (Olivier Award nomination for Best Lighting Design 1993)) 1992, Don Carlos (Lyric Studio) 1992, Billy Liar (RNT Mobil touring prodn) 1992, India Song (Theatr Clwyd) 1993, Julius Caesar (English Shakespeare Co) 1993, Bondagers (Traverse) 1993, The Three Lives of Lucie Cabrol (Theatre de Complicite) 1994, Death of a Salesman (Yorkshire Playhouse) 1994, Omma, Oedipus and the Luck of Thebes (Young Vic) 1994, The Magic Flute (Opera North) 1994, The Slab Boys Trilogy (Young Vic) 1994, Mosquito Coast (David Glass Mime Ensemble) 1994, Out of a House Walked a Man (Theatre de Complicite/RNT) 1994, Lucky (David Glass Mime Ensemble) 1995, Life with an Idiot (ENO) 1995, Death of the Carmelites (Guildhall Sch) 1995, Spring Awakening (RSC) 1995, Tartuffe (Royal Exchange) 1995, Werther (English Touring Opera) 1995, The Jungle Book (Young Vic) 1995, Ines de Castro (Scottish Opera) 1996, Don Giovanni (WNO) 1996, Henry IV (parts I & II, English Touring Theatre) 1996, A Christmas Carol (Lyric Hammersmith) 1996, The Mysteries (RSC) 1997, The Caucasian Chalk Circle (RNT) 1997; *Recreations* travel, cricket; *Style—* Ms Paule Constable; ✉ c/o Richard Haig, Performing Arts Management, 6 Windmill Street, London W1P 1HF (☎ 0171 255 1362, fax 0171 631 4631)

CONSTANT, Richard Ashley Meyricke; MBE (1983); s of Maj Ashley Henry Constant (d 1985), and Mabel Catherine (Kate), *née* Meyricke (d 1972); *b* 25 Nov 1954; *Educ* King's Sch Canterbury, RMAS, Univ of Durham (BA); *m* 1984, Melinda Jane, da of late H J Davies; 2 s (Llewelyn Ashley Meyricke b 1985, Tristam Ashley Meyricke b 1987), 2 da (Sophia b 1989, Rosanna (twin) b 1989); *Career* cmmnd Royal Green Jackets 1973, ret with the rank of Maj; merchant banker Robert Fleming & Co Limited 1985–89; md Gavin Anderson & Company UK Limited 1990–; non-exec dir: Austin Reed Group plc, Fibrowatt Ltd; *Recreations* shooting, fishing; *Clubs* IOD, Royal Green Jackets, Wig and Pen; *Style—* Richard Constant, Esq, MBE; ✉ Park Lodge, Aislaby, nr Whitby, North Yorkshire (☎ 01947 810250); Gavin Anderson & Co Ltd, 15–17 Eldon Street, London EC2M 7LA (☎ 0171 457 2345)

CONSTANTINE, David John; s of William Bernard Constantine, of Deganwy, North Wales, and Bertha, *née* Gleave; *b* 4 March 1944; *Educ* Manchester GS, Wadham Coll Oxford (BA, DPhil); *m* 9 July 1966, Helen Frances, da of Richard Stanley Best; 1 s (Simon Martin b 1 Oct 1972), 1 da (Mary Ann b 27 Nov 1968); *Career* sr lectr in German Univ of Durham 1979–80 (lectr 1969–79), fell in German Queen's Coll Oxford 1980–; fndr memb Durham Cyrenians charity for homeless (sec 1972–80); *Books* poetry: A Brightness to Cast Shadows (1980), Watching for Dolphins (1983, Alice Hunt Barlett Award), Madder (1987, Southern Arts Literature Prize), New and Selected Poems (1991), Caspar Hauser (1994); fiction: Davies (1985), Back at the Spike (1994); trans: Selected Poems of Friedrich Hölderlin (1990, new edn 1996), Goethe's Elective Affinities (1994); academic works: Early Greek Travellers and the Hellenic Ideal (1984, Runciman Prize), Hölderlin (1988); *Recreations* walking; *Style—* David Constantine, Esq; ✉ The Queen's College, University of Oxford, Oxford OX1 4AW

CONSTANTINE, Dennis; s of William Bernard Constantine (d 1953), of Accrington, Lancs, and Elsie, *née* Higson (d 1946); *b* 29 April 1926; *Educ* Accrington GS; *m* 1, 22 Dec 1949, Brenda Mary (d 1981), da of William J Rees; 2 da (Susan b 16 Jan 1951, Sharon b 29 Oct 1953); m 2, 20 Feb 1982, Elizabeth Joan Laverack (d 1996), da of Horace Pye; *Career* photographer; trainee quantity surveyor 1942–44, Nat Serv RAF 1944–47, ptnr Reilly & Constantine 1949–70, proprietor Constantine 1970–84; md: Constantine Colour Finishing Ltd 1970–86, Anthony Buckley & Constantine 1978–; exhibitions of portrait photography in Hong Kong, Singapore, Thailand and Aust, lectr to professional photographers throughout Europe, USA and Far East; pres and chm Inst of Incorporated Photograhers (now BIPP) 1962–63, pres Cncl Professional Photographers of Europe 1971–75, former chm Fellowship Ctee BIPP; Hon Master of Photography Professional Photographers of America 1975, Hon FBIPP 1980 (FBIPP 1962); *Recreations* walking, music, opera, travel; *Clubs* Oriental; *Style—* Dennis Constantine, Esq; ✉ Park Hall, Salford Priors, Worcs WR11 5SG (☎ 01789 490431); Anthony Buckley & Contantine Ltd, 109 Mount Street, London W1Y 5HE (☎ 0171 629 5235, fax 0171 499 7018); Upper Courtyard, Ragley Hall, Alcester, Warwickshire B49 5NH (☎ 01789 763953, fax 01789 763053)

CONSTANTINE, Joseph; s of Maj Robert Alfred Constantine, TD, JP (d 1968), and Marie Leonie Françoise Van Haaren (d 1993), eleventh in descent through female line from William the Silent, Count of Nassau in the Netherlands and Prince of Orange; *b* 12 Feb 1928; *Educ* Eton; *m* 1954, Mary Rose, da of late Harwood Lawrence Cotter, and Rosemary, Lady Ley (d 1977), yr da of late Capt Duncan Macpherson, RN, and sister of late Francis Cameron Macpherson of Cluny, 26 Chief of Clan Macpherson; 2 da (Annette (Hon Mrs Jonathan Boyd) b 1956, Susannah (Mrs Sten Bertelsen) b 1962); *Career* Lt Coldstream Gds 1946–48; Constantine Holdings Ltd: md 1965–92, pres 1992–; FRICS 1955; *Recreations* painting; *Clubs* Brooks's, Turf; *Style—* Joseph Constantine, Esq; ✉ 9 Canning Place, London W8 (☎ 0171 584 7640); The Priory, Knipton, Grantham, Lincs (☎ 01476 870238)

CONSTANTINE OF STANMORE, Baron (Life Peer UK 1981), of Stanmore in Greater London; Theodore Constantine; kt (1964), CBE (1956), AE (1945), DL (Greater London 1967); s of Leonard Constantine, of London, and Fanny Louise Constantine; *b* 15 March 1910; *Educ* Acton Coll; *m* 1935, Sylvia Mary (d 1990), yr da of Wallace Henry Legge-Pointing, of London; 1 s (Hon Roy b 1936), 1 da (Hon Jill (Hon

Mrs Murray) b 1938); *Career* sits as Conservative Peer in the House of Lords; served WWII RAuxAF; dir of industrial holding co 1956–59, chm of public companies 1959–85; chm Anscon Ltd; pres National Union of Cons and Unionist Assocs 1980– (chm 1967–68); High Sheriff Greater London 1967; Master Worshipful Co of Coachmakers 1975, Freeman City of London; *Recreations* reading, walking, watching motor racing; *Clubs* Carlton; *Style*— The Rt Hon Lord Constantine of Stanmore, CBE, AE, DL; ✉ Hunters Beck, Uxbridge Rd, Stanmore, Middx

CONSTANTINIDES, Prof Anthony George; s of George Anthony Constantinides, and Paraskeve Constantinides Skaliondas; *b* 1 Jan 1943; *Educ* The Pancyprian Gymnasium, Univ of London (BSc, PhD); *m* 21 Dec 1968, Pamela Maureen, da of Anthony Robert Bowman (ka 1940); 1 s (George Anthony b 21 Oct 1975); *Career* sr res fell the PO Res Dept 1968–70, prof in signal processing Imperial Coll of Sci and Technol 1983– (lectr then reader 1970–83); author of six books and over 200 papers in learned jls on aspects of digital signal processing; MIEEE 1978, FIEE 1985, FRSA 1986; Chevalier Palmes Academiques France; *Recreations* reading; *Style*— Prof Anthony Constantinides; ✉ Imperial College of Science Technology and Medicine, Dept of Electrical and Electronic Engineering, Exhibition Rd, London SW7 2BT (☎ 0171 589 5111)

CONSTANTINOU, Achilleas; s of Nicos Constatinou (d 1971), of London, and Efthymia, *née* Cleanthous; *b* 21 April 1948; *Educ* Arnos Secdy Modern Sch Southgate London, Waltham Forest Tech Coll, King's Coll London (LLB); *m* Androulla, da of George Georgallides; 3 s (Alexander Nicholas b 21 June 1981, Nicholas George b 3 May 1982, Marcus Aristos b 18 July 1990), 1 da (Lana Marie b 4 Aug 1984); *Career* started fashion business Aristos of London with late bro Aristos at 45 Carnaby St in 1966, joined family co full time in 1971, by 1973 owned 6 retail outlets in Carnaby St and Oxford St, a wholesale showroom in Great Portland St and headquarters in Marylebone, subsequently relocated showrooms to Mortimer St and subsequently to larger premises in Great Portland St and headquarters to Wood Green, was honoured by a royal visit by Princess Anne in 1992 to celebrate co's 25th anniversary; chm and md Ariella Fashions Ltd & Group of Cos 1985– (winner of two Women Fashion awards for Best Cocktail Dress and Best Evening Dress 1985); fndr Br Fashion Design Protection Assoc 1974 (which succeeded in gaining copyright protection extended to cover orignial fashion garment designs in 1980), advsr to Govt on amendments to Design Copyright and Patents Act 1988, UK rep EEC meeting of Assoc Européene des Industries de L'Habillement, fndr memb Fashion Indust Action Gp (responsible for formation of Br Fashion Cncl), fndr memb and dir Br Fashion Cncl (memb Exhibitors' Ctee), memb Advsy Bd London Fashion Exhbn, former chm Women's Wear Exec Ctee Br Knitting Clothing and Export Cncl; memb Gray's Inn; *Books* Memorandum on the Law of Copyright, Design Protection (contrib); *Style*— Achilleas Constantinou, Esq; ✉ Ariella Fashions Ltd, Aristos House, 25 Watsons Road, Wood Green, London N22 4TZ (☎ 0181 888 1213, fax 0181 889 8736)

CONTE HELM, Marie; *b* 13 Nov 1949, New York City; *Educ* City Univ of NY (BA), East West Center Univ of Hawaii (MA); *Career* lectr art history Leeward Community Coll Hawaii 1973–74, cultural offr Japan Info Centre Embassy of Japan London 1975–79, lectr in art history Sunderland Poly 1979–86, head Japanese Studies Div and reader in Japanese studies Univ of Sunderland 1986–94, reader in Japanese studies Univ of Northumbria 1994–; external examiner BA/MA in Japanese studies Univ of Sheffield 1992–; memb: British Assoc for Japanese Studies (hon sec 1992–94), Euro Assoc for Japanese Studies, Royal Soc for the Encouragement of Arts, Manufacturers and Commerce; memb Cncl Japan Soc 1992–96, memb Educn Ctee Japan Festival 1991 1989–91 (N Regnl Ctee 1988–91), memb Ctee Japan Language Assoc 1990–, Univ of Sunderland rep Anglo-Korean Network 1990–, chair Anglo-Japanese Women's Soc 1990–; memb Japan Studies Gp of UK-Japan 2000 Gp 1992–; *Books* Japan and the North East of England - From 1862 to the Present Day (1989, a Financial Times Book of the Yr 1989, Japanese edn 1991), The Japanese and Europe: Economic and Cultural Encounters (1996); author of numerous articles and reviews; *Style*— Ms Marie Conte Helm; ✉ Faculty of Arts and Design, University of Northumbria at Newcastle, Squires Building, Newcastle upon Tyne NE1 8ST (☎ 0191 227 3858, fax 0191 227 4559)

CONTI, Rt Rev Mario Joseph; *see:* Aberdeen, Bishop of (RC)

CONTI, Thomas A (Tom); s of Alfonso Conti (d 1961), of Paisley, Renfrewshire, and Mary McGoldrick (d 1979); *b* 22 Nov 1941; *Educ* Royal Scottish Acad of Music; *m* 1967, Katherine Drummond, da of Wilson George Drummond Tait, of Edinburgh; 1 da (Nina b 1973); *Career* actor and director; *Theatre* began 1960; London appearances incl: Savages (Royal Court and Comedy) 1973, The Devil's Disciple (RSC Aldwych) 1976, Whose Life Is It Anyway? (Mermaid and Savoy 1978, NY 1979), They're Playing Our Song (Shaftesbury) 1980, Romantic Comedy (Apollo) 1983, Jeffrey Bernard Is Unwell (Lyric) 1990, The Ride Down Mount Morgan (Wyndhams) 1991, Present Laughter (also dir) 1993, Chapter Two (Gielgud) 1996; as director: Last Licks (Broadway) 1979, Before the Party (Oxford Playhouse and Queen's) 1980, The Housekeeper (Apollo) 1982; *Television* incl: Madame Bovary, The Norman Conquests, Glittering Prizes, The Quick and the Dead (TV film), The Beatte Klarsfeld Story (mini-series), Wright Verdicts (USA) 1995; *Films* incl: Galileo 1974, Flame 1974, Eclipse 1975, Full Circle 1977, The Duelists 1977, The Wall 1980, Merry Christmas Mr Lawrence 1983, Reuben Reuben 1983, Miracles, Heavenly Pursuits, Beyond Therapy, Saving Grace, American Dreamer, Two Brothers Running, White Roses, Shirley Valentine, Someone Else's America 1994; *Awards* for Whose Life Is It Anyway?: Best Actor in a New Play SWET 1978, Best Stage Actor Variety Club of GB 1978, Tony for Best Actor 1979; *Clubs* Garrick; *Style*— Tom Conti Esq; ✉ c/o Chatto & Linnit, Prince of Wales Theatre, Coventry Street, London W1V 7FE (☎ 0171 930 6677, fax 0171 930 0091)

CONTRERAS, Dr (Carmen) Marcela; da of Dr Juan Eduardo Contreras (d 1993), of Coelemu, Chile, and Elena Mireya, *née* Arriagada; *b* 4 Jan 1942; *Educ* Dunalastair Br Sch for Girls Santiago Chile, Sch of Med Univ of Chile (clinical/immunology scholar, BSc, LMed, Medico-Cirujano, MD); *m* 1968, Dr Roberto Jaime Guiloff, s of Angel Guiloff; 1 s (Claudio b 10 Nov 1968), 1 da (Carolina b 1 May 1972); *Career* internship (gen med) Hosp San Juan de Dios Santiago Chile 1967–68, trg prog in internal med, immunology and immunohaematology (Univ of Chile) Univ Hosp J J Aguirre and Hosp San Juan de Dios Santiago 1968–72, lectr in immunology and immunohaematology Blood Bank and Centre of Immunohaematology Univ Hosp J J Aguirre Santiago 1971–72, Br Cncl scholar Royal Postgraduate Med Sch and MRC Blood Gp Unit London 1972–74, head Immunohaematology Lab North London Blood Transfusion Centre Edgware Middx 1974–78, sr registrar in haematology St Mary's Hosp London and Northwick Park Hosp Harrow Middx 1978–80; North London Blood Transfusion Centre London: dep dir 1980–84, chief exec/med dir 1984–95; exec dir London and SE Zone Nat Blood Serv 1995–; memb Cncl: Int Soc of Blood Transfusion (pres 1996–98), RCPath (chm Sub-ctee on Transfusion Med 1994–95); pres Section of Pathology RSM 1992–94; ed in chief Vox Sanguinis 1996–; hon sr lectr St Mary's Hosp London, hon memb MRC Blood Gp Unit; memb: Br Soc for Haematology, BMA, American Assoc of Blood Banks, Int Soc of Blood Transfusion, Br Blood Transfusion Soc, RSM (Sections of Pathology and Immunology), Euro Sch of Transfusion Med, Euro Cord Blood Banking Gp, UK Cord Blood Banking Gp; MRCPath 1988, FRCPEd 1992; *Books* Blood Transfusion in Clinical Med (jtly, 8 edn 1987, 9 edn 1993), ABC of Blood Transfusion (1990, 2 edn 1992), Blood Transfusion: The Impact of New Technologies (1990); author of over 300 pubns in the field of transfusion med; *Recreations* opera, theatre, walking, reading, training in developing countries; *Clubs* International Medical, Haematology Travellers'; *Style*— Dr Marcela Contreras; ✉ North London Blood Transfusion Centre, Colindale Avenue, London NW9 5BG (☎ 0181 200 4005/6, fax 0181 205 5017)

CONVILLE, David Henry; OBE (1983); s of Lt-Col Leopold Henry George Conville, CBE (d 1979), of Convillepur Farm, Sahiwal, Pakistan, and Katherine Mary, *née* Gispert (d 1973); *b* 4 June 1929; *Educ* Marlborough, St John's Coll Oxford, RADA; *m* 1, Jean Margaret Bury (d 1967); 1 da (Clare b 14 Oct 1959); m 2, 2 Jan 1970, Philippa Juliet Antonia, da of Alfred John Gordge (d 1959); 1 s (Leo b 23 Jan 1979); *Career* Nat Serv 1947–49, cmmnd Royal Welch Fus, 2 Lt 4 Bn Nigeria Regt Royal WAFF; Ipswich Rep Theatre 1952, Stratford Meml Theatre Co 1955 and 1957, fndr David Conville Prodns (toured 1959), first London prodns 1960, Toad of Toad Hall (West End) 1960–84, fndr New Shakespeare Co 1962, dir New Shakespeare Co at Open Air Theatre Regent's Park 1962–86, pres Soc of West End Theatre 1975, 1976 and 1983; plays written incl: The Wind in the Willows 1984, Look Here Old Son 1986, Obituaries 1988; awarded Coronation medal 1953; chm: Drama Centre 1982–89, The New Shakespeare Co; memb: Arts Cncl Drama Panel 1988–92, Soc of West End Theatres, Theatre Managers' Assoc; *Recreations* walking, reading, real tennis, wine; *Clubs* Garrick; *Style*— David Conville, Esq, OBE; ✉ The Old Farmhouse, Okeford Fitzpaine, Blandford, Dorset DT11 0RP

CONWAY, Dr Ashley V; *b* 7 Sept 1956; *Educ* St Edward's Sch Oxford, Univ of Southampton (BSc), Univ of London (PhD); *m* 7 July 1984, Martine Louise, *née* Jeronimus; 1 s (Joseph Jeronimus b 15 March 1989), 2 da (Emily Louise b 29 Aug 1987, Catherine May b 25 April 1993); *Career* psychologist specialising in application of hypnosis in treating anxiety and stress-related illness; sec Univ Psychology Soc 1977–79, hon psychologist Charing Cross Hosp 1985–, psychologist Devonshire Clinic London 1986–91, trauma conslt PPC UK Ltd 1993–; pt/t med res examining mind/body interactions 1985–, author of numerous published papers on related subjects in med and psychological jls; *Style*— Dr A V Conway; ✉ 10 Harley Street, London W1N 1AA (☎ 0171 467 8300, fax 0171 467 8312)

CONWAY, Dr David Ian; s of Jack and Gita Conway, of Salford; *b* 21 April 1948; *Educ* Manchester GS, Univ of Manchester (MB ChB, MD); *m* 23 Oct 1975, Pauline; 3 s (Jonathan b 1978, Benjamin b 1984, Duncan b 1988), 4 da (Rachel b 1979, Heather b 1981, Felicity b 1982, Rebecca b 1986); *Career* lectr obstetrics and gynaecology (specialising in infertility) Univ of Bristol 1980–84; conslt; Monklands Dist Gen Hosp Airdrie, Bellshill Maternity Hosp Bellshill Lanarkshire 1984–; FRCOG 1992 (MRCOG 1977); *Recreations* my family; *Style*— Dr David Conway; ✉ 53 Kirkintilloch Road, Lenzie, Glasgow, Scotland G66 4LB (☎ 0141 776 1463); Monklands District General Hospital, Monkscourt Ave, Airdrie, Lanarkshire, Scotland (☎ 01236 748748); Glasgow Nuffield Hospital, Beaconsfield Road, Glasgow (☎ 0141 334 9441)

CONWAY, Derek Leslie; MP (C) Shrewsbury and Atcham (majority 10,965); s of Leslie Conway, and Florence Gwendoline, *née* Bailes; *b* 15 Feb 1953; *Educ* Beacon Hill Boys' Sch; *m* 1980, Colette Elizabeth Mary, da of Charles Lamb; 2 s (Henry b 1982, Fredrick b 1985), 1 da (Claudia b 6 March 1989); *Career* memb Cons Pty Nat Exec 1972–81, nat vice chm Young Cons 1973–75; Parly candidate: (C) Durham Oct 1974, Newcastle upon Tyne East 1979; MP (C) Shrewsbury and Atcham 1983–; PPS: to Min of State for Wales 1988–91, to Min of State Dept of Employment 1992–93; asst Govt whip 1993–94; a Lord Cmmr HM Treasy (Govt whip) and memb Bd Treasy 1994–96, Vice-Chamberlain of HM Household (Govt whip) 1996–; memb Select Ctees: on Agriculture, on Tport, on Armed Forces Discipline 1990–91; vice-chm Defence Ctee 1991–93; borough cncllr 1974–78, ldr Tyne and Wear Met CC 1979–82 (memb 1977–83); memb: Bd Washington Devpt Corpn 1979–83, Bd Newcastle Airport 1979–82; Maj 5 Bn The LI TA; *Clubs* Beaconsfield, Shrewsbury; *Style*— Derek Conway, Esq, MP; ✉ House of Commons, London SW1A 0AA

CONWAY, Prof Gordon Richard; s of Cyril Gordon Conway (d 1977), of Kingston, Surrey, and Thelma, *née* Goodwin (d 1992); *b* 6 July 1938; *Educ* Kingston GS, Kingston Tech Coll, Univ of Wales Bangor (BSc), Univ of Cambridge (DipAgSc), Univ of West Indies Trinidad (DTA), Univ of California Davis (PhD); *m* 20 March 1965, Susan Mary, da of Harold Mumford, of Winchester, Hants; 1 s (Simon Goodwin b 10 Feb 1967), 2 da (Katherine Ellen b 2 March 1973, Zoe Martha (twin)); *Career* entomologist State of Sabah Malaysia 1961–66, statistician Inst of Ecology Univ of California 1966–69; Univ of London: res fell and lectr Dept of Zoology & Applied Entomology Imperial Coll 1970–76, reader in environmental mgmnt 1976–80, prof of environmental technol 1980–88, chm Centre for Environmental Technol 1980–86 (dir 1977–80), dir Sustainable Agric Prog Int Inst for Environment and Devpt 1986–88; rep for India, Nepal and Sri Lanka The Ford Foundation New Delhi 1989–92, vice chllr Univ of Sussex 1992–; visiting prof Imperial Coll 1989–; memb: Royal Cmmn on Environmental Pollution 1984–88, Educn and Trg Gp DTI 1993–; chm Bd IDS 1992–; memb Bd: Int Inst for Environment and Devpt London 1993–, Int Food Policy Research Inst Washington DC 1994–; dir: BOC Fndn London 1994–, Sussex Enterprise 1994–; chm Runnymede Cmmn on British Muslims and Islamaphobia 1996–; FIBiol; *Books* Pest and Pathogen Control (1980), After The Green Revolution (jtly, 1989), Unwelcome Harvest (jtly, 1991); *Recreations* travel, music; *Clubs* Reform; *Style*— Prof Gordon Conway; ✉ University of Sussex, Sussex House, Falmer, Brighton, E Sussex BN1 9RH (☎ 01273 678253, fax 01273 678335)

CONWAY, Dr (John) Kevin; s of William John Conway (d 1972), of Omagh, Co Tyrone, and Mary Theresa Conway (d 1971); *b* 31 Dec 1946; *Educ* Beragh PS Co Tyrone, Christian Bros' GS Omagh, Queen's Univ Belfast (BSc, PhD, dip in educn); *m* 8 Aug 1970, Winifred Mary, da of John R Cosgrove, and Joan Cosgrove; 3 s (Martin John b 16 Dec 1972, Simon Joseph b 29 April 1979, David Jonathan b 24 March 1981), 1 da (Mary Joan b 6 April 1975); *Career* British Sch of Brussels: Physics teacher 1973–, examinations offr 1975–, head Careers Dept 1977–80, Head Physics Dept 1979–80; head of Sixth Form Dane Court Sch Broadstairs 1980–82, vice princ St Brendan's Sixth Form Coll Bristol 1982–85, vice princ designate S Bristol Tertiary Coll 1985–86, coordinator Avon TVEI 1986, princ Greenhead Coll Huddersfield 1987–; *Books* 'A' Level Analysis for Added Value (1991); *Recreations* education; *Style*— Dr Kevin Conway; ✉ Greenhead Sixth Form College, Greenhead Road, Huddersfield HD1 4ES (☎ 01484 422032, fax 01484 518025)

CONWAY, Dr (David) Martin; s of Lt-Col Geoffrey Seymour Conway, MC (d 1984), of Portpatrick, Galloway, and Elsie, *née* Phillips (d 1992); *b* 22 Aug 1935; *Educ* Sedbergh, Gonville and Caius Coll Cambridge (BA, MA); *m* 10 March 1962, Ruth Fairey, da of Rev Richard Daniel (d 1983), of Audlem, Cheshire; 1 s (John b 1967), 2 da (Ann (Mrs Conway-Jones), Moira (Mrs Zheng)); *Career* int sec Student Christian Movement GB and Ireland 1958–61, study sec World Student Christian Fedn Geneva 1961–67, C of E's sec for Chaplaincies in Higher Educn London 1967–70, ed and pubns sec World Cncl of Churches Geneva 1970–74, asst gen sec Br Cncl of Churches London 1974–83, tutor in church and soc Ripon Coll Cuddesdon Oxford and dir Oxford Inst for Church and Soc 1983–86, pres Selly Oak Colls Birmingham 1986–97; ed: Oxford Papers on Contemporary Soc 1984–86, Christians Together newsletter 1983–91; vice chm Birmingham Diocesan Bd for Mission 1993–, chm Friends of the Church in China 1994–; *Books* The Undivided Vision (1966), Seeing Education Whole (1970), The Christian Enterprise in Higher Education (1971), Look Listen Care (1983), That's When the Body Works (1991); *Recreations* friends, travel, music; *Style*— Dr Martin Conway; ✉ President's House,

Selly Oak Colleges, Birmingham B29 6LQ (☎ 0121 472 2462); President's Office, Selly Oak Colleges, Birmingham B29 6LQ (☎ 0121 472 4231, fax 0121 472 8852, telex 334349 SELLYO G)

CONWAY, Robert David; s of Walter Conway, of Guildford; *b* 11 Dec 1949; *Educ* Univ of London (LLB); *m* 17 Jan 1976, Patricia Lock; 2 da (Anna b 6 Oct 1978, Laura b 20 Sept 1980); *Career* tax offr 1969, DPP 1973, called to the Bar Inner Temple 1974, SE circuit, lectr in law and legal conslt to Legal Protection Insur Co; writer and performer (as Walter Zerlin Jr); winner Edinburgh Festival Scotsman Award 1975 and 1980, own tv show on Granada, six plays published and performed worldwide; dir: Entertainment Machine Theatre Co, Coups De Theatre Ltd, Conway McGillivray Publishing House; legal advsr to A Fish Called Wanda, and Marlon Brando's A Dry White Season; *Books* Miss You've Dropped Your Briefs (cartoonist), The British Alternative Theatre Directory (ed yearly); *Recreations* art, music, swimming; *Style*— Robert Conway, Esq; ✉ 7 Stone Buildings, Lincoln's Inn, London WC2A 3SZ (☎ 0171 242 0961)

CONWAY, Robert John; s of Ernest Conway, and Jean Patricia; *b* 10 June 1951; *Educ* Univ of Salford (BSc); *m* 1 July 1972, Susan Mary; 1 s (Matthew James b 1975), 3 da (Claire Louise b 1977, Charlotte Elizabeth b 1979, Caroline Michelle b 1980); *Career* CA; ptnr Price Waterhouse; pres Southern Soc of Chartered Accountants 1996–97; FCA; *Style*— Robert Conway, Esq; ✉ Primavera, Goodworth Clatford, nr Andover, Hampshire (☎ 01264 323454); Price Waterhouse, The Quay, 30 Channel Way, Ocean Village, Southampton, Hants (☎ 01703 330077)

CONYNGHAM, 7 Marquess (I 1816); Frederick William Henry Francis Conyngham; also (sits as) Baron Minster (UK 1821), Earl Conyngham (I 1781), Baron Conyngham (I 1781), Viscount Conyngham (I 1789), Viscount Mount Charles (I 1797), Earl of Mount Charles and Viscount Slane (I 1816); patron of one living; s of 6 Marquess Conyngham (d 1974), by his 2 wife Antoinette Winifred, *née* Thompson (d 1966); *b* 13 March 1924; *Educ* Eton; *m* 1, 29 April 1950 (m dis 1970), Eileen Wren, o da of Capt Clement Wren Newsam; 3 s; m 2, 1971, Elizabeth Ann, yr da of late Frederick Molyneux Hughes, of Fareham, Hants, and formerly w of David Sutherland Rudd; m 3, 1980, Daphne Georgina Adelaide (d 24 Nov 1986), eldest da of R C Armour, and formerly w of C P V Walker; m 4, 29 May 1987, (Emma Christianne) Annabelle, o da of (Denys) Martin Agnew, of Keverstone Court, 95–97 Manor Road, Bournemouth BH13 BY; *Heir* s, Earl of Mount Charles, *qv*; *Career* late Capt Irish Gds; *Recreations* fishing, shooting, golf, tennis; *Clubs* Royal St George Yacht; *Style*— The Most Hon the Marquess; ✉ Myrtle Hill, Ramsey, Isle of Man

COODE-ADAMS, (John) Giles Selby; DL (Essex); s of Geoffery Coode-Adams (d 1986), and Cynthia Mildred, *née* Selby-Bigge; *b* 30 Aug 1938; *Educ* Eton; *m* 30 April 1960, Sonia Elisabeth, da of Laurence Frederick York (d 1965); 1 s (Ben b 19 Aug 1965), 1 da (Henrietta Guest b 5 Feb 1962); *Career* 2 Lt 16/5 Queen's Royal Lancers 1956–58; ptnr L Messel 1967– (joined 1959, taken over by Shearson Lehman Hutton 1984), md Lehman Brothers 1986–; chief exec Royal Botanic Gardens Kew Fndn, former memb Cncl Univ of Essex; Freeman: City of London, Worshipful Co of Merchant Taylors; *Recreations* fishing, music, gardening; *Clubs* Boodle's; *Style*— Giles Coode-Adams, Esq, DL; ✉ Lehman Brothers International, 1 Broadgate, London EC2 (☎ 0171 260 2122)

COOGAN, Ven Robert Arthur William; s of Ronald Dudley Coogan (d 1965), and Joyce Elizabeth, *née* Roberts (d 1971); *b* 11 July 1929; *Educ* Launceston HS, Univ of Tasmania (BA), Univ of Durham (DipTheol); *Career* asst curate St Andrew Plaistow 1953–56, rector Bothwell Tasmania 1956–62; vicar: St John N Woolwich 1962–73, St Stephen Hampstead 1973–77, St Stephen with All Hallows Hampstead 1977–85; priest i/c All Hallows Gospel Oak 1974–77; area dean: S Camden 1975–81, N Camden 1978–83; prebendary St Paul's Cathedral 1982–85, commissary for Bishop of Tasmania 1968–88, examining chaplain Bishop of Edmonton 1985–94, archdeacon of Hampstead 1985–94, ret; *Recreations* reading, gardening, travel; *Clubs* The Oriental; *Style*— The Ven Robert Coogan; ✉ 30 Marchwood Gate, Marchwood, Chichester, West Sussex PO19 4HA (☎ 01243 528828)

COOK, Prof Sir Alan Hugh; kt (1988); s of late Reginald Thomas Cook, OBE, and Ethel Cook; *b* 2 Dec 1922; *Educ* Westcliff HS for Boys, Corpus Christi Coll Cambridge (MA, PhD, ScD); *m* 1948, Isabell Weir Adamson, 1 s, 1 da; *Career* Univ of Cambridge: Jackson prof of natural philosophy 1972–90, head of Dept of Physics 1979–84, master of Selwyn Coll 1983–93; memb Science and Engrg Res Cncl 1984–88; FRS 1969, FRSE 1970, memb Soc Straniero Accad Naz dei Lincei (Rome) 1971; *Books* Gravity and the Earth, Global Geophysics, Interference of Electromagnetic Waves, Physics of the Earth and Planets, Celestial Masers, Interiors of the Planets, The Motion of the Moon, Gravitational Experiments in the Laboratory, Observational Foundations of Physics; *Recreations* travel, amateur theatre, painting, gardening; *Clubs* Explorers (NY), United Oxford and Cambridge; *Style*— Prof Sir Alan Cook, FRS, FRSE; ✉ 8 Wootton Way, Cambridge CB3 9LX (☎ 01223 356887)

COOK, Alistair Copland Campbell; s of George Arthur Campbell Cook (d 1978), of Edinburgh, and Margaret Maule, *née* McMurtrie (d 1987); *b* 3 July 1953; *Educ* Daniel Stewart's Coll Edinburgh, Univ of Aberdeen (BSc), Univ of Strathclyde (MBA); *m* 22 June 1979, Dr Glynis Elizabeth Cook, da of Douglas Cruickshank Watson; 3 s (Stuart b 9 Dec 1982, Richard b 7 Dec 1984, Graeme b 19 June 1988); *Career* articled clerk Touche Ross & Co Edinburgh 1976–80, mangr Price Waterhouse Hong Kong 1980–84, sr mangr Price Waterhouse London 1984–87; D'Arcy Masius Benton & Bowles Ltd London: fin dir and co sec 1987, gp fin dir 1989; chief fin offr DMB&B Holdings Ltd (UK, Ireland and Middle East) 1990–96; exec commercial dir and chief fin offr Ammirati Puris Lintas London 1996–; MICAS 1979, MIPA 1990; *Recreations* golf, Scottish paintings and watercolours; *Clubs* RAC, IOD, Hever Golf, Hong Kong Cricket; *Style*— Alistair Cook, Esq; ✉ Tylers, 47 Kippington Road, Sevenoaks, Kent TN13 2LL; Ammirati Puris Lintas, 84 Eccleston Square, London SW1A 1PX (☎ 0171 932 8888, fax 0171 932 8479)

COOK, Allan Vincent Cannon; s of Cyril Percy Cannon Cook (d 1957), and Jocelyne Marie Anne, *née* Cockell; *b* 28 Feb 1940; *Educ* Wimbledon Coll, LSE (BSc Econ); *Career* audit sr Knox Cropper & Co Chartered Accountants 1964–65 (articled clerk 1961–64); Unilever: accounting mangr then system analyst MacFisheries 1966–71, accountant Central Pensions Dept 1971–75, memb fin gp 1975–78, asst accounting principles offr 1978–79, seconded as sec International Accounting Standards Ctee (IASC) 1979–81; head of accounting res Shell International Petroleum Co 1982–90; chm Working Gp on Accounting Standards BIAC OECD; memb: Consultative Gp IASC, Accounting Standards Ctee 1987–90; tech dir Accounting Standards Bd 1990–; numerous contribs to learned jls; FCA 1974 (ACA 1964); *Recreations* theatre, music, walking; *Clubs* LSE; *Style*— Allan Cook, Esq; ✉ Accounting Standards Board, Holborn Hall, 100 Gray's Inn Rd, London WC1X 8AL (☎ 0171 404 8818, fax 0171 404 4497)

COOK, Beryl Frances; OBE (1996); da of Adrian Stephen Barton Lansley, and Ella, *née* Farmer-Francis; *b* 10 Sept 1926; *Educ* Kendrick Girls' Sch Reading; *m* 2 Oct 1948, John Victor Cook, s of Victor Harry Cook (d 1980); 1 s (John Lansley b 24 May 1950); *Career* artist; exhibitions incl: Plymouth Arts Centre 1975, Whitechapel Gallery London 1976, The Craft of Art (Walker Gallery Liverpool) 1979, Musée de Cahors 1981, Chelmsford Gallery Museum 1982, Portal Gallery London 1985, travelling retrospective exhibition (Plymouth Museum, Stoke-on-Trent, Preston, Nottingham and Edinburgh) 1988–89, Scunthorpe Museum and Art Gallery 1992, York City Art Gallery 1992, Portal Gallery 1993, anniversary exhibition Plymouth Arts Centre 1995; *Books* The Works (1978), Private View (1980), One Man Show (1981), Beryl Cook's New York (1985), Beryl Cook's London (1988), Bouncers (1991), Happy Days (1995); illustrated: Seven Years and a Day (1980), Bertie and the Big Red Ball (1982), My Granny (1983), Mr Norris Changes Trains (1990), The Loved One (1992); *Recreations* reading, travel; *Clubs* Lansdowne; *Style*— Mrs Beryl Cook, OBE; ✉ 3 Athenaeum St, The Hoe, Plymouth PL1 2RQ; Rogers Coleridge & White, 20 Powis Mews, London W11

COOK, Bob; *Career* writer; novels incl: Disorderly Elements 1985, Questions of Identity 1987, Faceless Mortals 1988, Paper Chase 1989, Fire and Forget 1990; *Style*— Bob Cook, Esq; ✉ c/o Richard Scott Simon Ltd, 43 Doughty Street, London WC1

COOK, (John) Brian; OBE (1988); s of John Wesley Cook (d 1967), of Leeds, Yorks, and Violet Mary Cook (d 1984); *b* 17 April 1931; *Educ* Leeds GS, BNC Oxford (BA, MA); *m* 1960, Barbara Avis, da of William Hugh Russell (d 1976), of London; 1 da (Barbara Ann b 1962); *Career* Nat Serv 2 Lt REME 1953–55; Royal Dutch Shell: joined Netherlands 1955, later engr Brunei and Sarawak, Indonesia 1961, Venezuela 1964, Italy 1970, transferred Nigeria 1972 (engrg mangr 1975); engrg mangr Shell Expro UK 1981–88 (formerly mangr Design and Tech Servs); chm Process Industs Div Inst of Mechanical Engrs 1988–91, hon pres Assoc of Br Offshore Indust 1989–94; Liveryman Worshipful Co of Engrs 1988; FRSA, FEng 1988, FIMechE 1975, FIEEE 1995; *Recreations* sailing, vintage cars; *Style*— Brian Cook, Esq, OBE, FEng; ✉ High Covert, Old Willingdon Road, Friston, East Sussex BN20 0AT (☎ 01323 422431)

COOK, Brian Francis; s of Harry Cook (d 1959), and Renia Maria, *née* Conlon (d 1962); *b* 13 Feb 1933; *Educ* St Bede's GS Bradford, Univ of Manchester (BA), Downing Coll and St Edmund's House Cambridge (BA, MA), Br Sch at Athens; *m* 18 Aug 1962, Veronica Mary Teresa, da of Bernard Dewhirst (d 1974); *Career* Nat Serv 1956–58, 16/15 The Queen's Royal Lancers; Dept of Greek and Roman Art Metropolitan Museum of Art NY: curatorial asst 1960, asst curator 1961–65, assoc curator 1965–69; keeper of Greek and Roman antiquities Br Museum 1976–93 (asst keeper 1969–76); writer and lectr on archaeology; corresponding memb German Archaeological Inst 1977, FSA 1971; *Books* Inscribed Hadra Vases in The Metropolitan Museum of Art (1966), Greek and Roman Art in the British Museum (1976), The Elgin Marbles (1984), The Townley Marbles (1985), Greek Inscriptions (1987, Dutch edn 1990, French edn 1994), The Rogozen Treasure (ed, 1989); *Recreations* reading, gardening; *Style*— B F Cook, Esq, FSA; ✉ 4 Belmont Ave, Barnet, Herts EN4 9LJ (☎ 0181 440 6590)

COOK, Charles Stuart; s of Norman Charles Cook (d 1994), of Wells, Somerset, and Dorothy Ida, *née* Waters (d 1994); *b* 19 Dec 1936; *Educ* King Edward VI Sch Southampton, Alleyn's Sch Dulwich, St Catherine's Coll Oxford (MA); *m* 28 July 1962 (m dis 1986), Jennifer, da of George Henry Baugh (d 1988), of nr Cowbridge, S Glamorgan; 2 s (Adam b 1966, Edward b 1969); *Career* Nat Serv 2 Lt The Buffs, The Royal East Kent Regt 1956–58, Capt TA List B 1961–74; asst master St Dunstans Coll London 1961–67; called to the Bar Lincolns Inn 1966; Hardwicke scholar 1963, Sir Thomas More bursary 1966, in practice 1967–, chm Med Appeals Tbnl 1979–90, recorder to the Crown Court 1987– (asst recorder 1981–87), jr of the Wales and Chester Circuit 1987–88; memb Llandaff PCC 1978–82; memb Criminal Bar Assoc 1988–; *Recreations* fine wines, photography, travel; *Style*— Charles Cook, Esq; ✉ 33 Park Place, Cardiff CF1 3BA (☎ 01222 233313, fax 01222 228294)

COOK, Christopher Paul; s of Edward Peter Cook, of Gt Broughton, N Yorks, and Joyce, *née* Layland; *b* 24 Jan 1959; *Educ* Barnard Castle Sch, Univ of Exeter/Exeter Coll of Art (BA, Combined Arts prize, Gladys Hunkin Poetry prize), Royal Coll of Art (J Andrew Lloyd scholar, MA, Anstruther award, John Minton Travel award), Accademia di Belle Arti Bologna (Italian Govt scholar); *m* Jennifer Jane, da of Edward John Mellings; 2 s (Matthew b 13 Jan 1983, Samuel b 3 Nov 1988); *Career* artist, poet; fell in painting Exeter Coll of Art 1989, sr lectr Univ of Plymouth (formerly Poly SW) 1992–; visiting lectr Royal Coll of Art 1990–; guest artist Stadelschule Frankfurt-am-Main 1991, visiting artist Academie van Beeldende Kunsten Rotterdam 1992, visiting fell Ruskin Sch Univ of Oxford 1993, distinguished visiting artist California State Univ Long Beach 1994, visiting artist BHU Vavanasi India 1994–96; *Solo Exhibitions* incl: Camden Arts Centre 1985, British Council Centre Amsterdam 1985, Spacex Gallery Exeter 1986, Galleria Maggiore Bologna 1987, Benjamin Rhodes Gallery 1988, 1990 and 1993, The Cleveland Gallery Middlesbrough 1989, Plymouth Arts Centre 1989, Stadelschule Frankfurt-am-Main 1991, Bath Contemporary Art Fair 1991, Kasteel van Rhoon Rotterdam 1992, Darlington Arts Centre 1992, RAM Museum Exeter 1992, Oldham Museum 1992, St Edmund Hall Oxford 1993, Northern Centre for Contemporary Art Sunderland 1994, Collins Gallery Glasgow 1995, Angel Row Nottingham 1995, Plymouth City Museum 1995, Galerie Helmut Pabst Frankfurt 1995, Jason & Rhodes Gallery 1996; *Gp Exhibitions* incl: The Sheffield Open (Mappin Gallery) 1985, The Camden Annual 1984 (first prizewinner) 1985 and 1986, Royal Over-Seas League Annual 1985 (prizewinner 1986 and 1987), Young Contemporaries (Whitworth Gallery Manchester) 1985, Tradition and Innovation in Printmaking Today (Milton Keynes and tour) 1986, The Human Touch (Fischer Fine Art) 1986, Due Pittori Inglesi (Associazione Italo-Brittanica Bologna) 1987, Romantic Visions (Camden Arts Centre) 1988, Bound Image Nigel Greenwood Gallery 1988, Figure 2 - A Personal Mythology (Welsh Arts Cncl tour) 1988, Richard Demarco Gallery Edinburgh 1989, Metropolitan Museum of Art New York, Real Life Stories (Cleveland Gallery Middlesbrough) 1989, Eros in Albion (Casa Masaccio San Giovanni Valdarno Italy) 1989, 3 Ways (Br Cncl/RCA tour to Eastern Europe and Africa) 1990–94, Modern Painters (Manchester City Art Gallery) 1990, Da Bacon a Oggi, Palazzo Vecchio Florence Italy 1991, Galerie im Stadthaus Bad Homburg Germany 1991, EAST (The Norfolk Gallery Norwich) 1991, A Collectors Choice (Bristol City Museum) 1992, Camouflage (5 Br Artists, 3 venue tour) LA 1994, 27e Festival International de la Peinture Cagnes-sur-Mer 1995, European Union Artists (Univ of Bangkok) 1995, de Peus a Terra (Galeria 4RT Barcelona) 1996; Brewhouse Open prize 1989, Lucy Morrison Meml prize (Royal Over-Seas League Annual) 1990; *Poetry* incl: New Nerves (1983), The Choosing and other Poems (1984), A Mythic Cycle (1989), A Lowdown Ecstasy (1991), Pilgrimmage III (Into Night) 1992; *Style*— Christopher Cook, Esq; ✉ c/o Jason and Rhodes Gallery, 4 New Burlington Place, London W1X 1SB (☎ 0171 434 1768)

COOK, Christopher William Batstone; s of Cecil Batstone Cook (d 1965), and Penelope, *née* Mayall; *b* 21 Jan 1951; *Educ* Eton; *m* 15 July 1978, Margaret Anne, da of Maj John Christopher Blackett Ord, of Whitfield Hall, Hexham, Northumberland; 2 s (Edward b 1982, Benjamin b 1983), 1 da (Emma b 1980); *Career* Lloyd's broker; dir C T Bowring & Co (Insurance) Ltd 1980–91, md Marsh & McLennan Worldwide 1988–91, chief exec Johnson and Higgins (Aviation) 1991–; *Recreations* shooting, stalking, fishing; *Style*— Christopher W B Cook, Esq; ✉ 45 Eland Road, London SW11 5JX (☎ 0171 228 5937); Johnson and Higgins, Aldgate House, Aldgate High Street, London EC3N 1AQ (☎ 0171 945 7441, fax 0171 945 7491)

COOK, Sir Christopher Wymondham Rayner Herbert; 5 Bt (UK 1886), of Doughty House, Richmond, Surrey; s of Sir Francis Ferdinand Maurice Cook, 4 Bt (d 1978), and Joan Loraine, *née* Ashton-Case (d 1995); *b* 24 March 1938; *Educ* King's Sch Canterbury; *m* 1, 1958 (m dis 1975), Malina, da of Aster Gunasekera, and former w of Cyril Wettasinghe, of Ceylon; 1 s (Richard Herbert Aster Maurice b 1959), 1 da (Priscilla Melina b 1968); m 2, 1975, Margaret, da of late John Murray, and former w of Ronald Miller; 1 s (Alexander James Frederick b 1980), 1 da (Caroline Emma b 1978); *Heir* s, Richard Herbert Aster Maurice Cook b 30 June 1959; *Career* dir Diamond Guarantees

Ltd 1980–91; *Style*— Sir Christopher Cook, Bt; ✉ La Fosse Equierre, Bouillon Road, St Andrew's, Guernsey GY6 8YN

COOK, (Jeremy) David; s of Thomas Brian Cook (d 1989), and Pauline Isabel Cook; *b* 18 May 1958; *Educ* Laurence Jackson Sch Guisborough, Prior Pursglove Coll, Univ of Keele (BA); *m* 21 Sept 1990, Katherine Elizabeth, da of Michael Bayer, of Chrishall, Herts; *Career* called to the Bar Gray's Inn 1982; *Recreations* travel, literature; *Style*— David Cook, Esq; ✉ Lamb Building, Temple, London EC4 7AS

COOK, David Kenneth; s of George Thomas Cook, and Beatrice, *née* Jackson (d 1990); *b* 21 Sept 1940; *Educ* Rishton Secdy Modern Sch Lancs, RADA; *Career* formerly actor; worked in TV (hosted children's prog Rainbow 1972) and in repertory in Dundee, Bristol Old Vic, Watford and Windsor; writer; memb: PEN, Soc of Authors, Writers' Guild, Actors' Equity; *Books* Albert's Memorial (1972), Happy Endings (1974, E M Forster Award 1977), Walter (1978, Hawthornden Prize 1978), Winter Doves (1979, shortlisted Arts Cncl Fiction Prize 1980), Sunrising (1984, Southern Arts Fiction Prize), Missing Persons (1986), Crying Out Loud (1988, shortlisted Whitbread Novel of the Year), Second Best (1991, Odd Fellows Social Concern Book Award 1992); *TV Plays* Willy (1972), Why Here?, Jenny Can't Work Any Faster, Mary's Wife (1980), Couples (series), Walter (C4, Special Jury Award Monte Carlo, runner-up Int Emmy award), Love Match (1986), Missing Persons (1990), Closing Numbers (1993, Special Jury Award Monte Carlo); *Films* Second Best (1994, Special Jury Award San Sebastian); *Style*— David Cook, Esq; ✉ c/o Deborah Rogers, Rogers Coleridge & White Ltd, 20 Powis Mews, London W11 1JN (☎ 0171 221 3717)

COOK, David Ronald; JP (1989); s of Charles Henry Cook, of Bristol, and Myrtle Ovington, *née* Harwood (d 1989); *b* 9 Nov 1943; *Educ* Thornbury GS; *m* 1, Frances Ann, *née* Leigh (d 1972); 2 da (Vicky Frances Leigh (Mrs Moss) b 24 April 1965, Jennifer Elaine Leigh b 9 Sept 1966); m 2, 21 June 1974, Angela Susan, da of Cecil Robert Cogdell (d 1988); 1 s (Charles David b 14 Aug 1978); *Career* articled clerk Parker Leader and Co Bristol 1960–65, audit sr Ricketts Cooper and Co 1965–69; ptnr: Burkett James and Co 1969–81, Pannell Kerr Forster (Bristol) 1981–96 (chm and managing ptnr 1985–95), N M G W forensic accountants 1996–; treas Bristol Referees Soc (RFU); FCA 1972 (ACA 1966), MInstD 1990; *Recreations* rugby football, squash, boating; *Clubs* Clifton, Redwood Lodge; *Style*— David Cook, Esq; ✉ Harwood House, Ham Lane, Dundry, Bristol BS18 8JA (☎ 0117 964 3763); N M G W, Crown House, 37/41 Prince Street, Bristol BS1 4PS (☎ 0117 927 7702, fax 0117 922 5191)

COOK, Derek Edward; TD; *b* 7 Dec 1931; *Educ* Denstone Coll, CCC Oxford (MA), Univ of Salford, Univ of Bradford, Huddersfield Tech Coll; *m*; 2 c; *Career* Nat Serv 1950–52, cmmnd Z Battery BAOR, W Riding Artillery 1952–68; with Tootal Ltd 1955–61, with John Emsley Ltd 1961–63, md A & S Henry & Co Ltd (Bradford) 1963–70, md Fibreglass Pilkington Ltd Bombay 1971–75 (chm 1976–79), chm and md Hindustan Pilkington Glass Works Ltd Calcutta 1976–79, dir R H Windsor Ltd India 1976–79, dir Killick Halco Ltd India 1977–79, chief exec Pilkington Brothers South Africa Ltd 1979 (chm 1981–84), chief exec Armourplate Safety Glass South Africa Ltd 1979 (chm 1981–84), dir Fibreglass South Africa Ltd 1979–82, chm Pilkington Glass Zimbabwe Ltd 1981–84, dir Pilkington Glass Ltd 1982 (chm 1984–85), dir Pilkington plc 1984–92, dir Flachglas AG 1985–89, dep chm Pilkington plc 1987–92 (gp md 1990–92), dir Libbey-Owens-Ford Co (USA) 1987–92, dir Minories Investment Tst plc 1993–; non-exec dir: Rowntree plc 1987–88, Charter Consolidated plc 1988–, Powell Duffryn plc 1989–, Leeds Permanent Building Society 1991–95, MFI (Furniture Gp) plc 1992–, Littlewoods Organisation plc 1992–, Kwik Save Group plc 1993–, Halifax Building Soc 1995–; memb Ct Univ of Leeds, dir Univ of Leeds Fndn 1989–; dir Breach Candy Hospital Tst 1974–79; memb Cncl: Indust and Parl Tst 1987–92, CBI 1988–92, Textile Inst 1994–; memb Cook Soc 1985–; govr The Cathedral Sch Bombay 1974–79; Holder of Royal Warrant of Appointment 1984–85; Freeman City of London, Liveryman Worshipful Co of Glass Sellers 1991–; FRSA, FSS, FTI, CText, CIMgt, FInstD; *Recreations* sailing, general sporting and country life interests; *Clubs* Oriental, Army & Navy, Cavalry & Guards, East India, RAC, Royal Ocean Racing, Royal Thames, Royal Yorkshire Yacht, Royal Bombay Yacht (cdre 1977–78), Leander, St James's (Manchester), Racquets (Manchester), Rand (Johannesburg), Country (Johannesburg); *Style*— Derek Cook, Esq, TD; ✉ Windmill Farm, Wrigley Lane, Over Alderley, nr Macclesfield, Cheshire SK10 4SA (☎ 01625 827985)

COOK, Francis (Frank); MP (Lab) Stockton North (majority 10,474); s of James and Elizabeth May Cook; *b* 3 Nov 1935; *Educ* Corby Sch Sunderland, De La Salle Manchester, Inst of Educn Leeds; *m* 1959 (sep), Patricia, da of Thomas Lundrigan; 1 s, 3 da; *Career* MP (Lab) Stockton N 1983– (sponsored by MSF), oppn whip 1987–91; memb Select Ctee: on Employment 1983–87, on Procedure of the House 1988–, on Defence 1992–; memb: CSCE Parly Assembly 1992–, N Atlantic Assembly 1988–; *Style*— Frank Cook, MP; ✉ House of Commons, London SW1A 0AA

COOK, Dr Gordon Charles; s of Charles Francis Cook (d 1983), of Petersfield, Hampshire, and Kate, *née* Grainger (d 1979); *b* 17 Feb 1932, Wimbledon; *Educ* Wellingborough GS, Kingston-upon-Thames GS, Raynes Park GS, Royal Free Hosp Sch of Med London (BSc, MB BS, MRCS, LRCP, MRCP, MD, DSc, Charlotte Brown prize, Cunning award, Legg award); *m* 1963, Elizabeth Jane, da of late Rev Stephen Noel Agg-Large, of Longparish, Hants; 1 s (David Charles Stephen b 10 June 1969), 3 da (Rosamund Elizabeth b 7 June 1967, Caroline Jane (twin) b 10 June 1969, Susanna Catherine b 23 July 1973); *Career* cmmnd RAMC (Capt), seconded Royal Nigerian Army 1960–62; various appts Royal Free, Hampstead Gen, Royal Northern, Brompton and St George's Hosps 1958–63, lectr Royal Free Hosp Sch of Med and Makerere UC Uganda 1963–69; prof of med and conslt physician: Univ of Zambia 1969–74, Univ of Riyadh 1974–75, Univ of Papua New Guinea 1978–81; sr MO MRC 1975–76, sr lectr in clinical scis London Sch of Hygiene and Tropical Med 1976–; hon conslt physician: Hosp for Tropical Diseases and UCLH 1976–, St Luke's Hosp for the Clergy 1988–; hon sr lectr in med UCL 1981–, hon lectr in clinical parasitology Bart's Med Coll 1992–; visiting prof Univs of Basrah, Mosul and Doha; memb Editorial Bd: Jl of Infection (ed 1995–), Transactions of the Royal Society of Tropical Medicine and Hygiene, Postgraduate Medical Jl; examiner RCP 1977–84, memb Cncl Fell Postgrad Med 1989– (vice pres 1996–), vice pres History of Med Section RSM 1994–96; pres: Royal Soc of Tropical Med and Hygiene 1993–95, Osler Club of London 1993–95; chm Erasmus Darwin Fndn Lichfield 1994–, memb Educnl Sponsored Books Tst (ESBT) 1996–; Frederick Murgatroyd meml prize RCP 1973; Freeman City of London, Liveryman Worshipful Soc of Apothecaries 1981; memb various professional bodies incl: RSM 1962, MRS 1965, Br Soc of Gastroenterology 1968, Physiological Soc 1971, Assoc of Physicians of GB and I 1973, Med Soc of London 1976, Br Soc for the Study of Infection 1982, Soc of Authors 1985 (memb Cncl Med Writers' Gp 1995–), JCHMT 1987–93; FRCP 1972, FRACP 1978, FLS 1989; *Books* Acute Renal Failure (jt ed, 1964), Tropical Gastroenterology (1980), 100 Clinical Problems in Tropical Medicine (jtly, 1987), Communicable and Tropical Diseases (1988), Parasitic Disease in Clinical Practice (1990), From the Greenwich Hulks to Old St Pancras: a history of tropical disease in London (1992), Gastroenterological Problems from the Tropics (ed, 1995), Travel - Associated Disease (ed, 1995), Manson's Tropical Diseases (ed 20 edn, 1996); *Recreations* walking, cricket, baroque and classical music, history (medical and scientific); *Clubs* Athenaeum, MCC, Baconian Club of St Albans (pres 1995–96); *Style*— Dr Gordon Cook; ✉ Department of Clinical Sciences, Hospital for Tropical Diseases, St Pancras Way, London NW1 0PE (☎ 0171 387 4411, fax 0171 388 7645, home ☎ 01727 869000)

COOK, Cdre Henry Home; s of George Home Cook (d 1920), of Westfield, Bowden, Cheshire, and Lilian Elena Anna Stewart, *née* Byng-Hall (d 1951); *b* 24 Jan 1918; *Educ* Pangbourne Coll; *m* 26 June 1943, Theffania (Fania), da of Arthur Percival Saunders (d 1956), of Latchmore Cottage, Gerrards Cross, Bucks and Highlands, Bolney, Sussex; 2 s (Martin b 1944, Charles b 1958), 2 da (Sarah b 1948, Alice b 1955); *Career* RN: Cadet 1936, Cdre 1973, head Br Def Staff Canada 1970–72, ADC to HM The Queen 1971–72, dir PR RN 1966–70; HM Naval Attaché 1963–66: Ankara, Teheran, Bagdad, Damascus, Amman; Cdr RNC Greenwich 1960–63; dir of admin Ellerman Gp Shipping Div 1973–80, dir Christopher Gold Assocs Ltd 1974–87, assoc advsr Industl Soc 1980–81, vice pres Inst Admin Mgmnt 1982– (chm 1981), gen cmmr of Income Tax 1982–92, dir PR Operation Raleigh 1984–87, PR conslt 1987–; vice pres The Chiltern Soc 1994– (chm 1988–93), hon sec Missions to Seamen Chalfont St Peter 1988–; memb Worshipful Co of Shipwrights 1968–, Freeman City of London 1967–; Dip Communication Advtg Mktg Fndn, FInstAM, MIPR; *Recreations* fishing; *Clubs* Wig & Pen; *Style*— Cdre Henry Home Cook; ✉ Ramblers Cottage, Layters Green, Chalfont St Peter, Bucks SL9 8TH (☎ 01753 883724)

COOK, James Robert; s of Robert James Cook (d 1961), of Hailsham, E Sussex, and Irene May Winsper, *née* Leyden; *b* 7 Dec 1945; *Educ* Co GS for Boys Bexhill-on-Sea E Sussex, Brighton Tech Coll; *m* 1; 2 s (Andrew Paul b 15 Sept 1968, Stephen John b 21 April 1970); m 2, 7 April 1990, Suzanne Valerie; *Career* audit sr: Douglas Wells & Co 1964–66, Coopers & Lybrand Deloitte 1967–69; fin accountant Overseas Containers Ltd 1969–73, chief accountant Frampton Property Group 1973–74; Blue Circle Industries PLC: mgmnt accountant 1974–85, gp pensions mangr 1984–95; dir AshakaCem PLC Nigeria 1996–; qualified first place (John C Latham prize) CACA finals 1966, awarded Jt Dip in Mgmnt Accounting Servs 1981; FCCA 1973 (ACCA 1968); *Recreations* church, music, theatre; *Style*— James Cook, Esq; ✉ 6 The Cuttings, Hampstead Norreys, Thatcham, Berks RG18 0RR (☎ 01635 202506); c/o Blue Circle Industries PLC, 84 Eccleston Square, London SW1V 1PX (☎ 0171 245 8165)

COOK, Dr John Barry; s of Albert Edward Cook, of Gloucester, and Beatrice Irene, *née* Blake (d 1978); *b* 9 May 1940; *Educ* Sir Thomas Rich's Sch Gloucester, King's Coll London (BSc, AKC), Guy's Hosp Med Sch Univ of London (PhD); *m* 1964, Vivien Margaret Roxana, da of Capt Victor Lamb, CBE, RN (d 1993), and Marjorie, *née* Metcalfe (d 1987); 2 s (David b 1967, Richard b 1972), 1 da (Susan b 1969); *Career* lectr in physics Guy's Hosp Med Sch 1964–65, sr sci master and head of Physics Dept Haileybury Coll 1965–72; headmaster: Christ Coll Brecon 1973–82, Epsom Coll 1982–92; dir Inner Cities Young People's Project 1992–95, princ King George VI & Queen Elizabeth Fndn of St Catharine's at Cumberland Lodge 1995–, chm The Childrens' Hospice Assoc for SE (CHASE) 1995–; *Books* Multiple Choice Questions in A-level Physics, Multiple Choice Questions in O-level Physics, Solid State Biophysics; *Recreations* most sports, philately, photography; *Style*— Dr John Cook; ✉ Cumberland Lodge, The Great Park, Windsor, Berks SL4 2HP (☎ 01784 432316, fax 01784 438507)

COOK, Lindsay Mary; da of Francis John Cook (d 1972), and Elsie Mary, *née* Gilliatt; *b* 24 July 1951; *Educ* Havelock Comp Sch Grimsby, The Open Univ (BA); *m* 1 May 1987, Tony Wilkinson, s of Ernest Wilkinson; 2 s (Rory b 14 Aug 1988, Gray b 27 Jan 1991); *Career* trainee journalist Grimsby Evening Telegraph 1969–74, reporter and consumer writer Morning Telegraph Sheffield 1974–76, freelance writer Sunday Times 1976–77, freelance contrib Money Mail (pt of Daily Mail) 1977–79, United Newspapers London 1977–86 (number 3 on newsdesk, features dept, dep London ed 1984), personal finance ed The Daily Telegraph 1986–89; The Times: money ed 1990–93, dep business ed 1993–94, business ed 1994–; Personal Finance Journalist of the Year 1987; *Books* The Money Diet, Three Months To Financial Fitness (1986); *Recreations* food, theatre; *Style*— Miss Lindsay Cook; ✉ The Times, 1 Pennington St, London E1 9XN (☎ 0171 782 5111, fax 0171 782 5112)

COOK, Malcolm Roderick Grant; s of Harold Cook, of Warwickshire, and Brenda Eileen, *née* Moore; *b* 29 Nov 1955; *Educ* Univ of Bath (BSc Econ); *m* Ann Cook; 1 da (Victoria Ann b 12 March 1989); *Career* chartered accountant; Arthur Young Chartered Accountants 1977–84, gp accountant F H Thomkins PLC 1984–86, business servs gp mangr Arthur Young 1986–87; Pannell Kerr Forster Birmingham: business servs gp mangr 1987–89, ptnr 1989–, managing ptnr 1991–; dir Birmingham Press Club Limited; MInstD, ACA; *Style*— Malcolm Cook, Esq; ✉ Pannell Kerr Forster, New Guild House, 45 Great Charles Street, Queensway, Birmingham, W Midlands B3 2LX (☎ 0121 212 2222, fax 0121 212 2300, mobile 0831 590025)

COOK, His Hon Judge Michael John; s of George Henry Cook (d 1947), and Nora Wilson, *née* Mackman; *b* 20 June 1930; *Educ* Leeds Grammar Sch, Worksop Coll, Leeds Univ; *m* 1, 1958, Anne Margaret Vaughan; 3 s, 1 da; m 2, 1974, Patricia Anne Sturdy; 1 da; *Career* Lt RA (Nat Serv Canal Zone); slr; sr ptnr Ward Bowie 1968–86, recorder Crown Ct 1980–86; circuit judge (SE Circuit) 1986–; designated child care judge Guildford County Ct, princ judge for civil matters in Surrey; author, lectr and former broadcaster; past pres London Slrs Litigation Assoc; memb Cncl Royal Med Fndn Freeman City of London; *Books* The Courts and You, Cook on Costs, Butterworth's Costs Service (gen ed), The Litigation Letter (gen ed), Butterworth's County Court Practice and Proceedings (contrib), Cordery on Solicitors, Butterworth's Personal Injury Service; *Recreations* horse riding, tennis, gardening, reading, theatre, travel; *Clubs* The Law Soc; *Style*— His Hon Judge Michael Cook; ✉ c/o Courts Administrator, Kingston Group, 10 Sundial Court, Tolworth Rise South, Surbiton, Surrey KT5 9NN (☎ 0181 335 3090)

COOK, Patrick Donald; s of Donald George Herbert Cook (d 1992), of Henley on Thames, Oxon, and Doreen Elizabeth, *née* Simpson; *b* 11 July 1956; *Educ* Abingdon Sch, Pembroke Coll Oxford (MA); *m* 10 Oct 1981, Caroline Elizabeth, da of John Andrew Graves, of Barnstaple, Devon; 3 da (Megan Elizabeth b 25 April 1986, Florence Emma b 4 Oct 1989, Imogen Amy b 25 Nov 1994), 1 s (Charles Patrick (twin) b 25 Nov 1994); *Career* admitted slr 1981; ptnr Osborne Clarke 1986–, licensed insolvency practitioner 1989–; memb: Law Soc 1981, Insolvency Lawyers Assoc 1989; *Recreations* sports (various), theatre, reading, gardening; *Style*— Patrick Cook, Esq; ✉ Withy Tree House, Stone Allerton, Axbridge, Somerset; Osborne Clark, 30 Queen Charlotte St, Bristol BS99 7QQ (☎ 0117 923 0220)

COOK, Prof Paul Derek; MBE (1985); s of James Walter Cook, and Florence, *née* Jefferay; *b* 12 March 1934; *Educ* Queen Mary Coll London (Sir John Johnson scholar, BSc, PhD); *m* 1954, Frances Anne, *née* James; 4 da; *Career* res scientist: MRC 1960–62, Middx Hosp Med Sch 1962–65; chm and md Scientifica-Cook Ltd 1962–; Brunel Univ: prof of laser technol 1986–, prof of laser physics 1986–91, prof of environmental sci 1992–; scientific advsr to: Min for the Environment and Countryside DoE 1990–92, Chm British Gas 1990–93; laser conslt BAe 1986–; responsible for design and devpt of numerous laser systems used in med and mil estabs throughout world, originator and inventor of Laser Guidance Systems for weapon alignment in Tornados; fndr pres The Br Sci and Technol Tst (helping disabled children worldwide) 1985–96, dep chm Conserve (Cons Govt Environmental Gp) 1990–92, originator Lena Appeal (sending med aid to sick children in Russia) 1991, envoy to Boris Yeltsin 1992; UK pres Japanese Zen Nippon Airinkai 1978–81; CEng, MIEE 1963; *Recreations* breeding and rearing exotic Japanese carp, cultivating Japanese bonzai; *Style*— Prof Paul Cook, MBE; ✉ Carlton

House, 78 Bollo Bridge Road, London W3 8AU; Department of Chemistry, Brunel University, Uxbridge, Middx UB8 3PH

COOK, Dr Peter John; CBE (1996); s of late John Cook, and Rose Cook, of Sale, Cheshire; *b* 15 Oct 1938; *Educ* Chorlton GS, Univ of Durham (BSc, DSc), ANU Canberra (MSc), Univ of Colorado Boulder (PhD); *m* 1961, Norma Irene; 2 s (John b 24 Nov 1964, Julian b 20 July 1968); *Career* geologist: Univ of Cambridge Gornergletcher Glaciological Expedition 1959, Univ of Durham Spitsbergen Expedition (ldr) 1960, Oil Search Gp Aust Bureau of Mineral Resources (BMR) 1961–64, Aust Nat Antarctic Res Expedition 1964–65, Phosphate Section BMR 1966–69; sr geologist Phosphate and Marine Geology BMR 1969–76, sr res fell in econ geology Res Sch of Earth Sciences ANU 1976–82 (chm of Faculty 1978–79, visiting fell 1982–90 and 1995), visiting fell Resource Systems Inst East-West Center Univ of Hawaii 1979, chief scientist BMR Div Continental Geology 1982–89, assoc dir BMR 1989–90, dir British Geological Survey 1990–; conslt: Astrogeology Div US Geological Survey 1967, Le Nickel Exploration 1977, Agrico Chemical Co 1980, Esso Exploration 1981–82; prof Institut de Geologie Universite Louis Pasteur Strasbourg 1989; chm: ACT Div Geological Soc of Aust 1972–73, Consortium for Ocean Geosciences of Aust Univs 1980–82, Cwlth-state Hydrogeological Ctee 1983–87, Tech Prog Int Sedimentological Congress 1983–86; memb: Indian Ocean Working Gp Int Union of Geology and Geophysics 1974–78, Geosciences Delgn to China Aust Acad of Sciences 1978, Cncl Aust Inst of Marine Sciences 1979–85, Advsy Ctee Centre for Remote Sensing Univ of NSW 1985–90, Review Ctee Dept of Geology James Cook Univ 1987, Advsy Cncl Aust Nuclear Sci and Technol Orgn 1986–90, Advsy Bd Inst of Engrg Surveying and Space Geodesy Univ of Nottingham 1990–, Geological Museum Advsy Panel Natural History Museum 1990–, Advsy Bd Univ of Manchester, Earth Sciences Ctee NERC 1991–, Advsy Bd Global Sedimentary Geology Prog 1991–, Bd Mineral Indust Research Orgn 1991–, Bd of Patrons Earth Centre Edinburgh 1992–, Earth Science and Technol Bd NERC 1994–; Adrian fell Univ of Leicester 1992–; chm UNESCO/IOC Prog of Ocean Sci in Relation to Non-Living Resources 1985–; pres: Aust Geoscience Cncl 1987–88, Euro Geo Surveys 1995–; memb: Int Assoc of Sedimentologists, Soc of Econ Palaeontologists, American Assoc of Petroleum Geologists, Geological Soc London, Geological Soc of Aust (chm 1972–73); *Publications* Sedimentology & Holocene History of a Tropical Estuary (1978), Phosphate Deposits of the World (1986), Australia: Evolution of a Continent (1990); author of 120 papers and articles in learned jls; *Recreations* skiing, walking, history, travel; *Clubs* Geological Soc; *Style—* Dr Peter J Cook, CBE; ✉ British Geological Survey, Keyworth, Nottingham NG12 5GG (☎ 0115 936 3226, fax 0115 936 3277)

COOK, Richard Herbert Aster Maurice; s (by 1 m) and h of Sir Christopher Cook, 5 Bt; *b* 30 June 1959; *Style—* Richard Cook, Esq

COOK, Rt Hon Robert Finlayson (Robin); PC (1996), MP (Lab) Livingston (majority 8,105); s of Peter Cook and Christina, *née* Lynch; *b* 28 Feb 1946; *Educ* Aberdeen GS, Univ of Edinburgh; *m* 1969, Margaret K Whitmore; 2 s; *Career* formerly: chm Edinburgh Corpn Housing Ctee, Scottish Assoc Labour Student Organisations, tutor-organiser with WEA; memb Tribune Gp; MP (Lab): Edinburgh Central 1974–1983, Livingston 1983–; oppn front bench spokesman on Treasury and econ affrs 1980–Nov 1983, Lab leadership campaign mangr for Rt Hon Neil Kinnock 1983, elected to Shadow Cabinet and front bench spokesman on European Community affrs Nov 1983–84, PLP campaign coordinator 1984–86, oppn front bench spokesman on trade and the City 1986–87, chief oppn spokesman on health and social security 1987–92, Lab leadership campaign mangr for Rt Hon John Smith 1992; chief oppn spokesman on: trade and indust 1992–94, foreign affrs 1994–; chair Lab Pty 1996–; *Style—* The Rt Hon Robin Cook, MP; ✉ House of Commons, London SW1A 0AA (☎ 0171 219 5120)

COOK, Roger James; s of Alfred Herbert Owen Cook (d 1968), and Linda May, *née* Kirk (d 1994); *b* 6 April 1943; *Educ* Hurlstone Agric Coll, Sydney Univ; *m* 1, 1966 (m dis 1974), Madeline Koh; m 2, 1982, Frances Knox; 1 da (Belinda Claire b 1985); *Career* TV and radio reporter ABC Aust 1960–66, TV and radio dir Warnock Sandford Advertising Aust 1966–68, reporter World at One and World This Weekend (BBC Radio 4) 1968–76, freelance documentary dir 1968–72, creator and presenter Checkpoint (Radio 4) 1973–85, presenter and reporter Time For Action/Reel Evidence (Radio 4) and investigative reporter Nationwide/Newsnight (BBC TV) 1972–84, reporter and presenter The Cook Report (Central) 1985–; awards: BPG award for outstanding contrib to radio 1978, Radio Personality of the Year 1979, McWhirter award for bravery 1980, Valiant for Truth award 1988, Radio and TV Industries Club ITV Prog of the Year (for the Cook Report) 1992; memb: NUJ 1968–, ACTT 1968–; *Books* What's Wrong With Your Rights? (with Tim Tate, 1988); *Recreations* walking, music, motor sport; *Style—* Roger Cook, Esq; ✉ Carlton Television, Central House, Broad St, Birmingham B1 2JP (☎ 0121 643 9898, fax 0121 616 1633)

COOK, Stephen Sands; s of John Stevenson Cook, and Elizabeth, *née* Brown; *b* 6 April 1960; *Educ* Duncanrig Sch East Kilbride, Univ of Aberdeen (LLB Hons, Dip LP); *m* 8 Aug 1981, Andrina, da of Henry Alexander Waters; 1 da (Kirsty Andrina b 2 Aug 1989), 1 s (Simon Stephen b 6 March 1996); *Career* trainee Moncrieff Warren Patterson Glasgow 1982–84, asst McGrigor Donald 1984–87, ptnr Herbert Smith London 1991–93 (asst 1987–91), head Company Dept McGrigor Donald 1994–96, ptnr Wiggin & Co 1996–; memb: Law Soc of Scotland 1984, Law Soc of Eng and Wales 1989; *Recreations* medieval history, walking the dog, wine, trying to learn the piano faster than my daughter; *Style—* Stephen Cook, Esq; ✉ Rossburn Farmhouse, Rossburn Lane, Blair Drummond, Stirlingshire; Wiggin & Co, 3 Albany Court Yard, Piccadilly, London W1V 9RA (☎ 0171 287 8833, fax 0171 287 8628)

COOK, Susan Lorraine (Sue); da of William Arthur Thomas, of Ickenham, Middx, and Kathleen May, *née* Prow; *b* 30 March 1949; *Educ* Vyner's GS Hillingdon, Univ of Leicester (BA); *m* 20 May 1981 (m dis 1987), John Christopher Williams, s of Leonard Williams (d 1988), of The Monkey Sanctuary, Looe, Cornwall; 1 s (Alexander Charles (Charlie) b 12 Oct 1982); *partner* since 1986, William James Macqueen; 1 da (Megan Jane Emily b 30 March 1988); *Career* radio prodr and broadcaster Capital Radio 1974–76, radio presenter of documentaries and topical features for BBC Radio Four and World Service, reporter and presenter for BBC TV's Nationwide 1979–83; presenter BBC TV: Pebble Mill at One, Breakfast Time, Out of Court, Holiday, Crimewatch UK (until 1995), Daytime Live, Having a Baby, Children in Need Appeal, That's the Way the Money Goes, Omnibus at the Proms, The Story of the London Sinfonietta, The Children's Royal Variety Performance; involved in work with charities helping children, animals and the elderly; patron: Parents at Work, Children's Liver Disease Fndn; tstee Citizenship Fndn, ambass Prince's Tst; *Books* Accident Action (jtly, 1978), Crimewatch UK (jtly, 1987), The Crimewatch Guide to Home Security and Personal Safety (1988); *Recreations* tennis, singing, spending time at home with the family; *Style—* Miss Sue Cook; ✉ c/o Ms S Freathy, Curtis Brown, Haymarket House, 28–29 Haymarket, London SW1Y 4SP (☎ 0171 396 6600)

COOK, Thomas Roger Edward; o s of Lt-Col Sir Thomas Cook, MP, JP (d 1970), of Sennowe Park, and Gweneth, o da of Spencer Evan Jones; ggs of Thomas Cook (d 1884); *b* 21 Aug 1936; *Educ* Eton, RAC Cirencester; *m* 1, 14 Sept 1960, Virginia (d 1978), yr da of Leslie Aked (d 1964), of Knaresborough, Yorkshire; m 2, Carola, da of Capt Roger Harvey (d 1976), of Ramsbury, Wilts; *Career* Lt Gren Guards 1954–56; farmer, forester and landowner; memb Rural Development Cmmn 1983–, High Sheriff Norfolk 1991–92; *Recreations* country pursuits, flying; *Clubs* The Air Sqdn, White's, Pratt's, Norfolk, Allsorts (Norfolk); *Style—* Thomas R E Cook, Esq; ✉ Sennowe Park, Guist, Norfolk NR20 5PB (☎ 01328 829202)

COOKE, *see:* Fletcher-Cooke

COOKE, Alan; s of Colin Cooke, and Shelia, *née* Harris; *b* 23 March 1966; *Educ* Tupton Hall Comp Sch; *m* Susan, *née* Richmond; *Career* table tennis professional; former memb BFL Grove England, currently memb Fontenay Club France; team Gold medallist Cwlth Championships 1985, 1989, and 1994, champion Nat Top 12 1987–90, team Silver medallist Euro Championships 1988 and 1992, Eng nat champion 1988, 1989 and 1996 (runner-up 1995), team Gold medallist and men's singles Gold medallist Cwlth Championships 1989, men's singles Silver medallist Cwlth Championships 1994 and 1995, former Cwlth champion; former world counter hitting record holder with Desmond Douglas (170 hits in one minute); *Style—* Alan Cooke, Esq; ✉ Pegasus, Seanor Lane, Lower Pilsey, Chesterfield, Derbyshire S45 8DQ; 28 Parwich Rd, North Wingfield, Chesterfield, Derbyshire S42 5JU (☎ 01246 852332)

COOKE, Rear Adm Anthony John; CB (1980); s of Rear Adm John Ernest Cooke, CB (d 1980), and Kathleen Mary, *née* Haward (d 1976); *b* 21 Sept 1927; *Educ* St Edward's Sch Oxford; *m* 1, 1951 (m dis 1994), Margaret Anne, da of Frederick Charles Hynard (d 1980); 2 s, 3 da; m 2, 1995, Patricia Sinclair, da of William Sinclair Stewart (d 1961), and Margaret Jane, *née* Foster; 1 step s, 2 step da; *Career* RN 1945, Cdre in Cmd Clyde Submarine Base 1973–75, Rear Adm 1976, sr naval memb directing staff RCDS 1975–78, Adm Pres RNC Greenwich 1978–80, ret; private sec to Lord Mayor of London 1981–92; Freeman: City of London, Worshipful Co of Shipwrights; Yr Bro Trinity House, OStJ 1990; *Style—* Rear Admiral Anthony Cooke, CB; ✉ 4 Amherst Road, Ealing, London W13 8ND

COOKE, Anthony Roderick Chichester Bancroft; yr twin s of Maj-Gen Ronald Basil Bowen Bancroft Cooke, CB, CBE, DSO (d 1971), and Joan (d 1989), da of late Maj Claude Chichester, of Tunworth Down House, Basingstoke; *b* 24 July 1941; *Educ* Ampleforth, London Business Sch (MSc); *m* 1972, Daryll, *née* Aird-Ross; 2 s, 1 da; *Career* chartered accountant 1964; chm and chief exec Ellerman Lines plc 1985–87 (dir 1976), chm and md Cunard Ellerman Ltd 1987–91, chief exec Andrew Weir & Co Ltd 1991–; pres Chamber of Shipping 1996–97; Liveryman Worshipful Co of Shipwrights; FCA 1964; *Style—* Anthony Cooke, Esq; ✉ Poland Court, Odiham, Hants RG29 1JL (☎ 01256 702060); 16 Ennismore Mews, London SW7 1AN (☎ 0171 589 0901); Andrew Weir & Co Ltd, Dexter House, 2 Royal Mint Court, London EC3N 4XX (☎ 0171 265 0808, fax 0171 956 1178, telex 887392)

COOKE, (Brian) Christopher; s of Samuel Burgess Ridgway Cooke (d 1978), and Diana, *née* Witherby; *b* 1 Feb 1951; *Educ* Westminster, Peterhouse Cambridge (MA); *Career* articled clerk then slr Bischoff & Co 1974–78, slr Bristows Cooke & Carpmael 1978–86, ptnr Linklaters & Paines 1989– (slr 1986–89); *Style—* Christopher Cooke, Esq; ✉ 5 Provost Road, London NW3 4ST (☎ 0171 722 6819), Linklaters & Paines, Barrington House, 59/67 Gresham St, London EC2V 7JA (☎ 0171 606 7080, fax 0171 606 5113)

COOKE, Christopher Edward Cobden; s of Reginald Garforth Cooke (d 1991), of Marlow, Bucks, and Phyllis Mary Blackburn, *née* Wilde (d 1992); *b* 18 April 1944; *Educ* King William's Coll IOM, Univ of Southampton (LLB); *m* 26 July 1969, (Greta) Yvonne, da of Raymond Vere Alberto (d 1979); 3 da (Lisa b 25 May 1971, Lucy b 11 March 1973, Lindy b 19 Jan 1977); *Career* slr; ptnr Rooks Rider (formerly Rooks & Co) London 1970– (currently sr ptnr); memb Int Ctee Soc of Tst and Estate Practitioners; memb: Law Soc 1969, Holborn Law Soc 1988, Int Tax Planning Assoc, Soc of Tst and Estate Practitioners; Freeman: City of London 1966, City of Monroe Louisiana 1986; Liveryman Worshipful Co of Makers of Playing Cards 1966; *Recreations* skiing; *Style—* Christopher Cooke, Esq; ✉ Rooks Rider, Challoner House, 19 Clerkenwell Close, London EC1R 0RR (☎ 0171 490 0774, fax 0171 490 1281, mobile tel 0835 225196)

COOKE, David Charles; s of Frederick John Edward Cooke (d 1969), of Clitheroe, Lancs, and Hilda, *née* Hughes; *b* 22 March 1938; *Educ* Accrington GS Lancs, Univ of Manchester (LLB); *Career* admitted slr 1961; asst slr: Hall Brydon & Co Manchester 1961–64, King & Partridge Madras India 1964–67; ptnr Pinsent & Co Birmingham (merged with Simpson Curtis to form Pinsent Curtis, May 1995) 1969– (asst slr 1967–69, ptnr 1969–87, sr ptnr 1987–94); sec W Midlands Devpt Agency 1986–; memb: Law Soc 1961–, Birmingham Law Soc 1967–; memb Cncl Birmingham C of C and Indust 1993–, memb West Midlands Regnl Cncl CBI 1993–; *Recreations* classical music, fell walking, fine arts, rugby union (watching), sheep; *Style—* David C Cooke, Esq; ✉ Pinsent Curtis, 3 Colmore Circus, Birmingham B4 6BH (☎ 0121 200 1050, fax 0121 626 1040)

COOKE, David John; s of Matthew Peterson Cooke, of Rugby, and Margaret Rose; *b* 23 Aug 1956; *Educ* Lawrence Sheriff Sch Rugby, Trinity Coll Cambridge (MA); *m* 31 March 1979, Susan Margaret, da of Albert Arthur George, of Rugby; 1 s (Stephen b 1984), 1 da (Helen b 1986); *Career* licensed insolvency practitioner; ptnr Banking and Insolvency Unit Pinsent Curtis slrs 1990– (ptnr 1982–); memb: Law Soc, Birmingham Law Soc, Insolvency Lawyers' Assoc; *Recreations* sailing, golf; *Clubs* Royal Dart Yacht, Law Society's Yacht, Olton Golf; *Style—* D J Cooke, Esq; ✉ Pinsent Curtis, 3 Colmore Circus, Birmingham B4 6BH (☎ 0121 200 1050, fax 0121 626 1040, telex 335101 PINCO G)

COOKE, Prof David John; s of John McKay Cooke, of Glasgow, and Esther Doonan, *née* Barch (1982); *b* 13 July 1952; *Educ* Larbert HS, Univ of St Andrews (BSc), Univ of Newcastle upon Tyne (MSc), Univ of Glasgow (DPhil); *m* 28 Sept 1979, Janet Ruth, da of Francis Salter; 2 da (Elizabeth b 2 Sept 1988, Esther Jane b 26 Feb 1991); *Career* basic grade clinical psychologist: Northumberland AHAs 1974–76, Greater Glasgow Health Bd 1976–78; sr clinical psychologist Gartnavel Royal Hosp Glasgow 1978–83; Douglas Inch Centre: princ clinical psychologist 1984, top grade clinical psychologist 1984– (with greater responsibility 1989–); prof of forensic psychology Dept of Psychology Glasgow Caledonian Univ 1992–; Cropwood fell Inst of Criminology Univ of Cambridge 1986; FBPsS 1986; *Books* Psychology in Prisons (with P Baldwin and J Howison, 1990), Treatment as an Alternative to Prosecution (1990), Psychological Disturbance in the Scottish Prison System: Prevalance, Precipitants and Policy (1994); *Recreations* sailing, cooking, opera; *Clubs* Clyde Canoe; *Style—* Prof David Cooke; ✉ Douglas Inch Centre, 2 Woodside Terrace, Glasgow G3 7UY (☎ 0141 211 8000, fax 0141 211 8005)

COOKE, Col Sir David William Perceval; 12 Bt (E 1661), of Wheatley Hall, Yorkshire; s of Sir Charles Arthur John Cooke, 11 Bt, of Fowey, Cornwall (d 1978), and Diana, *née* Perceval (d 1989); *b* 28 April 1935; *Educ* Wellington, RMA Sandhurst, Open Univ (BA 1983); *m* 30 March 1959, Margaret Frances, da of Herbert Skinner (d 1984), of Knutsford, Cheshire; 3 da (Sara Elisabeth Mary (Mrs Darren P Grosvenor) b 1960, Louise Diana Margaret b 1962, Catherine Faith Maria (Mrs Matthew Blakstad-Cooke) b 1968); *Heir* kinsman, Edmund Harry Cooke-Yarborough b 25 Dec 1918; *Career* 4/7 RDG 1955, RASC 1958, RCT 1965, ret 1990; dir Finance & Resources Bradford City Technology Coll 1990–91; conslt DC Research Consultancy 1992–; *Recreations* bird-watching, walking, social and local history, fishing; *Style—* Col Sir David Cooke, Bt; ✉ c/o Midland Bank, Knutsford, Cheshire WA16 6BZ

COOKE, Geoffrey Douglas (Geoff); OBE (1992); s of Douglas Bell Cooke (d 1987), and Emma, *née* Bailey (d 1982); *b* 11 June 1941; *Educ* Carlisle GS, St John's Coll York (CertEd, DipPE); *m* 10 Aug 1963, Susan Veronica; 2 s (Andrew Douglas James b 16 Dec 1972, David Charles Ian b 30 May 1976); *Career* sports coach and administrator; head of PE Dept: Ovenden Sch Halifax 1962–67, Temple Moor GS Leeds; PE advsr Leeds

City Cncl 1971–74, princ Leeds Athletic Inst 1974–83, princ offr Dept of Leisure Servs Leeds City Cncl 1983–88, chief exec Br Inst of Sports Coaches 1989–93, chief exec Nat Coaching Fndn 1995– (dir 1993–95); rugby: played as centre/fly-half captaining club and county 1962–72, coach Bradford RFC 1973–75, coach Yorkshire RUFC 1975–79 (chm of selectors 1980–85), mangr North of England RU 1985–87 (selector 1979–87), mangr England RU 1987–94, dir of rugby Bedford RFC 1996–; as mangr England: led tours to Australia/Fiji (twice) and Argentina, Grand Slam winners 1991 and 1992, World Cup runners-up 1991; mangr British Lions NZ 1993; also former minor cos cricketer; *Books* Rugby Union (1987), Skillful Rugby Union (1991); *Recreations* golf, skiing; *Clubs* Shipley Golf, Bradford & Bingley Rugby; *Style*— Geoff Cooke, Esq, OBE; ✉ National Coaching Foundation, 114 Cardigan Road, Headingley, Leeds LS6 3BJ (☎ 0113 274 4802, fax 0113 275 5019)

COOKE, George Venables; CBE (1978); s of William Geoffrey Cooke (d 1967), of Sandbach, Cheshire, and Constance Eva, *née* Venables (d 1976); *b* 8 Sept 1918; *Educ* Sandbach Sch Cheshire, Lincoln Coll Oxford (MA, DipEd); *m* 11 Oct 1941, Doreen, da of Harold Cooke (d 1984), of Sandbach, Cheshire; 1 s (Robin b 1946), 2 da (Susan (Mrs Wilson) b 1951, Prudence (Mrs Rushton) b 1954); *Career* WWII 1939–46, 7 Cheshire Regt TA, RMC Sandhurst, 10 Lancashire Fusiliers, HQ XIV Army, Maj; teacher Manchester GS 1947–51, prof asst (educn) W Riding of Yorks CC 1951–53, asst dir of educn Liverpool 1953–58, dep dir of educn Sheffield 1958–64, dir of educn Lindsey (Lincs) CC 1965–74, co educn offr Lincs CC 1974–78, gen sec Soc of Educn Offrs 1978–84 (pres 1975–76); chm Sec of States Advsy Ctee on Handicapped Children 1973–74, vice chm Nat Ctee of Enquiry into Special Educn (Warnock Ctee) 1974–78, memb Parole Bd 1984–87, chm Lincs and Humberside Arts 1987–91; Hon LLD Univ of Hull 1991; *Books* Education Committees (with P Gosden, 1986); *Recreations* golf, gardening; *Clubs* Royal Over-Seas League; *Style*— George Cooke, Esq, CBE; ✉ White House, Grange Lane, Riseholme, Lincoln LN2 2LQ (☎ 01522 522667)

COOKE, (John) Howard; s of Capt Jack Cooke, MC, of Exeter, Devon, and Ellen Jean, *née* Passmore; *b* 7 Jan 1952; *Educ* Exeter Sch, QMC London (LLB); *m* 1, 22 July 1972 (m dis 1983), Sally-Anne, da of Sydney Evans; m 2, 25 March 1983, Dr (Jayne) Elizabeth Mann; 2 da (Elena b 1983, Lauren b 1986); *Career* admitted slr 1976; conslt Frere Cholmeley Bischoff (ptnr 1980–95); memb Law Soc; *Recreations* country pursuits; *Style*— Howard Cooke, Esq; ✉ Frere Cholmeley Bischoff, 4 John Carpenter Street, London EC4Y 0NH (☎ 0171 615 8000, fax 0171 615 8080, telex 27623)

COOKE, Jean Esme Oregon; da of Arthur Oregon Cooke, and Dorothy Emily, *née* Cranefield (d 1981); *b* 18 Feb 1927; *Educ* Blackheath HS, Central Sch of Art and Crafts, Goldsmiths' Coll Sch of Art (Dip Art & Design), Camberwell Sch of Art, City and Guilds Coll of Arts, RCA; *m* 2 April 1953, John Randal Bratby; 3 s (David Johnathon Fernando b 1955, Jason Sovereign b 1959, Dayan Edvardo Joachim Jesse b 1968), 1 d (Wendy Dolores Carmen Hirondell b 1970); *Career* artist; lectr: Oxford Sch of Art, Royal Coll of Art 1964–74; Chantry Bequest Purchases 1969 and 1972; portraits: Dr Egon Wellesz, Dr Walter Oakshott for Lincoln Coll Oxford, Mrs Mary Bennett for St Hilda's Coll Oxford 1976, John Bratby for Royal Coll of Art Collection, John Bratby called Lilly Lilly on the Brow; self portrait: Tate, Royal Acad Collection; pres Friends of Woodlands Art Gallery; RA 1972 (memb Cncl 1972–74, sr hanger 1973 and 1974); *Recreations* Tai Chi, finding stones on the beach, riding a bike, swimming; *Clubs* Arts; *Style*— Miss Jean Cooke, RA; ✉ 7 Hardy Road, Blackheath, London SE3 7NS (☎ 0181 858 6288)

COOKE, Jeremy Lionel; QC (1990); s of Eric Edwin Cooke, of Warlingham, Surrey, and Margaret Lilian, *née* Taylor; *b* 28 April 1949; *Educ* Whitgift Sch Croydon, St Edmund Hall Oxford (open exhibition, MA, Rugby blues 1968 and 1969); *m* 24 June 1972, Barbara Helen, da of Geoffrey Curtis Willey, of Wallington, Surrey; 1 s (Samuel b 29 June 1984), 2 da (Emily b 3 June 1978, Josie b 28 March 1980); *Career* slr Coward Chance 1973–76; called to the Bar 1976, asst recorder 1994–; *Recreations* church congregation ldr, golf; *Style*— Jeremy Cooke, Esq, QC; ✉ 7 King's Bench Walk, Temple, London EC4Y 7DS (☎ 0171 583 0404, fax 0171 583 0950)

COOKE, John Arthur; s of Arthur Hafford Cooke, MBE (d 1987), Warden New Coll Oxford, and Ilse Cooke, *née* Sachs (d 1973); *b* 13 April 1943; *Educ* Dragon Sch Oxford, Magdalen Coll Sch Oxford, Univ of Heidelberg, King's Coll Univ of Cambridge (BA, MA), LSE; *m* 21 Feb 1970, Tania Frances, da of Alexander Cochrane Crichton; 1 s (Alexander b 1975), 2 da (Olga b 1972, Beatrice b 1977); *Career* asst princ Bd of Trade 1966, 2 then 1 sec UK Delgn to Euro Communities 1969–73, DTI 1973–76, Office of UK Perm Rep to Euro Communities 1976–77, DTI 1977–80, asst sec DTI 1980–84, seconded as asst dir to Morgan Grenfell & Co 1984–85, DTI 1985–, under sec Overseas Trade Div 2 DTI 1987–89, head Central Unit DTI 1989–92, dir Deregulation Unit 1990–92, head Int Trade Policy Div 1992–96, dir and advsr on trade policy DTI 1996–; leader UK del to ninth UN conf on trade and devpt 1996, chm OECD Trade Ctee 1996–; memb Cncl Marie Curie Meml Fndn 1992–; *Recreations* reading, travelling, looking at buildings; *Clubs* Utd Oxford and Cambridge, Cambridge Union; *Style*— John Cooke, Esq; ✉ Department of Trade and Industry, Kingsgate House, 66–74 Victoria St, London SW1E 6SW (☎ 0171 215 5000)

COOKE, Air Vice-Marshal John Nigel Carlyle; CB (1984), OBE (1954); s of Air Marshal Sir Cyril Bertram Cooke, KCB, CBE (d 1972), and (Elizabeth Amelia) Phyllis, *née* Davies (d 1994); *b* 16 Jan 1922; *Educ* Felsted, St Mary's Hosp Paddington (MD); *m* 1958, Elizabeth Helena Murray Johnstone; 2 s, 1 da; *Career* prof of aviation med 1974–79, dean of Air Force Med 1979–83, sr conslt RAF 1983–85, ret 1985; conslt CAA, conslt advsr to Sultan of Oman's Air Force 1985–90; conslt physician King Edward VII Hosp Midhurst 1988–; FRCP, FRCPEd, MFOM; *Recreations* fly fishing, gliding; *Clubs* RAF; *Style*— Air Vice-Marshal John Cooke, CB, OBE; ✉ 4 Lincoln Close, Stoke Mandeville, Bucks (☎ 01296 613852)

COOKE, Capt Jonathan Gervaise Fitzpatrick; OBE (1983); s of Rear Adm John Gervaise Beresford Cooke, CB (d 1976), and Helen Beatrice, *née* Cameron; *b* 26 March 1943; *Educ* Summerfields Oxford, Marlborough, RNC Dartmouth; *m* 9 April 1983, Henrietta Lorraine Deschamps, da of late Maj Saunders Edward Chamier, MC, of Green Hedges, Wadhurst, E Sussex; 1 s (Hugo b 1987), 2 da (Arabella b 1984, Serena b 1985); *Career* joined RN 1961; cmd three submarines (HMS Rorqual 1974–76, HMS Churchill 1981–82, HMS Warspite 1980–84), Cdr submarine sea trg 1984–86, Capt 3 Submarine Sqdn 1986–89, Br Naval Attaché Paris 1990–92, Royal Coll of Defence Studies 1993, Cdre MOD and ADC 1993–96; chief exec Leathersellers' Co 1996–; Yr Bro Trinity House 1994; Cdr de l'Ordre Nationale de Merite (France) 1992; *Recreations* tennis, reading, skiing, country sports; *Clubs* Naval and Military, Queen's; *Style*— Capt Jonathan Cooke, OBE, RN; ✉ Downstead House, Morestead, Winchester, Hants SO21 1LF (☎ 01962 777765); Leathersellers' Company, 15 St Helens Place, London EC3A 6DQ (☎ 0171 588 4615)

COOKE, (Patrick) Joseph Dominic; s of Patrick Cooke, of Galway, and Mary, *née* Naughton of Galway; *b* 9 Aug 1931; *Educ* St Joseph's Coll, Univ Coll Galway (BEng); *m* 31 Dec 1960, Margaret Mary, da of Dr Valentine Vincent Brown (d 1968); 2 s (Patrick Vincent b 11 Dec 1961, Robert Joseph b 11 Oct 1969), 4 da (Elizabeth Mary b 22 April 1963, Catherine Louise b 25 Aug 1964, Barbara Mair b 8 Jan 1966, Johanna Mair (twin) b 8 Jan 1966); *Career* graduate trainee United Steel Companies Ltd 1952–54, Workington Iron and Steel Co (Branch of United Steel Co) 1954–60, mgmnt conslt Urwick Orr 1961–73 (sr ptnr 1967–70, princ ptnr 1970–73), princ Cooke Management Consultants 1973–, non-exec dir EMAP plc 1984–, md The Daily Telegraph plc 1987–94 (non-exec dir and vice chm 1994–); MICE, MIMechE, CIMgt, FIMC (Stanford Smith award 1967); *Recreations* golf, gardening; *Style*— Joseph Cooke, Esq; ✉ The Telegraph plc, 1 Canada Square, Canary Wharf, London E14 5DT (☎ 0171 538 5000); Apt 305, Batiment le Terrasse, Parc Saint Roman, 7 Avenue de Saint Roman, MC 98000, Monaco

COOKE, His Hon (Richard) Kenneth; OBE (1945); s of Richard Cooke, and Beatrice Mary; *b* 17 March 1917; *Educ* Sebright Sch Wolverley, Univ of Birmingham; *m* 1, 1945, Gwendoline Mary Black (d 1984); m 2, 1985, Else Anni Hildegard Rowlands; *Career* Sqdn Ldr RAFVR 1939–45; admitted slr 1939, in private practice 1945–52, clerk to the justices 1952–70, metropolitan stipendiary magistrate 1970, recorder of the Crown Court 1972–80, circuit judge (SE Circuit) 1980–92; memb Lord Chllr's Advsy Ctee on Trg of Magistrates 1979–85; hon dep chm Magistrates' Assoc 1981–82 (chm Legal Ctee 1980–89), pres South West London Branch Magistrates' Assoc 1984–89, memb Advsy Bd Crime Concern 1990–; licensed reader Rochester Diocese 1970–; *Recreations* salmon and trout fishing; *Style*— His Hon Cooke, OBE; ✉ The Bridewell, 6 Liskeard Close, Chislehurst, Kent BR7 6RT (☎ 0181 467 3908)

COOKE, Martin James Paul; s of Lt-Col Cedric Paul Cooke (d 1974), and Katharine Norah Blanche *née* Lowick; *b* 25 Jan 1947; *Educ* Haileybury, Imperial Serv Coll; *m* 1, 19 Oct 1974 (m dis 1983), Janet Elizabeth, da of Alan Byrne, of Llanderffel, N Wales; 1 s (Nicholas b 1978), 1 da (Anna b 1976); m 2, 4 Jan 1985, Frances Mary, da of John Peter Jackson (d 1985), of Croydon; 3 s (Jonathan b 1986, Charles b 1988, Benedict b 1990), 1 da (Helena b 1994); *Career* CA; Touche Ross & Co 1969–72, ptnr Rensburg Stockbrokers 1976 (joined 1972), non-exec dir Radio City plc 1987–91, chm Northern Stock Exchange Conference 1988, dir BWD Rensburg Ltd 1988–; chm Chester Summer Music Festival 1979–81 (fin dir 1978–87), chm St Endellion Summer Festival 1990–; pres Liverpool Soc of CAs 1992–93; memb Stock Exchange 1973; FCA 1969, AIIMR 1973; *Recreations* sailing, music; *Clubs* Racquets (Liverpool), City Club (Chester); *Style*— Martin Cooke, Esq; ✉ Holywell Farm, Clutton, Tattenhall, Chester, Cheshire; B W D Rensburg Ltd, 100 Old Hall Street, Liverpool L3 9AB (☎ 0151 227 2030)

COOKE, Nicholas Huxley; s of Geoffrey Whitehall Cooke (d 1995), and Anne Heathorn, *née* Huxley (d 1989); *b* 6 May 1944; *Educ* Charterhouse, Worcester Coll Oxford (MA); *m* 27 June 1970, Anne, da of James Whittington Landon, DFC (d 1994); 2 s (James b 1983, Toby b 1986), 3 da (Fenella b 1973, Sophie b 1976, Caroline b 1978); *Career* dir (Scotland) British Trust for Conservation Volunteers 1978–84, dir Scottish Conservation Projects Trust 1984–; memb: Scottish Ctee for Euro Year of the Environment 1987–88, Forward Scotland 1987–, Assoc of Chief Offrs of Scot Voluntary Orgns 1989–; memb: Bd Scot Cncl for Voluntary Orgns, Scot Standing Conf of Vol Youth Orgns (SSCVYO); chm Lewis Stewart Meml Fund; pres Amateur Entomologists Soc 1975 (treas 1972–78); FRSA; *Recreations* outdoor conservation work, walking, photography, fly fishing; *Style*— Nicholas Cooke, Esq; ✉ Easter Stonefield, Port of Menteith, Stirling FK8 3RD (☎ 01877 382411); Scottish Conservation Projects Trust, Balallan House, 24 Allan Park, Stirling FK8 2QG (☎ 01786 479697, fax 01786 465359)

COOKE, (William) Peter; s of Douglas Edgar Cooke, MC (Lt Durham LI, d 1964), of Gerrards Cross, Bucks, and Florence May, *née* Mills (d 1986); *b* 1 Feb 1932; *Educ* Kingswood Sch Bath, Merton Coll Oxford (MA); *m* 22 April 1957, Maureen Elizabeth, da of Dr E A Haslam-Fox (d 1975) of Holmes Chapel, Cheshire; 2 s (Nicholas b 1959, Andrew b 1964), 2 da (Caroline b 1960, Stephanie b 1970); *Career* Nat Serv RA 1951; joined Bank of England 1955; seconded: to Bank for International Settlements Basle Switzerland 1958–59, as PA to md IMF Washington DC 1961–65, as sec City Takeover Panel 1968–69; Bank of England: first dep chief cashier 1970–73, advsr to Govrs 1973–76, head Banking Supervision 1976–85, assoc dir 1982–88; chm: City EEC Ctee 1973–80, Ctee on Banking Regulations and Supervisory Practices Bank for International Settlements Basle Switzerland 1977–88, Price Waterhouse World Regulatory Advsy Practice 1989–; dir: Safra Republic Holdings SA 1989–, Alexander & Alexander Services Inc 1994–, Financial Security Assurance (UK) Ltd 1994–, Bank of China International 1997–; chm Merton Soc 1979–95 (pres 1995–); govr: Pangbourne Coll 1982–, Kingswood Sch 1990–; memb: Mgmnt Ctee Eng Churches Housing Gp 1977–93, Bd The Housing Corp 1988– (dep chm 1994–), Cncl RIIA; dir: Church Housing Tst 1988–, Salzburg Seminar 1990–; *Recreations* music, golf, travel; *Clubs* Reform, Denham Golf; *Style*— Peter Cooke, Esq; ✉ Price Waterhouse, Southwark Towers, 32 London Bridge St, London SE1 9SY (☎ 0171 939 3000, fax 0171 378 0647, telex 884657/8)

COOKE, Peter Stephen; s of Henry Peter Cooke (d 1988), and Patricia Jean Cooke, *née* Wearing; *b* 13 April 1948; *Educ* Guildford Royal GS, Univ of Southampton (BSc); *m* 1, 24 July 1971 (m dis 1989), Patricia Ann, da of Robert Frederick Meredith; 2 da (Alexander b 1978, Amy b 1979); m 2, 15 July 1989, Elizabeth Margaret, da of Glyndwr Thomas; 1 s (George Henry b 1991); *Career* slr; legal advsr to Engrg Employers' Fedn 1978–83, ptnr Theodore Goddard 1984– (currently head Employment and Employee Benefits Gp); memb Worshipful Co of Slrs 1989; memb Law Soc; *Books* Croners Employment Law (1980), Croners Industrial Relations Law (contrib 1989); *Recreations* music, cycling and sailing; *Style*— Peter Cooke, Esq; ✉ 302 Cromwell Tower, Barbican, London EC2Y 8DD; Theodore Goddard, 150 Aldersgate St, London EC1A 4EJ (☎ 0171 606 8855, telex 884678, fax 0171 606 4390)

COOKE, Randle Henry; LVO (1971); s of Col H R V Cooke (d 1971), of Bridgnorth, Shropshire, and Mrs E F K Cooke (d 1978); *b* 26 April 1930; *Educ* Eton; *m* 19 Dec 1960, Clare, da of C J M Bennett, CBE, of London; 1 s (David b 27 May 1966), 1 da (Priscilla b 7 Nov 1961); *Career* 2 Lt 8 KRI Hussars 1949, served Korea with Regt and USAF (POW) 1950–53, ADC to GOC 7 Armoured Div 1955, regtl adj 1957, instr RMA Sandhurst 1960, Sqdn Cdr QRIH Malaya, Borneo and Germany 1963, GSO3 (SD) HQ 1 Div 1965, equerry to Duke to Edinburgh 1968–71, private sec to Lord Mayor of London 1972–74, dir personnel and admin Alginate Industries plc 1974–78; md: ARA International Ltd 1984–86, Mervyn Hughes International Ltd 1986–87; chm Randle Cooke and Associates recruitment conslts 1992– (md 1987–92); dep dir Treasurer's Dept Conservative Central Office 1992–95, fundraising dir Royal Botanic Gardens Kew 1995–; Freeman City of London 1971; *Recreations* most things to do with water; *Clubs* Cavalry and Guards', Caterpillar; *Style*— Randle Cooke, Esq, LVO; ✉ Chess House, Green Lane, Prestwood, Bucks HP16 0QA (☎ and fax 01494 862147); Royal Botanic Gardens Kew, Richmond, Surrey TW9 3AB (☎ 0181 332 5918, fax 0181 332 5901)

COOKE, Richard Kennedy Gordon; s of Alfred Gordon Cooke (d 1992), and Mary Eluned, *née* Mason; *b* 23 April 1950; *Educ* St Paul's Cathedral Choir Sch, Monkton Combe Sch, King's Coll Cambridge; *m* 31 May 1980, Alison Mary, da of Hon (Arthur) Maxwell Stamp (d 1984); 2 da (Florence Mary b 10 Sept 1982, Hannah Marian b 4 May 1984), 1 s (Maxwell Richard Gordon b 3 Nov 1985); *Career* conductor; conductor Cambridge Univ Chamber Orch and asst conductor Cambridge Univ Music Soc 1972–73, dir of choral music Tiffin Sch Kingston-upon-Thames 1974–81, conductor London Philharmonic Choir 1982–91, chorus master Opéra de Lyon 1992–95, conductor Royal Choral Soc 1995–; fndr Richard Cooke Singers 1989 (resident choir Aix-en-Provence Festival 1992); other appointments incl: dir of music St Columb Festival 1969–90, asst conductor Gemini Opera 1974–80, conductor Univ of Essex Choir 1981–, conductor Canterbury Choral Soc 1984–, asst chorus master London Symphony Chorus 1976–82; various conducting in Europe and Scandinavia incl: Gothenburg Symphony Orchestra, Opéra de Lyon, Aix-en-Provence Festival; Hon Doctorate Univ of Essex 1996; *Recordings* as conductor incl: Orff Carmina Burana (with RPO and Royal Choral Soc) 1995, Last Night of the Proms (with RPO and Canterbury Choral Soc) 1996; as chorus master incl:

Brahms Requiem (LPO under Klaus Tennstedt) 1986, Mahler Symphony No 8 (with LPO under Tennstedt, Grammy nomination) 1987, Cherubini Mass (with LPO under Riccardo Muti) 1987, Vaughan Williams Sea Symphony (with LPO under Bernard Haitink) 1989; *Recreations* cricket, reading, surfing, politics; *Style*— Richard Cooke, Esq; ✉ Sudbury House, Wrotham, nr Sevenoaks, Kent TN15 7AR (☎ 01732 882153, fax 01732 780861); c/o Magenta Music International, 4 Highgate High St, London N6 5JL (☎ 0181 340 8321, fax 0181 340 7823)

COOKE, His Hon Judge Roger Arnold; s of late Stanley Gordon Cooke, of Nether Alderley, Cheshire, and Frances Mabel, *née* Reading; *b* 30 Nov 1939; *Educ* Repton, Magdalen Coll Oxford (BA, MA); *m* 16 May 1970, Hilary, da of Eric Robertson, of Shorwell, IOW; 2 s (James b 1972, Thomas b 1975), 2 da (Elizabeth b 1973, Mary b 1979); *Career* called to Bar Middle Temple 1962 (Astbury scholar), ad eundem Lincoln's Inn 1967 (bencher 1994); practised at the Chancery Bar 1963–89, head of Chambers 1985–88, jt head of Chambers 1988–89, recorder 1987–89 (asst recorder 1982–87), circuit judge (SE Circuit) 1989–; pt/t students offr Lincoln's Inn 1976–80, hon sec Chancery Bar Assoc 1979–89; memb: Disciplinary Tbnls Bar 1988–89, Inns of Court Advocacy Training Ctee 1995–, memb Advocacy Studies Bd 1996–; churchwarden Little Berkhamstead 1979–94, memb Fin and Gen Purposes Ctee Broxbourne (C) Assoc 1986–89; govr The Pines Sch Hertford 1988–96 (chm 1990–95); Freeman (by purchase) City of London 1986; memb Inst Conveyancers 1983; *Recreations* gardening, photography, history, old buildings, food; *Clubs* Athenaeum, Royal Inst of GB; *Style*— His Honour Judge Roger Cooke; ✉ Central London County Court, 26 Park Crescent, London W1N 3PD

COOKE, Roger Malcolm; s of Sidney Cooke, and Elsie Cooke; *b* 12 March 1945; *Educ* Thames Valley GS; *m* 7 Sept 1968, Antoinette Mary; 1 s (Gregory b 22 Sept 1973), 1 da (Amanda b 4 June 1971); *Career* CA 1968; articled clerk Garner & Co Chartered Accountants 1962–68; Arthur Andersen: joined 1968, ptnr 1976–, head of London Tax Div 1979–89, area co-ordinator tax for Europe ME Africa and India 1989–93, head of UK tax practice and dep managing ptnr UK 1989–93, chief fin offr (world HQ) Arthur Andersen 1993–; FCA 1968, FTII 1969; *Recreations* cricket, tennis, football, skiing, squash; *Style*— Roger Cooke, Esq; ✉ Arthur Andersen & Co, 69 West Washington Street, Chicago 60610, Illinois, USA (☎ 00 1 312 507 2249, fax 00 1 312 372 8715)

COOKE, Prof Ronald Urwick; s of Ernest Oswald Cooke (d 1948), of Maidstone, Kent, and Lilian, *née* Mount (d 1949); *b* 1 Sept 1941; *Educ* Ashford GS, UCL (BSc, MSc, PhD, DSc); *m* 4 Jan 1968, Barbara Anne, da of Albert Henry Baldwin (d 1969), of Petts Wood, Kent; 1 s (Graham Stephen b 1971), 1 da (Emma Louise b 1974); *Career* Dept of Geography UCL: lectr 1961–75, reader 1975, prof and head of dept 1981–91, dean of arts 1991–92, vice provost 1991–93; vice-chllr Univ of York 1993–; Bedford Coll London: prof 1975–81, dean of sci 1978–80, vice princ 1979–80; co-fndr, dir and chm Geomorphological Services Ltd 1980–90; govr: Watford Boys' GS, Watford Girls' GS 1985–92; memb: RGS, Inst of Br Geographers (pres 1991–92), Geological Soc of London; *Books incl* Geomorphology in Deserts (with A Warren, 1973), Geomorphology in Environmental Management (with J C Doornkamp, 1974, 2 edn 1990), Arroyos and Environmental Change in the American Southwest (with R W Reeves, 1976), Environmental Hazards in Los Angeles (1984), Urban Geomorphology in Drylands (with D Brunsden, J C Doornkamp and DKC Jones, 1982), Desert Geomorphology (with A Warren and A S Goudie, 1993), Crumbling Heritage (with G Gibbs, 1993); *Clubs* Athenaeum; *Style*— Prof Ronald Cooke; ✉ The University of York, Heslington, York YO1 5DD (☎ 01904 432000)

COOKE, Simon Henry; s of George Bristow Cooke, DFC (d 1989), of Halstead, Essex, and Frances Evelina, *née* Hopkinson (d 1992); *b* 16 April 1932; *Educ* Marlborough, Gonville and Caius Coll Cambridge (MA); *m* 9 June 1956, Anne Gillian De Horne, da of Brig John Theodore De Horne Vaizey, of Halstead, Essex (d 1982); 3 s (Jonathan b 1959, Adam b 1960, Matthew b 1964); *Career* admitted slr 1957, ptnr Bristows Cooke & Carpmael 1960–96; chm Critchley Group plc 1979; non-exec dir: Biorex Laboratories Ltd, Lawsons (Whetstone) Ltd, Supreme Concrete Ltd; former dir: Bausch & Lomb UK Ltd, Trico Ltd, E Merck Ltd, Western Electric Co Ltd; chm Govrs Newport Free GS Essex; memb Law Soc; *Recreations* bird watching, skiing, shooting, travel, gardening; *Style*— Simon Cooke, Esq; ✉ Deers, Clavering, Saffron Walden, Essex CB11 4PX (☎ 01279 777342, fax 01279 777197)

COOKE, Stephen Giles; s of late Basil Cooke, and Dora Cynthia, *née* Richards; *b* 30 July 1946; *Educ* Stamford Sch, Leicester Coll of Art; *m* Jane Lesley, da of late Cowper Fredrick Ide; 2 s (Henry Stephen b 1975, James Cowper b 1979); *Career* articled clerk Clay Allison & Clark Worksop Notts, admitted slr 1971, ptnr Withers 1973– (joined 1971); dir The Ockenden Venture (refugee charity), dep chm London Handel Soc; *Books* Inheritance Tax and Lifetime Gifts (1987); *Recreations* gardening, tennis; *Style*— Stephen Cooke, Esq; ✉ The Pond House, Well, Hook, Hants RG29 1TL; Withers, 12 Gough Square, London EC4A 3DE (☎ 0171 936 1000, fax 0171 936 2589)

COOKE, Stephen Paul; s of James Armitage Cooke, of Junipers, Dunsfold, and Beryl Margaret, *née* Jarvis; *b* 8 April 1950; *Educ* Cranleigh Sch, Imperial Coll London (BSc, ARCS); *m* 23 Sept 1972, Penelope Anne, da of John Reginald Franklin, of Cranleigh, Surrey; 2 s (Alistair b 1976, Thomas b 1977), 1 da (Polly b 1986); *Career* ptnr Montagu Loebl Stanley & Co 1976, md Montagu Loebl Stanley Finance Services 1984, chief exec Gerrard Vivian Gray Ltd 1987–; dir: Gerrard & National Holdings plc, Hong Kong Investment Trust 1989–, Venturi Investment Trust 1990–, The Securities Inst 1992–94, London Stock Exchange, TT Group Holdings plc; AIIMR, FSI(Dip); *Recreations* tennis, horse racing; *Style*— Stephen Cooke, Esq; ✉ Gerrard Vivian Gray Ltd, Burne House, 88 High Holborn, London WC1V 6LS (☎ 0171 831 8883, fax 0171 831 9938, telex 887080)

COOKE, Prof Timothy; *b* 16 Sept 1947; *Career* house offr Royal Southern Hosp Liverpool 1973–74, demonstrator in anatomy Univ of Liverpool 1974–75, casualty offr Broadgreen Hosp Liverpool 1975–76 (SHO in orthopaedics 1975), registrar to Professorial Surgical Unit Liverpool Royal Infirmary 1976, registrar Wallasey Victoria Central 1976–77, registrar in paediatric surgery Alder Hey Children's Hosp 1977, research asst Dept of Surgery Liverpool Royal Infirmary 1978–79 (registrar to Professorial Surgical Unit 1977–78), registrar in surgery Professorial Unit Broadgreen Hosp 1979–80, lectr in surgery and hon sr registrar Univ of Southampton 1980–83; sr lectr in surgery and hon conslt surgn: Charing Cross and Westminster Med Sch 1983–86, Univ of Liverpool/Royal Liverpool and Broadgreen Hosps 1986–89; St Mungo prof of surgery and hon conslt surgn Royal Infirmary Glasgow 1989–; memb: Specialist Advsy Ctee in Gen Surgery, MRC Colorectal Cancer Ctee, UKCCCR Colorectal Cancer Ctee, Cncl Br Oncological Assoc, Exec Ctee Br Assoc of Cancer Research; author of numerous pubns in learned jls; memb Editorial Bd: Br Jl of Surgery (also memb Cncl), Br Jl of Cancer, Surgical Oncology, Current Practice in Surgery, GUT, Annals of the RCSEd; memb: Surgical Research Soc, Assoc of Surgns of GB and I, Br Breast Gp, RSM, Br Assoc for Cancer Research, Cell Kinetic Soc; *Style*— Prof Timothy Cooke; ✉ University Department of Surgery, Royal Infirmary, Queen Elizabeth Building, Alexandra Parade, Glasgow G31 2ER (☎ 0141 211 4870, fax 0141 211 4943)

COOKE OF ISLANDREAGH, Baron (Life Peer 1992), of Islandreagh, Co Antrim; Victor Alexander Cooke; OBE (1981), DL (Antrim 1970); s of (Norman) Victor Cooke, of Greenisland, Co Antrim; *b* 18 Oct 1920; *Educ* Marlborough, Trinity Coll Cambridge (MA); *m* 1951, Alison Sheila, only da of late Maj-Gen Francis Casement, DSO; 2 s (Michael John Alexander b 1955, James Victor Francis b 1960), 1 da (Victoria Sally (Mrs Nicholas Yonge) b 1956); *Career* Lt RN 1940–46; chm: Henry R Ayton Ltd Belfast 1970–89 (with firm 1946–89), Springvale EPS (formerly Polyproducts) Ltd 1964–, Belfast Savings Bank 1963, Harland & Wolff Ltd 1980–81 (dir 1970–87); dir NI Airports 1970–85; memb: Senate NI Parly 1960–68, NI Economic Cncl 1974–78; cmmr Irish Lights 1983–95 (chm 1990–92); CEng, FIMechE; *Clubs* Naval; *Style*— The Rt Hon Lord Cooke of Islandreagh, OBE, DL; ✉ c/o House of Lords, London SW1A 0PW

COOKE OF THORNDON, Baron (Life Peer UK 1995), of Wellington in New Zealand and of Cambridge in the County of Cambridgeshire; Sir Robin Brunskill Cooke; KBE (1986), kt (1977), PC (1977); s of Hon Mr Justice (Philip Brunskill) Cooke, MC (d 1956), and Valmai Digby Gore; *b* 9 May 1926; *Educ* Wanganui Collegiate Sch, Victoria Univ Coll Wellington NZ (LLM), Gonville and Caius Coll Cambridge (MA, PhD); *m* 1952, Phyllis Annette, da of Malcolm Balgownie Miller (d 1968), of Wellington; 3 s (Hon Philip Malcolm Brunskill b 1957, Hon Christopher Monckton Duthie b 1959, Hon Francis Morland Robin b 1965); *Career* called to the Bar New Zealand 1950, Inner Temple 1954 (hon bencher 1985), practised NZ 1955–72, QC 1964; judge: Supreme Ct of NZ 1972–76, Ct of Appeal of NZ 1976–96 (pres 1986–96), Ct of Appeal of Western Samoa and Supreme Ct of Fiji; visiting fell All Souls Coll Oxford 1990; cmmn memb Int Cmmn of Jurists 1993–, special status memb American Law Inst 1993–, life memb Lawasia 1988; hon fell Gonville and Caius Coll Cambridge, Hon LLD Victoria Univ 1989, Hon LLD Univ of Cambridge 1990, Hon DCL Univ of Oxford 1991; *Clubs* United Oxford and Cambridge University (London), Wellington (NZ); *Style*— The Rt Hon Lord Cooke of Thorndon, KBE; ✉ 4 Homewood Crescent, Karori, Wellington, New Zealand (☎ 00 644 4768 059); Lords of Appeal Corridor, House of Lords, London SW1A 0PW (☎ 0171 219 3352)

COOKE-PRIEST, Rear Adm Colin Herbert Dickinson; CB (1993); s of Dr William Hereward Dickinson Priest (d 1988), of Jersey, and Harriet Lesley Josephine, *née* Cooke; *b* 17 March 1939; *Educ* Marlborough, Britannia RNC Dartmouth; *m* 20 March 1965, Susan Mary Diana (Sue), da of Air Vice-Marshal John Forde Hobler, CB, CBE, of Queensland, Australia; 2 s (Nicholas b 1969, James b 1971), 2 da (Diana b 1966, Marina b 1974); *Career* Cdr RN 1973, CO HMS Plymouth 1975, CO HMS Berwick 1976, Capt 1980, CO HMS Boxer 1983, dir Maritime Tactical Sch 1985, CO HMS Brilliant and Capt (F) Second Frigate Sqdn 1987, Cdr RN Task Force Gulf 1988, Rear Adm 1989, Dep Asst Chief of Staff (Ops) SHAPE Belgium and maritime advsr SACEUR 1989, Flag Offr Naval Aviation 1990–93; nat dir Trident Trust 1994; gentleman usher to HM The Queen 1994; Freeman City of London 1986, Liveryman Worshipful Co of Coachmakers and Coach Harness Makers 1986, Upper Freeman Guild of Air Pilots and Air Navigators 1994; FRAeS 1992; *Recreations* narrow boating, tennis, golf; *Clubs* Army and Navy; *Style*— Rear Adm Colin Cooke-Priest, CB

COOKE-YARBOROUGH, Edmund Harry; s of George Eustace Cooke-Yarborough (d 1938), and Daphne Isabel, *née* Wrinch (d 1984); kinsman and hp of Sir David William Perceval Cooke, 12 Bt, *qv*; *b* 25 Dec 1918; *Educ* Canford, ChCh Oxford (BA, MA); *m* 1952, Anthea Katharine, da of John Alexander Dixon (d 1976), of Market Harborough; 1 s (Anthony Edmund b 1956), 1 da (Jane Anthea (Mrs Giles Vicat) b 1958); *Career* radar res for RAF 1940–48 (princ scientific offr TRE); AERE Harwell 1948–82: individual merit appointment as dep chief scientist 1955, head Instrumentation and Applied Physics Div 1957–80, chief res scientist 1980–82; dir E H Cooke-Yarborough Ltd 1986–; FEng 1980, FInstP, FIEE; *Books* An Introduction to Transistor Circuits (1957, second edn 1960); *Recreations* tracing archaeological alignments, digital computing, Stirling engines, motor cars; *Style*— Edmund Cooke-Yarborough, Esq, FEng; ✉ Lincoln Lodge, Longworth, nr Abingdon, Oxon

COOKSEY, Sir David James Scott; kt (1993); s of late Dr Frank Sebastian Cooksey, CBE, of Suffolk, and Muriel Mary, *née* Scott; *b* 14 May 1940; *Educ* Westminster, St Edmund Hall Oxford (MA, hon fell 1994); *m* 1973, Janet Clouston Bewley, da of Dr Ian Aysgarth Bewley Cathie, of Glos; 1 s (Alexander b 1976), 1 da (Leanda b 1974), 1 step da (Atlanta Wardell-Yerburgh); *Career* chm: Advent Ltd 1987– (md 1981–87), Bespak plc 1995– (dir 1993–); a dir of the Bank of England 1994–; dir: British Venture Capital Association 1983–89 (chm 1983–84), Isis Innovation Ltd 1992–95, William Baird plc 1995–; memb Innovation Advsy Bd DTI 1988–93; chm: Audit Cmmn for Local Govt and the NHS in England and Wales 1986–95, Local Govt Cmmn 1995–96; memb Cncl Univ of Southampton 1993–; govr Wellcome Tst 1995–; tstee: Mary Rose Tst 1993– (chm 1996–), CORDA 1993–; Liveryman Worshipful Co of Info Technologists; FRSA; *Recreations* sailing, performing and visual arts; *Clubs* Boodle's, Royal Yacht Squadron, Royal Thames Yacht; *Style*— Sir David Cooksey; ✉ Advent Ltd, 25 Buckingham Gate, London SW1E 6LD (☎ 0171 630 9811, fax 0171 828 1474)

COOKSON, Anthony John (Tony); s of John Cookson (d 1971), of Ipswich, and Joyce Creaser, *née* Hutchison; *b* 3 June 1940; *Educ* Northgate GS Ipswich; *m* 7 Oct 1967, Janet, da of Kenneth Noble (d 1992), of Ipswich; 1 s (John Alexander b 1978), 2 da (Samantha Jo b 1970, Tara Danielle b 1971); *Career* Hadleigh Industries Group plc: joined 1961, md 1971, gp chief exec 1987–; Freeman: City of London, Worshipful Co of Founders; FIMgt 1986; *Recreations* golf, skiing, travel, reading; *Clubs* Woodbridge Golf, Ski Club of Great Britain, RAC; *Style*— Tony Cookson, Esq; ✉ Hadleigh plc, Cromwell Court, No 5 Greyfriars Road, Ipswich, Suffolk IP1 1XG (☎ 01473 231031, fax 01473 232126)

COOKSON, Dame Catherine Ann; DBE (1993, OBE 1985); da of Catherine Fawcett; *b* 20 June 1906; *m* 1940, Thomas Henry Cookson; *Career* novelist; works trans into 21 languages; Catherine Cookson Fndn Univ of Newcastle estab 1985; Paul Harris fell Rotary Int Hexham 1985; Hon MA Newcastle upon Tyne 1983, Hon DLitt Univ of Sunderland; Freeman of South Shields 1978; memb: Writers' and Authors' Guild, Soc of Authors; *Books* incl: Kate Hannigan (1950), Maggie Rowan (1954), A Grand Man (1954, filmed as Jacqueline 1956), The Lord and Mary Ann (1956), Rooney (1957, filmed 1958), The Menagerie (1958), The Devil and Mary Ann (1958), Fenwick Houses (1960), Love and Mary Ann (1961), Life and Mary Ann (1962), Marriage and Mary Ann (1964), Mary Ann's Angels (1965), Matty Doolin (1965), Katie Mulholland (1967), Mary Ann and Bill (1967), Our Kate (autobiography, 1969), The Nice Bloke (1969), The Glass Virgin (1970), The Mallen Streak (1973), The Mallen Girl (1974), The Mallen Litter (1974), Our John Willie (1974), The Invisible Cord (1975), Go Tell It to Mrs Golightly (1977), The Cinder Path (1978), Tilly Trotter (1980), Tilly Trotter Wed (1981), Tilly Trotter Widowed (1982), A Dinner of Herbs (1985), Harold (1985), The Moth (1986), Catherine Cookson Country (memoirs, 1986), The Parson's Daughter (1987), The Cultured Handmaiden (1988), Let Me Make Myself Plain (personal anthology, 1988), The Harrogate Secret (1989), The Black Candle (1989), The Wingless Bird (1990), The Gillyvors (1990), My Beloved Son (1991), The Rag Nymph (1991), The House of Women (1992), The Maltese Angel (1992), The Year of the Virgins (1993), The Golden Straw (1993), Justice Is A Woman (1994), The Tinker's Girl (1994), The Obsession (1995), Plainer Still (1995), The Branded Man (1996); *As Catherine Marchant* Heritage of Folly (1962), Fen Tiger (1963), House of Men (1964), Martha Mary Crawford (1975), The Slow Awakening (1976), The Iron Façade (1977); *Clubs* PEN (English Centre); *Style*— Dame Catherine Cookson, DBE; ✉ c/o Sheil Land Associates Ltd, 43 Doughty St, London WC1N 2LF (☎ 0171 405 9351, fax 0171 831 2127)

COOKSON, Clive Michael; s of Richard Clive Cookson, and Ellen, *née* Fawwaz; *b* 13 Feb 1952; *Educ* Winchester, BNC Oxford (BA); *m* 8 April 1978, Caroline Davidson; 1 s (Robert b 9 Oct 1984), 1 da (Emma b 10 July 1986); *Career* journalist; trainee journalist Luton Evening Post Thomson Regional Newspapers 1974–76, American ed (in

Washington) Times Higher Education Supplement 1977–81 (science corr 1976–77), technol corr The Times 1981–83, sci and med corr BBC Radio 1983–87, sci ed Financial Times 1991– (technol ed 1987–90); Feature Writer of the Year (UK Technol Press Awards) 1988 and 1989, Glaxo Sci Writer of the Year 1994; *Style*— Clive Cookson, Esq; ✉ The Financial Times, 1 Southwark Bridge, London SE1 9HL (☎ 0171 873 4950, fax 0171 873 3950)

COOKSON, Prof Richard Clive; s of Clive Cookson (d 1971), of Nether Warden, Hexham, Northumberland, and Marion Amy, *née* James (d 1961); *b* 27 Aug 1922; *Educ* Harrow, Trinity Coll Cambridge (MA, PhD); *m* 4 Nov 1948, Ellen, da of Dr Amin Fawaz, of Lebanon; 2 s (Clive b 1952, Hugh b 1954); *Career* res fell Harvard Univ 1948, res chemist Glaxo Labs 1949–51, lectr Birkbeck Coll London 1951–57, prof of chemistry Univ of Southampton 1957–85; visiting prof Univ of California 1960; dir Cookson Chemicals Ltd 1986–94, chm Tocris Cookson Ltd 1994–; Freeman City of Newcastle upon Tyne; FRSC 1959, FRS 1968; *Style*— Prof R C Cookson, FRS; ✉ Northfield House, Coombe Bissett, Salisbury, Wilts SP5 4JZ

COOLING, (John) Michael; OBE, JP (1966); s of John William Cooling (d 1980), and Nellie, *née* Jones (d 1986); *b* 27 April 1920; *Educ* King's Coll Sch Wimbledon, Imperial Coll of Sci Technol & Med (BSc Eng); *m* 14 Feb 1952, Theresa Frances, da of John MacSharry; 2 s (John Breffni Marius b 17 Dec 1953, Michael Turlough Spencer b 5 Nov 1957), 1 da (Aoife Marie-Thérèse b 20 Sept 1960); *Career* Lieut (E) RN HMS Victorious HMS Fencer HMS Cleveland 1940–46; J Jeffreys and Co: design engr 1946–49, mangr McCann Ltd Dublin (subsid co) 1949–54, dir 1954–60, jt md 1960–73, chm 1968–73; chief engr & commercial dir of Belfour Kilpatrick 1973–79, chm and md of Heduco Ltd 1979–; dir: Beaumont (UK) Ltd 1987–96, Waste Gas Technology Ltd 1992–; pres: Heating and Ventilating Contractors Assoc 1969–70, CIBSE 1975–76 (gold medal 1987); hon fell American Soc of Heating Refrigeration and Air Conditioning Engrs 1984; memb: Worshipful Co of Fanmakers 1965, Worshipful Co of Plumbers 1975; FIMechE 1947, FCIBSE 1949, FIEE 1973, FEng 1985, FCGI 1986; *Recreations* golf; *Clubs* Royal Wimbledon Golf; *Style*— Michael Cooling, Esq, OBE, FEng; ✉ Valldemosa, 26 Conway Rd, Wimbledon, London SW20 8PA (☎ 0181 946 3432); Heduco Ltd, St George's House, 195/203 Waterloo Rd, London SE1 8XJ (☎ 0171 633 2380, fax 0171 261 9551)

COOMBE, Donald Howard; MBE (1992), JP (1973); er s of Howard James Coombe (d 1988); *b* 21 Oct 1927; *Educ* Northbrook C of E Sch Lee, Roan Sch Greenwich, Univ of The World (MA); *m* 5 June 1948, Betty Joyce, da of George William Adie (d 1938); 2 s (Richard Howard b 25 April 1953, David b 8 Oct 1958); *Career* RN 1942–47, hon cmmn to Adm Texas Navy 1976; chm: RTC Ltd (Lloyd's Brokers) 1971–; memb Lloyd's 1974; fndr chm: Coombe Tst Fund, Coombe Holiday Tst Fund; chm Victoria Wellesley Tst (all registered charities for Needy Children); life memb Royal Soc of St George; former cmmr Scouts Assoc; hon attorney-gen N Carolina, chm of bench 1982, cmmr Income Tax 1978–85; Freeman: City of London 1970, City of Dallas Texas 1976; Liveryman Worshipful Co of Poulters 1978; Order of St George (Sweden) 1974; *Books* The Geezer Wiv the Flahr; *Recreations* charity fundraising, social work, boxing; *Clubs* National Sporting; *Style*— Donald H Coombe, Esq, MBE, JP; ✉ Sunarise, Beckenham Place Park, Kent BR3 2BN (☎ 0181 658 2714, fax 0181 663 3932); Pelican House, One Hundred Tooley St, London SE1 2TH (☎ 0171 403 4446, fax 0171 403 1439)

COOMBE, His Hon Judge Gerald Hugh; s of Capt William Stafford Coombe (d 1962), and Mabel Florence, *née* Bullas (d 1983); *b* 16 Dec 1925; *Educ* Alleyn's Sch Dulwich, Hele's Sch Exeter, Exeter Coll Oxford (MA); *m* 17 Aug 1957, Zoe Margaret, da of Sidney Ivor Richards, of Penarth, S Wales; 1 s (Robert b 1960), 1 da (Fiona b 1963); *Career* RAF Navigator 256 and 85 Sqdns 1944–48 (crashed in Mosquito Night Fighter 1947); slr Whitehead Monckton and Co Maidstone 1953–86, HM coroner Maidstone Dist Kent 1962–86, recorder 1983–86, circuit judge (SE Circuit) 1986–; *Clubs* RAF; *Style*— His Hon Judge Gerald Coombe; ✉ The Law Courts, Barker Road, Maidstone ME16 8EQ

COOMBE, John David; s of Sidney Coombe; *b* 17 March 1945; *Educ* Haberdashers' Aske's, Univ of London (BSc); *m* 1970, Gail Alicia, *née* Brazier; 3 da; *Career* CA; gp treas The Charterhouse Group plc 1976–84, mangr fin and treasy Charter Consolidated plc 1984–86, md finance and main bd dir Glaxo Holdings plc 1992–95 (fin controller 1986–92), fin dir Glaxo Wellcome plc 1995–; *Style*— John Coombe, Esq; ✉ Langdon, Burtons Way, Chalfont St Gyles, Bucks HP8 4BW (☎ 01494 762240); Glaxo Wellcome plc, Lansdowne House, Berkeley Square, London W1X 6BQ (☎ 0171 493 4060, fax 0171 408 0228)

COOMBE, His Hon Judge Michael Ambrose Rew; s of John Rew Coombe (d 1985), of King's Langley, Herts, and Phyllis Mary (d 1980); *b* 17 June 1930; *Educ* Berkhamsted, New Coll Oxford (MA); *m* 7 Jan 1961, (Elizabeth) Anne, da of Tom Hull (d 1957); 3 s (Nicholas b Dec 1961, Jonathan b and d 1966, Peter b 1970), 1 da (Juliet b 1967); *Career* Nat Serv RAF; called to the Bar Middle Temple 1957, second prosecuting counsel to the Inland Revenue Central Criminal Ct and 5 Cts of London Sessions 1971, second counsel to the Crown Inner London Sessions 1971–74, first counsel to the Crown Inner London Crown Ct 1974, second jr prosecuting counsel to the Crown Central Criminal Ct 1975–77 (fourth jr 1974–75), recorder of the Crown Ct 1976–85, first jr prosecuting counsel to the Crown Central Criminal Ct 1977–78, a sr prosecuting counsel to the Crown at the Central Criminal Ct 1978–85, master of the Bench Middle Temple 1984–, circuit judge (SE Circuit) 1985, judge Central Criminal Ct 1986–; Freeman City of London 1986; *Recreations* theatre, antiquity, art and architecture, printing; *Style*— His Hon Judge Michael Coombe; ✉ Central Criminal Court, Old Bailey, London EC4M 7EH

COOMBES, Prof (Raoul) Charles Dalmedo Stuart; s of Col R C Coombes, MC, of Aldbourne, nr Marlborough, Wiltshire, and Doreen Mary, *née* Ellis; *b* 20 April 1949; *Educ* Douai Sch, St George's Hosp Med Sch (MB BS), UCL (PhD, MD); *m* 27 July 1984, Caroline Sarah, da of David Oakes, of Sunnyside, Cowley Hill Lane, St Helens, Merseyside; 2 s (Jack Raoul b 1985, Charles David b 1992), 2 da (Sophie Flora b 1987, Matilda Rose b 1989); *Career* med res fell MRC 1974–76; Royal Marsden Hosp: sr registrar 1976–78, sr lectr 1979–84, hon conslt 1979–; sr clinical scientist and hon sr lectr Ludwig Inst for Cancer Res 1979–88, head Clinical Oncology Unit St George's Hosp 1988–90, conslt med oncologist and hon sr lectr St George's Hosp Med Sch 1988–90; prof of med oncology and dir Cancer Res Campaign Laboratories, co-dir Cancer Servs Hammersmith Hosps Tst, dean of research Charing Cross and Westminster Med Sch; co-ordinator of nat and int trials for Int Collaborative Cancer Gp; memb: SW Thames Regnl Cancer Gp, Br Breast Gp 1988, Br Assoc Cancer Res 1988, American Assoc Cancer Res 1988; FRCP 1988 (MRCP 1973); *Books* Breast Cancer Management (ed, 1984), New Endocrinology of Cancer (1987); *Recreations* painting; *Style*— Prof Charles Coombes; ✉ Charing Cross and Westminster Medical School, St Dunstan's Rd, London W6 (☎ 0181 846 1418, fax 0181 846 1433)

COOMBS, Anthony Michael Vincent; MP (C) Wyre Forest (majority 10,341); s of Clifford Keith Coombs, of Stripes Hill House, Knowle, nr Solihull, W Midlands, and Celia Mary Gostling, *née* Vincent; *b* 18 Nov 1952; *Educ* Charterhouse, Worcester Coll Oxford (MA); *m* 21 Sept 1984, Andrea Caroline, da of Daniel Pritchard, of 11 Exeter Rd, Netherton Dudley, W Midlands; 1 s (Alexander Graham Daniel); *Career* fndr and md Grevayne Properties Ltd; MP (C) Wyre Forest 1987–; PPS: to Rt Hon David Mellor 1989–92, to Rt Hon Gillian Shephard as Sec of State for Educn and Employment 1995–96; asst govt whip 1996–; memb Nat Heritage Select Ctee 1994–96; vice chm: Back Bench Educn Ctee, Parliamentary Friends of Cyprus, All Party Human Rights Gp; *Recreations* tennis, golf, skiing, football, music; *Style*— Anthony M V Coombs, Esq, MP; ✉ Margaret Thatcher House, 35 Mill St, Kidderminster, Worcs DY11 6XB (☎ 01562 825459)

COOMBS, Brian William James; s of Ernest William Coombs (d 1982), of Weston-super-Mare, Avon, and Grace Lilian, *née* Horrell; *b* 2 July 1932; *Educ* Lewisham Sch; *m* 23 June 1956, Joyce Margaret, da of William Henry Higgs (d 1987), of Wednesbury, West Midlands; 2 s (James b 1960, Peter b 1963), 1 da (Ruth b 1966); *Career* RAF Statistics Branch 1954–56; Price Waterhouse & Co chartered accountants 1957–58, Aluminium Bronze Co Ltd 1958–60, co sec Halladay's Ltd 1960–66, mgmnt accountant Tubes Ltd (TI Group) 1966–69, sec and fin accountant TI Steel Tube Division Ltd 1970–73, fin dir TI Accles & Pollock Ltd 1973–84, fin dir Lewis Woolf Griptight Ltd 1985–90, chief fin offr L W G Holdings Ltd 1985–90, asst chief exec Trinity Centre (Birmingham) Ltd 1991–, int business conslt 1991–; vice chm Walsall HA; memb: London Business Sch Alumni Assoc, Birmingham Breakfast Rotary Club; FCA 1954, FCMA 1969; *Recreations* sculpture, genealogy, walking, classic cars; *Style*— Brian Coombs, Esq; ✉ 12 Gorway Rd, Walsall, West Midlands WS1 3BB (☎ 01922 21530); c/o Trinity Centre, Old Camp Hill, Birmingham B12 0JP (☎ 0121 772 0638, fax 0121 772 4815)

COOMBS, Derek Michael; s of Clifford Coombs (d 1975), and Elizabeth Mary, *née* Evans (d 1974); *b* 12 Aug 1937; *Educ* Bromsgrove Sch; *m* 2, 1986; Jennifer Sheila, *née* Lonsdale; 2 s; 1 s and 1 da by previous marriage; *Career* chm and md S & U plc 1976–; dir Metalrax Group plc 1975–, chm Prospect Publishing Ltd 1995–; named as one of the top 100 in The British Entrepreneur 1988; MP (C) Yardley 1970–74; political journalist, active pro-European and specialist in economic affrs; lectured at Party w/e conferences; govr Royal Hosp & Home for Incurables Putney; sponsor: Save the Children Fund, Live Music Now, Riding for the Disabled; *Recreations* friends, arts and media, skiing and walking; *Style*— Derek Coombs, Esq; ✉ Cheyne Row, London SW3

COOMBS, Prof Robert Royston Amos (Robin); s of late Charles Royston Amos, and Edris Owen Coombs (d 1972); *b* 9 Jan 1921; *Educ* Diocesan Coll Cape Town SA, Univ of Edinburgh (BSc), Royal Dick Veterinary Coll Edinburgh (MRCVS), Univ of Cambridge (PhD, ScD); *m* 13 Sept 1952, Anne Marion, da of Charles Geoffrey Blomfield; 1 s (Robert Christopher b 30 Aug 1954), 1 da (Rosalind Edris Lucy b 13 Jan 1956); *Career* WWII vol Royal Scots 1939, reserved occupation; Univ of Cambridge: Stringer fell King's Coll 1947–56, asst dir res Dept of Pathology 1948, reader in immunology 1962–65, fell Corpus Christi Coll 1962–, Quick prof of biology in immunology Immunology Div Dept of Pathology 1965–88, emeritus prof 1988–; foreign hon memb Royal Belgium Acad of Med 1991 (foreign corr 1979); hon memb: American Assoc of Immunologists 1973, Br Blood Transfusion Soc 1984, Br Soc for Immunology 1988, Br Soc of Allergy and Clinical Immunology 1988, Pathological Soc of GB and Ireland, Br Soc of Haematology 1993; Hon MD Linköping Sweden 1973, Hon Dr Med Vet Copenhagen 1979, Hon DSc Guelph Canada 1981, Hon DSc Edinburgh 1984; FRS 1965, FRCPath 1968, Hon FRCP 1973, Hon FRSM 1992; *Books* Serology of Conglutination (with A M Coombs and D G Ingram, 1961), Clinical Aspects of Immunology (co-ed with P G H Gell 1963, 1968, 1975); *Style*— Prof Robin Coombs, FRS; ✉ 6 Selwyn Gardens, Cambridge CB3 9AX (☎ 01223 352681)

COOMBS, Simon Christopher; MP (C) Swindon (majority 2,826); s of Ian Peter Coombs (d 1981), of Weston-super-Mare, and Rachel Margaret Anne, *née* Robins; *b* 21 Feb 1947; *Educ* Wycliffe Coll, Univ of Reading (BA, MPhil); *m* 1983, Kathryn Lee Coe Coombs; *Career* mktg exec Br Telecom and PO Telecommunications 1970–81, mktg mangr Telex Networks Br Telecom 1981–83; cncllr: Reading CBC 1969–72, Reading BC 1973–84 (chm Transportation Ctee 1976–83, vice chm Policy Ctee 1976–83, dep Cons ldr 1976–81, chief whip 1983); chm Wessex Young Cons 1973–76, chm Cons Party Wessex Area 1980–83, memb Nat Exec Cons Pty 1980–83; MP (C) Swindon 1983–, PPS to Min for Info Technol 1984, PPS to Min for the Environment 1984–85, PPS to Sec of State for Scot 1992–95, PPS to Pres of the Bd of Trade 1995–, chm All Pty Cable and Satellite TV Gp, treas Parly Information Technol Ctee, pres All Pty Food and Health Forum, memb Employment Select Ctee 1987–92; vice chm: All Pty Tourism Gp, All Party Manufacturing Gp, All Party Exports Gp; chm Cons Backbench Employment Ctee 1992, acting chm Cons Tourism Ctee 1992–; *Recreations* cricket, philately, music; *Clubs* Swindon Conservative; *Style*— Simon Coombs, Esq, MP; ✉ House of Commons, London SW1A 0AA

COOMBS, Stephen Geoffrey; s of Geoffrey Samuel Coombs, of Rotnoddie, nr Rothiemay, Aberdeenshire, and Joan Margaret, *née* Jones; *b* 11 July 1960; *Educ* Caldy Grange GS, RNCM, RAM; *Career* concert pianist; London debut Wigmore Hall 1975; performed at numerous festivals incl: Salisbury 1987, Henley 1988, Cheltenham 1988, Spoleto Italy 1988–90, Aldeburgh 1989–90, Radley 1990, Proms 1990, Three Choirs 1991, Bath 1993, Lichfield 1993 and 1995, Cardiff 1995, Sintra Portugal 1996; regular appearances throughout Europe; visiting lectr Univ of Central England 1994–96; Gold medal Int Liszt Concourse Hungary 1977, Worshipful Co of Musicians/Maisie Lewis award 1986; *Recordings* incl: The Hussey Legacy 1988, Complete Two Piano Works of Debussy 1989, Ravel Works for Two Pianos 1990, Mendelssohn Two Double Piano Concertos 1992, Arensky Piano Concerto in F Minor and Fantasy on Russian Folk Songs 1992, Bortkiewicz Piano Concerto No 1 1992, Arensky Suites for Two Pianos 1994, Glazunov Complete Piano Works 4 Vols 1995, Glazunov Piano Concertos Nos 1 & 2 (1996), Goedicke Concertstück (1996), Reynaldo Hahn Piano Concerto (1997), Massenet Piano Concerto (1997); *Recreations* genealogy, pubs, reading; *Style*— Stephen Coombs, Esq; ✉ c/o Wordplay, 11 Connaught Road, London E17 8QB

COONEY, Raymond George Alfred (Ray); s of Gerard Joseph (d 1987), of London, and Olive Harriet, *née* Clarke (d 1975); *b* 30 May 1932; *Educ* Alleyn's Coll Dulwich; *m* 8 Dec 1962, Linda Ann, da of Leonard Spencer Dixon (d 1985), of Epping; 2 s (Danny b 1964, Michael b 1966); *Career* actor, writer, producer, director; Nat Serv RASC 1950–52; acting debut Song of Norway (Palace Theatre) 1946; playwright: One For The Pot (1961), Chase Me Comrade (1964), Charlie Girl (1965), Not Now Darling (1967), Move Over Mrs Markham (1969), Why Not Stay for Breakfast? (1970), There Goes the Bride (1974), Run for your Wife (1983), Two into One (1984), Wife Begins at Forty (1985), It Runs In the Family (1989), Out of Order (1990), Funny Money (1993 (Olivier Award nomination for Best Comedy 1996)); also dir many of own plays; prodr: Lloyd George Knew My Father 1972, Say Goodnight to Grandma 1973, At the End of the Day 1973, The Dame of Sark 1974, A Ghost on Tiptoe 1974, Bodies 1980, Whose Life Is It Anyway? 1980, They're Playing Our Song 1980, Elvis 1981, Duet for One 1981, Children of a Lesser God 1982; fndr The Theatre of Comedy Co 1983 (artistic dir 1983–88); memb Actors' Equity; *Recreations* tennis, swimming; *Style*— Ray Cooney, Esq

COOPER, *see also:* Astley-Cooper

COOPER, Alan Guthlac; s of Jack Carr Cooper, of Harrogate, N Yorks, and Veronica Dora, *née* Ludolf; *b* 23 Aug 1955; *Educ* Brentwood Sch Essex, Univ of Durham (BA); *m* 17 July 1990, Carol, da of Alexander Beattie; 2 s (Matthew Guthlac b 30 Sept 1991, Samuel Alexander b 3 July 1993), 1 da (Rebecca Aimi b 26 May 1995); *Career* British Market Research Bureau Ltd 1977–80, sr researcher rising to planning dir Leo Burnett Advertising Ltd 1980–84, sr planner rising to assoc dir Gold Greenlees Trott Ltd 1984–88, bd/planning dir DDB Needham Ltd 1988; Simons Palmer Clemmow Johnson Ltd: bd/planning dir 1989–, head of planning 1993, chm Account Planning Gp 1996–; Lord Rothermere Radio Effectiveness Award 1982, IPA Advertising Effectiveness Award 1986 and 1994; memb MRS; *Books* Advertising Works (contrib Vol 4, 1987 and

Vol 8, 1995), Understanding Brands (1996); *Recreations* walking, cycling, swimming, enjoying my family; *Clubs* MCC; *Style—* Alan Cooper, Esq; ✉ 2 Stanbridge Road, Putney, London SW15 1DX (☎ 0181 788 9270); Simons Palmer Clemmow Johnson Ltd, 19–20 Noel Street, London W1V 3PD (☎ 0171 287 4455)

COOPER, Dr Andrew Michael; s of Peter Cooper, of Blythe Bridge, Stoke-on-Trent, and Eileen Mildred, *née* Billings; *b* 31 Oct 1958; *Educ* Longton HS Stoke-on-Trent, City of Stoke-on-Trent Sixth Form Coll, Univ of Leeds Sch of Med (MB ChB, MRCGP, Dip RCGP); *m* 1 July 1989, Ann, da of Roy Rossington; 1 s (Michael David Rossington b 20 Jan 1992); *Career* house offr Leeds Gen Infirmary 1982–83, SHO A&E Cardiff Royal Infirmary 1983–84, SHO Obstetrics and Gynaecology Llandough Hosp Cardiff 1984–85, S Glamorgan Vocational Trg Scheme for Gen Practice 1985–87, ptnr Fairwater Health Centre Cardiff 1987–; course organiser S Glamorgan Vocational Trg Scheme Univ of Wales Coll of Med Dept of Postgraduate Studies 1992–; RCGP: memb Welsh Cncl 1989–, memb Central Cncl 1990–95, treas SE Wales Faculty 1991–94, chm SE Wales Faculty 1994–, memb Patient Liaison Gp 1994–95; memb RCP/RCPsych Working Pty on Care of Elderly Patients with Mental Illness 1994–95; memb BMA 1982, MRCGP 1987, memb RSM 1989, memb Physicians for Human Rights (UK); *Recreations* golf, cricket, skiing, travel, music; *Clubs* Radyr Golf, Glamorgan CCC, St Fagan's Cricket; *Style—* Dr Andrew Cooper; ✉ Fairwater Health Centre, Plasmawr Road, Fairwater, Cardiff CF5 3JT (☎ 01222 566291, fax 01222 578870)

COOPER, Hon Artemis (Alice Clare Antonia Opportune); only da of 2 Viscount Norwich, CVO; *b* 22 April 1953; *m* 1 Feb 1986, Antony James Beevor, s of John Grosvenor Beevor, OBE (d 1987); 1 da (Eleanor Allegra Lucie (Nella) b 19 Jan 1990), 1 s (Adam John Cosmo b 10 Feb 1993); *Career* writer; tstee London Library 1994–; *Books* A Durable Fire: The Letters of Duff and Diana Cooper (ed, 1983), Cairo in The War 1939–45 (1989), Mr Wu and Mrs Stitch: The Letters of Evelyn Waugh and Diana Cooper (ed, 1991), Watching in the Dark - A Child's Fight for Life (1992), Paris after the Liberation 1944–49 (1994); *Style—* Ms Artemis Cooper; ✉ 54 St Maur Road, London SW6 4DP

COOPER, Dr Barrington Spencer; s of Maurice Lionel Cooper (d 1950), and Dena, *née* Orman (d 1959); *b* 15 Jan 1923; *Educ* Grocers' Co Sch, Queens' Coll Cambridge (BA), Bart's Med Sch London (MB BS, MRCGP), Cancer Meml Hosp NY Univ (fell), College Pacific (PhD); *m* 1, Fay Helena, *née* Harman; 1 da (Victoria Ann b 18 Feb 1957); m 2, 16 Dec 1988, Jane Eva Livermore Wallace, da of Edward Charles Livermore (d 1976), of Westhill, Buntingford, Herts; *Career* Capt RAMC 1947–49; formerly: house physician Whittington Hosp and Ashford Co Hosp, med registrar Oster House Hosp, clinical asst in psychiatry Bart's, London Jewish and Nat Hosp for Nervous Diseases, visiting physician Fndn for Manic Depression NYC, corr assoc WHO Psychosocial Centre Stockholm, psychosomatic investigator for WHO, med advsr various hosp projects and private cos; currently: chm Allied Med Diagnostic Services, visitor Boston Univ Med Sch, consulting physician Clinic of Psychotherapy and Rockerfeller Univ, visiting physician Strang Inst of Preventive Med NYC; med advsr: West One Prodns Inc, Fabyan Films Ltd, World Film Servs, New Media Med Univ; author of various specialist papers; dir Fabyan Ltd and Fabyan Films Ltd; independent film prodr: The One-Eyed Soldiers, The Doctor and the Devils, Le Voleur d'Enfants (co prodr); memb BAFTA; fndr Salerno Int Youth Orchestra Festival; fell Psychosomatic Res Soc; memb: Med Section Br Psychological Soc, Soc of Clinical Psychiatrists, Br Assoc of Counselling, Assoc of Family Therapy, London Jewish Hosp Soc, NY Acad of Scis; affiliate RCPsych; FRSH, FRSM, FAAAS; *Books* Helix (script, 1982), Travel Sickness (1982), Cockpits (1987), Consumer Guide to Prescription Medicines (1989, 2 edn 1993), Thomas Cook Health Passport (1989), Consumer Guide to Non-Prescription Medicines (1992, 3 edn 1996), Your Symptoms Diagnosed (1993, 2 edn 1996); *Recreations* film, music, theatre, fine arts, swimming, sailing; *Clubs* RSM, Regency; *Style—* Dr Barrington Cooper; ✉ Flat F, 21 Devonshire Place, London W1N 1PD (☎ 0171 935 0113, fax 0171 486 0505)

COOPER, Beryl Phyllis; QC (1977); o da of Charles Augustus Cooper (d 1981), and Phyllis Lillie, *née* Burrows (d 1988); *b* 24 Nov 1927; *Educ* Surbiton HS, Univ of Birmingham (BCom); *Career* called to the Bar Gray's Inn 1960, recorder of the Crown Court 1977–, dep High Ct judge 1980–, bencher 1988; sometime memb various statutory and legal ctees incl: Criminal Injuries Compensation Bd 1978, Nurses and Professions Allied to Medicine Pay Review Bd 1983–90; *Recreations* golf, swimming, theatre; *Clubs* English Speaking Union, Caledonian (Edinburgh); *Style—* Miss Beryl Cooper, QC; ✉ 8d South Cliff Tower, Eastbourne, Sussex; 9 Gough Square, London EC4A 3DE (☎ 0171 353 5371)

COOPER, Brian; s of Frederick Hubert Cooper, and Florence Mabel, *née* Field; *b* 1 Jan 1936; *Educ* St Albans Sch, De Havilland Aeronautical Tech Sch, Hatfield Poly, London Business Sch; *m* 21 Nov 1959, Marjorie Anne (Sue), da of Ronald John More (d 1973); 2 da (Jenny b 1962, Charlotte b 1967); *Career* Flying Offr RAF 1959–62; subsidiary co dir: Firth Cleveland GKN Gps (Germany, UK) 1962–74, Bowater Corpn Ltd (UK, France, Belgium, Holland, Germany) 1974–84; asst md Hargreaves Gp plc 1984–87, dir and md Coalite Gp plc 1987–89, non-exec dir Philip Harris Holdings plc, non-exec dir Silentnight Holdings plc 1994–, chief exec The N G Bailey Organisation Ltd; hon fell Brighton Poly 1987; CEng, MRAeS, FIMechE; *Recreations* squash, sailing, skiing; *Clubs* RAF; *Style—* Brian Cooper, Esq; ✉ The N G Bailey Organisation Ltd, Denton Hall, Ilkley, W Yorks LS29 0HH

COOPER, Dr Brian Thomas; s of Dr Andrew Matthew Cooper (d 1979), of West Wellow, Romsey, Hampshire, and Irene Elizabeth, *née* Roulston; *b* 20 May 1947; *Educ* Monkton Combe Sch Bath, Univ of Birmingham (BSc, MB ChB, MD); *m* 31 Aug 1973, Dr Griselda Mary Cooper, da of Dr Charles James Constantine Davey, of Box, Chippenham, Wiltshire; 1 da (Charlotte b 4 Aug 1987); *Career* lectr in med Univ of Bristol 1978–85, conslt physician Dunedin Hosp Dunedin NZ 1985–86, conslt physician Dudley Rd Hosp and Edgbaston Nuffield Hosp Birmingham, sr clinical lectr in med Univ of Birmingham 1987–; FRCP 1991 (MRCP 1974), MBSG 1979; *Books* Manual of Gastroenterology (1987); *Recreations* military history, classical music and opera, skiing; *Style—* Dr Brian Cooper; ✉ 36 Anstruther Rd, Edgbaston, Birmingham B15 3NW (☎ 0121 456 2174); Gastroenterology Unit, City Hospital, Dudley Rd, Birmingham B18 7QH (☎ 0121 554 3801 ext 4590)

COOPER, Prof Cary Lynn; s of Harry Cooper, of Los Angeles, California, USA, and Caroline Lillian, *née* Greenberg; *b* 28 April 1940; *Educ* Fairfax Sch Los Angeles, Univ of California (BS, MBA), Univ of Leeds (PhD); *m* 1, 1970 (m dis 1984), (Edna) June Taylor; 1 s (Hamish Scott b 1972), 1 da (Natasha Beth b 1974); m 2, 1984, Rachel Faith Davies; 2 da (Laura Anne b 1982, Sarah Kate b 1985); *Career* lectr in psychology Univ of Southampton 1967–73; UMIST: prof of mgmnt educn methods 1975–79, prof of organizational psychology 1979–, pro-vice-chllr 1995–; advsr: WHO and ILO 1982–84, Home Office (on police stress) 1982–84; memb Bd of Tstees American Inst of Stress 1984–, pres Br Acad of Mgmnt 1986–90, chm Professional Affairs Ctee OPD Int Assoc of Applied Psychology 1987–89, treas Int Fedn of Scholarly Assoc of Mgmnt 1990–92; ed Jl of Organizational Behaviour 1980–, co-ed Stress Medicine 1992–; chm Business and Management Panel HEFCE; Hon MSc Univ of Manchester 1979, hon prof of psychology Univ of Manchester 1986; Myers Lecture Br Psychological Soc 1986; memb American Psychosomatic Assoc, FRSA, FBPsS, FRSM; *Books* incl: T-Groups (jtly, 1971), Theories of Group Processes (1976), Developing Social Skills in Managers (1976), Stress at Work (jtly, 1978), Executives Under Pressure (1978), Behavioural Problems in Organisations (1979), Learning From Others in Groups (1979), The Executive Gypsy (1979), Current Concerns in Occupational Stress (1980), The Stress Check (1980), Improving Interpersonal Relations (1981), Psychology and Management (1982), Management Education (jtly, 1982), Stress Research (1983), Public Faces, Private Lives (jtly, 1984), Working Women (jtly, 1984), Psychology for Managers (jtly, 1984), Change Makers (jtly, 1985), Man and Accidents Offshore (jtly, 1986), International Review of Industrial and Organisational Psychology (jtly, 1986–95), (jtly, 1986), Pilots Under Stress (jtly, 1986), Women and Information Technology (jtly, 1987), Pressure Sensitive (jtly, 1988), High Flyers (jtly, 1988), Living with Stress (jtly, 1988), Early Retirement (jtly, 1989), Career Couples (jtly, 1989), Managing People at Work (jtly, 1989), Understanding Stress in Health Care Professionals (jtly, 1990), Stress Survivors (jtly, 1991), Industrial and Organizational Psychology Vols 1 and 2 (1991), Stress and Cancer (1991), Accidents and Stress in the Offshore Oil and Gas Industry (jtly, 1991), Relax: Dealing with Stress (jtly, 1992), Shattering the Glass Ceiling (jtly, 1992), Total Quality and Human Resource Management (jtly, 1992), Women's Career Development (jtly, 1992), Stress in the Dealing Room (jtly, 1993), The Workplace Revolution (jtly, 1993), Business Elites (jtly, 1994), Creating Healthy Work Organizations (jtly, 1994), Trends in Organizational Behavior (jtly, 1994), Work Psychology (jtly, 1995), Managing Mergers, Acquistions and Strategic Alliances (jtly, 1996), Handbook of Stress, Medicine, and Health (1996); *Recreations* raising children, trying to learn the piano, swimming, reading, following politics; *Clubs* St James'; *Style—* Prof C L Cooper; ✉ 25 Lostock Hall Rd, Poynton, Cheshire (☎ 01625 871 450); Manchester School of Management, UMIST, PO Box 88, Manchester M60 1QD (☎ 0161 200 3440, fax 0161 200 3518)

COOPER, David John; s of John Alec Cooper, of London, and Norma May, *née* Kennard; *b* 4 July 1951; *Educ* Green Sch, Univ of London (BEd); *m* 20 Jan 1979, Dr Winifred Dorothy Jane Cooper, da of William Harvey Cantrell (d 1974); 1 da (Laura Kirsten Jacqueline b 23 June 1982); *Career* analyst Unilever plc 1967–71, chemistry teacher Barking Abbey 1974–75, business devpt and mktg exec Baxter Inc 1975–79, mktg exec Smith and Nephew Ltd 1979–82, business devpt and mktg exec LIG Int Ltd, dir Pfizer Inc 1984–87, corporate financier Robert Fleming 1987–88, fndr and md David Cooper Associates (DCA) 1974–; Freeman City of London 1985, Liveryman Worshipful Co of Marketers 1985; FIMgt 1984, FInstD 1984, FCInstM 1984, MCInstB 1987, memb Soc Chem Indust; *Clubs* Athenaeum, Savage, City Livery Yacht (hon sec, Rear Cdre); *Style—* David Cooper, Esq; ✉ DCA, 52 Queen Anne Street, London W1M 9LA (☎ 0171 935 7374 and 0171 487 4686, fax 0171 935 8372, e-mail DAVIDCOOPER@DCA.TelMe.COM); Lou Cantou, CEPS, Roqueburn, 34390 France (☎ 00 33 6789 5499)

COOPER, Derek Anthony (Tony); s of Donald Cooper (d 1985), and Freda, *née* Sheridan (d 1991); *b* 11 Dec 1943; *Educ* Whitehaven GS, Univ of Edinburgh (BSc); *m* 23 Sept 1967, June, da of Thomas Iley; 2 da (Yvette b 23 March 1969, Nichola b 11 Feb 1971), 2 s (David b 4 Nov 1973, Edward Lois b 11 July 1989); *Career* forest offr Forestry Cmmn 1967–77; Inst of Professional Civil Servants: negotiations offr 1977–81, asst sec 1981–84, asst gen sec 1984–88, dep gen sec 1988–91; gen sec Engrs and Mangrs Assoc 1991–; dir Aid Transport Ltd; memb Energy Advsy Panel DTI; tstee: Power Aid Logistics, Hosp for Neuro Disability; FRSA; *Recreations* sailing, hill walking; *Style—* Tony Cooper, Esq; ✉ Engineers and Managers Association, Flaxman House, Gogmore Lane, Chertsey, Surrey KT16 9JS

COOPER, Derek Macdonald; OBE (1997); s of Stephen George Cooper (d 1958), and late Jessie Margaret Macdonald; *b* 25 May 1925; *Educ* Raynes Park Co Sch, Portree HS, Wadham Coll Oxford (MA); *m* 17 Oct 1953, Janet Marian, da of Robert Feaster; 1 s (Nicholas b 1957), 1 da (Penelope Jane b 1954); *Career* Leading Seaman RNVR 1943–47; broadcaster, journalist and author; prodr Radio Malaya 1950 (ret as controller of progs 1960), prodr Roving Report ITN 1960–61; radio progs incl: Today, Ten O'Clock Newstime, PM, Town and Country, A La Carte, Home This Afternoon, Frankly Speaking, Two of a Kind, You and Yours, Northbeat, New Worlds, Asian Club, Speaking for Myself, Conversations with Cooper, Friday Call, It's Your Line, The Food Programme, Offshore Britons, Person to Person, Meridien Book Programme; TV progs incl: World in Action, Tomorrow's World, Breathing Space, A Taste of Britain, The Caterers, World About Us, I Am An Engineer, Men and Materials, Apart from Oil, Money Wise, One in a Hundred, The Living Body, From the Face of the Earth, Scotland's Larder, This Food Business, Distilling Whisky Galore; columnist: Saga magazine, Scotland on Sunday; Glenfiddich Trophy as wine and food writer 1973 and 1980, Broadcaster of the Year 1984, Special Award Glenfiddich Awards 1996; fndr memb and first chm Guild of Food Writers 1985–88 (pres 1988–95); *Books* The Bad Food Guide (1967), The Beverage Report (1970), The Gullibility Gap (1974), Hebridean Connection (1977, revised edn 1991), Skye (3 edn 1989, 4 edn 1995), Guide to the Whiskies of Scotland (1979), Road to the Isles (1979, Scottish Arts Cncl award 1980, 2 edn 1990), Enjoying Scotch (with Diane Pattullo, 1980), Wine with Food (1980, 2 edn 1986), The Whisky Roads of Scotland (1982), The Century Companion to Whiskies (1983), Skye Remembered (1983), The World of Cooking (1983), The Road to Mingulay (1985, 2 edn 1988), The Gunge File (1986), A Taste of Scotch (1989), The Little Book of Malt Whiskies (1992); *Style—* Derek Cooper, Esq, OBE; ✉ 4 St Helena Terrace, Richmond, Surrey TW9 1NR (☎ 0181 940 7051)

COOPER, Wing Cdr Donald Arthur; CBE (1990), AFC (1961); s of Albert Arthur Cooper (d 1965), and Elizabeth Barbara, *née* Edmonds (d 1995); *b* 27 Sept 1930; *Educ* Queen's Coll Br Guiana, RAF Coll Cranwell, Open Univ (BA); *m* 5 April 1958, (Ann) Belinda, da of Adm Sir Charles Woodhouse, KCB, and Lady Woodhouse; 3 s (Andrew b 1959, Duncan b 1961, Angus b 1964); *Career* pilot on day fighter and trg sqdns RAF 1952–56, Empire Test Pilots Sch 1957, pilot Experimental Flying Dept RAE Farnborough 1958–60, RAF Staff Coll 1961 (airline tport pilot's licence: helicopters 1961, aeroplanes 1972), Sqdn Cdr CFS Helicopter Wing 1962–64, HQ Flying Trg Cmd 1964–66, Def Ops Requirements Staff MOD 1966–70, ret 1970; joined Accidents Investigation Branch Bd of Trade 1970, chief inspr Air Accident Investigations Branch Dept of Transport 1986–90; FRAeS 1984; *Recreations* amateur dramatics, walking, dancing; *Style—* Wing Cdr Donald Cooper, CBE, AFC; ✉ 7 Lynch Road, Farnham, Surrey GU9 8BZ (☎ 01252 715 519)

COOPER, Eileen; *b* 1953; *Educ* Goldsmiths' Coll London, Royal Coll of Art; *Career* artist; lectr St Martin's Sch of Art; *Solo Exhibitions* Air Gallery 1979, House Gallery 1981, Blond Fine Art 1982, 1983 and 1985, Artspace Gallery Aberdeen 1985, Castlefield Gallery Manchester 1986, Artsite Gallery Bath 1987, Benjamin Rhodes Gallery 1988, 1989 (Works on Paper) and 1990; *Gp Exhibitions* incl: New Contemporaries 1974 and 1976, Royal Acad Summer Show 1977, 1982 and 1984, Whitechapel Open 1982, 1983 and 1987, The Image as Catalyst (Ashindean Museum Oxford) 1984, Ten Years at Air 1985, The Int Festival of Painting Cagnes France 1985, Ljubljiana (Int Biennial of Graphic Art Yugoslavia) 1985 and 1987, Proud and Prejudiced (Twining Gallery NY) 1985, The Flower Show (Stoke on Trent Museum, touring) 1986, John Moores (Walker Art Gallery Liverpool) 1986, The Self Portrait - A Modern View (Artsite Bath, touring) 1987, Royal Over-Seas League Annual 1987 and 1988, Painters at the Royal Coll of Art (150 Annual Exhibition) 1988, Ikon Gallery Birmingham (touring) 1988, Athena Art Awards (Barbican) 1988, Figuring Out The 80s (Laing Gallery Newcastle) 1988, The New British Painting (Contemporary Arts Centre Cincinnati, touring) 1988, Figure 2: A Private Mythology (Aberystwyth Arts Centre, touring) 1988, Freedom (launch of illustrated book for Amnesty Int, Flowers East) 1988, Survival Int Auction (Harewood

House Leeds) 1989, Picturing People (Br Cncl tour Kuala Lumpur, Hong Kong and Singapore) 1989, 3 Ways (Royal Coll of Art/Br Cncl tour E Europe) 1990, Woodlands Art Gallery 1991, The Outsider Br Figuaration Now (Palazzo Vecchio Florence) 1991, Friends and Contemporaries (John Jones Gallery London) 1991, City Artists (Tobacco Dock London) 1991, Look Here Upon this Picture - And On This (touring show) 1992, Myth, Dream & Fable (Angel Row Gallery Notts) 1992, The New Patrons (Christies London) 1992, Innocence and Experience (S Bank Centre and Manchester Cty Art Gallery) 1992, Print Centre Editions (Pomery Purdy Gallery London) 1992, 20th C Women's Art (New Hall Cambridge) 1992, Aspects of British Figurative Art 1980–92 Crane Gallery London 1992, Drawings (Benjamin Rhodes Gallery); *Public Collections* Open Univ, Imperial Coll London, British Cncl, Kunsthalle Nuremberg (Purchase prize), Arts Cncl of GB, Contemporary Arts Soc, Cleveland Gallery, V & A Museum, Whitworth Art Gallery Manchester, Towner Art Gallery Eastbourne; installations: Staircase Project ICA London 1982; *Style*— Ms Eileen Cooper; ✉ c/o Benjamin Rhodes Gallery, 4 New Burlington Place, London W1X 1SB (☎ 0171 434 1768/9, fax 0171 287 8841)

COOPER, Rt Hon Sir Frank; GCB (1979, KCB 1974, CB 1970), CMG (1961), PC (1983); s of late Valentine H Cooper, of Fairfield, Manchester; *b* 2 Dec 1922; *Educ* Manchester GS, Pembroke Coll Oxford (hon fell 1976); *m* 1948, Peggie, da of F J Claxton; 2 s, 1 da; *Career* pilot RAF 1941–46; joined Civil Serv 1948, dep under sec of state MOD 1968–70, dep sec CSD 1970–73, perm under sec of state NI Office 1973–76, perm under sec of state MOD 1976–82, ret 1982; dir: Babcock 1983–89, Morgan Crucible 1983–94, N M Rothschild and Sons 1983–96; chm High Integrity Systems 1986–95; memb Cncl King's Coll London 1983–89 (govr 1982, fell 1987), visitor Univ of Loughborough 1988–; chm: King's Coll Med and Dental Sch 1984–89, Cranbrook Sch 1984–93 (govr 1982), Liddell Hart Tstees 1986–, Inst of Contemporary Br History 1986–, Imperial Coll London 1988– (govr 1982, vice chm 1984, fell 1988); vice pres Army Records Soc 1989– (vice chm 1986–88), memb Advsy Cncl on Public Records 1989–92; pres Assoc of Lancastrians in London 1991; *Clubs* Athenaeum, Naval and Military, RAF; *Style*— The Rt Hon Sir Frank Cooper, GCB, CMG; ✉ Delafield, 34 Camden Park Rd, Chislehurst, Kent BR7 5HG

COOPER, George John; s of Maj Sir Charles Eric Cooper, 5 Bt (d 1984), and his 2 wife, Mary Elisabeth, *née* Graham-Clarke; hp of bro, Sir William Daniel Charles Cooper, 6 Bt, *qv*; *b* 28 June 1956; *Educ* Harrow; *Career* vice chm IDDA; *Recreations* hunting, eventing, gardening; *Style*— George Cooper, Esq; ✉ Hinton House, Ablington, Bibury, Cirencester, Glos (☎ 012857 40233, fax 012857 40282)

COOPER, Gen Sir George Leslie Conroy; GCB (1984, KCB 1979), MC (1953), DL (1990); s of Lt-Col G C Cooper (d 1978), of Sudbury, Suffolk, and Yvonne Victoria, *née* Hughes (d 1978); *b* 10 Aug 1925; *Educ* Downside, Trinity Coll Cambridge; *m* 1957, Cynthia Mary, da of Capt Trevor Hume, of Old Harlow, Essex; 1 s (Timothy b 1958), 1 da (Clare b 1961); *Career* cmmnd RE 1945, Bengal Sappers and Miners 1945–48, Korea 1952–53, Lt-Col RE 4 Div 1966–68; instr: Sandhurst, Staff Coll Camberley; Cmd 19 Airportable Inf Bde 1969–71, dir Army Staff Duties 1976–79, GOC SE Dist 1979–81 (SW Dist 1974–75), Gen 1981, Adjt-Gen MOD 1981–84; Col Cmdt: RE 1980–93, RPC 1981–85; Col The Queen's Gurkha Engrs 1981–91; ADC Gen to HM The Queen 1982–84; Chief Royal Engr 1987–93; memb Bd of Mgmnt GEC UK, dir Mgmnt Devpt GEC 1985–86; chm: HGP Managing Agency Ltd 1990–91, Infantile Hypercalcaemia Fndn 1981–95, Knightstone Syndicate Management Ltd 1991–93, Quay Run-Off Services Ltd 1993, Princess Alexandra Hosp NHS Trust 1994–96; memb Cncl: National Army Museum 1981–95, Action Res 1983–95; *Recreations* shooting, gardening; *Clubs* Army and Navy, Essex, MCC; *Style*— Sir George Cooper, GCB, MC, DL; ✉ c/o Barclays Bank plc, 3–5 King Street, Reading, Berks RG1 2HD

COOPER, Granville John; s of Joseph Cooper, of Tibshelf, Derbys, and Edna May, *née* Slack (d 1989); *b* 1 May 1940; *Educ* Tupton Hall GS, Univ of N London (BSc); *Career* microwave engr GEC Applied Electronics Laboratories 1963–67, dep engrg mangr NATO Phase II Satellite Terminal Project 1968–69, project mangr Scottish Naval Satellite Communications (SATCOM) project 1971–73 (engrg mangr 1970–71), divnl mangr SATCOM Marconi Space and Defence Systems Ltd 1973–76, tech dir McMichael Ltd 1977–85 (joined 1976), md Vistek Electronics Ltd 1986–; memb: RTS, Soc of Motion Picture and Television Engrs; CPhys, FIEE, MIEEE, MInstP, FEng 1994; *Recreations* work, science, music, opera; *Style*— Granville Cooper, Esq, FEng; ✉ Vistek Electronics Ltd, Unit C, Wessex Road, Bourne End, Bucks SL8 5DT (☎ 01628 531221, fax 01628 530980)

COOPER, Dr Griselda Mary; da of Dr Charles James Constantine Davey, of Box, Corsham, Wilts, and Dr Gwyneth June Davey, *née* Pearson; *b* 8 April 1949; *Educ* Bath HS, Univ of Birmingham (MB ChB); *m* 31 Aug 1973, Dr Brian Thomas Cooper, s of Dr Andrew Matthew Cooper (d 1979); 1 da (Charlotte b 1987); *Career* sr lectr in anaesthesia Univ of Bristol 1981–87, conslt anaesthetist Dunedin Public Hosp NZ 1985–86, sr lectr in anaesthesia Univ of Birmingham 1988–; Royal Coll of Anaesthetists: fell, examiner, regnl advsr (W Midlands); *Recreations* walking, skiing, embroidery; *Style*— Dr Griselda Cooper; ✉ 36 Anstruther Road, Edgbaston, Birmingham B15 3NW (☎ 0121 456 2174), Birmingham Women's Hospital, QE Medical Centre, Edgbaston, Birmingham B15 2TG (☎ 0121 472 1377)

COOPER, (Samuel) James; *b* 15 Nov 1932; *Educ* Buckhurst Hill Sch, Imperial Coll London (BSc(Eng)); *m* 1960, Sheila A, *née* Schofield; 3 c; *Career* GD Branch RAF; Shell Chemical Co, Shellstar Ltd, mktg dir UKF Fertilizers Ltd (ret 1986); chm Gas Consumers' Cncl 1988–95; *Clubs* RAF; *Style*— James Cooper, Esq

COOPER, Hon Jason Charles Duff Bede; s and h of 2 Viscount Norwich; *b* 27 Oct 1959; *Educ* Eton, New Coll Oxford (BA), Oxford Brookes Univ (BA, Dip Arch); *Career* architect, designer, journalist; RIBA; *Recreations* piano, travel, skiing; *Style*— Jason Cooper; ✉ 14 Alexander Street, London W2 5NT

COOPER, Jilly; da of Brig W B Sallitt, OBE (d 1982), and Mary Elaine, *née* Whincup; *b* 21 Feb 1937; *Educ* Godolphin Sch Salisbury; *m* 7 Oct 1961, Leo Cooper, s of Leonard Cooper, of Norfolk; 1 s (Matthew Felix b 5 Sept 1968), 1 da (Emily Maud Lavinia b 13 June 1971); *Career* writer; former cub reporter Middlesex Independent Brentford 1955–57, followed by several jobs incl info offr, puppy fat model and switch board wrecker; newspaper columnist: Sunday Times 1969–82, Mail on Sunday 1982–87; memb Cncl Nat Canine Def League; *Books* author of 36 books incl: Class (1979), The Common Years (1984), Riders (1985), Rivals (1988), Polo (1991), The Man Who Made Husbands Jealous (1993), Araminta's Wedding (1993), Appassionata (1996); *Recreations* wild flowers, reading, mongrels, merry making and music; *Style*— Mrs Jilly Cooper; ✉ c/o Desmond Elliott, 38 Bury Street, St James's, London SW1 (☎ 0171 930 0097)

COOPER, Joan Davies; CB (1972); da of Valentine Holland Cooper (d 1941), of Manchester, and Louisa Wynnefred Cooper (d 1977); *b* 12 Aug 1914; *Educ* Fairfield HS nr Manchester, Univ of Manchester (BA), Nat Inst for Social Work; *Career* Teaching and Probation Serv 1937–41, asst dir of educn Derbyshire 1941–48, children's offr E Sussex 1948–65, chief inspr Children's Dept Home Office 1965–71, dir social work serv Dept of Health and Social Security 1971–76; vice pres Nat Children's Bureau 1963–, memb Social Sci Res Cncl 1972–76; chm: Nat Assoc for Care and Resettlement of Offender Ctee on Juvenile Crime 1977–85, Central Cncl for Educn and Trg of Social Workers 1984–87, Child Abuse Review Ctee E Sussex 1984–87, Care for the Carers E Sussex 1986–93 (pres 1993–), Int Expert Ctee on Access To Records 1987; pres: Ind Representation for Children in Need 1984–93, Gundreda Housing Assoc Lewes Sussex 1984–88; vice chm Lewes Tertiary Coll 1989–93; dir Retirement Security Ltd 1995–; hon visiting fell Univ of Sussex 1978–; Freedom City of Narvik (Norway) 1963; FRAnthropI 1972; *Books* Patterns of Family Placement (1978), Social Groupwork with Elderly People In Hospital (1980), The Creation of the British Personal Social Services (1983); *Recreations* walking and travel; *Clubs* University Women's; *Style*— Miss Joan Cooper, CB; ✉ 44 Greyfriars Court, Court Road, Lewes, Sussex BN7 2RF (☎ 01273 472604)

COOPER, John; s of Kenneth Cooper, of Manchester, and Irene, *née* Wright; *b* 29 April 1955; *Educ* Manchester GS, Royal Coll of Music (ARCM), King's Coll Cambridge (MA); *m* 5 Oct 1983, Jane Mary, da of late Alan Arthur Kingshotte, of Strawberry Hill, Middx; 1 da (Charlotte b 28 Aug 1984), 1 s (Benedict b 26 April 1988); *Career* admitted slr 1979, avocat au barreau de Paris 1992; ptnr Lovell White & King 1985–88 (articled clerk 1977), ptnr Lovell White Durrant 1988–; Freeman Worshipful Co of Slrs 1981; memb Law Soc; *Recreations* golf, horse racing, wine; *Style*— John Cooper, Esq; ✉ Lovell White Durrant, 65 Holborn Viaduct, London EC1A 2DY (☎ 0171 236 0066, fax 0171 236 0084); 37 Ave Pierre 1er de Serbie, 75008 Paris (☎ 00 33 1 49 52 04 26, fax 00 33 1 47 23 96 12)

COOPER, John Edwyn; s of Reginald Vincent Cooper, MBE, and Mildred Anne, *née* Clayton; *b* 18 Sept 1949; *Educ* Kingsbury Co GS, Univ of Hull (BSc); *m* 1, 1972 (m dis 1988), Patricia Anne, da of Wing Cdr Gordon F Turner, of Watford, Herts; m 2, 19 May 1988, Penelope Freda, da of Douglas Keith Walters (d 1968); 1 s (James Alexander b 10 March 1988); *Career* asst master in mathematics Hymers Coll Hull 1971–72, UK trg mangr Wang UK 1981–86, dir of educn NCR 1986–88, mgmnt info servs dir Wang UK 1988–92, dir of trg Bull Information Systems 1992–96, dir Profile International Consultancies 1995–; chm Exchange - West London HRD Network, memb Bd of Govrs Richmond-upon-Thames Coll; Freeman City of London 1982, memb Worshipful Co of Plumbers 1982; *Recreations* golf, food and wine; *Style*— John Cooper, Esq; ✉ Profile International Consultancies (☎ 01489 795595)

COOPER, John Gordon; s of John Gordon Cooper, of Wolverhampton, and Mary, *née* Hallam (d 1992); *b* 15 Sept 1958; *Educ* Regis Comp Sch, Univ of Newcastle (LLB, Butterworth Prize, badminton blue), Cncl of Legal Educn; *Career* writer and barrister (named in Bar Nat Directory as one of the most highly regarded barristers in London (top 40)); called to the Bar Middle Temple 1983, called to the Aust Bar NSW 1989, lawyer Clifford Chance 1989; legal advsr to: Shadow Treasy 1993–, Lab Pty 1994–; sec Lab Media Ctee, sec Lab Criminal Justice Ctee; writer: The Cure (Royal Court Theatre), Burning Point (Tricycle Theatre Kilburn), The Cured (Finborough Arms Theatre), The Law Lord (Screen Two film, BBC), The Advocates (3 part drama, Scottish TV), The Bill (contrib, Thames), Cutting Loose (LWT); contrib: Legal Eagles (BBC Radio WM), Presenter (BBC Radio), The Talking Show (C4), Street Legal (C4), Talkback (Sky TV); res diarist The Lawyer 1992–, various TV appearances as legal expert; contested (Lab): Surrey NW 1987, Amber Valley 1992; cnclr Watford 1990–94; chm Nat Exec League Against Cruel Sports 1995– (memb 1992–); memb: Bar Cncl (co-opted) 1981–84, Civic Theatre Tst Palace Theatre Watford 1991; fndr creative writing course Poly of Central London 1984; *Publications* Planning and Environmental Law Bulletin (1991); *Recreations* photography, swimming, football; *Clubs* Chelsea Arts, Mecklenburgh Health, Wolverhampton Wanderers FC; *Style*— John Cooper, Esq; ✉ Parsonage Farm, Dairy Way, Abbotts Langley, Herts WD5 0GJ (☎ 01973 908288)

COOPER, John Kaye; s of Ernest James Cooper, of Swillington, W Yorks, and Doreen Annie, *née* Kaye (d 1990); *b* 20 May 1947; *Educ* Rothwell GS, RSAMD; *m* 1 (m dis); 1 da (Gemma Lys b 1 Oct 1970); m 2, 1979, Charlotte Nerys Anne, da of Rev Canon Stephen Jackson; 2 s (Adam b 27 Oct 1980, Simon b 15 June 1982); *Career* cameraman Scottish Television 1967, floor mangr Thames Television 1968–72, prodn mangr Yorkshire Television 1972–76, drama prodr Tyne Tees Television 1976–77, prodr/dir Entertainment Dept London Weekend Television 1977–83, prodr/dir Limehouse Television 1983–84, controller of entertainment TVS 1984–87, independent prodr and md John Kaye Cooper Productions 1988–90, controller of entertainment London Weekend Television 1990–95, md The Talent Group 1995–; prodr numerous progs and series incl: Stanley Baxter Specials 1979–81 and Stanley Baxter series 1982 (BAFTA Best Light Entertainment Prog 1982), Russ Abbot's Madhouse 1981–84, Surgical Spirit (dir) 1988–89, Save the Children with Michael Crawford 1988, That's Showbusiness 1990, BAFTA Craft Awards 1990, Cluedo 1990, Royal Variety Performance 1991, 1993 and 1995, Time After Time 1994–95; exec prodr 1990–95: Gladiators, Barrymore, The Brian Conley Show, Hale and Pace, Br Comedy Awards; memb: RTS, BAFTA; *Recreations* golf, supporting Leeds United; *Style*— John Kaye Cooper, Esq; ✉ Talent Television Ltd, 235 Regent Street, London W1R 8AX (☎ 0171 434 1677, fax 0171 434 1577)

COOPER, Rear Adm John Spencer; OBE (1974); s of Harold Spencer Cooper, of Hong Kong (d 1972), and Barbara, *née* Highet (d 1974); *b* 5 April 1933; *Educ* St Edward's Sch Oxford, Clare Coll Cambridge (MA); *m* 13 Aug 1966, Jacqueline Street, *née* Taylor; 2 da (Philippa b 1967, Lucy b 1970); *Career* dir Trials (Polaris) 1976–78, sr UK Polaris rep Washington 1978–80, dir gen strategic weapon systems 1981–85, chief strategic systems exec 1985–88, ops mangr Ferranti Naval Systems 1988–93; *Recreations* sailing; *Style*— Rear Adm J S Cooper, OBE

COOPER, Joseph Elliott Needham; OBE (1982); s of Wilfred Needham Cooper (d 1949), of Westbury-on-Trym, and Elsie Goodacre, *née* Elliott (d 1963); *b* 7 Oct 1912; *Educ* Clifton, Keble Coll Oxford (MA); *m* 1, 15 Nov 1947, (Marjorie) Jean (d 1973), da of Gp Capt Sir Louis Greig, KBE, CVO, DL (d 1953), of Thatched House Lodge, Richmond Park; m 2, 4 July 1975, Carol Vivien Nelson (d 1996), da of Charles John Nelson Borg (d 1986), of Brighton; *Career* WWII: 66 Searchlight Regt RA, cmmnd 2 Lt 1941, Capt 1943, WO Sch Aircraft Recognition 1944, served GHQ AA Troops (21 Army Gp Rear) Normandy 1944, demobbed 1946; composer and arranger GPO Film Unit 1936–37, trained as concert pianist under Egon Petri, arrangement of Vaughan Williams Piano Concerto for 2 pianos (with co 1946, debut Wigmore Hall 1947, concerto debut Philharmonia Orch 1950, debut BBC Promenade Concerts Royal Albert Hall 1953); various piano recordings incl The World of Joseph Cooper; tours: India 1953, extensively Br Isles and continent; chm Face the Music BBC TV 1966–84, pres Dorking Halls Concertgoers Soc 1985–90; vice pres: 2 Care (formerly SOS Soc Old People's Homes) 1970–, Music Cncl English Speaking Union 1985–90; former pres Surrey Philharmonic Soc; memb: Music Panel Arts Cncl (chm Piano Sub Ctee) 1966–71, Ctee for an Organ St John's Smith Square 1986–92, Cncl Musicians Benevolent Fund 1987–90; tstee Countess of Munster Musical Tst 1975–80, govr Clifton Coll, pres Old Cliftonian Soc 1981–83, patron St George's Music Tst Bristol 1982–; solved the riddle of Elgar's Enigma Variations 1991; Freeman City of London, Liveryman Worshipful Co of Musicians 1963; ARCM; *Books* Hidden Melodies (1975), More Hidden Melodies (1976), Still More Hidden Melodies (1978), Facing the Music (autobiography, 1979); *Recreations* countryside, animals, church architecture; *Clubs* Garrick; *Style*— Joseph Cooper, Esq, OBE; ✉ Octagon Lodge, Ranmore, nr Dorking, Surrey RH5 6SX (☎ 01483 282658)

COOPER, Michael John; *b* 24 July 1937; *Educ* King's Sch Rochester, Univ of Exeter (BSc), Oberlin Coll Ohio, Int Mgmnt Devpt Inst Lausanne; *m*; 3 c; *Career* Nat Serv RAF 1955–57; Shell International Petroleum 1962–69: dist mangr Kumasi Ghana 1962–65, area desk Euro orgn Netherlands 1965–67, branch mangr Libya 1967–69; Panocean-Anco Ltd London 1970–83: project mangr 1970–72, mktg mangr 1972–74, mktg dir 1974–79, md 1979–83; chief exec Shipping & Energy Div Burmah Castrol PLC (previously Burmah Oil) 1983–91 (Main Bd dir 1986–91); DG British Diabetic Association 1992–; non-exec dir East Sussex Health Authy, visiting prof Univ of

Westminster, govr High Hurstwood Primary Sch East Sussex; recent previous appts incl: dir Energy Transportation Corporation Inc NY, dir Pakistan Petroleum Ltd Karachi, dir Premier Consolidated Oilfields PLC, dir UK Freight, Demurrage and Def Assoc, vice pres Inst of Petroleum, vice chm Indonesia Assoc; FRGS, MRIIA; *Recreations* the church, music, choir, cricket; *Clubs* Oriental; *Style*— Michael Cooper, Esq; ✉ Old Hall Cottage, High Hurstwood, Uckfield, East Sussex TN22 4AD (☎ 01825 733268); 130 Belgrave Road, London SW1V 2BL (☎ 0171 834 3891); Director-General, British Diabetic Association, 10 Queen Anne Street, London W1M 0BD (☎ 0171 323 1531, fax 0171 637 3644)

COOPER, Natasha; *see:* Wright, (Idonea) Daphne

COOPER, Neil Hunter; s of Keith Hunter Cooper (d 1977), and Margaret Anne, *née* Golden; *b* 30 June 1947; *m* Marion Louise, *née* Woodward; 1 s (Ewan Charles Hunter), 1 da (Louise Elizabeth Anne); *Career* Government Insolvency Service; Robson Rhodes: head Corp Recovery London 1986, ptnr i/c Nat Corp Recovery Dept 1990–; vice pres Assoc Europeenne de Practiciens des Procedures Collectives, memb Editorial Bd Insolvency Intelligence, vice pres INSOL (chm Steering Ctee Cross-Frontier), memb Int Advsy Bd Fed Agency on Insolvency in Russia; regular speaker at professional and commercial confs on insolvency law and practice; FCCA, FIPA, FSPI; *Books* Tolley's European Insolvency Guide, Recognition and Enforcement of Cross-Border Insolvency; *Recreations* classical music, opera, fly fishing, mountaineering, bird watching, photography; *Style*— Neil Cooper, Esq; ✉ Robson Rhodes, 186 City Road, London EC1V 2NU (☎ 0171 251 1644, fax 0171 253 4629)

COOPER, Dr Norman; s of Leonard John Cooper (d 1970), of Bridgend, S Wales, and Doris Eva, *née* Woof (d 1955); *b* 25 May 1930; *Educ* Bridgend GS, PhD, MBA, CDipAF; *m* Nancy; 1 s (David), 1 da (Jane); *Career* served Photographic Branch RAF, subsequently with May & Baker (photographic chemistry) and Ilford Ltd (quality control), fndr own mgmnt consultancy Norman Cooper Associates 1968 (currently sr ptnr), jt fndr The Skene Group 1974 (currently md); conslt and lectr worldwide; assessor in photographic sci and technol: BIPP, Jt Servs Sch of Photography; former pres Rotary Club of Aberdeen St Fittick and dist govr NE Scotland 1992–93; chm Advsy Ctee and tstee Aberdeen Int Youth Festival (organiser annual Skene Award), dir and vice chm Nat Youth Orch of Scotland, chm Enterprise Scotland; burgess Guild City of Aberdeen; Hon FBIPP 1987 (pres 1968, fell 1969); FFA, FIMgt; *Recreations* curling (sometime Scottish int player), watching rugby and cricket; *Clubs* Royal Northern and Univ; *Style*— Dr Norman Cooper; ✉ 16 Rubislaw Den South, Aberdeen AB15 4BB (☎ 01224 315154); The Skene Group, Rubislaw Den House, 23 Rubislaw Den North, Aberdeen AB12 4AL (☎ 01224 326221, fax 01224 310037)

COOPER, Patrick Ernest; s of Stuart Ranson Cooper (d 1966), and Lila Flemmich Cooper (d 1954); *b* 27 March 1935; *Educ* Wellesley House Broadstairs, Rugby; *m* 1963, Katrina Farnham, da of Frederick Windisch (d 1979), of Connecticut, USA; 2 da (Alexandra b 1967, Lila b 1970); *Career* Coldstream Guards 1953–55, cmmnd W Yorkshire Regt, served Malaysia and NI, TA 1955–61, ret Capt; accountant Cooper Bros, audit mangr Lybrand Ross Bros and Montgomery 1961–62, dir Clive Discount and Co Ltd 1967, chief exec Clive Holdings Group 1971–72 (chm 1972), dir of fin servs Sime Darby Holdings Ltd 1973, md Steel Bros and Co Ltd 1977 (dep chief exec and dep chm 1978), dep chm and chief exec Spinneys 1948 Ltd Jan 1980 (chm May 1980), chief exec Steel Bros Holdings plc 1984; dir: Steel Bros Holdings plc 1977–87, Steel Bros and Co Ltd 1977–87, Spinneys 1948 Ltd 1977–87, Goode Durrant plc 1988–92; non-exec dir: MK Electric Group 1983–88, Pubmaster Ltd 1993–; non-exec chm: De Morgan Group plc 1991–94, Alexon Group plc 1993–; tstee Southover Manor Educnl Tst Ltd; Swan Warden Worshipful Co of Vintners; *Recreations* golf, tennis, shooting, backgammon; *Clubs* Boodle's, Royal Ashdown Forest Golf, Royal St George's Golf; *Style*— Patrick Cooper, Esq; ✉ Glebe House, Fletching, Sussex TN22 3SP (☎ 01825 722104)

COOPER, Peter James; QC (1993); s of William James Cooper (d 1968), of Banbury, and Audrey Cooper; *b* 7 Oct 1947; *Educ* Peter Symonds Sch Winchester, Univ of Southampton (LLB); *m* 1978, Jenifer Ann, *née* Redway; 2 s (William James b 17 May 1979, Benjamin Peter b 23 Oct 1980); *Career* called to the Bar Gray's Inn 1974, memb chambers at 2 Harcourt Bldgs 1975–, recorder of the Crown Court 1993– (asst recorder 1989–93); *Recreations* golf, music; *Clubs* Midfearn Open Golf Soc; *Style*— Peter Cooper, Esq, QC; ✉ 2 Harcourt Buildings, 1 Floor Temple, London EC4 (☎ 0171 353 2112, fax 0171 353 8339)

COOPER, Philip Anthony Robert; s of Stanley Ernest Cooper, and Amy May, *née* Coleman; *b* 13 Jan 1950; *Educ* Felsted, Univ of Leeds (BSc), Univ of Cambridge (MA); *m* 17 July 1976, (Elizabeth) Jane, da of Dr Harold Leslie Keer Whitehouse; 1 s (Oliver Edward Keer b 1986), 2 da (Harriet Amy Jane b 1980, Emily Sarah Rose b 1982); *Career* lectr Sch of Architecture Univ of Cambridge 1974–78, engr Harris and Sutherland (London and Cambridge) 1978–, assoc and currently dir Harris and Sutherland International Ltd Consultant Civil and Structural Engineers, prof of structural design (first in UK) Univ of Leeds 1986–91; lectr Architectural Assoc 1993–; memb Univ of Cambridge Graduate Centre; MIStructE (memb Cncl); *Recreations* tennis, music, windsurfing; *Style*— Philip Cooper, Esq; ✉ 2 Pound Hill, Cambridge, Cambridgeshire CB3 0AE (☎ 01223 312055); Harris & Sutherland, 15 Sturton St, Cambridge CB1 2SN (☎ 01223 365731, fax 01223 361332)

COOPER, Philip John; CB (1989); s of Charles Cooper (d 1980), and Mildred Annie, *née* Marlow (d 1981); *b* 15 Sept 1929; *Educ* Deacons Sch Peterborough, Univ of Leicester (BSc); *m* 1, 1 Aug 1953, Dorothy Joan Chapman (d 1982), da of James Chapman (d 1970), of Rhos on Sea, N Wales; 2 da (Vivien Anne b 1954, Valerie Joan b 1957); m 2, 8 Aug 1986, Pamela Mary Coad (d 1988), da of Henry John Pysden (d 1979), of Durban, South Africa; m 3, 17 April 1993, Antoinette Erasmus, da of Carel Johannes Grové (d 1974), of Cape Town, South Africa; *Career* Nat Serv 2 Lt Royal Signals 1953–55; govt chemist 1952, Dept of Sci and Industl Res 1956–67, princ Miny of Technol 1967, PPS to Min for Industl Devpt 1972–73, under sec DOI and DTI 1979–89 (asst sec 1973–79), dir Warren Spring Lab DTI 1984–85; comptroller-gen The Patent Office DTI 1986–89; author of various papers on analytical and chemical matters; *Style*— Philip Cooper, Esq, CB; ✉ 12 The Lye, Tadworth, Surrey KT20 5RS

COOPER, Richard Arthur; *see:* Austin-Cooper, Richard Arthur Austin

COOPER, Richard Devereux Burcombe; s of late Alexander Burcombe Cooper, of Downleaze, Bristol, and Alma Gwendoline, *née* Harris; *b* 10 April 1943; *Educ* Clifton, The Taft Sch Watertown Connecticut USA, Trinity Coll Cambridge (MA); *m* 19 July 1975, Janet, da of Lt-Col Archibald Michael Lyle, DL, of Dunkeld, Perthshire; 3 da (Daisy b 17 Sept 1983, Hester b 21 Dec 1985, Tilly b 18 July 1988); *Career* ptnr Slaughter and May 1975– (slr 1968–); Eng int real tennis player: versus France 1967 and 1984, versus Australia 1969 and 1984; Cambridge blue: squash 1964, real tennis 1965; vice pres PHAB, former chm Tennis & Rackets Assoc Devpt and Young Professionals Prog; Freeman Worshipful Co of Goldsmiths 1986–; memb: Law Soc 1968, Hong Kong Law Soc 1986; *Recreations* music, tennis, shooting, travel, Chinese paintings, languages; *Clubs* Boodle's, Pratts, MCC, Queen's, Hawks', Jesters', Hong Kong, China; *Style*— Richard Cooper, Esq; ✉ 29 Lansdowne Gardens, London SW8 2EQ; Slaughter & May, 35 Basinghall Street, London EC2V 5DB (☎ 0171 600 1200, fax 0171 726 0038)

COOPER, Dr Richard Michael; s of late Harry Cecil Cohen, of London, and Sadie, *née* Speier; *b* 25 Nov 1940; *Educ* Belmont, Mill Hill Sch, Charing Cross Hosp (Gynaecology prize, Forensic Med prize); *m* Dawne Cooper, JP, da of late Alfred Matlow, and Phoebe, *née* Levy; 1 s (Adam b 31 July 1968), 2 da (Louise b 8 May 1972, Gabrielle b 22 Nov 1972); *Career* house appts at Charing Cross Hosp and Mount Vernon Hosp; princ in gen practice: 74 Brooksby's Walk London 1966–70, 71 Amhurst Park London 1970–76; in private practice 17 Harley St 1966–; med conslt: Bank of East Asia, Gambia High Cmmn, WPP Advertising, BDO Stoy Hayward; med examiner numerous insurance cos, conslt med offr Vardon plc and Pinnacle Insurance Cos; memb Cncl: Assurance Med Soc, Ind Doctors' Forum; FRSM 1969; fell: Assurance Med Soc, Hunterian Soc; *Recreations* family, broadcasting, fund raising and other communal activities, writing med articles; *Clubs* Old Millhillians, Knightsbridge Speakers'; *Style*— Dr Richard M Cooper; ✉ Wildbrook, 34 Uxbridge Rd, Stanmore, Middx HA7 3LQ (☎ 0181 954 8445/9291); 17 Harley St, London W1N 1DA (☎ 0171 580 3324, 0171 636 3126, fax 0171 436 0661)

COOPER, Sir Richard Powell; 5 Bt (UK 1905), of Shenstone Court, Shenstone, Co Stafford; s of Sir Francis (Frank) Ashmole Cooper, 4 Bt (d 1987), and Dorothy Frances Hendrika, *née* Deen; *b* 13 April 1934; *Educ* Marlborough; *m* 2 Oct 1957, Angela Marjorie, er da of late Eric Wilson, of Norton-on-Tees, Co Durham; 1 s (Richard Adrian b 1960), 2 da (Jane Alice b 1958, Belinda Gay b 1963); *Heir* s, Richard Adrian Cooper b 21 Aug 1960; *Career* farmer, economist, fund manager; *Recreations* foxhunting; *Clubs* Carlton, Buck's; *Style*— Sir Richard Cooper, Bt; ✉ Lower Farm, Chedington, Beaminster, Dorset DT8 3HY

COOPER, Robert; s of Alfred Cooper, of The Manor, Ogbourne Maisey, Marlborough, Wilts, and Marguerite Mary, *née* Bailey; *b* 18 Feb 1932; *Educ* Radley; *m* 1957 (m dis); 2 s (Alexander b 1960, Charles b 1961), 1 da (Carina b 1961); *Career* TA Capt RWY; pres: European Metal Recycling Ltd, Br Metals Fedn 1984 and 1985; Queen's Award for Export 1982 and 1986; memb Worshipful Co of Butchers; *Recreations* country pursuits (chm Vale of the White Horse Hunt); *Clubs* Cavalry and Guards'; *Style*— Robert Cooper, Esq; ✉ Ablington Manor, Bibury, Cirencester, Gloucestershire GL7 5NY (☎ 01285 740363); European Metal Recycling Ltd, Bridge House, Gipsy Lane, Swindon, Wiltshire SN2 6DZ (☎ 01793 532111, fax 01793 614214)

COOPER, Robert Francis; MVO (1975); s of Norman Cooper (d 1966), and Frances Cooper; *b* 28 Aug 1947; *Educ* Delamere Sch Nairobi, Worcester Coll Oxford (BA), Univ of Pennsylvania (MA); *Career* HM Dip Serv 1970, FCO 1970–71, Language Study 1971–73, Br Embassy Tokyo 1973–77, FCO 1979–82, seconded to Bank of England 1982–84, UK rep to EC Brussels 1984–87, head Far Eastern Dept FCO 1987–89, head of Policy Planning Staff 1989–92, currently minister British Embassy Bonn (cnsllr 1993–95); Order of the Sacred Treasure (4 Class, Japan) 1973; *Recreations* bicycles, bridge and the Bard; *Style*— Robert Cooper, Esq, MVO; ✉ c/o Foreign & Commonwealth Office, King Charles Street, London SW1A 2AH (☎ 0171 270 2911, fax 0171 270 3510)

COOPER, Robert George; CBE (1987); s of William Hugh Cooper, of Castlefinn, Co Donegal (d 1975), and Annie Cooper (d 1992); *b* 24 June 1936; *Educ* Foyle Coll Londonderry, Queen's Univ Belfast (LLB); *m* 2 Nov 1974, Patricia Frances, da of Gerald Nichol, of Belfast; 1 s (William Gerald b 1975), 1 da (Anne Cecilia b 1977); *Career* industl rels offr ICT 1958–64, sec NI Engrg Employers' Assoc 1964–72, jt political chm Alliance Pty of NI 1970–73 (fndr memb 1970, gen sec 1972–74), elected W Belfast memb NI Assembly 1973–75 (participant in Darlington and Sunningdale Constitutional Confs), min of Manpower NI Powersharing Govt 1974, elected W Belfast memb NI Constitutional Convention 1975–76; chm and chief exec Fair Employment Agency 1976–89, chm Fair Employment Cmmn 1990–; memb: Standing Advsy Cmmn on Human Rights 1976–, Equal Opportunities Cmmn for NI 1976–83; *Style*— Robert Cooper, Esq, CBE; ✉ Lynwood, 104 Bangor Road, Holywood, Co Down, N Ireland (☎ 01232 422071); Fair Employment Commission, Andras House, 60 Great Victoria Street, Belfast BT2 7BB (☎ 01232 240020, fax 01232 331544)

COOPER, Dr Robin Hayes; s of Dennis Joffre Cooper, and Marjorie, *née* Wilding; *b* 23 Dec 1947; *Educ* Corpus Christi Coll Cambridge (MA), Univ of Massachusetts (PhD); *m* 14 June 1985, Elisabet Britt, da of Gunnar Engdahl; 2 da (Anna Julia b 12 May 1986, Maria Emily b 19 March 1991); *Career* lectr in English language Univ of Freiburg 1969–71; Univ of Massachusetts: teaching asst in linguistics and TEFL 1971–73, res asst in natural language semantics 1973–75; asst prof Dept of Linguistics: Univ of Texas 1975–76, Univ of Massachusetts 1976–77; assoc prof Dept of Linguistics Univ of Wisconsin 1981–87 (asst prof 1977–81); docent Dept of Linguistics and Phonetics Lund Univ 1984–87; Univ of Edinburgh: reader Dept of Artificial Intelligence and Centre for Cognitive Science 1989–92 (lectr 1986–89), reader Centre for Cognitive Science 1992–95, prof of computational linguisitcs Gothenburgh Univ 1995–; princ investigator Human Communication Res Centre 1989–; Stanford Univ: Mellon fell in linguistics and philosophy 1980–81, fell Center for Advanced Study in the Behavioural Sciences 1981–82; Guggenheim fell 1986–87; FBA 1993; *Books* Quantification and Syntactic Theory (1983); *Recreations* childcare, music; *Style*— Prof Robin Cooper, FBA; ✉ Bigatan 1, S-431 39 Mölndal, Sweden (☎ 00 46 82 94 38); Department of Linguistics, Gothenburgh University, Renströmsgatan 6, S-41298, Göteborg, Sweden (☎ 00 46 31 773 2536, fax 00 46 31 773 4853, e-mail cooper@ling.gu.se, internet http://www.ling.gu.se/- cooper)

COOPER, (Hulbert) Rodney; s of Hulbert Francis Cooper (d 1959), of Bromley, Kent, and Dorothy Amy Burtt (d 1966); *b* 11 April 1933; *Educ* Bromley GS, Univ of London (BSc), Ravensbourne Coll of Art & Design, Central Sch of Art, Royal Naval Coll Greenwich; *m* 7 Oct 1961, (Mary) Anne, da of Aubrey George Eames (d 1962), of Bromley, Kent; 1 s (Matthew b 1963), 1 da (Nancy b 1967); *Career* Lt RN 1957–60, served HMS Ocean, port educn offr Chatham; sci advsr Br Pavilion Brussels World Fair 1956, res chemist A Wander Ltd 1960–63, designer Sir Basil Spence and Ptnrs 1963–70; BDP (Building Design Partnership) 1970–: assoc 1973–80, ptnr 1980–84, sr ptnr 1984–, chm of the interior, graphic and product design professions; external examiner: Univ of Wales Architectural Sch, Middx Univ; Govr Ravensbourne Coll of Design; FCSD 1975 (memb Cncl 1990); *Books* The Trade Report (1988), Specification (3 edn, 1989), contrib to architectural and design jls; *Recreations* cine photography, playing tenor saxophone, tennis, driving fast cars, making people laugh; *Style*— Rodney Cooper, Esq; ✉ Building Design Partnership, PO Box 4WD, 16 Gresse St, London W1A 4WD (☎ 0171 631 4733, fax 0171 631 0393, telex 25322)

COOPER, Ronald Edward (Ron); s of Walter Henry Cooper (d 1992), and Charlotte Mary Cooper; *b* 14 April 1943; *Educ* Westminster City GS, City Univ (BSc(MechEng)), MIT (Sr Exec Prog); *m* 7 Aug 1965, Valerie Jean; 3 da (Natasha Anne b 18 Nov 1968, Mandy Jane b 3 Aug 1970, Tamsin Joanne b 9 March 1972); *Career* design and devpt engrg apprentice Hilger & Watts Ltd 1959–67, systems analyst Rank Precision Industries 1967–69, project conslt Hoskyns Computer Consultancy 1969–71; Lucas Group: mangr systems analysis Lucas CAV 1971–73, supplies mangr Inline Pumps 1973–75, strategic planning mangr Lucas CAV 1975–78, product gen mangr Inline Pump Business Lucas CAV 1981–84 (factory mangr 1978–81), dir and gen mangr Fuel Injection Equipment UK Business 1984–87, dir and gen mangr Commercial Diesel Business 1987–89, dir and gen mangr Asian ops Lucas Car Diesel Systems 1989–91, best practice prog dir Lucas Automotive 1991–93; chief exec Royal Berks and Battle Hosps NHS Trust 1993–; *Recreations* golf, drawing and painting, sub-aqua, sailing, skiing, photography; *Style*— Ron Cooper, Esq; ✉ Royal Berkshire and Battle Hospitals NHS Trust, Royal Berkshire Hospital, London Road, Reading, Berks RG1 5AN (☎ 0118 987 7230, fax 0118 987 8042)

COOPER, Dr Rosemary Anne; da of Dr William Francis Cooper (d 1950), and Eileen Beryl, *née* Hall (d 1976); *b* 6 April 1925; *Educ* Westonbirt Sch, Cheltenham Coll, Girton Coll Cambridge, KCH Med Sch (MA, MB BChir, FRCP); *m* 14 Jan 1956, Walter van't Hoff, s of Robert van't Hoff (d 1979); 3 s (William b 1958, Hugh b 1960, Graham b 1961); *Career* med registrar: Westminster Hosp 1955–56, London Hosp 1959–62; Fulbright scholar 1956–57, res fell paediatrics Harvard Univ USA at Children's Med Centre Boston 1956–57, conslt clinical neurophysiologist North Staffordshire Hosp Centre 1958–89, sr res fell clinical neurophysiology Univ of Keele 1980–89; memb: Jt Ctee on Higher Med Trg 1976–84, Hon Advsy Neurology Panel Dept of Tport 1988–; pres: The Electroencephalographic Soc (now Br Soc for Clinical Neurophysiology) 1982–84, Assoc of Br Clinical Neurophysiologists 1984–87, Electrophysiological Technologists' Assoc 1987–92; FRCP 1977, FRSM; *Books* Sleep (ed, 1993); *Recreations* music, travel, sailing; *Clubs* Hardway Sailing, Trollope Soc, English Speaking Union, Cruising Assoc; *Style—* Dr Rosemary Cooper; ✉ Granida, 9 East Street, Hambledon, Hampshire PO7 4RX (☎ 01705 632382, fax 01705 632617)

COOPER, Maj-Gen Sir Simon Christie; KCVO (1991); s of Maj-Gen Kenneth Christie Cooper, CB, DSO, OBE (d 1981), of Dorset, and Barbara Mary, *née* Harding-Newman (d 1988); *b* 5 Feb 1936; *Educ* Winchester, Hamburg Univ; *m* 1967, Juliet Elizabeth, da of Cdr Geoffrey Inderwick Palmer, of Somerset; 1 s (Jonathan Francis Christie b 1969), 1 da (Venetia Elizabeth Somerset b 1971); *Career* cmmnd Life Gds 1956; served 1957–63: Aden, London, BAOR; Capt Adj Household Cavalry Regt 1963–65, ADC to CDS Earl Mountbatten of Burma 1965–66, Borneo Malaya 1966–67, Staff Coll 1968, BAOR 1969–75, CO Life Gds 1974–76, GSOI Staff Coll 1976–78, OC Household Cavalry and Silver Stick in Waiting 1978–81, cmdt RAC Centre 1981–82, RCDS 1983, dir RAC 1984–87, cmdt RMA Sandhurst 1987–89, Maj-Gen cmdg Household Div and GOC London Dist 1989–91; Master of the Royal Household 1992–; Hon Col Westminster Dragoons and Hon Col Royal Yeo 1987–; *Recreations* tennis, cricket, sailing, shooting, skiing; *Clubs* MCC; *Style—* Maj-Gen Sir Simon Cooper, KCVO; ✉ c/o Royal Bank of Scotland, Holts, Lawrie House, Farnborough, Hants GU14 7PQ

COOPER, Thomas Joshua; s of Duahne William Cooper (d 1993), of Yuma, Arizona, USA, and Nancy, *née* Roseman (d 1964); *b* 19 Dec 1946; *Educ* Humboldt State Univ Calif (BA, Secdy Teaching Credential, Community Teaching Credential), Univ of New Mexico Alberquerque (MA); *m* 1993, Catherine Alice, da of James Patrick Mooney, of Voorschoten, The Netherlands; 1 da (Laura Indigo b 4 March 1995); *Career* visual artist 1969–; teacher of photography Arcata HS Calif 1969, instr in photography Coll of the Redwoods Community Coll Eureka Calif 1970, teacher Dana Elementary Sch Nipomo Calif 1971, visiting lectr in photography Inst of American Indian Art Santa Fe New Mexico 1973, course dir for photographic studies and sr lectr in photography and history of photography Trent Poly Nottingham 1973–76, visiting asst prof of art Humboldt State Univ 1978–80, visiting artist Univ of Tasmania Sch of Art 1982; conductor of annual workshops: The Photographers Place Bradbourne 1982–, Salzburg Coll Salzburg Austria 1986–91; founding head Dept of Photography Sch of Fine Art Glasgow Sch of Art 1982–; memb: Photography Advsy Panel Scottish Arts Cncl 1986, Photography Bd CNAA 1986–87, Art Ctee Scottish Arts Cncl 1989–93; work in numerous public collections throughout world and in maj private collections in America, Britain, Europe and Australia; memb Soc for Photographic Educn 1969, fndr memb Scottish Soc for the History of Photography 1983, professional memb SSA 1984; *Major Exhibitions* incl: Images of our Mortality (Robert Self Gallery) 1977, A Quality of Dancing (Humboldt State Univ) 1984, American Photography: 1945–1980 (Barbican Art Gallery) 1985–86, The Hayward Annual (Hayward Gallery) 1985, John Weber Gallery NY 1988, 1990 and 1993, New North (Tate Gallery Liverpool) 1990, The Swelling of the Sea (Art Gallery and Museum Kelvingrove Glasgow) 1990, Kunst Europa (Heidelberg Kunstverein) 1991, Sojourn - Ten Years (Cairn Gallery) 1992, Seashore (Galerie Stadpark Krems Austria) 1993, Eight Photographers of the 90's (Laura Carpenter Fine Art, Santa Fe) 1993, Simply Counting Waves - 25 Years of Photographic Picture-Making by Thomas Joshua Cooper (Gulbenkian Fndn Centre for Modern Art Lisbon) 1994, Site Santa Fe - Longing and Belonging - From the Faraway Nearby (Mexico Museum of Fine Art Santa Fe) 1995, Two Artists - Thomas Joshua Cooper and Alfred Graf (Bregenz Austria) 1995, Light from the Darkroom - A Celebration of Scottish Photography (Edinburgh Festival Exhibition, Royal Scottish Acad and Nat Galleris of Scotland) 1995, Shadows in the Water (touring Bratislava, Slovakia, etc) 1995; *Awards* John D Phelan Award in Art & Literature 1970, maj photography bursary Arts Cncl of GB 1976, photography fell Nat Endowment of the Arts USA 1978, artists major bursary Scottish Arts Cncl 1994; *Publications* incl: Dialogue with Photography (1979, 2 edn 1992), Between Dark and Dark (1985), Dreaming the Gokstadt (1988), A Handful of Stones (1993), Simply Counting Waves - 25 Years of Photographic Picture-Making by Thomas Joshua Cooper (1994); *Recreations* cinema, reading, music (Renaissance, choral, country & western, operatic), athletics, barbeques, walking, wine; *Style—* Thomas Joshua Cooper, Esq; ✉ c/o Glasgow School of Art, 167 Renfrew Street, Glasgow G3 6RQ (☎ 0141 353 4500)

COOPER, William; s of Ernest Hoff (d 1960), of Crewe, and Edith Annie, *née* Summerfield (d 1979); *b* 4 Aug 1910; *Educ* Crewe Co Secdy Sch, Christ's Coll Cambridge (MA); *m* 3 Jan 1951, Joyce Barbara (d 1988), da of Rev William Frederick Harris, of Bristol; 2 da (Louisa b 1953, Catherine b 1955); *Career* Sqdn Ldr RAFVR 1940–46; asst cmmr Civil Serv Cmmn 1945–58; personnel conslt: UKAEA 1958–72, CEGB 1958–72, Cmmn of Euro Communities 1972–73; asst dir Civil Serv Selection Bd 1973–75, memb Bd of Crown Agents 1975–77, personnel advsr Millbank Tech Serv 1975–77; writer; adjunct prof of Eng lit Syracuse Univ London Centre 1977–90; fell Int PEN, FRSL; *Books* (as H S Hoff): Trina (1934), Rhea (1935), Lisa (1937), Three Marriages (1946); (as William Cooper): Scenes From Provincial Life (1950), The Struggles of Albert Woods (1952), The Ever-Interesting Topic (1953), Disquiet and Peace (1956), Young People (1958), C P Snow (Br Cncl Bibliographic Series, Writers and Their Work no 11, 1959), Prince Genji (a play, 1960), Scenes from Married Life (1961), Memoirs of a New Man (1966), You Want The Right Frame of Reference (1971), Shall We Ever Know (1971), Love on The Coast (1973), You're Not Alone (1976), Scenes from Metropolitan Life (1982), Scenes From Later Life (1983), From Early Life (1990), Immortality At Any Price (1991); *Recreations* swimming; *Clubs* Savile; *Style—* William Cooper, Esq; ✉ 22 Kenilworth Court, Lower Richmond Road, London SW15 1EW (☎ 0181 788 8326)

COOPER, Sir William Daniel Charles; 6 Bt (UK 1863), of Woollahra, New South Wales; s of Sir Charles Eric Daniel Cooper, 5 Bt (d 1984), and his 2 w, Mary Elisabeth, *née* Graham-Clarke; *b* 5 March 1955; *m* 22 Aug 1988, Julia Nicholson; *Heir* bro, George John Cooper, *qv*; *Career* dir: The Gdn Maintenance Serv, GMS Vehicles; *Style—* Sir William D C Cooper, Bt

COOPER, Maj-Gen William Frank; CBE (1972), MC (1945); s of Allan Cooper (d 1959), of Hazards, Shawford, Hants, and late Margaret Martha, *née* Pothelary; *b* 30 May 1921; *Educ* Sherborne; *m* 10 Aug 1945, Elisabeth Mary, da of George Finch (d 1918); 1 s (Allan George b 1950), 1 da (Gillian (Mrs Hewitt) b 1947); *Career* WWII cmmnd RE 1940, served N Africa and Italy, Staff Coll 1951, Co Field Sqdn RE Malayan Emergency, instr Staff Coll 1958–60, CRE 3 Div 1961–63, Lt-Col Staff HQ ME 1963–65, Brig Chief Engr 1968–70, Maj-Gen 1972–76; Mil advsr GKN Gp 1976–83, dir Gin Rectifiers' and Distillers' Assoc and Vodka Trade Assoc 1976–90; *Recreations* fly-fishing, bird watching, reading; *Clubs* Army and Navy; *Style—* Maj-Gen William F Cooper, CBE, MC; ✉ Neals, Aldbourne, Marlborough, Wilts SN8 2DW (☎ 01672 540716); 110 Kensington Park Rd, London W11 2PJ (☎ 0171 229 9222)

COORAY, His Hon Judge (Bulathsinhalage) Anura (Siri); s of Vincent Cooray (d 1965), of Kotte, Sri Lanka, and Dolly, *née* Manchanayake (d 1983); *b* 20 Jan 1936; *Educ* Christian Coll Kotte Sri Lanka, Univ of London; *m* 20 March 1957, Manel Therese, da of George Arthur Perera; 3 da (Carmalika Battolla b 31 Oct 1957, Sita Persaud b 21 July 1959, Samantha b 7 Aug 1966), 2 s (Vincent b 8 Aug 1961, Marlon b 6 July 1973); *Career* RAF Locking 1952–55, Royal Ceylon Air Force 1955–60; called to the Bar Lincoln's Inn 1968, practised Common Law Chambers Middle Temple and later dep head of Chambers 1 Gray's Inn Square, prosecuting counsel SE Circuit 1969–82, dep stipendary magistrate 1978–82, metropolitan stipendary magistrate (first non-white ever appointed) 1982, asst recorder 1985–88, recorder of the Crown Court 1988–90, memb Ctee of Magistrates 1990–91, circuit judge (SE Circuit, one of only two non-white judges nationally) 1991–; *Recreations* wine making, playing with grandchildren; *Style—* His Hon Judge Anura Cooray; ✉ Knightsbridge Crown Court, 1 Pocock Street, London SE1 0BT (☎ 0171 922 5800); 1 Gray's Inn Square, London WC1R 5AA (☎ 0171 405 8946); Kingsland, Etul Kotte, Sri Lanka (☎ 00 941 869223)

COOTE, Rev Bernard Albert Ernest; s of Albert Coote (d 1988, aged 100), of Steyning, Sussex, and Emma Jane, *née* Tye (d 1957); *b* 11 Aug 1928; *Educ* Steyning GS, Univ of London (BD); *m* 17 Aug 1957, Ann, da of Donovan Hopper; 2 s (John b 1958, Michael b 1960); *Career* RAF 1946–49; vicar Sutton Valence and E Sutton 1963–76, dir Royal Sch for the Blind Leatherhead 1976–90; chm Ctee on the Multihandicapped Blind 1984–90, vice chm Met Soc for the Blind 1991–; *Recreations* cricket, walking, travel, music; *Style—* The Rev Bernard Coote; ✉ 6 Coxham Lane, Steyning, West Sussex BN44 3LG

COOTE, Sir Christopher John; 15 Bt (I 1621), of Castle Cuffe, Queen's County, Ireland; s of Rear Adm Sir John Ralph Coote, 14 Bt, CB, CBE, DSC (d 1978), and Noreen Una, *née* Tighe (d 1996); *b* 22 Sept 1928; *Educ* Winchester, Christ Church Oxford (MA); *m* 23 Aug 1952, Anne Georgiana, yr da of Lt-Col Donald James Handford, RA (d 1980), of Guyers, Corsham, Wilts; 1 s (Nicholas Patrick b 1953), 1 da (Vanessa Jean b 1955); *Heir* s, Nicholas Patrick Coote b 28 July 1953; *Career* late Lt 17/21 Lancers; coffee and tea merchant 1952–; *Style—* Sir Christopher Coote, Bt

COOTE, Prof John Haven; s of Albert Ernest Coote (d 1967), of Enfield, and Gladys Mary Elizabeth, *née* Noble; *b* 5 Jan 1937; *Educ* Enfield GS, Chelsea Coll, Royal Free Hosp Sch of Med, Univ of London (BSc, PhD), Univ of Birmingham (DSc), Jagiellonian Univ Kracow (Dip of Faculty of Med, 1995); *m* 28 Dec 1974, Susan Mary, da of Dr William Hawkins Hylton (d 1989), of Clevedon; 1 s (Edward John b 1976), 2 da (Rachel Elizabeth b 1978, Naomi Caroline b 1981); *Career* Univ of Birmingham: lectr 1967, sr lectr 1970, reader 1977, prof of physiology and head of dept 1984, Bowman prof of physiology 1985, head Sch of Basic Med 1988–91; hon lectr Royal Free Hosp Sch of Med 1966; visiting prof: Tokyo 1974, Chicago 1988, Shanghai 1989, Heidelberg 1992; memb: Ctee Physiological Soc 1976–80, Soc for Experimental Biology 1976–; FBiol 1988, CBiol 1988, memb NY Acad of Sciences 1991; *Recreations* running, mountaineering (Birmingham Med Res Expeditionary Soc); *Clubs* Univ of London Graduate Mountaineering; *Style—* Prof John Coote; ✉ Department of Physiology, The Medical School, University of Birmingham, Birmingham B15 2TJ (☎ 0121 414 6915/6, fax 0121 414 6924, telex 338938 SPAHY G)

COOTE, Nicholas Patrick; s and h of Sir Christopher John Coote, 15 Bt, *qv*; *b* 28 July 1953; *Educ* Winchester; *m* 1980, Mona Rebecca, da of late Moushegh Bedelian; 1 s (Rory Alasdair b 3 April 1987), 1 da (Eleanor Marianne b 1984); *Career* British Airways; *Style—* Nicholas Coote, Esq

COPE, David Robert; s of Lawrence William Cope (d 1990), and Ethel Anne, *née* Harris (d 1980); *Educ* KCS Wimbledon, Univ of Cambridge (BA, MA), LSE (MSc); *m* 25 Aug 1992, Reiko, da of Junji Takashina (d 1989), of Higashi Fushimi, Japan; *Career* res offr UCL 1968–70, lectr Univ of Nottingham 1970–81, environmental team ldr Int Energy Agency Coal Res 1981–86, exec dir UK Centre for Econ and Environmental Devpt 1986–; prof of engrg economics Doshisha Univ Kyoto Japan 1997–98; memb: Depts of Environment and Trade and Indust Environmental Advsy Gp 1988–93, Cabinet Office Advsy Cncl on Sci and Technol Environment Ctee 1990–92, Dept of Environment Environmental Statistics Advsy Ctee and Academic Economists' Panels 1994–, Cncl Nat Soc for Clean Air and Environmental Protection, Packaging Standards Cncl 1994–96, Bd Inst for Sustainable Econ and Environmental Systems Washington State USA 1995–; external examiner Centre for Urban Planning and Environmental Mgmnt Univ of Hong Kong 1994–; *Books* Energy Policy and Land-Use Planning - an International Perspective (with P Hills and P James, 1984); *Recreations* hill walking, woodworking, classical music; *Style—* David R Cope, Esq; ✉ The UK Centre for Economic and Environmental Development, Suite E, 3 King's Parade, Cambridge CB2 1SJ (☎ 01223 367799, fax 01223 367794, e-mail 100345.1444@compuserve.com)

COPE, Rt Hon Sir John Ambrose; kt (1991), PC (1988); MP (C) Northavon (majority 11,861); s of late George Arnold Cope, MC, FRIBA, of Leicester; *b* 13 May 1937; *Educ* Oakham; *m* 1969, Djemila, da of Col P V Lovell Payne, of Martinstown, Dorset; 2 da; *Career* chartered accountant; Parly candidate (C) Woolwich E 1970; MP (C): South Glos 1974–83, Northavon 1983–; asst govt whip 1979–81, a Lord Cmmr of the Treasury 1981–83, dep chief whip and treas HM's Household 1983–87, min of state Dept of Employment and minister for Small Firms 1987–89, min of state Northern Ireland 1989–90, dep chm Conservative Party 1990–92, Paymaster Gen 1992–94; FCA; *Style—* The Rt Hon Sir John Cope, MP; ✉ House of Commons, London SW1A 0AA

COPE, Jonathan; *b* 1963; *Educ* White Lodge Royal Ballet Sch; *m* Maria Almeida; *Career* ballet dancer; princ Royal Ballet 1987–90 (joined 1982), business career 1990–92, returned to Royal Ballet 1992; leading roles (with Royal Ballet) incl: Prince in Swan Lake, The Sleeping Beauty and The Nutcracker, Solor in La Bayadère, Albrecht in Giselle, Romeo and Juliet, Le Baiser de la Fée, The Prince of the Pagodas, Cinderella, Palemon in Ondine, Serenade, Agon, Apollo, Opus 19/The Dreamer, The Sons of Horus, Young Apollo, Galanteries, The Planets, Still Life at the Penguin Café, The Spirit of Fugue, Concerto, Gloria, Requiem, A Broken Set of Rules, Pursuit, Piano, Grand Pas Classique, Monotones, Crown Prince Rudolph in Mayerling, Woyzeck in Different Drummer, Second Friend in The Judas Tree, Beliaev in A Month in the Country, Birthday Offering, La Valise, Air Monotones II, Fox in Renard, Fearful Symmetries, Symphony in C (partnering Sylvie Guillem), Duo Concertant, If This Is Still A Problem, Des Grieux in Manon, Illuminations; *Style—* Jonathan Cope, Esq; ✉ The Royal Ballet, Royal Opera House, Covent Garden, London WC2E 9DD (☎ 0171 240 1200, fax 0171 212 9121)

COPE, Wendy Mary; da of Fred Stanley Cope (d 1971), of Kent, and Alice Mary, *née* Hand; *b* 21 July 1945; *Educ* Farringtons Sch Chislehurst Kent, St Hilda's Coll Oxford (MA), Westminster Coll Oxford (DipEd); *Career* primary sch teacher: London Borough of Newham 1967–69, ILEA 1969–86 (seconded to Contact Newspaper as Arts and Reviews ed 1982–84, pt/t teacher 1984–86); freelance writer 1986–; Cholmondeley Award for Poetry 1987, Michael Braude Award American Acad of Arts and Letters 1995; FRSL; *Books* Making Cocoa for Kingsley Amis (1986), Twiddling Your Thumbs (1988), The River Girl (1991), Is That The New Moon? Poems by Women Poets (ed, 1988), Serious Concerns (1992), The Orchard Book of Funny Poems (1993); *Recreations* playing the piano, gardening; *Style*— Ms Wendy Cope, FRSL; ✉ c/o Faber & Faber, 3 Queen Square, London WC1N 3AU (☎ 0171 465 0045)

COPELAND, Col Christopher John Blanchard; s of Dr Francis John Copeland, of Rustington, West Sussex, and Betty, *née* Walker; *b* 12 July 1943; *Educ* Sherborne, RMA Sandhurst; *m* 9 Nov 1968, Penelope, da of Cdr M L Woollcombe, OBE, of Glebe Cottage, Fochabers, Scotland; 1 s (Nicholas b 26 April 1974), 1 da (Melanie b 25 August 1971); *Career* Adjutant 7 Para RHA 1973–75, Staff Coll 1976 Bty Comd 1978–80, Staff Coll instr Nigeria 1980–83, CO 1983–85, Chief of Staff 1987–91, Comd Gen Sp 1991–92, defence attache UAE 1993–; memb Ctee Br Ski Fedn; FBIM 1989; *Recreations* golf, skiing, sailing; *Clubs* Royal Ocean Racing; *Style*— Col Christopher Copeland; ✉ British Embassy Abu Dhabi, c/o FCO, King Charles Street, London SW1A 2AL

COPELAND, Prof John Richard Malcolm; s of Lorenzo Copeland (d 1982), and Kathleen Mary, *née* Hopkinson (d 1970); *b* 14 Oct 1932; *Educ* Newcastle under Lyme HS, Emmanuel Coll Cambridge (MA, MD, BChir), Univ of London (academic DPM); *m* 1963, Mary Bridget, da of Thomas O'Dwyer; 2 da (Caroline Mary Teresa b 1964, Veronica Anne Louise b 1965), 1 s (Andrew Thomas John b 1967); *Career* various house appts St Stephen's Hosp Chelsea, res med offr W End Hosp for Neurology and Neurosurgery London 1962–64, registrar in psychiatry Maudsley Hosp 1964–66; Inst of Psychiatry London: sr registrar 1966–68, lectr in psychiatry 1969–70, sr lectr 1970–76; Univ of Liverpool: prof and head Dept of Psychiatry 1976–, founding dir Inst of Human Ageing 1981–, hon conslt psychiatrist N Mersey Community Tst 1976–; hon lectr Guy's Hosp 1970–76; Sandoz lectr Basle 1990; Maudsley Bequest lectr RCPsych; advsr WHO; advsr and visiting prof Univ of Garounis (Libya) 1980–90; chm: Jt Ctee on Higher Psychiatric Trg in the Br Isles 1988–91, Mgmnt Ctee Euro Concerted Action on Depression in Older Age; memb: Advsy Bd on the Conferment of Titles Univ of London 1991–, Sci Ctee Int Inst of Psychosocial and Social Econ Res Univ of Limberg, Mgmnt Ctee Euro Concerted Action on Dementias, Steering Ctee MRC Cognitive Function and Ageing Study; Gold medal Yonsei Univ Coll of Med (Korea); memb: Br Geriatric Soc, Br Soc of Gerontology, Welsh Psychiatric Soc, Liverpool Psychiatric Soc, Int Psychogeriatric Assoc, World Fedn of Mental Health, Euro Psychogeriatric Assoc; FRCPsych 1977, FRCP 1980, FRSM; *Books* Psychiatric Diagnosis in New York and London (jtly, 1972), The Mind and Mood of Ageing: The Mental Health Problems of the Community Elderly in New York and London (jtly, 1983), Alzheimer's Disease: Potential Therapeutic Strategies (ed, 1992), Principles and Practice of Geriatric Psychiatry (sr ed, 1994); *Recreations* porcelain, skiing, Victorian house maintenance; *Clubs* United Oxford and Cambridge; *Style*— Prof John Copeland; ✉ University Department of Psychiatry, Royal Liverpool University Hospital, PO Box 147, Liverpool L69 3BX (☎ 0151 706 4141, fax 0151 709 3765, e-mail jrmcop@liverpool.ac.uk)

COPELAND, (Richard) Spencer Charles; s of Richard Ronald John Copeland, CBE, JP, DL (d 1958), of Stone, Staffs, and Ida, *née* Fenzi (MP for Stoke-on-Trent 1931–35, d 1964); *b* 18 Dec 1918; *Educ* St Peter's Ct Broadstairs Kent, Harrow, Alpine Coll Switzerland, Trinity Coll Cambridge (MA); *m* 1, 1940 (m dis), Sonia, da of late W J B Chambers, of Hoylake; 1 s (David Richard Michael b 1943); m 2, 1966, Jean, da of William Turner (d 1985), of Stoke-on-Trent; 1 s (William John Taylor b 1966), 1 adopted da (Elizabeth Anne b 1956); *Career* Lt RA LAA 1940–45; W T Copeland and Sons Ltd 1947 (later Spode Ltd): dir 1947, md 1955–66, chm 1966–71; dir Caverswall China Co Ltd 1975–81, dir Trelissick Investments Ltd 1975–86; fndr and fell Inst of Ceramics (now Inst of Materials) 1955, pres Br Ceramic Soc 1959–60, vice pres Assoc Euro de Ceramique 1960–62, memb Cncl Br Ceramic Research Assoc 1963–68 and 1971–72, pres Staffordshire Soc 1969–71, gen cmmr of Income Tax 1970–93, memb Cncl of Univ Coll North Staffordshire (now Univ of Keele) 1953–89, govr The Duchy GS Truro 1983–93; Hon MA Univ of Keele 1987; Freeman City of London, Liveryman Worshipful Co of Goldsmiths; hon life memb Royal Artillery Assoc 1966; life memb: Nat Tst 1958, Royal Instn of Cornwall 1974, Royal Yachting Assoc 1974; FRSA 1967; *Books* The Transactions of the British Ceramic Society (contrib, 1952 and 1955); published: The Copeland China Collection (by Vega Wilkinson, 1989), The Copelands of Kibblestone (by Vega Wilkinson, 1992); *Recreations* skiing, sailing; *Clubs* Royal Over-Seas League, Ski Club of GB, Royal Cwlth Yacht; *Style*— R Spencer C Copeland, Esq; ✉ Trelissick Mansion, Feock, Truro, Cornwall TR3 6QL (☎ 01872 862248)

COPELAND, Stephen Andrew; s of Derek Copeland, of Edleston, Cheshire, and Peggy, *née* Strangward; *b* 7 May 1946; *Educ* Nantwich GS, St Bartholomew's Hosp Med Sch London (MB BS); *m* 3 April 1972, Jennifer Ann, da of Dr John Almeyda, KSG (d 1986); 1 s (Matthew Scott b 17 March 1976), 1 da (Sara Clare b 26 Feb 1973); *Career* sr registrar Bart's 1975–79, clinical lectr Royal Nat Orthopaedic Hosp 1978, conslt orthopaedic surgn Royal Berkshire Hosp Reading 1979, memb Editorial Bd JBJS, hon memb American Shoulder Surgery Soc, ABC travelling fell, pres Br Shoulder and Elbow Soc, memb Int Bd of Shoulder Surgery, memb Cncl Orthopaedic Section RSM; developed own design of shoulder replacement; author of papers on shoulder surgery; *Books* Surgical Reconstruction in Rheumatoid Disease (1993), Operative Shoulder Surgery (1995), Shoulder Surgery (1996); *Recreations* tennis, windsurfing; *Style*— Stephen Copeland, Esq; ✉ Woodlands, Woodlands Rd, Harpsden, Henley-on-Thames, Oxfordshire RG9 4AA (☎ 0118 940 2114); Whitley Glebe, 11 Glebe Rd, Reading, Berks (☎ 0118 975 2097, fax 0118 940 1255)

COPEMAN, Dr Peter William Monckton; s of William Sydney Charles Copeman, CBE, TD, JP, MA, MD, FRCP (d 1970), and Helen, *née* Bourne (d 1980); head of the Copeman family, formerly of Sparham, Norfolk (*see* Burke's Landed Gentry, 18 edn, Vol III, 1972); *b* 9 April 1932; *Educ* Eton, CCC Cambridge (MA, MD, Copeman medal 1973), St Thomas's Hosp; *m* 19 May 1973, Lindsey Bridget, da of late David Vaughan Brims, of Heddon Hall, Heddon-on-the-Wall, Northumberland; 1 s (Andrew b 1980), 3 da (Mary b 1975, Louisa b 1977, Caroline b 1980); *Career* emeritus conslt physician i/c Dept of Dermatology Westminster and Westminster Children's Hosp; clinician, researcher and author; hon conslt dermatologist St Luke's Hosp for the Clergy London; Willan librarian Br Assoc of Dermatologists; cncllr The Game Conservancy, cnllr Arthritis & Rheumatism Cncl; patron Living of St James the Less Hadleigh Essex, patron, tstee and churchwarden St Mary's Bourne St London; Liveryman Worshipful Soc of Apothecaries; OStJ (memb Hosp Ctee); FRCP 1975; *Clubs* Athenaeum; *Style*— Dr Peter Copeman; ✉ 20 Spencer Park, London SW18 2SZ (☎ 0181 874 7549); 82 Sloane St, London SW1X 9PA (☎ 0171 245 9333, fax 0171 245 9232); Abshiel Farm, Morpeth, Northumberland NE65 8QN (☎ 01670 772268)

COPISAROW, Sir Alcon Charles; kt (1988); o s of late Dr Maurice Copisarow, of Manchester, and Eda Copisarow; *b* 25 June 1920; *Educ* Univ of Manchester, Imperial Coll London, Sorbonne (DSc); *m* 1953, Diana Elissa, yr da of Maj Ellis James Castello, MC, TD (d 1983); 2 s, 2 da; *Career* serv WWII Lt RN; HM cnsllr (scientific) Br Embassy Paris 1954–60, dir Dept of Scientific and Industl Res 1960–62, chief tech offr NEDC 1962–64, chief scientific offr Miny of Technol 1964–66, sr ptnr McKinsey and Co Inc 1966–76, former dir Br Leyland; memb: Br Nat Oil Corp, Touche Remnant Holdings, Press Cncl, Cncl Lloyd's; dep chm of Govrs ESU, tstee Duke of Edinburgh's Award, govr Benenden Sch; chm: Trinity Coll of Music London, Youth Business Initiative; first chm The Prince's Youth Business Tst; memb Admin Cncl Royal Jubilee Tsts; currently: special advsr Ernst & Young, dep chm Lloyd's Tercentenary Fndn (former chm), dir Windsor Festival, tstee Fndn for Manufacturing and Industry; patron Conseil National des Ingénieurs et des Scientifiques de France; Hon Freeman City of London, Liveryman Worshipful Co of Armourers and Brasiers; Hon FTCL; *Clubs* Athenaeum (chm), Beefsteak, White's; *Style*— Sir Alcon Copisarow; ✉ 25 Launceston Place, London W8 5RN

COPLAND, Dr Geoffrey Malcolm; s of Cyril Charles Copland (d 1984), and Jessie, *née* Ogden; *b* 28 June 1942; *Educ* Fitzmaurice GS Bradford upon Avon, Merton Coll Oxford (Open Postmastership, Harmsworth Sr Scholar, MA, DPhil); *m* 1, 1967, Janet Mary Todd; 1 da (Heidi Louise b 1970), 1 s (Alistair Hugh b 1973); m 2, 1985, Dorothy Joy Harrison; *Career* postdoctoral research Yale Univ USA 1967–69; Univ of London: postdoctoral research Queen Mary Coll 1969–71, lectr in physics Queen Elizabeth Coll 1971–80, dean of studies Goldsmiths Coll 1981–87; Univ of Westminster (formerly Poly of Central London): dep rector 1987–95, rector and vice-chllr 1995–; govr Greenhill Coll Harrow; tstee Thomas Wall Tst; MInstP 1974, FRSA 1990; *Publications* author of research papers and review articles in various academic jls; *Recreations* walking, gardening, cricket; *Clubs* Utd Oxford and Cambridge; *Style*— Dr Geoffrey Copland; ✉ University of Westminster, 309 Regent Street, London W1R 8AL (☎ 0171 911 5115, fax 0171 911 5103, e-mail coplang@wmin.ac.uk)

COPLAND, (William) Michael Ainslie; s of William Oranmore Copland (d 1980), of Tarporley, Cheshire, and Ethel Ainslie, *née* Bond; *b* 17 April 1947; *Educ* Sedbergh, St Catherine's Coll Oxford (MA), DMS; *m* 9 May 1970, Elizabeth Proctor, da of Edgar Anthony Francis; 1 s (Christopher Ainslie b 31 Jan 1974), 1 da (Sarah Elizabeth b 19 July 1975); *Career* editorial asst FMT Editorial & Writing Services Ltd 1970–73, PR mangr Inst of Mktg 1973–75, gp communications exec Giltspur Ltd 1975–77, dir of advtg and PR Burroughs Machines Ltd 1979–83 (PR mangr 1977–79), media rels mangr STC plc 1983–86, md A Plus Group Ltd PR 1992– (dir 1986–); chm Int Ctee PRCA; MCIM 1991; *Recreations* tennis, walking, Amnesty International; *Style*— Michael Copland, Esq; ✉ A Plus Group, New Tithe Court, 23 Datchet Road, Slough, Berks SL3 7PT (☎ 01753 790700, fax 01753 790701)

COPLAND-GRIFFITHS, Dr Michael Charles; s of Lt Cdr (Frederick) Charles Brandling Copland-Griffiths, MBE, of Bramley Cottage, Trowle House, Wingfield, Trowbridge, Wiltshire, and Mary Esmah Elizabeth, *née* Fry; *b* 7 Nov 1946; *Educ* Bradfield Coll, Anglo-Euro Coll of Chiropractic (Dr of Chiropractic); *m* 1, 28 Aug 1976 (m dis 1980), (Lorna) Penelope, da of John Napthine, of Spondon, Derbyshire; m 2, 6 Dec 1980, Noelle Mary (Penny), da of Herbert Bexon Spencer (d 1989), of Horton, nr Wimborne, Dorset; *Career* memb Faculty Anglo-Euro Coll of Chiropractic 1977–81 (memb Cncl 1978–80); Br Chiropractic Assoc: memb Cncl 1979–91 and 1993–, asst sec 1979–85, pres 1985–87, vice pres 1993–94, memb Fin & Gen Purposes Ctee 1986–88 and 1993–94 (chm 1986–87), chm Parly Ctee 1987–90 and 1994– (memb 1987–), President's Award for outstanding serv to the profession 1991, Western Provident Assoc Cup for servs to the chiropractic profession 1996; dir Chiropractic Registration Steering Group Ltd 1992– (chm 1994–); memb Advsy Ctee & Educn Ctee Inst of Complementary Med 1982–85, vice pres Anglo Euro Coll of Chiropractic Alumni Assoc 1982–91; Cncl for Complementary & Alternative Med: memb Ctee 1984–89, vice chm 1986–89; memb Bd of Advsrs Jl of Alternative and Complementary Med 1986–; Br rep Euro Chiropractors' Union 1986–87; *Books* Dynamic Chiropractic Today - The Complete and Authoritative Guide (1991); *Recreations* archaeology, post-medieval country pottery, history, natural history, British heritage, organic gardening, contemporary ceramics; *Style*— Dr Michael Copland-Griffiths; ✉ Trowle House, Wingfield, Trowbridge, Wilts BA14 9LE (☎ 01225 752199); Wingfield Chiropractic Clinic, Trowle House, Wingfield, Trowbridge, Wilts BA14 9LE (☎ 01225 752199, fax 01225 769842); Blandford Chiropractic Clinic, 11 Damory Court St, Blandford Forum, Dorset DT11 7QU (☎ 01258 455214); Chippenham Chiropractic Clinic, Emery House, Emery Lane, Chippenham, Wilts SN15 3JP (☎ 01249 447147, fax 01249 447661)

COPLEY, Matthew John; s of Dr Gordon John and Catherine Copley, of Surbiton, Surrey; *b* 4 Jan 1946; *Educ* Hollyfield Sch, chorister Kingston Parish Church; *Career* organ builder; trained as reed voicer Henry Willis & Sons 1961 (work incl tuning of Willis-built organs at St Paul's, Canterbury and Truro Cathedrals), reed voicer Grant Degens & Bradbeer 1967–72 (incl major installations at Univs of Sussex and York and New Coll Oxford); estab own business Organ Design Ltd 1974, has restored and rebuilt numerous older organs and built 12 new; lectr in organ building Merton Coll Surrey; *Recreations* gardening, photography, furniture and interior design, architecture, music and the reproducing piano; *Style*— Matthew Copley, Esq; ✉ Organ Design Ltd, 87a Maple Road, Surbiton, Kingston on Thames, Surrey KT6 4AW (☎ 0181 390 5059, fax 0181 339 9077)

COPLEY, Paul MacKriell; s of Harold Copley (d 1971), of Denby Dale, W Yorks, and Rene, *née* Hudson (d 1994); *b* 25 Nov 1944; *Educ* Penistone GS, Northern Counties Coll of Educn (Assoc Drama Bd Teachers' Cert); *m* 7 July 1972, (Primula) Natasha Mary Menzies, da of Lt-Col John Menzies Pyne (d 1965); *Career* actor and writer; *Theatre* incl: For King and Country 1976 (Actor of the Year in a New Play, Most Promising Actor), Sisters 1978, Whose Life is it Anyway? 1979, Rita Sue And Bob Too 1982, Other Worlds 1983, Fool in King Lear 1987 (with Anthony Quayle as Lear), Twelfth Night (tour of Iraq, Pakistan, Ethiopia, Sudan and Zimbabwe) 1987–88, Prin 1989, The Awakening 1990, I Thought I Heard a Rustling 1991, The Mortal Ash 1994, The Servant (Martini TMA Regional Theatre award for Best Actor in a Supporting Role) 1995, With Every Beat 1995, When we are Married 1996; *Television* incl: Days of Hope 1974, Chester Mystery Plays 1976, Treasure Island 1977, Travellers 1978, Cries from Watchtower 1979, Death of a Princess 1980, A Room for the Winter 1981, The Gathering Seed 1983, The Bird Fancier 1984, Dangerous Journey 1985, Oedipus at Colonus 1986, Gruey 1987, Young Charlie Chaplin 1988, Testimony of a Child 1989, Landmarks - Christopher Columbus 1990, Collision Course 1991, Stay Lucky 1991, Heartbeat 1992, Rides II 1992, Harry 1993, Cracker (series 1,2,3) 1993–95, A Pinch of Snuff 1993, Roughnecks 1994, Peak Practice (series 3) 1994, Sloggers 1995, This Life 1996; *Films* incl: Alfie Darling 1974, A Bridge Too Far 1976, Zulu Dawn 1979, Doll's Eye 1982, Ends and Means 1984, War and Remembrance 1987, The Pile Rats 1988, How's Business 1991, The Remains of the Day 1993, Jude 1996; *Radio* incl: The Marshalling Yard 1986, The Pilgrim's Progess 1988, Jesus 1990, The Fight For Barbara 1991, Tolkein's Smith of Wooton Major 1992, Vlad the Impaler 1992, That Summer 1993, Sons and Lovers 1994, The Snow Queen 1995, King St Junior 1996; audio book: Adam Bede (Penguin, 1996); *Writing* incl: Hitch (1976), Pillion (1977), Viaduct (1979), Tapster (1981), Fire Eaters (1984), Calling (1986), On Mayday (1987), Shakespeare in Africa (1990), Sally's Tree (1992), Tipperary Smith (1993), King St Junior (1996), Words Alive! (1996); *Recreations* swimming, motorcycling, travel, photography; *Style*— Paul Copley, Esq; ✉ c/o Kate Feast Management, 10 Primrose Hill Studios, Fitzroy Road, London NW1 8TR (☎ 0171 586 5502, fax 0171 586 9817); c/o Casarotto Ramsay Ltd, National House, 60–66 Wardour St, London W1V 3HP (☎ 0171 287 4450, fax 0171 287 9128)

COPLEY, His Hon Judge; Peter Edward; s of Edward Thomas Copley (d 1975), of London, and Florence Hilda, *née* Tidd (d 1971); *b* 15 Feb 1943; *Educ* Pinner County GS, Coll of Law; *m* 2, 1986, Janice Patricia, da of Edward George Webster; 1 da (Caroline b 12 September 1989); 2 c from previous m; 1 s (Lance b 22 August 1973), 1 da (Jane b 6 December 1975); *Career* articled clerk 1961–66, admitted slr 1966, recorder of the Crown Court 1992–95 (asst recorder 1989–92), circuit judge (SE Circuit) 1995–; *Recreations* sailing; *Clubs* Royal London Yacht, Island Sailing; *Style*— His Hon Judge Copley; ✉ Wood Green Crown Court, Woodall House, Lordship Lane, London N22 5LF

COPLIN, Prof John Frederick; CBE (1996); *b* 29 Oct 1934; *Educ* Bablake Sch Coventry, Imperial Coll London (BSc); *m* 1957, Jean Fowler; 3 s (Stephen b 1965, Richard b 1966, David b 1970); *Career* Rolls-Royce: joined as graduate apprentice Derby 1956, grad of the year 1958, chief designer RB211 1968–77, asst engrg dir Aero-Div 1977, dir of technol 1978, dir of design 1983, dir of new products engrg Rolls-Royce plc 1987, md Rolls-Royce Business Ventures Ltd 1988–91; currently UK advsr to Indonesian Min of State for Res and Technol Jakarta; Fellowship of Engrg: memb Cncl 1981–84, memb F & GP Ctee 1985–88; memb: Advsy Cncl for Applied R & D 1983–86, chm Aerospace Technol Bd MOD 1984–85 (memb 1980–83), Def Scientific Advsy Cncl MOD 1984–85; assoc fell Univ of Warwick, visiting prof of principles of engrg design Univ of Oxford 1989–91; recipient: Akroyd Stuart award 1966 (with G L Wilde) and 1985, James Clayton prize (with Frank Turner); FEng 1980, FCGI, FRAeS, FIMechE, FRSA; *Publications* author of numerous tech papers and articles worldwide; *Style*— Prof John Coplin, CBE, FEng; ✉ Jalan Kemang Timur V/2D, Jakarta 12730, Indonesia (☎ and fax 00 62 21 7992025)

COPPEL, Laurence Adrian; s of Henry Coppel (d 1979), of Belfast, and Anne Coppel (d 1964); *b* 15 May 1939; *Educ* Belfast Royal Acad, Queen's Univ Belfast (BSc); *m* 28 Oct 1964, Geraldine Ann, da of David Morrison (d 1991); 2 s (Kenton Andrew b 1968, Mark Hugo b 1972); *Career* exec dir: Singer & Friedlander Ltd 1971–91, Singer & Friedlander Group plc 1987–91; currently chm Nottingham Building Society (dir 1985–); dir: British Polythene Industries plc 1989–, Jenner Fenton Slade Group Ltd 1991–95, Wade Furniture Group Ltd 1991–, SOL Construction Holdings Ltd 1991–95; chm Landmatch plc 1993–95; non-exec memb Queen's Med Centre Univ Hosp NHS Tst 1993–; FCA; *Recreations* sailing, tennis, walking, music; *Style*— Laurence Coppel, Esq; ✉ Nottingham Building Society, 5–13 Upper Parliament Street, Nottingham NG1 2BX

COPPELL, Andrew Nicholson; s of William Edward Coppell, of Glasgow, and Mary Eliza Hill Foggo (d 1993); *b* 14 March 1939; *Educ* Queens Park Sr Secdy Sch, Univ of Glasgow (BSc, tennis blue, capt of Univ Tennis Club and Scottish Univs Team, W of Scotland and Scottish Doubles tennis champion); *m* 18 Sept 1964, Margaret, da of Robert Cunningham and Margaret Galloway, of Greenock; 2 da (Lynn b 28 April 1967, Heather b 3 Nov 1971); *Career* IBM UK Ltd: joined as graduate trainee 1961, variously programmer, analyst, data processing mangr, world trade info systems planning mangr, UK info servs mangr until 1972; Sedgwick Ltd: joined 1972, variously dir of systems, dir of systems and admin, dep chm of gp finance and admin, bd dir, dir of gp systems and chm of gp properties until 1985; dir of gp info servs Kleinwort Benson Group and dir Kleinwort Benson Ltd 1986–90; Lloyd's of London: gp head of systems 1990–92, dir of systems and ops 1993–, memb Lloyd's Market Bd 1993–; memb Worshipful Co of Information Technologists; MBCS; *Recreations* golf, tennis, secretary of Little Baddow United Reformed Church; *Style*— Andrew Coppell, Esq; ✉ Lloyd's of London, One Lime Street, London EC3M 7HA (☎ 0171 623 7100, direct line 0171 327 6152, fax 0171 327 6122)

COPPELL, Stephen James (Steve); s of James Coppell, and Christina Mary, *née* Howell; *b* 9 July 1955; *Educ* Quarry Bank Comp Liverpool, Univ of Liverpool; *m* 1981 (sep), Jane Eileen, *née* Humphreys; 1 s (Mark Stephen b 14 March 1986); *Career* former professional football player, currently manager; player: Tranmere Rovers 1973–75, Manchester Utd (over 400 appearances) 1975–84; England: 1 under 23 cap, 42 full caps 1978–83, played in World Cup Spain 1982; honours as player Manchester Utd: FA Cup 1977 (runners up 1976 and 1979), runners up League Cup 1983; Crystal Palace FC: mangr 1984–93 (resigned), promotion to Div 1 1989, runners up FA Cup 1990, relegated 1993; chief exec League Managers' Assoc 1993–95; rejoined Crystal Palace as tech dir 1995–96; mangr Manchester City FC 1996 (resigned); chm Professional Footballers' Assoc 1982–84, sometime contrib to football progs BBC TV, sometime columnist The Independent; *Books* Touch and Go (with Bob Harris, 1985); *Recreations* all sports; *Style*— Steve Coppell, Esq; ✉ c/o Manchester City Football Club, Maine Road, Moss Side, Manchester M14 7WN (☎ 0161 226 1191/2, fax 0161 227 9418)

COPPEN, Dr Alec James; s of Herbert John Wardle Coppen (d 1974), of London, and Marguerite Mary Annie, *née* Henshaw (d 1971); *b* 29 Jan 1923; *Educ* Dulwich, Univ of Bristol (MB ChB, MD, DSc), Maudsley Hosp, London Univ (DPM); *m* 9 Aug 1952, Gunhild Margareta, da of Albert Andersson, of Bastad, Sweden; 1 s (Michael b 1953); *Career* Br Army 1942–46; registrar then sr registrar Maudsley Hosp 1954–59, MRC Neuropsychiatry Res Unit 1957–74, MRC External Staff 1974–88; conslt psychiatrist: St Ebba's Hosp 1959–64, West Park Hosp Epsom 1964–90 (emeritus 1990); hon conslt St George's Hosp 1965–70, head WHO designated Centre for Biological Psychiatry UK 1974–88, memb Special Health Authy Bethlem Royal and Maudsley Hosp 1982–86; conslt WHO 1977–, examiner Royal Coll of Psychiatry 1973–77, Andrew Woods visiting prof Univ of Iowa 1981; lectr in: Europe, N and S America, Asia, Africa; memb Cncl and chm Res and Clinical Section RMPA 1965–70, chm Biology Psychiatry Section World Psychiatric Assoc 1972, pres Br Assoc Psychopharmacology 1975; ECNP Eli Lilly Award for outstanding research in neuropsychopharmacology 1991; author of numerous scientific papers on mental health; Freeman City of London 1980, Liveryman Worshipful Soc of Apothecaries 1985 (memb 1980); memb: Collegium Internationale Neuropsychopharmacologicum 1960 (memb Cncl 1979, pres 1990), RSM 1960, Br Pharmacological Soc 1977; hon memb: Mexican Inst of Culture 1974, Swedish Psychiatric Assoc 1977; corr memb American Coll Neuropsychopharmacology 1977, FRCP 1980 (MRCP 1975), distinguished fell APA 1981, Hon FRCPsych 1995 (FRCPsych 1971); *Books* Recent Developments in Schizophrenia (1967), Recent Developments in Affective Disorders (1968), Biological Psychiatry (1968), Psychopharmacology of Affective Disorders (1979), Depressive Illness: Biological and Psychopharmacological Issues (1981), 5-Hydroxytryptamine in Psychiatry (1991); *Recreations* golf, opera, photography; *Clubs* Athenaeum, The Harveian Soc, RAC; *Style*— Dr Alec Coppen; ✉ 5 Walnut Close, Epsom, Surrey KT18 5JL (☎ 01372 720800, fax 01372 742602)

COPPEN, Dr Michael James; s of Dr Alec James Coppen, of Epsom, Surrey, and Gunhild Margaretta, *née* Andersson; *b* 3 Dec 1953; *Educ* Epsom Coll, Royal Free Hosp Univ of London (MB BS); *m* 3 Sept 1983, Regina Poh Gek, da of Goh Choe Jim (d 1987); 1 s (Daniel James Michael b 25 Nov 1993), 1 da (Victoria Jade b 3 Sept 1991); *Career* sr house offr (later registrar) Guy's Hosp 1979–82, sr registrar UCH and Whittington Hosp 1982–87, conslt histopathologist Mayday Univ Hosp 1987–; FRCPath 1996 (MRCPath 1985); memb: Assoc Clinical Pathologists, British Soc of Clinical Cytology; *Articles* incl: Chronic Periaortitis Presenting As Common Bile Duct Obstruction (1991), Audit of Necropsies in a British District General Hospital (1992), Histoplasmosis of the Central Nervous System (1992), A Case of Warthin's Tumour with Co-existent Hodgkin's Disease (1993); pubns incl Evaluation of Buffy Coat Microscopy for the Early Diagnosis of Bacteraemia (1981); *Recreations* golf, reading, music; *Clubs* Royal Automobile, Hole in One; *Style*— Dr Michael Coppen; ✉ 5 Furlong House, 97 Tattenham Crescent, Epsom Downs, Surrey KT18 5NY (☎ 01737 357559); Department of Histopathology, Mayday Hospital, Mayday Road, Thornton Heath, Surrey (☎ 0181 401 3000 ext 5014)

COPPERWHEAT, Lee; s of Terence Copperwheat, of Luton, Beds, and Diana Frances Brooks, of St Just, Cornwall; *Career* fashion designer; estab (with Pamela Blundell) Copperwheat Blundell; Young Designer of the Yr (Lloyds Bank/Br Fashion Awards) 1994; *Style*— Lee Copperwheat; ✉ Copperwheat Blundell, 14 Cheshire Street, Shoreditch, London E2 6EH (☎ 0171 613 0651, fax 0171 729 8600)

COPPOCK, Surgn Rear Adm David Arthur; CB (1990); s of Oswald John Coppock of Fordingbridge (d 1979), and Ada Katherine, *née* Beaven (d 1979); *b* 19 April 1931; *Educ* Bishop Wordsworth Sch, Guy's Hosp (BDS), George Washington Univ (MSc); *m* 1, 31 May 1956, Maria Averil, *née* Ferreira (d 1985); 2 da (Phillipa (Mrs McIntyre) b 1957, Nicola (Mrs Tims) b 1959); m 2, 1990, Sally Annette Neville, *née* Cook; *Career* entered RN 1955; HM Ships: Eagle 1956, Tamar Hong Kong 1959, Hermes 1963, Rooke Gibraltar 1965; US Navy Exchange Bethesda MD 1972, dep dir of Naval Dental Serv 1980, Cmd dental surgn to C in C Naval Home Cmd 1983, dir Naval Dental Serv 1985, dir Def Dental Servs 1988–90, ret; QHDS 1985–90; memb Assoc of Professional Game Angling Instructors; *Recreations* fly fishing, tennis, golf; *Clubs* RSM; *Style*— Surgn Rear Adm David Coppock, CB; ✉ Breamore Lodge, West St, Hambledon, Hampshire PO7 4RW (☎ 01705 632566)

COPPOCK, Lawrence Patrick; s of Eric Francis Coppock, of Harrogate, and Betty Winifred, *née* Wilson; *b* 27 Jan 1952; *Educ* Royal GS, King George V GS; *m* 1 May 1982, Gillian Mary, da of Richard Charles Darby, of Stratford-on-Avon; 2 da (Katherine b 1984, Victoria b 1987), 1 s (Richard b 1993); *Career* chartered accountant Coopers & Lybrand 1971–75, sr analyst BL International 1976–78, fin controller Lex Service plc 1978–83, gp fin dir Heron Motor Group 1983–84, gp fin controller Heron Corporation plc 1985, fin and ops dir HP Bulmer Drinks Ltd 1986–88, sometime fin dir B & Q plc 1988; chm Broadreach Retail Services Ltd 1992–; memb local Cons Party, former treas Kyre Church Restoration; FCA 1980; *Recreations* skiing, walking; *Style*— Lawrence Coppock, Esq

COPPOCK, Prof (John) Terence; CBE (1987); s of Capt Arthur Leslie Coppock (d 1962), and Valerie Margaret, *née* Phillips (d 1981); *b* 2 June 1921; *Educ* Penarth County Sch, Queens' Coll Cambridge (BA, MA), Univ of London (PhD); *m* 6 Aug 1953, Sheila Mary (d 1990), da of Dr Gerard Burnett (d 1985); 1 s (John b 1960), 1 da (Helena b 1955); *Career* cmmnd Welch Regt 1941, serv ME 1942–46, Lt RA 1942; clerical offr Lord Chllr's Dept 1938–46, exec offr Miny of Works 1946–47, offr Customs and Excise 1947; UCL Dept of Geography: asst lectr 1950–52, lectr 1952–64, reader 1964–65; prof of geography Univ of Edinburgh 1965–86 (emeritus 1987); sec and treas Carnegie Tst for Univs for Scot 1986–, visiting prof of geography Birkbeck Coll 1986–95, fell UCL 1987–; vice pres RSGS 1975–, memb Scot Sport Cncl 1976–87, chm Exec Ctee Scot Field Studies Assoc 1977–80; MIBG 1948– (pres 1973–74), FRGS 1950, FBA 1975, FRSE 1976, FTS 1980, FRSA 1981, FRSGS 1988; *Books* The Changing Use of Land in Britain (with R H Best, 1962), An Agricultural Atlas of England and Wales (1964); *Recreations* badminton, walking, listening to music; *Style*— Prof J T Coppock, CBE, FRSE, FBA; ✉ 57 Braid Ave, Edinburgh EH10 6EB (☎ 0131 447 3443); Carnegie Trust for the Universities of Scotland, Cameron House, Abbey Park Place, Dunfermline, Fife KY12 7PZ (☎ 01383 622148, fax 01383 622149)

CORAH, (George) Nicholas; DL (Leics); s of Alfred Geoffrey Corah (d 1981), of Warnham, Sussex, and Evelyn Gladys, *née* Fleming (d 1975); *b* 23 Jan 1932; *Educ* Malvern Coll; *m* 11 June 1955, Penelope-Anne Grace, da of John Denis Daniels (d 1975); 1 da (Jacqueline), 3 s (Simon, Marcus, Benjamin); *Career* Nat Serv Cyprus and Egypt 1951–53; Corah plc: joined as mgmnt trainee 1953, mktg dir 1965–66, md 1966–69, chm and jt md 1969–80, exec chm 1980–88, non-exec chm 1988–89, ret from Corah plc 1989; regnl dir Lloyds Bank plc 1982–85, fndr chm Leicestershire Business Venture 1982–84, dep chm East Midlands Electricity plc 1991– (non-exec dir 1990–, memb E Midlands Electricity Bd 1984–90), non-exec dir Alliance & Leicester Building Society 1985– (non-exec dir Leicester Building Society 1978–85), non-exec dir East Midlands Development Company Ltd 1994–; memb Nat Mfrg Cncl CBI 1992–96, memb Exec and Cncl Industl Soc; memb Ct of Assts Worshipful Co of Framework Knitters (Past Master); High Sheriff of Leics 1996–97; CIMgt, FInstD, FRSA; *Recreations* the family, shooting, music, the English Home; *Clubs* Reform; *Style*— Nicholas Corah, Esq, DL; ✉ Wakerley Old Rectory, nr Oakham, Rutland, Leics LE15 8PA (☎ 01572 747734)

CORBEN, Carolyn Jessica; da of Cyril Lesley Corben, of Weymouth, Dorset, and Colette Mary, *née* Morris; *b* 13 Jan 1963; *Educ* Bournemouth and Poole Coll of Art & Design (dip), Goldsmiths' Coll (BA, Kingsley Howe meml award), RCA (MA, Worshipful Co of Gold and Silver Wyre Drawers prize); *Career* freelance embroidery and textile designer 1990–91, fndr memb The New RenaisCAnce (multi media co specialising in fashion and accessory design, display, styling and video prodn) 1991–; exhbns incl: Fouts and Fowler Gallery London 1991, Liberty London 1991, Premiere Classe Paris 1991, The World of The New RenaisCAnce (Royal Festival Hall and Parco Gallery Tokyo) 1992, Crafts in Performance (Crafts Cncl touring exhbn) 1993, In the Swim (Bremmerhaven Germany) 1993; TV and video work incl title sequences for BBC1, Ch4, S4C and Carlton, advtg work for British and Scottish Rail, W H Smith, TSB and Cusson's 'Pearl', window design for Liberty and Harvey Nichols London; *Style*— Ms Carolyn Corben; ✉ The New RenaisCAnce, 14 West Central Street, Bloomsbury, London WC1A 1JH (☎ 0171 240 8302, fax 0171 240 8306)

CORBEN, David Edward; s of Cyril Edward Corben, of Mayfield Cottage, Manor Rd South, Elmbridge, Surrey, and Florence Ethel Jessie, *née* Lewthwaite; *b* 5 March 1945; *Educ* St Paul's; *m* 1, 4 Jan 1969 (m dis), Fiona Elizabeth Macleod, da of Prof David Stern, of Teddington, Middx; 1 s (Mark b 1971), 1 da (Victoria b 1973); m 2, 7 May 1988, Miranda Davies, da of David McCormick, of Salisbury, Wilts; *Career* Lloyd's broker; Jardine Thompson Graham: dir 1971–, md 1976, chm 1986–; dir: JIB Group plc 1991–, Matheson and Co 1984–; memb Lloyd's; *Recreations* skiing, golf, tennis, motor racing, riding, rugby football; *Clubs* Roehampton; *Style*— David Corben, Esq; ✉ 42 Roedean Crescent, Roehampton, London SW15 5JU (☎ 0181 876 1969); Jardine Thompson Graham, Jardine House, 6 Crutched Friars, London EC3N 2HT (☎ 0171 528 4444)

CORBET, Prof Philip Steven; s of Alexander Steven Corbet (d 1948), of Tilehurst, Reading, Berks, and Irene Trewavas (d 1989), of Newlyn, Cornwall; *b* 21 May 1929; *Educ* Nelson Boys' Coll NZ, Dauntseys Sch W Lavington Wilts, Univ of Reading (BSc, DSc), Univ of Cambridge (PhD, ScD); *m* 1, 9 Feb 1957 (m dis 1979), Hildegard Gertrud, da of Otto Keller (d 1959), of Tübingen, W Germany; m 2, 15 Oct 1980 (m dis 1987), Laila Kristin Kjellström; 1 da (Katarina); m 3, 31 Dec 1987 (m dis 1995), Mary Elizabeth Canvin; *Career* zoologist E African Freshwater Fisheries Res Orgn Jinja Uganda 1954–57, entomologist E African Virus Res Orgn Entebbe Uganda 1957–62, res scientist Entomology Res Inst Canada Dept of Agric Ottawa Canada 1962–67, dir Res Inst Canada Dept of Agric Belleville Ontario Canada 1967–71, prof and chm Dept of Biology Univ of Waterloo Ontario Canada 1971–74, prof and dir Jt Centre for Environmental Scis Univ of Canterbury and Lincoln Coll Canterbury NZ 1974–78, prof Dept of Zoology Univ of Canterbury Christchurch NZ 1978–80, head Dept of Biological Scis Univ of Dundee 1983–86 (prof of zoology 1980–90, prof emeritus 1990–); visiting Cwlth prof Dept of Applied Biology Univ of Cambridge 1979–80, hon prof Univ of Edinburgh 1996–; memb NZ Environmental Cncl 1976–79, pres Br Dragonfly Soc 1983–92 (hon memb 1991); memb: Ctee for Scot Nature Conservancy Cncl 1986–90, Cncl Scot Wildlife Tst 1995–96; hon memb Int Odonatological Soc 1985; fell: Royal Entomological Soc 1950, fell Entomological Soc of Canada 1974 (pres 1971–72, Gold medal 1974); FInstBiol 1967, FRSTM&H 1985, FRSE 1987, FRSA 1991; *Books* Dragonflies (with C Longfield and N W Moore, 1960), A Biology of Dragonflies (1962), The Odonata of Canada and Alaska (with E M Walker, 1975), Behavior and Ecology of Dragonflies (1997); *Recreations* natural history, music; *Clubs* Arctic; *Style*— Prof Philip S Corbet, FRSE; ✉ Crean Mill, Crean, St Buryan, Cornwall TR19 6DH (☎ and fax 0131 650 5454);

Institute of Cell, Animal and Population Biology, University of Edinburgh, West Mains Rd, Edinburgh EH9 3JT (☎ 0131 650 5454, fax 0131 667 3210)

CORBETT, Gerald Michael Nolan; s of John Michael Nolan Corbett (d 1982), of Sedlescombe, Sussex, and Pamela Muriel *née* Gay; *b* 7 Sept 1951; *Educ* Tonbridge Sch, Pembroke Coll Cambridge (foundation scholar, MA), London Business Sch (MSc), Harvard Business Sch (exchange scholarship); *m* 19 April 1976, Virginia Moore, da of Neill Newsum, of Hindolveston, Norfolk; 1 s (John b 20 Jan 1981), 3 da (Sarah b 4 June 1979, Olivia b 13 Nov 1982, Josephine b 4 Oct 1984); *Career* conslt and case leader Boston Consulting Gp 1976–82; Dixons Gp plc: gp fin controller 1982–85, corporate fin dir 1985–87; gp fin dir Redland plc 1987–94, gp fin dir Grand Metropolitan plc 1994–; non-exec dir MEPC plc 1995–; govr: Abbots Hill Sch, Beechwood Park Sch; Freeman: City of London, Worshipful Co of Glaziers & Painters of Glass 1988; *Recreations* shooting, tennis, skiing; *Clubs* Downhill Only, MCC; *Style—* Gerald Corbett, Esq; ✉ Holtsmere End Farmhouse, Redbourn, Herts AL3 7AW; Grand Metropolitan plc, 8 Henrietta Place, London W1M 9AG (☎ 0171 518 5200, fax 0171 518 4612)

CORBETT, Nigel Stephen; s of Gerald Maurice Stephen Corbett (d 1992), of 34 Chester Row, London, and Elizabeth Mary Barber, *née* Lindsell; *b* 4 April 1942; *Educ* St George's Sch Windsor, Wellington; *m* 7 April 1966, Margaret, da of Douglas Theodore Freebody; 2 da (Charlotte-Anne b 8 Aug 1968, Tara Margaret b 7 Oct 1969); *Career* hotelier, restaurateur, nightclub owner; Rehearsal Room Night Club Royal Court Theatre 1964–66, Angelique Restaurant Discotheque King's Road Chelsea 1967–72, Françoise Club King's Road Chelsea 1969–79, Summer Lodge Country House Hotel 1979–; Cezar award Good Hotel Guide 1985, runner up Egon Ronay Hotel of the Year 1987, Holiday Which? Country House Weekend Hotel of the Year 1987, memb Relais et Chateaux 1992–; memb Yeovil Coll Catering Liaison Ctee; *Recreations* travel; *Style—* Nigel Corbett, Esq; ✉ Summer Lodge Country House Hotel, Evershot, Dorset DT2 0JR (☎ 01935 83424)

CORBETT, (Richard) Panton; s of Richard William Corbett, TD (d 1987), and Doris Vaughan, *née* Kimber (d 1991); *b* 17 Feb 1938; *Educ* Sunningdale, Eton, Aix en Provence Univ; *m* 1, 28 April 1962 (m dis 1973), Leila Francis, *née* Wolsten-Croft; 1 s (Oliver b 1965); m 2, 11 July 1974, Dame Antoinette Sibley, DBE, *qv*, da of E G Sibley (d 1991), of Birchington on Sea; 1 s (Isambard b 1980), 1 da (Eloise b 1975); *Career* 2 Lt Welsh Gds 1957; md Singer and Friedlander Holdings plc 1973–; dir: Saxon Oil plc 1980–86, First British American Corporation Ltd 1976–93, Interfinance and Investment Corporation 1974–80, Tex Holdings 1987–, Peninsula TV 1989–93, Haynes Publishing Group plc 1993–, South Staffordshire Water Holdings plc 1993–, Sterling Publishing Group PLC 1995–; chm Alternative Investment Market (AIM) London Stock Exchange; dir Royal Opera House Tst 1989–95, tstee Royal Ballet Benevolent Fund, memb Exec and chm Fin Ctee Royal Acad of Dancing; Freeman City of Shrewsbury 1979; *Recreations* tennis, shooting, opera, skiing, fishing, paragliding; *Clubs* Boodle's, Queen's; *Style—* Panton Corbett, Esq; ✉ 24 Chapel St, London SW1X 7BY (☎ 0171 235 4506); 2 Grove Farm, Longnor, nr Shrewsbury SY7 5PP; Singer & Friedlander Ltd, 21 New Street, Bishopsgate, London EC2M 4HR (☎ 0171 623 3000, fax 0171 626 3074, telex 886977)

CORBETT, Peter George; s of Dr John Hotchkins Corbett, and Patricia Kathleen, *née* Hope; *b* 13 April 1952; *Educ* Liverpool Coll, Liverpool Coll of Art and Design (fndn), Manchester Regnl Coll of Art and Design (BA); *Career* artist (oil on canvas); memb: Creative Minds Arts Gp Ctee 1978–81, New Age Festival Organising Ctee 1983 and 1984; lead singer and fndr memb rock band Aquarian 1983–85, composer Dr F and The TV Kids (Unity Theatre Liverpool) 1985, fndr memb Merseyside Contemporary Artists Mgmnt Ctee (formerly Liverpool Acad of Arts) 1988, chm and fndr memb Merseyside Visual Arts Festival (Visionfest) 1989–90; hon prof Academie des Sciences Humaines Universelles Paris 1993, life fell and hon prof of fine art Inst of Co-ordinated Research Victoria Aust 1994; memb: Nat Artists Assoc 1988–89 (chm Merseyside Branch), Design and Artists Copywright Soc, Abstract Artists Organisation London, Maison Internationale des Intellectuels Paris 1994; fndr memb Order of St Francis Liberal Catholic Church; *Exhibitions* incl: Centre Gallery Liverpool 1979, Liverpool Playhouse 1982, Acorn Gallery Liverpool 1985, Major Merseyside Artists Exhibition (Port of Liverpool Building) 1988, Merseyside Contemporary Artists Exhibition (Albert Dock Liverpool) 1988, Surreal Objects Exhibition (Tate Gallery Liverpool) 1989, Unity Theatre Liverpool 1990, Royal Liver Building Liverpool (2 person) 1991, Alternative 17 Exhibition (Merkmal Gallery Liverpool) 1991, Angelus Gallery Winchester (mixed) 1992, Senate House Gallery Liverpool Univ (one man) 1993, Acad of Arts Liverpool (two man) 1994, Vision Fest (open) 1994, Grosvenor Museum Exhibition Chester (open) 1995, Atkinson Gallery Southport (one man) 1995, The Three Month Gallery Liverpool (mixed) 1996; *Poetry Anthologies* included in: 'Voices of the Wind' and 'On the Other Side of the Mirror' (for Int Soc of Poets); *Publications* contrib to numerous creative jls; *Recreations* musical composition, playing the piano, meditation, yoga, contemporary dance; *Style—* Peter Corbett, Esq; ✉ Flat 4, 7 Gambier Terrace, Hope St, Liverpool L1 7BJ (☎ 0151 709 4045)

CORBETT, Peter Richard; s of John Lionel Garton Corbett, of Hampshire and Isle of Mull, and Susan Irene Sibil, *née* Wykeham (d 1995); *b* 25 Feb 1945; *Educ* Radley; *m* 23 March 1968, Margaret Catherine, da of Richard Holiday Pott, OBE (d 1968); 2 s (Richard b 1972, Charles b 1976), 1 da (Catherine (Mrs Edward Brooke) b 1969); *Career* ptnr Pearsons 1974–86, dir John D Wood and Co; FRICS; *Recreations* shooting, Dorset Horn sheep; *Style—* Peter R Corbett, Esq; ✉ Dene House, Binley, St Mary Bourne, Hampshire SP11 6HA

CORBETT, Maj-Gen Sir Robert John Swan; KCVO (1994), CB (1991); s of Robert Hugh Swan Corbett (d 1988), of Boughton Monchelsea, and Yalding Hill, Kent, and Patricia Elizabeth Cavan-Lambart (d 1988); *b* 16 May 1940; *Educ* Shrewsbury; *m* 23 Sept 1966, Susan Margaret Anne, da of Brig Michael James Palmer O'Cock, CBE, MC, of Kington Langley, Wilts; 3 s (Tom b 6 Dec 1967, Jonathan b 30 May 1969, Michael b 7 June 1973); *Career* cmmnd 1959, Staff Coll Camberley 1972–73, Cdr Gds' Independent Parachute Co 1973–75, Adj Sandhurst 1975–78, 2 i/c 1 Bn Ir Gds 1978–79, US Armed Forces Staff Coll 1979–80, Bde Maj (Lt Col) Household Div 1980–81, Co 1 Bn Ir Gds 1981–84, Chief of Staff Br Forces Falkland Islands 1984–85, Cdr 5 Airborne bde 1985–87, Royal Coll of Def Studies 1987, Dir Def Prog MOD 1987–88, GOC and Cmdt Br Sector Berlin until German Unification 1990, GOC London Dist and Maj-Gen cmdg Household Div 1991–94; Regtl Lt-Col Irish Gds 1988, Hon Col London Irish Rifles 1992; memb Beirat (Advsy Bd) Deutsche Bank Berlin 1990; sec The Dulverton Tst 1994–; Freeman City of London 1961, Liveryman Worshipful Co of Vintners 1975; Hon Citizen Pierrefeu France 1993; MIMgt; *Books* Berlin and the British Ally 1945–1990 (1993); *Recreations* reading, travel, English parish church architecture; *Clubs* Buck's, Pratt's, Cavalry and Guards'; *Style—* Maj-Gen Sir Robert Corbett, KCVO, CB; ✉ c/o RHQ, Irish Guards, Wellington Barracks, London SW1E 6HQ

CORBETT, Robin; MP (Lab) Birmingham Erdington (majority 4,735); s of Thomas Corbett, of West Bromwich, Staffs, and Margaret Adele Mainwaring; *b* 22 Dec 1933; *Educ* Holly Lodge GS Smethwick; *m* 1970, Val Hudson; 1 s, 2 da; *Career* journalist 1954–69, sr Lab advsr IPC Magazines Ltd 1969–74; Parly candidate (Lab): Hemel Hempstead 1966 and Feb 1974, West Derbyshire (by-election) 1967; MP (Lab): Hemel Hempstead Oct 1974–1979, Birmingham Erdington 1983–; communications conslt 1979–83; chm PLP Home Affairs Gp 1983–85, jt sec Aust and NZ Parly Gp 1983–, W Midlands Lab Whip 1984–85, memb Select Ctee on Home Affrs 1983–85; oppn front bench spokesman: on home affrs 1985–92, on broadcasting, media and national heritage 1992–94, on disabled rights 1994–95; vice chm: All-party Motor Industry Gp 1987–, Friends of Cyprus 1987–; memb Agricultural Select Ctee; memb Cncl: RCVS 1989–92, Save The Children 1987–90; *Recreations* walking, collecting bric-à-brac; *Style—* Robin Corbett, Esq, MP; ✉ House of Commons, London SW1A 0AA (☎ 0171 219 5096)

CORBETT, Timothy William Edward; er s of Richard William Corbett, TD (d 1987), of Longnor, nr Shrewsbury, and Doris Vaughan, *née* Kimber (d 1991); descended from the Ven Joseph Plymley, archdeacon of Shropshire (d 1830), who assumed the surname and arms of Corbett by Royal Licence 1804, o s to the Longnor estates which had been in possession of a cadet branch of the Corbets of Caus Castle since early in the 17th century (*see* Burke's Landed Gentry, 18 edn, vol II, 1969); *b* 6 Nov 1935; *Educ* Eton, Univ of Aix-en-Provence, RAC Cirencester; *m* 27 Feb 1965, (Iza) Priscilla, 2 da of Lt-Col Stephen S Murcott, of Bridgnorth, Shropshire; 2 s (James Edward Isham b 14 Aug 1971, Thomas Alexander Caradoc b 23 July 1983), 2 da (Sophie Louisa b 10 June 1966, Isabelle Sarah b 1 Feb 1968); *Career* farmer; chm Shropshire Branch Nat Farmers' Union 1979; memb Shropshire CC 1981–85, independent memb Shrewsbury & Atcham BC 1994–; High Sheriff of Shropshire 1996–97; *Recreations* skiing, shooting, windsurfing, bridge, humorous conversation; *Style—* Timothy Corbett, Esq; ✉ Dower House, Longnor, nr Shrewsbury, Shropshire (☎ 01743 718628)

CORBETT, William Jesse (Bill); s of William Jesse Corbett (d 1960), of Birmingham, and Dora, *née* Ruffles; *b* 21 Feb 1938; *Educ* Billesley Secdy Modern Sch; *Career* children's writer; formerly employed as: factory worker, merchant navy galley-boy, army physical trg instr, furniture remover, building worker; *Books* incl: The Song of Pentecost (Whitbread Prize, 1982), Pentecost and the Chosen One (1984), The End of the Tale (1985), Pentecost of Lickey Top (1987), The Bear Who Stood on His Head (1988), Dear Grumble (1989), Toby's Iceberg (1990), Little Elephant (1991), Duck Soup Farm (1992), The Dragon Brothers (1993), The Grandson Boy (1993), Hamish (1995); *Recreations* reading, music (loud symphonies), solitude; *Style—* Bill Corbett, Esq; ✉ Murray Pollinger Literary Agent, 222 Old Brompton Rd, London SW5 0BZ (☎ 0171 373 4711)

CORBIN, Jane; da of Aubrey George Corbin (d 1989), and Olive May, *née* Amery; *b* 16 July 1954; *Educ* King's Coll London (BA); *m*; 2 c; *Career* television correspondent and presenter; early career with Granada TV and Thames TV, foreign corr Channel 4 News 1983–88; BBC Television News & Current Affrs 1988–; sr corr Panorama (BBC1) 1988–; presenter: Behind the Headlines (BBC2) 1991–93, The Money Programme (BBC2) 1995–96; corr Election Night Special 1992, occasional presenter BBC news bulletins; *Assignments* for Channel 4 News incl: US presidential election 1984, assassination of Indira Gandhi (last journalist to interview her) and subseqent election of Rajiv Gandhi 1984–85, return of Benazir Bhutto to Pakistan 1988; for Panorama incl: fall of the Berlin Wall 1989, environmental effect of Chernobyl disaster 1990, Red Army's quashing of Azerbaijani rebellion, Cambodia ten years after Year Zero 1988, Iraqi weapons of mass destruction progs 1989–93, newly liberated Kuwait 1991, Iranian nuclear weapons prog 1993, Bosnia 1993, Norwegian involvement in Israeli/Palestinian peace accord (The Norway Channel) 1993, return of Yasser Arafat to Gaza 1994, investigation of war crimes at Srebrenica Bosnia 1996; *Awards* four RTS TV Journalism Awards, Rainier Award Monte Carlo TV Festival (for The Poisoned Land, The Dying Sea) 1990, Emmy nomination for Best Investigative Journalist (for Saddam's Secret Arms Ring) 1992; *Books* The Norway Channel (1994); *Recreations* sleeping, gardening, cooking; *Style—* Ms Jane Corbin; ✉ BBC Television, White City, 201 Wood Lane, London W12 7TS (☎ 0181 752 7100)

CORBY, Sir (Frederick) Brian; kt (1989); s of Charles Walter Corby (d 1984), of Raunds, Northants, and Millicent, *née* Pentelow; *b* 10 May 1929; *Educ* Kimbolton Sch, St John's Coll Cambridge (MA); *m* 1 Aug 1952, Elizabeth Mairi, da of Dr Archibald McInnes (d 1973); 1 s (Nicholas b 1960), 2 da (Fiona b 1955, Jane b 1957); *Career* chm: Prudential Corporation plc 1990–May 1995 (gp chief exec 1982–90), Prudential Assurance Co Ltd 1982–90, Mercantile and General Reinsurance Co plc 1985–90; dir Bank of England 1985–93, pres CBI 1990–92, pres NIESR 1994–; chm South Bank Bd 1990 ; chllr Univ of Herts 1992–96; Hon DSc City Univ London 1989; FIA 1955; Hon DLitt Cncl for Nat Academic Awards 1991; *Recreations* golf, gardening, reading; *Style—* Sir Brian Corby; ✉ Prudential Corporation plc, 142 Holborn Bars, London EC1N 2NH (☎ 0171 405 9222)

CORBY, Peter John Siddons; s of John Siddons Corby (d 1955), and Helen Anna, *née* Ratray (d 1974); *b* 8 July 1924; *Educ* Taplow GS; *m* 1, 1950 (m dis 1959), Gail Susan Clifford-Marshall; 2 s (Mark b 1950, Michael b 1951); m 2, 1960, Ines Rosemary, da of Dr George Anderson Mandow (d 1991); 1 s (John b 1962); *Career* RAFVR 1942–48, War Serv Aircrew 4 Gp Bomber Cmd, transferred Class E Reserve RAFVRT 1948, resigned 1951; created manufactured and marketed many products incl The Corby Electric Trouser Press (1961); non-exec dir various cos 1950–96; Freeman City of London 1977, Liveryman Worshipful Co of Marketors 1978; FInstD 1955, memb Lloyd's 1974–96; *Recreations* sailing, bridge; *Clubs* Oriental, Ocean Cruising, Yacht Club de France; *Style—* Peter Corby, Esq; ✉ The Sloop, 89 High St, Cowes, Isle of Wight PO31 7AW (☎ 01983 292188, fax 01983 291598)

CORBYN, Jeremy Bernard; MP (Lab) Islington North (majority 12,784); s of David Benjamin Corbyn, and Naomi Loveday, *née* Jocelyn; *b* 26 May 1949; *Educ* Adams GS Newport Shropshire; *m* Claudia Bracchitta; 3 s (Benjamin, Sebastian, Thomas); *Career* memb Haringey Borough Cncl 1974–83, NUPE area offr 1975–83; MP (Lab) Islington N 1983–, memb Select Ctee on Social Security 1991–; chm: London Gp of Lab MPs 1992–, PLP Health and Social Security Ctee 1985–89, PLP Northern Ireland Ctee 1985–89 and 1990–; *Recreations* running, gardening, reading, keeping chickens; *Style—* Jeremy Corbyn, Esq, MP; ✉ House of Commons, London SW1A 0AA

CORDINER, William Lawson (Bill); OBE (1995); s of Alex Lamb Cordiner (d 1964), of Edinburgh, and Jessie Lawson, *née* Brownlie (d 1970); *b* 9 March 1935; *Educ* Peterhead Acad, Boroughmuir Edinburgh; *m* 8 March 1958, Anne, da of Herbert Milton (d 1984); 1 s (Neil Stuart b 30 June 1974); *Career* Inland Revenue: joined 1952, seconded to E African Income Tax Dept 1960, resigned as sr collector 1967; HM Dip Serv: FCO 1967–68, accountant Saigon 1968–71, commercial attaché and vice consul Addis Ababa 1971–74, economic sec Kuwait 1974–76, commercial sec Baghdad 1976–78, seconded to DHSS Exports Promotion ME 1978–79, Rhodesia Dept FCO 1979–80, dep rep Br Govt Antigua and St Kitts Nevis (later Br High Cmmr's rep Antigua and Barbuda) 1980–83, consul (commercial) Seattle 1983–88, FCO 1988–90 (sec Br Delgn to Cwlth Heads of Govt Meeting Kuala Lumpur 1989), High Cmmr Kingdom of Tonga and consul Pacific Islands (US Territories South of the Equator) 1990–94, ret; Hon Ambassador of Goodwill Washington State (USA) 1987, Hon Citizen of Washington State (USA) 1987; *Recreations* golf, gardening, oil painting; *Clubs* Royal Cwlth Soc, Chateau des Vigiers Golf and Country (France); *Style—* Bill Cordiner, Esq, OBE; ✉ c/o FCO, King Charles St, London SW1

CORDINGLEY, Maj Gen John Edward; OBE (1959); s of Air Vice Marshal Sir John Walter Cordingley, KCB, KCVO, CBE (d 1977), and Elizabeth Ruth, *née* Carpenter (d 1938); *b* 1 Sept 1916; *Educ* Sherborne, RMA Woolwich; *m* 1, 8 Feb 1940 (m dis 1961), Ruth Pamela, yr da of Maj Sydney Alexander Boddam-Whetham, DSO, MC, RA (d 1925); 2 s (Michael, Maj Gen Patrick Cordingley, *qv*); m 2, 1961, Audrey Helen Anne, da of Maj Gen Frederick George Beaumont-Nesbitt, CVO, CBE, MC (d 1971), and formerly w of Maj Gordon Rennie (d 1984); 2 step da; *Career* cmmnd 2 Lt RA 1936, served WWII Europe and Far East, Bde Cdr 1961–62, IDC 1963, Dir Work Study MOD 1964–66, Dep Dir RA 1967–68, Maj-Gen RA BAOR 1968–71, ret; bursar Sherborne Sch 1971–73; Col Cmdt RA 1973–81, regtl comptroller RA 1975–82 and 1984–85; dir J W Carpenter 1977–89 (chm 1984–87); Liveryman Worshipful Co of Ironmongers; MIMgt, FInstD; *Recreations* golf, gardening; *Clubs* Army and Navy, Senior Golfers'; *Style*— Maj Gen John Cordingley, OBE; ✉ Church Farm House, Rotherwick, Nr Basingstoke, Hants RG27 9BG (☎ 0125 676 2734)

CORDINGLEY, Maj Gen Patrick Anthony John; DSO (1991); s of Maj Gen John Edward Cordingley, *qv*, and Ruth Pamela, *née* Boddam-Whetham; *b* 6 Oct 1944; *Educ* Sherborne, RMA Sandhurst; *m* 1968, Melissa, da of James Eric Crawley, OBE; 2 da (Antonia b 1972, Miranda b 1974); *Career* CO 5 Royal Inniskilling Dragoon Gds 1985–87 (cmmnd 1965), Bde Cdr 7 Armd Bde (Desert Rats) 1988–91, GOC 2nd Division 1992–96, sr Br Loan Serv Offr Sultanate of Oman 1996–; Bronze Star (US) 1991; Freeman: City of London, Worshipful Co of Ironmongers; OStJ 1992; FRGS; *Books* Captain Oates: Soldier and Explorer (1982), In the Eye of the Storm (1996); *Recreations* riding, windsurfing, skiing; *Clubs* Cavalry and Guards'; *Style*— Maj Gen Patrick Cordingley, DSO; ✉ Office of HH The Deputy Prime Minister for Security and Defence, PO Box 113, Muscat, Sultanate of Oman

CORDINGLY, Dr David Michael Bradley; s of Rt Rev Eric William Bradley Cordingly, MBE (d 1976), and Mary Eileen, *née* Mathews; *b* 5 Dec 1938; *Educ* Christ's Hosp, Oriel Coll Oxford (MA), Univ of Sussex (DPhil); *m* 8 May 1971, Shirley Elizabeth, da of Ian Gibson Robin and Shelagh Marian, *née* Croft; 1 s (Matthew), 1 da (Rebecca); *Career* graphic designer and typographer 1960–66, teacher in Jamaica 1966–67, exhibition designer British Museum 1968–71, keeper of Art Gallery and Museum Brighton 1971–78, asst dir The Museum of London 1978–80; Nat Maritime Museum: asst keeper 1980–86, keeper of pictures 1986–89, head of exhibitions 1989–93; writer and exhibition organiser 1993–; contrib articles: Burlington Magazine, The Connoisseur, Apollo Magazine, History Today; FRSA 1974; Order of the White Rose (Finland) 1986; *Books* Marine Painting in England (1974), Painters of the Sea (1979), The Art of the Van de Veldes (1982), Nicholas Pocock (1986), Captain James Cook, Navigator (ed, 1988), Pirates, Fact and Fiction (1992), Life among the Pirates: the Romance and The Reality (1995); *Style*— Dr David Cordingly; ✉ 2 Vine Place, Brighton, Sussex BN1 3HE

CORDREY, Peter Graham; s of Wing-Cdr Percival William George Cordrey, and Marjorie Joan, *née* Strickland; *b* 1 June 1947; *Educ* Wellingborough Sch, City Univ (MSc); *m* 1972, Carol Anne, da of Peter Lawrence Ashworth; 2 da (Joanne b 1979, Rowena b 1982); *Career* merchant banker and chartered accountant; head of banking Singer & Friedlander Ltd (dir Bank 1982); dir: First British American Corporation Ltd, Singer & Friedlander Leasing Ltd, Singer & Friedlander (Isle of Man) Ltd, Benchmark Group plc; *Recreations* tennis, golf, swimming; *Clubs* St George's Hill Tennis; *Style*— Peter Cordrey, Esq; ✉ Singer & Friedlander Ltd, 21 New Street, Bishopsgate, London EC2M 4HR (☎ 0171 623 3000, fax 0171 623 2122)

CORDY, Timothy Soames (Tim); s of John Knutt Cordy, and Margaret Winifred, *née* Sheward; *b* 17 May 1949; *Educ* Dragon Sch Oxford, Sherborne, Univ of Durham (BA), Univ of Glasgow (MPhil); *m* 1974, Dr Jill Margaret Tattersall; 2 c; *Career* asst city planning offr Leicester City Cncl 1980–85 (joined 1974), Communaute Urbaine de Strasbourg 1978–79, asst chief exec Bolton Municipal Borough Cncl 1985–87, chief exec Royal Soc for Nature Conservation 1987–94, dir Town and Country Planning Assoc 1994–; author of articles on housing renewal, local econ devpt and nature conservation; memb bd: UK 2000, Volunteer Centre UK; MRTPI 1976, FRSA 1991; *Recreations* music, food, France; *Style*— Tim Cordy, Esq; ✉ Town and Country Planning Association, 17 Carlton House Terrace, London SW1Y 5AS

CORDY-SIMPSON, Lt Gen Roderick Alexander; CB (1993), OBE (1984); s of Col John Roger Cordy-Simpson, CBE, MC (d 1979), of Shorne, Kent, and Ursula Margaret, *née* West; *b* 29 Feb 1944; *Educ* Radley; *m* 21 Dec 1974, Virginia Rosemary, da of Col Peter Jarrat Lewis (d 1983), of Thurston, Suffolk; 1 s (Angus b 1978), 1 da (Zoë b 1976); *Career* cmd 13/18 Royal Hussars 1983–86 (joined 1963), Cdr 4 Armoured Brigade 1988–90, chief of staff UN Bosnia Hercegovina 1992–93, chief of staff HQ BAOR 1993–94, GOC 1 Armoured Division 1994–96, Dep Cdr NATO Implementation Force Bosnia Hercegovina 1996–; *Recreations* skiing, shooting, reading; *Clubs* Cavalry and Guards; *Style*— Lt Gen Roderick Cordy-Simpson, CB, OBE; ✉ c/o Coutts & Co, 440 Strand, London WC2R 0QS

COREN, Alan; s of Samuel and Martha Coren; *b* 27 June 1938; *Educ* East Barnet GS, Wadham Coll Oxford, Univ of Yale, Univ of California at Berkeley; *m* 14 Oct 1963, Anne, da of Michael Kasriel (d 1981), of London; 1 s (Giles b 1969), 1 da (Victoria b 1972); *Career* writer/broadcaster; Punch: joined 1963, asst ed until 1966, literary ed 1966–69, dep ed 1969–77, ed 1978–87; TV critic The Times 1971–78, ed The Listener 1988–90; columnist: Daily Mail 1972–76, Mail on Sunday 1984–92, The Times 1988–, Sunday Express 1992–; contribs incl: Sunday Times, TLS, Observer, Spectator, Tatler; rector St Andrew's Univ 1973–76; Hon DLitt Nottingham 1993; *Books* The Dog It Was That Died (1965), All Except the Bastard (1969), The Sanity Inspector (1974), The Bulletins of Idi Amin (1974), Golfing for Cats (1974), The Further Bulletins of Idi Amin (1975), The Lady From Stalingrad Mansions (1977), The Peanut Papers (1977), The Rhinestone as Big as the Ritz (1979), Tissues for Men (1980), The Best of Alan Coren (1980), The Cricklewood Diet (1982), Present Laughter (1982), The Penguin Book of Modern Humour (ed, 1983), Bumf (1984), Something for the Weekend (1986), Bin Ends (1987), Seems Like Old Times (1989), More Like Old Times (1990), A Year in Cricklewood (1991), Toujours Cricklewood? (1993), Animal Passions (ed, 1994), A Bit on the Side (1995), The Alan Coren Omnibus (1996); The Pick of Punch (ed annual, 1979–89), The Punch Book of Short Stories: Book 1 (ed, 1979), Book 2 (1980), Book 3 (1981); TV series The Losers (1978); *Recreations* broadcasting, riding, bridge; *Style*— Alan Coren, Esq; ✉ Robson Books, Bolsover House, 5/6 Clipstone St, London W1P 7EB

COREN, Anne; da of Michael Maximilian Kasriel (d 1981), and Isabel, *née* Koss; *Educ* North London Collegiate Sch, Royal Free Hosp Sch of Med Univ of London (MB BS); *m* 14 Oct 1963, Alan Coren, *qv*, s of Sam Coren (d 1989); 1 s (Giles b 1969), 1 da (Victoria b 1972); *Career* Nat Heart Hosp, Charing Cross Hosp, sr registrar Middx Hosp, currently conslt anaesthetist Moorfields Eye Hosp; memb: Assoc of Anaesthetists, RSM; fell Coll of Anaesthetists, FFARCS; *Recreations* family life, travel, bridge; *Style*— Mrs Anne Coren; ✉ c/o Moorfields Eye Hospital, City Road, London EC1V 2PD (☎ 0171 435 8938)

CORFIELD, Rt Hon Sir Frederick Vernon; kt (1972), PC (1970), QC (1972); o s of late Brig Frederick Alleyne Corfield, DSO, OBE, IA (d 1939), of Chatwall Hall, Leebotwood, Salop, and Mary Graham, *née* Vernon (d 1968); *b* 1 June 1915; *Educ* Cheltenham, RMA Woolwich; *m* 1945, Elizabeth Mary Ruth, yr da of Edmund Coston Taylor, JP, of Arden, Church Stretton, Salop; *Career* WWII served RA (despatches, POW); called to the Bar Middle Temple 1945; bencher of the Middle Temple; MP (C) S Glos 1955–74, jt Parly sec Miny Housing and Local Govt 1962–64, min state BOT June-Oct 1970, min Aviation Supply 1970–71, min Aerospace DTI 1971–72; recorder of the Crown Ct 1979–87; vice chm Br Waterways Bd 1980–83 (memb 1974–83); dir: Mid-Kent Water Co, Mid Kent Hldgs plc (ret 1991); chm LAPDA 1975–89; *Books* Compensation & The Town & Country Planning Act 1959, The Community Land Act 1975, Compensation & The Compulsory Acquisition of Land (with R Carnwath, 1976); *Clubs* Army and Navy; *Style*— The Rt Hon Sir Frederick Corfield, QC; ✉ Wordings Orchard, Sheepscombe, nr Stroud, Glos GL6 7RE

CORFIELD, Eur Ing Sir Kenneth George; kt (1980); s of Stanley Corfield, and Dorothy Elizabeth, *née* Mason; *b* 27 Jan 1924; *Educ* Wolverhampton Poly; *m* 1960; 1 da; *Career* formerly with ICI Metals, md K G Corfield Ltd 1950–60; formerly: exec dir Parkinson Cowan, dep chm STC; dir Midland Bank 1979–91, tstee Sci Museum 1975–91, pres Telecommunications Engrg Mfrs' Assoc 1974–80, vice pres Engrg Employers' Fedn 1979–85; former memb Cncl: CBI, IOD; vice pres BIM 1978, first chm Br Engrg Cncl 1982–84, chm Standard Telephones and Cables plc 1979–85 (dir 1969–85), vice pres ITT Europe Inc 1967–85, sr offr International Telephone and Telegraph Corporation (UK) 1974–85, memb Advsy Cncl for Applied R&D 1981–84; dir: Britoil Ltd 1982–88; Octagon Group 1987–, Distributed Information Processing Ltd 1987–; chm Tanks Consolidated Investments PLC, memb Bd Companhia Do Caminho de Ferro de Benquela 1990–; memb Mgmnt Cncl Templeton Coll (Oxford Centre for Mgmnt Studies); Freeman City of London; Liveryman: Worshipful Co of Engrs, Worshipful Co of Scientific Instrument Makers; Hon DUniv Surrey 1976; Hon DSc: City Univ 1981, Univ of Bath 1982, Univ of London 1982, Aston Univ 1985; Hon DLL Univ of Strathclyde 1982, Hon DEng Univ of Bradford 1983, Hon Degree Open Univ 1985, Hon DSc Technology Loughborough Univ of Technol 1983; past pres IOD; Eur Ing, CEng, FEng 1979, FIMechE, CBIM; Hon FIEE; *Recreations* photography, music; *Clubs* Carlton; *Style*— Sir Kenneth Corfield, FEng; ✉ 8 John St, London WC1N 2ES

CORK, Dominic Gerald; *b* 7 Aug 1971; *Career* professional cricketer; Derbyshire CCC: debut 1990, county cap 1993; England: former memb U19 team, A team to West Indies 1991–92, A team to Aust, A team to S Africa, first team v W Indies 1995 (took hat-trick), first team tour S Africa 1995/96, memb squad World Cup India and Pakistan 1995, memb tour New Zealand 1997; 8 one day ints; Cricket Association Young Player of the Year 1991, Professional Cricketers' Assoc Player of the Year 1995; *Style*— Dominic Cork, Esq; ✉ Derbyshire CCC, County Ground, Nottingham Road, Derby DE2 6DA (☎ 01332 383211, fax 01332 290251)

CORK, Richard Graham; s of Hubert Henry Cork, of Bath, and Beatrice Hester, *née* Smale; *b* 25 March 1947; *Educ* Kingswood Sch Bath, Trinity Hall Cambridge (BA, MA, PhD); *m* 1970, Vena, da of James Jackson; 2 s (Adam James b 1974, Joe John b 1980), 2 da (Polly Beatrice b 1975, Katy Anna b 1978); *Career* author, critic, historian, exhibition organiser and broadcaster; art critic: Evening Standard 1969–77 and 1980–83, The Listener 1984–90, The Times 1991–; Lethaby lectr RCA 1974, ed Studio International 1975–79, Durning-Lawrence lectr UCL 1987, Slade prof of fine art Univ of Cambridge 1989–90, Henry Moore fell Courtauld Inst of Art 1992–95; John Llewelyn Rhys Meml Prize 1976, Sir Banister Fletcher Award 1985, Nat Art Collections Fund Award 1995; memb: Ctee Contemporary Art Soc, Fine Arts Advsy Ctee British Cncl, Editorial Bd Tate - The Art Magazine, Advsy Ctee Hayward Gallery; chm Visual Arts Advsy Panel Arts Cncl 1995; tstee Public Art Devpt Tst until 1996; *Exhibitions* organiser of various exhbns incl: Critic's Choice (Tooth Gallery) 1973, Beyond Painting and Sculpture (Arts Cncl) 1973, Vorticism and Its Allies (Hayward Gallery) 1974, Sculpture Now = Dissolution or Redefinition? (RCA) 1974, Art for Whom? (Serpentine Gallery) 1978, David Bomberg Retrospective (Tate Gallery) 1988, The Last Days of Mankind (Altes Museum Berlin) 1994, A Bitter Truth (Barbican Art Gallery) 1994; co-organiser: Arte Inglese Oggi (Palazzo Reale Milan) 1976, Un Certain Art Anglais (Musée d'Art Moderne Paris) 1979, British Art in the Twentieth Century (Royal Acad) 1987, The British Art Show 4 (Manchester, Edinburgh and Cardiff) 1995–96; *Books* Vorticism and Abstract Art in the First Machine Age (vol 1 1975, vol 2 1976), The Social Role of Art: Essays in Criticism for a Newspaper Public (1979), Art Beyond the Gallery in Early Twentieth Century England (1985), David Bomberg (1987), Architect's Choice: Art in Architecture in Great Britain since 1945 (with Eugene Rosenberg, 1992), A Bitter Truth: Avant-Garde Art and the Great War (1994); *Recreations* looking at art, enjoying my family; *Style*— Richard Cork, Esq; ✉ 24 Milman Rd, London NW6 6EG

CORK, Roger William; The Rt Hon the Lord Mayor of London; s of Sir Kenneth Russell Cork, GBE (d 1991), Lord Mayor of London 1978–79, and Nina, *née* Lippold; *b* 31 March 1947; *Educ* St Martin's Sch Northwood, Uppingham; *m* 9 May 1970, Barbara Anita Pauline (d 1996), da of Reginald Harper (d 1992), of Herne Bay; 1 s (Christopher b 1971), 2 da (Melissa b 1973, Georgina b 1974); *Career* chartered accountant; articled clerk Moore Stephens & Co 1965–69; ptnr: W H Cork Gully 1970 (joined 1969, W H Cork Gully changed to Cork Gully 1980 and associated with Coopers & Lybrand 1980), Cork Gully 1980–93, Coopers & Lybrand 1980–93, Moore Stephens 1994–, Moore Stephens Booth White 1995–; City of London: Freeman 1972, JP 1983–, Alderman Tower Ward 1983– (Common Councilman 1978–83), Sheriff 1992–93, Lord Mayor of London Nov 1996–Nov 1997; master Billingsgate Ward Club 1980–81, pres Tower Ward Club 1984– (fndr memb 1970); vice pres: Inst of Credit Mgmnt 1989– (chm 1985–87), City of London Branch Br Red Cross 1991– (jt chm City of London Christmas Market 1990–91); fndr pres Fedn of Euro Credit Mgmnt Assocs 1986; pres: City of London Branch Inst of Directors 1991– (chm 1987–91), Soc of Young Freemen 1994–; memb Exec Ctee Bucks Assoc of Youth Clubs, memb PCC St Mary at Hill, memb PCC and churchwarden St Olaves, churchwarden St Andrew Hubbard, tstee Tower Hill Tst, chm of tstees All Hallows Devpt Tst, memb City of London Archaeological Tst, chm of govrs St Dunstan's Coll Educnl Fndn 1991–; hon memb Ct HAC 1983–; Liveryman Worshipful Co of Bowyers (Master 1990–92); memb Ct of Assts: Worshipful Co of Chartered Accountants 1992–, Co of World Traders 1992–, Worshipful Co of Butchers 1996–; Hon Liveryman Worshipful Co of Environmental Cleaners 1993; OStJ; FCA, FIPA, FICM, FInstD; *Recreations* sailing, photography, DIY; *Clubs* Livery, Hardway Sailing, RYA; *Style*— The Rt Hon the Lord Mayor of London; ✉ Mansion House, London EC4N 8BH (☎ 0171 626 2500, fax 0171 623 9524); c/o Moore Stephens, 1 Snow Hill, London EC1A 2EN (☎ 0171 334 0334, fax 0171 528 9934, telex 884610 UNHARM, car 0860 311610); Rabbs, The Lee, Great Missenden, Bucks HP16 9NX (☎ 01494 837296)

CORK AND ORRERY, 14 Earl of (I 1620); John William Boyle; DSC (1945), VRD (1952); also Baron Boyle of Marston (GB 1711), Baron Boyle of Youghal (I 1616), Viscount Dungarvan (I 1620), Viscount Boyle of Kinalmeaky, Baron of Bandon Bridge and Baron Boyle of Broghill (I 1628), Earl of Orrery (I 1660); s of Hon Reginald Courtenay Boyle, MBE, MC (d 1946), and Violet, *née* Flower (d 1974); granted title, rank and precedence of an Earl's son 1967; suc bro 13 Earl of Cork and Orrery 1995; *b* 12 May 1916; *Educ* Harrow, King's Coll London (BScEng); *m* 16 Oct 1943, Mary Leslie, da of Gen Sir Robert Gordon-Finlayson, KCB, CMG, DSO (d 1956); 3 s (Viscount Dungarvan b 1945, Hon Robert William b 1948, Hon (Charles) Reginald b 1957); *Heir* s, Viscount Dungarvan, *qv*; *Career* sits as Baron Boyle of Marston in House of Lords; served WWII (despatches twice), Lt Cdr RNVR, six years active service with RN in western theatres; former conslt with Sir Alexander Gibb & Partners and others; CEng, FICE (ret), MIMechE (ret); *Recreations* country and family life, making and mending, reading; *Clubs* Lansdowne; *Style*— The Rt Hon the Earl of Cork and Orrery, DSC; ✉ Nether Craigantaggart, Dunkeld, Perthshire PH8 0HQ (☎ and fax 01738 710239)

CORK, CLOYNE AND ROSS, Bishop of 1988–; Rt Rev Robert Alexander Warke; s of Alexander Warke (d 1956), of Dublin, and Annie, *née* Pennington (d 1989); *b* 10 July 1930; *Educ* Mountmellick Nat sch, The King's Hosp, Univ of Dublin (BA, BD, capt 1st XI Hockey, capt Irish Univs' Hockey Team), Union Theol Seminary NY; *m* 10 Sept 1964, Eileen, da of George Skillen; 2 da (Jane b 24 Feb 1966, Ruth b 26 Oct 1968);

Career curate: Newtownards 1953–55, St Catherine's Dublin 1956–59, Rathfarnham Dublin 1959–64; Union Theol Seminary NY 1959–60; rector: Dunlavin (Co Wicklow) 1964–67, Drumcondra and North Strand Dublin 1968–71, Zion Parish Dublin 1971–80; archdeacon of Dublin 1980–88; *Books* St Nicholas, Church and Parish, Dunlavin (1967), Light at Evening Time (1986), Ripples in the Pool (1993); *Recreations* golf, reading, theatre; *Clubs* Rathfarnham Golf (Dublin); *Style*— The Rt Rev the Bishop of Cork, Cloyne and Ross; ✉ The Palace, Bishop Street, Cork, Republic of Ireland (☎ 00 353 21 316114, fax 00 353 21 273437); Cork, Cloyne and Ross Diocesan Office, 14 Cove Street, Cork, Republic of Ireland (☎ 00 353 21 272262, fax 00 353 21 968467)

CORKERY, Michael; QC (1981); s of Charles Timothy Corkery (d 1968), of London, and Nellie Marie, *née* Royal; *b* 20 May 1926; *Educ* King's Sch Canterbury; *m* 29 July 1967, Juliet Shore, da of Harold Glyn Foulkes (d 1966), of Shrewsbury; 1 s (Nicholas b 8 June 1968), 1 da (Charlotte b 29 May 1970); *Career* Lt Welsh Gds 1945–48; called to the Bar Lincoln's Inn 1949, bencher 1973, treasurer 1992; jr treasury counsel 1959–70, sr treasury counsel 1970, first sr treasury counsel Central Criminal Ct 1979–81; *Recreations* fishing, shooting, sailing, music, gardening; *Clubs* Cavalry and Guards', Hurlingham, Itchenor Sailing, Guards' Polo, Household Division Yacht, Friends of Arundel Cricket; *Style*— Michael Corkery, Esq, QC; ✉ 5 Paper Buildings, Temple, London EC4 (☎ 0171 583 6117)

CORKREY, Michael Christopher; s of Thomas Edward Lawrence Corkrey, of Moulsoe, Bucks, and Carole Martha, *née* Snape; *b* 24 Nov 1962; *Educ* Wootton Upper Sch, Bedford Coll of HE (DA), Leeds Poly (BA), Royal Acad Schs (post-dip in painting, Henfield Award, Worshipful Co of Painter-Stainers' Prize, De Segonzac Travelling Scholarship); *Career* artist; *Group exhibitions* John Player Portrait Award Exhbn (Nat Portrait Gall) 1986, 1987 and 1989, BP Portrait Award Exhbn (Nat Portrait Gall) 1990, 1991 and 1992, Three Young Painters (New Grafton Gall) 1990, Portrait Painters (Wyndham Fine Art) 1992, 1993 and 1994, Five (Atlantis Gall) 1993, Hunting/Observer Art Prizes Exhbn 1993, Hunting Group Art Prizes Exhbn 1994 and 1995, Figure it Out (Harrogate Art Gallery) 1996; *Portraits* incl: Jeffrey Bernard 1992, Keith Miller 1993, The Earl Spencer 1993; *Awards* Elizabeth Greenshield Fndn Award 1990, First Prize Hunting Gp Art Prizes 1994; *Style*— Michael Corkrey, Esq; ✉ 143 Kennington Park Road, London SE11 4JJ

CORLETT, Clive William; CB (1995); s of Frederick William Corlett (d 1973), of Bebington, Wirral, and Hanna Corlett; *b* 14 June 1938; *Educ* Birkenhead Sch, BNC Oxford (BA); *m* 15 Feb 1964, Margaret Catherine, da of John Mathew Jones (d 1977), of Moelfre, Anglesey; 1 s (Stephen b 1975); *Career* joined Inland Revenue 1960; seconded to: Civil Serv Selection Bd 1970, HM Treasy 1972–74 (as private sec to Chllr of the Exchequer) and 1979–81; Bd of Inland Revenue: under sec 1985–91, dep sec 1992–93, dir gen and cmmr 1993, dep chm 1994–; *Recreations* walking, theatre; *Style*— Clive W Corlett, Esq, CB; ✉ Board of Inland Revenue, Somerset House, Strand, London, WC2

CORLETT, The Rev Dr Ewan Christian Brew; OBE; s of Malcolm James John Corlett (d 1956), and Catherine Ann, *née* Brew (d 1964); *b* 11 Feb 1923; *Educ* King William's Coll IOM, Univ of Oxford (MA), Univ of Durham (PhD); *m* 1945, Edna Lilian, da of Arthur James Buggs, of Bromley, Kent; 3 s (Nigel, Brian, Malcolm); *Career* naval architect; chm and md Burness Corlett and Partners 1952–88 (naval architects and marine conslts); originator of and vice pres and naval architect to SS GB Project; ordained Sodor and Man: deacon 1991, priest 1992; asst curate Kirk Maughold, sec Diocesan Advsy Ctee and Diocesan church cmmr; tstee Nat Maritime Museum Greenwich 1975–92; past Prime Warden Worshipful Co of Shipwrights; pres Ramsey RNLI, hon vice pres Royal Inst of Naval Architects (past chm Cncl); World Ship Tst Award 1996; FEng 1978, FRINA, FIMarE, FRIN, FNI; *Recreations* yachting (yacht 'Stronnag'), model shipbuilding, astronomy, painting; *Clubs* Manx Sailing and Cruising; *Style*— The Rev Dr Ewan Corlett, OBE, FEng; ✉ Cottimans, Port-e-Vullen, Ramsey, Isle of Man IM7 1AP (☎ 01624 814009); BCH Ltd, Masonic Buildings, Ramsey, IOM (fax 01624 817248)

CORLEY, Sir Kenneth Sholl Ferrand; kt (1972); s of late Sidney Walter Corley, of London, and late A L Corley; *b* 3 Nov 1908; *Educ* St Bees Cumberland; *m* 1937, Olwen Mary, da of Maurice Hart Yeoman, of London; 1 s, 1 da; *Career* chm and chief exec Joseph Lucas (Industries) Ltd 1969–73 (joined 1927); Chevalier de la Legion D'Honneur; *Clubs* Royal Automobile; *Style*— Sir Kenneth Corley

CORLEY, Paul; *b* 1950; *Educ* Bablake Sch Coventry, Worcester Coll Oxford (BA); *Career* graduate trainee journalist Westminster Press 1972–75, sr feature writer Thomson Newspapers Newcastle upon Tyne 1975, journalist Look North BBC North East 1976–78, regnl features prodr BBC North East 1978–80, current affrs prodr BBC TV London 1980–82, prodr The Tube live music magazine prog (winner various int awards incl TV Times special award for innovaton) Tyne Tees TV Newcastle upon Tyne 1982–84, dir of progs and exec prodr of all network progs Border TV Carlisle 1984–91, dir of progs North East TV (bidding for NE franchise) 1991, controller of factual progs Carlton Television 1991–95, md Carlton Broadcasting 1995–96, controller of factual progs ITV Network 1996–; *Style*— Paul Corley, Esq; ✉ ITV Network Centre, 200 Gray's Inn Road, London WC1X 8HF (☎ 0171 843 8000, fax 0171 843 8157)

CORLEY, Peter Maurice Sinclair; s of James Maurice Corley (d 1975), and Barbara Shearer, *née* Sinclair; *b* 15 June 1933; *Educ* Marlborough, King's Coll Cambridge (MA); *m* 11 March 1961, Dr Marjorie Constance Corley, da of William John Doddridge (d 1982); 2 da (Carolyn b 1963, Rosalind b 1968); *Career* entered civil serv 1957, commercial sec Brussels 1969–71, dir gen Econ Cooperation Office Riyadh 1976–78, under sec DTI 1981–93, regnl policy conslt 1993–; *Recreations* bookbinding; *Clubs* Oxford and Cambridge; *Style*— Peter Corley, Esq; ✉ c/o Oxford and Cambridge Club, 71 Pall Mall, London SW1

CORLEY, Roger David; CBE (1993); s of Thomas Arthur Corley (d 1989), and Erica, *née* Trent; *b* 13 April 1933; *Educ* Hymers Coll Kingston upon Hull, Univ of Manchester (BSc); *m* 14 May 1964, Dr Brigitte, da of Leo Hubert Anton Roeder (d 1977); 3 s (Martin b 1966, Kevin b 1969, Steffan b 1971); *Career* Nat Serv Sub Lt RNVR 1954–56; Clerical Medical and General Life Assurance Society: joined 1956, investmt mangr 1961–72, actuary 1972–80, dir 1975–, dep gen mangr 1980–82, gen mangr 1982, md 1991–95; chm: Pharos SA, St Andrew's Group plc; dir: Lands Improvement Holding plc, Korea Asia Fund, Med Defence Union Ltd, Br Heart Fndn, City of Westminster Arts Cncl; memb Fin Services Cmmn (Gibraltar); Inst of Actuaries: fell 1960, memb Cncl 1976–94, hon sec 1980–82, vice pres 1985–88, pres 1988–90; memb Cncl Int Actuarial Assoc 1983– (vice pres 1990–); Freeman City of London 1979, memb Court Worshipful Co of Actuaries 1985– (Liveryman 1979, Sr Warden 1991–92, Master 1992–93); FIA 1960, AIIMR 1965, ASA 1970, DGVM 1975, FRSA 1990, CIMgt 1994; *Recreations* music, theatre, opera, visual arts, books, travel; *Clubs* Army and Navy, IOD, Gallio, Actuaries; *Style*— Roger Corley, Esq, CBE; ✉ Clerical, Medical and General Life Assurance Society, 15 St James's Square, London SW1Y 4LQ (☎ 0171 930 5474, fax 0181 731 7628)

CORMACK, Ian Donald; s of Andrew Gray Cormack (d 1993), of Falmouth, Cornwall, and Eliza Cormack; *b* 12 Nov 1947; *Educ* Falmouth GS, Pembroke Coll Oxford (BA, MA); *m* 14 Sept 1968, (Elizabeth) Susan (d 1994), da of Mark Tallack (d 1976), of Penryn, Cornwall; 1 s (James Mark Ian (Jamie) b 1975), 1 da (Sally Elizabeth b 1979); *Career* Citibank NA: joined 1969, dir SCAM 1976–78, head of Euro Trg Centre 1979, personnel dir N Europe 1980–84, head Financial Instns Gp UK 1984–88, head Financial Instns Gp Europe 1989–95, country corp offr UK 1993–, global indust head Investmt Indust 1996–; chm Citicorp UK Pension Fund 1980–89; Assoc of Payment Clearing Systems (APACS): memb Cncl 1985–, chm Risk Steering Gp 1990–91, memb Settlement Risk Gp 1991–93; London Stock Exchange: memb Securities Settlement Bd 1990–92, chm TAURUS Monitoring Gp 1992–93, memb CREST Task Force 1993; chm: Woolnoth Soc City of London 1990–92, CHAPS 1993–96; memb: Bd Cedel SA Luxembourg 1985–96, Clearing House Formation Ctee (LSE) 1989–91, Cncl ABSAL 1993–96, Advsy Gp Pembroke Coll Oxford (memb Chllr's City Promotion Panel 1995–); *Recreations* skiing, golf, fly-fishing, theatre; *Clubs* Bankers', RAC; *Style*— Ian Cormack, Esq; ✉ Holly Lodge, Lammas Lane, Esher, Surrey KT10 8PA (☎ 01372 467730); Citibank NA, Cottons Centre, Hays Lane, London (☎ 0171 500 5333, fax 0171 234 5277)

CORMACK, Dr John Francis; s of James E Cormack, of Chipping Norton, and Theresa, *née* Hill; *b* 27 April 1947; *Educ* St Joseph's Coll, London Hosp Med Coll, Corpus Christi Coll Cambridge; *m* 24 June 1978, Susan, *née* Hazelton; 1 da (Laura b 5 June 1980), 2 s (Ben b 13 Oct 1982, Marcus b 27 Nov 1987); *Career* sr ptnr in gen practice, med writer and bdcaster; hon press sec BMA, memb GMC; *Style*— Dr John Cormack; ✉ Drs Cormack and Allan, Greenwood Surgery, Tylers Ride, South Woodham Ferrers, Essex (☎ 01245 322443, fax 01245 321844)

CORMACK, Sir Patrick Thomas; kt (1995), MP (C) Staffordshire South (majority 22,633); s of Thomas Charles Cormack, of Grimsby, and Kathleen Mary Cormack; *b* 18 May 1939; *Educ* St James's Choir Sch Grimsby, Havelock Sch Grimsby, Univ of Hull; *m* 1967, Kathleen Mary, da of William Eric McDonald, of Aberdeen; 2 s; *Career* second master St James's Choir Sch Grimsby 1961–66, former English master and asst housemaster Wrekin Coll, head of History Dept Brewood GS Stafford; MP (C): Cannock 1970–74, Staffs S Feb 1974–; PPS to jt Parly Secs DHSS 1970–73; chm: All-Party Ctee Widows and One Parent Families 1974, Cons Pty Arts and Heritage Ctee 1979–83, All-Party Heritage Ctee 1979–, Br-Finnish Parly Gp 1992–, Br-Bosnian Parly Gp 1992–, Br-Croation Parly Gp 1992–; memb: Select Ctee Educn Science and Arts 1979–83, Speaker's Panel of Chairmen in the House of Commons 1983–; chm: House of Commons Works of Art Ctee 1987–, Cons Party Arts and Heritage Advsy Ctee 1988–; rector's warden St Margaret's Westminster 1978–90, Parly warden 1990–92; visiting parly fell St Antony's Coll Oxford 1994; memb: Faculty Jurisdiction Cmmn 1981–84, Royal Cmmn on Historical Manuscripts 1981–, Historic Buildings Cncl 1979–85, Cncl for Br Archaeology; tstee Historic Churches Preservation Tst, vice chm Heritage in Danger, memb Cncl of Winston Churchill Memorial Trust 1983–93, vice pres Soc of Antiquaries 1994; Freeman City of London, Liveryman Worshipful Co of Glaziers & Painters of Glass; hon citizen of Texas; FSA; *Books* Heritage in Danger (1976), Right Turn (1978), Westminster Palace and Parliament (1981), Castles of Britain (1982), Wilberforce the Nation's Conscience (1983), English Cathedrals (1984); *Recreations* visiting old churches, fighting philistines, not sitting on fences; *Clubs* Athenaeum; *Style*— Sir Patrick Cormack, MP, FSA; ✉ House of Commons, London SW1A 0AA (☎ 0171 219 5019/5514)

CORMACK, Prof Richard Melville; s of Dr William Sloan Cormack (d 1973), and Jean Wilson, *née* Niven (d 1982); *b* 12 March 1935; *Educ* Glasgow Acad, Univ of Cambridge (MA, Dip Math Stat), Univ of London (BSc), Univ of Aberdeen (PhD); *m* 1 Sept 1960, Edith, da of James Edward Whittaker, OBE (d 1973); 1 s (Andrew b 1963), 1 da (Anne b 1966); *Career* lectr in statistics Univ of Aberdeen 1956–66, sr lectr in statistics Univ of Edinburgh 1966–72, prof of statistics Univ of St Andrews 1972–94 (emeritus prof 1994–); visiting prof Univ of Washington 1964–65 and 1986; memb NERC 1983–89; Biometric Soc: Br sec 1970–77, int pres 1980–81, Br pres 1990–92; memb Cncl: RSS 1980–84, S Univs Cncl on Entrance 1982–89, Cncl Freshwater Biological Assoc 1978–83 and 1987–91; FRSE 1974, memb ISI 1972; *Books* The Statistical Argument (1971), vols 5 and 8 of ISEP Statistical Ecology Series (ed 1979); *Recreations* photography, music, hill walking; *Style*— Prof Richard Cormack, FRSE; ✉ School of Mathematical and Computational Sciences, University of St Andrews, North Haugh, St Andrews, Fife KY16 9SS (☎ 01334 463719, fax 01334 463748)

CORMACK, Prof Robert John; s of John Cormack (d 1979), and Christina, *née* Milne (d 1992); *b* 14 Dec 1946; *Educ* Montrose Acad, Univ of Aberdeen (MA); *m* 1973, Dr Elisabeth Charlotte Fischer, da of Ludwig Fischer; 1 da (Kelly Ann b 16 July 1976), 1 s (Nicholas John Ludwig b 17 May 1979); *Career* Brown Univ USA 1969–73 (Woodrow Wilson fell 1972–73); The Queen's Univ of Belfast: lectr in sociology 1973–87, sr lectr 1987–92, reader 1992–95, prof 1995–, dean Faculty of Economics and Social Sciences 1993–95, pro-vice-chllr 1995–; conslt Fair Employment Cmmn Standing Advsy Cmmn on Human Rights; expert contrib confs on HE Cncl of Europe; chm Belfast CAB 1989–93; *Books* Religion, Education and Employment (co-ed, 1983), Education and Social Policy in Northern Ireland (co-ed, 1987), Discrimination and Public Policy in Northern Ireland (co-ed, 1991), After the Reforms (co-ed, 1993); *Recreations* relaxing in Fermanagh; *Style*— Prof Robert Cormack; ✉ The Queen's University Belfast, University Road, Belfast BT7 1NN (☎ 01232 335339, fax 01232 237925, e-mail R.CORMACK@QUB.AC,UK)

CORMAN, Charles; *b* 23 Oct 1934; *Educ* St Paul's Sch, UCL (LLB), Univ of California at Berkeley (Fullbright scholar, LLM); *Career* assoc Goldstein Judd & Gurfein NY (attorneys) 1960; Titmuss Sainer Dechert (solicitors): articles 1955–58, asst slr 1959 and 1960–61, ptnr 1963–; *Style*— Charles Corman, Esq; ✉ Titmuss Sainer Dechert, 2 Serjeants' Inn, London EC4Y 1LT (☎ 0171 583 5353, fax 0171 353 3683)

CORNELL, Jim Scott; s of James William Cornell (d 1976), of Thirsk, and Annie, *née* Scott (d 1994); *b* 3 Aug 1939; *Educ* Thirsk GS, Bradford Inst of Technol; *m* 28 July 1962, Winifred Eileen, da of John Rayner (d 1974); *Career* British Rail: student civil engr 1959–64, asst divnl civil engr King's Cross 1974–76, divnl civil engr King's Cross 1976–78, divnl civil engr Newcastle 1978–81, asst regnl civil engr York 1981–83, regnl civil engr Scotland 1983–84, dep gen mangr Scotrail 1984–86, gen mangr Scotrail 1986–87, dir civil engrg 1988–92, md Regnl Railways 1992–93, md Infrastructure Servs 1993–96, exec dir Railway Heritage Tst 1996–; Inst of Civil Engrs Webb prize; CEng, FEng 1992, FCIT, FIIM, FPWI; *Recreations* tennis, golf, gardening; *Style*— Jim Cornell, FEng; ✉ Railway Heritage Trust, Melton House, 65/67 Clarendon Road, Watford, Herts WD1 1DP (☎ 01923 240250)

CORNER, (John) Michael; OBE (1990); s of Thomas Matthias Corner, of Bishop Auckland, Co Durham, and Winifred, *née* Bell; *b* 2 Oct 1939; *Educ* King James I GS Bishop Auckland, Univ of Manchester; *m* 3 Sept 1963, Gwendoline, da of Robert William Cook, of Bishop Auckland, Co Durham; 1 s (Adam b 1966); *Career* news ed Northern Echo Darlington 1966–68 (reporter 1960–64, chief reporter 1964–66); asst ed: Morning Telegraph Sheffield 1973–78 (night news ed 1968–73), The Star Sheffield 1978–82; ed: Sheffield Weekly Gazette 1982–83, The Star Sheffield 1983–92; dir: Sheffield Newspapers 1983–92, Sheffield Partnerships 1990–93, Destination Sheffield 1993–; PR conslt Jan Morris & Associates 1992, md Corner Communications Ltd 1992–; memb: Br Section of Int Press Inst 1984–90, Cncl of Cwlth Press Union 1989–91, BBC NE Advsy Cncl 1987–90, Cncl of Sheffield C of C 1988– (sr vice pres 1996–), Sheffield Indust Year Ctee and Indust Matters Ctee, Sheffield Image Ctee, Univ of Sheffield Chllrs Ctee on Br Assoc, Guild of Br Newspaper Eds 1982–92 and 1996–; tstee: Northern Radio, Five Weirs Walk, Child Helpline; winner Cwlth Press scholarship 1975; vice chm Parly and Legal Ctee Guild of Br Newspaper Eds 1989–90 (chm 1986–89); MInstD 1992 (vice chm Sheffield branch 1993–95, chm 1995–), MIPR; *Recreations* gardening; *Style*— Michael Corner, Esq, OBE; ✉ 11 Winchester Crescent, Sheffield S10 4ED; Corner Communications Ltd, Westbrook Court, 2 Sharrow Vale Road, Sheffield S11 8YZ (☎ 0114 268 7800, fax 0114 268 7770)

CORNES, John Addis; s of John Frederick Cornes; *b* 16 Aug 1944; *Educ* Eton, Univ of Oxford; *m* 1971, Veronica Mary Alicia; 2 c; *Career* dir: Capital House Unit Management Ltd, Capital House Investments Ltd, Brown Shipley PEP Ltd; dir West Downs School Ltd; chm: Gloucester 15 Ltd, Gloucester 13 Ltd; treas LEPRA; Liveryman Worshipful Co of Grocers; *Recreations* walking, watching sport; *Style—* John Cornes, Esq; ✉ Woodgates Farm, East Bergholt, Colchester, Essex

CORNESS, Sir Colin Ross; kt (1986); s of late Thomas Corness and Mary Evlyne, *née* Lovelace (d 1993); *b* 9 Oct 1931; *Educ* Uppingham, Magdalene Coll Cambridge (BA, MA), Harvard (AMP); *Career* Lt 3 Carabiniers (Prince of Wales) Dragoons Gds; called to the Bar 1956; chm: Redland plc 1977–95 (md 1967–82), Nationwide Building Society 1991–96, Glaxo Wellcome plc 1995– (non-exec dir 1994–); dir: W H Smith and Son plc 1980–87, Chubb and Son plc 1974–84 and Chubb Security plc 1992–, National Westminster Bank (SE Regnl Bd) 1982–86, Courtaulds plc 1986–91, Bank of England 1987–95, Gordon Russell plc 1985–89, S G Warburg Group plc 1987–95, Unitech plc 1987–95, Union Camp Corporation 1991–; memb: Nat Econ Devpt Ctee for Bldg 1981–84, Indust Devpt Advsy Bd 1982–84, Advsy Bd Br-American C of C 1987–91; pres: Nat Cncl of Bldg Materials Prods 1985–87, Inst of Roofing 1994–96; *Recreations* tennis, music, travel; *Clubs* Cavalry and Guards'; *Style—* Sir Colin Corness; ✉ Glaxo Wellcome plc, Lansdowne House, Berkeley Square, London W1X 6BQ (☎ 0171 493 4060, fax 0171 408 0228)

CORNFORD, Sir (Edward) Clifford; KCB (1977, CB 1966); s of John Herbert Cornford, of E Grinstead; *b* 6 Feb 1918; *Educ* Kimbolton Sch, Jesus Coll Cambridge; *m* 1945, Catherine, da of Frank Muir; 3 s, 3 da; *Career* Royal Aircraft Establishment 1938; chief exec and perm under sec of state MOD (Procurement Exec) 1975–77, chief of defence procurement 1977–80; FRAeS, FEng 1980; *Style—* Sir Clifford Cornford, KCB, FEng; ✉ The Spinney, 7 Ash Grove, Liphook, Hampshire GU30 7HZ (01428 722780)

CORNFORD, James Peters; s of John Cornford (d 1936), and Rachel Peters (d 1985); *b* 25 Jan 1935; *Educ* Winchester, Trinity Coll Cambridge (Earl of Derby student, sr scholar, MA History); *m* 1960, Avery Amanda, da of late B R Goodfellow; 1 s (Thomas b 1964), 3 da (Frances b 1965, Emma b 1968, Sophie b 1970); *Career* fell Trinity Coll Cambridge 1960–64, Harkness fell of Cwlth Fund 1961–62; research assoc Dept of Sociology Univ of California at Berkeley 1961, attached to Dept of Political Sci Univ of Chicago 1961–62; Univ of Edinburgh: lectr in politics 1964–68, prof of politics 1968–76, dir Outer Circle Policy Unit 1976–80, dir Nuffield Fndn 1980–88; visiting fell All Souls Coll Oxford 1975–76; dir Inst for Public Policy Research 1989–94, dir The Paul Hamlyn Foundation 1994–; dir Job Ownership Ltd 1979–; literary ed The Political Quarterly 1977–93, chm Political Quarterly Publishing Co 1993–; chm Cncl Campaign for Freedom of Info 1984–, tstee and chm S African Advanced Educn Project 1987–, chm Constitution Unit Faculty of Laws UCL 1995–; author of numerous reports and articles on political and constitutional subjects; FRHistS 1970; *Style—* James Cornford, Esq; ✉ 9 Wallingford Avenue, London W10 6QA (☎ 0181 968 6109); Paul Hamlyn Foundation, Sussex House, Upper Mall, London W6 9TA (☎ 0181 741 2812, fax 0181 741 2263)

CORNICK, Col Anthony Emlyn; s of late Alfred George Cornick, and late Tydvil, *née* Evans; *b* 19 Jan 1938; *Educ* Berkhamsted Sch, RMA Sandhurst; *m* 6 Aug 1966, Judith Cornick; 1 s (Simon Charles b 9 Aug 1969), 1 da (Clare Louise b 26 Oct 1967); *Career* Army 1956–94: Bn Cdr 1979–81 (despatches), plans policy staff SHAPE 1981–85, defence commitments staff MOD 1985–86, DA, NA, MA in Amman Jordan 1986–90, MLRS Int Corp 1990–94; clerk to the Tstees The Campden Charities 1994–; *Recreations* ornithology, music, travel, golf; *Style—* Col Anthony Cornick

CORNICK, Roger Courtenay; s of William Charles Cornick (d 1968), of Singapore, and Cynthia Avisa Louise, *née* Courtenay; *b* 13 Feb 1944; *Educ* various army schs in Egypt, Queen Elizabeth's Sch Crediton Devon; *m* 8 July 1995, Susan Mary (Susie); 2 da (Kate Elizabeth b April 1979, Victoria Rose b Feb 1981); *Career* trainee Royal Insurance Group 1963–68, rep Abbey Life Assurance Co 1968–70, asst dir Hambro Life Assurance Ltd 1970–77, dir Crown Financial Management Ltd 1977–80, ptnr Courtenay Manning Partners 1980–83, dep chm and gp mktg dir Perpetual plc 1982–; memb Exec Ctee Assoc of Unit Tsts and Investment Funds, tstee River and Rowing Museum; *Recreations* golf, tennis, skiing, theatre; *Clubs* Riverside, Royal Mid-Surrey Golf; *Style—* Roger Cornick, Esq; ✉ Perpetual plc, 47/49 Station Rd, Henley-on-Thames, Oxon RG9 1AF (☎ 01491 417000, fax 01491 578926, car 0831 212458)

CORNISH, Alan Stewart; s of Alfred Stewart Cornish (d 1980), of Orpington, Kent, and Ann Selina, *née* Westgate; *b* 27 April 1944; *Educ* Beckenham and Penge GS; *m* 8 March 1969, Daphne Elisabeth, da of Charles Gordon Saunders; 3 s (Nigel b 1972, Graham b 1975, Iain b 1982); *Career* gp fin controller Associated Communications Corporation plc 1975–82, vice pres Euro regnl office RCA Records 1982–84, gp chief exec Good Relations Group plc 1984–86, gp md Lowe Bell Communications Ltd 1986–89, chm and chief exec Deal Holdings Ltd 1989–90, chm Cornish Ltd 1989–, chief fin offr Hilton International 1992–95, gp chief exec Eurobell (Holdings) plc 1996–; dir Cable Communications Assoc; fndr memb Orpington Dist Guide Dogs for the Blind Assoc; London Borough of Bromley: cncllr 1974–80, dep ldr 1976–78, dep mayor 1978–79; FCMA 1976 (assoc 1971), FIMgt 1978, FInstD 1986; *Recreations* sport; *Clubs* local golf; *Style—* Alan Cornish, Esq; ✉ Aspens, 42 Oxenden Wood Road, Chelsfield Park, Orpington, Kent BR6 6HP (☎ 01689 856880, fax 01689 860091)

CORNISH, Anthony; s of Alfred Cornish, of Chingford, Essex; *b* 7 April 1935; *m* Linda Polan; 1 s (Simon); *Career* freelance dir and teacher 1984–; announcer and disc jockey Forces Bdcasting Serv Austria 1953–55, actor and stage mangr various repertory theatres 1955–58, artistic dir Civic Theatre Chesterfield 1959–62, radio drama prodr BBC Midland Region 1964–74, deviser and prodr weekly serial United, freelance dir Crescent Alexandra & Repertory Theatres Birmingham, artist in residence Tufts Univ Dept of Drama & Dance Medford USA 1969–70 and 1995–, dir Tufts Univ Jr Year Abroad Programme London 1971–77, literary and prodn mangr and assoc dir Haymarket Theatre Leicester 1974–76, freelance dir Shaw Theatre London and Bristol Old Vic 1977–80, drama supervisor Capital Radio London and visiting lectr Univ of Hull 1980–84; princ tutor Young Professional Dirs' Course Br Theatre Assoc 1989–90; memb: Cncl Dirs' Guild of GB, Guild of Drama Adjudicators; *Theatre* prodns incl: The Two Gentlemen of Verona, Tonight We Improvise, Tribeckett (all at Cornell Univ), House of Bernarda Alba (Webber Douglas Acad) 1988, 6 premieres by Andrew Davies and Vaclav Havel, Twelfth Night (Perishable Theatre) 1989, Take Back What's Yours (Warehouse Theatre) 1989, The Importance of Being Earnest (Pearl Theatre, NY) 1990, The Taming of the Shrew (Tomar, Portugal) 1990, Major Barbara (Pearl Theatre) 1990, As You Like It (Pearl Theatre) 1991, Manof Mode (Asolo Theatre Florida) 1992, Stage Door (Lillian Bayliss Theatre London) 1992, The Good Natur'd Man (Pearl Theatre) 1992; *Radio* co prodr The Forsyte Chronicles (BBC Radio 4) 1990, prodr and dir Shane (90 min adaptation for BBC Radio 4 launch of Cinema 100 series); *Style—* Anthony Cornish, Esq; ✉ Flat B, 63/65 Falcon Road, London SW11 2PG (☎ 0171 585 1508)

CORNISH, (Robert) Francis; CMG (1994), LVO (1978); s of C D Cornish; *b* 18 May 1942; *Educ* Charterhouse, RMA Sandhurst; *m* 1964, Alison Jane Dundas; 3 da; *Career* cmmnd 14/20 King's Hussars 1962; entered FCO 1968, Kuala Lumpur 1970, Jakarta 1971, first sec FCO 1973, Bonn 1976–80, asst private sec to HRH The Prince of Wales 1980–83, high cmmr Brunei 1983–1986, cnsllr (info) Washington and head of Br Info Servs NY 1986–90, head News Dept FCO 1990–93, sr British Trade Cmmr Hong Kong 1993–; *Clubs* Cavalry and Guards'; *Style—* Francis Cornish, Esq, CMG, LVO; ✉ c/o Foreign and Cwlth Office, King Charles St, London SW1

CORNISH, Prof Frederick Hector John; s of Robert Hector Cornish (d 1977), of Crediton, Devon, and Margaret Elizabeth, *née* Helmore (d 1975); *b* 29 June 1930; *Educ* Queen Elizabeth's GS, Crediton, Wadham Coll Oxford (MA, DPhil); *m* 4 Jan 1958, Monica Rosalie Hope; 2 s (John b 1961, Richard b 1965), 1 da (Rachel b 1959); *Career* Nat Serv instr Lt RN 1956–59; jr lectr in mathematics Univ of Oxford 1953–54, res fell Univ of BC Vancouver 1954–56, sr lectr Univ of Leeds 1965 (lectr 1959); Univ of York: prof of mathematics 1967–, head of Dept 1967–79, dep vice chllr 1975–78 and 1979–81, actg vice chllr 1978; memb: London Mathematical Soc, York Civic Tst; *Recreations* music, gardening, hill walking, DIY; *Style—* Prof Frederick Cornish; ✉ Lime Tree House, 99 Front St, Acomb, York YO2 3BU (☎ 01904 798022); Department of Mathematics, University of York, Heslington, York YO1 5DD (☎ 01904 433074)

CORNISH, James Easton; s of Eric Easton Cornish, of Scotland, and Ivie Hedworth, *née* McCulloch; *b* 5 Aug 1939; *Educ* Eton, Wadham Coll Oxford; *m* 1968, Ursula, da of Prof H R Pink, of German Fed Rep; 1 s (Toby b 1972); *Career* HM Dip Serv 1961–85: HM Embassy Bonn, BMG Berlin, HM Embassy Washington, Central Policy Review Staff; asst dir Phillips and Drew 1985–87, Co Nat West Securities 1987, dir NatWest Securities 1993; euro market strategist 1988–; *Recreations* reading; *Style—* James Cornish, Esq; ✉ c/o NatWest Securities, 135 Bishopsgate, London EC2M 3XT

CORNISH, Prof William Rodolph; s of Jack Rodolph Cornish (d 1978), and Elizabeth Ellen, *née* Reid; *b* 9 Aug 1937; *Educ* St Peter's Coll Adelaide, Univ of Adelaide (LLB), Univ of Oxford (BCL); *m* 25 July 1964, Lovedy Elizabeth, da of Edward Christopher Moule (d 1942); 1 s (Peter b 1968), 2 da (Anna b 1970, Cecilia b 1972); *Career* lectr in law LSE 1962–68, reader QMC London 1969–70, prof of English law LSE 1970–90, prof of law Univ of Cambridge 1990–95, dir Centre for Euro Legal Studies 1991–94, Herchel Smith prof of intellectual property law Univ of Cambridge 1995–; external academic memb Max Planck Inst for Patent Law Munich 1989–; FBA 1984; *Books* The Jury (2 edn, 1970), Law and Society in England 1750–1950 (1989), Intellectual Property: Patents, Copyright, Trade Marks and Allied Rights (3 edn, 1996); *Style—* Prof William Cornish, FBA; ✉ Magdalene College, Cambridge CB3 0AG

CORNOCK, Maj-Gen Charles Gordon; CB (1988), MBE (1974); s of Gordon Wallace Cornock (d 1978), of Warwicks, and Edith Mary, *née* Keeley; *b* 25 April 1935; *Educ* King Alfred Sch, RMA Sandhurst; *m* 1962, Kay, da of Cyril John Sidney Smith (d 1987), of Jersey; 2 s (Ian b 1963, James b 1966); *Career* cmmnd RA 1956, CO 7 Para RHA 1974–76 (despatches 1975), Cdr RA 3 Armd Div 1979–81, student Royal Coll of Def Studies 1982, Dep Cmdt Army Staff Coll Camberley, dir RA 1984–86, Chief of Staff Live Oak 1986–89; mangr England Jrs Hockey Team 1978–79; bursar Cranleigh Sch 1989–95; FIMgt; *Recreations* hockey, tennis, golf, skiing, water skiing; *Clubs* La Moye Golf, West Hill Golf; *Style—* Maj-Gen Charles Cornock, CB, MBE; ✉ Oranmore, Horseshoe Lane, Cranleigh, Surrey

CORNWALL, Archdeacon of; *see:* McCabe, Ven Trevor

CORNWALL-JONES, Mark Ralph; s of Brig Arthur Thomas Cornwall-Jones, CMG, CBE (d 1980), and Marie Joan Evelyn, *née* Hammersley-Smith; *b* 14 Feb 1933; *Educ* Glenalmond Coll, Jesus Coll Cambridge (MA); *m* 1959, Priscilla, da of Col Harold E Yeo (d 1957); 3 s (Adam b 1964, Matthew b 1967, Jason b 1969), 1 da (Kate b 1961); *Career* investmt mangr: The Debenture Corporation 1959–67, John Govett and Co Ltd 1967–90 (investmt dir 1983–88); chm: Ecclesiastical Insurance Group, Govett Oriental Investment Trust; dir: Halifax Financial Services Holdings, Updown Investment Co, Trades Union Fund Managers, and other cos; *Recreations* books, stalking, gardening, sailing, carpentry; *Clubs* Boodle's; *Style—* Mark Cornwall-Jones, Esq; ✉ Erin House, 3 Albert Bridge Rd, Battersea SW11 4PX; The Counting House, 53 Tooley St, London SE1 2QN

CORNWALLIS, 3 Baron (UK 1927); Fiennes Neil Wykeham Cornwallis; OBE (1963), DL (Kent 1976); only s of 2 Baron Cornwallis, KBE, KCVO, MC, JP, DL (d 1982), by his 1 w, Cecily (d 1943), da of Sir James Heron Walker, 3 Bt; *b* 29 June 1921; *Educ* Eton; *m* 1, 17 Oct 1942 (m dis 1948), Judith, o da of Lt-Col Geoffrey Lacy Scott, TD; 1 s, 1 da (decd); m 2, 1 June 1951, Agnes Jean, yr da of Capt Henderson Russell Landale; 1 s, 3 da; *Heir* s (by 1 w), Hon Jeremy Cornwallis; *Career* served WWII Lt Coldstream Gds (1941–44, then invalided); pres: Br Agric Contractors' Assoc 1952–54, Nat Assoc of Agric Contractors 1957–63 and 1986–; dir Planet Building Society 1968– (chm 1971–75); chm: Magnet and Planet Building Society 1975–79, Town and Country Building Society 1979–81 and 1990–92 (dir 1979–92), CBI Smaller Firms Cncl 1974–82 (chm 1979–82); pres English Apples and Pears Ltd; memb Bd of Tstees Chevening Estate 1979–; rep of Horticultural Co-operatives in EEC 1975–86; vice pres Fedn of Agric Co-operatives 1984–86; chm: FAC Fruit Forum 1972–89, Kingdom Quality Assur Scheme 1986–89, All Party Parly Br Fruit Gp 1994–; govr Sevenoaks Sch 1992, tstee E Malling Research Station; Pro Grand Master (Freemasons) United Grand Lodge 1982–91 (previously Dep Grand Master), Liveryman Worshipful Co of Fruiterers; FIHort; *Recreations* fishing, philately; *Clubs* Brooks's, Flyfishers' Pratt's; *Style—* The Rt Hon the Lord Cornwallis, OBE, DL; ✉ Ruck Farm, Horsmonden, Tonbridge, Kent TN12 8DT (☎ 01892 722267); 25B Queens' Gate Mews, London SW7 5QL (☎ 0171 589 1167)

CORNWELL, David John Moore; *see:* Le Carré, John

CORNWELL, Judy Valerie; JP (1985); da of Darcy Nigel Barry Cornwell (d 1967), of Australia, and Irene, *née* McCullen; *b* 22 Feb 1940; *Educ* Convent of Mercy Aust, Lewes GS Sussex; *m* 18 Dec 1960, John Kelsall Parry, *qv*, s of Edward Parry (d 1983), of Loughborough; 1 s (Edward Dylan b 20 June 1965); *Career* actress and author; pres: Relate (Brighton) 1988–94, Nat Assoc of Deaf Children (E Sussex); memb: Bd Inst of Alcohol Studies 1983–91, Bd West Pier Tst 1974–89, Cncl Equity 1982–85; memb: Equity 1955, Soc of Authors 1986, PEN 1989, Royal Soc of Literature 1994; *Television* Younger Generation plays 1961 (nominated Tommorrow's Star Actress Daily Mirror 1961), Call Me Daddy (winner Emmy award) 1967, Moody and Pegg 1974, Cakes and Ale 1974 (nominated Best Actress SFTA), The Good Companions 1980, Keeping Up Appearances (BBC) 1990–95; *Radio* The Navy Lark 1962; *Theatre* Oh! What A Lovely War 1963, RSC season at Stratford upon Avon 1972, Bed Before Yesterday (Lyric) 1976, Rose (NZ tour) 1981, The Government Inspector 1988, The Cemetery Club 1993; *Films* Wuthering Heights 1971, Santa Claus The Movie 1985; *Books* Cow and Cowparsley (1985), Fishcakes at the Ritz (1989), Seventh Sunrise (1993), Fear and Favour (1996); *Recreations* travel, philosophy, reading; *Style—* Ms Judy Cornwell, JP; ✉ c/o Ken McReddie Ltd, 91 Regent St, London W1R 7TB (☎ 0171 439 1456)

CORNWELL, Prof Keith John; *b* 4 April 1942; *Educ* Rickmansworth GS, Watford Tech Coll, City Univ (BSc, PhD), Heriot-Watt Univ (DEng); m; 2 c; *Career* apprentice then engrg designer J G Slatter Ltd 1959–65, Electricity Cncl res fell and latterly lectr Middlesex Poly 1965–70, sr lectr Dept of Mechanical Engrg Heriot-Watt Univ 1979–82 (lectr 1970–79), md KC Heat Pumps Ltd and KC Products Ltd 1982–86; Dept of Mechanical and Chemical Engrg Heriot-Watt Univ: reader and dir Energy Technol Unit 1986–87, head of dept 1989–93 (dep head 1988–89), dean of engrg 1993–95, dir of quality 1995–; CEng, FIMechE; author of over 60 pubns; *Style—* Prof Keith Cornwell; ✉ Department of Mechanical and Chemical Engineering, Heriot-Watt University, Riccarton, Edinburgh EH14 4AS (☎ 0131 449 5111, fax 0131 451 3129)

CORNWELL, Rupert Howard; s of Ronald Cornwell (d 1975), of Maidenhead, and Jean Margaret Cornwell; *b* 22 Feb 1946; *Educ* Winchester, Magdalen Coll Oxford (BA); *m* 1, April 1972, Angela Doria; 1 s (Sean b Oct 1974); m 2, March 1988, Susan Jean, da of Samuel Smith, of Edwardsville, Illinois; *Career* journalist; Reuters: joined London 1968, Paris 1969–72, Brussels 1969–70, Paris 1970–72; Financial Times: joined 1972, Foreign Desk 1972, Paris Bureau 1973–76, lobby corr Westminster 1976–78, Rome corr 1978–83, Bonn corr 1983–86; The Independent: joined 1986, Moscow corr 1987–91, Washington corr 1991–; Foreign Correspondent of the Year Granada 1988, David Holden prize 1989; *Books* God's Banker, The Life of Roberto Calvi (1983); *Recreations* foreign languages, cricket, travel; *Style—* Rupert Cornwell, Esq; ✉ Washington Correspondent, c/o The Independent, 1 Canada Square, Canary Wharf, London E14 5DL (☎ 0171 293 2000)

CORP, Ronald Geoffrey; s of Geoffrey Charles Corp, and Elsie Grace, *née* Kinchin; *b* 4 Jan 1951; *Educ* Blue Sch Wells, ChCh Oxford (MA); *Career* librarian, prodr and presenter BBC Radio 3 1973–87; composer; various choral works (published by Novello and Co Ltd), And All the Trumpets Sounded (cantata) performed 1989 (published by Stainer and Bell, 1993), Laudamus (cantata) performed 1994, Four Elizabethan Lyrics (cmmnd by Sainsburys for Choir of the Year, 1994, published OUP 1995); ed Upper Voice Series for OUP; conductor: New London Orchestra, New London Children's Choir, New London Collegium, London Choral Soc, Highgate Choral Soc; dir of choir (Jr Dept) RCM 1993–95; musical dir London Choral Soc 1985–, dir New London Collegium 1994–; various recordings for Hyperion Records with New London Orch (incl British Light Music Classics 1996), numerous recordings with New London Children's Choir (incl Britten for Naxos Records); involved with: BBC Singers, BBC Concert Orchestra; memb: Nat Fedn of Music Societies, Br Fedn of Young Choirs, Assoc of Br Choral Directors; *Books* The Choral Singer's Companion (1987); *Recreations* reading; *Style—* Ronald Corp, Esq; ✉ 41 Aberdare Gardens, London NW6 3AL (☎ 0171 625 4641, fax 0171 625 4876)

CORRALL, Dr Roger James Martin; s of Alfred James Corrall (d 1985), of Sutton Coldfield, and Amy Adeline, *née* Martin; *b* 4 Aug 1944; *Educ* Univ of Edinburgh (BSc, MB ChB, MD); *m* 19 Feb 1972, Rhona Lockyer, da of Maxwell Cameron McIntosh; 1 s (Euan James b 4 April 1974), 1 da (Fiona Helen b 1 Jan 1976); *Career* registrar in gen med diabetes and metabolic disorders Royal Infirmary Edinburgh 1970–71, clinical res fell in endocrinology Case Western Reserve Univ Cleveland Ohio 1971–73, sr registrar Edinburgh Northern Gp of Hosps 1975, hon clinical tutor Dept of Med Univ of Edinburgh 1975, conslt physician specialising in diabetes and endocrinology Bristol Royal Infirmary 1979–; author of in excess of 180 scientific pubns on diabetes, clinical endocrinology and hypoglycaemia; memb: Br Diabetic Assoc, Autonomic Research Soc, Euro Assoc for the Study of Diabetes, Euro Soc for Clinical Investigation; MRS, memb RSM, MRCP 1970, FRCPE 1984, FRCP 1985; *Recreations* music, theatre, the arts, wine, history, British countryside, dogs; *Style—* Dr Roger Corrall; ✉ 64 Pembroke Road, Clifton, Bristol BS8 3DX; Directorate of Medicine, Bristol Royal Infirmary, Bristol BS2 8HW (☎ and fax 0117 928 2768)

CORRICK, Philip; s of Frank Corrick, of Sidmouth, Devon, and Violet, *née* Willey (d 1991); *b* 30 March 1954; *Educ* Sidmouth Secdy Modern Sch, Exeter Coll (City & Guilds); *m* (m dis); *partner* Karen Geddes; *Career* jr sous chef Claridges Hotel London 1979–80, sous chef The Berkeley Knightsbridge 1980–84, exec chef Westbury Hotel London 1984–87, exec chef (all restaurants) Grosvenor House Park Lane 1989–90, exec chef Royal Automobile Club 1990–; affiliate memb Academie Culinaire de France 1986, memb Assoc Culinaire Française 1995; Trusthouse Forte Chef of the Year 1988, finalist Meilleur Ouvrier de Grande Bretagne 1991; *Recreations* music, swimming; *Clubs* Barnsdale Country; *Style—* Philip Corrick, Esq; ✉ 11 Chatsworth Close, Market Deeping, Peterborough PE6 8AZ (☎ 01778 380269); The RAC, 89–91 Pall Mall, London SW1Y 5HS (☎ 0171 930 2345, fax 0171 976 1086)

CORRIE, John Alexander; MEP (Cons) Worcs and Warwicks S (majority 1,204); s of John Corrie (d 1965), of Kirkcudbright, and Helen Brown; *b* 29 July 1935; *Educ* Kirkcudbright Acad, George Watson's Coll, Lincoln Agric Coll NZ; *m* 1965, Sandra, *née* Hardie; 1 s, 2 da; *Career* farmer Scotland (also NZ), national sheepshearing champion 1959; lectr: Br Wool Mktg Bd 1967–74, Agric Trg Bd 1969–74; Nuffield scholar in agric 1972; Parly candidate (Cons): N Lanark 1964, Central Ayr 1966; MP (Cons): Bute and N Ayr 1974–83, Cunninghame North 1983–87; Parly candidate (Cons) Argyll and Bute 1992; oppn whip 1975–76, PPS to George Younger as Sec of State for Scotland 1979–81, sec All-Pty Br-Turkish Ctee 1979–87, memb Select Ctee Scottish Affrs 1981–83, chm Scottish Cons Backbench Ctee 1981–83, ldr Cons Gp on Scottish Affrs 1982–87, sec Cons Backbench Fish-farming Ctee 1982–87, sec Cons Backbench Forestry Ctee 1982–85; MEP 1975–76 and 1977–79, MEP (Cons) Worcs and Warwicks S 1994–; rapporteur LOME IV, memb Devpt Ctee, memb Regnl Ctee; memb: Cncl of Europe and W Euro Union 1983–87, Cncl Nat Cattle Breeders' Assoc, Central Tport Consultative Ctee (London) 1989–94; dir Belted Galloway Soc 1987–93; chm Tport Users' Consultative Ctee (Scotland) 1989–94; dir Ayrshire Agric Soc 1990–94, sole rep from Scotland of Royal Agric Soc of England 1991–; Wilberforce award for humane work on abortion reform 1981; *Books* Forestry in Europe, The Importance of Forestry in the World Today, Fish Farming in Europe, Towards a Community Rural Policy (with Sir James Scott-Hopkins); *Recreations* shooting, fishing, tennis; *Style—* John Corrie, Esq, MEP; ✉ 98 High Street, Evesham, Worcestershire WR11 4HE (☎ 01386 40502)

CORRIE, His Hon Judge; Thomas Graham Edgar; s of John Alexander Galloway Corrie, OBE, MC (d 1986), of Chobham, Surrey, and Barbara Phyllis, *née* Turner; *b* 18 Dec 1946; *Educ* Eton, Brasenose Coll Oxford (BA); *m* 17 July 1971, Anna, da of John Logsdail; 2 da (Tamsin Laura b 12 Dec 1974, Alice Kate Marguerite b 6 Nov 1976), 1 s (Matthew John Galloway b 4 June 1981); *Career* called to the Bar Gray's Inn 1969, in practice 1971–94, circuit remembrancer 1988–94, recorder 1988–94, circuit judge (Midland & Oxford Circuit) 1994–; Freeman City of London; *Recreations* gardening, swimming, canal boating; *Clubs* Frewen (Oxford); *Style—* His Hon Judge Corrie; ✉ Northampton Combined Court Centre, 85–87 Lady's Lane, Northampton (☎ 01604 250131)

CORRIGAN, Thomas Stephen; s of Thomas Corrigan (d 1992), and Renée Victorine, *née* Chaborel (d 1994); *b* 2 July 1932; *Educ* Beulah Hill; *m* 1963, Sally Margaret, da of George Ernest Everitt (d 1980); 2 da (Caroline (Mrs Kenneth Clancy), Linda (Mrs Gerard Comyns)); *Career* CA; chm: Inveresk Group plc 1974–83 (md 1971–83), Havelock Europa plc 1983–89, Post Office Users' Nat Cncl 1984–94, Rex Stewart Group plc 1987–91, Rex Stewart Trust 1989–, Direct Mail Accreditation and Recognition Centre 1995–; also dir various other cos; pres Br Paper and Board Indust Fedn 1975–77, vice pres Euro Confedn of Pulp, Paper and Packaging Industries 1981–82; advsr Citizen's Charter Unit Cabinet Office 1994–; Master Worshipful Co of: Makers of Playing Cards 1978–79, Stationers and Newspaper Makers 1990–91, Marketors 1995; *Recreations* golf, tennis, bridge; *Clubs* MCC, Royal & Ancient, Walton Health Golf; *Style—* Thomas Corrigan, Esq; ✉ Woodend, The Chase, Kingswood, Tadworth, Surrey KT20 6HZ (☎ 01737 832709); 57 Marsham Court, Marsham Street, London SW1P 4JZ

CORRIN, His Hon Deemster; John William; CBE (1995); s of Evan Cain Corrin (d 1967), of IOM, and Dorothy Mildred, *née* Teare (d 1990); *b* 6 Jan 1932; *Educ* King William's Coll; *m* 1961, Dorothy Patricia, da of John Stanley Lace (d 1964), of IOM; 1 da (Jane b 1965); *Career* HM first deemster, clerk of the Rolls 1988–, HM attorney gen for IOM 1974–80, HM second deemster 1980–88, dep govr IOM 1988–; *Recreations* music, bridge, gardening; *Clubs* Ellan Vannin (IOM); *Style—* His Hon Deemster Corrin, CBE; ✉ 28 Devonshire Rd, Douglas, Isle of Man (☎ 01624 621806); Rolls Office, Douglas, Isle of Man (☎ 01624 685242)

CORRY, James Michael; s and h of Lt Cdr Sir William Corry, 4 Bt; *b* 3 Oct 1946; *Educ* Downside; *m* 1973, Sheridan Lorraine, da of Arthur Peter Ashbourne, of Crowland, Peterborough; 3 s (William James Alexander b 1981, Robert Philip John b 1984, Christopher Myles Anthony b 1987); *Career* various appts Shell-Mex and BP 1966–75 and BP 1975–; currently ops mangr Gas Dept BP Nederland BV Amsterdam; *Style—* James Corry, Esq; ✉ Aronskelkweg 40, 2241 WC Wassenaar, The Netherlands

CORRY, Viscount; John Armar Galbraith Lowry-Corry; s and h of 8 Earl Belmore, *qv*; *b* 2 Nov 1985; *Style—* Viscount Corry

CORRY, Lt Cdr Sir William James; 4 Bt (UK 1885), of Dunraven, Co Antrim; s of Sir James Perowne Ivo Myles Corry, 3 Bt (d 1987), and his 1 w, Molly Irene, *née* Bell; *b* 1 Aug 1924; *Educ* RNC Dartmouth; *m* 8 Dec 1945, Diana Pamela Mary, o da of Lt-Col James Burne Lapsley, MC, IMS; 4 s (James Michael b 1946, Timothy William b 1948, Nicholas John b 1958, Simon Miles b 1961), 2 da (Jane Susannah (Mrs John A Redman) b 1949, Patricia Diana (Mrs Mark Hassell) b 1956); *Heir* s, James Michael Corry b 3 Oct 1946; *Career* Lt Cdr RN (ret); *Style—* Lt Cdr Sir William Corry, Bt; ✉ East Hillerton House, Sreyton, Crediton, Devon EX17 5AD (☎ 013633 82407)

CORSAR, Col Charles Herbert Kenneth; LVO (1989), OBE (1981), TD 1960, DL (Midlothian 1975); s of Capt Kenneth Charles Corsar (d 1967), of Midlothian, and Winifred Paton, *née* Herdman (d 1989); *b* 13 May 1926; *Educ* Merchiston Castle Sch, King's Coll Cambridge (MA); *m* 25 April 1953, Hon Mary Drummond Buchanan-Smith (Hon Dame Mary Corsar, DBE, *qv*), da of Rt Hon Lord Balerno of Currie (see Debrett's Peerage and Baronetage); 2 s (George b 1954, David b 1957), 3 da (Kathleen b 1960 d 1960, Katharine b 1961, Mary b 1965); *Career* TA Col 1972–75, Hon ADC to HM The Queen 1977–81, Hon Col 1/52 Lowland Volunteers 1975–87, chm Lowland TA & VRA 1984–87; cncllr for Midlothian 1958–67, JP 1965, zone cmmr Home Def E Scotland 1972–75, pres Edinburgh Bn Boys' Bde 1969–87 (vice-pres UK 1970–91), chm Scottish Standing Conf of Voluntary Youth Orgns 1973–78, memb Scottish Sports Cncl 1972–75, chm Earl Haig Fund Scotland 1984–90; govr: Merchiston Castle Sch 1975–89, Clifton Hall Sch 1965–90; sec Royal Jubilee and Prince's Tsts (Lothians and Borders) 1977–93; sec for Scotland Duke of Edinburgh's Award Scheme 1966–87; Vice Lord-Lt Midlothian 1993–96; *Recreations* shooting, gardening, beekeeping; *Clubs* New (Edinburgh); *Style—* Col Charles H K Corsar, LVO, OBE, TD, DL; ✉ Burg, Torloisk, Ulva Ferry, Isle of Mull PA74 6NH (☎ 01688 500289); 11 Ainslie Place, Edinburgh EH3 6AS (☎ 0131 225 6318)

CORSAR, Hon Dame Mary Drummond; *née* Buchanan-Smith; DBE (1993); o da of Brig Baron Balerno, CBE, TD (Life Peer, d 1984), and Mary Kathleen, *née* Smith, of Pittodrie (d 1947); *b* 8 July 1927; *Educ* Westbourne, St Denis, Univ of Edinburgh (MA); *m* 25 April 1953, Col Charles Herbert Kenneth Corsar, LVO, OBE, TD, DL, *qv*, s of Kenneth Charles Corsar (d 1967), of Cairniehill; 2 s (George b 1954, David b 1957), 2 da (Katharine b 1961, Mary b 1965), and 1 da d in infancy (1960); *Career* dep chief cmmr Girl Guides Scotland 1972–77, chm WRVS Scotland 1982–88, chm WRVS 1988–93 (vice chm 1984–88); govr Fettes Coll 1982–, hon pres Scottish Women's Amateur Athletic Assoc 1973–91, memb Visiting Ctee Glenochil Young Offenders Inst 1972–92; memb: Convocation Heriot Watt Univ 1986–, Parole Bd for Scotland 1982–89; tstee TSB Fndn for Scotland 1992– (chm 1994–); *Recreations* hill walking, embroidery, the family; *Clubs* New (Edinburgh, assoc memb), Scottish Ladies Climbing; *Style—* The Hon Dame Mary Corsar, DBE; ✉ Burg, Torloisk, Ulva Ferry, Isle of Mull (☎ and fax 01688 500289)

CORSIE, Richard; s of Ronnie Corsie, of Edinburgh, and Joyce, *née* Brown; *b* 27 Nov 1966; *m* 24 June 1988, Suzanne Joyce, da of William Gillies Scott; *Career* bowls player; Scot indoor caps 1984–89, Bronze medal Cwlth Games Edinburgh 1986 and Auckland 1990, Hong Kong singles and pairs champion 1987 and 1988, Br singles champion 1988, Aust World Classic pairs champion 1988, World indoor bowls champion 1989 and 1991, Scottish pairs champion 1992, Worthing world Paris gold, World singles Silver, World team Gold 1992, World indoor singles champion 1993, Mazda Jack High singles champion 1993 and 1995, runner-up World indoor singles 1994 and 1995, Cwlth Games singles gold medalist 1994, winner World indoor pairs 1995; *Style—* Richard Corsie, Esq; ✉ 14 Ferguson Green, Musselburgh EH21 6XB

CORSTON, Jean Ann; MP (Lab) Bristol East (majority 2,692); da of Charles (Laurie) Parkin, and late Eileen Parkin; *b* 5 May 1942; *Educ* Yeovil Girls' HS, LSE (LLB 1989), Inns of Ct Sch of Law; *m* 1, 1961, Christopher Corston; 1 s, 1 da; m 2, 4 Jan 1985, Prof Peter Townsend, *qv*; *Career* called to the Bar Inner Temple 1990; organiser Taunton Lab Pty 1974–76, regnl organiser SW Regn Lab Pty 1981–85 (asst regnl organiser 1976–81), asst nat agent London 1985–86, sec Lab Pty Annual Conf arrangements 1985–86, MP (Lab) Bristol E 1992–; memb Select Ctee on: Agriculture 1992–95, Home Affrs 1995–; co-chair PLP Women's Gp 1992–, sec All Pty Parly Child Support Agency Monotoring Gp and Mature Women's Healthcare Gp, chair All Party Gp on Parenting, chair PLP Children and the Family Gp; memb: TGWU, Haldane Soc of Socialist Lawyers, Socialist Health Assoc, Co-op Party, ACTSA, One World; *Recreations* gardening, reading, walking; *Style—* Ms Jean Corston, MP; ✉ House of Commons, London SW1A 0AA

CORTAZZI, Sir (Henry Arthur) Hugh; GCMG (1984, KCMG 1980, CMG 1969); s of Frederick Edward Mervyn Cortazzi (d 1966), of Sedbergh, Yorks, and Madge, *née* Miller (d 1945); *b* 2 May 1924; *Educ* Sedbergh, Univ of St Andrews, Univ of London; *m* 3 April 1956, Elizabeth Esther, da of George Henry Simon Montagu (d 1976), of London; 1 s (William b 1961), 2 da (Rosemary b 1964, Charlotte b 1967); *Career* served RAF 1943–47; joined FO 1949, former cnsllr (Commercial) Tokyo, RCDS 1971–72, min (Commercial) Washington 1972–75, dep under sec of state FCO 1975–80, ambass to Japan 1980–84; dir: Hill Samuel Bank Ltd 1984–91, F & C Pacific Investment Trust 1984– (non-exec), GT Japan Investment Trust 1984– (non-exec); non-exec chm Thornton Pacific Investment Fund (SICAV) 1986–; advsr to: Mitsukoshi Ltd 1984–, NEC Corp Japan 1992–, Dai-ichi Kangyo Bank Japan 1992–, Bank of Kyoto 1992–, Wilde Sapte slrs London 1992–, PIFC 1993–, Matsuura Machinery Co Ltd 1996–; memb ESRC 1984–90, pres Asiatic Soc of Japan 1982 and 1983, chm Cncl Japan Soc London 1985–95 (hon chm 1995–96, hon vice pres 1996–), memb Ct Univ of Sussex 1985–92; Hon DUniv Stirling 1988, hon fell Robinson Coll Cambridge 1988; Yamagata Banto Prize Osaka 1991; Grand Cordon Order of the Sacred Treasure (Japan) 1995; *Books* translations from Japanese: Genji Keita - The Ogre and other stories of Japanese Salarymen (1972), The Guardian God of Golf and other humorous stories (1972), both reprinted as The Lucky One (1980); edited: Mary Crawford Fraser: A Diplomat's Wife in Japan - Sketches at the Turn of the Century (1982), Isles of Gold - Antique Maps of Japan (1983), Thoughts from a Sussex Garden (1984), Second Thoughts (1985), Japanese Encounter (1987, essays for Japanese students of English), Dr Willis in Japan - British Medical Pioneer 1862–1877 (1985), A British Artist in Meiji Japan (1991), Britain and Japan - Themes and Personalities (with Gordon Daniels, 1991), Mitford's Japan - The Memoirs and Recollections of the First Lord Redesdale, Richard Henry Brunton - Building Japan 1868–1876 (ed, 1991); Victorians in Japan - In and around the Treaty Ports (1987), Kipling's Japan (ed with George Webb, 1988), The Japanese Achievement (1990), Modern Japan: A Concise Survey (1993), Caught in Time: Japan (jt ed, 1994); various books (written and edited) translated into Japanese and various articles on Japanese themes in English and Japanese publications; *Recreations* music, opera, gardening; *Clubs* RAF; *Style—* Sir Hugh Cortazzi, GCMG; ✉ Ballsocks, Ballsocks Lane, Vines Cross, Heathfield, E Sussex TN21 9ET

CORVEDALE, Viscount; Benedict Alexander Stanley Baldwin; eldest s and h of 4 Earl Baldwin of Bewdley; *b* 28 Dec 1973; *Educ* Bryanston, Univ of Newcastle; *Style*— Viscount Corvedale; ✉ Manor Farm House, Godstow Road, Upper Wolvercote, Oxon OX2 8AJ (☎ 01865 552683)

CORY, Charles Raymond; CBE (1982); s of Charles Kingsley Cory (d 1967), and Ethel Muriel, *née* Cottam (d 1975); *b* 20 Oct 1922; *Educ* Harrow, ChCh Oxford; *m* 1, 19 Oct 1946, Vivienne Mary (d 1988), da of Maj John Fenn Roberts, MC (d 1971), of Kelowna, BC; 3 da (Elizabeth b 1948, Rosemary b 1950, Charlotte b 1953); m 2, 2 Sept 1989, Mrs Betty Horley, wid of Lt-Col Roy Horley; *Career* served WWII Lt RNVR N Atlantic, Channel, N Sea, C-in-C's commendation 1944; chm: John Cory and Sons Ltd 1965–91, Mountstuart Dry Docks 1962–66; vice chm: Br Tport Docks Bd 1970–80 (memb 1966), AB Electrical Products GR Ltd 1978–92; chm: S Glamorgan Health Authy 1974–84, Milford Haven Port Authy (formerly Conservancy Bd) 1982–94, Milford Dock Co 1990–94; memb Mgmnt Ctee RNLI 1954– (vice pres 1969, dep chm 1985–93); Church in Wales: memb 1960–, chm Fin Ctee 1975–88, dep chm Rep Body 1985–95 (hon treas 1988); chm: Welsh Cncl Mission to Seamen 1984–95, Cncl Univ of Wales Coll of Med 1988–; *Recreations* gardening, countryside; *Clubs* Cardiff and Country; *Style*— Raymond Cory, Esq, CBE; ✉ The Coach House, Llanblethian, Cowbridge, South Glamorgan (☎ 01446 772251)

CORY, Charlotte Angelica; da of Charles Peveril Phillips (d 1981), and Hilda May Flax, *née* Battle (d 1976); *b* 23 Sept 1956; *Educ* N London Collegiate Sch, Univ of Bristol (BA), Univ of York (DPhil); *m* April 1988, Robert William Cory; *Career* writer and woodcut artist; Judith E Wilson visiting fell Girton Coll Cambridge 1993–94; fndr memb UMPTY (millenium project for the growing of monkey puzzle trees); *Books* The Unforgiving (1991), The Laughter of Fools (1993), The Guest (1996); *Recreations* dogs, toy theatre, cultivating monkey puzzles and chocolate; *Clubs* University Women's (London), The Fox Boys (Manchester); *Style*— Charlotte Cory; ✉ c/o Faber & Faber Ltd, 3 Queen Square, London WC1N 3AU (☎ 0171 465 0045, fax 0171 465 0034)

CORY, Desmond; s of William Henry McCarthy (d 1937), of Hartland, Devon, and Iris Mary, *née* Chatfield; *b* 16 Feb 1928; *Educ* Steyning GS, St Peter's Coll Oxford (BA, MA), Univ of Wales (PhD); *m* 1956, Blanca Rosa, da of Francisco Poyatos; 4 s (John Francis b 1956, Alexander Justin b 1959, Richard Charles b 1962, David Anthony b 1964); *Career* language instr (later Centre dir) Int House Cordoba and Malaga (Spain) 1956–60, asst lectr (later lectr) in Eng (TEFL) UWIST Cardiff 1960–77, asst prof of Eng Univ of Qatar 1977–80; assoc prof of Eng: Univ of Bahrain 1980–85, Univ of Sanaa 1985–87; Eng language advsr to Miny of Educn Sultanate of Oman 1987–89, prof of Eng Eastern Mediterranean Univ Cyprus 1990–; author; *Fiction* The Name of the Game (1964), Deadfall (1965), Feramontov (1966), Timelock (1967), The Night Hawk (1969), Sunburst (1971), Take my Drum to England (1971), A Bit of a Shunt up the River (1974), The Circe Complex (1975), Bennett (1977), Lucky Ham (as Shaun McCarthy, 1979), The Strange Attractor (1991); *Children's Books* Ann and Peter in Southern Spain (1959), Belgrade Express (1960); *Anthologised Short Stories* Prince Milo (Winter's Crimes 7, 1975), Stumblebum the Wizard (Winter's Crimes 8, 1976), The Song of Fariq (Book Club Assoc, 1980); *Radio Plays* The Shaken Leaf (1955), Pilgrim at the Gate (1957), Pilgrim on the Island (1959), Orbit One (1964, all broadcast by the BBC); *Film Scripts* The Phoenix Sings (1956), Deadfall (1965), England Made Me (1976); *TV Plays and Series* The Circe Complex (ITV 1980), Gulf Diamonds (1980), The Doll (1980); contrib to various pubns incl: Kemsley Syndicate, Truth, Observer, Western Mail, Scotsman, London Magazine, Evening Standard, South Wales Echo, Diplomat, Gulf Mirror, Gulf Daily Observer; *Recreations* golf, tennis, travel; *Style*— Desmond Cory, Esq; ✉ Department of English, East Mediterranean University, PO Box 95, Gazi Magusa, Mersin 10, Turkey; c/o Macmillan Ltd, 4 Little Essex Street, London WC2R 3LF (☎ 0171 836 6633)

CORY, Sir (Clinton Charles) Donald; 5 Bt (UK 1919), of Coryton, Whitchurch, Co Glamorgan; s of Sir Clinton James Donald Cory, 4 Bt (d 1991), and Mary, *née* Hunt; *b* 13 Sept 1937; *Educ* Brighton Coll, abroad; *Heir* none; *Recreations* collecting Greek and Roman antiquities, student of classical studies; *Style*— Sir Donald Cory, Bt; ✉ 18 Cloisters Road, Letchworth, Herts SG6 3JS (☎ 01462 677206)

CORY, John; JP (Glam 1961), DL (Glam 1968); er s of John Herbert Cory (d 1939), of The Grange, St Brides-super-Ely, S Glam; *b* 30 June 1928; *Educ* Eton, Trinity Coll Cambridge; *m* 1965, Sarah Christine, er da of John Meade, JP, DL, of Maran Hassa, Itton, Gwent; 2 da; *Career* former dir John Cory and Sons Ltd, former chm Cardiff RDC; memb Representative Body of Church in Wales 1960–; jt MFH Glamorgan 1962–67; High Sheriff Glamorgan 1959–60, vice Lord Lt S Glam 1990–; KStJ; *Clubs* Cardiff and Country; *Style*— John Cory, Esq, JP, DL; ✉ The Grange, St Brides-super-Ely, Cardiff (☎ 01446 760211)

CORY-WRIGHT, Sir Richard Michael; 4 Bt (UK 1903), of Caen Wood Towers, Highgate, St Pancras, Co London and Hornsey, Middx; s of Capt (Anthony John) Julian Cory-Wright (ka 1944), and gs of Capt Sir Geoffrey Cory-Wright, 3 Bt (d 1969); *b* 17 Jan 1944; *Educ* Eton, Univ of Birmingham; *m* 1976 (m dis 1994), Veronica Mary, o da of James Harold Lucas Bolton; 3 s; *Heir* s, Roland Anthony Cory-Wright b 11 March 1979; *Style*— Sir Richard Cory-Wright, Bt; ✉ 21 Trenchard Close, Wallingford, Oxon OX10 9BB (☎ 01491 838844)

COSGRAVE, Dr Patrick John Francis; s of Patrick John Cosgrave (d 1952), of Dublin, and Margaret Anne, *née* Fitzgerald (d 1977); *b* 28 Sept 1941; *Educ* St Vincent's Sch Dublin, Univ Coll Dublin (BA, MA), Peterhouse Cambridge (PhD); *m* 1, 1965 (m dis 1974), Ruth, da of Prof Robin Dudley Edwards (d 1988), of Dublin; m 2, 1974 (m dis 1980), Norma Alicia Green, da of Douglas Cooper; m 3, 1981, Shirley, da of Gp Capt Ralph Ward; 1 da (Rebecca Jane b 9 Oct 1974); *Career* fndr and first ed London Office RTE 1968–69, desk offr CRD Home Office affrs 1969–70, political and dep ed Spectator 1970–75 (leader and feature writer 1975–79), features ed Telegraph Magazine 1974–76, special advsr to Rt Hon Margaret Thatcher 1975–79, managing ed Quartet Crime 1979–81, freelance writer and journalist 1982–; presenter: What the Papers Say (Granada), The Week In Westminster (Radio 4); Sacks lectr Oxford Centre for Postgraduate Hebrew Studies; memb: Cons Pty, Friends of the Union; *Books* The Public Poetry of Robert Lowell (1969), Churchill at War (1975), Cheyney's Law (1976), Margaret Thatcher - A Tory and her Party (1978, updated and reprinted as Margaret Thatcher - Prime Minister, 1979), The Three Colonels (1979), RA Butler - An English Life (1981), Adventure of State (1984), Thatcher - The First Term (1985), Carrington - A Life and a Policy (1985), The Lives of Enoch Powell (1989), The Strange Death of Socialist Britain (1992); contrib: The Spectator, The Times, Daily Telegraph, The Independent, Sunday Telegraph, Telegraph Magazine, Daily Express, Wall Street Journal, Literary Review, American Spectator, Encounter, National Review, New Law Journal, Le Point, Sunday Tribune (Dublin); *Recreations* dogs, watching cricket, roses, thrillers; *Style*— Dr Patrick Cosgrave; ✉ 44 Elms Crescent, London SW4 8QZ (☎ 0171 627 0306)

COSGROVE, Hon Lady; Hazel Josephine; da of Moses Aron Aronson (d 1978), of Glasgow, and Julia Tobias; *b* 12 Jan 1946; *Educ* Glasgow HS for Girls, Univ of Glasgow (LLB); *m* 17 Dec 1967, John Allan Cosgrove, s of Rev Dr Isaac Kenneth Cosgrove, DL, JP (d 1973); 1 da (Jillian Abigail b 1970), 1 s (Nicholas Joseph b 1972); *Career* advocate The Scottish Bar 1968–79, standing jr counsel to Dept of Trade 1977–79, QC (Scot) 1991; Sheriff of: Glasgow and Strathkelvin 1979–83, Lothian and Borders at Edinburgh 1983–96; temp judge Court of Session and High Court of Justiciary 1992–96; Senator Coll of Justice 1996–; memb Parole Bd for Scotland 1988–91, chm Mental Welfare Cmmn for Scotland 1991–96, vice chm Edinburgh Friends of Israel 1980–96; *Recreations* swimming, opera, foreign travel; *Clubs* New (Edinburgh); *Style*— The Hon Lady Cosgrove; ✉ Parliament House, Parliament Square, Edinburgh EH1 1RQ (☎ 0131 225 2595, fax 0131 225 8213)

COSH, (Ethel Eleanor) Mary; da of Arthur Lionel Strode Cosh (d 1952), of Bristol, and Ellen, *née* Janisch (d 1931); *Educ* Clifton HS Bristol, St Anne's Coll Oxford (BA, MA); *Career* freelance writer, historian, architectural historian and lectr; contrib to: The Times, TLS, Glasgow Herald, Country Life, Spectator; memb all nat conservation orgns, former ctee memb Soc of Architectural Historians of GB, vice chm Islington Soc, vice chm (former chm) Islington Archaeology and History Soc, tstee Islington Museum; FSA 1987; *Books* The Real World (1961), Inveraray and the Dukes of Argyll (with late Ian Lindsay, 1973, paperback edn, 1988), A Historical Walk through Clerkenwell (2 edn, 1987), With Gurdjieff in St Petersburg and Paris (with late Anna Butkovsky, 1980), A Historical Walk through Barnsbury (1981), The New River (3 edn, 1996), The Squares of Islington (Part I 1990, Part II 1993); *Recreations* architecture, opera, reading, historical research; *Style*— Mary Cosh, FSA; ✉ 10 Albion Mews, London N1 1JX (☎ 0171 607 9305)

COSSINS, John Brown; s of Albert Joseph Cossins (d 1995), of Fairway, Havering-atte-Bower, Romford, Essex, and Elizabeth Henrietta, *née* Brown (d 1989); *b* 15 Nov 1939; *Educ* Clark's Sch for Boys Ilford Essex, NE London Poly; *m* 9 March 1968, Christine Millicent, da of Henry George Avis, of Romford, Essex; 2 s (Alexander b 1969, Jonathan b 1971); *Career* Thomas Saunders Partnership 1962–: assoc 1968–74, ptnr 1974–88, jt managing ptnr 1988–, sr ptnr 1990–92; chm Thomas Saunder Partnership Ltd 1992–; ARIBA 1966, FCSD 1985; *Recreations* golf, gardening, shooting; *Style*— John B Cossins, Esq; ✉ Thomas Saunders Partnership Ltd, 90–98 Goswell Rd, London EC1V 7DB (☎ 0171 490 8899)

COSSONS, Sir Neil; kt (1994), OBE (1982); s of Arthur Cossons (d 1963), of Beeston, Notts, and Evelyn Edith, *née* Bettle (d 1986); *b* 15 Jan 1939; *Educ* Henry Mellish GS Nottingham, Univ of Liverpool (BA, MA); *m* 7 Aug 1965, Veronica, da of Henry Edwards (d 1986), of Liverpool; 2 s (Nigel b 1966, Malcolm b 1972), 1 da (Elisabeth b 1967); *Career* dep dir City of Liverpool Museums 1969–71; dir: Ironbridge Gorge Museum Tst 1971–83, Nat Maritime Museum 1983–86, Science Museum 1986–; pres: Museums Assoc 1981–82, Assoc of Ind Museums 1983– (chm 1977–83); cmmr Historic Bldgs and Monuments Cmmn (English Heritage) 1989–95 (memb Ancient Monuments Advsy Ctee 1984–); memb: BBC Gen Advsy Cncl 1987–90, Design Cncl 1990–94, Cncl Fndn for Manufacturing and Indust 1993–, Br Waterways Bd 1995–; govr: RCA 1989–, Imperial Coll of Sci Technol and Med 1989–93; tstee: Mary Rose Tst 1983–, HMS Warrior Tst 1988–; Freeman City of London 1983; memb Comité Scientifique Conservatoire National des Arts et Métiers 1991–; Hon: DSocSci Univ of Birmingham 1979 (hon prof 1994–), DUniv Open Univ 1984, LittD Univ of Liverpool 1989, DLitt Univ of Bradford 1991, DLitt Nottingham Trent Univ 1994, DUniv Sheffield Hallam Univ 1995, DLitt Univ of the West of England (UWE) 1995, DSc Univ of Leicester 1995; Norton Medlicott medal Historical Assoc 1991, President's medal Royal Acad of Engrg 1993; hon fell RCA; FSA 1968, FMA 1970, FRSA 1988, CIEE 1991, CIMgt 1996, Hon CRAeS 1996; *Books* Industrial Archaeology of the Bristol Region (with R A Buchanan, 1968), Industrial Archaeology (1975, 1987 and 1993), Ironbridge: Landscape of Industry (with H Sowden, 1977), The Iron Bridge: Symbol of the Industrial Revolution (with B S Trinder, 1979 and 1989), Making of the Modern World (ed, 1992); *Clubs* Athenaeum; *Style*— Sir Neil Cossons, OBE; ✉ The Old Rectory, Rushbury, Shropshire SY6 7EB (☎ 01694 771603); Science Museum, London SW7 2DD (☎ 0171 938 8003, fax 0171 938 8002)

COSTALL, Prof Brenda; da of John Costall, of Wellingore, Lincs, and Eileen Stella, *née* Austin; *b* 12 Sept 1947; *Educ* Kesteven & Grantham Girls' Sch, Univ of Bradford (BPharm, PhD, DSc); *m* 13 Dec 1969, Robert John Naylor, s of John Edwin Naylor; *Career* Univ of Bradford: research fell MRC 1972–73, lectr in pharmacology 1973–79, sr lectr in pharmacology 1979–83, reader in neuropharmacology 1983–85, prof of neuropharmacology 1985–, pro-vice-chllr (planning and resources) 1990–92, sr pro-vice-chllr (planning and resources) 1992–94, dep vice-chllr (with special responsibility for research, planning and resources) 1994–; memb: Br Pharmacological Soc (non-offr memb of Ctee), Brain Research Assoc, Collegium Internationale Neuro-Psychopharmacologicum, Euro Neurosciences Assoc of Psychopharmacology, Euro Coll of Neuropsychopharmacology, New York Acad of Scis; *Recreations* managing a large Georgian property, collecting antique furniture and paintings, love of arts including fashion and theatre; *Style*— Prof Brenda Costall; ✉ University of Bradford, Bradford, West Yorkshire BD7 1DP (☎ 01274 383016, fax 01274 395256)

COSTELLO, Dr John Francis; s of William Francis Costello (d 1987), of Dublin, and Sarah, *née* O'Donghue (d 1968); *b* 22 Sept 1944; *Educ* Belvedere Coll Dublin, Univ Coll Dublin, Mater Hosp Dublin (MB BCh, BAO, MD); *m* 1, 11 Nov 1972 (m dis 1986), Dr Christine White, da of Wilfred White, and Irene White; 3 s (Declan b 12 Aug 1973, Manus b 26 Feb 1976, Hugh b 5 July 1980); m 2, 5 July 1996, Susanna, da of late Nicholas Clarke; *Career* house staff Mater Hosp Dublin 1968–69, sr house offr St Stephen's Hosp, Royal Northern Hosp, Royal Postgrad Med Sch and Hammersmith Hosp 1970–72, registrar Brompton Hosp 1972–74, lectr Dept of Med Univ of Edinburgh and Royal Infirmary 1974–75, asst prof of med, attending physician and dir Pulmonary Function Laboratory San Francisco Gen Hosp and Univ of California 1975–77, conslt physician in gen med with special interest in respiratory disease King's Coll Hosp London 1978– (dir Dept of Thoracic Med 1982–), sr lectr in med King's Coll Sch of Med and Dentistry 1982–, clinical dir of acute servs Camberwell Health Authy 1988–91 (chm of conslts 1989–91), med dir and memb Bd King's Healthcare Tst 1992–94, dir Sackler Institute for Pulmonary Pharmacology 1993–; author of numerous scientific papers, reviews, books and chapters on aspects of respiratory disease; FRCP, FRCPI, FRSM (fndr pres Respiratory Section 1991–); *Recreations* running, golf, music; *Clubs* Carlton, Royal Wimbledon Golf; *Style*— Dr John Costello; ✉ 12 Melville Avenue, London SW20 0NS (☎ and fax 0181 879 1309); Department of Respiratory Medicine, King's College School of Medicine and Dentistry, Denmark Hill, London SE5 9RS (☎ 0171 346 3165, fax 0171 346 3589); Cromwell Hospital, Cromwell Road, London SW5 0TU (☎ 0171 370 4233)

COSTELLOE, Paul; *b* Dublin; *Educ* Blackrock Coll Dublin, design coll Dublin, Chambre Syndical Paris; *m*; 7 c; *Career* fashion designer; design asst Jacquest Sterel Paris 1969–71, designer Marks & Spencer 1972, chief house designer A Rinascente Milan 1972–74, designer Anne Fogerty NY, Pennaco NY and Trimfit Philadelphia 1974–79, own design house 1979–; company currently sells in the UK, Ireland, Europe, Scandinavia and N America under Paul Costelloe Collection and Dressage labels, flagship store Brompton Road and 5 franchise shops London; designer of new British Airways uniform 1994; memb London Designer Collection UK 1980–93; *Awards* Fil d'Or 1987, 1988 and 1989, nominee Br Designer of the Yr 1989, Woman's Jl Designer of the Yr 1990, Stazenbreau Designer of the Yr 1991; *Style*— Paul Costelloe, Esq; ✉ 27 Cheval Place, London SW7 1EW (☎ 0171 589 9484, fax 0171 589 9481); Head Office, Moygashel Mills, Dungannon, NI BT71 7PB (☎ 01868 722291, fax 01868 726433); Menswear Division, 91a Pelham Street, London SW7 (☎ 0171 589 7121)

COSTER, Malcolm David; *b* 29 June 1944; *Educ* Wimbledon County GS, King's Coll Univ of London (BSc); *Career* conslt Scicon 1966–71, systems and programming mangr Lloyds Register 1971–73, sr conslt, subsequently managing conslt, divnl mangr and gen mangr Scicon 1973–81, gp co-ordinator Systems (Worldwide) British Petroleum Co plc 1981–84, dir of Holdings and md (UK) James Martin Associates 1984–86; Coopers & Lybrand: ptnr and divnl ptnr in charge 1986–89, memb Bd 1990–94, exec ptnr i/c Mgmnt Consultancy 1990–94, exec ptnr i/c Business Devpt (UK) and chm Int Business Devpt Gp 1992–94; chm Unisys Ltd and pres Unisys Europe 1994–; non-exec dir: British Technology Group 1993–, Performing Rights Soc 1996–; Freeman City of London 1991, Liveryman Worshipful Co of Information Technologists 1992; CEng, MBCS, FRSA; *Recreations* golf; *Clubs* RAC, Cuddington; *Style*— Malcolm Coster, Esq; ✉ Unisys Europe-Africa, Bakers Court, Bakers Road, Uxbridge, Middx UB8 1RG (☎ 01895 862410, fax 01895 257630)

COSTER, Peter Lloyd; s of Charles Edward Coster, and Maude, *née* Wearing; *b* 19 Jan 1934; *Educ* East Barnet GS; *m* 8 May 1955, Sylvia Iris, da of Frederick Gordon Hills, of Enfield, Middx; 3 da (Tracey Susan (Mrs Perkins) b 22 July 1957, Sharon Elizabeth (Mrs Crofton-Diggins) b 18 April 1960, Sarah Jane (Mrs Dowling) b 23 July 1963); *Career* Midland Bank 1952, served Royal Marines 1952–54, The Scottish Life Assurance Co 1955–89, md C & G Guardian 1989–93; dir: Cheltenham & Gloucester Building Society 1990–93, Guardian Building Society 1983–90, Team Agencies plc 1986–87; chm: Network Properties Direct Ltd 1995–, Aspenden Education Ltd 1995–; Freeman City of London 1982, Liveryman Worshipful Co of Insurers 1983; JP Middx 1978–92; memb Magistrates' Assoc, MCIM 1978; *Recreations* golf, painting, gardening; *Clubs* RAC, Wig and Pen; *Style*— Peter Coster, Esq; ✉ Oxfootstone House, Brick Kiln Lane, South Lopham, Diss, Norfolk IP22 2JS (☎ and fax 01379 688211); Coastguard Cottage, Bacton, Norfolk

COTES, Peter (*né* Sydney Arthur Boulting); s of Walter Arthur Boulting, impressario and entrepreneur (d 1957), and Rose, *née* Bennett (d 1981); *b* 19 March 1912; *Educ* Latymer, privately educated, Italia Conti; *m* 1, 1937, Myfanwy, da of Taliasin Jones; m 2, 19 May 1948, Joan, da of Wallace and Rhoda Miller; *Career* theatrical/film producer and director; Mil Serv Queens Westminster, RAF, ENSA, Army Kinematograph Serv, Home Guard; controller/prodr and/or dir: New Lindsey Theatre Club 1946 (prodns transferred to West End), controller, The Library Theatre Manchester 1948 (in association with Arts Cncl of GB), New Boltons Theatre Club 1950–51 (prodns transferred to West End and Broadway); sr drama dir AR-TV 1955–58, supervising prodr drama Channel 7 Melbourne 1961, prodr Anglia TV 1964; prodr and writer numerous radio prodns 1980–88; co dir: Live Theatre, Peter Cotes Productions Ltd, Cotes Logan Productions, Brompton Theatre Co; memb: Medico-Legal Soc, Our Soc, TMA, Equity, ACTT, RSA; FRSA, Knight of Mark Twain; *Theatre* debut aged 4 in arms of Vesta Tilley (Portsmouth Hippodrome) and at age of 10 as page to Robert Loraine's Henry V at Theatre Royal Drury Lane (King George's Fund for Actors, 1924); boy actor in leading roles: Caravan (Queen's), Windmill Man (Victoria Palace), Peter Pan; other prodns incl: Pick Up Girl 1946, The Animal Kingdom 1947, Rocket to the Moon 1948, The Master Builder 1948, Miss Julie 1949, The Rising Wind 1949, Come Back Little Sheba 1951, The Biggest Thief in Town 1952, The Man 1952, The Father 1952, The Mousetrap 1952, A Pin to See the Peepshow 1953 (Broadway), Happy Holiday 1954, The Cardinal 1957, Hot Summer Night 1958, The Rope Dancers 1959, A Loss of Roses 1961, Hidden Stranger 1962 (Broadway), Paint Myself Black 1965, The Impossible Years 1966, Look, No Hands! 1971; prodr (with own co): Book of the Month (West End) 1954, The Old Ladies (from Hugh Walpole's novel, adapted by Rodney Ackland, with Flora Robson, Joan Miller and Joyce Carey in title roles, West End) 1967–70, Look No Hands 1971; *Television* incl: Woman in a Dressing Gown, The Haven, Look in any Window, What the Public Wants, Candida, The Infinite Shoeblack, Wild Justice, Shadow of the Vine; *Films* incl: The Right Person, The Young and the Guilty, Jane Clegg; *Books* No Star Nonsense (1949), The Little Fellow (1951), History of Amateur Theatre (1957), George Robey (1972), Circus: A World History (1976), The Barbirollis: A Musical Marriage (1983), Sincerely Dickie (1989), Thinking Aloud: Fragments of Autobiography (1993); contrib: The Guardian, The Times, Daily Telegraph, The Independent; *Clubs* Savage (life memb); *Style*— Peter Cotes, Esq; ✉ 7 Hill Lawn Ct, Chipping Norton, Oxon OX7 5NF (☎ 01608 641208)

COTIER, James Charles; s of James Charles Cotier (d 1992), of 81 Walsingham Rd, Southend-on-Sea, Essex, and Edna Roberts (d 1984); *b* 8 March 1949; *Educ* Wentworth Secdy Modern, Southend Art Coll; *m* 27 May 1987, Louise Roxane, da of David Hugh Jenkins; 2 da (Francesca Alice b 28 Dec 1987, Isabella Fleur 23 Nov 1990), 1 s (Louis Charles b 5 March 1994); *Career* advertising photographer 1974–; winner of: numerous D&AD awards, campaign press and poster awards, Creative Circle awards; exhibitor Hamilton's Gallery 1983; *Books* Nudes in Budapest (1991); *Recreations* photography, sky diving, cooking; *Style*— James Cotier, Esq; ✉ James Cotier Ltd, Studio 9, 12 Castlehaven Road, London NW1 8QW (☎ 0171 267 8112)

COTRAN, His Hon Prof Judge Eugene; s of Michael Cotran (d 1985), former Chief Justice of Cameroon, and Hassiba, *née* Khouri; *b* 6 Aug 1938; *Educ* Victoria Coll Alexandria Egypt, Univ of Leeds (LLM), Trinity Hall Cambridge (Dip Int Law, LLD); *m* 6 Oct 1963, Christiane, da of Homer Avierino (d 1972); 3 s (Marc b 1964, Patrick b 1966, Paul b 1972), 1 da (Layla b 1980); *Career* called to the Bar Lincoln's Inn 1959; lectr SOAS Univ of London 1962–77, judge High Ct Kenya 1977–82, practice in African Cwlth and int law; visiting prof in law (with ref to Africa and ME) and chm Centre for Islamic and ME Law SOAS Univ of London; recorder of the Crown Ct until 1992, circuit judge (SE Circuit) 1992–; int arbitrator; FCIArb; *Books* Re-statement of African Law (Kenya 1963), Case Book on Kenya Customary Laws (1987), Butterworth's Immigraton Law Service (gen ed, 1991), Yearbook of Islamic and Middle Eastern Law (gen ed, 1994–); also gen ed CIMEC book series; *Recreations* racing, swimming, bridge; *Style*— His Honour Professor Judge Eugene Cotran; ✉ 16 Hart Grove, London W5 3NB (☎ 0181 992 0432, fax 0181 992 7228); Southwark Crown Court, 1 English Grounds, off Battlebridge Lane, London SE1 2HU

COTTAM, Graeme Robin; s of Desmond Augustine Herbert Cottam, and Rosella Fothergill, *née* Smith; *b* 6 June 1955; *Educ* Reed's Sch Cobham Surrey, Univ of Bristol (LLB); *Career* called to the Bar Middle Temple 1978, Price Waterhouse 1979–, ptnr int tax servs (London); memb: Int Fiscal Assoc, American Bar Assoc; fell ICAEW 1993 (assoc 1983); *Recreations* theatre, opera, cinema, travel, pottering around the garden; *Style*— Graeme Cottam, Esq; ✉ Parson's Farm, Warren Corner, Froxfield, Hampshire GU32 1BJ (☎ 01730 827586); Price Waterhouse, No 1 London Bridge, London SE1 9QL (☎ 0171 939 4594, fax 0171 939 4377)

COTTAM, Harold; s of Rev Canon Frank Cottam (d 1974), and Elizabeth, *née* Wilson (d 1982); *b* 12 Oct 1938; *Educ* Bedford Sch; *m* 1962, Lyn, *née* Minton; 2 da (Hilary Anne b 25 Jan 1965, Rachel Marjorie b 21 May 1966); *Career* head of corp planning SmithKline Beecham UK 1964–66, commercial dir for Spain Simon Engineering Group 1966–68; Ernst & Young (and preceding firms): ptnr 1968–92, managing ptnr UK 1986–92, chm Ernst & Young pan-European consultancy gp 1992–93, chm Ernst & Young CASE Services (International) Paris 1992–93; chm: Haden MacLellan Holdings plc 1992–, Anglo United plc 1993–96, Rebus Group plc 1996–, Britannic Assurance plc 1996–; dir Allied Colloids Group plc 1992–; FCA (ACA 1960); *Recreations* music, tennis, farming; *Style*— Harold Cottam, Esq; ✉ Britannic Assurance plc, Moor Green, Moseley, Birmingham B13 8QF (☎ 0121 449 4444, fax 0121 449 0456)

COTTAM, Robert Gwynne; s of Maj-Gen the Rev A E Cottam, CB, CBE, MC (d 1964), of Robertsbridge, Sussex, and Margaret Eileen, *née* Haselden; *b* 5 June 1934; *Educ* Marlborough; *m* 7 Oct 1967, Morella Cumberland, da of Lt-Col Anthony Gerald Bartholmew Walker, of Stockbridge, Hants; 2 s (Charles b 1969, Henry b 1973), 1 da (Rosemary b 1971); *Career* Nat Serv 2 Lt E Surrey Regt 1953–54; mgmnt trg Watney Combe Reid Brewers 1955–59; with Grieveson Grant & Co Stockbrokers 1959–64; ptnr: W I Carr Sons & Co 1965–82, Grieveson Grant & Co 1982–86; dir Kleinwort Benson Securities 1987–94, ret; *Recreations* golf, racing, opera; *Clubs* MCC, City of London, Turf; *Style*— Robert Cottam, Esq; ✉ 7 Stanford Rd, London W8 5PP

COTTEE, Tony; *b* 11 July 1965; *Career* professional footballer (forward); 212 appearances (92 goals) West Ham Utd 1982–88; Everton FC: joined 1988 (for fee of just over £2m), scored 99 goals; rejoined West Ham 1994; 7 full England caps; *Style*— Tony Cottee, Esq; ✉ c/o West Ham FC, Boleyn Ground, Green Street, Upton Park, London E13 9AZ

COTTELL, Michael Norman Tizard; OBE (1988); s of Norman James Cottell (d 1973), of Southampton, and Eileen Claire Cottell (d 1997); *b* 25 July 1931; *Educ* Peter Symonds Sch Winchester, Univ Coll Southampton, Univ of Birmingham; *m* 1 June 1957, Joan Florence, da of Edward Clarence Dolton (d 1973), of Winchester; 2 s (Paul b 24 Feb 1959, Robert b 24 April b 1961); *Career* Nat Serv RE 1951–53, Suez Crisis 1956; highway engr 1948–67: Hants, Glos, Berks, Northants; asst to co surveyor Suffolk CC 1967–73, dep co surveyor E Sussex CC 1973–76; co surveyor: Northants 1976–84, Kent 1984–91; exec conslt Travers Morgan Ltd 1991–95; chm Aspen Associates 1996–; Lt Col Engrs and Tport Staff Corps RE (TA) 1989–; Liveryman: Worshipful Co of Paviors, Worshipful Co of Engineers; FEng 1990 (memb Cncl until 1994), FICE 1958 (MICE), FIHT 1954, MIMgt 1971, MASCE 1991; *Recreations* swimming, sailing, walking, music, travel, historic houses, theatre; *Clubs* RAC, Athenaeum; *Style*— Michael Cottell, Esq, OBE, FEng; ✉ Salcey Lawn, Harrow Court, Stockbury, Sittingbourne, Kent ME9 7UQ (☎ 01795 844132); Aspen Associates, Dippen Hall, Blindley Heath, Lingfield, Surrey RH7 6JX

COTTENHAM, 8 Earl of (UK 1850); Sir Kenelm Charles Everard Digby Pepys; 11 and 10 Bt (GB 1784 and UK 1801); also Baron Cottenham (UK 1836) and Viscount Crowhurst (UK 1850); s of 7 Earl (d 1968, 2 cous 7 times removed of Samuel Pepys, the diarist); *b* 27 Nov 1948; *Educ* Eton; *m* 1975, Sarah, yr da of Capt Samuel Richard Le Hunte Lombard-Hobson, CVO, OBE, RN; 2 s (Viscount Crowhurst, Hon Sam Richard b 26 April 1986), 1 da (Lady Georgina Marye b 9 Oct 1981); *Heir* s, Mark John Henry, Viscount Crowhurst b 11 Oct 1983; *Style*— The Rt Hon the Earl of Cottenham

COTTER, Sir Delaval James Alfred; 6 Bt (I 1763) of Rockforest, Cork, DSO (1944); s of Sir James Laurence Cotter, 5 Bt (d 1924); *b* 29 April 1911; *Educ* Malvern, RMC Sandhurst; *m* 1, 29 Sept 1943 (m dis 1949), Roma, o da of Adrian Rome, of Dalswinton Lodge, Salisbury, S Rhodesia, and wid of Sqdn Ldr Kenneth A Kerr MacEwen; 2 da (Sarah Gay Lisette (Mrs Michel Vigneron) b 1944, Charnisay Ann (Mrs Charles A H Gwyn) b 1946); m 2, 9 Dec 1952, Eveline Mary (d 1991), eld da of late Evelyn John Mardon, of Halsway Manor, Crowcombe, Somerset, and wid of Lt-Col John Frederick Paterson, OBE, RHA; *Heir* n, Patrick Laurence Delaval Cotter b 21 Nov 1941; *Career* late 13/18 Royal Hussars, NW Europe 1944–45; JP Wilts 1962–63; *Clubs* Army and Navy; *Style*— Sir Delaval Cotter, Bt, DSO; ✉ Green Lines, Iwerne Courtney, Blandford Forum, Dorset

COTTER, Patrick Laurence Delaval; s of Laurence Stopford Llewelyn Cotter (ka 1943, yr s of 5 Bt), and Grace Mary, *née* Downing; hp of unc, Sir Delaval Cotter, 6 Bt; *b* 21 Nov 1941; *Educ* Blundell's, RAC Cirencester; *m* 1967, Janet, da of late George Potter, of Goldthorne, Barnstaple, N Devon; 1 s (Julius Laurence George b 1968), 2 da (Jemima Grace Mary b 1970, Jessica Lucy Kathleen b 1972); *Career* antique dealer; *Style*— Patrick Cotter, Esq

COTTERELL, Henry Richard Geers (Harry); s and h of Sir John Henry Geers Cotterell, 6 Bt, *qv*; *b* 22 Aug 1961; *m* 5 July 1986, Carolyn Suzanne, elder da of John Moore Beckwith-Smith, of Maybanks Manor, Rudgwick, Sussex; 2 s (Richard John Geers b 1 May 1990, George Dominic Geers b 23 April 1994), 1 da (Poppy b 1988); *Career* cmmnd Blues and Royals 1981; memb Hereford and Worcester CC 1989–93; *Clubs* White's; *Style*— Harry Cotterell, Esq

COTTERELL, Sir John Henry Geers; 6 Bt (UK 1805) of Garnons, Herefordshire; DL (Hereford and Worcester); s of Lt-Col Sir Richard Charles Geers Cotterell, 5 Bt, CBE (d 1978), and 1 w, Lady Lettice, *née* Lygon (d 1973), da of 7 Earl Beauchamp, KG, KCMG, TD, PC, and Lady Lettice Grosvenor, da of late Earl Grosvenor, s of 1 Duke of Westminster; *b* 8 May 1935; *Educ* Eton, RMC Sandhurst; *m* 7 Oct 1959, (Vanda) Alexandra Clare, da of Maj Philip Alexander Clement Bridgewater; 3 s (Henry Richard Geers b 1961, James Alexander Geers b 1964, David George Geers b 1968), 1 da (Camilla Jane (Mrs Mark Houldsworth) b 1963); *Heir* s, Henry Richard Geers Cotterell, *qv*; *Career* offr Royal Horse Gds 1955–61; chm: Hereford and Worcs CC 1977–81, Radio Wyvern, Hereford Mappa Mundi Tst, Rural Voice, Rural Youth Tst, Herefordshire Community Health Tst; memb The Jockey Club, pres Nat Fedn of Young Farmers' Clubs 1986–91; *Style*— Sir John Cotterell, Bt, DL; ✉ Garnons, nr Hereford HR4 7JU (☎ 01981 590232, fax 01981 590406)

COTTESLOE, Cdr 5 Baron (UK 1874); Sir John Tapling Fremantle; 5 Bt (UK 1821), JP (Bucks 1984); Baron of the Austrian Empire (1816); s of Lt-Col 4 Baron Cottesloe, GBE, DL (d 1994), and his 1 w, Lady Elizabeth Harris (d 1983), da of 5 Earl of Malmesbury; *b* 22 Jan 1927; *Educ* Eton; *m* 26 April 1958, Elizabeth Ann, er da of Lt-Col Henry Shelley Barker, DSO (d 1970), of Rugby; 1 s (Hon Thomas Francis Henry b 1966), 2 da (Elizabeth (Betsy) Wynne (Hon Mrs Duncan Smith) b 1959, Hon Frances (Fanny) Ann (Hon Mrs Stanley) b 1961); *Heir* s, Hon Thomas Francis Henry Fremantle b 1966; *Career* joined RN 1944, Lt 1949, Lt Cdr 1957, Cdr 1962, ret 1966; chm Oxon-Bucks Div Royal Forestry Soc 1981–83; pres: Bucks County Show 1986 (chm 1977–82), Bucks Branch CLA (chm 1976–79), HMS Concord Assoc; dep pres RASE 1995–96; vice pres: Hosp Saving Assoc, BASC (previously WAGBI), Royal Agric Soc of England, Bucks Co Agric Assoc, Radcliffe tstee (chm 1997); govr Stowe Sch 1983–89; High Sheriff of Bucks 1969–70, Lord Lieut 1984–97; Hon Dr Univ of Buckingham 1993; KStJ 1984; *Recreations* shooting, crosswords, Sherlock Holmes, steam railways; *Clubs* Travellers', RN and Royal Albert (Portsmouth); *Style*— Cdr the Rt Hon the Lord Cottesloe, JP, RN (ret); ✉ The Old House, Swanbourne, Milton Keynes, Bucks MK17 0SH (☎ 01296 720263); The Estate Office, Home Farm, Swanbourne, Milton Keynes, Bucks MK17 0SW (☎ 01296 720256, fax 01296 720302)

COTTIER, Timothy Robin; s of Maj Gordon Cottier, of Conway, Wales, and Alice, *née* Moffat (d 1989); *b* 27 Dec 1953; *Educ* Merchant Taylors Sch; *m* 1980, Helen Adele, da of Douglas Constantine (d 1990), of St Clements, Jersey; 2 da (Sophia b 1983, Claudia b 1985); *Career* CA 1977; Price Waterhouse and Co Bahamas 1978–80, estab Corporate Finance Companies Leeds Trust plc and others 1981–90; chm: Lakeview Bank of the Bahamas 1979–82, Rini Tea Co plc 1980–90, Leeds Trust plc 1982–90 (chief exec), Nuwara Eliya Tea Plantations plc 1982–87, Sunwest Airlines Inc 1982–89, Swan Valley Minerals Pty 1983–89, Transmeridian Offshore Oil plc 1984–90, Amanda Hall Fashions Ltd 1984–91, Highlands Rubber and Coffee Ltd 1984–91, Charles Graham Textiles Ltd 1984–92, Western Reef Gold Mining Pty 1985–91, Antonia and Charlotte Interior Designs plc 1985–91, Larchfield Racing Syndicate Ltd 1985–90, Yacht Holidays plc 1984–91, Audiotext plc 1987–89, Leeds Corporate Finance Ltd 1989–94, Westpennant Ltd 1989–, Amcott Corporate Finance Ltd 1989–, Portland Exec Recruitment Ltd 1989–91; FCA 1982; *Recreations* shooting, sailing, gardening, golf, tennis, travel, architecture, antiques, reading; *Clubs* RAC, Public Schs, West Lancashire Yacht, Golf Del Sur-Golf; *Style*— Timothy Cottier, Esq; ✉ Amcott Corporate Finance Ltd, Amcott House, Montpellier Street, Harrogate, Yorks HG1 2NQ (☎ 01423 526526, fax 01423 521571)

COTTINGHAM, Barrie; s of John Cottingham, of Sheffield, and Eleanor, *née* Price; *b* 5 Oct 1933; *Educ* Carfield Sch Sheffield; *m* 5 Oct 1957, Kathleen, da of John Ernest Morton (d 1945), of Sheffield; 1 s (Nigel David b 13 Dec 1964), 1 da (Michelle Jayne b 5 Aug 1962); *Career* RAF 1955–57, cmmnd PO 1956; Coopers & Lybrand 1957–95: ptnr 1964, memb UK Bd 1974–93, exec ptnr i/c of the regions 1986–93; pres Sheffield and Dist Soc of CAs 1964, chm SIG plc 1993–; memb Bd: Cattles plc 1995–, Vibroplant plc 1996–; FCA 1955, ATII 1965; *Recreations* squash, golf, watching rugby and cricket, oil painting, opera; *Clubs* Naval and Military, Sheffield; *Style*— Barrie Cottingham, Esq; ✉ SIG plc, Hillsborough Works, Langsett Road, Sheffield, S6 2LW (☎ 0114 285 6300, fax 0114 285 6385)

COTTLE, Gerry; s of Reginald Brookes Cottle (d 1975), of Highbury, London, and Joan Miriam, *née* Ward, of Streatham, London; *b* 7 April 1945; *Educ* Rutlish Sch Wimbledon; *m* 7 Dec 1968, Betty, da of James Fossett (d 1972), of Henley-in-Arden; 1 s (Gerry b 1981), 3 da (Sarah b 1970, April b 1973, Juliette b 1976); *Career* ran away from school and joined a small circus becoming juggler and equestrian 1961, formed Gerry Cottle's Circus 1974; flew complete circus to Oman for Sultan's birthday 1976; overseas tours 1981–84: Bahrain, Iran, Shajah, Iceland, Hong Kong, Macau, Singapore, Malaysia; currently world's most travelled circus, touring 46 weeks a year, touring Moscow State Circus in UK 1995–96; memb: Variety Club of GB, Assoc of Circus Proprietors of GB 1973–, NOEA, IEAM; *Recreations* horse riding, collecting show business memorabilia; *Style*— Gerry Cottle, Esq; ✉ Woburn Park Farm, Addlestone Moor, Surrey KT15 2QF (☎ 01932 828888, fax 01932 859902)

COTTO, Mario; *b* 4 May 1938; *Educ* Univ of Turin; *Career* gen mangr London Branch Istituto Bancario San Paolo di Torino 1988–92 (joined bank 1957), chm and chief exec IMI Sigeco (UK) Ltd 1992–; chm Foreign Banks and Securities Houses Assoc 1992; *Clubs* RAC; *Style*— Mario Cotto, Esq; ✉ IMI Sigeco (UK) Ltd, IMI House, 8 Laurence Pountney Hill, London EC4R 0BE (☎ 0171 283 6264, fax 0171 283 9382)

COTTON, Dr Bernard Edward; CBE (1976); s of Hugh Harry Cotton (d 1963), and Alice Cotton; *b* 8 Oct 1920; *Educ* Sheffield City GS, Univ of Sheffield; *m* 1944, Stephanie Anne, da of Rev Arthur Evelyn Furnival (d 1960); 3 s; *Career* served WWII Lt Worcs Yeo 6 Airborne Div France and Normandy, Ardennes Rhine Airborne Landing; pres Samuel Osborn and Co Ltd 1978–79 (chm and chief exec 1969–78), dir Renold plc 1979–84; dep chm: Baker Perkins plc 1982–86, John Mountford Co Ltd Manchester 1984–87; chm Yorks and Humberside Econ Planning Cncl 1970–79, pres Yorks and Humberside Devpt Assoc 1973–84, memb BR Rail (Eastern Region) 1976–85; chm: Health Serv Supply Cncl 1980–85, South Yorkshire Residuary Body 1985–89; pro-chllr Univ of Sheffield 1983–87; Master Co of Cutlers in Hallamshire 1979; hon fell Sheffield City Poly 1980, Hon LLD Univ of Sheffield; *Recreations* gardening, quiet pursuits; *Style*— Dr Bernard Cotton, CBE; ✉ Stubbin House, Carsick Hill Road, Sheffield S10 3LU (☎ 0114 230 3082)

COTTON, Diana Rosemary (Mrs R B Allan); QC (1983); da of Arthur Frank Edward Cotton (d 1990), of Herts, and Muriel, *née* John (d 1986); *b* 30 Nov 1941; *Educ* Berkhamsted Sch for Girls, Lady Margaret Hall Oxford (exhibitioner, MA); *m* 1966, Richard Bellerby Allan, *qv*, s of John Bellerby Allan (d 1985), of Oxon; 2 s (Jonathan b 1972, Jeremy b 1974), 1 da (Joanna b 1977); *Career* called to the Bar Middle Temple 1964 (bencher 1990), memb Midland and Oxford Circuit, recorder of the Crown Court 1982–; memb: Criminal Injuries Compensation Bd 1989–, Criminal Injuries Compensation Appeals Panel 1996–; *Recreations* family, sport; *Style*— Miss Diana Cotton, QC; ✉ Devereux Chambers, Devereux Court, Temple, London WC2 (☎ 0171 353 7534)

COTTON, Ian Ellis; s of Dr William John Cotton (d 1988), and Kathleen, *née* Eliot (d 1992); *b* 2 Feb 1945; *Educ* Cranleigh Sch Surrey, New Coll Oxford (entrance scholar); *m* Almudena Maria Dolores Lucia, da of Michael John Binns; 2 da (Natalia Kathleen b 1993, Elena Elisabeth b 1996), 1 da by previous ptnr Myra Byron-Cox (Josephine b 1974); *Career* Univ of Oxford: ed and fndr Oxford Opinion, literary ed Isis; editorial trainee George Newnes Publishers 1966, Nova magazine 1967–68, freelance writer (Nova, Sunday Times Magazine) 1969–73, staff writer TV Times 1973–74, Mandrake column Sunday Telegraph 1974–78, freelance magazine writer (Observer, Cosmopolitan, Sunday Times Magazine) 1978–82, commissioning ed then asst ed You (Mail on Sunday magazine) 1982–86, freelance writer (Evening Standard, Sunday Times, Observer) 1986–; *Books* The Hallelujah Revolution (1995); *Recreations* walking, cricket; *Style*— Ian Cotton, Esq; ✉ 2 Common Barn Cottages, Remenham Hill, Henley-on-Thames, Oxon RG9 3ER (☎ 01491 577458, fax 01491 412413)

COTTON, His Hon John Anthony; s of Frederick Thomas Hooley Cotton, of Harrogate, and Catherine Mary Cotton; *b* 6 March 1926; *Educ* Stonyhurst, Lincoln Coll Oxford; *m* 1960, Johanna Aritia, da of Johan Adriaan van Lookeren Campagne, of Holland; 3 s, 2 da; *Career* called to the Bar 1949, dep chm W Riding of Yorks Quarter Sessions 1967–71, recorder of Halifax 1971, recorder of Crown Ct 1972, circuit judge 1973–93; memb Parole Bd 1995–; *Style*— His Hon John Cotton; ✉ Myrtle Garth, Rossett Beck Close, Harrogate, North Yorkshire

COTTON, John Nicholas; s of Sir John Cotton, KCMG, OBE, and Mary Bridget, *née* Connors; *b* 6 Aug 1941; *Educ* Downside, Merton Coll Oxford (MA); *m* 1 (m dis 1976), Caroline, da of Michael Stoop, MC; 1 s (Tanguy b 1969); m 2, Martine, da of Roland du Roy de Blicquy, of Brussels; 1 s (Edward b 1986), 1 da (Charlotte b 1981); *Career* Samuel Montagu London 1963–65, Spencer Thornton Belgium 1965–68, vice pres Loeb Rhoades Belgium 1968–72, exec dir Cogefon Belgium 1972–77; md: Edwin H Bradley Belgium 1977–80, Banque Belge Ltd London 1980–92; chm Queensborough Steel Co Ltd, vice chm Anglo-Belgian Chamber of Commerce 1992–; dir Mercury Asset Management plc 1993–; *Clubs* Boodle's, Eagle (Gstaad); *Style*— John Cotton, Esq; ✉ 19 Bourne St, London SW1 (☎ 0171 730 1685); Mercury Asset Management, 33 King William St, London EC4Y 9AR (☎ 0171 280 2800)

COTTON, Sir John Richard; KCMG (1969, CMG 1959), OBE (1947, MBE 1944); s of Julian James Cotton, ICS (d 1927), and Sophia Raffaela, *née* Ricciardi-Arlotta (d 1958); *b* 22 Jan 1909; *Educ* Wellington, RMC Sandhurst; *m* 1937, Mary Bridget, da of Nicholas Connors, of Stradbally, Co Waterford; 3 s (David, John, Brian); *Career* 8 Light Cavalry IA 1929–37, Maj; Indian Political Serv 1934–47: Aden 1934–35, HM Legation Addis Ababa 1935, Persian Gulf 1937–38, Rajputana 1939–41, Hyderabad 1941–44, Kathiawar 1944–46, Political Dept Delhi 1946–47; HM Foreign Serv 1947–69: Foreign Office 1948–51, cnsllr Madrid 1951–54, consul-gen Leopoldville 1954–57, cnsllr Brussels 1957–62, consul-gen Sao Paolo 1962–65, ambass Kinshasa Zaire 1965–69; adjudicator Immigration Tbnls 1970–81; *Recreations* golf, photography; *Clubs* Army and Navy; *Style*— Sir John Cotton, KCMG, OBE; ✉ Lansing House, Hartley Wintney, Hants RG22 8RY (☎ 01252 842681)

COTTON, Oliver; s of Robert Cotton, of London, and Ester, *née* Bonessen; *b* 20 June 1944; *Educ* Chiswick Poly, Drama Centre London; *m* 1, Catherine, *née* Stevens; 1 da (Abigail b 1969); m 2, Irene, *née* Gorst; 1 da (Sophie b 1986); *Career* actor and writer; stage debut Off Broadway NY 1966, The National Theatre 1966–68, repertory at Cheltenham and Watford 1969–72, Royal Court 1966–75, RSC 1975, NT 1975–79, RSC 1988–89, RNT 1990–91; *Theatre* prodns incl: Teddy in The Homecoming (Garrick) 1978, James Leeds in Children of a Lesser God (Albery) 1982, David in Benefactors (Vaudeville) 1984, David in That Summer (Hampstead) 1987, Butterfly Kiss (world premiere, Almeida) 1994, Dr Ostermark in Strindberg's The Father (tour) 1995; as writer Wet Weather Cover 1994–95, Frank in Educating Rita (tour) 1996, lead role in King Lear (Southwark Playhouse) 1996; *Television* incl: Cesare Borgia in The Borgias 1980, Ford in The Party 1987, Giles in Room at the Bottom 1988, Anderez in Boon 1989, Gregorie Rolf in Poirot 1989, Neville Nunn in Redemption 1991, Max Erstweiler in The Camomile Lawn 1991, Alan Cromer in Westbeach 1992 and 1993, Fireworks 1993, Space Cops 1994, Harry 1994, Sharpe's Battle 1994, The Story of Joseph 1994, Joseph Chamberlain in Rhodes 1995, Gregory Watling in Wokenwell 1996; *Films* incl: John the Disciple in The Day Christ Died 1979, Monks in Oliver Twist 1981, Priabin in Firefox 1982, Katis in Eleni 1985, Landis in Hiding Out 1987, Roccafino in The Sicilian 1987, Harana in Columbus - The Discovery 1992, King Heroac in Son of Pink Panther 1992, Paulo Lusano in The Innocent Sleep 1994, Charles Elliot in The Opium Wars 1996; as writer Singing for Stalin 1994–95; *Recreations* classical guitar, listening to music, talking, running, writing; *Style*— Oliver Cotton, Esq; ✉ c/o Markham & Froggatt Ltd, Julian House, 4 Windmill Street, London W1P 1HF (☎ 0171 636 4412, fax 0171 637 5233)

COTTON, Prof Roger Ernest; s of Frederick Stanley Cotton (d 1981), and Lillie, *née* Slater (d 1981); *b* 15 Sept 1926; *Educ* Derby Sch, Univ of London, Middx Hosp Med Sch (MB BS, MD); *m* 1, 12 May 1956 (m dis), Sheila Elizabeth Campbell (d 1986), da of Donald Logan (d 1968); 2 s (Andrew Robin b 1958, Richard John b 1961); m 2, 20 Oct 1989, Susan Veronica, *née* Towse; *Career* RAF med serv 1950–52; visiting prof of pathology N Western Univ Chicago USA 1959–60, sr lectr in pathology Middx Hosp 1960–63 (lectr 1952–59), emeritus pathologist City Hosp Nottingham 1990– (formerly pathologist 1963–90), special prof of diagnostic oncology Univ of Nottingham 1974–90, ed (fndn) Histopathology 1975–84, vice chm Nottinghamshire Health Authy 1977–81, int pres Int Acad of Pathology 1982–84; chm Crest Appeal and Nottingham Ctee Cancer Res Campaign; FRCPath 1973 (MRCPath 1963); *Books* Lecture Notes on Pathology (4 edn, 1992), A Colour Atlas of Respiratory Infections (with J Macfarlane and R G Finch, 1993); *Recreations* golf, gardening, music; *Style*— Prof Roger Cotton; ✉ 50 Broadgate, Beeston, Nottingham NG9 2FW (☎ 0115 925 8565)

COTTON, William Frederick (Bill); CBE (1989, OBE 1976); s of William Edward (Billy) Cotton, and Mabel Hope; *b* 23 April 1928; *Educ* Ardingly; *m* 1, 1950, Bernadine Maud Sinclair; 3 da; m 2, 1965, Ann Corfield, *née* Bucknall; 1 step da; m 3, 1990, Kathryn Mary, *née* Ralphs; *Career* jt md Michael Reine Music Co 1952–56; BBC TV: prodr Light Entertainment Dept 1956–62, asst head of light entertainment 1962–67, head of variety 1967–70, head of Light Entertainment Gp 1970–77, controller BBC1 1977–81, dep md 1981–82, md DBS 1982–84, chm BBC Enterprises 1982–86 and 1987–88 (vice chm 1986–87), md BBC Television 1984–88; chm Noel Gay TV and dir Noel Gay Organisation 1988–, non-exec dir Alba plc 1988–, non-exec chm Meridian Broadcasting Ltd 1996– (non-exec dep chm 1991–96); pres RTS 1992–95; JP Richmond 1976–84; FRTS; *Style*— Bill Cotton, Esq, CBE; ✉ Noel Gay Television, 1 Albion Court, Albion Place, Galena Road, London W6 0QT (☎ 0181 600 5200, fax 0181 600 5222)

COTTRELL, Sir Alan Howard; kt (1971); s of Albert Cottrell, and Elizabeth Cottrell, of Birmingham; *b* 17 July 1919; *Educ* Moseley GS, Univ of Birmingham; *m* 1944, Jean Elizabeth, da of Ernest William Harber; 1 s; *Career* former lectr and prof of physical metallurgy Univ of Birmingham, chief scientific advsr HM Govt 1971–74 (formerly dep chief); former vice pres Royal Soc, master Jesus Coll Cambridge 1974–86, vice chllr Univ of Cambridge 1977–79; memb Security Cmmn 1981–93; Hon DSc: Oxford 1979, Birmingham 1983; Hon LLD Cambridge 1996; Liveryman Worshipful Co of Goldsmiths; FRS 1955, FEng 1979; *Style*— Sir Alan Cottrell, FRS, FEng; ✉ 40 Maids Causeway, Cambridge CB5 8DD (☎ 01223 63806)

COTTRELL, Bryce Arthur Murray; s of Brig Arthur Foulkes Baglietto Cottrell, DSO, OBE (d 1962), of Ashford, Kent, and Mary Barbara, *née* Nicoll (d 1986); *b* 16 Sept 1931; *Educ* Charterhouse, CCC Oxford (MA); *m* 1955, Jeane Dolores, da of R P Monk (d 1942), of Coventry; 2 s, 2 da; *Career* memb Stock Exchange 1958, chm Phillips and Drew Stockbrokers 1985–88 (ptnr 1963–85); fell and funding dir CCC Oxford 1990–92; non-exec dir: Central Railway Group 1992–, Long Term Capital Ltd 1993–; govr St Leonards Mayfield Sch 1988–96; MSI 1992, CIMgt; *Recreations* railways, spectator sports, paintings; *Clubs* City of London; *Style*— Bryce Cottrell, Esq; ✉ The Portreeve's House, East Street, Tonbridge, Kent TN9 1HP (☎ and fax 01732 773277)

COTTRELL, David Vernon Swynfen; s of George Swinfen Cottrell (d 1960), of the Manor House, Bredon, Hereford & Worcester, and Dorothy Mary Catherine, *née* Liddell (d 1957); *b* 15 Nov 1923; *Educ* Eton, Windsor, Trinity Coll Cambridge; *m* 6 June 1950, Leontine Mariette (Marylena), da of Capt James Allan Dyson Perrins, MC (d 1974), of Waresley House, Hartlebury, Worcs; 1 s (Mark b 1955), 1 da (Sarah (Mrs Caulcutt) b 1953), 1 step s (Rupert b 1945), 1 step da (Rozanna (Mrs Hammond) b 1946); *Career* RNVR 1942–46; admitted slr 1951, conslt practising Birmingham, ret 1990; chm and dir: S J Bishop & Son Ltd IOW 1955–63, Waterloo House (Birmingham) Ltd 1957–, Temple St (Birmingham) Ltd 1957–88; dir Dares Brewery Ltd Birmingham 1960–63, fndr and life dir Newater Investments Ltd Birmingham 1963–, chm Tewkesbury Marina Ltd 1969– (md 1969–90); memb Cncl Assoc Brokers & Yacht Agents 1970–89, vice chm Nat Yacht Harbour Assoc 1984–90 (memb Cncl 1972–91, vice pres 1974–76, pres and chm 1979–82), chm Midlands Region Br Marine Indust Fedn 1988–90; High Sheriff Hereford & Worcs 1976; memb Cncl Lower Avon Navigation Tst 1951–, pres Gloucs Branch Inland Waterways Assoc 1976– (chm 1974–76); memb: Law Soc 1951–90, Yacht Brokers Designers and Surveyors Assoc 1975; *Recreations* yachting, shooting, landscape painting; *Clubs* Royal Yacht Sqdn (Cowes IOW), Royal Solent Yacht; *Style*— David Cottrell, Esq; ✉ The Tewkesbury Marina Ltd, Bredon Rd, Tewkesbury, Gloucestershire (☎ 01684 293737)

COTTRELL, (Patrick) Rupert; s of Patrick Nelson Hickman, of Hale Park, Fordingbridge, Hants, and Leontine Mariette, *née* Dyson-Perrins; gs of Sir Alfred Hickman, 2 Bt (see Peerage and Baronetage); assumed by Deed Poll 1953 the surname of Cottrell in lieu of that of Hickman; *b* 14 June 1945; *Educ* Gordonstoun; *m* 1, 19 Oct 1968 (m dis 1989), Claire, da of Lt-Col James Grey Round, OBE, JP, DL, of Birch, Colchester, Essex; 1 s (Nicholas Rupert b 21 Aug 1970), 1 da (Jessica Victoria b 19 April 1974); m 2, 17 July 1989, Anne, o da of late Arthur Holbrook, of Leics; *Career* Macnicol & Co 1964–65, Montagu Loebl Stanley 1965–68, Cazenove & Co 1968–80, ptnr Birch Farms 1975–89, dir Maronhart Ltd 1978–93; md Salamander Restorations 1980–; dir: Buzzacott Investment Management Ltd, Buzzacott Nominees Ltd 1984–90, Project 84 (Chelmsford) Ltd 1986–90, Bell Lawrie White 1990–92, Hill Samuel Private Client Management Ltd 1990–93, Henry Cooke Lumsden plc 1993–96; md Henry Cooke Lumsden (London) 1993–95; memb Cncl: FIMBRA 1986–90 (memb Membership Sub-Ctee 1987–90, memb Disciplinary Ctee 1988–89), Nat Assoc of Boys' Clubs 1985–91; chm Essex Assoc of Boys' Clubs 1985–91 (vice chm 1983); memb: Lloyd's, Securities Inst; *Recreations* reading, sailing, fishing, hunting, shooting; *Clubs* Royal Yacht Sqdn, Boodle's, Beefsteak, Jockey Club Rooms; *Style*— Rupert Cottrell, Esq; ✉ Ford Cottage, Exford, Somerset TA24 7PY

COTTS, Sir Richard Crichton Mitchell; 4 Bt (UK 1921), of Coldharbour Wood, Rogate, Sussex; er s of Sir (Robert) Crichton Mitchell Cotts, 3 Bt (d 1995), and Barbara

Mary Winefride, *née* Throckmorton (d 1982); *b* 26 July 1946; *Educ* Oratory Sch; *Heir* bro, Hamish William Anthony Mitchell Cotts b 1951; *Style*— Sir Richard Cotts, Bt

COUCH-SMITH, Lynda Beverley; da of John Couch, of Hove, E Sussex, and Brenda Cloak; *b* 5 Sept 1958; *Educ* Weydon Sch Farnham Surrey, West Hatch HS Chigwell Essex, London Coll of Printing (cert in radio journalism), London Acad of Music and Dramatic Art (cert of merit for spoken English, cert for reading); *Career* jr reporter and newsreader Swansea Sound 1978–80, sr reporter and prodr/presenter weekly arts prog Hereward Radio Peterborough 1980–82; GWR FM Radio (formerly Wiltshire Radio): sr reporter and presenter 1982–83, dep ed 1983, news ed 1983–86, head of news GWR FM and Brunel Classic Gold Radio 1986–92; former md Isle of Wight Radio Ltd 1992; Medical Radio award for most valued contrib to medicine on radio in UK for documentary Diabetes 1982; chm Businesswoman's Breakfast Club Swindon 1991–92; *Recreations* theatre, cinema, world travel, cooking, wine, gardening; *Style*— Miss Lynda Couch

COUCHMAN, Ernest Henry; s of Henry Ernest Couchman (d 1995), of Grays, Essex, and Eliza Gladys, *née* Glasson (d 1974); *b* 6 March 1939; *Educ* William Palmer Endowed Sch for Boys; *m* 14 Sept 1963, Patricia, da of Keith Robinson (d 1978); 1 s (James b 1968), 2 da (Caroline b 1972, Judith b 1978); *Career* CA; chief accountant Baird & Tatlock London Ltd 1965–68, head of business and professional studies Redditch Coll 1980–86, head of professional accounting studies SW London Coll 1986–88, Chart Foulks Lynch plc 1989–90, Matthew Boulton Coll 1990–95; lay pastor Studley Baptist Church 1978–84, lay pastor Dunnington Baptist Church 1995–; FCA; *Recreations* music; *Style*— Ernest H Couchman, Esq; ✉ 4 Stapleton Rd, Studley, Warwickshire (☎ 01527 85 2101)

COUCHMAN, James Randall; MP (C) Gillingham (majority 16,638); s of Stanley Randall Couchman (d 1992), and Alison Margaret Couchman (d 1994); *b* 11 Feb 1942; *Educ* Cranleigh Sch, King's Coll Newcastle upon Tyne; *m* 1967, Barbara Jean, da of Max Heilbrun (d 1956); 1 s, 1 da; *Career* Parly candidate (C) Chester le Street 1979, MP (C) Gillingham 1983–; PPS to: Sec of State for Social Security 1984–90, Min for Health 1986–88, Chllr of Duchy of Lancaster 1988–89, Sec of State for Social Security 1989–90, Lord Pres of Cncl and Ldr of The House 1995–; memb Select Ctee for: Social Services 1983–84, Northern Ireland 1995–; memb Public Accounts Ctee 1992–95, vice chm Parly Beer Club 1994–; memb Bexley Borough Cncl 1974–82, chm Bexley Social Servs 1975–78 and 1980–82, chm Bexley Health Authy 1981–83; dir Chiswick Caterers Ltd 1980–94; Liveryman Worshipful Co of Vintners; *Style*— James Couchman, Esq, MP; ✉ House of Commons, London SW1A 0AA (☎ 0171 219 3000)

COUCHMAN, Martin; s of Frederick Alfred James Couchman (d 1970), of Halstead, Kent, and Pamela Mary, *née* Argent; *b* 28 Sept 1947; *Educ* Sutton Valence, Exeter Coll Oxford (BA Jurisprudence); *m* 29 Oct 1983, Carolyn Mary Constance, da of Victor Frow Roberts (d 1987), of Childer Thornton, Cheshire; 3 s (Edmund Frederick Martin b 1985, William Thomas James b 1987, Nicholas Robert David b 1992), 1 da (Annie Elizabeth Constance b 1989); *Career* bldg indust 1970–77; Nat Econ Devpt Office: indust advsr 1977–84, head of admin 1984–87, on secondment as UK dir of Euro Year of the Environment 1987–88, sec to Nat Econ Devpt Cncl 1988–92; dep chief exec British Hospitality Assoc 1993–; FRSA 1987; *Recreations* amateur dramatics, Anglo-Saxon history, armchair archaeology; *Style*— Martin Couchman, Esq; ✉ The Old Rectory, Halstead, Sevenoaks, Kent TN14 7HG

COUGHLAN, Daniel Michael; s of Michael Joseph Coughlan, and Lilian Katherine, *née* Seymour; *b* 28 Aug 1941; *Educ* Drayton Manor County GS; *m* 5 June 1965, Jennifer Pamela, da of John Harmer (d 1970); 1 s (Mark Michael b Aug 1967), 1 da (Mandy-Diana b March 1972); *Career* gp prodn dir Sterling Publishing Group plc 1995–96; *Recreations* watching cricket, reading; *Clubs* Middlesex CCC, Uxbridge Cricket; *Style*— Daniel Coughlan, Esq; ✉ Pippins, 15 Pinewood Green, Iver Heath, Buckinghamshire

COULL, Prof Alexander (Alex); s of William Coull (d 1964), of Peterhead, and Jane Ritchie, *née* Reid (d 1969); *b* 20 June 1931; *Educ* Peterhead Acad, Univ of Aberdeen (BScEng, PhD, DSc), Cranfield Inst of Technol (MSc); *m* 27 Dec 1962, Frances Bruce, da of Francis T C Moir (d 1988), of Aberdeen; 1 s (Gavin b 1967), 2 da (Alison b 1964, Moyra b 1969); *Career* res asst MIT (USA) 1955, structural engr English Electric Co Ltd 1955–57; lectr in: engrg Univ of Aberdeen 1957–62, civil engrg Univ of Southampton 1962–66; prof of structural engrg Univ of Strathclyde 1967–76 (dean 1969–72), Regius prof of civil engrg Univ of Glasgow 1977–93 (dean of engrg 1981–84); chm Clyde Estuary Amenity Cncl 1981–86, govr Glasgow Poly 1987–93, past memb Ctee Inst of Structural Engrs (Scottish Branch); chm: Ctee on Tall Concrete and Masonry Bldgs, Cncl on Tall Bldgs and Urban Habitat 1984–93; FICE 1973, FIStructE 1973, FRSE 1971, FRSA 1989; *Books* ed: Tall Buildings (1967), Fundamentals of Structural Theory (1972), Tall Building Structures: Analysis and Design (1991); *Recreations* golf, skiing, hill-walking; *Clubs* Buchanan Castle Golf; *Style*— Prof Alex Coull, FRSE; ✉ 11 Blackwood Rd, Milngavie, Glasgow G62 7LB (☎ 0141 956 1655)

COULL, Maj-Gen John Taylor; CB (1992); s of John Sandeman Coull (d 1970), of Aberdeen, and Ethel Marjory, *née* Taylor; *b* 4 March 1934; *Educ* Robert Gordon's Coll Aberdeen, Univ of Aberdeen (MB ChB); *m* 27 Dec 1958, Mildred, da of Francis Thomson Macfarlane (d 1994); 3 s (Stephen John b 1960, Gordon David b 1962, Andrew Thomson b 1965); *Career* cmmnd RAMC 1960; conslt in gen surgery 1969, conslt in orthopaedic surgery 1972; advsr on orthopaedic surgery MOD 1977–86, conslt surgn BAOR 1986–88, QHS 1987–92, dir of surgery and conslt surgn to the Army and conslt surgn Royal Hosp Chelsea 1988–92, medico-legal advsr MOD (A) 1992–, Col Cmdt RAMC, Hon Col 202 Gen Hosp RAMC (V); author of articles on hip dislocation amputation and fracture fixation; contrib: Field Surgery Pocket Book, Rob Smith Surgery; FRCS, FRCSEd, FBOA (memb Cncl 1985–87), FRSM; *Recreations* house maintenance, woodwork, gardening; *Clubs* RSM; *Style*— Maj-Gen John Coull, CB; ✉ RAM College, Millbank, London SW1P 4RJ

COULSFIELD, Hon Lord; John Taylor Cameron; QC (Scot, 1973); s of John Reid Cameron, MA (d 1958), former Dir of Education, Dundee, and Annie Duncan, *née* Taylor (d 1982); *b* 24 April 1934; *Educ* Fettes Coll, CCC Oxford (MA), Edinburgh Univ (LLB); *m* 4 Sept 1964, Bridget Deirdre, da of Ian Caldwell Purston Sloan, The Black Watch (d 1940); *Career* admitted Faculty of Advocates 1960; lectr in public law Edinburgh Univ 1960–64; QC 1973; advocate-depute 1977–79; keeper of Advocates' Library 1977–87; judge Courts of Appeal of Jersey and Guernsey 1986–87; chm Medical Appeal Tribunals 1985–87; Scottish judge Employment Appeal Tribunal 1992–96; Senator of Coll of Justice with title of Lord Coulsfield 1987–; *Style*— The Hon Lord Coulsfield

COULSHED, Brig Dame (Mary) Frances; DBE (1953, CBE 1949), TD (1951); da of Wilfred Coulshed and Maud, *née* Mullin; *b* 10 Nov 1904; *Educ* Parkfields Cedars Derby, Convent of the Sacred Heart Kensington; *Career* ATS 1938–49, subsequently WRAC 1949–54; served WWII, NW Europe Campaign (despatches), Dep Dir Anti-Aircraft Cmd 1946–50, Dep Dir War Office 1950, Dir WRAC 1951–54, Brig, ret; ADC to HM The King 1951, ADC to HM The Queen 1952–54; Order of Leopold I of Belgium with Palm, Croix de Guerre with Palm 1946; *Style*— Brig Dame Frances Coulshed, DBE, TD; ✉ 49–51 Holton, West Heath Road, London NW3

COULSON, Sir John Eltringham; KCMG (1957, CMG 1946); er s of Henry John Coulson (d 1959), of Bickley, Kent; *b* 13 Sept 1909; *Educ* Rugby, CCC Cambridge; *m* 1944, Mavis Ninette, da of late Edwin Beazley, of Coleman's Hatch, Sussex; 2 s; *Career* Dip Serv: dep UK rep to UN NY 1950–52, asst under sec of state FO 1952–55, min Washington 1955–57, seconded to Paymaster Gen's Office 1957, ambass to Sweden 1960–63, dep under sec of state FO 1963–65, chief Dip Serv Admin 1965, sec gen EFTA 1965–72; pres Hants BRCS 1972–79; *Style*— Sir John Coulson, KCMG; ✉ The Old Mill, Selborne, Hants GU34 3LG (☎ 01420 51188)

COULSON, (Bevis) Michael Leigh; s of Capt Thomas William Bevis Coulson (d 1944), of Coulsdon, Surrey, and Vera, *née* Leigh; *b* 18 May 1945; *Educ* Charterhouse, Univ of Liverpool, City of London Coll (BSc), Drew Univ New Jersey, American Univ Washington DC; *m* 2 Oct 1971, Hilary Ann, da of Dr William Henry Cotton Croft; 3 da (Alice b 1978, Mary b 1981, Lisa b 1981); *Career* stockbroking investment analysis 1970–; head mining res Phillips & Drew 1982–86, dir and head Mining Dept Kitcat & Aitken 1986–90, chm Open Seas Ltd 1991–92, int mining dept and dir African Research Credit Lyonnais Laing 1992–94, head African Research Nedcor Securities 1994–; dir: Blue Sky Resources Ltd, InterAfrica Group Ltd; Freeman City of London 1985, memb Worshipful Co of Weavers 1985; memb Soc of Investmt Analysts 1975; MSI; *Recreations* cricket, football, horticulture; *Style*— Michael Coulson, Esq

COULSON-THOMAS, Prof Colin Joseph; s of Joseph Coulson Thomas, of Mullian, Cornwall, and Elsie, *née* Cannicott; *b* 26 April 1949; *Educ* Helston GS, LSE (Trevennon exhibitioner), London Business Sch (MSc), Univ of London (DPA, MSc(Econ)), Univ of Southern Calif (AM), Univ of SA (MPA), Aston Univ (PhD), DipM, DipCAM; *m* Margaret Anne, *née* Grantham; 2 da (Yvette May b 1978, Vivien Jane b 1980); *partner* Susan Coulson-Thomas, *née* Eppy; 1 s (Trystan Joseph b 1991); *Career* articled clerk Neville Hovey Gardner & Co 1970–73 (qualified CA 1973), student London Business Sch 1973–75, conslt Coopers and Lybrand Associates Ltd 1975–77, research exec IOD 1977–78; ed/publisher: Professional Administration (ICS) 1978–81, Casebook & Director (Casebook Publications Ltd) 1979–80; head of pubns and PR ICSA 1980–81, publishing dir (Periodicals) Longman Group Ltd 1981–84; Rank Xerox UK Ltd: mangr corp affrs 1984–87, corp affrs counsel 1987–93; chm: Adaptation Ltd 1994– (chm and chief exec offr 1987–94), Attitudes Skills and Knowledge Ltd 1994–, ASK Europe plc 1995–, ASK Multimedia Ltd 1995–, Policy Publications Ltd 1995–; corp affrs advsr BIM 1987–91, memb Home Office Partnership Advsy Bd 1993–94, leader and co-ordinator COBRA Project (EC) 1994–95; visiting research fell IT Inst Univ of Salford 1987–95, head of exec progs Univ of Southern Calif UK Prog 1987–88, dir of external affrs Euro Business Sch 1987–88, visiting fell Aston Business Sch 1988–93 (fndr dir Centre for the Professions 1988–89), sr visiting research fell City Univ Business Sch 1991–94, The Willmott Dixon prof of corp transformation and dean Faculty of Mgmnt Univ of Luton 1994–, sr assoc judge Inst Univ of Cambridge 1994–, Hooker distinguished visiting prof McMaster Univ 1995, visiting prof East China Univ of Science & Technology Shanghai 1996; memb Advsy Bd NI Graduate Mgmnt Devpt Programme 1994–; govr Moorfields Eye Hosp 1978–88, dep chm London Electricity Consultative Cncl 1980–86; memb: Cncl for Professions Supplementary to Med 1982–89, Nat Biological Standards Bd 1985–94; treas Central London Branch BIM 1977–79; chm: Crossbencher (Parly Liaison) Prog 1977–80, Public Affrs Ctee Inst of Mktg 1979–80; memb Ctee London Soc of CAs 1979–81, pres Soc of Co and Commercial Accountants 1984–85 (memb Cncl 1978–86), vice pres Soc of Conservative Accountants 1990– (sec 1978–83, chm 1983–90); memb Cncl IPR 1983–86 (chm Professional Practices Ctee 1985–86), memb Professional Devpt Ctee IOD 1989–; memb Cncl Conflict Res Soc 1974–76, treas The Beauchamp Lodge Settlement 1976–77, cncllr London Borough of Greenwich 1977–82, memb Greenwich Community Health Cncl 1977–80, govr Eltham Green, Kidbrooke, Roan and Charlton Schs 1977–81, memb Cncl Anglo-Brasilian Soc 1978–81; chm: Bow Group and Bow Publications 1982–83, Focus Group 1981–82 (pres 1983–86); memb Cncl: Royal Cwlth Soc 1981–85, Parly Info Technol Ctee 1987–96, Fndn for Sci and Technol 1987–92; tstee: Frontline Tst 1989–, Community Network 1989–; memb Advsy Panel Forum for Technol and Trg 1993–95, memb Nat Trade and Indust Forum 1993–; judge: Sword of Excellence Awards 1990–92, BT Award for Innovation in Electonic Trading 1993– (chm 1995–); Freeman City of London 1978; memb Worshipful Co of: Chartered Secs and Administrators 1978, Bakers 1984; FCA 1979, FCIS 1984, FSCA 1978, FCCA 1980, FMS 1984, FITD 1989, FIPR 1990, FIPM 1991, FRGS, FRSA; *Publications* A Guide to Business Schools (1975), Company Administration Made Simple (1975), Public Relations: A Practical Guide (1979), Public Relations is Your Business (1981), Marketing Communications (1983), The 'New Professionals' (BIM, 1988), The Responsive Organisation, People Management, the challenge of the 1990s (with Richard Brown, BIM, 1989), Too Old at 40? (BIM, 1989), Beyond Quality: Managing the Relationship with the Customer (with Richard Brown, BIM, 1990), The Complete Spokesperson (with Peter Bartram, 1990), The Flat Organisation: Philosophy and Practice (with Trudy Coe, BIM, 1991), Creating the Global Company - Successful Internationalisation (1992), Transforming the Company - Bridging the Gap Between Management Myth and Corporate Reality (1992), Creating Excellence in the Boardroom: A Guide to Shaping Directorial Competence and Board Effectiveness (1993), Developing Directors: Building An Effective Boardroom Team (1993), Business Restructuring and Teleworking (ed, 1994), Business Process Re-engineering: Myths and Realities (ed, 1994), The Responsive Organisation: Re-engineering new patterns of work (gen ed, 3 vols, 1995), The Competitive Network (exec ed, 1996); *Recreations* country houses, aviation, the music of the Rolling Stones and the Blues; *Clubs* City Livery, Royal Victoria League; *Style*— Prof Colin Coulson-Thomas; ✉ Adaptation Ltd, Rathgar House, 237 Baring Road, Grove Park, London SE12 0BE (☎ 0181 857 5907, fax 0181 857 5947); Faculty of Management, University of Luton, Putteridge Bury, Hitchin Road, Luton, Bedfordshire LU2 8LE (☎ 01582 482555, fax 01582 482689)

COULTHARD, David; *b* 27 March 1971; *Career* motor racing driver; achievements incl: Scottish Jr Kart champion 1983, 1984 and 1985, Scottish Open and Br Super 1 Kart champion 1986 and 1987, Scottish Open Kart champion 1988, first Formula Ford 1600 Championship 1989, fourth Br Vauxhall Lotus Challenge 1990, fifth GM Lotus Euroseries 1990, first Grand Prix (Silverstone) 1990, second Br Formula Three Championship 1991, winner Macau Grand Prix 1991, ninth European Formula 3000 Championship 1992, third Formula 3000 Championship 1993; Williams test driver 1993 and 1994, Formula One debut 1994, drove for Williams-Renault team 1994, signed for Williams-Renault for 1995 season, signed for McLaren International Ltd 1996 and 1997 seasons; Formula One career: 1 Grand Prix win, 7 pole positions; McLaren Autosport Young Driver of the Year 1990, ITV/Panasonic Young Sports Personality of the Year 1994, Daily Express Scottish Sports Personality of the Year 1994; *Style*— David Coulthard, Esq; ✉ c/o International Management Group, Pier House, Strand on the Green, Chiswick, London W4 3NN (☎ 0181 994 1444, fax 0181 994 9606)

COULTON, Very Rev Nicholas Guy; s of Nicholas Guy Coulton (d 1965), of Buckfastleigh, S Devon, and Audrey Florence Furneaux, *née* Luscombe; *b* 14 June 1940; *Educ* Blundell's, Cuddesdon Theol Coll Oxford, BD (London); *m* 28 Dec 1978, Edith Mary, da of John James Gainford, of Wolverhampton; 1 s (Andrew Nicholas Furneaux b 1981), 2 da (Katharine Ruth Finlay b 1983, Sarah Louise Luscombe b 1986); *Career* admitted slr 1962, asst slr Burges Salmon and Co Bristol 1962–65; curate Pershore Abbey Worcs with Birlingham Pinvin and Wick 1967–71, domestic chaplain to the Bishop of St Albans 1971–75, vicar St Paul's Church Bedford 1975–90, provost St Nicholas Cathedral Newcastle upon Tyne 1990–; chm North-East Cncl of Christians and Jews 1991–; *Recreations* gardening, reading, listening to music, historical exploration, rearing children, outdoor pursuits; *Style*— The Very Rev the Provost of Newcastle; ✉ The Cathedral Vicarage, 26 Mitchell Avenue, Jesmond, Newcastle upon Tyne NE2

3LA (☎ 0191 281 6554); The Cathedral Church of St Nicholas, Newcastle upon Tyne NE1 1PF (☎ 0191 232 1939, fax 0191 230 0735)

COUNSELL, Her Honour Judge; Hazel Rosemary; da of Arthur Henry Counsell, and Elsie Winifred Counsell; *b* 7 Jan 1931; *Educ* Clifton HS, La Châtellaine Switzerland, Bristol Univ; *m* 1980, Judge Peter Fallon, QC; *Career* called to the Bar 1956, Legal Dept Miny of Labour 1959–62, recorder Crown Court 1976–77, circuit judge (Western Circuit) 1978–; memb Matrimonial Causes Ctee 1983–87; govr Colston Girls Sch; *Style—* Her Hon Judge Counsell; ✉ The Law Courts, Small Street, Bristol BS1 1DA

COUPE, Barry Desmond; s of Harold Desmond Coupe (d 1992), of Talbot Woods, Bournemouth, and Alice, *née* Roberts; *b* 4 June 1951; *Educ* Canford Sch, Leeds Sch of Architecture (BA, Dip Arch); *m* 6 May 1978, Shan Patricia, da of James Ninian Reid Wilson, of Northbourne, Bournemouth; 2 s (Matthew b 6 Sept 1981, Benjamin b 11 Feb 1985); *Career* architect; Fitzroy Robinson & Ptnrs 1977–80, fndr ptnr Forum Architects 1980–; works incl: Nobelight Bldg 1983, leisure complex Whittaker House 1984, offrs' club RAF Mildenhall 1986, Beehive Shopping Centre Cambridge 1987, Bow Housing 1989, HQ Bldg Domino plc Cambridge 1987, The Quorum Development 1991, Wolverhampton Nuffield Hosp, Animal Hosp Animal Health Tst 1995, Animal Hosp Univ of Edinburgh 1996; Usafe Design award 1986, 1987, 1988 and 1989, Usafe Worldwide award 1986, Civic Tst award, commendation 1987; tstee Cambridge Children's Hospice; RIBA 1979; *Recreations* classic cars, cricket, photography, real tennis; *Clubs* Philanerers CC, Cambridge Univ Real Tennis, Tresco Cricket, Newmarket Real Tennis, Granta Rex 41; *Style—* Barry Coupe, Esq; ✉ Glebe Barn, Ashley, Newmarket, Suffolk CB8 9DU (☎ 01638 730751); Forum Architects, 38 Newmarket Road, Cambridge (☎ 01223 66616, fax 01223 66714)

COUPER, Dudley William Malcolm; s of Leslie Claude Couper (d 1962), of Farnham, Surrey, and Beatrice Ena, *née* Greengrass; *b* 9 April 1935; *Educ* Cranleigh Sch, Keble Coll Oxford (MA); *m* 3 June 1961, Jill, da of William Ronald Trumper (d 1965), of Devizes, Wilts; 1 s (Duncan b 1968), 2 da (Sarah b 1962, Joanna b 1963); *Career* admitted slr; Rowe and Maw: ptnr 1965–96, sr ptnr 1993–96, head of Property Dept 1968–94, fin ptnr 1969–90, chm Exec Ctee 1987–90; Cranleigh Sch: govr 1983–, chm Fin Ctee 1985–95, vice chm Governing Body 1992–95, chm Governing Body 1995–; memb Law Soc 1960; memb MCC; *Recreations* golf and sport of all kinds, travel, walking, gardening; *Clubs* Cowdray Park and Wildwood Golf; *Style—* Dudley Couper, Esq; ✉ Lansdowne, 20 Hurtmore Chase, Godalming, Surrey GU7 2RT (☎ 01483 419414, fax/messages 01483 419101)

COUPER, Dr Heather Anita; da of George Couper Elder Couper, of Bexhill on Sea, E Sussex, and Anita, *née* Taylor (d 1984); *b* 2 June 1949; *Educ* St Mary's GS, Univ of Leicester (BSc), Univ of Oxford; *Career* mgmnt trainee Peter Robinson Ltd 1967–69, res asst Cambridge Observatories 1969–70, lectr Greenwich Planetarium 1977–83, broadcaster and writer on astronomy and sci 1983–, Gresham prof of astronomy 1993–96; cmmr Millenium Cmmn 1994–; dir Pioneer Film and TV Productions 1988–; astronomy columnist The Independent, presenter of and contrib to many radio programmes incl Seeing Stars (BBC World Serv); pres: Br Astronomical Assoc 1984–86, Jr Astronomical Soc 1987–89; Hon DLitt Loughborough Univ 1991, Hon DSc Univ of Hertfordshire 1994; FRAS 1970; *Television* Channel 4: The Planets 1985, The Stars 1988; BBC 2: Horizon Special: A Close Encounter of the Second Kind 1992; Pioneer Productions: The Neptune Encounter (ITV) 1989, ET Please Phone Earth 1992, Space Shuttle Discovery 1993, Electric Skies 1994, Arthur C Clarke: The Visionary (Discovery Channel Europe) 1995, Wonders of Weather (Discovery Channel Europe and Learning Channel USA) 1995, Avalanche (Channel 4) 1995, On Jupiter (Discovery Channel America and Channel 4) 1995; *Books* 24 pubns incl: The Space Scientist series, The Universe, The Restless Universe, The Stars, The Planets, The Space Atlas, How the Universe Works, Guide to the Galaxy, Black Holes; *Recreations* travel, the English countryside, wine, food, music; *Clubs* Groucho, Rugby Club of London; *Style—* Dr Heather Couper; ✉ c/o Pioneer Productions, Pinewood Studios, Pinewood Road, Iver, Bucks SL0 0NH (☎ 01753 656159)

COUPER, Sir (Robert) Nicholas Oliver; 6 Bt (UK 1841); s of Maj Sir George Robert Cecil Couper, 5 Bt (d 1975), and Margaret Grace, *née* Thomas (d 1984); *b* 9 Oct 1945; *Educ* Eton, RMA Sandhurst; *m* 1, 1972 (m dis 1986), Kirsten (Curzon) Henrietta, da of Maj George Burrell MacKean, JP, DL (d 1983), of Loughanmore, Dunadry, Co Antrim; 1 s (James George b 1977), 1 da (Caroline Doune b 1979); m 2, 1991, Katrina Frances, da of Sir (Charles) Michael Walker, GCMG, *qv*, of Herongate House, W Chiltington, Pulborough, W Sussex; *Heir* s, James George Couper b 27 Oct 1977; *Career* Acting Maj Blues and Royals (ret); estate agent; ptnr Savills; dir: Aylesfords & Co, Lane Fox; currently in own property consultancy business; *Style—* Sir Nicholas Couper, Bt; ✉ 79 Devonshire Rd, London W4 2HU (☎ 0181 995 5603)

COUPLAND, (William) James; s of late William Arthur Coupland, and Patricia Anne, *née* Martin; *b* 25 May 1957; *Educ* Kings Coll Sch Wimbledon; *m* 13 Sept 1980, Helen Jane, da of Charles Alfred Everett; 3 s (Christopher Everett, Benjamin Jake b 1981, Joshua James b 1987); *Career* dir Shearson American Express Ltd 1982–92, md Shearson Lehman Metals Ltd 1985–93, dir Shearson Lehman Hutton Commodities Tokyo Ltd, sr vice pres Shearson Lehman Hutton Inc 1986–93, chm Shearson Lehman Hutton Commodities (now Lehman Brothers Commodities Ltd) 1987–93; dir The London Metal Exchange Ltd 1992–93, sr vice-pres Kidder Peabody International Ltd 1993–94, dir Deutsche Sharps Pixley Metals Ltd 1994–95; FRSA; *Recreations* tennis, golf, painting; *Style—* James Coupland, Esq; ✉ 5 Durrington Park, Wimbledon, London SW20 8NU

COUPLAND, Prof Rex Ernest; s of Ernest Coupland (d 1978), of Mirfield, Yorks, and Doris, *née* Threadgold; *b* 30 Jan 1924; *m* 14 July 1947, (Lucy) Eileen, da of William Sargent (d 1950), of Smallrice, Sandon, Staffs; 1 s (Michael Adam b 22 July 1953), 1 da (Lesley Diana Eileen b 11 Feb 1950); *Career* Nat Serv MD RAF 1948–50; house surgn Leeds Gen Infirmary 1947, lectr Univ of Leeds 1950–58, asst prof Univ of Minnesota 1955–56, Cox prof of anatomy Univ of St Andrews 1958–68, dean Faculty of Med Univ of Nottingham 1981–87 (Fndn prof of human morphology 1968–89); memb MRC Biological Res Bd 1964–70; chm: MRC Non-Ionizing Radiation Ctee 1970–89, Med Advsy Bd Crippling Diseases 1971–75; pres: Anatomical Soc GBI 1976–78, Br Assoc of Clinical Anatomists 1977–82; memb: Derby AHA 1978–81, Trent RHA 1981–88, Central Notts DHA 1988–90 (GMC 1981–88); FRSE 1970; *Books* The Natural History of the Chromaffin Cell (1965), Enterochromaffin and Related Cells (co ed with T Fujita, 1976), Peripheral Neuroendocrine Interaction (ed with WG Forssman, 1978), contrib numerous articles in learned jls; *Recreations* gardening, watercolour painting, shooting; *Clubs* RSM; *Style—* Prof Rex Coupland, FRSE; ✉ Foxhollow, Quaker Lane, Farnsfield, Notts NG22 8EE (☎ 01623 882028); The Magnetic Resonance Centre, University of Nottingham, University Park, Nottingham NG7 2RD (☎ 0115 951 5151)

COURAGE, Maj-Gen Walter James; CB (1994), MBE (1979); s of Walter Henry Phipps (d 1983), and Nancy Mary Gardner, *née* Reeves, and step s of Lt-Col Nigel Anthony Courage, MC (d 1964); *b* 25 Sept 1940; *Educ* Abingdon Sch, RMA Sandhurst; *m* 10 Oct 1964, Lavinia Patricia, da of John Emerson Crawhall Wood (d 1981); 1 s (Sebastian b 1 June 1971), 1 da (Camilla b 25 May 1969); *Career* cmmnd 5 Royal Inniskilling Dragoon Guards 1961, cmdg Regt 1982–84, Divnl Col Staff Coll 1984, cmdg 4 Armoured Bde 1984–88, Chief of Staff UN Force in Cyprus 1988–90, Chief Jt Serv Liaison Orgn and External Affairs Div British Forces in Germany 1990–95, DG TA 1995–96, ret; dir Business Devpt Germany Kroll Assoc; sr conslt Chemhill Germany; FIMgt; *Recreations* game shooting and county pursuits; *Clubs* Marylebone Cricket, Cavalry and Guards', I Zingari, International (Berlin); *Style—* Maj-Gen Walter Courage, CB, MBE; ✉ c/o Cavalry & Guards' Club, 127 Piccadilly, London W1

COURT, Clova; da of Ernest Cameron (d 1994), and Louise, *née* Grant; *b* 10 Feb 1960; *Educ* Watermount Sch Jamaica, Mons Hill Sch Dudley, Dudley Coll; *m* June 1988, Howard John Court, s of late Howard Lenard Court; *Career* athlete; int debut 1990; achievements: winner (heptathlon) Br Championships 1990–92, winner (60m hurdles) Br Championships 1993, winner (heptathlon) Europa Cup 1993, semi-finalist (100m and 60m hurdles) World Championships 1993, Silver medal (100m hurdles) Euro Clubs Championships 1993, winner (100m hurdles) Br Championships 1994; *Recreations* cooking, trying something new; *Style—* Ms Clova Court; ✉ c/o Birchfield Harriers, Alexander Stadium, Perry Barr, Birmingham B42 1BP (☎ 0121 344 4858)

COURT, Michael Edward (Mike); s of Edward George Bertram Court, of Sheperdswell, Kent, and Patricia Margaret, *née* Shipley; *b* 24 Jan 1956; *Educ* Dover GS, Univ Coll Oxford (MA); *partner* R Jackson; *Career* with various advertising agencies 1977–: intially with Leo Burnett, Wasey Campbell-Ewald (account handler rising to copywriter) 1977–79, Foote Cone & Belding 1979–81, Carter Hedger Mitchell (now Hedger Mitchell Stark); six months at TBWA; fndr ptnr Still Price Court Twivy D'Souza until 1989 (when sold to Interpublic), creative dir Young & Rubicam London 1990–93, ret; creative dir Court Burkitt & Company (formerly Burkitt Edwards Martin) 1995–; winner awards for: BA, London Transport, Irn Bru, Olivetti, Gatwick Express, Krupps, Mates Condoms, Red Mountain, Warburtons, Virgin Atlantic, RCN; memb D&ADA 1980; *Recreations* ships, ocean liners and cruises; *Style—* Mike Court, Esq; ✉ 33 Warrington Crescent, Maida Vale, London W9 1EJ (☎ 0171 289 6668); Court Burkitt & Company, 200 Tottenham Court Road, London W1P 9LA (☎ 0171 636 9801)

COURT-BROWN, Charles Michael; s of William Michael Court-Brown, OBE (d 1968), and Caroline Gordon Stephen, *née* Thom; *b* 3 Feb 1948; *Educ* George Watson's Coll Edinburgh, Univ of Aberdeen (BSc), Univ of Edinburgh (MD, MB ChB); *m* 6 July 1974, Jacqueline Yek Quen, da of To Leong Mok; 1 s (Michael b 1988), 1 da (Johanna b 1979); *Career* conslt orthopaedic surgn 1985–, sr lectr Dept of Orthopaedic Surgery Univ of Edinburgh 1985, conslt orthopaedic surgn Lothian Health Bd 1992–; fndr memb Br Trauma Soc; fell BOA, FRCS 1979, BORS 1983, FRCS (Ed Orth) 1984; *Books* External Skeletal Fixation (1984), Atlas of Intramedullary Nailing of the Tibia and Femur (1991); *Recreations* house building, cooking; *Style—* Charles Court-Brown, Esq; ✉ Royal Infirmary of Edinburgh, Lauriston Place, Edinburgh EH3 9YW (☎ 0131 536 3721, fax 0131 660 4227)

COURTAULD, Samuel; s of Major George Courtauld (d 1980), of Essex, and Claudine Suzanne, *née* Booth (d 1983); The Courtaulds were a Huguenot family from Ile d'Oleron near La Rochelle, came to England in 1690's, 3 generations were practising goldsmiths in London and subsequent predecessors became involved in weaving business and founded Courtaulds Ltd; *b* 14 March 1940; *Educ* Gordonstoun, McGill Univ Canada, Sorbonne; *m* 2 April 1963, Annette Susan (d 1995), da of Major Chandos Ormsby Jodrell Godwin-Williams (d 1985), of Kent; 1 s (Samuel b 1969), 3 da (Serena (Mrs Halbertsma) b 1964, Melissa (Mrs Jones) b 1965, Lucinda b and d 1968); *Career* late 2 Lt Grenadier Gds; stockbroker, James Capel & Co; Freeman City of London, Liveryman Worshipful Co of Goldsmiths; MSI; *Recreations* shooting, fencing, gardening, campanology; *Clubs* First Guards, White's; *Style—* Samuel Courtauld, Esq; ✉ Don Johns Farm, Earls Colne, Colchester, Essex (☎ 01787 222627); 55N Hans Road, London SW3 1RN (☎ 0171 589 6042); James Capel & Co, 6 Bevis Marks, London EC3A 7JQ (☎ 0171 336 5373)

COURTENAY, Lord; Hugh Rupert Courtenay; DL (Devon 1991); s and h of 17 Earl of Devon; *b* 5 May 1942; *Educ* Winchester, Magdalene Coll Cambridge; *m* 9 Sept 1967, Dianna Frances, elder da of late Jack Watherston, of Menslaws, Jedburgh, Roxburghshire; 1 s, 3 da (Hon Rebecca Eildon b 1969, Hon Eleonora Venetia b 1971, Hon Camilla Mary b 1974); *Heir* s, Hon Charles Peregrine Courtenay b 14 Aug 1975; *Career* chartered surveyor, farmer and landowner; former pres Devon Branch Country Landowners' Assoc; *Style—* Lord Courtenay, DL; ✉ Powderham Castle, nr Exeter, Devon EX6 8JQ (☎ 01626 890252)

COURTENAY-STAMP, (David) Jeremy; s of David Courtenay-Stamp, and Helen Annette, *née* Smith; *b* 25 April 1962; *Educ* Blundell's (scholar), LSE (LLB); *m* Elizabeth Ann, *née* Crawford; 2 da (Georgina Louise b 31 March 1993, Alexandra Isobelle b 22 April 1995); *Career* ptnr Macfarlanes 1992– (joined 1984); memb: Worshipful Co of Dyers, City of London Solicitors Co, Law Soc; ACA 1986; *Recreations* golf, scuba, skiing, sailing, tennis, squash; *Clubs* Chelsea Harbour; *Style—* Jeremy Courtenay-Stamp, Esq; ✉ Macfarlanes, 10 Norwich Street, London EC4A 1BD (☎ 0171 831 9222, fax 0171 831 9607)

COURTIS, John; s of Thomas Courtis (d 1976), of Stock, Ingatestone, Essex, and Marjorie May, *née* Dodson (m 2 Massey); *b* 14 July 1937; *Educ* Westminster; *m* 15 Jan 1966 (m dis 1995), Jane Margaret, da of William McCall-Smith (d 1970), of Weavers, Stradishall, Suffolk; 1 s (Neil Thomas b 1970), 1 da (Claudia Janet b 1969); *Career* cmmnd RAF 1960–63; Ford Motor Co 1963–67; dir: Reed Executive 1967–71, Executive Appointments Ltd 1971–74; chm: Courtis & McManus Ltd 1974–, DEEKO plc 1981–88, FRES 1986–87, Recruitment Soc 1991–93; FCA 1959; *Books* 44 Management Mistakes (1989), Marketing Services (1987), Interviews - Skills and Strategy (1988), Bluffers Guides (to Management 1986, Accountancy 1987, Photography 1988), Recruiting for Profit (1990), Getting A Better Job (1992), Recruitment Advertising: Right First Time (1994); *Recreations* writing, cooking; *Clubs* Savile, RAF; *Style—* John Courtis, Esq; ✉ Courtis & McManus Ltd, 72/75 Marylebone High St, London W1M 4AJ (☎ 0171 486 6849, fax 0171 487 4600)

COURTNEY, Diana Jean; da of Albert John Courtney, of Chiswick, London, and Sophia, *née* Fogg; *b* 20 March 1939; *Educ* Lourdes Mount Convent; *m* 1966 (m dis 1985), Edward John Charles, s of Edward George; 2 da (Nicola Diana b 9 Aug 1971, Antonia Jane b 17 April 1975); *Career* articled clerk Rexworthy Bonsor & Simons 1955–60; ptnr: Herbert Openheimer Nathan & Vandyk 1966–88 (slr 1961–66), Denton Hall 1988–; non-exec dir Bradford & Bingley Building Society; memb Cncl and pres City Property Assoc; memb: Law Soc 1960, Anglo American Real Property Inst, British Property Fedn, British Cncl of Offices; MInstD; FRSA; *Recreations* horse racing, gardening, opera, theatre; *Style—* Ms Diana Courtney; ✉ Denton Hall, Five Chancery Lane, Clifford's Inn, London EC4A 1BU (☎ 0171 242 1212, fax 0171 404 0087)

COURTNEY, Prof James McNiven; s of George Courtney (d 1972), of Glasgow, and Margaret, *née* McNiven (d 1980); *b* 25 March 1940; *Educ* Whitehall Sr Secdy Sch Glasgow, Univ of Glasgow (BSc), Univ of Strathclyde (PhD), Univ of Rostock (Dr sc nat); *m* 26 June 1965, Ellen Miller, da of James Copeland; 1 da (Margaret Ellen Louise b 28 March 1966), 2 s (James George b 28 June 1969, David William b 3 Aug 1975); *Career* rubber technologist: Maclellan Rubber Ltd 1962–65, Uniroyal Ltd 1965–66; Univ of Strathclyde: postgrad student 1966–69, lectr Bioengineering Unit 1969–81, sr lectr 1981–85, reader 1986–89, prof 1989–; sec treas: Int Soc for Artificial Organs 1994, Int Faculty for Artificial Organs 1995 (tenured prof 1992); Rudolf Virchow prize 1986, Univ of Rostock prize of honour 1987; EurChem 1994; FRSC 1977, FIM 1993; *Books* Artificial Organs (ed, 1977), Biomaterials in Artificial Organs (ed, 1984), Progress in Bioengineering (ed, 1989); *Recreations* football supporter (Glasgow Rangers); *Style—* Prof James M Courtney; ✉ 8 Maple Drive, Lenzie, Kirkintilloch, Glasgow G66 4EA

(☎ 0141 776 6726); Bioengineering Unit, Wolfson Centre, University of Strathclyde, 106 Rottenrow, Glasgow G4 0NW (☎ 0141 552 4400, fax 0141 552 6098)

COURTNEY, Keith; s of Raymond Courtney, of Newtownabbey, NI, and Margaret Faulkner, *née* McClelland; *b* 16 May 1966; *Educ* Boys' Model Sch, Univ of Ulster (BA); *m* 21 May 1994, Katherine Jane, da of Francis Allen Charles Barnard; *Career* art dir: GGT Advertising 1988–91 (accounts incl Cadbury's, Holstein Pils, Toshiba and Daily Mirror), Simons Palmer Denton Clemmow & Johnson 1991–93 (accounts incl Nike, BT and Greenpeace); sr art dir WCRS 1993–94 (accounts incl Carling, Radio Rentals, BMW and Canon), bd art dir Lowe Howard-Spink 1994–95 (accounts incl Stella, Heineken, Vauxhall and Reebok), creative dir K Advertising 1995– (accounts incl Pentax, Carlesberg, Cheltenham & Gloucester and Commercial Union); memb: Creative Directors' Forum, Soc for the Protection of Ancient Buildings; *Awards* D&AD Silver Award (Nike) and Silver nominations (Toshiba and Nike), British TV Gold Award (Toshiba) and Silver Award (BT), Campaign Press Silver Awards (Nike and Stella Artois), Creative Circle Silver Awards (Toshiba, Carling, Nike and Cadbury), Campaign Poster Silver Award (Nike); *Books* The Oldie Book of Cartoons (contrib, 1994); *Recreations* contemporary dance, collecting memorabilia; *Clubs* Michael's Piano Bar, Groucho's; *Style*— Keith Courtney, Esq; ✉ K Advertising, 83–89 Whitfield Street, London WC1 (☎ 0171 462 7777, fax 0171 462 7766)

COURTNEY, Nicholas Piers; s of Capt Frederick Harold Demming Courtney (d 1980), and Sybil, *née* Leigh-Pemberton (d 1972); *b* 20 Dec 1944; *Educ* The Nautical Coll Pangbourne, RAC Cirencester (Dip in Estate Mgmnt); *m* 30 Oct 1980, Vanessa Sylvia, da of John Bishop Hardwicke; *Career* land agent Greville Heygate & Co 1966–69, gen mangr The Mustique Co Mustique St Vincent W Indies 1970–74; contrib: The Times, Spectator, House & Gardens; ARICS 1967; *Books* incl: The Tiger (1980), Royal Children (1982), Sporting Royals (1983), The Very Best of British (1986), Princess Anne (1986), In Society (1987), Sisters-in-Law (1988), Windsor Castle (1989), The Mall (1989), Shakespeare's Stratford (1990), A Little History of Antiques (1994); *Recreations* shooting, gardening; *Clubs* Brooks's; *Style*— Nicholas P Courtney, Esq; ✉ 9 Kempson Road, London SW6 4PX

COURTNEY, Rohan Richard; s of Arthur Richard Courtney, of Chingford, London, and Cecelia, *née* Harrington; *b* 28 Jan 1948; *Educ* William Morris GS London; *m* 12 Jan 1974, Marilyn, da of Ernest Arthur Charles Goward (d 1972), of Waltham Cross, Herts; 1 s (Liam b 1975), 1 da (Siân b 1977); *Career* banker; National Provincial Bank London 1965–68; mangr: Rothschild Intercontinental Bank Ltd London 1968–75, Amex Bank Ltd London 1975–76; asst dir Amex Bancom Ltd Hong Kong 1976–78, md Euro Asian Fin (HK) Ltd Hong Kong 1978–80, sr mangr Creditanstalt Bankverein London 1980–82, gen mangr State Bank of New S Wales London 1982–90, md Rohan Courtney & Partners Ltd 1990–, gp chief exec Robert Fraser & Co Ltd 1991–92; chm: Sterling Trust plc 1992–94 (dir 1991–94), Swaine Adeney Brigg Ltd 1993–94, International Pacific Securities plc 1993–, West 175 Enterprises Inc 1996–; non-exec: dir Tullow Oil plc 1993–, Ian Business Group plc 1995–; memb The Britain-Australia Soc Bd of Mgmnt 1993–; Freeman City of London, Liveryman Worshipful Co of Woolmen; *Recreations* country pursuits; *Clubs* Royal Over-Seas League, East India, Bankers', Hong Kong CC; *Style*— Rohan Courtney, Esq; ✉ Deepwood, Lower Wood Road, Ludlow, Shropshire SY8 2JQ (☎ 01584 856548, fax 01584 856488); Tullow Oil Plc, 1st Floor, Ames House, 6 Duke of York Street, London SW1Y 6LJ (☎ 0171 976 2600, fax 0171 976 2611)

COURTOWN, 9 Earl of (I 1762); James Patrick Montagu Burgoyne Winthrop Stopford; also (sits as) Baron Saltersford (GB 1796), Baron Courtown (I 1758), Viscount Stopford (I 1762); s of 8 Earl of Courtown, OBE, TD, DL (d 1975); *b* 19 March 1954; *Educ* Eton, Berkshire Agric Coll, RAC Cirencester; *m* 6 July 1985, Elisabeth Dorothy, yr da of Ian Rodger Dunnett, of Pinders, Broad Campden, Glos; 1 s, 1 da (Lady Rosanna Elisabeth Alice b 13 Sept 1986); *Heir* s, James Richard Ian Montagu, Viscount Stopford b 30 March 1988; *Career* land agent; ARICS; Lord in Waiting (govt whip) 1995–; govt spokesman for Home Office Scotland and Transport; *Style*— The Rt Hon the Earl of Courtown; ✉ House of Lords, London SW1A 0PW

COUSE, Philip Edward; s of Oliver Couse (d 1969), of Birmingham, and Marion Couse (d 1968); *b* 24 March 1936; *Educ* Uppingham, Hackey Sch USA; *m* 1, May 1962 (m dis 1973); 2 s (James b 1963, Anthony b 1965), 1 da (Amanda b 1969); m 2, 13 April 1978, Carol Ann Pruitt, da of Ralph Johannessen (d 1985); 1 step da (Delaine Pruitt b 1969); *Career* CA; ptnr Coopers & Lybrand 1966–91; dir: Birmingham Heartlands Hosp NHS Tst 1992–, William King Ltd 1993–; pt/t cmmr Friendly Societies Cmmn 1992–; pres ICAEW 1989–90 (memb Cncl 1978–90); pres: Birmingham CAs Students Soc 1977–78, Birmingham and West Midlands Soc of CAs 1982–83; dir Hillstone Sch Tst Ltd Malvern 1971–86, pres Birmingham and Edgbaston Debating Soc 1977–78, chm Edgbaston C of E Coll for Girls Ltd 1982–88, chm Birmingham Repertory Theatre Fndn 1990–96, chm Birmingham Diocesan Bd of Fin 1992–; treas: Bishop of Worcester's Miny Fund 1970–90, CAs' Dining Club 1985–89 (pres 1989–91), Birmingham Eye Fndn (tstee) 1981–91; memb: Arthritis and Rheumatism Cncl W Midlands, Queen Elizabeth Hosp Birmingham Golden Jubilee Appeal Ctee 1987–89, Ctee Birmingham Nuffield Hosp Appeal 1990–92; dir Birmingham Repertory Theatre Ltd 1990–96, dir Ironbridge (Telford) Heritage Fndn Ltd 1991–; Liveryman Worshipful Co of CAs in England and Wales 1987; FCA 1961; *Recreations* music, woodwork, watching rugby football; *Clubs* RAC; *Style*— Philip Couse, Esq; ✉ 23 Frederick Road, Edgbaston, Birmingham B15 1JN

COUSINS, Capt Jack; s of Herbert Sidney Cousins (d 1954), of Leigh on Sea, Essex, and Mabel Irene Hilda, *née* Andrews (d 1968); *b* 2 Feb 1920; *Educ* Storrington Coll, Alleyn Ct Sch, Highfield Coll, Chalkwell Hall Sch, Westcliff HS, TS Mercury, Sir John Cass Coll Univ of London (Master Mariner Foreign Going); *m* 26 June 1948, Joyce Patricia (d 1969), da of Stanley Hennessy (d 1965), of Broomfield, Essex; 4 s (David b 1950, Roger b 1954, Simon b 1955, Andrew b 1958); *Career* Royal Dutch Shell Group 1936; Merchant Aircraft Carrier Amastra: 4 Offr 1940, 3 Offr 1941, 2 Offr 1942, 1 Offr 1943; Marine Offr/Master Basra Port Directorate Iraq 1948, Marine Supt's Dept Shaw Savill Line 1950; Port of London Authy 1951–80: harbour inspr, asst dockmaster, sr asst dockmaster, dep dockmaster Royal Docks, traffic co-ordinator/asst harbour master Port of London Authy; marine consIt 1980–95, int sports corr 1981–; memb and liaison offr Nat Union of Marine Aviation and Shipping Tport Offrs 1956; memb: Tech Ctee Hon Co of Master Mariners 1965–94, Perm Int Assoc of Navigation Congresses 1980– (Port of London rep 1957–); London Maritime Assoc: hon sec 1956–69, vice chm 1969, vice chm and hon treas 1980–92, vice pres 1992–; PR offr Essex Co Amateur Swimming Assoc (pres 1987), memb Exec Ctee and hon facilities sec Southern Cos Amateur Swimming Assoc 1976–94, vice pres and life memb Southend-on-Sea Swimming Club (chm Multi Nat Ctee); memb: Nat Swimming Pool Strategy Working Pty Sports Cncl 1976–90, Swimming Liaison Gp Eastern Sports Cncl 1976–94, Br Swimming Coaches Assoc 1980–; bronze ptnr Palace Theatre Tst Westcliff-on-Sea, patron Little Theatre Club; publicity offr TS Mercury Old Boys Assoc; life memb: Old Westcliffians Assoc RFC, Southend Airport Club, LSO Club, Les Amis d'Edith Piaf Paris, Nat Film Theatre Club, Br Film Inst, The Folio Soc; Freeman City of London 1969, Liveryman Hon Co of Master Mariners (memb 1959); *Recreations* swimming, skiing, theatre (former shareholder Really Useful Gp Ltd), philately, music, travel; *Style*— Capt Jack Cousins; ✉ Villa Valeta, 208 Carlton Ave, Westcliff-on-Sea, Essex SS0 0QD (☎ 01702 343779); Piz D'Err, Dischmastrasse 20, 7260 Davos Dorf, Switzerland

COUSINS, James Mackay (Jim); MP (Lab) Newcastle upon Tyne Central (majority 5,288); *b* 23 Feb 1944; *Educ* New Coll Oxford (scholar), LSE; *Career* contract researcher and lectr in steel shipbuilding and inner city job markets for trade unions, Cmmn on Industrial Rels and Depts of Employment and the Environment; MP (Lab) Newcastle upon Tyne Central 1987–; memb: Wallsend Borough Cncl 1969–73, Tyne and Wear CC 1973–86 (dep ldr 1981–86), CND, MSF; *Style*— Jim Cousins, Esq, MP; ✉ First Floor, 21 Portland Terrace, Newcastle-upon-Tyne NE2 1QQ; House of Commons, London SW1A 0AA

COUSINS, John Stewart; s of Leslie Raymond Cousins (d 1976), and Margaret Betty Kate, *née* Fry; *b* 31 July 1940; *Educ* Brentwood Sch, Britannia RNC Dartmouth, Jesus Coll Cambridge (MA); *m* 1, 26 Oct 1970 (m dis 1979), Anne Elizabeth, da of Patrick O'Leary (d 1976), of Llanishen, Glamorgan; 1 da (Charlotte b 1973); m 2, 28 Dec 1979, Geraldine Anne, da of Col Thomas Ivan Bowers, CBE, DSO, MC* (d 1980), of Yateley, Hants; *Career* RN 1958–62, cmmnd Sub Lt 1960, served Far East in HMS Belfast and HMS Maryton; Kleinwort Benson Ltd: joined 1966, Far East rep Tokyo 1970–73, md Hong Kong Branch 1973–78; fin advsr to chm Porodisa Gp Indonesia 1979–80, ptnr de Zoete and Bevan 1980–85, dir Barclays de Zoete Wedd Securities 1985–92, md Barclays de Zoete Wedd Equities Ltd, chief exec BZW Puget Mahé SA Paris; currently conslt and non-exec dir: Corney & Barrow Group plc, Baring Emerging Europe Trust plc, Korean Emerging Growth Fund PLC (chm), St David's Investment Trust PLC (chm); London advsr to Paris Stock Exchange; memb Panel on Takeovers and Mergers Hong Kong 1976–78; AMIIMR, MSI; *Recreations* racing, rugby, cricket, field sports; *Clubs* Brooks's, Caledonian; *Style*— John Cousins, Esq; ✉ 73 Redcliffe Gardens, London SW10 9JJ (☎ 0171 373 1919); Lamarie, 46140 Luzech, France (☎ 00 33 5 65 20 11 95)

COUSINS, (Herbert) Leslie; s of Herbert Leslie Cousins (d 1941), and Elsie Almer Joyce Cummings, *née* Becker; *b* 7 April 1942; *Educ* Bancroft's Sch; *m* 29 Jan 1966, Margaret, da of Horace Stanley John Phipps; 2 s (Robert Leslie b 30 Oct 1967, Jonathan Mark b 30 April 1970); *Career* Price Waterhouse: articled clerk London 1959, ptnr 1975–, sr client ptnr 1993–, chm Tstees PW (UK) Pension Fund 1988–; under sec DTI 1978–80; non-exec dir Property Services Agency 1988–91; memb: Advsy Ctee Central Statistical Office 1992–, Internal Audit Ctee Dept of Tport 1993–; FCA 1965; *Recreations* tennis, golf, roses; *Clubs* Effingham Golf, Clandon Regis Golf; *Style*— Leslie Cousins, Esq; ✉ Price Waterhouse, Southwark Towers, 32 London Bridge Street, London SE1 9SY (☎ 0171 939 3000, fax 0171 378 0647)

COUSINS, Eur Ing Raymond John Randal; s of Henry George Cousins (d 1983), and Freda Isabella, *née* Roberts; *b* 14 July 1938; *Educ* Alleyn's Sch, King's Coll London (BSc Engrg); *m* 28 Dec 1963, Ruth Imogen, da of William Charles Vigurs (d 1982); 2 da (Fiona Mary b 4 Oct 1967, Kirstie Ann b 6 Oct 1969); *Career* civil engr; sr ptnr Cyril Blumfield and Ptnrs 1988– (ptnr 1973–); vice chm Assoc of Consltg Engrs 1996– (chm Professional Court 1994–95, treas 1995–96); govr: Dulwich Coll 1991–95, Alleyn's Sch 1991–; tstee Dulwich Estates 1989– (dep chm 1995–); Master Worshipful Co of Woolmen 1993 (Liveryman 1973, clerk 1975–87, memb Court of Assts 1986–), asst clerk Worshipful Co of Engrs 1983– (memb Court of Assts 1983–); CEng, FICE, FIStructE, MConsE; *Recreations* golf, hill walking; *Clubs* Athenaeum, Dulwich and Sydenham Hill Golf; *Style*— Eur Ing Raymond J R Cousins; ✉ 33 Hitherwood Drive, London SE19 1XA (☎ 0181 670 4673); Cyril Blumfield & Partners, 192–198 Vauxhall Bridge Rd, London SW1V 1DX (☎ 0171 834 3631, fax 0171 630 9632)

COUSINS, Robin John; MBE (1980); s of Frederick Charles Cousins, of Baridon House, Knole Park, Almondsbury, and Edna Valerie Higgs; *b* 17 Aug 1957; *Educ* Henbury Comp Sch; *Career* ice skater; Bristol Ice Dance and Figure Skating Club 1968–80, nat primary champion 1969, nat jr champion 1972, nat sr champion 1976–79, int team memb 1973–80, Olympic team memb Innsbruck 1976, Olympic team memb Lake Placid 1980; Euro Championships: Bronze medal 1977, Silver medal 1979, Gold medal 1980; World Championships: Bronze medal 1978, Silver medal 1979, Silver medal 1980; Gold medal Olympic Games 1980, World freeskating champion 1978, 1979 and 1980, BBC Sports personality of the year 1980, peoples choice award sports 1980; world record for highest Axel jump (5.81 m) and back flip (5.48 m) at Richmond Ice Rink 1983; appearances incl: Holiday on Ice 1980–83, Skateaway (own series HTV) 1984, Robin Cousins Electric Ice (world tour) 1984, Robin Cousins Ice Majesty (world tour) 1986, Frank N Furter in The Rocky Horror Show (Duke of York's) 1995; various tv shows (incl Royal Command Performance); 11 Gold medals World Pro Skate Championships 1983–86, World professional Champion 1983, 1984 and 1986; currently: artistic dir Ice Castle International Training Center Calif, memb Bd of Dirs Foundation for International Ice Skating Advancement; *Style*— Robin Cousins, Esq, MBE; ✉ c/o Billy Marsh Associates Ltd, 174–178 North Gower Street, London NW1 2NB (☎ 0171 388 6858, fax 0171 388 6848)

COUTANCHE, Jurat the Hon John Alexander Gore; OBE (1997); s of Baron Coutanche (Life Peer, d 1973); *b* 25 May 1925; *Educ* Sherborne; *m* 1, 1 Sept 1949, Jean Veronica (d 1977), da of late Alexander Thomson Dawson, of Portelet House, Jersey; 1 s, 2 da; m 2, 1978, Gillian Margaret, da of late Brig John Douglas Fellowes Fisher, CBE; *Career* Lt Cdr RNR; former Jurat of Royal Court of Jersey and Lt Bailiff; *Clubs* Royal Channel Islands Yacht; *Style*— Jurat the Hon John Coutanche, OBE; ✉ Clos des Tours, St Aubin, Jersey, CI

COUTINHO, Graça (Mrs Manuel Castilho); *b* 26 Feb 1949; *Educ* Lisbon Fine Art Sch, St Martin's Sch of Art (ILEA scholarship, Gulbenkian scholarship); *m* Manuel Castilho, s of His Excellency Guilhere Castilho; 2 da (Branca b 15 March 1974, Sara b 12 Sept 1980); *Career* artist; *Solo Exhibitions* Modern Art Gallery Lisbon 1975 and 1983, Galeria Modulo (Oporto 1978, Lisbon 1980), Riverside Studios London 1979, Quadrum Gallery Lisbon 1986, Bertrand Gallery 1986, The Showroom Gallery London 1987, Todd Gallery London 1988 1989 and 1990, Calouste Gulbenkian Museum Lisbon 1989, Graça Fonseca Gallery Lisbon 1990 and 1991; *Gp Exhibitions* incl: Portuguese Contemporary Art (Lisbon 1975, San Paulo and Rio de Janeiro 1976), Lunds Kunsthall Lunds Sweden 1976, Beograd Belgrade 1977, Sao Paulo Biennale Brazil 1979, Paris Biennale 1980, Drawings (German Inst) Lisbon 1984, painting and a sculpture for Gaby Agis performance (Almeida Theatre) 1985, ARCO (Quadram Gallery Madrid) 1986, John Moores Exhibition Liverpool 1987 and 1989, Art Fair (Air Gallery London) 1988, Works on Paper (Todd Gallery London) 1990, Large Works/Gallery Artists (Art 91 Business Design Centre London) 1991; *Style*— Ms Graça Coutinho; ✉ Todd Gallery, 326 Portobello Rd, London W10 5RU (☎ 0181 960 6209)

COUTTS, Derek James; s of Donald James Coutts, and Margaret Joan Coutts; *Educ* William Morris Sch London, Colchester Art Sch, Royal Coll of Art London (ARCA); *children* 2 s (Jonathan James, Julien Mignonal); *Career* freelance photographer 1966–75, commercials dir 1975–; recipient of numerous advertising awards from D&AD, Cannes, etc; *Clubs* Groucho; *Style*— Derek Coutts; ✉ BFCS Ltd, 59 North Wharf Road, London W2 1LA (☎ 0171 402 5561, fax 0171 402 7738)

COUTTS, (Thomas) Gordon; QC (Scot 1973); s of Thomas Coutts (d 1976), and Evelyn Gordon Coutts; *b* 5 July 1933; *Educ* Aberdeen GS, Univ of Aberdeen (MA, LLB); *m* 1 Aug 1959, Winifred Katherine, da of William Alexander Scott (d 1982); 1 s (Julian b 1962), 1 da (Charlotte b 1964); *Career* passed Advocate 1959, standing junior counsel to Dept of Agric and Fisheries (Scot) 1965–73; chm: Industl Tbnls 1972, Med Appeal Tbnls 1984, VAT Tbnls 1990; temp judge Ct of Session Scot 1991–, vice pres (Scot) VAT and Duties Tbnls 1996–; called to the Bar Lincoln's Inn 1995; FCIArb; chm Faculty Services

Ltd 1989–93 (exec dir 1974–84); *Recreations* historical studies, travel, stamp collecting; *Clubs* New (Edinburgh), Bruntsfield Links Golf (Edinburgh); *Style*— T Gordon Coutts, Esq, QC; ✉ 6 Heriot Row, Edinburgh EH3 6HU (☎ and fax 0131 556 3042)

COUTTS, Herbert; s of the late Herbert Coutts, and the late Agnes, *née* Boyle; *b* 9 March 1944; *Educ* Morgan Acad Dundee; *m* 24 Dec 1970, Angela Elizabeth Mason, da of late Henry Smith; 1 s (Christopher b 10 Feb 1976), 3 da (Antonia b 17 Nov 1971, Naomi b 12 April 1977, Lydia b 31 Dec 1980); *Career* keeper of antiquities and bygones Dundee Museum 1968–71 (asst keeper 1965–68), supt of Edinburgh City Museum 1971–73, city curator Edinburgh City Museums and Galleries 1973–; maj projects: City of Edinburgh Art Centre (1980), Museum of Childhood Extension (1986), The People's Story Museum (1989), City of Edinburgh Art Centre Extension (1992); vice pres Museum Assts Gp 1967–70; memb: Govt Ctee on Future of Scotland's National Museums and Galleries 1978–80 (report published 1981), Cncl of Museums Assoc 1977–78 and 1986–88, Bd of Scottish Museums Cncl 1971–74 and 1986–88, Registration Ctee Museums and Galleries Cmmn 1989–, Bd Museums Training Inst 1995–; museums advsr to Convention of Scottish Local Authys 1986–90, tstee Paxton House 1988–, tstee E Lothian Community Devpt Tst 1989–; external examiner Univ of St Andrews 1993–; contested (Lab) S Angus 1970; SBStJ 1977, AMA 1970, FSA(Scot) 1965, FMA 1976; *Publications* Ancient Monuments of Tayside (1970), Tayside Before History (1971), Edinburgh - An Illustrated History (1975), Huntly House (1980), Lady Stair's House (1980); exhibition catalogues incl: Edinburgh Crafts (with R A Hill, 1973), Aince a Bailie Aye a Bailie (1974), Gold of The Pharaohs (ed, 1988), Dinosaurs Alive (ed, 1990), Sweat of the Sun - Gold of Peru (ed, 1990), Golden Warriors of the Ukranian Steppes (ed, 1993), Star Trek - The Exhibition (ed, 1995), Quest for a Pirate (ed, 1996), Gateway to the Silk Road: Cultural Relics from the Han to the Tang Dynasties from Xe'an China (ed, 1996); *Recreations* gardening, swimming, music, family; *Style*— Herbert Coutts, Esq; ✉ Kirkhill House, Queen's Rd, Dunbar, East Lothian, EH42 1LN (☎ 01368 863113); City Art Centre, 2 Market Street, Edinburgh, EH1 1DE (☎ 0131 529 3950)

COUVE DE MURVILLE, Most Rev Maurice Noël Léon; *see:* Birmingham, Archbishop of (RC)

COUZENS, Sir Kenneth Edward; KCB (1979, CB 1976); s of Albert Edward Couzens (d 1968), and May Phoebe, *née* Biddlecombe (d 1973); *b* 29 May 1925; *Educ* Portsmouth GS, Caius Coll Cambridge (BA), Univ of London (BA); *m* 1947, Muriel Eileen, da of Albert Fey (d 1943); 1 s, 1 da; *Career* dep sec Incomes Policy and Public Fin HM Treasy 1973–77 (joined 1951), second perm sec Overseas Fin 1977–82, perm sec Dept of Energy 1982–85; dep chm British Coal Corporation 1985–88; chm: Coal Products Ltd 1988–92, Credit Lyonnais Capital Markets Ltd 1991– (dir 1989–); memb Advsy Bd Nat Econ Res Assoc 1987–, cmmr Local Govt Cmmn for England 1993–95; *Recreations* gardening, reading, travelling; *Clubs* Reform; *Style*— Sir Kenneth Couzens, KCB; ✉ Coverts Edge, Woodsway, Oxshott, Surrey KT22 0ND (☎ 01372 843207)

COVE-SMITH, Dr (John) Rodney; s of Dr R Cove-Smith (d 1988), and Florence Margaret, *née* Harris (d 1989); *b* 26 Jan 1943; *Educ* Rugby, Gonville and Caius Coll Cambridge (MA, MB BChir, MD); *m* 26 April 1969, Jacqueline Mary (Dr Jackie Morgan), da of D K G Morgan, of Beckenham, Kent; 3 da (Julia Elizabeth b 1972, Andrea Lesley b 1975, Laura Suzanne b 1980); *Career* house surgn Peace Memorial Hosp Watford Herts 1967–68, house physician St Thomas's Hosp 1968–69; registrar: Dorset Co Hosp 1969–71, Nottingham City Hosp 1971–72; sr registrar in gen med and nephrology City Hosp Nottingham 1972–78, hon sr registrar in nephrology Guy's 1976–77, conslt physician and nephrologist S Tees Acute Hospitals NHS Tst 1978– (chief of med 1990–), clinical tutor Univ of Newcastle 1986–91; dep regnl advsr RCP (northern) 1996–; author various chapters and papers on renal med, particularly use of drugs in renal disease; memb: Renal Assoc, Euro Dialysis and Transplant Assoc, Br Transplant Soc; memb BMA, FRCP; *Recreations* sport (hockey, squash), music; *Style*— Dr Rodney Cove-Smith; ✉ Kirby House, Kirby-in-Cleveland, Middlesbrough, Cleveland TS9 7AN (☎ 01642 712618); Department of Nephrology, South Cleveland Hospital, Middlesbrough, Cleveland (☎ 01642 850850)

COVEN, Edwina Olwyn; CBE (1988), JP, DL (1987); da of Sir Samuel Instone, DL, and Lady Alice Instone; *Educ* St Winifred's Ramsgate, Queen's Coll London, Lycée Victor Duruy Paris, Marlborough Gate Secretarial Coll London; *m* 1951, Frank Coven; *Career* Private ATS (later Maj WRAC); army interpreter (French) serv UK and overseas incl: staff appts, Plans and Policy Div, Western Union Def Orgn (subsequently NATO), directorate manpower WO 1942–56; children's writer Fleetway Pubns 1959–84; gen features writer: She, Harper's, BBC Woman's Hour; performer and advsr children's and teenage ITV; memb Advsy Cncl BBC Radio London 1978–81; non-exec dir: TV-am 1985–93 (dep chm 1990–93), Crockfords plc 1993–95, Capital Corporation Plc 1995– (on expansion of Crockfords plc); stores conslt on promotion and fashion 1960–77, memb Advsy Ctee (Clothing and Footwear Sub Ctee) BSI 1971–73; chm Davbro Chemists 1967–71; JP Inner London N Westminster 1965–72 (dep chm 71–72), JP City of London 1969–88 (dep chm 1971–88), HM Lieut City of London 1981–, DL Greater London 1988–, chm City of London Police Ctee 1984–87 (dep chm 1983–84), memb Police Ctee AMA 1984–96, memb Jt Ctee of Mgmnt London Ct of Int Arbitration 1983–89; Dowgate Ward City of London: memb Ct of Common Cncl 1972–, elected alderman 1973 and 1974, dep 1975–; chief commoner City of London 1987–88; chm WRAC Assoc 1989–90 (memb Cncl 1973–90, vice pres 1984–88, vice chm 1985–89); memb: TAVRA City of London 1979–86, Assoc of Speakers 1975–, London Home Safety Cncl 1980–84; vice chm Cities of London and Westminster Home Safety Cncl 1984–89, vice pres Nat Orgn for Women's Mgmnt Educn 1983–90, chm Ctee for 800th Anniversary Mayoralty of Corpn of London 1988–90, memb Bd of Govrs City of London Sch 1972–77, chm Bd of Govrs City of London Sch for Girls 1978–81, memb Ct Univ of Sussex 1994–; Freeman Worshipful Co of Loriners 1967, Liveryman Worshipful Co of Spectacle Makers 1972, Hon Liveryman Worshipful Co of Lightmongers 1989; memb Royal Soc of St George 1972–, chm Vintry and Dowgate Wards Club 1977, Hon Capt of Police Salt Lake City 1986–; vice pres: Operation Raleigh 1989–94, FANY 1989–; FRSA 1988; Order of Wissam Alouite (Morocco) 1987, OStJ 1987; *Books* Tales of Oaktree Kitchen (2 edn, 1960); *Recreations* homemaking generally, lawn tennis, watching a variety of spectator sports; *Clubs* Hurlingham, Devonshire (Eastbourne); *Style*— Mrs Edwina Coven, CBE, JP, DL; ✉ 23 Tavistock, Devonshire Place, Eastbourne, E Sussex BN21 4AG (☎ 01323 416796)

COVENEY, Gerald Boore; s of Major Ronald Leslie Coveney, RE (d 1980), of Deepcut, Camberley, Surrey, and Hilary Elsie Boore; *b* 7 July 1938; *Educ* Farnham GS; *m* 1 Nov 1969, Shirley Rosemary Ann, da of Ronald Edmund Messenger, of Sussex; 2 s (Scott b 1971, Laurence b 1973); *Career* Lt-Sgt Platoon Instr Coldstream Gds; asst dir J Walter Thompson 1969–74; md: BMDC 1972–74, Lansdowne Marketing 1974–81, Lansdowne Euro 1981–84; chm and md Gerry Coveney and Associates ad agency 1984–92, pres Coveney Brand Communications 1992–94, chief exec Coveney Butler Communications 1994–; memb Cncl Inst of Grocery Distribution; assoc memb: Food and Drink Fedn, CIES (Int Chain Stores Assoc); former chm Strangers Gallery; memb: Lord's Taverners, Ctee Local Cons Assoc (former chm); former Cons cncllr; *Recreations* home and family, swimming; *Style*— Gerald B Coveney, Esq; ✉ Minden Lodge, Deepcut, Camberley, Surrey; Coveney Butler Communications, William Blake House, 8 Marshall Street, London W1V 2AJ (☎ 0171 734 0550, fax 0171 734 0709, car 01836 684583)

COVENEY, Prof James; s of James Coveney (d 1973), and Mary, *née* Sims (d 1976); *b* 4 April 1920; *Educ* St Ignatius Coll, Univ of Reading (BA), Univ of Strasbourg (Dr de l'Univ de Strasbourg); *m* 17 Sept 1955, Patricia Yvonne, da of Ernest Briggs Townsend; 2 s (Patrick John b 1956, Dr Peter Vivian Coveney, *qv* b 1958); *Career* served WWII, Flt Lt (Pilot) RAF; lecteur d'anglais Univ of Strasbourg 1951–53, lectr in French Univ of Hull 1953–58, asst dir Civil Serv Cmmn 1958–59, UN Secretariat NY 1959–61, NATO Secretariat 1961–64; Univ of Bath: sr lectr and head of modern languages 1964–68, prof of French 1969–85, emeritus prof 1985; visiting prof: Ecole Nationale d'Administration Paris 1974–85, Univ of Buckingham 1974–76, Bethlehem Univ 1985; conslt Univ of Macau 1988; memb: British-French Mixed Cultural Cmmn 1973–79, Bd of Govrs Br Inst in Paris 1975–79, Exec Ctee Cncl for the Advancement of Arab-British Understanding 1987–; corresponding memb Académie des Sciences Agriculture Arts et Belles Lettres Aix-en-Provence 1975; Chevalier de l'Ordre des Palmes Académiques 1978, Officier de l'Ordre National du Mérite 1986; *Books* incl: La Légende de l'Empereur Constant (1955), Glossary of French and English Management Terms (with S Moore, 1972), Le français pour l'ingénieur (with J Grosjean, 1974), Guide to French Institutions (with S Kempa, 1978), Harrap's French Business Management Terms (with S Moore, 1993); *Clubs* Travellers'; *Style*— Prof James Coveney; ✉ 40 Westfield Close, Bath BA2 2EB (☎ 01225 316670, fax 01225 469845)

COVENEY, Michael William; s of William Coveney, and Violet Amy, *née* Perry; *b* 24 July 1948; *Educ* St Ignatius Coll, Worcester Coll Oxford; *m* Susan Monica Hyman; 1 s (Thomas Geoffrey b 16 Dec 1977); *Career* ed Plays and Players 1975–78 (asst ed 1973–75), theatre critic and dep arts ed Financial Times 1981–89 (contrib 1972–80), theatre critic The Observer 1990–; *Books* The Citz (1990), Maggie Smith (1992), The Aisle is Full of Noises (1994), Knight Errant (with Robert Stephens, 1995), The World According to Mike Leigh (1996); *Recreations* music, travel, running; *Style*— Michael Coveney, Esq; ✉ The Observer, 119 Farringdon Road, London EC1R 3ER (☎ 0171 278 2332)

COVENEY, Dr Peter Vivian; s of Prof James Coveney, *qv*, of Bath, and Patricia Yvonne, *née* Townsend; *b* 30 Oct 1958; *Educ* Beechen Cliff Sch Bath, Lincoln Coll Oxford (BA), Princeton Univ NJ (Jane Eliza Procter fell), Merton Coll Oxford (sr scholar, MA), Keble Coll Oxford (Sir Edward P Abraham jr res fell, DPhil); *m* 9 May 1987, Samia Antonios Néhmé, da of Antonios Néhmé; 1 da (Elena b 22 Oct 1993); *Career* Wiener-Anspach fell Free Univ of Brussels Belgium 1985–86, sr coll lectr in physical chemistry Keble Coll Oxford 1987–88, lectr in physical chemistry Univ of Wales Bangor 1987–90; Schlumberger Cambridge Res Cambridge: prog ldr 1990–93, sr scientist 1993–; special invited lectr Dept Applied Mathematics & Theoretical Physics The Queen's Univ Belfast 1989–90, scholar in residence Inst for Science, Engrg & Public Policy Portland Oregon 1993, visiting fell in theoretical physics Wolfson Coll Oxford 1996–98; author of articles in scientific jls; holder of 3 patents for technical inventions; memb American Physical Soc (USA) 1985; CChem 1988, CPhys 1988, FRSC, FInstP; *Books* The Arrow of Time (with Roger Highfield, 1990), Frontiers of Complexity (with Roger Highfield, 1995); *Recreations* soccer, squash, swimming; *Style*— Dr Peter Coveney; ✉ Schlumberger Cambridge Research, High Cross, Madingley Road, Cambridge CB3 0EL (☎ 01223 325351, fax 01223 467004, e-mail coveney@cambridge.scr.slb.com)

COVENTRY, Archdeacon of; *see:* Russell, Ven (Harold) Ian Lyle

COVENTRY, 11 Earl of (E 1697); George William Coventry; also Viscount Deerhurst (I 1697); s of 10 Earl (ka 1940), and Hon Nesta Donne Philipps (who m 2, 1953, Maj Terence Fisher-Hoch), da of 1 and last Baron Kylsant; *b* 25 Jan 1934; *Educ* Eton, RMA Sandhurst; *m* 1, 22 March 1955 (m dis 1963), Marie Farquhar-Médart, da of William S Médart, of St Louis, USA; 1 s; m 2, 1969 (m dis 1975), Ann, da of Frederick William James Cripps; m 3, 1980 (m dis 1988), Valerie Anne Birch; m 4, 1992, Rachel Wynne, da of Jack and Louise Mason; *Heir* s, Viscount Deerhurst, *qv*; *Career* late 2 Lt Gren Gds; *Style*— The Rt Hon the Earl of Coventry; ✉ Earls Croome Court, Earls Croome, Worcester WR8 9DE (fax 01684 594222)

COVENTRY, Bishop of 1985–; Rt Rev Simon Barrington-Ward; s of Robert McGowan Barrington-Ward, DSO, MC (d 1948), of London, and Margaret Adele Barrington-Ward (d 1975); *b* 27 May 1930; *Educ* Eton, Magdalene Coll Cambridge (BA, MA), Westcott House Cambridge; *m* 13 Sept 1963, Jean Caverhill, da of Dr Hugh William Young Taylor, of Edinburgh; 2 da (Mary Caverhill b 1969, Helen McGowan b 1971); *Career* Nat Serv RAF 1949–50, PO 1949; lektor Free Univ Berlin 1953–54, chaplain Magdalene Coll Cambridge 1956; ordained: deacon 1956, priest 1957; lectr Univ of Ibadan Nigeria 1960–63, fell and dean Magdalene Coll Cambridge 1963–70, princ Crowther Hall, Selly Oak Colls 1970–75, gen sec Church Missionary Soc 1975–85; chm BSR Int Affairs and Devpt Ctee 1986–96; Chaplain to HM the Queen 1984–85; Prelate Order of St Michael and St George 1989–; memb House of Lords 1991–; Hon DD Wycliffe Hall Toronto 1983; FRAI; *Books* Love Will Out (1988), Why God? (1993), The Jesus Prayer (1996); *Recreations* walking, bicycling; *Style*— The Rt Rev the Lord Bishop of Coventry; ✉ Bishop's House, Davenport Rd, Coventry CV5 6PW (☎ 01203 672244)

COVERDALE, Stephen Peter; s of John Peter Coverdale, of Strensall, N Yorkshire, and Margaret Anne, *née* Cordukes; *b* 20 Nov 1954; *Educ* St Peter's Sch York, Emmanuel Coll Cambridge (Cricket blue); *m* 2 July 1977, Mary Jane, da of Michael Riddelsdell; 2 s (Paul Stephen b 24 July 1983, Duncan Philip b 14 Feb 1986), 1 da (Ruth Margaret b 12 Oct 1988); *Career* cricket administrator; player Yorkshire CCC 1973–82 (first class debut v Notts 1973), rep Young England v Young W Indies 1974; sec and mangr then chief exec Northamptonshire CCC 1985–; mangr: England A Tour to W Indies 1992, Young England Tour to India 1993; admitted slr, sports ed BBC Radio Leeds 1982–85; *Recreations* all sport, biographies, reading newspapers; *Style*— Stephen Coverdale, Esq; ✉ Northamptonshire CCC, County Ground, Wantage Road, Northampton NN1 4TJ (☎ 01604 32917, fax 01604 232855)

COWAN, Brig (James) Alan Comrie; CBE (1992, MBE 1956); s of Alexander Comrie Cowan, MC (d 1937), and Helen May Isobel, *née* Finlayson (d 1988); *b* 20 Sept 1923; *Educ* Rugby; *m* 2 Dec 1948, Jennifer Evelyn, da of Roland Evelyn Bland (d 1974), of Kingham, Oxon; 2 s (Anthony b 28 March 1953, Adrian b 16 Jan 1955), 1 da (Varian b 18 Oct 1950); *Career* cmmnd Rifle Bde 1942, served UK, Egypt and Italy 1942–45, regtl and staff appts in Egypt, Univ of Oxford, BAOR, Army Staff Coll, WO, Kenya, Malaya 1945–60, DS Army Staff Coll Camberley 1961–63, CO 1 Royal Leicesters (later 4 Royal Anglian) in UK, Aden and Malta 1964–66, GSO 1 17 Div Malaysia 1966–67, Col GS MOD London 1967–69, Cmd 8 Inf Bde NI 1970–71, DAG HQ UK Land Forces Wiltshire 1972–75; NI Office London 1975–80: princ for Industl Econ and Social Affrs 1975–78, asst sec 1978; sec Govt Hospitality Fund 1980–93; Freeman City of London 1985; *Recreations* current affairs, music, theatre, countryside; *Clubs* Army and Navy, MCC; *Style*— Brig Alan Cowan, CBE; ✉ c/o C Hoare & Co, 37 Fleet Street, London EC4P 4DQ

COWAN, Dr David Lockhart; s of Dr James Lockhart Cowan, JP, TD (d 1970), and Meryl Lockhart, *née* Cook; *b* 30 June 1941; *Educ* George Watson's Coll Edinburgh, Trinity Coll of Glenalmond Perthshire, Univ of Edinburgh (MB ChB); *m* 16 Sept 1966, Eileen May, da of Rev John William Gordon Masterton, of 19 Braid Ave, Edinburgh; 3 s (Christopher b 26 July 1967, Richard b 14 Oct 1969, Douglas b 31 May 1973), 1 da (Lindsey b 7 Jan 1971); *Career* chief resident prof Bryce Gen Hosp Toronto 1968–69; conslt otolaryngologist 1972–: City Hosp, Western Gen Hosp, Royal Hosp for Sick Children Edinburgh; hon sr lectr Univ of Edinburgh, hon sec Laryngology Section RSM; FRCSEd 1988; *Books* Paediatric Otolaryngology (1982), Logan Turner's Diseases of the Ear Nose and Throat (jtly, 1980), Coping with Ear Problems (1985); *Recreations* golf, sailing, all sports; *Clubs* Honourable Co of Edinburgh Golfers (Muirfield), Royal and Ancient (St Andrews), Bruntsfield Links Golfing Soc (Edinburgh), Elie Golf House; *Style*— Dr David Cowan; ✉ 28 Braid Hills Rd, Edinburgh EH10 6HY (☎ 0131 447 3424); 14 Moray Place, Edinburgh EH3 6DT (☎ 0131 225 4843)

COWAN, David Neville; s of Roy Neville Cowan (d 1987), of Heyshott, W Sussex, and Dorne Margaret, *née* Burgoyne-Johnson; *b* 21 May 1950; *Educ* Marlborough, Univ of Bath (BSc, BArch); *m* 23 Aug 1975, Gillian Judith, da of David Hay Davidson, OBE (d 1983), of Lymington, Hants; 2 s (Jonathan b 1979, Christopher b 1988); *Career* architect 1975; dir: David Cowan Associates 1989 (formed 1983), Charterfield Gp of Cos 1985; memb: Soc for the Protection of Ancient Bldgs, Panel of Architects Chichester Diocese; author of papers on designing for the elderly and disabled; RIBA 1976; *Recreations* skiing, badminton, riding; *Style*— David N Cowan, Esq; ✉ Oak Tree Cottage, Nursery Lane, Maresfield, E Sussex; David Cowan Associates Ltd, 9–10 Old Stone Link, Ship Street, East Grinstead, W Sussex (☎ 01342 410242)

COWAN, Prof (William) Maxwell; s of Adam Cowan (d 1981), and Jessie Sloan, *née* Maxwell (d 1986); *b* 27 Sept 1931; *Educ* Selbourne Coll East London SA, Univ of Witwatersrand SA (BSc), Univ of Oxford (BM BCh, MA, DPhil); *m* 31 March 1956, Margaret, *née* Sherlock; 2 s (Stephen Maxwell b 1959, David Maxwell b 1962), 1 da (Ruth Margaret b 1957); *Career* univ lectr Univ of Oxford 1958–66, assoc prof Univ of Wisconsin 1966–68, prof and dept head Washington Univ Sch of Medicine St Louis Missouri 1968–80, prof and vice pres Salk Inst La Jolla Calif 1980–86, vice chllr Washington Univ 1986–87, vice pres and chief scientific offr Howard Hughes Medical Inst Chevy Chase Maryland 1988–; Hon DSc: Emory Univ 1995, Northwestern Univ 1995; hon fell Pembroke Coll Oxford 1987 (fell 1960–66); fell American Acad of Arts and Scis 1976; memb: Inst of Medicine 1978, American Philosophical Soc 1987, Soc for Neuroscience (pres 1978); foreign memb Norwegian Acad of Scis; foreign assoc: Royal Soc of SA 1987, US Nat Acad of Scis 1981; FRS 1982; *Books* ed numerous vols on Neuroscience and Related Areas (1974); *Recreations* photography; *Style*— Prof Maxwell Cowan, FRS; ✉ 6337 Windermere Circle, North Bethesda, Maryland 20852, USA (☎ 00 1 301 493 9097); Howard Hughes Medical Institute, 4000 Jones Bridge Road, Chevy Chase, Maryland 20815, USA (☎ 00 1 301 215 8803, fax 00 1 301 215 8828)

COWAN, Michael John Julian; s of Kenneth Christopher Armstrong Cowan (d 1955), and Flora Muriel, *née* Stewart; *b* 24 June 1952; *Educ* Midhurst GS Sussex, Churchill Coll Cambridge (MA); *m* 26 Sept 1981, Hilary Jane, da of Albert Edward Slade (d 1987); 2 da (Eleanor Josephine, Philippa Rose), 1 s (Chrisopher David Andrew); *Career* investmt advsr NM Rothschild & Sons Ltd 1973–78, investmt dir Lazard Bros & Co Ltd 1979–87, princ Morgan Stanley International 1987–95, pres Silchester International Investors 1995–; *Recreations* golf, tennis, DIY; *Style*— Michael Cowan, Esq; ✉ Ranmoor, 5 Fairmile Ave, Cobham, Surrey KT11 2JA (☎ 01932 865400); Silchester International Investors, Heathcoat House, 20 Savile Row, London W1X 1AE (☎ 0171 468 5902, fax 0171 494 2717)

COWAN, Paul Adrian Dallas; s of E Cowan (d 1988), and Peggy Dallas, *née* Johnston; *b* 5 Aug 1951; *Educ* Oxted GS, London Coll of Printing and Design; *m* Jan 1979, Rosemary, *née* Nimmo; 3 da (Jo b 17 Sept 1980, Patty b 30 Nov 1983, Chrissy (twin) b 30 Nov 1983); *Career* tracing servs for detective agency 1970, messenger rising to account exec Ogilvy & Mather advtg agency 1971–73, sr account exec CPV Advertising 1973–74, account supr Ogilvy & Mather 1975–78; Saatchi & Saatchi: account supervisor 1978, account dir 1979–84, bd account dir 1984–86, gp account dir 1986–90; fndr md Cowan Kemsley Taylor 1990–; MIPA; *Recreations* flying, sailing, karate, cooking, family, advertising; *Style*— Paul Cowan, Esq; ✉ The Charterhouse, London; Seaview, IOW; Cowan Kemsley Taylor Ltd, 37 Dean Street, London W1V 5AP; (☎ 0171 734 9090, fax 0171 734 9097)

COWAN, Robert Christopher; s of Philip Leslie Cowan (d 1987), of Rustington, Sussex, and Anne Marie-Louise, *née* Cammiade; *b* 27 Aug 1949; *Educ* St Bonaventure's Sch, LSE; *m* 1975 (m dis 1981), Susan Ann Greenway; partner Carole Anne, da of Reginald Fowler; 1 s (Thomas Richard Faure b 1986), 2 da (Charlotte Ellen b 1985, Alannah Marie-Louise b 1989); *Career* reporter Leamington Spa Courier 1970–74, prodn ed Melody Maker 1974–76, features sub ed rising to chief features sub ed London Evening Standard 1976–86, chief features sub ed London Daily News 1986–87, The Times 1987–88, features ed The Scotsman 1988–90, Op-ed ed The Daily Telegraph 1990–96, focus ed The Sunday Telegraph 1996–; newspaper design award 1989 and 1990 for feature pages and regnl daily papers; *Recreations* tennis, music; *Clubs* The Park Langley; *Style*— Robert Cowan, Esq; ✉ Sunday Telegraph, 1 Canada Square, Canary Wharf, London E14 5DT (☎ 0171 538 6415, fax 0171 538 3810)

COWARD, David John; CMG (1965), OBE (1962); s of Robert James Coward (d 1962), of Exmouth, and Beatrice, *née* Masters (d 1961); *b* 21 March 1917; *Educ* Exmouth GS, Sch of Law; *m* 25 Sept 1954, Joan Margaret, da of Reginald Frank (d 1959), of Doncaster, Yorks; 3 da (Susan Fischel b 1957, Ruth Coward b 1960, Vivienne North b 1967); *Career* WWII RN 1939–47, served HMS King George V 1941–43, HMS Benbow sec to SBNO Trinidad 1943–46, ADC to Govr of Trinidad 1947, demobbed Lt Cdr RNVR; admitted slr 1938; Colonial Legal Serv Kenya: asst registrar general 1948, dep registrar general 1952, registrar general, public tstee and official receiver 1955–82 (permanent sec Miny of Justice and Constitutional Affrs Kenya 1963–64); Kenya Police Reserve 1949–63 (latterly as sr supt i/c Nairobi Area); chm Working Pty on the Future of the Company Secretarial Profession Kenya 1979–80, memb Accountants Registration Bd 1978–82, tstee Nat Museums of Kenya 1979–82; awarded Silver medal of the Int Olympic Ctee 1981 (for servs to the Olympic Movement); chm Storrington Branch Royal British Legion 1992–; Freeman City of London 1984, memb Worshipful Co of Chartered Secretaries and Administrators 1985; FCIS 1961, ACIArb 1984; *Recreations* golf, genealogy; *Clubs* Nairobi and Limuru (Kenya), West Sussex Golf; *Style*— David Coward, Esq, CMG, OBE; ✉ North Perretts, Spinney Lane, West Chiltington, West Sussex RH20 2NX (☎ 01903 742521)

COWARD, Vice-Adm Sir John Francis; KCB, DSO (1982); s of Reginald John Coward (d 1976), and Isabelle Marjorie Coward (d 1981); *b* 11 Oct 1937; *Educ* Downside, Britannia RNC Dartmouth; *m* 1963, Diana Taylor; 2 s (Simon b 21 May 1964, Rupert b 30 July 1968); *Career* joined RN 1954, served submarines; Flag Offr: Sea Trg 1987, First Flotilla 1989, Submarines 1991; Commandant RCDS 1992, ret 1994; Lt Govr and C-in-C of Guernsey 1994–; pres/patron numerous charities in Guernsey; *Recreations* sailing, golf, cricket; *Clubs* Royal Yacht Squadron, RNSA, Sloane (London); *Style*— Vice-Adm Sir John Coward, KCB, DSO; ✉ Government House, The Queen's Road, Guernsey, GY1 1GH (☎ 01481 726666, fax 014815 715919

COWARD, (John) Stephen; QC (1984); s of Frank Coward (d 1980), of Huddersfield, and Kathleen, *née* Bell; *b* 15 Nov 1937; *Educ* King James's GS Huddersfield, Univ Coll London (LLB); *m* 4 March 1967, Ann Lesley, da of Frederick Leslie Pye, of Leighton Buzzard, Beds; 4 da (Victoria b 1969, Sarah b 1971, Laura b 1974, Sophie b 1976); *Career* served RAF 1957–59; lectr in law and constitutional history UCL and Police Coll Bramshill 1962–64; called to the Bar Inner Temple 1964, recorder of the Crown Court 1980–, former head of chambers; memb Scaldwell Chamber Choir; *Recreations* wine, gardening, singing; *Clubs* Scaldwell; *Style*— Stephen Coward, Esq, QC; ✉ The Grange, Scaldwell, Northampton NN6 9JP (☎ 01604 880255, fax 01604 881997); 9 Bedford Row, London WC1R 4AZ (☎ 0171 242 3555, mobile 0585 562137)

COWDEN, Stephen (Steve); *b* 13 July 1952; *Educ* Allan Glen's Sch Glasgow, Univ of Edinburgh (LLB); *m* 1985; 1 s; *Career* slr Giggart Baillie & Gifford Glasgow 1974–77, Beecham Group plc 1977–90, co sec and gp legal offr Glaxo Wellcome plc 1996– (gp legal offr 1991–96); memb Law Soc of Scotland 1976; *Recreations* golf; *Style*— Steve Cowden, Esq; ✉ Glaxo Wellcome plc, Lansdowne House, Berkeley Square, London W1X 6BQ (☎ 0171 493 4060, fax 0171 408 0228)

COWDRAY, 4 Viscount (UK 1917); Sir Michael Orlando Weetman Pearson; 4 Bt (UK 1894); also Baron Cowdray (UK 1910); s of 3 Viscount Cowdray, TD, DL (d 1995), and his 1 w, Lady Anne Cowdray *née* Bridgeman, da of 5 Earl of Bradford; *b* 17 June 1944; *Educ* Gordonstoun; *m* 1, 1977 (m dis 1984), Ellen (Fritzi), da of late Hermann Erhardt, of Munich; m 2, 1 July 1987, Marina Rose, 2 da of John Howard Cordle, of Malmesbury House, The Close, Salisbury, and Mrs Venetia Caroline Ross Skinner, *née* Maynard; 1 s (Hon Peregrine John Dickinson b 27 Oct 1994), 3 da (Hon Eliza Anne Venetia b 31 May 1988, Hon Emily Jane Marina b 13 Dec 1989, Hon Catrina Sophie Lavinia b 13 March 1991); *Heir* s, Hon Peregrine John Dickinson Pearson b 27 Oct 1994; *Clubs* White's; *Style*— The Rt Hon Viscount Cowdray; ✉ Cowdray Park, Midhurst, W Sussex GU29 0AX

COWDREY, Christopher Stuart; s of Sir Colin Cowdrey, CBE, *qv*; *b* 20 Oct 1957; *Educ* Tonbridge Sch; *m* 1 Jan 1989, Christel Margareta, da of Carl-Johan Arne Holst-Sande, of Sweden; 2 s (Fabian Kruuse b 30 Jan 1993, Julius Lindahl b (twin) 30 Jan 1993); *Career* professional cricketer; Kent CCC: joined 1976, awarded county cap 1979, capt 1985–90, played in over 300 matches, left 1991; with Glamorgan CCC 1992, ret 1992; int career: played for Eng under 19 team versus W Indies 1974, capt Young Eng tour W Indies 1976, Eng debut in Bombay 1984, played in all 5 test matches in victorious Eng tour to India 1984–85, capt of Eng versus W Indies at Headingley 1988, 6 test matches, 3 one day ints; took a wicket on fourth ball in test match cricket bowling Kapil Dev and became the first man to take a wicket in his first over of test and one day int cricket; England XI tour to South Africa 1990; scored a century in first innings in the Benson & Hedges competition; *Books* Good Enough (with Jonathan Smith, 1986), What's Your Sport? (with David Lemmon, 1988); *Recreations* golf, writing, backgammon and all sports; *Style*— Christopher Cowdrey, Esq

COWDREY, Sir (Michael) Colin; kt (1992), CBE (1970); s of late Ernest Arthur Cowdrey, of Bangalore, India, and Kathleen Mary, *née* Taylor; *b* 24 Dec 1932; *Educ* Tonbridge, BNC Oxford; *m* 1, 1956 (m dis), Penelope Susan, da of late Stuart Chiesman, of Chislehurst, Kent; 3 s (1 of whom Christopher Cowdrey, *qv*), 1 da; m 2, 1985, Lady Herries of Terregles, *qv*; *Career* former cricketer; capt Kent CCC 1957–71 (awarded county cap 1951), 114 England test caps 1954–75 (capt 23 times), scored 107 centuries in first class cricket (22 in test matches); currently conslt Barclays Bank plc SE Region; memb Ctee MCC (pres 1986–87), chm Int Cricket Cncl 1989–93, pres The Lord's Taverners 1995, 1996 and 1997; Freeman City of London 1962; memb Ct of Assts Worshipful Co of Skinners (Master 1986); *Books* Cricket Today (1961), Time For Reflection (1962), Tackle Cricket This Way (1969), The Incomparable Game (1970), MCC - The Autobiography of a Cricketer (with Ian Wooldridge, 1976); *Recreations* golf; *Clubs* Boodle's, MCC; *Style*— Sir Colin Cowdrey, CBE; ✉ Angmering Park, Littlehampton, West Sussex BN16 4EX (☎ 01903 871423)

COWDRY, Quentin Francis; s of Brig Denzil Adrian Cowdry, of Woodbridge, Suffolk, and Fay Mary, *née* Willcocks; *b* 27 Feb 1956; *Educ* Woodbridge Sch Suffolk, Univ of Leicester (BA); *m* 27 Feb 1988, Zoë Laine, da of William McIntyre; *Career* graduate trainee reporter Nottingham Evening Post 1978–81, shipping reporter Southern Evening Echo 1981–84, reporter Sunday Telegraph 1984–86, reporter and lobby corr Daily Telegraph 1986–89, home affairs corr The Times 1989–91; consulting dir Affinity Consulting Ltd 1991–96; dir Paragon Communications PLC 1996–; *Recreations* shooting, fly fishing, skiing, keeping fit; *Style*— Quentin Cowdry, Esq; ✉ Paragon Communications plc, 142 Wardour Street, London W1V 4LL (☎ 0171 734 6030)

COWELL, His Hon Judge; Peter Reginald; s of Reginald Ernest Cowell, CBE (d 1982), of Lowmoor, Craddock, Cullompton, Devon, and Philippa Eleanor Frances Anne, *née* Prettejohn (d 1993); *b* 9 March 1942; *Educ* Bedford Sch, Gonville and Caius Coll Cambridge (MA); *m* 4 Aug 1975, Penelope Jane, da of Andrew John Presgrave Bowring (d 1987), of New Romney, Kent; 2 s (Nicholas b 1976, William b 1980), 1 da (Sarah b 1980); *Career* called to the Bar Middle Temple 1964, recorder of the Crown Court 1992–96 (asst recorder 1985), circuit judge (SE Circuit) 1996–; memb Senate Inns of Ct 1975–78; occasional memb Ctee: Thames Hare and Hounds Club, The Old Stagers; *Books* Cowell, A Genealogy (1986); *Recreations* running, acting, genealogy; *Style*— His Hon Judge Cowell; ✉ 3 New Square, Lincoln's Inn, London WC2A 3RS (☎ 0171 405 5577)

COWELL, Prof Raymond (Ray); DL (Notts 1996); s of Cecil Cowell (d 1970), and Susan, *née* Green; *b* 3 Sept 1937; *Educ* St Aidan's GS Sunderland, Univ of Bristol (scholarship, BA, PhD), Univ of Cambridge (postgrad CertEd, annual essay prize Educn Dept); *m* 14 Aug 1963, Sheila, da of George Bolton (d 1970); 1 s (Simon Jonathan b 1965), 1 da (Emma Victoria b 1968); *Career* asst English master Royal GS Newcastle upon Tyne 1962–66, sr lectr Trinity and All Saints Coll Leeds 1966–70, head of English Dept Nottingham Coll of Educn 1970–73, dep rector Sunderland Poly 1981–87 (dean 1974–80), dir and chief exec Nottingham Poly 1988–92, vice chllr Nottingham Trent Univ 1992–; chm Universities' and Colleges' Staff Devpt Agency 1993– (cncl memb 1992–); memb: CNAA 1974–77 and 1981–85, Unit for Devpt of Adult and Continuing Educn 1986–90, Mgmnt Ctee of Dirs of Polys 1989–91, Br Cncl Ctee for Int Co-operation in Higher Educn 1990–, Directing Gp OECD Prog on the Mgmnt of Higher Educn 1990–, Cncl Nat Cncl for Vocational Qualifications 1991–, Bd Higher Educn Business Enterprise (HEBE) 1993–95; chm: Staff and Educnl Devpt Assoc (SEDA) 1993–, Ctee of Vice-Chllrs and Princs (CVCP) Working Gp on Vocational Higher Educn 1993–96; bd memb: Greater Nottingham Trg and Enterprise Cncl 1990–93 (chm Strategic Forum), Nottingham City Challenge 1991–93, Cncl of Mgmnt Higher Educn International 1991–94, Arts Cncl of England 1996–; chm E Midlands Arts Bd 1995–; FRSA 1996; *Books* Twelve Modern Dramatists (1967), W B Yeats (1969), Edition of Richard II (1969), Critics on Yeats (1971), Critics on Wordsworth (1973), The Critical Enterprise (1975); *Recreations* music, theatre, golf; *Clubs* Athenaeum, RAC; *Style*— Prof Ray Cowell, DL; ✉ The Nottingham Trent University, Burton Street, Nottingham NG1 4BU (☎ 0115 941 8418, fax 0115 947 3523, telex 377534)

COWELL, Robert Douglas; s of Douglas Walter Cowell, of Newport, Gwent, and Gladys, *née* Williams; *b* 9 Feb 1947; *Educ* Newport GS Gwent, Balliol Coll Oxford (MA, PhD); *m* 1, 18 Oct 1969 (m dis 1984), Janice Carol; 2 da (Elizabeth Sarah b 1978, Julia Mary b 1980); m 2, 24 July 1986, Elizabeth Henrietta, da of Timothy Patrick Neligan, of Esher, Surrey; *Career* night shift foreman Turner & Newall Ltd 1972, investmt analyst Hoare Govett Ltd 1972–77, UK corporate devpt mangr Hanson Trust plc 1977–80, md Hoare Govett Securities (Hoare Govett) 1980–89, fndr ptnr Makinson Cowell 1989–; *Recreations* horse racing, golf; *Style*— Robert Cowell, Esq; ✉ Makinson Cowell, 16–18 St John's Lane, London, EC1M 4BS (☎ 0171 490 4977, fax 0171 490 5712)

COWEN, Alan Geoffrey Yale (Geoff); s of Alan Cowen (d 1975), and Agnes, *née* Yale (d 1960); *b* 24 Sept 1937; *Educ* St Edward's Coll Liverpool; *m* 22 Sept 1962, Eileen Frances, da of Reginald Altoft Johnston, of Henleaze, Bristol; 2 da (Sian b 18 March 1965, Sara b 17 May 1966); *Career* Nat Serv Sgt RAEC 1959–61; various appts in publishing 1962–, appointed md Phaidon Press 1987, chief exec Windsor Books International 1991; *Recreations* rugby; *Clubs* Maidenhead Rugby (fixture sec); *Style*—

Geoff Cowen, Esq; ✉ Egerton Cottage, 31 Furze Platt Rd, Maidenhead, Berks SL6 7NE (☎ 01628 29237); Windsor Books International, The Boundary, Wheatley Road, Garsington, Oxford OX44 9EJ (☎ 01865 361122, fax 01865 361133)

COWEN, Joseph; s of Denis Joseph Cowen (d 1986), and Hylda Yvette, *née* Burletson, of East Farndon Manor; *b* 30 April 1941; *Educ* Eton, Royal Agricultural Coll Cirencester; *m* 12 Sept 1970, Victoria Sarah, da of Brig Mark Stuart Ker Maunsell; 2 s (Philip Edward b 8 March 1972, Andrew Joseph b 7 Oct 1976); *Career* chartered surveyor and land agent; asst Davis & Bowring Kirkby Lonsdale 1963–65, Ingham & Yorke Clitheroe 1965–66; Fisher & Co (now Fisher Hoggarth): Evesham 1966–70, ptnr head office Market Harborough 1974– (joined 1970); RICS: chm Leics & Northants Branch 1984–85, memb Div Exec of Rural Practice Div 1988–93; FRICS (ARICS 1967); MFH Fernie 1972–; High Sheriff of Leics 1995–96; *Recreations* foxhunting, farming, all countryside matters, racing; *Clubs* Farmers'; *Style—* Joseph Cowen, Esq; ✉ Laughton Manor Farm, Laughton Hills, Lutterworth, Leics LE17 6QA (☎ 01858 880441); Fisher Hoggarth, 40 High Street, Market Harborough, Leics LE16 7NX (☎ 01858 410200, fax 01858 410207, mobile 0860 230346)

COWEN, Maurice Clifford; s of Bartley Cowen (d 1972), of London, and Joan Evelyn, *née* Homewood; *b* 29 Jan 1946; *Educ* Haverstock Sch, Univ of Sheffield (LLB, Edward Bramley Law prize); *m* 10 Aug 1968, Anne Margaret; 2 s (Matthew Duncan b 22 Jan 1974, Robert James b 30 Sept 1976); *Career* asst slr Slaughter and May 1970–72 (articled clerk 1968–70); Booth & Co: joined 1973, ptnr 1974–, head Company Law Dept 1989, jt sr ptnr 1993–; fndr memb: Leeds Fin Servs Initiative, Br-American Business Gp for the NE; memb Yorks and Humberside Cncl CBI; memb Law Soc 1970; *Recreations* literature, music, travel, fell walking; *Style—* Maurice Cowen, Esq; ✉ Booth & Co, Sovereign House, South Parade, Leeds LS1 1HQ (☎ 0113 283 2000, fax 0113 283 2060)

COWEN, Rt Hon Sir Zelman; AK (1977), GCMG (1977, CMG 1968), GCVO (1980), kt (1976), PC (1981), QC (1972); s of Bernard Cowen (d 1975), and Sara, *née* Granat (d 1989); *b* 7 Oct 1919; *Educ* Scotch Coll Melbourne, Melbourne Univ, New and Oriel Colls Oxford (BCL, MA, DCL); *m* 1945, Anna, da of Hyman Joseph Wittner (d 1974), of Melbourne; 3 s, 1 da; *Career* called to the Bar Gray's Inn 1947 (hon bencher 1978), barr Victoria 1951, QC Queensland (Aust) 1971; prof of public law and dean Faculty of Law Melbourne Univ 1951–66, vice chllr Univ of New England NSW 1967–70, Univ of Queensland 1970–77; govr gen of Australia 1977–82, chm Press Cncl (UK) 1983–88; provost Oriel Coll Oxford 1982–90, pro-vice chllr Univ of Oxford 1988–90; dir John Fairfax Holdings Ltd 1992– (chm 1992–94); pres Order of Australia Assoc 1992–95, nat pres Australia-Britain Soc 1993–95, chm Australian Nat Acad of Music 1995–; KStJ 1977, Knight Grand Cross of the Order of Merit of the Italian Republic 1989; *Style—* The Rt Hon Sir Zelman Cowen, AK, GCMG, GCVO, QC; ✉ Commonwealth Offices, 4 Treasury Place, East Melbourne, Victoria 3002, Australia (☎ 00 61 3 9650 0299, fax 00 61 3 9650 0301)

COWEY, Prof Alan; s of Harry Cowey, and Mary, *née* Boyle; *b* 28 April 1935; *Educ* Bede Sch Sunderland, Emmanuel Coll Cambridge (BA, MA, PhD, Athletics half blue); *m* 4 April 1959, Patricia, da of John Leckonby; 3 da (Lesley b 22 April 1963, Lisa b 16 June 1965, Jill b 19 April 1970); *Career* Rockefeller Fndn fell Univ of Rochester NY 1961–62, demonstrator in experimental psychology Cambridge 1962–66, Fulbright fell Harvard Univ 1966–67; Univ of Oxford: sr res offr 1967–68, Henry Head res fell of Royal Soc 1968–73, reader in experimental psychology 1973–81, prof of physiological psychology 1981–; fell: Emmanuel Coll Cambridge 1964–67, Lincoln Coll Oxford 1968–; MRC: chm Neurosciences Grants Ctee 1979–81 (memb 1974–77), chm Neurosciences Bd 1981–83 (memb 1979–83), memb Cncl 1981–85, dir Brain and Behaviour Res Centre 1990–96; pres: Euro Brain and Behaviour Soc 1986–88, Experimental Psychology Soc 1990–92; Spearman medal Br Psychological Soc 1967; FRS 1988; *Recreations* swimming, running, reading; *Style—* Prof Alan Cowey, FRS; ✉ Department of Experimental Psychology, University of Oxford, South Parks Road, Oxford, Oxon OX1 3UD (☎ 01865 271351, fax 01865 310447)

COWGILL, Brig Anthony Wilson; MBE (1945); s of Harold Wilson Cowgill (d 1965), and Hilda, *née* Garrett (d 1933); *b* 7 Nov 1915; *Educ* Bradford GS, Manchester GS, Univ of Birmingham (BSc), RCMS; *m* 2 April 1949, Joan Noel Mary, da of Peter James Stewart (d 1960); 1 s (Andrew Anthony b 1957), 1 da (Patricia Anne b 1951); *Career* cmmnd 1939, Def HQ Ottawa 1943–44, NW Europe 1944–45, GHQ India 1947, AHQ Pakistan 1948, Cwlth Div Korea 1953–54, MOD 1962–68, ret as Brig 1969; chief indust engr Rolls-Royce Ltd 1969–77, dir Br Mgmnt Data Fndn 1979–; headed Br Mgmnt Advanced Tech study teams to US, Japan and Europe 1980–92, chm Klagenfurt Conspiracy inquiry which cleared Harold Macmillan (late Earl of Stockton) and senior army officers of war crimes charges 1986–90; FIMechE, FIEE, Hon FMS, int fell American Soc for Advancement of Engrg, Int Technol Transfer award 1987; *Books* Management of Automation (1982), The Repatriations from Austria in 1945 (with Lord Brimelow and Christopher Booker, 1990), The Maastricht Treaty in Perspective (1992), Inward Investment and UK Links with the EC (1993); *Recreations* golf; *Clubs* Army and Navy, Beefsteak, RAC; *Style—* Brig Anthony Cowgill, MBE; ✉ Highfield, Longridge, Sheepscombe, Stroud, Glos GL6 7QU (☎ 01452 813211, fax 01452 812527)

COWIE, Alfred George Adam; s of Dr Alfred Cowie, DSO, TD (d 1987), of Aberdeen, and Edith Aileen Meldrum; *b* 22 Aug 1937; *Educ* Aberdeen GS, Leeds GS, Gonville and Caius Coll Cambridge (BA, MA), UCH (MB BChir); *m* 1 Aug 1959, Barbara Jean, da of Victor Henry Kelly (d 1979), of Brighton, Sussex; 2 da (Fiona b 30 March 1963, Alison (Mrs Marshall) b 13 Feb 1965); *Career* conslt surgn Hosp for Tropical Diseases London 1974, consit urologist UCH 1982 (sr lectr Dept of Surgery 1974, consit surgn 1974, teacher in surgery 1975), sr lectr Inst of Urology London 1982, consit urologist Middx Hosp 1984, hon consit surgn St Luke's Hosp for the Clergy 1984, clinical dir of surgery UCL Hosps, consit urologist Eastbourne District Hosp Tst 1995–; chm Regnl Trg Ctee NE Thames RHA, memb Ctee Bloomsbury Health Authy London; memb: BMA 1962, RSM 1984; FRCS 1984, FICS; *Recreations* hill walking, vintage cars, DIY; *Style—* Alfred Cowie, Esq; ✉ Vine Cottage, 4 Church Path, Hellingly, East Sussex BN27 4EZ; Eastbourne District General Hospital, King's Drive, Eastbourne, East Sussex BN21 2UD (☎ 01323 417400)

COWIE, Billy; s of James Reid Cowie, of Scotland, and Mary Thomson, *née* Lauchlan; *b* 21 Aug 1954; *Educ* Portobello Comp Secdy Sch, Univ of Edinburgh (BMus); *Career* music co-ordinator Univ of Brighton; artistic dir, choreographer and composer (with Liz Aggiss) for: The Wild Wigglers (formed 1982, performed ICA, Wembley Arena and Le Zenith Paris), Divas Dance Company (formed 1985, performances incl Torei en Veran Veta Arnold 1986–87, Eleven Executions 1988, Dorothy and Klaus 1989–91, Drool and Drivel They Care 1990 and French Songs 1991); cmmnd by: Extemporary Dance Theatre (for Dead Steps 1988–89), Carousel (for Banda Banda 1989 and La Soupe 1990); music for TV incl: Love Affair with Nature (Channel 4), Putting on the South (TVS), POV (ITV), ICA 40 Year Retrospective (BBC 2), Beethoven in Love (BBC 2); *Awards* incl: Special Award (Brighton Festival) 1989, ZAP Award for Dance (Brighton Festival) 1989, BBC Radio Award (Brighton Festival) 1990, Alliance & Leicester Award (Brighton Festival) 1990, Time Out/Dance Umbrella Award 1990, Best Contemporary Music Award (Brighton Festival) 1992, BBC 2 Dance for Camera Award 1993; *Recordings* incl: Youth in Asia, Beethoven in Love, Eleven Executions, Banda Banda, La Chanson Bien Douce, El Punal Entra en el Corazon, Ksiega Mych Marzen, Falling Apart at the Seams; *Recreations* cinema; *Style—* Billy Cowie, Esq; ✉ c/o School of Art, University of Brighton, Grand Parade, Brighton (☎ 01273 600900)

COWIE, Prof John McKenzie Grant; s of George Cowie (d 1985), and Helen Taylor, *née* Smith (d 1985); *b* 31 May 1933; *Educ* Royal HS, Univ of Edinburgh (BSc, PhD, DSc); *m* 6 Sept 1958, Agnes (Ann), da of James Campbell, of Edinburgh; 2 s (Graeme b 1969, Christian b 1970); *Career* asst lectr Univ of Edinburgh 1956–58, assoc res offr Nat Res Cncl of Canada 1958–67, lectr Univ of Essex 1967–69, prof of chemistry Univ of Stirling 1973–88 (sr lectr 1969–73), fndn prof of chem of materials Heriot-Watt Univ 1988–; vice chm Scottish Cncl for Disability; chm: Scottish Spinal Cord Injury Assoc, Br High Polymer Res Gp 1990–, Macro Group UK 1994–; hon pres: Stirling Assoc of Voluntary Orgns (formerly Cncl for Social Servs Stirling), Cncl for Disability Stirling; FRSE 1977, FRSC; *Books* Polymers: Chemistry and Physics of Modern Materials (1973, 2 edn 1991), Alternating Copolymers (1985); *Recreations* painting, reading, music; *Style—* Prof John Cowie, FRSE; ✉ Traquair, 50 Back Rd, Dollar, Clacks, Scotland FK14 7EA (☎ 01259 742031); Department of Chemistry, Heriot-Watt University, Edinburgh EH14 4AS (☎ 0131 451 3106, fax 0131 451 3180)

COWIE, Rev Dr Leonard Wallace; s of Rev Reginald George Cowie (d 1952), of Lincs, and Ella Constance, *née* Peerless; *b* 10 May 1919; *Educ* Royal GS Newcastle upon Tyne, Univ of Oxford (MA), Univ of London (MA, PhD); *m* 9 Aug 1949, Evelyn Elizabeth, da of Robert Trafford (d 1948), of Peterborough; 1 s (Alan b 1955); *Career* clerk in Holy Orders; lectr: St Mark and St John's Coll Chelsea 1945–68, Roehampton Inst of Higher Educn 1969–82; *Books* Henry Newman 1708–43 (1956), The March of the Cross (1962), Eighteenth-Century Europe (1963), Martin Luther (1969), The Reformation (1974), The French Revolution (1987), Lord Nelson, A Bibliography (1990), William Wilberforce, A Bibliography (1992), Edmund Burke, A Bibliography (1994), Sir Robert Peel, A Bibliography (1996); *Recreations* gardening, town walking; *Clubs* Athenaeum; *Style—* The Rev Dr Leonard W Cowie; ✉ 38 Stratton Road, Merton Park, London SW19 3JG (☎ 0181 542 5036)

COWIE, Sir Thomas (Tom); kt (1992), OBE (1982); s of Thomas Stephenson Knowles Cowie (d 1960), and Florence, *née* Russell (d 1984); *b* 9 Sept 1922; *Educ* Bede GS Sunderland; *m* 1, 1948, Lillas Roberts, *née* Hunnam (decd); 1 s (Thomas Andrew b 1950), 4 da (Elizabeth b 1951, Susan b 1953, Sarah b 1959, Emma b 1962); m 2, 1975, Mrs Diana Carole Wentworth Evans; 3 da (Alexandra b 1975, Charlotte b 1978, Victoria b 1982), 1 step s (Steven b 1964), 1 step da (Catherine b 1965); *Career* fndr chm T Cowie plc (and chief exec until 1991, now life pres); landowner (1620 acres); *Recreations* music, game shooting, walking; *Style—* Sir Tom Cowie, OBE; ✉ Broadwood Hall, Lanchester, Co Durham (☎ 01207 520 464)

COWIE, Hon Lord; William Lorn Kerr Cowie; s of late Charles Rennie Cowie, MBE, and Norah Slimmon Kerr; *b* 1 June 1926; *Educ* Fettes Coll, Clare Coll Cambridge, Glasgow Univ; *m* 1958, Camilla Henrietta Grizel, da of Randall Colvin Hoyle; 2 s, 2 da; *Career* Sub Lt RNVR 1944–47, advocate Scotland 1952, QC (Scot) 1967, appointed a senator of the Coll of Justice in Scotland with title of Lord Cowie 1977, ret 1994; judge Court of Appeal Botswana 1994; *Clubs* New (Edinburgh), RSAC Glasgow; *Style—* The Hon Lord Cowie; ✉ 20 Blacket Place, Edinburgh EH9 1RL (☎ 0131 667 8238)

COWIN, Thomas Eddie (Tom); OBE (1997); *b* 19 Aug 1945; *Educ* Gillingham GS, Trinity Hall Cambridge (MA), Univ of Leeds (Cert in English), Univ of Edinburgh (Dip in Applied Linguistics); *m* 1969, Jane Elizabeth, *née* Beams; 1 da, 1 s; *Career* English teacher in Turkey and Cyprus 1968–73, visiting prof of English Univ of Santa Caterina 1974–76; British Council: lectr English Language Inst 1976–77, asst English language offr Thailand 1977–79, dir of studies Barcelona 1979–83, dep dir Algeria 1983–87, projects offr India 1989, head HE Dept 1989–92 (HE advsr 1988–89), dir Ghana 1992–96, dir Bangladesh 1996–; *Recreations* travel, books, golf, archaeology; *Style—* Tom Cowin, Esq, OBE; ✉ c/o The British Council (Bangladesh), 10 Spring Gardens, London SW1A 2BN

COWLEY, 7 Earl (UK 1857); Garret Graham Wellesley; also Baron Cowley of Wellesley (UK 1828), Viscount Dangan (UK 1857); s of 4 Earl Cowley (d 1962), by his 2 w, Mary Elsie May; suc half n, 6 Earl, 1975; *b* 30 July 1934; *Educ* Univ of S California (BS), Harvard Univ (MBA); *m* 1, 1961 (m dis 1966), Elizabeth Susanne, da of late Haynes Lennon; 1 s, 1 da; m 2, 1968, Isabelle O'Bready; m 3, 1981, Paige Deming; *Heir* s, Viscount Dangan, *qv*; *Career* gp vice pres Bank of America NT and SA London; Int Investment Management Service 1980–85; dir Bank of America Int (London) 1978–85, dir various Bank of America Tst Cos; chm Cowley & Co financial and business consits 1985–90; investmt ptnr Thomas R Miller & Son (Bermuda) 1990–; memb Assoc of Cons Peers; *Style—* The Rt Hon the Earl Cowley; ✉ c/o House of Lords, London SW1A 0PW

COWLEY, Dr James; CBE (1984); *b* 18 Aug 1924; *Educ* Univ of London (BSc, PhD); *m* 1957, Jean Straughan; 2 s (John James b 1960, Martin Straughan b 1968); *Career* mechanical engrg apprentice Thomas Dryden and Sons Ltd Preston 1939–44, marine engr 1944–52 (Bibby Bros Liverpool, Hopemount Shipping Co, Lyle Shipping Co Glasgow, Shell Tankers); Dept of Transport Marine Survey Orgn: engr and ship surveyor 1952–61, princ engr and ship surveyor 1961–70, chief examiner of engrs 1970–73, chief surveyor 1973–76, engr surveyor-in-chief 1976–81, surveyor gen of ships 1981–88, ret 1988; non-exec chm The Maersk Co (IOM) Ltd 1988–, perm rep Republic of Vanuatu Int Maritime Orgn UN 1989–, marine consit 1990–; Euro Engr award 1980, Denny Gold Medal Inst of Marine Engrs 1982, Int Maritime Prize Int Maritime Orgn UN 1987; FEng 1983, hon FIMarE 1961, FIMechE 1963, hon fell Nautical Inst; *Recreations* ballroom dancing; *Style—* Dr James Cowley, CBE, FEng; ✉ 21 Stanstead Road, Caterham, Surrey CR3 6AD (☎ 01883 345774, fax 01883 341093); The Maersk Company (IOM) Ltd, Portland House, Station Road, Ballasalla, Isle of Man (☎ 01624 822667, fax 01624 822618)

COWLEY, John Henry Stewart; s of Kenneth Cyril Cowley (d 1983), of Douglas, IOM, and Daphne, *née* Leake; *b* 20 Feb 1947; *Educ* King William's Coll; *m* 1, 12 May 1971, Mary, da of late Geoffrey Whitehead, of Manchester; 1 s (George Edward Douglas b 1976), 1 da (Joanne Jane Caroline b 1973); m 2, 20 March 1986, Carolyn, da of Barry Walter Golding Thompson, of Tunbridge Wells; 1 s (Daniel Kenneth Gordon b 1986), 1 da (Charlotte Mary Frances b 1989); m 3, 28 Dec 1995, Gillian, da of John Arthur Holland, formerly of Southport, currently of Isle of Man; *Career* Heron and Brearley Ltd (became Isle of Man Breweries, reverted to Heron and Brearley 1996): dir 1972, chm and md 1983–92, non-exec dir 1992–, vice chm 1996–; dir: Okell and Son Ltd (brewers) 1972–, Bowring (IOM) Ltd 1984–, Castletown Brewery Ltd 1986–; memb Cncl IOM Chamber of Commerce 1985 (chm 1981–83, pres 1983–85); *Recreations* game shooting, sailing; *Clubs* Manx Automobile; *Style—* John Cowley, Esq; ✉ Rock Villa, Strathallaw Road, Onchan, Isle of Man IM3 1NN (☎ 01624 671808, fax 01624 671809); Heron and Brearley Ltd, Kewaigue, Douglas, Isle of Man IM2 1QG (☎ 01624 661120, fax 01624 661160)

COWLEY, Prof Roger Arthur; s of Cecil Arthur Cowley (d 1964), of Romford, Essex, and Mildred Sarah, *née* Nash; *b* 24 Feb 1939; *Educ* Brentwood Sch, Univ of Cambridge (BA, PhD); *m* 4 April 1964, Sheila Joyce, da of Charles Wells (d 1970), of Romford, Essex; 1 s (Kevin David b 1969), 1 da (Sandra Elizabeth b 1966); *Career* res fell Trinity Hall Cambridge 1963–64, res offr Atomic Energy Canada Ltd 1964–70, prof of physics Univ of Edinburgh 1970–88, prof of experimental philosophy Univ of Oxford 1988– (chm of physics 1993–96); FRSE 1971, FRS 1978; *Books* Structural Phase Transitions (1981); *Style—* Prof Roger Cowley, FRS, FRSE; ✉ Tredinnock, Harcourt Hill, Oxford

OX2 9AS (☎ 01865 247 570); Department of Physics, Clarendon Laboratory, Parks Road, Oxford OX1 3PU (☎ 01865 272224)

COWLING, Antony Brian (Tony); s of Albert Ernest Cowling (d 1987), of Swanley, Kent, and Georgina May Connell (d 1969); *b* 2 Jan 1936; *Educ* Bromley GS; *m* 1962, Renee Jacqueline Levy; 2 c (Didier Shaun b 1965, Danielle Julie b 1968); *Career* Nat Serv RAF 1958–60; research exec Benton & Bowles (ad agency) 1960–65, assoc dir Mass Observation (research agency) 1964–65, dir Taylor Nelson Ltd (research agency) 1965–89 (md 1974), chief exec Taylor Nelson AGB plc (Addison Consultancy Group until 1992) 1989– (joined as dir 1989); chm AMSO (Assoc of Market Survey Orgns) 1977–79 (sec/treas 1973–77), Home Office appointee Data Protection Tbnl 1987–; memb Market Res Soc, ESOMAR 1989; *Style*— Tony Cowling, Esq; ✉ Taylor Nelson AGB plc, 44 Upper High Street, Epsom, Surrey KT17 4QS (☎ 01372 739950, fax 01372 744100)

COWLING, (Thomas) Gareth; s of Clifford Cowling (d 1987), and Beryl Elizabeth, *née* Thomas; *b* 12 Nov 1944; *Educ* Eastbourne Coll; *m* 6 June 1970, Jill Ann, da of late Francis Neville Stephens; 1 s (Rupert b 13 Dec 1973), 1 da (Camilla b 16 March 1976); *Career* admitted slr 1969; asst Slrs Dept New Scotland Yard 1969–72, called to the Bar Middle Temple 1972, ad eundem Western Circuit 1972; stipendiary magistrate: Metropolitan Area 1988–89, Hampshire 1989; *Clubs* Hampshire; *Style*— Gareth Cowling, Esq; ✉ The Law Courts, Winston Churchill Ave, Portsmouth, Hants (☎ 01705 819421)

COWLING, Lester Norman; s of Norman Cowling (d 1972), of Kettering, and Muriel Cowling; *b* 7 Oct 1943; *Educ* Weymouth GS, Dover GS for Boys, Univ of Reading (BA); *Career* trainee journalist Daily Mirror Trg Scheme 1966–69, various positions rising to sub-ed Home Counties Newspapers 1969–73, variously business ed, features ed and sub-ed Northants Evening Telegraph (owned by EMAP) 1973–90, responsible for EMAP application for Northampton Independent Local Radio franchise 1983; KCBC Ltd: fndr exec chm responsible for successful ILR franchise application 1990, md 1993–94; dir Northamptonshire Broadcasting Company 1987–93; chm Mapeldown Ltd; bdcast conslt and freelance journalist 1994–; memb Local Advsy Bd Northants TEC; *Recreations* travel, theatre, reading; *Style*— Lester Cowling, Esq

COWLING, Maurice John; s of Reginald Frederick Cowling (d 1962), of London, and May, *née* Roberts (d 1963); *b* 6 Sept 1926; *Educ* Battersea GS, Jesus Coll Cambridge (BA); *Career* Capt Queen's Royal Regt British and Indian Armies; Univ of Cambridge: fell Jesus Coll 1950–53 and 1961–63, lectr in history 1961–76, fell of Peterhouse 1963–93 (emeritus fell 1993–), reader in history 1976–88; literary ed The Spectator 1970–71, prof of religion Columbia Univ NY 1989; Parly candidate (Cons) Bassetlaw 1958–59, memb Cambridgeshire and Isle of Ely CC 1966–70; *Books* Mill and Liberalism (1963), Disraeli Gladstone and Revolution (1967), The Impact of Labour (1971), The Impact of Hitler (1975), Conservative Essays (ed, 1979), Religion and Public Doctrine in Modern England (vol I 1980, vol II 1985); *Style*— Maurice Cowling, Esq

COWLING, Peter John; s of Harry Clifford Cowling, and Irene Charlotte, *née* Phillips; *b* 11 Nov 1944; *Educ* Bletchley GS, BRNC Dartmouth (Robert Roxburgh Meml Prize, Ronald McGraw Meml Prize, Graham Naval History Prize, Queen's Gold Medal); *m* 1979, Sara Anne, da of Alexander Fox; 2 da (Lucie Charlotte b 14 Jan 1981, Olivia Elizabeth Mary b 17 Dec 1983); *Career* served RN 1963–94; Capt HMS Naiad 1979–81, Capt 3 Destroyer Sqdn 1988–90, Capt RN Presentation Team 1990–91, Sr Naval Offr Middle East 1991, Dir Naval Operations 1991–94; dir RSA 1994–; chm Friends of the Benjamin Franklin House 1996–; *Recreations* gardening, sailing, tennis; *Style*— Peter Cowling, Esq; ✉ Royal Society for the Encouragement of Arts Manufactures and Commerce, 8 John Adam Street, London WC2N 6EZ (☎ 0171 930 5115, fax 0171 839 5805)

COWPE, William Arthur; s of Allan Cowpe (d 1974), and Margery Cowpe, of Worsley, Manchester; *b* 8 Nov 1945; *Educ* Hollings Coll Manchester (Dip Hotel & Catering); *m* 5 Aug 1972, Pauline Elizabeth, da of Frederick Trevor Holt; 2 da (Charlotte Elizabeth b 21 Feb 1976, Hannah Louise (twin)); 1 s (Richard William Allan b 12 May 1979); *Career* commis de cuisine: The Savoy London 1964–67, Hotel Chateau d'Ouchy Lausanne Switzerland 1967–68, Hotel Baur au Lac Zurich 1968; chef de partie Kur Hotel Bad Neuenahr Germany 1968–69; The Goring Hotel London: jr asst mangr 1969–70, sr asst mangr 1970–74, mangr 1974–78, gen mangr 1978–89, dir 1989–; chm Restoration Appeal St John's Church Waterloo; memb: Considerate Hoteliers City of Westminster, Union Soc of Westminster, Lords Taverners; memb Ctee Reunion des Gastronomes 1981, hon memb Acad of Food and Wine Service 1989; Master Innholder 1995, Freeman City of London 1995; FHCIMA 1995; *Recreations* golf, cricket, tennis; *Clubs* Farnham Golf, Bourne Tennis; *Style*— William Cowpe, Esq; ✉ The Goring, Beeston Place, Grosvenor Gardens, London SW1W 0JW (☎ 0171 396 9000, fax 0171 834 4393)

COWPER-COLES, Sherard Louis; LVO (1991); s of Sherard Hamilton Cowper-Coles (d 1968), of Sevenoaks, and Dorothy, *née* Short; *b* 8 Jan 1955; *Educ* Tonbridge (scholar), Hertford Coll Oxford (scholar); *m* 1982, Bridget Mary, da of Neil Emerson Elliott; 5 c (Henry Sherard b 27 Nov 1982, Rupert Neil b 16 Aug 1984, Minna Louise b 18 Feb 1986, Frederick Peter b 20 May 1987, Myles Philip b 21 March 1990); *Career* Foreign Office London 1977–78, Arabic language training 1978–80, third then second sec Br Embassy Cairo 1980–83, first sec Planning Staff FCO 1983–85, private sec to Perm Under Sec 1985–87, first sec Br Embassy Washington 1987–91, asst Security Policy Dept FCO 1991–93, efficiency scrutineer FCO May-Sept 1993, res assoc Int Inst for Strategic Studies 1993–94, head Hong Kong Dept FCO 1994–; Liveryman Worshipful Co of Skinners 1988; *Recreations* being in the country with my children; *Clubs* Institute of Contemporary Arts; *Style*— Sherard Cowper-Coles, Esq, LVO; ✉ Head of Hong Kong Department, Foreign & Commonwealth Office, Whitehall, London SW1A 2AH (☎ 0171 270 3000)

COWPERTHWAITE, Sir John James; KBE (1968, OBE 1960), CMG (1964); s of late John James Cowperthwaite of Edinburgh, and Jessie Wemyss Barron, *née* Jarvis; *b* 25 April 1915; *Educ* Merchiston Castle Sch, Univ of St Andrews, Christ's Coll Cambridge; *m* 1941, Sheila Mary, da of Alexander Thomson, of Aberdeen; 1 s; *Career* colonial admin service Hong Kong 1941, Sierra Leone 1942–45, fin sec Hong Kong 1961–72, int advsr Jardine Fleming and Co Ltd 1972–82; *Clubs* Hong Kong Jockey, Hong Kong Golf, Royal and Ancient Golf; *Style*— Sir John Cowperthwaite, KBE, CMG; ✉ 25 South St, St Andrews, Fife KY16 9QS (☎ 01334 474759)

COX, Alex; s of Jack Cox, of the Wirral, and Moyna Reese, *née* Hinton; *b* 15 Dec 1954; *Educ* Wirral GS, Worcester Coll Oxford (MA), Univ of Bristol, UCLA (Fullbright fell, MFA); *m* 14 Dec 1989, Cecilia Luzmila Montiel Ginocchio, da of late Mañuel Fernando Montiel Ruiz; *Career* film director: Sleep Is For Sissies 1980, Repo Man 1983, Sid and Nancy 1985, Straight To Hell 1986, Walker 1987, El Patrullero 1991, Death and the Compass 1992; presenter Moviedrome series (BBC2); hon citizen Tucson Arizona 1988; memb: BECTU (UK film union) 1985, STIC (Mexican film union) 1990; *Recreations* the desert; *Style*— Alex Cox, Esq

COX, His Honour (James) Anthony; s of Herbert Sidney Cox (d 1972), and Gwendolin Margaret Cox (d 1973); *b* 21 April 1924; *Educ* Cotham Sch Bristol, Univ of Bristol (LLB); *m* 1950, Doris Margaret, da of Vincent Percy Fretwell (d 1933); 3 s, 1 da; *Career* War Serv RM 1943–46; called to the Bar 1949, recorder of the Crown Court 1972–76, circuit judge 1976–94; *Recreations* cricket, golf, sailing, the arts; *Clubs* MCC, Somerset County Cricket, Royal Western Yacht, Yealm Yacht, Bigbury Golf; *Style*— His Hon Anthony Cox; ✉ Haldonhay, Lower Court Road, Newton Ferrers, Plymouth PL8 1DE

COX, Dr Anthony Robert; s of Robert George Cox, of Copperfields, Fetcham, Surrey, and Gladys, *née* Streatfield; *b* 30 Nov 1938; *Educ* Brockley Co Sch, Imperial Coll London (BSc, PhD); *m* 14 Sept 1963, Constance Jean, da of Charles Hammond (d 1974); 1 s (Mark Robert b 15 Feb 1970), 2 da (Helen Jane b 17 June 1964, Angela Jean b 15 Aug 1966); *Career* Royal Armament R & D Estab Sevenoaks: metallurgist 1960–69, exchange scientist US Naval Res Laboratory 1969–71, head of steel res 1971–75; asst dir Armour and Materials Branch Mil Vehicle Engrg Estab Chertsey 1975–80, asst dir of def sci MOD 1980–83, cnsllr (sci and technol) Br Embassy Washington DC 1983–87, head Div of Radiation Sci and Acoustics National Physical Laboratory 1987–92, cnsllr (sci and technol) Br Embassy Tokyo 1993–; MIM, CEng; *Recreations* sailing, squash, walking; *Style*— Dr Anthony Cox; ✉ British Embassy, 1 Ichibaneho, Chiyoda-ku, Tokyo 102, Japan

COX, Prof Antony Dawson; s of William Ronald Cox (d 1970), and Dorothy, *née* Gerrard (d 1961); *b* 2 Dec 1935; *Educ* Bryanston, Gonville and Caius Coll Cambridge (MA, MB BCh), St Thomas's Hosp London (MPhil); *m* 1 July 1961, (Pamela) Teresa, da of Capt Egerton Gervase Edward Harcourt-Vernon, MC (d 1976); 3 s (Simon b 1962, Nicholas b 1964, Hugo Francis b 1967); *Career* Nat Serv 2 Lt RA 1954–56; conslt in child and adolescent psychiatry Bethlem Royal and Maudsley Hosps London 1976–85, hon conslt in child and adolescent psychiatry to Br Army 1984–94, sr lectr Inst of Psychiatry London 1985–87, Mersey RHA prof of child and adolescent psychiatry at Univ of Liverpool (fndn chair) 1987–89, prof of child and adolescent psychiatry UMDS of Guy's and St Thomas's Hosps Univ of London 1990–; memb Human Fertilisation and Embryology Authy 1990–94, pres Psychiatry Section RSM 1996–97; memb BMA, FRSM, FRCPsych 1979, FRCP 1987; *Recreations* local and family history, music; *Style*— Prof Antony Cox; ✉ Flat 11, 92–94 Great Titchfield St, London W1P 7AG; Wensley Hall, Wensley, Matlock, Derbyshire

COX, Dr (Christopher) Barry; s of Herbert Ernest Cox (d 1983), and May, *née* Bell; *b* 29 July 1931; *Educ* St Paul's, Balliol Coll Oxford (BA, MA), St John's Coll Cambridge (PhD), Univ of London (DSc); *m* 6 April 1961, Sheila (d 1996), da of William Edward Morgan (d 1978); 2 s (Timothy b 1962, Justin b 1970), 1 da (Sally b 1964); *Career* King's Coll London: asst lectr in zoology 1956–59, lectr 1959–66, sr lectr 1966–69, reader 1969–76, prof 1976–96, head Dept of Zoology 1982–85, head Dept of Biology 1985–88, asst princ 1989–96; Harkness fell Cwlth Fund Harvard 1959, sr Fulbright fell Stanford 1989; formerly chm: Woodcote Residents Assoc, Action Ctee for Epsom, Epsom Protection Soc; Freeman City of London 1983; memb Palaeontological Assoc 1960–91 (vice pres 1980–81); *Books* Prehistoric World (1975), Biogeography: an Ecological & Historical Approach (5 edn, 1993), Macmillans Illustrated Encyclopaedia of Dinosaurs and Prehistoric Animals (1988), Atlas of the Living World (1989); *Recreations* theatre, tennis, gardening; *Style*— Dr Barry Cox; ✉ Forge Cottage, Ashtead, Surrey KT21 2BD (☎ 01372 273167)

COX, Barry Geoffrey; *b* 25 May 1942; *Educ* Tiffin Sch Kingston Surrey, Magdalen Coll Oxford (BA); *children* 2 s, 2 da; *Career* journalist with: The Scotsman 1965–67, Sunday Telegraph 1967–70; reporter and prodr Granada TV 1970–74; London Weekend Television: ed 1974–77, head of current affrs 1977–81, controller of features and current affrs 1981–87, dir of corp affrs 1987–94, special advsr to chief exec 1994; dir ITV Assoc 1995–; sec Br Exec Int Press Inst; FRTS; *Books* Civil Liberties In Britain (1975), The Fall of Scotland Yard (jtly, 1977); *Style*— Barry Cox; ✉ The Independent Television Association, 200 Gray's Inn Road, London WC1X 8XZ (☎ 0171 843 8000)

COX, Barry Stewart; s of Frederick G O Cox (d 1978), and Lilian Cox (d 1963); *b* 29 July 1945; *Educ* Bancroft's Sch Woodford Green Essex, Univ of Essex (BA Economics); *m* Patricia, da of Frank Moinet; 3 s (Ben b 11 June 1977, Toby b 26 April 1980, Oliver b 21 May 1984); *Career* graduate trainee rising to account dir/assoc bd dir J Walter Thompson 1967–76; Collett Dickenson Pearce & Partners 1976–88: joined as account dir, appointed to Bd 1979, head of client servs 1983–86, head of new business 1986–88; md and equity ptnr Stewart Smith Deighton Cox (formerly Elgie Stewart Smith) 1988–90; Publicis 1990–: progressively mgmnt supr, head of client serv then dir of business devpt, managing ptnr 1995–; fund raiser Assoc for Research into Stammering in Childhood (ARSC); MIPA, memb D&AD; *Recreations* golf, sailing, rugby; *Clubs* MCC, Richmond Golf, Richmond Rugby; *Style*— Barry Cox, Esq; ✉ 14 Sandy Lane, Teddington, Middlesex TW11 0DR (☎ 0181 977 0459); Publicis, 82 Baker Street, London W1M 2AE (☎ 0171 935 4426, fax 0171 487 5351)

COX, Prof (Charles) Brian; CBE (1990); s of Hedley Ernest Cox, (d 1988), and Rose, *née* Thompson (d 1938); *b* 5 Sept 1928; *Educ* Wintringham Secdy Sch, Pembroke Coll Cambridge (MA, MLitt); *m* 7 Aug 1954, Jean, da of Harold Willmer (d 1968); 1 s (Richard Hedley b 1955), 2 da (Sally Jean b 1958, Celia Willmer b 1960); *Career* Mil Serv 1947–49 (RAEC, WO II 1948); lectr Univ of Hull 1954–66; Univ of Manchester: prof of Eng lit 1966–76, John Edward Taylor prof of Eng lit 1976–93 (emeritus prof 1993), dean Faculty of Arts 1984–86, pro-vice chllr 1987–91; visiting assoc prof Univ of Calif Berkeley 1964–65, Brown fell Univ of the South Sewanee Tennessee 1980; visiting prof: King's Coll London 1993–95, Sheffield Hallam Univ 1993–; pres Nat Cncl for Educnl Standards 1984–89 (chm 1979–84); hon fell Westminster Coll Oxford 1993–; chair: North West Arts Bd 1994–, Arvon Fndn 1994–; memb Kingman Ctee 1987–88, chm Nat Curriculum Eng Working Gp 1988–89; co-ed: Critical Quarterly 1959–, Black Papers on Educn 1969–77; *Books* The Free Spirit (1963), Modern Poetry (ed with A E Dyson, 1963), Practical Criticism of Poetry (ed with A E Dyson, 1965), Joseph Conrad: The Modern Imagination (1974), Every Common Sight (1981), Two-Headed Monster (1985), Cox on Cox: An English Curriculum for the 1990s (1991), The Great Betrayal: Memoirs of a Life in Education (1992), Collected Poems (1993), The Battle for the English Curriculum (1995); *Recreations* Manchester Utd, walking; *Clubs* Lansdowne; *Style*— Prof Brian Cox, CBE; ✉ 20 Park Gates Drive, Cheadle Hulme, Cheshire SK8 7DF (☎ 0161 485 2162); Department of English, The University, Manchester M13 9PL (☎ 0161 275 2000)

COX, Brian Denis; s of Charles Cox, and Mary Ann Guillerline McCann; *b* 1 June 1946; *Educ* London Acad of Music and Dramatic Arts; *m* 1967 (m dis), Caroline Burt; 1 s (Alan), 1 da (Margaret); *Career* actor and director; *Theatre* Orlando in As You Like It (Birmingham and Vaudeville (London debut)) 1967, title role in Peer Gynt (Birmingham Rep) 1967, Ulfhejm in When We Dead Awaken (Assembly Hall Edinburgh) 1968, Steven in In Celebration (Royal Court) 1969, Gregers Werle in The Wild Duck (Edinburgh Festival) 1969, Alan in The Big Romance (Royal Court) 1970, Norman in Don't Start Without Me (Garrick) 1971, Knight of Riprafatta in Mirandolina (Gardner Centre Brighton) 1971, Brian Lowther in Getting On (Queen's) 1971, Gustav in The Creditors (Open Space Theatre) 1972, Eilert Lovborg in Hedda Gabler (Royal Court) 1972, Berowne in Love's Labours Lost (Playhouse Nottingham) 1972, title role in Brand (Playhouse) 1972, Sergeant Match in What The Butler Saw (Playhouse) 1972, D'Artagnan in The Three Musketeers (Playhouse) 1972, Proctor in Cromwell (Royal Court) 1973, Sergius in Arms and the Man (Royal Exchange Manchester) 1974, Sir Henry Harcourt Reilly in The Cocktail Party (Royal Exchange) 1975, Emigres (Nat Theatre Co, Young Vic) 1976, Theridamas in Tamburlaine the Great (NT) 1976, Brutus in Julius Caesar (NT) 1977, De Flores in The Changeling (Riverside Studios) 1978, title role in Herod (NT) 1978, Ireton in The Putney Debates (NT) 1978, Mickey in On Top (Royal Court) 1979, Vicomte Robert de Trivelin in Have You Anything to Declare? (Royal Exchange then Round House) 1981, title role in Danton's Death (NT) 1982, Edmund Darrell in Strange Interlude (Duke of York 1984, Nederlander Theatre NY 1985), D I Nelson in Rat in the Skull (Royal Court 1984, Public Theatre NY 1985), Paul Cash in Fashion (RSC, The Pit) 1988, title role in Titus Andronicus (Swan Theatre Stratford-upon-Avon and on tour in

Madrid, Paris and Copenhagen) 1988, The Taming of the Shrew (RSC, Theatre Royal), Johnny in Frankie and Johnny in the Clair-de-Lune (Comedy Theatre) 1989, title role in King Lear (NT, toured E and W Europe, Cairo and Tokyo) 1990–91, Richard III (RNT), Harold Hill in The Music Man (Open Air Theatre) 1995; as director prodns incl: The Man with a Flower in His Mouth (Edinburgh Festival) 1973, The Stronger (Edinburgh Festival) 1973, I Love My Love (Orange Tree) 1983, Mrs Warren's Profession (Orange Tree) 1989, The Crucible (Moscow Art Theatre, Riverside and Edinburgh) 1988–89, The Philanderer (Hampstead) 1991, The Master Builder (Royal Lyceum Edinburgh and Riverside) 1993/94, Richard III (Regent's Park) 1995; *Television* Laurent in Therese Raquin (Masterpiece Theatre PBS) 1981, Jemima Shore (Thames), Rat in the Skull (Central), Alas Smith and Jones (BBC), Perfect Scoundrels (TVS), The Cloning of Joanna May (Granada), Lost Language of the Cranes (BBC), Van der Valk (Thames), Redfox (Fitzroy Films), The Big Battalions, Six Characters in Search of an Author (BBC), Inspector Morse (Zenith), Sharpe's Rifles (Sharpe Films), Grushko (BBC) 1994, The Negotiator (BBC) 1994; *Film* Trotsky in Nicholas and Alexandra 1971, Steven Shaw in In Celebration 1975, Father Gora in Pope John Paul II (movie CBS) 1984, Dr McGrigor in Florence Nightingale (movie NBC) 1985, Dr Lektor in Manhunter 1986, Duffy in Shoot for the Sun 1986, Peter Kerrigan in Hidden Agenda 1990, Iron Will, Argyle in Braveheart 1994, Killearn in Rob Roy 1994, Chain Reaction 1996, The Glimmer Man 1996, Long Kiss Goodnight 1996, Kiss the Girl 1996, Desperate Measures 1996, Good Vibrations 1996; *Awards* Olivier Award Best Actor (Rat in the Skull) 1985, Drama Magazine Best Actor Award (Rat in the Skull) 1985, Olivier Award Best Actor in a Revival (Titus Andronicus) 1988, Drama Magazine Award (for work in the RSC 1987–88 season) 1988, International Theatre Institute Award 1989; *Publications* Salem to Moscow - An Actor's Odyssey (1991), The Lear Diaries (1993); *Recreations* keeping fit; *Style*— Brian Cox, Esq; ✉ Conway van Gelder Robinson Ltd, 18–21 Jermyn Street, London SW1Y 6HP (☎ 0171 287 0077, fax 0171 287 1940)

COX, Baroness (Life Peer UK 1982), of Queensbury in Greater London; Caroline Anne Cox; da of Robert John McNeill Love, MS, FRCS (d 1974), of Brickendon, Herts, and Dorothy Ida, *née* Borland; *b* 7 July 1937; *Educ* Channing Sch Highgate, London Univ (BSc, MSc Econ); *m* 1959, Murray Newell Cox, FRCPsych, s of Rev Roland Lee Cox, of London; 2 s (Hon Robin Michael b 1959, Hon Jonathan Murray b 1962), 1 da (Hon Philippa Ruth Dorothy b 1965); *Career* head Dept of Sociology N London Poly 1974–77, dir Nursing Education Research Unit Chelsea Coll London Univ 1977–83; sits as Cons Peer in House of Lords (deputy speaker 1986–), baroness-in-waiting and Govt whip 1985; chllr Bournemouth Univ 1992–; non-exec dir: Andrei Sakharov Fndn, PWS, pres: Christian Solidarity Internat (UK), Tushinskaya Children's Hosp Tst, Standing Conf of Women's Orgns, Inst of Admin Mgmnt; vice pres Royal Coll of Nursing; memb: Advsy Cncl Inst of Euro Def and Strategic Studies, Freedom Assoc; tstee: MERLIN (Medical Emergency Relief Int), Siberian Medical Univ, Smith & Nephew Fndn, Nuffield Provincial Hosps Tst; patron: Med Aid for Poland Fund, Youth With a Mission, London Bible Coll, Physicians for Human Rights UK, Premier Radio; hon fell Univ of Westminster; Hon PhD Polish Univ in London 1988, Hon DH Univ of Utah, Hon LLD CNAA; Hon Doctorate Univ of Yerevan, Armenia; Hon FRCS; Hon DSS Queen's Univ Belfast; William Wilberforce Award 1995; Cdr Cross of the Order of Merit Republic of Poland 1990; *Books* The Right to Learn (co-author with Dr John Marks, 1982), Sociology: An Introduction for Nurses, Midwives and Health Visitors (jt ed, 1983), Trajectories of Despair: Misdiagnosis and Maltreatment of Soviet Orphans (1991), Ethnic Cleansing in Progress: War in Nagorno Karabakh (jtly, 1993), Made to Care: The Case for Residential and Village Communities for People with a Mental Handicap (co-author, 1995); *Recreations* squash, campanology, hill walking; *Clubs* Royal Over-Seas League; *Style*— The Rt Hon Lady Cox; ✉ 1 Arnellan House, 144–146 Slough Lane, Kingsbury, London NW9 8XJ (☎ 0181 204 7336, fax 0181 204 5661); The White House, Wyke Hall, Gillingham, Dorset SP8 4WS (☎ 01747 823436)

COX, Charles; s of Harry Cox, of London, and Myra Emily, *née* Brooking; *b* 25 Sept 1949; *Educ* Stratford GS London; *m* 12 April 1975, Sandra Carol, da of Victor Anthony Willis Taylor (d 1974); 1 s (Peter b 1978), 1 da (Helen b 1976); *Career* CA; Turquands Barton Mayhew 1968–79, ptnr Pannell Kerr Forster 1984– (joined 1979); FCA 1972; *Recreations* memb PCC St Andrew's Church Hornchurch, jogging, reading, venture scout leader, running a youth club; *Clubs* RAC; *Style*— Charles Cox, Esq; ✉ Pannell Kerr Forster, New Garden House, 78 Hatton Garden, London EC1N 8JA (☎ 0171 831 7393, fax 0171 405 6736, telex 295 928)

COX, Christopher Charles Arthur; s of Col Harold Bernard Cox (d 1990), of Farnham, Surrey, and Ivie Vera, *née* Warren (d 1981); *b* 21 July 1944; *Educ* St Edward's Sch Oxford, Hertford Coll Oxford (BCL, MA); *m* 5 May 1984, Kathleen Susan Anne May, da of James Buist Mackenzie (d 1976), of Madrid, Spain; 2 da (Andrea b 1986, Georgina b 1987); *Career* admitted slr 1970; Coward Chance 1968–77, Spicer & Oppenheim 1981–84, ptnr Nabarro Nathanson 1986– (slr 1984–86); memb Tax Ctee ICC; Freeman City of London 1986; memb: Int Fiscal Assoc, VAT Practitioners' Gp; *Books* Partnership Taxation (jtly, 1979), Capital Gains Tax on Businesses (jtly, 1992); *Recreations* politics, mountain walking, music, theatre; *Style*— Christopher Cox, Esq; ✉ Nabarro Nathanson, 50 Stratton St, London W1X 6NX (☎ 0171 493 9933, fax 0171 629 7900, telex 8813144 G)

COX, Dennis William; s of Albert Cox (d 1978), and Margot, *née* Auerbach; *b* 27 Feb 1957; *Educ* Hornchurch GS, Westfield Coll London (exhibitioner, BSc Mathematics); *m* 31 Aug 1996, Lisette Mermod; 2 adopted da (Natalie b Nov 1981, Candace b Nov 1983); *Career* various positions rising to sr mangr banking and fin Arthur Young (now Ernst & Young) 1978–88, sr mangr banking and fin BDO Binder Hamlyn 1988–90, audit mangr Midland Bank rising to sr audit mangr (Compliance) HSBC Holdings plc 1991–; ICAEW: memb Cncl 1995–, memb Audit Faculty 1995–, memb Fin Servs Authorisation Ctee 1996–, memb Ctee Workplace 2000 1996–; Securities Inst: fndr memb Audit Discussion Gp 1994–, fndr memb Compliance Discussion Gp 1996–; pres S Essex Soc of Chartered Accountants 1994–95 (memb Main Ctee 1983–); MCIB 1988, FCA 1991 (ACA 1981), MSI 1992; *Publications* Banks: Accounts, Audit & Practice (Butterworths, 1993); also author of various articles in Butterworths Jl of Banking and Finance among others; *Recreations* hockey, travel, music, art; *Clubs* Upminster Hockey; *Style*— Dennis Cox, Esq; ✉ 7 Berkeley Drive, Hornchurch, Essex RM11 3PY (☎ 01708 451498); HSBC Holdings plc, 10 Lower Thames Street, London EC3R 6AE (☎ 0171 260 0210, fax 0171 260 9834)

COX, Rev Canon Eric William; s of Sydney Eric Cox (d 1979), of Beeston, Nottingham, and Maude Marie Cox; *b* 17 July 1930; *Educ* Henry Mellish GS Bulwell Notts, Bede Coll Durham (BA), Wells Theol Coll; *m* 7 Jan 1959, Jennifer Anne, da of Lt-Col the Rev Maurice James Fraser Wilson (d 1985), of Baschurch, Shropshire; 4 s (Peter b 1959, Timothy b 1960, Paul b 1963, Andrew b 1968), 1 da (Joanna b 1966); *Career* RAF 1949–51; ordained: deacon 1956, priest 1957; asst curate St Mary Magdalene Sutton-in-Ashfield 1956–59, asst chaplain Utd Anglican Church Brussels Belgium 1959–62; vicar: St Luke's Winnington Northwich Cheshire 1962–71, St Michael and All Angels Middlewich Cheshire 1971–95 (ret); rector St John Evangelist Byley-cum-Leese Cheshire 1973–95 (ret), rural dean Middlewich 1980–94, hon canon Chester Cathedral 1984–95 (canon emeritus 1995–); chm of govrs Sir John Deane's Coll Northwich; memb: Rotary Club of Northwich 1970–95 (pres 1984), Rotary Club of Wem 1995–; *Style*— The Rev Canon Eric Cox; ✉ Lovel Hollow, Church Road, Baschurch, Shrewsbury SY4 2EE (☎ 01939 261258)

COX, Sir Geoffrey Sandford; kt (1966), CBE (1959, MBE 1945); s of (Charles William) Sandford Cox, of Wellington, NZ, and Mary, *née* MacGregor; *b* 7 April 1910; *Educ* Southland HS NZ, Otago Univ NZ, Oriel Coll Oxford; *m* 1935, Cecily Barbara Talbot (d 1993), da of Alexander Turner, of Fernhurst, Sussex; 2 s (Peter, Patrick), 2 da (Rosamond, Evelyn); *Career* WWII served NZ Army in Med; journalist; formerly reporter: News Chronicle, Daily Express; ed and chief exec ITN 1956–68 (fndr News at Ten), dep chm Yorkshire TV 1968–71; chm: Tyne Tees TV 1972–74, UPITN Inc (USA) 1975–81, London Broadcasting Co 1977–81; ind dir The Observer 1981–89; *Books* Defence of Madrid (1937), The Red Army Moves (1941), Road to Trieste (1947), Race for Trieste (1978), See It Happen: The Making of ITN (1983), A Tale of Two Battles (1987), Countdown to War (1989), Pioneering Television News (1995); *Recreations* fishing, tracing Roman roads; *Clubs* Garrick; *Style*— Sir Geoffrey Cox, CBE

COX, Gilbert Henry; s of Cecil Henry Cox, of Bishop's Stortford, Herts; *b* 12 April 1936; *Educ* Newport GS Essex; *m* 1, (m dis), Pamela Edith, da of Ernest Walter Arthur Firman; 1 s (Timothy Henry b 29 Dec 1960); m 2, 11 Oct 1969 (m dis), Valerie Iris, da of Jack Henry Gilder; m 3, 27 May 1992, Brenda Margaret, da of Alex Seyderhelm; *Career* Associated Press Fleet Street 1952–55, freelance press photographer 1955–59, proprietor Cox Photography 1959–; pres BIPP 1993–94; Hon Professional Fame Photographer (Norway) 1986, Photographic Craftsman Professional Photographers of America 1991 (memb 1975); FBIPP 1975 (assoc 1970), FRPS 1976 (ARPS 1973); *Recreations* scuba-diving; *Style*— Gilbert Cox, Esq; ✉ Cox Photography, 3 Northgate End, Bishop's Stortford, Herts CM23 2ET (☎ 01279 652024 and 01279 505046)

COX, Sheriff Principal Graham Loudon; QC (Scot 1993); s of Rev Thomas Loudon Cox (d 1971), of Crail, and Leonainie Violet Rose, *née* Watson (d 1965); *b* 22 Dec 1933; *Educ* Hamilton Acad, Grove Acad Broughty Ferry, Univ of Edinburgh (Harry Dalgetty bursar, MA, LLB); *m* 1, 1959 (m dis 1975), June Mary Constance Gunner; 3 da (Sandra Mary Loudon b 6 Dec 1961, Elaine Margaret Munro b 31 Jan 1963, Susan Elizabeth Watson b 30 July 1965); m 2, 1977, Jean, da of Capt James Nelson (d 1974); *Career* admitted slr 1957 (apprentice slr 1954–56); Nat Serv 2 Lt RASC 1956, transferred to Directorate Army Legal Servs 1957, Capt 1957, T/Maj 1960, demobbed 1961; devilled to James P H Mackay (present Lord Chllr) 1961–62, called to Scottish Bar 1962, advocate depute 1967–68, sheriff at Dundee 1968–93, sheriff princ South Strathclyde, Dumfries and Galloway 1993–; Sheriffs' Assoc: sec 1987–91, vice pres 1991–92, pres 1992–93; memb Cncl Cwlth Magistrates' and Judges' Assoc 1991–94; *Recreations* golf, skiing, restoring interesting properties; *Clubs* Crail Golfing Society, Royal & Ancient Golf (St Andrews); *Style*— Sheriff Principal Graham Cox, QC; ✉ Crail House, Crail, Fife KY10 3SJ (☎ 01333 450270, fax 01333 450183); 13 Rochsolloch Farm Cottages, Victoria Place, Airdrie ML6 9BQ (☎ 01236 770158); Sheriff Principal's Chambers, Sheriff Court, Graham Street, Airdrie, Lanarkshire ML6 6EE (☎ 01236 751121, fax 01236 747497)

COX, Dr James (Jim); s of Dr Michael Ievers Cox, and Betty, *née* Firth; *Educ* Keswick Sch, Univ of Newcastle upon Tyne (MB BS, MD); *m* 1 Feb 1975, Fiona Mary; 1 da (Tamsin b 30 Oct 1978), 1 s (Charles b 8 July 1982); *Career* GP trainee Northumbria 1973–76, asst prof Dept of Family Practice Southern Illinois Univ Sch of Med Springfield Illinois 1976–78; GP: Morpeth Northumberland 1978–80, Caldbeck Cumbria 1980–; assoc advsr in gen practice Univ of Newcastle upon Tyne 1988–97; memb Irish Coll of Gen Practitioners 1985, FRCGP 1991 (memb Cncl 1990–); *Books* A-Z of the Human Body (conslt ed, 1987), The Good Health Fact Book (conslt ed, 1995); *Recreations* fell walking, sailing; *Style*— Dr Jim Cox; ✉ The Barn, Caldbeck, Wigton, Cumbria CA7 8DS; The Surgery, Friar Row, Caldbeck, Wigton, Cumbria CA7 8DS (☎ 016974 78254, fax 016974 78661)

COX, John; s of Leonard John Cox (d 1983), and Ethel Minnie May, *née* McGill; *b* 12 March 1935; *Educ* Queen Elizabeth's Hosp Bristol, St Edmund Hall Oxford (MA); *Career* stage dir; freelance work with occasional medium term contracts for theatre, opera and TV 1959–71; dir of prodns Glyndebourne 1972–82, gen administrator and artistic dir Scottish Opera 1982–86, prodn dir Royal Opera Covent Garden 1988–94, int freelance engagements; Evening Standard Award for Intermezzo, Olivier Award for Cosi Fan Tutte; hon fell St Edmund Hall Oxford 1992; *Recreations* horticulture, fine art; *Style*— John Cox, Esq; ✉ c/o Lies Askonas Ltd, 6 Henrietta Street, London WC2E 8LA (☎ 0171 405 1296, fax 0171 242 1831)

COX, John Colin Leslie; CBE (1994); s of Dr Leslie Reginald Cox, OBE, FRS (d 1965), and Hilda Cecilia Cox (d 1991); *b* 23 Oct 1933; *Educ* Univ Coll Sch London, Queens' Coll Cambridge (BA); *m* 16 April 1983, Avril Joyce, da of H A G Butt (d 1975), of Sibford Gower, Oxon; 1 s (Charles b 16 March 1987), 1 da (Victoria b 13 Dec 1983); *Career* Nat Serv 2 Lt 2/10 Princess Mary's Own Gurkha Rifles 1956–58, GSM Malaya 1958; Shell Gp: joined 1958, exec posts Shell Ghana 1962–65 and London 1966–67, personnel dir Shell Chemicals UK 1978–81, dir business devpt and chm subsid companies 1981–86, DG Chem Ind Assoc 1987–95, chief exec London First Centre 1995–; FRSA 1989; *Recreations* sailing, antiques, country pursuits, photography; *Clubs* Army and Navy, Hurlingham Leander (Henley on Thames), Royal Solent Yacht (IOW); *Style*— John C L Cox, Esq, CBE; ✉ c/o London First Centre, 1 Hobhouse Court, Suffolk Street, London SW1Y 4HH (☎ 0171 925 2000)

COX, John Edward; OBE (1993); s of Edward Ralph Cox, of Sutton-on-Sea, Lincolnshire, and Evelyn Lavinia Mary, *née* Pawley; *b* 18 Oct 1946; *Educ* The GS Brigg Lincs, Brasenose Coll Oxford (BA); *m* 17 Jan 1974, Diane, da of Bernard Sutcliffe (d 1985), of Hemingford Grey, Cambs; 1 da (Laura b 29 Jan 1976); *Career* called to the Bar Middle Temple; sales mangr: International Book Information Services Ltd 1968–71, The Open Univ 1971–76; md Open Univ Educational Enterprises Ltd 1976–81, mktg dir telepublishing Butterworth and Co Ltd 1981–83; md: Scholastic Publications Ltd 1983–90, B H Blackwell Ltd 1990–94, Carfax Publishing Company 1994–; memb Air Travel Trust Ctee, chm Air Tport Users' Ctee until 1992; MIMgt 1977, MCIT 1990, FInstD 1991; *Recreations* philately, conversation; *Style*— John Cox, Esq, OBE; ✉ The Pippins, 6 Lees Close, Whittlebury, Towcester, Northants NN12 8XF (☎ 01327 857908, fax 01327 858564); Carfax Publishing Company, Abingdon Science Park, Barton lane, Abingdon, Oxon OX14 3UE (☎ 01235 401000, fax 01235 401550)

COX, Prof John Lee; *b* 9 Oct 1939; *Educ* Univ of Oxford (MA, BM BCh, DM), The London Hosp; *m*; 3 c; *Career* house surgn The London Hosp 1966, house physician then SHO in chest and gen med St Charles' Hosp London 1966–68, SHO in gen med St Leonard's Hosp London 1968–69, locum registrar Paddington Chest Clinic Feb-April 1969, registrar Univ Dept of Psychiatry The London Hosp Dec 1969–72 (SHO April-Dec 1969), lectr Dept of Psychiatry Makerere Univ Kampala Uganda, hon lectr The London Hosp and hon conslt Butabika Hosp Kampala 1972–74, lectr Dept of Psychiatry The London Hosp 1974–75, sr lectr Dept of Psychiatry Univ of Edinburgh and hon conslt Royal Edinburgh Hosp and Western Gen Hosp 1975–76, prof of psychiatry Keele Univ 1986– (head of dept Sch of Postgraduate Med 1986–94), conslt psychiatrist City Gen Hosp Combined Health Care NHS Tst 1986–; dean RCPsych 1993– (former chm Gen Psychiatry Specialist Ctee); memb Regional Clinical Research Ctee and regional dir of R & D Advsy Gp W Midlands RHA; formerly WHO conslt Botswana and Br Cncl conslt Zimbabwe; fndr memb and past pres Marcé Soc (int soc for the prevention and mgmnt of postnatal mental illness), Marcé Medal 1996; DPM, FRCPEd 1985, FRCPsych 1986; *Books* Postnatal Depression: A Guide for Health Professionals (1986),

Transcultural Psychiatry (ed and contrib, 1986), Racial Discrimination and the Health Service (jt ed, 1989), Current Approaches: Childbirth as a Life Event (jt ed, 1989), Prevention of Postnatal Depression: uses and misuses of the Edinburgh Postnatal Depression Scale (jt ed); author of various book chapers and numerous academic pubns; *Style*— Prof John L Cox; ✉ Department of Psychiatry, School of Postgraduate Medicine, Thornburrow Drive, Hartshill, Stoke on Trent ST4 7QB (☎ 01782 716019, fax 01782 747319)

COX, (Edward) John Machell; s of Sqdn Ldr Edward Machell Cox (d 1992), and late Joan Edith, *née* Hewlett; *b* 18 Sept 1934; *Educ* Charterhouse, St Peter's Hall Oxford (MA); *m* 29 May 1965, Elizabeth Jean, da of Maj Anthony Frederick Halliday Godfrey (ka France 1939); 1 s (Charles Mark), 1 da (Victoria); *Career* Nat Serv Lt RASC 1953–55; CA; ptnr: Brown Peet & Tilly 1969–71, Howard Tilly 1971–88, Baker Tilly 1988–91; dir Campbell-Johnston Associates (Management Recruitment Consultants) Ltd; chm: North Kensington City Challenge Co Ltd, Brighter Kensington & Chelsea Scheme; vice chm NW London Mental Health NHS Trust, dir Octavia Hill Housing Trust (memb Mgmnt Ctee); Royal Borough of Kensington and Chelsea: cnclr 1974–, mayor 1986–87, chm Housing and Social Servs Ctee 1988–93, memb Policy and Resources Ctee 1993–, memb Planning and Conservation Ctee 1993–; interim DG Euro Script Fund 1992–93; Freeman City of London, Liveryman Worshipful Co of Fruiterers; FCA; *Clubs* Hurlingham; *Style*— E J M Cox, Esq; ✉ 13 St Ann's Villas, London W11 4RT (☎ and fax 0171 603 9828)

COX, Vice Adm Sir John Michael Holland; KCB (1982); s of late Thomas Cox, MBE, and Daisy Anne Cox; *b* 27 Oct 1928, Peking; *Educ* Hilton Coll Natal SA, RNC Dartmouth; *m* 1962, Anne Garden Farquharson, da of Donald Farquharson Seth Smith, MC, and formerly wife of Jacob, Viscount Folkestone (now 8 Earl of Radnor); 1 s, 1 da; *Career* HMS Britannia RNC 1946, ADC to Gen Sir Robert Mansergh C-in-C Allied Forces N Europe 1952 and to Govr of Victoria 1955, Cdr 1962, Capt 1968, naval attaché Bonn 1969, Cdr guided missile destroyer HMS Norfolk 1972, dir Naval Ops and Trade 1973–75, Cdre NATO Standing Naval Force Atlantic 1976–77, Rear Adm 1977, COS to C-in-C Naval Home Cmd 1977–79, Cdr Anti-Submarine Gp 2 and Flag Offr Third Flotilla 1979–82, Vice Adm 1981, Flag Offr Naval Air Cmd 1982–83, ret; dir: The Spastics Soc (now Scope) 1984–88, Soundalive 1988–; *Recreations* gardening, all sports; *Style*— Vice Adm Sir John Cox, KCB; ✉ c/o MOD Personnel Records, Whitehall, London SW1

COX, Ven John Stuart; s of Arthur Francis William Cox (d 1988), and Clarice Mildred, *née* Dadswell (d 1992); *b* 13 Sept 1940; *Educ* The Judd Sch Tonbridge, Fitzwilliam House Cambridge (MA), UC Rhodesia and Nyasaland (Rotary Int fellowship), Wycliffe Hall/Linacre Coll Oxford (BA), Univ of Birmingham (DPS); *m* 1 Feb 1964, Mary Diane, da of Jack Henry Watson Williams; 1 s (David John b 20 June 1969), 1 da (Elizabeth Diane b 13 Feb 1972); *Career* asst curate: St Mary Prescot Lancs 1968–71, St George Newtown Birmingham 1971–73; rector St George Newtown Birmingham 1973–78, selection sec Advsy Cncl for Church Miny 1978–83, canon residentiary Southwark Cathedral 1983–91, dir of ordinands and post-ordination trg Southwark 1983–91, vicar Roehampton Ecumenical Parish 1991–95, archdeacon of Sudbury 1995–; memb Gen Synod 1990–95; tstee: Anglican Gp Educnl Tst, Suffolk Historic Churches Tst; memb Cncl Missions to Seamen; *Books* Religion and Medicine Vol 1 (contrib, 1970), Say One for Me (contrib, 1992); *Recreations* reading, music, golf, gardening, theatre; *Style*— The Ven the Archdeacon of Sudbury; ✉ 84 Southgate Street, Bury St Edmunds, Suffolk IP33 2BJ (☎ 01284 766796, fax 01284 723163)

COX, Josephine; da of Bernard Brindle, and Mary Jane Brindle; *b* 15 July 1940; *m* Kenneth George Cox; 2 s (Spencer John, Wayne Kenneth); *Career* writer; former jobs incl: clerk to Milton Keynes Devpt Cncl, various secretarial positions, ptnr family landscaping co, teacher for 14 years, sociology/history lectr Bletchley Coll Milton Keynes; 18 novels as Josephine Cox, 4 novels as Jane Brindle; Superwoman of GB 1980; *Books* Her Father's Sins (1986), Let Loose the Tigers, Angels Cry Sometimes, Take This Woman, Outcast, Whistledown Woman, Alley Urchin, Vagabonds, Don't Cry Alone, Jessica's Girl, Nobody's Darling, Born to Serve, More Than Riches, A Little Badness, Living a Lie, The Devil You Know, A Time for Us, Cradle of Thorns (1997); as Jane Brindle: Scarlet, No Mercy, The Tallow Image, No Heaven No Hell, The Seeker (1997); *Recreations* horse-riding, swimming, walking, reading, creating board games; *Style*— Mrs Josephine Cox; ✉ c/o Sheil Land Associates, 43 Doughty Street, London WC1N 2LF (☎ 0171 405 9351, fax 0171 831 2127)

COX, Laura Mary; QC (1994); da of John Arthur Bryant (d 1972), of Wolverhampton, and Mary Eileen, *née* Clarke; *b* 8 Nov 1951; *Educ* Wolverhampton HS for Girls, Queen Mary Coll London (LLB, LLM); *m* 1970, David John Cox, s of Harry Cox; 3 s (Jonathan James b 25 April 1980, Leo John b 7 June 1983, Benjamin David b 19 May 1993); *Career* called to the Bar Inner Temple 1975, recorder of the Crown Court 1995– (asst recorder 1992–), head of chambers 1996; memb Ctee Employment Law Bar Assoc, chm Sex Discrimination Ctte Bar Cncl 1996–; memb: Assoc of Personal Injury Lawyers, Personal Injuries Bar Assoc, Industl Law Soc, Professional Negligence Bar Assoc, Administrative Law Bar Assoc, Assoc of Women Barristers; *Recreations* music, theatre, cinema, football, good food and wine; *Style*— Mrs Laura Cox, QC; ✉ First Floor, Cloisters Chambers, 1 Pump Court, Temple, London EC4Y 7AA (☎ 0171 583 0303, fax 0171 583 5597)

COX, Mark; MBE (1979); s of Leslie Cox, of Leicester, and Marion, *née* Ransome; *b* 5 July 1943; *Educ* Wyggeston GS, Millfield, Downing Coll Cambridge (capt Lawn Tennis Club); *m* 4 July 1966, Alison Jane Theresa, da of Reginald Findlay Stroud; 2 s (Julian b 12 Dec 1970, Steven b 3 Aug 1974), 1 da (Lorraine b 2 May 1976); *Career* tennis coach and commentator; former player: first represented GB King's Cup 1963, played 16 Davis Cup ties 1967–79 (singles: won 15, lost 6; doubles: won 8, lost 6), turned professional 1970, ranked GB number 1 six times; dir Rover Junior Tennis Initiative for LTA 1990–, currently tennis commentator BBC TV; formerly vice pres Assoc of Tennis Professionals; *Style*— Mark Cox, Esq, MBE; ✉ Lawn Tennis Association, The Queen's Club, Barons Court, W Kensington, London W14 9EG (☎ 0171 385 2366, fax 0171 381 5965)

COX, Neil Derek; s of Clifford Walter Ernest, and Meryl Rita, *née* Holland; *b* 1 Aug 1955; *Educ* King Edward VI GS Stafford, Glasgow Caledonian Univ (BSc); *m* 23 March 1981, Averin Moira, da of Philip Anthony Donovan; 1 s (Andrew b 1986), 2 da (Katy b 1984, Jocelyn b 1990); *Career* sr optometrist Moorfields and KCH London, private contact lens practice London; memb Cncl Int Glaucoma Assoc, lectured widely and published papers on clinical applications of contact lenses; Liveryman Worshipful Co of Spectaclemakers; FBCO 1978, FAAO 1991; *Recreations* wine, food, photography; *Style*— Neil D Cox, Esq; ✉ 28 Weymouth St, London W1N 3FA (☎ 0171 631 1046)

COX, Patrick Lathbridge; s of Terry Brian Cox, of Victoria, BC, Canada, and Maureen Patricia, *née* Clarke; *b* 19 March 1963; *Educ* Cordwainer's Coll Hackney (DATech); *Career* footwear designer; work included in collections of: Vivienne Westwood, John Galliano, Richard James, Alistair Blair, Lanvin, John Flett & Katherine Hamnett London and Paris 1985–92; exhibited in: Aust Nat Gallery, V & A; Accessory Designer of the Yr Br Fashion Awards 1994 and 1995; *Style*— Patrick Cox, Esq

COX, Paul William; s of Oliver Jasper Cox, CBE, of London, and Jean Denise, *née* Cooper; *b* 31 July 1957; *Educ* Port Regis Sch, Stanbridge Earls Sch, Camberwell Sch of Art And Crafts (BA), RCA (MA); *m* 28 Nov 1987, Julia Claire, da of Capt Peter Dale Nichol, RN (ret), of Hayling Island, Hants; 1 da (Harriet Claire b 16 Aug 1991), 1 s (Jack William b 22 July 1994); *Career* freelance artist and illustrator 1982–; contrib: The Times, Telegraph, Independent, Spectator, Punch, Sunday Times, Observer, Sunday Express, New Yorker, Vanity Fair; visiting lectr in illustration Camberwell Sch of Art and Crafts 1982–90, reportage illustrations for Blueprint 1984–89; watercolour drawings exhibitions: Workshop Gallery 1984, Illustrators' Gallery 1985, Chris Beetle's Gallery 1989 and 1993, Scandinavian Contemporary Art Gallery 1993; designed commemorative stamps for 600th anniversary of The Lord Mayor's Show 1989; hon memb Soc of Architect Artists 1993; *Books* illustrated: Experiences of an Irish RM (1984), The Common Years (1984), A Varied Life (1984), The Outing (1985), The Character of Cricket (1986), Romantic Gardens (1988), Evacuee (1988), Rebuilding The Globe (1989), Dear Boy (1989), Leave it to Psmith (1989), Three Men in a Boat (1989), The Cricket Match (1991), Honourable Estates (1992), Favourite Songs of Denmark (1993), Wind in the Willows (1993), The Russian Tea Room (1993), Rumpole (1994), Look Out London (1995), Jeeves and Wooster (1996); *Clubs* Chelsea Arts; *Style*— Paul Cox, Esq; ✉ Twytten House, Wilmington, East Sussex BN26 5SN (☎ 01323 871264, fax 01323 871265)

COX, Richard Hubert Francis; TD (1965); s of Hubert Eustace Cox (d 1961), of Kensington, and Joan Olive, *née* Thornton (d 1977); *b* 8 March 1931; *Educ* Stowe, St Catherine's Coll Oxford (BA); *m* 1, 1962 (m dis), Caroline, *née* Jennings; 3 c (Lorna Katherine b 1963, Ralph Pelham b 1964, Jeremy Philip b 1966); m 2, 1983 (m dis), Francesca, da of Toby Ralegh Head; *Career* foreign corr Sunday Times 1960–64, HM Dip Serv 1964–66, def corr Daily Telegraph 1966–72, md Thornton Cox publishers 1973–, novelist 1974–; Maj 44 Ind Parachute Bde (V) until 1978, bd memb CARE International UK 1985–, ctee memb Army Flying Assoc; *Books* non fiction: Pan Africanism in Practice (1964), Kenyatta's Country (1965); fiction: Operation Sealion (1974), Sam 7 (1976), Auction (1978), The Ice Raid (1983), Ground Zero (1984), The Columbus Option (1986), An Agent of Influence (1988), Park Plaza (1991), Eclipse (1996); travel: Kenya and Northern Tanzania (9 edn, 1997), Southern Africa (6 edn, 1995); *Recreations* flying, skiing; *Clubs* Army and Navy, Muthaiga Club, Aero Club of East Africa; *Style*— Richard Cox, Esq, TD; ✉ c/o Army and Navy Club, Pall Mall, London SW1

COX, Dr Robin Anthony Frederick; s of Ronald Frederick Cox (d 1986), of 6 Upcher Ct, The Esplanade, Sheringham, Norfolk, and Hilda Mary, *née* Johnson (d 1990); *b* 29 Nov 1935; *Educ* Ashby-de-la-Zouch GS, Gonville and Caius Coll Cambridge (MA, MB BChir), Guy's Hosp; *m* 8 Sept 1962, Maureen Jennifer, da of William Jackson Moore (d 1969), of N Walsham, Norfolk; 1 s (Andrew b 1967), 1 da (Fiona b 1964); *Career* conslt occupational physician; princ in med practice Gorleston on Sea Norfolk 1964–76, dir North Sea Med Centre 1972–76, med dir Phillips Petroleum Co Europe and Africa 1976–86; chief med offr: CEGB 1986–90, National Power 1990–92; corporate med advsr Prudential Assurance Co, med advsr Electricity Assoc; currently pres: Cambridge Bird Club (former chm), Int Assoc Physicians for Overseas Serv; formerly: pres Gorleston Rotary Club, chm Diving Med Advsy Ctee, vice dean Faculty of Occupational Med, memb Cncl Br Tst for Ornithology; Freeman City of London 1978, Liveryman Worshipful Soc of Apothecaries; FRCP, FFOM; Bronze medallist Royal Humane Soc 1974; *Books* Offshore Medicine (1982), Fitness for Work (1995); *Recreations* ornithology, fly fishing, gardening, photography, walking; *Clubs* RSM, British Ornithologists'; *Style*— Dr Robin Cox; ✉ Linden House, Long Lane, Fowlmere, Cambridgeshire SG8 7TG (☎ 01763 208636, fax 01763 208549)

COX, Simon Foster Trenchard; s of Foster Trenchard Cox (d 1996), of Godalming, Surrey, and Madeleine Winifred Needham, *née* Cooper (d 1989); *b* 17 Jan 1956; *Educ* Eton, Trinity Coll Oxford (MA); *m* 1 Feb 1992, Hania Katherine, da of Jan and Sophie Mier Jedrzejowicz; *Career* HAC 1980–88, cmmnd 1985; admitted slr 1980; Norton Rose: articled clerk 1978–80, slr 1980–88, ptnr 1988–; Freeman City of London Slrs Co; memb Law Soc 1980; tstee Needham Cooper Charitable Tst 1990–; *Recreations* water sports, running; *Clubs* HAC; *Style*— Simon Cox, Esq; ✉ Norton Rose, Kempson House, Camomile Street, London EC3A 7AN (☎ 0171 283 6000, fax 0171 283 6500)

COX, Stephen James; *b* 5 Dec 1946; *Educ* Univ of Birmingham (BA), Univ of Leeds (Dip ESL), Univ of Sussex (MA); *Career* English teacher Bolivia (VSO) 1965–66, British Cncl 1969–84 (incl postings Warsaw, Accra and London), educn attaché British Embassy Washington DC 1984–85, asst sec for int affrs Royal Soc 1985–91, dir gen Commonwealth Inst 1991–; chair Br Cncl Whitley Cncl Trades Union Side 1981–84; memb: Exec Ctee Great Britain-E Europe Centre 1988–91, Editorial Bd Round Table 1994–, Educn Ctee Royal Geographical Soc 1995–; FRGS, FRSA; *Recreations* cricket, visiting galleries; *Clubs* Royal Over-Seas League, Geographical Club, English Speaking Union; *Style*— Stephen Cox, Esq; ✉ Commonwealth Institute, Kensington High Street, London W8 6NQ (☎ 0171 603 4535, fax 0171 602 7374)

COX, Stephen Joseph; s of Leonard John Cox (d 1984), of Bristol, and Ethel Minnie May McGill (d 1980); *b* 16 Sept 1946; *Educ* St Mary Redcliffe Sch Bristol, Central Sch of Art and Design; *m* 1 June 1970, Judith, da of John Douglas Atkins, of Well Court Farm, Tyler Hill, nr Canterbury, Kent; 2 da (Pelé Delaney, Georgia Easterly); *Career* aculptor; Arts Cncl major awards 1978 and 1980, Br Cncl bursaries 1978 and 1979, Hakone Open Air Museum prize Japan 1985, Indian Triennale Gold medal 1986, Goldhill Sculpture prize Royal Acad 1988, Capital and Counties Art and Work award 1991; title of book by Henry Moore Fndn 1991, subject of book The Sulpture of Stephen Cox 1995; sr research fell Wimbledon Sch of Art 1995–96; *Solo Exhibitions* Tate Gallery, Lisson Gallery, Nigel Greenwood Gallery, 25 Festival dei Due Mondi Spoleto 1982, Bath Festival Artsite 1988, Arnolfini Gallery Bristol 1985 (touring to Museum of Modern Art Oxford, Midland Group Gallery Nottingham, also Amsterdam, Milan, Rome, Florence, Geneva, Basle, Paris, New Delhi (Br rep Indian Triennale 1986)), Museum of Egyptian Modern Art Cairo 1995, Stephen Cox: Surfaces and Stones of Egypt Henry Moore Inst 1995, Sight of Kephren Michael Hue-Williams Fine Art 1995, Royal Botanic Gardens Kew 1995–96, An Indian Decade 3 exhibitions - Art Today Gallery, Indian Cncl for Cultural Rels (ICCR) Ajanta Gallery and Jamali Kamali Gardens, Michael Hugh-Williams Fine Art 1996; *Group Exhibitions* Paris Biennale 1977, British Sculpture in the Twentieth Century (Whitechapel Art Gallery) 1981, Venice Biennale 1982 and 1984, New Art Tate Gallery 1983, Int Garden Festival Liverpool 1984, Int Survey of Painting and Sculpture (New York Museum of Modern Art) 1984, 40 Years of Modern Art 1945–85 (Tate Gallery), British Art in the 1980's (Brussels Museum of Modern Art), New Displays (Tate Gallery) 1992, Sculptors Drawings (Tate Gallery) 1994, Time Machine (British Museum) 1994–95 (travelling to Museo Egizio Torino), Hathill Fndn Goodwood; *Collections* Tate Gallery, V&A, Br Museum, Br Cncl, Walker Art Gallery Liverpool, Henry Moore Centre for Sculpture, Hunterian Art Gallery, Groningen Museum Netherlands, Peter Ludwig Collection FRG, Fogg Museum USA, Hakone Open Air Museum; *Installed Sculptures* Tondo: Ascension (Royal Festival Hall) 1983, Ganapathi & Devi (Broadgate London) 1989, Osirisisis (Stockley Park London) 1991, Hymn (Univ of Kent Canterbury) 1991, Mantra (Br Cncl building New Delhi) 1992, Echo (Fleet Place Ludgate), Reredos, altar, font and stations of the cross (Church of St Paul Haringay); *Commissions* Cairo Opera House (FCO cmmn) 1988–89, Br High Cmmn Canberra Aust (Tribute Sculpture, FCO cmmn) 1996, Newcastle Cathedral 1996, St Luke's Chelsea 1996; *Clubs* Chelsea Arts; *Style*— Stephen Cox, Esq; ✉ 154 Barnsbury Rd, London N1 OER

COX, Thomas Michael; MP (Lab) Tooting (majority 4,107); *b* 1930; *Educ* LSE; *Career* MP (Lab): Wandsworth Central 1970–74, Wandsworth Tooting 1974–83, Tooting 1983–; formerly asst Govt whip, a Lord Cmmr of the Treasury 1977–79, memb Cncl of Europe/Western Euro Union, vice chm Br Gp Inter-Parly Union; *Style*— Thomas Cox, Esq, MP; ✉ House of Commons, London SW1A 0AA

COX, Timothy John Lomas; TD (1971); s of Arthur Cox (d 1979), of Lower Willingdon, Sussex, and Winifred Mabel, *née* Lomas-Smith (d 1975); *b* 9 March 1939; *Educ* King's Sch Rochester; *m* 5 Sept 1970, Julia Rosemary, da of Henry Francis Workman (d 1988), of Grantown on Spey, Morayshire; 1 s (Adrian b 1974), 1 da (Rosemary b 1976); *Career* cmmnd 2 Lt RA TA 1959 (actg Maj 1970–), Central Vol HQ RA 1973–89 (Maj 1975–89); admitted slr 1962; ptnr Oswald Hickson Collier 1966–; memb various professional and mil assocs; Freeman City of London 1983, Freeman and Liveryman Worshipful Co of Painter Stainers; *Recreations* photography, country pursuits; *Style—* Timothy Cox, Esq, TD; ✉ Messrs Oswald Hickson Collier, 1 Pemberton Row, Fetter Lane, London EC4A 3EX (☎ 0171 583 5333, fax 0171 353 0743)

COX, Prof Timothy Martin; s of William Neville Cox, of Leics, and Joan Desirée, *née* Ward; *b* 10 May 1948; *Educ* The London Hosp Med Coll Univ of London (MSc, MD), Univ of Cambridge (MA, MD); *m* 1975, Susan Ruth, da of Harry Philips Mason, of Builth Wells, Powys; 3 s, 1 da; *Career* house physician and surgn Professorial Units The London Hosp 1971–72, jr lectr in morbid anatomy Bernard Baron Inst 1972–74, jr clinical posts United Oxford Hosp 1974–75, Wellcome Tst sr clinical fell 1979–85; Royal Post Grad Med Sch: jr clinical posts 1974, registrar, hon sr registrar and MRC res fell 1975–79, sr lectr 1985–87, sr lectr in haematology and conslt Dept of Med 1987–89; prof of med Univ of Cambridge and fell Sidney Sussex Coll 1989–; visiting scientist Dept of Biology MIT 1983–84, visiting prof Univ of Manchester 1994, Schorstein Meml lectr London Hosp Med Coll 1994, Bradshaw lectr RCP 1996; external examiner in med: Hong Kong 1990, Univ of London 1992–; memb Exec Ctee Assoc of Physicians of GB and Ireland 1995–97 (memb 1984); FRCP 1984; *Recreations* music, melanic moths; *Style—* Prof Timothy Cox; ✉ Department of Medicine, University of Cambridge School of Clinical Medicine, Addenbrooke's Hospital, Hills Rd, Cambridge CB2 2QQ (☎ 01223 336864)

COXON, Richard; *Educ* Royal Northern Coll of Music; *Career* tenor; studies with Robert Alderson; princ Scottish Opera 1993–96, freelance 1996–; performances with Scottish Opera incl: Alfredo in La Traviata, Trabuco in La Forza del Destino, Sailor in Tristan und Isolde, Jacquino in Fidelio, Nemorino in L'Elisir d'Amore, Narraboth in Salome, Flavio in Norma, Barbarigo in I due Foscari, Jiři in The Jacobin, Don Ottavio in Don Giovanni; other roles: Nemorino (Opera Northern Ireland and Opera Zuid Maastricht), Ralph Rackstraw in HMS Pinafore (National Operetta Company), Die Freunde von Salamanka (Edinburgh Int Festival 1993 and Aix-en-Provence Festival), Messiah (Royal Albert Hall), Alfredo in La Traviata (Opera Northern Ireland); oratorio and solo recitals with: Hallé Orch, Royal Scottish Nat Orch, BBC Scottish Symphony Orch, London Pops Orch, London Musici (world premiere of A Live Flame); *Awards* Webster Booth/Esso Award, Clonter Opera Prize, Ricordi Opera Prize, Peter Moores Foundation Award, Wolfson Tst Award; *Style—* Richard Coxon, Esq; ✉ IMG Artists Europe, Media House, 3 Burlington Lane, London W4 2TH (☎ 0181 747 9977, fax 0181 747 9131)

COXWELL-ROGERS, Col Richard Annesley; DL (Gloucestershire); s of Maj-Gen Norman Annesley Coxwell-Rogers, CB, CBE, DSO (d 1985), of Cheltenham, and Diana Mary, *née* Coston (d 1995); *b* 26 April 1932; *Educ* Eton, Sandhurst; *m* 21 Sept 1965, Martha Felicity, da of Col G T Hurrell, OBE (d 1989); 2 s (James b 1969, Edward b 1973); *Career* serv 15/19 The King's Royal Hussars 1952–82 (CO Regt 1973–75): Malaya, Germany, UK; Col 15/19 Hussars 1988–92; area appeals organiser Avon, Glos and Wilts Cancer Research Campaign 1982–93; Vice Lord-Lt Gloucestershire 1993–, High Sheriff for County of Gloucestershire 1994–95; *Recreations* hunting, shooting; *Clubs* Cavalry and Guards'; *Style—* Col Richard A Coxwell-Rogers, DL; ✉ Close Farm House, Coberley, Cheltenham, Glos GL53 9QZ (☎ 01242 870519, fax 01242 870200)

COYLE, Michael Thomas Patrick; s of Michael Coyle (d 1985), and Mary Elizabeth, *née* Skelly; *b* 21 Jan 1955; *Educ* Finchley Catholic GS, UEA (BA), Lancaster Gate Coll of Law; *Career* advertising exec; trainee rising to account mangr Young & Rubicam 1979–83, account mangr rising to account dir Saatchi & Saatchi 1983–88, Ogilvy & Mather 1988–89 (dir (Australia), client service dir, dep md), int bd dir Bates Dorland (formerly BSB Dorland) 1989–, regnl dir Bates Europe 1996–; *Recreations* reading, music, travelling, tennis, cricket, football, bobsleigh; *Clubs* Albanian Assoc, Queens; *Style—* Michael Coyle, Esq; ✉ 5 Maryon Mews, Hampstead Heath, London NW3 2PU (☎ 0171 262 5077, fax 0171 258 3757)

COYTE, Kenneth Anthony; s of Stanley Edward Coyte (d 1953), of Leeds, and Amy Vera, *née* Pote (d 1953); *b* 6 Feb 1932; *Educ* Blundell's, Sidney Sussex Coll Cambridge (MA); *m* 7 Jan 1956, Patricia Claire, da of William Macke (d 1979), of Cincinnati, Ohio, USA; 3 s (Anthony b 1958, Benjamin b 1963, Matthew b 1966), 3 da (Nerissa b 1956, Rebecca b 1961, Amy b 1962); *Career* 2 Lt RE 1950; film critic; Saturday Review NY 1955, TV reporter UP Movietone 1955–56, vice pres UP ITN 1968–80; World Wide TV News: pres 1980–92, dir UK Ltd 1980–, dir TV-AM News Ltd 1981–91, dir TCTV (USA) 1990–, exec chm 1992–; memb RTS, FRSA; *Style—* Kenneth Coyte, Esq; ✉ Worldwide Television News, Interchange, Oval Road, Camden Lock, London NW1 (☎ 0171 410 5200, fax 0171 413 8302)

CRABTREE, Maj-Gen Derek Thomas; CB (1983); s of late William Edward Crabtree, and Winifred Hilda Burton, *née* Wood; *b* 21 Jan 1930; *Educ* St Brendan's Coll Bristol; *m* 1960, Daphne Christine, *née* Mason, 1 s, 1 da; *Career* dir gen of Weapons (Army) MOD 1980–84; Col Duke of Edinburgh's Royal Regt (Berks and Wilts) 1982–87 and 1988–89; gen mangr Regular Forces Employment Assoc 1987–94; *Clubs* Army and Navy; *Style—* Maj-Gen Derek Crabtree, CB; ✉ 53 High Street, Shrivenham, Swindon SN6 8AW

CRABTREE, His Hon Judge; Jonathan; s of Charles Harold Crabtree (d 1981), of Stansfield Hall, Todmorden, Lancs, and Elsie Marion, *née* Gaukroger (d 1993); *b* 17 April 1934; *Educ* Bootham Sch, St John's Coll Cambridge (MA, LLM); *m* 1, 27 Aug 1957 (m dis 1974), Caroline Ruth Keigwin, da of Alan Edward Oliver (d 1983), of Lewes, Sussex; 2 s (Abraham John b 5 Aug 1963, Daniel Edward b 5 Dec 1965, d 1983), 3 da (Harriet Mary b 25 Nov 1958, Rose Charity b 10 Dec 1961, (Alice) Ann b 15 July 1964); m 2, 13 June 1980, Wendy Elizabeth, da of Douglas Robert Ward (d 1956); *Career* Seaman RN 1952–54; HM inspr of factories 1958–60, called to the Bar Gray's Inn 1960, recorder 1974–86, circuit judge (NE Circuit) 1986–; *Recreations* history and archaeology, cooking; *Style—* His Hon Judge Crabtree; ✉ Courts Administrator, 10 Floor, Pennine House, 20/2 Hawley St, Sheffield S1 2EA (☎ 0114 275 5866)

CRACE, Andrew Laurence Spencer; s of Harold Clarence Crace (d 1971), of Much Hadham, Herts, and Gladys Caroline, *née* Wise (d 1977); descendant of Edward Crace, coach designer and appointed keeper of pictures to the Royal Palaces 1790; John and Frederick Crace furniture/wallpaper designers and manufacturers concerned with the interior decoration of the Royal Opera House, Carlton House, The Royal Pavilion Brighton, the Palace of Westminster; *b* 28 May 1953; *Educ* Coll of Estate Mgmnt Reading (BSc); *Career* designer and retailer predominantly of furniture, garden products and buildings; proprietor: Alitag Plant Labels 1980, Andrew Crace Designs 1983, The Bronze Collection 1990–; ARICS 1980; *Recreations* travel and exploration, photography, sculpture, opera, music, gardening and dendrology, bricklaying; *Style—* Andrew L S Crace, Esq; ✉ Harefield House, Much Hadham, Herts SG10 6ER (☎ 01279 842685, fax 01279 843646)

CRACKNELL, Andrew; *b* 23 Oct 1946; *Career* exec creative dir Ammirati Puris Lintas (concurrently chm 1996–); *Clubs* Green Street; *Style—* Andrew Cracknell, Esq; ✉ Ammirati Puris Lintas, 84 Eccleston Square, London SW1V 1PX (☎ 0171 932 8665, fax 0171 932 8774)

CRACKNELL, Prof Arthur Philip; s of Christopher Theodore Cracknell (d 1969), of Ilford, and Phyllis Mary, *née* Staines (d 1985); *b* 18 May 1940; *Educ* Chigwell Sch Essex, Pembroke Coll Cambridge (MA), The Queen's Coll Oxford (DPhil), Univ of Singapore (MSc); *m* 13 April 1966, Margaret Florence, da of James Grant (d 1972), of Gateshead; 1 s (Christopher Paul b 15 April 1967), 2 da (Anne Patricia b 3 March 1972, Andrée Jacqueline b 30 Nov 1975); *Career* lectr in physics: Univ of Singapore 1964–67, Univ of Essex 1967–70; prof of theoretical physics Univ of Dundee 1978– (sr lectr 1970–74, reader 1974–78); ed International Journal of Remote Sensing 1983; former chm Remote Sensing Soc; FInstP 1970, FRSE 1976, FRSA 1992, FRSSoc 1995; *Books* Applied Group Theory (1968), The Fermi Surfaces of Metals (jtly, 1971), Ultrasonics (1980), Computer Programs for Image Processing of Remote Sensing Data (ed, 1982), Magnetism in Solids - Some Current Topics (ed jtly, 1982), Remote Sensing Applications in Marine Science and Technology (ed, 1983), Introduction to Remote Sensing (jtly, 1991), The Advanced Very High Resolution Radiometer (1997); author of numerous scientific res papers in scientific journals; *Recreations* reading, hill-walking, gardening; *Style—* Prof Arthur P Cracknell, FRSE; ✉ 54 Hamilton Street, Broughty Ferry, Dundee DD5 2RE; Department of Applied Physics and Electronic & Mechanical Engineering, University of Dundee, Dundee DD1 4HN (☎ 01382 344549, fax 01382 345415)

CRACKNELL, His Hon Judge; (Malcolm) Thomas; s of Percy Thomas Cracknell (d 1988), and Doris Louise Cracknell; *b* 12 Dec 1943; *Educ* Royal Liberty Sch Romford, Univ of Hull (LLB), King's Coll London (LLM); *m* 1, 1968 (m dis 1980) Ann; 1 s (Simon Anthony b 1970), 1 da (Rebecca Judith b 1972); m 2, 30 July 1988, Felicity Anne, da of Prof David M Davies, of Shotley Bridge; 1 da (Alexandra Flora Louise b 1990), 2 s (William David Thomas b 1992, Oliver George Thomas b 1994); *Career* lectr in law Univ of Hull 1968–74, barr 1970–89, asst rec 1984, recorder of the Crown Ct 1988, circuit judge (NE Circuit) 1989–, resident judge Hull Combined Court Centre 1994–; *Recreations* golf, cricket, gardening, walking, reading; *Style—* His Hon Judge Cracknell

CRACROFT-ELEY, Bridget Katharine; da of Lt-Col Sir Weston Cracroft-Amcotts, MC, DL (d 1975), of Hackthorn Hall, Lincoln, and Rhona, *née* Clifton-Brown, DL; *b* 29 Oct 1933; *Educ* Lincoln Girls' HS, Crofton Grange Sch Buntingford Herts; *m* 31 Oct 1959, Robert Peel Charles (Robin) Cracroft-Eley (d 1996) (who assumed the additional surname of Cracroft), s of Charles Ryves Maxwell Eley, OBE (d 1983), of East Bergholt Place, Suffolk; 1 s (William b 1963), 1 da (Annabel b 1961); *Career* worked for charities and voluntary orgns; parish cncllr and sch govr; High Sheriff of Lincolnshire 1989–90, Lord-Lt for Co of Lincolnshire 1995–; *Recreations* gardening, upholstery; *Style—* Mrs Robin Cracroft-Eley; ✉ Hackthorn Hall, Lincoln LN2 3PQ

CRADDOCK, (William) Aleck; LVO (1981); *b* 1924; *Educ* City of London Sch; *m* 1947, Olive Mary Brown; 1 s, 1 da; *Career* joined Druce and Craddock, Craddock and Tomkins Ltd (family firm) 1946; Harrods Ltd: joined as asst to Food Mangr 1954, dir 1964, dir and gen mangr 1970, asst md 1975, md 1980–84, chm 1981–86, dep chm 1987–88; dir: House of Fraser Ltd 1980–90, Cartier Ltd 1986–; vice chm Drapers Drapers Cottage Homes 1987–94 (pres Appeal 1985–86); pres Twenty Club 1988; Liveryman Worshipful Co of Cooks 1972; Cavaliere Ufficiale (Fourth Class) Order Al Merito Della Repubblica Italiana 1980; *Recreations* fell walking, water colour painting; *Clubs* Guards' Polo (life memb), Arts; *Style—* Aleck Craddock, Esq, LVO; ✉ 17 Tretawn Park, Mill Hill, London NW7 4PS

CRADDOCK, Malcolm Gordon; s of Gilbert Craddock, and Evelyn Marion, *née* Gordon; *b* 2 Aug 1938; *Educ* St Albans Sch, Queens' Coll Cambridge (MA); *m* 29 May 1965, Jenni, da of David Maclay; 2 s (Sam, Ben), 1 da (Emily); *Career* entered film industry 1962; asst dir to Joseph Losey 1964–66 (Accident, Modesty Blaise); dir: Mr Lewis 1965, The Beach 1967; film dir of TV commercials (Sunday Times awards) 1966–, founding ptnr and dir Picture Palace Prodns Ltd 1970–; prodr TV drama 1984–: Tandoori Nights (Channel Four) 1985–87, Ping Pong (Venice Int Film Festival) 1986, twenty one short films, 4 Minutes (winner Gold Award for Drama NY 1986), Firing the Bullets, Hunting the Squirrel and Pushed (Channel Four and ECA) 1989–90, When Love Dies (4 Play/Eurocops series Channel Four) 1990, The Orchid House (series, Channel 4) 1991, Sharpe's Rifles and Sharpe's Eagle (ITV) 1993, Little Napoleons (Channel Four) 1994, Sharpe's Company, Sharpe's Enemy and Sharpe's Honour (ITV) 1994, Karaoke Love Affair (NHK Tokyo) 1994, Sharpe's Sword, Sharpe's Gold and Sharpe's Battle (ITV) 1995, Sharpe's Regiment, Sharpe's Siege and Sharpe's Mission (ITV) 1996; *Recreations* tennis, watching Tottenham Hotspur FC; *Clubs* The Groucho; *Style—* Malcolm Craddock, Esq; ✉ 19 Edis Street, London NW1 8LE (☎ 0171 722 2745); Picture Palace Productions Limited, 53a Brewer Street, London W1R 3FD (☎ 0171 734 6630, fax 0171 734 8574)

CRADDOCK, Nigel Christopher; s of William Alfred Craddock (d 1976), of Harrogate, N Yorks, and Louisa Maud, *née* Edmanson (d 1974); *b* 30 Aug 1937; *Educ* Harrogate GS; *m* 24 Sept 1966, Penelope Jane, da of Laurence Sydney Stevens (d 1987), of Cirencester, Glos; 3 s (Alexander, James, Daniel); *Career* Nat Serv RAF 1956–58; dir: Hogg Robinson (UK) Ltd 1965–77, Barclays Insurance Services Co Ltd 1977–93, Spread Eagle Insurance Co Ltd 1986–93; sales dir Barclays Unit Trusts and Insurance 1985–86, md Barclays Insurance Brokers Int Ltd 1986–93, ret; non-exec dir PYV Ltd 1993–, dir Esprit Insurance Programs Limited 1995–; memb: Berkhamsted Cons Party, Worshipful Co of Insurers; FCII 1969, memb Soc of Fellows; *Recreations* golf, rugby, cricket, reading, walking, history (Open University); *Style—* Nigel Craddock, Esq; ✉ PYV Ltd, 7 Cavendish Square, London W1M 0NH (☎ 0171 323 1333)

CRADICK, (Christopher) Roger; s of Henry Cyril Cradick (d 1986), and Rita, *née* Perkin (d 1995); *b* 6 Nov 1932; *Educ* Penarth GS, Llandovery Coll; *m* 1, 15 June 1957, Mary Elizabeth, da of late Frederick John Stephenson; 2 s (Simon b 18 Jan 1960, Neil b 14 Jan 1965), 1 da (Sian Elizabeth b 7 July 1962); m 2, 2 Sept 1968, Gillian Susan, da of Ernest Whetter (d 1982); 1 s (Richard b 21 May 1970); *Career* admitted slr 1954, sr ptnr Morgan Bruce slrs until 1996, ret; dep dist registrar High Ct and dep Co Ct registrar High Ct and dep Co Ct registrar 1976–90, dep dist judge 1991–; chm: Social Security Appeals Tbnl 1979–85, Med Appeals Tbnl 1985–95, Registered Homes Tbnl 1995–; pres Cardiff and Dist Law Soc 1985–86, memb Bye Laws Revision Sub Ctee Law Soc; memb Law Soc 1956; *Recreations* rugby football (former referee), gardening; *Clubs* Old Penarthians RFC (vice pres); *Style—* Roger Cradick, Esq; ✉ St Andrews Rd, Dinas Powis, South Glamorgan CF6 4HB

CRADOCK, Rt Hon Sir Percy; PC (1993), GCMG (1983, KCMG 1980, CMG 1968); *b* 26 Oct 1923; *Educ* St John's Coll Cambridge; *m* 1953, Birthe Marie Dyrlund; *Career* HM Dip Serv: joined FO 1954, first sec Kuala Lumpur 1957–61, Hong Kong 1961, first sec Peking 1962, FO 1963–66, cnsllr and head of chancery Peking 1966–68, Chargé d'Affaires Peking 1968–69, head of planning staff FCO 1969–71, under-sec Cabinet Office 1971–75, leader UK Delgn Geneva Test Ban Discussions 1977–78, ambass E Germany 1976–78, ambass People's Republic of China 1978–83, continuing responsibility for negotiations over future of Hong Kong 1983–84; foreign policy advsr to the Prime Minister 1984–92; hon fell St John's Coll Cambridge 1982; *Publications* Experiences of China (1994); *Style—* The Rt Hon Sir Percy Cradock, GCMG; ✉ c/o Reform Club, 104 Pall Mall, London SW1Y 5EW

CRADOCK-HARTOPP, Lt Cdr Sir Kenneth Alston; 10 Bt (GB 1796), of Freathby, Leicestershire, MBE (1946), DSC (1952); s of Maj Louis Montague Cradock-Hartopp (d

1957), and Marjorie Somerville, *née* Watson (d 1971); suc cous, Sir John Edmund Cradock-Hartopp, 9 Bt (d 1996); *b* 26 Feb 1918; *m* 18 June 1942, Gwendolyn Amy Lilian, da of late Capt Victor Crowther Upton; 1 da (Christina (Mrs Thomas M Hickman) b 1948); *Heir* none; *Career* Lt Cdr (ret) RN; served WWII (cmd MTB Flotillas) and Korea (cmd HMNZ frigate Taupo 1951–52); chm Royal Naval Amateur Radio Soc 1984–87; FRGS 1949; Legion of Merit (USA) 1957; *Style—* Lt Cdr Sir Kenneth Cradock-Hartopp, Bt, MBE, DSC; ✉ Keepers, Yeovilton, Yeovil, Somerset BA22 8EX (☎ 01935 840240)

CRAFT, Prof Alan William; *b* 6 July 1946; *Educ* Rutherford GS Newcastle, Univ of Newcastle (MB BS, MD); *Career* postgrad trg in Newcastle Hosps, MRC trg fell Royal Marsden Hosp London 1976–77; conslt paediatrician: N Tyneside and Newcastle 1978–86, Royal Victoria Infirmary Newcastle 1986–91; James Spence prof of child health Univ of Newcastle 1993– (prof of paediatric oncology 1991–93); sec Int Paediatric Oncology Soc 1993– (memb 1980); memb Br Paediatric Assoc 1978; FRCP; *Style—* Prof Alan Craft; ✉ 2 Ruthven Court, Adderstone Crescent, Newcastle Upon Tyne NE2 2HH (☎ 0191 2816718); Department of Child Health, Royal Victoria Infirmary, Newcastle upon Tyne NE1 4LP (☎ 0191 202 3009, fax 0191 202 3022)

CRAFT, Prof Ian Logan; s of Reginald Thomas Craft, of Essex, and Mary Lois, *née* Logan; *b* 11 July 1937; *Educ* Owen Sch London, Univ of London, Westminster Hosp Med Sch (MB BS); *m* 19 Dec 1959, Jacqueline Rivers, da of John James Symmons (d 1985), of London; 2 s (Simon b 4 Sept 1964, Adrian b 1 Sept 1968); *Career* house offr Radiotherapy Dept and Dept of Obstetrics and Gynaecology Westminster Hosp 1961–62, sr house offr (later house surgn and house physician) St James Hosp Balham 1962–63, house surgn Hammersmith Hosp 1965, sr house offr (later surgical registrar) Professional Unit Westminster Hosp 1965–66, resident med offr Queen Charlotte's Hosp London 1967, gynaecological registrar (later resident registrar) Inst of Obstetrics and Gynaecology Chelsea Hosp for Women 1968–69, resident med offr Gen Lying-In Hosp London 1969, registrar Queen Mary's Hosp Roehampton 1970, sr registrar Westminster Hosp London 1970, rotational sr registrar Kingston Hosp Surrey 1971–72, sr lectr and hon conslt Queen Charlotte's Hosp and Chelsea Hosp for Women 1972–76, prof of obstetrics and gynaecology Royal Free Hosp Sch of Med 1976–82, dir of gynaecology Cromwell Hosp London 1982–85, dir of fertility and obstetrics studies Humana Hosp Wellington London 1985–90, dir London Gynaecology and Fertility Centre 1990–; visiting prof UCL; frequent lectr and prolific contrib to med literature; life memb: Zoological Soc, Nat Tst, English Heritage, RNLI, Friends of St Paul's Cathedral, Friends of Durham Cathedral, Byron Soc, Turner Soc, Walpole Soc; FRCS 1966, FRCOG 1986 (MRCOG 1970); memb: RSM, Br Fertility Soc, Harveian Soc (London); *Recreations* art, ceramics, sculpture, music, opera, theatre, most sports, antiquities; *Clubs* Heritage, Natural Pursuits, Ornithology; *Style—* Prof Ian Craft; ✉ 5 Devonshire Mews, North London W1N 1FR; The London Gynaecology and Fertility Centre, Cozens House, 112A Harley St, London W1 (☎ 0171 224 0707, fax 0171 224 3120)

CRAFT, Prof Maurice; s of Jack Craft (d 1952), of London, and Polly, *née* Lewis (d 1973); *b* 4 May 1932; *Educ* Colfe's GS, LSE (BScEcon), Sch of Educn Univ of Dublin (HDipEd), Inst of Educn Univ of London (AcadDipEd), Univ of Liverpool (PhD), Univ of Nottingham (DLitt); *m* 19 May 1957, Alma, da of Ellis Sampson (d 1975), of Dublin; 2 da (Anna b 1961, Naomi b 1964); *Career* Nat Serv 1953–55, cmmnd 2 Lt RAOC served Suez Canal Zone, appointed Acting Capt; head Dept of Sociology Edge Hill Coll of Educn 1960–67, sr lectr Univ of Exeter 1967–74, prof of educn La Trobe Univ Melbourne 1974–76, Goldsmiths' prof of educn Univ of London 1976–80, prof of educn Univ of Nottingham 1980–89 (pro-vice-chllr 1983–87, former Dean of Faculty and chm Sch of Educn), fndn dean of humanities and social science Hong Kong Univ of Sci and Tech 1989–94, research prof in educn Univ of Greenwich 1994–; author of numerous learned books, monographs and papers; UK del to UNESCO, Cncl of Europe and EEC Confs; vice chm CVU; memb: Exec Ctee UCET, CNAA; *Books* Family, Class and Education (1970), Linking Home and School (1980), Teaching in a Multicultural Society (1981), Change in Teacher Education (1984), Education and Cultural Pluralism (1984), Ethnic Relations and Schooling (1995), Teacher Education in Plural Societies (1996); *Recreations* music, walking; *Clubs* Royal Over-Seas League; *Style—* Prof Maurice Craft; ✉ University of Greenwich, Southwood Campus, Avery Hill Road, Eltham, London SE9 2HB (☎ 0181 331 8000)

CRAFTS, Prof Nicholas Francis Robert; s of Alfred Hedley Crafts, of Sutton-in-Ashfield, Notts, and Flora Geraldine Mary Crafts (d 1992); *b* 9 March 1949; *Educ* Brunts GS Mansfield Notts, Trinity Coll Cambridge (Wrenbury scholar, MA); *m* 29 March 1969, Barbara, da of Arthur Daynes (d 1992); 2 da (Rachel b 22 Oct 1969, Helen b 13 Aug 1971), 1 s (Adam b 26 Sept 1973); *Career* lectr in econ history Univ of Exeter 1971–72, lectr in economics Univ of Warwick 1972–77, fell and praelector in economics UC Oxford 1977–86; prof of econ history: Univ of Leeds 1987–88, Univ of Warwick 1988–95, LSE 1995–; visiting asst prof of economics Univ of California Berkeley 1974–76, visiting prof of economics Stanford Univ 1982–83; memb Cncl: Royal Econ Soc 1991–93, Econ History Soc 1992–; FBA 1992; *Books* British Economic Growth During the Industrial Revolution (1985), Can De-Industrialization Seriously Damage your Wealth? (1993); *Recreations* horse-racing; *Style—* Prof Nicholas Crafts, FBA; ✉ Department of Economic History, London School of Economics, Houghton Street, London WC2A 2AE

CRAGG, Anthony Douglas (Tony); s of late Douglas Roland Cragg, and late Audrey May, *née* Rutter; *b* 9 April 1949; *Educ* Wimbledon Sch of Art (BA), RCA (MA); *m* 1 (m dis), Ute Oberste-Lehn; 2 s (Daniel Anthony b 1979, Thomas Douglas b 1976); m 2, Tatjana Verhasselt; 1 s (John Eric b 1987), 1 da (Catharina Eve May b 1989); *Career* sculptor; Düsseldorf Kunstakademie: tutor 1978–88, prof 1988–, vice chllr 1988–; winner Von der Heydt prize 1988, winner Turner prize 1988; Chevalier des Arts et Lettres; RA 1994; *Solo exhibitons* incl: Lisson Gallery London 1979, Arnolfini Gallery Bristol 1980, Whitechapel Art Gallery London 1981, Nouveau Musée Lyon 1981, Musée d'Art et d'Industrie St Etienne 1981, Rijksmuseum Kröller-Müller Otterloo 1982, Marian Goodman NYC 1982, Badischer Kunstverein Karlsruhe 1982, Kunsthalle Bern 1983, Louisiana Museum of Modern Art 1984, Humlebaek Denmark 1984, Kölnischer Kunstverein Cologne 1984, Palais des Beaux-Arts Brussels 1985, ARC Musée d'Art Moderne de la Ville de Paris 1985, Kestner-Gesellschaft Hannover 1985, Staatsgalerie Moderner Kunst Munich 1985, The Brooklyn Museum NYC 1986, Hayward Gallery London 1987, Venice Biennale 1988, Stedelijk Van Abbe Museum Eindhoven 1989, Kunstsammlung Nordrhein-Westfalen Düsseldorf 1989, Newport Harbour Art Museum Newport Beach Calif 1990, Corcoran Gallery of Art Washington DC 1991, Power Plant Toronto 1991, Houston Contemporary Art Museum 1991, IVAM Valencia 1992, Tramway Glasgow 1992, CCA Glasgow 1992; *Group exhibitions* incl: Aperto '80 Venice Biennale 1980, Venice Biennale 1986, Dokumenta 8 Kassel 1987, Venice Biennale 1993, Recent British Sculpture from the Arts Cncl Collection (South Bank Centre London) 1993; *Style—* Tony Cragg, Esq, RA

CRAGG, Anthony John; s of Samuel Arthur Leslie Cragg, of St Leonard's on Sea, E Sussex, and Gwendolen Mary, *née* Pevler (d 1991); *b* 16 May 1943; *Educ* Hastings GS, Lincoln Coll Oxford (open scholar, BA); *m* 4 Sept 1971, Jeanette Ann, da of Alfred Richard Rix; 2 da (Alexandra Frances Helen b 14 Feb 1977, Susannah Rose b 14 April 1982); *Career* MOD: asst princ 1966, asst private sec to Perm Under Sec 1968–70, princ 1971, asst private sec to Sec of State for Defence 1974–76, seconded to FCO 1977–79, asst sec 1979, head of Naval Resource Planning Secretariat 1980–83, chief offr UK Sovereign Base Areas Cyprus 1983–85, Royal Coll of Defence Studies 1988, under sec 1990, chm Defence Orgn Planning Team 1991–92; asst sec gen NATO Brussels 1993–; *Recreations* swimming, walking, music, reading; *Style—* Anthony Cragg, Esq; ✉ Assistant Secretary General, NATO Headquarters, 1110 Brussels, Belgium (☎ 00 32 2 707 4111)

CRAGG, Bernard Anthony; *Career* fin dir Carlton Communications plc 1985– (formerly co sec); ACA; *Style—* Bernard Cragg, Esq; ✉ Carlton Communications plc, 25 Knightsbridge, London SW1X 2RZ (☎ 0171 663 6363, fax 0171 663 6360)

CRAIG, Surgn Rear Adm Alexander (Sandy); s of Rev Dr Albert Craig, and Agnes Nicol, *née* Wards; *b* 22 Nov 1943; *Educ* George Watson's Boys' Coll Edinburgh, Univ of Edinburgh (MB ChB); *m* 1968, Kathleen Margaret, *née* Elliott; 2 da (Rebecca Jane b 19 Feb 1970, Lucy Kate 11 Aug 1981), 1 s (Adam Elliott b 16 April 1972); *Career* with RN; Regtl MO 45 Commando RM 1969–72, Jt Servs Families Clinic Malta 1972–74, OC Med Sqdn CDO Log Regt RM 1974–78, MOD 1978–80, Nat Defence Coll Latimer 1981, Families Clinic Naples 1981–83, CSO to Dean of Naval Medicine 1983–86, PMO HMS Sultan 1986–87, CSO to SRA (OMS) 1987–89, MO i/c Inst of Naval Medicine Alverstoke 1989–90, dir Med Organisation MOD 1990–93, QHP 1992, Surgn Rear Adm (Support Med Servs) and Dean of Naval Medicine 1993–94, Med DG (Naval) 1994–97; FRSM 1994; *Recreations* travel, golf; *Style—* Surgn Rear Adm Sandy Craig; ✉ Medical Director General (Naval), Victory Building, HM Naval Base, Portsmouth, Hampshire PO1 3LS (☎ 01705 727800, fax 01705 727413)

CRAIG, Amanda Pauline; da of Denis Bathurst Craig, of Rome, and Zelda Rose Craig; *b* 22 Sept 1959; *Educ* Bedales, Clare Coll Cambridge (exhbner); *m* 1988, Robin John Cohen, s of L Jonathan Cohen; 1 da (Leonora Rose), 1 s (William Alexander); *Career* writer; freelance journalist The Times and The Sunday Times 1984–85, asst features ed Tatler 1986, novelist 1988–; freelance critic for Independent, Spectator etc; Young Journalist of the Year Award 1985, Catherine Pakenham Award 1987; memb Soc of Authors; *Books* Foreign Bodies (1990), A Private Place (1991), A Vicious Circle (1996); *Recreations* reading, gardening, opera; *Style—* Ms Amanda Craig; ✉ c/o Giles Gordon, Curtis Brown, Haymarket House, 28/29 Haymarket, London SW1Y 4SP (☎ 0171 396 6600, fax 0171 396 0110)

CRAIG, Dr Brian George; s of Very Rev Dr Williams Magee Craig, of Moira Co Down, and Maud, *née* Macrory; *b* 6 Sept 1953; *Educ* Portadown Coll, Queen's Univ Belfast (MD, BCh, BAO); *m* Jennifer, da of Albert Mawhinney, of 46 Princess Way, Portadown; 2 s (Adam b 1984, Matthew b 1986); *Career* sr registrar: cardiology Royal Victoria Hosp 1982–83, Hosp for Sick Children Toronto Canada (clinical fell in paediatric cardiology) 1983–85, paediatrics Royal Belfast Hosp for Sick Children 1985–86; conslt in paediatric cardiology Royal Belfast Hosp for Sick Children 1986–; memb: Ulster Paediatric Soc 1979–, Br Paediatric Cardiac Assoc 1987–, Br Paediatric Assoc 1988–, Irish Cardiac Soc 1988–, Br Cardiac Soc 1990, ctee Presbyterian Church, Boys Bde; Hon MD Queen's Univ Belfast; MRCP (UK) 1980; numerous publications in learned jnls; *Recreations* gardening, family, tennis; *Style—* Dr Brian Craig; ✉ 10 Plantation Ave, Lisburn, Co Antrim, N Ireland BT27 5BL (☎ 01846 671587); Royal Belfast Hospital for Sick Children, 180–184 Falls Rd, Belfast, N Ireland BT12 6BE (☎ 01232 240503 ext 2397)

CRAIG, Colin Fetherston; s of Rev Cuthbert Leslie Craig (d 1982), of Weardale, and Muriel, *née* Cole; *b* 29 Aug 1947; *Educ* Kent Coll Canterbury, Kingston Coll of Art; *m* 4 July 1989, Linda Jayne, da of Edward Howard; *Career* creative dir: Cogent Elliott Ltd 1975–78, Doyle Dane Bernbach Ltd 1978–79, Grierson Cockman Craig & Druiff Ltd 1979–86, Grey Ltd 1986–87; planning creative dir TBWA (formerly Holmes Knight Ritchie then TBWA Holmes Knight Ritchie) 1987–93; writer of music for TV and radio 1968–, lectr in TV technique, writer of screenplays for TV and cinema, writer of party political bdcasts for the Lib Dem Party, winner of over 60 nat and int TV awards, multi-instrumentalist, singer, conductor; memb: D & AD 1969, Songwriters' Guild 1978, PRS 1977; *Recreations* music, horticulture, cinema, church, dalmatians; *Clubs* Lansdowne; *Style—* Colin Craig, Esq; ✉ The Consulting Room, 6 Brewer Street, London W1R 3FP (☎ 0171 734 0031, fax 0171 734 0036)

CRAIG, David; *see:* Tucker, (Allan) James

CRAIG, Dr Edward John; s of Charles William Craig (d 1989), and Annie, *née* Taylor (d 1983); *b* 26 March 1942; *Educ* Charterhouse, Trinity Coll Cambridge (BA, PhD, cricket blue); *m* m 1, 1973 (m dis 1986), Isabel Nina, *née* Barnard; 2 da (Ellen Elizabeth b 23 June 1980, Claire Madeleine b 8 Aug 1982); m 2, 1987, Gillian Helen Elizabeth Edwards; *Career* Univ of Cambridge: res scholar Trinity Coll 1963–66 (sr scholar 1962–63), fell Churchill Coll 1966–, asst lectr in philosophy 1966–71, lectr 1971–92, reader in modern philosophy 1992–; visiting lectr Univ of Melbourne 1974, guest prof Univ of Heidelberg 1981; visiting prof: Univ of Hamburg 1977–78, Indian Inst of Advanced Study Shimla 1996; ed Ratio 1987–92, chief ed Routledge Encyclopedia of Philosophy 1991–; FBA 1993; *Books* David Hume: Eine Einführung in seine Philosophie (1979), The Mind of God and the Works of Man (1987), Knowledge and the State of Nature (1990), Was Wir Wissen Können (1993); *Recreations* music, golf; *Style—* Dr Edward Craig, FBA; ✉ Churchill College, Cambridge CB3 ODS

CRAIG, George Charles Graham; s of George Craig (d 1970), and Elizabeth Strachan, *née* Milne; *b* 8 May 1946; *Educ* Nottingham Univ (BA); *m* 9 March 1968, (Ethne) Marian, da of Herbert Henry Asquith Gallagher (d 1989); 2 s (Andrew b 9 June 1971, Robert b 13 July 1974), 1 da (Emily b 5 June 1978); *Career* asst princ Miny of Tport 1967; Welsh Office: private sec to Min of State 1971, princ 1973, princ private sec to Sec of State 1978, asst sec 1980, under sec 1986, princ establishment offr until 1994, head Tport Planning and Environment Gp 1994–; *Style—* George Craig, Esq; ✉ Welsh Office, Cathays Park, Cardiff CF1 3NQ (☎ 01222 823695)

CRAIG, Hugh Michael (Mike); s of Norman Craig (d 1991), of Dewsbury, and Irene Craig, *née* Shires (d 1985); *b* 11 March 1935; *Educ* Eastborough Sch Dewsbury, Wheelwright GS West Yorkshire; *m* 1, 1957 (dis 1980), Christine Thornes; 1 s (Philip Michael b 5 April 1960); m 2, 1984 Susan; 3 step c (Andrew Douglas Lawrie Craig, Eva Elisabeth Craig, Dawn Alice Craig); *Career* comedy writer, BBC producer, author and after dinner speaker 1966–; audit clerk 1951–53 (and 1957–59), nat service (RAF) 1953–57, Huntley & Palmer sales rep 1959–66; written for Harry Worth, Ken Dodd, Roy Castle, Richard Stilgoe, Morecambe and Wise, Jimmy Tarbuck, Hinge and Bracket, Des O'Connor, Selwyn Froggitt, Dave Allen and Frankie Howard; prodr: The Grumbleweed's Radio Show (for 15 yrs), It's A Funny Business (own interview show for 12 yrs); over 1200 series written/prodr incl: Jimmy Cricket, Gordon Kaye and Su Pollard; barker of The Variety Club of GB and Ireland; pres: Manchester Music Hall Assoc, Manchester Lunch and Laughter Club; scribe rat The Grand Order of Water Rats 1990–96; *Awards* TV & Radio Industries Club Award for Radio Programme of the Year (for The Grumbleweeds) 1984, Variety Club of GB Jesters Award for 25 yrs contrib to Comedy 1988, holder Rotary Int Club Paul Harris Award; *Books* Look Back With Laughter (vol 1, March 1996, vol 2, Dec 1996); *Recreations* golf, writing, speaking, opera; *Clubs* Artists, 1820 Club; *Style—* Mike Craig, Esq; ✉ Mike Craig Enterprises, 29 Park Road, Timperley, Cheshire WA14 5AS (☎ 0161 962 9555, fax 0161 969 6789, mobile 0831 356574); PO Box 102, Altringham, Cheshire WA14 5GA

CRAIG, Ian Wallace; s of Dr Daniel MacKinnon Craig, DSO (d 1982), and Phyllis Clifton, *née* Garrett (d 1994); *b* 7 Aug 1943; *Educ* Framlingham Coll Suffolk, RNEC Manadon Plymouth (Dip in Mech Engrg); *m* 16 Nov 1968, Jacqueline Wendy, da of Dr E J Grierson, of Saltash, Cornwall; 1 s (Andrew b 4 Jan 1970), 1 da (Juliet b 20 May

1972); *Career* HMS Albion 1967–69, HMS Ganges 1971–74, HMS Tiger 1974, RN Staff Coll 1975–78, marine engr offr HMS Ardent 1975–78, Cdr 1979, directorate of naval offrs appts (engrg) MOD(N) 1979–81, sqdn marine engr Offr to 4 Frigate Sqdn HMS Avenger 1981–83, Trg Cdr HMS Sultan 1983–85, exec offr BRNC Dartmouth 1985–85, Capt 1986, HM Naval Base Rosyth 1986–87, dep dir of naval manpower planning MOD(N) 1987–89, RCDS 1990, fleet marine engr offr 1991–92, SURFLOT (Surface Flotilla) marine engr offr 1992–93, Cdre 1993, dir of naval recruiting until 1995, ret as Capt 1995; Eur Ing, CEng, FIMechE, FIMarE, FIMgt; *Recreations* tennis, walking, sailing; *Clubs* RNSA; *Style—* Ian Craig, Esq; ✉ Plymouth

CRAIG, Sir (Albert) James Macqueen; GCMG (1984, KCMG 1981, CMG 1975); s of James Craig (d 1954), of Scone by Perth, and Florence, *née* Morris; *b* 13 July 1924; *Educ* Liverpool Inst HS, Queen's Coll Oxford, Magdalen Coll Oxford, Univ of Cairo; *m* 1952, Margaret Hutchinson; 3 s, 1 da; *Career* former lectr in Arabic Univ of Durham; HM Dip Serv: entered 1956, ambass Syria 1976–79, ambass Saudi Arabia 1979–84; visiting prof in Arabic Univ of Oxford 1985–91, lectr Pembroke Coll, sr assoc memb St Anthony's Coll Oxford 1992 (fell 1970–71); DG Middle East Assoc 1985–93 (pres 1993–); dir: Saudi-British Bank 1985–94, Hong Kong Egyptian Bank 1987–94 (advsr 1994–); advsr Hong Kong and Shanghai Bank 1985–92; chm Roxby Engineering International Ltd 1988–; vice chm Middle East International 1990–; hon fell Centre for Middle Eastern and Islamic Studies Univ of Durham 1986; pres British Soc for Middle East Studies 1987–94; tstee Karim Rida Said Fndn 1985–; OStJ 1984 (memb Cncl 1984–90); *Clubs* Travellers'; *Style—* Sir James Craig, GCMG; ✉ 33 Bury St, London SW1 (☎ 0171 839 2137)

CRAIG, John Egwin; OBE (1990); s of Thomas Joseph Alexander Craig, CIE (d 1969), and Mabel Frances, *née* Quinnell (d 1979); *b* 16 Aug 1932; *Educ* Charterhouse; *m* 27 June, 1959, Patricia, da of Exmo Senor Joao Costa Lopes (d 1980), of Sintra, Portugal; 3 s (Colin b 5 Dec 1960, Andrew b 15 June 1962, James b 12 Oct 1968); *Career* cmmnd Royal Irish Fusiliers 1950; Cooper Bros 1958–61, memb Cncl The Stock Exchange 1961–64; N M Rothschild & Sons Ltd: joined 1964, dir 1970–91, md 1981–84; dir Standard Chartered plc 1989–94; chm: Jupiter European Investment Trust plc, Belfast International Airport Holdings Ltd, Powerscreen International plc; dir: Jupiter International Group plc, Korea Liberalisation Fund Ltd, China Investment Trust plc, Int Fund for Ireland (UK govt appt); memb: Exec Ctee Br Bankers' Assoc 1982–89 (chm 1988–89), Deposit Protection Bd 1986–89; FCA, FRSA; *Clubs* Brooks's; *Style—* John Craig, Esq, OBE; ✉ Saxonbury House, Frant, Tunbridge Wells, Kent TN3 9HJ (☎ and fax 01892 750644); Jupiter International Group PLC, Knightsbridge House, 197 Knightsbridge, London SW7 1RB (☎ 0171 412 0703, fax 0171 581 3857)

CRAIG, John Frazer; CB (1994); s of John Fraser (d 1958), and Margaret Jane Gibson, *née* Mauchlen (d 1983); *b* 8 Nov 1943; *Educ* Robert Richardson GS Sunderland; *m* 1, 1963 (m dis 1972), Ann Bardo, *née* Pryor; 2 s (Robert b 1965, James b 1967), 1 da (Amanda b 1970); m 2, 1973, Janet Elizabeth, *née* Oswald; *Career* HM Customs and Excise 1961–69, NBPI 1969–70; Welsh Office: joined 1970, private sec to Perm Sec 1972–74, private sec to Sec of State 1980–82, asst sec 1982–85, under sec Indust Dept 1985–87, under sec/princ fin officer 1987–90, dep sec/dir econ affairs 1990–; *Style—* John Craig, Esq, CB; ✉ Welsh Office, Cathays Park, Cardiff CF1 3NQ (☎ 01222 825111)

CRAIG, (Robert) Peter; s of Robert Theodore Gilpin Craig (d 1986), of Alnmouth, Northumberland, and Jessie, *née* McKinstry; *b* 24 June 1940; *Educ* George Watson's Boys' Coll Edinburgh, Med Sch Univ of Durham (MB BS 1964), Univ of Newcastle (MD 1987); *m* 27 Aug 1971, Jean, da of Cecil and Ellen Toft; 1 s (Robert James Teucer b 4 Feb 1974), 2 da (Clare Elizabeth Honor b 13 July 1975, Ailsa Helen Louise b 30 Dec 1977); *Career* cmmnd 2 Lt Royal Artillery (TA) 1958, cmmnd 2 Lt (med cadet) Royal Army Med Corps 1963; house surgn then house physician Royal Victoria Infirmary Newcastle upon Tyne 1964–65; promoted Capt RAMC 1965; Regtl Med Offr: 49 Field Regt RA Hong Kong 1965–66, 1/2 Goorkhas Hong Kong and Brunei 1966–68; sr house offr: in gen and thoracic surgery then A & E med Cambridge Mil Hosp Aldershot 1968–69, in urology Queen Alexandra Mil Hosp (QAMH) London 1969–70, in orthopaedics Royal Herbert Hosp Woolwich 1970; promoted Maj RAMC 1970; registrar in gen and oncological surgery QAMH 1970–71, registrar in gen surgery Br Mil Hosp Dhekelia Cyprus 1971–74, sr registrar QAMH 1974–75, hon sr registrar Birmingham Accident Hosp 1975, sr research assoc Dept of Surgery Royal Victoria Infirmary Newcastle 1975–76, sr registrar in gen surgery Br Mil Hosp Rinteln W Germany 1976–77, sr registrar Guy's Hosp London 1977–78; promoted Lt Col RAMC 1978; conslt surgn: Mil Wing Musgrave Park Hosp Belfast 1978–79, Br Mil Hosp Hong Kong 1971–81, Queen Elizabeth Mil Hosp Woolwich (also sr lectr in mil surgery) 1981–86; CO Br Mil Hosp Rinteln 1987–89 (sr conslt in surgery and clinical tutor 1986–87), promoted Col 1987, Cdr Med HQ 4 Armd Div Herford W Germany 1989–90, promoted Brig 1990, cmd conslt surgn HQ BAOR Rheindahlen 1990–92, promoted Maj Gen 1992, Dir of Army Surgery MOD London 1992–93, Cdr Med HQ UKLF Wilton Wilts 1993–94, ret Army 1994; conslt in A & E med Wansbeck Gen Hosp Northumberland 1994–96; author of numerous papers in The Lancet, BJS and other jls; chm Jt Defence Med Servs/NHS Med Support Plan, memb Sub-Ctee on Trauma RCS; former memb: Gen Dental Cncl of Hong Kong, Cncl Royal Army Med Coll, Army Med Servs Exec Ctee; memb: Travelling Surgical Soc, BMA, Mil Surgical Soc (fndr memb); FRCS 1971, FFAEM 1994, FRSM, fell Assoc of Surgns of GB and I; QHS 1992–94; OStJ 1993; *Recreations* golf, bridge, gardening, travel, driving, undemanding reading; *Clubs* Northumberland Golf, Wildernesse Golf; *Style—* Mr R Peter Craig; ✉ c/o Drummonds, 49 Charing Cross, London SW1A 2DX

CRAIG, Stuart Bowen; s of Alexander Craig (d 1995), and Maureen Lydia Frances, *née* Frost; *b* 15 Aug 1943; *Educ* Kingston GS, Univ of Southampton (LLB); *m* 1967, Lynnard Graham, da of Geoffrey Clay Whitehurst (d 1944); 1 s (Nolan b 1969), 1 da (Natasha b 1971); *Career* dir: Kleinwort Benson Investmt Mgmnt Ltd 1978–86, Kleinwort Grieveson Investmt Mgmnt Ltd 1986–87, Fraser Green Ltd 1987–88, Nikko Fraser Green Ltd 1988–92, Singer & Friedlander Investment Management Ltd 1992–94, John Scott & Partners Investment Management Ltd 1995–; govr Kingston GS 1978–; tstee Charinco/Charishare 1978–; memb: Pensions Res Accountants Gp 1988–, Soc of Pension Conslts 1988–94 (memb Investmt Ctee 1988–91, memb Cncl 1991–92 and 1993–94, memb General Purposes Ctee 1993–94); FCA 1969, AIIMR 1971, MSI 1992 (memb Stock Exchange 1987); *Recreations* rowing, cycling, driving and off-roading, sailing, swimming, walking, food and wine; *Clubs* Weybridge Rowing (vice pres), Leander, Kingston Rowing, Marlow Rowing, All Wheel Drive, Land Rover Owners', Middlesex County RFU, Scotch Malt Whisky Soc, Surrey Walks, Tramp; *Style—* Stuart Craig, Esq; ✉ Little Spinney, Caenshill Rd, Weybridge, Surrey KT13 0SW (☎ 01932 848539); John Scott & Partners Investment Management Ltd, The Coach House, 81 High Street, Marlow, Bucks SL7 1AB (☎ 01628 471911, fax 01628 478550)

CRAIG, (Anne Gwendoline) Wendy; da of George Dixon Craig (d 1968), and Anne Lindsay; *b* 20 June 1934; *Educ* Durham HS for Girls, Darlington HS, Yarm GS, Central Sch of Speech Training and Dramatic Art; *m* 30 Sept 1955, John Alexander (Jack) Bentley (d 1994), s of John Bentley (d 1944); 2 s (Alastair b 5 April 1957, Ross b 10 Nov 1961); *Career* actress; vice pres The Leprosy Mission 1993–; Hon MA Teesside Univ 1994; *Theatre* incl: Ipswich Repertory Theatre 1953, Epitaph For George Dillon (Royal Court and Broadway) 1957, The Wrong Side of the Park 1960, The Gingerman, Ride A Cock Horse, I Love You Mrs Patterson, Finishing Touches, Peter Pan 1968, Breezeblock Park 1975, Beyond Reasonable Doubt (Queen's) 1987, Matters Matrimonial 1995; various pantomimes; *Television* incl: Not In Front Of The Children, And Mother Makes Three, And Mother Makes Five, Nanny, Butterflies, Laura and Disorder, Brighton Belles; *Films* incl: The Mindbenders, The Servant (British Academy nomination), The Nanny, Just Like A Woman, I'll Never Forget What's-Is-Name, Joseph Andrews; *Recordings* incl: Tales of Beatrix Potter (Gold disc), Show Me The Way 1988, I'm Growing 1990; *Awards* incl: BAFTA award Best Actress 1968, BBC Personality of the Year 1969 (ITV 1973); *Books* Happy Endings (1972), The Busy Mums Cook Book (1983), Busy Mums Baking Book (1986), Kid's Stuff (1988); *Recreations* walking, gardening; *Style—* Miss Wendy Craig; ✉ c/o Richard Hatton Ltd, 29 Roehampton Gate, London SW15 5JR (☎ 0181 876 6699, fax 0181 876 8278)

CRAIG, Rt Hon William; PC (NI 1963); s of late John Craig, of Milecross, Newtownards, Co Down, and Mary Kathleen, *née* Lamont; *b* 2 Dec 1924; *Educ* Dungannon Royal Sch, Larne GS, Queen's Univ Belfast; *m* 1960, Doris, da of Ewald Hilgendorff, of Hamburg; 2 s; *Career* served WWII RAF 1943–46; admitted slr 1952; MP: (U) Larne Div Antrim NI Parl 1960–73, (UU) Belfast E 1974–79; memb: (Vanguard U Progressive) N Antrim NI Assembly 1973–75, (United UU Coalition) E Belfast NI Constitutional Convention 1975–76; chief whip Parl of NI 1962–63; min of: Home Affairs 1963–64 and 1966–68, Health and Local Govt 1964, Devpt 1965–66; ldr: Ulster Vanguard 1972–78 (fndr 1972), Vanguard U Party 1973–77 (fndr 1973); memb: Cncl of Europe 1976–79, WEU 1976–79; *Style—* The Rt Hon William Craig

CRAIG-COOPER, Sir (Frederick Howard) Michael; kt (1991), CBE (1982), TD (3 bars), DL (Gtr London 1986); s of Frederick William Valentine Craig-Cooper (d 1975), and Elizabeth Oliver-Thompson Craig-Cooper, *née* Macdonald (later Mrs Carroll-Leahy); *b* 28 Jan 1936; *Educ* Horris Hill, Stowe, Coll of Law London; *m* 8 March 1968, Elizabeth Snagge, MVO, da of Leonard William Snagge (d 1971), and Eleanor Randolf Snagge (d 1983); 1 s (Peter b 3 March 1972); *Career* Nat Serv RA served combined ops UK Malta and Cyprus 1954–56, TA 1956–88 (cmd NGLO Unit 29 Commando Regt RA 1972–75); articled slr (to Sir Arthur Driver) Jaques & Co 1956–61, slr Allen & Overy 1962–64; Inco Ltd 1964–85: dir of cos in UK, Europe, Africa, ME and India 1972–84, conslt and non-exec dir UK and ME 1984–85; dir: Craig Lloyd Ltd 1968–, Paul Ray International 1984–91, Carré Orban & Partners Ltd 1989–93, Tichborne Enterprises Ltd 1993–, National Bank of Kuwait (International) plc 1993–, Whichford International Ltd 1994–96, Ely Place Holdings Ltd 1994–, Craigmyle and Company Ltd 1995–, WIB Publications Ltd 1996–; memb Cncl Mining Assoc of UK 1977–82, chm Disciplinary Appeal Ctee Chartered Inst of Mgmnt Accountants 1994–; chm Employers' Support Ctee TAVRA Gtr London 1987–90; Cons Party: Parly candidate (C) Houghton-Le-Spring 1966 and 1970, chm Chelsea Cons Assoc 1974–77 (pres 1983–95), pres Kensington and Chelsea Cons Assoc 1995–, treas Gtr London Area Nat Union of Cons and Unionist Assocs 1975–84 (memb 1975–91), chm Cons Nat Property Advsy Ctee 1986–93 (memb 1986–); Royal Borough of Kensington & Chelsea: cncllr 1968–74, memb Cncl 1968–78, Cons chief whip 1971–74, chm Fin Ctee 1972–74, memb Investmt Panel 1973–, Alderman 1974–78, Rep Lt Kensington and Chelsea 1987–; chm Order of St John for London 1990–94 (memb Chapter-General 1993–); tstee: Copper Devpt Tst Fund 1974–85, Order of Malta Homes Tst 1980–, The Orders of St John Tst 1988–; Freeman City of London 1964, Warden Worshipful Co of Drapers (Liveryman 1970, jr warden 1987–88, memb Ct of Assts 1987); memb: Law Soc 1962, Inst of Arbitrators (fell 1992); Offr Order of Merit with Swords of Sovereign Mil Order of Malta (1986), KStJ 1990 (OStJ 1978); *Books* Management Audit: How to Create an Effective Management Team (with Philippe De Backer, 1993), Maw on Corporate Governance (with Prof N N Graham Maw and Lord Lane of Horsell, 1994), Maximum Leadership: The World's Top Business Leaders Discuss How They Add Value to Their Companies (with Charles Farkas, Philippe De Backer and Lord Sheppard of Didgemere, 1995); *Recreations* admiring wife's gardening; *Clubs* Beefsteak, Pratt's, White's; *Style—* Sir Michael Craig-Cooper, CBE, TD, DL

CRAIG-MARTIN, Michael; s of Paul F Craig-Martin, of Dublin, and Rhona, *née* Gargan; *b* 28 Aug 1941; *Educ* The Priory Sch Washington DC, Fordham Univ NYC, Yale Univ (BA, BFA, MFA); *m* 25 May 1963 (sep), Janice Lucia, da of Franklin Hashey; 1 da (Jessica Clodagh b 10 dec 1963); *Career* artist; various teaching appts NY and England 1965–: artist in residence King's Coll Cambridge 1970–72, Goldsmiths' Coll London 1974–, Millard prof of fine art 1994–; tstee Tate Gallery 1989–94; *Solo Exhibitions* incl: Rowan Gallery London 1969–80, Inst of Modern Art Brisbane and touring in Australia 1978, Galeria Foksal Warsaw 1979 and 1994, Galerie Bama Paris 1980, Fifth Triennale India New Delhi 1982, Waddington Galleries London 1982, 1985, 1988, 1992 and 1993, A Retrospective 1968–89 (Whitechapel Gallery London) 1989, Galerie Claudine Papillon Paris 1990 and 1993, Projects 27 (Museum of Modern Art NYC) 1991, Musée des Beaux Arts Le Havre 1991, Pompidou Centre Paris 1994, Museum Sztuki Lodz Poland 1994, Museum of Contemporary Art Chicago 1995; *Gp Exhibitions* incl: 7 Exhibitions (Tate Gallery) 1972, The New Art (Hayward Gallery) 1972, Idea and Image in Recent Art (Art Inst of Chicago) 1974, Art as Thought Process (Serpentine Gallery London) 1974, IX Biennale des Jeunes Artistes (Paris) 1975, Sydney Biennale (Art Gallery of New S Wales) 1976 and 1990, Documenta VI (Kassel FDR) 1977, Un Certain Art Anglais (Paris) 1979, Aspects of British Art Today (Met Art Museum Tokyo and touring in Japan) 1982, Between Object and Image - Contemporary British Sculpture (Palacio de Velazquez Madrid and touring in Spain) 1986, Starlit Waters: British Sculpture, an International Art 1968–88 (Tate Liverpool) 1988, Wall to Wall (Serpentine) 1994, The Adventure of Painting (Kunstvereins Dusseldorf and Stuttgart) 1995; *Public Collections* incl: Tate Gallery, Museum of Modern Art NYC, Australian Nat Gallery Canberra, V&A, Musée des Beaux Arts Andre Malraux Le Havre, Haags Gemeentemuseum Netherlands, British Cncl, Arts Cncl of GB; *Commissions* incl: Midland Bank NY, Hasbro-Bradley UK Ltd London, Rosehaugh Stanhope Investments PLC for Broadgate London, Morgan-Stanley International Canary Wharf London public collections, New Tokyo Exhibition Center; *Publications* incl: Michael Craig-Martin: A Retrospective Exhibition 1968–89 (catalogue, Whitechapel Gallery, 1989), Michael Craig-Martin (catalogue, Musee des Beaux Arts Andre Malraux Le Havre, 1991); *Style—* Michael Craig-Martin, Esq; ✉ c/o Waddington Galleries, 11 Cork Street, London W1X 1PD (☎ 0171 437 8611); School of Visual Arts, Goldsmiths' College, London SE14 6NW (☎ 0171 919 7671)

CRAIG OF RADLEY, Marshal of the RAF Baron (Life Peer UK 1991), of Helhoughton in the county of Norfolk; Sir David Brownrigg Craig; GCB (1984, KCB 1981, CB 1978), OBE (1967); s of Maj Francis Brownrigg Craig (d 1943), of Dublin, and Olive Craig (d 1958); *b* 17 Sept 1929; *Educ* Radley, Lincoln Coll Oxford; *m* 1955, Elisabeth June, da of Charles James Derenburg (d 1976), of West Byfleet; 1 s (Hon Christopher Charles Bronwrigg b 28 March 1957), 1 da (Hon Susan Elisabeth b 26 April 1960); *Career* cmmnd RAF 1951, AOC No 1 Gp RAF Strike Cmd 1978–80, vice-chief of Air Staff 1980–82, AOC-in-C Strike Cmd and C-in-C UKAF 1982–85, Chief of Air Staff 1985–88, Chief of Def Staff 1988–91, Marshal of the RAF 1988; memb House of Lords Select Ctee on Science and Technology 1993–; *Clubs* RAF; *Style—* Marshal of the RAF the Lord Craig of Radley, GCB, OBE; ✉ House of Lords, London SW1A 0PW

CRAIGAVON, 3 Viscount (UK 1927); Sir Janric Fraser Craig; 3 Bt (UK 1918); s of 2 Viscount Craigavon (d 1974); *b* 9 June 1944; *Educ* Eton, London Univ (BA, BSc); *Heir* none; *Career* FCA; *Style—* The Rt Hon the Viscount Craigavon; ✉ 17 Launceston Place, London W8

CRAIGEN, James Mark (Jim); JP; eldest s of late James Craigen, of Glasgow, and late Isabel Craigen; *b* 2 Aug 1938; *Educ* Shawlands Acad Glasgow, Univ of Strathclyde, Heriot-Watt Univ (M Litt); *m* 20 March 1971, Sheena, da of late James Millar, of Linlithgow; *Career* compositor 1954–61, industl rels asst Scottish Gas Bd 1963–64, asst sec Scottish TUC 1964–68, asst sec Scottish Business Educn Cncl 1968–74; Glasgow City cncllr 1965–68, contested Ayr Constituency 1970, MP (Lab and Co-op) Glasgow Maryhill 1974–87, PPS to Sec of State Scot 1974–76, memb UK Delgn Cncl of Europe 1976–80, chm Select Ctee Employment 1982–83 (memb 1979–83), oppn front bench spokesman Scot 1983–85; hon vice pres Bldg Socs Assoc 1985–88, dir and sec Scot Fedn of Housing Assocs 1988–91; freelance writer, regular contrib Co-operative News; tstee Nat Museums of Scot 1985–91; CIMgt; *Books* Forward! Labour Politics in Scotland 1888–1988 (contrib, 1989); *Style*— Jim Craigen, Esq, JP

CRAIGMYLE, 3 Baron (UK 1929); Thomas Donald Mackay Shaw; s of 2 Baron Craigmyle (d 1944), and Lady Margaret Cargill Mackay (d 1958), da of 1 Earl of Inchcape; *b* 17 Nov 1923; *Educ* Eton, Trinity Coll Oxford (MA); *m* 22 Sept 1955, Anthea Esther Christine Theresa, da of late Edward Charles Rich, of 31 Yeomans Row, London SW3; 3 s (Hon Thomas Columba b 1960, Hon Justin Edward Magnus b 1965, Hon (Alexander) Joseph Ranald b 1971), 3 da (Hon Alison Margaret (Hon Mrs Heggs) b 1956, Hon Catriona Mary (Hon Mrs MacGreevy) b 1958, Hon Madeleine Claire b 1963); *Heir* s, Hon Thomas Columba Shaw, *qv*; *Career* chm Craigmyle and Co Ltd 1960–, dir Claridge Mills Ltd (chm 1971–93, Queen's award for Export 1982 and 1987); pres Br Assoc SMO Malta 1989–95; pres Catholic Union of GB 1993–; Liveryman Worshipful Co of Shipwrights; FRSA; KStJ, Kt Cdr with Star Order of Pius IX 1993; *Clubs* Royal Thames Yacht, Caledonian; *Style*— The Rt Hon Lord Craigmyle; ✉ 18 The Boltons, London SW10 9SY (☎ 0171 373 3533/5157); Scottas, Knoydart, Inverness-shire PH41 4PL (☎ 01687 642241)

CRAIK, Col Robert Rainey; OBE, TD, JP, DL (Lancs 1983); s of G B Craik of Tannadice, Angus, and Eleanor, *née* Rainey; *b* 25 March 1925; *Educ* Forfar Acad; *m* 1957, Sybil M Carr; 1 s (Timothy), 1 da (Susannah (Mrs Rupert Chenevix-Trench)); *Career* WWII served NW Europe and India, TA 1958–81; land surveyor and co dir; chm Westhoughton Cons Assoc 1977–83; chm: County of Lancaster Rifle Assoc 1970–79, NW of England and IOM TAVRA 1987–90, Liverpool Scottish Regtl Assoc 1992–96; Hon Col Cheshire ACF 1989–; High Sheriff Lancashire 1993–94; *Recreations* shooting, skiing, poetry, people; *Style*— Col Robert Craik, OBE, TD, JP, DL; ✉ Sage Cottage, The Spinney, Saxmundham, Suffolk IP17 1AR (☎ 01728 602354)

CRAIK, Prof Thomas Wallace; s of Thomas Craik (d 1969), of Warrington and Ada, *née* Atherton (d 1974); *b* 17 April 1927; *Educ* Boteler GS Warrington, Christ's Coll Cambridge (MA, PhD); *m* 25 Aug 1955 (m dis 1975), Wendy Ann, da of James Garfield Sowter (d 1980), of Kingston upon Thames; 1 s (Roger b 1956); *Career* lectr in English Univ of Leicester 1953–65, lectr then sr lectr Univ of Aberdeen 1965–72, prof Univ of Dundee 1973–77, prof Univ of Durham 1977–89, prof emeritus 1989–; *Books* The Tudor Interlude (1958), The Comic Tales of Chaucer (1964); ed: Massinger, The City Madam (1964), Massinger, A New Way to Pay Old Debts (1964), Sidney, Poetry and Prose (1965), Marlowe, The Jew of Malta (1966), Minor Elizabethan Tragedies (1974), Shakespeare, Twelfth Night (1975), Donne, Poetry and Prose (1986), Beaumont and Fletcher, The Maid's Tragedy (1988), Shakespeare, The Merry Wives of Windsor (1989), Shakespeare, King Henry V (1995); gen ed and contrib to The "Revels" History of Drama in English (1975–83); *Recreations* music, painting; *Style*— Prof T W Craik; ✉ 58 Albert St, Durham DH1 4RJ (☎ 0191 384 4528); School of English, University of Durham, Elvet Riverside, New Elvet, Durham DH1 3JT (☎ 0191 374 2000)

CRAKE, Paul Alexander; *b* 16 Nov 1962; *Educ* King Edward VII GS King's Lynn Norfolk, Univ of Southampton (BA), Dorset Business Sch Bournemouth Poly; *Career* Southampton City Cncl 1986–91 (latterly mktg mangr), head of mktg and communications Stirling District Cncl 1991–95, communication dir Design Cncl 1995–; FRSA; *Style*— Paul Crake; ✉ Design Council, Haymarket House, 1 Oxendon Street, London SW1Y 4EE (☎ 0171 208 2121, fax 0171 839 6033)

CRAM, Prof (William) John; s of Rev Frederick Charles Cram, of Harby, Leics, and Laura Mary, *née* Redhead (d 1991); *b* 6 Sept 1940; *Educ* Kingswood Sch, St John's Coll Cambridge (MA, PhD); *m* 25 July 1965, Patricia Jean, da of Reginald Middleditch (d 1987); 2 s (Nicholas b 1973, Roderick b 1976); *Career* sr res asst UEA 1967–68; Univ of Sydney Aust: lectr in biology 1969, sr lectr 1975, reader 1979–84; Univ of Newcastle upon Tyne: prof of plant biology 1984–, head Dept of Plant Biology 1984–88, head Dept of Biology 1988–91; author of numerous scientific papers; memb Plant Biology Ctee Soc for Experimental Biology 1984–87; hon sec Aust Soc of Plant Physiologists 1976–79, exec sec XIII Int Botanical Congress 1981, sec Nat Conf of Univ Profs 1992–; *Recreations* violin, running, gardening; *Style*— Prof John Cram; ✉ Department of Biological and Nutritional Sciences, Agriculture Building, University of Newcastle upon Tyne NE1 7RU (☎ 0191 222 7886, fax 0191 222 6720, e-mail W.J.CRAM@NCL.AC.UK)

CRAM, Stephen (Steve); MBE (1986); s of William Frank Cram, and Maria Helene, *née* Korte; *b* 14 Oct 1960; *Educ* Jarrow GS, Newcastle Poly (BA); *m* 17 Dec 1983, Karen Anne, da of John Andrew Waters; 1 da (Josephine), 1 s (Marcus); *Career* middle distance runner; Cwlth Games: Gold medal 1500m 1982 and 1986, Gold medal 800m 1986; World Championships Gold medal 1500m 1983; Euro Championships: Gold medal 1500m 1982 and 1986, Bronze medal 800m 1986; Olympic Games Silver medal 1500m 1984, memb Br Olympic Squad 1980 and 1988; world mile record holder, former world record holder 1500m and 2000m; athletics commentator: Eurosport, Sky TV, Radio 5 Live, BBC TV; PR conslt: BUPA, Ogden Sports Arenas; BAF rep Nat Olympic Ctee, memb Sports Cncl; charity work for NCH, patron Macmillan Cancer Relief; pres London and Southern England Branch Sunderland AFC Supporters' Assoc; hon fell Sunderland Univ; *Recreations* golf, football, snooker; *Clubs* Jarrow and Hebburn AC, Sunderland AFC; *Style*— Steve Cram, Esq, MBE; ✉ Tranwell House, Tranwell Woods, Morpeth, Northumberland NE61 6AQ (☎ 01670 503266)

CRAMER, Christopher Ranville (Chris); s of James Cramer, of Portsmouth, and Patricia Cramer (d 1993); *b* 3 Jan 1948; *Educ* Portsmouth Northern GS; *m* Helen Margaret; 1 da (Hannah Ruth b 24 Oct 1982); *Career* journalist Portsmouth News 1965–70; BBC: field prodr 1970–81 (various assignments incl Rhodesia ceasefire, held hostage at Iranian Embassy Siege London 1980), on secondment to estab new TV service for Sultan of Brunei 1975–77, dep foreign ed 1981–82, foreign ed then home ed 1982–86, news ed, intake ed then managing ed 1986–91, head of newsgathering BBC TV and Radio News 1991–96, vice pres and managing ed CNN International 1996–; FRTS 1993 (memb Cncl 1992–94); *Books* Hostage (1981); *Recreations* rowing, jogging; *Style*— Chris Cramer, Esq

CRAMMOND, Ian Ashley; s of Ronald Charles Crammond (d 1980), and Rosemary Joan Victoria, *née* Ashley; *b* 26 March 1951; *Educ* Magdalen Coll Sch Oxford, Pembroke Coll Cambridge (MA); *m* 1982, Wendy Ann, da of Huw Pritchard (d 1980); *Career* graduate trainee then account exec Leo Burnett Ltd 1972–74, account exec then account mangr Benton & Bowles 1974–76, account mangr then account dir Davidson Pearce Ltd 1976–82 (associate dir 1980–82), bd account dir Allen Brady & Marsh 1984–85, bd account dir Ogilvy & Mather London 1986–87 (account dir 1985–86); business devpt dir: Brunning Advertising (also client services dir) 1987–88, GGK London Ltd 1989–92 (dir of corp devpt 1992), chm and chief exec Crammond Dickens Lerner 1993–; 2nd IPA Advtg Effectiveness awards 1982 (commendation new prods and services); memb: IPA 1982, Mktg Soc 1986; *Books* Advertising Works 2 (contrib, 1982); *Recreations* photography, mountain walking; *Style*— Ian Crammond, Esq; ✉ Crammond Dickens Lerner, 27 Kingly Court, Kingly Street, London W1R 5LE (☎ 0171 434 0967, fax 0171 734 0102, e-mail cdl@eworld.com)

CRAMOND, Ronald Duncan; CBE (1987); s of Adam Cramond (d 1974), of Edinburgh, and Margaret Weir, *née* McAulay (d 1978); late wife Connie MacGregor direct descendant of John MacGregor, personal attendant and piper to Prince Charles Edward Stuart; *b* 22 March 1927; *Educ* George Heriot's Sch, Univ of Edinburgh (MA); *m* 18 March 1954, Constance Margaret (d 1985), da of John MacGregor, of Auchterarder (d 1964); 1 s (Kenneth b 1959), 1 da (Fiona b 1957); *Career* Royal Scots Europe 1949–51; private sec to Parly Under Sec Scottish Office 1956–57; post graduate fell in applied economics Univ of Glasgow 1963; Haldane medallist Royal Inst of Public Admin 1964; under sec Scottish Office 1971–83, dep chm Highlands and Islands Devpt Bd 1983–88; memb Scottish Tourist Bd 1985–88; cmmr Countryside Cmmn for Scotland 1988–92, tstee Royal Museum of Scotland 1985–96, chm Scottish Museums Cncl 1990–93, tstee Scottish Civic Tst 1988–95, chm Scottish Greenbelt Fndn 1992–; FIMgt; FSA (Scot); *Books* Housing Policy in Scotland; *Recreations* golf, hill walking, theatre; *Style*— Ronald D Cramond, Esq, CBE; ✉ Scottish Greenbelt Foundation, 375 West Regent Street, Glasgow G2 4NT

CRAMP, Prof Rosemary Jean; CBE (1987); da of Robert Raymond Kingston Cramp, of Hallaton, Leics, and Vera Grace, *née* Ractliffe (d 1965); *b* 6 May 1929; *Educ* Market Harborough GS, St Anne's Coll Oxford (MA, BLitt); *Career* lectr St Anne's Coll Oxford 1950–55; Univ of Durham: lectr 1955–60, sr lectr 1966–71, prof 1971–90, prof emeritus 1990–; visiting fell All Souls Coll Oxford 1992; conslt archaeologist Durham Cathedral, tstee Br Museum 1978–, cmmr Royal Cmmn of Ancient and Historical Monuments for Scotland 1974–, memb Redundant Churches Advsy Bd, memb Review Ctee for Export of Works of Art 1994–; vice pres Royal Archaeological Inst 1992–, memb Validation Panel Museum Trg Inst 1993–; former pres: Cncl Br Archaeology, Cumberland and Westmorland Antiquarian and Archaeological Soc; Hon DSc Durham 1995; FSA; *Books* Corpus of Anglo Saxon Stone Sculpture (vol 1 1984, vol 2 with R N Bailey 1988), Studies in Anglo Saxon Sculpture (1992); *Recreations* cooking, walking, reading; *Clubs* United Oxford & Cambridge Univ; *Style*— Prof Rosemary Cramp, CBE, FSA; ✉ 5 Leazes Place, Durham DH1 1RE (☎ and fax 0191 386 1843)

CRAMPIN, Peter; QC (1993); s of John Hames Crampin, of Bath, and Gwendoline Edith, *née* Richardson; *b* 7 July 1946; *Educ* St Albans Sch Univ Coll Oxford (open exhibitioner, MA); *m* 2 Oct 1975, Frida Yvonne, eld da of late Henri Helmut Schoemann; 1 s (Joseph Charles b 11 July 1990); *Career* admitted slr 1973, called to the Bar Middle Temple 1976, jt head of chambers, 2nd jr counsel to the Attorney-Gen in charity cases 1988–93, recorder 1995–; *Style*— Peter Crampin, Esq, QC; ✉ 11 New Square, Lincoln's Inn, London WC2A 3QS (☎ 0171 831 0081, fax 0171 405 2560)

CRAMPIN, Prof Stuart; s of Sydney Crampin (d 1968), of Tiptree, Essex, and Kate, *née* Ireson (d 1984); *b* 22 Oct 1935; *Educ* Maldon GS, KCL (BSc, Jelf medal), Pembroke Coll Cambridge (PhD, ScD); *m* 15 June 1963, Roma Eluned, da of Lloyd Williams; 2 da (Liss-Carin b 7 Sept 1964, Amelia Catharine b 26 Aug 1966); *Career* Nat Serv RAF 1954–56; res fell Seismological Inst Univ of Uppsala 1963–65, Gassiot fell in seismology NERC 1965–67, dep chief scientific offr Br Geological Survey 1986–92 (princ scientific offr 1967–76, sr princ scientific offr 1976–86), prof of seismic anisotropy Dept of Geology and Geophysics Univ of Edinburgh 1992–; fndr dir Edinburgh Anisotropy Project 1988–; organiser various int workshops on seismic anisotropy 1982–; Mombusho visiting prof Hokkaido Univ 1985; chm Cmmn on Wave Propagation in Real Media Int Assoc of Seismology and Physics of the Earth's Interior 1984–90; author of over 170 papers in int res jls; memb: Royal Astronomical Soc 1961, Seismological Soc of America 1963, American Geophysical Union 1981, Soc of Exploration Geophysicists 1982 (Virgil Kauffman Gold medal 1988), Euro Assoc of Exploration Geophysicists 1982 (Conrad Schlumberger award 1986), Euro Geophysical Soc 1985; FRSE 1986; *Recreations* hill walking, travelling, gardening; *Style*— Prof Stuart Crampin, FRSE; ✉ 4/7 Advocate's Close, Edinburgh EH1 1PS (☎ 0131 225 4771); Tullybelton Old Farm, Bankfoot, Perth PH1 4DH; Department of Geology and Geophysics, Grant Institute, West Mains Road, Edinburgh EH9 3JW (☎ 0131 650 4908, fax 0131 668 3184)

CRAMPTON, Peter Duncan; MEP (Lab) Humberside (majority 40,618); s of Edmund Crampton (d 1953), and Louisa, *née* Thurman (d 1967); *b* 10 June 1932; *Educ* Blackpool GS, Univ of Nottingham (BA), Univ of Birmingham (MA), Univ of Hull (Dip in W Euro Studies), Univ of London (PGCE); *m* Margaret Eva, da of George William McMillan (d 1954); 2 s (David b 1962, Robert b 1964); *Career* statistician Plessey Co 1955–56, geography teacher Coventry 1957–61, educn offr Uganda 1961–64; geography lectr: Tech Coll Birmingham 1964–70; Hull Coll of Educn 1970–85, pt/t lectr writer and Parly asst 1985–89; MEP (Lab) Humberside 1989–; chm: Euro Nuclear Disarmament 1984–86, CND Int Ctee 1988–90; *Books* Voices for One World (contrib, 1988); *Style*— Peter Crampton, Esq, MEP; ✉ 135 Westbourne Avenue, Hull HU5 3HU (☎ 01482 449337, fax 01482 449403)

CRAMPTON, Prof Richard John; s of John Donald Crampton (d 1988), of Kidderminster, Worcs, and Norah, *née* Haden; *b* 23 Nov 1940; *Educ* Queen Elizabeth's GS Hartlebury Worcs, Solihull Sch, Trinity Coll Dublin (MA), Sch of Slavonic and E Euro Studies Univ of London (PhD); *m* 10 July 1965, Celia Primrose Mary, da of Dermot Marshall Harriss (d 1943), of Nyasaland; 2 s (Will b 1969, Ben b 1972); *Career* prof of E Euro history Univ of Kent at Canterbury 1988–90 (lectr in history 1967–78, sr lectr 1978–88), prof of E Euro history St Edmund Hall Oxford 1996– (univ lectr 1990–96, fell 1990–); FRHistS; *Books* The Hollow Detente (1981), Bulgaria 1878–1918: A History (1983), A Short History of Modern Bulgaria 1987, Bulgaria (1989), Eastern Europe in the Twentieth Century (1994); *Recreations* reading, cooking, listening to music, bird watching; *Style*— Dr Richard Crampton; ✉ 4 Yew Tree Farm, Ascott-under-Wychwood, Chipping Norton, Oxon OX7 6AW (☎ 01993 831591); St Edmund Hall, Oxford OX1 4AR (☎ 01865 274151)

CRAMPTON, (Arthur Edward) Seán; MC (1943), GM (1944), TD (1946); eldest s of Joshua Crampton (d 1979), and Ethel Mary, *née* Dyas (d 1979); *b* 15 March 1918; *Educ* Vittoria Jr Sch of Art, Birmingham Central Coll of Art; *m* 1959, Patricia Elizabeth Cardew, eldest da of late Col Leslie John Cardew Wood; 1 s (Daniel), 4 da (Bridget, Katinka, Nicolette, Harriet); *Career* served WWII London Irish Rifles: Western Desert, Sicily (MC), Italy (GM), wounded; sculptor; memb Art Workers' Guild (master 1979); chm Bd of Govrs Camberwell Sch of Art 1983–88; govr London Inst 1986–89; author of innumerable works throughout UK and USA; FRBS (pres 1965–70); *Clubs* Athenaeum, Chelsea Arts; *Style*— Sean Crampton, MC, GM, TD; ✉ Rookery Farmhouse, Calne, Wilts SN11 0LH (☎ 01249 814068, fax 01249 816088)

CRAMSIE, Marcus James Lendrum; s of Arthur Vacquerie Cramsie, of Co Tyrone, NI, and Susan Doreen, *née* Lendrum; *b* 24 April 1950; *Educ* Charterhouse, Trinity Hall Cambridge (MA); *m* 19 March 1983, Carol Lesley; 1 s (Rory b 1990), 2 da (Camilla b 1984, Louise b 1986); *Career* Price Waterhouse 1972–76, Kleinwort Benson Ltd 1976–91 (dir 1986–91), dir Singer & Friedlander Holdings Ltd 1991–; FCA; *Recreations* golf, shooting, tennis; *Style*— Marcus Cramsie, Esq; ✉ 20 Lyford Rd, London SW18 3LG; Singer & Friedlander Ltd, 21 New St, London EC2M 4HR (☎ 0171 623 3000)

CRAN, James Douglas; MP (C) Beverley (majority 16,517); s of James Cran (d 1991), of Aberdeen, and Jane McDonald Cran (d 1986); *b* 28 Jan 1944; *Educ* Ruthrieston Sch Aberdeen (Dux medallion), Aberdeen Coll of Commerce, King's Coll Univ of Aberdeen

(MA); *m* 1973, Penelope Barbara, da of Richard Thomas Parker Wilson, of London; 1 da (Alexandra Penelope b 1981); *Career* researcher Cons Res Dept 1970–71, sec and chief exec Nat Assoc of Pension Funds 1971–79, W Midlands dir CBI 1984–87 (Northern dir 1979–84); MP (C) Beverley 1987–, memb House of Commons Select Ctee on Trade and Indust 1987–92, vice chm Cons Backbench NI Ctee 1992–95; PPS to Sir Patrick Mayhew as Sec of State for NI 1995–; memb: House of Commons Select Ctee on NI Affairs 1994–95, NI Grand Ctee 1996–; sec: Cons Backbench Constitutional Affrs Ctee 1988–90, Cons Backbench Euro Affrs Ctee 1989–91, St John All Pty Parly Gp 1992–93 (vice chm 1993–95), All Pty Anglo-Malta Gp 1992–94; memb Cncl Pensions Tstee Forum 1992–95; Maastricht rebel; conslt Lincoln National (UK) plc; winner Daily Mirror Nat Speaking Trophy 1969; OStJ; *Recreations* travelling, reading biographies and autobiographies; *Style*— James Cran, Esq, MP; ✉ House of Commons, London SW1A 0AA (☎ 0171 219 4445)

CRAN, Mark Dyson Gordon; QC (1988); s of Gordon Cran (d 1972), and Diana, *née* Mallinson; *b* 18 May 1948; *Educ* Gordonstoun, Millfield, Univ of Bristol (LLB); *m* 29 July 1983 (m dis 1986), Prudence Elizabeth, *née* Hayles; *Career* called to the Bar Gray's Inn 1973; in practice London; *Recreations* country sports, convivial disputation, wine and food, books and theatre; *Clubs* Brooks's, MCC; *Style*— Mark Cran, Esq, QC; ✉ Brick Court Chambers, 15–19 Devereux Court, London WC2R 3JJ (☎ 0171 583 0777, fax 0171 583 9401)

CRANBORNE, Viscount; Robert Michael James (Gascoyne-)Cecil; PC (1994), DL (Dorset 1988); also 13 Baron Cecil (E 1603), of Essendon, Co Rutland by writ in acceleration; s and h of 6 Marquess of Salisbury, *qv*; received a Writ in Acceleration summoning him to the House of Lords in his father's Barony of Cecil 1992; *b* 30 Sept 1946; *Educ* Eton, ChCh Oxford; *m* 1970, Hannah Ann, da of Lt-Col William Joseph Stirling of Keir, gs of Sir William Stirling-Maxwell, 9 Bt (a Baronetcy dormant since 1956); 2 s (Hon Robert Edward William b 1970, Hon James Richard b 1973), 3 da (Hon Elizabeth Ann b 1972, Hon Georgiana b 1977, Hon Katherine (twin) b 1977); *Heir* s, Hon Robert Edward William (Gascoyne-)Cecil b 18 Dec 1970; *Career* MP (C) Dorset S 1979–87; chm Afghanistan Support Ctee; PPS to Cranley Onslow as Min of State FCO April-May 1982 (when resigned to be free to criticise Govt's Ulster devolution plans), Parly under sec of state MOD 1992–94, Lord Privy Seal and ldr of the House of Lords 1994–; memb Blue Chip Tory Dining Club; *Style*— The Rt Hon Viscount Cranborne, PC, DL; ✉ The Manor House, Cranborne, Wimborne, Dorset

CRANBROOK, 5 Earl of (UK 1892); Gathorne Gathorne-Hardy; DL (Suffolk 1984); also Viscount Cranbrook (UK 1878), Baron Medway (UK 1892); s of 4 Earl, CBE (d 1978) by his 2 w, Dowager Countess Cranbrook, OBE, JP; *b* 20 June 1933; *Educ* Eton, Corpus Christi Coll Cambridge (MA), Univ of Birmingham (PhD); *m* 9 May 1967, Caroline, o da of Col Ralph George Edward Jarvis, of Doddington Hall, Lincoln, by his w Antonia Meade (*see* Peerage Earl of Clanwilliam); 2 s (John Jason (Lord Medway) b 1968, Hon Argus Edward b 1973), 1 da (Lady Flora b 1971); *Heir* s, Lord Medway, *qv* b 1968; *Career* sr lectr in zoology Univ of Malaya 1961–70, ed Ibis 1973–80; memb Sub Ctee F (Environment) Select Ctee on Euro Communities House of Lords 1979–90; chm: Stichting voor Eur Milieubeleid 1990–, English Nature (Nature Conservancy Cncl for Eng) 1991–; memb: Royal Cmmn on Environmental Pollution 1981–92, Natural Environment Res Cncl 1982–88, Broads Authy 1988–, Nat Conservancy Cncl 1990; non-exec dir Anglian Water 1987–89; dep chm Harwich Haven Authy 1995– (memb Bd 1989–95); Skinner and Freeman of City of London; Hon DSc Univ of Aberdeen; FIBiol, FLS, FZS, FRGS; OStJ; *Books* Mammals of Borneo (1965, 2 edn 1977), Mammals of Malaya (1969, 2 edn 1978), Birds of the Malay Peninsula (with D R Wells, 1976), Mammals of South East Asia (1987, 2 edn 1990), Key Environments: Malaysia (ed, 1988), Belalong: a tropical rainforest (with D S Edwards, 1994); *Style*— The Rt Hon the Earl of Cranbrook, DL; ✉ c/o English Nature, Northminster House, Peterborough PE1 1UA (☎ 01733 318363, fax 01733 898290)

CRANE, His Hon Judge; Peter Francis; s of Francis Roger Crane, of Northants, and Jean Berenice, *née* Hadfield (d 1987); *b* 14 Jan 1940; *Educ* Nottingham HS, Highgate Sch, Gonville and Caius Coll Cambridge (MA, LLM), Tulane Univ USA (LLM); *m* 1967, Elizabeth Mary, da of Noel Bawtry Pittman; 4 da (Anna b 1968, Kate b 1969, Rebecca b 1972, Lucy b 1974); *Career* barrister Midland and Oxford Circuit 1964–87, recorder 1982–87, circuit judge (Midland and Oxford Circuit) 1987–, resident judge Peterborough Combined Court 1992–; memb: Senate of the Inns of Court and the Bar 1983–86, Professional Conduct Ctee 1984–86, Bar Ctee 1985–86, Main Bd Judicial Studies Bd 1993–96; *Publications* Phipson on Evidence (co-ed 14 edn, 1990); *Recreations* reading, walking, gardening, wine; *Style*— His Hon Judge Crane; ✉ The Glebe House, Pytchley, Kettering, Northants NN14 1EW (☎ 01536 790322, e-mail pcrane@lix.compulink.co.uk)

CRANE, Robert Coutts; OBE (1992); s of William Crane (d 1980), of Stirlingshire, and Mary Shearer, *née* Coutts (d 1994); *b* 16 May 1935; *Educ* Denny HS, Inst of Chartered Accountants of Scotland (1957); *m* 1960, Anna Katerina Jephson, da of Capt John Arthur Jephson-Jones (d 1964), of Fife; 1 s (John b 1961), 1 da (Sheenagh b 1963); *Career* RNR Sub Lt 1958–59, Capt UDR 1971–73; dep accountant BP Refinery Grangemouth 1960–63; chief accountant, dep gen mangr Highland Printers Ltd 1963–67, md Belfast Telegraph Newspapers Ltd 1979–95 (accountant 1967, dep production mangr 1969, production mangr 1970, gen mangr Weekly Newspapers 1971 (asst md 1973)); md Chester Chronicle & Associate Newspapers Ltd 1976–78; FIMgt; *Recreations* trout fishing, photography, gliding; *Style*— Robert C Crane, Esq, OBE; ✉ Logwood Mill, 22 Logwood Rd, Ballyclare, Co Antrim BT39 9LR (☎ 01960 322487)

CRANE, (Thomas Peter) Robin; s of Thomas Taversham Crane (d 1987), and Lilian Crane (d 1995); *b* 8 Nov 1931; *Educ* Christ's Hosp; *m* 15 Aug 1955, Wendy Elisabeth, da of Lt-Col Frederick Skipwith (d 1960); 2 da (Jenni b 1958, Caroline b 1969); *Career* reg cmmn RASC 1950–57, resigned as Capt; maltster: Arthur Guinness & Co 1957–59, Sandars & Co 1959–67; film dir and prodr World About Us BBC (Majorca Observed, The Other Iceland, Rabbits - Wanted Dead or Alive?, Butterflies); Br Sponsored Film Festivals Gold Awards for: Event Horse 1975, The Colourmen 1984, Heritage of the Forest 1984; NY Film & TV Festival Silver Award for Mirror to the Fun 1984; chm: Sussex Wildlife Tst 1987–94, Royal Soc for Nature Conservation 1994–; FRES 1979; *Recreations* nature conservation, music, golf; *Style*— Robin Crane, Esq; ✉ Bridge Cottage, Well Lane, Midhurst, West Sussex GU29 9QQ

CRANE, Teresa Louise; da of Jack Goodsell (d 1964), of Hornchurch, and Teresa, *née* Overson; *b* 10 June 1938; *Educ* Hornchurch GS; *children* 1 s (Andrew Anthony b 1962), 1 da (Michele Jacqueline (Mrs Smith) b 1964); *Career* writer; vice pres Essex Red Cross; *Books* Molly (1980), A Fragile Peace (1981), The Rose Stone (1984), Sweet Songbird (1987), Hawthorne Heritage (1988), Tomorrow Jerusalem (1990), Green and Pleasant Land (1991), Strange are the Ways (1993), Freedom's Banner (1994), The Italian House (1995), The Raven Hovers (1996); *Recreations* reading, music, cooking, walking, travelling, grandchildren, although not necessarily always in that order; *Clubs* Arts; *Style*— Mrs Teresa Crane; ✉ Blake Friedmann Literary Agency, 37–41 Gower St, London WC1E 6HH (☎ 0171 631 4331, fax 0171 323 1274)

CRANFIELD, Richard William Lionel; s of Lionel Sydney William Cranfield (d 1965), of Tewin, Herts, and Audrey Cecil Martin, *née* Pank; *b* 19 Jan 1956; *Educ* Winchester, Fitzwilliam Coll Cambridge (MA); *m* 26 Sept 1981, Gillian Isabel, da of Archibald Spence Fleming (d 1979), of Graden, Kelso, Roxburghshire; 2 s (Edward, George), 2 da (Sophie, Henrietta); *Career* Lt HAC 1979–86; admitted slr 1980; ptnr Allen & Overy; Freeman City of London 1985, memb Worshipful Co of Merchant Taylors; memb Law Soc; *Recreations* golf, field sports; *Style*— Richard Cranfield, Esq; ✉ Allen & Overy, One New Change, London EC4M 9QQ (☎ 0171 330 3000, fax 0171 330 9999)

CRANLEY, Viscount; Rupert Charles William Bullard Onslow; s and h of 7 Earl of Onslow, *qv*; *b* 16 June 1967; *Educ* Eton; *Recreations* country sports; *Style*— Viscount Cranley; ✉ Temple Court, Clandon Park, Guildford, Surrey

CRANSTON, Prof Ross Frederick; s of Frederick Hugh Cranston, of Brisbane, Aust, and Edna Elizabeth, *née* Davies; *b* 23 July 1948; *Educ* Nundah State Sch, Wavell HS Brisbane, Univ of Queensland (BA, LLB), Harvard Univ (LLM), Univ of Oxford (DPhil); *m* 1, 5 March 1976 (m dis 1985), Dr (Barbara) Jane Stapleton, da of Colin Arthur Stapleton, of Sydney; m 2, 25 Aug 1988, Elizabeth Anna, da of Leslie Victor Whyatt, of Kent; 1 da (Imogen Molly); *Career* called to the Bar Gray's Inn 1976, asst recorder 1991–; lectr in law Univ of Warwick 1975–77, Aust Nat Univ 1978–86, prof of banking law Univ of London 1986–92, dir Centre for Commercial Law Studies Queen Mary and Westfield Coll London 1989–92 (dean Faculty of Laws 1988–91), Cassel prof of commercial law Univ of London 1993–; conslt Ctee of Inquiry concerning Public Duty and Private Interest 1979, memb Legal Advsy Panel Nat Consumer Cncl 1976–77 and 1987–; conslt: World Bank, IMF, UNCTAD, Cwlth Secretariat, Lord Woolf's Inquiry into Access to Justice 1994–96; Parly candidate (Lab) Richmond (Yorks) gen election 1992; pres SPTL 1992–93 (vice pres 1991–92); *Books* Regulating Business (1979), Law and Economics (jt ed, 1981), Consumers and the Law (2 edn, 1984), Delays and Efficiency in Civil Litigation (jtly, 1984), Legal Foundations of the Welfare State (1985), Law, Government and Public Policy (1987), The Single Market and the Law of Banking (ed, 3 edn, 1995), Banks, Liability and Risk (ed, 2 edn 1995), European Banking Law (ed, 1993), Principles of Banking Law (1997); *Clubs* Reform; *Style*— Prof Ross Cranston; ✉ Department of Law, London School of Economics and Political Science, Houghton Street, London WC2A 2AE (☎ 0171 405 7686, fax 0171 955 7366); 3 Veralum Buildings, Gray's Inn, London WC1R 5EA (☎ 0171 831 8441, fax 0171 831 8479)

CRANWORTH, 3 Baron (UK 1899); Philip Bertram Gurdon; s of Hon Robin Gurdon (ka 1942, s of late 2 Baron, KG, MC, who d 1964) and late Hon Yoskyl Pearson, da of 2 Viscount Cowdray (who m 2, Lt-Col Alistair Gibb, and m 3, 1 Baron McCorquodale of Newton, KCVO, PC); *b* 24 May 1940; *Educ* Eton, Magdalene Coll Cambridge; *m* 18 Jan 1968, Frances Henrietta, da of late Lord William Walter Montagu Douglas Scott, MC (s of 7 Duke of Buccleuch), and Lady Rachel Douglas-Home (da of 13 Earl of Home); 2 s (Hon (Sacha William) Robin b 1970, Hon (Brampton) Charles b 1975), 1 da (Hon Louisa-Jane b 1969); *Career* late Lt Royal Wilts Yeo; *Style*— The Rt Hon the Lord Cranworth; ✉ Grundisburgh Hall, Woodbridge, Suffolk

CRASTON, Rev Canon (Richard) Colin; s of Albert Edward Craston (d 1977), and Ethel Craston (d 1962); *b* 31 Dec 1922; *Educ* Preston GS, Univ of Bristol (BA), Univ of London (BD), Lambeth (DD); *m* 1, 10 July 1948, Ruth (d 1992); 1 s (Andrew b 4 Dec 1951), 1 da (Carolyn Edmonds b 17 Sept 1954); m 2, 14 May 1993, Rev Brenda H Fullalove; *Career* RN 1941–46; curate of Nicholas Durham 1951–54, team rector of St Paul with Emmanuel Bolton 1954–93, area dean Bolton 1972–92, chaplain to HM The Queen 1985–92, chm House of Clergy Diocese of Manchester 1982–94; memb: Standing Ctee Gen Synod 1976–95 (chm Business Sub-Ctee 1991–95), Crown Appointments Cmmn 1982–92; chm Anglican Consultative Cncl 1990–96 (vice chm 1986–90); *Books* Biblical Headship and the Ordination of Women (1986), Authority in the Anglican Communion (contrib, 1987), Open to the Spirit (ed, 1987), Anglicanism and the Universal Church (contrib, 1990), Robert Runcie - A Portrait By His Friends (contrib, 1990), By Word and Deed (ed, 1992); *Style*— The Rev Canon Colin Craston; ✉ 12 Lever Park Avenue, Horwich, Bolton, Lancashire BL6 7LE (☎ 01204 699972, fax 01204 690813)

CRATHORNE, 2 Baron (UK 1959); Sir Charles James Dugdale; 2 Bt (UK 1945), DL (Cleveland 1983); s of 1 Baron, TD, PC (d 1977), and Nancy, OBE (d 1969), da of Sir Charles Tennant, 1 Bt; *b* 12 Sept 1939; *Educ* Eton, Trinity Coll Cambridge; *m* 1970, Sylvia Mary, da of Brig Arthur Montgomery, OBE, TD; 1 s (Hon Thomas Arthur John Dugdale b 1977), 2 da (Hon Charlotte b 1972, Hon Katharine b 1980); *Heir* s, Hon Thomas Dugdale; *Career* with Sotheby and Co 1963–66, asst to Pres Parke-Bernet NY 1966–69, James Dugdale and Associates London (ind fine art consultancy serv) 1969–; fine art lectr; dir: Cliveden Hotel 1985–, Voyager Hotels Ltd 1989–; tstee National Heritage Memorial Fund 1992–95; chm: The Georgian Gp 1990–, Captain Cook Tst 1993–, Jt Ctee of the Nat Amenity Socs 1996–; contribs to Apollo and The Connoisseur; memb: Ct of the Univ of Leeds 1985–, Yarm Civic Soc 1987– (pres), Editorial Bd House Magazine 1983–, Cons Advsy Gp on the Arts and Heritage 1988–, Yorks Regnl Ctee Nat Tst 1974–84 and 1988–94; hon sec All Party Parliamentary Arts and Heritage Gp 1981–; pres: Cleveland Family History Soc 1988–, Cleveland Sea Cadets 1988–, Hambledon Dist CPRE 1988–, Cleveland Assoc of Nat Tst 1982–94; govr Queen Margaret's Sch York 1986–; patron: Attingham Tst for the Study of the Br Country House 1990–, Cleveland Community Fndn 1990–; FRSA (memb Cncl RSA 1982–88); *Books* Edouard Vuillard (1967), Tennants Stalk (jtly 1973), A Present from Crathorne (jtly, 1989), Cliveden, The Place and the People (1995); *Recreations* photography, travel, family life in the country; *Style*— The Rt Hon the Lord Crathorne, DL; ✉ Crathorne House, Yarm, Cleveland TS15 0AT (☎ 01642 700431); House of Lords, London SW1 (☎ 0171 219 5224)

CRATON, David Malcolm; s of George Edgar Maurice Craton (d 1946), and Edith, *née* Izzard (d 1973); *b* 9 May 1934; *Educ* Royal Wanstead Sch, Phillips Acad Andover Mass, LSE (Leverhulme scholar, BSc Econ); *m* 19 July 1958, Sheila Ann, *née* Ollis; 3 s (Jonathan Peter Michael b 15 June 1965, Paul Anthony Maurice b 14 Jan 1970, Timothy Charles Matthew (twin) b 1970), 2 da (Caroline Beverley b 1 May 1962, Sarah Elizabeth b 20 April 1967); *Career* Nat Serv RE 1953–55; prod mangr Morphy-Richards Ltd 1959–60, mktg exec Foote Cone & Belding 1960–61; General Electric Co: advtg mangr 1961–62, mktg mangr 1962–64, divisional mangr domestic appliances 1964–66; sales dir Remington Electric 1966–67, Bd dir (and md of subsids) Erwin Wasey (Inter Public) 1967–71, chm and chief exec CLK Group plc 1972–90 (estab as Craton Lodge & Knight Ltd 1972, public USM Co 1984), princ D Craton & Associates 1992, chm Innovation Management International 1990–92; MInstM 1971, MIMC 1986; *Recreations* riding, sailing, sheep farming, history; *Style*— David Craton, Esq

CRAUFURD, Sir Robert James; 9 Bt (GB 1781), of Kilbirney, N Britain; s of Sir James Gregan Craufurd, 8 Bt (d 1970), and Ruth Marjorie, *née* Corder; *b* 18 March 1937; *Educ* Harrow, Univ Coll Oxford (MA); *m* 1, 1964 (m dis 1987), Catherine Penelope, yr da of late Capt Horatio Westmacott, RN, of Torquay, Devon; 3 da (Caroline Anne b 1965, Penelope Jane b 1967, Veronica Mary b 1969); m 2, 1987, Georgina Anne, da of late John Dennis Russell, of Lymington, Hants; *Heir* none; *Career* memb London Stock Exchange 1969; *Style*— Sir Robert Craufurd, Bt; ✉ East Grove, Grove Road, Lymington, Hants SO41 3RF (☎ 01590 672406)

CRAVEN, Archdeacon of; *see:* Grundy, Ven Malcolm Leslie

CRAVEN, 9 Earl of (GB 1801); Benjamin Robert Joseph Craven; also Baron Craven (E 1665), Viscount Uffington (GB 1801); o s of 8 Earl of Craven (d following a motor accident 1990), and Teresa Maria Bernadette, da of Arthur John Downes, of Blackhall, Clane, Co Kildare; *b* 13 June 1989; *Style*— The Rt Hon the Earl of Craven

CRAVEN, Gemma; da of Gabriel Bernard Craven, of Leigh-on-Sea, Essex (formerly of Dublin), and Lillian Elizabeth Josephine, *née* Byrne; *b* 1 June 1950; *Educ* Loretto, St Bernard's Convent Westcliff-on-Sea, Bush Davies Sch; *m* 10 June 1988, David Beamish, s of Phillip Beamish, of Greasby, Wirral; *Career* actress; stage debut Let's Get a Divorce (Palace Theatre Westcliff) 1968, West End debut Anya in Fiddler on the Roof 1970; *Theatre* Chichester Festival Theatre 1974: R Loves J, Dandy Dick, The Confederacy, A Month in the Country; NT 1985–87: A Chorus of Disapproval, Jacobowsky and the Colonel, The Magistrate, Three Men on a Horse; other roles incl: Audrey! 1971, Trelawny 1972, The Threepenny Opera (Bristol Old Vic) 1975, Songbook 1979, They're Playing Our Song 1980–81 (SWET Award Best Actress in a Musical), Song and Dance 1982, Loot 1984 (City Limits Best Comedy Actress), Nellie Forbush in South Pacific (Prince of Wales) 1988–89, Private Lives 1991, Godspell (Barbican) 1993, Same Time Next Year 1993, Present Laughter 1994, Lunch Girls (Windsor Theatre Royal) 1995, The Darling Buds of May (nat tour) 1995, Calamity Jane (Sadler's Wells) 1996; *Television* incl: Boon, Pennies from Heaven, Emily, East Lynne, She Loves Me, The Marshal, The Man Who Cried; *Films* incl: The Slipper and the Rose 1976 (Variety Club Film Actress of the Year), Why Not Stay For Breakfast?, Wagner, Double X 1991, The Mystery of Edwin Drood 1993, Still Life 1993, The Words upon the Window Pane 1994; *Recreations* cooking; *Style*— Miss Gemma Craven; ✉ c/o Jan Kennedy, Billy Marsh Associates Ltd, 174–178 North Gower Street, London NW1 2NB (☎ 0171 388 6858, fax 0171 388 6848)

CRAVEN, Sir John Anthony; kt (1996); *Career* chm Deutsche Morgan Grenfell Group plc; non-exec dir Rothmans International BV 1991–, memb Conseil d'Administration Société Générale de Surveillance Geneva, former memb Securities and Investments Bd; *Style*— Sir John Craven; ✉ Deutsche Morgan Grenfell Group plc, 23 Great Winchester Street, London EC2P 2AX (☎ 0171 545 6100)

CRAVEN, Prof John Anthony George; s of George Marriot Craven (d 1989), and Dorothy Maude, *née* Walford; *b* 17 June 1949; *Educ* Pinner GS, King's Coll Cambridge (Kennedy Meml Scholar, Adam Smith Essay Prize, Stephenson Essay Prize, MA), MIT; *m* 1974, Laura Elizabeth, da of Prof John Loftis; 1 s (Matthew Thomas b 1978), 1 da (Rebecca Mary b 1981); *Career* Univ of Kent: lectr in economics 1971–76, sr lectr 1976–80, reader 1980–86, prof of economics 1986–, dean Faculty of Social Scis 1987–91, pro-vice-chllr 1991–93, dep vice-chllr 1993–96; vice-chllr Univ of Portsmouth 1997–; visiting assoc prof Univ of Guelph Canada 1982–83; memb: Royal Economic Soc 1971, Econometric Soc 1978; *Books* Distribution of the Product (1979), Introduction to Economics (1984, 2 edn 1989), Social Choice (1992); *Recreations* village cricket, choral singing, charity trustee; *Style*— Prof John Craven; ✉ Old Lynch Cottage, Brook Street, Eastry, Sandwich, Kent CT13 0HR (☎ 01304 611559); University of Portsmouth, Winston Churchill Avenue, Portsmouth PO1 2UP (☎ 01705 876543, fax 01705 843400)

CRAVEN, John Raymond; s of Bill Craven (d 1990), of Leeds, and Marie, *née* Noble (d 1989); *b* 16 Aug 1940; *Educ* Leeds Modern GS, Leeds Coll of Commerce; *m* 27 March 1971, Jean Marilyn, da of Alfred (Blackie) Howe, CBE (d 1974); 2 da (Emma Katherine b 30 Nov 1972, Victoria Jane b 12 April 1975); *Career* journalist and presenter; jr reporter The Harrogate Advertiser (later reporter The Yorkshire Post and freelance reporter for nat press); BBC: news writer 1965, TV reporter Points West (BBC Bristol) 1970, presenter Search (current affairs magazine for children) 1971, presenter and later ed John Craven's Newsround 1972–89, currently presenter Countryfile (weekly rural and environmental magazine); other TV credits incl: Swap Shop, Saturday Superstore, Breakthrough, Story Behind The Story; winner: BAFTA Award (for best children's TV documentary) 1975, Pye TV Award (for distinguished services to TV) 1983, TV Times Award (for top children's personality) 1983; patron: Rainforest Action Fund, Whale and Dolphin Conservation Soc; vice pres Wildlife Hosp Tst; pres: Young People's Tst for the Environment, Uphill Ski Club, Young Archaeologists Club, Chesham Light Opera Co; *Recreations* golf, swimming, walking in the countryside, aviation; *Style*— John Craven, Esq; ✉ c/o Unique Artistes Ltd, Crown House, 225 Kensington High Street, London W8 6SA (☎ 0171 937 3181, fax 0171 937 5847)

CRAVEN, Air Marshal Sir Robert Edward; KBE (1970, OBE 1954), CB (1966), DFC (1940); s of Gerald Craven, of Port Elizabeth, SA, and Edith Craven; *b* 16 Jan 1916; *Educ* Scarborough Coll; *m* 1940, Joan, da of Capt E S Peters; 1 s, 1 da; *Career* MN 1932–37, joined RAF 1937, 201, 210 and 228 Sqdns, cmd RAF Eastleigh and RAF Lyneham, Air Vice-Marshal 1965, SASO Flying Trg Cmd 1967, SASO Trg Cmd 1968–69, Cdr Maritime Air Forces (AOC 18 Gp) 1969–72, Air Marshal 1970, ret 1972; Order of Menelik (Ethiopia) 1955; *Clubs* RAF; *Style*— Air Marshal Sir Robert Craven, KBE, CB, DFC; ✉ Letcombe House, Letcombe Regis, Oxon

CRAWFORD, Alexander Hamilton; s of James Allison Crawford (d 1978), and Betsy Carroll, *née* Hughes (d 1950); *b* 15 Jan 1944; *Educ* Queen Mary's Sch Basingstoke Hants, Imperial Coll London (BSc), Open Univ Business Sch (Dip in Management), Farnborough Coll of Technol (intermediate dip in French); *m* 1, 6 Jan 1968 (m dis 1982), Lesley Sandra Jane; 1 s (Stephen Nicholas b 8 July 1981), 2 da (Alison Mary b 6 Jan 1971, Sarah Louise b 30 May 1973); m 2, 1 June 1982, Jennifer Mary Evans, *née* Stuart; *Career* managing ed IPC Sci & Technol Press 1967–72, sci ed Euro Physical Soc 1972–73, mathematics teacher Aldershot Manor Sch 1974–77, engr ed Electrical Review 1977–80, Euro ed Energy Developments 1981; ed: Health & Safety at Work 1982–87, Laboratory News 1987–92 and 1993–; managing ed: Laboratory Practice 1992, Laboratory News 1992; chm Nat Science Centre Project 1994–96 (dir 1993–96); memb: Rushmoor Borough Cncl 1976–85, Nat Consumer Cncl 1977–82, Hampshire CC 1981–82; MInstP 1970, MIMgt 1990, FRMS 1990, AIL 1992; *Recreations* swimming; *Style*— Alexander Crawford, Esq; ✉ 17 Cargate Avenue, Aldershot, Hampshire GU11 3EP (☎ 01252 314708); EMAP Maclaren, PO Box 109, Scarbrook Rd, Croydon CR9 1QH (☎ 0181 277 5304, fax 0181 277 5302, telex 946665)

CRAWFORD, Prof Alistair; s of John Gardiner Crawford (d 1991), of Fraserburgh, Aberdeenshire, and Mary Ann, *née* Holiday (d 1993), of Hull; *b* 25 Jan 1945; *Educ* Fraserburgh Acad, Glasgow Sch of Art (DA), Aberdeen Coll of Educn (Art Teacher's Cert); *m* 5 Nov 1971, Joan, da of Clifford Martin; *Career* art teacher Woodfarm HS Glasgow 1966–67, lectr in textile design Dept of Textile Industs Univ of Leeds 1968–71, sr lectr in graphic design Coventry Poly 1971–73; UCW Aberystwyth: lectr in graphic art 1974–83, sr lectr 1983–87, actg head Dept of Visual Art and curator of college collections 1986–90, reader 1987–90, prof of graphic art 1990–95, head Dept of Visual Art and keeper of college collections 1990–93, head School of Art 1993–95, research prof of art 1995–; painter, printmaker, photographer, art historian; fell Printmakers' Cncl of GB 1978, memb Euro Soc for the History of Photography 1981, MSTD 1977, FRSA 1983–86, MSIAD 1977–86 (ASIAD 1973), FRPS 1991, RCA 1994; *Exhibitions* solo incl: Curwen Gallery London 1981, Segno Grafico Venice 1981, Centro Iniziative Per l'Arte e la Cultura Palazzo Kechler Udine Italy 1981, Cartesius Gallery Trieste Italy 1982, Italian Journal (Curwen Gallery London) 1983, Printworks Gallery Chicago 1983, The Spirit of Place (Wales & Scot touring) 1986–88, Travel Journal (Tolquhon Gallery Aberdeenshire) 1992, Barcelona Tango Printworks Gallery Chicago 1994, It is in the Nature of My Gaze (Univ of Wales Aberystwyth) 1995; jt exhibitions incl: 4 times 20 (Oriel Theatre Clwyd Mold and touring, with Norman Ackroyd, David Hockney and Terry Willson) 1981–82, Vedute d'Italia/Alistair Crawford & Robert Greethem (Catherine Lewis Gallery UW Aberystwyth and Wales touring 1987–88 and Printworks Gallery Chicago 1988), Pivot - 16 artists using photography (Oriel Mostyn Llandudno and Wales touring) 1991–92; public collections incl: The Glasgow Sch of Art, The Nat Museum of Wales, Hunterian Museum & Art Gallery Glasgow, Welsh Arts Cncl, SW Thames Health Authy, Continental Bank Collection Chicago, Mazda Cars (UK), The Br Sch at Rome, P & O London, Newport, Leicester, Norwich & Hove Museums, Br Cncl, Nat Library of Wales, Imperial Coll London, Contemporary Art Soc of Wales, Frito-Lay Corporation Dallas, Eton Coll Windsor, The Getty Group Chicago, The Beckman Inst Univ of Illinois at Champaign, The Scottish Fisheries Museum Anstruther Fife; touring exhibitions designed and arranged incl: Elio Ciol photographer (Welsh Arts Cncl and N Wales Arts Assoc) 1977–81, John Thomas 1838–1905 photographer (Welsh Arts Cncl) 1977–81, Mario Giacomelli - a retrospective 1955–83 (Visiting Arts Unit of GB and Ffotogallery Cardiff) 1983–86, Carlo Bevilacqua Il Maestro (Visiting Arts Unit of GB and UW Aberystwyth) 1987–90, Mario Giacomelli (Printworks Gallery Chicago) 1995; *Awards* incl: Welsh Arts Cncl Design Award 1976, Welsh Arts Cncl/Editions Alecto Major Printmaking Award 1977, W Wales Arts Assoc Cmmn Award 1977, Welsh Arts Cncl Travel Award 1978, Br Cncl 1981, Sir Winston Churchill travelling fellowship in Photography 1982, Royal Nat Eisteddfod Gold Medal in Fine Art 1985, Royal Nat Eisteddfod Photography Prize 1989, Balsdon sr fell Br Sch at Rome 1995–96; *Publications* incl: John Thomas 1838–1905 Photographer (with Hilary Woollen, 1977), The Print Collection of the University College of Wales Aberystwyth (1984), Mario Giacomelli (1985), Elio Ciol - Italia Black & White (1986), Carlo Bevilacqua (1986), Elio Ciol - Assisi (1991), Will Roberts (1994), Kyffin Williams (1995); *Recreations* gardening; *Style*— Prof Alistair Crawford; ✉ School of Art, The University of Wales, Buarth Mawr, Aberystwyth, Dyfed SY23 1NE

CRAWFORD, HE Charles Graham; s of Graham Wellington James Crawford, of Hemel Hempstead, Herts, and Edith Ellen, *née* Orrah; *b* 22 May 1954; *Educ* St Albans Sch, St John's Coll Oxford (BA Jurisprudence), Lincoln's Inn (Part II Bar Exams), Fletcher Sch of Law and Diplomacy Boston USA (MA Law and Diplomacy); *m* 1990, Helen Margaret, *née* Walsh; 2 s (James b 1991, Robert b 1993); *Career* HM Dip Serv: Indonesia Desk FCO 1979–81, second then first sec (press/info) Belgrade 1981–84, Civil Aviation Desk then speechwriter FCO 1984–87, first sec (political) Pretoria/Cape Town 1987–91, Soviet then Eastern Dept FCO 1991–93, political cnsllr Moscow 1993–96, HM ambass to Bosnia and Herzegovina (Sarajevo) 1996–; *Recreations* chess, music; *Style*— HE Mr Charles Crawford; ✉ c/o Foreign & Commonwealth Office (Sarajevo), King Charles Street, London SW1A 2AH

CRAWFORD, Daniel Frank; s of Frank Lewis Crawford, and Edna, *née* Partington; *b* 11 Dec 1945; *m* 10 May 1985, Stephanie Crawford; 1 step da (Katey); *Career* manager and artistic dir King's Head Theatre 1970–; prodr/co-prodr of West End prodns incl: Kennedy's Children (Arts Theatre) 1975, Spokesong (Vaudeville) 1977, Fearless Frank (Princess, NYC) 1980, Mr Cinders (Fortune) 1983, Wonderful Town (Queen's) 1986, Easy Virtue (Garrick) 1988, Artist Descending a Staircase 1988, Being at Home with Claude (Vaudeville) 1990, Kvetch (Garrick, Evening Standard Award) 1991, September Tide (Comedy) 1993–94, Lust (Theatre Royal); dir: Spread a Little Happiness - The Work of Vivian Ellis (Whitehall and King's Head), Philadelphia Here I Come (Wyndham and King's Head); award winning King's Head prodns incl: Mr Cinders (with Denis Lawson), The Lady and the Clarinet (with Imelda Staunton), Da (Broadway, 4 Tony's), The Browning Version (with Nigel Stock), Hello and Goodbye (with Janet Suzman and Ben Kingsley); dir Cavalcade (nat tour); panel memb Vivian Ellis prize for New Musical Writing; *Clubs* Savage, Groucho; *Style*— Daniel Crawford, Esq; ✉ King's Head, 115 Upper St, Islington, London N1 1QN (☎ 0171 226 8561/1916/0364, fax 0171 226 8507)

CRAWFORD, Sir Frederick William; kt (1986), DL (W Midlands 1995); s of William Crawford (d 1955), and Victoria Maud, *née* Careless (d 1988); *b* 28 July 1931; *Educ* George Dixon GS Birmingham, Univ of London (BScEng, MSc, DSc), Univ of Liverpool (PhD, DipEd, DEng); *m* 21 Oct 1963, Béatrice Madeleine Jacqueline, da of Roger Hutter, of Paris; 1 s (Eric b 1968 d 1992), 1 da (Isabelle (Mrs Peter Sutton), b 1965); *Career* scientist NCB Mining Res Estab Middx 1956–57, sr lectr in electrical engrg Coll of Advanced Technol Birmingham 1958–59; Stanford Univ California 1959–82: prof of electrical engrg 1969–82, chm Inst for Plasma Res 1973–80; vice-chllr Univ of Aston 1980–96; non-exec dir: Legal & General Group plc 1988–, Rexam plc (formerly Bowater plc) 1989–, PowerGen plc 1990–; vice pres Parly and Scientific Ctee 1992–95, vice chm Ctee of Vice-Chllrs and Princs 1993–95; High Sheriff for W Midlands 1995–96; Freeman City of London 1986, Master Worshipful Co of Engrs (Liveryman 1987, Sr Warden 1994), memb Ct of Assts Worshipful Co of Info Technologists 1995 (Liveryman 1993); hon bencher Inner Temple 1996; FEng 1985, FInstP 1964, FAPS 1965, FIEE 1965, FIEEE 1972, FIMA 1978, CIMgt 1986; *Clubs* Athenaeum; *Style*— Sir Frederick Crawford, DL, FEng; ✉ Aston House, 1 Arthur Road, Edgbaston, Birmingham B15 2UW (☎ 0121 454 7545)

CRAWFORD, Maj-Gen Ian Campbell; CBE (1982); *b* 17 June 1932; *Educ* Dumfries Acad, Univ of Edinburgh (MB ChB); *m* 4 April 1959, Phyllis Mary; 1 s (Niall b 1967), 1 da (Fiona b 1960); *Career* conslt physician (Cardiology) Queen Elizabeth Mil Hosp Woolwich 1977–83 and 1985–90; dir Army Med and consltg physician to the Army 1990–92, hon physician to HM The Queen 1990–92; private consultant practice (cardiology and gen internal med) 1992–; FRCPE 1972, FRCP 1986; *Style*— Maj-Gen Ian C Crawford, CBE; ✉ The Arbour, Bobbing, Kent (☎ 01795 842292, fax 01795 843753); BUPA Alexandra Hospital, Impton Lane, Walderslade, Kent ME5 9PG (☎ 01634 687166, fax 01634 686162)

CRAWFORD, Prof James Richard; s of James Allen Crawford, of Hahndorf, S Australia, and Josephine Margaret, *née* Bond; *b* 14 Nov 1948; *Educ* Univ of Adelaide (BA, LLB, Stow scholar), Univ of Oxford (DPhil); *m* 1, Marisa Luigina, *née* Ballini; 2 da (Rebecca Jane b 5 Aug 1972, Emily Jessica Teresa b 17 Aug 1975); m 2, 1992, Patricia Hyndman; 2 da (Alexandra Vijayalalitha b 26 Sept 1992, Natasha Mihiri b 3 Jan 1994); *Career* Univ of Adelaide: lectr 1974–77, sr lectr 1977–82, reader 1982–83, prof of law (personal chair) 1983–86; cmmr Australian Law Reform Cmmn 1982–84 (pt/t cmmr 1984–90), Challis prof of int law Univ of Sydney 1986–92 (dean Faculty of Law 1990–92), Whewell prof of int law Univ of Cambridge 1992–, professorial fell of Jesus Coll Cambridge 1992–; barr of High Ct of Australia and of the Supreme Ct of NSW, memb of chambers 3 Verulam Place London; dir of studies Int Law Assoc London 1991–; memb: Advsy Ctee on the Australian Judicial System The Constitutional Cmmn 1985–87, Institut de Droit Int 1991 (assoc 1985), UN Int Law Cmmn 1992–96; judge on Admin Tbnl OECD 1993–; Hon Bencher Gray's Inn 1991–; *Publications include* The Creation of States in International Law (1981, Creative Scholarship award American Soc of Int Law), Australian Courts of Law (3 edn, 1993), The Rights of Peoples (ed, 1988); author and contrib to many law reports; *Recreations* cricket, reading, walking; *Style*— Prof James Crawford; ✉ Jesus College, Cambridge CB5 8BL (☎ 01223 339506, fax 01223 311668)

CRAWFORD, Lincoln; s of Norman Crawford (d 1983), and Ena Crawford (d 1972); *b* 1 Nov 1946; *Educ* Univ Tutorial Coll London, Brunel Univ (LLB); *m* 26 July 1976, Janet, da of John Clegg (d 1987); 3 s (Douglas Luke b 4 Dec 1978, Paul David b 26 Aug 1981, Jack Justin b 7 Sept 1988); *Career* called to the Bar 1977, currently asst recorder; advsr to Lord Scarman following Brixton disorders 1981, exec memb Prison Reform Tst; memb: Cmmn for Racial Equality 1984, Parole Bd 1985–88, Professional Standards Ctee Gen Cncl of the Bar, Br Boxing Bd of Control, Black-Jewish Forum; chm: Prince's Tst Sports Ctee 1989, Ind Adoption Serv; S of England chm Special Needs Appeals Panel FHEFC; vice chm Charta Mede Tst; participant Duke of Edinburgh Study Conf 1989, govr Hampstead Comprehensive Sch,; *Recreations* squash, swimming; *Clubs* Commonwealth; *Style*— Lincoln Crawford, Esq; ✉ 12 Kings Bench Walk, Temple, London EC4 (☎ 0171 583 0811, fax 0171 583 7228)

CRAWFORD, Dr Lionel Vivian; s of John Mitchell Crawford (d 1988), and Fanny May, *née* Barnett (d 1967); *b* 30 April 1932; *Educ* Rendcomb Coll nr Cirencester Glos, Emmanuel Coll Cambridge (sr scholar, MA, PhD); *m* 1957, Elizabeth Minnie, da of Charles Martin Green; 1 da (Lucy Elizabeth b 1969); *Career* Nat Serv 2/Lt 6 Bn REME 1950–52; Rockefeller Fndn travelling fell 1958–60 (visiting res fell Virus Laboratory Univ of California Berkeley 1958–59, Div of Biology California Inst of Technology Pasadena 1959–60), MRC staff memb Inst of Virology Glasgow 1960–68, visiting res fell Biological Laboratories Univ of Harvard 1963 and 1965, head Dept of Molecular Virology Imperial Cancer Res Fund Laboratories London 1968–88, chm Cellular and Molecular Biology Gp 1968–71, visiting res fell Cold Spring Harbor Laboratory Long Island NY, Eleanor Roosevelt Int Cancer fellowship to Dept of Biochemistry Stanford Univ California 1976–77, head of Imperial Cancer Res Fund Tumour Virus Gp Dept of Pathology Univ of Cambridge 1988–95; memb: Soc of Gen Microbiology, Euro Molecular Biology Orgn (memb Cncl 1973); FRSE 1970, FRS 1988; *Recreations* restoring old houses; *Style*— Dr Lionel Crawford, FRS, FRSE; ✉ Suffolk (☎ 01473 787251)

CRAWFORD, Michael; OBE (1987); *b* 19 Jan 1942; *Educ* St Michael's Coll Bexley, Oakfield Sch Dulwich'; *Career* actor 1955–; in original prodn of Britten's Noyes Fludde and of Let's Make an Opera; *Theatre* incl: Come Blow Your Horn (Prince of Wales) 1961, Travelling Light 1965, The Anniversary 1966, No Sex Please We're British (Strand) 1971, Billy (Drury Lane) 1974, Same Time Next Year (Prince of Wales) 1976, Flowers for Algernon (Queen's) 1979, Barnum (Palladium) 1981–83 and (Victoria Palace) 1985–86, The Phantom of the Opera (Her Majesty's 1986, NY 1988, Los Angeles 1989 (world tour of USA, Canada, Aust and UK)), The Music of Andrew Lloyd Webber 1991–92, EFX (MGM Grand Las Vegas) 1995; numerous radio and TV broadcasts; *Television* incl: Some Mothers Do 'Ave 'Em, Chalk and Cheese; *Films* incl: Soap Box Derby, Blow Your Own Trumpet, Two Left Feet, The War Lover, Two Living One Dead, The Knack 1964, A Funny Thing Happened on the Way to the Forum 1965, The Jokers, How I Won the War 1966, Hello Dolly 1968, The Games 1969, Hello and Goodbye 1970, Alice in Wonderland 1972, The Condorman 1980; *Awards* Tony Award for Best Actor in a Musical (for Phantom of the Opera) 1988; *Style*— Michael Crawford, Esq, OBE; ✉ c/o ICM Ltd, Oxford House, 76 Oxford Street, London W1N 0AX (☎ 0171 636 6565, fax 0171 323 0101)

CRAWFORD, Prof Michael Hewson; s of Brian Hewson Crawford, and Margarethe Bettina, *née* Nagel; *b* 7 Dec 1939; *Educ* St Paul's Sch, Oriel Coll Oxford (BA, MA), Br Sch at Rome (scholar); *Career* Jane Eliza Procter visiting fell Princeton Univ 1964–65; Christ's Coll Univ of Cambridge: res fell 1964–69, fell 1969–86, lectr 1969–86; prof of ancient history UCL 1986–; visiting prof: Univ of Pavia 1983, Ecole Normale Supérieure Paris 1984, Univ of Padua 1986, Sorbonne Paris 1989, Univ of San Marino 1989, Univ Statale Milan 1990, Univ of L'Aquila 1990, Univ of Pavia 1992; jt dir: Excavations of Fregellae 1980–86, Valpolcevera Project 1987–94, Veleia Project 1994–, S Martimo Project 1996–; chm Jt Assoc of Classical Teachers 1992–95 (chm Ancient History Ctee 1978–84), vice pres Roman Soc 1981–; ed: Papers of the Br Sch at Rome 1975–79, Jl of Roman Studies 1980–84; foreign memb Istituto Lombardo 1990, memb Academia Europaea 1995; FBA 1980; *Books* Roman Republican Coin Hoards (1969), Roman Republican Coinage (1974), Archaic and Classical Greece (with D Whitehead, 1982), Coinage and Money under the Roman Republic (1985), L'impero romana e la struttura economica e sociale delle province (1986), The Coinage of the Roman World in the Late Republic (with A Burnett, 1987), Medals and Coins from Budé to Mommsen (ed with C Ligota and J B Trapp, 1991), Antonio Agustín between Renaissance and Counter-reform (ed, 1993), Roman Statutes (ed, 1996); contribs to Annales, Economic History Review, Jl of Roman Studies; *Style*— Prof Michael Crawford; ✉ Department of History, University College, Gower Street, London WC1E 6BT (☎ 0171 380 7396)

CRAWFORD, (Robert) Norman; CBE (1973); s of William Crawford (d 1944), of Londonderry, and Annie Catherine, *née* Rexter (d 1942); *b* 14 June 1923; *Educ* Foyle Coll Londonderry, The Queen's Univ of Belfast (BComSc); *m* 1948, Jean Marie Patricia, da of Hugh Carson (d 1954), of Portrush; 1 s (David), 5 da (Jennifer, Catherine, Mary, Zelda, Emma); *Career* CA; md The McNeill Group (NI) Ltd 1960–68; chm: Nature Reserves Ctee 1965–87, NI Transport Holding Co 1968–75; dir and chief exec William Clark and Sons Ltd 1983–87; pres: NI Outward Bound Assoc 1975–92, NI C of C and Indust 1967–68, Belfast Branch BIM 1976–78; vice pres: S Belfast Scout Cncl 1984–95, Retirement Assoc of N Ireland; chm: R N Crawford and Co Business Advisors 1968–, Regnl Cncl BIM 1968–70, NI Wildlife Campaign; bd memb: UK Centre for Economic and Environmental Devpt 1985–92, Solway Heritage 1995–, Crichton Tst, Crichton Devpt Co; life memb: RSA, Ulster Wildlife Tst, RSPB; memb Senate of Queen's Univ Belfast 1968–93; *Clubs* Ulster Reform; *Style*— R Norman Crawford, Esq, CBE; ✉ 23 Corberry Mews, Maxwelltown, Dumfries DG2 7AX

CRAWFORD, Robert Gammie; CBE (1990); s of William Crawford (d 1980), of Aberdeen, and Janet Beveridge, *née* Gammie (d 1974); *b* 20 March 1924; *Educ* Robert Gordon's Coll Aberdeen; *m* 4 Sept 1947, Rita, da of August Daniel Veiss (d 1975), of Latvia; 1 da (Fiona b 1959); *Career* Flt Lt navigator RAF 1942–47; admitted slr 1950; ptnr Ince and Co (int shipping lawyers) 1950–73; dir: AVDEL plc 1983–94, Sturge Aviation Syndicate Management Ltd 1994–, L R Integrity Management Ltd (formerly Marine Offshore Management Ltd) 1994–96, Ockham Aviation Agencies Ltd 1996–; chm: Highlands and Islands Airports Ltd 1986–93, Independent Claims Services Ltd 1993–; memb Lloyd's 1975–95; memb Bd: Lloyd's Register of Shipping 1982–94, Civil Aviation Authy 1984–93; vice chm Port of London Authy 1985–92; chm UK War Risk Club 1982–; dir: UK Protection and Indemnity Club 1983–94 (chm 1984–91), UK Freight Demurrage Defence Club 1987–; farmer 1966–; Freeman City of London; FInstD; *Recreations* shooting, golf, reading, conversation; *Clubs* Royal Northern and University (Aberdeen); *Style*— Robert G Crawford, Esq, CBE; ✉ 9 London House, Avenue Rd, London NW8 7PX (☎ and fax 0171 483 2754); West Mains of Auchenhove, Lumphanan, Aberdeenshire AB31 4QT (☎ and fax 013398 83208/667)

CRAWFORD, Prof Robert MacGregor Martyn; s of Dr Crawford, Robert MacGregor Cleland (d 1981), and Bethia Rankyn, *née* Martyn (d 1976); *b* 30 May 1934; *Educ* Glasgow Acad, Univ of Glasgow (BSc), Liège (Docteur en Sciences Naturelles); *m* 20 June 1964, Barbara Elizabeth, da of Percy Hall (d 1979); 1 s (Magnus b 29 Oct 1971); *Career* prof of plant ecology Univ of St Andrews 1977– (lectr in botany 1962–72, reader 1972–77); FRSE 1974, FIBiol; *Books* Studies in Plant Survival (1989); *Recreations* photography, music; *Style*— Prof Robert Crawford, FRSE; ✉ Kincaple Cottage, St Andrews, Fife KY16 9SH (☎ 01334 850214); Sir Harold Mitchell Building, The University, St Andrews, Fife KY16 9AL (☎ 01334 463370, fax 01334 463366)

CRAWFORD, Robert William Kenneth; s of Hugh Merrall Crawford (d 1982), of West Bergholt, Colchester, Essex, and Mary, *née* Percival; *b* 3 July 1945; *Educ* Culford Sch, Pembroke Coll Oxford (BA); *m* 9 Dec 1975, Vivienne Sylvia, da of Boghdan Andre Polakowski; 1 s (Alistair b 1987), 1 da (Helen b 1984); *Career* Imperial War Museum: head res and info office 1971–89, keeper Dept of Photographs 1975–83, asst dir 1979–82, dep dir gen 1982–95, dir-gen 1995–; *Style*— R W K Crawford, Esq; ✉ Imperial War Museum, Lambeth Rd, London SE1 6HZ (☎ 0171 416 5206)

CRAWFORD, Sir (Robert) Stewart; GCMG (1973, KCMG 1966, CMG 1951), CVO (1955); s of Sir William Crawford, KBE (d 1950), and Marion Stewart, *née* Whitelaw; *b* 27 Aug 1913; *Educ* Gresham's, Oriel Coll Oxford; *m* 1938, Mary Katharine (d 1992), da of late Eric Corbett, of Witley, Surrey; 3 s (and 1 s decd), 1 da; *Career* Air Miny 1936; FO 1947, political resident Persian Gulf 1966–70, dep under sec FCO 1970–73, chm Ctee of Broadcasting Coverage 1973–74, BBC Gen Advsy Cncl 1975–84, Broadcasters' Audience Res Bd 1980–88; *Clubs* United Oxford & Cambridge Univ, Phyllis Court; *Style*— Sir Stewart Crawford, GCMG, CVO; ✉ 19 Adam Court, Bell St, Henley-on-Thames, Oxon (☎ 01491 574702)

CRAWFORD, Susan Louise (Mrs Jeremy Phipps); da of Lt Cdr Wilfrid Hornby Crawford, RN, and late Patricia Mary, *née* McCosh; *b* 11 May 1941; *Educ* St Denis Sch Edinbugh, Prior's Field Godalming, Studio Simi Florence Italy; *m* 12 Oct 1974, Jeremy Joseph Julian Phipps, s of Lt Alan Phipps (ka 1943); 1 s (Jake Shimi Alan b 29 Aug 1975), 1 da (Jemma Louise Rose b 21 July 1977); *Career* artist and equestrian portrait painter; portrait cmmns incl: HM The Queen (mounted), HRH The Prince of Wales (mounted), HM Queen Elizabeth the Queen Mother (for the Black Watch Regt), HRH The Princess Margaret, Countess of Snowdon (for The Royal Highland Fusiliers), HH The Sultan of Brunei, HRH The Princess Royal (mounted), nineteen Epsom Derby winners and steeplechasers incl Red Rum, Arkle and Desert Orchid; collections worldwide; work exhibited at: The Royal Scot Acad, The Nat Portrait Gallery, The Royal Acad of Arts, The Royal Soc of Portrait Painters, The Queen's Gallery, V&A, The National Gallery of Pahang Pinang Malaysia, Arthur Akermann & Son, The David Ker Gallery, The Tryon Gallery; *Style*— Ms Susan Crawford

CRAWFORD, Vice Adm Sir William Godfrey; KBE (1961), CB (1958), DSC (1941); s of Henry Edward Venner Crawford, JP (d 1937), of Wyld Court, Axminster, Devon; *b* 14 Sept 1907; *Educ* RNC Dartmouth; *m* 29 April 1939, Mary Felicity Rosa (d 1995), 2 da of Sir Philip Williams, 2 Bt (d 1958); 3 s (Edward, Alexander, James), 1 da (Prunella); *Career* Lt RN 1929, Rear Adm 1956, Imperial Def Coll 1956–58, flag offr Sea Training 1958–60, Vice Adm 1959, cdr Br Navy Staff and naval attaché Washington 1960–62, ret 1963; dir Overseas Offices BTA 1964–72; *Clubs* Royal Cruising; *Style*— Vice Adm Sir William Crawford, KBE, CB, DSC; ✉ Broadlands, Whitchurch Canonicorum, Bridport, Dorset DT6 6RJ (☎ 01297 489591)

CRAWFORD, His Hon Judge William Hamilton Raymund; QC (1980); s of Col Mervyn Crawford, DSO, JP, DL (d 1977), of Dunscore, Dumfriesshire, and Martha Hamilton, *née* Walker (d 1991); *b* 10 Nov 1936; *Educ* Winchester, Emmanuel Coll Cambridge; *m* 1965, Marilyn Jean, da of John Millar Colville; 1 s, 2 da; *Heir* Alexander Mervyn Colville Crawford; *Career* called to the Bar 1964, dep chm Agric Land Tbnl 1978, recorder Crown Ct 1979–86, circuit judge (NE Circuit) 1986–; *Recreations* fishing, shooting, hill farming; *Clubs* Naval and Military, Northern Counties; *Style*— His Hon Judge William Crawford, QC; ✉ c/o The Crown Court, Newcastle upon Tyne

CRAWFORD AND BALCARRES, 29 (and 12) Earl of (S 1398, 1651 respectively); Robert Alexander Lindsay; KT (1996), DL (Fife), PC (1972); also Lord Lindsay (of Crawford; *ante* 1143), Lord Lindsay of Balcarres (S 1633), Lord Lindsay and Balniel (S 1651), Baron Wigan of Haigh Hall (UK 1826), Baron Balniel (Life Peer UK 1974); Premier Earl of Scotland in precedence; maintains private officer-of-arms (Endure Pursuivant); s of 28 Earl, KT, GBE, FSA (d 1975), and Mary Katherine (d 1994), da of late Col the Rt Hon Lord Richard Cavendish, CB, CMG, PC (gs of 7 Duke of Devonshire); *b* 5 March 1927; *Educ* Eton, Trinity Coll Cambridge; *m* 27 Dec 1949, Ruth Beatrice, da of Leo Meyer-Bechtler, of Zürich; 2 s, 2 da; *Heir* s, Lord Balniel; *Career* Grenadier Gds 1945–49; MP (C): Hertford 1955–74, Welwyn and Hatfield Feb-Sept 1974; PPS to Fin Sec of Treasy 1955–57, min Housing and Local Govt 1957–60; memb Shadow Cabinet (Health and Social Security) 1967–70, min of state Def 1970–72, min of state Foreign and Cwlth Affrs 1972–74; chm Lombard North Central Bank 1976–80; vice-chm Sun Alliance Insurance Group 1975–91; dir: National Westminster Bank 1975–88, Scottish American Investment Trust 1978–88; first Crown Estate cmmr and chm 1980–85; pres RDCs Assoc 1959–65; chm: Nat Assoc for Mental Health 1963–70, Historic Buildings Cncl for Scotland 1976–83, Royal Cmmn on the Ancient and Historical Monuments for Scotland 1985–95; chm: Bd of Nat Library of Scotland 1990–, Jt Ctee NGS/RSA 1993–96; Lord Chamberlain to HM Queen Elizabeth The Queen Mother 1992–; *Style*— The Rt Hon the Earl of Crawford; ✉ House of Lords, London SW1A 0PW

CRAWFORD-SMITH, (Robert) Ian; s of Capt Brodie Crawford-Smith (d 1956), of Guildford, Surrey, and Catherine Galen Cowie, *née* Burns (d 1974); *b* 14 Dec 1931; *Educ* HS Harrow Middx; *m* 13 Aug 1955, Ann Sheila, da of Edmund Thomas Hudson (d 1984), of Holton Heath, Dorset; 1 s (Philip Duncan b 1960), 1 da (Joanna Louise b 1962); *Career* Royal Tank Regt 1950–52; underwriter Northern Assoc Co Ltd 1952–65, dir H Clarkson Insurance Holdings Ltd (later Clarkson Puckle Ltd) 1965–86, vice chm Birchgrey Ltd (promoters of Euro Open golf tournament and gen sports promoters) 1981–95, dir Berkeley (Insurance) Ltd 1986–95, insur conslt Hambros Bank 1986–95; memb: Family Practitioners Ctee 1960–73, Bucks Exec Ctee 1965–69, Round Table 1964–72, S Bucks Community Health Cncl; chm local hosps 1965–71; Freeman City of London, Liveryman Worshipful Co of Insurers; Chartered Insurance Practitioner, ACII 1956, FInstD 1980, FBIIBA; *Recreations* golf, wine, watching sport generally; *Clubs* IOD, MCC; *Style*— Ian Crawford-Smith, Esq; ✉ Cranford Chiltern Road, Chesham Bois, Amersham, Bucks HP6 5PH

CRAWLEY, Christine; MEP (Lab) Birmingham E (majority 55,120); *b* 1950; *Career* former drama teacher and youth theatre leader, town and dist cncllr in Oxon, Parly candidate (Lab) SE Staffs 1983; MEP (Lab) Birmingham East 1984–; Euro Parl: chair Women's Rights Ctee 1989–94, dep leader Euro Parly Labour Pty 1994–, memb Civil Liberties Ctee and Women's Rights Ctee; memb: Fabian Soc, Co-operative Party, CND, Mfrg Sci and Fin Union; *Recreations* Latin American literature, amateur dramatics, attending local football matches in Birmingham; *Style*— Ms Christine Crawley, MEP; ✉ Euro Office, 5 Barnsley Road, Edgbaston, Birmingham B17 8EB (☎ 0121 429 7117)

CRAWLEY, Frederick William; s of William Clement Crawley (d 1962), and Elsie Florence, *née* Valentine (d 1984); *b* 10 June 1926; *m* 1951, Ruth Eva, da of Dr Hans Jungmann (d 1970); 2 da (Nicola, Fiona); *Career* Lloyds Bank plc: jt gen mangr 1975, exec dir Lloyds Bank Int 1975–76, asst chief gen mangr 1977–78, dep chief gen mangr 1978–84, vice chm and chief exec offr Lloyds Bank California 1983–84, chief gen mangr 1985, dep chief exec 1985–87, dir 1985–88; dep chm RAF Benevolent Fund Enterprises Ltd 1988–; chm: Betta Stores plc 1989–92, Alliance & Leicester Building Society 1992–94 (formerly dep chm), Girobank plc (subsid of Alliance & Leicester) 1992–95 (formerly dep chm), Legal and General Recovery Investment Trust PLC 1994–; dir: Lloyds Development Capital Ltd 1987–92, Barratt Developments plc 1988–; hon treas RAF Benevolent Fund; FCIB, CIMgt; *Recreations* aviation, shooting, photography; *Style*— Frederick Crawley, Esq; ✉ 4 The Hexagon, Fitzroy Park, London N6 6HR (☎ and fax 0181 341 2279)

CRAWLEY, John; *b* 21 Sept 1971; *Career* professional cricketer; Cambridge Univ 1991–93 (capt 1992 and 1993), debut Lancashire CCC 1989; England U19: tour to Aust 1989/90, NZ 1990/91; England: test debut v S Africa 1994, memb team touring Aust 1994/95; *Style*— John Crawley, Esq; ✉ c/o Lancashire CCC, Old Trafford, Manchester M16 0PX (☎ 0161 848 7021)

CRAWLEY, Peter Stanbridge; s of William John Crawley (d 1965), and Grace Loelia, *née* Pegg; *b* 5 Dec 1923; *Educ* Univ Coll Sch Hampstead London; *m* 20 May 1950, Joan Elizabeth Spicer Crawley, FRCPE, da of Dr Percy Peter James Stewart, OBE (d 1924); 2 s (Richard b 1951, Patrick b 1952), 1 da (Jane b 1957); *Career* WWII RAC RASC Capt 1942–47; princ dir Faber & Faber Ltd 1964–73 (dir 1961–64), dir Faber Music Ltd 1965–73; ind publisher in assoc with Victor Gollancz Ltd 1973–; publisher: Master

Bridge Series, architectural history books; illustrated (photographs) many architectural history books; *Recreations* golf, reading, photography, music, bird-watching, ceramics; *Clubs* Savile; *Style—* Peter Crawley, Esq; ✉ Garth House, Hertingfordbury, Herts SG14 2LG (☎ 01992 582963, fax 01992 505014); Victor Gollancz Ltd, Wellington House, 125 Strand, London WC2R 0BB (☎ 0171 420 5555, fax 0171 240 7261)

CRAWLEY, Thomas Henry Raymond; s of Charles William Crawley (d 1992), of Cambridge, and Kathleen Elizabeth, *née* Leahy (d 1982); *b* 17 May 1936; *Educ* Rugby, Trinity Coll Cambridge (MA); *m* 22 April 1961, Felicity Merville, da of Gerald Ashworth Bateman (ret Cdr RN, d 1995); 1 s (Charles b 1965), 2 da (Alice b 1967, Tessa b 1969); *Career* Martin's Bank Ltd 1959–61; admitted slr 1965, slr Hong Kong 1986; ptnr: Turner Kenneth Brown 1967–94, Radcliffes Crossman Block 1994–; City of London Solicitors prize and Charles Steele prize 1964; Freeman City of London 1985, Liveryman Worshipful Co of Solicitors 1987; memb Law Soc Eng and Hong Kong; *Clubs* Travellers, Hong Kong; *Style—* Thomas Crawley, Esq; ✉ Radliffes Crossman Block, 5 Great College Street, London SW1P 3SJ (☎ 0171 222 7040, fax 0171 222 6208/6754)

CRAWLEY-BOEVEY, Sir Thomas Michael Blake; 8 Bt (GB 1784), of Highgrove, Glos; s of Sir Launcelot Valentine Hyde Crawley-Boevey, 7 Bt (d 1968), and Elizabeth Goodeth, da of Herbert d'Auvergne Innes; *b* 29 Sept 1928; *Educ* Wellington, St John's Coll Cambridge (MA); *m* 16 Feb 1957, Laura (d 1979), da of late Jan Pouwels Coelingh, of Wassenaar, Netherlands; 2 s (Thomas Hyde b 1958, William Walstan b 1960); *Heir* s, Thomas Hyde Crawley-Boevey b 26 June 1958; *Career* former shipping agent; ed: Money Which? 1968–76, Which? 1976–80 (ed-in-chief 1980–82); memb Cncl Insurance Ombudsman Bureau 1985–; *Books* Buying, Selling and Owning Shares (1987), Finance Your Future (1989); *Clubs* Gower and Swansea Bay Windsurfing, Grafham Water Sailing; *Style—* Sir Thomas Crawley-Boevey, Bt; ✉ Trebanau, Cilycwm, Llandovery, Dyfed SA20 OHP (☎ 01550 20496)

CRAWSHAW, Gillian Anne (Jill); da of William Sumner Crawshaw (d 1983), and Trudy, *née* Riding; *b* 13 Oct 1943; *Educ* West Kirby GS for Girls, St Anne's Coll Oxford (MA); *m* 1973, Stephen Rudolf Danos, s of Sir Laszlo Danos (d 1935); 2 s (Toby William Laszlo b 1974, Dominic Stephen Robert b 1977); *Career* freelance travel writer for numerous publications 1966–71; travel ed: Daily Mail 1971–82, Evening Standard 1982–87, Sunday Express and Sunday Express Magazine 1987–92, The European 1992–93; currently regular contrib to various magazines, radio and TV programmes incl: The Times, Independent on Sunday, (Glasgow) Herald, Landmark Travel TV, LBC, Talk Radio UK; sole travel contrib The Doomsday Book project; three times Travel Writer of the Year, commended Br Press Awards, twice awarded French Govt Writers' Awards; memb Br Guild of Travel Writers; *Books* Holidays with Children at Home & Abroad (1982); *Recreations* Oriental carpets, Georgian architecture, skiing, obsessional travel, food, deserts; *Style—* Mrs Jill Crawshaw; ✉ Pond House, 54 Highgate West Hill, London N6 6DA (☎ 0181 340 0307, fax 0181 348 3782)

CRAWSHAW, 4 Baron (UK 1892); Sir William Michael Clifton Brooks; 4 Bt (UK 1891), DL (Leics 1992); s of 3 Baron (d 1946), and Sheila, da of late Lt-Col P R Clifton, CMG, DSO; *b* 25 March 1933; *Educ* Eton, ChCh Oxford; *Heir* bro, Hon David Brooks, *qv*; *Career* sits as Cons Peer in House of Lords; Lord of the Manor of Long Whatton, patron of the living of Shepshed; pres: NW Leics Cons Assoc 1982–, Leics Disabled Assoc; vice pres Spinal Injuries Assoc; chm Quorn Hunt Ctee 1971–91; treas Loughborough Cons Assoc 1954–58; co cmmr Leics Boy Scouts 1958–77; *Clubs* Boodle's, MCC; *Style—* The Rt Hon the Lord Crawshaw, DL; ✉ Whatton, Loughborough, Leics (☎ 01509 842225, fax 01509 842268)

CRAWSHAY, Martin Richard Charles; s of Capt Walter Stanley Cubitt Crawshay (d 1955), of Norwich, Norfolk, and Elaine Grace (Betty), *née* Osborne (d 1972); *b* 16 Jan 1928; *Educ* Eton, RMA Sandhurst; *m* 24 Oct 1967, Joanna Deborah Grania, da of Maj Thomas Henry Bevan, MC (d 1964), of Castlebellingham, Co Louth; 1 s (Charles Martin b 1969); *Career* Adj: 16/5 The Queen's Royal Lancers 1956–57 (cmmnd 1948), Univ of Oxford OTC 1959–61; racing liaison exec Horserace Betting Levy Bd 1963–91, pres Nat Pony Soc 1992, pres Br Percheron Horse Soc 1993; hon memb and tstee Br Equine Veterinary Assoc; tstee and gardens co-ordinator Suffolk Red Cross 1991–; Freeman City of London, Liveryman Worshipful Co of Farriers; *Recreations* racing, shooting, croquet, wildlife; *Clubs* Cavalry and Guards; *Style—* Martin Crawshay, Esq; ✉ The Old Vicarage, Leavenheath, Colchester, Essex CO6 4PT (☎ 01787 210384)

CRAWSHAY, Col Sir William Robert; kt (1972), DSO (1945), ERD, TD, DL (Glam 1964, Monmouthshire 1970, Gwent 1974); s of Capt Jack William Leslie Crawshay, MC (d 1950; whose mother Mary was da of Sir John Leslie, 1 Bt), sometime of Caversham Park, Oxon, by his w Claire, *née* Stickelbaut (who m subsequently Hon George Egerton, 2 s of 5 Earl of Wilton); *b* 27 May 1920; *Educ* Eton; *m* 1950, Elisabeth Mary Boyd, da of Lt-Col Guy Franklin Reynolds, MC (d 1950); *Career* cmmnd (SR) 1 Royal Welch Fusiliers 1939, SOE France 1944–45, served WWII (despatches twice), Parachute Regt (TA) 1947–60, ADC to HM The Queen 1966–71, Hon Col 3 Royal Regt of Wales (Vol) Bn 1970–82; Vice-Lord Lt of Gwent 1979–95; served Arts Cncl of GB 1962–74, chm Welsh Arts Cncl 1968–74; pres: National Museum of Wales 1977–82, Wales Area Royal Br Legion 1974–88; chm Cncl Univ Coll Cardiff 1966–87; Chev Légion d'Honneur 1945, Croix de Guerre 1945; KStJ 1969; *Clubs* White's, Cardiff and County; *Style—* Col Sir William Crawshay, DSO, ERD, TD, DL; ✉ Llanfair Court, Abergavenny, Gwent (☎ 0187 384 0215)

CRAY, Rev Graham Alan; s of Alan Cray, of Little Paxton, Cambs, and Doris Mary Kathleen, *née* Hann (d 1963); *b* 21 April 1947; *Educ* Trinity Sch of John Whitgift Croydon, Univ of Leeds (BA Theol), St John's Coll Nottingham; *m* 14 July 1973, Jaqueline, *née* Webster; 2 da (Catherine Ann b 29 Sept 1979, Sarah Emma b 29 Dec 1982); *Career* curate St Mark's Gillingham Kent 1971–75, Northern co-ordinator Youth Dept Church Pastoral Aid Soc 1975–78, vicar St Michael-le-Belfrey York 1978–92, princ Ridley Hall Cambridge 1992–; memb: Governing Body SPCK, Advsy Ctee Anglican Renewal Ministries, Advsy Ctee Greenbelt Festivals, Organising Ctee Evangelical Anglican Leadership Conf; *Books* David Watson - A Portrait by his Friends (contrib, 1985), By My Spirit (contrib, 1988), In Spirit and Truth (contrib, 1989), The Gospel and Tomorrow's Culture (1994), To Proclaim Afresh (contrib, 1995), Building a Relational Society (contrib, 1996); *Recreations* listening to rock music, reading theology, following Test Cricket; *Style—* The Rev Graham Cray; ✉ The Principal's Lodge, Ridley Hall, Cambridge CB3 9HG (home ☎ 01223 358665, work ☎ 01223 353040, fax 01223 301287)

CREAGH, Giles Peter Vandeleur; TD (1967); s of Lt Cdr Giles Desmond Vandeleur Creagh, RNVR (d 1963), of Blo' Norton, Norfolk, and Olga, *née* Beckwith (d 1983); *b* 21 Nov 1927; *Educ* Marlborough, Clare Coll Cambridge (MA); *m* 1 Sept 1962, Jean Margaret Heather, da of Godfrey George Hoole (d 1980), of Krugersdorp, SA; 2 s (Desmond Giles Vandeleur b 1963, Henry Giles Vandeleur b 1965); *Career* Maj (TA) Suffolk Regt, JRRU, 23 SAS, Int Corps; slr and notary public; dir Bury St Edmunds Building Society 1969–88, local dir Cheltenham & Gloucester Building Society 1988–89, sr ptnr Greene & Greene Slrs 1981–94; registrar and legal sec Diocese of St Edmundsbury and Ipswich 1956–75, pres Suffolk and North Essex Law Soc 1984–85, chm Social Security Appeal Tbnls 1984–91; memb Gen Assembly of C of E 1959–65; *Clubs* United Oxford and Cambridge, Special Forces, Norfolk; *Style—* Giles Creagh, Esq, TD; ✉ The Old Rectory, Market Weston, Diss, Norfolk IP22 2PE

CREAN, Dr Gerard Patrick; s of Patrick Joseph Crean (d 1953), of Courtown Harbour, Co Wexford, Eire, and Katherine Frances, *née* Dunn (d 1960); *b* 1 May 1927; *Educ* Rockwell Coll Co Tipperary, Univ Coll Dublin (MB BCh, BAO), Univ of Edinburgh (PhD); *m* 20 Aug 1960, Janice Dodds, da of Thomas McKean Mathieson (d 1985), of Luanshya, Zambia; 1 s (Justin b 31 March 1964), 2 da (Kate b 19 May 1961, Stephanie b 10 Oct 1962); *Career* house offr Mater Misericordia Hosp Dublin 1953–54, clinical asst Dept of Med Royal Infirmary Edinburgh 1954–56; Western Gen Hosp Edinburgh: house offr 1954–56, registrar, sr registrar 1956–59, memb staff Clinical Endocrinology Res Unit MRC, hon conslt physician 1959–67; hon lectr Dept of Therapeutics Univ of Edinburgh 1964–67, conslt physician Southern Gen Hosp Glasgow 1967–92, conslt physician Ross Hall Hosp 1978–, hon lectr Univ of Glasgow 1967–92, visiting prof in physiology Univ of Pa USA 1972, dir Diagnostic Methodology Res Unit Southern Gen Hosp 1974–92; pres Br Soc of Gastroenterology 1986; memb: Br Soc of Gastroenterology, Scot Assoc of Physicians, Scot Soc of Experimental Med, Assoc of Physicians of GB and Ireland, Caledonian Soc of Gastroenterology, Prout Club, Glasgow Gastroenterology Club; fndr memb and pres Scottish Fiddle Orchestra; FRCP (Edinburgh 1965, Glasgow 1978, Ireland 1988); *Books* The Physiology of Gastric Secretion (contrib, 1967), Davidson's Principles and Practice of Medicine (contrib, 1971–90), An intergrated Textbook of Gastroenterology (contrib, 1971), Peptic Ulcer: Problem Areas in Diagnosis (contrib, 1983), Peptic Ulcer Disease (contrib, 1985); *Recreations* traditional fiddle playing, golf, history of Antarctic exploration; *Style—* Dr Gerard Crean; ✉ St Ronan's, Duchal Rd, Kilmacolm, Renfrewshire PA13 4AY (☎ 01505 872504)

CREASE, David Plaistow; s of Gilbert Crease, of Beckenham, Kent (d 1971), and Margaret Frances Plaistow (d 1981); *b* 22 July 1928; *Educ* Christ's Hosp, Gonville and Caius Coll Cambridge (MA), Edinburgh Coll of Art (Diploma); *m* 15 Aug 1969, Jane Rosemary, da of Harold Leonard Goodey, of Reading; 1 da (Hermione b 1970); *Career* architect Public Works Dept Hong Kong 1955–59, office of Oscar Niemeyer and in own practice Brasilia 1960–63, chief architect Design Unit Univ of York 1966–81 (awards incl 3 Medals and Civic Tst Award for housing schemes in Yorkshire), in own practice York 1981–; princ works incl: univ housing at Heslington York 1967–74, housing at Beverley Minster (commended by RIBA 1990), Bishop's Wharf York (Housing Design Award 1993), Minerva Mews Yarm Teesside 1995, housing at Owlthorpe Sheffield 1995; RIBA; *Recreations* hunting the clean boot (human scent) with bloodhounds; *Clubs* Pickering Liberal; *Style—* David P Crease, Esq; ✉ Deer Park, Scampston, Malton, N Yorks YO17 8HN; Crease Edmonds Strickland, Architects, Bishopgate House, Skeldergate Bridge, York YO2 1JH (☎ 01904 641289, fax 01904 621808)

CREASEY, Richard John; s of John Creasey, MBE (d 1973), and (Evelyn) Jean, *née* Fudge; *b* 28 Aug 1944; *Educ* Malvern; *m* 5 Jan 1968, Wendy; 2 s (Simon b 19 July 1972, Guy b 1 May 1974), 1 da (Sarah b 19 Jan 1980); *Career* Granada TV: researcher 1965–72, prodr 1972–74; ATV Network: prodr 1974–77, exec prodr 1977–78, head of documentaries 1978–81; Central TV: controller of features 1981–90, dir of special projects 1990–94; dir of factual progs Meridian Broadcasting 1992–94, creative dir The Digital Village 1995–; expedn ldr Ford London-New York Overland Challenge 1993–94; chm Soviet Br Creative Assoc 1989– (dep chm 1989), tstee and co fndr Television Tst for the Environment (TVE), vice chm Wildscreen Tst; *Recreations* family, sailing, reading; *Clubs* BAFTA; *Style—* Richard Creasey, Esq; ✉ 17 St Leonards Road, London SW14 7LY (☎ 0181 876 0375)

CREBER, Frank Paul; s of Dr Geoffrey Tremain Creber, of Wood Green, Fordingbridge, Hants, and Hilda, *née* Lewey; *b* 12 Jan 1959; *Educ* Dr Challoner's GS Amersham Bucks, Univ of Newcastle-upon-Tyne (BA), Chelsea Sch of Art (MA); *m* 1982, Marguerite Honor Blake, da of The Rev Canon Peter Douglas Stuart Blake; 2 s (Theodore Sebastion Peter b 1983, Nicholas Tremaine b 1986); *Career* artist; most important works: White Light/Yellow Light (1987), Within One Flame go Two As One (1987), Open State (1988), Man with Bird (1989), Cliff Dance (1990), The Bather (1991), White Rock (1991), The Family (1993), The Planets (1995); exhibitions incl: Barclays Bank Young Painters Competition (Henry Moore Gallery, RCA London) 1987, Picker Fellowship Show (Kingston Poly (now Kingston Univ)) 1988, two man show (Diorama Gallery London) 1988, solo show (Sue Williams Gallery Portobello Rd London) 1988, 1989, 1991 and 1992, Picker Fellows At Kingston (Watermans Art Centre Brentford) 1989, Artist of The Day (Flowers East London) 1989, two persons show (Paton Gallery) 1990, gp show (ROI at Lloyd's London) 1990, Painting Today (auction at Bonham's Knightsbridge) 1991, Where Art Meets Community (Tobacco Dock London) 1992, Bow's Arts (Sedgewick's Aldgate East London) 1992, Inner City Blues (gp show, Barbican Concourse Gallery) 1993, gp show (Great Banquet Exhibition Banqueting House Whitehall) 1995, gp show (Homerton Hosp London) 1996, solo show (Mosaic Highgate London) 1996; exhibitions organised and curated: Art Meets Community (Tobacco Dock London) 1992, gp show (Bow's Arts Gallery London) 1992, Inner City Blues (Barbican) 1993; works in collections: Unilever plc, Arthur Andersen & Co, Art for Hosps, Stanhope Construction Ltd, Leicestershire Collection, Int Business Machines; artist in residence The Bromley-by-Bow Centre London 1992–; awards: prizewinner Avon Open (Artsite Gallery Bath) 1984, prizewinner Brewhouse Open (Taunton) 1985, Herbert Read fellowship Chelsea Sch of Art 1986, jt winner Barclays Bank Young Painters award 1987, Picker fellowship Kingston Poly (now Kingston Univ) 1987–88; *Style—* Frank Creber, Esq; ✉ 49 Darnley Road, Hackney, London E9 6QH (☎ 0181 533 5104); The Bromley-by-Bow Centre, 1 Bruce Road, London E3 3HN (☎ 0181 980 4618, fax 0181 983 0372)

CREDITON, Bishop of 1996–; Rt Rev Richard Stephen Hawkins; s of John Stanley Hawkins (d 1965), and Elsie, *née* Briggs (d 1992); *b* 2 April 1939; *Educ* Exeter Sch, Exeter Coll Oxford (MA), St Stephen's House Oxford, Univ of Exeter (BPhil); *m* 1966, Valerie Ann, da of Leonard William Herneman; 2 s (Simon b 1967 (decd), Daniel b 1973), 2 da (Rebecca b 1968, Caroline b 1972 (decd)); *Career* team vicar Clyst Valley Team Ministry 1966–78, jt dir Exeter-Truro Ministerial Trg Sch and Bishop of Exeter's offr for ministry 1978–81, diocesan dir of ordinands 1979–81, archdeacon of Totnes 1981–88, bishop of Plymouth 1988–96; *Style—* The Rt Rev the Bishop of Crediton; ✉ 10 The Close, Exeter, Devon EX1 1EZ (☎ 01392 273509)

CREE, Helen; *b* 27 Feb 1954; *Educ* NCTJ proficiency cert in journalism; *Career* journalist Bletchley & Milton Keynes Gazette (Home Counties Newspapers Ltd) Luton Beds 1972–76, asst head of PR Scotland and Northern Ireland Automobile Assoc 1976–80, press and PRO Metal Box plc 1980–81, dir Struthers Public Relations Ltd 1981–83; PR Consultants Scotland: joined as dir of Edinburgh ops 1983, involved in MBO from Grant Forrest Gp 1985, co bought by Shandwick Gp 1989, subsequently i/c personnel and trg, md 1993–; MIPR (chm 1992–93), memb Mktg Soc; *Style—* Helen Cree; ✉ Shandwick Scotland, 9 Lynedoch Crescent, Glasgow G3 6EQ (☎ 0141 333 0557, fax 0141 332 7990, mobile 0836 790072)

CREED, Peter Howard; s of Sidney Howard Creed (d 1971), of Wolverhampton, and Gladys Marguerite, *née* Shaw (d 1977); *b* 27 June 1931; *Educ* Tettenhall Coll Wolverhampton; *m* 1956, Joan, da of Henry Francis (d 1986), of Wolverhampton; 2 s (Michael b 1958, Charles b 1962); *Career* SAC RAF 1954–56; joined Express and Star advertisement rep 1957; advertisement mangr: Shropshire Star 1964 (dir 1968–73), Express and Star 1973; gp advertisement dir The Midlands News Assoc Ltd 1980–91 (incl Express and Star, Shropshire Star and Shropshire Weekly Newspapers), Peter Creed Communications 1991–; dir Precision Colour Printing Ltd Telford 1981–84; chm Newspaper Advertising Conference Ctee 1977–83 (memb Advertising Ctee 1975–91); Newspaper Soc rep on Code of Advertising Practice Ctee for Advertising Standards

Authy 1985–91; govr Tettenhall Coll 1978–; *Recreations* cricket, golf, ardent Wolves Football Club supporter; *Clubs* Penn Cricket (Wolverhampton), Wrekin Golf; *Style—* Peter Creed, Esq; ✉ 218 Henwood Rd, Tettenhall, Wolverhampton, West Midlands WV6 8NZ (☎ 01902 752653)

CREEGOR, Vivien (Mrs Applebaum); da of Leonard Creegor (d 1996), and Stella, *née* Myers; *b* 10 April 1955; *Educ* Orange Hill Girls' GS, City of London Poly; *m* 27 May 1990, David Applebaum, s of Victor and Shirley Applebaum; *Career* presenter, newsreader, journalist; chm 3 UN confs on women's health for WHO (Geneva Switzerland, Beijing China (incl speeches by Hillary Clinton, Julius Nyrere and Jane Fonda); BBC Amateur Actress of the Year Award 1979; memb Greenpeace; *Television and Radio* BBC: prodn assistant Radio Drama Department 1977–80, announcer and newreader Radio 4 1980–81, presenter/reporter Points West Bristol TV News 1982–88, newsreader News After Noon BBC1 1984, sub-editor/scriptwriter TV News 1985–86, presenter/reporter Transit (Sports & Events) 1987, newsreader Newsview BBC2 1988; also for BBC: The Small Business Programme, Breakthrough, Radio 2 newsreader, abridger for A Book at Bedtime Radio 4, reader of morning story, numerous in-house videos; presenter Sky News 1989–; *Recreations* reading, writing, cinema; *Clubs* Groucho's; *Style—* Ms Vivien Creegor; ✉ c/o Fox Artist Management, Concorde House, 101 Shepherd's Bush Road, London W6 7LP (☎ 0171 602 8822, fax 0171 603 3956)

CREEK, Malcolm Lars; LVO (1980), OBE (1985); s of Edgar Creek (d 1977), of Edmonton, Alberta, Canada, and Lily, *née* Robertshaw (d 1950); *b* 2 April 1931; *Educ* Belle Vue Sch Bradford, Univ of London (BA); *m* 1 (m dis 1970), Moira; 1 s (Jeremy b 1960), 1 da (Helen b 1955); m 2, 17 July 1970, Gillian Mary, da of Arthur Ridley Bell (d 1989), of Bertram Drive North, Meols, Wirral; 1 s (Richard b 1975), 2 da (Alison b 1973, Sarah b 1974); *Career* Nat Serv 1950–52; FO 1950 and 1952–56, vice consul Mogadishu and Harar 1956–58, FO 1958–59, 2 sec Mexico City 1959–62 (Abidjan 1962–64, Santiago 1964–68), 1 sec and head of Chancery San Jose 1968–71 (Havana 1972–74), FO 1974–77, 1 sec Tunis 1978–81 (Lima 1981–85), high cmmr Vila Vanuatu 1985–88, consul-gen Auckland 1988–90; *Recreations* family history, tennis; *Style—* Malcolm Creek, Esq, LVO, OBE; ✉ 17 Bertram Drive North, Meols, Wirral, Merseyside L47 OLN (☎ 0151 632 5520)

CREER, Kenneth Ernest; MBE (1993); s of Ernest Lyons Creer (d 1989), of Isle of Man, and Robina, *née* Kelly (d 1975); *b* 29 Aug 1937; *Educ* Douglas HS Isle of Man, Salisbury Sch of Art Wiltshire, Central London Poly, Br Inst of Professional Photography; *m* 5 Dec 1964 (m dis 1996), Pauline Winifred, da of Leslie James Artis; 3 s (Colin Leslie b 12 Dec 1965, Peter b 21 May 1968, Paul Robin b 18 March 1976); m 2, 31 May 1996, Jean Maureen, da of Charles Lucas; *Career* apprentice photographer S R Keig Ltd Isle of Man 1954–57, photographer 16 Ind Parachute Bde 1957–60, photographic printer Speedy Photographic London 1960–61, sr photographer Metropolitan Police New Scotland Yard 1963–68 (photographer 1961–63); Metropolitan Police Forensic Sci Lab (now Forensic Sci Service): head Photographic Section 1968–, princ photographer 1969–83, chief photographer 1983–; responsible for the introduction of specialist criminological photographic techniques; lectr and author of numerous papers on criminological photographic matters; Richard Farrant Meml trophy for distinction in applied photography 1983; FBIPP 1983 (memb 1964), FRPS 1986; *Recreations* sailing, golf; *Style—* Kenneth Creer, Esq, MBE; ✉ Head of Serious Crimes Unit, Forensic Science Service Laboratory, 109 Lambeth Rd, London SE1 7LP (☎ 0171 230 6062)

CREER, (Dahlis) Virginia; da of Cdre Bruce Loxton, RAN (ret), of Sydney, Aust, and Dahlis Ailsa, *née* Robertson; *b* 4 Feb 1948; *Educ* Ascham Sch Sydney Aust, Univ of Sydney (BA); *m* 1971, David Victor Charles Creer, s of Victor Charles Hamish Creer; 1 s (Benjamin Fulke Matthew b 7 Sept 1976), 1 da (Camilla Dahlis Elizabeth b 12 July 1979); *Career* Mktg Div Unilever Ltd 1969–72, asst brand mangr then brand mangr Schweppes Ltd 1972–77 (mktg mangr 1976), account dir Grey Advertising Ltd 1978–80; Davidson Pearce Ltd: sr planner 1980, Bd dir 1982, agency devpt dir 1985–87, exec planning and devpt dir 1987–88; asst md BMP Davidson Pearce Ltd 1988–89, managing ptnr BMP DDB Needham Ltd 1989, md BMP 4 1990–; memb: Mktg Soc 1976, MRS 1980, IPA 1982, Forum 1992; *Recreations* running, riding, sailing; *Clubs* Women's Advertising Club of London; *Style—* Mrs Virginia Creer; ✉ BMP 4, 12 Bishops Bridge Rd, London W2 6AA (☎ 0171 258 3979, fax 0171 258 4455)

CREGEEN, Peter Geoffrey; s of Geoffrey Hugh Stowell Cregeen (d 1980), of Hove, and Viola Gertrude Dorothea, *née* Butler; *b* 28 Jan 1940; *Educ* St Christopher's Sch Hove, Hove Coll, Guildhall Sch of Music and Drama; *m* Carole, da of Frederick Walker; 3 da (Lucy b 5 May 1969, Maria b 23 Aug 1971, Emma b 6 April 1974), 1 s (Tom b (twin) 6 April 1974); *Career* actor Palace Theatre Watford 1959–60, dir and actor Salisbury Playhouse 1960–63 (returned as assoc artistic dir 1969), television dir 1964–87 for BBC (also prodr), ATV, Yorkshire TV, LWT (also prodr) and Thames TV (also prodr), exec prodr The Bill (Thames) 1988, head of drama series BBC Television 1989–93, prodr BBC 1994–95, prodn dir Stoll Moss Theatres 1995–; dir Ludlow Festival 1982–84; cncl memb: Dirs' Guild of GB 1988, RTS 1989–92, BAFTA 1992–96, bd memb: Actors Centre 1989–96 (chm 1995–96), TAPS 1994–96; FGSM; *Recreations* music, gardening; *Style—* Peter Cregeen, Esq; ✉ 2 Ormond Road, Richmond-upon-Thames TW10 6TH (☎ 0181 332 3081)

CREGGY, Stuart; JP (Westminster 1979); s of Leslie Creggy (d 1972), and Fay, *née* Schneider; *b* 27 May 1939; *Educ* Western Univ USA (MA), Law Soc Sch of Law; *Career* admitted slr 1963, cmmr for oaths 1969, currently sr ptnr Talbot Creggy & Co; chm Sussex Co Freeholds plc; memb: Variety Club of GB, Law Soc; fell Royal Philatelic Soc, FIMgt, FFA, ACIArb; *Recreations* swimming, philately; *Clubs* RAC; *Style—* Stuart Creggy, Esq, JP; ✉ 46 Viceroy Court, Prince Albert Road, St Johns Wood, London NW8 7PS (☎ 0171 586 4465); Talbot Creggy & Co, 38 Queen Anne St, London W1M 9LB (☎ 0171 637 8865, fax 0171 637 2630, car 0836 234008, 0836 234009, telex 8954619)

CRERAR, Lorne Donald; s of Ronald Crerar, of Wester Ross, and Isobel Scott, *née* Pollok; *b* 29 July 1954; *Educ* Kelvinside Acad, Univ of Glasgow (LLB Hons, Shaws Stewart Meml Prize and Bennet Miller Prize for Best Private Law Student); *m* 29 Oct 1994, Susan Mary, da Gerard Reilly; *Career* qualified slr 1978; Harper Macleod: ptnr 1985–, co-founding ptnr Business Law Div, head Commercial Property Dept and Banking Law Unit, also currently managing ptnr Harper Macleod; princ legal advsr several fin instns; pt/t visiting lectr Univ of Glasgow; NP; memb Law Soc of Scotland; *Recreations* hill-climbing, golf, First Div rugby referee; *Clubs* Western, Glasgow Art, Arlington Baths; *Style—* Lorne Crerar, Esq; ✉ Harper Macleod, 45 Gordon Street, Glasgow G1 3PE (☎ 0141 221 8888, fax 0141 226 4198)

CRESSWELL, Helen (Mrs Brian Rowe); da of Joseph Edward Cresswell, and Annie Edna, *née* Clarke; *b* 1934; *Educ* Nottingham Girls HS, King's Coll London (BA); *m* 1962, Brian Rowe; 2 da; *Career* freelance author and TV scriptwriter; *TV series* Lizzie Dripping 1973–75, Jumbo Spencer 1976, The Bagthorpe Saga 1980, The Secret World of Polly Flint 1986, Moondial 1988, Five Children and It (adaptation) 1991, The Return of the Psammead 1993, Amy 1993, The Watchers 1995, The Famous Five (co-adaptor) 1995, The Demon Headmaster (adaptation) 1996, The Phoenix and the Carpet (adaptation) 1997; author of numerous plays; *Publications* Sonya-by-the-Shire (1961), Jumbo Spencer (1963), The White Sea Horse (1964), Pietro and the Mule (1965), Jumbo Back to Nature (1965), Where The Wind Blows (1966), Jumbo Afloat (1966), The Piemakers (1967), A Tide for the Captain (1967), The Signposters (1968), The Sea Piper (1968), The Barge Children (1968), The Night-Watchmen (1969), A Game of Catch (1969), A Gift from Winklesea (1969), The Outlanders (1970), The Wilkeses (1970), The Bird Fancier (1971), At the Stroke of Midnight (1971), Lizzie Dripping (1972), The Bongleweed (1972), Lizzie Dripping Again (1974), Butterfly Chase (1975), The Winter of the Birds (1975), My Aunt Polly (1979), My Aunt Polly by the Sea (1980), Dear Shrink (1982), The Secret World of Polly Flint (1982), Ellie and the Hagwitch (1984), Ordinary Jack (1977), Absolute Zero (1978), Bagthorpes Unlimited (1978), Bagthorpes v The World (1979), Bagthorpes Abroad (1984), Bagthorpes Haunted (1985), Moondial (1987), Time Out (1987), Bagthorpes Liberated (1988), The Story of Grace Darling (1998), Two Hoots (1988), Whatever Happened in Winklesea? (1989), Rosie and the Boredom Eater (1989), Almost Goodbye Guzzler (1990), Hokey Pokey Did It! (1990), Meet Posy Bates (1990), Posy Bates Again (1991), Lizzie Dripping and The Witch (1991), The Bagthorpe Triangle (1992), The Return of the Psammead (1992), Posy Bates and the Bag Lady (1993), The Watchers (1993), Classic Fairy Tales (Retold (1993)), Giant (1994), Polly Thumb (1994), Stonestruck (1995), Mystery at Winklesea (1995), Mister Maggs (1995), The Little Sea Horse (1995), Bagthorpes Besieged (1996), Bag of Bones (1997), Sophie and the Sea Wolf (1997); *Recreations* watercolour painting, collecting books, antiques and coincidences, sundial watching; *Style—* Ms Helen Cresswell; ✉ Old Church Farm, Eakring, Newark, Notts NG22 0DA (☎ 01623 870 401)

CRESSWELL, Dr Lyell Richard; s of Jack Cecil Cresswell (d 1986), and Muriel Minnie, *née* Sharp (d 1982); *b* 13 Oct 1944; *Educ* Victoria Univ of Wellington NZ (BMus), Univ of Toronto (MusM), Univ of Aberdeen (PhD); *m* 4 Jan 1972, Catherine Isabel, da of Keith James Mawson, of Otaki, NZ; *Career* composer; works incl: Concerto for Violin and Orchestra (1970), Salm (1977), Prayer for the Cure of a Sprained Back (1979), The Silver Pipes of Ur (1981), Le Sucre du Printemps (1982), O! (1982), Concerto for Cello and Orchestra (1984), The Fallen Dog (1984), Our Day Begins at Midninght (1985), To Aspro Pano Sto Aspro (1985), Speak For Us Great Sea (1985), A Modern Ecstasy (1986), The Pumpkin Massacre (1987), Sextet (1988), Passacagli (1988), Ixion (1988), Voices of Ocean Winds (1989), Ylur (1990), Il Suono di Enormi Distanze (1993), Dragspil (1995); memb: Composers Guild of GB, Assoc of Professional Composers, Scottish Soc of Composers, Composers Assoc of NZ; various works recorded on Continuum label and Linn Records; *Recreations* illustrating the book of Ezekiel; *Style—* Dr Lyell Cresswell; ✉ 4 Leslie Place, Edinburgh, Scotland EH4 1NQ (☎ and fax 0131 332 9181)

CRESSWELL, Hon Mr Justice; Hon Sir Peter John; kt (1991); s of Rev Canon JJ Cresswell, and Madeleine, *née* Foley; *b* 24 April 1944; *Educ* St John's Sch Leatherhead, Queen's Coll Cambridge (MA, LLM); *m* 29 April 1972, Caroline, da of Maj Gen Sir Philip Ward, KCVO, CBE, DL, of Sussex; 2 s (Oliver b 11 Nov 1973 d 1988, Mark b 25 Sept 1975); *Career* called to the Bar Gray's Inn 1966, QC 1983, recorder of the Crown Court 1986–91, bencher Gray's Inn 1989, judge of the High Court of Justice (Queen's Bench Div) 1991–, judge in charge of the Commercial List 1993–94; chm London Common Law and Commercial Bar Assoc 1985–87, memb Senate of Inns of Ct and Bar 1981–86; chm: Gen Cncl of the Bar 1990 (memb 1987–90, vice chm 1989), Cncl Cystic Fibrosis Res Tst (Exec Ctee); hon memb Canadian Bar Assoc 1990; *Books* Encyclopaedia of Banking Law (1982–94); *Recreations* fly-fishing, river management, the Outer Hebrides; *Clubs* Flyfisher's; *Style—* The Hon Mr Justice Cresswell; ✉ Royal Courts of Justice, Strand, London WC2A 2LL

CRESWELL, Alexander Charles Justin; s of Sir Michael Justin Creswell, KCMG (d 1986), and Baroness Charlotte Mea thoe Schwartzenberg en Hohenlandsberg; *b* 14 Feb 1957; *Educ* Winchester, W Surrey Coll of Art & Design, Byam Shaw Sch of Drawing & Painting; *m* 4 July 1992, Mary Curtis, da of John Green, of Calamansac, Cornwall; *Career* artist; tutor The Prince of Wales's Summer Sch in Civil Architecture 1991–, tutor The Prince of Wales's Inst of Architecture London 1992–; pres Ewhurst Village Soc; *Exhibitions* contrib numerous gp exhbns 1982–; solo: White Horse Gallery London 1982, 1983 and 1984, Anima Gallery London 1983, Jonathan Poole Gallery London 1983, 1985 and 1987, Sally Le Gallais Gallery Jersey 1984, Addison Ross Gallery London 1984, 1985 and 1986, Crake Gallery Johannesburg 1984, Bulstrode Gallery London 1985, Brussels Europa Hotel 1985, Ritz Hotel London 1987, Fine Art Trade Guild Gallery London 1989, Arthur Andersen & Co London 1989, Spink & Son London 1991, 1994 and 1997, Atlantic Hotel Jersey 1991, Cadogan Gallery London 1992, China Club Hong Kong 1995; *Commissions* incl: The Royal Collection, Cawdor Castle Tourism Ltd, Parliamentary Art Coll, Duchy of Cornwall, Royal Bank of Scotland, The BBC, London Capital Club; *Books* The Silent Houses of Britain (1991); *Recreations* gardening, sailing, classic cars; *Clubs* Architecture, Art Workers Guild, Port Navas Yacht; *Style—* Alexander Creswell, Esq; ✉ Copse Hill, Ewhurst, Surrey (☎ 01483 277493)

CRESWELL, Brig David Hector Craig; s of Lt-Col John Hector Creswell, OBE, of Colchester, Essex, and Laurette Maxwell, *née* Craig; *b* 12 May 1942; *Educ* Wellington, RMA Sandhurst; *m* 30 Sept 1967, Pamela Mary Scott, da of Dr Denis Dearman Matthews (d 1986), of Winchester; 2 s (Edward b 1969, Nicholas b 1972); *Career* reg cmmn RA 1962, asst def attaché Copenhagen 1979–81, co 40 Field Regt RA 1981–84, directing staff Royal Mil Coll of Sci 1984–85, superintendent Proof and Experimental Estab Shoeburyness 1985–87, dir Rapier 1988–91; dir of mktg British Aerospace Defence plc 1991–; FIMgt 1986; *Recreations* sailing, golf, skiing, walking, reading; *Style—* Brig David Creswell; ✉ British Aerospace Defence plc, Dynamics Division, Six Hills Way, Stevenage, Herts SG1 2DA

CRETNEY, Dr Stephen Michael; Hon QC (1992); s of Fred Cretney (d 1980), and Winifred Mary Valentine, *née* Rowlands (d 1982); *Educ* The Manchester Warehousemen and Clerks Orphan Schs Cheadle Hulme, Magdalen Coll Oxford (DCL, MA); *m* 7 July 1973, Rev Antonia Lois, da of Cdr Anthony George Glanusk Vanrenen, RN, of Fordingbridge, Hants; 2 s (Matthew b 1975, Edward b 1979); *Career* Nat Serv 1954–56; admitted slr 1962, ptnr Macfarlanes 1964–65, Kenya Sch of Law Nairobi 1966–67, Univ of Southampton 1967–68, fell Exeter Coll Oxford 1968–78, law cmmr 1978–83, prof of law Univ of Bristol 1983–93 (dean of faculty 1984–88), fell All Souls Coll Oxford 1993–; FBA 1985; *Books* The Enduring Power of Attorney (with D Lush, 4 edn 1976), Principles of Family Law (with Prof J M Masson, 6 edn 1996), Elements of Family Law (3 edn, 1997); author of other legal texts and articles in learned jls; *Clubs* Utd Oxford and Cambridge Univ; *Style—* Dr Stephen Cretney, QC, FBA; ✉ All Souls College, Oxford OX1 4AL (☎ 01865 279379, fax 01865 279299)

CREW, Chief Constable Edward Michael; QPM; s of Joseph Edwin Crew (d 1993), and Cecilia Mary Crew (d 1995); *b* 13 Jan 1946; *Educ* Haberdashers' Aske's, RCDS; *m* Gillian Winifred Crew, da of Edward Frederick John Glover; 1 da (Lynne Gillian b 29 Jan 1969), 1 s (Duncan Edward b 10 March 1971); *Career* police constable rising to chief supt Metropolitan Police 1965–84 (cadet 1962–65), dep chief constable Kent Co Constabulary 1989–93 (asst chief constable 1984–89); chief constable: Northamptonshire Police 1993–96, West Midlands Police 1996–; memb ACPO 1984; *Recreations* memb Gideons, walking, gardening, doing-it-myself badly; *Style—* Chief Constable Edward Crew, QPM; ✉ West Midlands Police HQ, Lloyd House, Colmore Circus, Queensway, Birmingham B4 6NQ

CREWE, Candida Annabel; da of Quentin Hugh Crewe, *qv*, of London, and Angela Maureen Huth, *qv*; *b* 6 June 1964; *Educ* The Manor Sch Great Durnford Wilts, St Mary's Sch Calne Wilts, Headington Sch Oxford; *Career* bookshop asst 1983–86, jr ed Quartet Books Ltd London 1985–86, journalist weekly column London Evening Standard 1985–86; freelance journalist 1986–: The Spectator, The Guardian, The Independent, The Times, The Daily Telegraph, The Sunday Telegraph, The Observer, The Sunday

Times, Tatler, Harpers & Queen, Marie-Claire, You Magazine, The Evening Standard; *Awards* runner-up for Catherine Pakenham meml award for Journalism 1987, winner Catherine Pakenham award for Journalism 1990; memb PEN Int; *Books* Focus (1985), Romantic Hero (1986), Accommodating Molly (1989), Mad About Bees (1991), Falling Away (1996); *Recreations* photography; *Clubs* Groucho; *Style—* Miss Candida Crewe

CREWE, Prof Ivor Martin; s of late Francis Crewe, of West Didsbury, Manchester, and Lilly Edith, *née* Neustadtl; *b* 15 Dec 1945; *Educ* Manchester GS, Exeter Coll Oxford (MA), LSE (MSc); *m* 3 July 1968, Jill Barbara, da of Dr Theo Gadian, of Salford; 2 s (Ben b 1974, Daniel b 1977), 1 da (Deborah b 1972); *Career* asst lectr Dept of Politics Univ of Lancaster 1967–69, jr res fell Nuffield Coll Oxford 1969–71; Univ of Essex: lectr 1971, sr lectr 1974, dir ESRC data archive 1974–82, prof Dept of Govt 1982–, pro-vice chllr (academic) 1992–95, vice-chllr 1995–; co-dir British Election Study 1973–82, ed British Jl of Political Sci 1977–82 and 1984–92; commentator on elections and public opinion for Channel 4, The Guardian and The Observer; memb: Political Studies Assoc, American Political Studies Assoc; *Books* A Social Survey of Higher Civil Service (1969), Decade of Dealignment (1983), The British Electorate 1963–1987 (1991), SDP: The Birth, Life and Death of the Social Democratic Party (1995); *Recreations* opera, walking; *Style—* Prof I M Crewe; ✉ University of Essex, Colchester, Essex CO4 3SQ (☎ 01206 872000, fax 01206 879493, e-mail vc@essex.ac.uk)

CREWE, Quentin Hugh; s of Maj Hugh Dodds Crewe, CMG, TD, of HM Consular Serv (*né* Dodds but changed name by deed poll 1945) and Lady Annabel, da of 1 and last Marquess of Crewe, KG, PC, JP; *b* 14 Nov 1926; *Educ* Eton, Trinity Coll Cambridge; *m* 1, 1956, Martha Sharp; 1 s (Sebastian b 1958), 1 da (Sabrina b 1959); m 2, 1961 (m dis 1970), Angela Huth, *qv*; 1 da (Candida Crewe, *qv*), and 1 s decd; m 3, 1970 (m dis 1983), Susan, da of Capt Richard Cavendish, JP, DL (s of Col Rt Hon Lord Richard Cavendish, CB, CMG, yr bro of 9 Duke of Devonshire); 1 s (Nathaniel b 1971), 1 da (Charity b 1972); *Career* journalist (articles particularly on food) and author; has written for Queen, Vogue, Daily Mail, Sunday Times, Sunday Mirror, Sunday Telegraph, Spectator; *Books* A Curse of Blossom (1960), Frontiers of Privilege (1961), Great Chefs of France (1979), International Pocket Food Book (1980), In Search of the Sahara (1983), The Last Maharaja (1985), Touch the Happy Isles (1987), In the Realms of Gold (1989), Well, I Forget the Rest (1991), Foods from France (1993), Crewe House (1995); *Recreations* travel; *Style—* Quentin Crewe, Esq; ✉ 9 Bliss Mill, Chipping Norton, Oxon OX7 5JR (☎ 01608 642176, fax 01608 642178)

CREWE, Rosemary Anne (Romy); *see:* Newell, Rosemary Anne (Romy)

CREWE, Thomas Cavey; s of Henry Alexander Crewe (d 1959), of Christchurch, NZ, and Ethel Ina, *née* Gillman (d 1945); *b* 5 Oct 1925; *Educ* Christchurch Boys' HS, Univ of Otago (BDS); *m* 1, 5 April 1952, Gweneth Jessie (d 1986), da of Francis Frederick Jolly (d 1957), of Auckland, NZ; 1 s (Simon b 1958), 1 da (Rachel (Mrs Fairhead) b 1960); m 2, 17 June 1995, Linda Diane, da of James Albert Kressinger (d 1992), of Plymouth, Devon; *Career* RNZAF 1945; conslt oral and maxillofacial surgn 1959–90, civil conslt to RN 1970–90; memb Cncl IAOMS 1982–88; pres: BAOMS 1984–85, Oral Surgery Club of GB 1989–90; memb: Forensic Sci Soc, Br Assoc of Forensic Odontologists, RCS (FDS 1960), BDA, BAOMS, IAOMS, RN Med Club; FRSM; *Recreations* photography, travel, walking; *Clubs* RSM; *Style—* Thomas Crewe, Esq; ✉ 2 Torland Road, Hartley, Plymouth, Devon PL3 5TS (☎ 01752 772422)

CRIBB, Evelyn Francis Theodore; s of Canon Charles Theodore Cribb (d 1976); descended from John Evelyn (b 1620), the diarist, one of the original fellows of the Royal Soc; *b* 24 June 1929; *Educ* Marlborough, Christ's Coll Cambridge; *m* 1956 (m dis), Jane Howard, da of Ronald Le Grice Eyre (d 1940); 1 s (Nigel b 1958), 2 da (Philippa b 1961, Fiona b 1965); m 2, Annabelle Southon; *Career* called to the Bar Middle Temple 1954; appts with: General Motors, GEC, BOC; dir Freemans plc 1977–89 (co sec 1971–89); memb: Euro Cmmn's Advsy Ctee on Commerce and Distribution (rapporteur gen for consumer affairs) 1986–95, Copyright Tbnl 1990–, Isle of Man Copyright Tbnl 1992–; dir: Brixton Information Technology Centre 1981–89, Direct Mail Services Standards Bd 1983–93, Commercial Union Local Bd 1983–88, Business in the Community Cncl 1986–89; chm: Mailing Preference Serv 1987–89, Peckham Settlement, Cncl BASSAC 1983–85; memb CBI Cncl 1983–89, dep chm S London Business Initiative 1989–92; cncllr London Borough of Fulham (Cons ldr) 1959–62, tstee Freemans Tst 1979–; memb: Gen Ctee BACFI 1987–96, Ctee IOD (W Surrey Branch) 1993–; assoc memb Hockey Assoc; *Style—* Evelyn Cribb, Esq; ✉ The Squirrels, Fox Corner, Worplesdon, Guildford, Surrey GU3 3PP (☎ 01483 236278)

CRIBBINS, Bernard; s of John Edward Cribbins (d 1964), and Ethel, *née* Clarkson (d 1989); *b* 29 Dec 1928; *Educ* St Annes Elementary Sch Oldham Lancs; *m* 27 Aug 1955, Gillian Isabella, da of Maj Donald Victor Charles McBarnet (ka 1943); *Career* actor; serv 3 Bn (later 2/3 Bn) Parachute Regt Palestine 1947–48, 16 Div HQ Germany 1949; asst stage mangr student Oldham Repertory Theatre aged 14; vice pres SPARKS; *Theatre* West End debut in Comedy of Errors (Arts Theatre) 1956; performances incl: Harmony Close, Lady at the Wheel, New Cranks, And Another Thing, The Big Tickle, Hook Line and Sinker, Not Now Darling, There Goes The Bride, Run for Your Wife, Guys and Dolls, Anything Goes, Doolittle in My Fair Lady (Houston Grand Opera Texas), Lady Be Good (Regents Park Open Air Theatre), Prof Otto Marvuglia in La Grande Magia (RNT) 1995; *Television* own series: Cribbins, Cuffy, Langley Bottom; title role in Dangerous Davies, Good Old Days, Shillingbury Tales, High and Dry, Fawlty Towers, Call My Bluff; voices for The Wombles and Buzby; *Films* incl: The Railway Children 1971, Casino Royale, Two Way Stretch, Wrong Arm of the Law, She, Carry On Jack, Carry On Spying, The Water Babies, Carry On Columbus 1992; *Recordings* hit records incl: Right Said Fred, Hole in the Ground, Gossip Calypso; *Recreations* fishing, shooting, golf; *Style—* Bernard Cribbins, Esq; ✉ c/o James Sharkey Associates Ltd, 21 Golden Square, London W1R 3PA (☎ 0171 434 3801, fax 0171 494 1547)

CRICHTON, Charles Ainslie; s of John Douglas Crichton (d 1963), of Wallasey, and Hester Wingate *née* Ainslie (d 1959); *b* 6 Aug 1910; *Educ* Oundle, New Coll Oxford (BA); *m* 1, Dec 1936 (m dis), Pearl Allan; 2 s (David b 1938, Nicholas b 1943); m 2, Nadine Charlotte Haze; *Career* film writer and director: *Television* numerous credits incl: Danger Man, The Avengers, Black Beauty, Space 1999, Smuggler, Adventurer; *Films* incl: Dead of Night (co-dir) 1947; as dir: Hue and Cry 1947, Against the Wind, Another Shore, Dance Hall, The Lavender Hill Mob 1951, The Titfield Thunderbolt 1953, The Love Lottery, The Divided Heart, Law and Disorder, Floods of Fear, Battle of the Sexes 1959, Boy Who Stole a Million 1960, The Third Secret 1963, He Who Rides a Tiger 1965, A Fish Called Wanda 1987; *Recreations* fishing, photography; *Style—* Charles Crichton, Esq; ✉ 1 Southwell Gardens, London SW7 4SB (☎ 0171 373 6546)

CRICHTON, Viscount; John Henry Michael Ninian Crichton; s and h of 6 Earl of Erne; *b* 19 June 1971; *Educ* Sunningdale Sch, Shiplake Coll, L'Institut de Touraine Tours France; *Recreations* theatre, arts, tennis, shooting, fishing; *Clubs* Lough Erne Yacht; *Style—* Viscount Crichton; ✉ Flat 4, 40 Harcourt Terrace, London SW10; Crom Castle, Newtown Butler, Co Fermanagh, Northern Ireland

CRICHTON, Maurice Peter; CBE (1994); s of Maurice Crichton (d 1957), of Glasgow, and Jenny Shirra, *née* Ferguson (d 1964); *b* 4 June 1928; *Educ* Cargilfield Sch, Sedbergh; *m* 30 April 1959, Diana Russell, da of John Russell Lang, CBE (d 1993), of Tetbury, Glos; 3 s (Russell Lang b 1960, Maurice Peter b 1964, David Ferguson b 1968), 1 da (Caroline Anne b 1962); *Career* Nat Serv Royal Tank Regt 1947–49; ptnr Wilson Stirling & Co CAs Glasgow 1956, subsequently ptnr Touche Ross & Co, ret from practice 1986; dir Woolwich Building Society 1977–, chm Irvine Devpt Corp 1991–; Deacon Convener of Trades of Glasgow 1988–89; MICAS 1955; *Recreations* golf, shooting, music, trout fishing; *Clubs* Caledonian, Western (Glasgow); *Style—* Maurice Crichton, Esq, CBE; ✉ 26 Newtyle Road, Ralston, Paisley PA1 3JX (☎ 0141 889 3660, fax 0141 887 3277); The Marne, Grange Rd, Earlsferry, Leven, Fife (☎ 01333 330222)

CRICHTON, Nicholas; s of Charles Ainslie Crichton, and Vera Pearl McCallum, *née* Harman-Mills; *b* 23 Oct 1943; *Educ* Haileybury, Queens Univ Belfast (LLB); *m* 29 March 1973, Ann Valerie, da of Col John Eliot Jackson, of Lopcombe Corner, nr Salisbury, Wilts; 2 s (Simon b 25 Feb 1975, Ian b 12 Jan 1977); *Career* admitted slr 1970; asst slr Currey & Co 1970–71 (articled 1968–70), ptnr Nicholls Christie & Crocker 1974–86 (asst slr 1972–74); met stipendiary magistrate 1987–, recorder of the Crown Court 1995– (asst recorder 1991–95); *Recreations* cricket, golf, watching rugby, gardening, birdwatching, walking; *Style—* Nicholas Crichton, Esq; ✉ c/o Inner London Family Proceedings Court, 185 Marylebone Road, London NW1 5QG

CRICHTON-STUART, Lord Anthony; yr s of 6 Marquess of Bute (d 1993); *b* 14 May 1961; *Educ* Ampleforth, Univ of Durham; *m* 8 Sept 1990, Alison J, yr da of Keith Bruce, of Highgate, London; 2 da (Flora Grace b 10 Nov 1994, Eliza Rose b 7 March 1996); *Career* art expert; vice pres Old Master Paintings Dept Christie's; *Clubs* Brooks's; *Style—* The Lord Anthony Crichton-Stuart

CRICK, Prof Bernard Rowland; s of Harry Edgar Crick (d 1968), and Florence Clara, *née* Cook (d 1987); *b* 16 Dec 1929; *Educ* Whitgift Sch, UCL (BSc), LSE (PhD), Harvard Univ; *m* 18 Sept 1953 (m dis 1980), Joyce Pumpfrey Morgan; 2 s (Oliver, Tom); *Career* lectr LSE 1957–59; prof of politics: Univ of Sheffield 1965–71, Birkbeck Coll London 1971–84; hon fell Univ of Edinburgh 1984–, visiting fell Woodrow Wilson Centre 1995–96; literary ed The Political Quarterly 1993– (jt ed 1966–80), winner Yorks Post Book of the Year Award 1980; memb Cncl Hansard Soc 1962–92, hon pres Politics Assoc 1970–76, hon vice pres Political Studies Assoc 1994–; chm: The Political Quarterly Publishing Co 1980–93, Orwell Memorial Tst 1981, British Ctee of British and South African Conf 1991–94; Hon DSSc Queen's Univ Belfast 1988, Hon Dr of Arts Univ of Sheffield 1990; Hon DLitt: E London Univ 1990, Kingston Univ 1996; *Books* The American Science of Politics (1958), In Defence of Politics (1962, latest edn 1992), The Reform of Parliament (1964), Crime, Rape and Gin (1975), George Orwell, A Life (1980, latest edn 1992), Socialism (1987), Essays on Politics and Literature (1989), Political Thoughts and Polemics (1990); *Recreations* polemicising, book and theatre reviewing, hill walking; *Clubs* Savile, Univ of Edinburgh; *Style—* Prof Bernard Crick; ✉ 8A Bellevue Terrace, Edinburgh EH7 4DT (☎ and fax 0131 557 2517)

CRICK, Charles Anthony; s of Maurice Arthur Crick, TD (d 1979), of 42 Westwood Park Road, Peterborough, and Margaret Matilda, *née* Edney; *b* 7 May 1949; *Educ* Oundle Sch, UCL (LLB); *Career* admitted slr 1974, articled clerk and asst slr Allen and Overy 1972–80, asst slr Middleton Potts and Co 1980–81, ptnr D J Freeman and Co 1981–; Freeman City of London Slrs' Co 1986; memb Law Soc; *Recreations* golf, music, painting; *Clubs* Hunstanton Golf, The Addington Golf; *Style—* Charles Crick, Esq; ✉ D J Freeman, 43 Fetter Lane, London EC4A 1NA (☎ 0171 583 4055)

CRICK, Prof Francis Harry Compton; OM (1991); *b* 8 June 1916; *Educ* UCL (BSc), Caius Coll Cambridge (PhD); *m* 2, Odile, *née* Speed; 3 c; *Career* scientist with Admiralty 1940–47, Med Res Cncl student Strangeways Lab Cambridge 1947–49, Med Res Cncl Lab of Molecular Biology Cambridge 1949–77 (housed in Cavendish Lab until 1962), J W Kieckhefer distinguished res prof Salk Inst for Biological Studies La Jolla Calif and adjunct prof Psychology Dept Univ of Calif San Diego 1977–; pres The Salk Inst 1994–95; Protein Structure Project Brooklyn Poly NYC 1953–54, visiting prof Chemistry Dept Harvard Univ 1959, visiting lectr Rockefeller Inst NY 1959, visiting prof of biophysics Harvard Univ 1962, Ferkhauf Fndn visiting prof Salk Inst 1976–77; Warren Triennial Prize Lecture (with J D Watson) 1959, Lasker Award (with J D Watson and M H F Wilkins) 1960, Prix Charles Leopold Mayer French Academies des Sciences 1961, Research Corp Award (with J D Watson) 1961, Nobel Prize for Physiology or Medicine (with J D Watson and M H F Wilkins) 1962, Gairdner Fndn Award Toronto 1962, Royal Medal Royal Soc London 1972, Copley Medal Royal Soc London 1975, Michelson-Morley Award Cleveland Ohio 1981, Benjamin P Cheney Medal Spokane Washington 1986, Golden Plate Acad of Achievement Malibu Calif 1987, Joseph Priestly Award Dickinson Coll Carlisle Penn 1988, Wright Prize VIII Harvey Mudd Coll Claremont Calif 1988, Albert Medal for 1987 RSA London 1988; hon fell: Churchill Coll Cambridge 1965, Royal Soc of Edinburgh 1966, Caius Coll Cambridge 1976, Indian Acad of Sciences 1985, John Muir Coll Univ of Calif San Diego 1986, Inst of Biology London 1995, Tata Inst of Fundamental Research Bombay 1996; foreign hon memb American Acad of Arts and Sciences 1962, hon memb American Soc of Biological Chemists 1963, hon memb Royal Irish Acad 1964, foreign assoc Nat Acad of Sciences USA 1969, memb German Acad of Science Leopoldina 1969, foreign memb American Philosophical Soc Philadelphia 1972, hon memb Hellenic Biochemical and Biophysical Soc 1974, assoc foreign memb French Acad of Sciences 1978; FRS 1959; fell: UCL 1962, American Assoc for the Advancement of Sci 1966, Indian Nat Science Acad 1982, Rochester Museum NY 1984; *Style—* Prof Francis Crick, OM, FRS; ✉ The Salk Institute for Biological Studies, 10010 N Torrey Pines Road, La Jolla, CA 92037, USA

CRICK, Richard William; s of Cyril Albert Edden Crick (d 1988), of Easton-in-Gordano, Avon, and Blanche Helen, *née* Prewett; *b* 7 June 1946; *Educ* Clifton Coll, Brasenose Coll Oxford (MA); *m* 17 July 1971 (sep), Judith Margaret, da of Huw Jackson (d 1982), of Gateshead; 1 s (James b 1974), 1 da (Sally b 1977); *Career* accountant Deloitte Haskins and Sells 1967–71; banker: Hill Samuel & Co Ltd 1972–87 (dir 1981–87), md Hill Samuel Merchant Bank (SA) Ltd 1981–85, dir Barclays de Zoete Wedd Ltd 1988–, md Corp Finance Div Barclays Tokyo 1992–95, vice-chm Corp Finance Div Barclays de Zoete Wedd Ltd 1995–; FCA; *Recreations* golf, skiing, sailing, travel, wine; *Clubs* St Enodoc Golf, Wentworth Golf; *Style—* Richard W Crick, Esq; ✉ 2 Craven Hill Mews, London W2 3DY (☎ 0171 402 8096); Barclays de Zoete Wedd Ltd, Ebbgate House, 2 Swan Lane, London EC4R 3TS (☎ 0171 623 2323, fax 0171 956 4662)

CRICK, Ronald Pitts; s of Owen John Pitts Crick (d 1972), of Minehead, Somerset, and Margaret, *née* Daw (d 1970); *b* 5 Feb 1917; *Educ* Latymer Upper Sch London, King's Coll Hosp Med Sch; *m* 22 March 1941, Jocelyn Mary Grenfell, da of Leonard Adolph Charles Robins (d 1968), of Hendon; 4 s (Martin b 1942, Jonathan b 1948, Adrian b 1950, Humphrey b 1957), 1 da (Gillian b 1944); *Career* surgn South America route MN 1939–40, Surgn Lt RNVR Fleet Air Arm Atlantic, Indian Ocean, Pacific theatres 1940–46; King's Coll Hosp: ophthalmic registrar 1946–50, conslt ophthalmic surgn 1950–82, hon conslt ophthalmic surgn 1982–; Royal Eye Hosp: ophthalmic registrar 1946–50, conslt surgn 1950–69; conslt ophthalmic surgn Belgrave Hosp for Children 1950–66, examiner RCS 1961–68; King's Coll Med Sch: teacher of ophthalmology 1960–82, lectr emeritus in ophthalmology 1982–; memb Ophthalmic Speciality Ctee SE Thames Regnl Hosp Bd 1970–82; chm: Ophthalmic Trg Ctee SE Thames RHA 1973–82, Int Glaucoma Assoc 1974–; Duke-Elder Glaucoma Award American Soc of Contemporary Ophthalmology 1985, Alim Meml lectr Ophthalmological Soc of Bangladesh; MRCS, LRCP 1939, DOMS (RCS) 1946, FRCS 1950; memb Oxford Ophthalmological Congress 1943, FRSM 1950, charter memb Int Glaucoma Congress American Soc Contemporary Ophthalmology 1977; memb: Int Perimetic Soc 1974–, Euro Glaucoma Soc 1980–; FRCOphth 1989; *Books* The Computerised Monitoring of Glaucoma in Glaucoma-Contemporary International Concepts (J Bellows, 1979), The

Diagnosis of Chronic Simple Glaucoma in Glaucoma (J Cairns, 1985), All About Glaucoma (1981), A Textbook of Clinical Ophthalmology (1987, 2 edn 1996); *Recreations* motoring, sailing, swimming; *Clubs* RAC, Royal Motor Yacht; *Style*— Ronald Pitts Crick, Esq; ✉ Sandbanks House, Panorama Rd, Sandbanks, Poole, Dorset, BH13 7RD (☎ and fax 01202 707560); King's College Hospital, Denmark Hill, London SE5 9RS (☎ 0171 737 4000 ext 2934, ☎ and fax 0171 737 3265)

CRICKHOWELL, Baron (Life Peer UK 1987), of Pont Esgob in the Black Mountains and Co of Powys; (Roger) Nicholas Edwards; PC (1979); s of (Herbert Cecil) Ralph Edwards, CBE, FSA (d 1977), and Marjorie Ingham Brooke; *b* 25 Feb 1934; *Educ* Westminster, Trinity Coll Cambridge (BA, MA); *m* 1963, Ankaret, da of William James Healing, of Kinsham House, nr Tewkesbury, Glos; 1 s (Hon Rupert Timothy Guy b 1964), 2 da (Hon Sophie Elizabeth Ankaret b 1966, Hon Olivia Caroline b 1970); *Career* 2 Lt Royal Welch Fusiliers 1952–54; employed at Lloyd's by Wm Brandt's 1957–76 (memb Lloyd's 1968–), chief exec Insur Gp; dir: Wm Brandt's Ltd 1974–76, R W Sturge (Holdings) Ltd 1970–76, PA International and Sturge Underwriting Agency Ltd 1977–79, Globtik Tankers Ltd 1976–79, Ryan International plc and subsids 1987–89, Associated British Ports Holdings plc 1987, HTV Group plc 1987–; dep chm Anglesey Mining plc 1988–, chm ITnet Holdings Ltd 1996–; MP (Cons) for Pembroke 1970–87 (ret), memb Shadow Cabinet and Cons Front Bench spokesman on Welsh Affairs 1974–79, sec of State of Wales 1979–87; chm: Nat Rivers Authority Advsy Ctee 1988–89, Nat Rivers Authority 1989–96; memb Ctee The Automobile Assoc; pres: Univ of Wales Coll of Cardiff 1988–, Contemporary Art Soc for Wales 1988–93, South East Wales Arts Assoc 1987–94; *Recreations* fishing, gardening, collecting drawings & watercolours; *Clubs* Cardiff and County, Brooks's; *Style*— The Rt Hon Lord Crickhowell, PC; ✉ Pont Esgob Mill, Fforest Coal Pit, nr Abergavenny, Gwent NP7 7LS; 4 Henning St, London SW11 3DR

CRIGHTON, Prof David George; s of George Wolfe Johnston Crighton (d 1976), and Violet Grace, *née* Garrison; *b* 15 Nov 1942; *Educ* Watford Boys GS, St John's Coll Cambridge (BA, MA, ScD), Imperial Coll London (PhD); *m* 1, 2 March 1969 (m dis 1986), Mary Christine, da of Stanley James West, of Tamworth; 1 s (Benjamin b 23 April 1970), 1 da (Beth b 3 Oct 1971); m 2, 6 Sept 1986, Johanna Veronica, *née* Hol; *Career* prof of applied mathematics Univ of Leeds 1974–85; Univ of Cambridge: prof of applied mathematics 1986–, professorial fell St John's Coll 1986–, head Dept of Applied Mathematics and Theoretical Physics 1991–; author of various scientific papers in jls and conf proceedings on fluid mechanics, acoustics, wave theory and applied mathematics; pres EUROMECH-Euro Mechanics Soc 1993–; FRAeS 1982, FIMA 1986, FIOA 1988, FRS 1993; *Recreations* music, opera; *Style*— Prof David G Crighton, FRS; ✉ The Laurels, 58 Girton Rd, Cambridge CB3 0LN (☎ 01223 277100); University of Cambridge, DAMTP, Silver St, Cambridge CB3 9EW (☎ 01223 337860, fax 01223 337918/312984, telex 81240 G)

CRIGHTON, Dr Gordon Stewart; s of Allan Crighton (d 1971), of Balbeggie, Perthshire, and Margaret, *née* Stewart; *b* 29 April 1937; *Educ* Perth Acad, Univ of St Andrews (BSc); *m* 25 Aug 1962, Margaret, da of late James Stephen; 4 da (Suzanne Elizabeth b 18 Sept 1963, Isla Margaret b 16 March 1966, Heather Frances b 17 March 1967, Jennifer Rhona b 13 March 1968), 1 s (Andrew Gordon b 5 Feb 1965); *Career* Mott Hay & Anderson Consulting Engrs 1959–63 and 1965–66, Sir William Halcrow & Partners Consulting Engrs 1963–65 and 1967–78, L N Henderson & Associates Consulting Engrs 1966–67 and 1969–71, project mangr Kinhill Project Mangrs and Engrs 1971–72, project co-ordinator and chief resident engr Brian Colquhoun & Partners Consulting Engrs 1975–78, Valentine Laurie & Davies Consulting Engrs 1972–75 and 1978–82; Balfour Beatty 1982–93: head Civil Engrg Dept Project Engrg Div 1982–86, engrg dir Channel Tunnel 1986–92, engrg dir Kuala Lumpur Int Airport Malaysia 1992–93; project mangr construction (exec mangr) Mass Transit Railway Corporation 1993–; author of numerous symposiums on civil engrg worldwide; Hon DSc Univ of Kent 1992; fell American Soc of Civil Engrs 1982, FICE 1982, fell Instn of Engrs Hong Kong 1994, FEng 1995; *Recreations* golf; *Style*— Dr Gordon Crighton, FEng; ✉ 11 The Haystacks, High Wycombe, Bucks HP13 6PY (☎ 01494 440638); Mass Transit Railway Corporation, World Trade Square Tower, 123 Hoi Bun Road, Ngau Tau Kok, Hong Kong (☎ 00 852 2993 3528, 00 852 2758 5332)

CRIGMAN, David Ian; QC (1989); s of Jack Crigman (d 1987), and Sylvia, *née* Rich; *b* 16 Aug 1945; *Educ* King Edward's Sch Birmingham, Univ of Leeds (LLB); *m* 20 Aug 1980, Judith Ann, da of Mark Penny; 1 s (Sam Mark b 7 April 1982); *Career* called to the Bar Gray's Inn 1969, recorder of the Crown Court 1985–; *Recreations* writing, tennis, skiing; *Style*— David Crigman, Esq, QC; ✉ 1 Fountain Court, Steelhouse Lane, Birmingham B4 6DR (☎ 0121 236 5721, fax 0121 236 3639)

CRILL, Sir Peter Leslie; KBE (1995, CBE 1980), kt (1987); s of Sydney George Crill (d 1959, Connetable of St Clement 1916–58), of Jersey, and Olive, *née* Le Gros (d 1978); family were boatbuilders who came to Jersey from Mannheim in 1785; *b* 1 Feb 1925; *Educ* Victoria Coll Jersey, Exeter Coll Oxford (MA); *m* 1953, Abigail Florence Rosaline, da of Albert Ernest Dodd, JP (d 1949), of Dromara, NI; 3 da (Joanna b 1954, Anthea b 1956, Helena b 1958); *Career* called to the Bar Middle Temple 1949, called to Jersey Bar 1949; States of Jersey: dep for St Clement 1951–58, senator 1960–62, slr gen 1962–69, attorney gen 1969–75, dep bailiff 1975–86, bailiff 1986–95; hon fell Exeter Coll Oxford 1991; CStJ 1994; FICArb; *Recreations* riding, sailing; *Clubs* United Oxford and Cambridge Univ, Royal Yacht Squadron; *Style*— Sir Peter Crill, KBE; ✉ Beechfield House, Trinity, Jersey

CRIPPS, (Matthew) Anthony Leonard; CBE (1971), DSO (1943), TD (1947), QC (1958); s of Maj Hon Leonard Harrison Cripps, CBE (d 1959, 3 s of 1 Baron Parmoor), and Miriam Barbara, *née* Joyce (d 1960); hp of cousin, 4 Baron Parmoor; *b* 30 Dec 1913; *Educ* Eton, ChCh Oxford (MA); *m* 21 June 1941, (Dorothea) Margaret (d 1992), da of George Johnson-Scott (d 1964), of Hill House, Ashby-de-la-Zouch; 3 s (Seddon b 1942, Jeremy b 1943, James b 1956); *Career* 2 Lt to Lt-Col Royal Leics Regt TA 1933–45; called to the Bar Middle Temple 1938 (bencher 1965, dep treas 1982, treas 1983), Inner Temple 1961, Hong Kong 1974, Singapore 1987; recorder: Nottingham 1961–71, Crown Ct 1972–77; judge Ct of Arches 1969–80, dep sr judge Br Sovereign Bases Area Cyprus 1978–90; memb: Senate Four Inns of Ct 1967–71 and 1982–83, Bar Cncl 1967–69 and 1970–74; chm: Disciplinary Ctee Milk Mktg Bd 1956–90, IOM Agric Mktg Cmmn 1961–62, Home Sec's Advsy Ctee on Serv Parly Candidates 1966–90, Nat Panel Approved Coal Merchants Scheme 1972–90, Legal Advsy Ctee RSPCA 1977–90; memb Agric Wages Bd 1964–73; memb Miny of Agric Ctees of Inquiry: foot and mouth disease 1968–69, export of live animals for slaughter 1973–74; chm: Reigate Cons Assoc 1961–64, Res Ctee Soc of Cons Lawyers 1963–67, Cons Pty Res Ctee of Inquiry into discrimination against women in law and admin 1968–69; memb Exec Ctee Nat Union of Cons Assocs 1964–72, cmmr local govt election petitions 1978–82; pres Coal Trade Benevolent Assoc 1983; Worshipful Co of Fuellers: Jr Warden 1988, Sr Warden 1989, Master 1990–91; *Books* Agriculture Act (1947), Agricultural Holdings Act (1948), Cripps on Compensation (9 edn), Spice of Life (1992); *Recreations* travel, forestry, family life; *Clubs* Brooks's, Phyllis Court; *Style*— Anthony Cripps, Esq, CBE, DSO, TD, QC; ✉ Woodhurst, McCrae's Walk, Wargrave, Berks RG10 8LN (☎ 0118 940 3449); chambers: 1 Harcourt Buildings, Temple, London EC4Y 9DA (☎ 0171 353 9421/9151, fax 0171 353 4170, telex 8956718 CRIPPS G)

CRIPPS, Sir (Cyril) Humphrey; kt (1989); s of Sir Cyril Thomas Cripps, MBE (d 1979), and Amy Elizabeth, *née* Humphrey (d 1984); *b* 2 Oct 1915; *Educ* Northampton GS, St John's Coll Cambridge (MA); *m* 1942, Dorothea Casson, da of Reginald Percy Cook (d 1968); 3 s (Robert, John d 1989, Edward), 1 da (Eleanor d 1994); *Career* chm Pianoforte Supplies Ltd 1979– (md 1960–); chm: Air BVI 1971–86, Velcro Indust NV 1973–96, Cripps Fndn 1979–; memb: Northants CC 1963–74 (ldr Independents), New CC 1973–81; bd memb Northampton Devpt Corp 1968–85; life memb Ct Univ of Nottingham 1953–, fndn govr Bilton Grange Prep Sch 1957–80; govr: Northampton GS 1963–74, Northampton Sch for Boys 1977–81 (vice chm Fndn Tst 1970–81 and 1986–88, chm 1988–96), Northampton HS for Girls 1966–91 (chm 1972–84); tstee: Cripps Postgrad Med Centre Northampton Gen Hosp 1969–, Univ of Nottingham Devpt Tst 1990–93; memb Tsts for Fabric of Peterborough Cathedral 1975–95, pres Johnian Soc 1966; DL Northants 1986–96; hon fell: Cripps Hall Univ of Nottingham 1959, St John's Coll Cambridge 1966, Magdalene Coll Cambridge 1971, Selwyn Coll Cambridge 1971, Queens' Coll Cambridge 1979; Hon DSc Nottingham 1975, Hon LLD Cantab 1976; Liveryman: Worshipful Co of Wheelwrights 1957 (memb Ct 1970, Master 1982), Worshipful Co of Tallow Chandlers 1983; Freeman City of London 1957, High Sheriff Northamptonshire 1985–86; FCS, FRIC, CChem, FRSC; *Recreations* travel, photography, natural history (entomology-rhopalocera), philately; *Style*— Sir Humphrey Cripps; ✉ Bull's Head Farm, Eakley Lanes, Stoke Goldington, Newport Pagnell, Bucks MK16 8LP (☎ 01908 551223); Simplex Works, Roade, Northampton NN7 2LG (☎ 01604 862441)

CRIPPS, Michael Frederick; s of Maj Charles Philip Cripps, TD, of Sussex, and Betty Christine, *née* Flinn; *b* 22 Oct 1947; *Educ* Felsted, Medway Coll (HNC); *m* 23 April 1982, Carolyn Louise, da of Elie Gabriel Farah; 3 s (Alexander Timothy James (step s) b 1974, Nicholas Frederick b 1985, Christopher Philip b 1988); *Career* mgmnt conslt; dist mangr Johnson Group 1969–72, branch mangr Drake Conslts 1972–73; Cripps Sears Transearch (formerly Cripps Sears & Partners Ltd): ptnr 1973–78, chm and md 1978–; memb Ctee Japan Assoc; MIPM, FInstD 1985; *Recreations* sport generally - active rugby football player & supporter, people, travel, contemporary & classical live music; *Clubs* City of London, MCC; *Style*— Michael Cripps, Esq; ✉ Cripps Sears Transearch, Sardinia House, 52 Lincoln's Inn Fields, London WC2A 3LZ (☎ 0171 404 5701, fax 0171 242 0515)

CRIPPS, Philip Charles; s of Alan Derek Cripps (d 1958), and Winifred Mary Cripps (d 1958); *b* 29 Dec 1945; *Educ* Royal Pinner Sch, Harrow, Aston Univ (BA); *m* 24 June 1967, Jayne, da of Stanley Roney; 2 da (Michelle b 21 Jan 1971, Cara b 7 Jan 1975); *Career* chief exec Thameside Int Mgmnt Conslts 1977–; non-exec dir various companies 1979–; lectr UK, USA, Europe; *Recreations* squash, racquetball, water skiing; *Clubs* Lingfield Health, Maidenhead, Westhorpe Water Ski Marlow; *Style*— Philip C Cripps, Esq; ✉ Thameside International Management and Personnel Development Consultants, Broadway House, 21 Broadway, Maidenhead, Berkshire SL6 1NJ (☎ 01628 39254, moblie 0802 355114)

CRISFORD, John Northcote; s of George Northcote Crisford, CBE, and Effie Mary, *née* Saul; *b* 27 Sept 1915; *Educ* Brighton Coll; *m* 28 June 1947, Prunella Beatrice Evelyn, da of John Ridout-Evans (d 1971); 1 s (Timothy b 1951), 2 da (Mary b 1949, Felicity b 1959); *Career* WWII served RASC, Lancs Fusiliers, Intelligence Corps (India), Capt; advertising: Unilever Ltd, Lintas Ltd 1932–39; dep chief regnl offr Central Office of Info Cambridge 1947–48, UK info offr Sydney 1949–51, dep publicity mangr The Metal Box Co Ltd 1957–62, assoc dir Planned PR (subsidiary of Young and Rubicam Ltd) 1963–66, head of PR Br Tport Docks Bd 1966–77; chm Winsford Parish Cncl 1980–87, LEA govr Winsford Sch 1989–93; ed Four Parishes magazine 1989–93, established Nether Halse Books 1981 (publishes own poetry, local guide and history books, and a religious work); visiting lectr Br Tport Docks Bd Staff Coll 1968–77, lectures on poetry to clubs, schools etc 1984–; pres Winsford and Exton Branch Royal British Legion; memb IPR Examinations Bd 1962–67, govr Communication, Advertising and Mktg Educn Fndn 1969–72 (CAM Dip PR); memb PR Inst of Aust 1950–53, FRSA 1954, FIPR 1969 (memb Cncl 1959–61, 1963–65 and 1966–72, pres 1970–71); *Publications* incl: Public Relations Advances (1973), Management Guide to Corporate Identity (contrib, 1971), The Role of PR in Management (contrib, 1972); A Poet's Gift (1981), Were I a Giant (1983), Lot 201 (1984), A Gloria for Special Occasions (1988), William Dicker - a great Exmoor Schoolmaster (1992), Lawyer Lashbrooke - A 17th Century Westcountry Rogue (1994), The Divine Man - What Did He Say? (1994, awarded Crystal Mark by the Plain English Campaign 1996); *Recreations* writing, reading, psychical research; *Style*— John Crisford, Esq; ✉ Nether Halse, Winsford, Minehead, Somerset TA24 7JE (☎ 01643 85314); Nether Halse Books, Winsford, Minehead, Somerset TA24 7JE (☎ 01643 85314)

CRISP, Dr Adrian James; s of Bertram William Crisp, of Harrow Weald, Middx, and Mary Louise, *née* Butland; *b* 21 Nov 1948; *Educ* Univ Coll Sch London, Magdalene Coll Cambridge (MA, MB BChir, MD), UCH London; *m* 6 July 1974, Lesley Roberta, da of Archibald Shaw (d 1981), of Harrow, Middx; 1 s (Alasdair James Gavin b 1977, d 1990), 1 da (Alison Victoria b 1979); *Career* house offr and sr house offr UCH and Northwick Park Hosp Harrow 1974–78, med registrar UCH 1978–80, sr registrar Guy's Hosp 1980–85, res fell Massachusetts Gen Hosp and Harvard Univ 1982–83; Addenbrooke's Hosp Cambridge: conslt rheumatologist 1985–, dir Bone Density Unit 1989–91, postgrad clinical tutor 1990–; conslt rheumatologist: Newmarket Hosp 1985–, Princess of Wales Hosp Ely 1993–; assoc lectr Univ of Cambridge 1985–, dir of studies in clinical med and fell Churchill Coll Cambridge 1992–; memb Editorial Bd Rheumatology Review; memb: Br Soc for Rheumatology, Bone and Tooth Soc; DRCOG 1977, MRCP 1977, FRCP (London) 1991; *Publications* Oxford Textbook of Rheumatology (contrib), Blackwell's Textbook of Diabetes (contrib), Management of Common Metabolic Bone Disorders (jtly); *Recreations* military history, golf, pre 1960 British films; *Style*— Dr Adrian Crisp; ✉ Arran House, 19 Cambridge Rd, Little Abington, Cambridgeshire CB1 6BL (☎ 01223 891141); Addenbrooke's Hospital, Cambridge CB2 2QQ (☎ 01223 216254)

CRISP, Bernard David James; s of Bertie Bela Crisp (d 1968); *b* 11 June 1926; *Educ* Whitgift, Univ of Liverpool; *m* 1947, Lorna Jean, *née* Clarke (d 1996); *Career* Lt RNVR; md Cunard Travel (ret); dir: Cunard Line, Cunard Hotels; pres SSAFA (Central London); vice pres Br Maritime Charitable Fndn; chm: SSAFA Appeals Ctee, Passenger Shipping Assoc 1986–87; tstee Ex-Servs Mental Welfare Soc; Freeman City of London; FCIM, OStJ; *Recreations* writing, gardening; *Style*— Bernard Crisp, Esq; ✉ 2 Norfolk Ave, Sanderstead, Surrey

CRISP, John William Maxwell; s of John Francis Crisp (d 1949), of Berkshire, and Lady Dora Scott, *née* Fox; *b* 10 Nov 1929; *Educ* Eton; *m* 1956, Elizabeth Frances Mary, da of Capt H B Barclay, OBE, MC, of Kenya; 2 s (Hugh b 1958, William b 1960); *Career* 2 Lt King's Royal Rifle Corps 1949–50, Capt (TA) Queen's Westminster Rifles; chm: London Section Inst of Brewing 1964–66, Allied Brewing Trades Assoc 1970, Maltsters Assoc of GB 1973–74, Crisp Malting Ltd 1962–95, Anglia Maltings Holdings Ltd 1982–95; sec Hurlingham Polo Assoc; fell Inst of Brewing; *Recreations* shooting, sailing, walking; *Clubs* Lansdowne, Green Jackets; *Style*— John Crisp, Esq; ✉ Winterlake, Kirtlington, Kidlington, Oxon OX5 3HG (☎ 01869 350384, fax 01869 350625)

CRISP, (Edmund) Nigel Ramsay; *b* 14 Jan 1952; *Educ* Uppingham, St John's Coll Cambridge (MA); *m* 1 May 1976; 1 s, 1 da; *Career* Halewood Community Cncl 1973–76, Trebor Ltd 1977–81, Cambridgeshire Community Cncl 1981–86; unit gen mangr East Berks Health Authy 1986–92; chief exec: Heatherwood and Wexham Park Hosps NHS Tst 1992–93, Oxford Radcliffe Hosp NHS Tst 1993–; regional dir NHS exec for South Thames Region 1997–; licentiate Inst of Health Serv Mgmnt; *Style*— Nigel Crisp, Esq;

✉ Oxford Radcliffe Hospital NHS Trust, John Radcliffe Hospital, Headley Way, Headington, Oxford OX3 9DU (☎ 01865 741741)

CRISP, Sir (John) Peter; 4 Bt (UK 1913), of Bungay, Suffolk; s of Sir John Wilson Crisp, 3 Bt (d 1950), and Marjorie, *née* Shriver (d 1977); *b* 19 May 1925; *Educ* Westminster; *m* 5 June 1954, Judith Mary, yst da of Herbert Edward Gillett (d 1954), of Marlborough, Wilts, and niece of Sir Harold Gillett, 1 Bt; 3 s (John Charles b 1955, Michael Peter b 1957, Charles Frank b 1960), 1 da (Catherine Mary b 1962); *Heir* s, John Charles Crisp b 10 Dec 1955; *Career* slr (ret) Ashurst Morris Crisp and Co; *Style*— Sir Peter Crisp, Bt; ✉ Crabtree Cottage, Drungewick Lane, Loxwood, Billingshurst, W Sussex RH14 0RP (☎ 01403 752374)

CRISPE, Simon Leslie Hare; *b* 31 July 1955, New Zealand; *Educ* BArch (NZ); *m* 27 April 1979, Marianne Denise; 2 c; *Career* assoc dir Lister Drew and Associates (before acquistion by W S Atkins) 1989–91, tech dir W S Atkins 1993– (assoc architect 1992–93); projects incl: project mangr Chicacio Beach Resort Dubai 1993–95, project ldr BA World Cargo Centre UK 1995–; ARCUK, RIBA; *Recreations* motor sport, classic car restoration, wood carving and cabinet making; *Clubs* Daimler and Lanchester Owners', Porsche Club of GB; *Style*— Simon Crispe, Esq; ✉ W S Atkins, Woodcote Grove, Ashley Road, Epsom, Surrey KT18 5BW (☎ 01372 726140, fax 01372 740055)

CRITCHETT, Sir Ian George Lorraine; 3 Bt (UK 1908), of Harley St, Borough of St Marylebone; s of Sir (George) Montague Critchett, 2 Bt, MVO (d 1941), and Innes, *née* Wiehe (d 1982); *b* 9 Dec 1920; *Educ* Harrow, Clare Coll Cambridge (BA); *m* 1, 9 Oct 1948, Paulette Mary Lorraine (d 1962), eld da of late Col Henry Brabazon Humfrey; m 2, 10 Feb 1964, Jocelyn Daphne Margret, eld da of late Cdr Christopher Mildmay Hall; 1 s (Charles George Montague b 1965), 1 da (Xanthe Clare Lorraine b 1968); *Heir* s, Charles George Montague Critchett b 2 April 1965; *Career* RAFVR 1942–46; HM Dip Serv: FO 1948, 3 sec Vienna 1950, 2 sec Bucharest 1951, 2 sec Cairo 1956, 1 sec FO 1962, cnsllr FCO 1977, ret 1980; *Clubs* Travellers', MCC; *Style*— Sir Ian Critchett, Bt; ✉ Uplands Lodge, Pains Hill, Limpsfield, Oxted, Surrey RH8 0RF (☎ 01883 722371)

CRITCHLEY, Bruce; s of Brig Gen A C Critchley, CMG, CBE, DSO (d 1962), and Diana, *née* Fishwick (d 1996); *b* 9 Dec 1942; *Educ* Eton; *m* Hazel, da of Jack Bateman, of Somerset; 1 da (Georgina b 1976), 2 s (Thomas and Neil (twins) b 1977); *Career* broadcaster/journalist; previously with Blue Circle Industries 1962–69 and 1971–86 (British Car Auction 1969–70); freelance sports broadcaster 1986–; dir Critchley Pursuits; played golf for GB v USA (Walker Cup) 1969, played for Eng 1962 and 1969/70; *Books* Golf and all its Glory, Power Golf, Faldo: In Search of Perfection (1994); *Recreations* bridge, listening to classical music; *Clubs* Sunningdale Golf, Garrick; *Style*— Bruce Critchley, Esq; ✉ Doone, Ridgemount Road, Sunningdale, Berks SL5 9RL (home ☎ 01344 23194, business ☎ 01344 23526, fax 01344 872268)

CRITCHLEY, Dr Edmund Michael Rhys; s of Prof A Michael Critchley, and Dr Doris Critchley, *née* Rees; *b* 25 Dec 1931; *Educ* Stowe, Lincoln Coll Oxford (DM), KCH Med Sch, FRCP, FRCPEd; *m* 1964, Dr Mair, da of Ivor Bowen; 2 s (Giles b 1965, Hugo b 1967), 1 da (Helen b 1968); *Career* Capt RAMC; sr registrar UCH 1964–66, instr in neurology Univ of Lexington Med Centre 1966–68, conslt neurologist Preston and N Lancs 1968–96, hon prof of neurology Univ of Central Lancashire 1993–96, ret; examiner for MRCP; memb Cncl: Assoc Br Neurologists 1985–88, Royal Coll of Physicians 1988–96; pres N of England Neurological Assoc 1992; prospective Parly candidate (Lib Dem) Bolton NE 1996; *Books* Hallucinations and Their Impact on Art (1987), Speech and Language Disorders (1987), Neurological Emergencies (1988), Diseases of the Spinal Cord (1992), The Neurological Boundaries of Reality (1994); *Style*— Dr Edmund Critchley; ✉ 18 Merlin Rd, Blackburn, Lancs BB2 7BA (☎ 01254 260342)

CRITCHLEY, Sir Julian Michael Gordon; kt (1995), MP (C) Aldershot (majority 19,188); s of Dr Macdonald Critchley, CBE, and his 1 w Edna Auldeth, *née* Morris (d 1974); *b* 8 Dec 1930; *Educ* Shrewsbury, Sorbonne, Pembroke Coll Oxford (MA); *m* 1, 15 Oct 1955 (m dis 1965), Paula Joan, da of Paul Baron; 2 da (Julie b 20 Nov 1957, Susannah b 26 Sept 1961); m 2, April 1965, Mrs Heather Anne Goodrick, da of Charlie Moores (d 1949); 1 s (Joshua b 7 Sept 1970), 1 da (Melissa b 19 Jan 1967); *Career* writer, broadcaster, journalist; MP (C): Rochester and Chatham 1959–64, Aldershot 1970–97 (standing down); chm Bow Gp 1966–67, memb One Nation Gp of Cons MPs; dir Br Boxing Bd of Control; *Books* The Conservative Opportunity (ed, 1965), Collective Security (with O Pick, 1975), Warning and Response (1978), NATO and the Soviet Union in the 80s (1980), Westminster Blues (1985), Heseltine (1987), A View from Westminster (ed, 1987), Palace of Varieties (1989), Hung Parliament (1991), Floating Voter (1992), Some of Us (1992), Borderlands (with David Paterson, 1993), A Bag of Boiled Sweets (1994), Heseltine 11 (1994); *Recreations* collecting early Staffordshire pottery and porcelain, exploring Shropshire, watching boxing; *Style*— Sir Julian Critchley, MP; ✉ 19 Broad Street, Ludlow, Shropshire (☎ 01584 877084); House of Commons, London SW1A 0AA (☎ 0171 219 5170)

CRITCHLEY, Philip; CB (1990); s of Henry Stephen Critchley (d 1980), of Cumbria, and Edith Adela, *née* Currie (d 1980); *b* 31 Jan 1931; *Educ* Manchester GS, Balliol Coll Oxford (MA); *m* 1962, Stella Ann, da of Frederick John Barnes, of Kent; 2 s (Conrad b 1965, Brian b 1966), 1 da (Rachel b 1971); *Career* Nat Serv Intelligence Corps 1953–55, Corp BAOR; civil servant 1955–91; under sec DOE 1980–85, dir of network mgmnt and maintenance (highways) Dept of Tport 1990–91, pt/t advsr Dept of Tport 1991–94, pt/t conslt DOE and Martin Jack & Co 1994–; FRSA; *Recreations* philosophy, writing poetry; *Clubs* Blackheath Harriers, Oxford Union; *Style*— Philip Critchley, Esq, CB; ✉ Infield House, Kendall Ground, Lowick, Ulverston, Cumbria LA12 8ER (☎ 01229 885254)

CRITCHLEY, Tom; s of Leonard Critchley (d 1986), and Jessie, *née* Turner (d 1988); *b* 17 Aug 1928; *Educ* Sheffield Coll of Technol; *m* 15 Dec 1951, Margaret, da of Frederick Bland (d 1934); 1 s (Andrew b 1959); *Career* Davy-Ashmore Group 1951–66, Cammell Laird and Upper Clyde Groups 1966–69, JCB Group 1969–70, EMI Group 1970–80, head Investmt Casting Mission to Canada; sr ptnr Int Consultancy Practice 1980–85, under sec Dept of Health 1986–90, int business advsr 1990–; md: UK High Technology Co 1991–95, UK/Polish Jt Venture Polish Acad of Sciences 1991–95; head indust missions to Japan, SE Asia, Soviet Union and Poland 1988–91; UN advsr: Tanzanian Govt, High Cmmn for Refugees; chm Anglo Soviet Healthcare Gp 1988–91, memb Bd Nat Inst of Govt Purchasing USA 1977–78, UK del Int Fedn of Purchasing and Materials Mgmnt 1978–82, faculty memb Mgmnt Centre Europe 1980–86, dir Int Mgmnt Inst 1984–88; Chartered Inst of Purchasing and Supply: fell 1967, chm of Cncl 1974–75, pres 1977–78, chm External Affrs 1978–82, memb Int Cncl 1979–82; memb NHS Mgmnt Bd for Procurement and Distribution 1986–90, chm UK Leisure Trade Assoc 1990–93, dir of govt and regulatory affairs Pan-European Trade Fedn 1992–93, dir Ctee for Int Students Imperial Coll London 1996–, assoc UK Exec Search Co 1996–; *Recreations* competitive sports, live theatre, North American history; *Style*— Tom Critchley, Esq; ✉ 3 Lincoln Close, Stoke Mandeville, nr Aylesbury, Bucks HP22 5YS (☎ 01296 612511, fax 01296 614203)

CRITCHLOW, Howard Arthur (Harry); s of Arthur Critchlow, of Nottingham, and Edith Ellen, *née* Evans (d 1972); *b* 22 April 1943; *Educ* Nottingham HS, Univ of Sheffield (BDS); *m* 5 Dec 1970, Avril, da of George Pyne, of Sheffield; 1 s (Edward b 1972), 1 da (Bridget b 1974); *Career* conslt oral surgn 1976–: Glasgow Dental Hosp, Stobhill Gen Hosp, Royal Hosp for Sick Children Glasgow; res work in: cryosurgery, laser surgery, dental implants; memb BDA 1965, FBAOMS 1976, FDSRCS (Eng), FDSRCP (Glas); *Recreations* hill walking, running, gardening, DIY, keep fit; *Clubs* 41 Club; *Style*— Harry Critchlow, Esq; ✉ Glasgow Dental Hospital, 378 Sauchiehall St, Glasgow G2 3JZ (☎ 0141 211 9600)

CRITCHLOW, Prof Keith Barry; s of Michael Bernard Critchlow (d 1972), of London, and Rozalind Ruby, *née* Weston-Mann (d 1983); *b* 16 March 1933; *Educ* Summerhill Sch, St Martin's Sch of Art London (Inter NDD), RCA (ARCA); *m* Gail Susan, da of Geoffrey W Henebery; 1 s (Matthew Alexander), 4 da (Louise Penelope, Amanda Jane, Amelia Poppy, Dawn Kathy); *Career* Nat Serv RAF 1951–53; lectr at most art and architecture schools in the UK; teaching appts at: Harrow, Sir John Cass, Hornsey, Watford, Wimbledon, The Slade, The Royal Coll; appts abroad incl: Ghana, Kuwait, Sweden, Aust, India, USA, Canada, Jordan, Iran, Saudi Arabia; formerly: tutor and res dir The Architectural Assoc, tutor in painting Sch of the Royal Coll of Art, tutor Slade Sch, dir Visual Islamic Arts Unit Royal Coll of Art; currently dir Research Dept and dir of Visual Islamic and Traditional Arts The Prince of Wales's Inst of Architecture (where also directs annual Summer Sch in USA); fndr of own architectural design office; buildings designed in: USA, Kuwait, Saudi Arabia, Iran, UK (incl Krishnamurti Study Centre), India (incl SS Baba Inst of Higher Med Sciences Hosp Puttaparthi - second largest hosp in Asia); FRCA 1986 (Dr 1989), FDIH (USA) 1987; *Books* Order in Space (1969), Chartres Maze - A Model of the Universe?, Islamic Patterns - A Cosmological Approach, The Sphere, Soul & Androgyne, Into the Hidden Environment, Time Stands Still, The Whole Question of Health (with Jon Allen, 1995); *Recreations* painting, writing, geometry, walking, photography, meditation; *Style*— Prof Keith Critchlow; ✉ Director of Research, The Prince of Wales's Institute of Architecture, 14–15 Gloucester Gate, Regent's Park, London NW1 4HG (☎ 0171 916 7380, fax 0171 916 7381)

CRITTENDEN, Eur Ing Prof Barry David; s of Henry John Crittenden (d 1990), and Rosina Katie, *née* Hedley (d 1969); *b* 23 May 1947; *Educ* Chislehurst and Sidcup GS (Hugh Oddy meml prize), Univ of Birmingham (BSc, PhD); *m* 30 Oct 1971, Janet Mary, da of Raymond Charles Pinches; 1 da (Lucy Rosina b 2 April 1979), 1 s (Daniel Charles b 4 Aug 1981); *Career* chemical engr UKAEA Aldermaston 1971–73; Univ of Bath: lectr 1973–88, sr lectr 1988–91, reader 1991, prof of chemical engrg 1991–; dir Selectamaster Ltd 1988–; CEng, Eur Ing, FIChemE; *Books* Management of Hazardous and Toxic Wastes in the Process Industries (with S T Kolaczkowski, 1987), Waste Minimization: A Practical Guide (with S T Kolaczkowski, 1995); *Recreations* photography, cycling; *Style*— Eur Ing Prof Barry Crittenden; ✉ School of Chemical Engineering, University of Bath, Claverton Down, Bath BA2 7AY (☎ 01225 826501, fax 01225 826894)

CROAN, Sheriff Thomas Malcolm; s of John Croan (d 1951), of Edinburgh, and Amelia, *née* Sydney (d 1989); *b* 7 Aug 1932; *Educ* St Joseph's Coll Dumfries, Univ of Edinburgh (MA, LLB); *m* 2 April 1959, Joan Kilpatrick, da of George Law; 1 s (Nicholas Miles Law b 14 April 1960), 3 da (Gillian Carol Mary b 4 April 1963, Karen Margaret Sylvia 3 Aug 1965, Larissa Anne Sydney b 7 April 1973); *Career* admitted to Faculty of Advocates 1956, standing jr counsel to Queen and Lord Treasurer's Remembrancer 1963–64, standing jr counsel to Scottish Devpt Dept 1964–65 (for highways work 1967–69), advocate depute 1965–66, memb Legal Aid Supreme Court Ctee 1968–69, sheriff of Grampian, Highland and Islands (formerly Aberdeen, Kincardine and Banff) 1969–83, sheriff of N Strathclyde 1983–; *Recreations* sailing; *Style*— Sheriff Thomas Croan; ✉ Sheriff Court House, St Marnock Street, Kilmarnock KA1 1ED

CROCK, Henry Vernon; AO; s of Vernon John Crock (d 1963), of Perth, WA, and Annie, *née* Doyle (d 1973); *b* 14 Sept 1929; *Educ* St Louis Sch Perth WA, Univ of WA, Univ of Melbourne (MB, BS, MD, MS, Gold medallist Anatomy Dept); *m* 15 March 1958, Dr (Mary) Carmel, da of Sylvester Michael Shorten (d 1966), of Melbourne, Victoria, Aust, and Violet, *née* Haslett (d 1974); 2 s (Vernon Michael b 1963, Damian Luke b 1965), 3 da (Catherine Mary b 1958, Elizabeth Anne b 1960, Carmel Therese b 1962); *Career* St Vincent's Hosp Melbourne: jr res MO 1954, sr res MO 1955, sr surgical registrar 1957; sr demonstrator Anatomy Dept Univ of Melbourne 1956 (res tutor Newman Coll), Nuffield Dominions' clinical asst in Orthopaedic Surgery Nuffield Orthopaedic Centre Univ of Oxford 1957–60 (lectr in Orthopaedic surgery 1959–60), sr hon orthopaedic surgn St Vincent's Hosp Univ of Melbourne 1961–86, assoc prof Dept of Surgery Univ of Melbourne 1978–86 (special lectr in orthopaedic surgery 1961–86); memb Aust Rheumatism Assoc 1966–86; Aust Orthopaedic Assoc: memb 1961–, memb Victorian Bd of Studies 1968–80, memb Fed Exec Bd 1972–73, memb Fed Prog Ctee 1972–75, memb Fed Ctee for Continuing Educn 1974–76, sec for Registrar Training Prog Victorian Branch 1976–80; corresponding memb: Scoliosis Res Soc 1974–, Japanese Orthopaedic Assoc 1991–; rep (Aust) on Editorial Bd British Journal of Bone and Joint Surgery 1976–80; pres: Facet Club of Aust (Spinal Surgery) 1977–79, Int Soc for the Study of Lumbar Spine 1984–85; fndr memb Euro Spine Soc 1990; hon sr lectr in orthopaedic surgery Royal Postgrad Med Sch Hammersmith 1986–, hon res fell Anatomy Dept RCS 1986; LO Betts meml Gold medal Aust Orthopaedic Assoc 1976, Sir Alan Newton prize Royal Australasian Coll of Surgeons 1977, Wood-Jones Medal RCS 1983; FRCS 1957, FRACS 1961, FBOA 1989; *Books* The Blood Supply of the Lower Limb Bones in Man (1967), The Blood Supply of the Vertebral Column and Spinal Cord in Man (with Dr H Yoshizawa, 1977), Practice of Spinal Surgery (1984), The Conus Medullaris and Cauda Equina in Man (with Dr M Yamagishi and Dr M C Crock 1986), A Short Practice of Spinal Surgery (1993), An Atlas of Vascular Anatomy of the Skeleton and Spinal Cord (1996); many contribs to learned medical journals; *Recreations* collecting fine art, technical photography; *Clubs* The Melbourne, Associated; *Style*— Henry Crock, Esq, AO; ✉ Cromwell Hospital, Cromwell Rd, London SW5 OTU (☎ 0171 373 2591, fax 0171 373 9525)

CROCKARD, (Hugh) Alan; s of Hugh Crockard (d 1988), and Mary, *née* McKimm (d 1988); *b* 24 Jan 1943; *Educ* Royal Belfast Acad Instn, Queen's Univ Belfast (Sinclair Medal in Surgery); *m* 1978, Dr Caroline Orr; 2 s (Michael Charles b 30 Jan 1984, Thomas Hugh b 18 Jan 1987); *Career* Wellcome sr surgical fell 1973–74, Hunterian prof (treatment of head injury) RCS 1973–74, Fogarty int postdoctoral fell Chicago 1974–75, sr lectr in neurosurgery Queen's Univ Belfast 1974–78, conslt neurosurgn The Nat Hosp for Neurology and Neurosurgery 1978–, hon sr lectr Inst of Neurology London; dir Cerebral Oedema Research Gp 1980–93, co-fndr Br Cervical Spine Soc 1986, fndr Surgical Workshops for Anatomical Prosecution 1990, Hill workshop tutor RCS 1994; Calvert medal 1972, Morrow lectr Belfast 1984, Jameson medal (Neurosurgical Soc of Australasia) 1989, Lund Neurosurgical medal 1987, Olivacrona lectr 1995, Harrington medal 1995, Wylie McKissock medal 1996; numerous visiting professorships; sec Br Cervical Spine Soc; memb: Soc of Br Neurological Surgns, American Acad of Neurological Surgery, American Assoc of Neurological Surgns, Soc of Neurological Surgns, Hungarian Spine Soc; FRCSEd 1970, FRCS 1970; *Books* Trauma Care (with W M Odling-Smee, 1981), Neurosurgery: The Scientific Basis of Clinical Practice (with R Hayward and J T Hoff, 1992); also author of over 290 original articles; *Recreations* music, travel, sailing, skiing, photography; *Clubs* RSM; *Style*— Alan Crockard, Esq; ✉ Department of Surgical Neurology, The National Hospital for Neurology and Neurosurgery, Queen Square, London WC1N 3BG (☎ 0171 636 4191, fax 0171 722 3141)

CROCKER, Prof Alan Godfrey; s of Percival Thomas Crocker (d 1951), of Pontypridd, Mid Glamorgan, and (Alice) Maud, *née* Chown (d 1988); *b* 6 Oct 1935; *Educ* Pontypridd Boys' GS, Imperial Coll London (BSc, DSc), Univ of Sheffield (PhD); *m* 29 Dec 1959, Glenys Mary, da of Bernard Oddie, of Clitheroe, Lancs; 1 s (Gareth Richard b 1967); *Career* Univ of Surrey Dept of Physics: lectr 1959–65, reader 1965–81, prof 1981–, head of dept 1991–92; author of many papers in sci jls on defects in crystals and their influence on mechanical properties; chm: Cncl of Validating Univs, Br Assoc of Paper Historians, Gunpowder Mills Study Gp, Godalming Water Turbine Tst; past chm: Wind and Watermill Section Soc for the Protection of Ancient Bldgs, Univ Ctee validating degrees of Assoc Insts, Guildford Inst; pres Surrey Ind History Gp, vice pres Surrey Archaeological Soc; memb Exec Ctee Surrey Local Hist Cncl; FInstP 1967, FIM 1970–88, FSA 1989, CEng 1978; *Books* Catteshall Mill (with G M Crocker, 1981), Paper Mills of the Tillingbourne Valley (1988), The Diaries of James Simmons (with M Kane, 1990); *Recreations* industrial archaeology, hill walking; *Clubs* Soc of Antiquaries; *Style*— Prof Alan Crocker, FSA; ✉ 6 Burwood Close, Guildford, Surrey GU1 2SB (☎ 01483 565821); Department of Physics, University of Surrey, Guildford, Surrey GU2 5XH (☎ 01483 259401, telex 859331, fax 01438 259501, e-mail A.Crocker@surrey.ac.uk)

CROCKER, Dr John; s of Norman Kenneth Thornton Crocker, of Bexhill-on-Sea, E Sussex, and Olga Elspeth Crocker, *née* Robertson; *b* 18 June 1951; *Educ* Sevenoaks Sch Kent, Univ of Cambridge (MA, MD); *m* 29 Jan 1972, Catherine Barbara, da of Lord Tombs, of Honington, nr Shipston-on-Stour, Warwicks; 1 s (Stephen John b 16 Jan 1980); *Career* lectr in pathology Univ of Birmingham 1976–83, conslt histopathologist Birmingham Heartlands Hosp (formerly E Birmingham Hosp) 1983–, sr clinical lectr Univ of Birmingham 1993–, visiting sr clinical lectr Univ of Warwick 1994–; author of numerous papers, editorials, reviews and chapters on the pathology of malignant lymphomas, leukaemia and Hodgkin's disease; ed-in-chief Clinical Molecular Pathology; chm W Midlands Oncology Assoc, memb Br Lymphoma Gp; memb: Pathological Soc of GB and Ireland, Assoc of Clinical Pathologists; fell Royal Microscopical Soc; FRCPath 1993 (MRCPath 1981); *Books* Cell Proliferation in Lymphomas (1993), Molecular Biology in Histopathology (1994), The Biology of Disease (1995); *Recreations* classical music, literature, computing, geology; *Style*— Dr John Crocker; ✉ Chiltern, 226 Blossomfield Rd, Solihull, West Midlands B91 1NT; Histopathology Department, Birmingham Heartlands Hospital, Birmingham B9 5SS (☎ 0121 766 6611, fax 0121 766 8450)

CROCKETT, Pippa Beryl; da of Philip Henry Crockett, MBE, and Beryl, *née* Wright (d 1969); *b* 23 July 1955; *Educ* Abbotsholme Sch; *Career* dir: County Leatherwear 1976, Hustwick Ltd 1979; md: County Leatherwear (Tinter Ltd) 1987–, County Chamois Co Ltd 1987– (dir 1980); ptnr Heart of England Antiques 1987–; assoc memb Int Export Assoc 1978, FInstD 1991; *Recreations* sailing, skiing; *Style*— Miss Pippa Crockett; ✉ Chamant Manor, Old End, Appleby Magna, Derbyshire; County Chamois Co Ltd, John St Leatherworks, Glascote, Tamworth, Staffs B77 3EA (☎ 01827 63672, fax 01827 62365, car 0860 434003)

CROCKFORD, (Philip) David Vyvyan; s of Philip Theodore Clive Crockford (d 1950), and Muriel Mary, *née* Moorhouse (d 1988); *b* 21 Nov 1930; *Educ* Merchant Taylors', RMA Sandhurst; *m* 11 July 1953, Margaret Kathleen, da of Maj Charles Deane Cowper; 1 s (Adrian Robert Vyvyan b 27 April 1956), 2 da (Sarah Claire d'Ambrumenil b 25 Aug 1954, Charlotte Kathleen Winifred Joy b 2 March 1962); *Career* cmmnd RA 1951–55; formerly: sales and mktg IBM (UK) Ltd, PA mgmnt conslt; dir: Willis Faber & Dumas Ltd, Alexander Howden Underwriting Ltd; chm: C I de Rougemont & Co Ltd, C I de Rougemont Holdings Ltd; md Crockford Devitt Underwriting Agencies Ltd; memb Lloyd's; *Recreations* country pursuits, collecting antiquarian books; *Clubs* City University, Boodle's; *Style*— David Crockford, Esq; ✉ C I de Rougemont & Co Ltd, Marlon House, 71–74 Mark Lane, London EC3 (☎ 0171 481 9277)

CROFT, Col (Noel) Andrew Cotton; DSO (1945), OBE (1970); s of Rev Canon Robert William Croft (d 1947), of Kelvedon Vicarage, Essex, and Lottie Alice Bland, *née* Clayton (d 1962); *b* 30 Nov 1906; *Educ* Lancing, Stowe, ChCh Oxford (MA), Sch of Technol Manchester; *m* 24 July 1952, Rosalind (d 1996), da of Cdr A H de Kantzow, DSO, RN (d 1928); 3 da (Clare b 1953, Corinna b 1955, Julia b 1957); *Career* under mangr cotton trade Carlisle 1929–32; memb Br Trans-Greenland Expdn (Guinness Book of Records longest self-supporting dog-sledge journey) 1933–34; ADC to Maharajah of Cooch Behar India 1934–35; 2 i/c Oxford Univ Arctic expdn to North East Land 1935–36, Ethnological Expdn to Swedish Lapland 1937–38; res Cambridge Univ 1938–39; WWII Serv: Capt 1939, cmd WO mission to Russo-Finnish War 1939–40, Bde Intellngence Offr Ind Companies Norwegian Campaign 1940, advsr Admty Combined Ops 1940–41, Maj 1941, asst mil attaché Stockholm 1941–42, OC sea or parachute ops (Norway, Corsica, Italy, France, Denmark), Lt-Col 1945; asst dir of science WO 1945–48, WO rep Canadian Arctic Exercise 'Musk Ox' 1945–46, sr observer NW Frontier Trials India 1946–47, attached Canadian Army 1947–48, GSOI WO 1948–51, Col Br Jt Servs Mission USA 1952–54, sr liaison offr HQ Continental Armies, OC Inf Jr Ldrs Bn Plymouth 1954–57; cmdt: Army Apprentices Sch Harrogate 1957–60, Met Police Cadet Corps 1960–71; FRGS (BACK award 1945 and 1946, hon sec 1951, memb Cncl 1949–51, hon fell 1992), corresponding fell Arctic Inst of N America, life memb RIIA; Polar medal 1942 (Clasp Arctic 1935–36); *Books* Polar Exploration (1939, 2 edn 1947), Under The Pole Star (with AR Glen, 1937), A Talent For Adventure (1991); *Recreations* sailing, skiing, mountaineering, photography; *Clubs* Alpine, Special Forces (tstee), Arctic (memb and former sec); *Style*— Col Andrew Croft, DSO, OBE; ✉ The River House, 52 Strand-on-the-Green, London W4 3PD (☎ 0181 994 6359)

CROFT, Annabel; da of James Anthony Deriaz Croft, of Farnborough, Kent, and Susan Jane Croft; *b* 12 July 1966; *Educ* West Heath Sch Sevenoaks; *Career* TV presenter (formerly tennis player); started playing tennis aged 9, jr champion Under 12, 14 and 16 age gps, winner Jr Wimbledon 1985, Br no 1 1985/86, ret 1987; former presenter Treasure Hunt (C4) and Interceptor (ITV); presenter: Sssports (BBC) 1993, Sailaway (Anglia), Vauxhall Premier Trophy (Channel 4); guest presenter: Entertainment Show (Sky), This Morning (Granada); memb Equity; *Recreations* tennis, sailing, theatre, films, antiques; *Clubs* All England Lawn Tennis; *Style*— Miss Annabel Croft; ✉ c/o Lake-Smith Griffin Associates, 15 Maiden Lane, London WC2E 7NA (☎ 0171 836 1020, fax 0171 836 1040)

CROFT, Hon Bernard William Henry Page; s and h of 2 Baron Croft, *qv*, by his w, Lady Antoinette Fredericka Hersey Cecilia Conyngham (d 1959), da of 6 Marquess Conyngham; *b* 28 Aug 1949; *Educ* Stowe, Univ of Wales (BSc Econ); *m* 1993, Mary Elizabeth, da of James Richardson, of Co Tyrone; *Career* publishing; *Recreations* shooting, fishing, skiing; *Clubs* Hurlingham, Naval and Military; *Style*— The Hon Bernard Croft; ✉ Croft Castle, Leominster, Herefordshire HR6 9PW; 5 Comeragh Mews, London W14 9HW

CROFT, Charles Beresford; s of Arthur James Croft (d 1979), and Margaret Bays Conyers, *née* Wright; *b* 14 Jan 1943; *Educ* Worksop Coll, Leeds Univ Medical Sch (MB ChB Hon); *m* 23 March 1968, Hilary Louise Whitaker, da of Ronald Whitaker (d 1968); 1 da (Emma Louise b 1972); *Career* conslt surgn and assoc prof Albert Einstein Sch of Med NY 1974–79; conslt surgn: The Royal Nat Throat Nose and Ear Hosp London, The Nat Heart and Chest Hosp London 1979–; civil conslt in laryngology RAF 1983–; FRCS 1970, FRCSEd 1972; *Recreations* golf, tennis, sailing; *Clubs* Moor Park Golf, RSM; *Style*— Charles B Croft, Esq; ✉ Rye Lodge, 91 Copsewood Way, Northwood, Middx (☎ 01923 823793); 48 Crawford Street, London W1 (☎ 0171 262 7837); 55 Harley Street, London W1N 1DD (☎ 0171 580 2426)

CROFT, David; OBE; s of Reginald Sharland (d 1944), of Hollywood, and Anne, *née* Croft (d 1960); *b* 7 Sept 1922; *Educ* Rugby; *m* 2 June 1952, Ann Callender, da of Reginald Coupland (d 1983), 4 s (Nicholas b 26 March 1953, John b 11 May 1964, Richard b 18 Nov 1969, Tim b 10 Sept 1973); 3 da (Penelope b 10 April 1954, Jane b 16 July 1960, Rebecca (Mrs Simon Cadell) b 23 Jan 1962); *Career* WWII RA 1942, Dorset Regt 1944; served: N Africa, India, Malaya, WO; final rank Maj; actor 1946, BBC writer 1951–, script ed Rediffusion 1955; writer/dir: Tyne Tees 1960–61, BBC 1962; co-writer (with Jimmy Perry), prod and dir: Dad's Army, It Ain't' Alf Hot Mum, Are You Being Served?, Hi De Hi, 'Allo 'Allo, You Rang Milord 1994, Which Way to the War 1995, Oh Doctor Beeching! 1995; Desmond Davis Award 1981, RTS Award 1991; memb BAFTA; *Style*— David Croft, Esq, OBE; ✉ Honington Hall, Honington, nr Bury St Edmunds, W Suffolk IP31 1RB

CROFT, His Hon Judge; David Legh; QC (1982); s of Alan Croft (d 1965), of Dore, Sheffield, and Doreen Mary, *née* Mitchell (d 1991); *b* 14 Aug 1937; *Educ* Haileybury, Univ of Nottingham (LLB); *m* 27 July 1963, Susan Mary, da of George Richard Winnington Bagnall (d 1982), of Wickham, nr Newbury, Berks; 2 s (Rupert Legh b 1966, Jocelyn Harry b 1968); *Career* called to the Bar Middle Temple 1960, recorder of the Crown Court 1985, circuit judge (SE Circuit) 1987–; *Recreations* cooking; *Style*— His Hon Judge Croft, QC; ✉ The Law Courts, Barker Road, Maidstone ME16 8EQ

CROFT, Dr Desmond Nicholas; s of Dr Charles Richard Croft, TD (d 1981), of Plymouth, Devon, and Phyllis Mary, *née* Lee (d 1985); *b* 14 June 1931; *Educ* St John's Winnipeg, Westminster, Trinity Coll Oxford (BM BCh, MA, DM); *m* 1960, Dr (Hilary) Diana Russel Rendle, da of Hilary Cameron Russel Rendle (d 1944), of Singapore; 2 s (Charles b 1960, Nicholas b 1963), 1 da (Hilary b 1966); *Career* Nat Serv Capt RAMC, jr med specialist Br Mil Hosp Tripoli 1959–61; MRC fell 1963–64, Nuffield Fndn fell Boston USA 1964–65, sr conslt physician St Thomas' Hosp London 1994–96 (clinical dir of nuclear med 1969–92); pres Nuclear Med Section Union of Euro Med Specialists (UEMS) 1990–94 (fndr Euro Bd for Nuclear Med 1994), fndr Clinical Positron Emission Tomography (PET) Centre 1992, memb PET Mgmnt Ctee St Thomas and Guy's Hosp 1992–; pres Br Nuclear Med Soc 1976–78; examiner MD and MS Univ of London, fndr memb Euro Nuclear Med Soc 1974 and memb Int Sci Ctee 1980–86 (sec 1985), chm Medical and Surgical Offrs' Ctee St Thomas' Hosp 1986–89; tstee Florence Nightingale Museum 1995–; FRCP 1975, Hon FRCR 1986, FRSM; *Books* 127 contribs to scientific literature in British Medical Journal, Gut, Clinical Science, Nuclear Medicine Communications, European Journal of Nuclear Medicine and other learned jls; *Recreations* rowing, golf, fishing; *Style*— Dr Desmond Croft; ✉ Bourne House, Hurstbourne Priors, Whitchurch, Hampshire RG28 7SB (☎ 01256 89 2665); The Consulting Rooms, York House, 199 Westminster Bridge Road, London 7UT (☎ 0171 928 5485, fax 0171 928 3748)

CROFT, Giles Laurance; s of John Rothschild Croft, of The Cloisters, Perrymead, Avon, and Nikki, *née* Geal; *b* 20 June 1957; *Educ* Monckton Combe Sch, City of Bath Tech Coll; *Career* artistic director; dir Bath Young People's Theatre Co 1978–80, regnl ed Bananas magazine 1979–80, admin Le Metro Theatre Co Bath 1980–82, artistic dir Gate Theatre 1985–89, series ed Absolute Classics 1988–90, literary mangr Royal Nat Theatre 1989–95, artistic dir Palace Theatre Watford 1995–; many prodns as dir incl: Conversations with a Cupboard Man (Lyric Hammersmith) 1983, Written in Sickness (Upstream) 1984, Orphee (Upstream) 1984, Elmer Gantry (Gate) 1986, The Boxer (Edinburgh Festival) 1986, Naomi (Gate) 1987, The Infant (Gate) 1989, The Secret Life (BBC Radio 4) 1993; for Watford credits incl: Anna Karenina 1995, Foreign Lands 1996, Beethovens Tenth 1996; author of many short stories and articles (published and bdcast); memb Dirs' Guild of GB; FRSA; *Style*— Giles Croft, Esq; ✉ 26 Edgeley Road, London SW4 6ER; Palace Theatre, Clarendon Road, Watford, Herts (fax 01923 819664)

CROFT, 2 Baron (UK 1940); Sir Michael Henry Glendower Page Croft; 2 Bt (UK 1924); s of 1 Baron, CMG, TD, PC (d 1947), and Hon Nancy Beatrice Borwick, da of 1 Baron Borwick; *b* 20 Aug 1916; *Educ* Eton, Trinity Hall Cambridge; *m* 1948, Lady Antoinette Conyngham (d 1959), da of 6 Marquess Conyngham; 1 s, 1 da; *Heir* s, Hon Bernard Croft, *qv*; *Career* called to the Bar 1952; former dir Henry Page and Co and Ware Properties Ltd; underwriting memb Lloyd's 1971–; FRSA; OStJ; *Style*— The Rt Hon the Lord Croft; ✉ Croft Castle, nr Leominster, Herefordshire

CROFT, Sir Owen Glendower; 14 Bt (E 1671), of Croft Castle, Herefordshire; s of Sir Bernard Hugh Denman Croft, 13 Bt (d 1984), and Helen Margaret, *née* Weaver (d 1995); *b* 26 April 1932; *m* 1959, Sally Patricia, da of Dr Thomas Montagu Mansfield, of Brisbane, Australia; 1 s (Thomas Jasper b 1962), 2 da (Patricia Alice b 1960, Georgiana b 1964); *Heir* s, Thomas Jasper Croft, *qv*; *Style*— Sir Owen Croft, Bt; ✉ Salisbury Court, Uralla, NSW 2358, Australia

CROFT, Rodney John; s of Ronald Croft, of Bolton, Lancs, and Joan Constance, *née* Bolton; *b* 26 Feb 1944; *Educ* Bolton Sch, Selwyn Coll Cambridge and Middx Hosp Med Sch (MA, MB BChir, MChir, FRCS, FACS, Berkley fell); *m* 28 July 1973, Hazel Ann, da of late Bernard Dudley Cattermole, and late Eva Cattermole; 2 s (Alexander James b 25 Nov 1974, Alistair Charles b 7 April 1977), 1 da (Antonia Jane b 9 April 1980); *Career* house surgn Middx Hosp 1968, house physician Central Middx Hosp 1969, registrar Dept of Clinical Measurement Middx Hosp 1970, surgical registrar Ipswich Hosps 1971–73, surgical registrar in neurosurgery Maida Vale Hosp 1973; Central Middx and The Middx Hosps: surgical registrar 1973–75, sr surgical registrar 1975–80, research sr registrar 1976; North Middx Hosp: conslt general and vascular surgn 1980–, RCS surgical tutor 1983–89, undergraduate tutor 1986–; Royal Free Hosp Med Sch: clinical sub-dean 1988–, memb Cncl 1991–, School Medal 1993; assoc prof of surgery St George's Univ Grenada 1989–, hon sr lectr in surgery Univ of London 1994–; examiner in surgery (final MB BS) Univ of London 1989–; BSI rep ISO Ctee for Surgical Implants 1993–, memb CEN Ctee for Vascular Implants 1992–; pres Cambridge Univ Med Soc 1964–65; Capt RAMC TAVR 1972–74, Surgn Lt rising to Lt Cdr RNR 1974–83; Liveryman Worshipful Soc of Apothecaries, Freeman City of London; memb: BMA 1968, Int Soc of Chirugie 1976, Vascular Surgical Soc of GB and Ireland 1981, Military Surgical Soc 1988; FRSM 1975, fell Assoc of Surgns of GB and Ireland 1980; *Recreations* music (classical and jazz), rowing, skiing; *Clubs* Garrick, MCC, Lord's Taverners'; *Style*— Rodney J Croft, Esq; ✉ 127 Queen's Road, Buckhurst Hill, Essex IG9 5BH (☎ 0181 505 7813); Department of Surgery, North Middlesex Hospital, Sterling Way, London N18 1QX (☎ 0181 887 2401); 144 Harley Street, London W1N 1AH (☎ 0171 935 0023)

CROFT, Thomas Jasper; s and h of Sir Owen Glendower Croft, 14 Bt, *qv*, and Sally Patricia, da of Dr Thomas Montagu Mansfield; *b* 3 Nov 1962; *Educ* The Armidale Sch, Darling Downs Inst (Assoc Dip Mech Eng), Univ of Sydney (Advanced Dip Land Mgmnt); *m* 29 Jan 1989, Catherine Fiona, da of Graham William White; *Career* landscape co-ordinator; *Recreations* ornithology, bush walking, photography; *Style*— Mr T J Croft; ✉ Haldon, Havelock Road, Beechworth, Victoria 3747, Australia (☎ 00 61 057 282841)

CROFT, Sir Thomas Stephen Hutton; 6 Bt (UK 1818), of Cowling Hall, Yorks; s of Maj Sir John Archibald Radcliffe Croft, 5 Bt (d 1990), and Lucy Elizabeth, *née* Jupp; *b* 12 June 1959; *Educ* King's Sch Canterbury, UCL (BSc), RCA (MA); *Heir* uncle, Cyril Bernard Croft b 1918; *Career* architect; *Style*— Sir Thomas Croft, Bt; ✉ 52 Kelso Place, London W8 5QQ (☎ 0171 937 5518); Barn House, Rayham Farm, Rayham Road, Whitstable, Kent

CROFT BAKER, Michael Anthony; s of Alec Croft Baker (d 1989), and Violet Maryon, *née* Clark; *b* 27 April 1936; *Educ* City of London Sch, King's Coll Univ of London (LLB); *m* 25 May 1968, Yvonne, da of Capt Kenneth George Hall, of Grouville, Jersey, CI; 2 s (James, Edward); *Career* admitted slr 1960; ptnr: Theodore Goddard 1965–91, Allison & Humphreys 1991–; Freeman Worshipful Co of Solicitors 1967; memb: Law Soc 1957, City of London Club 1993; *Recreations* gardening, sport, music; *Style*— Michael Croft Baker, Esq; ✉ Byways, Gregories Farm Lane, Beaconsfield, Bucks HP9 1HJ; Allison &

Humphreys, East India House, 109–117 Middlesex Street, London E1 7JF (☎ 0171 570 6000, fax 0171 570 6060)

CROFTON, 7 Baron (I 1797); Guy Patrick Gilbert Crofton; 10 Bt (I 1758); s of 5 Baron Crofton (d 1974); suc bro, 6 Baron 1989; *b* 17 June 1951; *Educ* Theresianistische Akademie Vienna, Midhurst GS; *m* 1985, Gillian Susan Burroughs, o da of Harry Godfrey Mitchell Bass, CMG, of Reepham, Norfolk; 2 s (Hon (Edward) Harry Piers, Hon (Charles) Marcus George (twin) b 23 Jan 1988); *Heir* s, Hon (Edward) Harry Piers Crofton b 23 Jan 1988; *Career* Lt-Col 9/12 Royal Lancers (Prince of Wales's); currently defence attaché, Berne, Switzerland; *Clubs* Cavalry and Guards'; *Style—* The Rt Hon the Lord Crofton; ✉ c/o Home HQ, 9th/12th Royal Lancers, TA Centre, Saffron Road, Wigston, Leics LE8 2TU

CROFTON, Sir John Wenman; kt (1977); s of Dr William Mervyn Crofton; *b* 1912; *Educ* Tonbridge, Sidney Sussex Coll Cambridge (BA, MA, MD), St Thomas' Hosp London (MB BCh); *m* 1945, Eileen Chris Mercer, MBE; *Career* sr lectr in med Postgrad Med Sch of London 1947–51; Univ of Edinburgh: prof of respiratory diseases and tuberculosis 1952–77, dean Faculty of Med 1963–66, vice princ 1970–71; pres Royal Coll of Physicians Edinburgh 1973–76; Liveryman Worshipful Soc of Apothecaries; Dr (hc) Univ of Bordeaux 1994; FRCP, FRCPEd, FACP, FRACP, FRCPI, FFCM; *Style—* Sir John Crofton; ✉ 13 Spylaw Bank Rd, Edinburgh EH13 0JW (☎ 0131 441 3730)

CROFTON, Sir Malby Sturges; 5 Bt (UK 1838), of Longford House, Sligo (but name does not, at time of going to press, appear on the Official Roll of Baronets); s of Maj Sir (Malby Richard) Henry Crofton, 4 Bt, DSO (d 1962); *b* 11 Jan 1923; *Educ* Eton, Trinity Coll Cambridge; *m* 14 Jan 1961 (m dis 1966), Elizabeth Madeline Nina, da of Maj Rhys Clavell Mansel (d 1969), of Ropley Manor, Alresford, Hants; *Heir* kinsman, (Henry Edward) Melville Crofton, MBE b 15 Aug 1931; *Career* Mayor Royal Borough of Kensington and Chelsea 1978 (ldr Kensington Borough Cncl 1968–77), ptnr Messrs Fenn and Crosthwaite, memb London Stock Exchange 1957–75, memb GLC 1970–73 and (N Ealing) 1977; *Recreations* tennis, swimming, motoring, planting trees, farming; *Clubs* Cavalry and Guards', Hurlingham; *Style—* Sir Malby Crofton, Bt; ✉ Longford House, Co Sligo, Republic of Ireland

CROFTON, (Henry Edward) Melville; MBE (1970); s of Brig Roger Crofton, CIE, MC (d 1972), by his 2 w Dorothy Frances (d 1953), da of Col Henry Melville Hatchell, DSO; hp of kinsman, Sir Malby Crofton, 5 Bt, *qv*; *b* 15 Aug 1931; *Educ* Hilton Coll Natal, Trinity Coll Cambridge (BA); *m* 10 Dec 1955, Mary Brigid, twin da of late Gerald K Riddle, of Buttercombe, Ogwell, Newton Abbot, Devon; 2 s (Julian Malby b 1958, Nigel Melville b 1964), 1 da (Nicola Dorothy (Mrs Julian D P George) b 1961); *Career* princ admin offr HMOCS Nyasaland/Malawi 1956–72; industl trg advsr Overseas Development Administration 1974–91; conslt to Foreign Office Know How Fund for Eastern Europe and the Former Soviet Union 1991–; *Style—* Melville Crofton, Esq, MBE; ✉ Haldon, St Giles Hill, Winchester, Hants SO23 0JH

CROFTON, Dr Richard Wenman; s of Sir John Wenman Crofton, *qv*, and Eileen Chris Crofton, MBE; *b* 2 Oct 1947; *Educ* The Edinburgh Acad, Sidney Sussex Coll Cambridge, Univ of Edinburgh (MA, MB ChB); *m* 26 April 1975, Susan Anne, da of William Henry James (d 1979), of Beverley, Yorks; 1 s (David b 8 Aug 1978), 1 da (Eilidh b 17 Nov 1984); *Career* MRC res fell Dept of Therapeutics Univ of Edinburgh 1973–77, res fell Dept of Infectious Diseases Leiden Univ The Netherlands 1974–76, registrar Aberdeen Teaching Hosps 1977–79, lectr Dept of Med Univ of Aberdeen 1979–83, conslt physician Law Hosp Carluke 1983–; FRCPEd 1986, memb Br Soc of Gastroenterology; *Recreations* family life, the outdoors, bird watching; *Style—* Dr Richard Crofton; ✉ 22 Silverdale Crescent, Lanark, Lanarkshire ML11 9HW (☎ 01555 661394); Law Hospital, Carluke, Lanarkshire ML8 5ER (☎ 01698 361100)

CROHAM, Baron (Life Peer UK 1977), of London Borough of Croydon; Sir Douglas Albert Vivian Allen; GCB (1973, KCB 1967, CB 1963); s of Albert John Allen (ka 1918), of Croydon, Surrey; *b* 15 Dec 1917; *Educ* Wallington GS, LSE (BSc); *m* 1941, Sybil Eileen (d 1994), da of John Marco Allegro (d 1964), of Carshalton, Surrey; 2 s (Hon John Douglas b 1945, Hon Richard Anthony b 1950), 1 da (Hon Rosamund Sybil (Hon Mrs Sulyak) b 1942); *Career* perm sec: Treasy 1968–74, Civil Serv Dept 1974–77; dir: Pilkington plc 1978–92, Guinness Mahon & Co Ltd 1989–92; chm: British National Oil Corporation 1982–86 (dep chm 1978–82), Guinness Peat Group 1983–87, Trinity Insurance Ltd 1988–92; industl advsr to Govr Bank of England 1978–83; chm: Anglo-German Fndn 1981–, Review of Univ Grants Ctee 1985–87; *Recreations* woodwork; *Clubs* Reform, Civil Service; *Style—* The Rt Hon the Lord Croham, GCB; ✉ 9 Manor Way, South Croydon, Surrey CR2 7BT (☎ 0181 688 0496)

CROLL, Prof James George Arthur; s of Keith Waghorn Croll (d 1976), and Jean, *née* Campbell (d 1994); *b* 16 Oct 1943; *Educ* Palmerston North Boy's HS NZ, Univ of Canterbury Christchurch NZ (BE, PhD); *m* 16 Dec 1966, Elisabeth Joan, da of Robert Colston Sprackett (d 1993), of Auckland, NZ; 1 s (Nicolas James b 1974), 1 da (Katherine Elisabeth b 1978); *Career* asst engr NZ Miny of Works 1961–67, Chadwick prof of civil engrg and head Dept of Civil Engrg UCL 1992– (res fell 1967–70, lectr 1970–82, reader in structural engrg 1982–85, prof of structural engrg 1985–92); former: sec and chm Br Soc for Social Responsibility in Sci, sec Jt Br Ctee For Stress Analysis; CMath, FICE, FIStructE, FIMA, FEng 1990; *Books* Elements of Structural Stability (1973), Force Systems & Equilibrium (1975); *Recreations* music, sailing, skiing, cycling, painting; *Clubs* Hayling Island Sailing; *Style—* Prof James Croll, FEng; ✉ 36 Bisham Gardens, Highgate, London N6 4DD (☎ 0181 348 4753); Department of Civil and Environmental Engineering, University College London, London WC1E 6BT (☎ 0171 387 7050 ext 2233/071 380 7224, telex 296273 UCLENG G, fax 0171 380 0986)

CROLL, (Mary) Louise; CBE (1995); da of James Croll (d 1978), and Catherine, *née* Lucey (d 1988); *b* 10 Sept 1935; *Educ* St Anne's Convent GS Southampton Hants; *Career* joined FO 1953, Bahrain 1957–59, Addis Ababa 1959–61, UK Mission to UN New York 1961–63, FCO 1964–69, vice consul Bilbao 1969–71, second sec Lusaka 1971–75, FCO 1975–79, first sec Madrid 1979–83, FCO 1984–88, HM consul Florence and consul gen San Marino 1988–92, HM ambass San José 1992–95, ret; *Recreations* reading, art appreciation, travel; *Style—* Miss Louise Croll, CBE; ✉ c/o Foreign & Commonwealth Office, King Charles Street, London SW1A 2AH

CROMARTIE, 5 Earl of (UK 1861); John Ruaridh Grant Mackenzie; also Viscount Tarbat (UK 1861), Baron Castlehaven (1861), Baron MacLeod of Castle Leod (UK 1861); Chief of the Clan Mackenzie; s of 4 Earl of Cromartie, MC, TD (d 1989), and his 2 w, Olga, *née* Laurance (d 1996); *b* 12 June 1948; *Educ* Rannoch Sch Perthshire, Univ of Strathclyde; *m* 1, 1973 (m dis 1983), Helen, da of John Murray; 1 s (decd); m 2, 1985, Janet Clare, da of Christopher James Harley, of Strathpeffer; 2 s (Colin Ruaridh, Viscount Tarbat b 7 Sept 1987, Hon Alasdair Kenelm Stuart b 6 Dec 1989); *Heir* s, Viscount Tarbat b 7 Sept 1987; *Career* cross-bencher in House of Lords; explosives conslt, past editor Explosives Engineering; memb Inst of Explosive Engrs 1982, exec memb Mountaineering Cncl of Scotland 1994; *Books* Rock and Ice Climbs in Skye (SMT); part author: Cold Climbs, Classic Rock, Wild Walks and many magazine articles both in the climbing and explosives press; *Recreations* mountaineering, geology, art; *Clubs* Scottish Mountaineering, Army and Navy, Pratt's; *Style—* The Rt Hon the Earl of Cromartie; ✉ Castle Leod, Strathpeffer, Ross-shire IV14 9AA

CROMBIE, Prof Alexander Leaster; s of Richard Crombie (d 1987), and Annie Drummond (d 1983); *b* 7 Aug 1935; *Educ* Cork GS, Galashiels Acad, Univ of Edinburgh (MB ChB); *m* 26 Aug 1961, Margaret Ann, da of David Alexander Adamson (d 1981); 2 s (Richard David, David Alexander), 2 da (Pauline Ann, Louise Margaret); *Career* clinical tutor in ophthalmology Univ of Edinburgh 1964–67, MRC fell John Hopkins Univ Baltimore USA 1965–66, conslt ophthalmologist Royal Victoria Infirmary Newcastle upon Tyne 1967–95; Univ of Newcastle upon Tyne: prof of ophthalmology 1976–95, assoc dean Med Sch 1981–89, dean of med 1989–95; author of chapters in books on ophthalmology, medical ethics and medical education; former vice pres Coll of Ophthalmologists, former pres Age Concern Newcastle, tstee Northumbria Calvert Tst; FRCSEd 1964, FRCOphth 1989; *Recreations* golf, reading, music, art, walking; *Style—* Prof Alexander Crombie; ✉ 19 Graham Park Road, Gosforth, Newcastle upon Tyne (☎ 0191 285 2378); 6 The Granary, Dunbar, East Lothian, Scotland

CROMBIE, Alexander Llewellyn Wallace; s of James Wallace Crombie (d 1947), and Sarah Emily, *née* Morris; *b* 19 July 1943; *Educ* Ellesmere Coll, Worcester Coll For The Blind, Univ of Nottingham (LLB); *m* 8 April 1972, Caroline Cawood, da of David John Laurance; 2 s (Duncan b 1975, Hamish b 1978), 1 da (Sarah b 1973); *Career* admitted slr 1968, sr ptnr Crombie Collins 1971–88; ptnr Ironsides Ray & Vials 1988–92, sr ptnr Crobie Collins 1992–96; chm: Visually Impaired Cncl of Leics 1982–89 and 1991–96, Nat Library for the Blind 1982–87, Braille Chess Assoc 1987–93; memb Law Soc; *Style—* Alexander Crombie, Esq; ✉ Elton House, 47 High Street East, Uppingham, Leics LE15 (☎ 01572 823643, fax 01572 821502)

CROME, David Robert; s of Robert Crome (d 1962), and Margaret, *née* Williams; *b* 23 Nov 1937; *Educ* William Hulme's GS Manchester; *m* 28 Sept 1963, Sandra Joan, da of Albert Storrs, of Lowestoft; 3 da (Ruth Margaret (Mrs Selwyn-Crome) b 1964, Helen Jayne (Mrs Hardy) b 1965, Wendy May (Mrs Mobbs) b 1970); *Career* admitted slr 1960; sr ptnr Dunne & Crome 1974, princ magistrate (later chief magistrate and acting chief justice) Solomon Islands 1980–82, recorder of the Crown Court 1993–; full-time chm of Industl Tbnls 1990–; Parly candidate (Lib) Waveney Div 1966 and 1970; FCIArb 1973; *Recreations* sailing, singing (tenor), cycling; *Clubs* Royal Norfolk and Suffolk Yacht, Norfolk County; *Style—* David Robert Crome, Esq; ✉ Office of the Industrial Tribunals, Southgate Street, Bury St Edmunds, Suffolk IP33 2AQ (☎ 01284 762171)

CROMER, 4 Earl of (UK 1901); Evelyn Rowland Esmond Baring; also Baron Cromer (UK 1892), Viscount Cromer (UK 1899), and Viscount Errington (UK 1901); s of 3 Earl of Cromer, KG, GCMG, MBE, PC (d 1991), and Hon Esme Mary Gabrielle Harmsworth, CVO, da of 2 Viscount Rothermere; *b* 3 June 1946; *Educ* Eton; *m* 1, 1971 (m dis 1992), Plern Isarankura na Ayudhya; m 2, 1993, Shelley Hu, da of Hu Guo-qin, of China; 1 s (Alexander Rowland Harmsworth, Viscount Errington b 5 Jan 1994); *Heir* s, Viscount Errington; *Career* md: Inchcape China Ltd 1979–94, Inchcape Vietnam Ltd 1987–94, Inchcape Special Markets Ltd 1990–94; dir: Inchcape Pacific Ltd 1985–94, Schroder AsiaPacific Fund plc 1995–, Korea Asia Fund Ltd 1995–; dep chm: Land-Ocean Inchcape Int Container Transport Co Ltd (China) 1985–94, Motor Transport Co of Guangdong & Hong Kong Ltd (China) 1979–94; chm Lloyd George Standard Chartered China Fund Ltd (Hong Kong); dir: Jardine Fleming China Region Fund Inc (USA), China & Eastern Investments Ltd (Hong Kong), Lazard Vietnam Fund Ltd (Guernsey), Cluff Oil (Hong Kong) Ltd, Cluff Oil China Ltd (Hong Kong), Pacific Basin Bulk Shipping Inc (USA); memb St John's Cncl (Hong Kong) 1980–85; *Recreations* mountain climbing, deep sea diving; *Clubs* White's, Oriental, Hong Kong (Hong Kong); *Style—* The Rt Hon the Earl of Cromer; ✉ House of Lords, London SW1A 0PW

CROMIE, Stephen John Henry; s of Dr Brian William Cromie, of Kings Cliffe, Northants, and Heather Anne Howie, *née* Wood; *b* 13 Jan 1957; *Educ* Abingdon Sch, Downing Coll Cambridge (MA); *m* 28 Aug 1982, Marianne Frances, da of John Edward Burton, East Ewell, Surrey; 1 s (Jonathan b 1989), 1 da (Charlotte b 1996); *Career* admitted slr 1981; ptnr Linklaters & Paines 1987– (joined 1979); memb: Law Soc, City of London Slr's Co; *Books* International Commercial Litigation (jtly, 1990, 2 edn 1997), Merger Control in Europe (1991); *Recreations* wine, cooking, cycling; *Style—* S J H Cromie, Esq; ✉ Linklaters & Paines, Barrington House, 59/67 Gresham Street, London EC2V 7JA (☎ 0171 606 7080, fax 0171 606 5113)

CROMPTON, Prof David William Thomasson; s of Arthur Thomasson Crompton, of Bolton, Lancashire, and Gladys, *née* Mather; *b* 5 Dec 1937; *Educ* Bolton Sch, Univ of Cambridge (BA, MA, PhD, ScD); *m* 14 April 1962, Effie Mary, da of Robert Marshall (d 1989), of Stowmarket, Suffolk; 1 s (John b 1963), 2 da (Tessa b 1964, Virginia b 1967); *Career* Nat Serv 2 Lt King's Own Royal Regt 1956–58; lectr Univ of Cambridge 1968–85 (asst in res 1963–68), vice master Sidney Sussex Coll 1981–83 (res fell 1964–65, fell 1965–85), adjunct prof Div of Nutritional Sciences Cornell Univ NY 1981–; Univ of Glasgow: John Graham Kerr prof of zoology 1985, vice-dean of science 1993–; Scientific medal The Zoological Soc of London 1977; fndr memb Br Soc for Parasitology 1962, memb American Inst of Nutrition 1981, co ed Parasitology 1972–82; memb: Aquatic Life Sciences Ctee NERC 1981–84, WHO Expert Ctee for Parasitic Diseases 1985–; chm Co of Biologists Ltd 1994–, head of WHO Collaborating Centre for Soil-transmitted Helminthiases at Univ of Glasgow 1989–, md St Andrew's Clinics for Children 1992–, memb American Soc of Parasitology 1989; fell Royal Soc of Tropical Med and Hygiene 1986, FIBiol 1979, FZS 1980, FRSE 1989; *Books* An Ecological Approach to Acanthocephalan Physiology (1970), Parasitic Worms (with S M Joyner, 1980), Parasites and People (1984), Biology of the Acanthocephala (ed with B B Nickol), Ascariasis and its Public Health Significance (ed with M C Nesheim and Z S Pawlowski, 1985), Ascariasis and its Prevention and Control (ed with M C Nesheim and Z S Pawlowski, 1989), A Guide to Human Helminths (with Isabel Coombs, 1991); *Recreations* hill walking, fishing, books, terriers, especially bull terriers; *Style—* Prof David Crompton, FRSE; ✉ 7 Kirklee Terrace, Glasgow, Scotland G12 0TQ (☎ 0141 357 2631); Institute of Biomedical and Life Sciences, University of Glasgow, Glasgow G12 8QQ (☎ 0141 330 4914, fax 0141 330 5971, telex 777070)

CROMPTON, Prof Gareth; s of Edward Crompton (d 1986), of Drefach-Felindre, Dyfed, and Annie Jane, *née* Jones; *b* 9 Jan 1937; *Educ* Llandysul GS, Univ of Wales Coll of Med (MB BCh); *m* 12 June 1965, Valmai Gloria, da of Reginald Thomas Lalande (d 1969), of Barry, S Glamorgan; 1 da (Elspeth b 1974); *Career* county MO, county welfare offr and princ schs MO Anglesey CC 1966–73, area med offr Gwynedd Area Health Authy 1974–77, chief med offr Welsh Office 1978–89, prof of public health med Univ of Wales Coll of Med 1989–, chief admin med offr, dir of public health med and exec dir S Glam Health Authy 1989–96; chm Anglesey Disablement Advsy Ctee 1969–77, sec Fluoridation Study Gp Soc of Med Offrs of Health 1969–73, specialty advsr Health Serv Cmmr for England and Wales 1974–77; memb: Gen Med Cncl 1981–83 and 1987–89, Med Advsy Ctee to Registrar Gen 1988–90, Public Health Laboratory Service Bd 1991–, Gorsedd Beirdd Ynys Prydain 1996–; QHP 1984–87; DPH 1964, DRCOG 1962, FFCM 1976, FRCP 1986, FFPHM 1989; *Recreations* bowls, gardening, watching rugby football; *Clubs* Cardiff Athletic; *Style—* Prof Gareth Crompton; ✉ Temple of Peace and Health, Cathays Park, Cardiff CF1 3NW (☎ 01222 231021, fax 01222 371104)

CROMPTON, His Hon Judge; Ian William; s of Thomas Crompton (d 1992), Penmaenmawr, N Wales, and Hilda, *née* Kershaw (d 1994); *b* 28 June 1936; *Educ* Manchester GS, Victoria Univ of Manchester (LLB); *m* 11 July 1962, Audrey, da of William Hopewell; 2 s (Paul b 15 March 1965, Mark b 12 July 1967); *Career* asst slr: Manchester Co Magistrates' Court 1962–63 (articled clerk 1959–62), O'Collier Littler & Kilbeg Manchester 1963–65 (ptnr 1965–72); clerk to the Justices: Manchester Co Magistrates' Ct 1972–74, Eccles Magistrates' Ct 1974–83; dep stipendiary magistrate Manchester City Magistrates' Ct 1981–83, stipendiary magistrate Sheffield Magistrates'

Ct 1983–94, recorder NE Circuit 1990–94, circuit judge (Northern Circuit) 1994–; assoc Imperial Soc of Teachers of Dancing 1980–; *Recreations* golf and dancing; *Clubs* Hallamshire Golf (Sheffield); *Style*— His Hon Judge Crompton; ✉ c/o Northern Circuit Office, 15 Quay Street, Manchester M60 9FD

CROMPTON, Dr (Michael) Rufus; s of Clifford Crompton (d 1972), of Worthing, and Sarah Ashton, *née* Winterburn (d 1988); *b* 9 Sept 1931; *Educ* Shrewsbury, UCH London (MB BS, MD, PhD, DMJ); *m* 3 May 1972, (Yvonne) Anne, da of Bertram Pulford, of Epsom; 2 da (Yvette Selina Ashton b 10 Feb 1973, Danielle Dorothea Clare b 4 Jan 1977); *Career* sr registrar Nat Hosp Queens Square London 1957; Dept of Neurosurgery St George's Hosp London: sr registrar 1959, conslt neuropathologist 1963, conslt forensic pathologist 1970; providing forensic serv to Her Majesty's Coroner and the Met Police; memb: Br Assoc of Forensic Med 1963, Medico Legal Soc 1963; MRCS, LRCP, FRCPath; *Books* Closed Head Injury, Its Pathology and Legal Medicine (1985); *Recreations* supporting family riding activities; *Clubs* Hurlingham, Ham Polo; *Style*— Dr Rufus Crompton; ✉ Department of Forensic Medicine, St George's Hospital Medical School, London SW17 ORE (☎ 0181 672 9944 ext 55240–1)

CROMPTON, Sarah Melanie; da of Donald Walker Crompton (d 1982), and Mary, *née* Barnes; *b* 30 Aug 1957; *Educ* Headington Sch Oxford, Hertford Coll Oxford (BA), Univ Coll Cardiff (Dip in Journalism); *m* 1995, Icaro Kosak; *Career* features writer Coventry Evening Telegraph 1983–85 (reporter 1980–83), dep features ed Woman Oct 1986– April 1987 (researcher and features writer 1985–86), asst ed Woman's Own 1989–90 (features ed April 1987–89), asst ed Telegraph Magazine 1990–94, arts ed The Daily Telegraph 1994–; *Recreations* watching Manchester United and other forms of armchair sport; *Style*— Ms Sarah M Crompton; ✉ The Daily Telegraph, 1 Canada Square, Canary Wharf, London E14 5DT (☎ 0171 538 5000)

CROMWELL, 7 Baron (E 1375); Godfrey John Bewicke-Copley; s of 6 Baron Cromwell (d 1982; Barony abeyant 1497 to 1923, when abeyance terminated in favour of present Baron's gf, 5 Baron); *b* 4 March 1960; *m* 23 June 1990, Elizabeth A, da of John Hawksley; 1 da (Hon Helen Tatiana b 18 March 1995); *Heir* da, Hon Helen Tatiana Bewicke-Copley b 18 March 1995; *Style*— The Rt Hon the Lord Cromwell; ✉ c/o House of Lords, London SW1

CRONIN, Damian Francis; *Career* Rugby Union lock forward London Scottish RFC and Scotland; clubs: Bath RFC, Ilford Wanderers, Barbarians RFC, Penguins RFC, Bourges RFC, Anglo-Scots, currently playing for Wasps RFC; Scotland: debut v Ireland 1988, Grand Slam winners 1990, tour Zimbabwe 1988, tour Japan 1989, tour NZ 1990, World Cup 1991 and 1995, tour Aust 1992, 36 caps; memb British Lions' team touring NZ 1993; *Recreations* antiques and restoration, squash; *Style*— Damian Cronin, Esq

CRONIN, Tacey Marguerite (Mrs David Bain); da of Flt Lt Anthony Arthur Cronin (d 1972), and Margaret Elizabeth, *née* Roberts; *b* 28 June 1959; *Educ* Stamford HS, Bristol Univ (LLB); *m* 3 Jan 1987, David Ian Bain, s of Capt David Walter Bain (d 1975); 3 da (Athene Margaret b 1990, Esmé Rose b 1993, Cecily Mary b 1996); *Career* called to the Bar Middle Temple 1982; memb: Bar Cncl 1985–86, Gen Cncl of the Bar 1987; dir BMIF 1988–; *Recreations* theatre, golf, motor racing, travel; *Style*— Miss Tacey Cronin; ✉ Albion Chambers, Broad St, Bristol BS1 1DR (☎ 0117 927 2144, fax 0117 926 2569)

CRONIN, Vincent Archibald Patrick; s of Archibald Joseph Cronin (d 1981), the author, of Vevey, Switzerland, and Agnes Mary, *née* Gibson (d 1981); *b* 24 May 1924; *Educ* Ampleforth, Harvard, Trinity Coll Oxford (BA); *m* 25 Aug 1949, Chantal, da of Comte Jean De Rolland (d 1985), of Manoir De Brion, Dragey par Sartilly 50530, France; 2 s (James b 1956, Luan b 1959), 3 da (Sylvilie b 1951, Dauphine b 1962, Natalie b 1967); *Career* author; memb Cncl RSL 1976–86; *Books* incl: The Golden Honeycomb (1954), The Wise Man From the West (1955), The Last Migration (1957), A Pearl to India (1959), The Letter after Z (1960), Louis XIV (1964), Napoleon (1964), Four Women in Pursuit of an Ideal (1965), The Florentine Renaissance (1967), The Flowering of the Renaissance (1970), Catherine, Empress of all the Russias (1978), The View From Planet Earth (1981), Paris on the Eve (1989); *Recreations* swimming, tennis; *Clubs* Oxford and Cambridge; *Style*— Vincent Cronin, Esq; ✉ c/o HarperCollins, Ophelia House, Fulham Palace Rd, London W6

CROOK, Anthony Donald (Tony); s of Thomas Roland (d 1926), of Hoghton, nr Preston, Lancs, and Emily, *née* Allsup; *b* 16 Feb 1923; *Educ* Clifton, Sidney Sussex Coll Cambridge; *m* 28 June 1943, Dianne Ada, da of William Smith (d 1958), of Lincoln; 1 da (Carole Anne); *Career* RAF 1939–46 (despatches twice), Flt Lt 1945; formed racing car partnership with Raymond Mays 1945, won first post-war motor race to be held in Britain 1946, raced and distributed Bristol Cars made by Bristol Aeroplane Co; over 400 races incl: formula one and two, Grand Prix, and speed hill climbs 1946–55; bought (with the late Sir George White) Bristol Cars 1960 (by 1973 sole owner, md and chm); *Clubs* British Racing Drivers'; *Style*— Tony Crook, Esq; ✉ Bristol Cars Ltd, Head Office, 368–370 Kensington High Street, London W14 8NL

CROOK, Colin; s of Richard Crook (d 1970), and Ruth Crook (d 1971); *b* 1 June 1942; *Educ* Harris Coll Preston, Liverpool Poly; *m* 1965, Dorothy Jean, da of Alfred Edward Taylor, of Wallasey; 2 da; *Career* Motorola (USA) 1969–79, dir advanced systems gp ops MGR Microcomputers 1975–78; md: Zynar Holdings BV, Rank Precision Industries 1978–80, BT Telecom Enterprises; chm: HBS Ltd (UK) 1980–83, Nestar Systems (USA) 1980–83; memb Main Bd BT 1983–1984, sr vice pres Data General Corpn 1984–89, chm Corp Technol Ctee Citicorp NY USA 1990–; FEng 1981, MIEE, MIERE, MIEEE, MACM (USA); *Recreations* photography, sailing, reading, walking, travel; *Style*— Colin Crook, Esq, FEng; ✉ The Old School House, Harvest Hill, Hedsor, Bourne End, Bucks SL8 5JJ (☎ 0162 8527479); Citibank, 399 Park Ave, NY, NY 10043, USA

CROOK, 2 Baron (UK 1947), of Carshalton, Co Surrey; Douglas Edwin Crook; o s of 1 Baron Crook (d 1989), and Ida Gertrude Catherine, *née* Haddon (d 1985); *b* 19 Nov 1926; *Educ* Whitgift Middle Sch Croydon, Imperial Coll London (ACGI, BSc, DIC); *m* 15 Feb 1954, Ellenor, da of Robert Rouse (d 1962), of Sunderland; 1 s (Hon Robert Douglas Edwin b 29 May 1955), 1 da (Hon Catherine Hilary b 22 May 1960); *Heir* s, Hon Robert Douglas Edwin Crook, *qv*; *Career* CEng, MICE; *Style*— The Rt Hon Lord Crook; ✉ Ridgehill Barn, Etchinghill, Folkestone, Kent CT18 8DF (☎ 01303 863 353)

CROOK, Frances Rachel; da of Maurice Crook (d 1977), of London, and Sheila Sibson-Turnbull; *b* 18 Dec 1952; *Educ* Camden Sch London, Univ of Liverpool (BA), Univ of Lancaster (PGCE); 1 da (Sarah Rose Eleanor b 27 May 1988); *Career* campaign organiser Amnesty Int 1980–85, dir Howard League for Penal Reform 1985–; cnclr Barnet Borough 1982–90, govr Greenwich Univ; memb: Lab Party, CND, NUPE; *Style*— Ms Frances Crook; ✉ The Howard League, 708 Holloway Road, London N19 3NL (☎ 0171 281 7722)

CROOK, Prof (Joseph) Mordaunt; s of Austin Mordaunt Crook (d 1967), and Florence Irene, *née* Woolfendon (d 1986); *b* 27 Feb 1937; *Educ* Wimbledon Coll, BNC Oxford (MA, DPhil); *m* 1, 4 July 1964, Margaret Constance, da of James Mulholland (d 1974); m 2, 9 July 1975, Susan, da of Frederick Hoyland Mayor (d 1972); *Career* lectr Bedford Coll London 1965–75, res fell Warburg Inst 1970–71, reader in architectural history Univ of London 1975–81, Slade prof of fine art Univ of Oxford 1979–80, visiting fell BNC Oxford 1979–80, prof of architectural history Univ of London 1981–, visiting fell and Waynflete lectr Magdalen Coll Oxford 1985, visiting fell Gonville and Caius Coll Cambridge 1986, public orator Univ of London 1988–91; memb Historic Bldgs Cncl for Eng 1974–84, pres Soc of Architectural Historians (GB) 1980–84, memb Advsy Bd for Redundant Churches 1991–; Freeman Goldsmiths Co 1978 (Liveryman 1984); FSA, FBA; *Books* The British Museum (1972), The Greek Revival (1972), The History of The King's Works (1973–76), William Burges and the High Victorian Dream (1981), The Dilemma of Style: Architectural Ideas from the Picturesque to the Post-Modern (1987); *Recreations* strolling; *Clubs* Athenaeum, Brooks's; *Style*— Prof J Mordaunt Crook, FSA, FBA; ✉ Royal Holloway and Bedford New Coll, Egham, Surrey TW20 OEX

CROOK, Paul; s of William Giles Crook, of Poole, Dorset, and Helen Margaret, *née* Swales; *b* 6 March 1952; *Educ* Ruzawi Sch Zimbabwe, Peterhouse Sch Zimbabwe, Jesus Coll Cambridge (MA, LLB); *m* 11 Sept 1976, Dr Susan Jill, da of Dr Andrew Ernest Dossetor, of Newmarket, Suffolk; 2 s (John b 1988, Peter b 1990), 1 da (Anne b 1986); *Career* admitted slr 1978, ptnr Allen & Overy (based Paris) 1984–; Freeman City of London Slrs Co 1984; memb Law Soc; *Recreations* golf, hockey, skiing, squash, tennis; *Style*— Paul Crook, Esq; ✉ Allen & Overy, 21 rue Jean Goujon, 75008 Paris, France (☎ 00 33 1 49 53 06 37, fax 00 33 1 49 53 91 52, telex 6510179)

CROOK, Hon Robert Douglas Edwin; s and h of 2 Baron Crook, *qv*, of Carshalton, Co Surrey, and Ellenor, *née* Rouse; *b* 29 May 1955; *m* 29 May 1981, Suzanne Jane, da of Harold Robinson, of Farnsfield, Notts; 2 s (Matthew Robert b 28 May 1990, James Nicholas b 16 June 1992); *Style*— The Hon Robert Crook; ✉ 21 Doncella Street, The Gap, Queensland 4060, Australia

CROOKALL, Prof John Roland; s of Dr Robert Crookall (d 1981), and Gladys Kate, *née* Stoneham (d 1969); *b* 5 May 1935; *Educ* Dorking County GS, Willesden Coll of Technol (HNC), Imperial Coll (DIC), Univ of Nottingham (PhD); *m* 19 June 1965, Gretta Mary, da of Basil Blaxley Inger; 2 s (Barry Nicholas b 5 Oct 1966, Andrew Spencer b 1 Oct 1967), 1 da (Sheila Elizabeth Anne b 8 May 1972); *Career* performance and design engr aero-engines de Havilland Engine Co Ltd 1957–61 (engrg apprentice 1952–57), visiting lectr Willesden Coll of Technol 1958–62, PhD res Univ of Nottingham 1962–65, lectr and course mangr MSc course in prodn technol Imperial Coll London 1965–74; Cranfield Inst of Technol: prof of mfrg systems 1974–90, head Dept for Design of Machine Systems 1982–84, emeritus prof of mfrg 1990; int conslt in intellectual property and patents 1990–, fndr and chm Computer Integrated Manufacturing Inst Cranfield 1985–90, fndr and head Coll of Manufacturing Cranfield 1985–90, chm Bd CIM Technology Ltd 1985–90, chm CIRP (UK) Ltd 1988–91; memb numerous ctees and professional bodies incl: memb Advsy Ctee on Sci and Technol 1988–92, memb Parly and Scientific Ctee 1985–91, chm UK Bd Int Inst for Prodn Engrg Res (CIRP) 1988–91, memb and UK rep Int Fedn of Info Processing (IFIP); external examiner to 11 prodn and mechanical engrg courses within UK; memb Royal Coll of Organists, sr memb American Soc of Mfrg Engrs, assoc Chartered Inst of Patent Agents; FEng 1990, FCGI, CEng, FIMechE, AMIOD, MAE; *Awards* Instn of Mechanical Engrs: James Clayton fellowship 1962, James Clayton prize 1965, E Midlands Branch prize 1965; meritorious commendation Indust Year Awards DTI 1986, LEAD award SME (USA) 1991; *Books* Numerically Controlled Machine Tools (1970); author of over 100 papers on mfrg; *Recreations* music, organist St Peter de Merton Bedford; *Style*— Prof John R Crookall, FEng; ✉ 12 Hall Close, Harrold, Bedford MK43 7DU (☎ 01234 720475, fax 01234 720675)

CROOKE, Dr John Walter; s of William Grosvenor Crooke (d 1985), of Lincs, and Esmé Beatrice, *née* Greene (d 1989); *b* 7 July 1933; *Educ* Scunthorpe GS, UCH London (BSc, MB BS, DA, FRCA); *m* 28 Oct 1961, Mary Lynn, da of Angus Ernest Gibson (d 1980), of Lincoln; 1 s (James), 1 da (Heather); *Career* Nat Serv Capt RAMC, anaesthetist Br Mily Hosp Benghazi N Africa; conslt anaesthetist Royal Liverpool Univ Hosp Tst 1968–96, pt/t demonstrator Dept of Anaesthesia Univ of Liverpool 1978–96 (pt/t lectr Dept of Dental Surgery), ret; med rep Mersey Regnl Supplies Ctee, memb Assoc of Anaesthetists; fell Royal Coll of Anaesthetists; memb: HCSA, BMA; *Recreations* flying (PPL), car restoration, fishing, cycling; *Clubs* Aston Martin Owners, Lotus, RSPB; *Style*— Dr John W Crooke; ✉ The Pingles, 12 Park Avenue, Crosby, Liverpool L23 2SP (☎ 0151 924 5758)

CROOKENDEN, Lt-Gen Sir Napier; KCB (1970, CB 1966), DSO (1945), OBE (1954); 2 s of Col Arthur Crookenden, CBE, DSO (d 1962), and Dorothy, *née* Rowlandson; *b* 31 Aug 1915; *Educ* Wellington, RMC Sandhurst; *m* 3 Aug 1948, Hon Patricia Nassau, da of 2 Baron Kindersley, CBE, MC; 2 s, 2 da; *Career* Cheshire Regt 1935, CO 9 Para Bn 1944–46 and 16 Para Bde 1960–61, dir Land/Air Warfare 1964–66, Cmdt Royal Mil Coll of Science 1958–59, Col The Cheshire Regt 1969–71, GOC-in-C Western Cmd 1969–72, Col Cmdt Prince of Wales Div 1971–74; dir: SE Regnl Bd Lloyds Bank Ltd 1973–86, Flextech Ltd 1973–86; tstee Imperial War Museum 1973–83, chm SSAFA 1974–85, Lt HM Tower of London 1975–81; DL Kent 1979–95; *Books* Drop Zone Normandy (1976), Airborne at War (1978), Battle of the Bulge 1944 (1980); *Clubs* Army and Navy; *Style*— Lt-Gen Sir Napier Crookenden, KCB, DSO, OBE; ✉ Twin Firs, Four Elms, Edenbridge, Kent TN8 6PL (☎ 01732 700229)

CROOKENDEN, Simon Robert; QC (1996); s of Maj Spencer Crookenden, CBE, MC, of Kendal, Cumbria, and late Jean, *née* Dewing; *b* 27 Sept 1946; *Educ* Winchester, Corpus Christi Coll Cambridge (MA); *m* 20 Aug 1983, Sarah Anne Georgina Margaret, da of George Leonard Pragnell, of Cheltenham; 1 s (Thomas Henry b 19 Sept 1987), 2 da (Rebecca Jean b 9 Nov 1985, Alice Lily b 5 Aug 1991); *Career* called to the Bar Gray's Inn 1974; *Recreations* rowing; *Clubs* London Rowing; *Style*— Simon Crookenden, Esq, QC; ✉ Essex Court Chambers, 24 Lincoln's Inn Fields, London WC2A 3ED (☎ 0171 813 8000, fax 0171 813 8080)

CROOKS, Lee; s of Herbert James Crooks, and Joan, *née* Owen; *b* 18 Sept 1963; *Educ* Ainthorpe Jr HS, Sydney Smith HS; *m* 1, 4 July 1980 (m dis), Janet Hilary, *née* Taylor; 1 da (Emma Louise b 21 July 1982), 1 s (Stuart Andrew b 23 Oct 1984); m 2, 15 June 1994, Karen Norton; 1 s (Benjamin James b 15 June 1993), 1 da (Megan Leigh b 21 Aug 1989); *Career* rugby league player; city and co under 11 rep, city, co and nat under 16 capt; Hull RLFC: joined 1980, debut v Salford, 196 appearances; Leeds RLFC: joined 1987, debut v Leigh 1989, 55 appearances; Castleford RLFC: joined 1990, debut v St Helens, over 200 appearances; 3 Yorks caps; GB caps: 6 colts, 4 under 21, 1 under 24, 19 full; memb full int tours to Australasia 1984, 1988 and 1992; former painter and decorator; *Recreations* golf; *Style*— Lee Crooks, Esq; ✉ Castleford RLFC, Wheldon Rd, Castleford, West Yorks WF10 2SD (☎ 01977 552674, fax 01977 518007)

CROOKS, Stanley George; s of Wallace George Crooks (d 1978), and Alice Mary, *née* Clancy (d 1989); *b* 3 March 1925; *Educ* St Marylebone GS London, Univ of London (BSc, BSc Econ); *m* 22 July 1950, Gwendoline May, da of Arthur George Hatch; 1 s (Andrew b 1959), 1 da (Julia b 1961); *Career* Royal Artillery 1943–47 (service Burma 1944–45, Indochina 1945, Malaya 1946, Hong Kong 1947); Pirelli Group of Companies 1950–; md Pirelli General Ltd Southampton 1967–71 (joined 1950), gen mangr Société Internationale Pirelli Basle 1974–82 (dep gen mangr 1971–74), dir and gen mangr Pirelli Société Generale Basle 1982–87; chm: Pirelli Construction Co Ltd 1982–91, Pirelli Ltd 1987–91, Pirelli Focom Ltd 1987–91, Pirelli Tyres UK 1991–92; vice chm: Pirelli UK plc 1989–, Pirelli General plc 1994– (chm 1987–94); chm CBI Educn Policy Panel 1995–; vice chm Cncl Univ of Southampton 1987–96, chm Univ of Southampton Mgmnt Sch 1990–92; chm of govrs Southampton Inst of Higher Educn 1988–90; pres Southern Sci and Technol Forum 1977–93; Hon DSc Southampton 1977; FIEE 1965, CIMgt 1970; *Recreations* gardening, music, reading; *Style*— Stanley Crooks, Esq; ✉ Bournewood House, Bourne Lane, Twyford, Winchester, Hampshire SO21 1NX; Pirelli UK plc, 11 Berkeley Street, London W1X 6BU (☎ 0171 355 5080, fax 0171 355 5066)

CROOKSTON, Peter Christian; s of Robert Crookston (d 1969), and Nancy Hedley; *b* 30 Dec 1936; *Educ* Clegwell Sch Hebburn on Tyne, Newcastle upon Tyne Coll of Commerce; *m* 1, Julia Hampton (m dis 1974); 1 s (James b 21 Feb 1970); m 2, 31 March 1988, Zoe Zenghelis, da of John Tsakiris (d 1985), and Anastasia Gabriel (d 1994), of Herodotou 12, Athens, Greece; *Career* ed Nova magazine 1969–71; features ed: Sunday Times 1971–73, The Observer 1973–77; ed: The Observer Magazine 1977–82, Geo International 1988–90; dep ed Departures 1990–91, ed WORLD Magazine 1991–93, contributing ed Telegraph Magazine 1993–94, ed English Heritage magazine 1994–; *Books* Villain (1967), Village England (ed, 1979), Island Britain (ed, 1981), The Ages of Britain (ed, 1982); *Recreations* sailing, cycling; *Clubs* Chelsea Arts, Groucho; *Style—* Peter Crookston, Esq; ✉ 84 Portland Road, London W11 4LQ (☎ 0171 229 3373, fax 0171 243 1467)

CROOM-JOHNSON, Rt Hon Sir David Powell; kt (1971), PC (1984), DSC (1944), VRD (1953); 3 s of late Hon Sir Reginald Powell Croom-Johnson (d 1957), a sometime Judge of the High Court, and Ruby Ernestine, *née* Hobbs (d 1961); *b* 28 Nov 1914; *Educ* Stowe, Trinity Hall Cambridge (hon fell 1985); *m* 1940, Barbara Douglas (d 1994), da of Erskine Douglas Warren, of Toronto, Canada; 1 da (Deborah); *Career* barr 1938, QC 1958, recorder Winchester 1962–71, judge Courts of Appeal Jersey and Guernsey 1966–71, High Court judge (Queen's Bench Div) 1971–84, Lord Justice of Appeal 1984–89; *Clubs* Garrick; *Style—* The Rt Hon Sir David Croom-Johnson, DSC, VRD; ✉ 59 Coleherne Court, Old Brompton Road, London SW5 0EF (☎ 0171 373 2343)

CROPPER, Hilary Mary; da of Arnold Trueman, of Cheshire, and Madeline Emily, *née* Sutton; *b* 9 Jan 1941; *Educ* Univ of Salford (BSc); *m* 16 Sept 1963, Peter John Cropper, s of Samuel Cropper; 1 s (Carl St John b 1971), 2 da (Elizabeth b 1969, Charlotte b 1973); *Career* various sr mgmnt positions ICL 1970–85, chief exec FI Group plc 1985–, non-exec dir TSB Bank plc 1987–90; non-exec memb: Post Office Board 1990–96, British Overseas Trade Board 1992–96; govr Univ of Hertfordshire 1995–; Freeman: City of London 1987, Worshipful Co of Information Technologists 1987; CIMgt 1988; FBCS, FRSA; *Style—* Mrs Hilary Cropper; ✉ Woodlands, Parslows Hillock, Princes Risborough, Bucks (☎ 01494 488227); FI Gp plc, Campus 300, Maylands Ave, Hemel Hempstead, Herts HP2 7TQ (☎ 01442 233339, fax 01442 238400)

CROPPER, James Anthony; s of Anthony Charles Cropper (d 1967), of Tolson Hall, Kendal, and Philippa Mary Gloria, *née* Clutterbuck; *b* 22 Dec 1938; *Educ* Eton, Magdalene Coll Cambridge (BA); *m* 30 June 1967, Susan Rosemary, da of Col F J N Davis (d 1988), of Northwood, Middx; 2 s (Charles Michael Anthony b 1969, d 1974, Mark b 1974), 1 da (Sarah b 1972); *Career* dir: James Cropper PLC papermakers 1966– (chm 1971–), East Lancs Paper Group PLC 1982–84, NW Water Group PLC 1989–90; pres Br Paper and Bd Indust Fedn 1987–89; dir Cumbria Rural Enterprise Agency 1987–, chm govrs of Abbot Hall Art Gallery and Museum 1983–88; memb: S Westmorland RDC 1967–74, Lancs River Authy 1968–74, NW Water Authy 1973–80 and 1987–89, S Lakeland Dist Cncl 1974–77; High Sheriff of Westmorland 1971, Lord Lt of Cumbria 1994– (Vice Lord Lt 1991, DL 1986); Liveryman Worshipful Co of Stationers & Newspaper Makers; FCA; *Recreations* shooting, skiing, windsurfing; *Clubs* Brooks's; *Style—* James Cropper, Esq; ✉ Tolson Hall, Kendal, Cumbria (☎ 01539 722011); James Cropper PLC, Burneside Mills, Kendal, Cumbria (☎ 01539 722002)

CROPPER, Peter John; s of Samuel Duncan Cropper (d 1961), and Anna Southwell, *née* Parkinson (d 1990); *b* 7 Feb 1940; *Educ* Salford GS, Univ of Manchester; *m* 16 Sept 1963, Hilary Mary, da of Arnold Trueman, of Bollington, Cheshire; 1 s (Carl b Oct 1971), 2 da (Elizabeth b Dec 1969, Charlotte b Feb 1973); *Career* various tech and mgmnt appts AEI and English Electric 1960–68, software devpt mangr ICL 1968–75, gen mangr Computer Gp CWS Ltd 1975–80; md: STC IDEC Ltd 1980–85, STC Technology Ltd 1985–87; dir corporate info systems STC plc 1987–91, vice pres info systems Northern Telecom Ltd (following merger with STC plc) 1991–; Freeman City of London 1988, Liveryman Worshipful Co of Scientific Instrument Makers, Liveryman and memb Ct of Assts Worshipful Co of Information Technologists; CEng, FBCS, FIMgt; *Recreations* bridge, theatre; *Clubs* Naval and Military; *Style—* Peter Cropper, Esq; ✉ Woodlands, Pink Road, Parslows Hillock, Princes Risborough, Bucks HP27 0RJ (☎ and fax 01494 488727); Northern Telecom Ltd, Information Systems, Westacott Way, Maidenhead, Berks SL6 3QH (☎ 01628 432920, fax 01628 432980, e-mail peter.cropper@nt.com)

CROSBEE, Rachel; da of Roger Henry Fox, of Ashby de la Zouch, Leics, and Jennifer Jean Munro, *née* Betten; sis of Richard Fox, MBE, *qv*; *b* 6 May 1969; *Educ* Roundwood Park Secdy Sch Harpenden, Nottingham Sch of Physiotherapy; *m* 7 Nov 1992, David Crosbee; *Career* canoeist; competes in slalom K1 ladies, began with St Albans Club 1983, currently with Nottingham Club; achievements incl: fourth Jr Euro Championships 1987, team Silver medal Pre World Championships Maryland USA 1988, team Bronze medal Pre World Championships Taceu Yugoslavia 1990, team Bronze medal Pre World Championships Mezzana Italy 1992 (individual 9th), team Bronze medal World Championships Mezzana 1993, sixth World Cup Nottingham 1992, also competed in Olympic Games Barcelona 1992 and World Championships 1989, 1991 and 1993, first World Cup Nottingham 1994 (second overall), fourth World Championships Nottingham 1995 (Silver in team), competed Olympic Games Atlanta 1996, ninth place World Cup series 1996; ranked number 1 in GB 1992, 1994 and 1996; qualified physiotherapist 1990, currently sr physiotherapist General Hosp Nottingham; *Recreations* sports therapy, walking, running rivers; *Style—* Mrs Rachel Crosbee; ✉ c/o British Canoe Union, Adbolton Lane, West Bridgford, Nottingham NG2 5AS (☎ 0115 982 1100)

CROSBIE, Annette; *b* 12 Feb 1934; *Career* actress; *Theatre* Citizens Theatre Glasgow: View from a Bridge, The Crucible, Anne Frank, The Cherry Orchard, Guy Landscape (also Royal Court); Bristol Old Vic: Romeo and Juliet, The Tempest, A Taste of Honey, Caesar and Cleopatra; Comedy Theatre: Tinker, My Place, A Singular Man; other: Mr Bolfry (Aldwych), The Changeling (Royal Court), Twelfth Night (City of London Festival and tour), The Winslow Boy (New Theatre), The Family Dance (Criterion), Curse of the Starving Class (Royal Court), Corn is Green (Yvonne Arnaud Theatre Guilford), The Undertaking (Greenwich and Fortune), Tiger at the Gate (NT), Forty Years On (Chichester), Tramway Road (Lyric), Talk of the Devil (Palace Theatre Watford), Collier's Friday Night (Greenwich), Curtains (Whitehall), The Way South (Bush), I Thought I Heard A Rustling (Stratford Theatre Royal), Karate Billy Comes Home (Theatre Upstairs Royal Court); *Television* BBC: Catherine of Aragon in The Six Wives of Henry VIII (BAFTA Best Actress 1970), The Seagull, East Lynne, Auntie's Niece, Waste, Twelfth Night, Langrish Go Down, Find Me First, Henrick Ibsen, Of Mycenae and Men, Tolstoy, The Misanthrope, Jessie, Richard III, Pericles, Nobody's Property, Paying Guests, Watch With Mother, Take Me Home, Beyond the Pale, Summers Lease, Colin's Sandwich, One Foot in the Grave (2 series), Jute City; other: Queen Victoria and Edward VII (ATV, BAFTA and TV Times Best Actress 1975), The Portrait (LWT), Lilly Langtry (LWT), The House on the Hill (STV), Lowry - A Private View (Granada), Sunday Night Thriller (LWT), Charles Dilk Trilogy (Granada), Northern Lights (STV), The Pyramid Game (LWT), Off Peak (STV), Que Sera (TVS), Paradise Postponed (Euston Films), Taggart (STV), Game Set and Match (Granada), Bon Esperance (French TV), Heartbeat (Yorkshire), The Speaker of Mandarin (TVS); *Films* The Slipper and the Rose (Best Actress Evening News Drama Awards 1976), Hawk the Slayer, The Disappearance of Harry, Ordeal By Innocence, Final Warning, The Pope Must Die; *Style—* Ms Annette Crosbie; ✉ c/o Conway van Gelder Robinson Ltd, 18–21 Jermyn Street, London SW1Y 6HP (☎ 0171 287 0077, fax 0171 287 1940)

CROSBIE, Neil; s of James Steele Crosbie (d 1973), and Doreen, *née* Bell; *b* 28 Jan 1953; *Educ* Royal GS Newcastle upon Tyne, Aston Univ (BSc); *m* 2 Aug 1975, Christine Mary, da of John Fletcher Tully; 1 da (Ciaran b 9 March 1979), 2 s (Andrew b 1 Dec 1980, Iain b 9 May 1983); *Career* Forward Trust (Finance) Ltd 1973–74, Universities and Colleges Christian Fellowship 1975–79; British & Foreign Bible Society: joined as asst to Exec Dir 1979–81, customer servs mangr 1981–84, dir of admin 1984–88, personnel and admin dir 1988–91, exec dir/chief exec 1991–; memb ACENVO 1993; MIMgt 1985, MInstD 1995; *Recreations* reading, walking, sleeping; *Style—* Neil Crosbie, Esq; ✉ Chief Executive, Bible Society, Stonehill Green, Westlea, Swindon SN5 7DG (☎ 01793 418100, fax 01793 418118)

CROSBIE, William; s of Archibald Shearer Crosbie (d 1961), of Faucheong, Hankow, Huphe, China, and Mary Nicol, *née* Edgar (d 1948); *b* 31 Jan 1915; *Educ* Glasgow Acad, Glasgow Sch of Art/Univ (BA), Studio of Fernand Leger Paris, Academy de la Grande Chaumiere Paris; *m* 1, 2 Oct 1944, (Mary) Grace McPhail (d 1973); 2 da ((Mary) Pauline Elizabeth b 7 July 1947, Michelle Louise b 6 April 1951 d 24 April 1951); m 2, 6 June 1975, (Margaret) Anne, da of Sydney Roger (d 1976), of Persia; *Career* conscript MN 1942–45; artist studies in schs and studios in Paris, Brussels, Athens, Istanbul, Cairo, Rome, Florence; numerous exhbns since 1946, one man exhbns in Glasgow, Edinburgh, London, USA, Brussels and Hamburg; works in: Kelvingrove Galleries Glasgow, Arts Cncl, Scottish provincial galleries, Edinburgh City Arts Centre (mural) 1980, Scottish Gallery of Modern Art 1980, Sydney State Gallery Aust, Wellington NZ, Royal Collection UK, Refectory Fruit Market Gallery Edinburgh 1980, Nat Library of Scotland 1986, Scottish Nat Portrait Gallery 1995, various private collections; govr: Edinburgh Coll of Art 1972–75, Glasgow Sch of Art 1975–81; keeper RSA 1977–85; RGI 1975, RSA 1967 (hon prof); *Recreations* sailing, history (art and Medieval history); *Clubs* LSC, GAC; *Style—* William Crosbie, Esq; ✉ Rushes House, 10 Winchester Rd, Petersfield, Hants GU32 3BY (☎ 01730 266899)

CROSBY, John Rutherford; s of John Charles Crosby (d 1938), of Colchester, and Florence Nightingale, *née* Rutherford (d 1982); *b* 1 May 1933; *Educ* Univ of Durham (BA), Univ of London (MA), Univ Coll Cardiff (Dip in Personnel Mgmnt); *m* 10 March 1962, Rosalind Elizabeth, da of Gilbert Baynon Williams (d 1968); 2 s (Neil b 1966, David b 1968), 1 da (Sarah (Mrs Perrin) b 1963); *Career* personnel mgmnt appts with EMI and Costain Group 1958–68, sr conslt Hay MSL 1968–76, personnel dir British American Tobacco Co 1983–88 (head of personnel servs 1976–83), dir of gp personnel BAT Industries 1988–92; IPM: vice pres 1979–81, pres 1985–87, chm IPM servs 1985–87, chm IPM Advsy Ctee on Nominations 1987–89; memb: Cncl VSO 1983–92, Civil Serv Final Selection Bd 1984–, Business Liaison Ctee London Business Sch 1984–90, NEDO Steering Gp on Human Resource Devpt 1986–87, Employment Appeal Tbnl 1991–, Armed Forces Pay Review Body 1993–, Jt Steering Gp Social Servs Inspectorate 1993–; memb Bd: Ind Assessment and Research Centre 1988–, Legal Aid Bd 1994–; govr Centre for Int Briefing (Farnham Castle) 1983–, chm Croydon Coll 1993– (govr 1987, vice chm 1989–93), tstee Overseas Students Tst 1988–93; govr Univ of Westminster 1994–, memb Cncl Univ of Sussex 1995–; Freeman of Colchester 1971; CIPM 1980, CIMgt 1983, FInstD 1984; *Books* Handbook of Management Development (contrib 1986 and 1991); *Recreations* music (particularly opera), theatre, avoiding all gardening; *Clubs* Oriental, IOD; *Style—* John Crosby, Esq; ✉ 70 Woodcote Valley Rd, Purley, Surrey CR8 3BD (☎ 0181 660 2717)

CROSET, Paul John Francis; OBE (1967); s of Louis Paul Croset (d 1982), and May Eveline, *née* Garrett (d 1989); *b* 15 March 1919; *Educ* Rishworth Sch, Stamford Sch; *m* 26 Aug 1944 (m dis 1985), (Margaret) Vivien, da of William Suckling, of Radlett, Herts; 3 da (Jacqueline b 1946, Jane b 1948, Louise b 1956); *Career* served WWII Maj RE with BEF, BNAF, CMF; engr; chm and fndr Holset Engineering Co Ltd 1952–, md BHD Engineers 1959–73, chm Readicut International plc 1977–84 (dir 1969–89, dep chm 1984–89), local dir Barclay Bank plc Leeds 1977–84; dir: Cummins Engine Co Ltd 1981–84, Hepworth plc 1985–89; conslt to Dept of Engrg Univ of Warwick 1989–92; underwriting memb Lloyd's 1968–; Freeman City of London 1972, Liveryman Worshipful Co of Founders 1973; MSAE 1964, FRSA 1973, CIMgt 1980; *Recreations* fishing, shooting, horology; *Clubs* Army and Navy, RAC; *Style—* Paul Croset, Esq, OBE; ✉ Summer Court, 1 Otley Road, Harrogate, N Yorkshire HG2 ODJ (☎ 01423 568216)

CROSLAND, John David; *b* 17 Oct 1936; *Educ* Silcoates Sch, St Catharine's Coll Cambridge (MA); *m* 31 March 1967, Susan Jane Frances; 1 s (Timothy John Edward b 1970), 1 da (Jane Ellen Lucy b 1972); *Career* slr and merchant banker; dir Robert Fleming Holdings Ltd 1973–90, conslt Robert Fleming & Co Ltd 1990–92; non-exec dir: Bankers Investment Trust plc, Concentric plc, Fleming Japanese Investment Trust plc; *Style—* John Crosland, Esq; ✉ 17 Gerard Rd, Barnes, London SW13 9RQ; Stone Cottage, Marehill, Pulborough, W Sussex RH20 2ED; Bankers Investment Trust plc, 3 Finsbury Avenue, London EC2M 2PA (☎ 0171 410 4100, fax 0171 377 5742)

CROSLAND, Prof Maurice Pierre; s of David Crosland, and Berthe, *née* Mispoulet; *b* 19 March 1931; *Educ* Stationers' Sch, Univ of London (BSc, MSc, PhD); *m* 22 April 1957, Joan Mary, da of William Cooley; 3 s (Peter b 1959, Michael b 1962, Paul b 1966), 1 da (Margaret b 1964); *Career* visiting prof: Univ of California Berkeley 1967, Cornell Univ NY 1967–68; reader in history of sci Univ of Leeds 1969–74 (lectr 1963), visiting prof Univ of Pennsylvania 1971, prof of history of sci and dir of Unit for the History Philosophy and Social Rels of Sci Univ of Kent Canterbury 1974–94; hon ed Br Jl for History of Sci 1965–71, pres Br Soc for the History of Sci 1974–76, memb Int Acad of History of Sci 1976–; Dexter award American Chem Soc 1984; *Books* The Society of Arcueil: A View of French Science at the Time of Napoleon I (1967), Historical Studies in the Language of Chemistry (2 edn, 1978, Spanish trans 1988), Science in France in the Revolutionary Era Described by Thomas Bugge (1969), The Science of Matter: A Historical Survey (1971, 2 edn 1993), The Emergence of Science in Western Europe (1975, Italian trans 1979), Gay-Lussac, Scientist and Bourgeois (1978), French Translation (1992), Science under Control: The French Academy of Sciences 1795–1914 (1992), In the Shadow of Lavoisier: The Annales de Chimie and the Emergence of a New Science (1994), Studies in the Culture of Science in France and Britain since the Enlightenment (1995); *Recreations* listening to classical music, foreign travel, cycling; *Style—* Prof Maurice Crosland; ✉ History of Science, Rutherford College, University of Kent, Canterbury, Kent CT2 7NX (☎ 01227 764000)

CROSS, Prof Anthony Glenn; s of Walter Sidney Cross (d 1941), and Ada, *née* Lawson; *b* 21 Oct 1936; *Educ* High Pavement Sch Nottingham, Trinity Hall Cambridge (Wootton Isaacson scholar, MA, PhD) Harvard Univ (AM), UEA (D Litt); *m* 11 Aug 1960, Margaret, da of Eric Arthur Elson (d 1986); 2 da (Jane b 1964, Serena b 1967); *Career* Nat Serv 1955–57; Frank Knox meml fell Harvard Univ 1960–61, reader UEA 1972–81 (lectr 1964–69, sr lectr 1969–72); visiting fell: Centre for Advanced Study Univ of Illinois 1968–69, All Souls Coll Oxford 1977–78; Roberts prof of Russian Univ of Leeds 1981–85, prof of Slavonic studies Univ of Cambridge 1985–; memb Br Univs Assoc of Slavists (pres 1982–84); FBA 1989, fell Russian Acad for the Humanities 1996; *Books* N M Karamzin (1971), Russia Under Western Eyes (1971), Anglo-Russian Relations in the Eighteenth Century (1977), By the Banks of The Thames - Russians in Eighteenth Century Britain (1980), The Russian Theme in English Literature (1985), Anglophilia on the Throne - The British and Russians in the Age of Catherine the Great (1992), Anglo-Russica - Selected Essays on Anglo-Russian Cultural Relations (1993), Engraved in the Memory - James Walker and his Russian Anecdotes (1993), By the Banks of the

Neva: Chapters from the Lives and Careers of the British in Eighteenth-Century Russia (1996); *Recreations* food, travel, collecting books, watching cricket; *Style*— Prof Anthony Cross, FBA; ✉ Department of Slavonic Studies, University of Cambridge, Sidgwick Avenue, Cambridge, CB3 9DA (☎ 01223 335007, fax 01223 335062, e-mail agc28@cam.ac.uk)

CROSS, 3 Viscount (UK 1886); Assheton Henry Cross; s of 2 Viscount (d 1932), and Maud, da of late Maj-Gen Inigo Richmond Jones, CVO, CB (Maud's maternal gf was Hon Richard Charteris, 2 s of 9 Earl of Wemyss and March); *b* 7 May 1920; *Educ* Shrewsbury, Magdalene Coll Cambridge; *m* 1, 12 Jan 1952 (m dis 1957), Patricia Mary, da of Edward Pearson Hewetson, of Windermere; 2 da (Hon Venetia Clare b 1953, Hon Nicola b 1954); m 2, 1972 (m dis 1977), Mrs Victoria Webb; m 3, 1983, (m dis 1987), Mrs Patricia J Rossiter; *Heir* none; *Career* sits as Cons Peer in House of Lords; formerly Capt Scots Gds; *Clubs* Cavalry and Guards'; *Style*— The Rt Hon the Viscount Cross; ✉ Wildwood, Itchenor, Sussex

CROSS, Beverley; s of George Cross, theatrical mangr, and Eileen Williams, actress; *b* 13 April 1931; *Educ* Pangbourne, Balliol Coll Oxford; *m* 1975, Dame Maggie Smith, DBE, the actress; *Career* playwright, screenwriter and librettist; work incl: One More River, Strip The Willow, Boeing Boeing, Half a Sixpence, The Mines of Sulphur, Hans Anderson, The Great Society, Jorrocks, The Scarlet Pimpernel, The Rising of the Moon, Catherine Howard, Miranda; *Clubs* Garrick; *Style*— Beverley Cross, Esq; ✉ Curtis Brown Ltd, 28–29 Haymarket, London SW1Y 4SP

CROSS, Prof (Margaret) Claire; da of Frederick Leonard Cross (d 1964), of Leicester, and Rebecca *née* Newton (d 1984), of Leicester; *b* 25 Oct 1932; *Educ* Wyggeston GS Leicester, Girton Coll Cambridge (BA, PhD); *Career* co archivist for Cambridgeshire 1958–61, int fell American Assoc of Univ Women 1961–62, res fell Univ of Reading, currently prof Dept of History Univ of York (formerly lectr, sr lectr, reader); numerous pubns in jls; memb: Royal Historical Soc, Ecclesiastical History Soc, Historical Assoc; FRHistS; *Books* The Free Grammar School of Leicester (1953), The Puritan Earl - The Life of Henry Hastings (1966), The Royal Supremacy in the Elizabethan Church (1969), Church and People 1450–1660 - The Triumph of the Laity in the English Church (1976), York Clergy Wills 1520–1600 - 2: The Minister Clergy (1984), Urban Magistrates and Ministers - Religion in Hull and Leeds from the Reformation to the Civil War (1985), Law and Government under the Tudors - Essays Presented to Sir Geoffrey Elton on his Retirement (1988), York Clergy Wills 1520–1600 - 2: The City Clergy (1989), The End of Medieval Monasticism in the East Riding of Yorkshire (1993), Monks, Friars and Nuns in Sixteenth Century Yorkshire (ed with N Vickers, 1995); *Recreations* gardening; *Style*— Prof Claire Cross; ✉ 17 Pear Tree Court, York YO1 2DF (☎ 01904 654221); Dept of History, University of York, Heslington, York YO1 5DD (☎ 01904 430000 ext 2959)

CROSS, Denis Charles; s of late Lt Charles Philip Cross, RN; *b* 13 May 1938; *Educ* Downside, Balliol Coll Oxford; *m* 1963, Margaret McAdam, *née* Black; 3 da (Katharine, Felicity, (Margaret) Frances), 2 s (James, Thomas); *Career* dir of risk mgmnt Hambros Bank Ltd 1985– (joined 1961); *Style*— Denis Cross, Esq; ✉ 18 Bolingbroke Grove, London SW11 6EP (☎ 0181 673 8187); Hambros Bank Ltd, 41 Tower Hill, London EC3N 4HA (☎ 0171 480 5000)

CROSS, (John) Dennis; s of Colin Cross (d 1978), and Edith, *née* Griffiths (d 1938); *b* 16 June 1935; *Educ* Clacton-on-Sea Co HS; *m* 19 July 1958, Shirley Phyllis, da of late Henry Charles Paynter; 1 s (Jason Andrew b 9 April 1967), 1 da (Caroline Nicola b 22 July 1969); *Career* Nat Serv RAF 1958–60; articled clerk: Bensusan Butt Eves Colchester 1951–54, Moller Morton & Co London 1951–58; ptnr then sr ptnr Chater & Myhill 1962–67 (joined 1960), sr ptnr KPMG Peat Marwick Cambridge 1987–95, conslt KPMG 1995–; treas RNLI Cambridge (Silver badge 1988); ACA 1958, memb Insolvency Practitioners Assoc 1978; *Recreations* sailing, golf; *Clubs* Walton and Frinton Yacht, Cambridge Rutherford Rotary; *Style*— Dennis Cross, Esq; ✉ KPMG, Chater House, 37 Hills Rd, Cambridge CB2 1XL (☎ 01223 66692, fax 01223 842508)

CROSS, Gillian Clare; da of James Eric Arnold (d 1988), and Joan Emma, *née* Manton; *b* 24 Dec 1945; *Educ* N London Collegiate Sch for Girls, Somerville Coll Oxford (MA), Univ of Sussex (DPhil); *m* 1967, Martin Cross; 2 s (Jonathan b 1967, Anthony b 1984), 2 da (Elizabeth b 1970, Katherine b 1985); *Career* children's author; memb Soc of Authors; *Books* The Runaway (1979), The Iron Way (1979), Revolt at Ratcliffe's Rags (1980), Save Our School (1981), A Whisper of Lace (1981), The Demon Headmaster (1982), The Dark Behind the Curtain (1982), The Mintyglo Kid (1983), Born of the Sun (1983), On the Edge (1984), The Prime Minister's Brain (1985), Swimathon (1986), Chartbreak (1986), Roscoe's Leap (1987), A Map of Nowhere (1988), Rescuing Gloria (1989), Wolf (1990, Carnegie medal Library Assoc), The Monster from Underground (1990), Twin and Super-Twin (1990), Gobbo the Great (1991), Rent-a-Genius (1991), The Great Elephant Chase (1992, winner first prize Smarties Awards, Whitbread children's book award), The Furry Maccaloo (1992), Beware Olga! (1993), The Tree House (1993), Hunky Parker is Watching You (1994), What Will Emily Do? (1994), New World (1994), The Crazy Shoe Shuffle (1995), Posh Watson (1995), The Roman Beanfeast (1996), The Demon Headmaster Strikes Again (1996), Pictures in the Dark (1996); *Recreations* orienteering, playing the piano; *Style*— Mrs Gillian Cross; ✉ c/o Oxford Children's Books, Oxford University Press, Walton Street, Oxford OX2 6DP

CROSS, Air Chief Marshal Sir Kenneth Bryan Boyd; KCB (1959, CB 1954), CBE (1945), DSO (1943), DFC (1940); s of Pembroke H C Cross, of Eastoke Lodge, Hayling Island, and Jean, *née* Boyd; *b* 4 Oct 1911; *Educ* Kingswood Sch Bath; *m* 15 Jan 1945, Brenda Megan (d 1991), da of Wing Cdr Frank James Bickley Powell, of Hinton Cottage, Hinton, nr Melksham, Wilts; 2 s, 1 da; *Career* RAF 1930, AOCIC Bomber Cmd 1959–63, Air Chief Marshal 1965, AOCIC Tport Cmd 1963–66, ret 1967; dir Red Cross London Branch, ret 1981; *Clubs* RAF; *Style*— Sir Kenneth Cross, KCB, CBE, DSO, DFC; ✉ 12 Callow St, London SW3 6BE

CROSS, Martin Patrick Arthur; s of Patrick Arthur Cross, of Whitton, Middx, and Moira Vera, *née* Kenny; *b* 19 July 1957; *Educ* Cardinal Vaughan GS, Queen Mary Coll London, Inst of Educn London; *m* Christine, da of Francis Dowling; 2 da (Natasha b 24 Nov 1989, Lara b 18 Dec 1992), 1 s (Francis b 12 May 1994); *Career* amateur rower; clubs: London Rowing 1976–81, Thames Tradesmans 1982–; 18 consecutive GB caps 1977–94 (Britain's most capped rower); achievements incl: second coxless fours World Jr Championships 1975, Bronze medal coxless fours World Championships 1978 and 1979, Bronze medal coxless fours Olympic Games Moscow 1980, Gold medal coxed four Olympic Games LA 1984, Silver medal coxless pairs World Championships 1985, Gold medal coxed fours Cwlth Games 1986, fourth Olympic Games Seoul 1988, Bronze medal eights World Championships 1991, sixth Olympic Games Barcelona 1992; also 10 Henley wins and 3 Lucerne Golds; records: championship best coxed fours (6:01) World Championships Copenhagen 1987, GB best coxless fours (5:56) World Championships Tasmania 1990; history and politics teacher: Hounslow and ILEA 1979–81, Hampton Sch 1982– (dep head of VIth form 1994–97, head of VIth form 1997–); athlete rep to BOA 1984–94; memb: Nat Olympic Ctee 1985–94, Cncl Amateur Rowing Assoc 1988–, Cncl FISA 1992–; chm: Athletes Cncl BOA 1990–94, Athletes Cmmn FISA 1992–; chm Hampton Lab Pty 1991– (sec 1987–91, candidate local govt election 1990), press sec Twickenham CLP 1990–92; dir Rowing Promotion Ltd, rowing commentator Channel 4, EuroSport and BBC Radio 5; Rower of the Year 1991, Desborough Award for Services to BOA 1994; *Recreations* playing guitar in the parish folk group, living in French house whenever possible, writing, organizing regattas; *Clubs* Olympians (fndr memb); *Style*— Martin Cross, Esq; ✉ 8 Coombe Crescent, Hampton, Middx TW12 3PD (☎ and fax 0181 979 6159)

CROSS, Nicholas John; s of John Cross, CBE, of Ixworth, Suffolk, and Janet, *née* Devitt; *b* 13 Aug 1962; *Educ* Uppingham Sch Rutland, Univ of Cambridge (BA); *m* Non, da of Rt Hon John Morris, MP, QC; 2 s (Henry John Caradog b 14 June 1996, Llewelyn John Edmund b (twin) 14 June 1996); *Career* dir SRU Ltd mgmnt consultancy 1992–93 (joined 1984), int planning dir Bartle Bogle Hegarty Ltd advtg agency 1993–96, mktg dir (i/c advtg, direct mail catalogues and storecard ops) Selfridges Ltd dept store 1996–; memb Mgmnt Ctee Nat Youth Agency (formerly Nat Youth Bureau) 1988–93; *Recreations* shooting, sailing; *Clubs* Farmers'; *Style*— Nicholas Cross, Esq; ✉ 14 St Paul Street, London N1 7AB; Selfridges Ltd, 400 Oxford Street, London W1A 1AB (☎ 0171 629 1234)

CROSS, Philippa Jane (Pippa); da of Robert Lionel Cross (d 1977), and Jill Patricia Abbott, MBE, of Ipswich; *b* 13 May 1956; *Educ* Ipswich HS GPDST, St Anne's Coll Oxford; *m* 1982, Graham Ronald Lee; 1 da (Maisie Victoria Kelda b 2 May 1983), 1 s (Pierrot Robert Alexander b 6 Aug 1991); *Career* entertainments mangr Wembley Conf Centre 1977–80; Granada Television Manchester: mangr Drama Dept 1980–81, mangr features 1981–85; mangr factual progs TVS Television Maidstone 1985–88; Granada Television London: mangr Dir of Progs' Office 1988–90, prodn exec My Left Foot, prodn exec The Field, head of devpt feature films and films for TV 1990–, head of film 1993–, prodr Jack & Sarah, and August, exec prodr Some Kind of Life; *Recreations* horse riding, cinema, children (!); *Style*— Ms Pippa Cross; ✉ Granada Film, Granada Television Ltd, 36 Golden Square, London W1R 4AH (☎ 0171 494 6388, fax 0171 494 6360)

CROSS BROWN, Tom; s of Christopher James Cross Brown, and Georgina, *née* Forrester; *b* 22 Dec 1947; *Educ* Uppingham, BNC Oxford (MA), INSEAD (MBA); *m* 1972, Susan Rosemary, da of Col Mansel Halkett Jackson (d 1967); 1 s (Nicol b 1975), 3 da (Gemma b 1977, Amelia b 1982, Claire (twin) b 1982); *Career* md Lazard Brothers & Co Ltd 1994 (dir 1985), chief exec Lazard Brothers Asset Management Ltd 1994; non-exec dir Whitegate Leisure plc 1987–92; *Style*— Tom Cross Brown, Esq; ✉ Shipton Old Farm, Winslow, Buckingham MK18 3JL; Lazard Brothers & Co Ltd, 21 Moorfields, London EC2P 2HT

CROSSETT, Robert Nelson (Tom); s of Robert Crossett (d 1961), and Mary, *née* Nelson (d 1988); *b* 27 May 1938; *Educ* Campbell Coll Belfast, Queen's Univ Belfast (BSc, BAS), Lincoln Coll Oxford (DPhil), UEA; *m*; 2 c; *Career* cmmnd pilot Gen Duties Branch RAFVR; gp ldr Environmental Studies Aust Atomic Energy Cmmn Res Establishment Sydney 1966–69, sr sci offr ARC Letcombe Laboratory 1969–72, crop devpt offr Scot Agric Devpt Cncl 1972–75 (sec Crops Ctee), agric res advsr Sci Advsrs' Unit Dept of Agric and Fisheries Scot 1975–78; MAFF: sci liaison offr Horticulture and Soils 1978–84, head Food Sci Div 1984–85, chief scientist Fisheries and Food 1985–89; environment dir National Power 1989–91, gen sec Nat Soc for Clean Air and Environmental Protection 1992–97; DG Int Union of Air Pollution Prevention and Environmental Protection Assoc (IUAPPA) Jan 1997–; chm: Steering Gp on Food Surveillance 1985–89, AFRC 1985–89, CMO's Ctee on Med Aspects of Food Policy 1985–89, NERC 1985–89, Supervisory Bd of the Laboratory of the Govt Chemist 1985–89, Southern Regnl Environmental Protection Advsy Ctee of Environment Agency 1997–; memb: UK Govt Roundtable on Sustainable Devpt 1995–, Advsy Gp to Sec of State for Environment (on environmental mgmnt and audit) 1995–; *Publications* papers on plant physiology, marine biology and food science; *Recreations* walking, gardening, orienteering, boats; *Style*— Tom Crossett, Esq; ✉ IUAPPA, 136 North Street, Brighton BN1 1RG (☎ 01273 326313, fax 01273 735802)

CROSSLAND, Anthony; s of Ernest Thomas Crossland (d 1968), and Frances Edith Crossland (d 1969); *b* 4 Aug 1931; *Educ* High Pavement Sch Nottingham, ChCh Oxford (BMus, MA); *m* 3 Dec 1960, Barbara Helen, da of Herbert Pullar-Strecker (d 1976); 1 s (Nicholas Anthony James b 1962), 2 da (Caroline Sarah b 1964, Victoria Jane b 1967); *Career* asst organist: Christ Church Cathedral Oxford 1957–61, Wells Cathedral 1961–70; organist and master of the choristers Wells Cathedral 1971–96; pres Cathedral Organists' Assoc 1983–85; DMus (Lambeth) 1994; FRCO 1957, ARCM; *Recreations* photography, reading; *Style*— Anthony Crossland, Esq; ✉ Barton End, 10B Newtown, Bradford-on-Avon, Wiltshire BA15 1NE

CROSSLAND, Prof Sir Bernard; kt (1990), CBE (1980); s of Reginald Francis Crossland (d 1976), and Kathleen Mary, *née* Rudduck (d 1950); *b* 20 Oct 1923; *Educ* Simon Langton GS Canterbury, Derby Regnl Tech Coll, Univ Coll of Nottingham (BSc, MSc, PhD, DSc); *m* 25 July 1946, Audrey, da of Frank Elliott Birks (d 1961); 2 da (Jennifer b 1948, Mary Anne b 1952); *Career* tech asst Rolls Royce Ltd 1943–45 (apprentice 1940–44), lectr Luton Tech Coll 1945–46, sr lectr in mechanical engrg (formerly asst lectr and lectr) Univ of Bristol 1946–59; Queen's Univ of Belfast: prof and head Dept of Mechanical and Industl Engrg 1959–84, dean Engrg Faculty 1964–67, pro vice chllr 1978–82, emeritus prof of mechanical engrg 1984–; assessor King's Cross Underground Fire Investigation 1988; chm: NI Youth Careers Guidance Cmmn 1975–81, NI Manpower Cncl 1981–86, Bd of Engrs Registration 1983–86, NI Postgrad Awards Advsy Bd 1982–95, Public Hearing into the Bilsthorpe Colliery accident 1994; memb: NI Trg Cncl 1964–81, NI Econ Cncl 1981–85, AFRC 1981–87, NI Ind Devpt Bd 1982–87, Engrg Cncl 1983–88; Freeman City of London 1987, memb Worshipful Co of Engrs 1988; Hon DSc: Nat Univ of Ireland 1984, Univ of Dublin 1985, Univ of Edinburgh 1987, The Queens Univ Belfast 1988, Univ of Aston 1988, Cranfield Inst of Technol 1989; Hon DEng: Univ of Bristol 1992, Univ of Limerick 1993, Univ of Liverpool 1993; hon fell Univ of Luton 1994; FIMechE (pres 1986–87), Hon FWI (pres 1995–), Hon MASME, Hon FIEI, MRIA, FEng 1979, FRS 1979 (vice pres 1984–86); *Recreations* walking, music, travel; *Clubs* Athenaeum; *Style*— Prof Sir Bernard Crossland, CBE, FEng, FRS; ✉ 16 Malone Ct, Belfast BT9 6PA (☎ 01232 667 495); The Queen's University, Belfast BT7 1NN (☎ 01232 247 303, fax 01232 247 895, telex 74487)

CROSSLAND, Sir Leonard; kt (1969); s of Joseph William Crossland (d 1962), of Stocksbridge, Sheffield, and Frances Crossland; *b* 2 March 1914; *m* 1964, Joan (d 1996), da of Stanley Percival Brewer, of Bath; *Career* served WWII Europe (despatches twice); chm and dir Ford Motor Co Ltd 1968–72 (joined 1945); chm: Eaton Ltd 1972–82, Energy Research and Development Ltd 1974–; dir Eaton Corp (US) 1974–81; farmer (700 acres); Liveryman Worshipful Co of Glaziers & Painters of Glass; *Recreations* shooting, fishing, golf; *Clubs* RAC, City Livery, BRDC; *Style*— Sir Leonard Crossland; ✉ Abbotts Hall, Gt Wigborough, Colchester, Essex CO5 7RZ (☎ 01206 735456, fax 01206 735301)

CROSSLAND, Prof Ronald Arthur; s of Ralph Crossland (d 1972), of Nottingham, and Ethel, *née* Scattergood (d 1974); *b* 31 Aug 1920; *Educ* Nottingham HS, King's Coll Cambridge; *Career* served RA 1941–45, Lt 19 Field Regt RA (1st Div), served GB, Tunisia and Italy; Henry fell Yale Univ 1946–48, sr Student Ctee for Studentships in Oriental Languages and Literatures (Hittite philology) 1948–51, hon asst lectr in ancient history Univ of Birmingham 1950–51, lectr in ancient history King's Coll Newcastle upon Tyne, Univ of Durham 1951–58, Harris fell King's Coll Cambridge 1952–56, prof of Greek Univ of Sheffield 1958–82 (dean Faculty of Arts 1973–75, emeritus prof 1982); British Cncl visiting lectr in Czechoslovakia 1961, visiting prof of linguistics Texas Univ (Austin) 1962, Collitz visiting prof of linguistics Michigan Univ 1967, visiting fell in classics Victoria Univ of Wellington 1979; FSA; *Publications* Immigrants from the North (Cambridge Ancient History, revised edn, 1/2, Chapter XXVII 1971), Linguistic Problems of the Balkan Area (Cambridge Ancient History, revised edn, Chapter 20c 1982), Bronze Age Migrations in the Aegean (with Ann Birchall, 1973), Early Greek Migrations (in M Grant, editor Civilization of the Ancient Mediterranean, 1987); *Recreations* travel, music; *Style—* Prof Ronald Crossland, FSA; ✉ 59 Sherlock Close, Cambridge CB3 0HP (☎ 01223 358 085)

CROSSLEY, Barbara Jane; da of Jim Crossley (d 1956), and Lily, *née* Schofield; *b* 10 April 1952; *Educ* Cavendish GS Buxton, Univ of Lancaster (BA), Univ of Wales Coll of Cardiff (post grad dip); *m* June 1987, Barry Stocks; *Career* writer and journalist; *Books* Candyfloss Coast (1991, Virago), Rollercoaster (1994, Virago); *Style—* Ms Barbara Crossley; ✉ c/o Gregory & Radice, 3 Barb Mews, London W6 7PA (☎ 0171 610 4676, fax 0171 610 4686)

CROSSLEY, The Hon (Richard) Nicholas; TD (1974), DL (N Yorks 1988); s of 2 Baron Somerleyton, MC (d 1959), and Bridget, *née* Hoare (d 1983); *b* 24 Dec 1932; *Educ* Eton, RMA Sandhurst; *m* 1, 30 April 1958, Alexandra Ann Maitland (d 1990), da of Wing Cdr Charles Donald Graham Welch, of Graffham, Sussex; 1 s, 2 da; *m* 2, 30 June 1995, Mrs Priscilla Ann Kennedy, yr (twin) da of Maj Alastair Graham, MC (d 1975), of Middleton Quernhow, Ripon, N Yorks; *Career* farmer 1963–, MFH 1969; Capt 9 Queen's Royal Lancers (ret), Maj Queen's Own Yeo (TA), CO Queen's Own Yeo 1973–76, Bt-Col 1977, Col TA NE Dist 1978–81, ADC (TAVR) to HM The Queen 1980–84; memb HM Body Guard of Hon Corps of Gentlemen at Arms 1982–, Hon Col Queen's Own Yeomanry 1990–93; High Sheriff N Yorks 1989–90; area govr Ocean Youth Club 1985–, tstee for Stable Lads Welfare Tst 1984–93, pres The Nat Light Horse Breeding Soc 1992; *Recreations* hunting, shooting, stalking, sailing; *Clubs* Cavalry and Guards', Pratt's, Royal Yacht Squadron; *Style—* The Hon Nicholas Crossley, TD, DL, MFH; ✉ Westfield Farm, Norton, Malton, N Yorks YO17 9PL (☎ 01653 693272)

CROSSLEY, Sir Nicholas John; 4 Bt (UK 1909), of Glenfield, Dunham Massey, Co Chester; er s of Sir Christopher John Crossley, 3 Bt (d 1989), and his 1 w, Carolyne Louise, da of late L Grey Sykes; *b* 10 Dec 1962; *Heir* bro, Julian Charles Crossley b 11 Dec 1964; *Style—* Sir Nicholas Crossley, Bt

CROSSLEY, Paul Christopher Richard; CBE (1993); s of Frank Crossley (d 1948), and Myra, *née* Barrowcliffe (d 1979); *b* 17 May 1944; *Educ* Silcoates Sch Wakefield, Mansfield Coll Oxford; *Career* pianist; int concert career with world's leading orchs, ensembles, and conductors; solo recitalist and regular broadcaster; works specially written for him by leading composers incl: Adams, Berio, Gorecki, Henze, Takemitsu, Tippett; artistic dir London Sinfonietta 1988–94; sixteen TV progs on prominent composers; recordings incl: Liszt: A Recital 1983, Ravel: Complete Piano Music 1983, Fauré: Complete Piano Music 1983–87, Tippett: Sonatas 1–4 1985, Messiaen: Turangalila-Symphonie 1986, Messiaen Des Canyons aux Etoiles Oiseaux Exotiques, Couleurs de la Cité Celeste 1988, Poulenc: Complete Piano Music 1989, Stravinsky: Complete Music for Piano and Orchestra 1990, Adams: Eros Piano 1991, Takemitsu: Riverrun 1991, Debussy: Complete Piano Music 1993, Franck: Symphonic Variations 1994 and Piano Music 1994, Lutoslawski: Piano Concerto 1995; Hon Fell Mansfield Coll Oxford 1991; *Recreations* mah-jongg, reading; *Style—* Paul Crossley, Esq, CBE; ✉ Van Walsum Management, 26 Wadham Road, London SW15

CROSSLEY, Maj-Gen Ralph John; CB (1987), CBE (1981); s of Edward Crossley (d 1978), of Sussex, and Eva Mary, *née* Farnworth (d 1965); *b* 11 Oct 1933; *Educ* Felsted; *m* 1957, Marion Hilary, da of Herbert Wilfred Bacon (d 1975), of Salisbury; 1 s (Robin), 1 da (Amanda); *Career* Army Offr; Dep Cmdt RMC of Science 1982, Dir Gen Weapons (Army 1984), ret 1986; dir def policy Avon Rubber plc 1987–91; vice pres Hospital Savings Assoc 1994; chm Salisbury Health Care NHS Tst 1994; *Recreations* golf, reading, gardening, walking; *Clubs* Nat Tst; *Style—* Maj-Gen Ralph Crossley, CB, CBE; ✉ c/o Odstock Hospital, Salisbury, Wilts

CROSSLEY-HOLLAND, Kevin John William; s of Peter Charles Crossley-Holland of Dyfed, and Joan Mary Crossley-Holland, *née* Cowper, MBE; *b* 7 Feb 1941; *Educ* Bryanston, St Edmund Hall Oxford (MA); *children* 2 s (Kieran b 1963, Dominic b 1967), 2 da (Oenone b 1982, Eleanor b 1986); *Career* ed Macmillan & Co 1962–69, Gregory fell in poetry Univ of Leeds 1969–71, talks prodr BBC 1972, editorial dir Victor Gollancz 1972–77, lectr in English, Tufts in London program 1969–78, lektor Regensburg Univ 1979–80, Arts Cncl fellow in writing Winchester Sch of Art 1983 and 1984, visiting prof St Olaf Coll Minnesota 1987, 1988 and 1989, endowed chair in the humanities and fine arts Univ of St Thomas Minnesota 1991–95; editorial conslt Boydell and Brewer 1987–89; chm E Arts Assoc Literature Panel 1986–89; dir American Composers Forum, tstee Wingfield Coll; *Books* poetry: 6 vols incl Waterslain (1986), New and Selected Poems 1965–1990 (1991), The Language of Yes (1996); for children: The Green Children (1966, Arts Cncl award), Storm (1985, Carnegie medal), British Folk Tales (1987), Sleeping Nanna (1989), The Labours of Herakles (1993), Norse Myths (1993), Talk About Short (1997); translations from Old English: Beowulf (1968), The Exeter Book Riddles (revised edn 1993), The Norse Myths (1981), Pieces of Land (1972), The Stones Remain (1989); edited: The Anglo-Saxon World (1982), Folk-Tales of The British Isles (1985), The Oxford Book of Travel Verse (1986), Young Oxford Book of Folk-Tales (1997); opera: The Green Children (with Nicola LeFanu, 1990), The Wildman (with Nicola LeFanu, 1995); musical settings: A Knot of Riddles (with Sir Arthur Bliss), Riddles (with William Mathias), Pilgrim Jesus (with Stephen Paulus); *Recreations* music, walking, archaeology, travel; *Style—* Kevin Crossley-Holland, Esq; ✉ c/o Rogers, Coleridge and White Literary Agency, 20 Powis Mews, London W11 1JN (☎ 0171 221 3717, fax 0171 229 9084)

CROSSMAN, David; s of Henry William Crossman (d 1966), and Gertrude Edith Mary, *née* Glasscock (d 1996); *b* 12 Jan 1947; *Educ* Belmont Sch Tottenham, City Coll for Further Educn London; 1 s (Tom Dow-Smith b 1972); *Career* professional TV prodr and dir 1974–; credits incl: The Cannon and Ball Show 1979–81, Metal Mickey 1980–81, A Week in Politics 1982, Chips Comic 1983, The Pocket Money Programme 1984–85, The Editors 1990, Winners World 1992, Message in a Bottle 1994, Gaytime TV 1995, The Final Frontier 1996; memb Dirs' Guild of GB; *Recreations* photography, motoring, fatherhood; *Style—* David Crossman, Esq; ✉ Flat One, 58 Wickham Rd, Beckenham, Kent BR3 6RQ (☎ 0181 658 2012); Dareks Production House (fax 0181 658 2012)

CROSTHWAITE, Andrew Donald; s of Donald Rothery Crosthwaite, of Lytham, Lancashire, and Jean Mary, *née* Cavill; *b* 16 March 1957; *Educ* Manchester GS, Worcester Coll Oxford (BA); *children*; 2 s (Matthew Andrew b 14 May 1990, Sam Neil (twin)), 1 da (Katie Louisa b 19 Aug 1991); *Career* advtg exec; Ogilvy & Mather 1978–81, McCormick Publicis 1981–82, Doyle Dane Bernbach 1982–85; FCO Ltd: joined 1985, dir 1986, planning ptnr until 1993; dir of planning Euro RSCG (now Euro RSCG Wnek Gosper) following merger 1993–; *Recreations* hard work and clean living; *Style—* Andrew Crosthwaite, Esq; ✉ Euro RSCG Wnek Gosper, 11 Great Newport Street, London WC2H 7JA (☎ 0171 240 4111, e-mail acrosthw@eurorscg.co.uk)

CROSTHWAITE, Peregrine Kenneth Oughton; s of Kenneth Alan Crosthwaite, and Nora Elsie, *née* Oughton; *b* 24 March 1949; *Educ* St Paul's, Trinity Coll Oxford (MA); *m* 29 Oct 1982, Valerie Janet, yr da of Sir Albert Jonas Cahn, 2 Bt; 2 s (Nicholas Anthony b 22 Jan 1985, Thomas William b 23 Oct 1986), 1 da (Sally-Anne Claire b 8 May 1989); *Career* joined Fenn & Crosthwaite 1972 (merged with George Henderson to become Henderson Crosthwaite 1975), ptnr Henderson Crosthwaite 1979–89, currently chm Henderson Crosthwaite Institutional Brokers Ltd; memb: Worshipful Co of Merchant Taylors, Freeman City of London; memb London Stock Exchange 1975; *Recreations* cricket, squash, tennis, golf, skiing, music, books, theatre; *Style—* Peregrine Crosthwaite, Esq; ✉ 30 Larpent Ave, London SW15 6UU (☎ 0181 788 2073); Henderson Crosthwaite Institutional Brokers Ltd, 32 St Mary at Hill, London EC3P 3AJ (☎ 0171 623 9992, fax 0171 528 0884)

CROUCH, Prof Colin John; s of Charles John Crouch (d 1990), of Charlbury, Oxon, and Doris Beatrice, *née* Baker (d 1990); *b* 1 March 1944; *Educ* Latymer Upper Sch Hammersmith, LSE (BA), Univ of Oxford (DPhil); *m* 10 June 1970, Joan Ann, da of David Freedman (d 1972), of London E1; 2 s (Daniel b 1974, Ben b 1978); *Career* lectr in sociology: LSE 1969–70, Univ of Bath 1972–73; reader LSE 1980–85 (lectr 1973–79, sr lectr 1979–80); Univ of Oxford: fell and tutor in politics Trinity Coll 1985–, faculty lectr in sociology 1985–96, chm Sub-Faculty of Sociology 1987–89, proctor 1990–91, chm Social Studies Faculty Bd 1994, prof of sociology 1996–; prof of sociology Euro Univ Inst Florence 1995–; res interests in the comparative sociology of Western Europe; curator Bodleian Library 1990–95, delegate Oxford Univ Press 1992–; memb Standing Ctee of Ct of Govrs LSE 1980–84, jt ed The Political Quarterly 1985–95, chm Fabian Soc 1976 (memb Exec Ctee 1969–78); memb Oxford West and Abingdon Lab Pty, referee class 3 Oxfordshire Football Assoc; *Editor* Stress and Contradiction in Modern Capitalism (with Lindberg et al, 1975), Br Political Sociology Yearbook Vol III Participation in Politics (1977), The Resurgence of Class Conflict in Western Europe since 1968 vol I Nat Studies vol II comparative Analyses (with A Pizzorno, 1978), State and Economics in Contemporary Capitalism (1979), Int Yearbook of Organizations Democracy vol I Organizational Democracy and Political Processes (with F Heller, 1983), The New Centralism (with D Marquand, 1989), Corporatism and Accountability Organised Interests in Br Public Life (with R P Dore, 1990), European Industrial Relations: the Challenge of Flexibility (with G Baglioni, 1990), The Politics of 1992 (with D Marquand, 1990), Towards Greater Europe? (with D Marquand, 1992), Social Research and Social Reform (with A Heath, 1992), Ethics and Markets (with D Marquand, 1993), Organized Industrial Relations in Europe (with F Traxler, 1995), Reinventing Collective Action (with D Marquand, 1995), Les capitalismes en Europe (with W Streeck, 1996); *Books* The Student Revolt (1970), Class Conflict and the Industrial Relations Crisis (1977), The Politics of Industrial Relations (2 edn 1982), Trade Unions the Logic of Collective Action (1982), Industrial Relations and European State Traditions (1993); *Recreations* playing violin, listening to music, gardening; *Style—* Prof Colin Crouch; ✉ European University Institute, 50016 S Domenico di Fiesole, Florence, Italy (☎ 00 39 55 4685 441, fax 00 39 55 4685 201)

CROUCH, Sir David Lance; kt (1987), DL (Kent 1992); s of Charles Littler Stanley Crouch (d 1966), of Northwood, Middx, and Rosalie Kate, *née* Croom (d 1972); *b* 23 June 1919; *Educ* Univ Coll Sch; *m* 5 July 1947, Margaret Maplesden, da of Maj Sydney Maplesden Noakes, DSO, of Shorne, Kent; 1 s (Patrick b 19 May 1954), 1 da (Vanessa b 11 Oct 1951); *Career* served City of London Yeomanry (TA) 1938–43, RA 1943–46, Maj, attached RAF 1944–45, service in N Africa, Europe, Burma; joined: British Nylon Spinners 1946, ICI Ltd 1950–62; dir International Wool Secretariat 1962–64, chm: David Crouch & Co Ltd (Public Relations) 1964–89, Noble and Samson Ltd; dir: Pfizer Ltd 1969–88, Burson Marsteller Ltd 1972–83, Kingsway Public Relations 1985–89, Westminster Communications Group Ltd 1988–; Parly candidate (Cons) W Leeds 1959, MP (Cons) Canterbury 1966–87; chm: All Pty Gp for Chemical Industry 1968–87, All Pty Gp for Energy Studies 1982–87, Anglo-Egyptian Parliamentary Gp 1970–87, Br Gp Inter-Parly Union 1984–87, Advsy Ctee on Works of Art to the Speaker 1983–87; memb: Select Ctee for Nationalized Industries 1966–74, Public Accounts Ctee 1974–79, Select Ctee for Social Servs 1980–82; memb: SE Thames RHA 1970–84, Cncl Univ of Kent at Canterbury 1971–95, MRC 1984–87; pres The Kent Soc 1987–94; chm: Channel Theatre 1984–86, The Theatres Tst 1987–92; govr Kent Inst of Art and Design 1988–93, vice pres Crisis at Christmas; Hon DCL Univ of Kent at Canterbury 1987; *Books* A Canterbury Tale (1987); *Recreations* golf, painting; *Clubs* Athenaeum, MCC, Kent and Canterbury, Royal St George's Golf; *Style—* Sir David Crouch, DL; ✉ The Oast House, Fisher St, Badlesmere, Faversham, Kent (☎ 01227 730528)

CROUCH, Sunny; *b* 11 Feb 1943; *Educ* Univ of Lancaster (MA), Dip CIM, Dip MRS; *m*; *Career* mktg mgmnt Brocades (GB) Ltd 1966–72; course dir (Honours Degree in Business Studies) Univ of Portsmouth Business Sch 1972–83, visiting course dir (Mkt Res) Coll of Chartered Inst of Mktg 1977–83; mktg conslt 1972–83, chief mktg and tourism offr City of Portsmouth 1983–88 (Tourist Authy of the Year Award 1985, English Tourist Bd's first England for Excellence Award for Cities 1988), dir of mktg and public affrs London Docklands Devpt Corp 1988–; non-exec bd dir Melody Radio 1989–92; chm: DOBRIC Publications 1990–, TourEast London 1993–; vice pres Docklands Business Club 1989–; memb: Nat Cncl Tourism Soc 1989– (currently vice chm), Nat Exec Ctee Forum UK 1990–93, Industl and Economic Affrs Ctee Gen Synod C of E 1991–; govr: City of Portsmouth Girls' Sch 1977–88, Portsmouth Coll of Art, Design and FE 1984–88; Freeman City of London 1993; FCIM 1970, full memb MRS 1975, FTS 1985, MInstD 1990; *Publications* Mass Media and Cultural Relationship (jtly, 1975), Marketing Research for Managers (1984 and 1985, 2 edn 1996); *Style—* Mrs Sunny Crouch; ✉ London Docklands Development Corporation, Thames Quay, 191 Marsh Wall, London E14 9TJ (☎ 0171 512 8476, fax 0171 512 0244)

CROW, Dr Julie Carol; da of Dr Eric George Hemphill Carter, and Phyllis Elsie, *née* Crump; *b* 26 Feb 1942; *Educ* Chislehurst and Sidcup Girls GS, London Hosp Med Coll Univ of London; *m* 22 Jan 1966, Dr Timothy John Crow, s of Percy Arthur Crow; 1 s (Oliver b 10 April 1971), 1 da (Louise b 21 Feb 1974); *Career* house physician and surgn Aberdeen 1966; Univ of Aberdeen: lectr in pathology 1968–71, pt/t lectr 1971–73; Northwick Park Hosp: pt/t registrar 1975–76, pt/t sr registrar 1976–82, locum conslt histopathology 1983–85; sr lectr in histopathology Royal Free Hosp of Med 1985– (hon conslt); registrar Royal Coll of Pathologists 1996–; memb: BMA, MWF, IAP, Pathological Soc of GB and Ireland; FRCPath 1989; *Recreations* chinese brush painting, computer games, reading, watching TV; *Style—* Dr Julie Crow; ✉ 16 Northwick Circle, Kenton, Harrow, Middlesex HA3 0EJ; Department of Histopathology, Royal Free Hospital and School of Medicine, Pond St, London NW3 2QG (☎ 0171 830 2227, fax 0171 830 2529)

CROW, (Hilary) Stephen; CB (1995); s of Aubrey Everard Crow (d 1991), of Crowborough, Sussex, and Ivy Marion, *née* Warltier (d 1990); *b* 2 Sept 1934; *Educ* Leek HS, William Ellis Sch, St Catharine's Coll Cambridge (MA); *m* 8 April 1958, Margaret, da of Frederick Anderson (d 1961); 2 s (Andrew b 1962, Matthew b 1965), 1 da (Anne b 1958); *Career* Nat Serv RA Intelligence Corps 1952–54; various appts in Lancashire CC and Southport CBC 1957–72, divnl planning offr and princ asst co planning offr Hertfordshire CC 1972–76; DOE and Welsh Office: planning inspr 1976–88, chief planning inspr 1988–94; hon prof planning practice Dept of City and Regnl Planning Univ of Wales Cardiff 1995–; FRTPI (M) 1963, FRGS 1965, FRICS 1992; *Style—* Stephen Crow, Esq, CB; ✉ The Pines, Lyncombe Vale Road, Bath BA2 4LS (☎ 01225 337680)

CROWDEN, James Gee Pascoe; JP (Wisbech 1969); yr s of Lt-Col R J C Crowden, MC (d 1977), of Peterborough, and Nina Mary, *née* Gee (d 1981); *b* 14 Nov 1927; *Educ* Bedford Sch, Pembroke Coll Cambridge (MA); *m* 1955, Kathleen Mary (d 1989), wid of Capt F A Grounds, and da of late Mr and Mrs J W Loughlin, of Upwell; 1 s (decd); 1 step s; *Career* cmmnd Royal Lincs Regt 1947; chartered surveyor; sr ptnr Grounds & Co 1974–88; former pres Agric Valuers' Assocs of Cambs, Herts Beds and Bucks, Lincs, Norfolk and Wisbech; rowed in Oxford and Cambridge Boat Race 1951 and 1952 (pres 1952), Capt GB VIII Euro Championships Macon 1951 (Gold medallists), rowed 1950

Euro Championships (Bronze medal) and 1952 Olympics, coached 20 Cambridge crews 1953–75, steward Henley Royal Regatta 1960 (memb Ctee of Mgmnt 1965–92), memb Cncl Amateur Rowing Assoc 1957–77, chm Cambs Olympic Appeals 1984, 1988, 1992 and 1996; vice pres Br Olympic Assoc 1988–; pres: Cambs Fedn of Young Farmers 1971–73, Cambs Scouts 1992–, Cambs TAVRA and Cadet Ctee 1992–, E Anglia TAVRA 1996– (vice pres 1992–96), Old Bedfordians' Club 1996–; patron: Cambs Royal British Legion 1992–, Cambs Red Cross 1992–; Hon Coll Cambs ACF 1996–; govr: March GS 1960–70 (chm 1967–70), King's Sch Peterborough 1980–90, St Hugh's Sch Woodhall Spa 1981–92; chm Cncl Order of St Etheldreda 1992–; memb: Ely Diocesan Pastoral Ctee 1969–89, Ely Cathedral Fabric Ctee 1986–90; chm Appeal Exec Ctee Peterborough Cathedral 1979; High Sheriff Cambs and Isle of Ely 1970, Lord Lt Cambs 1992– (DL 1971, Vice-Lord Lt 1985–92); hon memb Ct Co of Watermen and Lightermen of the River Thames (Master 1991–92); hon fell Pembroke Coll Cambridge 1993; FCIArb 1977, FRSA 1990; KStJ 1992; *Recreations* rowing, shooting; *Clubs* East India, Devonshire, Sports and Public Schs, Hawks', Univ Pitt, Cambridge County, Leander, Sette of Odd Volumes; *Style*— J G P Crowden, Esq, JP; ✉ 19 North Brink, Wisbech, Cambs PE13 1JR (☎ 01945 583320)

CROWDER, Frederick Petre; QC (1964); s of Sir John Ellenborough Crowder (d 1961), and Florence Gertrude Petre (d 1981); *b* 18 July 1919; *Educ* Eton, ChCh Oxford; *m* 12 July 1948, Hon Patricia Winifred Mary, da of 25 Baron Mowbray, MC (d 1965) (also 26 Baron Segrave and 22 Baron Stourton); 2 s (Richard b 1950, John b 1954); *Career* served 1939–45 War as Maj Coldm Gds (N Africa, Italy, and Burma); called to the Bar Inner Temple 1948, master of the Bench 1971; SE Circuit, recorder of Gravesend 1960–67; Herts QS, chm 1963–71; contested (C) N Tottenham 1945; MP (C): Ruislip-Northwood 1950–74, Hillingdon, Ruislip-Northwood 1974–79; PPS to: Slr-Gen 1952–54, attorney-gen 1954–62; recorder of Colchester 1967–91; treas of Inner Temple 1991 (reader 1990); ret; *Clubs* Pratt's, Carlton; *Style*— Frederick P Crowder, Esq, QC; ✉ 8 Quarrendon St, SW6 3SU (☎ 0171 731 6342); c/o 2 Harcourt Bldgs, Temple EC4 (☎ 0171 353 2112)

CROWDER, Ven Norman Harry; s of Laurence Smethurst Crowder (d 1977), and Frances Annie, *née* Hicks; *b* 20 Oct 1926; *Educ* Nottingham HS, St John's Coll Cambridge (MA), Westcott House Theol Coll Cambridge; *m* 16 Dec 1971, Pauleen Florence Alison, *née* Styles; 1 s (Richard b 1973); *Career* curate St Mary's Radcliffe-on-Trent 1952–55, residential chaplain to Bishop of Portsmouth 1955–59; chaplain Canford Sch 1964–72 (asst chaplain 1959–64), vicar of St John's Oakfield Ryde IOW 1972–75, dir of religious educn Portsmouth Dio and residentiary canon of Portsmouth Cathedral 1972–85, archdeacon of Portsmouth 1985–93; *Recreations* water colours of J M W Turner, poetry of T S Eliot, conservation of elephants; *Clubs* MCC; *Style*— The Ven N H Crowder; ✉ 37 Rectory Road, Salisbury, Wiltshire SP2 7SD (☎ 01722 320052)

CROWDY, Maj-Gen Joseph Porter; CB (1984); s of Lt-Col Charles R Crowdy (d 1936), and Kate, *née* Porter; *b* 19 Nov 1923; *Educ* Gresham's Sch, Univ of Edinburgh (MB ChB); *m* 1948, Beryl Elisabeth Sapsford; 4 da; *Career* house surgeon Norfolk and Norwich Hosp 1947–48, joined RAMC 1949, dir Army Preventive Med 1978–81, cmdt and postgrad dean Royal Army Med Coll 1981–84, ret 1984, rep Col Cmdt RAMC 1987; QHP 1981–84, hon conslt in nutrition to the Army 1984–88; Liveryman Worshipful Soc of Apothecaries; FFPHM, MFOM; *Style*— Maj-Gen Joseph Crowdy, CB; ✉ Pepperdon Mine, Lustleigh, Newton Abbot, Devon TQ13 9SN (☎ 01647 277419)

CROWE, Brian Lee; CMG (1985); s of Eric Eyre Crowe (d 1952), and Virginia Bolling, *née* Teusler (d 1981); *b* 5 Jan 1938; *Educ* Sherborne Sch, Magdalen Coll Oxford; *m* 19 Jan 1969, Virginia, da of Col George Willis, MC, OBE (d 1980); 2 s (Alexander b 1972, Charles b 1975); *Career* FO 1961, Br Embassy Moscow 1962–64, FCO London 1965–68; Br Embassy: Washington 1968–73, Bonn 1973–76; head of Policy Planning Staff FCO London 1976–78, head of Chancery UK Perm Rep to EEC Brussels 1979–81, head of Euro Community Dept FCO London 1982–84, commercial min Br Embassy Washington 1985–89, ambass to Austria 1989–92, dep under sec of state FCO 1992–94, dir gen for External Relations Cncl of the EU Brusels 1994–; *Recreations* tennis, squash, winter sports; *Style*— Brian Crowe, Esq, CMG; ✉ Council of the EU, 170 Rue de la Loi, 1048 Brussels, Belgium (☎ 00 32 2 285 8552, fax 00 32 2 285 6218)

CROWE, David Edward Aubrey; s of Norman Ronald Aubrey Crowe (d 1983), and Barbara Lythgoe, *née* Jones; *b* 31 Aug 1939; *Educ* Cranleigh Sch Surrey, Christ Church Oxford (MA); *m* 8 June 1963, Helen Margaret, da of George Denis Dale (d 1983); 2 da (Sarah b 1967, Lucy b 1971); *Career* slr 1964; ptnr: HA Crowe and Co 1964–68, Gouldens 1968–89; dir TT Group plc 1992–; Parly candidate (Lib): Bromley 1970, Ravensbourne 1974; ldr Lib Gp Bromley Cncl 1974–78, vice chm London Lib Pty 1975, chm Bromley Consumer Gp 1978–79, cncllr (Lib Dem) Bromley Cncl 1994–; chm Beckenham and Bromley Nat Tst 1975–79 (hon sec 1979–88); memb Law Soc; *Recreations* opera, gardening; *Clubs* Oxford and Cambridge, National Liberal; *Style*— David Crowe, Esq; ✉ 73 Manor Way, Beckenham BR3 3LW (☎ 0181 650 8684, fax 0181 289 1457)

CROWE, Rev Canon Philip Anthony; s of Francis Frederick Crowe (d 1993), and Hilda, *née* Moss; *b* 16 Aug 1936; *Educ* Repton Sch Derbyshire, Selwyn Coll Cambridge (MA), Ridley Hall Cambridge; *Career* Nat Serv RA 1955–57; tutor in New Testament Greek and Mission Oak Hill Theol Coll 1962–65, ed Church of England Newspaper 1967–70, sec Bursary Scheme for Overseas Students 1967–70, sr staff memb St Martin-in-the-Bull Ring 1970–76, rector of Breadsall Derby 1977–88, Derby diocesan missioner 1977–83, tutor in ethics St John's Coll Nottingham 1986–88, princ Salisbury and Wells Theol Coll 1988–94, rector of Overton, Penley & Erbistock church in Wales 1995–; memb Soc for the Study of Christian Ethics; *Books* Pastoral Reorganisation (1978), Christian Baptism (1980), The Use and Abuse of Alcohol, A Whisper Will Be Heard (1994), Mission in the Modern World (contrib), Church and Sacraments (contrib); *Recreations* music, gardening, walking, squash, reading; *Style*— The Rev Canon Philip Crowe; ✉ 4 Sundorne, Overton-on-Dee, Wrexham LL13 0EB (☎ and fax 01978 710229)

CROWE, Dame Sylvia; DBE (1973, CBE 1967); da of Eyre Crowe; *b* 1901; *Educ* Berkhamsted, Swanley Hort Coll; *Career* served FANY and ATS 1939–45; designed gardens 1927–39, landscape architect in private practice 1945–; work as consult incl: Harlow and Basildon New Town Corporations, CEGB for Trawsfynydd and Wylfa Nuclear Power Stations, Forestry Cmmn, reclamation of land after 1952 floods, gardens for Univ of Oxford and Cwlth Inst London reservoirs at Bewl Bridge Wimbleball and Rutland Water; pres Inst of Landscape Architects 1957–59, vice pres Int Fedn of Landscape Architecture 1964 (sec 1948–59), hon fell Aust Inst of Landscape Architects 1978, chm Tree Cncl 1974–76; Hon DLitt Univ of Newcastle 1975, Hon LLD Univ of Sussex 1978, Hon DLitt Heriot-Watt Univ Edinburgh; hon fell Inst of Foresters, Hon FRIBA 1969; *Books* incl: Tomorrow's Landscape (1956), Garden Design (1958, 2 edn 1981), The Landscape of Power (1958), The Landscape of Roads (1960), Patterns of Landscape (1986); *Recreations* gardening, walking, countryside; *Style*— Dame Sylvia Crowe, DBE; ✉ 59 Ladbroke Grove, London W11 3AT (☎ 0171 727 7794)

CROWE, Victoria Elizabeth; da of Philip Farrands Crowe (d 1980), and Aziel, *née* Rowe; *b* 8 May 1945; *Educ* Kingston Sch of Art, Royal Coll of Art; *Career* artist; pt/t lectr Edinburgh Coll of Art; RSW 1982, ARSA 1987; *Solo Exhibitions* incl: The Scottish Gallery Edinburgh 1970, 1973, 1977, 1982 and 1995, Thackeray Gallery London 1983, 1985, 1987, 1989, 1991 and 1994, Mercury Gallery Edinburgh 1986, Fine Art Society Glasgow and Edinburgh 1988, Bruton Gallery Somerset 1989, Bruton Gallery Bath 1993; *Group Exhibitions* incl: Artist and Teacher (Fine Art Society Edinburgh and Glasgow), Contemporary Art from Scotland (tourng exhbn to Kendal, London, Sheffield, Middlesborough, Aberdeen, Inverness, Glasgow and Edinburgh), Light from the Window (Nat Gallery of Scotland), Portrait 84 (National Portrait Gallery London), Portraits on Paper (Scottish Arts Cncl touring exhbn) 1984–85, Sunday Times/Singer Friedlander Watercolour Exhbn 1988, 1990, 1991, 1992 and 1993, Scottish Art in the 20th Century (RWEA Bristol) 1991, Portrait of a Living Marsh (work from Artists for Nature Fndn Polish project, Zeist and touring exhbn throughout Europe and USA with book) 1993, Artists for Nature in Extremadura (touring exbhn throughout Europe and USA with book, 1995); numerous exhbns at RA London, RSA Edinburgh, Royal Scottish Watercolour Soc and Bath Art Fair; *Public Collections* incl: RCA, RA, Scottish Nat Gallery of Modern Art, Univ of Edinburgh, Contemporary Art Soc, NT for Scotland, Scottish Nat Portrait Gallery, City Art Centre Edinburgh, Nat Portrait Gallery London; *Commissioned Portraits* incl: R D Laing (for SNPG), Tam Dalyell MP, Lord Wemyss (for Nat Tst Scotland), kathleen Raine, Dame Janet Vaughn (Nat Portrait Gallery); *Awards* incl: Daler/Rowney Prize for Watercolour RA 1987, Hunting Gp major award 1988, Chris Beetles Prize RWS, Sir William Gillies Bequest RSA for travel and study in Italy 1992; *Style*— Ms Victoria Crowe; ✉ Bank House, Main Street, West Linton, Peebleshire, Scotland EH46 7EE

CROWE, HE The Hon William J, Jr; *b* 1925, Kentucky; *Educ* Oklahoma City, US Naval Acad (grad), Stanford Univ (MA), Princeton (PhD); *Career* former US mil career (Admiral); progressively: C-in-C US Naval Forces Europe, C-in-C Allied Forces Southern Europe, C-in-C US Pacific Cmd; chm Jt Chiefs of Staff Dept of Defense 1985–87 and 1987–89; counselor Center for Strategic and Int Studies Washington DC and prof of geopolitics Univ of Oklahoma 1989–94; chm President's Foreign Intelligence Advsy Bd (PFIAB) 1993–94; 1990–94: dir Cncl on Foreign Rels, chm Washington Inst of Foreign Affrs; dir: Texaco, Merrill Lynch, Pfizer, Norfolk and Southern, General Dynamics; American ambassador to the Court of James's 1994–; *Books* The Line of Fire (jtly), Reducing Nuclear Danger: The Road Away from the Brink (jtly); author of numerous articles on mil and foreign policy; *Style*— The Hon William J Crowe, Jr; ✉ The American Embassy, 24 Grosvenor Square, London W1A 1AE (☎ 0171 499 9000)

CROWLEY, Dermot Joseph; s of Jerome Crowley (d 1980), of Cork, Ireland, and (Mary) Agnes O'Sullivan; *b* 19 March 1947; *Educ* Colaiste Chriost Ri Cork, Univ Coll Cork; *m* 3 July 1982, Suzanne Laura, da of late Wilfred Smith; *Career* actor; *Theatre* NT appearances 1978–81 incl: Plough and the Stars, Elif in Brand, Macbeth, Careless in The Double Dealer, Rhon in Undiscovered Country, Oliver in As You Like It, Venticelo in Amadeus (also Her Majesty's), The Woman, Catesby in Richard III; at Bristol Old Vic: Richard Rowan in Exiles, Owen in Translations, Khelstakov in The Government Inspector; other appearances incl: Alan in Dark River (Orange Tree Richmond), Flann O'Brien in Flann O'Brien's Hard Life (Tricycle Kilburn), Roulstone in Observe the Sons of Ulster Marching Towards The Somme (Hampstead, won Best Supporting Actor Bass Charrington Theatre Awards 1987), Jim in The Strangeness of Others (NT), Pyotr Suslov in Summerfolk (Chichester Festival), Lovborg in Hedda Gabler (Hampstead), Michael Carney in A Whistle in the Dark (Abbey Theatre Dublin, Royal Court), Frank O'Farrel in Frauds (Abbey Theatre Dublin), The Hostage (RSC); *Television* for BBC: Juliet Bravo, Call Me Mister, Radio Testimony of a Child, Pictures, Casualty, Redundant, Hamlet, The Big Gamble, The Queen's Arms, The Sculptress, Do Not Disturb; fo LWT: Blue Money, Hercule Poirot, Ulysses; for Granada: El Cid, Victorian Scandals, The Double Dealer, Bulman; other credits incl: Hannay (Thames), Boon (Central), Echoes (Working Title), March on Europe (BBC Euro co-prodn), Minder (Euston Films), The Promise (RTE), Two Track Mind (Channel 4), Codename Kyril (HTV), Empty Nest (CBS), Call Red (Thames), Ellington (YTV); *Radio* incl: Morning Story, Hunchback of Notre Dame, Portraits of Monmartre, Ebb Tide; *Films* incl: Giro City, Return of the Jedi, Octopussy, Little Dorrit, Wilt, Son of the Pink Panther; *Recreations* playing Babu, swimming, chess; *Style*— Dermot Crowley, Esq; ✉ c/o Mayer & Eden Ltd, 34 Kingly Court, London W1R 5LE (☎ 0171 434 1242, fax 0171 287 5834)

CROWLEY, Graham Neil; s of Victor Matthew Crowley, and Veronica Mary, *née* Lee; *b* 3 May 1950; *Educ* St Martin's Sch of Art (DipAD), RCA (MA); *m* 16 Dec 1978, Sally Ann, da of Warwick Arthur Townshend; 2 s (Robin Merrick 1 Aug 1982, Pearse Max Gary 20 July 1985); *Career* artist; artist in residence Univ of Oxford 1982–83, memb Fine Art Faculty British Sch at Rome 1982–88, sr fell in painting S Glamorgan Inst of Higher Educn Cardiff 1986–89, drawing residency Riverscape Int Cleveland 1991–92; memb Advsy Bd ICA 1985–89, Fine Art Working Ctee Nat Advsy Bd DES 1987–88; *Solo Exhibitions* Air Gallery London 1982, Home Comforts (Museum of Modern Art Oxford and touring) 1983, Reflections (Riverside Studios) 1984, Night Life (ICA) 1984, Table Manners (Edward Totah Gallery London) 1984, Forum Zurich Art Fair 1984, Domestic Crisis (Totah Gallery NYC) 1986, In Living Memory and Other Paintings (Edward Totah Gallery) 1987, Law and Order (Cleveland Gallery Middlesborough) 1989, More Paintings About Speculating and Flower Arranging (Edward Totah Gallery) 1989, Ballads and Folk Songs - Paintings 1991–89 (Howard Gdns Gallery S Glam Inst of HE) 1990, Somewhere Else (Edward Totah Gallery) 1991, Northern Seen (Northern Centre for Contemporary Art Sunderland) 1992; *Gp Exhibitions* incl: John Moores Exhbn (Walker Art Gallery Liverpool) 1976, 1980, 1982, 1983, 1985, 1987 and 1993 (prize winner 1983), Drawing (Barbara Toll Gallery NYC) 1984, Venice Biennale (Anthony Reynolds Gallery) 1984, The Proper Study (Br Cncl New Delhi) 1985, Still Life - A New Life (Harris Museum and Art Gallery Preston and touring) 1985, Figuring Out the '80's (Laing Art Gallery Newcastle) 1988, The New British Painting (USA) 1988, Real Life Stories (Spacex Exeter) 1989–90, The New British Painting (Queen's Museum NYC) 1990, The Brew House Open Taunton (first prize) 1990, Riverscape (Middlesborough and Cleveland Galleries) 1993; *Murals* Brompton Hosp London 1982, Chandler's Ford Library 1983; *Work in Public Collections* Imperial War Museum, Museum of Auckland NZ, Arts Cncl Collection, Ipswich Museum, Leicester Educn Authy, Leeds Educn Authy, V&A, Br Cncl Collection, Contemporary Arts Soc, Kettles Yard Cambridge, Castle Museum Nottingham, Univ of Northumbria at Newcastle; *Books* Gogol's Overcoat (1984, ICA for Nighlife Exhbn); *Recreations* reading, motor cycling, classic motoring, gardening; *Style*— Graham Crowley, Esq; ✉ Bampton, 58 Lowther Hill, London SE23 1PY (☎ 0181 690 1726)

CROWLEY, Niall; Hon CBE (1993); *b* 18 Sept 1926; *Career* ptnr KPMG Stokes Kennedy Crowley CAs 1950– (managing ptnr 1969–77); chm: Cahill May Roberts Group plc, Aquaporte Holdings Ltd, Irish Life Assurance plc 1974–83, Allied Irish Banks plc 1977–89; dep chm Alliance & Leicester Building Society; dir: J Rothschild International Assurance plc, Scottish Amicable European, Girobank plc (subsid of Alliance & Leicester); fndr chm Financial Servs Indust Assoc in Ireland 1984–88 (memb Cncl 1984–), chm Br Irish Assoc 1994–; pres: Inst of Chartered Accountants of Ireland 1970–71, Dublin C of C 1983–84, Inst of Bankers Ireland 1987–88; New Zealand hon consul in Ireland 1991; *Style*— Niall Crowley, Esq, CBE; ✉ c/o Alliance & Leicester Building Society, 49 Park Lane, London W1Y 4EQ; 46 Upper Mount Street, Dublin 2, Ireland (☎ 00 353 1 676 2464, fax 00 353 1 676 2489)

CROWLEY, Dr Theresa Vivianne; da of Joseph Crowley, of Bucks, and Margaret Mary, *née* Heaton; *b* 4 Nov 1953; *Educ* Notre Dame London, Bedford Coll Univ of London (BSc), UCL (PhD); *m* 18 Aug 1979, Christopher Stephen Bainton, s of David Bainton, of Dorset; *Career* chartered psychologist and policy advsr; Austin Knight Ltd 1974–75, Department of Employment 1975–77 and 1983–85, Kiernan & Co (UK) Ltd 1978–83, Cabinet Office 1985–86 and 1991–, HM Treasy 1986–88, Industl Soc 1988–90, Policy

Studies Inst 1988–, Union Inst Ohio 1994–, King's Coll London 1995–; hon sec Div of Occupational Psychology Br Psychological Soc; associate fell Br Psychological Soc; *Books* Redundancy (1985), Beyond Redundancy (1992); many papers on employment, education, training and unemployment; *Recreations* riding, archaeology, the Western Mystery tradition; *Style—* Dr Theresa Vivianne Crowley; ✉ London; Pludérien, 56160 Séglien, France

CROWLEY-MILLING, Michael Crowley; CMG (1982); s of Thomas William Crowley-Milling (d 1954), of Colwyn Bay, N Wales and Gillian May, *née* Chinnery (d 1942); *b* 7 May 1917; *Educ* Radley Coll, St John's Coll Cambridge (MA); *m* 1957, Gee, da of William Gray Dickson (d 1983), of West Ferry, Dundee; *Career* electrical engr Metropolitan-Vickers Electric Co Ltd 1938–63: devpt of radar 1938–46, design and devpt of electron linear accelerators for physics med and irradiation purposes 1946–63; Directorate Daresbury Nuclear Physics Lab 1963–71; Euro Orgn for Nuclear Res (CERN) Geneva 1971–83: responsible for control system for Super Proton Synchrotron (SPS) 1971–76, SPS div leader 1977–78, dir Acceleration Program 1979–80, conslt 1981–85; SLAC Stanford Univ (USA) 1983–85; conslt: Los Alamos Nat Lab USA 1985–95, Elettra Lab Trieste 1988–92, SSC Lab Dallas USA 1991–94; dir Crowley Conslts 1984–; CEng, FIEE; *Books* Accelerator Control Systems (ed, 1986), Accelerator and Large Experimental Physics Control Systems (ed, 1990), John Bertram Adams - Engineer Extraordinary (1993), various articles in tech press on accelerators and control systems; *Recreations* vintage cars, sailing (yacht 'SPS'); *Clubs* VSCC, LPYC; *Style—* Michael Crowley-Milling, Esq, CMG; ✉ 15 Les Ruches, 1264 St Cergue, Switzerland

CROWSON, Richard Borman; CMG (1986); s of Clarence Borman Crowson (d 1980), of Gainsborough, and Cecilia May, *née* Ramsden (d 1973); *b* 23 July 1929; *Educ* Queen Elizabeth's GS Gainsborough, Downing Coll Cambridge (MA); *m* 1, 29 Feb 1960 (m dis 1974), Sylvia, *née* Cavalier; 1 s (Anthony b 26 Feb 1961), 1 da (Hilary b 3 March 1964); m 2, 21 May 1983, Judith Elaine, da of Marion Earl Clark, of Lincoln, Nebraska, USA; 1 step s (David b 5 Aug 1967); *Career* HM Colonial Serv Uganda 1955–62, FO 1962–63, 1 Sec (Commercial) Br Embassy Tokoyo 1963–68, dep high cmmr Barbados 1968–70, FCO 1970–74, cnsllr (Commercial & Aid) Br Embassy Jakarta 1975–77, cnsllr (Hong Kong Affairs) Br Embassy Washington (also accredited in Ottawa) 1977–82, cnsllr Br Embassy Berne 1983–85, Br high cmmr Mauritius and concurrently HM Ambass Fed Islamic Repub of the Comoros 1985–89; FCIS 1962; *Recreations* music, theatre; *Clubs* Royal Cwlth Soc; *Style—* Richard Crowson, Esq, CMG; ✉ 67 Crofton Rd, Orpington, Kent (☎ 01689 891320)

CROWTHER, Eric John Ronald; OBE (1977); s of Stephen Charles Crowther (d 1943), and Olive Beatrix, *née* Selby (d 1951); *b* 4 Aug 1924; *m* 1959, Elke Auguste Ottilie, da of Ludwig Winkelmann (d 1976), of Germany; 1 s (Edward b 1963), 1 da (Evelyn b 1961); *Career* served RN Med 1943–47; called to the Bar Lincoln's Inn 1951 (winner Inns of Court Contest in Advocacy 1950), in practice at Criminal Bar 1951–68, metropolitan stipendary magistrate 1968–89, recorder of the Crown Court 1983–96, resident magistrate Monsterrat 1996–; lectr: in English Br Cncl 1951–81, in elocution and advocacy Cncl of Legal Educn 1955–91, in evidence to RN 1968–89; chm Training Sub Ctee Inner London Magistrates 1981–89; ed Commonwealth Judicial Journal 1973–77; hon offr Int Students House 1981–; *Books* Advocacy for the Advocate (1984), Last in the List (1988), Look What's on the Bench! (1992); *Style—* Eric J R Crowther, Esq, OBE; ✉ c/o Lincoln's Inn, London WC2

CROWTHER, Joseph Stanley (Stan); s of Cyril Joseph Crowther (d 1970), of Rotherham and Florence Mildred, *née* Beckett; *b* 30 May 1925; *Educ* Rotherham GS, Rotherham Coll of Technol; *m* 1948, Margaret, da of Llewellyn Royston (d 1956), of Huddersfield; 2 s; *Career* journalist formerly with Yorkshire Evening Post; MP (Lab) Rotherham 1976–92, PPS to Min of State for Employment 1978–79, memb Trade and Indust Select Ctee 1979–92, memb Chm's Panel 1983–92; Mayor of Rotherham 1971–72 and 1975–76; chm Yorks and Humberside Devpt Assoc 1973–76, vice pres Town and Country Planning Assoc, pres Rotherham Arts Cncl; hon assoc Br Veterinary Assoc; *Style—* Stan Crowther, Esq; ✉ 15 Clifton Crescent South, Rotherham (☎ 01709 364559)

CROWTHER, His Hon Judge; Thomas Rowland; QC (1981); s of Dr Kenneth Vincent Crowther, of Gwent, and Winifred Anita, *née* Rowland (d 1992); *b* 11 Sept 1937; *Educ* Newport HS, Keble Coll Oxford (MA); *m* 1969, Gillian Jane, da of William Leslie Prince (d 1978); 1 s (Thomas b 1970), 1 da (Lucy b 1971); *Career* barr 1960, in practice Oxford Circuit 1960–69, in practice Wales and Chester Circuit 1970–84, jr of Wales and Chester Circuit 1974, recorder Crown Ct 1980–84, Crown Ct judge 1985; dir Gwent Area Broadcasting Ltd 1982–84; circuit judge (Wales and Chester Circuit) 1985–; *Recreations* garden, trout fishing, golf; *Clubs* Cardiff and County, Newport Golf; *Style—* His Hon Judge Crowther, QC; ✉ Lansor, nr Caerleon, Gwent NP6 1LS (☎ 01633 450224)

CROWTHER-ALWYN, Peter; s of Rev Vivian Crowther-Alwyn (d 1967), of Ipswich, Suffolk, and Jessie, *née* Hough; *b* 14 April 1944; *Educ* Rossall Sch Fleetwood Lancs; *m* 5 Nov 1977, Irene Elizabeth, da of James Stewart Young; 2 da (Victoria Louise b 13 Feb 1979, Alexandra b 15 April 1981); *Career* articled clerk Clark Son & Moyle Ipswich 1962–66, audit clerk Paterson & Thompson 1966–67, audit sr Coopers & Lybrand Birmingham 1967–68; Pannell Fitzpatrick & Co: audit sr Port of Spain Trinidad 1968–70, resident ptnr Grenada 1972–75 (resident mangr 1970–71), seconded to Monrovia Liberia 1976–77; Pannell Kerr Forster: ptnr and dir Monrovia Liberia 1977–79, ptnr Banjul The Gambia 1987–94 (resident ptnr 1978–87), fin and admin ptnr Central Admin UK 1988–91, int fin ptnr 1991–96, int fin dir 1996–; memb Exec Ctee Gambia C of C & Indust 1978–87, Royal Danish Consul Banjul The Gambia 1985–87; chm Fajara Club The Gambia 1986–87 (treas 1984–86, chm Admissions Ctee 1978–79), chm Royal Soc of St George Banjul (The Gambia) Branch 1984–87; FCA 1979 (ACA 1968), FIMgt 1990 (MIMgt 1972), MInstD 1988; *Recreations* model car collecting, watching television, reading; *Clubs* Royal Over-Seas League; *Style—* Peter Crowther-Alwyn, Esq; ✉ Lings Farm, 47 Main St, Keyworth, Notts NG12 5AA (☎ 0115 937 6646); Pannell Kerr Forster, Regent House, Clinton Avenue, Notts NG5 1AZ (☎ 0115 960 8171, fax 0115 969 1203, car 0831 094602)

CROXFORD, David; s of Frederick William Gordon Croxford (ka 1944), and Lucy May, *née* Williams; *b* 3 Oct 1937; *Educ* Hinchley Wood Co Sch Esher Surrey; *m* 5 July 1975, Victoria Wendy, da of Robert Francis Fort; *Career* CA 1962; trained and qualified with Hagley Knight & Co 1955–62, Tansley Witt & Co (now part of MacIntyre Hudson) 1962–64, Ogden Parsons & Co (now part of Coopers & Lybrand) 1964–67, mangr Bird & Partners 1968–71; Moore Stephens: sr and managerial positions Bermuda 1972–77, re-located to Jersey 1977, accounts controller 1977, special servs mangr 1979, ptnr 1980–95; ind practitioner 1996–; memb: ICAEW 1962, Jersey Soc of Chartered and Certified Accountants 1977, Jersey Assoc of Practising Chartered and Certified Accountants 1981, Jersey Taxation Soc 1986, IOD 1988, Soc of Practitioners of Insolvency 1992, Soc of Tst and Estate Practitioners 1996; Licensed Insolvency Practitioner 1989; *Recreations* singing (choral and sacred), golf, music, gardening; *Clubs* La Moye Golf (Jersey), Jersey Gilbert and Sullivan Soc, Jersey Amateur Dramatic, The Victoria (Jersey); *Style—* David Croxford, Esq; ✉ La Chaumiere, College Hill, St Helier, Jersey JE2 4RE (☎ 01534 872751, fax 01534 872752)

CROXFORD, Ian Lionel; QC (1993); s of Peter Patrick Croxford, BEM, and Mary, *née* Richardson; *b* 23 July 1953; *Educ* Westcliff HS for Boys, Univ of Leicester (LLB); *m* Sandra; 1 da, 1 s; *Career* called to the Bar Gray's Inn 1976 (Bacon scholar), ad eundem Lincoln's Inn; *Recreations* watching sport; *Style—* Ian Croxford, Esq, QC; ✉ 2–3 Gray's Inn Square, Gray's Inn, London WC1R 5JH (☎ 0171 242 4986, fax 0171 405 1166)

CROXON, Raymond Patrick Austen; QC (1983); *b* 31 July 1928; *Educ* Strand Coll and St Thomas's Hosp (MSR), King's Coll London (LLB); *m* 1952 (sep 1989), Monica Howard; 2 s, 2 da; *partner* Hara Marinou; *Career* served RAMC 1946–49; radiographer 1950–59, called to the Bar Gray's Inn 1960; publishing co 1960–63, practising barr 1963–, head of chambers; *Recreations* travel, walking, swimming, reading, listening to music, attending concerts and theatre, learning modern Greek language; *Clubs* Savage; *Style—* Raymond Croxon, Esq, QC; ✉ Chambers: 2 Salisbury Villas, Station Road, Cambridge CB2 2LA (☎ 01223 301517, fax 01223 359267)

CROYDON, Archdeacon of; *see:* Davies, Ven (Vincent) Anthony (Tony)

CROYDON, David John; s of John Farley Croydon, of Stourbridge, West Midlands, and Patricia Ethel, *née* Lloyd; *b* 26 Feb 1949; *Educ* King Edward VI GS Stourbridge, Univ of London (BA); *m* 29 July 1972, Catherine Mary, da of James Goddard, of Birmingham; 1 s (Luke James b 20 Jan 1981), 1 da (Madeleine Lucy b 26 June 1986); *Career* advertising exec 3M Corporation 1977–80, account mangr MSW Promotions 1980–81, account dir Counter Products Marketing 1981–86, fndr and md Marketing Principles Ltd (sales promotion consultancy) 1986–; memb: Sales Promotion Conslts Assoc, Inst of Sales Promotion; *Recreations* rugby football; *Clubs* Chinnor, Saracens, Middx; *Style—* David Croydon, Esq; ✉ Monks Hill, South Hills, Brill, Aylesbury, Bucks; Marketing Principles Ltd, Frewin Chambers, Frewin Court, Cornmarket, Oxford (☎ 01865 791854, fax 01865 791852, car 0836 334150)

CROYDON, Bishop of 1985–; Rt Rev Dr Wilfred Denniston Wood; *b* 1936; *Educ* Barbados WI, Codrington Coll Barbados; *m*; 3 s, 2 da; *Career* ordained (St Paul's Cathedral) 1962; curate St Stephen with St Thomas Shepherd's Bush 1962–67, hon curate and Bishop's offr in race rels 1967–74, vicar of St Laurence Catford 1974–82, archdeacon and borough dean of Southwark 1982–85; JP 1971–82; fndr memb: Jt Cncl for the Welfare of Immigrants, Shepherd's Bush Social and Welfare Assoc, Shepherd's Bush Credit Union, Shepherd's Bush Housing Assoc, Berbice Housing Co-op Assoc, Carib Housing Assoc; memb Bd Housing Corp 1986–95; former: memb Bd Shelter, moderator World Cncl of Churches' Prog to Combat Racism, memb Royal Cmmn on Criminal Procedure, memb Archbishop of Canterbury's Cmmn on Urban Priority Areas (produced report Faith in the City); pres Inst of Race Rels (former chm); *Books* Vicious Circle (with John Downing, 1968), Keep the Faith, Baby (1994); *Style—* The Rt Rev the Bishop of Croydon; ✉ St Matthew's House, 100 George Street, Croydon CR0 1PJ (☎ 0181 681 5496, fax 0181 686 2074)

CROZIER, Brian Rossiter; s of Robert Henry Crozier (d 1939), and Elsa, *née* McGillivray (d 1957); *b* 4 Aug 1918; *Educ* Lycée Montpellier France, Peterborough Coll Harrow, Trinity Coll of Music London; *m* 7 Sept 1940, Mary Lillian (Lila) (d 1993), da of Charles Augustus Samuel (d 1965); 1 s (Michael b 1948), 3 da (Kathryn-Anne (Mrs Choguill) b 1941, Isobel (Mrs Colbourn) b 1944, Caroline (Mrs Wyeth) b 1953); *Career* conslt and writer on int affairs; WWII aeronautical inspection 1941–43; music and art critic London 1935–39; reporter and sub-ed: Stoke-on-Trent, Stockport, London 1940–41, News Chronicle 1944–48; sub-ed and writer Sydney Morning Herald Aust 1948–51, correspondent Reuters 1951–52 (sub-ed 1943–44), features ed Straits Times Singapore 1952–53, leader writer and corr, ed of Foreign Report The Economist 1954–64, commentator for the BBC Overseas Servs 1954–65, chm Forum World Features 1965–74, co-fndr Inst for the Study of Conflict 1970 (dir 1970–79); contrib ed: National Review NY 1978–, Now! London 1980–81, The Times 1982–84; adjunct scholar Heritage Fndn Washington DC 1984–95, distinguished visiting fell Hoover Instn Stanford California 1996–; named in The Guinness Book of Records 1988 as the writer who has interviewed most heads of state and govt in the world (65) 1948–92 (now 67); *Books* The Rebels (1960), The Morning After (1963), Neo-Colonialism (1964), South-East Asia in Turmoil (1965), The Struggle for the Third World (1966), Franco (1967), The Masters of Power (1969), The Future of Communist Power (1970), De Gaulle (1973), A Theory of Conflict (1974), The Man Who Lost China (Chiang Kai-Shek) (1977), Strategy of Survival (1978), The Minimum State (1979), Franco: Crepúsculo de un hombre (1980), The Price of Peace (1980), Socialism Explained (jtly, 1984), This War Called Peace (jtly, 1984), The Andropov Deception (under pseudonym John Rossiter, 1984), The Grenada Documents (ed 1987), Socialism: Dream and Reality (1987), The Gorbachev Phenomenon (1990), Communism: Why Prolong its Death-Throes? (1990), Free Agent (autobiography, 1993), The KGB Lawsuits (1995), Le Phenixrouge (jtly, 1995); *Recreations* piano, taping stereo; *Clubs* RAC; *Style—* Brian Crozier, Esq; ✉ 18 Wickliffe Avenue, Finchley, London N3 3EJ (☎ 0181 346 8124, fax 0181 346 4599); 1AA Carlisle Place, London SW1P 1NP (☎ 0171 931 8046, 0171 828 5618)

CROZIER, John; *b* 28 June 1946; *Educ* Tiffin Sch, Univ of Bristol (BA), Kingston Poly (Dip in mgmnt studies); *m* (m dis); 2 c; *Career* Avon Cosmetics UK Ltd 1968–71 (job evaluation offr and personnel offr, sr personnel offr), personnel mangr Human Resources and Sales and Distribution Lyons Bakery Ltd 1971–73; Rank Xerox International Ltd: personnel mangr Midland and West 1973–75, personnel mangr UK Operations 1975–82, Euro personnel mangr 1978–82; Grand Metropolitan plc: personnel and communications dir Chef & Brewer 1982–84, personnel PR and Communications dir Grand Metropolitan Retailing Ltd 1984–86; Heidrick & Struggles International Inc 1986–88 (ptnr Euro Practice, exec search conslt); Lopex plc: exec dir 1988–, chm and chief exec Riley Advertising Ltd; MInstD 1985, MIPA; *Style—* John Crozier, Esq; ✉ Garden Flat, 59 The Avenue, Kew Gardens TW9 2AL (☎ 0181 940 7020); Lopex plc, 4 Red Lion Court, London EC4A 3EN (☎ 0171 353 3223)

CRUICKSHANK, Alexander Andrew Campbell; s of Alexander Cruickshank, FRCS (d 1980), and Eileen Bertha, *née* Coleman; *b* 30 Nov 1945; *Educ* Haileybury and ISC, Peterhouse Cambridge (MA); *m* 19 May 1973, Susan Mary, da of Alan Pearce Greenaway, JP; 2 s (David b 1976, Benjamin b 1982), 1 da (Sarah b 1974); *Career* Refinery and Distribution Planning Esso Petroleum Co 1967–72, Automated Real-Time Investments Exchange Ltd 1973–78, dir Orion Royal Bank Ltd 1985–88 (joined 1979), sr dir Continental Bank NA 1988–90, exec dir Sumitomo Finance International 1990–91, md Lion Gate Securities Ltd 1991–94, chief exec The Little Foundation 1994–; Liveryman Worshipful Co of Gardeners; *Recreations* golf, reading, gardening; *Clubs* St George's Hill Golf, City Livery, United Wards, City Pickwick (hon sec); *Style—* A A C Cruickshank, Esq; ✉ The Doone, Byfleet Rd, Cobham, Surrey KT11 1EA (☎ 01932 864714)

CRUICKSHANK, David John Ogilvie; s of Ogilvie Cruickshank, of Scotland, and Rosemary Elizabeth, *née* Philip; *b* 20 Feb 1959; *Educ* Waid Acad Anstruther Fife, Univ of Edinburgh (BCom); *m* 1984, Rona, da of Rowland Dalgliesh; 2 da (Lindsay Alexandra b 28 Aug 1990, Fiona Jacqueline b 4 June 1992); *Career* Touche Ross (now Deloitte & Touche): trainee chartered accountant Edinburgh 1979–82, tax mangr 1982–88, tax ptnr 1988–, ptnr i/c London Tax Practice 1995–; MICAS 1982; *Recreations* work, family, golf, travel, good company, current affairs; *Clubs* IOD, Pyrford Golf, Newtonmore Golf; *Style—* David Cruickshank, Esq; ✉ Deloitte & Touche, Hill House, 1 Little New Street, London EC4A 3TR (direct ☎ 0171 303 3638, direct fax 0171 583 6434)

CRUICKSHANK, Donald Gordon (Don); s of Donald Campbell Cruickshank, of Moray, Scotland, and Margaret Buchan *née* Morrison; *b* 17 Sept 1942; *Educ* Fordyce Acad, Univ of Aberdeen (MA), Manchester Business Sch (MBA); *m* 17 Oct 1964, Elizabeth Buchan, da of Alexander Watt Taylor, of Fraserburgh, Aberdeenshire,

Scotland; 1 s (Stewart b 1965), 1 da (Karen b 1969); *Career* McKinsey and Co Inc 1972–77, dir and gen mangr Sunday Times Times Newspapers Ltd 1977–80, dir Pearson Longman Ltd 1980–84, md Virgin Group plc 1984–89; chm Wandsworth District Health Authority 1986–89, chief exec NHS in Scotland 1989–93, dir-gen of telecommunications Office of Telecommunications 1993–; non-exec dir Christian Salvesen PLC 1993–95; *Recreations* opera, theatre, golf, sport; *Style*— Don Cruickshank, Esq; ✉ Office of Telecommunications, 50 Ludgate Hill, London EC4M 7JJ (☎ 0171 634 8801)

CRUICKSHANK, Dr John Gladstone (Ian); s of Prof John Cecil Cruickshank, MD (d 1956), of London, and Mabel Elizabeth, *née* Harvey; *b* 17 Oct 1930; *Educ* Highgate Sch, UCL (MB BS, MRCS, LRCP), Univ of Cambridge (MA), Univ of Birmingham (MD, MRCPath); *m* 27 Dec 1958, Margaret Montague, da of Lt-Col Charles Philip Heath, DSO (d 1989), of Cullompton, Devon; 1 s (John b 1967), 3 da (Isobel 1960, Catriona b 1961, Morag b 1963); *Career* RAF pilot offr 1948–50; lectr in pathology Univ of Cambridge 1957–64, lectr in microbiology Univ of Birmingham 1964–68, dean Faculty of Med Univ of Rhodesia 1973–75 (prof of med microbiology 1968–76), dir Public Health Laboratory Exeter 1988–95 (dep dir 1976–88); memb Cncl Univ of Rhodesia 1970–75, regnl rep RCPath 1986–88, visiting conslt WHO 1987; FRCPath 1978; *Recreations* reading, tennis, music, the countryside; *Style*— Dr Ian Cruickshank; ✉ Coombe Farm, Knowle, Cullompton, Devon EX15 1PT (☎ 01884 33533)

CRUICKSHANK OF AUCHREOCH, Martin Melvin; s of Brig Martin Melvin Cruickshank, CIE (d 1964), and Florence Watson Cruickshank (d 1976); *b* 17 Sept 1933; *Educ* Rugby, Eaton Hall, Corpus Christi Coll Cambridge; *m* 1 March 1958, Rona, da of Mary Fenella Paton of Grandhome (d 1949), of Grandhome House, Aberdeen; 3 s (Martin b 1960, Nicholas b 1961 d 1973, Paul b 1963), 1 da (Fenella b 1959); *Career* cmmnd Gordon Highlanders 1952, serv Malaya 1952–53 (despatches), Cyprus 1955–56, Germany 1960–61, Congo 1962 (Co cmd), Nigeria 1962–64 (chief instr Offr Cadet Sch, Bde Maj, Dep Cmdt Nigerian Military Coll), ret 1967; landowner; sec and past pres Strathfillan Golf Club; Order of St John in Scotland: memb Cncl 1970–75, memb Chapter 1970–, Sword Bearer 1977–96; KStJ 1982 (OStJ 1965, CStJ 1974); FRGS; *Recreations* travel (particularly deserts), bird watching, golf, music, oenology; *Clubs* Army and Navy, Optimists'; *Style*— M M Cruickshank of Auchreoch; ✉ Auchreoch, Crianlarich, Perthshire (☎ 01838 400218, fax 01838 400217)

CRUM EWING, Humphry John Frederick; s of Humphry William Erskine Crum Ewing (d 1985), and Winifred Mary, *née* Kyle (d 1988); *b* 11 May 1934; *Educ* Marlborough, Ch Ch Oxford (MA); *m* 1, 30 April 1964, Carolyn Joan Maule (d 1975), da of Lt-Col Ian Burn-Murdoch, OBE, IA (d 1963), and formerly w of 3 Baron Wrenbury; 1 s (Alexander b 1966), 2 da (Arabella b 1967, Nicola b and d 1969); m 2, 14 Feb 1980, Mrs Janet Angela Tomlinson, da of L R Bates (d 1965), of Leicester; *Career* public and int affrs conslt; pres Oxford Univ Cons Assoc 1956, Parly candidate (C) Swansea East 1959; chm: Ingersoll Group 1966–69, Rajawella Cos 1976–79; advsr to: Shadow Foreign Sec 1977–79, Min for Consumer Affrs 1981–83, Min for Higher Educn and Sci 1987–90, Min for Training 1990–92, Parly Sec Office of Public Servs & Sci 1992–93, Political Office of PM 1992, Academic Panel Staff Coll Camberley 1993–; treas Secs' and Assts' Cncl House of Commons 1990–94; fell Lancaster Univ Centre for Defence & Int Security Studies 1992–; ed Bailrigg Publications 1995–; Liveryman Worshipful Co of Clockmakers; *Recreations* bridge, cooking, travelling, collecting; *Style*— Humphry Crum Ewing, Esq; ✉ 63 Baker St, Reading, Berks RG1 7XY (☎ and fax 0118 958 5096)

CRUMPLIN, Michael Kenneth Hugh; s of Col W C D Crumplin (d 1994), and Muriel Elizabeth Kerr Barley (d 1970); *b* 12 Aug 1942; *Educ* Wellington, Middx Hosp Med Sch (MB BS); *m* 29 May 1965, Elizabeth Ann, da of Maj Guy William Walker Bunting; 2 s (Ian Douglas b 22 Sep 1970, Patrick Gordon b 17 June 1972), 1 da (Fiona Jane Kerr b 1 July 1977); *Career* house surgn and house physician: Middx Hosp 1965, Central Middx Hosp 1966; sr house offr Middx Hosp 1966, registrar in surgery Princess Margaret Hosp Swindon and Middx Hosp 1970–72, sr registrar United Birmingham Hosps 1973–77 (res fell and hon sr registrar 1972–73), conslt gen surgn Wrexham Maelor Hosp Tst 1977–; former RCS regnl advsr surgery N Wales; former chm: Court of Examiners RCS, Hosp Specialists and Conslts' Assoc, Editorial Bd British Journal of Surgery; former memb Cncl Assoc Surgns GB and I; FRCS; *Publications* author of numerous chapters and articles for med books and jls; *Recreations* Scottish country dancing, military history (Napoleonic Wars); *Clubs* East India; *Style*— Michael Crumplin, Esq; ✉ Greenridges, 57 Wynnstay Lane, Marford, Nr Wrexham, Clwyd LL12 8LH (☎ 01978 854701); Maelor General Hospital, Watery Rd, Wrexham, Clwyd (☎ 01978 291100)

CRUMPTON, Michael Joseph; CBE (1992); s of Charles E and Edith Crumpton; *b* 7 June 1929; *Educ* Poole GS, Univ Coll Southampton, Lister Inst of Preventive Med London (BSc, PhD); *m* 1960, Janet Elizabeth Dean; 1 s, 2 da; *Career* Nat Serv RAMC 1953–55; memb Scientific Staff Microbiological Research Estab Porton Wilts 1955–60, visiting scientist fellowship Nat Inst of Health Bethesda Maryland USA 1959–60, research fell Dept of Immunology St Mary's Hosp Med Sch London 1960–66, memb Scientific Staff Nat Inst for Med Res Mill Hill 1966–79 (head of Biochemistry Div 1976–79), dir of research (Laboratories) Imperial Cancer Research Fund Laboratories 1991–93 (dep dir of research 1976–91), dir Imperial Cancer Research Technology Ltd 1989–; non-exec dir Amersham International plc 1990–; visiting fell John Curtin Sch for Med Res ANU Canberra 1973–74, Biochemistry Soc visiting lectr Aust 1983; memb: WHO Steering Ctee for Encapsulated Bacteria 1984–91 (chm 1988–91), Cell Bd MRC 1979–83, Scientific Advsy Ctee Lister Inst 1986–91, Sloan Ctee General Motors Res Fndn 1986–88 (chm 1988), MRC AIDS Directed Prog Steering Ctee 1987–91, Scientific Ctee Swiss Inst for Experimental Cancer Res 1989–, DTI/SERC Biotech Jt Advsy Bd 1989–93; memb Cncl: Royal Inst 1986–90 (memb Davy Faraday Lab Ctee 1985–90, chm of Ctee 1988–90), MRC 1986–90, Royal Soc 1990–92, Inst of Cancer Res 1994–, Imperial Coll of Sci and Technol 1994–; memb Sci Cncl Celltech Ltd 1980–90; chm: Sci Advsy Bd Biomed Res Centre Univ of Br Columbia Vancouver 1987–91, DOH/HSE Advsy Ctee on Dangerous Pathogens 1991–; memb: Governing Body BPMF 1987–95, Governors Strangeways Res Lab 1993–; memb Editorial Bd: Biochemical Jl 1966–73 (dep chm 1969–72), Euro Jl of Immunology 1972–86, Immunochemistry 1975–79, Immunogenetics 1979–85, Biochemistry Int 1980–86, Molecular Biology and Medicine 1983–86, Human Immunology 1985–; regional ed Molecular Immunology 1982–86; sr treas Royal Soc Club 1988–89; memb: EMBO 1982–, Academia Europea 1996–; hon memb American Assoc of Immunology 1995; FRS 1979; *Publications* contrib to learned scientific jls; *Recreations* gardening, reading; *Style*— Michael Crumpton, Esq, CBE, FRS; ✉ 33 Homefield Road, Radlett, Herts WD7 8PX (☎ 01923 854675)

CRUSH, His Hon Judge; Harvey Michael; s of George Stanley Crush (d 1970), of Chislehurst, Kent, and Alison Isabel, *née* Lang (d 1992); *b* 12 April 1939; *Educ* Chigwell Sch Essex; *m* 1, 21 Aug 1965 (m dis 1982), Diana, da of Frederick Joseph Bassett (d 1965), of Coulsdon, Surrey; 1 s (Nicholas b 1 Dec 1967), 1 da (Emily b 21 May 1971); m 2, 9 Dec 1982, Margaret (Maggie) Rose, da of Nicholas Dixson (d 1986); *Career* admitted slr 1963; ptnr Norton Rose 1968–91, dir TOSG Trust Fund Ltd 1970–95; memb Supreme Court Rule Ctee 1984–88, recorder of the Crown Court 1992–95 (asst recorder 1987–92); circuit judge (SE Circuit) 1995–; vice pres City of London Law Soc 1989–91, memb Law Soc, chm Swanley & Dist CAB Mgmnt Ctee 1991–93 (memb 1991–); memb Local then General Ctee London Legal Aid Area 1969–82 (memb Area Ctee 1982–95); dir Br Assoc of Aviation Conslts 1991–95 (hon slr 1991–94); hon life memb Sevenoaks and Dist Motor Club (chm 1968–71); Liveryman: Worshipful Co of Slrs 1982 (memb Court of Assistants 1987–, Master 1994–95), Worshipful Co of Farriers 1984; Freeman Guild of Air Pilots and Air Navigators 1991; MRAeS 1980; *Recreations* flying, travel; *Style*— His Hon Judge Crush; ✉ Croydon Combined Court Centre, The Law Courts, Altyre Road, Croydon, Surrey CR9 5AB (☎ 0181 681 2533, fax 0181 760 0432)

CRUTCHLOW, John Adrian; s of James William Crutchlow, of Saffron Walden, Essex (d 1979), and Elsie Nellie, *née* King; *b* 30 March 1946; *Educ* Finchley County GS, North-Western Poly (HNC, post grad dip), Open Univ (BA); *m* 22 May 1971, Valerie Elizabeth, da of Claude Harold Farage (d 1964); *Career* Paymaster General's Office 1962–65; Met Police Civil Staff: exec offr (Fin Branch) 1965–69, higher exec offr 1969–74 (personnel/mgmnt servs 1969–71, admin/special projects 1971–74), princ (CID Secretariat, Bldg Section, asst dir of fin 1974–81), sr princ 1981–86 (dep dir of fin 1981–84, dep estab offr 1984–86), asst sec (dir of fin) 1986–92, asst under-sec of state (dir of fin) 1992, dep to Receiver for the Metropolitan Police District 1994, ret from Met Police; pres New Scotland Yard Civil Staff Assoc 1994; FIMgt 1991, FInstAM(Dip) 1995; *Recreations* reading, gardening, renovating old houses; *Style*— John Crutchlow, Esq

CRUTHERS, Sir James Winter; kt (1980); s of James William Cruthers (d 1992), and Kate Cruthers (d 1950); *b* 20 Dec 1924; *Educ* Perth Tech Coll; *m* 1950, Alwyn Sheila, da of late Jack Della; 1 s, 1 da; *Career* magazines ed Western Australia Newspapers Ltd 1953, chm and md TVW Enterprises Ltd 1975–81 (gen mangr 1958), chm Aust Film Cmmn 1981, dir News Corporation Ltd 1981–91, News America Holdings Inc 1985–91, Sky Television Ltd 1984–90, chm Westpre Ltd 1990–; Queen's Jubilee Medal 1977, W Aust Citizen of the Year 1980; *Style*— Sir James Cruthers; ✉ c/o Westpre Ltd, 34 Stirling Street, Perth 6001, Western Australia

CRUTTWELL, Christopher George; s of Reginald Quentin Cruttwell (d 1968), and Joan, *née* McCausland (d 1969); *b* 25 July 1932; *Educ* King's Sch Bruton, St John's Coll Oxford (BA); *m* 14 April 1971, Patricia Valerie, da of Albert George Long (d 1984); 1 s (Stephen John b 1972), 1 da (Elizabeth Ann b 1974); *Career* admitted slr 1959; ptnr Gouldens 1963–94 (conslt 1994–); memb: Law Soc, Royal Philatelic Soc; *Recreations* philately, hockey; *Style*— Christopher Cruttwell, Esq; ✉ 35 Old Lodge Lane, Purley, Surrey CR8 4DL (☎ 0181 668 3035); Gouldens, 22 Tudor St, London EC4Y 0JJ (☎ 0171 583 7777, telex 21520, fax 0171 583 3051)

CRWYS-WILLIAMS, Air Vice-Marshal David Owen; CB (1990); s of late Gareth Crwys-Williams, OBE, of Llangollen, Clwyd, and Frances Ellen, *née* Strange; *b* 24 Dec 1940; *Educ* Oakham Sch, RAF Coll Cranwell; *m* 1, 1963 (m dis 1972), Jennifer Jean, *née* Pearce; 1 da (Jacqueline Lara b 23 Feb 1967); m 2, 31 March 1973, Irene (Suzie), da of late D J T Whan, of Kendal, Cumbria; 1 s (Huw David b 20 Nov 1975), 2 da (Kirsty Jane b 20 Feb 1977, Claire Elizabeth b 4 Nov 1981); *Career* RAF Coll Cranwell 1958–61, commissioned as pilot 1961, 30 Sqdn Kenya 1961–63, 47 Sqdn RAF Abingdon 1964–66, ADC to C-in-C RAF Trg Cmd 1966–68, Sqdn Ldr 1969, OC 46 Sqdn RAF Abingdon 1969–71, OC Ops RAF Masirah Oman 1972, Army Staff Coll 1973, Personal Staff Offr to C-in-C Near East Air Force 1974–75, Wing Cdr 1975, OC 230 Sqdn RAF Odiham 1975–77, Personnel Offr MOD 1977–79, Gp Capt 1979, Dep Dir Air Plans MOD 1979–81, Station Cdr RAF Shawbury 1982–84, RCDS 1985, Air Cdre 1985, Dir of Air Support (later Dir of Air Staff Duties) 1986–88, Air Vice-Marshal 1988, Cdr Br Forces Falkland Islands 1988–89, Dir Gen RAF Personnel Services MOD 1989–92; md: Services Sound and Vision Corporation 1993–, Visua Ltd 1996–; chm: Columbia Communications Europe 1994–, Teleport International London 1994–, European Broadcasting Corporation 1995–; FIPD 1991, FIMgt 1993; *Recreations* building, fishing, walking; *Clubs* RAF; *Style*— Air Vice-Marshal David Crwys-Williams, CB; ✉ c/o Barclays Bank, PO Box 42, Abingdon, Oxon OX14 1GU

CRYAN, His Hon Judge; Donald Michael; s of Thomas Cryan, of Ireland, and Helen McBeath Munro (d 1974); *b* 18 Jan 1948; *Educ* Salvatorian Coll, UCL (LLB); *m* 1973, Pamela; 2 s; *Career* called to the Bar Inner Temple 1970 (bencher 1991), recorder 1993–96, circuit judge (SE Circuit) 1996–; memb Ctee: Barristers' Benevolent Assoc, Marshall Hall Tst, Legal Charities Garden Party; Freeman City of London 1978, Liveryman Worshipful Co of Fruiterers 1978; *Recreations* theatre and walking; *Clubs* RAC; *Style*— His Hon Judge Cryan; ✉ 4 Paper Buildings, Temple, London EC4

CRYSTAL, Alan Maurice; s of Leo Crystal, and Marion Crystal; *b* 2 Sept 1954; *Educ* Latymer Upper Sch London, King's Coll London, Westminster Med Sch London (MB BS); *m* 7 Sept 1980, Gillian Elizabeth, da of John Williams, MBE, of Canford Cliffs, Poole; 1 s (Edward James b 11 July 1991), 2 da (Charlotte Jayne b 16 May 1983, Stephanie Nicole b 18 March 1985); *Career* conslt gynaecologist and obstetrician Royal Berkshire Hosp Reading; FRCSEd 1983, FRCOG 1996; *Recreations* golf, tennis; *Style*— Alan Crystal, Esq; ✉ Eyot Wood, Bolney Road, Lower Shiplake, Henley-on-Thames RG9 3NS; 72 Berkeley Ave, Reading (☎ 0118 958 4711)

CRYSTAL, Prof David; OBE (1995); s of Samuel Cyril Crystal, of London, and Mary Agnes, *née* Morris; *b* 6 July 1941; *Educ* St Mary's Coll Liverpool, UCL (BA), Univ of London (PhD); *m* 1, 1 April 1964, Molly Irene (d 1976), da of Capt Robert Stack (d 1965); 2 s (Steven David b 1964, Timothy Joseph b 1969, d 1972), 2 da (Susan Mary b 1966, Lucy Alexandra b 1973); m 2, Hilary Frances, da of Capt Kenneth Norman (d 1990), of Cuffley, Herts; 1 s (Benjamin Peter b 1977); *Career* res asst Survey of English Usage UCL 1962–63, asst lectr linguistics Univ Coll of North Wales 1963–65; Univ of Reading: lectr 1965–69, reader 1969–75, prof of linguistics 1975–85; hon prof of linguistics Univ of North Wales (Bangor) 1985–; writer and ed of ref books 1985–; ed: Journal of Child Language 1974–85, The Language Library 1978–, Applied Language Studies 1980–84, Child Language Teaching and Therapy 1985–96, Linguistics Abstracts 1985–96; assoc ed Journal of Linguistics 1970–73, co-ed Studies in Language Disability 1974–, consulting ed English Today 1984–94, usage ed Great Illustrated Dictionary (Readers Digest, 1984); author of numerous pubns connected with the English language and linguistics; dir The Ucheldre Centre Holyhead 1990–; memb Bd Br Cncl 1996–; fell Coll of Speech Therapists 1983, FRSA 1983; *Books* incl: The Cambridge Encyclopedia of Language (1987, 2 edn 1997), The English Language (1988), The Cambridge Encyclopedia (ed, 1990, 3 edn 1997), The Cambridge Biographical Encyclopedia (ed, 1994), The Cambridge Encyclopedia of the English Language (1995); *Recreations* cinema, music, bibliophily; *Style*— Prof David Crystal, OBE; ✉ Akaroa, Gors Avenue, Holyhead, Anglesey LL65 1PB (☎ 01407 762764); PO Box 5, Holyhead, Anglesey LL65 1RG (fax 01407 769728)

CRYSTAL, Jonathan; s of Dr Samuel Cyril Crystal, OBE, of London, and Rachel Ethel, *née* Trewish; *b* 20 Dec 1949; *Educ* Leeds GS, QMC London (LLB); *m* Giselle Satya, *née* Veremie; 2 s (Petros, Jeremie), 1 da (Sophie); *Career* called to the Bar Middle Temple 1972; memb Hon Soc of Middle Temple; dir Tottenham Hotspur Football Club 1991–93; *Recreations* sports, travel; *Style*— J Crystal, Esq; ✉ Cloisters, 1 Pump Court, Temple, London EC4Y 7AA (☎ 0171 583 0303, fax 0171 583 2254)

CRYSTAL, Michael; QC (1984); s of Dr Samuel Cyril Crystal, OBE, of Leeds, and Rachel, *née* Trevish; *b* 5 March 1948; *Educ* Univs of London and Oxford (LLB, BCL); *m* 1972, Susan Felicia Sniderman; 1 s (Benjamin Joel b 1980), 1 da (Sara Jane b 1983); *Career* called to the Bar Middle Temple 1970, bencher 1993, dep judge of the High Ct 1995–; sr visiting fell Centre for Commercial Law Studies Queen Mary & Westfield Coll London 1987–, DTI inspr 1988–89 and 1992; govr Royal Shakespeare Co 1988–; author of various legal textbooks; hon fell Queen Mary & Westfield Coll 1996; *Recreations* theatre, music, travel, cricket; *Clubs* RAC, MCC; *Style*— Michael Crystal, Esq, QC; ✉ 3–4 South Square, Gray's Inn, London WC1R 5HP (☎ 0171 696 9900, fax 0171 696 9911)

CRYSTAL, Peter Maurice; s of Boris Leonard Crystal, of Leeds, and Pauline Mary, *née* Fox; *b* 7 Jan 1948; *Educ* Leeds GS, St Edmund Hall Oxford (MA), McGill Univ (LLM); *m* (m dis); 2 da (Emma, Anna); *Career* sr ptnr Memery Crystal slrs; Parly candidate: Leeds NE (SDP) 1983 and 1987, Fulham (Lib Dem) 1992; memb Law Soc; *Recreations* sports, travel; *Clubs* Reform, Athenaeum, Hurlingham; *Style—* Peter Crystal, Esq; ✉ Memery Crystal, 31 Southampton Row, London WC1B 5HT (☎ 0171 242 5905, fax 0171 242 2058, telex 298957)

CSÁKY, John; s of Alexander Csáky (d 1993), of Woolland House, Blandford Forum, Dorset, and Mary, *née* Baker (d 1982); *b* 31 Aug 1945; *Educ* Bedales Sch, Portsmouth Sch of Art, Royal Coll of Art (MA); *m* 1970 (m dis 1993), Iryna Pasznyk, da of Petro Pasznyk (d 1987), of Munich; 2 da (Taissa b July 1973, Roxi b March 1977); *Career* Wolff Olins Design Conslts 1970–71, Milton Keynes Development Corporation 1971–81, Special Projects Partnership 1980–85; Fitch plc: dir Leisure Div 1985–92, dir Seville office Spain (designing pavilions for Expo 92) 1990–92; John Csaky Associates 1992–; major design projects: Milton Keynes Bowl 1979, TT Tsui Chinese Gallery V&A Museum 1991, British Pavilion Expo 88 Brisbane 1988, Puerto Rico and Saudi Arabian Pavilions Expo 92 Seville 1992; FRGS, FCSD; *Recreations* travel, photography; *Style—* John Csáky; ✉ 24 Winchester Road, London NW3 3NT (☎/fax 0171 586 8770)

CÆSAR, Rev Canon Anthony Douglass; CVO (1991, LVO 1987); s of Rev Canon Harold Douglass Cæsar (d 1961), and Winifred Kathleen Cæsar; *b* 3 April 1924; *Educ* Cranleigh Sch, Magdalene Coll Cambridge (MA, MusB), St Stephen's House Oxford; *Career* Flying Offr RAF 1943–46; asst music master Eton 1948–51, precentor Radley 1952–59, asst curate St Mary Abbots Kensington 1961–65, asst sec ACCM 1965–70, chaplain Royal Sch of Church Music 1965–70, dep priest-in-ordinary to HM The Queen 1967–68 (priest-in-ordinary 1968–70), resident priest St Stephen's Church Bournemouth 1970–73, precentor and sacrist Winchester 1974–79 (residentiary canon 1976–79, hon canon 1979–91, canon emeritus 1991); sub dean of HM Chapels Royal, dep clerk of the Closet and sub-almoner, domestic chaplain to HM The Queen 1979–91 (extra chaplain 1991–), chaplain St Cross Hosp Winchester 1991–93; FRCO; *Style—* The Rev Canon Anthony Cæsar, CVO; ✉ Flat 2, Old Kiln, Yarbridge, Brading, Isle of Wight PO36 0BP (☎ 01983 406435)

CUBBON, Sir Brian Crossland; GCB (1984, KCB 1977, CB 1974); *b* 9 April 1928; *Educ* Bury GS, Trinity Coll Cambridge; *m* 1956, Elizabeth Lorin Richardson; 3 s, 1 da; *Career* Home Office 1951; perm under sec of state NI Office 1976–79, perm under sec of state Home Office 1979–88; *Clubs* United Oxford & Cambridge University, Beefsteak; *Style—* Sir Brian Cubbon, GCB; (☎ 01892 832534)

CUBEY, Dr (Robert) Bevis; s of Dr Donald Robert Cubey, of Whitley Bay, Northumberland, and Nita Margaret Howard, *née* Allen (d 1986); *b* 5 April 1938; *Educ* Rossall and St Catharine's Coll Cambridge (MA, MB BChir); *m* 22 Sept 1962, Ann Marples, da of Oscar Slack, of Burton-on-Trent; 1 s (Mark b 1966), 3 da (Fritha b 1965, Janet b 1973, Tanya b 1979); *Career* surgical specialist Masasi Dist Hosp Tanzania 1967–71; conslt ophthalmic surgn: Ipswich Suffolk 1976–84, W Cumbria 1984–92; ind ophthalmic surgn 1992– (designed and operates first UK mobile eye clinic Cumbria); scientific papers on surgical and ophthalmological topics; FRCSEd, FRCS, FRCSI, FRCOphth; *Recreations* after-dinner speaking, fell walking, singing, farming, gardening; *Style—* Dr Bevis Cubey; ✉ Hopebeck, Vale of Lorton, Cockermouth, Cumbria CA13 9UD (☎ 01900 85667); Cumbrian Independent Hospital, Branthwaite Rd, Workington, Cumbria CA14 4SS (☎ 01900 67111); Tarn Lodge Eye Hospital, Heads Nook, Carlisle CA4 9BT (☎ 01228 70114)

CUBITT, Sir Hugh Guy; kt (1983), CBE (1977), JP (Surrey 1964), DL (Gtr London 1978); s of Col Hon (Charles) Guy Cubitt, CBE, DSO, TD, DL (d 1979), 6 s of 2 Baron Ashcombe, and Rosamond Mary Edith, *née* Cholmeley (d 1984); *b* 2 July 1928; *Educ* RNC Dartmouth; *m* 26 June 1958, Linda Ishbel, da of Hon Angus Campbell, CBE, JP (d 1966), yr s of 1 Baron Colgrain; 1 s (Jonathan Guy b 1962), 2 da (Joanna Mary (Mrs Smyth-Osbourne) b 1960, Victoria Jane (Mrs Harding-Rolls) b 1964); *Career* Lt RN Korea 1949–50; memb Westminster City Cncl 1963–78 (alderman 1974, ldr 1972–77), Lord Mayor Westminster 1977–78; ptnr Cubitt and West 1962–79; dir: PSIT plc 1962–, National Westminster Bank plc 1977–90, Rea Brothers Gp plc 1995– (chm 1996–); chm: Housing Corp 1980–90, Lombard North Central 1980–91; cmmr English Heritage 1988–94; govr: Cranleigh Sch 1978–95 (chm 1980–95), West Heath Sch 1974–91 (chm 1978–91), Royal Acad of Music 1978–, Peabody Tst 1991–; chm: Anchor Tst 1991–, Housing Assoc Charitable Tst 1991–97; High Sheriff of Surrey 1983–84, chm S E Surrey Bench 1993–95 (Dorking Bench 1991–93); Freeman City of London 1975, Liveryman Worshipful Co of Needlemakers 1975–87; Hon FRAM 1985; FRICS 1970, FRSA; *Recreations* travel, photography, country sports; *Clubs* Boodle's; *Style—* Sir Hugh Cubitt, CBE, JP, DL; ✉ Chapel House, West Humble, Dorking, Surrey RH5 6AY (☎ 01306 882994)

CUCCIO, John; *b* 31 May 1947; *Educ* Liverpool Coll, Univ of Liverpool, Univ of South Florida; *Career* dental surgn Wimpole St 1977– (specialist in advanced restorative and cosmetic dentistry incl implants and guided tissue regeneration); cmmnd RADC(V) TA 1984; memb: BDA, Br Soc of Peridontology, Br Dental Implant Soc; *Recreations* hill walking, shooting, deer stalking; *Clubs* Naval and Military; *Style—* John Cuccio, Esq; ✉ 59 Wimpole Street, London W1M 7DE (☎ 0171 486 4433)

CUCKNEY, Baron (Life Peer UK 1995), of Millbank in the City of Westminster; Sir John Graham Cuckney; s of Air Vice-Marshal Ernest John Cuckney, CB, CBE, DSC (d 1965), and Lilian, *née* Williams; *b* 12 July 1925; *Educ* Shrewsbury, Univ of St Andrews; *m* 1960, Muriel, da of late Walter Scott Boyd; *Career* chm The Orion Publishing Group Ltd 1994–97; former chm: Royal Insurance Holdings plc, 3i Group plc, Westland Group plc, The Thomas Cook Group, John Brown PLC, Brooke Bond Group plc, International Military Services Ltd, Port of London Authority, Bd Mersey Docks and Harbour, Standard Industrial Trust; former dep chm TI Group plc, former vice chm Glaxo Wellcome plc; former dir: Brixton Estate plc, Lazard Bros & Co Ltd; *Style—* The Rt Hon Lord Cuckney; ✉ House of Lords, London SW1A 0PW

CUDDEFORD, Norman Allan; s of Charles Leonard Allan Cuddeford (d 1986), of Leigh-on-Sea, and Gwendoline May, *née* Hockley (d 1985); *b* 8 Jan 1933; *Educ* Felsted; *m* 1, 1963 (m dis 1975), Penelope Alexandra Cuddeford; 1 s (Alastair b 1964); m 2, 12 April 1975, Maria, da of Dr Erasmo Hoyo Hernandez, of Mexico City; 1 da (Vanessa b 1980), 1 step da (Ana Gabriela b 1971); *Career* Nat Serv RAF 1952–54, cmmnd 1953, later CO RAF Sennen (at that time the youngest CO in RAF); associated with Lloyd's of London since 1955; freelance sports commentator (covering athletics, cricket, tennis) BBC Radio 1965–; dir S B J Devitt Ltd 1988–; conslt: Meacock, Samuelson & Devitt Ltd (Lloyd's brokers), SBJ Stephenson Ltd, Steel Burrill Jones Ltd; memb Rottingdean Preservation Soc; Freeman City of London 1956, Liveryman Worshipful Co of Glass Sellers; *Recreations* travel, good company and convivial conversation, cricket; *Clubs* RAF, MCC, Lloyd's Motor, Rugby Club of London; *Style—* Norman Cuddeford, Esq; ✉ Point Clear, Lustrells Rd, Rottingdean, E Sussex (☎ 01273 304 943); 6 Kinburn St, London SE16; Steel Burrill Jones Ltd, 100 Whitechapel Rd, London E1 (☎ 0171 816 2000)

CUDLIPP, Baron (Life Peer UK 1974), of Aldingbourne, Co W Sussex; Hugh Kinsman Cudlipp; kt (1973), OBE (1945); s of William Cudlipp, of Cardiff; *b* 28 Aug 1913; *Educ* Howard Gdns Sch Cardiff; *m* 1; m 2, 1945, Eileen Ascroft (d 1962); m 3, 1963, Jodi, da of late John L Hyland, of Palm Beach, Florida, USA; *Career* Lab Whip House of Lords until Nov 1981 when resigned to join SDP (now Liberal Democrats); journalist, ed and publisher; Mirror Group newspapers 1935–40 and 1946–49; managing ed Sunday Express 1950–52, ed-in-chief Mirror Group newspapers 1952–63; chm: Daily Mirror Newspapers Ltd 1963–68, International Publishing Corporation 1968–73; former dir Associated TV Ltd; *Books* Publish and Be Damned! (1955), At Your Peril (1962), Walking on the Water (1976), The Prerogative of the Harlot (1980); *Recreations* music; *Clubs* Garrick; *Style—* The Rt Hon the Lord Cudlipp, OBE; ✉ House of Lords, London SW1A 0PW

CUDMORE, Harold; s of Harold Cudmore, and Sheila, *née* Coleman (d 1948); *b* 21 April 1944; *m* 20 Oct 1993, Lauren Eleanor Dagge; 1 da (Freya b 2 Sept 1994); *Career* sailor; skipper White Crusader Br Americas Cup challenger 1986–87, mangr successful Br Admiral's Cup team 1989, winner numerous regattas and world championships, advsr and coach America 3 (winning America's Cup) 1992, advsr and coach France America 95 (French challenger for America's Cup 1995); *Clubs* Royal Cork Yacht, Royal Thames Yacht, Royal Ocean Racing, Fort Worth Boat; *Style—* Harold Cudmore, Esq; ✉ 4 Queens Road, Cowes, Isle of Wight PO31 8BQ (☎ 01983 291376, fax 01983 291771)

CUENE-GRANDIDIER, Richard John Davis; s of Jean Alphonse Cuene-Grandidier, of Les Alluets-le-Roi, 78580 Maule, France, and Paula Susan, *née* Davis, of Ancenis-les-Bois, Riaille, France; *b* 13 Sept 1955; *Educ* Holmewood House, Downside; *m* 1, 13 June 1982 (m dis); 1 da (Sophie b 1985); m 2, 1 July 1989 (m dis); *Career* various appts Nat West Bank plc 1976–86; Société Générale: dep sr relationship mangr London 1987–89, sr relationship mangr London 1989–94, vice pres and sr relationship dir NY 1994–96, vice pres and foreign corp gp mangr NY 1996–; *Recreations* motor sport, flying, riding, shooting; *Clubs* Br Racing and Sport Car; *Style—* Richard Cuene-Grandidier, Esq; ✉ Apt 12A, 350 East 72 Street, New York, NY 100021, USA; Société Générale, 1221 Avenue of the Americas, New York, NY 10020, USA (☎ 00 1 212 278 6927, fax 00 1 212 278 7462)

CUFFLIN, Michael John; OBE (1984); s of Harry Bradshaw Cufflin (d 1963), of 70 Shanklin Drive, Leicester, and Annie Elizabeth, *née* Palmer (d 1985); *b* 21 Aug 1932; *Educ* Wyggeston Boys' GS Leicester, Worcester Coll Oxford (MA); *m* 23 April 1960, Susan Jenifer, da of William Pollard (d 1949), of Four Oaks, Sutton Coldfield; 2 s (Oliver b 3 March 1962, Edward b 1 Dec 1967), 2 da (Joanna b 27 Jan 1961, Lucy b 26 June 1963); *Career* stockbroker; P N Kemp-Gee and Co 1954–59, chm Wilshere Baldwin and Co 1986–94 (joined 1959), dir Albert E Sharp; chm: Br Aust Soc (Leics Branch), Leicester Cons Fedn; tstee Leicester GS Tst, hon treas Leics Co Nursing Assoc, vice chm Leicester Twinning Assoc, pres Leicester Cons Euro Cncl, memb Leicester CC 1967–89, Lord Mayor of Leicester 1984–85; *Recreations* gardening; *Clubs* The Leicestershire (pres 1991–96), Leicester Rotary; *Style—* Michael Cufflin, Esq, OBE; ✉ 7 Burlington Road, Leicester LE2 3DD (☎ 0116 270 3063); Albert E Sharp, 19 The Crescent, King St, Leicester LE1 6RX (☎ 0116 254 1344, fax 0116 255 0969)

CULE, Dr John Hedley; s of Walter Edwards Cule (d 1942), of Glamorgan, and Annie, *née* Russ (d 1940); *b* 7 Feb 1920; *Educ* Porth Co Sch, Kingswood Sch Bath, Trinity Hall Cambridge (MA, MD), King's Coll Hosp (MRCS, LRCP, FRCGP); *m* 23 March 1944, Joyce Leslie, da of Henry Phillips Bonser (d 1962); 2 s (Simon b 1949, Peter b 1951), 1 da (Myfanwy b 1955); *Career* WWII Capt RAMC served Italy (despatches) 1943–46; surgical registrar Addenbrooke's Hosp 1947, med registrar KCH 1948, princ NHS partnership Camberley 1948–71, psychiatrist St David's Hosp Carmarthen and Psychiatric Unit W Wales Gen Hosp 1972–86; lectr in history of med Univ of Wales Coll of Med 1972–; pres: Osler Club London 1972, History of Med Soc of Wales 1978–80, Br Soc for History of Med 1985–87 (vice pres 1984, treas 1972–82), Int Soc for History of Med 1992–96 (vice pres 1989–92); memb Cncl Harveian Soc 1964; chm Sanders Watney Tst (Driving for the Disabled) 1994– (vice-chm 1986–94); High Sheriff Co of Dyfed 1985–86; chm Welsh Branch Br Driving Soc 1986–94; emeritus fell American Osler Soc, Hon FRSM 1996; Freeman City of London 1964, Liveryman Worshipful Soc of Apothecaries 1962; FSA 1996; *Books* Wreath on the Crown (1967), A Doctor for the People (1980), Child Care through the Centuries (jt ed, 1986), The Great Maritime Discoveries and World Health (jt ed, 1991), Russia and Wales. Essays on the History of State Involvement in Health Care (jt ed, 1994); *Recreations* horse carriage driving trials, fly fishing; *Clubs* Royal Society of Medicine; *Style—* Dr John H Cule; ✉ Abereinon, Capel Dewi, Llandysul, Ceredigion SA44 4PP (☎ 01559 362229, fax 01559 362238)

CULHANE, Prof (John) Leonard; s of late John Thomas Culhane, and late Mary Agnes, *née* Durkin; *b* 14 Oct 1937; *Educ* Clongowes Wood Coll, Univ Coll Dublin (BSc, MSc), Univ Coll London (PhD); *m* 7 Sept 1961, Mary Brigid, da of late James Smith; 2 s (Simon b 22 Sept 1963, Laurence b 18 Feb 1966); *Career* Dept of Physics UCL: res asst 1963, lectr 1967, reader 1976, prof 1981–94, dir Mullard Space Sci Laboratory 1983–; head and prof Dept of Space and Climate Physics UCL 1994–; sr scientist Lockheed Palo Alto Laboratory 1969–70; author of more than 200 scientific papers on solar and cosmic X-ray astronomy, X-ray instrumentation and spectroscopy; memb: Cncl Univ of Surrey 1985–88, Astronomy Plan Sci Bd SERC 1989–93, Particle Physics and Astronomy Res Cncl 1996–; chm: Space Sci Prog Bd 1989–94, British Nat Ctee Space Res 1989–93, COSPAR Cmmn E 1994–; UK delegate and vice chm ESA SPC 1990–95; chm Space Innovations Ltd 1996–; memb: IAU, American Astronomical Soc, RAS; foreign memb Norwegian Acad of Sci and Letters 1996; FRS 1985; *Books* X-Ray Astronomy (with P Sanford, 1981); *Recreations* music, racing cars; *Style—* Prof J Leonard Culhane, FRS; ✉ 24 Warnham Road, Horsham, West Sussex RH12 2QU (☎ 01403 263475); Mullard Space Science Laboratory, University College London, Holmbury St Mary, Dorking, Surrey RH5 6NT (☎ 01483 274111, fax 01483 278312, telex 859185 UCMSSL G)

CULLEARN, David Beverley; s of Jack Cullearn (d 1944), of Bradford, and Gladys Irene, *née* Earnshaw; *b* 22 April 1941; *Educ* Grange GS Bradford, Leeds Sch of Archictecture (DipArch); *Career* architect and painter in watercolours; ptnr Edmund Kirby Liverpool, Manchester and London; awards: Structural Steel Design Award 1987, Malcolm Dean Design Award 1987, Office of the Year award (Volvo HQ) 1987–88, various Civic Tst Awards; exhibitions: Phillips Gallery, Manchester Art Gallery, Royal Acad; former chm Soc of Architect Artists; RIBA; *Recreations* mountain walking, horse racing, architecture, painting; *Style—* David Cullearn, Esq; ✉ High Royd, Northgate, Honley, Huddersfield HD7 2QL (☎ 01484 663 633); 8 King St, Manchester M2 6AQ (☎ 0161 832 3667, fax 0161 832 3795)

CULLEN, Prof Alexander Lamb; OBE (1960); s of Richard Henry Cullen, of Lincoln, and Jessie, *née* Lamb; *b* 30 April 1920; *Educ* Lincoln Sch, Imperial Coll London (BSc, PhD, DSc); *m* 24 Aug 1940, Margaret, da of Andrew Lamb, OBE, of Southgate, N London; 2 s (Michael b 1941, David b 1942), 1 da (Isobel b 1946); *Career* scientist Royal Aircraft Estab 1940–46; lectr and reader Univ Coll London 1946–55, prof and head Dept of Electrical Engrg Univ of Sheffield 1955–67, Pender prof of electrical engrg and head of dept 1967–80, sr fell SERC at UCL 1980–83, currently hon res fell UCL (hon fell 1994); hon prof NW Poly Univ Xian China; IEEE Microwave Career Award 1989; Hon DSc Chinese Univ of Hong Kong 1983, Hon DEng Sheffield Univ 1985, Hon DSc Univ of Kent at Canterbury 1986; FCGI 1964, FIEEE 1967, FEng 1977, FRS 1977, Hon FIERE 1987, Hon FIEE 1989; *Books* Microwave Measurement (with H M Barlow, 1950); *Recreations* music; *Style—* Prof Alexander Cullen, OBE, FRS, FEng; ✉ Department of Electronic and Electrical Engineering, University College London, Torrington Place, London WC1E 7JE (☎ 0171 387 7050, fax 0171 387 4350)

CULLEN, Prof Christopher Noel (Chris); s of Patricia, *née* Cody; *b* 25 Dec 1949; *Educ* N Manchester GS, Univ Coll of N Wales Bangor (BA, PhD); *Career* dir of clinical psychology servs to people with mental handicaps Salford HA 1983–86, SSMH chair of learning difficulties Univ of St Andrews 1986–95, prof Keele Univ 1995–; former chm Professional Affrs Bd Br Psychological Soc; fell Br Psychological Soc 1983; *Books* Human Operant Conditioning and Behaviour Modification (ed with G Davey, 1988); *Recreations* climbing, fell running; *Clubs* Mynydd Climbing; *Style*— Prof Chris Cullen; ✉ Psychology Department, Keele University, Staffordshire ST5 5BG

CULLEN, Donna-Maria; da of Richard Cullen, of Brentwood, Essex, and Joyce Margaret, *née* Hagger; *b* 18 April 1963; *Educ* Collegiate Jr and High Sch Port Elizabeth SA, Univ of Cape Town (MA); *m* 25 April 1992, Gary Assim; 2 s (b 1993 and 1996); *Career* PR executive; account exec Gwynne Hart Associates (latterly The Grayling Group of Companies) 1985–87, account mangr Kingsway Public Relations (latterly The Rowland Company) 1987–88; Lowe Bell Good Relations: account dir 1988–89, assoc dir 1989–90, bd dir 1990–, dep md 1994–96; asst to Sir Tim Bell Lowe Bell Consultants 1996–; FRSA; *Recreations* restaurants, reading, animal welfare; *Style*— Ms Donna-Maria Cullen; ✉ Lowe Bell Consultants, 7 Hertford Street, London W1 (☎ 0171 495 4044)

CULLEN, Rt Hon Lord; (William) Douglas Cullen; PC (1997); s of Sheriff Kenneth Douglas Cullen (d 1956), and Gladys Margaret, *née* Douglas-Wilson (d 1992); *b* 18 Nov 1935; *Educ* Dundee HS, Univ of St Andrews (MA), Univ of Edinburgh (LLB); *m* 1961, Rosamond Mary, da of William Henry Nassau Downer, OBE, of NI; 2 s, (Christopher, Adrian), 2 da (Sophia, Felicity); *Career* advocate 1960, standing jr counsel to HM Customs and Excise 1970–73, QC 1973, Advocate-Depute 1978–81, a senator Coll of Justice in Scotland (Lord of Session) 1986–97, Lord Justice Clerk of Scotland Jan 1997–; chm: Med Appeal Tbnl 1977–86, Ct of Inquiry into Piper Alpha Disaster 1988–90, Review of Business of the Outer House of the Ct of Session 1995, Tbnl of Inquiry into the shooting at Dunblane Primary Sch 1996; memb Royal Cmmn on Ancient and Historical Monuments of Scot 1987–; chm: Cncl The Cockburn Assoc (Edinburgh Civic Tst) 1984–86, Govrs St Margaret's Sch Edinburgh 1994–; Hon LLD Aberdeen Univ 1992, Hon DUniv Heriot-Watt Univ 1995; Hon FEng 1995, FRSE 1993; *Recreations* gardening, natural history; *Clubs* New (Edinburgh); *Style*— The Rt Hon Lord Cullen, FRSE; ✉ Court of Session, Parliament House, Edinburgh EH1 1RQ (☎ 0131 225 2595)

CULLEN, Sir (Edward) John; kt (1991); s of William Henry Pearson Cullen, and Ellen Emma Cullen; *b* 19 Oct 1926; *Educ* Univ of Cambridge (MA, MEng, PhD), Univ of Texas (MS); *m* 1954, Betty Davall Hopkins; 2 s, 2 da; *Career* dep chm Rohm and Haas (UK) Ltd until 1983; chm Health and Safety Cmmn 1983–93; pres: Inst of Chemical Engrs 1988–89, Fédération Européenne d'Associations Nationales d'Ingenieurs (FEANI) 1996–; memb: Cncl (now Senate) Engrg Cncl 1990–, Cncl Royal Acad of Engrg until 1994, HRH Duke of Edinburgh's Cwlth Study Conf Cncl 1990; chm: Br Nat Ctee for Int Engrg Affrs 1991–, Robens Inst Advsy Ctee 1993–; Hon DSc Univ of Exeter 1993; FEng 1987, FRSA 1988; *Recreations* gardening, swimming, reading, walking; *Clubs* IOD; *Style*— Sir John Cullen, FEng; ✉ 14 Gloucester Walk, Kensington, London W8 4HZ

CULLEN, Dr Michael Henry; s of Charles Gavin Cullen, and Olive, *née* Walker; *b* 29 March 1947; *Educ* Queen Elizabeth's Sch Barnet, Univ of Bristol (BSc, MB ChB, MD); *m* 1, 2 July 1972 (m dis 1988), Rosemary Elizabeth; 3 s (Matthew Jacob b 13 March 1974, Alexander James b 11 Dec 1976, Thomas Oliver b 7 May 1980); *m* 2, 20 Aug 1989, Alison Helen, da of David Machin; 1 da (Flora Ruth b 28 March 1991); *Career* conslt med oncologist Queen Elizabeth Hosp and sr clinical lectr in oncology Univ of Birmingham 1982–; clinical dir Oncology and Haematology Servs Univ Hosp Birmingham NHS Trust 1990–; author of pubns on: lung cancer, testicular cancer, lymphoma; memb: Int Assoc for the Study of Lung Cancer, Euro Assoc of Med Oncologists, Br Assoc for Cancer Res, MRC Working Pty on Testicular Tumours; memb Assoc of Cancer Physicians; FRCP 1988; *Recreations* tennis, skiing, wine tasting, classical guitar playing, fine art collecting; *Style*— Dr Michael Cullen; ✉ Priory Hospital, Edgbaston, Birmingham B5 7UG (☎ 0121 440 2323); Queen Elizabeth Hospital, Edgbaston, Birmingham B15 2TH (☎ 0121 627 2444, fax 0121 414 2496)

CULLEN, (Charles) Nigel; OBE (1987), TD (1976, and 2 Bars 1982 and 1990), DL (Notts 1991); s of Peter Carver Cullen (d 1990), of Mapperley Park, Nottingham, and Dorothy, *née* Woodward (d 1992); *b* 26 Sept 1944; *Educ* Trent Coll; *m* 15 April 1981, Brenda Suzanne, da of Flt Offr Franklin Paul Bowen, US Army, of Oklahoma, USA; 1 s (Stephen James b 1971), 1 da (Emily Josephine b 1979); *Career* TA: cmmnd 1964, platoon cdr 5/8 Bn Sherwood Foresters 1964–67, platoon cdr Mercian Vol 1967–72, co cdr 3 WFR 1972–78, GSO 2 V Notts 1978–81, 2 i/c 3 WFR 1981–83, SO 2 G3 V 54 Inf Bde 1984, CO 3 WFR 1984–87, SO 1 G3 V E Dist 1987–88, dep cdr 54 Inf Bde 1988–91; TA ColSPT DARC 1991–92; admitted slr 1970, ptnr Freeth Cartwright Hunt Dickins; NP; pres: Notts C of C and Indust 1991–92, Notts City Business Club 1989–90; chm Assoc of E Midlands C of C and Industry 1994–96; Dep Under Sheriff of Derbyshire; ADC (TA) 1991–93; memb: Notts Law Soc, The Notaries' Soc; memb Law Soc; *Recreations* bridge, theatre, photography; *Style*— Nigel Cullen, Esq, OBE, TD, DL; ✉ 10 Sefton Drive, Mapperley Park, Nottingham NG3 5ER (☎ 0115 960 6906); Freeth Cartwright Hunt Dickins, 20 Low Pavement, Nottingham NG1 7DL (☎ 0115 936 9369, fax 0115 962 3441)

CULLEN, Terence Lindsay Graham; QC (1978); s of Eric Graham Cullen (d 1962), of East Malling, Kent, and Jean Morrison Hunter, *née* Bennett (d 1987); *b* 29 Oct 1930; *Educ* RNC Dartmouth; *m* 23 Aug 1958, Muriel Elisabeth, da of Horace Rolfe; 3 s (Oliver James Graham b 1959, Henry Lindsay Alexander b 1963, Edmund William Hector b 1966); *Career* RN 1948–55; Prestige Group Ltd 1955–61; called to the Bar Lincoln's Inn 1961, bencher 1986; called to the Bar: Singapore 1978, Malaysia 1980, Hong Kong 1986, Bermuda 1991; *Recreations* opera, racing; *Style*— Terence Cullen, Esq, QC; ✉ 54 Canonbury Park North, London N1 2JT (☎ 0171 226 8263); 13 Old Square, Lincoln's Inn, London WC2A 3UA (☎ 0171 404 4800, fax 0171 405 4267)

CULLEN, Timothy William Brian (Tim); s of (James) Brian Cullen, CBE (d 1972), and (Sybil) Kathleen, *née* Jones (d 1991); *b* 23 March 1944; *Educ* King William's Coll Isle of Man, Trinity Coll Dublin (MA); *m* 19 July 1980, Nora Denise, da of Vytautas Meskauskas, of Pompano Beach, Florida; 1 s (Brian b 1986), 1 da (Jura b 1982); *Career* English teacher St Edward's Sch Florida 1967–69, press spokesman Ford Motor Co Ltd Warley England 1969–73, int press spokesman Ford Motor Co Dearborn Michigan 1973–75, int public affairs admin Continental Bank Chicago 1975–78, various external affairs posts World Bank Washington DC 1978–84, chief of external affairs Euro Office World Bank Paris 1984–90, chief of Media Rels Div and chief spokesman World Bank Washington DC 1990–96, sr advsr external affrs World Bank 1996–; pres Bd of Dirs Int Sch of Paris 1988–89, chm Int Multimedia Consortium for Environment and Devpt (IMCED) 1993–, memb Cncl Television Tst for the Environement (TVE) 1993–; *Books* Yugoslavia and The World Bank (1979); *Recreations* cooking, photography, fishing; *Clubs* East India; *Style*— Tim Cullen, Esq; ✉ 7012 River Rd, Bethesda MD 20817, USA (☎ 00 1 301 320 0024); World Bank, 1818 H Street, NW Washington DC 20433, USA (☎ 00 1 202 473 1782, fax 00 1 202 522 2421, telex WUI 64145 WORLDBANK, internet TCULLEN@Worldbank.org)

CULLEN OF ASHBOURNE, 2 Baron (UK 1920); Charles Borlase Marsham Cokayne; MBE (1945); s of 1 Baron Cullen of Ashbourne, KBE (d 1932, whose f was the celebrated G(eorge) E(dward) C(okayne), Clarenceux King of Arms and ed of The Complete Peerage); *b* 6 Oct 1912; *Educ* Eton; *m* 1, 2 July 1942 (m dis 1947), Valerie Catherine Mary, da of late William Henry Collbran; 1 da (Hon Julia Collbran (Hon Mrs Wigart) b 1943); *m* 2, 21 June 1948, Patricia Mary (d 1996), er da of Col S Clulow-Gray; *Heir* bro, Hon Edmund Cokayne; *Career* Maj RCS (TA), served WWII; one of HM Lts City of London 1976, a lord in waiting to HM (govt whip) 1979–82, dep speaker House of Lords 1982–91; amateur tennis champion 1947 and 1952; *Clubs* MCC, Swinley Forest Golf; *Style*— The Rt Hon the Lord Cullen of Ashbourne, MBE; ✉ 75 Cadogan Gardens, London SW3 2RB (☎ 0171 589 1981)

CULLEY, Kenneth (Ken); s of James Culley (d 1970), of Cheshire, and Lily Valentine, *née* Dale (d 1970); *b* 3 June 1942; *Educ* Kings Sch Macclesfield; *m* 1, 1964 (m dis 1984), Barbara May, da of Frank Hooley; 2 da (Alison Jane b 1966, Johanne Helen b 1968), 1 s (Nicholas James b 1971); *m* 2, 1985, Eleanor Pamela Broomhead, da of Dr David Alexander Whyte Fairweather; *Career* accountant Bradford & Bingley Building Society 1965–69, gen mangr Cheshire Building Society 1969–83, chief exec and dir Portman Building Society 1983–; dir The Building Societies Trust Ltd 1995–; memb Cncl: Building Socs Assoc 1986– (dep chm 1994–95, chm 1995–96), Int Union of Housing Fin Instns 1995–; memb Cncl of Mortgage Lenders 1994–; FCIB; *Recreations* fishing, riding, country pursuits; *Style*— Ken Culley, Esq; ✉ Coombesbury Cottage, Boxford, Newbury, Berks RG16 8DE (☎ 01488 608509, fax 01488 608806); Portman Building Society, Portman House, Richmond Hill, Bournemouth, Dorset BH2 6EP (☎ 01202 292444, fax 01202 558568)

CULLIMORE, Colin Stuart; CBE (1978); s of Reginald Victor Cullimore (d 1960), and May Maria, *née* Jay; *b* 13 July 1931; *Educ* Westminster, Univ of Grenoble, Nat Coll of Food Technol; *m* 1952, Kathleen Anyta, da of Edgar Lamming (d 1951); 1 s (Jeremy Stuart b 1953); *Career* cmmnd Royal Scots Fus, seconded Parachute Regt 1951, serv Cyprus, Egypt, Maj 1956, 10 Bn Parachute Regt (TA) 1960; gen mangr: Payne & Son Ltd 1960–65, J H Dewhurst Ltd 1969; md J H Dewhurst Ltd 1976–90, dir Albion Insurance Co Ltd 1973–92, dir of external affrs Vestey Group Cos 1990–92; chm: Retail Consortium Food Ctee 1973–74, Multiple Shops Fedn 1977–79, NAAFI 1993–96 (dir 1984–96); dep chm: Meat Promotion Exec 1975–78, Inst of Meat 1982–83; pres Br Retailers Assoc 1984–89 (vice pres 1979–84 and 1990–); vice chm: Retail Consortium 1985–88, Coll Distributive Trades 1976–79; vice pres Confedn of Euro Retailers 1982–88; memb: Lincoln Diocesan Bd of Fin 1993– (chm Resources Ctee 1994–95), Regtl Cncl Parachute Regt 1991–, Ctee for Commerce and Distribution of EEC 1984–91; memb Cncl Industry and Parliament Tst 1987–94; tstee: Airborne Assault Normandy Tst, Western United Group Pension Scheme 1987–; chm Reserve Forces Ulysses Tst 1992–96, dir Longhurst Housing Association Ltd 1996–; govr London Inst 1988–90; Freeman of City of London 1972, Liveryman and memb Ct Worshipful Co of Butchers; Gold medal of Inst of Meat 1956, Butchers' Co Gold medal 1956; CIMgt 1984, FInstD 1973, MRSH 1956, MInstM 1956, FRSA 1988; *Clubs* Naval and Military, IOD, Farmers'; *Style*— Colin Cullimore, Esq, CBE; ✉ Wyberton Park, Wyberton, Boston, Lincs PE21 7AF (☎ 01205 311423, fax 01205 354864)

CULLINAN, Edward Horder; CBE; s of Dr Edward Revill Cullinan, CBE (d 1965), and Dorothea Joy, *née* Horder; *b* 17 July 1931; *Educ* Ampleforth, Univ of Cambridge (BA), Architectural Assoc (AADipl), Univ of California at Berkeley; *m* Rosalind, *née* Yeates; 1 s (Thomas Edward b 1965), 2 da (Emma Louise b 1962, Kate b 1963); *Career* Nat Serv Lt RE 1949–51; architect in practice London 1959, fndr Edward Cullinan Architects 1968–; Bannister Fletcher prof Univ of London 1978–79; visiting critic 1973–85: Toronto, Cincinatti, MIT; Graham Willis prof Univ of Sheffield 1985–87, George Simpson prof Univ of Edinburgh 1987–89; sponsor Architects and Engrs for Social Responsibility; FRSA 1981, RA 1991 (ARA 1989), Hon FRIAS 1995; *Books* Edward Cullinan Architects (1984 and 1995); *Recreations* building, horticulture, silviculture, skiing, surfing; *Style*— Edward Cullinan, Esq, CBE, RA; ✉ Gib Tor, Quarnford, Buxton, Derbyshire SK17 0TA; Edward Cullinan Architects Ltd, The Wharf, Baldwin Terrace, London N1 (☎ 0171 704 1975, fax 0171 354 2739)

CULLINGHAM, Anthony Charles; s of Wallace Charles Cullingham, of Filbert House, Leicester, and Sheila Ann, *née* Foster; *b* 9 July 1957; *Educ* Guthlaxton GS Leics, Bristol Poly, Watford Coll, City Literary Inst; *m* Emma Claire, *née* Hancock; *Career* advtg copywriter: Saatchi & Saatchi 1979–82, Garland Compton 1982; sr writer Geers Gross 1982–85, sr writer/assoc dir Lintas Worldwide 1985–89, course dir Watford Copywriting/Art Direction Course 1989–; *Recreations* sport; *Clubs* KCS (Wimbledon), Leicester City FC; *Style*— Anthony Cullingham, Esq; ✉ West Herts College, Watford Campus, Hempstead Road, Watford WD1 3EZ (☎ 01923 257578)

CULLIS, Prof Charles Fowler; s of Prof Charles Gilbert Cullis (d 1941), of Wimbledon, London, and Winifred Jefford, *née* Fowler (d 1976); *b* 31 Aug 1922; *Educ* Stowe, Trinity Coll Oxford (BA, BSc, DPhil, MA, DSc); *m* 3 Sept 1958, (Marjorie) Elizabeth, da of Sir Austin Innes Anderson (d 1973), of Clandon, Surrey; 2 s (Jonathan b 1961, Philip b 1967), 2 da (Jane b 1963, Eleanor b 1965); *Career* ICI res fell Univ of Oxford 1947–50, lectr in physical chemistry Imperial Coll London 1950–59 (sr lectr in chemical engrg 1959–64), reader in combustion chemistry Univ of London 1964–66; City Univ: prof of physical chemistry, head Chemistry Dept 1973–84, pro-vice-chllr 1980–84, Saddlers res prof 1984–87, Leverhulme emeritus res fell 1987–89, currently emeritus prof; visiting prof Univ of California Berkeley 1966, visiting scientist CSIRO Sydney 1970, academic visitor NSW Institute of Technology Ltd 1974; cncllr Mid Sussex 1986–95; dir City Technology Ltd 1977–91 (Queen's Award for Technol 1982 and 1985, and for Export 1988); chm Safety in Mines Res Advsy Bd 1980–88; govr: City of London Poly 1982–84, Haywards Heath Coll 1986–96, Oathall Community Coll 1986–96; memb Cncl Univ of Sussex 1993–95; tstee Sino-British Fellowship Tst 1992–; Liveryman Worshipful Co of Bakers 1983–; FRSC 1958, FRSA 1983; *Books* The Combustion of Organic Polymers (1981), The Detection and Measurement of Hazardous Gases (1981), author of numerous original scientific papers; *Recreations* music, theatre, travel, golf; *Clubs* Athenaeum; *Style*— Prof Charles Cullis; ✉ Quinces, Courtmead Rd, Cuckfield, W Sussex RH17 5LP (☎ 01444 453513)

CULLIS, Michael Fowler; CVO (1955); s of Emeritus Prof Charles Gilbert Cullis (d 1941), of London, and Winifred Jefford Fowler (d 1976); *b* 22 Oct 1914; *Educ* Wellington, Brasenose Coll Oxford (scholar, MA); *m* 1968, Catherine Cameron, da of Alexander Cook Robertson (d 1988), of Arbroath, Scotland; *Career* mil intelligence Gibraltar 1939–40, min of Econ Warfare London, Spain and Portugal 1940–44, dip serv 1945–58, FO responsible for Austria 1945–50, first sec Oslo 1951–55, regnl information cnsllr for the Nordic countries Copenhagen 1955–58, advsr to Govr of Malta 1959–60; sr res fell Atlantic Inst Paris 1962–65; visiting prof Aachen and Bologna Univs; FCO dir of Arms Control and Disarmament 1967–74, conslt Non-Governmental Bodies 1975–79; candidate Euro Parly elections 1979; UK dir European Cultural Fndn Amsterdam 1983–92; fund-raiser Univ of Buckingham 1980–82; writer, lecturer and broadcaster, contrib to several books on int affairs; *Clubs* Athenaeum; *Style*— Mr Michael Cullis, CVO; ✉ Peel House, Buntingford, Herts SG9 9AE (☎ 01763 272209)

CULME-SEYMOUR, Cdr Sir Michael; 5 Bt (UK 1809), of Highmount, Co Limerick, and Friery Park, Devonshire; s of Vice Adm Sir Michael Culme-Seymour, 4 Bt, KCB, MVO (d 1925), and Florence Agnes Louisa, *née* Nugent (d 1956); *b* 26 April 1909; *m* 18 March 1948, Lady (Mary) Faith (d 1983), da of 9 Earl of Sandwich, and formerly wife of late Philip Booth Nesbitt; 2 s (decd), 1 step da (adopted) ((Caroline) Gemma (Mrs Nesbitt) b 1939); *Heir* cousin, Michael Patrick Culme-Seymour b 28 April 1962; *Career* joined RN 1926, ADC to Govr Gen of Canada 1933–35, served WWII in Atlantic, N

Africa and Far East (despatches), served IDC 1946–47, ret 1947; succeeded Rev Wentworth Watson to the Rockingham Castle Estates 1925, passed them to nephew Cdr L M M Saunders Watson 1969; farmer and landowner; memb Northants CC 1948–55, JP Northants 1949, DL Northants 1958–71, High Sheriff Northants 1966; Bledisloe Gold medal for Landowners 1972; memb Contemporary Art Soc, Historic Houses Assoc, Country Landowners' Assoc; *Clubs* Brooks's; *Style*— Cdr Sir Michael Culme-Seymour, Bt, RN; ✉ Wytherston, Powerstock, Bridport, Dorset DT6 3TQ

CULSHAW, Robert Nicholas; MVO (1979); s of late Ivan Culshaw, and Edith Marjorie Jose, *née* Barnard; *b* 22 Dec 1952; *Educ* Univ Coll Sch Hampstead, King's Coll Cambridge (MA); *m* 19 March 1977, Elaine Ritchie, da of Alan Clegg; 1 s (Robin Alexander b 20 June 1992); *Career* HM Diplomatic Serv: FCO 1974–75, MECAS 1975–76, Muscat 1977–79, Khartoum 1979–80, Rome 1980–84, FCO London 1984–88, dep head of mission and consul-gen Athens 1989–93, head News Dept and FCO spokesman 1993–95, min-cnsllr Washington 1995–; FRSA; *Recreations* singing, skiing, poetry; *Style*— Robert Culshaw, Esq, MVO; ✉ Trade Department, British Embassy, BFPO 2 (e-mail betrd@ tmn.com)

CULYER, Prof Anthony John; s of Thomas Reginald Culyer (d 1979), and Betty Ely, *née* Headland; *b* 1 July 1942; *Educ* Sir William Borlase's Sch Marlow, King's Sch Worcester, Univ of Exeter (BA), UCLA; *m* 26 Aug 1966, Sieglinde Birgit, da of Kurt Kraut (d 1947); 1 s, 1 da; *Career* Fulbright scholar 1964–65, lectr Univ of Exeter 1965–69; Univ of York 1969–: lectr, sr lectr, reader, prof of economics and head Dept of Economics and Related Studies 1986–, pro vice-chllr 1991–94, dep vice-chllr; visiting prof: Queens Univ Canada 1976, Trent Univ Canada 1985–86, Medis Inst Munich 1990, Toronto Univ Canada 1991 (hon prof 1991–); William Evans visiting prof Otago Univ NZ 1979, Woodward lectr Univ of Br Columbia Canada 1986, Perey lectr McMaster Univ Canada 1991, Champlain lectr Trent Univ Canada 1991; chm: NHS Task Force on Funding of R & D 1993–94, Methodology Panel NHS Technology Assessment R & D Programme; vice chm N Yorks Health Authy 1995–; memb: Central R & D Ctee for the NHS, Yorkshire Region R & D Ctee, Review Advsy Ctee on the London Special Health Authys 1993, Subject Area Panel (Economics) ESRC, Br Cncl Health Advsy Ctee, Central R & D Ctee Nat Working Gp on R & D in Primary Care 1996; professional conslt to: UK Dept of Health, OECD, EEC, WHO, Govt of Canada, Govt of NZ; memb Office of Health Economics: Editorial Policy Ctee, Editorial Bd; co-ed Journal of Health Economics 1982–; memb Editorial Bd: Br Med Jl, Med Law International, Clinical Effectiveness in Nursing, Jl of Medical Ethics; memb Conf of Heads of Univ Depts of Economics 1987–; memb Kenneth J Arrow Award Prize Ctee; memb and founding chm Health Economists Study Gp; memb: Royal EC Soc, Research Advsy Ctee Canadian Inst for Advanced Research, Acad Advsy Cncl Univ of Buckingham; church organist and choirmaster, memb Liturgy and Music Advsy Gp Diocese of York 1995–, chm North East Yorkshire Area Royal Sch of Church Music; *Publications incl* Health Economics (1973), Economics of Social Policy (1973), Benham's Economics (1973), Economic Policies and Social Goals (1974), Need and the National Health Service (1976), Annotated Bibliography of Health Economics (1977), Human Resources and Public Finance (1977), Economic Aspects of Health Services (1978), Measuring Health (1978), Political Economy of Social Policy (1980 and 1991), Economic and Medical Evaluation of Health Care Technologies (1983), Health Indicators (1983), Economics (1985), Public Finance and Social Policy (1985), International Bibliography of Health Economics (1986), Public and Private Health Services (1986), Health Care Expenditures in Canada (1988), Perspectives on the Future of Health Care in Europe (1989), Standards for Socioeconomic Evaluation of Health Care Products and Services (1990), Competition in Health Care (1990), The Economics of Health (1991); International Review of the Swedish Health Care System (1991), Recent Developments in Health Economics (1992), Equity in Health Care Policy (1992), Supporting Research and Development in the NHS (1994); also over 200 articles and pamphlets; *Recreations* music and gardening; *Style*— Prof Anthony Culyer; ✉ The Laurels, Barmby Moor, York, YO4 5EJ (☎ 01759 302639); Department of Economics and Related Studies, University of York, Heslington, York, YO1 5DD (☎ 01904 433762/433789/433752, fax 01904 433759, telex 57933 YORKUL, e-mail (janet) ajc17@ unix.york.ac.uk)

CUMANI, Luca Matteo; s of Sergio Cumani (d 1980), and Elena, *née* Cardini; *b* 7 April 1949; *Educ* Milan; *m* 1979, Sara Doon, da of Simon Patrick Conyngham Plunket; 1 s (Matthew Sergio Simon b 1981), 1 da (Francesca Deepsea b 1983); *Career* racehorse trainer; rider of 85 winners in Italy, France and UK incl Moet and Chandon on Meissen and Prix Paul Noel de la Houtre on Harland 1972, champion amateur Italy 1972; formerly asst trainer to: S Cumani, H R A Cecil 1974–75; first held trainer's licence 1976; horses trained incl: Kahyasi, Freeze The Secret, Old Country, Triple Tipple, Tolomeo, Commanche Run, Free Guest, Bairn, Embla, Then Again, Celestial Storm, Half a Year, Casey, Infamy, Markofdistinction, Barathea, Only Royale; races won incl: Ever Ready Derby, Irish Derby, St Leger, Italian Derby, Premio Roma (twice), Arlington Million, Rothmans International, E P Taylor Stakes, Juddmonte International Stakes, Phoenix Champion Stakes, St James's Palace Stakes (twice), Cheveley Park Stakes, Prix Royal Oak, Queen Elizabeth II Stakes, Sussex Stakes, Brent Walker Fillies Mile, Irish 2000 Guineas, Yorkshire Oaks (twice), Breeders Cup Mile; *Style*— Luca Cumani, Esq

CUMBERLAND, Prof David Charles; s of Frank Charles Cumberland, of Pleasington, nr Blackburn, Lancs, and Edna Constance, *née* Hodson; *b* 17 Aug 1944; *Educ* Queen Elizabeth GS Blackburn, Univ of Edinburgh Med Sch (MB ChB); *m* 26 Dec 1970, Marilyn Susan, da of Colin Rowley (d 1974); 2 da (Louise Helen b 21 Aug 1973, Melanie Claire b 9 April 1976); *Career* prof of interventional cardiology Univ of Sheffield and Northern General Hosp specializing in treatment of coronary artery disease by angioplasty and associated research; author of numerous articles in jls; memb: BMA, Br Cardiac Soc, Cncl of Br Cardiovascular Intervention Soc; fndr chm Br Coronary Angioplasty Gp; FRCR 1973, FRCPEd 1986, FACC 1993, FRCS 1994, FESC 1994; *Books* Recent Advances in Radiology and Medical Imaging (jtly, 1986), Endovascular Surgery (jtly, 1989), Laser Angioplasty (jtly, 1989); *Recreations* jiu jitsu, sailing, country walking; *Style*— Prof David Cumberland; ✉ Upper Hurst, Gatehouse Lane, Outseats, Hathersage S30 1BQ (☎ 01433 650946); Clinical Sciences Centre, Northern General Hospital, Sheffield S5 7AU (☎ 0114 271 5841, fax 0114 261 9587)

CUMBERLEGE, Baroness (Life Peer UK 1990), of Newick, Co E Sussex; Julia Frances Cumberlege; CBE (1985), DL (East Sussex 1986); da of Dr Lambert Ulrich Camm, of Appleton, Newick, Sussex, and Mary Geraldine Gertrude, *née* Russell (d 1962); *b* 27 Jan 1943; *Educ* Convent of the Sacred Heart Kent; *m* 14 Jan 1961, Patrick Francis Howard Cumberlege, s of Geoffrey Fenwick Jocelyn Cumberlege, DSO, MC (d 1979); 3 s (Hon (Christopher) Mark b 1961, Hon Justin Francis b 1964, Hon Oliver Richard b 1968); *Career* memb: Lewes Dist Cncl 1966–79 (ldr 1977–78), E Sussex CC 1974–85 (chm Social Servs Ctee 1979–82); JP 1973–85; memb E Sussex AHA 1977–81; chm: Brighton Health Authy 1981–88, Nat Assoc of Health Authys 1987–88, SW Thames RHA 1988–92; Parly under sec of state for health in House of Lords 1992–; memb: NHS Policy Bd 1989–, Cncl St George's Med Sch, Press Cncl 1977–83, Appts Cmmn 1984–90; chm: Review of Community Nursing for Eng 1985, Review of Maternity Servs for England 1993; vice pres RCN 1988, chm and govr several schs, memb Cncl Brighton Poly 1987–89 (memb Formation Ctee 1988–89); hon degree: Univ of Surrey, Univ of Brighton; Vice Lord Lt of E Sussex 1991; FRSA; *Clubs* RSM; *Style*— The Rt Hon Baroness Cumberlege, CBE, DL; ✉ Vuggles Farm, Newick, Lewes, E Sussex BN8 4RU (☎ 01273 400453, fax 01273 401084); House of Lords, London SW1A 0PW

CUMING, Frederick George Rees; s of Harold Albert Cuming (d 1976), of Welling, Kent; and Grace Madeleine, *née* Rees; *b* 16 Feb 1930; *Educ* Sidcup Sch of Art, RCA; *m* Oct 1962, Audrey, da of Eric Lee, of Ashton-under-Lyme; 1 s (Daniel Lee b 5 Nov 1964), 1 da (Rachel Joanna b 25 Aug 1971); *Career* Nat Serv Sgt RAEC 1949–51; painter; winner grand prix fine art Monaco Ingot Industl Expo, Sir Brinsley Ford award New English Arts Club, House and Garden Prize RA 1994; adviser New Metropole Arts Centre Folkestone, tstee Rye Art Gallery and Eastern Rooms Gallery; memb: Nat Tst, New English Arts Club 1960; ARCA 1964, RA 1974; *Gp Exhibitions* incl: Royal Soc of Portrait Painters, John Moores Liverpool, Leicester Gallery, Pictures for Schools, 12 Royal Academicians Chichester, Little Studio NY, Artists of Fame and Promise (Brandler Galleries Brentwood) 1993; *Solo Exhibitions* New Metropole Arts Centre Folkestone 1972–75, Jonleigh Guildford 1975, Thackeray London 1976, Chichester 1976, Grafton London 1983, 1985, 1987, 1988 and 1990, Drew Canterbury 1983–86, Easton Rooms Rye 1983, Nat Tst Fndn for Arts (Agnews), Salute to Turner (Agnews), Edinburgh Festival 1995; *Public Collections* incl: Royal Acad, Miny of Works, Monte Carlo Museum, Brighton and Hove Museum, St John's and Worcester Colls Oxford, New Metropole Arts Centre, Farringdon Tst, W H Smith, LWT; *Recreations* reading, music, travelling, walking; *Clubs* Chelsea Arts, Dover St Arts; *Style*— Frederick Cuming, Esq, RA; ✉ The Gables, Wittersham Rd, Iden, Rye, E Sussex TN31 7UY (☎ 01797 280322)

CUMMING, Alexander James; s of Alexander George Cumming (d 1980), of Aberdeen, and Jean Campbell Cumming (d 1995); *b* 7 March 1947; *Educ* Fordyce Acad Banffshire, Robert Gordon's Coll Aberdeen, Univ of Aberdeen (MA); *m* 1973, Margaret Ada, da of John Callan; 2 da (Louise b 1975, Victoria b 1982), 1 s (Iain b 1977); *Career* VSO Calcutta 1969–70, Wiggins Teape (papermakers) 1970–72, Glen Gordon (knitwear mfrs) 1972–74, BOC 1974–75, treas Grampian Health Bd 1975–93, dir of fin Scottish Heath Serv 1994, chief exec Aberdeen Royal Hosps NHS Tst 1994–; treas Lancstane Housing Assoc; memb: CIMA 1973, CIPFA 1974; *Recreations* sport, walking, music; *Style*— Alexander Cumming, Esq; ✉ Loanhead of Savoch, Auchnagatt, Ellon, Aberdeenshire; Aberdeen Royal Hospitals NHS Trust, Foresterhill House, Ashgrove Road West, Aberdeen AB9 8AQ (☎ 01224 681818, fax 01224 840597)

CUMMING, Prof Gordon; s of Charles Gordon Cumming (d 1982), and Clara, *née* Wright (d 1980); *b* 31 May 1922; *Educ* Worcestershire Co HS, Univ of London (BSc), Univ of Birmingham (MB ChB, PhD, DSc, FRCP), Columbia Univ New York; *m* 19 July 1951, Jean Edith, da of Arthur Dyke Peasnell (d 1983); 4 s ((Alasdair) Duncan Gordon b 4 Aug 1952, Bruce b 14 Jan 1960, Robert (twin), Andrew b 4 Aug 1962), 1 da (Fiona b 17 July 1956); *Career* house physician Med Professorial Unit Queen Elizabeth Hosp Birmingham 1956, house surgn Sorrento Maternity Hosp Birmingham 1957, asst RMO Gen Hosp Birmingham 1957, registrar Royal Postgraduate Med Sch 1958, lectr in med Univ of Birmingham 1959, res fell Coll of Physicians and Surgns NY 1960; Univ of Birmingham: lectr in med 1962–65, sr lectr 1965–67, reader in med 1967; conslt physician United Birmingham Hosps 1965, med dir Midhurst Med Res Inst 1973–90, faculty prof of clinical sci Univ of Surrey 1977, sr lectr Univ of London Cardiothoracic Inst 1979, treas MRS 1979, prof of thoracic med Univ of London 1984; visiting prof: Univ of Tokyo, Univ of Orange Free State, Univ of Natal; chm Info Ctee Nuffield Provincial Hospitals Tst; DHSS: memb Steering Ctee on Re-organisation of the NHS 1971–72, memb Computer Policy Ctee and Computer R & D Ctee 1971–74; chm: EHIS Ltd, EDBS Ltd; memb: Physiological Soc, MRS, Euro Soc of Clinical Investigation, Assoc of Physicians of GB and NI, Société Française de la Tuberculose et des Maladies Respiratoires, Fleischner Soc, Breathing Club, Mass Spectrometer Soc of Japan, American Physiological Soc; memb Cncl Br Lung Fndn 1985– (treas 1985–86), treas Med Res Soc 1978–, chm Visitors RCP Ctee on Postgraduate Educn; memb Editorial Bd: American Jl of Physiology 1968–72, Clinical Sci and Molecular Med 1970–75, Jl of Applied Physiology 1973–76, Lung 1980–88; over 100 articles published in learned jls; FRICS 1966 (ARICS 1944); *Books* The Medical Management of Acute Poisoning (1961), Structure and Function in the Human Lung (with L B Hunt 1964), Disorders of the Respiratory System (with S Semple 1970 and 1979), The Scientific Foundations of Respiratory Medicine (with J G Scaddin 1979), The Pulmonary Circulation in Health and Disease (with G Bonsignore 1980), The Lung in its Environment (with G Bonsignore 1982), Cellular Biology of the Lung (with G Bonsignore), Drugs and the Lung (with G Bonsignore 1983), Smoking and the Lung (with G Bonsignore 1984); *Recreations* skiing, making violins, music, business; *Style*— Prof Gordon Cumming; ✉ The Old Rectory, Poltimore, Devon EX4 0AR (☎ 01392 461410); Midhurst Medical Research Unit, Aldens Business Court, Alphington, Exeter (☎ 01392 76923)

CUMMING, Dr (William James) Kenneth; s of Wallace Cumming, of Manchester, and Kathleen Margurite, *née* Lavery; *b* 29 Aug 1946; *Educ* The Royal Belfast Acad Inst, The Queen's Univ of Belfast (BSc, MB BCh); *children* 2 da (Emma b 27 Dec 1973, Claire b 25 Aug 1975); *Career* registrar and sr registrar Newcastle upon Tyne 1972–79, conslt neurologist Withington Hosp Univ of Manchester 1979–96; pres NW Myasthenic Assoc, chm South Manchester Imaging PLC; Hon MD The Queen's Univ Belfast 1979, BAO 1971; memb Acad of Experts, MInstD; FRCP, FRCPI, fell Royal Acad of Med in Ireland; *Recreations* golf; *Clubs* East India; *Style*— Dr Kenneth Cumming; ✉ 5 Belstone Close, Bramhall, Cheshire SK7 3QA; Neuro Science Unit, Alexandra Hospital, Mill Lane, Cheadle SK8 2PX (☎ 0161 428 1072, fax 0161 428 3421)

CUMMING, Robert Alexander; s of Alexander Ian Cumming (d 1962), and Bery Mary Stevenson; *b* 31 May 1945; *Educ* Trinity Hall Cambridge (MA); *m* 7 June 1975, Alison Carolyn, da of John George Jenkins, CBE, *qv*; 2 da (Hester Chloe Mary b 2 June 1983, Phoebe Alice Elizabeth b 5 June 1988); *Career* called to the Bar Middle Temple (Harmsworth scholar) 1967, practising barrister 1967–69, Hambros Bank 1970–71, lectr Tate Gall 1974–78, dir Christie's Fine Arts Course 1978–88, chm Christie's Education 1988–; pres: Christie's Education Inc (USA), Christie's Éducation (France); tstee Christie's Educn Trust 1986–; memb: Exhbns Sub Ctee Arts Cncl 1984–88, Cncl Friends of the Tate Gall 1983–, Thames and Chiltern Regnl Ctee Nat Trust 1990–96; chm Contemporary Art Soc 1988–90; external examiner: Univ of London 1976–80, Univ of Glasgow 1988–92; writing awards: Silver Pencil Award Utrecht 1982, TES Sr Info Book Award 1983, Premio Europeo di Letteratura Giovainle Pier Paolo Vergerio Padua 1985; memb: Middle Temple 1967, Gray's Inn 1969; FRSA 1990; *Books* Macmillan Encyclopedia of Art (1977), Just Look (1979), Just Imagine (1982), Christie's Guide to Collecting (1984), Looking into Paintings (1985, with TV programme), Working with Colour (exhbn catalogue, 1985), The Colour Eye (1990), Discovering Turner (1990), Paolozzi Mythologies (exhbn catalogue, 1990), Annotated Art (1995); *Recreations* all things European, family life, making and collecting, golf, shooting, wine, investment and the stockmarket; *Clubs* Arts; *Style*— Robert Cumming, Esq; ✉ The Old Mill House, Maids Moreton, Buckingham MK18 7AR (☎ 01280 816226); Christie's Education, 63 Old Brompton Road, London SW7 3JS (☎ 0171 581 3933, fax 0171 589 0393)

CUMMING-BRUCE, Edward Simon Hovell-Thurlow; s of Rt Hon Sir Roualeyn Cumming-Bruce, *qv*, and Lady Sarah Cumming-Bruce, *née* Savile (d 1991); *b* 7 June 1958; *Educ* Ampleforth, Magdalen Coll Oxford (MA); *m* 1984, Antonia, da of C S Gaisford-St Lawrence, of Howth Castle, Dublin, Eire; 2 s (Michael b 1985, William b 1987), 1 da (Isabelle b 1990); *Career* Laurence Prust & Co (and successor firms) 1980–90; dir: Schroder Securities Ltd 1990–91, Kleinwort Benson Securities Ltd 1992–; *Recreations* fishing, shooting; *Style*— Edward Cumming-Bruce, Esq; ✉ Kleinwort Benson Securities Ltd, 20 Fenchurch St, London EC3 (☎ 0171 623 8000, fax 0171 929 2657)

CUMMING-BRUCE, Rt Hon Sir (James) Roualeyn Hovell-Thurlow; kt (1964), PC (1977); 3 s (twin) of late 6 Baron Thurlow; *b* 9 March 1912; *Educ* Shrewsbury, Magdalene Coll Cambridge (BA); *m* 4 Aug 1955, Lady (Anne) Sarah Alethea Marjorie Savile (d 1991), yst da of 6 Earl of Mexborough (d 1945); 2 s, 1 da; *Career* called to the Bar Middle Temple 1937, judge of High Court Family Div 1964–77, presiding judge NE Circuit 1971–74, a Lord Justice of Appeal 1977–85 (ret); *Clubs* Pratt's, United Oxford and Cambridge; *Style*— The Rt Hon Sir Roualeyn Cumming-Bruce

CUMMINGS, Constance; CBE (1974); da of Dallas Vernon Halverstadt (d 1922), of Seattle, USA, and Kate Logan, *née* Cummings (d 1957); *b* 15 May 1910; *Educ* St Nicholas Girls' Sch USA, Univ of London; *m* 3 July 1933, Benn Wolfe Levy, s of Octave George Levy (d 1947), of London; 1 s (Jonathan Cummings b 1949), 1 da (Jemima Madge b 1951); *Career* theatre, film, television and radio actress; credits incl: Mme Bovary 1938, Goodbye Mr Chips 1939, Romeo and Juliet, St Joan (Old Vic) 1939–40, organised many troop shows during the war years, Peter and the Wolf (Albert Hall) 1951, Lysistrata 1957, Rape of the Belt 1957, Who's Afraid of Virginia Woolf? 1964, Fallen Angels 1967, Hay Fever 1980, Crown Matrimonial 1988, Tête a Tête (USA) 1989; NT: Long Day's Journey into Night, The Cherry Orchard, Coriolanus; The Circle (Hong Kong Arts Festival), Mrs Warren's Profession (English-Speaking Theatre Vienna); NY: The Chalk Garden 1992, Wings; memb: Lab Pty, Arts Cncl, Cncl Br Actors' Equity, Exec Ctee Actors' Charitable Tst, RSA; *Recreations* anthropology, music, horticulture; *Style*— Miss Constance Cummings, CBE; ✉ 68 Old Church Street, London SW3 (☎ 0171 352 0437)

CUMMINGS, John Scott; MP (Lab) Easington (majority 26,390); s of George Cummings, and Mary, *née* Cain; *b* 6 July 1943; *Educ* Murton Cncl Sr Sch; *Career* colliery electrician Murton Colliery 1958–87, sec Murton Colliery Mechanics 1967–87, MP (Lab, NUM sponsored) Easington 1987–; memb: Cncl of Europe (memb Agric Sub-ctee), Western Euro Union; memb: Miners Gp of Lab MPs, Easington RDC (leader 1979–87), Northumbrian Water Authy 1977–83, Peterlee and Aycliffe Devpt Corp 1980–87; vice chm Coalfield Community Campaign 1984–87, hon pres Co Durham Branch Stonham Housing Assoc; *Recreations* Jack Russell terriers, walking, foreign travel, reading, socialising; *Clubs* Murton Victoria, Murton Demmi, Murton Ex Servicemens', Thornley Catholic, Peterlee Lab; *Style*— John Cummings, Esq, MP; ✉ Constituency Office, Seaton Holme, Easington Village, Co Durham (☎ 0191 527 3773, fax 0191 527 3655); House of Commons, London SW1A 0AA

CUMMINS, Andrew; *Career* formerly with BHP Ltd, McKinsey & Co and Elders IXL Ltd/Foster's Brewing Group Ltd, gp dir strategic devpt Inchcape plc 1992–; *Style*— Andrew Cummins, Esq; ✉ Inchcape plc, 33 Cavendish Square, London W1M 9HF (☎ 0171 546 0022, fa 0171 533 9102)

CUMMINS, Gus; s of Harold George Cummins (d 1986), of London, and Honor, *née* Bird (d 1978); *b* 28 Jan 1943; *Educ* Sutton Art Sch, Wimbledon Art Sch (NDD, sr drawing prize), RCA (MA); *m* 1968, Angela, da of Arthur C Braven; 2 s (Casper b 1968, Marcus b 1970), 1 da (Rosie b 1979); *Career* artist; taught pt/t 1969–: Hammersmith, Sutton, Croydon, Chelsea, Ravensbourne, Wimbledon, City & Guilds, RA Schs of Art; sculptural work for exhbn display during 1970's, exhibited paintings since 1970's; *Solo Exhibitions* Gardner Art Centre Brighton 1991, Stormont Studios Rye 1991, Metropole Art Centre Folkstone 1992, Brian Sinfield Gallery Oxford 1993, Hastings Museum Gallery 1993, Lamont Gallery London; two persons shows: Eastern Rooms Gallery Rye 1987, New Grafton Gallery London 1993, Star Gallery Lewes; *Gp Exhibitions* incl: London Gp 1981–, RA 1982–, Hastings Museum 1979–, Eastern Rooms Gallery Rye 1984–, Spirit of London 1983 and 1984, Odette Gilbert Gallery 1984 and 1985, paintings and sculptural installations Dordrecht Festival 1986, Lloyds of London Travelling 1986 and 1987, Gardner Art Centre Brighton Univ 1988, Hunting Group Mall Gallery 1989 and 1990, President's Choice RA and Arts Club 1989, Academicians Choice Mall Gallery and Eye Gallery Bristol 1990, Looking Glass Appeal (Riverside One London) 1990, Discerning Eye (Mall Gallery and tour) 1991–92, Barbican Centre 1992, New Grafton Gallery 1992, Singer Friedlander/Sunday Times Water Colour Competition Mall Gallery 1992; *Awards* Henry Moore Prize (London Gp) 1982, Second Prize Spirit of London 1983, Daler-Rowney Prize RA 1987, First Prize Hunting Gp Mall Gallery 1990. House & Garden Prize RA 1992, Blackstone Award RA 1992; memb Rye Soc of Artists 1979–, memb London Gp 1982; RA 1992; *Recreations* music, poetry, swimming, snooker; *Clubs* Chelsea Arts; *Style*— Gus Cummins, Esq, RA; ✉ Harpsichord House, Cobourg Place, Hastings, Sussex TN34 3HY (☎ 01424 426429)

CUMPSTY, Prof Nicholas Alexander; s of Norman Cumpsty (d 1980), and Edith A, *née* Hendry; *b* 13 Jan 1943; *Educ* Haberdashers' Aske's Hampstead, Imperial Coll London (BSc), Trinity Coll Cambridge (PhD); *m* 1, 1966, Annette Tischler (d 1982); 1 s (Daniel b 19 June 1970), 1 da (Megan b 7 June 1973); m 2, Mary Cecily Hamer, *née* Turner; 2 step da (Emily D Hamer b 7 Nov 1968, Camilla R Hamer b 26 July 1973); *Career* res fell Peterhouse Coll Cambridge 1966–69, sr noise engr Rolls Royce 1969–71; Univ of Cambridge: fell Peterhouse 1972–, prof of aerothermal technol 1989– (lectr then reader 1972–89), dir Whittle Laboratory; fell American Soc of Mechanical Engrs 1975; FIMechE 1992, FEng 1995; *Books* Compressor Aerodynamics (1989); *Recreations* reading, music, photography, walking, scuba-diving; *Style*— Prof Nicholas Cumpsty, FEng; ✉ Whittle Laboratory, University of Cambridge, Madingley Road, Cambridge CB3 0DY (☎ 01223 337598, fax 01223 337596)

CUNARD, Peter John; s of Basil Charles Henry Cunard (d 1962), of London, and Christine May, *née* Tremer (d 1995); *b* 21 Aug 1945; *Educ* Latymer Fndn; *m* 1970, Susan Margaret Ethel, da of James Coleridge; 2 s (Nicholas Peter b 30 Oct 1971, Sebastian James b 29 Dec 1972), 1 da (Catherine Jane b 27 Nov 1976); *Career* press offr Assoc Television 1964–69, press and PR offr English Stage Co Royal Court Theatre 1969, PR advsr Duke of Bedford 1969–73, head of PR Trust House Forte 1973–76, dir Durden-Smith Communications 1976–80, fndr and md Granard Communications 1980–90, chief exec The Rowland Co (after merger of Granard Communications with Kingsway PR) 1990–92, memb Exec Ctee Rowland Worldwide Ltd; ptnr Tolman Cunard Ltd (strategic conslts) 1991–, chm Cunard Communications Ltd 1992–; tstee Sick Children's Trust 1984, chm Devpt Ctee Public Relations Consultants Assoc 1985; MInstD 1980; *Books* Public Relations Case Book (1990); *Recreations* travel, photography, theatre studies, cricket; *Clubs* Lord's Taverners, Solus; *Style*— Peter Cunard, Esq; ✉ The Mill House, Stanningfield, Suffolk IP29 4RX

CUNDY, Rt Rev Ian Patrick Martyn; *see:* Peterborough, Bishop of

CUNINGHAME, *see:* Fairlie-Cuninghame, Montgomery Cuninghame

CUNLIFFE, Prof Barrington Windsor (Barry); CBE (1994); s of George Percival Windsor (d 1942), and Beatrice Emma, *née* Mersh; *b* 10 Dec 1939; *Educ* Northern GS Portsmouth, St John's Coll Cambridge (BA, MA, PhD, LittD); *m* 1, 1962 (m dis 1979), Frances Ann, *née* Dunn; 1 s (Daniel b 1962), 1 da (Charlotte b 1967); m 2, 4 Jan 1979, Margaret, da of late Robert Herdman, of Brockworth, Glos; 1 s (Thomas b 1981), 1 da (Anna b 1984); *Career* asst lectr Univ of Bristol 1963–66, prof of archaeology Univ of Southampton 1966–72, prof of Euro archaeology Univ of Oxford 1972–; memb: Roman Soc, Soc of Medieval Archaeology, Royal Archaeological Inst; vice pres: Soc of Antiquaries 1982–85 (pres 1991–95), Prehistoric Soc 1983–86; a govr Museum of London 1995–; Hon: DLitt Univ of Sussex 1983, DSc Univ of Bath 1984, DUniv The Open Univ 1995; FSA 1964, FBA 1979, correspondent memb Deutschen Archaologischen Instituts, hon memb Royal Irish Acad; *Books* The Cradle of England (1972), Rome and the Barbarians (1975), Rome and her Empire (1978), The Celtic World (1979), Roman Bath Discovered (1984), The City of Bath (1986), Greeks, Romans and Barbarians (1988), Iron Age Communities in Britain (1991), Wessex to AD 1000 (1993), The Oxford Illustrated Prehistory of Europe (1994), Iron Age Britain (1995); *Clubs* Athenaeum; *Style*— Prof Barry Cunliffe, CBE, FBA, FSA; ✉ Institute of Archaeology, 36 Beaumont St, Oxford (☎ 01865 278240)

CUNLIFFE, Sir David Ellis; 9 Bt (GB 1759), of Liverpool, Lancashire; s of Sir Cyril Henley Cunliffe, 8 Bt (d 1969), and Eileen M, *née* Parkins; *b* 29 Oct 1957; *Educ* St Alban's GS for Boys; *m* 1983, Linda Carol, da of John Sidney Batchelor, of Harpenden; 3 da (Emma Mary b 1986, Katherine Alice b 1990, Bridget Carol b 1991); *Heir* bro, Andrew Mark Cunliffe b 17 April 1959; *Career* business development manager; *Style*— Sir David Cunliffe, Bt; ✉ Sunnyside, Burnthouse Lane, Needham, nr Harleston, Norfolk IP20 9LN

CUNLIFFE, Hon Henry (Harry); s and h of 3 Baron Cunliffe, *qv*; *b* 9 March 1962; *Educ* Eton; *Career* retail mgmnt 1982–85: The Cathedral Shop, Heuston Copy; banking: business services mangr Norwest Bank Minnesota 1985–93, private banker Norwest Bank Minnesota 1994–; Freeman Worshipful Co of Goldsmiths; *Recreations* photography, sailing, tennis, eight-ball pool, magic; *Style*— The Hon Harry Cunliffe; ✉ 2524 Pillsbury Avenue South, Minneapolis, MN 55404, USA (☎ 612 872 1981)

CUNLIFFE, Lawrence Francis; MP (Lab) Leigh (majority 18,827); *b* 25 March 1929; *Educ* St Edmund's RC Sch Worsley Manchester, Ruskin Coll Oxford; *m* 1950 (m dis 1983), Winifred, da of William Haslem; 3 s, 2 da; *Career* engr NCB 1949–79; cncllr: Farnworth BC 1960–74, Bolton MDC 1974–79; MP (Lab) Leigh 1979–, oppn whip 1980–87; magistrate 1967–79; Hon Alderman Bolton Met Dist BC 1996; *Recreations* cricket, football, swimming, horse racing; *Style*— Lawrence Cunliffe, Esq, MP, JP; ✉ House of Commons, London SW1A 0AA

CUNLIFFE, 3 Baron (UK 1914); Roger Cunliffe; s of 2 Baron Cunliffe (d 1963), and his 1 w, Joan Catherine, da of late Cecil Lubbock (n of 1 Baron Avebury); *b* 12 Jan 1932; *Educ* Eton, Trinity Coll Cambridge (BA, MA), Architectural Assoc (AADipl), Open Univ; *m* 27 April 1957, Clemency Ann, da of late Maj Geoffrey Benyon Hoare, of Clover House, Aldeburgh, Suffolk; 2 s, 1 da; *Heir* s, Hon Henry Cunliffe; *Career* consltg architect; dir: Exhibition Consultants Ltd, International Merchandising Centre Ltd Nicosia; memb Bd Coll of Estate Management; chm Suffolk Craft Soc; Warden Worshipful Co of Goldsmiths; RIBA, MIMgt, MAPM; *Books* Office Buildings (with Leonard Manasseh, 1962), Tomorrow's Office (with Santa Raymond, 1996); *Recreations* making bread, planting trees, cycling; *Style*— The Rt Hon Lord Cunliffe; ✉ The Broadhurst, Brandeston, Woodbridge, Suffolk IP13 7AG

CUNLIFFE, William James; s of William Cunliffe, and Bertha, *née* Longworth; *b* 28 Dec 1939; *Educ* Univ of Manchester (BSc, MB ChB), Univ of London (MD); *m* 3 June 1963, (Elizabeth) Janet, da of Arthur Wheeler Wood; 2 s (David Neil b 14 May 1964, Timothy Peter b 28 April 1970), 1 da (Susan Deborah b 20 June 1967); *Career* sr registrar Dermatology Dept Royal Victoria Infirmary Newcastle Upon Tyne 1966–69 (registrar 1964–66), conslt dermatologist Gen Infirmary at Leeds 1969–, prof of dermatology, chm and dir Leeds Fndn for Dermatological Res 1981–; chm: Br Soc of Investigated Dermatology 1976–79, Yorkshire Dermatologists, Br Assoc of Dermatology and Therapy Sub Gp; sec and pres Euro Soc of Dermatological Res 1985–89; *Recreations* walking, gardening; *Style*— William Cunliffe, Esq; ✉ 47 Tredgold Avenue, Bramhope, Leeds LS16 9BS (☎ 0113 267 2326); Department of Dermatology, The General Infimary at Leeds, Great George St, Leeds LS1 3EX (☎ 0113 243 2799)

CUNNINGHAM, Andrew Edward Tarrant; s of Will Edward Dennis Cunningham (d 1980), and Muriel Iris, *née* Tarrant (d 1987); *b* 15 March 1945; *Educ* The King's Sch Canterbury; *m* 24 March 1973, Mary Vivien Swainson; 2 s (Anthony Paul b 6 Aug 1974, John Roger b 17 Nov 1976); *Career* ptnr Moore Stephens 1972– (articled clerk 1963, mangr 1971); Liveryman City Livery of Upholders 1977, Freeman Worshipful Co of Goldsmiths 1977, Liveryman Worshipful Co of Shipwrights 1993; FCA 1974 (ACA 1969); *Recreations* golf, music; *Clubs* Salisbury and South Wilts Golf; *Style*— Mr Andrew Cunningham; ✉ Moore Stephens, St Paul's House, Warwick Lane, London EC4P 4BN (☎ 0171 334 9191, fax 0171 248 3408)

CUNNINGHAM, Sir Charles Craik; GCB (1974, KCB 1961, CB 1946), KBE (1952), CVO (1941); s of late Richard Yule Cunningham, of Abergeldie, Kirriemuir, Angus, and Isabella, *née* Craik; *b* 7 May 1906; *Educ* Harris Acad Dundee, Univ of St Andrews (MA, BLitt, LLD); *m* 1934, Edith Louisa (d 1990), da of late Frank Coutts Webster, OBE; 2 da (Isobel, Margaret); *Career* joined Scot Office 1929, private sec to Sec of State for Scot 1935–39, Scot Home Dept 1939–57 (sec 1948–57); perm under sec Home Office 1957–66, dep chm UKAEA 1966–71; chm: Radiochemical Centre Ltd 1971–74, Uganda Resettlement Bd 1972–74; dir Securicor 1971–81; *Clubs* Reform, New (Edinburgh); *Style*— Sir Charles Cunningham, GCB, KBE, CVO; ✉ 25 Regent Terrace, Edinburgh EH7 5BS (☎ 0131 556 9614)

CUNNINGHAM, Lt-Gen Sir Hugh Patrick; KBE (1975, OBE 1966); s of Sir Charles Banks Cunningham, CSI (d 1967), of Campbelltown, Argyll and Grace, *née* Macnish; *b* 4 Nov 1921; *Educ* Charterhouse; *m* 1, 1955, Jill (d 1992), da of J S Jeffrey (d 1978), of E Knoyle, Wilts; 2 s, 2 da; m 2, 1996, Zoë, da of T S Andrew, of Cape Town, S Africa; *Career* 2 Lt RE 1942, GOC SW Dist 1971–74, ACGS (OR) MOD 1974–75, Lt-Gen 1975, Dep Chief of Def Staff (OR) 1976–78, ret; Col Cmdt RE 1976–81, Col Queen's Gurkha Engrs 1976–81, Col Bristol Univ OTC 1977–87; HM Lt Tower of London 1983–86; dir: Fairey Holdings 1978–87, Fairey Engineering 1981–86, MEL 1982–89, Trend Communications Ltd 1983–86; chm: LL Consultants 1983–89, The Trend Group 1986–89; Hon Memb of Ct Worshipful Co of Glass Sellers (Master 1980–81); pres Old Carthusian Soc 1982–87, govr Suttons Hosp in Charterhouse 1983–96, chm Port Regis Sch 1980–94 (visitor 1994–); *Clubs* Army and Navy, MCC; *Style*— Lt-Gen Sir Hugh Cunningham, KBE; ✉ Granary Mill House, Fontmell Magna, Shaftesbury, Dorset SP7 9JU (☎ 01747 812025, fax 01747 811965)

CUNNINGHAM, James Dolan (Jim); MP (Lab) Coventry SE (majority 1,311); s of Adam Cunningham, and Elizabeth, *née* Farrel; *b* 4 Feb 1941; *Educ* St Columbia HS, Tillicoultry Coll (Dips in Industrial Law and Soc Scis); *m* 1 March 1985, Marion, da of late Frank Muir Podmore; 1 s (Andrew), 1 da (Jeanette), 1 step da (Jacqueline (Mrs Stevenson)), 1 step s (Paul A Douglas); *Career* engr Rolls Royce until 1988; Coventry City Cncl: sometime vice-chm Fin Ctee, chm Leisure Ctee, vice-chm Tport and Highways Ctee, chief whip, dep ldr of the Cncl, and ldr 1988–92 (memb 1972–93); chief steward and shop steward MSF; sec then chm Coventry SE CLP; MP (Lab) Coventry SE 1992–; *Recreations* walking, reading, music, football, politics, history, archaeology, political philosophy; *Style*— Jim Cunningham, Esq, MP; ✉ 2nd Floor, 107 New Union St, Coventry CV1 2NT (☎ and fax 01203 553159); Room 310, 7 Millbank, London SW1P 3JA (☎ and fax 0171 219 6362)

CUNNINGHAM, Dr John; *b* 27 June 1949; *Educ* Magdalen Coll Sch Oxford, Trinity Hall Cambridge (BA), Oxford Univ Clinical Med Sch (Nuffield travel award, BM BCh, DM, MRCP); *Career* house physician and house surgn Radcliffe Infirmary Oxford 1974–74, SHO (rotating) Whittington Hosp London 1974–75, SHO (thoracic med) Brompton Hosp 1975, med registrar Cardiothoracic Dept Central Middx Hosp 1976–77, lectr in med Med Unit London Hosp Med Coll 1977–80, fell Div of Endocrinology and Metabolism Washington Univ Sch of Med St Louis Missouri USA 1980–82, conslt physician and nephrologist Royal London Hosp 1982–; Royal London Hosp Sch of Med:

hon sr lectr in med 1986–, sub-dean for student admissions 1990–; physician to The Royal Household 1993–; special tstee Royal London Hosp 1985–, recognised teacher Univ of London 1985–, Jan Brod Meml lectr Prague 1993; memb Editorial Bd: Nephrology Dialysis Transplantion 1993–, Int Procceedings Jl (Nephrology Section) 1993–; memb: RSM, American Soc of Nephrology, Med Res Soc, Renal Assoc, American Soc for Bone and Mineral Res, Euro Calcified Tissue Soc, Bone and Tooth Soc, Euro Dialysis and Transplant Assoc - Euro Renal Assoc, Int Soc of Nephrology; FRCP 1988; *Publications* author of chapters in med and scientific textbooks, invited reviews and over 60 original articles in scientific jls; *Recreations* music, various sports - active and passive; *Style*— Dr John Cunningham; ✉ Department of Nephrology, Royal London Hospital, Whitechapel Road, London E1 1BB (☎ 0171 377 7366, fax 0171 377 7003)

CUNNINGHAM, Rt Hon Dr John Anderson (Jack); PC (1993), MP (Lab) Copeland (majority 2,439), DL (Cumbria 1991); s of Andrew Cunningham; *b* 4 Aug 1939; *Educ* Jarrow GS, Bede Coll Univ of Durham (PhD); *m* 1964, Maureen; 1 s, 2 da; *Career* formerly research chemist Durham, then lectr and Trades Union official, cncllr Chester-Le-Street DC (chm Fin Ctee 1969–74); MP (Lab): Whitehaven 1970–83, Copeland 1983–; PPS to Rt Hon James Callaghan 1972–76, Parly under sec of state Dept of Energy 1976–79; front bench oppn spokesman on: Industry 1979–83, Environment 1983–92; memb Shadow Cabinet 1983–, shadow ldr House of Commons and Lab campaign coordinator 1989–92; chief oppn spokesman on: foreign and Cwlth affrs (shadow foreign sec) 1992–94, trade and industry 1994–95, National Heritage 1995–; *Recreations* gardening, fell walking, fly fishing, music, books, ornithology; *Style*— Rt Hon Dr Jack Cunningham, MP; ✉ House of Commons, London SW1A 0AA

CUNNINGHAM, John Roderick; s of John Cunningham (d 1952), of Kent, and Millicent, *née* Seal (d 1929); *b* 13 May 1926; *Educ* Beckenham Sch Kent, Queen's Univ Belfast (BSc(Econ)), FCIB; *m* 1964, Monica Rachel, da of Cedric George (d 1964), of Horley, Surrey; 1 s (Roderick b 1965), 2 da (Meryl b 1955 (from previous marriage), Clare b 1970); *Career* RAF Aircrew 1943–47; dir Coutts & Co 1980–87 (various exec posts 1950–80), chm Nikko Bank plc 1987–92; memb: Bd of Govrs Cordwainers' Coll 1981–92, Cncl City Branch IOD 1985–; chm and vice pres City Branch Royal Soc of St George 1990–, chm Tonbridge Cons Assoc 1990–; memb Ct of Assts Worshipful Co of Loriners 1975 (Master 1984); *Recreations* gardening in Southern Spain, City of London activities; *Clubs* IOD, City Livery; *Style*— John R Cunningham, Esq; ✉ Oak Lodge, 126 Pembury Road, Tonbridge, Kent TN9 2JJ (☎ 01732 352447)

CUNNINGHAM, Mark James; s of James Arthur Cunningham, and Carole Kathleen, *née* Wood; *b* 6 June 1956; *Educ* Stonyhurst, Magdalen Coll Oxford (BA), Poly of Central London (Dip in Law); *m* 19 July 1980 (m dis 1995); 2 s (Charles b 1984, Edward b 1989), 2 da (Clementine b 1981, Susannah b 1985); *Career* called to the Bar Inner Temple 1980, jr counsel to the Crown Chancery 1992; *Recreations* tennis, cricket, horses, food; *Style*— Mark Cunningham, Esq; ✉ 5 New Square, Lincoln's Inn, London WC2 3RJ (☎ 0171 404 0404, fax 0171 831 6016)

CUNNINGHAM, (Harold) Michael Clunie; s of Harold Cunningham, of Woodside, Bickerton, Cheshire, and Margaret Isabel, *née* McPherson; *b* 18 Nov 1947; *Educ* Rossall Sch, RMA Sandhurst; *m* 22 Dec 1970, Virginia Pamela Liege, da of Col Sir Thomas Butler, Bt, CVO, DSO, OBE (d 1994); 2 s (Charles Alexander Clunie b 9 Dec 1978, Rupert Jasper Clunie b 25 May 1984), 2 da (Sophia Louisa Caroline b 31 July 1973, Henrietta Maria Charlotte b 17 Dec 1975); *Career* cmmnd 2 Lt Queen's Own Hussars 1968, ret as Capt 1976; ptnr Neilson Hornby Crichton stockbrokers 1981–86 (joined 1976), dir Neilson Milnes 1986–91, exec dir Neilson Cobbold 1991–, exec chm Pennine Fund Managers Ltd 1994–; MSI (memb Stock Exchange 1981); *Recreations* field sports, fishing, sailing; *Style*— Michael Cunningham, Esq; ✉ Dolhyfryd, Lawnt, Denbigh, Clwyd (☎ 01745 814805); Neilson Cobbold Ltd, Martins Building, 4 Water St, Liverpool L2 3UF (☎ 0151 236 6666, fax 0151 236 4996)

CUNNINGHAM, Phyllis Margaret; da of Andrew Cunningham (d 1992), of Manchester; *b* 15 Sept 1937; *Educ* Chorlton Central Sch Manchester, Loreburn Coll Manchester (Dip in Business Studies), Univ of York; *Career* trainee admin Withington Hosp Manchester 1956–59, personal/res asst to Med Dir Geigy Pharmaceutical Co Manchester 1959–62, unit admin The Roosevelt Hosp NY 1962–64, planning offr The Royal Free Hosp London 1964–74, dep house govr and sec to the Bd The Royal Marsden Hosp London 1974–80; chief exec: The Royal Marsden Hosp Special Health Authy 1980–94, The Royal Marsden NHS Tst 1994–; govr Christ's Sch Richmond 1995–; Veuve Clicqout Businesswoman of the Year 1991; FRSA 1993; *Recreations* travel, gardening, sailing, theatre, music; *Clubs* Hosp Offrs'; *Style*— Miss Phyllis Cunningham; ✉ The Royal Marsden NHS Trust, Fulham Road, London SW3 6JJ (☎ 0171 352 8171, fax 0171 376 4809)

CUNNINGHAM, Roseanna; MP (SNP) Perth and Kinross (majority 7,311); da of Hugh Cunningham (d 1993), and Catherine, *née* Dunlay; *b* 27 July 1951; *Educ* Univ of West Australia (BA), Univ of Edinburgh (LLB), Univ of Aberdeen (Dip of legal practice); *Career* asst research offr SNP 1977–79, slr Dumbarton DC 1986 (trainee slr 1983–85); slr: Glasgow DC 1986–89, Ross Harper & Murphy Glasgow 1989–90; admitted Faculty of Advocates 1990; MP (SNP) Perth and Kinross 1995–; *Recreations* reading, arguing, music; *Style*— Ms Roseanna Cunningham, MP; ✉ House of Commons, London SW1A 0AA (☎ 0171 219 6424); 51 York Place, Perth (☎ 01738 444002, fax 01738 444602)

CUNNINGHAM, Tom; *b* 22 June 1965; *Career* drummer with Wet Wet Wet; 14 top twenty singles incl 3 no 1's (With A Little Help From My Friends 1988 (raised over £600,000 for Childline), Goodnight Girl 1992, Love Is All Around 1994); albums with Wet Wet Wet: Popped In Souled Out (1987, UK no 1), The Memphis Sessions (1988, UK no 3), Holding Back The River (1989, UK no 2), High On The Happy Side (1992, UK no 1), End Of Part One (compilation, 1994, UK no 1), Picture This (1995); participated in: Prince's Trust Rock Gala 1988, 1989 and 1990, concert for Nelson Mandela's 70th birthday 1988, John Lennon Tribute concert 1990; *Style*— Tom Cunningham, Esq; ✉ c/o Wet TM Ltd, 14/16 Speirs Wharf, Port Dundas, Glasgow G4 9TB (☎ 0141 353 1515, fax 0141 353 3852)

CUNNINGHAM, Tony; MEP (Lab) Cumbria and Lancs N (majority 22,988); s of Daniel Cunningham (d 1987), of Workington, and Bessie, *née* Lister; *Educ* Workington GS, Univ of Liverpool (BA); *m* 1985, Anne, da of Albert and Margaret Gilmore; 1 da (Angela b 1993), 1 step s (David b 1978), 1 step da (Marie b 1981); *Career* history teacher Alsager Comp Sch 1977–80, English teacher Mikunguni Trade Sch Zanzibar 1980–82, history teacher Netherhall Sch Maryport 1983–93, MEP (Lab) Cumbria and Lancs N 1994–; Mayor of Workington 1990–91, ldr Allerdale BC 1992–94; *Recreations* sport in general (co rep at cross-country), reading; *Style*— Tony Cunningham, Esq, MEP; ✉ Office A, Strawberry How Business Centre, Lorton Road, Cockermouth, Cumbria CA13 9QX (☎ 01900 826601)

CUNNINGHAM-JARDINE, Ronald Charles (Ronnie); s of Charles Frederick Cunningham (d 1973), of Jardine Hall, Lockerbie, and Dorothy Agnes Jessie, *née* Jardine (d 1964); *b* 19 Sept 1931; *Educ* Ludgrove, Eton, RMA Sandhurst; *m* 19 Sept 1958, (Constance Mary) Teresa, da of John Inglis (d 1959), of West Nisbet, Jedburgh; 1 s (John Charles b 11 Nov 1961), 1 da (Rachel Mary (Mrs Andrew Wardall) b 28 Dec 1963); *Career* served Royal Scots Greys 1950–58, ret Capt; Lord Lt Dumfries & Galloway Region (Dists of Nithsdale and Annandale & Eskdale) 1991– (Vice Lord Lt 1988–91); pres Lockerbie Branch Royal Br Legion 1974–, chm BFSS Dumfries & Galloway 1988–93; sec and chm Dumfriesshire Hunt 1960–88; *Recreations* all country sports; *Clubs* White's; *Style*— Ronald Cunningham-Jardine, Esq; ✉ Fourmerkland, Lockerbie, Dumfriesshire DG11 1EH (☎ 01387 810226, fax 01387 811375, car 0860 914947)

CUNYNGHAME, Sir Andrew David Francis; 12 Bt (NS 1702), of Milncraig, Ayrshire; s of Sir (Henry) David St Leger Brooke Selwyn Cunynghame, 11 Bt (d 1978), and Hon Pamela Margaret (d 1991), da of late 5 Baron Stanley of Alderley; *b* 25 Dec 1942; *Educ* Eton; *m* 1, 1972, Harriet Ann, da of Charles Thomas Dupont, of Montreal, Canada; 2 da (Ann Marie Albinia b 1978, Tania Albinia Pamela Jean b 1983); m 2, 19 Aug 1989, Isabella, da of late Edward Everett Watts, Jr; *Heir* bro, John Philip Henry Michael Selwyn Cunynghame b 1944; *Career* former chm City Vintagers Ltd; senior ptnr Chipchase Cunynghame; Liveryman Worshipful Co of Pattenmakers; FCA; *Clubs* Brooks's; *Style*— Sir Andrew Cunynghame, Bt; ✉ 12 Vicarage Gardens, London W8 4AH

CUNYNGHAME, John Philip Henry Michael Selwyn; s of Sir (Henry) David St Leger Brooke Selwyn Cunynghame, 11 Bt (d 1978); hp of bro, Sir Andrew David Francis Cunynghame, 12 Bt, *qv*; *b* 9 Sept 1944; *Educ* Eton; *m* 1981, Marjatta, da of Martti Markus, of Muhos, Finland; 1 s (Alexander b 1985), 1 da (Niina Kaarina b 1983); *Career* dir Nobilo Vineyards of NZ; memb Ct of Assts Worshipful Co of Pattenmakers; *Style*— John Cunynghame Esq; ✉ 26d Belgrave Road, London SW1V 1RG (☎ 0171 828 0559, fax 0171 834 7699)

CUPITT, Rev Don; s of late Robert Cupitt, of Wendover, Bucks, and Norah Cupitt; *b* 22 May 1934; *Educ* Charterhouse, Trinity Hall Cambridge (BA), Westcott House Cambridge; *m* 28 Dec 1963, Susan Marianne, da of Frank Cooper Day (d 1941); 1 s (John b 1965), 2 da (Caroline b 1966, Sally b 1970); *Career* Nat Serv 2 Lt Royal Signals 1956–57; curate St Philip's Salford 1959–62, vice princ Westcott House Cambridge 1962–65; Emmanuel Coll Cambridge: dean 1965–91, asst univ lectr 1968–73, univ lectr 1973–96; Hon DLitt Univ of Bristol 1985; *Books* Christ and the Hiddenness of God (1971), Crisis of Moral Authority (1972), The Leap of Reason (1976), Jesus and the Gospel of God (1979), The Debate about Christ (1979), Taking Leave of God (1980), The Sea of Faith (1984, BBC TV series 1984), Only Human (1985), The Long-Legged Fly (1987), The New Christian Ethics (1988), Radicals and the Future of the Church (1989), The Worlds of Science and Religion (1976), Who Was Jesus? (with Peter Armstrong, 1977, BBC TV documentary, 1977), The Nature of Man (1979), Explorations in Theology (1979), The World to Come (1982), Life Lines (1986), Creation out of Nothing (1990), What is a Story? (1991), The Time Being (1992), After All (1994), The Last Philosophy (1995), Solar Ethics (1995); *Recreations* hill-walking; *Style*— The Rev Don Cupitt; ✉ 62 Humberstone Road, Cambridge CB4 1JF; Emmanuel College, Cambridge CB2 3AP (☎ 01223 334267, fax 01223 334267)

CURBISHLEY, Alan Charles; s of William George Curbishley, of Barkingside, Essex, and Cordielia Maud, *née* Foley (d 1982); *b* 8 Nov 1957; *Educ* South West Ham Tech Sch for Boys; *m* 15 July 1983, Carol, da of Robert Henry John Watson; 1 da (Claire b 14 March 1985), 1 s (Michael Alan b 27 July 1988); *Career* professional football manager (former player); 94 appearances West Ham Utd 1974–79, 154 appearances Birmingham City 1979–83, 32 appearances Aston Villa 1983–84, 67 appearances Charlton Athletic 1984–87, 120 appearances Brighton & Hove Albion 1987–90; Charlton Athletic: rejoined as player 1990, jt player mangr (with Steve Gritt) 1991–95 (30 appearances), sole mangr June 1995–; England caps: 8 schoolboy, 10 youth under 18 (World Youth Cup winners 1975), 1 under 21; club honours: runners-up medal Euro Cup Winners' Cup West Ham Utd v Anderlecht 1976, promotion to Div 1 Birmingham City 1980, promotion to Div 1 Charlton Athletic 1986, promotion to Div 2 Brighton & Hove Albion 1988; FA full coaching licence 1991; Barclays Mangr of the Month: Oct 1991, March 1992, Aug 1992; Endsleigh League Mangr of the Month Aug 1993; *Style*— Alan Curbishley, Esq; ✉ Charlton Athletic Training Ground, Sparrows Lane, New Eltham, London SE9 2JR (☎ 0181 859 8888, fax 0181 294 2095)

CURIEL, Raul Morris; s of Isaac Curiel Segura, of Montevideo, Uruguay, and Clara, *née* Margounato; *b* 31 March 1946; *Educ* Colegio Nacional Jose P Varela Scdy Sch Montevideo Uruguay, Univ de la Republica Montevideo Uruguay, Iowa State Univ USA (BArch), Univ of Minnesota USA (MArch); *m* 26 May 1976, Linda, da of Ronald Webb; 2 da (Alessandra Stephanie b 5 May 1985, Melanie Jane b 30 May 1989); *Career* formerly architect Sao Paulo Brazil, dir The Fitzroy Robinson Partnership UK 1983– (architectural asst 1978–83); major architectural projects incl: The Standard Chartered Bank, Sedgwick House, HQ for the Moscow Narodny Bank, interiors for London HQ of Drexel Burnham Lambert, a mixed conservation/new office building at 75 King William St, numerous business parks; awarded: AIA merit award, selected design Sch of Architecture ISU 1971, selected design UNESCO's Int Design Competition 1972, Mason's award 1990 and Tiler's and Bricklayer's award 1990 for building at 75 King William St; memb: IAB 1977, RIBA 1979; *Recreations* theatre, reading, swimming, viewing buildings, sketching; *Style*— Raul Curiel, Esq; ✉ The Fitzroy Robinson Partnership, 77 Portland Place, London W1N 4EP (☎ 0171 636 8033)

CURL, Prof James Stevens; s of George Stevens Curl (d 1974), of Hillhall, Co Down, and Sarah, *née* McKinney (d 1995); *b* 26 March 1937; *Educ* Cabin Hill, Campbell Coll, Queen's Univ, Belfast Coll of Art, Oxford Sch of Architecture, UCL (DipArch, DipTP, PhD); *m* 1, 1960 (m dis 1986), Eileen Elizabeth, da of John Blackstock (d 1984), of Belfast; 2 da (Dr Astrid James b 1962, Ingrid b 1964); m 2, 1993, Prof (Stanisława) Dorota Iwaniec, *qv*, da of Count Kazimierz Czartorycki (d 1944), of Krasiczyn, nr Przemysl, Poland; *Career* architect, town planner, antiquarian, architectural historian; architectural ed Survey of London 1970–73, conslt architect to Scottish Ctee for European Architectural Heritage Year 1973–75, sr architect Herts CC 1975–78, research prof of architectural history Centre for Conservation Studies De Montfort Univ Leicester 1995– (sr lectr 1978–88, prof of architectural history Dept of Architecture 1988–95); visiting fell Peterhouse Cambridge 1991–92; vice pres Friends of Kensal Green Cemetery; memb: Salisbury Gp, Fabric Advsy Ctee Leicester Cathedral; author of numerous articles and reviews; Liveryman Worshipful Co of Chartered Architects; RIBA, MRTPI, ARIAS, FSAScot, FSA 1974; *Books* The Victorian Celebration of Death (1972), The Erosion of Oxford (1977), The Egyptian Revival (1982), The Life and Work of Henry Roberts 1803–76, Architect (1983), English Architecture (1987), The Londonderry Plantation 1609–1914 (1986), Victorian Architecture (1990), The Art and Architecture of Freemasonry (1991, Sir Banister Fletcher Award 1992), Classical Architecture (1992), Encyclopaedia of Architectural Terms (1993), Georgian Architecture (1993), A Celebration of Death (1993), Egyptomania (1994), Victorian Churches (1995); *Recreations* music, opera, travel, literature, food, wine, poetry, painting; *Clubs* Art Workers' Guild, Authors'; *Style*— Prof James Stevens Curl, FSA; ✉ 2 The Coach House, Burley-on-the-Hill, Oakham, Rutland LE15 7TE (☎ 01572 755880); 15 Torgrange, Holywood, Co Down BT18 0NG (☎ 01232 425141); Centre for Conservation Studies, De Montfort University, The Gateway, Leicester LE1 9BH (☎ 0116 253 2781)

CURL, His Hon Judge; Philip; s of Dr Oliver Curl, and Joan, *née* Crooks; *b* 31 Oct 1947; *Educ* Radley, Univ of Southampton (LLB); *m* 22 Oct 1983, Nicola Ruth, da of late Richard Quentin Gurney; 2 da (Olivia Elisabeth b 17 Jan 1986, Eleanor Rose b 16 May 1989); *Career* called to the Bar Gray's Inn 1970, recorder 1995–96 (asst recorder 1991), circuit judge (SE Circuit) 1996–; *Recreations* playing and watching sport, art, travel; *Clubs* MCC, Norfolk (Norwich); *Style*— His Hon Judge Curl; ✉ Norwich Combined Courts Centre, Bishopgate, Norwich NR3 1UR

CURLE, Sir John Noel Ormiston; KCVO (1975, CVO 1956), CMG (1966); s of Maj William Sidney Noel Curle, MC (d of wounds 1918), of Melrose; *b* 12 Dec 1915; *Educ* Marlborough, New Coll Oxford; *m* 1, 1940 (m dis 1948), Diana, da of Cdr Ralph H Deane, RN; 1 s, 1 da; m 2, 1948, Pauline, da of Hylton Welford, of Hylton, Co Durham, and wid of Capt David Roberts; 1 step-s (decd), 2 step-da; *Career* served WWII Irish Gds Capt 1941; entered Dip Serv 1939; ambass to: Liberia 1967–70, Guinea 1968–70, the Philippines 1970–72; vice marshal of the Diplomatic Corps 1972–75, ret; dir of protocol Hong Kong 1976–85; advsr for Coronation of the King of Swaziland 1986; *Style*— Sir John Curle, KCVO, CMG; ✉ Appletree House, nr Aston-le-Walls, Daventry, Northants NN11 6UG (☎ 0129 586 211)

CURLING, David Antony Bryan; s of Bryan William Richard Curling, of Fullerton Manor, nr Andover, Hants, and late Elizabeth Mary, da of Maj Sir Eric Bonham, 3 Bt, CVO, JP (d 1937), and sis of Sir Antony Bonham, 4 Bt (UK 1852), DL, *qv*; *b* 27 Jan 1943; *Educ* Eton; *m* 19 Oct 1970, Jennifer, *née* Schlesinger; 2 da (Charlotte Chloe b 18 April 1972, Antonia Jessica b 20 March 1974); *Career* Dixon Wilson Tubbs & Gillet 1962–66, Peat Marwick Mitchell Johannesburg 1967–68, Union Acceptances Pty Ltd Johannesburg 1969–70; Williams de Broë plc: joined 1971, appointed dir 1974–; *Recreations* sailing; *Clubs* Royal Yacht Squadron, Bembridge Sailing (Cdre 1985–86); *Style*— David Curling, Esq; ✉ Williams de Broë plc, 6 Broadgate, London EC2M 2RP (☎ 0171 588 7511, fax 0171 588 1702)

CURLING, Robert Douglas (Rob); s of Col John Douglas Forsyth Curling, OBE (d 1971), and Winifred Jill, *née* Waddell; *b* 8 Sept 1957; *Educ* Cranleigh; *Career* freelance presenter; casually employed 1975–76; BBC: joined as vaults boy (latterly film examiner) BBC Film Library 1976, newsreader/co-presenter London Plus (BBC South East) 1987; freelance with the BBC 1987–; former reader news bulletins BBC Breakfast News, narrator A Balancing Act (BBC 2) 1987, presenter Issues (two series, BBC 2, first series nominated BAFTA) 1987–89, researcher, writer and presenter Noticeboard (renamed Behind the Screen, BBC 1 and 2) 1987–89; co-presenter: Into Music (BBC 2) 1988, Bazaar (series) 1989, Railwatch (BBC 1) 1989, Air Show '90 & Farnborough '90 1990 (and International Air Tattoo 1991); presenter 15 Minutes From Now and co-presenter Living Now (BSB's Now channel) 1990–91, presenter The Geography Programme (BBC 2) 1991–92, co-presenter International Boat Show 1992, host Turnabout (quiz, BBC 1) 1990–; co-presenter and sports corr Newsroom South East 1987–95; conf host various cos and presenter of corporate videos; *Recreations* playing tennis and cricket, DIY, playing drums, trumpet and piano, countryside; *Clubs* Lord's Taverners; *Style*— Rob Curling, Esq; ✉ c/o Agent, Anita Land, Simpson Fox Associates, 52 Shaftesbury Avenue, London W1V 7DE (☎ 0171 434 9167)

CURNOCK, Dr David Anthony; s of George Henry Reginald Curnock, of Bramcote Hills, Nottingham, and Vera Marjorie, *née* Bucknell; *b* 17 Aug 1946; *Educ* Chigwell Sch Essex, St John's Coll Cambridge (MA, MB BChir), Charing Cross Hosp Med Sch; *m* 13 Nov 1971, Anne Elizabeth, da of John Ruff, of Holmbury-St-Mary, Surrey; 1 s (Michael b 1982), 3 da (Ruth b 1972, Elizabeth b 1974, Esther b 1980); *Career* lectr in child health Univ of Benin Nigeria 1977–79, sr registrar of paediatrics Derbys Children's Hosp and Nottingham City Hosp 1979–82, conslt paediatrician Nottingham City Hosp 1982–; FRCP 1989; *Recreations* printing, railway history; *Style*— Dr David Curnock; ✉ 39 Sevenoaks Crescent, Bramcote Hills, Nottingham NG9 3FP; Department of Paediatrics, City Hospital, Nottingham NG5 1PB (☎ 0115 969 1169)

CURNOW, (Elizabeth) Ann Marguerite; QC (1985); da of Cecil Curnow (d 1944, as Japanese POW), and Doris, *née* Behr (d 1964); *b* 5 June 1935; *Educ* St Hilda's Sch Whitby, King's Coll London (LLB), Sorbonne (Cours de Civilisation Française); *m* 28 Sept 1981, His Hon Judge (William) Neil Denison, QC, *qv*; 3 step s; *Career* called to the Bar Gray's Inn 1957, prosecuting counsel to the Crown Middx Crown Court 1972–77, sr prosecuting counsel to the Crown Central Criminal Court 1981– (jr prosecuting counsel 1977–81), recorder of the Crown Court, bencher Gray's Inn 1985; *Recreations* music (especially opera), tapestry, Burmese cats, gardens; *Style*— Miss Ann Curnow, QC; ✉ 6 King's Bench Walk, Temple, London EC4Y 7DR (☎ 0171 583 0410, fax 0171 353 8791)

CURNOW, Barry John; s of Stuart John Curnow (d 1986), and Margaret Agnes (Daisy), *née* Parkhouse; *b* 19 May 1948; *Educ* Sutton HS Plymouth, Univ of Exeter (BA), Univ of London (MA); *m* 1, 23 Oct 1971, Patricia Margaret, da of Dr D R L Newton; m 2, 24 Dec 1987, Penelope Ann, da of Henry S J de Haas, of Tywardreath, Cornwall; *Career* independent mgmnt conslt; personnel mangr GLC 1969–73, joined Hay-MSL 1974, gp md Hay-MSL Management Consultants 1984–86, chief exec Hay Management Consultants Asia HK 1986–87, worldwide dir Hay Group 1987–90, chm and chief exec MSL Group International 1987–91, fndr dir Future Perfect 1987 (exec chm 1991–), non-exec dir and advsr to several cos, chm Independent Counselling and Advsy Servs (ICAS) Ltd 1991–, princ Maresfield Curnow Sch of Mgmnt Consulting 1991–; pres: UK Inst of Personnel Mgmnt 1991–92 (vice pres pay and employment conditions 1984–86, former chm Croydon and S London Branch), Inst of Mgmnt Conslts 1996–97 (chm Professional Standards Ctee 1992–96); conducted res at The Mgmnt Coll Henley 1974–83; Freeman City of London, Liveryman Worshipful Co of Chartered Secs and Admins, memb Guild of Mgmnt Conslts; assoc Chartered Inst of Mktg; CIPD, FIMC, FIMgt, FCIS, FInstD, FRSA; *Books* Managing Third Age Careers - The Corporate Challenge (with John McLean Fox, 1994), Curnow on Consulting (1995), The Chance to Live More Than Once (companion vol to Third Age Careers - The Corporate Challenge, with John McLean Fox, 1996), Consultant 2000 (1997); articles in various pubns; *Recreations* amateur radio licence G3UKI 1965; *Style*— Barry Curnow, Esq; ✉ Maresfield Curnow School of Management Consulting, 10 Maresfield Gardens, London NW3 5SU (☎ 0171 431 6085 and 0171 435 0592)

CURPHEY, Dr (Robert) Norman; s of John Cubbon Curphey (d 1966), of Ramsey, Isle of Man, and Isabel Margaret, *née* Killip (d 1991); *b* 18 May 1943; *Educ* Ramsey GS, Charing Cross Hosp Med Sch Univ of London (MB BS, MRCS, LRCP); *m* 21 Sept 1968, Jennifer, da of Roy Skudder (d 1982), of 31 Old Church Rd, Playing Place, Truro; 2 da (Juliet b 1972, Sarah b 1973); *Career* sr registrar Leeds Gen Infirmary 1973–76, conslt radiologist Royal Cornwall Hosp Teliske 1976–; dir Cornwall Breast Screening Serv; FRCR 1975; *Recreations* golf, gardening; *Style*— Dr Norman Curphey; ✉ Chy-an-Gwens, Moresk Road, Truro, Cornwall TR1 1BW (☎ 01872 77908); Mammography Unit, Royal Cornwall Hospital (Treliske), Truro, Cornwall TR1 3LJ (☎ 01872 74242)

CURRAN, Edmund Russell; s of William John Curran (d 1973), of Dungannon, N Ireland, and Elizabeth, *née* Russell (d 1945); *b* 29 Sept 1944; *Educ* Royal Sch Dungannon N Ireland, Queen's Univ Belfast (BSc, DipEd); *m* 1, 1969 (m dis 1992), Romaine, da of William Carmichael; 2 s (Jonathan William b 18 Sept 1973, Andrew Edmund Simon b 13 Oct 1975), 2 da (Cathryn Ruth b 1 Sept 1975, Claire Susannah b 10 March 1978); m 2, 1994, Pauline Beckett, da of Jack Beckett; *Career* Belfast Telegraph: grad trainee journalist 1966–67, reporter, feature writer then ldr writer 1967–72, asst ed 1973–74, dep ed 1974–88; ed Sunday Life (Belfast) 1988–92 (seconded as ed Wales on Sunday 1991), ed Belfast Telegraph 1993–; UK Regnl Newspaper Ed of the Year 1992; *Recreations* tennis, golf; *Clubs* Belfast Boat, Belvoir Park Golf; *Style*— Edmund Curran, Esq; ✉ Belfast Telegraph, 124 Royal Avenue, Belfast BT1 1EB (☎ 01232 264400, fax 01232 554517)

CURRAN, Sir Samuel Crowe; kt (1970); s of John Hamilton Curran (d 1959); *b* 23 May 1912; *Educ* Univ of Glasgow (MA, BSc, PhD, DSc), Univ of Cambridge (PhD); *m* 1940, Joan Elizabeth, da of Charles Millington Strothers (d 1975); 4 children; *Career* scientist and educationalist; former chief scientific advsr to Sec of State for Scotland, chief scientist UKAEA 1955–59; princ: Royal Coll of Sci and Technol 1959–64, Univ of Strathclyde 1964–80; visiting prof in energy studies Univ of Glasgow 1980–90; fell Univ of Strathclyde 1992–; hon fell St John's Coll Cambridge 1972–; scientific advsr: Thorburn Associates, Plant Safety Ltd; inventions incl: scintillation counter 1944, gas-filled proportional counter 1947; Cdr Order of St Olav Norway 1965, Cdr Polonia Restituta Poland 1970; FRSE 1947, FRS 1953, FEng 1983; *Recreations* golf, horology; *Clubs* Caledonian; *Style*— Sir Samuel Curran, FRS, FRSE, FEng; ✉ 93 Kelvin Court, Glasgow G12 0AH (☎ 0141 334 8329)

CURRAN, Stephen William; s of Dr Richard Desmond Curran, CBE (d 1985, Capt RNVR), and Marguerite Claire, *née* Gothard; *b* 9 March 1943; *Educ* Marlborough House School, Wellington College, RMA Sandhurst; *m* 21 June 1969, Anne Beatrice, da of Harry Grumbar, of Rats Castle, Roughway, nr Tonbridge, Kent; 1 s (Charles b 1972), 1 da (Louise b 1979); *Career* Lt 1 The Queen's Dragoon Gds 1963–66; Permutit Co Ltd 1966–67, Bowater Co Ltd 1967–71, analyst Grumbar and Sée 1971–75, managing consl Coopers and Lybrand Assocs 1975–79, project fin mangr NCB Pension Funds 1979–81, chief exec Candover Investments plc 1991– (dep chief exec 1981–90); FCCA 1973; *Recreations* skiing, swimming, tennis, running; *Clubs* Cavalry and Guards', Hurlingham; *Style*— Stephen Curran, Esq; ✉ c/o Candover Investments plc, 5th Floor, 20 Old Bailey, London EC4M 7LN (☎ 0171 489 9848, fax 0171 248 5483)

CURRAN, Susan; da of Norman Griffin, of Lincoln, and Maureen, *née* McGinnity; *b* 14 May 1952; *Educ* Abbeydale GS for Girls Sheffield, Univ of Sussex (BA); *m* 1, 1976 (m dis 1980), Timothy Curran; m 2, 1980 (m dis 1987), Raymond Curnow; 2 s (Rufus Lawrence b 7 Nov 1980, Evan Giles b 14 Dec 1982); *Career* underwriter FM Insurance Co 1973–78, dir and sec Probit Consultancies Ltd 1979–87, freelance writer 1985–, md Rampant Horse Ltd 1993–95; memb Norwich City Cncl (Lab) 1990–95; *Books* fiction: The Mouse God (1987), The Heron's Catch (1989), Mrs Forster (1991), Mine (1994), Communion With Death (1995); non-fiction incl: How to Write a Book and Get it Published (1990), The Penguin Computing Book (with Ray Curnow, 1983), Word Processing for Beginners (1984), Business Applications for the BBC Micro (1984); *Recreations* politics, cooking, collecting contemporary art, other people; *Style*— Ms Susan Curran; ✉ 140 Whitehall Road, Norwich, Norfolk NR2 3EW (☎ 01603 665843, fax 01603 661589)

CURRIE, Andrew Buchanan; s of Buchanan Currie, of Loughborough, Leics, and Wilma Drysdale, *née* Livingston; *b* 16 April 1954; *Educ* Loughborough GS, Univ of Birmingham (BA); *Career* employment res exec Inst of Dirs 1983–86, sr account exec Profile Public Relations 1986–88, dep dir and head of res Shopping Hours Reform Cncl 1988–94, ed Making Sense of Shopping 1988–94, asst dir of public affrs BAA plc 1994–; *Recreations* opera, reading, writing; *Style*— Andrew Currie, Esq; ✉ 115 Northside, Clapham Common, London SW4 9SW; BAA plc, 130 Wilton Road, London SW1V 1LQ (☎ 0171 932 6735, fax 0171 932 6783)

CURRIE, (Joseph) Austin; s of John Currie (d 1979), of Mullaghmarget, Dungannon, Co Tyrone, and Mary Currie, *née* O'Donnell (d 1984); *b* 11 Oct 1939; *Educ* Edendork PES, St Patrick's Acad Dungannon, Queen's Univ Belfast (BA); *m* 13 Jan 1968, Annita, *née* Lynch; 2 s (Dualta b 1971, Austin b 1974), 3 da (Estelle b 1968, Emer b 1979, Caitriona b 1970); *Career* lectr, conslt, writer, broadcaster; MP N Ireland 1964–72, memb N Ireland Assembly 1973–75, min of Housing Local Govt and Planning 1974; memb: NI Constitutional Convention 1975–76, NI Assembly 1980–84; elected TD (Fine Gael) for Dublin West 1989–, min of state Depts of Health, Justice and Educn 1994–; appointed to Anglo-Irish Inter Parly Gp 1989, Irish presidential candidate 1990; front bench spokesperson on equality and law reform 1994–; *Recreations* golf, snooker, Gaelic football; *Style*— J Austin Currie, TD; ✉ Tullydraw, Ballyowen Lane, Lucan, Co Dublin, Ireland

CURRIE, Brian Murdoch; s of William Murdoch Currie (d 1984), and Dorothy, *née* Holloway; *b* 20 Dec 1934; *Educ* Blundell's (open scholar), Oriel Coll Oxford (open scholar, MA); *m* 21 Oct 1961, Patricia Maria, da of Capt Frederick Eaton-Farr (d 1945); 3 s (Murdoch b 1964, Lachlan b 1967, Gregor b 1975), 1 da (Lucinda b 1966); *Career* Subaltern RTR 1957–59; Arthur Andersen: articled clerk 1959–62, qualified CA 1962, ptnr 1970–90, managing ptnr London 1977–82; fin memb HMSO Bd 1972–74, inspr Dept of Trade 1978–81; memb: Restrictive Practices Ct 1979–, Take-over Panel (occasional) 1989–; dep chm Fin Reporting Cncl 1996–; ICAEW: memb Cncl and Mgmnt Ctee 1988–, vice chm Fin Reporting and Auditing Group 1990–92, chm Practice Regulation Directorate 1992–93, chm CAs Jt Ethics Ctee 1994–95, vice pres 1994–95, dep pres 1995–96, pres 1996–97; chm Public Sector Liaison Gp of Accounting Standards Ctee 1984–86; memb Euro Ctee of Br Invisibles 1991–95; lay memb GDC; tstee Oriel Coll Devpt Tst 1979–94; memb Ct of Assts Worshipful Co of Chartered Accountants; fell Inst of Ops Mgmnt (memb Nat Cncl 1970–73), FIMC; *Recreations* Exmoor and natural history; *Clubs* Athenaeum, Pluralists; *Style*— Brian Currie, Esq; ✉ Westbrook House, Bampton, Devon EX16 9HU (☎ 01398 331418)

CURRIE, Sir Donald Scott; 7 Bt (UK 1847); s of George Donald Currie (d 1980), and Janet, *née* Scott; suc unc, Sir Alick Bradley Currie, 6 Bt (d 1987); *b* 16 Jan 1930; *m* 1, 1948 (m dis 1951), Charlotte, da of Charles Johnstone, of Mesa, Arizona, USA; 1 s (Donald Mark b 1949, d 1994), 2 da (Julia Ann (Mrs Eugene R Gangaware) b 1950, Janet Sue (Mrs Robert E Buck) b (twin) 1950); m 2, 30 April 1952, Barbara Lee (d 1993), da of A P Garnier, of California; 1 s (Gary Dwayne b 1953), 2 da (Tina Marie (Mrs Linneman) b 1955, Kathren Evelyn (Mrs Earl Avara) b 1959); m 3, 10 Dec 1994, Barbara Lou Lebsack, da of Joshua I Fenn, of Kansas; *Heir* gs, Mark Donald Currie b 1970; *Career* US Dept of the Interior; US Nat Park Serv; *Style*— Sir Donald Currie, Bt

CURRIE, Edwina; MP (C) Derbyshire South (majority 4,658); da of late Simon Cohen; *b* 13 Oct 1946; *Educ* Liverpool Inst, St Anne's Coll Oxford (MA), LSE (MSc); *m* 1972, Raymond Frank Currie, *qv*; 2 da; *Career* teacher and lectr 1972–81, head Dept of Business Studies Bromsgrove Sch 1978–81; city cncllr Birmingham 1975–86; memb: Birmingham AHA 1975–82, Birmingham Community Rels Cncl 1979–83; chm: Birmingham Social Servs Ctee 1979–80, Central Birmingham Health Authy 1981–83, Birmingham Housing Ctee 1982–83; MP (C) Derbyshire South 1983–, memb Select Ctee on Social Servs 1983–86, Parly private sec to Keith Joseph Sec of State for Educn 1986, Parly under sec DHSS, Min for Women's Health 1986–88; elected nat chm Cons Gp for Europe 1995, vice-chm European Movement 1995, jt chm Future of Europe Tst; columnist Today Newspaper 1990–91; Assoc of Speakers Clubs Speaker of the Year 1990; Campaigner of the Year Spectator Parliamentarian of the Year Awards 1994; *Books* Life Lines (1989), What Women Want (1990), Three Line Quips (1992), A Parliamentary Affair (1994), A Woman's Place (1996); numerous articles and short stories; *Recreations* family, writing, domestic arts; *Clubs* Swadlincote Cons (Derbys); *Style*— Mrs Edwina Currie, MP; ✉ House of Commons, London SW1A OAA

CURRIE, Ian Hamilton; s of John Currie (d 1984), and Vera Matilda Currie, *née* Lea; *b* 9 March 1948; *Educ* Portsmouth Northern GS; *m* 22 Feb 1972, Catherine Helen, da of Ernest William Pink (d 1983); 2 da (Victoria Catherine b 1979, Jacqueline Neoma b 1983); *Career* fin dir Gieves Group plc; dir: Gieves & Hawkes Ltd, Gieves & Hawkes International Ltd; chm: Chivers Press Ltd, Roundabout Garages Ltd, Pullinger Interiors and Furnishings Ltd; FCA (England and Wales) 1970; *Recreations* cruiser sailing; *Clubs* Portchester Sailing (cdre); *Style*— Ian Currie, Esq; ✉ 2 Church Rd, Hayling Island, Hants (☎ 01705 462966, fax 01705 461240, car 0836 270166)

CURRIE, James McGill; s of late David Currie, of Kilmarnock (Scotland), and Mary, *née* Smith; *b* 17 Nov 1941; *Educ* St Joseph's Sch Kilmarnock, Blairs Coll Aberdeen, Royal Scots Coll, Valladolid (Spain), Univ of Glasgow (MA); *m* 27 June 1968, Evelyn Barbara, da of Alexander Malcolm Macintyre, of Glasgow; 1 s (Alister John b 1971), 1 da (Jennifer b 1973); *Career* civil servant; asst princ Scot Home and Health Dept 1968–72, Scot Educn Dept 1972–75; asst sec: Tport Policy 1977–80, Industl Devpt 1981–82; cnsllr for Social Affrs and Tport at UK Perm Representation to EEC in Brussels 1982–86, dir Euro Regnl Devpt Fund of Euro Cmmn (Brussels) 1987–89, chef de cabinet to Sir Leon Brittan 1989–92, dep ambass at EC Delgn to US in Washington 1993–96, dir gen Customs and Indirect Taxation (DG XXI) 1996–; *Recreations* guitar, tennis, good food; *Style—* James M Currie, Esq; ✉ European Commission (DG XXI), 200 Rue de la Loi, 1049 Brussels, Belgium

CURRIE, Kenneth Alexander (Ken); s of Alexander Currie, of Barrhead, and Georgina, *née* Ruddie; *b* 9 March 1960; *Educ* Barrhead HS, John Nielson Sch Paisley, Paisley Coll of Technol, Glasgow Sch of Art (Elizabeth Greenshields Fndn scholar, Cargill scholar, BA, Dip of Postgrad Studies, Newberry medal); *m* July 1992, Marie Barbour; 1 da (Eilidh Barbour b 27 Dec 1993); *Career* artist; *Solo Exhibitions* Art and Social Commitment (with Keith Ross, Glasgow Arts Centre) 1982, New Work from Glasgow (Arnolfini, Bristol) 1986, Third Eye Centre Glasgow 1988, Raab Galerie Berlin 1988, Story from Glasgow (Kelvingrove Museum, Glasgow) 1990, Raab Gallery London 1991, Raab Gallery Berlin 1993, Galerie Christian Dam Copenhagen 1994, Raab Boukamel Gallery London 1995; *Group Exhibitions* incl: New Image Glasgow (Third Eye Centre and tour) 1985–86, New Art New World (Christie's) 1986, A Cabinet of Drawing (Gimpels Fils) 1986, The Vigorous Imagination (Scottish Nat Gallery of Modern Art) 1987, Art History (Hayward Gallery) 1987, Obsessions (Raab Gallery) 1987, The Lion Rampant: New Scottish Paintings & Photography (Artspace, San Francisco) 1988–89, Scottish Art since 1900 (Scottish Nat Gallery of Modern Art and Barbican Art Gallery) 1989–90, Metamorphosis (Raab Gallery) 1989–90, Glasgow's Great British Art Exhibition (Art Gallery and Museum Kelvingrove) 1990, Mischaire le Carte Immague Speculare (Gian Ferrari Arte Contemporanea) 1990–91; *Works in Public Collections* Scottish Arts Cncl Edinburgh, Scottish Nat Gallery of Modern Art, Macmaster Univ Art Gallery Toronto, Br Cncl, Aberdeen Art Gallery, Nottingham Castle Museum, City of Manchester Art Gallery, Glasgow museums and art galleries; *Style—* Ken Currie, Esq; ✉ Raab Gallery, 9 Cork Street, London

CURRIE, Raymond Frank (Ray); s of William Murdoch Currie (d 1984), and Dorothy, *née* Holloway (d 1995), of South Molton, Devon; *b* 11 May 1945; *Educ* Blundell's, The Loomis Sch Windsor Connecticut, Corpus Christi Coll Cambridge (exhibitioner, BA); *m* 1 July 1972, Edwina Currie, MP, *qv*, da of Simon Cohen; 2 da (Deborah Josephine b 30 Oct 1974, Susannah Elizabeth b 19 May 1977); *Career* Arthur Andersen: articled clerk 1967–70, qualified ACA 1970 (FCA 1974), London 1970–73, fndr memb Birmingham practice 1973–79, dir of training 1979–96; dir Tower House Training Ltd 1996–; memb Bd of Accreditation of Educn Courses CCAB 1985–95 (chm 1992–95); ICAEW: chm Dist Training Bd 1986–90, memb Educn and Training Directorate 1989–, chm Educn & Assessment Ctee 1995–, memb Cncl 1994–; memb Business & Mgmnt Studies Ctee CNAA 1986–91; MITD 1983, MIPM 1987; *Recreations* all sports - playing some slowly, following all enthusiastically, reading, cinema; *Clubs* Reform, Le Beaujolais, MCC, Yorkshire CCC, Swadlincote Conservative; *Style—* Ray Currie, Esq; ✉ Tower House Training Ltd, The Tower House, Findern, Derby DE65 6AP (☎ 01283 704794, fax 01283 703920); Flat 1 EE, 1 Carlisle Place, London SW1P 1NP (☎ 0171 828 6057)

CURRIE-CATHEY, (Vernon Howard) Peter; s of Edward Stanley Currie-Cathey, and Eileen Peggy, *née* Fryer; *b* 21 Aug 1941; *Educ* Sloane GS; *m* 2 Feb 1963, Jean Sylvia, *née* Rice; 2 s (James Vernon b 24 April 1967, Stuart Alex b 25 Sept 1969); *Career* former ptnr Nigel Rose & Ptnrs (chartered quantity surveyors) currently conslt; Freeman City of London, memb Worshipful Co of Arbitrators; FRICS 1964, FCIArb 1973; *Recreations* badminton; *Style—* Peter Currie-Cathey, Esq; ✉ Nigel Rose & Partners, 6 Broad St, Wokingham, Berks RG11 1AB (☎ 0118 977 4702, fax 0118 977 4829)

CURRIE OF MARYLEBONE, Baron (Life Peer UK 1996), of Marylebone in the City of Westminster; David Anthony Currie; s of Kennedy Moir Currie (d 1972), of London, and Marjorie, *née* Thompson; *b* 9 Dec 1946; *Educ* Battersea GS, Univ of Manchester (BSc), Univ of Birmingham (M Soc Sci), Univ of London (PhD); *m* 9 July 1975 (m dis), Shaziye, da of Hussein Gazioglu, of Nicosia, Cyprus; 2 s (Hon James Mehmet b 9 April 1978, Hon Timothy Timur b 8 May 1982); m 2, 24 March 1995, Angela Mary Piers Dumas; *Career* Hoare and Govett Co 1971–72, Economic Models 1972; QMC London: lectr 1972–79, reader 1979–81, prof of economics 1981–88; London Business Sch: prof of economics 1988–, dir of Centre for Economic Forecasting 1988–95, dep princ 1992–95; memb: HM Treasy Panel of Independent Forecasters 1992–95, Advsy Bd for the Research Cncls 1992–93, Advsy Cmmn RPI 1992–; tstee Joseph Rowntree Reform Tst 1991–; memb Royal Econ Soc; *Books* Advances in Monetary Economics (ed, 1985), The Operation and Regulation of Financial Markets (ed, 1986), Macroeconomic Interactions between North and South (ed, 1988), Macroeconomic Policies in an Interdependent World (ed, 1989), Rules, Reputation and Macroeconomic Policy Coordination (1993), EMU: Problems in the Transition to a Single European Currency (ed, 1995), North-South Linkages and International Macroeconomic Policy (ed, 1995); *Recreations* music, literature, swimming; *Style—* The Rt Hon Lord Currie of Marylebone; ✉ London Business School, Sussex Place, Regents Park, London NW1 4SA (☎ 0171 262 5050, fax 0171 402 0718 and 0171 724 6069, telex 27461 LONBISKOL G)

CURRY, Rt Hon David Maurice; PC (1996), MP (C) Skipton and Ripon (majority 19,330); s of Thomas Harold Curry and late Florence Joan, *née* Tyerman; *b* 13 June 1944; *Educ* Ripon GS, CCC Oxford, Kennedy Sch of Govt Harvard (Kennedy scholar); *m* 1971, Anne Helene Maud Roullet; 1 s, 2 da; *Career* reporter: Newcastle Journal 1967–70, Financial Times 1970–79 (trade ed, international companies ed, Brussels correspondent, Paris correspondent, European news ed); sec Anglo-American Press Assoc of Paris 1978–79, fndr Paris Cons Assoc 1977; European Parliament: MEP (EDG) NE Essex 1979–89, chm Agric Ctee 1982–84 (yst ctee chm in Euro Parliament's history), Cons spokesman Budget Ctee 1984–, rapporteur gen EEC Budget 1987; MP (C) Skipton and Ripon 1987–, min of state MAFF 1992–93 (Parly sec 1989–92); min of state DOE: for planning and local govt 1993–94, for local govt, housing and urban regeneration 1994–; *Books* The Food War: the EEC-US Conflict in Food Trade (1982); *Recreations* digging, windsurfing; *Style—* The Rt Hon David Curry, MP; ✉ Newland End, Arkesden, Essex CB11 4HF (☎ 01799 85368); Constituency office: 19 Otley St, Skipton, N Yorks BD19 1DY (☎ 01756 792092)

CURRY, Jilly Mary; da of (Thomas) Peter Ellison Curry, QC, *qv*, of Hurlands, Dunsfold, Surrey, and Pamela Joyce, *née* Holmes; *b* 29 Nov 1961; *Educ* Royal Naval Sch Haslemere, Queen Anne's Sch Caversham; *m* 1990, Robin Wallace, *qv*; 1 s (Lloyd Ellison b 13 Feb 1995); *Career* freestyle skier; memb of freestyle ski team 1984, first Br girl to win a world cup skiing event, Gold medal for the combined freestyle event at World Cup La Clusaz France 1990, competed Winter Olympics Albertville (4th in Aerials event) 1992 and Lillehammer 1994; *Recreations* tennis, squash, water-skiing, trampolining, foreign languages; *Style—* Miss Jilly Curry; ✉ Thatches, 103 High Street, Codford St Peter, Wilts BA12 0NE

CURRY, John Arthur Hugh; s of Col Alfred Curry (d 1975), and Mercia, *née* Friedlander; *b* 7 June 1938; *Educ* KCS Wimbledon, St Edmund Hall Oxford (MA, rugby and tennis blues), Harvard Graduate Sch of Business Admin (MBA); *m* 1962, Anne Rosemary, *née* Lewis; 3 s, 1 da; *Career* chartered accountant; chm ACAL plc 1986–; non-exec dir: Unitech plc until 1996, Dixons Group plc, Foreign & Commonwealth Smaller Companies PLC; Liveryman Worshipful Co of Chartered Accountants; FCA; *Recreations* tennis, rugby, travel; *Clubs* All England Lawn Tennis and Croquet (chm), Int Lawn Tennis Club of GB, Queens; *Style—* John Curry, Esq; ✉ Stokewood Park House, Droxford, Hants SO32 3QY

CURRY, Mark Preston; s of Arthur Stanley Curry (d 1967), and Lily Parker; *b* 27 Aug 1961; *Educ* Brigshaw Comp Sch W Yorks; *Career* actor and television presenter; *Theatre* incl: extensive theatre work since 1988 incl: Billy in Billy Liar (nat tour) 1988, Move Over Mrs Markham, Alastair Spenlow 1989–90, How The Other Half Loves, Fancourt Babberley in Century Prodn of Charley's Aunt (nat tour) 1992, Tassell in Theatre Royal Windsor's celebration prodn of The Happiest Days of Your Life Autumn 1993, co-starred in Woman in Black (Fortune) June-Dec 1994, Noises Off (Mobil Touring Theatre) 1995, Gordon in Nevilles Island (Manchester Library Theatre) 1996, Vernon in They're Playing our Song (Haymarket Basingstoke) 1996, Don Luckwood in Singin' in the Rain (Theatre Royal Haymarket) 1996; *Television* roles incl: Tim in Sounding Brass (ATV) 1979, Bread (BBC) 1990, Close to Home 1990, London's Burning 1990; as presenter incl: Junior Showtime (YTV) 1969–74, Calendar Kids (YTV) 1977–78, Get Set For Summer (BBC) 1981–83, The Saturday Picture Show (BBC) 1984–86, Screen Test 1984–85, Make 'Em Laugh (BBC) 1984–85, Treasure Houses (BBC) 1984–85, Blue Peter (BBC) 1986–90, Get Grammar series (BBC TV Schs) 1993, Record Breakers (BBC) 1994–96; appeared in two children's Royal Variety Performances and The Queen Mother's 90th Birthday Gala (Palladium) 1990; *Radio* presenter BBC Radio 5: On Your Marks 1990–92, Weekend Edition 1992–93; memb BBC Radio Wimbledon commentary team 1991, 1992 and 1993 (for TV 1995); *Awards* incl: winner TV & Radio Industries Club Award for Blue Peter 1987 and On Your Marks 1991, Sony nomination On Your Marks 1991, BAFTA nomination for best Children's Prog for Blue Peter 1988; *Recreations* tennis; *Style—* Mark Curry, Esq; ✉ c/o Jon Roseman Agencies Ltd, 46 Sutton Court Road, London W4 4NL (☎ 0181 742 0552, fax 0181 742 0554)

CURRY, (Thomas) Peter Ellison; QC (1973); s of Maj F R P Curry, RA (d 1955), and Sybil, *née* Woods (d 1996); *b* 22 July 1921; *Educ* Tonbridge, Oriel Coll Oxford (MA); *m* 30 March 1950, Pamela Joyce, da of Gp Capt A J Holmes, AFC (d 1950); 2 s (Guy b 1952, Iain b 1953), 2 da (Fleur b 1956, Jilly Mary Curry, *qv*, b 1959); *Career* enlisted 1939, offr cadet 1940, OCTU Bangalore and Deolali India 1941, 1 Indian Field Regt Indian Artillery (India, North West Frontier, Burma, Assam) 1941–44, air trg course Peshawar 1944, Capt Air Force Devpt Centre Amesbury 1944, air directorate War Office GSO 3 1945–46; called to the Bar Middle Temple 1953, QC 1966 (resigned 1967), slr Freshfields 1967, returned to Bar 1970, bencher Middle Temple 1979, head of chambers; pres Aircraft and Shipbuilding Industries Arbitration Tbnl 1978–80; GB athletics rep Olympic Games 1948, Br 3000m steeplechase champion 1948, winner Oxford and Cambridge Cross Country 1947 and 1948; squash: represented Army, Oxford Univ, Sussex; asst scoutmaster Stepney Sea Scouts 1946; chm: Walston House Boys and Girls' Club 1951, Cobham Cons Assoc 1958; vice chm Barristers Benevolent Assoc 1990–91 (treas 1964–71 and 1984–90), chm Chancery Bar Assoc 1980–85, tstee Stable Lads Welfare Tst 1986–92; *Recreations* lawn tennis, gardening, farming, the turf; *Clubs* Army & Navy; *Style—* Peter Curry, Esq, QC; ✉ Hurlands, Dunsfold, Surrey (☎ 01483 200356); 5 Victoria Grove Mews, London W2; 4 Stone Buildings, Lincoln's Inn, London WC2 (☎ 0171 242 5524, fax 0171 831 9152/0483 200 356)

CURRY, Stephen Robert; s of Stanley Curry (d 1964), of Clitheroe, Lancashire, and Norah, *née* Rowlinson; *b* 17 Oct 1942; *Educ* Clitheroe Royal GS, Manchester Coll of Commerce (journalism course); *m* Angela, *née* Blackshaw; 1 s (Michael b 27 Jan 1970); *Career* journalist; The Blackburn Times 1959–62, Lancashire Evening Post 1963, sports reporter Head Office United Newspapers London 1964–66, chief football writer Daily Express 1980– (football reporter 1966–80); *Style—* Stephen Curry, Esq; ✉ Daily Express, Ludgate House, 245 Blackfriars Rd, London SE1 9UX (☎ 0171 928 8000/071 922 7141, car 0831 237 057)

CURTEIS, Ian Bayley; s of late John Richard Jones, of Lydd, Kent, and late Edith Marion Pomfret Cook, *née* Bayley; *b* 1 May 1935; *Educ* Slough GS, Univ of London; *m* 1, 8 July 1964 (m dis 1985), Mrs Joan MacDonald; 2 s (Tobit b 1966, Mikol b 1968); *m* 2, 12 April 1985, Joanna Trollope, *qv*, da of A G C Trollope, of Overton, Hants; 2 step da (Louise b 1969, Antonia b 1971); *Career* TV playwright, dir, actor; BBC TV script reader 1956–63, staff dir (drama) BBC and ATV 1963–67 (dir of plays by John Betjeman, John Hopkins, William Trevor and others); chm Ctee on Censorship Writers' Guild of GB 1981–85, tstee Joanna Trollope Charitable Tst 1995–; author of numerous newspaper articles and speeches on the ethics and politics of British broadcasting; FRSA 1984; *TV Plays* incl: Beethoven, Sir Alexander Fleming (BBC entry at Prague Festival 1973), Mr Rolls and Mr Royce, Long Voyage out of War (trilogy), The Folly, The Haunting, Second Time Round, A Distinct Chill, The Portland Millions, Philby, Burgess and Maclean (Br entry Monte Carlo Festival 1978, BAFTA nomination Best Play of the Year), Hess, The Atom Spies, Churchill and the Generals (Grand Prize for Best Programme of 1981 New York Int Film and TV Festival and BAFTA nomination Best Play of the Year), Suez 1956 (BAFTA Nomination Best Play of the Year), Miss Morison's Ghosts (British entry Monte Carlo Festival), BB and Lord D, The Mitford Girls; *Screenplays* Andre Malraux's La condition Humaine (1982), Lost Empires (adapted from J B Priestley), Graham Greene's The Man Within (TV), The Nightmare Years (TV 1990), The Zimmerman Telegram (1991), Gorbachev (1992), The Choir (BBC serial, 1993), Yalta (BBC, 1995); *Published Plays* A Personal Affair, Long Voyage out of War (1971), Churchill and the Generals (1979), Suez 1956 (1980), The Falklands Play (1987); *Recreations* avoiding television; *Clubs* Garrick, Beefsteak; *Style—* Ian Curteis, Esq; ✉ c/o Campbell's Office, Coutts & Co, 440 Strand, London WC2R 0QS

CURTIS, Prof Adam Sebastian Genevieve; s of Herbert Lewis Curtis, DSM (d 1974), of London, and Nora, *née* Stevens (d 1954); *b* 3 Jan 1934; *Educ* Aldenham, King's Coll Cambridge (MA), Univ of Edinburgh (PhD); *m* 3 May 1958, Ann, da of William Park (d 1993), of Berwick upon Tweed; 2 da (Penelope Jane b 1961, Susanna Clare b 1964); *Career* lectr in zoology UCL 1962–67 (hon res asst Dept of Anatomy 1957–62); Univ of Glasgow: prof of cell biology 1967–, head Molecular and Cellular Biology Div 1994–95; pres Scot Sub-Aqua Club 1972–75, memb Cncl RSE 1983–86, pres Soc for Experimental Biology 1991–93; FIBiol 1968, FRSE 1969; *Books* The Cell Surface (1967), Cell-Cell Recognition (ed, 1978); *Recreations* gardening, sports diving, making mosaics; *Style—* Prof Adam Curtis, FRSE; ✉ 2 Kirklee Circus, Glasgow G12 0TW (☎ 0141 339 2152); Laboratory of Cell Biology, University of Glasgow, Glasgow G12 8QQ (☎ 0141 330 5147, fax 0141 330 4501)

CURTIS, Anthony Samuel; s of Emanuel Curtis (d 1979), of London, and Eileen, *née* Freedman; *b* 12 March 1926; *Educ* Midhurst GS, Merton Coll Oxford (BA, MA); *m* 3 Oct 1960, Sarah, *qv*; 3 s (Job b 1961, Charles b 1963, Quentin b 1965); *Career* served RAF 1945–48; lectr Br Inst of Sorbonne 1950–51, freelance journalist and critic (The Times, New Statesman, BBC) 1952–55, on staff Times Literary Supplement 1955–58 (dep ed 1959–60), Harkness fell in journalism at Yale and elsewhere USA 1958–59, literary ed Sunday Telegraph 1960–70; Financial Times: arts and literary ed 1970–72, literary ed 1972–89, chief book critic 1989–94; theatre articles London Magazine; numerous broadcasts on Radio 3 and 4, author of features and radio plays, reg appearances on

Critics Forum; Br Cncl lectr France & India; memb Soc of Authors (tstee pension fund), treas Royal Lit Fund; FRSA 1990; *Publications include* The Pattern of Maugham (1974), Somerset Maugham (biography, 1977), The Rise and Fall of the Matinée Idol (ed, 1977), The Critical Heritage - Somerset Maugham (ed with John Whitehead, 1987), The Nonesuch Storytellers - Somerset Maughan (ed and intro, 1990); *Recreations* correspondence chess, backgammon; *Clubs* Garrick, Travellers', Beefsteak; *Style—* Anthony Curtis, Esq; ✉ 9 Essex Villas, London W8 7BP (☎ 0171 937 7798)

CURTIS, Prof Charles David; s of Flt Lt Charles Frederick Curtis, and Kate Margaret, *née* Jackson (d 1988); *b* 11 Nov 1939; *Educ* High Storrs GS Sheffield, Imperial Coll London, Univ of Sheffield (BSc, PhD); *m* 24 Nov 1963, Diana Joy, da of Lionel Sidney Saxty (d 1990), of Holmfirth Grove, Sheffield; 2 da (Sarah b 1965, Kate b 1968); *Career* Univ of Sheffield 1965–88 (successively lectr, reader, prof); Univ of Manchester: head of Dept 1989–92, prof 1992–, research dean Faculty of Science and Engrg 1994–; visiting prof UCLA 1970–71, industl fell Marathon Oil Co Denver 1973, CSPG visiting prof Univ of Calgary 1981, visiting prof Tongji Univ Shanghai China 1984, res assoc Br Petroleum Res Centre 1987–88, conslt BP Research International 1988–94, conslt ENRICERCHE Milan 1994–; various pubns in jls; cncl memb Natural Environment Res Cncl 1990–93; memb: Scientific and Educn Ctees Royal Soc 1977–89, CNAA 1980–89, Radioactive Waste Management Advsy Ctee 1994–, Geological Soc of London; FGS 1977 (pres 1992–94); *Recreations* mountaineering, gardening, writing; *Style—* Prof Charles Curtis; ✉ Townhead Cottage, Edale Road, Hope S30 2RF; Department of Earth Sciences, University of Manchester, Oxford Rd, Manchester M13 9PL (☎ 0161 275 3802, fax 0161 275 3947)

CURTIS, Maj Edward Philip; s of Maj Gerald Edward Curtis (d 1975), of Cwmbach Lodge, Glasbury-on-Wye, via Hereford, and Philippa, *née* Alcock (d 1975); hp of kinsman, Sir William Peter Curtis, 7 Bt, *qv*; *b* 25 June 1940; *Educ* Bradfield, RMA Sandhurst; *m* 1978, Catherine Mary, da of Henry Armstrong, of Christchurch, NZ; 2 s (George Edward b 1980, Patrick James b 1986), 2 da (Henrietta Rose b 1979, Clementine Z b 1983); *Career* Maj 16/5 The Queen's Royal Lancers, served Germany BAOR, Far E, Mid E, UK, cmmnd 1961; Staff Offr 7 Armd Bde 1968–70, Adj 16/5 Lancers 1971, Sqn Ldr 16/5 Lancers 1971–73, Co Cdr RMA Sandhurst 1973–75, Staff Offr HQ 38 Gp RAF 1976–77, ret 1977; stockbroker Harris Allday Lea and Brooks; MSI (Dip); *Recreations* shooting, fishing, cricket, squash, philately, bridge; *Clubs* MCC, Free Foresters, I Zingari, Salmon and Trout; *Style—* Maj Edward Curtis; ✉ Lower Court, Bitterley, Ludlow, Shropshire SY8 3HF (☎ 01584 891052); office (☎ 01584 872391, fax 01584 876884)

CURTIS, Most Rev (Ernest) Edwin; CBE (1976); s of Ernest John Curtis (d 1937), of Stalbridge, Dorset, and Zoe, *née* Tite (d 1927); *b* 24 Dec 1906; *Educ* Foster's Sch Sherborne, Univ of London, Royal Coll of Science (BSc, Dip Ed), Wells Theol Coll; *m* 1, 24 Dec 1937, Dorothy Anne (d 1965), da of John Hill; 1 s (Robert b 17 April 1940), 1 da (Audrey (Mrs Buckingham) b 16 Dec 1938); m 2, 7 Feb 1970, Evelyn Mary, da of Herbert Josling; *Career* sr maths master Lindisfarne Coll Westcliff-on-Sea 1928–31, civil chaplain and princ St Paul's Theol Coll Mauritius 1937–45; vicar: All Saints Portsea 1947–55, St John's Lockheath 1955–66; rural dean Alverstoke Portsmouth 1965–66; bishop: Mauritius and Seychelles 1966–73, Mauritius 1973–76; archbishop of Anglican Province of Indian Ocean 1973–76; hon asst bishop of Portsmouth 1976–; *Style—* The Most Rev Archbishop Edwin Curtis, CBE; ✉ 5 Elizabeth Gardens, Havenstreet, Ryde, Isle of Wight PO33 4DU (☎ 01983 883049)

CURTIS, James William Ockford; QC (1993); s of Eric William Curtis, MC, of Bedford, and Margaret Joan, *née* Blunt, of Bedford; *b* 2 Sept 1946; *Educ* Bedford Sch, Worcester Coll Oxford (MA jurisprudence); *m* 1985, Genevra Fiona Penelope Victoria Caws, QC, *qv*, da of Richard Byron Caws, CBE, *qv*; 1 da (Polly Joanna Sarah Clare b 26 Nov 1987); *Career* called to the Bar Inner Temple 1970, pupillages with William Gage (now Hon Mr Justice Gage), and Neil Denison (now The Common Serjeant of London), recorder of the Crown Court 1991–; *Recreations* farming, field sports, skiing, classics; *Clubs* Reform, Flyfishers'; *Style—* James Curtis, Esq, QC; ✉ 6 King's Bench Walk, Temple, London EC4Y 7DR (☎ 0171 583 0410, fax 0171 353 8791)

CURTIS, John Gilbert; s of late Col A G Curtis; *b* 2 Oct 1932; *Educ* Charterhouse, Worcester Coll Oxford; *m* 1963, Susan Judith, *née* Whitefield; 2 s; *Career* Lt Royal Green Jackets; dir Matheson and Co Ltd 1967–; past master Worshipful Co of Leathersellers; *Clubs* Oriental; *Style—* John Curtis, Esq; ✉ Clayhurst, Odiham, Hants RG29 1JG; Matheson and Co Ltd, 3 Lombard St, London EC3V 9AQ (☎ 0171 528 4000)

CURTIS, Paul Francis; s of Thomas Joseph Curtis (d 1943), of Oxford, and Kathleen Mary, *née* Philips; *b* 15 Nov 1940; *Educ* S Bonaventures GS, LSE (BSc (Econ), dep pres of Union); *m* 24 Aug 1968, Maria Victoria, da of Adam Manduke; 1 s (Rupert Paul b 1 Sept 1977); *Career* Euro merchandising mangr Electric Storage Battery Co 1963–66, advtg exec Philips Electrical Ltd 1966–67, brands mangr Ranks Hovis McDougall Ltd 1967–69, sr brands mangr Van den Berghs 1969–70, mktg dir Mars Confectionery Slough Berks 1970–85, exec dir and pres int mktg International Distillers & Vintners 1985–96, gp mktg dir Grand Metropolitan plc 1996–; non-exec dir Royal Doulton plc 1996–; memb: Cncl ISBA, Advsy Ctee ITC; *Recreations* shooting, theatre, Yorkshire; *Style—* Paul Curtis, Esq; ✉ Grand Metropolitan plc, 8 Henrietta Place, London W1M 9AG (☎ 0171 518 5300, fax 0171 518 4676)

CURTIS, Penelope; da of Adam S G Curtis, of Glasgow, and Ann, *née* Park; *b* 24 Aug 1961; *Educ* Westbourne Sch, Corpus Christi Coll Oxford (BA), Courtauld Inst Univ of London (MA, PhD); *Career* Tate Gall Liverpool 1988–94, head Henry Moore Centre for the Study of Sculpture 1994–; *Exhibitions* curator (Tate Gall Liverpool): Modern British Sculpture from the Collection 1988, Strongholds - New Art from Ireland 1991, Barbara Hepworth - A Retrospective 1994; *Style—* Dr Penelope Curtis; ✉ Centre for the Study of Sculpture, Henry Moore Institute, 74 The Headrow, Leeds, West Yorks LS1 3AA (☎ 0113 246 9469, fax 0113 246 1481)

CURTIS, Penelope Jane Hamilton (Mrs Christopher Crouch); da of Thomas Curtis, of Buckland, Surrey, and Nancy Frances Mary, *née* Pearson; *b* 20 Feb 1957; *Educ* St Michael's Sch Oxted Surrey, Univ of Exeter (LLB, Lloyd Parry prize, Maxwell law prize); *m* 22 Aug 1987, Christopher Charles Crouch, s of Francis Harry Anson Crouch; 2 da (Alexandra b 1991, Serena b 1994); *Career* Freshfields: articled clerk 1979–81, slr 1981–87; N M Rothschild: head Compliance Dept 1987–, dir 1989–; memb City of London Slrs Co, Freeman City of London; memb Law Soc; *Recreations* theatre, opera, walking; *Style—* Ms Penelope Curtis; ✉ 6 Earls Court Gardens, London SW5 0TD; N M Rothschild & Sons Ltd, New Court, St Swithin's Lane, London EC4P 4DU (☎ 0171 280 5000, fax 0171 929 1643)

CURTIS, Hon Mr Justice; Hon Sir Richard Herbert Curtis; kt (1992); *b* 24 May 1933; *Educ* Shrewsbury, Oxford Univ (MA); *Career* called to the Bar Inner Temple 1958, recorder of the Crown Ct 1974–89, QC 1977; hon recorder City of Hereford 1981–92, bencher Inner Temple 1985–, a pres Mental Health Review Tbnls 1983–92, recorder City of Birmingham and sr circuit judge Oxford and Midland Circuit 1989–92; judge of the High Court of Justice (Queen's Bench Div) 1992–; presiding judge Wales and Chester Circuit 1994–; *Style—* The Hon Mr Justice Curtis; ✉ Royal Courts of Justice, Strand, London WC2A 2LL

CURTIS, Sarah; JP (Inner London, 1978); da of Dr Carl Myers (d 1963), of Preston, Lancs, and Ruth, *née* Stross (d 1973); *b* 21 May 1936; *Educ* Roedean (scholar), Sorbonne, St Hugh's Coll Oxford (exhibitioner, MA, pres OU Lib Club); *m* 3 Oct 1960, Anthony Curtis, *qv*; 3 s (Job b 1961, Charles b 1963, Quentin b 1965); *Career* Times Educnl Supplement 1958–59, The Times 1959–61, freelance journalist and reviewer (The Times, New Society, TES, TLS, Financial Times, Guardian, New Statesman & Society, BBC Radio 4 and World Service) 1961–, educn and info offr Family Planning Assoc SW London 1971–73, res project dir Wandsworth Cncl for Community Relations 1975–76, ed Adoption & Fostering (jl of British Agencies for Adoption & Fostering) 1976–87, ed RSA Journal and head of communications RSA 1989–95; Parly candidate (Lib) Enfield N Feb and Nov 1974; memb: Exec Bd UK Ctee for UNICEF 1971–84, Lord Chllr's Advsy Ctee on JPs for Inner London 1982–89, Mgmnt Ctee Ind Adoption 1988–; chm Youth and Family Cts Inner London; FRSA 1995; *Books* New Orbits (jt author, 1959), High Time for Radicals (jt author, 1960), Thinkstrip series (1976–79), Looking at Handicap (ed, 1982), It's Your Life series (jt author, 1983), From Asthma to Thalassaemia (ed, 1986), St Hugh's - 100 Years of Women's Education in Oxford (contrib, 1986), Juvenile Offending (1989); *Recreations* reading novels, gardening and cooking; *Style—* Mrs Sarah Curtis; ✉ 9 Essex Villas, London W8 7BP (☎ 0171 937 7798)

CURTIS, Stephen Russell; s of Barry Russell, and Joyce Muriel, *née* Smith; *b* 27 Feb 1948; *Educ* Forest Sch London, Univ of Exeter (BA); *m* 1972, Gillian Mary, *née* Pitkin; 3 s, 1 da; *Career* asst statistician Business Statistics Office 1970–72; DTI: joined 1972, statistician Export Statistics 1975–78, statistician 1978–83, chief statistician 1983–85; Business Statistical Office: registrar of Cos 1985–90, chief exec 1988–90; chief exec DVLA 1990–95, chief exec designate Employment Tbnl Serv 1996, md Companies and Info Div Jordans Ltd 1997–; *Recreations* walking, travel, photography; *Clubs* Civil Service; *Style—* Stephen Curtis, Esq; ✉ Jordans Ltd, 21 St Thomas Street, Bristol BS1 6JS

CURTIS, Timothy Stephen (Tim); s of Bruce Curtis, of Malvern, Worcs, and Betty Holliday, *née* Roebuck; *b* 15 Jan 1960; *Educ* Royal GS Worcester, Hatfield Coll Durham, Magdalene Coll Cambridge (Cricket blue); *m* 21 Sept 1985, Philippa Neild, da of David Neild Cornock-Taylor; 1 da (Jennifer May b 9 Feb 1991), 1 s (Andrew b 17 Feb 1993); *Career* professional cricketer; Worcestershire CCC: first class debut 1979, awarded county cap 1984, vice capt 1990–92, capt 1992–95; England NCA under 19 tour Canada 1979; 5 Test match appearances: 2 v W Indies (Headingley, Oval) 1988, 3 v Aust (Edgbaston, Old Trafford, Trent Bridge) 1989; honours: Co Championship 1988 and 1989, Refuge Assurance League 1987 and 1988, winners Benson and Hedges Cup 1991 (runners-up 1990 and 1994), winners Nat West Trophy 1994 (runners-up 1988); schoolmaster Royal GS Worcester during two winter terms, chm Professional Cricketers' Assoc 1989–; *Recreations* all sports, gardening, reading novels, socialising; *Style—* Tim Curtis, Esq; ✉ Worcestershire CCC, County Ground, New Road, Worcester (☎ 01905 422694)

CURTIS, Sir William Peter; 7 Bt (UK 1802), of Cullands Grove, Middlesex; s of Sir Peter Curtis, 6 Bt (d 1976), and Joan Margaret, *née* Nicholson; *b* 9 April 1935; *Educ* Winchester, Trinity Coll Oxford (MA), RAC Cirencester; *Heir* kinsman, Maj Edward Philip Curtis b 25 June 1940; *Career* late 16/5 Lancers; *Style—* Sir William Curtis, Bt

CURTISS, Air Marshal Sir John Bagot; KCB (1980, CB 1979), KBE (1982); s of Maj E F B Curtiss, RFC; *b* 6 Dec 1924; *Educ* Radley Coll, Wanganui Collegiate Sch NZ, Worcester Coll Oxford; *m* 1946, Peggy Drughorn, da of Edward Bowie; 3 s (Peter, Simon, Jonathan), 1 da (Patricia); *Career* RAF 1942, flying Bomber and Fighter Cmds 1942–74, Dir Gen Orgn RAF 1975–77, Cmdt Staff Coll 1977–80, AOC No 18 Gp 1980–83, Air Cdr Falklands Campaign 1982; dir and chief exec Soc of Aerospace Cos 1984–89; chm: Meml Fund For Disaster Relief USA Branch 1990–, Pathfinders Disaster Relief Organisation 1995–; pres: Cncl Air League 1985–, Aircrew Assoc 1986–; Liveryman Worshipful Co of Coachmakers & Coach Harness Makers; chm RAF Oxford & Cambridge Soc 1982–; CIMgt 1981, FRAeS 1984; *Clubs* RAF, MCC, Pilgrims, Colonels (pres); *Style—* Air Marshal Sir John Curtiss, KCB, KBE; ✉ 13–17 Ironmonger Row, London EC1V 3QN (☎ 0171 250 1700, fax 0171 250 1511)

CURTOIS, Brian Richard; s of Leslie Howard Curtois (d 1991), of Leigh-on-Sea, Essex, and Marjorie Joyce Louise, *née* Fenton (d 1966); *b* 30 Dec 1936; *Educ* Dulwich; *m* 29 Sept 1962, Brenda Rosemary, da of late Donald Osman Copeland; 1 s (Martin Ralph b 25 Nov 1964), 1 da (Jennifer b 18 Feb 1967); *Career* journalist; Hornchurch News 1957, Ilford Recorder 1957–59, Nottingham Evening News 1959–61, Press Association 1961–64; BBC: gen reporter 1964–70, political reporter 1970–74, dep political ed later chief political corr 1974–88, memb BBC Commons TV Project team 1988–89, chief Parly commentator 1988–92; lecturer and conslt; *Recreations* cricket, music, theatre, walking; *Clubs* Essex County Cricket; *Style—* Brian Curtois, Esq; ✉ 45 Lake Rise, Romford, Essex RM1 4DZ

CURWEN, Michael Jonathan; s of Dr Montague Curwen, and Thelma, *née* Freiberger; *b* 13 Nov 1943; *Educ* Clifton, Queen's Coll Oxford (BA); *m* 28 June 1970, (Helena) Sandra, da of Dr Charles Norman Faith; 1 s (Robert b 1974), 1 da (Nicola b 1971); *Career* called to the Bar Inner Temple 1966, recorder of the Crown Court 1989–; *Recreations* theatre, golf, gardening; *Style—* Michael Curwen, Esq; ✉ 10 Raeburn Close, London NW11 6UG; 6 Pump Court, Temple, London EC4Y 7AR (☎ 0171 583 6013, fax 0171 353 0464)

CURZON, Prof Martin Edward John; s of Stanley Arthur Curzon, of Selsdon, Surrey, and Antoinette Carmela, *née* Davies; *b* 11 May 1940; *Educ* Univ of London (BDS, PhD), Univ of Rochester (MS); *m* 1, 1964 (m dis 1992), Jennifer Anne; 3 s (Richard Martin b 1967, Thomas Paul b 1972, Neil Simon b 1974); m 2, 1994, Anne; *Career* extern Govt of BC 1965–66, lectr Univ of Bristol 1968–70, sr dental offr Govt of Canada 1970–73, chm Oral Biology Eastman Dental Center 1973–83 (fell 1966–68), prof Univ of Leeds 1983–; pres: Br Paedodontic Soc 1987–88, Euro Acad of Paediatric Dentistry 1990–94; memb: BDA, ORCA, EAPD, CAPD, AAPD, IADR, FDS 1993; *Books* Trace Elements and Dental Disease (1983); *Recreations* fell walking, gardening; *Style—* Prof Martin Curzon; ✉ 488 Otley Road, Adel, Leeds (☎ 0113 267 4709); Department of Paediatric Dentistry, University of Leeds, Clarendon Way, Leeds LS2 9LU (☎ 0113 233 6138, fax 0113 233 6140)

CURZON, Lady Mary Gaye Georgiana Lorna; *née* Curzon; da of 6 Earl Howe, CBE; *b* 21 Feb 1947; *m* 1, 1971 (m dis 1976), (Kevin) Esmond Peter Cooper-Key (d 1985), s of Sir Neil Cooper-Key, former MP; 1 da (Pandora b 1973); m 2, 1977 (m dis 1987), John Austen Anstruther-Gough-Calthorpe, s of Brig Sir Richard Anstruther-Gough-Calthorpe, 2 Bt, CBE (d 1985); 1 s (Jacobi b 1983), 2 da (Georgiana b 1978, Isabella b 1980); m 3, 29 Jan 1988, Jeffrey Bonas, s of late Harry Bonas, of Grangewood Hall, Netherseale, Burton-on-Trent; 1 da (Cressida b 1989); m 4, 17 Dec 1996, Christopher Shaw; *Style—* Lady Mary Gaye Curzon; ✉ The Old Rectory, Ovington, Alresford, Hants (☎ 01962 732821)

CURZON, Hon Peter Ghislain Nathaniel; s (by 1 m) and h of 3 Viscount Scarsdale, *qv*; *b* 6 March 1949; *Educ* Ampleforth; *m* 1983 (m dis), Karen Jackson; 1 da (Danielle b 1983); *Career* landowner (75 acres); *Recreations* The Cresta Run, skiing, golf; *Style—* The Hon Peter Curzon; ✉ Battle Barn Stud Farm, Sedlescombe, E Sussex

CUSACK, Mark Paul John; s of Capt Robert Joseph Cusack, of Dublin, and Olive Mary, *née* Byrne; *b* 28 Feb 1958; *Educ* St Paul's Sch Dublin, Trinity Coll Dublin (BBS); *m* July 1990, Susan Jane Williams; 2 da (Jessica Ruth b July 1991, Rebecca Sophie b Oct 1993); *Career* Arthur Andersen & Co 1979–83, dir and head UK res Hoare Govett Securities 1988–90 (conglomerates analyst 1985–88, construction analyst 1983–85), dir Hoare Govett Corporate Finance 1990–91, fin conslt 1991–92, dir BZW Research 1992–95, exec dir UBS Research 1995–; FCA; *Recreations* squash, tennis, golf; *Clubs* Queens, Riverside, Fitzwilliam (Dublin); *Style—* Mark P Cusack, Esq

CUSACK, Niamh; da of Cyril Cusack (d 1993), and Maureen (d 1977); *b* 20 Oct 1959; *Educ* Scoil Lorcan Dublin, Colaiste Iosagain, Royal Acad of Music, Guildhall Sch of Music and Drama; *Career* actress; *Theatre* Gate Theatre Dublin: Hester Worsley in A Woman of No Importance, Irina in Three Sisters, Nora in A Doll's House; RSC: Desdemona in Othello, Juliet in Romeo and Juliet, Jane Hogarth in The Art of Sucess; West Yorkshire Playhouse: Pegeen Mike in The Playboy of the Western World, Gemma in Captain Swing; Lady Mary in The Admirable Crichton (Theatre Royal Haymarket), Gustchen in The Tutor (Old Vic), Nora Clitheroe in The Plough and the Stars (Young Vic), Irina in Three Sisters (Royal Exchange Manchester), Helena in The Faerie Queen (Aix-en-Provence); *Television* Lucky Sunil, Poirot, Till We Meet Again, Jeeves and Wooster, Heartbeat; *Films* Paris By Night, Fools of Fortune, The Playboys; *Awards* Irish Life Award, Irish Post Award; *Recreations* walking, cooking, reading, dreaming; *Style*— Ms Niamh Cusack; ✉ Peters Fraser & Dunlop Ltd, 503 The Chambers, Chelsea Harbour, Lots Road, London SW10 0XF (☎ 0171 352 4446, fax 0171 352 7356)

CUSACK, Sinead Mary; da of the actor Cyril James Cusack (d 1993), and his 1 w, Maureen, *née* Kiely (d 1977); *m* 23 March 1977, Jeremy Irons, *qv*; 2 s (Samuel b 16 Sept 1978, Maximilian b 17 Oct 1985); *Career* actress; *Theatre* for RSC incl: Lady Amaranth in Wild Oats, Lisa in Children of the Sun, Isabella in Measure For Measure, Celia in As You Like It, Evadne in The Maid's Tragedy, Lady Anne in Richard III, Portia in The Merchant of Venice, Daisy in The Custom of the Country, Ingrid in Peer Gynt, Kate in Taming of the Shrew, Beatrice in Much Ado About Nothing, Roxanne in Cyrano de Bergerac, Lady Macbeth in Macbeth; other credits incl: Desdemona in Othello (Ludlow Festival), Raina in Arms And The Man (Oxford Festival), Alice in Aristocrats (Hampstead), Masha in The Three Sisters (Gate Dublin and Royal Court), Ruth in Map of the Heart (Globe), Grace in Faith Healer (Royal Court); *Television* for BBC incl: Playboy of the Western World, Menace - The Solarium, Shadow of a Gunman, George Sand - Notorious Woman, Affairs of the Heart, Quiller, Love's Labour Lost, Trilby, Supernatural - Ghost in Venice, The Kitchen, The Henhouse, Twelfth Night, Tales From Holywood, Oliver's Travels (also film), Have Your Cake and Eat It; other credits incl: The Eyes Have It (ATV), Romance: The Black Knight (Thames), Scoop (LWT), God on the Rocks (Channel 4); *Films* Alfred the Great, Tamlyn, David Copperfield, Hoffman, Revenge, Horowitz in Dublin Castle, The Last Remake of Beau Geste, Rocket Gibraltar, Venus Peter, Waterland, Bad Behaviour, Cement Garden, The Sparrow, Flemish Board, Stealing Beauty; *Style*— Ms Sinead Cusack; ✉ c/o Markham & Froggatt Ltd, 4 Windmill St, London W1P 1HF (☎ 0171 636 4412, fax 0171 637 5233)

CUSENS, Prof Anthony Ralph; OBE (1989); s of James Henry Cusens (d 1964), and May Edith, *née* Thomas (d 1988); *b* 24 Sept 1927; *Educ* St John's Southsea, UCL (BSc, PhD); *m* 25 July 1953, Pauline Shirin, da of Herbert James German (d 1973); 3 da (Deborah b 1954, Rebecca b 1955, Sarah b 1962); *Career* res engr Br Cast Concrete Fedn 1952–54; sr lectr: Royal Military Coll of Sci Shrivenham 1954–56, Univ of Khartoum 1956–60; prof of structural engrg Asian Inst of Technol Bangkok 1960–65; prof of civil engrg: Univ of Dundee 1965–78, Univ of Leeds 1979–92, conslt Brian Clancy Partnership 1993–; chm UK Certification Authy for Reinforcing Steels 1994–; pres: Concrete Soc 1983–84, IStructE 1991–92; Hon DSc Aston Univ 1993; FICE 1966, FIStructE 1967, FRSE 1974, FEng 1988; *Books* Bridge Deck Analysis (1975); *Recreations* golf; *Clubs* East India, Pannal Golf; *Style*— Prof Anthony Cusens, OBE, FEng; ✉ Old Hall Cottage, Bramham, Wetherby, W Yorks LS23 6QR (☎ 01937 845527, fax 01937 841066)

CUSHING, Philip Edward; *Educ* Highgate Sch, Christ's Coll Cambridge; *Career* formerly with Norcros plc then LEGO Group, chief exec international ops Norton Opax until 1990; Inchcape plc: joined as chief exec Inchcape Berhad 1990, main bd dir 1992–, dir i/c testing servs, shipping servs and buying servs 1992–95, also i/c mktg and distribution 1994–95, md 1995–; non-exec dir Bunzl plc; MCIM; *Style*— Philip Cushing, Esq; ✉ Inchcape plc, 33 Cavendish Square, London W1M 9HF (☎ 0171 546 0022, fax 0171 546 0010)

CUSINE, Prof Douglas James; s of James Fechney Cusine (d 1987), of Johnstone, Renfrewshire, and Catherine, *née* McLean (d 1975); *b* 2 Sept 1946; *Educ* Hutchesons' Boys' GS Glasgow, Univ of Glasgow (LLB); *m* 21 July 1973, Marilyn Calvert, da of George Ramsay (d 1988), of Johnstone, Renfrewshire; 1 s (Graeme b 2 Jan 1984), 1 da (Jane b 19 Sept 1981); *Career* admitted slr 1971; lectr in private law Univ of Glasgow 1974–76; Dept of Conveyancing Univ of Aberdeen: lectr 1976–82, sr lectr 1982–90, head of dept 1987–, prof 1990–; memb and examiner for Law Soc of Scotland 1988–; memb Lord President's Advsy Cncl for Messengers at Arms and Sheriff Offrs 1989–, chm Bd of Examiners Soc of Messengers at Arms and Sheriff Offrs 1990–92; memb Cncl Law Soc; *Books* The Impact of Marine Pollution (jt ed, 1980), Scottish Cases and Materials in Commercial Law (jt ed, 1987), A Scots Conveyancing Miscellany (ed, 1988), New Reproductive Techniques: A Legal Perspective (1988), Law and Practice of Diligence (jtly, 1990), Standard Securities (1991), Missives (jtly, 1993), Requirements of Writing (jtly, 1995); *Recreations* swimming, walking, bird watching; *Style*— Prof Douglas Cusine; ✉ Department of Conveyancing and Professional Practice of Law, University of Aberdeen, Taylor Building, Old Aberdeen AB9 2UB (☎ 01224 272415, fax 01224 272442, telex 73458 UNIABNG)

CUSK, Rachel Emma; da of Peter Cusk, of Bury St Edmunds, and Carolyn, *née* Woods; *b* 8 Feb 1967; *Educ* St Mary's Convent Cambridge, New Coll Oxford (BA); *m* 1995, Josh Hillman, s of Dr Mayer Hillman; *Career* freelance journalist/book reviewer 1993–; judge literary competitions for: Whitbread, London Arts Bd, Elle Magazine, Charleston Tst, Ascham Literary Endowment Fund, Fourth Estate; patron UN Year for Tolerance 1995; *Books* Saving Agnes (1993, Whitbread First Novel Award 1993), The Temporary (1995), The Country Life (1997); various short stories; *Recreations* piano, walking; *Style*— Ms Rachel Cusk; ✉ c/o The Wylie Agency, 36 Parkside, 52 Knightsbridge, London (☎ 0171 234 6394)

CUSSANS, Emma Katherine de Cusance; da of Anthony de Cusance Cussans, of Gillingham, Dorset, and Cecilia Anne, *née* Ratcliffe; *b* 20 July 1953; *Educ* St Mary's Convent Shaftesbury Dorset, Holland Park Comp London, Univ of Manchester (BA); *m* 19 Oct 1985 (m dis 1996), Michael Geoffrey Stuart Tolkien, s of Stuart Frederick Gerald Tolkien (d 1978), of Staverton, Devon; 2 s (Edward Michael de Cusance b 6 April 1990, Oliver Bertram de Cusance (twin) b 6 April 1990); *Career* Yachting Monthly Magazine: features ed 1981–85, organiser Outside Events Yachting Monthly Triangle Race 1986, 1988, 1990 and 1992, organiser Yachting Monthly Classic Yacht Rally 1989, 1991 and 1993, organiser Yachting Monthly Ocean Cruising Club Long Term Cruising Symposium 1991; co-ordinator Yachting World Centenary Celebrations 1994; ed: Tall Ships News 1983–, West Country Cruising 1988, East Coast Rivers 1989; memb: Topsham Museum Soc, Topsham Soc, Devon Valuation Tbnl; memb Yachting Journalists Assoc 1982; *Publications* Fodor's Guide to Great Britain (South-West); *Recreations* sailing, gardening, dog walking; *Clubs* Royal Western Yacht of England, Royal Torbay Yacht, Topsham Sailing; *Style*— Ms Emma Cussans; ✉ Ford Rise, Lower Broad Oak Road, West Hill, Ottery St Mary, Devon EX11 1UD (☎ and fax 01404 815984)

CUSSINS, Peter Ian; s of Philip Cussins (d 1976), of Newcastle upon Tyne, and Doreen Cussins; *b* 18 March 1949; *Educ* Bootham Sch York, Univ of London (BSc); *m* 18 Sept 1973, Vandra Jean, da of Maynard Stubley, of Alnmouth, Northumberland; 1 s (Jabin b 1980), 3 da (Abigail b 1976, Alexandra b 1978, Lydia b 1983); *Career* chm: Cussins Homes Ltd 1973–, Cussins Investment Properties Ltd 1981–, Cussins Commercial Developments Ltd 1981–, Cussins Property Group plc 1981–; *Recreations* golf, fishing; *Style*— Peter I Cussins, Esq; ✉ West Bitchfield Tower, Belsay, Newcastle upon Tyne NE20 0JP; Cussins Property Group plc, Great North Rd, Gosforth, Newcastle upon Tyne NE3 2DA (☎ 0191 2850 567)

CUSTIS, Patrick James; CBE (1981); er s of Alfred William Custis (d 1945), of Dublin, and Amy Custis; *b* 19 March 1921; *Educ* The High Sch Dublin; *m* 1954, Rita, yr da of Percy William Rayner (d 1968), of Bognor Regis; 1 s; *Career* CA; Josolyne Miles Co CAs 1946–51, RTZ 1951–55, Glynwed International 1956–67, fin dir Guest Keen and Nettlefolds (GKN) 1974–81 (joined 1967), ret; dir: New Court Property Fund Managers Ltd 1978–91, Lloyds Bank Midlands and N Wales Regnl Bd 1979–91, Prisons Bd (Home Office) 1980–85, Associated Heat Services plc 1981–90, Wolseley plc 1982–90, Leigh Interests plc 1982–96 (chm 1994–96), Birmingham Technology Ltd 1983–93, MCD Group plc (chm) 1983–86, Wyko Group plc 1985–94, Benford Concrete Machinery plc 1985–86; chm Midlands Indust Gp of Fin Dirs 1977–80, co-opted memb Cncl ICAEW 1979–85, memb Monopolies and Mergers Cmmn 1981–82; pres Wolverhampton Soc of CAs 1985–86; Liveryman Worshipful Co of CAs in England and Wales; FCA, FCMA, FCIS, JDipMA, FRSA; *Recreations* gardening, walking, reading; *Clubs* Royal Over-Seas League; *Style*— Patrick Custis, Esq, CBE; ✉ West Barn, Westmancote, Tewkesbury, Glos GL20 7ES (☎ 01684 772865)

CUSWORTH, Leslie (Les); s of Cecil Cusworth (d 1982), and Jean Cusworth, of Normanton, West Yorkshire; *b* 31 July 1954; *Educ* Normanton GS; *m* 24 July 1976, Marcia Jean Ann, da of Norman Hobbs; 2 da (Hannah Jean b 14 Dec 1982, Sarah Ann b 28 Dec 1987); *Career* Rugby Union fly half Leicester FC and England (12 caps); clubs: Leicester FC 1978–90 (365 appearances, 946 points scored, record no of drop goals in a season (25) 1975), Barbarians RFC 1978–90; England: debut v NZ 1979, Five Nations debut v France 1982; coach to England Rugby 7's (winners World 7's 1993), asst coach to England A XV; physical educn teacher 1976–83, dir P & G Bland Insurance Brokers 1983–; *Recreations* golf, snooker, squash; *Style*— Les Cusworth, Esq; ✉ 14 Stoughton Drive, Evington, Leicester LE5 6AN (☎ 0116 273 8030); Leicester Football Club, Aylestone Rd, Leicester (☎ 0116 254 1607, fax 0116 254 1607)

CUSWORTH, (George Robert) Neville; s of George Ernest Cusworth (d 1966), of Bad Homburg, Germany, and Violet Helene, *née* Cross (d 1969); *b* 14 Oct 1938; *Educ* St Paul's, Keble Coll Oxford (MA), Courtauld Inst (Cert in Euro Art), Stanford Univ California; *m* 6 Sept 1963, (Vivien) Susan, da of Philip Glynn Grylls, of Worthing, Sussex; 1 s (Nicholas b 20 March 1964), 1 da (Juliet b 30 Jan 1966); *Career* Butterworth Group: chief exec 1987–, chm 1990–; chm Bowker-Saur Ltd 1989–92, dir Reed Publishing Ltd 1989–93, chm Butterworth-Heinemann Ltd 1990–93, chief exec Professional Div Reed International Books Ltd 1990–95, dir and chm Legal Div Reed Elsevier plc 1995–, dir Elsevier NV 1995–; dir Int Electronic Publishing Research Centre 1985–88, memb Cncl Publishers' Assoc 1988–91, chm Bd Book House Trg Centre 1989–93; Freeman City of London 1982, Liveryman Worshipful Co of Stationers and Newspapers 1984; *Recreations* theatre, heraldry, art history, walking; *Clubs* Garrick; *Style*— Neville Cusworth, Esq; ✉ Butterworths, Halsbury House, 35 Chancery Lane, London WC2A 1EL (☎ 0171 400 2500)

CUTHBERT, Prof Alan William; s of Thomas William Cuthbert (d 1989), and Florence Mary, *née* Griffin (d 1970); *b* 7 May 1932; *Educ* Deacon's GS Peterborough, Leicester Coll of Technol (BPharm), Univ of St Andrews (BSc), Univ of London (PhD), Univ of Cambridge (MA); *m* 22 April 1954, Harriet Jane (Hetty), da of Charles McLagan Webster (d 1969); 2 s (Adrian b 1960, Bruce b 1962); *Career* Instr Lt RN 1953–56; Univ of Cambridge: reader in pharmacology 1973–79, prof of pharmacology and head Pharmacology Dept 1979–, master Fitzwilliam Coll 1991–; author of over 200 scientific papers; Hon DSc: De Montfort Univ 1993, Aston Univ 1995; Hon LLD Univ of Dundee 1995; elected Academia Europaea 1996, memb Academie Royal de Medicine de Belgique 1996; FRS 1982; *Recreations* growing orchids, travelling, tennis, working; *Clubs* Royal Society Club, Hawks; *Style*— Prof Alan Cuthbert, FRS; ✉ Master's Lodge, Fitzwilliam College, Cambridge CB2 ODG (☎ 01223 332029); Department of Pharmacology, Tennis Court Rd, Cambridge CB2 1QJ (☎ 01223 334004, fax 01223 334040, e-mail awc1000@cam.ac.uk)

CUTHBERT, Michael William; s of Thomas Cuthbert (d 1977), of Coventry, and Thelma Josephine, *née* O'Hehir; *b* 6 July 1956; *Educ* Archbishop Ullathorne RC Comp Sch, UCL (LLB); *m* 29 July 1989, Stephanie Edith, da of David Henry Tate (d 1994), of Leigh, Surrey; 1 da (Caroline Isabella Louise b 13 Aug 1991); *Career* slr; Slaughter and May: articled clerk 1978–80, asst slr 1980–82; Clifford Turner: asst slr 1982–86, ptnr 1986–87; ptnr Clifford Chance London 1987–89 and 1993– (ptnr New York 1989–93); memb: Law Soc 1980, City of London Solicitors' Co; Slr of the Supreme Ct of: the Judicature of Eng and Wales 1980, Hong Kong 1986; *Recreations* opera, food and wine, the cinema; *Clubs* Raffles; *Style*— Michael Cuthbert, Esq; ✉ Clifford Chance, 200 Aldersgate Street, London EC1A 4JJ (☎ 0171 600 1000, fax 0171 600 5555, telex 887847)

CUTHBERT, Stephen Colin (Steve); s of Colin Samuel Cuthbert (d 1975), formerly of Sanderstead, Surrey, and Helen Mary Cuthbert, *née* Scott (d 1986); *b* 27 Oct 1942; *Educ* Trinity Sch of John Whitgift, Univ of Bristol (BSc); *m* 1, 22 Feb 1969 (m dis 1986), Jane Elizabeth, da of late David Bluett, of Sydney, Australia; 2 s (Simon b 1974, Ian b 1974), 1 da (Nicola b 1971); m 2, 27 Oct 1987, Susan Melanie, da of Kenneth Gray, of Brighton; 1 step s (Christopher b 1982), 2 step da (Joanna b 1971, Nicola b 1974); *Career* md Brent International plc 1980–93 (dir 1976–93), DG The Chartered Inst of Mktg 1994–; chm CBI Southern Region 1992–83 (vice chm 1990); *Recreations* cruising sailing, family interests; *Style*— Steve Cuthbert, Esq; ✉ The Chartered Institute of Marketing, Moor Hall, Cookham, Maidenhead, Berkshire SL6 9QH (☎ 01628 427001, fax 01628 427009)

CUTHBERTSON, Eric Ian; WS (1963); s of Ranald Ker Cuthbertson (d 1983), of Edinburgh, and Agnes Thomson, *née* Mitchell (d 1967); *b* 17 Nov 1934; *Educ* Edinburgh Acad, Sedbergh, Univ of Edinburgh; *m* 17 Nov 1962, Shona Campbell Aitken, da of Francis Aitken Wright (d 1959); 1 da (Fiona b 1967); *Career* slr 1963–; dir: Scottish Equitable Policyholders Trust Ltd, Inverteviot Properties (Edinburgh) Ltd, Scotia Campbell Marine Ltd; *Recreations* shooting, fishing, mountain walking, gardening; *Clubs* Bruntsfield Links Golf; *Style*— Eric I Cuthbertson, Esq, WS; ✉ 102 Ravelston Dykes, Edinburgh (☎ 0131 337 7629); 21 Melville Street Lane, Edinburgh EH3 7QB (☎ 0131 225 7500, fax 0131 220 1231)

CUTHBERTSON, Iain; s of Sir David Paton Cuthbertson (d 1989), and Jean Prentice, *née* Telfer (d 1987); *b* 4 Jan 1930; *Educ* Glasgow Acad, Aberdeen GS, Univ of Aberdeen (MA); *m* 1, (m dis 1988), Anne Kristen (d 1996); m 2, Janet Mary Smith; *Career* actor; visiting stage dir and tutor in Scot voice Royal Scot Acad of Music and Drama, former hon pres Scot Community Drama Assoc, rector Univ of Aberdeen 1975–78; Hon LLD Univ of Aberdeen 1978, FRSAMD 1982; *Theatre* Citizens' Theatre Glasgow: Othello, Serjeant Musgrave's Dance, Armstrong's Last Goodnight, The Crucible, Cat on a Hot Tin Roof, Enemy of the People; Edinburgh Festival: The Baikie Charivari, The Hidden King, The Wallace, The Four Sons of Aymon (narrator); Arts Theatre: Ronald Duncan season, Abelard and Heloise, This Way to the Tomb; tours incl: Dr Angelus, Candida, The Caine Mutiny, Scagnarelle; other credits incl: Pitlochry Festival Theatre season 1961, Long John Silver (Metropole Glasgow), Serjeant Musgrave's Dance and Shelley (Royal Court), A Drunk Man Looks at a Thistle (narrator, The Old Athenaeum Glasgow) 1992; as admin: gen mangr and dir of prodns Citizens' Theatre Glasgow 1962–65, assoc dir Royal Court Theatre London 1965 (dir/trans first prodn of Ubu Roi), dir Perth

Theatre, admin Playhouse Theatre Nottingham; *Television* series incl: The Borderers, Sutherlands Law, Budgie, Charles Endell Esq, Supergran; guest appearances in series: Ripping Yarns, Campion, Inspector Morse, Dr Who, Z Cars, Juliet Bravo, The Onedin Line, The Duchess of Duke Street, The Standard; other credits incl: City Lights, Rab C Nesbitt, Scotch on the Rocks, Darwin, The Glass Mountain, Lytton's Diary, We The Accused, The Mourning Brooch, The Glory Boys, Danger UXB, Diamond Crack Diamond, The House with the Green Shutters, The Spirit of Man, Permanent Red, Antonia Jane's Mid-Life Crisis, Anthony and Cleopatra, The Justice Game, The Fasting Girl, Black Beauty, Tom Brown's Schooldays, Vice Versa, Children of the Stones, The Ghost of Motley Hall, The Caledonian Cascade, The Queen's Realm, Casualty, Oliver's Travels; *Opera* Ariadne auf Naxos (Scottish Opera); *Films* incl: The Railway Children, Up the Chastity Belt, The Assam Garden, A Perfect Spy, Gorillas in the Mist, Scandal, Let Him Have It; *Publications* reviews, criticisms and articles on subjects incl: theatre, books, food, National Trust for Scotland, castellated houses, sailing; also poetry and trans of plays for performance; *Recreations* sailing, driving, playing on word processors; *Clubs* Athenaeum, Royal Highland Yacht, National Trust for Scotland (life memb); *Style*— Iain Cuthbertson, Esq; ✉ c/o Janet Welch Personal Management, 32 Hill St, Richmond, Surrey TW9 1TW (☎ 0181 332 6544, fax 0181 332 6527)

CUTHBERTSON, District Judge; Peter; s of Peter Brentley Cuthbertson, and Edna, *née* Stockdale; *b* 3 March 1949; *Educ* Robert Richardson's GS Ryhope, Pembroke Coll Oxford (MA, chm Blackstone Soc); *m* 26 May 1971, Carole Margaret, da of Sydney White and Margaret Alice Humphrey White; 1 da (Caroline Helen b 7 Feb 1976), 1 s (Timothy Peter b 18 Aug 1979); *Career* admitted slr 1973; Latimer, Hinks, Marsham & Little (now Latimer Hinks): articled to late Eric Nelson Marsham 1971–73, ptnr 1975–92; district judge 1992–; memb Law Soc; *Recreations* golf, sailing, theatre, tennis, walking in Lake District; *Clubs* Oxford Union Society, Barnard Castle Golf; *Style*— District Judge Cuthbertson; ✉ Sunderland County Court, John Street, Sunderland, Tyne & Wear SR1 1RB

CUTLER, (John) Derek; s of (Joseph) Thomas Cutler (d 1962), of Oldbury, Worcs, and Winifred, *née* Skidmore (d 1984); *b* 2 Aug 1932; *Educ* Oldbury GS, Birmingham Sch of Architecture; *m* 5 May 1958, Peggy Maureen, da of Herbert William Merrett (d 1984), of Bordon, Hants; 2 s (Timothy John b 1962, James Ewen b 1967), 1 da (Jacqueline Ann b 1960); *Career* Nat Serv RE 1958–60; architect; sr ptnr Phillips Cutler Phillips Troy 1985–87 (ptnr 1962–85), md PCPT Architects Ltd 1987–; memb Birmingham Architectural Assoc; RIBA 1958, FRSA 1966; *Recreations* jazz, theatre; *Style*— Derek Cutler, Esq; ✉ PCPT Architects Ltd, 61 St Paul's Square, Birmingham B3 1QR (☎ 0121 236 7070, fax 0121 236 7717)

CUTLER, Sir Horace Walter; kt (1979), OBE (1963), DL (Gtr London 1981); eldest s of Albert Benjamin Cutler, and Mary Ann Cutler; *b* 28 July 1912; *Educ* Harrow GS; *m* 1957, Christiane, da of Dr Klaus Muthesius; 1 s, 3 da (and 1 s from previous m); *Career* former Mayor of Harrow, ldr of oppn GLC 1974–77 (dep ldr 1964–67 and 1973–74), memb Harrow West GLR 1964–86; ldr: GLC 1977–81, oppn 1981–82, contested (C) Willesden East 1970; *Books* The Cutler Files (autobiog, 1982); *Style*— Sir Horace Cutler, OBE, DL; ✉ Hawkswood, Hawkswood Lane, Gerrards Cross, Bucks SL9 7BN (☎ 01753 663182)

CUTLER, Ivor; *m* (m dis); 2 s (Jeremy, Daniel); *Career* RAF (VR) 1942–43, trained as air navigator (grounded for dreaminess); humorist; aged 6 sang My Love is Like a Red Red Rose by Robert Burns and won sch prize, apprentice fitter Rolls Royce 1940, first aid and storeman Winsor Engrg Co 1943–45, teacher 1948–80 (South Sch Paisley 1948–50, A S Neill's Summerhill 1950–51, ILEA 1952–80), first gig at Blue Angel London 1957 (unmitigated failure), started writing poetry aged 42 (wasn't any good until 48); Music: 270 songs, music for Ken Russell's Diary Of A Nobody BBC2; Records: Dandruff (with Phyllis King, 1974), Velvet Donkey (with Phyllis King and Fred Frith, 1975), Jammy Smears (with Phyllis King, 1976), Women Of The World (1984), Privilege (with Linda Hirst, David Toop and Steve Beresford, 1984), Gruts (1986), Prince Ivor (1986), Life In A Scotch Sitting Room Volume 2 (1996), A Wet Handle (1996), Ludo (1997); TV: The Acker Bilk Band Show, Magical Mystery Tour, Offbeat for Tired Music Lovers, Up Sunday, Dave Allen in search of the great British eccentric, Innes Book of Records, Old Grey Whistle Test; Radio: Monday Night At Home, John Peel 1970–, Start The Week, Andy Kershaw, Pye Radio Award for Humour 1980–81; BBC Radio 3 plays 1979– incl: Silence, Ivor Cutler & The Mermaid, Ivor Cutler & The Mole, Ivor Cutler & The Princess, Ivor Cutler & His Dad, Ivor Cutler & A Barber, A Miner Is Approached by Ivor Cutler, A Sheet Metalworker is Approached by Ivor Cutler, King Cutler (series with Phyllis King) 1990, A Stuggy Pren (series) 1994, A Jelly Mountain (series) 1996; Radio 4 series: Ivor Cutler has 15 1990, Cutler the Lax 1991; Performances incl: The Royal Festival Hall, Coliseum, Rainbow, Theatre Royal Drury Lane, a tour with Van Morrison; cartoons: Observer, Private Eye, Sunday Times, International Times; Poetry: Many Flies Have Feathers (1972), A Flat Man (1977), Private Habits (1981), Large et Puffy (1984), Fresh Carpet (1986), A Nice Wee Present From Scotland (1988), Fly Sandwich (1991), Is that your Flap, Jack? (1992), A Stuggy Pren (1994), A Wet Handle (1996); Short Stories (illustrated by Martin Honeysett): Life in a Scotch Sitting Room Volume 2 (1984), Gruts (1986), Fremsley (1987), Glasgow Dreamer (1990); Short Stories (illustrated by author): Gruts (1962), Cockadoodledon't!!! (1966); Children's Stories (illustrated by Helen Oxenbury): Meal One (1971), Balooky Klujypop (1973), The Animal House (1976); Herbert-Five Stories (illustrated by Patrick Benson, 1988), Grape Zoo (illustrated by Jill Barton, 1991), Doris the Hen (illustrated by Claudio Muñoz, 1992), The New Dress (illustrated by Claudio Muñoz, 1995); Philosophy: Befriend a Bacterium (illustrated by Martin Honeysett, 1992); regular illustrated poetry columnist Scotland on Sunday magazine; quotes about Ivor Cutler incl: The demeanour and voice of the weariest human ever to be cursed with existence (Music Week), Ivor Cutler spends a lot of time in his bedroom (Observer Magazine); ambition: to disappear without any help; memb: PRS, MCPS, PPL, PLR; *Recreations* dishing out sticky labels to deserving persons; *Style*— Ivor Cutler; ✉ c/o BBC, Broadcasting House, London W1A 1AA

CUTLER, His Hon Judge; Keith Charles; s of Henry Walter Cutler, of Woburn Sands, Bucks, and Evelyn Constance, *née* Butcher; *b* 14 Aug 1950; *Educ* Rickmansworth GS, Cedars Sch, Univ of Bristol (LLB); *m* 30 Aug 1975, Judith Mary, da of Ronald Philip Haddy (d 1974); 1 s (James b 1982), 1 da (Anna b 1985); *Career* called to the Bar Lincoln's Inn 1972; asst recorder 1989, recorder 1993–96, circuit judge (Western Circuit) 1996–; memb Hon Soc of Lincoln's Inn; *Clubs* RAC; *Style*— His Hon Judge Cutler; ✉ 3 Pump Court, Temple, London EC4Y 2AJ (☎ 0171 353 0711, fax 0171 353 3319)

CUTLER, Timothy Robert (Robin); CBE (1995); s of Frank Raymond Cutler (d 1943), and Jeannie Evelyn, *née* Badenoch (d 1973); *Educ* Banff Acad, Univ of Aberdeen (BSc); *m* 1958, Ishbel Wingate MacFarlane, da of James Primrose; 1 s (David Richard b 19 Nov 1960), 1 da (Gillian Elizabeth Jane b 2 June 1964); *Career* Nat Serv RE 1956–58; Colonial Forest Serv Kenya 1958–64, NZ Forest Service 1964–87; Miny of Forestry: asst sec 1987–88, chief exec 1988–90; DG Forestry Cmmn for GB 1990–95; Hon DSc Univ of Aberdeen; memb: NZ Inst of Forestry, Cwlth Forestry Assoc; FICFor 1993; *Recreations* tennis, golf, travel, gardening; *Clubs* Commonwealth Trust, Edinburgh Breakfast Rotary; *Style*— Robin Cutler, Esq, CBE; ✉ 14 Swanston Road, Edinburgh EH10 7BB

CUTTS, John William; s of William George Cutts (d 1951), of London, and Ingeborg Ernestine, *née* Walter; *b* 27 Sept 1950; *Educ* Dean Close Sch Cheltenham, Univ of Sussex (BSc), INSEAD Fontainebleau (MBA); *m* 18 Sept 1976 (m dis); 4 da (Samantha Mady Nicola b 23 Feb 1985, Dominique Lara Elisabeth b 24 July 1986, Tatiana Rebecca Sara b 5 Feb 1988, Natasha Tara Josephine b 21 Jan 1991); *Career* apprentice Rolls Royce Ltd 1968–72, technical export mangr Ansafone Ltd 1973–75, gen mangr H & B Real Gewerbebau GmbH 1976–79, gen mangr Eupic Services BV (property investment) 1979–81, md mergers and acquisitions Amsterdam Rotterdam Bank NV 1981–88, dir Euro mergers and acquisitions Corporate Fin Dept Samuel Montagu & Co Ltd 1988–92, md corporate fin West Merchant Bank Ltd 1992–; non-exec chm: BPL Holdings Ltd, Friedland Group Ltd; non-exec dir Orbis International; chm INSEAD Alumni Fund; *Recreations* opera, sailing; *Clubs* Royal Thames Yacht, Hurlingham; *Style*— John Cutts, Esq; ✉ West Merchant Bank Ltd, 33–36 Gracechurch St, London EC3V 0AX (☎ 0171 623 8711, fax 0171 444 7766)

CYMERMAN, Anthony; s of Alfred Cymerman, of Highgate, London, and Annette, *née* Loufer; *b* 4 Dec 1944; *Educ* La Sainte Union Convent, Hargrave Park Sch, Dame Alice Owen's Sch, Univ of Leeds (BChD); *m* 28 March 1976, Cherry, da of Maj R Keal, MBE; 1 s (James Alexander b 9 June 1977), 1 da (Kate Elizabeth b 28 Dec 1981); *Career* qualified from Leeds Dental Sch 1970, assoc London 1970–72, started own private practice in Harley St 1971 (second practice in NW London 1974); conslt BUPA and Private Patients Plan 1982; former memb: Camden and Islington FPC (now FHSA), Camden and Islington Local Dental Ctee, Camden and Islington Dental Serv Ctee, Dental Advsy Ctee UCH, Fedn London Area LDCS; hon tutor London Hosp Dental Sch 1986; memb: BDA 1970, RSM 1987; *Recreations* cricket, clay pigeon shooting; *Clubs* MCC; *Style*— Anthony Cymerman, Esq; ✉ 25 Dartmouth Park Hill, London NW5 1HP (☎ 0171 485 2505, mobile 0860 683861)

CZERNIN, Hon Mrs ((Mary) Hazel Caridwen); *née* Scott-Ellis; eldest da of 9 Baron Howard de Walden and 5 Baron Seaford and Lady Howard de Walden, *née* Countess Irene Harrach (d 1975); *b* 12 Aug 1935; *m* 20 Nov 1957, Joseph Czernin, s of late Count Franz Josef Czernin (of the family granted title of Count (*Reichsgraf*) of the Holy Roman Empire by the Emperor Ferdinand III 1652 with the predicate 'Hoch und Wohlgeboren (High and well-born)'; 1 s, 5 da; *Career* co-heiress to Barony of Howard de Walden; *Style*— The Hon Mrs Czernin; ✉ White Oak House, Highclere, Newbury, Berks RG20 9RJ; 47 Queens Gate Gardens, London SW7 5ND

D

d'ABO, Jennifer Mary Victoria; da of Maj Michael William Vernon Hammond-Maude, and Jacqueline Rosamond Mary, *née* Patrick (d 1963); *b* 14 Aug 1945; *Educ* Hatherop Castle, Mademoiselle Anita Paris, Queen's Secretarial Coll; *m* 1 (m dis), David Morgan-Jones; 1 da (Sophy b 1967); m 2 (m dis), Peter Egbert Cadbury, *qv*; 1 s (Joel b 1971); m 3 (m dis 1987), Robin d'Abo; *Career* proprietor Wavey Line Grocery Store 1976–77; dir: Burlingtons Furnishing Co Ltd 1977–80, Jean Sorelle Ltd 1980–82, Dollar Air Servs 1982–86, Stormgard plc 1985–87, Pentos plc 1987–88, Averys of Bristol 1988–92, London Docklands Devpt Corp 1985–88, Channel Four TV Co Ltd 1986–87; chm: Ryman Group plc 1981–87, Levelmill Investments Ltd 1987–, Roffey Bros Ltd, Moyses Stevens Investments Ltd 1989–, T Parker & Sons Ltd 1990–, Wulfsohn & James Ltd 1990–; tstee Natural History Museum 1988–; memb Doctors and Dentists' Remuneration Review Body 1989–91; memb Industl Devpt Bd for NI 1992–95, pres Nat Events Ctee Imperial Cancer Research Fund 1993–, memb Bd Imperial Cancer Research Fund 1993–; CIMgt 1985, FRSA 1986, FInstM 1987; *Style*— Mrs Jennifer d'Abo; ✉ Moyses Stevens International, Quill Street, Hanger Lane, London W5 1PG (☎ 0181 998 1177, fax 0181 998 2277)

D'ALBIAC, James Charles Robert; s of Air Marshal Sir John D'Albiac, KCVO, KBE, CB, DSO (d 1963), and Lady Sibyl Mary, *née* Owen; *b* 14 Oct 1935; *Educ* Winchester, Magdalen Coll Oxford (BA); *m* 2 May 1964, Carole Ann, da of Robert Percy Garner (d 1988); 1 da (Jane Sibyl b 22 Sept 1966); *Career* Nat Serv 2 Lt Lincolnshires serv Malaya 1954–56; stockbroker, ptnr Rowe & Pitman stockbrokers London 1968–86; dir: Mercury Asset Management 1986–91, Jupiter Tyndall Group plc 1991–95; MSI, AIIMR; *Recreations* golf, chess; *Clubs* Berkshire Golf, Huntercombe Golf, United Oxford & Cambridge Univ; *Style*— James D'Albiac, Esq; ✉ 65 Pont Street, London SW1X 0BD

D'AMICO, Marcus; s of Vincent D'Amico, and Patricia, *née* Carr; *b* 4 Dec 1965; *Educ* Reading Blue Coat Sch, Windsor Coll; *Career* actor; *Theatre* incl: Barry in The Boys Next Door (Hampstead and Comedy Theatre), Louis in Angels in America (RNT), Eric in An Inspector Calls (Royale, Broadway), Leo in Design for Living (Gielgud), Cain in Cain (RSC) 1995–96; *Television* incl: David Ware in Trainer (2 series, BBC), Michael in Tales of the City (Channel 4), Gary in SWALK (Channel 4); *Radio* Little Women; *Film* incl: Guy in Hope Machine 1995, Hand-O in Full Metal Jacket, Wayne in The Silent Twins (BBC), Colin in Last Summer's Child (BBC); *Awards* Time Out Award Best Actor (for The Boys Next Door) 1991; nominations incl: Olivier Best Actor Award (for Angels in America) 1992, Theatre World Award and Drama Desk Award Best Supporting Actor (for An Inspector Calls) 1994; *Style*— Marcus D'Amico, Esq; ✉ c/o William Morris Agency (UK) Ltd, 31/32 Soho Square, London W1V 6DG (☎ 0171 434 2191, fax 0171 437 0238)

d'ANCONA, John Edward William; CB (1994); s of Adolph d'Ancona (d 1970), of Malta, and Margaret Simpson Gilbert, *née* Arnott (d 1977); *b* 28 May 1935; *Educ* St Edward's Coll Malta, St Cuthbert's GS Newcastle, King's Coll Durham (BA, DipEd); *m* 27 Dec 1958, (Mary) Helen, da of Sqdn Ldr Ralph Taylor Hunter (d 1957), of Newcastle upon Tyne; 3 s (Matthew R b 1968, Patrick D b 1972, Michael P b 1974); *Career* teacher 1959–61; Civil Serv: asst princ Miny of Educn 1961–64, PPS to Min of State for Educn 1964–65; princ: Miny of Educn 1965–67, Miny of Technol 1967–70, DTI 1970–74; asst sec Dept of Energy 1974–81, under sec and dir gen Offshore Supplier Office Dept of Energy 1981–94 (conslt 1994–); *Recreations* cricket, philately, winebibbing; *Style*— John d'Ancona, Esq, CB

D'ARCY, Robert John Bruce; s of Cecil Vivian Robert D'Arcy (d 1995), of Holbrook, Ipswich, and Margery Mary, *née* Bailey (d 1987); *b* 12 Aug 1942; *Educ* Marlborough, Univ of Munich, Coll of Estate Management; *m* 22 Nov 1969, Janet Maxwell, da of Maxwell Heron Matheson (d 1978), of Woodbridge, Suffolk; 2 s (Justin b 6 Sept 1971, Toby b 26 Jan 1977), 2 da (Annabel (twin) b 6 Sept 1971, Charlotte b 12 Jan 1973); *Career* chartered surveyor; Chestertons 1966–68, Donaldsons 1968–69, ptnr James Crichton and Co 1969–; FRICS; *Recreations* sailing, shooting; *Clubs* Royal Thames Yacht; *Style*— Robert D'Arcy, Esq; ✉ The Old Rectory, Bredfield, Woodbridge, Suffolk IP13 6AX (☎ 01394 385223)

d'ASCOLI, Bernard; s of Georges d'Ascoli, of Aubagne, France, and Marcelle, *née* Thermes; *b* 18 Nov 1958; *Educ* Marseille Conservatoire; *partner*, Eleanor Harris; 1 s (Stéphane b 1996); *Career* pianist; debuts: Queen Elizabeth Hall, Barbican and Royal Festival Hall 1982, Concertgebouw Amsterdam 1984, Houston USA 1985, The Proms Royal Albert Hall 1986, Tokyo 1988, Paris 1989; performed as soloist with: RPO, LPO, Philharmonia, BBC Symphony Orch, CBSO, Chamber Orch of Euro; played under conductors incl: Paavo Berglund, Andrew Davis, Sergiu Comissiona, Kurt Sanderling, Sir Yehudi Menuhin, Andrew Litton, Yevgeny Svetlanov, Michel Plasson, Sir John Pritchard; various int tours; *Recordings* Liszt Sonata, La Legierezza; Franck: Prelude Chorale and Fugue (1982); Schuman: Carnaval, Papillons, Fantasie Stücke op 111 (1989); Chopin: 4 Ballades, Nocturne in C Sharp Minor, Berceuse, Tarantelle, Andante Spianato and Grande Polonaise (1990); *Awards* Best Young Talent in France 1976, First Prize Int Maria Canals Competition Barcelona 1978, Chopin Prize Santander 1980, Third Prize Leeds Int Piano Competition 1981; prize winner: Marguerite Long Competition Paris, Bach Competition Leipzig, Chopin Competition Warsaw; *Recreations* philosophy, psychology, sport; *Style*— Bernard d'Ascoli, Esq; ✉ c/o Clarion/Seven Muses, 47 Whitehall Park, London N19 3TW (☎ 0171 272 4413, fax 0171 281 9687)

D'CRUZ, Trevlyn Raphael; s of Samuel Patrick D'Cruz (d 1961), Kathlyn, *née* Belletty (d 1965); *b* 30 Aug 1938; *Educ* Goethals Sch; *m* 4 Jan 1964, Jill Ann, da of John Hudson Rogers; 1 s (Jaimie Simon b 20 Nov 1964), 1 da (Emma Claire b 27 Aug 1966); *Career* articled clerk to N N Pampel 1955–60, chartered accountant Baker Todman & Co 1961–65, Morgan Crucible Co 1966–70; publisher: New English Library 1970–81, Hodder & Stoughton 1981–84; md Accountancy Business Group 1985–; chm Merton Women's Aid (refuge) 1987–; FCA 1966; *Recreations* reading, opera; *Style*— Trevlyn D'Cruz, Esq; ✉ 9 Allfarthing Lane, London SW18 2PG (☎ 0181 874 1951); Institute of Chartered Accountants in England and Wales (ICAEW), Accountancy Business Group, 40 Bernard St, London WC1N 1LD (☎ 0171 920 8920)

D'EYNCOURT, *see:* Tennyson-d'Eyncourt

D'JANOEFF, Alexander Constantine Basil; s of Constantine V D'Janoeff (d 1986), of Windsor, and Margarita, *née* Rotinoff; *b* 27 March 1952; *Educ* Eton, Strasbourg Univ France; *m* 22 June 1991, Hon Anne, da of 9 Baron Rodney (d 1992); *Career* qualified CA 1977; Coopers & Lybrand: joined 1972, Paris Office 1977–80, London Office 1980–85, seconded Schroder Ventures (Mgmnt Buy Out Fund) 1985, Corp Fin Dept Coopers & Lybrand 1986–96, ptnr 1986–96, dir i/c Euro Corp Fin 1989–96, chm French Market Sector Gp 1990–96; md merchant banking CS First Boston 1996–; FCA, FRSA; *Recreations* golf, mountain walking in Switzerland; *Clubs* Brooks's, Annabel's, Guards' Polo; *Style*— Alexander D'Janoeff, Esq; ✉ C S First Boston, One Cabot Square, London E14 4QS (☎ 0171 516 3232, fax 0171 516 3477)

D'OLIER-LEES, John Cathcart; s of John Rutherford D'Olier-Lees (d 1972); descends from Sir John Lees,1 Bt successively Usher of Black Rod, Sec of State for War and sec to PO in Ireland d 1811; hp of kinsman, Sir Thomas Harcourt Ivor Lees, 8 Bt, *qv*; *b* 12 Nov 1927; *m* 1957, Wendy Garrold, yr da of late Brian Garrold Groom, of Edinburgh; 2 s (Trevor John Cathcart b 1961, James Scott Lewis b 1963); *Career* formerly Lt 2 Bn Border Regiment and SAS Regiment (Artists Rifles) TA; *Clubs* Naval and Military; *Style*— John D'Olier-Lees, Esq; ✉ The Cottage, 58 Southampton Road, Ringwood, Hants

D'OYLY, Hadley Gregory; s and h of Sir Nigel D'Oyly, 14 Bt, *qv*; *b* 29 May 1956; *Educ* Milton Abbey; *m* 1, 1978 (m dis 1982), Margaret Mary Dent; m 2, 17 May 1991, Annette Frances Elizabeth, yst da of Maj Michael White, of Farnham Royal, Bucks; 1 da (India Dolores b 1992); *Career* furniture/interior/exterior designer; md Bookman Design International Ltd; currently reading theology at King's Coll London; *Recreations* squash, motor racing; *Style*— Hadley D'Oyly, Esq; ✉ Flat B, 37 New North Road, Islington, London N1 6JB

D'OYLY, Sir Nigel Hadley Miller; 14 Bt (E 1663), of Shottisham, Norfolk; s of Sir Hastings D'Oyly, 11 Bt (d 1950), and his 2 w Evelyn; suc half bro Sir John Rochfort D'Oyly, 13 Bt (d 1986); *b* 6 July 1914; *Educ* Radley, RMC Sandhurst; *m* 27 Oct 1939, Dolores (d 1971), da of Robert H Gregory, of New Lodge, Crowhurst, Sussex; 1 s (Hadley Gregory b 1956), 2 da (Carol Dolores (Mrs Charles Pearce) b 1942, Sherry Angela (Mrs R Mumford) b 1946); *Heir* s, Hadley Gregory D'Oyly, *qv*; *Career* served WWII, Maj, The Royal Scots, Hong Kong, France, War Office; civil engr, md OPS (London) & Co; *Recreations* rugby, tennis, swimming, photography; *Clubs* Ski Club of GB, Knights'; *Style*— Sir Nigel D'Oyly, Bt; ✉ New Lodge, Crowhurst, nr Battle, E Sussex TN33 9AB (☎ 01424 830278)

D'SOUZA, Dr Frances Gertrude Claire; da of Robert Anthony Gilbert Russell (d 1979), of Ardingly Farm, Sussex, and Pauline Wilhelmina, *née* Parmet (d 1988); *b* 18 April 1944; *Educ* St Mary's Princethorpe Warwicks, UCL (BSc), Univ of Oxford (DPhil); *m* 1, 1959 (m dis 1973), Stanislaus Joseph D'Souza; 2 da (Christa Claire b 1960, Heloise b 1962); m 2, 1985 (m dis 1994), Martin John Griffiths; *Career* clinical asst Autistic Unit Marlborough Day Hosp 1965–67, Ford Fndn research fell Wellcome Inst of Comparative Physiology 1973–77, pt/t lectr Dept of Anthropology LSE 1974–80, sr lectr in physical anthropology Dept of Humanities Oxford Poly 1977–79, res dir Relief and Development Inst 1983–86 (fndr dir 1979–83), independent research conslt on relief and devpt 1986–87, academic visitor Dept of Biological Sciences Univ of Oxford 1987–88, dir Article 19 Int Centre against Censorship 1989–; advsr to: Inter-Action, Robert F Kennedy Meml, Oxford Civil Liberties Soc; memb: Cncl Save the Children Fund, Int Inst of Communications 1989–; fndr memb: Afghan Support Ctee, AfghanAid 1981–89, Int Broadcasting Tst, Cncl for Arms Control 1982–85, Int Alert 1982–92, Int Freedom of Expression Exchange (IFEX) 1992 (convenor 1994); *Publications* author of numerous scientific papers, journalism and human rights pubns; regular broadcaster; *Recreations* music, especially opera, string quartets and Mahler, serious walking, shiatsu; *Style*— Dr Frances D'Souza; ✉ Article 19, Lancaster House, 33 Islington High Street, London N1 9LH (☎ 0171 278 9292, fax 0171 713 1356)

D'SOUZA, Mavis Mathilda Ursula; da of John Paul Martin D'Souza (d 1982), of London, and Mildred Amelia, *née* Fernandes (d 1994); *b* 14 March 1947; *Educ* St Joseph's Convent Sch Dar-Es-Salaam Tanzania, Univ of London (LLB); *Career* called to the Bar Middle Temple 1975, ed-in-chief Lloyd's Law Reports 1995– (ed 1976–94); memb: Bar Assoc of Commerce Fin and Indust 1976, Int Bar Assoc 1986, Inst of Chartered Shipbrokers 1987; *Recreations* country walking, reading; *Style*— Miss Mavis D'Souza; ✉ LLP Ltd, 69–77 Paul Street, London EC2 (☎ 0171 553 1000)

da COSTA, Aires Anthony (Tony); s of Antonio Vincente da Costa (d 1957), of Nairobi, Kenya, and Maria Estel Isabel Aida, *née* dos Martrez e Souza; *b* 23 June 1943; *Educ* St Francis de Sales Coll Nagpur (MB BS, MD, FRCP); *m* 22 April 1972, Yvonne Mae, da of Edward Clark, of Northumbria; 1 s (Oliver b 1977); *Career* res fell Northwestern Univ Chicago 1970–73, conslt neuropathologist NW Thames RHA 1974–78, conslt Leeds and Yorks RHA 1978–; author of numerous papers on neurophysiology in learned jls; memb EEG Soc, fell N of England Neurological Assoc, examiner Electroencephalography and Clinical Neurophy Examining Bd, memb Assoc of Br Clinical Neurophysiologists; memb BMA, FRCP (Canada); *Books* Textbook of General Medicine (contrib, 1983); *Recreations* rowing, motor sport, photography; *Style*— Tony da Costa, Esq; ✉ St James's University Hospital, Beckett St, Leeds LS9 7TF (☎ 0113 243 3144, fax 0113 228 3804)

DACIE, Sir John Vivian; kt (1976); s of John Charles Dacie; *b* 20 July 1912; *Educ* King's Coll Sch, King's Coll Hosp (MD); *m* 1938, Margaret Kathleen Victoria, *née* Thynne; 3 s, 2 da; *Career* sr lectr then reader Br Postgrad Medical Sch 1946–57, prof of haematology London Univ 1957–77; author; FRS 1967, Hon FRSM 1984; *Books* Haemolytic Anaemias, Practical Haematology; *Recreations* entomology, music; *Style*— Sir John Dacie, FRS; ✉ 10 Alan Rd, Wimbledon, London SW19 7PT (☎ 0181 946 6086)

DACK, Simon Edward; s of Michael Dack (d 1979), and Florence Dack; *b* 26 Jan 1959; *Educ* Caterham, Worthing HS; *Career* photographer; Worthing Gazette 1976–80, Keystone Press Agency 1980–82; Brighton Evening Argus 1983–; assignments covered incl: Brixton riots 1981, Brighton bombing 1984, Oxfam and leprosy feature India, rescue of children by Sally Becker from Mostar Bosnia 1993, street children in Romania feature 1994; winner Ilford Features Photographer of the Year 1992 (commended 6 times), BT Southern News Photographer of the Yr 1994; *Clubs* Nelson Golf Society; *Style*— Simon Dack, Esq; ✉ c/o Picture Desk, Brighton Evening Argus, Argus House, Crowhurst Road, Hollingbury, Brighton BN1 8AR (☎ 01273 544544)

DACKER, Philip Andrew; s of Frederick Andrew Dacker (d 1992), and Margaret Chisholm, *née* Greig; *b* 20 June 1949; *Educ* Edinburgh Acad, Univ of Edinburgh (LLB); *m* 30 Dec 1972, Ellinor Lindsay (Lyn), da of Dr Hugh McLeod Tunstall MacDonald; 1

da (Vicki b 16 Dec 1989); *Career* apprentice J & F Anderson WS Edinburgh 1970–72, asst slr Alexander Hendry & Son Denny 1972–73; Dundas & Wilson: asst slr 1973–76, ptnr Commercial Property Dept 1976, managing ptnr 1991–96, ptnr Banking Gp 1996–; memb Bd Lothian Young Enterprise; memb: Law Soc of Scotland 1973, Int Bar Assoc, IOD; NP 1978, WS 1978; *Recreations* golf, travel; *Clubs* Bruntsfield Links (Edinburgh); *Style—* Philip Dacker; ✉ Partner, Dundas & Wilson, Saltire Court, 20 Castle Terrace, Edinburgh EH1 2EN (☎ 0131 228 8000, fax 0131 228 8888)

DACRE, Myles Randell; s of Peter Dacre, and Joan, *née* Hill; *b* 8 Feb 1958; *Educ* Univ Coll Sch, Camberwell Sch of Art, Univ of Reading (BA Graphic Communication); *Career* sr art dir Corporate Annual Reports 1982–86, assoc dir Addison Design 1986–88; md: Citigate Design 1988–93, Lloyd Northover Citigate 1993–; *Style—* Myles Dacre, Esq; ✉ Lloyd Northover Citigate, 8 Smarts Place, London WC2B 5LW (☎ 0171 430 1100, fax 0171 430 1490)

DACRE, Nigel; s of Peter Dacre, and Joan, *née* Hill; *b* 3 Sept 1956; *Educ* Univ Coll Sch Hampstead London, St John's Coll Oxford (MA); *m* Dr Jane Elizabeth Dacre, da of Peter Verrill; 1 s (Robert b 1989), 1 da (Claire b 1986); *Career* graduate trainee BBC 1978, BBC Bristol 1980, TV journalist News at Ten ITN 1982, prog ed World News ITN 1987, newsroom ed ITN General Election Special 1987, ed European Elections Special 1989, exec prodr News At One and News at 5:40 1990–92, head of programme output and exec prodr News at Ten 1992–93, ed ITN News on ITV 1995– (dep ed 1994–95); *Books* ITN Budget Factbook (ed, 1985); *Style—* Nigel Dacre, Esq; ✉ Independent Television News, 200 Gray's Inn Rd, London WC1X 8XZ (☎ 0171 833 3000)

DACRE, Paul Michael; s of Peter Dacre, and Joan, *née* Hill; *b* 14 Nov 1948; *Educ* Univ Coll Sch London, Univ of Leeds (BA); *m* Kathleen, da of Charles James Thomson; 2 s (James Charles b 21 May 1984, Alexander Peter b 6 Aug 1987); *Career* Daily Express: reporter Manchester 1970–71, reporter, feature writer and assoc features ed London 1971–76, NY corr 1976–79; Daily Mail: bureau chief NY 1980, dep news ed London 1981, news ed 1983, asst ed news and foreign 1986, asst ed features 1987, exec ed 1988, assoc ed 1989–91; ed: Evening Standard 1991–92, Daily Mail 1992–; *Style—* Paul Dacre, Esq; ✉ The Daily Mail, Northcliffe House, 2 Derry St, London W8 5TT (☎ 0171 938 6000)

DACRE, Baroness (E 1321); Hon Rachel Leila; *née* Brand; da of 4 Viscount Hampden, who was also 26 Baron Dacre, following whose death (1965) the Viscountcy passed to his bro while the Barony fell into abeyance between the two surviving daughters, till terminated in favour of Rachel, the elder, 1970; *b* 24 Oct 1929; *m* 26 July 1951, Hon William Douglas-Home (d 1992); 1 s, 3 da; *Heir* s, Hon James Thomas Archibald Douglas-Home b 16 May 1952; *Style—* The Rt Hon Lady Dacre; ✉ Derry House, Kilmeston, Alresford, Hants SO24 0NR

DACRE OF GLANTON, Baroness; Lady Alexandra Henrietta Louisa; *née* Haig; da of Field Marshal 1 Earl Haig; *m* 1, 10 June 1941 (m dis 1954), Rear Adm Clarence Dinsmore Howard-Johnston, CB, DSO, DSC; 2 s, 1 da; m 2, 4 Oct 1954, Hugh Trevor-Roper, *see* Dacre of Glanton, Baron; *Career* chm: Music Therapy Charity 1969–82, Edinburgh Festival Guild 1960–80, Border Regn; organiser Oxford Subscription Concerts 1962–80; patron Cambridge Univ Opera Society; *Recreations* music, painting, interior decoration, gardening; *Style—* The Rt Hon the Lady Dacre of Glanton; ✉ The Old Rectory, Didcot, Oxon OX11 7EB

DACRE OF GLANTON, Baron (Life Peer UK 1979), of Glanton, Co Northumberland; Hugh Redwald Trevor-Roper; s of Dr Bertie William Edward Trevor-Roper; *b* 15 Jan 1914; *Educ* Charterhouse, ChCh Oxford; *m* 4 Oct 1954, Lady Alexandra Haig, da of Field Marshal 1 Earl Haig, the WWI Gen; *Career* sits as Cons Peer in House of Lords; former tutor ChCh Oxford, Regius prof of modern history Oxford 1957–80, nat dir Times Newspapers 1974–88, master Peterhouse Cambridge 1980–87; *Clubs* Garrick, Beefsteak; *Style—* The Rt Hon the Lord Dacre of Glanton; ✉ The Old Rectory, Didcot, Oxon OX11 7EB

DADA, Feroze Ahmad; s of Ahmad Valimohamed Dada, of Pakistan, and Halima; *b* 21 April 1952; *Educ* St Patrick's Sch Karachi, Univ of Karachi (BCom); *m* 4 Feb 1984, Farida, da of H L A Maung, of Burma; 1 s (Nadir b 1990), 1 da (Sumaya b 1986); *Career* sr ptnr Freeman & Partners Chartered Accountants 1981–; dir: FSI Group plc 1986–, Brook Hotels PLC 1994–, Reyker Investments Ltd 1995–; FCA 1983, ATII 1978, ACIArb 1996; *Books* Interest Relief for Companies (1981); *Recreations* cricket; *Clubs* Brondesbury Cricket; *Style—* F A Dada, Esq; ✉ Northfield, 158 Totteridge Lane, Totteridge, London N20 8JJ (☎ 0181 446 7846); Freeman & Partners Chartered Accountants, 30 St James's Street, London SW1A 1HB (☎ 0171 925 0770, fax 0171 925 0726)

DAFFERN, Allan Lister; s of Lister Daffern, of Keighley, and Anne Marguerite, *née* Stewart; *b* 8 Aug 1939; *Educ* Bellevue GS Bradford; *m* Madeleine, da of late Albert Cyril Yeo; 1 s (Richard), 2 da (Jane, Sarah); *Career* Nat Serv RAEC 1960–62; trainee Royal Insurance 1955–60, md: Life & Pensions Co Bartlett Insurance Brokers 1972–85 (joined 1963), life & pensions brokerage Rattray Daffern & Partners Ltd (co sold to Willis Corroon 1987) 1985–87; regnl md Willis Wrightson Financial Planning Ltd 1988–89, chief exec Willis Consulting Ltd 1989–91, chief exec Willis Corroon Financial Planning Ltd 1992–; dep chm Fin Servs Ctee Br Insurance & Investmt Brokers Assoc 1984–89, dir Personal Investment Authy 1993–, dir Investors Compensation Scheme 1995–; FCII 1960, Assoc Pensions Mgmnt Inst 1983; *Recreations* golf, fell walking, travel, Yorkshire cricket; *Clubs* Yorkshire CCC, Masham Golf; *Style—* Allan Daffern, Esq; ✉ The Carrs, Darley, Harrogate, N Yorkshire HG3 2QQ (☎ 01423 780384); Willis Corroon Financial Planning Ltd, 30 Park Place, Leeds LS1 2SP (☎ 0113 245 9077, fax 0113 242 6824)

DAFIS, Cynog Glyndwr; MP (Plaid Cymru) Ceredigion and Pembroke North (majority 3,193); s of late Rev George Davies, and Annie Davies; *b* 1 April 1938; *Educ* Aberaeron County Secdy Sch, Neath Boys' GS, UCW Aberystwyth; *m* 1 Jan 1962, Llinos Iorwerth, da of Iorwerth and Eluned Jones; 2 s, 1 da; *Career* teacher of English and Welsh Pontardawe Coll of FE 1960–62, head of English Newcastle Emlyn Secdy Modern Sch 1962–80, teacher of English Aberaeron Comp Sch 1980–84, head of English Dyffryn Teifi Comp Sch Llandysul 1984–91, res offr Dept of Adult Continuing Educn UC Swansea 1991–92; MP (Plaid Cymru) Ceredigion and Pembroke N 1992–; *Recreations* literature, music, walking, jogging; *Style—* Cynog Dafis, Esq, MP; ✉ Crugyreryr Uchaf, Talgarreg, Llandysul, Dyfed; House of Commons, London SW1A 0AA

DAFTER, Raymond Maurice (Ray); s of Maurice Henry Dafter, of Swindon, Wilts, and Dorothy Joan, *née* Vincent; *b* 22 April 1944; *Educ* Marlborough GS, The Coll Swindon, Harvard Univ; *m* 25 Sept 1965, Christine, da of William Charles Richard Franklin (d 1976), of Swindon, Wilts; 2 da (Yvonne Louise b 5 May 1968, Claire Rachel b 13 Dec 1970); *Career* journalist: Evening Advertiser Swindon 1961–64, Evening Post Bristol 1964–70, Financial Times London 1970–83; central dir Public and Overseas Relations Electricity Cncl London 1983–88, dep chief exec and head of consultancy Valin Pollen Ltd 1988–90, corp affairs dir Enterprise Oil plc 1990–; FInstPet 1978; *Books* Running Out of Fuel (1978), Scraping the Barrel (1980), Winning More Oil (1982); *Recreations* sailing, music, flying, walking; *Style—* Ray Dafter, Esq; ✉ Wolsey Oast, Claygate Rd, Laddingford, Kent (☎ 01892 730376)

DAGGER, John Frederick Hannay; s of Richard Leslie Dagger, MD (d 1973), of Newcastle upon Tyne, and Iris, *née* Hannay (d 1973); *b* 13 July 1927; *Educ* Uppingham; *m* 19 June 1948, Patricia Anne, da of Charles Edward Thompson (d 1979), of Sheffield; 1 s (Richard b 1950), 1 da (Sarah b 1953); *Career* Capt Coldstream Gds 1945–52 (Malaya 1948–50); tea planter S India 1952–56, dir Hopfactors (UK) Ltd 1963–86 (joined 1957); genealogist; Freeman City of London 1994; memb AGRA 1984; *Recreations* walking, looking up old relatives; *Style—* John Dagger, Esq; ✉ Oak House, Horsmonden, Tonbridge, Kent TN12 8LP (☎ 01892 722272, fax 01892 722671)

DAGLESS, Prof Erik Leslie; s of Alec W Dagless, and Johanne, *née* Petersen (d 1976); *b* 4 Nov 1946; *Educ* Orton Longueville GS, Univ of Surrey (BSc, PhD); *m* 23 Aug 1969, Christine Annette, da of Leslie Lansbury; 2 s (Niels b 1973, Stephen b 1975), 1 da (Helen b 1972); *Career* lectr Univ Coll Swansea 1971–78, sr lectr UMIST 1981 (lectr 1978–81); Univ of Bristol: prof of microelectronics 1982–, head of dept 1985–88, dean Faculty of Engrg 1988–91, Leverhulme Tst Royal Soc Senior Res Fell 1991–92; hon ed Part E IEE Proceedings, conslt ed ESES Addison Wesley; memb Exec Ctee UCNS 1989–92; FIEE; *Books* Introduction to Microprocessors (1979); *Style—* Prof Erik Dagless; ✉ Department of Electrical and Electronic Engineering, Merchant Venturer's Building, Woodland Road, Bristol BS8 1UB (☎ 0117 954 5205)

DAGWORTHY, Wendy; *Educ* Medway Coll of Art, Hornsey Coll of Art (DipAD); *Career* fashion designer with Radley (Quroum) 1971, designer/dir own label Wendy Dagworthy Ltd 1972–88 (outfit exhibited at V&A), freelance designer and conslt for Laura Ashley 1992; has exhibited internationally (London, Milan, NY, Paris), participating designer The Courtelle Awards, Fashion Aid and many other charity shows; dir London Designer Collections 1982–90, conslt to CNAA Fashion/Textiles Bd 1982, judge RSA Bd 1982; lectr at numerous colls since 1972 incl: Bristol, Kingston, Liverpool, Manchester, Newcastle and Lancashire Polys, Gloucester and Medway Colls of Art & Design, Salisbury Coll of Art, RCA; external assessor (fashion courses) for numerous colls incl: St Martin's Sch of Art 1986–88, Swire Coll of Design Hong Kong Poly 1989; judge of art and design projects, awards and competitions for various cos incl: Br Wool Textile Corp, Br Fashion Awards, Tissavel Fur, BP, Courtelle Awards, Lennard's Bursary Award, Fil d'Or Int Linen Award Monte Carlo 1985, Irish Designer Awards 1988, Smirnoff Awards 1989, Lloyd's Bank Fashion Challenge (chm) 1990–91, Nat Nescafe Design Competition 1991, ICI Fibres Tactel Awards Paris 1992, The Clothes Show Competition 1993; course dir (BA Hons Fashion) Central St Martin's Coll of Art and Design 1989–, course and document advsr Birmingham Poly 1991; has appeared regularly on TV and radio shows nationwide; hon memb Fashion Acts; *Style—* Ms Wendy Dagworthy; ✉ Central St Martin's School of Art, 107–109 Charing Cross Road, London WC2H 0DU (☎ 0171 753 9090)

DAGWORTHY PREW, Wendy Ann; da of Arthur Sidney Dagworthy (d 1972), of Gravesend, Kent, and Jean Annie, *née* Stubbs; *b* 4 March 1950; *Educ* Northfleet Secdy Sch for Girls, Medway Coll of Design, Hornsey Coll of Art (BA); *m* 4 Aug 1973, Jonathan William Prew, s of Capt William Sidney Augustus Prew (d 1962), of Somerset and Africa; 2 s (Augustus Art b 17 Sept 1987, Somerset Sidney b 14 July 1990); *Career* designer/dir Wendy Dagworthy Ltd 1972–; lectr various colls, coll external assessor BA Hons degree in fashion and textiles, course dir BA Hons degree in fashion Central St Martin's Coll of Art & Design 1989–; dir London Designer Collections 1982, conslt CIYAA Fashion/Textiles Bd 1982–, judge Art and Design Projects various mfrs, memb RSA Bd; participating designer Fashion Aid Albert Hall; exhibitor V&A; seasonal exhibitor: London, Milan, NY, Paris; various TV appearances; Fil D'Or Int Linen Award; memb Br Fashion Cncl; *Recreations* dining out, theatre, horse racing, reading, painting, cooking; *Clubs* Chelsea Arts, Groucho; *Style—* Ms Wendy Dagworthy Prew; ✉ 18 Melrose Terrace, London W6 (☎ 0171 602 6676)

DAHRENDORF, Baron (Life Peer UK 1993), of Clare Market in the City of Westminster; Sir Ralf Dahrendorf; KBE (1982); s of Gustav Dahrendorf (d 1954), and Lina, *née* Witt (d 1980); *b* 1 May 1929; *Educ* Hamburg Univ (DPhil), LSE (PhD); *m* 1980, Ellen Joan, da of James Krug, of NY; *Career* lectr Saarbrücken 1957; prof of sociology: Hamburg 1958–60, Tübingen 1960–64, Konstanz 1966–69 (vice-chm Funding Ctee Konstanz Univ 1964–66); Parly sec of state FO 1969–70, memb EEC Cmmn Brussels 1970–74, dir LSE 1974–84, non-exec dir Glaxo Holdings PLC 1984–, warden St Antony's Coll Oxford 1987–97, dir and chm Newspaper Publishing plc 1992–93; memb: Hansard Soc Cmmn on Electoral Reform 1975–76, Royal Cmmn on Legal Servs 1976–79; tstee Ford Fndn 1976–88; Hon DLitt: Reading, Dublin, Malta; Hon LLD: Manchester, Wagner Coll NY, York (Ontario), Columbia NY; Hon DHL: Kalamazoo Coll, Johns Hopkins Univ Baltimore; Hon DSc: Ulster, Bath, Bologna; Hon DUniv: Open Univ, Maryland, Surrey; Hon Dr: Université Catholique de Louvain; Hon DSSc: Queen's Belfast, Univ of Birmingham; Hon Dr in International Relations The American Univ Washington, Hon Dr in Sociology Univ of Urbino; Hon Degree Univ of Buenos Aires, Hon DPhil Univ of Haifa in Isreal, Hon Dr Université René Descartes Paris; Hon MRIA; hon fell: Imperial Coll, LSE; Grand Cross de l'Ordre du Mérite (Sénégal) 1971, Grosses Bundesverdienstkreuz mit Stern und Schulterband (W Germany) 1974, Grand Croix de l'Ordre du Mérite (Luxembourg) 1974, Grosses Goldenes Ehrenzeichen am Bande für Verdienste (Austria) 1975, Grand Croix de l'Ordre de Léopold II (Belgium) 1975; FBA, FRSA; *Clubs* Reform, Garrick; *Style—* The Rt Hon Lord Dahrendorf, KBE; ✉ St Antony's College, Oxford OX2 6JF

DAICHES, Prof David; CBE (1991); s of Salis Daiches (d 1945), and Flora Levin (d 1983); *b* 2 Sept 1912; *Educ* George Watson's Coll Edinburgh, Univ of Edinburgh (MA, Vans Dunlop scholar, Eliot prize) Balliol Coll Oxford (Elton exhibitioner, DPhil); *m* 1, 28 July 1937, Isobel Janet (d 1977), da of William Mackay (d 1941), of Scotland; 1 s (Alan Harry b 1939), 2 da (Jennifer Rachel b 1941, Elizabeth Mackay b 1946); m 2, 22 Dec 1978, Hazel Margaret Newman (d 1986); *Career* second sec Br Embassy Washington DC USA 1943–46; Bradley fell Balliol Coll Oxford 1936–37, prof of English Cornell Univ USA 1946–51, univ lectr in English and fell Jesus Coll Cambridge 1951–61, prof of English and dean Sch of English and American Studies Univ of Sussex 1961–77, dir Inst for Advanced Studies in the Humanities Univ of Edinburgh 1981–86; former pres: Soc of Authors in Scotland, Assoc for Scottish Literary Studies, Saltire Soc (now hon pres); Hon LittD Brown Univ 1968, Docteur de L'Université Sorbonne 1973; Hon DLitt: Univ of Edinburgh 1976, Univ of Sussex 1978, Univ of Stirling 1980, Univ of Glasgow 1987, Univ of Bologna 1989, Guelph Univ 1990; hon fell Sunderland Poly 1977; FRSE 1981, FRSL; *Books* incl: The Novel and The Modern World (1939), The King James Bible: A Study of its Sources and Development (1941), Robert Burns (1950), A Critical History of English Literature (1960), The Paradox of Scottish Culture (1964), Walter Scott and his World (1971), God and the Poets (1984); *Recreations* music, talking; *Clubs* Scottish Arts, New Club (Edinburgh); *Style—* Prof David Daiches, CBE, FRSE; ✉ 22 Belgrave Crescent, Edinburgh EH4 3AL

DAICHES, Lionel Henry; QC (Scotland 1956); s of Rev Dr Salis Daiches (d 1945), of Edinburgh, and Flora Levin (d 1983); *b* 8 March 1911; *Educ* George Watson's Coll Edinburgh, Univ of Edinburgh (MA, LLB); *m* 1947 (m dis 1973), Dorothy Bernstein; 2 s (Michael, Nicholas); *Career* N Staffs Regt 1940–46, Maj J A G Staff, 1 Army N Africa, Italy (including Anzio Beachhead); admitted to Faculty of Advocates 1946, standing jr counsel Bd of Control Scotland 1950–56; fell Int Acad of Trial Lawyers 1976; *Books* Russians at Law (1960); *Recreations* talking, globe trotting; *Clubs* New (Edinburgh), Scottish Arts (Edinburgh); *Style—* Lionel Daiches, Esq, QC; ✉ 10 Heriot Row, Edinburgh EH3 6HU (☎ 0131 556 4144); Parliament House, Parliament Square, Edinburgh EH1 1RF (☎ 0131 226 2881)

DAIN, David John Michael; CMG (1991); s of late John Gordon Dain, and Joan, *née* Connop; *b* 30 Oct 1940; *Educ* Merchant Taylors', St John's Coll Oxford (MA); *m* 28 June 1969, Susan Kathleen, da of J Richard F Moss, OBE, of Cambridge; 1 s (Christopher b

1977), 4 da (Sarah b 1974, Penelope b 1979, Tessa and Sophie (twins) b 1981); *Career* HM Dip Serv 1963–: Sch of Oriental and African Studies (Persian Studies), Br Embassy Tehran 1964, oriental sec Kabul 1965–68, Cabinet Office 1969–72, Bonn 1972–75, FCO 1975–78, head of Chancery Athens 1978–81, dep high cmmr Nicosia 1981–85, head Western Euro Dept FCO 1985–89, attached to Office of the Min for the Civil Serv 1989–90, high cmmr Cyprus 1990–94, dir for Asian affairs (asst under sec of state) 1994–; fell Inst of Linguists; Royal Order of Merit (Norway) 1988; *Recreations* tennis, bridge, walking, sailing, natural history, flying, fishing; *Clubs* United Oxford and Cambridge Univ, Oxford Union, Royal Over-Seas League; *Style—* David J M Dain, Esq, CMG; ✉ c/o FCO, King Charles Street, London SW1A 2AH

DAIN, John Stewart; s of Dr Basil Guy Dain (d 1976), of Acocks Green, Birmingham, and Veronica Mary, *née* Price (d 1969); *b* 27 Dec 1937; *Educ* Uppingham; *m* 15 Aug 1964, Carol Gail, da of Leigh Walter Denis Clulee; 2 s (Mark St John b 28 June 1967, Justin Leigh b 3 May 1970); *Career* articled clerk Newman Biggs & Co CAs Birmingham 1956–62, Deloitte Plender Griffiths London 1962–64, Withnall Carlyle Bridgewater & Scurrah Birmingham 1964–65, Dain & Co 1965–95 (successively mangr, ptnr, managing ptnr then sr ptnr); company sec and jt dep chm Business Link (Staffs) Ltd; pres and past chm Burton upon Trent Enterprise Agency, past chm Tamworth and Lichfield Gp of CAs, former memb Audit Registration Ctee Inst of CAs, memb Enterprise Gp ICAEW, senator Jr Chamber Int, past pres Burton upon Trent Jr Chamber and past regnl chm and nat treas Br Jr Chamber, treas and past pres Burton upon Trent C of C and Indust, memb Cncl E Mercia C of C, memb Exec Ctee Staffs Devpt Assoc and chm Staffs Fin Exchange, chm Barton-under-Needwood Youth and Community Advsy Ctee, past chm Barton-under-Needwood Parish Cncl, past chm Assoc of Staffs Sports Cncls, chm Grey Gables (old people's home), chm St Giles Hospice Whittington Lichfield, vice chm Burton Hosps NHS Tst; FCA 1962, FCCA 1981, FIMgt 1980; *Recreations* walking, hockey, rugby, photography; *Clubs* The Burton (treas), Burton upon Trent Rugby, Holland Sports (past chm), Barton-under-Needwood Hockey, Bretby Rotary (fndr pres and past sec), The Rocket (past pres); *Style—* John Dain, Esq; ✉ 32 Captains Lane, Barton-under-Needwood, Burton upon Trent, Staffordshire DE13 8EZ (☎ and fax 01283 712613)

DAINTITH, Prof Terence Charles; s of Edward Daintith (d 1942), and Irene, *née* Parsons; *b* 8 May 1942; *Educ* Wimbledon Coll, St Edmund Hall Oxford (BA, MA), Univ of Nancy (Leverhulme Euro scholar); *m* Christine Anne, da of Sqdn Ldr Charles Edward Bulport; 1 s (Edward Charles b 1967), 1 da (Alexandra b 1968); *Career* called to the Bar 1966; assoc in law Univ of Calif 1963–64, lectr in constitutional law Univ of Edinburgh 1964–72 (dir of studies in law 1970–72), visiting prof Faculty of Law Univ of Aix Marseilles III France 1975, prof of public law and head Dept of Public Law Univ of Dundee 1972–83 (fndr and dir Centre for Petroleum and Mineral Law Studies 1977–83), prof of law Euro Univ Inst Florence 1981–87; Univ of London: prof of law 1988–, dir Inst of Advanced Legal Studies 1988–95, dean Insts of Advanced Study 1991–94, dean Sch of Advanced Study 1994–; Parsons scholar Univ of Sydney 1988; ed Jl of Energy and Nat Resources Law 1983–92; tstee: Hamlyn Tst 1988–, Petroleum and Mineral Law Educn Tst 1989–95; memb Academia Europaea 1989 (convenor legal ctee 1993–96); *Publications* Report on the Economic Law of the United Kingdom (1974), United Kingdom Oil and Gas Law (with G D M Willoughby, 1977, 2 edn 1984), The Legal Character of Petroleum Licences (ed and contrib, 1981), European Energy Strategy - The Legal Framework (with L Hancher, 1986), Contract and Organisation - Social Science Contributions to Legal Analysis (with G Teubner 1986), The Legal Integration of Energy Markets (with S Williams, 1987), Law as an Instrument of Economic Policy - Comparative and Critical Approaches (1988), Harmonization and Hazard - Regulating Workplace Health and Safety in the European Community (with G R Baldwin, 1992), Implementing EC Law in the United Kingdom: Structures for Indirect Rule (1995); *Recreations* cycling, curling and carpentry; *Clubs* Athenaeum; *Style—* Prof Terence Daintith; ✉ School of Advanced Study, University of London, Senate House, Malet Street, London WC1E 7HU (☎ 0171 636 8000, ext 3450)

DAINTON, Baron (Life Peer UK 1986), of Hallam Moors in South Yorkshire; Dr Sir Frederick Sydney Dainton; kt (1971); s of George Whalley, and Mary Jane Dainton; *b* 11 Nov 1914; *Educ* Central Sch Sheffield, St John's Coll Oxford (MA, BSc), Sidney Sussex Coll Cambridge (PhD, ScD); *m* 1942, Barbara Hazlitt, JP, PhD, o da of late Dr W B Wright, of Manchester; 1 s (Hon John Bourke b 10 Sept 1947), 2 da (Hon Mary Crawford (Hon Mrs Whitehead) b 15 Feb 1950, Hon Rosalind Hazlitt (Hon Mrs Conway) b 11 April 1952); *Career* fell and praelector St Catharine's Coll Cambridge 1945–50, H O Jones lectr in physical chemistry Univ of Cambridge 1947–50, vice chllr Univ of Nottingham and hon dir Cookridge High Energy Radiation Res Centre Univ of Leeds 1965–70 (prof of physical chemistry 1950–65), Dr Lee's prof of chemistry Univ of Oxford 1970–73, chllr Univ of Sheffield 1979–; chm: Advsy Ctee on Sci and Tech Information 1966–70, Nat Libraries Ctee 1969–70, Cncl Scientific Policy Advsy Bd for the Res Cncls 1969–73, Univ Grants Ctee 1973–78, Harkness Fellowship UK Selection Ctee 1974–81, Nat Radiological Protection Bd 1978–85, Br Library Bd 1978–85, Royal Postgrad Med Sch 1979–89, Edward Boyle Meml Tst 1982–; govr: Henley Admin Staff Coll 1974–89, LSE 1980–; tstee: Br Museum (natural history) 1974–84, Wolfson Fndn 1979–88; cmmr Museums and Galleries 1983–91; hon fell: St Catharine's Coll Cambridge, St John's Coll Oxford, RCP, Royal Soc of Chemistry, RCR, BIR, Library Assoc, LSE, QMC (now Queen Mary and Westfield Coll), Birkbeck Coll, Goldsmiths' Coll, RPMS; privilegiate St Hilda's Coll Oxford 1994–; pres RPMS 1990–; visiting prof: Toronto 1949, Notre Dame 1952, MIT 1959, Melbourne 1959, Cornell 1961, Alberta 1962; foreign memb: Royal Soc of Sci Sweden, American Acad of Arts and Sci, Acad of Scis Göttingen, Acad Mediterranae della Scienze, American Philosophical Soc; Hon ScD: Łódź, Dublin; Hon DSc: Bath, Loughborough, Heriot-Watt, Warwick, Strathclyde, Exeter, Belfast, Manchester, E Anglia, Leeds, McMaster, Uppsala, Liverpool, Ulster, Salford, Reading, Kent; Hon LLD: Nottingham, Aberdeen, Sheffield, Cambridge, London; Hon DCL Oxford; Hon DLitt CNAA; Davy Medal Royal Soc, Tilden and Faraday Medals Royal Soc of Chemistry, Crookshank Medal RCR, Syvanus Thompson Medal BIR, John Snow Medal Coll of Anaesthetists, Firth Medal Forensic Science Soc, Semenov Centenary Medal Russian Acad of Sci; prime warden Worshipful Co of Goldsmiths 1982–83 (memb Ct of Assts); Knight Cdr Order of Merit Poland; Hon FRSE 1996; FRSC 1938, FRS 1957, FRCP 1979, FRCR 1984, FLA 1986; *Books* Chain Reactions (1956 and 1966, in Polish and Chinese translations), Photochemistry and Reaction Kinetics (jt ed and contrib, 1967), Choosing a British University (1980), Universities and the National Health Service (1983); *Recreations* walking, colour photography; *Clubs* Athenaeum; *Style—* The Rt Hon Lord Dainton, FRS; ✉ 36 Charlbury Road, Oxford OX2 6UX (☎ 01865 510568)

DAKERS, Dr Lionel Frederick; CBE (1983); s of Lewis Dakers (d 1978), and Eleanor, *née* Hooper (d 1976); *b* 24 Feb 1924; *Educ* Rochester Cathedral Choir Sch, pupil of Sir Edward Bairstow (organist of York Minster), Royal Acad of Music, DMus (Lambeth); *m* 21 April 1951, Mary Elisabeth, da of Rev Claude Williams (d 1963); 4 da (Rachel, Mary, Juliet, Felicity); *Career* WWII, served RAEC 1942–47; asst organist St George's Chapel Windsor 1950–54, asst music master Eton 1952–54; organist: Ripon Cathedral 1954–57, Exeter Cathedral 1957–72; dir Royal Sch of Church Music 1972–89, chm Salisbury Diocesan Advsy Ctee 1990–, Lay Canon Salisbury Cathedral 1993–; Hon MusD Exeter 1991; FRCO 1945, FRAM 1962, FRCM 1980; *Books* Church Music at the Crossroads (1970), A Handbook of Parish Music (1979), Making Church Music Work (1978), Music and the Alternative Service Book (ed, 1980), The Chorister's Companion (ed, 1980), The Psalms - Their Use and Performance Today (1980), The Church Musician as Conductor (1982), Church Music in a Changing World (1984), Choosing - and Using - Hymns (1985), New Church Anthem Book (ed, 1992), Places where they sing (1995); *Recreations* book collecting, gardening, continental food, travel; *Clubs* Athenaeum; *Style—* Dr Lionel Dakers, CBE; ✉ 6 Harcourt Terrace, Salisbury, Wiltshire SP2 7SA (☎ 01722 324880)

DALBY, Ven (John) Mark Meredith; s of William Dalby, and Sheila Mary, *née* Arkell; *b* 3 Jan 1938; *Educ* King George V Sch Southport, Exeter Coll Oxford (MA), Ripon Hall Oxford, Univ of Nottingham (PhD); *Career* ordained: deacon 1963, priest 1964; curate: Hambleden Bucks 1963–68, Fawley, Fingest, Medmenham and Turville Bucks 1965–68; vicar of St Peter Spring Hill Birmingham 1968–75, rural dean of Birmingham City 1973–75, sec Ctee for Theol Educn and selection sec Advsy Cncl for the Church's Min (now Advsy Bd of Min) 1975–80, hon curate of All Hallows Tottenham 1975–80, vicar of St Mark Worsley 1980–84, team rector of Worsley 1984–91, rural dean of Eccles 1987–91, archdeacon of Rochdale 1991–; examining chaplain to the Bishop of Manchester 1980–; memb: Gen Synod of C of E 1985–95, Liturgical Cmmn 1986–95; *Recreations* travel, local and family history, philately; *Clubs* Royal Commonwealth Society; *Style—* The Ven the Archdeacon of Rochdale; ✉ 21 Belmont Way, Rochdale, Lancs OL12 6HR (☎ and fax 01706 48640)

DALDRY, Stephen David; s of Patrick Daldry (d 1976), and Cherry, *née* Thompson; *b* 2 May 1961; *Educ* Huish GS Taunton, Univ of Sheffield (BA); *Career* artistic director; appt incl: Metro Theatre 1984–86, artistic assoc Crucible Theatre Sheffield 1986–88 (trainee dir (Arts Cncl) 1985–86), Gate Theatre London 1989–92, Royal Court Theatre London 1992–; prodn incl: Damned for Despair (Gate Theatre (winner best dir London Fringe Awards and Critics' Circle)), An Inspector Calls (NT (winner best dir, Olivier Awards, Evening Standard Awards, Critics' Circle Awards, Drama Desk Awards, Tony Awards)), Machinal (RNT (winner best dir Olivier Awards)), Judgement Day (Old Red Lion Theatre (winner best dir London Fringe Awards)), Ingoldstadt (Gate Theatre (winner best dir London Fringe Awards and Time Out Awards)), Figaro gets Divorced (Gate Theatre (winner best dir Time Out Awards)), The Kitchen (Royal Court) 1995; memb: Equity, Soc of Dirs (USA); *Style—* Stephen Daldry, Esq; ✉ c/o The Royal Court Theatre, Sloane Square, London SW1W 8AS (☎ 0171 730 5170, fax 0171 730 4705)

DALE, Celia Marjorie (Mrs Guy Ramsey); da of James Dale (d 1985), of London, and Marguerite, *née* Adamson (d 1981), of London; *Educ* privately; *m* 1938, Guy Ramsey (d 1959), s of Cecil Ramsey; 1 s (Simon b 1944); *Career* reviewer, publishers' advsr, author; winner Crime Writers' Assoc Veuve Cliquot Short Story award; memb Crime Writers' Assoc 1979; *Books* The Least of These (1943), To Hold the Mirror (1945), The Dry land (1952), The Wooden O (1953), Trial of Strength (1955), A Spring of Love (1960), Other People (1964), A Helping Hand (1966), Act of Love (1969), A Dark Corner (1971), The Innocent Party (1973), Helping with Inquiries (1979), A Personal Call and Other Stories (1986), Sheeps Clothing (1988); author of numerous short stories, radio, and television recordings; *Recreations* reading, conversation, travel; *Style—* Ms Celia Dale; ✉ Curtis Brown, Haymarket House, 28/29 Haymarket, London SW1Y 4SP (☎ 0171 396 6600, fax 0171 396 0110)

DALE, Iain Leonard; OBE (1989); s of Leonard H Dale, CBE, DL (d 1986), fndr of Dale Electric International plc 1935, and Doris Anne Smithson (d 1984); *b* 9 June 1940; *Educ* Scarborough Coll Yorkshire; *m* Maria, da of Josef Lanmuller (d 1973), of Pottendorf-Landegg, Lower Austria, Austria; 3 s (Jonathan Iain b 1963, Paul Josef b 1967, David Leonard b 1969); *Career* creative dir Streets Advertising 1969–71, md Hicks Oubridge Public Affairs 1971–74; chm: Dale Electric International plc 1992–94 (dir 1972–94), Dale Power Systems plc 1992–94; dir: Ottomotores Dale Sa De Cv (Mexico) 1981–94, Dale Electric Power Systems Ltd (Thailand) 1985–94, Witt & Busch Ltd (Nigeria) 1986–94; chm TR Pacific Investment Trust plc 1994– (dir 1990–); non-exec dir: Chevalier International Holdings Ltd Hong Kong 1992–, Silvermines Group plc 1995–, Bowman Power Systems Ltd 1995–; chm Assoc of Br Generating Set Manufacturers 1984–85; chm: South East Asia Trade Advsy Gp (SEATAG) 1988–92, Southern Asia Advsy Group (SAAG) 1994–, Br Cncl's Professional Involvement Project 1994–; memb: NEDO Generating Set Sub Gp 1982–87, Nat Cncl CBI 1984–94 (memb Fin and Gen Purpose Ctee 1992–93), Latin American Trade Advsy Gp 1985–92, Br Overseas Trade Bd 1992–, Bd of Govrs SOAS Univ of London 1992–94, Foreign & Cwlth Office Business Panel 1994–; pres Scarborough Economic Action Ltd 1994–; memb Company of Merchant Adventurers of City of York; CIMgt; *Recreations* walking, photography; *Clubs* RAC; *Style—* Iain L Dale, Esq, OBE; ✉ Grove House, Low Marishes, Malton, N Yorks YO17 0RQ (☎ 01904 621295, fax 01904 620218)

DALE, John; s of Kenneth Dale, of Cleethorpes, and Eileen, *née* Minchin; *b* 1 May 1946; *Educ* Wintringham GS Grimsby; *Career* Daily Mail 1968–78, The Observer 1978–79, Now! magazine 1979–81; ed Take a Break magazine 1991–; memb Br Soc of Magazine Eds 1991; *Books* The Prince and The Paranormal (1985); *Style—* John Dale, Esq; ✉ Take a Break, 25–27 Camden Road, London N1 9LL (☎ 0171 284 0909)

DALE, Laurence Vincent; s of George Robert Dale, of Keymer, Sussex, and Thelma Jean, *née* Singleton; *b* 10 Sept 1957; *Educ* Brighton Hove & Sussex GS, Guildhall Sch of Music and Drama, Salzburg Mozarteum; *Career* tenor; memb Royal Opera Co Covent Garden 1980–81, professional debut as Camille in The Merry Widow (ENO) 1981; awarded Medaille de la Ville de Paris for contrib to French culture; *Roles* incl: Don José in Peter Brooke's La Tragedie de Carmen (cr role) 1981, title role in Orfeo (ENO 1983, Salzburg Festival 1993), Ulysses (ENO) 1989, Don Ottavio in Don Giovanni (Nice, Munich, Salzburg Festival, WNO, Berlin, Marseille, Genova), Ferrando in Cosi fan Tutte (WNO, Holland Festival, Frankfurt, Berlin), Alfredo in La Traviata (WNO), Fenton in Falstaff (Brussels, Aix-en-Provence, NY, Milano, Covent Garden, Buenos Aires), Eisenstein in Die Fledermaus (WNO), Tamino in The Magic Flute (Vienna Staatsoper, Salzburg, Zurich, Brussels, Toronto, Stuttgart, Berlin, Opera Bastille Paris), Romeo in Gounod's Romeo and Juliet (Basel, Zurich), Idamante in Idomeneo (Holland Festival), Ramino in La Cenerentola (Glyndebourne, Marseille), Pelléas et Mélisande (Lausanne), Belfiore in La Finta Giardiniera (Salzburg Festival debut) 1992, title role in Werther (Lille and Paris) 1993, Debussy's Rodrigue et Chimene (world premiere Lyon Opera) 1993; *Recordings* incl: Recital of French Opera and Opera-Comique Arias (under Kenneth Montgomery, 1988), Gounod's St Cecilia Mass, Mozart's Mass in C Minor, Honegger's Le Roi David, Debussy's Rodrigue et Chimene, Purcell's The Fairy Queen, Berlioz Prix de Rome Cantatas, Monteverdi's Orfeo, Chausson's La Tempete; *Style—* Laurence Dale, Esq; ✉ Musicaglotz, 11 Rue Le Verrier, 75006 Paris (☎ 00 33 1 42 34 5340, fax 00 33 1 40 46 9377)

DALE, Prof Peter Grenville Hurst; s of Thomas Calvert Dale (d 1964), of Ambleside, N Brunton, Gosforth, Newcastle upon Tyne, and Phyllis, *née* Addison; *b* 14 Feb 1935; *Educ* Dame Allan's Boys' Sch, Rutherford Coll, King's Coll Univ of Durham (DipArch), Leeds Metropolitan Univ (MA); *m* 1 (m dis 1985); 3 s (Ruarigh b 1966, Patrick b 1968, Robert b 1971); m 2, 14 Sept 1988, Elizabeth Josephine Mary, da of Lt Cdr Reginald Galer, RN (ret), of Pembroke, Dyfed; *Career* chartered architect; former posts in: Kingston upon Thames, Surrey Co, Gateshead Borough, Newcastle City; asst dir Lothian Region 1974–77, Co architect Humberside 1977–87, self-employed 1987–; sr lectr Leeds Metropolitan Univ 1987–96, external prof Univ of Leeds 1994–; author of 5 RIBA open learning packages in practice mgmnt, briefing processes, price control, selecting contractors and tendering procedures; memb Cncl ARCUK (vice chm 1994), chm ARCUK/RIBA Jt Validation Panel 1996–, former memb Cncl SCALA and RIAS; RIBA: twice former hon treas, vice pres, memb Cncl, memb Educn Ctee, former chm Yorks Region, twice former pres Humberside Branch; former dep chm Lothian Region Children's Panels; memb Independant Tribunal Serv; project mangr CISC/NCVQ Future of the Built Environment; chm: BSI Tech Ctee for Contractor Standards in EC (also Euro delegate), Govt Advsy Panel for DOE Res; memb Whole Indust Res Strategy Gp DOE; parish clerk to St Faith under St Paul's; memb: Worshipful Co of Chartered Architects 1988 (Jr Warden and memb Ct of Assts), Worshipful Co of Parish Clerks; Freeman City of London 1990; RIBA 1961, FRIAS 1971, FRSA 1992, MBAE 1994; *Recreations* painting, golf, fishing, shooting; *Clubs* Athenaeum; *Style*— Prof Peter G H Dale; ✉ 19 Mile End Park, Pocklington, York YO4 2T (☎ and fax 01759 302996)

DALE, Stephen Hugh; s of Frederick Francis George Dale, of Lewes, Sussex, and Margaret Brenda Nancy, *née* Beales; *b* 12 July 1955; *Educ* Bolton Sch, Univ of Manchester (BA); *m* Corinne Jenny, *née* David; 1 da (Claire Jenny Margaret b Nov 1994); *Career* chartered accountant Deloitte Haskins & Sells Manchester 1976–80 (articled clerk 1976–79); Price Waterhouse: joined Tax Dept Manchester 1980, specialised in VAT and transferred to London office 1983, ptnr 1989– (Paris office 1991–); ICAEW: memb Tax Ctee, chm VAT Ctee 1988–96; memb: VAT Practitioners Gp 1983–91 (memb Exec Ctee), Jt VAT Ctee 1996–; pres Indirect Tax Ctee FEE 1993–; memb VAT Ctee Centre Français du Commerce Extérieur 1994–, pres Int VAT Assoc 1994–96 (tech sec 1996–), memb Conseil d'Administration de la Pratique de la TVA; ACA 1980; *Books* Advanced VAT Planning, Property and Financial Services (1989); *Recreations* music, walking, golf; *Style*— Stephen Dale, Esq; ✉ Price Waterhouse, Juridique et Fiscal, Tour AIG, Paris La Defense, France (☎ 00 33 1 41 26 41 61, fax 00 33 1 41 26 41 26)

DALE, Thomas Edward (Tom); DL (Essex 1996); s of Leonard George Dale (d 1964), of St Osyth, Essex, and Sybil Eileen Mary, *née* Stevenson (d 1988); *b* 14 March 1931; *Educ* Gosfield Sch Halstead, LSE (BSc), Inst of Educn Univ of London (PGCE); *Career* Nat Serv RA 1950–52; teacher 1952–54, warden Cambridge Int Centre 1960–66; organising sec Liberal International (Br Gp) 1967–, PA to Ldr of Lib Pty 1967–76, int offr Lib Pty 1977–85; dir: TEAM Promotions Ltd 1986–, Mercialodge Ltd 1987–; Parly candidate: (Lib) Harwich 1959, 1964, 1966 and 1969, (Alliance) Centl Suffolk 1987; pres Harwich Lib Assoc (now Lib Dem), pres N Essex Lib Democarats; former chm E Regnl Lib Pty, former exec memb ELDR Brussels, pres Univ of London Union 1957–58 (dep 1956–57), sec LSE SU 1955–56, govr LSE 1981–87; Essex CC: rep Brightlingsea Div 1965–67, 1973–77 and 1981–, vice chm P & R Ctee 1993–94 and 1995–, chm of Council 1994–95 (vice chm 1993–94), dep ldr of Council 1993–95 and 1995–, chm Heritage and Culture Bd 1996–; ldr Lib Dem Gp 1989–93 (dep ldr 1981–89 and 1993–94), spokesman on highways and agric estates 1981–89, spokesman on property 1993–; chm ACC Consumer Affrs Ctee 1986–87 and 1988–89; overseas fund raising dir Fight for Sight Appeal 1990–91; memb: Tendring DC 1979–95 (chm P & R Ctee 1991–95), St Osyth PC 1979–87, E Anglia Tourist Bd 1986–, Kent and Essex Sea Fisheries Cmmn 1986–, Environment Agency Essex Flood Def Ctee 1989–, Brightlingsea Town Cncl 1991– (mayor 1996); govr: Gosfield Sch (former chm), Colchester Inst 1981–93; sec Hampden Educnl Tst; Freeman Cinque Port Liberty of Brightlingsea; *Recreations* theatre, films, travel; *Clubs* National Liberal (memb Gen Ctee); *Style*— Tom Dale, Esq, DL; ✉ Flat 1, 2 Barking Road, London E6 3BP (☎ 0181 470 8640, fax 0181 470 3301); 45 Campernell Close, Brightlingsea, Colchester, Essex CO7 0TB (☎ 01206 305552)

DALE, Sir William Leonard; KCMG (1965); s of late Rev William Dale; *b* 1906; *Educ* Hymers Coll Hull; *m* 1966, Mrs Gloria Finn, *née* Spellman; 1 da (Rosemary Lincoln (Mrs Simon Alfred Hallgarten)); *Career* barr 1931; entered Colonial Office 1935; legal advsr: Govt of Libya 1951–53, Miny of Educn 1954, Cwlth Rels Office 1961–66, Gen Cncl UNRWA Beirut 1968–73; int legal conslt; *Books* Law of the Parish Church, Legislative Drafting: A New Approach, The Modern Commonwealth, Time Past Time Present; *Clubs* Travellers'; *Style*— Sir William Dale, KCMG; ✉ 20 Old Buildings, Lincoln's Inn, WC2A 3UP (☎ 0171 242 9365)

DALE-THOMAS, Philippa Mary; da of Peter Alan Dale-Thomas, of Taunton, Somerset, and Thirle Wynette Alpha, *née* Tribe; *b* 5 March 1960; *Educ* Cheltenham Ladies' Coll, Cambridge Coll of Arts and Technol (HND); *Career* bd dir: Edelman Public Relations 1989–93 (joined 1982), Fishburn Hedges 1993–; IPR Awards for: public affairs 1987 and 1991, commerce and indust 1989 and 1990, internal communications 1989, long-term PR programmes 1991; MIPR 1988, MInstD 1989; *Recreations* horse riding, scuba diving, playing the piano; *Style*— Miss Philippa Dale-Thomas; ✉ Fishburn Hedges, 1 Northumberland Avenue, Trafalgar Square, London WC2B 5BW (☎ 0171 839 4321, fax 0171 839 2858)

DALES, Alistair Robert Harry; s of Ronald Harrold Dales, and Dorothy Helen, *née* Walton (d 1988); *b* 26 May 1949; *Educ* Hymers Coll Hull; *m* Aug 1971, Janis Ann, da of late George Moses; 1 da (Rachel Helen b 13 Feb 1980), 1 s (Benjamin Thomas b 18 Dec 1981); *Career* articled clerk then chartered accountant Hodgson Harris & Co Hull 1966–72, Price Waterhouse Brussels 1972–76; J P Morgan: vice pres Brussels 1976–84, vice pres Amsterdam 1984–85, vice pres London 1985–89; Nationwide Building Society: gen mangr internal audit 1989–91, divnl dir mortgage and insurance 1991–92, divnl dir fin 1992, gp fin dir 1993–; FCA 1971; *Recreations* reading, gardening, golf; *Style*— Alistair Dales, Esq; ✉ Nationwide Building Society, Nationwide House, Pipers Way, Swindon, Wilts SN38 1DL (☎ 01793 455340, fax 01793 455341)

DALES, Richard Nigel; CMG (1992); s of Kenneth Richard Frank Dales, TD (d 1989), of Southwold, Suffolk, and Olwen Mary, *née* Preedy; *b* 26 Aug 1942; *Educ* Chigwell Sch, St Catharine's Coll Cambridge (MA); *m* 10 Sept 1966, Elizabeth Margaret, da of Edward Owen Martin (d 1966), of Loughton, Essex; 1 s (Jeremy b 1973), 1 da (Eleanor b 1976); *Career* entered FO 1964, third sec Yaoundé Cameroon 1965–67, FCO 1968–70, second sec 1969, second (later first) sec Copenhagen 1970–73, asst private sec to Sec of State for Foreign and Cwlth Affrs 1974–77, first sec Head of Chancery and HM Consul Sofia 1977–81, asst S Asian Dept FCO 1981–82, cnsllr Copenhagen 1982–86, dep high cmmr Harare 1986–89, Head of Southern Africa Dept (later Central and Southern African Dept) FCO 1989–91, seconded to Recruitment and Assessment Services Agency as resident chm (FCO) CSSB 1991–92, high cmmr Zimbabwe 1992–95, dir (Africa and The Commonwealth) FCO 1995–; *Recreations* music, walking; *Clubs* United Oxford and Cambridge University; *Style*— Richard Dales, Esq, CMG; ✉ c/o Foreign and Commonwealth Office, King Charles St, London SW1A 2AH

DALEY, Michael John William; s of Desmond William Daley, of Cockfosters, Herts, and Alma Joan, *née* Ellen; *b* 23 Sept 1953; *Educ* Hatfield Sch; *m* 1993, Elizabeth Jane, *née* Hobson; 1 s (Nicholas William b 28 May 1995); *Career* S G Warburg & Co Ltd 1973–77, Credit Suisse First Boston Ltd 1977–86 (asst mangr 1979, mangr 1982), dir Credit Suisse First Boston Asset Management Ltd 1984–86, vice pres and head Fixed Income Group Morgan Stanley International 1986–91, exec dir Morgan Stanley Asset Management Ltd 1988–91; md: Hubbard & Daley Ltd 1991–92, Strategic Value Management Ltd 1992–; dir Guinness Flight Global Asset Management Ltd 1994–; FInstD 1984, MIMgt 1986, MSI 1993; *Recreations* golf, skiing, mountaineering, motoring, shooting; *Clubs* Carlton, RAC; *Style*— Michael Daley, Esq; ✉ Strategic Value Management Ltd, 37 Woodstock Road, London W4 1DT (☎ 0181 995 0724)

DALGETY, Hon Mr Justice; Ramsay Robertson; s of late James Robertson Dalgety, of Dundee, and Georgia Alexandra, *née* Whyte; *b* 2 July 1945; *Educ* Dundee HS, Univ of St Andrews (LLB); *m* 13 Nov 1971, Mary Margaret, da of late Rev Neil Cameron Bernard, of Edinburgh; 1 s (Neil b 1975), 1 da (Caroline b 1974); *Career* Advocate at the Scottish Bar 1972–85, QC (Scot) 1986–91, judge of the Supreme Ct Tonga 1991–; dir and chm: Archer Transport Ltd and Archer Transport (London) Ltd 1982–85, Venture Shipping Ltd 1983–85; dir: Scottish Opera Ltd 1980–90, Scottish Opera Theatre Trust Ltd 1987–90; memb: Faculty of Advocates 1972, IOD 1982–89; cncllr City of Edinburgh DC 1974–80, chm Opera Singers' Pension Fund London 1991– (tstee 1983–, dep chm 1987–91); temp sheriff 1987–91, dep traffic cmmr for Scotland 1988–93, dep chm Edinburgh Hibernian Shareholders' Assoc 1990–92; *Recreations* boating, golf, cricket, football, opera, travel; *Clubs* Surrey County Cricket, Nuku'alofa (Tonga); *Style*— Hon Mr Justice Dalgety; ✉ Apartment N, 116 Queensferry Road, Edinburgh EH4 2BT (☎ 0131 332 1417); Supreme Court, PO Box 11, Nuku'alofa, Kingdom of Tonga, South Pacific (☎ chambers 00 676 23599, home 00 676 23348, fax 00 676 23098)

DALGLEISH, Prof Angus George; s of Ronald Dalgleish, and Eileen Anna Dalgleish; *b* 14 May 1950; *Educ* Harrow Co GS for Boys, UCL (MRC scholar, BSc, MD), UCH (MB BS); *m* 28 Sept 1984, Judy Ann, da of Geoffrey Riley; 1 s (Tristan Amadeus b 7 Dec 1988); *Career* house surgn in general surgery and orthopaedics and locum casualty offr St Stephen's Hosp 1975, house physician in general med and oncology Poole District Hosp 1975, flying doctor serv Queensland 1976–77, general med registrar Princess Alexandra Hosp Brisbane 1978–80 (resident MO 1977–78), general med registrar Princess Alexandra Hosp and cardio-thoracic registrar Prince Charles Hosp 1980–81, registrar in radiotherapy Queensland Radium Inst Royal Brisbane Hosp 1981–82, sr registrar in oncology Royal Prince Alfred Hosp Sydney 1982–83, sr registrar in clinical immunology and haematology Clinical Immunological Research Centre Univ of Sydney and Kanematsu Inst Royal Prince Alfred Hosp 1983–84, clinical res fell Inst of Cancer Research and hon sr registrar Royal Marsden Hosp 1984–86, clinical scientist MRC/CRC and hon conslt physician, immunologist and oncologist Northwick Park Hosp 1986–88, head Retrovirus Research Gp CRC 1988–91, head of clinical virology, sr lectr and hon conslt physician Royal London Hosp Med Coll 1991–, prof and fndn chair of oncology St George's Hosp Med Sch 1991–; conslt Glaxo Wellcome; tstee London Youth Cancer Holiday Tst; FRCPath 1995 (MRCPath 1992), FRACP 1984, FRCP 1993 (MRCP 1984); *Publications* author of numerous medical pubns and chapters in books; *Recreations* windsurfing, skiing, opera; *Style*— Prof Angus Dalgleish; ✉ Divison of Oncology, St George's Hospital Medical School, Cranmer Terrace, Tooting, London SW17 0RE (☎ 0181 725 5815)

DALGLISH, Kenneth Mathieson (Kenny); MBE; *b* 4 March 1951; *Career* professional football manager; played for Celtic and Liverpool (manager 1986–91); honours with Celtic: Scottish League champions 1972–74 and 1977, Scottish Cup winners 1972, 1974, 1975 and 1977, Scottish League Cup winners 1975; with Liverpool: European Cup 1978, 1981 and 1984 (runners-up 1985), Div 1 champions 1979, 1980, 1982, 1983, 1984, 1986, 1988 and 1990, FA Cup 1986 and 1989, League Cup 1981–84; Blackburn Rovers FC: manager 1991–95 (promoted Premier League 1992, Premier League Champions 1995), dir of football 1995–96; manager Newcastle Utd FC 1997–; Scotland: 102 full caps; Football Writers' Footballer of the Year 1979, PFA Player of the Year 1983, Manager of the Year 1986 and 1988; Freeman City of Glasgow; *Style*— Kenny Dalglish, MBE; ✉ c/o Newcastle United Football Club, St James's Park, Newcastle-upon-Tyne NE1 4ST (☎ 0191 201 8400)

DALHOUSIE, 16 Earl of (S 1633); Simon Ramsay; KT (1971), GCVO (1979), GBE (1957), MC (1944), JP (Angus 1967), DL (1951); also Lord Ramsay of Dalhousie (S precedence of 1618), Lord Ramsay and Keringtoun (S 1633) and Baron Ramsay of Glenmark (UK 1875); s of 14 Earl of Dalhousie (d 1928), and Lady Mary Heathcote-Drummond-Willoughby (d 1960), da of 1 Earl of Ancaster; suc bro, 15 Earl of Dalhousie 1950; *b* 17 Oct 1914; *Educ* Eton, Ch Ch Oxford; *m* 26 June 1940, Margaret Elizabeth Mary, CStJ, da of Brig-Gen Archibald Stirling of Keir, JP, DL, MP (d 1931); 3 s, 2 da; *Heir* s, Lord Ramsay, *qv*; *Career* 4/5 Bn Black Watch, Maj 1942; Lieut Royal Co of Archers (Queen's Body Guard for Scotland) 1956; MP (C) Angus 1945–50, Cons whip 1946–48, Lord-Lt 1967–89; govr gen Fedn of Rhodesia and Nyasaland 1957–63; Lord Chamberlain to HM Queen Elizabeth The Queen Mother 1965–92; chllr Univ of Dundee 1977–92; *Recreations* gardening, fishing; *Clubs* White's; *Style*— The Rt Hon the Earl of Dalhousie, KT, GCVO, GBE, MC, JP, DL; ✉ 199 Cranmer Court, London SW3 (☎ 0171 352 6477); Brechin Castle, Brechin, Angus DD9 6SG (☎ 01356 622176)

DALITZ, Prof Richard Henry; s of Frederick William Dalitz (d 1959), of Melbourne, Aust, and Hazel Blanche, *née* Drummond (d 1970); *b* 28 Feb 1925; *Educ* Scotch Coll, Ormond Coll, Univ of Melbourne (BA, BSc), Trinity Coll Cambridge (PhD); *m* 8 August 1946, Valda, da of William Victor Giffen Suiter (d 1970), of Melbourne, Aust; 1 s (Rodric b 10 Nov 1947), 3 da (Katrine b 4 Aug 1950, Heather b 22 March 1960, Ellyn b 24 March 1964); *Career* res asst in physics Univ of Bristol 1948–49, reader in mathematical physics Univ of Birmingham 1955–56 (lectr 1949–55), prof of physics Enrico Fermi Inst for Nuclear Studies Univ of Chicago 1956–66, Royal Soc res prof Univ of Oxford 1963–90 (prof emeritus 1990); visiting fell Churchill Coll Cambridge 1962–63, fell All Souls Coll Oxford 1964–90 (emeritus fell 1990); memb: Sigma Xi 1954, Planetary Soc 1988, BAAS 1988, Maćica Serbska (Bautzen) 1993; fell American Physical Soc 1959, corr memb Aust Acad of Sci 1978, foreign memb Polish Acad of Sci 1980, foreign fell Nat Acad of Sci India 1990, foreign assoc US Nat Acad of Sci 1991; Hon DSc Univ of Melbourne 1991; FRS 1960, FRSA 1962, FInstP (London) 1970; *Books* K Mesons and Hyperons: Reports on Progress in Physics (1957), Strange Particles and Strong Interactions (1962), Nuclear Interactions of the Hyperons (1965), Quark Models for the Elementary Particles: High Energy Physics (contrib, 1966), Nuclear Energy Today and Tomorrow (contrib, 1971), Dr Paul Dirac (with R E Peierls, 1987), A Breadth of Physics (with R B Stinchcombe, 1988), The Collected Works of P A M Dirac 1924–48 (1995); *Recreations* biographical researches, study of Sorbian (Wendish) language, history and emigration, travelling hopefully; *Style*— Prof Richard Dalitz, FRS; ✉ 28 Jack Straw's Lane, Oxford, Oxon OX3 0DW (☎ 01865 62531); Department of Theoretical Physics, 1 Keble Rd, Oxford OX1 3NP (☎ 01865 273966, fax 01865 273947, telex 83295 NUCLOX G)

DALKEITH, Countess of; Lady Elizabeth Marian Frances; *née* Kerr; 4 da of 12 Marquess of Lothian, KCVO, *qv*; *b* 8 June 1954; *Educ* London Sch of Economics (BSc); *m* 31 Oct 1981, Earl of Dalkeith, *qv*; 2 s, 2 da; *Career* radio journalist BBC; chm The Scottish Ballet 1990–95, memb Dumfries and Galloway Health Bd 1987–90, patron CRUSAID Scotland, tstee Nat Museums of Scotland 1991–; *Recreations* music, reading, theatre, television; *Style*— Countess of Dalkeith; ✉ Dabton, Thornhill, Dumfriesshire; 24 Lansdowne Road, London W11

DALKEITH, Earl of; Richard Walter John Montagu Douglas Scott; s and h of 9 and 11 Duke of Buccleuch and Queensberry, KT, VRD, JP, *qv*; *b* 14 Feb 1954; *Educ* Eton, Christ Church Oxford; *m* 31 Oct 1981, Lady Elizabeth Marian Frances, *qv*, 4 da of 12 Marquess of Lothian, *qv*; 2 s (Lord Eskdaill, Hon Charles David Peter b 1987), 2 da (Lady Louisa Jane Therese b 1982, Lady Amabel Clare Alice b 1992); *Heir* s, Walter John Francis Montagu Douglas Scott (Lord Eskdaill) b 2 Aug 1984; *Career* dir Border Television 1989–90; dist cncllr Nithsdale 1984–90, memb Nature Conservancy Cncl 1989–91, nat memb for Scot ITC (formerly IBA) 1990–95, dep chm 1996–; pres: East of Eng Agric Soc 1990–91, Royal Smithfield Club 1992; chm (SW) Scot Natural Heritage 1992–95, memb Millenium Cmmn 1994–; *Style*— Earl of Dalkeith, DL; ✉ Dabton,

Thornhill, Dumfries (☎ 01848 330467); 24 Lansdowne Rd, London W11 3LL (☎ 0171 727 6573)

DALLAGLIO, Lawrence; *b* 10 Aug 1972; *Educ* Ampleforth Coll, Kingston Univ; *Career* professional rugby union flanker; Wasps RFC: joined 1990, played for colts, Under-21, students, and A team, currently capt 1st XV 1995–; England: colts, Under-21, students, A team, memb winning 7's team World Cup Murrayfield 1993, won first cap (as replacement) v S Africa 1995, first full cap v Western Samoa 1995, 8 full caps (as at Dec 1996); Player of the Year RFU 1995–96; *Style—* Lawrence Dallaglio, Esq; ✉ c/o Rangers Stadium, South Africa Road, Shepherds Bush, London W12 7PA; c/o James Grant Media Group Ltd, Syon Lodge, London Road, Syon Park, Middlesex TW7 5BH (☎ 0181 232 4100, fax 0181 232 4101)

DALLAS, Michael John Linwood; s of Linwood Forbes Dallas (d 1982), and Helen, *née* Ralston (d 1990); *b* 2 Feb 1944; *Educ* Diocesan Coll Cape Town, Univ of Cape Town (BCom); *m* 28 April 1973, Elizabeth, da of John McGill Dick; 2 s (James Robert Linwood b 9 March 1976, Edward John McGill b 1 Aug 1979); *Career* Coopers & Lybrand: trainee Cape Town, joined London office 1969, ptnr 1985–, ptnr i/c Public Service Audit Dept 1993–; memb: S African Inst of CAs 1968, Public Sector Liaison Ctee Accounting Standards Bd 1991–, CIPFA 1992, FRSA 1996; *Recreations* walking, antiques, the Cotswolds, skiing; *Style—* Michael Dallas, Esq; ✉ Coopers & Lybrand, 1 Embankment Place, London WC2N 6NN (☎ 0171 213 5235, fax 0171 213 5221)

DALLING, Robert; s of John Dalling, and Mary Watson, *née* Youngson; *b* 17 Nov 1942; *Educ* Ardrossan Acad, Univ of Glasgow (MB ChB); *m* 27 March 1972, Lorna MacLean, da of John Stoddart; 1 s (Jonathan b 8 May 1979), 2 da (Claire b 2 March 1974, Jane b 22 Dec 1976); *Career* conslt surgn Stobhill Hosp Glasgow 1978–; Burgher of City of Glasgow, memb of Incorporation of Tailors Glasgow; FRCSEd 1972, FRCSGlas 1984; *Style—* Robert Dalling, Esq; ✉ 287 Southbrae Drive, Glasgow G13 1TR Scotland (☎ 0141 959 2338); Department of Surgery, Stobhill Hospital, Glasgow G21 3UW (☎ 0141 558 0111)

DALLOW, Peter Raymond; s of Henry Pownall Dallow (d 1969), and Annie Louise, *née* Taylor (d 1928); *Educ* Bishop Vesey's GS Sutton Coldfield; *m* 1945, Margaret Doreen Brandwood; 1 s (John Roderick b 4 Jan 1948), 1 da (Sally Ann (Mrs Kirkman) b 24 Sept 1955); *Career* served WWII Capt RA in UK Egypt and Italy 1940–46, Maj Army Cadet Force 1948–56, paymaster TA, Maj The Queen's Own Warwickshire and Worcestershire Yeomanry 1960–67; qualified chartered accountant H H Sherwood & Co 1948 (ptnr 1951–67), sr ptnr Sherwood Thompson & Co Tamworth Staffs 1967–87; dir NADFAS Enterprises Ltd 1992–95; memb: Cncl ICAEW 1977–87, Nat Cncl and Fin Ctee The Carr-Gomm Soc Ltd 1990–93, Fin Ctee NADFAS 1990–94; pres: The Birmingham and W Midlands Soc of Chartered Accountants 1976–77 (memb Ctee 1966–87), The Birmingham Chartered Accountant Students' Soc 1978–79; The Assoc of Accounting Technicians: fndr memb and memb Cncl 1980–88, pres 1983–84; memb Yardley Cons Assoc 1948–55, fndr chm Acocks Green Young Cons 1949–52; Solihull Cons Assoc: memb 1955–, hon treas 1971–72, chm 1972–75, pres and tstee 1995–; govr and treas St George's C of E Comp Sch Newtown Birmingham 1991–95, treas Home-Start Saltley; FCA; *Recreations* music, opera; *Clubs* Naval & Military, The Birmingham; *Style—* Peter R Dallow, Esq; ✉ 4 Parklands, Blossomfield Road, Solihull, West Midlands B91 1NG (☎ 0121 705 3726)

DALLY, Dr Ann Gwendolen (Mrs Philip Egerton); da of Claud Mullins (d 1968), and Gwendolen Mullins; *b* 29 March 1926; *Educ* Oxford HS, Somerville Coll Oxford (exhibitioner, BA, MA), St Thomas' Hosp London (MB BS, DObstRCOG, MD); *m* 1, 1950 (m dis 1969), Peter John Dally, s of Capt Arthur Thomas Dally, RN; 6 c (Simon b 1951, d 1989, Mark b 1952, Emma b 1954, Jane b 1956, John b 1959 d 1994, Adam b 1961); m 2, 1959, Philip Wellsted Egerton, s of Arthur Egerton; *Career* psychiatrist, medical journalist and medical historian; former positions: St Thomas' Hosp, St James' Hosp Balham, Wandsworth Hosp Group; in private practice 1956–; ed Maternal And Child Care 1965–70, res fell Wellcome Inst for the History of Medicine 1990–; pres Assoc of Ind Doctors in Addiction; Research Prize 1956; memb: BMA 1950, RSM 1958; *Books* A Child is Born (1966), Intelligent Person's Guide to Modern Medicine (1966), Cicely, the Story of a Doctor (1968), Mothers, their Power and Influence (1976), The Morbid Streak (1977), Why Women Fail (1978), Inventing Motherhood: The Consequences of an Idea (1981), A Doctor's Story (1990), Women Under The Knife (1991); *Recreations* country, family life; *Clubs* RSM, BMA; *Style—* Dr Ann Dally; ✉ Flat 6, 40/41 Wimpole Street, London W1M 7AF (☎ 0171 935 1768); Wiblings Farm, Graffham, Petworth, W Sussex GU28 0PU (☎ 01798 867279)

DALMENY, Lord; Harry Ronald Neil Primrose; s and h of 7 Earl of Rosebery, *qv*; *b* 20 Nov 1967; *m* 18 June 1994, Caroline J, eldest da of Ronald Daglish and of Mrs William Wyatt-Lowe; *Clubs* Pitt, St Moritz Toboganning, Beefsteak; *Style—* Lord Dalmeny; ✉ Dalmeny House, South Queensferry, West Lothian EH30 9TQ

DALRYMPLE, *see:* Hamilton-Dalrymple

DALRYMPLE, Hon Colin James; JP, DL (Midlothian); 4 and yst s of Lt-Col 12 Earl of Stair, KT, DSO, JP, DL (d 1961); *b* 19 Feb 1920; *Educ* Eton, Trinity Coll Cambridge; *m* 1, 25 Aug 1945 (m dis 1954), Pamela Mary, only da of Maj Lamplugh Wickham, CVO; 1 da; m 2, 12 March 1956, Fiona Jane, only da of late Adm Sir Ralph Alan Bevan Edwards, KCB, CBE; 1 s, 2 da; *Career* served WWII Scots Guards Italy, ret Maj; pres Scottish Landowners Fedn 1991–96, memb Queen's Body Guard for Scotland (Royal Co of Archers); *Recreations* landowning and farming; *Clubs* New (Edinburgh); *Style—* The Hon Colin Dalrymple, JP, DL; ✉ Oxenfoord Mains, Dalkeith, Midlothian, Scotland EH22 2PF

DALRYMPLE, Hon Hew North; TD, DL (Ayrshire); s of 12 Earl of Stair (d 1961); bro of 13 Earl of Stair; *b* 27 April 1910; *Educ* Eton; *m* 1, 20 June 1938, Mildred Helen (d 1980), da of Hon Thomas Henry Frederick Egerton (d 1953), 3 s of 3 Earl of Ellesmere (5 Earl became 6 Duke of Sutherland); 1 s (Robert Hew b 1946); m 2, 20 Jan 1983, Helen Margaret Wilson, da of late James Phillips, of Albany, Ballantrae; *Career* formerly Capt 2 Bn Black Watch (TA), served N Africa and Burma (twice wounded); memb Queen's Body Guard for Scotland (Royal Co of Archers); *Style—* The Hon Hew Dalrymple, TD, DL; ✉ Castlehill, Ballantrae, Ayrshire KA26 0LA (☎ 01465 831238)

DALRYMPLE, James Stewart; s of Andrew Dalrymple (d 1973), of Motherwell, Scotland, and Margaret, *née* Craig; *b* 19 Aug 1941; *Educ* Dalziel HS Motherwell; *m* 13 Dec 1971, Margaret Elizabeth, *née* Stevenson; 1 s (William b 24 Aug 1971), 1 da (Jean Eileen b 13 Feb 1973); *Career* jr reporter Hamilton Advertiser 1960–61; news reporter: Scottish Daily Record Glasgow 1961–63, Scottish Daily Express Glasgow 1963–65; crime reporter Daily Express London 1965–70, mangr Mirror Group Newspapers Trg Scheme 1970–81, London ed Scottish Daily Record 1981–86; writer: The Independent 1986–89, The Independent on Sunday 1989–90, The Sunday Times 1990–; Granada 'What The Papers Say' Reporter of the Year 1988, UK Press Awards Feature Writer of the Year 1991; *Recreations* golf; *Style—* James Dalrymple, Esq; ✉ 18 Garthlands, Maidenhead, Berks SL6 7PJ (☎ 01628 20276)

DALRYMPLE, Robert Gordon; s of Ian Murray Dalrymple (d 1989), and Joan Margaret, *née* Craig; *b* 1 March 1943; *Educ* Rugby, Trinity Coll Cambridge (MA); *m* 1970 (m dis); 1 s (Alexis Murray Lucien b 1974), 2 da (Friday Alexandra Sophie Kennet b 1972, Miranda Victoria-Jane b 1975); *Career* PR exec; journalist: United Newspapers 1969, City and Industrial Publicity Services 1969–72; business and fin affrs mangr BL Motor Corp 1972–75, sec gen Indust Ctee for Packaging and the Environment 1975–76; dir: Universal McCann 1976–81, Grandfield Rork Collins 1981–91; fndr dir Cardew & Co 1991–95; writer and journalist as Robert Pilgrim; corp communications and mgmnt conslt; ptnr Aveling Partners 1995–, devpt dir Inst of Clinical Hypnosis 1995–; former chm Ealing Arts Cncl, memb Cncl World Wide Fund For Nature; *Books* Education in England (1970), England is a Foreign Country (1971), How African was Egypt? (ed, 1973), The Political Pound (ed, 1983), Robert Pilgrim's London (1987), Robert Pilgrim's Endangered Species (1988), Resuming the Egg (1989); *Recreations* cricket, broadcasting, writing; *Clubs* Naval and Military; *Style—* Robert Dalrymple, Esq; ✉ 28 Tantallon Road, London SW12 8DG (☎ and fax 0181 673 2230); Aveling Partners, Russell Chambers, The Piazza, Covent Garden, London WC2E 8AA (☎ 0171 240 1505, fax 0171 240 4443); Institute of Clinical Hypnosis (☎ 0181 675 1598)

DALRYMPLE-CHAMPNEYS, Lady; Norma Hull; da of late Col Richard Hull Lewis, and wid of A S Russell, MC, DSc; *Educ* Univ of Oxford (MA); *m* 1974, as his 2 w, Capt Sir Weldon Dalrymple-Champneys, 2 Bt, CB, DM, FRCP (d 14 Dec 1980, when title became extinct); *Career* hon res fell (formerly fell and librarian) Somerville Coll Oxford, hon fell Oriel Coll Oxford, Leverhulme emeritus fell 1974; Rose Mary Crawshaw prize Br Acad 1990; *Books* Studies in Memory of Gabrielle Enthoven (contrib chapter Sarah Baker - Governess-General of the Kentish Theatre, 1952), The Notebook of Thomas Bennet (1956), Bibliography of William Cowper (1963), Poems of William Cowper (1967), The Complete Poetical Works of George Crabbe, 3 vols (1987); *Style—* Lady Dalrymple-Champneys

DALRYMPLE-HAMILTON OF BARGANY, Capt North Edward Frederick; CVO (1961, MVO 1954), MBE (1953), DSC (1943), JP (1980), DL (Ayrshire 1973); s of Adm Sir Frederick Hew George Dalrymple-Hamilton of Bargany, KCB (d 1974, gs of 10 Earl of Stair, KT, JP, DL) by his w Gwendolen, 3 da of Sir Cuthbert Peek, 2 Bt; *b* 17 Feb 1922; *Educ* Eton; *m* 1, 23 July 1949, Hon Mary Helen (d 1981), da of Rt Hon David John Colville, GCIE, TD, PC, 1 Baron Clydesmuir (d 1954); 2 s (North John Frederick b 1950, James Hew Ronald b 1955); m 2, 9 April 1983, Geraldine Inez Antoinette, da of late Maj Frank Harding (who m 1, 1955, Maj Rowland Beech, MC (d 1972); 2 da); *Career* entered RN 1940, served WWII and Korea, Cdr 1954, cmdg HMS Scarborough 1958, exec offr HM Yacht Britannia 1959–60, Capt 1960, cmdg HMS Tenby and Capt (F) 17 Frigate Sqdn 1963, dir Naval Signals MOD 1965, Capt Adm Surface Weapons Estab 1967, ret 1970; Lt Queen's Body Guard for Scotland (Royal Co of Archers); *Clubs* New (Edinburgh), Pratt's, MCC; *Style—* Capt North Dalrymple-Hamilton of Bargany, CVO, MBE, DSC, JP, DL, RN; ✉ Lovestone House, Bargany, Girvan, Ayrshire KA26 9RF (☎ 01465 871227)

DALRYMPLE-HAY, Sir James Brian; 6 Bt (GB 1798); s of Lt-Col Brian George Rowland Dalrymple-Hay (d 1943); suc cous, Sir Charles John Dalrymple-Hay, 5 Bt, CVO (d 1952); *b* 19 Jan 1928; *Educ* Blundell's; *m* 12 April 1958, Helen Sylvia, da of late Stephen Herbert Card, of Reigate, Surrey; 3 da (Fiona Louise (Mrs Richard Norcross) b 1963, Charlotte Ann b 1966, Lucie Helen b 1969); *Heir* bro, John Hugh Dalrymple-Hay b 16 Dec 1929; *Career* Lt RM 1948; sole principal of firm of estate agents 1955–68, ptnr in firm of estate agents 1968–85; *Style—* Sir James Dalrymple-Hay, Bt; ✉ The Red House, Church St, Warnham, nr Horsham, W Sussex

DALRYMPLE-HAY, John Hugh; s of Lt-Col Brian George Rowland Dalrymple-Hay (d 1943); hp of bro Sir James Brian Dalrymple-Hay, 6 Bt, *qv*; *b* 16 Dec 1929; *Educ* Blundell's; *m* 6 Oct 1962, Jennifer Phyllis Roberta, da of late Brig Robert Johnston, CBE, of London; 1 s (Malcolm John Robert b April 1966); *Career* late Capt Royal Scots Fusiliers; *Recreations* golf, skiing, sailing; *Style—* John Dalrymple-Hay, Esq; ✉ Little Meadow, Forty Green Rd, Knotty Green, Beaconsfield, Bucks HP9 1XL

DALRYMPLE-WHITE, Sir Henry Arthur Dalrymple; 2 Bt (UK 1926) of High Mark, Co Wigtown; DFC (1941) and bar (1942); s of Lt-Col Sir Godfrey Dalrymple Dalrymple-White, 1 Bt (d 1954, s of Gen Sir Henry Dalrymple White, KCB, who cmd 6 Inniskilling Dragoons throughout Crimean War and was maternal gs of Sir Hew Dalrymple, 1 Bt), by his w Hon Catherine Mary, da of 12 Viscount Falkland; *b* 5 Nov 1917; *Educ* Eton, Magdalene Coll Cambridge, London Univ; *m* 17 Sept 1948 (m dis 1956), Mary, only da of Capt Robert Henry Cunciffe Thomas, 8th Royal Hus, by his wife Cynthia, 2nd da of Capt Francis Sandford; 1 s; *Heir* s, Jan Hew Dalrymple-White, *qv*; *Career* Wing-Cdr RAFVR, served WW II; *Style—* Sir Henry Dalrymple-White, Bt, DFC; ✉ c/o Aero Club of East Africa, PO Box 40813, Nairobi, Kenya

DALRYMPLE-WHITE, Jan Hew; s and h of Sir Henry Arthur Dalrymple Dalrymple-White, 2 Bt, *qv*; *b* 26 Nov 1950; *Educ* Stowe, Huddersfield Polytechnic, Univ of Stirling; *Style—* Jan Dalrymple-White, Esq

DALTON, Sir Alan Nugent Goring; kt (1977), CBE (1969), DL (Cornwall 1982); s of Harold Goring Dalton, and Phyllis Marguerite, *née* Ash; *b* 26 Nov 1923; *Educ* King Edward VI Sch Southampton; *Career* md: English Clays, Lovering and Pochin and Co Ltd 1961–84; chm English China Clays plc 1984–89 (dep chm 1968–84); dir: Sun Alliance and London Assurance Group 1976–89, National Westminster Bank plc (Western Bd) 1977–91, dir Westland plc 1980–85; chm BR (Western) Bd 1978–92, chm Devon & Cornwall Development Co 1988–91; CIMgt; *Recreations* sailing, painting, reading; *Clubs* Royal Yacht Squadron, Royal Western Yacht Eng; *Style—* Sir Alan Dalton, CBE, DL

DALTON, Andrew Searle; s of Frederick James Searle Dalton (d 1953), and Mary, *née* Whittaker (d 1973); *b* 18 May 1949; *Educ* Oundle, Magdalen Coll Oxford; *m* 16 Oct 1982, Jennie Kelsey, da of Edward Webb Keane, of New York; 2 s (Frederick Victor Burdell b 1986, Benjamin Edward Alexander b (twin) 1986), 2 da (Abigail Mary b 1985, Elizabeth Ann b 1992); *Career* S G Warburg Group plc 1972–95, dir Mercury Asset Management Group plc 1986–, vice chm Mercury Asset Management plc; cncllr Royal Borough of Kensington and Chelsea (memb Educn and Libraries Ctee, tstee N Kensington Amenity Tst); chm Kensington and Chelsea Conservative Assoc; hon treas Lindley Educnl Tst, memb Cncl Oakhill Theological Coll; tstee: Kingham Hill Tst, Ridley Hall Cambridge, Wycliffe Hall Oxford; farmer; Liveryman Worshipful Co of Grocers; *Clubs* Carlton; *Style—* Andrew Dalton, Esq; ✉ 9 Lansdowne Crescent, London W11 2NH (☎ 0171 221 9335); Mercury Asset Management plc, 33 King William St, London EC4R 9AS (☎ 0171 280 2800, fax 0171 280 2820); Crofts, Castle Douglas, Kirkcudbrightshire DG7 3HX (☎ and fax 01556 650235)

DALTON, Annie; da of late Cecil Henry James Dalton, and Audrey Beryl, *née* Harris; *b* 18 Jan 1948; *Educ* Felixstowe Secdy Mod, Ipswich Civic Coll, Univ of Warwick (BA); *m* (m dis); 1 da (Anna Rachel b 1 Jan 1971), 1 adopted da (Maria Jane b 5 Nov 1976), 1 adopted s (Reuben Alexander 24 Nov 1973); *Career* children's writer; currently writer in residence HMP Wellingborough, writer's exchange in Jamaica; *Books* Nightmaze (shortlisted Carnegie Award 1990), The Alpha Box, Swan Sister, Naming the Dark, The Real Tilly Beany (commended for Carnegie Award 1992), The Afterdark Princess (winner Nottingham Oak Children's Book Award 1991); *Style—* Ms Annie Dalton; ✉ c/o Curtis Brown, 4th Floor, Haymarket House, 28–29 Haymarket, London SW1Y 4SP (☎ 0171 396 6600)

DALTON, Vice Adm Sir Geoffrey Thomas James Oliver; KCB (1986); s of Jack Roland Thomas Dalton (d 1981), of Epsom, Surrey, and Margaret Kathleen, *née* Oliver (d 1978); *b* 14 April 1931; *Educ* Reigate GS, RNC Dartmouth; *m* 30 March 1957, Jane Hamilton, da of Colin Hamilton Baynes (d 1976), of Suffolk; 4 s (Alastair b 1964, David b 1966, Richard b 1970, Antony b 1971); *Career* joined RN 1949; cmd: HMS Maryton 1958–60, HMS Relentless 1966–67, Cdr 1966, HMS Nubian 1969–70, Capt 1972, HMS Jupiter and Seventh Frigate Sqdn 1977–79, HMS Dryad (Sch of Maritime Ops) 1979–81;

Rear Adm 1981, Asst Chief of Naval Staff (Policy) 1981–84, Vice Adm 1984, Dep Supreme Allied Cdr Atlantic 1984–87; sec gen MENCAP 1987–90; pres Royal British Legion 1993–, pres and chm Ex-Serv Fellowship Centres 1993–, vice chm Regular Forces Employment Assoc 1993–, govr Queen Mary and Westfield Coll 1992–; Freeman City of London 1953, Master Worshipful Co of Drapers 1996 (memb Ct of Assts 1989); FIMgt 1987; *Recreations* tennis, gardening, fishing, walking, motorcycling; *Clubs* Royal Over-Seas League; *Style—* Vice Adm Sir Geoffrey Dalton, KCB; ✉ Farm Cottage, Catherington, Hants PO8 OTD (☎ 01705 592369)

DALTON, Robert Anthony (Tony); *Educ* Dame Allan's Boys' Sch Newcastle-upon-Tyne; *m* Joanne; 1 s (Simon), 1 da (Julia); *Career* mktg mangr Van Den Berghs Ltd (Unilever) 1958–71, sales and mktg mangr Littlewoods 1971–73, dep chm Saatchi & Saatchi Advertising and chm and chief exec Ted Bates (Saatchi & Saatchi) 1973–88, chm and chief exec FCB Advertising until 1992, subsequently self employed in creative and mktg servs consultancy, dep chm Saatchi & Saatchi Advertising (London) 1995–96 (non-exec dir Laing Henry until bought by Saatchi & Saatchi 1995), sr exec Saatchi & Saatchi (New York) 1997–; FIPA; *Recreations* opera, theatre, literature, sport, horse racing; *Clubs* RAC, Mosimanns, Harry's Bar; *Style—* Tony Dalton, Esq; ✉ Saatchi & Saatchi, 375 Hudson Street, New York, NY 10014–3660, USA (☎ 00 1 212 463 2000)

DALTON, Robin Ann; da of Dr Robert Agnew Eakin (d 1965), of Sydney, Aust, and Lyndall Everad, *née* Solomon (d 1950); *b* 22 Dec 1920; *Educ* Frensham NSW Aust, SOAS Univ of London; *m* 1, 8 Oct 1940 (m dis 1942), Ian (John) Gordon Spencer, of Queensland, Aust; m 2, 1 May 1953, Emmet Michael Dalton (d 1957), s of Maj-Gen James Emmet Dalton, MC (d 1978), of Dublin; 1 da (Lisa Maria b 1954), 1 s (Seamus Emmet b 1956); m 3, 22 June 1993, William Edward Cranston Fairchild; *Career* special advsr and press offr Thai govt 1953–58, literary agent Robin Dalton Assocs Ltd 1965–87, dir International Famous Agency (now ICM) 1972–75; entered film indust 1984, project developer Nineteen Eighty-Four 1984, exec prodr Emma's War 1985; prodr Madame Sousatzka 1988, Country Life 1993–94, Oscar and Lucinda 1996; life memb Anglo-Thai Soc; *Books* Aunts up the Cross (as Robin Eakin 1963, reprinted 1980), Australia Fair? (chapter in anthology, 1984), numerous magazine and newspaper articles; *Style—* Mrs Robin Dalton; ✉ 127 Hamilton Terrace, London NW1 9QR (☎ 0171 328 6169, fax 0171 624 4420)

DALTON, Timothy; *b* 21 March 1946; *Educ* RADA; *Career* actor; *Theatre* began career in regnl theatre: lead roles in The Merchant of Venice, Richard II, The Doctor's Dilemma, St Joan; London debut as Malcolm in Little Malcolm and His Struggle Against the Eunuchs (Royal Court); other roles incl: Arthur in A Game Called Arthur, Edgar in King Lear, Berowne in Love's Labours Lost (Aldwych), Prince Hal in Henry IV (parts I and II), King Henry in Henry V (Roundhouse), Romeo in Romeo and Juliet, The Samaritan (Shaw), Black Comedy and White Liars, The Vortex (Greenwich), Lord Byron in Lunatic Lover and Poet (Old Vic) 1980, Mark Antony in The Romans (New Mermaid), Hotspur in Henry IV (part I (Barbican)) 1981–82, Antony & Cleopatra 1986, The Taming of the Shrew (Haymarket) 1986, A Touch of the Poet (with Vanessa Redgrave, Young Vic) 1988; *Television* incl: Candida (BBC), Five Finger Exercise, Centennial (mini-series), Charlie's Angels, Mr Rochester in Jane Eyre (BBC) 1982, The Master of Ballantrae (HTV), Mistral's Daughter 1984 (US mini-series, with Lee Remick, Stephanie Powers & Stacey Keach), Florence Nightingale (US mini-series, with Jaclyn Smith, Timothy West), Sins (mini-series, with Joan Collins) 1985, Philip von Joel in Framed (mini-series, Anglia), In the Company of Wolves (Anglia) 1993, Rhett Butler in Scarlett (mini-series, Sky TV) 1994, Salt Water Moose (movie comedy, USA/Canada) 1995, Johnny Loves Suzy (Field of Blood) 1996, The Reef (CBS) 1996; *Films* incl: King of France in The Lion Winter (with Peter O'Toole & Katherine Hepburn), Prince Rupert in Cromwell (with Alec Guinness & Richard Harris), Heathcliffe in Wuthering Heights, Darnley in Mary Queen of Scots (with Vanessa Redgrave & Glenda Jackson (Brit Film Award nomination)), Charles Lord in Permission to Kill (with Dirk Bogarde & Ava Gardner), Juan de Dios in The Man Who Knew Love, lead in Sextette (with Mae West, Tony Curtis & Ringo Starr), Col Christie in Agatha 1978 (with Dustin Hoffman & Vanessa Redgrave), Prince Barin in Flash Gordon 1979, Chanel Solitaire (with Marie-France Pisier) 1980, Dr Rock in The Doctor and the Devils 1985, Basil St John in Brenda Starr (with Brooke Shields) 1986, Hawks 1987, James Bond in The Living Daylights 1987 and Licence to Kill 1988, The King's Whore 1989, Neville Sinclair in The Rocketeer (Touchstone) 1990, The Beautician and the Beast (Paramont) 1996; *Style—* Timothy Dalton, Esq; ✉ c/o James Sharkey Associates Ltd, 21 Golden Square, London W1R 3PA (☎ 0171 434 3801, fax 0171 494 1547)

DALY, Alexander (Alec); CBE; *b* 1 March 1936; *Educ* Univ of Edinburgh; *Career* formerly with ICL, various positions rising to head of truck mfrg ops Ford Motor Co 1962–78; GKN plc: joined as exec chm GKN Sankey 1978, main bd dir 1986–94, latterly md Engineered and Agritechnical Products; CBI: dep dir-gen 1994–, chm National Mfrg Cncl 1995–; chm: Brent International plc, Cray Electronics plc; non-exec dir Robert Bosch (UK) Ltd 1994–; Freeman: Worshipful Co of Glaziers, City of London; CIMgt, FIMI, FRSA; *Recreations* reading, rugby football, theatre; *Clubs* RAC; *Style—* Alec Daly, Esq, CBE; ✉ Confederation of British Industry, Centre Point, 103 New Oxford Street, London WC1A 1DD (☎ 0171 379 7400)

DALY, Barbara Susan (Mrs Laurence Tarlo); OBE; da of Philip Daly (d 1985), and Eva, *née* Sapherson (d 1971); *b* 24 March 1944; *Educ* Leeds Coll of Art; *m* 16 March 1982, Laurence Joel Frederic Tarlo, s of William Tarlo, of Long Island, NY; *Career* make-up artist: BBC 1964–68, freelance 1968–86; md Colourings Ltd 1986–91; films incl: A Clockwork Orange, Barry Lyndon; make-up conslt to HRH The Princess of Wales; memb Ctee Orgn for Trg; patron: Skin Treatment and Res Tst Westminster Hosp, Nat Assoc Drama for Visually Handicapped, HOPE for Children; memb BAFTA 1987; *Books* Daly Beauty, Make-up Made Easy, New Looks From Barbara Daly; *Recreations* Eastern philosophy, riding; *Style—* Ms Barbara Daly, OBE

DALY, His Eminence Cardinal Cahal Brendan; *see:* Armagh, Cardinal Archbishop of (RC)

DALY, Francis D; s of Edward M Daly, of Montenotte, Cork (d 1983), and Clare, *née* Egan (d 1987); *b* 16 Sept 1943; *Educ* Glenstal Abbey, Univ Coll Cork (BCL); *m* 21 Feb 1970, Patricia Mary, da of the late H P O'Connor, of Cork; 2 s (Teddy b 14 Nov 1970, Ken b 22 April 1972), 2 da (Aiveen b 14 Nov 1973, Alex b 6 Oct 1976); *Career* admitted slr 1966; ptnr Ronan Daly Jermyn 1970– (joined 1966), chm Allied Metropole Hotel plc; pres Law Soc of Ireland 1996–97; *Recreations* golf, sailing; *Clubs* Cork Golf, Cork Constution RFC, Schull Sailing; *Style—* Francis D Daly, Esq; ✉ Cleveland, Blackrock Rd, Cork; Corthna, Schull, Co Cork (☎ 00 353 21 294 279); Ronan Daly Jermyn, 12 South Mall, Cork (☎ 00 353 21 272 333, fax 00 353 21 273 521)

DALY, HE James; CVO (1994); s of late Maurice Daly, and Christine Daly; *b* 8 Sept 1940; *Educ* St Thomas More Chelsea, UCL (BScEcon); *m* 1990, Dorothy Lillian, *née* Powell; 2 s; *Career* served RM 1958–67; HM Dip Serv: joined FO 1968, third sec Accra 1971–73, third sec Moscow 1973–76, second sec Karachi 1976–78, first sec FCO 1978–79, first sec Sofia 1979–86, consul-gen Paris 1986–92, cnsllr and consul-gen Moscow 1992–95, high cmmr Vanuatu 1995–; *Recreations* reading, music, walking; *Clubs* Lansdowne, National Liberal; *Style—* HE Mr James Daly, CVO; ✉ c/o Foreign & Commonwealth Office (Vila), King Charles Street, London SW1A 2AH

DALY, Margaret Elizabeth; da of Robert Bell (d 1978), of Belfast, and Evelyn Elizabeth, *née* McKenna; *b* 26 Jan 1938; *Educ* Methodist Coll Belfast; *m* 1964, Kenneth Anthony Edward Daly, s of Edward Joseph Daly (d 1983), of Ireland; 1 da (Denise b 1971); *Career* trade union official ASTMS 1959–70, conslt Cons Central Office 1976–79, dir Cons Trade Union Orgn 1979–84, MEP (EPP) Somerset and Dorset West 1984–94 (Hon MEP 1994); dir Margaret Daly Associates 1996–; prospective Cons Parly candidate Weston-super-Mare 1995–; memb Bd Traidcraft Exchange, memb Mgmnt Corp Cannington Coll, pres Centre for Trade Unions (Europe); fell Indust and Parliament Tst; *Clubs* Soroptimist; *Style—* Mrs Margaret Daly; ✉ Margaret Daly Associates, The Old School House, Aisholt, Bridgwater, Somerset TA5 1AR (☎ 01278 671688, 01278 671684)

DALY, Prof Michael de Burgh; s of Dr Ivan de Burgh Daly, CBE, FRS (d 1974), of Long Crendon, Bucks, and Beatrice Mary, *née* Leetham (d 1976); *b* 7 May 1922; *Educ* Loretto, Gonville and Caius Coll Cambridge (MA, MD, ScD), St Bartholomew's Hosp London; *m* 4 Sept 1948, (Beryl) Esmé, da of Wing Cdr Alfred James Nightingale (d 1948), of London; 2 s (Colin de Burgh b 10 Sept 1950, Nigel de Burgh b 20 March 1954); *Career* house physician St Bartholomew's Hosp London 1947–48, lectr in physiology UCL 1948–54, pt/t extramural contract Miny of Supply (now MOD) Porton Wilts 1949–51, Rockefeller Fndn travelling fell in med Univ of Pennsylvania USA 1952–53, Royal Society Locke res fell at Dept of Physiology UCL 1955–58, chair in physiology Univ of London at St Bartholomew's Hosp Med Coll London 1958–84, visiting lectr Swedish Univs 1959–60, visiting prof of physiology Univ of NSW Aust 1966, Ethel Mary Baillieu fell Baker Med Res Inst Melbourne 1976, G L Brown lectr Physiological Soc 1985–86, distinguished visitor in physiology Royal Free Hosp Sch of Med 1984–; film William Harvey and the Circulation of the Blood (awarded Gold Medal of BMA); treas St Bartholomew's Hosp Med Sch 1983–84 (govr 1970–96), co-ed Journal of Physiology 1956–63 and 1984–89, chm Monographs Bd of Physiological Soc 1981–87 (memb 1979–87), chm Benevolent Fund Ctee Physiological Soc 1995–96 (memb 1992–95); awarded: Schafer Prize in Physiology UCL 1953, Thruston Medal Gonville and Caius Coll Cambridge 1958, Sir Lionel Whitby Medal Univ of Cambridge 1963; memb Underwater Physiology Sub Ctee of Med Res Cncl RN Personnel Res Ctee 1975–84, chm Personnel Res Ethical Ctee Miny of Def (RN) 1990– (memb 1975–90), chm Armed Servs Conslt Approval Bd in Applied Physiology and Aviation Med 1989–; memb: Physiological Soc 1951–86 (hon memb 1986–), Soc of Experimental Biology 1965–, Undersea and Hyperbaric Med Soc 1972–88, European Underwater Baromedical Soc 1972–, Br Heart Fndn Res Fund Ctee 1982–85; FRSM 1958, FRCP 1978; *Books* Peripheral Arterial Chemoreceptors and Respiratory-Cardio-Vascular Integration (1997); also author of many pubns in sci jls; *Recreations* model engineering; *Clubs* RSM; *Style—* Prof Michael Daly; ✉ 7 Hall Drive, Sydenham, London SE26 6XL (☎ 0181 778 8773); Department of Physiology, Royal Free Hospital School of Medicine, Rowland Hill St, London NW3 2PF (☎ 0171 794 0500, fax 0171 433 1921)

DALY, Michael Francis; CMG; s of late William Daly, and late Hilda Daly; *b* 7 April 1931; *Educ* Downside, Gonville and Caius Coll Cambridge; *m* 1, 1963, Sally Malcolm Angwin (d 1966); 1 da; m 2, 1971, Juliet Mary Siragusa, *née* Arning; 1 step da; *Career* Transreef Indust & Investmt Co SA 1955–66, Gen Electric Co London 1966; HM Dip Serv: first sec FCO 1967, first sec (commercial) Rio de Janeiro 1969, first sec (info) and head of chancery Dublin 1973, asst head Cultural Rels Dept FCO 1976, cnsllr consul gen and head of chancery Brasilia 1977–78, ambass Ivory Coast Upper Volta and Niger 1978–83, head W African Dept FCO and non resident ambass Chad 1983–86, ambass Costa Rica and non resident ambass to Nicaragua 1986–89, ambass Bolivia 1989–91; sec The Margaret Mee Amazon Tst 1993–; *Clubs* Johannesburg Country, Canning; *Style—* Michael Daly, Esq, CMG; ✉ 45 Priory Rd, Kew, Surrey TW9 3DQ (☎ 0181 940 1272)

DALYELL, Hon Mrs (Kathleen Mary Agnes); *née* Wheatley; da of Baron Wheatley (Life Peer, d 1988); *b* 17 Nov 1937; *Educ* Convent of Sacred Heart, Queens Cross Aberdeen, Univ of Edinburgh; *m* 26 Dec 1963, Tam Dalyell, MP, *qv*; 1 s, 1 da; *Career* teacher of history; memb Historic Buildings Cncl of Scotland 1975–87, dir Heritage Education Tst 1987–, memb Ancient Monuments Bd of Scotland 1989–, chm Bo'ness Heritage Tst 1988–95, tstee Paxton Tst 1988–92, cmmr Royal Fine Art Cmmn for Scotland 1992–; *Recreations* reading, travel, hill walking; *Style—* The Hon Mrs Dalyell; ✉ The Binns, Linlithgow EH49 7NA

DALYELL, (Sir) Tam; 11 Bt (NS 1685), of the Binns (but does not use title); MP (Lab) Linlithgow (majority 7,026); s of Lt-Col Gordon Loch Dalyell, CIE, and (Dame) Eleanor Isabel Dalyell of The Binns, *de jure* Baronetess (d 1972); *b* 9 Aug 1932; *Educ* Eton, King's Coll Cambridge, Univ of Edinburgh; *m* 26 Dec 1963, Hon Kathleen Mary Agnes, *qv*, da of Baron Wheatley (Life Peer, d 1988); 1 s (Gordon Wheatley b 26 Sept 1965), 1 da (Moira Eleanor b 25 May 1968); *Heir* s, Gordon Wheatley Dalyell b 26 Sept 1965; *Career* Nat Serv Royal Scots Greys 1950–52; King's Coll Cambridge 1952–56, teacher Bo'ness Acad 1956–60, seconded to British India Steam Navigation Co as dir of studies on Ship Sch Dunera 1960–62, MP (Lab) Linlithgow 1962–; memb: Public Accounts Ctee, Select Ctee on Sci and Technol 1965–68, Nat Exec Ctee of Lab Pty 1986–87, Educn Inst of Scot; ldr Parly Union Delgn to: Brazil 1976, Zaire 1990; weekly columnist New Scientist 1967–; Hon DSc Univ of Edinburgh 1994; *Books* Case for Ship Schools (1960), Ship School Dunera (1962), Devolution: the End of Britain? (1978), One Man's Falklands (1983), A Science Policy for Britain (1983), Misrule - How Mrs Thatcher Misled Parliament (1987), Dick Crossman: A Portrait (1989); *Style—* Tam Dalyell, Esq, MP; ✉ Binns, Linlithgow, Scotland EH49 7NA; House of Commons, London SW1A 0AA

DALZEL-JOB, Lt Cdr Patrick; DL (1979); s of Capt Ernest Dalzel Job (ka 1916), and Ethel, *née* Griffiths (d 1970); *b* 1 June 1913; *Educ* Berkhamsted Sch, Switzerland; *m* 26 June 1945, Bjorg (d 1986), da of Erling Bangsund (d 1977), of Tromso, Norway; 1 s (Iain b 1946); *Career* Lt Cdr (removed whole civilian population from Narvik before German bombing, received personal thanks of King of Norway), special ops in enemy-occupied territory, ret 1956; writer; author of From Arctic Snow to Dust of Normandy 1991 (Norwegian and British TV, British Radio, inspired Norwegian Liberation Cantata 1995); former youth organiser Duke of Edinburgh's Award; Knight (1 class) Royal Norwegian Order of St Olav with Swords; *Recreations* sailing (to Arctic Russia in 1939), skiing; *Clubs* Special Forces; *Style—* Lt Cdr Patrick Dalzel-Job, DL; ✉ Nead-an-Eoin, by Plockton, Ross-shire, Scotland (☎ 01599 544244, fax 01599 544443)

DALZIEL, Ian Martin; s of John Calvin Dalziel (d 1983), and Elizabeth Roy, *née* Bain; *b* 21 June 1947; *Educ* Daniel Stewart's Coll Edinburgh, St John's Coll Cambridge, Université Libre de Bruxelles, London Business Sch; *m* 1972, Nadia Maria Iacovazzi; 4 s; *Career* Mullens & Co 1970–72, Manufacturers Hanover Ltd (London and NY) 1972–83, co fndr and dep md Adam & Co Group plc 1983–92; chm: Continental Assets Trust plc 1989–, CFC-Daum 1995–; dir: Lepercq-Amcur Fund NV 1988–, VICORP NV 1995–; chm: CSI Inc 1992–, Venturi SA 1992–; cncllr London Borough of Richmond upon Thames 1978–79; MEP (EDG) Lothians 1979–84; *Recreations* golf, skiing, shooting, tennis; *Clubs* Brooks's, New (Edinburgh), Royal and Ancient Golf (St Andrews); *Style—* Ian Dalziel, Esq; ✉ 7 Cours de Rive, 1204 Geneva, Switzerland (☎ 00 41 22 310 45 22, fax 00 41 22 310 45 25)

DALZIEL, Malcolm Stuart; CBE (1984); s of Robert Henderson Dalziel (d 1979), and Susan Aileen, *née* Robertson (d 1981); *b* 18 Sept 1936; *Educ* Banbury GS, St Catherine's Coll Oxford (MA); *m* 1961, Elizabeth Anne, da of Major Philip Collins Harvey (d 1977); 1 s (Rory b 1974), 2 da (Caroline, Annabel); *Career* Nat Serv 1955–57, Lt The

Northamptonshire Regt; The British Cncl: SOAS 1960, educn offr Lahore Pakistan 1961–63, regnl dir Penang Malaysia 1963–67, regnl rep Lahore 1967–70, rep Sudan 1970–74, dir Mgmnt Serv Dept and dep controller Estabs Div 1974–79, controller Higher Educn Div 1983–87; cnsllr cultural affairs British Embassy Cairo 1979–83, sec Int Univ and Poly Cncl 1983–87; dep chm Cncl for Educn in the Cwlth 1990– (memb Exec Ctee 1983–), affiliate Queen Elizabeth House Int Devpt Centre Oxford Univ; dir CERES (Conslts in Econ Regeneration in Europe Servs) 1988–, int funding conslt 1991–; memb Ct Univ of Essex 1983–88; *Recreations* theatre, ballet, rugby football, walking; *Clubs* United Oxford and Cambridge, Northampton CCC (vice pres); *Style—* Malcolm Dalziel, Esq, CBE; ✉ 368 Woodstock Rd, Oxford OX2 8AE (☎ and fax 01865 558969)

DALZIEL, Dr Maureen; *b* 7 April 1952; *Educ* Notre Dame HS Glasgow, Univ of Glasgow (MB ChB), MFCM 1985, FFPHM 1990; *m*; *Career* jr hosp doctor Glasgow and Lanarkshire Hosps 1976–79, GP E Kilbride Glasgow 1979–81, registrar then sr registrar in public health med Brent and SW Herts HAs 1981–85, assoc dir NW Thames RHA 1989 (conslt in public health med 1985–89); chief exec: SW Herts DHA 1990–93 (dir of public health 1989–90), Hillingdon Health Agency 1993–95; regnl dir of public health N Thames RHA 1995–; sr lectr in public health med London Sch of Hygiene and Tropical Med 1989–90 (lectr 1981–85); memb: Nat Specialist Commissioning Advsy Gp 1996–, Nat Steering Gp Considering Interface Between Clinicians and Research 1996–, CMO Working Gp on Health of the Nation 1996–, Steering Ctee UK Cochrane Centre 1996–; numerous articles in learned jls and papers presented at nat confs; *Recreations* skiing, reading novels and biographies, golf (Par 3), watching old films; *Style—* Dr Maureen Dalziel; ✉ North Thames Regional Office, 40 Eastbourne Terrace, Paddington, London W2 3QR (☎ 0171 725 5419)

DAMANT, David Cyril; s of William Alexander Arthur Damant (d 1983), and Mary Edith Damant; *b* 15 March 1937; *Educ* Queens' Coll Cambridge; *Career* former ptnr: Investment Research Cambridge, Quilter Goodison 1982–86; md Paribas Asset Management (UK) Ltd 1987–91; chm: MAP Fund Managers Ltd 1991–93, Credit Suisse Investment Management Group 1993–; pres Euro Fedn of Fin Analysts Socs 1995–; chm Soc of Investmt Analysts 1980–82 (fell 1986), memb Bd Int Accounting Standards Ctee 1986– (del to Russian Int Advsy Bd on Accounting and Auditing 1992–, memb Exec Ctee 1995–), memb UK Accounting Standards Ctee 1987–90, treas Inst for Quantitative Investment Research 1988–, del Euro Communities Accounting Advsy Forum 1991–, co chm Int Co-ordinating Ctee Fin Analysts Assocs; *Recreations* opera, food & wine; *Clubs* Beefsteak, Garrick, City of London; *Style—* David Damant, Esq; ✉ Agar House, 12 Agar St, London WC2N 4HN (☎ 0171 379 6926, fax 0171 379 8254); 16 Orchard St, Cambridge CB1 1JT (☎ 01223 357768); 357 Herengracht, 1016BA Amsterdam, The Netherlands (☎ 00 31 20 622 0060, fax 00 31 20 622 1624); Credit Suisse Investment Management Group, Beaufort House, 15 St Botolph St, London EC3A 7JJ (☎ 0171 426 2626, fax 0171 375 1161)

DANCE, Charles Walter; s of Walter Dance (d 1950), of Birmingham, and Eleanor, *née* Perks (d 1985); *b* 10 Oct 1946; *Educ* Widey Tech Sch Plymouth, Plymouth Sch of Art, Leicester Coll of Art and Design; *m* 18 July 1970, Joanna Elizabeth Nicola Daryl, da of Francis Harold Haythorn, of Plymstock, Devon; 1 s (Oliver b 1974), 1 da (Rebecca b 1980); *Career* actor 1970–; *Theatre* seasons at repertory theatres: Leeds, Oxford, Windsor, Swindon, Chichester, Greenwich; joined Royal Shakespeare Company 1975; leading roles in RSC prodns incl Richard III, As You Like It, Henry IV Parts 1 and 2, Henry V, Henry VI Part 2, The Changeling, Perkin Warbeck, The Jail Diary of Albie Sachs, title roles in Henry V and Coriolanus; *Television* incl: The Fatal Spring, Rainy Day Women, The Secret Servant, The Jewel in the Crown (BAFTA Best Actor nomination), First Born, Out on a Limb, The Macguffin, Saigon - The Last Day, Rebecca, Goldeneye, In the Presence of Mine Enemies; *Radio* Frederick Delius in The Paradise Garden Attained, Sydney Carton in A Tale of Two Cities; *Films* For Your Eyes Only, Plenty, The Golden Child, Good Morning Babylon, Hidden City, White Mischief, Pascali's Island, China Moon, Alien 3, La Valle de Pietra, Century, Last Action Hero, Kabloonak, Exquisite Tenderness, Shortcut to Paradise, Undertow, Michael Collins, Space Truckers; *Style—* C W Dance, Esq; ✉ c/o ICM, Oxford House, 76 Oxford Street, London W1N 0AX (☎ 0171 636 6565); c/o William Morris Agency Inc, 151 El Camino Drive, Beverley Hills, California 90212, USA

DANCY, Dr (Christopher) Mark; s of Prof John Christopher Dancy, of Mousehole, Cornwall, and Angela Dawn, *née* Bryant; *b* 16 July 1948; *Educ* Winchester, Trinity Coll Oxford, St Thomas's Hosp London (BA, BM BCh); *m* 30 June 1974, Susanna, da of Lt Cdr Cedric Collingwood Wake-Walker, of Rogate, nr Petersfield, Hants; 1 s (Luke b 1983), 2 da (Arabella b 1977, Martha b 1979); *Career* dir of med Central Middx Hosp 1989 (conslt cardiologist 1987); conslt cardiologist St Mary's Hosp Paddington and Central Middx Hosp; hon clinical sr lectr St Mary's Hosp Med Sch 1987; FRCP 1994 (MRCP 1976); *Recreations* sailing, choral singing; *Style—* Dr Mark Dancy; ✉ Central Middlesex Hospital, Acton Lane, London NW10 7NS (☎ 0181 453 2151, fax 0181 965 1837)

DAND, Dr Ian William; s of William Slight Dand (d 1988), and Mary Audrey Beryl, *née* Hepworth; *b* 14 Feb 1941; *Educ* Bishop Vesey's GS Sutton Coldfield, Univ of Glasgow (BSc, PhD); *m* 1 April 1971, Rosemary Patterson, da of late Lt Cdr Arthur Winter; 2 s (James Alexander b 1973, John Ross Patterson b 1977); *Career* tech apprentice John I Thornycroft & Co 1959–64; Ship Div National Physical Laboratory: sr scientific offr 1970–76, princ scientific offr 1976–81, sr princ scientific offr (IM) 1981; sr scientist NMI Ltd 1982–85, mangr Vessel Hydrodynamics Gp British Maritime Technology Ltd 1985–94, dir BMT SeaTech Ltd 1994–; Silver Medal RINA 1976 and 1982; companion Nautical Inst 1976, FRINA 1993, FEng 1994, FRSA 1996; *Recreations* occasional cricket, woodwork, model-making, sketching, DIY; *Style—* Dr Ian Dand, FEng; ✉ BMT SeaTech Ltd, Haslar, Gosport, Hampshire PO12 2AG (☎ 01705 335021, fax 01705 335018)

DANDO, Jill; da of Herbert Jack Howard Dando, of Weston-super-Mare, N Somerset, and Jean, *née* Hockey (d 1986); *b* 9 Nov 1961; *Educ* Worle Sch Weston-super-Mare, Broadoak Sch Weston-super-Mare; *Career* reporter Weston Mercury 1980–85 (NCTJ cert 1982), reporter/presenter BBC Radio Devon 1985–87, prodr TSW 1987, presenter BBC South West 1988, presenter BBC News and Current Affrs (BBC Breakfast News, Six O'Clock News, Nine O'Clock News) 1988–; other credits: Holiday, Crimewatch UK, Summer Holiday, Songs of Praise, Safari UK; *Recreations* theatre, reading biographies, walking, antiques; *Style—* Ms Jill Dando; ✉ c/o Speakeasy, 90 St Marys Road, Market Harborough, Leics LE16 7DX (☎ 01858 461961)

DANDY, David James; s of James Dandy, of Gt Shelford, Cambs, and Margaret, *née* Coe (d 1984); *b* 30 May 1940; *Educ* Forest Sch, Emmanuel Coll Cambridge, London Hosp Med Coll (MD MChir, MA, FRCS); *m* 17 Sept 1966, (Stephanie) Jane, da of Harold Vaughan Essex (d 1985), of Wellington, Somerset; 1 s (James b 1971), 1 da (Emma b 1973); *Career* sr fell Toronto Gen Hosp Canada 1972–73, conslt orthopaedic surgn Addenbrooke's Hosp Cambridge and Newmarket Gen Hosp 1975–, assoc lectr Faculty of Clinical Med Univ of Cambridge 1975–, civilian advsr in knee surgery RN and RAF 1980–; Br Orthopaedic Assoc: fell 1975, Robert Jones prize 1991, Naughton Dunn meml lecture 1991, memb Cncl 1992–94; RCS: James Berry prize 1985, Hunterian prof 1994, memb Cncl 1994–; pres: Int Arthroscopy Assoc 1989–91, Br Orthopaedic Sports Trauma Assoc 1993–95, Br Assoc of Surgery of the Knee; vice pres elect Br Orthopaedic Assoc 1996; dir: Int Soc of Knee, Euro Soc of Knee and Arthroscopy 1984–; Freeman: City of London, Worshipful Soc of Apothecaries 1987; FRCS; *Books* Arthroscopy of the Knee (1973), Arthroscopic Surgery of the Knee (1981), Arthroscopy of the Knee - A Diagnostic Atlas (1984), Essentials of Orthopaedics and Trauma (1989); *Recreations* gardening, writing; *Clubs* East India, RSM; *Style—* Mr David Dandy; ✉ The Old Vicarage, Great Wilbraham, Cambs CB1 5JF (☎ 01223 880006, fax 01223 881779); Addenbrooke's Hospital, Hills Rd, Cambridge CB2 2QQ (☎ 01223 216103)

DANDY, Gillian Margaret (Gill); da of George Thomas Dandy, and Marjorie Walker Dandy, of Westbrook, nr Devizes, Wilts; *b* 17 Aug 1957; *Educ* NCHEE Dip in Home Economics; *Career* trainee account exec rising to account mangr Harrison Cowley Public Relations Ltd Birmingham 1980–83, account exec rising to assoc dir Leslie Bishop Company Ltd London 1983–90, bd dir i/c food and retail Shandwick Communications Ltd London 1990–96, dir of devpt and PR London Bible Coll 1996–; memb: Inst of Home Economics, Mktg Soc; MIPR; *Recreations* travel, skiing, theatre, active memb of St Barnabas Church Kensington and London Bible Coll; *Style—* Miss Gill Dandy; ✉ 56 Southerton Road, Hammersmith, London W6 0PH (☎ 0181 748 0809); London Bible College, Green Lane, Northwood, Middx HA6 2UW

DANEMAN, Paul Frederick; s of Frederick Daneman (d 1930), and Dorothy, *née* Almenrader; *b* 26 Oct 1925; *Educ* Haberdashers' Aske's, Sir William Borlase's Sch Marlow, Univ of Reading, RADA; *m* 1, 1952 (m dis 1965), Susan, *née* Courtney; m 2, 10 Oct 1965, Meredith Frances, da of late Thomas Kinmont; 2 da (Sophie b 1965, Flora b 1973); *Career* actor; RAF Bomber Cmd 1943–47; *Theatre* first professional appearance 1947, Bristol Old Vic 1950, Birmingham Rep 1951–52, Old Vic 1953–55 (Toby Belch, Tullus Aufidius in Coriolanus, Justice Shallow in Henry IV), original Vladimir in Waiting for Godot 1955, Faulkland in The Rivals, Dubedat in The Doctor's Dilemma (Saville) 1956, Old Vic 1957–58 (Henry VI, Fool in King Lear), Cusins in Major Barbara (Royal Court) 1958, Old Vic 1961–62 (Dr Faustus, Bastard in King John, Richard III, Malvolio in Twelfth Night), Arthur in Camelot (Drury Lane) 1965, Captain Hook in Peter Pan 1967, Rolfe in Hadrian VII (Haymarket) 1969, Don't Start Without Me (Garrick) 1971, Double Edge (Vaudeville) 1975, title role in Macbeth 1976, Shut Your Eyes and Think of England (Apollo) 1979; *Television* incl: Richard III in An Age of Kings 1960, Not in Front of the Children 1970, Spy Trap 1972–74, Never a Cross Word 1971, Stay with Me till Morning 1980, The Two Gentleman of Verona 1983, Antigone 1984–85, Hold the Dream 1987, Roman Holiday 1987, Perfect Spy 1988, Blore MP 1989, GBH 1991, Thatcher, The Final Days 1992; *Films* incl: Zulu 1966, How I Won the War 1967, Oh! What a Lovely War 1966; *Books* If I Only had Wings (1995); *Recreations* painting, reading; *Style—* Paul Daneman, Esq; ✉ c/o Chatto & Linnit, Prince of Wales Theatre, Coventry Street, London W1V 7FE (☎ 0171 930 6677, fax 0171 930 0091)

DANG, Mohinder Singh; s of Mohan Singh, of Amristar, Punjab, India, and Shakuntal, *née* Kaur; *b* 2 April 1946; *Educ* Med Coll Amristar (MB BS), Punjab Univ (MS Ophth), Univ of Dublin (DO); *m* 5 Dec 1975, Sona Singh, da of Aya Ram (d 1989); 1 s (Rickey b 21 Oct 1979 d 1979), 2 da (Neetika b 24 Jan 1977, Tarana b 11 May 1982); *Career* sr house offr: Charing Cross Hosp London 1973, Canterbury Hosp 1973–74; registrar in ophthalmology: Birkenhead Hosp 1974–78, Bournemouth Hosp 1978–80; sr registrar in ophthalmology Manchester Royal Eye Hosp 1980–83; conslt in ophthalmology: Darlington Meml NHS Tst 1983– (memb Unit Mgmnt Bd, former chm Med Exec Ctee, chm Med Staff Ctee), Friarage NHS Tst Northallerton N Yorks, SW Durham NHS Tst 1983–; memb various working gps and ctees Darlington Health Authy, memb UK, Euro and Int Intraocular Implant Socs; author of numerous articles in jls; memb Exec: Sikh Community Gp Darlington, Overseas Doctors Assoc UK, Indian Doctors of Cleveland; hon res fell Indian Cncl of Medical Res 1970–72; Masters in Surgery (Ophth) 1973; FRCSEd 1979, FCOphth 1988, FRCOphth 1993; *Recreations* walking, reading, travel, golf; *Style—* Mohinder Singh Dang, Esq; ✉ Mussoorie House, Compton Grove, Darlington, Co Durham (☎ 01325 486371); Consultant Ophthalmic Surgeon, Memorial Hospital, Darlington, Co Durham (☎ 01325 380100, fax 01325 743801)

DANGAN, Viscount; Garret Graham Wellesley; s (by 1 m) and h of 7 Earl Cowley, *qv*; *b* 30 March 1965; *m* 30 June 1990, Claire L, o da of Peter Brighton, of Grasmere, Stow Bridge, King's Lynn, Norfolk; 1 s (Hon Henry Arthur Peter b 3 Dec 1991); *Career* banker; traded options Hoare Govett Ltd, money markets Banque Indosuez, latterly with Geldermann Ltd; *Clubs* Brooks's; *Style—* Viscount Dangan; ✉ c/o Brooks's, St James's Street, London SW1

DANIEL, Sir Goronwy Hopkin; KCVO (1969), CB (1962); s of David Daniel; *b* 21 March 1914; *Educ* Pontardawe Secdy Sch, Amman Valley Co Sch, UCW Aberystwyth, Jesus Coll Oxford (DPhil); *m* 28 March 1940, Lady Valerie Lloyd George; 1 s, 2 da; *Career* lectr Dept of Econs Univ of Bristol 1940–41, temp clerk House of Commons (attached to Select Ctee Nat Expenditure) 1941–43, Miny of Town & Country Planning 1943–47, chief statistician Miny of Fuel and Power 1947, under sec 1955–64, perm under sec of state Welsh Office 1964–69; princ UCW Aberystwyth 1969–79, vice chllr Univ of Wales 1977–79; dep chm Bank of Wales 1984–90 (dir 1972–); HM Lt for Dyfed 1979–89; former chm HGTAC; former memb: Gen Advsy Cncl BBC, Welsh Languange Cncl, SSRC; chm: Welsh Fourth TV Channel Authy 1981–86, Meml Coll of the Welsh Independents 1985–90, Powers and Functions Working Pty Univ of Wales 1988–89; dep chm Prince of Wales' Ctee 1980–86; hon memb Gorsedd of Bards; Hon Freeman City of London; hon fell Jesus Coll Oxford; Hon LLD Wales; *Clubs* Travellers'; *Style—* Sir Goronwy Daniel, KCVO, CB; ✉ Cae Ffynnon, 67 St Michael's Road, Llandaff, Cardiff (☎ 01222 553150)

DANIEL, His Hon Judge Gruffydd Huw Morgan; DL (Gwynedd 1993); s of Prof John Edward Daniel (d 1962), and Catherine Megan Parry-Hughes (d 1972); *b* 16 April 1939; *Educ* Ampleforth, Univ Coll of Wales (LLB), Inns of Court Sch of Law; *m* 10 Aug 1968, Phyllis Margaret Bermingham, da of Walter Ambrose Bermingham, of Clifden, Connemara, Eire (d 1988); 1 da (Antonia Siwan Bermingham); *Career* Nat Serv 1958–60 (volunteered), served 24 Foot the South Wales Borderers, cmmnd 2 Lt 23 Foot the Royal Welch Fusiliers, Capt 6/7 RWF 1965, served MELF (Cyprus) and UK; called to the Bar Gray's Inn 1967, recorder 1980–86, in practice Wales and Chester Circuit, circuit jr 1975, asst parly boundary cmmr for Wales 1981–82 (Gwynedd Enquiry) and 1985, liaison judge for Gwynedd 1988–96 (dep liaison judge 1984–88), dep liaison judge N Wales 1996–, circuit judge (Wales and Chester Circuit) 1986–, dep sr judge (non-resident) Sovereign Base Areas Cyprus 1995–, tstee Royal Welch Fusiliers Museum 1995–, Hon Col 6 (Cadet) Bn RWF 1996–; *Recreations* shooting, sailing, gardening; *Clubs* Reform, Royal Anglesey Yacht, Bristol Channel Yacht; *Style—* His Honour Judge Daniel, DL; ✉ Rhiw Goch, Halfway Bridge, Bangor, Gwynedd LL57

DANIEL, (Reginald) Jack; OBE (1958); s of Reginald Daniel Daniel, and Florence Emily, *née* Woods; *b* 27 Feb 1920; *Educ* Royal Naval Engrg Coll Keyham, RNC Greenwich; *Career* warship and submarine designer; dir Submarine Design and Prodn 1970–74, dir gen Ships and head of Royal Corps of Naval Constructors MOD 1974–79, bd memb Br Shipbuilders and dir of technol Warships 1979–84, conslt and Canadian project dir VSEL plc 1984–91; FEng 1976 (fndr fell), FRINA, FIMarE, RCNC; *Style—* Jack Daniel, Esq, OBE, FEng; ✉ Meadowland, Cleveland Walk, Bath BA2 6JU

DANIEL, Sir John Sagar; kt (1994); *b* 31 May 1942; *Educ* Christ's Hosp Sussex, St Edmund Hall Oxford (open scholar, BA, MA), Univ of Paris (NATO scholar, Joliot-Curie scholar, DSc), Thorneloe Coll (ATh), Concordia Univ (MA); *m* 1966, Kristin Anne Swanson; 1 s, 2 da; *Career* assoc prof Dept of Metallurgical Engrg Univ of Montreal 1971–73 (asst prof 1969–71), dir of studies Télé-Université Univ of Quebec 1974–77 (co-ordinator 1973–74), vice pres Learning Servs Athabasca Univ Alberta 1978–80, vice rector academic affrs Concordia Univ Montreal 1980–84, pres Laurentian Univ Ontario 1984–90, vice chancellor The Open Univ 1990–; assoc cmmr Nat Cmmn on Educn 1992–93; pres: Canadian Soc for the Study of HE 1982–83 (vice pres and prog chm 1981–82), Int Cncl for Distance Educn 1982–85 (prog chm 12th World Conf Vancouver 1978–82), Canadian Assoc for Distance Educn 1988–89; memb Editorial Bd: Distance Education 1980–90, Canadian Jl of Higher Education 1980–90, Jl of Distance Education 1988–90, British Jl of Educational Technology 1988–90; numerous opening and keynote addresses at int conferences; vice pres Organizing Ctee World Jr Athletics Championships Sudbury 1986–88, dir Milton Keynes and N Bucks Trg and Enterprise Cncl 1990–95; tstee Carnegie Fndn for the Advancement of Teaching 1993–; memb Cncl: Fndn International Baccalaureate 1992–, Univ of Buckingham 1994–, Coll of St Mark and St John 1994–96, Central Sch of Speech and Drama 1994–; memb: Nat Defence Coll Canada 1989–90, HE Quality Cncl 1992–94, Advsy Cncl Royal Naval Engrg Coll 1993–, Conseil d'Administration Centre National d'Education à Distance 1994–, Br North American Ctee 1995–; reader C of E Diocese of St Albans; hon fell St Edmund Hall Oxford 1990; hon life memb: Canadian Assoc for Distance Educn 1990, Int Cncl for Distance Educn 1988; Distinguished Young Memb Award American Soc for Metals 1973, Frank Oppenheimer Award American Soc for Engrg Educn Annual Conf NY 1974, Cwlth of Learning Award of Excellence 1995; Hon DLitt Deakin Univ Aust 1985, Hon DSc Royal Mil Coll St Jean Canada 1988, Hon DEd CNAA 1992, Hon LlD Univ of Waterloo Canada 1993, Hon DSc Open Univ of Sri Lanka 1994; Officier de l'Ordre des Palmes Académique (France) 1992 (Chevalier 1986); *Publications* author of numerous articles in professional jls; *Style*— Sir John Daniel; ✉ Wednesden House, Aspley Guise, Milton Keynes MK17 8DQ; The Open University, Walton Hall, Milton Keynes MK7 6AA (☎ 01908 653214, fax 01908 655093, telex 825061, e-mail j.s.daniel@open.ac.uk)

DANIEL, Prof Nicholas; s of Jeremy Daniel, of Wood Green, Hants, and Margaret Louise (Billie) *née* Tomkins (d 1993); *b* 9 Jan 1962; *Educ* Salisbury Cathedral Sch, Purcell Sch, RAM; *m* 1986, Joy, *née* Farrall; 2 s (Alastair William b 23 May 1994, Patrick Nicholas b 1 March 1996); *Career* oboist; prof GSM (fell 1995); winner BBC Young Musician of the Year 1980; duo with Julius Drake 1980–; regularly appears with: Lindsay Quartet, Brindisi Quartet, Vanburgh String Quartet; debut BBC Proms 1992; recent performances incl: debut Japan and USA, Pinchas Zuckerman, Camerata Roman Sweden, Scottish Chamber Orch, European Community Chamber Orch, Orch of the Mozarteum Salzburg, Eng Chamber Orch, Lucerne Festival Strings Evian Festival; 1996 premieres incl: works by John Taverner, Diana Burrell, Howard Skempton; works specially composed by Michael Berkeley, Sir Harrison Birtwistle, Sir Peter Maxwell Davies, Oliver Knussen, Colin Matthews, David Matthews, Thea Musgrave, Sir Michael Tippett; 17 CDs on Chandos, Collins, Hyperion, Virgin, Leman Classics; Artist of the Week BBC Radio 3 1996; memb: Liedloff Continuum Network, Natural Nurturing Network, Assoc of Radical Midwives, Nat Childbirth Tst, The Informed Parent; ARAM 1986, FFSM 1995; *Recreations* Star Trek, cooking, walking, theatre, ballet, cinema, music, home birth; *Style*— Prof Nicholas Daniel; ✉ c/o Upbeat Management, Sutton Business Centre, Restmor Way, Wallington, Surrey SM6 7AH (☎ 0181 773 1223, fax 0181 669 6752)

DANIEL, Paul Wilson; s of Alfred Daniel, of Drayton Basset, Staffs, and Margaret, *née* Poole; *b* 5 July 1958; *Educ* King Henry VIII Sch Coventry, King's Coll Cambridge, Guildhall Sch of Music and Drama; *m* 1988, Joan Rodgers, *qv*; 2 da (Eleanor Elizabeth b 4 Sept 1990, Rose Imogen b 14 May 1993); *Career* conductor; music dir Opera Factory London 1980–90, music dir Opera North and princ conductor English Northern Philharmonia (Opera North orch) 1990–, music dir designate ENO; studied with Sir Adrian Boult and Sir Edward Downes; conducted numerous major international orchs incl: LSO, London Philharmonic, Royal Philharmonic, BBC Symphony, London Sinfonietta, CBSO, RLPO, Scottish Chamber Orch, Hallé Orch, Nat Youth Orch, Czech Philharmonic, National Orch of Belgium, Royal Flanders Philharmonic, Ensemble Intercontemporain, Musique Vivante (Paris), Ensemble Modern (Germany); operas conducted with Opera North incl: Verdi's Jérusalem (Br stage première) and Attila, Dukas' Ariane et Barbe-Bleue, Tippet's King Priam, Don Giovanni, Boris Godunov (BBC Proms 1992), Don Carlos, Wozzeck, Schrecker's Der Ferne Klang, Britten's Gloriana (at Royal Opera House Covent Garden), Debussy's Pelléas et Mélisande, Janáček's Jenufa; other operas conducted incl: numerous for ENO incl Figaro's Wedding 1992, King Priam (Nancy Opera, the opera's French première, awarded French Critics' Prize); co-presenter Channel 4/Opera North TV series Harry Enfield's Guide to Opera 1993 (also conducted accompanying EMI recording); *Recordings* with various artists and orchs incl: LSO and John Williams (Sony Classics), Scottish Chamber Orch and Evelyn Glennie (BMG), English Northern Philharmonia and Opera North companion to Harry Enfield's Guide to Opera (EMI); *Style*— Paul Daniel, Esq; ✉ Opera North, Grand Theatre, 46 New Briggate, Leeds LS1 6NU (☎ 0113 243 9999, fax 0113 244 0418); Harrison/Parrott Ltd, 12 Penzance Place, London W11 4PA (☎ 0171 229 9166, fax 0171 221 5042)

DANIEL, Philip Louis; 2 s of Oscar Louis Wood Moore (d 1931), and Louisa Ann, *née* à Court (d 1919); name changed by Deed Poll from à Court Moore 1945; *b* 23 June 1919; *Educ* Cardinal Vaughan Meml Sch Kensington, LSE (BA); *Career* OTC (RA) Univ of London 1937–39, cmmnd RA 1940, Capt 1942, served Burma and India 1942–45, Maj 1944, SO HQ SEAC 1944–45 (Supreme Allied Cdr's Commendation 1945), Maj RARO 1945–69; asst princ Miny of Food 1948, served Overseas Food Corp Tanganyika, private sec to Sir Laurence Helsby and others 1950–52, Air Miny 1953, asst sec Dept of Econ Affrs 1965, dep chm SE Econ Planning Bd 1968; DOE: head London Geographical Planning Div 1972–78, New Towns Div 1978–79, memb Planning Inspectorate 1980–89; chm: Int Ctee Newman Assoc of GB 1960–84 (pres 1969–71), Issues Ctee Catholic Union of GB 1980–, Clifton Episcopal Cmmn of Inquiry 1989, Catholic Cncl for Polish Welfare 1994–; memb Cncls: Town and Country Planning Assoc 1982–89 and 1991–, Keston Research 1980–, Reigate Soc 1987–; hon memb Phi Kappa Theta Fairfield Conn USA 1971; Freeman City of London 1972 (memb Guild of Freeman 1974), Liveryman Worshipful Co of Scriveners 1978; FIMgt 1980; KSG (HH Pope Paul VI) 1975 (Knight Cdr with Star (Pope John Paul II) 1996), Knight Order of Holy Sepulchre of Jerusalem 1980 (Grand Officer 1991, archivist 1993), Knight's Cross Order of Polonia Restituta 1991; *Books* articles incl: Can World Poverty Be Abolished? (World Justice Vol XI), A Nation's Shame: Three Decades of London Housing (1971); A Short History of the Order of the Holy Sepulchre (1994); *Recreations* motoring, fencing, theatre, historical and economic writing; *Clubs* Army and Navy, Players' Theatre; *Style*— Philip Daniel, Esq; ✉ Meadhouse, 37 Somerset Rd, Redhill, Surrey RH1 6LT

DANIEL, Dr Reginald; s of Reginald Daniel (d 1988), and Alice, *née* Youell (d 1993); *b* 7 Dec 1939; *Educ* Palmers Sch Grays Essex, Univ of London, Westminster Hosp Med Sch (MB BS, LRCP, FRCS, fell Royal Coll of Ophthalmologists, DO, AKC, ECFMG); *m* Carol; 1 s (Lorne Piers b 23 July 1968), 1 da (Claire Suzanne b 2 Dec 1969); *Career* conslt ophthalmic surgn Guy's and St Thomas's Hosps, ophthalmic private practice Harley Street and London Bridge Hosp; lectr Univ of London; author of many ophthalmic papers in professional jls; Freeman City of London, Liveryman Worshipful Co of Spectacle Makers; memb: BMA, Euro Intraocular Implant Soc, American Academy of Ophthalmology, Contemporary Soc of Ophthalmologists in USA, Moorfield Hosp Surgns' Assoc; *Recreations* golf, tennis, skiing; *Clubs* City of London Livery; *Style*— Dr Reginald Daniel; ✉ 152 Harley St, London W1N 1HH (☎ 0171 935 3834, fax 0171 224 2574)

DANIEL, Ronald George Daniel (Ron); s of Percy Daniel (d 1977), and Nellie, *née* Chalmers (d 1949); *b* 15 Oct 1942; *Educ* Br Sch of Niteroi Brasil, Anglo-American Sch Rio de Janeiro; *m* Anjula Helen; 1 s (Alexis Louis Warren b 7 March 1968), 1 da (Eliena May Josephine b 10 Aug 1972); *Career* theatre dir; fndr Teatro Oficina Sao Paulo 1959, actor Byre Theatre St Andrews 1964, joined Victoria Theatre Stoke on Trent 1965, dir Sophocles' Electra and Plautus' Pot of Gold 1966, dir Goldsmith's She Stoops to Conquer 1977, joined RSC 1966, full time dir Victoria Theatre Stoke on Trent 1967–72 (prodns incl: Coriolanus, Major Barbara, Hamlet, Time Travellers), freelance dir 1972–77 (prodns incl: The Long and the Short and the Tall, Measure for Measure, Man is Man, Puntila and His Servant Matti), artistic dir The Other Place RSC 1977 (prodns incl: 'Tis a Pity She's a Whore, Pericles, Timon of Athens, Peer Gynt), assoc dir RSC (prodns incl: A Midsummer Night's Dream, The Tempest, Hamlet, Romeo and Juliet, A Clockwork Orange, Richard II); assoc artistic dir American Repertory Theatre Boston 1992 (prodns incl: Hamlet, The Seagul, Henry IV parts 1 and 2, Dream of the Red Spider, Silence, Cunning and Exile, The Cherry Orchard); head of acting and directing programmes Inst of Advanced Theatre Trg Harvard; lectr and teacher; *Style*— Ron Daniels, Esq; ✉ c/o William Morris Agency, 31/32 Soho Square, London W1V 5DG (☎ 0171 434 2191)

DANIEL, William Wentworth; CBE (1997); s of George Taylor Daniel, and Margaret Elizabeth, *née* Hopper; *b* 19 Nov 1938; *Educ* Univ of Manchester (BA, MSc); *m* 1, 22 Sept 1961 (m dis 1974), Lynda Mary, *née* Garrett; m 2, 6 July 1990, Eileen Mary, *née* Loudfoot (d 1996); *Career* asst lectr Univ of Manchester 1962–63, directing staff Ashorne Hill Mgmnt Coll Warwickshire 1963–65, research offr Research Services Ltd London 1965–67, res fell Univ of Bath 1967–68, dir The Policy Studies Inst (formerly Political and Economic Planning London) 1986–93 (res fell 1968–83, dep dir 1983–86); memb: Econ and Social Res Cncl (ESRC) 1992–96, Ctee of Experts European Fndn for the Improvement of Living and Working Conditions (EFILWC) 1992–96; *Books* incl: Racial Discrimination in England (1968), The Right to Manage? (1972), Sandwich Courses in Higher Education (1975), Where Are They Now? - A Follow up Survey of the Unemployed (1977), Maternity Rights - The Experience of Women (1980), Workplace Industrial Relations in Britain (1983), Workplace Industrial Relations and Technical Change (1987), The Unemployed Flow (1990); *Recreations* golf, tennis; *Clubs* National Liberal, Bude & North Cornwall Golf; *Style*— William Daniel, Esq, CBE; ✉ Chyvarton, Higher Upton, Bude, North Cornwall; Flat 2, 64 Queensway, London W2 3RL; 3 Rotherwood, 8 Maer Down Road, Bude, North Cornwall EX23 8NG (☎ and fax 01288 356678)

DANIELL, Gillian Mary; da of John Averell Daniell, of Lutterworth, Leicestershire, and Nancy Helen Law; *b* 23 Feb 1947; *Educ* The Sch of Sts Mary and Anne Bromley, Loughborough Coll of Art, Slade Sch of Fine Art (Dip in Theatre Design), Goldsmiths Coll of Art (BA), RCA (MA); *m* 1972 (m dis 1987), Vaughan, s of Herman Grylls; 1 da (Sarah Hope b 22 June 1979); *Career* theatre designer, television producer and artist; memb: CNAA (examiner for fine art BA Hons) 1984–87, Soc of Br Theatre Designers 1989–; pt/t lectr variously at: Portsmouth Poly, Croydon Coll of Art, Homerton Coll Cambridge, London Coll of Printing; currently at: The London Inst, Central, Saint Martins, Univ of Greenwich, The Chinese Univ of Hong Kong; *Exhibitions* incl: Young Contemporaries 1969, mixed show RCA 1970 and 1971, mixed show Trinity Coll Cambridge 1971, Art Spectrum Alexandra Palace London 1971, Past students of the Environmental Media Dept RCA 1972, mixed staff show Croydon Coll of Art 1973, Art Into Landscape exhbn Serpentine Gall 1974 (awarded second prize); Scaling Up Guild Hall Manchester 1986; *Theatre* fndr Calliope Theatre Co Williamstown Mass; co-designer and dir: The Zoo Story (Royal Court) 1970, Fallen Woman 1985; designer credits incl: As Cuecas (The Bloomers 1975, German Inst Lisbon Portugal 1985), The Winter Dancers (Royal Court) 1977; freelance designer for Durham Theatre Co Darlington 1982–85; Liverpool Playhouse: Rat In The Skull 1987, Macbeth 1988, Second Lady 1988, Of Mice And Men (also UK tour) 1989; other prodns incl: Diary of A Somebody - The Orton Diaries (NT) 1987, Monopoly (The Old Red Lion) 1987, Two Acts Of Love (Prince of Wales Theatre) 1987, The Orton Diaries (The King's Head) 1987, Every Good Boy Deserves Favour (Queen Elizabeth Hall) 1987, A Slice of Saturday Night (The King's Head and The Arts Theatre) 1989; *Television* documentary prodr, formed own TV prodn co 1982; *Awards* nomination for Best Design in Charrington London Fringe Award (for Slice of Saturday Night) 1990; *Style*— Ms Gillian Daniell; ✉ 79 Mortimer Road, London N1 5AR (☎ 0171 254 4579)

DANIELL, Sir Peter Averell; kt (1971), TD (1950), DL (Surrey 1976); s of late Roger Henry Averell Daniell; *b* 8 Dec 1909; *Educ* Eton, Trinity Coll Oxford (MA); *m* 18 July 1935, Leonie Mayne, da of late Henry Beauchamp Harrison; 2 s (Roger b 1939, James b 1949), 1 da (Celia (Mrs Prideaux) b 1936); *Career* KRRC 1939–45; sr ptnr Mullens and Co, ret 1973; sr govt broker 1963–73; memb Ct of Assts Worshipful Co of Drapers (Master 1980); *Clubs* Brooks's, Alpine; *Style*— Sir Peter Daniell, TD, DL; ✉ Glebe House, Buckland, Surrey (☎ 01737 842320)

DANIELS, George; MBE (1982); s of George Daniels, and Beatrice, *née* Cadou; *b* 19 Aug 1926; *m* 1964, Juliet Anne, *née* Marryat; 1 da; *Career* served 2 Bn E Yorks Regt 1944–47; author, watchmaker, horological consultant; began professional horology 1947–, restoration of historical watches 1956–, hand watch-making to own designs 1969–; chm Horological Industries Ctee 1982–96; memb Ct of Assts Worshipful Co of Clockmakers (Master 1980); Victor Kullberg Medal Stockholm Watch Guild 1977, Gold Medal Br Horological Inst 1981, Tompion Gold Medal 1981, City & Guilds Insignia Award (Hons) 1986, City & Guilds Gold Medal for Craftmanship 1991; Hon DSc City Univ 1994; hon fell and Gold Award recipient of American Watchmakers Inst 1987; *Books* English and American Watches (1965), The Art of Breguet (1975, 2nd edition 1978), Watchmaking (1981), Sir David Salomon's Collection (1981), Practical Watch Escapement (1994); *Recreations* vintage cars, fast motorcycles, opera, Scotch whisky; *Clubs* Athenaeum, Lansdowne, RAC; *Style*— George Daniels, Esq, MBE; ✉ Riversdale, Jurby Road, Ramsay, Isle of Man

DANIELS, Jack; s of David John, of Swanage, Dorset, and Margaret Ann, *née* Owen; *b* 8 June 1963; *Educ* Lode Heath Comp Sch Solihull W Mids, Warblington Comp Sch Havant Hants, Portsmouth Coll of Art (OND), Bournemouth Coll of Art (HND); *m* 9 July 1988, Teresa Ann, da of Bernard Appleby; 2 s (Jake b 11 Jan 1989, Jaxon b 29 July 1991); *Career* former apprentice electrical engr; photographer (specialising in animal portraits) 1988–; editorial cmmns for: Sunday Times, Daily Telegraph, The Observer, Daily Mail, The Field, GQ, The New Scientist, Country Life, Elle, Evening Standard, Esquire, BBC Wildlife, etc; advtg cmmns for clients incl: Cadbury's, Farleys, Citroen Austria, Birmingham Mint, Spillers Pet Foods, British Coal, Twickenham Rugby Club, Nationwide Building Society, National Westminster Bank, Jacobs Bakeries, Budget Car Hire, Nickelodeon TV, Pentax, Prudential, The Prince's Youth Business Trust, British Gas, Nissan, Logitech, IBM, Nat Canine Defence League, Our Price, TSB; other cmmns for book covers and record sleeves; work published throughout Europe, USA and Far East; contrib Tony Stone Worldwide Picture Library; has exhibited at Association, Special Photographers, Photographers, Hamilton's, Barbican, Royal Photographic and Smith's Galleries; memb Assoc of Photographers 1988; *Awards* Zig-Zag/Pentax Photographer of the Yr 1988, Gold medal Royal Photographic Soc 133rd Print Awards 1989, Merit Assoc of Photographers 11th Awards 1993; *Recreations* sea fishing, target shooting, computing, visiting The Square and Compass; *Clubs* Tennessee Squire, Dorchester Pistol and Rifle, Wessex Gun, Christchurch Gun, Swanage Gun, Glastonbury '95 Vets, Square and Compass Hat (Worth Matravers, Dorset); *Style*— Jack Daniels, Esq; ✉ (home ☎ 01929 427429, fax 01929 427471, mobile 0831 356719); c/o Ms Jo Clark, 13 Prowse Place, London NW1 9PN

DANIELS, Patrick Deane; s of Gerald Ernest Deane Daniels (d 1942), and Marcelle Barbara Mary Daniels; *b* 20 April 1940; *Educ* St George's Coll Weybridge Surrey, Univ of Durham (LLB), Coll of Law; *m* Heide Marie, da of Friedrich Mumm (d 1944); 1 s (Mark Frederick), 1 da (Nina Marie); *Career* asst slr Bulcraig and Davis 1965–66 (articled clerk 1962–65), attended course in German law and worked in Germany 1966–67, asst slr Freshfields 1968–72, ptnr Simmons and Simmons 1973– (asst slr 1972–73); ctee memb: City of London Law Soc 1992–, Br-German Jurists' Assoc 1992–; memb: Law Soc, Br Inst of Int and Comparative Law; memb Ct of Assts City of London Slrs' Co 1995 (Freeman and Liveryman 1990); *Publications* Tolley's Company Law (contrib), Management of Interest Rate Risk, Management of Currency Risk (1989); *Recreations* walking, swimming, arts, wine; *Clubs* Carlton; *Style*— Patrick Daniels, Esq; ✉ Simmons & Simmons, 21 Wilson Street, London EC2M 2TQ (☎ 0171 628 2020, fax 0171 628 2070)

DANIELS, (Newton Edward) Paul; s of Handel Newton Daniels, and Nancy, *née* Lloyd; *b* 6 April 1938; *Educ* Sir William Turner's GS Coatham Redcar; *m* 1, 26 March 1960 (m dis 1975); 3 s (Paul Newton b 9 Sept 1960, Martin b 19 Aug 1963, Gary b 15 March 1969); m 2, 2 April 1988, Debbie, *née* McGee; *Career* Nat Serv Green Howards 1957–59, served Hong Kong; magician and entertainer; clerk (later internal auditor) local govt, mobile grocery business (later shop owner), turned professional 1969, TV debut Opportunity Knocks 1970; subsequent TV series incl: The Paul Daniels Magic Show, Odd One Out, Every Second Counts, Wizbit (childrens series), Wipeout, Secrets; theatre: It's Magic (Prince of Wales) 1980–82, An Evening With Paul Daniels (Prince of Wales) 1983; Christmas season Savoy 1989; summer seasons: Great Yarmouth 1979, Bournemouth 1980, Blackpool 1983; appeared in 5 Royal Variety Shows; winner: Magician of the Year Award, Hollywood's Acad of Magical Arts Golden Rose of Montreux Trophy 1985 (for Paul Daniels Easter Magic Show BBC); memb: Inner Magic Circle, The Grand Order of Water Rats; *Books* Paul Daniels Magic Book (1980), More Magic (1981), Paul Daniels Magic Annual (1983), 77 Popular Card Games and Tricks (1985), The Paul Daniels Magic Showcase (1992), 50 Easy Card Tricks (1993); *Recreations* photography, golf, tennis; *Clubs* The Magic Circle; *Style*— Paul Daniels, Esq; ✉ P O Box 250, Uxbridge, Middx UB9 5DX (☎ 01302 321 233, fax 01895 834 891)

DANIELS, Prof Peter George; s of Frederick James Daniels, of Ilford, Essex, and Eileen Bertha, *née* Galley; *b* 30 Sept 1950; *Educ* Ilford Co HS, Univ of Bristol (BSc), UCL (PhD, DSc); *m* 12 July 1975, Anne Elizabeth, da of Robert Latham, of Hammersmith, London; 1 s (Geoffrey b 1989), 1 da (Katherine b 1986); *Career* Dept of Mathematics City Univ: lectr 1977, reader 1981, prof of applied mathematics 1985–, head of Dept 1987–; *Recreations* soccer, gardening; *Style*— Prof Peter Daniels; ✉ Department of Mathematics, City University, Northampton Square, London EC1V OHB (☎ 0171 477 8450, fax 0171 477 8597)

DANKWORTH, John Philip William; CBE (1974); *b* 20 Sept 1927; *Educ* Monoux GS, RAM; *m* 18 March 1958, Clementine Dinah (Cleo Laine, *qv*); 1 s (Alex b 1960), 1 da (Jackie b 1963); *Career* musician, closely involved with post-war devpt of Br jazz 1947–60; pops music dir LSO 1985–90, princ guest pops conductor San Francisco Orch 1987–89; cmmnd compositions incl: Improvisations (with Matyas Seiber) 1959, Escapade (Northern Sinfonia Orchestra) 1967, Tom Sawyer's Saturday (Farnham) 1967, String Quartet 1971, Piano Concerto (Westminster Festival) 1972, Grace Abounding 1980, The Diamond and The Goose 1981, Reconciliation (for silver jubilee of Coventry Cathedral) 1987, Woolwich Concerto (clarinet concerto for Emma Johnson) 1995, Lady in Waiting (Houston Ballet), Man of Mode (RSC), Edward II (Nat Theatre); film scores incl: We Are the Lambeth Boys, The Criminal, Saturday Night and Sunday Morning 1964, Darling, The Servant 1965, Modesty Blaise, Sands of Kalahari, Morgan, Return From the Ashes (Academy Award nomination) 1966, Accident 1969, Salt and Pepper 1969, Fathom 1969, 10 Rillington Place 1971, The Last Grenade 1971; musical theatre incl: Boots with Strawberry Jam (with Benny Green) 1968, Colette (starring Cleo Laine) 1979; TV theme for the Avengers series; numerous records incl: Echoes of Harlem, Misty, Symphonic Fusions; Variety Club of GB show business personality award (with Cleo Laine); Hon MA Open Univ 1975; Hon DMus: Berklee Sch 1982, Univ of York 1993; FRAM 1973; Liveryman Worshipful Co of Musicians; *Recreations* driving, household maintenance; *Style*— John Dankworth, CBE; ✉ The Old Rectory, Wavendon, Milton Keynes, Bucks MK17 8LT (☎ 01908 583151, fax 01908 584414)

DANN, Clifford Thomas; s of George Dann (d 1971), of Hellingly, Sussex, and Grace Sophia, *née* Hook (d 1970); *b* 17 July 1927; *Educ* Hailsham Co Sch, Univ of London (BSc); *m* 1, 14 Aug 1948 (m dis 1988), Bronwen Annie, da of the late Gordon Gauld, of Coventry; 1 s (Vyvian b 1959 d 1994), 1 da (Angela b 1951); m 2, 21 Nov 1988, Patricia Anne Purdon, da of The Very Rev Ivan Delacherois Neill, CB, OBE; 3 step s (Charles, Richard, Philip); *Career* chartered surveyor; fndr and sr ptnr Clifford Dann & Partners 1956–94 (conslt 1994–); dir: Individual Life Insurance Co Ltd 1972–76, Network Data Ltd 1981–83; RICS: chm Jr Orgn 1957–58, memb Cncl 1958–61 and 1973–87, chm Sussex Branch 1973–74, chm Public Affrs Ctee 1975–80, chm Policy Review Ctee 1980–82, pres 1983–84; Int Fedn of Surveyors: UK del 1958–82 and 1990–93, chm Town Planning Cmmn 1974–75; pres The Charter Soc 1994–, hon treas Cwlth Assoc of Surveying and Land Economy (CASLE) 1995–; lectr on arbitration practice; chm: Lewes Round Table 1958, Sussex Area World of Property Housing Tst 1965–72, League of Friends of Chailey Heritage (physically disabled children) 1978–, The Chailey Challenge Appeal 1991–; memb: The Speaker's Appeal for St Margaret's Westminster Ctee, Friends of Lewes Ctee 1957–63, Lewes Old People's Welfare Ctee 1962–68; govr: Lewes Tech Coll 1967–73, Univ of Brighton 1989– (vice chm 1994–); pres Lewes C of C 1965, memb Surrey and Sussex Rent Assessment Panel 1965–72; Freeman City of London 1979, Liveryman Worshipful Co of Chartered Surveyors; memb FIABCI 1960–85, FRICS 1957 (ARICS 1949); *Publications* author of numerous articles in professional jls incl: International Economic Factors in Urban Development (1962), Community Land Scheme (1971–75), Real Estate Arbitration in the UK (1992), Professional Ethics (1996); *Recreations* music, organ, choir training, gardening, DIY, travelling abroad; *Style*— Clifford Dann, Esq; ✉ The Old Jewellers, 176 High Street, Uckfield, E Sussex TN22 1AU (☎ and fax 01825 760020)

DANN, Jill; da of Maj Harold Norman Cartwright, MC (d 1955), of Solihull, Warwicks, and Marjorie Alice, *née* Thornton (d 1972); *b* 10 Sept 1929; *Educ* Solihull HS for Girls, Univ of Birmingham (LLB), St Hilda's Coll Oxford (BCL), Inner Temple; *m* 12 July 1952, Anthony John Dann (Tony), s of Sydney William Henry Dann (d 1988), of Chippenham, Wilts; 3 s (Christopher b 1954, Michael b and d 1956, Timothy b 1961), 2 da (Jennie b 1957, Rachel b 1961); *Career* barr; broadcaster and dir ARK 2 Television Ltd; vice chm House of Laity Gen Synod, church cmmr, tstee Church Urban Fund, vice chair Trinity Coll Bristol, former Mayoress of Chippenham, pres Cheltenham and Gloucester Coll of HE; *Recreations* reading, grandchildren; *Style*— Mrs Jill Dann; ✉ The Riverbank, Reybridge, Lacock, Wiltshire SN15 2PF (☎ and fax 01249 730205)

DANN, Trevor John; *b* 6 Nov 1951; *Educ* Nottingham HS, Univ of Cambridge (MA); *m* 5 Feb 1991, Maureen Patricia, *née* Gunn; 1 da (Celia b 22 Nov 1992), 1 s (Henry b 25 June 1994); *Career* prodr: BBC Radio 1974–83, BBC TV progs incl Live Aid and Whistle Test 1983–88; freelance TV prodr 1988–91, managing ed BBC Greater London Radio 1991–93 (prog organiser 1988–91), md Confederate Broadcasting 1993–95, head of prodn BBC Radio 1 1995–; *Clubs* Notts County Supporters; *Style*— Trevor Dann, Esq; ✉ BBC Radio 1, Broadcasting House, London W1A 1AA (☎ 0171 765 5407, fax 0171 765 2471)

DANTZIC, Roy Matthew; s of David A Dantzic, of Whitecraigs, Glasgow, and Renee, *née* Cohen; *b* 4 July 1944; *Educ* Brighton Coll Sussex; *m* 3 June 1969, Diane, da of Abraham Clapham (d 1984), of Whitecraigs, Glasgow; 1 s (Toby Alexander b 15 Feb 1975), 1 da (Emma Lucy b 23 Sept 1973); *Career* Coopers & Lybrand 1962–69, Kleinwort Benson Ltd 1970–72, Drayton Corporation Ltd 1972–73, Samuel Montagu & Co Ltd 1974–80 (dir 1975), fin dir Britoil plc (formerly Br National Oil Corporation) 1980–84; dir: Pallas Group SA 1984–85, Wood Mackenzie & Co 1985–89, Stanhope Properties plc 1989–95, Merrill Lynch International Ltd 1995–96; md: Port Greenwich Ltd 1996–97, BG plc Property Div 1997–; non-exec chm Premier Portfolio Group plc 1985–94; non-exec dir: British Nuclear Fuels plc 1987–91, Moor Park (1958) Ltd 1980–90, Saxon Oil plc 1984–85, Total Oil Holdings Ltd 1995–96, Airplanes Ltd 1996–, AeroUSA Inc 1996–; govr Brighton Coll 1990–, pt/t memb CEGB 1984–87; FICAS 1969; *Recreations* golf, theatre, sitting in the shade; *Clubs* MCC, Moor Park Golf; *Style*— Roy Dantzic, Esq; ✉ BG plc, Property Divison, Heron House, 322 High Holborn, London WC1V 7PW

DANVERS, Ivor Colin; s of Charles Danvers (d 1948), of London, and Violet, *née* Broughton (d 1970); *b* 14 July 1932; *Educ* Central Sch of Speech and Drama; *m* 3 Sept 1956, Henrietta, da of John Bruce Holmes (d 1968), of London; 1 s (Thomas Asher b 1 Sept 1965), 1 da (Lindsey b 24 Aug 1958); *Career* actor; Nat Serv RAF 1950; dir Richmond Theatre Surrey 1966–70; active supporter SPARKS and Aid for the Crippled Child; *Theatre* incl: The Mousetrap (Ambassadors) 1960, Robert and Elizabeth (Lyric) 1964, The Waiting Game (Arts) 1965, Give a Dog a Bone (Westminster) 1967, Norman Conquests (Globe and Apollo) 1975, Journey's End (Mermaid and Cambridge) 1972, Touch of Danger (Whitehall) 1989, Me and My Girl (Adelphi) 1990, Romeo and Juliet, Taming of the Shrew (Regents Park Theatre) 1993; *Television* incl: The Little Door, Minder, Terry and June, Love from Italy, No Place like Home, Angels, Softly Softly, The World Walk, Purple People Eater, Howards Way (as Gerald Urquhart) 1985–90, Keeping up Appearances; *Recreations* chess, bridge, golf; *Clubs* Richmond Golf, Stage Golf (pres 1987); *Style*— Ivor Danvers, Esq; ✉ c/o Felix de Wolfe, Mansfield House, 376–378 The Strand, London WC2R 0LR (☎ 0171 379 5767, fax 0171 836 0337)

DANVILLE, Comte Norbert Leon; s of Comte André Danville, Croix de Guerre (d 1986), of Paris, and Valentine, *née* de Topolsky (d 1979); *b* 26 Nov 1947; *Educ* Ecole Alsacienne Paris, Law Sch (Paris Panthéon), Sciences Po Paris; *m* 1 (m dis 1988), Annick Jousset; m 2, 24 Oct 1988, Madame Ines Voute, da of Jean Sapinno, of Geneva, Switzerland; 1 step da (Melissende Voute b 1980), 1 da (Anne-Laure b 1989), 1 s (Charles b 1993); *Career* 19 Sqdn Cavalry Regt at Les Invalides Paris 1973–74; with: Compagnie Finançière Edmond de Rothschild Paris 1974–78, Barclays Bank SA France 1978–82, BAII (London) 1982–89; md Acteon (Paris) 1990–93, chm Compagnie Européenne de Gestion et d'Investissements (EUROGI) 1994–, dir CODELOG 1995–; cncllr Franco-British Chamber of Commerce; memb: Franco-Swiss Chamber Geneva, The French Benevolent Soc London; FInstD; *Clubs* Overseas Bankers', RAC, Annabel's; *Style*— Comte Norbert Danville; ✉ EUROGI, 21 Avenue George V, 75008 Paris, France (☎ 00 33 1 53 67 72 72, fax 00 33 1 53 67 72 73)

DANZIGER, Daniel Justin Guggenheim (Danny); s of Edward Joseph Danziger, of Palm Beach, Los Angeles, and Gigi, *née* Guggenheim; *b* 1 Feb 1953; *Educ* Harrow, Rollins Coll Florida (BA); *m* (m dis 1991), Victoria Constance Baillieu; *Career* author and journalist; formerly with family businesses, writer Sunday Express then Sunday Times; columnist: The Independent 1990–95, Daily Mail 1996–; nominated Columnist of the Year 1991; *Books* The Happiness Book (1980), All in a Day's Work (1987), Eton Voices (1988), The Cathedral (1989), The Noble Tradition (1990), Lost Hearts (1992), The Orchestra (1995); *Recreations* swimming, golf, collecting watches; *Clubs* Wentworth Golf, RAC, Epicurean Soc, Hillcrest CC; *Style*— Danny Danziger, Esq; ✉ c/o Curtis Brown, Haymarket House, 28–29 Haymarket, London SW1Y 4SP (☎ 0171 390 6600, fax 0171 396 0110)

DANZIGER, Nick; s of Harry Lee Danziger, and Angela, *née* King; *b* 22 April 1958; *Educ* Switzerland, Chelsea Art Sch (BA, MA); *Career* photographer; visiting lectr various arts schs and univs 1980–; numerous solo exhbns USA, Japan, Europe, appearances in nat and int newspapers and magazines; fndr orphanage Kabul Afghanistan; FRGS 1982; *Television* incl: War Lives & Videotape (BBC) 1991, Adventures in the Land of Splaj (Channel 4) 1993, Down & Out in Paris and London (Channel 4) 1993, French Letters (Channel 4) 1994, Postcards from the Edge (Channel 4) 1996; *Awards* Winston Churchill Memorial Tst Fellowship 1982, winner Prix Italia (best tv documentary for War Lives & Videotape) 1992, fell in photography Nat Museum of Photography Film & Television 1994; *Books* Danziger's Travels (1987), Danziger's Adventures (1992), Danziger's Britain (1996); *Style*— Nick Danziger, Esq; ✉ c/o Mark Lucas, Lucas Alexander Whiteley, 47 Emperor's Gate, London SW7 4HJ (☎ 0171 373 9258)

DARBY, Catherine; da of Harry Peters, of Caernarvon, North Wales, and Vera, *née* Knight; *b* 3 March 1935; *Educ* Caernavon GS, UCNW (scholarship, DipEd, Ida Esling award); *m* 1 (m dis), Malcolm Black, s of Vernor Black; m 2 (m dis), George Ratcliffe; 3 c (Martin Peters b 1958, Rachel Peters b 1963, Emily Peters b 1965); *Career* teacher of retarded children 1956–58; author 1958–; *Publications* incl: Moon Chalice Series (6 vols, 1975–), Falcon Series (12 vols, 1976–), A Dream of Fair Serpents (1979), Sabre Series (6 vols, 1980–), Rowan Series (6 vols, 1982–), a further 100 novels under other pseudonyms (Maureen Peters, Veronica Black, Levanah Lloyd, Belinda Grey, Sharon Whitby and Elizabeth Law), 15 magazine serials, 25 short stories, 12 articles; *Recreations* travel, tapestry work, study of occult, reading; *Style*— Ms Catherine Darby; ✉ c/o Robert Hale Ltd, Clerkenwell House, 45–47 Clerkenwell Green, London EC1R OHT (☎ 0171 251 2661)

DARBY, Dr David James William; s of William Darby (d 1971), of Cairo, and Sylvia Aitken (d 1975); *b* 14 June 1935; *Educ* Downside, Royal London Hosp Med Sch Univ of Lodon (MB BS, DO, MRCS, LRCP, memb Univ of London Boxing Team); *m* 1, 1958 (m dis 1966), Fern Linker; 2 s (Mark Benedict b 1958, Hugh David b 1960), 1 da (Fiona Fern Mary b 1961); m 2, 1975, Charlotte Elizabeth, da of Leslie Baines, OBE; *Career* St John's Hosp Jerusalem 1963; ophthalmologist: Royal London Hosp 1964–70, Westminster Hosp 1965–84, Moorfield Eye Hosp 1969–; in private practice 1970–; med offr ABA 1975–; memb Ct of Dirs Soc for Relief of Widows and Orphans of Medical Men 1975–; memb BMA 1960, FRSM 1970, MRCOphth 1989; author of Common Causes of Visual Loss in the Elderly (Br Jl of Geriatric Med, 3 Vols, 1983); *Recreations* shooting, fishing, boating, golf; *Clubs* The Royal Society of Medicine, The Elite (fndr memb), Saints & Sinners, Harlequin RFC, Royal Automobile; *Style*— Dr David Darby; ✉ 73 Harley St, London W1N 1DE (☎ 0171 487 4025/4145); 28 Beaumont St, London W1N 1FE (☎ 0171 935 8752)

DARBY, (Elizabeth Ann) Foxy; *née* Foxon; da of Lt-Col Arthur Denham Foxon, DSO, TD, and Vera Mae, *née* Newsome; *b* 2 Feb 1952; *Educ* Westonbirt Sch, Kingston Coll of Art (DipAD), RCA (MA); *m* 1 Oct 1983, Keith Harry Darby, s of Harry Darby (d 1970), of Hagley, Worcs; 3 s (Harry b 1986, Randel b 1987, Edward b 1990), 1 da (Leonora Ann b 1992); *Career* personal design asst to John Stefanidis 1977–79; dir: Fanny Foxon Ltd (interior design) 1979–83, Country Fittings Ltd 1983–96; design dir Triumph Holdings Ltd 1986–96; *Recreations* Jack Russell terriers, horse-riding, designing, reading books on architecture, houses and gardens; *Style—* Mrs Keith Darby; ✉ Warnell Hall, Sebergham, Cumbria

DARBY, Gavin J; *b* 15 Feb 1956; *Educ* Cranleigh Sch, Univ of Manchester (BSc Mgmnt Science); *m*; 2 da, 1 s; *Career* early positions in brands and mktg mgmnt with Spillers and S C Johnson; Coca-Cola: joined as mktg mangr (later mktg dir) 1984, devpt assignment Coca-Cola Enterprises (USA) 1988–89, ops dir UK 1989–91, based Brussels (responsible for Denmark, Holland, Belgium and Luxembourg) 1991–93, pres Northwest Europe Div 1993– (responsible for above and France), based UK (adding Br and Irish businesses to territories) 1995–, also sr vice pres Coca-Cola International and memb Euro Operating Bd; *Recreations* golf, current affairs and economics; *Style—* Gavin Darby, Esq; ✉ Coca-Cola Northwest Europe, 1 Queen Caroline Street, London W6 9HQ (☎ 0181 237 3228, fax 0181 237 3720)

DARBY, George; s of late Norman Darby, and Joanna Eleanor, *née* Willock; *b* 20 July 1942; *Educ* Bolton Sch, Univ of Nottingham (BA); *m* 1, Constance Elizabeth Smith; 2 s (Antony Peter b 9 Feb 1969, Christopher David b 31 May 1978), 2 da (Susanne Clare b 28 Sept 1966, Amanda Zoe b 21 Nov 1975); m 2, Helene Marie Feger; 1 da (Stephanie Kate b 22 April 1996); *Career* Westminster Press grad trainee Keighley News 1963–64; sub-ed: Northern Echo 1964–65, Daily Mirror 1966–68; The Sunday Times 1968–85: personal asst to Harold Evans (ed), editorial mangr, asst ed, assoc managing ed features, assoc magazine ed, chief asst to Frank Giles (ed), exec features ed, seconded as ed The Times Royal Wedding Magazine 1981 and The Times Bicentenary Magazine 1984; managing ed then ed Sunday Today 1985–86, dep ed Today 1987, exec ed The Observer Magazine 1987–88, conslt ed The Independent Magazine 1988, dep ed The Telegraph Magazine 1988–96, editorial projects dir The Telegraph Group Ltd 1996–; adjunct prof Univ of Missouri Sch of Journalism 1985–86, proprietor Jigsaw Productions design consultancy 1970–; *Books* various ghosted autobiographies; ed: The Sunday Times Bedside Book (1983 and 1984), Thalidomide Children and the Law (1977); contrib Pictures on a Page (by Harold Evans, 1978); *Style—* George Darby, Esq; ✉ The Telegraph Group Ltd, 1 Canada Square, London E14 5DT (☎ 0171 538 5000)

DARBY, Dr Michael Douglas; s of Arthur Douglas Darby, of The Old Rectory, Ilketshall St Margaret, Nr Bungay, Suffolk, and Ilene Doris, *née* Eatwell (d 1986); *b* 2 Sept 1944; *Educ* Rugby, Univ of Reading (PhD); *m* 26 Aug 1977, Elisabeth Susan, da of Leslie Robert Done; *Career* asst to Barbara Jones 1963; V&A: Textiles Dept 1964–72, prints and drawings 1973–76, exhibitions offr 1977–83, dep dir 1984–87; surveyor gen Carroll Fndn 1990–94; memb: Crafts Cncl 1984–87, IOW Advsy Ctee English Heritage 1986–, Cncl The Nat Tst 1989–92, Cncl Royal Entomological Soc 1988–90; FRES 1977, FRGS 1984, FRSA 1989, AMA 1990; *Books* Stevengraphs (jtly, 1968), Marble Halls (jtly, 1973), Early Railway Prints Victoria and Albert Museum (1974, 1979), The Islamic Perspective (1983), British Art in the V and A (1983), John Pollard Seddon (1983); author of numerous articles in popular and learned jls; *Recreations* books, beetles, drawing; *Style—* Dr Michael Darby; ✉ The Old Malthouse, Sutton Mandeville, Salisbury, Wilts SP3 5ND

DARBY, Dr Peter George; s of Cecil George Darby (d 1987), and Ethel Mary, *née* Steele (d 1985); *b* 21 June 1934; *Educ* Pinner Co Sch, Univ of London St George's Hosp Med Sch (MB BS), Univ of Liverpool (DMRD); *m* 31 Oct 1959, Sheila Karen Rosemary, da of Hans Marius Kjeldsen (d 1982), of Wallingford, Berks; 2 s (Simon b 1961, Christopher b 1963), 1 da (Naomi (Mrs Watkins) b 1967); *Career* Nat Serv Capt RAMC 1959–61, Regtl MO LI Somerset and Cornwall; house surgn St George's Hosp 1958, GP 1961–70, registrar in radiology Liverpool Hosps 1970–73, sr registrar Bristol Hosps 1973–76, conslt radiologist Swindon 1976–; memb Ctee: Wessex RHA, Swindon DHA; memb: Parish Church S Cerney, Harnhill Centre Christian Healing Cirencester; MRCR 1973 (memb Ctee), LRCP, MRCS; *Style—* Dr Peter Darby; ✉ Meadow View, Cricklade Rd, S Cerney, Cirencester, Glos (☎ 01285 860328); Department of Diagnostic Radiology, Princess Margaret Hosptal, Okus Rd, Swindon, Wilts SN1 4JU (☎ 01793 536231)

DARBY, Sir Peter Howard; kt (1985), CBE (1973), QFSM (1970); s of the late William Cyril Darby, and Beatrice, *née* Colin; *b* 8 July 1924; *Educ* Coll of Advanced Technol Birmingham; *m* 1948, Ellen Josephine, *née* Glynn; 1 s, 1 da; *Career* chief offr London Fire Brigade 1977–80, HM's chief inspr of Fire Servs 1980–87; dir Argus Alarms; chm: Certifire, FS Nat Examinations Bd, Bd of Govrs St James Secdy Modern Sch Barnet; Freeman City of London, Liveryman Worshipful Co of Basketmakers; FIFireE 1968, CBIM 1983; CStJ 1982; *Recreations* golf, fishing, sailing; *Clubs* Livery, Candlewick Ward, City of London; *Style—* Sir Peter Darby, CBE, QFSM; ✉ 10 Moor Lane, Rickmansworth, Herts WD3 1LG

DARBYSHIRE, (John) Anthony Charles; s of (Leslie) Noel Darbyshire (d 1981), of Normanton, Derbyshire, and Marjorie Darbyshire (d 1947); *b* 7 May 1939; *Educ* Uppingham, Keble Coll Oxford (BA, MA), McGill Univ Montreal; *m* 1, 3 June 1967 (m dis 1982), (Faith) Lorraine, da of Noel William Hempsall, of Walesby, Notts; 1 s (Markham Noel Charles b 10 June 1968); m 2, 28 Aug 1982, Sheena Nanette Mabel, da of Capt Thomas Wilson Taylor, of Barnby Moor, Retford, Notts; 1 s ((John) Hamish McGregor b 26 Sept 1984), 1 da (Keturah Mona Ellen b 8 Dec 1986); *Career* prodn mangr John Darbyshire & Co Ltd 1964–66, conslt Urwick Orr & Ptnrs 1966–67, chm AH Turner Gp Ltd 1967–90, princ Anthony Darbyshire & Assocs 1990–; memb: Mgmnt Ctee Br Vehicle Rental & Leasing Assoc 1980–90, Cncl CBI 1982–90 (Smaller Firms Cncl 1979–89, E Midlands Regnl Cncl 1980–90); chm Bassetlaw Industry Assoc 1986–89 (memb Mgmnt Ctee 1986–), memb Nat Exec Bd Young Enterprise 1989–90 (chm Notts area Bd 1986–90), chm N Notts Trg and Enterprise Cncl 1989–90, dir N Notts Bus Link 1995–96; tstee Comino Fndn 1993–; FInstD 1976, FRSA 1988, CIMgt 1989 (MIMgt 1971, FIMgt 1983); *Recreations* skiing, golf, gardening and preserving the quality of life; *Style—* Anthony Darbyshire, Esq; ✉ Barnby Moor House, Barnby Moor, Retford, Notts DN22 8QX (☎ 01777 700440)

DARBYSHIRE, David Glen; s of Thomas Leslie Darbyshire (d 1979), and Alice, *née* Moss; *b* 20 May 1944; *Educ* Wigan GS, Liverpool Coll of Art, Univ of Newcastle upon Tyne (BA, BArch); *m* 7 July 1973 (m dis 1990), Jane Helen; 1 da (Kate); *Career* architect Ryder and Yates Ptnrs 1972–75, princ architect Washington Devpt Corp 1975–79, ptnr Jane and David Darbyshire 1979–87; Civic Tst Award for Dukes Cottages Backworth; Civic Tst Commendation for: Church St Cramlington, St John's Green Percy Main; winner of: St Oswald's Hospice Special Category Regnl Ltd Competition and Civic Tst Award, RIBA Nat Award Building of the Year 1988, The Times/RIBA Community Enterprise Scheme Commendation, Housing Design Award for Collingwood Ct Morpeth 1989; princ Darbyshire Architects 1987–; RIBA; *Recreations* music, mechanical engineering, fine art; *Clubs* Bristol Owners'; *Style—* David Darbyshire, Esq; ✉ 10 Lily Crescent, Jesmond, Newcastle upon Tyne (☎ 0191 281 0501); Darbyshire Architects, Hawthorn Cottage, Hawthorn Rd, Gosforth, Newcastle upon Tyne NE3 4DE (☎ 0191 284 2813)

DARBYSHIRE, David Stewart; s of Wing Cdr Rupert Stanley Darbyshire (ka 1941), and Ann, *née* Todd; *b* 14 Nov 1940; *Educ* Radley, Oriel Coll Oxford (MA); *m* 24 Jan 1970, Elizabeth, da of Eric Watts; 1 s (Rupert b 1975), 2 da (Sophie b 1973, Alice b 1978); *Career* Capt SAS AVR 1964–70; called to the Bar 1965, in practice 1965–66; Arthur Andersen: London 1966–72, Paris 1972–79, ptnr 1976–, Leeds 1979–85, London 1985–94, Moscow 1994–; treas Hakluyt Soc 1989; vice pres Federation des Experts Comptables Européens 1990, memb Ordre des Experts Comptables and Compagnie des Commissaires aux Comptes 1977; FCA 1970, ATII 1971; *Recreations* sailing, hill-walking; *Clubs* Royal Thames Yacht, Sea View Yacht; *Style—* David Darbyshire, Esq; ✉ 11 Warwick Square, London SW1V 2AA; Hutton Mount, Ripon, N Yorks HG4 5DR; Arthur Anderson, Staraya, Basmannaya 14, 103064 Moscow, Russia (☎ 00 7 502 222 4600, fax 00 7 502 222 4603)

DARBYSHIRE, Jane Helen; *née* Wroe; OBE (1994); da of Gordon Desmond Wroe (d 1994), of Brixham, S Devon, and Patricia, *née* Keough; *b* 5 June 1948; *Educ* Dorking GS, Univ of Newcastle (BA, BArch); *m* 1, 7 July 1973 (m dis), David Glen Darbyshire, s of Thomas Darbyshire (d 1980), of Wigan, Lancs; 1 da (Kate b 1979); m 2, 25 July 1993, Michael Murray Walker; *Career* chartered architect in private practice; ptnr Jane and David Darbyshire 1979–87, princ Jane Darbyshire Associates 1987–94, dir Jane Darbyshire and David Kendall Ltd 1995–; exhibitor Women in Architecture (RIBA) 1983, winner St Oswalds Hospice Design Competition 1981, exhibitor DLI Museum Durham 1981; Civic Tst: award for restoration 1982, commendation for Cramlington Housing 1983, commendation for flat refurbishment Percy Main 1986, award for St Oswalds Hospice Gosforth Newcastle upon Tyne 1987; award for housing design Morpeth 1988, Nat RIBA award 1988, Building of the Year Award 1988, Nat Housing Design award 1989, 2 housing design awards 1991, RIBA award for St Cuthbert's Church Durham 1991, Civic Tst Award 1992 and 1993; features: Channel 4 Design Matters, BBC Townscape; Civic Tst assessor, RIBA Awards assessor 1984–, memb Bd Tyne and Wear Urban Devpt Corp 1993–, external examiner Univ of Newcastle upon Tyne 1992–; *Recreations* music, art, history of architecture, horses; *Style—* Ms Jane Darbyshire, OBE; ✉ Hallgarth, Allendale, Northumberland; Jane Darbyshire and David Kendall Ltd, Millmount, Ponteland Rd, Newcastle upon Tyne

DARCH, Jonathan Robert (Jon); s of John Darch, of Bristol, and Dorothy Winifred, *née* Fry; *b* 30 March 1958; *Educ* Bristol GS, Univ of Manchester (BA); *Career* traffic mangr Radio West 1981–83, sales exec then sales mangr Signal Radio Stoke-on-Trent 1983–87, sales dir Marcher Sound Wrexham 1987–90, chief exec Sunset Radio Manchester 1990–91, dir Minster Sound Radio plc York 1994– (gen mangr 1992–); *Recreations* watching Bristol City FC and Gloucestershire CCC lose!; *Style—* Jon Darch, Esq; ✉ Minster Sound Radio plc, PO Box 123, Dunnington, York YO1 5ZX (☎ 01904 488888)

DARCY DE KNAYTH, Baroness (18 in line, E 1332); Dame Davina Marcia Ingrams; *née* Herbert; DBE (1996); da of 17 Baron Darcy de Knayth, *né* Hon Mervyn Herbert, 2 s of 4 Earl of Powis by his w (Violet) Countess of Powis, in whose favour the abeyance existing in the Barony of Darcy de Knayth was terminated in 1903, and Vida, da of late Capt James Harold Cuthbert, DSO; *b* 10 July 1938; *m* 1 March 1960, Rupert George Ingrams (k in a motor accident 28 Feb 1964), s of Leonard St Clair Ingrams, OBE, and bro of Richard Ingrams, *qv*; 1 s, 2 da; *Heir* s, Hon Caspar Ingrams; *Career* sits as Independent in House of Lords; *Style—* The Lady Darcy de Knayth, DBE; ✉ Camley Corner, Stubbings, Maidenhead, Berks (☎ 01628 822935)

DARELL, Guy Jeffrey Adair; s and h of Sir Jeffrey Lionel Darell, 8 Bt, MC, *qv*; *b* 8 June 1961; *Educ* Eton, RMC Sandhurst; *m* 1988, (Justine) Samantha, da of Mr Justice T Reynolds, of Sydney, NSW, Australia; 1 s (Harry Thomas Adair b 10 May 1995), 2 da (Sophia Elizabeth Alexandra b 22 Nov 1989, Amelia Flora Frances b 7 Jan 1993); *Career* cmmnd Coldstream Guards 1981; insur broker with Minet Lloyds Holdings Ltd 1984–93 (dir Minets 1988–93), dir Fenchurch Insurance Brokers 1993–; *Style—* Guy Darell Esq; ✉ 5 Norland Square, London W11 4PX (☎ 0171 228 9036)

DARELL, Brig Sir Jeffrey Lionel; 8 Bt (GB 1795), of Richmond Hill, Surrey, MC (1945); o s of Col Guy Marsland Darell, MC (d 1947), 3 s of 5 Bt; suc cous, Sir William Oswald Darell, 7 Bt (d 1959); *b* 2 Oct 1919; *Educ* Eton, RMC Sandhurst; *m* 30 June 1953, Bridget Mary, da of Maj-Gen Sir Allan Henry Shafto Adair, 6 Bt, GCVO, CB, DSO, MC; 1 s (Guy Jeffrey Adair b 1961), 2 da (Katherine Mary (Mrs Richard J Astor) b 1954, Camilla Viola (Mrs Henry R T Adeane) b 1956); *Heir* s, Guy Jeffrey Adair Darell, *qv*; *Career* Brig (ret) Coldstream Guards, served WWII 1939–45 (The Coats Mission 1940–41), Lt-Col 1957, cmd 1 Bn Coldstream Guards 1957–59, AAG War Office 1959–61, Coll Cdr RMA Sandhurst 1961–64, Regimental Lt-Col cmdg Coldstream Guards 1964, cmd 56 (London) Inf Bde TA 1965–67, vice pres Regular Commissions Bd 1968–70, Cmdt Mons Officer Cadet Sch 1970–72, ADC to HM The Queen 1973–74; tstee and memb London Law Trust 1981–; High Sheriff of Norfolk 1985–86; *Clubs* Army and Navy, MCC; *Style—* Brig Sir Jeffrey Darell, Bt, MC; ✉ Denton Lodge, Harleston, Norfolk (☎ 01986 788206)

DARESBURY, 4 Baron (UK 1927), of Walton, Co Chester; Sir Peter Gilbert Greenall; 5 Bt (UK 1876), DL (Cheshire 1994); eldest s of 3 Baron Daresbury (d 1996), and his 1 w, Margaret Ada, *née* Crawford; *b* 18 July 1953; *Educ* Eton, Univ of Cambridge (MA), London Business Sch (Sloan fellowship); *m* 11 Sept 1982, Clare Alison, da of Christopher Nicholas Weatherby, MC, of Whaddon House, Whaddon, Bucks; 4 s (Hon Thomas Edward b 1984, Hon Oliver Christopher b 1986, Hon Toby Peter b 1988, Hon Jonathan James (Jake) b 1992); *Heir* s, Hon Thomas Edward Greenall b 6 Nov 1984; *Career* md The Greenalls Group plc, chm Aintree Racecourse Co Ltd, non-exec dir First Leisure PLC; High Sheriff of Cheshire 1992; *Clubs* Jockey, White's, Turf, MCC, Royal & Ancient; *Style—* The Rt Hon the Lord Daresbury, DL; ✉ Hall Lane Farm, Daresbury, Warrington, Cheshire WA4 4AF (☎ 01925 740212); The Greenalls Group plc, Wilderspool House, Greenalls Avenue, Warrington, Cheshire WA4 6RH (☎ 01925 651234)

DARGAN, Dr Michael Joseph; *b* 14 Sept 1918; *Educ* Patrician Brothers Ballyfin, Trinity Coll Dublin; *m* Catherine (Blanche) O'Rourke; 2 s, 3 da; *Career* former chm: Aer Lingus (and chief exec), CRH plc, Bank of Ireland Fin Ltd, Intercontinental Hotels (Ireland) Ltd, Fitzwilton Group, Atlantic Mills Ltd, Pigs & Bacon Cmmn, Posts and Telegraphs Review Gp, Irish Mgmnt Inst; former dir: Bank of Ireland, Burlington Industs Inc (USA); chm: Robert J Goff plc, Int Bloodstock Holdings; owner Athasi Stud, ptnr Eyrefield House Stud; life fell Int Acad of Mgmnt; *Clubs* Irish Turf, Royal Dublin Soc, Royal Dublin Golf, Royal Irish Automobile; *Style—* Dr Michael Dargan; ✉ 3 Carleton Villas, Ballsbridge, Dublin 4

DARKAZALLY, Mamoun Al; s of Abdul Hadi (d 1986), and Farizeh Arabi; *b* 9 Oct 1942; *Educ* Univ of New York (BS), New York Univ Graduate Sch of Business (MBA); *m* 2 June 1971, Vivian, da of William Ram (d 1968); 1 s (Anwar b 1973); *Career* Chase Manhattan Bank: NY 1973–74, Beirut 1974–75; Commercial Bank of Qatar 1975–79, dep gen regnl mangr Al Saudi Banque London 1981– (Paris 1979–81), dep gen mangr and head Private Banking Banque Française de l'Orient 1990–92; dir: Lonworld Investment 1992–, London Gate Investment 1995–; dir Arab Bankers' Assoc, chm Syrian Arab Assoc UK 1988–; MInstD; *Style—* Mamoun Al Darkazally, Esq; ✉ 7a Inverness Gardens, London W8 4RN (☎ 0171 221 1874); London Gate Ltd, 54 Knightsbridge Court, 12 Sloane Street, London SW1X 9LQ (☎ 0171 235 9990, fax 0171 235 9995)

DARKE, Christopher (Chris); s of late Derek Herbert Darke, and Helen Navina, *née* Davies; *b* 5 Aug 1949; *m* 1, Marian Darke, *qv*; 1 s (Cerith James), 1 da (Joanna Siân); m 2, Lorraine Julie; 1 da (Ellen Cordelia); *Career* engrg draughtsman 1970–77, TU offr AUEW-TASS 1977–82, nat offr AUEW-TASS/MSF 1982–92, gen sec Br Air Line Pilots' Assoc (BALPA) 1992–; *Recreations* flying, travel, reading, gardening; *Style—* Chris Darke, Esq; ✉ British Air Line Pilots' Association, 81 New Road, Harlington, Hayes, Middx UB3 5BG (☎ 0181 476 4000, fax 0181 476 4077)

DARKE, Geoffrey James; s of Harry James Darke (d 1983), and Edith Annie Darke (d 1973); *b* 1 Sept 1929; *Educ* Prince Henry's GS Worcs, Birmingham Sch of Architecture

(DipArch); *m* 1959, Jean Yvonne, da of Edwin Rose (d 1971); 1 s (Christopher), 2 da (Elizabeth, Sarah); *Career* cmmnd RE 1954–56, Malaya; sr architect Stevenage New Town Devpt Corp 1952–58, private practice 1958–61, ptnr Darbourne & Darke Architects and Landscape Planners 1961–87 (work incl several large cmmns, particularly public housing also commercial and civic bldgs), fndr Geoffrey Darke Associates 1987–; successes in nat and int competitions incl: Stuttgart 1977, Hanover 1979, Bolzano 1980, Hanover (Misburg) 1982; memb Union of Int Architects Co-ordinating Gp 1982–; RIBA: memb Cncl 1977–83, chm Competitions Working Gp 1979–84, memb EC Affrs Ctee 1990–, RIBA rep Access Ctee for Eng 1992–; memb Aldeburgh Festival Snape Maltings Fndn 1979–; ARIBA, FRSA; numerous medals and awards for architectural work; co-recipient (with John Darbourne) Fritz Schumacher award for servs to architecture and town planning (Hamburg) 1978; *Recreations* music; *Style*— Geoffrey Darke, Esq; ✉ Geoffrey Darke Associates, Neptune House, 43 King Street, Aldeburgh, Suffolk IP15 5BY (☎ 01728 452275)

DARKE, Marian; da of Herbert Pearce, of Cardiff, and Margaret, *née* Forbister; *b* 19 May 1948; *Educ* Cardiff HS for Girls, Univ of Birmingham (BA); *m* 1976 (m dis 1982), Chris Darke, *qv*; 1 s (Cerith James b 23 May 1977), 1 da (Joanna Siân b 17 July 1978); *Career* French teacher: Washwood Heath Comp Sch Birmingham 1972–77, Hollyfield Sch Kingston-upon-Thames 1980–96, Kingston-upon-Thames LEA 1996–; NUT: memb Nat Exec 1989–, sr vice pres 1992, national pres 1993–94; convenor Cncl for Educnl Advance 1995–; *Style*— Ms Marian Darke; ✉ The National Union of Teachers, Hamilton House, Mabledon Place, London WC1H 9BD (☎ 0171 388 6191)

DARKE, Marjorie Sheila; *b* 25 Jan 1929; *Educ* Worcester GS for Girls', Leicester Coll of Art and Technol; *m* 12 July 1952; 2 s (b 1955 and 1957), 1 da (b 1959); *Career* textile designer John Lewis Partnership 1950–54, writer 1962–; memb: Soc of Authors, Int PEN; *Books* for young adults: Ride the Iron Horse (1973), The Star Trap (1974), A Question of Courage (1975), The First Midnight (1977), A Long Way to Go (1978), Comeback (1981), Tom Post's Private Eye (1982), Messages and Other Shivery Tales (1984), A Rose From Blighty (1990); for children: Mike's Bike (1974), What Can I Do? (1975), Kipper's Turn (1976), The Big Brass Band (1976), My Uncle Charlie (1977), Carnival Day (1979), Kipper Skips (1979), Imp (1985), The Rainbow Sandwich (1989), Night Windows (1990), Emma's Monster (1992), Just Bear and Friends (1996); *Style*— Ms Marjorie Darke; ✉ c/o Rogers Coleridge & White Ltd, Literary Agency, 20 Powis Mews, London W11 1JN (☎ 0171 221 3717)

DARKE, Simon Geoffrey; s of Dr Geoffrey Darke (d 1995), of Leicester, and Margaret Winifred, *née* Wadsworth (d 1987); *b* 14 Dec 1941; *Educ* Downside, London Hosp Med Coll (MB BS, MRCP, LRCS, FRCS, MS); *m* 31 Jan 1970, Patricia Elizabeth, da of Philip Wreaks Mason, CBE (d 1975); 2 s (Nicholas Gregory Simon b 18 June 1974, Christopher Michael Mason b 4 June 1979), 1 da (Tiffanie Jane b 18 Aug 1972); *Career* London Hosp: house surgn 1965, rotating surgical resistrar 1969–71, lectr to surgical unit 1971–72, sr registrar 1973–76, lectr professional surgical unit 1976–77; Addenbrooke's Hosp Cambridge: accident offr 1967–68, sr house offr 1968; surgical registrar Bethnal Green Hosp 1968–69; sr registrar: Whipps Cross Hosp 1972–73, London Hosp 1973–75; conslt vascular and gen surgn: E Dorset Health Authy, Royal Bournemouth Hosp and Poole Gen Hosp 1977–; numerous presentations and lectures to learned socs, numerous pubns in med jls; memb, pres-elect and former sec Vascular Surgical Soc GB and Ireland, fndr exec memb and former treas Euro Soc Vascular Surgery, memb Assoc of Surgns; *Publications* contrib book chapters on vascular surgery; *Recreations* tennis, fishing, shooting, skiing; *Style*— Simon Darke, Esq; ✉ Oaks, 6 Leicester Rd, Branksome Park, Poole, Dorset BH13 6BZ (☎ 01202 761870; Royal Bournemouth Hospital, Bournemouth, Dorset (☎ 01202 303626)

DARLEY, Julian Robin; s of John James Darley (d 1974), and Kathleen Mary, *née* Wilkinson (d 1993); *b* 28 Dec 1937; *Educ* Caterham, Downing Coll Cambridge (MA); *Career* early appointments in UK, USA and Germany incl md Strongwork Diving Ltd 1978–79, gen mangr Abu Dhabi Liquefaction Co 1983–85, chief exec BP Engineering & Technical Centre 1986–90, pres BP Exploration Alaska Inc 1990–94, head of gp research and engrg British Petroleum Co plc 1994–; non-exec dir AMEC plc 1996–; pres Pipeline Industries Guild 1989; winner Cncl Medal Instn of Chemical Engrs 1989; Freeman Worshipful Co of Tallow Chandlers; FIChemE 1988, FEng 1996; *Recreations* outdoors, wildlife, fishing, walking, reading; *Clubs* Athenaeum; *Style*— Julian Darley, Esq, FEng; ✉ British Petroleum Co plc, Research & Engineering Centre, Chertsey Road, Sunbury on Thames, Middlesex TW16 7LN (☎ 01932 764444, fax 01932 763283)

DARLEY, Kevin Paul; s of Clifford Darley, of Wolverhampton, West Midlands, and Dorothy Thelma, *née* Newby; *b* 5 Aug 1960; *Educ* Colton Hills Comp Sch; *m* 22 Nov 1982, Debby Ford, da of Donald Ford; 2 da (Lianne Kerry b 1983, Gemma Louise b 1988); *Career* flat race jockey; apprenticed to Reg Hollinshead 1976, rode out claim 1978, Champion apprentice 1978 (70 winners), retained by owner Peter Savill 1989–; first winner Dust-Up Haydock 1977, first group winner Borushka Gp 2 Park Hill Stakes 1983, Cock of the North 1990, 1992 and 1993, 154 winners 1995 season, first Gp 1 winner River North Aral Pokal Gp 1 1994, winner first Classic French Derby Chantilly (riding Celtic Swing) 1995; *Recreations* gardening, listening to music (Phil Collins & Genesis), DIY, shooting, fishing; *Style*— Kevin Darley, Esq; ✉ Castle Garth, Sheriff Hutton, York YO6 1RG (☎ 01347 878383)

DARLEY, Sylvia Juliet; OBE (1987); da of Thomas Bladworth Darley (d 1983), of Cantley Hall, Doncaster, and Gladys Gordon Norrie Darley (d 1987); *b* 15 March 1923; *Educ* Southover Manor Sch Lewes, Doncaster Tech Coll; *Career* served WRNS 1943–46; sec (later mangr) to Sir Malcolm Sargent 1947–67; fndr and chief exec Malcolm Sargent Cancer Fund for Children 1967–95 (pres 1995–), fndr Malcolm Sargent Cancer Fund for Children in Aust (NSW 1984, Victoria 1988, Western Aust 1990); dir Charity Christmas Card Cncl (chm 1981–86, dep chm 1986–91); dir Malcolm Sargent Festival Choir; *Recreations* music, cooking, bird-watching, organising concerts; *Style*— Miss Sylvia Darley, OBE; ✉ President, Malcolm Sargent Cancer Fund for Children, 26 Lamont Road, London SW10 0JE (☎ 0171 352 6805)

DARLING, Alistair Maclean; MP (Lab) Edinburgh Central (majority 2,126); s of Thomas Young Darling (d 1995), and Anna Darling; *b* 28 Nov 1953; *Educ* Loretto, Univ of Aberdeen (LLB); *m* 12 Nov 1986, Margaret McQueen Vaughan; 1 s (Calum), 1 da (Anna); *Career* slr 1978–82, passed advocate 1984; memb Lothian Regnl Cncl 1982–87, chm Lothian Region Tport Ctee 1986–87; MP (Lab) Edinburgh Central 1987–; oppn front bench spokesman on: home affairs 1988–92, Treasy and economic affrs 1992–96; shadow chief sec to the Treasy 1996–; memb Lab Pty's Economic Cmmn 1994–; govr Napier Coll Edinburgh 1985–87; *Style*— Alistair Darling, Esq, MP; ✉ House of Commons, London SW1A 0AA (☎ 0171 219 4584)

DARLING, Sir Clifford; GCVO (1994), kt (1977); s of Charles and Aremelia Darling; *b* 6 Feb 1922; *Educ* Acklins Public Sch, several public schs in Nassau; *Career* senator 1964–67, dep speaker House of Assembly 1967–69, Min of State 1969, Min of Labour and Welfare 1971, Min of Labour and National Insurance 1974–77, speaker House of Assembly 1977, MP Bahamas 1977–92, Governor-General The Bahamas 1992–94; past chm Tourist Advsy Bd; memb: Masonic Lodge, Elks Lodge; *Style*— Sir Clifford Darling, GCVO; ✉ PO Box N-1050, Nassau, Bahamas

DARLING, Rt Rev Edward Flewett; *see:* Limerick and Killaloe, Bishop of

DARLING, Hon (Robert) Julian Henry; s and h of 2 Baron Darling; *b* 29 April 1944; *Educ* Wellington, RAC Cirencester; *m* 1970, Janet Rachel, da of J Mallinson; 2 s, 1 da; *Career* chartered surveyor in private practice specialising in rural estate devpt; farmer; memb Exec Ctee Nat Assoc of Prison Visitors 1993–; vice chm Norfolk Mental Health Care NHS Tst 1994–; *Recreations* fishing, gardening; *Clubs* Norfolk; *Style*— The Hon Julian Darling; ✉ Intwood Hall, Norwich, Norfolk NR4 6TG (☎ 01603 454554, office ☎ 01603 250450, fax 01603 250520)

DARLING, Gen Sir Kenneth Thomas; GBE (1969, CBE 1957), KCB (1963, CB 1957), DSO (1945); eld s of (George) Kenneth Darling, CIE (d 1964), of Dial House, Aldeburgh; *b* 17 Sept 1909; *Educ* Eton, RMC; *m* 1941, Pamela Beatrice Rose (d 1990), eld da of Maj Henry Denison-Pender, DSO, OBE, MC (d 1967), of Hook, Hants; *Career* 2 Lt 7 Royal Fus 1929, served WWII, 6 Airborne Div NW Europe (wounded), cmd 5 Parachute Bde Java 1946, cmd Airborne Forces Depot 1948, cmd 16 Independent Parachute Bde 1950, COS 1 Corps 1955, COS 2 Corps 1956, Dep Dir of Staff Duties WO 1957, Maj-Gen 1958, Dir of Ops Cyprus 1958–60, Dir of Inf WO 1960–62, Lt-Gen 1962, GOC 1 Corps 1962–63, Col Royal Fus 1963–68, GOC-in-C Southern Cmd 1964–66, Gen 1967, Col Cmdt Para Regt 1965–67, C-in-C Allied Forces N Europe 1967–69, Col Royal Regt of Fus 1968–74, ADC (Gen) to HM The Queen 1968–69; *Recreations* riding, hunting; *Clubs* Army & Navy; *Style*— Gen Sir Kenneth Darling, GBE, KCB, DSO; ✉ Vicarage Farmhouse, Chesterton, Bicester, Oxon OX6 8UQ (☎ 01869 252092)

DARLING, 2 Baron (UK 1924); Robert Charles Henry Darling; DL (Somerset 1972, Avon 1974); s of Maj Hon John Darling, DSO (s of 1 Baron); suc gf 1936; *b* 15 May 1919; *Educ* Wellington, Sandhurst; *m* 15 Aug 1942, Bridget Rosemary Whishaw, da of Rev Francis Cyprian Dickson; 1 s, 2 da; *Heir* s, Hon Julian Darling, FRICS; *Career* served WWII, Italy, Maj; chief exec Royal Bath and West & South Counties Soc 1961–79; dir Bristol Waterworks 1978–90; regnl dir Lloyds Bank 1979–89; *Recreations* fishing, gardening; *Style*— The Rt Hon Lord Darling, DL; ✉ Puckpits, Limpley Stoke, Bath, Somerset (☎ 01225 722146)

DARLINGTON, Rear Adm Sir Charles Roy; KBE (1965); s of Charles Arthur Darlington (d 1962), of Stoke-on-Trent, and Alice, *née* Edwards, of Prestatyn (d 1919); *b* 2 March 1910; *Educ* Orme Sch Newcastle-under-Lyme, Univ of Manchester (BSc); *m* 1, 1935, Nora Dennison (d 1993), da of James Wright, of Maulds Meaburn, Westmorland; 1 s, 1 da; m 2, 14 March 1995, Lucille Patricia, da of Frederick Charles Bailey, of Southsea, Hants; *Career* joined RN 1941, served WWII, HMS Valiant in Med and E Indies, HMS Excellent, HMS Implacable and HMS Vanguard, Instr Capt 1956, Rear Adm 1960, dir Naval Educn Serv 1960–65, ret; memb staff Haileybury 1965–75; *Recreations* maths, cricket, chess; *Style*— Rear Adm Sir Charles Darlington, KBE; ✉ 11 Freestone Rd, Southsea, Hants

DARLINGTON, Gavin Leslie Brook; s of Arthur Brook Darlington, and Pamela Leslie, *née* Roberts; *b* 27 June 1949; *Educ* Rugby, Downing Coll Cambridge (LLB); *m* 11 April 1977, Pavla Ann, da of Karel Kucek; 1 s (Nicholas James b 7 Jan 1986), 1 da (Georgina Ruth b 19 Nov 1989); *Career* Freshfields: articled clerk 1972–74, asst slr 1974–80, ptnr 1980–; memb: Law Soc, Int Bar Assoc; *Recreations* gardening, golf, swimming, theatre, cinema; *Style*— Gavin Darlington, Esq; ✉ 65 Fleet Street, London EC4Y 1HT

DARLINGTON, Jonathan Philip; s of John Oliver Darlington, of Kidderminster, and Bernice Constance Elizabeth, *née* Murphy; *b* 1 Feb 1956; *Educ* King's Sch Worcester, Univ of Durham, Royal Acad of Music; *m* 8 Dec 1979, Katherine Theresa, da of Lt Col Anthony Wynter Lister; 2 s (William John Anthony b 8 Aug 1988, Edmund Harry b 2 April 1992); *Career* conductor and pianist; has conducted various major orchs and opera cos, particularly in France, given numerous concerts as pianist and chamber musician; dep music dir Paris Opera 1992–94, first res conductor Düsseldorf Opera 1997–; Radio France 1980–82, Nancy Opera 1982–83; conductor: The Marriage of Figaro (Paris Opera debut) 1991, A Midsummer Night's Dream (Paris Opera, also tour to Bolshoi) 1991, The Barber of Seville (Paris Opera), Swan Lake (Paris Opera, also video recording) 1992, The Nutcracker (Paris Opera) 1993, The Magic Flute (Paris Opera) 1994, Das Lied von der Erde (Paris Opera) 1994, Marriage of Figaro (Lausanne) 1995, Metropolitan Opera NY (with Paris Opera Ballet) 1996; Chevalier des Arts et des Lettres 1992; *Recreations* mountaineering, skiing, wind-surfing, reading, chamber music; *Style*— Jonathan Darlington, Esq; ✉ c/o ICM Artists (London) Ltd, Oxford House, 76 Oxford Street, London W1N 0AX (☎ 0171 323 3223, fax 0171 636 3528)

DARLINGTON, Stephen Mark; s of John Oliver Darlington, MBE, and Bernice Constance Elizabeth, *née* Murphy; *b* 21 Sept 1952; *Educ* King's Sch Worcester, ChCh Oxford (MA); *m* 12 July 1975, Moira Ellen, da of Noel Edward Lionel Hill; 3 da (Rebecca b 1979, Hannah b 1981, Olivia b 1985); *Career* asst organist Canterbury Cathedral 1974–78, master of music St Albans Abbey 1978–85, artistic dir Int Organ Festival 1979–85, organist and student in music ChCh Oxford and lectr Univ of Oxford 1985–; FRCO; *Recreations* travel, wine, canoeing; *Style*— Stephen Darlington, Esq; ✉ Christ Church, Oxford OX1 1BY (☎ 01865 276195)

DARLOW, Paul Manning; s of Brig Eric William Townsend Darlow, OBE, of New Inn Cottage, East End, Witney, Oxon, and Joan Elsie Darlow, JP, *née* Ring; *b* 7 Feb 1951; *Educ* St Edward's Sch Oxford, Mt Hermon Sch Massachussets, King's Coll London (LLB); *Career* called to the Bar Middle Temple 1973, recorder of the Crown Court 1994–; *Style*— Paul Darlow, Esq; ✉ St John's Chambers, Small Street, Bristol BS1 1DW (☎ 0117 921 3456, fax 0117 929 4821)

DARNLEY, 11 Earl of (I 1725); Adam Ivo Stuart Bligh; sits as Baron Clifton of Leighton (E 1608); also Baron Clifton of Rathmore (I 1721), Viscount Darnley (I 1723); s of 9 Earl of Darnley (d 1955), and his 3 w, Rosemary, da of late Basil Potter; suc half-bro, 10 Earl, 1980; *b* 8 Nov 1941; *Educ* Harrow, Ch Ch Oxford; *m* 14 Oct 1965, Susan Elaine, JP, da of Sir Donald Forsyth Anderson (d 1973), by his w Margaret, sis of Sir Harry Llewellyn, 3 Bt, CBE, DL, *qv*; 1 s, 1 da (Lady Katherine Amanda b 1971); *Heir* s, Lord Clifton of Rathmore; *Style*— The Rt Hon Earl of Darnley; ✉ Netherwood Manor, Tenbury Wells, Worcs WR15 8RT

DARRAGH, Dr Paul Mervyn; TD; *b* 20 Feb 1947; *Educ* Queen's Univ Belfast (MB BCh, MD, PhD), Univ of Edinburgh (MSc, Dip in Community Med), DCH; *m* April 1973, Heather Isobel; 1 s (Peter Edward John b 1979), 1 da (Alison Jane b 1977); *Career* princ in gen practice NI 1975, asst chief administrative med offr Eastern and Social Servs Bd NI 1979, sr lectr The Queen's Univ Belfast and conslt in public health med Royal Victoria Belfast 1980–; prison visitor, chm Bd of Govrs Edenbrooke PS; sec Townsend St Presbyterian Church, chm Townsend Outreach Centre, co-dir Townsend Enterprise Park; FRCP (Ireland) 1989, FFPHM (RCP) 1989, AFOM (Ireland); *Recreations* sailing; *Style*— Dr Paul Darragh; ✉ Royal Victoria Belfast, Department of Epidemiology and Public Health, Mulhouse, Grosvenor Road, Belfast BT12 6BA (☎ 01232 240503)

DART, Geoffrey Stanley; s of Wilfrid Stanley Dart, of Torquay, and Irene Jean, *née* Crews; *b* 2 Oct 1952; *Educ* Devonport HS, Torquay Boys' GS, St Peter's Coll Oxford (scholar, MA); *m* 17 Aug 1974, Rosemary Penelope, da of late Gordon Frederick Hinton; 1 s (Thomas James b 15 Nov 1978), 1 da (Rebecca Clare b 17 Oct 1980); *Career* civil servant; researcher Electricity Cncl 1974–77, various positions Dept of Energy 1977–84, cabinet sec Cabinet Office 1984–85, princ private sec to Sec of State for Energy 1985–87; Dept of Energy: asst sec Electricity Div 1987–89, asst sec Offshore Safety Div 1989–91, head Finance Branch 1991–92; DTI: asst sec Competitiveness Div 1992–94, dir De-Regulation Unit 1994, head Regnl Devpt Div 1995–96, dir Simplification Project 1996–; non-exec dir Laing Engineering Ltd 1991–95, dir European Investment Bank 1994–; *Recreations* reading, listening to music, films, football, cricket; *Style*— Geoffrey

Dart, Esq; ✉ Simplification Project Team, Department of Trade and Industry, 1 Victoria Street, London SW1H 0ET (☎ 0171 215 2510, fax 0171 215 5603)

DARTMOUTH, 9 Earl of (GB 1711); Gerald Humphry Legge; also Baron Dartmouth (E 1682) and Viscount Lewisham (GB 1711); s of 8 Earl, CVO, DSO, RN (d 1962), and Roma, Countess of Dartmouth; *b* 26 April 1924; *Educ* Eton; *m* 1, 21 July 1948 (m dis 1976), Raine, da of Alexander George McCorquodale (d 1964), and who m 2, 1976, 8 Earl Spencer, LVO (d 1992), and 3, 1993, Comte Jean-François de Chambrun; 3 s, 1 da; m 2, 1980, Mrs Gwendoline May Seguin, da of late Charles René Seguin; *Heir* s, Viscount Lewisham, *qv*; *Career* served WWII Capt Coldstream Guards (despatches); chm: Ocean Wilsons Holdings plc until 1995, Anglo-Brazilian Soc until 1994; Hon LLD Dartmouth Coll USA; FCA; *Clubs* Buck's, Boodle's; *Style*— The Rt Hon the Earl of Dartmouth; ✉ The Manor House, Chipperfield, King's Langley, Herts (☎ 01923 264498)

DARWALL-SMITH, Lucy Ellen; da of Herbert Francis Eade, and Anne Barbara, *née* Forbes; *b* 1 June 1955; *Educ* Micklefield Sch for Girls; *m* 5 Aug 1978, (Randle) Philip Ralph Darwall-Smith, s of Randle Frederic Hicks Darwall-Smith; 1 da (Daisy b 26 Nov 1985); *Career* assoc dir Lopex 1979–81, md Darwall Smith Associates Ltd 1981–; MInstD, MRCA; *Recreations* theatre, ballet, food, friends; *Clubs* Commonwealth, Sloane; *Style*— Mrs Lucy Darwall-Smith; ✉ Middleham House, Ringmer, nr Lewes, East Sussex BN8 5EY (☎ 01273 813503, fax 01273 814019); Darwall Smith Associates Ltd, 44–46 St John Street, London EC1M 4DT (☎ 0171 490 1100)

DARWALL SMITH, Her Hon Judge; Susan Patricia; da of George Kenneth Moss, JP (d 1991), and Jean Margaret, *née* Johnston; *b* 27 Oct 1946; *Educ* Howell's Sch Denbigh; *m* 15 Sept 1968, Simon Crompton Darwall Smith, s of Randle Frederick Hicks Darwall Smith; 2 da (Belinda Claire b 1 Aug 1972, Emma Louise b 7 Nov 1974); *Career* called to the Bar Gray's Inn 1968, in practice Western Circuit 1968–92, recorder 1986–92, circuit judge (Western Circuit) 1992–; govr The Redmaids' Sch Bristol 1990–; *Recreations* travel, opera, ballet, theatre, gardening; *Clubs* Army & Navy; *Style*— Her Hon Judge Darwall Smith; ✉ Bristol Crown Court, The Law Courts, Small Street, Bristol BS1 2HL

DARWEN, 3 Baron (UK 1946), of Heys-in-Bowland, W Riding of Yorkshire; Roger Michael Davies; eldest s of 2 Baron Darwen (d 1988), and Kathleen Dora, *née* Walker; *b* 28 June 1938; *Educ* Bootham Sch York; *m* 1961, Gillian Irene, da of Eric G Hardy, of Valley View, Leigh Woods, Bristol; 2 s (Hon Paul b 1962, Hon Benjamin b 1966), 3 da (Hon Sarah b 1963, Hon Naomi b 1965, Hon Mary b 1969); *Heir* s, Hon Paul Davies b 1962; *Style*— The Rt Hon the Lord Darwen; ✉ Labourer's Rest, Green Street, Pleshey, Chelmsford, Essex

DARWENT, Rt Rev Frederick Charles; JP; s of Samuel Darwent (d 1957), and Edith Emily, *née* Malcolm (d 1968); *b* 20 April 1927; *Educ* Warbreck Sch Liverpool, Ormskirk GS, Wells Theol Coll; *m* 1, 1949, Edna Lilian (d 1981), da of David Waugh and Lily Elizabeth, *née* McIndoe; 2 da (twins); m 2, 1983, Mrs Roma Evelyn Fraser, elder da of John Michie and Evelyn, *née* Stephen; *Career* served with Royal Inniskilling Fusiliers Far East 1945–48; banker Williams Deacon's (later Williams and Glyn's, now merged with Royal Bank of Scotland) 1943–61; ordained Dio of Liverpool: deacon 1963, priest 1964; curate of Pemberton Wigan 1963–65 (i/c St Francis Kitt Green 1964–65); rector: Strichen 1965–71, New Pitsligo 1965–78, Fraserburgh 1971–78; canon St Andrew's Cathedral Aberdeen 1971, dean of Aberdeen and Orkney 1973–78, bishop of Aberdeen and Orkney 1978–92, ret; Burgess of Guild of the City of Aberdeen 1985, chm The Missions to Seamen Scotland 1987–96 (treas 1996–); Hon LTh St Mark's Inst of Theology; *Recreations* amateur stage (acting and producing), music (especially jazz), calligraphy; *Clubs* The Club of Deir (Aberdeenshire), Rotary International; *Style*— The Rt Rev F C Darwent, JP; ✉ 107 Osborne Place, Aberdeen AB25 2DD (☎ 01224 646497)

DARWIN, (George) Erasmus; e s of William Robert Darwin (d 1970; gs of Charles Darwin); *b* 11 Feb 1927; *Educ* Winchester, Trinity Coll Cambridge (MA); *m* 5 Oct 1956, Shuna Mary, da of George Ronald Service, of Kinfauns House, by Perth (d 1961); 2 s, 1 da; *Career* Babcock & Wilcox Ltd 1957–78, chief exec Richardsons Westgarth Group 1978–82, chm Home Grown Produce (Holdings) Ltd 1979–; elected Common Cncl City of London 1995–; *Recreations* sailing, bridge; *Clubs* Savile; *Style*— Erasmus Darwin, Esq; ✉ 3A Pembroke Gardens, London W8 (☎ 0171 602 6474); Home Grown Produce (Holdings) Ltd, 204 Central Markets, London EC1A 2LL (☎ 0171 236 3884, fax 0171 827 6527)

DARWIN, Philip Waring; s of William Robert Darwin (d 1971), and Sarah Monica, *née* Slingsby (d 1987); *b* 23 Oct 1929; *Educ* Winchester, Trinity Coll Cambridge (BA); *Career* Nat Serv 2 Lt 3 The Kings Own Hussars 1948–49; CA 1955; Moores Carson & Watson 1952–55, Schweppes Ltd 1955–57, Schweppes (USA) Ltd 1957–60 (vice pres 1958–60); Laurence Prust & Co: ptnr 1962–83, sr ptnr 1974–83, dir 1986–90; chm The Smaller Companies Investment Trust plc, memb Bd Stolt Neilsen SA; Liveryman Worshipful Co of Drapers; *Clubs* Savile; *Style*— P W Darwin, Esq; ✉ 4 Gore St, London SW7 5PT (☎ 0171 584 8842); c/o Stolt Nielsen Ltd, Aldwych House, 71–91 Aldwych, London WC2B 4HN (☎ 0171 611 8981, fax 0171 611 8965)

DAS, Dr Sankar Kumar; s of D Das (d 1974), of Calcutta, India, and late Nilima, *née* Roy Chondbury; *b* 1 Dec 1933; *Educ* Univ of Calcutta (MB BS, MRCP); *m* 26 Nov 1977, Enakshi, da of P K Roy (d 1976); 1 s (Shumit b 1 June 1979), 1 da (Priya b 27 Feb 1984); *Career* med registrar Victoria Hosp Blackpool 1964–66, fell of internal, chest and nuclear med and asst instr in med VA Hosp Milwaukee Wisconsin USA 1966–69, sr med registrar King's Coll Hosp and St Francis Hosp London 1970–74; conslt physician in geriatric med: Manor Hosp Derby and Derby City Hosp 1974–77, St Helier Gp Hosp and London Borough of Sutton 1977–; hon sr lectr Univ of London 1977–, recognised teacher St George's Hosp Tooting 1977–; conslt Specialists' Assoc; inventor of: hind paddle walker Mk I, II and III, exercising machine, DAK mobile Mk I and II walking frames, disc computer for analytical prog on geriatric med, clinical audi urinary incontinence gadgets (male and female); memb Panel on Residential Accommodation Sutton Borough; memb: Br Geriatric Soc 1966, Royal Inst of GB, Br Geriatric Soc, American Coll of Chest Physicians, NY Acad of Scis 1992; FRSH 1966, FRCP 1974, FCCP (USA) 1974; fell: Int Biographical Assoc 1980, Int Youth in Achievement 1980; *Books* Lecture Notes on Medical Infirmities, Europe (1981), Fits, Faints and Falls (1985), contrib to med jls and author of papers on computers in medicine; *Recreations* flying, polo, horse riding, cricket; *Style*— Dr Sankar Das; ✉ 62 Rose Hill, Sutton, Surrey SM1 3EX (☎ 0181 644 1639); St Helier Hospital, Wrythe Lane, Carshalton, Surrey SM5 1AA (☎ 0181 644 4343)

DASGUPTA, Prof Partha Sarathi; s of Prof Amiya Dasgupta (d 1992), of Santiniketan, India, and Shanti, *née* Dasgupta; *b* 17 Nov 1942; *Educ* Univ of Delhi (BSc), Univ of Cambridge (BA, Stevenson prize, PhD); *m* 29 June 1968, Carol Margaret, da of Prof James Edward Meade; 2 da (Zubeida b 11 Jan 1974, Aisha b 3 July 1983), 1 s (Shamik b 13 Aug 1977); *Career* supernumery fell Trinity Hall Cambridge 1971–74 (res fell 1968–71); LSE: lectr 1971–75, reader 1975–78, prof of economics 1978–84; Univ of Cambridge: prof of economics 1985–, fell St John's Coll Cambridge 1985–, Frank Ramsay prof of economics 1994–; prof of economics, prof of philosophy and dir Programme in Ethics in Society Stanford Univ Calif 1989–92; visiting asst prof Carnegie-Mellon Univ 1968–69, visiting fell Delhi Sch of Economics 1970–71, Ford visiting prof Inst of Economic Growth Univ of Delhi 1981; visiting prof: Jawaharlal Nehru Univ 1978, Stanford Univ 1983–84 (visiting assoc prof 1974–75), Harvard Univ 1987, Princeton Univ 1988; memb Cncl: Econometric Soc 1984–90, European Soc for Populaton Economics 1987–91, Royal Economic Soc 1988–93, European Economic Assoc 1989–93; assoc ed: Jl of Development Economics 1972–76, Social Choice and Welfare 1984–96, Jl of Environmental Economics and Management 1985–89; memb Panel of Experts of Environmental Health WHO 1975–85, prog dir for applied economic theory and econometrics Centre for Public Policy Res London 1984–86 (res fell 1983–93), res advsr UNU/World Inst for Devpt Economics 1991–94, chm Beijer Int Inst of Ecological Economics Royal Swedish Acad of Sciences 1991–, memb Scientific Bd Santa Fe Inst 1991–96, sr res fell Inst for Policy Reform Washington DC 1992–94; foreign hon memb American Acad of Arts and Sciences 1991, foreign memb Royal Swedish Acad of Sciences 1991, hon fell LSE 1994; fell Econometric Soc 1975; FBA 1989; *Books* Guidelines for Project Evaluation (with S A Marglin and A K Sen, 1972), Economic Theory and Exhaustible Resources (with G M Heal, 1979), The Control of Resources (1982), Environmental Decision-Making (jt ed, 1984), Economic Organizations as Games (jt ed, 1986), The Economics of Bargainning (jt ed, 1987), An Inquiry into Well-Being and Destitution (1993); author of numerous articles in jls, lectrs and reviews; *Clubs* MCC; *Style*— Prof Partha Dasgupta, FBA; ✉ 1 Dean Drive, Holbrook Road, Cambridge CB1 4SW (☎ 01223 212179); University of Cambridge, Sidgwick Avenue, Faculty of Economics, Cambridge CB3 9DD (☎ 01223 335207)

DASH, John Raymond; s of Walter Charles Samuel Dash (d 1977), of Cwmbran, Gwent, and Elsie Mildred, *née* Crump; *b* 6 April 1959; *Educ* W Monmouth GS, Univ of Bradford; *Career* prodr Pennine Radio Bradford 1981–83, presenter and sports ed Gwent Broadcasting 1983–85, presenter Two Counties Radio Bournemouth 1985–87; Red Dragon Radio Cardiff: presenter 1987–92, head of music 1990–92, head of progs 1992, dir of progs 1992–95; prog dir Piccadilly Radio Manchester 1995–; barker Variety Club of GB; memb Radio Acad; *Style*— John Dash, Esq; ✉ Piccadilly Radio Ltd, 127–131 The Piazza, Piccadilly Plaza, Manchester M1 4AW (☎ 0161 236 9913)

DASHWOOD, Prof Arthur Alan; s of Alan Stanley Dashwood (d 1941), and Dorothy Mary Dashwood; *b* 18 Oct 1941; *Educ* Michaelhouse Sch Natal SA, Rhodes Univ Grahamstown SA (BA), Oriel Coll Oxford (MA); *m* Julie Rosalind, *née* Pashley; *Career* called to the Bar 1969; legal sec Ct of Justice of the Euro Communities 1978–80, prof of law Univ of Leicester 1980–87, dir Legal Serv Cncl of the EU 1987–94, prof of Euro law and dir Centre for Euro Legal Studies Univ of Cambridge 1995–; fell Sidney Sussex Coll Cambridge 1995–; *Books* Wyatt & Dashwood's European Community Law (with D Wyatt); also author of numerous articles in legal periodicals; *Recreations* fishing; *Style*— Prof Arthur Dashwood; ✉ Centre for European Legal Studies, University of Cambridge, Faculty of Law, 10 West Road, Cambridge CB3 9DZ (☎ 01223 330093, fax 01223 330095)

DASHWOOD, Cyril Francis; s of Cyril Russell Dashwood, CBE (d 1962), of Slough, and Laura Louise, *née* Steward (d 1959); *b* 15 March 1925; *Educ* Cranleigh Sch; *m* 20 Sept 1958, Prudence Elizabeth, da of Arnold George Oliver Williams, of Amersham; 2 s (Richard b 1961, William b 1968), 1 da (Joanna b 1964); *Career* Flt Lt RAF 1943–47; CA; conslt Moores Rowland (formerly sr ptnr); vice pres Hockey Assoc 1988– (hon treas 1983–92), chm Nat Hockey Fndn; memb Cncl English Sinfonia Orchestra 1982–, govr Dr Challoners GS 1995–, former chm Broad St Ward Club; Freeman: City of London 1985, Worshipful Co of CAs 1986; FCA 1950; *Recreations* music, sport, gardening; *Clubs* MCC; *Style*— Cyril Dashwood, Esq; ✉ Ruthwell, Oakway, Chesham Bois, Bucks HP6 5PQ (☎ and fax 01494 725103); Moores Rowland, Cliffords Inn, Fetter Lane, London EC4A 1AS (☎ 0171 831 2345, fax 0171 831 6123)

DASHWOOD, Edward John Francis; s (by 1 m) and h of Sir Francis John Vernon Hereward Dashwood, 11 Bt, *qv*; *b* 25 Sept 1964; *Educ* Eton, Univ of Reading (BSc); *m* 10 April 1989, Lucinda Nell, o da of Gerrard Herman Francis Miesegaes and Mrs D Parker; 2 s (George Francis b 17 June 1992, Robert Edward b 15 Nov 1993), 1 da (Victoria Lucinda b 21 March 1991); *Career* land agent, landowner; ARICS; *Recreations* shooting, fishing, tennis; *Style*— E J F Dashwood, Esq; ✉ West Wycombe Park, Bucks (☎ 01494 524412, fax 01494 471617)

DASHWOOD, Sir Francis John Vernon Hereward; 11 Bt (Premier Bt of GB, cr 1707), of West Wycombe, Buckinghamshire; s of Sir John Lindsay Dashwood, 10 Bt, CVO (d 1966); *b* 7 Aug 1925; *Educ* Eton, ChCh Oxford (MA), Harvard Business Sch; *m* 1, 3 May 1957, Victoria Ann Elizabeth Gwynne (d 1976), o da of Maj John Frederick Foley, Baron de Rutzen (d 1944) (whose ancestor Augustus, Col in the Army of the Grand Duchy of Lithuania, obtained an acknowledgement of nobility from King Wladislaw IV of Poland *ante* 1677), of Slebech Park, Pembrokeshire, by his w Sheila Victoria Katrin (now Lady Dunsany), da of Sir Henry Philipps, Bt, of Picton Castle; 1 s (Edward John Francis b 1964), 3 da (Emily Jane (Mrs Charles W L Naper) b 1958, Georgina Helen (Mrs Charles H J Weld) b 1960, Caroline Sarah b 1962); m 2, 1977, Marcella Teresa Guglielmina Maria, formerly w of Giuseppe Sportoletti Baduel, wid of Jack Frye, CBE, and da of Marcellino Scarafina; 1 step s (Marco Sportoletti Baduel b 1966); *Heir* s, Edward John Francis Dashwood b 25 Sept 1964; *Career* landowner and farmer; Parly candidate (C) W Bromwich 1955 and Gloucester 1957; High Sheriff Bucks 1976; chm Bucks Branch CLA 1980; Liveryman Worshipful Co of Vintners; *Books* The Dashwoods of West Wycombe, The Great Lloyds Robbery; *Recreations* shooting, tennis, bridge; *Clubs* White's; *Style*— Sir Francis Dashwood, Bt; ✉ West Wycombe Park, High Wycombe, Bucks HP14 3AJ (☎ 01494 523720)

DASHWOOD, Sir Richard James; 9 Bt (E 1684), of Kirtlington Park, Oxfordshire, TD (1987); s of Sir Henry George Massy Dashwood, 8 Bt (d 1972), and Susan Mary (d 1985), da of late Maj Victor Robert Montgomerie-Charrington; *b* 14 Feb 1950; *Educ* Eton; *m* 1984 (m dis 1993), Kathryn Ann er da of Frank Mahon, of Barretts Farm, Eastbury, Newbury, Berks; 1 s (Frederick George Mahon b 1988); *Heir* s, Frederick George Mahon Dashwood b 29 Jan 1988; *Career* Lt 14/20 King's Hussars 1969, TA & VR 1973– (Major 1992); ptnr Harris Allday Lea & Brooks Stockbrokers; *Clubs* Boodle's; *Style*— Sir Richard Dashwood, Bt; ✉ Ledwell Cottage, Sandford St Martin, Oxon OX7 7AN (☎ 01608 683267)

DAUBENEY, Philip Edward Giles; s of Cyril Walter Philip Daubeney (d 1969), and Emily Margaret, *née* Gleed; *b* 27 March 1938; *Educ* Hardyes Sch Dorchester, Balliol Coll Oxford (MA); *m* 12 Aug 1961, Heather Margaret; 1 s (Piers Edward Francis b 25 March 1964), 1 da (Clare Elizabeth b 19 April 1966); *Career* served as 2 Lt Parachute Regt 1956–58; ICI 1961–93: ICI md India 1983–90, regnl chief exec ICI African and Eastern Region 1990–93; chief exec Electricity Assoc 1993–; chm: S Africa Business Assoc 1993–, S Africa Area Advsy Gp BOTB 1993–95; *Recreations* gardening, sailing, water colours; *Clubs* Oxford and Cambridge; *Style*— Philip Daubeney, Esq; ✉ Durmast House, Burley, Hants BH24 4AJ; The Electricity Association, 30 Millbank, London SW1P 4RD (☎ 0171 963 5896, fax 0171 963 5980)

DAUBNEY, Christopher Paul (Chris); s of Rev Kenneth Crocker Daubney (d 1992), of Alton, Hants, and Evelyn Blanche, *née* Knight (d 1987); *b* 14 Sept 1942; *Educ* Clifton, St John's Coll Cambridge (BA, MA); *Career* various posts BBC 1964–73; IBA: princ engr quality control 1973–81, head of quality control 1981–83, head of engrg info servs 1984–87, head Engrg Secretariat 1987, asst dir of engrg (policy and projects) 1987–88; chief engr Channel 4 1988–96, with Samsung 1996–; CEng 1973, FIEE 1990 (MIEE 1973), MIOA 1978; *Recreations* walking, swimming, family life; *Style*— Chris Daubney, Esq

DAULBY, Charles William (Bill); s of Philip Daulby (d 1989), and Mary, *née* Wilkinson (d 1995); *b* 8 June 1947; *Educ* Colne GS, Univ of Sheffield (BA); *m* 1, 4 Aug 1970 (m dis 1995), Christine Anne, da of Fred Spencer (d 1987), of Colne, Lancs; 2 da (Emma b 1974, Kate b 1977); m 2, 20 April 1996, Valerie Ann, da of Edwin Davis (d

1976); *Career* dir: Nissan UK Holdings Ltd 1989–93, AFG Holdings Ltd 1989–93; md: Automotive Leasing Ltd 1990–, Commercial Vehicle Management Ltd 1994–; MInstD; *Recreations* golf; *Style*— Bill Daulby, Esq; ✉ Automotive Leasing Ltd, Dominion House, Dominion Way, Rustington, W Sussex BN16 3HG (☎ 01903 858300 fax 01903 859442)

DAUNCEY, Brig Michael Donald Keen; DSO (1945), DL (Gloucester 1983); s of Thomas Gough Dauncey (d 1965), of Crowthorne, Berks, and Alice, *née* Keen (d 1988); the name Dauncey was first recorded in Uley, Glos, c1200s; *b* 11 May 1920; *Educ* King Edward's Sch Birmingham; *m* 1945, Marjorie Kathleen, da of Hubert William Neep (d 1967); 1 s (John), 2 da (Gillian, (Margaret) Joy); *Career* cmmnd 22nd (Cheshire) Regt 1941, seconded to Glider Pilot Regt 1943, Arnhem 1944 (wounded, taken prisoner, later escaped), MA to GOC-in-C Greece 1946–47, seconded to Para Regt 1947–49, Staff Coll 1950, instr RMA Sandhurst 1957–58, CO 1st Bn 22nd (Cheshire) Regt 1963–66 (BAOR and UN Peace-keeping Force Cyprus), DS Plans JSSC 1966–68, Cmdt Jungle Warfare Sch 1968–69, Cmdt Support Weapons Wing Sch of Inf Netheravon 1969–72, Brig 1973, def and mil attaché Br Embassy Madrid 1973–75, ret from Army 1976; Col 22nd (Cheshire) Regt 1978–85, Hon Col 1 Cadet Bn Glos Regt (ACF) 1981–90; pres The Glider Pilot Regtl Assoc 1994–; *Recreations* rough shooting, travelling, tennis, under-gardener; *Clubs* Army & Navy; *Style*— Brig Michael Dauncey, DSO, DL; ✉ Uley Lodge, Uley, nr Dursley, Glos GL11 5SN (☎ 01453 860216)

DAVAN WETTON, Hilary John; s of Eric Davan Wetton, CBE (d 1986), of Nairn, and Valerie, *née* Edwards (d 1970); *b* 23 Dec 1943; *Educ* Westminster, Royal Coll of Music, Brasenose Coll Oxford; *m* 1, 19 Sept 1964, Elizabeth Jane Tayler; 3 da (Charlotte, b 1966, Venetia b 1969, Fenella b 1972); m 2, 5 Jan 1989, Alison Mary Moncrieff, da of Prof Alexander Kelly; 1 s (Alexander b 1991), 1 da (Camilla b 1995); *Career* dir of music: St Albans Sch 1965–67, Cranleigh Sch 1967–74, Stantonbury Educn Campus and Music Centre 1974–79, St Paul's Girls Sch 1979–94, Tonbridge Sch 1994–; conductor: St Albans Choral Soc 1965–67, Guildford Choral Soc 1968–, Woking Symphony Orch 1971–74, Milton Keynes Chorale 1974–79, Milton Keynes City Orch (formerly Chamber Orch) 1975–, The Holst Singers of London 1978–91, Birmingham Schools' Symphony Orch 1983–85, Scottish Schools' Orch 1984–95, Buckinghamshire Youth Orch 1985–89, Wren Orch 1989–, Canticum 1992–94, Edinburgh Youth Orch 1994–; guest conductor with orchs in Australia, Bulgaria, Denmark, Iceland, Norway, Singapore and USA; performances on Radio 3 (with Ulster Orch and BBC Concert Orch), BBC 2 and Thames Television; conslt for Classic FM Masterclass 1994–; author of articles in Music and Musicians, Musical Times, Choir and Organ and Classic FM Magazine; Hon MA Open Univ 1983, Hon DMus De Montfort Univ 1994; memb RSA; *Recordings* with LPO 1988: Mozart Jupiter Symphony, Holst Planets, Elgar Enigma Variations; other recordings incl: Vaughan Williams 5 Tudor Portraits and Holst Golden Goose (with Philharmonia and Guildford Choral Soc), Holst Choral Symphony (with RPO and Guildford Choral Soc, winner of Diapason D'Or 1994), works by Britten, Bliss and Holst (with Holst Singers), 5 CDs of 19th century British symphonists (with Milton Keynes City Orch); *Recreations* tennis; *Clubs* Garrick; *Style*— Hilary Davan Wetton, Esq; ✉ Hartlake Roundels, Hartlake Road, Golden Green, Kent TN11 0BL (☎ 01732 773182); c/o Richard Haigh, Performing Arts Management, 6 Windmill Street, London W1P 1HF (☎ 0171 255 1362, fax 0171 631 4631)

DAVENPORT, *see:* Bromley-Davenport

DAVENPORT, Brian John; QC (1980); s of late Robert Cecil Davenport, FRCS, and Helen Elizabeth, *née* Mayfield (d 1990); *b* 17 March 1936; *Educ* Bryanston Sch, Worcester Coll Oxford; *m* 1969, Erica Tickell, yr da of Prof E N Willmer; 2 s, 1 da; *Career* called to the Bar Gray's Inn 1960; jr counsel to: ECGD 1970–74, Dept of Employment 1972–74, Bd of Inland Revenue 1974–80; law cmmr 1981–88; joined Inner Temple (ad eundem) 1978, bencher of Gray's Inn 1984; *Style*— Brian Davenport, Esq, QC; ✉ 43 Downshire Hill, London NW3 1NU (☎ 0171 435 3332)

DAVENPORT, Hugo Benedick; s of (Arthur) Nigel Davenport, *qv*, and Helena Margaret, *née* White (d 1979); *b* 6 June 1953; *Educ* Westminster, Univ of Sussex (BA); *m* 10 Aug 1988, Sarah, da of Hugh Mollison; 1 s (Bram); *Career* Visnews Ltd 1976–77, Liverpool Daily Post and Echo 1977–80, freelance journalist 1980–81, NI corr The Observer 1984–85 (reporter and feature writer 1981–84), feature writer Mail On Sunday 1985–87, film critic Daily Telegraph 1989–90 (news feature writer 1987–89), freelance writer-broadcaster 1996–; prize for population and environmental reporting Population Inst Washington 1988; *Recreations* reading, walking, drawing, music; *Style*— Hugo Davenport, Esq; ✉ 6 Ann's Close, Kinnerton Street, London SW1X 8EG (☎ and fax 0171 235 0559)

DAVENPORT, James Kinder (Jamie); s of John Grenville Kinder Davenport, of Falkirk, Scotland, and Audrey Willis, *née* Kirby; *b* 18 July 1955; *Educ* George Heriot's Sch Edinburgh, Trinity Coll Cambridge (BA); *m* 7 July 1979, (Deborah) Sian, da of Dr J Quentin Hughes; 2 s (Benjamin Kinder b 31 Oct 1981, John James (decd) b 9 July 1987), 3 da (Gemma Louise b 21 May 1984, Lily Clare b 30 Jan 1989, Laura Frances b 11 April 1991); *Career* advertising exec; account exec Grey Advertising 1977–79; account exec then assoc dir: Geers Gross Ltd 1979–84, Foote Cone & Belding 1984–86; TBWA (TBWA-Holmes Knight Ritchie since 1990): dir 1986–87, client service dir 1987–89, chief exec UK 1989–90, dir TBWA/HKR 1990–92; sr ptnr Attinger Jack Advertising 1993–; MIPA; *Recreations* family, friends and the dinner table; *Style*— Jamie Davenport, Esq

DAVENPORT, Prof John; s of William Kenneth Davenport, of Coventry, and Eda Bessie, *née* Taylor; *b* 12 Feb 1946; *Educ* Bablake Sch Coventry, St Mary's Hosp Med Sch, Univ of London (BSc, DSc), Univ of Southampton (MSc), Univ Coll Wales (PhD); *m* 1970, Julia Lesley, *née* Ladner; 2 da (Emma b 9 Nov 1973, Kate b 19 April 1976); *Career* demonstrator Dept of Marine Biology Univ Coll Wales 1970–72; Unit of Marine Invertebrate Biology NERC: higher scientific offr 1972–74, sr scientific offr 1974–80, princ scientific offr 1980–83; Univ Coll of N Wales: sr lectr Sch of Animal Biology 1987–88 (lectr 1983–87), reader Sch of Ocean Sciences 1989–91 (sr lectr 1988–89); dir Univ Marine Biological Station and chair Marine Biology Univ of London 1991–; memb Bd and Cncl Scottish Assoc for Marine Science, memb Bd Western Region Scottish Environmental Protection Agency; FIBiol 1987, FRSE 1995; *Books* Animal Osmoregulation (with J C Rankin, 1981), Environmental Stress and Behavioural Adaptation (1985), Animal Life at Low Temperature (1992); author of numerous articles in scientific jls; *Recreations* skiing, sailboarding, walking, birding; *Style*— Prof John Davenport, FRSE; ✉ University Marine Biological Station, Isle of Cumbrae KA28 0EG (☎ 01475 530581, fax 01475 530260, e-mail jdavenport@udcf.gla.ac.uk)

DAVENPORT, John Martin; s of Eric Davenport (d 1961), of Hook Heath, Surrey, and Winifred Mary, *née* Elder; *b* 16 Oct 1931; *Educ* Uppingham, Oriel Coll Oxford (MA); *m* 14 Sept 1957, Wendy Angela, da of Claude Wyatt, of Bournemouth; 2 s (Philip b 1961, Peter b 1966); *Career* exec dep chm F & C Pacific Investment Trust plc 1985–89; exec dir: Foreign & Colonial Management Ltd 1970–89, Community Hospitals Group plc 1981–91; non-exec dir Granville Investment Management 1991– (exec dir 1989–91); FCA; *Recreations* railways, gardening; *Clubs* MCC; *Style*— John Davenport, Esq; ✉ Mint House, 77 Mansell Street, London E1 8AF (☎ 0171 488 1212)

DAVENPORT, (Arthur) Nigel; s of Maj Arthur Davenport, MC, of Sidney Sussex Coll, Cambridge; *b* 23 May 1928; *Educ* Cheltenham, Trinity Coll Oxford; *m* 1, 1951 (m dis 1962) Helena Margaret, *née* White (d 1979); 1 s (Hugo Benedick, *qv*), 1 da (Laura); m 2, 1972 (m dis 1980), Maria Aitken, *qv*, da of Sir William Aitken, KBE, MP (d 1964, n of 1 Baron Beaverbrook), and former w of Mark Durden-Smith; 1 s (Jack); *Career* actor; served RASC and with Br Forces Network in Germany 1946–48; late memb OUDS; memb original English Stage co Royal Court Theatre (appearing in 14 prodns); pres Equity 1986–92 (vice pres 1978–80 and 1982–86); *Theatre* began acting 1951; most recently Murder is Easy (co dir, Duke of York) 1993; touring 1986–94 incl: King Lear, The Old Country, Sleuth, The Constant Wife; *Television* incl: George III in The Prince Regent, South Riding, Howards Way; *Film* over 40 appearances incl: A Man for All Seasons, Virgin Soldiers, Mary Queen of Scots, Chariots of Fire; *Recreations* gardening, travel; *Style*— Nigel Davenport, Esq; ✉ c/o Green and Underwood Ltd, 2 Conduit Street, London W1R 9TG (☎ 0171 493 0308)

DAVENPORT, Philippa; da of David Drummond (d 1993), and Helen, *née* Meagher; *b* 25 May 1940; *Educ* St Mary's Convent Ascot, Assumption Convent Paris; *m* 1972, Michael Murphy; *Career* food and cookery writer; formerly memb Old Masters Dept Christies Fine Art Auctioneers, property devpt Sardinia, asst to Orson Welles then Joseph Losey (incl script reading and choosing locations) until 1972, freelance food and cookery writer 1972–; devised and developed Good Cooking (Marshall Cavendish) 1974; contrib to Financial Times 1973–, Evening Standard, Sunday Times, Good Housekeeping, Country Living 1985–; fndr memb Guild of Food Writers 1985; *Awards* Glendfiddich Award for Food Writing 1988 and 1995, Restaurateurs' Food Writers Award 1993, Michael Smith Award (for writing about fine English foods) 1994, Maria-Luigia Duchessa di Parma Int Award for Journalism 1995, Guild of Food Writers Magazine Cookery Writing Award 1996, Glenfiddich Cookery Writing Award 1996; *Books* Good Cooking on a Budget (1974), 100 Great Dishes Made Easy (1980), Davenport's Dishes (1980), Cooking for Family and Friends (1982), Country Cook (1987); *Recreations* eating, travelling, rubbernecking, gardening, reading, cinema; *Style*— Miss Philippa Davenport; ✉ Selkley House, Whittonditch, Ramsbury, Marlborough, Wiltshire SN8 2QA

DAVENPORT-HANDLEY, Sir David John; kt (1980), OBE (1962), JP (Rutland 1948), DL (Leics 1974); s of John Davenport-Handley (d 1943); *b* 2 Sept 1919; *Educ* RNC Dartmouth; *m* 1943, Leslie Mary, da of Wing Cdr Sydney Mansfield Goldsmith, RAF; 1 s, 1 da; *Career* Lt RN, ret 1947; chm: Clipsham Quarry Co 1947–, Rutland and Stamford Cons Assoc 1952–65, Rutland Petty Sessional Div 1957–84, E Mids Area Cons Assoc 1971–77 (treas 1965–71), Nat Union of Cons and Unionist Assocs 1979–80 (vice chm 1977–79); High Sheriff Rutland 1954, Vice Lord-Lt Rutland 1972 (DL 1962); tstee Oakham Sch 1970–86, memb Parole Bd 1981–84, pres E Mids Area Cons Cncl 1987–93, chm Rutland Historic Churches Preservation Tst 1987–, pres Nat Union of Cons and Unionist Assocs 1990–91; *Recreations* gardening, music; *Clubs* English Speaking Union; *Style*— Sir David Davenport-Handley, OBE, JP, DL; ✉ Clipsham Hall, Oakham, Rutland, Leics

DAVENTRY, 3 Viscount (UK 1943); Francis Humphrey Maurice FitzRoy Newdegate; JP (Warwickshire 1960); father assumed by Royal Licence the additional surname of Newdegate 1936; s of Cdr the Hon John Maurice FitzRoy Newdegate, RN (d 1976), s of 1 Viscountess Daventry (d 1962), and Hon Mrs John FitzRoy Newdegate; *b* 17 Dec 1921; *Educ* Eton; *m* 1959, Hon Rosemary, da of Lt-Gen 1 Baron Norrie, GCMG, GCVO, CB, DSO, MC (d 1977); 2 s, 1 da; *Heir* s, Hon James FitzRoy Newdegate; *Career* Capt Coldstream Gds 1943 (served in Africa and Italy), ADC to Viceroy of India 1946–48; High Sheriff Warwicks 1970, Lord-Lt Warwickshire 1990–96 (DL 1970, vice Lord-Lt 1974–90); KStJ 1990; *Clubs* Boodle's; *Style*— The Rt Hon the Viscount Daventry, JP; ✉ Temple House, Arbury, Nuneaton, Warwicks CV10 7PT (☎ 01203 383514)

DAVEY, Andrew Paul (Andy); s of Peter Anthony Cecil Davey, of Bristol, and Joan Venville, of Elverstoke, Hants; *b* 12 July 1962; *Educ* W Sussex Coll of Design (Dip, Advanced Coll Dip in Industl Design), Royal Coll of Art (MDes Industl Design); *Career* product designer; ptnr MWA Product Design Consultants London 1986–89, fndr princ TKO Product Design Consultants London 1990–; clients incl: Canon Inc (Japan), NEC Corp (Japan), Sanyo Electric Co Ltd (Japan and UK), Sony Corporation (Japan), Hasbro Europe (UK and Europe), Seiko Corporation (Japan), Oxford Instruments (UK), AXIS Incorporated (Japan); lectr on design issues in Japan and at venues incl: CSD, Design Museum, Central St Martins, ICA and V&A in London; featured in various articles and pubns incl: AXIS (int design mag Tokyo), The Best of British Design (Internos Books) 1992, The I.D. 40 (int design mag NY) 1996 and Terence Conran on Design 1996; various appearances on TV incl: Raising the Phoenix (ITV) 1986, Design Sense (BBC 2) 1989 and Rough Guide to Design (BBC 2) 1992, BBC Design Awards (BBC 2) 1996; memb: CSD, Design Museum, DBA, D&AD; work in the perm collection of Design Museum London (Taurus telephone, lighting and furniture); *Awards* D&AD Award for Most Outstanding Br Product for Working Environments (Taurus desk phone) 1989, D&AD Award for Most Outstanding Product for the Home 1990, finalist Design Week Awards 1991, Miny for Int Trade and Indust (Japan) Grand Prize and Chairman's Prize (System K kitchenware) 1991, D&AD Award for Most Outstanding Product for Health and Leisure (AXIS eyewear) 1993, Best Product Design and jt Designer of the Yr BBC Design Awards (freeplay clockwork radio for Third World) 1996, winner Best of Category (consumer products) I.D. Magazine 1996; *Exhibitions* incl: Design it Again (Design Cncl London) 1988, British by Design (Design Cncl London) 1991–92, Br Cncl touring exhbn 1992–93, British Design - Catalyst for Commercial Success (Design Center Singapore) 1993, Designed in One, Made in the Other - New Products of Collaboration Between Britain and Japan (Design Museum London) 1994, 'thinkteck!' (Tokyo Design Network collaborative exhbn and symposium Design Museum London) 1995; *Recreations* yachting, skiing, multimedia, old cars; *Style*— Andy Davey, Esq; ✉ TKO Product Design Consultants, 17–18 Great Sutton Street, Clerkenwell, London EC1V 0DN (☎ 0171 490 2505, fax 0171 490 2502)

DAVEY, Jon Colin; s of Frederick John Davey (d 1991), and Dorothy Mary, *née* Key (d 1969); *b* 16 June 1938; *Educ* Raynes Park GS; *m* 1962, Ann Patricia, da of Maj Stanley Arthur Streames (d 1977); 2 s (Simon b 1964, Jonathan b 1967), 1 da (Jennifer b 1972); *Career* asst sec Broadcasting Dept Home Office 1981–85 (asst sec of Franks Ctee on Official Secrets 1971–72, sec of Williams Ctee on Obscenity and Film Censorship 1977–79, sec of Hunt Inquiry into Cable Expansion and Broadcasting Policy 1982); dir gen Cable Authy 1985–90, dir Cable and Satellite Independent Television Commission 1991–96, memb British Screen Advsy Cncl 1990–96, dir Communications Equity Associates Int Ltd 1996–; hon fell Soc of Cable Telecommunication Engrs 1994; *Recreations* music, lawn-making, English countryside; *Style*— Jon Davey, Esq; ✉ 71 Hare Lane, Claygate, Esher, Surrey KT10 0QX (☎ 01372 810106)

DAVEY, Prof Kenneth Jackson; s of Reginald Alfred Davey (d 1962), and Vera Elizabeth, *née* Jackson (d 1973); *b* 7 Dec 1932; *Educ* Silcoates Sch, Merton Coll Oxford (MA), Univ of Birmingham (MSocSc); *m* 18 Aug 1962, Beryl Joyce, da of John Iliff Herbert (d 1975); 2 s (Guy b 1964, Julian b 1966), 1 da (Stephanie b 1971); *Career* RA 1954–56: 2 Lt 1955, Lt 1956; HM Overseas Admin Serv in Uganda 1957–69, dir of studies E African Staff Coll 1970–72; Inst of Local Govt Studies Univ of Birmingham 1972–: assoc dir 1974–83, prof of devpt admin 1981–, dir 1983–89; conslt to govts of: Kenya 1975–76, Indonesia 1978–, Pakistan 1981–82; conslt to World Bank on urban fin 1982– (in Bangladesh, Brazil, China, Jordan, Kenya, Mexico, Russia, South Africa, Tanzania, Turkey and Uganda); co-ordinator British assistance to local govt reform in Czech Republic, Slovakia and Hungary 1991–; vice chm Cncl Malvern Coll 1994–; FRSA 1988; *Books* Taxing a Peasant Society (1974), Financing Regional Government (1983), Strengthening Municipal Government (1989), Urban Management (1996); *Recreations* choral singing, walking; *Style—* Prof Kenneth Davey; ✉ Cross House, Powick, nr Worcester WR2 4RP (☎ 01905 830286); Institute of Local Government Studies, University of Birmingham, PO Box 363, Birmingham B15 2TT (☎ 0121 414 5011, fax 0121 414 4989, telex 3337 UOBHAM)

DAVEY, Nigel Thomas; s of Leslie Douglas, and Elsie Alice, *née* Hummerston; *b* 8 May 1947; *Educ* Ilford Co HS, Trinity Coll Cambridge (MA); *m* 19 Aug 1972, Ruth Mary; 3 s (James b 1975, Andrew b 1977, Richard b 1979); *Career* CA; ptnr: Spicer & Oppenheim 1980–90, Touche Ross (now Deloitte & Touche) 1990–; FCA 1972, FTII 1994; *Books* The Business of Partnerships (with P J Oliver, 1991), Ray: Partnership Taxation (with M Parry-Wingfield, 1996); *Recreations* tennis, badminton, music; *Style—* Nigel Davey, Esq; ✉ 31 Middleton Rd, Shenfield, Brentwood, Essex CM15 8DJ (☎ 01277 211954); Deloitte & Touche, Hill House, 1 Little New St, London EC4A 3TR (☎ 0171 936 3000, fax 0171 583 8517, telex 884739 TRLNDN G)

DAVEY, Peter John; s of John Davey (d 1981), and Mary, *née* Roberts; *b* 28 Feb 1940; *Educ* Oundle, Univ of Edinburgh (BArch); *m* 1968, Carolyn Frances, da of Maj Francis Hervey Pulford (d 1978); 2 s (Pelham Francis John b 1977, Meredith William Thorold b 1979); *Career* architect, journalist, writer and critic; dir: EMAP Architecture 1994–, EMAP Construct 1995–; publishing dir Architectural Research Quarterly 1995–; managing ed Architects' Journal 1978–82, ed The Architectural Review 1982–; memb Cncl RIBA 1990–93 (vice pres and hon librarian 1991–93); Knight (first class) Order of White Rose of Finland 1991; *Books* Arts and Crafts Architecture (1982, new edn 1995); contrib to many professional jls; *Clubs* Athenaeum; *Style—* Peter Davey, Esq; ✉ 44 Hungerford Rd, London N7 9LP; The Architectural Review, 151 Rosebery Avenue, London EC1 (☎ 0171 505 6701)

DAVEY, Richard H; s of Hubert H Davey, and May, *née* Harding; *b* 22 July 1948; *Educ* Lancing, Lincoln Coll Oxford (BA); *m* 5 c (Anna b 17 Jan 1974, Edward b 30 July 1981, Nicholas b 10 Feb 1984, Benedict b 31 Aug 1989, Thomas b 14 Sept 1991); *Career* Slater Walker 1970–76, NM Rothschild & Sons 1976–83, dir Exco International plc 1983–87; md Merrill Lynch International 1987–89, corp fin dir N M Rothschild & Sons 1989–; *Style—* Richard Davey, Esq; ✉ N M Rothschild & Sons Limited, New Court, St Swithins Lane, London EC4 (direct ☎ 0171 280 5071)

DAVEY, Dr Ronald William; s of Frederick George Davey, and Cecilia Beatrice, *née* Lawday; *b* 25 Oct 1943; *Educ* Trinity Sch of John Whitgift, King's Coll London, King's Coll Hosp Med Sch; *Career* consulting physician in homeopathy and sress mgmnt; princ in NHS 1970–77, dep md dir Pharmakon Clinics 1977–79, private med practice 1980, clinical asst Royal London Homeopathic Hosp and Tunbridge Wells Homeopathic Hosp 1981–85, physician to HM The Queen 1986–; hon med dir Blackie Fndn Tst 1980–, tstee conslt and vice chm of Res Cncl for Complementary Medicine 1987–89; lectr: Faculty of Homeopathy, Missionary Sch of Medicine 1987–89; visiting res fell Marie Curie Meml Fndn 1978–79, Blackie fell Nat Heart and Lung Inst 1978–90 (currently visiting res fell); memb rep of Laing Charities to Chair of Complementary Med Univ of Exeter; patron: Natural Medicines Soc, NW Friends of Homoeopathy; assoc Br Med Acupuncture Soc; FRSM; *Publications* contrib numerous articles to various med pubns 1979–92; *Recreations* riding, skiing, reading, music, ballet and opera; *Clubs* RSM; *Style—* Dr Ronald Davey; ✉ 1 Upper Wimpole St, London W1M 7TD (☎ 0171 580 5489, fax 0171 224 1094)

DAVEY SMITH, Prof George; *b* 9 May 1959; *Educ* Univ of Oxford (MA), Univ of Cambridge (MB BChir), London Sch of Hygiene and Tropical Med (MSc), Univ of Cambridge (MD), MFPHM 1992; *Career* clinical research fell and hon clinical med offr Welsh Heart Prog 1985–86, Wellcome research fell in clinical epidemiology Univ Coll and Middx Sch of Med Dept of Community Med 1986–89, lectr in epidemiology London Sch of Hygiene and Tropical Med 1989–92, sr lectr in public health and epidemiology and hon sr registrar then conslt in public health med Dept of Public Health Univ of Glasgow 1992–94, prof of clinical epidemiology Univ of Bristol and hon conslt in public health med Avon Health 1994–; hon research fell: Dept of Epidemiology and Public Health UCL, Social Statistics Research Unit City Univ London, Centre for Health Economics Univ of York; hon sr research fell Dept of Public Health Univ of Glasgow; conslt ODA/Govt of India Nat AIDS Control Prog; memb: Steering Ctee Nat Fitness Survey 1987–91, MRC Health Servs and Public Health Research Bd Grants Ctee; memb Editorial Bd: Sociology of Health and Illness, Jl of Epidemiology and Community Health; editorial advsr Social Sci and Med, author of numerous pubns in academic jls and book chapters; memb: Int Epidemiological Assoc, Soc for Social Med (memb Exec Ctee), Br Sociological Assoc; *Style—* Prof George Davey Smith; ✉ Department of Social Medicine, University of Bristol, Canynge Hall, Whiteladies Road, Bristol BS8 2PR (e-mail zetkin@bristol.ac.uk)

DAVID, Helen Ruth; da of Anthony Frank Littman, and Valerie Ann, *née* Singer; *b* 25 July 1955; *Educ* Brighton and Hove GS for Girls, Eastbourne Coll of Art and Design, Camberwell Sch of Arts and Crafts (BA), St Martin's Sch of Art; *m* 15 Aug 1987, Colin Michael David, s of late Walter David; 1 s (Oliver Louis b 24 Feb 1989), 1 da (Isabelle Valentine Shelly b 14 Feb 1991); *Career* design dir Helen David English Eccentrics 1983– (designing hand-printed luxury fashion and scarves), external assessor Glasgow Sch of Art 1988–90, external assessor St Martin's Sch of Art 1993–96, visiting lectr RCA; memb CNAA 1987–, memb RSA 1996; *Books* English Eccentrics - The Textile Designs of Helen Littman (1991); *Recreations* theatre, music; *Style—* Mrs Helen David; ✉ Helen David English Eccentrics, The Postmen's Office, 30 Leighton Road, London NW5 2QE (☎ 0171 284 2524, fax 0171 284 2530)

DAVID, Hugh Housdon; s of James Frederick David (d 1990), and Marjorie Grace, *née* Housdon; *b* 22 May 1954; *Educ* GS, Stockwell Coll, Inst of Educn Univ of London (BEd); *Career* English teacher Ramsden Sch Orpington Kent 1976–82, dir Fulcrum Theatre 1982–84; freelance writer 1982–; contrib: The Times, The Independent, The Independent on Sunday, Times Educational Supplement, London Evening Standard; columnist History Today 1987–93; memb Awards Panel Royal TV Soc 1986 and 1988; *Play* Coping (London 1982, BBC Radio 1985); *Documentary* The Last Night For Ever (BBC Radio 1983); *Books* The Fitzrovians (1988), Heroes, Mavericks and Bounders (1991), Stephen Spender - A Portrait with Background (1992), On Queer Street (1997); *Recreations* reading, theatre; *Style—* Hugh David, Esq; ✉ Flat D, 37 Albert Square, London SW8 1BY (☎ 0171 587 0935, fax 0171 587 0935)

DAVID, Joanna; da of Maj John Almond Hacking, and Davida Elizabeth, *née* Nesbitt; *b* 17 Jan 1947; *Educ* Altrincham GS, Elmhurst Ballet Sch, Royal Acad of Dancing, Webber Douglas Acad of Dramatic Art; *partner* (since 1972), Edward Charles Morice Fox, *qv*; 1 s (Frederick Samson Robert Morice b 5 April 1989), 1 da (Emilia Rose Elizabeth b 31 July 1974); *Career* actress; memb Ctee: Ladies' Theatrical Guild, Unicorn Theatre for Children, RADA; *Theatre* incl: Chichester Festival Theatre 1971, Family Reunion 1973 and Uncle Vanya 1977 (Royal Exchange Manchester), Cherry Orchard 1983 and Breaking the Code 1986 (Theatre Royal Haymarket), Stages (RNT) 1992; *Television* incl: War and Peace, Sense and Sensibility, Last of the Mohicans, Duchess of Duke Street, Rebecca, Carrington and Strachey, Fame is the Spur, First Among Equals, Paying Guests, Unexplained Laughter, Hannay, Children of the North, Secret Friends, Inspector Morse, Maigret, Rumpole of the Bailey, Darling Buds of May, The Good Guys, Sherlock Holmes - The Cardboard Box, Pride and Prejudice, A Touch of Frost, Bramwell; *Films* Mill on the Floss 1996; *Style—* Miss Joanna David; ✉ c/o Michael Whitehall Ltd, 125 Gloucester Road, London SW7 4TE (☎ 0171 244 8466, fax 0171 244 9060)

DAVID, Baroness (Life Peer UK 1978), of Romsey, City of Cambridge; Nora Ratcliff David; JP (Cambridge City 1965); da of George Blockley Blakesley, JP (d 1934); *b* 23 Sept 1913; *Educ* Ashby-de-la-Zouch Girls' GS, St Felix Southwold, Newnham Coll Cambridge (MA); *m* 1935, Richard William David, CBE (d 1993), s of Rev Ferdinand Paul David (d 1955); 2 s (Hon Nicholas Christopher b 1937, Hon (Richard) Sebastian b 1940), 2 da (Hon Teresa Katherine (Hon Mrs Davies) b 1944, Hon Elizabeth Sarah (Hon Mrs Forder) b 1947); *Career* sits as Lab Peer in House of Lords, dep chief oppn whip 1983–87 and oppn spokesman for environment and local govt in Lords 1983–86, oppn spokesman for educn 1979–83 and 1986–; former Cambridge city cncllr, Cambs co cncllr 1974–78; memb: Bd Peterborough Devpt Corp 1976–78, EC Select Ctee 1991–94, EC Agric Ctee; Baroness-in-Waiting to HM The Queen 1978–79; hon fell: Newnham Coll Cambridge 1986, Anglia Higher Educn Coll 1989; Hon DLitt Staffordshire Univ 1994; *Recreations* swimming, theatre, reading, travel; *Style—* The Rt Hon Baroness David, JP; ✉ 50 Highsett, Cambridge CB2 1NZ (☎ 01223 350376); Cove, New Polzeath, nr Wadebridge, Cornwall (☎ 01208 863310); House of Lords, London SW1 (☎ 0171 219 3159)

DAVID, Peter Howard; s of George Maurice David (d 1969), and Ruth, *née* Bloch; *b* 7 Sept 1951; *Educ* Liverpool Coll, Univ of London (BA); *m* 1 July 1978, Celia, da of Norman Binns; 1 s (Ian George b 8 Jan 1980), 1 da (Tessa b 12 Feb 1982); *Career* formerly on staff The Teacher Newspaper; The Times Higher Education Supplement: chief reporter until 1981, Washington ed 1981–83; Washington ed Nature 1983–84; The Economist: tech corr 1984, on foreign staff 1985, int ed 1986–93, business affrs ed 1993–; *Books* Star Wars and Arms Control (1984), Triumph in the Desert (1990); *Clubs* RAC; *Style—* Peter David, Esq; ✉ The Economist, 25 St James's Street, London SW1A 1HG (☎ 0171 830 7040)

DAVID, His Hon Judge Sir Robert Daniel George (Robin); kt (1995), QC (1968), DL (Cheshire, 1972); s of Alexander Charles Robert David (d 1967), and Edrica Doris Pole, *née* Evans (d 1978); *Educ* Christ Coll Brecon, Ellesmere Coll Salop; *m* 1944, Edith Mary, *née* Marsh; 2 da (Mary Edrica Ann b 20 Oct 1946 d 24 Sept 1990, Nancy Elizabeth b 19 May 1949); *Career* Capt RA 1943–47; called to the Bar 1949, circuit judge (Wales & Chester Circuit) 1972–; Cheshire QS: dep chm 1961, chm 1967, full time chm 1968; dep chm Agric Land Tbnl (Wales) 1965–68, cmmr of assize 1970, memb Parole Bd of England & Wales 1971–74, pres Mental Health Review Tbnl (Mersey Regn) 1983–95; *Books* The Magistrate in the Crown Court (1982); *Style—* His Hon Judge Sir Robin David, QC, DL; ✉ Chester Crown Court The Castle, Chester (☎ 01244 317606)

DAVID, Timothy James; s of Herman Francis David (d 1974), of Wimbledon, and Mavis Jean, *née* Evans; *b* 3 June 1947; *Educ* Stonyhurst, New Coll Oxford (MA), Univ of Rhodesia (Grad CertEd), Univ of London; *m* 24 Feb 1996, Rosemary, da of Josef and Prudence Kunzel; *Career* vol teacher Southern Rhodesia 1965–66, New Coll Oxford 1966–69, headmaster St Peter's Community Secdy Sch Salisbury and memb Conf of The Heads of African Secdy Schs 1970–71, Univ of Rhodesia 1972, Br Cncl 1973, educn dir Help the Aged 1974 (concurrently pt/t London Univ); HM Dip Serv: entered FCO by open competition 1974, second later first sec Dar es Salaam 1977–80, Cwlth Coordination Dept FCO 1980–82 (sec to UK Delgn to Cwlth Heads of Govt Meeting 1981), UK Mission to UN NY 1982, on loan to Central and Southern Africa Dept ODA 1983–84, UK Mission to UN Geneva 1985–88, head of Int and Planning Section and dep head Aid Policy Dept ODA 1988–89, cnsllr and head of Narcotics Control and Aids Dept FCO 1989–91, ambass to Fiji and high cmmr to Nauru and Tuvalu 1992–95, concurrently high cmmr to Kiribati 1994–95, counsellor Middle East Dept 1995, dep high cmmr to Zimbabwe 1996–; UK dir Tuvalu Tst Fund 1992–95, memb Cncl Univ of the S Pacific 1993–95, patron Save the Children (Fiji) 1993–95; *Recreations* friends, reading, music, travel, tennis, squash, walking; *Clubs* Commonwealth Trust Harare, All England Lawn Tennis and Croquet; *Style—* Tim David, Esq; ✉ c/o FCO, King Charles Street, London SW1A 2AH

DAVID, Wayne; MEP (Lab) South Wales Central (majority 86,082); s of David Haydn David, of Bridgend, Mid Glam, and Edna Amelia, *née* Jones; *b* 1 July 1957; *Educ* Cynffig Comp Sch, Univ Coll Cardiff (BA, PGCE FE, Charles Morgan prize in Welsh history), Univ Coll Swansea; *m* 8 June 1991, Catherine Thomas; *Career* teacher of history Brynteg Comp Sch 1983–85, tutor organiser Workers' Educn Assoc Mid Glamorgan 1985–89; MEP (Lab): South Wales 1989–94, South Wales Central 1994–; treas Euro Parly Lab Party (formerly Br Lab Gp) 1989–91, first vice pres Euro Parl Regnl Policy Ctee 1992–94, ldr Euro Parly Lab Pty 1994–; vice pres: Socialist Gp in Euro Parliament 1994–, Cardiff Br UN Assoc, Assoc of County Cncls and Assoc of Dist Cncls; memb: One World Action, Nicaraguan Solidarity Campaign; fell Cardiff Univ 1995; *Recreations* music, reading; *Style—* Wayne David, Esq, MEP; ✉ Tŷ Cathway, Bryn Rhedyn (off The Rise), Tonteg, Pontypridd, Mid Glam (☎ 01443 217810); South Wales Central European Office, 42 Charles Street, Cardiff, South Glamorgan CF1 4RN (☎ 01222 342848, fax 01222 342981)

DAVID-WEILL, Michel Alexandre; s of Pierre David-Weill, and Berthe, *née* Haardt; *b* 23 Nov 1932; *Educ* Institut de Sciences Politiques Paris, Lycée Français New York; *m* 1956, Helene Lehideux; 4 da; *Career* Brown Brothers Harriman 1954–55, Lehman Brothers New York 1955–56; Lazard Frères & Co New York: joined 1956, ptnr 1961–, sr ptnr 1977–; Lazard Brothers & Co London: dir 1965–, chm 1990–91, dep chm 1992–; ptnr Lazard Frères et Cie Paris 1965–, chm Lazard Frères & Co LLC 1995–; non-exec dir Pearson plc 1970–; Chevalier Legion d'Honneur; *Clubs* Knickerbocker (NY), Brook (NY), Creek (Locust Valley); *Style—* Michel David-Weill, Esq; ✉ Lazard Freres & Co, 30 Rockefeller Plaza, New York, NY 10020, USA (☎ 00 1 212 632 6000, fax 00 1 212 632 6060); Lazard Brothers & Co Ltd, 21 Moorfields, London EC2P 2HT (☎ 0171 588 2721, fax 0171 628 2485)

DAVIDGE, Christopher Guy Vere; OBE (1982), DL (1994); s of (Cecil) Vere Davidge (d 1981), of Little Houghton, Northants, and his 1 w, (Ursula) Catherine (d 1948), yr da and co-heir of Christopher Smyth, JP, DL (d 1934); *see* Burke's Landed Gentry, 18 edn, vol II, 1969; *b* 5 Nov 1929; *Educ* Eton, Trinity Coll Oxford (MA); *m* 1, 1 Feb 1963, Winifred Marian, da of John Stanley Crome; m 2, 1 June 1993, Jill Annette, da of Ewart William Girdler; *Career* dir Mixconcrete (Holdings) plc 1964–82 (md 1964–69), chm various private cos 1960–; memb Cncl Lloyd's 1982–88, dir Lloyd's of London Press Ltd 1985–91 (chm 1989–91); High Sheriff of Northants 1988–89; rowed for: Eton 1947–48, Oxford 1949–52 (pres OUBC 1950–51), GB 1952–63; steward Henley Royal Regatta 1967–, chm Leander Club 1968–78; chef de mission GB team Olympic Games 1976; vice pres: Br Olympic Assoc 1976– (vice chm 1972–76), Cwlth Games Cncl 1990– (hon treas 1969–74, vice chm 1974–90); pres Amateur Rowing Assoc 1977–85; memb Cncl FISA (Medal of Honour 1973, chm Regattas Cmmn 1976–90); chm St Andrew's Hosp Northampton 1994– (govr 1969–, vice chm 1991–94, chm of tstees 1991–); chm of govrs and tstee: Maidwell Hall Sch Northampton 1979–94, Three Shires Hosp Northampton 1981–; pres Northamptonshire Branch Britsh Red Cross 1992–94; chm Northamptonshire Record Soc 1989–; Freeman: City of London, Worshipful Co of Watermen; *Recreations* rowing, gardening, restoration of old houses; *Clubs* Leander, Vincent's; *Style—* Christopher Davidge, Esq, OBE, DL; ✉ Little Houghton House, Northampton (☎ 01604 890234)

DAVIDOVITZ, (Robert Hyman) Colin; BEM (1954); s of Lambert Samuel Davidson, and Rose-Marie Davidson; *b* 18 Aug 1930; *Educ* Tynecastle Secdy Sch Edinburgh; *m* 20

Sept 1958, Catherine, da of Archibald Callaghan; 2 s (Philip b 1961, Robert b 1964), 2 da (Judith b 1959, Theresa b 1963); *Career* RN: boy telegraphist 1946, telegraphist 1948, leading telegraphist (special) 1951, PO telegraphist (PROV) 1954; Assoc-Rediffusion telerecordist 1955, sr engr Scottish TV 1957; Southern TV: sr engr 1958, prodn mangr 1964, prodn controller 1975; West Midland studio controller ATV/Central 1981, dir ops TV-am 1987–92, dir Kingsway Production Services Ltd 1992–; cncllr Eastleigh BC 1996–; pres Catenians Southampton 1976; *Recreations* photography, painting, yachting; *Style*— Colin Davidovitz, Esq, BEM; ✉ 55 Kingsway, Chandlers Ford, Hants SO5 1FH (☎ 01703 251342)

DAVIDSON, Alan Ingram; s of late Joseph Davidson, of Aberdeen, and late Jean, *née* Dunbar; *b* 25 March 1935; *Educ* Robert Gordon's Coll Aberdeen, Univ of Aberdeen (MB ChB, ChM); *m* 14 Oct 1967, Margaret Elizabeth, da of McKay Eric Robertson, of Inverness, Scotland; 1 s (Ranald b Nov 1968), 1 da (Lindsay b April 1970); *Career* Nat Serv Capt RAMC 1960–62; conslt surgn and hon sr lectr Aberdeen Royal Infirmary 1974–; DObstRCOG 1963, FRCSEd 1968; *Recreations* gardening; *Clubs* University, Royal Northern; *Style*— Alan Davidson, Esq; ✉ Green Roofs, 20 Hillview Rd, Cults, Aberdeen, Scotland (☎ 01224 867347); Aberdeen Royal Infirmary, Foresterhill, Aberdeen, Scotland (☎ 01224 681818)

DAVIDSON, Andrew Scott Rutherford; s of Andrew Rutherford Davidson, of Edinburgh (d 1967), and Jean, *née* McKenzie (d 1983); *b* 18 Nov 1929; *Educ* Merchiston Castle Sch Edinburgh; *m* 2 Sept 1960, Dorothy Mowat Proudfoot, da of Dr Charles Crighton Robson, MC (d 1958); 1 s (Charles b 1966), 2 da (Katharine (Mrs Nick Allen) b 1962, Sarah b 1964); *Career* Capt Royal Scots 1950; joined Bank of Scotland 1951, gen mangr (England) 1977–89; non-exec dir: The British Linen Bank Ltd 1978–89, Kellock Ltd 1981–92, The Canada Life Assurance Co of GB Ltd 1990–, Canada Life Unit Trust Managers Ltd 1990–96, Bank of Scotland London Bd 1989–91; chm Bankers' Benevolent Fund 1980–89; Freeman City of London 1978; FCIBS; *Recreations* golf, fishing, rugby, bird watching; *Clubs* MCC, Walton Heath Golf; *Style*— Andrew Davidson, Esq; ✉ Dawes Mead, Leigh, Reigate, Surrey RH2 8NN (☎ 01306 611281)

DAVIDSON, Anthony Beverley (Tony); s of Dr Ronald Beverley Davidson (d 1972), and Edna Robina Elizabeth, *née* Cowan; *b* 25 Dec 1947; *Educ* Morgan Acad Dundee, Univ of St Andrews (MA); *m* 21 Dec 1971, Avril Rose, da of John Pearson Duncan, of Dundee; 2 s (Ronald John b 1975, Duncan Anthony b 1982), 2 da (Amanda Beverley b 1977, Laura Rose b 1979); *Career* CA 1974; mangr Deloitte Haskins & Sells (Edinburgh) 1970–75, sr mangr Whitelaw Wells & Co 1975–76, chief accountant Highways Dept Lothian Regnl Cncl 1976–77, chief inspr TSB (Tayside and Central Scotland) 1977–79, head Inspection Div TSB Gp 1979–82, gen mangr TSB (Tayside and Central Scotland) 1982–83, sr exec dir TSB Scotland plc 1987–90 (gen mangr 1983–87); md UAP Provincial Insurance plc 1990–; FCMA 1975, FCIBS 1984; *Recreations* golf, photography; *Clubs* Gullane Golf, Wentworth Golf, Windermere golf; *Style*— Tony Davidson, Esq; ✉ The Whim, Victoria Rd, Windermere, Cumbria LA23 2DL (☎ 015394 46271); UAP Provincial Insurance plc, Stramongate, Kendal LA9 4BE (☎ 01539 723415, fax 01539 794196)

DAVIDSON, Arthur; QC (1978); *b* 7 Nov 1928; *Educ* Liverpool Coll, King George V Sch Southport, Trinity Coll Cambridge; *Career* served Merchant Navy; called to the Bar Middle Temple 1953; Parly candidate (Lab) Blackpool South 1955, Preston North 1959, Hyndburn 1983; MP (Lab) Accrington 1966–83, PPS to Slr-Gen 1968–70, Parly sec Law Offrs Dept 1974–79; oppn spokesman on: defence 1980–81, legal affairs 1981–83 (front bench spokesman 1982–83); memb: Cncl Consumers' Assoc 1970–74, Exec Ctee Soc of Labour Lawyers 1981–, Home Affairs Select Ctee 1980–83; formerly chm: PLP Home Affairs Gp; legal dir: Associated Newspaper Holdings 1987–90, Mirror Group Newspapers 1991–; memb: Nat Fabian Soc, Cncl Nat Youth Jazz Orch; chm: House of Commons Jazz Club 1973–83; *Style*— Arthur Davidson Esq, QC; ✉ 1 Pump Court, Temple, London EC4Y 7AA (☎ 0171 583 0303, fax 0171 583 5597/2254)

DAVIDSON, Hon Lord; Charles Kemp Davidson; s of Rev Donald Davidson, DD (d 1970), of Edinburgh, and Charlotte Davidson; *b* 13 April 1929; *Educ* Fettes, Univ of Oxford (MA), Univ of Edinburgh (LLB); *m* 1960, Mary, OBE (1994), da of Charles Mactaggart, MC (d 1984), of Argyll; 1 s (Donald), 2 da (Caroline, Louise (Mrs Andrew Hanson)); *Career* Nat Serv 2 Lt Argyll Sutherland Highlanders 1953–55; Faculty of Advocates: admitted 1956, keeper Advocates Library 1972–76, vice dean 1977–89, dean 1979–83; QC (Scot) 1969; procurator to Gen Assembly of the Church of Scot 1972–83, senator of the Coll of Justice 1983–96, dep chm Boundary Cmmn for Scot 1985–96, chm Scot Law Cmmn 1988–96; FRSE 1985; *Style*— The Hon Lord Davidson, FRSE; ✉ 22 Dublin Street, Edinburgh EH1 3PP (☎ 0131 556 2168)

DAVIDSON, Christopher William Sherwood (Bill); s of Thomas Leigh Davidson, of Ilkley, W Yorks, and Donaldine, *née* Brown (d 1982); *b* 29 July 1940; *Educ* Uppingham, Univ of Nottingham (BA); *Career* articles with R K Denby (later Sir Richard Denby) 1962–65, admitted slr 1966; asst slr: Winkworth & Pemberton Westminster 1966–67, Coward Chance 1968–70; ptnr Ashton Hill & Co Nottingham 1971–75, gp slr and co sec NUS Services Ltd 1975–77; co sec: Endsleigh Insurance Services Ltd 1968– (legal advsr 1966–), NUS Services Ltd 1971–; fndr (later sr ptnr) Christopher Davidson & Co 1977–; memb Law Soc; *Recreations* cooking and crime fiction; *Style*— Bill Davidson, Esq; ✉ The Old Rectory, Kemerton, Nr Tewkesbury, Gloucestershire GL20 7HY (☎ 01386 725244); Christopher Davidson & Co, 2/3 Oriel Terrace, Oriel Road, Cheltenham, Gloucestershire GL20 7HY (☎ 01242 581481, fax 01242 221 210)

DAVIDSON, Clare Louise; da of Dr Walter Eardley Freeling Davidson (d 1984) and Viola Joan, *née* Howard, of London; *b* 30 May 1943; *Educ* Ashford HS for Girls, LAMDA; *m* 1969 (m dis 1986), Viggo Richard Kihl; 1 s (Thomas Eardley b 1972), 1 da (Emily Broun b 1974); *partner*, Johann Valentyn Budding; *Career* freelance director, acting and voice coach: LAMDA, privately, Riverside Studios, Morley Coll, The Actors' Centre; lectr: Guildhall Sch, RADA; acting coach to: Sting, Lulu, Dudley Moore, Stephen Rea; fndr Clare Davidson Acting Program 1992, dir Fndn Course British American Drama Acad 1989–92 (dean 1988–89); memb: Equity 1963, Directors' Guild of GB 1983 (fndr memb Cncl 1983–85); *Theatre* dir 1973–; prodns incl: Up in Sweden (King's Head), The Maids (Dublin Festival and Lyric Hammersmith), Happy Days (Belfast Festival and Warehouse), Boesman and Lena (Field Day Theatre Co and Hampstead), Miss Julie (Lyric Hammersmith and Duke of York's), Little Eyolf (Lyric Hammersmith) 1985, Five Finger Exercise (Cambridge Theatre Co), Hedda Gabler (Rogeland Theatre Stavanger and Bloomsbury) 1986, Peer Gynt (Cambridge Theatre Co) 1987, Atonement (Lyric Hammersmith) 1987, Alpha Beta (Man in the Moon) 1988, Shona (Pentameters) 1989, A Midsummer Night's Dream 1990, Hay Fever 1991, Master Harold and the Boys 1992, The Three Sisters 1993; *Films* dialogue coach on numerous prodns incl: Chitty Chitty Bang Bang, Brimstone and Treacle, The Bride, Accident, The Power of One; *Style*— Ms Clare Davidson

DAVIDSON, Dr Duncan Lewis Watt; s of Lewis Davidson, CBE, DD (d 1981), and Jean Davidson; *b* 16 May 1940; *Educ* Knox Coll Jamaica, Univ of Edinburgh (BSc, MB ChB); *m* 22 July 1964, Anne Veronica McDougall, da of Dr Arthur Maiden, OBE, of St Andrews, Fife; 4 s (Simon Lewis Tweedie b 9 July 1965, Mark Oliver Tweedie (twin) b 9 July 1965, (Julian) Anthony b 6 Feb 1967, Peter Duncan b 2 June 1970), 1 da (Kathleen Anne b 2 Jan 1978); *Career* various appts in med and neurology in Edinburgh and Montreal Canada 1966–76, conslt neurologist Tayside Health Bd and hon sr lectr in med Univ of Dundee 1976–; FRCPE 1979; *Books* Neurological Therapeutics (with Jar Lenman, 1981); *Recreations* golf, gardening, photography; *Style*— Dr Duncan Davidson; ✉ Brooksby, Queens Terrace, St Andrews, Fife KY16 9ER (☎ 01334 476108); Department of Neurology, Dundee Royal Infirmary, Dundee DD1 9ND (☎ 01382 660111)

DAVIDSON, Edward Alan; QC (1994); s of Alan Thomas Davidson (d 1977), of Sheffield, and Helen Muriel, *née* Johnston (d 1952); *b* 12 July 1943; *Educ* King's Sch Canterbury, Gonville and Caius Coll Cambridge (scholar, Tapp Postgraduate scholar, MA, LLB); *m* 19 May 1973, Hilary Jill, da of Norman S Fairman; 2 s (Mark b 14 June 1976, Philip b 27 Aug 1978); *Career* called to the Bar Gray's Inn 1966 (Atkin & Birkenhead scholar), in practice Chancery Bar 1968–; memb: Chancery Bar Assoc, Professional Negligence Bar Assoc; *Recreations* tennis, bridge, gardening; *Style*— Edward Davidson, Esq, QC; ✉ 4 Stone Buildings, Lincoln's Inn, London WC2A 3XT (☎ 0171 242 5524, fax 0171 831 7907)

DAVIDSON, Erick Stanley; s of Stanley Davidson, of East Allenby House, Horncliffe, Northumberland, and Agnes Sanderson Turnbull, *née* Mackay; *b* 10 Feb 1949; *Educ* Berwick-upon-Tweed GS, Hull Sch of Architecture, Newcastle Coll of Art (Business Studies and Design Dip); *m* 1977, Yvonne Jean Grace, da of Archibald Dickson (d 1981); 2 da (Carolyne b 1 May 1978, Linsey b 2 April 1982); *Career* mangr Marks & Spencer 1971–72, asst to MD of Pubns RIBA 1972–74, business mangr The Jenkins Group 1974–76, mktg dir Ads Graphics 1976–78, fndr chm and md The Tayburn Group 1978–; govr St George's Sch for Girls Edinburgh, memb Young Presidents' Orgn Scotland, asst Merchant Co of Edinburgh; *Recreations* golf; *Clubs* Dun Whinny-Gleneagles, Dunbar; *Style*— Erick Davidson, Esq; ✉ Beech House, Dalrymple Crescent, Edinburgh EH9 2NX (☎ 0131 667 7421); The Tayburn Group, 15 Kittle Yards, Causewayside, Edinburgh EH9 1PJ (☎ 0131 662 0662, fax 0131 662 0606)

DAVIDSON, Ian; MP (Lab) Glasgow Govan (majority 4,125); *Educ* Jedburgh GS, Galashiels Academy, Univ of Edinburgh (MA), Jordanhill Coll Glasgow; *m*; 1 s, 1 da; *Career* MP (Lab) Glasgow Govan 1992–; jt vice-chm Defence Ctee; memb Backbench: Overseas Aid Ctee, Trade & Industry Ctee; chm Shipbuilding Sub Ctee, vice-chm Aerospace Sub Ctee; memb All Pty Country Gps: America, Canada, ANZAC, Zimbabwe, South Africa, Japan; *Recreations* running, swimming, rugby union; *Style*— Ian Davidson, Esq, MP; ✉ House of Commons, London SW1A 0AA (☎ 0171 219 3000)

DAVIDSON, His Hon Judge Ian Thomas Rollo; QC (1977); s of Dr Robert Davidson (d 1970), and Margaret Miller Davidson (d 1980); *b* 3 Aug 1925; *Educ* Fettes, Corpus Christi Coll Oxford (BA); *m* 1, 1954, Gyöngyi (m dis 1982), da of Prof Csaba Anghi; 1 s (Stuart), 1 da (Amanda); m 2, 1984, Barbara Ann, da of Jack Watts; 1 s (Alasdair); *Career* War Serv RAC 1943–47, Lt Derbyshire Yeo; called to the Bar Gray's Inn 1955, asst lectr UCL 1959–60, dep recorder Nottingham 1971, recorder of the Crown Ct 1974, circuit judge (Midland and Oxford Circuit) 1984–; *Recreations* music, golf, photography; *Clubs* Forty, Nottinghamshire Services, Muswell Hill Golf, Nottinghamshire Golf; *Style*— His Hon Judge Ian Davidson, QC; ✉ 15 Park Valley, The Park, Nottingham NG7 1BS (☎ 0115 947 0672)

DAVIDSON, Jim; *b* 13 Dec 1954; *Educ* St Andrew's Sch Charlton; *Career* entertainer, comedian and TV presenter; *Theatre* stage performances incl: Britannia Pier Great Yarmouth 1986, 1989 and 1991, Princess Theatre Torquay 1987, 1988, 1990 and 1992, Cardiff 1987, Cinderella (Apollo Oxford, Hippodrome Bristol, Alhambra Theatre Bradford) 1985, 1986 and 1989, Dick Whittington (London Palladium) 1980, Cinderella (Dominion Theatre London) 1988, Back on The Road Tour 1990, Buttons in Sinderella (Cambridge Theatre) 1993/94; many cabaret and club engagements; *Television* shows incl: New Faces (debut ITV) 1976, What's On Next, The Jim Davidson Show (five series, TV Times Award Funniest Man on TV 1980), Up The Elephant And Round The Castle (four series), Home James (four series), Stand Up Jim Davidson, Jim Davidson Special 1984, Jim Davidson's Falkland Specials 1985, Jim Davidson In Germany 1986, Jim Davidson's Comedy Package 1987, Wednesday At Eight 1988, Telethon 1988, Big Break 1991–, The Generation Game 1995–; *Videos* incl: The Unedited Jim Davidson Live, Something Old, Something New, Something Borrowed, Something...; *Recordings* LPs incl: The Jim Davidson Album, A Dirty Weekend with Jim Davidson, Another Dirty Weekend; *Books* incl: Too Risky, Too Frisky, Jim Davidson Gets hooked, Jim Davidson's True Brit; *Style*— Jim Davidson, Esq

DAVIDSON, 2 Viscount (UK 1937); John Andrew Davidson; s of 1 Viscount Davidson, GCVO, CH, CB, PC (d 1970), and Hon Dame Frances Davidson, DBE (Baroness Northchurch, d 1985); *b* 22 Dec 1928; *Educ* Westminster, Pembroke Coll Cambridge; *m* 1, 30 June 1956 (m dis 1974), Margaret Birgitta (who m 2, 1974, as his 2 w, 4 Viscount Colville of Culross), da of Maj-Gen Cyril Henry Norton, CB, CBE, DSO; 4 da (1 decd); m 2, 1975, Pamela Joy Dobb, da of John Vergette; *Heir* bro, Hon Malcolm Davidson, *qv*; *Career* served with Black Watch and 5 Bn KAR 1947–49; dir Strutt & Parker (Farms) Ltd 1960–75; lord-in-waiting 1985–86; Capt Queen's Body Guard of the Yeomen of the Guard (dep chief whip in House of Lords) 1986–91; memb: Cncl CLA 1965–75, RASE 1973–75; *Style*— The Viscount Davidson; ✉ House of Lords, London SW1A 0PW

DAVIDSON, Dr John Forsyth; s of late John F Davidson, of Lumphanan, Aberdeenshire, and Jane C, *née* Morton; *b* 11 Jan 1934; *Educ* Robert Gordon's Coll Aberdeen, Univ of Aberdeen (MB); *m* Laura G, *née* Middleton; 1 s (Graeme J F), 1 da (Fiona J (Mrs McMillan)); *Career* conslt haematologist in administrative charge Dept of Haematology Glasgow Royal Infirmary and Associated Hosps Glasgow 1990– (conslt haematologist 1969–), hon clinical sr lectr Univ of Glasgow 1990– (hon clinical lectr 1971–90), hon conslt haematologist Univ of Strathclyde 1992–; formerly: memb Cncl, memb Exec, Trg and Fin Ctees, memb Standing Advsy Ctee on Haematology and memb Scottish Affrs Ctee RCPath, memb Cncl and memb Standing Ctee on Educn and Specialists Standards RCPEd, pres, sec, memb Ctee and chm Haemostasis and Thrombosis Task Force Br Soc for Haematology, chm Steering Ctee NEQAS in Blood Coagulation UK Nat Quality Assurance Schemes, memb Faculty of Med and Senate Univ of Glasgow, memb Ctee Scottish Nat Blood Transfusion Assoc, chm Int Ctee Int Soc for Fibrinolysis and Thrombolysis, Surgn Ltd RN; currently: sec Jt Ctee on Haematology RCPath and RCP, coll examiner and memb Haematology Examiners Ctee RCPath, memb Br Ctee for Standards in Haematology Br Soc for Haematology (former sec), chm Jt Working Pty on Quality Assurance, memb Nat Quality Assurance Advsy Panel for Haematology and memb Steering Ctee NEQAS in Gen Haematology UK Nat Quality Assurance Schemes, memb Advsy Ctee on Haematology and Blood Transfusion and accreditation inspr in haematology and blood transfusion Clinical Pathology Accreditation Ltd, examiner Univs of Glasgow and London, memb Nat Panel of Specialists in Haematology (Sec of State for Scotland appointment), independent conslt on review in health complaints procedure and professional rep on Sec of State paragraph 190 appeals (Sec of State appointment); author or co-author of over 180 pubns, chapters or review articles in the field of haematology; formerly advsr to Ed British National Formulary, currently memb, ed and chm Editorial Bd and co-ed-in-chief Fibrinolysis Int Soc for Fibrinolysis and Thrombolysis; FRCPEd, FRCPGlas, FRCPath; *Style*— Dr John F Davidson; ✉ Craigiebank, 20 Roman Road, Bearsden, Glasgow G61 2SL (☎ 0141 942 3356); Department of Haematology, Glasgow Royal Infirmary University NHS Trust, Castle Street, Glasgow G4 0SF (☎ 0141 211 4669, fax 0141 211 4931)

DAVIDSON, Prof John Frank; s of John Davidson, and Katie Davidson; *b* 7 Feb 1926; *Educ* Heaton GS Newcastle, Trinity Coll Cambridge (BA, PhD, ScD); *m* 1948, Susanne Hedwig Ostberg; 1 s, 1 da; *Career* Mechanical Devpt Dept Rolls Royce Derby 1947–50

(apprentice 1947); Univ of Cambridge: res fell Trinity Coll 1949–53, res in Engrg Laboratory 1950–52, univ demonstrator in chemical engrg 1952–54, univ lectr 1954–75, fell and steward Trinity Coll 1957, prof of chemical engrg and head Dept of Chemical Engrg 1975–78, Shell prof of chemical engrg 1978–93, vice master Trinity Coll Cambridge 1992–96; visiting prof: Univ of Delaware 1960, Univ of Sydney 1967, MIT 1981, Univ of Delaware 1981 (also Oregon and Houston), Univ of Notre Dame Indiana 1988; visiting lectr Univs of Cape Town and Johannesburg 1964, Wilhelm lectr Princeton 1988; memb: Ct of Enquiry for Flixborough Disaster 1974–75, Advsy Ctee on Safety of Nuclear Instalations HSE 1977–87, Advsy Cncl for Applied Res and Devpt 1980 (memb Jt Working Pty on Biotechnology), Governing Body AFRC Inst of Engrg Res 1982, Advsy Bd AFRC Inst of Food Res 1986; foreign assoc US Nat Acad of Engrg 1976, fell Indian Nat Sci Acad 1990; FIChemE (pres 1970–71), MIMechE, fndr FEng 1976 (memb Acid Emmissions Ctee 1985), FRS 1974 (vice pres 1989); Hon DSc Univ of Aston 1989; Docteur Honoris Causa de l'Institut National Polytechnique de Toulouse 1979, Int Fluidization Award of Achievement (Engrg Fndn Conf Banff) 1989; *Books* Fluidization Particles (with D Harrison, 1963), Fluidization (1971, 2 edn with R Clift and D Harrison, 1985); *Recreations* hill walking, gardening, mending bicycles and other domestic artifacts; *Style*— Prof John Davidson, FRS, FEng; ✉ 5 Luard Close, Cambridge CB2 2PL (☎ and fax 01223 246104); University of Cambridge, Department of Chemical Engineering, Pembroke St, Cambridge CB2 3RA (☎ 01223 334799)

DAVIDSON, Dr John Knight; OBE (1990); s of John Rose Davidson (d 1973), of Edinburgh, and Edith Jane, *née* Good (d 1965); *b* 17 Aug 1925; *Educ* George Watsons Coll Edinburgh, Univ of Edinburgh; *m* 25 June 1955, Edith Elizabeth, da of Archibald McKelvie (d 1963), of Edinburgh; 2 s (Alastair b 1958, Neil b 1959), 1 da (Fiona b 1956); *Career* Capt RAMC ME Cmd 1949–51, 2 i/c 35 Field Amb 1 Gds Bde 1951; radiology training Edinburgh and St Bart's London, conslt radiologist in admin charge Western Infirmary and Gartnavel Gen Glasgow 1967–90, hon clinical lectr Univ of Glasgow 1967–90; conslt: US Navy 1974–89, French Navy 1978, several diving cos, National Hyperbaric Centre Aberdeen 1990–92; currently conslt advsr in diving and compressed air med; non-exec dir Yorkhill NHS Tst Glasgow 1993–95; dep pres Glasgow and Renfrewshire BRCS 1988–93; Scot Cons and Unionist Assoc: exec memb 1991–, memb Health Policy Ctee 1991– (chm 1991–96); memb: MRC Decompression Panel (Bone Disease) 1965–92, Cncl Med and Dental Union of Scotland 1971–95, Med Advsy Gp BBC Scot 1988–; RCR: memb Cncl 1971–74 and 1984–87, chm Examining Bd 1976–79, chm Standing Scot Ctee 1985–89, Scot Sub Ctee on Distinction Awards 1982–84; Rohan Williams prof Australasia 1977, Aggarwal Meml Oration India 1988; memb Editorial Bd Euro Jl of Radiology 1990–96; hon memb Scot Radiology Soc 1995; hon fell: Royal Aust Coll of Radiology 1979, American Coll of Radiology 1992, International Skeletal Soc 1994 (fndr memb, Medal 1992), Med and Dental Def Union of Scot 1996; memb: RCR, BMA, BIR; FRCPEd, FRCPGlas; *Books* Aseptic Necrosis of Bone (1976), numerous radiology pubns; *Recreations* golf, bridge, painting, hill-walking, skiing; *Clubs* R&A, Glasgow Art, Pollok Golf, Buchanan Bridge; *Style*— Dr John K Davidson, OBE; ✉ 15 Beechlands Avenue, Netherlee, Glasgow G44 3YT

DAVIDSON, John Roderick; yr s of (Alexander) Ross Davidson (d 1977), of Portsmouth, and Jessie Maud, *née* Oakley (d 1984); *b* 29 Jan 1937; *Educ* Portsmouth Northern GS, Univ of Manchester (BA, Wadsworth Memorial award); *Career* advsr to students Chelsea Sch of Art 1966–68, asst sch sec Royal Post Grad Med Sch 1968–74; Imperial Coll London: asst sec 1974–77, personnel sec 1977–85, admin sec 1985–89; Univ of London: clerk of the Senate 1989–94, clerk of the Council 1994–, dir of admin 1991–; memb Univ of London Examinations and Assessment Cncl 1991–; dir: London East Anglian Group Ltd 1991–96, SAUL Trustee Company Ltd 1993–, London Area South Eastern Library Region 1995–, Senate House Services Ltd 1996–; govr Charterhouse 1994–; memb Soc of Genealogists 1988–; *Recreations* opera, theatre, genealogy; *Style*— John Davidson, Esq; ✉ 10 Lansdowne, Carlton Drive, London SW15 2BY (☎ 0181 789 0021); University of London, Senate House, Malet St, London WC1E 7HU (☎ 0171 636 8000, fax 0171 631 0118)

DAVIDSON, Dr (William) Keith Davidson; CBE (1982), JP (Glasgow 1962); s of James Fisher Keith Davidson (d 1978), of Bearsden, Glasgow, and Martha Anderson, *née* Milloy (d 1956); *b* 20 Nov 1926; *Educ* Coatbridge Secdy Sch, Univ of Glasgow; *m* 6 Feb 1952, Dr Mary Waddell Aitken, da of Dr George Jamieson (d 1967), of Chryston; 1 s (Keith b 1954), 1 da (Mhairi b 1956); *Career* Med Offr 1 Bn RSF 1950, Maj 2 i/c 14 Field Ambulance 1950–51, Med Offr i/c Holland & Belgium 1952; gen med practitioner 1953–90; DPA Univ of Glasgow 1965, chm Glasgow Local Med Ctee 1971–75, chm Scottish Gen Med Servs Ctee 1972–75, memb Scottish Cncl on Crime 1972–75, dep chm Gen Med Servs Ctee (UK) 1975–79, memb Scottish Med Practices Ctee 1968–80, chm Scottish Cncl BMA 1978–81, vice pres BMA 1983–, memb Gen Med Cncl 1984–94, hon pres Glasgow Eastern Med Soc 1984–85, chm Scottish Health Servs Planning Cncl 1984–89, memb Scottish Health Servs Policy Bd 1985–89, memb Gtr Glasgow Health Bd 1989–91; chm: Strathclyde AIDS Forum 1990–92, Gtr Glasgow Health Bd AIDS Forum 1990–93, Gtr Glasgow Health Bd Drugs & Alcohol Forum 1990–93; chm Chryston HS Bd 1995– (vice chm 1990–95); Elder Church of Scotland 1956–; session clerk: Ruchazie Parish Church 1961–71, Stepps Parish Church 1983–; SBStJ 1976; memb Bonnet Makers and Dyers Craft; fell BMA 1975, FRCGP 1980; *Recreations* gardening; *Style*— Dr Keith Davidson, CBE, JP; ✉ Dunvegan, Stepps, Glasgow G33 6DE (☎ 0141 779 2103, fax 0141 779 4513)

DAVIDSON, Keith Thomas; s of Thomas Middleton Davidson (d 1980), of Northampton, and Victoria Irene, *née* Geary (d 1995); *b* 12 Sept 1932; *Educ* Whitgift Sch S Croydon, Univ of London (LLB); *m* 1, 1962 (m dis 1983), Susan Jennifer; 1 da (Catherine Mary (Mrs Perold) b 12 Aug 1964); m 2, 1989, Jessie McLeod; 2 step da (Margaret Belle Sinclair (Mrs Simes) b 24 Dec 1963, Rosemary Sinclair (Mrs Lundie) b 20 Aug 1967), 1 step s (Roderick Sinclair b 1 March 1970); *Career* slr; articled to Bennett Welch & Co London SE19 1950–55, admitted slr 1955, Nat Serv RASC (studied Air Law at Inst of Advanced Legal Studies) 1955–57, asst slr Herbert Smith & Co London 1957–60, estab in-house legal dept De La Rue Co plc London 1960, asst slr Frere Cholmeley 1960–63; ptnr Company/Commercial Dept Phipps & Troup Northampton 1964–69 (asst slr 1963), Phipps & Troup merged to become Becke Phipps Northampton 1969 (appointed head Company/Commercial Dept 1969), Becke Phipps merged to become Hewitson Becke & Shaw 1989, sr ptnr Hewitson Becke & Shaw 1991–94; memb Law Soc 1957; cncllr Northampton Co Borough Cncl 1965–72; memb C of E: Church Assembly 1965–70, Gen Synod 1970–, Bishops' Cncl 1982–, Gen Synod Legal Aid Ctee 1985–91, Peterborough Diocesan Synod 1965– (lay chm 1982–88), Diocesan Bd for Devpt Miny 1989–; lay reader C of E 1961–; memb: Gen Ctee British & Foreign Bible Soc 1977–89, Finance Ctee Northampton Red Cross 1985–; non-exec dir Northants Health Authy 1994–96; chm of tstees Northampton Municipal Charities; *Recreations* walking; *Clubs* Northampton and County; *Style*— Keith Davidson, Esq; ✉ The Poplars, Sandy Lane, Church Brampton, Northants NN6 8AX (☎ 01604 845489); c/o Hewitson Becke & Shaw, 7 Spencer Parade, Northampton NN1 5AB (☎ 01604 233233, fax 01604 27941)

DAVIDSON, Lionel; *b* 31 March 1922; *m* 1, 1949, Fay Jacobs (d 1988); 2 s (Philip b 1952, Nicolas b 1962); m 2, 1989, Frances Ullman; *Career* author; *Books* The Night of Wenceslas (1960, Best First Novel award Authors' Club 1961, Gold Dagger award CWA 1961), The Rose of Tibet (1962), A Long Way to Shiloh (1966, Gold Dagger award CWA 1967), Making Good Again (1968), Smith's Gazelle (1971), The Sun Chemist (1975), The Chelsea Murders (1977, Gold Dagger award 1978), Under Plum Lake (1980), Kolymsky Heights (1994); work also includes TV, films and children's books; *Style*— Lionel Davidson, Esq; ✉ c/o Curtis Brown Ltd, 4th Floor, Haymarket House, 28–29 Haymarket, London SW1Y 4SP (☎ 0171 396 6600)

DAVIDSON, Malcolm Alexander; s of Robert Stanley Davidson (d 1987), and Hilda, *née* Capewell (d 1975); *b* 30 Nov 1933; *Educ* Prescot GS; *m* 31 July 1958, Patricia Edna, da of Raymond Parker Lenton (d 1982); 1 s (Alasdair Malcolm b 1965), 1 da (Fiona Sarah b 1967); *Career* Nat Serv Queen's Own Cameron Highlanders 1952–54; md Littlewoods Pools 1987–93, dir The Littlewoods Organisation 1987–93, Intertoto bd memb 1991–93; tstee Fndn for Sport and the Arts 1991–; FRSA 1991; *Recreations* shooting, golf, tennis, swimming, music; *Clubs* Heswall Golf; *Style*— Malcolm A Davidson, Esq; ✉ c/o Littlewoods Pools, Walton Hall Ave, Liverpool L67 1AA (☎ 0151 525 3677, 0151 342 3920)

DAVIDSON, Hon Malcolm William Mackenzie; s of 1 Viscount Davidson, *qv*; *b* 28 Aug 1934; *Educ* Westminster, Pembroke Coll Cambridge (MA); *m* 1970, Evelyn Ann Carew, widow of Alan George Perfect, WS, and da of William Blackmore Storey; 1 s ((John) Nicolas Alexander b 1971), 1 da (Sophie Ann Frances b 1973); *Career* 2 Bn Black Watch 1954–55; Taylor Woodrow 1958–63, archaeology 1964–66, antique dealer and valuer City Fine Arts 1968, London Fine Art Valuation Consultancy 1980–87, Sotheby's rep S Spain 1988–94; pres Met Public Gardens Assoc 1986–91; *Clubs* Pratt's, Bath & County, Puffins; *Style*— The Hon Malcolm Davidson; ✉ Las Cuadras, Monte de la Torre, Apdo 58, 11370 Los Barrios, Prov de Cadiz, Spain (☎ and fax 34 56 63 02 34)

DAVIDSON, Dr Marilyn Joy; da of Wallace Eyre, and Joyce Mary, *née* Robinson, of Queniborough, Leics; *b* 22 Nov 1951; *Educ* Melton Mowbray Upper Sch Leics, Bolton Inst of Technol Bolton Lancs (ext BA Univ of London), Barnet Coll London (CertEd), Univ of Queensland Brisbane Australia (MA), UMIST (PhD); *m* (m dis); 1 da (Fern Eyre-Morgan b 8 Oct 1986), 1 s (Lloyd Eyre-Morgan b 16 Aug 1988); *Career* lectr Dept of Community Studies Barnet Coll of Further Educn 1974–75, tutor in psychology Univ of Queensland Australia 1975–79, guest psychology lectr and supervisor Dept of Mgmnt Sciences UMIST 1980–83, guest lectr Univ of Manchester and Manchester Business Sch 1980–84, sr lectr in organisational psychology UMIST Manchester Sch of Mmgnt 1989– (lectr 1984–89); ed Women in Management Review 1991–96, assoc ed Occupational and Organizational Psychology; assoc editorial memb: Gender, Work and Organisations, The International Review of Women and Leadership; CPsychol, FBPsS (memb Div of Occupational Psychology, memb Div of Psychology Women Section), FRSA; *Books* with C L Cooper: High Pressure: The Working Lives of Women Managers (1982), Stress and the Woman Manager (1983), Working Women - An International Survey (1984), Women in Management (1984), Women and Information Technology (ed, 1987), The Stress Survivors (1991), Shattering the Glass Ceiling - The Woman Manager (1992), European Women in Business and Management Europe 1992 (ed, 1993); others: Reach for the Top: A Woman's Guide to Success in Business and Management (1985), Vulnerable Workers - Psychological and Legal Issues (ed with J M Earnshaw, 1991), Women in Management - Current Research Issues (ed with R Burke, 1994); author of numerous articles and chapters in jls and pubns; *Recreations* playing 'cello, horse-riding, theatre, cinema; *Style*— Dr Marilyn Davidson; ✉ Manchester School of Management, UMIST, PO Box 88, Manchester M60 1QD (☎ 0161 200 3449, fax 0161 200 3505)

DAVIDSON, Neil Forbes; QC (Scot 1993); *b* 13 Sept 1950; *Educ* Univ of Stirling (BA), Univ of Bradford Mgmnt Centre (MSc), Univ of Edinburgh (LLB, LLM); *m* 1980, Regina Anne, *née* Sprissler; *Career* analyst J & A Scrimgeour 1972; admitted to Faculty of Advocates 1979; dir: Scot Cncl for Int Arbitration 1990–, City Disputes Panel 1994–; *Books* Judicial Review in Scotland (1986); *Style*— Neil Davidson, Esq, QC; ✉ c/o Advocates' Library, Parliament House, Parliament Square, Edinburgh EH1 1RF (☎ 0131 226 5071, fax 0131 225 3642)

DAVIDSON, Dr Neil McDonald; s of John Mackinnon Davidson (d 1980), and Alice Mary Stewart, *née* McDonald (d 1993); *b* 15 May 1940; *Educ* Merton Coll Oxford (MA, DM), St Thomas's Hosp London; *m* 31 Dec 1963, Jill Ann, da of Ernest Ripley; 3 s (Angus b 1966, Alastair b 1970, Calum b 1981), 1 da (Fiona b 1967); *Career* lectr then sr lectr in med Ahmadu Bello Univ Zaria Nigeria 1969–74, conslt physician Eastern Gen Hosp Edinburgh 1979–92, hon sr lectr Univ of Edinburgh 1979–92 (lectr then sr lectr in med 1975–79), asst dir of studies (med) Edinburgh Postgrad Bd for Med 1985–92; chief of internal med NWAF Hosp Tabuk Saudi Arabia 1992–95, visiting prof of med Royal Coll of Surgns in Ireland 1992–95, head Dept of Med Zayed Military Hosp Abu Dhabi 1995–96, sr conslt physician Armed Forces Hospital Kuwait 1996–; author of papers on peri-partum cardiac failure, endocrinology and metabolism, tropical diseases; memb GMC 1989–94, FRCPE 1982, FRCP 1984; *Recreations* collecting antique maps, Munro-bagging; *Style*— Dr Neil Davidson; ✉ 43 Blackford Rd, Grange, Edinburgh EH9 2DT (☎ 0131 667 3960, fax 0131 662 9320)

DAVIDSON, Nicholas Ranking; QC (1993); s of Brian Davidson, CBE (d 1995), and Priscilla Margaret, *née* Chilver (d 1981); *b* 2 March 1951; *Educ* Winchester (scholar), Trinity Coll Cambridge (exhibitioner, BA, vice pres Union Soc); *m* 7 Sept 1978, Gillian Frances, da of Michael Leslie Watts; 2 da (Alexandra Frances Priscilla b 20 July 1983, Elizabeth Frances Hermione b 9 April 1989); *Career* called to the Bar Inner Temple 1974 (Inner Temple scholar, cert of honour, Treasurer's prize, Hughes Parry prize); dep chm Professional Negligence Bar Assoc 1996– (treas 1990–95); govr St Mary's Sch Ascot 1996–; *Recreations* bridge, music, skiing; *Style*— Nicholas Davidson, Esq, QC; ✉ 4 Paper Buildings, Temple, London EC4Y 7EX (☎ 0171 353 3366, fax 0171 353 5778, mobile 0850 878438)

DAVIDSON, Peter John; s of John Frank Davidson, and Susanne, *née* Ostberg; *b* 25 July 1954; *Educ* Perse Sch, Trinity Coll Cambridge (sr scholar, MA), IMD, INSEAD; *Career* process engr; ICI Agricultural Division Billingham: process engr Projects & Engrg Dept 1977–81, NITRAM plants mangr 1981–83, ammonia section mangr res 1983–86, res mangr 1986–89; process engrg mangr ICI Engineering 1989–94, gp research and technol mangr Tioxide PLC 1994–; non-exec dir Paras Ltd; corporate memb Inst of Chemical Engrs and Chartered Engrs 1983, FICE, MEng, FEng 1992, FRSA 1995; *Recreations* hillwalking, planning gardens, skiing, sailing, watercolours, cooking; *Style*— Peter Davidson, Esq, FEng; ✉ 25 The Green, Hurworth on Tees, Darlington DL2 2AA (☎ 01325 721613); Tioxide Group Services, West Site, Haverton Hill Road, Billingham, Cleveland TS23 1PS (☎ 01642 376811, fax 01642 376398)

DAVIDSON, (Charles) Peter Morton; s of Dr William Philip Morton Davidson (d 1978), of Northumberland, and Muriel Maud, *née* Alderson (d 1987); *b* 29 July 1938; *Educ* Harrow, Trinity Coll Dublin (MA, LLB); *m* 15 Sept 1966, Pamela Louise, da of Harry Campbell-Rose, of Natal; *Career* called to Bar Inner Temple 1963; contested (C) N Battersea Gen Election 1966, chm London Rent Assessment Panel 1973–84, pt/t immigration appeals adjudicator 1976–84; memb London Borough Cncl: Wandsworth 1964–68, Merton 1968–71; met stipendiary magistrate 1984–, recorder of the Crown Court 1991–; chm of Family Panel 1991–; *Recreations* music, travel; *Clubs* Hurlingham; *Style*— Peter Davidson, Esq; ✉ Camberwell Green Magistrates Court, 15 D'Eynsford Road, London SE5 7UP

DAVIDSON, Richard John; s of Arthur Vincent Davidson, of Folkestone, Kent, and Mary Anne Rutter, *née* Douglas; *b* 2 Sept 1946; *Educ* Fettes, Worcester Coll Oxford (BA, MA); *m* 30 April 1977, Alison Elizabeth, *née* Wager; 2 s (Thomas Henry b June 1980, Peter John b Feb 1982); *Career* slr; Baker & McKenzie London: articled clerk 1968–70, slr 1970–72, assoc (Chicago) 1972–74, ptnr 1975–95, memb Exec Ctee 1990–94; memb Law Soc; *Recreations* painting, sculpting; *Clubs* Arts; *Style*— Richard Davidson, Esq

DAVIDSON, Prof Robert; s of George Braid Davidson (d 1970), and Gertrude May, *née* Ward (d 1978); *b* 30 March 1927; *Educ* Bell Baxter Sch Cupar Fife, Univ of St Andrews (MA, BD); *m* 22 Aug 1952, Elizabeth May, *née* Robertson; 4 s (Robert Ward b 1953, Donald George b 1955, John Alexander b 1970, Scott b 1973), 3 da (Joyce Elizabeth b 1958, Olive May b 1962, Elizabeth May b 1966); *Career* lectr: in biblical studies Univ of Aberdeen 1952–60, in Hebrew and Old Testament Univ of St Andrews 1960–66, in Old Testament Univ of Edinburgh 1966–72; prof of Old Testament language and literature Univ of Glasgow 1972–91 (princ Trinity Coll 1982–91, Kerr lectureship 1983); Edward Cadbury lectureship Univ of Birmingham 1988–89; Moderator of Gen Assembly of the Church of Scot 1990; Hon DD: Univ of Aberdeen 1985, Univ of Glasgow 1993; FRSE 1989; *Books* The Bible Speaks (1959), Pelican Guide to Modern Theology (vol 3, 1970), The Old Testament (1964), The Bible in Religious Education (1979), The Courage to Doubt (1983), Wisdom and Worship (1990), A Beginner's Guide to the Old Testament (1992), Go By The Book (1995); commentaries: Genesis 1–11 (1973), Genesis 12–50 (1979), Jeremiah 1 (1983), Jeremiah 2 (1985) Ecclesiastes and Song of Songs (1986); *Recreations* music, gardening; *Style*— Prof Robert Davidson, FRSE; ✉ 30 Dumgoyne Dr, Bearsden, Glasgow G61 (☎ 0141 942 1810); Department of Biblical Studies, University of Glasgow, G12 8QQ (☎ 0141 339 8855 ext 4607)

DAVIDSON, Roderick Macdonald; JP (1976); s of Dr Stephen Moriarty Davidson, of Plymouth, and Kathleen Flora, *née* Macdonald; *b* 2 Jan 1938; *Educ* Clifton, St John's Coll Cambridge; *m* 17 June 1961, Jane Margaret, da of late Dr Basil Stanley Kent, of Kingsclere; 1 s (Michael b 1965), 2 da (Emma b 1963, Juliet b 1969); *Career* Nat Serv RM 1956–58, cmmnd 1957; dir Albert E Sharp (stockbroker); non-exec dir Close Bros VCT 1996; cncllr Bristol City Cncl 1969–74; memb Antient Soc of St Stephens Ringers Dolphin Canynges; tax cmmr 1978, High Sheriff of Avon 1981–82; memb Worshipful Co of Curriers; MSI; *Recreations* golf, fishing, music; *Clubs* MCC, Clifton, Thurlestone Golf, Bristol and Clifton Golf; *Style*— Roderick Davidson, Esq, JP; ✉ Albert E Sharp, 2 Trinity Street, College Green, Bristol BS1 5TE (☎ 0117 926 0051)

DAVIDSON, Air Vice-Marshal Rev Sinclair Melville; CBE (1968); s of James Stewart Davidson (d 1961), and Anne Sinclair, *née* Cowan (d 1938); *b* 1 Nov 1922; *Educ* Bousfield Sch Kensington, RAF Cranwell, RAF Tech Coll, Chichester Theol Coll; *m* 1944, Jean Irene, *née* Flay; 1 s (and 1 s decd); *Career* served WWII, RAF (despatches), psa 1956, air staff Air Miny 1957–60, jssc 1960, Asst Cmdt RAF Locking 1963–64, chm Jt Signal Bd (ME) 1965, idc 1968, dir Signals (Air) MOD 1969–71, Air Offr Wales and Station Cdr RAF St Athan 1972–74, asst chief Def Staff (Signals) 1974–75; sec Inst of Electronic and Radio Engrs 1977–82; ordained 1982, priest i/c Parish of Holy Trinity High Hurstwood 1983–88; Liveryman Worshipful Co of Scientific Instrument Makers; CEng, FIEE, FRAeS; *Recreations* parish affairs, maintenance of home and garden; *Clubs* RAF; *Style*— Air Vice-Marshal Rev Sinclair Davidson, CBE; ✉ Trinity Cottage, High Hurstwood, Uckfield, East Sussex (☎ 01825 732151)

DAVIDSON DAVIS, Philomena Mary; da of Thomas Oliver Grant Davidson, violinist (d 1985), and Mary Bridget Bourke; *b* 24 March 1949; *Educ* City & Guilds of London Art Sch (Edward Stott travel scholarship, Dip in Sculpture), Royal Acad Schs London (RAS Dip in Sculpture, Gold Medal for Sculpture, Bronze medal for work from the figure); *m* 7 Dec 1974, Michael Frank Davis; 2 da (Lucy Victoria b 3 June 1977, Ruth Alexandra b 18 Jan 1982); *Career* sculptor; studied Japanese language arts and architecture Japan 1973–76, opened Bronze Foundry Milton Keynes 1980, opened current studio Hanslope 1987; exhibitions: Royal Acad Summer Exhibition, Royal West of England Acad Annual Show, Westminster City Gallery, Bircham Gallery, Margam Sculpture Park, Woodlands Gallery; dir Chelsea Harbour Sculpture 1993 and 1996, md The Sculpture Co Ltd 1994; first woman pres Royal Soc of Br Sculptors 1990–96 (assoc 1984, fell 1990), FRSA 1990, RWA 1996; *Recreations* swimming, pilates, reading biographies; *Clubs* Arts; *Style*— Ms Philomena Davidson Davis; ✉ Longstreet Studio, 19 Hartwell Road, Hanslope, Milton Keynes (☎ 01908 315841, fax 01908 611363)

DAVIDSON KELLY, (Charles) Norman; s of (Frederick) Nevill Davidson Kelly (d 1976), of Edinburgh, and Mary Lyon Campbell (Molly), *née* MacLeod (d 1993); *b* 3 June 1945; *Educ* Edinburgh Acad, Exeter Coll Oxford (BA), Univ of Edinburgh (LLB); *m* 2 Sept 1972, Annabella Daphne Pitt, da of Herbert Alasdair Pitt Graham, of the Bahamas; 1 s (John b 1977), 1 da (Suzanna b 1979); *Career* law apprentice/asst slr W & J Burness, WS Edinburgh; slr with Ivory & Sime Edinburgh, co sec Oil Exploration (Holdings) Ltd 1974–79, corp devpt dir LASMO plc 1986–94, gp gen mangr Business Devpt BHP Petroleum Ltd 1995–; memb Bd Sidro SA 1990–; *Recreations* sheep breeding; *Clubs* Puffins; *Style*— Norman Davidson Kelly, Esq; ✉ Little Boarhunt, Liphook, Hants GU30 7EE; BHP Petroleum Ltd, Devonshire House, Piccadilly, London W1X 6AQ (☎ 0171 499 9555); 120 Collins Street, Melbourne, Victoria 3000, Australia (☎ 00 61 3 9652 6666)

DAVIE, *see:* Ferguson Davie

DAVIE, Alan; CBE (1972); *b* 28 Sept 1920; *Educ* Edinburgh Coll of Art (DA); *m* 1947, Janet Gaul, 1 da; *Career* painter, poet, musician, silversmith and jeweller; numerous solo and group exhibitions worldwide since 1946 incl: London, Edinburgh, New York, Florida, Arizona, Perth, Delphi, Geneva, Hong Kong, Sweden; solo shows: Paris 1982, 1987 and 1988, ACA Gallery Munich 1994; retrospective exhibitions: Edinburgh Festival and RSA Galleries 1972, Braunschweig and Karlsrhue Germany 1972, SW Arts touring Scotland 1988–89, 54 Years of Paintings (McLellen Galleries Glasgow and Talbot Rice Gallery Univ of Edinburgh) 1992, Bristol RWA Galleries 1992, touring exhibition to Scotland, Brussels, Brazil, Argentina, Columbia, Venezuela, Chile, Mexico, Peru and Costa Rica 1992–94, Barbican London 1993, Ireland Kilkenny Castle (ACA Gallery NY, Bineth Gallery Tel Aviv, Brighton Univ); work included in: Br Painting 1700–1960 (Moscow), Br Painting and Sculpture 1960–70 (Washington), Br Paintings (Hayward Gallery) 1974, 25 years of Br Art (RA London) 1977, Retro Gouaches (Br Cncl Brussels) 1992, Il Mago (Art Gallery & Museum Glasgow) 1993; many works in public collections worldwide; external assessor Art Degrees 1967–; music concerts and broadcasts with Tony Oxley Sextet 1974–75; Monographs Alan Davie (Lund Humphries, 1967 and 1991), Alan Davie: The Quest for the Miraculous (Lund Humphries, 1993); Gregory fell Univ of Leeds, sr fell RCA London; Guthrie Award (Royal Scot Acad Edinburgh) 1942; graphic prizes: Krakow 1966, Ibiza Museum 1976; Best Foreign Painter (VII Bienal de Sao Paulo) 1963, Saltire Award 1977; Hon DLitt: Herriott Watt Univ Edinburgh 1994, Univ of Hertfordshire 1995; HRSA, RWA; *Recreations* sailing, underwater swimming, music; *Style*— Alan Davie, Esq, CBE; ✉ Gamels Studio, Rush Green, Hertford SG13 7SB (☎ 01920 463684, fax 01920 484406)

DAVIE, Jonathan Richard; s of Richard Davie, of Wimbledon, and Anne Christine Margaret, *née* Wilmot; *b* 21 Sept 1946; *Educ* Tonbridge, Univ of Neuchatel; *m* 13 Sept 1986, Belinda Mary, da of Wing Cdr M V Blake; 2 da (Samantha Jane b 4 Jan 1991, Francesca Louise b 23 Aug 1995)); *Career* articled to J Dix Lewis Caesar Duncan & Co (now Robson Rhodes) CAs 1965–69; Wedd Durlacher Mordaunt & Co: joined 1969, memb Stock Exchange 1974, ptnr 1976–86, sr dealing ptnr 1986; main bd dir Barclays de Zoete Wedd Holdings 1986– (md Fixed Income 1986–91), chief exec BZW Global Equities 1991–; FCA (ACA 1970); *Recreations* golf, tennis, skiing; *Clubs* City of London, Queen's, Royal and Ancient, Royal St George's Golf, Prestwick Golf, Berkshire Golf, Sunningdale Golf, Rye Golf; *Style*— Jonathan Davie, Esq; ✉ BZW Securities Ltd, Ebbgate House, 2 Swan Lane, London EC4R 3TS (☎ 0171 623 2323, fax 0171 956 4118)

DAVIE, (Stephen) Rex; CB (1993); s of Sydney Charles Davie (d 1986); *b* 11 June 1933; *Educ* Ilfracombe GS; *m* Sept 1955, Christine; 1 s (Stephen Mark), 1 da (Ruth Nicola); *Career* exec offr Inland Revenue 1951, Office of Minister for Science 1962, NEDO 1967, Civil Serv Dept 1970, asst sec 1979, sr sec Security Cmmn 1979–89, under sec Cabinet Office 1989–93 (joined 1983), head Working Party on CPS and SFO 1994–95; memb: Cncl on Tbnls 1995–, Civil Serv Appeal Bd 1995–; vice chm Inst of Cancer Research 1995– (memb Cncl 1993–); *Recreations* reading, travel, gardening; *Clubs* Athenaeum, Civil Service; *Style*— Rex Davie, Esq, CB; ✉ 2 Linnet Close, Basingstoke, Hants RG22 5PD (☎ 01256 27851, fax 01256 814576)

DAVIE, Dr Ronald; s of Thomas Edgar Davie (d 1956), and Gladys May, *née* Powell; *b* 25 Nov 1929; *Educ* King Edward VI GS Aston Birmingham, Univ of Reading (BA), Univ of Manchester (CertEd, Dip in Teaching the Deaf), Univ of Birmingham (Dip in Educnl Psychology), Univ of London (PhD); *m* 3 Aug 1957, Kathleen, da of William Wilkinson (d 1976); 1 s (Neil Adrian John b 1961), 1 da (Alison Catherine (Mrs Gray) b 1960); *Career* educnl and child psychologist; county educnl psychologist Isle of Wight 1961–64, co-dir Nat Child Devpt Study 1968–71, dep dir and dir of res Nat Children's Bureau 1972–73 (princ res offr 1965–68), prof of educnl psychology Univ Coll Cardiff 1974–81, dir Nat Children's Bureau 1982–90, consulting psychologist 1990–, visiting prof Oxford Poly 1991–, hon res fell UCL 1991–, visiting fell Univ of Newcastle upon Tyne; chm Policy Ctee Nat Assoc for Special Educn Needs, patron Action for Special Educnl Needs, vice pres Young Minds, memb Cncl Caldecott Community; Hon DEd, FBPsS, hon memb BPA; FRSA; *Books* 11,000 Seven-Year-olds (1966), Living with Handicap (1970), From Birth To Seven (1972), Children Appearing Before Juvenile Courts (1977), Change in Secondary Schools (1985), Child Sexual Abuse: The Way Forward After Cleveland (1989), Listening to Children in Education (1996), The Voice of the Child (1996); *Recreations* photography, antiques, calligraphy; *Style*— Dr Ronald Davie; ✉ Bridge House, Upton, Caldbeck, Cumbria CA7 8EU (☎ 016974 78364)

DAVIES, Prof Alan; *b* 17 Feb 1931; *Educ* Corpus Christi Coll Oxford (MA), Dept of Educn Univ of Oxford (DipEd), Univ of Birmingham (PhD), Univ of Edinburgh (Dip Gen Linguistics); *Career* English teacher various English and African schs 1955–62, sr res assoc Univ of Birmingham 1962–65; Univ of Edinburgh: lectr 1965–72, sr lectr 1972–85, co-dir Inst for Applied Language Studies 1979–85, head Dept of Applied Linguistics 1985–90 and 1993–94, reader 1985–92, prof 1992–, head Planning and Budgetary Unit 1992–94; seconded as prof of English Tribhuvan Univ Kathmandu 1969–71; Univ of Melbourne: visiting prof Dept of Linguistics and Language Studies and dir Language Testing Centre Nat Languages and Literacy Inst of Australia 1990–91; co-ed: Applied Linguistics 1984–89, Language Testing 1992–; chm Br Assoc of Applied Linguistics 1976–79, sec gen Assoc Internationale de Linguistique Appliquée 1978–81; memb: Br Assoc of Applied Linguistics, Australian Assoc of Applied Linguistics; *Books* Principles of Language Testing (1990), The Native Speaker in Applied Linguistics (1991), author of over 100 book chapters, articles and reviews; *Style*— Prof Alan Davies; ✉ Department of Applied Linguistics, University of Edinburgh, 14 Buccleuch Place, Edinburgh EH8 9LN (☎ 0131 650 3497, fax 0131 650 6526)

DAVIES, Air Marshal Sir Alan Cyril; KCB (1979, CB 1974), CBE (1967); s of Richard Davies, of Maidstone; *b* 31 March 1924; *m* 1949, Julia Elizabeth Ghislaine, da of James Russell, of Forres; 2 s (and 1 s decd); *Career* joined RAF 1941, cmmnd 1943, cmd Jt Anti-Submarine Sch Flight 1952–54, cmd Air Sea Warfare Devpt Unit 1958–59, cmd No 201 Sqdn 1959–61, Air Warfare Coll 1962, dep dir Operational Requirements MOD 1964–66, cmd RAF Stradishall Suffolk 1967–68, dir Air Plans MOD 1969–72, asst Chief of Air Staff MOD 1972–74, dep COS HQ Allied Air Forces Central Europe 1974–77, dep C-in-C RAF Strike Command 1977, dir Int Mil Staff NATO Brussels 1978–81, head RAF Support Area Economy Review Team 1981–83; co-ordinator Anglo/American Rels MOD 1984–94; Corps of Commissionaires: dir 1984–89, chm 1989–91, pres 1993–94; *Clubs* RAF; *Style*— Air Marshal Sir Alan Davies, KCB, CBE; ✉ 10 Crispin Close, Caversham, Berks RG4 7JS

DAVIES, Dr Alun Grier; CBE (1980); s of Thomas Davies (d 1957), of Beth-Horon, Penygroes, Llanelli, and Sarah Ann, *née* Edwards (d 1978); *b* 16 Sept 1914; *Educ* Amman Valley GS, Univ of Wales Aberystwyth (BA); *m* 29 June 1940, Claudia Eleanor, da of John Evans (d 1948), of Penygraig, Aberdyfi, Gwynedd; 1 s (Gareth); *Career* called to the Bar Gray's Inn 1945, HM inspr of taxes Inland Revenue 1936–47, taxation controller Consolidated Zinc Corp 1947–65, exec dir RTZ Corporation plc 1965–79, int conslt 1979–87; Univ of Wales: memb Ct 1980–, memb Audit Ctee 1990–93; Univ of Wales Aberystwyth: memb Ct 1973–, memb Cncl 1974–, hon treas Cncl 1980–91, memb Audit Ctee 1990–; memb Central Fin Bd Methodist Church 1960–88, memb Bd Int Bureau of Fiscal Documentation Amsterdam 1975–88; pres: Christian Assoc of Business Execs 1977–82, Int Fiscal Assoc 1979–83 (hon pres 1993–); cncl memb: IOD 1966–84, CBI 1970–73; chm of Tax Ctees: IOD 1965–78, CBI 1970–73; Freeman City of London 1975, Liveryman Worshipful Co of Loriners 1975; Hon LLD Univ of Wales 1991; fell Univ of Wales Aberystwyth 1996; FInstD, FTII; *Books* Man the World Over (1947), Render unto Caesar (1966); *Recreations* wine tasting, freelance journalism; *Clubs* Reform; *Style*— Dr Alun G Davies, CBE; ✉ 7 Craigleith, 41 Grove Rd, Beaconsfield, Bucks HP9 1PT (☎ 01494 671 601); The Toft, Aberdyfi, Gwynedd LL35 0PY (☎ 01654 767463)

DAVIES, Sir Alun Talfan; kt (1976), QC (1961); s of Rev William Talfan Davies, of Gorseinon, Swansea; *b* 22 July 1913; *Educ* Gowerton GS, University Coll of Wales Aberystwyth (LLB), Gonville and Caius Coll Cambridge (MA, LLB); *m* 1942, Eiluned Christopher, da of Humphrey R Williams, of Stanmore, Middx; 1 s, 3 da; *Career* called to the Bar Gray's Inn 1939, bencher 1969; recorder of: Merthyr Tydfil 1963–68, Swansea 1968–69, Cardiff 1969–71; a recorder of the Crown Court 1972–86, hon recorder of Cardiff 1972–86, judge of Court of Appeal Jersey and Guernsey 1969–83; memb Criminal Injuries Compensation Bd 1976–85; pres: Royal Nat Eisteddfod of Wales 1979–82, Ct Welsh Nat Opera 1978–1981, Welsh Centre of Int Affrs 1986–90; chm Bank of Wales 1991– (dep chm 1973–91, dir 1971–73), former vice chm HTV Group Ltd (also chm Welsh Bd); chm Tstees Aberfan Fund 1967–90; hon professorial fell UCW Aberystwyth 1971, hon fell Trinity Coll Carmarthen, Hon LLD UCW (Aberystwyth) 1973; *Style*— Sir Alun Davies, QC; ✉ 10 Park Road, Penarth, S Glamorgan (☎ 01222 701341)

DAVIES, Prof Alwyn George; s of Rev John Lewis Davies (d 1986), of Hunstanton, Norfolk, and Victoria May, *née* Rowe; *b* 1926; *Educ* Hamonds GS Swaffham Norfolk, UCL (BSc, PhD, DSc); *m* 11 Aug 1956, Margaret, da of Geoffrey Drake (d 1980), of Menai Bridge, Anglesey; 1 s (Stephen b 1960), 1 da (Sarah b 1958); *Career* lectr Battersea Poly 1949, prof of chemistry UCL 1969– (lectr 1953, reader 1964); fell UCL 1991; FRSC; FRS 1989; *Books* Organic Peroxides (1961); *Style*— Prof Alwyn Davies, FRS; ✉ 26 South Approach, Moor Park, Northwood, Middx HA6 2ET (☎ 01923 823528); Chemistry Department, UCL, 20 Gordon Street, London WC1H 0AJ (☎ 0171 387 7050, fax 0171 380 7463, e-mail a.g.davies@ucl.ac.uk)

DAVIES, Andrew Wynford; *b* 20 Sept 1936; *Educ* Whitchurch GS Cardiff, UCL; *m* 1960; *Career* author, screenwriter and playwright; *Awards* Guardian Children's Fiction Award 1979, Boston Globe Horn Award 1979, Broadcasting Press Guild Award 1980 and 1990, Pye Colour TV Award Best Children's Writer 1981, RTS Writer's Award 1986 and 1987, BAFTA Writer's Award 1989, Primetime Emmy Award 1991, Writers' Guild Award 1991, BAFTA Award 1993, Hon DLitt Univ of Coventry 1994; *Television* scripts/adaptations: To Serve Them All My Days 1979 (from R F Delderfield novel, BBC1), A Very Peculiar Practice 1986–87, Mother Love 1989, House of Cards (from

Michael Dobbs novel) 1990, Filipina Dreamers 1991, The Old Devils (from Kingsley Amis novel) 1992, Anglo-Saxon Attitudes 1992, A Very Polish Practice 1992, To Play the King (Michael Dobbs, BBC1) 1993, Middlemarch (from Jane Austen novel, BBC1) 1994, Pride and Prejudice (Jane Austen, BBC1) 1995, Game On (with Bernadette Davis) 1995, The Final Cut (Michael Dobbs, BBC1) 1995, Daniel Deronda (from George Eliot novel, BBC) 1996, Emma (Jane Austen, ITV) 1996, Wilderness (with Bernadette Davis) 1996, Moll Flanders (Defoe, ITV) 1996; *Stage Plays* Rose 1981, Prin 1990; *Films* Circle of Friends 1995; *Fiction* A Very Peculiar Practice (1986), The New Frontier (1987), Getting Hurt (1989), Dirty Faxes (1990), B Monkey (1992); *Children's books* The Fantastic Feats of Dr Boox (1972), Conrad's War (1978), Marmalade and Rufus (1981), Marmalade Atkins in Space (1981), Educating Marmalade (1982), Danger Marmalade at Work (1983), Marmalade Hits the Big Time (1984), Alfonso Bonzo (1987), Poonam's Pets (with Diana Davies, 1990), Marmalade on the Ball (1995); *Recreations* tennis, food, alcohol; *Style—* Andrew Davies, Esq; ✉ c/o The Agency, 24 Pottery Lane, London W11 4LZ (☎ 0171 727 1346, fax 0171 727 9037)

DAVIES, Anna Elbina; *see:* Morpurgo Davies, Prof Anna

DAVIES, Rear Adm Anthony; CB (1964), CVO (1972); s of James Arthur Davies (d 1939), and Margaret Davies (d 1971); *b* 13 June 1912; *Educ* RNC Dartmouth, Open Univ (BA); *m* 1940, Lilian Hilda Margaret (d 1980), da of Sir Harold Martin Burrough, GCB, KBE, DSO (d 1977); 2 s, 2 da; *Career* joined RN 1926, dep dir RN Staff Coll 1956–57, Far East Fleet Staff 1957–59, dep dir Naval Intelligence 1959–62, head Br Def Liaison Staff Canberra Australia 1963–65; warden St George's House Windsor Castle 1966–72; *Style—* Rear Adm Anthony Davies, CB, CVO; ✉ 11A South St, Aldbourne, Marlborough, Wilts (☎ 01672 540418)

DAVIES, Ven (Vincent) Anthony (Tony); s of Vincent Davies, of Knighton, Leicester, and Maud Mary Cecilia, *née* Hackett; *b* 15 Sept 1946; *Educ* Green Lane Boys' Secdy Modern, Charles Keene Coll Leicester, Brasted Place Theol Coll, St Michael's Theol Coll Llandaff; *Career* Walkers (Organ Builders) Ltd 1961, Messrs Pearce & Son jewellers Leicester 1962–63, Furse (Wholesale) Electrical Ltd Leicester 1963–67, works study offr Leicester Mercury 1967–69, Theol Coll 1969–73, curate St James Owton Manor (Dio of Durham) 1973–76, curate St Faith Wandsworth (Dio of Southwark) 1976–78 (vicar 1978–81), vicar St John Walworth 1981–94, rural dean of Southwark and Newington 1988–93, archdeacon of Croydon and canon of Southwark Cathedral 1994–; *Recreations* swimming, walking, architecture, history, Italy; *Style—* The Ven the Archdeacon of Croydon; ✉ Croydon Area Episcopal Office, St Matthew's House, 100 George Street, Croydon, Surrey CR0 1PE (☎ 0181 681 5496, fax 0181 686 2074)

DAVIES, Capt Eur Ing Anthony John (Taff); s of Albert Joseph Davies, of Metheringham, Lincs, and Gladys, *née* Blackbourn; *b* 29 Oct 1936; *Educ* Minster Sch Southwell; RNCs: Dartmouth, Manadon, Greenwich; *m* 12 Sept 1959, Mary Josephine, da of Leonard John Crook (d 1983), of Paignton, Devon; 2 s (Timothy John Peter b 1964, Roderick James Lindsay b 1967); *Career* RN: joined 1953, Cdr 1972, Capt 1979, fleet weapon engr offr 1981–83, RCDS 1984, dir ship refitting policy MOD(N) 1985–87, Capt HMS Collingwood 1987–88; md Davies Management Ltd 1989–; sr conslt: ICS (UK) Ltd 1996–, McGraw Consultancy Malaysia; dir: Sussex Training (West), Sussex Downs Enterprise Agency; memb Sussex Enterprise; cncllr East Wittering Ward Chichester DC 1991– (memb various ctees); memb Ct Univ of Sussex; memb American Soc for Quality Control; CEng, FIMarE 1977, FIEE 1980, FIMgt 1985, Eur Ing, FEANI 1990, FIQA 1994; *Recreations* walking, sailing, golf; *Clubs* RN Sailing Assoc, West Wittering Sailing, Batti-Wallah's Soc, RN Royal Marines Mountaineering, Goodwood Golf; *Style—* Capt Eur Ing Taff Davies, RN; ✉ North House, Chapel Lane, West Wittering, Chichester, West Sussex PO20 8QG (☎ 01243 513414, fax 01243 511373, mobile 0831 491166)

DAVIES, Barry; *b* 24 Oct 1940; *Educ* Cranbrook Sch Kent, Univ of London; *m* Penny; 1 da (Giselle), 1 s (Mark); *Career* sports broadcaster; cmmnd RASC (broadcaster Br Forces Network Cologne) 1962; with BBC Radio and corr The Times 1963–66; joined ITV (first TV football commentary Chelsea vs AC Milan 1966), covered 1966 World Cup and 1968 Olympic Games; joined BBC 1969; has covered Olympic Games, World Cup, Cwlth Games and Wimbledon; sports commentated and presented: football, tennis, boat race, hockey, ice hockey, ice skating, badminton, gymnastics, water skiing, cycling and volleyball; presenter Maestro (series, BBC); *Style—* Barry Davies, Esq; ✉ c/o Geoffrey Irvine, API Personality Management Ltd, 141–143 Drury Lane, London WC2B 5TB (☎ 0171 379 4625, fax 0171 836 1735)

DAVIES, Dr Bethan; da of Ben Davies (d 1980), of Gravesend, Kent, and Enid, *née* Thickens (d 1974); *b* 15 Sept 1927; *Educ* GS for Girls Gravesend, UCL W London Hosp Med Sch (MRCS, LRCP), Univ of Manchester (MEd); *m* 1, 8 April 1950 (m dis 1965), Ralph Schwiller, s of Isidore Schwiller (d 1956), of London; 1 s (John b 28 Oct 1953); m 2, 6 Sept 1986, Prof (Henry John) Valentine Tyrrell; *Career* CMO and SC MO Southampton 1960–72; conslt in audiological med: Charing Cross Hosp 1974–93, Cromwell Hosp 1984–; pres W London branch NDCS, jt pres BACDA; memb: BSA, BAAP; hon FCPCH; *Recreations* book collecting (antiquarian children's); *Style—* Dr Bethan Davies; ✉ Fair Oaks, Coombe Hill Rd, Kingston on Thames, Surrey KT2 7DU (☎ 0181 949 6623)

DAVIES, Betty Alicia; JP (Nottingham 1971); da of Charles William Pearl (d 1975), of Nottingham, and Alice, *née* Stevenson; *Educ* Haywood Sch Nottingham, Guildhall Sch of Music and Drama (LGSM); *m* 3 April 1954, Barry Douglass Davies, s of Cecil Vivien Davies (d 1972), of Bidston, Cheshire; *Career* fashion/textile designer and mktg and mgmnt conslt; princ: Betty Davies Scottish Fashion International 1990– (design and project mgmnt of ceremonial and corp wear); public memb Press Cncl 1983–90; memb Ct Univ of Nottingham, memb Bd of Govrs Nottingham Girls HS 1987–94, govr Edinburgh Coll of Art 1989–; chm Nottingham Cncl for Voluntary Serv 1981–84; winner Scottish Style award 1989; MIMgt 1982; *Recreations* musical, theatrical, collecting paintings of contemporary woman artists, seal watching; *Style—* Mrs Betty Davies, JP; ✉ Baileys Garden, Nottingham NG3 5BW (☎ 0115 960 4412); 53 George Street, Edinburgh EH2 2HT (☎ 0131 220 2755, fax 0131 220 1008); North Cottage, Woodstock, Oxon (☎ 01993 811321)

DAVIES, Prof (John) Brian; s of John Kendrick Davies (d 1966), and Agnes Ada Davies (d 1971); *b* 2 May 1932; *Educ* Univ of Cambridge (MA), Univ of London (MSc, PhD, DSc); *m* 11 Aug 1956, Shirley June, da of Frederick Ralph Abrahart; 1 s (Jeremy b 1960), 2 da (Fiona b 1961, Nicola b 1970); *Career* res scientist Mullard Res Laboratories 1955–63, lectr Univ of Sheffield 1963–67; Univ Coll London: sr lectr 1967–70, reader 1970–85, prof 1985–, dean of engrg 1989–91; FIEE 1982, FEng 1988, FIEEE 1995; *Books* Electromagnetic Theory (vol 2, 1972); *Recreations* cross country skiing, music, mountaineering; *Style—* Prof Brian Davies, FEng; ✉ 14 Gaveston Drive, Berkhamsted, Herts HP4 1JE (☎ 01442 864954); Department of Electrical Engineering, University College, Torrington Place, London WC1E 7JE (☎ 0171 387 7050, fax 0171 387 4350, telex 296273)

DAVIES, Air Vice-Marshal (David) Brian Arthur Llewelyn; s of Cyril Graham Vincent Davies (d 1978), of Dyfed, and Iris Ann Thomas; *b* 4 Feb 1932; *Educ* UCL, Univ Coll Hosp Med Sch (BSc, MB BS); *m* 24 May 1958, Jean Mary, da of Edwin Rupert Goate (d 1978), of Beccles, Suffolk; 2 s (Christopher b 1959, Nicholas b 1961); *Career* dep dir of med personnel Miny of Def 1980–82, OC RAF(H) Wegberg W Germany 1982–85, cmdt Central Med Estab 1985–87, dep PMO Strike Cmd 1987–89, PMO RAF Support Cmd 1989–91; QHP 1990–92; memb: BMA, Faculty of Public Health Med; MFOM; *Recreations* skiing, gardening, travel; *Clubs* RAF, RSM; *Style—* Air Vice-Marshal Brian Davies, RAF (ret); ✉ c/o Royal Bank of Scotland, 127–128 High Holborn, London WC1

DAVIES, Brigid Catherine; *see:* Gardner, Brigid Catherine

DAVIES, Bryan; MP (Lab) Oldham Central and Royton (majority 8,606); s of George William Davies (d 1989), and Beryl Davies; *b* 9 Nov 1939; *Educ* Redditch Co HS, UCL (BA), Inst of Educn LSE (BSc); *m* 1963, Monica Rosemary Mildred, da of Jack Shearing (d 1980); 2 s (Roderick Gareth b 1964, Gordon Huw b 1966), 1 da (Amanda Jane b 1969); *Career* teacher Latymer Sch 1962–65, lectr Middx Poly 1965–74; Parly candidate (Lab) Norfolk Central 1966, MP (Lab) Enfield North Feb 1974–1979, Parly candidate (Lab) Newport West 1983, MP (Lab) Oldham Central and Royton 1992–; sec Parly Lab Pty 1979–92; PPS: to dep PM 1975–76, Dept of Educn 1976, Treasy 1977; Govt whip 1979; memb Select Ctee on: Overseas Devpt 1975–78, Public Expenditure 1975–78, Nat Heritage 1992–93; shadow higher educn min 1993–; memb Med Res Cncl 1977–79; *Recreations* literature, sport; *Style—* Bryan Davies, Esq, MP; ✉ House of Commons, London SW1A 0AA (☎ 0171 219 4064)

DAVIES, Bryn; CBE, DL (Mid Glamorgan 1992); s of Gomer Davies (d 1959), and Annie Mary, *née* Phillips (d 1986); *b* 22 Jan 1932; *Educ* Cwmlai Secdy Sch; *m* 1, 1956 (widowed); 2 s (Nigel b 22 April 1957, Gareth b 5 Jan 1960); m 2, 1991, Kathy Davies; *Career* Nat Serv RAMC; trade union official Agric Workers' Union 1956–91, chm Mid Glamorgan HA 1978–94; chm Rhondda/Taff Ely Macmillan Fund Cancer Relief Appeal (hon life memb); vice chm Princess of Wales Hosp Scanner Appeal, tstee Heart Res Inst Appeal; *Recreations* golf, gardening, watching rugby; *Clubs* Pyle RFC (vice pres), Bridgend RFC (patron), Pyle and Kenfie Golf; *Style—* Bryn Davies, Esq, CBE, DL; ✉ 3 Lias Cottages, Porthcawl, Mid Glamorgan (☎ 01656 785851)

DAVIES, Chris; MP (Lib Dem) Littleborough and Saddleworth (majority 1,993); *b* 7 July 1954; *Educ* Cheadle Hulme Sch Stockport, Gonville and Caius Coll Cambridge (MA), Univ of Kent at Canterbury; *m* 27 Oct 1979, Carol; 1 da; *Career* chm Housing Liverpool City Cncl 1982–83, marketing and communications conslt 1983–95, MP (Lib Dem) Littleborough and Saddleworth 1995–; *Recreations* fell running; *Style—* Chris Davies, Esq, MP; ✉ 4 Higher Kinders, Greenfield, Oldham OL3 7BH (☎ 0161 628 4778); House of Commons, London SW1A 0AA (☎ 0171 219 5877)

DAVIES, Dr Christopher (Chris); s of William Alfred Davies (decd), and Rose Phoebe, *née* Beaupré; *b* 4 Oct 1946, Derby; *Educ* Forest Fields GS, Univ of Manchester (BSc, PhD); *m* 1984 (sep), Jean Margaret, *née* Fletcher; 1 s (Paul Alexander b 2 Sept 1973), 2 da (Jennifer Eiriann b 11 March 1977, Rosanne Lucy b 27 Aug 1981); *Career* Cambridge Consultants Ltd: engr analogue electronics 1972–77, gp ldr Communications and Processing Gp 1977–85, ops mangr Physics and Electronic Technol Business Unit 1985–88, dir Electronics Div 1988–94, dir Product Devpt Business Unit 1994–; *Recreations* windsurfing, reading, people-watching; *Clubs* Graffham Water Sailing; *Style—* Dr Chris Davies; ✉ Cambridge Consultants Ltd, Science Park, Milton Road, Cambridge CB4 4DW (☎ 01223 420024, fax 01223 423373, e-mail Christopher.Davies@camcon.co.uk)

DAVIES, Colin Godfrey; *b* 1934; *Educ* Kings Sch Bruton, Loughborough Univ of Technology (BSc); m; 2 s; *Career* cmnd offr RAF 1952–54; bank official National Provincial Bank 1951–55; Cable and Wireless plc: technician rising to sr mangr commercial and technical fields 1955–77, chief engr Long Distance Servs Abu Dhabi 1978–79, mangr Int Servs Qatar 1980–82, general mangr Qatar 1983–87, dir of Corp Technol 1988–90; DG Projects and Engrg CAA 1990–; CEng, FIEE, FRAeS; *Recreations* sport; *Style—* Colin Davies, Esq; ✉ National Air Traffic Services, CAA House, 45–59 Kingsway, London WC2B 6TE (☎ 0171 832 5776, fax 0171 832 6478)

DAVIES, Cyril James; CBE, DL; s of James Davies (d 1967), of Newcastle-upon-Tyne, and Frances Charlotte, *née* Baker (d 1960); *b* 24 Aug 1923; *Educ* Heaton GS Newcastle-upon-Tyne; *m* Elizabeth Hay Leggett, da of James William Hay (d 1954), of Newcastle; 2 s (Nigel b 1950, Chistopher b 1954), 2 da (Elizabeth b 1952, Julia b 1958); *Career* WWII Lt (A) RNVR Fleet Air RN 1942–46; city treas: Newcastle upon Tyne 1969–74, Tyne and Wear 1974–80; chief exec City of Newcastle-upon-Tyne 1980–86; memb Newcastle Univ Cncl; dir: Theatre Royal Tst, Arts Marketing, Peoples Theatre; tstee: William Leech Charity, Rothley Charity; treas Heaton Methodist Church; *Recreations* gardening, music, theatre, walking; *Style—* Cyril Davies, Esq, CBE, DL; ✉ 36 Lindisfarne Close, Jesmond, Newcastle-upon-Tyne NE2 2HT (☎ 0191 281 5870)

DAVIES, 3 Baron (UK 1932), of Llandinam, Co Montgomery; David Davies; s of 2 Baron Davies (ka 1944), by his w, Ruth Eldrydd (d 1966), da of Maj W M Dugdale, CB, DSO, of Glanyrafon Hall, Llanyblodwell, Shropshire; *b* 2 Oct 1940; *Educ* Eton, King's Coll Cambridge; *m* 1972, Beryl, da of W J Oliver; 2 s (Hon David Daniel, Hon Benjamin Michael Graham b 7 July 1985), 2 da (Hon Eldrydd Jane b 1973, Hon Lucy b 1978); *Heir* s, Hon David Daniel Davies b 23 Oct 1975; *Career* chm Welsh National Opera Co 1975–; CEng, MICE; *Style—* The Rt Hon the Lord Davies; ✉ Plas Dinam, Llandinam, Powys

DAVIES, Dr David Denison; s of Samuel Davies (d 1958), and Ethel Mary, *née* Dennison (d 1980); *Educ* Salt GS, Univ of Leeds (MRCS, LRCP), Univ of London (PhD); *m* 26 Feb 1977, Kay; 1 s (Edward b 1978), 1 da (Philippa b 1980); *Career* res fell Anaesthetics Res Dept RCS London 1967–70, conslt anaesthetist Central Middx Hosp London 1970–; memb: Anaesthetic Res Soc, Pain Soc; author of numerous publications on gas chromatography, pharmacokinetics of anaesthetic agents, morbidity and mortality in anaesthesia and pain therapy; FRCA, FRSM; *Books* Gas Chromatography in Anaesthesia: Thesis (1975); *Recreations* history, painting, traditional jazz; *Style—* Dr David Denison Davies; ✉ 10 Beaufort Place, Bray, Maidenhead, Berks SL6 2BS (☎ 01628 71003); Dept of Anaesthetics, Central Middx Hosp, Acton Lane, London NW10 7NS (☎ 0181 965 5733)

DAVIES, Prof Sir David Evan Naunton; kt (1994), CBE (1986); s of David Evan Davies (d 1935), and Sarah, *née* Samuel (d 1982); *b* 28 Oct 1935; *Educ* West Monmouth Sch, Univ of Birmingham (MSc, PhD, DSc); *m* 1, 21 July 1962, Enid (d 1990), da of James Edwin Patilla; 2 s (Christopher James b 1965, Michael Evan b 1967); m 2, 19 Nov 1992, Jennifer Eason Rayner; *Career* lectr and sr lectr Univ of Birmingham 1961–67, hon sr princ sci offr Royal Radar Estab Malvern 1966–67, asst dir Res Dept BR Derby 1967–71, vice provost UCL 1986–88 (prof of electrical engrg 1971–86), vice-chllr Loughborough Univ of Technol 1988–Sept 1993, chief scientific advsr MOD Sept 1993–; pres Royal Acad of Engrg 1996–; memb and chm of numerous ctees of: MOD, DES, Cabinet Office; Rank Prize for Optoelectronics 1984, Callendar Medal (Inst of Measurement and Control) 1984, Centennial Medal (Inst of Electrical and Electronic Engrs USA) 1984, Faraday Medal (IEE) 1987; Hon DSc: Univ of Loughborough 1994, Univ of Bradford 1995; Hon DEng: Univ of Birmingham 1994, South Bank Univ 1994; FIEE 1967, FEng 1979, FRS 1984; author of over 150 publications mainly concerned with radar and fibre optics; *Style—* Prof Sir David Davies, CBE, FRS, FEng; ✉ Church Hill House, Church Lane, Danehill, Sussex RH17 7EY; 5 Prince Regent Mews, Netley Street, London NW1; Chief Scientific Adviser, Ministry of Defence, Main Building, Whitehall, London SW1A 2HB (☎ 0171 218 9000)

DAVIES, Sir David Henry; kt (1973); s of David Henry Davies; *b* 2 Dec 1909; *Educ* Brierley Hill Sch Ebbw Vale; *m* 1934, Elsie May, da of Joseph Battrick; 1 s, 1 da (and 1 da decd); *Career* gen sec Iron & Steel Trades Confedn 1967–75 (asst gen sec 1953–66); hon sec Br Section Int Metalworkers' Fedn 1960–75, hon treas Br Lab Party 1965–67 (chm 1963), vice chm Nat Dock Labour Bd 1966–68, chm Euro Coal and Steel Community Consultative Ctee 1973; memb: Gen Cncl TUC 1967–75, English Industl Estates Corp 1971–75, Industl Arbitration Bd 1974; first chm Welsh Devpt Agency 1976–79; *Style—* Sir David Davies; ✉ 82 New House Park, St Albans, Herts (☎ 01727 856513)

DAVIES, David Johnston; s of John Edwardes Davies (d 1948), and Margaret Frances, *née* Morrison; *b* 28 May 1948; *Educ* Royal Masonic Sch for Boys, Univ of Sheffield (BA(Econ)), Univ of Oxford (CertEd); *m* July 1977, Susan Anne, *née* Cuff; 2 da (Amanda Jane b March 1980, Caroline Frances b April 1983); *Career* Thomson Regional Newspapers (Belfast Telegraph) 1970–71, BBC corr and presenter 1971–94 (variously BBC TV News political corr, BBC TV News educn corr, presenter/corr Grandstand and Match of the Day, assignments incl General Elections and World Cups), dir public affrs Football Association 1994–; memb: RTS 1985–, Football Writers Assoc 1990–; Duke of Edinburgh's Gold Award 1965, Clear Speaking Award Birmingham Inst for the Deaf 1993; *Recreations* family, watching cricket, tennis, theatre; *Clubs* Lancashire CCC; *Style—* David Davies, Esq; ✉ The Football Association, 16 Lancaster Gate, London W2 3LW (☎ 0171 314 5264)

DAVIES, David Michael (Dai); *b* 10 June 1947; *Educ* St Bartholomew's Hosp (MB BS, MRCS, LRCP, cert for higher educn surgical trg in plastic surgery); *m* 3 c; *Career* conslt plastic surgn; house physician Bart's London 1971, sr house offr Birmingham Accident Hosp 1972, lectr Dept of Anatomy Bart's Med Sch 1973, sr house offr Bart's 1973–74, registrar gen surgery and orthopaedics St Albans City Hosp 1974–76, plastic surgery Queen Victoria Hosp East Grinstead 1976–78 (Burns res fell and hon sr registrar 1976–77), registrar NE Thames Regnl Plastic Surgery Unit St Andrew's Hosp Billericay 1978–79, sr registrar Dept of Plastic Surgery Frenchay Hosp Bristol 1979–81, overseas visiting fell in microsurgery Royal Melbourne Hosp 1979–81; conslt plastic surgn: W Middx Univ Hosp Isleworth 1981–88, Hammersmith Hosp 1981– (also hon sr lectr), St Mary's Hosp 1987–, Charing Cross Hosp Fulham 1988– (also hon sr lectr); teacher Univ of London 1985–; pres Plastic Surgical Section RSM 1996 (sec 1985–86), sec NW Thames Advsy Ctee on Plastic Surgery 1988–90; former ed plastic surgery section of Surgery jl 1987–93; memb: BMA, Br Assoc of Plastic Surgns, Br Assoc of Aesthetic Plastic Surgns (memb Cncl 1988–90, archivist 1989, sec 1990–93), Br Microsurgical Soc (sec 1984), Assoc of Head & Neck Oncologists of GB, Joseph Soc (Euro Acad of Facial Surgery), Examiners of Royal Coll of Surgns; Thackray scholar in microvascular surgery (Br Assoc of Plastic Surgns) 1978; FRCS 1975, FRSM; *Books* ABC of Plastic Surgery (1985), Safe Cosmetic Surgery (1996); author of numerous papers in Br Jl of Surgery, Br Med Jl and Br Jl of Plastic Surgery; *Style—* Dai Davies, Esq; ✉ 55 Harley St, London W1N 1DD (☎ 0171 631 3927, fax 0171 636 6573)

DAVIES, Prof David Protheroe; s of Rev Canon William John Davies (d 1987), and Mary Annie Maureen, *née* Lewis; *b* 19 July 1939; *Educ* Christ Coll Brecon, Corpus Christi Coll Cambridge (MA), CCC Oxford (MA, BD); *m* 1963 (m dis 1992), Brenda Lloyd, da of late William Huw Owen; 1 da (Siwan Eleri b 1972); *Career* ordained: deacon 1964, priest 1965; asst curate St Mary's Swansea 1964–67; St David's Univ Coll Lampeter: lectr 1967–76, sr lectr 1976–86, dean Faculty of Arts 1977–81, dean Faculty of Theology 1981–91 (previously 1975–77), prof of theology 1986–, dep princ 1988–94, pro-vice-chllr 1994–; memb Ct and Cncl Univ of Wales; chm and dir Cwmni'r Gannwyll (ind TV Co), memb Central Religious Advsy Ctee (BBC and IBA); *Books* Yr Efengylau A'r Actau (1978), Diwinyddiaeth Ar Waith (1984), Against the Tide (1995); *Recreations* sport, acting; *Style—* Prof D P Davies; ✉ Rhiw, Maesycrugiau, Pencader, Dyfed SA39 9LG (☎ 01559 395252); Department of Theology and Religious Studies, University of Wales, Lampeter, Dyfed SA48 1ED (☎ 01570 424708, fax 01570 423641, telex 48475)

DAVIES, Rt Hon (David John) Denzil; PC (1978), MP (Lab) Llanelli (majority 19,270); s of G Davies; *b* 9 Oct 1938; *Educ* Queen Elizabeth GS Carmarthen, Pembroke Coll Oxford; *m* 1963, Mary Ann Finlay, of Illinois; 1 s, 1 da; *Career* lectr Univ of Chicago 1963, lectr in law Univ of Leeds 1964; called to the Bar Gray's Inn 1964; MP (Lab) Llanelli 1970–, memb Public Accounts Ctee, PPS to Sec of State for Wales 1974–76, min of state Treasury 1976–79; oppn front bench spokesman on: Treasury matters 1979–81, defence and disarmamemt 1981–88; shadow Welsh sec 1983, chief opposition spokesman on defence 1985–88 (resigned); *Style—* The Rt Hon Denzil Davies, MP; ✉ House of Commons, London SW1A 0AA (☎ 0171 219 5197)

DAVIES, Derek; s of John Davies (d 1965), and Alice, *née* Heap (d 1996); *b* 27 Oct 1933; *Educ* Bolton Sch, Trinity Hall Cambridge (MA, MB BChir); *m* 2 May 1959, Barbara Jean, da of William Helsby (d 1969); 2 s (Christopher b 1960, Timothy b 1969), 2 da (Alison b 1964, Amanda b 1967 d 1980); *Career* sr med house offr Manchester Royal Infirmary 1960–62 (resident clinical pathologist 1959–60); med registrar: Derbyshire Royal Infirmary 1962–63, UCH 1963–65; lectr then sr lectr in clinical endocrinology Victoria Univ of Manchester 1968–88 (hon conslt 1972–88), conslt physician Manchester Royal Infirmary 1988–95 (med clinical dir 1991–94), chm Clinical Bd Manchester Central Hosps and Community Care NHS Tst 1991–92; ret; pt/t med chm Pensions Appeal Tribunals (England & Wales); FRSM, FRCP, fell Manchester Med Soc; *Style—* Derek Davies, Esq; ✉ 32 Barrow Bridge Rd, Smithills, Bolton, Lancs BL1 7NJ (☎ 01204 847129)

DAVIES, Derek Lewis; CBE (1996); s of Glyndwr Lewis, and Lily May, *née* Jones; *b* 28 Sept 1933; *Educ* Birmingham Central Coll of Tech; *m* 2 Oct 1954, Barbara Joy, da of Charles Barwick; 2 s (Jeremy b 1960, Robert b 1966); *Career* Lt Royal Mil Police 1954–56; GEC: student apprentice Birmingham 1950–54, chief engr Pakistan 1958–62, dir Overseas Servs 1973–81, dir Electrical Projects 1981–86; sales mangr Foster Transformers Ltd 1962–67, sales dir Ottermill Switchgear 1967–73, chm Drake & Scull Holdings plc 1986–89, dir Simon Engineering plc 1987–93, dir Magnolia Group plc 1993–; memb NEDO Airports Ctee 1985, chm UK Airports Gp 1984–86, chm North West Industl Devpt Bd 1989–, chm Stockport Health Cmmn 1994–96; Lt Col The Engr & Tport Staff Corps RE (TA); Freeman Worshipful Co of Feltmakers; FRSA, ARAeS; *Recreations* rugby, golf; *Clubs* Athenaeum, St James's (Manchester); *Style—* Derek Davies, Esq, CBE; ✉ Peartree Cottage, Birdingbury, Warwickshire CV23 8EN (☎ and fax 01926 632325)

DAVIES, Dickie; *b* 30 April 1933; *Educ* Oldershaw GS Wallasey; *m* Liz; 2 s (Daniel and Peter (twins)); *Career* served RAF and Merchant Navy; joined Southern TV as announcer and newsreader 1960, presenter World of Sport (ITV) 1965–85; other programmes presented incl: Olympic Games 1980, Sportsworld, Sun TV Awards, int snooker events, world championship boxing contests, European and World Athletics Championships, World Gymnastics Championships, Jigsaw (one series, Channel 4), Sportsmasters (several series, ITV), The World of Golf (one series, ITV), World Snooker Masters (Sky TV), Panasonic Sports Awards (ITV), Bobby Charlton's Scrapbook (current series for BSkyB), currently sports presenter for Classic FM; guest appearances on: Celebrity Squares, Celebrity Sweepstake, the Russell Harty Show, Saturday Scene, Play It Again, Budgie, Husband of the Year, Look Alive, the Pyramid Game, Mind Your Language, Give Us A Clue, Babble, The Six O'Clock Show, Child's Play and Cluedo; frequent conference presenter and after-dinner speaker; subject of This Is Your Life 1975; *Style—* Dickie Davies, Esq; ✉ c/o API Personality Management, 141–143 Drury Lane, London WC2B 5TB (☎ 0171 379 4625, fax 0171 836 1735)

DAVIES, Donald; CBE (1978, OBE 1973); s of Wilfred Lawson Davies (d 1972), and Alwyne Davies; *b* 13 Feb 1924; *Educ* Ebbw Vale GS, Univ Coll Cardiff (BSc); *m* 1948, Mabel, da of John Henry Hellyar (d 1960); 2 da; *Career* conslt mining engr; memb National Coal Bd 1973–84 (area dir 1967–73); chm: NCB Opencast Exec 1973–83, NCB Ancillaries 1979–87; FIMinE; *Recreations* golf, fishing; *Clubs* RAC; *Style—* Donald Davies, Esq, CBE; ✉ Wendy Cottage, Dukes Wood Ave, Gerrards Cross, Bucks (☎ 01753 885083)

DAVIES, Edward Rodney; *b* 25 May 1955; *Educ* Leeds GS, Univ of Manchester (LLB Hons), Coll of Law, King's Coll London MSc; *m* Juliet; *Career* admitted slr 1982; ptnr specialising in construction and engrg law Masons slrs Manchester 1989–; trained as mediator American Arbitration Assoc (San Francisco); course lectr in construction and engrg law, visiting research fell UMIST; memb: Law Soc 1982, American Arbitration Assoc 1994; *Recreations* walking; *Style—* Edward Davies, Esq; ✉ Masons, World Trade Centre, Exchange Quay, Manchester M5 3EJ (☎ 0161 877 3777, fax 0161 877 6869)

DAVIES, Elsa Myfanwy; da of Mary, *née* Williams; *Educ* Univ of Wales (Teacher's Cert), Open Univ (BA), Univ of London (DipEd, MA); *Career* teacher Glamorgan CC 1965–70, dep head London Borough of Hillingdon 1970–74; head teacher: Surrey CC 1974–83, London Borough of Hillingdon 1983–87; mangr Inst of Management 1988–91, dir National Playing Fields Assoc 1991–; conslt to various bodies incl: Univ of London, Moorhead State Univ Minnesota, Univ of Ulster, Univ of Leicester, Manchester Poly, Brighton Poly, BBC Enterprises, Welsh Consumer Cncl, The Spastics Soc (now Scope), National Foundation for Education and Research, Commission of the European Communities; lectr to various orgns, local authorities and colleges incl: Capita Training, The Engineering Cncl, The Industrial Soc, Surrey, Hants, Essex and Sheffield Local Authys, Univ of Antwerp, Univ of Birmingham, Kingston Poly, Poly of Wales, Mid Kent Coll of HE; memb: Cncl for Nat Academic Awards Educnl Orgn, Mgmnt Bd and Initial Teacher Educn Bd 1985–91, Nat Curriculum Working Gp on Design and Technol 1989–91, Cncl Advsy Centre for Educn 1977–90 (former chm), Cncl British Educnl Mgmnt and Admin Soc 1980–92, ESU 1980– (Page scholar 1981), UK/US Teacher Exchange Ctee Central Bureau for Educnl Visits and Exchanges 1981–92 (former vice chm), Euro Forum for Educn Mgmnt 1981–92, Commonwealth Cncl for Educnl Admin 1981–92, Educn 2000 1983, Court Univ of Wales Coll of Cardiff 1989–92, Organising Ctee Educn Mgmnt Int Intervisitation Prog 1990, Cncl Action for Govrs Info and Trg Sponsorship Ctee 1990–91, Working Gp Human Resource Devpt Partnership 1990–91, Belgravia Breakfast Club 1991–, Lady Taverners 1992–, London Businesswomen's Network 1992–, City of London Sport and Recreation Cncl 1992–94, Shadow Sec of State's Nat Lottery Gp 1996; hon advsr World Educn Fellowship (GB) 1977– (former chm), external examiner Wales Poly 1985–91; FIMgt 1987, FRSA 1989 (memb Examinations Bd Educnl Policy Ctee and chm Advsy Ctee on Initial Educn 1990); author of several chapters and articles in educnl pubns; *Clubs* Westminster Dining, Glamorgan CCC; *Style—* Mrs Elsa Davies; ✉ National Playing Fields Association, 25 Ovington Square, London SW3 1LQ (☎ 0171 584 6445, fax 0171 581 2402)

DAVIES, HE Emrys Thomas; CMG (1987); s of Evan William Davies (d 1954), and Dinah, *née* Jones; *b* 8 Oct 1934; *Educ* Parmiters Fndn Sch London, Sch of Slavonic Studies Cambridge, Sch of Oriental & African Studies London, Inst of Fine Arts Hanoi Univ; *m* 1960, Angela Audrey, da of Paul Robert Buchan May (d 1952); 1 s (Robert), 2 da (Victoria, Elizabeth); *Career* RAF 1953–55; HM Dip Serv: served Peking and Shanghai 1956–59, FO 1959–60, Political Residence Bahrain 1960–62, UN Gen Assembly NY 1962, FO 1962–63, asst political advsr to Hong Kong Govt 1963–68, Br High Cmmn Ottawa 1968–71, FCO 1972–76, commercial cnsllr HM Embassy Peking 1976–78 (in charge 1976 and 1978), Univ of Oxford Business Summer Sch 1977, NATO Defense Coll Rome 1979, dep high cmmr Ottawa 1979–82, Diplomatic Serv overseas inspr 1982–83, dep perm rep to OECD Paris 1984–87, HM ambass Hanoi Vietnam 1987–90, Br high cmmr to Barbados, Antigua and Barbuda, St Kitts and Nevis, Dominica, St Lucia, St Vincent and the Grenadines and Grenada 1991–94, ret; head UK Delgn to the EC Monitoring Mission Zagreb Jan-April 1995, sec gen Tripartite Cmmn for the Restitution of Monetary Gold Brussels June 1995–; *Books* Albigensians and Cathars (trans); *Recreations* golf, theatre, painting, walking; *Clubs* Cwlth Tst, Cambridge Univ Centre, Glamorgan CCC, Bath Golf; *Style—* Emrys Davies, Esq, CMG; ✉ Taringa, 1 Bloomfield Park, Bath BA2 2BY

DAVIES, Frank John; CBE (1993); s of Lt-Col F H Davies (d 1991), of Lincoln, and Veronica Josephine Davies (d 1943); *b* 24 Sept 1931; *Educ* Monmouth Sch, UMIST; *m* 1956, Sheila Margaret, da of Geoffrey Bailey (d 1938), and Frances Bailey (d 1971); 3 s (James, Stephen, Jonathan); *Career* gp chief exec and md Rockware Gp plc 1983–93; dir: BTR Nylex Ltd 1991–94, Ardagh plc, Saltire plc; chm Bardon Group plc 1994–; chm: Nuffield Orthopaedic Centre NHS Tst 1990–, Health and Safety Cmmn 1993–; pres: Glass Mfrs Fedn 1986 and 1987, Fedn Europeene de Verre D'Emballage 1988–89; vice pres St John's Ambulance Oxon 1973–; memb: Oxon Health Authy 1983–91, Cncl CBI 1986–93, Packaging Standards Cncl 1992–93; Freeman: City of London, Worshipful Co of Basketmakers, Worshipful Co of Glass Sellers; OStJ 1987, CIMgt, FRSA; *Recreations* NHS, gardening, music, history, theatre; *Clubs* Carlton, RAC; *Style—* Frank Davies, Esq, CBE; ✉ Stonewalls, Castle Street, Deddington, Oxon OX15 0TE (☎ 01869 338131); c/o Health and Safety Commission, Rose Court, 2 Southwark Bridge, London SE1 9HS

DAVIES, Gareth; CBE (1992); s of Lewis Davies (d 1985), of S Devon, and Margaret Ann, *née* Jones; *b* 13 Feb 1930; *Educ* King Edward's GS Aston Birmingham; *m* 12 Sept 1953, Joan Patricia, da of Edmond Charles Prosser (d 1986), of NZ; 1 s (Mark b 1959); *Career* chm (formerly also gp chief exec) Glynwed International plc and subsidiary cos 1986– (joined 1969); non-exec dir: Midland Independent Newspapers plc 1994–, Lloyd Chemist PLC 1995–; chm Ironbridge Gorge Devpt Tst, memb Bd W Midlands Devpt Agency; Liveryman Worshipful Co of Plumbers; FCA, CIMgt; *Recreations* music, opera; *Style—* Gareth Davies, Esq, CBE; ✉ 4 Beech Gate, Roman Road, Little Aston Park, Sutton Coldfield, W Midlands; Glynwed International plc, Headland House, 54 New Coventry Road, Sheldon, Birmingham B26 3AZ (☎ 0121 742 2366, telex 336608, fax 0121 742 7372)

DAVIES, (David) Gareth; s of John Davies (d 1978), and Annie Ceridwen, *née* Evans (d 1949); *b* 7 Feb 1939; *Educ* Aberdare GS for Boys, Univ of Wales Coll of Cardiff (BA); *m* 1963, Sonia Eileen, da of Harry Ludlow; 1 s (Ioan Geraint b 14 March 1968); *Career* museum asst in charge Chelmsford and Essex Museum 1964–65, asst curator Colchester and Essex Museum 1965–70, dir Verulamium and City Museum St Albans 1970–86, dir Cncl of Museums in Wales 1986–96; advsr Govt Reviewing Ctee for the Export of Works of Art, ctee memb Soc of Museum Archaeologists, councillor at large Museums' Assoc, sec Contemporary Art Soc for Wales, chm Glam/Gwent Archaeological Tst; memb Ct of Govrs Univ Coll Swansea; author of numerous articles and papers; FMA 1979 (AMA 1970), FSA 1978; *Recreations* rugby and cricket (spectator), theatre, reading and music, food and wine, walking; *Style—* Gareth Davies, Esq, FSA; ✉ 1 Court Cottages, Michaelston Road, St Fagans, Cardiff, South Glam CF5 6EN (☎ 01222 595206)

DAVIES, His Hon Judge Gareth Lewis; s of David Edward Davies (d 1960), of Slwch, Bronllys, Brecon, and Glynwen Lewis (d 1992); *b* 8 Sept 1936; *Educ* Brecon Co GS, Univ of Wales (LLB); *m* 1962; 2 da (Sally b 1963, Lucy 1965), 2 s (Simon b 1967, Jonathan b 1967); *Career* qualified slr 1962, ptnr Ottaways St Albans 1965–90, recorder 1983–90, circuit judge (SE Circuit) 1990–; *Recreations* sailing instructor, ski guide, cycling, classic cars; *Style—* His Hon Judge Gareth Davies; ✉ Bronllys Castle, Bronllys, Brecon, Powys LD3 0HL (☎ 01874 711826); St Albans Crown Court, 4 Bricket Road, St Albans, Herts AL1 3HY

DAVIES, (David) Garfield; CBE (1996); s of David John Davies (d 1976), of Bridgend, Glamorgan, and Lizzie Ann, *née* Evans (d 1993); *b* 24 June 1935; *Educ* Heolgam Secdy Modern Bridgend, Bridgend Tech Coll, Port Talbot Sch of Further Educn; *m* 12 March 1960, Marian, da of Raymond Jones, of Trelewis, nr Treharris, Glamorgan; 4 da (Helen Claire b 16 Jan 1961, Susan Karen b 22 May 1962, Karen Jayne b 16 June 1965, Rachel Louise b 24 Jan 1969); *Career* Nat Service Sr Aircraftsman RAF 1956–58; British Steel Corp: jr operative Corp 1950–51, apprentice electrician 1951–56, electrician 1958–69; Union of Shop Distributive and Allied Workers (USDAW): area organiser 1969–73, dep divnl offr 1973–78, nat offr 1978–86, gen sec 1986–; TUC: memb Gen Cncl 1986–, memb Employment Appeal Tribunal 1991–, chm Int Ctee TUC 1992–; cncllr Penybont RDC 1966–69; JP Ipswich 1972–78; *Style*— Garfield Davies, Esq, CBE; ✉ 64 Dairyground Road, Bramhall, Stockport, Cheshire SK7 2QW (☎ 0161 439 9548); Union of Shop, Distributive & Allied Workers, 188 Wilmslow Road, Fallowfield, Manchester M14 6LJ (☎ 0161 224 2804, fax 0161 257 2566)

DAVIES, Gavyn; OBE (1979); s of W J F Davies, of Southampton, and M G Watkins; *b* 27 Nov 1950; *Educ* Taunton's Sch Southampton, St John's Coll Cambridge (BA), Balliol Coll Oxford; *m* 1989, Susan Jane Nye; 1 da (Rosie b 31 Jan 1990), 1 s (Ben b 14 March 1995); *Career* econ advsr Policy Unit 10 Downing St 1974–79, UK economist Phillips and Drew 1979–81; chief UK economist: Simon and Coates 1981–86, Goldman Sachs 1986– (ptnr 1988–); memb HM Treasy independent panel of economic forecasting advisers 1992–; visiting prof LSE 1988–; *Recreations* sport; *Style*— Gavyn Davies, Esq, OBE; ✉ Goldman Sachs, Peterborough Court, 133 Fleet Street, London EC4A 2BB (☎ 0171 774 1000, fax 0171 774 1181)

DAVIES, (John) Geoffrey; s of Leonard Churchman Davies (d 1990), of Cardiff, and Olive Winnifred Davies; *b* 12 May 1942; *Educ* Oundle, Univ of London (BSc(Econ)); *m* 15 July 1978, Penelope Antoinette Jeanne, *née* Cracroft-Rice; 1 s (Benjamin John b 5 Oct 1979); *Career* apprentice then prodn mangr British Ropes 1961–67, mgmnt conslt Inbucon AIC 1968–71, mangr Messrs Man Judd 1975–76 (articled clerk 1971–74); Touche Ross (now Deloitte & Touche): jt ptnr in charge Jersey 1977–, regnl ptnr in charge Touche Ross UK Offshore Region 1991–; FCA (ACA 1974); *Recreations* swimming, walking, boating, cycling, reading and wine; *Clubs* Cardiff & County, Victoria, United; *Style*— Geoffrey Davies, Esq; ✉ Deloitte & Touche, PO Box 403, Lord Coutanche House, 66–68 Esplanade, St Helier, Jersey JE4 8WA (☎ 01534 37770, fax 01534 34037)

DAVIES, Capt Geoffrey Franklin; TD (1964); s of Franklyn George Davies (d 1952), of Kidderminster, Worcs, and Doris, *née* Thatcher (d 1987); *b* 13 Jan 1930; *Educ* King Charles I Sch Kidderminster, King Edward VI Sch Stourbridge, Univ of Birmingham (LLB); *m* 1, 19 June 1954 (m dis 1970), Barbara Mary, da of Maj William Horace Cooper (d 1965), of The Old Rectory, Hagley, W Midlands; 1 s (Nigel William b 16 Nov 1956), 1 da (Jayne Elizabeth b 1 Sept 1958); m 2, 31 Oct 1970 (m dis 1972), Barbara Jean, da of James Skillen, of USA; 1 s (James Skillen b 12 Aug 1971); m 3, 30 July 1977, Barbara (Bobby) Joyce, da of Harold Williams (d 1959), of Chaddesley, Corbett, Worcs; *Career* cmmnd 2 Lt RASC 1953, Capt RASC later RCT 1956, served with 110 Tport Column until 1964; admitted slr 1952; sr ptnr: Thursfields 1956–95 (now conslt), Desmond & Holder Worcester 1987–; former chm WM Cooper & Sons (Builders), sec John Brecknell Charity 1956–, cases sec and/or pres NW and SE Shropshire Branch NSPCC 1956–, memb Kidderminster Borough Cncl (chm two ctees) 1970–76, chm Kidderminster Cons 200 Club 1970–83, form prov Aide de Campe Knights Templar Worcs, vice pres Stourport Boat Club, former prov sr Grand Warden Worcs; memb Law Soc 1952; *Recreations* rowing, golf; *Clubs* Leander, Worcester Rowing, Kidderminster Golf; *Style*— Capt Geoffrey F Davies; ✉ Drayton Lodge, Drayton, Belbroughton, nr Stourbridge, W Midlands (☎ 01562 730240)

DAVIES, George William; s of George Davies (d 1987), of Southport, Lancs, and Mary, *née* Wright; *b* 29 Oct 1941; *Educ* Bootle GS, Univ of Birmingham; *m* 1, 25 Sept 1965 (m dis 1985), Anne Margaret, da of Maj Donald Dyson Allan, of Hants; 3 da (Melanie b 8 Aug 1966, Emma b 23 Sept 1968, Alexandra b 7 Sept 1973); m 2, 7 Dec 1985 (m dis 1992), Mrs Elzbieta (Liz) Krystyna Devereux-Batchelor, da of Stanislaw Ryszard Szadbey; 2 da (Lucia b 22 May 1988, Jessica b 2 June 1989), m 3, 16 Oct 1992, Fiona Teresa, da of Donovan Karl Shead, of Hants; 2 s (George Jeremy b 19 Feb 1992, Barnaby Charles b 9 Dec 1993); *Career* stock merchandise controller Littlewoods Stores 1967–72, School Care (own business) 1972–75, Party Plan and Pippadee Lingerie 1975–81; J Hepworth & Son 1981–88: responsible for launch of Next Feb 1982, jt gp md 1984, chief exec 1985, chm and chief exec 1987–88; chm and md The George Davies Partnership plc 1989, md George Clothing (part of Asda Group plc) 1995–, fndr S'porter (themed designer clothing for football clubs) 1996; memb Ct Univ of Leics 1988–; Hon degree Liverpool Poly 1989, Hon DDes Nottingham Trent Univ 1996; FRSA 1987, sr fell RCA 1988; *Books* incl: What Next? (1989); *Recreations* golf, tennis, squash; *Clubs* Formby Golf, Blackwell Golf; *Style*— George Davies, Esq; ✉ George Clothing, Magna House, Hunter Boulevard, Magna Park, Lutterworth, Leics LE17 4XN (☎ 01455 553090, fax 0116 265 8525)

DAVIES, Geraint Talfan; s of Aneirin Talfan Davies, OBE (d 1980), of Cardiff, and Mary Anne, *née* Evans (d 1971); *b* 30 Dec 1943; *Educ* Cardiff HS For Boys, Jesus Coll Oxford (MA); *m* 9 Sept 1967, Elizabeth Shan, da of Thomas Vaughan Yorath of Cardiff; 3 s (Matthew b 1969, Rhodri b 1971, Edward b 1974); *Career* asst ed Western Mail 1974–78, head of news and current affairs HTV Wales 1978–82, asst controller of programmes HTV Wales 1982–87, dir of programmes Tyne Tees TV 1987–90, controller BBC Wales 1990–; chm Newydd Housing Assoc 1975–78; tstee: Tenovus Cancer Appeal 1984–87, Br Bone Marrow Donor Appeal 1987–; memb: Mgmnt Ctee Northern Sinfonia 1989–90, Prince of Wales Ctee 1993–95, NCVQ 1996–; chm Inst of Welsh Affairs 1992–, govr Welsh Coll of Music and Drama 1993–; dir: Northern Stage Co 1989–90, The Newcastle Initiative 1989–90; *Style*— Geraint Talfan Davies, Esq; ✉ BBC Wales, Broadcasting House, Llandaff, Cardiff CF5 2YQ (☎ 01222 572888, fax 01222 555286, telex 265781)

DAVIES, Prof Sir Graeme John; kt (1996); s of Harry John Davies, and Gladys Edna, *née* Pratt; *b* 7 April 1937; *Educ* Sch of Engrg Univ of Auckland NZ, Univ of Cambridge (MA, ScD); *m* Florence Isabelle; 1 s (Michael b 1960), 1 da (Helena b 1961); *Career* lectr Dept of Metallurgy and Materials Sci Univ of Cambridge 1962–77, fell St Catharine's Coll Cambridge 1967–77, prof Dept of Metallurgy Univ of Sheffield 1978–86, vice-chllr Univ of Liverpool 1986–91; chief exec: Univs Funding Cncl 1991–93, Polys and Colls Funding Cncl 1992–93, Higher Educn Funding Cncl for Eng 1992–95; princ and vice-chllr Univ of Glasgow Oct 1995–; dir Univs Superannuation Scheme Ltd; author and co-author of more than 120 sci papers on forming processes, welding, solidification and casting, mechanical properties of materials; Rosenhain medal Inst of Metals 1982; Freeman City of London 1987, Liveryman Worshipful Co of Ironmongers 1989; CEng, FIM, FIMechE, FRSA, FEng 1988, FRSE 1996; *Books* Solidification and Casting (1973), Texture and the Properties of Materials (co-ed, 1976), Solidificacao e Fundicao das Metals e Suas Ligas (jtly, 1978), Hot Working and Forming Processes (co-ed, 1980), Superplasticity (jtly, 1981), Essential Metallurgy for Engineers (jtly, 1985); *Recreations* birdwatching; *Clubs* Athenaeum; *Style*— Prof Sir Graeme Davies, FRSE, FEng; ✉ University of Glasgow, Glasgow G12 8QQ (☎ 0141 339 8855)

DAVIES, Prof Graham Arthur; s of Evan Henry Davies (d 1978), and Esther Alice, *née* Powell (d 1979); *b* 2 July 1938; *Educ* Wolverhampton Municipal GS, Univ of Birmingham (BSc, PhD), Univ of Manchester (DSc, Sir John Cadman Medal, Moulton Medal IChemE); *m* July 1963, Christine Pamela, da of Frederick Charles Harris; 1 s (Andrew Simon Craig), 1 da (Joanna Elizabeth); *Career* Procter & Gamble Ltd Newcastle-upon-Tyne 1963–65; UMIST: lectr in chemical engrg 1965–70, sr lectr 1970–76, reader 1976–88, prof 1988–, head Dept of Chemical Engrg 1993–; FIChemE, CEng, FEng 1995; *Books* Recent Advances in Liquid-Liquid Extraction (co-author, 1970), Science & Practice of Liquid-Liquid Extraction (1993); *Recreations* golf; *Style*— Prof Graham Davies, FEng; ✉ Chemical Engineering Department, UMIST, PO Box 88, Manchester M60 1QD (☎ 0161 200 4342)

DAVIES, (Stephen) Howard; s of Thomas Emrys Davies, and (Eileen) Hilda, *née* Bevan (d 1991); *b* 26 April 1945; *Educ* Christ's Hosp, Univ of Durham (BA), Univ of Bristol; *m* Susan, da of Rt Rev Eric St Q Wall (former Bishop of Huntingdon); 2 da (Hannah Clare b 1973, Katherine Sian (Kate) b 1978); *Career* theatre director; assoc dir Bristol Old Vic 1971–73 (prodns incl: Troilus and Cressida, Candida, Spring Awakening), fndr memb Avon Touring Co, asst dir RSC 1974; freelance dir 1974–76: The Caucasian Chalk Circle (Birmingham Rep), The Threepenny Opera (York Rep), The Iceman Cometh (RSC Aldwych), Man is Man (RSC); assoc dir RSC 1976–86, fndr and dir The Warehouse RSC 1977–82 (prodns incl: Piaf, Good, Les Liaisons Dangereuses), visiting dir National Theatre 1987–88 (prodns incl: The Shaughraun, Cat on a Hot Tin Roof, The Secret Rapture), assoc dir Royal National Theatre 1989– (prodns incl: Hedda Gabler, The Crucible, Piano, A Long Day's Journey into Night, Mary Stuart); *Recreations* travel, hill-walking, watching rugby; *Style*— Howard Davies, Esq; ✉ c/o Royal National Theatre, South Bank, London SE1 9PX (☎ 0171 928 2033, fax 0171 620 1197)

DAVIES, Howard John; s of Leslie Powell Davies (d 1989), of Rochdale, Lancs, and Marjorie, *née* Magowan; *b* 12 Feb 1951; *Educ* Manchester GS, Memorial Univ of Newfoundland, Merton Coll Oxford (MA), Stanford Univ Calif (MS in Mgmnt Sci); *m* 30 June 1984, Prudence Mary, da of Eric Phillipps Keely, CBE (d 1988), of Findon; 2 s (George b 1984, Archibald b 1987); *Career* FO 1973–74, private sec to HM Ambass Paris 1974–76, HM Treasy 1976–82, McKinsey and Co 1982–85, special advsr to Chllr of the Exchequer 1985–86, re-joined McKinsey and Co 1986–87, controller Audit Cmmn for Local Authorities and the NHS (formerly for Local Authorities) 1987–92, dir gen CBI 1992–95; dep govr Bank of England Sept 1995–; non-exec dir GKN plc until Aug 1995; *Recreations* cricket, writing; *Clubs* Barnes Common Cricket; *Style*— Howard Davies, Esq; ✉ Bank of England, Threadneedle Street, London EC2R 8AH (☎ 0171 601 4444, fax 0171 601 5901)

DAVIES, Hugh Llewelyn; CMG (1994); s of Vincent Ellis Davies, OBE, of 12 St Swithuns Close, East Grinstead, Sussex, and Rose Trench, *née* Temple (d 1993); *b* 8 Nov 1941; *Educ* Rugby, Churchill Coll Cambridge (BA); *m* 21 Sept 1968, Virginia Ann, da of Hugh Lucius; 1 s (Jonathan b 1973), 1 da (Charlotte b 1970); *Career* HM Dip Serv: FO 1965, Chinese language studies Hong Kong 1966–68, second sec and HM consul Peking 1969–71, China Desk FCO 1971–74, first sec (econ) Br Embassy Bonn 1974–77, head of chancery Br High Cmmm Singapore 1977–79, asst head Far Eastern Dept FCO 1979–82, secondment Barclays Bank Int 1982–83, commercial cnsllr Br Embassy Peking 1984–87, dep perm UK rep OECD Paris 1987–90, head Far East Dept FCO 1990–93, sr Br trade cmmr Hong Kong 1993, Br sr rep on the Sino-British Jt Liaison Gp Hong Kong 1993–; *Recreations* travel, sports, art, gardens; *Clubs* Hong Kong, Hong Kong Country, China; *Style*— Hugh Davies, Esq, CMG; ✉ c/o Foreign & Commonwealth Office (UKREP JLG Hong Kong), King Charles Street, London SW1A 2AH

DAVIES, Hugh Seymour; s of Harold Escott Davies (d 1992), of Wanborough, Wilts, and Joan Mary, *née* Seymour (d 1995); *b* 23 April 1943; *Educ* Westminster, Univ of Oxford (BA); *m* 5 Sept 1981, Pamela Judith, da of Anthony Michael Bailey (d 1957); 1 da (Rebecca b 1986); *Career* composer, instrument inventor, performer and musicologist; asst to the composer Karlheinz Stockhausen in Cologne 1964–66, conslt researcher Electronic Music Studio Goldsmiths' Coll Univ of London 1986–91 (dir 1967–86), conslt Music Dept Gemeentemuseum The Hague 1986–; compositions incl: Shozyg I + II 1968, Meldoci Gestures 1978, Strata 1987, Inventio 1994; major performances incl: Stockhausen's performing gp 1964–66, BBC Proms 1969 and 1986, Stockholm Festival for Electroacoustic Music 1989; ctee memb: Macnaghten Concerts 1968–71, Arts Cncl New Activities 1969–70, Electroacoustic Music Assoc 1977–84; memb Bd of Dirs Artist Placement Gp 1975–89; Hon Citizenship City of Baltimore USA 1988; *Books* International Electronic Music Catalog (1968); chapters in: Poésie Sonore Internationale (1979), Electronic Music for Schools (1981), Nuova Atlantide (1986), Echo - The Images of Sound (1987), Vitalité et contradictions de l'avant-garde: Italie-France 1909–1924 (1988), Nordic Music Days 100 Years (1988), Piano (1988), Musiques Electroniques (1990), Companion to Contemporary Musical Thought (1992), Medzinárodné Fórum Elektroakustickej Hudby (1993), Francesco Balilla Pratella (1995); The New Grove Dictionary of Musical Instruments (300 entries 1984), five other dictionaries; *Style*— Hugh Davies, Esq; ✉ 25 Albert Rd, London N4 3RR (☎ 0171 272 5508)

DAVIES, (Edward) Hunter; s of John Davies (d 1958), of Cambuslang, and Marion, *née* Brechin (d 1987); *b* 7 Jan 1936; *Educ* Creighton Sch Carlisle, Carlisle GS, Univ of Durham; *m* 1960, Margaret Forster, *qv*; 1 s, 2 da; *Career* author, broadcaster, publisher; journalist Sunday Times 1960–84 (ed Sunday Times Magazine 1975–77); columnist: Punch 1979–89, Stamp News 1981–86, Evening Standard 1987, The Independent 1989–95; presenter BBC Radio Four's Bookshelf 1983–86; memb: Br Library Consultative Gp on Newspapers 1987–89, Bd Edinburgh Book Festival 1990–95; pres Cumbria Wildlife Tst 1994–; *Books* fiction incl: Here We Go Round the Mulberry Bush (1965, filmed 1968), A Very Loving Couple (1971), Flossie Teacake's Fur Coat (1982), Come on Ossie! (1985), Saturday Night (1989), Striker (1992); non-fiction incl: The Other Half (1966), The Beatles (1968, 2 edn 1985), The Glory Game (1972, 2 edn 1985), A Walk Around the Lakes (1979), William Wordsworth (1980), Father's Day (1981, TV series 1983), The Joy of Stamps (1983), The Good Guide to the Lakes (also publisher, 1984, 4 edn 1993), In Search of Columbus (1991), Hunting People (1994), Teller of Tales (1994), Wainwright (1995), Living on the Lottery (1996); *Recreations* collecting stamps, Lakeland books; *Style*— Hunter Davies, Esq; ✉ 11 Boscastle Rd, London NW5 (☎ 0171 485 3785); Grasmoor House, Loweswater, Cockermouth, Cumbria

DAVIES, Huw Humphreys; s of William Davies (d 1984), of Llangynog, and Harriet Jane, *née* Humphreys (d 1991); *b* 4 Aug 1940; *Educ* Llandovery Coll, Pembroke Coll Oxford (MA); *m* 1966, Elizabeth Shân, da of William Harries; 2 da (Elin Mari b 25 April 1969, Catrin Humphreys b 23 Sept 1971); *Career* prog dir and prodr TWW 1964–68; HTV Wales: programme dir and prodr 1968–78, asst controller of programmes 1978–79, controller of programmes 1979–81, dir of programmes 1981–89, chief exec 1987; gp dir of TV HTV Group 1989–94, pres HTV International 1994–96; fndr independent TV prodn co Square Circle 1996–; memb Gorsedd of Bards; FRSA 1989; *Recreations* walking, reading, swimming; *Style*— Huw Davies, Esq; ✉ 27 Victoria Road, Penarth, Cardiff CF64 3HY

DAVIES, His Hon Judge Ian Hewitt; TD; s of Rev John Robert Davies (d 1968), and Gwendoline Gertrude, *née* Garling (d 1978); *b* 13 May 1931; *Educ* Kingswood Sch, St John's Coll Cambridge (MA); *m* 31 July 1962, Molly Cecilia Vaughan, da of Brig Charles Hilary Vaughan Vaughan, DSO (d 1978); *Career* Nat Serv 1950–51, cmmnd KOYLI, served 3 Bn Parachute Regt, TA 1951–71, Lt-Col; called to the Bar Inner Temple 1958, circuit judge (SE Circuit) 1986–; *Recreations* lawn tennis, sailing; *Clubs* Boodle's, MCC, Hurlingham; *Style*— His Hon Judge Ian Davies, TD; ✉ c/o Central Criminal Court, Old Bailey, London EC4M 7EH

DAVIES, Hon Islwyn Edmund Evan; CBE (1986), JP (Powys), DL (Powys 1983); s of 1 Baron Davies; *b* 10 Dec 1926; *Educ* Gordonstoun; *m* 1959, Camilla Anne, elder da of late Col Lawrence William Coulden, of Hadley Wood, Herts; 3 s; *Career* Hon LLD (Wales); FRAgS; *Style*— The Hon Islwyn Davies, CBE, JP, DL; ✉ Perthybu, Sarn, Newtown, Powys (☎ 01686 670620)

DAVIES, Dr Ivor John; s of David Howell Davies, of Penarth, S Glam, and Gwenllian, *née* Phillips (d 1990); *b* 9 Nov 1935; *Educ* Penarth Co Sch, Cardiff Coll of Art (NDD), Swansea Coll of Art (ATD), Univ of Lausanne, Univ of Edinburgh (PhD); *Career* artist; teacher of art and craft Little Ealing Secdy Modern Boys Sch London 1957–59, asst teacher of Eng Univ of Lausanne and Gymnases 1959–61, pt/t lectr in history of art Extra Mural Dept Cardiff 1961–63, lectr i/c History of Art 19th and 20th Century Dept of Fine Art Univ of Edinburgh 1963–78, first curator Talbot Rice Art Centre Univ of Edinburgh 1971–78, lectr in history of art and head School of Cultural Studies Faculty of Art and Design Gwent Coll of Higher Educn Newport 1978–88; lectr and external examiner for numerous bodies; author of numerous articles and reviews in art magazines; involved in destruction-in-art, multi-media and experimental theatre in the 1960s; memb: AICA (Int Assoc of Art Critics), GWELED (Welsh arts movement), AAH (Assoc of Art Historians); vice pres Royal Cambrian Acad 1995– (memb 1992–); *Exhibitions* solo exhbns since 1963 incl: Oriel (Welsh Art Cncl Gallery Cardiff) 1974, City Art Gallery Leeds 1975, Talbot Rice Art Centre Univ of Edinburgh 1972, 1973, 1974 and 1977, Holsworthy Gallery New King's Road London 1980 and 1981, Newport Museum and Art Gallery 1987, Max Rutherson/Roberts Gallery Bond St London 1989, Jeddah Saudi Arabia 1990, Mandarin Hong Kong 1992, Wrexham Library touring exhibition 1991–93, Victoria Art Gallery Bath 1993; numerous gp exhbns nationally and internationally 1953–93; *Work in Public Collections* incl: Welsh Arts Cncl, Scottish Arts Cncl, City Art Gallery, Leeds, Nat Museum of Wales, Arts Cncl of GB, Newport Museum and Art Gallery, the Deal Collection Dallas; *Recreations* languages; *Style*— Dr Ivor Davies; ✉ 99 Windsor Rd, Penarth, South Glamorgan, Wales CF64 1JF (☎ 01222 703492)

DAVIES, (David) John; s of J N J Davies (d 1978), of Epsom, and P Davies, *née* Williams (d 1983); *b* 17 March 1933; *Educ* Christ's Coll Cambridge (MA); *m* 29 Oct 1960, Pauline Margot, s of E R Owen (d 1955), of Ashtead; 2 s (Gordon Howard b 1964, Richard James b 1967 d 1988); *Career* analyst Cazenove and Co 1968–71, managing ptnr and md Quilter Goodison Co 1981–86 (joined 1971, ptnr 1973), dep md Paribas Ltd 1987–91; chm: The Epic Interactive Media Co Ltd 1993–96, Priestmere Ltd; Freeman: City of London, Worshipful Co of Upholders; MSI (Dip), MIMgt, FRSA, FInstD; *Recreations* water sports and Chinese culture; *Clubs* Carlton; *Style*— John Davies, Esq; ✉ Paddock Cottage, Downsway, Tadworth, Surrey KT20 5DH (☎ 01737 212317)

DAVIES, John; s of John Charles Davies (d 1987), of Birmingham, and Kathleen Anne, *née* Snipe; *b* 12 July 1946; *Educ* Bournville Boys' Tech Sch Birmingham; *m* 6 Nov 1971, Jacqueline, da of William Springall Wheeler; 1 s (Charles William b 26 Nov 1974), 3 da (Alison Jane b 29 April 1976, Nicola Kate b 23 March 1978, Lucy Anne b 25 June 1980); *Career* trainee investment analyst Midland Assurance Ltd Birmingham 1964–67; investment analysis: J M Finn & Co (Stockbrokers) 1968–71, Nat Coal Bd Pension Fund 1971–73; Confederation Life Insurance Co: asst mangr equity investmt 1973–74, mangr pension investmts 1974–76, mangr segregated funds investmts 1976–79, dep investmt mangr 1979–82; investmt mangr 3i Group plc 1982–84, md 3i Asset Management Ltd 1984–; govr and trustee St Michael Sch Sunninghill; AIIMR 1970, MSI; *Recreations* music, reading, hill walking; *Clubs* Girt Clog Climbing; *Style*— John Davies, Esq; ✉ 3i Asset Management Ltd, 91 Waterloo Road, London SE1 8XP (☎ 0171 928 3131, fax 0171 928 0058)

DAVIES, Prof John Christopher Hughes (Christie); s of Christopher George Davies (d 1984), and Marian Eileen, *née* Johns (d 1975); *b* 25 Dec 1941; *Educ* Dynevor Sch, Emmanuel Coll Cambridge (BA, MA, PhD); *Career* tutor in economics Univ of Adelaide Aust 1964, radio prodr BBC Radio 3 prog 1967–69, lectr in sociology Univ of Leeds 1969–72, visiting lectr in sociology Indian univs incl Univ of Bombay and Univ of Delhi 1973–74, prof of sociology Univ of Reading 1984– (lectr then sr lectr then reader 1972–84), distinguished scholars interdisciplinary lectr Inst of Humane Studies George Mason Univ Virginia 1986, visiting lectr Jagiellonian Univ of Krakow Poland 1991; *Books* Wrongful Imprisonment (with R Brandon, 1973), Permissive Britain (1975), Censorship and Obscenity (with R Dhavan, 1978), Ethnic Humor Around the World (1990); *Recreations* travel, geology, art exhibitions, jokes; *Clubs* Union Soc (Cambridge, pres 1964); *Style*— Prof Christie Davies; ✉ Department of Sociology, University of Reading, Whiteknights, Reading, Berks RG6 2AA (☎ 0118 931 8518, fax 0118 931 8922)

DAVIES, John David; s of David Mervyn Davies (d 1976), of Coventry, and Sarah Jane Davies; *b* 29 Oct 1936; *Educ* King Henry VIII Sch Coventry, NW London Poly (ALA), Loughborough Univ (MLS); *m* 1959, Susan, *née* Blackburn; 1 s (Michael David b 6 April 1961), 2 da (Jennifer Ann b 23 July 1963, Helen Elizabeth b 29 July 1965); *Career* Nat Serv RN 1955–57; worked in public libraries 1958–66; British Council: librarian posts in Thailand, Lebanon, Nigeria and London 1966–80, dir Central Information Servs 1980–83, dir Systems Dept 1983–85, dep dir Germany 1985–92, dir Singapore 1992–; *Recreations* music, theatre, bridge, skiing, walking; *Clubs* Tanglin, Barn Theatre, Welwyn Garden City; *Style*— John Davies, Esq; ✉ The British Council, 30 Napier Road, Singapore 1025

DAVIES, Dr John Douglas (Jack); s of Maj William Herbert Douglas Davies, RAMC (d 1987), and Ethel Mary Sheila, *née* Smith (d 1984); *b* 10 Aug 1936; *Educ* St Paul's, Univ of London (MB BS, MD); *m* 1 June 1963, (Patricia) Maureen, da of Thomas Addison (d 1969); 1 s (Dr William Alexander Douglas Davies b 1967), 3 da (Penelope Jane b 1964, Rachel Laura b 1966, Antonia Ruth b 1969); *Career* sr registrar Bart's 1966–72, conslt sr lectr in pathology Univ of Bristol and Bristol Royal Infirmary 1972–, dir Regional Breast Pathology Unit Southmead Hosp 1989–; lectr in cellular pathology Bristol Poly and West of Eng Univ 1975–; visiting prof and lectr Univs of Ghana, Benghazi, Aix-Marseilles, Budapest, Lahore and Med Acad Jinan China; external examiner: RCS, RCPath, Univs of London, Sheffield, Manchester and Wales 1982–, Worshipful Soc of Apothecaries London 1990–93, Utd Examining Bd 1994–; author of over 300 medico-scientific papers on breast and elastic pathology; vice pres Academicals CC; memb Editorial Bd and book review ed W of Eng Med Jl 1989–92, hon ed Journal of Current Oncology 1994–, ed Assoc of Clinical Pathologists Histopathology Broadsheets 1994–, memb Editorial Bd Journal of Clinical Pathology 1995–; chm Information Gp RCPath Breast Pathology Advsy Ctee 1990–, memb Ctee Pathological Soc GB 1983–87, chm SW Regnl Histopathology Gp 1983–88, memb Cncl and postgrad educn sec Assoc of Clinical Pathologists 1984–92, memb RCPath Acad Activity Ctee 1989–92, pres Wessex Assoc of Clinical Pathologists 1990–93, vice pres Assoc of Clinical Pathologists 1995–96; LRCP 1961, MRCPath 1969, FRCPath 1980, MRCS 1961; *Books* Periductal Mastitis (1971), Vascular Disturbances in A G Stansfeld's Lymph Node Biopsy Interpretation (1985, 2 edn 1992), Guidelines for Course Organisers (1990), Evaluation of Radiography Cabinets (1991); *Recreations* fly-fishing, dog walking, wood watching; *Clubs* RSM, Academicals Cricket; *Style*— Dr J D Davies; ✉ 20 Clifton Park, Clifton, Bristol BS8 3BZ (☎ 0117 973 4294); Llwyn-y-celyn, Llanwrda, Carmarthenshire SA19 8EP (☎ 01550 777223); Regional Breast Pathology Unit, Southmead Hospital, Bristol BS10 5NB (☎ 0117 950 5050 ext 4169, fax 0117 950 9690)

DAVIES, John Howard; CBE (1984), DL (Clwyd 1986); s of Rev William Hugh Davies (d 1981), of Cardiff, and Mary Eunice, *née* Thomas (d 1971); *b* 6 May 1926; *Educ* Holyhead Co Sch, UCW, Poitiers Univ France (BA, DipEd); *m* 5 Oct 1954, Elizabeth, da of James Jenkins, JP (d 1965), of Carmarthen; 3 s (Jonathan b 1956, Mark b 1958, Timothy b 1960); *Career* Capt Royal Welch Fusiliers 1944–48, cmmnd Indian Mil Acad; served: India, Burma, Malaya, Sumatra; Colonial Educn Serv North Nigeria 1952–56, dist educn offr Notts 1957–58, dep dir of educn Montgomeryshire 1958–66; dir of educn: Flintshire 1970–74 (dep dir of educn 1966–70), Clwyd 1974–85; chm: Welsh Fourth Channel Authy (S4C) 1986–93, Cncl UCW Bangor, Clwyd Appeal Fund for Hosp Scanner Equipment; memb: Cncl and Ct UCW, Cncl UCW (Coll of Med); hon memb Gorsedd of Bards 1985; FRSA 1980; *Recreations* golf, gardening; *Style*— John Howard Davies, Esq, CBE, DL; ✉ Staddle Stones, Hendy Rd, Mold, Clwyd (☎ 01352 700110)

DAVIES, John Howard; s of Jack Davies, screenwriter (d 1994), and Dorothy Davies; *b* 9 March 1939; *Educ* Haileybury and ISC, Univ of Grenoble; *Career* former child actor; credits incl: Oliver Twist (title role), The Rocking Horse Winner, Tom Brown's Schooldays (title role); BBC Television: prodn asst 1967–69, prodr 1969–77, head of comedy 1977–82, head of light entertainment 1982–85; produced and directed series incl: The World of a Beachcomber, All Gas and Gaiters, The Goodies, Steptoe and Son, early episodes of Monty Python's Flying Circus (winner BAFTA award), The Good Life, The Other One, Fawlty Towers (winner BAFTA award); later responsible for series incl: Yes Minister, Not The Nine O'Clock News, To the Manor Born, Butterflies, Hi-De-Hi, Only Fools and Horses, Just Good Friends,' Allo 'Allo; also prodr Blackadder pilot; Thames Television: prodr and dir 1985–88, controller of light entertainment 1988–92; produced and directed series incl: Executive Stress, All in Good Faith, We'll Think of Something and Andy Capp, No Job for a Lady, Hope it Rains, Mr Bean (winner Montreux Golden Rose, Press Prize and City of Montreux Comedy Prize, International Emmy, Banff Award); currently independent TV prodr and dir (through J.H.D. Ltd); dir: Men Behaving Badly pilot, The Vicar of Dibley Easter Special (BBC); *Style*— John Howard Davies, Esq; ✉ J.H.D. Ltd, The Cat, 35 Catslip, Nettlebed, Oxon RG9 5BL (☎ and fax 014191 641743)

DAVIES, Wing Cdr John Irfon; MBE (1963); s of Thomas Mervyn Davies, of Porthcawl, and Mary Margaret, *née* Harris (d 1988); *b* 8 June 1930; *Educ* Stanley Sch, Croydon Poly; *m* 20 Dec 1950, Jean Marion, da of late John Bruce Anderson, of Darlington; 1 da (Jane b 1957); *Career* RAF 1948, cmmnd 1950, Flying Coll 1956, Staff Coll 1963, Coll of Air Warfare 1970, MOD 1970–72 (and 1964–66), Cabinet Office 1972–74; Welsh Office: princ Housing Div 1974–76, private sec to Sec of State for Wales 1976–78, asst sec agric policy 1978–82, asst sec housing policy 1983–84, under sec housing health and social policy 1985–86, under sec and head Agric Dept 1986–90; dir Sallingbury Casey (Wales) 1990–92; lay memb GMC 1990–, sec Univ of Wales Review Bd 1990–92, chm Health Promotion Authy for Wales 1992–; *Recreations* golf, music, fishing; *Clubs* Radyr Golf, RAF, Cardiff and County; *Style*— Wing Cdr John I Davies, MBE; ✉ Friston, 15 Windsor Rd, Radyr, Cardiff CF4 8BQ (☎ 01222 84267)

DAVIES, Prof John Kenyon; s of Harold Edward Davies (d 1990), of Cardiff, and Clarice Theresa, *née* Woodburn (d 1989); *b* 19 Sept 1937; *Educ* Manchester GS, Wadham Coll Oxford (BA), Merton Coll Oxford (MA), Balliol Coll Oxford (DPhil); *m* 1, 8 Sept 1962 (m dis 1978), Anna Elbina Laura Margherita, da of A Morpurgo (d 1939), of Rome; m 2, 5 Aug 1978, Nicola Jane, da of Dr R M S Perrin; 1 s (Martin b 1979), 1 da (Penelope b 1981); *Career* Harmsworth scholar Merton Coll Oxford 1960–63, jr fell Centre for Hellenic Studies Washington DC 1961–62, Dyson jr fell Balliol Coll Oxford 1963–65, lectr Univ of St Andrews 1965–68, fell in ancient history Oriel Coll Oxford 1968–77, Rathbone prof of ancient history and classical archaeology Univ of Liverpool 1977–, pro vice chllr Univ of Liverpool 1986–90, Leverhulme research prof 1995–; ed: Journal of Hellenic Studies 1973–77, Archaeological Reports 1972–74; chm: St Patrick's Isle (IOM) Archaeological Tst 1982–85, NW Archaeological Tst 1982–91; auditor CVCP Academic Audit Unit 1990–93; FBA 1985, FSA 1986, FRSA 1988; *Books* Athenian Propertied Families 600–300 BC (1971), Democracy and Classical Greece (1978, 2 edn 1993), Wealth and the Power of Wealth in Classical Athens (1981), The Trojan War: its historicity and context (jt ed with L Foxhall, 1984); *Recreations* choral singing; *Clubs* Royal Over-Seas League; *Style*— Prof John K Davies; ✉ 20 North Rd, Grassendale Park, Liverpool L19 0LR (☎ 0151 427 2126); School of Archaeology, Classics and Oriental Studies, University of Liverpool, Abercromby Square, PO Box 147, Liverpool L69 3BX (☎ 0151 794 2400, fax 0151 794 2442, telex 627095 O UNILPL G)

DAVIES, Jonathan; MBE (1995); s of Leonard Davies (d 1976), of Trimsaran, and Diana, *née* Rees; *b* 24 Oct 1962; *Educ* Gwendraeth GS; *m* 11 Aug 1984, Karen Marie, da of Byron J Hopkins; 1 s (Matthew Scott b 20 July 1988); *Career* rugby union outside-half; *Rugby Union* clubs: Trimsaran, Neath RFC, Llanelli RFC until 1989 (when turned professional), Cardiff RFC 1995–; Wales: debut v Eng 1985, memb World Cup Squad (6 appearances) 1987, memb Triple Crown winning team 1988, tour NZ (2 test appearances) 1988, 29 caps, sometime capt; also played for Barbarians RFC; *Rugby League* threequarters (position); clubs: joined Widnes RLFC (world record transfer fee) 1989, free transfer Warrington RLFC 1993–95 (when reverted to Union); Wales: memb nat side (semi-finalists World Cup 1995); GB: 6 caps (memb tour NZ 1990, former capt); *Books* Jonathan (1989); *Video* The Jonathan Davies Story (1990); *Recreations* any sport; *Style*— Jonathan Davies, Esq, MBE; ✉ Cardiff Rugby Football Club, Cardiff Arms Park, Westgate Street, Cardiff

DAVIES, Prof Kay Elizabeth; CBE (1995); *b* 1 April 1951; *Educ* Somerville Coll Oxford (Kirkaldy Prize, MA, DPhil); *m*; 1 c; *Career* Guy Newton jr research fell Wolfson Coll Oxford 1976–78, Royal Soc Euro post-doctoral fell Service de Biochimie Centre d'Etudes Nucleaires de Saclay Gif-sur-Yvette France 1978–80; St Mary's Hosp Med Sch Dept of Biochemistry: Cystic Fibrosis research fell 1980–82, MRC sr research fell 1982–84; John Radcliffe Hosp Oxford: MRC sr research fell Nuffield Dept of Clinical Med 1984–86, MRC external staff Nuffield Dept of Clinical Med 1986–89, MRC external staff Molecular Genetics Gp Inst of Molecular Med and univ research lectr Nuffield Dept of Clinical Med 1989–92; MRC research dir MRC Clinical Scis Centre Royal Post Graduate Med Sch Hammersmith and prof of molecular genetics Univ of London 1992–94, MRC external staff head Molecular Genetics Gp Inst of Molecular Med John Radcliffe Hosp Oxford 1994–95; Dept of Biochemistry Univ of Oxford: prof of genetics 1995–, assoc head for external relations 1996–; fell Univ of Oxford: Green Coll 1989–92 and 1994–95, Keble Coll 1995–, Somerville Coll (hon) 1995; Bristol-Myers visiting prof USA 1986, James and Jean Davis Prestige visiting prof Univ of Otago NZ 1996; memb: Advsy Ctee Euro Cell and Tissue Bank 1989–, Med Ethics Advsy Gp Lambeth Palace 1994–, Scientific Advsy Panel CIBA Fndn 1994–, Genetics Interest Gp Wellcome Tst 1996–; founding ed Human Molecular Genetics 1992–; memb numerous Editorial Bds incl: Jl of Biotherapeutics and Gene Therapy 1994–, Gene Therapy 1994–, Molecular Medicine Society 1994–, Molecular Medicine Today 1994–; memb: Academia Europaea, EMBO, Biochemical Soc, Genetics Soc, Euro Human Genetics Soc; 7th Annual Colleen Giblin distinguished lectr Columbia Univ USA 1992, distinguished lectr Mayo Clinic 1994; Annual Medal Int Inst of Biotechnology 1993, Wellcome Tst Award 1996; Hon DSc Univ of Victoria BC 1990; MRCPath, Hon MRCP 1995; *Books* Molecular Analysis of Inherited Diseases (with A P Read, 1988, revised edn 1992), Human Genetics Diseases. A Practical Approach (ed, 1988), Genome Analysis. A Practical Approach (ed, 1988), The Fragile X Syndrome (ed, 1989), Application of Molecular Genetics to the Diagnosis of Inherited Disease (ed, 1989), Genome Analysis Review (ed with S Tilghman, 7 vols, 1990–94); also author of numerous articles for learned jls; *Style*— Prof Kay Davies, CBE; ✉ Genetics Laboratory, Department of Biochemistry, South Parks Road, Oxford OX1 3QU (☎ 01865 275324, fax 01865 275215)

DAVIES, Kenneth Seymour; s of George Seymour Davies, of Eastcote, Middx, and (Isobel) Dorothy, *née* Corfield (d 1995); *b* 11 Feb 1948; *Educ* St Nicholas GS Northwood; *m* 15 May 1971, Brenda Margaret, da of William George Cannon (d 1987), of Ruislip, Middx; 4 s (Mark b 1972, Peter b 1974, Robert b 1976, Trevor b 1982), 1 da (Kirsty b 1980); *Career* CA 1970; ptnr Pannell Kerr Forster 1974–; hon treas Willing Wheels Club (cancer charity); FCA; *Recreations* gardening, walking; *Style*— Ken Davies, Esq; ✉ Braunston, 15 Berks Hill, Chorleywood, Herts WD3 5AG (☎ 01923 282156); Pannell Kerr Forster, 78 Hatton Garden, London EC1N 8JA (☎ 0171 831 7393, fax 0171 405 6736, telex 295928)

DAVIES, Laura Jane; MBE (1988); da of David Thomas Davies, and Rita Ann, *née* Foskett; *b* 5 Oct 1963; *Educ* Fullbrook Co Secdy Sch; *Career* professional golfer; memb Curtis Cup Team 1984, Br Open Ladies Golf champion 1986, US Open champion 1987, memb winning European Solheim Cup team 1992; over 40 tournament wins in professional career 1985–; currently ranked world no 1; memb Golf Fndn; *Recreations* all sport, music; *Style*— Miss Laura Davies, MBE

DAVIES, (Robert) Leighton; QC (1994); s of Robert Brinley Davies (d 1978), of Cwmparc, Rhondda, Mid Glamorgan, and Elizabeth Nesta, *née* Jones; *b* 7 Sept 1949; *Educ* Rhondda County GS Porth, CCC Oxford (BA, BCL, boxing blue); *m* 25 Aug 1979, Linda Davies, da of David Fox, of Cwmparc, Rhondda, Mid Glamorgan; 2 s (Rhoss b 30 May 1980, Greg b 9 Jan 1991), 1 da (Rhia b 12 Nov 1985); *Career* called to the Bar Gray's Inn 1975; practising barr in Cardiff 1975–, recorder of the Crown Court 1994– (asst recorder 1990); memb: Greenpeace, The Criminal Bar Assoc 1988; *Recreations* fly fishing, gardening, watching rugby football; *Style*— Leighton Davies, Esq, QC; ✉ Bryn Corun, Glyncoli Road, Treorchy, Rhondda, Mid-Glamorgan CF42 6SB (☎ 01443 774559); 9/10 Park Place, Cardiff CF1 3DP (☎ 01222 382731, fax 01222 222542)

DAVIES, (Edward) Leslie; s of Robert Davies (d 1956), of North Ferriby, and Mabel Joyce, *née* Roberts (d 1965); *b* 23 Dec 1931; *Educ* Ruthin Sch, Jesus Coll Oxford (MA); *m* 4 Feb 1995, Pauline Ann Molyneux; *Career* admitted slr 1956, ptnr Ivesons 1960–; pres Hull Inc Law Soc 1965–, memb Cncl Law Soc of England and Wales 1976– (chm Educn and Trg Ctee 1983–86); govr Coll of Law 1983–; Under Sheriff Kingston upon Hull 1965; memb Law Soc 1960; *Recreations* golf; *Clubs* Royal Over-Seas League, Brough Golf (pres, former capt); *Style*— Leslie Davies, Esq; ✉ 30 Parkfield Avenue, North Ferriby, East Yorkshire HU14 3AL (☎ 01482 631312); Ivesons, PO Box 119, 19 Bowlalley Lane, Hull HU1 1YL (☎ 01482 326511, fax 01482 228008)

DAVIES, Dr Lindsey Margaret; da of Dr Frank Newby, of Horsham, Sussex, and Margaret, *née* Thomsett; *b* 21 May 1953; *Educ* Univ of Nottingham (BMedSci, MB BS, Post Grad Cert in Child Health, MFCM, MHSM, FFPHM); *m* 21 Sept 1974 (m dis 1994), Dr Peter Davies; 2 s (James b 11 July 1979, Adam b 30 Sept 1980); *Career* house surgn Mansfield Gen Hosp 1975, house physician Nottingham City Hosp 1976, clinical med offr (child health and occupational med) Nottingham HA 1977–80, sr clinical med offr (community child health) Nottingham DHA 1981–83, registrar then sr registrar in community med Trent RHA 1983–85, dir of public health Southern Derbyshire HA 1985–90 (seconded as visiting scholar Georgetown Univ Oct-Dec 1988), dir of public health Nottingham HA 1990–93; NHS Exec: head Public Health Div 1993–94, regional dir of public health 1994–; special lectr Univ of Nottingham Med Sch 1991–; memb various Dept of Health working parties; memb Cncl and Cncl Exec BMA 1991–93 (chm Ctee for Public Health Med and Community Health 1992–93); author of various articles in learned jls; *Style*— Dr Lindsey Davies; ✉ Regional Director of Public Health, NHS Executive, Trent Regional Office, Fulwood House, Old Fulwood Road, Sheffield S10 3TH (☎ 0114 263 0300)

DAVIES, Ven Lorys Martin; s of Evan Tudor Davies (d 1952), of St Clears, Dyfed, and Eigen Morfydd, *née* Davies; *b* 14 June 1936; *Educ* St Mary's C of E Sch, Whitland GS, St David's Coll Univ of Wales (Organ exhibitioner, Philips history scholar, BA), Wells Theol Coll; *m* 8 Oct 1960, Barbara Ethel, da of Charles David Walkley; 2 s (Christopher Martin b 6 Oct 1961, Stephen Mark b 22 Sept 1964); *Career* asst curate St Mary's Tenby 1959–61, chaplain Brentwood Sch 1962–66, chaplain and head of dept Solihull Sch 1966–68, vicar of Moseley (St Mary's) Birmingham 1968–81; chaplain: Uffculme Clinic 1968–71, Sorrento Maternity Hosp 1968–81, Moseley Hall Hosp 1968–81; residentiary canon Birmingham Cathedral 1981–92, diocesan dir of ordinands 1982–90, chm House of Clergy 1990–92, archdeacon of Bolton 1992–; chm: Elisabeth Dowell Housing Assoc 1969–91, Robert Stevens Tst 1973–, Freda and Howard Ballance Tst 1982–; memb Birmingham Rotary Club 1982–90; JP Birmingham 1978–92; ALCM; *Recreations* sport, music, theatre, reading, travel; *Style*— The Ven the Archdeacon of Bolton; ✉ 45 Rudgwick Drive, Brandlesholme, Bury, Lancs BL8 1YA (☎ and fax 0161 761 6117)

DAVIES, Maldwyn Thomas; s of Mervyn Davies (d 1985), of Merthyr Tydfil, Mid Glam, S Wales, and Ceinwen, *née* Williams (d 1983); *b* 24 Oct 1950; *Educ* Welsh Coll of Music and Drama Cardiff (LRAM, ARCM, LWCMD, Silver medal), Univ Coll Cardiff (BMus); *m* 5 August 1978, Christine Margaret, da of Howard Jestyn Powell; 2 da (Bethan Catherine b 18 January 1985, Elin Angharad b 22 March 1987); *Career* tenor; appearances at festivals: Edinburgh, Bath, Windsor, Hong Kong, Florence, Bergen, Vienna; concerts: BBC Welsh Symphony, LSO, Scot Nat Orchestra, BBC Philharmonic, The Philharmonia, Acad of St Martin-in-the Fields, LPO, London Mozart Players, most maj UK choral socs incl Bach Choir, Huddersfield Choral Soc; princ contract Royal Opera House Covent Garden 1980–82 (roles in Billy Budd and Alceste and many small roles); other opera performances incl: Cosi Fan Tutte (Lyric Opera of Qld), L'Isola Disabitata (Wexford Festival), Das Rheingold (The Ring Cycle Bayreuth Festival), The Seraglio (Kent Opera), Alceste (Geneva), The Seraglio, The Magic Flute and Cosi Fan Tutte (Scot Opera), debut A Midsummer Marriage (ENO), Don Giovanni (Opera New Zealand); records extensively for BBC; *Recordings* Boughton's The Immortal Hour, Bridge's The Christmas Rose, Haydn's Nelson Mass, Handel's The Messiah and Alcina, Stainer's The Crucifixion, Mozart's Requiem; *Recreations* DIY, fishing, films; *Style*— Maldwyn Davies, Esq; ✉ 43 Frobisher, Haversham Park, Bracknell, Berkshire RG12 7WQ (☎ and fax 01344 423155); Robert Gilder & Co, Enterprise House, 59–65 Upper Ground, London SE1 9PQ (☎ 0171 928 9008, fax 0171 928 9755)

DAVIES, Mandy Joanna; da of Dr Brian Christopher Beaumont Pickles, of Sutton Coldfield, W Midlands, and Angela, *née* Probyn-Skinner; *b* 29 Sept 1966; *Educ* Arthur Terry Sch Sutton Coldfield, Bedford Coll of Higher Educn (BA); *Career* int hockey player; memb Sutton Coldfield Ladies Hockey Club 1982–; England: under 18's 1985, under 21's 1986–87, sr debut v Spain 1988, 69 caps, played in Four Nations Tournament Spain 1988 and 5–match series Holland 1989, memb Euro Cup squad 1991 (Gold medallists), Capt Home Counties 1993–, S Africa tour 1993; GB: 71 caps 1990–, played in Four Nations Tournament Aust and NZ 1990, reserve GB Olympic Squad 1992, Champions' Trophy 1993, World Cup 1994, Olympic Qualifying Tournament Cape Town 1995, Olympic Games Atlanta (fourth place) 1996; formerly under 18's county rep: athletics, hockey, netball; formerly area rep: swimming, cross country; currently sr property admin Britannic Assurance; *Recreations* skiing, sailing, golf; *Style*— Mrs Mandy Davies; ✉ 17 Longdon Drive, Four Oaks, Sutton Coldfield, W Midlands B74 4RF (☎ 0121 353 9357); Britannic Assurance, Moor Green, Moseley, Birmingham B13 8QF (☎ 0121 449 4444)

DAVIES, Mark Edward Trehearne; s of Denis Norman Davies, of Slinfold, Sussex, and Patricia Helen, *née* Trehearne; *b* 20 May 1948; *Educ* Stowe; *m* 1, 8 June 1974 (m dis 1984), Serena Barbara, *née* Palmer; m 2, 20 Nov 1987, Antonia Catherine, da of Jeremy Barrow Chittenden, of Lytes Cary Manor, Somerset; 2 s (Hugo b 5 Oct 1989, another b 24 Sept 1996), 2 da (Sophia b 13 May 1988, Mollie b 18 March 1993); *Career* commodity broker Ralli International 1969, fndr Inter Commodities 1972 (awarded Queen's Award for Export Achievement 1981); chief exec: GNI Ltd 1972–, GNI Holdings Ltd 1976–, Gerrard & National Holdings PLC 1995– (dir 1986–); dir: GNI Property Development Ltd (formerly Inter Commodities Trading Ltd) 1976–, GNI Freight Futures Ltd 1981–, ICV Ltd 1981–, Inter Commodities Ltd 1982–, GNI Wallace Ltd 1986–, GNI Inc 1989–, Trifutures 1989–, The Rank Foundation 1991–, Warwick Racecourse Company Ltd 1993–, LM Moneybrokers Ltd 1994–, GNI Fund Management Ltd 1995–; chm Franklin Property & Investments Ltd 1994–, Admington Hall Farms; *Books* Trading in Commodities (co-author, 1974); *Recreations* hunting, racing; *Clubs* White's; *Style*— Mark Davies, Esq; ✉ 26 Chester Street, London SW1; GNI Ltd, Cannon Bridge, Atrium Building, 25 Dowgate Hill, London EC4R 2GN (☎ 0171 337 3500, fax 0171 337 3501, car 0385 356456)

DAVIES, Melvyn John (Mel); s of William John Davies, of Rhiwderin, Gwent, and Ruby Rosalia Davies; *b* 27 Aug 1948; *Educ* Duffryn Comp Sch, Newport Tech Coll; *m* 6 Sept 1980, Rosalie Rhonda, da of James Iorwerth James; 2 s (Gregory James b 12 Sept 1987, Jonathan William b 24 Jan 1990); *Career* co dir and racehorse owner; total 46 race wins, 17 by Barnbrook Again: Queen Mother Champion 2m chase (twice), Arlington Premier Final, Gerry Fielden Hurdle, Ladbroke Hurdle Leopardstown, Comton Brothers Chase, Hurst Park Chase, 5 times winner Newbury, 5 times winner Cheltenham incl South Wales Showers Caradon Mira Silver Trophy; records held by Barnbrook Again: 2m course Newbury, 2 1/2m course Cheltenham; sponsor of 12 races Cheltenham, 5 races Chepstow, and 40 at other courses; presenter Channel 4 racing Newmarket 1990; formerly apprentice plumber then plumber, fndr md South Wales Shower Supplies (t/a Faucets); raised money towards res into children's cancer illnesses and for Spinal Injuries Assoc; nominated for S Wales Young Businessman award 1988; memb Cncl Racehorse Owners' Assoc 1994; *Recreations* horse-racing, former Newport County FC devotee, various charities; *Style*— Mel Davies, Esq; ✉ Cayo House, Raglan, Gwent NP5 2HJ; 4 and 5 Court Road, Cwmbran, Gwent NP44 3AS (☎ 01633 872828, fax 01633 872264)

DAVIES, (Albert) Meredith; CBE (1982); s of Rev E A Davies; *b* 30 July 1922; *Educ* Stationers' Co's Sch, Keble Coll Oxford, RCM, Accademia di St Cecilia Rome; *m* 1949, Betty Hazel, *née* Bates; 3 s, 1 da; *Career* conductor: Royal Choral Soc 1972–85, Leeds Philharmonic Soc 1975–83; princ Trinity Coll of Music 1979–88; *Style*— Meredith Davies, Esq, CBE; ✉ 40 Monmouth St, Bridgwater, Somerset TA6 5EJ

DAVIES, Sir (David Herbert) Mervyn; kt (1982), MC (1944), TD (1946); s of Herbert Bowen and Esther Davies; *b* 17 Jan 1918; *Educ* Swansea GS; *m* 1951, Zita Yollanne Angelique Blanche Antoinette, da of Rev E A Phillips, of Bale, Norfolk; *Career* served WWII 18 Bn Welch Regt, 2 London Irish Rifles in Africa and Europe; admitted slr 1939, Travers Smith scholar and Daniel Reardon prize, called to the Bar Lincoln's Inn 1947, QC 1967, circuit judge 1978–82, justice of the High Court (Chancery Div) 1982–93; *Style*— Sir Mervyn Davies, MC, TD; ✉ 3 Stone Buildings, Lincoln's Inn, London WC2 (☎ 0171 242 8061); The White House, Great Snoring, Norfolk (☎ 01328 820 575)

DAVIES, Prof (Cyril Thomas) Mervyn; s of Cyril Thomas Davies (d 1993), of Bridgnorth, Shropshire, and Florence Davies (d 1985); *b* 2 Dec 1933; *Educ* Univ of London (BSc), Univ of Edinburgh (PhD, DSc); *m* 30 March 1963, Jacqueline Grace, da of Raymond John Morgan, of Lyme Regis; 2 s (Jonathan b 16 March 1965, James Davies b 26 April 1966), 1 da (Susanna Davies b 17 Oct 1970); *Career* lectr Univ of Edinburgh 1962–65, lectr and res scientist MRC 1965–79, visiting prof Univ of Milan 1968–69, conslt WHO 1969, prof of physiology Dar es Salaam Tanzania 1970–72, visiting res prof Stockholm Sweden 1973, visiting prof Copenhagen Denmark 1975, dir Med Res Cncl Unit Queens Med Centre Nottingham 1979–85, fndn prof of sport and exercise scis Univ of Birmingham 1986–94 (emeritus prof 1994); sec Int Paediatric Work Physiology Gp 1976, physiological conslt to Sports Cncl 1977–78, memb Editorial Bd European Jl of Applied Physiology 1977; memb Physiological Soc; *Recreations* gardening, bridge, squash racquets, golf, reading; *Clubs* Edgbaston Priory (Birmingham), Edgbaston Golf; *Style*— Prof Mervyn Davies; ✉ The Coach House, Pumphouse Lane, Barnt Green, Bromsgrove, Worcs B60 1QW (☎ 0121 445 4745)

DAVIES, (John) Michael; s of Vincent Ellis Davies, OBE, of East Grinstead, W Sussex, and late Rose Trench, *née* Temple; *b* 2 Aug 1940; *Educ* King's Sch Canterbury, Peterhouse Cambridge (BA); *m* 1971, Amanda Mary, da of Hedley Wilton Atkinson, of Shaldon, Devon; 2 s (William b 1976, Harry b 1982), 1 da (Anna b 1973); *Career* House of Lords: clerk Parliament Office 1964, seconded to Civil Serv as private sec to Leader of House and Chief Whip House of Lords 1971–74, establishment offr and sec to Chm of Ctees 1974–83, princ clerk Overseas and European Office 1983–85, clerk of Private Bills and Examiner of Petitions for Private Bills 1985–88, reading clerk and clerk of Public Bills 1988–91, clerk asst and clerk of Public Bills 1991–94, clerk asst and princ finance offr 1994–97, clerk of the Parliaments 1997–; sec: Soc of Clerks-at-the-Table in Cwlth Parliaments (jt ed The Table) 1967–83, Statute Law Ctee 1974–83; *Style*— Michael Davies, Esq; ✉ 26 Northchurch Terrace, London N1 4EG; House of Lords, London SW1 (☎ 0171 219 3181)

DAVIES, Sir (Alfred William) Michael; kt (1973); s of Alfred Edward Davies (d 1958), of Stourbridge, Worcs; *b* 29 July 1921; *Educ* King Edward's Sch Birmingham, Univ of Birmingham; *m* 1947, Margaret, da of Robert Ernest Jackson, of Sheffield; 1 s, 3 da; *Career* called to the Bar Lincoln's Inn 1948, QC 1964, dep chm Northants Quarter Sessions 1963–71; recorder: Grantham 1963–65, Derby 1965–71, Crown Ct 1972–73; ldr Midland Circuit 1968–71, jt ldr Midland and Oxford Circuit 1971–73; judge of the High Ct of Justice (Queen's Bench Div) 1973–91; chm Mental Health Review Tribunal for Birmingham Area 1965–71, chllr Diocese of Derby 1971–73, chm Hospital Complaints Procedure Ctee 1971–73; *Style*— Sir Michael Davies; ✉ c/o Child & Co, 1 Fleet Street, London EC4Y 1BD

DAVIES, (Angie) Michael; *b* 23 June 1934; *Educ* Shrewsbury, Queens' Coll Cambridge (MA); *m* 1960, Jane Priscilla; 2 children; *Career* chm and chief exec Imperial Foods and dir Imperial Group until May 1982; chm: Tozer Kemsley and Millburn Holdings plc 1985–86 (non-exec dir 1982–86), Worth Investment Trust plc 1986–95 (non-exec dir 1984–95), Bredero Properties plc 1986–94, Perkins Foods plc 1987–, Calor Group plc 1988– (non-exec dir 1987–), Berk Ltd 1988–95, Wiltshier plc 1988–95, National Express Group Ltd 1992–, Simon Engineering plc; dep chm: TI Group plc 1990–93 (non-exec dir 1984–93), Manpower plc 1989–92 (non-exec dir 1987–92), GPA Group plc 1993–; non-exec dir: The Littlewoods Organisation plc 1982–88, British Airways plc 1983–, Avdel plc 1983–94, TV-am plc 1983–89, Worcester Group 1991–92; FCA; *Style*— A Michael Davies, Esq; ✉ Little Woolpit, Ewhurst, Cranleigh, Surrey (☎ 01483 277344); 7 Lowndes Close, London SW1 (☎ 0171 235 6134)

DAVIES, Prof (John) Michael; s of Alfred Ernest Davies (d 1975), of Walsall, and Mavis Muriel, *née* Wildgoose (d 1979); *Educ* Queen Mary's GS Walsall, Univ of Manchester (BSc, PhD, DSc); *m* 24 June 1967, Anthea Dorothy, da of Rex Henry Percy,

MBE, DL, of Guildford; 1 s (Peter b 18 Nov 1972), 1 da (Claire b 16 Oct 1974); *Career* lectr Univ of Manchester 1962–65, engr Ove Arup & Partners Edinburgh 1965–70, visiting prof Univ of Karlsruhe 1980–81; Univ of Salford: reader 1971–80, prof of civil engrg 1981–95, chm Civil Engrg Dept 1988–91; prof of structural engrg Univ of Manchester 1995–; memb: Br Standards Ctees, Ctee Euro Convention for Constructional Steelwork (chm 1991–); ctee coordinator Int Bldg Cncl 1985–89; FIStructE 1976, FICE 1977; *Books* Manual of Stressed Skin Diaphragm Design (with E R Bryan, 1982), Plastic Design to BS 5950 (with B A Brown, 1996); *Recreations* tennis, golf, skiing; *Style—* Prof Michael Davies; ✉ 83 Park Road, Hale, Altrincham, Cheshire WA15 9LQ (☎ 0161 980 2838); Manchester School of Engineering, University of Manchester, Manchester M13 9PL (☎ 0161 275 4434, fax 0161 275 4361)

DAVIES, Michael Thomas (Mike); *b* 16 Aug 1947; *Educ* Aston Univ (BSc); *Career* former divnl md British Alcan Aluminium, exec dir (Main Bd) Williams Holdings plc 1988– (joined 1986); *Style—* Mike Davies, Esq; ✉ Williams Holdings PLC, Pentagon House, Sir Frank Whittle Road, Derby DE21 4XA (☎ 01332 202020, fax 01332 348283)

DAVIES, Nicola Velfor; QC (1992); *b* 13 March 1953; *Educ* Bridgend Girls' GS, Univ of Birmingham (LLB); *Career* called to the Bar Gray's Inn 1976; *Style—* Nicola Davies, QC; ✉ 3 Serjeants Inn, London EC4Y 1BQ (☎ 0171 353 5537, fax 0171 353 0425)

DAVIES, Rev Noel Anthony; s of Rev Ronald Anthony Davies (d 1967), of Pontycymer, Glamorgan, and Anne, *née* Morgans; *b* 26 Dec 1942; *Educ* Garw GS Pontycymer Glamorgan, UCNW Bangor (BSc), Mansfield Coll Oxford (BA Theol); *m* 10 Aug 1968, Patricia, da of John Cyril Barter (d 1986), of Lyme Regis; *Career* min Welsh Congregational Church Glanaman Dyfed 1968–77; gen sec: Cncl of Churches for Wales and Cmmn of The Covenanted Churches in Wales 1977–90, Cytun: Churches Together in Wales 1990–; chm Cncl of Welsh Congregational Union 1990–93, moderator Churches' Cmmn on Mission 1991–95, memb numerous Churches' ctees at Welsh and Br levels incl Cncl of Churches for Britain and I, also involved in World Cncl of Churches; *Publications* Wales: Language, Nation, Faith and Witness (1996), Wales: A Moral Society? (jt ed with Bishop Rowan Williams, 1996); also author of collections of prayers and meditations in Welsh; *Recreations* gardening, music, West Highland terriers, Oriental cooking; *Style—* The Rev Noel Davies; ✉ Cytun: Churches Together in Wales, 21 St Helens Road, Swansea, W Glamorgan SA1 4AP (☎ 01792 460876)

DAVIES, Noel Anthony Thomas; s of Thomas Herbert Davies, of Abergavenny, Gwent, and Vera May, *née* Smith (d 1995); *b* 1 Jan 1945; *Educ* Hereford Cathedral Sch (George Robertson Sinclair music scholar), RCM (ARCM organ performance, ARCM piano accompaniment, Michael Mudic Award for opera conducting); *Career* conductor; studied under Melville Cook, Hubert Dawkes and Sir Adrian Boult; specialises in operas by Mozart, Verdi, Puccini and operas of Eastern Europe; English Nat Opera (formerly Sadler's Wells Opera): repetiteur 1967, conducting debut 1969, res conductor 1974–; conductor ENO tour to Metropolitan Opera NY; guest appearances with Houston Grand Opera, Iceland Opera, Bergen Festival, Bayerische Staatsoper Munich, The Australian Opera; ed several works by Handel which have had been performed internationally; charity work incl: Catholic Stage Guild, Cardinal Hume Centre (for young people at risk in London), Terrence Higgins Tst, various other charities for AIDS sufferers; *Books* Handel's Xerxes (co-ed with Sir Charles Mackerras, Chester Music Ltd); *Recreations* cuisine, British countryside, supporter of West Ham United FC; *Style—* Noel Davies, Esq; ✉ 6c Maitland Place, London E5 8TR (☎ and fax 0181 985 9138)

DAVIES, Col Norman Thomas; OBE (1996, MBE 1970), JP (NE Hants 1984); s of Edward Ernest Davies (d 1937), and Elsie, *née* Scott; *b* 2 May 1933; *Educ* Holywell, RMA Sandhurst, Open Univ (BA); *m* 1961, Penelope Mary, da of Peter Graeme Agnew, of Cornwall; 1 s (Peter), 1 da (Clare); *Career* cmmnd RA 1954, served Malaya, Germany and UK 1954–64, mil asst to COS Northern Army Gp 1968–69, cmd C Battery RHA, 2 i/c 3 Regt RHA 1970–72, GSO I (DS) Staff Coll Camberley and Canadian Land Forces Cmd and Staff Coll 1972–74, cmd 4 Field Regt RA 1975–77, mil dir of studies RMC of Sci Shrivenham 1977–80 (Col 1977); registrar Gen Dental Cncl 1981–96; memb EC Advsy Ctee on the Trg of Dental Practitioners 1983–96; hon memb BDA 1990; *Recreations* rugby union, gardening, wine, fly-fishing, household maintenance; *Clubs* RSM; *Style—* Col N T Davies, OBE, JP; ✉ Lowfields Cottage, London Rd, Hartley Wintney, Hants (☎ 01252 843303)

DAVIES, Owen Handel; s of David Trevor Davies, and Mary Davies; *b* 22 Sept 1949; *Educ* Hazelwick Comp, Magdalene Coll Cambridge; *m* Caroline Jane Davies; 1 s (Jack Andrew Bowen 30 May 1982), 1 da (Mary Laura Caroline b 22 Feb 1988); *Career* called to the Bar Inner Temple 1973, jt head of chambers 2 Garden Ct Middle Temple; ed LND Journal; memb: Amnesty Int Lawyers' Gp, Environmental Law Assoc, Administrative Law Assoc, Criminal Bar Assoc, Liberty, Immigration Law Practitioners' Assoc, Haldane Soc; *Publications* articles and pamphlets on law and disarmament incl: The Illegality of Nuclear Warfare, A Tax on Peace; *Style—* Owen Davies, Esq; ✉ 2 Garden Court, Middle Temple, London EC4Y 9BL (☎ 0171 353 1633, fax 0171 353 4621, mobile 0860 746050)

DAVIES, Eur Ing Owen Mansel; s of D Mansel Davies, of Penarth, South Glamorgan, and Margaret Phyllis, *née* Hunt; *b* 3 June 1934; *Educ* Swansea GS, Clifton Coll, Peterhouse Cambridge (BA, MA); *m* 1960, Elisabeth Jean Leedham; 1 s (Timothy Mansel b 8 May 1963), 2 da (Catherine Elisabeth b 30 July 1961, Susan Margaret b 12 July 1966); *Career* Nat Serv Lt RA 1953–55; BP International technologist Aden Petroleum Refinery 1960–64, process engr London 1965–68, project engr BP Italia Rome 1969, mangr Catalytic Branch BP Trading Ltd 1970–72, mangr Projects Div Refineries Dept BP Trading Ltd 1972–75, md BP SE Asia Singapore 1975–78, pres Sohio Construction Co San Francisco 1978–80, gen mangr Projects London 1981–88, gen mangr Business Services BP Engineering London 1988–92, ind conslt 1992–; memb Northamptonshire Police Authy 1995–; FInstPet 1978, FIChemE 1985, FEng 1989, CEng, Eur Ing; *Recreations* sailing, gardening, photography; *Style—* Eur Ing Owen Davies, FEng; ✉ 63 High Street, Braunston, Daventry, Northants NN11 7HS (☎ and fax 01788 890076)

DAVIES, Patrick Taylor; CMG (1978), OBE (1967); s of Andrew Taylor Davies (d 1983), and Olive Kathleen Mary, *née* Hobson (d 1972); *b* 10 Aug 1927; *Educ* Shrewsbury, St John's Coll Cambridge (MA), Trinity Coll Oxford; *m* 1959, Marjorie Eileen, da of late Arthur Wilkinson; 2 da (Jennifer, Susan); *Career* entered HM Colonial Admin Serv Nigeria 1952, perm sec Kano State 1970–79, chief inspr Area Cts 1972–79; *Style—* Patrick Davies, Esq, CMG, OBE; ✉ Rose Cottage, Childs Ercall, Shropshire TF9 2DB (☎ 01952 840255)

DAVIES, Prof Paul Charles William; s of Hugh Augustus Robert Davies, of London, and Pearl Vera, *née* Birrell; *b* 22 April 1946; *Educ* Woodhouse GS Finchley, UCL (BSc, PhD); *m* 1, 13 July 1968 (m dis 1972), Janet Elaine, *née* Hammill; m 2, 28 July 1972, Susan Vivien Corti, da of Corti Woodcock (d 1958); 1 s (Charles Hugh Aidan b 1981), 1 da (Annabel Rebecca Eleanor b 1977); *Career* formerly: lectr in applied mathematics King's Coll London, prof Dept of Physics Univ of Newcastle upon Tyne; currently prof of natural philosophy Univ of Adelaide S Aust (formerly prof of mathematical physics); former govr Dame Allan's Schs Newcastle upon Tyne, vice pres Teilhard de Chardin Centre; ABC Eureka Prize for the Promotion of Science 1991; Advance Australia Award 1993, Templeton Prize for Progress in Religion 1995; FInstP 1984, FAIP 1990; *Books* non-fiction: The Physics of Time Asymmetry (1974 and 1977), Space and Time in the Modern Universe (1977), The Forces of Nature (1979, 2 edn 1986), The Search for Gravity Waves (1980), The Runaway Universe (1978), The Edge of Infinity (1981), The Accidental Universe (1982), Quantum Fields in Curved Space (with N D Birrell, 1982), God and the New Physics (1983), Quantum Mechanics (1984), Superforce (1984), The Ghost in the Atom (with J R Brown, 1986), The Cosmic Blueprint (1987), Superstrings (with J R Brown, 1988), The New Physics (ed, 1989), The Matter Myth (1991), The Mind of God (1992), The Last Three Minutes (1994), Are We Alone? (1995), About Time (1995); fiction: Fireball (1987); numerous tech papers incl: Scalar Particle Production in Schwarzschild and Rindler Metrics (1975), The Thermodynamic Theory of Black Holes (1977), Perturbation Technique for Quantum Stress Tensors in a General Robertson-Walker Spacetime (with W G Unruh, 1979), Journey through a Black Hole (with I G Moss, 1989); *Recreations* travel, making radio and television programmes; *Style—* Prof Paul Davies; ✉ The University of Adelaide, Department of Physics & Mathematical Physics, Australia 5005 (☎ 00 61 8 8303 5685, fax 00 61 8 8232 6541, telex UNIVAD AA 89141)

DAVIES, (Rowland) Peter; s of Peter Davies (d 1975), of Mold, Flintshire, and Freda Emily, *née* Roberts (d 1952); *b* 27 Oct 1934; *Educ* Alun GS Mold, UCNW Bangor (BA, DipEd), Univ of Lancaster (MA); *m* 1959, Marian, da of Robert Owens; 1 s (Christopher Mark b 1962), 1 da (Siân Lyn b 1965); *Career* Nat Serv RAEC Cyprus 1956–58; Caludon Castle Comp Sch for Boys Coventry: asst teacher of history 1958–64, dep housemaster 1960–64; Settle HS West Riding of Yorks: head of history 1964–72, head of Sixth Form 1970–72; dep headmaster Radyr Comp Sch S Glamorgan 1972–76, head designate Mynydd Isa HS Clwyd 1974–76, headmaster Nether Stowe Comp Sch Lichfield Staffs 1976–82, headmaster Thomas Alleyne's HS Uttoxeter Staffs 1982–92, seconded headteacher into industry Univ of Warwick 1992–93; dir Staffordshire (Education-Business) Partnership 1993–96; memb SHA 1977–93; represented N Wales at hockey 1956 and S Warwickshire at rugby 1963; *Books* Mixed Ability Grouping (1975), Mixed Ability Teaching (contrib, 1980); *Recreations* hockey, jogging, golf, fell walking; *Style—* Peter Davies, Esq; ✉ 7 Thornhill Close, Barton-under-Needwood, Burton-upon-Trent, Staffs DE13 8DJ (☎ 01283 712582)

DAVIES, Dr Peter David Owen; s of Herbert Lewis Owen Davies, of Caldy, Wirral, and Mary Ann Lockerbie, *née* Curry (d 1983); *b* 30 April 1949; *Educ* Marlborough, UC Oxford, St Thomas' Hosp London (MA, BM BCh, FRCP, DM); *m* 1975, Eleanor Mary Baskerville, da of David Mynors; 3 s (Richard b 1976, Edward b 1978, Michael b 1985), 1 da (Mary b 1982); *Career* various jr posts London Hosps until 1978, clinical offr MRC Tuberculosis and Chest Diseases Unit Brompton Hosp 1978–80, subsequently various posts Cardiff 1980–88, conslt respiratory physician Aintree Hosps and Cardiothoracic Centre Liverpool 1988–; licenced reader (Anglican Church) Dio of Chester; memb: BMA 1973, Br Thoracic Soc 1979, American Thoracic Soc 1987; *Books* Clinical Tuberculosis (ed); also author of papers on many aspects of tuberculosis particularly epidemiological; *Style—* Dr Peter Davies; ✉ Tuberculosis Research Unit, Cardiothoracic Centre, Thomas Drive, Liverpool L14 3PE (☎ 0151 228 1616, fax 0151 228 7688)

DAVIES, Peter Donald; s of Stanley Davies, of Aberystwyth, Dyfed, and Dorothy Margaret, *née* Addicott (d 1987); *b* 14 May 1940; *Educ* Ardwyn Sch Aberystwyth, Guy's Hosp Univ of London (MB BS); *m* 23 May 1965 (m dis 1989), Penelope Anne, da of Wilfred Reginald Dawes; 2 da (Lucy Bronwen b 1969, Emma Sian b 1971); *Career* lectr in experimental ophthalmology Inst of Ophthalmology London 1967–70, resident Moorfields Eye Hosp 1970–74, sr registrar Middx Hosp and Moorfields Eye Hosp 1974–78, conslt ophthalmic surgn Norwich Health Dist 1978–, initiated the devpt of out-patient cataract surgery in the UK 1983–, author of pubns on ophthalmology and corneal surgery; FRCS 1973; *Recreations* horse riding, shooting; *Style—* Peter Davies, Esq; ✉ Consulting Rooms, Hill House, BUPA Hospital, Old Watton Rd, Colney, Norwich NR4 7SZ (☎ 01603 456181 ext 408)

DAVIES, Peter Douglas Royston; CMG (1994); s of late Douglas Frederick Davies, of Christchurch, Dorset, and late Edna Matilda, *née* Dingle; *b* 29 Nov 1936; *Educ* Brockenhurst Co HS Hants, LSE (BSc); *m* 28 Jan 1967, Elizabeth Mary Lovett, da of Dr Leslie Williams (d 1956); 1 s (Simon Leslie Peter b 1968), 2 da (Eleanor Catherine b 1971, Jane Olivia b 1974); *Career* FO (now FCO): joined 1964–66, second sec Nicosia 1966–67, FO 1967–68, first sec Budapest 1968–71, FCO 1971–74, consul Rio de Janeiro 1974–78, cnsllr The Hague 1978–82, dep high cmmr Kuala Lumpur 1982–85, RCDS 1986, head Arms Control and Disarmament Dept FCO 1987–91, consul gen and DG Trade and Investment Canada Toronto 1991–96; fndr Peter Davies and Assocs (Canada) 1996–; *Recreations* reading, golf, skiing; *Style—* Peter Davies, Esq, CMG; ✉ Peter Davies and Associates, 158 Crescent Road, Toronto M4W 1V2, Canada

DAVIES, Peter Lewis Morgan; OBE (1978); s of David Morgan Davies (d 1962), and Annie Lee, *née* Jones (d 1983); *b* 15 Feb 1927; *Educ* Fishguard Co Sch; *m* 23 May 1953, Gwenith, da of Thomas Devonald Thomas Cilgerran (d 1969), of Cilgerran; *Career* Lt Welch Regt and Royal Welch Fusiliers 1944–48; Midland Bank plc 1943–51; Barclays Bank Int Ltd: Bahamas 1952–55, Nigeria 1955–67, Libya 1968–70, Zambia 1970–79, mangr Kaunda Square Kitwe (northern area mangr), alternate dir Barclays Zambia Ltd; team ldr World Bank Mission to Indonesia 1979–80, dir Pembrokeshire Business Initiative 1986– (md 1983–86), business cncllr Welsh Devpt Agency 1986–89, advsr The Prince's Youth Business Tst 1993–95; Br Exec Serv Overseas: Turks and Caicos Is 1982–83, Fiji 1990; memb: TAVRA Wales Regnl Ctee and Assoc 1988–93, Nat Employers' Liaison Ctee Wales; county treas Royal Br Legion Pembrokeshire, hon patron 4 Bn Royal Regt of Wales 1987–93; chm: Fin Ctee Last Invasion Bicentenary Ctee, Friends of the Community Fishguard and Goodwick 1992–, Fishguard and Goodwick Branch Pembrokeshire Cons and Unionist Assoc 1995–; FIMgt 1973; *Recreations* photography, philately; *Style—* Peter Davies, Esq, OBE; ✉ Court House, Tower Hill, Fishguard, Pembrokeshire SA65 9LA (☎ 01348 873 793)

DAVIES, Maj-Gen Peter Ronald; CB (1991); s of Lt-Col Charles Henry Davies, of Crookham Village, Hants, and Joy, *née* Moore; *b* 10 May 1938; *Educ* Llandovery, Welbeck, RMA Sandhurst; *m* 12 Sept 1960, (Rosemary) Julia, da of David Felice (d 1961), of Douglas, IOM; 1 s (Tristan David Henry b 1961), 1 da (Cecily Harriet (Mrs Richard Eaton) b 1963); *Career* cmmnd Royal Signals 1958, served BAOR Berlin, Cyprus, Borneo and UK 1958–72, Bde Maj 20 Armd Bde 1973–74, Instr Staff Coll Camberley 1975–76, CO 1 Armd Div Signal Regt 1976–79, Col GS SD HQ UKLF 1979–82, Bde Cdr 12 Armd Bde 1982–84, RCDS 1985, Dep Cmdt and Dir of Studies Army Staff Coll 1985–86, Cdr Communications BAOR 1987–90, GOC Wales 1990–91; Col King's Regt (8th, 63rd, 96th) 1986–94, Chm Regtl Cncl and King's Liverpool and Manchester Regts' Assoc 1986–94, Col Cmdt Royal Signals 1991–96; dir gen RSPCA 1991–, exec dir World SPA 1992–, exec dir Euro Gp for Animal Welfare 1992–, chm Freedom Food Ltd 1994–; conslt Int Strategic Planning Advsy Bd Andrew Corporation USA 1991–92; govr Welbeck Coll 1980–81, tstee Llandovery Coll 1992–, memb Exec Ctee Forces Help Soc and Lord Robert's Workshops 1994–96; CIMgt 1994 (FIMgt 1991), FIPD 1991, FZS 1994; *Recreations* music, wine, perpetual motion, Welsh nostalgia; *Clubs* Buck's, Army and Navy, Fadeaways; *Style—* Maj-Gen Peter Davies, CB; ✉ RSPCA Headquarters, Causeway, Horsham, West Sussex RH12 1HG (☎ 01403 264181, fax 01403 241048)

DAVIES, Ven Philip Bertram; s of Rev Bertram Davies (d 1970), and Nancy Jonsson, *née* Nicol (d 1978); *b* 13 July 1933; *Educ* Lancing Coll, Cuddesdon Theol Coll; *m* 29 June 1963, (Elizabeth) Jane, da of The Ven John Farquhar Richardson (d 1991); 2 s (Simon Philip b 1964, Matthew James b 1968), 2 da (Sarah Jane b 1966, d 1973, Eleanor Mary b 1974); *Career* supt Travancore Tea Estates Co S India 1957–58 (asst supt 1954–57), asst sales mangr Lewis's Ltd Manchester 1959–61; asst curate St John the Baptist

Atherton Lancs 1963–66, vicar St Mary Magdalen Winton Eccles 1966–71, rector St Philip with St Stephen Salford 1971–76, vicar Christ Church Radlett Herts 1976–87, rural dean Aldenham 1979–87, archdeacon of St Albans 1987–; *Recreations* fishing, gardening, bridge; *Style*— The Ven the Archdeacon of St Albans; ✉ 6 Sopwell Lane, St Albans, Herts AL1 1RR (☎ 01727 857973)

DAVIES, Quentin; MP (C) Stamford and Spalding (majority 22,869); s of Dr Michael Ivor Davies, and Thelma Davies; *b* 29 May 1944; *Educ* Dragon Sch, Leighton Park, Gonville and Caius Coll Cambridge (BA), Harvard (Frank Knox Fell); *m* 1983, Chantal, da of Lt-Col R L C Tamplin, Military Knight of Windsor; 2 s (Alexander, Nicholas); *Career* HM Dip Serv: third sec FCO 1967–69, second sec Moscow 1969–72, first sec FCO 1973–74; Morgan Grenfell & Co Ltd: asst dir 1974–78, dir and pres Morgan Grenfell France SA 1978–81, dir and head of Euro Corp Fin 1981–87, conslt 1987–93; MP (C) Stamford and Spalding 1987–; memb: Euro Standing Ctee 1990–, Treasy Select Ctee 1992–, Standards and Privileges Ctee 1996–; dir Dewe Rogerson International 1987–, advsr NatWest Markets 1993–; *Recreations* reading, walking, riding, skiing, travel; *Clubs* Beefsteak, Brooks's, Travellers', Constitutional (Spalding), S Lincs Cons (Bourne); *Style*— Quentin Davies, Esq, MP; ✉ c/o House of Commons, London SW1A 0AA

DAVIES, Dr Rachel Bryan; da of John Edwards (d 1960), and Gweno, *née* Davies Bryan (d 1981); *b* 6 Oct 1935; *Educ* Friends' Sch Sibford, Friends' Sch Sidcot, Univ Coll of Wales Aberystwyth (LLB), QMC London (LLM), King's Coll London (PhD); *m* 1958, Geraint Tim Davies, s of David Evan Davies; 1 s (Siôn b 1967), 4 da (Angharad b 1960, Crisiant b 1963, Manon b 1965, Rhianon b 1968); *Career* called to the Bar Gray's Inn 1965; res asst Law Faculty Melbourne Univ 1958–62, lectr in law Kingston Poly 1965–67, law reporter The Times 1975–81, commercial law reporter Financial Times 1981–92; chm Rent Tbnls 1981–86, exec and consultative ed Kluwer Law Publishing 1985–89, chm Industl Tbnls 1992– (pt/t chm 1986–92), vice pres Univ of Wales Swansea 1994–, memb Cncl and Ct of Govrs Univ of Wales 1995–; De Lancey and De La Hantey prize for medico-legal journalism 1981; FRSA 1990; *Recreations* walking, music, reading; *Style*— Dr Rachel Davies; ✉ Gelli Heblyg, Llangynwyd, Maesteg, Pen-y-Bont ar Ogwr CF34 0DT (☎ 01656 739115)

DAVIES, Prof (Robert) Rees; CBE (1995); s of William Edward Davies (d 1967), of Corwen, Gwynedd, and Sarah Margaret, *née* Williams (d 1986); *b* 6 Aug 1938; *Educ* Ysgol y Berwyn Bala, UCL (BA), Merton Coll Oxford (DPhil); *m* 29 July 1966, Carys, da of Ifor Lloyd Wynne (d 1970), of Wrexham, Clwyd; 1 s (Prys b 11 April 1972), 1 da (Manon b 25 May 1968); *Career* lectr: Univ Coll Swansea 1961–63, UCL 1963–76; prof of history Univ Coll of Wales Aberystwyth 1976–95 (vice princ 1988–91), Chichele prof of medieval history Univ of Oxford 1995–; asst ed and review ed History 1963–73, James Ford special lectr Univ of Oxford 1988, Wiles lectr Queen's Univ Belfast 1988, visiting fell Magdalen Coll Oxford 1992, Br Acad Wolfson research prof 1993–95; chm Ancient Monuments Bd for Wales 1995– (memb 1978–, dep chm 1993–95); memb: Cncl Nat Museum of Wales 1987–90, Cncl Historical Assoc 1990–92; chm: Nat Curriculum History Ctee for Wales 1988–90, Br Nat Ctee Int Congress of Historical Sciences 1992–; convenor History at Univs Def Gp 1990–92; jt winner Wolfson Literary award for History 1987, Norton Medlicott medal Historical Assoc 1994; pres: Royal Historical Soc 1992–96 (vice pres 1988–92), Assoc of History Teachers of Wales 1994–; hon fell: UC Swansea, UC Aberystwyth; FRHistS 1968, FBA 1987; *Books* Lordship and Society in the March of Wales (1978), Conquest, Coexistence and Change: Wales 1063–1415 (1987), Domination and Conquest: The experience of Ireland, Scotland and Wales 1100–1300 (1990), The Revolt of Owain Glyn Dŵr (1995), Welsh Society and Nationhood (ed, 1985), The British Isles 1100–1500 (ed, 1988); *Recreations* walking, music; *Style*— Prof Rees Davies, CBE, FBA; ✉ All Souls College, University of Oxford, Oxford OX1 4AL (☎ 01865 279379, fax 01865 279299)

DAVIES, Prof (Eurfil) Rhys; CBE (1990); s of Daniel Haydn Davies (d 1957), and Mary, *née* Jenkins (d 1961); *b* 18 April 1929; *Educ* Rhondda GS, Llandovery Coll, Clare Coll Cambridge (BA, MA, MB BChir), St Mary's Hosp London; *m* 15 Dec 1962, Zoë Doreen, da of Stanley Ivan Victor Chamberlain (d 1984); 3 s (Matthew b 1966, Huw b 1968, d 1995, Timothy b (twin) 1968); *Career* Nat Serv Capt RAMC 1954–56, regtl MO 24 Regt 1955–56; conslt radiologist Utd Bristol Hosps 1966–81, prof of clinical radiology Univ of Bristol 1981–93 (head of Clinical Sch 1991–93), prof emeritus 1993; civilian conslt in radiodiagnosis to the RN 1988–96; pres Br Nuclear Med Soc 1972–74; memb: Admin of Radioactive Substances Advsy Ctee 1978–83, Bristol and Weston Health Authy 1984–86, Ionising Radiation Advsy Ctee 1995–; Royal Coll of Radiologists: registrar 1976–81, warden 1984–86, pres 1986–89, memb Working Gp on Ionising Radiation (H & SE) 1987–95; memb: GMC 1989–93, Ct Univ of Bath 1989–93, Clinical Standards Advsy Gp 1991–93; hon fell Faculty of Radiologists RCSI 1976; FRSM, FFR 1964, FRCPE 1972, FRCR 1976, FDSRCS 1989; memb: BMA, Br Inst of Radiology; *Books* Radionuclides in Radiodiagnosis (jtly 1974), Nuclear Medicine: Applications in Surgery (ed with W E G Thomas, 1988); *Recreations* walking, theatre, wine; *Style*— Prof Rhys Davies, CBE; ✉ 19 Hyland Grove, Westbury on Trym, Bristol BS9 3NR (☎ 0117 950 1532)

DAVIES, His Hon Judge Rhys Everson; QC (1981); Evan Davies (d 1986), of Neath, W Glam, and Nancy Caroline, *née* Everson (d 1947); *b* 13 Jan 1941; *Educ* Cowbridge and Neath GS, Univ of Manchester (LLB); *m* 9 Feb 1963, Katharine Anne, da of Walter William Yeates; 1 s (Mark Everson b 24 July 1965), 1 da (Carolyn Alison (Mrs Balston) b 16 Feb 1969); *Career* called to the Bar Gray's Inn 1964, in practice on N Circuit 1964–90, recorder 1980–90, sr circuit judge, resident judge for Manchester and hon recorder of Manchester 1990–; bencher Gray's Inn 1993; chm Greater Manchester Area Criminal Justice Liaison Ctee 1992–; memb Ct and Cncl Univ of Manchester 1993–; *Recreations* music, walking; *Style*— His Hon Judge Rhys Davies, QC; ✉ Manchester Crown Court, Crown Square, Manchester M3 3FL

DAVIES, Richard James Guy; s of George Glyn Davies, MBE, of Frinton-on-Sea, Essex, and Cynthia Joan, *née* Franklin; *b* 7 Dec 1953; *Educ* Felsted, St Catharine's Coll Cambridge (MA); *m* 19 July 1980 (m dis 1992); 2 s (Michael b 1985, Christopher b 1987); *Career* with Lazard Bros & Co Ltd 1976–93, chief exec LET Ventures Ltd 1993–95; British Linen Bank Ltd: joined as dir 1995, head of corp fin 1995–; *Recreations* sailing, music, literature; *Clubs* Royal Burnham Yacht; *Style*— Richard Davies, Esq; ✉ Rookery Farm, Nayland Road, West Bergholt, Essex CO6 3DE (☎ 01206 271303); British Linen Bank Ltd, 8 Frederick's Place, London EC2R 8AT (☎ 0171 601 6840, fax 0171 600 1383)

DAVIES, Prof Robert; s of Thomas Stephen Davies (d 1985), of Abercynon, Glam, and Winifred Gertrude, *née* Taylor (d 1985); *b* 5 Jan 1935; *Educ* Mountain Ash GS, Univ of Birmingham; *m* 30 March 1959, (Sylvia) Meriel, da of Richard Westwood Rhodes (d 1985), of Hagley, W Midlands; 1 da (Sylvia Anne (Mrs Warwick)); *Career* tech offr ICI 1957–60, dep chief engr Bilston Foundries 1960–61; Univ of Birmingham: lectr 1965–71, sr lectr 1971–78, reader in engrg plasticity 1978–82, prof of mechanical engrg 1982–96, dep dean faculty of engrg 1987–90; author of 80 papers on: metal forming, powder metallurgy, adhesive bonding, laser technol; memb Nat Tst; CEng 1965, MIMechE 1965, MIM 1975, memb RSPB; *Books* Developments in High Speed Metal Forming (1970); *Recreations* antiques, ornithology; *Style*— Prof Robert Davies; ✉ High Crest, Rowney Green, Alvechurch, Birmingham B48 7QP (☎ 0121 445 2283)

DAVIES, Prof Robert James; s of Canon Dilwyn Morgan Davies, of Ilmington, Warwickshire, and Kate, *née* Maltby (d 1987); *b* 24 Feb 1943; *Educ* St Johns Sch Leatherhead, St Catharine's Coll Cambridge (MA, MB BS, MD); *m* 1, 1969 (m dis 1979); 2 s (Mark b 10 Oct 1972, James b 27 May 1975); m 2, June 1981, Karen, da of Dennis Stanley Seymour Henley, of Bexley; *Career* res fell Brompton Hosp London 1971–73, lectr in med St Thomas's Hosp London 1973–76, med res Univ of Tulane New Orleans USA 1976–77; St Bartholomew's Hosp London: conslt physician 1977–, dir Asthma and Allergy Res Dept 1981–, conslt in charge Dept of Respiratory Med 1987–, prof of respiratory med 1991– (reader 1983–90); dir Gen and Emergency Medicine Royal Hosps Tst 1994–96, dir of R & D Royal Hosps NHS Tst 1996–; third vice pres Int Assoc for Allergy and Immunology 1994– (treas 1985–94), pres Br Soc for Allergy and Clinical Immunology 1987–90, chm Br Allergy Fndn 1991–; medal of Faculty of Med Univ of Montpellier France 1981; FRCP 1982, fell American Acad of Allergy and Immunology 1984; *Publications* Respiratory Medicine (ed, 1988–94), Allergy - The Facts (ed, 1989); *Recreations* hill walking, snooker; *Clubs* Athenaeum; *Style*— Prof Robert J Davies; ✉ Department of Respiratory Medicine, The London Chest Hospital, Bonner Road, London E2 9JX (☎ 0181 983 2404, fax 0181 983 2274)

DAVIES, Robert John; s of Prof William Davies (d 1988), of Aberystwyth, and Janet, *née* Robinson; *b* 12 Oct 1948; *Educ* King Edward VII Sch Sheffield, HS of Stirling, Univ of Edinburgh (LLB); *m* 28 Aug 1971, Eileen Susan, da of George Littlefield (d 1952); 1 s (Christopher b 1978); *Career* fin dir Ford Motor Company Spain 1983–85 (various positions UK and USA 1970–83), dir and mgmnt conslt Coopers & Lybrand Associates 1985–87, fin dir Wedgwood Limited 1987–88, gp chief fin offr and dir Waterford Wedgwood plc 1989–91, gp fin dir Ferranti International plc 1991–93, fin dir East Midlands Electricity plc 1994–; FCMA 1976; *Recreations* golf; *Style*— Robert Davies, Esq; ✉ East Midlands Electricity plc, Corporate Office, PO Box 444, Wollaton, Nottingham NG8 1EZ (☎ 0115 901 0101, fax 0115 901 8019, mobile 0850 775707)

DAVIES, Robert Stephen; s of Richard George Davies (d 1968), and Megan, *née* Matthews (d 1992); *b* 23 Feb 1945; *Educ* Bridgend GS; *m* 25 July 1970, Philippa Mary, da of Herbert Woodley (d 1971); 2 s (Charles b 1972, Nicholas b 1975), 2 da (Lucy b 1982, Katy (twin) b 1982); *Career* audit mangr Mann Judd 1969–71 (articled clerk 1965–69), mgmnt conslt 1971–72, supervisor budgets and planning Gulf Oil Int London 1974–76 (sr fin analyst 1972–74), mangr fin and servs Gulf Oil Refining Ltd 1976–78, fin dir Gulf Oil Switzerland AG 1978–80, dir of logistics and supply Gulf Oil (GB) Ltd 1995– (fin dir 1980–95); fndr memb Jaguar Car Club, memb Cncl Cheltenham Ladies' Coll; FCA 1969; *Recreations* music, antique furniture, vintage cars, tennis; *Clubs* Bentley Drivers', Oil Industries Club, Vintage Sports Car Club; *Style*— Robert Davies, Esq; ✉ Rosehill, New Barn Lane, Cheltenham, Glos (☎ 01242 225302, fax 01242 225404); Gulf Oil (GB) Ltd, Rosehill, New Barn Lane, Cheltenham, Glos GL52 3LA

DAVIES, Prof Rodney Deane; CBE (1995); s of Holbin James Davies (d 1990), of Naracoorte, S Aust, and Rena Irene, *née* March (d 1982); *b* 8 Jan 1930; *Educ* Adelaide HS, Univ of Adelaide (BSc, MSc), Univ of Manchester (PhD, DSc); *m* 3 Jan 1953, (Valda) Beth, da of Arthur Roy Treasure (d 1988); 2 s (Warwick b 1953 d 1977, Stewart b 1960), 2 da (Rosalyn b 1955, Claire b 1957); *Career* Univ of Manchester: asst lectr 1953–56, lectr 1956–63, sr lectr 1963–67, reader 1967–76, prof of radio astronomy 1976–, dir Nuffield Radio Astronomy Laboratories 1988–; visiting astronomer Radio Physics Div CSIRO Sydney Australia 1963 (res offr 1951–53); memb various bds and ctees SERC, pres Royal Astronomical Soc 1987–89 (sec 1978–86), memb various ctees Int Astronomical Union; FRS 1992, FRAS 1956, FInstP, CPhys 1972; *Books* Radio Studies of the Universe (with H P Palmer, 1959), Radio Astronomy Today (with H P Palmer and M I Large, 1963), The Crab Nebula (co ed with F G Smith, 1971); *Recreations* gardening and fell walking; *Style*— Prof Rodney Davies, CBE, FRS; ✉ Parkgate House, Fulshaw Park, Wilmslow, Cheshire SK9 1QG (☎ 01625 523592); University of Manchester, Nuffield Radio Astronomy Laboratories, Jodrell Bank, Macclesfield, Cheshire SK11 9DL (☎ 01477 571321, fax 01477 571618, telex 36149)

DAVIES, (Anthony) Roger; s of (Richard) George Davies of Bridgend, Glamorgan (d 1968), and Megan, *née* Matthews (d 1992); *b* 1 Sept 1940; *Educ* King's Coll Univ of London (LLB, AKC); *m* 23 Sept 1967, Clare, da of Cdr William Arthur Walters, RN; 2 s (George b 1974, Hugo (twin) b 1974), 1 da (Antonia b 1972); *Career* called to the Bar Gray's Inn 1965; Lord Justice Holker sr scholar, in practice South Eastern Circuit, met stipendiary magistrate 1985, recorder of the Crown Ct; *Recreations* music, history, reading; *Clubs* Travellers'; *Style*— Roger Davies, Esq; ✉ c/o Horseferry Rd Magistrates Court, London SW1

DAVIES, Roger Guy; s of Cyril Graham Davies, OBE (d 1974), and Hettie Susannah, *née* Lewis; *b* 5 Nov 1946; *Educ* Kingswood Sch, Fitzwilliam Coll Cambridge (MA); *m* 30 May 1970, Diana June, da of Harold Charles Perks (d 1967); 3 s (Tom b 23 Sept 1973, William b 8 Nov 1974, Edward b 17 Dec 1977), 1 da (Georgina b 18 Oct 1982); *Career* ptnr Allen & Overy: articled clerk 1970–72, asst slr 1972–76, ptnr 1976–, Freeman Worshipful Co of Slrs; memb Law Soc; *Recreations* golf, tennis, shooting, music; *Clubs* Ashridge Golf, Oxford and Cambridge Golfing Soc, Hawks'; *Style*— Roger Davies, Esq; ✉ Corner Farm, Gaddesden Row, Hemel Hempstead, Herts HP2 6HN; Allen & Overy, One New Change, London EC4M 9QQ (☎ 0171 330 3000, fax 0171 330 9999)

DAVIES, Ronald (Ron); MP (Lab) Caerphilly (majority 22,672); s of late Ronald Davies; *b* 6 Aug 1946; *Educ* Bassaleg GS, Portsmouth Polytechnic, Univ Coll of Wales Cardiff; *m* 1981, Christina Elizabeth Rees; 1 da (Angharad Rees b 14 May 1986); *Career* sch teacher 1968–70, tutor/organiser WEA 1970–74, further educn advsr Mid-Glamorgan LEA 1974–83; MP (Lab) Caerphilly 1983–, oppn whip 1985–87; oppn spokesman on: agric and rural affrs 1987–, food 1989–; chief oppn spokesman on: agriculture 1992, Wales 1992–; elected memb Shadow Cabinet 1992–, shadow sec of state for Wales 1992–; cncllr Bedwas and Machen UDC and Rhymney Valley DC 1969–83; *Style*— Ron Davies, Esq, MP; ✉ House of Commons, London SW1

DAVIES, Rt Rev Roy Thomas; *see:* Llandaff, Bishop of

DAVIES, (Robert) Russell; s of John Gwilym Davies, of Llanbedr, Merioneth, and Gladys, *née* Davies; *b* 5 April 1946; *Educ* Manchester GS, St John's Coll Cambridge (scholar, BA, Tiarks German award); *m* 23 March 1972, Judith Anne, da of Noel Stephen Slater; 1 s (Steffan John b 5 Feb 1979); *Career* freelance journalist and broadcaster; TV actor and presenter (5 Series) 1970–71, cartoonist Liberal News 1971, caricaturist Times Literary Supplement 1972–74; The Observer: football reporter 1973–76, film critic 1973–78, contracted writer 1983–88; sports columnist New Statesman 1978–79, TV critic Sunday Times 1979–83 (columnist 1978–), dep ed Punch 1988 (contrib 1976–92); sports columnist: Sunday Telegraph 1989–94, Daily Express 1996–; radio critic Sunday Telegraph 1996–; radio incl: documentaries on American culture for Radio 3, biographies of jazz and blues figures, plays for radio, Midweek 1979–81, sports documentaries, radio series (When Housewives had the Choice, Radio Fun, Seven Deadly Singsongs, What An Institution, Quad Wrangles, Turns of the Century, Word of Mouth); television incl: What The Papers Say, What The Papers Say Annual Awards 1989–97, presenter Saturday Review, presenter Jazz Week and Jazz On a Summer's Day weekend BBC2, music documentaries BBC2 (Laughing Louie, Duke Ellington and his Famous Orchestra, Le Jazz Hot, The Lowest of the Low, Buddy Bolden's Children, A Musical Nation?, The Honky Tonk Professor), Statements (arts series BBC Wales), Knowing My Place (HTV); formerly: librettist Love And The Ice Cream Vendor (Roundhouse and South Bank Show LWT), actor Charles Charming's Challenges (Apollo Theatre); recorded The World of Buddy Bolden (with Humphrey Lyttelton) 1986; memb Br Actors Equity; *Books* Peregrine Prykke's Pilgrimage (illustrator, 1976), Vicky (with Liz Ottaway, 1987), Ronald

Searle (1990), The Diaries of Kenneth Williams (ed), The Kenneth Williams Letters (ed), Foreign Body: The Secret Life of Robert Maxwell (1996); *Recreations* jazz and jazz history, trombone, tuba, bass saxophone and piano playing, comic art, cartooning, tidying up; *Style*— Russell Davies, Esq; ✉ c/o Peters, Fraser and Dunlop, 5th Floor, The Chambers, Chelsea Harbour, Lots Road, London SW10 0XF (☎ 0171 344 1000)

DAVIES, Ryland; s of Gethin Davies, and Joan Davies; *b* 9 Feb 1943; *Educ* Royal Manchester Coll of Music (studied with Frederic R Cox, OBE); *m* 1, 1966 (m dis 1981), Anne Elizabeth Howells; m 2, 1983, Deborah Rees; 1 da (Emily); *Career* tenor, operatic prodr and voice teacher; debut as Almaviva in The Barber of Seville WNO 1964, debut as prodr L'Elisir d'Amore 1991; pt/t prof of singing RNCM 1987–94; performed at venues incl Covent Garden, Glyndebourne, NY Met, Milan, Paris, Vienna, Salzburg, Berlin, Hamburg, Stuttgart, Buenos Aires, Bonn; worked with orchs incl: London Symphony, London Philharmonic, English Chamber Orch, Chicago Symphony, Philadelphia Orch, Vienna Symphony, Boston Symphony, Cleaveland Symphony, Bavarian Radio Orch; worked under conductors incl: Sir John Pritchard, Sir Colin Davis, Sir Charles Mackerras, Daniel Barenboim, Sir Georg Solti, Richard Bonynge, Simon Rattle, Andrew Davis, Erich Leinsdorf, Karl Böhm, Zubin Mehta, Claudio Abbado, Herbert von Karajan, Bernard Haitink, James Levine, John Eliot Gardiner; made numerous recordings, given performances on radio, TV and film; Boyce and Mendelssohn Fndn scholarship 1964, John Christie award 1965; fell Royal Manchester Coll of Music 1971, fell Welsh Coll of Music and Drama 1996; *Roles* incl: Belmonte in Die Entführung aus dem Serail (Glyndebourne), Fenton in Falstaff (Scottish Opera), Ferrando in Così Fan Tutte (Covent Garden, Met Opera NY), Flamand in Capriccio (Glyndebourne), Tamino in The Magic Flute (Glyndebourne, WNO, Scottish Opera), Essex in Britten's Gloriana (Sadler's Wells), Hylas in The Trojans, Don Ottavio in Don Giovanni (Covent Garden), Cassio in Otello, Ernesto in Don Pasquale (Covent Garden), Lysander in A Midsummer Night's Dream (Covent Garden, Glyndebourne), The Prince in The Love for Three Oranges (Glyndebourne), Eisenstein in Die Fledermaus (ENO), Nemorino in L'Elisir d'Amore (Covent Garden), Le Duc, Chérubin and Basilio in Le Nozze di Figaro (Covent Garden), Arbace in Idomeneo (Met Opera NY); *Style*— Ryland Davies, Esq; ✉ Elm Cottage, Loseberry Road, Claygate, Surrey KT10 9DQ (☎ and fax 01372 463762)

DAVIES, Sharron Elizabeth; MBE (1993); da of Terry Davies, and Sheila, *née* Conybeare; *b* 1 Nov 1962; *Educ* Kelly Coll Devon; *m* Derek Redmond, *qv*; 1 s (Elliott Anthony Mark b 4 Nov 1993); *Career* swimmer; memb Br Olympic Team 1976 (youngest memb), 1980 (Silver medal 400m individual medley) and 1992, Bronze medal 400m European Championships 1977, Gold medals 200m and 400m individual medley Cwlth Games 1978, Bronze medal 4 x 100m freestyle relay Cwlth Games 1990; has broken over 200 Br records; Sportswoman of the Year 1978 and 1980; interior design and fashion conslt; Amazon in Gladiators (ITV) 1995–96, presenter The Big Breakfast (Planet 24 for Channel 4) 1996–; *Style*— Ms Sharron Davies, MBE; ✉ The Big Breakfast, c/o Planet 24 Ltd, The Planet Building, Thames Quay, 195 Marsh Wall, London E14 9SG

DAVIES, Simon; s of Arthur Rees Davies (d 1982), of Newcastle-Emlyn, Cardiganshire, and Catherine Elizabeth, *née* Jones (d 1991); *b* 12 March 1937; *Educ* Cardigan GS, Coll of Estate Mgmnt (pres SU); *m* 24 Oct 1959 (m dis 1989), Anja Ilse, *née* Körner; 1 s (Michael Stephen b 1 April 1960, d 1978), 1 da (Kathleen Anja b 1 June 1964); m 2, March 1990, Sheila Jane, *née* Henderson; *Career* md Kemp and Hawley Ltd Chartered Surveyors; hon memb Gorsedd of Bards; Freeman City of London; FRICS; FCIArb; *Recreations* rugby, opera; *Style*— Simon Davies, Esq; ✉ 9 Hyde Park Crescent, London W2 2PY; 13 Monmouth St, London WC2H 9DA (☎ 0171 405 8161, fax 0171 836 2214)

DAVIES, Dr Stevie; da of Henry James Davies (d 1974), of Swansea, and Mona Joan Davies; *b* 2 Dec 1946; *Educ* Priory Girls' GS Shrewsbury, Univ of Manchester (BA, MA, PhD); *m* 1; 1 s (Robin Harry b 1980), 2 da (Emily Jane b 1977, Grace Hannah (twin) b 1980); m 2, 1990, Frank Regan; *Career* lectr in English lit Univ of Manchester 1971–84; author and pt/t tutor 1984–; sr research fell Roehampton Inst; memb Milton Soc of America; memb Greenpeace, involved in the peace movement and feminism; Arts Cncl Writer's Award 1996; *Books* literary criticism: Emily Brontë: The Artist as a Free Woman (1983), Images of Kingship in 'Paradise Lost' (1983), The Idea of Woman in Renaissance Literature (1986), Emily Brontë (1988), Virginia Woolf's 'To the Lighthouse' (1989), Shakespeare's 'Twelfth Night' (1993), John Donne (1994), Emily Brontë: Heretic (1994), Henry Vaughan (1995); novels: Boy Blue (1987, Fawcett Soc Book Prize 1989), Primavera (1990), Arms and the Girl (1992), Closing the Book (1994, longer short-list for Booker Prize, short-list for Fawcett Soc Prize 1994), Four Dreamers and Emily (1996); *Recreations* playing piano, listening to music, reading; *Style*— Dr Stevie Davies

DAVIES, Susan Elizabeth (Sue); OBE; da of Stanworth Wills Adey (d 1980), and Joan Mary Margaret Charlesworth (d 1967); *b* 14 April 1933; *Educ* Nightingale-Bamford NY USA, Eothen Caterham Surrey, Triangle Secretarial Coll; *m* 11 Sept 1954, John Ross Twiston Davies, s of John Harold Twiston Davies (d 1990); 2 da (Joanna Lyn Twiston b 27 Dec 1955, Stephanie Jane Twiston b 27 March 1956, d 1988); *Career* photography; Municipal Jl 1953–54, various voluntary jobs, Artists Placement Gp 1966–67, ICA 1967–70, fndr and dir Photographers' Gallery 1971–91 (first photography gallery in Europe), photography consIt 1991–; Progress medal Royal Photographic Soc 1982, Kulturpreis German Photographic Soc 1990; memb: CNAA Photography Ctee 1982–86, CNAA Design Panel 1986–88; Hon FRPS 1980; *Recreations* jazz, gardens, grandchildren; *Clubs* Chelsea Arts; *Style*— Mrs Sue Davies, OBE; ✉ 53 Britwell Rd, Burnham, Bucks SL1 8DH (☎ and fax 01628 662677)

DAVIES, Terence; s of Thomas Davies (d 1952), of Liverpool, and Helen, *née* O'Brien; *b* 10 Nov 1945; *Educ* Sacred Heart RC Boys' Sch, Coventry Drama Sch, Nat Film and TV Sch; *Career* actor, writer and director (film) 1973–; shipping office clerk 1960–61, unqualified book-keeper and accountant 1961–63; dir: The Terence Davies Trilogy (7 int prizes), Distant Voices Still Lives (17 int prizes), The Long Day Closes (2 int prizes); *Books* Hallelujah Now (novel, 1983), A Modest Pageant (1992); *Recreations* reading, listening to music, dining, humour; *Style*— Terence Davies, Esq; ✉ c/o Nigel Britten, Nigel Britten Management, Garden Studios, 11–15 Betterton Street, Covent Garden, London WC2H 9BP

DAVIES, Thomas; s of David Charles Davies (d 1967), and Henrietta Florence, *née* Sutton (d 1984); *b* 25 June 1932; *Educ* Pinner County GS; *m* 1959, Ursula Jane, da of Leonard Theodore Freeman; 3 da (Virginia Jane (Mrs R B Stevens) b 1962, Gillian Karina b 1964, Kristina Louise b 1968); *Career* Sydenham & Co (now Kidsons Impey) Chartered Accountants: articled 1952–57, qualified 1958, opened Hereford office 1960, ptnr 1967– (currently ptnr i/c Hereford office); FCA; *Recreations* game fishing, walking, ornithology, crosswords; *Style*— Thomas Davies, Esq; ✉ Hunters Moon, Breinton, Hereford HR4 7PB (☎ 01432 266746); Kidsons Impey, Elgar House, Holmer Rd, Hereford HR4 9SF (☎ 01432 352222, fax 01432 269367)

DAVIES, Tudor Griffith; *b* 2 Dec 1951; *Educ* Barry Boys GS, Manchester Univ (BSc); *m* 26 July 1980, Julia Alison, *née* Harvey; 4 s (William, Gwyn, Rhodri, Steffan), 1 da (Sally); *Career* corporate recovery ptnr Arthur Young CAs 1984–88, currently chief exec Hicking Pentecost plc, non-exec dir Scottish Highland Hotels plc; ACA; *Recreations* fishing, rugby football; *Style*— Tudor Davies, Esq; ✉ Hicking Pentecost plc, 19 Stanwell Road, Penarth, South Glamorgan CF64 2EZ (☎ 01222 711333, fax 01222 711666)

DAVIES, (William) Vivian; s of Walter Percival Davies, of Llanelli, Dyfed, and Gwenllian, *née* Evans; *b* 14 Oct 1947; *Educ* Llanelli GS, Jesus Coll Oxford (BA, MA), Queen's Coll Oxford (Randall-MacIver student in archaeology); *m* 1, 30 Oct 1970 (m dis 1994), Janet Olwen May, da of Laurie Frederick Foat, DFM, of Llanelli, Dyfed; 1 s (Thomas Dafydd Robert b 30 June 1974), 1 da (Elen Mai b 24 May 1971); m 2, 11 Aug 1996, Renée Frances, da of Lester Friedman, of Los Angeles, USA; *Career* Egyptologist; dep keeper Dept of Egyptian Antiquities Br Museum 1981–88 (asst keeper 1974–81), visiting prof of Egyptology Univ of Heidelberg 1984–85, keeper of Egyptian Antiquities Br Museum 1988–; hon librarian Egypt Exploration Soc 1975–85, reviews ed Journal of Egyptian Archaeology 1975–85, gen ed EES Publications 1989–; chm Sudan Archaeological Research Soc 1991–; memb: Governing Cncl Br Inst in Eastern Africa 1989–, German Archaeological Inst 1992–; FSA 1980; *Books* Egyptian Sculpture (with T G H James, 1983), Saqqara Tombs (with A B Lloyd and A J Spencer, 1984), Problems and Priorities in Egyptian Archaeology (ed with J Assmann and G Burkard, 1987), Egyptian Hieroglyphs (1987), Catalogue of Egyptian Antiquities in the British Museum VII Axes (1987), Egypt and Africa Nubia from Prehistory to Islam (ed, 1991), Biological Anthropology and the Study of Ancient Egypt (ed with Roxie Walker, 1993), Time Machine, Ancient Egypt and Contemporary Art (ed with James Putnam, 1994), Egypt, the Aegean and the Levant (ed with Louise Schofield, 1995); *Style*— Vivian Davies, Esq, FSA; ✉ Department of Egyptian Antiquities, British Museum, London WC1B 3DG (☎ 0171 323 8306, fax 0171 323 8303)

DAVIES, Prof Wendy Elizabeth; da of late Douglas Charles Davies, and Lucy, *née* Evans; *b* 28 Aug 1942; *Educ* Maynard Sch, Univ of London (BA, PhD); *Career* historian; lectr Univ of Birmingham 1970–76; UCL: lectr 1977–81, reader 1981–85, prof 1985–, head of dept 1987–92, dean 1991–95, pro-provost 1996–; visiting fell All Souls Coll Oxford 1986; memb: Cncl Soc for Medieval Archaeology 1983–86, Ancient Monuments Bd for Wales 1994–; a govr Museum of London 1995–; FRHistS 1979, FSA 1988, FBA 1992; *Books* An Early Welsh Microcosm (1978), The Llandaff Charters (1979), Wales in the Early Middle Ages (1982), Small Worlds, The Village Community in Early Medieval Brittany (1988), Patterns of Power (1990), The East Brittany Survey, Field Work and Field Data (1994); *Recreations* gardening, early music; *Style*— Prof Wendy Davies; ✉ History Department, University College London, Gower Street, London WC1E 6BT (☎ 0171 391 1348)

DAVIES, Rev Dr William Rhys; s of Rhys Thomas Davies (d 1936), and Alice, *née* Swift (d 1995); *b* 31 May 1932; *Educ* Blackpool GS, Hartley Victoria Theol Coll Manchester, Univ of Manchester (MA, PhD), BD (London External); *m* 9 Nov 1955, Barbara Constance, da of Allan Topping (d 1978); 1 s (Michael b 27 June 1957), 1 da (Helen b 20 Feb 1964); *Career* methodist minister: Middleton Manchester 1955–60, Fleetwood 1960–65, Stockton on Tees 1965–66, Warrington (serving as sr lectr in religious studies Padgate Coll 1966–79); supt methodist minister Bradford Mission 1979–83, princ Cliff Coll Calver Sheffield 1983–94, ret; supernumerary methodist minister; pres Methodist Conf 1987–88, moderator Free Church Federal Cncl 1991–92; consIt ed Dunamis Magazine 1972–95; chm Methodist Ctee for Relations with People of Other Faiths 1988–; memb: Cncl of Mgmnt Evangelical Alliance 1985–91, Cncl Garden Tomb Assoc (Jerusalem) 1992–95; *Books* Gathered into One (1975), Spirit Baptism and Spiritual Gifts in Early Methodism (1973), What About the Charismatic Movement? (1980), Rocking the Boat (1986), Spirit Without Measure (1996); *Recreations* reading, sport; *Style*— The Rev Dr William Davies; ✉ 25 Grange Avenue, Thornton Cleveleys, Lancashire FY5 4PA (☎ 01253 864678)

DAVIES-SCOURFIELD, Brig Edward Grismond Beaumont; CBE (1966, MBE 1951), MC (1940), DL (1984); s of Henry Gwyn Davies-Scourfield (d 1934), of Sussex, and Helen Mary, *née* Newton (d 1973); *b* 2 Aug 1918; *Educ* Winchester, RMC Sandhurst; *m* 24 Nov 1945, Diana Lilias, da of Sir Nigel Davidson, CBE (d 1961), of Sussex; 1 s (Gwyn b 1959), 1 da (Susan b 1948); *Career* army offr, ret 1973; cmmnd 2 Lt KRRC 1938, Despatches 1945, CO 1 Bn Rifle Bde 1960 (Lt-Col), Bde Col Royal Green Jackets 1962, Brig Cdr Br Jt Servs Trg Team Ghana 1964, Dep Cdr NEARELF 1966, cmd Salisbury Plain Area 1970; gen sec Nat Assoc of Boys Clubs (vice pres) 1973–82, memb E Hants Ctee CPRE, chm Hants Army Benevolent Fund 1983–92, tstee regtl funds 1971–89, church warden 1975–88 and 1994–95; *Books* In Presence of my Foes: Travels and Travails of a P.O.W (1991); *Recreations* racing, shooting, tennis, walking; *Clubs* Army and Navy, Mounted Infantry; *Style*— Brig E G B Davies-Scourfield, CBE, MC, DL; ✉ c/o Lloyds Bank plc, Cox's & King's Branch, PO Box 1190, 7 Pall Mall, London SW1Y 5NA

DAVIS, *see:* Lovell-Davis

DAVIS, *see:* Hart-Davis

DAVIS, Albert Edward; s of Albert Ellerd Davis (d 1954), of Luton, Beds, and Kate Elizabeth, *née* Sell (d 1962); *b* 15 July 1928; *Educ* Luton GS; *m* 1 March 1952, Rhona, da of Walter Maurice Temple-Smith (d 1980), of Harpenden, Herts; 1 s (Andrew Albert b 1956); *Career* sr ptnr Davis & Co (certified accountants) 1964– (joined 1945, jr ptnr 1950–64); dir Beacon Private Trust 1960–; memb: City of London Branch Royal Soc of St George, United Wards Club City of London, Farringdon Ward Club, Ward of Cheap Club; Freeman City of London 1984, Liveryman Worshipful Co of Arbitrators 1984; FTII 1951, FCCA 1952, FCIArb 1968; *Recreations* music, walking, travel, horticulture; *Clubs* City Livery; *Style*— Albert Davis, Esq

DAVIS, Andrew Frank; CBE (1992); *b* 2 Feb 1944; *Educ* Royal Coll of Music, King's Coll Cambridge (organ scholar); *Career* conductor; continuo player for Eng Chamber Orch and Acad of St Martin-in-the-Fields, studied conducting with Franco Ferrara in Rome; Festival Hall debut 1970 conducting BBC Symphony Orch; asst conductor The Philharmonia Orch 1973–77, princ guest conductor Royal Liverpool Philharmonic Orch 1974–77, music dir Toronto Symphony Orch 1975–88 (conductor laureate 1988–), music dir Glyndebourne Festival Opera 1988–, chief conductor BBC Symphony Orch 1989– (incl tours to Hong Kong, Europe and Japan); has worked with other orchs incl: Berlin Philharmonic, Frankfurt Radio Symphony, Tonhalle, Stockholm Philharmonic, Israel Philharmonic, NY Philharmonic, Boston, Chicago and Philadelphia Orchs, LA Philharmonic; appeared at venues incl: Paris Opera, Royal Opera House Covent Garden, Met Opera NY, Chicago Lyric Opera, La Scala Milan, BBC Proms (conductor Last Night 1993–), All Saints' Day Concert Musikverein Vienna, various Br and Euro festivals, numerous other venues in N America, Europe and Far East; work for Glyndebourne Festival Opera incl: Eugene Onegin, Falstaff, Ariadne auf Naxos, Don Giovanni, Katya Kabanova 1988, Jenufa 1989, Tippett's New Year 1990, The Marriage of Figaro 1991, La Clemenza di Tito 1991, The Magic Flute 1991, Peter Grimes 1992, Pique Dame 1992; other operatic work incl: The Marriage of Figaro (Chicago Lyric Opera), La Clemenza di Tito (Chicago Lyric Opera), Peter Grimes (Bavarian Staatsoper) 1991; awarded Royal Philharmonic Soc/Charles Heidsieck Conductor's Award 1990; *Recordings* incl: all Dvorak Symphonies (with The Philharmonia), Mendelssohn Symphonies (with Bavarian Radio Symphony Orch), Tippett The Mask of Time (with BBC Symphony Orch, following Euro premiere BBC Proms 1984, winner Gramophone Record of the Year 1987, Grand Prix du Disque 1988), Shostakovich Violin Concertos, Brahms Piano Concertos, Nielsen Symphonies 4 and 5, various by Elgar, Vaughan Williams, Britten, Delius and Tippett; over 25 recordings with Toronto Symphony Orch incl: Strauss Four Last Songs and Salome final scene, Holsts Planets Suite, Handel Messiah; *Style*—

Andrew Davis, Esq, CBE; ✉ c/o Harold Holt Ltd, 31 Sinclair Road, London W14 0NS (☎ 0171 603 5148, fax 0171 603 0019, telex 22339 HUNTER)

DAVIS, (Richard) Anthony; s of Joseph David Davis (d 1970), of Talley, Dyfed, and Blanche Marie, *née* Stephenson (d 1991); *b* 20 May 1945; *Educ* Ruthin; *m* 11 July 1981, Wendy Hilary, da of Eric Curme, of Rodborough, Gloucestershire; *Career* articled clerk in private practice Birmingham 1963–66, personnel mgmnt Britannic Assurance Birmingham 1966–70; mktg communications 1970–, in private practice 1973–; ed British Commercial and Industrial Property 1974–76, ctee memb Silver Jubilee Expo Hyde Park London 1977, ptnr Davenports London 1982–; tstee Langley House Trust; Parly candidate Solihull 1970; visiting lectr: Birbeck Coll London, South Bank Univ Business Sch London; memb Cncl Inst of PR 1988–90 (MIPR 1974–92); Freeman: City of London 1987, Horners' Co 1993; MCIM 1991, MIMgt 1991, FRSA 1992; *Recreations* music, classical guitar, watercolours, gardening, food, photography; *Style—* Anthony Davis, Esq; ✉ Davenport Marketing, Clerkenwell House, 45–47 Clerkenwell Green, London EC1R 0HT (☎ 0171 490 8410, fax 0171 738 6198)

DAVIS, Col Anthony Wilmer; OBE (1994, MBE 1972); s of Brig Thomas William Davis, OBE (d 1982), of Sea Point, South Africa, and Margot Caddy, *née* Mackie (d 1983); *b* 11 Aug 1930; *Educ* Bryanston; *m* 28 June 1957, Susan Ward, da of Stephen Edgar Hames (d 1985), of Prestbury, Cheshire; 1 s (Simon b 1959), 1 da (Fiona b 1961); *Career* RMA Sandhurst 1949–51, cmmnd Manchester Regt 1951, Staff Coll Camberley 1961, Armed Forces Staff Coll Norfolk Virginia USA 1968, Bde Maj Berlin Inf Bde 1969–71, CO King's Regt 1972–74, Directing Staff Nat Def Coll Latimer 1975–77, Col GS Staff Coll Camberley 1978–81; Comptroller and Sec Forces Help Soc and Lord Roberts Workshops 1982–96, ret; FIMgt 1980; *Recreations* golf, classical music; *Style—* Col A W Davis, OBE

DAVIS, (John) Barry; s of Wilfred John Davis (d 1973), of Birmingham, and Edna Olive, *née* Chester (d 1988); *b* 6 Jan 1936; *Educ* George Dixon GS Birmingham; *m* 10 Sept 1960, Brenda Margaret, da of William Henry Barnes; 1 da (Elizabeth Jayne b 20 Jan 1972); *Career* articled clerk Jacob Cavenagh & Skeet Chartered Accountants Birmingham 1952–57, qualified 1958; ptnr Neville Russell Birmingham 1965–96 (joined when Dixon Hopkinson 1958), sole practitioner in private practice 1996–; methodist local preacher; hon consul Finland; FCA (ACA 1958), MIPA, MSPI, LLCM, ALCM; *Recreations* classical music, opera, ballet, gardening; *Clubs* Birmingham Consular Association, Birmingham Organists Association; *Style—* Barry Davis, Esq; ✉ 31 Mirfield Road, Solihull, West Midlands B91 1JH (☎ and fax 0121 705 4937)

DAVIS, Dr Brian Elliott; *b* 1944; *Educ* Univ of Sussex (BSc), Univ of Sheffield (PhD); *m*; 3 c; *Career* with Esso 1970–86; Nationwide Building Society: joined 1986, gen mangr 1987, dir Link 1987–, gen mangr Nationwide Anglia (following merger) 1987–89, resource dir 1989–92, ops dir 1992–94, chief exec 1994–; chm Bldg Socs Assoc 1996–; FRSA 1990, CIMgt 1993; *Recreations* squash and amateur dramatics; *Style—* Dr Brian Davis; ✉ Nationwide Building Society, Nationwide House, Pipers Way, Swindon, Wilts SN38 1NW

DAVIS, Maj-Gen Brian William; CB (1985), CBE (1980, OBE 1974); s of late Edward William Davis, MBE, and Louise Jane, *née* Webber; *b* 28 Aug 1930; *Educ* Weston super Mare GS, Mons Offr Cadet Sch Aldershot; *m* 1954, Margaret Isobel Jenkins; 1 s, 1 da; *Career* cmmnd RA 1949, Lt-Col Staff Coll Camberley 1969–71, CO 32 Light Regt RA serving in BAOR NI and UK 1971–74, Col logistic plans and ops HQ BAOR 1975, Brig 1975, Cdr RA 3 Div 1976–77, RCDS 1978, COS NI 1979–80, C-in-C Mission to Soviet Forces Germany 1981–82, Maj-Gen 1982, COS Logistic Exec (Army) MOD 1982–83, Vice QMG 1983–85, ret 1985; head of public affairs RO plc 1985–94; dep pres Army Rugby Union 1984–88; *Recreations* rugby, cricket, fishing; *Clubs* Army & Navy, Special Forces, HAC, MCC, Somerset CCC, Piscatorial Soc, Fadeaways; *Style—* Maj-Gen Brian Davis, CB, CBE; ✉ c/o Royal Bank of Scotland, Laurie House, Victoria Rd, Farnborough, Hants

DAVIS, Calum; s of Roy Albert George Davis, of Pigeon House Corner, Rockford, Ringwood, Hants, and Catherine Jessie Davis, of Oban, Scotland; *b* 18 June 1951; *Educ* Taunton Sch, Canterbury Sch of Architecture (DipArch); *m* 20 Aug 1977 (m dis 1996); 1 s (Jamie b 1981), 1 da (Josie b 1984); *Career* architect; sr ptnr Architon Group Practice architects and planning consultants; dir: Architon Developments Ltd 1986, Architon Services Ltd 1986, Trefoil Properties Ltd 1988; Architects Registration Cncl UK 1979; RIBA 1979; Eng trialist under 19 rugby 1969; rep: SW Eng Schs rugby 1969, S Eng under 19 rugby 1969; *Recreations* golf, skiing, conservation of historic buildings; *Clubs* RAC; *Style—* Calum Davis, Esq; ✉ The Stone House, 21 Rose Hill, Dorking, Surrey RH4 2EA (☎ 01306 883946); Architon Group Practice, Architon House, 7 Ashley Rd, Epsom, Surrey KT18 5AQ (☎ 01372 745600, fax 01372 745016, mobile 0831 837908)

DAVIS, Carl; *b* 28 Oct 1936; *m* Jean Boht, *qv*; 2 da (Hannah b 1 Jan 1972, Jessie b 3 May 1974); *Career* composer and conductor; studied with: Paul Nordoff and Hugo Kauder NY, Per Norgaad Copenhagen; asst conductor New York City Opera 1958; Chevalier des Arts et des Lettres (France) 1983; *Musical theatre* Diversions (Obie Prize Best Review) 1958, Twists (Arts Theatre London) 1962, The Projector and Cranford (Theatre Royal Stanford East), Pilgrim (Edinburgh Festival), The Wind in the Willows (Haymarket) 1985, Alice in Wonderland (Hammersmith) 1987, The Vackees (Haymarket) 1987; *Incidental music for theatre incl* The Prospect Theatre Co, The National Theatre, The Royal Shakespeare Co; *Ballet* A Simple Man 1987, Lipizzaner 1988, Liaison Amoureuses (Northern Ballet Theatre) 1988, Madly, Badly, Sadly, Gladly, David and Goliath, Dances of Love and Death (London Contemporary Dance Theatre), The Picture of Dorian Gray (Sadler's Wells Royal Ballet), A Christmas Carol (Northern Theatre Ballet) 1992, The Savoy Suite (English Nat Ballet) 1993, Alice in Wonderland (English Nat Ballet) 1995; *Music for TV incl* The Snow Goose (BBC TV) 1971, The World at War (Thames TV, Emmy Award) 1972, The Naked Civil Servant (Thames TV) 1975, Our Mutual Friend (BBC TV) 1978, Hollywood (Thames TV) 1980, Churchill - The Wilderness Years (Southern TV) 1981, Silas Marner (BBC TV) 1985, Hotel du Lac (BBC TV) 1986, The Accountant (BAFTA Award) 1989, The Secret Life of Ian Fleming 1989, Separate but Equal 1991, The Royal Collection 1991, A Year in Provence 1992, Fame in the 20th Century - Clive James 1992, Ghengis Cohn 1993, Thatcher - The Downing Street Years 1993, Message for Posterity (Dennis Potter) 1994, Pride and Prejudice 1995, Oliver's Travels 1995, British Film Music (BBC) 1995, European Cinema 1995, Celtic Symphony 1996; *Operas for TV* The Arrangement, Who Takes You to The Party, Orpheus in the Underground, Peace; *Film music* The Bofors Gun 1969, The French Lieutenant's Woman (BAFTA award) 1981, Champions 1984, The Girl in a Swing 1988, Rainbow 1988, Scandal 1988, Frankenstein Unbound 1989, The Raft of the Medusa 1991, The Trial 1992, The Voyage 1993, Widow's Peak 1994, series of Thames Silents incl Napoleon, The Wind, The Big Parade, Greed, The General, Ben Hur, Intolerance, Safety Last, The Four Horsemen of Apocalypse 1992, Wings 1993, Waterloo 1995; *Concert works* Music for the Royal Wedding, Variations on a Bus Route, Overture on Australian Themes, Clarinet Concerto 1984, Lines on London Symphony 1984, Fantasy for Flute and Harpsichord 1985, The Searle Suite for Wind Ensemble, Fanfare for Jerusalem 1987, The Glenlivet Fireworks Music 1988, Norwegian Brass Music 1988, Variations for a Polish Beggar's Theme 1988, Pigeons Progress 1988, Jazz Age Fanfare 1989, Everest 1989, Landscapes 1990, The Town Fox (text by Carla Lane) 1990, A Duck's Diary 1990, Paul McCartney's Liverpool Oratorio (with Paul McCartney) 1991; *Recordings incl* Christmas with Kiri (with Kiri Te Kanawa) 1986, Beautiful Dreamer (with Marylin Horne) 1986, The Silents 1987, Ben Hur 1989, A Simple Man 1989, The Town Fox and Other Musical Tales (text by Carla Lane) 1990, Paul McCartney's Liverpool Oratorio 1991, Liverpool Pops At Home 1995, Pride and Prejudice 1995; *Style—* Carl Davis, Esq

DAVIS, Charles Harvey; s of Albert Davis, and Renate, *née* Loeser; *b* 6 April 1949; *Educ* Westminster, St Bart's Hosp; *m* 18 Dec 1973, Frances Margaret Laura, da of Brig Don Grant, of Jersey, CI; 1 s (Freddie b 1983), 1 da (Sanjana b 1970); *Career* formerly sr registrar Nat Hosp for Nervous Diseases; conslt neurosurgn 1986–: NW RHA, Preston Health Authy, Burnley Health Authy, Blackpool Health Authy; fndr memb Br Cervical Spine Soc, memb Soc of Br Neurosurgns, FRCS; *Books* Biology of Brain Tumour (contrib, 1985), Diseases of the Spinal Cord (contrib, 1992); *Recreations* gardening; *Style—* Charles Davis, Esq; ✉ The Old Vicarage, 220 Brockholes View, Preston PR1 4XJ (☎ 01772 791003); Fulwood Hall Hospital, Midgery Lane, Fulwood, Preston (☎ 01772 704111)

DAVIS, Sir Charles Sigmund; kt (1965), CB (1960); s of Maurice Davis (d 1943); *b* 22 Jan 1909; *Educ* Trinity Coll Cambridge; *m* 1940, Pamela Mary, da of Kenneth Dawson, OBE (d 1957); 2 da (Caroline, Elizabeth); *Career* HG 1940–45; called to the Bar Inner Temple 1930, legal advsr to MAFF and The Forestry Cmmn 1957–74, counsel to the Speaker House of Commons 1974–83; chm of Cncl Nat Soc for Cancer Relief 1983–85 (tstee 1983–89), vice pres Cancer Relief Macmillan Fund 1989–; LRAM, ARCM; *Recreations* music; *Style—* Sir Charles Davis, CB; ✉ 9 Beech Court, 33B Arterberry Road, Wimbledon, London SW20 8AG (☎ 0181 879 0394)

DAVIS, Christine Agnes Murison; da of William Russell Aitken, of Dunblane, and Betsy Mary, *née* Murison; *b* 5 March 1944; *Educ* Ayr Acad, Univ of St Andrews (MA), Univ of Aberdeen (dip in Educn); *m* 27 July 1968, Robin John Davis; 2 da (Marion Elizabeth b 11 Oct 1969, Alison Joan b 11 Oct 1969); *Career* history teacher: Cumbernauld HS 1967–68, Stirling HS 1968–69, supply work 1971–75; HM Inst Cornton Vale 1979–87; memb: Dunblane Town Cncl (Dean of Guild 1974–75) 1972–75, Perth and Kinross Joint CC 1972–75, Scottish Examination Bd 1982–86, North of Scotland Hydro Electric Bd 1980–90, Scottish Economic Cncl 1987–95, Scottish Ctee of the Cncl on Tribunals 1989–95, Hansard Soc Cmmn on Election Campaigns 1990–91; memb Ctee: Central Region Valuation Appeal 1975–89, Legal Aid Central 1980–87, Information Technol Awareness 1983–84; chm: Electricity Consultative Cncl for the North of Scotland District 1980–90 (memb 1974–77, dep chm 1978–79), Scottish Legal Aid Bd 1991– (memb 1986–89 and 1990–91), Scottish Agricultural Wages Bd 1995– (memb 1990–95); vice chair Information Technol Year Scottish Ctee 1981–82; dir and tstee: Nat Energy Fndn 1990–, Energy Action Scotland 1992–; tstee Joseph Rowntree Charitable Tst 1996–; *Recreations* embroidery, walking, gardening; *Clubs* Scottish Arts, Penn; *Style—* Christine Davis; ✉ 24 Newton Crescent, Dunblane, Perthshire FK15 0DZ (☎ 01786 823226, fax 01786 825633); Scottish Legal Aid Board, 44 Drumsheugh Gardens, Edinburgh EH3 7SW (☎ 0131 226 7061, fax 0131 220 4878)

DAVIS, Christopher Brian; s of Brian Lewis Davis, of Spain, and Susan Patricia, *née* Cooke; *b* 24 Sept 1958; *Educ* Abberley Hall Sch, Malvern, Central London Poly; *m* 17 Aug 1985, Bridget Jane, da of Ralf Edward Harding; 1 s (James Christopher b 27 April 1986), 2 da (Victoria Jane b 5 May 1988, Georgina Lucy b 24 July 1991); *Career* formerly comedy magician (appearances incl the Royal Command Windsor, entertaining the troops in the Falkland Islands, and various TV and theatre venues); md John Partridge clothing mfrs 1983–92 (sold co), returned to theatre; BKCEC export award 1989 and 1990, Queen's Award for Export 1991, runner up Observer Young Business Man of the Year; memb: Magic Circle, Equity Freeman City of London, Freeman Worshipful Co of Woolmen; *Recreations* shooting, drinking sherry in front of log fires; *Clubs* Groucho, Annabel's; *Style—* Christopher Davis, Esq; ✉ c/o Carol Hayes & Assocs, 31 Great Malborough Street, London W1V 1HA (☎ 0171 287 1911)

DAVIS, Christopher John Dusser; s of John Frank Davis (d 1988), and Pamela Mary Wilson, *née* Boyle; *b* 28 June 1941; *Educ* Bradfield Coll Berks, ChCh Oxford (MA); *m* 15 Aug 1969, Linda Lee, da of late Lee Oberholtz; 1 s (Benjamin James b 28 May 1977); *Career* ed Hamlyn Goup 1968–72, managing ed Mitchell Beazley 1972–74; Dorling Kindersley: ed dir 1974–82, publishing dir 1982–, dep chm 1987–; hon dep marshal Ford County Historical Assoc Dodge City Kansas USA 1975; *Books* North American Indian (1969), World Soccer (1972, 2 edn 1974), Olympic Games (1972); *Recreations* arts, sport, travel, dogs, wine; *Clubs* Groucho, 2 Brydges; *Style—* Christopher Davis, Esq; ✉ Dorling Kindersley Holdings PLC, 9 Henrietta Street, London WC2E 8PS (☎ 0171 753 3534, fax 0171 753 3588)

DAVIS, Clive Timothy; s of Sherman Alexander Davis, of Bath, and Betty Mavis, *née* Savery; *b* 8 Oct 1959; *Educ* Culverhay Comp Sch, St Catherine's Coll Oxford (BA); *m* 2 May 1986, Mohini, da of Mohanbhai Patel; 2 s (Shivan Clive b 7 Sept 1990, Krishan Alexander b 11 March 1993); *Career* journalist; books ed West Indian World newspaper 1981–85 (gen reporter and arts ed 1981–82), BBC News trainee 1982–84, sub ed BBC Radio News 1984–86, freelance feature writer and gen reporter The Guardian 1985–86, feature writer London Daily News 1986–87, writer The Times 1987–; feature writer Sunday Times 1994–; based New York 1994–; writer and presenter: Richard Wright - A Native Son (Radio 4 documentary), Eyewitness - William L Shirer (Radio 4 documentary); *Recreations* piano; *Style—* Clive Davis, Esq; ✉ 2 Apsley Cottages, Lower Road, Cookham, Berks SL6 9EZ; The Times, 1 Pennington St, London E1 9XN

DAVIS, Sir Colin Rex; kt (1980), CBE (1965); s of Reginald George Davis (d 1944), of Weybridge, Surrey, and Lillian; *b* 25 Sept 1927; *Educ* Christ's Hosp, Royal Coll of Music; *m* 1, 1949 (m dis 1964), April Cantelo; 1 s, 1 da; m 2, 1964, Ashraf Naini, da of Abeolvahab Naini Assar (d 1978); 3 s, 2 da; *Career* formerly conductor: BBC Scottish Orchestra, Sadler's Wells (musical dir 1961–65); chief conductor BBC Symphony Orchestra 1967–71, conducted Bayreuth 1977, musical dir Royal Opera House Covent Garden 1971–86; princ guest conductor: Boston Symphony Orchestra 1972–84, LSO 1975–95, New York Philharmonic 1998; princ conductor LSO 1995–; music dir Bayerischer Rundfunk Orchestra Munich 1983–92; Freeman City of London 1992; hon conductor Dresden Staatskapelle 1990, Commendatore of Republic of Italy 1976, Chev de la Legion d'Honneur 1982, Cdr's Cross of the Order of Merit of Fed Republic of Germany 1987, Cdr L'Ordre des Lettres (France) 1990, Bayerischen Verdienstorden 1992, Cdr First Class Order of the Lion of Finland 1992, Royal Philharmonic Gold Medal 1996; winner Pipesmoker of the Year (32nd recipient) 1996; *Recreations* reading, gardening, knitting; *Clubs* Athenaeum; *Style—* Sir Colin Davis, CBE; ✉ 39 Huntingdon St, London N1 1BP; c/o Columbia Artists Management Inc, 165 W 57th St, New York, NY 10019, USA

DAVIS, David; *b* 14 June 1935; *Educ* William Ellis Sch Highgate, Univ of London (BSc); *m* 2 July 1958; *Career* ptnr Cohen Arnold & Co (chartered accountants) 1961–70, fin advsr and lectr 1970–; non-exec dir 1971–: Daejan Holdings plc, City & Country Properties plc, Metropolitan Properties Ltd; headmaster Pardes House GS E Finchley 1979–85, memb House Ctee Bearsted Meml Hosp until closure 1977; FCA, ATTI; *Recreations* walking, kiting, gardening, computer studies; *Style—* David Davis, Esq; ✉ 158–162 Shaftesbury Ave, London WC2 (☎ 0171 836 1555)

DAVIS, David Henry; s of Harry Joseph Davis (d 1986), of London, and Madge May, *née* Rosen; *b* 25 July 1936; *Educ* Streatham GS, Brighton Coll, Pitmans Coll; *m* 21 June 1959, Beryl Maureen, da of Harry Lancer; 1 s (Jonathan Anthony Bruce b 19 March 1963); *Career* trainee South London Advertiser 1952–53; reporter: Croydon Times 1953–56, Kentish Express 1956–57; sub ed Press Assoc/Reuters 1957–62, chief sub ed

Universal News Services 1962–64, business reporter The Times 1964–68; Daniel J Edelman Ltd (PR): dir 1968, dep md 1969–76, md 1976–80, chm 1980–85; chm Daniel J Edelman Europe Ltd 1985–92; dir: Medialink 1992–, dir Key Communications 1992–95; chm ION International Ltd 1995–, vice chm ION Systems Inc 1995–; non-exec chm Chambers Cox PR 1995–; vice chm PR Conslts Assoc 1985; tstee Montessori St Nicholas Centre, memb Crafts Cncl, Home Office lay visitor; MIPR 1982; *Recreations* watching sport, my family; *Clubs* The Carlton, Press (Paris); *Style—* David Davis, Esq; ✉ 67 Albion Gate, Albion Street, Hyde Park, London W2 (☎ 0171 262 5295)

DAVIS, Rt Hon David Michael; PC (1997), MP (C) Boothferry (majority 17,535); s of Ronald Alexander Davis, and Elizabeth, *née* Brown; *b* 23 Dec 1948; *Educ* Bec GS, Univ of Warwick (BSc), London Business Sch (MSc), Harvard Univ (AMP); *m* 28 July 1973, Doreen, da of Alfred John Cook; 1 s (Alexander b 1987), 2 da (Rebecca b 1974, Sarah b 1977); *Career* strategic planning dir Tate & Lyle plc 1984–87 (non-exec dir 1987–90); MP (C) Boothferry 1987–; Govt whip 1989–93, Parly sec Office of Public Service and Science 1993–94, min of state for Europe FCO 1994–; dir Globe Investment Trust plc 1989–90; *Recreations* flying, mountaineering, writing; *Style—* The Rt Hon David Davis, MP; ✉ House of Commons, London SW1A 0AA

DAVIS, David William; s of George Henry Davis, of Beaconsfield, and Lucy Ada, *née* Tylee (d 1959); *b* 29 Oct 1942; *Educ* Emanuel Sch; *m* 25 Nov 1967, Jennifer, da of Wilfred Snell; 1 s (Kenneth b 28 May 1971), 1 da (Jacqueline b 25 Feb 1970); *Career* CA 1966; ptnr: Fryer Sutton Morris & Co 1967–, Fryer Whitehill & Co 1971–, Clark Whitehill 1982–; FCA 1975; *Recreations* badminton, bridge; *Style—* David Davis, Esq; ✉ Blue Hills, Ibstone, Bucks HP14 3XT (☎ 01491 638245); Clark Whitehill, 25 New Street Square, London EC4A 3LN (☎ 0171 353 1577, fax 0171 583 0543, telex 887422, car tel 0860 632 382)

DAVIS, Derek Richard; s of Stanley Lewis Davis, OBE, of Malta, and Rita Beatrice Rachel, *née* Rosenheim; *b* 3 May 1945; *Educ* Clifton, Balliol Coll Oxford (BA); *m* 25 Jan 1987, Diana, da of Ellis Levinson, of Chelsea; 1 s (Joshua b 1990), 1 da (Rebecca b 1988); *Career* asst princ Bd of Trade 1967, princ DTI 1972; Dept of Energy: asst sec 1977, under sec 1985; head Oil and Gas Div DTI 1992, DG British National Space Centre 1993–; *Style—* Derek Davis, Esq; ✉ British National Space Centre, Bridge Place, 88/89 Eccleston Square, London SW1V 1PT (☎ 0171 215 0877, fax 0171 215 0804)

DAVIS, Donald Conway; s of George Davis (d 1981), of Liverpool, and Edna Ruth, *née* Conway; *b* 19 March 1932; *Educ* Quarry Bank HS; *m* 1965, Edwina Margaret Lawson, da of Edwin Lawson Spence (d 1955), of Lancs; 1 s (Simon b 1971), 3 da (Alexandra b 1966, Lucinda b 1968, Emily b 1986); *Career* 2 Lt Army 1955–57; gp dir: Liverpool Daily Post & Echo Ltd (publishing and printing) 1962–69, Harrison & Son Ltd (printing) 1969–73; gp md Pitman plc (publishing and printing) 1973–82, exec chm Security Holdings Ltd (printing) 1983–86, md Hunter Print Group plc (printing) 1986–89; currently chm: Contemporary Printers Ltd, TH Brickell & Son Ltd; Liveryman Worshipful Co of Stationers and Newspaper Makers; FCA, FRSA; *Recreations* sailing, golf, cricket and rugby; *Clubs* Hon Artillery Co, Royal Thames Yacht, Marylebone Cricket, Beaconsfield Golf, Wasps Rugby Football, Lancs Co Cricket, RSA; *Style—* Donald Davis, Esq; ✉ Austenwood, Austenwood Common, Gerrards Cross, Buckinghamshire SL9 8NL (☎ 01753 882816)

DAVIS, Prof Donald Henry; s of Henry William Davis (d 1978), and Georgina Rose, *née* Marshall (d 1984); *b* 28 Nov 1934; *Educ* Sir George Monoux GS, UCL (BSc, PhD); *m* 2 Sept 1961, Anne Elizabeth, da of Harold Thomas Grinstead (d 1988); 1 s (Timothy John), 1 da (Claire Elizabeth); *Career* res assoc Univ of Chicago 1961–62; UCL: res asst Physics Dept 1959–61 and 1962–63, lectr 1963–72, reader Physics and Astronomy Dept 1972–86, prof 1986–; memb: RSPB, WWF; CPhys, FInstP 1971; *Recreations* bridge, photography, gardening; *Style—* Prof Donald Davis; ✉ Department of Physics and Astronomy, University College London, Gower Street, London WC1E 6BT (☎ 0171 380 7151, fax 0171 380 7145)

DAVIS, Prof Edward Arthur; s of Edward Davis (d 1988), and Elizabeth, *née* Smith; *b* 26 Nov 1936; *Educ* Univ of Birmingham (BSc), Univ of Reading (PhD), Univ of Cambridge (MA); *m* 30 Oct 1960, Christine Elizabeth, da of Philip Edwyn Riley (d 1987); 2 s (Philip b 1962, Andrew b 1964); *Career* res asst prof Physics Dept Univ of Illinois USA 1963–64, scientist Xerox Corp Rochester NY USA 1964–67, lectr Physics Dept Univ of Cambridge 1973–80 (Royal Soc Mr and Mrs John Jaffé Donation res fell Cavendish Laboratory 1968–73), dean Faculty of Sci Univ of Leicester 1987–90 (prof of experimental physics 1980–); CPhys, FInstP, fell American Physical Soc; *Books* Electronic Properties of Non-Crystalline Materials (with N F Mott, 1971, 2 edn 1979), Science in the Making Vol 1 (1995); *Recreations* flying light aircraft, tennis, rock climbing, golf; *Style—* Prof Edward Davis; ✉ Physics Department, University of Leicester, University Road, Leicester LE1 7RH (☎ 0116 252 3571/5, fax 0116 252 2770, telex 341664 LUXRAY G)

DAVIS, Evan Harold; s of Quintin Visser Davis, of Leatherhead, Surrey, and Hazel Noreen, *née* Groves; *b* 8 April 1962; *Educ* The Ashcombe Sch Dorking, St John's Coll Oxford (MA, ed Cherwell 1983), Kennedy Sch of Government Harvard Univ (MPA); *Career* research offr Inst for Fiscal Studies 1984–86, Harvard Univ 1986–88, research fell Centre for Business Strategy London Business Sch 1988–92, co-ordinator corporate policy research Inst for Fiscal Studies 1992–93, economics corr BBC 1993–; memb Advsy Cncl Social Market Fndn 1994–; *Books* The Penguin Dictionary of Economics (with G Bannock and R Baxter, 1987); *Style—* Evan Davis; ✉ Room 3071, BBC Broadcasting House, London W1A 1AA (☎ 0171 765 4105, fax 0171 636 4808, mobile 0385 306219)

DAVIS, Frank; s of Julius Davis (d 1970), of Hampstead Garden Suburb, and Dinah, *née* Benjamin; *b* 8 June 1920; *Educ* London Poly, Inns of Ct Sch of Law; *m* 4 Jan 1945, Irene, da of Isaac Lipman (d 1964); 2 s (Malcolm, Richard); *Career* Special Servs; memb Lloyd's of London 1979, md various companies; former ldr Finchley Borough Cncl (cncllr 1956–65, Mayor 1963–64), cncllr London Borough of Barnet 1964–71 and 1990– (Dep Mayor 1993–94); Parly candidate: Finchley 1966, Acton 1968; changed name temporarily to Frank Liberal Davis, forcing amendment to Representation of the People Act 1949, which prohibited appearance of party affiliations on ballot papers; resigned from Lib Party 1970, joined Conservative Party 1987; campaigned successfully for Unsolicited Goods Act and Rating of Empty Properties Act, also Public Bodies (Admissions) Act 1960, compelled private clubs tenanting cncl land for golf and other sports to ban discrimination against Jews 1963–70; JP 1970–92 (dep chm Inner London Magistrates 1986–89); memb Appeals Tbnls Dept of Social Servs and Dept of Employment 1970–90, lay judge of Crown Ct (appeals and committals) 1985–92; memb: Trades Advsy Cncl 1951–87, Bd of Deputies 1957–70; govr Tel Aviv Univ; memb Arsenal FC, fndr Wingate FC, chm Wingate Charity Tst, fndr memb and vice pres Maccabi Assoc; memb Hon Soc of Gray's Inn 1953; Order of Independence Uganda 1964; *Recreations* travel, horticulture; *Clubs* Rotary Int; *Style—* Frank Davis, Esq, JP; ✉ 20 Connaught Drive, Finchley, London NW11 6BJ

DAVIS, Grahame Watson; s of William Henry, of Chatham, Kent (d 1944), and Georgina, *née* Watson (d 1985); *b* 9 Sept 1934; *Educ* King's Sch Rochester; *m* 29 Aug 1963, Wendy Lovelace Davis, JP, da of Antony Lovelace Wagon, of Rochester (d 1978); 1 s (Piers b 1971), 1 da (Helena b 1966); *Career* slr; formerly sr ptnr Hextall Erskine & Co London, chm Industl Tbnls 1993–; memb The Law Soc; *Recreations* golf, cricket; *Clubs* Wig and Pen, Castle, The Roffen; *Style—* Grahame W Davis, Esq; ✉ c/o Office of Industrial Tribunals, Tufton House, Tufton Street, Ashford, Kent TN23 1RJ

DAVIS, Sir (Ernest) Howard; kt (1978), CMG (1969), OBE (1960); s of Edwin Howard Davis; *b* 22 April 1918; *Educ* Christian Bros Sch Gibraltar, Coll of St Joseph Blackpool, Univ of London; *m* 1948, Marie, da of Gustave Bellotti; 2 s; *Career* dep govr Gibraltar 1971–78; *Style—* Sir Howard Davis, CMG, OBE; ✉ Flat 6, Mount Pleasant, South Barrack Road, Gibraltar (☎ 00 350 70358)

DAVIS, Dr Ian Robert; s of David Davis (d 1988), of Paignton, S Devon, and Theodora, *née* Rawson; *b* 2 March 1937; *Educ* Northern Poly (DipArch), Georgia Inst of Technol, Univ Coll Univ of London (PhD); *m* 8 July 1961, Judith Margaret, da of Roy Cardwell (d 1975), of Bognor, Sussex; 1 s (Simon b 1969), 2 da (Amanda b 1962, Caroline b 1964); *Career* architect in practice 1961–70, princ lectr Sch of Architecture Oxford Poly 1970–89; advsr UN Post-Disaster Shelter Provision Reconstruction and Disaster Preparedness 1975–93, memb Nat Acad of Sci Int Ctee on the Implications of Disaster Assistance Washington DC 1976–79, leader Housing and Hazards Section Int Karakoram Expedition, chm Int Panel on Disaster Risk Reduction 1981–86, dir Disaster Mgmnt Centre 1982–89, dir Int Training and Research Centre (INTRAC) 1991–96; memb Nat Coordination Ctee on the Int Decade for Nat Disaster Reduction (IDNDR) 1990–; md International Development and Emergency Relief Conslts Ltd (IDRC) Oxford Centre for Disaster Studies (OCDS) 1993–; dir Safe Trust 1995–; Sasakawa-DHA (UN) Disaster Prevention Award 1996; visiting fell: Cranfield Univ 1993, Univ of York 1995; hon fell Oxford Brookes Univ 1991; RIBA, FRGS; *Books* Shelter and Disaster (1978), Disasters and Small Dwelling (ed, 1982), Dunroamin - The Suburban Semi and Its Enemies (with P Oliver and I Bentley, 1982, reprinted 1994), Disasters and the Small Dwelling - Perspectives for the UN IDNDR (ed with Yasemin Aysan, 1992), Christian Perspectives on Disaster Management (ed with Michael Wall, 1993), At Risk: Natural Hazards and People's Vulnerability and Disasters (with P Blaikie, T Cannon and B Wisner, 1994), Building for Safety Compendium (with A Clayton, 1994), Developing Building for Safety Programmes (with Y Aysan, A Clayton, A Cory and D Sanderson, 1995), Disaster Mitigation, Preparedness and Response. An Audit of UK Assets (with D Sanderson, J Twigg and B Cowden); *Recreations* photography, painting, music, travel; *Style—* Dr Ian Davis; ✉ 97 Kingston Rd, Oxford OX2 6RL (☎ 01865 56473, fax 01865 516865); Oxford Centre for Disaster Studies (OCDS), PO Box 137, Oxford OX4 1BB (☎ 01865 202772, fax 01865 202848)

DAVIS, James Gresham; CBE (1988); s of Col Robert Davis, OBE, JP (d 1963), and Josephine, *née* Edwards (d 1976); *b* 20 July 1928; *Educ* Bradfield, Clare Coll Cambridge (MA); *m* 24 Nov 1973, Adriana Johanna (Hanny), da of Evert Verhoef (d 1978), and Petronella Verhoef-Stuy, of Rhoon, Holland; 3 da (Mariske b 1974, Katrina b 1978, Charlotte b 1980); *Career* RN 1946–49; P & O Steam Navigation Co: joined 1952, Calcutta 1953–54, Kobe (Japan) 1954–56, Hong Kong 1956–57, dir P & O Lines 1967–72; chm: British Rail Anglian Bd 1988–92, Bromley Shipping plc 1989–94, TIP Europe plc 1990–93; dir: Kleinwort Benson Ltd 1973–88, DFDS Ltd 1975– (chm 1984–95), DFDS Travel Ltd 1975–, Pearl Cruises of Scandinavia Inc 1982–86, Rodskog Shipbrokers (Hong Kong) Ltd 1983–88, Associated British Ports Holdings plc 1983–, Transport Development Group plc 1984–91, Sedgwick Marine & Cargo Ltd 1988–, Global Ocean Carriers Ltd 1988– (chm 1996–), British International Freight Association 1989–, Hempel Paints Ltd 1992–, Trinitas Services Ltd 1993–, Tsavliris Salvage (International) Ltd 1994–, 2M Invest Copenhagen 1996–; memb Advsy Bd: J Lauritzen A/S Copenhagen 1981–85, DFDS A/S Copenhagen 1981–85; advsr Tjaerborg (UK) Ltd 1985–87; pres: Chartered Inst of Tport 1981–82, World Ship Soc 1969, 1971, 1984, 1985 and 1986, Harwich Lifeboat (RNLI) 1984–, Inst of Freight Forwarders Ltd 1984–86, National Waterways Tport Assoc 1986 92, Inst of Supervisory Mgmnt 1989–93, Inst of Chartered Shipbrokers 1990–92 (vice pres 1988–90), Inst of Export 1995– (vice pres 1991–95); vice pres Br Maritime League 1984–89; chm: International Maritime Industries Forum 1981–, Simpler Trade Procedures Bd (SITPRO) 1987–, Danish-UK C of C 1992–; pt/t memb Br Transport Docks Bd 1981–83; memb Cncl: The Marine Soc 1986– (chm Cncl 1987–93), Missions to Seamen 1981–, Bureau Veritas 1989–; tstee National Maritime Museum 1993–, govr World Maritime Univ (chm Friends of the World Maritime Univ 1985–); memb: Baltic Exchange 1973, Greenwich Forum 1982; Freeman City of London 1986, Liveryman and Asst to the Court Worshipful Co of Shipwrights, Sr Warden Co of World Traders 1995– (Master 1996), Younger Brother Trinity House; FCIT 1969, Hon FNI 1985, Hon FInstFF 1986, FRSA 1986, FISM; *Recreations* golf, family, ships; *Clubs* Brooks's, Hurlingham, Golfers, Harwich and Dovercourt Golf, Royal Calcutta Golf, Fanlingerers, Holland Park Lawn Tennis; *Style—* James Davis, Esq, CBE; ✉ 115 Woodsford Square, London W14 8DT (☎ 0171 602 0675); Summer Lawn, Dovercourt, Essex CO12 4EF (☎ 01255 502981)

DAVIS, James Patrick Lamert; s of (Walter) Patrick Carless Davis (d 1996), and Jane, *née* Lamert (d 1988); *b* 23 Sept 1946; *Educ* Charterhouse, Balliol Coll Oxford; *m* 18 May 1974, Sally Anne, da of Noel Kemball; 1 s (Andrew b 23 March 1978), 3 da (Nicola b 23 March 1980, Sarah b 9 June 1982, Clare b 30 June 1986); *Career* Freshfields: articled clerk 1969, ptnr 1976–, ptnr i/c Singapore Office 1980–84; *Recreations* fishing, golf; *Clubs* MCC, Singapore Cricket, Berkshire Golf; *Style—* James Davis, Esq; ✉ Freshfields, 65 Fleet St, London EC4Y 1HS (☎ 0171 936 4000, fax 0171 832 7001)

DAVIS, John; s of Alfred Davis (d 1972), and Amelia Redman (d 1951); *b* 27 Aug 1934; *m* 20 March 1954, Jean Doris, da of Horace George Newson (d 1964); *Career* film producer and director; served WWII Fleet Air Arm 1942–46; entered films 1950, formed View Finder Films Ltd 1960, writer and dir of documentaries and TV commercials, prodn assoc Go To Blazes; prodr: Girl in the Headlines, Daylight Robbery, Indiscreet, Kidnapped, 20,000 Leagues Under the Sea; dir Cry Wolf, prodn assoc Murphy's War; prodr and dir Danger Point; co-writer: Obsession, The Linsky Witness; prodn mangr: The Beast Must Die, Sherlock Holmes, Murder By Degree, Can I Help You?, Silver Dream Racer, Remembrance; writer: Grand Babylon Hotel, The End of Love; prodn supervisor: Gilbert and Sullivan Operas, Indiana Jones and The Temple of Doom, Lace II, The Two Mrs Grenvilles; prodn mangr: Never Say Never Again, King David; assoc prodr: Nineteen Eighty Four, Half Moon Street, Taffin, Inspector Morse, Moi General de Gaulle, The Quare Fellow, The Old Curiosity Shop; line prodr Spooks, prodn supervisor About Face, exec in charge of prodn Soldier Soldier (New Zealand); rep Completion Bd Fifty Fifty; dir: Bryanston Films Ltd, Bryanston Seven Arts Ltd; *Clubs* Savile; *Style—* John Davis, Esq; ✉ 20 Brockley Avenue, Stanmore, Middlesex HA7 4LX (☎ 0181 958 6115, fax 0181 958 7568); Higher Hayne, Roadwater, W Somerset (☎ 01984 40555)

DAVIS, Prof John Allen; s of Maj H E Davis, MC, RA, and Mary, *née* Allen; *b* 6 Aug 1923; *Educ* Blundell's, St Mary's Hosp Univ of London (Gold Medal, MB BS), MD (Cantab), FRCP Lond; *m* 1957, Madeleine Elizabeth Vinicombe (d 1991), da of Wing Cdr Harry Ashlin; 3 s (Henry b 1958, Arthur b 1959, William b 1963), 2 da (Mary b 1961, Ruth b 1967); *Career* serv BAOR 1948–50; house physician St Mary's Hosp London 1946–47, house physician Hosp for Sick Children Great Ormond St London 1949–50, registrar Paediatric Dept St Mary's Hosp 1951–52, exchange sr asst Children's Hosp Med Centre Boston and teaching fell Harvard Univ 1953, sr registrar Paediatric Unit St Mary's Hosp 1957–59 (Unit Home Care Scheme 1954–57), res fell Nuffield Oxford 1959–60, sr lectr Postgrad Med Sch Hammersmith, reader in paediatrics Inst of Child Health Univ of London, children's physician Hammersmith Hosp 1967, prof of paediatrics and child health Univ of Manchester 1967–79, prof of paediatrics and fell Peterhouse Cambridge 1979–88 (emeritus 1988–); external examiner Univs of: Sheffield,

Oxford, Newcastle, London, Leicester, Hong Kong, Singapore; patron: Soc for Reproductive and Infant Psychology, Arts for Health, Child Psychotherapy Tst, Squiggle Fndn; former pres Euro Soc for Paediatric Res; Dawson Williams Meml Prize BMA 1986, James Spence Medallist BPA 1991, Gold Medal Hunterian Soc 1995; FRCP (former second vice pres); *Recreations* collecting and painting watercolours, gardening, reading, music; *Style*— Prof John Davis; ✉ Fourmile House, 1 & 3 Cambridge Road, Great Shelford, Cambridge CB2 5JE

DAVIS, Sir John Gilbert; 3 Bt (UK 1946), of Barrington Hall, Co Cambridge; s of Sir Gilbert Davis, 2 Bt (d 1973); *b* 17 Aug 1936; *Educ* Oundle, RNC Dartmouth; *m* 16 Jan 1960, Elizabeth Margaret, da of Robert Smith Turnbull, of Falkirk; 1 s (Richard Charles b 1970), 2 da (Wendy Elizabeth b 1962, Linda Mary b 1964); *Heir* s, Richard Charles Davis b 11 April 1970; *Career* exec vice pres Abitibi Price Inc Toronto until 1990, former chm Abitibi Price Sales Corporation NY; currently developing a recycled pulp plant in Chateau Thierry France under name of Greenfield Paper Company Ltd; *Recreations* squash, golf, reading, piano; *Clubs* Toronto, Rosedale Golf, Donalda; *Style*— Sir John Davis, Bt; ✉ 5 York Ridge Road, Willowdale, Ontario M2P 1R8, Canada

DAVIS, John Patrick; s of Ralph Patrick Davis, of Chaldon, Surrey, and Vivian Hilda, *née* Braund; *b* 12 June 1944; *Educ* Tonbridge, Univ of Nottingham (BSc); *m* 5 Aug 1972, Fenella Irene, da of Guy Charles Madoc, CBE, KPM, of Ramsey, Isle of Man; 1 s (Michael b 23 June 1975), 1 da (Rosemary b 11 June 1976); *Career* gen mangr mech engrg Redpath Dorman Long Ltd 1979–83, chm Intelek plc 1990– (chief exec and gp md 1985–90); CEng 1971, FIEE 1986, FIMechE 1992, MIWeldE 1983; *Recreations* mountain walking, bee keeping; *Style*— John Davis, Esq; ✉ The Old Vicarage, Bourton, Swindon, Wiltshire SN6 8HZ; Intelek plc, PO Box 25, South Marston Industrial Estate, Swindon, Wiltshire SN3 4TR (☎ 01793 827000, fax 01793 827578)

DAVIS, Kenneth John; s of Kenneth John Davis, of Saltdean, Sussex, and Ethel Viola, *née* Miller; *b* 10 March 1943; *Educ* Addey and Stanhope GS; *m* 18 Feb 1967, Janette Doreen, da of John Henry Lighton; 1 s (Anthony Lee b 1971), 1 da (Elizabeth Ann b 1974); *Career* Alexander Stenhouse Ltd: regnl dir 1982–85, mktg dir 1985–86, chief operating offr (all UK and Eire branches) 1986–87, chief exec offr 1988–92; dir Cowick Hall Insurance Services 1983–; chief exec Alexander & Alexander Europe 1992–, pres Alexander & Alexander International Inc (and chm of the Global Retail Co) 1995–; Freeman City of London, memb Worshipful Co of Insurers; FCII; *Books* Marketing Insurance - A Practical Guide (jtly, 1986); *Recreations* sailing; *Clubs* Little Ship; *Style*— Kenneth Davis, Esq; ✉ Alexander & Alexander Ltd, 10 Devonshire Square, London EC2M 4LE (☎ 0171 621 9990, fax 0171 621 9950, telex 920368 ASLDN G)

DAVIS, Air Vice-Marshal (Robert) Leslie; CB (1984); s of Sidney Davis; *b* 22 March 1930; *Educ* Wolsingham GS, Bede Sch Collegiate Sunderland Co Durham; *m* 1956, Diana, *née* Bryant; 1 s, 1 da; *Career* Cdr RAF Staff and Air Attaché, Br Defence Staff Washington DC 1977–80, Administrator of the Sovereign Base Areas and Cdr Br Forces and AOC Cyprus 1980–83, ret 1983; chm Durham Branch SSAFA, hon county rep RAF Benevolent Fund; *Clubs* RAF; *Style*— Air Vice-Marshal Leslie Davis, CB; ✉ High Garth Farm, Witton-le-Wear, Co Durham DL14 0BL

DAVIS, Lindsey Margaret; da of William Alfred Davis, of Addington, Kent, and late Joan Margaret, *née* Barker; *b* 21 Aug 1949; *Educ* King Edward VI HS for Girls Birmingham, Lady Margaret Hall Oxford (MA); *Career* civil servant Property Services Agency 1972–85, full time writer 1986–; memb: Soc of Authors, Crimewriters' Assoc, The Detection Club; shortlisted for Georgette Heyer Historical Novel prize 1985, 1986 and 1988; winner Crimewriters' Assoc (CWA) Dagger in the Library award 1995; author of various romantic serials for Woman's Realm; *Books* incl The Falco series: The Silver Pigs (1989, Authors' Club Best First Novel award 1990), Shadows in Bronze (1990), Venus in Copper (1991), The Iron Hand of Mars (1992), Poseidon's Gold (1993), Last Act in Palmyra (1994), Time to Depart (1995), A Dying Light in Corduba (1996); c No Alibi (contrib author, 1995); *Recreations* home improvement (it needs it!), dressmaking, theatre; *Style*— Ms Lindsey Davis; ✉ c/o Heather Jeeves Literary Agency, 9 Dryden Place, Edinburgh EH9 1RP (☎ 0131 668 3859)

DAVIS, Margaret Ann McLeod Leo (Meg); da of John Alexander Bede McLeod Davis (d 1976), of Montréal, Quebec, Canada, and Barbara Ann Lusby; *b* 26 Sept 1957; *Educ* École Classique Sécondaire Villa Maria, McGill Univ (BA); *m* 25 Oct 1990, J Pimblett; *Career* Phoenix Theatre Montréal 1978–80, dir MBA Literary Agents 1988– (joined 1984); co fndr Paradox Theatre Montréal; *Recreations* trombone, cigars, late night philosophy; *Style*— Ms Meg Davis; ✉ MBA Literary Agents Ltd, 45 Fitzroy St, London W1P 4HR (☎ 0171 387 2076, fax 0171 387 2042)

DAVIS, Dr Mark Herbert Ainsworth; s of Christopher Ainsworth Davis (d 1951), and Frances Emily Davis, JP, *née* Marsden, of Loughborough, Leics; *b* 1 May 1945; *Educ* Oundle, Clare Coll Cambridge (BA, MA, ScD), Univ of Calif Berkeley (MS, PhD); *m* 15 Oct 1988, Jessica Isabella Caroline, da of Robert Sinclair Smith, of Broadstairs, Kent; *Career* res asst Electronics Res Laboratory Univ of California Berkeley 1969–71; Imperial Coll London: lectr 1971–79, reader 1979–84, prof of system theory 1984–95; dir and head of research and product devpt Tokyo-Mitsubishi International plc 1995–; visiting prof Imperial Coll London 1995–; sometime visiting prof: Harvard Univ, MIT, Univ of Oslo; FSS 1985, fell Inst of Mathematical Statistics 1994; *Books* Linear Estimation and Stochastic Control (1977), Stochastic Modelling and Control (1985), Markov Models and Optimization (1993); *Recreations* classical music (violin and viola); *Style*— Dr Mark Davis; ✉ 11 Chartfield Ave, London SW15 6DT (☎ 0181 789 7677); Tokyo-Mitsubishi International plc, 6 Broadgate, London EC2M 2AA (☎ 0171 577 2714, fax 0171 577 2888)

DAVIS, Martin Mitchell; s of Kenneth Bertram Davis (d 1983), of Alcester, Warwickshire, and Emily Mary Tillett, MBE, *née* Gateley; *b* 30 May 1943; *Educ* Ampleforth, Univ Coll Oxford (MA); *m* 21 June 1975, Caroline Ann, da of John James Yorke Scarlett (d 1984), of Kingsbridge, S Devon; 3 s (Edmund b 1976, Leo b 1977, Thomas b 1979), 1 da (Agnes b 1982); *Career* slr; ptnr Wiggin and Co Cheltenham 1974–77, subsequently fndr Davis & Co (now Davis Gregory); chm Cheltenham Cncl of Churches 1977–78, pres Cheltenham Legal Assoc 1987–88, ctee memb Glos and Wilts Law Soc 1987–92; tstee: Summerfield Charitable Tst 1989–, Glenfall House Tst 1993–95; chm Glos and Wilts Branch Soc of Tst and Estate Practitioners 1991–95, memb Devpt Ctee Cheltenham Arts Festivals 1992–95, vice chm Gloucester Branch CPRE 1993–; co-fndr Christian Ecology Gp 1980; hon fell Cheltenham and Glos Coll of HE 1995; memb Law Soc; *Recreations* walking, cycling, photography, listening to music; *Clubs* Pax Christi, Cyclists Touring; *Style*— Martin Davis, Esq; ✉ 25 Rodney Rd, Cheltenham (☎ 01242 235202, fax 01242 224716, e-mail mmd@davisg.thenet.co.uk)

DAVIS, Martyn Paul; s of Max Parsken Davis (d 1995), of London, and Patricia Gladys, *née* Wall (d 1965); *b* 1 Sept 1929; *Educ* Highgate Sch, LSE (BScEcon), Poly Sch of Mgmnt, Harvard Business Sch; *Career* sales trainee Coutinho Caro & Co 1953–53, publicity controller Buland Publishing Co 1953–54, assoc dir Robert Brandon & Partners 1954–56, sr account exec T Booth Waddicor & Partners 1957–59, head of mktg servs Coll for the Distributive Trades London (secondments to Saatchi & Saatchi and IPC Magazines) 1960–89, mktg communications conslt 1989–; Freeman City of London 1984, Liveryman Worshipful Co of Marketors 1985; fell CAM Fndn (memb 1954), FCIM (memb 1958), FIPR (memb 1956); *Books* A Career in Advertising (1963), Handbook for Media Representatives (1967), Business-to-Business Marketing & Promotion (1989), The Effective Use of Advertising Media (1996); *Recreations* swimming and weight training, the arts, opera, ballet, classical music, good food; *Style*— Martyn P Davis, Esq

DAVIS, Melanie Ruth; da of Cyril Searle, of Woodford, Essex, and Ita, *née* Bursztyn; *b* 31 Aug 1958; *Educ* Caterham Co Sch Essex, London Sch of Fashion, Ravensbourne Coll of Art (BA); *Career* designer: Polly Peck plc 1979–80, Fitrite 1980–81; managing and design dir Pamplemousse 1982–; *Recreations* skiing, linguistics, aerobics, art, travel; *Clubs* Champneys Health; *Style*— Mrs Melanie Davis; ✉ Pamplemousse, 54 Eastcastle Street, London W1N 8AB (☎ 0171 436 8494, fax 0171 436 3456)

DAVIS, Dr Michael; s of Harry Tyrrell Davis (d 1970), of London, and Joan, *née* Latcham; *b* 8 July 1943; *Educ* Charterhouse, St Thomas's Hosp Med Sch Univ of London (MB BS, MD, MRCP); *m* 1, 5 Dec 1970 (m dis 1994), Elizabeth Maureen, da of Hedley Victor Billing (d 1984); 2 s (Justin b 10 May 1974, Julian b 29 Jan 1978), 1 da (Joelle b 18 May 1972); m 2, 2 Sept 1994, Catherine Susan Jones; 1 da (Annabelle b 7 Jan 1996); *Career* jr hosp posts 1967–74, sr lectr and conslt physician Liver Unit King's Coll Hosp 1974–82; conslt physician: Dudley Rd Hosp Birmingham 1982–86, Royal United Hosp Bath 1986–; clinical examiner RCP 1989–; author scientific papers and chapters med textbooks relating to gastroenterology; memb Br Soc of Gastroenterology 1972, FRCP 1984; *Books* Drug Reactions and the Liver (1981), Therapy of Liver Disease (1989); *Recreations* woodwork, music, walking; *Style*— Dr Michael Davis; ✉ Royal United Hospital, Combe Park, Bath BA1 3NG (☎ 01225 824131, fax 01225 825516)

DAVIS, Michael Edward; s of Capt Raymond Norris Davis, of Sevenoaks, Kent, and Margaret, *née* Pierce; *b* 14 Aug 1951; *Educ* Sevenoaks Sch, Univ of London (BA); *m* 17 Aug 1974, Helen Frances, da of William Podmore, OBE, JP, of Consall Hall, Wetley Rocks, Stoke on Trent, Staffs; 1 s (Paul Michael William b 4 July 1983), 1 da (Laura Helen Margaret b 2 Feb 1986); *Career* admitted slr 1977, ptnr Herbert Smith 1986– (joined 1975); Freeman Worshipful Co of Slrs; memb: Law Soc, Int Bar Assoc, Acad of Experts, Soc of Construction Law; *Recreations* horse riding, water skiing, travel, landscaping, rugby football; *Style*— Michael Davis, Esq; ✉ Herbert Smith, Exchange House, Primrose St, London EC2A 2HS (☎ 0171 374 8000)

DAVIS, Michael R (Mike); s of S H S Davis (d 1989), of Watlington, Oxon, and B H Davis, *née* Back; *b* 6 Jan 1948; *Educ* Winchester, Sorbonne; *m* 1, 1975 (m dis 1985), Angela, *née* Fortune; 2 da (Kate b 1978, Sophie b 1981); m 2, 1994, Suzette, *née* Knittl; *Career* advtg exec; Foote Cone & Belding London 1967–69; Young & Rubicam: Milan Italy 1970, London 1971–76, Tokyo Japan 1976–78, dir London 1978–81; dir Holdings Bd Wight Collins Rutherford & Scott plc 1981–84, dir of client servs TBWA London 1984–87, md Leagas Shafron Davis 1987–, work consists of managing ad agency gp and nat and int advtg campaigns; MIPA, memb Mktg Soc; *Recreations* fly fishing, music; *Style*— Michael Davis, Esq; ✉ Leagas Shafron Davis, Metropolis House, 22 Percy Street, London W1P 9FF (☎ 0171 528 8888)

DAVIS, Nigel Anthony Lamert; QC (1992); s of (Walter) Patrick Carless Davis (d 1996), of Roehampton, and Jane, *née* Lamert (d 1987); *b* 10 March 1951; *Educ* Charterhouse, Univ Coll Oxford (MA); *m* (m dis 1992), Sheila Ann Gillies Nickel; 3 da (Louisa Mary and Katherine Elizabeth (twins) b 6 Dec 1980, Marianna Jane b 10 July 1984); *Career* called to the Bar Lincoln's Inn (Hardwicke scholar, Kennedy scholar) 1975, Treasury jr counsel 1985; *Clubs* MCC, Vincent's (Oxford), Riverside; *Style*— Nigel Davis, QC; ✉ 7 Stone Buildings, Ground Floor, Lincoln's Inn, London WC2A 3SZ (☎ 0171 405 3886, fax 0171 242 8502)

DAVIS, Norman Harold; s of Tobias Davis (d 1990), and Sybil, *née* Bernstein (d 1984); *b* 16 July 1931; *Educ* Strodes Fndn Egham Surrey; *m* 10 June 1956, Evelyn, da of Harry Lester (d 1954); 1 s (Robin b 1961); *Career* CA, sr ptnr Lane Heywood Davis CAs 1955–, fin dir Yale & Valor plc 1969–87, chm Dixor Strand plc 1978–86, dir Apollo Watch Products plc 1989–92; former chm: Lighting and Leisure Industries plc, George H Hurst plc; former dir: Henara plc, Phoenix Mining and Finance plc; vice pres Jewish Care; A Digest on Individual Voluntary Organsiations; *Clubs* Oriental; *Style*— Norman H Davis, Esq; ✉ 30 Church Mount, Hampstead Garden Suburb, London N2 0RP (☎ 0181 455 8977); Lane Heywood Davis, Anchor Brewhouse, 50 Shad Thames, Tower Bridge City, Tower Bridge, London SE1 2YB (☎ 0171 403 4403, fax 0171 357 6357, car 0850 867 800)

DAVIS, Peter Anthony; s of Montague Davis, of London, and Goldie Davis; *b* 2 Nov 1946; *Educ* Haberdashers' Aske's, Univ of E Anglia (BA); *m* 4 Sept 1992, Carole Virginie, da of Jacques Leprette, ambass France; 4 s (Andrew b 8 April 1980, Simon b 11 March 1985, Stephen b (twin) 11 March 1985, Timothy Scott b 21 June 1995), 1 da (Lucie b 11 Sept 1993); *Career* Price Waterhouse: Audit Practice 1968–72, Management Consultants 1973–, ptnr 1980–, ptnr in charge Europe 1992 (France 1989), memb Bd European Mgmnt 1992–; FCA 1972, FIMC 1979; *Recreations* golf, cricket, tennis; *Style*— Peter Davis, Esq; ✉ 22 Randolph Crescent, London W9 1DR (☎ 0171 286 8401); Price Waterhouse Management Consulting Ltd, Southwark Towers, 32 London Bridge Street, London SE1 9SY (☎ 0171 939 3000, fax 0171 638 1358)

DAVIS, Peter Anthony; *b* 10 Oct 1941; *Educ* Winchester Coll, Lincoln Coll Oxford (MA Law); *m*; 2 s (b 1975 and 1977); *Career* gen audit ptnr Price Waterhouse 1974–80 (joined 1963), exec dep chm Harris Queensway 1980–87; Sturge Holdings PLC: gp fin dir 1988–93, dep chm 1991–93; dir gen National Lottery (OFLOT) 1993–; non-exec dir: Symphony Group PLC 1984–87, Horne Brothers PLC 1984–89, Avis Europe PLC 1987–89, Abbey National Building Society then Abbey National plc 1982–94 (dep chm 1988–94), Provident Financial plc 1994–, Equitable Life Assurance Society 1995–; memb Cncl ICAEW 1989–95 (chm Bd for Chartered Accountants in Business 1990–93); Liveryman Worshipful Co of Chartered Accountants; FCA (ACA 1967); *Recreations* tennis, fishing, football, theatre; *Style*— Peter Davis, Esq; ✉ Office of the National Lottery, 2 Monck Street, London SW1P 2BQ (☎ 0171 227 2000)

DAVIS, Sir Peter John; kt (1997); s of John Stephen Davis, and Adriantje, *née* de Baat; *b* 23 Dec 1941; *Educ* Shrewsbury; *Career* mgmnt trainee and salesman Ditchburn Organisation 1959–65, mktg and sales General Foods Ltd 1965–72, Fitch Lovell Ltd 1973–76, mktg dir and md Key Markets 1973–76, dir and asst md J Sainsbury plc 1976–86, chm Reed International plc 1990–94 (chief exec 1986–92), chief exec and co-chm Reed Elsevier plc (following merger) 1993–94 (resigned); memb Supervisory Bd: Elsevier NV 1993–94, Aegon NV 1993–94; gp chief exec Prudential Corporation plc 1995– (non-exec dir 1994–95); non-exec dir The Boots Company plc 1991–; chm: Adult Literacy and Basic Skills Agency, Nat Advsy Cncl for Educn and Training Targets 1993–, Business in the Community (BITC) 1997–; dep chm Business in the Community, vice pres Chartered Inst of Mktg; tstee: Royal Opera House 1994–, Victoria & Albert Musuem 1994–; govr Duncombe Sch Hertford; *Recreations* sailing, swimming, opera, wine; *Clubs* Trearddur Bay Sailing (Cdre 1982–84); *Style*— Sir Peter Davis; ✉ Prudential Corporation plc, 142 Holborn Bars, London EC1N 2NH

DAVIS, Peter Kerrich Byng; s of Frank C Davis, MC (d 1979), and Barbara, *née* Hartshorne; *b* 4 May 1933; *Educ* Felsted, Univ of London, St Thomas' Hosp Med Sch (MB BS); *m* 24 April 1965, Jennifer Anne, da of Brig-Gen (Creemer) Paul Clarke (d 1971); 1 s (Paul b 14 Aug 1966), 1 da (Emma b 9 Aug 1968); *Career* sr registrar in plastic surgery Churchill Hosp Oxford 1968–71; conslt plastic surgn 1971–: St Thomas' Hosp London (now emeritus), Queen Mary's Hosp Roehampton, Kingston Hosp; Br Assoc of Aesthetic Plastic Surgns: memb 1977–, vice pres 1981, pres 1982–84, hon sec 1988–91; memb: BMA 1959, BAPS 1971, RSM 1971, ICPRS 1971, ISAPS 1979; *Books* Operative Surgery (contrib, 1982), Maxillo - Facial Injuries (contrib, 1985 and 1996); *Recreations* fishing; *Style*— Peter Davis, Esq; ✉ 97 Harley St, London W1 (☎ 0171 486 4976, car tel 0860 333472)

DAVIS, Peter Robert Christian; OBE (1993); s of Robert Henry Davis (d 1990), and Ruth Anna Louise, *née* Larsen; *b* 25 Feb 1949; *Educ* Archbishop Tenison's GS, S W London Coll (HNC, Dip in Mktg); *m* Nov 1984, Anne Klitgaard, da of Finn Bertelsen; 1 da (Sarah Maria Klitgaard b 26 April 1985), 1 s (Thomas Caspar b 11 June 1988); *Career* Inco Europe Ltd: sales asst German Div 1967–69, asst to Customer Servs Mangr 1969–73; asst to Product Mangr Metal Box Ltd 1973–75, mktg co-ordinator Medical Products 3M UK plc 1976–77, product mangr then gp project mangr Dylon International Ltd 1977–84, special advsr to Rt Hon Kenneth Baker DOE 1984–86, head Home Affairs Cons Res Dept 1986–87, head General Election Media Monitoring Unit Cons Central Office 1992, dir of Mktg Membership and Overseas Affairs RIBA 1988–93, currently chief exec The Industry Cncl for Packaging and the Environment (Incpen); Tidy Br Gp: memb Cncl 1993–, dir and tstee 1996–; cncllr (Cons) Lambeth 1978–84, dep ldr Lambeth Cncl 1982, chm Cons Greater London Area Local Govt Ctee 1988–91, chm Croydon S Cons Assoc 1995–; FCIM (MCIM 1973); *Recreations* walking, reading, gardening, European history; *Style*— Peter Davis, Esq, OBE; ✉ 64 Woodcote Valley Road, Purley, Surrey CR8 3BD (☎ 0181 668 3915); The Industry Council for Packaging and the Environment Inc, Tenterden House, 3 Tenterden Street, London W1R 9AH (☎ 0171 409 0949)

DAVIS, Reginald; *m* 20 June 1948, Audrey Fields; 1 da (Marilyn b 1952); *Career* served RN and Fleet Air Arm WWII as photographer, active serv Far East; photographer specialising in royalty and celebrities; has accompanied the Br Royal Family on more than fifty state visits and has photographed membs of eighteen royal families, has an international colour library comprising 37,000 photographs; first and second prizes Encylopaedic Britannica Awards for Colour Photography 1962, first prize Rothmans Award for Colour Photography 1971; decorated Order of Taj Iran 1978; FRPS 1971, fell Br Inst 1975, FBIPP, FMPA 1980; *Books* Royalty of the World (1969), Princess Anne A Girl of Our Time (1973), Elizabeth Our Queen (1977), Royal Families of the World (1978), The Prince of Wales (1978), Monarchy in Power (1978), The Persian Prince (1979), The Royal Family of Thailand (1981), The Royal Family of Luxembourg (1989); *Recreations* gardening, videoing, rotary; *Clubs* Hendon Rotary (pres 1989–90); *Style*— Reginald Davis, Esq; ✉ 64 Totteridge Village, London N20 8PS (☎ 0181 445 3131, fax 0181 446 8886)

DAVIS, Hon Mr Justice; Sir (Dermot) Renn; kt (1981), OBE (1971); s of Capt Eric Renn Davis, OBE (d 1945), of Highlands Hotel, Molo, Kenya, and Norah Alexandrina, *née* Bingham (d 1967); *b* 20 Nov 1928; *Educ* Prince of Wales Sch Nairobi, Wadham Coll Oxford (BA); *m* 1984, Mary Helen Farquharson, da of Brig Thomas Farquharson Ker Howard, DSO (d 1963), of Goldenhayes, Woodlands, Hants, and wid of William James Pearce; *Career* barr; crown counsel Kenya 1956–62, attorney gen Solomon Is and legal advsr Western Pacific High Cmmn 1962–73, Br Judge Anglo-French Condominium of the New Hebrides 1973–76; chief justice: Solomon Is and Tuvalu 1976–80, Gibraltar 1980–86, Falkland Is 1987–; judge Br Atlantic Territory 1988–; justice of appeal Ct of Appeal: Gibraltar 1989–, St Helena 1991–, Br-Indian Indian Ocean Territory 1991–; *Clubs* United Oxford and Cambridge Univ, Muthaiga Country (Nairobi); *Style*— Sir Renn Davis, OBE; ✉ c/o Barclays Bank plc, 30 High Street, Hungerford, Berks RG17 0NQ

DAVIS, Richard Charles; s of Joseph Arthur Davis, of Fairford, Glos, and Dorothy Ellen, *née* Head; *b* 15 May 1949; *Educ* Queen's Coll Taunton, Univ of Leeds (LLB); *m* 21 Sept 1974, Margaret Jane, da of William Dixon, OBE; 1 s (James William Richard b 14 March 1984), 1 da (Sarah Margaret b 8 Sept 1981); *Career* admitted slr 1974, ptnr Eversheds (formerly Eversheds Hepworth & Chadwick) 1982– (joined 1979); memb Law Soc; *Recreations* art, music, travel, sailing; *Style*— Richard C Davis, Esq; ✉ The Gables, Bishop Thornton, Harrogate, N Yorks HG3 3JR (☎ 01423 770172); Eversheds, Cloth Hall Court, Infirmary Street, Leeds LS1 2JB (☎ 0113 243 0391, fax 0113 245 6188)

DAVIS, Richard Henry; s of Ralph Davis, of Cornwall, and Joyce Amelia, *née* Danziger, of London; *Educ* Univ Coll Sch, Ealing Coll of Higher Educ; *m* 11 Sept 1974, Suzanne Jane, da of Cyril Roy Biggs; 1 s (Mark Walton b 26 Dec 1976), 1 da (Charlotte Anne Mary b 6 Dec 1983); *Career* Connaught Hotel 1966–67, Grand Metropolitan 1968–69, Rank Hotels Royal Lancaster 1969–74, EMI Leisure Ltd 1975–79 (banqueting mangr and food & beverage mangr Selfridge Hotel), gen mangr Royal Westminster Hotel, mgmnt conslt IHLC 1980–82, md Dukes Hotel 1982–89, mgmnt conslt R H Davis 1990, dir Hotel Development Associates Ltd, formerly gen mangr Brown's Hotel; memb UK team Culinary Olympics Budapest 1968; Master Innholder 1987, Freeman City of London 1987; FHCIMA; *Recreations* sailing, swimming, reading, music; *Clubs* RAC; *Style*— Richard Davis, Esq

DAVIS, Rodney Colin; s of (Arthur) Cyril Gordon Davis (d 1993), and Phyllis Eleanor Margaret Griffiths, *née* Roberts (d 1977); *b* 9 July 1940; *Educ* Churcher's Coll Petersfield, King's Coll London (LLB), Tulane Univ New Orleans USA (LLM); *m* 4 Sept 1965, Elizabeth Jeanne, da of Arthur William Richards, of Englefield, Sturminster Newton, Dorset; 1 s (Ian b 1968), 1 da (Sarah b 1970); *Career* asst slr Durham CC 1965–70, asst clerk Berks CC 1970–74; ptnr: Coward Chance 1979–87 (asst slr 1974–79), Clifford Chance 1987–95; memb City of London Slrs' Co; *Recreations* gardening; *Style*— Rodney Davis, Esq; ✉ Mead Furlong, Reading Road, Cholsey, Wallingford OX10 9HG (☎ 01491 651215, fax 01491 651938)

DAVIS, Roger O'Byrne; s of Paul Patterson Davis (d 1984), of Burnham Market, Norfolk, and Mabel Beryl Davis; *b* 1 Aug 1943; *Educ* Wrekin Coll Wellington Shropshire; *Career* articled clerk Chantrey Button & Co 1960–66; Cooper Brothers & Co (now Coopers & Lybrand); joined 1966, ptnr 1975, seconded to HM Treasy 1975–77, currently head of audit practice; FCA; *Books* Adding Value To The External Audit (1990); *Recreations* walking, sailing, music; *Style*— Roger Davis, Esq; ✉ Coopers & Lybrand, 1 Embankment Place, London WC2N 6NN (☎ 0171 213 4531)

DAVIS, Sandra Sharon; da of Josef Martin Davis, and Milly Edith Davis; *b* 3 July 1956; *Educ* South Hampstead HS, Univ of Sussex (BA), Univ of Aix-en-Provence, Coll of Law; *m* 6 Sept 1987, Avron Woolf Smith, of South Africa; 2 s (Zakari Louis Smith b 5 Sept 1989, Elliott Nathan Smith b 8 Dec 1991); *Career* Mishcon de Reya (formerly Victor Mishcon & Co): articled clerk 1979–81, ptnr 1984–, staff ptnr 1993–96, also currently head of Family Dept; memb: Slrs' Family Law Assoc, Lord Chllr's Child Abduction Panel, Holborn Law Soc; fell Int Acad of Matrimonial Lawyers; FRSA; *Books* International Child Abduction (1993); *Recreations* photography, travel, theatre, art, family; *Style*— Ms Sandra Davis; ✉ Mishcon de Reya, 21 Southampton Row, London WC1B 5HS (☎ 0171 440 7000)

DAVIS, Prof Stanley Stewart; s of William Stanley Davis, of Warwick, and Joan, *née* Lawson; *b* 17 Dec 1942; *Educ* Warwick Sch, Univ of London (BPharm, PhD, DSc); *m* 24 Nov 1984, Lisbeth, da of Erik Illum (d 1986), of Denmark; 3 s (Benjamin b 1970, Nathaniel b 1974, Daniel b 1984); *Career* lectr Univ of London 1967–70, sr lectr Aston Univ 1970–75, Lord Trent prof of pharmacy Univ of Nottingham 1975–; chm: Pharmaceutical Profiles Ltd, Danbiosyst (UK) Ltd); FRSC, FRPharmS; *Books* Imaging in Drug Research (1982), Microspheres in Drug Therapy (1984), Site Specific Drug Delivery (1986), Delivery Systems for Peptides (1987), Polymers for Controlled Drug Delivery (1987), Pharmaceutical Applications of Cell and Tissue Culture in Drug Transport (1991); *Recreations* skiing, tennis, painting; *Style*— Prof Stanley Davis; ✉ 19 Cavendish Crescent North, The Park, Nottingham NG7 1BA; Department of Pharmaceutical Sciences, Univ of Nottingham, University Park, Nottingham (☎ 0115 951 5121)

DAVIS, Steven Ilsley; s of Lt-Col George Ilsley Davis, of Tinmouth, Vermont, and Marion Brown Davis; *b* 6 Nov 1934; *Educ* Phillips Acad Mass, Amherst Coll Mass (BA), Harvard Business Sch (MBA); *m* 27 Feb 1960, Joyce Ann, da of Theodore S Hirtz (d 1962), of NY; 2 s (Andrew Tinmouth b 1962, Christopher Stamer b 1963), 1 da (Stephanie b 1975); *Career* private US Army Reserve 1958; asst vice pres JP Morgan & Co 1959–66, US Agency for Int Devpt 1966–68, first vice pres Bankers Trust Co 1968–72; md: First International Bankshares Ltd 1972–79, Davis International Banking Consultants 1979–; asst dir US Govt Agency for Int Devpt 1966–68; Hon Phi Beta Kappa Amherst Coll; *Books* The Eurobank (1975), The Management of International Banks (1979), Excellence in Banking (1985), Managing Change in the Excellent Banks (1989); *Recreations* skiing, tennis, hiking; *Clubs* Roehampton; *Style*— Steven Davis, Esq; ✉ 66 South Edwardes Square, London W8 (☎ 0171 602 6348); Davis International Banking Consultants, 9 North Audley Street, London W1 (☎ 0171 495 2288, fax 0171 839 9250)

DAVIS, Terence Anthony Gordon (Terry); MP (Lab) Birmingham Hodge Hill (majority 7,068); s of Gordon Davis; *b* 5 Jan 1938; *Educ* King Edward VI GS Stourbridge, UCL, Univ of Michigan; *m* 1963, Anne, *née* Cooper; 1 s, 1 da; *Career* Parly candidate (Lab): Bromsgrove 1970, 1971 (by-election), 1974 (twice), Birmingham Stechford March 1977 (by-election); MP (Lab): Bromsgrove 1971–74, Birmingham Stechford 1979–83, Birmingham Hodge Hill 1983–; oppn front bench spokesman: Health Serv 1981–83, Treasy and Econ Affrs 1983–86, Indust 1986–87; memb: Public Accounts Ctee 1987–94, Advsy Cncl on Public Records 1989–94, Cncl of Europe Assembly 1992–, Western European Union Assembly 1992–; memb MSF, former memb Yeovil RDC, business exec (MBA) and motor indust mangr; *Style*— Terry Davis, Esq, MP; ✉ c/o House of Commons, London SW1

DAVIS, Sir Thomas Robert Alexander Harries; KBE (1980); s of Sidney Thomas Davis; *b* 11 June 1917; *Educ* King's Coll Auckland, Otago Univ Med Sch (MB ChB), Sch of Tropical Medicine Sydney Univ (DTM & H), Harvard Sch of Public Health (MPH); *m* 1, 1940, Myra Lydia Henderson; 3 s; m 2, 1979, Pa Tepaeru Arika (d 1989); *Career* chief MO Cook Islands Med Serv 1948–52 (MO and surgical specialist 1945–48), Res Staff Dept of Nutrition Harvard Sch 1952–55, chief Dept of Environmental Med Arctic Aero-Med Laboratory Fairbanks Alaska 1955–56, dir Environmental Med Div Army Med Res Laboratory NNrt Knox 1956–61 (qualified space surgn NASA 1960), res dir US Army Res Inst of Environmental Med Natick 1961–63, res exec Arthur D Little Inc Cambridge Mass 1963–71, in private med practice 1974–; formed Democratic Pty of Cook Islands 1971, premier Cook Islands 1978–87 (in oppn 1972–78); patron: Cook Islands Sports' Assoc (Men's Olympic Ctee), Boxing Assoc; visiting dir Bishop Museum Hawaii; hon memb: Maritime Amateur Radio Club 1952, Alaska Territorial Med Assoc 1956; Cert of Appreciation Army Ballistic Missile Agency 1958, Silver Jubilee Medal 1977, Order of Merit (FRG) 1978, Papua New Guinea Independence Medal 1985; Pa Tuterangi Ariki 1979; memb: NZ Med Assoc 1945, Cook Islands Library and Museum Soc 1946 (past pres), RSM 1960, Cook Islands Med and Dental Assoc 1970 (past pres), Cook Islands Voyaging Soc (pres 1992–), Cook Islands Yachting Fedn (pres 1995–); fell Royal Soc of Tropical Med and Hygiene 1949, FRSH; *Books* Doctor to the Islands (1954), Makutu (1956), Island Boy (1992), Vaka (1992), author of numerous scientific pubns; *Clubs* Avatiu Sports (patron), Lions (past pres), Harvard (Boston USA), Rarotonga Sailing (patron), Avatiu Cricket (patron), Wellington (NZ); *Style*— Sir Thomas Robert Davis, KBE; ✉ PO Box 116, Rarotonga, Cook Islands

DAVIS, Victor Lionel; s of Alfred Lionel Davis (d 1952), and Elizabeth Jane, *née* Beer (d 1994); *Educ* Alleyn's Sch Dulwich (LCC scholarship); *Career* editorial copy boy Daily Express 1945–47; Nat Serv Army 1947–49; reporter Streatham News 1950–56, reporter/night news ed Daily Sketch and night news ed The People 1956–60; Daily Express: reporter, foreign corr and news ed 1960–65, NY Bureau 1965–67, show business ed 1967–86; showbusiness ed The Mail on Sunday 1986–94; life memb NUJ 1950; *Books* The Ghostmaker (1996); also author of a number of published short stories; *Recreations* staying curious; *Style*— Victor Davis, Esq; ✉ 52 Campden Street, Kensington, London W8 7ET (☎ 0171 229 3836)

DAVIS, William; *b* 6 March 1933; *Educ* City of London Coll; *m* 1967, Sylvette Jouclas; *Career* broadcaster, columnist and author; formerly financial ed: Evening Standard, Sunday Express, The Guardian; presenter BBC TV's Money Programme 1967–69, ed Punch 1969–79, ed High Life (British Airways in-flight magazine) 1973–, dir Fleet Holdings and Morgan Grampian 1979–81, ed-in-chief Financial Weekly 1980–81, dir Thomas Cook 1988–, chm Br Tourist Authy and the Eng Tourist Bd 1990–93, dir British Invisibles 1990–93, non-exec chm Allied Leisure 1993–, chm and editorial dir Premier Magazines 1992–; memb Devpt Cncl The Nat Theatre 1990–92; Knight Order of Merit of the Italian Republic; *Books* Three Years Hard Labour, Merger Mania, Money Talks, Have Expenses Will Travel, It's No Sin to be Rich, The Best of Everything (ed), Money in the 1980s - How to Make it, How to Keep it, The Rich, Fantasy, The Corporate Infighter's Handbook, The Supersalesman's Handbook, The Innovators, Children of the Rich, The Lucky Generation, A Positive View of the 21st Century; *Style*— William Davis, Esq; ✉ c/o High Life Magazine, Haymarket House, 1 Oxendon Street, London SW1Y 4EE

DAVIS-GOFF, Sir Robert William; 4 Bt (UK 1905), of Glenville, Parish of St Patrick's, Co Waterford; s of Sir Ernest William Davis-Goff, 3 Bt (d 1980); *b* 12 Sept 1955; *Educ* Cheltenham; *m* 1978, Nathalie Sheelagh, da of Terence Chadwick, of Lissen Hall, Swords, Co Dublin; 3 s (William Nathaniel b 1980, Henry Terence Chadwick b 1986, James Sammy Chadwick b 1989), 1 da (Sarah Chadwick b 1982); *Heir* s, William Nathaniel Davis-Goff b 20 April 1980; *Career* picture dealer, property mgmnt; *Recreations* shooting; *Style*— Sir Robert Davis-Goff, Bt; ✉ Seafield, Donabate, Co Dublin, Republic of Ireland

DAVISON, Prof Alexander Meikle (Sandy); RD (1985); s of John Christal Davison, of Riding Mill, Northumberland, and Alison Meikle, *née* Goodfellow; *b* 31 Jan 1940; *Educ* Daniel Stewart's Coll Edinburgh, Univ of Edinburgh (BSc, MB ChB, MD); *m* 10 June 1960, Marion Elizabeth Stewart, da of James George Somerville; 2 s (Andrew b 1960, Iain b 1967), 1 da (Pamela b 1965); *Career* Surgn Lt Cdr RNR princ med offr HMS Ceres 1987–94; conslt renal physician St James' Univ Hosp 1974–, prof of renal med Univ of Leeds 1996– (sr clinical lectr 1984–); ed emeritus Nephrology Dialysis Transplantation monthly jl, contrib to Davidsons Textbook of Med, ed and contrib Oxford Textbook of Clinical Nephrology; pres elect Int Soc for Artificial Organs; memb: Cncl European Renal Assoc, Medical Appeal Tbnl; FRCPEd (memb Cncl), FRCP; *Books* Dialysis Review (ed, 1978), Synopsis of Renal Diseases (1981), Mainstream Medicine, Nephrology (1988); *Recreations* gardening, shooting; *Style*— Prof Sandy Davison, RD; ✉ 9 Lidgett Park Road, Leeds LS8 1EE (☎ 0113 266 1042, fax 0113 236 9905); Department of Renal Medicine, St James's University Hospital, Leeds LS9 7TF (☎ 0113 243 3144, direct line 0113 283 6983, fax 0113 242 8870)

DAVISON, Clive Phillip; s of Maj Laurence Napier Davison (d 1966), and Rosa Rachel Louisa, *née* Parker (d 1994); *b* 14 March 1944; *Educ* Grange Sch Christchurch Dorset, Poly of the South Bank, Thames Poly; *m* 1, 1968 (m dis 1982), Sandra, da of Thomas Keith Lord, of Billericay, Essex; m 2, 27 Sept 1993, Jane Elise, da of Roger Howorth, of West Moors, Dorset; 1 s (Alexander Napier b 2 Oct 1988), 1 da (Hannah Louise b 26 Jan 1990); *Career* chartered architect, assoc Trehearne & Norman Preston & Partners

1974–77, ptnr Trehearnes 1977–79, design and site supervisor of Min of P T T Riyadh 1977–83, co sec and dir I M Coleridge Ltd 1987, princ Davison Associates; designer of various hosp and healthcare projects for NHS trusts; RIBA; *Recreations* squash, guitar, reading, skiing; *Style—* Clive Davison, Esq; ✉ 3 Croft Rd, Christchurch, Dorset BH23 3QQ (☎ 01202 479341); Davison Associates, Priory Chambers, 6 Church St, Christchurch, Dorset (☎ 01202 470176, fax 01202 487627)

DAVISON, (George) Gordon; s of George Robert Davison (d 1984), and Winifred Margaret, *née* Collie (d 1982); *b* 30 Nov 1934; *Educ* King's Sch Tynemouth, King's Coll Univ of Durham (BSc); *m* 1, 30 Dec 1961, Anne; 1 da (Susan b 1970), 1 s (Peter b 1974); m 2, 4 July 1969, Judith Agnes; *Career* chm Berghaus Ltd 1966–93 (sold to Pentland Group plc 1993), md LD Mountain Centre Ltd 1993–; ptnr Dene Associates (Consultants) 1993–; *Recreations* climbing, skiing, windsurfing, diving, squash; *Style—* Gordon Davison, Esq; ✉ 3 Benthall, Beadnell, Northumberland NE67 5BQ (☎ 01665 720366); LD Mountain Centre Ltd, 34 Dean Street, Newcastle upon Tyne NE1 1PG (☎ 0191 232 23561, fax 0191 222 0082)

DAVISON, Ian Frederic Hay; *b* 30 June 1931; *Educ* LSE (BSc(Econ)), Univ of Michigan; *Career* managing ptnr Arthur Andersen & Co 1966–82, dep chm and chief exec Lloyd's of London 1983–86; chm: Hong Kong Securities Review Ctee 1987–88, Credit Lyonnais Capital Markets 1988–91, Storehouse plc 1990–96, The National Mortgage Bank 1992–, Newspaper Publishing plc 1993–94, McDonnell Information Systems plc 1993–; non-exec dir: Cadbury Schweppes plc 1990–96, Chloride Group plc; chm: Sadler's Wells Fndn 1995–, Cncl Royal Coll of Art 1996–; memb Cncl ICAEW; FCA; *Books* A View of the Room, Lloyd's, Change and Disclosure (1987); *Recreations* music, opera, gardening; *Clubs* Athenaeum; *Style—* Ian Hay Davison, Esq; ✉ 25 James Street, London W1M 5HY

DAVISON, Timothy Paul; s of John Paul Davison (d 1991), of Newcastle upon Tyne, and Patricia Davison; *b* 4 June 1961; *Educ* Kenton Sch Newcastle, Univ of Stirling (BA), Univ of Glasgow (MBA), Inst of Health Servs Mgmnt (DipHSM); *m* 1980, Hilary Williamson, *née* Gillick; 1 s (Ruairidh James b 20 Feb 1990); *Career* NHS nat mgmnt trainee 1983–84, gen servs mangr Stirling Royal Infirmary 1984–86, patient servs mangr Royal Edinburgh Hosp 1986–88, hosp admin Glasgow Royal Infirmary 1988–90, sector gen mangr Gartnavel Royal Hosp 1990–91, unit gen mangr Glasgow Mental Health Unit 1991–94, chief exec Gtr Glasgow Community & Mental Health Servs NHS Tst 1994–; assoc memb IHSM; *Recreations* tennis, golf, military and political history; *Clubs* Thorn Park Lawn Tennis, Bearsden Golf; *Style—* Timothy Davison, Esq; ✉ Greater Glasgow Community & Mental Health Services NHS Trust, Gartnavel Royal Hospital, Great Western Road, Glasgow G12 0XH (☎ 0141 211 3764, fax 0141 334 0952)

DAVOUD, Nicole Matilde; OBE (1994, MBE 1982); da of Jacques Gellert (d 1991), and Lara Gellert, of Brussels; *b* 6 Oct 1939; *Educ* Lyceo Nacional No 1 Buenos Aires, Univ of Buenos Aires; *m* 31 March 1960, Raymond Davoud, *qv*; 1 s (Alexander Joseph b 5 April 1966); *Career* fndr and dir Nicole Davoud Associates (qualitative research conslts) 1963–74, re-directed to vol sector due to Multiple Sclerosis; fndr Crack MS (young arm of Multiple Sclerosis Soc) 1974–76, memb Cncl Multiple Sclerosis Soc 1976–80, memb Ctee Int Year of Disabled 1979–82, memb N London Ctee for Employment of People with Disabilities 1991–, memb Presidential Working Party Disability Appeal Tbnl 1991–92, memb Disability Living Allowance Advsy Bd 1995–; memb MRS 1970–95; *Publications* Multiple Sclerosis and Its Effect on Employment (1980), Part Time Employment - Time For Recognition, Organisation and Legal Reform (1980), Where Do I Go From Here? (autobiography, 1985), Disability Employment Credit - The Way Ahead (1990), Employing People With Disabilities - Employers' Perspective (1992), Welfare to Work: Disability Perspective (1996); *Recreations* meditation, friends and the arts; *Style—* Mrs Nicole Davoud, OBE

DAVOUD, Raymond Israel; s of Benjamin Davoud (d 1982), and Lilly, *née* Ely (d 1992); *b* 27 Dec 1931; *Educ* St Paul's, Trinity Coll Cambridge (MA), McGill Univ Montreal (MCom); *m* 31 March 1960, Nicole Matilde Davoud, OBE, *qv*; 1 s (Alexander Joseph b 5 April 1966); *Career* int mktg conslt 1964–; memb: Mktg Soc, Mktg Cncl; MCIM, MMRS, FICA; *Recreations* bridge, gardening, classic cars; *Style—* Raymond Davoud, Esq; ✉ Raymond Davoud & Associates, 22 Kingsgate Ave, London N3 3BH (☎ 0181 346 4879, car 0860 464323)

DAVSON, *see:* Glyn, Bt, Sir Anthony

DAVSON, Christopher Michael Edward; s of Sir Edward Rae Davson, 1 Bt, KCMG (d 1937); hp to bro Sir Anthony Glyn, 2 Bt, *qv*; *b* 26 May 1927; *Educ* Eton; *m* 1, 2 June 1962 (m dis 1972), Evelyn Mary, o da of late James Wardrop; 1 s (George Trenchard Simon b 1964); m 2, 1975, Kate, da of Ludo Foster, of Greatham Manor, Pulborough, Sussex; *Career* Capt, formerly Welsh Guards; formerly fin dir of cos in the Booker McConnell Group; Liveryman Worshipful Co of Musicians; *Recreations* archaeology; *Style—* Christopher Davson, Esq; ✉ 4 Mermaid St, Rye, Sussex TN31 7JA

DAWBARN, Sir Simon Yelverton; KCVO (1980), CMG (1976); s of Frederic Dawbarn, and Maud Louise, *née* Mansell; *b* 16 Sept 1923; *Educ* Oundle, CCC Cambridge; *m* 1948, Shelby Montgomery, *née* Parker; 1 s, 2 da; *Career* WWII Reconnaissance Corps; FCO 1949–53 and 1961–71; served: Brussels, Prague, Tehran, Algiers, Athens; FCO 1971–75, head of W African Dept and non-resident ambass to Chad 1973–75, consul-gen Montreal 1975–78, ambass to Morocco 1978–82, ret; *Style—* Sir Simon Dawbarn, KCVO, CMG

DAWBER, George Arthur; s of Arthur Dawber (d 1986), of Calgary Canada, and Gladys, *née* Garrett (d 1989); *b* 15 Sept 1939; *Educ* Alma Park, UMIST; *m* 19 March 1966, Glenys, da of Eric Ernest Whalley; 1 s (Howard Jason b 20 May 1972), 2 da (Zoë Cordelia b 29 July 1970, Aimie Camilla b 9 March 1980); *Career* professional photographer: nat serv station photographer RAF, trained in photographic transmissions 1956–59, professional cricketer Lancashire CCC 1959–60, industl photographer 1960–70, general photographer 1970–75, freelance with own studio 1975– (specialising in wedding, portrait and PR photography), former princ lectr Fuji Professional Sch of Photography UK (has lectured widely UK and Overseas), course dir Photo Trg Overseas; memb Admissions and Qualifications Bd BIPP (nat pres BIPP 1983–84) and Master Photographers Assoc; *Awards* winner Kodak Bride of the Year Competition, winner Kodak Portraits in Uniforms Competition, awarded Craftsmen Degree of Professional Photographers of America (CrPhotog) and Presidential award for services to his profession 1984; FBIPP, FMPA; *Style—* George Dawber, Esq; ✉ The Cottage, 159 Dialstone Lane, Offerton, Stockport, Cheshire SK2 6AU (☎ 0161 483 3114, studio fax 0161 483 6063)

DAWE, Roger James; CB (1988), OBE (1970); s of Harry James, and Edith Mary, *née* Heard; *b* 26 Feb 1941; *Educ* Hardye's Sch Dorchester, Fitzwilliam House Cambridge; *m* 1965, Ruth Day, da of Frederic Jolliffe; 1 s (Mark b 1968), 1 da (Caroline b 1971); *Career* joined Miny of Lab 1962; private sec to: PM 1966–70, Sec of State for Employment 1972–74; under sec MSC 1981–84, dep sec Dept of Employment 1985–92, dep sec Dept of Educn 1992–95, DG for further and higher educn and youth trg Dept of Educn and Employment 1995–; *Recreations* tennis, soccer, theatre, music; *Style—* Roger Dawe, Esq, CB, OBE; ✉ Department for Education and Employment, Sanctuary Buildings, Great Smith Street, London SW1P 3BT (☎ 0171 925 6210)

DAWES, Prof Edwin Alfred; s of Harold Dawes (d 1939), of Goole, Yorks, and Maude, *née* Barker (d 1967); *b* 6 July 1925; *Educ* Goole GS, Univ of Leeds (BSc, PhD, DSc); *m* 19 Dec 1950, Amy, da of Robert Dunn Rogerson (d 1980), of Gateshead; 2 s (Michael b 1955, Adrian b 1963); *Career* lectr in biochemistry Univ of Leeds 1950 (asst lectr 1947–50), sr lectr in biochemistry Univ of Glasgow 1961–63 (lectr 1951–61); Univ of Hull: Reckitt prof of biochemistry 1963–92 (emeritus 1993), dean of sci 1968–70, pro vice chllr 1977–80, dir Biomedical Res Unit 1981–92; ed Biochemical Journal 1958–65, ed in chief Journal Gen Microbiology 1976–81; Fedn of Euro Microbiological Socs: ed-in-chief FEMS Microbiology Letters, pubns mangr 1982–90, archivist 1990–; chm Sci Advsy Ctee Yorks Cancer Res Campaign 1978– (campaign dep chm 1987–); visiting lectr Biochemical Soc Aust and NZ 1975, American Med Alumni lectr Univ of St Andrews 1980–81; hon vice pres: The Magic Circle London (memb 1959–, historian 1987–), Scot Conjurers' Assoc 1973–, Scot Assoc Magical Soc 1996–; pres: Br Ring Int Brotherhood of Magicians 1972–73, Hull Lit and Philosophical Soc 1976–77 (memb Cncl 1973–); memb Hall of Fame Soc of American Magicians 1984; chm Fndn Ctee Philip Larkin Soc 1995–; Hon DSc Univ of Hull 1992; FRSC 1956, FIBiol 1964; *Books* The Great Illusionists (1979), Isaac Fawkes: Fame and Fable (1979), Quantitative Problems in Biochemistry (6 edn, 1980, trans into 6 languages), Biochemistry of Bacterial Growth (jtly, 3 edn 1982), The Biochemist in a Microbial Wonderland (1982), Vonetta (1982), The Barrister in The Circle (1983), The Book of Magic (1986, re-issued as Making Magic, 1992), Microbial Energetics (1986), The Wizard Exposed (1987), Philip Larkin: the Man and His Work (contrib, 1989), Henri Robin: Expositor of Science and Magic (1990), Novel Biodegradable Microbial Polymers (ed, 1990), Molecular Biology of Membrane-Bound Complexes in Phototrophic Bacteria (ed, 1990), The Magic of Britain (1994), Charles Bertram: The Court Conjurer (1996); *Recreations* conjuring, book-collecting; *Style—* Prof Edwin Dawes; ✉ Dane Hill, 393 Beverley Road, Anlaby, E Riding HU10 7BQ (☎ 01482 657998); Department of Biological Sciences, University of Hull, Hull, E Riding HU6 7RX (☎ 01482 465316, fax 01482 466443)

DAWES, Ewan David; JP (1975 Northumberland); s of Joseph Dawes (d 1965), of Ashington, Northumberland, and Florence, *née* Woodgate (d 1982); *b* 6 Nov 1937; *Educ* King Edward VI GS Morpeth, Univ of Manchester (DipArch); *m* 8 Aug 1963, Joan Elizabeth, da of James Bland Tomlin (d 1978), of Ashington, Northumberland; 2 da (Jan b 1966, Lyn b 1967); *Career* ptnr in private practice 1960–; memb Jt Technical Ctee Working Gp on Design and Build Tendering Procedures 1981–82; ARIBA 1963; memb: UMIST 1960, Architects in Industry and Commerce 1972; FRSA 1983, FIMgt 1983; *Recreations* golf; *Style—* Ewan D Dawes, Esq, JP; ✉ MDP Architects, Robson House, 29 Newgate Street, Morpeth, Northumberland NE61 1AT (☎ 01670 510077, fax 01670 510088)

DAWES, Howard Anthony Leigh; s of George Roland Dawes (d 1965), of Weatheroak Hall, nr Alvechurch, Worcs, and (Phyllis) Kathleen, *née* Reeves; *b* 4 Aug 1936; *Educ* Uppingham; *m* 1 (m dis); 1 s, 3 da; m 2, Aug 1991, Judith Ann, *née* Bolton; *Career* chm and chief exec: Dawes Trust Ltd 1965–, Neville Industrial Securities 1965–88; dir Velcourt Group plc 1968–; chm Nuffield Hosp 1984–89; past chm Ctee of Friends of Birmingham Museums and Galleries, hon treas Birmingham Cons Assoc 1968–76, memb Midland Industl Cncl 1977–, chm Scientific Instrument Soc 1994–; chm Pershore Abbey Appeal 1991–; Freeman City of London, Liveryman Worshipful Co of Glaziers; FCA, FRAS 1960, FRSA 1975; *Recreations* history of science; *Clubs* Kildare Street (Dublin), Buckland; *Style—* Howard Dawes, Esq; ✉ Craycombe House, nr Fladbury, Worcestershire WR10 2QS (☎ 01386 860692); PO Box 15, Pershore, Worcestershire WR10 2RD (☎ 01386 861075, fax 01386 861074)

DAWES, Rt Rev Peter Spencer; s of late Jason Spencer Dawes, and late Janet, *née* Blane; *b* 5 Feb 1928; *Educ* Aldenham, Hatfield Coll Univ of Durham (BA); *m* 4 Dec 1954, Ethel; 2 s (Michael b 1959, Daniel b 1964), 2 da (Janet b 1956, Mary b 1968); *Career* ordained: deacon 1954, priest 1955; curate: St Andrew Islington, St Ebbes Oxford 1954–60; tutor Clifton Theological Coll 1960–65, vicar Good Shepherd Romford 1965–80, examining chaplain to Bishop of Chelmsford 1970, archdeacon West Ham 1980–88, bishop of Derby 1988–95, ret; memb: Gen Synod 1970, Standing Ctee 1975; *Style—* The Rt Rev Peter Dawes; ✉ 45 Arundell, Ely, Cambs CB6 1BQ

DAWICK, Viscount; Alexander Douglas Derrick Haig; s and h of 2 Earl Haig, OBE; *b* 30 June 1961; *Educ* Stowe, Cirencester; *Clubs* The New Club; *Style—* Viscount Dawick; ✉ Third Farm, Melrose, Roxburghshire TD6 9DR

DAWID, Prof (Alexander) Philip; s of Israel Dawid, and Rita, *née* Abel; *b* 1 Feb 1946; *Educ* City of London Sch, Trinity Hall and Darwin Coll Cambridge (MA, Dip Math Statistics, ScD); *m* 18 March 1974, (Fatemeh) Elahe, da of Mohamed Ali Madjd; 1 s (Jonathan b 10 May 1975), 1 da (Julie b 29 July 1979); *Career* prof of statistics The City Univ 1978–81, prof UCL 1982– (lectr 1969–78, reader 1981–82); medicines cmmr 1988–91; ed Biometrika 1992–96; memb Int Statistical Inst 1978, fell Inst of Mathematical Statistics 1979, Chartered Statistician 1993; *Recreations* music; *Style—* Prof Philip Dawid; ✉ Department of Statistical Science, University College London, Gower St, London WC1E 6BT (☎ 0171 380 7190)

DAWKINS, Dr Ceridwen Elizabeth; da of Dr Herbert Charles Cole, of Abingdon, Oxon, and Elsie May, *née* Williams; *b* 22 June 1952; *Educ* St Helen & St Katharine Sch Abingdon, Univ of Bristol (BSc, MB ChB); *m* 16 July 1977 (m dis 1989), Dr Richard William Spence, s of Dr William Ormerod Spence (d 1977), of Bristol; 3 da (Dawn b 1980, Michaela (twin) b 1980, Eleanor b 1983); m 2, 29 Sept 1990, Martin Scott Dawkins, s of Thomas George Desmond Dawkins, of Somerset; *Career* conslt chem pathologist Dept of Chem Pathology Frenchay Hosp Bristol 1986–; ACB 1979, FRCPath 1996, ACP 1986; *Recreations* skiing, fell walking, gardening; *Style—* Dr Ceridwen Dawkins; ✉ Department of Chemical Pathology, Frenchay Hospital, Bristol BS16 1LE (☎ 0117 970 2043, fax 0117 957 1866, e-mail 106001.3357@Compuserve.com)

DAWKINS, Prof (Clinton) Richard; s of Clinton John Dawkins, and Jean Mary Vyvyan, *née* Ladner; *b* 26 March 1941; *Educ* Oundle, Balliol Coll Oxford (MA, DPhil, DSc); *m* 1; m 2; 1 da (Juliet Emma); m 3, 1992, Hon Sarah Ward (the actress Lalla Ward), only da of 7 Viscount Bangor (d 1993), and formerly w of Tom Baker; *Career* asst prof of zoology Univ of Calif Berkeley 1967–69; Univ of Oxford: univ lectr in zoology and fell New Coll 1970–90, univ reader in zoology 1990–95, Charles Simonyi prof in public understanding of sci 1995–; Royal Soc of Literature award 1987, Los Angeles Times literary prize 1987, Silver medal Zoological Soc of London 1989, Michael Faraday award Royal Soc of London 1990, Royal Instn Christmas lectures 1991, Nakayama prize 1993; Hon DLitt: Univ of St Andrews 1995, Australian Nat Univ Canberra 1996; hon fell Regent's Coll London 1988; *Books* The Selfish Gene (1976, 2nd edn 1989), The Extended Phenotype (1982), The Blind Watchmaker (1986), River Out of Eden (1995), Climbing Mount Improbable (1996); *Style—* Prof Richard Dawkins; ✉ New College, Oxford OX1 3BN (☎ 01865 279555)

DAWKINS, Simon John Robert; s of Col William John Dawkins, and Mary, *née* King; *b* 9 July 1945; *Educ* Solihull Sch, Univ of Nottingham (BA), Queens' Coll Cambridge (PGCE), Birkbeck Coll London (MA); *m* 25 July 1968, Janet Mary, da of Gordon Harold Stevens; 1 s (Thomas Peter James b 16 Nov 1974), 1 da (Sarah Mary Louise b 2 Oct 1972); *Career* formerly head of econs and housemaster Dulwich Coll, currently headmaster Merchant Taylors' Sch Crosby Liverpool; *Recreations* sport, gardening; *Clubs* E India; *Style—* Simon Dawkins, Esq; ✉ Brackenwood, St George's Rd, Hightown, Liverpool (☎ 0151 929 3546); Merchant Taylors' School, Crosby, Liverpool L23 (☎ 0151 928 3508)

DAWN, Elizabeth; da of Albert Butterfield (d 1984), of Leeds, Yorks, and Annie, *née* Shaw (d 1975); *b* 8 Nov 1939; *Educ* St Patrick's, Corpus Christi Leeds; *m* 1, 1957; 1 s (Graham b 1958); m 2, Donald Ibbetson, s of Arthur Ibbetson; 3 da (Dawn b 1963, Ann b 1967, Julie b 1968); *Career* actress; Kisses at Fifty (BBC) 1972, Speech Day (BBC)

1972, Leeds United (BBC) 1973, Sunset Across The Bay (BBC) 1974, How's Yer Father (Granada) 1974, Sam (BBC) 1974, Z Cars (BBC) 1974, Village Hall 1974, Crown Court 1975, Green Hill Pals 1975, Larry Grayson Special 1975, Lie Detector (commercial) 1975; Vera Duckworth in Coronation Street (Granada) 1974–; Royal Variety Show (Palladium) 1989; London a recorded Passing Strangers with Joe Longthorne 1994; patron: Booth Hall Hosp, Manchester Taxi Drivers' Assoc; *Recreations* charity work with mentally handicapped children; *Style*— Ms Elizabeth Dawn; ✉ c/o Arena Entertainments, Regent's Court, 39 Harrogate Road, Leeds, Yorkshire LS7 3PD (☎ 0113 239 2222, fax 0113 239 2016)

DAWNAY, Caroline Margaret; da of Capt Oliver Payan Dawnay, CVO (d 1988), of Longparish and Wexcombe, and Lady Margaret Boyle, da of 8 Earl of Glasgow; *b* 22 Jan 1950; *children* 1 s (Hugo Ronald Alexander MacPherson b 28 Jan 1980); *Career* dir A D Peters & Co Ltd Writers' Agents 1981–94 (joined 1977, merger to form Peters Fraser & Dunlop 1988), dir June Hall Agency 1989–93, dir Peters Fraser & Dunlop 1993–; pres Assoc of Authors' Agents 1994–, treas Assoc of Authors' Agents 1991–94; *Clubs* 2 Brydges Place; *Style*— Miss Caroline Dawnay; ✉ 14 Sterndale Rd, London W14 0HS; Peters Fraser & Dunlop, Fifth Floor, The Chambers, Chelsea Harbour, Lots Rd, London SW10 0XF (☎ 0171 344 1000)

DAWNAY, Hon Mrs (Iris Irene Adele); *née* Peake; LVO (1959); da of 1 Viscount Ingleby (d 1966), and Lady Joan, *née* Capell, Vicountess Ingleby (d 1979); *b* 23 July 1923; *m* 25 March 1963, as his 2 w, Oliver Payan Dawnay, CVO (d 1988), s of Maj-Gen Guy Dawnay, CB, CMG, DSO, MVO (d 1952), of Longparish House, Hants, *see* Viscount Downe; 1 da (Emma b 1964); *Career* lady-in-waiting to HRH The Princess Margaret 1952–62; *Style*— The Hon Mrs Dawnay, LVO; ✉ Wexcombe House, Marlborough, Wilts (☎ 01264 731229); Flat 5, 32 Onslow Square, London SW7 (☎ 0171 584 3963)

DAWNAY, (Charles) James Payan; s of Capt Oliver Payan Dawnay, CVO (d 1988), and Lady Margaret Stirling Aird, *née* Boyle; *b* 7 Nov 1946; *Educ* Eton, Trinity Hall Cambridge (MA); *m* 10 June 1978, Sarah, da of Edgar David Stogdon, MBE, of Little Mead, Witchampton, Wimborne, Dorset; 1 s (David b 1985), 3 da (Alice b 1979, Olivia b 1981, Fenella b 1988); *Career* dir S G Warburg 1984–87, dir Mercury Asset Management Group plc 1987–91, chm Mercury Fund Managers Ltd 1987–91, dir Martin Currie Investment Management Ltd 1992–; *Recreations* fishing, collecting; *Clubs* Brooks's, Pratt's, New (Edinburgh); *Style*— C J P Dawnay, Esq; ✉ Symington House, by Biggar, Lanarkshire ML12 6LW (☎ 01899 308211); Martin Currie Investment Management Ltd, Saltire Court, 20 Castle Terrace, Edinburgh EH1 2ES (☎ 0131 229 5252)

DAWOOD, Nessim Joseph; s of late Yousef Dawood, and late Muzli, *née* Toweg; *b* 27 Aug 1927; *Educ* Univ of Exeter, Univ of London; *m* 1949, Juliet, *née* Abraham; 3 s; *Career* Arabist; md The Arabic Advertising and Publishing Co Ltd London 1958–; dir: Contemporary Translations Ltd 1962–, Bradbury Wilkinson (Graphics) Ltd 1975–86; Middle East conslt, author of occasional book reviews in national newspapers; FIL 1956–93; *Books* The Thousand and One Nights (trans, 1954), The Koran (trans 1956, 42 edn 1997), Aladdin and Other Tales (trans 1957), The Muqaddimah of Ibn Khaldun (ed, 1967), Tales from the Thousand and One Nights (trans 1973, 20 edn 1995), Arabian Nights (illustrated children's edn 1978), Sindbad the Sailor, Aladdin and Other Tales (1989), The Koran (trans with Arabic parallel text, 1990); *Recreations* theatre; *Clubs* Hurlingham; *Style*— Nessim J Dawood, Esq; ✉ 1 Hyde Park Gate, London SW7 5XE (☎ 0171 584 7000, fax 0171 584 5544)

DAWS, Andrew Michael Bennett; s of Victor Sidney Daws (d 1978), and Doris Jane Daws (d 1996); *b* 11 March 1943; *Educ* King's Sch Grantham, Univ of Exeter (LLB), Coll of Law; *m* 1, 1969 (m dis 1979), Edit, *née* Puskas; m 2, 27 Aug 1981, Phoebe, da of Clifford Hughes; 2 s (Harry Arthur Victor Bennett b 1986, Guy Cromwell George Bennett b 1990), 1 da (Constance Clemency Jane Bennett b 1984); *Career* admitted slr 1967, ptnr Denton Hall 1975–; *Recreations* golf, squash; *Clubs* Royal Mid-Surrey Golf; *Style*— Andrew M B Daws, Esq; ✉ Denton Hall, 5 Chancery Lane, Clifford's Inn, London, EC4A 1BU (☎ 0171 242 1212, fax 0171 404 0087, telex 263567 BURGIN G)

DAWSON, Sir Anthony Michael; KCVO (1993); s of Leslie Joseph Dawson, and Mable Annie, *née* Jayes; bro of John Leonard Dawson, CVO, *qv*; *b* 8 May 1928; *m* 1956, Barbara Anne Baron, da of late Thomas Forsyth, MD; 2 da; *Career* physician: St Bartholomew's Hosp 1965–86 (consulting physician 1986–), King Edward VII Hosp for Officers 1968–96, physician to HM The Queen 1982–93 (to the Royal Household 1974–82), head HM Med Household 1989–93; vice chm Bd of Mgmnt King's Fund for London 1983–93, treas RCP 1985–91 (censor 1977–78), chm Med Coll of St Bart's Hosp Tst 1985–, vice chm Exec Ctee Royal Med Benevolent Fund 1993–96, chm Ctee of Mgmnt Royal Med Benevolent Fund 1996–; treas The British Digestive Fndn 1992–; special tstee Bart's and St Mark's Hosp 1994–, tstee Distressed Gentlefolk's Aid Assoc 1994–; chm Cncl British Heart Fndn 1993–, memb Cncl Med Insurance Agency 1993–, memb Cncl Queen Mary and Westfield Coll Univ of London 1995–; Liveryman Worshipful Co of Barbers; FRCP; *Style*— Sir Anthony Dawson, KCVO; ✉ Thorpe View, The Green, Culworth, Banbury, Oxon OX17 2BB

DAWSON, Lt-Col Herbrand Vavasour; DL (N Yorks 1988); s of Maj John Vavasour Dawson (d 1935), and Charlotte Gerda, *née* Romilly (d 1980); *b* 13 June 1918; *Educ* Winchester, RMC Sandhurst; *m* 19 Dec 1942, Grizelda Louise, da of Maj George Mitchell Richmond (d 1957), of Kincairney, Murthly, Perthshire; 1 s (Christopher b 1943), 1 da (Catherine b 1944); *Career* cmmnd Queen's Own Cameron Highlanders 1938; served: France 1939–40, Sicily 1943, Holland and Germany 1944–45, GSO III HQ BAOR 1946–48; student Staff Coll 1950, Bde Maj 155 Inf Bde 1951–53, DAAG HQ Scottish Cmd 1957–60, cmd 4/5 Bn Queens Own Cameron Highlanders 1960–62, AAG HQ Northern Cmd, ret Lt-Col 1968; N Yorks CC: memb 1973–93, vice chm 1985–89, chm 1989–90, chm Public Protection Ctee 1981–93, hon alderman 1994; chm Nat Parks Ctee Assoc of County Cncls 1993 (vice chm 1989–93), pres Yorks Agric Soc 1994; *Recreations* skiing; *Style*— Lt-Col Herbrand Dawson, DL; ✉ Weston Hall, Otley, Yorks (☎ 01943 462430)

DAWSON, Sir Hugh Michael Trevor; 4 Bt (UK 1920), of Edgwarebury, Co Middlesex; s of Maj Sir (Hugh Halliday) Trevor Dawson, 3 Bt (d 1983), and Caroline Jane, *née* Acton; *b* 28 March 1956; *Educ* at home; *Heir* bro, Nicholas Antony Trevor Dawson, *qv*; *Style*— Sir Hugh Dawson, Bt; ✉ 11 Burton Court, Franklin's Row, London SW3

DAWSON, John A L; s of James Lawrence Dawson (d 1984), and Olive Joan, *née* Turner; *b* 6 Feb 1950; *Educ* Mill Hill Sch, Univ of Southampton (British Rail engrg scholar); *m* 18 June 1980, Frances Anne Elizabeth, *née* Whelan; 2 da (Alice Anne Louise b 27 June 1983, Grace Emily Rose b 3 July 1987); *Career* DOE 1972–76, Dept of Tport 1976–81, overseas tport conslt 1981–85, dir of tport London Regnl Office Dept of Tport 1985–88, chief road engr Scottish Devpt Dept 1988, dir of roads Indust Dept Scottish Office 1989–95, gp public affrs dir AA 1995–; MICE 1976, FIHT 1987; *Recreations* touring; *Clubs* Dalmahoy Golf and Country (Edinburgh), Royal Scottish Automobile (Glasgow); *Style*— John Dawson, Esq; ✉ Group Director Public Affairs, Automobile Association, Norfolk House, Priestley Road, Basingstoke, Hampshire RG24 9NY (☎ 01256 492966, fax 01256 494911, telex 858538 AABAS G)

DAWSON, John Leonard; CVO (1992); s of late Leslie Joseph Dawson, and Mabel Annie Jayes; bro of Sir Anthony Dawson, KCVO, *qv*; *b* 30 Sept 1932; *Educ* King's Coll Hosp London (MB MS); *m* 1958, Rosemary Brundle; 2 s, 1 da; *Career* surgn: Bromley Hosp, King Edward VII Hosp for Offrs, King's Coll Hosp, to HM's Royal Household 1975–83, to HM The Queen 1983–90 (sergeant surgn 1990–91); dean Faculty of Clinical Med King's Coll Sch of Med and Dentistry 1989–93, ret 1994; Liveryman Worshipful Co of Barbers; FRCS; *Style*— John Dawson, Esq, CVO; ✉ 107 Burbage Rd, Dulwich, London SE21 7AF

DAWSON, (Archibald) Keith; s of Wilfred Joseph Dawson, MBE, of Scarborough, and Alice Marjorie Dawson (d 1985); *b* 12 Jan 1937; *Educ* Scarborough HS for Boys, Nunthorpe GS, Queen's Coll Oxford (MA, DipEd); *m* 16 Dec 1961, Marjorie, da of Arthur George Blakeson (d 1977), of Wetherby; 2 da (Eleanor Margaret b 1965, Katharine Elizabeth b 1967); *Career* Nat Serv RAF 1955–57; teacher Ilford Co HS For Boys 1961–63, head of history Haberdashers' Aske's Sch 1965–71 (history teacher 1963–65), headmaster The John Mason Sch Abingdon 1971–79, princ Scarborough Sixth Form Coll 1979–84, princ King James's Coll of Henley 1984–87, headmaster Haberdashers' Aske's Sch 1987–96; memb HMC; FRSA; *Books* Society and Industry in the Nineteenth Century - A Documentary Approach (with Peter Wall, 1968), The Industrial Revolution (1971); *Recreations* walking, swimming, cricket, theatre, music; *Clubs* East India, Public Schools; *Style*— Keith Dawson, Esq

DAWSON, Lynne; da of Francis Lewis Dawson, of Newton-on-Ouse, Yorks, and Rita, *née* Slater; *Educ* Easingwold Sch Yorks, Guildhall Sch of Music and Drama London, Britten-Pears Sch Snape; *Career* soprano; worked as French translator and interpreter until 1978; has performed with orchs incl: Berlin Philharmonic, Vienna Philharmonic, Boston Symphony, San Francisco Symphony, all major Br orchs; concert venues incl: Lincoln Center NY, La Scala Milan, Colon Buenos Aires, Aix-en-Provence Festival, Salzburg Festival, Edinburgh Festival, Royal Albert Hall, Wigmore Hall, South Bank; *Operatic performances* incl: Purcell's Fairy Queen (Aix-en-Provence Festival) 1989, Constanze in Mozart's Die Entführung aus dem Serail (La Monnaie Brussels) 1990, Teresa in Berlioz' Benvenuto Cellini (Amsterdam Opera) 1991, Countess in the Marriage of Figaro (Strasbourg Festival) 1991, Fiordiligi Cosi Fan Tutte (Naples) 1992, Amenaide in Rossini's Tancredi (Berlin State Opera) 1994, Pamina in The Magic Flute (Berlin Staatsopera) 1995; *Recordings* over 50 recordings incl: Bach's B Minor Mass, Beethoven Choral Symphony, Gluck's Iphigenie en Aulide, Handel's Messiah, Haydn's Creation, Mozart's C Minor Mass, Requiem, Don Giovanni and Die Entführung aus dem Serail, Orff's Carmina Burana; *Recreations* gardening; *Style*— Miss Lynne Dawson; ✉ c/o IMG Artists Europe Ltd, Media House, 3 Burlington Lane, Chiswick, London W4 2TH (☎ 0181 233 5800, fax 0181 742 8758)

DAWSON, Mark Patrick; s of Douglas George Damer Dawson; *b* 19 Oct 1941; *Educ* Wellington; *m* 1, 1970 (m dis 1983), Carol Anne, da of John Dudley Groves; 2 s; m 2, 1987 (Constance) Clare Power, *née* Mumford; *Career* Lt Essex Yeo; chm and md Pickford Dawson & Holland Ltd 1970–78; md: Jardine Matheson Insurance Brokers UK Ltd 1978–79, Jardine Matheson Underwriting Agencies Ltd 1979; dep chm: Jardine Lloyd's Underwriting Agencies Ltd (formerly Jardine Glanvill Underwriting Agencies Ltd) 1991–95 (md until 1990), Jardine Lloyd's Advisers Ltd 1994–95 (conslt 1995–96); *Clubs* Boodle's, Hurlingham; *Style*— Mark Dawson, Esq; ✉ Cooks Green, Lamarsh, Bures, Suffolk CO8 5DY

DAWSON, Michael John; OBE (1986); *b* 20 Jan 1943; *Educ* King James's GS Knaresborough; *m*; 2 da; *Career* formerly with: Cawood Wharton, Yorkshire Dyeware & Chemical Molecular Metals, Denys Fisher; chm: Tunstall Group plc 1980– (joined 1970), Mion Electronics plc 1993–; non-exec dir Eurocopy plc 1995–; The Prince's Youth Business Tst: chm N Yorks Bd 1986–, tstee 1996–; memb: Bd YORTEK 1985– (chm 1985–90), Cncl Univ of York 1990–, York Minster Fund High Steward's Cncl 1992–; chm Voice of Yorkshire 1995–; FCCA 1970; *Recreations* game fishing, horses, travel, cookery; *Clubs* Reform, Merchant Adventurers', Merchant Taylors'; *Style*— Michael Dawson, Esq, OBE; ✉ The Doctor's House, Askham Bryan, York YO2 3QS (☎ 01977 661234)

DAWSON, Nicholas Antony Trevor; s of Sir (Hugh Halliday) Trevor Dawson, 3 Bt (d 1983); hp of bro, Sir Hugh Michael Trevor Dawson, *qv*; *b* 17 Aug 1957; *Style*— Nicholas Dawson Esq

DAWSON, (Joseph) Peter; s of Joseph Glyn Dawson (d 1980), and Winifred Olwen, *née* Martin (d 1957); *b* 18 March 1940; *Educ* Bishop Gore GS Swansea, UC Swansea (BSc); *m* 1964, Yvonne Anne Charlton, da of Charlton Smith (d 1974), of London; 1 s (Alex b 1972), 1 da (Jo-Anne b 1969); *Career* Trade Union official; negotiating sec Assoc of Teachers in Tech Insts 1974–75; Nat Assoc of Teachers in Further and Higher Educn (NATFHE): negotiating sec 1976–79, gen sec 1979–89, asst sec (membership) 1989–91, asst sec (pensions and membership services) 1991–93; memb Euro Ctee World Confedn of Organisations of Teaching Profession (WCOTP) 1983–93, gen sec Euro Trade Union Ctee for Educn (ETUCE) 1991–93 (memb Exec Bd 1984–93), co-ordinator for Europe Education International (EI) 1993–; hon fell Coll of Preceptors 1984; FRSA 1987; *Recreations* theatre, cricket, association football; *Clubs* Surrey CCC; *Style*— Peter Dawson, Esq; ✉ EI, International Trade Union House, 155 Boulevard Emile Jacqmain, 1210 Brussels, Belgium (☎ 00 32 2 224 0611, fax 00 32 2 224 0606)

DAWSON, Prof Peter; s of Frederick Dawson, of Sheffield, and May, *née* Pierrepoint; *b* 17 May 1945; *Educ* Firth Park Sch Sheffield, King's Coll London (BSc, PhD), Westminster Med Sch (MB BS); *m* 20 July 1968, Hilary Avril, da of Kenneth Reginald Sturley, of Amersham, Bucks; 1 s (James b 1978), 1 da (Kate b 1976); *Career* sr house offr in: gen and renal med Hammersmith Hosp 1979–80, medical oncology Royal Marsden Hosp 1980; registrar in radiology Guy's Hosp 1980–82, sr registrar in radiology Middx Hosp 1982–85, prof of diagnostic radiology Royal Postgrad Med Sch and Hammersmith Hosp 1996– (reader and hon conslt 1985–96); author of various scientific med res papers; pres British Inst of Radiology, memb Faculty Bd of Radiodiagnosis Royal Coll of Radiologists; MInstP 1966, MRCP 1980, FRCR 1984, FRCP 1994; *Recreations* grand opera, wine, snooker; *Style*— Prof Peter Dawson; ✉ Beechers, Green Lane, Chesham Bois, Amersham, Bucks HP6 5LQ (☎ 01494 728222); Hammersmith Hosp, Dept of Radiology, Du Cane Rd, London W12 0HS (☎ 0181 383 4956, fax 0181 743 5409)

DAWSON, Prof Sandra June Noble; *née* Denyer; da of Wilfred Denyer, of Corton Denham, Sherborne, Dorset, and Joy Victoria Jeanne, *née* Noble; *b* 4 June 1946; *Educ* Dr Challoner's Sch Amersham Bucks, Univ of Keele (BA); *m* 23 Aug 1969, Henry Richards Currey Dawson, s of Horace Dawson (d 1952), of Sotik, Kenya; 1 s (Tom Stephen John b 1983), 2 da (Hannah Louise Joy b 1976, Rebecca Annie Brenda b 1978); *Career* Imperial Coll London: res offr 1969–70, lectr then sr lectr 1971–90, prof of organisational behaviour 1990–95; KPMG prof of mgmnt studies and dir Judge Inst of Mgmnt Studies Univ of Cambridge 1995–, fell Jesus Coll Cambridge 1995–; chm Riverside Mental Health Tst 1992–95; non-exec dir: Public Health Lab Serv 1996– (memb Strategic Review Gp 1994–), Fleming Claverhouse Investment Tst, Cambridge Econometrics; memb: Res Strategy Bd Offshore Safety Div HSE 1990–95, N Thames NHS Regnl R & D Ctee 1994–95; *Books* Analysing Organisations (1986, 2 edn 1992), Safety at Work: The Limits of Self Regulation (1988), Managing in the NHS: a Study of Senior Executives (1995); *Recreations* music, walking; *Style*— Prof Sandra Dawson; ✉ The Judge Institute of Management Studies, University of Cambridge, Trumpington Street, Cambridge CB2 1AG (☎ 01223 339700)

DAWSON, William Strachan; s of John Oliver Hanbury Dawson, of South Cadbury, Somerset, and Elizabeth Sutherland, *née* Strachan; *b* 10 Sept 1955; *Educ* Winchester, Selwyn Coll Cambridge (MA); *m* 8 Sept 1984, Alison Jill, da of John Eric Aldridge, of

Bentley Wood, Halland, nr Lewes, E Sussex; 2 s (Henry b 1988, Archie William b 1994), 1 da (Lucinda b 1986); *Career* admitted slr 1980, ptnr Simmons & Simmons 1986–; *Books* contrib Tolley's Company Acquisitions Handbook (1989, 4 edn 1996),; *Recreations* golf, skiing, food, classical music; *Clubs* Roehampton; *Style*— William Dawson, Esq; ✉ Simmons & Simmons, 21 Wilson Street, London EC2M 2TX (☎ 0171 628 2020, fax 0171 628 2070)

DAWSON PAUL, Anthony; s of Joseph Dawson Paul (d 1976), and Eugenie Flavie, *née* Ozanne (d 1968); *b* 17 June 1935; *Educ* Charterhouse; *m* 22 Nov 1969, Merrill Anne, da of Brig Herbert Anthony Brakes, MBE (d 1987); 2 s (Andrew b 2 July 1972, Nicholas b 9 Aug 1974); *Career* sr ptnr Dennis Murphy Campbell (stockbrokers) 1984– (joined 1955, ptnr 1961–84), dir The Average Tst plc; chm and vice pres of the Putney Soc, memb City of London Livery Ctee 1987–89; Master The Worshipful Co of Salters 1996; FCIS; *Clubs* City of London; *Style*— Anthony Dawson Paul, Esq; ✉ 14 Dover Park Drive, Roehampton, London SW15 5BG (☎ 0181 789 0011); Dennis Murphy Campbell, 6 Broad Street Place, London EC2M 7DA (☎ 0171 638 0033, fax 0171 638 1318)

DAWTRY, Sir Alan; kt (1974), CBE (1968, MBE (Mil) 1945), TD (1948); s of Melancthon Dawtry, of Sheffield; *b* 8 April 1915; *Educ* King Edward VII Sch Sheffield, Univ of Sheffield; *Career* served WWII, France, N Africa and Italy (despatches twice), Lt-Col; admitted slr 1938, asst slr Sheffield 1938–48; dep town clerk: Bolton 1948–52, Leicester 1952–54; town clerk: Wolverhampton 1954–56, Westminster 1956–77; memb Metrication Bd 1969–74, Clean Air Cncl 1960–75; chm Sperry Rand Ltd 1977–86, Sperry Rand (Ireland) Ltd 1977–86, pres London Rent Assessment Panel 1979–86; FIMgt, FRSA; awarded numerous foreign decorations; *Style*— Sir Alan Dawtry, CBE, TD; ✉ 901 Grenville House, Dolphin Square, London SW1 (☎ 0171 798 8100)

DAY, Bernard Maurice; CB (1987); s of Maurice James Day (d 1959), of Chingford, Essex, and May Helen, *née* Spicer (d 1972); *b* 7 May 1928; *Educ* Bancroft's Woodford Green Essex, LSE (BScEcon); *m* 11 Feb 1956, (Ruth Elizabeth) Betty, da of Richard Stansfield (d 1957), of Walton-on-Thames; 2 s (Keith b 1961, Geoffrey b 1965), 1 da (Christine b 1959); *Career* Intelligence Corps and RA 1946–48, cmmnd RA 1948; cabinet sec Cabinet Office 1959–61, sec Meteorological Office 1965–70, estab offr Cabinet Office 1970–72; MOD: head air staff sec 1972–74, under sec central staffs and air force 1974–84, under sec fleet support 1985–88, ret 1988; panel chm Civil Serv Selection Bd 1988–96 (res chm 1984–85), chm Standing Ctee St Mary Oatlands Parish Church, ctee memb Elmbridge Mental Health Assoc; *Recreations* swimming, carpentry; *Clubs* Cwlth Tst; *Style*— Bernard Day, Esq, CB; ✉ 26 The Riverside, Graburn Way, East Molesey, Surrey

DAY, Dr Christopher Duncan; s of Roger William Elmsall Day (d 1984), and Kathleen Margaret, *née* Bell (d 1996); *b* 19 July 1941; *Educ* Hymers Coll Hull, Kings Coll Univ of Durham (MB BS); *m* 1, 5 Nov 1966, Pamela (d 1979), da of William Corbet Barnsley (d 1981), of Newcastle upon Tyne; 1 s (William b 1977), 1 da (Elizabeth b 1972); m 2, 21 Aug 1982, Rosemary Ann, da of Charles Darby, of Datchet, Berks; *Career* house offr in surgery and med Newcastle upon Tyne Gen Hosp 1964–65, sr house offr in anaesthetics Dudley Rd Hosp Birmingham 1965–66, registrar and sr registrar in anaesthetics Sheffield Hosps 1966–70, conslt in anaesthetics 1970–; med dir Chesterfield and N Derbyshire Royal Hosp NHS Tst 1993–; memb: CSA, AAGBI; *Style*— Dr Christopher Day; ✉ Alghero, 44 Matlock Rd, Walton, Chesterfield, Derbs S42 7LE (☎ 01246 270942); Chesterfield and N Derbyshire Royal Hospital, Chesterfield Rd, Calow, Chesterfield, Derbs S44 5BL (☎ 01246 277271, fax 01246 276955)

DAY, Colin Norman; *Career* sr advsr Henderson Investors; pt/t chm Grandfield Ltd (formerly Grandfield Rork Collins PR), ind dir WED Ltd; vice chm Govrs Anglia Poly Univ; memb CIPFA; magistrate; *Style*— Colin Day, Esq; ✉ Henderson Investors, 3 Finsbury Avenue, London EC2M 2PA (☎ 0171 410 4100)

DAY, Darren C; s of Terence Graham, of Essex, and Anne, *née* Wilkins; *b* 17 July 1968; *Educ* Sir Charles Lucas Sch Colchester; *Career* singer, actor and television host; semi-professional snooker player 1984; memb Variety Club of GB, patron BLISS (Colchester); *Theatre* lead roles incl: Joseph and the Amazing Technicolor Dreamcoat (London Palladium 1993, nat tour/Bristol Hippodrome/Manchester Place 1994), Great Expectations (Theatr Clwyd 1993, two nat tours 1994–96), Copacabana (Prince of Wales) 1995, Summer Holiday (Blackpool Opera House 1996, nat tour 1997); *Television* appeared in the Children's Royal Variety Performance (Dominion) 1991 and 1993; as host incl: Teen Win Lose or Draw (ITV) 1993, Children's Royal Variety Performance (youngest ever host, London Palladium) 1994, Just Kidding (Sky 1) 1995–, You Bet (ITV) 1996–; *Recordings* Godspell (TER) 1993; released on RCA Records 1996 incl: Summer Holiday Medley, The Next Time, Summer Holiday Album 1997; *Awards* Sir James Carreras Award for Outstanding New Talent (Variety Club of GB) 1995; *Recreations* gynasium, snooker, cinema; *Clubs* Arts; *Style*— Darren Day, Esq; ✉ c/o James Grant Media Group Ltd, Syon Lodge, London Road, Syon Park, Middlesex TW7 5BH (☎ 0181 232 4100, fax 0181 232 4101)

DAY, Sir Derek Malcolm; KCMG (1984, CMG 1973); s of Alan W Day (d 1968), and Gladys, *née* Portlock (d 1974); *b* 29 Nov 1927; *Educ* Hurstpierpoint Coll Sussex, St Catharine's Coll Cambridge (MA); *m* 1955, Sheila, da of George Nott (d 1955), of Newnhan Bridge, Worcs; 3 s (William Day, *qv*, Richard, Nicholas), 1 da (Katharine); *Career* HM Foreign Serv: entered 1951, third sec Br Embasssy Tel Aviv 1953–56, private sec to Ambass Rome 1956–59, second then first sec FO 1959–62, first sec HM Embassy Washington 1962–66, first sec FO 1966–67, asst private sec to Sec of State for Foreign Affrs 1967–68, head of Personnel Ops Dept FCO 1969–72, cnsllr Br High Cmmn Nicosia 1972–75, HM ambass to Ethiopia 1975–78, asst under sec FCO 1979, dep under sec of state FCO 1980, chief clerk 1982–84, Br high cmmr Ottawa 1984–87; dir Monenco Ltd Canada 1988–92, chm Crystal Palace Sports and Leisure Ltd 1993–; memb Cncl Canada-UK C of C 1988–93, cmmr Cwlth War Graves Cmmn 1987–92, vice chm BRCS 1988–94; chm Governing Body Hurstpierpoint Coll Sussex 1987, govr Bethany Sch 1988; *Clubs* Hawks (Cambridge), United Oxford & Cambridge; *Style*— Sir Derek Day, KCMG; ✉ Etchinghill, Goudhurst, Kent

DAY, Dr Kenneth Arthur; s of Arthur Day (d 1989), and Irene Laura, *née* Pope (d 1993); *b* 18 July 1935; *Educ* Greenford Co GS, Bristol Univ Med Sch (MB ChB, DPM); *m* 1, 27 June 1959 (m dis 1993), Sheila Mary, da of Albert Torrance (d 1971); 2 s (Paul Vincent b 1961, Matthew Charles b 1964), 1 da (Caroline b 1960); m 2, 6 Nov 1993, Diana Ruth, da of John Snowden Lee (d 1993); *Career* registrar Barrow Hosp Bristol 1962–66, registrar and sr registrar Dept of Psychiatry Univ of Newcastle 1966–69, conslt psychiatrist Northern RHA and Newcastle Health Authy 1969–92, sr lectr Dept of Psychiatry Univ of Newcastle 1986–, conslt psychiatrist and med dir Northgate and Prudhoe NHS Tst Morpeth 1992–; Mental Health Act cmmr 1987–94; vice pres Int Assoc for the Scientific Study of Mental Deficiency 1992–96 (sec 1985–92), vice chm Mental Retardation Section World Psychiatric Assoc 1989–96 (sec 1983–89), vice pres Euro Assoc for Mental Health in Mental Retardation 1993–; Dept of Health (formerly DHSS): memb Hosp Advsy Serv 1972, sci advsr 1981–87, memb Standing Med Advsy Ctee 1984–88, memb Nat Devpt Team 1977–86, med memb Mental Health Review Tbnl 1988–, memb Hosp Advsy Gp Reed Ctee on Mentally Disordered Offenders; RCPsych: memb Cncl, Ct of Electors, Fin & Exec Ctee and numerous other ctees, chm Section for Psychiatry of Mental Handicap 1983–87; pres Northern Region Mencap 1978–90, WHO advsr on mental handicap to the People's Republic of China 1991; Winston Churchill Meml Fellowship 1972, Burden Gold medal and Res prize 1985–86, Blake Marsh lectr RCPsych 1989, WHO Fellowship 1990; writer and presenter The Special Child YTV 1977 and The Special Child Teenage Years YTV 1979; conslt and writer BBC TV series incl: Homes from Home 1976, Accident of Birth 1978, Aspects of Mental Handicap 1979, The Handicapped Family 1979, Let's Go 1979, 1980 and 1982; winner Animal Portraits category Wildlife Photographer of the Year 1989; Freeman City of London 1989, Liveryman Worshipful Soc of Apothecaries 1993 (Yeoman 1988); FRCPsych 1978 (fndn memb 1972), FRSM 1983, hon offr and fell Int Assoc for the Scientific Study of Intellectual Disability 1996; *Publications* The Special Child (1977), The Special Child - The Teenage Years (1979), Behaviour Problems in The Mental Handicapped: An Annotated Bibliography (1988), numerous scientific papers, articles and chapters on mental handicap; photographs published in natural history books and magazines; *Recreations* squash, badminton, tennis, golf and other sports, natural history, painting, carving, photography; *Clubs* City Livery; *Style*— Dr Kenneth Day; ✉ 28 Percy Gardens, Tynemouth, Tyne and Wear NE30 4HQ; Northgate Hospital, Morpeth, Northumberland NE61 3BP (☎ 01670 394070)

DAY, Lucienne; da of Felix Conradi (d 1957), of Croydon, Surrey, and Dulcie Lilian, *née* Duncan-Smith; *Educ* Convent Notre Dame De Sion Worthing Sussex, Croydon Sch of Art, RCA; *m* 5 Sept 1942, Robin Day, OBE, *qv*, s of Arthur Day (d 1956), of High Wycombe, Bucks; 1 da (Paula b 1954); *Career* teacher Beckenham Sch of Art 1942–47, freelance designer 1948– (dress fabrics, furnishing fabrics, carpets, wallpapers, table-linen); cmmnd by: Heal's Fabrics, Edinburgh Weavers, Cavendish Textiles, Tomkinsons, Wilton Royal, Thos Somerset, firms in USA, Scandinavia and Germany; designed china decoration for Rosenthal China Bavaria 1956–68, currently designing silk mosaic tapestries; conslt (with Robin Day) John Lewis Partnership 1962–87; work in permanent collections incl: V & A, Trondheim Museum Norway, Cranbrook Museum Michigan, Röhsska Museum Gothenburg Sweden, Musée des Arts Decoratifs Montreal, Art Inst of Chicago, Whitworth Art Gallery Univ of Manchester; awards incl: Design Cncl Awards 1957, 1960 and 1968, American Inst of Dirs First Award 1950; Triennale Di Milano: Gold Medal 1951, Gran Premio 1954, Hon Doctorate of Design Univ of Southampton 1995; memb: Rosenthal Studio-Line Jury 1960–68, Ctee Duke of Edinburgh Prize for Elegant Design 1960–63, Cncl RCA 1962–67, Design Bursary Juries RSA; RDI 1962 (Master 1987–89), ARCA 1940, FSIAD 1955; *Recreations* plant collecting in Mediterranean regions, gardening; *Style*— Mrs Lucienne Day; ✉ 49 Cheyne Walk, Chelsea, London SW3 5LP (☎ 0171 352 1455)

DAY, Prof Michael Herbert; s of Herbert Arthur Day (d 1962), and Amy Julienne, *née* Bradwin (d 1970); *b* 8 March 1927; *Educ* Sevenoaks Sch, Royal Free Hosp Sch of Med Univ of London (MB BS, MRCS, LRCP, PhD, DSc, FCSP); *m* 12 April 1952, José Ashton, da of Joseph Hankins (d 1985); 1 s (Jeremy Paul); *Career* RAF 1945–48, served England and ME; prof of anatomy and dir dept St Thomas's Hosp Med Sch 1972–89; invited lectures incl: Harvard Univ Cambridge Mass, Yale Univ New Haven Conn, The Leakey Fndn for Anthropological Res, Univ of Surrey, LSE, The Royal Free Hosp Sch of Med; named lectures: The Bennett Lecture of Leicester Literary and Philosophical Soc 1977, The Osman Hill Meml Lecture 1978, The Louis Leakey Meml Lecture 1984; Chartered Soc of Physiotherapy: memb Fellowships Advsy Bd 1977–88, memb Cncl 1977–93, memb Working Pty on Rules of Professional Conduct and Ethics 1983–86; memb and nat del Exec Ctee of Perm Cncl Int Union of Anthropological and Ethnological Sciences 1983–93, pres World Archaeological Congress 1986–90, numerous undergrad and postgrad examinerships at home and abroad; chm: The Bill Bishop Meml Tst, The Leakey Tst, Govrs Int Students House 1990– (govr 1984–); fell: Royal Anthropological Inst (pres 1979–83), The Linnean Soc; memb: Anatomical Soc of GB and I (vice pres 1980), Soc for the Study of Human Biology, Primate Soc of GB (pres 1976–79), Int Primatological Union, American Assoc of Physical Anthropology; *Books* Guide to Fossil Man (4 edn 1986); *Recreations* real tennis, fly fishing, sub-aqua diving; *Clubs* Athenaeum, MCC; *Style*— Prof Michael Day; ✉ 26 Thurlow Road, Hampstead, London NW3 5PP (☎ 0171 435 0899, fax 0171 794 4657); The Machan, Carradale, Argyll, Scotland (☎ 01583 3714); The Manyatta, Emerald Ridge, St Peter, Barbados, W Indies (246 422 0726); Department of Palaeontology, Natural History Museum, Cromwell Rd, London SW7 5BD (☎ 0171 938 9314, e-mail m.day@ulcc.ac.uk)

DAY, Michael John; *b* 6 Feb 1944; *Educ* Univ of Liverpool (BSc); *m* 26 Feb 1966, Susan, *née* Holmes; 1 s (Philip John b 21 Sept 1970), 1 da (Tanya Jane b 22 April 1969); *Career* actuary; ptnr Duncan C Fraser & Co 1972–86, chm Heywood & Partners Ltd 1983–90, dir William M Mercer Ltd 1986–95, consltg actuary 1995–; FIA 1970; *Style*— Michael Day, Esq; ✉ Theakston, Quarry Road, Hinderton, South Wirral L64 7UA (☎ 0151 336 7170)

DAY, Sir Michael John; kt (1992), OBE (1980); s of Albert Day, of London, and Ellen Florence, *née* Itter (d 1973); *b* 4 Sept 1933; *Educ* Univ Coll Sch, Selwyn Coll Cambridge, LSE; *m* 30 July 1960, June Marjorie, da of Dr John William Mackay (d 1958), of Whitehaven, Cumberland; 1 s (Christopher b 1965), 1 da (Lisa (Mrs Gordon Clark) b 1963); *Career* Nat Serv RA; probation offr Surrey 1960–64, sr probation offr W Surrey 1964–67, asst princ probation offr Surrey 1967–68; chief probation offr: Surrey 1968–76, W Midland 1976–88; chm: Chief Probation Offrs' Conference 1974–77, Assoc of Chief Offrs of Probation 1983–88, Cmmn for Racial Equality 1988–April 1993; *Recreations* countryside, gardening, music, books; *Style*— Sir Michael Day, OBE; ✉ Thornhill, Oldbury, Bridgnorth, Shropshire

DAY, Prof Nicholas Edward; s of John King Day, of 1 Pearson Rd, Holt, Norfolk, and Mary Elizabeth, *née* Stinton (d 1993); *b* 24 Sept 1939; *Educ* Greshams Sch, Univ of Oxford (BA, Jr Univ prize), Univ of Aberdeen (PhD); *m* 19 Sept 1961, Jocelyn Deanne, da of Henry George Broughton (d 1988); 1 s (Owen John b 5 May 1965), 1 da (Sheenagh Louise b 4 April 1963); *Career* res fell Univ of Aberdeen 1962–66, fell Australian Nat Univ 1966–69, statistician then head Unit of Biostatistics and Field Studies Int Agency for Res on Cancer Lyon 1969–86, cancer expert Nat Cancer Inst USA 1978–79, dir MRC Biostatistics Unit Cambridge 1986–89 (hon dir 1989–), prof of public health Univ of Cambridge 1989–; chm MRC Ctee on the Epidemiology and Surveilance of Aids 1988–92; fell: Churchill Coll Cambridge 1986–91, Hughes Hall Cambridge 1991–; fell Royal Statistical Soc; *Books* Statistical Methods in Cancer Research Vol 1 (1980) and Vol 2 (1988), Screening For Cancer of the Uterine Cervix (1986), Screening For Breast Cancer (1988); *Recreations* sea fishing, tree growing; *Style*— Prof Nicholas Day; ✉ Porch House, Haddenham, Ely, Cambs CB6 3TJ (☎ 01353 740472); Institute of Public Health, Robinson Way, Cambridge CB2 2SR (☎ 01223 330314, fax 01223 330330)

DAY, Prof Peter; *b* 20 Aug 1938; *Educ* Maidstone GS, Wadham Coll Oxford (Gibbs prize in chemistry, MA, DPhil); *m* 1964, Frances Mary Elizabeth, *née* Anderson; 1 da (Alison b 1968), 1 s (Christopher b 1971); *Career* jr res fell St John's Coll Oxford 1963–65, departmental demonstrator Inorganic Chemistry Laboratory Oxford 1965–68, fell and tutor in organic chemistry St John's Coll Oxford (jr dean 1967–70, vice pres 1974), lectr in inorganic chemistry Univ of Oxford 1965–88, dir Institut Laue-Langevin Grenoble 1989–91, (Br assoc dir 1988–89), dir and resident prof of chemistry Royal Institution of GB 1991–94, Fullerian prof Royal Inst 1994–; visiting prof UCL 1991–, ad hominem prof of solid state chemistry Univ of Oxford 1988–91; fell Royal Soc of London 1986; professeur associé Faculté des Sciences Université de Paris-Sud Orsay 1975, guest prof H C Ørsted Inst Univ of Copenhagen 1978, visiting fell Res Sch of Chemistry Australian Nat Univ Canberra 1980; visiting appts at res laboratories: Cyanamid Euro Res Inst Geneva 1962, Bell Laboratories Murray Hill NJ 1966, IBM Res Laboratories San Jose

Calif 1974, Xerox Corp Webster Res Center Rochester NY 1978; memb Cncl: Parly and Scientific Ctee 1991–, COPUS 1991–; chm Royal Soc Res Grant Bd for Chemistry 1992– (memb 1983–85 and 1991–); Br Cncl: memb Science Advsy Ctee 1991–, chm Anglo-French Advsy Ctee 1992–; Royal Soc of Chemistry: memb Dalton Div Cncl 1983–88, vice pres 1986–88, books & review ctee 1984–85; memb numerous ctees SERC 1976–; memb: Nat Ctee on Superconductivity 1987–89, Univ of Oxford Superconductivity Gp 1988–91 (chm steering ctee 1987), ISIS Science Advsy Cncl 1988–91 (chm Experimental Selection Panel (Structures) 1988); memb numerous int science ctees; memb Editorial Advsy Bds: Nouveau Journal de Chimie, Synthetic Metals, Review of Solid State Sciences, Dictionary of Inorganic Compunds, Journal of Materials Chemistry, Chemistry of Materials; ed seven chemistry books; rep govr Sevenoaks Sch Kent 1977–88; memb Academia Europaea 1992–; hon fell: Wadham Coll Oxford 1991–, Indian Acad Sci 1994, St John's Coll Oxford 1996–; Hon DSc Univ of Newcastle 1994; FRS 1986; *Style*— Prof Peter Day, FRS; ✉ The Royal Institution, 21 Albemarle Street, London W1X 4BS (☎ 0171 409 2992, fax 0171 629 3569)

DAY, Sir Robin; kt (1981); s of late William Day; *b* 24 Oct 1923; *Educ* Bembridge Sch, St Edmund Hall Oxford (pres Oxford Union 1950); *m* 1965 (m dis 1986), Katherine Mary, *née* Ainslie, of Perth, W Australia; 2 s; *Career* called to the Bar 1952, TV and radio journalist; ITN 1955–59, Panorama BBC 1959–88, World at One 1978–87, Question Time BBC TV 1979–89; chm Hansard Soc for Parly Govt 1981–83; hon bencher Middle Temple, hon fell St Edmund Hall; *Publications* Television: A Personal Report (1961), The Case for Televising Parliament (1963), Day by Day (1975), Grand Inquisitor (memoirs, 1989), ...But With Respect - Memorable TV Interviews (1993); *Clubs* Garrick, RAC; *Style*— Sir Robin Day; ✉ c/o Capron Productions, Gardiner House, Broomhill Road, London SW18 4JQ

DAY, Robin; OBE (1983); s of Arthur Day (d 1956), of High Wycombe, Buckinghamshire, and Mary, *née* Shersby (d 1956); *b* 25 May 1915; *Educ* High Wycombe Sch of Art, RCA; *m* 5 Sept 1942, Lucienne Day, *qv*, da of Felix Conradi (d 1957), of Croydon, Surrey; 1 da (Paula b 1954); *Career* princ of own design practice 1940–; worldwide success with design of seating for sports stadia, concert halls, airports, etc; interior design of Super VC10 aircraft; jt first prize NY Museum of Modern Art competition for design of furniture, Gold medal Milan Triennale exhbn 1951, Design Centre award 1957, 1961, 1965 and 1966, Design medal CSID 1957; ARCA, RDI 1959; *Recreations* walking, mountaineering, ski touring; *Clubs* Alpine, Climbers, Eagle Ski; *Style*— Robin Day, Esq, OBE, RDI; ✉ 49 Cheyne Walk, London SW3 5LP (☎ 0171 352 1455)

DAY, Rosemary; da of Albert Rich (d 1985), and Alice, *née* Wren; *b* 20 Sept 1942; *Educ* Christ's Hosp, Bedford Coll Univ of London (BA); *m* (m dis); *Career* asst dir gen GLC 1979–82 (joined 1964), dir of admin London Tport 1983–87, chief exec Data Networks plc 1986–88, ops dir Allied Dunbar Assurance plc 1988–94; non-exec dir: Nationwide Anglia Building Society 1983–88, London Buses Ltd 1988–93, London Tranport 1993–, Milk Marketing Bd 1993–94, Legal Aid Advsy Ctee 1993–94, Senior Salaries Review Body 1994–; chm London Ambulance Serv Trust 1996–, chm Govt Offices Mgmnt Bd 1996; chm Joyful Co of Singers 1987 (Gran Premio Citta D'Arezzo 1994); ATII 1980, FRSA 1983, CIMgt 1988; *Recreations* singing, conversation, the arts; *Style*— Mrs Rosemary Day; ✉ 452 Kings Road, London SW10 0LQ (☎ 0171 352 7050, fax 0171 351 7058)

DAY, Stephen Peter; CMG (1989); s of Frank William Day (d 1956), and Mary Elizabeth Day (d 1968); *b* 19 Jan 1938; *Educ* Bancroft's Sch Essex, CCC Cambridge (MA); *m* 24 Feb 1965, Angela Doreen, da of William Attwood Waudby, of Kenya; 1 s (Richard b 1972), 2 da (Belinda b 1966, Philippa b 1968); *Career* HMOCS; political advsr South Arabian Fedn 1961–67, first sec Political Adviser's Office Singapore 1970, first sec (press) UK mission to UN New York 1972–75, cnsllr Beirut 1977–78, consul-gen Canadian Prairie Provinces 1979–81, ambass Doha 1981–84, head of ME Dept FCO 1984–86, attached to household of HRH The Prince of Wales 1986, ambass Tunisia 1987–92, sr Br trade commissioner Hong Kong 1992–93, dir Cncl for the Advancement of Arab-British Understanding 1993–94; chm: British-Tunisian Soc 1994–, Palestine Exploration Fund 1995–; dir Claremont Associates 1994–; govr Qatar Acad; *Recreations* walking, reading; *Clubs* Hong Kong; *Style*— Stephen Day, Esq, CMG; ✉ Oakfield Cottage, 92 West End Lane, Esher, Surrey KT10 8LF (☎ and fax 01372 464138)

DAY, Stephen Richard; MP (C) Cheadle (majority 15,778); s of late Francis Day, and Annie, *née* Webb; *b* 30 Oct 1948; *Educ* Otley Secdy Mod Sch, Park Lane Coll of FE, Leeds Poly; *m* 2, 5 Nov 1982, Frances, da of late James Raywood Booth, of Hove Edge, nr Brighouse, W Yorks; 1 s by previous m (Alexander b 1973); *Career* sales clerk William Sinclair & Sons 1965–70 (asst sales mangr 1970–77); sales rep: Larkfield Printing Co 1977–80, A H Leach & Co 1980–84; sales exec: PPI Chromacopy 1984–86, Chromagene Ltd 1986–87; conslt Chromagene Photo Labs 1987; former memb: Otley Town Cncl, Leeds City Cncl; Parly candidate (C) Bradford 1983, MP (C) Cheadle 1987–; successfully sponsored Motor Vehicles - Wearing of Seat Belts by Children Act 1988, memb Select Ctee on Social Security, co chm PACTS; graduate memb Inst of Export 1972–92, conslt NALGO Section UNISON 1990–, co-chair All Pty West Coast Main Line Group, exec memb Cwlth Party Assoc (UK branch); *Recreations* music, films, Roman history; *Clubs* Royal Wharfedale, Cheadle Hulme Royal British Legion, Cheadle and Gatley Cons, Cheadle Hulme Cons; *Style*— Stephen Day, Esq, MP; ✉ House of Commons, Westminster SW1A 0AA (☎ 0171 219 6200 and 0161 486 6875)

DAY, Timon Richard; s of Peter Leonard Day, and Lois Elizabeth, *née* Stockley; *b* 16 March 1951; *Educ* St Paul's, Univ of Exeter (BA); *m* 31 March 1979, Zuzannah; 1 s (Matthew Peter b 15 Aug 1988); *Career* mkt res trainee RSGB Ltd until 1974, mkt res Mass Observation 1974–76, teacher at French Lycée Paris 1976–78, fin journalist Investors Review 1978–80, freelance journalist 1980–81; fin journalist: Financial Info Co 1981–83, Scotsman Newspapers 1983–87, Mail on Sunday 1987–89 (business ed 1989–); winner NFSE Small Business Journalist of the Year award 1990; *Recreations* tennis, walking, cycling, cinema; *Clubs* Campden Hill Lawn Tennis; *Style*— Timon Day, Esq; ✉ Mail on Sunday, City Office, Northcliffe House, Derry Street, London W8

DAY, William Michael; s of Sir Derek Day, KCMG, *qv*, of Goudhurst, Kent, and Sheila, *née* Nott; *b* 26 June 1956; *Educ* Tonbridge Sch Kent, Univ of Exeter (BA Politics); *m* 1986, Kate Susanna, da of Bill Gardener; 1 s (Rupert b 7 Sept 1987), 2 da (Eleanor b 21 April 1989, Susanna b 6 Dec 1991); *Career* Save the Children Fund: Uganda 1983, Ethiopia 1983–84, Sudan 1984; prodr/presenter BBC World Serv for Africa 1985–87, relief co-ordinator Oxfam Ethiopia 1987–88, grants dir Africa Charity Projects/Comic Relief 1988–94, dir Opportunity Trust 1994–96, chief exec CARE International UK 1996–; non-exec dir South Kent Hosps NHS Tst 1994–; memb: Central Appeals Ctee BBC 1992–, Grants Cncl Charities Aid Fndn 1990–94; *Style*— William Day, Esq; ✉ CARE International UK, 36–38 Southampton Street, London WC2E 7AF (☎ 0171 379 5247, fax 0171 379 0543, e-mail day@uk.care.org)

DAY-LEWIS, Daniel; s of Cecil Day-Lewis, CBE (Poet Laureate, d 1972), by his 2 w, Jill Balcon, actress, da of late Sir Michael Balcon, film prodr; yr half-bro of Sean Day-Lewis, *qv*; *Educ* Bristol Old Vic Theatre Sch; *children* 1 s (Gabriel b 1996); m, 1996, Rebecca Miller, da of Arthur Miller, of USA; *Career* actor; *Theatre* Bristol Old Vic Co: The Recruiting Officer, Troilus and Cressida, Funny Peculiar, Old King Cole, A Midsummer Night's Dream (transferred to Old Vic), Class Enemy, Edward II, Oh! What A Lovely War; Little Theatre Co: Look Back in Anger, Dracula; other roles incl: Guy Bennet in Another Country (Queen's) 1982, Romeo in Romeo and Juliet (RSC tour) 1983–84, Mayakovsky in The Futurists (NT) 1986, title role in Hamlet (NT) 1989; *Television* Shoestring, Artemis II, The Lost Traveller, The Sugar House, Beyond the Glass, How Many Miles to Babylon, Thank You PG Woodhouse, Dangerous Corner, My Brother Jonathan, Insurance Man; *Films* Gandhi 1981, The Saga of HMS Bounty 1983, My Beautiful Launderette 1985, A Room With A View 1985, Nanou 1985, The Unbearable Lightness of Being 1986, Stars and Bars 1987, My Left Foot 1988, Ever Smile New Jersey 1988, Last of the Mohicans 1991, Age of Innocence 1992, In the Name of the Father 1993, The Crucible 1995; *Awards* Best Supporting Actor NY Critics' Awards for My Beautiful Launderette and A Room With A View 1986; Best Actor Awards for My Left Foot incl: Oscar 1990, BAFTA 1990, Evening Standard Film Awards 1989, Rehab Entertainment Awards 1989, Boston Soc of Film Critics 1989, NY Critics 1990, LA Critics 1990, Nat Soc of Film Critics 1990, London Critics Film Circle 1990, Montreal Critics 1990, Dublin Independent 1990; Variety Club Best Film Actor Award for Last of the Mohicans 1992; *Style*— Daniel Day-Lewis, Esq; ✉ c/o Julian Belfrage Associates, 46 Albemarle Street, London W1X 4PP (☎ 0171 491 4400, fax 0171 493 5460)

DAY-LEWIS, Sean Francis; s of Cecil Day-Lewis, Poet Laureate 1967–72 (d 1972), of London, and Constance Mary, *née* King (d 1975); *b* 3 Aug 1931; *Educ* Allhallows Sch Devon; *m* 1960, Gloria Ann (Anna), da of James Henry Mott (d 1980); 1 s (Finian b 1966), 1 da (Keelin b 1963); *Career* Nat Serv RAF 1949–51; ed: Bridport News 1952–53, Southern Times Weymouth 1953–54, Herts Advertiser St Albans 1954–56, Express and Star Wolverhampton 1956–60; arts ed Socialist Commentary 1966–71, TV and radio ed Daily Telegraph 1960–86 (ed 1970), TV ed London Daily News 1986–87; freelance writer and commentator on broadcasting matters 1987–; *Books* Bulleid - Last Giant of Steam (1964), C Day-Lewis - An English Literary Life (1980), One Day In The Life of Television (ed, 1989), TV Heaven (1992); *Recreations* music, ball games, country life; *Style*— Sean Day-Lewis, Esq; ✉ Restorick Row, Rosemary Lane, Colyton, Devon EX13 6LW (☎ 01297 553039)

DAYKIN, Dr Andrew Philip; s of Philip William Daykin, of St Albans, Herts, and Eileen Elizabeth, *née* Sales (d 1985); *b* 27 Dec 1950; *Educ* St Albans Sch, Univ of Oxford (MA), St Mary's Hosp Med Sch (MB BS); *m* 10 Sept 1977, Chrystal Margaret, da of Anthony George Mitsides, of London; 2 da (Eleni b 1981, Ariana b 1983); *Career* sr house offr Whittington Hosp London 1977, sr house offr and registrar in anaesthetics St Mary's Hosp London 1978–81, sr registrar Winchester and Southampton Hosps 1981–86, clinical fell in anaesthesia Ottawa Children's Hosp Canada 1984; Taunton and Somerset Hosp: conslt anaesthetist and dir of intensive care 1986–, dir of anaesthetics 1994–; MRCP 1978, FFARCS 1980; *Recreations* canoeing, sailing; *Style*— Dr Andrew Daykin; ✉ Priors Lodge, Blagdon Hill, Taunton, Somerset TA3 7SH (☎ 01823 421588); Musgrove Park Hospital, Taunton, Somerset TA1 5DA (☎ 01823 333444)

DAYKIN, Christopher David; CB (1993); s of John Francis (d 1983), and Mona, *née* Carey; *b* 18 July 1948; *Educ* Merchant Taylors', Pembroke Coll Cambridge (MA); *m* 1977, Kathryn Ruth, da of Harold William Tingey; 2 s (Jonathan b 1982, Jeremy b 1984), 1 da (Rachel b 1981); *Career* Govt Actuary's Dept: 1970, 1972–78 and 1980–, princ actuary 1982–84, directing actuary 1985–89, govt actuary 1989–; princ (Health and Social Servs) HM Treasy 1978–80; FIA 1973 (pres 1994–96); VSO Brunei 1971; *Recreations* travel, photography, language; *Style*— Christopher Daykin, Esq, CB; ✉ Government Actuary's Department, 22 Kingsway, London WC2B 6LE (☎ 0171 211 2620, fax 0171 211 2650)

DAYMOND, Dr Terence John; s of late Deric Alfred Daymond, of Verwood, Dorset, and Ethel Anne, *née* Bird; *b* 24 Feb 1942; *Educ* Rutlish Sch, Univ of Edinburgh (MB ChB, MRCP), DipObstRCOG, Dip Phys Med; *m* 18 Jan 1969, Jacqueline Mary, da of Bernard Joffre Martin, of Wisbech, Cambridgeshire; 1 s (Benjamin b 1983), 3 da (Carolyn b 1969, Joanna b 1971, Charlotte b 1986); *Career* acting CMO Dhariwal nr Amritsar Punjab India 1969–70, med registrar King's Lynn Norfolk 1971–73, rheumatology registrar Aylsham Norfolk 1973–76, sr registrar in rheumatology Royal Victoria Infirmary Newcastle upon Tyne 1976–79, conslt in rheumatology and rehabilitation City Hosps Sunderland 1979, lectr in med Univ of Newcastle upon Tyne, hon lectr Dept of Pharmacy Sunderland Univ, hon physician Sunderland SCOPE; pres: Sunderland Branch Nat Back Pain Soc, Washington Branch Arthritis Care; FRCP 1987; memb BMA, BSR; *Books* Treatment in Clinical Medicine Rheumatic Disease (with Hilary H Capell, T J Daymond, W Carson, 1983); *Recreations* swimming; *Style*— Dr Terence Daymond; ✉ Ivy Lodge, 25 Front Street, Whitburn, Sunderland SR4 7JB (☎ 0191 529 3912); Department of Rheumatology, District General Hopital, Sunderland SR4 7TP (☎ 0191 565 6256)

DAZELEY, Peter William; s of late William Henry George Dazeley, of W Kensington, and Freda Kathleen, *née* Ward, MBE; *b* 29 June 1948; *Educ* Holland Park Comp; *m* (m dis); *Career* photographer specialising in prodn of creative images for leading advtg and design cos; life memb Assoc of Photographers (formerly AFAEP); *Recreations* golf, squash; *Clubs* Queens, Coombe Hill Golf; *Style*— Peter Dazeley, Esq; ✉ Peter Dazeley, The Studios, 5 Heathmans Rd, Parsons Green, Fulham, London SW6 4TJ (☎ 0171 736 3171, fax 0171 731 8876)

de BLANK, Justin Robert; s of William de Blank (d 1974), and Agnes Frances, *née* Crossley (d 1973); *b* 25 Feb 1927; *Educ* Marlborough, Corpus Christi Coll Cambridge (BA), Royal Acad Sch of Architecture; *m* 1972 (m dis 1976), Mary Jacqueline Dubois Godet; m 2, 1977, Melanie Alexandra Margaret, da of Col Robert James Thompson Irwin, MC; 3 da (Polly Bartna b 17 Sept 1977, Martha Louise b 15 Dec 1979, Clementine Rose b 27 May 1982); *Career* Edible Fats Div Unilever (van den Berghs and Jurgens Ltd) 1953–58, J Walter Thompson advertising 1958–66 (mangr Paris Office 1962–64), dir Conran Design Group 1966, fndr chm and md Justin de Blank Provisions Ltd 1967–93, opened first specialist London food shop 1968 and first restaurant Duke Street 1972; fndr: de Blank Restaurants (partnership with Catering & Allied Ltd) 1987–95, Justin de Blank Foods Ltd (partnership with Carter Corp NY) 1993–; other retail and catering outlets opened ICA, Nat Gallery, etc; dir: Kitchen Range Foods Ltd 1972–, The Original Porters Provisions Company 1993–; opened (with wife) Shipdham Place country restaurant (Egon Ronay star, Michelin red M) 1979–89; *Recreations* gardening, golf, tennis, sailing, historic buildings; *Clubs* Annabel's, Royal West Norfolk Golf; *Style*— Justin de Blank, Esq; ✉ 12 Trigon Road, London SW8 1NH (☎ 0171 582 2996)

de BLOCQ van KUFFELER, John Philip; s of Capt F de Blocq van Kuffeler, of Royal Netherlands Navy, and Stella, *née* Hall; *b* 9 Jan 1949; *Educ* Atlantic Coll, Clare Coll Cambridge (MA); *m* 3 April 1971, Lesley, da of Dr E M Callander; 2 s (Hugo b 1974, Alexander b 1979), 1 da (Venetia b 1977); *Career* CA 1973; Peat Marwick Mitchell & Co 1970–77 (assignments UK, Holland, Germany, Egypt), head of corporate fin Grindlay Brandts Ltd 1980–82 (mangr 1977–80); Brown Shipley & Co Ltd: dir 1983–91, head of corporate fin 1983–88, memb Exec Ctee 1985–91, head of investmt banking UK and USA 1986–88; gp chief exec Brown Shipley Holdings plc 1988–91, chief exec Provident Financial plc 1991–; non-exec dir: Campbell & Armstrong plc 1986–, Finsbury Smaller Companies Trust plc 1992–; memb Ctee Issuing Houses Assoc 1984–88; FCA; *Recreations* fishing, shooting, tennis; *Style*— John de Blocq van Kuffeler, Esq; ✉ Provident Financial plc, Colonnade, Sunbridge Road, Bradford, West Yorks BD1 2LQ (☎ 01274 731111, fax 01274 393369)

de BOER, Anthony Peter (Tony); CBE (1982); s of late Goffe de Boer, and late Irene Kathleen, *née* Grist; *b* 22 June 1918; *Educ* Westminster; *m* 19 Jan 1942, Pamela Agnes Nora, da of Frank Bullock (decd); 1 s (Christopher); *Career* Nat Serv sapper (AA) RE

1939–40, 2 Lt Indian Army 6 Gurkha Rifles 1940–43, Major RIASC 1944–46; Royal Dutch Shell Group: joined 1937, served China Sudan Egypt Ethiopia Aden Palestine 1946–58, area coordinator Africa Middle E 1959–63, chm Shell Trinidad 1963–64, md mktg Shell Mex & BP 1964–67; dep chm Wm Cory & Son 1968–71, dir Nat Bus Co 1969–83, chm Anvil Petroleum (Attock Oil) 1974–85, dir Chloride Gp 1976–85, dir Burmah Oil 1978–85, chm Tomatin Distillers 1978–85, memb Policy Ctee Price Waterhouse 1979–86; dir Brighton and Hove Albion FC 1969–72, chm Keep Britain Tidy Gp 1969–79 (vice pres 1980–), memb Cncl Univ of Sussex 1969–91 (memb Ct 1991–), chm Br Road Fedn 1972–87 (vice pres 1988–), memb Cncl CBI 1980–83, vice chm RAC 1985–89, vice pres Ind Schs Careers Orgn 1989–; Freeman City of London, memb Worshipful Co of Coach Makers and Coach Harness Makers; CIMgt 1974; *Recreations* sport, theatre, gardening; *Clubs* Royal Automobile, Garrick; *Style*— Anthony de Boer, Esq, CBE

de BOINVILLE, Simon Murdoch Chastel; s of Charles Alfred Chastel de Boinville (d 1985), of Farnham, Surrey, and Frances Anne, *née* Morrison (d 1984); *b* 16 March 1955; *Educ* Radley, RAC Cirencester; *m* 4 Oct 1980, Shaunagh Elisabeth, da of Dermott Bibby Magill, of Baughurst, Hants; 3 s (Reuben b 1986, d 1988, Nicolai b 1989, Lucian b 1991), 1 da (Cornelia b 1988); *Career* ptnr Cluttons Chartered Surveyors 1989–91 (joined 1979), dir John D Wood & Co (Residential and Agricultural) Ltd 1991–96; FRICS; *Recreations* gardening, fishing; *Clubs* Farmers'; *Style*— Simon de Boinville, Esq; ✉ Grantham Farm, Baughurst, Tadley, Hants RG26 5JT (☎ 0118 981 5821)

de BONO, Prof David Paul; s of Joseph Edward de Bono, CBE (d 1973), of St Julians, Malta GC, and Josephine, *née* Burns; *b* 19 Jan 1947; *Educ* St Edwards Coll Malta, Downside, Trinity Hall Cambridge (MA, MD), St George's Hosp London; *m* 2 Jan 1971, Anne Mary, da of Flt Lt John Fingleton (d 1985), of Preston, Lancs; 2 s (John b 1972, Joseph b 1975); *Career* fell Trinity Hall Cambridge 1973–76, clinical lectr Univ of Oxford 1976–79, conslt physician Royal Infirmary of Edinburgh 1979–89; Univ of Leicester: Br Heart Fndn prof of cardiology 1989–, head Dept of Med 1996–; memb: Br Heart Fndn 1986–89, Cncl Br Cardiac Soc 1995–; FRCPE 1982, FRCP(Lond) 1990, FESC 1994; *Recreations* model aeroplanes, sailing; *Style*— Prof David de Bono; ✉ 75 Station Rd, Cropston, Leicestershire LE7 7HG (☎ 0116 236 4140); Department of Cardiology, University of Leicester, Glenfield Hospital, Groby Rd, Leicester LE3 9QP (☎ 0116 256 3038 or 0116 256 3021, fax 0116 287 5792)

de BONO, Edward Francis Charles Publius; s of late Prof Joseph Edward de Bono, CBE, of St Julian's Bay, Malta, and Josephine, *née* Burns; *b* 19 May 1933; *Educ* St Edward's Coll Malta, Royal Univ of Malta (BSc, MD), ChCh Oxford (Rhodes scholar, DPhil), Univ of Cambridge (PhD); *m* 1971, Josephine Hall-White; 2 s; *Career* Univ of Cambridge: asst dir of res Dept of Investigative Med 1963–76, lectr in med 1976–83; fndr and dir Cognitive Research Trust Cambridge 1971–83, sec gen Supranational Independent Thinking Orgn (SITO) 1983–, fndr Int Creative Forum 1990–; TV series: de Bono's Course in Thinking (BBC), The Greatest Thinkers (WDR Germany); lectured extensively worldwide; *Books* incl: The Use of Lateral Thinking (1967), Lateral Thinking; A Textbook of Creativity (1970), Wordpower (1977), de Bono's Thinking Course (1982), Six Thinking Hats (1985), Letters to Thinkers (1987), I am Right, You are Wrong (1990), Handbook for the Positive Revolution (1991), Six Action Shoes (1991), Teach Your Child to Think (1992); *Recreations* travel, toys, thinking; *Clubs* Athenaeum; *Style*— Dr Edward de Bono; ✉ Cranmer Hall, Fakenham, Norfolk; L2 Albany, Piccadilly, London W1V 9RR

de BOTTON, Gilbert; *b* 16 Feb 1935; *Educ* Victoria Coll Alexandria Egypt, Columbia Univ NYC (MA); *m* 1, 6 July 1962 (m dis 1988) Jacqueline, *née* Burgauer; 1 da (Miel b 27 Feb 1968), 1 s (Alain b 20 Dec 1969); m 2, 17 Dec 1990, Hon Mrs Janet Green, da of Lord Wolfson of Marylebone, formerly wife of Michael Green; *Career* UFITEC SA Union Financière (Zurich) 1960–68, md Rothschild Bank AG (Zurich) 1968–82, chm Global Asset Management London 1983–; tstee Tate Gallery 1985–92, chm Int Cncl Tate Fndn; *Recreations* art, literature; *Clubs* Carlton, Athenaeum; *Style*— Mr Gilbert de Botton; ✉ 1 Eaton Close, London SW1W 8JX; Suot Mulin, St Moritz, Switzerland; Global Asset Management Ltd, GAM House, 12 St James's Place, London SW1A 1NX (☎ 0171 493 9990, fax 0171 493 0715, telex 296099 GAMUK)

de BRANT, Peter; s of Col Alexander Baron Brant (d 1952), and Vivian Waldo, *née* Story (d 1944); *b* 31 Jan 1930; *Educ* Highgate Sch, Lausanne Univ, Univ of Cambridge (MA), Harvard Univ, Architecural Assoc Sch of Architecture (Dip); *m* 1, 4 June 1965 (m dis 1973), Gillian, da of Capt H R Temperley, HAC (d 1940); 1 da (Sophia); m 2, 30 May 1993, Diana Ho Siok Min; *Career* architect; assoc RMJM Ptnrship 1964–78; projects incl: Univ of Bath, new Hereford and Worcester Co HQ, Free Univ of Iran; currently conslt de Brant Joyce and Ptnrs (ptnr 1978); projects incl: Univ of Teaching Hosp Nsuka Nigeria, Open Univ of Nigeria, specialist hosps in Saudi Arabia, listed building redevelopments UK, palaces (Saudi Arabia, UK, Brunei, Oman, Qatar); fell Linaean Soc 1980; *Recreations* archaeology, enviromental studies; *Style*— Peter de Brant, Esq; ✉ Bury Court, Jacobstow, Cornwall (☎ 0128 884 360); de Brant Joyce and Partners, 13 Harley St, London W1M 9LD (☎ 0171 637 9865)

DE BURGH, Chris John (*né* Davison); s of Charles John Davison, of Wexford, Ireland, and Maeve Emily, *née* de Burgh; *b* 15 Oct 1948; *Educ* Marlborough, Trinity Coll Dublin (MA); *m* Diane Patricia, da of Arthur Morley; 2 s (Hubie Christopher b 29 March 1988, Michael Charles Arthur b 30 Oct 1990), 1 da (Rosanna Diane b 17 April 1984); *Career* singer and songwriter; has released 15 albums to date, debut album Far Beyond These Castle Walls 1974, most recent album Beautiful Dreams 1995; single The Lady in Red, album Into the Light (both 1986) and album Flying Colours reached number one in UK, USA and elsewhere; toured extensively in Europe, Aust, Japan, UK and Ireland; winner of over 80 Gold, Silver and Platinum discs since 1976 in USA, Canada, England, Ireland, W Germany, Belgium, Holland, Switzerland, Austria, Norway, Sweden, Spain, S Africa, Aust, Hong Kong, Brazil, Denmark, France and Israel; other awards incl: Beroliner award (W Germany), Bambi award (W Germany), Midem Int Trophy (France), ASCAP award (UK and America, 1987, 1988, 1990 and 1991), IRMA awards (Ireland 1985–1990); *Recreations* swimming, scuba diving, golf, fine wine collecting, antiques, persian rugs; *Style*— Chris De Burgh, Esq; ✉ Mismanagement, 754 Fulham Rd, London SW6 5SH (☎ 0171 731 7074, fax 0171 736 8605)

DE BURGH, Lydia Anne; da of Capt Charles De Burgh, DSO, RN (d 1973), of Seaforde, and Isabel Caroline Berkeley, *née* Campbell (d 1969); *b* 3 July 1923; *Educ* privately, Byam Shaw Sch of Art; *Career* WRNS 1942 (ULTRA), Br Red Cross 1943–45; professional portrait, wildlife and landscape painter; apprenticed to late Sonia Mervyn RP; exhibitions at: Royal Soc of Portrait Painters, Royal Soc of Br Artists, Royal Birmingham Soc, Royal Ulster Acad of Art, Glasgow Inst of Fine Arts, Soc of Wildlife Artists London, Soc of Equestrian Artists, Ulster Watercolour Soc; solo exhbns incl: NI Office, Vose Gallery Boston Mass 1957, HQ NI 1975 and 1978, Gordon Gallery London, Wildlife Gallery Eastbourne; retrospective exhib Down County Museum then The Malone Gallery Belfast 1993; cmmns incl: Princess Alice HRH The Duchess of Gloucester 1954, HM The Queen 1955, 1956 and 1959 (portrait used as a Caribbean Afro-Commonwealth stamp 1993), HRH the late Princess Royal 1956 and 1957, the late Marquess and Marchioness of Headfort, African wildlife in Kenya for Rowland Ward Ltd, Crossroads of Sport (Sportsmans Gallery NY) 1960–70, Maze Prison 1972; lectr worldwide, numerous interviews on BBC; HRUA 1985 (ARUA 1956), memb Ulster Watercolour Soc, memb Chelsea Art Soc 1956–72; *Books* Lydia's Story (1991, recorded for Blind and Disabled Listening Libraries RNIB 1993); *Recreations* travelling, reading, gardening, fine arts, fashion; *Style*— Lydia De Burgh, HRUA; ✉ 4 Church Court, Castlewellan Road, Clough, Downpatrick, Co Down BT30 8QX

de CANDOLE, (Mark) Andrew Vully; s of Eric Armar Vully de Candole, CMG, CBE (d 1989), and Elizabeth Marion, *née* Constable-Roberts; *b* 15 April 1953; *Educ* Marlborough Coll; *Career* md City Gate Estates Plc 1985–90, md Pathfinder Group 1991–; non-exec dir Queen Victoria Hospital NHS Trust 1994–96; *Recreations* garden design, riding, skiing, sailing; *Style*— Andrew de Candole, Esq; ✉ Groombridge Place, Groombridge, Nr Tunbridge Wells, Kent TN3 9QG (☎ 01892 863999, fax 01892 863996)

de CHAMBRUN, *see:* Chambrun

de CHASSIRON, HE Charles Richard Lucien; s of Brig H E C de Chassiron (d 1974), and Deane, *née* Richardson (d 1996); *b* 27 April 1948; *Educ* Rugby, Jesus Coll Cambridge (MA), JFK Sch of Govt Harvard Univ (MPA); *m* 28 Sept 1974, Britt-Marie Sonja, da of Nils G Medhammar; 1 s (Hugo b 1976), 1 da (Anna b 1975); *Career* FCO: joined 1971, Stockholm 1972–75, Maputo 1975–78, Salisbury 1980, Brasilia 1982–85, head of S American Dept 1988–89, cnsllr (econ and commercial) Rome 1989–94, ambass Estonia 1994–; memb UK Delgn at Lancaster House Rhodesia Conf 1979; *Recreations* walking, history of art; *Style*— HE Mr Charles de Chassiron; ✉ c/o FCO (Tallinn), King Charles Street, London SW1A 2AH (☎ 00 372 631 3353)

de CHAZAL, Paul André; s of Claude de Chazal (d 1993), of Funchal, Madeira, and Simone, *née* de Cunha; *b* 25 Sept 1942; *Educ* Downside, Madrid Univ, Sidney Sussex Coll Cambridge (BA); *m* 27 May 1978, Donatienne, da of late Jean-Louis Dierckx de Casterlé, of Brussels, Belgium; 2 da (Mélusine b 1979, Julie b 1982); *Career* Simmons & Simmons: asst slr London 1967–69, ptnr 1969–, ptnr i/c Brussels 1969–71, ptnr London, Brussels, Hong Kong, Paris, NY, Lisbon, Milan, Abu Dhabi and Shanghai; admitted slr Supreme Court of Judicature Hong Kong 1981; dir: British-American Insurance Co Ltd Nassau Bahamas 1972–88, Windsor Group Ltd 1987–88, Windsor Life Assurance Co Ltd 1978–88, Hamilton Insurance Co Ltd and Hamilton Life Assurance Co Ltd 1983–; memb: Law Soc, City of London Slrs' Co, AIPPI, Belgian-Luxembourg Chamber of Commerce (memb Cncl and hon gen sec), Exec Ctee Anglo-Portuguese Soc 1986–89, French Chamber of Commerce, Portuguese Chamber of Commerce, US Chamber of Commerce, Japan Assoc, Japan Soc, Union Internationale des Avocats, Inter-Pacific Bar Assoc, L'Association des Juristes Franco-Britanniques; *Clubs* Wisley Golf, Dragon; *Style*— Paul de Chazal, Esq; ✉ Simmons & Simmons, 21 Wilson Street, London EC2M 2TX (☎ 0171 628 2020, fax 0171 628 2070, telex 888562)

de CLIFFORD, 27 Baron (E 1299); John Edward Southwell Russell; er s of 26 Baron de Clifford, OBE, TD (d 1982), by his 1 w, Dorothy Evelyn (d 1987), da of Ferdinand Meyrick, MD, of Kensington Court, London, and Kate Meyrick the nightclub owner; *b* 8 June 1928; *Educ* Eton, RAC Cirencester; *m* 27 June 1959, Bridget Jennifer, yst da of Duncan Robertson, of Llantysilio Hall, Llangollen, by his w Joyce (aunt of Sir Watkin Williams-Wynn, 11th Bt,, *qv*); *Heir* bro, Hon William Russell; *Career* farmer, ret; *Clubs* Naval & Military; *Style*— The Rt Hon Lord de Clifford; ✉ Riggledown, Pennymoor, Tiverton, Devon EX16 8LR (☎ 01363 866301)

de COURCY, Anne Grey; da of Maj John Lionel Mackenzie Barrett (d 1940), of Tendring, Essex, and Evelyn Kathleen Frances, *née* Ellison-Macartney; *Educ* Wroxall Abbey Leamington Spa; *m* 1, 1951, Michael Charles Cameron Claremont Constantine de Courcy (d 1953), elder son of Lt Cdr Hon Michael John Rancé de Courcy, RN (d 1940); m 2, 24 Jan 1959, Robert Armitage, 2 s of Gen Sir (Charles) Clement Armitage, KCB, CMG, DSO, DL, of Downington House, Lechlade, Glos; 1 s (John b Dec 1959), 2 da (Sophy b June 1961, Rose b March 1964); *Career* Evening News: writer, columnist, woman's ed 1972–80; Evening Standard: writer, columnist, section ed 1982–92; Daily Mail 1993–; *Books* Kitchens (1973), Starting From Scratch (1975), Making Room at the Top (1976), A Guide to Modern Manners (1985), The English in Love (1986), 1939 - The Last Season (1989), Circe - The Life of Edith, Marchioness of Londonderry (1992); *Recreations* reading, writing, swimming, gardening; *Style*— Ms Anne de Courcy; ✉ Daily Mail, Northcliffe House, 2 Derry Street, Kensington, London W8 5TT (☎ 0171 938 7178, fax 0171 937 4463)

de COURCY, Nevinson Russell; s of Nevinson William de Courcy (d 1919), and Grace, *née* Russell (d 1967); gggs of Adm Hon Michael de Courcy, 3 s of 25(20) Baron Kingsale; hp to kinsman, 30 Baron, Premier Baron of Ireland; *b* 21 July 1920, (posthumously); *m* 23 July 1954, Nora Lydia (d 1994), da of James Plint, of Great Crosby, Lancs; 1 s (Nevinson Mark, b 11 May 1958), 1 da (Katherine Grace, b 26 April 1955); *Career* served WWII RE; MICE, MIMARINE; *Style*— Nevinson de Courcy Esq; ✉ 15 Market Rd, Remuera, Auckland 5, NZ

de COURCY LING, John; CBE (1990); s of late Arthur Norman Ling (d 1973), of Warwick, and Veronica, *née* de Courcy (d 1987), of Painestown Co Kildare; *b* 14 Oct 1933; *Educ* King Edward's Sch Edgbaston, Clare Coll Cambridge (MA); *m* 4 July 1959, Jennifer Rosemary, da of Stanley Haynes (d 1957); 1 s (Adam b 12 Aug 1960), 3 da (Julia (Lady Wigan) b 31 Oct 1961, Patricia b 15 Jan 1963, Catherine b 16 Jan 1965); *Career* 2 Lt Royal Ulster Rifles 1955, Lt on active serv Cyprus 1957–58; joined FO 1959; a private sec to successive Mins of State: Lord Harlech 1960–61, Joseph Godber 1961–63; second sec Santiago 1963–66, first sec Nairobi 1966–69, chargé d'affaires Chad 1973, cnsllr HM Embassy Paris 1974–77, ret FO 1978; farmer: Bellehatch Park Henley-on-Thames 1977–85, Glyme Valley Chipping Norton 1985–; MEP (C) Warwickshire 1979–89, Cons chief whip 1979–83, memb Exec Ctee Nat Union of Cons Assocs 1979–83, vice chm Devpt Aid Ctee 1984–87, chm EEC Delgn to Israel 1979–82; memb Cncl: Lloyd's 1985–88, RIIA 1990–94; pres Henley-on-Thames Agric Assoc 1980–81; memb Catholic Bishops' Ctee on Europe 1986–; tstee Maison Française Oxford 1992–; chm/dir various cos concerned with construction, publishing and reinsurance 1990–; contrib: The Tablet, Sunday Times; *Books* Famine and Surplus (with T R McK Sewell, 1985), Tales of Imperial Decline (1992), Epires Rise and Sink (1996); *Recreations* sailing, skiing, opera, bridge; *Clubs* Beefsteak, Leander (Henley-on-Thames), Royal Leamington Spa Conservative, Chipping Norton Golf; *Style*— John de Courcy Ling, Esq, CBE; ✉ Lamb House, Bladon, Woodstock, Oxford OX20 1RS (☎ 01993 811654)

DE FEO, Joseph; s of Ralph and Jean De Feo; *b* 31 May 1947; *Educ* Adelphi Univ New York (BA, MBA, MS); *m* Anna Julie; 1 s (Christian Joseph), 1 da (Danielle Julie); *Career* asst mangr Computer Ops Interstate Stores Inc 1969–71, systems programmer Chemical Bank New York 1971–72, mangr Systems Software Blyth & Co Inc 1972, sr systems programmer Federal Reserve Bank of New York 1972–74, vice pres Info Servs Smith Barney, Harris Upham 1974–77, vice pres Int Bank Servs Chase Manhattan Bank 1982–84 (vice pres Bank Support Servs 1977–82), vice pres Systems Devpt and User Support Gp Goldman Sachs & Co 1984–87, dir Gp Systems and Ops Morgan Grenfell & Co Ltd 1988–89, dir Gp Ops and Technol Barclays Bank plc 1989–96, chief exec Open Group 1996– (former non-exec dir); author of numerous articles in indust and mgmnt pubns and nat newspapers, frequent lectr and speaker; memb Cncl APACS, fndr memb Group of 20, chm CHAPS Clearing Co (formerly Cheque and Credit Clearing Co); non-exec dir Nat IT Skills Forum; sr rep for Barclays Gp in SWIFT; *Style*— Joseph De Feo, Esq; ✉ The Open Group, Apex Plaza, Forbury Road, Reading, Berks RG1 1AX (☎ 01734 508311)

de FERRANTI, Sebastian Basil Joseph Ziani; er s of Sir Vincent Ziani de Ferranti, MC (d 1980), and Dorothy Hettie Campbell, *née* Wilson (d 1993); *b* 5 Oct 1927; *Educ* Ampleforth; *m* 1, 9 April 1953, Mona Helen, da of T E Cunningham; 1 s, 2 da; m 2,

1983, Naomi Angela Rae; *Career* 4/7 Dragoon Gds 1947–49; Brown Boveri Switzerland and Alsthom France 1949–50, chm Ferranti plc 1963–82 (dir 1954, md 1958–75); dir: British Airways Helicopters 1982–84, GEC plc 1982–, Nat Nuclear Corp 1984–88; lectures: Granada Guildhall 1966, Royal Institution 1969, Louis Blériot Paris 1970, Faraday 1970–71; pres: Electrical Res Assoc 1968–69, BEAMA 1969–70, Centre for Educn in Sci Educn and Technol Manchester and Region 1972–82; chm Int Electrical Assoc 1970–72; memb: Nat Defence Industs Cncl 1969–77, Cncl IEE 1970–73; tstee Tate Gallery 1971–78, chm Civic Tst for the North West 1978–83, cmmr Royal Cmmn for Exhibition of 1851 1984–, vice pres RSA 1980–84, chm Hallé Concerts Soc 1988–; High Sheriff of Cheshire 1988–89; Liveryman: Worshipful Co of Wheelwrights, Guild of Air Pilots and Air Navigators; Hon DSc: Univ of Salford 1967, Cranfield Inst of Technol 1973; hon fell UMIST; *Clubs* Cavalry and Guards, Pratt's; *Style*— Sebastian de Ferranti, Esq; ✉ Henbury Hall, Macclesfield, Cheshire SK11 9PJ (☎ 01625 422101)

de FONBLANQUE, John Robert; CMG (1993); s of Maj-Gen Edward Barrington de Fonblanque (d 1981), of Lyndhurst, Hants, and Elizabeth Flora Lutley, *née* Sclater; *b* 20 Dec 1943; *Educ* Ampleforth, King's Coll Cambridge (MA), LSE (MSc); *m* 24 March 1984, Margaret, da of Harry Prest; 1 s (Thomas b 1985); *Career* HM Dip Serv 1968–: second sec Jakarta 1969–71, first sec UK rep to EC 1971–77, princ HM Treasy 1977–79, FCO 1979–83, asst sec Cabinet Office 1983–85, cnsllr Delhi 1986–87, cnsllr and head of Chancery UK Rep to EC 1988–93, visiting fell Royal Inst for International Relations 1993, dir for international orgns 1994–; *Recreations* mountain walking; *Style*— John R de Fonblanque, Esq, CMG; ✉ c/o FCO, King Charles Street, London SW1A 2AH

de FRANCIA, Prof Peter Laurent; s of Laurent Fernand de Francia (d 1937), of Paris, and Alice, *née* Groom; *b* 25 Jan 1921; *Educ* Univ of London (BA), Slade Sch; *m* 1980 (m dis 1988), Jenny Franklin; *Career* Army Service 1940–45; Canadian Govt Exhibition Commision Ottowa 1948–50, prodr BBC TV London 1952–54, Dept of Art History St Martin's Sch London 1954–61, Dept of Art History RCA 1961–69, princ Dept of Fine Art Goldsmiths' Coll 1970–72, prof of painting RCA 1972–86; various exhibitions 1958–80 (Milan, London, Amsterdam, Prague, New York, Edinburgh and London); recent exhibitions: Forum Gallery NY 1983, Camden Arts Centre London 1987, Pomeroy Purdy Gallery London 1989, London Frith St Gallery 1989; contrib to Art History Exhibition Hayward Gallery London 1987–88; works in public collections: V & A, Br Museum, Tate Gallery, Museum of Modern Art NY, Graves Art Gallery Sheffield, City Gallery Birmingham, Museum of Modern Art Prague; FRCA; *Books* Léger, the Great Parade (1969), The Life and Work of Ferdinand Léger (1983), "Untitled" (1989); *Style*— Prof Peter de Francia; ✉ 44 Surrey Square, London SE17 2JX (☎ 0171 703 8361); Lacoste, Vaucluse, France (☎ 00 33 90 75 91 12)

DE FREYNE, 7 Baron (UK 1851); Francis Arthur John French; s of 6 Baron, JP, DL (d 1935), by Victoria, da of Sir John Arnott, 2 Bt; *b* 3 Sept 1927; *m* 1, 30 Jan 1954 (m dis 1979); 2 s (Hon Fulke b 1957, Hon Patrick b 1969), 1 da (Hon Vanessa b 1958); m 2, 1978, Sheelin Deirdre, da of Col Henry O'Kelly, DSO, of Co Wicklow, and wid of William Walker Stevenson; *Heir* s, Hon Fulke Charles Arthur John French; *Career* Knight of Malta; *Style*— The Rt Hon Lord De Freyne; ✉ c/o House of Lords, London SW1A 0PW

DE GELSEY, Alexander Henry Marie; CBE (1989), DL (Kent, 1991); s of Baron Henry de Gelsey (d 1963), and Marguerite, *née* Lieser (d 1965); bro of William de Gelsey, *qv*; *b* 24 June 1924; *Educ* RC Univ Sch Budapest, Trinity Coll Cambridge; *m* 5 Feb 1969, Romy, da of Frederick Edgar Cairns (d 1972), of Oxford; 1 da (Annabel b 1975); *Career* chm Sericol International Ltd 1955–, memb SE Thames RHA 1984–88, chm E Kent Enterprise Agency 1985–; dep chm East Kent Initiative 1991–; memb: Kent Economic Devpt Bd 1986–91, Kent Investments Ltd 1986–91, Southern Bd BR 1988–92, Special Health Authy 1989–92, Kent Community Housing Tst 1990–, Governing Cncl Univ of Kent 1989–, Thanet Healthcare Tst 1992–; chm Br-Hungarian Small Business Fndn 1991–; hon consul of the Republic of Hungary 1990–; *Recreations* shooting, boating, travelling, walking; *Style*— Alexander De Gelsey, Esq, CBE, DL; ✉ 22 South Terrace, London SW7 2TD (☎ 0171 581 2541, fax 0171 584 4156); Boughton Church House, Faversham, Kent ME13 9NB (☎ 01227 751202, fax 01227 750962)

DE GELSEY, William Henry Marie; s of Baron Henry de Gelsey (d 1963), formerly of Hungary, and Marguerite, *née* Lieser (d 1965); bro of Alexander De Gelsey, CBE, DL, *qv*; *b* 17 Dec 1921; *Educ* Roman Catholic Univ Public Sch Budapest, Trinity Coll Cambridge (MA); *Career* investment banker (exec dir) Hill Samuel and Co Ltd 1959–71, md Orion Bank Ltd 1971–80, dep chm Orion Royal Bank Ltd 1980–88, sr advsr to Managing Bd Creditanstalt-Bankverein (Vienna and London) 1988–; *Recreations* travelling; *Clubs* Annabel's, Mark's, Harry's Bar; *Style*— William de Gelsey, Esq; ✉ Creditanstalt, c/o Schottengasse 6, 1010 Vienna, Austria (☎ 00 431 53131 1919, fax 00 431 319 6525); Creditanstalt, c/o 125 London Wall, London EC2V 7AH (☎ 0171 417 4902, fax 0171 417 4909); Palais Saint-Pierre, 32 Boulevard d'Italie, Monte-Carlo, MC 9800 Monaco

de GLANVILLE, Philip (Phil); *b* 1 Oct 1968; *Educ* Bryanston Sch, Univ of Durham, St Catherine's Coll Oxford (Dip SocSci); *Career* professional rugby union centre; former clubs: Durham Univ RFC (capt final year), Oxford Univ RFC (Blue 1990); currently with Bath RFC 1990– (capt 1995–); England: won first cap v S Africa 1992, memb squad World Cup South Africa 1995 (3 appearances), capt 1996–, 17 full caps (as at Dec 1996); honours with Bath FC: winners Pilkington Cup four times, winners Courage Div One five times (three times winners League and Cup double); *Style*— Phil de Glanville, Esq; ✉ c/o Bath RFC, The Recreation Ground, Bath, Avon; c/o James Grant Media Group Ltd, Syon Lodge, London Road, Syon Park, Middlesex TW7 5BH (☎ 0181 232 4100, fax 0181 232 4101)

de GREY, Michael John; *b* 6 Sept 1942; *m* 1, 1966 (m dis 1988), Carolyn Blackie; 2 da (Rachel Emma b 1969, Helen Sarah b 1971); m 2, 1989, Charlotte Ashe; 1 da (Annabel Louise b 1994); *Career* schoolmaster Elstree Sch 1961, district mangr Courages Brewery 1962–70, concerts mangr Victor Hochhauser Ltd 1970–72, gen mangr London Mozart Players 1972–81, gen mangr Royal Choral Soc 1976–79, admin dir London Sinfonietta 1981–88 (admin dir Opera Factory 1985–88), conslt SE Arts and London Handel Orch 1988–89, gen mangr LAMDA 1989, head of mktg Soundalive Tours 1990–91, chief exec Nat Youth Orch of GB 1991–; dir: Assoc of Br Orchs 1984–89, LPO 1987–89; memb Music Advsy Panel SE Arts 1986–90; *Style*— Michael de Grey, Esq; ✉ National Youth Orchestra of Great Britain, 32 Old School House, Britannia Road, Kingswood, Bristol BS15 2DB (☎ 0117 960 0477, fax 0117 960 0376)

de GREY, Spencer Thomas; s of Sir Roger de Grey, KCVO, PPRA (d 1995), and Flavia, *née* Irwin; *b* 7 June 1944; *Educ* Eton, Churchill Coll Cambridge (MA, DipArch); *m* 3 Sept 1977, Hon (Amanda) Lucy, da of Baron Annan, OBE (Life Peer), *qv*; 1 da (Georgia Catherine b 22 Aug 1988), 1 s (Felix Nicholas b 29 Aug 1992); *Career* architect London Borough of Merton 1969–73; Foster & Partners (formerly Foster Associates): joined 1973, estab Hong Kong office 1979, dir responsible for Third London Airport at Stansted and Sackler Galleries Royal Acad 1981, design ptnr 1991–; projects as design ptnr incl: Commerzbank HQ (Frankfurt), Lycée Albert Camus (Fréjus), EDF regional operational centre (Bordeaux), Law Faculty Univ of Cambridge, Great Court British Museum, new med bldg Imperial Coll London, Nat Botanical Gardens for Wales; lectr at home and abroad incl Le Louvre Paris and RIBA London; tstee Royal Botanical Gardens Kew 1995–; ARCUK 1969, RIBA 1993; *Recreations* music, theatre, travel; *Style*— Spencer de Grey, Esq; ✉ Foster & Partners, Riverside 3, 22 Hester Road, London SW11 4AN (☎ 0171 738 0455, fax 0171 738 1107)

de GRUCHY, Nigel Ronald Anthony; s of Robert Philip de Gruchy (d 1994), and Dorothy Louise, *née* Cullinane (d 1991); *b* 28 Jan 1943; *Educ* De La Salle Coll Jersey, Univ of Reading (BA), Univ of London (PGCE), Universite de Paris (Cert Pratique de Langue Français), L'Alliance Français (Cert de Français Parlé et du Diplôme de Langue Française); *m* 1970, Judith Ann, da of Delore Berglund, of Minn USA; 1 s (Paul b 7 Dec 1975); *Career* TEFL Berlitz Schs Santander 1965–66, Versailles 1966–67, student of French/tutor in English Paris 1967–68, head of Econs Dept St Joseph's Acad ILEA 1968–78; Nat Assoc of Schoolmasters Union of Women Teachers: sec London Assoc and memb Nat Exec 1975–78, asst sec 1978–82, dep gen sec 1982–89, gen sec 1990–; memb: Gen Cncl TUC 1990–, Exec Bd Education International 1993–; contribs Career Teacher; *Recreations* golf, music, reading, sport, travel; *Style*— Nigel de Gruchy, Esq; ✉ NASUWT, 5 King Street, Covent Garden, London WC2E 8HN (☎ 0171 379 9499, fax 0171 497 8262)

de GUINGAND, Anthony Paul; s of Paul Emile de Guingand (d 1976), and Olwyn Doreen, *née* Witts; *b* 7 Aug 1947; *Educ* Ampleforth; *m* 24 Nov 1973, Diana Mary, da of John Harrington Parr; 2 s (Marcus b 1977, Peter b 1982), 1 da (Emily b 1979); *Career* exec dir International Commodities Clearing House Ltd 1973–86; md London Traded Options Market 1986–92, md of fin and admin LIFFE 1992–; memb Ctee London Soc of CAs (chm London Business Bd); FCA; *Recreations* rugby, golf; *Style*— Anthony de Guingand; ✉ LIFFE, Cannon Bridge, London EC4R 3XX

de HAAS, Margaret Ruth; da of Joseph de Haas, of Charter Way, London, and Lisalotte Herte, *née* Meyer; *b* 21 May 1954; *Educ* Townsend Girls' Sch Bulawayo Zimbabwe, Univ of Bristol (LLB); *m* 18 May 1980, Iain Saville Goldrein, s of Neville Clive Goldrein, of Torreno, of Blundellsands, Crosby, Liverpool; 1 s (Alastair Philip b 1 Oct 1982), 1 da (Alexandra Ann b 22 Feb 1985); *Career* called to the Bar Middle Temple 1977, practising N Circuit, asst recorder; memb: Br Insur Law Assoc, Professional Negligence Bar Assoc, Family Law Bar Assoc; FRSA; *Books* Property Distribution on Divorce (2 edn with Iain S Goldrein, 1985), Personal Injury Litigation (with Iain S Goldrein, 1985), Domestic Injunctions (1987), Butterworths Personal Injury Litigation Service (with Iain S Goldrein), Family Court Practice (contrib, 1992), Structured Settlements (jt ed-in-chief with Iain S Goldrein, 1993), Medical Negligence (with Ian S Goldrein, 1996); *Recreations* family, swimming, law, theatre; *Style*— Miss Margaret de Haas; ✉ 5th Floor, Corn Exchange, Fenwick St, Liverpool L2 7QS (☎ 0151 227 5009, fax 0151 236 1120, car 0836 583257); 12 King's Bench Walk, Temple, London EC4Y 7EL (☎ 0171 583 0811, fax 0171 583 7228); 4 Linden Ave, Blundellsands, Crosby, Liverpool L23 8UL (☎ 0151 924 2610)

de HAMEL, Christopher Francis Rivers; s of Dr Francis Alexander de Hamel, and Joan Littledale, *née* Pollock; *b* 20 Nov 1950; *Educ* Otago Univ NZ (BA), Univ of Oxford (DPhil); *m* 1, 1978 (m dis 1989); 2 s; m 2, 1993, Mette Tang Simpson, *née* Svendsen; *Career* Sotheby's: cataloguer of medieval manuscripts 1975–77, asst dir 1977–82, dir western & oriental manuscripts 1982–; Hon LittD St John's Univ Minnesota 1994; FSA 1981, FRHistS 1986; *Books* Glossed Books of the Bible and the Origins of the Paris Booktrade (1984), A History of Illuminated Manuscripts (1986, 2 edn 1994), Medieval & Renaissance Manuscripts in New Zealand (with M Manion and V Vines, 1989), Syon Abbey, the Library of the Bridgettine Nuns and their Peregrinations after the Reformation (1991), Scribes and Illuminators (1992); various reviews, articles and catalogues; *Clubs* Grolier (NY), Association Internationale de Bibliophilie (Paris); *Style*— Christopher de Hamel, Esq, FSA; ✉ Sotheby's, 34/35 New Bond St, London W1A 2AA (☎ 0171 408 5330, fax 0171 408 5960)

de HAVILLAND, John Anthony; s of Maj-Gen Peter Hugh de Havilland, CBE, DL (d 1989), and Helen Elizabeth Wrey (d 1976), da of William Whitmore Otter-Barry, of Horkesley Hall, Colchester; *b* 14 April 1938; *Educ* Eton, Trinity Coll Cambridge; *m* 1964, Hilary Anne, da of Robert Ewen MacKenzie (d 1993), of Ulceby, Lincs; 1 s (Piers b 1970), 2 da (Lucinda b 1965, Victoria b 1968); *Career* joined J Henry Schroder Wagg & Co Ltd 1959 (md 1971–90), ret 1990; chm Nat Rifle Assoc 1990–, capt England VIII 1979–93, shot for England 1961–96, winner Match Rifle Championship at Bisley nine times since 1963; *Recreations* shooting and rifle shooting; *Style*— John de Havilland, Esq; ✉ Cottesloe Lodge, Bisley Camp, Brookwood, Surrey GU24 0NY

de HOGHTON, Sir (Richard) Bernard Cuthbert; 14 Bt (E 1611), of Hoghton Tower, Lancashire, DL (Lancs); s of Sir Cuthbert de Hoghton, 12 Bt (d 1958), and half-brother of Sir (Henry Philip) Anthony Mary de Hoghton, 13 Bt (d 1978); *b* 26 Jan 1945; *Educ* Ampleforth, McGill Univ Montreal (BA), Birmingham Univ (MA); *m* 1974, Rosanna Stella Virginia, da of Terzo Buratti, of Florence; 1 s (Thomas James Daniel Adam b 1980), 1 da (Elena Susannah Isabella b 1976); *Heir* s, Thomas James Daniel Adam de Hoghton b 11 April 1980; *Career* landowner; investment banker with Teather & Greenwood & Co, Turner and Newall & Co Ltd 1967–71; sr exec: Vickers da Costa & Co 1971–77, de Zoete & Bevan & Co 1977–86 (ptnr 1984–86); dir: BZW Securities Ltd 1986–89, Brown Shipley & Co 1990–94; lay rector of Preston; memb: Country Lanowners' Assoc, Historic Houses Assoc; patron: Int Spinal Research Tst, Auto-Cycle Union; MSI (dip), assoc European Soc of Investment Analysts; Knight SMO Malta, Knight Constantinian Order of St George; *Recreations* skiing, shooting, tennis; *Clubs* Royal Over-Seas League; *Style*— Sir Bernard de Hoghton, Bt, DL; ✉ Hoghton Tower, Hoghton, Preston, Lancs PR5 0SH (☎ 01254 852986, fax 01254 852109)

de JONGH, Nicholas; s of Cyril Windsor de Jongh (d 1981), of Esher, Surrey, and Margaret, *née* Whitelaw (d 1990); *b* 13 Jan 1938; *Educ* St Edward's Sch Oxford; *m* 7 June 1975, Elizabeth Jane, da of Dr Richard Norman (d 1961), of Fakenham, Norfolk; 1 s (Alexander b 1977), 1 da (Miranda b 1982); *Career* Nat Serv Army 1956–58; dir Engrg Employers Fedn 1979–94 (joined 1975), corp dir public affrs GKN plc 1994–; memb various orgns involved in promotion of careers in engrg; FRSA 1986; *Recreations* writing, gardening, pictures; *Clubs* Carlton; *Style*— Nicholas de Jongh, Esq; ✉ 22 Campion Rd, London SW15 6NW (☎ 0181 785 6928); Netherfield, The Street, Sharrington, Norfolk NR24 2AB; GKN plc, 7 Cleveland Row, London SW1A 1DB (☎ 0171 930 2424, fax 0171 839 3638)

de JONQUIERES, Guy; s of Maurice de Fauque de Jonquières, of London, and late Pauline de Jonquières; *b* 14 May 1945; *Educ* Lancing, Exeter Coll Oxford; *m* 1977, Diana Elizabeth, da of T V N Fortescue; 2 s (Alexander b 1981, Julian b 1983); *Career* graduate trainee Reuters 1966–68; Financial Times: staff corr 1968–80 (Paris, Washington, Saigon, NY, Brussels), electronics indust corr 1980–86, int business ed 1986–; *Recreations* reading, travel; *Style*— Guy de Jonquières, Esq; ✉ The Financial Times, 1 Southwark Bridge, London SE1 9HL (☎ 0171 873 3651, fax 0171 405 5700)

de la BÉDOYÈRE, Comtesse Michael; Charlotte; *née* Halbik; *b* 24 Nov 1931; *Educ* The Old Palace Mayfield Sussex; *m* 1960, as his 2 w, Comte Michael de la Bédoyère, sometime ed Catholic Herald and gs through his f of Alexis Huchet, Marquis de la Bédoyère (who m 1869 Hon Mildred Greville-Nugent, da of 1 Baron Greville); Charles Huchet de la Bédoyère was cr Comte 1710 and was Procureur-Général of the Bretagne Parlement, while another Huchet was cr Comte 1815 by Napoleon; Bertrand Huchet, Seigneur de la Huchetais and Sec of State to Jean V, Duke of Brittany, m c 1420 Jeanne de la Bédoyère, Dame de la Bédoyère; Comte Michael was gs through his mother of Dr A Thorold, sometime Bishop of Winchester; 2 c; *Career* md and chm Search Press Ltd/Burns & Oates Ltd (publishers to the Holy See since 1842), dir Women's Health Concern; MInstD; *Recreations* gardening, swimming, photography; *Style*— Comtesse

Michael de la Bédoyère; ✉ Spey House, Mayfield, E Sussex; Wellwood, North Farm Rd, Tunbridge Wells, Kent TN2 3DR (☎ 01892 510850)

de la BEDOYERE, Count Quentin Michael Algar; s of Count Michael de la Bedoyere (d 1973), and Catherine, *née* Thorold (d 1959); *b* 23 Nov 1934; *Educ* Beaumont Coll Old Windsor Berks, LAMDA; *m* 28 July 1956, Irene Therese Philippa, da of late Martyn Gough; 2 s (Guy Martyn Thorold b 28 Nov 1957, Raoul Maurice Greville Huchet, *qv* b 20 Aug 1959), 3 da (Catherine Christina Mansel b 20 April 1961, Camilla Louise Nugent b 27 Sept 1963, Christina Sibyl Montagu b 15 April 1966); *Career* Nat Serv 2 Lt RASC 1953–55; Jacqmar Ltd 1956–57; Sun Life of Canada: sales rep 1957, field mgmnt 1960, London Head Office 1972, field trg offr 1972–76, mktg offr 1976–79, dir mktg devpt and PR 1980, vice pres individual product mktg 1984, vice pres planning and devpt 1987–90, vice pres product mgmnt 1990–94, md Sun Life of Canada Unit Managers Limited 1994– (dir 1990–); *Books* The Doctrinal Teaching of the Church (1963), The Family (1975), Barriers and Communication (1976), The Remaking of Marriages (1978), Managing People and Problems (1988), How to Get Your Own Way in Business (1990), Getting What You Want (1994); *Recreations* freelance writing, public speaking, motorcycling, grandchildren; *Style*— Count de la Bedoyere; ✉ 10 Edge Hill, Wimbledon, London SW19 4LP (☎ and fax 0181 946 7166)

de la BÉDOYÈRE, (Count) Raoul Maurice Greville Huchet; s of Count Quentin de la Bedoyere, *qv*, of London, and Irene, *née* Gough; *b* 20 Aug 1959; *Educ* KCS Wimbledon, Wimbledon Coll, Univ of Birmingham (BA); *m* 24 Nov 1989, Sally Jean, da of Frank Carswell; 1 da (Eléonore Frances Kallisto b 2 April 1993), 1 s (Zacharie Adam Kronos b 28 Jan 1996); *Career* media sales VNU Publications 1982–84, media buyer Foote Cone and Belding advtg 1984–86, media planner Davidson Pearce 1986–87, bd account planner Gold Greenlees Trott 1991–92 (media planner 1987–91); planning dir: Woollams Moira Gaskin O'Malley 1994–95 (account planner 1992–94), Burkitt Edwards Martin 1995; account planner Bates Dorland 1995–; *Recreations* motorcycling on my Ducati, scuba diving, decorative painting; *Style*— Raoul de la Bédoyère, Esq

DE LA BERE, Sir Cameron; 2 Bt (UK 1953), of Crowborough, Co Sussex; s of Sir Rupert De la Bère, 1 Bt, KCVO (d 1978), Lord Mayor of London 1952–53, and Marguerite (d 1969), eldest da of Lt-Col Sir John Humphery; *b* 12 Feb 1933; *Educ* Tonbridge and abroad; *m* 20 June 1964, Clairemonde, only da of Casimir Kaufmann, of Geneva; 1 da (Réjane (Mrs Michel Lacoste) b 1965); *Heir* bro, Adrian De la Bère b 17 Sept 1939; *Career* jeweller; Liveryman Worshipful Co of Skinners; *Clubs* Société Litéraire (Geneva), Hurlingham; *Style*— Sir Cameron De la Bère, Bt; ✉ 1 Avenue Theodore Flournoy, 1207 Geneva, Switzerland (☎ 00 41 22 786 00 15)

de la MARE, Prof Albinia Catherine; OBE (1993); da of Richard Herbert Ingpen de la Mare (d 1986), and Amy Catherine, *née* Donaldson (d 1968); sis of Giles de la Mare, *qv*; *b* 2 June 1932; *Educ* Queens Coll Harley St London, Lady Margaret Hall Oxford (BA, MA), Warburg Inst Univ of London (PhD); *Career* asst librarian Bodleian Library Oxford 1964–88 (temp cataloguer 1962–64), prof of palaeography King's Coll London 1989–; memb: Civil Def Corps 1965–68, Nat Voluntary Civil Aid Oxford 1968, Comité International de Paléographie Latine 1986– (memb Bureau 1991–); hon fell Lady Margaret Hall Oxford 1989; FRHistS, FBA 1987, FSA 1990; *Books* Catalogue of the Italian Manuscripts of Major J R Abbey (with J Alexander, 1969), Catalogue of the Lyell Manuscripts in the Bodleian Library Oxford (1971), Handwriting of Italian Humanists I (1973), Miniatura Fiorentina del Rinascimento (contrib, 1985); *Recreations* gardening, listening to music, travel; *Style*— Prof Albinia de la Mare, OBE, FBA, FSA; ✉ Department of English, King's College, London WC2R 2LS (☎ 0171 873 2916, fax 0171 873 2257)

de la MARE, (Walter) Giles Ingpen; s of Richard Herbert Ingpen de la Mare (d 1986), of Much Hadham, Herts, and Amy Catherine, *née* Donaldson (d 1968); bro of Prof Albinia de la Mare, OBE, FBA, FSA, *qv*; *b* 21 Oct 1934; *Educ* Eton, Trinity Coll Oxford (MA); *m* 10 Aug 1968, Ursula Alice, da of Nigel Oliver Willoughby Steward, OBE (d 1991), of Cullompton, Devon; 1 s (Joshua b 1969), 1 da (Catherine b 1971); *Career* Nat Serv RN 1953–55, Midshipman RNVR 1954 (Sub Lt 1955); dir: Faber and Faber Ltd 1969–, Faber Music Ltd 1977–87, Geoffrey Faber Holdings Ltd 1990–, Giles de la Mare Publishers 1995–; Publishers Assoc: chm Univ Coll and Professional Publishers Cncl 1982–84, memb Cncl 1982–85, chm Copyright Ctee 1988, chm Freedom to Publish Ctee 1992–95; memb: Freedom to Publish Ctee Int Publishers Assoc 1993–96, Stefan Zweig Ctee Br Library 1986–95; literary tstee Walter de la Mare 1982–; *Books* The Complete Poems of Walter de la Mare (ed, 1969), Publishing Now (contrib gen chapter, 1993), Short Stories 1895–1926 by Walter de la Mare (ed, 1996); *Recreations* music (performance and listening), art and architecture, photography, exploring remote places; *Clubs* Garrick; *Style*— Giles de la Mare, Esq; ✉ c/o Faber and Faber Ltd, 3 Queen Square, London WC1N 3AU (☎ 0171 465 0045)

de la RUE, Sir Andrew George Ilay; 4 Bt (UK 1898), of Cadogan Square, Chelsea, Co London; s of Sir Eric Vincent de la Rue, 3 Bt (d 1989), and his 1 w, Cecilia (d 1963), da of Maj Walter Waring, DL, MP (d 1930); *b* 3 Feb 1946; *Educ* Millfield; *m* 1984, Tessa Ann, er da of David Dobson, of Stragglethorpe Grange, Lincoln; 2 s (Edward Walter Henry b 25 Nov 1986, Harry William John b 27 July 1989); *Heir* s, Edward Walter Henry de la Rue b 25 Nov 1986; *Style*— Sir Andrew de la Rue, Bt; ✉ Stragglethorpe Grange, Brant Broughton, Lincs (☎ 01636 626505); 27 Kersley Street, London SW11 (☎ 0171 585 1254)

de la TOUR, Frances; da of Charles de la Tour (d 1983), and Moyra de la Tour, *née* Fessas (now Mrs Silberman); family of the painter Georges de la Tour (d 1652); *b* 30 July 1945; *Educ* Lycee Francais de Londres, Drama Centre London; *children* 1 da (Tamasin Kempinski b 12 Nov 1973), 1 s (Josh Kempinski b 7 Feb 1977); *Career* actress; *Theatre* RSC 1965–71: various roles incl Helena in Peter Brook's prodn of A Midsummer Night's Dream; other credits incl: Violet in Small Craft Warnings (Hampstead and Comedy (Best Supporting Actress Plays and Players Awards)) 1973, Ruth Jones in The Banana Box (Apollo) 1973, Isabella in The White Devil (Old Vic) 1976, Eleanor Marx in Landscape of Exiles (Half Moon) 1978, title role in Hamlet (Half Moon) 1979, Stephanie in Duet for One (Bush and Duke of York's (Standard Best Actress, Critics' Best Actress, SWET Best Actress in a New Play Awards)) 1980, Jean in Skirmishes (Hampstead) 1982, Sonya in Uncle Vanya (Haymarket) 1982, Josie in A Moon for the Misbegotten (Riverside and Mermaid (SWET Best Actress in a Revival Award)) 1983, title role in St Joan (NT) 1984, Dance of Death (Riverside) 1985, Sonya and Masha in Chekhov's Women (Lyric) 1985, Brighton Beach Memoirs (NT) 1986, Lillian (Lyric and Fortune) 1986, Facades (Lyric Hammersmith) 1988, Regan in King Lear (Old Vic) 1989, Olga Knipper in Chekhov's Women (Moscow Lytcée Theatre and a special performance at Moscow Arts Theatre) 1990, When She Danced 1991 (Globe (Best Supporting Actress Olivier Awards 1992)), The Pope and the Witch (Comedy) 1992, Greasepaint (Lyric Hammersmith) 1993, Les Parents Terribles (RNT (nominated Olivier Award for Best Actress)) 1994, Three Tall Women (Wyndham's) 1995, The Fire Raisers (Riverside Studios) 1995, Blinded by the Sun (RNT) 1996; *Television* incl: Play for Today (BBC) 1973 and 1975, Rising Damp (series, YTV) 1974–76, Flickers (series, ITV) 1980, Duet for One 1985 (BBC (BAFTA Best Actress nomination)), Ghengis Cohn (TV film) 1994, Dennis Potter's Cold Lazarus (BBC/Channel 4 TV Film); *Films* incl: Rising Damp 1979 (Standard Best Film Actress Award 1980); *Style*— Ms Frances de la Tour; ✉ c/o Kate Feast Management, 10 Primrose Hill Studios, Fitzroy Road, London NW1 8TR (☎ 0171 586 5502, fax 0171 586 9817)

DE LA WARR, 11 Earl (GB 1761); William Herbrand Sackville; also Baron De La Warr (E 1299 and 1570), Viscount Cantelupe (GB 1761), and Baron Buckhurst (UK 1864); er s of 10 Earl De La Warr, DL (d 1988); *b* 10 April 1948; *Educ* Eton; *m* 1978, Anne, *née* Leveson, former w of Earl of Hopetoun (s of 3 Marq of Linlithgow); 2 s (Lord Buckhurst b 1979, Hon Edward b 1980); *Heir* s, William Herbrand Thomas, Lord Buckhurst b 13 June 1979; *Career* farmer, Shetland Pony breeder and stockbroker; Mullens & Co 1976–81, Credit Lyonnais Laing 1981–; pres Sussex Youth Assoc; *Recreations* country pursuits; *Clubs* White's, Turf; *Style*— The Rt Hon the Earl De La Warr; ✉ Buckhurst Park, Withyham, E Sussex; 14 Bourne St, London SW1

de LANGE, Rabbi Dr Nicholas Robert Michael; s of George Douglas de Lange, of London, and Elaine, *née* Jacobus; *b* 7 Aug 1944; *Educ* Christ Church Oxford (MA, DPhil, James Mew Rabbinic Hebrew prize), Leo Baeck Coll London (Rabbinic dipl); *m* 6 Sept 1990, Patricia, *née* Touton-Victor; *Career* Parkes Library fell Univ of Southampton 1969–71; Univ of Cambridge: lectr in Rabbinics 1971–95, fell Wolfson Coll 1984–, reader in Hebrew and Jewish studies 1995–; memb: Br Assoc for Jewish Studies 1974– (past pres), Cncl Jewish Historical Soc of England 1975–, Ctee The Translators Assoc 1990–93, Soc of Authors; founding ed (with Judith Humphrey) Bulletin of Judeo-Greek Studies 1987–; *Books* Origen and the Jews (1976), Apocrypha - Jewish Literature of the Hellenistic Age (1978), Origène - Philocalie 1–20 (with Marguerite Harl, 1983), Atlas of the Jewish World (1984), Judaism (1986), Greek Jewish Texts from the Cairo Genizah (1996); trans from the Hebrew of 11 Amos Oz books; author of numerous articles in jls and pubns; *Recreations* travel, phellology (study and collection of corks); *Style*— Rabbi Dr Nicholas de Lange; ✉ Faculty of Divinity, The Divinity School, St John's Street, Cambridge CB2 1TW (☎ 01223 332590, fax 01223 332582)

de LASZLO, Damon Patrick; only s of Patrick David de Laszlo (d 1980), and Deborah, *née* Greenwood (d 1980), da of 1 Viscount Greenwood PC, KC, and gs of Philip de Laszlo (d 1937), the portrait painter; *b* 8 Oct 1942; *Educ* Gordonstoun; *m* 1972, Hon Sandra Daphne, da of 2 Baron Hacking (d 1971); 2 s (Robert b 1977, William b 1979), 1 da (Lucy b 1975); *Career* co dir; chm Economic Res Cncl 1980–, chm Harwin plc; memb Bd Fedn of Electronic Industries; *Recreations* shooting, scuba diving, economics; *Clubs* Boodle's, City of London; *Style*— Damon de Laszlo, Esq; ✉ A2 Albany, Piccadilly, London W1V 9RD (☎ 0171 437 1982); Pelham Place, Newton Valance, Alton, Hampshire GU34 3NQ (☎ 01420 588212)

de LÉZARDIÈRE, Comte Alec; *b* 16 Dec 1948; *Educ* Ecole Polytechnique Paris, Univ of Stanford (MBA); *m* Isabelle; 2 s (Charles b 13 June 1980, Joachim b 16 May 1984), 2 da (Angelique b 17 Jan 1983, Ludivine b 16 Jan 1989); *Career* Paribas Ltd: joined 1974, an md 1989–, currently head of equities; *Recreations* opera, golf, shooting, skiing; *Clubs* Jockey (Paris), Automobile (Paris), Wentworth; *Style*— Comte Alec de Lezardiere, Esq; ✉ Head of Equities, Paribas Capital Markets Group, 33 Wigmore St, London W1H 0BN (☎ 0171 895 2655, fax 0171 895 2555)

de LISI, Benedetto (Ben); s of Vincent Michael de Lisi, of 711 Blydenburgh Rd, Hauppauge, Long Island, NY, USA, and Palma Aida, *née* Afflitto; *b* 31 May 1955; *Educ* Hauppauge HS Hauppauge Long Island NY, Suffold Community Coll Long Island NY, Pratt Inst of Fine Arts Brooklyn NY USA; *Career* fashion designer; fndr: Benedetto Inc menswear 1980–82, Ci Boure restaurant Belgravia (with ptnr J L Journade) 1982, Benedetto Ltd producing Ben de Lisi label 1982–91; fndr dir BDL (Design) Ltd 1991–; IWS Freestyle Awards 1987, nominated Most Innovative Designer of the Year 1990, winner Glamour category British Fashion Awards 1994 and 1995 (nominated 1992); *Style*— Ben de Lisi, Esq; ✉ 6a Poland Street, Soho, London W1V 3DG (☎ 0171 734 0089, fax 0171 494 0651)

de LISLE, Everard John Robert March Phillipps; DL (Leics 1980); s of Maj John Adrian Frederick March Phillipps de Lisle, DL (d 1961), of Stockerston Hall, Leics, and Elizabeth Muriel Smythe, *née* Guinness (d 1974); *b* 8 June 1930; *Educ* Eton, RMA Sandhurst; *m* 2 April 1959, Hon Mary Rose Peake, da of 1 Viscount Ingleby, PC (d 1966), of Snilesworth, Northallerton, Yorks; 2 s (Charles b 1960, Tim de Lisle, *qv*, b 1962), 1 da (Rosanna b 1968); *Career* cmmd RHG (The Blues) 1950, Capt 1954, Maj 1960, ret 1962; London Stock Exchange 1963– (memb 1965); tstee Henry Smith Charity 1981–; High Sheriff Leics 1974, vice Lord Lt Leics 1990; *Recreations* shooting, tennis, swimming; *Clubs* MCC, Leicestershire Far and Near; *Style*— Everard de Lisle, Esq, DL; ✉ Stockerston Hall, Oakham, Leics LE15 9JD (☎ 01572 822404, fax 01572 822177); 11 Buckingham Court, Kensington Park Road, London W11 3BP (☎ 0171 229 4120)

DE L'ISLE, Maj 2 Viscount (UK 1956), of Penshurst, Co Kent; Philip John Algernon Sidney; 10 Bt (UK 1806), of Castle Goring, Co Sussex, and 8 Bt (UK 1818), of Penshurst Place, Co Kent, MBE (1977), DL (Kent 1996); also Baron De L'Isle and Dudley (UK 1835); o s of 1 Viscount De L'Isle, VC, KG, GCMG, GCVO, PC (d 1991), and his 1 w, Hon Jacqueline Corinne Yvonne, *née* Vereker (d 1962), da of FM 6 Viscount Gort, VC, GCB, CBE, DSO, MC; *b* 21 April 1945; *Educ* Tabley House Cheshire; *m* 15 Nov 1980, Isobel Tresyllian, da of Sir Edmund Gerald Compton, GCB, KBE; 1 s (Hon Philip William Edmund b 2 April 1985), 1 da (Hon Sophia Jacqueline Mary b 25 March 1983); *Heir* s, Hon Philip William Edmund b 2 April 1985; *Career* cmmnd Grenadier Gds 1966, served BAOR, NI and Belize, GSO3 Ops/SD HQ 3 Inf Bde NI 1974–76, ret 1979, Hon Col 5 Bn Princess of Wales Royal Regt (Queen's and Royal Hampshires) 1992–; farmer and landowner; memb Ctee CLA Kent (chm 1983–85); Freeman City of London, Liveryman Worshipful Co of Goldsmiths; *Clubs* White's, Pratt's; *Style*— The Viscount De L'Isle, MBE, DL; ✉ Penshurst Place, Penshurst, Tonbridge, Kent TN11 8DG (☎ 01892 870307)

de LISLE, Timothy John March Phillipps (Tim); s of Everard de Lisle, *qv*, of Stockerston, Leics, and Hon Mary Rose, *née* Peake, da of 1 Viscount Ingleby (d 1966); *b* 25 June 1962; *Educ* Eton, Worcester Coll Oxford (exhibitioner, BA); *m* 1991, Amanda, da of Clive Barford, of Aldworth, Berks; 1 s (Daniel b 24 Jan 1994); *Career* freelance journalist 1979–86, fndr Undergraduate Tutors 1983–87; The Daily Telegraph: diary reporter 1986–87, chief rock critic 1986–89, gen reporter 1987, news feature writer 1987–89, ed Weekend Section 1989–90; arts ed The Times 1989; The Independent on Sunday: cricket corr 1990–91, arts ed 1991–95; freelance arts and sports writer 1995– (cricket columnist The Independent, arts feature writer The Independent on Sunday and The Daily Telegraph, contrib Harpers & Queen, The Economist, The Sunday Telegraph Magazine); ed Wisden Cricket Monthly 1996–; memb NUJ 1983–; *Publications* Lives of the Great Songs (ed, 1994, revised and expanded edn, 1995); *Recreations* swimming, television, books, films; *Clubs* Cricket Writers', Eton Ramblers; *Style*— Tim de Lisle, Esq; ✉ 63 College Cross, London N1 1PT (☎ 0171 619 0014, fax 0171 619 0015)

DE LOS ANGELES, Victoria; *b* 1 Nov 1923; *Educ* Escoles Milá i Fontanals de la Generlitat de Catalumya Barcelona, Conservatorio de Liceo Barcelona (hons grad completed the 6 year course in 3 years); *m* 1948, Enrique Magriná (dec'd); 2 s; *Career* lyric soprano, opera and concert artiste; concert debut de la Musica Catalana Barcelona 1944, opera debut Gran Teatro del Liceo Barcelona 1945, concert and opera tours of Europe, North America, Central and S America, South Africa, Middle and Far East, Aust, New Zealand, Thailand, Korea, Philippines, Singapore, Hong Kong and most E European countries 1945–; repertoire of over 1000 German Lieder, French art songs and Spanish songs; operatic repertoire incl: Marriage of Figaro, Lohengrin, Tannhäuser, Die Meistersinger, Trautatz, Cavelleria Rusticana, I Pagliacci, La Boheme, Madame Butterfly, Manon; first prize Concord International Geneva 1947, Gold medal Barcelona 1958, medal Premio Roma 1969, numerous French, Italian and Dutch awards; Gold disc for 5 million records sold; Hon Doctorate Univ of Barcelona; Cross of Lazo de Dama Spain, Condecoracion Banda de la Orden Civil de Alfonso X (El Sabio) Spain; *Style*— Miss V De Los Angeles; ✉ Avenida de Pedralbes 57, 08034 Barcelona, Spain; c/o Nicholas Curry, Clarion/Seven Muses, 47 Whitehall Park, London N19 3TW (☎ 0171 272 4413, fax 0171 281 9687)

DE LOTBINIÈRE, *see:* Joly de Lotbinière

de MAULEY, 6 Baron (UK 1838); Gerald John Ponsonby; s of 5 Baron de Mauley (d 1962); *b* 19 Dec 1921; *Educ* Eton, Ch Ch Oxford (BA, MA); *m* 1954, Helen, widow of Lt-Col Brian Abdy Collins, OBE, MC, and da of Hon Charles Sholto Douglas (d 1960, 2 s of 19 Earl of Morton); *Heir* bro, Hon Thomas Maurice Ponsonby, *qv*; *Career* Lt Leics Yeo, Capt RA, served 1939–45 (France); called to the Bar Middle Temple; *Style*— The Rt Hon Lord de Mauley; ✉ Langford House, Little Faringdon, Lechlade, Glos

de MEL, (John Chitrapri) Lalith; *b* 6 May 1937; *Educ* St Joseph's Coll Colombo Sri Lanka, Peterhouse Cambridge; *m* Shiranee; 1 da (Chiara); *Career* early career as research economist, lectr in economics and with Shell Sri Lanka; Reckitt & Colman plc: joined as mktg dir Sri Lanka 1964, various devpt projects with subsid Atlantis SA Brazil, md Reckitt & Colman Sri Lanka 1971–77, regnl dir Asia and Far E (based at corp head office London) 1977, i/c corp devpt in Far E (based Singapore) 1989–91, main bd dir i/c Asia, Far E and Australasia (based London) 1991–96, also i/c Africa 1994–96, gp dir of pharmaceuticals worldwide 1996–; *Clubs* Oriental, Lambourne Golf, Royal Colombo Golf; *Style*— Lalith de Mel, Esq; ✉ Reckitt & Colman plc, One Burlington Lane, London W4 2RW (☎ 0181 994 6464)

de MILLE, His Hon Judge Peter Noël; s of Noël James de Mille (d 1995), and Ailsa Christine, *née* Ogilvie; *b* 19 Nov 1944; *Educ* Fettes Coll, Trinity Coll Dublin (BA, LLB); *m* 17 Dec 1977, Angela Mary, da of Peter Cooper; 1 da (Charlotte Elizabeth b 17 June 1981); *Career* called to the Bar Inner Temple 1968, recorder of Crown Court (Midland and Oxford Circuit) 1987–92, circuit judge (Midland and Oxford Circuit) 1992–; *Recreations* music, theatre, sailing; *Clubs* Aldeburgh Yacht; *Style*— His Honour Judge de Mille; ✉ 5 Fountain Court, Steelhouse Lane, Birmingham B4 6DR (☎ 0121 606 0500, fax 0121 606 1501)

de MOLLER, June Frances; *b* 25 June 1947; *Educ* Roedean, Hastings Coll, Université de la Sorbonne; *m* 1967 (m dis 1980); *Career* md Carlton Communications Plc 1993– (dir 1983–); non-exec dir: Anglian Water plc 1992–, Riverside Mental Health NHS Trust 1992–96, Judge Inst Advsy Bd 1996–; *Recreations* reading, riding, tennis, the arts, memb Rare Breed Society; *Style*— Mrs June de Moller; ✉ Carlton Communications Plc, 25 Knightsbridge, London SW1X 7RZ (☎ 0171 663 6363, fax 0171 663 6300)

de MONTMORENCY, Sir Arnold Geoffroy; 19 Bt (I 1631), of Knockagh, Co Tipperary; s of James Edward Geoffrey de Montmorency (d 1934); suc cous, Sir Reginald d'Alton Lodge de Montmorency, 18 Bt, 1979; *b* 27 July 1908; *Educ* Westminster, Peterhouse Cambridge (MA, LLM); *m* 20 April 1949 (m annulled 1953), and remarried 1972, Nettie Hay, da of William Anderson of Morayshire; *Heir* none; *Career* War Serv RASC 1939–45 (Maj 1944–45); called to the Bar Middle Temple 1932, chm (pt/t) Industl Tbnls 1975–81, former chm Contemporary Review Cmmn; Parly candidate (Lib): Cambridge 1959, Cirencester and Tewkesbury 1964; fndr and pres Friends of Peterhouse; *Books* Integration of Industrial Legislation (1984); *Clubs* Nat Liberal; *Style*— Sir Arnold de Montmorency, Bt

de MOUBRAY, Anthony Jankowski; s of Josef Orzel-Jankowski, VM (d 1967), and Barbara, *née* de Moubray (d 1964), of Aberdour, Fife; *b* 2 Oct 1946; *Educ* King's Sch Canterbury; *m* 13 Oct 1969, Danielle Marian, da of H L A Green; 1 s (Arran b 1970), 2 da (Selena b 1972, Barbara b 1979); *Career* chartered architect; sr ptnr Lee Evans de Moubray International; dir/tstee Sounds New Ltd; conslt: Portland Shipping Co, Southern Water plc; former chm Canterbury Chapter RIBA; fell Architects and Surveyors Inst, ARIBA; *Recreations* music, theatre, skiing; *Style*— Anthony de Moubray, Esq; ✉ Norham Grange, Selling, Nr Faversham, Kent (☎ 01227 752721, fax 01227 456345); Villa Aroca, Avenue d'Alsace, Le Rayol-Canadel, Var, France

de NAHLIK, Wing Commander Andrew Julius Adolph; s of Wiktor Nahlik (d 1963), and Marja, *née* Rucker; *b* 27 Feb 1920; *Educ* Tech Univ of Lwow Poland (BEng), Univ of Bath (Dip industl admin); *m* 8 July 1943, Anne Ella Renee, da of Maj H Milton (d 1969); 2 s (Christopher Andrew Victor b 28 June 1945, Philip Adam Charles b 1 June 1950); *Career* Polish Air Force serv France 1940, UK 1940–47 (interpreter, fighter pilot, flying instr, staff offr); RAF 1947–68: RAF Eastleigh Nairobi 1961–65, dir of studies Cmd and Staff Sch RAF Ternhill 1965–67, dir Sr Offrs Mgmnt Courses RAF Upavon, ret Wing Cdr 1968; personnel devpt mangr Satchwell Controls (GEC) 1969–72, manpower devpt mangr Bristol Myers Co 1973–83; freelance lectr and conslt on deer mgmnt, head Br Deer Soc Ctee (developing a syllabus of deer mgmnt studies for Univs and Colls) 1986–89; co-ordinator and lectr Woodland Deer Mgmnt Courses RAC Cirencester; MIMgt, MIPM; fell Br Deer Soc 1993; Cross of Merit with Swords (Poland) 1942; *Books* Wild Deer (1958), Deer Management (1978), Revised Wild Deer (1987), Principles and Methods of Deer and Habitat Management (1992); *Recreations* deer stalking, game shooting, fly fishing, photography; *Clubs* Royal Air Force; *Style*— Wing Commander Andrew de Nahlik; ✉ 3 Mount Pleasant, Kilmington, Warminster, Wilts BA12 6RC (☎ 01985 844749)

DE NARDIS DI PRATA, Mainardo; s of Balduccio de Nardis di Prata, of London, and Simonetta Vallarino Gancia; *b* 24 Nov 1960; *Educ* Bedales, Univ Bocconi Milan (Economics); *m* 2 July 1988, Christiana Clerici di Cavenago; 2 s (Alberico b 14 Feb 1992, Gaerardo b 19 March 1994); *Career* McCann Erickson Rome 1980–81, Young and Rubicam Milan 1981–83, fndr ptnr Alberto Cremona 1983–85, vice chm Medianetwork Group Italy 1987–93 (merged with CIA 1993), md CIA Group Europe Holdings and chm various gp cos in Europe 1993–; currently exec dir F W Gancia & C SpA Calelli Italy; chm MNI (Assoc of Euro Media Independents) 1988–93; *Books* La Mappa dei Media in Europa (The Map of European Media); *Recreations* ski, sailing, classic cars; *Clubs* Il Clubino Milan Italy (affiliated to Boodle's London); *Style*— Mainardo de Nardis Di Prata, Esq; ✉ 2 Kelso Place, London W8 5QD (☎ 0171 937 8696, fax 0171 937 6367); CIA Group Europe Holdings, 1 Paris Garden, London SE1 8NU (☎ 0171 803 2254, fax 0171 261 1226, mobile 0385 504362)

de NAVARRO, Michael Antony; QC (1990); s of Alma José Maria de Navarro (d 1979), of Broadway, Worcs, and Agnes Dorothy McKenzie, *née* Hoare (d 1987); *b* 1 May 1944; *Educ* Downside, Trinity Coll Cambridge (BA); *m* 20 Dec 1975, Jill Margaret, da of Charles Walker, of Southwell, Notts; 1 s (Antony Charles b 1980), 2 da (Katharine Mary b 1978, Frances Anne b 1982); *Career* called to the Bar Inner Temple 1968, recorder Western Circuit 1990–; *Recreations* opera, cricket; *Clubs* MCC; *Style*— Michael de Navarro, Esq, QC; ✉ 2 Temple Gardens, Temple, London EC4Y 9AY (☎ 0171 583 6041, fax 0171 583 2094, telex 885040)

de NORMANN, John Anthony; OBE (1989); s of Sir Eric de Normann, KBE, CB (d 1982), of Surrey, and Winifred Scott, *née* Leigh (d 1968); *b* 25 Jan 1923; *Educ* Westminster, ChCh Oxford (MA); *m* 1959, Diana, da of Charles Phipps (d 1960), of Wilts; 2 s (Roderick b 1959, Anthony b 1961); *Career* Capt RA Far East 1942–45; ICI 1947–80, chm Farrow Gp 1970–80; cncllr: Economic and Social Consultative Assembly, European Community Brussels 1982–90; dir Nat Cncl of Building Material Prodrs 1975–95; memb Bd BSI 1984–86, chm Wilts Archaeologial and Natural History Soc 1990–93; *Recreations* book collecting, gardening, travel, motoring; *Clubs* White's; *Style*— John A de Normann, Esq, OBE; ✉ Lower Leaze, Box, nr Corsham, Wilts SN13 8DU (☎ 01225 742786)

de OSUNA, HE Sheelagh Marilyn; da of Henry Wells Macnaughton-Jones, and Cynthia, *née* Swan; *b* 25 March 1948, Pointe-à-Pierre, Trinidad; *Educ* St Michael's Sch Limpsfield Surrey, Univ of Sussex (BA Int Rels), Universidad Javeriana Bogota Colombia (Dip in Spanish Language), Centro Internacional de Idiomas Cordoba Spain (Dip in Spanish Language), Sch of Advanced Int Studies Washington DC (Dip), Int Law Inst Georgetown Univ (Dip); *children* 1 da (Natasha b 1 Feb 1977); *Career* diplomat of the Republic of Trinidad and Tobago; entered Foreign Serv 1970, second sec Perm Mission to the UN Geneva 1970–71, Foreign Serv offr I Miny of External Affrs 1971–72, first sec and consul Caracas 1972–77, Foreign Serv offr II then III Political and Economic Div Miny of External Affrs 1977–79, cnsllr (trade/economic affrs) Washington 1979–88, Foreign Serv offr III then IV Miny of External Affrs and Int Trade 1988–92 (dep and actg dir Int Economic Rels Div 1988–91, dir Marine and Legal Affrs Div 1991–92), dep high cmmr to the Ct of St James's 1992–95, ambass for trade Miny of Trade and Indust 1995–96, high cmmr to the Ct of St James's 1996–; *Recreations* opera, scuba diving, cooking; *Style*— HE Mrs Sheelagh de Osuna; ✉ High Commission of the Republic of Trinidad and Tobago, 42 Belgrave Square, London SW1X 8NT (☎ 0171 245 9351, fax 0171 823 1065)

de PASS, David Vincent Guy; s of Lt Cdr John Gerald Irvine de Pass, RN (d 1981), and Marie Elizabeth, *née* Eberhardt (d 1988); *b* 27 Aug 1949; *Educ* Harrow, George Washington Univ (MCL), LSE (LLM); *m* 14 April 1982 (m dis 1987), Angela, da of Peter Shand Kydd, of Ardencaple, Isle of Seil, Oban, Argyll; *Career* admitted slr 1973; admitted to the Bar of Dist of Columbia 1978, ptnr and head of private client dept Holman Fenwick & Willan 1986–; pubns in law jls and magazines, contrib to legal precedents book; memb: Law Soc, Phi Delta Phi Legal Fraternity; *Recreations* cricket, philately, music; *Clubs* Harrovian Rifle Assoc, Harrow Wanderers, Hurlingham; *Style*— David de Pass, Esq; ✉ Holman Fenwick & Willan, Marlow House, Lloyds Avenue, London EC3N 3AL (☎ 0171 488 2300, fax 0171 481 0316, HFWLON 8812247)

de PEYER, David Charles; *b* 25 April 1934; *Career* dir-gen Cancer Research Campaign 1984–96, ret; *Style*— David de Peyer, Esq

de PIRO, His Hon Alan Caesar Haselden; QC (1965); s of Joseph William de Piro (killed 1942), of Singapore, and Louise Bell Irvine; *b* 31 Aug 1919; *Educ* Repton, Trinity Hall Cambridge (MA); *m* 1, 1947, Mary Elliot (decd); 2 s; m 2, 1964, Mona Ursula Addington; 1 step s, 1 step da; *Career* Capt RA, served W Africa 1940–44; barr 1947, dep chm Warwicks QS and Bedford QS 1967–72, master of the Bench Middle Temple 1971–, reader 1989; recorder 1972–82, circuit judge (Midland and Oxford Circuit) 1983–91; vice pres and co-pres Union Internationale des Avocats 1968–73, memb Cncl Int Bar Assoc 1967–86; FCIArb 1978; *Recreations* canals, gardening, conversation; *Clubs* Hawks' (Cambridge); *Style*— His Hon Alan de Piro, QC; ✉ Toll House, Bascote Locks, Leamington Spa, Warwicks CV33 0DT; 23 Birmingham Road, Stoneleigh, Warwicks CV8 3DD

de QUINCEY, Paul Morrison; s of Ronald Anthony de Quincey, and Margaret Winifred Claire, *née* Dingley (d 1990); *b* 23 June 1954; *Educ* Sutton HS Plymouth, Univ of Leeds (MA, PGCE); *m* 1 May 1976, Teresa Elizabeth Patricia, *née* Casabayo; 1 da (Lara Claire b 8 April 1983), 1 s (Thomas Anthony b 16 Oct 1985); *Career* English teacher Esan Teacher Trg Coll Nigeria 1976–78, English master Wakefield Girls' HS 1979–81; British Council: asst rep Korea 1981–84, conslt 1984–87, asst rep Algeria 1987–91, dep dir Czechoslovakia 1991–93, dir Venezuela 1993–; *Recreations* fishing, shooting, tennis, squash; *Style*— Paul de Quincey, Esq; ✉ The British Council, Torre La Noria, Piso 6, Paseo Enrique Eraso, Las Mercedes/Sector San Roman, Caracas 1065, Venezuela

DE RAMSEY, 4 Baron (UK 1887); John Ailwyn Fellowes; DL (1993 Cambs); s of 3 Baron De Ramsey, KBE, TD, DL (d 1993), and Lilah Helen Suzanne, *née* Labouchere (d 1987); *b* 27 Feb 1942; *Educ* Winchester; *m* 1, 1973 (m dis 1983), Phyllida Mary, da of Philip Athelstan Forsyth; 1 s (Hon Freddie John b 1978); m 2, 1984, Alison Mary, er da of Sir Archibald Birkmyre, 3 Bt, *qv*; 1 s (Hon Charles Henry b 1986), 2 da (Hon Daisy Lilah b 1988, Hon Flora Mary b 1991); *Heir* s, Hon Freddie John Fellowes b 31 May 1978; *Career* farmer; dir Cambridge Water Co 1974–94 (chm 1983–89), pres CLA 1991–93, Crown Estate cmmr 1994–, chm Environment Agency 1995–; FRAgS 1993; *Recreations* fishing; *Clubs* Boodle's; *Style*— The Rt Hon Lord De Ramsey, DL; ✉ Abbots Ripton Hall, Abbots Ripton, Huntingdon, Cambs PE17 2PQ

de ROS, 28 Baron (E 1264); Peter Trevor Maxwell; Premier Baron of England; s of 27 Baroness de Ros (d 1983), and Cdr David Maxwell, RN; gs of Hon Mrs (Angela) Horn; *b* 23 Dec 1958; *Educ* Headfort Sch Kells, Stowe, Down HS Downpatrick; *m* 5 Sept 1987, Angela Siân, da of late Peter Campbell Ross; 1 s (Finbar James b 14 Nov 1988), 2 da (Katharine Georgiana Maxwell b 26 Oct 1990, Jessye Maeve Maxwell b 8 July 1992); *Heir* s, Hon Finbar James Maxwell b 14 Nov 1988; *Style*— The Rt Hon the Lord de Ros

DE ROTHSCHILD, *see:* Rothschild

de ROTHSCHILD, Edmund Leopold; CBE (1997), TD (and 2 Bars); s of Maj Lionel Nathan de Rothschild, OBE, JP (d 1942), of Exbury House, Exbury, nr Southampton, and Marie-Louise, *née* Beer; bro of Leopold de Rothschild, CBE, *qv*; *b* 2 Jan 1916; *Educ* Harrow, Trinity Coll Cambridge (MA); *m* 1, 22 June 1948, Elizabeth (d 1980), da of Marcel Lentner, of Vienna; 2 s (Nicholas David b 10 Oct 1951, David Lionel (twin) b 28 Nov 1955), 2 da (Katherine Juliette b 11 July 1949, Charlotte Henrietta b 28 Nov 1955); m 2, 26 April 1982, Anne Evelyn, JP, widow of J Malcolm Harrison, OBE; *Career* Maj RA (TA), served WWII, BEF, BNAF, CMF, France, N Africa, Italy (wounded); merchant banker; dir Rothschild Continuation Ltd 1975–95 (ptnr 1946, sr ptnr 1960–70, chm 1970–75); chm AUR Hydropower Ltd 1980–91; dep chm British Newfoundland Corp Canada 1963–69 (dir 1953–63); dep chm Churchill Falls (Labrador) Corp (Canada) 1966–69; pres Assoc of Jewish Ex-Servicemen and Women, pres Res into Ageing; HM Govt tstee Freedom from Hunger Campaign 1965–, vice pres Queens Nursing Inst; memb: Asia Ctee BNEC 1970–71 (chm 1971), Cncl Royal Nat Pension Fund for Nurses until 1996; Freeman City of London, Liveryman Worshipful Co of Fishmongers 1949; Hon LLD Memorial Univ of Newfoundland 1961, Hon DSc Salford 1983; Order of the Sacred Treasure (first class) Japan 1973; *Books* Window on the World (1949); *Recreations* fishing, gardening, golf; *Clubs* White's, Portland; *Style*— Edmund de Rothschild, Esq, CBE, TD; ✉ New Court, St Swithin's Lane, London EC4P 4DU (☎ 0171 280 5000, fax 0171 929 1643, telex 888031); Exbury House, Exbury, nr Southampton, Hants SO45 1AF (☎ 01703 893145)

de ROTHSCHILD, Baron Eric Alain Robert David; s of Baron (James Gustave Jules) Alain de Rothschild (d 1982), and Mary Germaine, *née* Chauvin du Treuil; *b* 3 Oct 1940; *Educ* Lycée Janson de Sailly Paris France, Polytechnicum of Zürich; *m* 21 Dec 1983, (Donna) Maria Beatrice, da of Don Alfonso Caracciolo di Forino (d 1990); 2 s (James Alain Robert Alexandro b 7 Dec 1985, Piétro Noé Genaro b 21 March 1991), 1 da (Anna Saskia Esther b 29 April 1987); *Career* managing ptnr Chateau Lafite Rothschild 1974–; chm: Paris Orleans SA 1975–, Rothschild Continuation Ltd London 1977–; dir: N M Rothschild & Sons Ltd London 1978, N M Rothschild Asset Management Ltd London 1989–, Chalone Inc San Francisco 1989–; ptnr Rothschild et Compagnie Banque 1987–; *Style*— Baron Eric de Rothschild; ✉ Rothschild & Co Banque, 17 Avenue Matignon, 75008 Paris, France (☎ 00 33 1 40 74 40 74, fax 00 33 1 45 63 78 86)

de ROTHSCHILD, Sir Evelyn Robert Adrian; kt (1989); s of Anthony de Rothschild, DL (d 1961, 3 s of Leopold de Rothschild, CVO, JP, 1 cousin Edmund de Rothschild, *qv*), and Yvonne, da of late Robert Cahen d'Anvers, of Paris; *b* 29 Aug 1931; *Educ* Harrow, Trinity Coll Cambridge; *m* 1, 1966 (m dis 1971), Jeanette (d 1981), da of Ernest Bishop; m 2, 1973, Victoria, da of Lewis Schott; 2 s (Anthony b 1977, David b 1978), 1 da (Jessica b 1974); *Career* chm: N M Rothschild & Sons Ltd, Economist Newspaper 1972–89 (dir until 1992); former non-exec directorships incl: IBM UK Ltd, Chemical Investment Bank Ltd, Manufacturers Hanover Ltd, The Daily Telegraph; govr LSE, pres St Mary's Hosp Med Sch; *Style*— Sir Evelyn de Rothschild; ✉ Ascott, Wing, Leighton Buzzard, Beds; N M Rothschild & Sons Ltd, New Court, St Swithin's Lane, London EC4P 4DU (☎ 0171 280 5000, fax 0171 220 7108)

de ROTHSCHILD, Leopold David; CBE (1985); 2 s of Maj Lionel de Rothschild, OBE, JP (d 1942); bro of Edmund de Rothschild, CB, TD, *qv*; *b* 12 May 1927; *Educ* Harrow, Trinity Coll Cambridge; *Career* dir: Sun Alliance & London Insurance 1982–95, N M Rothschild & Sons 1970–, Bank of England 1970–83; chm: English Chamber Orchestra and Music Soc Ltd, Bach Choir; tstee: Glyndebourne Arts Tst, Nat Museum of Sci and Indust 1987–; chm cncl Royal Coll of Music 1988–; memb Cncl Winston Churchill Meml Tst; Hon DUniv York 1991; Liveryman Worshipful Co of Musicians; FRCM; Order of Francisco de Miranda 1 class (Venezuela) 1978, Gran Oficial Order de Merito (Chile) 1993, Ordem Nacional Do Cruzeiro Do Sul (Brazil) 1993, Order of the Aztec Eagle Encomienda (Mexico) 1994; *Style*— Leopold de Rothschild Esq, CBE; ✉ N M Rothschild & Sons, New Court, St Swithin's Lane, London EC4P 4DU (☎ 0171 280 5000, fax 0171 929 1643)

de SAINTE CROIX, Dr Geoffrey Ernest Maurice; *b* 8 Feb 1910; *Educ* UCL (BA), Univ of Oxford (DLitt, MA); *m* 3 Sept 1959, Margaret, *née* Knight; 2 s; *Career* ancient historian; J H Gray lectr Univ of Cambridge 1973, Gregynog lectr Univ Coll of Wales Aberystwyth 1986, Townsend lectr Cornell Univ USA 1988; contrib to numerous learned jls; fell: New Coll Oxford 1953–77 (hon fell 1985), UCL 1987; memb Assoc of Univ Teachers, FBA 1972; *Books* Studies in the History of Accounting (jtly, 1956), The Crucible of Christianity (jtly, 1969), The Origins of the Peloponnesian War (1972), Debts, Credits, Finance and Profits (jtly, 1974), Studies in Ancient Society (jtly, 1974), The Class Struggle in the Ancient Greek World, From the Archaic Age to the Arab Conquests (1981, Isaac Deutscher Meml Prize 1982, revised edn 1983, Spanish edn 1988); *Style*— Dr G E M de Ste. Croix, FBA; ✉ Evenlode, Stonesfield Lane, Charlbury, Oxford OX7 3ER (☎ 01608 810453)

de SALABERRY, Count Pascal; s of Comte de Salaberry (d 1993), of France, and Gilberte, *née* Burrus (d 1992); *b* 15 Nov 1941; *Educ* Univ of Paris, Univ of Geneva; *Career* Banque Transatlantique Paris 1969–77, Ivory & Sime plc Edinburgh 1978–91; chm Sumitrust Ivory & Sime Ltd 1989–91 (md 1987); non-exec dir: Continental Assets Trust plc 1990, European Assets Trust NV 1991, Indépendance et Expansion SA 1992, Evalfi SA 1995; *Recreations* sports, bridge, backgammon, antiques; *Clubs* Jockey (Paris), Automobile Club de France (Paris); *Style*— Comte Pascal de Salaberry; ✉ 4 rue Paul Baudry, F75008 Paris, France

de SALIS, 9 Count (Holy Roman Empire 1748, cr by Francis I); John Bernard Philip Humbert de Salis; TD; also Hereditary Knight of the Golden Spur (1571); s of 8 Count de Salis (Lt-Col Irish Gds, d 1949), of Lough Gur, Co Limerick, and (Mary) Camilla, *née* Presti di Camarda (d 1953); descended from Peter, 1 Count de Salis-Soglio (1675–1749), Envoy of the Grisons Republic to Queen Anne; Jerome, 2 Count de Salis, was naturalised Br by Act of Parliament 1731 following his marriage to Mary, da and co-heiress of the last Viscount Fane; an earlier member of the family, Feldzeugmeister Rudolph von Salis, was cr a Baron of the HRE by the Emperor Rudolf II in 1582 for gallantry against the Turks; through Sophia, da of Adm Francis William Drake, w of Jerome, 4 Count de Salis, the family is heir-gen of Sir Francis Drake; the 8 Count's mother was Princess Hélène de Riquet, da of Prince Eugène de Caraman-Chimay (Prince of Chimay 1527 HRE by Maximilian I, Belgium 1889 by Leopold II), who was a descendant of Jean de Croy killed at Agincourt 1415 and gs of Thérèse de Cabarrus (Madame Tallien); *b* 16 Nov 1947; *Educ* Downside, CCC Cambridge (LLM); *m* 1, 1973 (m dis and annulled); m 2, Marie-Claude, 3 da of Col René-Henri Wüst, Swiss Army, of Zürich and Geneva; 1 s (Count John-Maximilian Henry b 3 Nov 1986), 2 da (twins b 20 Dec 1995); *Heir* s, Count John-Maximilian Henry de Salis b 3 Nov 1986; *Career* late Brevet Maj 9/12 Royal Lancers (Prince of Wales's), special offr Panzergrenadiers Swiss Army; called to the Bar Gray's Inn; delegate Int Ctee Red Cross Missions in Middle East, Africa, head of delgn Iraq 1980–81, Thailand 1981–84, special envoy in Lebanon 1982; ptnr Gautier Salis et Cie Geneva 1989–, vice chm Bank Lips Zurich 1996–; ambass of the Order of Malta: to Thailand 1986–, to Cambodia 1993–; pres Swiss Assoc of the Order of Malta 1995–; Knight of Honour and Devotion Sov Mil Order of Malta 1974, Gold Medal with Swords (Beirut) 1982, Knight of Justice Constantinian Order of St George, Knight Grand Cross Order of the White Elephant (Thailand), Knight Grand Cross of the Order of Merit of the Order of Malta with Swords; *Recreations* melancholia; *Clubs* Cavalry and Guards', Travellers', Beefsteak, Cercle de la Terasse (Geneva), Royal Bangkok Sports; *Style*— The Count de Salis, TD; ✉ Maison du Bailli, CH-1422 Grandson, Switzerland (☎ 00 41 24 445 1466, fax 00 41 24 445 3403); Gautier, Salis & Cie, 4 rue Jean-Petitot, CH-1204 Geneva, Switzerland (☎ 00 41 22 318 3030, fax 00 41 22 318 3050)

de SAUMAREZ, 7 Baron (UK 1831); Sir Eric Douglas Saumarez; er twin s of 6 Baron de Saumarez (d 1991), and Joan Beryl (Julia), *née* Charlton; *b* 13 Aug 1956; *Educ* Milton Abbey, Univ of Nottingham, RAC Cirencester; *m* 1, 14 July 1982 (m dis 1990), Christine Elizabeth, yr da of Bernard Neil Halliday, OBE, of Woodford Green, Essex; 2 da (Claire b 1984, Emily b 1985); m 2, 4 Sept 1991, Susan, *née* Hearn; *Heir* bro, Hon Victor Thomas Saumarez b (twin) 13 Aug 1956; *Career* farmer; *Recreations* shooting, fishing, flying; *Style*— The Rt Hon the Lord de Saumarez; ✉ Shrubland Park, Coddenham, Ipswich, Suffolk IP6 9QQ (☎ 01473 830449, fax 01473 832202)

de SAVARY, Peter John; *Educ* Charterhouse; *m* 1 (m dis), Marcia (now the Hon Lady (John) Astor); 2 da (Lisa, Nicola); m 2, 1985 (m dis 1986), Alice, *née* Simms; m 3, 1986, (Lucille Lana), *née* Paton; 3 da (Tara, Amber, Savannah Havana Noelle); *Career* entrepreneur (petroleum, property and maritime interests); America's Cup challenger 1983 and 1987; chm The Carnegie Club; Tourism Personality of the Year (English Tourist Bd) 1988; *Recreations* sailing, riding, carriage driving; *Clubs* St James's, Royal Thames Yacht, Royal Burnham Yacht, Royal Torbay Yacht, Royal Corinthian Yacht, Port Pendennis Yacht (Cdre); *Style*— Peter de Savary Esq; ✉ Skibo Castle, Clashmore, Dornoch, Sutherland IV25 3RQ

de SILVA, (George) Desmond Lorenz; QC (1984); s of Edmund Frederick Lorenz de Silva, MBE (d 1994), of Kandy, Sri Lanka, and Esme Norah Gregg de Silva (d 1982); *b* 13 Dec 1939; *Educ* privately; *m* 5 Dec 1987, HRH Princess Katarina of Yugoslavia, o da of HRH Prince Tomislav of Yugoslavia, and HGDH Princess Margarita of Baden, and ggggda of Queen Victoria; 1 da (Victoria Marie Esme Margarita b 6 Sept 1991); *Career* called to the Bar: Middle Temple 1964, Sierra Leone 1968, Gambia 1981, Gibraltar 1992; dep circuit judge 1976–80, head of chambers; memb: Home Affrs Standing Ctee Bow Gp 1982, Editorial Advsy Bd Crossbow 1984; vice pres St John Ambulance London (Prince of Wales Dist) 1984–; councilman City of London (Ward of Farringdon Without) 1980–95; landowner (Taprobane Island in the Indian Ocean); Freeman City of London, Liveryman Worshipful Co of Fletchers, Liveryman Worshipful Co of Gunmakers; KStJ 1994 (CStJ 1985, OStJ 1980); *Recreations* politics, shooting, travel; *Clubs* Brooks's, Carlton, City Livery, Orient (Colombo); *Style*— Desmond de Silva Esq, QC; ✉ 28 Sydney Street, London SW3; Taprobane Island, Weligama Bay, Weligama, Sri Lanka; 2 Paper Buildings, Temple, London EC4Y 7ET (☎ 0171 936 2611)

de SILVA, Harendra Aneurin Domingo; QC (1995); s of Annesley de Silva (d 1978), of Colombo, Sri Lanka, and Maharani of Porbandar (d 1989); *b* 29 Sept 1945; *Educ* Millfield, Queens' Coll Cambridge (MA, LLM); *m* 10 June 1972, Indira; 1 s (Nihal Ceri b 17 Jan 1979), 1 da (Ayesha Annette b 30 July 1975); *Career* called to the Bar Middle Temple 1970, recorder of the Crown Court; *Recreations* golf, bridge, tennis; *Clubs* Roehampton; *Style*— Harendra de Silva, Esq, QC; ✉ 2 Paper Buildings, Temple, London EC4Y 7ET (☎ 0171 936 2611)

DE SILVA, Dr Stephanie Gwendoline; da of Muthumadinage Piyasena (d 1990), of Sri Lanka, and Esther, *née* Dabare (d 1989); *b* 11 Dec 1938; *Educ* Methodist Coll Colombo Sri Lanka, Med Sch Univ of Colombo Sri Lanka; *m* 19 Oct 1967, Ariyapala De Silva, s of K A De Silva (d 1971), of Sri Lanka; 1 da (Gitanjali Tania b Aug 1968); *Career* conslt psychiatrist Hounslow and Spelthorne Community Tst (based West Middlesex Hosp Isleworth) 1981– (sr registrar 1978–80), clinical tutor and regnl tutor for NW Thames RHA 1985; chairperson Med Exec Ctee Leavesden Hosp 1988; NHS Meritorious Service Award 1991; MRCPsych, FRCPsych 1992; *Style*— Dr Stephanie De Silva; ✉ 12 Grove Road, Northwood, Middlesex (☎ 01923 821356); West Middlesex Hospital, Twickenham Road, Isleworth, Hounslow, Middlesex (☎ 0181 560 0991 ext 6190)

de SOUZA, Christopher Edward; s of Denis Walter de Souza, of Woolhampton, Berks, and Dorothy Edna, *née* Woodman (d 1984); *b* 6 June 1943; *Educ* Prior Park Coll Bath, Univ of Bristol, Old Vic Theatre Sch Bristol; *m* 1971 (m dis 1981), Robyn Ann Williams; *partner* Elinor Ann Kelly; 2 s (Tristan Edward b 17 June 1987, Sebastian Denis b 19 April 1993); *Career* broadcaster, also composer, opera producer and director; head of music St Bernadette's Sch Bristol 1966–70, staff prodr Sadler's Wells/ENO 1971–75, arts prodr BBC Radio London 1975–79, music prodr BBC Radio 3 1980–86, prodr BBC Promenade Concerts 1987–88, presenter BBC Radio 3 1988–95 (progs incl On Air 1992–93 and own prog Tuning Up focusing on young musicians 1990–92, awarded NY Radio Show Silver Medal 1992); also occasional presenter BBC Radio 5 until 1994 and on television; fndr dir Liszt Festival of London 1977; prodr: over 100 operas for BBC Radio, Abbey Opera, Northern Ireland Opera, Handel Opera, Opera East, Royal Coll of Music, Aldeburgh Festival, Bologna Festival, Krakow Festival and Miami Festival; dir Br stage premières of: Liszt's Don Sanche 1977, Virgil Thompson's The Mother of Us All 1979, Pfitzner's Palestrina 1983, Gretry's William Tell 1984; regular competition adjudicator, contributed articles to The Listener, Music and Musicians, Musical Times, The Strad, BBC Proms Guides 1992 and 1993; chm: SE Branch Composers' Guild of GB 1974–76, AVANTI (agency for young musicians) 1985–91; memb: Park Lane Group 1984–92, Redcliffe Concerts 1985–90, British Youth Opera 1986–; memb: Equity, Composers' Guild of GB, Performing Rights Soc, Royal Soc of Musicians, Royal Phiharmonic Soc; *Compositions* incl: 8 Epithalamia for Organ (1966–71), Sonata for Flute and Piano (1974), Maharajahs (music for BBC2 series), Four Brecht Songs (1991), Six-foot Cinderella (music for BBC2), Symphonic Suite from Britten's music for The Rescue, The Ides of March for A Cappella Chorus (1993); *Recordings* incl first modern prodn of Liszt's opera Don Sanche (produced at Liszt Festival of London 1977, BBC Studio Recording with BBC Scottish Symphony Orch); *Books* A Child's Guide to Looking at Music (1980); *Recreations* entertaining, travel, languages, painting, drawing, photography, swimming; *Clubs* Royal Over-Seas League; *Style*— Christopher de Souza, Esq; ✉ Westbrook Farm Cottage, Boxford, nr Newbury, Berks RG20 8DL (☎ 01488 608503); c/o Music International, 13 Ardilaun Rd, London N5 2QR (☎ 0171 359 5183, fax 0171 226 9792)

de SOUZA, Edward James; s of Edward Valentine De Souza (d 1946), and Annie Adeline Swift, *née* Calvert (d 1992); *b* 4 Sept 1932; *Educ* Blackfriars Laxton, RADA; *m* Miranda, da of Philip Connell; 2 s (Timothy James b 26 Feb 1961, Jonathan Job b 16 Aug 1962), 2 da (Emma Louise b 22 Dec 1963, Rebecca Kate b 31 Aug 1967); *Career* actor; *Theatre* incl: Dream (Stratford-upon-Avon), Alls Well (Stratford-upon-Avon), Private Lives (Duke of York), Dirty Linen (Arts), Night and Day (Phoenix), The Philanthropist (Mayfair), The Hot House (Ambassadors), Galileo (Almeida), Moonlight (Almeida, Comedy Theatre), Amadeus (Her Majesties), The School for Scandal (Chichester); NT: Players, Venice Preserved, The Dream, Le Cid; most recently Troilus and Cressida (Stratford-upon-Avon) 1996; *Television* incl: Marriage Lines, After Henry, One Foot In The Grave, Count of Monte Christo; *Films* incl: The Spy Who Loved Me, Phantom of the Opera, Kiss of the Vampire, 39 Steps; most recently Jane Eyre 1996; *Radio* Man in Black (Fear On Four); *Recreations* golf, gardening, water colours; *Clubs* Stage Golfing Soc; *Style*— Edward de Souza, Esq; ✉ c/o Sally Long Innes, ICM Ltd, Oxford House, 76 Oxford Street, London W1N 0AX (☎ 0171 636 6565, fax 0171 323 0101)

DE STEMPEL, Sophie Christina; da of Baron Michael De Stempel, of Crosfield Road, Hampstead, and Cristina MacDonald; *b* 31 Dec 1960; *Educ* Lady Eden's Sch London, Convent of the Sacred Heart Woldingham, City and Guilds Sch of Art Kennington; *Career* artist; exhibitions incl: Gallery 24 Powis Terrace 1985, Conway Hall 1986, Albemarle Gallery 1987, The Mall Galleries 1988, and many mixed shows; most important works: The Unmade Bed 1986 (Saatchi collection), Profile of Gillian Melling 1988 (Catherine Parma collection), interior 1989 (Berry collection), Interior Bathroom 1989 (Saatchi collection), India Jane Birley 1990 (Pigoztsi collection), India Jane in an Interior 1990–91 (Saatchi collection); *Style*— Sophie De Stempel; ✉ c/o Houldsworth Fine Art, 124 Barlby Road, London W10 6BL

de SWIET, (Eleanor) Jane; da of Mr R M Hawkins, of Worcester, and Mrs J R Hawkins, *née* Fawn; *b* 18 Aug 1942; *Educ* Cheltenham Ladies' Coll (head girl), Girton Coll Cambridge (MA), Univ of London Inst of Educn (PGCE); *m* 12 Sept 1964, Dr Michael de Swiet, *qv*; 2 s (Thomas Michael b 12 May 1970, Charles Richard b 12 Dec 1972), 1 da (Harriet Kate b 18 Aug 1968); *Career* Classics teacher: Francis Holland Sch 1965–67, St Paul's Girls' Sch 1967–70, Queen's Coll 1975–84 (also head of careers), City of London Sch for Girls 1984–89 (head of Classics and head of 4 and 5 years); headteacher The Henrietta Barnett Sch 1989–; dir Smallpeice Enterprises Ltd; treas Assoc of Girls' Maintained Schs, pres Jt Assoc of Classics Teachers, assoc memb Girls' Schs Assoc; memb: SHA, Ramblers' Assoc, Nat Trust, Highgate Soc, Highgate Literary and Scientific Inst; *Recreations* Yorkshire, fell walking, reading, collecting glass, music and theatre; *Style*— Mrs E J de Swiet; ✉ 60 Hornsey Lane, London N6 5LU (☎ and fax 0171 272 3195); The Henrietta Barnett School, Central Square, London NW11 7BN (☎ 0181 458 8999, fax 0181 455 8900)

de SWIET, Dr Michael; s of John de Swiet, of Trewen Pentrych, Cardiff, and Mary Marguerite, *née* Smith; *b* 15 Aug 1941; *Educ* Cheltenham, Univ of Cambridge (MD); *m* 12 Sept 1964, (Eleanor) Jane de Swiet, *qv*, da of Richard Miles Hawkins, of Weston Hill House, Broadwas on Teme, Worcs; 2 s (Thomas Michael b 12 May 1970, Charles Richard John b 12 Dec 1972), 1 da (Harriet Kate b Aug 1968); *Career* sr house offr Nat Hosp for Nervous Diseases 1968; UCH: house physician 1966–67, sr house offr 1967–68, res fell 1968–70; res fell Univ of California San Francisco 1970–71, registrar Radcliffe Infirmary Oxford 1971–73; conslt physician 1973–: Queen Charlotte's Hosp, UCH and Northwick Park Hosp; academic sub dean Royal Postgrad Med Sch Inst of Obstetrics and Gynaecology; MRCP 1968, FRCP 1981, FRCOG 1992; *Books* Basic Science in

Obstetrics Gynaecology (co-ed, 2 edn 1992), Medical Disorders in Obstetric Practice (3 edn, 1995); *Recreations* the arts, gardening, woodwork, walking; *Style—* Dr Michael de Swiet; ✉ 60 Hornsey Lane, London N6 5LU; Queen Charlotte's Hospital, Goldhawk Rd, London W6 0XG (☎ 0181 740 3905, fax 0181 740 3922, car 0142 6914418)

de THAME, Gerard; s of Brian de Thame, of Bewdley, Worcs, and Marie-Jeanne, *née* Pitesche; *b* 24 June 1958; *Educ* Malvern, Hereford Art Coll, Brighton Poly (BA), Chelsea Sch of Art (MA); *Career* sculptor 1978–85 (Rome scholar 1983–84, Mark Rothko travel award to California, New Mexico and Arizona 1984–85), commercials and video dir 1986–; pop videos directed incl: Black's 'Wonderful Life' (NY Festival Silver Award 1987, Diamond Award for Best Male Video 1988, Golden Lion Award Cannes 1988), Tanita Tikaram's 'The Cathedral Song' (D&AD Music Video of the Year and Best Direction of the Year 1989) and 'Twist in My Sobriety' (Diamond Award for Best Male and Female Video 1989), Sting's 'Why Should I Cry'; commercials directed for clients incl: Pimms (Summertime), First Direct, ICL, McEwans Lager, Toshiba (numerous Creative Circle awards for 'Nicam TV' 1991), Tennent's Lager (Mobius Award and 1st prize Int Advtg Festival for 'Tennent's Galore' 1992), British Telecom 'Hawking' (BTA Golden Arrow 1994); included in Direction magazine's 20 top commercials dirs 1991; memb: D&AD, Dirs' Guild of America, ACCT; *Clubs* Groucho, Upstairs at 58; *Style—* Gerard de Thame, Esq; ✉ Gerard de Thame Films Ltd, 16–18 Hollen Street, London W1V 3AD (☎ 0171 437 3339, fax 0171 437 3338, mobile 0860 621725)

de TRAFFORD, Sir Dermot Humphrey; 6 Bt (UK 1841), of Trafford Park, Lancs; VRD; s of Sir Rudolph Edgar Francis de Trafford, 5 Bt, OBE (d 1983), and his 1 w, June Isabel, MBE (d 1977), only da of Lt-Col Reginald Chaplin; *b* 19 Jan 1925; *Educ* Harrow, ChCh Oxford (MA); *m* 1, 26 June 1948 (m dis 1973), Patricia Mary, o da of late Francis Mycroft Beeley, of Long Crumples, nr Alton, Hants; 3 s (John Humphrey b 1950, Edmund Francis b 1952, Gerard Thomas Joseph b 1968), 6 da (Mary Annette b 1949, Elizabeth Eugenie (Mrs John A Langdon) b 1951, Patricia Clare (Mrs P W U Corbett) b 1955, Victoria Mary (Mrs Andrew Roberts) b 1958, (Cynthia) June Bernadette (Mrs Nicholas C Kirkman) b 1958, (Antonia) Lucy Octavia (Mrs David Carotti) b 1966); m 2, 1974, Xandra Carandini, da of Lt-Col Geoffrey Trollope Lee, and former w of Roderick Walter (d 1996); *Heir* s, John Humphrey de Trafford b 12 Sept 1950; *Career* md GHP Group Ltd 1961 (chm 1966–77), dep chm Imperial Continental Gas Assoc 1972–87 (dir 1963–87), chm Low & Bonar plc 1982–90 (dep chm 1980); vice pres IOD 1993–95 (formerly chm); CIMgt, FRSA; *Recreations* gardening, golf; *Clubs* White's, Royal Ocean Racing; *Style—* Sir Dermot de Trafford, Bt, VRD; ✉ The Old Vicarage, Appleshaw, nr Andover, Hants (☎ 01264 772357, fax 01264 773062)

de TRAFFORD, John Humphrey; eldest s and h of Sir Dermot Humphrey de Trafford, 6 Bt, VRD, *qv*, and his 1 w, Patricia Mary, *née* Beeley; *b* 12 Sept 1950; *Educ* Ampleforth, Univ of Bristol (BSc); *m* 1975, Anne, da of Jacques Faure de Pebeyre; 1 s (Alexander Humphrey b 28 June 1978), 1 da (Isabel June b 1980); *Career* vice pres American Express Europe Ltd 1987–92, vice pres and gen mangr American Express International (Taiwan) Inc 1992–94, vice pres American Express Travel Related Services Inc 1994–96, sr vice pres, head Consumer Servs Gp and country mangr for the UK and Ireland American Express 1996–; *Clubs* Royal Ocean Racing; *Style—* John de Trafford, Esq; ✉ American Express Ltd, Portland House, Stag Place, Victoria, London SW1E 5BZ (☎ 0171 925 4636)

de VALOIS, Dame Ninette, *née* Edris Stannus; OM (1992), CH (1980), DBE (1951, CBE 1947); 2 da of Lt-Col Thomas Robert Alexander Stannus, DSO, JP (d of wounds 1917, Anglo-Irish Protestant family settled in Ireland ca 1618), and Elizabeth Graydon, *née* Smith (d 1961); *b* 6 June 1898; *m* 5 July 1935, Dr Arthur Blackall Connell; *Career* fndr dir Royal Ballet 1931–63 (previously Sadler's Wells Ballet), fndr Royal Ballet Sch; former ballerina; prima ballerina Covent Garden Royal Opera Season 1919 and 1928, with Diaghilev's Ballet Russes 1923–26; choreographer: Job, Rake's Progress, Checkmate, Don Quixote; pres London Ballet Circle until 1981; Chev of the Legion of Honour (France) 1950; Royal Albert Medal 1963, Erasmus Prize Fndn Award 1974; *Books* Invitation to the Ballet (1937), Come Dance With Me (1957), Step By Step (1977); *Style—* Dame Ninette de Valois, OM, CH, DBE; ✉ c/o Royal Ballet School, 153 Talgarth Rd, London W14 (☎ 0181 748 6335/3123)

de VASCONCELLOS, Josefina; MBE (1985); da of late H H de Vasconcellos, and Freda, *née* Coleman; *Educ* Royal Acad Schs; *m* 1930, Delmar Banner (d 1983); *Career* sculptor; works incl: High Altar and Statue (Varengeville Normandy) crozier for Bristol Cathedral 1948, National War Meml (Battle of Britain Museum Aldershot) 1955, life size Mary and Child (St Paul's Cathedral) 1955, The Flight into Egypt (for St Martin in the Fields, now in Cartmel Priory) 1958, Winged Victory Crucifix (Clewer Church and Canongate Kirk Edinburgh) 1964, Lord Denning (portrait in bronze) 1969, life size Virgin and Child (Blackburn Cathedral) 1974, Reredos (Wordsworth Chapel) 1988, life size twin bronzes Reconciliation (one in ruins of Coventry Cathedral and one in Peace Park Hiroshima); fndr memb Soc of Portrait Sculptors, invited one man exhibition Manchester Cathedral Christmas 1991; fndr Adventure Base for Disabled Youngsters, The Harriet Tst; Hon DLitt Univ of Bradford 1977; FRBS, ret memb IPI; *Recreations* music, small garden; *Clubs* Royal Over-Seas League; *Style—* Ms Josefina de Vasconcellos, MBE; ✉ The Old Wash House Studio, Peggy Hill, Ambleside, Cumbria LA22 9EG (☎ 015394 33794)

de VERE, Alison Frances; da of George Reginald Johnstone de Vere (d 1950), and Alison Frances, *née* Mansfield (d 1993); *b* 16 Sept 1927; *Educ* Brighton Art Sch, Royal Acad Sch of Painting; *m* July 1947 (m dis 1957), Karl Martin Weschke; 1 s (Benjamin de Vere Weschke b 25 April 1956); *Career* designer Halas and Batchelor Cartoons Ltd 1951–56, TV commercial dir Guild TV Ltd 1958–66, designer 1961–66, designer for decor TV Cartoons Ltd 1967–69, designer and animator Wyatt-Cattaneo Productions Ltd 1970–80, independent 1981–; films incl Psyche and Eros (film collaboration with Karl Weschke for Channel Four) 1994; *Awards* Gold award for Br Industl and Scientific Films 1968 (for design direction and animation of WHO film False Friends), Special Jury award Annecy Festival 1975 (for film Cafe Bar), Grand Prix Annecy Festival 1979 (for film Mr Pascal), second prize Los Angeles Film Festival (for Channel Four drama Silas Marner), Best TV Film prize and Critics prize Annecy 1987 (for Channel Four film The Black Dog), Best Film prize Hans Andersen Festival Odense Denmark 1989; memb: The Theosophical Soc 1967, L'Association Internationale du Film D'Animation; *Recreations* writing poetry; *Style—* Ms Alison de Vere; ✉ Alison de Vere Animation Ltd, 70 Causewayhead, Penzance, Cornwall TR18 2SR (☎ 01736 331846)

de VESCI, 7 Viscount (I 1776); Thomas Eustace Vesey; 9 Bt (I 1698); also Baron Knapton (I 1750); s of 6 Viscount de Vesci (d 1983), by his w Susan Ann (d 1986), da of late Ronald Owen Lloyd Armstrong-Jones, MBE (and sis of Earl of Snowdon, *qv*); *b* 8 Oct 1955; *Educ* Eton, Univ of Oxford; *m* 5 Sept 1987, Sita-Maria Arabella, o da of Brian de Breffny (d 1989), of Castletown Cox, Co Kilkenny, and Maharaj Kumari Jyotsna Devi Dutt, da of late Maharajadhiraja Bahadur Uday Chand Mahtab, KCIE, of Burdwan; 2 s (Hon Damian Brian John b 1985, Hon Oliver Ivo b 16 July 1991), 1 da (Hon Cosima Frances b 1988); *Heir* s, Hon Oliver Ivo Vesey b 16 July 1991; *Career* timber grower and farmer; dir Aanoor Bagley India; *Clubs* White's; *Style—* The Rt Hon the Viscount de Vesci; ✉ 14 Rumbold Road, London SW6 2JA

de VILLIERS, Hon Alexander Charles; s and h of 3 Baron de Villiers, *qv*; *b* 29 Dec 1940; *m* 1966; *Style—* The Hon Alexander de Villiers

de VILLIERS, 3 Baron (UK 1910); Arthur Percy de Villiers; s of 2 Baron de Villiers (d 1934); *b* 17 Dec 1911; *Educ* Diocesan Coll SA, Magdalen Coll Oxford; *m* 9 Nov 1939 (m dis 1958), Edna Alexis Lovett, da of Dr A D MacKinnon, of Wilham Lake, BC, Canada; 1 s, 2 da; *Heir* s, Hon Alexander Charles de Villiers; *Career* called to the Bar Inner Temple 1938; Auckland Supreme Ct 1949; farmer, ret; *Clubs* Cwlth Tst; *Style—* The Rt Hon the Lord de Villiers; ✉ PO Box 66, Kumeu, Auckland, New Zealand (☎ 00 64 9 411 8173)

de VINK, Peter Henry John; s of Dr Ludovicus Petrus Hendricus Josephus de Vink (d 1987), and Catharina Louisa Maria, *née* Van Iersel; *b* 9 Oct 1940; *Educ* Univ of Edinburgh (BCom); *m* 1, 27 May 1967 (m dis 1993), Jenipher Jean, da of Ranald Malcolm Murray-Lyon, MD (d 1969); 1 s (Patrick b 1971), 1 da (Natalie b 1970); m 2, 23 Sept 1994, Julia Christine Quarles van Ufford; *Career* Nat Serv 1961–63, cmmnd Dutch Army; dir Ivory & Sime 1975 (joined 1966, ptnr 1969), fndr dir Edinburgh Financial & General Holdings Ltd 1978–; dir: Viking Resources Oil & Gas Ltd 1972–88, Viking Resources Tst plc 1972–88, Wereldhave NY 1973–90, Benline Offshore Contractors Ltd 1974–96, Albany Oil & Gas Ltd 1987–91, Capital Copiers (Edinburgh) Ltd 1989–90, Screen Consultants NV 1994, Oxford Philanthropic 1994–96; memb: Exec Scot Cncl (Devpt and Ind) 1981–90, Bd of Govrs Napier Univ, Scottish Industrial Development Advsy Bd, Scottish Ctee of the Game Conservancy Cncl, Scottish Cons Bd of Fin; *Recreations* shooting, golf, fishing; *Clubs* New (Edinburgh); *Style—* Peter H J de Vink, Esq; ✉ Edinburgh Financial & General Holdings Ltd, 7 Howe St, Edinburgh EH3 6TE (☎ 0131 225 6661, fax 0131 556 6651, car tel 0836 700956, portable 0836 702335)

de VOGÜÉ, Count Ghislain Alain Marie Melchior; s of Comte Robert Jean de Vogüé, and Anne, *née* d'Eudeville; *b* 11 Aug 1933; *Educ* Univ of Le Havre; *m* 1 July 1960, Catherine Marie Monique, *née* Fragonard; 1 s (Marc b 14 Dec 1979), 1 da (Laurence b 1 Feb 1976); *Career* mgmnt attache Banque de l'Union Europeenne 1959–64, md Moet et Chandon Epernay 1969–75 (joined 1965), vice chm of bd Moet-Hennessy Paris 1988–94 (dir 1976–), chm M & C London Ltd, chm Domaine Chandon (USA); memb Bd: LVMH, Moet et Chandon (France), Jas Hennessy (France), Imprimerie FPGV (France), Bodegas Chandon Buenos Aires (Argentina), Chandon do Brasil Sao Paolo (Brazil), Domaine Chandon Pty (Australia), FEVS, Chandon SA (Spain); *Recreations* music, tennis, skiing, golf, sailing; *Style—* Count Ghislain de Vogüé; ✉ 13 Grosvenor Crescent, London SW1X 7EE; 174 Boulevard St Germain, 75006 Paris

de VOIL, Paul Walter; s of late Pfarrer Paul Vogel, and late Maria Christine, *née* Hurfeld; adopted s of late Very Rev Walter Harry de Voil, of Carnoustie; *b* 29 Sept 1929; *Educ* Fettes, Hertford Coll Oxford; *m* 26 July 1952, Sheila, da of late William George Danks, of Elsecar; 1 s (Nicholas b 1962), 1 da (Sally b 1960); *Career* Flying Offr RAF 1950–53; taxation conslt and lectr; Inland Revenue 1953–60, Ford Motor Co 1960–63, Herbert Smith & Co 1964–69, Baker Sutton & Co 1969–78, Lonrho plc 1978–87, Arthur Young (now Ernst & Young) 1987–89, Paul de Voil & Co 1990–95; pt/t chm VAT Tbnls 1992–, dep special cmmr of income tax 1993–; non-stipendiary Anglican deacon 1992, priest 1993; Freeman: City of London 1969, Worshipful Co of Slrs 1969; memb: FTII 1964, Law Soc 1967; *Books* de Voil on Tax Appeals (1969), de Voil on Value Added Tax (1972); *Recreations* wine, music, statues, bright-eyed love; *Clubs* RAF; *Style—* Paul de Voil, Esq (on ecclesiastical matters The Rev Paul de Voil); ✉ Water Lane Barn, Denston, Newmarket, Suffolk CB8 8PP (☎ and fax 01440 820181)

de VRIES, Edo Barend Philip; s of Philip De Vries (d 1954), of Hilversum, Netherlands, and Ella, *née* Troetel (d 1980); *b* 13 Nov 1925; *Educ* Gymnasium Haganum, Prinses Beatrix Lyceum Glion Switzerland, Univ of Utrecht (LLM); *m* 1, 21 Dec 1949 (m dis 1961), Anne Eliza, da of Harry Hyman Tels (d 1940), of Rotterdam; 2 da (Harriet (Mrs Hermans) b 1950, Elizabeth (Baroness Van Utenhove) b 1954); m 2, Mary McHugh (d 1968); 1 s (Philip b 1966); m 3, 1969 (m dis 1988), Sonya Beasley; 1 da (Clare b 1969); m 4, 1992, Janet Erskine; *Career* voluntary WWII serv 1944–45; barr; mangr Int Legal Dept Royal Dutch-Shell Group Venezuela (various positions 1949–68); practising memb Tax Bar; *Books* Taxation of Trades in the United Kingdom (1975); *Recreations* sailing, piano playing, DIY, music; *Clubs* RAF Yacht; *Style—* Edo de Vries, Esq; ✉ 1 Appleton Road, Catisfield, Fareham, Hampshire PO15 5QH (☎ 01329 314141, fax 01329 315678)

de WAAL, Sir Henry (Constant Hendrik); KCB (1989, CB 1977), QC (1988); 3 s of late Hendrik de Waal; *b* 1 May 1931; *Educ* Tonbridge, Pembroke Coll Cambridge; *m* 1964, Julia Jessel; 2 s; *Career* called to the Bar Lincoln's Inn 1953, bencher 1989, Law Cmmn 1969–71, Parly Counsel 1971–81, second Parly counsel 1981–86, first Parly Counsel 1987–91; hon fell Pembroke Coll Cambridge; *Style—* Sir Henry de Waal, KCB, QC; ✉ 62 Sussex St, London SW1

de WAAL, Rt Rev Hugo Ferdinand; *see:* Thetford, Bishop of

de WECK, Paul Louis; s of Eugene P de Weck (d 1984), of Wimbledon, and Mary Eileen, *née* French; *b* 6 May 1937; *Educ* Beaumont Coll, Old Windsor; *m* 27 April 1963, Ann Eileen, da of Wilfrid Frederick John Ward (d 1973), of Worcester Park; *Career* Nat Serv 1955–57, sr Aircraftman RAF, Photographic Reconaissance Course; joined Charles Gee and Co 1958– (ptnr 1969, second sr ptnr); md C & H (Hauliers) Ltd 1970–; chm Gee Trailers Ltd, dir Gee Property Services Ltd; memb Baltic Exchange 1970–; Freeman City of London 1978, memb Worshipful Co of Gardeners 1978; FInstFF 1974, FICS 1987; *Recreations* gardening, horse racing, swimming, riding, photography; *Clubs* Beaufort Hunt, Racehourse Owners' Assoc, Longbourn Ward, Castle Baynard Ward; *Style—* Paul de Weck, Esq; ✉ Nettleton Lodge, Nettleton, Chippenham, Wilts (☎ 01249 782556); Charles Gee and Co, Knightrider House, Knightrider Street, London EC4V 5BH (☎ 0171 815 3505, fax 0171 815 3506)

de WILDE, (Alan) Robin; QC (1993); s of Capt Ronald Cedric de Wilde (d 1985), and Dorothea Elizabeth Mary, *née* Fenningworth; *b* 12 July 1945; *Educ* Dean Close Sch, RAF Coll Cranwell; *m* 16 April 1977, Patricia Teresa, da of Gerald Ivan Bearcroft (d 1980), and Kathleen Mary, *née* O'Toole (d 1975); 3 s; *Career* called to the Bar Inner Temple 1971, bencher 1996; chm Professional Negligence Bar Assoc 1995–; Liveryman Worshipful Co of Bowyers; *Style—* Robin de Wilde, Esq, QC; ✉ 199, Strand, London WC2R 1DR

DE WITT, Ronald Wayne; s of James Goldwyn De Witt, of Saskatoon, Canada, and Una Doreen, *née* Lane; *b* 31 March 1948; *Educ* Sch of Advanced Nursing Wellington NZ (Dip Nursing), Univ of Humberside (BA Business, MA Health Mgmnt); *Career* student nurse Misericordia Hosp 1967–70, staff nurse Winnipeg Children's Hosp 1970, charge nurse Stoke Mandeville Hosp 1971–73 (staff nurse 1971), nursing offr Queen Mary Hosp Roehampton 1973–75, asst princ nurse Auckland Hosp 1980–83 (supervisor 1975, sr supervisor 1976–80), dir of nursing Green Lane Hosp Auckland 1983–86, chief nurse Auckland Health 1988–90 (dep chief nurse 1986–88), district mangr Auckland City 1989–90, gen mangr Auckland Hosp 1990–91, chief exec Royal Hull Hosp NHS Tst 1991–; Dow Coring Int Award for Plastic Surgery 1973; MHSM; *Style—* Ronald De Witt, Esq; ✉ Royal Hull Hospitals NHS Trust, Hull Royal Infirmary, Anlaby Road, Hull HU3 2JZ (☎ 01482 674200, fax 01482 674857)

DE WOLFE, Earl Felix; s of Meyer De Wolfe (d 1976), and Regina, *née* Van Leer (d 1979); *b* 1 July 1914; *Educ* UCS; *m* 23 June 1967, Brenda, da of Bernard Duggleby (d 1980), of Hull; 2 da (Victoria b 1965, Caroline b 1968); *Career* WWII Flt Lt RAF 1941–45; theatrical and literary agent 1938–; chm Personal Mangrs Assoc 1970–77; *Style—* Earl De Wolfe, Esq; ✉ Flat L, 10 Hyde Park Mansions, London NW1 5BG (☎ 0171 723 3508); Manfield House, 1 Southampton Street, London WC2R 0LR (☎ 0171 379 5767, fax 0171 836 0337)

de ZULUETA, Dr Felicity Ines Soledad (Mrs Kahya); da of Dr Julian de Zulueta, and Gillian Owtram de Zulueta; *b* 26 March 1948; *Educ* UEA (BSc), Univ of Cambridge (MA), Univ of Sheffield (MB ChB); *m* 30 Sept 1977, Sedat Kahya, s of late Samuel Kahya, of Istanbul, Turkey; 1 s (Damian Samuel Hakan b 10 Nov 1979); *Career* private psychotherapist, qualified gp analyst; sr house offr, registrar and sr registrar Maudsley Hosp where trained in psychotherapy, trained at Tavistock Clinic in family therapy, clinical lectr in traumatic studies and hon conslt psychiatrist in forensic psychiatry (running a trauma clinic in Maudsley Hosp) 1996–, pt/t conslt psychotherapist Charing Cross Hospital London, hon sr lectr Univ of London; memb: Med Section Amnesty Int, Inst of Group Analysis, Int Soc for Traumatic Stress Studies; MRCPsych; *Books* From Pain to Violence: the traumatic roots of destructiveness (1993); also contrib chapters to various books; *Recreations* travelling, photography, walking, scuba diving; *Style—* Dr Felicity de Zulueta; ✉ Institute of Psychiatry, 16 De Crespigny Park, Denmark Hill, London SE5 8AF (☎ 0171 703 5411)

DE ZULUETA, Paul Gerald; *see:* Torre Diaz, Count of

DEACON, John; s of John James Deacon, and Anne, *née* Turner; *b* 30 March 1938; *Educ* E Grinstead Co GS; *m* 1968, Christine Whitney; 1 da (Amanda Christine b 1970), 1 s (Jonathan Christopher b 1972); *Career* Nat Serv RAF 1956–59; commercial planning mangr Philips Records 1965–69 (joined 1960), commercial dir A & M Records 1973–79 (gen mangr 1969–73), DG BPI 1979– (memb Cncl 1971–79); chm Br Record Indust Tst 1991–; memb: Advsy Ctee Nat Sound Archive 1983–, City Technol Colls Tst 1989–; govr Br Performing Arts & Technol Sch Croydon 1991–; first recipient Br Record Indust Award 1992; FRSA 1992; *Recreations* music, reading, gardening; *Clubs* Sussex CCC; *Style—* John Deacon, Esq; ✉ The British Phonographic Industry Ltd, 25 Savile Row, London W1X 1AA (☎ 0171 287 4422, fax 0171 287 2252)

DEACON, John Richard; s of Arthur Henry Deacon, and Lilian Deacon; *b* 19 Aug 1951; *Educ* Gartree HS, Beauchamp GS Leicester, Chelsea Coll; *m* Veronica; 5 s (Michael, Robert, Joshua, Cameron, Luke), 1 da (Laura); *Career* guitarist and songwriter; first band Opposition, joined Queen 1971 (with Freddie Mercury (d 1991), Brian May, *qv*, Roger Taylor, *qv*); albums: Queen (1973, Gold), Queen II (1974, Gold), Sheer Heart Attack (1974, Gold), A Night at the Opera (1975, Platinum), A Day at the Races (1976, Gold), News of the World (1977, Gold), Jazz (1978, Gold), Live Killers (1979, Gold), The Game (1980, Gold), Flash Gordon Original Soundtrack (1980, Gold), Greatest Hits (1981, 9 times Platinum), Hot Space (1982, Gold), The Works (1984, Platinum), A Kind of Magic (1986, double Platinum), Live Magic (1986, Platinum), The Miracle (1989, Platinum), Queen at the Beeb (1989), Innuendo (1991, Platinum), Greatest Hits Two (1991), Made in Heaven (1995); number 1 singles: Bohemian Rhapsody (1975 and 1991), Under Pressure (1981), Innuendo (1991); numerous tours worldwide, performed at Live Aid Concert Wembley Stadium 1985; voted Best Band of the Eighties ITV/TV Times 1990, Br Phonographic Indust award for Outstanding Contribution to Br Music 1990; *Style—* John Deacon, Esq; ✉ Queen Productions Ltd, 46 Pembridge Road, London W11 3HN (☎ 0171 727 5641)

DEAKIN, John; s of Keith John Deakin, of Bedford, and Kathleen Irene, *née* Stenning; *b* 4 March 1965; *Educ* Sharnbrook Sch Beds, Bedford Coll of Higher Educn, South Notts Coll West Bridgford, Nottingham Law Sch, Nottingham Trent Univ; *m* 7 Sept 1991, Mary Elizabeth; 1 da (Charlotte Mary b 6 Sept 1995); *Career* rowing cox; began coxing Star Club Bedford 1978–79, coxed fastest club eight from the provinces 1982–84, memb Notts Co Rowing Assoc 1986–, rep GB in lightweight eights and placed fifth at World Championships Copenhagen 1987, won lightweight competitions 1987 (Mannheim, Amsterdam, Nottingham and Bronze at Lucerne), won lightweight eights 1989 (Nottingham), Ladies Plate Henley in re-row against Harvard in record time, competitions won 1990 (Thames Cup Henley Royal Regatta, Silver medal Lucerne, Bronze medal World Championships Lake Barrington Tasmania), won lightweight eight Duisberg 1991, fifth lightweight eight World Championships 1991, ninth coxed four Olympic Games 1992, fifth lightweight eights World Championships 1993, World champion lightweight eights 1994, Prince Philip Cup Henley, Lucerne and Paris 1994, Br lightweight eight record 5mins 31secs World Championships 1994, Gold in coxed fours and eights Italy 1995, Silver medal lightweight eights World Championships Finland 1995, Gold lightweight eight Lucerne 1995, nat champ men's, women's and lightweight eights 1996, fourth lightweight eights World Championships Scotland 1996; currently law student; ARA Bronze award for coaching 1992; *Recreations* theatre, cinema, football, collecting books, watches and wine; *Style—* John Deakin, Esq; ✉ 39 Exchange Rd, West Bridgford, Nottingham; Nottinghamshire County Rowing Association, National Watersports Centre, Holme Pierrepont, Nottingham (☎ 0115 982 1212)

DEAKIN, Michael; s of Sir William Deakin, DSO, *qv*, and Margaret, *née* Beatson Bell; bro of Prof Nicholas Deakin, CBE, *qv*; *b* 21 Feb 1939; *Educ* Bryanston, Universite d'Aix Marseilles, Emmanuel Coll Cambridge (MA); *Career* writer, documentary and film maker; fndr ptnr Editions Alecto (fine art publishers) 1960–64, prodr BBC Radio Current Affairs Dept 1964–68, prodr then editor Documentory Unit Yorkshire TV 1968–81; prodns incl: Out of Shadow into the Sun - The Eiger, Struggle for China, Whicker's World - Way Out West, Johnny Go Home (Br Acad award, 1976), David Frost's Global Village, The Frost Interview - The Shah, Act of Betrayal 1987, Not a Penny More, Not a Penny Less 1989, Secret Weapon 1990, Doomsday Gun 1993, The Good King 1994; fndr memb TV-am Breakfast Time Consortium 1980; TV-am: dir of progs 1982–84, memb Bd 1984–85, conslt 1984–87; dir Griffin Productions Ltd 1985–, sr vice pres Paramount/Revcom 1987–93; *Books* Restif de la Bretonne - Les Nuits de Paris (translated with Nicholas Deakin, 1968), Gaetano Donizetti (1968), Tom Grattan's War (1970), The Children on the Hill (1972, 9 edn 1982), Johnny Go Home (with John Willis, 1976), The Arab Experience (with Antony Thomas, 1975, 2 edn 1976), Flame in the Desert (1976), I Could Have Kicked Myself (with David Frost, 1982), Who Wants to be Millionaire (with David Frost, 1983), If You'll Believe That You'll Believe Anything... (1986); *Recreations* motorcyling, eating, music, dalmations; *Clubs* BAFTA; *Style—* Michael Deakin, Esq; ✉ Griffin Productions, 15 Bloomsbury Square, London SW1 (☎ 0171 312 3707, fax 0171 312 3708)

DEAKIN, Prof Nicholas Dampier; CBE (1997); s of Sir William Deakin, DSO, *qv*, and Margaret, *née* Beatson Bell; bro of Michael Deakin, *qv*; *b* 5 June 1936; *Educ* Westminster Sch, Milton Acad Massachusetts, Christ Church Coll Oxford (BA, MA), DPhil (Sussex) 1972; *m*; 3 c, 3 step c; *Career* civil servant (admin class) 1959–63: asst princ Home Office, private sec to Minister of State 1962–63; asst dir Nuffield Survey of Race Rels 1963–68, res fell Centre for Multi-Racial Studies Univ of Sussex 1969–71, lectr Sch of African and Asian Studies Univ of Sussex 1971–72, head Social Studies then Central Policy Unit GLC 1972–80; Univ of Birmingham: prof of social policy and admin 1980–, head Dept Social Admin 1980–91, dean Faculty of Commerce and Social Science 1986–89 (dep dean 1984–86); public orator 1992–95; visiting fell Adlai Stevenson Inst of Int Affrs Univ of Chicago 1972, visitor Centre for Environmental Studies 1971–72 (then memb Res Advsy Ctee), memb Social Affrs Ctee Econ and Social Res Cncl 1982–86 (vice chm 1984–86), scientific advsr Personal Servs DHSS 1986–91; chm: Birmingham Standing Conf for the Single Homeless 1983–86, Cncl for Voluntary Service Nat Assoc 1982–85, Nat Cncl for Vol Orgns Cmmn on Future of Vol Sector in England 1995–96 (report published as Meeting the Challenge of Change 1996); memb Exec Ctee Nat Cncl for Voluntary Orgns 1982–85 and 1988–91; govr: Royal Inst of Public Admin 1981–88, Family Policy Studies Centre 1984–; memb Ctee W Midlands Low Pay Unit 1983–84; regular lectr for Civil Serv; external examiner: UCL, Univ of Glasgow, Brunel Univ, Southampton Univ, Univ of Edinburgh, Univ of Exeter, Univ of Bath, LSE, Univ of Nottingham, Loughborough Univ; author of numerous articles in various learned publications; DPhil Univ of Sussex 1972; *Publications include* Colour and Citizenship (co-author, 1969), Colour and the British Electorate (ed, 1965), Policy Change in Government (ed, 1986), The Politics of Welfare (1987, 2 edn 1994), The Enterprise Culture of the Inner Cities (co-author, 1993), contrib The Yearbook of Social Policy in Britain (eds Catherine Jones and June Stevenson, 1984), contrib Party Ideology in Britain (eds L J Tivey and A W Wright, 1989), Consuming Public Services (with A W Wright, 1990), The Costs of Welfare (jt ed and contrib, 1993); *Style—* Prof Nicholas Deakin, CBE; ✉ Department of Social Policy and Social Work, University of Birmingham, PO Box 363, Birmingham B15 2TT

DEAKIN, Pippa Caroline; da of (Iver) Tim Deakin, of The Homestead, Botesdale, Diss, Suffolk, and (Elizabeth) Joyce, *née* Knuckey; *b* 30 Oct 1965; *Educ* The Manor House Great Durnford Wilts, Princess Helena Coll Temple Dinsley Hitchen Herts; *Career* hotelier; teacher Hill House prep sch 1982, nursery sch teacher 1983–86, governess and nursery sch teacher abroad 1986–91, fndr proprietor Pippa Pop-Ins (first children's nursery hotel) 1992–; England Tourist Bd England for Excellence award 1992, Which? Hotel Guide London Hotel of the Yr 1994, nominated as Entrepreneur of the Year by BAWE for most orginal new business, representing GB in the FCEM World Awards 1996; govr Princess Helena Coll Herts 1993–, tstee St Nicholas Montessori Centre London/Int 1996–; memb Br Assoc of Women Entrepreneurs, Hon FRSA 1995; *Recreations* riding, skiing, sailing, the Arts, charity fund-raising and illustration for children; *Style—* Miss Pippa Deakin; ✉ Pippa Pop-Ins Company Ltd, 430 Fulham Road, London SW6 1DU (☎ 0171 385 2458/7, fax 0171 385 5706, car 0374 119319)

DEAKIN, Sir (Frederick) William Dampier; kt (1975), DSO (1943); s of Albert Witney Deakin, of Aldbury, Tring, Herts; *b* 3 July 1913; *Educ* Westminster Sch, Ch Ch Oxford; *m* 1, 1935 (m dis 1940), Margaret Ogilvy, da of Sir Nicholas Beatson Bell, KCSI, KCIE (d 1936); 2 s (Prof Nicholas Deakin, CBE, *qv*, Michael Deakin, *qv*); m 2, 1943, Livia Stela, da of Liviu Nasta, of Bucharest; *Career* fell and tutor Wadham Coll Oxford 1936–49, seconded to SOE War Office 1941, led first Br Mission to Tito 1943, first sec HM Embassy Belgrade 1945–46, res fell Wadham Coll 1949, warden St Antony's Coll Oxford 1950–68, ret; hon fell: Wadham Coll 1961, St Antony's Coll 1969; hon student Ch Ch Oxford 1979; Grosse Verdienstkreuz 1958, Chev de la Légion d'Honneur 1953; Hon FBA 1981; *Clubs* Beefsteak, White's, Brooks's; *Style—* Sir William Deakin, DSO; ✉ 83330 Le Beausset, Le Castellet, Var, France

DEAKINS, Eric Petro; s of Edward Deakins (d 1970), of London, and Gladys Frances, *née* Townsend (d 1964); *b* 7 Oct 1932; *Educ* Tottenham GS, LSE (BA); *m* 21 July 1990, Alexandria Victoria Anne, da of Michael Richard Weaver; 1 s (Tom b 1991), 1 da (Sophie b 1992); *Career* Nat Serv 2 Lt RASC 1953–55; memb Tottenham Borough Cncl 1958–61 and 1962–63; MP (Lab): West Walthamstow 1970–74, Walthamstow 1974–87; Parly under sec: Trade 1974–76, Health & Social Security 1976–79; divnl gen mangr FMC Ltd 1969–70 (exec 1956–69), political and trade conslt 1987–; memb Cncl: World Devpt Movement 1980–92, Population Concern 1983–; *Books* A Faith to Fight For (1964), You and Your MP (1987), What Future for Labour? (1988); *Recreations* writing, cinema, squash, football; *Style—* Eric Deakins, Esq; ✉ 36 Murray Mews, London NW1 9RJ (☎ 0171 267 6196, fax 0171 267 3151)

DEALTRY, Prof (Thomas) Richard; s of George Raymond Dealtry (d 1966), of York, and Edith, *née* Gardiner (d 1990); *b* 24 Nov 1936; *Educ* Cranfield Inst of Advanced Technol (MBA); *m* 17 Sept 1963 (m dis 1982), Pauline Sedgwick; 1 s (Roger Paul b 7 June 1968), 1 da (Claire Elizabeth b 1 Nov 1972); *Career* Nat Serv 1959–61, Capt RAEC 1960; under sec Scottish Office and Industl Advsr for Scotland 1977–78, regnl dir and conslt industl advsr Gulf Orgn for Industl Consulting Arabian Gulf Territories Orgn 1978–82, business and mgmnt devpt conslt 1982–, company broker and prof in strategic mgmnt at Int Mgmnt Centre Buckingham 1982–; CEng, MIME, MCIM; *Recreations* golf, rugby union; *Style—* Prof Richard Dealtry; ✉ 43 Hunstanton Ave, Harborne, Birmingham B17 8SX (☎ 0121 427 6949, fax 0121 427 8491, e-mail prof.dealtry@dial.pipex.com)

DEAN, Beryl (Mrs Phillips); MBE (1975); da of Herbert Charles Dean (d 1950), of Bromley, Kent, and Marion, *née* Petter (d 1946); *b* 2 Aug 1911; *Educ* Bromley HS, Royal Sch of Needlework, Bromley Sch of Art, RCA; *m* 22 June 1974, Wilfrid Maurice Phillips, s of Capt William George Phillips (d 1968), of Northampton; *Career* actg head Eastbourne Sch of Art 1939–45, designer and maker of ballet costumes 1939–46, tutor Hammersmith Coll of Art 1947–66, freelance ecclesiastical designer and embroiderer 1956–89; designs: Chelmsford Cathedral 1954–86 (red frontal, vestments, goldbanner, large hanging), Emmanuel Coll Cambridge 1961 (altar frontal), Guildford Cathedral 1965 (cope, mitre), Canterbury Cathedral 1966– (cope, mitre, copes for Dean and Chapter), St George's Chapel Windsor Castle 1970–75 (five large panels), Resurrection cope and mitre 1980, large panel Twelfth Night 1987; lectr Stanhope Inst of Adult Educn 1964–78; examples of work exhibited in GB and USA, Royal exhibitioner RCA, organiser Exhibition Br Ecclesiastical Embroidery St Paul's Cathedral Crypt 1990; memb Soc of Authors, FSDC, ARCA; *Books* Ecclesiastical Embroidery (1958), Church Needlework (1961), Ideas for Church Embroidery (1968), Creative Appliqué (1970), Embroidery in Religion and Ceremonial (1981), Church Embroidery (1982), Church Needlework (new edn, 1990), Designing Stitched Textiles for the Church (1993), Rebecca Compton and Elizabeth Thomson. Pioneers of Stitching in the 1930's (1996); *Recreations* gardening; *Style—* Beryl Dean, MBE; ✉ 59 Thornhill Square, London N1 1BE (☎ 0171 607 2572)

DEAN, Brian; s of Thomas Brown Dean (d 1959), of Jarrow, and Florence, *née* Shaw; *b* 10 July 1937; *Educ* Dame Allan's Boys' Sch Newcastle, Univ of Edinburgh (MB ChB), Univ of Liverpool (MCh); *m* 24 March 1962, (Catherine) Margaret, da of Thomas Day McNeill Scrimgeour, MBE (d 1969), of Burntisland Fife; 3 da (Rosalyn Gresham b 1962, Alison Handley b 1966, Joanna b 1970); *Career* conslt surgn Fife Orthopaedic Serv 1970–; clinical dir Orthopaedics/Accident and Emergency Serv 1993–95; memb Aberdour Angling Club (pres 1980–81), memb Rotary Club (pres of Dunfermline 1987–88), pres Fife Branch BMA 1982–83; memb BMA, fell BOA, FRCSEd; *Recreations* game fishing, yachting, modelling; *Style—* Brian Dean, Esq; ✉ Queen Margaret Hospital, Dunfermline, Fife (☎ 01383 623623)

DEAN, Christopher Colin; MBE (1981); s of Colin Gordon Dean, of Nottingham, and Mavis Pearson; step s of Mary Betty Chambers; *b* 27 July 1958; *Educ* Calverton Manor Sch, Sir John Sherbrooke Sch, Colonel Frank Seely Sch Nottingham; *m* 15 Oct 1994, Jill Ann, da of Robert Trenary, of USA; *Career* ice skater; with Sandra Elson: Br Primary Ice Dance champion 1972, Br Jr Ice Dance champion 1974; partnership with Jayne Torvill, *qv* 1975–; achievements incl: first int win St Gervais 1976, Br champions 1978, 1979, 1980, 1981, 1982, 1983 and 1994; Euro champions: Innsbruck 1981, Lyon 1982, Budapest 1984, Copenhagen 1994; World champions: Hartford USA 1981, Copenhagen 1982, Helsinki 1983, Ottawa 1984; Gold medal Olympic Games Sarajavo 1984 (fifth place Lake Placid 1980), Bronze medal Olympic Games Lillehammer 1994; World Professional Ice Dance champions 1984, 1985 and 1990; first professional tour 1984, co-fndr skating co with Jayne Torvill (tour Eng, Aust, USA and Canada) 1985, TV special Fire & Ice (LWT) 1986, tour with IceCapades USA 1987, fndr co of Soviet skaters (tour UK, USSR, Aust, USA and Canada) 1988, choreographer winning routines for Paul and Isabelle Duchesnay World Championships Munich 1991, recorded Bladerunners (Omnibus, BBC)

1991, tour Aust with Soviet co 1991; re-entered int competition 1994, third Professional World Tour 1994; world record holders for most number of perfect 6.0 scores in skating competition (Olympic Games 1984), only couple to attain Gold Star Ice Dance Test 1983, BBC Sports Personality and Team winners 1983 and 1984, awarded Jacques Favart Trophy Int Skating Union 1986; Hon MA Nottingham Trent Univ; *Recreations* motor racing, cars, motorbikes, theatre, dance, cinema; *Style*— Christopher Dean, Esq, MBE; ✉ c/o Debbie Turner, PO Box 32, Heathfield, E Sussex TN21 0BW

DEAN, John Lawrence; s of John Eric Dean (d 1975); *b* 24 Sept 1961; *Educ* Eastcliffe GS Newcastle upon Tyne, Chelsea Sch of Art, Manchester Poly; *m* 1, 1990 (m dis 1993), Linda Sharon, *née* Cash; 1 da (Rosie Anna); m 2, 1994, Denise Gabrielle, da of Thomas Byrne; *Career* jr copywriter Saatchi & Saatchi advtg 1982–86, copywriter rising to gp head/bd dir WCRS 1986–90, gp head/bd dir Still Price Lintas 1990–93, fndr ptnr Addition Marketing until Sept 1993, jt bd creative dir Butterfield Day Devito Hockney Nov 1993–; *Awards* Creative Circle Gold Award for Most Promising Beginner 1983, numerous others incl British TV, Campaign Press & Poster, Cannes Lions, NY Festival, D&AD, One Show, etc, 1983–; memb D&AD; *Recreations* golf, skiing, writing; *Style*— John Dean, Esq; ✉ Butterfield Day Devito Hockney, 47 Marylebone Lane, London W1M 5FN (☎ 0171 224 3000, fax 0171 935 9865)

DEAN, Dr Paul; CB (1981); s of Sydney Dean (d 1969), and Rachel, *née* Kurshnirsky; *b* 23 Jan 1933; *Educ* Hackney Downs GS, QMC London (BSc, PhD); *m* 10 Oct 1961, Sheila Valerie, da of Reuben Gamse (d 1973); 1 s (Grahame Clive b 29 Aug 1965), 1 da (Andrea Rachel b 14 Sept 1962); *Career* Nat Physical Laboratory: theoretical physicist 1957–66, head Central Computer Unit 1967, supt Div Quantum Metrology 1969–74, dep dir 1984–76, dir 1977–90; under sec Dept of Indust 1976–77 (pt/t head Div 1979–81); writer and advsr; memb Int Ctee Weights and Measures 1985–90; chm: Conslt Ctee on Ionizing Radiation 1987–90; pres Br Measurement and Testing Assoc 1990–95; chm EUROMET 1988–90, fell QMC 1984 (later QM and Westfield Coll); FInstP 1970, FIMA 1969; *Recreations* chess, music, computing, bridge, mathematics, astronomy; *Style*— Dr Paul Dean, CB

DEAN, Peter Henry; CBE (1993); s of Alan Walduck Dean, and Gertrude, *née* Bürger; *b* 24 July 1939; *Educ* Rugby, Univ of London (LLB); *m* 31 July 1965, Linda Louise, da of The Rev William Edward Keating; 1 da (Amanda b 1967); *Career* admitted slr 1962; RTZ Corporation plc: joined 1966, sec 1972–74, dir 1974–85; freelance business conslt 1985–96; dep chm Monopolies and Mergers Cmmn 1990–97 (memb 1982–97), Investment Ombudsman 1996–; non-exec dir: Associated British Ports Holdings plc 1980–, Liberty Life Assurance Co Ltd 1986–95, Seeboard plc 1993–96; chm English Baroque Choir 1985–89, chm Cncl of Mgmnt Highgate Counselling Centre 1991– (memb 1985–); memb Law Soc; *Recreations* music (especially choral singing), skiing; *Clubs* Ski Club of GB; *Style*— Peter Dean, Esq, CBE; ✉ 52 Lanchester Road, Highgate, London N6 4TA (☎ 0181 883 5417, fax 0181 365 2398); Office of the Investment Ombudsman, 6 Frederick's Place, London EC2R 8BT (☎ 0171 796 3065)

DEAN, Raymond Frank (Ray); s of Mario Frank Dean (d 1957), and late Leah Marsh Shannon; *b* 29 July 1936; *Educ* Britannia HS Vancouver, Guildford Coll of Art Surrey; *m* 26 Oct 1971, Anne Elisabeth, *née* Young; *Career* engine room apprentice RCN 1953–56; draughtsman Alcan Canada 1956–59 (chief shop steward Utd Steelworkers of America); photographer 1961–; assignments incl: still photography for Oscar winning documentary Dylan Thomas by Jack Howells, first exhibition Wig & Pen Club, work published by Br Jl of Photography and Photography Magazine; theatre and ballet photography incl: The Royal Opera House, Nureyev, Fonteyn, Marcel Marceau, Le Coq Mime, Comedie Francaise; design work for Derek Jarman incl: The Devils, Jazz Calendar; jt fndr Job Magazine 1973–84; int industl photographer; clients incl: Shell International, Elf Oil, Buitoni, Honeywell, Design Magazine, British Steel, Coutts Bank, Hill Samuel, Lloyd's, Alcan, Michelin, ICI; *Recreations* France and Scotland, eating, drinking, taking pictures; *Style*— Ray Dean, Esq; ✉ 4 Newton Grove, Chiswick, London W4 1LB (☎ 0181 994 0779, fax 0181 995 6421)

DEAN, Stafford Roderick; s of Eric Edwin Dean, and Vera Standish, *née* Bathurst; *b* 20 June 1937; *Educ* Epsom Coll, RCM (opera scholar); *m* 1, 1963, Carolyn Joan, *née* Lambourne; 4 s (Russell Edwin b 9 Feb 1966, Mark Roderick b 24 Aug 1967, Warwick Ashcroft b 19 March 1969, Ashley Jameson b 15 Aug 1974); m 2, 1981, Anne Elizabeth, *née* Howells; 1 s (Matthew Stafford Howells b 12 May 1981), 1 da (Laura Elizabeth Howells b 27 April 1983); *Career* bass; with Glyndebourne Chorus and Opera For All 1962–64, Sadler's Wells Opera 1964–69, Covent Garden Opera 1969– (now guest singer); Sadler's Wells Opera debut as Zuniga in Carmen 1964, Royal Opera House debut as Masetto in Don Giovanni 1969, int debut as Leporello in Don Giovanni Stuttgart 1971, performed with all major Euro and American opera cos (especially in prodns of Mozart repertoire); *Performances* recent operatic roles incl: Alfonso d'Este in Lucrezia Borgia (Covent Garden), Osmin in Die Entführung aus dem Serail (Scot Opera, Hamburg, Geneva), Bottom in A Midsummer Night's Dream (Covent Garden), Rangoni in Boris Godunov (Covent Garden, Orange, Florence), Rocco in Fidelio (Scottish Opera), The Count in Jacobin (Scottish Opera), The King of Portugal in Ones de Castro (Scottish Opera), Waldrov in Arabella, Dr Bartolo in Le Nozze di Figaro (Covent Garden), Don Alfonso in Cosi fan Tutte (Madrid, Lisbon, Covent Garden); recital repertoire incl: Beethoven 9th Symphony and Missa Solemnis, Mozart, Verdi and Penderecki Requiems, Shostakovich 14th Symphony; *Style*— Stafford Dean, Esq; ✉ c/o Allied Artists, 42 Montpelier Square, London SW7 1JZ (☎ 0171 589 6243, fax 0171 581 5269)

DEAN, Timothy Nicholas; s of Geoffrey Dean, of Penzance, Cornwall, and Hilda, *née* Floyd; *b* 23 April 1956; *Educ* Dr Challoner's GS, Guildhall Sch of Music and Drama (ATCL), Univ of Reading (BA), RCM (ARCM); *m* 1981, Ruth Mary, da of Dr Peter Reid Duncan; 3 s (Jonathan Andrew b 26 Sept 1983, Thomas Carey b 28 Dec 1986, Duncan Matthew b 26 Dec 1992); *Career* head of music/chorus master Kent Opera 1983–90, asst music dir D'Oyly Carte Opera Co 1990–91, music dir The Opera Co Tunbridge Wells 1991–94, head of opera RSAMD 1994–; music dir British Youth Opera 1987–, conductor London Bach Soc 1988–90; conducting debuts: ENO 1991, Scottish Opera 1991; festival appearances incl: City of London, Bath, Spitalfields, Aldeburgh, Covent Garden, Stour, Cheltenham, Brighton, Canterbury; conductor: Queen Elizabeth Hall, Purcell Room, Sadlers' Wells, Theatre Royal Drury Lane, Royal Opera House Covent Garden, St John's Smith Square, Wigmore Hall, St Martin-in-the-Fields, St James's Palace, Chequers, 10 Downing Street; FRSA; *Recreations* walking, reading, theatre, racquet sports; *Style*— Timothy Dean, Esq; ✉ Braeval, 4 Ellergreen Road, Bearsden, Glasgow G61 2RJ (☎ 0141 942 8121); Royal Scottish Academy of Music and Drama, 100 Renfrew Street, Glasgow G2 3BD (☎ 0141 332 4101, fax 0141 353 0372); British Youth Opera, c/o South Bank University, 103 Borough Road, London SE1 0AA (☎ 0171 815 6090/1/2/3, fax 0171 815 6094

DEAN, Winton Basil; s of Basil Herbert Dean, CBE (d 1978), of London, formerly of Little Easton Manor, Dunmow, Essex, and Esther, *née* Van Gruisen (d 1983); *b* 18 March 1916; *Educ* Harrow, King's Coll Cambridge (MA); *m* 4 Sept 1939, Hon Mrs (Thalia Mary) Dean, da of 2 Baron Craigmyle (d 1944); 1 s (Stephen b 1946), 2 da (Brigid b 1943, d 1945, Diana b and d 1948), 1 adopted da (Diana b 1955); *Career* Admty (Naval Intelligence) 1944–45; memb: Music Panel Arts Cncl 1957–60, Ctee Handel Opera Soc 1955–60, Cncl Royal Musical Assoc 1965– (vice pres 1970–); Ernest Bloch prof of music 1965–66, Regent's lecturer Univ of California Berkeley 1977, Matthew Vassar lecturer Vassar Coll Poughkeepsie NY 1979; memb Mgmnt Ctee Halle Handel Soc 1979– (vice pres 1991–); kuratorium Göttingen Handel Festival 1981–; translated libretto of Weber's opera Abu Hassan (performed Cambridge, Arts Theatre 1938), ed (with Sarah Fuller) Handel's opera Julius Caesar (performed Birmingham 1977); Hon DMus (Cantab) 1996; Hon RAM 1971, FBA 1975, corresponding memb American Musicological Soc 1989; *Books* The Frogs of Aristophanes (translation of songs and choruses to music by Walter Leigh, 1937), Bizet (1948, 3 revised edn 1975), Handel's Dramatic Oratorios and Masques (1959), Shakespeare and Opera (in Shakespeare and Music, 1964), Handel and The Opera Seria (1969), Beethoven and Opera (in The Beethoven Companion, 1971), Handel, Three Ornamented Arias (ed, 1976), The Rise of Romantic Opera (ed, 1976), The New Grove Handel (1982), French Opera, Italian Opera and German Opera in the Age of Beethoven 1790–1830 (in New Oxford History of Music vol VIII, 1982), Handel's Operas 1704–1726 (with J M Knapp, 1987, revised edn 1995), Essays on Opera (1990); *Recreations* shooting, naval history; *Clubs* English Speaking Union; *Style*— Dr Winton Dean, FBA; ✉ Hambledon Hurst, Godalming, Surrey GU8 4HF (☎ 01428 682644)

DEAN OF BESWICK, Baron (Life Peer UK 1983), of West Leeds in the Co of West Yorks; Joseph Jabez Dean; s of John and Annie Dean, of Manchester; *b* 3 June 1922; *m* 1945, Helen, da of Charles Hill; issue; *Career* MP (Lab) Leeds W 1974–83; *Style*— The Rt Hon Lord Dean of Beswick; ✉ House of Lords, London SW1

DEAN OF HARPTREE, Baron (Life Peer UK 1993), of Wedmore in the County of Somerset; Sir (Arthur) Paul Dean; kt (1985), PC (1991); s of Arthur Dean (d 1961), of Weaverham, Cheshire; *b* 14 Sept 1924; *Educ* Ellesmere Coll, Exeter Coll Oxford (MA, BLitt); *m* 1, 1957, Doris Ellen (d 1979), da of Frank Webb (d 1960), of Sussex; m 2, 1980, Mrs Margaret Frances (Peggy) Parker, *née* Dierden; *Career* WWII Capt Welsh Gds, ADC to Cdr 1 Corps BAOR; former farmer; CRD 1957, resident tutor Swinton Cons Coll 1956–57, asst dir CRD 1962–64, Parly candidate (C) Pontefract 1962; MP (C): N Somerset 1964–83, Woodspring 1983–92; oppn front bench spokesman on health and social security 1969–70, Parly under-sec DHSS 1970–74, chm Cons Health and Social Security Ctee 1979–82; memb: Commons Servs Select Ctee 1979–82, Exec Ctee Cwlth Parly Assoc UK Branch 1975–92, Commons Chm's Panel 1979–82; second dep chm House of Commons and dep chm Ways and Means 1982–87, first dep chm Ways and Means and dep speaker 1987–92; dep speaker House of Lords 1995–; memb exec ctee Assoc of Conservative Peers 1995–; formerly: memb Church in Wales Governing Body, govr BUPA, chm Cons Watch-Dog Gp for Self-Employed; dir: Charterhouse Pensions, Watney Mann and Truman Hldgs; govr Cwlth Inst 1981–89, pres Oxford Univ Cons Assoc; *Clubs* Oxford Carlton (pres), Oxford and Cambridge; *Style*— The Rt Hon Lord Dean of Harptree, PC; ✉ c/o House of Lords, London SW1A 0PW

DEAN OF THORNTON-LE-FYLDE, Baroness (Life Peer UK 1993), of Eccles in the County of Greater Manchester; Brenda Dean; da of Hugh Dean, of Thornton, Cleveleys, Lancs; *b* 29 April 1945; *Educ* St Andrews Eccles, Stretford GS; *m* 30 April 1988, Keith Desmond McDowall, CBE, *qv*; *Career* admin sec Manchester Branch SOGAT 1959–71 (asst branch sec 1971, sec 1976), gen sec SOGAT 1985–91 (pres 1983–85), dep gen sec GPMU 1991–92; chm Ind Ctee for the Supervision of Standards of Telephone Information Servs 1993–; non-exec Bd memb Univ Coll Hosps London 1993–; memb: Women's Nat Cmmn (co chm 1975–78), NEDC 1985–92, BBC Gen Advsy Cncl 1985–89, TUC Gen Cncl 1985–92, TUC Econ Ctee 1987–92, Cncl City Univ 1991–, Cncl Assoc of Business Sponsorship of the Arts 1989–, Advsy Ctee Carnegie 3rd Age Enquiry, Press Complaints Cmmn 1993–, Bdcasting Complaints Cmmn 1993–94, Armed Forces Pay Review Body 1993–94; govr Ditchley Fndn 1992–; non-exec dir: Inveresh plc 1993–, Chanselan Phipps Group plc 1994–; Hon MA Univ of Salford 1986, Hon BA City Univ 1993; hon fell Lancashire Poly 1991; *Recreations* reading, cooking, sailing; *Style*— The Rt Hon Lady Dean of Thornton-le-Fylde; ✉ House of Lords, London SW1A 0PY

DEANE, Derek; s of Gordon Shepherd, and Margaret, *née* Seager; *Career* sr princ Royal Ballet 1980–89 (joined 1972, later choreographer), dep artistic dir/res choregrapher Teatro dell'Opera Rome 1990–92, artistic dir English National Ballet and English National Ballet Sch 1993–; prodns for English Nat Ballet incl: restaging of Marius Petipa's Grand Pas from Paquita, Giselle 1994, Alice in Wonderland 1995; choreographer for Royal Ballet and Birmingham Royal Ballet; various prodns in USA, France, Japan, Australia, S Africa; subject of BBC television documentary 1995; *Style*— Derek Deane, Esq; ✉ English National Ballet, Markova House, 39 Jay Mews, London SW7 2ES (☎ 0171 581 1245, fax 0171 225 0827)

DEAR, Sir Geoffrey James; kt (1997), QPM (1982), DL (1985); s of Cecil William Dear, and Violet Mildred, *née* Mackney; *b* 20 Sept 1937; *Educ* Fletton GS, UCL (LLB); *m* 1958, Judith Ann (d 1996), da of J W Stocker (d 1972), of Peterborough; 1 s (Simon b 1963), 2 da (Catherine b 1961, Fiona b 1966); *Career* joined Peterborough Combined Police after cadet serv 1956, various posts rising to supt Mid Anglia Constabulary 1970–72, asst chief constable Nottinghamshire Constabulary 1972, dep asst cmmnr Met Police 1980–81, asst cmmr Met Police 1981–85, chief constable West Midlands Police 1985–90, HM inspr of constabulary 1990–; Queen's Commendation for Bravery 1979; fell UCL 1990; FRSA 1989; *Recreations* field sports, rugby football, fell walking, music, reading, gardening; *Clubs* East India; *Style*— Sir Geoffrey Dear, QPM, DL; ✉ Government Buildings, Whittington Rd, Worcester WR5 2PA (☎ 01905 359564)

DEARDEN, James; s of late Basil Dearden, and Melissa Stribling Dearden (d 1992); *b* 1949; *Educ* New Coll Oxford (BA); *Career* started as prodn asst in film indust 1967, cutting room trainee rising to film editor in commercials and documentaries 1971–76; writer prodr and dir: The Contraption 1978 (first short film), Diversion (Gold plaque Chicago Film Festival 1980); writer and dir: The Cold Room 1983 (Special Jury prize Oxford Film Festival 1984), Pascali's Island 1987 (selected as an offical Br entry 1988 Cannes Film Festival), A Kiss Before Dying 1991; writer of several screenplays incl Fatal Attraction (Academy Award nomination); *Style*— James Dearden, Esq; ✉ c/o ICM Ltd, Oxford House, 76 Oxford Street, London W1N 0AX (☎ 0171 636 6565, fax 0171 323 0101)

DEARDEN, Dr (Norman) Mark; s of Norman Gerald Dearden, of Leeds, and Mary Isobel Emily, *née* Mosby; *b* 30 June 1953; *Educ* Lord William's GS, Univ of Leeds (BSc, MB ChB); *m* 6 Sept 1986, Margaret Ruth, da of Eric Burkinshaw; 2 s (Paul b 1988, Richard b 1989); *Career* jr doctor Leeds 1977–81, lectr in anaesthetics Univ of Leeds 1981–84, conslt neuro anaesthetist and pt/t sr lectr in anaesthetics Edinburgh 1985–92, conslt anaesthetist and clinical sr lectr in anaesthesia Leeds 1992–; contrib to: Lancet, BMJ, Br Jl of Anaesthesia, Br Jl of Hospital Medicine, Jl of Neurosurgery, Jl of Neurosurgical Anaesthesiology, Anaesthesia, Current Opinion in Anaesthesiology, Current Anaesthesia and Critical Care, Jl of Physiology, Br Jl of Intensive Care, Jl of Neurotrauma, Behavioural Brain Res, Clinical and Laboratory Haematology, Care of the Critically Ill, Jl of Anatomy, Jl of Neurology Neurosurgery and Psychiatry; Br rep on the Intensive Care Gp of The World Fedn of Neurology; memb: Yorks Soc of Anaesthetists 1980, Intensive Care Soc 1983, Scottish Soc of Anaesthetists 1985, E of Scotland Soc of Anaesthetists 1985, World Fedn of Neurologists 1988, Euro Intensive Care Soc 1989, Exec Euro Brain Injury Consortium (EBIC); *Books* Brain Protection (1983), The Clinical Use of Hypnotic Drugs in Head Injury (contrib), Advances in Brain Resuscitation (1991), Management of Brain Edema in Head Injury (contrib), Réanimation et Neurologie (contrib, 1995), Neurochemical Monitoring in the Intensive Care Unit (contrib, 1995); *Recreations* horticulture, DIY; *Style*— Dr Mark Dearden; ✉ Nan Tan

House, Dixon Lane, Wortley, Leeds LS12 4AD; Department of Anaesthesia, Leeds General Infirmary, Great George Street, Leeds LS1 3EX (☎ 0113 243 2799, fax 0113 231 6821)

DEARDEN, Michael Bailey (Mike); s of John Skelton Dearden (d 1963), and Doris Dearden (d 1969); *b* 15 Sept 1942; *Educ* Manchester GS, Merton Coll Oxford (BSc); *m* 16 July 1964, Monica Tatiana, da of Gordon Hewlett Johnson; 1 s (Jonathan Michael b 31 Jan 1965), 1 da (Kathryn Tatiana b 2 Feb 1969); *Career* Castrol Ltd: mktg mangr 1980–84, chief exec Castrol Malaysia 1984–86, gen mangr New Ventures Castrol Ltd 1986–88, regnl dir Castrol Ltd 1988–91; chief exec Foseco International 1991–95, chemicals dir (main bd) Burmah Castrol plc 1995–; Liveryman Worshipful Co of Coachmakers and Coach Harness Makers; ACIM 1965, MIMC 1975; *Recreations* gardening, bridge, rugby, travel, reading; *Clubs* United Oxford and Cambridge University; *Style*— Mike Dearden, Esq; ✉ Burmah Castrol plc, Burmah Castrol House, Pipers Way, Swindon, Wilts SN3 1RE (☎ 01793 452083, fax 01793 512640)

DEARDEN, Neville; s of Maj Issac Samuel Dearden (d 1979), and Lilian Anne, *née* Claxton (d 1983); *b* 1 March 1940; *Educ* Rowlinson Tech Sch Sheffield, King Alfred Coll Winchester, Univ of Southampton; *m* 1, 4 April 1963, Jean Rosemary, da of Walter Francis Garratt, of Sheffield; 2 s (Adrian b 1968, David b 1970), 1 da (Karen b 1966); m 2, 3 May 1980, Eileen Bernadette, da of Dr William John Sheehan; 4 s (Michael b 1981, Patrick b 1984, Ciaran b 1987, Liam b 1990); *Career* head of Science Dept Lafford Sch Lincolnshire 1961–67; md: W Garratt & Son Ltd 1972–78, M & H Fabrications Ltd 1972–77; chief exec S W Fabrications Ltd 1980–84, md Sheffield Brick Group plc 1982–87, chief exec Pan Computer Systems Ltd 1982–85; chm: Parker Winder and Achurch Ltd 1983–85, C H Wood Security Ltd 1983–; Smith Widdowson Eadem Ltd: chm 1983–, md 1986–; md F G Machin Ltd 1983–; chief exec: JCL Engineering Services Ltd, Crompton Engineering (Lancs) Ltd 1989; Comyn Ching Ltd: gp manufacturing dir 1990–, gp sales and mktg dir 1995–; independent dir Marshall Bros (Bury) Ltd 1993; dir SRC Advanced Systems Ltd 1996–, sr conslt Quantum Enterprise Development 1996–; FIMgt, FIIM, FICM, FInstD, DMS; *Recreations* game and sea fishing, boating, practical craft work; *Clubs* Birmingham Press, De La Salle Assoc, Sheffield RUFC, Royal Yachting Assoc; *Style*— Neville Dearden, Esq; ✉ SRC Advanced Systems Ltd, Roseland House, 80 Bushey Wood Road, Dore, Sheffield S17 3QB (☎ and fax 0114 236 4386, e-mail 100016.3474@compuserve.com)

DEARING, Sir Ronald Ernest (Ron); kt (1984), CB (1979); s of Ernest Henry Ashford Dearing (d 1941), and M T Dearing; *b* 27 July 1930; *Educ* Doncaster GS, Univ of Hull (BSc), London Business Sch (Sloane fell); *m* 1954, Margaret Patricia, *née* Riley; 2 da; *Career* regnl dir N Region DTI 1972–74, under sec DTI and Dept of Industry 1972–76, dep sec Dept of Industry 1976–80; chm: Post Office 1981–87 (dep chm 1980–81), Camelot Group plc 1994–95; gp chm Nationalised Industs Chairmen's Gp 1983–84; non-exec dir: Prudential Corp 1987–91, Whitbread Co plc 1988–90, Ericsson Ltd 1988–93, Br Coal Corp 1988–91, IMI plc 1988–; chm: Co Durham Devpt Corp 1987–90, CNAA 1987–88, Polys and Colls Funding Cncl 1988–92, Northern Devpt Corp 1990–94, Fin Reporting Cncl 1989–93, Review Ctee on Accounting Standards, Universities Funding Cncl 1991–92, Sch Curriculum and Assessment Authy 1993–, Nat Curriculum Cncl, Sch Examinations and Assessment Cncl 1993, Higher Educn Funding Cncl for England 1992–93; chllr Univ of Nottingham; first pres Inst of Direct Mktg 1994–; tstee: TRAC, The Sascha Lasserson Meml Tst; patron Music in Allendale; Hon DEng Univs of Durham and Hull, Hon FEng 1992; *Recreations* music, gardening, car boot sales; *Style*— Sir Ron Dearing, CB, Hon FEng; ✉ The School Curriculum and Assessment Authority, Newcombe House, 45 Notting Hill Gate, London W11 3JB

DEAS, Roger Stewart; s of George Stewart (d 1983), of Motherwell, and Winifred Mary, *née* Ogden; *b* 1 Aug 1943; *Educ* The HS of Glasgow, Univ of Glasgow (BSc); *m* 27 June 1970, Carole, da of Percy Woodward, of Nottingham; 2 da (Angela Elizabeth b 1972, Wendy Jane b 1974); *Career* fin dir: Brown Bros Ltd 1974–81, Currys Group plc 1981–85, Heron Corporation plc 1985–86; nat fin ptnr Coopers & Lybrand 1986–95; md Bridewell Group plc 1995–; FCMA 1986 (ACMA 1974); *Recreations* sailing; *Clubs* Royal Motor Yacht; *Style*— Roger Deas, Esq; ✉ Island View, 10 Chaddesley Glen, Canford Cliffs, Poole, Dorset BH13 7PY (☎ 01202 709394); The Bridewell Group plc, Bridewell House, Reading, Berks RG1 1JG (☎ 0118 960 7550)

DEAVE, John James; s of Charles John Deave (d 1970), of London, and Gertrude Debrit, *née* Hunt (d 1972); *b* 1 April 1928; *Educ* Charterhouse, Pembroke Coll Oxford (MA); *m* 16 Aug 1958, Gillian Mary, now Rev G M Deave (Deacon 1987), da of Adm Sir Manley Power, KCB, CBE, DSO (d 1981), of Norton Cottage, Yarmouth, IOW; 1 s (Jonathan b 1959), 1 da (Victoria b 1961); *Career* called to the Bar Gray's Inn 1952, recorder of the Crown Court, chm Med Appeal Tbnl; *Recreations* gardening, history; *Clubs* Notts United Services; *Style*— John Deave, Esq; ✉ Greensmith Cottage, Stathern, Melton Mowbray, Leics (☎ 01949 603 40); 1 High Pavement Chambers, Nottingham (☎ 0115 941 8218)

DEAYTON, (Gordon) Angus; s of Roger Davall Deayton, of Caterham, Surrey, and Susan Agnes, *née* Weir; *b* 6 Jan 1956; *Educ* Caterham Sch Surrey, New Coll Oxford (BA); *Career* writer and broadcaster; with Oxford Revue at Edinburgh Festival 1978 and 1979, memb Hee Bee Gee Bees pop parody gp 1979–85, writer and performer Radio Active (BBC Radio 4) 1980–87 (various awards incl from BPG and Sony); writer/performer: Brunch (Capital Radio) 1985–88, Uncyclopaedia of Rock (Capital Radio) 1986–87 (Monaco Radio award 1986), Rowan Atkinson Stage Show (UK, Aust and NY) 1986–90, Alexei Sayle's Stuff (BBC2) 1988–91, One Foot in the Grave (BBC1) 1989–96, KYTV (BBC2) 1989–93 (Grand Prix and Silver Rose of Montreux 1992), TV Hell (BBC2) 1992; host Have I Got News For You (BBC2) 1990–; writer and presenter: In Search of Happiness (BBC1) 1995, End of the Year Show (BBC1) 1995; presenter BAFTA Awards 1996; other awards incl: Newcomer of the Year TV Comedy Awards 1991, Best TV Performance in a non-acting role BPG Awards 1992, New Talent of the Year TV and Radio Indust Club Awards 1992, BBC TV Personality of the Year TV and Radio Indust Club Awards 1995; *Books* Radio Active Times (1986), The Uncyclopaedia of Rock (1987), In Search of Happiness (1995); *Recreations* soccer (former Crystal Palace FC triallist), tennis, skiing; *Clubs* Groucho, Soho House; *Style*— Angus Deayton; ✉ Talkback, 33 Percy St, London W1V 9FG (☎ 0171 631 3940)

DEBENHAM, Sir Gilbert Ridley; 3 Bt (UK 1931), of Bladen, Co Dorset; s of Sir Ernest Ridley Debenham, 1 Bt, JP (d 1952); suc bro, Sir Piers Kenrick Debenham, 2 Bt, 1964; *b* 28 June 1906; *Educ* Eton, Trinity Coll Cambridge; *m* 1 April 1935, Violet Mary (Mollie) (d 1994), da of His Honour Judge (George Herbert) Higgins (d 1937); 3 s (George Andrew b 1938, d 1991, William Michael b 1940, Paul Edward b 1942), 1 da (Virginia Mary (Mrs Purchon) b 1936); *Heir* gs, Thomas Adam Debenham b 28 Feb 1971; *Career* former consultant psychiatrist NHS, farmer (ret); *Style*— Sir Gilbert Debenham, Bt; ✉ Tonerspuddle Farm, Dorchester, Dorset DT2 7JA (☎ 01929 471 245)

DEBENHAM TAYLOR, John; CMG (1967), OBE (1959), TD (1967); s of John Francis Taylor (d 1941), and Harriett Beatrice, *née* Williams (d 1973); *b* 25 April 1920; *Educ* Whitgift, Aldenham; *m* 1966, Gillian May, da of Cyril Bernard James (d 1981), of Sussex; 1 da (Catharine Jessica b 1972); *Career* Maj RA (TA) Finland, Middle East and SE Asia 1939–45; HM Dip Serv: FO 1946, control cmmn Germany 1947–49, second sec Bangkok 1950, acting consul Songhkla 1951–52, vice consul Hanoi 1952–53, FO 1953–54, first sec Bangkok 1954–56, FO 1956–58, Singapore 1958–59, FO 1960–64, cnsllr Kuala Lumpur 1964–66, FO 1966–69, cnsllr Washington 1969–72 and Paris 1972–73, FCO 1973–77, ret 1977; industl conslt 1978–95; *Recreations* walking, reading, history; *Clubs* Naval and Military; *Style*— John Debenham Taylor, Esq, CMG, OBE, TD; ✉ The East Wing, Gunton Hall, Hanworth, Norfolk NR11 7HJ

DEBERE, (Greville) David; s of David Debere (d 1937), of London, and Patricia, *née* Crone (d 1991); *b* 22 Aug 1935; *Educ* Lancing; *m* 4 Nov 1967, Margaret Anne Silvester, da of Sir Cyril Haines, KBE (d 1988); 1 s (Nicholas b 1972), 1 da (Stephanie b 1970); *Career* admitted slr 1959, asst slr Coward Chance 1960–67, ptnr Brecher & Co 1969–82, subsequently asst dir Slrs' Complaints Bureau of Law Soc (joined 1983), currently sr legal officer Office of the Banking Ombudsman; memb Assoc Cricket Umpires; memb Law Soc 1960; *Recreations* sport, cricket umpiring, bridge; *Clubs* MCC, Middx CC; *Style*— David Debere, Esq; ✉ Office of the Banking Ombudsman, 70 Gray's Inn Road, London WC1X 8NB (☎ 0171 404 9944)

DEBLONDE, Eric; *b* 24 April 1951; *m* Evelyne Blondel; 1 s (Olivier b 24 Jan 1978); *Career* chef; Henri IV Restaurant Dunkirk 1967–69, second de cuisine Hotel de Dieppe Rouen 1972 (joined 1969, CAP de cuisine 1970–72), mil serv 1972–73, second de cuisine Auberge de l'Ecu de France Rouen Aug-Sept 1973, chef saucier Inn on the Park London 1973–74, chef garde mangr Hôtel du Golf Crans Sur Sierre Switzerland 1974–75, chef rôtisseur Belles Rives Juan les Pins May-Sept 1975, sous chef Inn on the Park London 1975–76, chef de cuisine La Marine Caudebec en Caux 1976, exec chef Hotel Tunis Hilton Tunisia 1977–79 (1 sous chef 1976–77), chef de cuisine Le Kilal Château Baie de St Tropez March-Nov 1979, chef de cuisine Frantei Bordeaux 1980–86, exec chef Four Seasons Inn on the Park 1986–; chef Challenge Anneka (BBC Television) 1994; recent awards incl: Grand Prix de l'Académie Nationale de Cuisine, Craft Guild of Chefs Banqueting Award 1995; pres Association Culinaire Francaise 1992–, memb Académie Culinaire de France; Chevalier de l'Ordre du Merite Agricole 1995, Maître Cuisinier de France 1996, vice consul Ordre des Canardiers GB; *Style*— Eric Deblonde, Esq; ✉ The Four Seasons Hotel, Hamilton Place, Park Lane, London W1A 1AZ (☎ 0171 499 0888, fax 0171 499 5572)

DEBY, John Bedford; QC (1980); s of late Reginald Bedford Deby, and late Irene, *née* Slater; *b* 19 Dec 1931; *Educ* Winchester, Trinity Coll Cambridge (MA); *Career* called to the Bar Inner Temple 1954; recorder of the Crown Court 1977–95, bencher Inner Temple 1986; *Style*— John Deby, Esq, QC; ✉ 11 Britannia Rd, London SW6 2HJ (☎ 0171 736 4976)

DECIES, 7 Baron (I 1812); Marcus Hugh Tristam de la Poer Beresford; only s of 6 Baron Decies (d 1992), and his 2 w, Diana, *née* Turner Cain; *b* 5 Aug 1948; *Educ* St Columba's Coll, Univ of Dublin (MLitt); *m* 1, 1970 (m dis 1974), Sarah Jane, only da of Col Basil Gunnell; m 2, 1981, Edel Jeanette, da of late Vincent Ambrose Hendron, of Dublin; 2 s (Hon Robert Marcus Duncan de la Poer b 14 July 1988, Hon David George Morley Hugh de la Poer b 4 May 1991), 1 da (Hon Louisa Katherine de la Poer b 23 Oct 1984); *Heir* s, Hon Robert Marcus Duncan de la Poer Beresford b 14 July 1988; *Career* FCIArb; *Clubs* MCC, Kildare St and University (Dublin); *Style*— The Rt Hon Lord Decies; ✉ Straffan Lodge, Straffan, Co Kildare, Ireland

DEE, Michael James Damian; s of Kenneth William Dee (d 1977), of Bath, and Dorothy Josephine, *née* Whittern-Carter; *b* 12 June 1946; *Educ* Douai Coll, Univ of Edinburgh (BSc); *m* 28 April 1973, Pamela Sarah, da of Cecil George Moore, of Jersey; 4 da (Samantha b 1974, Joanna b 1976, Nicola b 1977, Belinda b 1980); *Career* dir Damian Investment Tst 1972–73, md Europlan Financial Services 1976–, chm Europlan Holdings Ltd 1984–; FInstD; *Recreations* sailing, golf; *Clubs* Royal Channel Islands Yacht, La Moye Golf; *Style*— Michael Dee, Esq; ✉ Le Fromentel, La Grande Route de la Cote, St Clement, Jersey JE2 6SD, Channel Islands; Europlan Holdings Ltd, Lister House, The Parade, St Helier, Jersey JE2 3QQ, Channel Islands (☎ 01534 505800, telex 4192334 wyvern G, fax 01534 505805)

DEECH, Ruth Lynn; da of Josef Asher Fraenkel (d 1987), of London, and Dora, *née* Rosenfeld (d 1989); *b* 29 April 1943; *Educ* Christ's Hosp, St Anne's Coll Oxford (BA), Brandeis Univ USA (Fulbright award, MA); *m* 23 July 1967, Dr John Stewart Deech, s of Max Deech; 1 da (Sarah Rosalind Phyllis b 13 Nov 1974); *Career* legal asst Law Cmmn 1966–67, called to the Bar 1967, res asst to Leslie Scarman (now Rt Hon Lord Scarman) 1967–68, asst prof of law Univ of Windsor Canada 1968–70, fell and tutor in law St Anne's Coll Oxford 1970–91, pupillage 1981, princ St Anne's Coll Oxford 1991–; visiting prof Osgoode Hall Law Sch York Univ Canada 1978; Univ of Oxford: sr proctor 1985–86, memb Hebdomadal Cncl 1986–, chm Admissions Ctee 1993–; visiting lectr Faculty of Law Cape Town Univ 1994; memb Ctee of Inquiry into Equal Opportunities on the Bar Vocational Course 1993–94, memb Exec Cncl of Int Soc of Family Law, chm Human Fertilisation and Embryology Authy 1994–; govr: Carmel Coll Wallingford 1980–90, Oxford Centre for Hebrew and Jewish Studies 1994–; chm Stuart Young awards 1988–, tstee Jewish Continuity 1994–; hon bencher Inner Temple 1996–; *Recreations* after dinner speaking, music, entertaining; *Style*— Mrs Ruth Deech; ✉ St Anne's College, Oxford OX2 6HS (☎ 01865 274800, fax 01865 274895)

DEEDES, Maj-Gen Charles Julius (John); CB (1968), OBE (1953), MC (1944); s of Gen Sir Charles Deedes, KCB, CMG, DSO (d 1968), of Budleigh Salterton, Devon, and Eve Mary, *née* Dean-Pitt; *b* 18 Oct 1913; *Educ* Oratory Sch, RMC Sandhurst; *m* 4 Sept 1939, Beatrice Elaine (Betty), da of H M Murgatroyd (d 1961), of Brockfield Hall, York; 3 s (Charles (Michael) Julius b 1941, Christopher b 1944, Jeremy b 1955); *Career* cmmnd KOYLI 1933, regtl appts 1939–44, serv NW Europe, Caribbean, Italy (wounded), asst mil sec GHQ ME 1946–48, CO Glider Pilot Regt 1949–50, GSO 1 WO 1951–54, CO 1 Bn KOYLI 1954–56, serv Kenya, Aden, Cyprus, Col Gen Staff WO 1957–59, Bde Cdr 150 Inf Bdes TA 1959–62, dep dir staffs duties MOD 1963–65, chief of staff HQ Eastern Cmd 1965–68, Col KOYLI 1966–70, COS HQ Southern Cmd 1968, Dep Col LI (Yorks) 1970–72; treas: Thirsk and Malton Cons Assoc, Ryedale Cons Assoc; FIMgt 1968; Norwegian Military Cross 1940; *Recreations* horticulture, modern history; *Style*— Maj-Gen John Deedes, CB, OBE, MC; ✉ Lea Close, Brandsby, York YO6 4RW (☎ 01347 888239)

DEEDES, Hon Jeremy Wyndham; s of Baron Deedes, MC, PC, DL, *qv*, and Evelyn Hilary, *née* Branfoot; *b* 24 Nov 1943; *Educ* Eton; *m* 1973, Anna Rosemary, da of late Maj Elwin Gray; 2 s (George William b 28 Feb 1976, Henry Julius b 8 June 1978); *Career* reporter: Kent & Sussex Courier 1963–66, Daily Sketch 1966–69; dep ed Daily Express 1976–79, managing ed Evening Standard 1979–85 (ed Londoner's Diary 1970–76), managing ed Today 1985–86; Daily and Sunday Telegraph: exec ed 1986–92, editorial dir 1992–96; md Telegraph Group 1996–; memb Horserace Totalisator Bd 1992–; *Recreations* cricket, racing, cabinet making; *Clubs* Boodle's; *Style*— The Hon Jeremy Deedes; ✉ Hamilton House, Compton, Newbury, Berkshire RG16 0QJ (☎ 01635 578 695); The Daily Telegraph, 1 Canada Square, Canary Wharf, London E14 5DT (☎ 0171 538 5000)

DEEDES, Baron (Life Peer UK 1986), of Aldington, Co Kent; William Francis; MC (1944), PC (1962), DL (Kent 1962); s of Herbert William Deedes, JP, of Saltwood Castle (which was sold 1925) and Sandling Park (which was sold 1897), and Melesina Gladys, JP, 2 da of Philip Chenevix Trench, gs of Richard Chenevix Trench, yr bro of 1 Baron Ashtown; *b* 1 June 1913; *Educ* Harrow; *m* 1942, Evelyn Hilary, da of Clive Branfoot, of Stonegrave, Yorks; 1 s (Hon Jeremy Wyndham b 1943) and 1 s decd (Julius Brook b 1947 d 1970), 3 da (Hon Juliet Evelyn Mary b 1948, Hon Victoria Frances Jill (Hon Mrs Southey) b 1950, Hon Lucy Rose (Hon Mrs Crispin Money-Coutts) b 1955); *Career* served WWII Maj KRRC (TA); ed The Daily Telegraph 1974–86; memb Historic Bldgs Cncl England 1958–62, parly select cttee on Race Relations and Immigration

1970–74, MP (C) Ashford 1950–74, min without portfolio 1962–64, Parly under sec Home Office 1955–57, Parly sec Miny of Housing and Local Govt 1954–55; *Clubs* Carlton, Beefsteak, Royal and Ancient; *Style*— The Rt Hon Lord Deedes, MC, PC, DL; ✉ New Hayters, Aldington, Kent (☎ 01233 720269)

DEEGAN, Terence Leslie (Terry); s of Gilbert Leslie Deegan (d 1970), and Doris Elsie, *née* Barnet; *b* 26 Sept 1942; *Educ* Dartford GS; *m* Susan Philippa; 1 s (Paul b 24 Sept 1969), 2 da (Tara Joanna b 18 Nov 1982, Naomi Rachel b 12 Aug 1985); *Career* with Customs & Excise 1959–67, full time union official Customs & Excise Group (Trade Union) 1967–71, asst sec Soc of Civil and Public Servants 1971–80; Communication Managers Assoc (CMA): dep gen sec 1980–89, elected gen sec 1989– (re-elected 1994); memb Exec Cncl Euro Ctee of Postal Telegraph and Telephone Int (PTTI), exec memb Euro Ctee Postal Comité Paritaire; ed CMA News 1989–; *Recreations* theatre, poultry keeping, walking, cycling and family; *Clubs* Lansdowne (London), Theatre Royal Bath; *Style*— Terry Deegan, Esq; ✉ Communication Managers' Association, CMA House, Ruscombe Business Park, Twyford, Reading, Berks RG10 9JD (☎ 01734 342300, fax 01734 342087)

DEELEY, Michael; s of John Hamilton-Deeley (d 1979), and Josephine Frances Anne, *née* Deacon; *b* 6 Aug 1932; *Educ* Stowe; *m* 1, 1955 (m dis 1967), Teresa Harrison, 1 s (Manuel b 4 Jan 1964), 2 da ((Catherine) Anne b 26 Aug 1956, Isobel b 16 July 1957); m 2, 16 Jan 1970, Ruth Vivienne Emilie, da of Vivian George Stone-Spencer of Brighton, Sussex; *Career* Nat Serv 1950–52, 2 Lt IRWK serv Malaya 1951–52; film prodr; md: Br Lion Films 1972–76, EMI Films Ltd 1976–79; pres EMI Films Inc (USA) 1977–79, chm and chief exec offr Consolidated Entertainment Inc 1984–90, head of int TV Island World 1991–92; prodr of more than thirty motion pictures incl: The Deer Hunter (Best Film Oscar 1978), The Italian Job, Convoy, Murphy's War, The Man Who Fell to Earth, Blade Runner, Robbery, A Gathering of Old Men (NAACP Image Award); dep chm Br Screen Advsy Cncl; fndr memb: PM's Working Party on the Film Indust (1974), Interim Action Ctee on the Film Indust; memb Motion Picture Acad Arts & Sciences (US), ACTT; *Recreations* sailing; *Clubs* Garrick, Wianno, New York Yacht; *Style*— Michael Deeley, Esq; ✉ PO Box 397, Osterville, Mass 02655, USA

DEELEY, Patricia Anne; da of Walter Edgar Jones (d 1983), and Ellen Elizabeth, *née* Goddard (d 1973); *b* 30 Sept 1944; *Educ* St Joseph's Convent Kenilworth, Univ of Bristol (LLB); *m* 9 July 1966, Peter Anthony William Deeley, s of William Deeley; 3 da (Aleanor Elizabeth Jude b 28 Sept 1976, Anna Shahida Jude b 10 Aug 1982, Rosemary Lucy Jude b 27 Nov 1984); *Career* called to the Bar Lincoln's Inn 1970, head of chambers 1992–, recorder of the Crown Ct 1993–; non-exec dir Walsgave Hosps NHS Tst, memb Ct Univ of Warwick; memb Br Assoc of Lawyer Mediators; *Recreations* food, friends, flowers; *Style*— Mrs Patricia Deeley; ✉ Priory Chambers, 2 Fountain Court, Steelhouse Lane, Birmingham, West Midlands B4 6DR (☎ 0121 236 3882, fax 0121 233 3205)

DEELEY, Peter Anthony William; s of George William Deeley (d 1985), of Warwicks, and Bridie Deeley, of Balsall Common, nr Coventry; *b* 30 Aug 1942; *Educ* Ratcliffe Coll Leics, Coventry Poly; *m* 9 July 1966, Patricia Ann, da of Walter Edgar Jones (d 1983), of Coventry; 3 da (Eleanor Elizabeth Jude b 28 Sept 1976, Anna Shahida Jude b 10 Aug 1982, Rosemary Lucy Jude b 27 Nov 1984); *Career* dep md GW Deeley Ltd 1968 (joined 1958); chm Deeley Group Ltd 1985; pres Builder Employers' Confedn (Coventry) 1970–; vice chm: Coventry Hosps Tst (chm 1992–), Coventry Tech Coll; Freeman City of Coventry 1963; memb Inst of Bldg; *Recreations* golf, walking; *Style*— Peter Deeley, Esq; ✉ Eathorpe Hall, Eathorpe, nr Leamington Spa CV33 9DF (☎ 01926 632755); Deeley Group Ltd, William House, Torrington Ave, Coventry (☎ 01203 462521, fax 01203 469533)

DEERHURST, Viscount; Edward George William Omar Coventry; s (by 1 m) and h of 11 Earl of Coventry, *qv*; *b* 24 Sept 1957; *Style*— Viscount Deerhurst

DEERING, Peter Henry; JP (1972); s of William John Deering (d 1962), and Margaret Florence Deering (d 1991); *b* 25 Feb 1931; *Educ* N London Poly Sch of Architecture; *m* 9 Aug 1952, Fay Constance, da of Walter Frederick Sermons (d 1984); *Career* Nat Serv 1955–56; assoc Martin Hutchinson (architect) 1949–67, ptnr David Hogg and Ptnrs (architects) 1973–; memb: Pensions Appeal Tbnl 1993–, Middx Justices Advsy Ctee 1990–, Bd of Visitors Pentonville Prison 1980–92 (chm 1989–91), Mental Health Review Tbnl 1994–; chm Haringey PSA 1990–94; Freeman City of London; *Recreations* cricket, bowls; *Clubs* MCC, Cricketers Club of London, Myddelton House CC; *Style*— Peter Deering, Esq, JP; ✉ 11 Lambourne Gardens, Enfield, Middx EN1 3AD (☎ 0181 363 4093); David Hogg and Partners, 20 Crawford Place, London W1H 1JE (☎ 0171 724 5720)

DEERY, Dr Alastair Robin Stewart; s of late Sgt-Major Michael John Stewart Deery, MM, and Isabella Stout, *née* Murray; *b* 5 Oct 1953; *Educ* Alleynes Sch, Univ of London (BSc, MB BS); *m* 1, 24 Dec 1981 (m dis 1993), Dr Clare Constantine Davey, da of Dr Charles James Constantine Davey; m 2, April 1994, Dr Valerie Thomas, da of David Thomas; 1 s (Andrew), 1 da (Charlotte); *Career* house offr UCH London 1979, sr house offr Manchester 1980, registrar in histopathology Western Infirmary Glasgow 1981–83, sr registrar in histopathology and cytopathology Charing Cross Hosp London 1984–86, conslt, hon sr lectr in histopathology and cytopathology and dir cytopathology unit Royal Free Hosp London 1986– (chm of pathology 1994–96, unit trg dir 1996–); memb: Br Soc of Clinical Cytology, Pathological Soc of UK, BMA; FRCPath 1996 (Royal Coll tutor in pathology 1996–); *Recreations* collecting writing instruments, skiing; *Style*— Dr Alastair Deery; ✉ Cytopathology Unit, Academic Department of Histopathology, Royal Free Hospital School of Medicine, Pond Street, Hampstead, London NW3 2QG (☎ 0171 830 2944)

DeFREITAS, Phillip Anthony Jason (Phil); s of Martin DeFreitas, and Sybil DeFreitas; *b* 18 Feb 1966, Dominica; *Educ* Willesden HS London; *m* 10 Dec 1990, Nicola; 1 da (Alexandra Elizabeth Jane b 5 Aug 1991); *Career* professional cricketer; Leicestershire CCC 1985–88 (capped 1986), Lancashire CCC 1989–94 (capped 1989), Derbyshire CCC 1994–; honours with Lancs: Sunday League champions 1989, NatWest Trophy winners 1990 (Man of the Match), Benson & Hedges Cup winners 1990; overseas teams: Port Adelaide S Aust 1985, Mossman Sydney 1988; England: over 44 test matches 1986–, over 102 one day internationals; tours and tournaments: Aust 1986/87, World Cup 1987, Sharjah Cup 1987, Pakistan, Aust and NZ 1987/88, India and W Indies 1989/90, Nehru Cup 1989, Aust 1990/91, NZ and Aust (incl World Cup) 1991/92, Aust 1994/95, S Africa 1996 (memb squad 7 match one day series), World Cup 1996; *Recreations* golf, gardening, family; *Style*— Phil DeFreitas, Esq; ✉ c/o Derbyshire CCC, County Cricket Ground, Nottingham Road, Derby DE2 6DA

DEFRIEZ, Alistair Norman Campbell; s of Norman William Defriez, and Helen Catherine, *née* Maclean (d 1991); *b* 2 Nov 1951; *Educ* Dulwich Coll, Univ Coll Oxford (Open Gladstone scholar, MA); *m* 1978, Linda Phillips; 1 da (Rachel Philippa b 1982), 2 s (Richard Alistair James b 1984, Henry Alistair William b 1985); *Career* Coopers & Lybrand 1973–78, dir SBC Warburg (formerly S G Warburg & Co Ltd) 1987– (joined 1978), on secondment as dir-gen Panel on Takeovers and Mergers 1996–; FCA 1978 (ACA 1976); *Recreations* golf, rugby, music, reading; *Clubs* Royal Mid-Surrey Golf, London Scottish RFC, Bankers'; *Style*— Alistair Defriez, Esq; ✉ The Panel on Takeovers and Mergers, PO Box 226, The Stock Exchange Building, London EC2P 2JX (☎ 0171 382 9026, fax 0171 638 1554)

DEGEN, Dr Richard Mark; s of William Degen (d 1986), of Vienna, and Bertha, *née* Weinlös; *b* 18 Feb 1938; *Educ* Christ's Coll GS, King's Coll London, Royal Dental Hosp London (BDS, Prosthetics prize 1958, Baldwin scholar 1960, Dolamore prize 1960, LDS RCS 1961), Charing Cross Hosp London, St George's Hosp London; *m* 1973, Bernice Janet, da of Cyril Roles; 3 s (Jonathan Howard b 24 Feb 1965, Antony Craig b 6 Dec 1966, Robbie Benjamin b 21 July 1976), 1 da (Danielle Lisbeth b 30 March 1978); *Career* dental surgeon NHS 1961, oral surgery, dental reconstruction and conscious sedation specialist in private practice 1966–; demonstrator in conservative dentistry Royal Dental Hosp Sch of Dental Surgery London; memb: Br Soc of Med and Dental Hypnosis 1983, Soc for Advancement of Anaesthesia in Dentistry 1986; The Royal Humane Soc Award 1971; peer review convenor and teacher RCS; *Recreations* private aviation, electronics, swimming; *Style*— Dr Richard M Degen; ✉ 135 Harley Street, London W1N 1DJ (☎ 0171 486 2207, fax 0181 455 9099)

DEGG, Garry William; s of George William Degg (d 1977), of Stoke-on-Trent, and Anne, *née* Wright (d 1990); *b* 2 May 1944; *Educ* Hanley HS Stoke-on-Trent, Stoke-on-Trent and Manchester Colls of Commerce (HNC); *m* 1964, Jennifer Ann, da of Joseph Lamb; 1 da (Deborah Julie b 14 Feb 1965), 1 s (Anthony Steven b 25 Nov 1969); *Career* admin trainee rising to personnel supervisor Midlands Electricity Board 1960–68, dep power station admin offr Pembroke Power Station CEGB 1968–70, sr personnel offr then personnel mangr NORWEB Manchester 1970–77, personnel mangr then dir of info systems and personnel SWEB Bristol 1977–87; Midlands Electricity plc (formerly Midlands Electricity Board) Birmingham: dir of Corp Servs and bd sec 1987–90, exec dir corp servs 1990–93, exec dir ops 1993–; ACIS 1965; *Recreations* music, sports enthusiast; *Style*— Garry Degg, Esq; ✉ Midlands Electricity plc, Mucklow Hill, Halesowen, West Midlands B62 8BP (☎ 0121 423 2345, fax 0121 422 3311, car 0831 575859)

DEGHY, Julian; s of Guy Deghy, of London (d 1992), and Mari, *née* Hooper; *b* 16 Oct 1960; *Educ* St Clement Danes GS for Boys; *Career* freelance photographic asst 1980–82, photographic asst to James Cotier, *qv* 1983–86, freelance photographer 1987–; various exhbns incl Assoc of Photographers Awards exhbn 1993 (Merit Colour Series Section); memb Assoc of Photographers 1987; *Recreations* racing, theatre, music, travel, food and wine; *Clubs* Chelsea Arts; *Style*— Julian Deghy, Esq; ✉ 43 Carol Street, London NW1 0HT (☎ 0171 267 7635, fax 0171 267 8706)

DEHN, Conrad Francis; QC (1968); s of Curt Gustav Dehn (d 1948), of London, and Cynthia Doris, *née* Fuller (d 1987); *b* 24 Nov 1926; *Educ* Charterhouse, ChCh Oxford (BA, MA); *m* 1, 1954, Sheila, da of William Kilmurray Magan (d 1967), of London; 2 s (Hugh b 1956, Guy b 1957), 1 da (Katharine b 1959); m 2, 1978, Marilyn, da of Peter Collyer (d 1979), of Oxon; *Career* RA 1945–48, best cadet Mons Basic OCTU 1946, 2 Lt 1947; called to the Bar Gray's Inn 1952 (bencher 1977), recorder of the Crown Court 1974–, head of Fountain Court Chambers 1984–89, dep High Ct judge 1988–96, treas Gray's Inn 1996; dir Bar Mutual Insur Fund 1988–; chm: London Univ Disciplinary Appeals Ctee 1986–, Advsy Ctee Gen Cmmrs of Income Tax Gray's Inn 1994–; *Recreations* theatre, living in France, walking; *Clubs* Reform; *Style*— Conrad Dehn, Esq, QC; ✉ Fountain Court, Temple, London EC4Y 9DH (☎ 0171 583 3335, telex 8813408 FONLEG G, fax 0171 353 0329)

DEHN, Thomas Clark Bruce; s of Harold Bruce Dehn, and Jean Margaret Henderson, *née* Ewing; *b* 6 March 1949; *Educ* Harrow, RAF Coll Cranwell, St Bartholomew's Hosp Med Coll London (MB BS, MS, FRCS, LRCP); *m* 15 Sept 1984, (Dorothea) Lorraine, da of Gilbert Maurice Baird, of Dunbartonshire; 2 da (Henrietta b 1986, Emily b 1988); *Career* gen surgn; conslt gen surgn Royal Berkshire Hosp Reading, clinical lectr in surgery Nuffield Dept of Surgery John Radcliffe Hosp Oxford 1984–88, lectr in surgery St Bartholomew's Hosp Med Coll 1980–84; conslt surgn Royal Berks Hosp Reading 1990–; examiner in surgery Faculty of Dental Surgns RCS 1990–; memb: Hosp Jr Staff Ctee 1987–88, Cncl Section of Surgery RSM 1993–, RCS Comparative Audit Serv Ctee 1992–, MRC Working Pty on Oesophageal Cancer 1994–, Grey Turner Surgical Club 1994–, Br Oesophageal Gp 1994–, Br Soc of Gastroenterologists, Assoc of Surgns of GB and I; Freeman City of London, Liveryman and Steward Worshipful Co of Distillers; *Recreations* flying, rowing and shooting; *Style*— Thomas Dehn, Esq; ✉ Department of Surgery, Royal Berkshire Hospital, Reading, Berkshire RG1 5AN (☎ 0118 987 8623)

DEL MAR, Michael Bernard; s of Richard Oscar Del Mar (d 1995), of Milford-on-Sea, Hants, and Millicent, *née* Shewell (d 1997); *b* 6 June 1946; *Educ* Marlborough Coll, Univ of Birmingham (BSc); *m* 9 Jan 1971, Anthea Noël, da of Paul Ian Van Der Gucht (d 1993), of Herriard, Hants; 3 s (Dominic b 7 Dec 1972, Sam b 11 April 1974, Oliver b 1 Oct 1976); *Career* ptnr L Messel 1978–86, exec dir Shearson Lehman Hutton Securities 1988–90, dir SG Warburg Securities; *Recreations* fishing, gardening; *Style*— Michael Del Mar, Esq; ✉ SBC Warburg, 1 Finsbury Avenue, London EC2M 2PP (☎ 0171 606 1066)

DELACÔTE, Jacques; *Educ* Paris Conservatory, Musikakademie Vienna (under Prof Swarowsky); *Career* conductor; orchestral debut Bruckner Symphony No 9 NY Philharmonic; maj int orchs conducted incl: Vienna Philharmonic, Vienna Symphony, Israel Philharmonic, Orchestre de Paris, Orchestre National de France, Bavarian Radio Orch Munich, San Francisco Symphony, Montreal Symphony, LSO, LPO, RPO, Cleveland Orch, Scottish Nat and Chamber Orch, English Chamber Orch, Nat Orch of Belgium, Royal Danish Orch, BBC London, Rias Berlin, Tokyo Philharmonic, Yomiuri Nippon Symphony; operatic debut Madame Butterfly Vienna State Opera; maj int operatic cos worked with incl: Deutsche Oper-am-Rhein Düsseldorf, Zürich Opera, Royal Danish Opera, Royal Opera House Covent Garden (incl Far East tour to South Korea and Japan), Chatelet Theatre Paris, Paris Opera, Hamburg State Opera, Munich State Opera, Deutsche Oper Berlin, Scottish Opera, WNO, Teatro Liceo Barcelona, Teatro Colon Buenos Aires; recent operatic appearances incl: Royal Opera House (Turandot and Samson et Dalila), Carmen with Placido Domingo, ENO, Pittsburgh, Montreal, Toronto, Earl's Court London and tour to Japan, Sydney and Melbourne, Chicago Opera, Flandern Festival, Orange Festival, Macerata Festival; debut Henry Wood Promenade Concerts 1986; operatic recordings for: EMI (with Samuel Ramey and José Carreras), Philipps (with José Carreras and Montserrat Caballé), Tring (with RPO); *Style*— Jacques Delacôte, Esq; ✉ c/o IMG Artists, Media House, 3 Burlington Lane, Chiswick, London W4 2TH

DELACOURT-SMITH OF ALTERYN, Baroness (Life Peer UK 1974); Margaret Rosalind; da of F J Hando; *b* 5 April 1916; *Educ* Newport High Sch, St Anne's Coll Oxford; *m* 1939, Lord Delacourt-Smith, PC (Life Peer, d 1972); 1 s, 2 da; m 2, 1978, Prof Charles Blackton; *Career* cncllr of Royal Borough of New Windsor 1962–65, JP 1962–67; *Style*— The Rt Hon the Lady Delacourt-Smith; ✉ House of Lords, London SW1

DELAMERE, 5 Baron (UK 1821); Hugh George Cholmondeley; s of 4 Baron Delamere (d 1978, whose gf 2 Baron was fifth cous of 1 Marquess of Cholmondeley) and his 1 w, Phyllis, da of Lord George Montagu Douglas Scott (3 s of 6 Duke of Buccleuch); *b* 18 Jan 1934; *Educ* Eton, Magdalene Coll Cambridge (MA Agric); *m* 1964, Ann Willoughby, da of Sir Patrick Gilbert Renison, GCMG, and formerly w of Michael Tinné; 1 s; *Heir* s, Hon Thomas Patrick Gilbert Cholmondeley b 19 June 1968; *Career* farmer; sr settlement officer Kinangop 1962–63; landowner (57,000 acres); *Recreations* racing, shooting, flying; *Clubs* Pitt, Muthaiga Country, Jockey (Kenya); *Style*— The Rt Hon the Lord Delamere; ✉ Soysambu, Elmenteita, Kenya; Delamere Estates Ltd, Private Bag, Nakuru, Kenya (☎ operator 155 to connect with Elmenteita 28)

DELAMORE, Dr Irvine William; s of William Delamore (d 1968), and May, *née* Wright; *b* 16 July 1930; *Educ* Spalding GS, Univ of Edinburgh (MB ChB, PhD); *m* 8 Dec

1955, (Hilda) Rosemary, Edgar Frank Thomas (d 1984); 2 da (Catherine b 1957, Wendy b 1958); *Career* surgn Lt RNVR 1955–57; Damon Runyon res fell Yale Univ Med Sch 1960–61, visiting WHO prof Baroda Med Sch India 1963–64, conslt physician Blackburn Royal Infirmary 1966–69, hon conslt physician Manchester Royal Infirmary 1989– (conslt physician 1970–89); memb: Br Soc for Haematology, Worshipful Soc of Apothecaries, Assoc of Physicians; FRCPE 1968, FRCPath 1974, FRCP(London) 1981; *Books* Haematological Aspects of Systemic Disease (1990), Myeloma and other Paraprotein Disorders (1986), Leukaemia (1986); *Recreations* golf, gardening, photography, reading; *Style*— Dr Irvine Delamore; ✉ Fisher House, Rivington, Bolton, Lancs BL6 7SL (☎ and fax 01204 696437); BUPA Hospital, Russell Rd, Whalley Range, Manchester M16 8AJ (☎ 0161 226 0112)

DELANEY, Francis James Joseph (Frank); 5 s of Edward Joseph Delaney (d 1968), of Tipperary, Ireland, and Elizabeth Josephine, *née* O'Sullivan (d 1990); *b* 24 Oct 1942; *Educ* Abbey Schs Tipperary, Rosse Coll Dublin; *m* 1, 1966 (m dis 1980), Eilish, *née* Kelliher; 3 s (Edward b 1968, Bryan b 1971, Owen b 1976); m 2, 1988, Susan, *née* Collier; *Career* writer, TV and radio broadcaster, journalist; work incl: RTE News Dublin, current affrs with BBC N Ireland, BBC TV and BBC Radio 4; *Books* James Joyce's Odyssey (1981), Betjeman Country (1983), The Celts (1986), A Walk in the Dark Ages (1988), My Dark Rosaleen (novella 1989), Legends of the Celts (1989), The Sins of the Mothers (novel, 1992), A Walk to the Western Isles (1993), Telling the Pictures (novel, 1993), A Stranger in their Midst (novel, 1995); *Clubs* Athenaeum, Chelsea Arts; *Style*— Frank Delaney, Esq; ✉ c/o Harper Collins Publishers, 77–85 Fulham Palace Road, London W6 8JB

DELANEY, Dr John Christopher; s of John Lawrence Delaney (d 1985), and Isabel, *née* Garroch; *b* 16 Feb 1941; *Educ* St Anselms Coll Birkenhead, Univ of Liverpool (MB ChB); *m* 24 July 1965, Julia Margaret Delaney, JP, da of Ernest Emmett Cotter (d 1994), of Liége House, Upton, Wirral; 2 s (Andrew John b 1968, Simon Gerard James b 1971), 1 da (Susan Mary b 1966); *Career* conslt physician Arrowe Park Hosp Wirral 1976–, dist tutor RCP 1986, pubns on asthma and aspirin sensitivity; chm: Wirral Dist Conslts Ctee, Med Bd Wirral Hosps, Dist Med Audit Ctee Wirral; club doctor Tranmere Rovers FC; memb: Br Thoracic Soc, BMA; FRCP 1984 (MRCP 1971); *Recreations* golf, gardening, reading, watching soccer; *Style*— Dr John Delaney; ✉ Chelline, 12 West Close, Noctorum, Birkenhead, Merseyside (☎ 0151 677 2500); Arrowe Park Hospital, Upton, Wirral (☎ 0151 678 5111, car 0860 596747)

DELANEY, Laurance; s of Charles Gerald Delaney (d 1981), and Irene, *née* Jenkins; *b* 8 May 1956; *Educ* Stebon Heath Secdy Sch; *m* 1975, Joyce Lynne, da of Richard Peter Johns; 1 s (Simon Leigh b 15 June 1978), 1 da (Vicky Louise b 3 Jan 1981); *Career* rugby union player; Llanelli Sch Boys 1971–72, New Dock Stars Youth 1972–75, over 501 appearances Llanelli RFC 1977–; Wales caps: 3 youth 1974–75, 7 B 1985, 11 full 1989– (incl 4 World Cup appearances 1991); 5 appearances Barbarians; *Recreations* green bowling, fishing; *Style*— Laurance Delaney, Esq; ✉ c/o Llanelli RFC, Strady Park, Llanelli, Dyfed

DELANEY, Theo John Samuel; s of Barry John Samuel Delaney, of Hamilton Terrace, London, and Brenda Jean, *née* Darby; *b* 31 Dec 1965; *Educ* Shene Sch, Richmond Coll; *Career* prodn runner John Clive & Co 1984–86, prodn asst Berkofsky Barrett Productions 1986–87, news ed Direction Magazine (Haymarket Publishing) 1988–89; film dir: Tony Kaye Films 1990–91 (film prodr 1989–90), Spots Film Services 1991–96, Tomboy Films 1996–; *Awards* Bronze (NY Advtg Festival) 1990, Gold (Creative Circle Awards) 1990, Silver Lion (Int Advtg Festival Cannes) 1990 and 1991, work accepted for D&AD Annual 1992, Best New Director (Saatchi and Saatchi New Directors Showcase/Int Advtg Festival Cannes) 1993; memb D&AD 1992; *Clubs* Groucho; *Style*— Theo Delaney, Esq; ✉ Tomboy Films, 40–41 Foley Street, London W1P 7LD

DELBRIDGE, Richard; s of Tom Delbridge, and Vera, *née* Lancashire; *b* 21 May 1942; *Educ* LSE (BSc), Univ of California Berkeley (MBA); *m* 19 March 1966, Diana Genevra Rose, da of H W Bowers-Broadbent; 1 s (Mark b 1973), 2 da (Roseanna b 1970, Cressida b 1982); *Career* CA 1966; Arthur Andersen: articled clerk 1963–66, mgmnt conslt 1968–, ptnr 1974–76; sr vice pres and gen mangr London office J P Morgan & Co Inc 1987–89 (int operations 1976–79, comptroller 1979–85, asst gen mangr 1985–87), gp fin dir Midland Bank plc 1989–92, gp fin dir HSBC Holdings plc (following takeover of Midland Bank) 1993–95, dir and chief fin offr National Westminster Bank plc 1996; bd memb The Securities Assoc 1988–89; FCA 1972; *Recreations* hill walking, books; *Style*— Richard Delbridge, Esq; ✉ 48 Downshire Hill, London NW3 1NX; National Westminster Bank, 41 Lothbury, London EC2P 2BP (☎ 0171 726 1333, fax 0171 726 1511)

DELL, David Michael; CB (1986); s of Montague Roger Dell (d 1980), and Aimée Gabrielle, *née* Gould (d 1964); *b* 30 April 1931; *Educ* Rugby, Balliol Coll Oxford (MA); *Career* 2 Lt Royal Signals, serv Egypt and Cyprus 1954–55; Admty 1955–60, MOD 1960–65, Miny of Technol 1965–70; DTI: joined 1970, under sec 1976–83, dep sec 1983, dir Industl Devpt Unit 1984–87, dir Euro Investmt Bank 1984–87, chief exec Br Overseas Trade Bd 1987–91; dir Nesbit Evans Group 1991–93; *Clubs* RAC, St Stephen's Constitutional, Leeds; *Style*— David M Dell, Esq, CB; ✉ 18 Shouldham Street, London W1

DELL, Rt Hon Edmund Emanuel; PC (1970); s of Reuben Dell, and Frances Dell; *b* 15 Aug 1921; *Educ* Owen's Sch London, Queen's Coll Oxford (MA); *m* 1963, Susanne Gottschalk; *Career* Lt RA serv Euro 1944–45; memb Manchester City Cncl 1953–60, pres Manchester and Salford Trades Cncl 1958–61, MP (Lab) Birkenhead 1964–79, Parly sec Miny of Technol 1966–67, Parly under sec of state Dept of Econ Affrs 1967–68; min of state: BOT 1968–69, Dept of Employment and Productivity 1969–70; chm Commons Public Accounts Ctee 1973–74 (acting chm 1972–73), paymaster-gen 1974–76, sec of state trade and pres BOT 1976–78, memb Ctee Three Wise Men investigation into working of EEC instns 1978–79; chm: Hansard Soc Cmmn on Paying for Politics 1979–80, Ctee on Int Business Taxation 1982, Working Pty on Co Political Donations 1985 (Hansard Soc and Const Reform Centre); chm and chief exec Guinness Peat Group 1979–82, chm C4 TV Co Ltd 1980–87, dir Shell Transport and Trading Co plc 1979–92; chm: Public Fin Fndn 1984–91, Prison Reform Tst 1988–93, London C of C and Indust 1990–92 (pres 1991–92), Commercial Educn Tst 1989–92; dep chm Govrs Imperial Coll 1988–91; hon fell Fitzwilliam Coll Cambridge 1986; FRHistS 1996; *Publications* The Good Old Cause (ed with J E C Hill, 1949), Brazil: The Dilemma of Reform (Fabian pamphlet, 1964), Political Responsibility and Industry (1973), Report on European Institutions (with B Biesheuvel and R Marjolin, 1979), The Politics of Economic Interdependence (1987), A Hard Pounding: Politics and Economic Crisis 1974–76 (1991), The Schuman Plan and the British Abdication of Leadership in Europe (1995), The Chancellors (1996); articles in learned journals; *Recreations* listening to music; *Style*— The Rt Hon Edmund Dell; ✉ 4 Reynolds Close, NW11 7EA (☎ 0181 455 7197)

DELL, Dame Miriam Patricia; ONZ (1993), DBE (1980, CBE 1975), JP (1975); da of Gerald Wilfred Matthews (d 1940, family arrived NZ 1824) and Ruby Miriam, *née* Crawford (d 1948); *b* 14 June 1924; *Educ* Epsom Girls' GS, Auckland Univ (BA), Auckland Teachers' Training Coll (Teaching Cert); *m* 1946, Dr Richard Kenneth Dell, QSO; 4 da; *Career* teacher 1945–47, 1957–58 and 1961–71; nat chm Young Wives 1956–58; memb: Exec Cncl for Equal Pay and Opportunity 1966–76, various sub ctees Standards Assoc 1967–70, Joint Ctee on Women's Employment Nat Devpt Cncl 1969–74; convener and tutor Hutt Valley Marriage Guidance Cncl 1971 (tutor 1964–70); memb: Exec Environment and Conservation Organisation 1971–78 (chm 1988–), Ctee of Inquiry into Equal Pay 1971–72, Nat Exec Nat Marriage Guidance Cncl 1972–76; fndr memb Hutt Valley Branch Fedn Univ Women, chairwoman Ctee on Women 1974–81; memb: Nat Cmmn for UNESCO 1974–85, Nat Cncl Urban Devpt Assoc 1975–78, Steering Ctee and conslt Nat Cmmn for IYC 1977–79, Social Security Appeal Authority 1974–; pres Inter-Church Cncl of Public Affairs 1982–90 (vice-pres 1979–82); Nat Cncl of Women of NZ: rep for Mothers' Union Wellington Branch 1957, fndr memb Hutt Valley Branch 1958, pres 1966–68, vice pres Bd of Offrs 1967–70, nat pres 1970–74, co-opted memb Parly Watch Ctee 1974–, convener Physical Environment Standing Ctee 1974–78, convener Status of Women Standing Ctee 1978–79; Int Cncl of Women: vice convener Standing Ctee on Physical Environment 1973–76, vice pres 1976–79, pres 1979–86, hon pres 1986–88, memb Ctee of Honour 1986–; nat co-ordinator Int Women's Yr (IWY) 1975, memb Museum of New Zealand Project Devpt Bd 1988–91, memb Social Responsibility Cmmn and convener Public Affairs Unit (Anglican Church) 1989–91, dep chair Wellington Conservation Bd 1989–, chairwoman Suffrage Centennial Year Tst 1991–94, memb Ctee to Review Honours System in NZ 1995–; has organised numerous workshops, leadership training courses and seminars nationally and internationally and has represented NZ at many overseas conferences; Adele Ristori prize 1976, Queen's Silver Jubilee medal 1977, New Zealand Commemorative medal 1990, Suffrage Centennial medal 1993; *Recreations* gardening, handcraft; *Style*— Dame Miriam Dell, ONZ, DBE, JP; ✉ 98 Waerenga Rd, Otaki, NZ (☎ 00 64 6 364 7267); 275 Cockayne Road, Ngaio, Wellington, NZ (☎ and fax 00 64 4 479 4581)

DELL, Ven Robert Sydney; s of Sydney Edward Dell (d 1957), and Lilian Constance, *née* Palmer (d 1968); *b* 20 May 1922; *Educ* Harrow Co Sch, Emmanuel Coll Cambridge (MA), Ridley Hall; *m* 1953, Doreen Molly, da of William Layton (d 1957); 1 s (Christopher James b 1965), 1 da (Katharine Julia b 1961); *Career* ordained 1948, vice-princ Ridley Hall Cambridge 1957–66, vicar of Chesterton Cambridge 1966–73, archdeacon of Derby 1973–92 (archdeacon emeritus 1992), hon canon of Derby Cathedral and examining chaplain to Bishop of Derby 1973–92, canon residentiary of Derby Cathedral 1981–92; memb of the Gen Synod of the Church of Eng 1978–85; hon fell Univ of Derby 1993; *Recreations* travel and writing; *Style*— The Ven Robert Dell; ✉ 7 Moss Drive, Haslingfield, Cambridge (☎ 01223 872194)

DELLA SALA, Prof Sergio; *b* 23 Sept 1955; *Educ* Univ of Milan Medical Sch (MD, PhD), Univ of California at Berkeley (pre-med); *Career* Univ of Milan: registrar in neurology 1980–84, conslt in neurology 1987–93, head of Neuropsychology Unit 1989–93; prof of psychology Univ of Aberdeen 1994–; *Style*— Prof Sergio Della Sala; ✉ Department of Psychology, University of Aberdeen, King's College, Aberdeen AB24 2UB (fax 01224 273426)

DELLIÈRE, John Peter; s of Robert Fernand George Dellière, of Haslemere, Surrey, and Elaine Gorton, *née* Hobbs; *b* 6 Aug 1944; *Educ* Whitgift Sch; *m* 28 June 1969, Elizabeth Joan, da of Gordon Keith Harman, of Lower Kingswood, Surrey; 3 s (Christian John b 10 Jan 1972, James Peter b 26 Aug 1976, Michael Robert Gordon b 2 Oct 1979); *Career* Mellors Basden & Co (City Accountants) 1963–68, Arthur Andersen & Co 1968–70, dir The White House (Linen Specialists) Ltd 1970, md The White House Ltd and subsidiary cos 1982– (dir 1980–, jt md 1982–85); memb Cncl Bond St Assoc 1977–96 (chm 1981–83); FCA 1979 (ACA 1967), ATII 1967; *Recreations* golf, tennis; *Clubs* RAC, Monte's; *Style*— John Dellière, Esq; ✉ Stable Cottage, Mill Lane, Ripley, Surrey GU23 6QT (☎ 01483 224975); The White House Ltd, 51 New Bond St, London W1Y 0BY (☎ 0171 629 3521, fax 0171 629 8269, mobile 0836 206362)

DELLIPIANI, Dr Alexander William; s of William Alexander Dellipiani (d 1965), of Gibraltar, and Lourdes, *née* Pallas (d 1982); *b* 25 Oct 1934; *Educ* Gibraltar GS, Univ of Edinburgh (MB ChB, MD); *m* 29 Sept 1962, Dorothy Sheila Lenore, da of Allan Inglis, CMG (d 1984), of Edinburgh; 1 s (John b 13 Jan 1973), 3 da (Elizabeth b 7 May 1964, Jane b 27 April 1968, Louise b 7 Dec 1970); *Career* house offr The Royal Infirmary Edinburgh 1959–60, sr lectr The Med Sch Baroda India 1965–66, lectr Dept of Therapeutics Univ of Edinburgh 1964–68 (res fell 1960–64), conslt physician N Tees Gen Hosp and hon sr lectr Univ of Newcastle upon Tyne 1968–96; univ postgrad med tutor N Tees Dist 1973–76, regnl advsr RCP(Ed) 1976–95 (examiner MRCP II 1970–), conslt physician Cleveland Constabulary 1986–; memb Vocational Trg Sub-Ctee Med Newcastle until 1995; chm: N Tees Dist Med Exec Ctee 1976–78, Gen Hosp Staff Ctee 1980–84; memb: N Regnl Res Ctee 1982–90, Northern RHA 1982–90, N Regnl Med Ctee 1982–90; fell RMS Edinburgh 1959, MBSG 1964, memb British Soc of Digestive Endoscopy 1972; FRCP, FRCPE; *Books* contrib: Coronary Care in The Community (1977), Intestinal Stomas (1978), Disease of the Gut and Pancreas (1994); *Style*— Dr Alexander W Dellipiani; ✉ Lynton, 17 Maltby Rd, Thornton, Middlesbrough, Cleveland TS8 9BU (☎ 01642 590470); North Tees General Hospital, Hardwick, Stockton on Tees, Cleveland TS19 8PE (☎ 01642 617617)

DELLOW, Jeffrey (Jeff); s of Ernest Dellow (d 1966), of Heworth, County Durham, and Edith, *née* Greenwell; *b* 19 Jan 1949; *Educ* Bill Quay Sch, St Martin's Sch of Art, Maidstone Coll of Art, Slade Sch of Fine Art (Cheltenham Fellowship); *m* June 1976, Paula Jean Alison, da of Lt Col Roy Cleasby, MBE; 1 da (Bryony Grace b 27 Jan 1987); *Career* artist; lectr: Hull Coll of Art 1977–86, Roehampton Inst London 1978–80, N E London Poly 1978–86, Slade Sch of Fine Art (postgrad painters) 1980–82, Winchester Sch of Art 1982–86, Central Sch of Art 1982–84; head of painting and print lectr Hull of Coll of Art 1986–88, head of painting Kingston Univ 1988–; visiting artist: RAF Bruggen W Germany 1974–75, Hull Coll of Art 1977, NE London Poly 1978, Roehampton Inst London 1978, Maidstone Coll of Art 1979, Slade Sch of Fine Art 1979, Manchester Poly Fine Art 1980, Norwich Sch of Art 1981, Winchester Sch of Art 1981; work in collections incl: Arts Cncl of GB, Unilever, James Capel, Coopers & Lybrand, Arthur Andersen & Co, BASF UK; *Exhibitions* incl: John Moores 10 Liverpool 1976, Drawing in Action Arts Cncl Touring Show 1978–79, Open Attitudes Museum of Modern Art Oxford 1979, Small Works by Younger Br Artists 1980, Small Works Roehampton Inst 1980, Sculpture and Painting from the Greenwich Studios Woodlands Gallery Blackheath 1981, Opening Show Hull Artists Assoc 1982, Small Works (Newcastle upon Tyne Poly Gallery 1982), Whitechapel Open 1983–91, Marseille Art Present Artis Gallery Marseille, Maison du Peuple Gardance France 1983, 100 Artists The Showroom Gallery London 1984, Drawings and Watercolours Hull Coll of Art 1984, Greenwich Festival Studio Open 1985–93, Summer in the City Ikon Gallery Birmingham 1985, Three Painters Arteast Gallery collective 1986, solo show New Paintings Castlefield Gallery 1987, Three Abstract Painters Todd Gallery 1987, Art for Sale Minories Gallery 1988, Idylls Todd Gallery Summer Show 1989, Bath Art Fair 1989, John Moores 16 Liverpool 1989, Art 90 Islington Art Fair 1990, Todd Soho Gallery 1990, Olympia Art Fair 1990, Creative Assets Harris Museum Preston 1990, Works on Paper Todd Gallery 1990, Pachipamwe III Nat Gallery of Zimbabwe Harare 1990, Broadgate Art Week 1990, John Moores 17 (prizewinner) 1991, Whitechapel Studio Open 1992, Greenwich Studios Painting and Sculpture Woodlands Gallery Blackheath 1992, Leeds Poly Artists Symposium/Workshop 1992, Watercolour Curwen Gallery (Windmill St, London), Sunday Times Singer & Friedlander Watercolour Competition Mall Galleries (London), Sans Frontiers Waterman Art Centre 1993, solo exhibition Recent Paintings Cafe Gallery London 1995; *Awards* Boise travelling scholarship, Arts Cncl of GB minor bursary, prizewinner Athena Art Awards Barbican 1988; *Style*— Jeff Dellow, Esq; ✉ Kingston University, School of Fine Art, Knights Park, Kingston upon Thames KT1 2QJ (☎ 0181 547 2000)

DELMAR-MORGAN, Michael Walter; s of Curtis Delmar Morgan (d 1987), and Susan Henrietta, *née* Hargreaves Brown; *b* 1 March 1936; *Educ* Eton; *m* 17 Feb 1962, Marjorie, da of John Kennedy Logan (d 1984); 1 s (Benjamin b 1966), 2 da (Katharine b 1968, Alexandra b 1971); *Career* banker; dir: Brown Shipley & Co Ltd 1966–88, Columbus Financial Services Ltd 1989–, Columbus Asset Management Ltd 1989–; vice chm St Dunstan's (The Blinded Servicemen's Charity); *Recreations* sailing; *Clubs* Royal Yacht Sqdn; *Style—* Michael W Delmar-Morgan, Esq

DELROY-BUELLES, Konrad; s of Josef and Margarethe Buelles, of Aachen, Germany; *b* 6 Sept 1941; *Educ* Aachen TH Germany, Antioch Coll Ohio USA (BA); *m* Ingrid, da of Barnet Delroy; 2 da (Marnie b 12 June 1979, Ilana b 10 March 1981); *Career* mgmnt trainee Legler Italy 1966–69; Burlington Industries Inc: mgmnt trainee NY 1969–70, various managerial appts US, UK and Switzerland 1970–86; md Eismann International Ltd 1983–; md B B Burlington, dir Kim Von Herzog Properties Ltd; *Recreations* squash, gardening; *Style—* Konrad Delroy-Buelles, Esq; ✉ Eismann International Ltd, Margarethe House, Eismann Way, Phoenix Park Industrial Estate, Corby, Northants NN17 1ZB (☎ 01536 407010, fax 01536 406512)

DELTEIL, Christian Claude; s of Roger Delteil, and Catherine, *née* Fluxa; *b* 13 May 1954; *m* 9 Jan 1978, Geneviève Petit-Roche; 1 s (Sébastien b 31 Dec 1985), 1 da (Lauriane b 19 May 1979); *Career* Military Serv as chef of Admiral Brest; apprentice in Caborg France, commis chef then chef de partie Le Gavroche London 1975–76, chef de partie The Connaught 1976–77, sous chef then head chef Chewton Glen Hotel New Milton Hants 1978–82, chef and proprieter L'Arlequin 1982–, currently chef Cutty Catering Specialist Ltd; awards: one Michelin Star 1983, two stars Egon Ronay 1983, Restaurant of the Year Egon Ronay 1989; memb Académie Culinaire de France; *Recreations* karate, deep sea diving; *Style—* Christian Delteil, Esq; ✉ c/o Cutty Catering Specialist Ltd, 57 Sandgate Street, London SE15 (☎ 0171 358 1617, fax 0171 635 9760)

DELVIN, Dr David George; s of William Delvin, of Ayrshire, and Elizabeth, *née* Falvey, of Kerry; *b* 28 Jan 1939; *Educ* St Dunstan's Coll, King's Coll Hosp Univ of London; *m* 1 (m dis), Kathleen, *née* Sears; 2 s, 1 da; m 2, Christine Campbell Webber; *Career* TV doctor and writer; dir The Medical Information Service; memb GMC until 1995, med conslt to NAFPD, conslt ed Gen Practitioner, vice chm Med Journalist Assoc, winner Best Book award of American Med Writers' Assoc, Consumer Columnist of the Year; LRCP, MRCS, DRCOG, MRCGP; Médaille de la Ville de Paris; *Recreations* scuba, running, opera; *Clubs* Royal Soc of Medicine; *Style—* Dr David Delvin; ✉ c/o Coutts & Co, 2 Harley St, London W1

DELVIN, Lord; Sean Charles Weston Nugent; does not at present use courtesy title; s and h of 13 Earl of Westmeath; *b* 16 Feb 1965; *Educ* Ampleforth; *Career* computer analyst; *Style—* Sean Nugent, Esq

DEMARCO, Prof Richard; OBE (1984); s of Carmine Demarco (d 1975), of Edinburgh, and Elizabeth Valentine Fusco (d 1982); *b* 9 July 1930; *Educ* Holy Cross Acad Edinburgh Coll of Art, Moray House Teachers Coll; *m* 1956, Anne Carol, da of Robert Muckle; *Career* artist, arts organiser, bdcaster, lectr; art master Duns Scotus Acad Edinburgh 1956–67, illustrator of BBC pubns 1958–61, fndr memb and vice chm Traverse Theatre Club 1963–67, dir Traverse Art Gallery 1963–67; artistic dir: Richard Demarco Gallery 1966–, Euro Youth Parl 1993–; tstee Kingston-Demarco Euro Cultural Fndn 1993–, dir Demarco Euro Art Fndn 1993– (tstee 1992); introduced avant-garde visual art to Edinburgh Festival Prog 1967 and presented avant-garde art from abroad 1968–92; responsible for promotion of nat and int art and theatre; visiting lectr at over 150 schs of art and univs, prof Univ of Kingston 1993– (Stanley Picker fell and lectr Kingston Poly 1991); artist represented in over 1600 collections; illustrator of books incl: The Edinburgh Diary 1980, The Royal Mile 1990, Literary Edinburgh 1992; regular broadcaster TV and radio in Britain, N America and Poland; progs incl: One Man's Week (1971), Images (5 progs Grampian TV, 1974), The Demarco Dimension (1988), The Green Man (BBC Omnibus, 1990), Portrait of Richard Demarco (BBC2, 1991); pubns incl: The Artist as Explorer (1978), The Road to Meikle Seggie (1978), The Celtic Consciousness (1978), A Life in Pictures (1994); weekly columnist: Edinburgh and Lothian Post 1987–89, Sunday Times (Scotland) 1988; dir Sean Connery's Scot Int Educn Tst 1972, memb Bd of Govrs Carlisle Sch of Art 1973–77, contrib ed Studio International 1982–84; external examiner: Stourbridge Sch of Art 1987–89, Wolverhampton Sch of Art 1990; LLD (hc) Univ of Dundee 1996; Scot Arts Cncl award for services to the Arts in Scotland 1975, Br International Theatre Inst Award 1992, Polish International Theatre Inst Award (Stanislaw Witkiewicz Award) 1992, Hon DFA Atlanta Coll of Art 1993; The Gold Order of Merit of the Polish People's Republic 1976, The Order of Cavaliere della Repubblica d'Italia 1988, Chevalier de L'Ordre des Arts et des Lettres de France 1991; Cdr Hospitiller Order of St Lazarus of Scotland 1996; memb Association International des Critiques d'Art, memb SSA, RSW, Hon FRIAS 1991; *Recreations* exploring The Road to Meikle Seggie towards the Hebrides in the footsteps of the Roman Legions, St Servanus and the Celtic Saints, and the medieval scholars, onwards into the Mediterranean and Eastern Europe; *Clubs* Scottish Arts (Edinburgh), Polish; *Style—* Prof Richard Demarco, OBE; ✉ 23A Lennox St, Edinburgh EH4 1PY (☎ 0131 343 2124); The Richard Demarco European Art Foundation, 3 York Lane, Edinburgh EH1 3HY (☎ 0131 557 0707, fax 0131 552 5972); Kingston University, Millenium House, Eden Street, Kingston-upon-Thames, Surrey KT1 1BL (☎ 0181 547 2000, fax 0181 547 7789)

DEMERY, Edward Peter; s of Peter Demery, and Cecilia Gwyneth Nepean, *née* Clifford-Smith; *b* 12 Dec 1946; *Educ* Bradfield; *m* 16 Jan 1971, Alexandra, da of Harold Paillet Rodier of Leatherhead, Surrey; 1 s (Rupert b 1972), 1 da (Miranda b 1973); *Career* dir Clifford-Smith (Underwriting Agencies) Ltd 1976–85; Justerini & Brooks Ltd wine merchants: joined 1967, dir 1977–, sales dir 1986–93, md 1993–; Clerk of the Royal Cellars 1992–; memb Worshipful Co of Vintners; *Recreations* golf, cricket, tennis; *Clubs* I Zingari, Band of Brothers, Royal and Ancient, Royal St George's Golf, Boodle's; *Style—* Edward Demery, Esq; ✉ 72 Vineyard Hill Road, Wimbledon, London SW19 7JJ (☎ 0181 946 7056); Justerini & Brooks Ltd, 61 St James's Street, London SW1A 1LZ (☎ 0171 493 8721, fax 0171 499 4653, telex 264 470 WINEJB G)

DEMIDENKO, Nikolai; s of Anatoli Antonovich Demidenko; *b* 1 July 1955; *Educ* Moscow Conservatoire; *m* Julya Borisovna Dovgiallo; *Career* pianist; studied with Dmitri Bashkirov; visiting prof: Univ of Surrey, Yehudi Menuhin Sch; medallist: Concours International de Montreal 1976, Tchaikovsky Int Competition 1978; performances incl: Br debut with Moscow Radio Symphony Orch 1990, Piano Masterworks series Wigmore Hall 1993; 1994–95 appearances incl: Hollywood Bowl, Berlin with Berliner Symphoniker, Royal Festival Hall with RPO and Yuri Temirkanov, various Scottish venues with Scottish Chamber Orch, Toronto, Haskil-Kempff Festival Luxembourg, St John's Smith Square for BBC, Belfast, Chester and Ribble Valley Festivals, complete Mussorgsky song cycles with Anatoli Safiulin St John's Smith Square, Rouen and Verbier Festival, Int Piano Series Royal Festival Hall, Gramophone Award Winners Festival Wigmore Hall; 1995–96 season incl: Celebrity Recital Series Barbican, Scriabin Concerto with Netherlands Radio Philharmonic, Prokofiev Second Concerto with LPO, Gershwin Rhapsody in Blue with BBC Philharmonic Orch, series with Israel Philharmonic, tour of Australia for ABC, Int Piano Festival Singapore, Gramophone Award Winners Festival Wigmore Hall; 1996–97 season incl: recitals in Amsterdam, Istanbul, Munich, Prague, Toronto, Warsaw, Bristol, Windsor Festival, Barbican Great Orchs of the World Series (with Moscow Philharmonic), Polish Radio Symphony Orch, Orchestre Philharmonique de Luxembourg; *Recordings* for Hyperion Records incl: works by Bach-Busoni, Chopin, Liszt, Medtner Second and Third Piano Concertos with BBC Scottish Symphony Orch (winner Gramophone Award 1992), Rachmaninov Music for Two Pianos with Dmitri Alexeev (nominated Classic CD Instrumental Award 1995), Live at Wigmore double album, Tchaikovsky First Piano Concerto, Scriabin Piano Concerto (winner Classic CD Award 1994), Weber Concertos, Clementi Sonatas, Mussorgsky Song Cycles, Schubert Impromptus, Prokofiev's 2 and 3 Piano Concerto (with London Philharmonic and Alexander Lazaren); *Style—* Nikolai Demidenko, Esq; ✉ c/o Georgina Ivor Associates, 28 Old Devonshire Road, London SW12 9RB (☎ 0181 673 7179, fax 0181 675 8058)

DEMPSEY, (James) Andrew Craig; s of James Dempsey (d 1982), and Gladys, *née* Cook (d 1993); *b* 17 Nov 1942; *Educ* Ampleforth, Univ of Glasgow; *m* 4 April 1966, Grace, da of Dr Ian MacPhail; 1 s (Colin b 1971), 1 da (Catherine b 1976); *Career* exhibition organiser Arts Cncl of GB 1966–71, keeper Dept of PR Victoria & Albert Museum 1971–75, assoc curator Hayward Gallery 1993– (asst dir 1975–93); *Recreations* reading, walking, travelling; *Style—* Andrew Dempsey, Esq; ✉ Hayward Gallery, South Bank Centre, London SE1 (☎ 0171 921 0876, fax 0171 928 0063)

DEMPSEY, Dr Brenda Mary; da of George Kenneth Price (d 1972), of Birkenhead, Cheshire, and Doris Hamill, *née* Crawford (d 1977); *b* 22 July 1927; *Educ* Birkenhead HS GPDST, Univ of Liverpool Med Sch (MB ChB); *m* 1, 26 Jan 1952, John Anthony Dempsey (d 1982), s of George Barlow Dempsey, MC (d 1959), of Willaston, Wirral, Cheshire; 2 s (David C b Aug 1956, Christopher John b Aug 1964), 2 da (Alison M b April 1958, Carolyn M b Oct 1961); m 2, June 1985, Barry Walker Kay; *Career* Royal Free Hosp: resident anaesthetist 1952, registrar anaesthetist 1954–57, sr registrar 1957; resident anaesthetist Queen Charlotte's Maternity Hosp and Chelsea Hosp for Women 1952–53, anaesthetist The Nethersole Hosp Hong Kong 1958–60; conslt anaesthetist: Elizabeth Garret Anderson Hosp 1961–72, Prince of Wales Hosp Tottenham 1961–72, Ashford Dist Gen Hosp Ashford Middx 1972–92; subsequently temp conslt anaesthetist Heatherwood and Wexham Park Hosp Tst until 1997; memb Rotary Inner Wheel Staines; FFARCS 1955; *Recreations* managing a livery stables and riding school, swimming; *Style—* Dr Brenda Dempsey; ✉ Lyfords Meadow, 127 Lock's Ride, Ascot, Berks SL5 8RX (☎ 01344 882129)

DEMPSEY, Michael Bernard; s of John Patrick Dempsey (d 1993), latterly of Ramsgate, Kent, and Britannia May, *née* Thompson (d 1993); *b* 25 July 1944; *Educ* Bishop Ward RC Secdy Mod Dagenham Essex; *m* 1, 21 Oct 1967 (m dis 1988), Sonja, da of George Mathew Green; 1 da (Polly b 15 Oct 1969), 2 s (Joe and Ben (twins) b 2 Jan 1972); m 2, 15 Aug 1989, Charlotte Antonia, da of David Elliot Richardson; 2 da (Daisy b 2 May 1990, Fleur May b 15 July 1994); *Career* asst designer Chevron Studio 1963–64, in-house designer Bryan Colmer Artist Agents 1964–65, freelance designer 1965–66, designer Cato Peters O'Brien 1966–68; art dir: William Heinemann Publishers 1968–74, William Collins/Fontana Publishers 1974–79; fndr ptnr Carroll & Dempsey 1979–85, chm and creative dir CDT Design (formerly Carroll Dempsey & Thirkell) 1985–; memb D&AD 1968 (memb Exec 1996–, pres 1997–), FCSD 1980, RDI 1994; *Awards* D&AD Silver 1981 (most outstanding technical lit) and 1984 (most outstanding book jacket), D&AD Gold and Silver 1985 (most outstanding book design), 2 D&AD Silvers 1989 (most outstanding annual report and album covers), 2 D&AD Silvers 1992 (most outstanding corp ID and logo), CSD Minerva Award 1993 (most outstanding corp ID); *Books* Bubbles - Early Advertising Art of A & F Pears (1978), The Magical Paintings of Justin Todd (1978), Pipe Dreams - Early Advertising Art of The Imperial Tobacco Company (1982); *Recreations* architecture, art history, cinema, photography, theatre, opera; *Style—* Michael Dempsey, Esq; ✉ 114 de Beauvoir Road, London N1 4DJ (☎ 0171 241 1361); CDT Design Ltd, 21 Brownlow Mews, London WC1N 2LA (☎ 0171 242 0992, fax 0171 242 1174)

DEMPSTER, Alastair Cox; *b* 22 June 1940, Glasgow; *Educ* Paisley GS; *m* Kathryn; 2 s (Stuart b 4 June 1968, Ross b 6 Nov 1971); *Career* Royal Bank of Scotland plc: various branch banking appts W of Scotland 1955–62, Branch Dept (Inspection and Advances) Head Office 1962–68, exec asst Head Office 1968–70, asst personnel mangr 1970–72, rep New York Office 1972–73, rep SE Asia Office Hong Kong and md Royal Scot Finance Co Ltd 1973–77, controller, supt then asst gen mangr International Div 1977–86; TSB Group plc: dir of commercial banking and international/exec dir 1986–91, chief exec TSB Bank Channel Islands Ltd 1991–92 (dep chm 1992–), chief exec TSB Bank Scotland plc 1992–; dir Scottish Homes; pres Chartered Inst of Bankers in Scotland, immediate past chm Ctee of Scottish Clearing Bankers; dir: Office of the Banking Ombudsman, Scottish Fin Enterprise; chm The Caledonian Fndn; memb: Scottish Cncl CBI, Scottish Cncl Devpt and Industry Bd Exec Ctee, Ct of Heriot-Watt Univ (convener Audit Ctee), Bd of Govrs Edinburgh Art Coll; a High Constable City of Edinburgh; FCIBS; *Recreations* golf, tennis, bridge, world affairs, reading, gardening; *Clubs* Luffness New Golf; *Style—* Alastair Dempster, Esq; ✉ TSB Bank Scotland plc, Henry Duncan House, 120 George Street, Edinburgh EH2 4TS (☎ 0131 225 4555, fax 0131 220 0240)

DEMPSTER, John William Scott; s of Dr David Dempster (d 1981), of Plymouth, and Mary Constance, *née* Simpson (d 1985); *b* 10 May 1938; *Educ* Plymouth Coll, Oriel Coll Oxford (MA); *Career* civil servant; dep sec Dept of Tport, princ private sec to the Sec of State for the Environment 1976–77; finance offr Dept of Tport 1977–81, princ establishment and finance offr Lord Chancellor's Dept 1981–84; Dept of Tport: head of marine directorate 1984–89, princ establishment and fin offr 1989–91, currently dep sec Aviation, Shipping and Int Directorate (grade 2); *Recreations* mountaineering, sailing (part owner of yacht Carolina); *Clubs* Royal Southampton Yacht, Alpine; *Style—* John Dempster, Esq, CB; ✉ Aviation Shipping & International Directorate, DOT, Great Minster House, 76 Marsham Street, London SW1P 4DR

DEMPSTER, Maj Malcolm Maclagan; s of Henry Maclagan Dempster (d 1983), and Ruth Appleby, *née* Rowan; *b* 17 March 1940; *m* (m dis 1984); 1 da (Sarah Georgina b 1982); *Career* qualified aeronautical engr HM Forces, served Malayan and Borneo conflicts (incl secondment to Ghurkha Forces), cmmnd 1974, PSO Staff of Flag Offr Naval Air Cmd 1977–79, SO MOD Procurement 1979–81, SO HQ 1 Br Corps Germany 1981–83, cmd appt UK 1983–85, SO MOD responsible for NATO Air (Army) matters 1985–88; UK del: NATO Advsy Gp on Aeronautical Res and Devpt 1986–88, NATO Ctee for Future Aircraft and Equipment Requirements 1986–88, NATO Air Forces Ctee for Int Interoperability 1985–88 (chm 1988), Int Aeronautical Ctee for Standardisation 1986–88; md: Goldenlogic Ltd 1988–91, Express Thurston Helicopters Ltd 1989–91, Anglo Turkish Ltd 1992–; vice pres (UK) Octrin Corporation; dir Express Aviation Marketing 1989–91, commercial dir Spearhead Envotech Ltd 1991–; conslt on aeronautical matters to Crown Agents 1989; chief exec Biggin Hill Airport Business Assoc, co-opted memb Biggin Hill Int Air Fair Ctee 1988–91; SERC visiting tutor to univ PhD courses; MInstD, MRAeS; *Publications* author of various scientific and tech articles; *Recreations* golf, music, country pursuits, a constant battle with a 200 year old country property and a chateau in France; *Clubs* IOD, Stringfellow's; *Style—* Maj Malcolm Dempster; ✉ 9 Richard Place, Knightsbridge, London W2 (☎ 0171 589 4200); Well Cottage, Monxton, Andover, Hants SP11 8AS (☎ 01264 710535); The Chateau, St Philbert sur Orne, Normandy, France

den BRINKER, Prof Carl Siegmund; s of Hermanus Maria den Brinker (d 1975); *b* 29 March 1930; *Educ* St Franciscus Coll Rotterdam, Univ of Bath (MSc); *m* 1965, Margaret, da of Frank Todd (d 1990); 1 s, 3 da; *Career* physicist Texas Instruments Ltd 1961–75, dir Mackintosh Consultants 1976–78, tech dir Redifon Ltd 1978–90, dir Rediffusion Electronics 1985–89, scientific conslt 1990–, dir (scientific) Hillard Communications Systems Ltd 1991–93; visiting prof Univ of Westminster 1991–95; memb Cncl for Nat Academic Awards 1978–84, vice pres IERE 1984–87, memb Communications Tech Ctee Def Scientific Advsy Cncl 1984–90; author of several scientific papers and patents; Freeman City of London, Master Worshipful Co of Scientific Instrument Makers 1991, Freeman Worshipful Co of Glaziers and Painters of Glass; CPhys, CEng, FInstP, FIEE, FRSA; *Recreations* music, theatre, Saxon and Romanesque church architecture; *Style—* Prof Carl den Brinker; ✉ 55 Underhill Rd, London SE22 0QR (☎ 0181 693 5970)

DENBIGH AND DESMOND, 12 and 11 Earl of (E1622 and I 1622); Alexander Stephen Rudolph Feilding; also Baron Feilding, Viscount Feilding (both E 1620), Baron Feilding, Viscount Callan (both I 1622), and Baron St Liz (E1663); o s of 11 Earl of Denbigh and 10 Earl of Desmond (d 1995), and Caroline Judith Vivienne, *née* Cooke; *b* 4 Nov 1970; *Educ* Stowe; *m* 27 Jan 1996, Suzanne Jane, yr da of Gregory R Allen, of Mudberry House, Centry Road, Brixham, Devon; *Heir* kinsman, William David Feilding b 1939; *Style—* The Rt Hon the Earl of Denbigh and Desmond; ✉ Newnham Paddox, Monks Kirby, nr Rugby, Warwickshire CV23 0RX (☎ 01788 832173)

DENCH, Dame Judith Olivia (Judi); DBE (1988, OBE 1970); da of Dr Reginald Arthur Dench (d 1964), of York, and Eleanora Olave Dench; *b* 9 Dec 1934; *Educ* The Mount Sch York, Central Sch of Speech and Drama; *m* 5 Feb 1971, Michael Williams, *qv*; 1 da (Finty b 24 Sept 1972); *Career* actress and director; fndr memb Surrey Soc CPRE; Hon DLitt: Univ of York 1978, Univ of Warwick 1980, Univ of Birmingham 1989, Loughborough Univ 1991, Open Univ 1992, Univ of London 1994; assoc memb RSC 1969–; *Theatre* stage roles for RSC incl: The Gift of the Gorgon, The Cherry Orchard, Measure for Measure, A Midsummers Night's Dream, Penny for a Song, Twelfth Night, The Winter's Tale, The Comedy of Errors, Macbeth (SWET Best Actress Award), Pillars of the Community, Juno and the Paycock (SWET, Standard, Plays and Players and Variety Club Awards), Waste; roles in the West End incl: The Promise, Cabaret, The Wolf, The Good Companions, The Gay Lord Quex, Pack of Lies (SWET and Plays & Players Best Actress Award), Mr and Mrs Nobody, The Plough and the Stars; roles at RNT incl: The Importance of Being Earnest (Evening Standard Best Actress Award), Other Places (Standard, Plays & Players and Drama Awards), Antony and Cleopatra (Olivier, Drama Magazine, and Evening Standard Best Actress Awards), Entertaining Strangers, Hamlet, The Sea, The Seagull, Absolute Hell (Olivier Award for Best Actress 1996) 1995, A Little Night Music (Olivier Award for Best Actress in a Musical 1996) 1995; as dir: Much Ado About Nothing, Look Back in Anger (Renaissance Theatre Co), Macbeth (Central School), The Boys from Syracuse (Regent's Park, Best Revival of a Musical Olivier Awards 1992), Romeo and Juliet (Regent's Park) 1993; *Television* incl: Marching Song, Hillda Lessways, Pink Streek and Sealing Wax, An Age of Kings, Major Barbara, Talking to a Stranger (BAFTA Best TV Actress Award), A Fine Romance (BAFTA Best TV Actress Award), Going Gently (BAFTA Best TV Actress Award), Saigon Year of the Cat, The Browning Version, Mrs & Mrs Edgehill (ACE Award for Best Actress), Absolute Hell, As Time Goes By; *Films* incl: Four in the Morning (BAFTA Award for Most Promising Newcomer), Wetherby, A Room With a View (BAFTA Award for Best Supporting Actress), 84 Charing Cross Road, A Handful of Dust (BAFTA Award for Best Supporting Actress), Henry V, Jack & Sarah 1995, M in Goldeneye 1995; *Style—* Dame Judi Dench, DBE; ✉ c/o Julian Belfrage Associates, 46 Albemarle Street, London W1X 4PP (☎ 0171 491 4400, fax 0171 493 5460)

DENHAM, 2 Baron (UK 1937); Sir Bertram Stanley Mitford Bowyer; 10 Bt (E 1660), of Denham, and 2 Bt (UK 1933), of Weston Underwood; PC (1981), KBE (1991); s of 1 Baron Denham (d 1948), and Hon Daphne Freeman-Mitford (d 1996, aged 100), da of 1 Baron Redesdale; suc to Btcy of Denham on death of kinsman 1950; *b* 3 Oct 1927; *Educ* Eton, King's Coll Cambridge; *m* 14 Feb 1956, Jean, da of Kenneth McCorquodale, MC, TD; 3 s, 1 da; *Heir* s, Hon Richard Grenville George Bowyer; *Career* late Lt Oxford and Bucks LI; a Lord-in-Waiting to HM The Queen 1961–64 and 1970–71, Capt of Yeomen of the Gd (dep chief whip in House of Lords) 1971–74, Capt Hon Corps Gentlemen-at-Arms 1979–91 (govt chief whip House of Lords), oppn dep chief whip 1974–78, oppn chief whip 1978–79; conslt (non-slr) to Reid Minty solicitors 1991–; memb Countryside Cmmn 1993–; *Books* The Man Who Lost His Shadow (1979), Two Thyrdes (1983), Foxhunt (1988), Black Rod (1997); *Clubs* White's, Pratt's, Garrick; *Style—* The Rt Hon the Lord Denham, PC, KBE; ✉ The Laundry Cottage, Weston Underwood, Olney, Bucks MK46 5JZ (☎ 01234 711535)

DENHAM, Gary George; s of Maurice Denham, and Patricia Denham; *b* 4 July 1951; *Educ* Bennets End Secdy Sch; *m* 6 May 1972, Vivienne, da of Roy Howlett; 4 s (Nathan b 10 Dec 1975, Jacob b 3 Oct 1979, Joshua b 31 Aug 1983, Elijah b 13 June 1986), 1 da (Krsna b 14 June 1977); *Career* art dir The Kirkwood Company advtg agency 1971–73, head of art Maisey Mukerjee Russell 1973–74; art dir: French Gold Abbott 1974–76, Greys Sydney Aust 1976–77; freelance art dir/photographer 1977–83; art dir: Bartle Bogle Hegarty 1983–84, Boase Massimi Pollitt 1984–86; head of art Holmes Knight Ritchie 1986–87, jt creative dir Aspect Hill Holliday 1987–89, art dir/gp head Bartle Bogle Hegarty 1989–92, head of art CME KHBB 1992–95, sr creative Leagas Delaney 1995, freelance art dir/photographer/painter 1995–; awards incl: Bronze Irish Int Advtg Awards, Silver Campaign Press Awards, Gold Pegasus (Readers Digest) Awards, Gold NY Art Dirs Show; photography exhibited: New Australian Photography 1977, Venezia 1979, Pompidou Centre 1980; work in The Polaroid Collection Boston USA; memb D&AD 1975; *Recreations* gardening, painting; *Style—* Gary Denham, Esq

DENHAM, John; MP (Lab) Southampton Itchen (majority 551); *b* 15 July 1953; *Educ* Woodroffe Comp Lyme Regis, Univ of Southampton (BSc); *m* Ruth Dixon; 1 s, 1 da; *Career* formerly: campaign offr Friends of the Earth and War on Want, conslt to various devpt orgns, head of youth affairs Br Youth Cncl; MP (Lab) Southampton Itchen 1992– (contested Southampton Itchen 1983 and 1987); elected memb: Hampshire CC 1981–89 (dep ldr and spokesperson on educn), Southampton City Cncl 1989–93 (chair Housing Ctee); memb MSF; *Recreations* cricket, gardening, cooking, family; *Style—* John Denham, Esq, MP; ✉ House of Commons, London SW1A 0AA (☎ 0171 219 3000)

DENHAM, Maurice; OBE (1992); s of Norman Denham (d 1931), of Beckenham, Kent, and Winifred, *née* Lillico (d 1942); *b* 23 Dec 1909; *Educ* Tonbridge Sch; *m* 3 Dec 1936, Margaret (d 1971), da of late Laurie Dunn; 2 s (Christopher William b 6 June 1939, Timothy Maurice b 13 Dec 1946), 1 da (Virginia Margaret b 5 May 1948); *Career* actor; served The Buffs, RA 1940–45; weekly rep work in Hull, Croydon and Brighton 1934–37, Busman's Honeymoon (Comedy Theatre) 1938–39, Hayfever (TV, Laburnham Grove) 1938–40 (first broadcast 1938), ITMA 1939, Much Binding in the Marsh 1946; *Theatre* incl: Fallen Angels 1949, Ambassadors 1949, All Shaw's One Act Plays (Arts) 1951, Dock Brief (Hammersmith Lyric) 1958, What Shall We Tell Caroline (Garrick) 1958, The Andersonville Trial (Mermaid) 1961, King John (Old Vic) 1961–62, Macbeth (Old Vic) 1961–62, The Lovers of Viorne (Royal Court) 1971, Uncle Vanya (Hampstead) 1979–80, Serebriakov 1979–80; *Radio* numerous broadcasts incl: A Tale of Two Cities, Dr Manette, The Forsyte Chronicles, James; *Television* progs incl: Talking to a Stranger, Father, The Old Men at the Zoo, All Passion Spent, Miss Marple, Black Tower, The Trial of Klaus Barbie, Behaving Badly, Inspector Morse, Lovejoy, Memento Mori, Sherlock Holmes, Peak Practice 1993–94, The Bill, Prisoners of Time, Pie in the Sky 1995; *Film* over 100 appearances incl: Doctor at Sea, Easter, The Purple Plain, Blore, 84 Charing Cross Road, Martin; *Recreations* golf, conducting gramophone records; *Clubs* Garrick, Green Room; *Style—* Maurice Denham, Esq, OBE; ✉ c/o Julian Belfrage Associates, 46 Albemarle Street, London W1X 4PP (☎ 0171 491 4400, fax 0171 493 5460)

DENHAM, Dr Michael John; s of Ernest William Denham (d 1989), and Lila Beatrice, *née* Sword (d 1974); *b* 17 March 1935; *Educ* King Edward VI Sch Norwich, City of Norwich Sch, Downing Coll Cambridge, Westminster Med Sch (MA, MD, FRCP); *m* 31 Oct 1965, Sheila Ann, da of David Rodger (d 1976); 1 s (Nicholas b 1973), 2 da (Tessa b 1970, Susan b 1976); *Career* conslt physician in geriatric med Northwick Park Hosp and Clinical Res Centre 1973–; RCP censor and examiner: for membership 1985–, for Dip of Geriatric Med 1989–; lectr and examiner: for health visitors Stevenage Coll 1979–88, for health visitors and dist nurses Univ of Hertfordshire 1989–; ed jl Care of the Elderly 1989–95, author numerous articles on care of the elderly; sec Br Geriatrics Soc 1979–81 (pres 1992–94), annual secondments to NHS Advsy Serv 1981–91, med advsr to Research into Ageing 1983–90; *Books* Treatment of Medical Problems in the Elderly (ed, 1980), Care of the Long Stay Elderly Patient (ed 1983, 2 edn 1990), Blood Disorders in the Elderly (jt ed, 1985), Infections in the Elderly (ed, 1986), Health Visiting and the Elderly (jt ed 1987, 2 edn 1991), Drugs in Old Age (jt ed, 1990); *Recreations* swimming, reading, DIY, air shows, gardening; *Style—* Dr Michael Denham; ✉ Northwick Park Hospital, Watford Rd, Harrow, Middx HA1 3UJ (☎ 0181 864 3232)

DENHAM, Pamela Anne; da of Matthew Gray Dobson (d 1970), and Jane, *née* Carter (d 1962); *b* 1 May 1943; *Educ* Central Newcastle HS, Kings Coll Univ of London (BSc, PhD); (m dis 1980), Paul Denham (d 1988); m 2, Brian Murray (d 1993); *Career* Miny of Technol 1967–70, subsequently DTI, currently under sec and regnl dir Government Office for the North East; Hon LLD Univ of Sunderland 1994; FRSA; *Recreations* walking, skiing, cooking, reading; *Style—* Mrs Pamela Denham; ✉ Government Office for the North East, Stanegate House, 2 Groat Market, Newcastle upon Tyne NE1 1YN (☎ 0191 235 7201)

DENHAM-DAVIS, Colin John; s of Cecil John Denham-Davis (d 1957), of Chelsea, and Gwendolene Lilian (Gill), *née* Stimson (d 1978); *b* 13 May 1930; *Educ* Marlborough, St John's Coll Cambridge (Hockey blue); *m* 1958, Alison Apphia, da of Col E F W Mackenzie, MC, OBE; 3 da (Virginia Apphia b 1960, Melanie Jane b 1962, Charlotte Lilian b 1964), 1 s (Andrew John b 1967); *Career* Capt 2nd Royal Tank Regt 1952–54; various positions rising to md J A Davis & Son Ltd 1955–69, Diehl Golightly Ltd/Management Audit Ltd conslts 1970–73; merchandise dir: Kay Co Ltd 1978–82 (merchandise mangr 1973–78), GUS Home Shopping 1982–87; jt chm Polikoff Universal Wales (menswear manufacturing) 1985–88; mktg dir: Kay Co Ltd 1987–92, GUS Home Shopping 1992–94; dir Brewery Arts Cirencester 1991–; chm Star Centre for Disabled Youth Cheltenham 1992–; FRSA; *Clubs* MCC, Free Foresters; *Style—* Colin Denham-Davis, Esq; ✉ Ampney House, Ampney Crucis, Cirencester, Glos GL7 5SA (☎ 01285 851236, fax 01285 850885)

DENHOLM, (James) Allan; CBE (1992); s of James Denholm (d 1959), and Florence Lily Keith, *née* Kennedy (d 1972); *b* 27 Sept 1936; *Educ* Hutchesons' Boys' GS Glasgow; *m* 10 Sept 1964, Elizabeth Avril, da of John Stewart McLachlan (d 1994), of Duni, South Broomage Ave, Larbert, Stirlingshire; 1 s (Keith b 7 Sept 1966), 1 da (Alison b 24 May 1969); *Career* dir: William Grant and Sons Ltd 1975–, Scottish Mutual Assurance Soc 1987– (dep chm 1992–), Abbey National plc 1992–, Abbey National Life plc 1993–; dir Scottish Cremation and Burial Reform Soc 1980–; pres Inst of Chartered Accountants of Scotland 1992–93; chm: Glasgow Jr C of C 1972–73, E Kilbride Devpt Corp 1983– (memb 1979–); visitor Incorp of Maltmen in Glasgow 1980–81, pres 49 Wine and Spirit Club of Scotland 1983–84, tstee Scottish Cot Death Tst 1985–, dir Weavers' Soc of Anderson 1987 (preses 1994–95), pres Assoc of Deacons of the Fourteen Incorporated Trades of Glasgow 1994–95, collector The Trades House of Glasgow 1996–97, dir The Merchants House of Glasgow 1996–, memb Advsy Bd The Salvation Army 1996–, dir The Soc of Deacons and Free Preseses of Glasgow 1996–; elder New Kilpatrick Parish Church Bearsden; CA 1960, FSA Scotland 1987, FRSA 1992; *Recreations* shooting, golf; *Clubs* Royal Scottish Automobile; *Style—* J Allan Denholm, Esq, CBE; ✉ Greencroft, 19 Colquhoun Drive, Bearsden, Glasgow G61 4NQ (☎ and fax 0141 942 1773); William Grant & Sons Ltd, Strathclyde Business Park, Motherwell ML4 3AN (☎ 01698 843843)

DENHOLM, John Clark; s of Robert Denholm (d 1986), of Lower Largo, Fife, and Ann King, *née* Clark; *b* 10 Sept 1950; *Educ* Buckhaven HS, Univ of St Andrews (MA); *m* 16 Dec 1978, Julia Margaret, da of Ben Gregory; 1 s (Michael b 19 Sept 1988), 1 da (Katy b 16 April 1986); *Career* product mangr The Boots Co Nottingham 1972–76, brand mangr Scottish & Newcastle Breweries 1976–80, account dir Hall Advertising 1980–84, chm The Leith Agency Edinburgh 1995– (md 1984–95), gp md Silvermills (holding co) 1995–; MIPA 1986; *Recreations* golf; *Style—* John Denholm, Esq; ✉ The Leith Agency, The Canon Mill, Canon Street, Edinburgh EH3 5HE (☎ 0131 557 5840, fax 0131 557 5837)

DENINGTON, Baroness (Life Peer UK 1978), of Stevenage, Herts; Dame Evelyn Joyce Denington; DBE (1974, CBE 1966); da of Philip Charles Bursill, of Woolwich; *b* 9 Aug 1907; *Educ* Blackheath HS, Bedford Coll London; *m* 1935, Cecil Dallas Denington, s of Richard Denington, of Wanstead; *Career* journalist 1927–31, teacher 1933–50; gen sec Nat Assoc of Lab Teachers 1937–47; memb: St Pancras Borough Cncl 1945–59 (chm Staff Ctee, Planning Ctee and Gen Purposes Ctee), LCC 1946–65 (vice chm Housing Ctee 1949–60, chm Devpt & Mgmnt Sub-Ctees 1949–60, chm New & Expanding Towns Ctee 1960–65), GLC 1964–77 (chm Cncl 1975–76, dep ldr opposition 1967–73, chm Housing Ctee 1964–67, chm Tport Ctee 1973–75), Stevenage Devpt Corpn 1950–80 (chm 1966–80), Central Housing Advsy Ctee 1955–73 (memb Sub-Ctee producing Parker Morris report and chm Sub-Ctee producing Our Older Homes Report), SE Econ Planning Cncl 1966–79; memb and chm of various bds of mgmnt and govr of schs in St Pancras and Islington 1945–73, chm London Coll for the Garment Trades (Coll of Fashion), memb and chm of Govrs Ardale Sr Boys' Approved Sch, chm Hornchurch Children's Home; memb: Sutton Dwellings Housing Tst 1976–82, Shackleton Housing Assoc 1976–82, N Br Housing Assoc 1976–88, St Pancras Housing Assoc 1977–78, Gtr London Secdy Housing Assoc 1978–83, Sutton (Hastoe) Housing Assoc 1981–88, St Edward's Housing Assoc 1983–87; memb and a vice pres Town & Co Planning Assoc; Freeman City of London; Hon FRIBA, Hon MRTPI; *Style—* The Rt Hon Baroness Denington, DBE; ✉ Flat 3, 29 Brunswick Square, Hove, E Sussex

DENISON, Edward Allan Kitson; OBE (1986), TD (and clasp); s of Wing Cdr Amos Allan Denison, MBE, MC (d 1976), of Devon, and Margery, *née* Morton (d 1975); *b* 13 Sept 1928; *Educ* St Peter's York, Brasenose Coll Oxford (MA, BCL); *m* 18 May 1957, Mary Hey, da of William Peacock, of Malton, N Yorks; 1 s (Mark b 1960) 1 da (Clare b 1962); *Career* cmmnd W Yorks Regt 1947, served occupation of Austria TA 1948–67, Lt-Col 3 Bn Prince of Wales's Own 1965–67 (Hon Col 1993–), Yorks and Humberside TA&VRA; slr and conslt in private practice; formerly head of Legal Dept to Shepherd Building Group plc and first chm Legal Group to Bldg Employers' Confedn; non-exec dir and former dir: Univ of Leeds Fndn, many public and private cos; public appts: N Riding CC 1970–74, N Yorks CC 1973–81 (ldr 1977–81); memb: ACC Fin Ctee 1977–81, Yorks & Humberside Econ Planning Cncl 1970–79, Yorks Humberside & E Midlands Industl Devpt Bd 1981–85; former chm and pres Thirsk and Malton and Ryedale Cons Assoc, pres N Yorks Euro Cons Assoc; chm Bd of Govrs St Peter's Sch; chm N Yorks Cancer Relief Macmillan Fund; boxed for Oxford Univ 1950–51, memb Headingley RUFC 1950–56; *Recreations* shooting, skiing, tennis, travel; *Clubs* Army and Navy,

Vincent's; *Style*— Edward A K Denison, Esq, OBE, TD; ✉ The Old Vicarage, Bossall, York; Chancery House, 141–143 Holgate Rd, York (☎ 01904 610820, fax 01904 646972)

DENISON, John Law; CBE (1960, MBE Mil 1945); s of Rev Herbert Bouchier Wiggins Denison (d 1968), of Bexhill, Sussex; *b* 21 Jan 1911; *Educ* Brighton Coll, Royal Coll of Music, St George's Sch Windsor Castle; *m* 1, 1936 (m dis 1946), Anne Claudia Russell, da of Col Claude Russell Brown, CB, DSO (d 1939); m 2, 1947, Evelyn Donald (d 1958), da of John Moir; 1 da; m 3, 1960 Audrey Grace Burnaby (d 1970), da of Brig-Gen Frederick Gilbert Bowles, RE (d 1947); m 4, 1972, Françoise Henriette Mitchell (d 1985), da of Maître Garrigues; *Career* served WWII 1939–45 (despatches); music dir Arts Cncl of GB 1948–65, dir South Bank Concert Halls 1965–76; chm: Cultural Programme, London Celebrations, Queen's Silver Jubilee 1977; memb Cncl Royal Coll of Music 1970–91; chm: Royal Concert (in aid of musical charities) 1976–87, Arts Educn Schs 1976–91; hon memb Royal Philharmonic Soc 1989 (hon treas 1976–89); FRCM, Hon RAM, Hon GSM; Cdr Order of Lion (Finland), Chev dans l'Ordre des Arts et des Lettres (France); FRSA; *Clubs* Garrick, Army and Navy; *Style*— John Denison, Esq, CBE; ✉ 9 Hays Park, nr Shaftesbury, Dorset SP7 9JR

DENISON, (John) Michael (Terence Wellesley); CBE (1983); s of Gilbert Dixon Denison (d 1959), and Marie Louise, *née* Bain (d 1915); maternal gf A W Bain on Kimberley diamond rush 1871, founded A W Bain & Sons Insurance Brokers Leeds 1874 (now Bain-Hogg), Lord Mayor of Leeds 1913; *b* 1 Nov 1915; *Educ* Wellesley House Broadstairs, Harrow (entrance exhibitioner), Magdalen Coll Oxford (BA); *m* 29 April 1939, Dulcie Winifred Catherine (the actress Dulcie Gray, *qv*), da of Arnold Savage Bailey, CBE (d 1935); *Career* actor since 1938–; Army 1940–46; Capt Intelligence Corps: NI, ME, Greece, UK; cncllr Equity 1949–77 (vice pres 1952, 1961–63, 1974); dir: Allied Theatre Prodns 1966–75, Play Co of London 1970–74, New Shakespeare Co 1971–; 115 theatrical prodns of which more than 50 in London, 15 films, innumerable radio and TV plays (including 80 as Boyd QC); Queen's Jubilee Medal 1977; FRSA; *Books* The Actor and His World (1964), Overture and Beginners (1973), Double Act (1985); articles for the Dictionary of National Biography on Sir Noel Coward, Sir Peter Daubeny, Peter Bridge (1985–86) and Glen Byam Shaw (1993); *Recreations* golf, painting, watching cricket, gardening, motoring; *Clubs* MCC, Richmond Golf; *Style*— Michael Denison, Esq, CBE; ✉ Shardeloes, Amersham, Buckinghamshire HP7 ORL

DENISON, His Hon Judge; (William) Neil; QC (1980); s of William George Denison (d 1963), of Jersey, and Jean Brodie, *née* Riddell (d 1996); *b* 10 March 1929; *Educ* Queen Mary's Sch Walsall, Univ of Birmingham (LLB), Hertford Coll Oxford (BCL); *m* 1, 1955; 3 s; m 2, 1981, Elizabeth Ann Marguerite Curnow, QC, *qv*; *Career* called to the Bar Lincoln's Inn 1952 (bencher 1993), Colonial Legal Serv Tanganyika 1958–63, recorder of the Crown Ct 1979–85, circuit judge (SE Circuit) 1985–; Liveryman Worshipful Co of Wax Chandlers 1988, Common Serjeant of London 1993; *Books* The Law of Tanganyika (1964); *Recreations* walking, reading rubbish; *Clubs* Garrick; *Style*— His Hon Judge Denison, QC; ✉ Central Criminal Court, Old Bailey, London EC4M 7EH (☎ 0171 248 3277)

DENISON-PENDER, Hon Robin Charles; yr s of 2 Baron Pender, CBE (d 1965) and bro of 3 Baron; *b* 7 Sept 1935; *Educ* Eton; *m* 7 May 1966, Clare Nell, only da of Lt-Col James Currie Thomson, MBE, TD, JP, DL, of Stable Court, Walkern, Herts; 2 s, 1 da; *Career* late 2 Lt 11 Hussars 1954–56; vice pres Royal Albert Hall 1970–83, chm The Knole Club 1985–95; High Sheriff Kent 1993–94; memb Worshipful Co of Founders; MSI; *Recreations* golf, gardening, tennis; *Clubs* White's; *Style*— The Hon Robin Denison-Pender; ✉ Jessups, Mark Beech, Edenbridge, Kent TN8 5NR (☎ 01342 850684)

DENMAN, 5 Baron (UK 1834); Sir Charles Spencer Denman; 2 Bt (UK 1945), of Staffield, Co Cumberland; CBE (1976), MC (1942), TD; s of Hon Sir Richard Denman, 1 Bt (d 1957); suc cous, 4 Baron, 1971; *b* 7 July 1916; *Educ* Shrewsbury; *m* 11 Sept 1943, Sheila Anne (d 1987), da of Lt-Col Algernon Bingham Anstruther Stewart, DSO; 3 s, 1 da; *Heir* s, Hon Richard Thomas Stewart Denman; *Career* served WWII Duke of Cornwall's LI (TA), Maj 1943, served India, M East and Mediterranean; contested Leeds Central (C) 1945; formerly chm Marine & General Mutual Life Assurance Soc, formerly dir Consolidated Gold Fields and other cos; vice pres Middle East Assoc; memb Ctee of Middle East Trade, formerly memb Ctee on Invisible Exports; tstee: Kitchener Memorial Fund, Arab Br Charitable Fndn; formerly govr Windlesham House School; formerly dir: Close Bros Gp, British Water, Wastewater Ltd; chm Saudi British Soc; pres: Royal Soc for Asia Affairs, NZ-UK C of C; cncl memb Inst for Study of Conflict; *Clubs* Brooks's; *Style*— The Rt Hon Lord Denman, CBE, MC, TD; ✉ c/o House of Lords, London SW1A 0PW

DENMAN, Prof Donald Robert; s of Robert Martyn Denman (d 1915), of Finchley, and Letitia Kate, *née* Barnes (d 1968); *b* 7 April 1911; *Educ* Christ's Coll Finchley, Univ of London (BSc, MSc, PhD), Univ of Cambridge (MA); *m* 12 April 1941, (Jessie) Hope, da of Richard Henry Prior (d 1919); 2 s (Jonathan b 1949, Richard b 1951); *Career* WWII serv Air Miny RAF (Civil) 1939–41, dep exec Cumberland War Agric Ctee 1941–46; chartered surveyor in private practice 1937–39; Univ of Cambridge: land agent 1946–48, lectr 1948–68, head Dept of Land Econ 1962–78, prof of land econ 1968–78, fell Pembroke Coll 1962–78, emeritus prof and fell 1978–; established land econ tripos and dept at Univ of Cambridge, undertook similar pioneering work in other univs UK and overseas; patron Small Farmers' Assoc; memb: Land Decade Educnl Cncl, ctees RICS, ctees Cwlth Assoc of Surveying and Land Econ; chm Cwlth Human Ecology Cncl, memb Advsy Panel Aims of Indust, fndr Human Ecology Fndn, advsr Govt of Iran 1968–74; memb: Agric Improvement Cncl, Cncl Nat Academic Awards, Nat Cmmn UNESCO, Ecology Cmmn, Int Union for Conservation of Nature; memb Ely Church Assembly; Hon DSc Univ of Kumasi 1979; hon fell: Royal Swedish Acad of Forestry and Agric 1971, Ghana Inst of Surveyors 1970; FRICS (gold medallist); Distinguished Order of Hamayoun Imperial Ct of Persia 1974; *Books* over 40 publications incl: Origins of Ownership (1958), Land Use and the Constitution of Property (1969), Land Use: An Introduction to Proprietary Land Use Analysis (1976), The Place of Property (1978), Land in a Free Society (1980), Markets Under the Sea (1983), After Government Failure (1987), A Half and Half Affair: Chronicles of a Hybrid Don (1993); *Recreations* travel; *Clubs* Carlton, Farmers'; *Style*— Prof Donald Denman; ✉ 12 Chaucer Road, Cambridge CB2 2EB (☎ 01223 357725)

DENMAN, Hon Richard Thomas Stewart; s and h of 5 Baron Denman, MC; *b* 4 Oct 1946; *Educ* Milton Abbey; *m* 18 April 1984, (Lesley) Jane, da of John Stevens, of 2 Shakespear Drive, Hinckley, Leics; 1 s (Robert b 19 Dec 1995), 3 da (Natasha Anne b 1986, Philippa Jane b 1987, Louisa Clare b 1993); *Career* chartered accountant; articled to Deloitte 1966; ACA; *Clubs* Brooks's; *Style*— The Hon Richard Denman

DENMAN, Sir (George) Roy; KCB (1977, CB 1972), CMG (1968); s of Albert Denman, of Marlborough, Wilts; *b* 12 June 1924; *Educ* Harrow GS, St John's Coll Cambridge; *m* 1966, Moya, da of John M Lade; 1 s, 1 da; *Career* served WW II as Maj Royal Signals, BOT 1948, served in HM Embassy Bonn and UK delgn to Geneva 1957–61 and 1965–67, under-sec BOT 1967–70; memb: negotiating delgn EEC 1970–72, BOTB 1972–75; dep sec: DTI 1970–74, Dept of Trade 1974–75; second perm sec Cabinet Office 1975–77, dir-gen External Affairs EEC 1977–82, EC ambass to US 1982–89, business fell Kennedy Sch Harvard 1989–90, conslt in int trade; *Style*— Sir Roy Denman, KCB, CMG; ✉ Avenue de Tervuren 194B, Boîte 15, B-1150 Brussels, Belgium (☎ 00 32 2 770 1521)

DENNEHY, Constance Mauguerita; da of Denis Franklyn Dennehy (d 1944), of Christchurch, NZ, and Constance, *née* Dennehy (d 1951); *b* 29 Dec 1931; *Educ* Villa Maria Convent, Canterbury Univ Coll NZ, Univ of Otago NZ (MB ChB); *Career* conslt child psychiatrist Hosps for Sick Children 1971–94, hon sr lectr St Bartholomew's Hosp 1972–; FRCPE, FRCPsych, DPM, FRSM, FRGS; *Style*— Miss Constance Dennehy; ✉ 18 Montpelier Grove, London NW5 2XD (☎ and fax 0171 485 4210); 14 Devonshire Place, London W1

DENNER, Dr (William) Howard Butler; s of William Ormonde Ralph Denner, of Merthyr Tydfil, and Violet Evelyn, *née* Arscott (d 1984); *b* 14 May 1944; *Educ* Cyfarthfa Castle GS, Univ Coll of Wales Cardiff (BSc, PhD); *m* 16 July 1966, Gwenda, da of Trevor Williams; 2 da (Siân Emily b 16 Aug 1972, Angela Mair b 6 Jan 1976); *Career* res assoc: Univ of Miami 1968–69, Univ of Cardiff 1969–72; MAFF: sr scientific offr 1972–74, grade 7 1974–84, head Food Composition and Info Unit 1984–89, head Food Science Div 1989–92, chief scientist (Food) 1992–95; sec Food Additives and Contaminants Ctee 1974–84, sec Ctee Toxicity of Chemicals in Food, Consumer Products and the Environment 1978–84, memb and vice chm FAO/WHO Expert Ctee on Food Additives 1978–85; chm: Codex Ctee on Fats and Oils 1987–92, Steering Gp on Chemical Aspects of Food Surveillance 1992–95, Steering Gp on Microbiological Surveillance of Food 1992–94; assessor: Advsy Ctee on Novel Foods and Processes 1985–92, Advsy Ctee on Genetic Modification 1985–92, Advsy Ctee on Microbiological Safety of Food 1990–95; scientific govr British Nutrition Fndn 1992–95; *Photographic Career* freelance photographer 1996–; lectr and judge E Anglian Fedn of Photographic Alliance of Great Britain 1978–88, judge Essex Int Salon of Photography 1987–88, solo exhbn Half Moon Gallery London 1974, numerous photographs in Int exhbns, newspapers and books; AFIAP 1972; *Recreations* golf, gardening; *Style*— Howard Denner, Esq; ✉ 33 Waldegrave Gardens, Upminster, Essex RM14 1UT

DENNES, John Mathieson; s of Norman Dennes (d 1964), of Devizes, Wilts, and Muriel Evelyn Thomas (d 1985); *b* 19 May 1926; *Educ* Rugby, Christ's Coll Cambridge (MA); *m* 5 April 1961, Verity Ann Mary, da of Lt-Col Leslie Rushworth Ward, MC, RA (d 1977), of Harleston, Norfolk; 4 s (Jonathan b 1962, Thomas b 1963, Adam b 1964, William b 1966); *Career* Mil Serv 1944–47, Intelligence Corps (Far East); slr; sr ptnr Waltons & Morse (ret); non-exec dir: Eversure Underwriting Agency Ltd 1990–, Holman Managed Syndicates Ltd 1993–; annual subscriber to Lloyd's 1989–; *Recreations* choral music, industrial archaeology, driving, good food and wine; *Style*— John M Dennes, Esq; ✉ Trevanion, Portloe, Truro, Cornwall TR2 5RG

DENNETT, Angelina Brunhilde; da of Leonard Arthur Dennett (d 1978), and Antonia Augustine Elizabeth Dennett; *b* 11 June 1956; *Educ* Ridgeway Secdy Sch, West Kent Coll, City of London Poly (BA), Univ of London (LLM); *m* 15 Aug 1989, David Thomas Fish; 1 s (Thomas Henry Dennett Fish b 8 Aug 1992), 1 da (Clementine Alexandra Dennett Fish b 20 March 1994); *Career* called to the Bar Middle Temple 1980; awards incl: Middle Temple Blackstone Pupillage award 1981, Malcolm Wright Pupillage award 1981; memb Family Law Bar Assoc; *Style*— Ms Angelina Dennett; ✉ Manchester House Chambers, 18–22 Bridge St, Manchester M3 3BZ (☎ 0161 834 7007, fax 0161 834 3462)

DENNING, Baron (Life Peer UK 1957), of Whitchurch, Co Southampton; Alfred Thompson Denning; kt (1944), PC (1948), DL (Hants 1978); s of Charles Denning (d 1941), of Whitchurch, Hants, and Clara, *née* Thompson; *b* 23 Jan 1899; *Educ* Andover GS, Magdalen Coll Oxford; *m* 1, 28 Dec 1932, Hilda Mary Josephine (d 1941), da of late Rev Frank Northam Harvey; 1 s; m 2, 27 Dec 1945, Joan Daria (d 1992), da of John Vinings Elliott-Taylor, and wid of John Matthew Blackwood Stuart, CIE; *Career* barr Lincoln's Inn 1923, KC 1938, bencher 1944; chllr: Dio of Southwark 1937–44, London 1942–44; recorder of Plymouth 1944, judge of the High Ct of Justice 1944–48, Lord Justice of Appeal 1948–57, Lord of Appeal in Ordinary 1957–62, Master of the Rolls 1962–82, ret; hon master of the bench: Middle Temple 1972, Gray's Inn 1979, Inner Temple 1982; chm Royal Cmmn on Historical Manuscripts until 1982, pres Nat Marriage Guidance Cncl until 1983; conducted Profumo Inquiry 1963; treas Lincoln's Inn 1964; hon fell: Magdalen Coll Oxford, Univ Coll London; author, broadcaster; DL (Hants) 1978, ret; Hon LLD: Ottawa 1955, Glasgow 1959, Southampton 1959, London 1960, Cambridge 1963, Leeds 1964, McGill 1967, Dallas 1969, Dalhousie 1970, Wales 1973, Exeter 1976, Columbia 1976, Tilburg (Netherlands) 1977, W Ontario 1979, British Columbia 1979, Sussex 1980, Buckingham 1983, Nottingham 1984; Hon DCL Oxford 1965; *Publications* Smith's Leading Cases (joint ed, 1929), Bullen and Leake's Precedents (1935), Freedom under the Law (Hamlyn Lectures, 1949), The Changing Law (1953), The Road to Justice (1955), The Discipline of Law (1979), The Due Process of Law (1980), The Family Story (1981), What Next in the Law (1982), The Closing Chapter (1983), Landmarks in the Law (1984), Leaves From My Library (1986); *Style*— The Rt Hon Lord Denning, PC; ✉ The Lawn, Whitchurch, Hants (☎ 01256 892144)

DENNING, (Charles Henry) David; s of late Lt-Gen Sir Reginald Denning, KCVO, KBE, CB, of Delmonden Grange, Hawkhurst, Kent, and Eileen Violet, OBE, *née* Currie (d 1992); *b* 1 May 1933; *Educ* Winchester; *m* 21 June 1958, Patricia Margaret (d 1996), da of Cdr Nigel Loftus Henry Fane (d 1974); 2 s (James Henry b 1959, Guy William b 1962), 2 da (Sophia Jane b 1964, Venetia Mary b 1966); *Career* cmmnd 11 Hussars 1952, demobbed 1954, Territorial Offr City of London Yeo 1954–57; underwriting memb Lloyd's 1960–92; dir: B W Noble Ltd Insurance Brokers 1968–74, C T Bowring Insurance Ltd 1973–74; chm The Copenhagen Reinsurance Co UK Ltd 1974–, memb Exec Ctee and former chm London Insurance and Reinsurance Market Assoc (formerly Reinsurance Offices Assoc) 1993–95; *Recreations* shooting, farming; *Style*— David Denning, Esq; ✉ Bewl Bridge Farm, Lamberhurst, Kent TN3 8JJ (☎ 01892 890876)

DENNING, (Michael) John; s of Frederick Edward Denning (d 1985), of Bath, and Linda Agnes Albertine, *née* Young (d 1953); *b* 29 Nov 1934; *Educ* Benedicts; *m* 12 March 1966, Elizabeth Anne, da of Ralph William Beresford, of High Clere, Ben Rhydding, Ilkley, Yorks; 1 s (Simon b 1969), 2 da (Jacqueline b 1968, Nicola b 1972); *Career* owner of Burghope Manor (13th century); chm: Hammerton Holdings Ltd, Gentry Homes; fndr The Heritage Circle of Historic Country Houses, lectr and after-dinner speaker on the stately homes of GB, organiser of tours for overseas gps to visit and stay in stately homes; *Recreations* shooting, travel; *Style*— Michael Denning, Esq; ✉ Burghope Manor, Winsley, Bradford-on-Avon, Wiltshire BA15 2LA (☎ 01225 723557/722695, fax 01225 723113)

DENNING, Dr the Hon Robert Gordon; only child of Baron Denning, PC; *b* 3 Aug 1938; *Educ* Winchester, Magdalen Coll Oxford (MA, PhD); *m* 30 Dec 1967, Elizabeth Carlyle Margaret, da of E R Chilton, of Oxford; 2 children; *Career* 2 Lt KRRC 1957–58; fell and tutor in inorganic chemistry Magdalen Coll Oxford 1968–; *Style*— Dr the Hon Robert Denning; ✉ Magdalen College, Oxford OX1 4AU

DENNINGTON, Dudley; s of John Dennington (d 1962), and Beryl, *née* Hagon (d 1944); *b* 21 April 1927; *Educ* Clifton, Imperial Coll London (BSc); *m* 1951, Margaret Patricia, da of Andrew Mackenzie Stewart (d 1976); 2 da; *Career* 2 Lt RE; mangr George Wimpey 1959–65, traffic cmmr and dir of devpt GLC 1970–72 (chief engr 1965–70), sr ptnr Bullen and Partners 1988–92 (ptnr 1972–92); visiting prof King's Coll London 1978–80; vice pres ICE 1990–92; FCGI, FEng 1985, FICE, FIStructE; *Recreations* painting; *Clubs* Reform; *Style*— Dudley Dennington, Esq, FEng

DENNIS, Maj-Gen Alastair Wesley; CB (1985), OBE (1973); s of Ralph Dennis, and Helen, *née* Henderson; *b* 30 Aug 1931; *Educ* Malvern, RMA Sandhurst; *m* 1957, Susan Lindy Elgar; 1 s, 2 da; *Career* Col GS Cabinet Office 1974–75, Cdr 20 Armd Bde 1976–77, Dep Cmdt Staff Coll 1978–80, Dir Defence Policy (B) MOD 1980–82, Dir Mil Assistance

Overseas MOD 1982–85, Col 16/5 The Queen's Royal Lancers 1990–93, Col The Queen's Royal Lancers 1993–95; sec Imperial Cancer Res Fund 1985–91, chm Assoc Med Res Charities 1987–91, govr and memb Cncl Malvern Coll 1987–93; *Recreations* golf, gardening, bees; *Style—* Maj-Gen Alastair Dennis, CB, OBE; ✉ c/o Barclays Bank, 2 Market Place, Wallingford, Oxon OX10 0EJ

DENNIS, Prof Ian Howard; s of Flt Lt Bernard Cecil Dennis (d 1982), of Altrincham, Cheshire, and Jean Harrison, *née* Dennis; *b* 17 Sept 1948; *Educ* Manchester GS, Queens' Coll Cambridge (MA); *m* 17 July 1982, Dr Susan Mary Bower, da of Ivan William Bower (d 1989), of Southsea, Hants; 1 s (Robert William b 1984), 1 da (Katherine Mary b 1986); *Career* called to the Bar Gray's Inn 1971; lectr in law Cncl of Legal Educn 1971–73; UCL: lectr 1974–82, reader 1982–87, prof 1987–; Allen, Allen and Hesley visiting professorial fell Univ of Sydney 1995; special conslt Law Cmmn 1986–87 (memb criminal codification team 1981–89), memb Cncl Soc of Pub Teachers of Law; chm of Govrs Burleigh Co Infant Sch Crawley Down W Sussex; *Books* Odgers Principles of Pleading and Practice (with D B Casson, 1975), Codification of the Criminal Law, a Report to the Law Commission (with J C Smith and E J Griew, 1985); *Recreations* chess, swimming, wine, mountain walking; *Style—* Prof Ian Dennis; ✉ Faculty of Laws, University College London, Bentham House, Endsleigh Gardens, London WC1H 0EG (☎ 0171 391 1431)

DENNIS, Rt Rev John; patron of sixty-one livings, three Archdeaconries and twenty-four honorary Canonries; the See was founded 1914; s of Hubert Ronald Dennis (d 1990), of Ipswich, and Evelyn Neville-Polley (d 1982); *b* 19 June 1931; *Educ* Rutlish Sch Merton, St Catharine's Coll Cambridge (MA); *m* 28 Aug 1956, Dorothy Mary, da of Godfrey Parker Hinnels (d 1975); 2 s (John David b 1959, Peter Hugh b 1962); *Career* RAF 1950–51; curate: St Bartholomew's Armley Leeds 1956–60, Kettering 1960–62; vicar: the Isle of Dogs 1962–71, John Keble Mill Hill 1971–79; area dean W Barnet 1979–86, prebendary St Paul's Cathedral 1977–79, bishop suffragan Knaresborough 1979–86, bishop of St Edmundsbury and Ipswich 1986–96; diocesan dir of Ordinands Diocese of Ripon 1980–86, episcopal guardian of Anglican Focolarini 1981–96, chaplain Third Order of Soc of St Francis 1989–95; co chm Anglican-Oriental Orthodox Forum 1989–96, English Ctee Anglican-RC Relations 1989–92; memb House of Lords 1991–; *Recreations* cycling, walking, gardening, wood carving, reading; *Clubs* RAF; *Style—* The Rt Rev John Dennis; ✉ 15 Mackenzie Road, Cambridge CB1 2AN

DENNIS, Dr John Stephen; s of Patrick John Dennis (d 1990), and Audrey, *née* Martin (d 1971); *b* 26 Sept 1955; *Educ* Churchfields Sch Swindon, Selwyn Coll Cambridge (nat engrg scholar, BA, N Carolina State Univ prize, College Book prize, res scholar, PhD); *m* 5 Sept 1981, Ruth Dennis, MRCVS, da of Rev Dr John Wall; *Career* lectr Dept of Chemical Engrg Univ of Cambridge 1984–88, self employed conslt chem engr 1989–, mangr LINK Biochemical Engrg Prog 1989–, biochemical engrg co-ordinator SERC 1991–; Steetley Award Inst of Energy 1989; memb Ctee Biotechnology Gp SCI; corporate memb IChemE 1986, CEng 1986; *Publications* author of numerous articles and symposia on combustion, heat transfer, fluidisation and biochemical engrg; *Recreations* rowing (formerly memb Cambridge Univ 2nd VIII), sculling, running, reading; *Style—* Dr John Dennis; ✉ 20 High Street, Stetchworth, Newmarket, Suffolk CB8 9TJ (☎ 01638 508171, fax 01638 508344)

DENNIS, Leslie (Les); *né* Heseltine; s of Leslie Heseltine (d 1982), of Liverpool, and Winifred, *née* Grimes (d 1977); *b* 12 Oct 1953; *Educ* Quarry Bank GS; *m* 1, 1 May 1974 (m dis), Lynne Mary, da of Ronald Charles Thomas Webster; 1 s (Philip James Heseltine b 22 Dec 1979); m 2, 4 June 1994, Amanda Holden; *Career* entertainer; shows incl: Russ Abbot's Madhouse (LWT) 1982–85, Les & Dustin's Laughter Show (BBC) 1986–86, Russ Abbot Show (BBC) 1986–91, Les Dennis Laughter Show (BBC) 1987–91, host Family Fortunes (Central TV) 1987–, Maurice in Intimate Relations (film), and numerous guest spots on variety and chat shows; stage: summer seasons since 1979, Royal Variety Performance 1984; pantomimes incl: Cinderella (New Theatre Hull), Mother Goose (Swansea Grand Theatre), Babes in the Wood (Theatre Royal Newcastle), Sleeping Beauty (Edinburgh) 1993; lead in Me and My Girl (Adelphi Theatre) 1992, lead in Don't Dress For Dinner (tour); memb Variety Golfing Soc; *Recreations* golf, tennis, cinema, theatre, running, eating; *Style—* Les Dennis, Esq; ✉ c/o Mike Hughes, Prince of Wales Theatre, Coventry Street, London W1V 8AS (☎ 0171 930 9161)

DENNIS, Dr Richard Benson; s of Alfred Benson Dennis, of Weymouth, Dorset, and Valentine Betty, *née* Smith; *b* 15 July 1945; *Educ* Weymouth GS, Univ of Reading (BSc, PhD); *m* 17 Dec 1971, Beate, da of Wilhelm Stamm (d 1974), of W Germany; 2 da (Andrea b 1974, Angela b 1976); *Career* Alexander von Humboldt fell Munich Univ W Germany 1976–78, sr lectr Heriot-Watt Univ 1978–91 (lectr 1971), fndr Mütek GmbH W Germany 1980, md Edinburgh Instruments Ltd 1983–, dir Edinburgh Sensors Ltd 1987–; memb Cncl of Mgmnt and treas UK Trade Assoc for Lasers and Electro-optics, memb Scottish Consultative Cncl on the Curriculum 1990–94; chm Sch Bd Balerno HS 1989–93; *Recreations* bridge, golf; *Clubs* Carlton Bridge, Dalmahoy Country; *Style—* Dr Richard Dennis; ✉ Moorside, 8 Ravelrig Hill, Balerno, Edinburgh EH14 7DJ (☎ 0131 449 5392); Edinburgh Instruments Ltd, Riccarton, Currie, Edinburgh EH14 4AS (☎ 0131 449 5844, fax 0131 449 5848, telex 7255 EDINST, e-mail sales@edinst.com)

DENNIS, Rodney John; s of William Gordon Dennis, of SA, and Shiela Dennis; *b* 7 Nov 1952; *Educ* Univ of Cape Town SA (BBusSci (Econ Hons)); *m* 27 Aug 1979, Pamela Mary, *née* Hartnady; *Career* chief investment offr Prudential Portfolio Managers Ltd March 1996–; *Recreations* flying, sailing, skiing, reading, music; *Style—* Rodney Dennis, Esq; ✉ Prudential Portfolio Managers Ltd, 142 Holborn Bars, London EC1N 2NH (☎ 0171 548 3065, fax 0171 548 3588)

DENNIS, Ronald (Ron); s of Norman Stanley Dennis (d 1986), of Woking, Surrey, and Evelyn, *née* Reader; *b* 1 June 1947; *Educ* Guildford Tech Coll (Vehicle Technol Course); *m* 31 Dec 1985, Lisa Ann, da of Gary K Shelton; 1 s (Christian Shelton b 27 Oct 1990), 2 da (Charlotte Victoria b 25 Aug 1987, Francesca Olivia b 11 Nov 1993); *Career* apprentice Thomson & Taylor, owner/mangr Project Four team (winning ProCar Championship 1979 and Formula 3 Championship 1979–80), fndr co with McLaren team 1980 (now in ptnrship with Techniques d'Avant Garde); McLaren Formula 1 racing team: winners Constructors' Cup 1984–85 and 1988, 1989, 1990 and 1991, seven driving championships in nine years to 1992; dir: TAG McLaren Group (md), McLaren International Ltd (md), TAG McLaren Marketing Services, McLaren Cars Ltd, TAG Electronic Systems Ltd, Woodhurst Equipment Ltd, Project Four Ltd, Upper Crust Ltd; memb: Formula One Constructors' Assoc, Fedn Internationale du Sport Automobile Formula One Cmmn; dir Friends of the Royal Botanic Gardens Kew; Hon DTech De Montfort Univ 1996; *Recreations* golf, shooting, snow and water skiing; *Clubs* Morton's, Tramp, St James's, British Racing Drivers'; *Style—* Ron Dennis, Esq; ✉ McLaren International Ltd, Woking Business Park, Albert Drive, Woking, Surrey GU21 5JY (☎ 01483 728211, fax 01483 720157)

DENNISTON, Rev Robin Alastair; s of late Alexander Guthrie Denniston, CMG, CBE; *b* 25 Dec 1926; *Educ* Westminster, ChCh Oxford (MA), Univ of Edinburgh (MSc); *m* 1, 1950, Anne Alice Kyffin (d 1985), da of Dr A Geoffrey Evans (d 1951); 1 s, 2 da; m 2, 1987, Dr Rosa Susan Penelope Beddington; *Career* 2 Lt 66 Airborne Light Regt RA, serv UK; md Hodder & Stoughton Ltd 1968–72 (previously promotion mangr, editorial dir), dep chm George Weidenfeld & Nicolson 1973, non-exec chm A R Mowbray & Co 1974–; chm: Sphere Books 1975–76, Thomas Nelson & Sons 1975–78, Michael Joseph 1975–78, George Rainbird Ltd 1975–78; dir Thomson Pubns Ltd and Hamish Hamilton Ltd 1975–78; acad publisher OUP 1978, Oxford publisher 1983–88; ordained: deacon 1978, priest 1979; priest i/c Gt and Little Tew 1987–90 and 1995–, min i/c St Serf's Burntisland Fife and St Columba's Aberdour Fife 1990–93; *Books* Partly Living (1967), Anatomy of Scotland (co-ed, 1992); *Recreations* espionage studies, trees, music; *Style—* The Rev Robin Denniston; ✉ 112 Randolph Avenue, London W9 1PQ

DENNY, Sir Anthony Coningham de Waltham; 8 Bt (I 1782), of Castle Moyle, Kerry; s of Rev Sir Henry Lyttelton Lyster Denny, 7 Bt (d 1953); *b* 22 April 1925; *Educ* Clayesmore, Anglo-French Art Centre, Regent St Polytech Sch of Architecture; *m* 1 Sept 1949, Anne Catherine, er da of late Samuel Beverley; 2 s (Piers Anthony de Waltham b 1954, Thomas Francis Coningham b 1956), 1 adopted da (Sophy Elinor Sisophanh b 1974); *Heir* s, Piers Anthony de Waltham Denny b 14 March 1954; *Career* serv RAF (air crew) 1943–47; designer; ptnr in Verity and Beverley (Architects and Designers), offices in: London, Tetbury, Gloucestershire and Lisbon, Portugal; memb Fabric Advsy Ctee Gloucester Cathedral; hereditary Freeman of Cork; MCSD, FRSA; *Clubs* Arts; *Style—* Sir Anthony Denny, Bt; ✉ The Priests House, Muchelney, Langport, Somerset TA10 0DQ (☎ 01458 252621)

DENNY, Anthony Miles; only child of Sir (Jonathan) Lionel (Percy) Denny, GBE, MC, Lord Mayor of London 1965–66 (d 1985), and Doris (d 1985), da of Robert George Bare, of Putney; *b* 14 Dec 1925; *m* 28 June 1952 (m dis 1969), Pamela Diana, only child of late Capt Thomas Hamilton Denny, MBE, IA (d 1959), a collateral of the Denny of Castle Moyle barts; 1 s, 1 da; *Career* memb City of London Ct of Common Cncl; HM Lt for City of London 1980–; Liveryman Worshipful Co of Vintners, memb Ct of Assts Worshipful Co of Barbers (Master 1978–79); Knight Order of St John; *Clubs* City Livery, Guildhall; *Style—* Anthony Denny, Esq; ✉ 87 The Straight Bit, Flackwell Heath, High Wycombe, Bucks HP10 9NE

DENNY, Sir Charles Alistair Maurice; 4 Bt (UK 1913), of Dumbarton, Co Dunbarton; s of Sir Alistair Maurice Archibald Denny, 3 Bt (d 1995), and Elizabeth Hunt, da of Maj Sir (Ernest) Guy Richard Loyd, 1 Bt, DSO; *b* 7 Oct 1950; *Educ* Wellington Coll, Univ of Edinburgh; *m* 1981, Belinda (Linda) Mary, yr da of James Patrick McDonald, of Dublin; 1 s (Patrick Charles Alistair b 1985), 1 da (Georgina Mary b 1989); *Heir* s, Patrick Charles Alistair Denny b 2 Jan 1985; *Recreations* golf, racing, gardening; *Clubs* Royal and Ancient Golf St Andrews; *Style—* Sir Charles Denny, Bt; ✉ Farthing Cottage, Lamberhurst, Kent TN3 8HD

DENNY, John Ingram; s of Thomas Ingram Denny, of Macclesfield, Cheshire, and Claire Dorothy, *née* Lewis; *b* 28 May 1941; *Educ* Normain Coll Chester, Poly of N London (DipArch), Univ of Reading (MSc); *m* 2 June 1967, Carol Ann Frances, da of Walter James Hughes, of St Leonards, Bournemouth, Hants; 1 s (Paul b 7 Oct 1969), 2 da (Louise (Mrs Adrian Myers) b 23 July 1971, Sarah b 31 Jan 1974); *Career* sr ptnr HOK Cecil Denny Highton chartered architects (joined 1970, elected ptnr 1971); responsible for following cmmns: the refurbishment, remodelling and restoration of the FCO Whitehall and the old War Office, the interior design for the Home Sec's Office Queen Anne's Gate, over 20 projects for V & A, Natural History and Science Museums; memb Assoc of Conslt Architects, ARIBA, FRSA; *Recreations* golf, photography; *Clubs* Reform; *Style—* John Denny, Esq; ✉ HOK Cecil Denny Highton, Axtell House, 23/24 Warwick Street, London W1R 6DH (☎ 0171 734 6831, fax 0171 734 0508)

DENNY, Jonathan Molesworth; s of Maj Noel Nigel Molesworth Denny, MC (d 1993), of Wokingham, Berks, and Margaret Louise Denny (d 1996); *b* 28 Aug 1953; *Educ* Charterhouse, Univ of Southampton (LLB); *m* 20 May 1978, Annette Clare, da of Peter Raymond Underwood Easteal (d 1986); 2 s (Timothy Peter Noel b 1985, James Rupert Simon b 1990), 1 da (Charlotte Lois Clare b 1983); *Career* admitted slr 1977; managing ptnr Cripps Harries Hall 1990– (joined 1980, ptnr 1982); memb Law Soc; *Recreations* cricket, tennis, skiing, golf, viticulture, military history; *Style—* Jonathan Denny, Esq; ✉ Cripps Harries Hall, Seymour House, 11–13 Mount Ephraim Road, Tunbridge Wells, Kent TN1 1EN (☎ 01892 515121, fax 01892 544878)

DENNY, Piers Anthony de Waltham; er s and h of Sir Anthony Coningham de Waltham Denny, 8 Bt, *qv*; *b* 14 March 1954; *Educ* King Alfred Sch, Westfield Coll London; *m* 1987, Ella Jane, o da of Peter P Huhne, of Earls Court; 2 da (Matilda Ann b 1988, Isabel Margaret b 1990); *Style—* Piers Denny, Esq

DENNY, Richard William Geoffrey; s of Rev Sir Henry Lyttelton Lyster Denny, 7 Bt (d 1953), of Castle Moyle, Kerry, and Joan Dorothy Lucy, *née* Denny (d 1976); bro of Sir Anthony Denny, 8 Bt, *qv*, and Robyn Denny, distinguished modern painter; *b* 4 Feb 1940; *Educ* Royal Masonic Sch Bushey Herts, Plumpton Coll of Agric Sussex; *m* 1, 24 Feb 1961 (m dis 1978), Andrée Suzanne Louise, eldest da of Marcel Louis Parrot; 4 s (Lyster b 1961, Walter b 1963, Giles b 1964, Julius b 1966); m 2, 24 Aug 1984, Linda May Denny, da of Maximilian Magnun, of Calcutta, India; *Career* int conference speaker on motivation; md Denny Farms Ltd 1967–, co-fndr and dir Leadership Development Ltd 1974, lectures worldwide on selling, motivation and people mgmnt 1974–, fndr, chm and md Results Training Ltd 1979–91, chm and md Man Management Ltd 1979–; *Videos* writer and presenter world's first video sales course on professional selling 1983 (now called Win at Sales), Dare to be Great 1986, writer and presenter The Professional Manager video course; *Books* Selling to Win (1988), Motivate to Win (1993), Speak for Yourself (1994); *Recreations* farming, sailing, squash, hunting, skiing; *Style—* Richard Denny, Esq; ✉ Foxcote Court, Moreton-in-Marsh, Gloucestershire GL56 0NJ; Man Management Ltd, PO Box 16, Moreton-in-Marsh, Gloucestershire (☎ 01608 651597)

DENNY, Ronald Maurice; s of Maurice Ellis Louis Denny (d 1981), and Ada Beatrice, *née* Bradley; *b* 11 Jan 1927; *Educ* Gosport County Sch; *m* 7 Nov 1952, Dorothy, da of William Hamilton (d 1933); 1 s (Andrew b 1964), 2 da (Jane b 1957, Elizabeth b 1958); *Career* Rediffusion plc: chief exec 1979–89, chm 1985–89 (ret); dir: BET plc 1982–89 (ret), Thames Television 1980–89, Electrocomponents plc 1984–95, GSS Ltd Malta 1991–; memb Philharmonia Orchestra Tst 1984–92; CEng, FIEE 1948, FRSA 1985, Hon RCM 1984; *Recreations* music, reading; *Clubs* Athenaeum, Arts; *Style—* Ronald Denny, Esq; ✉ 19 Nichols Green, London W5 2QU (☎ 0181 998 3765, fax 0181 248 7934)

DENNYS, Nicholas Charles Jonathan; QC (1991); s of John Edward Dennys, MC (d 1973), and Hon Lavinia Yolande Lyttelton; *b* 14 July 1951; *Educ* Eton, BNC Oxford (BA); *m* 19 Feb 1977, Frances Winifred, da of Rev Canon Gervase William Markham, of Morland, Penrith, Cumbria; 4 da (Harriet b 5 Feb 1979, Sophie b 2 Feb 1981, Romilly Mary b 31 March 1984, Katharine b 14 July 1986); *Career* called to the Bar Middle Temple 1975; *Recreations* golf, windsurfing, reading; *Style—* Nicholas Dennys, Esq, QC; ✉ 1 Atkin Bldgs, Gray's Inn, London WC2 (☎ 0171 404 0102)

DENOON DUNCAN, Russell Euan; s of Douglas Denoon Duncan (d 1955), of Johannesburg, and Ray, *née* Reynolds (d 1981); *b* 11 March 1926; *Educ* Michaelhouse Natal SA; *m* 28 Jan 1956, Caroline Jane Lloyd, da of Noel Wynne Spencer Lewin (d 1980), of London; 2 s (James b 1957, Angus b 1960); *Career* SA Artillery 1943–45; served: Egypt, Italy; admitted attorney SA 1949, admitted slr 1961; ptnr Webber Wentzel, Johannesburg 1952–61; Cameron Markby Hewitt (formerly Markbys): ptnr 1963–90, sr ptnr 1987–90, conslt 1990–; chm National Australia Group (UK) Limited 1987–92; vice pres Br Hungarian Law Assoc 1991–94, pres Br Polish Legal Assoc 1995– (vice chm 1989–91, chm 1991–95); former chm Thames Ditton Residents' Assoc; Freeman Worshipful Co of Slrs 1987; offr Order of Merit of Poland; FInstD; *Recreations* mountain walking, tennis, painting; *Clubs* City of London, City Law, Royal Tennis Ct, Rand, Johannesburg Country; *Style—* Russell Denoon Duncan, Esq; ✉ Rose Cottage, Watts Rd, Thames Ditton, Surrey KT7 0BX (☎ 0181 398 5193, fax 0181 398 9282)

DENSHAM, (Peter) Ryan Cridland; s of Humphrey Ashley (d 1979), and Mary Constance, *née* Cridland; *b* 8 Feb 1949; *Educ* Clifton; *m* Melinda Jane, da of Peter Lowell Baldwin; 2 s (Henry b 1982, George b 1987), 1 da (Emily b 1980); *Career* CA; with Chalmers Impey & Co London 1967–73 (articled clerk 1967–71), with Thornton Baker (now Grant Thornton) 1973–83 (ptnr 1979), ptnr Price Waterhouse 1983–; ACA 1971; *Recreations* fishing, sailing, golf, skiing; *Style—* Ryan Densham, Esq; ✉ Price Waterhouse, 31 Great George Street, Bristol BS1 5QD (☎ 0117 929 1500)

DENT, Jeremy Francis; s of Cdr Adrian James Dent, of Sway, Hants, and Diane Elizabeth, *née* Buxton; *b* 24 Jan 1952; *Educ* Bradfield Coll, Univ of Southampton (BSc); *Career* trainee accountant Peat Marwick McLintock 1974–77; lectr in accounting: Univ of Southampton 1977–82, London Business Sch 1982–88; prof of accounting Manchester Business Sch 1988–90; reader in accounting LSE 1991–; visiting prof: Stockholm, Copenhagen, Turku, Sydney FCA 1977; *Style—* Jeremy Dent, Esq; ✉ 2 Keble House, Manor Fields, London SW15 3LS (☎ 0181 785 2828); London School of Economics & Political Science, Houghton St, London WC2A 2AE (☎ 0171 955 7430, fax 0171 955 7420, telex 24655)

DENT, Sir John; kt (1986), CBE (1976, OBE 1968); s of Harry F Dent; *b* 5 Oct 1923; *Educ* King's Coll London (BSc); *m* 1954, Pamela Ann, da of Frederick G Bailey; 1 s; *Career* chm CAA 1982–6; dir: Engineering Group Dunlop Ltd Coventry 1968–76, Dunlop Holdings Ltd 1970–82, Industrie Pirelli Spa 1978–81, Dunlop AG 1979–82, Pirelli Gen 1980–92, Pirelli Ltd 1985–92; md Dunlop 1978–82; pres: Inst of Travel Mgmnt 1986–94, Int Fedn of Airworthiness 1987–89; FEng 1980; *Style—* Sir John Dent, CBE, FEng; ✉ Hellidon Grange, Hellidon, Daventry, Northants (☎ 01327 260589)

DENT, Sir Robin John; KCVO (1992); s of Rear Adm John Dent, CB, OBE (d 1973); *b* 25 June 1929; *Educ* Marlborough; *m* 2 Oct 1952, Hon Ann Camilla Denison-Pender, da of 2 Baron Pender, CBE (d 1965); 2 da (Annabel Jane (Mrs Meade) b 15 Oct 1954, Jennifer Ann (Mrs Martin Smith) b 27 May 1957); *Career* Bank of England 1949–51, M Samuel & Co 1951–65, dir Hill Samuel & Co Ltd 1965–67, md Baring Bros & Co Ltd 1967–86, dir Barings plc 1985–89, chm Mase Westpac Ltd 1989–93; dir TR City of London Trust plc 1977–; chm: Exec Ctee Br Bankers' Assoc 1984–85, Public Works Loan Bd 1990–; memb: Bd Cancer Res Campaign 1967–95, Advsy Ctee Hong Kong & Shanghai Banking Corp 1974–81, Deposit Protection Bd 1982–85; dep chm Export Guaranty Advsy Cncl 1983–85; treas King Edward's Hosp Fund for London 1974–92, special tstee St Thomas' Hosp 1988–, chm Florence Nightingale Museum Tst 1994–; *Clubs* White's; *Style—* Sir Robin Dent, KCVO; ✉ 44 Smith St, London SW3 4EP (☎ 0171 352 1234)

DENT-YOUNG, David Michael; CBE (1977); s of Lt Col John Dent-Young, TD (d 1955), of Nutley, Bath, and Olivette, *née* De Bruyn (d 1939); *b* 25 March 1927; *Educ* St Aidans Coll Grahamstown SA, Camborne Sch of Mines Cornwall (ACSM); *m* 12 July 1951, Patricia, da of James Edward McKeon, of Bath; 3 da (Jane (Mrs N Frere) b 1952, Sarah (Mrs G Hawkins) b 1954, Nicola (Mrs P Holman) b 1964); *Career* mining engr Nigerian Alluvials Ltd 1951–53; AO Nigeria Ltd: mining engr 1953–57, area engr 1957–65, dist supt 1964–67, sr supt 1967–71; chm and md Amalgamated Tin Mines of Nigeria Ltd 1973–80 (md 1980–83), dir Bisichi Mining plc 1983–; govr Jos Sch of Mines; memb until 1983: Nigerian Chamber of Mines, Nigerian Employers Consultative Assoc, Nigerian Mining Employers Assoc, Consultative Ctee Restoration & Reclamation, Bd of Mgmnt Kaduna Poly Nigeria; pres Plateau Horticultural Soc (Nigeria); CEng, FIMM; Nigerian Medal of Independance 1961; *Recreations* gardening, photography, swimming; *Clubs* Royal Cwlth Soc; *Style—* David Dent-Young, Esq, CBE; ✉ The Cloisters Cottage, Perrymead, Bath BA2 5AY (☎ 01225 837677); Bisichi Mining plc, 8–10 New Fetter Lane, London EC4A 1NQ (☎ 0171 236 3539, fax 0171 248 2850)

DENTON, Dr Anthony Albert; CBE (1997); *b* 14 March 1937; *Educ* Downing Coll Cambridge (MA), Imperial Coll London (PhD, DIC); *Career* graduate apprenticeship Quasi-Arc Co Bilston and Gateshead 1958–60, design engr British Oxygen Company 1960–63, lectr in mechanical engrg Imperial College London (City & Guilds Coll) 1963–66, conslt W D Noble & Co London 1960–71, md Noble Denton & Associates Ltd 1977–80 (tech dir 1971–77), chm Noble Denton International Ltd 1981–; hon visiting prof Dept of Civil Engrg City Univ London; memb Editorial Bd Offshore Engineer 1983–, former memb Advsy Panel Risk Management and Loss Control; Royal Acad of Engrg: memb Cncl 1990–92, vice pres 1992–95, hon sec Int Affrs 1992–95, chm Int Ctee 1992–95 (memb 1987–91); IMechE: memb Cncl 1987–, pres 1993–94; pres IMechIE 1996–; memb Cncl Inst of Materials 1995–; chm Sea Ops Gp Cmmn on Concrete Sea Structures Int Fedn of Prestressed Concrete (FIP) 1974–89; Marine Technology Directorate: memb Educn and Trg Ctee 1986–88, memb Bd of Mgmnt 1996–; memb: Ctee Offshore Engrg Soc ICE 1987–89, Parly Gp for Engrg Devpt; ind advsr IACMST; author of over 50 technical papers on stress analysis, offshore oil and gas platforms, risk and safety; also author of two patents on tubular welding electrode manufacture (now lapsed); Liveryman Worshipful Co of Blacksmiths, Freeman City of London; CEng, MASME, FCGI, FEng 1983, FIMechE (pres 1993–94), FRINA, FInstD, FRSA; *Recreations* motoring, rugby; *Clubs* Oriental, Royal Northern and University; *Style—* Dr Anthony Denton, CBE, FEng; ✉ Chairman, Noble Denton International Ltd, Noble House, 131 Aldersgate Street, London EC1A 4EB (☎ 0171 606 4961, fax 0171 606 6570, telex 296928)

DENTON, Charles Henry; s of Alan Denton; *b* 20 Dec 1937; *Educ* Reading Sch, Univ of Bristol (BA); *m* 1961, Eleanor Mary, *née* Player; 1 s, 2 da; *Career* deckhand 1960, advtg trainee 1961–63, BBC TV 1963–68, freelance TV prodr with Granada, ATV and Yorkshire TV 1969–70, dir Tempest Films Ltd 1969–71, md Black Lion Films 1979–81, controller of progs ATV 1977–81 (head of documentaries 1974–77), dir of progs Central Independent TV 1981–84, dir Central Independent Television plc 1981–87, chief exec Zenith Productions 1984–93, head of drama BBC TV 1993–96; chm: Zenith North Ltd 1988–93, Action Time Ltd 1988–93; chm PACT until 1993, govr Br Film Inst 1993–, memb Arts Cncl of England 1996–; FRSA 1988, FRTS 1988; *Style—* Charles Denton, Esq; ✉ c/o BBC Films, Television Centre, Wood Lane, London W12 7RJ (☎ 0181 743 8000)

DENTON, Prof Sir Eric James; kt (1987), CBE (1974); s of George Denton; *b* 30 Sept 1923; *Educ* Doncaster GS, St John's Coll Cambridge (ScD), UCL; *m* 1946, Nancy Emily, da of Charles Wright; 2 s, 1 da; *Career* lectr in physiology Univ of Aberdeen 1948–56, physiologist Marine Biological Assoc Laboratory Plymouth 1956–74 (dir 1974–87), Royal Soc res prof Univ of Bristol 1964–74; FRS; *Style—* Prof Sir Eric Denton, CBE, FRS; ✉ Fairfield House, St Germans, Saltash, Cornwall PL12 5LS (☎ 01503 230204); The Laboratory, Citadel Hill, Plymouth, Devon PL1 2PB (☎ 01752 222772)

DENTON, Kenneth Raymond; s of Stanley Charles Denton (d 1957), of Rochester, and Lottie Bertha Rhoda, *née* Dorrington (d 1972); *b* 20 Aug 1932; *Educ* Rochester Tech and Sch of Art, Medway Coll of Art and Design; *m* 5 Oct 1957, Margaret, da of Thomas Nesbitt (d 1969), of Crossnenagh, Keady, Co Armagh, NI; 3 s (Colin b 1959, Martin b 1960, Nigel b 1961); *Career* Nat Serv RASC, transferred to REME 1952–54; freelance designer and decorative artist 1954–63; designs incl: domestic interiors and furniture, interiors and inn-signs for major brewing cos, Bd Room for Grants of St James; lectr 1963–67 (Royal Sch of Mil Engrg, Maidstone Coll of Art, Medway Coll of Design, Erith Coll of Art), landscape and marine artist 1967–; exhibitions in UK, Europe, Canada and USA, 40 one man shows, shared exhbitions with Patrick Hall, Leslie Moore and Enzo Plazzotta; work in many private and public collections, numerous TV and radio appearances; memb Cncl and Publishing, Selection and Hanging Ctees RSMA; FBID 1963, RSMA 1976, FCSD 1987, FRSA 1989, memb Int Soc of Marine Painters Florida 1992; *Books* A Celebration of Marine Art - 50 Years of the Royal Society of Marine Artists (jt prodr and writer); *Recreations* classical music, piano playing; *Style—* Kenneth Denton, Esq; ✉ Priory Farm Lodge, Sporle, King's Lynn, Norfolk PE32 2DS (☎ 01760 722084)

DENTON, Nicholas John (Nick); s of John Richard Denton, and Jennifer Jane, *née* Forbes; *b* 18 Oct 1955; *Educ* Winchester, Magdalene Coll Cambridge (MA); *m* 23 March 1991, Katie, da of Michael Benzecry; 1 s (Toby John b 19 May 1993), 1 da (Rebecca Louisa b 2 June 1995); *Career* Dewe Rogerson Ltd: account dir London 1981–86, dir Australia 1986–87; corp affrs mangr Eurotunnel plc 1987–88, dir Shandwick Consultants Ltd 1988–; *Recreations* tennis, history, reading, opera, walking; *Style—* Nick Denton, Esq; ✉ Shandwick Consultants Ltd, Aldermary House, 10–15 Queen Street, London EC4N 1TX (☎ 0171 329 0096, fax 0171 329 6009)

DENTON, Prof Richard Michael (Dick); s of Arthur Benjamin Denton (d 1968), of Chippenham, Wilts, and Eileen Mary, *née* Evans; *b* 16 Oct 1941; *Educ* Wycliffe Coll Stonehouse Glos, Christ's Coll Cambridge (MA, PhD), Univ of Bristol (DSc); *m* 1965, Janet Mary, *née* Jones; 2 da (Sally Catherine b 1967, Hannah Rachel b 1972), 1 s (Stephen Richard b 1969); *Career* Dept of Biochemistry Univ of Bristol: MRC Metabolism Control Gp 1966–72, lectr 1973–78, reader 1978–87, prof of biochemistry (personal chair) 1987–, head of dept 1995–; MRC sr research leave fellowship 1984–88; memb: MRC Grants Ctee and Physiological Systems Bd 1977–85, Research Ctee Br Diabetic Assoc 1986–92 (chm 1990–92), Molecular and Cell Biology Panel Wellcome Tst Research Ctee 1993–96; R D Lawrence lecture Br Diabetic Assoc 1981; memb Biochemical Soc 1965; *Publications* over 220 research papers in Nature, Biochemical Jl and other int research jls on topics incl molecular basis of the control of metabolism by insulin and other hormones; *Recreations* family, fell walking, keeping fit, cooking, reading; *Style—* Prof Dick Denton; ✉ Department of Biochemistry, University of Bristol, Bristol BS8 1TD (☎ 0117 928 7433, fax 0117 928 8274, e-mail r.denton@bristol.ac.uk)

DENTON OF WAKEFIELD, Baroness (Life Peer UK 1991), of Wakefield in the County of West Yorkshire; Jean Denton; CBE (1990); da of late Charles J Moss, and Kathleen, *née* Tuke; *b* 29 Dec 1935; *Educ* Rothwell GS, LSE (BSc); *Career* info exec BBC News Div (Home and Overseas) 1958, communications exec Procter & Gamble 1959–61, mktg conslt and asst ed Retail Business Economist Intelligence Unit 1961–64, market investigations Women's Magazines Div IPC 1964–66, res Hotel and Catering Dept Univ of Surrey 1966–68, professional racing/rally driver 1968–71 (competed in Europe & Middle East, successfully completed London-Sydney Marathon and World Cup Rally to Mexico, twice British Women Racing Driver's Champion); mktg dir: Huxford Gp 1971–78, Heron Motor Gp 1978–80; md Herondrive 1980–85, dir external affairs Austin Rover Gp 1985–86, dir Burson-Marsteller 1986–92, dep chm Black Country Development Corporation 1987–92; memb Bd: British Nuclear Fuels plc 1987–92, Triplex Lloyd plc 1989–92, London & Edinburgh Insurance Group 1989–92, Think Green 1988–91, North West Television 1991, UK 2000 1986–89; memb: Interim Advsy Ctee on Teachers Pay and Conditions 1989–91, The Engrg Cncl 1986–92 (chm Fin Ctee), The RSA Cncl 1990–91, Sch Teachers Review Body 1991–92; a Baroness-in-Waiting 1991–92, Parly under-sec of state DTI 1992–93, Parly sec of state for environment 1993–94, min for economy and agric NI 1994–; co chm Women's Nat Ctee 1992–; pres: FORUM UK, Women on the Move Against Cancer; former chm Mktg Gp of GB; former memb Hansard Soc's Cmmn on Women at the Top; Hon DLett Bradford 1993, Hon DH King's Coll Pennsylvania 1994; Freeman City of London 1982; FCInstM 1972, FIMI 1974, FRSA 1987, CIMgt 1988; *Clubs* British Women Racing Drivers (vice pres); *Style—* The Rt Hon Baroness Denton of Wakefield, CBE; ✉ House of Lords, London SW1A 0PW (☎ 0171 219 3000, fax 0171 735 2642)

DENYER, Prof Peter Brian; s of Robert Ralph Denyer, of Littlehampton, Sussex, and Evelyn May, *née* Swinbank; *b* 27 April 1953; *Educ* Worthing Tech HS, Loughborough Univ of Technol (BSc), Univ of Edinburgh (PhD); *m* 20 July 1977, Fiona Margaret Lindsay, da of Ernest William Reoch, of Edinburgh; 2 da (Kate b 1982, Kirsty b 1984); *Career* design engr Wolfson Microelectronics Inst Edinburgh 1976–80; Univ of Edinburgh: lectr 1981–86, reader 1986, prof chair of integrated electronics 1986–; md Vision Group plc 1990–; head devpt team the 'Peach' (smallest video camera in the world); *Books* Introduction to MOSLSI Design (1983), VLSI Signal Processing - A Bit-Serial Approach (1985), Bit-Serial VLSI Computation (1988); *Recreations* walking, family, plumbing; *Style—* Prof Peter Denyer; ✉ Vision Group plc, 31 Pinkhill, Edinburgh EH12 7BF (☎ 0131 539 7111, fax 0131 539 7141)

DENYER, Roderick Lawrence; QC (1990); s of Oliver James Denyer (d 1982), and Olive Mabel, *née* Jones; *b* 1 March 1948; *Educ* Grove Park GS for Boys Wrexham, LSE (LLM); *m* 21 April 1973, Pauline; 2 da (Hannah b 4 March 1978, Alexandra b 10 Feb 1981); *Career* barr; lectr in law Univ of Bristol 1971–73, called to the Bar 1970, recorder of the Crown Court, head of chambers; Personal Injury Litigation and Children (1993), various pubns in legal jls; *Recreations* cricket, 1960s pop music; *Style—* Roderick Denyer, Esq, QC; ✉ St John's Chambers, Small Street, Bristol BS1 1DW (☎ 0117 921 3456, fax 0117 929 4821)

DENYER, Stephen Robert Noble; s of Wilfred Denyer, of Sherborne, Dorset, and Joy Victoria Jeanne, *née* Noble; *b* 27 Dec 1955; *Educ* Fosters GS Sherborne, Univ of Durham (BA); *m* 3 Sept 1988, Monika Maria, da of Heinrich Christoph Wolf, of Lübeck, Germany; 2 s (Martin, Timothy), 1 da (Helen); *Career* slr; ptnr Allen & Overy (specialising in Central and Eastern Europe and in corp fin work) 1986–; chm Int Bar Assoc's Eastern Euro Forum; memb: Central and Eastern Euro Panel of Br Invisibles, Exec Ctee Br-Polish Legal Assoc; Freeman Worshipful Co of Slrs 1986; memb Law Soc 1980; memb Int Bar Assoc 1987; *Recreations* walking, travel, gardening; *Style—* Stephen Denyer, Esq; ✉ Allen & Overy, One New Change, London EC4M 9QQ (☎ 0171 330 3000, fax 0171 330 9999)

DENZA, Eileen; CMG (1984); da of Alexander Young (d 1995), of Aberdeen, and Ellen Duffy (d 1981); *b* 23 July 1937; *Educ* Univ of Aberdeen (MA), Univ of Oxford (MA), Harvard Univ (LLM); *m* 1966, John Denza, *qv*; 2 s (Mark b 1969, Paul b 1971), 1 da (Antonia b 1967); *Career* asst lectr in law Univ of Bristol 1961–63, called to the Bar Lincoln's Inn 1963, asst legal advsr FCO 1963–74, legal cnsllr FCO 1974–86, legal advsr to UK Representation to Euro Community 1980–83, pupillage and practice at Bar 1986–87, second counsel to the Chm of Ctees, counsel to Euro Communities Ctee House of Lords 1987–95, sr reseach fell UCL 1996– (tutor 1990–96); memb: European Community Law Section Advsy Bd Br Inst of Int and Comparative Law, Advsy Bd Inst of European Public Law Univ of Hull; FRSA; *Books* Diplomatic Law (1976); contributor to: Satow, Diplomatic Practice, Essays in Air Law, Airline Mergers and Co-operation in the European Community, Consular Law and Practice, Institutional Dynamics of European Integration, The European Union and World Trade Law; *Recreations* music; *Style—* Mrs Eileen Denza, CMG

DENZA, John; s of Luigi Carlo Denza (d 1991), of Hampstead, and Joyce Mary, *née* Withers (d 1952); *b* 4 May 1930; *Educ* Winchester, Corpus Christi Coll Cambridge (MA); *m* 1966, Eileen Denza, *qv*; 2 s (Mark b 1969, Paul b 1971), 1 da (Antonia b 1967); *Career* chartered accountant; with Spicer & Pegler until 1958, Cooper Brothers & Co 1958–61; Finnie Ross Welch (merged with Stoy Hayward 1992): joined 1961, ptnr 1963–94; Liveryman Worshipful Co of Haberdashers 1953 (also currently hon asst), Freeman City of London; FCA 1968 (ACA 1956); *Recreations* music; *Clubs* Hurlingham; *Style*— John Denza, Esq; ✉ 85 Redington Road, London NW3 7RR (☎ 0171 435 0984)

DERĘGOWSKI, Prof Jan Bronisław; s of Jan Deręgowski (d 1964), and Szczęsława Helena, *née* Enskajt (d 1987); *b* 1 March 1933; *Educ* schooling abroad and N Copernicus Polish Coll, Univ of London (BSc, BA, PhD), Univ of Aberdeen (DSc); *m* 14 August 1958, Eva Loft, da of Eiler Gudmund Nielsen; 2 s (Sven Marek b 2 Dec 1966, Niels Tadeusz b 12 Feb 1969), 1 da (Anna Halina b 16 Nov 1978); *Career* various engrg appts 1960–65, Miny of Overseas Devpt research fell Univ of Zambia 1965–69; Univ of Aberdeen: lectr 1969–77, sr lectr 1977–81, reader 1981–88, prof 1988–; memb Soc Polonaise des Sciences et des Lettres a l'Etranger 1990; fell Netherlands Inst for Advanced Studies; FBPsS, FRSE 1994; *Books* Illusions, Patterns and Pictures (1980), Distortion in Art: The Eye and the Mind (1984), Perception and Artistic Style (co-author, 1990); *Recreations* reading, history of the Grand Duchy of Lithuania, Polish language; *Style*— Prof Jan Deręgowski, FRSE; ✉ Department of Psychology, University of Aberdeen, King's College, Old Aberdeen, Aberdeen AB9 2UB (☎ 01224 272247 and 01224 272228, fax 01224 273426)

DERAMORE, 6 Baron (UK 1885); Sir Richard Arthur de Yarburgh-Bateson; 7 Bt (UK 1818); yr s of 4 Baron Deramore (d 1943), and bro of 5 Baron (d 1964); *b* 9 April 1911; *Educ* Harrow, St John's Coll Cambridge (MA), Architectural Assoc Sch; *m* 28 Aug 1948, Janet Mary, da of John Ware, MD; 1 da; *Heir* none; *Career* served as Navigator/Flt Lt RAFVR 1940–45; chartered architect; salaried ptnr Arthur William Kenyon 1938–39; ptnr: H G Cherry and Ptnrs 1952–65, Cherry and Deramore 1965–70; practised as Arthur Deramore in Bucks then Yorks 1970–82; memb Cncl Architectural Assoc 1951–54; pres: 14 Sqdn Reunion Assoc, Vale of Pickering Art Club, York Area Prayer Book Soc; FRIBA (ARIBA 1937); *Recreations* watercolour painting, writing; *Clubs* RAF, RAC; *Style*— Rt Hon Lord Deramore; ✉ Heslington House, Aislaby, Pickering, N Yorks YO18 8PE (☎ 01751 473195)

DERBY, Archdeacon of; *see:* Gatford, Ven Ian

DERBY, 19 Earl of (E 1485); Edward Richard William Stanley; 12 Bt (E 1627); also Baron Stanley of Bickerstaffe (UK 1832) and Baron Stanley of Preston (UK 1886); s of Hon Hugh Henry Montagu Stanley (d 1971, gs of 17 Earl of Derby), and Mary Rose (who m 2, A William A Spiegelberg) da of late Charles Francis Birch, of Rhodesia; suc uncle, 18 Earl of Derby, MC, DL (d 1994); *b* 10 Oct 1962; *Educ* Eton, RAC Cirencester; *m* 21 Oct 1995, Hon Caroline Emma Neville, da of 10 Baron Braybrooke, *qv*; *Heir* bro, Hon Peter Hugh Charles Stanley b 1964; *Career* cmmnd Grenadier Gds 1982–85; dir incl: Fleming Private Fund Management Ltd 1991–, Fleming Private Asset Management Ltd 1992–, Fleming Private Nominees Ltd 1992–, Haydock Park Racecourse Co Ltd 1994–; pres: Liverpool C of C 1995–, Royal Liverpool Philharmonic Soc 1995–, Royal Lytham & St Annes Golf Club 1995–; tstee: Nat Museums and Galleries on Merseyside 1995–, Aintree Racecourse Charitable Appeal Tst 1995–; hon vice pres BFSS 1995–; patron: Friends of Liverpool Cathedral 1995–, RNLI 1995–; life pres Rugby Football League 1996; *Clubs* White's, Turf, Jockey Club Rooms; *Style*— The Rt Hon the Earl of Derby; ✉ Knowsley, Prescot, Merseyside L34 4AF (☎ 0151 489 6147, office fax 0151 489 6148); 1 Netherton Grove, Chelsea, London SW10 9TQ (☎ 0171 814 2700, fax 0171 814 2850)

DERBY, Bishop of 1995–; Rt Rev Jonathan Sansbury Bailey; s of Walter Eric Bailey (d 1994), of Port Erin, IOM, and Audrey Sansbury, *née* Keenan; *b* 24 Feb 1940; *Educ* Quarry Bank HS Liverpool, Trinity Coll Cambridge (MA); *m* 1965, Susan Mary, da of Maurice James Bennett-Jones (d 1980); 3 s (Mark, Colin, Howard); *Career* curate: Sutton Lancs 1965–68, Warrington 1968–71; warden Marrick Priory 1971–76, vicar Wetherby Yorks 1976–82, archdeacon of Southend 1982–92, Bishop's offr for indust and commerce Dio of Chelmsford 1982–92, suffragan bishop of Dunwich 1992–95, Clerk of the Closet to HM The Queen 1996–; *Recreations* beekeeping, carpentry, music, theatre; *Clubs* United Oxford and Cambridge Univ; *Style*— The Rt Rev the Bishop of Derby; ✉ Derby Church House, Derby DE1 3DR (☎ 01332 346744, fax 01332 295810)

DERBY, Peter Jared; s of Samuel Jonathan James Derby (d 1974), of Belfast, and Frances Emma, *née* Leckie; *b* 21 Feb 1940; *Educ* Inchmarlo Sch, Royal Belfast Academical Inst, Queen's Univ Belfast (BSc); *m* 3 Aug 1968, Rosemary Jane, da of Charles Euan Chalmers Guthrie (d 1985), of Edinburgh; 1 s (Andrew b 1971), 2 da (Lucy b 1969, Polly b 1973); *Career* jt asst actuary Scottish Widows Fund 1965–67 (joined 1961), ptnr Wood Mackenzie and Co 1970–86 (joined 1967); dir: Hill Samuel and Co Ltd 1986–88, Ashton Tod McLaren 1988–89, Quilter & Co Ltd 1989–; sidesman Christ Church Shamley Green; memb Guildry of Brechin Angus 1973; Freeman: City of London, Worshipful Co of Actuaries 1979–; FFA 1965, AIA 1968, memb Stock Exchange 1970; *Recreations* golf, tennis, squash, skiing, music; *Clubs* Travellers', New (Edinburgh), Woking Golf; *Style*— Peter J Derby, Esq; ✉ Haldish Farm, Shamley Green, Guildford GU5 0RD (☎ 01483 898 461); Quilter & Co Ltd, St Helen's, 1 Undershaft, London EC3A 8BB (☎ 0171 662 6262, fax 0171 726 8826, telex 883719)

DERBYSHIRE, Sir Andrew George; kt (1986); s of late Samuel Reginald Derbyshire; *b* 7 Oct 1923; *Educ* Chesterfield GS, Queens' Coll Cambridge (MA), Architectural Assoc (AADipl); *m* Lily Rhodes, *née* Binns, widow of Norman Rhodes; 3 s, 1 da; *Career* physicist and architect; Admty Signals Estab and Bldg Res Station 1943–46; Farmer & Dark (Marchwood and Belvedere power stations) 1951–53, West Riding Co Architect's Dept 1953–55, asst city architect Sheffield 1955–61, currently pres RMJM Ltd (formerly Robert Matthew, Johnson-Marshall & Partners, joined 1961); chm RSA Art for Architecture Scheme 1994–; memb: Cncl RIBA 1950–72 and 1975–81 (sr vice pres 1980), NJCC 1961–65, Bldg Indust Communications Res Ctee 1964–66 (chm Steering Ctee), DOE Planning and Tport Res Advsy Cncl 1971–76, Standing Cmmn on Energy and the Environment 1978–, Construction Indust Cncl 1990–94; pt/t memb CEGB 1973–84; memb Bd: PSA 1975–79, London Docklands Devpt Corp 1984–88, Construction Indust Sector Gp NEDC 1988–92; Hoffman Wood prof of architecture Univ of Leeds 1978–80, external prof Dept of Civil Engrg Univ of Leeds 1981–85, Gresham prof of rhetoric Gresham Coll 1990–92; many pubns and broadcasts on professional consultancy, planning and building new towns and univs, new forms of public tport, physical planning in the developing world and the function of sci in architecture and planning; Hon DUniv York 1972; hon fell Inst of Advanced Architectural Studies Univ of York 1994–; FRIBA, FRSA 1981 (chm Art for Architecture Project 1994–), Hon FIStructE 1992; *Recreations* family and garden; *Style*— Sir Andrew Derbyshire; ✉ 4 Sunnyfield, Hatfield, Herts AL9 5DX (☎ 01707 265903, fax 01707 275874)

DERBYSHIRE, Benjamin Charles Edward; s of Sir Andrew George Derbyshire, *qv*, and Lily, *née* Binns; *b* 15 May 1953; *Educ* Bryanston, Hatfield GS, Sch of Architecture Birmingham Poly, Sch of Architecture Univ of Cambridge (DipArch); *m* 14 April 1979, Annie Anoja Sapumali, da of I D S Weerawardina; 1 s (Albert Guy Devakumara b 24 April 1987), 1 da (Millicent Grace Ranjani b 15 Jan 1990); *Career* architect; Hunt Thompson Assocs: joined 1976, assoc 1979–, ptnr 1986–; projects incl: new housing Ponler Street and Isledon Village, refurbishments Lansdown Drive Hostel, Sandringham buildings, St Olave's Mansions, Northwood Tower, Woolwich Common Estate and Watney Market, redevelopments Waltham Forest Housing Action Tst and Culverwell Rd Bristol; chm USER Research 1991– (fndr dir 1989); memb: RIBA Community Architecture Gp 1983–87, Campaign Gp Business in the Community Professional Firms Gp 1990–, Ctee Nat Tenants' Resource Centre 1991–, Bd Prince's Trust 1992– (memb Ctee Faith in Estates 1986–87); contrib to architectural pubns; RIBA 1977, FRSA 1993; *Awards* Civic Trust award and NE Thames Architecture Award (for Ponler Street housing), Times/RIBA Community Enterprise Commendations (for Newquay House and Isledon Road housing), Housing Project Design Award, Waltham Forest Design Award and Commendation and Brickwork Design Award (for Northwood Tower and Waltham Forest); *Recreations* walking, cycling, music; *Style*— Benjamin Derbyshire, Esq; ✉ Hunt Thompson Associates, 79 Parkway, London NW1 7PP (☎ 0171 495 8555, fax 0171 485 1232)

DERBYSHIRE, Prof Edward; s of Edward Derbyshire (decd), of Timonium, Maryland, USA, and Kathleen, *née* Wall; *b* 18 Aug 1932; *Educ* Alleyne's GS Stone Staffs, Univ of Keele (BA, DipEd), McGill Univ Montreal (MSc), Monash Univ (PhD); *m* 2 June 1956, Maryon Joyce, da of Arthur John Lloyd (decd), of Keele, Staffs; 3 s (Edmund Lloyd b 20 Jan 1959, Edward Arthur b 13 April 1965, Dominic Giles b 17 Nov 1968); *Career* RAEC 1954–56; lectr in geography Univ of NSW Aust 1960–62, sr lectr in geography Monash Univ Aust 1965–66 (lectr 1963–65); Univ of Keele: lectr in physical geography 1967–70, sr lectr 1970–74, reader 1974–84, prof of geomorphology 1984; Univ of Leicester: prof of physical geography 1985–90, res prof 1990–92, prof emeritus 1991–; res prof of physical geography Royal Holloway Coll Univ of London 1991–, hon res prof Gansu Acad of Scis People's Repub of China 1991–, Belle Van Zuylen prof Univ of Utrecht 1992; pres Br Geomorphological Res Gp 1982–83 (hon sec 1971–75), pres Section E Br Assoc for the Advancement of Sci 1989–90, sec gen Int Union for Quaternary Res (INQUA) 1991–95, ed Quaternary Perspectives, chm Int Geological Correlation Prog (UNESCO/IUGS) 1996–; FGS (1974), FRGS (1980); Antarctic Serv Medal USA 1974; *Books* The Topographical Map (1966), Climatic Geomorphology (ed, 1973), Geomorphology and Climate (ed, 1976), Geomorphological Processes (with J R Hails and K J Gregory, 1980); *Recreations* photography, music, poetry, painting; *Style*— Prof Edward Derbyshire; ✉ Department of Geography, Royal Holloway College London, Egham, Surrey TW20 0EX (☎ 01784 443656, fax 01273 748919)

DERBYSHIRE, Eileen; da of Frank Derbyshire (d 1976), of Manchester, and Mary Edna, *née* Taylor (d 1993); *b* 6 Oct 1931; *Educ* Manchester HS for Girls, Northern Sch of Music; *m* 1 April 1965, Thomas Wilfrid Holt, s of George Wrangham Holt; 1 s (Oliver Charles Thomas b 22 May 1966); *Career* actress; first bdcast in 1948, has taken part in numerous radio prodns; first appeared in rep 1952 (toured with Century Theatre and others); plays role of Emily Bishop in Coronation Street (joined in first yr 1960); LRAM; *Style*— Miss Eileen Derbyshire; ✉ c/o Granada Television Ltd, Granada TV Centre, Quay Street, Manchester M60 9EA

DERBYSHIRE, Hugh Bernard; *m*; 2 c; *Career* High Sheriff Hereford & Worcs 1995–96; *Style*— Hugh Derbyshire, Esq; ✉ c/o Hereford City Council, St Owen Street, Hereford HR1 2PJ

DERBYSHIRE, Nicholas Crawford (Nick); s of Arnold Clifford Derbyshire (d 1974), of Oxford, and Eileen, *née* Crawford; *b* 20 July 1943; *Educ* St Edward's Sch Oxford, Sch of Architecture Gloucester Coll of Art and Design (Dip Arch), Manchester Business Sch (Dip Business Studies), Hochschule Für Gestaltung Ulm Germany; *m* 18 July 1970, Winifred, da of Donald Blenkinsop; 2 s (William George b 1971, Thomas Henry b 1974); *Career* architect; British Rail: joined Regnl Architects' Office York 1970, southern regnl architect 1986–89, architect for Network SE 1989–91, dir Architecture and Design Gp 1991–95; dir Nick Derbyshire Design Associates Ltd 1995–; visiting prof Dept of Design Nottingham Trent Univ 1996–; *Awards* Civic Tst Award 1976 and FT Architectural Award 1978 (for Bradford Transport Interchange), FT Architectural Award (for travel centre at Newcastle station) 1986, Civic Tst Award (for scheme at Poole station) 1990, RICS Building Conservation Award and Lord Montagu Trophy (for Liverpool St Station) 1992; RIBA; FRSA; *Books* Liverpool Street: A Station for the Twenty-First Century (1991); *Recreations* sailing, hillwalking; *Clubs* 300; *Style*— Nick Derbyshire, Esq; ✉ Nick Derbyshire Design Associates Ltd, East Side Offices, King's Cross Station, London N1 9AP (☎ 0171 922 4922, fax 0171 922 4924)

DERHAM, Dr Kenneth Walter; s of Kenneth Reginald Derham, of Southampton, and Edith Sybil, *née* Harden; *b* 16 May 1949; *Educ* Univ of Essex (PhD), Univ of Bath (BSc); *m* 16 April 1977, Janet Mary, da of Edgar Victor Garton (d 1984), of Enfield; 1 da (Anna Rose b 1980); *Career* commissioning ed Elsevier Applied Sci Publishers 1974–77, sr ed Plenum Publishing Co 1977–; md: Plenum UK & Euro 1978–91, Plenum Publishing Co Ltd 1991–; memb: Br Computer Soc, Royal Soc of Chemistry; CChem; *Style*— Dr Kenneth Derham; ✉ Plenum Publishing Company Ltd, 101 Back Church Lane, London E1 1LU (☎ 0171 264 1910, fax 0171 264 1919)

DERING, Christopher John; s of Dr John Charles Dering, of Southampton, and Annette Joan, *née* Green; *b* 21 Sept 1964; *Educ* Weymouth GS, Exeter Coll Oxford (scholar, Maxwell Law Prize, Slaughter & May Contract Prize, proxime accessit Martin Wronker Prize, BA, MA); *m* 18 July 1987, Julie Ann, da of late Harry Alfred Killick; 1 da (Lucy Ann b 18 May 1993); *Career* lectr in law Exeter Coll Oxford 1986–88, called to the Bar Middle Temple 1989, admitted slr 1992, ptnr Masons 1992– (joined 1989); *Books* Jersey Law Reports (ed, 1987–88), Service Level Agreements (contrib, 1993), Eco-Management and Eco-Auditing (contrib and co-ed, 1993); *Recreations* caravanning; *Style*— Christopher Dering, Esq; ✉ 4 Meitner Close, Bramley, Hampshire (☎ 01256 880702, fax 01256 880926); Masons, 30 Aylesbury Street, London EC1R 0ER (☎ 0171 490 4000, fax 0171 490 2545, car 0831 195933, mobile 0385 280034)

DERMOTT, William; CB (1984); s of William and Mary Dermott; *b* 27 March 1924; *Educ* Univ of Durham (MSc); *m* 1946, Winifred Joan Tinney; 1 s, 1 da; *Career* agric scientist Univ of Durham and Wye Coll Univ of London 1943–46, MAFF 1976 (sr sci specialist and dep chief sci specialist 1971–76), head of Agric Sci Serv 1976–84, pres Br Soc of Soil Sci 1981–82, actg dir gen ADAS 1983–84; *Style*— William Dermott, Esq, CB; ✉ 22 Chequers Park, Wye, Ashford, Kent TN25 5BB (☎ 01233 812694)

DERNIE, Frank William; s of James Harry Dernie (d 1973), and Monica Mary, *née* Pacey; *b* 3 April 1950; *Educ* Kirkham GS, Imperial Coll London (BScEng); *m* 20 July 1974, Sheenagh Virginia, da of Ian Robertson; 3 da (Kirsty Miranda b 31 Dec 1976, Hannah Jane b 2 April 1978, Virginia Mary b 28 Feb 1980), 1 s (James Ian Robertson b 27 June 1982); *Career* motorsport designer; chief engr Hesketh Racing 1976–78, head of R & D Williams Grand Prix Engineering 1978–88, tech dir Team Lotus 1988–90, chief engr Benetton Formula Ltd 1992–95, conslt tech dir Ligier 1990–; *Style*— Frank Dernie, Esq; ✉ Greystacks, Denchworth Road, Wantage, Oxon OX12 9AU (☎ 01235 768505); Ligier Sports, Technopole de la Nievre, 58470 Magny Cours, France

DERRINGTON, John Anthony; CBE; s of late John Derrington; *b* 24 Dec 1921; *Educ* Battersea Poly (BSc), Imperial Coll London (DIC); *m* 1971, Beryl June, *née* Kimber; 1 s, 3 da; *Career* chartered civil engrg conslt, formerly with Sir Robert McAlpine & Sons; former pres ICE; FEng 1979; *Recreations* gardening, travel, reading; *Style*— John Derrington, Esq, CBE, FEng; ✉ 3 Gorham Ave, Rottingdean, Brighton BN2 7DP

DERRY AND RAPHOE, Bishop of 1980–; Rt Rev James Mehaffey; s of John Mehaffey (d 1991), of Portadown, Co Armagh, NI, and Sarah, *née* McKerr (d 1994); *b* 29 March 1931; *Educ* Portadown Coll, Trinity Coll Dublin (MA, BD), Queen's Univ Belfast (PhD); *m* 21 July 1956, Thelma Patricia, da of Charles Frederick Leord Jackson (d 1991); 2 s (Philip Jackson b 19 Aug 1957 d 1993, Timothy James b 28 June 1962), 1 da (Wendy Marguerite b 27 Sept 1958); *Career* asst curate: St Patrick's Ballymacarrett Belfast 1954–56, St John's Deptford London 1956–58; asst curate Down Parish Church and minor canon of Down Cathedral Downpatrick 1958–60, bishop's curate St Christopher's Belfast 1960–62; incumbent: of Kilkeel Co Down 1962–66, of St Finnian's Belfast 1966–80; canon missioner of Down and Dromore Dio 1976–80; *Style*— The Rt Rev the

Bishop of Derry and Raphoe; ✉ The See House, 112 Culmore Road, Londonderry BT48 8JF, NI (☎ 01504 351206); Diocesan Office, London Street, Londonderry, NI (☎ 01504 262440, fax 01504 352554)

DERRY-EVANS, Robert Stephen; *b* 2 March 1952; *Educ* Univ of Oxford (MA Classics); *Career* McKenna & Co: asst slr 1977–84, ptnr Hong Kong 1984–89, ptnr London 1989–94, managing ptnr 1994–; author of numerous articles and speaker at confs worldwide; memb: Law Soc, Law Soc of Hong Kong, Int Bar Assoc; *Style*— Robert Derry-Evans, Esq; ✉ McKenna & Co, Mitre House, 160 Aldersgate Street, London EC1A 4DD (☎ 0171 606 9000, fax 0171 606 9100)

DERVAIRD, Hon Lord; John Murray; QC (Scotland 1974); s of John Hyslop Murray (d 1984), of Beoch, Stranraer, and Mary, *née* Scott (d 1993); *b* 8 July 1935; *Educ* Cairnryan Sch, Edinburgh Acad, CCC Oxford (MA), Univ of Edinburgh (LLB); *m* 30 July 1960, Bridget Jane, 2 da of Sir William Maurice Godfrey, 7 Bt (d 1974); 3 s (Alexander Godfrey b 12 Feb 1964, William John b 21 Oct 1965, David Gordon b 4 June 1968); *Career* Lt Royal Signals 1954–56; advocate 1962, QC (Scotland) 1974, memb Scottish Law Cmmn 1979–88; chm: Agric Law Assoc 1981–85 (vice pres 1985–91), Scottish Cncl of Law Reporting 1978–88, Scottish Lawyers Euro Gp 1975–78, Med Appeal Tribunals 1978–79 and 1985–88, Scottish Ctee on Arbitration 1986–, Scot Cncl for International Arbitration 1989–; Lord of Session (Senator of the Coll of Justice) 1988–89; Univ of Edinburgh: Dickson Minto prof of company law 1990–, dean Faculty of Law 1994–96; designated by UK to Panel of Arbitrators for Int Centre for Settlement of Investment Disputes 1996–; hon pres Advocates Business Law Gp 1988–, vice pres Comité Européen de Droit Rural 1989–93; memb City Disputes Panel 1994–; chm: Scottish Ensemble (formerly Scottish Baroque Ensemble) 1990–, Luss Estates Tst 1991–; tstee David Hume Inst 1992–; grand chaplain Von Poser Soc of Edinburgh 1994–; FCIArb 1991; *Books* Stair Encyclopedia of Scots Law - Title 'Agriculture' (1987), Corporate Law - The European Dimension (contrib, 1991), Butterworths European Law Vol 1 - Companies (contrib, 1992), Handbook International Commercial Arbitration (Scotland) (1995); *Recreations* music, farming, gardening, birdwatching, curling; *Clubs* New (Edinburgh), Puffins (Edinburgh), Aberlady Curling; *Style*— The Hon Lord Dervaird; ✉ 4 Moray Place, Edinburgh EH3 6DS (☎ 0131 225 1881, fax 0131 220 0644); Auchenmalg House, Auchenmalg, Wigtownshire DG8 0JR (☎ 01581 500205); Wood of Dervaird Farm, Glenluce, Wigtownshire (☎ 01581 300222)

DERWENT, Henry Clifford Sydney; s of Clifford Sydney Derwent (d 1995), of Daventry, Northants, and Joan Kathleen, *née* Craft; *b* 19 Nov 1951; *Educ* Berkhamsted Sch, Worcester Coll Oxford; *m* 26 Nov 1988, Rosemary Patricia Jesse, da of Reginald Meaker; 2 da (Olivia Christiana Maud b 28 June 1989, Romola Henrietta Rose b 8 Nov 1993), 1 step da (Rachel Patricia Alice Milnes-Smith b 5 March 1978); *Career* DOE and PSA 1974–85 (seconded to Midland Bank 1984), Dept of Tport 1986–96 (various posts 1986–92, dir Nat Roads Policy 1992–96, seconded to SBC Warburg 1996); *Recreations* music, riding, watercolours; *Style*— Henry Derwent, Esq; ✉ c/o Executive Agencies Division, Department of Transport, 76 Marsham Street, London SW1P 4DR (☎ 0171 271 4878, fax 0171 271 5887)

DERWENT, Richard Austin; *b* 28 Sept 1953; *Educ* Merry Oak Comp, Richard Taunton Coll; *Career* Deloitte Haskins & Sells audit jr and sr Southampton 1972–79, audit sr London 1979–81; audit mangr Brooking Knowles & Lawrence 1981–82, audit mangr Rawlinson & Hunter 1982–84, sr tech mangr Pannell Kerr Forster 1984–86, sr tech mangr Clark Whitehill 1986–91, freelance writer, lectr and conslt 1991–; chm Fin Reporting Discussion GP LSCA 1989–90 (sec 1988–89); memb Fin Reporting Ctee ICAEW 1990–96; contrib chapters to ICAEW Annual Surveys and numerous articles in accountancy jls; FCA; *Publications* Charities (ICAEW Indust Accounting and Auditing Guide, princ author), Corporate Governance Handbook (exec ed); *Recreations* bridge, swimming, music, watching sport (esp golf); *Style*— Richard A Derwent, Esq; ✉ 22 Kenton Way, Goldsworth Park, Woking, Surrey GU21 3QG (☎ 01483 723721)

DERWENT, 5 Baron (UK 1881); Sir Robin Evelyn Leo Vanden-Bempde-Johnstone; 7 Bt (GB 1796), LVO (1957), DL (N Yorkshire 1991); s of 4 Baron Derwent, CBE (d 1986), and Marie Louise, *née* Picard (d 1985); *b* 30 Oct 1930; *Educ* Winchester, Clare Coll Cambridge (MA); *m* 12 Jan 1957, Sybille Marie Louise Marcelle, da of Vicomte de Simard de Pitray (d 1979); 1 s (Hon Francis Patrick Harcourt b 1965), 3 da (Hon Emmeline Veronica Louise (Hon Mrs Winterbotham) b 1958, Hon Joanna Louise Claudia (Hon Mrs Matthews) b 1962, Hon Isabelle Catherine Sophie b 1968); *Heir* s, Hon Francis Patrick Harcourt Johnstone, *qv*, b 1965; *Career* 2 Lt Kings Royal Rifle Corps 1949–50, Lt Queen Victoria's Rifles (TA Res) 1950–53; second sec FO 1954–55 and 1958–61, private sec to Br Ambass Paris 1955–58, second sec Mexico City 1961–65; first sec: Washington 1965–68; FO 1968–69; N M Rothschild & Sons Ltd 1969–85, md Hutchison Whampoa (Europe) Ltd 1985–; dir: F and C (Pacific) Investment Trust, Scarborough Building Society; chm Thorstone Land & Property; memb N York Moors Nat Park Authy 1996–; Chev Legion of Hon 1957, Officier de l'Ordre Nationale du Mérite (France) 1978; *Recreations* shooting, fishing; *Clubs* Boodle's; *Style*— The Rt Hon the Lord Derwent, LVO, DL; ✉ Hackness Hall, Scarborough, N Yorks; 30 Kelso Place, London W8 5QG

DERX, Donald John; CB; *b* 1928; *Educ* Tiffin Sch Kingston, St Edmund Hall Oxford (BA); *Career* asst princ Bd of Trade 1951, Cabinet Office 1954–55, Colonial Office 1957–65, Industl Policy Div Dept of Economic Affrs 1965–68, dir Treasy Centre for Administrative Studies 1968–70, dep sec Dept of Employment 1972–84 (joined 1971); dir Policy Studies Inst 1984–86, head of gp corp affrs Glaxo Holdings plc 1986–90, non-exec dir Glaxo Wellcome plc 1991–; *Style*— Donald Derx, Esq, CB; ✉ Glaxo Wellcome plc, Lansdowne House, Berkeley Square, London W1X 6BP (☎ 0171 493 4060)

DESAI, Baron (Life Peer UK 1991), of St Clement Danes in the City of Westminster; Meghnad Jagdishchandra Desai; s of Jagdishchandra Chandulal Desai (d 1984), of Baroda, India, and Mandakini, *née* Majmundar (d 1989); *b* 10 July 1940; *Educ* Univ of Bombay (BA, MA), Univ of Pennsylvania (PhD 1964); *m* 27 June 1970, Gail Graham, da of George Ambler Wilson, CBE (d 1978), of Brandon House, North End Avenue, London NW3; 1 s (Hon Sven b 18 Sept 1975), 2 da (Hon Tanvi b 12 April 1972, Hon Nuala b 2 Jan 1974); *Career* assoc specialist Dept of Agric Econ Univ of California 1963–65; LSE: lectr 1965–77, sr lectr 1977–80, reader 1980–83, prof 1983–, head of LSE Devpt Studies Institute 1990–, dir LSE Centre for the Study of Global Governance 1992–; memb: Cncl Royal Econ Soc 1991–, Exec Ctee Fabian Soc 1991–92; chm Islington South and Finsbury Constituency Lab Pty 1986–92; pres Assoc of Univ Teachers in Economics 1987–90; Hon DSc Kingston Univ 1992; FRSA 1991; *Books* Marxian Economic Theory (1974), Applied Econometrics (1976), Marxian Economics (1979), Testing Monetarism (1981), Cambridge Economic History of India vol 2 (co-ed, 1983), Agrarian Power & Agricultural Productivity in South Asia (co-ed, 1984), Lectures on Advanced Econometric Theory (ed, 1988), Lenin's Economic Writings (ed, 1989); *Recreations* reading, politics; *Clubs* Reform; *Style*— The Rt Hon Lord Desai; ✉ 606 Collingwood House, Dolphin Square, London SW1V 3NF; London School of Economics, Houghton Street, London WC2A 2AE (☎ 0171 955 7489, fax 0171 955 7591)

DESMOND, Denis Fitzgerald; CBE (1989), DL (Co Londonderry 1992); s of Maj James Fitzgerald Desmond, JP, DL, of Ballyarton House, Killaloo, Londonderry, and Harriet Ivy, *née* Evans (d 1972); *b* 11 May 1943; *Educ* Castle Park Dublin, Trinity Coll Glenalmond Perthshire; *m* 25 July 1965, Annick Marie Marguerite Francoise, da of M Jean Faussemagne, of Nancy, France; 1 da (Stephanie b 1970); *Career* 2 Lt and Lt RCT (TA) 1964–69; chm and md Desmond & Sons Ltd Londonderry 1970– (dir 1966–70), chm Adria Ltd Strabane 1976–81, dir Ulster Development Capital Ltd Belfast 1985–90, regnl dir Nationwide Anglia Building Society 1986–90, dir Ulster Bank Ltd 1990–; High Sheriff Co Londonderry 1974, ADC to Govr NI 1967–69; Hon DSc: Queen's Univ Belfast 1987, Univ of Ulster 1991; *Recreations* fishing, tennis; *Style*— Denis Desmond, Esq, CBE, DL; ✉ Desmond & Sons Ltd, Drumahoe, Londonderry BT47 3SD (☎ 01504 44901, fax 01504 311447, telex 74402)

DESMOND, Denis John; s of Patrick Desmond, of Worcester, and Doreen Desmond (d 1985); *b* 30 Oct 1949; *Educ* Ratcliffe Coll Leicester, Univ of Liverpool (BA); *m* 30 March 1973, Elizabeth Mary, da of Gerard Corcoran, of Altrincham, 1 s ((Christopher) Liam), 1 da (Laura Jane); *Career* called to the Bar Middle Temple 1974; *Style*— Denis Desmond, Esq; ✉ 6 Fountain Court, Steelhouse Lane, Birmingham (☎ 0121 233 3282, fax 0121 236 3600, car tel 0860 631111)

DESSELBERGER, Ulrich; s of Dr Hermann Desselberger (d 1985), and Henriette Albers; *b* 22 July 1937; *Educ* Ludwig Georgs Gymnasium Darmstadt Germany, Free Univ Berlin (MD); *m* 15 April 1965, Elisabeth Martha Maria, da of Dr Bernhard Wieczorek (d 1976), and Hanne Blümel (d 1968); 2 s (Matthias b 1967, Jona b 1969), 2 da (Susanne b 1966, Mirjam Ruth b 1971); *Career* res asst Dept of Pathology Virchow Hosp and Klinikum Westend W Berlin 1967–69, res asst and conslt Dept of Virology Hannover Med Sch 1970–76, Fulbright res fell and visiting res asst prof Dept of Microbiology Mount Sinai Med Center NY 1977–79, sr lectr Dept of Virology Univ of Glasgow and hon conslt Greater Glasgow Health Bd UK 1979–88; conslt virologist and dir: Regional Virus Laboratory E Birmingham Hosp 1988–91, Clinical Microbiology and Public Health Laboratory Addenbrooke's Hosp Cambridge 1991–; memb: NY Acad of Sciences, American Soc for Microbiology, American Soc for Virology, Soc for Gen Microbiology UK, Deutsche Gesellschaft für Hygiene und Mikrobiologie; FRCPath, FRCPG; *Style*— Ulrich Desselberger, Esq; ✉ Clinical Microbiology and Public Health Laboratory, Level 6, Addenbrooke's Hospital, Hills Rd, Cambridge CB2 2QW (☎ 01223 216816, fax 01223 242775)

DESSER, Arnold; s of Max Desser, of Winnipeg, Canada, and Clara, *née* Gosman; *b* 1 April 1945; *Educ* Univ of Manitoba (BA), Queen's Univ Ontario Canada (postgrad fell), Nanjing Coll of Traditional Chinese Med China (CAc), Westminster Pastoral Fndn, Centro Milanese di Terapia della Famiglia Italy; *Career* managing ed Arthur Mee's Children's Encyclopedia 1974–76, freelance photojournalist 1973–82, res conslt The Movie magazine 1977–82, conslt to The Museum of the Moving Image London 1984, sr lectr and clinic dir London Sch of Acupuncture and Traditional Chinese Med 1986–, acupuncturist Marylebone Health Centre 1987–93, course organiser Marylebone Centre Tst 1989–93; memb Br Acupuncture Cncl, site examiner Br Acupuncture Accreditation Bd 1986–; *Books* Who's Who in the Movies (with Ann Lloyd and David Robinson, 1983); *Recreations* T'ai Chi, Qi Gong, films; *Style*— Arnold Desser, Esq; ✉ City Health Centre, 36 Featherstone St, London EC1 (☎ 0171 251 4429)

DETHRIDGE, David John; s of Thomas Henry John Dethridge, and Eileen Elizabeth, *née* Pain; *b* 25 June 1952; *Educ* Kingston GS, King Edward's Sch Bath, Queen's Coll Oxford (MA); *m* 13 Aug 1988, Alexandra, da of Peter Neville Metcalfe; 3 s (Christopher b 27 Jan 1990, Samuel b 12 April 1992, Jonathan b 12 March 1994); *Career* called to the Bar Lincoln's Inn 1975; head of Chambers 12 Old Square Lincoln's Inn 1986–91 (memb 1977); memb Cncl: Latimer House Oxford, Church Soc; former memb Nat Ctee Lawyers' Christian Fellowship; *Style*— David Dethridge, Esq; ✉ Verulam Chambers, Peer House, Verulam Street, London WC1X 8LX (☎ 0171 813 2400)

DETSINY, (Anthony) Michael; s of Rudolph Detsiny, JP (d 1987), and Edith, *née* Scheff (d 1993); *b* 25 July 1941; *Educ* Highgate Sch; *m* 2 Dec 1967, Angela Hazel, da of Francis Charles Cornell (d 1977); 2 s (Warren Rodney b 1969, Stephen Charles b 1978), 1 da (Hazel Karen b 1972); *Career* dir: Cadbury Ltd 1977–83, Allied Breweries 1983–86; md The Creative Business Ltd 1986–91, chm and chief exec Foote Cone and Belding (London) 1991–96, dir The Marketing and Communications Business 1996–; *Recreations* gardening, reading; *Clubs* Lansdowne; *Style*— Michael Detsiny, Esq; ✉ The Willows, Moor End Common, Frieth, nr Henley-on-Thames, Oxon (☎ 01494 881176)

DETTORI, Lanfranco (Frankie); s of Gianfranco Dettori, and Maria, *née* Nieman; *b* 15 Dec 1970; *Career* flat race jockey; apprenticed to Luca Cumani, champion apprentice 1990 (100 winners), retained by John Gosden; major races won: Queen Elizabeth II Stakes 1990, World Young Jockey Championship Japan 1992/93, Ascot Gold Cup (twice), French Derby (on Polytain) 1992, Nunthorpe Stakes 1993, Prix de L' Abbeye de Longchamp, Sussex Stakes, Fillies Mile, Heinz 57, Irish Derby (on Balanchine) 1994, The Oaks (on Balanchine) 1994 and (on Moonshell) 1995, St Leger (on Classic Cliché) 1995 and (on Shantou) 1996, King George VI and Queen Elizabeth Diamond Stakes (on Lammtarra) 1995, Prix de l'Arc de Triomphe (on Lammtarra) 1995, 2,000 Guineas (on Mark of Esteem) 1996; winner Golden Spurs Award 1989, Derby Award 1990; winner all seven races on one card at Ascot 28 Sept 1996; Cartier Award of Merit 1996; champion jockey 1994 and 1995; *Recreations* football, swimming, snooker, sport in general; *Style*— Frankie Dettori, Esq; ✉ c/o Peter Burrell, The School Office, 47 The Street, Kirtling, Newmarket, Suffolk CB8 9PB

DEUCHAR, Patrick Lindsay; s of David Deuchar, and Marian, *née* Davies; *b* 27 March 1949; *Educ* Christ's Hosp, Wiltshire Coll of Agriculture; *m* 1 (m dis), Gwyneth; 1 s (David Lindsay b 3 March 1976), 1 da (Patricia Margaret b 5 April 1978); *partner* Liz Robertson, *qv*; 1 da (Briony Elizabeth Veronica b 4 July 1991); *Career* unit mangr farm in Berks 1968–70, journalist and info offr Agric Div IPC Business Press 1970–71; PR offr The Royal Show 1971–74, PR mangr Earl's Court & Olympia exhibition halls 1974–78, own PR consultancy 1978–81, dir London Office World Championship Tennis 1983–89 (joined as Euro PR dir 1981), chief exec Royal Albert Hall 1989–, md Royal Albert Hall Developments Ltd 1989–; winner Int Facility Mangr of 1993 (Performance Magazine); bd dir: London First 1994– (memb Visitors Cncl 1995–), Trafalgar Square 2000; tstee: Cardiff Bay Opera House 1993–96, Albert Meml Tst 1994–; memb Cncl Royal Coll of Music 1995–; chm SPARKS (sporting charity) 1992–, memb Nat Fundraising Ctee The Muscular Dystrophy Gp, barker Variety Club of GB 1992, memb Ctee Royal Marsden Hosp Appeal 1990–92; Freeman Worshipful Co of Armourers & Braziers 1966; MInstD 1986, FRSA 1992; *Style*— Patrick Deuchar, Esq; ✉ Chief Executive, Royal Albert Hall, Kensington Gore, London SW7 2AP (☎ 0171 589 3203, fax 0171 225 0899)

DEUTSCH, André; CBE (1989); s of Bruno Deutsch (d 1967), and Maria, *née* Havas (d 1984); *b* 15 Nov 1917; *Career* trainee Nicholson & Watson Publishers 1942–45, Allan Wingate (Publishers) Ltd 1945–50 (latterly md); André Deutsch Ltd: chm and md 1951–84, jt chm and md 1984–87, pres 1987–91, resigned; chm Aurum Press 1992; FRSA; *Recreations* publishing, talking; *Clubs* Garrick, Groucho; *Style*— André Deutsch, Esq, CBE

DEUTSCH, Antonia Sara; da of Ronald Leopold Deutsch, of Ilmington, Warwickshire, and Jill Patricia, *née* Davis; *b* 24 June 1957; *Educ* The Abbey Sch Worcestershire, The Sorbonne; *m* 31 May 1980, Colin David Guy Robinson, s of Guy Martyn Robinson; 1 s (Oscar Charles Thomas b 4 Nov 1989), 1 da (Eliza Alice Louise b 10 Aug 1991); *Career* photographic asst 1981–84, freelance photographer specialising in people, landscapes and black and white images 1984–; awards incl: Assoc of Photographers Silver Award 1989, Gold and Merit Awards 1991 and Judges' Choice 1996, Ilford Print of the Year 1989; memb Assoc of Photographers (formerly AFAEP) 1988; *Recreations* photography, independent rough travel, family; *Style*— Ms Antonia Deutsch; (☎ mobile 0836 344 972)

DEUTSCH, Renée; da of Maurice Deutsch, and Matilda Deutsch; *b* 2 Aug 1944; *Educ* Hendon Co GS, Northern Poly Sch of Architecture; *m* (m dis); m 2, 10 June 1995, Robert Cooper; *Career* architecture and design for 10 years, mgmnt consultancy for 6 years; appeals coordinator (3 years): Almeida Theatre, Half Moon Theatre, London Contemporary Dance; head of consumer PR Dennis Davidson Assocs, vice pres and md Consumer Products Div The Walt Disney Co Ltd until 1991, ind mktg conslt 1991–93, md The Licensing Syndicate Ltd 1993–; *Recreations* performing arts, visual arts, reading, tennis; *Clubs* Groucho; *Style—* Ms Renée Deutsch; ✉ 93A Camden Mews, London NW1 9BU (☎ 0171 482 4347); The Licensing Syndicate Ltd, Euston House, 81–103 Euston St, London NW1 2ET (☎ 0171 388 3111, fax 0171 387 7324)

DEVA, Niranjan Joseph (Nirj); DL (Greater London) 1985, MP (C) Brentford and Isleworth (majority 2,086); s of late Thakur Dr Kingley de Silva Deva Aditya, and Rita de Silva Deva, da of Sen Dr M G Perera, MVO; *b* 11 May 1948; *Educ* St Joseph's Coll Columbo, Univ of Loughborough (Hons Degree Aeronautical Engrg); *m* Indra, da of late Romy Govindia; 1 step s; *Career* company dir and scientific advsr, memb Cncl RCS 1977–79, chm Bow Gp 1981 (sec Foreign Affrs Ctee 1985–87), former advsr to Viscount Whitelaw and Rt Hon David Howell, MP, memb Nat Consumer Cncl 1985–88, chm DTI/NCC Ctee on deregulation of Euro air tport 1985–87, contested election (C) Hammersmith 1987; MP (C) Brentford and Isleworth 1992–; memb: Euro Standing Ctee B 1992–, All-Pty Mfrg Gp 1993–; memb Standing Ctee on: Immigration Bill 1992–, Parly Admin (Ombudsman) 1993–; jt sec Cons Pty Aviation Ctee 1992–; PPS Scottish Office 1996–; author of various articles and pamphlets on Chile, Zimbabwe, Rhodesia, enterprise zones, air tport, deregulation; *Recreations* tennis, riding, reading; *Clubs* Carlton, Hownslow Conservative; *Style—* Nirj Joseph Deva, Esq, DL, MP; ✉ House of Commons, London SW1A 0AA (☎ 0171 219 3000, internet http://www.the-commons.com/deva, e-mail deva.mp@commons.u-net.com); constituency office: 433 Chiswick High Road, London W4 4AU (☎ 0181 994 1406)

DEVANEY, John F; *b* 1946; *Educ* BEng, Univ of Harvard (Advanced Mgmnt Prog); *Career* Perkins Engines: graduate trainee 1968–76, project mangr Canton Ohio 1976–78, dir quality control then dir mfrg UK 1978–82, dir sales and business devpt Engines Div 1982–83, pres Engines Div 1983–88, gp vice pres European Components Group (now Perkins Group) Peterborough 1988; gp vice pres Enterprises Group Toronto 1988–89, chm and chief exec offr and gp vice pres Kelsey-Hayes Corporation Romulus Michigan 1989–92; Eastern Group plc (formerly Eastern Electricity plc): md 1992–95, chief exec 1993–95, exec chm 1995–, dir subsids Egas Ltd, Powerhouse Retail Ltd, EA Technology Ltd; pres Electricity Assoc 1994–95; non-exec dir: Midland Bank plc 1994–, Penske Transportation Inc USA; CEng, FIEE, FIMechE; *Clubs* Reform; *Style—* John Devaney, Esq; ✉ Eastern Group plc, Wherstead Park, PO Box 40, Wherstead, Ipswich, Suffolk IP9 2AQ (☎ 01473 688688, fax 01473 554410)

DEVAS, Michael Campbell; MC (1945); only s of Geoffrey Charles Devas, MC (d 1971; whose mother was Edith, da of Lt-Col Hon Walter Campbell, 3 s of 1 Earl Cawdor), by his w Joan (d 1975), great niece of Rt Hon Sir Henry Campbell-Bannerman, the Liberal PM (1906–08); *b* 6 June 1924; *Educ* Eton; *m* 1, 28 June 1952 (m dis 1966), Patience Merryday, da of late Sir Albert Gerald Stern, KBE, CMG (d 1966); 1 s, 1 da; m 2, 12 Oct 1967, Gillian Barbara, da of late Col H M P Hewett, of Chipping Warden, nr Banbury, and formerly w of Charles Arthur Smith-Bingham; 1 s; *Career* served Welsh Gds NW Europe 1942–47, Capt 1946; banker; joined M Samuel & Co 1947, dir 1960; dir Kleinwort Benson Ltd 1965–86; chm: Colonial Mutual Life Assurance (UK Bd) 1982–94, Kleinwort Charter Investment Trust plc until 1992; dir Dover Corporation (USA) 1967–94; Liveryman Worshipful Co of Drapers; *Recreations* sailing, skiing; *Clubs* White's, Royal Yacht Sqdn; *Style—* Michael Devas, Esq, MC; ✉ Hunton Court, Maidstone, Kent (☎ 01622 820307)

DEVAUX, His Hon Judge; John Edward; s of Henry Edward Devaux (d 1988), and Anne Elizabeth Devaux (d 1984); *b* 25 March 1947; *Educ* Beaumont Coll, Univ of Bristol (LLB); *m* 1979, Fiona Mary, *née* O'Conor; 2 da; *Career* called to the Bar Lincoln's Inn 1970, recorder of the Crown Court 1989–93, circuit judge (SE Circuit) 1993–; *Style—* His Hon Judge Devaux; ✉ Ipswich Crown Court, The Courthouse, Civic Drive, Ipswich, Suffolk IP1 2DX (☎ 01473 213841)

DEVENPORT, Rt Rev Eric Nash; s of Joseph Samuel Devenport (d 1964), and Emma Devenport (d 1947); *b* 3 May 1926; *Educ* St Chad's Sch, Open Univ, Kelham Theol Coll; *m* 19 April 1954, Jean Margaret, da of Cliff Richardson (d 1985); 2 da (Rachel Mary b 1956, Clare Helen b 1962); *Career* curate: St Mark Leicester 1951–54, St Matthew Barrow-in-Furness 1954–56; succentor Leicester Cathedral 1956–59; vicar: Shepshed 1959–64, Oadby 1964–73; leader of mission Leicester 1973–80, hon canon Leicester 1973–80, bishop of Dunwich 1980–92, area chaplain Actors' Church Union 1980–92 (chaplain 1973–92), chaplain of St Mark Florence and St Peter Siena, acting archdeacon in Italy and Malta, auxiliary bishop in Europe 1992–; chm: Hospital Chaplaincies Cncl 1985–90, Diocesan Communications Offrs Ctee 1985–92, chm BBC Radio Suffolk 1989–92; Liveryman Worshipful Co of Framework Knitters 1980–; *Recreations* theatre, painting; *Clubs* Royal Commonwealth Soc; *Style—* The Rt Rev Eric Devenport; ✉ Via Maggio 16, 50125 Florence, Italy (☎ and fax 00 39 55 29 47 64)

DEVERALL, Philip Brook; s of William James Deverall, of Lyme Regis, Dorset, and Marion, *née* Brook (d 1983); *b* 30 April 1937; *Educ* Lymm GS Cheshire, UCL (MB BS); *m* 10 June 1961, Ann Beaumont, da of Frank Henry Drury (d 1961); 2 s (Stephen Charles b 16 July 1962, James Joseph b 6 March 1976), 1 da (Helen Catherine b 10 Feb 1965); *Career* house physician and surgn UCH London 1960–61, sr house surgn Barnet Hosp 1961–63, cardio vascular fell Univ of Alabama USA 1968–70, conslt heart surgn Leeds Hosp 1970–77 (registrar in surgery 1963–65, registrar 1965–68, chm and dir Cardiac Dept), conslt heart surgn Guy's Hosp 1977; author of numerous scientific articles and chapters in books; memb: Br Cardiac Soc, American Heart Assoc, Soc of Thoracic Surgns, Soc of Thoracic Surgns USA; hon memb Soc of Cardiovascular Surgns of Asia 1987; *Recreations* travel, theatre, music; *Style—* Philip Deverall, Esq; ✉ 3 Northfield Close, Bromley, Kent BR1 2WZ (☎ 0181 467 5418); Suite 303, Emblem House, London Bridge Hospital, London SE1 2PR (☎ 0171 486 7753, fax 0171 935 4416); 21 Upper Wimpole St, London W1M 7TA (☎ 0171 935 2847, fax 0171 935 4416)

DEVERELL, Maj-Gen John Freegard (Jack); OBE (1987, MBE 1979); s of Harold James Frank Deverell (d 1986), of Bath, and Joan Beatrice, *née* Carter; *b* 27 April 1945; *Educ* King Edward's Sch Bath, RMA Sandhurst, RNC Greenwich; *m* 15 Dec 1973, Jane Ellen, da of Gerald Tankerville Norris Solomon, of Hindon, Wilts; 1 s (Simon b 21 Oct 1978), 1 da (Emma b 23 Nov 1976); *Career* RMA Sandhurst 1964–65, cmmnd Somerset and Cornwall Light Infantry 1965, Cmd 3 Bn Light Infantry 1984–86, Dir of Studies Royal Mil Coll of Sci 1986–88, Cdr UK Mobile Force 1988–90, DG Army Manning and Recruitment 1993–95, Cmdt Royal Mil Acad Sandhurst 1995–; FRSA; *Recreations* cricket, golf, horses; *Clubs* Cavalry and Guards', I Zingari, Free Foresters, Mounted Infantry; *Style—* Maj-Gen J F Deverell, OBE; ✉ Academy Headquarters, Royal Military Academy, Sandhurst GU15 4PQ

DEVEREUX, Alan Robert; CBE (1980), DL; s of Donald Charles Devereux, and Doris Louie Devereux; *b* 18 April 1933; *Educ* Colchester Sch, Clacton Co HS, Mid-Essex Tech Coll; *m* 1, 1959, Gloria Alma, *née* Hair (d 1985); 1 s (Iain b 1964); m 2, 1987, Elizabeth, *née* Docherty; *Career* chief exec offr Scotros PLC 1970–80; dir: Scottish Mutual Assurance Society 1972–, Walter Alexander PLC 1980–90, Gleneagles PLC 1990–; chm: Hambros Scotland Ltd 1984–90, Scottish Ambulance Serv NHS Tst 1994–; fndr dir Quality Scotland Fndn 1991–; chm: CBI Scotland 1977–79, Scottish Tourist Bd 1980–90; memb Br Tourist Authy 1980–90; CEng, MIEE; *Recreations* reading, work, charities; *Clubs* E India, Devonshire, Sports and Public Schools; *Style—* Alan Devereux, Esq, CBE, DL; ✉ South Fell, 24 Kirkhouse Road, Blanefield, Stirlingshire G63 9BX (☎ 01360 770464, fax 01360 771133)

DEVEREUX, Richard; s of Austin Augustus Devereux (d 1970), of Lincoln, and Vera Evelyn, *née* Whylde; *b* 3 April 1956; *Educ* Bishop King Sch Lincoln, Portsmouth Coll of Art (scholar, DipAD); *m* 20 Aug 1977, Christine Anne, da of Stanley Holmes; 1 da (Hannah Galadriel b 22 March 1988); *Career* artist; *Solo Exhibitions* Recent Works (Axis Gallery Brighton) 1979, Recent Works (Hiscock Gallery Portsmouth) 1980, Circles (Usher Art Gallery Lincoln) 1984, Assembled Rites (Artsite Bath) 1987, On Sacred Ground (Cairn Gallery Glos) 1988, Beyond the Hall of Dreams (New Art Centre London) 1989, In Stillness and In Silence (Usher Art Gallery Lincoln then The Gallery Cork Street London) 1994, Primordium (Cairn Gallery Glos) 1994–95; *Selected Group Exhibitions* Rufford Arts Centre Notts 1982, Ogle Gallery Cheltenham 1984, Sculpture to Touch (Usher Gallery Lincoln, Ferens Gallery Hull, Normanby Hall Scunthorpe) 1986, 20th Century Br Sculpture (Roche Court Wilts) 1988–96, New Art Centre London 1989 and 1990, The Journey (Lincoln) 1990, Southampton City Art Gallery 1990, Shared Earth (Peterborough Art Gallery, plus 6 venue tour) 1991–92, 20th Century Br Sculpture (Millfield Sch Somerset) 1992, The Solstice (Cairn Gallery Glos) 1992, Painting the Earth (The Gallery at John Jones London) 1993, ARCO (Madrid Spain) 1994, Art 25! (Basel Switzerland) 1994, Art 26! (Basel Switzerland) 1995, Alchemy (Bury St Edmonds Art Gallery and Ickworth House Suffolk) 1995, Art 27 (Basel Switzerland) 1996; *Collections incl* Tate Gallery, Bodleian Library Oxford, Nat Library of Scotland, Trinity Coll Dublin, The Nat Tst and various private collections UK and abroad; *Published Limited Edition Books* Quiet Flame (1986), Assembled Rites (1987), The Bowl of Grain (1989–90), In Stillness and In Silence (1991), From the Angel's Palm (1992), Marked by Ritual (1992), Travaux Publics (1996); subject of several articles in various pubns; *Style—* Richard Devereux, Esq; ✉ 21 North Parade, Lincoln, Lincolnshire LNI 1LB (☎ and fax 01522 887621); c/o New Art Centre, 168 Sloane Street, London SW1X 9QF (☎ 0171 235 5844, fax 0171 823 1624)

DEVEREUX, Robert Charles Debohun; s of Herbert Morris Devereux (d 1949), and Fanny Rosemary Devereux (d 1980); *b* 15 Dec 1928; *Educ* Repton, Univ of Cambridge (MA); *m* 23 Oct 1954, Anna-Mary, da of Henry Edmund Theoderic Vale (d 1969); 1 s (Charles b 3 June 1956), 2 da (Christina b 13 April 1958, Jane b 12 June 1961); *Career* Nat Serv RE 1947–49 Egypt; Wellcome plc: joined 1953, chief engr 1958, gen prodn mangr 1964–69, ops dir 1972–92; dir Care Britain 1992–; memb Chem Industs Assoc Trade Affrs Bd 1959–69, pres NW Kent Post Grad Med Centre 1972–77; CEng, MIMechE, FIMgt; *Recreations* reading, gardening; *Clubs* RAC; *Style—* Robert Devereux, Esq; ✉ Lone Oak, Parkfield, Sevenoaks, Kent TN15 0HX

DEVEREUX, Vanessa Gay; da of Edward James Branson, of Tanyard Farm, Shamley Green, Guildford, Surrey, and Evette Huntley, *née* Flindt; sis of Richard Charles Nicholas Branson, *qv*; *b* 3 June 1959; *Educ* Box Hill Sch, New Acad of Art Studies; *m* 1983, Robert Devereux, s of Humphrey Devereux; 3 s (Noah Edward b 1987, Louis-Robert de Lacey b 1991, Ivo Edmund Bouchier b 9 March 1995), 1 da (Florence b 1989); *Career* with: Posterbrokers 1981–83, Picturebrokers 1983–86; proprieter Vanessa Devereux Gallery 1986–; fndr Portobello Contemporary Art Festival; *Recreations* theatre, cinema, sport, food; *Style—* Mrs Vanessa Devereux; ✉ 5 Ladbroke Terrace, London W11 3PG (☎ 0171 229 6485, fax 0171 727 7582)

DeVILLE, Sir (Harold Godfrey) Oscar; kt (1990), CBE (1979); s of Harold DeVille (d 1980); *b* 11 April 1925; *Educ* Burton-on-Trent GS, Trinity Coll Cambridge (MA), Univ of London (PhD 1995); *m* 1947, Pamela Fay, da of late Capt Rowland Ellis; 1 s; *Career* Lt RNVR 1943–46; personnel mangr Ford Motor Co 1949–65; BICC Ltd: gen mangr central personnel rels 1965–70, dir 1971, exec vice chm 1978–80, exec dep chm 1980–84; chm Meyer International plc 1987–91 (dir 1984); memb: Cmmn on Industl Rels 1971–74, Central Arbitration Ctee 1976–77, Cncl ACAS 1976–91, Cncl CBI 1977–85; memb Cncl and fell: Inst Manpower Studies 1971–91, Indust Soc 1977–84; chm: Iron and Steel Econ Devpt Ctee 1984–86, Govt Review of Vocational Qualifications 1985–86, memb Bd BR 1985–91; memb Cncl Univ of Reading 1985–91, chm Nat Cncl for Vocational Qualifications 1986–90; *Recreations* genealogy, fell-walking; *Style—* Sir Oscar DeVille, CBE

DEVINE, (John) Hunter; s of John Hunter Devine (d 1982), of Lenzie, Scotland, and Joan Margaret, *née* Hislop; *b* 1 Dec 1935; *Educ* Lenzie Acad; *m* 25 Jan 1964 (m dis 1989), Gillian, da of Edwin John Locke (d 1982), of Chester; 2 s (Oliver John Hunter b 1968, Gavin Richard b 1970); *Career* London sec Scottish Amicable Life Assurance Soc 1964–70 (actuarial trainee 1953–64), pension sales mangr Scottish Amicable 1971–75, dir Leslie & Godwin (Life and Pensions) Ltd 1975–78, Godwins Ltd 1978–86; md: Godwins Central Servs Ltd 1978–81, Godwins Central Ltd 1982–86; chm Godwins Ltd 1993– (md 1987–92); chm Assoc of Consulting Actuaries 1995–; memb Worshipful Co of Actuaries 1982; Freeman City of London 1983; FFA 1964, FPMI 1977, ASA 1980, FInstD 1988; *Recreations* football (int Scottish amateur 1956–60, GB Olympic Team Rome 1960), golf, theatre, travel; *Clubs* Queens Park Football, Hindhead Golf; *Style—* Hunter Devine, Esq; ✉ Godwins Ltd, Briarcliff House, Kingsmead, Farnborough, Hants GU14 7TE (☎ 01252 544484, fax 01252 378546, car tel 0468 286878)

DEVINE, Rt Rev Joseph; *see:* Motherwell, Bishop of (RC)

DEVINE, Magenta; da of Gerald Joseph Taylor, of Marbella, and Valerie Rose, *née* Hill (d 1988); *b* 4 Nov 1960; *Educ* St Helens Public Sch, Dr Challoner's Girls Sch Bucks, High Wycombe Art Coll; *Career* press offr Tony Brainsby PR Co and columnist for Gay News 1980–85, formed own co organising PR for Sigue Sigue Sputnik 1985–87, reporter/dir Network 7 C4 1987–88; presenter: RoughGuide BBC 2 1988–95, Reportage BBC 2 1988–90, 01 (London Arts and Entertainment Show, Thames TV) 1990–91, direct half hour documentary series Youth Dept BBC 1993–94; presenter various radio shows; feature writer for: Today, The Mail and The Guardian; *Recreations* collecting sculpture (especially Zimbabwean), avoiding my accountant and bank manager, inventing jet lag cures, reading, lazing on the sofa, watching TV and avoiding work, finding new sorts of unhealthy food to eat, not going to the gym, feeling guilty about all of the above; *Clubs* Groucho's; *Style—* Ms Magenta Devine; ✉ c/o Speak Limited, 46 Old Compton Street, London W1V 5PB

DEVINE, Prof Thomas Martin; *b* 30 July 1945; *Educ* Univ of Strathclyde (BA, PhD, DLitt); *m*; 2 s (twins), 3 da; *Career* Univ of Strathclyde: asst lectr in econ history 1969–70, lectr in history 1970–78, sr lectr 1978–83, reader in Scottish history 1983–88, prof of Scottish history 1988–, chm Dept of History 1989–92, dean Faculty of Arts and Social Scis 1993–94, dir Research Centre in Scottish History 1993–, dep princ 1994–; Univ of Guelph Canada: visiting prof of Scottish history 1983 and 1988, adjunct prof of Scottish history Faculty of Graduate Studies 1989–; British Acad/Leverhulme Tst sr research fell 1992–93; Sr Hume Brown Prize in Scottish History Univ of Edinburgh 1976, chm Cncl of Econ and Social History Soc of Scotland 1984–88 (memb Cncl 1989–90); ed Scottish Economic and Social History 1981–86; convener Section Ctee Archaeology and Historical Studies RSE 1994– (memb 1993–); memb: Cncl Scottish History Soc 1976–79, Cncl Scottish Catholic Historical Soc 1977–82 (convenor of Cncl 1991–95), Company of Scottish History 1981–, Bd of Govrs St Andrew's Coll of Educn 1990–95; tstee Nat Museums of Scotland 1995–; FRHistS 1980, FRSE 1992 (Henry Duncan Prize and lectr

1993), FBA 1994; *Books* The Tobacco Lords: A Study of the Tobacco Merchants of Glasgow and their Trading Activities 1740–1790 (1975), Lairds and Improvement in the Scotland of the Enlightenment (ed, 1979), Ireland and Scotland 1600–1850: Parallels and Contrasts in Economic and Social Development (with D Dickson, 1983), Farm Servants and Labour in Lowland Scotland 1770–1914 (1984), A Scottish Firm in Virginia: William Cunninghame and Co 1767–1777 (1984), People and Society in Scotland 1760–1830 (ed with R Mitchison, 1988), The Great Highland Famine: Hunger, Emigration and the Scottish Highlands in the Nineteenth Century (1988, Agnes Muir MacKenzie Prize Saltire Soc 1991), Improvement and Enlightenment (ed, 1989), Conflict and Stability in Scottish Society 1700–1850 (ed, 1990), Irish Immigrants and Scottish Society in the Eighteenth and Nineteenth Centuries (1991), Scottish Emigration & Scottish Society (ed, 1992), The Transformation of Rural Scotland: Social Change and Agrarian Development 1660–1815 (1994), Clanship to Crofter's War: The Social Transformation of the Scottish Highlands (1994), Scottish Elites (ed, 1994), Industry, Business and Society in Scotland since 1700 (ed with A J G Cummings, 1994), Glasgow, Vol I, Beginnings to 1830 (ed with G Jackson, 1995), Exploring the Scottish Past: Themes in History of Scottish Society (1995), Scotland in the Twentieth Century (with R J Finlay, 1996); also author about 70 book chapters and contribs to learned jls; *Recreations* foreign travel, relaxing, exploring the Scottish Highlands and Islands; *Style*— Prof Thomas M Devine, FRSE, FBA; ✉ Room 5.26, Livingstone Tower, University of Strathclyde, Glasgow G1 1XH (☎ 0141 552 4400 ext 4494)

DEVITT, Sir James Hugh Thomas; 3 Bt (UK 1916), of Chelsea, Co London; s of Lt-Col Sir Thomas Gordon Devitt, 2 Bt (d 1995), and his 3 w, Janet Lilian, da of late Col Hugh Sidney Ellis, CBE, MC; *b* 18 Sept 1956; *Educ* Sherborne, Corpus Christi Coll Cambridge (MA); *m* 20 April 1985, Susan Carol, er da of Dr (Adrian) Michael Campbell Duffus, of Woodhouse Farm, Thelbridge, Crediton, Devon; 2 s (Jack Thomas Michael b 1988, William James Alexander b 1990), 1 da (Gemma Florence b 1987); *Heir* s, Jack Thomas Michael Devitt b 29 July 1988; *Career* chartered surveyor Devitts; ARICS; *Clubs* Ipswich Town FC; *Style*— Sir James Devitt, Bt

DEVLIN, (Hugh) Brendan; CBE (1994); s of Maj John Joseph Devlin, OBE (d 1993), and Kathleen Claire, *née* Maxey (d 1966); *b* 17 Dec 1932; *Educ* Trinity Coll Dublin (BA, MB BCh, BAO, MA, MD, MCh), St Thomas' Hosp London; *m* 13 Sept 1958, Ann Elizabeth, da of Maj Robert Arthur Heatley (d 1947); 5 s (Timothy Robert Devlin, MP, *qv*, John Paul (d 1972), James Brendan, Peter Leonard, Brendan Michael William); *Career* demonstrator in anatomy Trinity Coll Dublin 1958, surgical registrar Sir Patrick Dun's Hosp Dublin 1959–63, sr surgical registrar St Thomas' Hosp London 1963–70, conslt surgn N Tees Gen Hosp 1970–94 (hon conslt 1994–), lectr in clinical surgery Univ of Newcastle upon Tyne 1970–94, dir Surgical Epidemiology and Audit Unit Royal Coll of Surgns Eng 1994–; Arris and Gale lectr RCS 1970, Colles lectr RCSI 1985, visiting prof Univ of Illinois 1991, Bradlaw oration Faculty of Dental Surgery RCS 1996, Bradshaw lectr RCS 1996, Hunterian orator RCS 1997; memb: Jt Conslts Ctee Dept of Health 1988–93, Mgmnt Ctee King Edward's Hosp Fund for London 1988–96, Ct of Examiners RCSI 1976–88; chm Examinations Ctee United Examining Bd for UK 1992–; RCS: memb Cncl 1986–, chm Examinations Bd 1992–95, sec Nat Confidential Enquiry into Perioperative Deaths 1992–; chm Audit Working Gp Acad of Med Royal Colls 1995, pres Br Assoc of Day Surgery 1994–96; vice chm Br Jl of Surgery 1978–93; hon fell: Assoc of Surgns of Poland (Rydygier Medal 1989), Assoc of Surgns of India (Chatterjee lectr 1984); FRCSI 1960, FRCS 1961, FACS 1985, FRCSEd 1988; *Books* Stoma Care Today, Medicine (1985), Management of Abdominal Hernias (1988, 2 edn 1997), The Report(s) of the National Confidential Enquiry into Perioperative Deaths (1988, 1990, 1991, 1993, 1995 and 1996); numerous other scientific pubns; *Recreations* gardening, walking, music; *Clubs* RSM, Kildare Street and University (Dublin); *Style*— Brendan Devlin, Esq, CBE; ✉ Fir Tree House, Hilton, Yarm TS15 9JY (☎ 01642 590246, secretary ☎ and fax 01642 597076); Flat 4, 64 St George's Square, London SW1V 3QT (☎ 0171 821 8846)

DEVLIN, His Hon Keith Michael; s of Francis Michael Devlin (d 1996), of Goring, Sussex, and Norah Devlin (d 1996); *b* 21 Oct 1933; *Educ* Price's Sch, Univ of London (LLB, MPhil, PhD); *m* 12 July 1958, Pamela Gwendoline, da of Francis James Phillips (d 1984), of Inverkeithing, Fife, Scotland; 2 s (Stephen b 1964, Philip b 1966), 1 da (Susan b 1968); *Career* cmmnd Nat Serv 1953–55; called to the Bar Gray's Inn 1964; dep chief clerk Met Magistrates' Cts Serv 1964–66, various appts as a dep met stipendiary magistrate 1975–79; asst recorder 1980–83, recorder 1983–84, circuit judge (SE Circuit) 1984–95, dep circuit judge 1995–; liaison judge Beds 1990–93, resident judge Luton Crown Ct 1991–93; a chm Mental Health Review Tbnl 1991–93 and 1995–; Brunel Univ: univ lectr in law 1966–71, reader in law 1971–84, assoc prof of law 1984–96 professorial research fell 1996–, memb Ct 1984–88; memb Ct Univ of Luton 1994–; fell Netherlands Inst for Advanced Study in the Humanities and Social Sciences Wassenaar 1975–76, memb Consumer Protection Advsy Ctee 1976–81; Magistrates' Assoc: memb Legal Ctee 1974–88, vice chm 1984–88, co-opted memb Cncl 1980–88, a vice pres Buckinghamshire branch 1994–; JP Inner London (Juvenile Ct Panel) 1968–84 (chm 1973–84); jt fndr and ed Anglo-American Law Review 1972–84; Liveryman and Warden Worshipful Co of Feltmakers (memb Ct of Assts 1991–); memb Royal Instn (memb Fin Ctee 1987–, memb Cncl 1994–); FRSA; *Publications* Sentencing Offenders in Magistrates' Courts (1970), Sentencing (Criminal Law Library No 5, with Eric Stockdale, 1987), articles in legal journals; *Recreations* Roman Britain, watching cricket, fly-fishing; *Clubs* Athenaeum, MCC, Hampshire Cricket; *Style*— His Hon Keith Devlin; ✉ Aylesbury Crown Court, Market Square, Aylesbury, Bucks HP20 1XD (☎ 01296 434401)

DEVLIN, Roger William; s of William Devlin, of Lancs, and Edna, *née* Cross; *b* 22 Aug 1957; *Educ* Manchester GS, Wadham Coll Oxford (MA); *m* 1983, Louise Alice Temlett, da of John Frost Tucker, of Somerset; 2 da (Sophie Victoria Temlett b 29 Nov 1989, Grace Katherine b 4 March 1993); *Career* dir: Hill Samuel & Co Ltd 1986–91, Corning Europe 1991–93, First Residential Properties 1991–, Henry Ansbacher & Co Ltd 1994– (head of corp fin); non-exec chm The Monitor Group Ltd 1994–; *Recreations* golf, horse racing; *Clubs* Worplesdon, Royal St George's Golf; *Style*— Roger Devlin, Esq; ✉ 12 The Orchard, Chiswick, London W4 (☎ 0181 747 9856); Henry Ansbacher & Co Ltd, One Mitre Square, London EC3A 5AN (☎ 0171 283 2500, fax 0171 626 9707)

DEVLIN, Stuart Leslie; AO (1988), CMG (1980); *b* 9 Oct 1931; *Educ* Gordon Inst of Technol Geelong, Royal Melbourne Inst of Technol, RCA; *m* 1986, Carole; *Career* goldsmith, silversmith and designer; Royal Warrant as Goldsmith Jeweller to HM The Queen 1982; Freeman City of London 1966, Prime Warden Worshipful Co of Goldsmiths 1996–97; DesRCA (Silversmith), DesRCA (Industl Design-Engrg); *Style*— Stuart Devlin, Esq, AO, CMG; ✉ Southbourne Court, Copsale, Southwater, West Sussex (☎ 01403 733000)

DEVLIN, Hon Timothy; 3 s of Baron Devlin, PC (Life Peer, d 1992); *b* 28 July 1944; *Educ* Winchester, Univ Coll Oxford; *m* 31 Jan 1967, Angela, er da of A J G Laramy; 2 s (Sebastian b 1973, Fabian b 1975), 2 da (Miranda b 1969, Esmeralda b 1971); *Career* journalist; former news ed TES, reporter The Times 1971–73 (educn corr 1973–77), nat dir ISIS 1977–84, PR dir IOD 1984–86, assoc dir Charles Barker Traverse-Healy 1986–89, fndr Tim Devlin Enterprises (educational PR consultancy); *Books* What Must We Teach (with Lady Warnock, 1977), Public Relations and Marketing for Schools (with Brian Knight, 1990), Old School Ties (with Hywel Williams, 1992); *Style*— The Hon Timothy Devlin; ✉ Ramsons, Maidstone Rd, Staplehurst, Kent TN12 0RD (☎ 01580 893176)

DEVLIN, Timothy Robert (Tim); MP (C) Stockton South (majority 3,369); s of (Hugh) Brendan Devlin, CBE, *qv*, and Ann Elizabeth, *née* Heatley; gs of Maj John Joseph Devlin, OBE; *b* 13 June 1959; *m* 1, 1987 (m dis 1989); m 2, 9 Nov 1991, Carol-Anne, da of Edmund Aitken; *Career* with Cons Res Dept 1981, accountant 1981–84, called to the Bar Lincoln's Inn 1985; MP (C) Stockton S 1987–; PPS: to Sir Nicholas Lyell, QC, MP as Attorney Gen 1992–94, to Anthony Nelson, MP as Min of Trade 1995–; chm Northern Gp of Cons MPs, pres Northern Cons Trade Unions, sec All Pty Chemical Industry Gp; memb: Cwlth Parly Assoc, GB-East Europe Centre, Cncl Cons Gp for Europe, Cncl Franco-Br Parly Gp, Stockton-on-Tees Cons Assoc, Soc of Cons Lawyers, Bow Gp; former chm LSE Cons, chm Islington N Cons Assoc 1986 (sec 1985); memb Bd of Tstees NSPCC 1994–96; patron: Opera Nova, Stockton Vocal Union, Stockton Music Festival, Rare Breeds Survival Tst; govr Yarm Sch; *Style*— Tim Devlin, Esq, MP; ✉ House of Commons, London SW1A 0AA (☎ 0171 219 3000); Constituency Office: 2 Russell Street, Stockton-on-Tees, Cleveland TS18 1NS (☎ 01642 605035)

DEVNEY, (Constance) Marie; CBE (1978, OBE 1973); da of Dr Richard Swanton Abraham; *b* 1 April 1934; *Educ* Pendleton HS, Bedford Coll London; *m* 1, 1960 (m dis 1976), Thomas Michael Valentine Patterson; m 2, 1984, Barrie Spencer Devney; *Career* TGWU: nat woman officer 1963–76, nat officer 1976–84; chm Gen Cncl of TUC 1974–75 and 1977 (memb 1963–84); memb: Hotel and Catering Training Bd 1966–86, Central Arbitration Ctee 1975–94, Equal Opportunities Cmmn 1976–84, Legal Aid Advsy Ctee 1986–90; dir Remploy 1968–86, memb Banking Ombudsman Cncl 1992–; chm Cncl Queen's Coll Harley St; *Style*— Mrs Marie Devney, CBE; ✉ 34 York House, Upper Montagu St, London W1H 1FR

DEVON, 17 Earl of (E 1553); Sir Charles Christopher Courtenay; 13 Bt (I 1644), JP (Devon 1950); patron of four livings; s of Rev the 16 Earl of Devon (d 1935); *b* 13 July 1916; *Educ* Winchester, RMC; *m* 29 July 1939, Sybil Venetia, da of Capt John Vickris Taylor, JP (d 1956), and formerly wife of 6 Earl of Cottenham; 1 s, 1 da; *Heir* s, Lord Courtenay, *qv*; *Career* Capt Coldstream Gds (RARO), WWII 1939–45 (wounded, despatches), Actg Maj 1942; *Style*— The Rt Hon the Earl of Devon, JP; ✉ Stables House, Powderham Castle, Exeter EX6 8JQ (☎ 01626 890253)

DEVONPORT, 3 Viscount (UK 1917); Sir Terence Kearley; 3 Bt (UK 1908); also Baron Devonport (UK 1910); s of 2 Viscount Devonport (d 1973); *b* 29 Aug 1944; *Educ* Aiglon Coll Switzerland, Selwyn Coll Cambridge (BA, DipArch, MA), Univ of Newcastle (BPhil); *m* 7 Dec 1968 (m dis 1979), Elizabeth Rosemary, 2 da of late John G Hopton, of Chute Manor, Andover; 2 da (Hon Velvet b 1975, Hon Idonia b 1977); *Heir* kinsman, Chester Dagley Hugh Kearley, *qv*; *Career* architect: David Brody NY USA 1967–68, London Borough of Lambeth 1971–72, Barnett Winskill Newcastle upon Tyne 1972–75; landscape architect Ralph Erskine Newcastle 1977–78, in private practice 1979–84; forestry mangr 1973–, farmer 1978–; md Tweedswood Enterprises 1979; dir various other cos 1984–; chm Millhouse Developments Ltd 1989–; memb: Lloyd's 1976–90, Int Dendrology Soc 1978–, TGEW Northern Advsy Ctee 1978–92, TGUK Nat Land Use and Environment Ctee 1984–87, CLA Northern Advsry Ctee 1980–85; pres: Arboricultural Assoc 1995–, Forestry Cmmn Ref Panel 1987–93; RIBA, ALI, FRSA 1996; *Recreations* nature, travel, the arts, good food, trees, music, country sports; *Clubs* Beefsteak, Farmers', RAC, MCC, Royal Over-Seas League, Northern Counties (Newcastle); *Style*— The Rt Hon the Viscount Devonport; ✉ Ray Demesne, Kirkwhelpington, Newcastle upon Tyne, Northumberland NE19 2RG

DEVONSHIRE, 11 Duke of (E 1694); Andrew Robert Buxton Cavendish; KG (1996), MC (1944), PC (1964); also Baron Cavendish of Hardwicke (E 1605), Earl of Devonshire (E 1618), Marquess of Hartington (E 1694), Earl of Burlington and Baron Cavendish of Keighley (both UK 1831); s of 10 Duke of Devonshire, KG, MBE, TD (d 1950), and Lady Mary Gascoyne-Cecil, GCVO, CBE (d 1988), da of 4 Marquess of Salisbury, KG, PC; *b* 2 Jan 1920; *Educ* Eton, Trinity Coll Cambridge; *m* 19 April 1941, Hon Deborah Mitford (*see* Devonshire, Duchess of); 1 s, 2 da (Lady Emma Tennant, Lady Sophia Morrison, *qqv*); *Heir* s, Marquess of Hartington, *qv*; *Career* served WWII as Capt Coldstream Gds; contested Chesterfield (C) 1945 and 1950 (pres Chesterfield Cons Assoc 1982); Parly under sec of state for Cwlth rels 1960–62, min of state Cwlth Rels Office 1962–1964, min of state Colonial Affrs 1963–64; former exec steward Jockey Club, memb Horserace Totalisator Bd 1977–86; vice Lord-Lt Derbys 1957–87, chllr Univ of Manchester 1965–86; chm Grand Cncl Br Empire Cancer Campaign 1956–81; former pres: Royal Hosp and Home Putney, Lawn Tennis Assoc; former nat pres Cons Friends of Israel; Liveryman Worshipful Co of Fishmongers, hon memb Ct of Assts Worshipful Co of Farriers; KStJ; *Books* Park Top: A Romance of the Turf (1976); *Clubs* Brooks's, White's, Pratt's; *Style*— His Grace the Duke of Devonshire, KG, PC, MC; ✉ Chatsworth, Bakewell, Derbyshire DE45 1PP (☎ 01246 582204); 4 Chesterfield St, London W1X 7HG (☎ 0171 499 5803)

DEVONSHIRE, Duchess of; Hon Deborah Vivien; *née* Mitford; 6 da of 2 Baron Redesdale (d 1958), and sis of Nancy, Pamela, Unity and Jessica Mitford, also of Hon Lady Mosley; *b* 31 March 1920; *Educ* private; *m* 19 April 1941, 11 Duke of Devonshire, *qv*; 1 s, 2 da; *Career* dir: Chatsworth House Tst, Cavendish Hotel Baslow, Devonshire Arms Hotel Bolton Abbey; ptnr Chatsworth Carpenters; pres of many local charitable orgns; *Books* The House: A Portrait of Chatsworth (1982), The Estate: A View From Chatsworth (1990), Farm Animals (1990), Treasures of Chatsworth (1990); *Style*— Her Grace the Duchess of Devonshire; ✉ Chatsworth, Bakewell, Derbyshire DE45 1PP (☎ 01246 582204, fax 01246 582937)

DEVONSHIRE, His Hon Judge; Michael Norman; TD (1969); s of Maj Norman George Devonshire (d 1983), of Tunbridge Wells, and Edith, *née* Skinner (d 1965); *b* 23 May 1930; *Educ* The Kings Sch Canterbury; *m* 31 March 1962, Jessie Margaret, da of Meirion Roberts (d 1974), of Tywyn, Merioneth; *Career* 2 Lt RA 1953–55; TA 1956–69: Queen's Own Royal West Kent Regt, Queen's Regt; admitted slr 1953, Master of Supreme Ct (Taxing Office) 1979–91, recorder of Crown Ct 1987, circuit judge (SE Circuit) 1991–; pres London Slrs' Litigation Assoc 1974–76, chm Advsy Ctee on Justices of Peace for SE London 1995–; memb Cncl RYA 1978–92 and 1993–96, chm RYA SE Regnl Assoc 1993–; chm Int Regulations Ctee Int Sailing Fedn (formerly Int Yacht Racing Union); memb: Pleasure Navigation Cmmn, Union Internationale Motor Nautique; FCIArb 1968; *Recreations* sailing; *Clubs* Royal Thames Yacht, Hoo Ness Yacht, Bough Beech Sailing (cdre 1976–79); *Style*— His Hon Judge Devonshire, TD; ✉ Law Courts, Altyre Road, Croydon, Surrey CR9 5AB

DEWAR, *see:* Beauclerk-Dewar

DEWAR, Rt Hon Donald Campbell; PC (1996), MP (Lab) Glasgow Garscadden (majority 13,340); s of Dr Alasdair Dewar, of Glasgow; *b* 21 Aug 1937; *Educ* Glasgow Acad, Glasgow Univ; *m* 1964 (m dis 1973), Alison Mary, da of Dr James S McNair, of Glasgow; 1 s, 1 da; *Career* MP (Lab): Aberdeen South 1966–70, Glasgow Garscadden 1978–; PPS to the Pres of the BOT 1967, chm Commons Select Ctee on Scottish Affrs 1979–81, oppn front bench spokesman on Scottish affrs 1981–83, memb Shadow Cabinet 1984–, chief oppn spokesman on Scottish affrs 1983–92, chief oppn spokesman on social security 1992–95, shadow chief whip 1995–; *Style*— The Rt Hon Donald Dewar, MP; ✉ 23 Cleveden Rd, Glasgow G12 0PQ (☎ 0141 334 2374); House of Commons, London SW1A 0AA (☎ 0171 219 3000)

DEWAR, Hamish Richard John; s of Richard John Gresley Dewar (d 1991), of Hay Hedge, Bisley, nr Stroud, Glos, and Andrena Victoria Dewar; *b* 15 Jan 1956; *Educ* Sherborne, Downing Coll Cambridge (MA); *m* 21 May 1983, Anna Maria, da of Patrick

Cloonan, of Sawbridgeworth, Herts; 2 s (Lachlan b 18 July 1987, Mungo b 25 Feb 1991), 1 da (India b 3 Jan 1989); *Career* specialist in conservation and restoration of paintings; studied under Richard Maelzer at Edward Speelman Ltd 1977–81, own practice 1982–; main restoration works incl: David with Head of Goliath by Guido Reni, Seed of David (altar piece from Llandaff Cathedral) by D G Rossetti, Angel di Soto by Picasso, The Light of the World by Holman Hunt; *Recreations* golf; *Clubs* Sunningdale Golf; *Style*— Hamish Dewar, Esq; ✉ The Gray House, Chadlington, Oxon OX7 3LX (☎ 01608 676332); 14 Mason Yard, Duke Street, St James's, London SW1Y 6BU (☎ 0171 930 4004)

DEWAR, Ian Peter Furze; s of late John Thompson Dewar, and Joan Eileen, *née* Furze; *b* 2 March 1947; *Educ* Eltham GS, Coll for Distributive Trades (Dip Mktg); *m* 1 Feb 1975, Wendy Jane, da of Brian Palmer; 2 s (Oliver John b 1985, Francis James b 1987); *Career* advtg exec; Brunnings Yorks 1979–82; dir: THB & W 1982–84, O & M Direct 1984–85, Grey Direct 1989–94; fndr: Dewar Coyle Maclean 1985–89, Faxed Facts Ltd 1993–94, Dewar Direct Ltd 1995–, Inference Consultants Ltd 1995–; fndr memb IDM 1994; MInstM 1970, MIPA 1989; *Recreations* food and drink; *Clubs* Pinball Owners' Assoc; *Style*— Ian Dewar, Esq; ✉ 48 Palace Road, East Molesey, Hampton Court, Surrey KT8 9DW

DEWAR, Robert James; CMG (1969), CBE (1964); s of Dr Robert Scott Dewar (d 1939); *b* 1923; *Educ* Glasgow HS, Univ of Edinburgh, Wadham Coll Oxford; *m* 1947, Christina Marianne, da of late Olaf August Ljungberger, of Stockholm; 2 s, 1 da; *Career* Colonial Forest Serv Nigeria and Nyasaland 1944–60, chief conservator of forests Nyasaland 1961–64, perm sec Natural Resources Malawi 1964–69, memb staff World Bank 1969–84, chief of Agric Div Regnl Mission for E Africa 1974–84, conslt to the World Bank 1984–86; vice chm The Zimbabwe Tst; *Recreations* golf, angling, gardening; *Clubs* Cwlth Trust, New Cavendish; *Style*— Robert Dewar Esq, CMG, CBE; ✉ Hawkshaw, Comrie Road, Crieff, Perthshire PH7 4BJ (☎ 01764 654830)

DEWAR DURIE, Andrew Maule; DL (Dunbartonshire 1996); s of Lt-Col Raymond Varley Dewar Durie of Durie, of Court House, Pewsey, Wiltshire, and Wendy, *née* Frances St John Maule; bro of Christian Dewar Durie, *qv*; *b* 13 Nov 1939; *Educ* Cheam Sch Berks, Wellington Coll Berks; *m* 25 Aug 1972, Marguerite Jamila, da of Graf Kunata Kottulinsky, of Vienna, Austria; 2 s (James Alexander b 26 April 1978, Philip Antony b 29 Aug 1986), 1 da (Nicola Louise b 19 Sept 1974); *Career* cmmnd Argyll & Sutherland Highlanders 1958–68; served: UK, BAOR, SE Asia, Aden; ret Capt 1968; White Horse Distillers 1968–83: dir 1973–82, sr export dir 1982–83; int sales dir Long John International (Whitbread & Co plc) 1983–88; James Burrough Distillers: Euro sales dir 1988, dep md 1988–89, md 1989–90, chief exec offr 1990–91; md Allied Distillers Ltd (subsid of Allied Domecq PLC) 1991–; vice chm CBI Scotland Cncl 1996; memb Incorporation of Maltmen 1995, Liveryman Worshipful Co of Distillers 1986; *Recreations* sailing, tennis, rough shooting, skiing; *Clubs* Army & Navy; *Style*— Andrew Dewar Durie, Esq, DL; ✉ Finnich Malise, Croftamie, West Stirlingshire G63 0HA (☎ 01360 660257); Allied Distillers Ltd, 2 Glasgow Rd, Dumbarton G82 1ND (☎ 01389 765111, fax 01389 742112, telex 777221 ALDIST)

DEWAR DURIE, Christian Frances; da of Lt-Col Raymond Varley Dewar Durie of Durie, of Pewsey, Wilts, and Frances, *née* St John Maule; sis of Andrew Dewar Durie, *qv*; *b* 6 Aug 1945; *Educ* Downe House Newbury, Belfast Coll of Art, St Martin's Sch of Art (DipAD Hons); *Career* asst designer H & M Rayne 1966–70, gp designer Euromanik Ltd 1970–73, fashion co-ordinator André Peters-Louis Ferraud 1974–75, fashion dir Nigel French Enterprises Ltd 1975–78, managing ed Prism Fashion Publications 1978–81, owner and dir Parasol Associates 1981–; hon sec The Friends of Castle Sychrov (UK) 1990–; Winston Churchill Memorial Tst travel fellowship 1969; FRSA 1967; *Recreations* skiing, travel, theatre, literature, art; *Style*— Miss Christian Dewar Durie; ✉ Parasol Associates, 3 King's House, 400 King's Road, London SW10 0LL (☎ 0171 351 3236)

DEWAR OF THAT ILK AND VOGRIE, YOUNGER, Col Michael Kenneth O'Malley; o s and h of Lt-Col (Kenneth) Malcolm Joseph Dewar of that Ilk and Vogrie, OBE, Chief of the Name and Arms of Dewar, and Alice Maureen, *née* O'Malley; *b* 15 Nov 1941; *Educ* Downside, Pembroke Coll Oxford (BA, MA), RMA Sandhurst; *m* 6 July 1968, Lavinia Mary, o da of late Dr Jack Souttar Minett, of Stony Stratford, Bucks; 3 s (Alexander Malcolm Bretherton b 1970, James Michael Bretherton b 1973, Edward Jack Bretherton b 1978), 1 da (Katharine Victoria Lavinia b 1981); *Career* cmmnd 2 Lt The Royal Green Jackets 1962, psc, Lt-Col 1982, CO Light Division Depot 1985–87, Col 1987, Col Defence Studies Staff Coll Camberley 1987–90 (ret); dep dir Int Inst for Strategic Studies 1990–94, dir The Albemarle Connection 1995–; Knight of Honour and Devotion SMO Malta 1988; *Books* Internal Security Weapons and Equipment of the World (1978), Brush Fire Wars, Campaigns of the British Army since 1945 (1984, revised 1987), The British Army in Northern Ireland (1985), Weapons and Equipment of Counter-Terrorism (1987), The Art of Deception in Warfare (1989), The Defence of the Nation (1989), An Anthology of Military Quotations (1990), Northern Ireland Scrapbook (jtly, 1986), Campaign Medals (jtly, 1987), War in the Streets (1992), The Gulf War: A Photographic History (1992); *Clubs* Naval and Military; *Style*— Col Michael Dewar of that Ilk and Vogrie, Younger; ✉ c/o Barclays Bank plc, 50 Jewry St, Winchester, Hants SO23 8RG; Bates Dorland Ltd, 121–141 Westbourne Terrace, London W2 6JR (☎ 0171 262 5077)

DEWE, Roderick Gorrie (Roddy); s of Douglas Percy Dewe (d 1978), and Rosanna Clements Gorrie (d 1971); *b* 17 Oct 1935; *Educ* abroad, Univ Coll Oxford (BA); *m* 1964, Carol Anne, da of Michael Beach Thomas (d 1941), of Herts; 1 s (Jonathan 1967), 1 da (Sarah b 1965); *Career* chm Dewe Rogerson Group Ltd (fndr 1969); memb Bd of Mgmnt PRCA; *Recreations* golf, travel; *Clubs* City of London; *Style*— Roddy Dewe, Esq; ✉ 55 Duncan Terrace, London N1 8AG (☎ 0171 359 7318); Booking Hall, Southill Station, nr Biggleswade, Beds (☎ 01462 811 274); Dewe Rogerson Group Ltd, 3 1/2 London Wall Buildings, London Wall, London EC2M 5SY (☎ 0171 638 9571, fax 0171 638 7091, telex 883610)

DEWE MATHEWS, Bernard Piers; CBE (1996), TD (1965); s of Denys Cosmo Dewe Mathews (d 1985), of London, and Elizabeth Jane, *née* Davies (d 1937); *b* 28 March 1937; *Educ* Ampleforth, Harvard Business Sch; *m* 10 Feb 1977, Catherine Ellen, da of Senator John Ignatius Armstrong (d 1977), of NSW, Aust; 1 s (Charles-Frederick (Freddie) b 1985), 3 da (Jacqueline b 1978, Laura b 1979, Chloe b 1982); *Career* Nat Serv 2 Lt Malaya 1956–57, TA Maj 21 SAS Regt 1957–67; Edward Moore & Sons CAs 1957–62, BP Co Ltd 1962–65, Coopers & Lybrand & Assocs 1965–69, dir and head Int Projects Div J Henry Schroder & Co Ltd 1978– (joined 1969), dir Thames Power Ltd 1988–91; govr St Paul's Girls' Prep Sch 1988–93, cncl memb London C of C 1986–87; memb: SEATAG 1985–89, OPB 1989–95, EGAC 1993–, Outward Bound Mgmnt Ctee 1996–; FCA 1972 (ACA 1962); *Recreations* music, opera, skiing, landscape gardening; *Clubs* Garrick; *Style*— Bernard Dewe Mathews, Esq, CBE, TD; ✉ 112 Castelnau, Barnes, London SW13 9EU (☎ 0181 741 2592); J Henry Schroder & Co Ltd, 120 Cheapside, London EC2V 6DS (☎ 0171 382 6682, fax 0171 382 3949, telex 885029)

DEWEY, Sir Anthony Hugh; 3 Bt (UK 1917), of South Hill Wood, Bromley, Kent; JP (1961); s of Maj Hugh Grahame Dewey, MC (d 1936), and gs of Rev Sir Stanley Daws Dewey, 2 Bt (d 1948); *b* 31 July 1921; *Educ* Wellington, RAC Cirencester; *m* 22 April 1949, Sylvia Jacqueline Rosamund, da of late Dr John Ross MacMahon, of Branksome Manor, Bournemouth; 2 s (Rupert Grahame b 1953, Charles Ross b 1960), 3 da (Delia Mary (Mrs Nicholas J Wingfield-Digby) b 1951, Carola Jane (Mrs Robert H Sutton) b 1955, Angela Rosamund (Mrs Ivan Hicks) b 1957); *Heir* s, Rupert Grahame Dewey b 29 March 1953; *Career* Capt RA NW Europe 1940–46; farmer Somerset; *Clubs* Army and Navy; *Style*— Sir Anthony Dewey, Bt, JP; ✉ The Rag, Galhampton, Yeovil, Somerset BA2 7AJ (☎ 01963 440213)

DEWEY, Prof John Frederick; s of John Edward Dewey (d 1982), of London, and Florence Nellie Mary, *née* Davies; *b* 22 May 1937; *Educ* Bancrofts Sch, Univ of London (BSc, DIC, PhD), Univ of Cambridge (MA, ScD), Univ of Oxford (MA, DSc); *m* 4 July 1961, Frances Mary, da of William Blackhurst (d 1971), of Wistow, Cambs; 1 s (Jonathan Peter 1965), 1 da (Ann Penelope b 1963); *Career* lectr: Univ of Manchester 1960–64, Univ of Cambridge 1964–70; prof: Albany Univ New York 1970–82, Univ of Durham 1982–86, Dept of Earth Sciences Univ of Oxford 1986–; memb Academy of Europe 1989; FGS 1960, FRS 1985; *Recreations* watercolour painting, model railways, tennis, skiing, cricket; *Style*— Prof John Dewey, FRS; ✉ Sherwood Lodge, 93 Bagley Wood Rd, Kennington, Oxford OX1 5NA (☎ 01865 735525); Department of Earth Sciences, Parks Rd, Oxford OX1 3PR (☎ 01865 272021)

DEWEY, Rupert Grahame; er s and h of Sir Anthony Hugh Dewey, 3 Bt, *qv*; *b* 29 March 1953; *m* 23 Oct 1978, Suzanne Rosemary, da of late Andrew Lusk, of Fordie, Comrie, Perthshire; 2 s (Thomas Andrew b 27 Jan 1982, Oliver Nicholas b 1984), 1 da (Laura Kate b 1988); *Career* ptnr Wood & Awdry Wansbroughs (solicitors) Bath; *Style*— Rupert Dewey, Esq; ✉ Church Farm House, Wellow, Bath BA2 8QS

DEWHIRST, Timothy Charles; DL (E Yorkshire); s of Alistair Jowitt Dewhirst, CBE, of Driffield, N Humberside, and Hazel Eleanor, *née* Reed; *b* 19 Aug 1953; *Educ* Worksop Coll; *m* 15 July 1978, Prudence Rosalind, da of Frank Geoffrey Horsell, of Knaresborough, N Yorks; 1 s (Charles Alistair Geoffrey b 4 June 1980), 1 da (Samantha Prudence b 26 June 1983); *Career* chm Dewhirst Group plc (clothing and toiletry mfrs) 1993– (chief exec 1986–93); vice chm BCIA 1990–; memb Cncl BATC 1993–; *Recreations* shooting, fishing, sailing; *Style*— Timothy C Dewhirst, Esq, DL; ✉ Nafferton Heights, Nafferton, nr Driffield, N Humberside YO25 0LD; Dewhirst Group plc, Dewhirst House, Westgate, Driffield, N Humberside YO25 7TH (☎ 01377 252561, fax 01377 252030)

DEWHURST, Prof Sir (Christopher) John; kt (1977); s of late John Dewhurst; *b* 2 July 1920; *Educ* St Joseph's Coll Dumfries, Victoria Univ Manchester; *m* 1952, Hazel Mary Atkin; 2 s, 1 da; *Career* formerly prof of obstetrics and gynaecology Univ of London at Queen Charlotte's Hospital for Women, dean Inst of Obstetrics and Gynaecology 1979–85; Hon DSc Sheffield, Hon MD Uruguay; Hon FACOG, Hon FRCSI, Hon FCOG (SA), Hon FRACOG, FRCOG, FRCSE; *Style*— Prof Sir John Dewhurst; ✉ 21 Jack's Lane, Harefield, Middx UB9 6HE (☎ 0189 582 5403)

DEWHURST, Philip Anthony; s of Alfred John Dewhurst, and Rosalind Georgina Dewhurst; *b* 25 Sept 1949; *Educ* Mark Hall Sch; *m* Joan Catherine; 1 da (Grace b 14 June 1983), 1 s (Tom b 27 March 1987); *Career* mgmnt trainee then copywriter Longman Group Ltd 1968–71, int publicity controller Evans Publishing Ltd 1971–73; PRO: Havering London BC 1973–76, Hackney London BC 1976–77; head of PR and publicity City of Canterbury 1977–80, PRO Surrey CC 1980–84; dir of public affrs: Chemical Industries Assoc 1984–88, Sterling Public Relations 1988–92; md public affrs GCI Group 1992–94, gen mangr GCI Europe 1993–94; chief exec The Rowland Company (Saatchi & Saatchi PR) 1994–95, dir of corp affrs Railtrack plc 1995–; FIPR 1989, FRSA 1989; *Recreations* art, travel; *Style*— Philip Dewhurst, Esq; ✉ Railtrack plc, 40 Bernard Street, London WC1N 1BY (☎ 0171 344 7100)

DEWS, Peter; s of John Dews (d 1961), and Edna, *née* Bloomfield (d 1976); *b* 26 Sept 1929; *Educ* Queen Elizabeth GS Wakefield, Univ Coll Oxford (BA, MA); *m* 1960, Ann, da of Arthur Stanley Rhodes (d 1982); *Career* schoolmaster 1952–54; dir sound and TV BBC 1954–64; dir: Ravinia Festival Chicago 1964 and 1970, Birmingham Repertory Theatre 1966–72, Hadrian VII Birmingham 1967, London 1968, NY 1969, Chichester Festival Theatre 1978–80, Stratford Ontario 1973, 1981 and 1984; awarded: Antoinette Perry (Tony) Award Broadway 1969, Guild of TV Drama Prodrs and Dirs Award for Best Drama Prodn (An Age of Kings) 1960; Hon DLitt Univ of Bradford; *Style*— Peter Dews, Esq; ✉ 8 Capstan Row, Deal, Kent CT14 6NE (☎ 01304 368937)

DEXTER, Colin; *b* 29 Sept 1930; *Educ* Stamford Sch, Christ's Coll Cambridge (MA); *m* 30 March 1956, Dorothy; 1 s (Jeremy b 1962), 1 da (Sally b 1960); *Career* author; Nat Serv; sr asst sec Univ of Oxford Delegacy of Local Examinations 1966–87; five times crossword champion of Ximenes and Azed Competitions; Hon MA (by incorporation) Univ of Oxford 1966; memb: Crime Writers' Assoc, Detection Club; *Books* Inspector Morse crime novels: Last Bus to Woodstock (1975), Last Seen Wearing (1976), The Silent World of Nicholas Quinn (1977), Service of All The Dead (Silver Dagger Award CWA, 1979), The Dead of Jericho (Silver Dagger Award CWA, 1981), The Riddle of the Third Mile (1983), The Secret of Annexe 3 (1986), The Wench is Dead (Gold Dagger Award CWA, 1989), The Jewel That Was Ours (1991), The Way Through the Woods (Gold Dagger Award CWA, 1992), Morse's Greatest Mystery (1993), The Daughters of Cain (1994), Death is Now My Neighbour (1996); *Recreations* crosswords, reading; *Style*— Colin Dexter, Esq; ✉ 456 Banbury Rd, Oxford OX2 7RG

DEXTER, Edward Ralph (Ted); s of Ralph Marshall Dexter (d 1974), and Elise Genevieve, *née* Dartnall (d 1974); *b* 15 May 1935; *Educ* Radley, Jesus Coll Cambridge (cricket capt); *m* 1963, Susan Georgina, da of Thomas Cuthbert Longfield; 1 s (Thomas), 1 da (Genevieve); *Career* Nat Serv 2 Lt 11 Hussars Malaya 1956–57 (Malaya Campaign Medal); cricket player 1958–68 (capt Sussex 1960–65 and England 1962–65), freelance journalist 1965–88, sports promotion conslt 1978–, currently ptnr Ted Dexter & Associates (PR); chm England Ctee TCCB 1989–93 (resigned); Parly candidate (C) Cardiff 1965; *Recreations* golf; *Clubs* MCC, Sunningdale Golf, Royal & Ancient Golf; *Style*— Ted Dexter, Esq; ✉ 20a Woodville Gardens, Ealing, London W5 2LQ (☎ 0181 998 6863)

DEXTER, Mariella Lisa; *b* 6 Aug 1953; *Educ* Sutton HS GPDST, Univ of Sussex (BA), King's Fund Coll London (DipHSM); *Career* English language asst Lycée Paul Cezanne Aix-en-Provence 1973–74, admin asst Central Register and Clearing House Ltd London 1975–76, nat admin trainee NW Thames RHA 1976–78, dep hosp administrator Central Middx Hosp 1978–82, dep divnl administrator Banstead Hosp Sutton 1982–83, unit administrator Mental Health Unit Victoria Health Authy 1984–85; Riverside Health Authy: unit gen mangr Mental Health 1985–88, dir of policy devpt 1988–90, unit gen mangr Charing Cross Hosp 1990–91, dep chief exec Riverside Health (directly managed unit) 1991; unit gen mangr Acute Unit Gloucestershire Health Authy 1991–93, chief exec Gloucestershire Royal NHS Trust 1993–; preceptor/mentor IHSM students 1980–, guest speaker and lectr various confs on health service mgmnt and related issues; *Style*— Ms Mariella Dexter; ✉ Gloucestershire Royal NHS Trust, Gloucestershire Royal Hospital, Great Western Road, Gloucester GL1 3NN (☎ 01452 528555, fax 01452 394737)

DEXTER, Prof (Thomas) Michael; s of Thomas Richard Dexter (d 1976), and (Gertrude) Agnes, *née* Depledge (d 1991); *b* 15 May 1945; *Educ* Manchester Central GS, Univ of Salford (BSc, DSc), Univ of Manchester (PhD); *m* 10 Aug 1966 (m dis 1978), (Frances) Ann, da of John Sutton, of Hurdsfield, nr Macclesfield; 2 s (Alexander Michael b 1972, Thomas b 1987), 2 da (Katrina Ann (twin) b 1972, Rachel b 1985); *Career* visiting fell Sloan Kettering Inst NY USA 1976–77, sr scientist Paterson Laboratories Manchester 1977–87 (scientist 1973), life fell Cancer Res Campaign 1978–, head of Dept of Experimental Haematology Paterson Inst for Cancer Res Manchester 1982–, prof of haematology (personal chair) Univ of Manchester 1985–, dep dir Paterson Inst 1994–, pres Int Soc for Experimental Haematology 1988–89, Gibb Res Fell 1992–; author of 250 papers in jls; memb: Scientific Ctee Leukaemia Res Fund 1985–88, Grants Ctee Cancer Res Campaign 1986–93, Ctee on Effects of Ionising Radiation 1988–93, Scientific Advsy Bd Biomedical Res Center Univ of Br Columbia 1988–91, Steering Ctee

Electro-Magnetic Fields National Grid 1989–, Scientifc Ctee Gunnar Nilsson Res Tst Fund 1991–; memb Editorial Bd of 10 scientific jls; memb: Ctee SERC 1991–94, Ctee AFRC (now BBSRC) 1991–94, Cncl MRC 1993–96 (chm MCMB 1994–96, chm Human Genome Coordinating Ctee 1996–), Ctee on Med Affects of Radiations in the Environment (COMARE) 1993–, World Ctee IACRLD 1994–, Cncl Royal Society 1995–96; MRCPath 1987, Hon MRCP 1994 FRS 1991; *Recreations* folk-singing, poetry & gardening; *Style*— Prof Michael Dexter, FRS; ✉ Holly Barn, Pedley Hill, Adlington, Cheshire SK10 4LB; Paterson Institute for Cancer Research, Christie Hospital & Holt Radium Institute, Withington, Manchester M20 9BX (☎ 0161 446 3231, telex 9349999 TXLINK G - quote MBX 614458123 as first line of text, fax 0161 446 3033)

DEXTER, Sally Julia; da of Edward Dexter, of Sonning Common, Reading, and Retha Joan, *née* Roginson; *b* 15 April 1960; *Educ* Chiltern Edge Sch Sonning Common, King James's Coll Henley on Thames, Nat Youth Theatre, LAMDA; *Career* actress; *Theatre* NT 1985–88 incl: Hermione in The Winter's Tale, Octavia in Antony and Cleopatra, Sarah Eldridge in Entertaining Strangers, Fanny Margolies in The American Clock, Mizi in Dalliance, Polly Peachum in The Threepenny Opera, Miss Prue in Love for Love; RNT 1992 incl: The Recruiting Officer and A Midsummer Night's Dream; Open Air Theatre Regent's Park 1989 incl: Acerbita in The Swaggerer, Olivia in Twelfth Night, Titania in A Midsummer Night's Dream; RSC 1990–91 incl: Catalena in The Last Days of Don Juan, Regan in King Lear, Helen in Troilus and Cressida; other credits incl: Bunny in Babes in Arms (LAMDA) 1984, Princess Winnifred in Once Upon A Mattress (Watermill Theatre, Newbury) 1985, title role in Lady Betty (Cheek by Jowl) 1989, Nancy in Oliver (The Palladium) 1994–95; *Television* incl: A Touch of Frost, The Plant (Screen One); *Recordings* The Art of Love (readings from the Kamasutra, CD and cassette); *Awards* winner Olivier Award for Most Promising Newcomer 1986, nominated Olivier Award for Best Actress in A Musical (for Oliver) 1995; *Recreations* walking, talking, eating, hot baths, horse riding, ceroc dancing; *Style*— Ms Sally Dexter; ✉ c/o ICM Ltd, Oxford House, 76 Oxford Street, London W1N 0AX (☎ 0171 636 6565, fax 0171 323 0101)

DEYERMOND, Prof Alan David; s of Maj Henry Deyermond (d 1966), and Margaret, *née* Lawson (d 1958); *b* 24 Feb 1932; *Educ* Quarry Bank HS Liverpool, Victoria Coll Jersey, Pembroke Coll Oxford (MA, BLitt, DLitt); *m* 30 March 1957, Ann Marie, da of William Bracken (d 1943), and Mary, *née* Burke (d 1985); 1 da (Ruth Margaret b 1971); *Career* Westfield Coll (latterly Queen Mary & Westfield Coll) London: asst lectr 1955–58, lectr 1958–66, reader 1966–69, sr tutor 1967–72, prof of Spanish 1969–, dean Faculty of Arts 1972–74 and 1981–84, vice princ 1986–89; assoc dir Inst of Romance Studies Univ of London 1991–93; visiting prof: Univ of Wisconsin USA 1972, UCLA 1977, Princeton Univ USA 1978–81, Univ of Victoria Canada 1983, Northern Arizona Univ USA 1986, Johns Hopkins Univ USA 1987, Univ Nacional Autónoma de México 1992; pres Assoc Internacional de Hispanistas 1992–; sidesman St Peter's Church St Albans, tstee Kentish's Educnl Fndn (chm 1992–); corresponding fell: Medieval Acad of America 1979, Real Academia de Buenas Letras de Barcelona 1982; memb Hispanic Soc of America 1985, Premio Internacional Elio Antonio de Nebrija 1994, FSA 1987, FBA 1988; *Books* incl: The Petrarchan Sources of "La Celestina" (1961, 2 edn 1975), Epic Poetry and the Clergy - Studies on the "Mocedades de Rodrigo" (1969), A Literary History of Spain - The Middle Ages (1971), "Lazarillo de Tormes" - A Critical Guide (1975), Historia y crítica de la literatura española: Edad Media (1980, first supplement 1991), El "Cantar de Mio Cid" y la épica medieval española (1987), Tradiciones y puntos de vista en la ficción sentimental (1992); *Recreations* dog walking, psephology, vegetarian cookery; *Style*— Prof Alan Deyermond, FBA; ✉ 20 Lancaster Road, St Albans, Herts AL1 4ET (☎ 01727 55383); Department of Hispanic Studies, Queen Mary and Westfield College, Mile End Road, London E1 4NS (☎ 0171 775 3138 or 0171 975 5061, fax 0181 980 5400, e-mail a.d.deyermond@qmw.ac.uk)

DEYES, Anthony Francis (Tony); s of William Francis Deyes (d 1948), and Marjorie, *née* Ridgway; *b* 9 July 1944; *Educ* Kingswood Sch Bath, KCL (BA), Inst of Educn Univ of London (PGCE), Univ of Aston (MPhil), Middlesex Poly (MBA); *m* 1968, Maya, da of Emil Koch; 3 s (Philip Francis b 27 Feb 1969 d 1971, Marcus Eugene b 11 March 1972, Robert Anthony b 21 Feb 1973); *Career* teacher King's Sch of English Bournemouth 1968–69, dir Language Inst Univ of Deusto Bilbao 1973–76 (lectr in English and linguistics 1969–73); British Council: dir Coimbra 1976–77, dir of studies Lisbon 1977–80, visiting prof of linguistics Catholic Univ of Sao Paulo 1980–85, sr advsr English Language Div 1987–90 (conslt 1985–87), dir Rio de Janeiro 1990–93, dir and cultural attaché Ecuador 1993–; author of over 60 articles in professional and academic jls; *Recreations* reading, swimming, golf, amateur dramatics, music (opera and Mozart), walking, speech-making; *Style*— Tony Deyes, Esq; ✉ The British Council, Avenida Amazonas, 1646 y Orellana, Casilla 17–07–8829, Quito, Ecuador

DHANDSA, Dr Narinder S; s of Shiv Dhandsa (d 1971), and Samitar Dhandsa; *b* 29 Feb 1956; *Educ* Gillingham GS Kent, St Thomas' Hosp Med Sch (MB, BS); *Career* jr hosp doctor NHS 1979–82, chief exec Associated Nursing Services plc 1984–; currently dir: Rickshaw Restaurants Ltd, Vigour Ltd; *Recreations* skiing, golf, art; *Style*— Dr Narinder Dhandsa; ✉ Associated Nursing Services plc, No 1 Battersea Square, Battersea, London SW11 3PZ (☎ 0171 924 3026, fax 0171 924 2559)

DHARGALKAR, Suresh Dinkar; LVO (1994); s of Dinkar Laxman Dhargalkar (d 1979), of Bombay, India, and Sushila, *née* Belwalkar (d 1993); *b* 16 Dec 1934; *Educ* Hind Vidhylaya HS Bombay, Sch of Architecture Sir J J Sch of Art Bombay, Sch of Architecture Regent Street Poly London, Poly Coll of Architecture and Advance Building Technol London; *m* 3 Aug 1962, Hildegard (d 1991), da of Oswald Bente (d 1964); 2 s (Hans b 1963, Martin b 1967 d 1985); *Career* architectural asst in private architectural practice: Bombay 1952–55, London 1955–70; architect in private practice London 1970–74, princ architect with PSA/DOE for Royal Palaces 1979–90 (architect 1975–79), actg conslt architect project mangr with Royal Household 1995– (superintending architect 1990–95); special interest in environmental control for preservation of historic artefacts, lighting and precaution against fire and theft in historic bldgs, palaces and museums; works undertaken in restoration and new works at: Windsor Castle, St James's Palace, Hampton Court Palace, British Museum, National Maritime Museum; active participant in organising seminars for conservation of cultural historic properties for ICCROM (int centre for the study of preservation and restoration of cultural property Rome) until 1989 (Cert 1984); Freeman City of London 1965; corp memb RIBA 1970, memb ARCUK 1970; *Recreations* travel, cooking, watercolour painting, philately; *Style*— Suresh Dhargalkar, Esq, LVO; ✉ 3 Elmer Gardens, Edgware, Middlesex HA8 9AR (☎ 0181 952 3075); Royal Philatelic Collection, Buckingham Palace, London SW1A 1AA (☎ 0171 930 4832, fax 0171 839 5950)

DHASMANA, Janardan Prasad; s of Govind Ram Dhasmana, of Dehradun, India, and Savitri Dhasmana; *b* 15 Jan 1942; *Educ* Lucknow Univ India (BSc, MB BS, MS); *m* 2 Dec 1965, Lakshmi, da of Ram Prasad Joshi (d 1986); 1 s (Devesh b 6 Oct 1973), 1 da (Divya b 25 July 1970); *Career* surgical registrar The Wellingdon Hosp New Delhi 1968–71; Bristol Royal Infirmary: registrar in cardiothoracic surgery 1975–78, sr registrar 1978–85, conslt 1986–; clinical res fell Univ of Alabama 1980–81, sr registrar in cardiac surgery Royal Hosp for Sick Children Gt Ormond St London 1982–83; memb: Soc of Thoracic and Cardiovascular Surgeons of GB and Ireland, Br Cardiac Soc, Euro Assoc of Cardio-thoracic Surgery, BMA, Cardiac Surgery Res Club, Royal Soc of Med Soc of SW Surgns of Eng, W Country Chest Physicians; FRCS England 1975, FRCSEd 1975, FRCS (C/Th) 1982; *Recreations* photography, sports watching, music; *Style*— Janardan P Dhasmana, Esq; ✉ Consultant Cardiothoracic Surgeon, Bristol Royal Infirmary, Bristol BS2 8HW (☎ 0117 928 2146, fax 0117 928 3871)

DI PALMA, Vera June; OBE; da of William Di Palma (d 1949), and Violet May, *née* Pryke; *b* 14 July 1931; *Educ* Haverstock Central Sch, Burghley Girls' Sch; *m* 4 July 1973, Ernest Brynmor Jones (d 1995); *Career* accountant in public practice 1947–64, tax accountant Dunlop plc 1964–67, sr lectr City of London Poly 1967–71, tax conslt 1971–80, chm Mobile Training Ltd 1978–; memb VAT Tbnl 1977–, public works loan cmmr 1978–, dep chm Air Travel Tst Ctee 1986–, non-exec memb S Warwicks Health Authy 1991–93; FCCA 1956 (pres 1980–81), FTII 1960; *Books* Capital Gains Tax (1972), Your Fringe Benefits (1978); *Recreations* tennis, dancing, dog walking, gardening; *Style*— Ms Vera Di Palma, OBE; ✉ Temple Close, Sibford Gower, Banbury, Oxon OX15 5RX (☎ 01295 780222); Mobile Training Ltd, Green Acres, Sibford Gower, Banbury, Oxon OX15 5RX (☎ 01295 788115, fax 01295 780366, mobile 0802 323143)

DI STEFANO, Arturo Damiano; s of Salvatore Di Stefano, of Aintree, Liverpool, and Nicolina, *née* Tiso; *b* 25 Feb 1955; *Educ* Cardinal Allen GS, Liverpool Poly, Goldsmiths' Coll London (BA), RCA (MA, Unilever award), Accademia Albertina Turin (Italian Govt scholar); *m* 30 Oct 1987, Jan, da of John Frederick Greenhalgh; *Career* artist; *Solo Exhibitions* incl: 04 Gallery Oxford 1985, Pomeroy Purdy Gallery London 1987, 1989, 1991 and 1993, Gabriele Fasolino Gallery Turin 1987, Helmut Pabst Gallery Frankfurt 1991, Paintings & Prints 1981–92 (Walker Art Gallery Liverpool) 1993, Purdy Hicks Gallery London 1993; *Gp Exhibitions* incl: Leicester Exhibition (Beaumanor Hall) 1983–89, Royal Acad Summer Show 1983–84, Whitechapel Open 1984–85, Young Masters (Solomon Gallery London) 1986, Six Artists (Groucho Club London) 1986, Pupils of Peter de Francia (Camden Arts Centre) 1987, Blasphemies, Ecstasies, Cries (Serpentine Gallery London) 1989, En Série (John Hansard Gallery Southampton) 1989, Cutting Edge (Manchester Art Gallery) 1989, 3 Ways (Br Cncl/RCA touring) 1990, Jeune Peinture 1990 (Grand Palais Paris) 1990; Br Cncl award 1986 and 1991; work in collections of: Arthur Andersen London, Unilever London; *Style*— Arturo Di Stefano, Esq; ✉ c/o Purdy Hicks Gallery, 65 Hopton Street, London SE1 9GZ (☎ 0171 237 6062)

DIAMAND, Peter; Hon CBE (1972); *b* 1913, Dutch citizen; *Educ* Schiller-Realgymnasium Berlin, Univ of Berlin; *m* 1, 1948 (m dis 1971), Maria Curcio; m 2 (m dis 1979), Sylvia Rosenberg; 1 s; *Career* arts administrator; sec Artur Schnabel 1934–39; dir: Holland Festival 1948–65, Edinburgh Int Festival 1966–78; artistic advsr: Orchestre de Paris 1976–, Teatro alla Scala (Milan) 1977–78; dir and gen mangr RPO 1978–81, dir Mozart Festival Paris 1981–87; Hon LLD Univ of Edinburgh; Knight Oranje Nassau (Holland), Cdr des Arts et des Lettres France 1985, Offr Grand Cross of Merit (Austria), Commendatore (Italy); *Style*— Peter Diamand, Esq, CBE; ✉ 28 Eton Court, Eton Ave, London NW3 3HJ (☎ and fax 0171 586 1203)

DIAMOND, His Hon Judge Anthony Edward John; QC (1974); s of Arthur Sigismund Diamond (d 1978), and Gladys Elkah Diamond (d 1945); *b* 4 Sept 1929; *Educ* Rugby, Corpus Christi Coll Cambridge (MA); *m* 21 Dec 1965, Joan Margaret, da of Thomas Gee; 2 da (Emma b 1966, Lucy b 1971); *Career* 2 Lt RA 1948–49; called to the Bar Gray's Inn 1953; practised as barr at Commercial Bar 1958–90, dep High Ct judge 1982–90, head of chambers 4 Essex Court 1984–90, recorder Crown Ct 1985–90, bencher Gray's Inn 1985, circuit judge (SE Circuit) 1990–; memb Independent Review Body under Colliery Review Procedure 1983–90, chm Appeal Tbnl under Banking Act 1985–90, judge i/c Central London County Ct Business List 1994–; *Recreations* the visual arts; *Style*— His Hon Judge Anthony Diamond, QC; ✉ 1 Cannon Place, London NW3 1EH (☎ 0171 435 6154); Central London County Court, 13 14 Park Crescent, London W1N 3PD

DIAMOND, Prof Aubrey Lionel; s of Alfred Diamond (d 1951), of London, and Millie, *née* Solomons (d 1963); *b* 28 Dec 1923; *Educ* Central Fndn Sch London, LSE (LLM); *m* 26 Nov 1955, Eva Marianne, da of Dr Adolf Bobasch (d 1976), of London; 1 s (Paul b 1960), 1 da (Nicola b 1958); *Career* RAF 1943–47; Dept of Law LSE 1957–66, ptnr Lawford & Co 1959–71 (conslt 1986–), prof of law QMC London 1966–71, law cmmr 1971–76, dir Inst of Advanced Legal Studies 1976–86, prof of law Notre Dame Univ (USA) 1987–, co dir London Law Centre 1987–; visiting prof: Stanford Univ, Univ of Virginia, Tulane Univ, Melbourne Univ, Univ of East Africa; advsr on security interests DTI 1986–88; pt/t chm Indust1 Tbnls 1984–90, dep chm Data Protection Tbnl 1985–96; memb: Latey Ctee on Age of Majority 1965–67, Cncl Law Soc 1976–92; vice pres Inst of Trading Standards Admin 1975–, pres Br Insurance Law Assoc 1988–90; chm Hamlyn Tst 1977–88; Hon DCL The City Univ 1992; hon fell: LSE 1984, QMC (now Queen Mary and Westfield) 1984; Hon MRCP 1990, Hon QC 1992; *Books* The Consumer, Society and the Law (with Lord Borrie, 1963), Introduction to Hire-Purchase Law (1967), Commercial and Consumer Credit (1982), A Review of Security Interests in Property (1989); *Style*— Prof Aubrey Diamond, QC; ✉ University of Notre Dame, London Law Centre, 7 Albemarle Street, London W1X 4NB (☎ 0171 493 9002, fax 0171 408 4465)

DIAMOND, Prof Derek Robin; s of Lord Diamond, *qv*, of Little Chalfont, Bucks, and Sadie, *née* Lyttleton; *b* 18 May 1933; *Educ* Harrow County GS, Univ of Oxford (MA), Northwestern Univ of Illinois (MSc); *m* 12 Jan 1957, Esme Grace, da of Richard Bryant Passmore (d 1982); 1 s (Andrew Richard b 1961), 1 da (Stella Ruth b 1963); *Career* lectr in geography Univ of Glasgow 1957–68, prof of geography (specialising in urban and regnl planning) LSE 1982– (reader in regnl planning 1968–82), hon prof of human geography Inst of Geography Beijing 1990; vice pres Town and Country Planning Assoc, past pres Inst of Br Geographers, hon pres Regional Studies Assoc, hon memb RTPI 1989; FRGS; *Books* Regional Policy Evaluation (1983), Infrastructure & Industrial Costs in British Industry (1989); *Recreations* philately; *Clubs* Geographical; *Style*— Prof Derek Diamond; ✉ 9 Ashley Drive, Walton-on-Thames, Surrey KT12 1JL (☎ and fax 01932 223280); London School of Economics and Political Science, Houghton Street, London WC2A 2AE (☎ 0171 955 7496, fax 0171 955 7412)

DIAMOND, Baron (Life Peer UK 1970); John Diamond; PC (1965); s of late Rev Solomon Diamond, of Leeds, and Henrietta Diamond; *b* 30 April 1907; *Educ* Leeds GS; *children* 2 s, 2 da; *Career* former dir: Sadler's Wells Trust Ltd, London Opera Centre; MP (Lab) Manchester 1945–51, Gloucester 1957–70; chief sec to the Treasury 1964–70 (memb of Cabinet 1968–70); dep chm of ctees House of Lords 1974; chm: Royal Cmmn on the Distribution of Income and Wealth 1974–79, Indust and Parliament Tst 1976–82; hon treas Fabian Soc; elected SDP ldr in House of Lords 1982–88; *Style*— Rt Hon Lord Diamond, PC; ✉ Aynhoe, Doggetts Wood Lane, Chalfont St Giles, Bucks

DIAMOND, (Peter) Michael; OBE (1996); s of William Howard Diamond (d 1979), and Dorothy Gladys, *née* Powell (d 1961); *b* 5 Aug 1942; *Educ* Bristol GS, Queens' Coll Cambridge (MA); *m* 1968, Anne Marie; 1 s (Benjamin b 1969), 1 da (Candida b 1972); *Career* chief arts and museums offr Bradford 1976–80, chm Yorkshire Sculpture Park 1978–81, memb Craft Cncl 1981–84, dir Birmingham Museums & Art Gallery 1980–95, memb Cncl Aston Univ 1983–92, bd memb Museums Trg Inst 1990–93; Hon DSc Univ of Aston 1993; FRSA 1990; *Style*— Michael Diamond, Esq, OBE; ✉ 40 Jordan Rd, Four Oaks, Sutton Coldfield, W Midlands B75 5AB (☎ 0121 308 3287)

DIBB-FULLER, Edwin; *b* 1946; *Educ* Brixton Sch of Building London; *Career* sr engr Alan Marshall and Partners consltg engrs 1970–77, project leader and sr structural engr BBC (responsible for design of regnl television studios in Manchester, Bristol, Glasgow and Belfast) 1977–85, profession chm Southern Region and ptnr Building Design Partnership 1985–93 (responsible for the design of several commercial projects incl

London HQ Morgan Guarantee Company of NY); dir Oscar Faber consltg engrs 1993–; CEng, FIStructE; *Style—* Edwin Dibb-Fuller, Esq; ✉ Oscar Faber Consulting Engineers, 23 Middle Street, London EC1A 7JA (☎ 0171 600 1388)

DIBBEN, Kenneth Francis; s of Stanley Cyril Dibben (d 1978), and Edna Florence, *née* Hobbs (d 1977); *b* 13 Feb 1929; *Educ* King Edward VI Sch Southampton, Worcester Royal GS, Univ of Southampton (BCom); *m* 1962, Dora Mary Bower, *née* Tunbridge; 1 s (Gye b 1975); *Career* dir: Hambros Bank 1970–78, Hambros Pacific Ltd Hong Kong 1973–78, K F Dibben & Co, Higginson & Partners Ltd 1992–93, University of Southampton Holdings Ltd 1989–, Southampton Student Halls I-IV Plc 1993–, Universities Superannuation Scheme 1985– (chm Audit Ctee), Chilworth Manor 1991–; chm: ESU Dartmouth House Club Ltd 1977–90, Kalamazoo PLC 1989–91 (dir 1978–91), Kalamazoo Inc (USA) 1988–91, Marsham Court Management Co 1989–94, Public Access Terminals 1992–, The Global Group PLC 1993–94, Chilworth Centre 1993–, Hammond Bridge 1996–; ind corp fin advsr 1978–; memb: Univs Authorities Panel 1981–93, Fin Ctee Wessex Med Tst 1993–, Bd Univs and Colls Employers' Assoc 1993–; treas Univ of Southampton 1982–; hon treas: Fountain Soc 1989–, Furniture History Soc 1990–; tstee The Mitchell City of London Charity 1979–; former hon treas Wider Share Ownership Cncl; Parly candidate (C) Barking 1959; Freeman City of London, Liveryman Worshipful Co of Chartered Accountants; FCA, CIMgt, FCT, FRSA; *Clubs* Carlton, Hong Kong (HK), ESU; *Style—* Kenneth Dibben, Esq; ✉ 3 Marsham Court, Marsham Street, London SW1P 4JY (☎ 0171 821 9153, fax 0171 630 8273); Naish Priory, East Coker, Somerset BA22 9HQ (☎ 01935 862201)

DIBBLE, Robert Kenneth; s of Herbert William Dibble (d 1973), and Irene Caroline Dibble (d 1995); *b* 28 Dec 1938; *Educ* Westcliff HS for Boys; *m* 26 Aug 1972, Teresa Frances, da of James Vincent MacDonnell; 4 s (William b 5 July 1973, Thomas b 12 April 1975, Edward b 7 Feb 1979, Matthew b 31 Dec 1980); *Career* RNC Dartmouth 1955–58, HMS Belton 1958–59, Lt HM Yacht Britannia 1959–60, HMS Caesar 1961–62, Russian interpreter's course 1962–64, mixed manned ship USS Claude V Ricketts 1964–65, long communications course 1965–66, Sqdn Communications Offr HMS Ajax 1966–67, Lt Cdr HMS Hampshire 1967–68, head of electronic warfare HMS Mercury 1968–70, def fell Kings Coll London 1970–71, Staff Ops Offr to Sr Naval Offr W Indies 1971–72, Cdr naval staff and head of electronic warfare policy MOD 1972–75, i/c HMS Eskimo 1975–76, DS Maritime Tactical Sch 1976–77; admitted slr 1980; slr Linklaters and Paines 1980–81 (articled clerk 1978–80), ptnr Wilde Sapte 1982–; Freeman: City of London, City of London Solicitors' Co, Worshipful Co of Shipwrights; *Recreations* family, tennis, music, reading, languages; *Style—* Robert Dibble, Esq; ✉ Wilde Sapte, 1 Fleet Place, London EC4M 7WS (☎ 0171 246 7000, fax 0171 246 7777, telex 887793)

DIBDIN, Michael John; s of Frederick John Dibdin, of Chichester, W Sussex, and Peigi, *née* Taylor; *b* 21 March 1947; *Educ* Friends' Sch Lisburn Co Antrim NI, Univ of Sussex (BA), Univ of Alberta Canada (MA); *m* 1, 1971 (m dis 1986), Benita, *née* Mitbrodt; 1 da (Moselle b 1975); m 2, 1987 (m dis 1995), Sybil Claire, da of John Guy Tempest Sheringham; 1 da (Emma Yvette b 1988); *Career* author; *Books* The Last Sherlock Holmes Story (1978), A Rich Full Death (1986), Ratking (winner Gold Dagger award CWA, 1988), The Tryst (1989), Vendetta (1990), Dirty Tricks (1991), Cabal (1992), The Dying of the Light (1993), The Picador Book of Crime Writing (ed, 1993), Dead Lagoon (1994), Dark Spectre (1995), Così fan tutti (1996); *Recreations* walking, wine, music; *Clubs* Groucho; *Style—* Michael Dibdin, Esq; ✉ c/o Pat Kavanagh, Peters Fraser and Dunlop, The Chambers, Chelsea Harbour, London SW10 OXF (☎ 0171 344 1000, fax 0171 352 7356 and 0171 351 1756)

DICE, Brian Charles; OBE (1997); s of Frederic Dice, MC, of Minehead, Somerset (d 1979); *b* 2 Sept 1936; *Educ* Clare Coll Cambridge (MA); *m* 22 May 1965, Wendy, da of De Warrenne Harrison (d 1983); 2 da (Nicola b 1968, Melissa b 1971); *Career* Cadbury Schweppes plc 1960–86 (dir 1979–86), chief exec Br Waterways Bd 1986–96; *Style—* Brian Dice, Esq, OBE; ✉ 28 Stratton Road, Beaconsfield, Bucks HP9 1HS

DICK, Alastair Campbell; s of David Norwell Dick (d 1992), and Margaret Marshall Shaw, *née* Mudie (d 1990); *b* 31 March 1937; *Educ* Blaydon GS, King's Coll Durham (BSc); *m* Oct 1958, Pamela Edith Thornton; 3 s (Michael Campbell b Aug 1959, Gavin Jeremy b Aug 1963, Jonathon Neil b Oct 1965); *Career* scientific offr (DSIR) Road Research Laboratory 1958–62, traffic engr Newcastle upon Tyne 1962–64, lectr in highway and traffic engrg Univ of Newcastle upon Tyne 1964–68, assoc then exec dir Freeman Fox Wilbur Smith & Associates (later Freeman Fox & Associates, now Halcrow Fox Associates) 1968–75, chief exec Alastair Dick & Associates 1975–94, dir of gp planning National Express Group plc 1994–; FIHT 1972, FICE 1981, FCIT 1994, FEng 1994; *Clubs* RAC; *Style—* Alastair Dick, Esq, FEng; ✉ April Cottage, Garden Close, Leatherhead, Surrey KT22 8LU (☎ 01372 374965); National Express Group plc, 13 Regent Street, London SW1Y 4LR (☎ 0171 930 0979, fax 0171 839 2894)

DICK, (John) Antony; s of Cdre John Mathew Dick, CB, CBE (d 1981), and Anne Moir, *née* Stewart; *b* 23 March 1934; *Educ* Trinity Coll Glenalmond, Worcester Coll Oxford (BA); *m* 15 May 1967, Marigold Sylvia, da of Rev Cecil B Verity; 1 s (Crispin b 1971), 2 da (Amy-Clare b 1972, Jasmine b 1974); *Career* RN 1952–54; qualified CA 1956; investmt mangr: Iraq Petroleum Co Ltd 1961–67, J Henry Schroder Wagg and Co Ltd 1967–68; md Kingsdrive Investment Management Ltd 1969–70; dir GT Management plc 1970–91; non-exec dir: USDC Investment Trust 1987–93, S R Pan European Investment Trust 1987–, Foreign & Colonial Eurotrust 1989–, Makepeace Ltd 1988–, The Technology Broker Ltd 1990–, Saracen Value Trust 1993–, Hotspur Investments 1993–95, Chescor Indian Investment Trust 1994–, Aquarian Explosion Wall Co 1994–, Invesco Tokyo Trust 1995–; *Recreations* sailing, psychological astrology; *Style—* Antony Dick, Esq; ✉ 26 Chalcot Square, London NW1 8YA (☎ and fax 0171 722 5126)

DICK, Brian Booth; s of James Dick, and Doris Ethel, *née* Booth; *b* 20 Dec 1943; *Educ* Kilmarnock Acad; *m* 19 Oct 1966, Caryl Anne, da of James McClure; 1 s (Alistair b 25 Oct 1972), 2 da (Laura b 26 Oct 1967, Susanna b 19 May 1969); *Career* sec: Crown Continental Merchant Bank Jamaica 1971–74, Caribbean Bank 1974–76; fin dir and sec: Lyle Shipping plc 1976–83, Noble Grossart Ltd 1983–; MICAS; *Recreations* golf, skiing, music, family; *Clubs* Royal Burgess Golfing Soc, Merchants of Edinburgh Golf; *Style—* Brian Dick, Esq; ✉ 2 Ravelston House Rd, Edinburgh EH4 3LW (☎ 0131 332 1120); Noble Grossart Ltd, 48 Queen St, Edinburgh EH2 3NR (☎ 0131 226 7011, fax 0131 226 6032)

DICK, (Raphael) Christopher Joseph; CBE; s of Capt Henry Pfeil Dick (d 1951), and Marie Louise Armandine Cornslie, *née* Van Cutsem (d 1993); *b* 3 July 1935; *Educ* Downside; *Career* cmmnd RTR 1954, IRTR 1954–60, Staff Coll 1965–67 (staff 1972–76), Sqdn Ldr 13/18 Hussars 1968–70, CO 3 RTR 1976–78, Col 1981–83, Brig 1984–88; dir: Linguaphone Inst 1988–93, PKL Ltd 1993–; memb RUSI; *Recreations* skiing, swimming, walking, sailing; *Clubs* Naval and Military; *Style—* Christopher Dick, CBE; ✉ 14 Rivermill, 151 Grosvenor Road, London SW1V 3JN; PKL, 2 Jubilee Place, London SW3 3TQ (☎ 0171 352 8111, fax 0171 351 1608)

DICK, Frank William; OBE (1989); s of Frank Dick, of Edinburgh, and Diana May, *née* Sinclair; *b* 1 May 1941; *Educ* Royal HS Edinburgh, Loughborough Coll (DLC), Univ of Oregon (BSc); *m* 1, 1970 (m dis 1977), Margaret Fish; 1 s (Frank Sinclair Shacklock b 3 Oct 1972); m 2, 18 Feb 1980, Linda Elizabeth, da of Frank Brady; 2 da (Erin Emma Louise b 18 July 1981, Cara Charlotte Elizabeth b 18 May 1985); *Career* dep dir of physical educn Worksop Coll 1965–69, nat athletics coach for Scotland 1970–79, dir of coaching Br Athletics Fed 1979–94 (resigned), coaching conslt 1995–; athletics coach: Euro Cup 1979–93, Olympic Games 1980–92, Euro Championships 1982–90, World Championships 1983–93; coach to: Daley Thompson (athletics) 1983–92, Boris Becker (conditioning tennis) 1986–89, Jeff Thompson (conditioning karate) 1986–, Mark MacLean (conditioning squash) 1987–, Gerhard Berger (conditioning Formula 1) 1990–, Katarina Witt (conditioning skating) 1991–; chm Br Assoc of Nat Coaches 1985–86; pres: Euro Athletics Coaches Assoc 1985–, Br Inst of Sports Coaching 1990–91; FBISC 1989; *Books* Sports Training Principles (1980, 1989 and 1995), Winning (1992); *Recreations* music, public speaking, jogging; *Style—* Frank Dick, Esq, OBE; ✉ The Highland, East Hill, Sanderstead, Surrey CR2 0AL (☎ 0181 651 4858, fax 0181 657 3247); 22 Suffolk Street, London SW1Y 4HS (☎ 0171 930 0003, fax 0171 930 1443)

DICK, Prof George Williamson Auchinvole; s of Rev David A Dick (d 1965), and Blanche, *née* Spence (d 1945); *b* 14 Aug 1914; *Educ* Royal HS Edinburgh, Univ of Edinburgh (MD, DSc), Johns Hopkins Univ Baltimore USA (MPH); *m* 6 June 1941, Brenda Marian, da of Samuel Cook; 2 s (Bruce b 3 Feb 1948, John-Mark b 24 Aug 1953), 2 da (Alison b 18 June 1950, Caroline b 14 April 1952); *Career* WWII Lt RAMC 1940, Capt RAMC graded specialist 1941, E Africa Cmd 1942–46 (Maj, specialist in pathology, OC Mobile Lab Br and Italian Somaliland and reserved areas, Mobile Res Unit), Lt-Col OC Med Div No IEA Gen Hosp; pathologist Colonial Med Res Serv 1946–51; fell 1947–48: Rockefeller Fndn, Johns Hopkins Univ (res fell 1948–49); scientific staff MRC 1951–54, prof of microbiology Queen's Univ Belfast 1955–65, dir Bland-Sutton Inst 1966–73, Bland-Sutton prof of pathology Middlesex Hosp Med Sch Univ of London 1966–73; asst dir Br Postgrad Med Fedn 1973–81, postgrad dean SW Thames RHA 1973–81, prof of pathology Univ of London 1966–81, hon lectr and hon conslt Inst of Child Health 1973–81, chm MARC Ltd 1981–90; pres Inst of Med Laboratory Technol (now Inst of Biomedical Science) 1966–76, treas RCPath 1973–78, pres Rowhook Med Soc 1975–94; memb: Mid Downs Health Authy W Sussex 1981–84, Jt Bd Clinical Nursing Studies 1982–85; chm DHSS/Regnl Librarians Ctee 1982–90, examiner Med Schs (UK, Dublin, Nairobi, Kampala, Riyadh, Jeddah), assessor HNS and CMS S London Coll, ret; Liveryman Worshipful Soc of Apothecaries; memb: RSM, BMA, Int Epidemiol Soc, Pathology Soc of GB (and Ireland); FRCPE, FRCP, FRCPath, MPH, Hon FLA; *Books* Immunology (1978, re-issued as Practical Immunisation 1986, Indonesian ed 1989), Immunology of Infectious Diseases (ed, 1979, Russian edn 1980), Health on Holiday and Other Travels (1982); author of over 200 scientific papers on yellow fever, arbor viruses, polio, hepatitis, multiple sclerosis and others; *Recreations* epidemiology of infectious diseases and prevention, travel, gardening, natural history; *Style—* Prof George Dick; ✉ Waterland, Rowhook, Horsham, W Sussex RH12 3PX (☎ 01403 790549, fax 01403 269180)

DICK, Dr Jeremy Peter Rose; s of Peter Dick, and Diana, *née* George (d 1983); *b* 29 Sept 1953; *Educ* Marlborough (exhibitioner), King's Coll Cambridge (exhibitioner, MA), KCH (MB BChir, FRCP, PhD); *m* 21 Sept 1985, Bridget Mary, da of Roger Gates; 1 s (Andrew b 1988), 2 da (Madeleine b 1989, Catherine b 1994); *Career* SHO Douera Hosp Algeria and house physician St Luke's Hosp Guildford 1977–78, house surgn KCH and SHO St Nicholas Hosp Plumstead 1978–79, SHO Maudsley Hosp, KCH and Brompton Hosp 1979–80, registrar in cardiology Papworth Hosp and registrar in nephrology Addenbrooke's 1980–81, SHO in neurology Nat Hosp 1982–83, res registrar in neurology Maudsley Hosp and KCH 1983–86, registrar in neurology N Manchester Gen Hosp and Manchester Royal Infirmary 1987–89, sr registrar in neurology Charing Cross Hosp 1989–91, conslt in neurology Royal London Hosp, Newham Gen Hosp and St Andrew's Hosp 1991–; Pfizer prize for res in clinical med Manchester Med Soc 1989; memb Assoc of Br Neurologists; FRSM; *Recreations* squash, golf, skiing; *Clubs* Jesters, Royal Cinque Ports Golf; *Style—* Dr Jeremy Dick; ✉ Department of Neurology, The Royal London Hospital, Whitechapel Road, London E1 1BB (☎ 0171 377 7421, fax 0171 377 7008)

DICK, Stewart John Cunningham; s of John David Cunningham Dick, of Edinburgh (d 1990), and Jessie Anderson Calder (d 1985); *b* 14 Jan 1946; *Educ* George Watson's Coll Edinburgh, Univ of Edinburgh (MA, LLB); *m* 12 April 1974, Alison Aileen Mackintosh, *née* Dickson; *Career* Wallace and Sommerville (became Whinney Murray) 1968–72, MICAS 1972, dir of corp banking Brown, Shipley and Co Ltd 1980–92 (joined 1972), dir and head of banking Henry Ansbacher & Co Ltd 1993–; non-exec dir Hampshire Trust plc; *Recreations* gardening, golf; *Clubs* Caledonian, RAC; *Style—* Stewart Dick, Esq; ✉ Ardmore, Woodlands Road, West Byfleet, Surrey KT14 6JW (☎ 01932 342755); Henry Ansbacher & Co Ltd, One Mitre Square, London EC3A 5AN (☎ 0171 283 2500)

DICKEN, Air Vice-Marshal Michael John Charles Worwood; CB (1990); s of Air Cdre Charles Worwood Dicken, CBE (d 1971), and Olive Eva, *née* Eustice; *b* 13 July 1935; *Educ* Sherborne, St Peter's Hall Oxford, RAF Coll Cranwell; *m* 31 March 1962, Jennifer Ann, da of Maj James Aeneas Dore, of the HAC; 1 s (Timothy James d 1989), 2 da (Joanna Louise, Jemma Catherine); *Career* cmmnd 1958, served Cyprus and Far E, RAF Staff Coll 1971, asst def advsr Canberra 1972–74, Uxbridge 1974–76, Nat Def Coll 1977, RAF Coningsby 1978–79, directing staff RAF Staff Coll 1980–82, OC RAF Hereford 1982–84, HQ 1 Gp 1984–85, dir of personnel (airmen) RAF 1985–88, air offr admin and air offr cmdg Support Gp 1989–92; private sec to The Rt Hon the Lord Mayor of London 1992–; Liveryman Worshipful Co of Scriveners; *Style—* Air Vice-Marshal Michael Dicken, CB

DICKENS, Barnaby John; s of Archie Bernard Dickens, and June Mary McNeile; *b* 9 June 1954; *Educ* Dulwich, Trinity Coll Cambridge (scholar, MA); *m* 13 Oct 1983, Lucy Anne, da of Sir Oliver Nicholas Millar, GCVO, FBA, *qv*; 3 s (Roland Oliver Porter b 9 April 1979, Max John Porter b 27 Aug 1981, Archie Dickens b 2 March 1994), 1 da (Marnie Dickens b 13 Nov 1985); *Career* account exec: The Creative Business 1977–78, WS Crawford 1978–79; Public Advertising Cncl LA 1980, account dir Marsteller 1984 (account mangr 1981), Bd account dir GGK London 1986–92, md Crammond Dickens Lerner 1993–; *Recreations* badminton, my family; *Style—* Barnaby Dickens, Esq; ✉ Crammond Dickens Lerner & Partners Ltd, 5–7 Carnaby Street, London W1V 1PG (☎ 0171 434 0967)

DICKENS, Christopher Roger (Chris); *b* 12 Aug 1944; *m* Elizabeth Jane; 2 s (James Christopher b 7 March 1978, Michael Harry b 19 June 1989), 1 da (Samantha Lee b 2 Jan 1976); *Career* early mktg experience with retail grocery co, later Nat Accounts Div Elida Gibbs (Unilever Group Co), formerly sales group head LWT and numerous postions with J Walter Thompson (latterly media mangr and head of outdoor), media dir Leo Burnett 1978 (vice chm 1983–84), dep chm Young & Rubicam (with mgmnt responsibility for UK and Euro media resource) 1984–87 (worldwide media dir with responsibilty for media operation NY office 1987–88), exec dir sales and md publishing British Satellite Broadcasting Limited 1988–90, re-joined Young & Rubicam (London) as worldwide media dir 1990–95 (group chm UK 1991–94), proprietor Chris Dickens Communications (int communications consultancy) 1996–; memb numerous advtg indust ctees and frequent presenter media seminars and confs; chm Postar Ltd (outdoor advertisers' audience research body) 1996–; *Style—* Chris Dickens, Esq; ✉ Chris Dickens Communications, 68 South Lambeth Road, London SW8 1RL (☎ 0171 582 3086)

DICKENS, Dr Diana Margaret; da of Frederick George Young, OBE (d 1981), of Bath, Somerset, and Nora Evelyn, *née* Evans; *b* 7 April 1938; *Educ* Sheffield HS, Univ of Bristol (MB ChB); *m* 6 June 1964, Anthony John Gilmore Dickens, s of George Edward Dickens, of Bristol, Avon; 1 s (Stephen James Gilmore b 4 June 1970), 1 da (Sandi b 23 Aug 1967); *Career* conslt psychiatrist Leavesden Hosp Watford 1974–85, gen mangr Rampton Hosp Retford Notts 1989–93 (med dir 1985–89), project mangr Forensic

Services Trent RHA 1993–95, clinical dir Dept of Mental Health Bassetlaw 1996– (consl in learning disability 1995–); vice pres RCPsych 1989–91, memb Standing Med Advsy Ctee 1988–92; FRSM, FRCPsych; *Recreations* golf, music, literature, art and design; *Style—* Dr Diana Dickens; ✉ 18 Ranmoor Court, Graham Road, Sheffield S10 3DW (☎ 0114 230 8713)

DICKENS, Prof (Arthur) Geoffrey; CMG (1974); s of Arthur James Dickens (d 1957), of Hull, and Gertrude Helen, *née* Grasby (d 1979); *b* 6 July 1910; *Educ* Hymers Coll Hull, Magdalen Coll Oxford (BA, MA), Univ of London (DLit); *m* 1 Aug 1936, Molly (d 1978), da of Capt Walter Bygott, RE (d 1959); 2 s (Peter Geoffrey b 1940, Paul Jonathan b 1945 d 1994); *Career* served RA 1940–45, 2 Lt 1941, Lt 1942, Capt 1943; fell Keble Coll Oxford 1933–49; prof of history: Univ of Hull 1949–62 (pro vice chllr 1959–62), King's Coll London 1962–67 (FKC 1967), Univ of London 1967–77; dir Inst of Historical Res 1967–77, foreign sec Br Acad 1968–78; pres: Central London Branch Historical Assoc 1980–, Hornsey Hist Soc 1982–92, German History Soc 1980–89; hon vice pres: Royal Historical Soc 1977–, The Historical Assoc 1978–; Hon DLitt: Kent, Sheffield, Leicester, Liverpool, Hull (all 1977); FBA 1966, FSA 1963, FRHistS 1947; Order of Merit (Cdr's Class) of Federal Republic of Germany 1980; *Books* 17 books and numerous articles on the Renaissance and Reformation period and local history, mainly Yorkshire; *Recreations* studying modern British painting (ca 1900–50); *Style—* Prof Geoffrey Dickens, CMG, FSA, FBA; ✉ 401 Carole House, Oldfield Estate, Fitzroy Road, London NW1 8UA (☎ 0171 586 0595)

DICKENS, Roger Joseph; CBE (1997), DL (W Midlands 1993); s of William Herbert Dickens (d 1961), of Digbeth, and Gladys Lilian, *née* James; *b* 17 Jan 1948; *Educ* Tipton GS; *m* 11 July 1981, Laraine, da of Stanley Johnson; 1 s ((Roger) James b 18 June 1982); *Career* CA; articled clerk J H Rock & Co Dudley, qualified 1969; KPMG Peat Marwick (formerly Peat Marwick Mitchell & Co): joined 1969, ptnr 1976, sr ptnr Birmingham 1986, regnl sr ptnr 1991, memb UK Bd 1991, memb Asia Pacific Bd 1994, dep sr ptnr UK 1996–; memb Cncl CBI West Midlands, vice chm and memb Cncl Birmingham C of C and Industry; chm W Midlands Industl Developement Board; Freeman City of London 1989, memb Worshipful Co of Gunmakers 1989; ATII, FCA; *Recreations* shooting; *Clubs* RAC, Mark's; *Style—* Roger Dickens, Esq, CBE, DL; ✉ KPMG, 2 Cornwall Street, Birmingham B3 2DL (☎ 0121 232 3000, fax 0121 236 6473)

DICKER, Col Geoffrey Seymour Hamilton; CBE (1965), TD (1953), DL (1963); s of Capt Arthur Seymour Hamilton Dicker, MBE (d 1974), of Oakley House, Acle, Norfolk, and Margaret Kathleen, *née* Walley (d 1971); *b* 20 July 1920; *Educ* Haileybury, King's Coll Cambridge; *m* 1942, Josephine Helen, da of F G Penman (d 1963), of Inwood, Bushey, Herts; 1 s, 2 da (1 decd); *Career* joined Royal Signals 1940, Adj 6 Armoured Divnl Signals 1943–45, GSO (2) AFHQ Caserta 1945–46 (MBE, despatches), cmmnd TA 1948, Hon Col 54 (E Anglian) Signal Regt (TA) 1960–67, Hon Col 36 (E) Signal Regt (V) 1979–85, ADC (TA) to HM The Queen 1965–70, vice chm Cncl of TA and VR Assocs 1975–80, Hon Col Cmdt RCS 1970–80, chm Reserve Forces Assoc 1976–83, vice pres (UK) Inter-Allied Confed of Reserve Offrs 1976–83; CA 1950; treas Univ of East Anglia 1973–85, pro chllr and chm of Council 1985–90; chm Eastern Region Bd Eagle Star Insurance Co 1969–86, pres Great Yarmouth Cons Assoc 1969–86, ptnr Lovewell Blake & Co of Gt Yarmouth, Lowestoft, Norwich and Thetford (ret 1983); Provincial Grand Master Norfolk United Grand Lodge of Freemasons 1980–95, Dep Grand Master Mark Grand Lodge 1986–93; treas Scientific Exploration Soc 1987–90; Hon DCL Univ of E Anglia 1985; *Recreations* sailing; *Clubs* Norfolk (pres 1992), Army and Navy, Royal Norfolk and Suffolk Yacht (Cdre 1978–80), Norfolk Broads Yacht (Cdre 1959–62); *Style—* Col Geoffrey Dicker, CBE, TD, DL; ✉ The Hollies, Strumpshaw, Norwich NR13 4NS (☎ 01603 712357)

DICKETTS, Simon Charles Hedley; s of Brian John Dicketts, of Glastonbury, Somerset, and Daphne Francis, *née* Little; *b* 13 Sept 1954; *Educ* Corchester Sch Corbridge Northumberland, St Edward's Sch Oxford; *Career* porter Christies auctioneers 1975, employed at J Walter Thompson 1976–80; Saatchi & Saatchi: joined as copywriter 1985, creative gp head 1985–92, jt creative dir 1992–95 (resigned); founding memb and jt creative dir M&C Saatchi 1995–; awards incl: 3 Gold Lions Cannes Film Advtg Awards, 12 Campaign Press Silver Awards; memb D&AD; *Recreations* food, wine, bridge, tennis, snooker; *Clubs* Mortons, The Ship Snooker; *Style—* Simon Dicketts, Esq; ✉ M&C Saatchi Ltd, 34–36 Golden Square, London W1R 4EE (☎ 0171 543 4500, fax 0171 543 4501)

DICKIE, Brian James; s of Robert Kelso Dickie (d 1994), and Harriet Elizabeth, *née* Riddell (d 1969); *b* 23 July 1941; *Educ* Haileybury, Trinity Coll Dublin; *m* 1, 1968, Victoria Teresa Sheldon, da of Edward Christopher Sheldon Price, of Glos; 2 s (Patrick b 1969, Edward b 1974), 1 da (Eliza b 1970); m 2, 1989, Nancy Gustafson; *Career* artistic dir Wexford Festival 1967–73, admin Glyndebourne Touring Opera 1967–81, gen admin Glyndebourne 1981–88, gen dir Canadian Opera Company 1989–93, currently artistic cnsllr Opéra de Nice; Liveryman Worshipful Co of Musicians; *Clubs* Garrick; *Style—* Brian Dickie, Esq; ✉ c/o L'Opéra de Nice, 4 Rue St François de Paule, F-06000 Nice, France

DICKIE, Col Charles George; TD (1975); s of Rev Robert Pittendreigh Dickie (d 1934), of Longriggend, Lanarks, and Margaret, *née* Brock (d 1962); *b* 21 Jan 1932; *Educ* Uddingston GS; *m* 5 Oct 1956, Jane Mitchell, da of William Marshall (d 1968); 1 s (Stuart b 28 Feb 1963), 2 da (Dianne b 8 May 1961, Susan b 6 Feb 1965); *Career* Nat Serv RA 1950–52; TA 1952–56 and 1963–82, RARO 1983–; RASC until 1965, subsequently RCT then staff appts SOI Liaison, US/UK L of C, Tport Branch NW Dist; Col (TA) Non-infantry HQ NW Dist; ADC (TA) to HM The Queen 1980–83; DL Merseyside 1983–88; co sec Liverpool Building Society (Birmingham Midshires Building Society 1982–92) 1972–92, chm Abbeyfield (Wolverhampton) Society Ltd 1996– (treas 1992–96); pres CBSI 1989–91 (dep pres 1988–89, memb Cncl 1980–93); civil rep W Midlands Region Forces Employment Assoc 1987–94, chm TA & VRA NW Eng 1992–96, chm SSAFA West Mids Central 1995–; treas: Mersey Synod Utd Reformed Church 1980–84, Ludlow Constituency Cons Assoc 1992–96; FCIB, FCIBS; *Clubs* Army & Navy, Inst of the RCT, Birmingham; *Style—* Col C G Dickie, TD; ✉ The Malthouse, Folley Rd, Ackleton, Shropshire WV6 7JL (☎ 01746 783420, fax 01746 783506)

DICKIE, Dr Nigel Hugh; s of John Dickie, OBE, of Oxshott, Surrey, and Inez Campbell, *née* White; *b* 4 Oct 1956; *Educ* King's Coll Sch Wimbledon, Queen Elizabeth Coll London (BSc, The Copping prize in Nutrition, PhD); *m* 24 Aug 1986, Alison Susan May, da of John Michael Duffin; 2 s (Andrew James John b 27 Feb 1988, Alexander Stuart b 8 Oct 1990); *Career* nutritionist Van den Berghs and Jurgens Ltd 1982–83, conslt nutritionist Slimming Magazine, Slimming Magazine Clubs and various leading food companies 1983–85, md Holmes & Marchant Counsel Group (formerly Counsel Ltd, PR co) 1992– (dir 1985); Freeman City of London 1989; memb: Nutrition Soc 1978, Br Dietetic Assoc 1985, Soc of Chem Indust 1985; FRSH 1991, FIFST 1991; *Recreations* good food and wine, family and home; *Style—* Dr Nigel Dickie; ✉ Holmes & Marchant Counsel, 15–17 Huntsworth Mews, London NW1 6DD (☎ 0171 402 2272)

DICKINS, Julian Grahame; s of Grahame John Dickins, of Newbury, Berks, and Claire Daisy, *née* Myers; *b* 31 Dec 1957; *Educ* St Bartholomew's Sch Newbury, Univ of Southampton (LLB), Coll of Law Guildford; *Career* admitted slr 1983; ptnr Penningtons 1986– (joined 1983); memb: PCC St Michael's and All Angels Church Enborne Berks, Newbury Dramatic Soc, Law Soc 1983; *Recreations* amateur dramatics, church organ, piano; *Clubs* Rotary; *Style—* Julian Dickins, Esq; ✉ Penningtons, 9 London Rd, Newbury, Berkshire RG14 1DH (☎ 01635 523344, fax 01635 523444)

DICKINS, Rob; s of Percy Charles Dickins, of London, and Sylvia Marjorie, *née* Jones; *b* 24 July 1950; *Educ* Ilford Co HS, Loughborough Univ (BSc); *Partner* Cherry Gillespie (actress); *Career* Warner Bros Music (now Warner Chappell Music): promotion mangr, professional mangr 1973–74, md 1974–79 (signed The Sex Pistols, Vangelis, Madness and Whitesnake); head of int WB Music 1979–83, chm WEA Records UK 1983 (signed Howard Jones 1983 whose first album sold over 2 million world-wide), estab two-label structure WEA and East West (with Ramon Lopez chm Warner Int), fndr Blanco Y Negro Records (with Geoff Travis), currently chm Warner Music (UK) Ltd; memb Cncl BPI (former chm); *Recreations* Victorian art, gardening, writing; *Clubs* Groucho; *Style—* Rob Dickins, Esq; ✉ Warner Music UK, The Warner Building, 28 Kensington Church Street, London W8 4EP (☎ 0171 937 8844, fax 0171 938 3901)

DICKINSON, (Vivienne) Anne (Mrs Basil Phillips); da of Oswald Edward (d 1956), of Mapperley Park, Nottingham, and Ida Ismay Harris (d 1984); *b* 27 Sept 1931; *Educ* Nottingham Girls HS; *m* 1, 15 March 1951 (m dis 1961), John Kerr Large, s of Maj Thomas Large (d 1959), of Cotgrave, Notts; m 2, 22 June 1979, David Hermas Phillips (d 1989); m 3, 19 March 1993, Basil Phillips, OBE; *Career* exec Crawford 1960–64; promotions ed: Good Housekeeping 1964–65, Harpers Bazaar 1965–67; dir: National Magazine Co 1967–68, Benson PR Ltd 1968–70 (md 1970–71); bought Kingsway PR Ltd (formerly Benson PR) 1971 (sold to Saatchi & Saatchi 1985), exec chm Rowland Co 1990 (ret), dir The Birkdale Group PLC 1991–, chm Leedex Cornerstone 1991–93; chm Woman of the Year Lunch 1983–85 (vice chm 1987–90), vice chm PRCA 1978–82 and 1990, PR Professional of the Year 1988; chm: Family Welfare Assoc 1990–94, Counsellors in Public Policy 1992–93, Bd of Mgmnt PRCA 1992–95, Graduate Appoints Ltd 1993–94; Freeman City of London 1990, Liveryman Worshipful Co of Marketors 1990; FIPR 1986, CIMgt 1986, FInstD 1987, MInstM 1979; *Recreations* riding; *Style—* Miss Anne Dickinson; ✉ St Mary's House, Church Square, Rye, Sussex

DICKINSON, Brian Henry Baron; s of Alan E F Dickinson (d 1978), and Ethel M Dickinson (d 1980); *b* 2 May 1940; *Educ* Leighton Park Sch Reading, Balliol Coll Oxford (BA); *m* 26 May 1971, Sheila Minto; *Career* MAFF: asst princ 1964–68, princ 1968–75; asst sec Dept of Prices and Consumer Protection 1975–78; MAFF: asst sec 1978–84, grade 3 1984–, under sec (food safety) 1989–96, under sec (animal health) 1996–; *Style—* Brian Dickinson, Esq; ✉ Ministry of Agriculture, Fisheries and Food, Government Buildings (Toby Wing), Hook Rise South, Tolworth, Surbiton, Surrey KT6 7NF (☎ 0181 330 8141, fax 0181 330 8140)

DICKINSON, (Paul) Bruce; s of Bruce Dickinson, of Aachen, Germany, and Sonja, *née* Hartley; *b* 7 Aug 1958; *Educ* Oundle, King Edward VII GS Sheffield, QMC London (BA); *m* 1, 1984 (m dis 1987), Jane Barnett; m 2, Paddy Bowden, da of late Col Walter Bowden, of USA; 2 s (Austin Matthew, Griffin Michael), 1 da (Kia Michelle); *Career* singer, songwriter, broadcaster and author; first professional group Samson: joined 1979, 4 albums, UK tour, left 1981; Iron Maiden: joined 1981, 11 albums, world tour with each album, left 1993; 4 solo albums and 3 world tours since 1990; awarded over 100 Gold and Platinum Discs, No 1 single Bring Your Daughter to the Slaughter 1991; film soundtrack credits: Nightmare on Elm Street, Incubus; TV acting debut in The Paradise Club (BBC) 1990, dir various music videos; presenter Bruce Dickinson Rock Show (Radio 1) 1995, winner Silver Sony Radio Award 1994; charity involvements incl: Prince's Tst concert, NSPCC, Make A Wish Fndn USA, Rock Aid Armenia, various drug and alcohol rehabilitation clinics; qualified nat fencing referee and amateur coach, winner Nat Team Foil Championships with Hemel Hempstead Club 1989, ranked no 7 in UK 1989; *Books* The Adventures of Lord Iffy Boatrace (1990), The Missionary Position (1992); *Recreations* flying, fencing, railways; *Style—* Bruce Dickinson, Esq; ✉ c/o The Sanctuary Group plc, The Colonnades, 82 Bishop's Bridge Rd, London W2 6BB (☎ 0171 243 0640, fax 0171 243 0470)

DICKINSON, Prof Harry Thomas; s of Joseph Dickinson (d 1979), and Elizabeth Stearman, *née* Warriner (d 1979); *b* 9 March 1939; *Educ* Gateshead GS, Univ of Durham (BA, DipEd, MA), Univ of Newcastle (PhD), Univ of Edinburgh (DLitt); *m* 26 Aug 1961, Jennifer Elizabeth, da of Albert Galtry, of Kilham, E Yorks; 1 s (Mark James b 1967), 1 da (Anna Elizabeth b 1972); *Career* Earl Grey fell Univ of Newcastle 1964–66; Univ of Edinburgh: asst lectr 1966–68, lectr 1968–73, reader 1973–80, prof of Br history 1980–; concurrent prof of history Nanjing Univ China 1987–; author of many historical essays and articles, ed History; FRHistS; *Books* The Correspondence of Sir James Clavering (1967), Bolingbroke (1970), Walpole and the Whig Supremacy (1973), Politics and Literature in the Eighteenth Century (1974), Liberty and Property (1977), Political Works of Thomas Spence (1982), British Radicalism and the French Revolution (1985), Caricatures and the Constitution (1986), Britain and the French Revolution (1989), The Politics of the People in Eighteenth-Century Britain (1995); *Style—* Prof Harry Dickinson; ✉ 44 Viewforth Terrace, Edinburgh EH10 4LJ (☎ 0131 229 1379); History Department, University of Edinburgh, Edinburgh EH8 9JY (☎ 0131 650 3785, fax 0131 650 3784)

DICKINSON, Very Rev the Hon Hugh Geoffrey; s of Hon Richard Sebastian Willoughby Dickinson, DSO (d 1935), of Washwell House, Painswick, Glos; raised to the rank of a baron's son, which would have been his had his father survived to succeed to the title, 1944; *b* 17 Nov 1929; *Educ* Westminster, Trinity Coll Oxford, Cuddesdon Theol Coll; *m* 29 June 1963, Jean Marjorie, da of Arthur Storey, of Leeds; 1 s, 1 da; *Career* ordained 1956; chaplain: Trinity Coll Cambridge 1958–63, Winchester Coll 1963–69; bishop's advsr for adult education Coventry Diocese 1969–77, vicar of St Michael's St Albans 1977–86, dean of Salisbury 1986–96; *Style—* The Very Rev the Hon Hugh Dickinson; ✉ 22 St Peter's Road, Cirencester, Glos GL7 1GR (☎ 01285 657710)

DICKINSON, Prof (Christopher) John; s of Reginald Ernest Dickinson (d 1978), of London, and Margaret, *née* Petty (d 1983); *b* 1 Feb 1927; *Educ* Berkhamsted Sch, Univ of Oxford (MSc, MA, DM), UCH Med Sch; *m* 26 June 1953, Elizabeth Patricia, da of William Patrick Farrell (d 1985), of London; 2 s (Mark John b 1956, Paul Tabois b 1965), 2 da (Emma Elizabeth b 1955, Caroline Margaret b 1958); *Career* Capt RAMC (jr med specialist) 1955–56; house appts UCH 1953–54; Middx Hosp: med registrar 1957–58, res fell 1959–60; Rockefeller fell Cleveland Clinic USA 1960–61; UCH 1961–75: lectr, sr lectr, conslt; prof of med St Bartholomew's Hosp Med Coll 1975–92 (now emeritus); memb: Med Res Cncl 1986–90, Assoc of Physicians; former chm: Med Res Soc, Assoc Clinical Profs of Med; former vice pres RCP; former sec: Harveian Soc, Euro Soc Clinical Investigation; MRCP 1956, FRCP 1968, ARCO 1987, FRSA 1994; *Books* Electrophysiological Technique (1950), Clinical Pathology Data (1951 & 1957), Clinical Physiology (1959, 5 edn, 1985), Neurogenic Hypertension (1965), Computer Model of Human Respiration (1977), Software for Educational Computing (1980), Neurogenic Hypertension II (1990); *Recreations* theatre, opera, playing the organ; *Clubs* Garrick; *Style—* Prof John Dickinson; ✉ Griffin Cottage, 57 Belsize Lane, London NW3 5AU (☎ 0171 431 1845); Wolfson Institute of Preventive Medicine, Charterhouse Square, Medical College of St Bartholomew's Hospital, London EC1M 6BQ (☎ 0171 982 6219, fax 0171 982 6270)

DICKINSON, Prof John Philip; s of George Snowden Dickinson (d 1974), of Morecambe, and Evelyn, *née* Stobbart; *b* 29 April 1945; *Educ* Univ of Cambridge (BA, MA), Univ of Leeds (MSc, PhD); *m* 17 Feb 1968, Christine, da of Maurice Houghton (d 1980), of Morecambe; 1 s (Anthony), 2 da (Rachel, Vanessa); *Career* lectr: Univ of Leeds 1968–71, Univ of Lancaster 1971–75; sr lectr: Univ of Western Aust 1975–80, Univ of

Dundee 1980–81; prof of accounting Univ of Stirling 1981–85; Univ of Glasgow: prof of accounting and fin 1985, head Dept of Accounting and Fin 1987–91, dir Glasgow Business Sch 1987–89, dean Faculty of Law and Fin Studies 1989–92; princ King Alfred's Coll Winchester 1992–, dist organiser Christian Aid 1989–92; chm Br Accounting Assoc 1994–95; FASA CPA 1976, FIMgt 1980, FRSA 1980, FCIS 1992 (ACIS 1976); *Books* Statistics for Business Finance and Accounting (1976), Portfolio Theory (1974), Risk and Uncertainty in Accounting and Finance (1974), Portfolio Analysis and Capital Markets (1976), Management Accounting: An Introduction (1988), Statistical Analysis in Accounting and Finance (1990); *Recreations* photography, travel, languages, poetry; *Style—* Prof John Dickinson; ✉ Holm Lodge, St James' Lane, Winchester, Hants SO22 4NY (☎ 01962 862280, fax 01962 877669); King Alfred's College, Winchester, Hants SO22 4NR (☎ 01962 827221, fax 01962 879033)

DICKINSON, Lorna; da of Michael Eugene Dickinson, of Sidmouth, Devon, and Barbara, *née* Benfield; *b* 20 Dec 1958; *Educ* Homelands Sch Derby, Univ of Warwick (BA); *m* 4 June 1983, Michael Ingham, BBC football corr; *Career* currently exec prodr Entertainment/Features LWT; credits incl: Sunday Sunday, The Late Clive James, An Audience with Mel Brooks, An Audience with Billy Connolly, The World According to Smith and Jones, Clive James meets Katharine Hepburn, The Dame Edna Experience, Aspel and Company, The Trouble with Michael Caine (Gold Award New York Int Film & TV Festival), The Trouble with Joan Collins, The Trouble with Agatha Christie, Two Rooms - A Celebration of the Songs of Elton John and Bernie Taupin (prodr and dir), 30 Years of James Bond (prodr and dir), BAFTA 1994 and 1996, An Audience with Bob Monkhouse, An Audience with Ken Dodd, Schofield in Hawaii (Prospect Pictures), Robin Williams in the Wild with the Dolphins (Tigress), Page Three (Original), An Audience with Freddie Starr, One in a Million; *Style—* Ms Lorna Dickinson; ✉ c/o LWT, The London Television Centre, Upper Ground, London SE1 9LT (☎ 0171 261 3618/3062)

DICKINSON, Patric Laurence; s of John Laurence Dickinson, and April Katherine, *née* Forgan, of Stroud, Glos; *b* 24 Nov 1950; *Educ* Marling Sch, Exeter Coll Oxford (MA); *Career* res asst Coll of Arms 1968–78, Rouge Dragon Pursuivant of Arms 1978–89, Richmond Herald 1989–, treas Coll of Arms 1995–, Earl Marshal's sec 1996–; called to the Bar Middle Temple 1979; hon treas: English Genealogical Congress 1975–91, Bar Theatrical Soc 1978–; hon sec and registrar Br Record Soc 1979–, pres Oxford Union Soc 1972, vice pres Assoc of Genealogists and Record Agents (AGRA) 1988–; *Recreations* music, cycling, swimming, walking, talking, attending memorial services; *Clubs* Brooks's; *Style—* P L Dickinson, Esq; ✉ College of Arms, Queen Victoria St, London EC4V 4BT (☎ 0171 236 9612)

DICKINSON, Prof Peter; s of Frank Dickinson (d 1978), and Muriel, *née* Porter; *b* 15 Nov 1934; *Educ* The Leys Sch, Queens' Coll Cambridge (MA), Juilliard Sch of Music NY, Univ of London (DMus); *m* 29 July 1964, Bridget Jane, da of Lt Cdr Edward Philip Tomkinson, DSO (ka 1942); 2 s (Jasper b 1968, Francis b 1971); *Career* composer; recorded works incl: piano concerto and organ concerto, Outcry, Mass of the Apocalypse, The Unicorns, Rags, Blues and Parodies, Songcycles, Surrealist Landscape, American Trio; pianist; recorded works largely with sister Meriel Dickinson (mezzo); academic posts incl: prof Univ of Keele 1974–84 (now emeritus), prof of music Goldsmiths Univ of London 1991–; numerous contribs to books periodicals and BBC radio; bd memb Trinity Coll of Music 1984; memb: Assoc of Professional Composers, Sonneck Soc USA, RSM; LRAM, ARCM, FRCO, FRSA, Hon FTCL; *Books* Twenty British Composers (ed, 1975), The Music of Lennox Berkeley (1989); *Recreations* rare books; *Clubs* Garrick; *Style—* Prof Peter Dickinson; ✉ c/o Novello & Co, 8–9 Frith Street, London W1V 5TZ

DICKINSON, Hon Peter Malcolm de Brissac; s of Hon Richard Sebastian Willoughby Dickinson, DSO (s of 1 Baron Dickinson); raised to the rank of a Baron's s 1944; *b* 16 Dec 1927; *Educ* Eton, King's Coll Cambridge; *m* 1, 25 April 1953, Mary Rose (d 1988), elder da of Vice Adm Sir Geoffrey Barnard, KCB, CBE, DSO, of Bramdean, Alresford, Hants; 2 da (Philippa Lucy Ann b 1955, Polly b 1956), 2 s (John Geoffrey Hyett b 1962, James Christopher Meade b 1963); m 2, 3 Jan 1992, J C Robin McKinley, of Blue Hill, Maine, USA; *Career* author; asst editor Punch 1952–69; chm Mgmnt Ctee Soc of Authors 1978–80; has published numerous children's books and detective novels; *Style—* The Hon Peter Dickinson; ✉ Bramdean Lodge, Bramdean, nr Alresford, Hants SO24 0JN

DICKINSON, 2 Baron (UK 1930); Richard Clavering Hyett Dickinson; s of Hon Richard Sebastian Willoughby Dickinson, DSO (d 1935) and gs of 1 Baron (d 1943); *b* 2 March 1926; *Educ* Eton, Trinity Coll Oxford; *m* 1, 1957 (m dis), (Margaret) Ann, da of Brig Gilbert R McMeekan, CB, DSO, OBE, JP (d 1982); 2 s; m 2, 1980, Rita Doreen Moir; *Heir* s, Hon Martin Hyett Dickinson b 30 Jan 1961; *Style—* Rt Hon Lord Dickinson; ✉ Painswick House, Painswick, Stroud, Glos (☎ 01452 813646)

DICKINSON, Robert Henry; s of Robert Joicey Dickinson (d 1981), and Alice Penelope, *née* Barnett (d 1985); *b* 12 May 1934; *Educ* Harrow, Christ Church Oxford (MA); *m* 3 Aug 1963, Kyra Irina, da of Laurence Boissevain; 1 s (Robert Alexander b 23 June 1964), 2 da (Emma b 19 March 1967, Laura b 23 May 1970); *Career* admitted as slr 1960, currently sr ptnr Dickinson Dees Slrs; chm: Northern Rock Building Society, Grainger Trust PLC, Kavli Ltd, Northern Investors PLC, Minet Group Pension & Life Assurance Scheme; dep chm Tyne Tees Televison Holdings PLC; dir: Northern Venture Managers Ltd, Yorkshire-Tyne Tees Television Holdings PLC, Reg Vardy PLC; *Clubs* Boodle's, Pratt's, Northern Counties; *Style—* Robert Dickinson, Esq; ✉ Styford Hall, Stocksfield-on-Tyne, Northumberland NE43 7TX; Cross House, Westgate Road, Newcastle upon Tyne, Tyne and Wear NE99 1SB (☎ 0191 261 1911, fax 0191 261 5855)

DICKINSON, Simon Clervaux; s of Peter Dickinson, of Northumberland, and Anne, *née* Chayter; *b* 26 Oct 1948; *Educ* Aysgarth Sch, Harrow (art scholar, first cricket and football XIs); *m* Hon Jessica, da of 2 Baron Mancroft (d 1987); 2 da (Phoebe Victoria b 27 Sept 1984, Octavia Jessica b 18 Feb 1986), 1 s (Milo Clervaux Mancroft b 28 June 1989); *Career* art dealer; Christies: joined 1968, dir 1974–93, sr picture dir 1990–93; proprietor Simon Dickinson Ltd and Simon Dickinson Inc 1993–; paintings discovered/re-discovered incl: Titian's Portrait of Giacomo Delfino 1977 (last previously recorded in 16th century), Watteau's Allegory of Spring 1983, Van Dyck's Portrait of Ann Carr 1983, Constable sketch for The Young Waltonians 1984, Guido Reni's Portrait of St James the Greater 1988, Claude Landscape 1989, Titian's Venus and Adonis 1991 (subsequently sold to Getty Museum for £7.5m), Hendrick Goltzius' The Crucifixion 1991 (missing since 1604), Guido Reni self-portrait 1992; *Recreations* gardening, shooting, fishing, tennis; *Clubs* White's, Boodle's; *Style—* Simon Dickinson, Esq; ✉ Simon Dickinson Ltd, 58 Jermyn Street, London SW1Y 6LX (☎ 0171 493 0340, fax 0171 493 0793)

DICKINSON, Stephen; s of Rev Arthur Edward Dickinson (d 1989), and Ada Violet, *née* Hickey (d 1972); *b* 12 Oct 1934; *Educ* Aysgarth, St Edward's Sch Oxford, King's Coll Newcastle, Univ of Durham (BA); *m* 23 March 1968, Mary Elisabeth, da of Maj Richard Quintin Gurney (d 1980), of Bawdeswell Hall, East Dereham, Norfolk; 2 s (Michael Edward b July 1969, James Stephen b May 1971); *Career* Nat Serv Flying Offr RAF 1957–59; chartered accountant 1962; CA Br Virgin Islands 1963–74, md Grainger Trust plc Newcastle upon Tyne; *Recreations* field sports, farming, cricket; *Clubs* Whites, Northern Counties, RAF; *Style—* Stephen Dickinson, Esq; ✉ Crow Hall, Bardon Mill, Hexham, Northumberland NE47 7BJ (☎ 01434 344495, fax 01434 344115); Grainger Trust plc, Chaucer Buildings, 57 Grainger St, Newcastle upon Tyne NE1 5LE (☎ 0191 261 1819, fax 0191 232 7874)

DICKS, Terence Patrick (Terry); MP (C) Hayes and Harlington (majority 53); s of Frank and Winifred Dicks; *b* 17 March 1937; *Educ* Univ of Oxford, LSE; *m* (m dis); 1 s, 2 da; *Career* clerk: Imperial Tobacco Co Ltd 1952–59, Miny of Labour 1959–66; admin offr GLC 1971–85, cncllr Hillingdon BC 1974–87; Parly candidate Bristol S 1979, MP (C) Hayes and Harlington 1983–, former memb Select Ctee on Tport; *Style—* Terry Dicks, Esq, MP; ✉ House of Commons, London SW1

DICKSON, Dr Donald Harold Wauchope; s of William Hamilton Dickson (d 1966), of Belfast, and Marie, *née* Hayes (d 1963); *b* 16 Oct 1924; *Educ* Foyle Coll Derry, Belfast Royal Acad, Queen's Univ Belfast (Dunville (1946–48) and Larmor (1947–48) research studentships, PhD 1949, cricket blue); *m* 15 Sept 1951, (Verena) Audrey (d 1991), da of Leonard Edwin Arthur Naylor (d 1972), of Iver, Bucks; 1 s (Andrew Charles Patrick b 11 July 1956); *Career* res chemist Glaxo Laboratories Ltd London 1950–54, mgmnt liaison exec and prodn controller Parke Davis & Co London 1954–60, head Dept of Chemistry Malvern Coll 1960–64, head N Antrim Further Educn Area 1964–85; CP Snow fell Univ of Texas at Austin USA 1987– (Humanities Res Centre Award 1991); Abbeyfield Soc: area chm N Antrim and N Derry 1968–85, memb Nat Cncl UK 1975–86, memb Fin and Gen Purposes Ctee UK 1981–86; Assoc of Principals of Colls: memb Salaries Superannuation and Servs UK 1974–85, chm NI 1979–80, memb UK Nat Cncl 1977–80 and 1983–85, hon memb UK 1986; govr Belfast Royal Acad 1977–79, memb Bd of Educn Centre New Univ of Ulster 1977–84; FRSC 1964; *Recreations* writing C P Snow's biography, veteran athletics (UK rep in 100, 200 and 400m IX World Championships Finland 1991, 100, 200 and 400m and 300m hurdles Euro Veteran Championships Norway 1992), rugby football (1 XV Queen's Univ Belfast 1943–45 and Belfast Royal Acad 1949–50), cricket (Ulster Schs XI 1943, N Down 1 XI 1950); *Clubs* Savage, MCC, XL, Leprechauns, Royal Portrush and Portstewart Golf, Soc of Authors, Crustaceans (Edinburgh); *Style—* Dr Donald Dickson; ✉ 3 Meldreth, Coley Ave, Woking, Surrey GU22 7BS (☎ 01483 761106)

DICKSON, Prof Gordon Ross; s of Thomas Winston Dickson (d 1962), and Florence, *née* Carruthers (d 1978); *b* 12 Feb 1932; *Educ* Tynemouth HS, King's Coll Durham (BSc, DPhil); *m* 1, Dorothy Olive (d 1989), da of (John) Wilfred Stobbs (d 1958); 2 s (Stephen Ross b 1957, John Raymond b 1962), 1 da (Kay b 1964); m 2, Nov 1991, Vicky Craigoe Adams; *Career* tutorial res student Univ Sch Agric King's Coll Newcastle upon Tyne 1953–56, asst farm dir Cncl King's Coll Nafferton Stocksfield-on-Tyne 1956–58, farms mangr Fitzalan-Howard Estates Arundel W Sussex 1958–71, princ Royal Agric Coll Cirencester 1971–73, prof of agric Univ of Newcastle upon Tyne 1973–; chm: Agric Wages Bd England & Wales 1981–84, North of England Advsy Ctee of Forestry Cmmn 1987–, Grain Co Ltd 1995–; dep chm Home-Grown Cereals 1983–94; memb: Agric & Vet Sci Sub Ctee UGC 1974–86, Min of Agric Advsy Cncl 1976–79; memb and dep chm Central Cncl Agric & Hort Co-op 1972–82; FRAgS, FIAgrM; *Recreations* sport, art; *Clubs* Farmers'; *Style—* Prof Gordon Dickson; ✉ The West Wing, Bolam Hall, Morpeth, Northumberland NE61 3ST (☎ 01661 881 696); Department of Agriculture, The University, Newcastle upon Tyne, NE1 7RU (☎ 0191 222 6869, fax 0191 222 7811)

DICKSON, Dr James Holms; s of Peter Dickson (d 1973), and Jean, *née* Holms (d 1951); *b* 29 April 1937; *Educ* Bellahouston Acad Glasgow, Univ of Glasgow (BSc), Univ of Cambridge (MA, PhD); *m* 6 June 1964, Camilla Ada, da of George Bruce Lambert (d 1970); 1 s (Peter b 1965), 1 da (Kate b 1968); *Career* fell (former res fell) Clare Coll Cambridge 1963–70, sr res asst Univ of Cambridge 1961–70; Univ of Glasgow: joined as lectr in botany 1970, later sr lectr, currently reader in botany; botanist Royal Soc expedition to Tristan da Cunha 1961, ldr Trades House of Glasgow expedition to Papua New Guinea 1987; investigator of bryophytes found with Tyrolean Iceman 1994–95; pres: Nat History Soc Glasgow, Botanical Soc Scotland; conslt to Britoil Exhibition Glasgow Garden Festival 1988; FLS 1964, FRSE 1993 (Neill Medal 1996); *Books* Bryophytes of the Pleistocene (1973), Wild Plants of Glasgow (1991), A Naturalist in the Highlands - James Robertson and his Life and Travels in Scotland (with Prof Douglas Henderson, 1994); *Recreations* gardening; *Style—* Dr James Dickson, FRSE; ✉ 113 Clober Rd, Milngavie, Glasgow, Scotland (☎ 0141 956 4103); Department of Environmental and Evolutionary Biology, University of Glasgow (☎ 0141 330 4364, fax 0141 330 5971)

DICKSON, Dr Jennifer; da of John Liston Dickson (d 1975), of Cape Town, SA, and Margaret Joan, *née* Turner (d 1980); *b* 17 Sept 1936; *Educ* Eunice HS for Girls Bloemfontein SA, Goldsmiths' Coll Sch of Art London, Atelier 17 Paris; *m* 13 April 1961, Ronald Andrew Sweetman; 1 s (William David (Bill) b 17 Aug 1965); *Career* artist, photographer, garden historian; teacher Eastbourne Sch of Art 1959–62, directed and developed Printmaking Dept Brighton Coll of Art 1962–68, graphics atelier Saidye Bronfman Centre Montreal 1970–72; sessional instr: Concordia Univ Montreal 1972–79, Université d'Ottawa 1980–85; head Dept of Art History Saidye Bronfman Centre Montreal 1985–88; visiting artist: Ball State Univ 1967, Univ of WI 1968, Univ of Wisconsin 1972, Ohio State Univ 1973, W Illinois Univ 1973, Haystack Mountain Sch of Crafts Maine 1973, Queen's Univ 1977–78; subject of CBC Special TV progs 1980, 1982, 1990 and 1995; fndr memb: Br Printmakers' Cncl, Print & Drawing Cncl Canada; Hon LLD Univ of Alberta 1988; fell Royal Soc of Painter-Etchers & Engravers, RA 1976 (ARA 1971), CM 1995; *Exhibitions* incl: The Secret Garden 1975, The Earthly Paradise 1980 and 1981, The Last Silence (Canadian Museum of Contemporary Photography) 1993 and on tour 1995; *Public Collections* incl: Nat Gallery of Canada Ottawa, Nat Film Bd of Canada, Metropolitan Museum NY, V & A London, The Hermitage Museum St Petersburg, Bibliotheque Nationale Paris; *Awards* incl: Prix de Jeunes Artistes pour Gravure Biennale de Paris 1963, Special Purchase Award World Print Competition (San Francisco Museum of Art) 1974, Biennale Prize 5th Norwegian Int Print Biennale 1980; *Books* The Hospital for Wounded Angels (1988), The Royal Academy Gardener's Journal (1991); *Recreations* opera, film, visiting gardens; *Style—* Dr Jennifer Dickson, CM, RA; ✉ 20 Osborne Street, Ottawa, Ontario K1S 4Z9, Canada (☎ 00 1 613 730 2083, fax 00 1 613 730 1818, studio ☎ 00 1 613 233 2315); Wallack Galleries, 203 Bank St, Ottawa, Ontario K2P 1W7, Canada (☎ 00 1 613 235 4339, fax 00 1 613 235 0102)

DICKSON, Jeremy David Fane; s of Lt-Col J D L Dickson, MC (d 1959), and Elizabeth Daphne, *née* Fane; *b* 23 June 1941; *Educ* Marlborough, Emmanuel Coll Cambridge (MA); *m* 9 Oct 1965, Patricia, da of Laurence Cleveland Martin (d 1980); 1 s (James David Laurence b 30 Jan 1970), 1 da (Lucy Camilla b 25 June 1971); *Career* ptnr Coopers & Lybrand 1977 (chm Worldwide Insur Gp), chm Insur Ctee Fedn des Experts Comptables Euro; FCA; *Recreations* golf, cricket, shooting, philately; *Clubs* MCC, Royal Wimbledon Golf, Hunstanton Golf; *Style—* Jeremy Dickson, Esq; ✉ 8 Alan Rd, Wimbledon, London SW19 7PT (☎ 0181 946 5854); Coopers & Lybrand, 1 Embankment Place, London WC2N 6NN (☎ 0171 212 5156, fax 0171 212 5510)

DICKSON, Michael Douglas (Mike); s of Dr (William) Powell Greenlie Dickson (d 1986), of Lancaster, and Muriel Constance, *née* MacKinnon; *b* 25 Jan 1948; *Educ* Sedbergh, Coll for Distributive Trades London (HNC Business Studies); *m* 30 Aug 1986, Elizabeth Anne, da of Graham George Giles; 2 s (Edward Alexander Dickson b 4 Sept 1987, William George Dickson b 20 June 1989); *Career* KMP Partnership advtg agency London 1967–71, bdcaster Radio Hong Kong 1971, Lintas London 1972–76, TBWA 1976–80, dep md Astral Advertising 1980–82, dir Aspect Advertising 1982–85, ptnr Edwards Martin Thornton 1985–88, mgmnt bd dir DMB&B 1988–; memb Mktg Soc

1980; *Publications* Marketing: Communicating with the Consumer (contrib, 1992); *Recreations* sailing (former vice chm Sigma Class Assoc); *Clubs* Royal Ocean Racing; *Style*— Mike Dickson, Esq; ✉ Meadowbrook Cottage, Marsh, nr Aylesbury, Bucks HP17 8SP (☎ 01296 615597); D'Arcy Masius Benton & Bowles, 123 Buckingham Palace Road, London SW1W 9DZ (☎ 0171 630 0000, fax 0171 630 0033, mobile 0802 348800)

DICKSON, Murray Graeme; CMG (1961); s of late Norman Bonnington Dickson, OBE, and late Anne, *née* Higgins; *b* 19 July 1911; *Educ* Rugby, New Coll Oxford (MA), Univ of London (DipEd); *Career* ordinary seaman MN 1934–35, War Serv with Force 136 SE Asia, Maj; Prison Serv (Borstals) 1935–40, joined Educn Dept Govt of Sarawak 1947, dir of educn Sarawak 1955–66, UNESCO advsr on educn to Govt of Lesotho 1967–68; *Books* A Sarawak Anthology · Understanding Kant's Critique of Pure Reason 19 Tales from Herodotus (1989), The Best of Thucydides, Conflict and Chivalry in the 14th C; *Clubs* Royal Cwlth Soc; *Style*— Murray Dickson, Esq, CMG; ✉ 1 Hauteville Court Gardens, Stamford Brook Ave, London W6 0YF

DICKSON, Niall Forbes Ross; s of Sheriff Ian Anderson Dickson (d 1982), and Margaret Forbes, *née* Ross (d 1981); *b* 5 Nov 1953; *Educ* Glasgow Acad, Edinburgh Acad, Univ of Edinburgh (MA, DipEd), Moray House Coll (CertEd); *m* 1979, Elizabeth Selina, da of James Mercer Taggart, of Lisburn, Co Antrim; 2 da (Jennifer Margaret b 1982, Julia Amy Victoria b 1987), 1 s (Andrew James Ross b 1984); *Career* teacher Broughton HS Edinburgh 1976–78, publicity offr National Corporation for the Care of Old People 1978–79, head of publishing Age Concern England 1980–82 (press offr 1979–80); ed: Therapy Weekly 1982–83, Nursing Times 1983–88; BBC: health corr 1988–90, chief social affairs corr 1990–95, social affrs ed 1995–; visiting fell Office for Public Mgmnt 1994–; winner Business and Professional Periodical of the Year Award 1985 and 1988; memb NUJ; *Books* Ageing in the 80's · What Prospects for the Elderly? (1981); *Recreations* tennis, golf; *Clubs* Reform, Pall Mall, London; *Style*— Niall Dickson, Esq; ✉ BBC Television Centre, Wood Lane, London W12 7RJ (☎ 0181 576 4926, fax 0181 749 9016, mobile 0860 539503, pager 0181 840 7000 no 0352810)

DICKSON, Prof Peter George Muir; s of William Muir Dickson (d 1956), of London, and Regina, *née* Dowdall-Nicolls (d 1968); *b* 26 April 1929; *Educ* St Paul's, Worcester Coll Oxford (BA, MA, DPhil, DLitt); *m* 27 Oct 1964, Ariane Flore, da of Ennemond Raoul Marie Faye, of Clifton Down, Bristol; 1 da (Olimpia b 1975); *Career* res fell Nuffield Coll Oxford 1954–56, tutor St Catherine's Soc Oxford 1956–60, fell St Catherine's Coll Oxford 1960–, prof of early modern history Univ of Oxford 1989–96 (reader in modern history 1978–89, emeritus prof 1996); FBA 1988, FRHistS 1970; *Books* The Sun Insurance Office 1710–1960 (1960), The Financial Revolution in England 1688–1756 (1967), Finance and Government Under Maria Theresia 1740–1780 (1987); *Recreations* tennis, cinema; *Style*— Prof P G M Dickson, FBA; ✉ Field House, Iffley, Oxford OX4 4EG (☎ 01865 779599); St Catherine's Coll, Oxford OX1 3UJ (☎ 01865 271700)

DICKSON, Sheriff Robert Hamish; WS (1969); s of Sheriff Ian Anderson Dickson, WS (d 1982), of Cleveden Gardens, Glasgow, and Margaret Forbes, *née* Ross (d 1981); *b* 19 Oct 1945; *Educ* Glasgow Acad, Drumtochty Castle, Glenalmond Coll, Univ of Glasgow (LLB); *m* 12 Aug 1976, Janet Laird, da of Alexander Campbell (d 1987), of Dykehead Schoolhouse, Port of Menteith; 1 s (Graeme Ross Campbell b 13 Nov 1977); *Career* legal asst Edinburgh 1969–71, ptnr Brown Mair Gemmill & Hislop Solicitors 1973–86 (joined 1971), Sheriff of S Strathclyde, Dumfries and Galloway at Airdrie 1988– (floating Sheriff 1986–88); *Recreations* golf, music, reading; *Clubs* Elie Golf House, Glasgow Golf; *Style*— Sheriff Robert Dickson, WS; ✉ Airdrie Sheriff Court, Graham Street, Airdrie ML6 6EE (☎ 01236 751121)

DICKSON, Ruth Marjorie; MBE; da of Col Randolf Nelson Greenwood, MC, JP (d 1977), and Beatrice Marion, *née* Montfort-Bebb (d 1949); *b* 9 Feb 1923; *Educ* St Margarets Welwyn Herts, Eastbourne Coll (Dip Domestic Econ); *m* 12 May 1944, Col David E Livingstone Dickson, TD, DL (d 1984), s of Frederick Livingstone Dickson (d 1960); 2 s (Duncan Charles Livingstone b 1945, Malcolm James Livingstone b 1949); *Career* ATS 1940, cmmnd 1941, discharged 1943; fndr Ruth Dickson Tst for Disabled 1974–; pres: Stone Handicapped Club, Stafford Multiple Sclerosis Club; former memb and chm Stone RDC (joined 1958), memb Stafford Borough Cncl 1974–, Mayor 1974–75, JP until 1991; *Recreations* gardening, gundogs; *Style*— Mrs Ruth Dickson, MBE; ✉ Hill Cottage, Barlaston, Stoke on Trent ST12 9DQ (☎ 01782 372434)

DIDSBURY, (Michael) Peter Townley; s of William Didsbury (d 1975), and Edith Pomfrett, *née* Brown (d 1995); *b* 10 April 1946; *Educ* Hymers Coll Hull, Balliol Coll Oxford (Elton exhibitioner), Univ of Durham (MPhil); *m* Patricia Ann, da of Leonard Cooley; 1 da (Sarah Louise b 10 June 1983); *Career* schoolmaster Humberside Educn Authy 1974–80, archaeologist Humberside CC Archaeology Unit 1987–96, freelance archaeological conslt 1996–; *Books* The Butchers of Hull (1982), The Classical Farm (1987), That Old-Time Religion (1994); *Awards* Poetry Book Soc Recommendation for The Classical Farm 1987 and for That Old-Time Religion 1994, The Cholmondely Award for Poetry 1989; *Style*— Peter Didsbury, Esq; ✉ c/o Bloodaxe Books, PO Box 1SN, Newcastle upon Tyne NE99 1SN

DIEHL, His Hon Judge John Bertram Stuart; QC (1987); s of Ernest Henry Stuart Diehl, of Swansea, and Caroline Pentreath *née* Lumsdaine; *b* 18 April 1944; *Educ* Bishop Gore Sch Swansea, UCW Aberystwyth (LLB); *m* 29 July 1967, Patricia; 2 s (Robert b 1973, Stephen b 1975); *Career* asst lectr and lectr Univ of Sheffield 1965–69, called to the Bar Lincoln's Inn 1968, recorder 1984, circuit judge (Wales and Chester Circuit Office) 1990–; *Recreations* squash, golf; *Clubs* Bristol Channel Yacht; *Style*— His Hon Judge J B S Diehl, QC; ✉ c/o The Crown Court, Law Courts, St Helen's Road, Swansea

DIEPPE, Prof Paul; *b* 20 May 1946; *Educ* Caterham Sch, St Bartholomew's Hosp London; *m* 14 Aug 1971, Elizabeth Anne; 2 da (Clare Rachel b 29 April 1974, Victoria Louise b 30 April 1977); *Career* registrar Guy's Hosp 1973–74, sr registrar Bart's 1976–78 (res fell 1974–76); Univ of Bristol: sr lectr in med 1978–86, ARC prof of rheumatology 1987–, dean Faculty of Med 1995–; FRCP 1983; *Books* Crystals and Joint Disease (1983), Rheumatological Medicine (1985), Slide Atlas of Rheumatology (1985), Arthritis (1988), Rheumatology (1993); *Recreations* sailing; *Style*— Prof Paul Dieppe; ✉ Faculty of Medicine, Senate House, Tyndall Avenue, Bristol BS8 1TH (☎ 0117 928 8333, fax 0117 934 9854)

DIERDEN, Kenneth Norman (Ken); s of Norman William Dierden (d 1984), of Havant, and Marjorie Harvey, *née* Nicholas; *b* 26 Feb 1952; *Educ* Bancrofts Sch Woodford Green, Univ of Southampton (BA); *m* 28 Aug 1976, Margaret Ann, da of Walter Roland Charles Hayward, of Stoke-on-Trent; 1 da (Isabella b 1988); *Career* Freshfields Slrs 1980– (ptnr 1987–); chm Assoc of Pension Lawyers 1995–; memb Worshipful Co of Slrs; memb Law Soc, ATII; *Books* Tolley's Company Law (contrib, 1988), Tolley's Director's Handbook (contrib, 1990), The Guide to the Pensions Act 1995 (ed, 1995); *Recreations* hockey; *Style*— Ken Dierden, Esq; ✉ Freshfields, 65 Fleet St, London EC4Y 1HS (☎ 0171 936 4000, fax 0171 832 7001, telex 889292)

DIGBY, Baroness; Dione Marian; *née* Sherbrooke; DBE (1991), DL (Dorset 1983); da of Rear Adm Robert St Vincent Sherbrooke, VC, CB, DSO (d 1972), of Oxton Lodge, Notts, and Rosemary Neville, *née* Buckley; *b* 23 Feb 1934; *Educ* Southover Manor Sch; *m* 18 Dec 1952, 12 Baron Digby, *qv*; 2 s, 1 da; *Career* chm: Dorset Assoc of Youth Clubs 1966–75, Dorset Community Cncl 1977–79, Standing Conference of Rural Community Cncls and Cncls of Voluntary Service 1977–79, Dorset Small Industries Ctee of COSIRA 1982–85; govr Dorset Coll of Agric 1977–83; W Dorset Dist cncllr representing Cerne Valley 1976–86; memb: Wessex Water Authority 1983–89 (chm Avon and Dorset Customer Consultative Ctee), BBC/IBA Central Appeals Advsy Ctee 1975–80, SW Arts Management Ctee 1980–86, Bath Festival Cncl of Management 1971–81 (chm 1976–81), Arts Cncl of GB 1982–86 (chm Trg Ctee, vice chm Dance Panel, memb Music Panel), South Bank Bd 1985–88 (govr 1988–90); non-exec dir National Westminster Bank Western Advsy Bd 1986–92; memb: Bd Nat Rivers Authority 1989–96 (chm Southern Regnl Advsy Bd), Univ of Exeter Cncl 1981–95; tstee: Tallis Scholars Tst 1984–, Royal Acad of Music Fndn 1985–; chm South and West Concerts Bd 1989–; memb Bd of Mgmnt Bournemouth Orchestras Ltd 1989–; govr Sherborne Sch 1987–; fndr, chm and hon sec Summer Music Soc of Dorset 1963–; pres: Joseph Weld Hospice Tst, Dorset Opera, Dorset Craft Guild, Cncl Bournemouth Orchestras, Dorset Youth Assoc; *Recreations* skiing, sailing, tennis; *Style*— The Rt Hon the Lady Digby, DBE, DL; ✉ Minterne, Dorchester, Dorset DT2 7AU (☎ 01300 341370, fax 01300 341747)

DIGBY, 12 Baron (I 1620 and GB 1765); Edward Henry Kenelm Digby; JP (1959); s of 11 Baron, KG, DSO, MC (d 1964), and Hon Pamela, *née* Bruce (d 1978), da of 2 Baron Aberdare; bro-in-law of late Averell Harriman; *b* 24 July 1924; *Educ* Eton, Trinity Coll Oxford, RMC; *m* 18 Dec 1952, Dione Marian, DBE, DL (Dorset 1983), yr da of Rear Adm Robert St Vincent Sherbrooke, VC, CB, DSO; 2 s (Hon Henry Noel Kenelm b 1954, Hon Rupert Simon b 1956), 1 da (Hon Zara Jane (Hon Mrs Percy) b 1958); *Heir* s, Hon Henry Noel Kenelm Digby, *qv*; *Career* Capt Coldstream Gds 1947, ADC to C-in-C Far E Land Forces 1950–51; Hon Col 4 Bn Devonshire and Dorset Regt 1992–96; dir Paccar (UK) Ltd; memb Dorchester RDC 1962, cncllr Dorset CC 1966–81 (vice chm 1974–81); Lord-Lt for Dorset 1984– (DL 1957, Vice Lord-Lt 1965–84); chm RAS of the Cwlth 1967–79, dep chm SW Econ Planning Cncl 1972–79, chm Dorset Magistrates' Cts Ctee 1984–; pres: Royal Bath and W Soc 1976, Cncl St John for Dorset 1984–, Eastern Wessex TAVRA 1993–96, Relate (Dorset), Wessex Branch IOD, Dorset SSAFA; patron Dorset BRCS; KStJ 1984; *Recreations* skiing, tennis; *Clubs* Pratt's; *Style*— The Rt Hon the Lord Digby, JP; ✉ Minterne, Dorchester, Dorset DT2 7AU (☎ 01300 341370)

DIGBY, Hon Henry Noel Kenelm; s and h of 12 Baron Digby, *qv*; *b* 6 Jan 1954; *Educ* Eton; *m* 12 July 1980, Susan E, er da of Peter Watts, of 6 Albert Terrace Mews, SW1; 1 s (Edward St Vincent Kenelm b 5 Sept 1985), 1 da (Alexandra Jane Kira b 13 March 1987); *Career* gp fin controller Jardine Davies (Manila) 1980–81, asst treas Jardine Matheson & Co Ltd 1981–84, investmt mangr Jardine Fleming & Co Ltd Hong Kong 1984–, dir Jardine Fleming Investmt Mgmnt Ltd 1989; ACA; *Recreations* skiing, tennis; *Style*— The Hon Henry Digby; ✉ Jardine Fleming Holdings Ltd, 46th Floor, Jardine House, 1 Connaught Place, Hong Kong

DIGBY-BELL, Christopher Harvey; s of Lt-Col Horatio Arthur Digby-Bell, of Chichester, Sussex, and Elizabeth Margaret Ann, *née* Cochrane; *b* 21 June 1948; *Educ* Marlborough; *m* 7 Sept 1974, Claire, da of Stephen Sutherland Pilch, of Finchampstead, Berkshire; 2 s (Timothy b 1981, William b 1984), 1 da (Melissa b 1980); *Career* admitted slr 1972; Taylor & Humbert 1966–82, managing ptnr Taylor Garrett 1987–89 (joined 1982); Frere Cholmeley Bischoff: joined as ptnr 1989, sometime mktg and business devpt ptnr, currently int ptnr; hon legal advsr Down's Syndrome Assoc 1990; memb Law Soc 1972; *Recreations* cricket, golf, collecting cricket prints, photography, cooking, cinema, pop music, playing the drums, American football; *Clubs* MCC, Leander, Stewards (Henley), Berkshire Golf; *Style*— Christopher Digby-Bell, Esq; ✉ Frere Cholmeley Bischoff, 4 John Carpenter Street, London EC4Y 0NH (☎ 0171 615 8000, fax 0171 615 8080, telex 27623 Freres G)

DIGGLE, Prof James; s of James Diggle, and Elizabeth Alice, *née* Buckley; *b* 29 March 1944; *Educ* Rochdale GS, St John's Coll Cambridge (Henry Arthur Thomas scholar, Pitt scholar, Browne scholar, Allen scholar, BA, MA, PhD, LittD, Hallam prize, Montagu Butler prize, 2 Browne medals, Porson prize, Members' Latin essay prize, Chllr's classical medal); *m* 8 June 1974, Sedwell Mary, da of Preb Frederick Alexander Routley Chapman (d 1988); 3 s (Charles James b 1975, Julian Alexander b 1977, Nicholas Marcel b 1978); *Career* Univ of Cambridge: fell Queens' Coll 1966–, librarian Queens' Coll 1969–77, asst lectr in classics 1970–75, praelector Queens' Coll 1971–73 and 1978–, lectr in classics 1975–89, univ orator 1982–93, chm Faculty of Classics 1989–90 (librarian 1975–81), reader in Greek and Latin 1989–95, prof of Greek and Latin 1995–; pres Cambridge Philological Soc 1996–98 (hon sec 1970–74, jt ed Proceedings 1970–82), jt ed Cambridge Classical Texts and Commentaries 1977–, chm Classical Jls Bd 1990–97 (treas 1979–90); FBA 1985; *Books* The Phaethon of Euripides (1970), Flavii Cresconii Corippi Iohannidos... Libri VIII (jt ed, 1970), The Classical Papers of A E Housman (jt ed, 1972), Studies on the text of Euripides (1981), Euripidis Fabulae (vol 2 1981, vol 1 1984, vol 3 1994), The Textual Tradition of Euripides' Orestes (1991), Cambridge Orations 1982–93: A Selection (1994), Euripidea: Collected Essays (1994); *Style*— Prof James Diggle; ✉ Queens' College, Cambridge CB3 9ET (☎ 01223 335527, fax 01223 335522)

DIGGLE, Maj Peter John; s of Lt-Col Wadham Heathcote Diggle, DSO, OBE, MC (d 1958), of Eden House, Malton, Yorks, and Nancy, *née* Conran (d 1958); *b* 17 July 1921; *Educ* Stowe, Trinity Coll Cambridge; *m* 17 Sept 1959, Anna Sylvia, da of Freiherr von der Lancken-Wakenitz (d 1956), of Seidlitzhof, Krefeld; 2 s (Richard b 1961, William b 1962); *Career* Maj Gren Gds 1940–52, served NW Europe and Malaya; dir: J M Potter Ltd 1953–62, R C Carr Ltd, J Senior Ltd and J Haig Ltd 1962–66, City Jewellers Ltd 1965–66; fndr Diamond Investment Concept 1968, dir Inter Diamond Brokers SA 1972–76, chm Amalgamated Diamond Brokers 1976–86, dir Public Servants Housing Fin Assoc Home Ownership Club 1984–, dir Minibars (UK) Ltd 1989–; patron Harrogate Abbeyfield Soc, pres Household Div Assoc Yorks Branch, chm Sydney Smith Appeal; *Recreations* tennis, shooting, equitation; *Clubs* Army and Navy, Shikar; *Style*— Maj Peter Diggle; ✉ The Old Brewery, Thornton le Clay, York YO6 7TE (☎ 01653 81334)

DIGNAN, Maj-Gen (Albert) Patrick; CB (1978), MBE (1952); s of Joseph William Dignan (d 1964), and Rosetta Weir (d 1978); *b* 25 July 1920; *Educ* Christian Brothers Sch Dublin, Trinity Coll Dublin (MA, MD); *m* 1952, Eileen, da of James John White (d 1956); 2 s, 1 da; *Career* Brig and Consulting Surgeon FARELF 1969–71, sr consultant surgeon and asst prof of Military Surgery Queen Alexandra Military Hosp Millbank 1972–73, dir Army Surgery and consulting surgeon to the Army 1973–78, QHS 1974–78; hon consultant surgeon Royal Hosp Chelsea, hon consultant Oncology and Radiotherapy Westminster Hosp 1975–78, consultant in Accident and Emergency Medicine Ealing Hosp 1978–79; memb Acad of Med Singapore 1970–71, pres Army Medical Bds 1980–90; fell Assoc of Surgns of GB and Ireland, FRCS, FRCSI, FRSM; *Books* A Doctor's Experiences of Life (1994); *Recreations* gardening, golf; *Style*— Maj-Gen Patrick Dignan, CB, MBE; ✉ Ramridge Dene, 182 Beckenham Hill Rd, Beckenham, Kent BR3 1SZ (☎ 0181 658 7690)

DILHORNE, 2 Viscount (UK 1964); Sir John Mervyn Manningham-Buller; 5 Bt (UK 1866); also Baron Dilhorne (UK 1962); s of 1 Viscount Dilhorne, sometime Lord High Chllr and Lord of Appeal in Ordinary (d 1980, ggs of Sir Edward M-B, 1 Bt, who was bro of 1 Baron Churston) by his w Lady Mary Lindsay (4 da of 27 Earl of Crawford and Balcarres); *b* 28 Feb 1932; *Educ* Eton, RMA Sandhurst; *m* 1, 8 Oct 1955 (m dis 1973), Gillian Evelyn, er da of Col George Cochrane Stockwell, JP; 2 s, 1 da (Hon Mary Louise (Hon Mrs Cowan) b 1970); m 2, 17 Dec 1981, Dr Susannah Jane Eykyn, *qv*, da of late Cdr W C Eykyn, RN, and former w of Colin Gilchrist; *Heir* s, Hon James Edward Manningham-Buller, *qv*; *Career* Lt Coldstream Gds 1952–57, served Egypt, Germany, Canal Zone; cncllr Wilts CC 1964–66; called to the Bar 1979; md Stewart Smith (LP&M) Ltd 1970–74; memb: Jt Parly Ctee on Statutory Tribunals 1981–88, EEC Select Ctee (Law & Institutions) 1986–89; chm VAT Tbnl 1989–; fell Inst of Taxation (memb Cncl

1969–82); *Recreations* skiing, opera singer (bass), shooting; *Clubs* Buck's, Pratt's, Royal St George's, Swinley Forest Golf, Beefsteak; *Style*— The Rt Hon Viscount Dilhorne; ✉ 164 Ebury St, London SW1N 8UP (☎ 0171 730 0913); 4 Breams Buildings, London EC4A 1AQ (☎ 0171 353 5835)

DILKE, Sir John Fisher Wentworth; 5 Bt (UK 1862), of 76 Sloane Street, Chelsea; s of Sir Fisher Wentworth Dilke, 4 Bt, Major (TA), Lloyd's underwriter (d 1944), of Lepe Point, Exbury, Hants, and Ethel Lucy (d 1959), da of W K Clifford, FRS; *b* 8 May 1906; *Educ* Winchester, New Coll Oxford; *m* 1, 15 Sept 1934 (m dis 1949), Sheila, o da of Sir William Seeds, KCMG (d 1973), sometime ambass to Brazil and Russia; 2 s (Charles John Wentworth b 1937, Timothy Fisher Wentworth b 1938); m 2, 28 Dec 1951, Iris Evelyn, only child of late Ernest Clark, of London; *Heir* s, Rev Charles John Wentworth Dilke b 21 Feb 1937; *Career* HM Foreign Service 1929–32, sub editor and foreign correspondent for The Times 1936–39, rejoined Foreign Service 1939; *Style*— Sir John Dilke, Bt; ✉ Ludpits, Etchingham, E Sussex

DILKS, Prof David Neville; s of Neville Ernest Dilks, and Phyllis, *née* Follows; *b* 17 March 1938; *Educ* Worcester Royal GS, Hertford Coll Oxford (BA), St Antony's Coll Oxford; *m* 15 Aug 1963, Jill, da of John Henry Medlicott (d 1971), of Shrewsbury; 1 s (Richard b 1979); *Career* research asst to: Sir Anthony Eden (later Earl of Avon) 1960–62, Marshal of the RAF Lord Tedder 1963–65, Rt Hon Harold Macmillan (later Earl of Stockton) 1964–67; asst lectr then lectr LSE 1962–70; Univ of Leeds: prof of international history 1970–91 (visiting fell All Souls' Coll Oxford 1973), chm Sch of History 1974–79, dean Faculty of Arts 1975–77, dir Inst for Int Studies 1989–91; vice-chllr Univ of Hull 1991–; memb Univs Funding Cncl 1989–91; tstee: Ferens Educn Tst 1991–, Imperial War Museum 1983–90, Edward Boyle Meml Tst 1981–, Heskel and Mary Nathaniel Tst 1986–90, Lennox-Boyd Meml Tst 1984–91; pres Int Ctee for the History of the Second World War 1992–; Freeman City of London 1979, Liveryman Worshipful Co of Goldsmiths 1984; Médaille de Vermeil (French Acad) 1994, Hon Doctorate of History Russian Acad of Scis Moscow 1996; FRHistS, FRSL; *Books* Curzon in India (vol 1 1969, vol 2 1970), The Diaries of Sir Alexander Cadogan (ed, 1971), The Conservatives (contrib, 1977), Retreat from Power (2 vols, ed and contrib, 1981), Neville Chamberlain (vol 1, 1984), Barbarossa: The Axis and the Allis (ed jtly, 1994), Grossbritannien und der deutsche Widerstand (ed jtly and contrib, 1994); *Clubs* Brooks's, Royal Over-Seas League; *Style*— Prof David Dilks; ✉ Vice-Chancellor's Office, University of Hull, Cottingham Road, Hull HU6 7RX (☎ 01482 341454, fax 01482 466557)

DILLON, Andrew Patrick; s of Patrick and Kathleen Dillon, of Altrincham, Cheshire; *b* 9 May 1954; *Educ* St Ambrose Coll Hale Barns Cheshire, N Cheshire Coll of FE Altrincham, Univ of Manchester (BSc Geography); *m* Alison, *née* Goodbrand; 2 da (Emily b 3 Jan 1993, Kate b 7 March 1995); *Career* asst admin Bolton Royal Infirmary 1978–81, unit admin Queen Elizabeth Hosp for Children London 1981–83, dep unit admin The London Hosp Whitechapel 1983–86, unit gen mangr The Royal Free Hosp London 1986–91, chief exec St George's Healthcare NHS Tst London 1991–; memb: Nat Cncl NHS Tst Fedn 1995–, Health Servs Accreditation Bd 1995–; MHSM 1975; *Recreations* family, cycling, walking in the Lake District; *Style*— Andrew Dillon, Esq; ✉ St George's Healthcare NHS Trust, St George's Hospital, Blackshaw Road, London SW17 0QT (☎ 0181 725 1635, fax 0181 725 2559)

DILLON, Rt Hon Lord Justice; Sir (George) Brian Hugh Dillon; kt (1979), PC (1982); s of Capt George Crozier Dillon, RN (d 1946); *b* 2 Oct 1925; *Educ* Winchester, New Coll Oxford; *m* 1954, Alisoun Janetta Drummond, da of Hubert Samuel Lane, MC (d 1962); 2 s, 2 da; *Career* called to the Bar Lincoln's Inn 1948, QC 1965, bencher Lincoln's Inn 1973, high court judge (Chancery) 1979–82, Lord Justice of Appeal 1982–94, memb Supreme Ct Rule Ctee 1986–; *Style*— Rt Hon Sir Brian Dillon; ✉ Bridge Farm House, Grundisburgh, Woodbridge, Suffolk IP13 6UF

DILLON, 22 Viscount (I 1622); Harry Benedict Charles Dillon; also Count Dillon (Fr cr of Louis XIV 1711 for Hon Arthur Dillon, 3 s of 7 Viscount and father of 10 and 11 Viscounts, who was Col proprietor of the Dillon Regt, promoted to Lt-Gen in the Fr service, govr of Toulon, and cr titular Earl Dillon 1721/22 by the Chevalier de St Georges, otherwise known as the Old Pretender or, to his supporters, James III); s of 21 Viscount Dillon (d 1982); *b* 6 Jan 1973; *Heir* unc, Hon Richard Dillon; *Style*— Rt Hon the Viscount Dillon; ✉ c/o 28 Canning Cross, London SE5 8BH

DILLON, Viscountess; (Mary) Jane; *née* Young; *Educ* Royal Coll of Art (MDes); *m* 1972, 21 Viscount Dillon (d 1982); 1 s (Henry, 22 Viscount Dillon, *qv*), 1 da (Hon Beatrice Inès Renée b 28 Dec 1978); *Career* furniture designer; design conslt to furniture manufacturers in UK, Italy, Spain, Germany and USA; tutor Industl Design Sch RCA 1994–; external assessor to various BA courses in UK; nominated for Delta de Plata award 1979 for Actis office chair range produced by Casas of Barcelona Spain (designed in collaboration with husband); FRSA 1994; *Style*— Rt Hon Viscountess Dillon; ✉ 28 Canning Cross, London, SE5 8BH (☎ 0171 274 3430, fax 0171 274 8731)

DILLON, Martin; s of Gerard Dillon, and Maureen, *née* Clarke; *b* 2 July 1949; *Educ* St Finian's Belfast, Montfort Coll Hants, St Malachy's Coll Belfast; *m* 1, Aug 1973 (m dis 1984), Mildred Matilda, da of Albert Smyth; m 2, 1986, Katherine, da of Patrick Bannon; 1 da (Nadia b Feb 1987), 1 step s (Crawford Anderson); *Career* journalist and author; journalist Belfast Telegraph 1972–73; BBC: news reporter 1974–75, arts prodr 1975–78, ed gen progs 1979–86, ed topical features radio 1986–88, ed topical features television 1988; *Books* Political Murder in NI (1973), Rogue Warrior of the SAS: A Biography of Lt-Col Paddy 'Blair' Mayne (1987), The Shankill Butchers: A Case Study of Mass Murder (1989), The Dirty War (1990), Killer in Clowntown (1992); *Plays* for TV and radio incl: The Squad, The Waiting Room, The Dog; *Recreations* flyfishing; *Style*— Martin Dillon, Esq

DILLWYN-VENABLES-LLEWELYN, *see also:* Venables-Llewelyn

DILLY, Prof (Peter) Noel; GM, RD; s of George Frederick Dilly (d 1979), of Walsall, and Annie Winifred, *née* Fox (d 1982); *b* 25 Dec 1935; *Educ* Howardian HS Cardiff, UCH (MB BS), RCS (Dip in Ophthalmology); *m* 1, 22 Nov 1967 (m dis), Muriel Daphne, *née* Holmshaw; 1 s (Stephen George b 22 May 1968); m 2, 5 July 1979, Susan Ann, *née* Butcher; 1 da (Sarah Ann b 26 Sept 1981), 1 s (Simon George b 8 July 1983); *Career* res asst to Prof J Z Young FRS, 1960–62, house surgn UCH 1966 (house physician 1965–66), lectr in anatomy UCL 1966–67, res asst MIT USA 1969–70, sr lectr in anatomy UCL 1970–74, prof and chm Dept of Structural Biology St George's Hosp Med Sch 1974–; hon res assoc Dept of Chemistry UCL 1975–, hon assoc specialist in ophthalmology St George's Hosp 1989– (hon occulist 1984–89); yachtmaster ocean examiner RYA 1983; MRIN; fell Royal Coll of Ophthalmologists (FRCOphth); *Recreations* anything dangerous, polar exploration and deep ocean cruising, Himalayan mountaineering (4 expeditions), potholing and caving, astronomical telescope building; *Clubs* Alpine, Medway Yacht, Walton and Frinton Yacht, Wimbledon Park Golf; *Style*— Prof Noel Dilly, GM, RD; ✉ 11 Westwood Park, Forest Hill, London SE23 3QB (☎ 0181 699 7876); Department of Anatomy, St George's Hospital Medical School, Cranmer Terrace, London SW17 0RE (☎ 0181 725 5207, fax 081 725 3326)

DILNOT, Andrew William; s of A W J Dilnot, and P J Dilnot, *née* Ozmond; *b* 19 June 1960; *m* Catherine, *née* Morrish; 2 da (Rosemary b 29 Sept 1990, Julia b 30 March 1993); *Career* Inst for Fiscal Studies: research asst rising to sr research offr 1981–86, dir of personal sector research 1987–90, dep dir 1990–91, dir 1991–; coll lectr in economics LMH Oxford 1987–88, dir of studies and coll lectr in economics Exeter Coll Oxford 1988–89; hon research fell Univ Coll London 1985–, visiting fell Australian Nat Univ Canberra 1986, visiting prof of social economics (Downing Meml fell) Melbourne Univ 1989, regular lectr Civil Service Coll and numerous confs; pt/t presenter Analysis (BBC Radio 4), regular contrib to TV and radio news and current affrs progs, also articles in national broadsheets; special advsr to House of Lords Select Ctee enquiries into harmonisation of European social security systems and withholding tax on investmt income; memb: Social Security Advsy Ctee 1992–, Cncl Royal Economic Soc 1993–, Fiscal Studies Task Force of the Effect of the Tax System on Innovative Activity Office of Sciene and Technol 1993–94, Retirement Income Enquiry (Anson Ctee) 1994–, Costs of Continuing Care Enquiry (Barclay Ctee) 1995–; *Books* The Reform of Social Security (1984), The Economics of Social Security (1989), Pensions Policy in the UK: An Economic Analysis (1994); also author of numerous book chapters, articles, reports and other papers; *Style*— Andrew Dilnot, Esq; ✉ The Institute for Fiscal Studies, 7 Ridgmount Street, London WC1E 7AE (☎ 0171 636 3784, fax 0171 323 4780)

DILS, Prof Raymond Ronald; s of François Gommaire Dils, of Birmingham (d 1970), and Minnie Dils (d 1968); *b* 16 March 1932; *Educ* Univ of Birmingham (BSc, PhD, DSc); *m* 29 Oct 1966, Joan Agnes, da of George Crompton (d 1945), of Stoke-on-Trent; 2 da (Ruth, Rachael); *Career* lectr Dept of Biochemistry Univ of Birmingham 1962–69, sr lectr then reader Dept of Biochemistry Univ of Nottingham Med Sch 1969–76, prof of biochemistry and physiology Univ of Reading 1976–; author of approx 100 papers in jls; vice pres Thames Valley Branch WEA; memb: Nutrition Soc, Biochemical Soc, Soc for Endocrinology; FRIC, FIBiol, CChem, CBiol; *Recreations* theatre, reading, travel; *Style*— Prof Raymond Dils; ✉ School of Animal and Microbial Sciences, University of Reading, Whiteknights, PO Box 228, Reading RG6 6AJ (☎ 0118 931 8015)

DILWORTH, Stephen Patrick Dominic; s of Patrick Dilworth, of London, and Ida Dilworth; *b* 20 Oct 1951; *Educ* St Joseph's Acad Blackheath, Open Univ (BA); *children*: 1 s (Nicholas b 1981), 1 da (Laura b 1982); *Career* regnl mangr Leeds Permanent Building Soc: Thames Valley 1982–86, London 1986–88; asst gen mangr of mktg Town and Country Building Soc 1988–92, Stephen Dilworth Marketing Consultancy 1992–94, head of corp affrs Bank of Ireland (GB) 1994–; dir: Soho Ltd, Yamada International plc; chm Soho Housing Assoc; FCBSI 1977, MCIM 1992, AIPR 1992, FCIB 1993; *Books* More Than A Building Society (1987); *Recreations* squash, golf, films, football, history, economics; *Clubs* RAC; *Style*— Stephen Dilworth, Esq; ✉ 12 Tovey Close, London Colney, Herts AL2 1LF (☎ 01727 826364, fax 01727 827342); Bank of Ireland (☎ 0118 960 5318)

DIMBLEBY, David; s of Richard Dimbleby, CBE (d 1965), and Dilys, *née* Thomas; *b* 28 Oct 1938; *Educ* Charterhouse, ChCh Oxford, Paris Univ, Perugia Univ; *m* 1967, Josceline Rose, *qv*, da of Thomas Gaskell; 1 s, 2 da; *Career* freelance broadcaster and newspaper proprietor; news reporter BBC Bristol 1960–61; presenter and interviewer on network programmes incl: Quest (religion), What's New (science for children), In My Opinion (politics), Top of the Form 1961–63; documentary films incl: Ku-Klux-Klan, The Forgotten Million, Cyprus - The Thin Blue Line 1964–65, South Africa - The White Tribe 1979 (RTS supreme documentary award), The Struggle for South Africa 1990 (US Emmy award, Monte Carlo Golden Nymph award), US-UK Relations - An Ocean Apart (7 films) 1988; special corr CBS News New York, film reports (and documentary film Texas-England) for 60 minutes 1966–68, commentator Current Events 1969, presenter 24 Hours (BBC1) 1969–72, chm The Dimbleby Talk-In 1971–74, films for Reporter at Large 1973, Election Campaign Report 1974; presenter: Panorama (BBC1) 1974–77 and 1980–82 (reporter 1967–69), People and Power 1982–83, BBC General Election Results programmes 1979, 1983, 1987 and 1992, This Week Next Week 1984–86, Question Time 1994–; live commentary on public occasions incl: State Opening of Parliament, Trooping the Colour, wedding of Prince Andrew and Sarah Ferguson, Queen Mother's 90th birthday parade (RTS outstanding documentary award), meml services incl Sir Laurence Olivier (RTS outstanding documentary award); chm: Wandsworth Borough News Ltd 1986– (md 1979–86), Dimbleby and Sons Ltd 1986– (md 1966–86); *Books* An Ocean Apart (with David Reynolds, 1988); *Style*— David Dimbleby, Esq; ✉ 14 King St, Richmond, Surrey TW9 1NF

DIMBLEBY, Jonathan; s of Richard Dimbleby, CBE (d 1965), and Dilys, *née* Thomas; *b* 31 July 1944; *Educ* UCL (BA); *m* 1968, Bel Mooney, *qv*; 1 s (Daniel Richard b 1974), 1 da (Katherine Rose b 1980); *Career* freelance journalist, broadcaster and author; TV and radio reporter BBC Bristol 1969–70, World at One (BBC Radio) 1970–71, This Week (Thames TV) 1972–78 and 1986–88, prodr and presenter Jonathan Dimbleby in South America (Thames) 1979, Jonathan Dimbleby in Evidence - The Police 1980 (Thames), The Bomb (Thames) 1980, The Eagle and the Bear (Thames) 1981, The Cold War Game (Thames) 1982, The American Dream (Thames) 1984, Four Years On - The Bomb (Thames) 1984, assoc ed and presenter First Tuesday series (Thames) 1982–85, ed documentary series Witness (Thames) 1986–88, presenter and ed Jonathan Dimbleby on Sunday (TV-am) 1985–86, presenter On the Record (BBC TV) 1988–93, writer and presenter Review of the Year 1989 and 1990 and Russia at the Rubicon (BBC) 1990, interview with President Gorbachev (BBC) 1990, Election Call (BBC) 1992, chm Any Questions? (BBC Radio) 1987–, presenter Any Answers? (BBC Radio) 1988–, co-deviser and host The Brain Game (Channel 4) 1992, writer and presenter Charles - The Private Man, The Public Role (Central) 1994, presenter Jonathan Dimbleby (LWT) 1995–; pres Cncl for Protection of Rural England 1992–; memb: VSO, Richard Dimbleby Cancer Fund; *Awards* incl Soc of Film and TV Arts Richard Dimbleby Award (for most outstanding contrib to factual TV) 1974; *Books* Richard Dimbleby (1975), The Palestinians (1979), The Prince of Wales: A Biography (1994); *Recreations* music, sailing, tennis; *Style*— Jonathan Dimbleby, Esq; ✉ c/o David Higham Associates Ltd, 5–8 Lower John St, London W1R 4HA

DIMBLEBY, Josceline Rose; da of late Thomas Josceline Gaskell; *b* 1 Feb 1943; *Educ* Cranborne Chase Sch Dorset, Guildhall Sch of Music; *m* 1967, David Dimbleby, *qv*; 1 s, 2 da; *Career* cookery writer for Sainsbury's 1978–, cookery ed Sunday Telegraph 1982–, regular contrib to BBC Good Food Magazine 1993–; regular demonstrator annual BBC Cooking & Kitchen shows and others, occasional TV incl Masterchef and Good Food Prog (both BBC); André Simon Award 1979, Glenfiddich Cookery Writer of the Year Award 1993; *Books* A Taste of Dreams (1976), Party Pieces (1977), Josceline Dimbleby's Book of Puddings, Desserts and Savouries (1979), Favourite Food (1983), The Essential Josceline Dimbleby (1989), The Practically Vegetarian Book (USA edn, 1995); for Sainsbury's: Cooking for Christmas (1978), Family Meat and Fish Cookery (1979), Cooking with Herbs and Spices (1979), Curries and Oriental Cookery (1980), Salads for all Seasons (1981), Marvellous Meals with Mince (1982), Festive Food (1982), Sweet Dreams (1983), First Impressions (1984), The Josceline Dimbleby Collection (1984), Main Attractions (1985), A Traveller's Tastes (1986), The Josceline Dimbleby Christmas Book (1987), The Josceline Dimbleby Book of Entertaining (1988), The Cook's Companion (1991), The Almost Vegetarian Cookbook (1994), The Christmas Book (1994); *Recreations* singing, travel; *Style*— Mrs Josceline Dimbleby; ✉ 14 King Street, Richmond, Surrey TW9 1NF (☎ 0181 940 6668, fax 0181 332 1356)

DIMMOCK, Prof Nigel John; s of Herbert Douglas Dimmock (d 1987), of Brookwood, Surrey, and Doreen Agnes, *née* Robinson (d 1984); *b* 14 April 1940; *Educ* Woking GS, Univ of Liverpool (BSc), Univ of London (PhD); *m* 1, 27 April 1963 (m dis), Jennifer Ann, da of John Glazier, of Bulawayo, Zimbabwe; 2 s (Nicholas b 1 Feb 1964, Simon b 26 Dec 1965), 1 da (Samantha b 1 Nov 1967); m 2, 30 Oct 1987, Jane Elizabeth Mary, da of Dr Samuel Ballantine, of Leicester (d 1985); *Career* virologist and teacher; MRC Salisbury 1961–66, Aust Nat Univ Canberra 1966–71; Univ of Warwick: lectr 1971, sr lectr 1975, reader 1982, prof 1986; visiting res fell: Melbourne 1977, Munich 1979, Vancouver 1981, Perth Aust 1987; memb: Med Advsy Ctee Multiple Sclerosis, Br Soc of Immunologists, Soc for Gen Microbiology; ed Jl of Gen Virology 1980–88; *Books* Introduction to Modern Virology (with S B Primrose, 1987, 2 edn 1994), Neutralization of Animal Viruses (1993), Mims' Pathogenesis of Infectious Disease (jtly, 1995); *Recreations* theatre, books, working with wood, road running; *Style*— Prof Nigel Dimmock; ✉ Department of Biological Sciences, University of Warwick, Coventry CV4 7AL (☎ 01203 523593, fax 01203 523568)

DIMMOCK, Rear Adm Roger Charles; CB (1988); s of Frank Charles Dimmock (d 1992), and Ivy Annie May, *née* Archer (d 1989); *b* 27 May 1935; *Educ* Price's Sch; *m* 1958, Lesley Patricia Reid; 3 da (Sandra b 1959, Jacqueline b 1960 d 1987, Nicola b 1963); *Career* entered RN 1953; pilot's wings FAA 1954, USN 1955, qualified flying instr 1959; Master Mariner Foreign Going Cert of Serv 1979; served RN Air Sqdns and HM Ships Bulwark, Albion, Ark Royal, Eagle, Hermes, Anzio, Messina, Murray, Berwick (i/c), Naiad (i/c); CSO to FO Carriers and Amphibious Ships 1978–80; cmd RNAS: Culdrose 1980–82, HMS Hermes 1982–83; dir Naval Air Warfare MOD 1983–84, Naval Sec 1985–87, Flag Offr Naval Air Cmd 1987–88; chm tstees Fleet Air Arm Museum 1987–88; dir: Archer Mullins Ltd 1990–, Charnauds Ltd 1992–; pres: RN Hockey Assoc 1985–90, Combined Services Hockey Assoc 1987–93, Denmead-Hambledon Branch RNLI 1981–; memb Ctee of Mgmnt RNLI 1987–; memb IOD 1994–; *Recreations* hockey umpire, cricket, squash, golf, family and friends; *Clubs* Royal Naval, Royal Albert Yacht; *Style*— Rear Adm Roger Dimmock, CB; ✉ Beverley House, 19 Beverley Grove, Farlington, Portsmouth, Hants PO6 1BP

DIMSON, Prof Elroy; s of David Dimson, of London, and Phyllis, *née* Heilpern; *b* 17 Jan 1947; *Educ* Univ of Newcastle upon Tyne (BA), Univ of Birmingham (MCom), Univ of London (PhD); *m* 1 July 1969, Dr Helen Patricia Dimson, da of Max Sonn, of Whitley Bay; 3 s (Jonathan Ashley b 1971, Benjamin Simon b 1979, Daniel Marc b 1986), 1 da (Susanna Rachel b 1973); *Career* Tube Investments 1969–70, Unilever Ltd 1970–72; currently prof of fin London Business Sch (joined 1972, dean MBA Progs 1986–90, chair Fin Faculty 1992–94); chm The German Investment Trust plc; dir: Hoare Govett Indices Ltd, Mobil Trustee Co Ltd; bd memb: Journal of Banking and Finance, Journal of Investing, Advances in Finance Investment and Banking; formerly visiting prof: Univ of Chicago, Univ of California (Berkeley), Univ of Hawaii, Euro Inst Brussels, Bank of England; advsr: SIB, Stock Exchange; *Books* Risk Measurement Service (with Paul Marsh, 1979–) Cases in Corporate Finance (with Paul Marsh, 1988), Stock Market Anomalies (1988), author of numerous published papers; *Style*— Prof Elroy Dimson; ✉ London Business School, Sussex Place, Regents Park, London NW1 4SA (☎ 0171 262 5050, fax 0171 724 3317, telex 27461, e-mail Edmimson@lbs.lon.ac.uk)

DIMSON, Gladys Felicia; CBE (1976); da of late I Sieve; *Educ* Laurel Bank Sch Glasgow, Univ of Glasgow, LSE; *m* Dr Samuel Barnet Dimson, MD, FRCP (d 1991); 1 da (Wendy); *Career* memb: GLC for Battersea North 1970–85 (former chm GLC Housing Ctee), ILEA 1970–85, Bd Shelter, Cncl of Toynbee Hall 1983–91; chm: Toynbee Housing Assoc 1976–88, E London Housing Assoc 1979–94, Boleyn and Forest Housing Soc 1976–88; tstee: Sutton Housing Tst 1982–90, Shelter Housing Aid Centre; co-pres Na-amat (int orgn of working women and volunteers) 1993–; FRSA 1976; *Style*— Mrs Gladys Dimson, CBE

DIN, Russhied Ali; s of Matab Ali Din, of Rawalpindi, Pakistan, and Hilda Rose, *née* Dring (d 1985); *b* 8 April 1956; *Educ* Ordsall Secdy Modern, Salford Coll of Technol, Birmingham Poly (BA); *Career* designer: City Industrial Shopfitters 1978, Fitch & Co 1979, Italy Studios Giardi Rome 1980, Thomas Saunders Architects 1981, Peter Glynn Smith Assoc 1982–84 (BAA Gatwick refurbishment 1983), Allied Int Designers 1984–86; formed DIN Associates 1986– (became Ltd Co 1988); design conslt to Next Retail plc 1987 (incl Department X concept Oxford St 1988), top office exhibition 1988, designed theatre set and costumes for Leicester Haymarket Theatre 1991; other projects incl: Conran Habitat USA 1991, Polo Ralph Lauren Paris 1991; external assessor Kingston Poly and Ecole Superiure D'Arts Graphiques & D'Architecture Interiure (ESAG); Young Business Person of the Year (Observer and Harvey Nichols) 1991; MCSD 1991; *Recreations* equestrian pursuits, tennis; *Style*— Russhied Din, Esq; ✉ DIN Associates Ltd, 32 St Oswalds Place, London SE11 5JE (☎ 0171 582 0777)

DINAN, Prof Timothy; *b* 25 July 1955; *Educ* MD (NUI), PhD (London), DSc (NUI), MA (NY); *Career* currently prof and head Dept of Psychological Med St Bartholomew's Hosp London; author of over 100 peer reviewed papers on neuroendocrine aspects of depression and on the treatment of resistant depression; FRCPsych 1994, FRCPI 1995; *Style*— Prof Timothy Dinan; ✉ Department of Psychological Medicine, St Bartholomew's Hospital, West Smithfield, London EC1A 7BE (☎ 0171 601 8138, fax 0171 601 7969, e-mail T.G.DINAN@mds.qmw.ac.uk)

DINARDO, Carlo; s of Nicandro Dinardo (1987), and Rosaria, *née* Iannacone; *b* 5 July 1939; *Educ* St Patrick's HS Coatbridge Scotland, Paddington Tech Coll, Tech Coll Coatbridge Scotland, Univ of Strathclyde; *m* 30 Aug 1962, Irene Rutherford, da of William James Niven (d 1977), of Helensburgh; 1 s (Mark b 27 April 1967), 2 da (Karen b 24 Oct 1965, Lorraine b 7 Aug 1973); *Career* fndr ptnr own practice of consulting engrs 1969; princ: Dinardo & Ptnrs 1978–, Dinardo Partnership 1990–; dir Scottish Conslts Int 1987–90; memb Ctee: Educn Task Gp Inst of Structural Engrs 1987–, Industl Trg Advsy Bd Paisley Coll of Technol, Inst of Engrg and Shipping Scotland 1994–; memb Bd of Govrs of Westbourne Sch for Girls Glasgow 1984–91; CEng 1965, MIStructE 1965, MICE 1967, FIStructE 1976, FICE 1976, MIHT 1979, FInstPet 1979, ACIArb 1980, FGS 1982, FIHT 1982, MConsE 1984, MASCE 1991, FEANI, FHKIE 1992; *Publications* author of papers published in learned jls; *Recreations* golf, skiing, fishing, rugby, curling, historical travels; *Clubs* Royal Northern & Univ (Aberdeen), Buchanan Castle Golf (Drymen), Glasgow Golf, Royal Aberdeen Golf; *Style*— Carlo Dinardo, Esq; ✉ Tighness, Kirkhouse Rd, Killearn, Glasgow G63 9ND (☎ 01360 550298); Dinardo Partnership Ltd, Mirren Court, 119 Renfrew Rd, Paisley, Renfrewshire PA3 4EA (☎ 0141 889 1212, fax 0141 889 5446, car tel 0860 836757)

DINEEN, Michael Laurence; s of John Leonard Dineen, of Winchester and Kendal, and Nancy Margaret, *née* Carter; *b* 17 July 1949; *Educ* Brockenhurst GS, Keble Coll Oxford (BA in PPE), Magdalene Coll Cambridge (LLB); *Career* lectr Dorset Inst of Higher Educn 1974–78, called to the Bar Inner Temple 1977 (practising barr 1978–); memb Panel of Arbitrators Western Circuit Arbitration 1993–; wine treas Western Circuit 1990–93; *Recreations* wine and food, talking, walking; *Clubs* Reform, Hampshire (Winchester); *Style*— Michael Dineen, Esq; ✉ 18 Carlton Crescent, Southampton, Hants SO15 2XR (☎ 01703 639001, fax 01703 339625); All Saints Chambers, 9–11 Broad St, Bristol BS1 2HP

DINGEMANS, Rear Adm Peter George Valentin; CB (1990), DSO; s of Dr George Albert Dingemans (d 1993), of Grenofen, Steyning, Sussex, and Marjorie Irene, *née* Spong; *b* 31 July 1935; *Educ* Brighton Coll; *m* 25 March 1961, Faith Vivien, da of Percy Michael Bristow (d 1986); 3 s (Timothy George b 1962, James Michael b 1964, Piers Anthony b 1966); *Career* entered RN 1953, jr offr HMSs Vanguard, Superb and Ark Royal 1953–58, 1 Lt Woolaston 1958–60, torpedo anti-sub offr HMS Yarmouth 1963, OIC Leading Rating's Leadership Course 1964, CO HMS Maxton 1965–67, RAF staff course Bracknell 1968, 1 Lt HMS Torquay 1969–70, staff of Flag Offr 2 i/c Far East Fleet, MOD Directorate of Naval Plans 1971–73, CO HMS Berwick and HMS Lowestoft 1973–74, MOD staff asst COS (policy) 1974–76, Capt Fishery Protection then Mine Counter Measure 1976–78, RCDS 1979, CO HMS Intrepid Falkland Islands Conflict 1980–82, Cdre Amphibious Warfare, Rear Adm 1985, Flag Offr Gibraltar 1985–87, COS to C in C Fleet 1987–90; dir: Argosy Asset Management plc 1990–91, Ivory & Sime plc 1991–92; head of benefits payroll and insurances Slaughter & May slrs 1992–; pres: Br Legion (Cowfold) 1991–, Royal Naval Assoc (Horsham) 1994–, pres Old Brightonian Assoc 1995; chm of tstees Royal Naval Club of 1765 and 1785 1995; Freeman City of London, Liveryman Worshipful Co of Coachmakers and Coach Harness Makers; *Recreations* family and friends, tennis, shooting; *Clubs* Naval and Military, City Livery; *Style*— Rear Adm Peter Dingemans, CB, DSO; ✉ c/o Lloyds Bank Ltd, Steyning, Sussex

DINGLE, Dr John Thomas; s of T H Dingle (d 1990), and Violet, *née* Tolman; *b* 27 Oct 1927; *Educ* King Edward Sch Bath, Univ of London (BSc, DSc), Univ of Cambridge (PhD); *m* 11 July 1953, Dorothy Vernon; 2 s (Jonathan b 1957, Timothy b 1959); *Career* Mil Serv RN 1946–49; res asst Royal Nat Hosp for Rheumatic Diseases Bath 1951–59; Strangeways Research Laboratory: sr res asst 1959, head Physiology Dept 1969, dep dir (MRC external staff) 1971–79, chm Pathophysiology Laboratory 1976–, dir 1979–93; Corpus Christi Coll Cambridge: fell 1968–93, warden of Leckhampton 1981–86, steward of Estates 1987–93; pres Hughes Hall Cambridge 1993–; chm Editorial Bd The Biochemical Jl 1976–82, pres Br Connective Tissue Soc 1980–86, pres Cambridge Univ Rugby Union Football Club 1990– (treas 1983–90); *Awards* Heberden medal 1978, Steindler award 1980; author of numerous papers in scientific learned jls; *Recreations* rugby, sailing; *Clubs* Hawks, Farmers, Royal Dart Yacht Club; *Style*— Dr John Dingle; ✉ Walnut Tree Cottage, 38 Church St, Gt Shelford, Cambridge CB2 5EL; Rheumatology Research Laboratory, Addenbrookes Hospital, Cambridge; Hughes Hall, Cambridge (☎ 01223 334890)

DINGLEY, Gerald Albert; s of Albert Dingley, and Cecélia, *née* Frost; *Educ* Henry Compton Sch for Boys, LSE; *m* 1957, Christine, da of Alexander Wait; 1 s (Mark), 1 da (Tina); *Career* formerly served RAF; md Pentax UK Ltd 1979–, pres/dir gen Pentax France SA 1982–; FCIM, MREconS; *Style*— Gerald Dingley, Esq; ✉ Pentax UK Ltd, Pentax House, Heron Drive, Langley, Slough SL3 8PN (☎ 01753 792792)

DINGWALL-SMITH, Ronald Alfred; CB (1977); *b* 24 Feb 1917; *Educ* Alleyn's Sch, LSE; *m* 1 June 1946, (Margaret) Eileen; 1 s (Richard b 1951), 1 da (Gillian (Mrs Waters) b 1947); *Career* served WWII Maj gen list 1939–47; clerical offr MOT 1934–35, auditor Exchequer and Audit Dept 1935–47; Scottish Educn Dept: asst princ 1947–49, admin princ 1949–56, asst sec 1956–65; under sec Scottish Devpt Dept 1965–70, princ fin offr Scottish Office 1970–78; sr res fell Univ of Glasgow 1979–81; memb Bd St Vincent Drilling 1979–80; chm Hanover (Scotland) Housing Assoc Group 1988–92 (memb 1979–92); memb Cmmn Local Authy Accounts in Scotland 1980–85, govr Moray House Co of Educn Edinburgh 1980–87; *Recreations* golf, bowls, gardening; *Clubs* Braid Bowling (Edinburgh); *Style*— Ronald Dingwall-Smith, CB; ✉ 3 Frogston Terrace, Edinburgh EH10 7AD (☎ 0131 445 2727)

DINKEL, Emmy Gerarda Mary; da of John Jacob Keet (d 1937), of Orsett, Grays, Essex, and Mary, *née* Hartoch (d 1951); *b* 5 Sept 1908; *Educ* Palmer's Coll Grays Essex, Southend-on-Sea Coll of Art, Royal Coll of Art; *m* 25 Oct 1941, Prof Ernest Michael Dinkel (d 1983), s of Charles Dinkel (d 1944), of Huddersfield, Yorks; 2 s (John Michael Antony b 9 Oct 1942 (d 15 Aug 1991), Philip Charles Christian Dinkel, *qv* b 3 Oct 1946); *Career* teacher of embroidery and design to Evening Insts London 1932–34, arts and crafts teacher Sherborne Sch for Girls 1934–37, freelance illustrator and designer 1937–39, sr instr Coll of Art Gt Malvern 1939–41, supply teacher Edinburgh 1957–61; princ works incl: Dream Children, Funeral of Mozart, Babe Eternal, Jane Eyre, Hungarian Peasant Women, Precious Bane, Flight to Freedom and Peace, The Dream Cloud, Aconites in Duntisbourne; signs work Emmy G M Dinkel-Keet; exhibitions incl: RA, RSA, RWA and other galleries; RA exhbn White Sails In the Harbour reproduced in Country Life June 1990; memb Cirencester Civic Soc; ATD 1930, ARCA 1933, ARWA 1977, RWA 1987; *Style*— Mrs E G M Dinkel; ✉ 1 The Mead, Cirencester, Glos GL7 2BB (☎ 01285 653682)

DINKEL, Philip Charles Christian; s of Prof Ernest Michael Dinkel (d 1983), and Emmy Gerarda Mary Dinkel, *qv*, *née* Keet; *b* 3 Oct 1946; *Educ* Ampleforth, Architectural Association Sch of Architecture; *m* 3 Oct 1981, Lucia, *née* Stevens; 2 s (Henry b 5 Oct 1988, Theodore b 15 June 1990), 1 da (Charlotte b 7 Feb 1986); *Career* architect; Sir Hugh Casson Project architect for Hobhouse Ct Trafalgar Square 1973–77 (Civic Trust award 1981), in private practice specialising in conservation work, commercial and residential projects in UK, Albania and Far East 1977–; AA prize 1970; fndr and first chm Lloyd's of London WRG 1994; RIBA; *Recreations* the arts, cello, conservation matters; *Clubs* Roehampton, RAC; *Style*— Philip Dinkel, Esq; (☎ 0171 789 6669, fax 0171 789 6476)

DINKIN, Anthony David; QC (1991); s of Hyman Dinkin, of London, and Mary, *née* Hine (d 1992); *b* 2 Aug 1944; *Educ* Henry Thornton GS Clapham, Coll of Estate Mgmnt Univ of London (BSc); *m* 20 Oct 1968, Derina Tanya, da of Benjamin Green (d 1994); *Career* called to the Bar Lincoln's Inn 1968, examiner in law Univ of Reading 1985–92, recorder of the Crown Court 1989–; memb Anglo-American Real Property Inst; *Recreations* gardening, theatre, music, travel; *Clubs* Players; *Style*— Anthony Dinkin, Esq, QC; ✉ 2–3 Gray's Inn Square, London WC1R 5JH (☎ 0171 242 4986, fax 0171 405 1166)

DINSDALE, Owen Malcolm; s of Malcolm George Frank Dinsdale, and Suzanne, *née* van Rooyen; *b* 15 Jan 1947; *Educ* King Edward VII Sch Johannesburg, Univ of Witwatersrand; *m* 9 July 1972, Bernice, da of William Greenblatt; 3 s (Tarquin Ian b 24 April 1974, Ryan Stuart b 22 Nov 1976, Ewan Anthony b 5 May 1980); *Career* md Telerama Redifussion 1979–81; md: Barlow Manufacturing Co 1984–86 (gen mangr 1981–84), Imperial Cold Storage 1986–87, Gerber Foods Holdings 1987–88; chief exec Acsis Group plc until 1994, currently dir Premier Health Group plc; *Recreations* fly fishing, hockey, tennis, golf; *Clubs* Country (Johannesburg), Wanderers; *Style*— Owen Dinsdale, Esq; ✉ Ridge End, 82 West Hill, Aspley, Guise, Bedfordshire MK17 8DX (☎ 01908 583318)

DINSDALE, Reece; s of Alan Dinsdale, and Sally, *née* Walker; *b* 6 Aug 1959; *Educ* Normanton GS; *Career* actor; *Theatre* incl: Beethoven's Tenth (West End) 1983, Red Saturday (Royal Court) 1984, Observe the Sons of Ulster (Hampstead) 1986, Woundings (Royal Exchange Manchester) 1986, Don Carlos (Royal Exchange Manchester) 1987, Old Years Eve (RSC) 1987–88, Boys Mean Business (Bush) 1989, Wild Oats (West Yorkshire Playhouse) 1990, Playboy of the Western World (West Yorkshire Playhouse) 1991, Racing Demon (RNT and tour) 1991, Revengers Tragedy (West Yorkshire Playhouse) 1992, A Going Concern (Hampstead) 1993, Morning and Evening (Hampstead) 1995; *Television* incl: Threads (BBC) 1984, Home To Roost (YTV) 1985–89, Coppers (BBC) 1987, Storyteller (Channel 4) 1987, Take Me Home 1988, Haggard (YTV) 1988–89, Young Catherine (Consolidated Films) 1990, Full Stretch (SelecTV) 1992, Thief Takers (Carlton) 1995–96, Bliss (Carlton) 1995; *Film* incl: Winter Flight 1984, A Private Function 1984, ID 1994, Hamlet 1996, Romance and Rejection 1996; *Style*— Reece Dinsdale, Esq; ✉ c/o William Morris Agency (UK) Ltd, 31/32 Soho Square, London W1V 6DG (☎ 0171 434 2191, fax 0171 437 0238)

DINWIDDIE, Ian Maitland; s of Lauderdale Maitland Dinwiddie (d 1978), and Frances Lilian Pedrick; *b* 8 Feb 1952; *Educ* Sherborne Sch Dorset, Univ Exeter (BA); *m* 1978,

Sally Jane, da of Leslie Ronald Croydon; 1 s (Andrew b 1984), 2 da (Laura b 1981, Lucy b 1991); *Career* audit mangr Arthur Young & Co 1972–82, fin controller Arbuthnot Savory Milln Holdings Ltd 1982–86, gen mangr Savory Milln Ltd 1986; fin dir: Arbuthnot Latham Bank Ltd 1987, Guinness Mahon Holdings plc until 1990; currently fin dir Allen & Overy Slrs; *Recreations* sailing; *Style*— Ian Dinwiddie, Esq; ✉ Allen & Overy, One New Change, London EC4M 9QQ (☎ 0171 330 3000, fax 0171 330 9999)

DINWIDDIE, Dr Robert; s of Noel Alexander Williamson Dinwiddie (d 1994), of Dumfries, Scotland, and May Stirling, *née* Kennedy (d 1996); *b* 23 Feb 1945; *Educ* Dumfries Acad, Univ of Aberdeen (MB ChB); *m* 23 Oct 1971, Mary McCalley, da of James Saunderson (d 1984), of Dumfries, Scotland; 1 s (Robert b 1973), 1 da (Jane b 1974); *Career* conslt paediatrician: Queen Charlotte's Maternity Hosp London 1977–86, Great Ormond St Hosp for Children London 1977–; hon sr lectr Inst of Child Health Univ of London 1977–; author of numerous scientific pubns on paediatrics especially cystic fibrosis and the chest; memb RSM, DCH, FRCP; *Books* The Diagnosis and Management of Paediatric Respiratory Disease (1990); *Recreations* gardening, walking, running; *Clubs* RSM; *Style*— Dr Robert Dinwiddie; ✉ 1 Circle Gardens, Merton Park, London SW19 3JX; Great Ormond St Hospital for Children, Great Ormond St, London WC1N 3JH (☎ 0171 405 9200, fax 0171 829 8634)

DIPLOCK, Prof Anthony Tytherleigh; s of Bernard Diplock, and Elsie Diplock; *b* 24 July 1935; *Educ* Univ of Bristol (BSc), Univ of London (PhD), DSc (London); *m* 1, 1957 (m dis 1979); 1 s, 1 da; *m* 2, 1980, Lynn Christine, *née* Richards; 1 s; *Career* memb rising to head Biochemistry Res Dept Vitamins Ltd Tadworth (subsequently Beecham Res Laboratories) 1956–67, sr lectr rising to reader in biochemistry Royal Free Hosp Med Sch Univ of London 1967–77, prof and head Dept of Biochemistry Guy's Hosp Med Sch 1977–84, chm Div of Biochemistry United Med and Dental Schs of Guy's and St Thomas's Hosps 1984–; hon prof of biochemistry Xi'an Med Univ China 1985–; Univ of London: memb Senate 1980–93, dean Faculty of Med 1986–91, memb Ct 1989–93, memb Cncl 1993–95; memb Cncl: BPMF 1988–91, Hunterian Inst RCS 1989–92, Royal Free Hosp Sch of Med 1989–95, Roedean Sch 1989–; memb: Cwlth Scholarships Cmmn 1991–, Tea Cncl Advsy Bd 1995–; Antioxidant Research Prog mangr MAFF 1994–; Evian Health Award 1988, Caroline Walker Award 1993; *Publications* Fat-Soluble Vitamins (1985); approx 225 papers in scientific jls; *Style*— Prof Anthony T Diplock; ✉ International Antioxidant Research Centre, Division of Biochemistry and Molecular Biology, United Medical and Dental Schools, Guy's Hospital, London SE1 9RT (☎ 0171 955 4521, fax 0171 403 7195)

DISKI, Jenny; da of James Simmonds (d 1966), of London and Banbury, Oxford, and René, *née* Rayner; *b* 8 July 1947; *Educ* St Christopher Sch Letchworth Herts, King Alfred Sch Golders Green London, UCL; *m* Dec 1976, Roger Diski, s of Ralph Marks; 1 da (Chloe b 1 July 1977); *Career* author; formerly shop asst, Eng and history teacher Haggerston Sch Hackney 1973–77 (free sch teacher 1972–73), home tutor ILEA 1977–83, teacher Islington Sixth Form Centre 1985–89; *Books* Nothing Natural (Methuen), Rainforest (Methuen and Penguin), Like Mother (Bloomsbury and Vintage), Then Again (Bloomsbury and Vintage), Happily Ever After (Hamish Hamilton), Monkey's Uncle (Weidenfeld and Nicolson, 1994), The Vanishing Princess (Phoenix, 1996), The Dream Mistress (Weidenfeld & Nicholson, 1996); *Television plays* A Fair and Easy Passage (Channel 4), Seduction (Channel 4), Murder in Mind (BBC1); *Style*— Ms Jenny Diski; ✉ c/o A P Watt, 20 John Street, London WC1N 2DR (☎ 0171 405 6774)

DISLEY, John Ivor; CBE (1979); s of Harold Disley, and Marie Hughes; *b* 20 Nov 1928, Corris, Gwynedd; *Educ* Oswestry HS, Loughborough Coll; *m* 1958, Sylvia Cheeseman; 2 da; *Career* former Br steeplechase record holder and former Welsh mile record holder; Bronze Medal winner Helsinki Olympics 1952, Sportsman of the Year 1955; vice chm Sports Cncl 1974–82; dir: Reebok UK Ltd 1984–95, London Marathon Ltd; memb Royal Cmmn on Gambling 1976–78; *Books* Tackle Climbing, Orienteering, Expedition Guide, Your Way with Map & Compass; *Recreations* mountaineering, running; *Clubs* Climbers, Southern Navigators, Olympians; *Style*— John Disley, Esq, CBE; ✉ Hampton House, Upper Sunbury Rd, Hampton, Middlesex (☎ 0181 979 1707, fax 0181 941 1867)

DISPENZA, Adriano; s of Mario Dispenza, of St Laurent du Var, France, and Lina, *née* Inzirillo; *b* 24 Sept 1948; *Educ* Queen Mary Coll (BSc), Paris (Dip Faculté de Droit et Sciences Economiques); *m* 12 March 1979, Rallia Jean, da of John Adam Hadjipateras, of Greece; 1 da (Carolina b 5 March 1981); *Career* Morgan Grenfell & Co Ltd 1973–77, Amex Bank Ltd 1977–79, md First Chicago Ltd 1979–88, md Merrill Lynch Int Ltd; *Recreations* reading, travel, crosswords; *Clubs* RAC; *Style*— Adriano Dispenza, Esq; ✉ 36 Abbey Lodge Park Road, London NW8 7RJ (☎ 0171 724 6881, fax 0171 723 5737)

DISS, Eileen (Mrs Raymond Everett); da of Thomas Alexander Diss, and Winifred, *née* Irvine; *b* 13 May 1931; *Educ* Ilford Co HS, Central Sch of Art and Design; *m* 18 Sept 1953, Raymond Terence Everett, s of Elmo Terence Everett; 2 s (Timothy Patrick b 1959, Matthew Simon Thomas b 1964), 1 da (Danielle Claire b 1956); *Career* BBC TV designer 1952–59, freelance designer 1959–; designs for BBC incl: Maigret, Cider with Rosie; designs for ITV incl: The Prime of Miss Jean Brodie, Porterhouse Blue, Jeeves and Wooster; theatre designs for Nat Theatre and W End Theatres; feature films: Joseph Losey's A Doll's House 1972, Sweet William 1978, Harold Pinter's Betrayal 1982, Secret Places 1984, 84 Charing Cross Road 1986, A Handful of Dust 1988, August 1994 (dir Anthony Hopkins); BAFTA Awards: 1961, 1965, 1974 and 1992; RDI 1978, FRSA; *Style*— Miss Eileen Diss; ✉ 4 Gloucester Walk, London W8 4HZ (☎ 0171 937 8794)

DISS, Paul John; s of John Richard Diss, and Margaret Mary, *née* Finn; *b* 30 Nov 1951; *Educ* St Joseph's Coll Stoke-on-Trent, St Joseph's Coll Ledsham Cheshire, St Mary's Coll Toddington Glos, St Catharine's Coll Cambridge (BA); *m* 20 Sept 1980, Janice Marie, da of Thomas Ronald Fletcher; 1 da (Nicola Lesley b 31 May 1985), 2 s (Jonathan Mark b 14 Nov 1987, Matthew Stephen b 22 Feb 1990); *Career* slr Linklaters & Paines 1976–77 (articled clerk 1974–76), ptnr Stephenson Harwood 1982– (slr 1977–81 and 1984–), Stephenson Harwood & Lo (Hong Kong) 1981–84; Freeman City of London Slrs' Co 1986; memb Law Soc; *Recreations* collecting books; *Style*— Paul Diss, Esq; ✉ Stephenson Harwood, One St Paul's Churchyard, London EC4M 8SH (☎ 0171 329 4422, fax 0171 606 0822)

DITCHBURN, (John) Blackett Dennison; s of Thomas Dennison Ditchburn, and Elaine, *née* Walton; *b* 7 Jan 1957; *Educ* Strode's Sch Egham, Walthamstow Tech Coll, NE London Poly (HNC Surveying); *m* 1985, Judy, da of Jack Regis, of Northwood, Middx; 1 da (Hayley Juliette b 31 March 1987), 1 s (Loic Jack Dennison b 2 Nov 1988); *Career* advtg exec; land surveyor 1973–80, Murray Evans Associates (PR) 1980–82, Political Research and Communications (lobbyists) 1982–83, account mangr Granard Communications 1983–85, account dir Aspect Hill Holliday 1985–86; Prudential Corporation 1986–94: advtg and sponsorship mangr 1986–89, advtg mangr 1989–91, corp communications mangr 1991–94; dir of communication strategy TMD Carat Advertising 1994–; prepared CBI's response to the Bdcasting Green Paper 1989; regular speaker at mktg confs; memb: Exec Ctee ISBA 1988–94 (vice chm 1991–94), Special Issues Ctee Advtg Assoc 1990–94; memb Mktg Soc 1992, assoc memb D&AD 1993; *Books* Superbiking (1983); *Recreations* cooking, reading, anything on wheels; *Style*— Blackett Ditchburn, Esq; ✉ TMD Carat Advertising Ltd, New London House, 172 Drury Lane, London WC2B 5QR (☎ 0171 611 8000, fax 0171 611 8010)

DIX, Prof Gerald Bennett; s of Cyril Dix (d 1984), and Mabel Winifred, *née* Bennett (d 1970); *b* 12 Jan 1926; *Educ* Altrincham GS, Univ of Manchester (BA, DipTP), Harvard (Master Landscape Arch); *m* 1, 1956 (m dis 1963); 2 s (Stephen b 1957, Graham b 1959); *m* 2, 1963, Lois, da of John Noel Nichols (d 1966); 1 da (Kate b 1964); *Career* RAF 1944–47; asst lectr Univ of Manchester 1951–53 (studio asst in arch 1950–51), chief asst to Sir Patrick Abercrombie and city planning offr Addis Ababa 1954–56, sr planning offr Singapore 1957–59, acting planning advsr Singapore 1959, sr res fell Ghana 1959–63, sr planner BRS/ODA UK Govt 1963–65, prof of planning Univ of Nottingham 1970–75 (lectr then sr lectr 1966–70); Univ of Liverpool: Lever prof 1975–88 (currently emeritus), pro vice chllr 1984–87, hon sr fell 1988–; hon sr res fell Chinese Res Acad of Environmental Scis 1989, hon cncl memb Assoc for Protection of Mountain Summer Resort Miny of Civil Affrs China 1991; planning and landscape conslt; memb: E Midlands Econ Planning Cncl 1973–75, Historic Areas Advsy Ctee English Heritage 1986–88; pres World Soc for Ekistics 1987–91; Hon DEng Dong-A Korea 1995; ARIBA 1950–87 and 1994–, FRTPI, FRSA; *Books* Ecology and Ekistics (ed, 1977), Third World Planning Review (fndr ed, 1978–90); *Recreations* travel, photography, cooking; *Clubs* Athenaeum; *Style*— Prof Gerald Dix; ✉ 13 Friars Quay, Norwich NR3 1ES (☎ 01603 632433, fax 01603 665659); Department of Civic Design, University of Liverpool, PO Box 147, Liverpool L69 3BX (☎ 0151 794 3108, fax 0151 708 3125, telex 62709 UNILPL G)

DIX, Wing Cdr Kenneth John Weeks; OBE (1975), AFC (1958), QC (1967); s of Eric John Dix (d 1982), of Dorset, and Kate, *née* Weeks (d 1986); *b* 12 Sept 1930; *Educ* HMC Canford Dorset, RAF Colls Cranwell, Bracknell, Manby (PSC, AWC); *m* 1, 1953 (m dis); m 2, 1969 (m dis); 1 s (Michael b 1956), 1 da (Linda b 1954); *Career* RAF 1948–83 (Europe, ME, Far E, USA), ret with rank of Wing Cdr; conslt for electronic def systems and mil advsr (Eldecon), specialist in aviation, navigation, weapons and reconnaissance systems; dir Electronic Defence Assoc; represented various counties, RAF and Combined Servs at rugby and athletics; Queen's Commendation 1967; MRAeS, MIMgt, MIEE, memb BHS; *Recreations* fly fishing, horse riding, shooting, studying antiques; *Clubs* RAF, Royal Over-Seas League; *Style*— Wing Cdr Kenneth J W Dix, OBE, AFC, QC, RAF; ✉ 41 Lincoln Park, Amersham, Bucks HP7 9EZ (☎ 01494 725562); c/o Lloyds Bank, Bournemouth BH1 1ED

DIXON, Prof Adrian Kendal; s of Kendal Dixon, and Annette, *née* Darley; *b* 5 Feb 1948; *Educ* Uppingham, King's Coll Cambridge (MA, MB BChir, MD), Bart's Med Coll (Golf purple); *m* 1979, Anne Hazel, *née* Lucas; 2 s (Charles Kendal b 21 Jan 1981, Thomas Christopher b 12 March 1987), 1 da (Emily Louise b 3 Feb 1983); *Career* jr hosp posts Bart's, Nottingham Gen Hosp and Hosp for Sick Children Great Ormand St 1972–79, lectr in radiology and hon conslt radiologist Addenbrooke's Hosp Cambridge 1979–94, prof of radiology Univ of Cambridge 1994–; fell Peterhouse Cambridge 1986–; FRCR 1978, FRCP 1991; *Books* Body CT (1983), Human Cross Sectional Anatomy (1991); *Recreations* family, golf; *Style*— Prof Adrian Dixon; ✉ Radiology 219, Addenbrooke's Hospital, Cambridge CB2 2QQ (☎ 01223 336890)

DIXON, Prof Anthony Frederick George (Tony); s of George Edward Dixon (d 1988), and Rose Emma, *née* Middlemiss (d 1986); *b* 4 May 1932; *Educ* E Ham GS, UCL (BSc), Jesus Coll Oxford (DPhil); *m* 20 Aug 1957, (Theodora) June, da of Michael Phil Theodore White, of E Harling, Norfolk; 1 s (Keith b 1965), 1 da (Fiona b 1963); *Career* Univ of Glasgow: asst lectr 1957–59, lectr 1959–69, sr lectr 1969–74; prof of biology: Univ of East Anglia 1974–, Nat Univ of La Plata Argentina Sept-Nov 1994; Gregor Mendel Gold Medal 1992; MBES 1952, FRES 1979; *Books* Biology of Aphids (1973), Simulation of Lime Aphid Population Dynamics (with N D Barlow, 1980), Cereal Aphid Populations: Biology Simulation and Prediction (with N Carter and R Rabbinge, 1982), Aphid Ecology (1985); *Recreations* reading; *Style*— Prof Tony Dixon; ✉ 20 Newfound Drive, Cringleford, Norwich, Norfolk NR4 7RY; School of Biological Sciences, University of East Anglia, Norwich NR4 7TJ (☎ 01603 592260, telex 975334)

DIXON, Dr Bernard; s of Ronald Dixon (d 1962), and Grace Peirson (d 1994); *b* 17 July 1938; *Educ* Queen Elizabeth GS Darlington, King's Coll Univ of Durham (BSc), Univ of Newcastle upon Tyne (PhD); *m* 1963 (m dis 1987), Margaret Helena Charlton; 2 s, 1 da; *Career* formerly res fell Univ of Newcastle, dep ed World Medicine 1966–68, ed New Scientist 1969–79 (dep ed 68–69); European ed: The Sciences 1980–85, Science 1980–86, The Scientist 1986–89; ed: Biotechnology 1989–, Med Science Research 1989–; columnist Br Med Jl; conslt American Soc for Microbiology 1995–; memb Bd: Speculations in Sci and Technol, World Journal of Biotechnology, Biologist; vice pres Gen Section Br Assoc for Advancement of Sci; memb: European Environmental Res Organisation, CSS 1982–90; chm Programme Ctee Edinburgh Int Sci Festival; Hon DSc Univ of Edinburgh 1996; FIBiol 1982 (CBiol); *Books* What is Science For (1973), Beyond the Magic Bullet (1978), Invisible Allies (1976), Health and the Human Body (1986), Ideas of Science (1984), How Science Works (1989), Science and Society (1989), From Creation to Chaos (1989), Our Genetic Future (1992), Genetics and the Understanding of Life (1993), Power Unseen - How Microbes Rule the World (1994); *Style*— Dr Bernard Dixon; ✉ 139 Cornwall Rd, Ruislip Manor, Middx HA4 6AW (☎ 01895 632390, fax 01895 678645)

DIXON, Brian Ringrose; s of Reginald E Dixon (d 1978), of Market Weighton, and Marianne, *née* Ringrose; *b* 4 Jan 1938; *Educ* Pocklington Sch; *m* 8 Oct 1966, Mary Annette, da of Sidney Robertson (d 1982), of Hawick; 2 s (James b 1971, John b 1973); *Career* Barclays Bank plc: asst mangr Scarborough 1971–73, asst mangr Grimsby 1973–76, asst dist mangr York dist 1976–79, mangr Berwick upon Tweed 1979–83, Scot dir 1983–; memb: Exec Cncl Scottish Cncl Devpt and Indust, Royal Highland and Agric Soc of Scot, Ct Univ of Strathclyde; ACIB; *Recreations* rugby, gardening, golf, walking, cricket; *Style*— Brian R Dixon, Esq; ✉ Barclays Bank plc, Scotland Director's Office, 5th Floor, 90 St Vincent Street, Glasgow G2 5UQ (☎ 0141 221 9585, fax 0141 204 3232, telex 777286)

DIXON, Christopher John Arnold; TD; s of Hubert John Dixon, MC (d 1972), of Wimbledon, and Mary Frances (d 1960); *b* 17 Aug 1928; *Educ* Rugby; *m* 8 Oct 1955, Ethelwyn Ada, da of Lt-Col J H Mousley, DSO, TD (d 1959), of Middleton Tyas, Yorks; 3 s (Anthony b 1958, Timothy b 1962, Michael b 1963), 1 da (Phyllida b 1960); *Career* Nat Serv and Short Serv Cmmn 2 Lt RA 1947–50, Maj TA 1951–60; ptnr Norton Rose 1960–95 (joined 1951); memb Law Soc 1955; *Recreations* sailing; *Clubs* City Univ, RA Yacht; *Style*— Christopher Dixon, Esq

DIXON, David Michael; CVO (1991); s of Rev James Eric Dixon, MC (d 1955), of Surrey, and Florence, *née* Pye (d 1980); *b* 1 May 1926; *Educ* Whitgift Sch, Univ of Oxford (MA), Harvard Law Sch (Cwlth Fund fell, LLM); *m* 1953, Alison Mary, da of Sir Leonard Sinclair (d 1984), of Surrey; 2 s, 1 da; *Career* RAFVR 1945–47; slr; conslt Withers 1991– (ptnr 1957–90, sr ptnr 1982–86), hon legal advsr Br Olympic Assoc 1977–; hon sec Cwlth Games Fedn 1982–; chm ELF Exploration UK plc; memb Ct of Assts Worshipful Co of Fletchers; *Recreations* sport, travel; *Clubs* Brooks's, Hurlingham, RAC, Achilles, Vincent's (Oxford); *Style*— David Dixon, Esq, CVO; ✉ 10 Peek Crescent, London SW19 5ER (☎ 0181 946 4125); ELF Exploration UK plc, 30 Buckingham Gate, London SW1E 6NN (☎ 0171 963 5000, fax 0171 963 5197)

DIXON, Rt Hon Donald (Don); PC (1996), MP (Lab) Jarrow (majority 17,907); s of late Christopher Albert Dixon, and Jane Dixon; *b* 6 March 1929; *Educ* Ellison Street Elementary Sch Jarrow; *m* Doreen Morad; 1 s, 1 da; *Career* shipyard worker 1947–74, branch sec GMWU 1974–79, cncllr S Tyneside MDC 1963–; MP (Lab) Jarrow 1979–, formerly Lab dep chief whip until 1996; *Recreations* football, boxing, reading; *Clubs* Jarrow Labour, Ex Servicemen's (Jarrow), Hastings (Hebburn); *Style*— The Rt Hon Don Dixon, MP; ✉ 1 Hillcrest, Jarrow, Tyne and Wear NE32 4DP (☎ 0191 897635); House of Commons, London SW1A 0AA (☎ 0171 219 3000)

DIXON, Sir Ian Leonard; kt (1996), CBE (1991); s of late Leonard Frank Dixon; *b* 3 Nov 1938; *Educ* SW Essex Co Tech Sch, Harvard Business Sch; *m* 1961, Valerie Diana, da of late Alexander Barclay; 2 s, 1 da; *Career* chartered builder; chm Willmott Dixon Ltd 1971–; cncllr Beds CC 1977–85; memb Nat Cncl CBI 1984–96 (chm Eastern Region 1988–90); chm: N Herts HA 1984–87, Riverside HA 1990–92, Beds TEC 1990–92, Construction Industry Cncl 1991–94, Construction Indust Bd 1996–; memb Construction Industry Trg Bd 1993–95; memb Cncl Univ Coll London 1991–96; govr: Univ of Anglia 1990–95, Univ of Luton 1994–; tstee The Bedford Charity 1977–86; Construction Man of the Year 1992, Construction Achievement Award 1989–94; Hon PhD Anglia Univ 1992; hon memb American Inst of Constructors 1989; hon fell: Inst of Building Control 1994, Inst of Structural Engineers 1995; FCIOB (pres 1989–90), CIMgt, FRSA; *Recreations* rugby, shooting, philately; *Clubs* The Carlton; *Style*— Sir Ian Dixon, CBE; ✉ Wain Wood Edge, Hitchin Road, Preston, Herts SG4 7TZ; Flat 2, 106 Park Street, Mayfair, London W1Y 3RB

DIXON, James Wolryche; s of late Michael Wolryche Dixon, of Crowborough, Sussex, and Barbara Mary, *née* Eccles; *b* 20 Feb 1948; *Educ* Lancing, CCC Oxford (MA); *Career* RAFVR actg PO Univ of Oxford Air Sqdn 1966–69; articled with Barton Mayhew & Co 1969, ptnr Ernst & Young 1984–95; FCA 1972, FRSA 1988; *Books* Vat Guide and Casebook (conslt ed, 1 edn), Tax Case Analysis (contrib), Vat Planning (contrib); *Recreations* cycling, photography, bridge, cooking; *Clubs* United Oxford and Cambridge Univ; *Style*— James Dixon, Esq; ✉ 48 Lytton Grove, Putney, London SW15 2HE (☎ 0181 780 9431, e-mail 106342.1071@compuserve.com)

DIXON, (David) Jeremy; s of Joseph Lawrence Dixon, and Beryl Margaret, *née* Braund; *b* 31 May 1939; *Educ* Merchant Taylors', AA Sch of Architecture (AADipl); *m* 1964, Fenella Mary Anne Clemens; 1 s, 2 da; *Career* architect: Alison & Peter Smithson 1966–67, Frederick MacManus & Partners 1967–71, Milton Keynes Development Corporation 1971–73; in private practice: Cross Dixon Gold Jones & Samson 1973–76, Jeremy & Fenella Dixon 1972–89, Jeremy Dixon BDP 1983–89, Jeremy Dixon Edward Jones and Jeremy Dixon Edward Jones BDP 1989–; awards won for projects incl: Northamptonshire Co offices 1973, Tate Gallery coffee shop 1981, Royal Opera House Covent Garden project 1983, housing Ashmill St Marylebone London 1984, study centre Darwin Coll Cambridge 1989, A Gateway for Venice (Venice Biennale) 1991; present clients incl: Henry Moore Fndn, Darwin Coll Cambridge, Univ of Portsmouth, Robert Gordon Univ Aberdeen, J Sainsbury plc, Nat Portrait Gallery 1994, Oxford Business Sch 1996; work regularly published and exhibited; formerly external examiner RIBA and memb various architectural juries; teacher: AA Sch 1972–82, RCA 1980–83, UC Dublin (visiting critic) 1989–90 and 1990–91; RIBA; *Recreations* walking in English landscape, contemporary sculpture and painting, music; *Style*— Jeremy Dixon; ✉ Jeremy Dixon Edward Jones, 41 Shelton Street, London WC2H 9HJ (☎ 0171 240 7044, fax 0171 240 7114)

DIXON, John Graham; s of Francis Brian Dixon (d 1985), of Bramhall, Cheshire, and Doris Brenda, *née* Leigh; *b* 2 July 1946; *Educ* The King's Sch Macclesfield; *m* 2 Jan 1993, Rosemary Weston; *Career* CA; Thornton Baker (now Grant Thornton) Manchester 1964–70; Peat Marwick Mitchell (now KPMG): London Office 1971–74, Manchester Office 1974–, ptnr 1976–; hon treas Lancashire and Cheshire Fauna Soc; FCA; *Recreations* ornithology, golf; *Clubs* St James's (Manchester), Manchester Literary and Philosophical Soc; *Style*— John Dixon, Esq; ✉ KPMG, St James' Square, Manchester M2 6DS (☎ 0161 838 4000, fax 0161 838 4040)

DIXON, Sir Jonathan Mark; 4 Bt (UK 1919), of Astle, Chelford, Co Palatine of Chester; s of Capt Nigel Dixon, OBE, RN (d 1978), and Margaret Josephine, da of late Maurice John Collett; suc unc, Sir John George Dixon, 3 Bt (d 1990); *b* 1 Sept 1949; *Educ* Winchester, Univ Coll Oxford (BA 1972, MA 1987); *m* 1978, Patricia Margaret, da of James Baird Smith; 2 s (Mark Edward b 29 June 1982, Timothy Nigel b 3 Jan 1987), 1 da (Katherine Anne b 1980); *Heir* s, Mark Edward Dixon b 29 June 1982; *Recreations* fishing; *Style*— Sir Jonathan Dixon, Bt; ✉ 19 Clyde Road, Redland, Bristol BS6 6RJ

DIXON, Hon Mrs Andrew; Karen Elizabeth; MBE (1996); da of late Hugh Charles Straker, and Elaine Felicia, *née* Peat; *b* 17 Sept 1964; *Educ* St Anne's HS Wolsingham, St Godric's Coll Hampstead; *m* 14 Dec 1991, Hon Andrew Wynne Valerian Dixon, s of 3 Baron Glentoran, CBE, DL, *qv*; *Career* int 3-day-event rider; jr Euro Champion 1982, Most Outstanding Young Rider of the Year 1982, Young Riders Euro Silver medallist 1983, int competition Badminton and Burghley 1984–96, Heineken int champion Punchestown 1988 (first champion) and 1994; memb Br Equestrian 3 Day Event team: Seoul Olympics (Silver medallist) 1988, Euro Championships Burghley (fourth) 1989, World Championships Stockholm (Silver medallist) 1990, Euro Championships Punchestown Ireland (team Gold medallist and individual Bronze medallist) 1991, Barcelona Olympics (individual sixth) 1992, World Championships (team Gold medallist and individual Bronze medallist) 1994, Atlanta Olympics 1996; Br Open and National champion 1994; vice pres Riding for the Disabled, public speaker, instr and demonstrator; memb Br Horse Soc; *Recreations* swimming, tennis, skiing; *Style*— The Hon Mrs Andrew Dixon, MBE; ✉ Wycliffe Grange, Wycliffe, nr Barnard Castle, Co Durham

DIXON, Kenneth Herbert Morley; CBE (1996); s of Arnold Morley Dixon (d 1975); *b* 19 Aug 1929; *Educ* Cranbrook Sch Sydney Aust, Univ of Manchester (BA), Harvard Business Sch (AMP); *m* 1955, Patricia Oldbury, *née* Whalley; 2 s (Michael, Giles b 1969); *Career* Lt Royal Signals BAOR Cyprus 1947–49; Calico Printers Association Ltd 1952–56; Rowntree & Co: joined 1956, mktg UK Confectionery Div 1966, dir Rowntree Mackintosh Ltd and dep chm UK Confectionery Div 1970, chm UK Confectionery Div 1973, dep chm Rowntree Mackintosh Ltd 1978, chm Rowntree Mackintosh plc (Rowntree plc from 1987) 1981–89; vice chm Legal and General Group plc 1986–94 (dir 1984–94), dir Yorkshire Tyne-Tees Television Holdings plc (formerly Yorkshire Television Holdings plc) 1989–, dep chm Bass PLC 1990–94 (dir 1988–96, chm Remuneration and Audit Ctees); memb: Cncl for Indust and Higher Educn 1986–, Cncl Nat Forum for Mgmnt Educn and Devpt 1987–; pt/t memb British Railways Bd 1990–; Univ of York: memb Hon Degrees Ctee 1983–, memb Fin Ctee 1986, chm Jt Ctee on Jarratt Report 1986, memb Policy and Resources Ctee 1987–, memb Ctee on Appts to Court and Cncl 1988–, pro chllr 1987–, chm Cncl 1990 (memb Cncl 1983); chm Open Univ Visiting Ctee 1990; FRSA, CIMgt; *Recreations* reading, music, fell walking; *Style*— Kenneth Dixon, Esq, CBE; ✉ c/o Yorkshire Tyne-Tees Television Holdings plc, The Television Centre, Leeds LS3 1JS

DIXON, Peter John; s of George Edward Dixon, and Violet Jose, *née* Bell; *b* 4 Feb 1949; *Educ* King Edward VI GS, Wellingborough GS, LSE (BSc), London Inst of Educn (postgrad CertEd), Brunel Univ (MEd); *m* 28 July 1973, (Elizabeth) Susan, da of Joseph Arthur Butterworth; 2 s (Simon Peter b 29 Sept 1979, Nicholas Jonathan b 8 Nov 1981); *Career* head of history and integrated studies Hayes Co GS 1972–80, chef and proprietor White Moss House Cumbria 1980–; winner of food and wine awards in all leading guide books; Master Chef of GB; *Recreations* walking, squash, wine tasting, bridge, chess; *Style*— Peter Dixon, Esq; ✉ White Moss House, Rydal Water, Grasmere, Cumbria LA22 9SE (☎ 01539 435295)

DIXON, Peter Vibart; s of Meredith Vibart Dixon (d 1967), of Surrey, and Phyllis Joan, *née* Hemingway (d 1982); *b* 16 July 1932; *Educ* Radley, King's Coll Cambridge (MA); *m* 1955, Elizabeth Anne Howie, da of Dr Max Davison (d 1970), of Surrey; 3 s (Patrick, Henry, Nigel); *Career* Nat Serv RA 1950–51; various posts: HM Treasy, Office of the Lord Privy Seal, Colonial Office, Civil Serv Cmmn; econ cncllr Br Embassy Washington 1972–75, press sec and head of Info Div HM Treasy 1975–78, under sec (industl policy) HM Treasy 1978–82, sec to NEDC 1982–87; dir of planning and admin Turner Kenneth Brown (slrs) 1988–92, chm Merton Sutton and Wandsworth Family Health Servs Authy 1995–96; FRSA; *Clubs* Utd Oxford & Cambridge Univ; *Style*— Peter Dixon, Esq; ✉ 23 Spencer Hill, Wimbledon, London SW19 4PA (☎ 0181 946 8931)

DIXON, Prof Richard Newland; s of Robert Thomas Dixon (d 1985), of Borough Green, Kent, and Lilian, *née* Newland (d 1973); *b* 25 Dec 1930; *Educ* Judd Sch Kent, King's Coll London (BSc), St Catharine's Coll Cambridge (PhD, ScD); *m* 18 Sept 1954, Alison Mary, da of Gilbert Arnold Birks (d 1966), of Horsforth, Leeds; 1 s (Paul b 1959), 2 da (Joan b 1961, Sheila b 1962); *Career* post doctoral fell Nat Res Cncl of Canada 1957–59, ICI fell lectr in chem Univ of Sheffield 1959–69, Sorby res fell Royal Soc 1964–69; Univ of Bristol: prof of chemistry 1969–96, dean of sci 1979–82, pro-vice chllr 1989–92, Alfred Capper Pass prof of chemistry 1990–96 (emeritus 1996); Leverhulme emeritus fell 1996–; visiting scholar Stanford Univ USA 1982–83; non-exec dir United Bristol Healthcare NHS Tst 1994– (vice chm 1995–); memb: Faraday Cncl of Royal Soc of Chem (vice pres 1989–), SERC Ctees; CChem 1976, FRSC 1976, FRS 1986; *Books* Spectroscopy and Structure (1965), Theoretical Chemistry (Vol 1 1971, Vol 2 1973, Vol 3 1975); *Recreations* mountain walking, travel, theatre, concerts, photography; *Style*— Prof Richard Dixon, FRS; ✉ 22 Westbury Lane, Bristol BS9 2PE (☎ 0117 968 1691); School of Chemistry, University of Bristol, Cantock's Close, Bristol BS8 1TS (☎ 0117 928 7661 fax 0117 925 1295)

DIXON-SMITH, Baron (Life Peer UK 1993), of Bocking in the County of Essex; Robert William (Bill) Dixon-Smith; DL (Essex 1986); 2 s of Dixon Smith (d 1995) of Lascelles, Braintree, Essex, and his 1 w, (Alice) Winifred, *née* Stratton (d 1976); *b* 30 Sept 1934; *Educ* Oundle, Writtle Agric Coll; *m* 13 Feb 1960, Georgina Janet, da of George Cook, of Halstead, Essex; 1 s (Hon Adam William George b 11 Jan 1963), 1 da (Hon Sarah Jane (*see* Christopher Henry St John Hoare) b 16 Dec 1960); *Career* Nat Serv 2 Lt King's Dragoon Gds 1955–57; farmer; memb Essex CC 1965–93 (chm 1986–89), memb Assoc of CCs 1983–93 (chm 1992–93), memb Local Govt Mgmnt Bd 1991–93, chm Anglia Poly Univ 1992–93 (Hon Dr 1994), memb Cncl Essex Univ 1991–94, govr Writtle Coll 1967–94 (chm of govrs 1973–85, fell 1993); memb: Select Ctee for Science and Technology, House of Lords 1994–, Select Ctee for European Communities, Sub-ctee 4 1994–; Freeman City of London 1988, Liveryman Worshipful Co of Farmers 1991; *Recreations* shooting, fishing, golf; *Style*— The Rt Hon Lord Dixon-Smith, DL; ✉ Lyons Hall, Braintree, Essex CM7 6SH (☎ 01376 326834)

DJUKANOVIC, Srdja (Chunky); s of late Jovo Djukanovic and Zorka, *née* Plavsic; *b* 6 Sept 1923; *Educ* Banja Luka (Bosnia), Zagreb (Croatia), Belgrade (Serbia); *m* 1948, Inez, yst da of John and Eleanor Price-Stephens, of Abercarn, S Wales; 1 s, 3 da; *Career* news and feature photographer; memb Special Ops Unit Jugoslav Resistance 1941–45, Italy 1945–47, arrived UK 1947 (took Br citizenship 1964), Bevin boy 1947–49, operating theatre technician 1949–55, freelance photographer 1955–64, staff photographer Daily Telegraph 1964–89, freelance photographer 1989–; pubns through syndications of Camera Press Ltd in 87 countries worldwide, contrib to all maj Euro and US magazines and TV current affairs progs and all UK daily and Sunday newspapers; subjects covered incl: Royal Family (Br and Euro), politicians, TU VIPs and equestrian events; *Exhibitions* Br Press Photo Awards 1965, World Press Photo Awards (The Hague) 1968, Photographers' Gallery London, Royal Collection Windsor Castle Royal Mews (permanent), Tom Blau Gallery (Camera Press London); memb Br Equestrian Writers' Assoc; *Publications incl* Princess Anne, Champion of Europe (with Bernard Foyster, 1973), Anne and Mark (with Judith Campbell, 1975), Margaret Thatcher - First Ten Years (with Lady Olga Maitland, 1989); Eventing (illustration photos, by Judith Campbell, 1976), Mark Phillips - Man and His Horses (illustration section photos, by Angela Rippon, 1982), Riding Through My Life (contrib, by HRH The Princess Royal, 1991), All the Queen's Men (illustrations section, by Brian Hoey, 1992); *Style*— Srdja Djukanovic, Esq; (☎ 0181 464 1231, mobile 0860 204378)

DOBASH, Prof Rebecca Emerson; da of I M Emerson, and Helen, *née* Cooper; *b* 3 Feb 1943; *Educ* Arizona State Univ (BA, MS), Washington State Univ (PhD); *m* 5 June 1965, Russell P Dobash, s of Paul Dobash; *Career* formerly: lectr and reader Univ of Stirling, prof in Sch of Social and Admin Studies Univ of Wales Coll of Cardiff; currently prof of social research Faculty of Economic and Social Scis Univ of Manchester; co fndr and co dir Violence Research Centre; memb: Int Sociological Assoc, Br Sociological Assoc, American Sociological Assoc, Soc for the Study of Social Problems; awards for outstanding research and pubns Int Soc of Victimology and American Soc of Criminology, August Vollmer Award; fell: Rockefeller Centre Bellagio Italy 1981 and 1992, Univ of Melbourne 1996; *Books* Violence Against Wives (1979), The Imprisonment of Women (1986), Women, Violence and Social Change (1992), Women Viewing Violence (1992), Gender and Crime (1995), The Simulated Client (1996), Research Evaluation and Programmes for Violent Men (1996); *Recreations* travel, food; *Style*— Prof Rebecca Emerson Dobash; ✉ School of Social Policy and Social Work, University of Manchester, Oxford Road, Manchester M13 9PL (☎ 0161 275 4490, fax 0161 275 4922, e-mail Dobash@Manchester.AC.UK)

DOBBIE, Dr Robert Charles (Bob); CB (1996); *b* 16 Jan 1942; *Educ* Dollar Acad, Univ of Edinburgh (BSc), Univ of Cambridge (PhD); *m* 18 Sept 1964, Elizabeth Charlotte, *née* Barbour; 3 s; *Career* ICI fell Univ of Bristol 1967–68, lectr in chemistry Univ of Newcastle upon Tyne 1968–76, tutor Open Univ 1975–85; DTI: princ 1976–83, asst sec 1983–90, under sec 1990–95 (on secondment to DOE 1990–92); under sec Cabinet Office 1995–; author 40 research pubns in chemistry 1964–78; *Recreations* theatre, malt whisky, mountains; *Style*— Dr Bob Dobbie, CB; ✉ Office of Public Service, Cabinet Office, Horse Guards Road, London SW1A 2AS (☎ 0171 270 6464, fax 0171 270 6500)

DOBBIN, Rev Dr Victor; MBE (1980), QHC (1993); s of Vincent Dobbin (d 1995), of Bushmills, and Annie, *née* Doherty (d 1957); *b* 12 March 1943; *Educ* Bushmills GS, Magee Univ Coll, Trinity Coll Dublin (MA), Queen's Univ Belfast (PhD); *m* Aug 1967, Rosemary, *née* Gault; 1 s (Nigel b 1975), 1 da (Anona b 1973); *Career* Royal Army Chaplains Dept: joined 1972, D warden RAChD Centre 1982–86, sr chaplain 3 Armd Div 1986–89, staff chaplain BAOR 1989–91, ACG Southern Dist 1991–95, Chaplain Gen Feb 1995–; Hon DD Presbyterian Theol Faculty in Ireland 1995; *Style*— Rev Dr V Dobbin, MBE, QHC; ✉ c/o MOD Chaplains (Army), Trenchard Lines, Upavon, Pewsey, Wilts SN9 6BE

DOBBS, Michael John; s of Eric William Dobbs (d 1990), and Eileen, *née* Saunders (d 1974); *b* 14 Nov 1948; *Educ* Hertford GS, Christ Church Coll Oxford (MA), Fletcher Sch of Law and Diplomacy USA (PhD, MALD); *Career* novelist; advsr Mrs Margaret Thatcher 1977–79, dep chm Saatchi & Saatchi 1983–91; govt special advsr Dept of Employment, DTI and Duchy of Lancaster 1981–87, chief of staff Conservative Party 1986–87, jt dep chm Cons Pty 1994–95; *Books* Salt on the Dragon's Tail (PhD thesis, 1975), House of Cards (1989, televised 1991), Wall Games (1990), Last Man to Die (1991), To Play the King (1992, televised 1993), The Touch of Innocents (1994), The Final Cut (1995), Goodfellowe MP (1997); *Recreations* new places, losing weight, genealogy, books; *Style*— Michael Dobbs, Esq; ✉ Bilshay Dairy Farmhouse, Dottery, Bridport, Dorset DT6 5HR (☎ 01308 425808, fax 01308 427069)

DOBBS, Sir Richard Arthur Frederick; KCVO (1991); o s of Maj Arthur Frederick Dobbs, JP, DL (d 1955), of Castle Dobbs, memb Senate of N Ireland 1929–33 and

1937–55, and Hylda Louisa, *née* Higginson (d 1957); descended from Robert Dobbs, of Batley, Yorkshire, whose gs John Dobbs went to Ireland in 1596 (*see* Burke's Irish Family Records); *b* 2 April 1919; *Educ* Eton, Magdalene Coll Cambridge (MA); *m* 28 Aug 1953, Carola Day, da of Gp Capt Christopher Clarkson (d 1994), of Connecticut, USA; 4 s (Andrew b 28 May 1955, Nigel, Matthew, Nicholas), 1 da (Sophia (Mrs Adam Foucar)); *Career* T/Capt Irish Gds (Supplementary Reserve), served WWII; called to the Bar Lincoln's Inn 1947, memb Midland circuit 1951–55; HM Lord Lt Co Antrim 1975–94 (DL 1957–59, Lt 1959–75); *Clubs* Cavalry and Guards'; *Style*— Sir Richard Dobbs, KCVO; ✉ Castle Dobbs, Carrickfergus, Co Antrim, Northern Ireland BT38 9BX (☎ 01960 372238)

DOBBS, Prof (Edwin) Roland; s of Albert Edwin Dobbs (d 1961), and Harriet, *née* Wright (d 1994); *b* 2 Dec 1924; *Educ* Ilford Co HS, Queen Elizabeth's GS Barnet, UCL (BSc, PhD, DSc); *m* 7 April 1947, Dorothy Helena, da of late Alderman A F T Jeeves, of Stamford, Lincs; 2 s (Richard Alexander Edwin b 1952, Jeremy Francis Roland b 1964), 1 da (Helena Jane b 1949); *Career* radar res offr Admty 1943–46; lectr in physics Queen Mary Coll Univ of London 1949–58, assoc prof of physics Brown Univ USA 1959–60 (res assoc in applied maths 1958–59), AEI fell Cavendish Laboratory Univ of Cambridge 1960–64, prof and head Dept of Physics Univ of Lancaster 1964–73; Univ of London: Hildred Carlisle prof of physics Bedford Coll 1973–85, prof and head Dept of Physics Royal Holloway and Bedford New Coll 1985–90, vice dean Faculty of Sci 1986–88, dean Faculty of Sci 1988–90, emeritus prof of physics 1990; visiting prof: Brown Univ 1966, Wayne State Univ 1969, Univ of Tokyo 1977, Univ of Delhi 1983, Cornell Univ USA 1984, Univ of Florida 1989, Univ of Sussex 1989–; memb: Physics Ctee SRC 1970–73, Nuclear Physics Bd SRC 1974–77, Paul Instrument Fund Ctee Royal Soc 1984–; chm Solid State Physics Sub Ctee Sci and Engrg Res Cncl 1983–86, sec The Templeton Lectures 1991–; memb Ripe Church PCC 1991–; FInstP 1964 (hon sec 1976–84), FIOA 1977 (pres 1976–78); *Books* Electricity and Magnetism (1984), Electromagnetic Waves (1985), Basic Electromagnetism (1993), Solid Helium Three (1994); *Recreations* travel, gardening, music; *Clubs* Athenaeum, Physical Soc Club; *Style*— Prof Roland Dobbs; ✉ c/o School of Chemistry, Physics and Environmental Sciences, University of Sussex, Falmer, Brighton BN1 9QJ (☎ 01273 606755, fax 01273 678097)

DOBBY, David Lloyd; s of William Lloyd Dobby, of Walmer, Deal, Kent, and Susan Kathleen, *née* Jobson (d 1986); *b* 6 April 1936; *Educ* St Dunstan's Coll Catford, Regent St Poly (DipArch); *m* 17 March 1967, Lesley Madeline, da of Frederic William Herron (d 1991), and Ivy Elizabeth *née* Cartwright, of Walmer, Deal, Kent; 2 da (Anna b 19 March 1969, Liz b 27 July 1971); *Career* architect 1965; CWS 1957–59, Ronald Ward & Partners 1959–61, Raymond Spratley & Partners 1961–63, Douglas Marriott & Partners 1963–65, James Munce Partnership 1965–68, Rush & Tompkins Group 1968–73; ptnr in private practice 1973–86: John Floydd Partnership, Dobby Foard & Ptnrs, DY Davies Dobby Foard; dir of practice DY Davies plc 1986–88, md Sargent & Potiriadis 1988–89, chartered architect mgmnt consit Practice and Quality Assurance 1990–, exec assoc Watkins Gray International 1990–91; author and illustrator 1991–; memb RIBA Conservation Forum 1995–; House of the Year Design award 1970 and 1972; designs incl: First Bush Bank W Africa, theme park Florida, new railway village Ashford Kent, Rush & Tompkins HQ offices Sidcup, Chatham House Duke of York St St James's, first jt Greek Orthodox and Anglican chapel in UK 1994; parish cncllr 1978–86; treas local ballet sch 1980–85, memb Dover Girls' GS PTA 1980–86, branch chm Dover and Deal Cons Assoc 1992–; ed The Golf Club Secretary 1996–; Freeman City of London 1981, Liveryman Worshipful Co of Joiners and Ceilers 1981; RIBA 1965, LicIQA 1990 (QA assessor 1991); *Books* Royal Cinque Ports - A Personal Record (1992), Golf on the Kent Coast (1993); *Recreations* golf, reading, politics, writing; *Clubs* Royal Cinque Ports, Folio Soc; *Style*— David Dobby, Esq; ✉ 10 Jarvist Place, Kingsdown, nr Deal, Kent CT14 8AL (☎ 01304 373331)

DOBBY, John Michael; s of Herbert Charles Dobby (d 1982), of Dover, and Gwendoline Dobby; *b* 21 Nov 1941; *Educ* Nautical Sch Mercury, City of London Coll; *m* 23 July 1966, Janet Constance, da of Albert Victor Williams; 3 s (Timothy James b 2 Jan 1968, Simon John b 30 March 1970, Martin Jason b 5 June 1972); *Career* apprentice timber importer 1959; Meyer International plc: md subsid Gabriel Wade (Southern) Ltd 1976–80 (dir 1972–80), gen mangr Meyer Merchants 1980–82, jt md Jewson Ltd 1983 (now chm), dir MI Nederland 1984–, dir Van Hoorebeke et Fils 1985–, chm Pont Meyer NV 1993– (dir 1986–), also chm Meyer Forest Products Ltd, chief exec Meyer International plc 1993– (dir 1983–); fell Inst of Wood Sci; *Recreations* swimming, gardening, sailing; *Clubs* RAC, RYA; *Style*— John Dobby, Esq; ✉ Hill Rise, High Street, Meonstoke, Hants SO32 3NH (☎ 01489 878657); Meyer International PLC, Aldwych House, 81 Aldwych, London WC2B 4HQ (☎ 0171 400 8888)

DOBIE, Alan Russell; s of Robert George Dobie (d 1985), and Sarah, *née* Charlesworth (d 1965); *b* 2 June 1932; *Educ* Wath GS, Barnsley Art Sch, London Old Vic Theatre Sch; *m* 1, 1955 (m dis 1961), Rachel Roberts; m 2, 1963 (m dis 1985) Maureen Stobie; 3 da (Casey b 1964, Emelia b 1966, Natasha b 1968); *Career* actor; *Theatre* 41 prodns with Old Vic Assoc London and Bristol 1952–56; to date 112 stage prodns incl: Jimmy Porter in Look Back in Anger (Royal Court and tour) 1957, Bill Walker in Major Barbara (Royal Court) 1958, Col in Live Like Pigs (Royal Court) 1958, Bernard Ross in No Concern of Mine (Westminster) 1958, Private Hurst in Sergeant Musgrave's Dance (Royal Court) 1959, Ulrich Brendal in Rosmersholme (Comedy Theatre) 1960, Louis Flax in Tiger and the Horse (Queens) 1960, title role in Macbeth (Ludlow Castle) 1961, Donald Howard in The Affair (Strand) 1961, Thomas Becket in Curtmantle (RSC Aldwych) 1962, Corporal Hill in Chips with Everything (Royal Court and Broadway) 1963, Bill Maitland in Inadmissible Evidence (Wyndham) 1965, title role in Benito Cereno (Mermaid) 1967, Thomas More in Man For All Seasons (Manitoba) 1968, title role in Hamlet (Manitoba) 1973, Prospero in The Tempest (Edinburgh Festival) 1978, Bottom in A Midsummer Night's Dream (Edinburgh Festival) 1978, Stephan Von Sala in The Lonely Road (London Old Vic) 1984, Atticus Finch in To Kill A Mockingbird (Mermaid) 1989, Haakon Werle in The Wild Duck (Phoenix) 1990, Eichman in Brother Eichman (Library Theatre Manchester) 1990, Nat in I'm Not Rappaport (tour) 1992, Jack in Dancing at Lughnasa (Garrick) 1994, The Judge in Rough Justice (Apollo) 1994, Marcelus/Player King/Grave Digger in Hamlet (Geilgud Theatre) 1995, Black Chiffon (tour); *Television* numerous roles incl: Face in The Alchemist (BBC) 1961, Faustus in Dr Faustus (BBC) 1961, David Corbet in The Planemakers (ATV) 1964, Kurt in Dance of Death (ATV) 1965, The Brothers in The Corsican Brothers (ATV) 1965, William The Conqueror in Conquest (BBC) 1966, Neckludou in Ressurrection (BBC) 1968, Robespierre in Danton (BBC) 1970, Andrei Bolkonski in War & Peace (BBC) 1971, Synavski in Trial of Synavski & Daniel (CBC) 1974, Martin Ellis in Double Dare (BBC) 1976, Stephen Blackpool in Hard Times (Granada) 1976, Cribb in Waxwork (Granada) 1978, Judge Brack in Hedda Gabler (YTV) 1980, Charles Clement in Gericault (BBC) 1982, Rabbi Moses in The Disputation (Channel 4) 1984; *Radio* contrib to 56 radio progs and 160 documentary commentaries; *Films* 7 film incl: Charge of the Light Brigade (as Mog) 1967, A Long Days Dying (as Helmut) 1967; *Recreations* art work, skiing, DIY; *Style*— Alan Dobie, Esq; ✉ c/o Vernon Conway Ltd, 5 Spring Street, London W2 3RA (☎ 0171 262 5506, fax 0171 402 4834)

DOBIE, Brig Joseph Leo; CBE (1969); s of David Walter Dobie (d 1943); *b* 26 Sept 1914; *Educ* Tynemouth HS, Univ of Durham (BSc), Mil Coll of Sci; *m* 1940, Joan Clare, da of Frank Watson (d 1982); 1 s, 3 da; *Career* 2 Lt RE (TA) 1937, Tyne Electrical Engrs RE (TA), Lt RAOC 1938, REME 1942, served WWII; Cmdt Army Apprentices' Sch Aborfield 1962–65 (Col), DDEME 1 Br Corps Germany 1965–66 (Brig), inspr of REME MOD 1966–69 (Brig); exec external rels and mktg ERA 1970–74; dir external activities and exec special projects IEE London 1974–82, dir Michael Shortland Assocs (conslts in computer aided engrg) 1982–87; CEng, FIEE; *Recreations* golf, gardening; *Clubs* Liphook Golf; *Style*— Brig Joseph Dobie, CBE; ✉ Findings, Tower Road, Hindhead, Surrey GU26 6ST (☎ 01428 605469)

DOBIE, Margaret Graham Campbell; OBE (1989); da of Robert Latta, JP (d 1936), of Kirkudbrightshire, and Janet Annie, *née* Campbell (d 1964); *b* 2 Dec 1928; *Educ* Dumfries Acad, Univ of Edinburgh (MA); *m* 27 June 1953, James Tait Johnstone Dobie, DSC, s of William Gardiner Murchie Dobie, MBE; 3 s (Robert b 23 July 1955, Alan b 24 Feb 1958, James b 14 Aug 1964); *Career* chair: Children's Panel Advsy Gp 1985–88, Valuation Appeal Panel Dumfries and Galloway 1986–, South West Scotland Screen Cmmn 1994–96; memb Broadcasting Cncl for Scotland 1987–91, hon vice pres Scottish Assoc for the Study of Delinquency 1992– (vice chair 1989–92); *Recreations* tennis, skiing, travel; *Style*— Mrs Margaret Dobie, OBE; ✉ Garthland, 8 New Abbey Road, Dumfries DG2 7ND (☎ 01387 254595)

DOBKIN, His Hon Judge; Ian James; s of Morris Dobkin (d 1979), of Leeds, and Rhoda, *née* Saipe; *b* 8 June 1948; *Educ* Leeds GS, Queen's Coll Oxford (Hastings exhibitioner, MA); *m* Oct 1980, Andrea Ruth, da of Jack Dante; 2 s (Matthew Jacob b 6 July 1983, Jonathan Edward b 4 Aug 1985); *Career* called to the Bar Gray's Inn 1971, in practice NE Circuit 1971–95, recorder of the Crown Court 1990–95 (asst recorder 1986–90), circuit judge (NE Circuit) 1995–; Parly candidate (Cons) Penistone 1978 and 1979; United Hebrew Congregation Leeds: vice pres 1981–84 and 1992–96, pres 1984–88 and 1996–; vice chm Leeds Hillel Fndn, memb Advsy Ctee Leeds Centre for Criminal Justice Studies Univ of Leeds 1987–; *Recreations* crosswords, music, theatre, reading; *Clubs* Moor Allerton Golf (Leeds), Yorks CCC; *Style*— His Hon Judge Dobkin; ✉ 6 Sandmoor Drive, Leeds LS17 7DG; Leeds Crown Court, Oxford Row, Leeds LS1

DOBLE, Denis Henry; s of Percy Claud Doble, of Canterbury, and Dorothy Grace, *née* Petley; *b* 2 Oct 1936; *Educ* Dover GS, New Coll Oxford (MA); *m* 18 July 1975, Patricia Ann, da of Peter Robinson (d 1985); 1 da (Katie b 1979), 1 s (Robin b 1981); *Career* Colonial Office 1960–65; HM Dip Serv 1965–96, ret: second sec Br Embassy Brussels 1966–68, first sec (devpt) Br High Cmmn Lagos 1968–72, S Asian Dept FCO 1972–75, first sec (econ) Br Embassy Islamabad 1975–78, first sec Br Embassy Lima 1978–82, E African Dept FCO 1982–84, actg dep high cmmr Bombay 1985, dep high cmmr Calcutta 1985–87, dep high cmmr Kingston 1987–91, consul-gen Amsterdam 1991–96; SBStJ 1972; *Recreations* tennis, cricket, cinema, colonial history; *Clubs* MCC; *Style*— Denis Doble, Esq; ✉ 5 Poplar Court, Station Road, Pulborough, West Sussex RH20 1AU

DOBLE, HE John Frederick; OBE (1981); s of Cdr Douglas Doble, RN (d 1972), of Ashbrittle, Somerset, and Marcella, *née* Cowan; *b* 30 June 1941; *Educ* Sunningdale Sch, Eton, RMA Sandhurst, Hertford Coll Oxford (BA); *m* 1 Dec 1975 (m dis 1992), Isabella, da of Col W H Whitbread, TD (d 1995), of Haslemere, Surrey; 1 da (Iona) Louisa b 20 July 1977); *Career* Capt 17/21st Lancers 1959–69 (on exchange with Lord Strathcona's Horse, Royal Canadians 1967–69); HM Dip Serv: FCO Arabian Dept 1969–72, Beirut 1972–73, UK del NATO Brussels 1973–77, FCO Commonwealth Coordination Dept 1977–78, Maputo 1978–81, FCO Info Dept 1981–83; Barclays Bank International 1983–85; consul gen: Edmonton 1985–89, Johannesburg 1990–94; high cmmr Swaziland 1996–; Liveryman Worshipful Co of Merchant Taylors 1971; *Recreations* horse and water sports, history, manual labour; *Clubs* Royal Over-Seas League, Poplar Blackwell and Dist Rowing; *Style*— HE Mr John Doble, OBE; ✉ c/o Foreign and Commonwealth Office (Mbabane), King Charles Street, London SW1A 2AH

DOBLE, Michael John; s of Brian Sinclair Doble (d 1979), and Margaret Ingham, *née* Eastwood; *b* 31 Oct 1951; *Educ* St George's Sch Harpenden, Coll of Law; *m* 8 Sept 1984, Nandika Shankari, da of Dr Victor Thevathasan; 2 s (George Michael b 28 Aug 1985, Edward Oliver b 8 Nov 1987), 2 da (Harriett Victoria Rose b 27 Apr 1993, Anna Elizabeth b 26 Nov 1994); *Career* slr; articled clerk Denton Hall & Burgin, ptnr Denton Hall 1981–; *Recreations* golf, cricket, country sports; *Clubs* MCC, Tanglin, Royal Blackheath Golf, Radyr Golf; *Style*— Michael Doble, Esq; ✉ Denton Hall, Five Chancery Lane, Clifford's Inn, London EC4A 1BU (☎ 0171 242 1212, fax 0171 404 0087); c/o Denton Hall, Beach Road No 08–05, Gateway East, Singapore 89721 (☎ 00 65 291 1219, fax 00 65 293 8102)

DOBSON, *see:* Howard-Dobson

DOBSON, Andrew Charles; s of Raymond Dobson, FRICS, of Rowlands Gill, Tyne and Wear, and Dr Mary Dobson, *née* Meikle; *b* 20 Feb 1956; *Educ* Oundle, St Catharine's Coll Cambridge (MA), Coll of Law Guildford; *m* 10 Aug 1985, Janet Margaret, da of Eric Shiells (decd); 1 s (Patrick Archie Shiells b 18 Jan 1988), 2 da (Alexandra Emma b 30 Dec 1989, Laura Poppy b 19 Nov 1991); *Career* litigation slr Macfarlanes 1980–86 (joined 1978), litigation ptnr Knapp Fishers 1986–87, head Commercial Litigation Lawrence Graham 1987–92 and 1995– (ptnr 1987–); memb: Law Soc 1980, Int Bar Assoc 1990; *Style*— Andrew Dobson, Esq; ✉ Lawrence Graham, 190 Strand, London WC2R 1JN (☎ 0171 379 0000, fax 0171 379 6854)

DOBSON, Prof (Richard) Barrie; s of Richard Henry Dobson (d 1967), and Mary Victoria Dobson; *b* 3 Nov 1931; *Educ* Barnard Castle Sch, Wadham Coll Oxford (BA, DPhil); *m* 19 June 1959, Narda, da of Maurice Leon (d 1981); 1 s (Richard Mark b 1 Dec 1961), 1 da (Michelle Jane b 19 Feb 1963); *Career* lectr in medieval history Univ of St Andrews 1958–64; Univ of York: lectr, sr lectr, reader 1964–76, prof of history 1978–88; prof of medieval history Univ of Cambridge 1988–; pres: Jewish Historical Soc of England 1990–91, Surtees Soc 1987–, Ecclesiastical History Soc 1991–92; chm York Archaeological Tst 1990–; memb Merchant Taylors' Co City of York 1979; FRHistS 1974, FSA 1979, FBA 1988; *Books* The Peasants Revolt of 1381 (1971), Durham Priory 1400–1450 (1973), The Jews of York and the Massacre of 1190 (1974), York City Chamberlains Accounts 1396–1500 (1980), Church and Society in the Medieval North of England (1996); *Recreations* hill walking, swimming; *Style*— Prof Barrie Dobson, FSA, FBA; ✉ Christ's College, Cambridge CB2 3BU (☎ 01223 334900)

DOBSON, Prof Christopher Martin; s of Arthur Dobson (d 1973), and Mabel, *née* Pollard; *b* 8 Oct 1949; *Educ* Abingdon Sch, Keble Coll Oxford (scholar, BSc, MA, Gibbs award), Merton Coll Oxford (sr scholar, DPhil); *m* 1977, Dr Mary Janet Dobson, da of Dr Derek Justin Schove; 2 s (Richard James b 16 Aug 1982, William Thomas b 11 March 1986); *Career* research fell Inorganic Chemistry Lab Univ of Oxford 1975–77, asst prof of chemistry Harvard Univ and visiting scientist MIT USA 1977–80; Univ of Oxford: lectr Brasenose Coll 1980–, fell Lady Margaret Hall 1980–, univ lectr in chemistry 1980–95, reader 1995–96, prof (Aldrichian praelector) of chemistry 1996–, dep dir Oxford Centre for Molecular Sciences 1989–; author of over 250 papers in learned jls; Corday Morgan Medal and Prize Royal Soc of Chemistry 1983, int research scholar Howard Hughes Med Inst USA 1992, Leverhulme Tst sr research fell Royal Soc 1993; memb: Royal Soc of Chemistry 1973, Biochemical Soc 1988; CChem, FRSC 1996, FRS 1996; *Recreations* gardening, family, friends; *Style*— Prof Christopher Dobson, FRS; ✉ Cripps Barn, Otmoor Lane, Beckley, Oxfordshire OX3 9UX (☎ 01865 351548); New Chemistry Laboratory, University of Oxford, South Parks Road, Oxford OX1 3QT (☎ 01865 275916, fax 01865 255921)

DOBSON, Vice Adm Sir David Stuart; KBE (1992); s of Eric Walter Dobson, and Ethel, *née* Pethurst; *b* 4 Dec 1938; *Educ* RNC Dartmouth; *m* 22 Dec 1962, Joanna Mary, da of late A T Counter; 2 s (Ben b 1964 Shaun b 1966), 1 da (Rebecca b 1970); *Career* RN: CO HMS Amazon 1975–76; Cdr Fleet Air Arm Appointer 1976–78; Capt, Naval and Air Attaché Athens 1979–82; SNO Falkland Islands 1982–83; CO HMS Southampton and Capt 5th Destroyer Sqdn 1983–85; Capt of the Fleet 1985–88; Rear Adm and Naval Sec 1988–90; Vice Adm 1991, COS Allied Naval Forces Southern Europe; ret 1994; sec gen Inst for Investment Mgmnt and Research 1996–; FIPD; *Recreations* hill walking, bird watching, choral singing, tennis; *Clubs* Army and Navy; *Style—* Vice Admiral Sir David Dobson, KBE; ✉ c/o Lloyds Bank, 5 The Square, Petersfield

DOBSON, Frank Gordon; MP (Lab) Holborn and St Pancras (majority 10,824); s of James William Dobson, and Irene Shortland, *née* Laley; *b* 15 March 1940; *Educ* Archbishop Holgate's GS York, LSE; *m* 1967, Janet Mary, da of Henry Alker, and Edith; 3 children; *Career* former administrator CEGB and Electricity Cncl; asst sec Cmmn for Local Admin 1975–79; MP (Lab, RMT sponsored): Holborn and St Pancras South 1979–83, Holborn and St Pancras 1983–; oppn front bench spokesman on: educn 1981–83, health 1983–87, energy 1989–92; shadow leader of the House and Lab Pty campaign co-ordinator 1987–89; chief oppn spokesman on: employment 1992–93, transport and London 1993–94, environment and London 1994–; *Style—* Frank Dobson, MP; ✉ 22 Great Russell Mansions, Great Russell Street, London WC1B 3BE; House of Commons, London SW1A 0AA

DOBSON, John Lancaster; s of Louis Charles Dobson (d 1971), of Heywood, Lancs, and Constance, *née* Lancaster; *b* 5 July 1941; *Educ* Bury GS, UMIST (BSc), Univ of Exeter (CertEd), Univ of Leeds (MA); *m* 1970, Katharine Mary, da of Rev William Henry Peter Hills; 2 s (Jeremy William Louis b 1974, Patrick John David b 1975); *Career* educn offr Miny of Educn W Nigeria 1964–69; British Council: lectr in science teaching Univ Coll of Cape Coast Ghana 1970–74 (asst lectr 1969–70), asst rep Islamabad 1974–78, regnl rep Sabah 1978–82, educn offr Adult and Community Educn 1983–86, dep dir Educn Dept 1986–89, rep Bandar Seri Begawan 1989–91, dir E Malaysia 1991–96; *Recreations* photography, reading, walking, model making, narrow gauge railway preservation; *Style—* John Dobson, Esq; ✉ Argoed, Garndolbenmaen, Gwynedd LL51 9RX

DOBSON, Michael William Romsey; s of Sir Denis Dobson, KCB, OBE, QC (d 1995), of London, and Lady Mary Elizabeth, *née* Allen; *b* 13 May 1952; *Educ* Eton, Trinity Coll Cambridge (MA); *Career* Morgan Grenfell Group plc: joined 1973, NY 1978–80, dir Morgan Grenfell Investment Services Ltd London 1980–84, md NY 1984–88, head of int investmt London 1985–86, md Morgan Grenfell Asset Management 1987– (chm 1988–89), gp chief exec Deutsche Morgan Grenfell Group plc 1989–; dir: Anglo and Overseas Trust plc 1987–, The Overseas Investment Trust plc 1987–; *Style—* Michael Dobson, Esq; ✉ Deutsche Morgan Grenfell Group plc, 23 Great Winchester Street, London EC2P 2AX (☎ 0171 588 4545, fax 0171 826 6155)

DOBSON, Nigel Hewitt; s of George Hewitt Dobson (d 1984), of Beckenham, Kent, and Ethel Grace, *née* Boxshall; *b* 13 Aug 1949; *Educ* St Dunstan's Coll; *Career* Whinney Murray & Co (now Ernst & Young) 1968–: Ernst & Ernst St Louis Missouri 1974–75, Corporate Advsy Servs Div Whinney Murray 1976–93, seconded Corporate Fin Dept Midland Bank 1978–80, ptnr 1981–, i/c Restructuring and Reorganisation Servs 1994–; FCA (ACA 1972), MSI 1993; *Recreations* sailing, gardening, reading; *Style—* Nigel Dobson, Esq; ✉ 5 Samuel Court, 44 Kelsey Park Ave, Beckenham, Kent BR3 2UN (☎ 0181 658 3115); Minnis Bay, Birchington, Kent; Ernst & Young, Becket House, 1 Lambeth Palace Rd, London SE1 7EU (☎ 0171 931 3090)

DOBSON, Roger Swinburne; OBE (1987); s of Sir Denis William Dobson (d 1996), and Thelma Swinburne (d 1964); *b* 24 June 1936; *Educ* Bryanston, Trinity Coll Cambridge (MA), Stanford Univ California (DEng), Golden Gate Univ; *m* Deborah Elizabeth Sancroft, da of Richard James Burrough; 1 s (William b 27 April 1977), 1 da (Serena b 5 July 1979); *Career* Binnie & Ptnrs 1959–69; Bechtel Ltd: joined 1969, gen mangr PMB Systems Engineering 1984–86, md Laing Bechtel Petroleum Development Ltd 1986–90; DG and Sec Inst of Civil Engineers 1990–; dep chm Thomas Telford Services Ltd 1990–; chm: Computer Aided Design Working Gp Process Plant Econ Devpt Cncl 1982–87, Energy Indust Cncl 1987–90; memb: Construction Indust Sector Gp (NEDO) 1988–92, DTI Action for Engrg Initiative 1994–96; dir Year of Engrg Success 1996–; memb Br Computer Soc 1969; FICE 1990 (MICE 1963), FEng 1993; *Publications* Some Applications of a digital computer to Hydraulic Engineers (1967), Effective CADCAM Data Exchange (1985), Offshore Structural Design Advances & Trends (1986), Keynote Address (CADCAM Data Exchange Tech Centre, 1986), Cost Effective R & D for Topsides Development (1987), Private Participation in Infrastructure Projects (1989); *Recreations* sailing, tennis, squash, gardening; *Clubs* Royal Ocean Racing, Royal Thames Yacht; *Style—* R S Dobson, Esq, OBE, FEng; ✉ The Institution of Civil Engineers, 1 Great George Street, London SW1P 3AA (☎ 0171 665 2002, fax 0171 222 0267, e-mail dobson_r@ice.org.uk)

DOBSON, Susan Angela (Sue); da of Arthur George Henshaw (d 1994), and Nellie, *née* Flower (d 1978); *b* 31 Jan 1946; *Educ* Holy Family Convent, Assumption Convent Ramsgate, Ursuline Convent Westgate on Sea, NE London Poly (BA, Dip HE); *m* 1966 (m dis 1974), Michael Dobson; *Career* fashion, cookery and beauty ed Femina 1965–69, contributing ed Fair Lady 1969–71; ed: SA Inst of Race Rels 1972, Wedding Day and First Home 1978–81, Successful Slimming 1981, Woman & Home 1982–94; ed-in-chief Choice 1994–; memb: British Soc of Magazine Editors, British Guild of Travel Writers, Bd Plan International UK; *Books* The Wedding Day Book (1981, 2 edn 1989); *Recreations* travel, books, photography, theatre, music, exploring Britain; *Style—* Ms Sue Dobson; ✉ Choice Publications Ltd, Apex House, Oundle Road, Peterborough, Cambs PE2 9NP (☎ 01733 555123, fax 01733 898487)

DOCHERTY, Dr David; s of David Docherty (d 1972); *b* 10 Dec 1956; *Educ* St Mungo's Acad Glasgow, Univ of Strathclyde (BA), LSE (PhD, MSc); *m* 1992, Kate, da of Sir Murray (now Rt Hon Lord Justice) Stuart-Smith, *qv*; 1 da (Flora b 17 Oct 1993); *Career* fell Broadcasting Research Unit 1984–89, research dir Broadcasting Standards Cncl 1989–91; BBC Television: head of bdcasting analysis 1991–93, head of planning and strategy 1993–95, controller of planning and strategy 1995–96, dir of strategy and channel devpt 1996–; *Books* The Last Picture Show (1989), Keeping Faith? Channel 4 and its Audience (1989), Running the Show: 21 Years of London Weekend Television (1990), Violence in Television Fiction (1991); *Style—* Dr David Docherty; ✉ 16 Avondale Park Gardens, London W11 (☎ 0171 243 8208); BBC Television Centre, Wood Lane, London W12 7RJ (☎ 0181 576 7289)

DODD, Jeremy Russell; s of John Russell Dodd, and Hilda, *née* Walker (d 1990); *Educ* Ruthin Sch N Wales, Nat Cert and Dip of Journalism; *m* 23 March 1963, Sylvia Ann, *née* Thorpe; *Career* indentured apprentice Chester Chronicle Ltd 1955–58, gen reporter Kemsley Ltd/Eastern Counties Newspapers Ltd 1958–63; Northcliffe Newspapers Ltd: specialist writer/chief reporter/dep news ed Scunthorpe Evening Telegraph 1963–69, dep news ed Grimsby Evening Telegraph 1963–73; asst PRO Derbyshire CC 1973–74, PRO Cambridgeshire CC 1974–81, chief info offr Anglian Water Authy 1981–88, head of PR Anglian region Nat Rivers Authy 1988–92, head of corp rels Anglian Water plc 1992–94; formerly: nat sec Local Govt Gp IPR, PR advsr E Anglia Consultative Ctee for Local Authys, visiting lectr in PR Fire Serv Staff Coll; Churchill travelling fell 1977, IPR Sword of Excellence 1988; FInstPR 1990 (MIPR 1976), MIMgt; *Publications* numerous articles and papers on PR/water indust and local govt issues; *Recreations* walking, swimming, listening to jazz, enjoying good wine; *Style—* Jeremy Dodd, Esq; ✉ Pawprints, 1a Sheringham Way, Orton Longueville, Peterborough, Cambs PE2 7AH (☎ and fax 01733 230419)

DODD, Kenneth Arthur (Ken); OBE (1982); s of late Arthur Dodd, and Sarah Dodd; *b* 8 Nov 1932; *Educ* Holt HS Liverpool; *Career* singer, comedian, actor, entertainer; professional debut Empire Theatre Nottingham 1954, London Palladium debut 1965 (created record by starring in own 42 week season), appeared in over 20 pantomimes, Shakespearean debut as Malvolio in Twelfth Night (Liverpool) 1971; records incl: Tears (number 1 for 6 weeks), Love Is Like a Violin, Happiness; *Recreations* racing, soccer, reading, people; *Style—* Ken Dodd, Esq, OBE; ✉ 76 Thomas Lane, Knotty Ash, Liverpool L14 5NX

DODD, William Atherton; CMG (1983); s of Frederick Dodd (d 1979) of Mayfield, Newton Lane, Chester, and Sarah, *née* Atherton (d 1976); *b* 5 Feb 1923; *Educ* City GS Chester, Christ's Coll Cambridge (MA, CertEd); *m* 10 Aug 1949, Marjorie, da of Maj Reginald Charles Penfold, MC (d 1970), of Reckerby, Queens Park, Chester; 2 da (Patricia b 1954, Janet b 1957); *Career* WWII Capt 8 Gurkha Rifles 1942–45; sr history master Ipswich Sch 1947–52, educn offr Miny of Educn Tanganyika/Tanzania 1952–65, under sec ODM 1980–83 (advsr 1970–77, chief educn advsr 1978–83), conslt Univ of London Inst of Educn 1983–91 (lectr 1965–70); tstee Amar (Marsh Arabs) Appeal; UK rep UNESCO Exec Bd 1983–85; *Books* Primary School Inspection in New Countries (1968), Society Schools and Progress in Tanzania (with J Cameron, 1970), Teacher at Work (1970); *Recreations* walking, music, watching cricket; *Clubs* MCC, Kent CR, Sevenoaks Vine, Sevenoaks Probus; *Style—* William Dodd, Esq, CMG; ✉ 20 Bayham Road, Sevenoaks, Kent TN13 3XD (☎ 01732 454238)

DODDS, Denis George; CBE (1977); s of Herbert Yeaman Dodds (d 1941), of Newcastle upon Tyne, and Violet Katherine Dodds (d 1928); *b* 25 May 1913; *Educ* Rutherford Coll Newcastle upon Tyne, Armstrong Coll Durham, Univ of London (LLB); *m* 27 Feb 1937, Muriel Reynolds (Pearly), da of Edward Smith (d 1950), of Durham; 2 s (Michael Edward b 9 Sept 1937, Gareth Yeaman b 26 June 1943), 3 da (Philippa Helen b 30 Aug 1944, Jaqueline Eira b 4 March 1947, Stephanie Eileen b 20 Feb 1951); *Career* Lt RNVR 1940–46; served: destroyers, light coastal forces, naval trg; admitted slr 1936; dep town clerk Cardiff 1946–48, sec and slr S Wales Electricity Bd 1948–57, industl relations advsr Electricity Cncl 1957–60, chm Merseyside and N Wales Electricity Bd 1962–77 (dep chm 1960–62); memb Electricity Cncl 1962–77: chm Nat Jt Ctee for Managerial Pay and Conditions, vice chm Nat Jt Industl Cncl for Pay and Conditions of Manual Employees; chm: Port of Preston Advsy Bd 1977–79, Br Approval Serv for Electric Cables Ltd 1981–93, Merseyside C of C and Indust 1976–78; memb: CBI Cncl Wales 1962–78, NW Econ Planning Cncl 1971–79, Nat Advsy Cncl for Employment of Disabled People 1981–92; cmmr for Boy Scouts Penarth S Wales 1950–57, gen sec Bristol Free Churches Housing Assoc 1983–94, memb Westbury-on-Trym PCC 1984–87; CIEE 1960, FIMgt 1960–77; *Recreations* music, gardening; *Clubs* Cwlth Soc; *Style—* Denis Dodds, Esq, CBE; ✉ Corners, 28 Grange Park, Westbury-on-Trym, Bristol BS9 4BP (☎ 0117 962 1440)

DODDS, Nigel Alexander; s of Joseph Alexander Dodds, of Enniskillen, Co Fermanagh, and Doreen Elizabeth, *née* McMahon; *b* 20 Aug 1958; *Educ* Portora Royal Sch, St John's Coll Cambridge (univ scholarship and McMahan studentship, BA, Winfield prize for law), Inst of Professional Legal Studies Belfast; *m* 17 Aug 1985, Diana Jean, da of James Harris, of Loughbrickland, Banbridge, Co Down; 2 s ((Nigel Andrew) Mark b 5 Aug 1986, Andrew James Joseph b 5 Jan 1990); *Career* called to the Bar NI 1981; pty sec Ulster Democratic Unionist Party; elected memb Belfast City Cncl 1985–, Lord Mayor of Belfast 1988–89 and 1991–92; vice pres Assoc of Local Authorities of NI 1988–89; memb: Senate Queen's Univ Belfast 1988–93, NI Forum 1996–; *Style—* Nigel Dodds, Esq; ✉ City Hall, Belfast (☎ 01232 320202)

DODDS, (John) Nigel William; *b* 18 June 1949; *Educ* Barnard Castle Sch, Univ of Nottingham (LLB), Coll of Law; *Career* admitted slr 1973; ptnr Alderson Dodds; memb Cncl Law Soc 1994–; memb Law Soc 1973; *Style—* Nigel Dodds, Esq; ✉ Alderson Dodds, 4/8 Stanley Street, Blyth, Northumberland NE24 2BU (☎ 01670 352293, fax 01670 354166)

DODDS, Sir Ralph Jordan; 2 Bt (UK 1964), of West Chiltington, Co Sussex; s of Sir (Edward) Charles Dodds, 1 Bt, MVO (d 1973); *b* 25 March 1928; *Educ* Winchester, RMA Sandhurst; *m* 9 Oct 1954, Marion, da of Sir Daniel Thomas Davies, KCVO (d 1966), of 36 Wimpole St, London; 2 da (Caroline (Mrs David Pegg) b 1956, Arabella (Mrs Philip H M Dymoke) b 1961); *Heir* none; *Career* Capt 13/18 Royal Hussars; underwriting memb of Lloyd's 1964; insur broker: Bray Gibb & Co (later Stewart Wrightson (UK) Ltd 1958–83), Willis Faber & Dumas 1983–90; Liveryman Worshipful Soc of Apothecaries; *Clubs* Cavalry & Guards', Hurlingham; *Style—* Sir Ralph Dodds, Bt; ✉ 49 Sussex Square, London W2

DODDS-PARKER, Sir (Arthur) Douglas; kt (1973); only s of Arthur Percy Dodds-Parker, FRCS (d 1940, assumed additional surname and arms of Dodds by Royal Licence 1903), and Mary, *née* Wise (d 1934); *b* 5 July 1909; *Educ* Winchester, Magdalen Coll Oxford (MA); *m* 6 April 1946, Aileen Beckett, only da of Norman Beckett Coster (d 1929), of Paris, and wid of Capt Ellison Murray Woods, IG; 1 s; *Career* Sudan Political Serv 1930–39; served WWII Grenadier Gds (despatches), specially employed in Ethiopia and Special Ops 1940–45; co dir 1946–; MP (C) Oxfordshire (Banbury Div) 1945–59, MP (C) Cheltenham 1964–74, MEP 1973–74; under sec of state for Foreign and Cwlth Affrs 1953–57, chm Cons Parly Imperial Affairs Ctee 1950–53; chm: Cons Parly Foreign and Cwlth Ctee 1970–73, Euro Atlantic Gp 1970–74; Freeman City of London 1986; Légion d'Honneur (France), Croix de Guerre avec Palme (France); *Recreations* fishing, walking; *Clubs* Leander, Vincents, Special Forces (chm and pres 1975–81); *Style—* Sir Douglas Dodds-Parker; ✉ 9 North Court, Great Peter Street, London SW1P 3LL

DODGSON, Paul; s of Flt Lt Reginald Dodgson, RAF, and Kathleen Slyvia, *née* Jay; *b* 14 Aug 1951; *Educ* Tiffin Sch Kingston, Univ of Birmingham; *m* 20 Feb 1982, Jan, da of Geoffrey Hemingway (d 1966); 1 s (William Geoffrey b 1 Feb 1991), 2 da (Eleanor b 17 Sept 1984, Laura b 22 July 1986); *Career* called to the Bar Inner Temple 1975, in practice criminal law, recorder of the Crown Ct 1996– (asst recorder 1992–96); *Recreations* sailing; *Clubs* Hardway Sailing, Bar Yacht, Surrey Cricket; *Style—* Paul Dodgson, Esq; ✉ 1 Hare Court, Temple, London EC4Y 7BE (☎ 0171 353 5324, fax 0171 353 0667)

DODSON, Hon Christopher Mark; s and h of 3 Baron Monk Bretton, *qv*; *b* 2 Aug 1958; *Educ* Eton, Univ of S Calif (MBA); *m* 1988, Karen, o da of B J McKelvain, of Fairfield, Conn, USA; 2 s (Benjamin b 1989, James b 1994), 1 da (Emma b 1990); *Career* pres and fndr Applied Digital Technology Beverly Hills California USA; *Style—* The Hon Christopher Dodson

DODSON, Sir Derek Sherborne Lindsell; KCMG (1975, CMG 1963), MC (1945), DL (Lincoln 1987); s of Charles Sherborne Dodson, MD (d 1956), of Leadenham, Lincoln, and Irene Frances, *née* Lindsell (d 1977); *b* 20 Jan 1920; *Educ* Stowe, RMC Sandhurst; *m* 29 Nov 1953, Julie Maynard (d 1992), o child of Hon Maynard Bertram Barnes (d 1970), of Washington DC, USA; 1 s (Gerald b 1957), 1 da (Caroline b 1955); *Career* served 1939–48 in RSF, mil asst to Br Cmmr Allied Control Cmmn for Bulgaria 1945–46; private sec to Min of State FO 1955–58, consul Elisabethville 1962–63, cnsllr and consul-gen Athens 1966–69; ambass: Hungary 1970–73, Brazil 1973–77, Turkey

1977–80; special rep to Sec of State for Foreign and Cwlth Affairs 1980–95; chm: Anglo Turkish Soc 1982–95, Beaver Guarantee Ltd 1984–86; dir Benguela Railway Co 1984–92 (conslt 1992–); Grand Cross of Cruzeiro do Sul (Brazil) 1976; *Recreations* walking, reading, history; *Clubs* Boodle's, Travellers'; *Style*— Sir Derek Dodson, KCMG, MC, DL; ✉ 47 Ovington Street, London SW3 2JA (☎ 0171 589 5055); Gable House, Leadenham, Lincoln LN5 0PN (☎ 01400 272212)

DODSON, Joanna; QC (1993); da of Jack Herbert Dodson, and Joan Muriel, *née* Webb; *b* 5 Sept 1945; *Educ* James Allen's Girls' Sch, Newnham Coll Cambridge (MA); *m* 1974 (m dis 1981); *Career* called to the Bar Middle Temple 1971; memb: SE Circuit, Family Law Bar Assoc; *Style*— Miss Joanna Dodson, QC; ✉ 14 Gray's Inn Square, Gray's Inn, London WC1R 5JP (☎ 0171 242 0858, fax 0171 242 5434)

DODSON, (Peter) Mark Loveys; s of Peter Sidney Dodson, of Colchester, and Elizabeth Katherine Loveys, *née* Davis; *b* 6 Oct 1957; *Educ* St Helena Sch Colchester, Colchester Inst of HE (Dip); *m* 28 Dec 1991, Sarah Margaret McGregor, da of Derek Charles Ralph Burn; *Career* chef; Portman Hotel London 1978–79, Old Court House Hotel Jersey 1979–80, Portman Hotel London 1980–81, sous chef Le Talbooth Dedham Essex 1981–83, head chef The Waterside Inn Bray 1988– (joined 1983, sous chef 1986–88); memb Academie Culinaire de France 1988; *Awards* second prize Mouton Rothschild Menu Competition 1986, Domaines Drouhin Prix des Deux Cartes 1993; *Books* Advanced Practical Cookery (contrib, 1995); *Recreations* record collecting, sport; *Style*— Mark Dodson, Esq; ✉ Roux Waterside Inn, Ferry Road, Bray, Berkshire SL6 2AT (☎ 01628 20691)

DODSON, Richard Charles; s of John Summerville Dodson, of Woodford Green, Essex, and Muriel Edith, *née* Bunce; *b* 2 Jan 1951; *Educ* Buckhurst Hill County HS, UCL (BSc); *m* 14 April 1979, Barbara, da of Allan Carrington, of Kenilworth, Warwickshire; 1 s (Lee b 1968); *Career* media res dir Foote Cone and Belding Ltd 1984–87 (media res mangr 1972), md Telmar Communications Ltd 1988–, pres Telmar Group Inc NY 1989–; treas Woodford Green CC; FIPA 1987; *Recreations* racing horses, cricket, bridge; *Style*— Richard Dodson, Esq; ✉ 15 Fairlight Ave, Woodford Green, Essex IG8 9JP (☎ 0181 491 6626); Curlew Cottage, Talland St, Polperro, Cornwall; Telmar Communications Ltd, 46 Chagford St, London NW1 6EB (☎ 0171 224 9992, fax 0171 723 5265, car 0850 599052)

DODSWORTH, *see:* Smith-Dodsworth

DODSWORTH, Geoffrey Hugh; JP (Herts); s of late Walter J J Dodsworth, and Doris, *née* Baxter; *b* 7 June 1928; *Educ* St Peter's Sch York; *m* 1, 1949, late Isabel Neale; 1 da (Helen b 1958); m 2, 1971, Elizabeth Ann, da of Dr Alan W Beeston, of Liverpool; 1 s (Simon b 1972), 1 da (Mary b 1974); *Career* dir Grindlays Bank Ltd 1976–80, chief exec Grindlay Brandts Ltd 1977–80, chm Oceanic Financial Services Ltd 1985–86 (pres and chief exec 1982–85), dep chm Oceanic Finance Corp Ltd 1985–86 (pres and chief exec 1982–85), pres Jorvik Finance Corp Ltd 1986, dir County Properties Group plc 1987–88, currently chm Dodsworth & Co Ltd (formed 1988), dir of various other cos; memb York City Cncl 1959–65, JP York 1961, MP (Cons) Herts SW 1974–79; Liveryman Worshipful Co of Shipwrights; FCA; *Recreations* riding; *Clubs* Carlton; *Style*— Geoffrey Dodsworth Esq, JP; ✉ Well Hall, Well, Bedale, N Yorks DL8 2PX (☎ 01677 470223); 78 Cliffords Inn, Fetter Lane, London EC4A 1BX (☎ 0171 831 8926, fax 0171 831 9142)

DODSWORTH, Prof (James) Martin; s of Walter Edward Dodsworth, and Kathleen Ida, *née* MacNamara; *b* 10 Nov 1935; *Educ* St George's Coll Weybridge, Univ of Fribourg, Wadham Coll Oxford (BA, MA); *m* 14 April 1968, Joanna, da of Wiktor Slawosz Rybicki; 1 s (Samuel James b 1968); *Career* lectr in English Birkbeck Coll Univ of London 1961–67, lectr, sr lectr then prof of English Royal Holloway Coll Univ of London 1967–; poetry reviewer The Guardian 1969–88, ed English 1976–87; pres The English Assoc 1992–95 (chm 1987–92), Cncl for Univ Eng (co fndr with Dr Gordon Campbell) 1988–90; *Books* The Survival of Poetry (ed, 1970), Hamlet Closely Observed (1985), English Economis'd (ed, 1989), Penguin History of Literature Vol 7: The Twentieth Century (ed, 1994); *Recreations* reading, eating and drinking, short walks; *Style*— Prof Martin Dodsworth; ✉ Royal Holloway, University of London, Egham Hill, Egham, Surrey TW20 OEX

DODSWORTH, Robert Leslie (Bob); DL; s of Harold Dodsworth (d 1985), and Elizabeth Alice, *née* Harding (d 1994); *b* 7 Sept 1936; *Educ* Barnard Castle Sch, Univ of Durham; *m* 11 April 1964, Hazel Joan, da of Augustus Stuart Moyse, of 41 Hardwick Close, Ipswich, Suffolk; 2 s (John b 1967, Simon b 1971), 1 da (Sarah b 1967 d 1970); *Career* CA; gp chief exec Ransomes plc engrs Ipswich 1977–93; dir: Spirax-Sarco Engineering plc, Ipswich Building Society; chm Christchurch Park Hosp; CIAgrE, CIMgt; *Recreations* golf, genealogy; *Clubs* Ipswich & Suffolk, Woodbridge Golf, Ipswich Golf; *Style*— Bob Dodsworth, Esq, DL; ✉ Alnesbourne House, 3 Valley Close, Woodbridge, Suffolk IP12 1NQ (☎ 01394 386849, fax 01394 383844)

DODWELL, Christina; da of Christopher Bradford Dodwell, of Sussex, and Evelyn, *née* Beddow; *b* 1 Feb 1951; *Educ* Southover Manor Lewes, Beechlawn Coll Oxford; *m* 1991, Stephen Hobbs; *Career* explorer and author; 3 year journey through Africa by horse 1975–78; 2 year journey through Papua New Guinea by horse and canoe 1980–81, presenter BBC film River Journey-Waghi 1984 (winner BAFTA award); memb Madagascar Consulate, chm Dodwell Tst; Freedom Sepik River region of Papua New Guinea 1984, winner Mungo Park medal Royal Scottish Geographical Soc 1989; FRGS 1982, FRSA 1985; *Books* Travels with Fortune (1979), In Papua New Guinea (1982), An Explorers Handbook (1984), A Traveller in China (1986), A Traveller on Horseback (1987), Travels with Pegasus (1989), Beyond Siberia (1993), Madagascar Travels (1995); *Recreations* fossil hunting, walking; *Style*— Ms Christina Dodwell; ✉ Hodder Headline, 338 Euston Road, London NW1 3BH (☎ 0171 873 6000, fax 0171 873 6024)

DODWORTH, Air Vice-Marshal Peter; CB (1994), OBE (1982), AFC (1971); s of Eric Albert Dodworth (d 1988), of Southport, and Edna, *née* Barker (d 1988); *b* 12 Sept 1940; *Educ* Southport GS, Univ of Leeds (BSc); *m* 1963, Kay, da of Hugh Parry; 4 s (Antony b 18 March 1965, Christopher b and d 1965, Bruce b 6 Aug 1967, Jonathan b 6 Feb 1976); *Career* cmmnd RAF 1961, flying trg (Jet Provosts and Vampires) 1961–63, No 54 Sqdn (Hunters) 1963–65, No 4 Flying Trg Sch (Gnats) 1965–67, advanced instr Central Flying Sch (Gnats) 1967–69, Harrier Conversion Team 1969–72, Air Staff HQ RAF Germany 1972–76, OC Ops Wing RAF Wittering (Harriers) 1976–79, Nat Defence Coll 1980, Air Cdr Belize 1980–82, Directing Staff RAF Staff Coll 1982–83, Stn Cdr RAF Wittering 1983–85, Cmd Gp Exec HQ Allied Air Forces Central Europe Ramstein Germany 1985–87, RCDS 1987, Dir of Personnel MOD 1988–91, Defence Attaché and head of Br Defence Staff Br Embassy Washington DC 1991–94, head Operations Branch Implementation Team 1994, Sr Directing Staff (Air) RCDS 1994–96; ret; *Recreations* golf, DIY, reading, gardening; *Clubs* RAF (chm 1994–); *Style*— Air Vice-Marshal Peter Dodworth, CB, OBE, AFC

DOE, Canon Francis Harold; s of Spencer F Doe (d 1922), and Ellen Mary, *née* Yerrill (d 1968); *b* 2 June 1922; *Educ* Secdy & Southwark Ordination Course; *m* 3 Sept 1955, (Elinor) Jill, da of Capt David Houseman (d 1956), of Middlesex; 1 s (Michael b 3 March 1959), 1 da (Amanda b 24 Oct 1960); *Career* curate: Sompting 1971–74, Stopham and Hardham 1974–78; priest i/c Sutton Bignor and Barlavington 1978–81, vicar Warnham 1981–87, rector Stopham and Fittleworth 1987–92, rural dean Petworth 1988–92, canon and prebendary Chichester Cathedral 1990–92 (canon emeritus 1992), priest i/c Stansted (and Forestside) 1992–94; asst to Archdeacon of Horsham 1973–; sec of friends and memb Exec Ctee Sussex Historic Churches Tst 1995–; life fell Imperial Soc of Teachers of Dancing; *Recreations* watching cricket, sailing; *Clubs* Forty, Sea View Yacht; *Style*— Canon Francis Doe; ✉ 30 School Hill, Warnham, Horsham, West Sussex RH12 3QN (☎ and fax 01403 218291)

DOE, Rt Rev Michael; *see:* Swindon, Bishop of

DOEH, Doran Moshe Asher; s of Benjamin Benzion Doeh (d 1985), and Pearl, *née* Kerner (d 1984); *b* 14 May 1948; *Educ* Dartmouth Coll USA (Reynolds scholar, BA), Univ of Oxford (MA), Univ of London (LLB); *m* 6 May 1981, Rosalind Susan, da of Denis Grenville Church; 3 s (Anthony Alexander b 1982, Maximilian David b 1984, Benjamin Benedict b 1986); *Career* called to the Bar 1973; legal advsr: Burmah Oil North Sea Limited 1975–76, The British National Oil Corporation 1977–82, Britoil PLC 1982–86; admitted slr 1987; ptnr in charge Moscow office Allen & Overy 1995– (joined 1986); hon assoc Centre for Petroleum and Mineral Law and Policy Univ of Dundee; memb: Law Soc, Int Bar Assoc, RIIA; *Recreations* cooking, wine, opera; *Clubs* United Oxford & Cambridge University; *Style*— Doran Doeh, Esq; ✉ Allen & Overy, One New Change, London EC4M 9QQ (☎ 0171 330 3000, fax 0171 330 3999); Dimitrovsky Pereulok 9, 103031 Moscow, Russian Federation (☎ 00 7 501 258 3111, fax 00 7 501 258 3113)

DOERR, Michael Frank; s of Frank Reginald Doerr, of W Wimbledon, and Florence May, *née* Wright (d 1993); *b* 25 May 1935; *Educ* Rutlish Sch; *m* 24 May 1958, Jill, da of William Garrett; 1 s (Kevin Michael b 17 May 1961), 1 da (Suzanne Jill b 10 March 1964); *Career* Friends' Provident Life Office: joined 1954, pensions actuary 1962–68, life mangr 1968–73, gen mangr mktg and sales 1973–80, ops dir 1980–87, dep md 1987–92, chief exec 1992–; chm: Preferred Direct Assurance Co Ltd 1992–, FP Asset Management Ltd 1995–; also dir: Endsleigh Insurance Services Ltd 1980–94, Seaboard Life Insurance Co Canada 1987–92, Friends' Provident Life Assurance Cos Ireland and Australia 1990–92, Eureko BV Netherlands 1992–, Friends Vilas-Fischer Trust Co (NY) 1996–; FIA 1959 (main prize for best student); *Recreations* tennis, golf, sailing, chess, bridge, theatre; *Clubs* Carlton, RAC, Goodwood Country, Chichester Yacht; *Style*— Michael Doerr, Esq; ✉ Friends' Provident Life Office, Pixham End, Dorking, Surrey RH4 1QA (☎ 01306 740123, fax 01306 888572)

DOGGART, Anthony Hamilton (Tony); s of James Hamilton Doggart (d 1989), of Albury, Surrey, and his 2 w Leonora Margaret, *née* Sharpley (d 1994); *b* 4 May 1940; *Educ* Eton, King's Coll Cambridge (MA); *m* 1 May 1964, Caroline Elizabeth, da of Nicholas Gerard Voute, of The Hague; 1 s (Sebastian Hamilton b 6 April 1970), 1 da (Nike Henrietta b 16 March 1972); *Career* head of Special Business Dept Save & Prosper Gp 1970–74, pres First Investment Annuity Co of America 1974–78, int exec vice pres Insur Co of N America 1978–80, fin dir Save & Prosper Gp 1986–94 (sales dir 1980–86); chief exec: Jardine Fleming Unit Trusts 1994, Fleming European Fund Management Div 1994–; called to the Bar Middle Temple 1962 (memb Lincoln's Inn); vice chm The Crafts Cncl, involved with Waterboatmen Ltd; *Books* Tax Havens and Offshore Funds (Economist Intelligence Report, 1972); *Recreations* skiing, water skiing, wild mushrooms, oak furniture; *Clubs* Garrick, Brooks's, City of London, Hurlingham; *Style*— Tony Doggart, Esq; ✉ 23 Ovington Gardens, London SW3 1LE (☎ 0171 584 7620); Fleming Fund Management (Luxemburg) SA, European Bank and Business Centre, Route de Trèves, L-2633, Luxembourg (☎ 00 352 3410 2001, fax 00 352 3410 2111)

DOGGART, John Victor; s of John Doggart, of Macclesfield, and Sara Doggart; *b* 9 May 1941; *Educ* Uppingham, Clare Coll Cambridge (MA), UCL (MA); *partner* Zoë, da of Air Cdre James Coward, of Canberra, Australia; 1 da (Tamzin b 1973); *Career* architect: Robert Matthew Johnson Marshall 1962, Urban Resources Administration (NY) 1966, Richard and Su Rogers (now Richard Rogers Assocs) 1967–69; energy conslt Milton Keynes Development Corp 1970–80, ptnr ECD Partnership (architects and energy conslts) 1980–95, md ECD Energy and Environment Ltd 1995–; memb: Nat Energy Rating Ctee, BREEAM Steering Ctee, Energy Systems Trade Assoc; CEng, MInstE; *Recreations* canoeing, sailing, skiing, jigsaws, reading; *Style*— John Doggart, Esq; ✉ ECD Energy and Environment Ltd, 11–15 Emerald St, London WC1N 3QL (☎ 0171 405 3121, fax 0171 405 1670)

DOHERTY, Dr Ciaran Conor; s of John Doherty, and Kathleen, *née* Hunter; *b* 29 March 1948; *Educ* St Mary's CBS GS Belfast, Queen's Univ of Belfast (MB, MD, MRCP); *m* Kathleen Mary, da of John Michael Collins, of Belfast; 1 s (Conor b 1981), 2 da (Karen b 1978, Catherine b 1981); *Career* NI kidney res fell 1976–78, clinical fell in nephrology Univ of S California 1979–81, conslt renal physician Belfast City Hosp and Royal Victoria Hosp 1981–, special lectr Dept of Med Queen's Univ of Belfast 1983– (jr tutor 1973–75, clinical teacher in nephrology 1981–), postgrad clinical tutor Belfast Post Grad Med Centre 1985–90; author and co author of 55 papers on kidney disease; pres Irish Nephrology Soc 1986–88, NI rep and cncl memb Nat Assoc of Clinical Tutors 1986; memb Assoc of Physicians of GB and NI 1988, fell Royal Acad of Med in Ireland 1990, FRCP 1992, FRCPI 1992; *Books* Peptic Ulcer and Chronic Renal Failure (1978); *Clubs* Corrigan; *Style*— Dr Ciaran Doherty; ✉ Regional Nephrology Unit, Belfast City Hospital Tower, Lisburn Rd, Belfast BT9 5JY (☎ 01232 329241)

DOHERTY, Kenneth (Ken); s of Anthony Doherty (d 1983), and Rose, *née* Lawler; *b* 17 Sept 1969; *Educ* Westland Row CBS; *Career* snooker player; turned professional 1990; amateur career: memb Rep of Ireland Sr Int team 1984–88 (Jr Int team 1984–87), Irish Jr champion 1983–86, World Jr champion 1987, Irish Amateur Sr champion 1987 and 1989, World Amateur Sr champion 1989; winner: B & H Masters 1990, Regal Welsh Masters 1993, Regal Scottish Masters 1993, Irish Professional Championships 1993, Pontins Professional International 1993 and 1994; runner up: Rothmans Grand-Prix 1993, Skoda Grand-Prix 1994; nominee Texaco Sportstar of the Year 1990, 1992 and 1993; *Recreations* golf, movies, swimming, soccer; *Style*— Ken Doherty, Esq; ✉ Team Sweater Shop, Kerse Road, Stirling FK7 7SG (☎ 01786 462634)

DOHERTY, Prof Peter Charles; s of Eric C Doherty, and Linda M Doherty; *b* 15 Oct 1940; *Educ* Univ of Queensland (BVSc, MVSc), Univ of Edinburgh (PhD); *m* 1965, Penelope Stephens; 2 s; *Career* veterinary surgeon; veterinary offr Animal Res Inst Brisbane 1963–67, scientific offr then sr scientific offr Dept of Experimental Pathology Moredun Res Inst Edinburgh 1967–71, postdoctoral fell then res fell Dept of Microbiology John Curtin Sch of Med Res ANU Canberra 1972–75 (prof and head Dept of Experimental Pathology 1982–88), assoc prof then prof Wistar Inst Philadelphia 1975–82, chm Dept of Immunology and Michael F Tamer Chair in Biomedical Res St Jude Children's Res Hosp Memphis 1988–, prof Depts of Paediatrics and Pathology Univ of Tennessee Memphis 1991–; licentiate RCVS; memb: American Assoc of Immunologists, American Assoc of Pathologists, various editorial bds; Paul Ehrlich Prize (West Germany) 1983, Gairdner Int Award for Med Sci (Canada) 1986, Alumnus of Year Univ of Queensland 1993, Lasker Award for Basic Med Research 1995, DVSc (hc) Univ of Queensland 1995, DSc (hc) Australian Nat Univ 1996; FAA 1983, FRS 1987; *Publications* author of numerous articles in learned journals, book chapters and reviews; *Recreations* walking, reading; *Style*— Prof Peter Doherty, FRS; ✉ 1389 Vinton Avenue, Memphis, Tennessee 38104, USA (☎ 901 725 9522); Department of Immunology, St Jude Children's Research Hospital, 332 North Lauderdale, Memphis, Tennessee 38101–0318 (☎ 901 522 0470, fax 901 522 8570)

DOIG, Caroline May; o da of Lt George William Lowson Doig (d 1942), and May Desson Doig, *née* Keir; *b* 30 April 1938; *Career* house offr and registrar Dundee, gen surgery trg Darlington and Durham, sr house offr in paediatric surgery Glasgow, further paediatric surgery trg Hosp for Sick Children Gt Ormond St London and Hosp for Sick Children Edinburgh; currently: sr lectr in paediatric surgery Univ of Manchester, conslt

Booth Hall Children's Hosp and St Mary's Hosp Manchester; sometime memb: Paediatric Speciality Trg Gp NHS 1976–78, Surgical Div Manchester DHA, N Manchester AHA 1990, Admissions Ctee Univ of Manchester, Univ of Manchester Working Pty on Clinical Academic Provision 1991, Cncl of Manchester Med Soc 1980–83 and 1990–93, Cncl of Paediatric Section RSM 1984–87, Med Advsy Bd Br Cncl 1990–; RCSEd: memb Cncl 1984–94 and 1996–, examiner primary 1980–, examiner part II 1982–, memb Sci and Educn Sub Ctee 1985–89 and 1990–94, memb Nominations Ctee 1994–, memb Devpt Ctee 1995–, memb Fin Ctee 1996–, chm Paediatric Surgical Advsy Bd until 1993, examiner in Singapore 1987 and 1994, Kuwait 1989, Kuala Lumpur 1990, Hong Kong 1990 and 1993, Singapore 1994; Gen Med Cncl: memb 1989–, memb Overseas Review Appeal Bd 1990–91, chm Overseas Ctee 1994– (memb 1990–); Med Women's Fedn: memb 1962–, memb Cncl 1980–87, memb Exec 1981–87, nat pres 1985–86, memb Sub Ctee on Postgrad Trg, memb Med Educn and Ethical Ctee, former liaison offr, former sec/treas Manchester and Dist Branch; Mason Brown lecture RCSEd 1989; memb: Br Assoc of Paediatric Surgns, Assoc of Surgns of GB and I, Assoc of Coloproctology, Br Soc of Gastroenterology, Br Paediatric Soc of Gastroenterology, Scot Paediatric Surgical Soc, Manchester Med Soc, Manchester Paediatric Club; FRSA; *Publications* Colour Atlas of Inguinal Hernias and Hydroceles in Infants and Children (1983), Recent Advances in Surgery (contrib, 1988), Gastroenterology, Clinical Science and Practice (contrib various chapters in vols I and II, 1993), Constipation (contrib, 1994); *Recreations* golf, swimming, gardening, theatre and cooking; *Clubs* Lansdowne; *Style*— Miss Caroline Doig; ✉ 3 Vernon Rd, Salford M7 4NW; Booth Hall Children's Hospital, Charlestown Rd, Blackley, Manchester M9 2AA (☎ 0161 741 5198, fax 0161 741 5609)

DOIG, John; s of David Doig (d 1994), and Mary (Mamie), *née* Maguire (d 1991); *b* 2 Aug 1958; *Educ* Holyrod Sch Glasgow, St Mary's Music Sch Edinburgh (first pupil enrolled at request of Lord Menuhin); *Career* violinist; BBC Symphony Orch 1975–78, princ first violin BBC Philharmonic Orch 1979–81; Scottish Opera Orch: co ldr 1986–88, guest ldr and dir 1988–90, ldr 1990–; fndr and dir Scottish Bach Consort 1994– (memb Bd of Dirs), fndr and artistic dir Killearn Series 1994; performances with Scottish Chamber Orch incl: Flanders Festival, Edinburgh Int Festival, BBC Proms, Carnegie Hall NY; *Recordings* with Scottish Chamber Orch: Bach Brandenburg Concerto No 2, Stravinsky Apollon Masagète, Tchaikovsky/Stravinsky Entr'Acte From The Sleeping Beauty (world premiere), Tchaikovsky Mozartiana, Britten Young Apollo and Les Illuminations; *Recreations* horse riding, dogs, water sports, country walks; *Style*— John Doig, Esq; ✉ Endrick Mews, Killearn, Stirlingshire G63 9ND (☎ 01360 550588); Scottish Opera, Theatre Royal, Glasgow; Scottish Bach Consort, 66 Main Street, Killearn, Stirling G63 9ND (☎ 01360 550824)

DOIG, (Robertson) Lindsay; s of Isaac Doig (d 1977), of Dundee, and Jean Ann Durno, *née* Robertson (d 1986); *b* 30 Aug 1938; *Educ* Univ of St Andrews (MB ChB), Univ of Dundee (ChM); *m* 24 Sept 1966, Roslyn, da of James Mayo Buchanan (d 1989), of Toorak, Melbourne; 3 s (Geoffrey b 1971, Roger b 1974, Colin b 1978); *Career* lectr in surgery and sr surgical registrar St Thomas' Hosp 1968–76, surgn to the Gen Infirmary Leeds and hon sr lectr in surgery Univ of Leeds 1976–; former tutor RCS; fell: Assoc of Surgns, Vascular Surgical Soc, RSM; memb: Br Assoc of Endocrine Surgns, Leeds Medico-legal Soc (memb Ctee, pres 1990–93), Leeds Medico-Chirurgical Soc; Freeman City of London 1978, Liveryman Worshipful Soc of Apothecaries; FRCSEd 1967, FRCS 1969; *Recreations* shooting, history, fine arts, music; *Clubs* Cheselden; *Style*— R Lindsay Doig, Esq; ✉ Strathleven, 439 Harrogate Road, Leeds, W Yorkshire LS17 7AB (☎ 0113 268 0053); General Infirmary at Leeds LS1 3EX (☎ 0113 243 2799); Mid-Yorkshire Nuffield Hospital, Leeds LS18 4HP (☎ 0113 258 8756); BUPA Hospital, Leeds LS8 1NT (☎ 0113 269 3939)

DOIG, Peter; *b* 1959; *Educ* Wimbledon Sch of Art, St Martin's Sch of Art (BA), Chelsea Sch of Art (MA); *Career* artist; tstee Tate Gallery 1996–; *Solo Exhibitions* Metropolitan Gallery 1984, The Naked City (Air Gallery) 1986, Articule (Montreal) 1990, Whitechapel Artist Award (Whitechapel Gallery) 1991, Victoria Miro Gallery 1994, Enterprise (NY) 1994; *Group Exhibitions* New Contemporaries (ICA) 1982 and 1983, Things as They Are (Riverside Studios) 1985, Into the Nineties (Mall Galleries) 1990, Barclays Young Artist Award (Serpentine Gallery) 1991, Inside a Microcosm (Laure Genillard Gallery) 1992, New Voices (Centre Albert Borschette) 1992, Moving into View (Royal Festival Hall) 1993, Twelve Stars (Barbican Centre) 1993, Projet Unite Firminy (Firminy Vert) 1993, John Moores Liverpool Exhbn 18 (1st prize) 1993, Prix Eliette von Karajan (tour, 1st prize) 1994, Unbound: Possibilities in Painting (Hayward Gallery) 1994, New Voices (Br Cncl tour to Spain) 1994, Enterprise 1994, Imprint '93 (Cabinet Gallery) 1994, Here and Now (Serpentine Gallery) 1994, Turner Prize (Tate Gallery) 1994; *Work in Collections* Contemporary Arts Soc, John Moores, Br Cncl, Arts Cncl, Euro Parliament; *Style*— Peter Doig, Esq; ✉ c/o Victoria Miro Gallery, 21 Cork Street, London W1X 1HB (☎ 0171 734 5082, fax 0171 494 1787)

DOLBY, Dr Richard Edwin; s of James Edwin Dolby (d 1991), of Northampton, and Kathleen Florence, *née* Clarke (d 1978); *b* 7 July 1938; *Educ* Northampton GS, Selwyn Coll Cambridge (BA, MA, PhD); *m* Jean Elizabeth; 2 da (Catherine Julia b 30 Aug 1965, Elizabeth Jane b 1 July 1968); *Career* Nat Serv REME 1956–58, graduate trainee Alcan Industries 1962–63, GEC Hirst Research Laboratories 1963–65; The Welding Institute: joined as res metallurgist 1965, head of Materials Dept 1978–80, res mangr 1980–86, dir Research & Technol 1986–; Pfeil prize Inst of Metals 1972, Sir William Larke Medal The Welding Inst 1982, Brooker Medal The Welding Inst 1990; chm Materials Engrg Div Inst of Metals 1988–; chm: Res Strategy Study Gp Int Inst of Welding 1989–, Ctee on Nuclear Plant Structural Integrity UKAEA 1989–; FIM 1977, FWeldI 1977, FEng 1987; *Recreations* golf, philately, gardening; *Style*— Dr Richard Dolby, FEng; ✉ 25 High St, Burwell, Cambridge CB5 OHD (☎ 01638 741305); The Welding Institute, Abington Hall, Abington, Cambridge CB1 6AL (☎ 01223 891162)

DOLL, Prof Sir (William) Richard Shaboe; CH (1996), kt (1971), OBE (1956); s of Henry William Doll, and Amy Kathleen, *née* Shaboe; *b* 28 Oct 1912; *Educ* Westminster, St Thomas' Hosp (DM, MD, DSc, FRCP); *m* 1949, Joan Mary Faulkner, da of Charles William Duncan Blatchford; 1 s, 1 da; *Career* served WWII RAMC; dir Statistical Res Unit MRC 1961–69, Regius prof of med Univ of Oxford 1969–79, first warden Green Coll Oxford 1979–83; chm: Adverse Reaction Sub-Ctee Ctee for the Safety of Medicines 1970–76, UK Coordinating Ctee Cancer Research 1972–77; vice pres Royal Soc 1970–71; memb: MRC 1970–74, Royal Cmmn on Environmental Pollution 1973–79, Standing Cmmn Energy and Environment 1978–82; RCP lectr: Milroy 1953, Marc Daniels 1969; orator Harveian 1982; hon fell 1982–: LSHTM, RSM, BMA; Hon DSc: Reading, Newcastle, Newfoundland, Belfast, Stoney Brook, Harvard, London, Oxford, Oxford Brooke's; Hon DM Tasmania; Hon MD: Birmingham, Bergen; Buchanan Medal Royal Society 1972, Gold Medal RIPH&H 1977, Gold Medal BMA 1983, Royal Medal Royal Society 1986; Hon: FRCGP, FRCOG, FRCR; FRS 1966; *Style*— Prof Sir Richard Doll, CH, OBE; ✉ 12 Rawlinson Rd, Oxford OX2 6UE (☎ 01865 58887, fax 01865 557241)

DOLLERY, Prof Sir Colin Terence; kt (1987); *b* 14 March 1931; *Educ* Lincoln Sch, Univ of Birmingham (Queen's scholar, BSc, MB ChB, Leith Newman prize in pathology); *m*; 1 s, 1 da; *Career* house physician: Queen Elizabeth Hosp Birmingham 1957 (house surgn 1956), Hammersmith Hosp London 1957, Brompton Hosp London 1958; Hammersmith Hosp: med registrar 1958–60, sr registrar 1960–63, conslt physician 1963–; Royal Postgraduate Med Sch: asst lectr in med 1960–61, tutor in med 1961–63, lectr in clinical therapeutics 1963–66, hon dir Med Research Cncl Clinical Pharmacology Research Gp 1966–67, sr lectr in clinical therapeutics Dept of Med 1967–69, prof of clinical pharmacology 1969–87, prof and chm Dept of Med 1987–91, dean 1991–96; dir of R&D Hammersmith, Queen Charlotte's and Chelsea Hosps London 1991–94, pro-vice chllr for med and dentistry Univ of London 1992–; Dept of Health: memb Ctee on Safety of Meds 1966–75, conslt advsr on clinical pharmacology to Chief MO 1979–81; Univ Grants Ctee: memb Med Sub-ctee 1971–80, chm Panel on Pharmacy 1973–77, memb Ctee and chm Med and Dental Sub-ctees 1984–89; memb: Univs Funding Cncl (concurrently chm Med Ctee) 1989–91, Med Ctee CVCP 1992–; first chm Cncl of Deans of UK Med Schs and Faculties 1992–93; memb: MRC (concurrently chm Physiological Systems Bd) 1982–84, Panel of Independent Assessors Nat Health and Med Research Cncl of Australia 1984–; chm: Clinical Pharmacology Section Br Pharmacological Soc 1970–75, Clinical Pharmacology Section Int Union of Pharmacology, Organising Ctee First World Conf on Clinical Pharmacology 1980; pres Int Union of Pharmacology 1987–90 (memb Cncl 1978–81, vice pres 1981–84); memb: Expert Advsy Panel on Drug Evaluation WHO 1982–, Int Cncl of Scientific Unions 1990–93, Univ Grants Ctee Hong Kong 1989– (chm Med Sub-ctee 1990–, memb Institutional Devpt Sub-ctee 1993–); visiting professorships: McMaster Univ Ontario 1972, Univ of Calif LA 1973, Univ of Queensland 1974, Med Univ of S Carolina 1976, Mayo Med Sch Minnesota 1977, Flinders Univ Adelaide, Beijing Med Univ 1987, Harvard Univ 1989, Univ of Chicago 1991, Mount Sinai Hosp NY 1992; numerous named lectures; non-exec dir Life Sciences plc 1988–, conslt Zeneca plc 1992–; memb: MRS, Research Defence Soc, Physiological Soc, Br Cardiac Soc, Br Pharmacological Soc, Assoc of Physicians of GB and I, Euro Soc for Clinical Investigation (past pres); FRCP, FRSM; Chev dans l'Ordre National du Merite (France) 1976, hon memb Assoc of American Physicians 1981, Int Soc of Hypertension Astra Award 1986, Hon MD Liege (Belgium) 1986, Hon DSc Birmingham 1988; *Publications* numerous papers in scientific jls concerned with high blood pressure and drug action; *Style*— Prof Sir Colin Dollery; ✉ Royal Postgraduate Medical School, Hammersmith Hospital, Du Cane Road, London W12 0NN (☎ 0181 740 3200, fax 0181 740 3203)

DOLLOND, Steven; s of Charles Dollond; *b* 28 Nov 1943; *Educ* Quintin Sch, Lincoln Coll Oxford (MA), Harvard Business Sch (MBA); *Career* called to the Bar Middle Temple; private office of Ldr of the Opposition 1968–70, contested (C) Eton and Slough Feb and Oct 1974; mgmnt conslt Arthur D Little 1972–77, mktg dir Br Technol Gp 1977–86, conslt Strategy International 1988–, chief exec Decatur Management 1994–; *Recreations* exotic travel; *Clubs* Carlton; *Style*— Steven Dollond, Esq; ✉ 804 Grenville House, Dolphin Square, London SW1V 3LR (☎ 0171 798 5638)

DOLMAN, Julian Henry; s of Arthur Frederick Dolman (d 1976), of Newport, Monmouthshire, and Margaret Mary, *née* McKinnon; *b* 16 Sept 1939; *Educ* Sherborne, St Catharine's Coll Cambridge (MA); *m* 1, 29 Nov 1962 (m dis 1974), Juliet, da of James White, of Charmouth; 2 da (Catherine b 1964, Sarah b 1966); m 2, 21 Sept 1974, Susan Jennifer, da of Roy Frederick Palmer, of Little Aston, Sutton Coldfield; 2 s (Charles b 1975, Edward b 1976); *Career* admitted slr 1966, ptnr Wall James and Davies; memb Law Soc Panel of Specialist Planning Lawyers 1991–; legal assoc Royal Town Planning Inst 1992–; author of numerous articles on town planning law and occasional lectr at univs; Freeman City of London 1979; memb Law Soc 1966; *Recreations* Africana 1840–52, history, gardening; *Style*— Julian Dolman, Esq; ✉ Forge Mill Farm, Shelsley Beauchamp, Worcs WR6 6RR; Wall James and Davies, 19 Hagley Road, Stourbridge, W Mids DY8 1QW (☎ 01384 371 622, fax 01384 374 057)

DOLMETSCH, Dr Carl Frederick; CBE (1953); s of Dr (Eugène) Arnold Dolmetsch, Chev de la Légion d'Honneur (d 1940), and Mabel, *née* Johnston (d 1963); *b* 23 Aug 1911; *Educ* privately, studied violin with Carl Flesch and Antonio Brosa; *m* 24 Feb 1937 (m dis 1961), Mary Douglas (d 1996), da of James Alexander Ferguson (d 1963), of Over Courance, by Lockerbie, Dumfriesshire; 2 s (François b 1940, Richard b 1945 d 1966), 2 da (Jeanne b 1942, Marguerite b (twin) 1942); *Career* musician; first public concert aged 7 and first tour aged 8; tours incl: Alaska, Australia, Austria, Belgium, Canada, Colombia, Denmark, France, Germany, Italy, Japan, Netherlands, NZ, Sweden, Switzerland, USA; dir: Soc of Recorder Players 1937–, Haslemere Festival of Early Music and Instruments 1940–, Dolmetsch Int Summer Sch 1971–; chm: Arnold Dolmetsch Ltd 1963–78 (md 1940–76), Dolmetsch Musical Instruments 1982–; memb Art Workers Guild 1953– (Master 1988); hon fell Trinity Coll of Music 1950; Hon DLitt Univ of Exeter 1960; hon fell London Coll of Music 1963; ISM; *Books* author of many edns of music and books on recorder playing; *Recreations* ornithology, natural history; *Style*— Dr Carl Dolmetsch, CBE; ✉ Dolmetsch Musical Instruments, 107 BRI, Haste Hill, Haslemere, Surrey GU27 3AY (☎ 01428 643235, fax 01428 654920, telex 858485 DEVCOM G)

DOLTON, David John William; s of Walter William Dolton (d 1969), and Marie Frances Duval, *née* Rice (d 1995); *b* 15 Sept 1928; *Educ* St Lawrence Coll Kent; *m* 1, 1959, Patricia Helen, da of late Maj Ernest G Crowe; 1 s (Kevin b 1964), 1 da (Catherine b 1961); m 2, 1986, Rosalind Jennifer, da of Harold Victor Chivers, of Bath, Avon; *Career* 2 Lt Royal Artillery 1946–48; Delta Metal Group 1950–76: commercial dir Extrusion Div, dir admin and personnel Rod Div 1967–76, also various non-exec directorships; chief exec Equal Opportunities Cmmn 1976–78, asst gen mangr UK National Employers Mutual General Insurance Ltd, dir and asst gen mangr NEM Business Services Ltd 1980–89; mgmnt conslt 1989–; govr The Queen's Coll Birmingham 1974–88; reader emeritus Diocese of Gloucester; Liveryman Worshipful Co of Gold and Silver Wyre Drawers; FCIS, FIMgt, FIPD; *Recreations* music, reading, hill walking, travel, photography; *Style*— David Dolton, Esq; ✉ Arrabon, Cirencester Road, South Cerney, Cirencester, Glos GL7 6HT (☎ 01285 862600)

DOMINGO, Rashid; MBE (1987); s of late Achmat Domingo, of Cape Town, SA, and Rukea Domingo; *b* 24 June 1937; *Educ* Trafalgar HS Cape Town, Univ of Cape Town (BSc); *m* 1962, Moreeda, *née* Maureen Virginia Sheffers; 1 s, 1 da; *Career* prodn mangr: Seravac Laboratories 1961–67, Miles Seravac Laboratories 1967–71; md Biozyme Laboratories Ltd 1971–95; MIBiol, CChem, CGIA, FRCS, FBS, FInstD, FInstM; *Style*— Rashid Domingo, Esq, MBE; ✉ 43 Plas Derwen View, Abergavenny, Gwent NP7 9SX (☎ 01495 859668)

DOMINIAN, Dr Jacob (Jack); MBE (1994); s of Charles Joseph Dominian, and Mary, *née* Scarlatou; *b* 25 Aug 1929; *Educ* Lycee Leonin Athens, St Mary's HS Bombay, Stamford GS, Fitzwilliam House Cambridge (MA, MB BChir), Exeter Coll Oxford (MA); *m* 23 June 1955, Edith Mary, da of John Smith (d 1961), of N Shields; 4 da (Suzanne Mary b 1957, Louise Regina b 1958, Elise Aline (Mrs Milne) b 1961, Catherine Renee b 1964); *Career* Nat Serv RAOC 1948–49; conslt physician then sr house offr Radcliffe Infirmary 1957–58, sr registrar Maudsley Hosp 1958–64, conslt physician Central Middlesex Hosp 1965–88; dir One Plus One Marriage & Partnership Research 1971–; memb: Catholic Marriage Advsy Cncl, Church of England's Cmmn on Marriage; Hon DSc Univ of Lancaster 1976; memb: BMA, RSM; FRCPEd, FRCPsych; *Books* Christian Marriage (1967), Marital Breakdown (1968), The Church and the Sexual Revolution (1971), Cycles of Affirmation (1975), Authority (1975), Proposals for a New Sexual Ethic (1977), Marriage Faith Love (1981), The Capacity to Love (1985), Sexual Integrity (1987), God, Sex and Love (with Hugh Montefiore, 1989), Passionate and Compassionate Love (1991), Marriage (1995); *Recreations* writing, music, theatre; *Style*— Dr Jack Dominian, MBE; ✉ Pefka, The Green, Croxley Green, Rickmansworth, Herts WD3 3JZ (☎ 01923 720972); 10 Harley Street, London W1

DOMINICZAK, Dr Marek Henryk; s of Dr Tadeusz Dominiczak, of Gdansk, Poland, and Dr Aleksandra Dominiczak; *b* 12 March 1951; *Educ* Copernicus HS Gdansk, Med Acad of Gdansk (MB, PhD); *m* 26 Dec 1976, Dr Anna Felicja Dominiczak, da of Prof Jakub Penson (d 1971); 1 s (Peter b 1985); *Career* conslt pathologist St Luke's Hosp Malta 1979–82, registrar and sr registrar Glasgow Royal Infirmary 1982–85, conslt biochemist West Glasgow Hosps Univ NHS Tst 1985–, hon sr lectr Univ of Glasgow 1990– (hon lectr 1986–90); special prof: Univ of Oslo 1974, Rockefeller Univ NY 1989; coordinator EC TEMPUS: Jt Euro Project 1991–93 and Jt Euro Network 1994–, Structural Jt Euro Project 1994–; memb: Br Diabetic Assoc, Assoc of Clinical Biochemists, Br Hyperlipidaemia Assoc, American Assoc for Clinical Chem; FRCPath; *Books* Joint European Project Management Handbook (1994); *Recreations* tennis, photography; *Clubs* University College; *Style—* Dr Marek Dominiczak; ✉ Department of Biochemistry, Gartnavel General Hospital, Glasgow G12 0YN (☎ 0141 211 2788, fax 0141 211 3452)

DON, Robert Seymour; s of Air Vice-Marshal Francis Percival Don, OBE, DL (d 1964), of North Elmham, Norfolk, and Angela Jane, *née* Birkbeck (d 1995); *b* 5 April 1932; *Educ* Eton, Trinity Coll Cambridge (MA); *m* 2 July 1955, Judith Henrietta, da of Geoffrey Nicholas Holmes, of Shotesham All Saints, Norfolk; 4 da (Charlotte b 1956, Joanna Mary (Mrs Thomas Fitzalan Howard) b 1958, Fiona b 1962, Henrietta b 1965); *Career* Nat Serv 1 The Royal Dragoons 1950–52, TA Fife and Forfar Yeomanry 1953–54; John Harvey & Sons Ltd 1957–65, RS Don Ltd and Hicks & Don Wine Merchants, owner Elmham Park Vineyard & Winery 1970–; former chm: English Vineyards Assoc, Norfolk Fruit Growers Assoc; churchwarden St Mary the Virgin North Elmham; Master of Wine; *Books* Off the Shelf (1967), Teach Yourself Wine (1968); *Recreations* shooting, fishing, deer stalking, skiing, photography; *Clubs* Cavalry & Guards'; *Style—* Robert Don, Esq; ✉ Elmham House, North Elmham, Dereham, Norfolk NR20 5JY (☎ 01362 668363/668571, fax 01362 668573)

DON, Robin Cameron; s of John Buttercase Don (d 1970), of Newport-on-Tay, Fife, Scotland, and Elizabeth Seath, *née* Fairbairn (d 1986); *b* 9 June 1941; *Educ* Bell Baxter HS Cupar Fife; *Career* theatre designer; trained to be a blacksmith and engr; apprentice to theatre designer Ralph Koltai 1967–71; designs for Open Space Theatre 1971–77: Four Little Girls, Othello, Tooth of Crime, How Beautiful with Badges, The Taming of the Shrew, And They Put Handcuffs on the Flowers, Sherlock's Last Case, Measure for Measure, Hamlet, The Merchant of Venice; designs for other prodns: Mary Queen of Scots (Scot Opera) 1977, Bartholomew Fair (Round House) 1978, Les Mamelles de Tiresias (RAM/Opera North 1978, ENO 1979), Eugene Onegin (Aldeburgh 1979, Ottawa 1982, San Francisco Opera 1986), The Marriage of Figaro (Opera North) 1979, A Midsummer Night's Dream (Aldeburgh 1980, Royal Opera House Covent Garden 1986), The Flying Dutchman (Opera North) 1980, The Ticket of Leave Man (NT) 1981, Shakespeare's Rome (Mermaid) 1981, Hotel Paradiso (NT of Iceland) 1981, The Trumpet Major (RNCM and WNO) 1981, The Last Elephant (Bush) 1981, Cosi Fan Tutti (NIOT Belfast) 1981, The Birthday Party (Pitlochry) 1981–82, Song and Dance (Palace London) 1982, Madame Butterfly (Opera North) 1982, L'Elisir d' Amore (NIOT Belfast) 1982, The Midsummer Marriage (San Francisco Opera) 1983, Peter Grimes (WNO 1983, Aust Opera Sydney 1986), Twelfth Night (RSC Stratford 1983 and RSC Barbican 1984), The Boyfriend (Old Vic) 1984, Tamerlano (Opera de Lyon) 1984, When I Was a Girl I Used to Scream and Shout (Bush 1984, Edinburgh Festival 1985, Sydney and Whitehall 1986), Giasone (Buxton Festival) 1984, Kiss of the Spiderwoman (Bush) 1985, On The Edge (Hampstead) 1985, Chicago (NT of Iceland) 1985, Man of Two Worlds (Westminster) 1985, Don Quixote (NY City Opera) 1986, More Light (Bush) 1987, Norma (Covent Garden) 1987, Carmen (Sydney) 1987, La Forza del Destino (Toronto) 1987, Fat Pig (Haymarket Leicester) 1987, Spookhouse (Hampstead) 1987, The Brave (Bush) 1988, Ziegfeld (London Palladium) 1988, A Walk in the Woods (Comedy) 1988, Cavalleria Rusticana (Sydney) 1989, Hidden Laughter (Vaudeville) 1990, The Rocky Horror Show (Piccadilly) 1990, Macbeth (Santiago Ballet) 1991, The Magic Flute (Iceland) 1991, (Sweden) 1992, Someone Who'll Watch Over Me (Hampstead Theatre 1992, Broadway 1992, Dublin 1993), Beautiful Thing (Bush) 1993, Eugene Onegin (Iceland) 1993, Black Comedy (Zurich) 1993, The Rocky Horror Show (Minneapolis) 1993, Il Pagliacci (Sydney) 1994, Darwin's Flood (Bush) 1994, The Knocky (Royal Court) 1995, The Winter Guest 1995 (Almeida, West Yorkshire Playhouse (nominated TMA Regional Theatre Awards for Best Design)), The Maiden Stone (Hampstead) 1995, Boom Bang A Bang (Bush) 1995, Hamlet (Royal Lyceum Theatre Co Edinburgh) 1995, Les Enfants du Paradis (RSC) 1996; dir Int Scenography Course Central St Martin's Sch of Art and Design London 1990–; memb: Exec Ctee Soc of Br Theatre Designers 1975–91, British Theatre Design 1979–1983, British Theatre Design 1983–87; winner Golden Troika (for Eugene Onegin) at Prague Quadriennale 1979; *Recreations* exploration of natural phenomena; *Style—* Robin Don, Esq; ✉ c/o MLR Ltd, 200 Fulham Road, London SW10 9PN (☎ 0171 351 5442, fax 0171 351 4560)

DON-WAUCHOPE, Sir Roger Hamilton; 11 Bt (NS 1667), of Edmonstone and Newton; elder s of Sir Patrick George Don-Wauchope, 10 Bt (d 1989), and Ismay Lilian Ursula, *née* Hodges; *b* 16 Oct 1938; *Educ* Hilton Coll Natal, Durban and Pietermaritzburg Univ; *m* 14 Dec 1963, Sallee, yr da of Lt-Col Harold Mill-Colman, OBE, ED, of Durban, S Africa; 2 s, 1 da; *Heir* s, Andrew Craig Don-Wauchope b 18 May 1966; *Career* ptnr Deloitte & Touche CAs S Africa 1972– (joined 1959); CA(SA), HDipTax; *Clubs* Victoria (chm), Maritzburg Country, Durban Country, Old Hiltonian (nat chm); *Style—* Sir Roger Don-Wauchope, Bt; ✉ Newton, 53 Montrose Drive, Pietermaritzburg 3201, Natal, S Africa (☎ 00 27 331 471107, fax 00 27 331 450285)

DONACHIE, Prof William David; s of Charles Donachie (d 1966), and Jessie, *née* Leiper; *b* 27 April 1935; *Educ* Dunfermline HS, Univ of Edinburgh (BSc, Sir David Baxter scholar, PhD); *m* 1965, Dr Millicent Masters; 1 s (David b 1974); *Career* asst lectr in genetics Univ of Edinburgh 1958–61; research assoc in biochemical scis Princeton Univ 1962–63; lectr in genetics Univ of Edinburgh 1963–65; on staff: MRC Microbial Genetics Research Unit Hammersmith Hosp 1965–68, Molecular Genetics Unit Edinburgh 1968–74; Univ of Edinburgh: sr lectr in molecular biology 1974–80, reader 1980–93, prof of bacterial genetics 1993–; visiting prof: Univ of Copenhagen 1978, Univ of Paris (VII) 1988; memb Academia Europaea 1989; *Recreations* natural history, drawing, t'ai chi, gardening and other good things; *Style—* Prof William D Donachie; ✉ Institute of Cell and Molecular Biology, University of Edinburgh, Darwin Building, King's Buildings, Mayfield Road, Edinburgh EH9 3JR (☎ 0131 650 5354, fax 0131 668 3870)

DONAGHY, Roger; s of George Gerald Donaghy (d 1989), of Portadown, Co Armagh, NI, and Florence, *née* Thompson; *b* 10 Feb 1940; *Educ* Portadown Tech Coll, Univ of Adelaide; *m* 17 Nov 1962, Rachael, da of Joseph Watson, of Portadown, Co Armagh, NI; 1 da (Nina Diane b 1968); *Career* reporter and feature writer Portadown Times 1955–61, feature writer Advocate Newspapers Tasmania 1961–63, TV reporter and industl corr Aust Broadcasting Corp Adelaide 1961–65; BBC World Serv News 1966–: journalist, duty ed, newsroom ed; FDR memb Rotary Club of Danson; *Recreations* golf, travel, reading, photography; *Style—* Roger Donaghy, Esq; ✉ 41 Bean Rd, Bexleyheath, Kent (☎ 0181 303 5109); BBC, Bush House, Strand, London WC2 (☎ 0171 240 3456)

DONALD, Dr Alastair Geoffrey; CBE (1993, OBE 1982); s of Dr Pollok Donald (d 1955), of Edinburgh, and Henrietta Mary, *née* Laidlaw (d 1975); *b* 24 Nov 1926; *Educ* Edinburgh Acad, CCC Cambridge (MA), Univ of Edinburgh (MB ChB); *m* 3 April 1952, (Edna) Patricia, da of Richard Morrison, WS (d 1944); 2 s (Ian Pollok b 1955, William b 1960), 1 da (Patricia Mary b 1953); *Career* Sqdn-Ldr Med Branch RAF 1952–54; GP Edinburgh 1954–, lectr Dept of Gen Practice Univ of Edinburgh 1960–70; RCGP: vice chm Cncl 1976–77, chm Bd of Censors 1979–80, chm Cncl 1979–82, chm Int Ctee 1987–91, pres 1992–94; past chm and provost SE Scotland Faculty, radio doctor BBC Scotland 1976–78; chm: UK Conf of Postgrad Advrs in Gen Practice 1978–80, Court of Dirs The Edinburgh Acad 1978–85 (dir 1957–85), Jt Ctee on Postgrad Trg for Gen Practice 1982–85, Armed Servs Gen Practice Approval Bd 1986–, Scottish Ctee Action on Smoking and Health 1986–93, Med Advsy Gp BBC Scotland 1988–; specialist advsr to House of Commons Social Servs Ctee 1986–87; vice chm Med & Dental Defence Union Scotland 1991–; James MacKenzie Medal RCP Edinburgh 1983, Hippocrates Medal 1994; James MacKenzie lectr RCGP 1985, Bruce Meml lectr 1987; pres: Rotary Club Leith 1957–58, Edinburgh Academical Club 1978–81; FRCGP 1971, FRCPE 1981, Hon FRCPAS (Glasgow) 1993; *Recreations* golf; *Clubs* Hawks' (Cambridge), Univ of Edinburgh Staff; *Style—* Dr Alastair Donald, CBE; ✉ 30 Cramond Rd North, Edinburgh EH4 6JE (☎ 0131 336 3824); Leith Mount, 46 Ferry Rd, Edinburgh EH6 4AE (☎ 0131 554 0558)

DONALD, Chris Mark; s of Hugh Ernest James Donald, of Newcastle upon Tyne, and late Kathleen Evelyn, *née* Rickard; *b* 25 April 1960; *Educ* Heaton Comp Newcastle, Newcastle Coll of Arts; *m* 15 May 1988, Dolores Clare, da of Charles Doherty; 1 s (Dale Thomas b 30 Sept 1989), 1 da (Jamie Clare b 15 Sept 1991); *Career* clerical offr DHSS Central Office Newcastle 1978–80, founded Viz Magazine 1979, ed Viz 1979–, student Newcastle Coll of Arts 1981–82, set up House of Viz to publish Viz full time 1984 (signed publishing agreement Virgin Books 1985 then John Brown Publishing Ltd 1987); Br Magazine Publishing Awards Youth Magazine Ed of the Year 1989; *Books* Viz: The Big Hard One (1986), Viz: The Big Hard Number Two (1987), Viz: The Big Pink Stiff One (1988), Viz: Holiday Special (1988), Viz: The Dog's Bollocks (1989), The Viz Book of Crap Jokes (1989), The Billy the Fish Football Yearbook (1989), Viz: The Spunky Parts (1990), Viz: The Sausage Sandwich (1991), Viz: The Fish Supper (1992), Viz: The Pork Chopper (1993), The Viz Book of Absolute Shite for Boys and Girls (1993), Viz: The Pan Handle (1994), The Viz Book of Top Tips (1994), Viz: The Bell End (1995), Top Tips Two (1995), Viz: The Turtle's Head (1996), Viz Letterbocks (1996), Viz: The Joy of Sexism (1996); *Recreations* railway station restoration, Newcastle United supporter, signwriting; *Style—* Chris Donald, Esq; ✉ House of Viz, PO Box 1PT, Newcastle upon Tyne NE99 1PT (☎ 0191 281 8177, fax 0191 281 9048)

DONALD, George Malcolm; s of George Donald, of Bieldside, Aberdeen, and Margaret, *née* Tait (d 1947); *b* 12 Sept 1943; *Educ* Robert Gordons Coll Aberdeen, Aberdeen Acad, Edinburgh Coll of Art (Andrew Grant scholar, post grad scholar, DA), Benares Hindu Univ (travelling scholar), Hornsey Coll of Art (CertEd), Univ of Edinburgh (MEd); *m* 1969 (m dis 1986); 1 da (Saskia b 1971), 1 s (Ninian Fraser b 1973); *Career* artist and printmaker; dir Centre for Continuing Studies Edinburgh Coll of Art; visiting prof Chinese Acad of Fine Art China 1993 and 1994; memb: SSA, Printmaker's Workshop; RSA 1992; *Solo Exhibitons* 57 Gall 1971, Pool Theatre Gall 1972, Shed 50 Gall 1974, Edinburgh Scottish Gall 1981, Bohun Gall 1984, Chine Collé 1984 and 1987, Open Eye Gall 1985, Peacock Printmakers' Gall 1985, Glasgow Print Workshops Gall 1985, Helsinki Festival 1985, Finnish Assoc of Printmakers' Gall 1985, Galerija Fakulteta Likovnih Umetnosti 1987, From the Edge (tour) 1990, New Paintings from China (Open Eye Gall) 1991, Christopher Hull Gall 1992, Far East - New Paintings from China and Japan (Open Eye Gall) 1993, 9 Translations from the Chinese 1994, New Paintings (Open Eye Gall) 1995; *Group Exhibitions* Marjorie Parr Gall 1968 and 1971, Edinburgh Int Festival 1968, Pernod Exhbn 1968, Scottish Graphics (57 Gall) 1971, Int Graphics (Carnegie Festival) 1971, Richard Demarco Gall 1972, Goosewell Gall 1972, McLellan Galls 1974, Mall Gall 1974, Among the Quiet Weavers (Weavers' Workshop) 1974, 20 x 57 Exhbn (57 Gall) 1975, Compass Gall 1975 and 1981, Young Scottish Artists (Scottish Gall) 1976, Scottish Print Open (Scottish Arts Cncl) 1976, New Prints (Printmakers' Workshop) 1976, Alamo Gall 1978, Scottish Gall 1978, Photo-Graphic (Printmakers' Workshop) 1979, Contemporary Papermakers (City Art Centre Edinburgh) 1980, UCF Gall 1981, Print Annual 2 (PMW) 1981, NY Festival City Gall 1983, Open Eye Gall 1983 and 1986, Mercury Gall 1983, 1984 and 1986, Sue Rankin Gall 1984 and 1987, Fine Art Soc 1984 and 1985, Nicholson Gall 1986, Charter House Gall 1986, Christopher Hull Gall 1987 and 1990, Smiths Galls 1987, Sarajevo Winter Festival 1988, Graphica Creativa 90 (Alvar Aalto Museum) 1990, One Hundred Years of Scottish Printmakers (Hunterian Museum) 1990, Bohun Gall 1990, Images of the Orient (Kingfisher Gall) 1990, Cormund Gall 1990, Gallery 41 1992, RSW (annually) 1992–, RSA (annually) 1992–, Open Eye Gall 1992, Loomshop Gall 1993; *Works in Collections* V & A, Nat Library of Scotland, Hunterian Museum, Scottish Arts Cncl, BBC, Nuffield Fndn, Miro Fndn Mallorca; *Awards* Latimer Award RSA 1970, Guthrie Award RSA 1973, Gillies prize RSA 1982, May Marshall Brown Award RSW 1983; *Recreations* fiddling, pottering, travelling; *Style—* George Donald, Esq, RSA; ✉ Edinburgh College of Art, Lauriston Place, Edinburgh EH3 9DF (☎ 0131 221 6111, fax 0131 221 6109)

DONALD, Hugh Robertson; s of Robert Donald, of Edinburgh, and Anne Mary, *née* Dovall (d 1994); *b* 5 Nov 1951; *Educ* Melville Coll Edinburgh, Univ of Edinburgh (LLB Hons); *m* 16 Aug 1975, Margaret Grace; 1 s (Euan Christopher b 6 July 1979), 1 da (Morag Elizabeth b 21 July 1981); *Career* Shepherd & Wedderburn: apprentice 1973–75, slr 1975–77, ptnr 1977–, managing ptnr 1994, chief exec 1995–; chm Family Mediation Scotland; WS 1979; *Recreations* walking, gardening, family; *Style—* Hugh Donald, Esq; ✉ Chief Executive, Shepherd & Wedderburn WS, Saltire Court, 20 Castle Terrace, Edinburgh EH1 2ET (☎ 0131 228 9900, fax 0131 228 1222, e-mail desk@shepwedd.co.uk)

DONALD, Ian Francis; s of Harold Gordon Donald (d 1975), of Cape Town, SA, and Jean Dorian, *née* Graham (d 1947); *b* 20 Aug 1928; *Educ* St Peter's Coll Adelaide S Aust; *m* 20 Nov 1958, Sonia Evelyn, da of James Bruce Leask, CBE (d 1980), of Pangbourne, Berks; 1 s (Adrian Francis b 1963), 1 da (Caroline Bruce b 1968); *Career* jt md Firth Cleveland Ltd 1960–72, dep chm Guest Keen & Nettlefolds plc (now GKN plc) 1972–88; chm: Allen West Ltd Ayr 1985–89, United Engineering Steels Ltd 1986–92; dir Hall Engineering (Holdings) plc 1987–, vice chm Gwent Community NHS Tst 1993–; chm: Hayward Fndn, Charles Hayward Tst; High Sheriff of Gwent 1996–97; FInstD; *Recreations* shooting, fishing, sailing; *Clubs* Royal Thames Yacht, RAC; *Style—* Ian Donald, Esq; ✉ Rockfield Farm, Monmouth, Gwent NP5 4NH (☎ 01600 713217, fax 01600 714715)

DONALD, John Alistair; *b* 6 Dec 1928; *Educ* Farnham GS, Farnham Sch of Art, RCA (travel scholarship); *m* (m dis); 4 s, 1 da; *Career* Nat Serv 1947–49; self-employed designer, goldsmith and silversmith; design conslt: Hadley Co 1956–75, Antler Luggage 1958–68, Halex hairbrushes 1960–65; exhibitor with Goldsmiths Co NY 1960, fndr own workshop Bayswater 1960; proprietor: retail shop and workshop Cheapside 1968–, retail shop (with Tecla Pearls) Bond St London 1969–72, additional workshop Sussex 1970; external assessor to various maj arts and crafts schs, chief assessor Chamber of Mines jewellery competition SA 1972 and 1973; work incl: civic and presidential regalia, silver for Birmingham Cathedral, Oxford & Cambridge Colls and City Livery Cos; work in the private collections of: HRH The Queen Mother, HRH Princess Margaret, HRH Prince Charles, Duchess of Gloucester, Queen Margarethe of Denmark, Rt Hon Mrs Thatcher; former offices incl: Sheriff of Nottingham, Mayor of Lincoln, Sheriff City of London;

Warden Worshipful Co of Goldsmiths (Freeman 1959, Liveryman 1972); *Recreations* golf; *Style—* John Donald, Esq; ✉ 120 Cheapside, London EC2V 6DR (☎ 0171 606 2675)

DONALDSON, Dr Alexander Ivan (Alex); s of Basil Ivan Samuel Donaldson, of Dublin, and Dorothy Cunningham, *née* Brown; *b* 1 July 1942; *Educ* Dublin HS, Sch of Veterinary Medicine Trinity Coll Dublin (foundation scholar, MA, MVB, ScD); *m* 1966, Margaret Ruth Elizabeth, da of Scott McDermot Swan; 1 da (Kerry Michele b 24 May 1969), 1 s (Michael Richard b 12 Feb 1971); *Career* post grad student Ontario Veterinary Coll Univ of Guelph 1965–69, postdoctoral fell Animal Virus Res Inst (now BBSRC Inst for Animal Health) 1969–71, asst prof Ontario Veterinary Coll Univ of Guelph 1972–73; BBSRC (formerly AFRC) Inst for Animal Health: veterinary res offr 1973–76, princ veterinary res offr 1976–89 (head of World Reference Laboratory for Foot and Mouth Disease 1985–89), head of Pirbright Laboratory and Div of Epidemiology 1989–; memb: BVA, RCVS, Soc for Gen Microbiology, Veterinary Res Club, Assoc of Veterinary Teachers and Res Workers, Soc for Veterinary Epidemiology and Preventative Med; *Awards* Commonwealth Bureau of Animal Health Prize and Evans Veterinary Med Prize 1964, Stevenson, Turner and Boyce Award 1966, RASE Res Medal 1988, Barei Prize (Italy) 1994; *Recreations* reading, photography, windsurfing; *Style—* Dr Alex I Donaldson; ✉ Pirbright Laboratory, Institute for Animal Health, Ash Road, Pirbright, Woking, Surrey GU24 0NF (☎ 01483 232441, fax 01483 232448)

DONALDSON, Antony Christopher; s of Sqdn Ldr John William Donaldson, DSO, AFC (ka 1940), and Sheila Richardson, *née* Atchley; *b* 2 Sept 1939; *Educ* Charterhouse, Regent Street Poly, Slade Sch, UCL; *m* 1960, Patricia Anne, da of Charles William Marks; 2 s (Matthew John b 1961, Lee b 1963); *Career* artist; teacher Chelsea Sch of Art 1962–66, Harkness fell USA; recents cmmns incl: bronze and iron screen Yohji Yamamoto London 1987, bronze entrance doors Joyce Hong Kong 1988, fountain Horselydown Square, Tower Bridge Piazza London, Michael Baumgarten for Berkeley House 1988–91 and torso Anchor Ct Horselydown Square 1989–91, aquarium wall and doors Arnold Chan Isometrics London 1990, wall piece Emmanuelle Khanh Paris 1990, bronze entrance doors Tina Tan Leo Ngee-Ann City Singapore 1993, sculpture entrance lobby Park Hyatt Hotel Tokyo, architect Kenzo Tange 1992–94; work in public collections incl: Arts Cncl of GB, Bradford City Art Gallery, Contemporary Art Soc London, Govt Art Collection, Olinda Museum Brazil, Tate Gallery, Ulster Museum Belfast, Walker Art Gallery Liverpool; *Exhibitions* solo incl: Rowan Gallery London 1963, 1965, 1966, 1968, 1970, 1979 and 1981, Nicholas Wilder Gallery Los Angeles 1968, Galleria Milano Milan 1971, Galerie du Luxembourg Paris 1973, 1976 and 1977, Bonython Gallery Adelaide Australia 1983, Juda Rowan Gallery London 1984, Daniel Gervis Paris 1985, Corcoran Gallery Los Angeles 1985, Mayor Rowan Gallery London 1989, Daniel Gervis Cannes 1992; group incl: Young Contemporaries (London) 1958, 1959, 1960 and 1961, John Moores Open (Walker Art Gallery Liverpool) 1963, The New Generation (Whitechapel Art Gallery) 1964, 4ieme Biennale des Jeunes Artistes Musee d'Art Moderne Paris 1965, Recent British Painting (Peter Stuyvesant Fndn Collection) 1967, Pittsburgh Int 1967, Art for Industry (RCA) 1969, Contemporary Prints (Ulster Museum Belfast) 1972, British Pop Art (Birch and Conran Fine Art London) 1987; *Films* Soft Orange 1969, Pix 1972; *Style—* Antony Donaldson, Esq; ✉ c/o Neffe-Degandt, 32a St George Street, London W1R 9FA

DONALDSON, (William) Blair MacGregor; s of Dr William Donaldson, of Edinburgh, and Janet Thompson, *née* Orr (d 1970); *b* 24 Dec 1940; *Educ* The Edinburgh Acad, Univ of Edinburgh (MB ChB), FRCS, FRCOphth, DO; *m* 27 July 1966, Marjorie Stuart, da of Hugh Gordon Mackay (d 1958); 1 da (Lesley Elizabeth b 1972); *Career* jr hosp appts in Tasmania and Scotland 1966–79, conslt ophthalmic surgn, sr univ lectr 1979– (special interest in microsurgical instrument design and devpt); memb: BMA, SOC, MECA; *Recreations* silversmithing, oil painting, antique restoration, skiing, golf; *Style—* Blair Donaldson, Esq; ✉ Kindrochit Lodge, Braemar, Deeside, Aberdeenshire; 45 Carlton Place, Aberdeen (☎ 01224 641166)

DONALDSON, David Torrance; QC (1984); s of Alexander Walls Donaldson, of Glasgow, and Margaret Merry, *née* Bryce; *b* 30 Sept 1943; *Educ* Glasgow Acad, Gonville and Caius Coll Cambridge (MA), Univ of Freiburg (DrJur); *m* 31 Dec 1985, Therese Marie Madeleine, da of Pierre Arminjon; *Career* fell Gonville and Caius Coll Cambridge 1965–1969, called to the Bar Gray's Inn 1968, recorder of the Crown Court; *Style—* David Donaldson, Esq, QC; ✉ 2 Hare Court, Temple, London EC4Y 7BH (☎ 0171 583 1770, fax 0171 583 9269)

DONALDSON, Prof Gordon Bryce; s of Alexander Walls Donaldson, of Glasgow, and Margaret Merry, *née* Johnston; *b* 10 Aug 1941; *Educ* Glasgow Acad, Univ of Cambridge (major open scholar, English Electric scholar, MA, PhD); *m* 15 Aug 1964, Christina, da of John Alexander Martin; 1 s (Ian Martin b 21 July 1966), 1 da (Anne Dunlop b 14 Oct 1968); *Career* lectr in physics Univ of Lancaster 1966–75, visiting scientist Univ of California Berkeley (Fulbright scholar) 1975; Univ of Strathclyde: lectr 1976–78, sr lectr 1978–85, head Dept of Applied Physics 1984–86, personal prof 1985–88, prof of applied physics 1988–, head Dept of Physics and Applied Physics 1993–; visiting prof Univ of Virginia Charlottesville 1981; nat co-ordinator for superconductivity SERC/DTI 1990–93; FInstP, CPhys, FRSE 1991; *Publications* author of over 100 scientific papers concerned chiefly with the science and applications of superconductivity, including chapters (some co-authored) in: Active and Passive Thin Film Devices (1978), Superconducting Electronics (1990), Concise Encyclopaedia of Magnetic and Superconducting Materials (1992), The New Superconducting Electronics (1993); *Style—* Prof Gordon B Donaldson, FRSE; ✉ 108 Springkell Avenue, Pollokshields, Glasgow G41 4EW (☎ 0141 427 3668); Department of Physics and Applied Physics, John Anderson Building, University of Strathclyde, Glasgow G4 0NG (☎ 0141 553 4134, fax 0141 552 7143)

DONALDSON, Hugh Montgomery; s of Dr Ian Montgomery Kerr Donaldson (d 1968), of Glasgow, and Annie Meek May, *née* Ferrier; *b* 21 Dec 1941; *Educ* Kelvinside Acad Glasgow, Univ of Glasgow (BSc), Univ of Strathclyde (MSc); *m* 8 Oct 1965, (Shirley) Rosemary, da of Shirley Edwin McEwan (Sem) Wright; 2 s (Richard Ian Montgomery b 14 Oct 1966, Nicholas Phillip Kerr b 19 Sept 1968), 1 da (Susannah Jane b 29 Nov 1971); *Career* sandwich apprentice Fairfield Shipbuilding and Engineering Co Ltd 1959–63; ICI: various maintenance research jobs Nobel Div until 1971 (joined as engr 1964), Organics Div 1971–73, area engr Huddersfield works 1973–76, project gp mangr Engrg Dept 1976–78, works engr Huddersfield Works 1978–81, chief engr ICI plc Engrg Dept NW and Fine Chemicals 1981–85, ops dir ICI Organics Div and Fine Chemicals Manufacturing Organisation 1985–90, gen mangr (personnel) ICI plc 1991–93, gen mangr (corp res) Zeneca Plc (following demerger from ICI) 1993–95; dir Atic Industries Bombay 1988–91; chief exec Holliday Chemical Holdings Plc 1995–, dir Fletcher Joseph Ltd 1994–; MIChemE 1985, FEng 1989, FIMechE 1989; *Recreations* sailing, golf, jogging, gardening; *Style—* Hugh M Donaldson, Esq, FEng; ✉ Holliday Chemical Holdings Plc, Leeds Road, Huddersfield HD2 1UH (☎ 01484 421841)

DONALDSON, Prof Iain Malcolm Lane; s of Archibald Thomson Donaldson (d 1981), of Edinburgh, and Milly, *née* Bailey (d 1986); *b* 22 Oct 1937; *Educ* Fettes, Univ of Edinburgh (MB ChB, BSc), Univ of Oxford (MA, by special resolution); *m* 18 July 1961, Jean Patricia, da of John Patrick Maule, OBE, of Edinburgh; 1 s (David b 1971); *Career* jr med and res posts Univ of Edinburgh 1962–69, Anglo-French res scholar Université de Paris 1969–70, res offr Laboratory of Physiology Univ of Oxford 1973–79 (MRC clinical res fell 1970–73), fell and tutor in med St Edmund Hall Oxford 1973–79 (emeritus fell 1979–), prof of zoology Univ of Hull 1979–87, prof of neurophysiology Univ of Edinburgh 1987–; author of papers on the physiology of the central nervous system; MRCP 1965, FRCPEd 1981 (MRCPEd 1965); *Recreations* studying the past; *Style—* Prof I M L Donaldson; ✉ Centre for Neuroscience, University of Edinburgh, Appleton Tower, Crichton Street, Edinburgh EH8 9LE (☎ 0131 650 3526, fax 0131 650 4579)

DONALDSON, Prof John Dallas; s of John Donaldson (d 1988), of Elgin, and Alexandrina Murray Ross, *née* Dallas (d 1985); *b* 11 Nov 1935; *Educ* Elgin Acad, Univ of Aberdeen (BSc, PhD), Univ of London (DSc); *m* 22 March 1961, Elisabeth Ann, da of George Edmond Forrest, of Eastbourne; 1 s (Richard b 1969), 2 da (Claire b 1962, Sarah b 1965); *Career* asst lectr Univ of Aberdeen 1958–61, chemistry lectr Chelsea Coll London 1961–72, reader in inorganic chemistry Univ of London 1972–80; City Univ: prof of industl chemistry 1980–90, dir Industl & Biological Chemistry Res Centre 1988–91; prof and head Dept of Chemistry Brunel Univ 1990–; dir Environmental Chemistry Centre Brunel 1991–; chm: J D Donaldson Research Ltd 1984–, Hopeman Associates (Scientific & Environment Consultants) Ltd 1991–; dir Oxford Forecasting Services Ltd 1994–; memb Nat Ctee for Chemistry 1985–89; tstee Zimbabwe Tech Mgmnt Trg Tst 1983–94; Freeman City of London 1982, Liveryman Worshipful Co of Pewterers 1983 (Freeman 1981); FRSC 1959, CChem, FRSA 1986, fell Soc of Industl Chemistry; *Books* Symmetry & Sterochemistry (with S D Ross, 1972), Cobalt in Chemicals (with S J Clark and S M Grimes, 1986), Cobalt in Medicine Agriculture and the Environment (with S J Clark and S M Grimes, 1986), Cobalt in Electronic Technology (with S J Clark and S M Grimes, 1988); *Clubs* Roehampton; *Style—* Prof John Donaldson; ✉ 21 Orchard Rise, Richmond, Surrey TW10 5BX (☎ 0181 876 6534); Dept of Chemistry, Brunel University, Uxbridge, Middx UB8 3PH (☎ 01895 274000, fax 01895 256502)

DONALDSON, Dame (Dorothy) Mary; GBE (1983), JP (Inner London 1960); da of Reginald George Gale Warwick (d 1956), and Dorothy Alice Warwick (d 1979); *b* 29 Aug 1921; *Educ* Portsmouth HS for Girls (GPDST), Wingfield Morris Orthopaedic Hosp, Middx Hosp (SRN); *m* 1945, Lord Donaldson of Lymington (Life Peer), *qv*; 1 s, 2 da; *Career* chm Women's Nat Cancer Control Campaign 1967–69; memb: Inner London Juvenile Ct Panel 1960–65, Ct of Common Cncl 1966–75, ILEA 1968–71, City Parochial Fndn 1969–75, NE Met Regnl Hosp Bd 1970–74, Cities of London and Westminster Disablement Advsy Ctee 1974–, NE Thames RHA 1976–81, Governing Body Charterhouse Sch 1980–84, Ctee The Automobile Association 1985–89; vice pres Br Cancer Cncl 1970, Counsel and Care for the Elderly 1980–; govr: London Hosp 1971–74, City of London Sch for Girls 1971–75, Berkhampstead Schs 1976–80, Gt Ormond Street Hosp for Sick Children 1978–80; chm: Cncl Banking Ombudsman 1985–94, Interim Licensing Authy In Vitro Fertilisation and Human Embryology 1985–91; Sheriff City of London 1981–82, Lord Mayor of London 1983–84; hon fell Girton Coll Cambridge 1983; memb Guild of Freemen City of London, alderman City of London (Coleman St Ward) 1975–91, Freeman City of Winnipeg, Liveryman Worshipful Co of Gardeners, Hon Freeman Worshipful Co of Shipwrights 1985, Hon Liveryman Worshipful Co of Fruiterers 1985; Hon DSc City Univ; hon memb CIArb; Order of Oman 1981, IPR President's Medal 1984, Grand Officier de L'Ordre National du Mérite 1984, DStJ 1983; FRCOG (ad eundem) 1991; *Recreations* sailing, skiing, gardening; *Clubs* Royal Cruising, Royal Lymington Yacht; *Style—* Dame Mary Donaldson, GBE, JP; ✉ 123 Shakespeare Tower, Barbican, London EC2Y 8DR

DONALDSON, Hon Michael John Francis; o s of Baron Donaldson of Lymington, PC (Life Peer), *qv*, and Dame (Dorothy) Mary Donaldson, *qv*; bro of Mrs Jenny Williams, *qv*; *b* 16 Nov 1950; *Educ* Stanbridge Earls; *m* 11 Nov 1972, Judith Margaret, da of late Edgar William Somerville, Garsington, Oxford; 2 s (William Michael Somerville b 29 Aug 1977, James John Francis (twin) b 29 Aug 1977); *Career* negotiator with Knight Frank & Rutley London 1969–71; dir: Edwood Property Co Ltd 1972–75, Nab Properties Ltd 1972–80; md and chm Marquis & Co commercial property surveyors and valuers 1975–; Incorporated Soc of Valuers and Auctioneers: chm SW London branch 1982–85, memb Nat Cncl 1985–96; Freeman City of London, Liveryman Worshipful Co of Cutlers; ASVA, ARVA, ACIArb 1973, FSVA, IRRV 1981, MAE 1995; *Recreations* sailing, skiing; *Clubs* Royal Southampton Yacht, Guildford Coastal Cruising; *Style—* The Hon Michael Donaldson; ✉ Windlesham, Surrey GU20 6LT (☎ 01344 26909, fax 01344 22006); Marquis & Co, 61 Richmond Road, Twickenham, Middx TW1 3AW (☎ 0181 891 0222, fax 0181 891 1767)

DONALDSON, Air Vice-Marshal Michael Phillips; MBE (1973); s of George Millar Donaldson (d 1986), of Chislehurst, Kent, and Mabel, *née* Phillips; *b* 22 July 1943; *Educ* Alice Deal Junior High (USA), Chislehurst and Sidcup GS; *m* 27 June 1970, Mavis, da of Albert Charles Cornish; 1 da (Sarah b 14 Dec 1974), 1 s (Duncan b 16 July 1979); *Career* joined RAF 1962, pilot and weapons instr No 23 Sqdn RAF Leuchars then No 226 OCU RAF Coltishall (Lightnings) 1965–69, USAF Florida (F-106s) 1970–73, pilot and weapons instr No 29 Sqdn then No 228 OCU RAF Coningsby (F-4 Phantoms) 1974–77, Army Staff Coll 1978, personal staff offr to Dep C-in-C Allied Forces Central Europe 1979–80, RAF Operational Requirements MOD 1980–83, OC 19 Sqdn RAF Wildenrath (Phantoms) 1983–85, OC 23 Sqdn RAF Stanley Falkland Is (Phantoms) 1985, dep personal staff offr to Chief of the Defence Staff 1986–87, OC RAF Wattisham (Phantoms) 1987–89, RCDS 1990, Sr Air Staff Offr No 11 Gp 1990–93, Cmdt RAF Staff Coll 1993–96, ret; princ Yorkshire Coast Coll of FE 1996–; memb RUSI; life vice pres RAF Squash Rackets Assoc; *Recreations* music, history, squash, rugby, tennis, golf; *Clubs* RAF; *Style—* Air Vice-Marshal Michael Donaldson, MBE; ✉ 83 Lincoln Road, Bassingham, Lincoln LN5 9JR (☎ 01522 789068)

DONALDSON, Prof Simon Kirwan; s of Peter Eden Kirwan Donaldson, and Edith Jane, *née* Stirland; *b* 20 Aug 1957; *Educ* St Faith's Sch Cambridge, Sevenoaks Sch, Pembroke Coll Cambridge (Sailing blue), Worcester Coll Oxford; *m* (Ana) Nora, *née* Hurtado; 2 s (Andres b 1984, Nicholas b 1993), 1 da (Jane b 1987); *Career* Univ of Oxford: jr res fell All Souls Coll 1983–85, Wallis prof of mathematics 1985–; FRS 1986; *Books* The Geometry of 4–Manifolds (with P B Kronheimer, 1990, OUP); *Recreations* sailing; *Style—* Prof Simon Donaldson, FRS; ✉ The Mathematical Institute, 24–29 St Giles, Oxford (☎ 01865 273540, fax 01865 273583)

DONALDSON, Hon Thomas Hay; o s of Baron Donaldson of Kingsbridge, OBE (Life Peer), and Frances Annesley, *née* Lonsdale (d 1994); *b* 1 June 1936; *Educ* Eton, Cincinnati Univ USA, Trinity Coll Cambridge (BA); *m* 1962, Natalie, da of late Basil Wadkovsky, of Miami Beach; 2 s, 4 da; *Career* with Empire Trust Co NY 1958–62, W E Hutton and Co NY 1962–63; Morgan Guaranty Trust Co of NY London Office 1963–96: vice pres 1972–90, Euro credit offr 1982–91, md 1990–96, chm Euro Credit Policy Ctee 1991–94, sr credit advsr Europe 1994–96; dir Abbey National Treasury Services PLC 1994–; memb: Fin Panel Second Severn Crossing 1991–, Advsy Panel Regulatory Bd of Lloyds; FCIB; *Books* Lending in International Commercial Banking, The Medium Term Loan Market (with J A Donaldson), Understanding Corporate Credit, How to Handle Problem Loans, Thinking About Credit, Credit Risk and Exposure in Securitisation and Transactions, Project Lending, The Treatment of Intangibles, Credit Control in Boom and Recession, More Thinking About Credit; *Recreations* bridge, reading, writing, shooting; *Clubs* Brooks's; *Style—* The Hon Thomas Donaldson; ✉ The Old Lodge, Mayertorne, Wendover Dean, Wendover, nr Aylesbury, Bucks HP22 6QA (☎ and fax 01296 622309)

DONALDSON OF KINGSBRIDGE, Baron (Life Peer UK 1967), of Kingsbridge, Co Buckingham; John George Stuart Donaldson; OBE (1944); s of Rev Stuart Alexander Donaldson (d 1915), master of Magdalene Coll Cambridge, by his wife Lady Albinia Frederica Hobart-Hampden (d 1932), sis of 7th Earl of Buckinghamshire; *b* 9 Oct 1907; *Educ* Eton, Trinity Coll Cambridge; *m* 20 Feb 1935, Frances Annesley, the writer Frances Donaldson (d 1994), da of Frederick Lonsdale, the playwright (d 1954); 1 s (Hon Thomas Hay b 1 June 1936), 2 da (Hon Rose Albinia (Hon Mrs Deakin) b 4 Nov 1937, Hon Catherine Frances (Hon Mrs Jennings) b 18 Nov 1945); *Career* WWII with RE 1939–45 in France, Italy, Iraq, Iran, Sicily, Italy, France and Germany, retiring as Lt-Col; assisted at the founding of and in planning, building and running the Pioneer Health Centre at Peckham 1932–39; farming in Warwicks, Glos and Bucks 1945–65; sits as Lib Democrat in House of Lords; Parly under-sec of state (Lab) N Ireland 1974–76, min for the arts Dept of Educn and Science 1976–79; dir: Royal Opera House Covent Garden 1958–74, Sadler's Wells Opera 1962–74; chm: Nat Cncl for the Care and Resettlement of Offenders 1965–74 (pres 1974–), Fedn of Zoos 1971–74; chm: Hotels Catering NEDO 1972–74, Confedn of Art & Design Instns 1982–84; *Clubs* Brooks's; *Style*— The Rt Hon the Lord Donaldson of Kingsbridge, OBE; ✉ c/o House of Lords, London SW1A 0PW

DONALDSON OF LYMINGTON, Baron (Life Peer UK 1988), of Lymington in the County of Hampshire; John Francis Donaldson; kt (1966), PC (1979), QC (1961); s of Malcolm Donaldson (d 1973), by his 1 w, Evelyn Helen Marguerite, eld da of late Maj Alistair Gilroy, 11 Hussars; *b* 6 Oct 1920; *Educ* Charterhouse, Trinity Coll Cambridge (MA); *m* 1945, Dame (Dorothy) Mary Donaldson, *qv*; 1 s (Hon Michael Donaldson, *qv* b 1950), 2 da (Hon Margaret-Ann b 1946, Hon Jennifer (Mrs Jenny Williams, *qv*) b 1948); *Career* served WWII Royal Signals and Gds Armd Div Signals, Control Cmmn for Germany (Legal Div); called to the Bar Middle Temple 1946, Bencher 1966, Treasurer 1986, High Court judge (Queen's Bench) 1966–79, Lord Justice of Appeal 1979–82, Master of the Rolls and chm Lord Chllr's Advsy Cncl on Public Records 1982–92; chm: Financial Law Panel 1993–, Inquiry into Coastal Pollution from Shipping 1993–94, Lord Donaldson's Assessment (Derbyshire) 1995; pres: Chartered Inst of Arbitrators 1980–83, Br Maritime Law Assoc 1979–, Br Insurance Law Assoc 1979–81; govr Sutton's Hosp in Charterhouse 1981–85; visitor: Nuffield Coll Oxford and UCL 1982–92, London Business Sch 1987–92; former memb Gen Cncl Bar 1956–61 and 1962–66, dep chm Hants QS 1961–66, memb Cncl on Tbnls 1965–66, pres Nat Industl Rels Court 1971–74; hon memb Law Soc 1994; Hon DUniv Essex 1983; Hon LLD: Univ of Sheffield 1984, Nottingham Trent Univ 1992; hon fell Trinity Coll Cambridge 1983; FCIArb 1980 (pres 1980–83); *Style*— The Rt Hon the Lord Donaldson of Lymington, PC; ✉ House of Lords, London SW1 (☎ (home) 0171 588 6610)

DONCASTER, Archdeacon of; *see:* Holdridge, Ven Bernard Lee

DONEGALL, 7 Marquess of (I 1791); Dermot Richard Claud Chichester; LVO; sits as Baron Fisherwick (GB 1790); also Viscount Chichester of Carrickfergus and Baron Chichester of Belfast (I 1625), Earl of Donegall (I 1647), Earl of Belfast (I 1791), Baron Templemore (UK 1831); Hereditary Lord High Admiral of Lough Neagh and Govr of Carrickfergus Castle; s of 4 Baron Templemore, KCVO, DSO, OBE, PC, JP, DL (d 1953), and Hon Clare Meriel Wingfield (d 1969), da of 7 Viscount Powerscourt; suc kinsman, 6 Marquess of Donegall 1975, having suc as 5 Baron Templemore 1953; *b* 18 April 1916; *Educ* Harrow, RMC; *m* 16 Sept 1946, Lady Josceline Gabrielle Legge, da of 7 Earl of Dartmouth, GCVO, TD (d 1958); 1 s, 2 da; *Heir* s, Earl of Belfast, *qv*; *Career* 2 Lt 7 Hussars 1936 (POW 1941–44), Maj 1944, served in Egypt, Libya, Italy; one of HM's Body Guard, Hon Corps of Gentlemen at Arms 1966; grand master Masonic Order Ireland, sr grand warden England, grand warden United Grand Lodge (Masonic) 1982–, Standard Bearer HM Body Guard of Hon Corps of Gentleman at Arms 1984–86; *Recreations* shooting, fishing; *Clubs* Cavalry & Guards', Kildare St (Dublin); *Style*— Most Hon Marquess of Donegall, LVO; ✉ Dunbrody Park, Arthurstown, Co Wexford, Republic of Ireland (☎ 00 353 51 389104)

DONERAILE, 10 Viscount (I 1785); Richard Allen St Leger; also Baron Doneraile (in the process of establishing right to the Peerages at time of going to press); s of 9 Viscount Doneraile (d 1983), and Melva, Viscountess Doneraile; *b* 17 Aug 1946; *Educ* Orange Coast Coll California; *m* 1969, Kathleen Mary, da of Nathaniel Simcox; 1 s, 1 da (Hon Maeve b 1974); *Heir* s, Hon Nathaniel St Leger b 13 Sept 1971; *Career* air traffic control specialist Missippi Univ; *Style*— Rt Hon Viscount Doneraile; ✉ 405 Eve Circle, Placentia, California 92670, USA

DONKIN, Dr Robert Arthur; s of Arthur Donkin (d 1967), of Loansdean, Morpeth, Northumberland, and Elisabeth Jane, *née* Kirkup (d 1969); *b* 28 Oct 1928; *Educ* Univ of Durham (BA, PhD), Univ of Cambridge (MA, LittD); *m* 13 Sept 1970, Jennifer, da of Joseph Edward Kennedy (d 1968), of Michael's Fold, Grasmere, Westmorland; 1 da (Lucy b 1977); *Career* Nat Serv Lt RA 1953–55; King George VI Meml fell Univ of Calif Berkeley 1955–56, asst lectr Dept of Geography Univ of Edinburgh 1956–58, lectr Dept of Geography Univ of Birmingham 1958–70, Leverhulme res fell 1966, visiting prof of geography Univ of Toronto 1969; Univ of Cambridge: fell Jesus Coll 1972–, tutor Jesus Coll 1975–85, lectr in the geography of Latin America 1971–90, reader in historical geography 1990–; Sauer lectr Univ of Calif Berkeley 1995; memb Hakluyt Soc 1967; FRAI 1969, FRGS 1975, FBA 1985; *Books* The Cistercian Order in Europe - A Bibliography of Printed Sources (1969), Spanish Red - An Ethnogeographical Study of Cochineal and the Opuntia Cactus (1977), The Cistercians - Studies in the Geography of Medieval England and Wales (1978), Agricultural Terracing in the Aboriginal New World (1979), Manna - An Historical Geography (1980), The Peccary - With Observations on the Introduction of Pigs to the New World (1985), The Muscovy Duck, Cairina Moschata Domestica (1989), Meleagrides - An Historical and Ethnogeographical Study of the Guinea Fowl (1991); *Style*— Dr Robert Donkin, FBA; ✉ 13 Roman Hill, Barton, Cambridge (☎ 01223 262 572); Jesus College, Cambridge CB5 8BL

DONLEAVY, James Patrick Michael; s of Patrick John Donleavy (d 1957), of NY, and Margaret, *née* Walsh (d 1987); *b* 23 April 1926; *Educ* Fordham Prep Sch NYC, Roosevelt HS Yonkers, Manhattan Prep Sch NYC, Naval Acad Prep Sch Port Deposit Maryland, Trinity Coll Dublin; *m* 1, 1949 (m dis 1969), Valerie, da of John McMichael Heron (d 1950), of Ilkley, Yorks and Port-e-Vullen, IOM; 1 s (Philip b 22 Oct 1951), 1 da (Karen b 31 March 1955); m 2, 1969 (m dis 1988), Mary Wilson Price; 1 s (Rory b 27 July 1980), 1 da (Rebecca b 28 Dec 1979); *Career* WWII US Navy 1944–46; author and playwright; painting exhbns Anna-Mei Chadwick Gallery 1989, 1991 and 1994; *Novels* The Ginger Man 1955, A Fairy Tale of New York 1961, A Singular Man 1963, The Saddest Summer of Samuel S 1966, The Beastly Beatitudes of Balthazar B 1968, The Onion Eaters 1971, The Destinies of Darcy Dancer Gentleman 1977, Schultz 1980, Leila 1983, JP Donleavy's Ireland In All Her Sins and In Some of Her Graces 1986, A Singular Country 1989, Are You Listening Rabbi Low 1987, That Darcy, That Dancer, That Gentleman 1990, The Lady Who Liked Clean Rest Rooms 1996, Wrong Information is Being Given Out at Princeton 1997; *Plays* What They Did in Dublin with The Ginger Man (with introduction) 1961, Fairy Tales of New York 1960, A Singular Man 1964, The Saddest Summer of Samuel S 1967, The Beastly Beatitudes of Balthazar B 1981; *Short stories* Meet My Maker The Mad Molecule 1964; *Manuals* The Unexpurgated Code: A Complete Manual of Survival and Manners, De Alfonce Tennis: The Superlative Game of Eccentric Champions, Its History, Accoutrements, Rules, Conduct and Regimen 1984; *Autobiography* The History of the Ginger Man: An Autobiography (1994), An Author and his Image and Other Pieces (1997); *Recreations* farming, De Alfonce tennis; *Clubs* Kildare St and Univ (Dublin), NY Athletic; *Style*— J P Donleavy, Esq; ✉ Levington Park, Mullingar, Co Westmeath, Ireland

DONNACHIE, Prof Alexander; s of Cdr John Donnachie, RNVR (d 1979), of Kilmarnock, Scotland, and Mary Ramsey, *née* Adams; *b* 25 May 1936; *Educ* Kilmarnock Acad, Univ of Glasgow (BSc, PhD); *m* 9 April 1960, Dorothy, da of Thomas Paterson (d 1979), of Kilmarnock, Scotland; 2 da (Susan b 1963, Lynn b 1965); *Career* lectr UCL 1963–65 (DSIR res fell 1961–63), res assoc CERN Geneva 1965–67, sr lectr Univ of Glasgow 1967–69; Univ of Manchester: prof of physics 1969–, head of theoretical physics 1975–85, dean Faculty of Sci 1985–87, dir Physical Laboratories 1989–94, dean Faculty of Sci and Engrg 1994–97; CERN: chm SPS Ctee 1988–93, memb Res Bd 1988–95, memb Scientific Policy Ctee 1988–93, memb Cncl 1989–94; sec C11 Cmmn IUPAP 1987–90, memb SERC 1989–94 (chm Nuclear Physics Bd 1989–93); FInstP; *Books* Electromagnetic Interactions of Hadrons Vols 1 and 2 (1978); *Recreations* sailing, walking; *Style*— Prof Alexander Donnachie; ✉ Physics Department, University of Manchester, Manchester M13 9PL (☎ 0161 275 4200, fax 0161 275 4218, telex JODREL G36149)

DONNACHIE, Ian Louis; s of Louis Donnachie, and Dorothy, *née* Green; *b* 4 June 1947; *Educ* DBA, MMS, MHSM, DipHSM, Graduate Program Hosp Mgmnt Chicago; *m* (m dis); 2 da (Samantha, Elspeth); *Career* chief exec St James's Univ Hosp NHS Tst Leeds 1981–90, chief exec Riverside Hospitals London and memb Cncl Charing Cross and Westminster Med Sch Univ of London 1990–94, chief exec Bradford Health and Bradford FHSA 1994–; memb Nat Cncl Inst of Health Servs Mgmnt, tstee and memb Bd NHS Mgmnt Advsy Serv, editorial advsr Journal of Health Care Management, memb HRH Duke of Edinburgh's Sixth Cwlth Study Conf Australia, dir and memb Bd Martin House Children's Hospice; *Recreations* sculpture, theatre, walking, reading; *Style*— Ian Donnachie, Esq; ✉ 2 Rossett Green Lodge, Rossett Green Lane, Harrogate, N Yorks HG2 9LL (☎ 01423 879707); Bradford Health Authority, New Mill, Victoria Road, Saltaire, Shipley, W Yorks BD18 3LD (☎ 01274 366112, fax 01274 366102)

DONNE, David Lucas; s of late Dr Cecil Lucas Donne, of Wellington, NZ, by his w Marjorie Nicholls Donne; *b* 17 Aug 1925; *Educ* Stowe, ChCh Oxford (MA Natural Sciences), Syracuse Univ; *m* 1, 1957, Jennifer Margaret Duncan (d 1975); 2 s, 1 da; m 2, 1978, Clare, da of Maj F J Yates; *Career* called to the Bar Middle Temple 1949; with Charterhouse Group 1953–64, William Baird 1964–67; chm: Dalgety 1977–86 (dep chm 1975–77), Crest Nicholson PLC 1973–92, Steetley PLC 1983–92 (dep chm 1979–83), Asda Group PLC 1986–88, Argos PLC 1990–95; dir: Royal Trust Bank 1972–93 (dep chm 1989–93), Sphere Investment Tst 1982–95 (chm 1989–95), Guinness Flight Extra Income Tst 1995–, Marathon Asset Management 1995–; memb: Nat Water Cncl 1980–83, Bd British Coal (formerly NCB) 1984–87, Stock Exchange Listed Cos Advsy Ctee 1987–91; tstee: Royal Opera House Devpt Land Tst 1985–90, The Game Conservancy 1987–91; Liveryman Worshipful Co of Gunmakers; *Recreations* shooting, opera, sailing; *Clubs* Royal Thames Yacht; *Style*— David Donne, Esq; ✉ 8 Montagu Mews North, London W1H 1AH

DONNE, Sir Gaven John; KBE (1979); s of Jack Alfred Donne, and Mary Elizabeth Donne; *b* 8 May 1914; *Educ* Palmerston North Boys' HS, Hastings HS, Victoria Univ Wellington NZ, Auckland Univ NZ; *m* 1946, Isabel Fenwick, da of John Edwin Hall; 2 s, 2 da; *Career* barr and slr 1938; stipendiary magistrate 1958–75, puisne judge Supreme Court of Western Samoa 1970–71; chief justice: Western Samoa 1972–75, Niue 1974–82, Cook Islands 1975–82; memb Court of Appeal Western Samoa 1975–82, rep of HM The Queen in the Cook Islands 1975–84; chief justice: Nauru 1985–, Tuvalu 1985–; memb Court of Appeal of Kiribati 1986–; *Style*— Sir Gaven Donne, KBE; ✉ Supreme Court Nauru; Otaramarae, RD4, Rotorua, NZ

DONNE, Sir John Christopher; kt (1976); s of Leslie Victor Donne (d 1960), of Hove, and Mabel Laetitia Richards, *née* Pike; *b* 19 Aug 1921; *Educ* Charterhouse; *m* 1945, Mary Stuart, da of George Stuart Seaton (d 1938); 3 da; *Career* admitted slr 1949, NP; conslt Donne Mileham & Haddock 1985–91; pres Sussex Law Soc 1969–70; chm: SE Regnl Hosp Bd 1971–74, SE Thames RHA 1973–83, NHS Trg Authy (for England and Wales) 1983–86; govr: Guy's Hosp 1971–74, Guy's Hosp Med Sch 1974–83; governing tstee Nuffield Provincial Hosp Tst 1975–; memb: Ct Univ of Sussex 1979–87, Mgmnt Ctee King Edward Hosp Fund for London 1982–84; memb Ct of Assts Worshipful Co of Broderers (Master 1983–84); FRSM; *Recreations* music, photography, gardening; *Clubs* Pilgrims, MCC, Army and Navy, Butterflies; *Style*— Sir John Donne; ✉ The Old School House, Acton Burnell, Shrewsbury, Shropshire SY5 7PG (☎ and fax 01694 731647)

DONNELLAN, Declan Michael Dominic Martin; s of Thomas Patrick John Donnellan, of Ballinlough, Co Roscommon, Eire, and Margaret Josephine Donnellan; *b* 4 Aug 1953; *Educ* St Benedict's Ealing, Queens' Coll Cambridge (MA); *Career* called to the Bar Middle Temple 1977; artistic dir Cheek By Jowl Theatre Co 1981–, assoc dir of Royal Nat Theatre 1989–; prodns incl: Macbeth and Philoctetes (Finnish Nat Theatre), The Duchess of Malfi (Wyndhams) 1995, Martin Guerre (Prince Edward) 1996; RNT: Fuente Ovejuna, Peer Gynt, Angels in America, Sweeney Todd; winner of 7 Laurence Olivier Awards incl Best Director of a Play (for As You Like It 1995); *Style*— Declan Donnellan, Esq; ✉ Cheek By Jowl, Alford House, Aveline St, London SE11 5DQ (☎ 0171 793 0153, fax 0171 735 1031)

DONNELLY, Alan John; MEP (Lab) Tyne & Wear (majority 88,380); s of John Donnelly, of Jarrow, and Josephine, *née* Anderson; *b* 16 July 1957; *Educ* Springfield Comp Sch, Sunderland Poly; *m* 1979 (m dis 1982), Hazel Cameron; 1 s (Jonothan Alan b 21 July 1980); *Career* nat fin dir GMB 1987–89 (regnl offr 1978–87), dir Unity Trust Bank 1987–89; MEP (Lab) Tyne and Wear 1989–; Euro Parl: sec EPLP 1989–91, vice pres Ctee for Relations with Japan 1989–91, rapporteur on German unification 1990, pres Euro Parliament Delgn Ctee for Rels with USA 1992–; memb: Lab Party 1974– (sec Jarrow CLP 1976–81), South Tyneside Met Borough Cncl 1980–84, Fabian Soc; hon fell Univ of Sunderland 1993; Knight Cdr Medal of the Order of Merit (Germany) 1991; *Recreations* tennis, swimming, music, reading; *Style*— Alan Donnelly, Esq, MEP; ✉ 1 South View, Jarrow, Tyne & Wear NE32 5JP (☎ 0191 489 7643, fax 0191 489 0643); European Parliament, Rue Belliard, Brussels (☎ 00 32 2 284 5202)

DONNELLY, Brendan Patrick; MEP (Cons) Sussex S and Crawley (majority 1,746); s of Patrick Aloysius Donnelly, of N London, and Mary Josephine, *née* Barrett (d 1986); *b* 25 Aug 1950; *Educ* St Ignatius Coll Tottenham, Christ Church Oxford (MA); *Career* Theodor-Heuss travelling scholar 1974–76, FO including posting to Bonn 1976–82, private sec to Chm Br Cons Euro Parl (Lord Plumb) 1982–86, memb cabinet Cons Euro Cmmr (Lord Cockfield) 1986–87, political conslt 1987–90, Cons candidate Euro elections London W 1989, special advsr to ldr of Cons Euro Parl (Sir Christopher Prout) 1990–94, MEP (C) Sussex S and Crawley 1994–; *Recreations* cricket watching, modern languages, modern history; *Clubs* Carlton, Middlesex CC, Sussex CC; *Style*— Brendan Donnelly, MEP; ✉ Conservative Association, 72 High Street, Brighton BN2 1RP (☎ 01273 626614, fax 01273 626693)

DONNELLY, (Joseph) Brian; s of Joseph Donnelly (d 1986), and Ada Agnes, *née* Bowness (d 1971); *b* 24 April 1945; *Educ* Workington GS, Queen's College Oxford (BA, MA), Univ of Wisconsin (MA); *m* 20 Aug 1966 (m dis 1994), Susanne; 1 da (Kathryn Charlotte b 27 Oct 1970); *Career* HM Dip Serv: 2 sec Republic of Ireland Dept FCO 1973, 1 sec UK mission to UN NY 1975, head of chancery Br High Cmmn Singapore 1979, asst head Personnel Policy Dept FCO 1982, deputy to chief scientific advsr Cabinet Office 1985, cnsllr and consul gen Br Embassy Athens 1988, Royal Coll of Defence

Studies 1990–91, head Non-Proliferation and Defence Dept FCO 1991–95, min UK Delgn to NATO Brussels 1995–; *Recreations* travel, reading, watching any sports, cinema; *Clubs* MG Owners; *Style*— Brian Donnelly, Esq; ✉ c/o Foreign and Commonwealth Office (UKDel NATO), King Charles Street, London SW1A 2AH

DONNELLY, Dougie; s of Robert Donnelly, of Glasgow, and Jane, *née* Wright; *b* 7 June 1953; *Educ* Hamilton Acad, Univ of Strathclyde (LLB); *m* 22 Aug 1980, Linda, da of David A Sommerville; 3 da (Kim b 20 Aug 1982, Laura b 9 Dec 1985, Lisa b 3 Oct 1991); *Career* booker MAC Entertainments Glasgow 1974–76, Radio Clyde 1976–92 (presenter Mid Morning Show, Rock Show, Music Week and Sunday File), presenter, commentator and reporter BBC TV Sport 1976–; coverage incl: Olympic Games, World Cup, European Football Championships, Commonwealth Games; presenter: Grandstand, Sportscene, Friday Night with Dougie Donnelly, Embassy World Snooker Championship, International Survival of the Fittest, World Indoor Bowls Championship, Embassy World Darts Championship, Benson & Hedges Snooker Masters; sports videos presenter and writer; *Awards* incl: Scottish TV Personality of the Year 1982, Scottish Radio Personality of the Year 1979, 1982 and 1985, Best Dressed TV Presenter 1985; *Recreations* golf, reading, music, socialising; *Clubs* Variety, Lord's Taverners (Scottish pres 1988–91); *Style*— Dougie Donnelly, Esq; ✉ c/o BBC TV Sport, Queen Margaret Drive, Glasgow G12 8DG (☎ 0141 338 2800, fax 0141 338 2409)

DONNELLY, James Thomas; s of Thomas Donnelly, and Margaret, *née* Nugent; *b* 21 Aug 1931; *Educ* Kilashee, Castleknock Coll, Trinity Coll Dublin (MA); *m* 31 April 1966, Lelia Ann, da of James Ivan McGuire, QC; 3 s (Christopher b 3 Aug 1970, Nicholas b 1 June 1972, James b 13 May 1976), 1 da (Lelia 15 May 1979); *Career* md: J & J Hunter Belfast 1956, Bryanstown Holdings 1962, Whitecliff Holdings 1963; chm Downtown Radio Ltd (Belfast ILR station) 1979–, dir Radio 2000 Dublin 1989–; cncl memb Belfast C of C underwriting memb Lloyds 1979; *Recreations* sailing, golf; *Clubs* Royal Irish Yacht, Royal Belfast Golf, Royal Alfred Yacht; *Style*— James Donnelly, Esq; ✉ Crawfordsburn, Co Down, Northern Ireland (☎ 01247 853255); J & J Hunter Ltd, Balmoral Rd, Belfast, Northern Ireland BT12 6PX (☎ 01232 618535)

DONNELLY, Dr Peter Duncan; *b* 27 Jan 1963; *Educ* Univ of Edinburgh (MB ChB), DA (RCS Eng), Univ of Stirling (MBA), Univ of Wales Coll of Med (MPH), MHSM, MFPHM, PMD (Harvard), CertPHC (RCSEd); *m* Joan; 2 s (Calum b 1992, Alistair b 1994); *Career* Capt (RAMC) TA attached 1/51 Highland Regt Perth 1988–89; HO: in gen surgery Leith Hosp Edinburgh 1985–86, in gen med Bangour Gen Hosp 1986; SHO: in A&E Broomfield Hosp Chelmsford 1986–87, in anaesthetics and intensive care Western Gen Hosp Edinburgh 1987–88, in psychiatry Liff Hosp Dundee 1988; anaesthetic locums Aug-Sept 1988, NHS MDG scholar Stirling MBA Prog 1988–89; Morgannwg HA: registrar 1989–90, sr registrar 1990–92, conslt in public health med 1992–93, actg dir of planning and procurement 1993–94, dep chief admin MO/dep dir of public health med 1994–96, dir of public health and exec memb HA Bd 1996–; sr lectr in public health med Univ of Wales Coll of Med 1992–96 (lectr 1989–92), hon sr lectr in public health med Univ of Wales Coll of Med and Univ of Wales Swansea 1996–; hon MO Brathay/Earthquest Yukon Expdn 1988; *Books* Climate and Health (contrib, 1993), Releasing Resources for Health Gain (contrib, 1995); also author of various articles and editorials; *Style*— Dr Peter D Donnelly; ✉ Director of Public Health, Morgannwg Health Authority, 41 High Street, Swansea SA1 5LT (☎ 01792 458066)

DONNELLY, Peter Lane; Baron of Duleek (Feudal Barony, dating from temp Henry II), Co Meath, Ireland; s of Col Paul J Donnelly Jr, of Oyster Bay, Long Island, New York, USA, and Marian, *née* Kinsley; *b* 18 March 1947; *Educ* Georgetown Univ Washington DC, Fordham Univ Law NY (Juris Doctor), New York Univ Graduate Sch of Business, Templeton Coll Oxford; *m* 1 (m dis 1982), Joyce Arbon; m 2, 23 May 1983, Georgina Mary, da of late Dennis Dallamore, of Johannesburg, SA; 2 s (Sebastian Peter Sumner b 1986, Octavian Xavier Buttemer b 1989); *Career* vice pres The European-American Bank & Tst Co NY 1969–77, ptnr Kuhn Loeb Lehman Brothers Int NY 1977–82, md (Int) The First Boston Corp NY 1982–86, md (Europe) Prudential-Bache Capital Funding London 1986–91, sr advsr FirstCorp (Johannesburg) 1991–93, dir FNB of Southern Africa (UK) Ltd 1992–93; sr advsr European Privatisation and Investment Corp (Vienna) 1991–, gen mangr UK and Western Europe ABSA Bank Limited Johannesburg 1994–; dir: ABSA Trust Jersey 1994–, ABSA Manx Holdings Isle of Man 1995–; *Recreations* lawn tennis, royal tennis, painting; *Clubs* Piping Rock (NY), Union (NY), Rand (Johannesburg), Brooks's, Queen's, Wentworth, St Moritz Tobogganing, Bembridge Sailing; *Style*— Peter Donnelly, Esq; ✉ 57 Chesilton Road, London SW6; The Ledge House, Foreland Fields Road, Bembridge, Isle of Wight; Hyla Brook Farm, Reading, Vermont, USA; 45 Imbezane Drive, Southbroom, Republic of South Africa

DONNER, Clive; s of Alex Donner (d 1981), of London, and Deborah, *née* Taffel (d 1976); *b* 21 Jan 1926; *m* 1971, Jocelyn, da of Bertie Rickards; *Career* film and theatre director; asst film ed 1941, film ed 1951–55, freelance film dir 1956–; teacher London Film Sch (then London Sch of Film Technique) 1968–74; memb: Panel BFI Lectures 1950–60, Cncl BAFTA 1970–73; *Theatre* incl: The Formation Dancers (Arts & Globe Theatre) 1964, Notts Playhouse Shakespeare and Pinter 1970–71, The Front Room Boys (Royal Court) 1971, Kennedy's Children (Kings Head, Arts Theatre, The Golden Theatre NY) 1975, The Picture of Dorian Gray (adapted by John Osborne, Greenwich Theatre) 1975; *Films* as editor incl: Scrooge 1951, The Card, Meet Me Tonight, Genevieve 1952, The Million Pound Note 1953, The Purple Plain, I Am A Camera 1955; as director incl: The Secret Place 1952, Some People 1962, The Caretaker (Silver Bear Berlin Film Festival) 1963, Nothing But The Best 1963, What's New Pussycat? (Jean Georges Auriol/Paul Gilson Award) 1965, Luv 1967, Here We Go Round the Mulberry Bush 1967, Alfred the Great 1969, Rogue Male 1976, The Three Hostages 1977, She Fell Among Thieves 1977, The Thief of Baghdad 1978, Oliver Twist 1981, The Scarlet Pimpernel 1982, Arthur the King 1983, To Catch a King 1983, A Christmas Carol 1984, Dead Man's Folly 1986, Babes in Toyland 1986, The Best Kept Secret (Motor Neurone Assoc Silver Award Br Med Cncl), Stealing Heaven 1988, Not A Penny More Not A Penny Less 1989, Coup de Foudre (Love at First Sight) 1990, Arrivederci Roma 1990, First Love Second Chance 1990, Gumshoe Waltz 1990, For Better and For Worse 1992, Charlemagne 1994; *Recreations* classical music (particularly opera), popular music, reading, walking anywhere from the streets of London to the Australian sea shore; *Style*— Clive Donner, Esq

DONNER, John Melville; s of Gerald Melville Donner (d 1964), and Pearl, only da of Sir Frank Bernard Sanderson, 1 Bt (d 1965); *b* 18 July 1930; *Educ* Stowe, RMA Sandhurst; *m* 1952, Patricia Mary, da of Barnet Thomas Jenkins (d 1941); 1 s (Rupert b 1955), 1 da (Annabel b 1958); *Career* Coldstream Gds 1948–53 and 1956 (Suez), T/Capt; Lloyd's of London: joined (with Arbon Langrish) 1955, elected memb 1964, non-underwriting memb 1995; md Fenchurch Insurance Holdings plc 1969–74; Donner Underwriting Agencies Ltd: chm 1976–90, pres 1990–92, conslt 1992–94; chm: JD Underwriting Agencies Ltd 1979–90, RD Underwriting Agencies 1980–91, CD Underwriting Agencies Ltd 1983–89, Western Bloodstock Ltd 1987–92, Stirling Underwriting Agencies 1988–92, Donner Names Assoc Ltd 1995–; dir: Alexander Syndicate Management Ltd 1982–94, West Somerset Railway plc 1991–, Wildae Restorations Ltd 1994–; Queen's Award for Export 1983 and 1988; chm Bd of Govrs St Michael's Sch Tawstock 1974–92; Freeman City of London 1977, Liveryman Worshipful Co of Plaisterers; *Recreations* motoring with old vehicles, the countryside, restoration and preservtion, travel, food and wine; *Clubs* Carlton, Bentley Drivers', Rolls-Royce Enthusiasts'; *Style*— John Donner, Esq; ✉ 39 Bramerton St, London SW3 (☎ 0171 352 9964); Heddon Oak House, Crowcombe, Taunton, Somerset TA4 4BJ (☎ 01984 618651, fax 01984 618393)

DONOHOE, Brian; MP (Lab) Cunninghame South (majority 10,680); s of George Donohoe, and Catherine Donohoe; *b* 10 Sept 1948; *Educ* Irvine Royal Acad, Kilmarnock Tech Coll (ONC); *m* 16 July 1973, Christine, da of Raymond Pawson; 2 s; *Career* draughtsman Ailsa Shipyard 1970–77 (engrg apprentice 1965–70), Hunterston Nuclear Power Stn 1977, draughtsman ICI Organics Div 1977–81, dist offr NALGO 1981–92, MP (Lab) Cunninghame S 1992–; convener Political and Educn Ctee TASS 1969–81, sec Irvine Trades Cncl 1973–82, chm Cunninghame Industl Devpt Ctee 1975–85, treas Cunninghame S Constituency Lab Pty 1983–91, memb Transport Select Ctee 1993–; *Recreations* gardening; *Style*— Brian H Donohoe, Esq, MP; ✉ House of Commons, London SW1A 0AA (☎ 0171 219 6230, constituency 01294 276844, mobile 0374 646600, pager 01426 264094)

DONOUGHMORE, 8 Earl of (I 1800); Richard Michael John Hely-Hutchinson; sits as Viscount Hutchinson of Knocklofty (UK 1821); also Baron Donoughmore of Knocklofty (I 1783) and Viscount Donoughmore of Knocklofty (I 1797); s of Col 7 Earl of Donoughmore (d 1981), and Jean, Countess of Donoughmore, MBE, *née* Hotham (d 1995); *b* 8 Aug 1927; *Educ* Winchester, New Coll Oxford (BM BCh, MA); *m* 1 Nov 1951, Sheila, da of late Frank Frederick Parsons and Mrs Roy Smith-Woodward; 4 s; *Heir* s, Viscount Suirdale; *Career* Capt RAMC 1954–56; fin conslt, company dir; chm Hodder Headline plc (formerly Headline Book Publishing plc) until 1997; *Recreations* fishing, shooting, racing; *Clubs* Jockey (Paris); *Style*— The Rt Hon the Earl of Donoughmore; ✉ The Manor House, Bampton, Oxon OX18 2LQ

DONOUGHUE, Baron (Life Peer UK 1985), of Ashton, Co Northants; Bernard Donoughue; s of Thomas Joseph Donoughue and Maud Violet, *née* Andrews; *b* 8 Sept 1934; *Educ* Northampton GS, Lincoln Coll Oxford (BA), Harvard Univ, Nuffield Coll Oxford (MA, DPhil); *m* 1959 (m dis 1990), Carol Ruth, da of late Abraham Goodman; 2 s (Hon Paul Michael David b 1969, Hon Stephen Joel b 1969), 2 da (Hon Rachel Anne b 1965, Hon Kate Miriam b 1967); *Career* lectr, sr lectr, reader LSE 1963–74, sr policy advsr to PM 1974–79, devpt dir Economist Intelligence Unit 1979–81, asst ed The Times 1981–82, head of res and investmt policy Grieveson Grant & Co 1984–86 (ptnr 1983), dir Kleinwort Benson Securities 1986–88, exec vice chm London and Bishopsgate International Investment 1988–91, oppn House of Lords spokesman on Treasury matters and energy 1991–, on National Heritage 1993–; memb: Advsy Bd Wissenschaftszentrum Berlin 1978–90, Cncl LSE, Cncl LSO, London Arts Bd 1991–; assoc memb Nuffield Coll Oxford; hon fell: Lincoln Coll Oxford, LSE, RCA; Hon LLD Univ of Leicester; FRHistS; *Books* Trade Unions in a Changing Society (1963), British Politics and the American Revolution (1964), The People into Parliament (with W T Rogers, 1966), Herbert Morrison: Portrait of a Politician (with G W Jones, 1973), Prime Minister (1987); *Style*— The Rt Hon the Lord Donoughue

DONOVAN, Ian Alexander; s of Ivar Kirkwood Donovan (d 1983), and Marion Sutherland, *née* Esslemont (d 1995); *b* 19 Dec 1945; *Educ* Malvern, Univ of Birmingham (MB ChB, MD); *m* 3 May 1975, Rosamund Mary, da of Reginald Vickors, of the Crescent, Hagley, Worcs; 1 s (Robert b 1985), 2 da (Amy b 1980, Lorna b 1982); *Career* sr lectr in surgery Univ of Birmingham 1979–87, conslt surgn W Midlands RHA 1987–; memb: Cncl Assoc of Surgns GB and Ireland, Advsy Ctee Admin of Radioactive Substances DHSS, Ct of Examiners Royal Coll of Surgns of Eng; hon sec W Midland Surgns Soc, RCS regnl advsr W Midlands Region; memb: Surgical Res Soc, Br Soc of Gastroenterology; FRCS; *Recreations* golf, photography, family; *Clubs* Edgbaston Golf, East India; *Style*— Ian Donovan, Esq; ✉ Birmingham Nuffield Hospital, Edgbaston, Birmingham (☎ 0121 456 2000)

DONOVAN, Ian Edward; s of John Walter Donovan (d 1986), and Ethel Molyneux Studdy Hooper (d 1990); *b* 2 March 1940; *Educ* Leighton Park Sch Reading; *m* 26 July 1969, Susan Betty da of William Harris (d 1993), of Abbotsbury, Dorset; 2 s (Christopher George b 1971, James William b 1974); *Career* fin dir: Lucas Girling Koblenz 1978–81, Lucas Electrical 1982–84; CAA: gp dir fin and central servs 1985–88, memb for fin 1986–88; dir and gp controller Smiths Industries Aerospace & Defence Systems Ltd 1988–; memb Cncl Soc of Br Aerospace Companies 1995–; hon treasurer The Air League; *Recreations* sailing, golf, flyfishing, music; *Style*— Ian E Donovan, Esq; ✉ Lawn Farm, Church Lane, Tibberton, Droitwich, Worcs WR9 7NW; 11 Sussex House, 220 Kew Rd, Kew, Richmond, Surrey

DONOVAN, Jason Sean; s of Terence Patrick Donovan, of Melbourne, Australia, and Susan Margaret, *née* Menlove (now Mrs McIntosh); *b* 1 June 1968; *Career* actor and singer; *Theatre* Joseph in Joseph and the Amazing Technicolor Dreamcoat (London Palladium) 1991–92 and 1992–93; *Television* first appearance Skyways (Network 7 Aust) 1979, I Can Jump Puddles (Aust Broadcasting Corp) 1979, Neighbours 1985–89, Heroes 1988, Shadows of the Heart 1990; *Albums* Ten Good Reasons (5 platinum disc) 1989, Between the Lines 1990, Joseph and the Amazing Technicolor Dreamcoat (cast album from the musical) 1991; hit singles: Nothing Can Divide Us 1988, Especially For You (duet with Kylie Minogue) 1988, Too Many Broken Hearts 1989, Sealed With A Kiss 1989, Everyday 1989, Hang On To Your Love 1990, Another Night 1990, Rhythm of the Rain 1990, Doing Fine 1990, Any Dream Will Do 1991, Happy Together 1991; sold more singles in the UK than any other act 1989, singer on Band aid single Do They Know It's Christmas 1989; *Tours* concert tours: Aust, Far East, Europe; *Awards* Logie Awards (Aust): Best New Talent 1987, Most Popular Actor 1988, Most Popular Actor in a Mini Series 1990; Smash Hits Awards: Most Fanciable Male 1989, Best Album 1989, Best Male Singer 1989, Best Male Artist of the Year 1990; *Recreations* surfing, reading biographies; *Style*— Jason Donovan, Esq; ✉ c/o Jonathan Altaras Associates Ltd, 27 Floral Street, London WC2E 9DP (☎ 0171 836 8722, fax 0171 836 6066)

DONOVAN, Judith; CBE (1997); da of Ernest Nicholson, of Bradford, and Joyce, *née* Finding; *b* 5 July 1951; *Educ* St Joseph's Coll Bradford, Woking Girls' GS, Univ of Hull (BA); *m* 12 Nov 1977, John Patrick Donovan, s of William Donovan, of Darlington; *Career* mktg trainee Ford Motor Co 1973–75, account mangr J Walter Thomson 1976, advertising mangr Grattan 1977–82, chm Judith Donovan Associates 1982–; pres Bradford Jr C of C 1980, memb Cncl Bradford C of C 1989–; chm Bradford Business Club 1985, chm Bradford TEC 1990–, dir Direct Mktg Assoc 1991–; govr Friends of Bradford Art Galleries & Museums 1984–89, dir Northern Ballet Theatre 1990–; fndr patron Women Mean Business, patron Small Business Bureau; memb Forum; MInstM 1977, MIMgt 1978, MCAM 1979, MInstD 1983, memb Mktg Soc 1987, FRSA 1995; *Recreations* reading, the Western Front, pets; *Clubs* The Naval, Westminster Dining; *Style*— Mrs Judith Donovan, CBE; ✉ 42 Heaton Grove, Bradford, W Yorks BD9 4EB (☎ 01274 543 966); Judith Donovan Associates, Phoenix House, Rushton Avenue, Bradford, W Yorkshire BD3 7BH (☎ 01274 656222, fax 01274 656167, car 0836 610683)

DONOVAN, Paul James Kingsley; s of Brian Donovan, of Croydon (d 1992), and Enid Constance, *née* Shaylor (d 1992); *b* 8 April 1949; *Educ* Queen Elizabeth's GS Barnet, Oriel Coll Oxford (MA); *m* 27 Oct 1979, Hazel Margaret, da of William Hubert Case (d 1987), of Kenya; 1 s (Toby b 1981), 2 da (Emily b 1987, Mary b 1989); *Career* journalist and writer; trainee Mirror Group Newspapers 1970–73, night news ed and reporter Sunday Mirror 1973–78, reporter, showbusiness writer and critic Daily Mail 1978–85, showbusiness ed, TV critic and media corr Today 1986–88; self-employed 1988–; radio columnist Sunday Times 1988–, TV previewer Hello! 1988–, occasional broadcaster;

memb: Radio Acad, Oxford Soc; *Books* Roger Moore (1983), Dudley (1988), The Radio Companion (1991); *Recreations* reading, music, walking; *Style*— Paul Donovan, Esq; ✉ 11 Stile Hall Gardens, London W4 3BS (☎ 0181 994 5316); office (☎ 0181 747 8387, fax 0181 747 4850)

DONOVAN, Prof Robert John; s of Francis Alexander Donovan (d 1991), of Sandbach, Cheshire, and Ida, *née* Brooks; *b* 13 July 1941; *Educ* Sandbach Sch, UCW (BSc), Univ of Cambridge (PhD); *m* 20 June 1964, Marion, da of William Colclough (d 1952); 1 da (Jane Frances); *Career* res fell Gonville and Caius Coll 1966–70; Univ of Edinburgh: lectr in physical chemistry 1970, reader 1974, appointed to personal chair of physical chemistry 1979, head Dept of Chemistry 1984–87 and 1995–, chair of chemistry 1986–; visiting scientist Max-Planck Inst für Strömungsforshung Göttingen 1975, JSPS sr visiting fell Inst of Molecular Sci Okazaki Japan 1982 (visiting fell 1983 and 1989), visiting fell Aust Nat Univ Canberra 1993; author numerous pubns; SERC: chm Laser Facility Ctee 1988–92, chm Facilities Cmmn 1993–95; FRSE 1976, FRSC 1980; *Recreations* riding, skiing and hill walking; *Style*— Prof Robert Donovan, FRSE; ✉ Department of Chemistry, The University of Edinburgh, West Mains Road, Edinburgh EH9 3JJ (☎ 0131 650 4722, fax 0131 650 6453)

DOOLEY, Wade Anthony; s of late Geoffrey Dooley, of Warrington, Cheshire, and Ethel Beatrice, *née* Wright; *b* 2 Oct 1957; *Educ* Bolton Boys' Sch, Beamont Boys' Sch Warrington, Lancashire Police Cadet Coll Preston; *m* 25 Oct 1980, Sharon Diane, da of late Sidney Corrie; 2 da (Sophie Helen b 14 Nov 1989, Sara Eleanor b 18 March 1992); *Career* former rugby union lock forward; clubs: Preston Grasshoppers RUFC 1975–94, Fylde RUFC, Barbarians RFC; rep: British Police, Lancashire B, Lancashire North; England: debut v Romania 1985, Five Nations debut v France 1985, memb World Cup squad 1987, toured Argentina 1990, memb Grand Slam winning team 1991 and 1992, memb runners-up team World Cup 1991, 55 caps, ret 1993; memb Br series winning (2–1) Lions tour Aust 1989 (2 test appearances) and NZ 1993; police offr Blackpool 1975–; *Books* The Tower and the Glory (autobiography, 1992); *Recreations* music (everything except jazz and country & western), eating out, fell walking, passion for gardening, relaxing with wife and daughters; *Style*— Wade Dooley, Esq

DOONICAN, Val; né Michael Valentine; 8 child of John Doonican (d 1941), of Waterford, Ireland, and Agnes, *née* Kavanagh (d 1983); *b* 3 Feb 1929; *Educ* De La Salle Coll Waterford; *m* 1 April 1962, Lynnette Rae; 2 da (Sarah, Fiona); *Career* entertainer/singer-guitarist; first professional job at seaside hotel in Southern Ireland 1947, worked with piano-playing ptnr supplying music and songs for Dublin radio show 1949, memb The Four Ramblers singing quartet until 1959, contrib weekly musical show BBC until 1964, subsequently hosted own TV series The Val Doonican Music Show until 1987; 3 Royal Variety Show appearances, sometime host of own show London Palladium and American TV; record sales number many millions, latterly subject of own video Songs From My Sketchbook; various awards incl: BBC Personality of the Year (Variety Club of GB), Showbusiness Personality of the Year, Radio Personality of the Year; *Autobiographies* The Special Years (1980), Walking Tall (1985); *Recreations* golf, sketching; *Clubs* Beaconsfield Golf; *Style*— Val Doonican, Esq; ✉ c/o Bernard Lee Management, Moorcroft Lodge, Fairleigh Common, Warlingham, Surrey CR3 9PE (☎ 01883 625667)

DORAN, Dr Barry Reginald Harewood; s of Walter Reginald Doran (d 1987), of Worcester Park, Surrey, and Dorothy Maud, *née* Harewood (d 1986); *b* 11 Feb 1940; *Educ* Raynes Park Co GS, St Bartholomew's Hosp Univ of London (MB BS); *m* 25 March 1966, Sheila, da of George Batterby, of Brundall, Norwich; 3 s (Andrew b 1966, Timothy b 1970, Michael b 1971); *Career* res asst RCS 1971–72, hon lectr in anaesthetics Victoria Univ of Manchester 1972–, dir Intensive Therapy Unit Manchester Royal Infirmary 1977– (conslt anaesthetist 1972–); inaugural chm Northern Critical Care Soc; memb: Anaesthetic Res Soc, Intensive Care Soc, Manchester Med Soc; FFARCS 1969; *Books* contrib: Surgery of the Mouth and Jaws, Cash's Textbook of Physiotherapy, Practical Anaesthesia for Surgical Emergencies; *Recreations* shooting; *Clubs* Ollerton; *Style*— Dr Barry Doran; ✉ Intensive Therapy Unit, Manchester Royal Infirmary, Oxford Road, Manchester M13 9WL (☎ 0161 276 4715)

DORAN, Nigel John Leslie; *b* 11 March 1950; *Educ* Trinity Coll Glenalmond, St Edmund Hall Oxford (MA), Univ of London (ext, LLM); *m* Julia; *Career* corp tax ptnr Macfarlanes 1988–; memb City of London Slrs' Co; ACCA, AIB, ATII; *Books* Taxation of Corporate Joint Ventures (1993 and 1996); *Recreations* golf; *Clubs* Coombe Hill Golf; *Style*— Nigel Doran, Esq; ✉ Macfarlanes, 10 Norwich Street, London EC4A 1BD (☎ 0171 831 9222)

DORCHESTER, Bishop of 1988–; Rt Rev Dr Anthony John Russell; *b* 25 Jan 1943; *Educ* Uppingham, Univ of Durham (BA), Trinity Coll Oxford (DPhil), Cuddesdon Theol Coll Oxford; *m* 1967, Sheila Alexandra; 2 s (Jonathan b 1971, Timothy b 1981), 2 da (Alexandra b 1969, Serena b 1975); *Career* ordained: deacon 1970, priest 1971; curate Hilborough Gp of Parishes 1970–73, rector Preston on Stour, Atherstone on Stour and Whitchurch 1973–88, canon theologian Coventry Cathedral 1977–78, chaplain to HM The Queen 1983–88, dir Arthur Rank Centre (Nat Agric Centre) 1983–88, area bishop of Dorchester Dio of Oxford 1988–; memb Gen Synod 1980–88, chaplain RASE 1982–91 (vice pres 1991–), hon chaplain Royal Agric Benevolent Inst 1983–; memb: Archbishops' Cmmn on Rural Affairs 1988–90, Rural Devpt Cmmn 1991–; *Books* Groups and Teams in the Countryside (ed, 1975), The Clerical Profession (1980), The Country Parish (1986), The Country Parson (1993); *Clubs* United Oxford & Cambridge Univ; *Style*— The Rt Rev the Bishop of Dorchester; ✉ Holmby House, Sibford Ferris, Banbury, Oxfordshire OX15 5RG (☎ 01295 780583)

DORÉ, Katharine Emma; da of Robert Edward Frederick Doré, of West Somerset, and Estelle Margaret, *née* Smith; *b* 13 Feb 1960; *Educ* St Brandon's Sch for Girls, Central Sch of Speech & Drama; *Career* freelance stage mangr and admin; cos worked for 1981–88 incl: Leicester Haymarket, Whirligig Children's Theatre, Scottish Ballet, English Touring Opera (now City of Birmingham Opera), Watermans Arts Centre; co dir (with Matthew Bourne) Adventures in Motion Pictures (modern dance co) 1988–; winner Barclays New Stages Award for Adventures in Motion Pictures 1990; *Recreations* contemporary arts; *Style*— Ms Katharine Doré; ✉ AMP, AMP House, 396 St John Street, London EC1V 4NJ (☎ 0171 833 5803, fax 0171 713 6040)

DORE, Prof Ronald Philip; CBE (1989); s of Philip Brine Dore, and Elsie Constance Dore; *b* 1 Feb 1925; *Educ* Poole GS, SOAS, Univ of London (BA); *m* 1957, Nancy Macdonald; 1 s, 1 da; *Career* lectr in Japanese Instns SOAS London 1951, prof of Asian Studies Univ of BC 1956, reader then prof of sociology LSE 1961 (hon fell 1980), fell IDS 1969–82, asst dir Tech Change Centre 1982–86; Imperial Coll London: visiting prof 1982–86, dir Japan-Europe Indust Res Centre 1986–91; adjunct prof MIT 1989–94, sr research fell Centre for Economic Performance LSE 1992–; memb Accademia Europaea, hon foreign memb American Acad of Arts and Scis 1978, hon foreign fell Japan Acad 1986; Order of the Rising Sun (3rd Class) Japan 1988; FBA 1975; *Books* City Life in Japan (1958), Land Reform in Japan (1959, 2 edn 1984), Education in Tokugawa Japan (1963, 2 edn 1983), Aspects of Social Change in Modern Japan (ed, 1967), British Factory, Japanese Factory (1973), The Diploma Disease (1976), Shinohata: Portrait of a Japanese Village (1978), Community Development: Comparative Case Studies in India, the Republic of Korea, Mexico and Tanzania (ed with Zoe Mars, 1981), Energy Conservation in Japanese Industry (1982), Flexible Rigidities: Structural Adjustment in Japan (1986), Taking Japan Seriously: A Confucian Perspective on Leading Economic Issues (1987), Japan and World Depression, Then and Now: Essays in Memory of E F Penrose (ed jtly, 1987), How the Japanese Learn to Work (with Mari Sako, 1988), Corporatism and Accountability: Organized Interest in British Public Life (ed jtly, 1990), Will the 21st Century be the Age of Individualism? (1991), The Japanese Firm: The Sources of Competitive Strength (ed jtly, 1994), Japan Internationalism and the UN (1996); *Style*— Prof Ronald Dore, CBE, FBA; ✉ 157 Surrenden Road, Brighton, East Sussex BN1 6ZA (01273 501370)

DOREY, Prof Anthony Peter (Tony); s of H W Dorey, of Wishford, Wilts, and N E Dorey, *née* Fancy; *b* 16 July 1938; *Educ* Brockenhurst GS, Univ of Cambridge; *m* 24 Sept 1960, Valerie; 1 s (Mark b 1963), 1 da (Juliet (Mrs Burd) b 1965); *Career* res physicist Philips 1960–65, lectr in physics Univ of Loughborough 1965–67, lectr and sr lectr in electronics Univ of Southampton 1967–83, prof Univ of Lancaster 1983–; MInstP, FIEE, MIEEE (USA); *Books* contrib to: Moderne Methoden und Hilfsmittel der Ingenieur Ausbildung (ed G Buzdugan, 1978), VLSI 89 (ed G Musgrave, 1989), Design and Test for VLSI and WSI Circuits (ed R Massara, 1989), Developments in Integrated Circuit Testing (ed D Miller, 1987); *Recreations* fell walking, singing; *Style*— Prof Tony Dorey; ✉ Honeytrek, Post Horse Lane, Hornby, Lancs LA2 8RH; Engineering Department, Univ of Lancaster, Bailrigg, Lancaster LA1 4YR (☎ 01524 593014, fax 01524 594207)

DOREY, Sir Graham Martyn; kt (1993); s of late Martyn Dorey, and late Muriel, *née* Pickard; *b* 15 Dec 1932; *Educ* Kingswood Sch Bath, Ecole des Roches Verneuil, Univ of Bristol (BA), Univ of Caen (Cert d'Études Juridiques); *m* 5 Sept 1962, Penelope Cecile, da of late Maj E A Wheadon, ED; 2 s (Robert b 1970, Martyn b 1972), 2 da (Suzanne b 1963, Jane b 1964); *Career* advocate of the Royal Court 1960, slr-gen Guernsey 1973, attorney-gen Guernsey 1977, dep bailiff Guernsey 1982–92, bailiff of Guernsey 1992–, pres Ct of Appeal Guernsey 1992–, judge Court of Appeal Jersey 1992–; people's dep States of Guernsey 1970–73; CStJ 1992; *Recreations* sailing, maritime history; *Style*— Sir Graham Dorey; ✉ Royal Court, Guernsey (☎ 01481 726161)

DOREY, Prof Howard Anthony; s of Stanley Cyril Dorey (d 1960), of Sevenoaks, and Mildred, *née* Boulton (d 1936); *b* 26 Aug 1930; *Educ* Sevenoaks Sch, Univ of Nottingham (BSc); *m* 10 May 1958, Althea Corinne Corbett, da of Dennis Tom Maynard; 3 da (Tessa Karen b 8 April 1961, Lynn Yvette b 3 March 1963, Meryl Ginette b 3 Aug 1964); *Career* Fairey Aviation Heston 1952–59; Schlumberger Inst Farnborough (aka Solartron) 1960–91: team ldr 1960, chief res engr 1972, dir 1988–91; prof of microsystems technol Dept of Electrical and Electronic Engrg Imperial Coll London 1991–; FIEE 1974, FInstP 1980, FInstMC 1990, FEng 1994; *Recreations* West Surrey Scottish Dancing Group (sec), music, theatre; *Style*— Prof Howard Dorey, FEng; ✉ Department of Electrical and Electronic Engineering, Imperial College of Science Technology and Medicine, Exhibition Road, London SW7 2BT (☎ 0171 594 6301, fax 0171 823 8125)

DORIGO, Anthony Robert (Tony); s of Roberto Dorigo, and Rosemary Anne, *née* Stankovic; *b* 31 Dec 1965; *Educ* Thornton Park HS Adelaide Aust, Seacombe HS Adelaide Aust; *m* 14 Feb 1988, Heather, da of Nicol Rystant Morris; 2 s (Luke b 28 July 1988, Todd Robert b 3 Jan 1991), 1 da (Sasha Rose b 12 April 1994); *Career* professional footballer; 111 league appearances Aston Villa 1984–87 (signed as apprentice July 1982), 200 appearances Chelsea 1987–91 (joined for a fee of £475,000), transferred to Leeds Utd (for £1.3m) 1991– (League Championship winners 1992); England caps: 11 under 21, 4 B, 15 full, memb squad World Cup Italy 1990 (played in third/fourth place play-off v Italy), memb squad Euro Championships Germany 1988 and Sweden 1992; Player of the Year: Aston Villa 1986–87, Chelsea 1987–88, Leeds 1991–92; *Recreations* golf; *Style*— Tony Dorigo, Esq; ✉ c/o Leeds Utd FC, Elland Rd, Leeds, West Yorks LS11 0ES (0113 271 6037)

DORKEN, (Anthony) John; s of late Oscar Roy Dorken, of Birmingham, and Margaret, *née* Barker; *b* 24 April 1944; *Educ* Mill Hill Sch, King's Coll Cambridge (MA); *m* 1972, Satanay, da of Fawzi Mufti; 1 da (Marina Charlotte b 1976), 1 s (Adam Alexander b 1981); *Career* VSO Libya 1965–66, asst princ Bd of Trade 1967–71, private sec to Parly Under Sec of State for Industry 1971–72, princ Dept of Trade and latterly Dept of Energy 1972–77, seconded to Cabinet Office 1977–79, asst sec Dept of Energy 1980–86, seconded to Shell UK Exploration and Production 1986–89, dir of resource mgmnt Dept of Energy 1989–92, dep DG Office of Gas Supply 1992–93, head Consumer Affairs Div DTI 1993–96; *Recreations* reading, walking, music, squash, tennis; *Clubs* Stormont Lawn Tennis and Squash Rackets (hon treas); *Style*— John Dorken, Esq; ✉ 10 Connaught Gardens, London N10 3LB (☎ 0181 372 6213)

DORKING, Archdeacon of; *see:* Wilson, Ven Mark John Crichton

DORKING, Bishop of 1996–; Rt Rev Ian James Brackley; s of Frederick Arthur James Brackley (d 1987), of Westcliff-on-Sea, Essex, and Ivy Sarah Catherine, *née* Bush (d 1980); *b* 13 Dec 1947; *Educ* Keble Coll Oxford, Cuddesdon Theol Coll; *m* 12 June 1971, Penelope (Penny) Ann, da of Arthur William Saunders; 2 s (Christopher James b 7 April 1972, Alexander Jonathan b 1 Aug 1975); *Career* ordained deacon 1971, priest 1972; asst curate St Mary Magdalene with St Francis Lockleaze Bristol 1971–74; Bryanston Sch Blandford Dorset: asst chaplain 1974–76, chaplain 1976–80, master i/c cricket 1975–80; vicar St Mary's E Preston with Kingston 1980–88, rural dean Arundel and Bognor 1982–87, team rector St Wilfrid's Haywards Heath 1988–96, rural dean Cuckfield Deanery 1989–95; proctor in convocation and memb Gen Synod 1990–95; *Recreations* cricket, pipe organs, theatre, reading; *Style*— The Rt Rev the Bishop of Dorking; ✉ 13 Pilgrims Way, Guildford, Surrey GU4 8AD (☎ 01483 570829, fax 01483 567268)

DORMAN, Sir Philip Henry Keppel; 4 Bt (UK 1923), of Nunthorpe, Co York; s of Richard Dorman (d 1976), and Diana Keppel, *née* Barrett; suc kinsman, Sir Charles Geoffrey Dorman, 3 Bt, MC (d 1996); *b* 19 May 1954; *Educ* Marlborough, Univ of St Andrews; *m* 1, 12 April 1982 (m dis 1992), Myriam Jeanne Georgette, da of late René Bay, of Royan, France; 1 da (Megan Bay Keppel b 1984); m 2, 15 June 1996, Sheena Alexandra Faro; *Heir* none; *Career* tax accountant; *Recreations* golf; *Clubs* MCC, Waterhall Golf (Brighton); *Style*— Sir Philip Dorman, Bt; ✉ 15 Wilbury Road, Hove, East Sussex BN3 3JJ (☎ 01273 724641)

DORMAND OF EASINGTON, Baron (Life Peer UK 1987), of Easington, Co Durham; John Donkin Dormand; s of Bernard and Mary Dormand, of Haswell, Co Durham; *b* 27 Aug 1919; *Educ* Bede Coll Durham, Loughborough Coll, St Peter's Coll Oxford, Harvard Univ; *m* 1963, Doris, da of Thomas Robinson, of Houghton-le-Spring, Co Durham; 1 step s, 1 step da; *Career* former teacher, educn advsr and dist educn offr; MP (Lab) Easington 1970–87, asst govt whip 1973, ld cmmr of Treasury 1974–81, chm PLP 1981–87; House of Lords 1987– (memb Liaison and Procedure Ctees and Shadow Cabinet); memb: Peterlee Lab Club, Easington Working Men's Club; hon fell St Peter's Coll Univ of Oxford; *Recreations* music, sport, films; *Style*— The Lord Dormand; ✉ House of Lords, London SW1A 0PW (☎ 0171 219 5419)

DORMANDY, Prof John Adam; s of Paul Szeben, and Klara, *née* Engel; *b* 5 May 1937; *Educ* St Paul's, Univ of London (MB BS); *m* 29 Jan 1983, Klara Dormandy, da of Prof I Zarday; 1 s (Alexis b 1969), 1 da (Xenia b 1972); *Career* conslt vascular surgn St George's Hosp, hon sr lectr in surgery and prof of vascular scis Univ of London; awarded: Fahreus Medal, Hamilton Bailey Prize, Hunterian Professorship of RCS; chm: section on clinical measurement RSM, Venous Forum RSM; ed jls on various aspects of circulatory disease; chm Euro Consensus on Critical Limb Ischaemia; DSc 1990; FRCSE 1974, FRCS 1975; *Books* Clinical Haemorheology (1987), Critical Limb Ischaemia (1990); *Recreations* skiing, squash; *Style*— Prof John Dormandy; ✉ Department of

Vascular Surgery, St James' Wing, St George's Hospital, Blackshaw Rd, London SW17 (☎ 0181 767 8346, fax 0181 682 2550)

DORMENT, Richard; *b* 15 Nov 1946; *Educ* Georgetown Prep Sch Garrett Park Maryland, Princeton Univ (BA cum laude), Columbia Univ NYC (Faculty fell 1968–72, MA, MPhil, PhD); *m* 1, 1970 (m dis 1981), Kate Ganz; 1 s (Anthony Ganz b 1975), 1 da (Lily Sophia b 1977); m 2, 1985, Harriet Waugh; *Career* asst curator of paintings Philadelphia Museum of Art 1973–76; guest curator for the exhbn Alfred Gilbert - Sculptor and Goldsmith (Royal Acad of Arts London) 1985–86; art critic: Country Life 1986, Daily Telegraph 1986–; frequent contrib: Times Literary Supplement, NY Review of Books; guest curator James McNeill Whistler Exhbn (Tate Gallery, Musée d'Orsay, Nat Gallery of Art Washington DC) 1994–95; memb: Advsy Ctee Govt Art Collection 1995–, Reviewing Ctee on the Export of Works of Art 1995–; tstee Watts Gallery; winner Hawthornden Prize for art criticism 1992; *Books* Alfred Gilbert (1985), British Painting in the Philadelphia Museum of Art (1986), James McNeill Whistler (with Margaret MacDonald, 1994); *Style*— Richard Dorment, Esq; ✉ 10 Clifton Villas, London W9 2PH (☎ 0171 266 2057)

DORMER, Robin James; s of Dudley James Dormer (d 1983), and Jean Mary, *née* Brimacombe; *b* 30 May 1951; *Educ* Int Sch of Geneva Switzerland, Univ Coll of Wales Aberystwyth (LLB); *Career* Coward Chance 1976–80; admitted slr 1980, memb legal staff Law Cmmn 1980–87, asst Parly Counsel Office 1987–90, asst slr Solicitor's Office Dept of Health 1992– (joined 1990); memb Terrence Higgins Tst (ldr Legal Servs Gp 1993–95); *Style*— Robin Dormer, Esq; ✉ Office of the Solicitor, Department of Health, New Court, 48 Carey St, London WC2A 2LS (☎ 0171 412 1467, fax 0171 412 1238)

DORRELL, Rt Hon Stephen James; PC (1994), MP (C) Loughborough (majority 10,833); s of Philip George Dorrell (d 1994) and Christine Dorrell; *b* 25 March 1952; *Educ* Uppingham, BNC Oxford; *m* 1980, Penelope Anne (Annette) Wears Taylor, da of James Taylor, of Windsor; 1 s (Philip James Andrew b 13 Nov 1992), 1 da (Alexandra b 11 July 1988); *Career* PA to Rt Hon Peter Walker MP 1974; export dir family clothing firm; Parly candidate (C) Kingston-upon-Hull E Oct 1974, MP (C) Loughborough 1979–, PPS to Rt Hon Peter Walker MP (Sec of State for Energy) 1983–87, asst Govt whip 1987–88, a Lord Cmmr of HM Treasy (govt whip) 1988–90, Parly under sec of state Dept of Health 1990–92, financial sec to Treasury 1992–94, sec of state for Nat Heritage 1994–, sec of state for Health 1995–; *Recreations* walking, reading; *Style*— The Rt Hon Stephen Dorrell, MP; ✉ House of Commons, London SW1A 0AA (☎ 0171 219 3000)

DORRIAN, Leeona June; QC (Scot 1994); da of Thomas Michael Dorrian (d 1975), of Edinburgh, and June Sylvia, *née* Neill; *b* 16 June 1957; *Educ* Cranley Sch Edinburgh, Univ of Aberdeen (LLB); *Career* admitted to Faculty of Advocates 1981, standing jr counsel to Health & Safety Exec in Scotland 1987–94, advocate depute 1988–91, standing jr counsel to Dept of Energy 1991–94; *Clubs* Scottish Arts (Edinburgh), Royal Scottish Automobile (Glasgow), Royal Forth Yacht (Edinburgh); *Style*— Miss Leeona Dorrian, QC; ✉ 23 Dundas Street, Edinburgh EH3 6QQ (☎ 0131 556 2256); c/o Advocates' Library, Parliament House, Edinburgh EH1 1RF (☎ 0131 226 5071, fax 0131 225 3642)

DORSET, Archdeacon of; *see:* Walton, Ven Geoffrey Elmer

DORWARD, David Campbell; s of David Gardyne Dorward (d 1971), of Craigton House, Monikie, and Margaret Edward, *née* Boyle; *b* 7 Aug 1933; *Educ* Morgan Acad, Univ of St Andrews (MA), RAM (GRSM); *m* 11 June 1968, Janet, da of Donald Offord; 1 s (Alan Michael b 15 Aug 1978), 2 da (Helen Marianne b 19 Nov 1972, Frances Imogen b 15 July 1974); *Career* Royal Philharmonic Soc prizewinner 1958, music prodr BBC Edinburgh 1962–91; freelance composer 1991–; composed: concerto for wind and percussion 1960, Symphony No 1 1961, four string quartets 1963–72, violin concerto 1965, cello concerto 1966, piano concerto 1976, viola concerto 1981, Symphony No 2 1995; many other chamber and orchestral works; incidental music for radio, television, theatre and film; arts advsr Lamp of Lothian 1967–, memb Scottish Arts Cncl 1972–78, conslt dir Performing Rights Soc 1985–90; memb: ISM, Composers' Guild Soc of Professional Composers; *Recreations* drawing and painting, photography, trying to program home computers, being alone, reading, walking; *Style*— David Dorward, Esq; ✉ 10 Dean Park Crescent, Edinburgh EH4 1PH (☎ 0131 332 3002)

DOSSOU-NAKI, HE Honorine; *b* 14 March 1946, Port-Gentil, Gabon; *Educ* Lycée Léon MBA Libreville Gabon, Université de Poitiers (BA), Université de Paris X Nanterre (LLB); *m* Samuel Dossou-Aworet; 5 c; *Career* Gabonese diplomat; dir of co-operation and asst sec gen Miny of Foreign Affrs 1975–76, asst dir Pres's Office 1976–80, ministerial rep Miny of Info and the Post Office May-Aug 1980, sec of state Miny of Foreign Affrs 1980–90, int affrs advsr to Pres 1990–93, perm rep and ambass of the Republic of Gabon to the UN Geneva 1993–94, ambass to the Ct of St James's 1996–; memb Ctee and Political Office Gabonese Democratic Party (PDG); chm of the Bd: Agricultural Soc of Port-Gentil 1989–, Gabonese Inst of Aid and Devpt 1992–; memb: French Inst of Int Relations, Assoc of Human Rights, Assoc of Gabonese Women Lawyers; Cdr: Equatorial Star of Gabon, Order of the King of Spain; Offr of Merit (France), Medal of Honour Gabon Police, Chev Order of Merit (Mauritius); *Recreations* sailing, tennis, jogging, gardening; *Style*— HE Madame Honorine Dossou-Naki; ✉ Embassy of the Republic of Gabon, 27 Elvaston Place, London SW7 5NL (☎ 0171 823 9986, fax 0171 584 0047)

DOTRICE, Roy; s of Louis Dotrice and Neva, *née* Wilton; *b* 26 May 1925; *Educ* Dayton Acad, Intermediate Sch Guernsey; Elizabeth Coll; *m* 1946, Kay Newman; 3 da (Michèle (m 1987 Edward Woodward, the actor), Karen (m 1994 Ned Nalle, Exec Vice Pres Universal TV), Yvette (m 1985, John E R Lumley)); *Career* actor; with Royal Shakespeare Co 1957–65, over 30 West End performances; 6 Broadway appearances incl 3 one-man shows: Winston Churchill, Abraham Lincoln, Brief Lives (in Guinness Book of World Records as longest running solo performance (1770 shows)); Best Actor awards for: Brief Lives (TV) UK 1969, The Caretaker USA 1966; Tony nomination for A Life 1981; recent films: The Cutting Edge, Lounge People, Amadeus, Eliminators, Corsican Brothers, The Scarlett Letter; recent Br TV: For the Greater Good; recent American TV: Beauty and the Beast, Going to Extremes, Wings, The Equaliser, LA Law, Picket Fences; *Recreations* fishing, riding, golf; *Clubs* Garrick, Players'; *Style*— Roy Dotrice Esq; ✉ c/o Bernard Hunter Associates, 13 Spencer Gardens, London SW14 7AH (☎ 0181 878 6308, fax 0181 392 9334)

DOUBLE, Michael Stockwell; s of Cyril William Stockwell Double (d 1942), and Alice Elizabeth Ellen, *née* Smith (d 1987); *b* 3 March 1935; *Educ* Christ's Hosp, Pembroke Coll Cambridge (MA); *m* 26 Feb 1966, Julia, da of Harold Ashwell Westrope (d 1961); 2 da (Lucy b 1967, Clare b 1970); *Career* Nat Serv Royal Corps of Signals; CA; dir: The Tussaud's Group Ltd 1981–, Warwick Castle Ltd 1987–, Chessington World of Adventures Ltd 1987–, Port Aventura SA Spain 1994–; FCA; *Recreations* sailing, theatre, walking; *Clubs* Island Cruising; *Style*— Michael Double, Esq; ✉ The Tussaud's Group Ltd, Maple House, 149 Tottenham Court Road, London W1P 0DX (☎ 0171 312 1131, fax 0171 465 0864)

DOUBLEDAY, John Vincent; s of Gordon Vincent Doubleday (d 1993), of Goat Lodge Farm, Great Totham, Maldon, Essex, and Margaret Elsa Verder, *née* Harris (d 1992); *b* 9 Oct 1947; *Educ* Stowe, Goldsmiths' Coll Sch of Art; *m* 1969, Isobel Jean Campbell, da of Maj Frederick Robert Edwin Durie (d 1995), of Argyll; 3 s (Robert b 1974, Edwin b 1977, James b 1979); *Career* artist; *Exhibitions* incl: Waterhouse Gallery 1968–69 and 1970–71, Richard Demarco Gallery Edinburgh 1973, Laing Art Gallery Newcastle, Bowes Barnard Castle 1974, Pandion Gallery NY, Aldeborough Festival 1983; *Portraits/Portrait Sculpture* incl: Baron Ramsey of Canterbury 1974, King Olav of Norway 1975, Prince Philip Duke of Edinburgh, Earl Mountbatten, Golda Meir 1976, Maurice Bowra 1979, Lord Olivier, Mary and Child Christ (Rochester Cathedral), Caduceus (Harvard Mass), Isambard Kingdom Brunel (two works in Paddington and Bristol), Charlie Chaplin (Vevey 1982, and London), Beatles (Liverpool), Dylan Thomas (Swansea 1984), Commando Memorial 1986, Arthur Mourant (St Helier Museum Jersey 1990), Sherlock Holmes (Town Square Meiringen 1991), Graham Gooch (Chelmsford 1992), Johann Pflug (Biberach 1994), Nelson Mandela (United World Colls 1996); *Work in Public Collections* Ashmolean, Br Museum, Herbert F Johnson NY, Tate Gallery, V & A, Nat Museum of Wales; *Recreations* marine conservation; *Style*— John Doubleday, Esq; ✉ Goat Lodge, Goat Lodge Rd, Gt Totham, Maldon, Essex (☎ 01621 892085);

DOUEK, Ellis Elliot; s of Cesar Douek, of London, and Nelly, *née* Sassoon; *b* 25 April 1934; *Educ* English Sch Cairo Egypt, Westminster Med Sch (MRCS, LRCP); *m* 1, 1964; 2 s (Daniel b 1965, Joel b 1967); m 2, 1994, Gill Green; *Career* Capt RAMC 1960–62; registrar ENT Royal Free Hosp 1965, sr registrar King's Coll Hosp 1968, conslt otologist Guy's Hosp 1970; FRCS 1967, RSM, BAO; *Books* Sense of Smell and Its Abnormalities (1974); contrib chapters in: Textbook of Otology and Laryngology 1988, Robbs Surgery 1976; *Recreations* painting; *Clubs* Athenaeum; *Style*— Ellis Douek, Esq; ✉ 1–24 Reynolds Close, London NW11 (☎ 0181 455 6427); 97 Harley St, London W1N 1DF (☎ 0171 935 7828, fax 0171 224 6911)

DOUGAL, Malcolm Gordon; s of Eric Gordon Dougal (d 1970), and Marie, *née* Wildermuth; *b* 20 Jan 1938; *Educ* Ampleforth, Queen's Coll Oxford (MA); *m* 1, 1964 (m dis 1995); 1 s (Gordon b 17 June 1982); m 2, 30 Sept 1995, Mrs Brigid J C Pritchard, *née* Turner; *Career* 2 Lt Royal Sussex Regt served Korea and Gibraltar 1956–58; De Havilland Aircraft 1961–64, Ticket Equipment Ltd (Plessey) 1964–66, Harris Lebus 1967–69, FCO London 1969–72; first sec: Br Embassy Paris 1972–76, Br Embassy Cairo 1976–79; FCO London 1979–81, HM Consul Gen Lille France 1981–85, Dep High Cmmr Br High Cmmn Canberra Aust 1986–89, Royal Coll of Def Studies London 1990, dir FCO/DTI Jt Directorate (Overseas Trade Services) 1991–94, HM consul gen San Francisco 1994–; memb: RSPB, Nat Tst; *Recreations* natural history, books, wine, history; *Style*— Malcolm Dougal, Esq; ✉ Foreign & Commonwealth Office (San Francisco), Whitehall, London SW1A 2AH

DOUGLAS, Alasdair Ferguson; s of George Douglas, of Perth, Scotland, and Christina, *née* Ferguson; *b* 16 March 1953; *Educ* Perth Acad, Univ of Edinburgh (LLB), QMC London (LLM); *m* Kathryn Veronica Cecile, da of Cecil Kennard, OBE (d 1971); 1 s (Robert Ferguson), 1 da (Alice Jane); *Career* admitted slr 1981; managing ptnr Travers Smith Braithwaite 1995– (ptnr 1985–95); memb Worshipful Co of Slrs; memb: Law Soc, Law Soc of Scotland; *Books* contrib: Tolley's Tax Planning, Tolley's Company Law; *Recreations* reading, cooking; *Style*— Alasdair Douglas, Esq; ✉ Travers Smith Braithwaite, 10 Snow Hill, London EC1A 2AL (☎ 0171 248 9133, fax 0171 236 3728, telex 887117)

DOUGLAS, Prof Alexander Shafto (Sandy); CBE (1985); s of Maj Quentin Douglas, RE (d 1974), of Kensington, London, and Edith Dorothy, *née* Ingram (d 1965); *b* 21 May 1921; *Educ* Marlborough, Coll of Estate Mgmnt (BSc), Trinity Coll Cambridge (BA, MA, PhD); *m* 18 Dec 1945, Audrey Mary Brasnett, da of Reginald George Parker (d 1983), of Mildenhall, Suffolk; 1 s (Malcolm b 1956), 1 da (Shirley (Mrs Mauger) b 1953); *Career* WWII Royal Signals: Signalman 1941, offr cadet 1942, 2 Lt India 1943, Lt 1943 (served 2 Div Kohima), released 1946; visiting prof Univ of Illinois USA 1953–54, fell and jr bursar Trinity Coll Cambridge 1955–57, dir Univ of Leeds Computing Laboratory 1957–60, tech dir CEIR UK Ltd (now EDS - SCICON) 1960–68, chm Leasco Systems and Research Ltd 1968–69, prof LSE 1969–84 (emeritus prof 1984–), non-exec dir The Monotype Corporation 1973–78, chm Specialist Information Services Ltd (consultancy) 1983–, pt/t visiting prof Middx Business Sch Middx Poly 1987–91; govr Int Cncl for Computers and Communications 1981–, dir UK Cncl Computers for Devpt 1987–90, advsr Sci and Technol Parly Ctees 1970–76; memb Defence Sci Advsy Cncl 1971–88, Sci Advsy Ctee Br Cncl 1978–88; Freeman City of London 1965, Liveryman Worshipful Co of Wheelwrights 1965, Liveryman Worshipful Co of Info Technologists 1986; FBCS (fndr memb 1956, pres 1972), FIMA 1964, ACIArb 1986, MBAE 1988, CEng 1990, CMath 1991, FRSA; *Books* Second Report of the Secretary General on the Application of Computers to Development (jtly, 1973); *Recreations* tennis, bridge, philately; *Clubs* City Livery (memb Cncl 1989–, vice pres 1993, pres 1994); *Style*— Prof Alexander Douglas, CBE; ✉ 9 Woodside Ave, Walton-on-Thames, Surrey KT12 5LQ (☎ 01932 881662, fax 01932 224923)

DOUGLAS, Anthony Jude (Tony); s of Arthur Sydney Douglas (d 1976), and Margaret Mary, *née* Farey; *b* 14 Dec 1944; *Educ* Cardinal Vaughan GS, Univ of Southampton (BA); *m* 24 Aug 1968, Jacqueline, *née* English; 2 da (Amy Jane b 2 Oct 1978, Laura Claire b 28 May 1984); *Career* Lintas Advertising: graduate trainee 1967, various account mgmnt posts, client serv dir 1980; D'Arcy McManus & Masius (D'Arcy Masius Benton & Bowles since merger 1985): gp account dir 1982, jt md 1985, jt chm and chief exec 1987–95; chief exec COI 1996–; FIPA, memb Mktg Soc; *Recreations* jogging, walking, reading, travel; *Clubs* RAC, St James's; *Style*— Tony Douglas, Esq; ✉ Central Office of Information, Hercules Road, London SE1 7DU (☎ 0171 261 8210)

DOUGLAS, (William) Barry; s of Barry Douglas (d 1988), and Sarah Jane, *née* Henry; *b* 23 April 1960; *Educ* RCM (with John Barstow, further study with Maria Curcio); *Career* concert pianist; debut London 1981, Gold medal Tchaikovsky Int Piano Competition Moscow 1986; worldwide concert career; tours: USA, Japan, Far East, USSR, Europe; subject of TV documentary After The Gold, appeared in Dudley Moore's TV series Concerto; former visiting fell Oriel Coll Oxford; Hon DMus Queen's Univ Belfast; FRCM 1988; *Recordings* Tchaikovsky Piano Concerto Nos 1, 2 and 3, Mussorgsky Pictures at an Exhibition, Brahms Piano Quintet in F Minor, Beethoven Hammerklavier, Brahms Piano Concerto No 1, Tchaikovsky Sonata in G, Liszt Piano Concertos, Prokofiev Sonatas 2 and 7, Berg Sonata, Liszt Sonata in B Minor, Beethoven Sonata Op 53, 57, 90, Rachmaninov Piano Concerto No 2; *Recreations* driving, reading, food and wine; *Style*— Barry Douglas, Esq; ✉ c/o IMG Artists, Media House, 3 Burlington Lane, London W4 2TH (☎ 0181 233 5800, fax 0181 233 5801)

DOUGLAS, Donald Macleod; s of Alexander Douglas (d 1973), of Falkirk, Scotland, and Florence, *née* Breakspear (d 1974); *b* 7 March 1933; *Educ* Falkirk HS, Edinburgh Coll of Art (travelling scholarship), RADA (scholarship); *m* 1968 (m dis 1991), Angela, *née* Galbraith; 3 da (Amy b 1971, Eliza b 1973, Joanna b 1975); *Career* actor; stage debut RSC 1960; repertory cos incl: Glasgow Citizens, Bristol Old Vic, Birmingham, Manchester, Leatherhead, Newcastle; *Theatre* West End Plays: Poor Bitos (Duke of York's), Boys in the Band (Wyndham's), Savages (Comedy), Gotcha (Shaw); RSC 1978–79: Merchant of Venice, Wild Oats, The Churchill Play; Stephen Joseph Co 1989: The Revengers Comedies, June Moon; others incl: Mr Cinders (Fortune) 1983, The Three Estates (Edinburgh Festival 1986, Warsaw), Absurd Person Singular (Whitehall) 1990–91, Medea (NY) 1994; *Television* incl: Rob Roy, Red Gauntlet, Middlemarch, Sense and Sensibiltity, War and Peace, Poldark, Poirot, Taggart, The Bill, Eastenders; *Films* incl: A Bridge Too Far, Give My Regards to Broad Street, She's Been Away; *Recreations* gardening, riding, painting; *Style*— Donald Douglas, Esq; ✉ c/o Joan Brown Associates, 3 Earls Road, London SW14 7JH (☎ 0181 876 9448, fax 0181 878 4403)

DOUGLAS, Gavin Stuart; RD (1970), QC (Scot 1971); s of late Gilbert Georgeson Douglas, and Rosena Campbell Douglas; *b* 12 June 1932; *Educ* South Morningside Sch,

George Heriot's Sch, Univ of Edinburgh (MA, LLB); *Career* Nat Serv RNVR; qualified as slr 1955; admitted Faculty of Advocates 1958, pt/t sub-ed The Scotsman 1957–61, memb Lord Advocate's Dept London (Parly draftsman) 1961–64, resumed practice at Scottish Bar 1964, jr counsel to BOT 1965, counsel to Scottish Law Cmmn 1965–96, chm Industl Tbnls 1966–78, counsel to Sec of State for Scotland under Private Legislation Procedure (Scotland) Act (1936) 1969–75 (sr counsel under that Act 1975–), ed Session Cases (7 volumes) 1976–82; Hon Sheriff in various Sheriffdoms 1965–71, Temp Sheriff 1990–; *Recreations* skiing, golf; *Clubs* Univ Staff (Edinburgh), Army and Navy; *Style*— Gavin Douglas, Esq, RD, QC; ✉ Parliament House, Parliament Square, Edinburgh EH1 (☎ 0131 226 5071)

DOUGLAS, Lord Gawain Archibald Francis; s of 11 Marquess of Queensberry (d 1954), by his 3 w (Mimi, Marchioness of Queensberry, d 1992); *b* 23 May 1948; *Educ* Downside, Royal Acad of Music (LRAM); *m* 1971, Nicolette, da of Col Frank Eustace (d 1976), of Hong Kong; 1 s (Jamie b 1975), 5 da (Dalziel b 1971, Elizabeth b 1974, Natasha b 1976, Margarita b 1978, Mary-Anne b 1981); *Career* former prof of pianoforte Blackheath Conservatoire of Music, music prof Kent Rural Music Sch Canterbury, concert recitalist, accompanist and duettist in company with wife; *Recreations* tennis, swimming, writing short stories and poems, books; *Clubs* Polish Hearth, Walmer Lawn Tennis; *Style*— The Lord Gawain Douglas; ✉ 2 Archery Square, Walmer, Deal, Kent (☎ 01304 375813)

DOUGLAS, Dr (John) Graham; s of Dr Keith Douglas, of Menston, nr Ilkley, and Mavis Douglas; *b* 20 Oct 1949; *Educ* Bradford GS, Univ of Edinburgh (BSc(Hons), MB ChB), FRCP FSAS; *m* 1 Oct 1977, Alison, da of John Menzies, of Dalkeith, Edinburgh; 1 s (Jamie b 5 Oct 1980), 1 da (Catriona Douglas b 7 June 1983); *Career* jr med and surgical house offr Edinburgh Royal Infirmary 1974–75, SHO and registrar in gen medicine, gastroenterology and renal medicine Eastern Gen Hosp and Edinburgh Royal Infirmary 1975–81, sr registrar in chest med and infection Edinburgh Royal Infimary and Northern Gen Hosp 1981–86, conslt physician with an interest in thoracic med and infection Aberdeen 1986–; author of 80 scientific publications on gen and thoracic med and infection; *Recreations* hillwalking, cycling, golf, skiing, DIY, history; *Style*— Dr Graham Douglas; ✉ Respiratory Unit, Aberdeen Royal Infirmary, Aberdeen AB25 2ZN (☎ 01224 681818 ext 58305)

DOUGLAS, Prof Ian; s of Prof Ronald Walter Douglas, of West Hill, Ottery St Mary, Devon, and Edna Maud, *née* Cadle; *b* 2 Dec 1936; *Educ* Merchant Taylors', Balliol Coll Oxford (BLitt, MA), Aust Nat Univ (PhD); *m* 16 Nov 1963, Maureen Ann, da of Frank Bowler (d 1988); 2 s (David b 1965, d 1981, Aidan b 1967), 1 da (Fiona b 1972); *Career* Nat Serv Bombardier RA 1956–58; lectr Univ of Hull 1966–71, prof of geography Univ of New England Armidale NSW Aust 1971–78, prof of physical geography Univ of Manchester 1979–; dir Salford and Trafford Groundwork Tst 1993–; pres Inst of Aust Geographers 1978; chm: Br Geomorphological Res Gp 1980–81, UK/MAB Urban Forum 1993–; organiser first Int Conf On Geomorphology Manchester 1985; MIWEM 1975; *Books* Humid Landforms (1977), The Urban Environment (1983), Environmental Change and Tropical Geomorphology (co-ed, 1985); *Recreations* walking in rainforests, swimming, gardening; *Style*— Prof Ian Douglas; ✉ 21 Taunton Road, Sale, Cheshire M33 5DD (☎ 0161 973 1708); School of Geography, University of Manchester M13 9PL (☎ 0161 275 3642, fax 0161 273 4407)

DOUGLAS, Prof James; s of James Douglas (d 1936), of Edinburgh, and Margaret Helen Douglas (d 1933); *b* 4 July 1932; *Educ* Heriot Watt Coll, Paris Conservatoire, Mozarteum Salzburg, Hochschule Munich; *m* 1, 1959, Mary Henderson Irving (d 1967); 2 s (Stephen James b 1961, Gavin John b 1962); m 2, 16 April 1968, Helen Torrance Fairweather; 1 da (Katharine Helen b 1971); *Career* composer, accompanist, organist; prof L'Académie des Sciences Universelles Paris 1992–; dir: Eschenbach Editions 1986–, Caritas Records 1989–; compositions incl: 12 symphonies, 12 string quartets, 20 orchestral works, chamber music, piano music, organ music, choral music and over 200 songs; operas: Mask, The King, Molière, Cuthbert; recordings: Visions of Glory (1990); organ music: Symphony, A Vision (1992, re-issued 1997), Flute Music (1992, re-issued 1997), Organ Music vol II (1993, re-issued 1997); memb: ISM, Music Publishers' Assoc, Performing Right Soc; *Books* The Music of Hermann Reutter (1966); *Recreations* reading, cloud watching; *Clubs* New Cavendish; *Style*— Prof James Douglas; ✉ 28 Dalrymple Crescent, Edinburgh EH9 2NX (☎ and fax 0131 667 3633)

DOUGLAS, Dr James Frederick; s of Capt Rev James Douglas, CF (ka 1944), and Annie Hildegarde, *née* Harte; *b* 22 Sept 1938; *Educ* Portora Royal Sch Enniskillen, Wadham Coll Oxford (MA, BM BCh, BCL), Queen's Univ of Belfast (MB BCh); *m* 27 April 1973, Giselle Sook An Lim; 4 s (Jeremy b 1975, Timothy b 1978, Andrew b 1981, Stephen b 1983, d 1984); *Career* lectr Coll of Law 1963–64, called to the Bar Middle Temple 1964, houseman Royal Victoria Hosp Belfast 1969–70, nephrologist 1972, conslt Belfast City and Royal Victoria Hosps 1975, sr nephrologist Belfast City Hosp 1988–; author of various pubns on: renal transplantation, renal failure, renal toxicology, the law and renal failure; memb: Renal Assoc, Euro Dialysis and Transplantation Assoc; FRCP 1987 (MRCP 1973); *Recreations* astronomy, chess, golf; *Style*— Dr James Douglas; ✉ Department of Nephrology, Belfast City Hospital, Lisburn Rd, Belfast (☎ 01232 329241 ext 2218/3010)

DOUGLAS, James Murray; CBE (1985); s of Herbert Douglas (d 1968), and Amy Crawford Murray (d 1976); *b* 26 Sept 1925; *Educ* Morrisons Acad Crieff, Univ of Aberdeen (MA), Balliol Coll Oxford (BA); *m* 1950, Julie, da of Hermann Kemmner (d 1969); 1 s (Michael b 1952), 1 da (Kathleen b 1954); *Career* RAF Flt Lt 1944–47; entered Civil Serv 1950, Treasy 1960–63, asst sec Miny of Housing and Local Govt 1964, sec Royal Cmmn on Local Govt 1966–69, dir gen CLA 1970–90; vice pres Confedn of Euro Agric 1971–88, chm Environment Ctee 1988–90; sec Euro Landowning Orgns Gp 1972–87; memb: Econ Devpt Ctee for Agric 1972–90, Cncl CBI 1986–89; dir Booker Countryside 1990–93; memb: NW Kent Branch Oxford Univ Soc, N Kent Decorative and Fine Arts Soc, Kent Ctee CLA 1991–; author of various articles on local govt and landowning; *Recreations* golf, music, reading, films, theatre; *Clubs* Utd Oxford & Cambridge Univ, Chislehurst Golf; *Style*— James Douglas, Esq, CBE; ✉ 1 Oldfield Close, Bickley, Kent BR1 2LL (☎ 0181 467 3213)

DOUGLAS, John Robert Tomkys; OBE; s of Sir Robert McCallum Douglas, OBE, and Millicent Irene Tomkys, *née* Morgan (d 1980); *b* 24 July 1930; *Educ* Oundle, Univ of Birmingham (BSc); *m* 12 Oct 1957, Sheila Margaret, da of Miles Varey (d 1963), of Liverpool; 2 s (Philip b 1960, Jonathan b 1962), 1 da (Alison b 1958); *Career* Nat Serv RE 1953–55, Lt 1955; civil engr; dir various cos in Douglas Group 1953–91; chm: Robert M Douglas Holdings plc 1978–91 (md 1976–87), Tilbury Douglas plc 1991–96, Birmingham Regeneration Ltd 1992–96 (dir 1987–92), Heartlands Development Services Ltd 1992–96 (dir 1989–92); dir Construction Indust Trg Bd 1990–95; ldr Sutton Coldfield Crusaders 1956–81, gen cmmr for Income Tax 1968–92, memb Ct of Govrs Univ of Birmingham 1972–, pres Birmingham Chamber of Indust and Commerce 1992–93 (memb Cncl 1981–95), tstee TSB Foundation for England and Wales 1986–93, pres Fedn of Civil Engrg Contractors 1987–90 (chm 1974–75), memb Comité de Direction of Fédération de L'Industrie Européenne de la Construction 1992–94 (treas 1992–94); Liveryman Worshipful Co of Paviors; FIHT (MIHT 1967), FCIOB 1973, FRSA 1982, CIMgt 1983; *Recreations* music, theatre, sailing; *Clubs* Caledonian, Royal Engineer Yacht, Royal Motor Yacht; *Style*— John Douglas, Esq, OBE; ✉ Threave, 2 Brudenell Avenue, Poole, Dorset BH13 7NW (☎ and fax 01202 706662)

DOUGLAS, Keith Humphrey; s of Arthur Ernest Douglas (d 1977), and Gladys Kittie, *née* Dyson (d 1926); *b* 11 May 1923; *Educ* Claremont Sch, Leamington Tech Coll; *m* 1944, Joan Lilian, da of Harry Sheasby (d 1976), of Leamington Spa; 2 s (Russell b 1948, Alistair b 1957); *Career* chm and md Keith Douglas (Motor Sport) 1964–, dir GKN Group 1966–85, chm KDA Ltd 1985–, md International Motor Sports Ltd 1994–96; assoc dir PE International 1986–; memb Govt to Govt Study Team Indonesian automotive sector 1991–92; commentator: Silverstone 1962–, ITV 1964–66; pres Nottingham Sports Car Club 1966–71, vice chm RAC Br Motorsports Cncl 1975–95, vice pres Br Motor Racing Marshals Club 1975–96, dir RAC Motor Sports Assoc 1979–94, driver discipline and inspr of racing driver schs RAC British Motor Sports Cncl, tstee RAC Motor Sports Trg Tst; FCIM, MSAE, AMIMechE; *Recreations* classic car rallies, motor sport commentating, game fishing, music, charity work for motor industry fund (BEN, organiser Jaguar 75, life govr 1989); *Clubs* RAC, BRDC, JDC, JCC, Guild of Motoring Writers, Thursday (organiser); *Style*— Keith Douglas, Esq; ✉ 281 Four Ashes Rd, Dorridge, Solihull, W Midlands B93 8NR (☎ and fax 01564 773202)

DOUGLAS, Kenneth; CBE (1991); s of John Carr Douglas (d 1948), and Margaret Victoria, *née* Allen (d 1980); *b* 28 Oct 1920; *Educ* Sunderland Tech Coll (Dip Naval Arch), CEng; *m* 1942, Doris, da of Thomas Henry Southern Lewer (d 1958); 1 s (Colin), 2 da (Gloria, Sally); *Career* tech asst Ship Div NPL 1945–46, mangr Vickers Armstrong Naval Yard Newcastle upon Tyne 1946–53, dir and gen mangr William Gray & Co Ltd 1953–58, md Austin & Pickersgill Ltd 1958–69 and 1979–83, chm Kenton Shipping Services Darlington 1968–77, md Upper Clyde Shipbuilders Ltd 1969–73, chm Simons Lobnitz Ltd and UCS Training Co 1969–73, dep chm Govan Shipbuilders 1971–73, chm Douglas (Kilbride) Ltd 1972–77, chm and md Steel Structures Ltd 1974–76, ship repair mktg dir Br Shipbuilders 1978–79; memb Bd of River Wear Cmmrs 1959–69; chm: Wear Shipbuilders Assoc 1965–66, Wearside Productivity Assoc 1965–66; external examiner (DMS) Rutherford Coll 1965–69, memb Advsy Ctee (Naval Arch) Univ of Newcastle 1965–69, govr Stow Coll Glasgow 1969–73, chm of govrs Univ of Sunderland (formerly Sunderland Poly) 1982–93; memb: Tyne and Wear Residuary Bd 1985–88, Bd Polys and Colls Employees Forum 1987–90; hon fell Univ of Sunderland 1993; author of papers to learned instns on mgmnt, mktg and costing in shipbuilding and standardisation in ship design; formerly: memb Baltic Exchange, MNECInst, FRINA, FRSA, MBIM, MInstD; *Clubs* Sunderland, Ashbrooke; *Style*— Kenneth Douglas, Esq, CBE; ✉ 60 Durham Road, East Herrington, Sunderland, Tyne and Wear SR3 3LZ

DOUGLAS, Margaret Elizabeth; OBE (1994); *b* 22 Aug 1934; *Educ* Parliament Hill GS London; *Career* BBC: joined as sec 1951, later worked in Current Affairs Dept, chief asst to Dir Gen 1983–87, chief political advsr 1987–93; supervisor of Parly Broadcasting House of Commons 1993–; *Recreations* watching politics and football; *Style*— Miss Margaret Douglas, OBE; ✉ House of Commons, London SW1A 0AA (☎ 0171 219 3000)

DOUGLAS, Prof Neil James; s of Prof Sir Donald Douglas (d 1993), and Margaret Diana, *née* Whitley; *b* 28 May 1949; *Educ* Glenalmond Coll, Univ of St Andrews (scholar), Univ of Edinburgh (MB ChB, MD); *m* 16 July 1977, Dr Susan McLaren Galloway, da of Dr Thomas McLaren Galloway; 1 s (Sandy Donald b 6 Jan 1983), 1 da (Kirsty McLaren b 21 Feb 1985); *Career* lectr in med Univ of Edinburgh 1974–83, MRC fell Univ of Colorado 1980–81; Univ of Edinburgh: sr lectr in med 1983–91, reader in med/respiratory med 1991–95, prof of respiratory and sleep med 1995–; physician Royal Infirmary Edinburgh 1983–, dir Scottish Nat Sleep Labs 1983–; Royal Coll of Physicians Edinburgh: dir of continuing med educn 1993–, dean 1995–; formerly: chm Editorial Bd Clinical Sci, hon sec Br Thoracic Soc, chm Br Sleep Soc; *Style*— Prof Neil Douglas; ✉ Respiratory Medicine Unit, Department of Medicine, Royal Infirmary, Edinburgh EH3 9YW (☎ 0131 536 3252, fax 0131 536 3255, e-mail N.J.Douglas@ed.ac.uk)

DOUGLAS, Rodney Hugh Rovery; s of Hugh Rovery Douglas, of Egham, Surrey, and Florence Alice, *née* Haggerty; *b* 18 Nov 1933; *Educ* Willesden Co GS, UCL (BSc); *m* 4 June 1960, Elise Margaret, da of Capt Bertram Vautier (d 1970), of Egham; 2 s (Graham b 1962, Adrian b 1964), 1 da (Heather b 1970); *Career* cmmnd RAF 1956–59, Flt Lt (airfield construction); served 5001 Sqdn: Malta, Libya, Cyprus, Aden; cmmnd Maj RE (TA, Engr and Tport Staff Corps) 1985, Lt-Col 1989, Col 1995; memb Mersey River Bd 1954–56; dir responsible for airport highway and public health projects Sir Frederick Snow & Partners Ltd (conslt engrs) 1959–95 (conslt 1995–); former pres Woking and Dist Scot Soc; CEng (civil), FICE, FInstHT, MConsE; *Recreations* yacht cruising, Scottish dancing; *Clubs* RAF, Cruising Assoc; *Style*— Rodney Douglas, Esq; ✉ Saltwood, Onslow Crescent, Woking, Surrey GU22 7AU (☎ 01483 829092); Sir Frederick Snow and Partners Ltd, Ross House, 144 Southwark St, London SE1 0SZ (☎ 0171 928 5688, fax 0171 928 1774, telex 917478 Snowmen London)

DOUGLAS, Dr (William) Stewart; s of William Douglas (d 1988), of Beith, Ayrshire, and Jane Goldie, *née* Guy; *b* 21 Feb 1945; *Educ* Spier's Sch, Univ of Glasgow (MB ChB); *m* 10 Jan 1986, Margaret Ross, da of James Russell Scott (d 1986), of Giffnock, Glasgow; *Career* conslt dermatologist; house offr: in med Ballochmyle Hosp 1968–69, in surgery Royal Infirmary Dumfries 1969; Ure scholar Univ of Glasgow Dept of Med 1969–70; Glasgow Royal Infirmary: sr house offr in med 1970–72, registrar in dermatology 1972–73 and 1974–75; lectr Univ of Nairobi Kenya 1973–74, sr registrar Aberdeen Royal Infirmary 1975–77, lectr Univ of Aberdeen 1975–77, conslt dermatologist to Lanarkshire Health Bd 1977–93, conslt dermatologist Monklands and Bellshill Hosps Tst 1993–; hon sec Scottish Dermatological Soc 1981–83; MRCP 1972, FRCPGlas 1983; *Recreations* sailing, skiing, cycling; *Style*— Dr Stewart Douglas; ✉ 102 Brownside Road, Cambuslang, Glasgow G72 8AF (fax 0141 641 3026); Department of Dermatology, Monklands Hospital, Airdrie ML6 0JS Lanarkshire (☎ 01236 748748)

DOUGLAS, Sue; *see:* Douglas Ferguson, Susan Margaret

DOUGLAS, Torin Stuart; s of Stuart Douglas (d 1994), of Reigate, and Hazel Joyce, *née* Smith (d 1989); *b* 24 Sept 1950; *Educ* Eastbourne Coll, Univ of Warwick (BA); *m* 6 Oct 1973, Carol Sheila, da of Kenneth Douglas Winstanley; 2 s (Richard Torin Winstanley b 18 Oct 1981, Michael Stuart b 6 March 1985), 1 da (Eleanor Frances b 20 April 1991); *Career* trainee journalist D C Thomson 1972–73, media writer then features ed Campaign 1973–76, information offr IBA 1976–78, assoc ed Marketing Week 1978–82, ed Creative Review 1980–82, advtg and mktg writer The Times 1982–84, advtg and media writer The Economist 1982–84, presenter Advertising World LBC Radio 1984–89, media page columnist The Independent 1988–89, media corr BBC News and Current Affairs 1989–; columnist Marketing Week 1980–, also contrib to Sunday Times, The Observer, The Guardian, Radio Times, Punch and The Listener; Mktg Soc Journalism Award 1983, Magazine Publishing Awards Best Business Columnist 1987; chm Bdcasting Press Guild 1996–97; memb NUJ; *Books* The Complete Guide to Advertising (1985); *Style*— Torin Douglas, Esq; ✉ BBC News and Current Affairs, Room 3116, Broadcasting House, Portland Place, London W1A 1AA (☎ 0171 765 4503, fax 0171 636 4295)

DOUGLAS, Rt Hon Sir William Randolph; KCMG (1983), kt (1969), PC (1977); s of William P Douglas; *b* 24 Sept 1921; *Educ* Bannatyne Sch, Verdun HS Quebec, McGill Univ (BA), LSE (LLB); *m* 1951, Thelma Ruth (d 1992), da of Ernest Gershon Gilkes; 1 s, 1 da; *Career* called to the Bar Middle Temple 1947, slr-gen Jamaica 1962 (formerly asst attorney-gen), Puisne Judge (Jamaica) 1962, chief justice (Barbados) 1965–86; High Cmmr for Barbados in London 1991–94; *Style*— The Rt Hon Sir William Douglas, KCMG

DOUGLAS AND CLYDESDALE, Marquess of; Alexander Douglas Douglas-Hamilton; s and h of 15 Duke of Hamilton and (12 of) Brandon, *qv*; *b* 31 March 1978; *Style—* Marquess of Douglas and Clydesdale

DOUGLAS FERGUSON, Susan Margaret; da of Kenneth Frank Douglas, of London, and Vivienne Mary, *née* Harris; *b* 29 Jan 1957; *Educ* Tiffin Girls' Sch Kingston Surrey, Univ of Southampton (BSc); *m* 26 July 1994; 1 s (Felix b 1994), 1 da (Freya b 1995); *Career* Arthur Andersen & Co Mgmnt Consultancy 1978–79, Mims Magazine Haymarket Publishing 1979–80; reporter: Sunday Express Johannesburg 1980–81; Mail on Sunday 1982–87: med corr, features ed, asst ed, assoc ed; asst ed Daily Mail 1987–91, dep ed Sunday Times 1992–95, ed Sunday Express 1996; *Recreations* riding; *Style—* Ms Susan Douglas Ferguson; ✉ Flat 2, 46 Lexington Street, London W1

DOUGLAS-HAMILTON, Rt Hon Lord James Alexander; PC (1996), QC (1996), MP (C) Edinburgh W (majority 879); 2 s of 14 Duke of Hamilton and Brandon, KT, GCVO, AFC, PC (d 1973); *b* 31 July 1942; *Educ* Eton, Balliol Coll Oxford (MA, Boxing blue, pres Union, pres Cons Assoc), Univ of Edinburgh (LLB); *m* 1974, Hon Priscilla Susan (Susie), *née* Buchan, da of 2 Baron Tweedsmuir (d 1996); 4 s (John Andrew b 1978, Charles Douglas b 1979, James Robert b 1981, Harry Alexander (twin) b 1981); *Career* offr TAS 6/7 Bn Cameronians Scottish Rifles 1961–66, TAVR 1971–73, Capt 2 Bn Lowland Volunteers; advocate 1968–74; Parly candidate (C) Hamilton Feb 1974, MP (C) Edinburgh W Oct 1974–; Scottish Cons whip 1977, a Lord Cmmr of the Treasy 1979–81, PPS to Malcolm Rifkind MP 1983–87 (as Min FO 1983–86, as Sec of State for Scotland 1986–87), Parly under sec of state for home affrs and environment 1987–92 (incl local govt at Scottish Office 1987–89, additional responsibility for local govt fin 1989–Sep 1990 and for the Arts in Scotland Sept 1990–92), Parly under sec of state for educn and housing Scottish Office 1992–95, min of state for home affrs and health (with responsibility for roads & tport and construction) Scottish Office 1995–; memb Scottish Select Ctee on Scottish Affrs 1981–83; hon sec: Cons Parly Constitutional Ctee, Cons Parly Aviation Ctee 1983–; chm Scottish Parly All-Pty Penal Affrs Ctee 1983; hon pres Scottish Amateur Boxing Assoc 1975; pres: Royal Cwlth Soc (Scotland) 1979–87, Scottish Nat Cncl UN Assoc 1981–87, Int Service Rescue 1995–; Hon Air Cdre No 2 (City of Edinburgh) Maritime HQ Unit 1995–; life memb Nat Tst for Scotland (memb Cncl 1977–82); disclaimed hereditary peerage (Earldom of Selkirk) Nov 1994; *Books* Motive for a Mission: The Story Behind Hess's Flight to Britain (1971), The Air Battle for Malta: the Diaries of a Fighter Pilot (1981), Roof of the World: Man's First Flight over Everest (1983), The Truth About Rudolf Hess (1993); *Recreations* golf, forestry, debating, history, boxing; *Style—* The Rt Hon Lord James Douglas-Hamilton, QC, MP; ✉ House of Commons, London SW1A 0AA (☎ 0171 219 4399, sec 0171 219 4206)

DOUGLAS-HOME, Lady (Lavinia) Caroline; DL (Berwicks 1983); eldest da of Baron Home of the Hirsel, KT, PC (d 1995), formerly 14 Earl of Home; *b* 11 Oct 1937; *Career* woman of the bedchamber (temp) to HM Queen Elizabeth The Queen Mother 1963–65, lady-in-waiting (temp) to HRH The Duchess of Kent 1966–67; tstee Nat Museum of Antiquities of Scotland 1982–85; FSA (Scot); *Recreations* antiquities, fishing; *Style—* The Lady Caroline Douglas-Home, DL; ✉ Heaton Mill House, Cornhill-on-Tweed, Northumberland TD12 4XQ (☎ and fax 01890 882303)

DOUGLAS-MANN, Bruce Leslie Home; s of late Leslie Douglas-Mann, MC, of Torquay, and Alice Home Douglas-Mann (d 1993); *b* 23 June 1927; *Educ* Upper Canada Coll Toronto, Jesus Coll Oxford; *m* 1955, Helen, da of Edwin Tucker, of Dulwich; 1 s, 1 da; *Career* admitted slr 1954; sr ptnr Douglas-Mann & Co 1964–; MP (Lab): Kensington N 1970–74, Merton Mitcham and Morden 1974–82 (resigned from Lab Pty 1981), joined SDP, sat as Ind Social Democrat, resigned seat 1982; refought on SDP/Lib Alliance ticket 1982, 1983 and 1987; chm SHELTER 1990–93 (chm Exec Ctee 1987–90, memb Bd 1974–), vice pres Bldg Socs Assoc 1973–90, pres or vice pres Social Environmemt and Resources Assoc 1973–80; chm: PLP Housing and Construction Gp 1974–79, PLP Environment Gp 1979–81 (vice chm 1972–79), Parly Select Ctee on Environment 1979–82, Soc of Lab Lawyers 1974–80; former memb Kensington & Chelsea Cncl; chm Arts Cncl Tst for Special Funds; *Style—* Bruce Douglas-Mann, Esq; ✉ Douglas-Mann & Co, 33 Furnival Street, London EC4A 1JQ (☎ 0171 405 7216, fax 0171 831 9906)

DOUGLAS MILLER, Robert Alexander Gavin; s of Maj Francis Gavin Douglas Miller (d 1950), and Mary Morison, *née* Kennedy; *b* 11 Feb 1937; *Educ* Harrow, Univ of Oxford (MA); *m* 9 March 1963, Judith Madeleine Smith, da of Richard Michael Desmond Dunstan, OBE, of Firbeck, nr Worksop, Notts; 3 s (Andrew Gavin b 30 Sept 1963, Robert Peter b 15 Jan 1965, Edward James b 20 May 1966), 1 da (Emma Lucy Jane b 8 Jan 1969); *Career* served in 9 Lancers 1955–57; joined Jenners Edinburgh 1962: md 1972, chm and md 1982–; chm and md Kennington Leasing; dir: First Scottish American Investmt Tst, Northern American Tst, Bain Clarkson Ltd, Edinburgh C of C; chm Outreach Tst, memb Kyle of Sutherland Fishery Bd landowner (5850 acres); *Recreations* fishing, shooting, gardening; *Clubs* New (Edinburgh); *Style—* Robert Douglas Miller, Esq; ✉ Bavelaw Castle, Balerno, Midlothian (☎ 0131 449 3972); Jenners, 48 Princes St, Edinburgh EH2 2YJ (☎ 0131 225 4791)

DOUGLAS-PENNANT, Hon Nigel; yr s of 5 Baron Penrhyn (d 1967), by his 2 w, and hp of bro, 6 Baron Penrhyn, DSO, MBE; *b* 22 Dec 1909; *Educ* Eton, Clare Coll Cambridge; *m* 1, 6 Sept 1935, Margaret Dorothy (d 1938), da of Thomas George Kirkham; 1 s; m 2, 20 July 1940, Eleanor Stewart (d 1987), eldest da of late Very Rev Herbert Newcome Craig, Dean of Kildare; 1 s, 1 da; m 3, 21 Oct 1993, Stella Mary Wingfield Digby, wid of The Rev J R Wingfield Digby (d 1983); *Career* formerly Maj RM; *Style—* The Hon Nigel Douglas-Pennant; ✉ Brook House, Glemsford, Sudbury, Suffolk

DOUGLAS-SCOTT-MONTAGU, Hon Ralph; s (by 1 m) and h of 3 Baron Lord Montagu of Beaulieu by 1 wife; *b* 13 March 1961; *Educ* Millfield, Brockenhurst Sixth Form Coll, Central Sch of Art and Design; *Career* graphic designer; *Books* The Producers' Guide to Graphics (book and video) (1986), The Graphics Guide (1988); *Clubs* BBC; *Style—* The Hon Ralph Douglas-Scott-Montagu; ✉ Palace House, Beaulieu, Brockenhurst, Hants SO42 7ZN

DOULTON, John Herbert Farre; s of Alfred John Farre Doulton, CBE, TD (d 1996), of Salcombe, Devon, and Vera Daphne, *née* Wheatley; *b* 2 Jan 1942; *Educ* Rugby, Keble Coll Oxford (MA); *m* 26 April 1986, Margaret Anne, da of Rev Cecil Ball (d 1959); *Career* asst master and housemaster Radley Coll 1966–88, princ Elizabeth Coll Guernsey 1988–; memb: Guernsey Deanery Synod, Admiralty Interview Bd; *Recreations* walking, travel, architecture, photography, boats, gardening, DIY; *Style—* John Doulton, Esq; ✉ Brantwood, Forest Rd, St Martin's, Guernsey, Channel Islands (☎ 01481 38995); Elizabeth College, Guernsey, CI (☎ 01481 726544, fax 01481 714839)

DOURO, Marquess of; (Arthur) Charles Valerian Wellesley; s and h of 8 Duke of Wellington, KG, LVO, OBE, MC; *b* 19 Aug 1945; *Educ* Eton, Ch Ch Oxford; *m* 3 Feb 1977, Antonia (chm Guinness Trust, pres Royal Hosp and Home Putney), da of HRH Prince Frederick von Preussen (d 1966, s of HIH Crown Prince Wilhelm, s and h of Kaiser Wilhelm II), and Lady Brigid Ness; 2 s (Earl of Mornington, Lord Frederick Charles b 30 Sept 1992), 3 da (Lady Honor b 25 Oct 1979, Lady Mary b 16 Dec 1986, Lady Charlotte b 8 Oct 1990); *Heir* s, Earl of Mornington b 31 Jan 1978; *Career* chm: Dunhill Holdings plc 1991–93 (dep chm 1990–91), Framlington Group PLC 1994–, Sun Life London Ltd 1995, Sun Life & Provincial plc 1996–; dep chm: Thames Valley Broadcasting 1975–84, Deltec Panamerica SA 1985–89, Guinness Mahon Holdings plc 1988–91, Vendôme Luxury Group PLC 1993–; dir: Transatlantic Holdings plc 1983–85, Sun Life Corporation plc 1988–96, GAM Worldwide Inc, Rothmans International plc 1990–93, Eucalyptus Pulp Mills 1979–88; MEP (C) for Surrey West 1979–89, Parly candidate Islington N (C) 1974; *Style—* Marquess of Douro; ✉ Vendôme Luxury Group PLC, 27 Knightsbridge, London SW1X 7YB (☎ 0171 838 8500, fax 0171 838 8540); The Old Rectory, Stratfield Saye, Reading RG7 2DA; Apsley House, Piccadilly, London W1V 9FA

DOUSE, Anthony Clifford; s of Clifford Redvers Douse (d 1968), of Nottingham, and Lilian Beatrice, *née* Wells (d 1952); *b* 18 Aug 1939; *Educ* Mundella GS Nottingham, RADA; *m* 6 July 1968, Diana Margaret, da of Walter Stanley Thompson; 1 da (Diana Helen b 1 Dec 1984); *Career* actor; memb editorial staff Howard Baker Amalgamated Press (early 1960s); *Theatre* incl: NT: State of Revolution, Strife, Richard III, The Fruits of Enlightenment, Major Barbara, The Fawn, Antigone, Wild Honey, Neaptide, Man Beast and Virtue, Once in a While the Odd Thing Happens; Royal Court: A Collier's Friday Night, The Duchess of Malfi, King Lear; other theatre incl: RSC 1991, 1992 and 1993, Major Barbara (Chichester Festival), Timon of Athens (Leicester), various work in repertory; *Television* incl: Lovejoy, Van der Valk; *Films* incl Prick Up Your Ears; *Recreations* reading; *Style—* Anthony Douse, Esq; ✉ c/o Acting Associates, 15 Falcon Road, London SW11 2PJ (☎ 0171 924 3728)

DOUSE, Raymond Andrew; s of Reginald Conrad Raymond Douse, of Eastbourne, and Patricia *née* Heatherley; *b* 10 May 1947; *Educ* Downside, New Coll Oxford (BA); *m* 1, 1974 (m dis 1995), Christine Hayes; 2 s (Nicholas b 1977, Christopher b 1986), 1 da (Olivia b 1980); m 2, 1996, Orla Dunne; *Career* investment banker; dir Hill Samuel & Co Ltd 1980–85; md: MMG Patricof & Co Ltd 1985–89, dir Daiwa Europe Ltd; *Recreations* golf, music, horse racing; *Style—* Raymond A Douse, Esq; ✉ 94 Arthur Rd, Wimbledon, SW19; Daiwa Europe Ltd, 5 King William St, London EC4N 7AX (☎ 0171 548 8251)

DOVE, Anthony Charles; s of Ian Mayor Dove (d 1972), of Blackpool, and Joan Beatrice, *née* Hadley (d 1992); *b* 22 July 1945; *Educ* Rugby, St John's Coll Cambridge (MA, McMahon studentship); *m* 1 June 1974, Susan Elizabeth, da of Joseph Cant; 3 da (Caroline Jane b 4 Aug 1977, Charlotte Elizabeth b 25 Oct 1982, Rebecca Joan b 8 March 1984); *Career* Simmons & Simmons: articled clerk 1967–69, asst slr 1969–73, ptnr 1973–; memb Law Soc; *Recreations* music; *Clubs* Holmes Place, Barbican; *Style—* Anthony Dove, Esq; ✉ Simmons & Simmons, 21 Wilson St, London EC2M 2TX (☎ 0171 628 2020, fax 0171 628 2070)

DOVE, John; s of Anthony Dove, and Betty Margaret, *née* Curran; *b* 24 July 1944; *Educ* Ampleforth, Univ of Durham (BA), Univ of Manchester (Dip in Drama); *Career* theatre director; Arts Cncl trainee dir under Philip Hedley Birmingham 1971–72, assoc dir to Jane Howell Northcott Theatre Exeter 1973–74 (co dir Bingo), freelance dir 1974–84 (worked with Richard Eyre at Nottingham, Richard Cotterell at Bristol Old Vic, Toby Robertson at Old Vic), assoc dir Hampstead Theatre 1984–; *Productions* for Hampstead Theatre incl: A Little Like Drowning (Plays and Players Award), Ask for the Moon, The Daughter in Law, The Awakening, Hedda Gabler, Bold Girls (Evening Standard Award), A Colliers Friday Night, Flight into Egypt; other recent prodns incl: Rafts and Dreams (Royal Court), Goodnight Siobhan (Royal Court), A Muse of Fire (Edinburgh Festival), adaptation of Angelic Avengers for Denmark, Backstroke in a Crowded Pool (Bush Theatre, Susan Smith Blackburn Award), Democracy (Bush Theatre), Someone Who'll Watch Over Me (West Yorkshire Playhouse), Morning and Evening (Hampstead), Crossing the Equator (Bush), The Soldiers Song (Theatre Royal Stratford East); *Recreations* painting, music, athletics, writing; *Style—* John Dove, Esq; ✉ c/o Hampstead Theatre, Swiss Cottage Centre, London NW3 (☎ 0171 722 9224)

DOVE, Martin David John; s of John Edward Dove, and Ann Nomori, *née* Ireson; *b* 29 April 1959; *Educ* Helsby GS, Adams GS, Kings Coll Univ of London (BA, AKC); *m* 11 April 1987, Sharon Rose Elizabeth, da of Roy William Rogers Edmonds; 2 da (Rachael Alice Rose b 1 Sept 1989, Eleanor Rebecca Ann b 30 July 1991), 1 s (William David John b 16 Nov 1993); *Career* Coopers and Lybrand London 1980–86, Cwlth Devpt Corp London 1986–89, Industl Venture Co Ltd Thailand 1989–91, South Western RHA 1991–94, dir of fin Royal United Hospital Bath NHS Tst 1994–; memb St Mary's Church Wotton; Freeman City of London 1980, Liveryman Worshipful Co of Leathersellers 1984; FCA 1993 (ACA 1983); *Recreations* squash, hockey; *Style—* Martin Dove, Esq; ✉ Rosemary, 3 Coombe Road, Wotton-under-Edge, Gloucestershire GL12 7LU

DOVER, Den; MP (C) Chorley (majority 4,246); s of Albert Dover (d 1971), and Emmie, *née* Kirk (d 1971); *b* 4 April 1938; *Educ* Manchester GS, Univ of Manchester (BSc); *m* 1989, Kathleen, da of John Thomas Fisher (d 1986); 1 s and 1 da (by previous m); *Career* civil engr; chief exec Nat Building Agency 1971–72, projects dir Capital and Counties Property plc 1972–75, contracts mangr Wimpey Laing Iran 1975–77, dir of Housing Construction GLC 1977–79; MP (C) Chorley 1979–; *Recreations* cricket, hockey, golf; *Style—* Den Dover, Esq, MP; ✉ 30 Countess Way, Euxton, Chorley, Lancs; 166 Furzehill Rd, Boreham Wood, Herts

DOVER, Sir Kenneth James; kt (1977); s of Percy Henry James Dover (d 1978), and Dorothy Valerie Anne Healey (d 1973); *b* 11 March 1920; *Educ* St Paul's, Balliol Coll Oxford (MA, DLitt), Merton Coll Oxford; *m* 1947, Audrey Ruth, da of Walter Latimer (d 1931); 1 s, 1 da; *Career* served WWII RA; tutorial fell Balliol Coll Oxford 1948–55; Univ of St Andrews: prof of Greek 1955–76, dean Faculty of Arts 1960–63 and 1973–75, chllr 1981–; visiting lectr Harvard Univ 1960, Sather visiting prof Univ of California 1967, prof-at-large Cornell 1983–89, prof of classics Stanford Univ California (Winter Quarter) 1987–92; hon fell Balliol Coll Oxford 1977, hon fell Merton Coll Oxford 1980; hon foreign memb American Acad of Arts and Sciences 1979–, foreign memb Royal Netherlands Acad of Arts and Sciences 1979–; pres: Soc for Promotion of Hellenic Studies 1971–74, Classical Assoc 1975, Corpus Christi Coll Oxford 1976–86 (hon fell 1986), Br Acad 1978–81; Hon LLD: Birmingham 1979, St Andrews 1981; Hon DLitt: Bristol, London 1980, St Andrews 1981, Liverpool 1983, Durham 1984; Hon DHL Oglethorpe 1984; FBA 1966, FRSE 1975; *Books* Greek Word Order (1960), Greek Popular Morality in the time of Plato & Aristotle (1974), Commentaries on various classical Greek texts, Greek Homosexuality (1978), Greek and the Greeks (1987), The Greeks and their Legacy (1988), Marginal Comment (memoirs, 1994); papers in learned journals; *Recreations* gardening, historical linguistics; *Clubs* Athenaeum; *Style—* Sir Kenneth Dover, FRSE, FBA; ✉ 49 Hepburn Gdns, St Andrews, Fife KY16 9LS (☎ 01334 473589); University of St Andrews, North Haugh, St Andrews, Fife KY16 9QQ

DOVER, Michael Grehan; s of Maj E J Dover (d 1983), and Ida, *née* Grehan; *b* 22 Oct 1948; *Educ* The King's Sch Canterbury, Trinity Coll Dublin (BA); *m* 1972, Ruth, da of Capt T A Pearson (d 1972); 2 s (Alexander b 1975, Linden b 1983), 1 da (Katherine b 1979); *Career* publisher Weidenfeld Publishers Ltd 1987 (editorial dir 1982), dir Orion Publishing Group Ltd 1992–; *Clubs* Chelsea Arts, London Rowing, Kildare St and University (Dublin); *Style—* Michael Dover, Esq; ✉ 27 Fulham Park Gdns, London SW6 4JX (☎ 0171 731 0818); Weidenfeld and Nicolson, Orion House, 5 Upper St Martin's Lane, London WC2H 9EA (☎ 0171 240 3444)

DOVER, Bishop of 1992–; Rt Rev (John) Richard Allan Llewellin; s of John Clarence Llewellin (d 1991), of Long Compton, Warwicks, and Margaret Gwenllian, *née* Low; *b* 30 Sept 1938; *Educ* Clifton Coll Bristol, Fitzwilliam Coll Cambridge (MA), Westcott House Theol Coll; *m* 24 July 1965, Jennifer Sally, da of Edward Terence House (d 1981), of Chard, Somerset; 1 s (David b 1966), 2 da (Sarah b 1968, Helen b 1970); *Career* slr 1960–61; curate Radlett 1964–68, asst priest Johannesburg Cathedral 1968–71, vicar Waltham Cross 1971–79, rector Harpenden 1979–85, bishop of St Germans 1985–92; *Recreations* sailing, DIY; *Style*— The Rt Rev the Bishop of Dover; ✉ Upway, 52 St Martin's Hill, Canterbury, Kent CT1 1PR (☎ 01227 464537, fax 01227 784985)

DOVER, Prof William Duncan; s of Joseph Dover (d 1940), and Sarah Jane Graham, *née* Wilson (d 1989); *Educ* Bishopshalt Sch, Univ of Surrey (DipTech), UCL (PhD); *m* 27 July 1968, Dilys, da of John Richard Edwards (d 1989); 1 s (James William b 1973), 1 da (Elizabeth Mary b 1976); *Career* asst Faculté Polytechnique De Mons Belgium 1966–67, lectr City Univ London 1967–69, Shell prof of mechanical engrg UCL 1987– (lectr 1969–78, reader 1978–83, prof of mechanical engrg 1983–87); dir: Dover & Partners Ltd 1979–86, UCL NDE Centre 1985–, TSC Ltd 1985–, NDE Technology Ltd 1994–; visiting prof City Univ 1985–; CEng, FIMechE, fell Br Inst of Nondestructive Testing; *Books* Fatigue and Crack Growth in Offshore Structures (ed, 1986), Fatigue of Offshore Structures (ed, 1989), Fatigue of Large Scale Threaded Connections (ed, 1989), Non Destructive Testing of Materials; 180 tech and sci papers; *Recreations* golf, swimming, skiing; *Style*— Prof William Dover; ✉ Coniston House, Orchehill Avenue, Gerrards Cross, Buckinghamshire SL9 8QH (☎ 01753 886097); NDE Centre, Department of Mechanical Engineering, University College London, Torrington Place, London WC1E 7JE (☎ 0171 380 7184, fax 0171 383 0831, telex 296273)

DOW, (John) Christopher Roderick; s of Warrender Begernie Dow (d 1950), of Shoreham-by-Sea; *b* 25 Feb 1916; *Educ* Bootham Sch York, Brighton Hove and Sussex GS, UCL; *m* 1960, Clare Mary Keegan; 1 s, 3 da; *Career* economist; dep dir Nat Inst of Econ and Social Res 1954–62, sr econ advsr HM Treasy 1962–63 (econ advsr 1945–54), asst sec-gen Orgn for Econ Co-operation and Devpt 1963–73, dir Bank of England 1973–81, advsr to Govr of Bank of England 1981–84; visiting fell NIESR 1984–; FBA 1982; *Books* The Management of the British Economy 1945–60 (1964), A Critique of Monetary Policy (with I D Saville, 1988); *Clubs* Garrick, Reform; *Style*— Christopher Dow, Esq, FBA; ✉ c/o Reform Club, 104 Pall Mall, London SW1

DOW, Rear Adm Douglas Morrison; CB (1991), DL (City of Edinburgh 1996); s of George Torrance Dow, and Grace Morrison, *née* MacFarlane; *b* 1 July 1935; *Educ* George Heriot's Sch, BRNC Dartmouth; *m* 1959, Felicity Margaret Mona, *née* Napier; 2 s; *Career* joined RN 1952, served on Staff of C-in-C Plymouth 1959–61, HMS Plymouth 1961–63, RN Supply Sch 1963–65, Staff of Cdr Far E Fleet 1965–67, HMS Endurance 1968–70, BRNC Dartmouth 1970–72, Cdr 1972, asst dir of Offr Appts 1972–74, sec to Cdr Br Navy Staff Washington 1974–76, HMS Tiger 1977–78, NDC Latimer 1978–79, Capt 1979, CSO (A) to Flag Offr Portsmouth 1979, sec to Controller of the Navy 1981, Capt HMS Cochrane 1983, Cdre HMS Centurion 1985, RCDS 1988, Rear Adm 1989, DG Naval Personal Servs MOD 1989–92; director The National Trust for Scotland 1992–; chm RN Rugby Union 1985–91, chm Combined Servs RFC 1989–91; FIMgt 1986; *Recreations* rugby, fly-fishing, shooting, golf, gardening; *Clubs* New (Edinburgh); *Style*— Rear Adm Douglas Dow, CB, DL; ✉ The National Trust for Scotland, 5 Charlotte Square, Edinburgh EH2 4DU (☎ 0131 226 5922, fax 0131 243 9501)

DOW, Rt Rev (Geoffrey) Graham; *see:* Willesden, Bishop of

DOWD, George Simon Edmund; s of George Francis Edmund Dowd, of Scarborough, Yorks, and Lily, *née* Clay; *b* 9 Nov 1946; *Educ* Scarborough HS for Boys, Univ of Liverpool Med Sch (MB ChB, FRCS, MCh (Orth), MD); *m* Angela Christine, da of John Anthony Sedman; 3 da (Olivia Jayne b 13 Oct 1975, Caroline Suzanne b 19 Oct 1977, Charlotte Louise b 12 Nov 1980; *Career* house surgn and physician David Lewis Northern Hosp Liverpool 1971–72, lectr in orthopaedics Univ of Liverpool 1978–81; sr lectr and conslt orthopaedic surgn: Royal Liverpool Hosp and Royal Liverpool Children's Hosp 1981–82, Univ of London and Royal Nat Orthopaedic Hosp 1982–87, conslt orthopaedic surgn St Bartholomew's Hosp and sr lectr Univ of London 1987–; Hunterian prof RCS 1985; ABC travelling fell, Heritage visiting prof Calgary Canada 1986; Norman Roberts medal 1978, President's medal BR Orthopaedic Res Soc 1986; memb BMA, Br Orthopaedic Assoc, Br Orthopaedic Res Soc; *Publications* author of Multiple Choice Questions In Orthopaedics and Trauma (1987), papers on trauma, arthritis and knee disorders in leading med jls; *Recreations* sailing, tennis and travel; *Style*— George Dowd, Esq; ✉ St Bartholomew's Hospital, West Smithfield, London EC1A 7BE (☎ 0171 601 8888); 134 Harley St, London W1N 1AH (☎ 0171 486 7912); Wellington Knee Surgery Unit, Wellington Hospital, Wellington Place, London NW8 9LR (☎ 0171 586 5959)

DOWD, James (Jim); MP (Lab) Lewisham West (majority 1,809); s of late James Dowd, and Elfriede Dowd; *b* 5 March 1951; *Educ* Sedgehill Comp Sch London, London Nautical Sch; *Career* apprentice Post Office telephone engr 1967–72, station mangr Heron Petrol Stations 1972–73, telecommunications engr Plessey 1973–92; London Borough of Lewisham: cncllr 1974–94, sometime chm Fin Ctee, dep mayor 1987 and 1991, mayor 1992; former memb Lewisham and N Southwark DHA; Parly candidate (Lab) Beckenham 1983, MP (Lab) Lewisham W 1992– (also contested 1987), London whip 1993–95, memb Shadow NI Team 1995–; memb: Lab Pty 1970–, Co-op Pty, Greenpeace, CND, Int Fund for Animal Welfare, MSF; *Style*— Jim Dowd, Esq, MP; ✉ House of Commons, London SW1A 0AA (☎ 0171 219 4617, fax 0171 219 2686)

DOWDEN, Richard George; s of Peter John Dowden, of Fairford, Gloucs, and Eleanor Isabella, *née* Hepple; *b* 20 March 1949; *Educ* St George's Coll, Bedford Coll London (BA); *m* 3 July 1976, (Mary Catherine) Penny, da of Stanley William Mansfield (d 1977); 2 da (Isabella Catherine b 1981, Sophie Elizabeth b 1983); *Career* sec Cmmn for Int Justice and Peace RC Bishops Conf 1972–75, ed Catholic Herald 1976–79, journalist The Times 1980–86, Africa ed The Independent 1986–94, dip ed The Independent 1994, foreign affairs writer The Economist 1995–; *Style*— Richard Dowden, Esq; ✉ 7 Highbury Grange, London N5 2QB; The Economist, 25 St James's Street, London SW1A 1HG (☎ 0171 830 7071)

DOWDESWELL, Lt-Col (John) Windsor; MC (1943), TD (1947), DL (Tyne & Wear 1976); s of Maj Thomas Reginald Dowdeswell (d 1967), and Nancy Olivia, *née* Pitt (d 1966); *b* 11 June 1920; *Educ* Malvern; *m* 1948, Phyllis Audrey, da of Donald Gomersal Horsfield (d 1972); 1 s (Patrick), 1 da (Bridget (Mrs Tyrrell)); *Career* cmmnd RA (TA) 1938, WWII RA 50 Div; served: France and Belgium 1940, ME 1941–43, Sicily 1943, NW Europe 1944–46; Lt Col cmdg 272 (N) Fd Regt RA(TA) 1963–66, Hon Col 101 (N) Field Regt RA (V) 1981–86; md Engineering Co 1960–63; magistrate Gateshead 1955–90, chm Gateshead Health Authy 1984–93; Vice Lord-Lt Tyne and Wear 1987–93; *Clubs* Northern Counties, Newcastle; *Style*— Lt-Col Windsor Dowdeswell, MC, TD, DL; ✉ 40 Oakfield Rd, Gosforth, Newcastle NE3 4HS (☎ 0191 285 2196)

DOWDING, 3 Baron (UK 1943); Piers Hugh Tremenheere Dowding; s of 2 Baron Dowding (d 1992), and his 2 w, Alison Margaret, *née* Bannerman; *b* 18 Feb 1948; *Educ* Fettes, Amherst Coll Mass (BA); *m* 1973, Noriko Shiho; 2 da (Hon Rosemary June b 25 Sept 1975, Hon Elizabeth Yuki b 16 Feb 1989); *Heir* bro, Hon Mark Denis James Dowding b 1949; *Career* assoc prof of English Okayama Shoka Univ 1977–; *Style*— The Rt Hon Lord Dowding

DOWELL, Sir Anthony James; kt (1995), CBE (1973); s of Arthur Henry Dowell (d 1976), and Catherine Ethel, *née* Raynes (d 1974); *b* 16 Feb 1943; *Educ* Hampshire Sch, Royal Ballet Sch; *Career* Royal Ballet: sr princ 1967–, asst to dir 1984–85, assoc dir 1985–86, dir 1986–; *Clubs* Marks; *Style*— Sir Anthony Dowell, CBE; ✉ The Royal Opera House, Covent Garden, London, WC2E 7QA (☎ 0171 240 1200)

DOWELL, Prof John Derek; s of William Ernest Dowell, of Ellistown, Leicester, and Elsie Dorothy, *née* Jarvis; *b* 6 Jan 1935; *Educ* Coalville GS Leicestershire, Univ of Birmingham (BSc, PhD); *m* 19 Aug 1959, Patricia, da of Lesley Clarkson, of Maltby, Yorkshire; 1 s (Simon Jeremy b 1964), 1 da (Laura b 1962); *Career* research fell Univ of Birmingham 1958–60, research assoc CERN Geneva 1960–62, lectr in physics Univ of Birmingham 1962–68, visiting scientist Argonne National Laboratory USA 1968–69, sr lectr Univ of Birmingham 1970–73 (lectr 1969–70), scientific assoc CERN Geneva 1973–74, prof of elementary particle physics Univ of Birmingham 1980– (sr lectr 1974–75, reader 1975–80), scientific assoc CERN Geneva 1985–87; chm SERC Particle Physics Ctee 1981–85 (memb Nuclear Physics Bd 1974–77 and 1981–85), chm CERN LEP Ctee 1993–96, chm Rutherford Appleton Laboratory Users Advsy Ctee 1993–, chm ATLAS Collaboration Bd (CERN) 1996–98, memb CERN Scientific Policy Ctee 1982–90 and 1993–96, UK memb Euro Ctee for Future Accelerators 1989–93; memb: BBC Sci Consultative Gp 1992–94, Ct Univ of Warwick 1992–, DESY Extended Scientific Cncl 1992–, Particle Physics and Astronomy Research Cncl 1994–; author of over 150 papers in scientific jls; memb American Physical Soc; FRS 1986, FInstP 1987 (Rutherford medal and prize 1988), CPhys 1987; *Recreations* piano, amateur theatre, squash, skiing; *Style*— Prof John Dowell, FRS; ✉ 57 Oxford Road, Moseley, Birmingham B13 9ES (☎ 0121 449 3332); School of Physics and Space Research, The Universtiy of Birmingham, Birmingham B15 2TT (☎ 0121 414 4658, fax 0121 414 6709)

DOWER, Prof Michael Shillito Trevelyan; CBE (1996); s of John Gordon Dower (d 1947), and Pauline, *née* Trevelyan (d 1988); *b* 15 Nov 1933; *Educ* The Leys Sch Cambridge, St John's Coll Cambridge (MA), UCL (DipTP); *m* 1 Sept 1960, Nan, da of late Allan Done; 3 s (John b 1961, Daniel b 1964, Alexander b 1968); *Career* town planning asst LCC 1957–60, town planner Civic Trust 1960–65, amenity and tourism planner UN Special Fund Ireland 1965–67, dir Dartington Amenity Res Trust 1967–81, dir Dartington Inst 1981–85, nat park offr Peak Park Joint Planning Bd 1985–92, DG Countryside Cmmn 1992–96, prof of countryside planning Cheltenham and Gloucester Coll of HE 1996–; memb: UK Sports Cncl 1965–72, English Tourist Bd 1969–76; fndr chm Rural Voice 1980–82, vice pres European Cncl for the Village and Small Town 1990– (pres 1986–90); Hon DSc Univ of Plymouth; Freeman City of Dallas Texas, Conseilleur d'Honneur de la Connêtablie de Guyenne; ARICS, MRTPI, FRSA, Hon FLI; *Books* Fourth Wave: The Challenge of Leisure (1965), Hadrian's Wall: A Strategy for Conservation and Visitor Services (1976), Leisure Provision and People's Needs (co-author, 1981); *Recreations* walking, landscape painting, dry-stone walling, travel; *Style*— Prof Michael Dower, CBE; ✉ CCRU, Cheltenham and Gloucester College, Swindon Road, Cheltenham, Glos GL50 4AZ (☎ 01242 543553, fax 01242 532997)

DOWER, Robert Charles Philips (Robin); s of John Gordon Dower (d 1947), and Pauline Dower, CBE, JP, *née* Trevelyan; *b* 27 Oct 1938; *Educ* The Leys Sch Cambridge, St John's Coll Cambridge (MA), Univ of Edinburgh (BArch), Univ of Newcastle (DipLD); *m* 4 Nov 1967, Frances Helen, da of Henry Edmeades Baker, of Owletts, Cobham, Kent; 1 s (Thomas b 1971), 2 da (Beatrice b 1974, Caroline b 1976); *Career* architect, landscape designer; Yorke Rosenberg Mardall London 1964–71, in private practice as princ Spence & Dower (chartered architects) Newcastle-upon-Tyne 1974–; memb: Northumberland and Newcastle Soc 1971– (vice chm 1994–), Northern Cncl for Sport and Recreation 1976–86, Countryside Cmmn for England and Wales 1982–91, Diocesan Advsy Ctee (Newcastle Diocese); minister's nominee to Northumberland Nat Park 1978–81, Cathedrals Fabric Cmmn for England nominee to Fabric Ctee Durham Cathedral 1991; ARIBA 1965; *Recreations* wood engraving, lettering inscriptions, walking, gardening; *Style*— Robin Dower, Esq; ✉ Cambo House, Cambo, Morpeth, Northumberland NE61 4AY (☎ 01670 774297); c/o Spence & Dower, 1 Osborne Road, Newcastle-upon-Tyne NE2 2AA (☎ 0191 281 5318)

DOWIE, Iain; s of Robert Dowie, of Hatfield, Hertfordshire, and Ann, *née* Taylor; *b* 9 Jan 1965; *Educ* Onslow Sch Hatfield, Hatfield Poly (MEng); *m* Deborah Ann, *née* Scattergood; 1 s (Oliver Robert Philip); *Career* professional footballer; formerly schoolboy player Southampton; Luton Town 1988–91, West Ham Utd 1991, Southampton 1991–95, Crystal Palace 1995, West Ham 1995–; over 30 caps Northern Ireland; Zenith Data Systems Cup runners-up medal Southampton 1992; environmental engr Air Weapons Div British Aerospace 1983–88; *Recreations* poetry, golf, travel, music, movies; *Style*— Iain Dowie, Esq; ✉ c/o West Ham FC, Boleyn Ground, Green Street, Upton Park, London E13 9AZ

DOWLEY, (Laurence) Justin; s of Laurence Edward Dowley, of Great Bowden, Leicestershire, and Virginia, *née* Jorgensen; *b* 9 June 1955; *Educ* Ampleforth, Balliol Coll Oxford (MA); *m* 11 Oct 1986, Emma, da of Martin Lampard, of Theberton, Suffolk; 2 s (Myles b 1989, Finn b 1992), 2 da (Laura b 1987, Florrie b 1994); *Career* Price Waterhouse 1977–80, Morgan Grenfell & Co Ltd 1981– (now dir); govr St Francis of Assisi Sch Notting Hill; ACA 1980; *Clubs* Royal West Norfolk Golf, MCC, Boodle's, City of London; *Style*— Justin Dowley, Esq; ✉ Morgan Grenfell & Co Ltd, 23 Great Winchester St, London EC2P 2AX (☎ 0171 588 4545, fax 0171 826 6180)

DOWLING, Prof Ann Patricia; da of Mortimer Joseph Patrick Dowling, of Birchington, Kent, and Joyce, *née* Barnes; *b* 15 July 1952; *Educ* Ursuline Convent Sch Westgate Kent, Girton Coll Cambridge (MA, PhD); *m* 31 Aug 1974, Dr Thomas Paul Hynes, s of Thomas Hynes; *Career* Sidney Sussex Coll Cambridge: research fell 1977–78, dir of studies in engrg 1979–90, fell 1979–; Univ of Cambridge: asst lectr in engrg 1979–82, lectr 1982–86, reader in acoustics 1986–93, dep head Engrg Dept 1990–93 and 1996–, prof of mechanical engrg 1993–; non-exec dir DRA 1995–; tstee Ford of Britain Trust 1993–; govr Felsted Sch 1994–; winner A B Wood Medal Inst of Acoustics 1990; memb AIAA 1990; fell: Inst of Acoustics 1989, Cambridge Philosophical Soc 1993; CEng 1990, FIMechE 1990, FEng 1996; *Books* Sound and Sources of Sound (with J E Ffowcs Williams, 1983), Modern Methods in Analytical Acoustics (with D G Crighton et al, 1992), contribs to various scientific jls; *Recreations* opera, flying light aircraft; *Style*— Prof Ann Dowling, FEng; ✉ Engineering Department, University of Cambridge, Trumpington Street, Cambridge CB2 1PZ (☎ 01223 332739, fax 01223 332662)

DOWLING, Dame Jean Elizabeth; DCVO (1978); da of Capt William Taylor (ka 1917), and late Margery, *née* Alchin; *b* 7 Nov 1916; *m* 25 Nov 1993, Ambrose Francis Dowling, MVO, MBE, TD; *Career* joined Office of Private Sec to HM The Queen 1958, chief clerk 1961–78; *Recreations* music, walking, looking at old buildings; *Style*— Dame Jean Dowling, DCVO; ✉ Church Cottage, Frittenden, Cranbrook, Kent TN17 2DD

DOWLING, Kenneth; CB (1985); s of Alfred Morris Dowling (d 1963), and Maria Theresa, *née* Berry (d 1952); *b* 30 Dec 1933; *Educ* King George V GS Southport; *m* 1957, Margaret Frances, da of Alfred Cyril Bingham (d 1974); 2 da (Angela, Catherine); *Career* RAF 1952–54; called to the Bar Gray's Inn 1960; Immigration Branch Home Office 1954–61; DPP's Dept: legal asst 1961, sr legal asst 1966, asst slr 1972, asst dir 1976, princ asst dir 1977, dep dir 1982–85; *Recreations* golf, reading; *Clubs* Ryde Golf (Isle of Wight); *Style*— Kenneth Dowling, Esq, CB

DOWLING, Prof Patrick Joseph; s of John Dowling (d 1951), of Dublin, and Margaret, *née* McKittrick; *b* 23 March 1939; *Educ* Christian Brothers Sch Dublin, Univ Coll Dublin (BE), Imperial Coll London (DIC, PhD); *m* 14 May 1966, Dr Grace Carmine Victoria Dowling, da of Palladius Mariano Agapitus Lobo, of Zanzibar; 1 s (Tiernan b 7 Feb 1968), 1 da (Rachel b 8 March 1967); *Career* bridge engr Br Constructional Steelwork Assoc 1965–68; Imperial Coll London: res fell 1966–74, reader 1974–79, British Steel prof of steel structures 1979–94, head Civil Engrg Dept 1985–94; vice-chllr and chief exec Univ of Surrey 1994–; fndr ptnr Chapman & Dowling 1981–94; Steel Construction Inst: memb Exec Ctee and Cncl 1985–, vice chm 1996–; pres Inst of Structural Engrs 1994–95, memb Senate Engrg Cncl 1996–; memb Cncl Royal Holloway Univ of London

1991–95; Gustave Trasenster Medal, Assoc des Ingénieurs Sortis de L'Université de Liege; Hon LLD Nat Univ of Ireland 1995, Hon DSc Vilnius Tech Univ Lithuania 1996; FIStructE 1978, FICE 1979, FEng 1981, FRINA 1985, FGGI 1989, FRS 1996; *Publications include* ed: Journal of Constructional Steel Research, Steel Plated Structures (1977), Buckling of Shells in Offshore Stuctures (1982), Design of Steel Structures (1988), Constructional Steel Design (1992); *Recreations* reading, travelling, sailing; *Clubs* Athenaeum, Chelsea Arts, National Yacht Club of Ireland; *Style*— Prof Patrick Dowling, FEng, FRS; ✉ Vice Chancellor, University of Surrey, Guildford, Surrey GU2 5XH (☎ 01483 259249, fax 01483 259518, e-mail p.dowling@surrey.ac.uk)

DOWLING, Robert Harry; s of Alan Sidney Victor Dowling (d 1991), and Daisy Tulip Dowling, of Sudbury, Suffolk; *b* 2 May 1946; *Educ* Stoneleigh W Tech Sch; *m* 1966, Caroline, da of Arthur Charles Gowan Frapwell; 1 s (Samuel b 21 Nov 1972), 1 da (Alexandra Harriet b 3 June 1981); *Career* photographer; trainee colour technician Time Life Laboratories London 1964–66, fndr mangr in-house colour line for Donaldson Pegram Studios (formerly Zolton Glass) 1966–68, fndr own studio 1968 (early cmmns for children's books, album covers and PR photography mainly for CBS records), shift towards pan-Euro advtg campaigns ca 1970, worked from studios in Amsterdam and London 1974–76, subsequent experience incl stills photographer on Ridley Scott commercials and dir of drama documentary (writer Michael Deakin, Yorkshire TV) 1976 (BISFA Award of Special Merit and Gold Award Miami Film Festival), shift towards TV commercials and music promos late 70's (incl Status Quo and Sky), jtly estab photographic studio Covent Garden for use in maj advtg campaigns (Heinz, Smirnoff, Colmans and Guinness) 1979, sabbatical NZ and USA 1983–84, estab new studio Clerkenwell to promote personal work 1984, latterly returned to work on TV commercials and film incl work for BBC and TV Espania; *Awards* Sun Life Award for Excellence in Photography, Best Automotive Ad of the Yr NY, other awards for Singapore Airlines and Chivas Reagal (Asia, Aust and USA), winner 2 awards Br Business Calendar Awards 1989 incl Kodak Trophy for Best Photography, AFAEP Gold Award for Pink Floyd album cover A Momentary Lapse of Reason 1989; *Books* Rare Breeds (1994); *Recreations* flying (PPL); *Style*— Robert Dowling, Esq; ✉ Robert Dowling Productions Ltd, The Old Forge Works, Sparrows Green, Wadhurst, East Sussex TN5 6SJ (☎ 01892 784700, fax 01892 784770, mobile 0585 275863)

DOWN, Sir Alastair Frederick; kt (1978), OBE (1944, MBE 1942), MC (1940), TD (1951); s of Capt Frederick Edward Down (d 1959); *b* 23 July 1914; *Educ* Marlborough; *m* 1947, Maysie Hilda (Bunny), da of Capt Vernon Mellon; 2 s, 2 da; *Career* WWII (despatches twice), 8 Army and 1 Canadian Army as Lt-Col and Col; CA 1938; dep chm and md BP Co Ltd 1962–75, pres BP Group in Canada 1957–62, chm and chief exec Burmah Oil Co Ltd 1975–83; *Recreations* shooting, golf, fishing; *Style*— Sir Alastair Down, OBE, MC, TD; ✉ Brieryhill, Hawick, Roxburghshire TD9 7LL

DOWN, Ashley Gordon; s of John Ernest Frank Down (d 1959), of Sydney, Aust, and Lois Marie, *née* Whitelaw (d 1992); *b* 17 Nov 1938; *Educ* Brisbane Boys' Coll, Univ of Queensland (BEcon), Harvard Business Sch; *m* 1, 21 April 1970 (m dis 1983) Ferelith Alison, da of Maj Mark Palmer, of Surrey; 1 s (John Mark Palmer b 1979), 1 da (Selina Eleanor b 1975); m 2, 8 Oct 1984, Christine Stanton, *née* McRoberts; m 3, 26 Sept 1996, Josephine Mary, yst da of Michael Minoprio, of London; *Career* sec Brisbane Stock Exchange 1959–67 (asst sec 1957–59), White Weld & Co (NY) 1967–69, ptnr i/c corp fin James Capel & Co (London) 1969–83, chm Prudential Bache Capital Funding (London) 1983–89; dir: M&G Group plc 1979–, Clive Discount plc 1984–89; hon treas Esmee Fairbairn Charitable Tst 1990–96 (tstee 1976–); memb Cncl: Wildfowl and Wetland Tst 1990–96 (hon treas 1992–96), Badminton Tst 1993–; Liveryman Worshipful Co of Gunmakers; *Recreations* country sports; *Clubs* Brooks's, City of London, MCC, Australian, Cook Soc; *Style*— Ashley Down, Esq; ✉ 652 Bd Eugene Brieux, 83530 Agay, St Raphael, France

DOWN, Lesley-Anne; da of P J Down, of London, and Isabella, *née* Gordon-Young; *b* 17 March 1955; *Educ* Professional Childrens Sch; *m* 1, 1982 (m dis 1985), William Friedkin; 1 s (Jack b 1982); m 2, 1986, Don E FauntLeRoy, s of Donald FauntLeRoy; *Career* actress 1967–; *Theatre* incl: The Marquise, Hamlet, Great Expectations, Pygmalion; *Television* incl: The Snow Queen, Upstairs Downstairs, The One and Only Phyliss Dixie, Heartbreak House, Unity Mitford, The Hunchback of Notre Dame, The Last Days of Pompeii, Arch of Triumph, North And South (books 1, 2 and), Indiscreet, Ladykillers, Nightwalk, Frog Girl, The Brewery; *Film* incl: The Smashing Bird I Used to Know, All the Right Noises, Countess Dracula, Assault, Scalawag, Tales from Beyond The Grave, Brannigan, The Pink Panther Strikes Again, A Little Night Music, The Betsy, Hanover Street, The Great Train Robbery, Rough Cut, Sphinx, Scenes from A Goldmine, Nomads, Munchie Strikes Back, The Unfaithful, Meet Wally Sparks; *Awards* nominee Golden Globe Best Actress for North And South; winner: Evening Standard Award Best New Actress for The Pink Panther Strikes Again, Bravo Award Best Actress for North And South; *Style*— Ms Lesley-Anne Down; ✉ c/o William Morris Agency (UK) Ltd, 31/32 Soho Square, London W1V 6DG (☎ 0171 434 2191, fax 0171 437 0238)

DOWN, Michael Kennedy; s of John Down (d 1952), and Irene Beryl, *née* Kennedy (d 1982); *b* 4 Feb 1930; *Educ* Sevenoaks Sch; *m* Barbara Joan, *née* West; 1 s (Ian b 1962), 2 da (Clare b 1958, Laura b 1960); *Career* Nat Serv RAF 1948–50; CA 1955; Moores Rowland (formerly Edward Moore & Sons): articled clerk 1950–55, ptnr 1960, jt managing ptnr 1974–85, exec dir Moores Rowland Int 1980–93; tstee The Ulverscroft Fndn 1996–; Freeman City of London, Master Worshipful Co of Glovers; FCA; *Recreations* travel, country life; *Style*— Michael Down, Esq; ✉ Heronshaw, Oldbury Lane, Ightham, Kent TN15 9DE (☎ 01732 882508)

DOWN, Rt Rev William John Denbigh; s of William Leonard Frederick Down (Flying Offr, RAFVR), and late Beryl Mary, *née* Collett; *b* 15 July 1934; *Educ* Farnham GS, St John's Coll Cambridge (BA, MA), Ridley Hall Theol Coll Cambridge; *m* 29 July 1960, Sylvia Mary, da of Martin John Aves (d 1985); 2 s (Andrew b 1962, Timothy b 1975), 2 da (Helen (Mrs Burn) b 1964, Julia b 1968); *Career* chaplain: RANR 1972–74, HMAS Leeuwin Fremantle W Aust 1972–74; ordained: deacon 1959, priest 1960; asst curate St Paul's Church Fisherton Anger Salisbury, asst chaplain The Missions to Seamen S Shields 1963–64 (sr chaplain 1964–65), port chaplain The Missions to Seamen Hull 1965–71, sr chaplain The Missions to Seamen Fremantle W Aust 1971–74, gen sec The Missions to Seamen London 1976–90 (dep gen sec 1975), chaplain St Michael Paternoster Royal City of London 1976–90, bishop of Bermuda 1990–95, asst bishop of Leicester and priest i/c St Mary Humberstone 1995–; Hon Canon: Holy Trinity Cathedral Gibraltar 1985, St Michael's Cathedral Kobe Japan 1987; Freeman City of London 1981; Hon Chaplain: Worshipful Co of Carmen 1978 (Hon Liveryman 1981), Worshipful Co of Farriers 1983 (Hon Liveryman 1986), Worshipful Co of Innholders 1983–90; Hon Memb Hon Co of Master Mariners 1989; FNI 1991; *Books* On Course Together (1989); *Recreations* golf, watching cricket, ships and seafaring, walking; *Clubs* MCC (assoc memb), Royal Cwlth Soc; *Style*— The Rt Rev William Down; ✉ St Mary's Vicarage, 56 Vicarage Lane, Humberstone, Leicester LE5 1EE (☎ 0116 276 7281)

DOWN AND CONNOR, Bishop of (RC) 1991–; Most Rev Patrick Joseph Walsh; s of Michael Walsh (d 1966), and Nora, *née* Hartnett (d 1988); *b* 9 April 1931; *Educ* St Mary's Christian Brothers GS, Queen's Univ Belfast (MA), Christ's Coll Cambridge (MA), Pontifical Lateran Univ Rome (STL); *Career* teacher St MacNissi's Coll Garron Tower 1958–64, chaplain Queen's Univ Belfast 1964–70, pres St Malachy's Coll Belfast 1970–83, aux bishop of Down and Connor 1983–91; *Recreations* walking, music, theatre; *Style*— The Most Rev the Bishop of Down and Connor; ✉ Lisbreen, 73 Somerton Road, Belfast BT15 4DE (☎ 01232 776185, fax 01232 779377)

DOWN AND DROMORE, 96 Bishop of 1986–; Rt Rev Gordon McMullan; s of Samuel McMullan (professional footballer, d 1952), and Annie McMullan (d 1979); *b* 31 Jan 1934; *Educ* Queen's Univ Belfast (BSc(Econ), PhD), Ridley Hall Cambridge (Dip in Religious Studies), Trinity Coll Dublin (MPhil), Geneva Theol Coll (THD), Univ of the South Sewanee USA (DMin), Harvard Divinity Sch (Merrill Fell, 1997); *m* 1957, Kathleen, da of Edward Davidson (d 1965); 2 s; *Career* ordained 1962, archdeacon of Down 1979–80, bishop of Clogher 1980–86; chm BBC Religious Advsy Ctee (N Ireland) and memb Central Religious Advsy Ctee for Bdcasting (BBC/ITC) 1987–93; *Books* A Cross and Beyond (1976), We Are Called... (1977), Everyday Discipleship (1979), Reflections on St Mark's Gospel (1984), Growing Together in Prayer (1990), Reflections on St Luke's Gospel (1992–94); *Recreations* association football, rugby football, cricket; *Style*— The Rt Rev the Bishop of Down and Dromore; ✉ The See House, 32 Knockdene Park South, Belfast BT5 7AB, N Ireland (☎ 01232 471973)

DOWNE, 11 Viscount (I 1681); John Christian George Dawnay; DL (North Yorkshire 1981); sits as Baron Dawnay of Danby (UK 1897); er s of 10 Viscount Downe, OBE, JP, DL (d 1965); *b* 18 Jan 1935; *Educ* Eton, Christ Church Oxford; *m* 16 Sept 1965, Alison Diana, da of Ian Francis Henry Sconce, OBE, TD, of Brasted Chart, Kent; 1 s, 1 da (Hon Sarah Frances b 2 April 1970); *Heir* s, Hon Richard Henry Dawnay b 9 April 1967; *Career* served as Lt Grenadier Gds 1954; landowner and industl mangr electronics indust; chm: York Ltd 1980–92 (pres 1993–), Sensor Dynamics Ltd 1990–, Aaston Ltd 1991–; dir: Masterlock Ltd 1988–, Yorkshire Bank PLC 1990–; chm: Ctee Nat Railway Museum 1985–96, N Yorks Ctee Rural Devpt Cmmn (non-exec) 1986–; vice chm Scarborough Theatre Trust Ltd 1984–; pres: N York Moors Historical Railway Tst 1970–, Yorkshire Rural Community Cncl 1977–, Aston Martin Owners' Club 1980–, Friends of the Nat Railway Museum 1988– (chm 1977–85), Yorks and Humberside Tourist Bd 1993–; memb: Fin and Gen Purposes Ctee CLA, N Yorks Nat Parks Ctee 1969–; tstee: Nat Museum of Science and Industry 1985–96, Burton Constable Fndn 1992–; Liveryman Worshipful Co of Scientific Instrument Makers; Hon Col (Y) Tport Regt RLC (V) 1984–95; *Recreations* analogue circuit design and railways (selectively); *Clubs* Pratt's; *Style*— The Rt Hon the Viscount Downe, DL; ✉ Wykeham Abbey, Scarborough, N Yorks (☎ 01723 862404); 5 Douro Place, London W8 (☎ 0171 937 9449)

DOWNER, Prof Martin Craig; s of Dr Reginald Lionel Ernest Downer (d 1937), of Shrewsbury, and Eileen Maud Downer, *née* Craig (d 1962); *b* 9 March 1931; *Educ* Shrewsbury, Univ of Liverpool (LDS, RCS), Univ of London (DDPH, RCS), Univ of Manchester (PhD, DDS); *m* 1961, Anne Catherine, da of R W Evans, of Cheshire; 4 da (Stephanie b 1962, Caroline b 1965, Diana b 1968, Gabrielle b 1972); *Career* area dental offr Salford 1974–79; chief dental offr: Scottish Home and Health Dept 1979–83, DHSS 1983–90; prof of dental health policy Eastman Inst of Dental Surgery 1990–; hon sr lectr Univs of Edinburgh and Dundee 1979–83; memb: WHO, Expert Panel on Oral Health; *Books* contributor: Cariology Today (1984), Strategy for Dental Caries Prevention in European Countries (1987), Evolution in Dental Care (1990), Risk Markers for Oral Diseases 1 - Dental Caries (1991), Cariology for the Nineties (1993), Oral Health Promotion (1993), Introduction to Dental Public Health (co-author, 1994); *Style*— Prof Martin Downer; ✉ Department of Dental Health Policy, Eastman Dental Institute for Oral Health Care Sciences, 256 Gray's Inn Road, London WC1X 8LD (☎ 0171 915 1192/3)

DOWNES, George Robert; CB (1967); s of Philip George Downes (d 1919), of Burnham on Crouch, and Isabella, *née* Webster (d 1967); *b* 25 May 1911; *Educ* King Edward's GS Birmingham, Grocers' Sch London; *m* 24 May 1947, Edna Katherine, da of William Longair Millar (d 1969), of Ringwood; 2 da (Alison b 1948, Marianne b 1951); *Career* RNVR in destroyers 1942–45 (Lt 1943); GPO: asst surveyor 1937, asst princ 1939, princ 1946; princ private sec Lord Pres of Cncl 1948–50, Lord Privy Seal 1951, asst sec 1951, Imperial Defence Coll 1952; GPO: dep regnl dir London 1955, dir London Postal Region 1960, dir postal servs 1965, dir ops and overseas 1967–71; dir of studies Royal Inst of Public Admin 1973–94, vice pres Abbeyfield N London Ex-Care Soc 1990– (chm 1977–90); *Recreations* music, gardening; *Style*— George Downes, Esq, CB; ✉ Orchard Cottage, Frithsden, Berkhamsted, Herts HP4 1NW (☎ 01442 866620)

DOWNES, Justin Alasdair; s of Patrick Downes (d 1978), and Eileen Marie, *née* Mackie; *b* 25 Sept 1950; *Educ* The Oratory; *Career* dir: Financial Strategy 1980–85, Streets Financial Strategy 1985–86; fndr Financial Dynamics Ltd 1986–87; dir: London Financial News 1996–, Rizwan Nash Ltd 1996–, various private cos; memb Somerset CC 1976–; memb Cncl Family Holidays Assoc 1990; *Style*— Justin Downes, Esq; ✉ 20 Pont Street, London SW1X 0AA (☎ 0171 235 3234); 45 Beech Street, London EC2Y 8AB (☎ 0171 628 5222)

DOWNES, Prof Kerry John; OBE (1994); s of Ralph William Downes (d 1993), and Agnes Mary, *née* Rix (d 1980); *b* 8 Dec 1930; *Educ* St Benedict's Ealing, Courtauld Inst of Art (BA, PhD); *m* 1962, Margaret, da of John William Walton (d 1963); *Career* librarian: Barber Inst of Fine Arts, Univ of Birmingham 1958–66; prof of history of art Univ of Reading 1978–91 (lectr 1966, reader 1971, prof emeritus 1991–); memb Royal Cmmn on Historical Monuments of Eng 1981–93; Hon DLitt Birmingham 1995; FSA 1962; *Books* Hawksmoor (1959 and 1969), Vanbrugh (1977 and 1987), Wren (1971, 1982 and 1988), Rubens (1980), English Baroque Architecture (1966), St Paul's Cathedral (1988); *Recreations* music, drawing, microchips, procrastination; *Style*— Prof Kerry Downes, OBE, FSA

DOWNES, His Hon Judge; Paul Henry; s of Eric Downes, of Clwyd, and Lavinia, *née* Starling; *b* 23 Nov 1941; *Educ* Ducie HS Manchester, Coll of Commerce UMIST, Coll of Law London, Inns of Court Sch of Law; *m* 1, Joyce; 2 s (Andrew Paul b 21 May 1965, Nicholas John b 22 Oct 1969), 1 da (Alison Jayne b 22 May 1968); m 2, Beverly Jill, da of Jack Cowdal; 1 s (Christopher Francis (Kit) b 26 May 1986); *Career* dep magistrates clerk: Manchester 1956–62, Sheffield 1962–63, Nottingham 1967–69; county prosecuting advocate Suffolk 1969–72, in practice at Bar Norwich 1972–95, recorder of the Crown Court 1993–95 (asst recorder 1991), circuit judge (SE Circuit) 1995–; *Recreations* music, chamber choir singing, playing instruments, reading, sailing; *Clubs* Norfolk (Norwich), Sloane; *Style*— His Hon Judge Downes; ✉ Norwich Combined Court Centre, Bishopgate, Norwich NR3 1UR (☎ 01603 761776)

DOWNES, Peter James; s of Harry Downes (d 1986), and Hilda, *née* Short (d 1990); *b* 7 May 1938; *Educ* Manchester GS, Christ's Coll Cambridge (MA, scholar), Univ of London (PGCE); *m* 21 Aug 1965, Pamela, da of Robert Charles Sterry; 2 s (Michael John b 8 Nov 1968, Christopher Paul b 28 May 1972); *Career* sr French master Manchester GS 1966–72 (French master 1960–66), head of linguistic studies Banbury Sch 1972–75; headteacher: Henry Box Sch Witney Oxon 1975–82, Hinchingbrooke Sch 1982–96; freelance educnl conslt 1997–; pres SHA 1994–95 (memb Nat Exec 1989–); chm Jt Cncl of Languages Assocs Conference 1985–87, Chev dans l'Ordre des Palmes Académiques; Hon FCP; FRSA 1991; *Books* Le Français d'Aujourdhui (1966–69), French for Today (1977–80), Vive la Différence (1989), Local Financial Management in Schools (1989); ed of over 70 titles; *Recreations* music, sport (cricket, volleyball), walking; *Clubs* Huntingdon Rotary; *Style*— Peter Downes, Esq; ✉ 42 Huntingdon Road, Brampton, Huntingdon, Cambs PE18 8PA (☎ 01480 450294)

DOWNEY, Sir Gordon Stanley; KCB (1984, CB 1980); s of Capt Stanley William Downey (d 1940), of London, and Winifred, *née* Dick (d 1970); *b* 26 April 1928; *Educ* Tiffin's Sch, LSE (BSc); *m* 7 Aug 1952, Jacqueline Norma, da of Samuel Goldsmith (d 1972), of London; 2 da (Alison b 1960, Erica b 1963); *Career* 2 Lt RA 1946–48; Miny of Works 1951–52, Treasy 1952–78 (on loan to Miny of Health 1961–62), dep head of Central Policy Review Staff 1978–81, Comptroller and Auditor Gen 1981–87; special advsr to Ernst & Young (formerly Ernst & Whinney) 1988–90; complaints cmmr Securities Assoc 1989–90; chm: delegacy King's Coll Med and Dental Sch 1989–91, FIMBRA 1990–93, Personal Investment Authy (PIA) 1992–93; memb bd Business Performance Gp LSE 1989–94, readers' rep Independent and Independent on Sunday 1990–95; Parly cmmr for standards 1995–; memb Cncl CIPFA 1982–87; *Recreations* visual arts, tennis; *Clubs* Army and Navy; *Style*— Sir Gordon Downey, KCB; ✉ 137 Whitehall Court, London SW1A 2EP (☎ 0171 321 0914)

DOWNHILL, Ronald Edward; s of John Edward Downhill (d 1986), of Burghfield Common, Berkshire and Lily, *née* Darraugh; *b* 11 Aug 1943; *Educ* Hyde Co GS Cheshire; *m* 1969, Olwen Elizabeth, da of Ronald Siddle; 3 da (Helen Louise b 1972, Rebecca Clare Elizabeth b 1975, Victoria Ruth b 1984); *Career* called to the Bar 1968, admitted slr 1974; Inland Revenue: Chief Inspector's Branch 1960–64, Estate Duty Office 1964–69, Slr's Office 1969–74; self employed tax conslt in ptnrship 1977–82, tax specialist Berwin Leighton (joined 1974, ptnr 1976–77 and 1982–); memb Revenue Law Ctee of Law Soc 1989; memb: Law Soc 1974, STEP 1993; ATII 1978; *Recreations* watching soccer, theatre; *Style*— Ronald Downhill, Esq; ✉ Berwin Leighton Solicitors, Adelaide House, London Bridge, London EC4R 9HA (☎ 0171 623 3144, fax 0171 623 4416)

DOWNIE, James; s of James Downie (d 1991), of Edinburgh, and Margaret Meikle Downie; *b* 9 Oct 1944; *Educ* Boroughmuir Sr Sedcy Sch, Edinburgh Coll of Art (scholar); *m* Mary McLeod, da of Dennis McTernan; 2 da (Fiona b 3 Aug 1971, Kirsty b 27 April 1974); *Career* trainee litho artist Waddie & Co printers 1962–67; subsequently with: Waterstons Printers 1967–68, McLehose Printers 1968–69; art dir McCallum Advertising Edinburgh 1969–71; creative dir: Hall Advertising Edinburgh 1975–89 (art dir 1971–75), The Leith Agency Edinburgh 1991–95 (creative ptnr 1989–91), Silvermills Group (parent co) 1995–96, Faulds Advertising 1996–; awards incl: 3 D&AD Silvers, 5 Clios, various Campaign Press and Poster, ILR Radio, Roses and Scottish Ad awards; *Recreations* golf, football, walking; *Style*— James Downie, Esq; ✉ Faulds Advertising, Sutherland House, 108 Dundas Street, Edinburgh EH3 5DQ (☎ 0131 557 6003)

DOWNIE, Robert MacKenzie (Robin); s of Robert Thom Downie (d 1978), and Margaret Jean, *née* Livingston; *b* 7 Dec 1950; *Educ* Glasgow HS; *m* 16 Sept 1985, Frances Catherine, da of Harold Bremner Reid; 2 s (Adam Robert b 3 Aug 1989, Marcus MacKenzie b 12 Jan 1991), 1 da (Rhoda Frances Margaret b 22 May 1993); *Career* Mann Judd Gordon CAs Glasgow 1968–79, ptnr Neville Russell 1979–; govr RSAMD 1988–, chm Scottish Crusaders 1990–94, memb Incorporation of Wrights Glasgow 1990; MICAS 1973 (convenor Area Trg Ctee 1987–91); *Clubs* RSAC; *Style*— Robin Downie, Esq; ✉ Neville Russell, 90 Vincent Street, Glasgow, Scotland G2 5UB (☎ 0141 226 4924, fax 0141 204 1338)

DOWNIE, Prof Robert Silcock; s of Capt Robert Mackie Downie (d 1980), of Glasgow, and Margaret Barlas, *née* Brown (d 1974); *b* 19 April 1933; *Educ* HS of Glasgow, Univ of Glasgow (MA), Queen's Coll Oxford (BPhil); *m* 15 Sept 1958, Eileen Dorothea, da of Capt Wilson Ashley Flynn (d 1942), of Glasgow; 3 da (Alison, Catherine, Barbara); *Career* Russian linguist Intelligence Corps 1955–57, lectr in philosophy Univ of Glasgow 1959–69, visiting prof of philosophy Syracuse NY USA 1963–64, prof of moral philosophy Univ of Glasgow 1969–, Stevenson lectr in medical ethics 1986–88; FRSE 1986; *Books* Government Action and Morality (1964), Respect for Persons (1969), Roles and Values (1971), Education and Personal Relationships (1974), Caring and Curing (1980), Healthy Respect (1987), Health Promotion (1990), The Making of a Doctor (1992), Francis Hutcheson (1994), The Healing Arts: An Illustrated Oxford Anthology (1994), Palliative Care Ethics (1995); *Recreations* music; *Style*— Prof Robert Downie, FRSE; ✉ 17 Hamilton Drive, Glasgow G12 8DN; Kilnaish, By Tarbert, Argyll (☎ 0141 339 1345); Department of Philosophy, University of Glasgow, Glasgow G12 8QQ (☎ 0141 330 4273, fax 0141 330 4112)

DOWNING, Dr Anthony Leighton; s of Sydney Arthur Downing, and Frances Dorothy Downing; *b* 27 March 1926; *Educ* Arnold Sch Blackpool, Univ of Cambridge, Univ of London; *m* 1952, Kathleen Margaret Frost; 1 da; *Career* dir Water Pollution Res Laboratory 1966–73, ptnr Binnie & Partners consulting engrs 1974–86, self-employed consultant 1986–96, dir Binnie Environmental Ltd 1991–95; FEng 1991, FIChemE, FIBiol, Hon FCIWEM, MIE (Malaysia), FRSA; *Recreations* golf; *Clubs* Knebworth Golf, United Oxford and Cambridge Univ; *Style*— Dr Anthony Downing, FEng; ✉ 2 Tewin Close, Tewin Wood, Welwyn, Herts AL6 0HF (☎ 01438 798474, fax 01438 798592)

DOWNING, Dr David Francis; s of Alfred William Downing (d 1963), and Violet Winifred, *née* Wakeford (d 1989); *b* 4 Aug 1926; *Educ* Bristol GS, Univ of Bristol (BSc, PhD), Univ of California Los Angeles, Open Univ (BA 1996); *m* 1948, Margaret, da of Raymond Llewellyn (d 1958); 1 s (Jonathan b 1962), 1 da (Anna b 1961); *Career* Army Lt Royal Welsh Fusiliers 1944–48; fell Univ of California Los Angeles 1955–57, lectr Dept of Agric and Horticulture Univ of Bristol 1957–58, Chem Def Establ MOD 1958–63 and 1966–68, scientific liaison offr Br Embassy Washington DC USA 1963–66, cnsllr (scientific) Br High Cmmn Ottawa Canada 1968–73, asst dir Royal Armaments R & D Estab MOD 1973–78; cnsllr (scientific) Br Embassy Moscow USSR 1978–81, asst dir resources and programmes MOD 1981–83, attaché (Def R & D) Br Embassy Washington DC USA 1983–87; pt/t chm Defence Research Agency Recruitment Bd, govr Sarum Coll, reader Salisbury Cathedral (Archbishops' Dip for Readers); FRSA; *Recreations* cross country skiing, arctic art, bird watching; *Clubs* Army & Navy; *Style*— Dr David Downing; ✉ 13 The Close, Salisbury, Wilts SP1 2EB

DOWNING, John; MBE (1992); *b* 17 April 1940; *Career* photographer; apprentice photographic printer Daily Mail 1956–61; Daily Express: perm freelance photographer 1962–64, staff photographer 1964–, chief photographer 1985–; maj news events covered incl: Vietnam, Beirut, The Falklands, Nicaragua, Afghanistan, The Gulf, Bosnia, Somalia and Rwanda; *Awards* Rothman's Br Press Pictures of the Year (human interest) 1971, runner up (news feature) World Press Photo Competition 1972 and 1978, Ilford Br Press Photographer of the Year 1977, 1979, 1980, 1981, 1984, 1988 and 1989, IPC Br Press Photographer of the Year 1977 and 1980 (runner-up 1991), UN Photography Gold Medal 1978, Photokina Gold Medal 1978, Martini Royal Newspaper Photographer of the Year 1990, Kodak Feature Photographer of the Year 1992/93; fndr Press Photographers' Assoc (now Br Press Photographers' Assoc) 1984 (pres until 1986); memb NUJ; *Style*— John Downing, Esq, MBE; ✉ c/o Picture Desk, Daily Express, Ludgate House, 245 Blackfriars Road, London SE1 9UX (☎ 0171 922 7171)

DOWNING, Paul Nicholas; s of Sydney Edward Downing (d 1982), of Berkhamsted, and Gladys, *née* Miles; *b* 19 March 1947; *Educ* Berkhamsted Sch, Univ of Essex; *m* 1; 1 da (Charlotte); m 2, 5 April 1991, Anne Theresa, da of Michael Anthony Gregory, OBE, of Dipley Common, Hants; 1 s (Max), 1 da (Holly); *Career* slr; ptnr Clifford Chance 1980–90, managing ptnr Pinsent Curtis London 1991–96, currently head of Price Waterhouse European Associated Law Firms; non-exec dir Auto Suture UK Ltd; memb: Law Soc, Int Bar Assoc; *Recreations* riding, scuba diving, skiing, tennis; *Clubs* The Hurlingham, Ski Club of GB, LTA; *Style*— Paul Downing, Esq; ✉ 22 Parkside Gardens, Wimbledon, London SW19 5EU (☎ 0181 946 7331); Price Waterhouse, No 1 London Bridge, London SE1 9QL (☎ 0171 939 1660, fax 0171 939 1661)

DOWNING, Richard; s of John Clifford Downing, of Stourbridge, and Greta Irene, *née* Kelley; *b* 8 Feb 1951; *Educ* King Edward VI Sch Stourbridge, Univ of Birmingham (BSc, MB ChB, MD); *m* 24 July 1976, Stella Elizabeth, da of Stefan Kolada, of Chaddesley Corbett, Worcs; 2 s (Benjamin Louis b 1978, Thomas Kolada b 1982), 2 da (Alice Elizabeth Gwendoline b 1984, Lily Anastazia b 1991); *Career* lectr in anatomy Univ of Birmingham 1976–77, res assoc Washington Univ St Louis USA 1977–78; surgical registrar: Birmingham AHA 1979–80, Worcester Royal Infirmary 1980–83; sr lectr and hon conslt in surgery Univ of Birmingham 1986–90 (lectr 1983–86), conslt vascular surgn Worcester Royal Infirmary 1990–; author of pubns on vascular surgery and pancreatic islet transplantation; examiner Faculty of Dental Surgery RCS, advsr in surgery Int Hosps Gp 1987–90; memb: BMA, Br Diabetic Assoc, Br Transplantation Soc, Euro Soc Vascular Surgery, Pancreatic Soc GB and Ireland, Surgical Vascular Soc GB and Ireland; FRCS 1980; *Recreations* antique books, the countryside; *Style*— Richard Downing, Esq; ✉ Department of General Surgery, Worcester Royal Infirmary, Ronkswood, Worcester WR5 1HN (☎ 01905 760725)

DOWNS, Sir Diarmuid; kt (1985), CBE (1979); s of John Downs, and Ellen *née* McMahon; *b* 23 April 1922; *Educ* Gunnersbury Catholic GS, Univ of London; *m* 1951, Mary Carmel, *née* Chillman; 1 s, 3 da; *Career* Ricardo Consulting Engineers plc: joined 1942, md 1967–84, chm 1976–87; dir Gabriel Communications Ltd (formerly Universe Publications Ltd) 1986–93; pres IMechE 1978–79; pro-chancellor Univ of Surrey 1992– (chm Cncl 1989–89); memb: Bd of Br Cncl 1987–93, Ct Univ of Sussex 1989–; FEng 1979, FRS 1985; *Recreations* theatre, literature, music; *Clubs* Hove; *Style*— Sir Diarmuid Downs, CBE, FRS, FEng; ✉ The Downs, 143 New Church Rd, Hove, E Sussex BN3 4DB (☎ 01273 419 357)

DOWNSHIRE, 8 Marquess of (I 1789); (Arthur) Robin Ian Hill; also Earl of Hillsborough (I 1751 and GB 1772, which sits as), Viscount Hillsborough (I 1717), Viscount Fairford (GB 1772), Viscount Kilwarlin (I 1771), Baron Harwich (GB 1756), and Baron Hill (I 1717); Hereditary Constable of Hillsborough Fort; s of Capt Lord (Arthur) Francis Henry Hill, The Greys Reserve (d 1953, s of 6 Marquess of Downshire), and Sheila (d 1961), yst da of Lt-Col Stewart MacDougall of Lunga; suc uncle, 7 Marquess, 1989; *b* 10 May 1929; *Educ* Eton; *m* 1, 5 Oct 1957, Hon Juliet Mary Weld-Forester (d 1986), da of 7 Baron Forester; 2 s (Earl of Hillsborough b 1959, Lord Anthony Ian b 1961), 1 da (Lady Georgina Mary b 1964); m 2, 18 Sept 1989, Mrs Diana Marion Hibbert, 2 da of Rt Hon Sir Ronald Hibbert Cross, 1 and last Bt, PC, KCMG, KCVO (d 1968), and former w of James Richard Emery Taylor; *Heir* s, Earl of Hillsborough, *qv*; *Career* 2 Lt Royal Scots Greys; farmer, FCA; *Recreations* shooting, travel; *Clubs* White's; *Style*— The Most Hon the Marquess of Downshire; ✉ Clifton Castle, Ripon, N Yorks HG4 4AB (☎ 01765 689326, fax 01765 689974); 162 Cranmer Court, Whiteheads Grove, London SW3 3HF (☎ 0171 581 1903)

DOWNTON, Dr Christine Veronica; da of Henry Devereux Downton (d 1962), and Christina Vera, *né e* Threadgold; *b* 21 Oct 1941; *Educ* Caerphilly GS, LSE (BSc, Phd); *Career* investmt banker; ptnr Pareto Ptnrs; former dir Investment Mgmnt Regulatory Orgn; chief exec offr: Archimedes Assocs, County NatWest Investment Management; sr conslt to the pres Federal Reserve Bank of NY, asst dir N M Rothschild, asst advsr Bank of England; govr: Kingston Univ, London Sch of Economics and Political Science; *Recreations* reading, walking; *Style*— Dr Christine V Downton; ✉ Pareto Partners, 271 Regent Street, London W1R 8PP

DOWNWARD, Maj-Gen Peter Aldcroft; CB (1979), DSO (1967), DFC (1952); s of Aldcroft Leonard Downward (d 1969), and Mary Rigby, *née* Halton (d 1978); *b* 10 April 1924; *Educ* King William's Coll IOM; *m* 1, 1953, Hilda Hinckley Wood (d 1976); 2 s (Jeremy, Julian); m 2, 1980, Mary Boykett Procter, *née* Allwork; *Career* enlisted The Rifle Bde 1942, cmmnd S Lancs Regt (PWV) 1943, seconded Parachute Regt, NW Europe 1944–45, India and SE Asia 1945–46, Palestine 1946, Berlin Airlift 1948–49, Army pilot Korea 1951–53, Cdr 1 Bn The Lancs Regt (PWV) South Arabia 1966–67, Cdr Berlin Inf Bde 1971–74, Cdr Sch of Infantry 1974–76, GOC W Midland Dist 1976–78; Col The Queen's Lancashire Regt 1978–83, Col Cmdt The King's Div 1979–83; Hon Col Liverpool Univ OTC 1979–89; Lt-Govr Royal Hosp Chelsea 1979–84; dir Oxley Devpts Co 1984–89; chm Museum of Army Flying 1984–88; pres Br Korean Veterans' Assoc 1987–; pres Assoc of Service Newspapers 1987–; govr Military Knights of Windsor 1989–; *Recreations* sailing, shooting, skiing; *Style*— Maj-Gen Peter Downward, CB, DSO, DFC; ✉ The Mary Tudor Tower, Windsor Castle, Berks SL4 1NJ (☎ 01753 868286)

DOWNWARD, Sir William Atkinson; kt (1977), JP (1973); s of George Thomas Downward (d 1915); *b* 5 Dec 1912; *Educ* Manchester Central HS, Manchester Coll of Technol; *m* 1946, Enid, da of late Alderman Charles Wood; *Career* memb Manchester City Cncl 1946, Lord Mayor of Manchester 1970–71, alderman Manchester 1971–74, Lord Lt Greater Manchester 1974–77; DL Lancs 1971; memb Ct of Govrs Univ of Manchester 1969–96, chm Manchester Overseas Students Welfare Conference 1972–87, dir Manchester Royal Exchange Theatre Co 1976–89; pres Greater Manchester Fedn of Boys Clubs 1978–; Hon LLD Manchester 1977; *Style*— Sir William Downward, JP; ✉ 23 Kenmore Rd, Northenden, Manchester M22 4AE (☎ 0161 998 4742)

DOWSETT, Prof Charles James Frank; s of Charles Aspinall Dowsett (d 1957), and Louise, *née* Stokes (d 1983); *b* 2 Jan 1924; *Educ* Owen's Sch Islington, St Catherine's Soc Oxford, Peterhouse Cambridge (MA, PhD), École Nationale des Langues Orientales Vivantes Paris, Institut Catholique Paris; *m* 23 Sept 1949, Friedel (d 1984), da of Friedrich Lapuner (d 1958), of Kalweitschen, East Prussia; *Career* reader in Armenian SOAS London 1965 (lectr 1954–65), Calouste Gulbenkian prof of Armenian studies Univ of Oxford and fell Pembroke Coll 1965–91, emeritus prof and emeritus fell Pembroke Coll 1991–; visiting prof Univ of Chicago 1976; cncl memb: Royal Asiatic Soc 1972–76, Philological Soc 1973–77; bd memb Marjory Wardrop Fund for Georgian Studies; contrib various articles to specialist and learned pubns; FBA 1978; *Books* The History of the Caucasian Albanians by Movses Daskhurantzi (1962), The Penitential of David of Gandjak (1962), Kütahya tiles and pottery from the Armenian Cathedral of St James Jerusalem Vol 1 (with John Carswell, 1972), Sayat-Nova, An 18th-Century Troubadour (1996); books for children (under pen-name Charles Downing): Russian Tales and Legends (1956), Tales of the Hodja (1964), Armenian Folktales and Fables (1972); *Style*— Prof Charles Dowsett, FBA; ✉ 21 Hurst Rise Rd, Cumnor Hill, Oxford OX2 9HE

DOWSON, Antony Peter; s of John Robert Dowson, and Sheila Margret, *née* Horstead; *b* 27 Jan 1958; *Educ* Royal Ballet School, White Lodge Richmond Park, ARAD, PDTC; *m* 17 March 1990 (m dis), Fiona Jane Chadwick, *qv*; 1 da (Emily b 23 April 1991); *Career* currently teacher English National Ballet Sch, former princ dancer Royal Ballet Co; leading roles with Royal Ballet incl: Mayerling, Manon, Sleeping Beauty, La Fille Mal Gardee, Prince of the Pagodas; *Recreations* watching football, Chelsea FC, listening to music, cooking; *Style*— Antony Dowson, Esq; ✉ c/o English National Ballet School, Carlyle Building, Hortensia Road, London SW10 0QS

DOWSON, Prof Duncan; CBE (1989); s of Wilfrid Dowson (d 1970), of Kirkbymoorside, Yorks, and Hannah, *née* Crosier (d 1987); *b* 31 Aug 1928; *Educ* Lady Lumley's GS Pickering Yorks, Univ of Leeds (BSc, PhD, DSc); *m* 15 Dec 1951, Mabel, da of Herbert Strickland (d 1961), of Kirkbymoorside, Yorks; 2 s (David Guy b 1953, Stephen Paul b 1956, d 1968); *Career* Sir W G Armstrong Whitworth Aircraft Co 1952–54; Dept of Mechanical Engrg Univ of Leeds 1954–: lectr 1954–63, sr lectr 1963–65, reader 1965–66, prof of fluid mechanics and tribology 1966–93, dir Inst of Tribology 1967–86, head of dept 1967–92, pro vice chllr 1983–85, dean for int relations 1988–93, prof emeritus 1993, research prof 1995–98; visiting prof Univ of NSW Sydney 1975; memb: Educn and Sci Working Pty on Lubrication Educn and Res 1972–76, Orthopaedic Implant Ctee DHSS 1974–77, Regnl Sci Ctee YRHA 1977–80, Res Ctee Arthritis and Rheumatism Cncl 1977–85, various SERC ctees 1987–90; memb Cncl IMechE 1988– (vice pres 1988–90, dep pres 1990–92, pres 1992–93); Liveryman Worshipful Co of Blacksmiths; Hon DTech Chalmers Univ of Technol Göteborg Sweden 1979; Docteur (hc) Institut National Des Sciences Appliquées de Lyon France 1991, Hon DSc Univ of Liège Belgium 1996; FIMechE 1973, FEng 1982, FRS 1987, FRSA (chm Yorks Region 1992–), FCGI 1996; fell: ASME, ASLE; memb Royal Swedish Acad of Engrg Sci 1986; *Books* Elastohydrodynamic Lubrication (second edn, 1977), History of Tribology (1979), Biomechanics of Joints and Joint Replacements (1981), Ball Bearing Lubrication (1981); *Recreations* walking; *Style—* Prof Duncan Dowson, CBE, FRS, FEng; ✉ Ryedale, 23 Church Lane, Adel, Leeds LS16 8DQ (☎ 0113 267 8933m fax 0113 281 7039); Department of Mechanical Engineering, The University of Leeds, Leeds LS2 9JT (☎ 0113 233 2153, fax 0113 242 4611, telex 556473 UNILDS G)

DOWSON, Dr Jonathan Hudson; s of John Heaton Dowson (d 1994), and Margot Blanche, *née* Hudson, of Brinton, Norfolk; *b* 19 March 1942; *Educ* The Leys Sch Cambridge, Queens' Coll Cambridge (MA, MB BChir, MD), St Thomas' Hosp, Univ of Edinburgh (DPM, PhD); *m* 29 Dec 1965, Lynn Susan, *née* Dothie; 2 s (James b 1968, Jonathan b 1972), 1 da (Emma b 1967); *Career* lectr in psychiatry Univ of Edinburgh 1973–75 (lectr in anatomy 1969–72), conslt psychiatrist Addenbrooke's Hosp Cambridge 1977–, lectr in psychiatry Univ of Cambridge 1977–, visiting prof Univ of Florida 1983; examiner: Univ of Cambridge 1988–, RCPsych 1981– (regnl advsr 1990–95); papers on ageing, brain lipopigment, personality disorders and drugs in psychiatry; fell commoner Queens' Coll Cambridge 1985; *Books* Personality Disorders: Recognition and Clinical Management (with A T Grounds, CUP, 1995); *Recreations* squash, theatre; *Clubs* United Oxford and Cambridge Univ; *Style—* Dr Jonathan Dowson; ✉ Old Vicarage, Church Lane, Sawston, Cambridge; Department of Psychiatry, Level 4, Addenbrooke's Hospital, Hills Rd, Cambridge CB2 2QQ (☎ 01223 336965)

DOWSON, Sir Philip Manning; kt (1980), CBE (1969); s of Robert Manning Dowson, of Geldeston, Norfolk; *b* 16 Aug 1924; *Educ* Gresham's Sch Holt, Univ Coll Oxford, Clare Coll Cambridge (MA), Architectural Assoc (AADipl), RIBA, FSIAD; *m* 1950, Sarah Albinia, da of Brig Wilson Theodore Oliver Crewdson, CBE (d 1961), by his w Albinia Joane, 2 da of Sir Nicholas Henry Bacon, 12 Bt, of London; 1 s, 2 da; *Career* Lt RNVR 1943–47; architect; Ove Arup and Partners: joined 1953, sr ptnr 1969–89, conslt 1989–; fndr ptnr Arup Associates architects and engrs 1963; memb Royal Fine Art Cmmn 1970–, tstee The Thomas Cubitt Tst 1978–, memb Bd of Tstees Royal Botanic Gardens Kew 1983–95, tstee The Armouries 1984–89; pres The Royal Academy of Arts 1993– (ARA 1979, RA 1986); Royal Gold Medal for Architecture RIBA 1981; hon fell: Clare Coll Cambridge, Royal Coll of Art, Duncan Jordanstone Coll of Arts, American Instn of Architects; *Style—* Sir Philip Dowson, CBE, PRA; ✉ Royal Academy of Arts, Piccadilly, London W1V 0DS (☎ 0171 494 5690)

DOXAT, Charles; s of John Nicholas Doxat, of Camberley, Surrey, and Margaret Jane, *née* Weston; *b* 12 March 1942; *Educ* Westminster; *m* 16 March 1963, Susan, da of John Eric Moore; 1 s (Jake b 23 June 1965), 1 da (Colette b 18 Aug 1963); *Career* trainee rising to account rep J Walter Thompson London 1960–67, mktg mangr Food Brokers Ltd 1967–68, md Sunquick Soft Drinks Ltd 1968–70, account dir J Walter Thompson London 1970–73, dir client servs and planning Dorland Advertising Ltd 1973–84; md: Foote Cone & Belding Ltd 1984–86, Doxat Chapman & Partners Ltd 1986–88; dep chm Burton Wisgard Doxat Ltd 1988–90; currently ptnr Advertising Planning and Management Ltd; holder of several British titles and records in swimming and triathlon; *Recreations* triathlon, golf; *Clubs* Otter Swimming, Serpentine Running, Wig & Pen, Lansdowne, Royal Wimbledon Golf; *Style—* Charles Doxat, Esq; ✉ 6 Molyneux St, London W1H 5HU; A P & M Ltd, 4 Goodwins Court, London WC2N 4LL (☎ 0171 240 0727, fax 0171 240 0354)

DOYE, Paul Frederick; s of Herbert Walter Charles Doye (d 1946), and Hilda Katie Louise, *née* Edwards; *b* 6 July 1940; *Educ* Hassenbrook Sch Essex; *m* 15 Sept 1962, Brenda Marion Kelway, da of Henry Tongeman (d 1975), of Stanford-le-Hope, Essex; 3 s (Stephen b 1964, Philip b 1967, Jonathan b 1971), 1 da (Ruth b 1966); *Career* dir: Keyser Ullmann Ltd 1969–81, Charterhouse Bank Ltd 1980–; non-exec dir: Petrocon Group plc 1972–88, Lonrho plc 1979–83, Rexmore plc 1995–; memb Cncl Africa Inland Mission Int; *Style—* Paul F Doye, Esq; ✉ 22 Monkhams Drive, Woodford Green, Essex (☎ 0181 505 1418); Charterhouse Bank Ltd, 1 Paternoster Row, London EC4 (☎ 0171 248 4000)

DOYLE, Anthony Paul (Tony); MBE (1988); s of Bernard James Doyle, of Ashford, Middx, and Agnes, *née* Laker; *b* 19 May 1958; *Educ* Salesian Coll Chertsey Surrey; *m* 9 Feb 1980, Anne Margaret, da of O P D'Rozario; 1 s (George Edward b 20 July 1992), 1 da (Gemma Clare b 8 Nov 1995); *Career* former professional cyclist; world professional pursuit champion 1980 and 1986, Euro Madison champion 1984, 1985, 1987, 1988, 1989 and 1990, Euro Omnium champion 1988 and 1989; 13 UK nat titles, 4 Silver and 3 Bronze medals World Championships, 23 six day wins, 2 Bronze medals Cwlth Games 1978, respresented UK Olympic Games Moscow 1980, Silver medal Cwlth Games 1994; chm Clarence Wheelers Cycling Club; dir of track racing Br Cycling Fedn 1995–96 (pres 1996); *Style—* Tony Doyle, Esq, MBE

DOYLE, (Frederick) Bernard; s of James Hopkinson Doyle, and Hilda Mary, *née* Spotsworth; *b* 17 July 1940; *Educ* Univ of Manchester, Harvard Business Sch (MBA); *m* Ann, *née* Weston; 2 s (Stephen Francis, Andrew John), 1 da (Elizabeth Ann); *Career* chartered engr; mgmnt conslt London, Brussels and USA 1967–72, Booker McConnell 1973–81 (dir 1979, chm Engrg Div to 1981); chief exec: SDP 1981–83, Welsh Water Authy 1983–87; dir ops MSL International (UK) Ltd 1988–90 and 1994–, md Hamptons 1990–94; CIMgt, FICE, FIWES, FRSA; *Recreations* reading, theatre, bird watching, walking, sailing; *Style—* Bernard Doyle, Esq; ✉ 38A West Road, Bromsgrove, Worcs B60 2NQ; MSL International (UK) Ltd, Quadrant Court, 50 Calthorpe Road, Edgbaston, Birmingham B15 1TH (☎ 0121 454 8864)

DOYLE, Dr David; RD (1973, and bar 1983); s of Edward Doyle, of Edinburgh, and Mary Stevenson, *née* Shand; *b* 28 Sept 1937; *Educ* George Heriot's Sch Edinburgh, Univ of Edinburgh (MD); *m* 1, 24 Oct 1964, Janet Caryl (d 1984), da of late Stanley Maurice Gresham Potter, of Nottingham; 5 s (Michael b 1966, Stanley b 1968, Edward b 1970, Arthur b 1972, Quintin b 1977); m 2, 28 Sept 1996, Catherine Ford Whitley, wife of late John Whitley, da of late Dr A G Cruickshank, of Edinburgh; *Career* RAFVR 1958–61, Univ of Edinburgh Air Sqdn, RAuxAF 1962–67, RNR 1967–; house offr in med and surgery Edinburgh Royal Infirmary 1961–62, anatomy demonstrator Univ of Edinburgh 1962–63, sr house offr in surgical neurology Edinburgh 1963; appts in academic pathology and neuropathology 1963–71: Edinburgh, King's Coll Hosp London; conslt neuropathologist Glasgow 1971–; Dip in Forensic Med, Cert in Aviation Med; CBiol, FIBiol, MRAeS, FFPathRCPI, FRCPEd 1996; *Recreations* Highland bagpiping, flying, climbing with Kate; *Clubs* RSM, Royal Scottish Piping Soc, Glasgow Highland; *Style—* Dr David Doyle, RD; ✉ Institute of Neurological Sciences, Glasgow G51 4TF (☎ 0141 201 2050, fax 0141 201 2998)

DOYLE, Ian Thomas; s of James Doyle (d 1994), of Glasgow, and Catherine Forgie Workman (d 1989); *b* 13 March 1940; *Educ* Whitehill Sr Secondary Sch Glasgow; *m* 2 Sept 1961 (m dis 1980), Maureen Marshall, da of Samuel Sunderland; 1 s (Lee Grant Marshall b 30 March 1968), 1 da (Gillian Stuart b 10 April 1967); m 2, 15 Oct 1982, Irene Dick Scott, da of Peter Dick; *Career* fndr and dir Doyle Cruden Group 1967–, fndr and chm Cuemasters Ltd 1988–; snooker players managed incl: Stephen Hendry 1985–, Fergal O'Brien, Mark Williams, Darren Morgan, Martin Clark, Nigel Bond, Gary Wilkinson, Dennis Taylor, Alain Robidoux, Ken Doherty, Joe Swail and David Gray; golfer managed: Dean Robertson; *Recreations* motor racing, golf and sport generally; *Style—* Ian Doyle, Esq; ✉ Cuemasters Ltd, Kerse Rd, Stirling FK7 7SG (☎ 01786 462634, fax 01786 450068)

DOYLE, Leo Mark; s of Raymond Harold Doyle, MBE (d 1965), and Jean Audrey, *née* Mattingly, of Gwynedd; *b* 22 Jan 1960; *Educ* Hailsham Comp Sch E Sussex, City Univ (BSc); *Career* economist; floor cleaner Hellingly Psychiatric Hosp 1978–79, City Univ 1979–82, housekeeping asst Eastbourne Dist Gen Hosp 1982–83; Kleinwort Benson Ltd: computer programmer 1983–84, econometrician 1984–87 (independently constructed Kleinwort Benson's model of the UK economy), economist/econometrician 1987–, dir Kleinwort Benson Securities 1993–; winner The Independent newspaper Golden Guru Award for UK forecasting 1990, Kleinwort economic model came second in Financial Times 5–yr forecasting survey; *Recreations* conservation work, worm farming, walking, cycling, designing board games; *Style—* Leo Doyle, Esq; ✉ Kleinwort Benson Securities, 20 Fenchurch Street, London EC3P 3DB (☎ 0171 956 8074)

DOYLE, Prof Peter; s of Archibald Edward Doyle (d 1979), of Widnes, and Mary, *née* Hemlet; *b* 23 June 1943; *Educ* West Park GS, Univ of Manchester (MA), Carnegie-Mellon Univ USA (MSc, PhD); *m* 8 Sept 1973, Sylvia Mary, da of Jeremiah Augustus Kenny, of Canley; 2 s (Benjamin Hollis b 6 Nov 1978, Hugo William b 8 June 1985); *Career* lectr London Business Sch 1971–73, prof of mktg Univ of Bradford 1973–84, prof INSEAD 1978–79, prof of mktg and strategic mgmnt Univ of Warwick 1984–; author of over 100 articles and books on mktg and business strategy; FInstM, fell CAM Fndn; *Books* Inflation (with R J Ball, 1969), Marketing Management & Strategy (1974), Case Studies in International Marketing (1982); *Recreations* tennis, running; *Clubs* Lansdowne; *Style—* Prof Peter Doyle; ✉ Hurst House, Stratford Road, Henley-in-Arden, Warwickshire B95 6AB (☎ 01564 792960); 41 Gloucester Walk, London; Warwick Business School, University of Warwick, Coventry CV4 7AL (☎ 01203 523911, fax 01203 523719, mobile 0385 396116)

DOYLE, Dr Peter; CBE (1992); s of Peter Doyle (d 1969), and Joan, *née* Murdoch (d 1987); *b* 6 Sept 1938; *Educ* Eastwood Secdy Sch Clarkson Glasgow, Univ of Glasgow (BSc, PhD); *m* 7 Aug 1962, Anita, *née* McCulloch; 1 da (Elaine b 13 Sept 1965, 1 s (Alan b 28 Feb 1967); *Career* ICI plc: joined ICI Pharmaceuticals Div 1963, head of Chemicals Dept ICI Pharmaceuticals Div 1975–77, research dir then R&D dir ICI Plant Protection Div (now ICI Agrochemicals) 1977–86, dep chm and technical dir ICI Pharmaceuticals 1986–89, gp research and technol dir and main bd dir 1989–93; exec dir Zeneca Group plc (following its demerger from ICI) 1993– (i/c R & D, safety, health and environment, mfrg and E & W Europe); visiting prof Univ of Strathclyde Graduate Business Sch 1991, Royal Soc Zeneca lectr 1993; chm Steering Ctee Cambridge Interdisciplinary Research Centre for Protein Engrg 1990–95, vice pres Cncl Royal Instn 1991; memb: Cncl Univ Coll London 1985–, Cncl Centre for the Exploitation of Sci and Technol 1989–, PM's Advsy Cncl on Sci and Technol 1989–94, MRC 1990–94, SERC Nat Ctee on Superconductivity 1990–94, Steering Ctee Oxford Interdisciplinary Research Centre for Molecular Sciences 1990–93, Bd of Dirs AFRC Rothstamsted Experimental Station 1991–, Cncl Salters' Inst of Industl Chemistry 1993–, Standing Gp on Health Technol Central R&D Ctee NHS 1994–, Royal Cmmn on Environmental Pollution 1994–; Hon DSc: Univ of Glasgow 1992, Univ of Nottingham 1993, Univ of Sussex 1995; Hon LLD Univ of Dundee 1994; memb Cncl of Assts Worshipful Co of Salters 1996 (Freeman 1982, Liveryman 1983, Renter Warden 1994–95); FRSE 1993; *Style—* Dr Peter Doyle, CBE, FRSE; ✉ Zeneca Group plc, 15 Stanhope Gate, London W1Y 6LN (☎ 0171 304 5000, fax 0171 304 5192)

DOYLE, Philip John; s of Albert Edward Doyle (d 1980), and Veronica Mary, *née* Jackson; *b* 30 Sept 1951; *Educ* West Park GS St Helens Lancs, Queens' Coll Cambridge (foundation scholar); *m* 1 July 1972, Anne Elizabeth, da of Francis William Frankland Dobby; 1 da (Lorna Mary b 19 June 1978), 2 s (Edward Francis b 22 Nov 1980, Howard William b 7 April 1984); *Career* Arthur Andersen: joined 1972, ptnr 1983–, head of Tax Div (London) 1993–; FCA 1977; *Recreations* walking, tennis, cricket, loafing around, completed London Marathon 1993; *Clubs* RAC; *Style—* Philip Doyle, Esq; ✉ Arthur Andersen, 1 Surrey Street, London WC2R 2PS (☎ 0171 438 3450, fax 0171 831 1133)

DOYLE, Sir Reginald Derek Henry; kt (1989), CBE (1980); s of John Henry Doyle (d 1966), and Elsie, *née* Palmer; *b* 13 June 1929; *Educ* Aston Commercial Coll; *m* 12 Dec 1953, June Magretta, da of Bertram Stringer (d 1940); 2 da (Amanda Jayne b 3 May 1959, Wendy Louise b 13 March 1963); *Career* RN 1947–54; Fire Bdes 1954–84; chief fire offr: Worcester City and Co 1973, Hereford and Worcester 1974–77, Kent 1977–84; Home Office Fire Serv Inspr 1984–87, HM Chief Inspr of Fire Servs 1987–94, ret; memb Company of Fire Fighters; CIMgt 1989, FIFireE 1973, OStJ 1991; *Recreations* shooting, swimming; *Clubs* Kent Rotary; *Style—* Sir Reginald Doyle, CBE; ✉ Glebe Croft, Marley Rd, Harrietshan, Kent ME17 1BS

DOYLE, Prof William; s of Stanley Joseph Doyle (d 1973), of Scarborough, Yorks, and Mary Alice, *née* Bielby; *b* 4 March 1942; *Educ* Bridlington Sch, Oriel Coll Oxford (MA, DPhil); *m* 2 Aug 1968, Christine, da of William Joseph Thomas (d 1969), of Aberdare, Glam; *Career* sr lectr in history Univ of York 1978–81 (asst lectr 1967–69, lectr 1969–78), prof of modern history Univ of Nottingham 1981–85, prof of history Univ of Bristol 1986–; visiting prof: Columbia S Carolina 1969–70, Bordeaux 1976, Paris 1988; visiting fell All Souls Coll Oxford 1991–92; pres Soc for the Study of French History 1992–95; Hon DUniv Université de Bordeaux III France; FRHistS; *Books* The Parlement of Bordeaux and the End of the Old Regime 1771–90 (1974), The Old European Order 1660–1800 (1978), Origins of the French Revolution (1980), The Ancien Regime (1986), The Oxford History of the French Revolution (1989), Officers, Nobles and Revolutionaries (1995), Venality. The Sale of Offices in Eighteenth Century France (1996); *Recreations* books, decorating, travelling about; *Clubs* Athenaeum, United Oxford and Cambridge Univ; *Style—* Prof W Doyle; ✉ Linden House, College Road, Lansdown, Bath, Somerset BA1 5RR; Department of Historical Studies, University of Bristol, 13 Woodland Rd, Bristol BS8 1TB (☎ 0117 928 7932)

DOYNE, Capt Patrick Robert; s of Col Robert Harry Doyne (d 1965), of Somerset, and Verena Mary, *née* Seymour (d 1979); *b* 9 Oct 1936; *Educ* Eton; *m* 7 Dec 1963, Sarah Caroline, da of Brig James Erskine Stirling, DSO, DL (d 1968), of Inverness-shire; 1 s (Timothy b 1966), 1 da (Lucinda b 1964); *Career* Capt Royal Green Jackets 1955–69 (served in Kenya, Malaya, Germany, Cyprus and USA); Lloyd's underwriter 1968–, Lloyd's broker 1969–74; in food indust 1974–83, dir Stacks Relocation 1988–; investmt advsr: Hill Samuel 1988–91, Prosperity Financial Services Group 1991–92; sec SCGB 1983–86, county chm Warwickshire BFSS 1995–; High Sheriff Warwickshire 1987; *Recreations* country sports, cricket; *Clubs* Boodle's, Pratt's, MCC; *Style—* Capt P R Doyne; ✉ Woodlands, Idlicote, Shipston-on-Stour, Warwickshire CV36 5DT (☎ 01608 661594, fax 01608 663887)

DRABBLE, Jane; da of Walter Drabble, of Hilton, Dorset, and Molly, *née* Boreham; *b* 15 Jan 1947; *Educ* Clayton Hall GS Newcastle under Lyme, Plympton GS Plymouth, Univ of Bristol (BA); *Career* BBC: studio mangr BBC Radio 1968–73, prodr Radio Current Affrs 1973–75, asst prodr, prodr, then sr prodr TV Current Affrs 1975–86, ed London Plus 1986–87, ed Everyman 1987–91, asst md Network TV 1991–94, concurrently head of factual progs Network TV 1993–94, dir of educn and memb Bd of Mgmnt 1994–; *Recreations* music, theatre, walking, sailing; *Style*— Ms Jane Drabble; ✉ BBC White City, 201 Wood Lane, London W12 7TS (☎ 0181 752 5252)

DRABBLE, Margaret; CBE (1980); da of His Honour John Frederick Drabble, QC (d 1982), by his w Kathleen, *née* Bloor; *b* 5 June 1939; *Educ* The Mount Sch York, Newnham Coll Cambridge; *m* 1, 1960 (m dis 1975), Clive Walter Swift, *qv*; 2 s, 1 da; m 2, 1982, Michael Holroyd, CBE, *qv*; *Career* author; Hon DLitt: Univ of Sheffield, Univ of East Anglia 1994; *Books* A Summer Birdcage (1962), The Garrick Year (1964), The Millstone (1966), Wordsworth (1966), Jerusalem the Golden (1967), The Waterfall (1969), The Needle's Eye (1972), London Consequences (ed with B S Johnson, 1972), Arnold Bennett - A Biography (1974), The Realms of Gold (1975), The Genius of Thomas Hardy (ed, 1976), New Stories 1 (co-ed, 1976), The Ice Age (1977), For Queen and Country (1978), A Writer's Britain (1979), The Middle Ground (1980), The Oxford Companion to English Literature (ed fifth edn, 1985), The Radiant Way (1987), The Concise Oxford Companion to English Literature (with Jenny Stringer, 1987), A Natural Curiosity (1989), Safe As Houses (1989), The Gates of Ivory (1991), Angus Wilson: A Biography (1995), The Witch of Exmoor (1996); *Style*— Ms Margaret Drabble, CBE; ✉ c/o Peters Fraser & Dunlop, 5th Floor, The Chambers, Chelsea Harbour, London SW10 0XF (☎ 0171 344 1000)

DRABBLE, Phil Percy Cooper; OBE (1993); s of Dr Edward Percy Drabble, and Madeline Ursula, *née* Steele; *b* 14 May 1914; *Educ* Bromsgrove, Univ of London; *m* 6 Sept 1939, Jessie Constance, da of George Thomas; *Career* engrg indust 1938–61, dir George Salter & Co Ltd; author and broadcaster 1961–, presenter (every programme in every series) One Man and His Dog 1976–93; best known for his campaigns for responsible multi-use of the countryside for wildlife and people, TV series My Wilderness Reprieved; contrib to jls incl: Country Times, Derbyshire Life, Trust, Burton Daily Mail, Daily Telegraph, Express and Star, Shropshire Star, Country Talk, Country Living; lectr Foyles Lecture Agency 1964; professional naturalist managing a wildlife reserve of 90 acres (specialising in badgers and herons); author of over 20 books on dogs, rural and environmental topics; Phil Drabble Award for Commitment to Youth (created by Earl Howe, Forestry Min) 1993; Countryside Award 1970, Centres of Excellence Award Forestry Authy 1992, 1993, 1994 and 1995; *Recreations* encouraging young naturalists; *Style*— Phil Drabble, Esq, OBE; ✉ Goat Lodge, Abbots Bromley, Rugeley, Staffs WS15 3EP (☎ 01283 840 345)

DRABBLE, Richard John Bloor; QC (1995); s of His Honour Frederick John Drabble, QC (d 1982), and Kathleen Marie, *née* Bloor (d 1984); *b* 23 May 1950; *Educ* Leighton Park Sch Reading, Downing Coll Cambridge (BA); *m* 31 May 1980, Sarah Madeleine Hope, da of Lt Cdr John David Walter Thomas Lewis (d 1966); 3 s (William b and d 1981, Frederick b 1982, Samuel b 1985); *Career* called to the Bar Inner Temple 1975, jr counsel to the Crown Common Law 1992–95; *publications* Halsburys Laws Social Security (contrib), Goudie & Supperstone Judicial Review (contrib), numerous articles; *Recreations* reading, walking; *Style*— Richard Drabble, Esq, QC; ✉ 4 Breams Buildings, London EC4A 1AQ (☎ 0171 353 5835, fax 0171 430 1677)

DRABU, Dr Yasmin Jeelani (Mrs Naqushbandi); da of Dr Ghulam Jeelani Drabu, of Hale, Cheshire, and Ayesha Jeelani, *née* Ashai; *b* 21 June 1950; *Educ* N Manchester GS, Univ of Manchester Med Sch (MB ChB); *m* 17 Aug 1975, Dr Khalid Naqushbandi, s of Ghulam Nabi Naqushbandi, of Srinagar Kashmir; 3 da (Lara Hennah b 3 Feb 1981, Shama b 10 Oct 1983, Sabah (twin) b 10 Oct 1983); *Career* sr registrar UCH 1980–82, conslt microbiologist N Middx Hosp 1982–; Royal Free Hosp: hon sr lectr 1989–, clinical dir of pathology 1993–95, clinical dir of diagnostic and therapy servs 1995–; memb Kashmiri Assoc of GB; DCH, FRCPath; *Style*— Dr Yasmin Drabu; ✉ Department of Microbiology, North Middlesex Hospital, Sterling Way, London N18 1QX (☎ 0181 887 2892, fax 0181 887 4227)

DRAGUN, Richard Eugenjusz; s of Jan Dragun (d 1996), of Anlaby, nr Hull, and Genowefa, *née* Hulnicka (d 1990); *b* 13 May 1951; *Educ* Marist Coll Hull, London Coll of Printing (DipAD); *Career* designer Nat Car Park Ltd 1973–74, dir Design Research Unit Ltd 1980–89 (designer 1974–80, assoc 1980–89); seconded pt/t: conslt and designer British Mass Transit Consultants, Taipe Metro project Taiwan 1986–87, sr designer Baghdad Metro project 1981–84; ptnr BDP Design 1989–; exhibition and museum design incl: Nat Sound Archive London (permanent exhibition), Spaceworks (Nat Maritime Museum London), Charing Cross Station (London Transport), History and Culture of Oman (Smithsonian Inst Washington DC), Gulf Cooperation Cncl (Summit Conf Exhibition Oman), Nat History Museum and Travelling Exhibitions for Miny of Heritage and Culture (Sultanate of Oman); conslt JV Gp (Dar Es Salaam, Int Trade Fair 1989–); work selected for pubn and exhibition in UK Graphic Design 1984–85, Best in Exhibition Design, Best in Retail Identity Design 1996, Graphis Diagrams (Switzerland), Design (Republic of China), World Graphic Design (Japan); author of various articles; memb Governing Body of Southwark Coll, chm Art and Design Consultative Ctee 1988–92, MCSD 1978; *Recreations* swimming, squash, flying, modern prints, books; *Style*— Richard Dragun, Esq; ✉ Building Design Partnership, PO Box 4WD, 16 Gresse Street, London W1A 4WD (☎ 0171 631 4733, fax 0171 631 0393)

DRAKAKIS-SMITH, Prof David William; s of William Smith (d 1966), of Liverpool, and Jessica, *née* Hughes (d 1990); *b* 18 Nov 1942; *Educ* Univ of Wales (BA, MA), Univ of Hong Kong (PhD); *m* 29 Dec 1967, Angela, da of Emmanuel Jean Drakakis, of Cardiff; 1 s (Emmanuel David b 1976), 1 da (Chloe b 1974); *Career* univ lectr: Glasgow 1967–88, Hong Kong 1968–73, Durham 1973–75; res fell Aust Nat Univ 1975–80; prof: Univ of Keele 1980–94, Univ of Liverpool 1994–; chm Inst of Br Geographers, Developing Areas Res Gp; FRSA; *Books* Urbanisation Housing and the Development Process (1981), Urbanisation in the Developing World (ed and contrib, 1986), Multinationals and the Third World (co-ed, 1986), The Third World City (1987), Cities and Economic Development in the Periphery and Semi-Periphery (ed, 1989), Pacific Asia (1992), Urban and Regional Development in Southern Africa (ed, 1992), Economic and Social Change in Pacific Asia (ed and contrib, 1993); *Recreations* golf, cricket, football, art; *Style*— Prof David Drakakis-Smith; ✉ Department of Geography, University of Liverpool, Liverpool L69 3BX (☎ 0151 794 2851, fax 0151 794 2866, e-mail drakis@liverpool.ac.uk)

DRAKE, *see:* Rivett-Drake

DRAKE, Hon Sir (Frederick) Maurice Drake; kt (1978), DFC (1944); s of Walter Charles Drake (d 1980), of Harpenden; *b* 15 Feb 1923; *Educ* St George's Sch Harpenden, Exeter Coll Oxford; *m* 1954, Alison May, da of William Duncan Waterfall, CB (d 1970), of Harpenden; 2 s, 3 da; *Career* served WWII, Flt Lt RAF; called to the Bar Lincoln's Inn 1950, bencher 1976, QC 1968, dep chm Beds QS 1966–71, recorder of the Crown Court 1972–78, standing sr counsel to Royal Coll of Physicians 1972–78, judge of the High Court of Justice (Queen's Bench Div) 1978–95, presiding judge Midland and Oxford Circuit 1979–83, treas Lincoln's Inn 1997–; memb Parole Bd 1984–86 (vice chm 1985–86), nominated judge Service Pensions Appeals 1986–95; hon alderman St Albans DC; *Recreations* music, opera, gardening, travel; *Style*— The Hon Sir Maurice Drake, DFC; ✉ c/o Royal Courts of Justice, Strand, London WC2A 2LL (☎ 0171 936 6259)

DRAKES, David Hedley Foster; s of Donald Frank Drakes (d 1986), and Kathleen, *née* Caldecott; *b* 20 Sept 1943; *Educ* Wyggeston GS for Boys Leicester, St Catharine's Coll Cambridge (exhibitioner, MA); *m* Patricia Margaret Mary, da of Edward Henshall; *Career* advtg account mangr: Doyle Dane Bernbach London 1966–70, Aalders Marchant Weinreich London 1970–72; fndr and dir Intellect Games 1973–76, md Marketing Solutions Limited 1977–82, fndr managing ptnr and majority shareholder The Marketing Partnership Limited 1983–; past chm: Inst of Sales Promotion, The Sales Promotion Consits Assoc; memb: Mktg Soc 1978, MRS 1989; *Recreations* opera, ballet, theatre, playing squash; *Clubs* RAC; *Style*— David Drakes, Esq; ✉ The Marketing Partnership Ltd, 69 Hatton Garden, London EC1N 8JT (☎ 0171 831 9190, fax 0171 831 1852)

DRAKES, Paul William Foster; s of Donald Frank Drakes (d 1986), and Kathleen, *née* Caldicott; *b* 6 Nov 1950; *Educ* Wyggeston GS; *m* 1, 1973 (m dis 1980), Janet Bell; 2 s (Oliver b 30 Dec 1975, William b 3 Jan 1979); m 2, 1981, Stephanie Anne, da of Melvyn Moffatt; 2 s (Jonathan b 18 Dec 1986, Harry b 4 July 1989); *Career* trainee Sun Life Co Leicester 1967, mgmnt trainee Dunlop Leicester 1967, trainee media planner and buyer Gee Advertising Leicester 1968, media planner and buyer C R Cassons London 1969, media gp head Allardyce Hampshire 1970, media gp head The Media Department Ltd 1973–; Primary Contact Ltd: media mangr 1973, media dir and Bd dir 1976, account gp head 1986, dir of client servs 1988; client servs dir ACGB Nottingham 1991; fndr ptnr Drakes Jardine Ltd 1992–; MIPA; *Recreations* with 4 sons and 2 at boarding school (Oakham) little time for hobbies, watching sons is main occupation, all other time devoted to starting the new company; *Style*— Paul Drakes, Esq; ✉ The Old Rectory, Plumtree Road, Cotgrave, Nottingham NG12 3HT (☎ 0115 989 4210); Drakes Jardine Ltd, Chartwell House, 67/69 Hounds Gate, Nottingham NG1 6BB (☎ 0115 950 7800, fax 0115 950 7333)

DRANSFIELD, Graham; s of Gordon Dransfield, of Linthwaite, Huddersfield, and Barbara, *née* Booth; *b* 5 March 1951; *Educ* Colne Valley HS Huddersfield, St Catherine's Coll Oxford (coll scholar, BA, Soccer blue); *m* 21 June 1980, Helen Frances, da of Lawrence Demchy; 1 da (Louise Jane b 14 Feb 1981), 1 s (Mark Lucas b 21 Dec 1984); *Career* articled clerk then asst slr Slaughter & May 1974–82; Hanson plc: slr 1982–86, co sec 1986, assoc dir 1989, dir 1992–; memb Law Soc 1976; *Recreations* squash, tennis, running, cycling, golf; *Clubs* Beckenham CC, Addington Golf; *Style*— Graham Dransfield, Esq; ✉ Hanson plc, 1 Grosvenor Place, London SW1X 7JH (☎ 0171 245 1245, fax 0171 245 9939, car 0836 205604)

DRAPER, Gerald Carter; OBE (1974); s of Alfred Henderson Draper (d 1962), and Mona Violanta, *née* Johnson (d 1982); *b* 24 Nov 1926; *Educ* Avoca Sch, Trinity Coll Dublin (MA); *m* 1951, Winifred Lilian, *née* Howe; 1 s (Alan), 3 da (Valerie, Hilary, Shirley); *Career* dir commercial ops BA 1978–82, md BA Intercontinental Servs Div May-Aug 1982; dir: BA Associated Cos 1972–82, Br Intercontinental Hotels Ltd 1976–82; chm Br Airtours Ltd 1978–82, ret from BA Bd 1982, chm Silver Wing Surface Arrangements Ltd 1971–82; dep chm: Trust House Forte Travel Ltd 1974–82, ALTA Ltd 1977–82, Hoverspeed UK Ltd 1984–86 (also md); chm: Govt Advsy Ctee on Advertising 1978–83, Draper Assocs Ltd 1983–87, Marketors' Hall Ltd; govr Coll of Air Training 1983–84; memb Bd: Communications Strategy Ltd 1983–86, AGB (TRI) Ltd 1983–85, Br Travel and Educnl Tst Ltd, Centre for Airline and Travel Marketing Ltd; chm: Outdoor Advertising Assoc of Gt Britain 1985–92, BR (Southern) Bd 1990–92; memb Ct of Assts Worshipful Co of Marketors (Master 1990); FCIM, FIT; *Recreations* shooting, golf, sailing; *Clubs* Burhill Golf, City Livery; *Style*— Gerald Draper, Esq, OBE; ✉ Old Chestnut, Onslow Road, Burwood Park, Walton-on-Thames, Surrey (☎ and fax 01932 228612); 13B La Frenaie, Cogolin, Var, France

DRAPER, Rev Dr Ivan Thomas; s of Thos George Draper (d 1966), and Ethel Alice, *née* Pearson (d 1962); *b* 11 Sept 1932; *Educ* Bemrose Sch, Univ of Aberdeen (MB ChB); *m* 4 July 1956, Muriel May, da of John Monro (d 1955); *Career* res fell Dept of Med Johns Hopkins Hosp Baltimore USA 1962–63, conslt neurologist rising to sr conslt neurologist Inst of Neurological Scis Glasgow 1965–94, ret; hon asst curate St Bride's Episcopal Church Glasgow, former pres Scottish Ornithologists Club, memb Cncl Scottish Cncl for Spastics, FRCPE 1966, FRCPG 1976; *Books* Lecture Notes on Neurology (6 edn, 1986); *Recreations* fishing, books, ornithology; *Style*— Rev Dr Ivan T Draper

DRAPER, Prof Paul Richard; s of James Krishen Draper, of York, and Dorothy Jean Draper; *b* 28 Dec 1946; *Educ* Univ of Exeter (BA), Univ of Reading (MA), Univ of Stirling (PhD); *m* Janet Margaret, *née* Grant; 1 s (Timothy James Jonathan b 29 Sept 1977), 1 da (Lucy Jane Jessica b 30 April 1980); *Career* research fell Univ of Stirling 1972–73, lectr Univ of St Andrews 1973–75, lectr Univ of Edinburgh 1976–78; Univ of Strathclyde: Esmée Fairbairn sr lectr 1978–86, prof 1988–, head Dept of Accounting & Finance 1990–95, vice dean Strathclyde Business Sch 1993–; Research Prize Inst for Quantitative Investment (with G Brown and E McKenzie) 1992; *Books* The Scottish Financial Sector (with I Smith, W Stewart and N Hood, 1988), The Investment Trust Industry in the UK (1989); *Recreations* rural living, home computing; *Style*— Prof Paul Draper; ✉ 19 Upper Gray Street, Edinburgh EH9 1SN (☎ 0131 667 4087); Department of Accounting and Finance, University of Strathclyde, Curran Building, 100 Cathedral Street, Glasgow G4 0LN (☎ 0141 552 4400 ext 3889, fax 0141 552 3547)

DRAPER, Peter Sydney; CB (1994); s of Sydney George Draper (d 1961), and Norah, *née* Taylor (d 1982); *b* 18 May 1935; *Educ* Haberdashers' Aske's, Regent Poly (Dip in Mgmnt Studies); *m* 1959, Elizabeth Ann, da of John George Frederick French; 3 s (Stephen John b 1961, Derek Peter b 1963, Christopher David b 1965); *Career* GCHQ Foreign Office 1953–56; Miny of Tport: exec offr 1956–63, higher exec 1963–69, princ 1969–71; Property Services Agency DOE: dir Estate Mgmnt Overseas 1971–74, asst sec 1975, head Staff Resources Div 1975–78, asst dir Home Regnl Servs 1978–81, Royal Coll of Defence Studies 1981–82, dir Eastern Region 1982–85, dir Defence Servs 1985–87, princ estab offr 1987–93, princ estab and fin offr 1993–95, ret; *Recreations* gardening, golf; *Clubs* Saffron Walden Golf; *Style*— Peter Draper, Esq, CB; ✉ Langdale, 22 Brewery Road, Pampisford, Cambs CB2 4EN (☎ 01223 835949)

DRAPER, Prof Ronald Philip; s of Albert William Draper, and Elsie, *née* Carlton; *b* 3 Oct 1928; *Educ* Nottingham Boys' HS, Univ of Nottingham (BA, PhD); *m* 19 June 1950, Irene Margaret; 3 da (Anne Elizabeth b 1957, Isabel Frances b 1959, Sophia Mildred b 1964); *Career* PO-Flying Offr RAF 1953–55; lectr in English Univ of Adelaide 1955–56; Univ of Leicester: asst lectr 1957–58, lectr 1958–68, sr lectr 1968–73; Univ of Aberdeen: prof of English 1973–94, Regius Chalmers prof of English 1987–94, head of dept 1984–92, prof emeritus 1994–; *Books* D H Lawrence (1964), D H Lawrence: The Critical Heritage (ed, 1970), Hardy: the Tragic Novels (ed 1975, revised 1991), George Eliot: The Mill on the Floss and Silas Marner (ed, 1978), Tragedy Developments in Criticism (ed, 1980), Lyric Tragedy (1985), Shakespeare: 'The Winter's Tale' Text and Performance (1985), D H Lawrence: Sons and Lovers (1986), Thomas Hardy: Three Pastoral Novels (ed, 1987), Shakespeare's Twelfth Night (1988), The Literature of Region and Nation (ed, 1989), An Annotated Critical Bibliography of Thomas Hardy (with Martin Ray, 1989), The Epic Developments in Criticism (ed, 1990), A Spacious Vision: Essays on Hardy (ed with Phillip V Mallett, 1994); *Dramatic Scripts* The Canker and the Rose (with P A W Collins, Mermaid Theatre 1964), DHL: A Portrait of D H Lawrence (with Richard Hoggart, Nottingham Playhouse 1967, New End Theatre Hampstead 1978, BBC TV 1980); *Recreations* reading, walking, listening to music; *Style*— Prof Ronald Draper; ✉ Maynestay, Catbrook, Chipping Campden, Glos GL55 6DJ (☎ 01386 840796)

DRAYCOTT, Douglas Patrick; QC (1965); s of George Draycott, and Mary Ann, *née* Burke; *b* 28 Aug 1918; *Educ* Wolstanton GS, Oriel Coll Oxford (MA); *m* 1 (m dis 1974), Elizabeth Victoria, da of F H Hall; 2 s (Philip b 1947, Simon b 1950), 3 da (Julia b 1954, Charlotte b 1957, Emma b 1961); m 2, 2 March 1979, Margaret Jean Brunton, da of Andrew Watson Speed; *Career* RTR Europe 1939–46, liaison offr to War Cabinet (Historical Section); called to the Bar Middle Temple 1950, master of the Bench 1972, leader Midland and Oxford circuit 1979–83; *Recreations* inland waterways; *Style*— Douglas Draycott, Esq, QC; ✉ 11 Sir Harry's Rd, Edgbaston, Birmingham B15 2UY (☎ 0121 440 1050); 4 Kings Bench Walk, London EC4Y 7DL (☎ 0171 353 3581); 5 Fountain Court, Birmingham B4 6DR (☎ 0121 606 0500)

DRESCHER, Derek Peter; s of Clifford Drescher (d 1966), and Joan Ringrose, *née* Jackson; *b* 13 March 1940; *Educ* Pocklington Sch, Univ of Birmingham; *m* 11 April 1966, Gillian Mary, da of Ronald Harry Eden, of Oxford; 2 da (Lucy, Alison); *Career* lighting designer Lincoln and Oldham Repertory Theatre Cos 1961–63; BBC Radio: studio mangr 1963–71, music prodr 1971–89, sr prodr (Jazz) 1989–; documentaries incl: Constant Lambert, Jelly Roll Morton, Charlie Parker, Little Titch, Max Roach, Miles Davis (The Phoenix, nominated for Sony award 1991), George Russell (The Invisible Guru), billy Mayerl (A Formula for Success); series incl: Man-Woman of Action, Desert Island Discs (1976–86), Jazz Today, Concerto, Highway to Heaven, Before the Blues (won Sony award for best specialist music prog 1988), This Week's Composer (Duke Ellington), Play as I Please (Humphrey Lyttelton), Touch of Genius (George Shearing), Impressions, A Man for All Music (André Previn), Misterioso (Thelonious Monk); *Books* Desert Islands Lists (with Roy Plomley, 1984); *Recreations* theatre, music, travel, books, photography; *Style*— Derek Drescher, Esq; ✉ 10 Fortismere Ave, Muswell Hill, London N10 3BL (☎ 0181 883 8081); BBC, Broadcasting House, Portland Place, London W1A 1AA (☎ 0171 765 4327)

DRESSER, Hilary Sarah; da of Clive Dresser, and Wilhelmina, *née* Stratton; *b* 12 April 1968; *Educ* Millfield, Univ of Kingston (BSc); *Career* former sprint canoeist; currently sports and leisure mangr Seeboard plc; achievements: semi-finalist World Championship Duisberg 1995, silver medallist K2 Copenhagen Int regatta 1995, silver medallist K2 and K4 Paris Int regatta 1995, bronze medallist K2 Poznan Int regatta 1995, Br Nat record holder 1994 and 1995, winner Br Nat Championships 1995; memb Olympic team Barcelona 1992; memb Br team: World Marathon Championships 1994, World Championships Mexico 1994; ret from sprint canoeing 1996; *Recreations* piano, clarinet, guitar, running, swimming, cinema; *Clubs* Richmond Canoe; *Style*— Miss Hilary Dresser

DREW, Dan Hamilton; s of Daniel Edward Drew (d 1974), of Petworth, Sussex, and Rena Frayer, *née* Hamilton (d 1990); *b* 31 Jan 1938; *Educ* Stubbington House and Tonbridge; *m* 1, 1963 (m dis), Carol Ann, da of Dr Robert Gibson Miller, of Helston, Cornwall; 1 s (Angus b 1967), 1 da (Xanthe b 1966); m 2, 1976, Beverley, da of Alan Lestocq Roberts (d 1981), of Graffham, Sussex; 1 da (Frances b 1979); *Career* CA; gp fin dir Interlink Express plc 1982–92; chm Bath and Wessex Opera Ltd 1992–; *Recreations* shooting, fishing; *Style*— D H Drew, Esq; ✉ Lower Poswick, Whitbourne, Worcester WR6 5SS (☎ 01886 821275, car 0831 411530)

DREW, Dorothy Joan; da of Francis Marshall Gant (d 1956), of Reading, Berkshire, and Wilhelmina Frederica, *née* Dunster (d 1982); *b* 31 March 1938; *Educ* The Sch of St Helen and St Katharine, Univ of London (LLB); *m* 12 Dec 1959, Patrick Drew, s of Alec Charles Drew (d 1967), of Reading, Berks; 2 s, 1 da; *Career* called to the Bar Gray's Inn 1981, pt/t chm Social Security Appeal Tbnls 1986–92; adjudicator Immigration Appeals Tbnl 1989–93, special adjudicator 1993–; chm Child Support Appeals Tbnl 1993–94; JP Reading 1975–95; *Recreations* music, theatre, golf; *Style*— Mrs Dorothy Drew; ✉ Handpost, Swallowfield, Berks RG7 1PY; 13 Draycott Ave, London SW3

DREW, Joanna Marie; CBE (1985); *b* 28 Sept 1929; *Career* Arts Council of GB 1952–88: asst dir Exhibitions 1970, dir of Exhibitions 1975, dir of Art 1978–86; dir Hayward Gallery and regnl exhibitions South Bank Centre 1987–92; memb Cncl RCA 1979–82; Officier L'Ordre des Arts et Lettres 1988 (Chevalier 1979), Officier de L'Ordre National du Mérite 1994 (Chevalier 1990); *Style*— Miss Joanna Drew, CBE

DREW, Prof John Sydney Neville; s of John William Henry Drew (d 1989), and Kathleen Marjorie, *née* Wright (d 1991); *b* 7 Oct 1936; *Educ* King Edward's Sch Birmingham, St John's Coll Oxford (MA), Fletcher Sch of Law and Diplomacy, Tufts Univ (AM); *m* 22 Dec 1962, Rebecca Margaret Amanda, *née* Usher; 2 s (Jason b 1965, David b 1972), 1 da (Emma b 1967); *Career* Lt Somerset LI 1955–57; HM Dip Serv 1960–73, dir of mktg and exec programmes London Business Sch 1973–79, dir of corp affairs Rank Xerox 1979–84, dir of Euro affrs Touche Ross Int 1984–86, head of UK Offices Euro Cmmn 1987–93; visiting prof of Euro mgmnt: Imperial Coll of Sci and Technol 1987–90, Open Univ 1992–; visiting prof of Euro business mgmnt Univ of Durham 1995–, co-dir Durham Inst for Change; dir: Europa Times 1993–94, The Change Group International PLC 1996–; pres Inst of Linguists 1993–, dep chm Enterprise Support Group 1993–95; Sloan fell London Business Sch 1970, assoc fell Templeton Coll Oxford 1982–87; Hon MBA Univ of Northumbria 1991; *Books* Doing Business in the European Community (1979, 3 edn 1991), Networking in Organisations (1986), Europe 1992 - Developing an Active Company Approach to the European Market (1988), Readings in International Enterprise (1994); *Recreations* travel, reading, golf, family life; *Clubs* United Oxford and Cambridge; *Style*— Prof John Drew; ✉ 49 The Ridgeway, London NW11 8PQ (☎ 0181 455 5054)

DREWRY, Dr David John; s of Norman Tidman Drewry (d 1984), of Grimsby, Lincs, and Mary Edwina, *née* Wray (d 1993); *b* 22 Sept 1947; *Educ* Havelock Sch Grimsby, Queen Mary Coll London (BSc), Emmanuel Coll Cambridge (PhD); *m* 10 July 1973, Gillian Elizabeth, da of Clifford Francis Holbrook (d 1979); *Career* Univ of Cambridge: Sir Henry Strakosh fell 1972, sr asst in res 1978–83, asst dir of res 1983; dir Scott Polar Res Inst, dir Br Antarctic Survey 1987–94, dir of science and technology and dep chief exec NERC 1994–; fell Queen Mary and Westfield Coll 1991–, visiting fell Green Coll Oxford 1995–, visiting prof Univ of London 1996–; vice pres Comité Arctique Int 1989–94, memb Cncl of Mangrs of Nat Antarctic Programmes (chm 1989–91); tstee Antarctic Heritage Tst, patron Robert Gordon Fndn; US Antarctic Serv Medal 1979, Polar Medal 1986, Gold Medal (Prix de la Belgica) Royal Acad of Belgium 1995; Hon DSc: Robert Gordon Univ 1993, Univ of Humberside 1994; memb: Int Glaciological Soc 1969 (vice pres 1991–96), Royal Geographical Soc (vice pres 1990–93, Cuthbert Peek Award 1979); FRGS 1972; *Books* Antarctica: Glaciological and Geophysical Folio (1983), Glacial Geologic Processes (1986); *Recreations* music, walking, skiing, gastronomy; *Style*— Dr David Drewry; ✉ Natural Environment Research Council, Polaris House, Northstar Avenue, Swindon, Wilts SN2 1EU (☎ 01793 411654, fax 01793 411780, e-mail d.j.drewry@nerc.ac.uk)

DREYER, Adm Sir Desmond Parry; GCB (1967, KCB 1963, CB 1960), CBE (1957), DSC (1940); s of Adm Sir Frederic Charles Dreyer, GBE, KCB (d 1956), of Winchester, by his w Una Maria, da of Rev J T Hallett; *b* 6 April 1910; *Educ* RNC Dartmouth; *m* 1, 1934, Elisabeth (d 1958), da of Sir Henry Getty Chilton, GCMG (d 1954); 1 s, 1 da (and 1 s decd); m 2, 12 Dec 1959, Marjorie Gordon (widow of Hon Ronald George Whiteley, OBE, yr s of 1 Baron Marchamley), da of Ernest Jukes, of Rickmansworth; *Career* RN 1924, served HMS Ajax, Coventry, Cairo and Duke of York and at Admty WWII, Capt 1948, COS to C-in-C Med 1955–57, Rear-Adm 1958, ACNS 1958–59, Flag Offr (Flotillas) Med 1960–61, Vice-Adm 1961, Flag Offr Air (Home) 1961–62, Cdr Far E Fleet 1962–65, Adm 1965, Second Sea Lord and chief Naval Personnel 1965–67, chief advsr (personnel and logistics) to Sec of State for Def 1967–68, ret 1968; first and princ Naval ADC to HM The Queen 1965–68; memb: Nat Bd for Prices and Incomes 1968–71, Armed Forces Pay Review Body 1971–79; pres RN Benevolent Tst 1970–78, Not Forgotten Assoc 1973–91, Regular Forces Employment Assoc 1978–82, Offrs' Pension Soc 1978–84; Gentlemen Usher to the Sword of State 1973–80; JP 1968–80, High Sheriff Hants 1977, DL Hants 1985; *Recreations* dry fly fishing, golf; *Clubs* Army & Navy; *Style*— Adm Sir Desmond Dreyer, GCB, CBE, DSC; ✉ Brook Cottage, Cheriton, Nr Alresford, Hants SO24 0QA (☎ 01962 771215)

DREYER, Capt Jeremy Chilton; LVO (1996); s of Adm Sir Desmond Dreyer, GCB, CBE, DSC, of Alresford, Hants, and Elisabeth, *née* Chilton (d 1958); *b* 24 May 1935; *Educ* Winchester; *m* 6 Aug 1960, Antoinette Marion (Toni), da of William Cornwall Stevens (d 1983), of Trevessa, Princes Risborough, Bucks; 2 s (Michael b 20 March 1963, Benjamin b 13 July 1967), 2 da (Katherine b 9 Nov 1961, d 1980, Sophie b 3 May 1970); *Career* RN 1953, qualified Signal Communications 1963; cmd: HMS Falmouth 1970–72, HMS Exeter 1980–82; Capt 5th Destroyer Sqdn, Cdre Dep Chief Allied Staff to C-in-C Eastern Atlantic 1982–85, ret 1985; asst clerk of the course Ascot Racecourse 1985–95; *Recreations* shooting, fishing, golf, tennis, skiing; *Style*— Capt Jeremy Dreyer, LVO, RN; ✉ Old Mill Cottage, Droxford, Hants SO32 3QS (☎ 01489 877208, fax 01489 877169)

DRIFE, Prof James Owen; s of Thomas John Drife (d 1993), of Bourach, The Knowe, Ancrum, Jedburgh, and Rachel Coldwell, *née* Jones (d 1986); *b* 8 Sept 1947; *Educ* Muirkirk JS Sch, Cumnock Acad, Univ of Edinburgh (BSc, MB ChB, MD); *m* 16 June 1973, Diana Elizabeth, da of Prof Ronald Haxton Girdwood, of 2 Hermitage Drive, Edinburgh; 1 s (Thomas b 20 Dec 1975), 1 da (Jennifer b 23 Nov 1977); *Career* house offr Edinburgh Royal Infirmary 1971–72, MRC res fell Edinburgh 1974–76, registrar Eastern Gen Hosp Edinburgh 1976–79, lectr Univ of Bristol 1979–82, sr lectr Univ of Leicester 1982–90, prof of obstetrics and gynaecology Univ of Leeds 1990– (dean of students 1996–), hon conslt obstetrician and gynaecologist Leeds Gen Infirmary 1990–; UK ed European Journal of Obstetrics and Gynaecology 1985–95; co-ed: Contemporary Reviews in Obstetrics and Gynaecology, British Journal of Obstetrics and Gynaecology 1994–; hon sec Blair-Bell Res Soc 1988–91; memb: GMC, Cncl RCOG, Midwifery Ctee UKCC, Cases Ctee Med Protection Soc 1985–94 (dir Med Claims Mgmnt Servs); FRCSEd 1981, FRCOG 1990 (MRCOG 1978); *Books* Dysfunctional Uterine Bleeding and Menorrhagia (ed, 1989), Micturition (co-ed, 1990), HRT and Osteoporosis (co-ed, 1990), Antenatal Diagnosis (co-ed, 1991), Prostalandins and the Uterus (co-ed, 1992), Infertility (co-ed, 1992), Contraception (co-ed, 1993); *Recreations* songwriting; *Clubs* RSM, National Liberal; *Style*— Prof James Drife; ✉ Department of Obstetrics and Gynaecology, D Floor, Clarendon Wing, Belmont Grove, Leeds LS2 9NS (☎ 0113 292 3888, fax 0113 292 6021)

DRINKWATER, Sir John Muir; kt (1988), QC (1972); s of John Drinkwater, OBE, Cdr RN (d 1971), and Edith Constance St Clair, *née* Muir (d 1978); *b* 16 March 1925; *Educ* RNC Dartmouth; *m* 10 Oct 1952, Jennifer Marion (d 1990), da of Edward Fitzwalter Wright (d 1956), of Morley Manor, Derby; 1 s (Jonathan Dominick St Clair b 1956); 4 da (Jane Fairrie b 1954, Joanna Elizabeth b 1958, d 1995, Juliet Caroline Leslie b 1961, Jessanda Katharine Jemima b 1964); *Career* HM Submarines 1943–47, Flag Lt to C-in-C Portsmouth and first Sea Lord 1947–50, Lt Cdr 1952, invalided 1953; called to the Bar Inner Temple 1957, recorder Crown Ct 1972, memb Parly Boundary Cmmn for England 1975–79, Income Tax cmmr, bencher Inner Temple, ret; dir BAA plc; *Clubs* Garrick, Pratt's; *Style*— Sir John Drinkwater, QC; ✉ Meysey Hampton Manor, Cirencester, Gloucestershire GL7 5JS (☎ 01285 851366); 27 Kilmaine Rd, London SW6 7JU (☎ 0171 381 1279); Le Moulin De Lohitzun, 64120 St Palais, France (☎ 00 1 33 59 65 76 04)

DRISCOLL, Fiona Elizabeth Lawrence; da of James Patrick Driscoll, *qv*, and Jeanne L Williams; *b* 27 April 1958; *Educ* Sorbonne (Diploma), Somerville Coll Oxford (MA); *m* 1992, Suresh Hiremath; *Career* mktg advsr Republican Campaign NY 1976, fin servs broker FPC 1976–80, mgmnt conslt Deloitte Haskins and Sells 1980–84, account dir Collett Dickenson Pearce 1984–87, sr conslt Lowe Bell Communications 1987–94, jt md The Rowland Company 1994–95, chief exec Ogilvy Adams Rinehart 1995–; memb: Nat Youth Cncl 1975, Bd 300 Group 1993– (chair 1994–); librarian (vice pres) Oxford Union 1979; *Style*— Ms Fiona Driscoll; ✉ Ogilvy Adams Rinehart, Chancery House, Chancery Lane, London WC2 (☎ 0171 404 3494)

DRISCOLL, James Patrick; s of Henry James Driscoll (d 1965), of Cardiff, and Honorah, *née* Flynn (d 1962); *b* 24 April 1925; *Educ* Coleg Sant Illtyd Cardiff, Univ Coll Cardiff (BA); *m* 16 April 1955, Jeanne Lawrence, da of James Idris Williams; 1 s (Jonathan James b 20 Sept 1961), 1 da (Fiona Elizabeth Driscoll, *qv*, b 27 April 1958); *Career* asst lectr Univ Coll Cardiff 1951–53, res fell Cncl of Europe 1953, Br Iron & Steel Fedn 1953–67 (latterly econ dir), md corp strategy British Steel Corporation 1967–80, chm and md Woodcote Consultants Ltd 1980–90, sr ptnr Woodcote Consultancy Services 1990–; chm Lifecare NHS Tst 1990–94, policy advsr Nationalised Industries' Chairmen's Gp 1990– (dir 1975–90); dep chm Univ Cons Fedn 1949–50, nat dep chm Young Cons 1950, Parly candidate (C) Rhondda West 1950, dep chm Nat Union of Students 1951–53; fell and memb: Ct of Govrs Univ Coll Cardiff (now Univ of Wales Coll of Cardiff) 1970–, CBI Cncl 1970–94; observer NEDC 1975–92; chm Econ Ctee Int Iron & Steel Inst 1972–74; FREconS, FRSA; *Recreations* travel, reading; *Style*— James Driscoll, Esq; ✉ Foxley Hatch, Birch Lane, Purley, Surrey CR8 3LH (☎ 0181 668 4081, fax 0181 763 2972)

DRISCOLL, Dr James Philip (Jim); s of Reginald Driscoll, and Janetta Bridget Driscoll; *b* 29 March 1943; *Educ* St Illtyd's Coll Cardiff, Univ of Birmingham (BSc, PhD), Manchester Business Sch; *m* 1969, Josephine Klapper; 2 s, 2 da; *Career* teacher St Illtyd's Coll Cardiff 1964, res Joseph Lucas Ltd 1968–69; British Steel Corporation: sr res offr 1969–72, Supplies Dept 1972–75, mangr Divnl Supplies 1975–78, project proposals mangr 1978–80, regnl mangr (Industry) S Wales 1980–82; econ and industl advsr to Sec of State for Wales, seconded at under-sec level Welsh Office Indust Dept 1982–85; Mgmnt Consultancy Div Coopers & Lybrand: assoc dir 1985–87, dir 1987–90, ptnr 1990–; CEng, MIChemE 1975, MInstGasE 1975, MInstE 1975; *Publications* author of various tech papers; *Recreations* family, sport; *Clubs* Cardiff Athletic, Peterston FC (Cardiff); *Style*— Dr Jim Driscoll; ✉ 6 Cory Crescent, Wyndham Park, Peterston-super-Ely, S Glamorgan (☎ 01446 760372)

DRISCOLL, Mark Robert; s of Leo Driscoll, and Katherine Driscoll; *b* 5 Oct 1949; *Educ* Colston's Sch Bristol, King's Coll London (BA); *m* 9 Oct 1981, Elspeth Margaret, da of David Cayley, of Cirencester, Glos; 1 s (William), 1 da (Anna); *Career* BBC: studio mangr 1971, exec prodr World Service 1986, ed foreign assignments Newsnight 1990, foreign duty ed 1992–; *Recreations* allotmenting; *Style*— Mark Driscoll, Esq; ✉ BBC Television, London W12

DRIVER, Sir Antony Victor; kt (1986); s of Arthur William Driver (d 1966), and Violet Clementina, *née* Brown (d 1986); *b* 20 July 1920; *Educ* King's Coll London (BSc(Eng)); *m* 16 Oct 1948, Patricia, da of Alfred Tinkler (d 1950); 3 s (Andrew Charles b 1952, James Antony b 1954, Robert Patrick b 1957); *Career* WWII Lt RA 1 Airlanding Light Regt 1 Airborne Div 1941–45; Shell-Mex & BP Ltd 1947–75; BP Oil Ltd 1975–80 (dir 1978–80), dir Hoogovens (UK) Ltd 1980–88 (chm 1986–88); dir: Oil Industries Club Ltd, Surrey Assoc of Youth Clubs and Surrey PHAB Ltd; memb Inst of Cancer Res, chm SW Thames RHA 1982–88; tstee Breakthrough (breast cancer charity) 1995–; Liveryman Worshipful Co of Tallow Chandlers 1972, Freeman City of London; CEng, FIMechE,

FInstPet, FIMgt; *Recreations* travel, wine, gardening, pyrotechnics; *Style*— Sir Antony Driver

DRIVER, Charles Jonathan (Jonty); s of Rev Kingsley Ernest Driver (d 1964), and Mrs Phyllis Edith Mary Baines, *née* Gould; *b* 19 Aug 1939; *Educ* St Andrew's Grahamstown, Univ of Cape Town (BA, BEd), Trinity Coll Oxford (MPhil); *m* 1967, Ann Elizabeth, da of Dr Bernard Albert Hoogewerf, of Chislehurst (d 1958); 2 s (Dominic b 1968, Thackwray b 1969), 1 da (Tamlyn b 1972); *Career* pres Nat Union of S African Students 1963–64; house master Int Sixth Form Centre Sevenoaks Sch 1968–73, dir of sixth form studies Matthew Humberstone Sch 1973–78, princ Island Sch Hong Kong 1978–83, headmaster Berkhamsted Sch 1983–89, master Wellington Coll Berks 1989–, ed Conference and Common Room (Periodical) 1993–; FRSA; *Books* Elegy for a Revolutionary (1968), Send War in Our Time, O Lord (1969), Death of Fathers (1971), A Messiah of the Last Days (1973); poetry: I Live Here Now (1973), Occasional Light (with Jack Cope, 1980), Hong Kong Portraits (1986), In the Water-Margins (1994); biography: Patrick Duncan, S African and Pan-African (1980); *Recreations* long-distance running, rugby, reading; *Style*— C J Driver, Esq; ✉ The Master, Wellington College, Crowthorne, Berks RG11 7PU (☎ and fax 01344 772261)

DRIVER, Christopher Prout; s of late Dr Arthur Driver; *b* 1 Dec 1932; *Educ* Rugby, ChCh Oxford; *m* 1958, Margaret Elizabeth, *née* Perfect; 3 da; *Career* writer and ed; Guardian staff 1960–68, ed The Good Food Guide 1969–82; The Guardian: food and drink ed 1984–88, co-ed personal page 1988–94; *Books* A Future for the Free Churches? (1962), The Disarmers (1964), The Exploding University (1971), The British at Table 1940–80 (1983), Pepys at Table (1984), Poems: 1951–1996, Music for Love (1994), Music (often written); *Style*— Christopher Driver, Esq; ✉ 6 Church Rd, Highgate, London N6 4QT (☎ 0181 340 5445)

DRIVER, David John; s of Denis Alan Driver (d 1968), of Cambridge, and Mona Eileen, *née* Scott; *b* 4 Aug 1942; *Educ* Perse Sch Cambridge, Cambridge Sch of Art; *m* 27 Nov 1976, Sara Penelope, da of Ashley Rock; 1 s (Paul Robert Thomas b 28 Dec 1979, Helen Rachel b 5 April 1984); *Career* freelance illustrator and designer for various publications since 1963 incl: Town, Queen, Vogue, Penguin Books, Observer Magazine, Sunday Times, Harpers Bazaar (re-design 1969), The Listener (re-design 1980); art ed Farm and Country (Thomson Organisation) 1963–67, asst art ed Woman's Mirror (IPC) 1967–68, art dir Cornmarket Press 1968–69, art ed and dep ed Radio Times 1969–81, freelance art dir Francis Kyle Gallery 1979–, head of design and asst ed The Times (News International) 1981–; designer of Royal Mail Christmas stamps 1991; winner various awards incl: Gold & Silver awards for Radio Times D&AD 1976, Editorial Award of Excellence Soc of Newspaper Design Awards (USA) 1987 and 1989, Newspaper Design Awards 1989 and 1994, Colour Newspaper of the Year and Features Design awards 1992; *Books* The Art of Radio Times (ed, compiler and designer, 1981); designer: Graham Greene Country (by Paul Hogarth and Graham Greene), The Windsor Style (by Suzy Menkes), The Mediterranean Shore (by Paul Hogarth and Lawrence Durrell); *Recreations* cricket; *Style*— David Driver, Esq; ✉ The Times, Times Newspapers Ltd, 1 Pennington Street, London E1 9XN (☎ 0171 782 5000, fax 0171 782 5639)

DRIVER, (James) Donald; OBE (1991); s of John Driver (d 1970), of Lancs, and Dorothea Leslie Driver (d 1987); *b* 20 Dec 1924; *Educ* Clitheroe Royal GS, Univ of Manchester; *m* 1948, Delia Jean, da of James Wilkinson, of Clitheroe; 1 s (John b 1952), 2 da (Susan b 1950, Joanna b 1957); *Career* Lt HM RM 1942–46; admitted slr 1948, private practice until 1970; gp legal advsr Investors in Industry plc (3i) 1973–83; chm: Meggitt plc 1985–91 (dir until 1996), Data Guild Ltd 1984–96, Travellers Fare Ltd 1989–92, Dixon Motors plc (formerly Plateau Mining plc) 1991–; dir Dollar Air Services Ltd 1988–93; *Recreations* sailing, cycling, skiing; *Style*— Donald Driver, Esq, OBE; ✉ Littlefield, Dedswell Drive, West Clandon, Guildford, Surrey GU4 7TQ (☎ 01483 222 518, fax 01483 225 313)

DRIVER, Sir Eric William; kt (1979); s of William Weale Driver, and Sarah Ann Driver; *b* 19 Jan 1911; *Educ* Strand Sch London, King's Coll London (BSc); *m* 1, 1938 (m dis), Winifred Bane; 2 da; m 2, 1972, Sheila Mary Johnson; *Career* civil engr ICI Ltd 1938–73 (ret as chief civil engr Mond Div); chm Mersey Regional Health Authy 1973–82; *Recreations* walking, gardening, travel; *Clubs* Budworth Sailing; *Style*— Sir Eric Driver; ✉ Conker Tree Cottage, Great Budworth, Cheshire (☎ 01606 892209)

DRIVER, Olga Lindholm; *see:* Aikin, Olga Lindholm

DROGHEDA, 12 Earl of (I 1661); Henry Dermot Ponsonby Moore; also Baron Moore (I 1616 and UK 1954, by which latter title he sits in House of Lords) and Viscount Moore (I 1621); s of 11 Earl of Drogheda, KG, KBE (d 1989), and Joan Eleanor, *née* Carr (d 1989); *b* 14 Jan 1937; *Educ* Eton, Trinity Coll Cambridge (BA); *m* 1, 15 May 1968 (m dis 1972), Eliza, da of Stacy Barcroft Lloyd, Jr, of Philadelphia; m 2, 1978, Alexandra, da of Sir Nicholas Henderson, GCMG; 2 s (Benjamin Garrett Henderson, Viscount Moore b 1983, Hon Garrett Alexander b 1986), 1 da (Lady Marina Alice b 1988); *Heir* s, Viscount Moore b 21 March 1983; *Career* Lt Life Gds 1957; photographer (professional name Derry Moore); *Books* The Dream Come True, Great Houses of Los Angeles (with Brendan Gill, 1980), Royal Gardens (with George Plumptre, 1982), Stately Homes of Britain (with Sybilla Jane Flower, 1982), Washington, Houses of the Capital (with Henry Mitchell, 1982), The English Room (with Michael Pick, 1984), The Englishwoman's House (with Alvilde Lees-Milne, 1984), The Englishman's Room (with Alvilde Lees-Milne, 1986), The Gardens of Queen Elizabeth The Queen Mother (with the Marchioness of Salisbury, 1988); *Clubs* Brooks's; *Style*— The Rt Hon the Earl of Drogheda; ✉ 40 Ledbury Rd, London W11 2AB (☎ 0171 229 5950, fax 0171 221 8135)

DROMGOOLE, June Kell; da of Robert Bonar Valentine (d 1982), of Dundee, and Alexandrina, *née* Kell (d 1958); *b* 1 Aug 1947; *Educ* Harris Acad Dundee, WRAC Coll Camberley; *m* 1, 1977 (m dis 1991), Peter Morrow; 1 s (Jamie Richard b 25 Aug 1980); m 2, 3 Aug 1991, Patrick Dromgoole, *qv*; *Career* 2 Lt WRAC 1966–68; with Global Television Services Ltd 1968–70, asst ITV Network buyer Granada Television Ltd 1970–73, dir of sales (and 50 per cent shareholder) AML International Ltd 1973–84, md Southbrook International Television Co 1985–87, chief operating offr Palladium International Television Ltd 1987–90, head of purchased progs BBC Television 1990–; memb BAFTA; *Recreations* French food and wine, theatre, cinema; *Style*— Mrs June Dromgoole; ✉ BBC Television, Centre House, Wood Lane, London W12 7RJ (☎ 0181 225 6721, fax 0181 749 0893)

DROMGOOLE, Nicholas; s of Nicholas Arthur Dromgoole (d 1994, aged 104), and Violet Alice Georgina, *née* Brookes; bro of Patrick Dromgoole, *qv*; *b* 3 Dec 1935; *Educ* Dulwich, St Edmund Hall Oxford (MA), Sorbonne (Dip); *m* (m dis 1988), Lesley Collier; *Career* headmaster: Grenville Coll N Devon, Pierrepont Sch Surrey; head of dept (formerly dean of Arts Faculty twice) London Guildhall Univ (formerly City of London Polytechnic) 1961–92; dance critic Sunday Telegraph 1965–; contrib of features to: Daily Telegraph, Country Life, Dancing Times, Dance and Dancers; chm Inst of Choreology 1969–87, Dance Section Critics Circle 1980–86; memb: Drama Advsy Ctee British Council, Dance and Performing Arts Ctees, Council for National Academic Awards; hon fell Inst of Choreology; *Books* Sibley and Dowell (1976); *Clubs* Garrick; *Style*— Nicholas Dromgoole, Esq; ✉ Sunday Telegraph, 1 Canada Square, Canary Wharf, London E14 5DT (☎ 0171 538 5000)

DROMGOOLE, Patrick Shirley Brookes Fleming; s of Nicholas Arthur Humphrey Dromgoole (d 1994, aged 104), and Violet Alice Georgina, *née* Brookes; bro of Nicholas Dromgoole, *qv*; *b* 30 Aug 1930; *Educ* Dulwich, Univ Coll Oxford (MA); *m* 1, 1960 (m dis 1991), Jennifer Veronica Jill, da of S O Davis, of Weymouth; 2 s (Sean, Dominic), 1 da (Jessica); m 2, June Dromgoole, *qv*, formerly Morrow; *Career* actor and variously employed London and Paris 1947–51; BBC drama prodr/dir 1954–63; freelance theatre, film and TV dir 1963–69; HTV Group: programme controller HTV Ltd 1969–81, asst md 1981–87, md 1987–88, chief exec HTV Group plc 1988–91; chm Portman Dromgoole Productions (PDP) 1992–; FRTS, FRSA; *Recreations* travel, field sports, oenophilia; *Clubs* Savile, Groucho, Castel's (Paris); *Style*— Patrick Dromgoole, Esq; ✉ Penkill Castle, Girvan, Ayrshire KA26 9TQ

DROMORE, Bishop of (RC) 1976–; Most Rev (Francis) Gerard Brooks; s of Bernard Brooks (d 1938), of Rathfriland, and Mary Elizabeth (May) Brooks (d 1935); *b* 14 Jan 1924; *Educ* St Colman's Coll Newry, St Patrick's Coll Maynooth (Nat Univ Ireland) (BSc, BD, Doctorate in Canon Law), Pontifical Univ Rome, Rota Court Rome, Gregorian Univ Rome; *Career* ordained priest Maynooth 1949; pres (headmaster) St Colman's Coll Newry 1972 (appointed to teaching staff 1953), canon Diocesan Chapter 1972; chm Irish Hierarchy's Fin Cmmn 1979–; *Recreations* formerly gardening, swimming; *Style*— The Most Rev the Bishop of Dromore; ✉ Bishop's House, 42 Armagh Road, Newry, Co Down, Northern Ireland BT35 6PN (☎ 01693 62444, fax 01693 60496)

DRONKE, Prof (Ernst) Peter Michael; s of A H R Dronke, and M M Dronke, *née* Kronfeld; *b* 30 May 1934; *Educ* Victoria Univ NZ (MA), Magdalen Coll Oxford (MA), Univ of Cambridge (MA); *m* 1960, Ursula Miriam, *née* Brown; 1 da; *Career* res fell Merton Coll Oxford 1958–61; Univ of Cambridge: lectr in medieval Latin 1961–79, fell Clare Hall 1964–, reader 1979–89, prof of medieval Latin lit 1989–; guest lectr Univ of Munich 1960, guest prof Centre d'Etudes Médiévales Poitiers 1969, Leverhulme fell 1973, W P Ker lectr Univ of Glasgow 1976, guest prof Univ Autònoma Barcelona 1977, visiting fell Humanities Res Centre Canberra 1978, visiting prof of medieval studies Westfield Coll 1981–86, Matthews lectr Birkbeck Coll 1983, Carl Newell Jackson lectr Harvard Univ 1992, O'Donnell lectr Univ of Toronto 1993, Barlow lectr Univ Coll London 1995; co ed: Mittellateinisches Jahrbuch 1977–, Premio Internazionale Ascoli Piceno 1988; author of essays in learned jls and symposia; hon pres Int Courtly Literature Soc 1974, corresponding fell Real Academia de Buenas Letras 1976; FBA 1984; *Books* Medieval Latin and the Rise of the European Love-Lyric (2 volumes, 1965–66), The Medieval Lyric (1968), Poetic Individuality in the Middle Ages (1970), Fabula (1974), Abelard and Heloise in Medieval Testimonies (1976), Barbara et Antiquissima Carmina (with Ursula Dronke, 1977), Bernardus Silvestris Cosmographia (ed, 1978), Introduction to Francesco Colonna Hypnerotomachia (1981), Women Writers of the Middle Ages (1984), The Medieval Poet and his World (1984), Dante and Medieval Latin Traditions (1986), Introduction to Rosvita, Dialoghi Drammatici (1986), A History of Twelfth Century Western Philosophy (1988), Hermes and the Sibyls (1990), Latin and Vernacular Poets of the Middle Ages (1991), Intellectuals and Poets in Medieval Europe (1992), Verse with Prose from Petronius to Dante (1994), Nine Medieval Latin Plays (1994); *Recreations* music, film, Brittany; *Style*— Prof Peter Dronke, FBA; ✉ 6 Parker Street, Cambridge CB1 1JL (☎ 01223 359942); Clare Hall, University of Cambridge, Cambridge CB3 9AL (☎ 01223 332360)

DRUCKER, Dr Henry Matthew; s of Arthur Drucker (d 1980), and Frances, *née* Katz; *b* 29 April 1942; *Educ* Rutherford HS New Jersey USA, Allegheny Coll USA (BA), LSE (PhD); *m* 29 March 1975, Nancy Livia, da of Edwin Harold Newman, of NY; *Career* sr lectr in politics Univ of Edinburgh 1979–86 (lectr 1967–78); dir: Development Office Univ of Oxford 1987–93, Campaign for Oxford 1988–93; non-exec dir Corporate Culture 1993–94, exec dir Oxford Philanthropic 1994–; memb: Political Studies Assoc, Hansard Soc, Inst of Charity Fund-Raising Mangrs; author; *Books* Doctrine and Ethos in the Labour Party (George Allen and Unwin, 1979), The Political Uses of Ideology (Macmillan, 1974), Breakaway: The Scottish Labour Party (EUSPB, 1978), Multi-Party Britain (Macmillan, 1979), The Politics of Nationalism and Devolution (with Gordon Brown, MP, Longman, 1980), John P Mackintosh on Scotland (ed, Longman, 1982), The Scottish Government Year Book (ed, with N L Drucker, 1976–83), Developments in British Politics 1 (jt gen ed, Macmillan, 1983, revised edn 1984), Developments in British Politics 2 (jt gen ed, Macmillan, 1986); *Style*— Dr Henry Drucker; ✉ 36 Windmill Road, Headington, Oxford OX3 7BX (☎ 01865 744300, fax 01865 744600)

DRUMLANRIG, Viscount; Sholto Francis Guy Douglas; s and h of 12 Marquess of Queensberry; *b* 1 June 1967; *Style*— Viscount Drumlanrig

DRUMM, Rt Rev Mgr Walter Gregory; er s of Owen Drumm (d 1995), and Kathleen, *née* Garrett (d 1986); *b* 2 March 1940; *Educ* St Aloysius' Coll Highgate, Balliol Coll Oxford (MA), Beda Coll Rome; *Career* tutor 1962–66, ordained 1970, asst priest St Paul's Wood Green 1970–73, chaplain Univ of Oxford 1973–83, parish priest Our Lady of Victories Church Kensington 1983–87, rector Pontifical Beda Coll Rome 1987–91, prelate of honour to HH The Pope 1988; *Clubs* Oxford and Cambridge; *Style*— The Rt Rev Mgr Walter Drumm; ✉ Cathedral Clergy House, 42 Francis Street, London SW1P 1QW

DRUMMOND, Archibald Craig; s of Robert Dunlop Drummond (d 1981), and Margaret Cranston, *née* Craig (d 1996); *b* 12 Aug 1941; *Educ* Eastwood HS, Ross Hall Scottish Hotel Sch Glasgow (Dip Hotel Mgmnt, BA); *m* Kay Scott, da of William Hepburn (d 1961); 1 da (Lynn Diane b 17 Feb 1966), 1 s (Graeme Craig b 26 April 1967); *Career* trainee Grosvenor House London 1962–65, dep mangr Grosvenor House Hotel Sheffield 1965–68, mangr Dudley Hotel Hove Sussex 1968–72, mangr Atholl Palace Hotel Pitlochry Perthshire Feb 1972 - Sept 1972, mangr North Stafford Hotel Stoke on Trent 1972–74, gen mangr The Grand Hotel Manchester 1974–82, gen mangr Post House Hotel Manchester 1982–86, gen mangr RAC Country Club Epsom 1986–; dep chm Hotel and Catering Trades Ctee Manchester Chamber of Commerce 1984–86; memb: Syllabus Ctee City & Guilds 1980–93 (moderating examiner 1980–93), Professional Advsy Ctee Tameside Coll of Technol 1980–86, Ctee NW Region Hotel and Catering Trades Benevolent Assoc 1981–86, Professional Advsy Ctee E Surrey Coll of Technol 1993–96; regnl assessor Southern Region City & Guilds 1986–93 (London and SE 1987–93); memb: Epsom C of C, Rusper Residents' Assoc; Master Innholder 1979 (chm 1990–91), memb Acad Culinaire Française 1984, memb Clus Secs & Mangrs Assoc 1996; Freeman City of London 1979; FHCIMA 1976 (memb 1962); *Recreations* golf, gardening, foreign travel, wines; *Clubs* Royal Scottish Automobile, W Sussex Golf, Glasgow Southern RFC; *Style*— Archibald Drummond, Esq; ✉ 14 East Street, Rusper, Horsham, West Sussex RH12 4RB (☎ 01293 871566); RAC Country Club, Woodcote Park, Epsom, Surrey KT18 7EW (☎ 01372 276311, fax 01372 276117)

DRUMMOND, David James; s of James Drummond, of Edinburgh, and Audrey Joan, *née* Morrison; *b* 4 Aug 1956; *Educ* George Watson's Coll Edinburgh, Univ of Edinburgh (BMus), RNCM Manchester; *m* 1, 25 June 1983 (m dis 1988), Jane Caroline, da of Derek Tregilges, of Perranporth, Cornwall; m 2, 9 April 1994, Elizabeth Kate, da of Tom Hutchinson; *Career* staff conductor and chorus master Stora Teatern Gothenburg Sweden 1982–84 (conducted Katerina Ismailova, The Turn of the Screw, Don Giovanni, Spöket på Canterville, Lo Sposo Senza Moglie), asst chorus master Eng Nat Opera 1984–88 (conducted Die Fledermaus, The Mikado, The Magic Flute), chorus master Scottish Opera 1988–90 (conducted Street Scene); currently: freelance conductor Kharkov Phiharmonic Orch, London Mozart Players and Salomon Orch, dir of Music & Opera UCL, musical dir Lorndon Oriana Choir and Artesian Orch; researched and conducted world premiere version Cesar Franck's opera Hulda 1994; *Recreations* squash, golf, hill-walking, football, languages, travel; *Style—* David Drummond, Esq; ✉ 1 Archer Road, South Norwood, London SE25 4JN (☎ and fax 0181 656 8796)

DRUMMOND, Sir John Richard Gray; kt (1995), CBE (1990); s of late Capt A R G Drummond, and Esther, *née* Pickering; *b* 25 Nov 1934; *Educ* Canford, Trinity Coll Cambridge (MA); *Career* writer and bdcaster; RNVR 1953–55; BBC Radio and TV: joined 1958, asst head Music and Arts, controller of music 1985–91, controller Radio 3 1987–91, dir BBC Proms 1985–95; programmes produced incl: Tortelier Master Classes 1964, Leeds Piano Competition 1966 (first prize Prague Festival 1967), Diaghilev 1967, Kathleen Ferrier 1968, Music Now 1969, Spirit of the Age 1975, The Lively Arts 1976–78; dir Edinburgh Int Festival 1978–83, vice chm Br Arts Festivals Assoc 1981–83 (vice pres 1994–), dir European Arts Festival 1992, pres Kensington Soc 1985–, chm Nat Dance Co-ordinating Ctee 1986–95; govr Royal Ballet 1986–, memb Theatres Tst 1989–; FRSA, FRCM; *Books* A Fine and Private Place (with Joan Bakewell, 1977), The Turn of the Dance (with N Thompson, 1984); *Clubs* New (Edinburgh); *Style—* Sir John Drummond, CBE; ✉ 61c Campden Hill Court, London W8 7HL (☎ 0171 937 2257)

DRUMMOND, Maldwin Andrew Cyril; OBE (1990), JP (1963), DL (Hampshire 1976); s of Maj Cyril Augustus Drummond, JP, DL (d 1945), of Cadland House, and Mildred Joan, *née* Humphreys (d 1976); *b* 30 April 1932; *Educ* Eton, RAC Cirencester, Univ of Southampton; *m* 1, 1955 (m dis 1977), Susan, da of Sir Kenelm Cayley; 2 da (Frederica (Mrs Templer) b 1957, Annabella (Mrs Villers) b 1959); m 2, 1 Jan 1978, Gillian Vera (Gilly), da of Gavin Clark, of Fawley, Hampshire; 1 s (Aldred b 1978); *Career* Nat Serv The Rifle Bde 1950–52, Capt Queen Victoria's Rifles TA 1952–65; farmer and owner Manor of Cadland; dir: Rothesay Seafoods 1968–92, Ocean Sound Ltd 1985–91, Southampton Harbour Bd and Br Tports Docks Bd 1965–75, Southern Water Authy 1983–86; chm: Bldg Ctee STS Sir Winston Churchill 1964–66, Sail Trg Assoc 1967–72, Warrior (formerly Ships) Preservation Tst 1979–91, Maritime Tst 1980–89, Boat Ctee RNLI 1984–92, New Forest 9th Centenary Tst 1987–94, New Forest Ctee 1990–, Heritage Coast Forum 1988–; past pres Hampshire Field Club and Archaeological Soc, pres Shellfish Assoc of GB and NI 1987–; tstee: Mary Rose Tst 1976–91, Royal Naval Museum 1986–; memb Ctee of Mgmnt RNLI 1971–; memb: New Forest DC 1957–65, Hampshire CC 1965–75; verderer of the New Forest 1961–90, countryside cmmr 1980–86, High Sheriff of Hampshire 1980–81; Freeman City of London 1986, Prime Warden Worshipful Co of Fishmongers (memb Ct 1986); Hon DSc Univ of Bournemouth 1994; younger bro Trinity House 1991–; FRGS, FRSA; *Books* Conflicts in an Estuary (1973), Secrets of George Smith Fisherman (ed and illustrator, 1973), Tall Ships (1976), Salt-Water Palaces (1979), The Yachtsman's Naturalist (with Paul Rodhouse, 1980), The New Forest (with Philip Allison, 1980), The Riddle (1985), West Highland Shores (1990), John Bute, An Informal Portrait (ed, 1996); *Recreations* sailing; *Clubs* Royal Yacht Squadron (cdre 1991–96), Royal Cruising, White's, Pratt's, Leander; *Style—* Maldwin Drummond, Esq, OBE, JP, DL; ✉ Cadland House, Fawley, Southampton (☎ 01703 891543); Manor of Cadland, Cadland House, Fawley, Southampton SO45 1AA (☎ 01703 892039, fax 01703 243308); Wester Kames Castle, Isle of Bute PA20 0QW (☎ 01700 503983)

DRUMMOND, Prof Michael Frank; s of Kenneth John Drummond (d 1973), and Ethel Irene, *née* Spencer; *b* 30 April 1948; *Educ* Atherstone GS, Univ of Birmingham (BSc, MCom), Univ of York (DPhil); *m* 8 June 1973, Margaret, da of James Brennan, of Tamworth, Staffs, 1 s (Thomas b 1980), 1 da (Kate b 1987); *Career* Univ of Birmingham: lectr 1978–84, sr lectr 1984–86, prof of health services management 1986–90; Univ of York: prof of economics 1990–, dir Centre for Health Economics 1995–; memb: North Warwickshire Health Authy 1982–90, Med Comm 1988–91; *Books* Principles of Economic Appraisal in Health Care (1980), Studies in Economic Appraisal in Health Care (1981), Economic Appraisal of Health Technology in the European Community (1987), Methods for the Economic Evaluation of Health Care Programmes (1987); *Recreations* running, travel; *Style—* Prof Michael Drummond; ✉ Centre for Health Economics, University of York, Heslington, York YO1 5DD (☎ 01904 433709, fax 01904 433644, e-mail chedir@york.ac.uk)

DRUMMOND, Rev Norman Walker; s of Edwin Payne Drummond (d 1971), of Greenock, and Jean Drummond, *née* Walker (d 1992); *b* 1 April 1952; *Educ* Merchiston Castle Edinburgh, Fitzwilliam Coll Cambridge (MA), New Coll Edinburgh (BD); *m* 1976, Lady Elizabeth Helen Kennedy, da of 7 Marquess of Ailsa; 3 s (Andrew b 1977, Christian b 1986, Ruaraidh b 1993), 2 da (Margaret b 1980, Marie Clare b 1981); *Career* ordained as minister of the Church of Scot, cmmnd to serv as Chaplain to HM Servs Army 1976; chaplain: Depot Parachute Regt and Airborne Forces 1977–78, 1 Bn The Black Watch (Royal Highland Regt) 1978–82, Fettes Coll 1982–84, to Moderator of Gen Assembly of Church of Scot 1980; headmaster Loretto Sch 1984–95, min of Kilmuir and Stenscholl Isle of Skye 1996–; chaplain to HM The Queen in Scotland, memb Queen's Body Guard for Scotland (Royal Co of Archers); BBC nat govr and chm Bdcasting Cncl for Scot, chm Ronald Selby Wright Christian Leadership Tst; pres: Edinburgh Battalion The Boys' Brigade, Victoria League for Overseas Students in Scot; govr Gordonstoun Sch; *Books* The First 25 Years - the Official History of the Kirk Session of The Black Watch (Royal Highland Regiment), Mother's Hands; *Recreations* rugby football, cricket, golf, curling, traditional jazz; *Clubs* MCC, Free Foresters, New (Edinburgh), Hawks' (Cambridge); *Style—* The Rev Norman Drummond; ✉ The Manse, Staffin, Isle of Skye IV51 9JE

DRUMMOND-MORAY OF ABERCAIRNY, William George Stirling Home; Laird of Abercairny; 2 (but eldest surviving) s of Maj James Drummond-Moray, twenty-first of Abercairny, and of Ardoch, Perthshire, JP, DL, by his w Jeanetta (twin da of Lt-Col Lord George Scott, OBE, JP, DL, 3 s of 6 Duke of Buccleuch & (8 of) Queensberry); *b* 22 Aug 1940; *Educ* Eton, RAC Cirencester; *m* 1, 7 Jan 1969 (m dis 1991), (Angela) Jane, da of Lt Cdr Michael Baring, RN (d 1954); 3 da (Anna b 1971, Frances b 1974, Georgina b 1979); m 2, 1991, Emma Moyra Rattray, er da of Capt James Rattray of Rattray; 1 da (Caroline b 1992); *Career* estate mangr; *Recreations* shooting, polo; *Style—* William Drummond-Moray of Abercairny; ✉ Abercairny, Crieff, Perthshire (☎ 01764 653114)

DRUMMOND-MURRAY OF MASTRICK, (William Edward) Peter Louis; s of Edward John Drummond-Murray of Mastrick (d 1976), and Eulalia Ildefonsa Wilhelmina Heaven (d 1988); *b* 24 Nov 1929; *Educ* Beaumont Coll; *m* 12 June 1954, Hon Barbara Mary Hope, 4 and yst da of 2 Baron Rankeillour, GCIE, MC (d 1958); 4 s, 1 da; *Career* dir Utd and Gen Tst and other cos; stockbroker; chief exec Hosp of St John and St Elizabeth London 1978–82; Slains Pursuivant of Arms to the Lord High Constable of Scotland the Earl of Erroll 1981–; Kt of Honour and Devotion SMOM 1971, Grand Cross of Obedience 1984, Chllr Br Assoc SMOM 1977–89, Delegate of Scotland and the Northern Marches 1989–; pres Murray Clan Soc; CStJ 1977, KStJ 1988; *Recreations* archaeology, genealogy, heraldry, baking, brewing, bookbinding, bookplate collecting; *Clubs* New (Edinburgh), Puffin's (Edinburgh); *Style—* Peter Drummond-Murray of Mastrick, Slains Pursuivant of Arms; ✉ 67 Dublin St, Edinburgh, EH3 6NS (☎ 0131 556 2913)

DRUMMOND OF MEGGINCH, Capt Humphrey; MC (1945); formerly Humphrey ap Evans, changed name by decree of Court of Lord Lyon 1966; s of Maj James John Pugh Evans, MBE, MC (d 1974), of Lovesgrove, Aberystwyth; *b* 18 Sept 1922; *Educ* Eton, Trinity Coll Cambridge; *m* 2 June 1952, Cherry Drummond, Lady Strange (16th holder of the peerage), *qv*; 3 s, 3 da; *Career* served 1942–45 with 1 Mountain Regt; Indian Political Serv 1947; gen sec Cncl for Preservation of Rural Wales 1947–51, Welsh rep of Nat Tst 1949–54; Gold Staff Offr coronation of HM Queen Elizabeth II; author and magazine contributor; fndr Kilspindie Basset Hounds; chm Soc of Authors (Scot) 1975–81; proprietor: The Historical Press, Scottish Salmon Fisheries; Freeman City of London; *Books* Our Man in Scotland, The Queen's Man, The King's Enemy, Falconry, Falconry For You, Falconry in the East, Nazi Gold, Balkan Assault (ed); *Recreations* Pre-Raphaelitism, mechanical musical instruments; *Clubs* Garrick; *Style—* Capt Humphrey Drummond of Megginch, MC; ✉ Tresco, 160 Kennington Road, London SE11 (☎ 0171 735 3681); Megginch Castle, Errol, Perthshire PH2 7SW (☎ 01821 642222, fax 01821 642708)

DRUMMOND YOUNG, James Edward; QC (Scot 1988); s of Duncan Drummond Young, MBE, DL, of Edinburgh, and Annette, *née* Mackay; *b* 17 Feb 1950; *Educ* John Watson's Sch Edinburgh, Sidney Sussex Coll Cambridge (BA), Harvard Law Sch (Joseph Hodges Choate Meml fell, LLM), Univ of Edinburgh (LLB); *m* 1991, Elizabeth Mary, da of John Campbell-Kease, of Connel, Argyll; *Career* admitted to Faculty of Advocates 1976, standing jr counsel Bd of Inland Revenue 1986–88; *Books* The Law of Corporate Insolvency in Scotland (with J B St Clair, 2 edn 1992), Stair Memorial Encyclopaedia of the Laws of Scotland (contrib, 1989); *Recreations* music, travel; *Clubs* New (Edinburgh); *Style—* James Drummond Young, Esq, QC; ✉ 14 Ainslie Place, Edinburgh EH3 6AS (☎ and fax 0131 225 6393); Advocates' Library, Parliament House, Edinburgh EH1 1RF (☎ 0131 226 5071, fax 0131 225 3642, telex 727856 FACADV 6)

DRURY, David Robert; s of Albert Drury (d 1970), of Leeds, and Anne, *née* Crewe (d 1970); *Educ* Temple Moor GS Leeds, Leeds Coll of Art (BA); *m* 1, 1970 (m dis), Pamela Mary, da of George Ratcliffe; 1 s (Benjamin b 4 Sept 1975), 1 da (Rebecca b 8 Jan 1977); m 2, 1984 (m dis), Janet Elizabeth, da of Reginald Carter; 1 s (Samuel b 23 Sept 1984); 2 da by Judith Anne Hayes (Bethan b 29 July 1991, Rhiannon b 8 Dec 1993); *Career* film and television director and producer; dir: Forever Young (Enigma/Goldcrest) 1984, Intrigue (Columbia TV) 1988, Children of the North (BBC) 1990 (winner RTS Award for best series), The Secret Agent (BBC) 1992, Bad Company (BBC Birmingham) 1993 (winner Samuelson Int Film and TV Award for best series), Prime Suspect III (Granada) 1993 (winner BAFTA Award for best drama series, American Critics Award and Banff TV Festival Award for best series, Emmy for best mini-series), Shannongate (Burlington Films) 1994, Rhodes (Zenith Prodns) 1995; prodr: City 1981; prodr/dir: Minter (winner New York Film Festival Award for best documentary, 1981), Citizen Bull 1982, Home and Away (Granada TV) 1984; film dir: Defence of the Realm (Enigma) 1986 (selected for dirs' fortnight Cannes Film Festival, winner Rimini Film Festival Award for best dir, Madrid Film Festival Award best film), Terra Roxa (Film Effekt) 1986, Split Decisions (New Century) 1988; *Recreations* my children, my boat, painting, writing; *Clubs* Groucho; *Style—* David Drury, Esq; ✉ c/o ICM Ltd, Oxford House, 76 Oxford Street, London W1N 0AX (☎ 0171 636 6565, fax 0171 323 0101)

DRURY, Very Rev John Henry; s of Henry Drury, and Barbara Drury; *b* 23 May 1936; *Educ* Bradfield, Trinity Hall Cambridge (MA), Westcott House Cambridge; *m* 1972, (Frances) Clare, da of Rev Prof Dennis Eric Nineham, of Oxford; 2 da; *Career* curate St John's Wood London 1963, chaplain Downing Coll Cambridge 1966, chaplain and fell Exeter Coll Oxford 1969, resident canon Norwich Cathedral and examining chaplain to Bishop of Norwich 1973, vice dean Norwich 1978, lectr in religious studies Univ of Sussex 1979–82, dean of chapel King's Coll Cambridge 1982–91, dean of Christ Church Oxford 1991–; Liveryman Worshipful Co of Dyers; *Books* Tradition and Design in Luke's Gospel (1976), The Parables in the Gospels (1985), Critics of the Bible (1989), The Burning Bush (1990); *Recreations* music, drawing; *Style—* The Very Rev the Dean of Christ Church; ✉ The Deanery, Christ Church, Oxford OX1 1DP (☎ 01865 276161)

DRURY, John Kenneth; s of John Kenneth Drury, of Paisley and Elizabeth Laird McNeil, *née* Pattison; *b* 23 Jan 1947; *Educ* Paisley GS, Univ of Glasgow (MB ChB, PhD); *m* 16 July 1974, Gillian Ruth Alexandra, da of Dr Thomas Gilmore, of Paisley; 1 s (Colin b 1981), 1 da (Sarah b 1978); *Career* res fell Inst of Physiology Univ of Glasgow, conslt gen surgn with interest in peripheral vascular surgery and clinical dir of gen surgery Victoria Infirmary NHS Tst Glasgow 1987–, hon clinical sr lectr Univ of Glasgow 1987– (memb Faculty of Med 1992–95, memb Univ Senate 1993–), examiner in fellowship RCS Glasgow, author of papers on gen and vascular surgery; memb: Ctee Paisley RNLI, Cncl Southern Med Soc; FRCS 1978; memb: Vascular Soc GB 1987, European Soc of Vascular Surgery; *Recreations* yachting, squash, golf, skiing; *Style—* John Drury, Esq; ✉ 10 Main Road, Castlehead, Paisley, Renfrewshire PA2 6AJ (☎ 0141 8894512); Department of Surgery, Victoria Infirmary, Langside, Glasgow G42 9TY (☎ 0141 649 4545)

DRURY, Jolyon Victor Paul; s of Alfred Paul Dalou Drury (d 1987), and Enid Marie, *née* Solomon (d 1996); *b* 19 Nov 1946; *Educ* Tonbridge Sch, Pembroke Coll Cambridge (exhibitioner, DipArch, MA); *m* 25 April 1975, Christine Evelyn Cary, da of Dr John Gilson, CBE; 2 s (Adrian John Jolyon b 24 Nov 1977, Charles Worthington Paul b 26 May 1981); *Career* Arup Associates 1971–75, fndr Jolyon Drury Consultancy 1975; memb Cncl Inst of Materials Management 1988–93; RIBA 1972, FIMH 1984, FILog 1993 (memb Cncl); *Publications* Building and Planning for Industrial Storage and Distribution (with Peter Falconer, 1975), Factories, Planning, Design and Modernisation (1981), Automated Warehouses (1988); *Recreations* small holding, France, etchings; *Clubs* Arts; *Style—* Jolyon Drury, Esq; ✉ Jolyon Drury Consultancy Ltd, Regent House, 190A Three Bridges Road, Crawley RH10 1LN (☎ 01293 510515, fax 01293 541525)

DRURY, Martin Dru; s of Walter Neville Dru Drury, TD, of Edenbridge, Kent, and Rae, *née* Sandiland; *b* 22 April 1938; *Educ* Rugby; *m* 5 Jan 1971, Elizabeth Caroline, da of the Hon Sir Maurice Bridgeman, KBE (d 1980), of Selham, Sussex; 2 s (Matthew b 8 Aug 1972, Joseph b 18 June 1977), 1 da (Daisy b 6 Sept 1974); *Career* broker at Lloyd's 1959–65, assoc dir Mallett & Son (Antiques) Ltd 1970–73 (dir 1965–70); The National Trust: historic bldgs rep and advsr on furniture 1973–81, historic bldgs sec 1981–95, dep DG 1992–95, DG 1996–; chm Landmark Tst 1992–95, dir Arundel Castle Tst Ltd 1987–95; vice chm Attingham Summer Sch, memb Exec Ctee The Georgian Gp 1976–94; memb Ct Worshipful Co of Goldsmiths; FSA; *Clubs* Brooks's, Pratt's; *Style—* Martin Drury, Esq, FSA; ✉ The National Trust, 36 Queen Anne's Gate, London SW1 (☎ 0171 222 9251, telex 8950997 NTRUST G)

DRURY, Prof Sir (Victor William) Michael; kt (1989), OBE (1978); s of George Leslie Drury (d 1936), of Bromsgrove, and Trixie, *née* Maddox; *b* 5 Aug 1926; *Educ* Bromsgrove Sch, Univ of Birmingham (MB ChB, MRCS, LRCP); *m* 7 Oct 1950, Joan, da of Joseph Williamson, of Winsford, Cheshire; 3 s (Mark b 9 May 1952, Simon b 17 March 1958, James b 27 July 1960), 1 da (Linda b 19 July 1954); *Career* Capt (surgical specialist) RAMC 1951–53, civilian conslt to Army 1985–91; travelling fell Nuffield 1965, GP Bromsgrove 1953–91, emeritus prof of gen practice Univ of Birmingham 1991; visiting prof Canterbury NZ 1984, Jeffcote professorship Westminster and Charing Cross 1989–92; memb: GMC 1984–94, SCOPME 1989–95; pres RCGP, chm Age Concern Eng 1992–95 (vice-pres 1995), chm Centre for Advancement of Interprofessional Educn 1994–; govr Bromsgrove Sch 1990–; FRCGP 1970, FRCP 1988, FRACGP 1988, FCPCH 1989; *Books* Introduction to General Practice (1979), Treatment A Handbook of Drug Therapy (46 instalments 1978–92), Treatment & Prognosis (1989), The Receptionist (3 edn, 1995), Medical Secretary's Handbook (6 edn, 1992), The New Practice Manager (3 edn, 1994); *Recreations* gardening, bridge, talking; *Style—* Prof Sir Michael Drury, OBE; ✉ Rossall Cottage, Church Hill, Belbroughton, nr Stourbridge, W Mids DY9 0DT (☎ and fax 01562 730229)

DRURY, Stephen Patrick; s of Patrick Keith Drury (d 1992), and Anne Rosemary, *née* Major-Lucas; *b* 20 May 1954; *Educ* Charterhouse, Oriel Coll Oxford (MA); *m* 25 June 1983, Deborah Ann, da of late Wilfred McBrien Swain, OBE; 2 s (Patrick b 1984, Benjamin b 1993), 1 da (Frances b 1987); *Career* called to the Bar 1977, admitted slr 1980, admitted slr Hong Kong 1984, ptnr Holman Fenwick & Willan 1985– (joined 1978); visiting lectr in ship fin law Business Sch City Univ 1990–; memb Cncl: Amateur Rowing Assoc 1980–84, Hong Kong Amateur Rowing Assoc 1984–87; Freeman City of London, Liveryman Worshipful Co of Merchant Taylors 1988; *Books* Arrest of Ships (vol 6, 1987); *Recreations* rowing, golf; *Clubs* Kingston Rowing, Royal Hong Kong Yacht, Effingham Golf, Lansdowne; *Style*— Stephen Drury, Esq; ✉ Holman Fenwick & Willan, Marlow Hse, Lloyds Ave, London EC3N 3AL (☎ 0171 488 2300, fax 0171 481 0584, telex 8812247)

DRYBURGH, Dr Frances Joan; da of Thomas Stewart Neilson (d 1980), of Largs, Scotland, and Alice Smith, *née* Nicol; *b* 16 Nov 1938; *Educ* Stirling HS, Univ of Glasgow (BSc, MB ChB); *m* 2 July 1965, Eric Campbell Dryburgh, s of James Dryburgh (d 1987); 2 s (Keith b 1967 d 1983, Gordon b 1969); *Career* conslt clinical biochemist Glasgow Royal Infirmary 1981– (sr registrar 1973–80); former pres Scot Western Assoc Med Women's Fedn, memb Soroptimist Int GB and Ireland, memb Nat Assoc of Clinical Biochemists (Mastership in Clinical Biochemistry 1981); FRCP (Glasgow) 1990, FRCPath 1993; *Style*— Dr Frances Dryburgh; ✉ 19 Quadrant Rd, Newlands, Glasgow G43 2QP (☎ 0141 637 3509); Department of Pathological Biochemistry, Royal Infirmary, Castle St, Glasgow (☎ 0141 211 4630, fax 0141 553 1703, telex 779234 HLAGLA)

DRYDEN, Sir John Stephen Gyles; 11 Bt (GB 1733), of Ambrosden, Oxfordshire; and 8 Bt (GB 1795), of Canons-Ashby, Northamptonshire; s of Sir Noel Percy Hugh Dryden, 10 Bt (d 1970; 6 in descent from Sir Erasmus Dryden, 6 Bt, bro of the poet John Dryden), and Rosamund Mary, *née* Scrope (d 1994); *b* 26 Sept 1943; *Educ* The Oratory Sch; *m* 1970, Diana Constance, da of Cyril Tomlinson, of Highland Park, Wellington, NZ; 1 s (John Frederick Simon b 1976), 1 da (Caroline Diana Rosamund b 1980); *Heir* s, John Frederick Simon Dryden b 26 May 1976; *Style*— Sir John Dryden, Bt; ✉ Spinners, Fairwarp, Uckfield, Sussex

DRYSDALE, Thomas Henry; s of Ian Drysdale, and Rosalind Marion, *née* Gallie; *b* 23 Nov 1942; *Educ* Cargilfield, Glenalmond, Univ of Edinburgh (LLB); *m* 1967, Caroline, da of Dr Gavin Shaw; 1 s, 2 da; *Career* solicitor; ptnr Shepherd & Wedderburn WS 1967– (managing ptnr 1988–94); dep keeper HM Signet 1991–; chm: John Watson's Trust, Educnl Advsy Ctee The Clark Fndn for Legal Educn; memb Exec Ctee Scottish Cncl of Law Reporting; dir Edinburgh Slrs' Property Centre 1976–89 (chm 1981–88); *Recreations* skiing, walking, reading; *Clubs* New (Edinburgh), Scottish Ski; *Style*— T H Drysdale, Esq, WS; ✉ Shepherd & Wedderburn WS, Saltire Court, 20 Castle Terrace, Edinburgh EH1 2ET (☎ 0131 228 9900)

DU CANN, Charlotte Jane Lott; da of Richard Dillon Lott du Cann, QC (d 1994), and Charlotte Mary, *née* Sawtell; *b* 20 June 1956; *Educ* Felixstowe Coll, Birmingham Univ (BA); *Career* shopping ed Vogue 1979–81; freelance writer 1981–: The Observer, Sunday Express mag, Time Out, Harpers & Queen; features writer The World of Interiors 1984, style ed The Magazine 1984–85, shopping and beauty ed Tatler 1986–87, contributing ed Elle 1987–88, fashion ed Independent 1988–90; currently writing for: Elle, Sunday Times, The Guardian, New Statesman and Society; *Books* Offal and The New Brutalism (1984), Vogue Modern Style (1988); *Recreations* poetry and cooking; *Style*— Ms Charlotte du Cann

DU CANN, Col the Rt Hon Sir Edward Dillon Lott; KBE (1985), PC (1964); er s of Charles Garfield Lott du Cann, barr-at-law (d 1983); *b* 28 May 1924; *Educ* Colet Court, Woodbridge Sch, St John's Coll Oxford (MA); *m* 1, 1962 (m dis 1990), Sallie Innes, da of James Henry Murchie (d 1967), of Ainways, Caldy, Cheshire; 1 s, 2 da; m 2, 1990, Jenifer Patricia Evelyn (d 1995), wid of Sir Robin Cooke, and da of Evelyn King, MP (d 1995), of Embley Manor, Romsey, Hants; *Career* served RNVR 1939–45, latterly i/c HMMTB 5010; Parly candidate (C): W Walthamstow 1951, Barrow in Furness 1955; MP (C) Taunton Div of Somerset Feb 1956–87, economic sec to the Treasy 1962–63, min of state BOT 1963–64; chm Select Ctees on: Public Expenditure 1971–73, Public Accounts 1974–79, Treasy and Civil Serv Affrs (fndr chm) 1979–83; memb Select Ctees on: House of Lords Reform 1962, Privileges 1974–87; chm: Cons Pty Orgn 1956–67, 1922 Ctee 1972–84, Liaison Ctee of Select Ctee Chairmen (fndr chm) 1974–83, All Pty Maritime Affrs Gp (fndr chm) 1984–87, Public Accounts Cmmn (fndr chm) 1984–87; pres: Anglo-Polish Cons Soc 1972–74, Nat Union Cons Unionist Assocs 1981–82; memb Lord Chllr's Advsy Ctee on Public Records 1961–62, vice chm Br-American Parly Gp 1978–81, pres Cons Parly EC Reform Gp 1985–87; jt sec: UN Parly Gp 1961–62, Cons Parly Fin Gp 1961–62; led Br Parly Delgns to USA 1980 and 1982 and China 1982; fndr Unicorn Group Unit Trusts 1957; chm: Unicorn Group 1957–62 and 1964–72, Association of Unit Trust Managers 1961, Keyser Ullmann 1972–75, Cannon Assurance 1972–80, Lonrho plc 1984–91 (dir 1972–91); dir Bow Group Publications 1979–84; vice pres Br Insur Brokers 1978–, pres Inst of Freight Forwarders 1988–89, govr Hatfield Coll Univ of Durham 1988–92; dep chm Family Planning Int Ctee, vice chm Wider Share Ownership Ctee 1970–; chm Burke Club 1968–79; visiting fell Univ of Lancaster Business Sch 1970–82; Hon Col 155 Wessex Regt RCT (Vols) 1972–82 (retains hon rank of Col), hon life memb Inst of RCT 1983; Master Worshipful Co of Fruiterers 1990 (Upper Warden 1989, Renter Warden 1988), first Freeman Taunton Deane Borough 1977; *Books* incl: Investing Simplified (1959), The Case for a Bill of Rights, How to Bring Public Expenditure Under Parliamentary Control, Time to Hoist the Red Ensign, Two Lives (1995), The Wellington Caricatures (1996), A New Competition Policy; *Clubs* Carlton, Pratt's, House of Commons Yacht (Cdre 1962, Adm 1974), Royal Western Yacht Club of England Co; *Style*— Col the Rt Hon Sir Edward du Cann, KBE; ✉ 6 Old Pye House, 15–17 St Ann's Street, London SW1P 2DE

du CROS, Sir Claude Philip Arthur Mallet; 3 Bt (UK 1916), of Canons, Middlesex; s of Capt Sir Philip Harvey du Cros, 2 Bt (d 1975), and Matilde Dita, *née* Mallet (d 1993); *b* 22 Dec 1922; *m* 1, 1953 (m dis 1974), Christine Nancy (d 1988), da of F E Bennett, of Spilsby, Lincs, and former w of George Tordoff; 1 s (Julian Claude Arthur Mallet b 1955); m 2, 1974 (m dis 1982), Margaret Roy, da of late Roland James Frater, of Gosforth, Northumberland; *Heir* s, Julian Claude Arthur Mallet du Cros b 23 April 1955; *Career* farmer; *Style*— Sir Claude du Cros, Bt; ✉ Longmeadow, Ballaugh Glen, Ramsey, Isle of Man

du CROS, Julian Claude Arthur Mallet; s and h of Sir Claude Philip Arthur Mallet du Cros, 3 Bt, *qv*; *b* 23 April 1955; *Educ* Eton; *m* 1984, Patricia M, o da of Gerald A Wyatt, of Littlefield School, Liphook, Hants; 1 s (Alexander Julian Mallet b 25 Aug 1990), 1 da (Henrietta Mary b 1988); *Style*— Julian du Cros Esq

DU-FEU, Vivian John; *Educ* Univ of Cardiff; *Career* admitted slr 1979, early career in Employment Law, joined Eversheds Phillips & Buck (now Eversheds) 1983, currently chm Eversheds Employment Law Gp; pt/t lectr in labour law Univ of Cardiff 1983–87 (pt/t tutor 1981–83), currently pt/t lectr in labour law (LLM degree course) Univ of Cardiff; dir Principle Training Ltd; memb Croner Editorial Advsy Bd; FIPM; *Books* The Conduct of Proceedings Before Industrial Tribunals, Protecting Your Business and Confidential Information (Croner, co-author 1992), Collective Labour Law (Croner, co-author 1992), Procedure in Industrial Tribunal Cases (Croner, co-author 1992), Flexible Working Practices (Croner, contrib 1996), Employment Law in the NHS (Cavandish, co-author 1996); *Style*— Vivian Du-Feu, Esq; ✉ Eversheds, Fitzalan House, Fitzalan Road, Cardiff CF2 1XZ (☎ 01222 471147, fax 01222 464347, DX 33016 Cardiff)

Du NOYER, Paul Anthony; s of Anthony George Du Noyer, of Liverpool, and Jean, *née* Moran; *b* 21 May 1954; *Educ* Bootle Salesian Coll, Wigan Tech Coll, LSE (BScEcon); *m* 25 June 1977, Una Mary O'Farrell, da of Edward Farrell; 2 s (Edward Paul b 22 Feb 1984, Daniel Paul b 25 June 1992); *Career* freelance journalist 1978–80, asst ed New Musical Express 1983–85 (staff writer 1980–83), ed Q magazine 1990–92 (asst ed 1986–90), ed Mojo magazine 1993–95; *Style*— Paul Du Noyer, Esq; ✉ c/o Mojo magazine, 4 Winsley Street, London W1N 7AR (☎ 0171 436 1515, fax 0171 323 0276)

du PLESSIS, Jan Petrus; *b* 22 Jan 1954; *Career* with International Div Rembrandt Group Ltd 1981–88, fin dir Compagnie Financière Richemont AG Switzerland (ultimate parent co of Rothmans International) 1988–, dir Richemont International Ltd 1990–; *Style*— Jan du Plessis, Esq; ✉ Richemont International Ltd, Chalfont House, Oxford Road, Denham, Uxbridge, Middlesex UB9 4DU (☎ 01895 837356)

du PRÉ, Ian Alastair; s of Gareth Kirkham du Pré (d 1996), of Jersey, CI, and (Elizabeth) Sheila Mary, *née* Dodd (d 1996); *b* 30 Oct 1945; *Educ* Sherborne; *m* 5 Dec 1981, Sabine, da of Guy de Brabandère (d 1961); 1 da (Pascale b 5 March 1983); *Career* articled clerk Ernst & Young 1964–69, accountant Lippincott & Margulies 1969–70, dir Douglas Llambias Associates 1970–77, ptnr Coopers & Lybrand 1977–; FCA; *Recreations* cricket, works of Anthony Trollope; *Clubs* MCC; *Style*— Ian du Pré, Esq; ✉ Coopers & Lybrand, Embankment Place, London WC2N 6NN (☎ 0171 583 5000, fax 0171 822 4652, telex 887470)

du VIVIER, Dr Anthony Wilfred Paul; s of Maj Paul Edward du Vivier (d 1967), and Joan Beryl, *née* Swann; *b* 16 June 1944; *Educ* Ampleforth, Bart's Med Sch (MD), FRCP; *m* 13 Aug 1977, Judith Vivienne, da of late Cdr Reginald Sidney Brett, RN; *Career* conslt dermatologist King's Coll Hosp London 1978–; *Clubs* RSM; *Style*— Dr Anthony du Vivier; ✉ Department of Dermatology, King's College Hospital, London SE5 9RS (☎ 0171 346 3258/3579); 115a Harley Street, London W1N 1DG (☎ 0171 935 6465, fax 0171 935 5014)

DUBBINS, Dr Paul Arthur; s of Reginald Walter Dubbins, and Ruth, *née* Hurrell (d 1970); *b* 28 Sept 1949; *Educ* Thorpe GS, King's Coll London (BSc), King's Coll Hosp London (MB BS); *m* 23 Sept 1972, Margaret, da of Leslie Spink (d 1989); 1 s (Jacob b 1977), 1 da (Natalie b 1979); *Career* house offr posts London and Farnham 1973–74, SHO in med Frimley Park Hosp 1975, sr registrar in diagnostic radiology King's Coll Hosp 1978–79 (registrar 1975–78), asst prof Thomas Jefferson Univ Hosp Philadelphia 1979–81, conslt radiologist Plymouth Hosps Tst (formerly Plymouth Gen Hosp) 1981–; sr lectr Univ of Plymouth, external examiner South Bank Univ; eighth Barry B Goldberg lectr 1990; postgraduate regional educn advsr RCR 1993–; memb Cncl: Br Med Ultrasound Soc 1991–95 (hon treas 1995–), RCR 1994–; FRCR 1978; *Books* Urogenital Ultrasound - a Text Atlas (1994), Ultrasound in Gastroenterology (1994); area ed Jl of Clinical Ultrasound 1991–95, Euro ed Ultrasound Int 1994–; *Recreations* travel, reading, music; *Clubs* Plymouth Medical Wine Tasting; *Style*— Dr Paul Dubbins; ✉ Department of Medical Imaging (X-Ray West), Derriford Hospital, Derriford Road, Plymouth, Devon PL6 8DH (☎ 01752 763265, fax 01752 792853)

DUBLIN, Archbishop of, Bishop of Glendalough, and Primate of Ireland and Metropolitan 1996–; Most Rev Walton Newcombe Francis Empey; s of Francis Fullerton Empey (d 1957), of The Rectory, Enniscorthy, Co Wexford, and Mildred May, *née* Cox; *Educ* Pertora Royal Sch Enniskillen Co Fermanagh, Trinity Coll Dublin (BA, BD); *m* Louise Eleanora, da of John Hall; 3 s (Patrick b 3 May 1961, Karl b 9 June 1963, Kevin b 7 Dec 1966), 1 da (Sheila b 7 Nov 1972); *Career* curate asst Glenageary Dublin 1958–60, bishop's curate Grand Falls NB Canada 1960–63; rector: Madawaska Parish NB Canada 1963–66, Stradbally Co Laois 1966–71; dean of St Mary's Cathedral Limerick 1971–81, bishop of Limerick and Killaloe 1981–85, bishop of Meath and Kildare 1985–96; hon citizen Repub of Madawaska; *Recreations* reading, fishing, walking, watching rugby; *Style*— The Most Rev the Archbishop of Dublin; ✉ The See House, 17 Temple Road, Milltown, Dublin 6, Ireland (☎ 00 353 1 4977849, fax 00 353 1 4976355)

DUBOWITZ, Prof Victor; s of Charley Dubowitz, and Olga, *née* Schattel; *b* 6 Aug 1931; *Educ* Beaufort W Central HS S Africa, Univ of Cape Town (BSc, MB ChB, MD), Univ of Sheffield (PhD); *m* 10 July 1960, Lilly Magdalena Suzanne, *née* Sebok; 4 s (David b 1963, Michael b 1964, Gerald b 1965, Daniel b 1969); *Career* res assoc histochemistry Royal Postgrad Med Sch 1958–60, clinical asst Queen Mary's Hosp for Children Carshalton 1958–60, lectr clinical pathology Nat Hosp for Nervous Diseases 1960–61, lectr child health Univ of Sheffield 1961–65 (sr lectr 1965–67), reader child health and developmental neurology Univ of Sheffield 1967–72, prof of paediatrics Univ of London 1972–, hon consIt paediatrician Hammersmith Hosp 1972–, dir Muscle Res Centre 1972–; FRCP 1972; Cdr Order Constantine the Great 1980, Arvo Ylppo Gold Medal Finland 1982; *Books* Developing and Diseased Muscle A Histochemical Study (1968), The Floppy Infant (2nd edn, 1980), Muscle Biopsy - A Modern Approach (2nd edn, 1985), Gestational Age of the Newborn - A Clinical Manual (1977), Muscle Disorders in Childhood (2nd edn, 1995), Neurological Assessment of the Preterm and Full-term Infant (1981), A Colour Atlas of Muscle Disorders in Childhood (1989), A Colour Atlas of Brain Disorders in the Newborn (1990); *Recreations* sculpting, hiking; *Style*— Prof Victor Dubowitz; ✉ Department of Paediatrics, Royal Postgraduate Medical School, Ducane Rd, London W12 (☎ 0181 740 3295, fax 0181 740 8281)

DUCAT-AMOS, Air Cmdt Barbara Mary; CB (1974), RRC (1971); da of Capt George William Ducat-Amos (d 1942), master mariner, and Mary, *née* Cuthbert (d 1974); *b* 9 Feb 1921; *Educ* The Abbey Sch Reading, Nightingale Training Sch, St Thomas's; *Career* trained SRN and CMB (pt 1) St Thomas's Hosp, dep matron RAF Hosp Nocton Hall 1967–68, sr matron RAF Hosp Changi Singapore 1968–70, princ matron MOD (RAF) 1970–72, matron-in-chief Princess Mary's RAF Nursing Serv and dir RAF Nursing Servs 1972–78, Queen's Hon Nursing Sister 1972–78, nursing offr (sister) Cable and Wireless plc 1978–85; nat chm Girls' Venture Corps Air Cadets 1982–91 (vice pres 1991–); Cdr (Sister) Order of St John of Jerusalem 1975; *Recreations* music, theatre, travel; *Clubs* RAF; *Style*— Air Cmdt Barbara Ducat-Amos, CB, RRC; ✉ c/o Barclays Bank, Wimbledon Village Branch, Wimbledon Group, PO Box 850, 37 Wimbledon Hill Road, London SW19 7LA

DUCHESNE, Brig (Peter) Robin; OBE (1978); s of Herbert Walter Duchesne (d 1978), of Mochdre, Clwyd, and Irene, *née* Cox (d 1979); *b* 25 Sept 1936; *Educ* Colwyn Bay GS, RMA Sandhurst, RMC of Sci, Royal Navy Staff Coll; *m* 30 March 1968, Jennifer MacLean, da of Brian Elphinstone Gouldsbury, of Piddlehinton, Dorset; 1 s (Charles b 7 April 1974), 1 da (Emma b 1 Oct 1977); *Career* cmmnd RA 1956, 101 Airborne Div USA 1963–64, Capt instr RMA Sandhurst 1965–67, CO 49 Field Regt RA 1975–77, Dir Staff Army Staff Coll Camberley 1977–79, Cdr Mil Advsy Team Ghana 1979–81, Cdr Arty 1 Armd Div Brig 1981–83, D/Cdr and COS UN Force Cyprus 1984–86; memb UN Assoc, chm ISTA 1996–, memb STA Cncl, sec gen RYA 1986–, skipper jt serv entry Whitbread Round the World Race 1978; memb Nat Olympic Ctee; chm Marine Conservaton Soc; FIMgt 1987; *Recreations* sailing, walking, most sports; *Clubs* RORC; *Style*— Brig Robin Duchesne, OBE; ✉ Lake Lodge, Farnham, Surrey GU10 2QB (☎ 01252 793901); Royal Yachting Association, RYA House, Romsey Rd, Eastleigh, Hants SO50 4YA (☎ 01703 629962, fax 01703 629924, e-mail admin@rya.org.uk)

DUCIE, 7 Earl of (UK 1837); David Leslie Moreton; also Baron Ducie (GB 1763) and Baron Moreton (UK 1837); s of 6 Earl of Ducie (d 1991), and Alison May, *née* Bates; *b* 20 Sept 1951; *Educ* Cheltenham, Wye Coll London (B Sc Agric); *m* 1975, Helen, da of M L Duchesne, of Brussels; 1 s (James Berkeley, Lord Moreton b 1981), 1 da (Lady Claire Alison b 1984); *Heir* s, James Berkeley, Lord Moreton b 6 May 1981; *Style*— The Rt Hon the Earl of Ducie; ✉ Talbots End Farm, Cromhall, Glos

DUCKWORTH, His Hon Judge; Brian Roy; DL (Lancs); s of Eric Roy Duckworth (d 1972); *b* 26 July 1934; *Educ* Sedbergh, Univ of Oxford (MA); *m* 1964, Nancy Carolyn, da of Christopher Holden (d 1972); 3 s, 1 da; *Career* called to the Bar 1958, recorder of the Crown Court 1972–83, circuit judge (Northern Circuit) 1983–, liaison judge to Chorley and S Ribble Magistracy 1992–; hon pres S Cumbria Magistracy 1987–92; memb: Lancs Probation Ctee 1990–, Lord Lieutenants' Magistracy Ctee 1992–, Ctee of Cncl of Circuit Judges 1996–; chm Samlesbury Hall Tst 1992–; *Recreations* golf, sailing, gardening; *Clubs* Pleasington Golf; *Style*— His Hon Judge Duckworth, DL; ✉ c/o The Crown Court, Openshaw Place, Ringway, Preston, Lancs PR1 2LL

DUCKWORTH, Edward Richard Dyce; s and h of Sir Richard Dyce Duckworth, 3 Bt, *qv*; *b* 13 July 1943; *Educ* Marlborough, Cranfield; *m* 1976, Patricia, only da of Thomas Cahill, of Eton, Berks; 1 s (James Dyce b 1984), 1 da (Helen Dyce b 1987); *Career* engineer and management conslt; *Recreations* tennis, fishing; *Style*— Edward Duckworth Esq

DUCKWORTH, John Clifford; s of late Harold Duckworth, and A H Duckworth, *née* Woods; *b* 27 Dec 1916; *Educ* KCS Wimbledon, Univ of Oxford; *m* 1942, Dorothy Nancy, *née* Wills; 3 s; *Career* md National Research Development Corporation 1959–70, currently non-exec dep chm Lintott plc (formerly chm); tstee Sci Museum; FEng 1976 (fndr fell); *Style*— John Duckworth, Esq, FEng; ✉ Huefield, Helford Passage, Falmouth TR11 5LD

DUCKWORTH, Judith Josa (Judy); JP (1973), DL (1994); da of Francis Reynolds Verdon (d 1960), and Beatrice Baxendale, *née* Airey (d 1977); *b* 23 Jan 1933; *Educ* St Mary's Sch Ascot, Paris Acad, London Sch of Fashion; *m* 11 June 1959, Peter William Trevor Duckworth; 2 da (Frances Silcock b 28 June 1961, Louise Verdon Silcock b 16 Aug 1967), 1 s (Jeremy Silcock b 4 Aug 1965); *Career* teacher Garden House Sch 1955–59; former pres: Lune Valley branch RNLI, Garstang branch NSPCC; currently govr Bleasdale Primary Sch; High Sheriff for Co of Lancashire 1994–95; *Recreations* gardening and country pursuits; *Style*— Mrs J J Duckworth, JP, DL; ✉ Bleasdale Tower, Garstang, nr Preston, Lancs PR3 1UY (☎ 01995 603352)

DUCKWORTH, (David) Keith; OBE (1984); s of Frank Duckworth (d 1945), of Blackburn, Lancs, and Emma, *née* Hardman; *b* 10 Aug 1933; *Educ* Giggleswick Sch Settle Yorks, City and Guilds Coll, Imperial Coll London (BSc, ACGI); *m* 1, 1959, Dorothy Ursula, da of Victor Cassal; 1 s (Roger Frank b 4 Aug 1965), 1 da (Patricia Karen b 20 Sept 1962); m 2, 1986, Gillian Mary Cockeril; *Career* Nat Serv Aircrew RAF 1950–52; gearbox devpt engr Lotus Engineering 1956–57, freelance racing mechanic 1957–58; Cosworth Engineering Ltd (sold to UEI plc 1980): fndr 1958, chief designer, chief engr and chm 1958–80, chief engr and chm Cosworth and non-exec dir UEI plc 1980–88; designer Ford Cosworth DFV Grand Prix Engine 1966 (winning 155 Formula 1 races, powering 12 drivers to world championships); winner: RAC Diamond Jubilee Trophy, Ferodo Gold Trophy (twice), two Br Design Awards (for DFV engine and Sierra Cosworth); FCGI 1989; *Recreations* helicopter flying, microlights, water and jet skiing, motorcycling, off road sporting vehicles; *Style*— Keith Duckworth, Esq, OBE; ✉ c/o Cosworth Engineering Ltd, St James Mill Rd, Northampton NN5 5JJ

DUCKWORTH, Sir Richard Dyce; 3 Bt (UK 1909), of Grosvenor Place, City of Westminster; s of Sir Edward Dyce Duckworth, 2 Bt (d 1945); *b* 30 Sept 1918; *Educ* Marlborough; *m* 5 Sept 1942, Violet Alison (d 1996), da of Lt-Col George Boothby Wauchope, DSO (d 1952), of Highclere, Newbury, by his wife Violet Adelaide, widow of Capt Merveyn Crawshay (ka 1914), da of Capt Edward von Mumm; 2 s (Edward Richard Dyce b 1943, Antony George Dyce b 1946); *Heir* s, Edward Richard Dyce Duckworth b 13 July 1943; *Career* retired East India merchant; *Style*— Sir Richard Duckworth, Bt; ✉ Dunwood Cottage, Shootash, Romsey, Hants

DUCKWORTH, Roger Peter Terence; s of Ronald Duckworth (d 1966), of Blackburn, Lancs, and Bessie, *née* Smith (d 1980); *b* 16 Jan 1943; *Educ* Accrington GS; *m* 12 June 1965, Marion, da of William Henry Holden (d 1981), of Blackburn, Lancs; 1 s (Myles b 1972), 1 da (Laurel b 1970); *Career* chm and chief exec offr: Tensar International Ltd, Netlon Ltd and the Netlon Group of Cos; ACMA; *Recreations* music, fell walking, theatre; *Clubs* Farmers; *Style*— Roger Duckworth, Esq; ✉ Netlon Ltd, New Wellington Street, Mill Hill, Blackburn, Lancs BB2 4PJ (☎ 01254 262431, fax 01254 680008)

DUCKWORTH-CHAD, Anthony Nicholas George; DL (Norfolk 1994); s of A J S Duckworth (d 1993), of Southacre House, King's Lynn, Norfolk; *b* 20 Nov 1942; *Educ* Eton, RAC Cirencester; *m* 6 May 1970, Elizabeth Sarah, da of Capt C B H Wake-Walker of East Bergholt Lodge, Suffolk; 2 s (James b 1972, William b 1975), 1 da (Davina b 1978); *Career* farmer and landowner; memb: Walsingham RDC 1963–74, North Norfolk DC 1974–95 (chm 1987–89); chm Norfolk branch Country Landowners' Assoc 1977–78, govr Greshams Sch 1974–; High Sheriff Norfolk 1992; memb Ct of Assts Worshipful Co of Fishmongers; *Recreations* country sports; *Clubs* Whites, Pratts; *Style*— Anthony Duckworth-Chad, Esq, DL; ✉ 5 Cumberland St, London SW1V 4LS; Pynkney Hall, East Rudham, King's Lynn, Norfolk PE31 6TF

DUDBRIDGE, Prof Glen; s of George Victor Dudbridge, and Edna Kathleen, *née* Cockle; *b* 2 July 1938; *Educ* Bristol GS, Magdalene Coll Cambridge (BA, MA, PhD), New Asia Inst of Advanced Chinese Studies Hong Kong; *m* 16 Sept 1965, Sylvia Lo Fung-Young, da of Lo Tak-Tsuen (d 1981); 1 s (Frank b 1967), 1 da (Laura b 1968); *Career* Nat Serv RAF 1957–59; jr res fell Magdalene Coll Cambridge 1965, fell Wolfson Coll Oxford 1966–85 (emeritus fell 1985); visiting assoc prof: Yale Univ 1972–73, Univ of California at Berkeley 1980; fell Magdalene Coll and prof of Chinese Univ of Cambridge 1985–89; Univ of Oxford: lectr in modern Chinese 1965–85, fell Univ Coll 1989–, prof of Chinese 1989–, Shaw prof of Chinese 1994–; hon research prof Chinese Acad of Social Scis 1996; FBA 1984; *Books* The Hsi-yu chi: a study of antecedents to the 16th century Chinese novel (1970), The legend of Miao-shan (1978, Chinese edn 1990), The Tale of Li Wa: study and critical edn of a Chinese story from the 9th century (1983), Religious Experience and Lay Society in T'ang China (1995); *Style*— Prof Glen Dudbridge, FBA; ✉ Institute for Chinese Studies, Walton Street, Oxford OX1 2HG (☎ 01865 280387, fax 01865 280431)

DUDDERIDGE, John Webster; OBE (1962); s of William George Dudderidge (d 1945), of Cheddon Fitzpaine, Somerset, and Mary Ethel, *née* Webster (d 1962); *b* 24 Aug 1906; *Educ* Magnus GS Newark-on-Trent, Univ Coll Nottingham (BSc); *m* 25 July 1936, (Gertrude Louisa) Evelyn (d 1991), da of Rev Frederick S Hughes (d 1920), of N China Mission, Peking, China; 2 s (John b 1937, Philip b 1949), 2 da (Ruth b 1938, Hilary b 1944); *Career* asst master Manor House Sch London 1929–31, asst master and house master Haberdashers' Aske's Sch 1931–69; British Olympic Assoc: memb Cncl 1949–69, memb Exec Ctee 1969–73, dep chm 1973–77, vice pres 1977–; Br Canoe Union: fndr memb 1936, sec for racing 1936–49, hon gen sec 1939–59, hon treas 1941–43, pres 1959–77, hon life pres 1977–, Award of Honour 1961; Int Canoe Fedn: memb Bd 1938–80, vice pres 1946–48, hon memb 1980–; Award of Honour 1962, Gold medal 1980; vice pres Open Canoe Assoc of GB 1980–; pres Cambridge Canoe Club 1994–; hon sec/treas Cwlth Canoeing Fedn 1968–84; memb Cncl for Eng Cwlth Games Fedn 1976–83; memb Ctee of Advsrs Sports Aid Fndn 1976–80 (statutory memb 1980–); memb Br Olympic Canoeing Team 1936, mangr Br Canoe Racing Team 1938–58, int official 1948–81, tstee Jubilee Canoeing Fndn 1986–; author of numerous articles on canoes and canoeing for magazines, jls, almanacks and encyclopaedias; memb: Beds and Cambs Wildlife Tst, CPRE, Nat Tst, SLD, Soc of Friends (Quakers); *Recreations* canoeing, walking, gardening, reading; *Clubs* Royal Canoe, Canoe Camping (vice pres 1972–), Olympians; *Style*— John Dudderidge, Esq, OBE; ✉ Tyros, 15 Lacks Close, Cottenham, Cambridge CB4 4TZ (☎ 01954 251752)

DUDDING, Richard Scarbrough; s of Sir John Scarbrough Dudding (d 1986), and Enid Grace, *née* Gardner; *b* 29 Nov 1950; *Educ* Cheltenham Coll, Jesus Coll Cambridge (MA); *m* 11 July 1987, Priscilla Diana, *née* Russell; 2 s (Edwin Charles Scarbrough b 19 Sept 1987, John Russell b 4 April 1989); *Career* DOE: joined 1972, private sec to Rt Hon John Smith 1976–78, seconded to Overseas Containers Ltd 1983–85, sec to Ctee of Enquiry into Conduct of Local Govt 1985–86, head of Fin, Gen and Housing Div 1986–88, Water Privatisation Team 1989–90, dir Central Fin 1990–93, dir Pollution Control and Waste 1993–96, princ establishments offr 1996–; *Recreations* golf, gardening, walking; *Style*— Richard Dudding, Esq; ✉ 3 Dora Road, London SW19 7EZ; Department of the Environment, 2 Marsham Street, London SW1P 3EB

DUDGEON, Gus; s of Patrick Boyd Dudgeon, and Elizabeth Louise, *née* Crighton; *b* 30 Sept 1942; *Educ* Haileybury and Imperial Service Coll, Summerhill; *m* 3 April 1965, Sheila, da of George Arthur Bailey; *Career* record prodr (formerly sound engr); founded own prodn co 1968; hits incl: Space Oddity (David Bowie), Je T'Aime (Sounds Nice), co-produced with Paul McCartney The Urban Spaceman (Bonzo Dog Doo Dah Band); prodr of all Elton John records 1969–76 and 1986–; singles incl: Your Song, Rocket Man, Crocodile Rock, Daniel, Saturday Night's Alright for Fighting, Yellow Brick Road, Don't Go Breaking My Heart, Nikita; has produced for other artists incl: Joan Armatrading, Chris Rea, Elkie Brooks, Jennifer Rush, Kiki Dee, The Beach Boys, Bruce Hornsby and XTC, Michael Ball, Fairport Convention and Judith Durham (ex-Seekers), Barbara Dickson; Silver discs: Run for Home 1978, Back and Fourth 1978, Magic in the Air 1978; Gold disc Whatever Happened to Benny Santini 1978; Platinum disc (Germany) Heart over Mind 1987 and all Elton John Records; NME Best Br Produced Record 1973, Top Albums Prodr 1974 and 1975, NOI Pop Prodr Billboard magazine 1975; fndr memb Br Prodrs' Guild (now Re-Pro); *Recreations* theatre, gardening, collecting rhinos, water-skiing, excellent food, Mercedes-Benzes, Aston Martins, and of course music; *Style*— Gus Dudgeon, Esq; ✉ c/o Tony English, Russells, Regency House, 1–4 Warwick Street, London W1R 5WB (☎ 0171 439 8692, fax 0171 287 0314)

DUDLESTON, Barry; s of Percy Dudleston (d 1979), and Dorothy Vera, *née* Jones; *b* 16 July 1945; *Educ* Stockport Sch; *m* 1, (m dis); 1 s (Matthew Barry b 12 Sept 1988), 1 da (Sharon Louise b 29 Oct 1968); m 2, 19 Oct 1994, Louise Wendy; *Career* cricket umpire; professional cricketer: Leicestershire CCC 1965–80, Gloucestershire CCC 1981–83; represented Rhodesia 1976–79; first class record: 295 matches, 32 centuries, highest score 202 v Derbyshire 1979; shared Leics record partnership 1st wicket 390 with J Steele v Derbyshire 1979; first class umpire 1984–, appointed to Test Match Panel 1991– (debut 4th Test England v W Indies Edgbaston 1991); *Clubs* MCC; *Style*— Barry Dudleston, Esq; ✉ Sunsport Tours Ltd, Hamilton House, 66 Palmerston Road, Northampton NN1 5EX (☎ 01604 31626)

DUDLEY, Anne Jennifer; da of William James Beckingham, of Brighton, and Dorothy Thelma Beckingham; *Educ* Eltham Hill GS, RCM (Performer's Dip, BMus), King's Coll London (MMus); *m* 1978, Roger Dudley, s of Leonard William Dudley; 1 da (Angela b 7 April 1992); *Career* musician, composer, arranger, prodr; keyboard player and arranger with: ABC (Lexicon of Love album), Wham! (Young Guns, Bad Boys and Everything She Wants), Malcolm McLaren (co-wrote Buffalo Gals and other tracks on Duck Rock), Frankie Goes to Hollywood (Two Tribes and The Power of Love); fndr memb Art of Noise (performed, wrote and co-produced all five albums); freelance arranger and musician with: Phil Collins, Paul McCartney, Wet Wet Wet, Dusty Springfield, Wham, Lisa Minelli, Lloyd Cole, Rod Stewart, Marc Almond, Seal, Tina Turner, Cher, Elton John, Pulp, Boyzone, Jaz Coleman of Killing Joke (songs From the Victorious City 1990); solo album Ancient and Modern 1995; composer of soundtracks for cinematic feature films incl: Hiding Out, Buster, Wilt, Silence Like Glass, Say Anything, Mighty Quinn, The Pope Must Die, Disorderlies, The Miracle, The Crying Game, Knight Moves, When Saturday Comes, The Grotesque, Hollow Reed; composer of soundtrack music for TV: Jeeves and Wooster 1990–93, Krypton Factor, Down to Earth, Anna Lee, Kavanagh QC; composer of music for TV and cinema commercials incl: Spanish Sherries, Volvo, World Wildlife Fund, Commercial Union, Reebok, Guinness; Grammy Award for Peter Gunn 1988, Midsummer Award for Volvo (Twister) 1996; memb BAFTA; *Style*— Anne Dudley; ✉ Air Edel Associates, 18 Rodmarton Street, London W1H 3FW (☎ 0171 486 6466, fax 0171 224 0344)

DUDLEY, Baroness (14 in line, E 1439); Barbara Amy Felicity Hamilton; *née* Lea-Smith; da of 12 Baron Dudley (d 1936); suc bro, 13 Baron, 1972; *b* 23 April 1907; *m* 1, 1929, Guy Raymond Hill Wallace (d 1967); 3 s, 1 da; m 2, 1980, Charles Anthony Crosse Hamilton; *Heir* s, Hon Jim Anthony Hill Wallace b 9 Nov 1930; *Style*— The Rt Hon the Lady Dudley; ✉ Hill House, Napleton Lane, Kempsey, Worcs WR5 3PY (☎ 01905 820253)

DUDLEY, Bishop of 1993–; Rt Rev Dr Rupert William Noel Hoare; s of Julian Hoare, and Edith, *née* Temple; *b* 3 March 1940; *Educ* Dragon Sch, Rugby, Trinity Coll Oxford (MA), Kirchliche Hochschule Berlin, Fitwilliam House and Westcott House Cambridge (MA), Univ of Birmingham (PhD); *m* Jan 1965, Gesine Pflüger; 3 s (Christopher, Martin, Nicholas), 1 da (Rebecca); *Career* curate St Mary's Oldham 1964–67, ordained priest 1965, lectr Queen's Coll Birmingham 1968–72, canon theologian Coventry Cathedral 1970–75, rector Parish of the Resurrection Beswick E Manchester 1972–78, canon residentiary Birmingham Cathedral 1978, princ Westcott House Cambridge 1981–93; *Recreations* walking, gardening (sometimes); *Style*— The Rt Rev the Bishop of Dudley; ✉ Bishop's House, 366 Halesowen Road, Cradley Heath, W Midlands B64 7JF (☎ 0121 550 3407, fax 0121 550 7340)

DUDLEY, 4 Earl of (UK 1860); William Humble David Ward; also Baron Ward of Birmingham (E 1664) and Viscount Ednam (UK 1860); s of 3 Earl of Dudley, MC (d 1969), by his 1 w, Lady Rosemary, *née* Sutherland-Leveson-Gower, RRC (d 1930), da of 4 Duke of Sutherland; *b* 5 Jan 1920; *Educ* Eton, Christ Church Oxford; *m* 1, 1946 (m dis 1961), Stella, da of Miguel Carcano, KCMG, KBE, sometime Argentinian Ambass to UK; 1 s, 2 da (twins); m 2, 1961, Maureen, da of James Swanson; 1 s, 5 da; *Heir* s, Viscount Ednam, *qv*; *Career* sits as Cons in House of Lords; 2 Lt 10 Hussars 1941, Capt 1945; ADC to The Viceroy of India 1942–43; memb House of Lords Ctee on Euro Secdy Legislation 1972–74 (chm Sub-Ctee on EEC Economics, Finance and Regnl Policy 1973–74); pres Baggeridge Brick Co Ltd; *Clubs* White's, Pratt's, Royal Yacht Sqdn; *Style*— The Rt Hon the Earl of Dudley; ✉ Vention House, Putsborough, Georgeham, N Devon (☎ 01271 890631/890632); 6 Cottesmore Gdns, London W8 (☎ 0171 937 5671)

DUDLEY, William Stuart; s of William Stuart Dudley, and Dorothy Irene, *née* Stacey; *b* 4 March 1947; *Educ* Highbury GS, St Martin's Sch Art (BA), Slade Sch of Art UCL (Post Grad Dip Fine Art); *Career* theatre designer; assoc designer RNT 1981– (res stage designer 1970–81); hon pres Tower Theatre 1988, hon dir Irish Theatre Co London; fndr memb folk band Morris Minor and the Austin Seven 1980; memb Soc of Br Theatre Designers, RDI 1989; *Theatre* RNT incl: Lavender Blue, Larkrise to Candleford, Lost Worlds, The World Turned Upside Down, Undiscovered Country (SWET Award),

Dispatches, Don Quixote, Schweyk in the Second World War, Cinderella, The Mysteries, The Real Inspector Hound, The Critic (Olivier Award for Best Costume Design 1993), Entertaining Strangers, Waiting for Godot, Cat on a Hot Tin Roof, The Shaughraun, The Changeling, Bartholomew Fair, The Voysey Inheritance, The Crucible, The Coup, Pygmalion, The Rise and Fall of Little Voice, On The Ledge, Johnny on a Spot; most recently: Under Milk Wood 1995, Wild Oats 1995, Mary Stuart 1996; RSC incl: Ivanov, That Good Between Us, Richard III, A Midsummer Night's Dream; Royal Court incl: Small Change, The Fool, Hamlet, Edmund, Kafka's Dick, Etta Jenks; other prodns incl: Hamlet (Neue Schauspielhaus Hamburg), The Ship, I Claudius, Mutiny!, Kiss me Kate, Girlfriends, Matador, Heartbreak House, My Night with Reg; *Opera* WNO incl: Anna Christie, The Barber of Seville, Indomeneo; Royal Opera House incl: Don Giovanni, Tales of Hoffman, Der Rosenkavalier, The Cunning Little Vixen; other opera incl: Billy Budd (Metropolitan Opera), The Ring (Bayreuth) 1983, Un Ballo in Maschera (Salzburg Festival) 1989, Lucia di Lammermoor (Lyric Opera of Chicago), The Big Picnic (Harland and Wolff, Glasgow), Lucia di Lammermoor (Opera National de Paris); *Television* Persuasion (BBC (BAFTA Award for Production Design 1996)); *Recreations* playing the concertina and the cajun accordian; *Style—* William Dudley, Esq; ✉ c/o Royal National Theatre, Upper Ground, London SE1 9PX

DUDLEY-WILLIAMS, Sir Alastair Edgcumbe James; 2 Bt (UK 1964), of City and Co of the City of Exeter; s of Sir Rolf Dudley Dudley-Williams, 1 Bt (d 1987); *b* 26 Nov 1943; *Educ* Pangbourne Coll; *m* 1972, Diana Elizabeth Jane, twin da of Robert Henry Clare Duncan, of Haslemere, Surrey; 3 da (Marina Elizabeth Catherine b 1974, Lorna Caroline Rachel b 1977, Eleanor Patricia Rosemary b 1979); *Heir* bro, Malcolm Philip Edgcumbe Dudley-Williams, *qv*; *Career* field salesman Hughes Tool Co Texas 1962–64, oil well driller Bay Drilling Corporation (Louisiana) 1964–65; driller: Bristol Siddeley Whittle Tools Ltd 1965–67, Santa Fe Drilling Co (N Sea and Libya) 1967–72, Inchcape plc 1972–86, Wildcat Consultants 1986–; chm Pirrie Hall Ctee Brook 1990–92; memb: Stewards Enclosure Henley Royal Regatta, Standing Cncl Baronetage; *Recreations* gardening, fishing, shooting; *Clubs* Royal Cornwall Yacht; *Style—* Sir Alastair Dudley-Williams, Bt; ✉ c/o The Old Manse, South Petherton, Somerset TA13 5DB

DUDLEY-WILLIAMS, Malcolm Philip Edgcumbe; yr s of Sir Rolf Dudley Dudley-Williams, 1 Bt (d 1987); bro and hp of Sir Alastair Edgcumbe James Dudley-Williams, 2 Bt, *qv*; *b* 10 Aug 1947; *Educ* Pangbourne Nautical Coll; *m* 1973, Caroline Anne Colina, twin da of Robert Henry Clare Duncan, of Haslemere, Surrey; 2 s (Nicholas Mark Edgcumbe b 1975, Patrick Guy Edgcumbe b 1978), 1 da (Clare Helen Colina b 1982); *Style—* Malcolm Dudley-Williams, Esq; ✉ 9 Bowerdean Street, London SW6 3TN

DUERDEN, Prof Brian Ion; s of late Cyril Duerden, of Burnley, Lancs, and Mildred, *née* Ion; *b* 21 June 1948; *Educ* Nelson GS, Univ of Edinburgh (BSc, MB ChB, MD); *m* 5 Aug 1972, Marjorie, da of late Thomas Blakey Hudson, of Brierfield, Burnley, Lancs; *Career* house offr thoracic surgery and infectious diseases City Hosp Edinburgh 1972–73, lectr and hon registrar in bacteriology Univ of Edinburgh Med Sch 1973–76; Univ of Sheffield Med Sch: lectr and hon sr registrar in med microbiology 1976–79, sr lectr and hon conslt in med microbiology 1979–83; prof and hon conslt microbiologist and infection control doctor Children's Hosp Sheffield 1983–90; Univ of Wales Coll of Med: prof of med microbiology 1991–, dir Cardiff Public Health Laboratory 1991–95, dir of med microbiology S Glamorgan 1991–95, dep dir Public Health Laboratory Service Bd 1995–; chm Editorial Bd Jl of Med Microbiology 1987– (ed in chief 1982–), memb Editorial Ctee Reviews Med Microbiology; chm Assoc of Profs of Med Microbiology 1994– (hon sec 1989–); memb: Nat Quality Assur Advsy Panel 1986–91, Microbiology Advsy Ctee 1988–94, Advsy Ctee on Dangerous Pathogens 1991–94, Jt Dental Ctee MRC 1989–93; Royal Coll of Pathologists: memb Cncl 1986–89 and 1990–93, examiner 1981–, memb Exec Ctee 1990–93, chm microbiology examiners 1994–; memb: Soc of Anaerobic Microbiology 1976 (chm 1989–93), Assoc of Med Microbiologists 1983 (hon sec 1984–87), Pathological Soc of GB and I (memb Ctee 1981–); FRCPath 1990 (MRCPath 1978), corresponding fell Infectious Diseases Soc of America; *Books* Short Textbook of Medical Microbiology (5 edn, 1983), A New Short Textbook of Microbial and Parasitic Infection (1987), Topley and Wilson's Principles of Bacteriology, Virology and Immunity (contrib 7 edn, 1983–84, ed and contrib 8 edn 1990), Anaerobes in Human Disease (1991), Medical and Environmental Aspects of Anaerobes (1992), Microbial and Parasitic Infection (1993), Medical and Dental Aspects of Anaerobes (1995); *Recreations* cricket, photography, travel, music; *Style—* Prof Brian Duerden; ✉ Pendle, Crossway Green, Chepstow, Gwent NP6 5LU; Department of Medical Microbiology and Public Health Laboratory, University of Wales College of Medicine, Heath Park, Cardiff CF4 4XN (☎ 01222 742168, fax 01222 742169)

DUFF, Alistair David Buchanan; s of Maj David Kerr Duff, FRSE, Croix de Guerre (d 1963), of Tighnabruaich House, Argyll and Muriel Kerr, *née* Cavaghan (d 1988); *b* 19 July 1928; *Educ* George Watson's Coll Edinburgh, Univ of Edinburgh; *m* 1 Feb 1958, Cynthia Mary, da of Maurice Stork Hardy (d 1974), of Cleughhead, Annan, Dumfriesshire; 1 s (Roderick b Oct 1963), 1 da (Carolyn b Aug 1962); *Career* Nat Serv RA Malaya 1947–49; vice chm Cavaghan & Gray Ltd Carlisle 1977–88 (dir 1957–63, md 1963–77); chm: TSB Cumbria 1971–75 (joined 1968), TSB Lancs and Cumbria 1976–83 (memb Central Bd 1976–86, dep chm NW Regnl Bd 1984–89); dir Carlisle Race Course Co 1978–; chm Br Bacon Curers Fedn 1975–76; gen cmmr of taxes 1977–; *Recreations* shooting, horse racing, sailing; *Clubs* Farmers', Border and County; *Style—* Alistair Duff, Esq; ✉ Monkcastle, Southwaite, Carlisle, Cumbria CA4 OPZ (☎ 01697 473273)

DUFF, Rt Hon Sir (Arthur) Antony; GCMG (1980, KCMG 1973, CMG 1964), CVO (1972), DSO (1944), DSC (1943), PC (1980); yr s of Adm Sir Arthur Allan Morison Duff, KCB, JP, DL (d 1952, ggs of Robert William Duff, whose mother was Lady Helen Duff, da of 1 Earl of Fife, ancestor of Dukes of Fife. Robert's f was Vice Adm Robert Duff of Logie and Fetteresso, one of 23 children of Patrick Duff of Craigston by his 2nd wife (he had 36 altogether)); *b* 25 Feb 1920; *Educ* RNC Dartmouth; *m* 1944, Pauline Marion, da of Capt R H Bevan, RN, and widow of Flt Lt J A Sword; 1 s ((Robin) Antony Duff, *qv*), 1 step s, 2 da; *Career* served RN 1937–46; entered Foreign Service 1946; first sec: FO 1952, Paris 1954, FO 1957, Bonn 1960; cnsllr Bonn 1962–64, ambass to Nepal 1964–65, Cwlth Office 1965–68, dep high cmmr Kuala Lumpur 1969–72, high cmmr Kenya 1972–75, dep under sec of State FCO 1975–80, dep to Perm Under Sec of State 1977–80; dep govr Southern Rhodesia 1979–80, dep sec Cabinet Office 1980–84, DG Security Serv 1985–87, ret; *Clubs* Army and Navy; *Style—* The Rt Hon Sir Antony Duff, GCMG, CVO, DSO, DSC; ✉ c/o National Westminster Bank, PO Box 25, 130 Commercial Road, Portsmouth, Hants PO1 1ES

DUFF, Prof (Robin) Antony; s of The Rt Hon Sir Antony Duff, GCMG, CVO, DSO, DSC, *qv*, of Dorset, and Lady Duff, *née* Pauline Bevan; *b* 9 March 1945; *Educ* Sedbergh, ChCh Oxford (BA); *Career* visiting lectr Univ of Washington Seattle USA 1968–69, currently prof Dept of Philosophy Univ of Stirling (joined 1970); research readership British Acad 1989–91; FRSE 1996; *Books* Trials and Punishments (1986), Intention, Agency and Criminal Liability (1990), Criminal Attempts (1996); *Style—* Prof Antony Duff, FRSE; ✉ Department of Philosophy, University of Stirling, Stirling FK9 4LA (☎ 01786 467555, fax 01786 451335)

DUFF, Dr Keith Leslie; s of Leslie Alexander George Duff, of London, and Elsie Muriel Janet, *née* Evans (d 1990); *b* 16 July 1949; *Educ* Haberdashers' Aske's, Univ Coll Cardiff (BSc), Univ of Leicester (PhD); *m* 21 June 1975, Janet, da of Dr William Smith Russell, of Leicester; 2 da (Katy b 9 Nov 1977, Elizabeth b 22 July 1979); *Career* Geology and Physiography Section Nature Conservancy Cncl: joined 1975, dep head 1978–85, head Earth Sci Conservation 1985–87; asst chief scientist Nature Conservancy Cncl 1987–91, chief scientist Nature Conservancy Cncl for England (English Nature) 1991–; Geologists' Association: memb Cncl 1976–85, sec Field Meetings 1978–82, vice pres 1982–85, hon memb 1996; Inst of Geologists: memb Cncl 1987–90, sec External Rels Ctee 1987–90; memb: Geological Soc (Conservation Ctee 1977–89, memb Cncl 1994–), Palaeontographical Soc (memb Cncl 1979–82), Environmental Advsy Bd Shanks and McEwan plc 1989–, Euro Working Gp on Earth Science Conservation 1988– (fndr memb); assessor Marine Sciences Ctee NERC 1988–91; memb Editorial Bd Geology Today 1985–; ldr several geological study tours to Western USA for Centre for Extra-Mural Studies Univ of London and GA 1981–92; dir Nat Stone Centre 1985–88; hon res fell Dept Geology Univ of Leicester; Foulerton award; CGeol 1990; *Books* Bivalvia of the Lower Oxford Clay of Southern England (1978), New Sites for Old (ed, 1985), Fossils of the Oxford Clay (contrib, 1991); author of numerous papers and articles in jnls; *Recreations* golf, skiing, travel; *Clubs* Toft Hotel Golf, City and Counties, Peterborough; *Style—* Dr Keith Duff, Esq; ✉ Nature Conservancy Council for England, Northminster House, Peterborough PE1 1UA (☎ 01733 318318, fax 01733 68834)

DUFF, Linda; da of Sean Duff, of Dublin, and Rita, *née* Ryan; *b* 17 July 1961; *Educ* St Mary's Holy Faith Convent Sch Dublin; *Career* editorial and advtg asst Irish Press newspapers 1979, asst Hot Press music magazine 1979, editorial asst Smash Hits 1980–85, contrib to Peter Powell Show Radio 1 1984, freelance journalist 1985–90 (contrib to London Evening Standard, The Sun, Daily Mirror), Problems Problems agony column Daily Mirror 1988–90, presenter The Night is Young live chat show LBC Radio 1988–90, own column The People 1989, freelance contrib to Cosmopolitan and Options magazines 1988–90; Daily Star: pop ed 1990–, Rave supplement ed 1993–; presenter Vibe weekly show BBC Radio 5 1991–92; memb: BRIT Awards Voting Acad, NUJ; *Books* The Molson Guide to What's Hot and What's Not (1989); *Recreations* partying, asking rude questions; *Clubs* Smashing, St Moritz (London), Ministry of Sound, POD (Dublin); *Style—* Ms Linda Duff; ✉ Rave Desk, Express Newspapers, Ludgate House, 245 Blackfriars Rd, London SE1 9UX (☎ 0171 928 8000, fax 0171 922 7962)

DUFF, Prof Michael John Benjamin; s of George Benjamin Duff (d 1976), and Joan Emily, *née* Reynolds; *b* 17 Jan 1933; *Educ* Emanuel Sch Wandsworth, UCL (BSc, PhD); *m* 20 April 1963, Susan Mary, da of Alfred Jones (d 1986); 1 s (Robert Michael b 1967), 1 da (Charlotte Fiona b 1964); *Career* devpt engr EMI Electronics Ltd 1956–58; Dept of Physics and Astronomy UCL: res asst 1958–62, lectr 1962–77, reader 1977–84, prof 1985–; hon sec Br Pattern Recognition Soc 1976–84, chm BPRA 1984–86, pres Int Assoc for Pattern Recognition 1990–92 (sec 1984–90); CEng 1966, FIEE 1981, FRSA 1986, FIAPR 1994; *Books* numerous pubns incl: Conference on Recent Developments in Cloud Chamber and Associated Techniques (ed with N Morris, 1956), Computing Structures for Image Processing (ed, 1983), Modern Cellular Automata (with K Preston, 1984), Intermediate-Level Image Processing (ed, 1986); *Recreations* travelling, music, gardening, photography; *Style—* Prof Michael Duff; ✉ Bramham Cottage, 66 Weston Park, Thames Ditton, Surrey KT7 0HL

DUFF, Samuel; s of Rev Samuel Noel Duff, and Emily McKinney, *née* Douther; *b* 20 Feb 1946; *Educ* Rainey Endowed Sch Magherafely, Univ of Edinburgh; *m* 8 Nov 1969, Patricia Katherine Fleming, da of Donald Morris Miller (d 1961), of Dale, Halkirk, Caithness; 2 s (Innes Noel b 1975 (decd), Andrew Samuel b 1977), 2 da (Louise Emma Jane b 1971, Iona Katherine b 1973); *Career* vet; asst: RS Cowie Ptnrs Keith 1970–77, AE Orr 1977–78; ptnr Orr Duff and Howat 1978–; pres Scottish Metropolitan Div BVA 1990–91; memb: BVA, SPVS, BCVA, BEVA; *Style—* Samuel Duff, Esq; ✉ Redriggs, Newtown, Ceres, Fife KY15 5LZ (☎ 01334 828345, fax 01334 828922)

DUFF, Rev Timothy Cameron; s of Timothy Duff (d 1974) of Tynemouth, and Marjory Magdalene, *née* Cameron; *b* 2 Feb 1940; *Educ* Royal GS Newcastle upon Tyne, Caius Coll Cambridge (MA, LLM); *m* 23 June 1966, Patricia, da of Capt John Munby Walker DLI (d 1955), of N Shields; 2 s (John b 1968, James b 1970), 1 da (Emma b 1973); *Career* admitted slr 1965, sr ptnr Hadaway and Hadaway 1988–; sec and clerk to tstees Tyne Mariners Benevolent Inst 1984–; dir: Tynemouth Building Society 1985–94, Universal Building Society 1994–; ordained deacon 1993, priest 1994, hon curate and non-stipendiary min Parish of Tynemouth Priory 1993–; memb Ecclesiastical Law Soc; *Recreations* sailing, reading, outdoor pursuits; *Clubs* Green Wyvern Yacht; *Style—* The Rev Timothy Duff; ✉ 26 The Drive, Tynemouth, Northumberland NE30 4JW (☎ 0191 257 1463, fax 0191 296 1904)

DUFF GORDON, Sir Andrew Cosmo Lewis; 8 Bt (UK 1813), of Halkin, Ayrshire; s of Sir Douglas Frederick Duff-Gordon, 7 Bt (d 1964, whose ggf, Sir William Duff Gordon, 2 Bt, was paternal gs of 2 Earl of Aberdeen); *b* 17 Oct 1933; *m* 1, 1967 (m dis 1975), Grania Mary, da of Fitzgerald Villiers-Stuart, of Dromana, Villerstown, Co Waterford; 1 s (Cosmo Henry Villiers b 1968); m 2, 1975, Eveline (Evie) Virginia Soames, *qv*, yst da of Samuel Soames, of Boxford House, Newbury; 3 s (William Andrew Lewis b 1977, Thomas Francis Cornewall b 1979, Frederick Samuel Douglas b 1981); *Heir* s, Cosmo Henry Villiers Duff-Gordon b 18 June 1968; *Clubs* City Univ, Sunningdale Golf, Kington Golf; *Style—* Sir Andrew Duff Gordon, Bt; ✉ 27 Cathcart Rd, London SW10; Downton House, Walton, Presteigne, Powys (☎ 01544 21223)

DUFFELL, Michael Royson; s of Roy John Duffell (d 1979), of Lenham, Kent, and Ruth Doris, *née* Gustafsson; *b* 19 June 1939; *Educ* Dulwich; *m* 1963, Gisela, *née* Rothkehl; 1 s (Christian Royson b 2 Feb 1964), 1 da (Julie Royson b 20 Oct 1969); *Career* reception mangr Hyde Park Hotel 1966–69, gen mangr Grosvenor Hotel Chester 1969–76, controller of the Household to HM King Hussein of Jordan 1976–80, dir and gen mangr The Ritz 1980–84; md: Cunard Hotels and The Ritz 1984–88, Hotel Atop the Bellevue Philadelphia USA 1988–90, The Chesterfield Hotel Palm Beach Florida 1991–92; pres Service Concepts Marketing Inc Palm Beach Florida 1990, gen mangr The Biltmore Hotel Miami Florida 1992–93, dir Rave Productions Inc 1993–, dir of the households to Leslie Wexner 1993–; fndr memb and first pres Savoy Gastronomes; *Recreations* tennis, golf, skiing; *Style—* Michael Duffell, Esq; ✉ 26 Brechin Place, London SW7 4QA; One Whitebarn Road, New Albany, Ohio 43054, USA (☎ 00 1 614 939 3097, fax 00 1 614 939 3062)

DUFFELL, Sir Peter Royson; KCB (1992), CBE (1988, OBE 1981), MC (1966); s of Roy John Duffell (d 1979), of Lenham, Kent, and Ruth Doris, *née* Gustaffson; *b* 19 June 1939; *Educ* Dulwich; *m* 9 Oct 1982, Ann Murray, da of Col Basil Bethune Neville Woodd (d 1975), of Rolvenden, Kent; 1 s (Charles Basil Royson b 20 Oct 1986), 1 da (Rachel Leonie Sylvia b 9 April 1985); *Career* cmmnd 2 KEO Gurkha Rifles 1960, attended Staff Coll Camberley 1971, Brigade Maj 5 Brigade 1972–74, MA to C in C UKLF 1976–78, Cmdt 1 Bn 2 KEO Gurkha Rifles 1978–81, Col GS MOD 1981–83, Cdr Gurkha Field Force 1984–85, COS 1 (BR) Corps 1986–87, RCDS 1988, Efficiency Unit Cabinet Office, Cdr Br Forces Hong Kong 1989–92, Inspr Gen of Doctrine and Trg 1992–95; chief exec Titmuss Sainer Dechert 1995–; Col Royal Gurkha Rifles 1995–; govr Sandroyd Sch 1995–; FRGS 1975, FRAS 1992; *Recreations* family, golf, collecting pictures, reading, skiing, elephant polo, travel, photogrpahy, wine; *Clubs* Travellers', Pratt's; *Style—* Sir Peter Duffell, KCB, CBE, MC; ✉ c/o Travellers' Club, 106 Pall Mall, London SW1Y 5EP

DUFFERIN AND AVA, Marchioness of; Serena Belinda Rosemary (Lindy); *née* Guinness; da of Gp Capt Loel Guinness, OBE (d 1988), and his 2 w, Lady Isabel

Manners, yr da of 9 Duke of Rutland; *b* 25 March 1941; *m* 21 Oct 1964, 5 and last Marquess of Dufferin and Ava (d 1988); *Career* writer and artist; *Recreations* gardening, nature conservation, golf; *Style*— The Most Hon the Marchioness of Dufferin and Ava; ✉ Clandeboye, Bangor, Co Down, N Ireland; 4 Holland Villas Rd, London W14

DUFFERIN AND CLANDEBOYE, 11 Baron (I 1800); Sir John Francis Blackwood; also 12 Bt (I) of Ballyleidy, and 8 Bt (UK 1814) (claim to the Irish titles is yet to be proved); s of 10 Baron Dufferin and Clandeboye (d 1991), and Margaret, *née* Kirkpatrick; *b* 18 Oct 1944; *Educ* Barker Coll Hornsby, Univ of NSW (BArch); *m* 1971, (Annette) Kay, da of Harold Greenhill, of Seaforth, Sydney, NSW; 1 s (Hon Francis Senden b 6 Jan 1979), 1 da (Hon Freya Jodie b 1975); *Heir* s, Hon Francis Senden Blackwood b 6 Jan 1979; *Career* architect in private practice; ARAIA; *Style*— The Rt Hon Lord Dufferin and Clandeboye; ✉ 169 Anson Street, Orange, NSW 2800, Australia

DUFFETT, Christopher Charles Biddulph; s of Capt Charles Henry Duffett, CBE, DSO (d 1981), and Leonora Biddulph; *b* 23 Aug 1943; *Educ* Bryanston, Peterhouse Cambridge (MA), Wharton Sch Univ of Pennsylvania (MBA); *m* 1973, Jennifer Edwards; 2 s (Samuel Owen Salisbury b 1975, Daniel Charles William Biddulph b 1977); *Career* Nat Devpt Office 1965–67, S G Warburg and Co Ltd 1969–71, Inco Ltd NY 1971–74, treas Inco Europe Ltd 1974–77, gp treas Rank Organization Ltd 1977–79, gp fin dir The Economist Newspaper Ltd 1979–88, chief exec offr The Law Debenture Corp plc 1988–; FCT; *Recreations* gardening, sailing, walking; *Clubs* Royal Ocean Racing, City of London; *Style*— Christopher Duffett, Esq; ✉ The Law Debenture Corporation plc, Princess House, 95 Gresham Street, London EC2V 7LY (☎ 0171 606 5451)

DUFFETT, Michael Terence; s of Francis Duffett (d 1993), of Beckenham, Kent, and Marjorie, *née* McCarthy (d 1988); *b* 1 Aug 1939; *Educ* Hill School Stillness, Central Poly, London Coll of Printing and Graphic Art; *m* Janet, da of Stanley Spencer; 4 da (Rachel b 1 Dec 1966, Emma b 24 Feb 1968, Rebecca b 9 May 1969, Sarah b 19 April 1970); *Career* photographer of fine art/museum and gallery photographic mgmnt; med photographer Royal Nat Orthopaedic Hosp 1959, photographer for Tate Gallery 1962, freelance commercial photographer and design conslt 1967–70, conslt to Slater Walker 1970, advsr on creation of new Photographic Dept Tate Gallery 1974, princ photographer Photographic Dept Tate Gallery 1977–, began collection of photographic equipment (1860–1960) 1977, lectr 1979–, head of photography Tate Gallery 1984–94, chief Govt photographer 1985–, organiser and mangr photographic recording prog of 30,000 Turner watercolours and drawings for the Clore Gallery 1985–, undertook complete photographic survey of entire collection Dulwich Picture Gallery 1988 and Bedford Coll; currently conslt carrying out quality survey of photographic colour images Tate Gallery; judge: Kodak Ltd Exposure Project 1989, 1990 and 1991, BIPP Nat Print Competition 1990, Inst of Med and Biological Illustrators 1990; chm and fndr Assoc for Historical and Fine Art Photography 1986; exhibitions incl: Guildhall 1961, Gallery Las 1963, Kings Gallery 1964, Kings Road Gallery 1972; ARPS 1965, FRSA 1987, FBIPP 1988; *Style*— Michael Duffett, Esq; ✉ 1 Queens Rd, Beckenham, Kent BR3 4JN (☎ 0181 650 2944)

DUFFETT, Roger Hugh Edward; s of Dr Edward Cecil Duffett (d 1984), and Cicely, *née* Haw (d 1960); *b* 20 Jan 1936; *Educ* Sherborne, Peterhouse Cambridge (scholar, MA); *m* 24 Oct 1959, (Angela) Julie, da of Herald Mills Olden (d 1975); 1 s (Simon Edward b 28 May 1964 d 1991), 1 da (Sarah Julie b 7 March 1967); *Career* Nat Serv cmmnd RA 1954–56; BP: res chemist 1959–64, mathematical computer modelling 1964–71, corp planning 1971–78, crude oil contract negotiator 1978–79, orgns and systems conslt 1979–87; conslt for various orgns incl Cambridge LEA, UNICEF and Riding for the Disabled 1987–88, sec Royal Coll of Surgns of Eng 1988–; Riding for the Disabled Assoc: memb Mgmnt Ctee 1990–, memb Cncl and Med Advsy Ctee 1994–; memb Mgmnt Ctee Home for Active Elderly Clare Park Farnham 1977–82, dir Quinta Nursing Home Farnham 1983–88; *Recreations* golf, coarse gardening, creative brain teasers; *Style*— Roger Duffett, Esq; ✉ The Royal College of Surgeons of England, 35–43 Lincoln's Inn Fields, London WC2A 3PN (☎ 0171 405 3474, fax 0171 831 9438)

DUFFIELD, Rachel Elizabeth; *b* 14 March 1958; *Educ* Midhurst GS Sussex, W Sussex Coll of Design Worthing, Wolverhampton Poly (coll scholar, Tim Turner Freer Media travelling scholar, BA); *Career* Orbis Publishing Group: picture res asst 1982–83, picture researcher books and magazines 1983–84, picture ed and head of dept 1984–85; picture ed and head of dept Macdonald & Co publishers (following takeover of Orbis) 1985–87, illustrations research controller Octopus Publishing Group 1987–90, picture coordinator and head of stills British Satellite Broadcasting Ltd 1990–91, chief exec Design and Artists Copyright Soc (and DACS rep on Br Copyright Cncl) 1991–; memb Confédération Internationale d'Auteurs Graphiques et Plastiques Ctees on Tariff Structure and Cable and Satellite Bdcasting; non-exec dir Educnl Recording Agency; *Style*— Ms Rachel Duffield; ✉ Design and Artists Copyright Society, Parchment House, Northburgh Street, London EC1 (☎ 0171 336 8811, fax 0171 336 8822)

DUFFIELD, Vivien Louise; CBE (1989); da of Sir Charles Clore (d 1978), and Francine, *née* Halphen (d 1993); *b* 26 March 1946; *Educ* French Lycée London, Cours Victor Hugo Paris, Heathfield Sch Ascot, LMH Oxford (MA); *m* 1969 (m dis 1976), John Duffield; 1 s (George Lincoln b 1973), 1 da (Arabella Elizabeth b 1971); *Career* chm Clore Fndn UK and Israel 1978–; NSPCC: memb Centenary Appeal Ctee 1983, memb Fin Devpt Ctee 1985; Royal Opera House Trust: dir 1985–, dep chm 1988–95, chm 1995–, chm Devpt Appeal 1996; dir Royal Opera House 1990–; vice chm: Wishing Well Appeal Great Ormond St Hosp 1987–, Cancer Appeal Royal Marsden Hosp 1990–; chm Eureka children's museum Halifax 1986–, dir Royal Ballet 1990–; tstee Dulwich Picture Gallery; benefactor of the year NACF; fell King's Coll London (FKC); Hon DPhil Weizmann Inst 1985, Hon RCM Royal Coll of Music 1987, Hon DLitt Univ of Buckingham 1990; *Recreations* skiing, shooting, opera, ballet; *Style*— Mrs Vivien Duffield, CBE; ✉ c/o The Clore Foundation, Unit 3, Chelsea Manor Studios, Flood St, London SW3 5SR

DUFFY, Carol Ann; OBE (1995); da of Francis Duffy, and Mary, *née* Black; *b* 23 Dec 1955; *Educ* St Joseph's Convent Stafford, Stafford Girls' HS, Univ of Liverpool (BA); *Career* freelance writer and poet; *Awards* Eric Gregory Award 1984, C Day Lewis fellowship 1982–84, Somerset Maugham Award 1988, Dylan Thomas Award 1990, Scottish Arts Cncl Book Award of Merit 1985 and 1990, Whitbread Award for Poetry 1993; *Books* Standing Female Nude (1985), Selling Manhattan (1987, 4 edn 1994), The Other Country (1990), Mean Time (1993), Selected Poems (1994), Anvil New Poets (ed, 1994); *Style*— Ms Carol Ann Duffy, OBE; ✉ c/o Anvil Press, Neptune House, 70 Royal Hill, London SE10 8RT (☎ 0171 469 3033)

DUFFY, Dr Francis Cuthbert (Frank); CBE (1997); s of John Austin Duffy (d 1944), and Annie Margaret, *née* Reed; *b* 3 Sept 1940; *Educ* St Cuthbert's GS Newcastle upon Tyne, Architectural Assoc Sch London (AADipl), Univ of California (MArch), Princeton (MA, PhD); *m* 4 Sept 1965, Jessica Mary, da of Philip Bear, of Chiddingstone, Kent; 3 da (Sibylla b 1966, Eleanor b 1969, Katya b 1970); *Career* asst architect Nat Bldg Agency 1964–67, Harkness fell of the Cwlth Fund 1967–70 (in USA), estab and head of London Office JFN Assoc 1971–74, currently chm DEGW International Ltd architects (fndr ptnr 1974); fndr and chm Bldg Use Studies 1980–88, fndr and chief ed Facilities (newsletter) 1984–90, conslt on the working environment to many cos and instns; pres Architects' Council of Europe 1994, PRIBA 1994–95; FRSA; *Books* Planning Office Space (jtly, 1976), The Orbit Study (princ author, 1984), Orbit 2 (jtly, 1985), The Changing City (jtly, 1989), The Changing Workplace (1992), The Responsible Workplace (jtly, 1993); *Clubs* Architectural Association, Athenaeum, Princeton (NY); *Style*— Dr Francis Duffy, CBE; ✉ DEGW International Ltd, 8 Crinan Street, London N1 9SQ (☎ 0171 239 7777, fax 0171 278 3613); 195 Liverpool Road, London N1 0RF (☎ 0171 837 3064); 3 The Terrace, Walberswick, Suffolk (☎ 01502 723814)

DUFFY, Prof John Alastair; s of John Duffy (d 1952), of Birmingham, and Edna Frances, *née* Walker; *b* 24 Sept 1932; *Educ* Solihull Sch Warwicks, Univ of Sheffield (BSc, PhD), Univ of Aberdeen (DSc); *m* 19 Dec 1959, Muriel Florence Lyon, da of Edward Ramsay (d 1977), of Hamilton; 1 s (Alastair b 1965), 1 da (Penelope b 1968); *Career* res chemist Albright & Wilson 1958–59, lectr Wolverhampton Poly 1959–61, sr lectr NE Wales Inst 1961–65, lectr, sr lectr, reader then prof of chem Univ of Aberdeen 1966–; quality assessor for Scottish Higher Educn Funding Cncl 1993–94; conslt: Schott Glaswerke W Germany 1984–86, Br Steel Corp 1986–89; author of 150 scientific pubns; chm NE Scotland Section Royal Soc of Chemistry 1978–81; FRSC, CChem; *Books* General Inorganic Chemistry (1966), Bonding, Energy Levels and Bands in Inorganic Solids (1990); *Recreations* music, romantic opera; *Style*— Prof John Duffy; ✉ 35 Beechgrove Terrace, Aberdeen AB15 5DR (☎ 01224 641752); Department of Chemistry, The University, Aberdeen (☎ 01224 272901, telex 73458 UNIABN G, fax 01224 272921, e-mail j.a.duffy@abdn.ac.uk)

DUFFY, Most Rev Joseph Augustine; *see:* Clogher, Bishop of (RC)

DUFFY, Mark Peter; s of Arthur Peter Duffy, and Mary Louise Marsland; *b* 8 Nov 1956; *Educ* Liverpool Inst, Peterhouse Cambridge (MA); *Career* investmt analyst W Greenwell and Co 1980–85, dir S G Warburg Securities 1985–95, exec dir SBC Warburg 1995–; *Publications* Rothmans International (1984), BAT and Financial Services (1985), RJR Nabisco - Profile of a New Group (1986), Tobacco Stocks and Diversification (1988), BAT the Dollar and Farmers Group (1988), Unilever and Personal Products (1989), How Important are the New Cigarette Markets (1991), Risk and Reward in Food Manufacturing (1992), Crisis and Compromise: CAP and GATT Reform (1992), BAT in Perspective (1993), Value in Food Manufacturing (1994), FET and Dividend Flow (1994), Tobacco Stocks & Markets (1995), Tobacco Litigation - the Investment Risk (1995); *Style*— Mark Duffy, Esq; ✉ SBC Warburg Securities, 1 Finsbury Ave, London EC2M 2PA (☎ 0171 606 1066)

DUFFY, Maureen Patricia; da of Grace Wright; *b* 1933; *Educ* Trowbridge HS, Sarah Bonnell HS for Girls, King's Coll London (BA); *Career* author, playwright and poet; co fndr Writers' Action Gp; chm: Authors Licensing and Collecting Soc 1980–95, Br Copyright Cncl 1989–, Copyright Licensing Agency 1996–; pres Writers' Guild of GB 1986–89 (jt chm 1977–88); vice pres: Euro Writers Congress 1991–, Beauty Without Cruelty; FRSL; *Books* incl: Illuminations (1991), Occam's Razor (1993), Henry Purcell (1994); *Style*— Ms Maureen Duffy; ✉ 18 Fabian Rd, London SW6 7TZ (fax 0171 385 2468)

DUFFY, Sir (Albert Edward) Patrick; kt (1991); s of James Duffy (d 1973), and Margaret Duffy (d 1992); *b* 17 June 1920; *Educ* LSE (BSc, PhD), Columbia Univ NY (PhD); *Career* Lt Fleet Air Arm RN 1940–46; economist; lectr Univ of Leeds; MP (Lab): Colne Valley 1963–66, Sheffield Attercliffe 1970–92; Parly under sec of state for def (Navy) 1976–79, former chm Select Ctee on Trade and Indust, Lab Parly Econ Affairs Fin Gp and Lab Def Gp, oppn spokesman on def 1979–80 and 1983–92, pres North Atlantic Assembly 1988–90 (memb 1979–, vice pres 1987), dep chm Atlantic Cncl of the UK 1994–; *Clubs* Trades & Labour (Doncaster), Naval; *Style*— Sir Patrick Duffy; ✉ 153 Bennetthorpe, Doncaster, S Yorks

DUFFY, Patrick G; s of Dr J B Duffy, and Mrs E C Duffy; *b* 8 Jan 1949; *Educ* (BCh, BOA); *m* 13 July 1987, Dr Zara Anne, *née* McClenahan; 2 s (Frederick b 16 July 1989, Peter b 12 July 1991), 2 da (Emmylene b 28 Oct 1993, Sarah-Jane b 24 Aug 1995); *Career* conslt paediatric urologist The Hosps for Sick Children Gt Ormond St London, sr lectr in paediatric urology Inst of Urology London; memb: BMA, RSM, FRCSI; *Recreations* sailing, squash, music; *Style*— Patrick Duffy, Esq; ✉ 13 Rookfield Ave, London N10 3TS; Portland Consulting Suite, 234 Great Portland Street, London W1N 5PH (☎ 0171 390 8322, fax 0171 390 8324)

DUFFY, Philip Edmund; s of Walter Duffy (d 1991), and Ellen Dalton (d 1995); *b* 21 Jan 1943; *Educ* St Edward's Coll W Derby, Royal Manchester Coll of Music (GRSM, ARMCM), Univ of London; *Career* master of the music Liverpool Metropolitan Cathedral 1966–96; memb Cncl Royal Sch Church Music; hon fell Guild of Church Musicians 1994; ISM 1966; KSG 1981; *Recreations* reading, theatre, walking; *Style*— Philip Duffy, Esq; ✉ 2 South Court, Wexford Road, Oxton L43 9TD

DUFFY, Simon; *b* 27 Nov 1949; *Educ* Univ of Oxford (BA), Harvard Business Sch (Harkness fell, MBA); *Career* analyst N M Rothschild and Sons 1973–76, analyst Shell UK 1978–80, conslt Bain and Company 1980–82, gen mangr planning and treasy Consolidated Gold Fields plc 1982–86, dir of corp fin Guinness PLC 1986–89, ops dir Guinness subsid United Distillers Ltd 1989–92, gp fin dir EMI Group plc (formerly Thorn EMI) 1992–; non-exec dir: Gartmore plc, Intellectual Property Inst; FRSA; *Style*— Simon Duffy; ✉ EMI Group plc, 4 Tenterden Street, Hanover Square, London W1A 2AY (☎ 0171 355 4848, fax 0171 495 1309)

DUFFY, Terence John; s of John Edward Duffy (d 1989), of Birkenhead, Cheshire, and Theresa, *née* Williamson (d 1963); *b* 24 Aug 1947; *Educ* St Anselm's Coll Cheshire, Jesus Coll Cambridge (BA, MA), New Coll Oxford (BM BCh); *m* 6 Aug 1971, Rowena Siriol, da of Henry Vaughan-Roberts, BM, of Conwy, N Wales; 1 s (Elliot Edward Vaughan b 1977), 1 da (Alexandra Margaret Theresa (Sasha) b 1983); *Career* house appts Bedford and Oxford 1972–73, demonstrator in anatomy Univ of Cambridge 1973–74 (supervisor Jesus Coll 1973–74), sr house offr and registrar Bedford and Cambridge Hosp 1974–78, registrar Swansea 1978–79, Wellcome res fell Cambridge 1979–80, lectr in surgery Univ of Cambridge and fell Jesus Coll 1980–84, sr lectr in surgery Univ of Keele 1984–89, conslt in gen and breast surgery N Staffs Hosp 1984–; numerous pubns on gen and transplant surgery 1978–; memb: Br Transplant Soc, W Midlands Surgical Soc, BMA 1969, BTS 1980, BASO 1990; FRCS 1977, FRSM 1989; *Recreations* music, sport; *Style*— Terence Duffy, Esq; ✉ North Staffordshire Hospital Centre, City General Hospital, Newcastle Rd, Stoke-on-Trent, Staffs (☎ 01782 718741)

DUGDALE, Hon David John; s of 1 Baron Crathorne, PC, TD (d 1977); *b* 4 May 1942; *Educ* Eton, Trinity Coll Cambridge; *m* 1972, Susan Louise, da of Maj L A Powell (d 1972); 1 s, 1 da; *Career* farmer and engr; High Sheriff for Co of Cleveland 1995; *Recreations* building, photography, shooting; *Style*— The Hon David Dugdale; ✉ Park House, Crathorne, Yarm, North Yorkshire TS15 0BD (☎ 01642 700225, work 01642 700295)

DUGDALE, Lady; Dame Kathryn Edith Helen; DCVO (1984, CVO 1973), JP (Shropshire 1964), DL (Shropshire 1995); da of Col Rt Hon Oliver Frederick George Stanley, MC, PC, MP (d 1950), and Lady Maureen Vane Tempest Stewart (see Londonderry); gda of 17 Earl of Derby; and Lady Alice Montagu, da of Duke of Manchester; *b* 4 Nov 1923; *m* 1956, Sir John Robert Stratford Dugdale, KCVO (d 1994), s of Sir William Francis Stratford Dugdale, 1 Bt (d 1965); 2 s (Edward Stratford b 1959, Henry Stratford b 1963), 2 da (Elizabeth Alice b 1957, Mary b 1961); *Career* woman of the bedchamber to HM The Queen 1955– (temporary extra 1961–71); *Style*— Lady Dugdale, DCVO, JP, DL; ✉ Tickwood Hall, Much Wenlock, Shropshire TF13 6NZ (☎ 01952 882644)

DUGDALE, Keith Stuart; JP (1967); s of George Dugdale (d 1954), of Norwich, and Dorothy Elizabeth, *née* Parkerson (d 1970); *b* 27 Sept 1930; *Educ* Gresham's Sch Holt, Magdalen Coll Oxford (MA); *m* 1957, Angela Marion, *née* Willey, DL Norfolk 1992; 2 s

(Christopher John b 1966, Jeremy Keith b 1969), 1 da (Hilary Ruth b 1964); *Career* CA; Martin & Acock: articled clerk 1951, ptnr 1956–94; pt/t memb VAT Tbnls 1992–; chm Norfolk and Norwich Triennial Festival 1977–82, pres E Anglian Soc of CAs 1978–79, vice chm Norfolk Family Health Servs Authy 1990–96, memb E Norfolk Health Authy 1996–, chm Norwich Bench 1996–; FCA 1955; *Recreations* book collecting, music, gardening; *Clubs* Norfolk; *Style*— Keith Dugdale, Esq, JP; ✉ Beck House, Kelling, Holt, Norfolk NR25 7EL (☎ 01263 588389, fax 01263 588594)

DUGDALE, (William) Matthew Stratford; s and h of Sir William Stratford Dugdale, 2 Bt, CBE, MC, *qv*; *b* 22 Feb 1959; *m* 1990, Paige Sullivan, da of late Thomas Haines Dudley Perkins; 2 s (William Stratford b 15 Aug 1992, Nathaniel Francis Stratford b 29 Aug 1996), 2 da (Clementine Alexandra Louise b 1991, Fernanda Elizabeth Grace b 15 April 1994); *Style*— Matthew Dugdale, Esq; ✉ Merevale Hall, Atherstone, Warwickshire CV9 2HG

DUGDALE, Sir William Stratford; 2 Bt (UK 1936), of Merevale and Blyth, Co Warwick; CBE (1982), MC (1943), JP (Warwicks 1951), DL (1955); s of Sir William Francis Stratford Dugdale, 1 Bt (d 1965); *b* 29 March 1922; *Educ* Eton, Balliol Coll Oxford; *m* 1, 13 Dec 1952, Lady Belinda Pleydell-Bouverie (d 1961), da of 7 Earl of Radnor, KG, KCVO; 1 s ((William) Matthew Stratford b 1959), 3 da (Laura (Hon Mrs Arthur Hazlerigg) b 1953, Matilda (Mrs Marcus May) b 1955, Charlotte (Hon Mrs Gerard Noel) b (twin) 1955); m 2, 17 Oct 1967, Cecilia Mary, da of Lt-Col Sir William Malcolm Mount, 2 Bt, ED, DL (d 1993); 1 s (Thomas Joshua Stratford b 1974), 1 da (Adelaide Margaret Victoria Jane b 1970); *Heir* s, (William) Matthew Stratford Dugdale b 22 Feb 1959; *Career* Capt Grenadier Gds 1944, served in Africa and Italy (despatches); slr 1949; chm: Trent River Authy 1965–73, Severn Trent Water Authy 1974–84, Nat Water Cncl 1982–84, General Utilities PLC 1988–; dir Phoenix Assurance 1985 (and other cos); chm Aston Villa FC 1973–81; High Sheriff Warwicks 1971–72; High Steward of Stratford-upon-Avon 1976–; *Clubs* Brooks's, White's, MCC, Jockey; *Style*— Sir William Dugdale, Bt, CBE, MC, JP, DL; ✉ Blyth Hall, Coleshill, Birmingham B46 2AD (☎ 01675 462203, fax 01675 465071); Merevale Hall, Atherstone, Warwicks (☎ 01827 713143, fax 01827 718090); 24 Bryanston Mews West, London W1 (☎ and fax 0171 262 2510)

DUGGAN, Prof Arthur William; s of Bernard Morgan Duggan, of Brisbane, Australia, and Margaret, *née* Bell; *b* 14 June 1936; *Educ* Univ of Queensland (BSc, MB BS, MD), Aust Nat Univ (PhD); *m* 4 July 1961, (Gwyndolyn) Helen, da of William Nathan Randall (d 1980); 2 s (Peter b 1962, Richard b 1964), 1 da (Anne b 1969); *Career* med practice Queensland Aust 1961–67 (med res 1968–70), CJ Martin fell Nat Health Med Res Cncl of Aust 1971–73, sr fell in pharmacology Inst of Advanced Studies Aust Nat Univ 1974–87, prof of vet pharmacology Univ of Edinburgh 1987–, RSM Fndn visiting prof 1989–; pres Aust Pain Soc; FRSE 1994; *Recreations* golf; *Style*— Prof Arthur Duggan, FRSE; ✉ 5C Strathalmond Rd, Edinburgh EH4 8AB; Department of Preclinical Vet Sciences, University of Edinburgh, Summerhall, Edinburgh EH9 1QH (☎ 0131 650 6100)

DUGGAN, HE Gordon Aldridge; CMG; *b* 12 Aug 1937; *Educ* Liverpool Collegiate Sch, Lincoln Coll Oxford; *m* 1969, Erica, *née* Anderssen; 1 s, 2 da; *Career* joined Foreign Office 1963, High Cmmn Canberra 1966–69, E African Dept Cwlth Coordination Dept FCO 1969–72, press and information offr Embassy Bonn 1972–74, first sec and head of Chancery Embassy Jakarta 1974–76, first sec High Cmmn Canberra 1976–79, asst S American Dept FCO 1979–80, commercial and economic cnsllr High Cmmn Lagos 1981–84, consul-gen and dir of Br export promotion in Switzerland Zurich 1985–88, head Commercial Mgmnt and Exports Dept 1988–89, on secondment as dir of project devpt Northern Engineering Industries PLC 1989–90, high cmmr to Singapore 1991–; *Clubs* Oxford and Cambridge; *Style*— HE Mr Gordon Duggan, CMG; ✉ c/o FCO (Singapore), King Charles Street, London SW1A 2AH

DUGGIN, Thomas Joseph (Tom); s of Joseph Duggin (d 1986), of Bury, Lancs, and Alice Lilian, *née* Mansfield; *b* 15 Sept 1947; *Educ* Thornleigh Salesian Coll; *m* 1, 1968 (m dis); 2 s (Nicholas James b 1973, Alistair Richard b 1975); m 2, 1983 (m dis); *Career* HM Dip Serv: joined 1967, desk offr Cwlth Policy and Planning Dept FCO 1967–68, desk offr Protocol Dept FCO 1969, third sec (commercial) Oslo 1969–73, third, later second sec (commercial) Bucharest 1973–76, asst private sec Private Office FCO 1976–79, second sec (Chancery/info) Bangkok 1979–82, first sec S America Dept FCO 1982–85, head of Chancery and consul La Paz 1985–88, head of Chancery Mexico City 1989–91, high cmmr to Vanuatu 1992–95, head of Security Dept FCO 1995–; *Recreations* golf, reading, music, tennis; *Style*— Tom Duggin, Esq; ✉ c/o Foreign and Commonwealth Office, King Charles Street, London SW1A 2AH

DUGUID, Ian McIver; s of John Duguid (d 1980), and Georgina, *née* McIver (d 1983); *b* 16 April 1926; *Educ* Aberdeen GS, Univ of Aberdeen (MB ChB, MD, DSc 1995), Univ of London (DO, PhD); *m* 1961 (m dis 1995); 2 s (Graham b 1963, Stewart b 1967); *Career* awarded scholarship to the Centre National de la Recherche Scientifique at the Fondation Opthalmologique de Rothschild (Paris) 1955; formerly sr ophthalmic surgn Charing Cross, Westminster and Moorfields Eye Hosps London; Liveryman Worshipful Soc of Apothecaries; FRCS 1961 (examiner in ophthalmology RCS London), FRCOphth 1988; Offr de l'Ordre National du Merite (1986); *Recreations* rugby, cars; *Style*— Ian Duguid, Esq; ✉ 73 Harley St, London W1N 1DE (☎ 0171 935 5874, fax 0171 224 5210)

DUGUID, Keith Paris; s of John Paris Duguid (d 1971), of Walsall, Staffs, and Gladys May, *née* Cooksey (d 1985); *b* 19 Jan 1942; *Educ* Chuckery Secdy Sch Walsall, Wednesbury Tech Coll Staffs, Manchester Coll of Sci & Technol; *m* 11 Sept 1965, Ann Moll, da of Charles Davis; 1 s (Angus John Paris b 3 June 1975), 2 da (Sally Ann b 22 Jan 1969, Rebecca b 15 June 1971); *Career* trainee then medical photographer Dept of Medical Illustration Manchester Royal Infirmary 1958–63; Dept of Medical Illustration and AV Services Westminster Hosp Medical Sch 1966–85 (med photographer, sr med photographer, dep to dir, head of Dept), dir Dept of Medical Illustration Univ of Aberdeen 1985–; lectr in UK USA and ME, examiner in med photography and AV to RPS, BIPP and Inst of Med Illustrators, ed Journal of Audiovisual Media in Medicine 1982–92, memb Editorial Bd Journal of Educational Technology Abstracts, author of over 40 papers; awards: Presidential award BIPP 1990, Norman K Harrison award Inst of Med Illustrators, Harold E Louis Research Film award BMA; FRPS, FBIPP, hon fell Inst of Med Illustrators; *Books* Essential Clinical Signs (jtly, 1990), Illustrated Cases in Acute Clinical Medicine (jtly, 1994); *Recreations* gardening, painting; *Style*— Keith Duguid, Esq; ✉ University of Aberdeen, Department of Medical Illustration, University Medical Buildings, Foresterhill, Aberdeen AB25 2ZD (☎ 01224 681818 ext 53813, fax 01224 404951)

DUKE, Prof Chris; s of Frederick Alexander Duke, of London, and Edith, *née* Page; *b* 4 Oct 1938; *Educ* Eltham Coll, Jesus Coll Cambridge (BA, CertEd, MA), King's Coll London (PhD); *m* 1 (m dis 1981), Audrey Ann, *née* Solomon; 1 s (Stephen b 1968), 2 da (Annie b 1970, Cathy b 1972); m 2, Jan 1982, Elizabeth Ann, da of E Lloyd Sommerlad, of Sydney, Aust; 2 s (Alex b 1978, Paul b 1981); *Career* lectr: Woolwich Poly 1961–66, Univ of Leeds 1966–69; fndr dir of continuing educn Australian National Univ 1969–85, fndn prof, chm of continuing educn and dir of open studies Univ of Warwick 1985–96 (pro-vice-chllr 1991–95), dep vice-chllr Univ of NSW and UWS Nepean pres 1996–; ed Int Jl of Univ Adult Educn 1971–96, author of various books; vice chm Universities Assoc for Continuing Educn 1994–96 (sec 1989–94), various other int and local continuing educn positions; Hon DLitt Keimyung Univ Korea; FACE, FRSA; *Recreations* gardening, bird-watching, living; *Style*— Prof Chris Duke; ✉ 26 Nepean Road, Emu Plains, Penrith, NSW, Australia; University of Western Sydney Nepean, PO Box 10, Kingswood, NSW 2747, Australia (☎ 00 61 47 360 229, fax 00 61 47 364 186, e-mail C.duke@uws.edu.au)

DUKE, Neville Frederick; DSO (1943), OBE (1953), DFC (1942 and two bars 1943, 1944), AFC (1948); s of Frederick Herbert Duke; *b* 11 Jan 1922; *Educ* Convent of St Mary, Judd Sch Tonbridge; *m* 1947, Gwendoline Dorothy, da of Stanley Fellows; *Career* RAF fighter pilot and test pilot 1940–48; served WWII: UK, W Desert, N Africa; CO 145 Sqdn Italy 1944, Sqdn Ldr, ret RAF 1948; CO 615 Sqdn RAuxAF 1950–51; chief test pilot Hawker Aircraft Ltd 1948–56, md Duke Aviation, mangr Aircraft Operating Unit Dowty Group, tech advsr consIt and chief test pilot Miles Aviation Ltd; test pilot: Brooklands Aerospace Group, Lovaux Ltd, Croplease Ltd, Aeronautic Ltd; MC (Czech) 1946; Queen's Commendation 1955; hon fell Soc of Experimental Test Pilots 1991; FRAeS; *Recreations* flying (private owner), fishing, sailing; *Clubs* Royal Cruising, Royal Naval Sailing Assoc, Royal Lymington Yacht, Bournemouth Flying, Old Sarum Flying; *Style*— Neville Duke, Esq, DSO, OBE, DFC, AFC; ✉ 3 Vitre Gardens, Lymington, Hants SO41 3NA

DUKE, Timothy Hugh Stewart; s of William Falcon Duke (d 1954), of Sway, Hants, and Mary Cecile, *née* Jackson; *b* 12 June 1953; *Educ* Uppingham, Fitzwilliam Coll Cambridge (BA); *Career* Peat Marwick Mitchell & Co 1974–81; College of Arms: research asst 1981–89, Rouge Dragon Pursuivant of Arms 1989–95, Chester Herald of Arms 1995–; Liveryman Worshipful Co of Broderers 1987; hon sec Harleian Soc 1994–; *Clubs* Travellers'; *Style*— Timothy Duke, Esq, Chester Herald of Arms; ✉ College of Arms, Queen Victoria Street, London EC4V 4BT (☎ 0171 236 7728, fax 0171 248 6448)

DULSON, Robert Pace (Bob); s of Henry Dulson (d 1985), of Newcastle-Under-Lyme, and Irene May Dulson, MBE, *née* Walley; *b* 31 July 1946; *Educ* Newcastle HS Staffordshire; *m* 2 Feb 1974, Angela, da of Albert Askey, of Leek, Staffordshire; *Career* journalist Northcliffe Newspapers 1970–78; BBC: publicist 1978, sr publicity offr 1985–88, chief press offr 1988–89, head of corporate press relations 1989–; *Recreations* music, theatre, gardening, DIY enthusiast; *Style*— Bob Dulson, Esq; ✉ Room 111, Henry Wood House, 3 and 6 Langham Place, London W1A 1AA (☎ 0171 765 3684)

DULVERTON, 3 Baron (UK 1929); Sir (Gilbert) Michael Hamilton Wills; 4 Bt (UK) 1897; s of 2 Baron Dulverton, CBE, TD, DL (d 1992), and his 1 w Judith Betty, *née* Leslie Melville (d 1983); *b* 2 May 1944; *Educ* Gordonstoun; *m* 1980, Rosalind Johnny Maria, da of late J van der Velde, of Rozenburg, Holland, and late Mrs R D Oliver, of Lochside, Kelso, Roxburghshire; 1 s (Hon Robert Anthony Hamilton b 20 Oct 1983), 1 da (Hon Charlotte Alexandra Hamilton b 1981); *Heir* s, Hon Robert Anthony Hamilton Wills b 20 Oct 1983; *Career* farmer, forester and industrialist; dir: West Highland Woodlands Ltd, Batsford Estate Co, Cotswold Houses Ltd; dep chm Thwaites Ltd; tstee: Batsford Fndn, Dulverton Tst; *Style*— The Rt Hon the Lord Dulverton; ✉ c/o House of Lords, London SW1A OPW

DUMA, Alexander Agim; s of Dervish Duma, of West Horsley, Surrey, and Naftali, *née* Andoni (d 1966); *b* 30 March 1946; *Educ* UCL (LLB); *m* 1980 (m dis 1983), Mary Gertrude, da of Surgn-Col E W Hayward, of Oxon; *Career* called to the Bar Gray's Inn 1969; Parly candidate (C) 1979, GLC candidate (C) Bermondsey 1977; dir: Blackfriars Settlement 1977–84 and 1986–89, Barclays de Zoete Wedd Ltd 1983–87, Chase Investment Bank Ltd 1987–89, Smith New Court Corporate Finance Ltd 1989–92 (consIt 1992–94), Equity & General plc 1987–90, Torday & Carlisle plc 1988–92, The New Plastics Co Ltd 1990–94, Lady Clare Ltd 1994–, Opera Players Ltd; chm: Oldavon Ltd (dir 1988–), Poundfloat Ltd 1992–95; consIt Granville & Co Ltd 1992–94, UK rep Deloitte & Touche Albania 1993–95; memb Cncl Newcomen Collett Fndn 1977–94, pres Bermondsey Cons Assoc 1979–83; hon consul Republic of Albania 1992–94; FCA; *Clubs* Carlton; *Style*— Alexander Duma, Esq; ✉ 13 Coulson St, London SW3 3NG (☎ 0171 823 7422, fax 0171 581 0982)

DUMAS, Dr Angela Mary Piers; *b* 29 June 1948; *Educ* Interior Design Dept Hammersmith Coll of Art & Bldg (Cert of Art and Design), Sch of Environmental Design RCA (MA), Univ of London (PhD); *children* 1 s (b 1967); *Career* designer Pentagram int design consultancy 1976–77, dir Dumas Baker Design Consultancy 1977–85, design mgmnt consIt British Railways Bd 1988–90; research dir Design Cncl 1995– (pt/t interim mangr for research 1994–95); Centre for Design Mgmnt London Business Sch: res fell 1985–88, consIt on the mgmnt of design 1988–91, dir 1991–; visiting fell London Business Sch, course planner Leicester Poly and Chelsea Sch of Art 1977–85; CNAA: memb and vice chm Three Dimensional Design Bd 1983–87, memb Ctee for Art and Design 1987–89; external examiner in design Univ of Ulster, memb Res Ctee PCFC 1989–90, reviewed design degree for Hong Kong Poly 1990, external examiner (BA Design Mgmnt) De Montfort Univ Leicester 1993, sr research assoc Judge Inst of Mgmnt Studies Univ of Cambridge; presenter at various int confs and author of various papers on design mgmnt; FRSA 1987, FCSD 1993; *Style*— Dr Angela Dumas; ✉ Design Council, Haymarket House, 1 Oxenden Street, London SW1Y 4EE (☎ 0171 208 2121, fax 0171 930 6483)

DUMAS, Col (John) Jeremy; OBE (1991); s of Lt-Col John Roger Dumas, Andover, Hants, and Hermione Elizabeth, *née* Parry; *b* 6 June 1942; *Educ* Radley; *m* 26 Feb 1966, Elizabeth Jane, da of Maj-Gen W Odling, CB, OBE, MC, of Fingringhoe, Colchester, Essex; 1 s (Richard John b 19 Dec 1967), 2 da (Alethea (Leafy) b 7 Jan 1970, Emily b 13 Jan 1972); *Career* cmmnd RA 1962, Capt 1969, Maj 1975, Lt-Col 1983, defence attaché Beirut 1989–90, Col 1991, defence attaché Damascus 1991–94, defence advsr Kingston Jamaica 1994–; *Recreations* offshore sailing, skiing; *Clubs* Army and Navy, West Mersea Yacht; *Style*— Col Jeremy Dumas; ✉ c/o Foreign & Commonwealth Office (Kingston), King Charles Street, London SW1A 2AH

DUMFRIES, Johnny; *see:* Bute, 7 Marquess of

DUMMETT, (Agnes Margaret) Ann; da of Arthur William Chesney (d 1949), and Kitty Mary, *née* Ridge (d 1988); *b* 4 Sept 1930; *Educ* Guildhouse Sch Pimlico London, Ware GS, Somerville Coll Oxford (exhibitioner, BA, MA); *m* 1951, Michael Anthony Eardley Dummett, *qv*, s of George Herbert Dummett (d 1971); 4 s (Christopher b 1952, Andrew b 1953, Paul b 1960, Philip b and d 1963), 3 da (Susanna b 1957, Judith b 1958 d 1960, Tessa b 1958); *Career* community rels offr Oxford City 1966–69, various res posts and temp teacher 1969–77, res worker Jt Cncl for the Welfare of Immigrants 1978–84, dir Runnymede Tst 1984–87, pt/t consIt on Euro policies to Cmmn for Racial Equality 1990–; formerly memb Catholic Bishops' Cmmn for Racial Justice, memb Govt Ctee of Inquiry into the Educn of Ethnic Minority Gps (Rampton/Swann Ctee) 1979–85; *Books* A Portrait of English Racism (1973), Citizenship and Nationality (1976), A New Immigration Policy (1978), British Nationality (with Ian Martin, 1982), Towards a Just Immigration Policy (ed, 1986), Subjects, Citizens, Aliens and Others (with Andrew Nicol, 1990); author of numerous articles and chapters in symposia; *Recreations* theatre going, walking in cities; *Clubs* Royal Cwlth Soc; *Style*— Mrs Ann Dummett; ✉ 54 Park Town, Oxford OX2 6SJ; Commission for Racial Equality, Elliot House, 10–12 Allington St, London SW1E 5EH (☎ 0171 828 7022, fax 0171 630 7605)

DUMMETT, Prof Michael Anthony Eardley; s of George Herbert Dummett (d 1970), and Mabel Iris, *née* Eardley-Wilmot (d 1980); *b* 27 June 1925; *Educ* Sandroyd Sch, Winchester, ChCh Oxford; *m* 1951, Ann Dummett, *qv*, *née* Chesney; 3 s, 2 da (1 s and 1 da decd); *Career* Univ of Oxford: fell All Souls Coll 1950–79 (sr res fell 1974–79, emeritus fell), reader philosophy of mathematics 1962–74, Wykeham prof of logic 1979–92 (emeritus prof), fell New Coll Oxford 1979–92 (emeritus fell); author of books on philosophy, voting theory and tarot; Hon DPhil Univ of Nijmegen 1983; Hon DLitt:

Univ of Caen 1993, Univ of Aberdeen 1993; FBA 1968–81 and 1995–; *Books include* Truth and Other Enigmas (1978), The Game of Tarot (1980); *Recreations* playing exotic card games; *Style*— Prof Michael Dummett, FBA; ✉ 54 Park Town, Oxford OX2 6SJ (☎ and fax 01865 558698); New College, Oxford (☎ 01865 279555)

DUMPER, Rt Rev Anthony Charles (Tony); s of Lt Charles Frederick Dumper, MC (d 1965), and Edith Mary, *née* Ribbins (d 1966); *b* 4 Oct 1923; *Educ* Surbiton GS, Christ's Coll Cambridge (BA, MA), Westcott House Cambridge; *m* 5 June 1948, Sibylle Anna Emilie, da of Paul Hellwig (d 1945), of Germany; 2 s (Peter Nicholas b 1951, Michael Richard Thomas b 1956), 1 da (Hildegard Sarah Sibylle b 1954); *Career* ordained 1947, archdeacon N Malaya 1955–64, dean Singapore 1964–70, rural dean Stockton on Tees 1970–77, bishop of Dudley 1977–93, hon asst bishop Birmingham 1993–; memb CND; *Books* Vortex of the East (1962); *Recreations* walking, gardening, reading; *Style*— The Rt Rev Tony Dumper; ✉ 117 Berberry Close, Bournville, Birmingham B30 1TB (☎ 0121 458 3011)

DUMVILLE, Prof David Norman; s of Norman Dumville (d 1958), and Eileen Florence Lillie, *née* Gibbs (d 1996); *b* 5 May 1949; *Educ* St Nicholas GS Northwood, Emmanuel Coll Cambridge (open entrance exhibitioner, sr scholar, MA), Univ of Edinburgh (PhD, Jeremiah Dalziel Prize); *m* 1, 23 Nov 1974, Sally Lois, *née* Hannay (d 1989); 1 s (Elliott Thomas b 19 July 1978); m 2, 29 Dec 1990, Prof Yoko Wada; 1 step s (Taro b 29 Oct 1989); *Career* Univ of Wales fell Dept of Welsh Univ Coll of Swansea 1976–77, asst prof Dept of English Univ of Pennsylvania 1977–78; Univ of Cambridge: univ lectr Dept of Anglo-Saxon, Norse & Celtic 1978–91, reader in early mediaeval history and culture of the British Isles 1991–95, prof of palaeography and cultural history 1995–; Girton Coll Cambridge: fell, Coll lectr and dir of studies in Anglo-Saxon, Norse and Celtic 1978–, (moral) tutor 1980–82, memb Cncl 1981–82, memb various Coll ctees; external dir of studies in Anglo-Saxon, Norse and Celtic Emmanuel Coll and St Catharine's Coll Cambridge 1978–85, Fitzwilliam Coll Cambridge 1991–; visiting prof and Pepys lectr Center for Medieval and Renaissance Studies UCLA 1995, distinguished visiting prof of medieval studies Univ of California at Berkeley 1997, visiting fell Huntington Library San Marino California 1984; vice-pres Centre Int de Recherche et de Documentation sur le Monachisme Celtique (Daoulas) 1986–; Br Acad research reader in the humanities 1985–87, research conslt Centre for Research and Scholarship St David's Univ Coll Univ of Wales 1987–, research assoc Sch of Celtic Studies Dublin Inst for Advanced Studies 1989–; memb Ed Advsy Bd: Anglo-Saxon Studies in Archaeology and History 1978–85, Toronto Mediaeval Texts and Translations 1978–, Cambridge Medieval Celtic Studies 1980–93 and Cambrian Medieval Celtic Studies 1993–; memb jt Br Acad and Royal Historical Soc Ctee on Anglo-Saxon Charters 1986–90 and 1993–; O'Donnell lectr in Celtic Studies: Univ of Oxford 1977/78, Univ of Edinburgh 1980/81, Univ of Wales 1982/83; FRHistS 1976, FSA 1983, FRSAIre 1989; *Books* Chronicles and Annals of Mediaeval Ireland and Wales: the Clonmacnoise-group Texts (with K Grabowski, 1984), Britain's Literary Heritage: The Early and Central Middle Ages c650–c1200 AD (1986), Histories and Pseudo-histories of the Insular Middle Ages (1990), Wessex and England from Alfred to Edgar. Six Essays on Political, Cultural, and Ecclesiastical Revival (1992), Liturgy and the Ecclesiastical History of Late Anglo-Saxon England: Four Studies (1992), English Caroline Script and Monastic History: Studies in Benedictinism AD 950–1030 (1993), Saint Patrick AD 493–1993 (jtly, 1993), Britons and Anglo-Saxons in the Early Middle Ages (1993); also author of numerous reviews and articles in learned jls; *Recreations* travel in North America, politics and other arguments; *Style*— Prof David Dumville; ✉ Girton College, Cambridge CB3 0JG (☎ 01223 338999, fax 01223 338896)

DUNALLEY, 7 Baron (I 1800); (Henry) Francis Cornelius Prittie; s of 6 Baron Dunalley (d 1992), and (Mary) Philippa, *née* Cary; *b* 30 May 1948; *Educ* Gordonstoun, Trinity Coll Dublin (BA), Bedford Coll London (CQSW); *m* 1978, Sally Louise, er da of late Ronald Vere, of Heaton Chapel, Cheshire; 1 s (Hon Joel Henry b 1981), 3 da (Hon Rebecca Louise b 1979, Hon Hannah Beatrice b 1983, Hon Rachel Sarah b 1987); *Heir* s, Hon Joel Henry Prittie b 29 April 1981; *Career* probation offr: Inner London Probation Serv 1977–80, Buckinghamshire Probation Serv 1980 83, Oxfordshire Probation Serv 1983–; *Style*— The Rt Hon the Lord Dunalley; ✉ 25 Stephen Rd, Oxford OX3 9AY (☎ 01865 61914)

DUNANT, Sarah; da of David Dunant, and Estelle, *née* Joseph; *Educ* Godolphin and Latymer Girls Sch, Newnham Coll Cambridge (BA); *m* 2 da (Zoe b 12 March 1987, Georgia b 30 Dec 1990); *Career* prodr BBC Radio 3 and 4 1974–76; freelance journalist, writer and broadcaster 1976–; presenter The Late Show (BBC2), co-writer Thin Air (BBC1), presenter Chain Reaction (BBC Radio 4); also appeared on other Radio 4 progs, BBC World Service and Capital Radio, contrib to The Listener; lectr Goldsmith's Coll 1985–86; *Books* Exterminating Angels (jtly, 1983), Intensive Care (jtly, 1986), Snow Storms In A Hot Climate (1988), Birth Marks (1991), Fatlands (1993), War of the Words (ed, 1994), Under My Skin (1995), The Age of Anxiety (ed, 1996), Transgressions (1997); *Recreations* travel; *Style*— Ms Sarah Dunant; ✉ Aitken & Stone Ltd, 29 Fernshaw Road, London SW10 0TG (☎ 0171 351 7561, fax 0171 376 3594)

DUNBAR, *see:* Hope-Dunbar

DUNBAR, Sir Archibald Ranulph; 11 Bt (NS 1700), of Northfield, Moray; s of Maj Sir (Archibald) Edward Dunbar, 10 Bt, MC (d 1969); *b* 8 Aug 1927; *Educ* Wellington, Pembroke Coll Cambridge, Imperial Coll of Tropical Agric Trinidad; *m* 1974, Amelia Millar Sommerville, da of late Horace Campbell Davidson, of Currie, Midlothian; 1 s (Edward Horace b 1977), 2 da (Harriet Sophie b 1974, Stephanie Clare b 1975); *Heir* s, Edward Horace Dunbar b 18 March 1977; *Career* Colonial Serv: entered 1953, agric offr Uganda, ret 1970; Hon Sheriff Sheriff Ct Dist of Moray; Kt of Honour and Devotion SMOM 1989; *Books* A History of Bunyoro-Kitara (1965), Omukama Chwa II Kabarega (1965), The Annual Crops of Uganda (1969); *Recreations* swimming, military modelling, model railways; *Clubs* New (Edinburgh); *Style*— Sir Archibald Dunbar, Bt; ✉ The Old Manse, Duffus, Elgin, Scotland IV30 2QD (☎ and fax 01343 830270)

DUNBAR, Sir Drummond Cospatrick Ninian; 9 Bt (NS 1698), of Durn, Banffshire; MC (1943); s of Sir George Alexander Drummond, 8 Bt (d 1949); *b* 9 May 1917; *Educ* Radley, Worcester Coll Oxford (BA 1938); *m* 1957, Sheila Barbara Mary, da of John Berkeley de Fonblanque; 1 s (Robert Drummond Cospatrick); *Heir* s, Robert Drummond Cospatrick Dunbar, Younger of Durn b 17 June 1958; *Career* served WWII Maj Black Watch; served: Middle E 1942–43, N Africa 1943, Sicily 1943, Normandy 1944 (twice wounded); Maj Black Watch, ret 1958; *Style*— Sir Drummond Dunbar, Bt, MC

DUNBAR, Ian; CB (1993); s of Thomas Dunbar (d 1993), of Woodford Green, Essex, and Rose, *née* Hook (d 1977); *b* 6 Jan 1934; *Educ* Buckhurst Hill County HS, Univ of Keele (BA, Dip in Social Studies), Reed Coll Portland USA, LSE (Dip in Applied Social Studies); *m* 11 June 1966, Sally Ann, da of Charles Maurice Hendrickson; 1 da (Tanya b 18 May 1968), 2 s (Alexander b 12 Nov 1970, Thomas b 4 July 1972); *Career* HM Prison Service: joined 1959, Leyhill Prison 1960–65, Prison Service Coll 1965–70, dep govr Long Lartin Prison 1970–72, govr Usk Borstal and Detention Centre 1972–74, Prison Dept (4 Div) Home Office 1974–78, govr Wormwood Scrubs 1983–85 (Feltham Borstal 1978–79, Wakefield Prison 1979–83), regnl dir of SW Region 1985–90, dir of inmate admin 1990–94, ret; *Books* Sense of Direction (1985); *Recreations* bee-keeping, gardening, photography, walking, reading; *Style*— Ian Dunbar, Esq, CB; ✉ c/o HM Prison Service, Headquarters, Cleland House, Page Street, London SW1P 4LN

DUNBAR, Sir James Michael; 14 Bt (NS 1694), of Mochrum, Wigtownshire; er s of Sir Jean Ivor Dunbar, 13 Bt (d 1993), and his 1 w, Rose Jeanne, *née* Hertsch; *b* 17 Jan 1950; *m* 1, 1978 (m dis 1989), Margaret Marie, da of Albert Jacobs; 2 s (Michael Joseph b 5 July 1980, David Scott b 22 May 1983), 1 da (Stacy Beth b 29 July 1985); m 2, 1989, Margaret Elizabeth, da of Gordon Talbot; 1 da (Cassandra Talbot b 23 July 1991); *Heir* s, Michael Joseph Dunbar b 5 July 1980; *Career* Col USAF; *Style*— Sir James Dunbar, Bt

DUNBAR, (William) John; OBE (1986); s of Capt William George Dunbar (d 1980), and Margaret May, *née* Probin (d 1939); *b* 19 May 1931; *Educ* Prior Park Bath; *m* 1958 (m dis 1989), Maureen Ann, da of Col C Harris, OBE, MC (d 1966); 2 s (Simon b 1959, Richard b 1960), 2 da (Catherine b 1961 d 1984, Anna b 1964); m 2, 1989, Gillian Beatrix, da of Joseph Dean Morley (d 1984); *Career* Nat Serv 2 Lt Trieste Italy 1953–55, chief fin offr Olayan Saudi Holdings 1978–80, chief exec BSC (Industry) Ltd 1980–85, gp md BETEC PLC 1985–92, exec dir Clayhithe PLC 1986–92, md Olayan Europe Ltd 1993–; non-exec dir: European Business Development Ltd 1971–, Business in the Community Ltd 1987–, Frigoscandia Ltd 1988–, Strand Associates Ltd 1994–; Freeman City of London 1959; FCMA, FBCS, FInstD, FIMgt; *Recreations* tennis, running, skiing, travel; *Clubs* IOD; *Style*— John Dunbar, Esq, OBE; ✉ Olayan Europe Ltd, 140 Piccadilly, London W1V 9FH (☎ 0171 235 4802, fax 0171 414 0408)

DUNBAR, John Greenwell; s of John Dunbar; *b* 1 March 1930; *Educ* UCS London, Balliol Coll Oxford (MA); *m* 1974, Elizabeth Mill Blyth; *Career* sec Royal Cmmn on the Ancient and Historical Monuments of Scotland 1978–90; memb Ancient Monuments Bd for Scotland 1978–90; FSA, FSA Scot, Hon FRIAS; *Books* The Architecture of Scotland (revised edn, 1978), Accounts of the Masters of Works 1616–1649 (vol 2, jt ed, 1982); *Clubs* New (Edinburgh); *Style*— John Dunbar, Esq, FSA; ✉ Patie's Mill, Carlops, by Penicuik, Midlothian EH26 9NF (☎ 01968 660250)

DUNBAR, Robert Drummond Cospatrick; s and h of Sir Drummond Dunbar, 9 Bt; *b* 17 June 1958; *Educ* Harrow, Ch Ch Oxford; *m* 1994, Sarah Margaret, da of Robert Brooks, of Hattingley, Hants; 1 s (Alexander b 1 March 1995); *Career* investment mangr, slr; AMSIA; *Clubs* Hurlingham; *Style*— Robert Dunbar, Esq; ✉ 32 Westover Road, London SW18 2RQ

DUNBAR OF HEMPRIGGS, Dame Maureen Daisy Helen; Btss (NS 1706), of Hempriggs, Caithness-shire; da of Courtenay Edward Moore (decd), s of late Jessie Mona Duff (who m Rev Canon Courtenay Moore), da of de jure 5 Bt; suc kinsman, Sir George Cospatrick Duff-Sutherland-Dunbar, 7 Bt, 1963; assumed name of Dunbar 1963, and recognised in the name of Dunbar of Hempriggs by Lyon Court 1965; *b* 19 Aug 1906; *Educ* Headington Sch Oxford, RCM (LRAM); *m* 1940, Leonard James Blake (d 1989), former dir of music Malvern Coll; 1 s (Richard Francis b 1945), 1 da (Eleanor Margaret (Mrs Michael Constable) b 1949); *Heir* s, Richard Francis Dunbar of Hempriggs, yr b 8 Jan 1945; *Career* music teacher; *Style*— Lady Dunbar of Hempriggs, Btss; ✉ 51 Gloucester St, Winchcombe, Cheltenham, Glos (☎ 01242 602122)

DUNBOYNE, 28 Baron (18 by Patent) (I 1324 and 1541) Patrick Theobald Tower Butler; VRD; s of 27 Baron (d 1945), and Dora Isolde Butler (d 1977), da of Cdr F F Tower, OBE, RNVR; *b* 27 Jan 1917; *Educ* Winchester, Trinity Coll Cambridge (MA); *m* 29 July 1950, Anne Marie, o da of late Sir Victor Alexander Louis Mallet, GCMG, CVO; 1 s, 3 da; *Heir* s, Hon John Fitzwalter Butler; *Career* 2 Lt (Supp Res) Irish Gds 1939, Lt 1940–44 (POW 1940–43, King's Badge), Refugee Dept Foreign Office 1945–46; called to the Bar: Middle Temple 1949 (Harmsworth scholar), Inner Temple 1962, King's Inns Dublin 1966; practised from London 1949–71, rec Hastings 1961–71; dep chm: Kent QS 1963–71, Middx QS 1962–65, Inner London QS 1971; circuit judge 1972–86; Archbishop of Canterbury's commissary gen for Canterbury Diocese 1959–71; fndr sec Bar Lawn Tennis Soc 1950–62; fndr sec Irish Peers Assoc 1963–71, fell Irish Genealogical Res Soc (pres 1971–91); Lt RNVR 1951–58, RNR 1958–60; *Books* The Trial of J G Haigh (Notable British Trials Series, 1953), Recollections of the Cambridge Union 1815–39 (jtly, 1953), Butler Family History (1966, 8 edn 1993), Happy Families (1983); *Recreations* lawn tennis, Butler genealogies; *Clubs* Irish, All England Lawn Tennis, Int Lawn Tennis of GB (pres 1973–83), 45 (pres 1974–91), Union (Cambridge, pres 1939), Pitt (Cambridge); *Style*— The Rt Hon Lord Dunboyne, VRD; ✉ 36 Ormonde Gate, London SW3 4HA (☎ 0171 352 1837)

DUNCAN, Alan J C; MP (C) Rutland and Melton (majority 25,535); *b* 31 March 1957; *Educ* Merchant Taylors', St John's Coll Oxford (Pres Oxford Union 1979, cox Coll First Eight), Harvard Univ (Kennedy scholar); *Career* with Shell International Petroleum 1979–81, in Singapore 1984–86, oil trader and conslt on oil supply and refining industs 1989–92; Parly candidate (C) Barnsley W and Penistone 1987, MP (C) Rutland and Melton 1992–; PPS to: Min of State for Health Dec 1993–Jan 1994 (resigned), Dr Brian Mawhinney as Chm Cons Pty 1995–; Freeman City of London, Liveryman Worshipful Co of Merchant Taylors; *Books* Saturn's Children, How the State Devours Liberty, Prosperity and Virtue (with Dominic Hobson, 1995); An End to Illusions (1993); *Recreations* fishing, shooting; *Style*— Alan Duncan, Esq, MP; ✉ House of Commons, London SW1A 0AA

DUNCAN, Dr Allan George; *b* 17 Oct 1940; *Educ* Robert Gordon's Coll Aberdeen, Univ of Aberdeen (BSc), New Coll Oxford (DPhil); *Career* chemical engrg researcher: UCLA 1966–67, US Nat Bureau of Standards 1967–69, UKAEA Harwell 1969–79; DOE: various positions rising to dep chief inspr Radiochemical Inspectorate 1979–87, various positions rising to dir and chief inspr HM Inspectorate of Pollution (HMIP) 1987–96, head of radioactive substances regulation Environment Agency 1996–; memb: EC Network of Environmental Regulators 1993–, Euratom Scientific and Tech Ctee 1994–, Environmental Assessment and Advsy Panel UK Accreditation Service 1994–; author various articles in scientific jls; memb Inst of Environmental Mgmnt 1995; *Style*— Dr Allan Duncan; ✉ Environment Agency, Rio House, Waterside Drive, Aztec West, Almondsbury, Bristol BS12 4UD (☎ 01454 624069, fax 01454 624409)

DUNCAN, Prof Archibald Alexander McBeth; s of Charles George Duncan (d 1978), of Edinburgh, and Christina Helen, *née* McBeth (d 1973); *b* 17 Oct 1926; *Educ* George Heriot's Sch Edinburgh, Univ of Edinburgh (MA), Balliol Coll Oxford (BA); *m* 21 Aug 1954, Ann Hayes, da of William Ewart Hayes Sawyer (d 1969); 2 s (Alastair David b 1958, Ewen James b 1960), 1 da (Beatrice Jane b 1956); *Career* lectr Balliol Coll Oxford 1950–51; lectr in history: Queen's Univ Belfast 1951–53, Univ of Edinburgh 1953–61; Leverhulme research fell 1961–62, prof of Scottish history and literature Univ of Glasgow 1962–93; hon professorial research fell Univ of Glasgow 1993–; clerk of Senate Univ of Glasgow 1978–83; memb Royal Cmmn on the Ancient and Historical Monuments of Scotland 1969–92; FRHistS 1960, FRSE 1982, FBA 1987; *Books* Scotland, The Making of the Kingdom (1975), Scotland from Earliest Times to 1603 (by W C Dickinson, 3 edn revised by A A M Duncan 1977), Regesta Regum Scotorum V, The Acts of Robert I 1306–29 (1988); *Recreations* swimming; *Style*— Prof A A M Duncan, FRSE, FBA; ✉ 17 Campbell Drive, Bearsden, Glasgow G61 4NF (☎ 0141 942 5023); Department of Scottish History, 9 University Gardens, Glasgow G12 8QH

DUNCAN, Arthur Henry (Bill); *b* 11 Jan 1933; *Educ* external degree; *m* 3 Sept 1960, Carol Elizabeth, *née* Gillmore; 2 s (Angus James b 10 June 1963, Bruce Maxwell b 21 March 1970); *Career* formerly with Distillers Co (Biochemicals) Ltd; Unilever: joined as research scientist 1959, various devpt and mfrg mgmnt appts in the UK, Netherlands, Italy and Australia, latterly involved in introdn of total quality mgmnt, ret 1993; chm Wirral Hosp NHS Tst 1992– (vice chm 1990–92); former chm constituency Cons Assoc, govr various schs; CChem, MRSC; *Recreations* fell walking, golf; *Style*— Bill Duncan, Esq; ✉ Wirral Hospital NHS Trust, Arrowe Park Road, Upton, Wirral, Merseyside L49 5PE (☎ 0151 678 5111)

DUNCAN, Prof Christopher John; s of Jack William Duncan (d 1982), of Selsdon, and Muriel Agnes, *née* Kirlew (d 1966); *b* 23 Feb 1932; *Educ* Trinity Sch of John Whitgift Croydon, Queen Mary Coll London (BSc, PhD); *m* 6 Sept 1958, Jennifer Jane, da of Ernest John Powell (d 1964), of Bickley, Kent; 3 s (Stephen b 1959, James b 1962, Alastair b 1962); *Career* reader in animal physiology Univ of Durham 1964–70, prof of zoology Univ of Liverpool 1970– (lectr in zoology 1958–64); memb Cncl, symposium convener and pubn offr Soc for Experimental Biology 1987–91, govr Liverpool Poly 1985–89, memb Cncl and chm NW Gp Inst of Biol; FIBiol 1980, scientific fell Zoological Soc of London 1980, FRSA 1989; *Books* Molecular Properties and Evolution of Excitable Cells (1967), Calcium in Biological Systems (ed, 1976), Secretory Mechanisms (ed, 1979), Calcium, Oxygen Radicals and Cellular Damage (ed, 1991); *Recreations* sailing, gardening, reading; *Style*— Prof Christopher Duncan; ✉ 3 Eddisbury Road, West Kirby, Wirral, Merseyside L48 5DR; School of Biological Sciences, Derby Building, University of Liverpool, PO Box 147, Liverpool L69 3BX (☎ 0151 794 4987, fax 0151 708 6502, telex 627095 UNILPL G)

DUNCAN, Geoffrey Stuart; s of Alexander Sidney Duncan (d 1956), and Gertrude Ruth, *née* Page; *b* 10 April 1938; *Educ* The GS Hemel Hempstead, Univ of London (BSc), Univ of Exeter (MA); *m* 14 July 1962, Shirley Bernice Matilda, da of Lawson Tate Vanderput (d 1970); 1 s (Paul Lawson b 12 Oct 1965), 1 da (Anna Ruth b 24 Nov 1968); *Career* Nat Serv 1959–64, short serv cmmn as Lt RAEC 1960–64, served Br, Singapore, Brunei; schoolteacher and tech coll lectr 1964–72, LEA advsr and offr 1972–82; Gen Synod Bd of Educn and Nat Soc for Promoting Religious Educn: schs sec and dep sec 1982–90, gen sec 1990–; pt/t tutor WEA 1968–71, pt/t cnsllr Open Univ 1971–72; govr Coll of St Mark and St John Plymouth, dir Urban Learning Fndn, diocesan reader Dio of Chichester; *Books* contrib to: Faith for the Future (1986), Schools for Tomorrow (1988); *Recreations* campanology, trying to play the piano; *Clubs* Naval and Military; *Style*— Geoffrey Duncan, Esq; ✉ 17 Carlton Road, Seaford, East Sussex BN25 2LE (☎ 01323 893587); Church House, Great Smith St, London SW1P 3NZ (☎ 0171 222 9011, fax 0171 233 2592)

DUNCAN, George; s of William Duncan (d 1966), and Catherine Gray, *née* Murray; *b* 9 Nov 1933; *Educ* Holloway Co GS, LSE (BScEcon), Wharton Sch of Fin, Pennsylvania Univ (MBA); *m* 1965, Frauke Ulricke; 1 da (Fiona b 1969); *Career* chief exec: Truman Hanbury Buxton Ltd 1967–71, Watney Mann Ltd 1971–72, Yule Catto & Co Ltd 1973–75; vice chm International Distillers & Vintners Ltd 1972; chm: Lloyds Bowmaker Ltd 1976–86 (dir 1973–86), ASW Holdings plc 1986–, HMC Group plc 1986–94, Whessoe plc 1987– (dir 1986–), Humberside Finance Group Ltd 1987–89, Rubicon Group plc 1992–95, Higgs & Hill plc 1992–, Laporte plc 1995– (dir 1987–); dir: BET plc 1981–96, Lloyds Bank 1982–87, Haden plc 1974–85 (dep chm 1984–85), TR City of London Trust plc 1977–, Associated British Ports Holdings plc 1986–, Newspaper Publishing plc 1986–93, Dewe Rogerson Group Ltd 1987–95, Calor Group plc 1990–; chm CBI Cos Ctee 1980–83, memb President's Ctee CBI 1980–83; Freeman City of London 1971; FCA; *Recreations* skiing, opera; *Style*— George Duncan, Esq; ✉ 30 Walton Street, London SW3 1RE

DUNCAN, Ian Alexander; s of late Kenneth George Duncan, and Peggy Pauline, *née* Stuchbury; *b* 21 April 1946; *Educ* Central GS Birmingham, Coll of Commerce Birmingham; *m* Carol Hammond, da of late William Wilford Smith; 2 s (Adam Harvey b 1966, Alexander James b 1975), 1 da (Tavira Caroline b 1975); *Career* certified accountant, founding fell Assoc of Corp Treasurers, formerly fin dir Pentos plc (resigned Pentos and all subsids 1984); dep chm and md (finance) Tomkins PLC (and subsids and assocs) 1984–; *Recreations* field sports, the Arts, travel, flying helicopters, scuba diving; *Style*— Ian A Duncan, Esq; ✉ Tomkins PLC, East Putney House, 84 Upper Richmond Rd, London SW15 2ST (☎ 0181 871 4544, fax 0181 874 3882)

DUNCAN, Ian McIntosh; *b* 25 Nov 1931; *Educ* Royal HS Edinburgh; *m* 14 June 1958, Marjorie Anne, da of Robert Brown (d 1968); 3 s (Callum b 1960, Neil b 1962, Andrew b 1964); *Career* Imperial Chemical Industries 1957–72 (various appts from works accountant to head Profits and Forecasting Group), Cavenham Ltd 1972–82 (various appts from gp controller to dir), GO Holdings Management Inc 1983–88 (chm, pres and chief exec), md fin and admin Guinness plc 1990–93; non-exec dir Era Group plc 1990–; *Recreations* tennis, golf, badminton; *Style*— Ian Duncan, Esq; ✉ 14 Wrensfield, Hemel Hempstead, Hertfordshire HP1 1RN (☎ 01442 251980)

DUNCAN, Jacqueline Ann; JP (South Westminster 1976); da of late Sonia Whitaker, *née* Bromley; *b* 16 Dec 1931; *Educ* Convent of the Sacred Heart Brighton, House of Citizenship London; *m* 1, 1955 (m dis 1963), Michael Inchbald; 1 s (Courtenay Charles b 1958), 1 da (Charlotte Amanda b 1960); m 2, 5 June 1974, Brig Peter Trevenen Thwaites (d 1991); m 3, 10 Feb 1994, Col Andrew Duncan, LVO, OBE; *Career* fndr and princ: Inchbald Sch of Design 1960–, Inchbald Sch of Fine Arts 1970–, Inchbald Sch of Garden Design 1972–; memb: Monopolies Cmmn 1972–75, Whitford Ctee on Copyright and Design 1974–76, London Electricity Conservation Cncl 1973–76, Visiting Ctee RCA 1986–90; tstee St Peter's Res Tst 1987–90; cncllr Westminster City Cncl (Warwick Ward) 1974–78; acting pres Int Soc of Interior Designers (London Chapter) 1987–90; fell Int Soc of Interior Designers 1994 (chm 1990–92); *Books* Directory of Interior Designers (1966), Bedrooms (1968), Design & Decoration (1971); *Recreations* arboriculture, fishing, historical research; *Clubs* Cavalry and Guards', Guards' Polo; *Style*— Mrs Andrew Duncan, JP; ✉ Inchbald School of Design, 32 Eccleston Square, London SW1V 1PB (☎ 0171 630 9011, fax 0171 976 5979)

DUNCAN, Sir James Blair; kt (1981); s of John Duncan, and Emily MacFarlane Duncan; *b* 24 Aug 1927; *Educ* Whitehill Sch Glasgow; *m* 1974, Betty Psaltis; *Career* chm: Transport Development Group plc 1975–92, BoAlloy Industries Ltd 1992–; memb LTE (pt/t) 1979–82, vice pres Scottish Cncl 1983– (memb 1976–); chm: London Exec Ctee 1983–, London C of C 1986–88, London C of C and Indust Commercial Educn Tst 1992–; pres: Inst of Rd Tport Engrs 1984–88, Chartered Inst of Tport 1980–81; dir British Road Fedn 1992–, tstee Rees Jeffreys Road Fund 1992; Liveryman Worshipful Co of Carmen (Award of Merit 1992), Freeman The Co of Watermen and Lightermen; CA (Scotland), FCIT, CIMgt, FRSA 1977, Hon FIRTE; *Publications* various papers on transport matters; *Recreations* travel, reading, golf, swimming, theatre; *Clubs* Caledonian, RAC; *Style*— Sir James Duncan; ✉ 17 Kingston House South, Ennismore Gardens, London SW7 1NF

DUNCAN, John; s of John Duncan (d 1976), of Henfield, Sussex, and Doris Annie, *née* Withers (d 1980); *b* 20 April 1936; *Educ* Steyning GS; *m* (m dis); 2 s (Alistair John b 12 Feb 1959, Graham Michael b 23 July 1961); *Career* National Westminster Bank (formerly Westminster Bank): various positions rising to dep mangr City of London 1952–74, chief info offr and dep head of public affrs 1974–79; dir of PR Dewe Rogerson Ltd 1979–83, divnl vice pres (public affrs) American Express Travel Related Servs Europe, ME and Africa 1983–86, gp corp affrs dir Inchcape plc 1986–95; corp affrs conslt and author 1995–; FCIB, FIPR; *Books* How to Manage Your Bank Manager (1982); *Recreations* sport, particularly golf and cricket, theatre, music, travel; *Clubs* RAC, MCC; *Style*— John Duncan, Esq; ✉ 34 Prebend Street, London N1 8PS (☎ and fax 0171 359 8259, mobile 0831 857850)

DUNCAN, Kathleen Nora; da of George James Denis Dale (d 1983), and Nellie Logan, *née* Jamieson; *b* 26 Sept 1946; *Educ* Christ's Hosp, St Aidan's Coll Durham (BA), Poly of Central London (Dip Arts Admin); *m* 11 Jan 1975 (m dis 1983), Neil Stuart Duncan; *Career* head of arts servs London Borough of Havering 1971–73, dep dir SE Arts 1974–76, chief exec Composers and Authors Soc of Hong Kong 1977–79, gen mangr Archer Travel Hong Kong 1979–82, int mktg dir Boosey & Hawkes Music Publishers Ltd 1983–86, mktg dir Order of St John 1986–89, mktg conslt The Performing Rights Soc Ltd 1989–90, dir gen Lloyds TSB Foundation for England and Wales 1990–; almoner and govr Christ's Hosp; *Recreations* music, travel, walking; *Style*— Mrs Kathleen Duncan; ✉ 148 Cranmer Court, London SW3 3HF (☎ 0171 589 6777); Lloyds TSB Foundation for England and Wales, PO Box 140, St Mary's Court, 20 St Mary at Hill, London EC3R 8NA (☎ 0171 204 5272, fax 0171 204 5275)

DUNCAN, Kenneth Sandilands (Sandy); OBE; s of Dr William Arthur Duncan (d 1946), of Eastbourne, Sussex, and Ethel Mary, *née* Edwards (d 1969); *b* 26 April 1912; *Educ* St Andrew's Eastbourne, Malvern, New Coll Oxford (BA); *m* 1, 4 June 1941, Katharine Beatrice, *née* Darwall (d 1955); 1 s (Andrew Duncan b 1943); m 2, June 1957 (m dis 1966), Dorothy, *née* Wentworth; *Career* WWII 2 Lt 176 Field Battery RA 1940, lectr OCTU Ilkley Yorks 1942–44, Asst Staff Capt, RA 3 Br Inf Div 1944–45, lectr WO Sch of Mil Admin No 1 Trg Wing, Maj (non substantive) reverting to Capt; master Bradfield 1935–38, gen sec Univs Athletics Union 1949–51, hon sec Achilles Club (Oxford and Cambridge blues and half blues) 1948–87, gen sec Cwlth Games Cncl for Eng 1948–72, hon sec Cwlth Games Fedn 1948–82, gen sec Br Olympic Assoc 1948–75 (consIt/librarian); Double Blue (Oxon) Athletics 1931, Soccer 1935, competed GB Int Athletics 1932–37; winner: Silver medal 4 x 110 yds relay Cwlth Games 1938, Gold medal 4 x 110 yds World Univ Games (Paris) 1937; Chef de Mission of 12 GB Olympic Teams (summer and winter) 1952–72; Olympic Order 1984, The White Rose and Lion of Finland 1952; *Books* The Oxford Book of Athletic Training (1957), Athletics - Do it This Way (1952); *Clubs* Royal Over-Seas League; *Style*— Sandy Duncan, Esq, OBE; ✉ Alexander House, 23 Courtfield Gardens, Earls Court, London SW5 0PF (☎ 0171 341 0037); The British Olympic Association, 1 Wandsworth Plain, London SW18 1EN (☎ 0181 871 2677, fax 0181 871 9104, telex 932312 BOA G)

DUNCAN, Michael Greig; s of Alec Greig Duncan (d 1979), and Betty, *née* Shaw; *b* 9 Sept 1957; *Educ* King Williams Coll IOM, Downing Coll Cambridge (BA); *m* 2 July 1983, Fiona Helen, da of Michael John Carlisle Glaze, CMG; 2 s (Rory b 8 March 1985, Adam b 12 June 1989), 1 da (Chloe b 14 Oct 1986); *Career* admitted slr 1981, ptnr Allen & Overy 1987– (asst slr 1981–86); memb City of London Law Soc; *Style*— Michael Duncan, Esq; ✉ Allen & Overy, One New Change, London EC4M 9QQ (☎ 0171 330 3000, fax 0171 330 9999)

DUNCAN, Dr Nicholas Hugh; s of Maj Dr Peter Duncan (d 1979), of Gorton, Manchester, and Pauline May, *née* Hughes; *b* 9 Sept 1954; *Educ* William Hulme's GS, Royal Victoria Med Sch Manchester (MB ChB); *m* 25 July 1984, Claire, da of Dennis Cooper (d 1979), of Malpas, Cheshire; 1 s (Ashley James b 1986), 1 da (Laura Alice b 1991); *Career* sr registrar in anaesthesia Ahmadu Bello Univ Kaduna Nigeria 1982–83, sr registrar in anaesthesia Univ of Cambridge 1983–85, conslt in anaesthesia and intensive care Queen Elizabeth Hosp Kings Lynn Norfolk 1986–; FFARCS 1982; *Recreations* flying, shooting, skiing, windsurfing; *Style*— Dr Nicholas Duncan; ✉ Consultant in Anaesthesia and Intensive Care, Dept of Anaesthesia, Queen Elizabeth Hospital, Gayton Rd, King's Lynn, Norfolk PE30 4ET (☎ 01553 766266)

DUNCAN, Dr Peter Watson; s of Arthur Alexander Watson Duncan, of Edinburgh, and Catherine Bowes, *née* Williamson; *b* 14 April 1954; *Educ* George Heriot's Sch, Univ of Edinburgh (MB ChB); *m* 16 April 1983, Fiona Margaret, da of Arthur Murray Grierson, of Tetbury, Glos; 1 s (Ian b 27 Feb 1987), 2 da (Meg b 3 April 1985, Jane b 18 Aug 1989); *Career* registrar in anaesthetics Royal Infirmary of Edinburgh 1979–82; sr registrar in anaesthetics: Newcastle upon Tyne 1982–85, Univ of Natal Durban 1983–84; Royal Preston Hosp: conslt in anaesthetics and intensive care 1985–, clinical dir (anaesthetics) 1991–; chm Assoc of North West Intensive Care Units 1996–; memb Intensive Care Soc; FRCA 1981; *Recreations* photography, music; *Style*— Dr Peter Duncan; ✉ Royal Preston Hospital, Sharoe Green Lane, Preston, Lancs (☎ 01772 710555)

DUNCAN, Richard; *see:* Rudin, Richard Duncan

DUNCAN, Roderick Kenneth; s of Kenneth George Duncan, DCM (d 1979), and Peggy Pauline, *née* Stutchbury; *b* 9 Feb 1949; *Educ* Central GS for Boys Birmingham, Birmingham Coll of Commerce; *m* 23 Sept 1972, Susan Deborah, da of Lionel William Lane, of Solihull; 2 s (Matthew James b 9 May 1978, Alistair Scott b 19 Nov 1980); *Career* sales dir County Unit Trusts Ltd 1985–87, investmt sales dir Aetna International (UK) Ltd 1987–, dir Aetna Unit Trusts Ltd 1987–, dep md Schroder Unit Trusts Ltd 1989–, dir Schroder Investment Management Ltd 1995–; ACIS 1972; *Recreations* golf, gardening; *Style*— Roderick Duncan, Esq; ✉ Hedges, Crest Hill, Peaslake, Surrey; Schroder Unit Trusts Ltd, Queen Victoria Street, London EC4

DUNCAN, Stanley Frederick St Clare; CMG (1983); s of Stanley Gilbert Scott Duncan; *b* 13 Nov 1927; *Educ* Latymer Upper; *m* 1967, Jennifer Bennett; 2 da; *Career* HM Dip Serv: India Office 1946, CRO 1947, private sec to Parly Under Sec of State 1954, 2 sec Ottawa 1954–55, Br Govt information offr Toronto 1955–57, 2 sec Wellington 1958–60, 1 sec CRO 1960, seconded to Central African Office 1962–64, 1 sec Nicosia 1964–67, FCO 1967–70, head of Chancery and 1 sec Lisbon 1970–73, consul-gen then chargé d'affaires Mozambique 1973–75, political cnsllr Brasilia 1976–77, head of Consular Dept FCO 1977–80, Canadian Nat Def Coll Kingston Ontario 1980–81, ambass to Bolivia 1981–85, high cmmr Malta 1985–87, ret; UN observer at South African elections 1994; FRGS; Offr Mil Order of Christ (Portugal); *Style*— Stanley Duncan, Esq, CMG; ✉ Tucksmead, Longworth, Oxon OX13 5ET

DUNCAN-JONES, Dr Richard Phare; s of Austin Ernest Duncan-Jones, and Elsie Elizabeth Duncan-Jones; *b* 14 Sept 1937; *Educ* King Edward's Sch Birmingham, King's Coll Cambridge (MA, PhD); *m* 1986, Julia Elizabeth, *née* Poole; *Career* Gonville and Caius Coll Cambridge: W M Tapp research fell 1963–67, domestic bursar 1967–84, official fell 1967–, coll lectr and dir of studies in classics 1984–; memb Inst for Advanced Study Princeton 1971–72; FBA 1992; *Books* The Economy of the Roman Empire (1974, 2 edn 1982), Structure and Scale in the Roman Economy (1990), Money and Government in the Roman Empire (1994); also author of articles in learned jls; *Recreations* walking, wine tasting, continental cinema; *Style*— Dr Richard Duncan-Jones, FBA; ✉ Gonville and Caius College, Cambridge CB2 1TA (☎ 01223 332394)

DUNCAN MILLAR, Ian Alastair; CBE (1978), MC (1945), DL (1960); s of late Sir James Duncan Millar; *b* 22 Nov 1914; *Educ* Gresham's, Univ of Cambridge (MA); *m* 1945, Louise Reid, da of W McCosh (d 1937); 2 s, 2 da; *Career* Sir Alexander Gibb & Partners consulting civil engrs 1936–40 and 1945–52; served Corps of Royal Engrs 1940–45, Maj, wounded (despatches); contested (Lib) Parly elections: Banff 1945, Kinross and W Perthshire 1949 and 1963; Perthshire and Kinross: cncllr 1946–79, convenor 1975–78; regnl cncllr and convenor Tayside 1974–78, depute chm N of Scotland Hydro Electric Bd 1970–72 (memb 1957–72); dir: Macdonald Fraser and Co 1961–86, Tay Dist Salmon Fisheries Bd 1962–80 and 1986–93, Hill Farming Res Orgn 1966–78; chm: United Auctions (Scot) Ltd 1967–74, Consultative Ctee on Freshwater and Salmon Fisheries Act 1981–86; vice pres Scot Landowners Fedn 1985–90; memb Royal Co of Archers (Queen's Bodyguard for Scotland) 1956–; former JP; MICE 1939, CEng, FIFM 1988; *Books* A Countryman's Cog (1990), A Bit of Bredalbane (1995); *Recreations* learning about and catching salmon, the land of Scotland; *Clubs* Royal Perth Golfing Soc; *Style*—

I A Duncan Millar, Esq, CBE, MC, DL; ✉ Reynock, Remony, Aberfeldy, Perthshire PH15 2HR (☎ 01887 830400)

DUNCAN SMITH, (George) Iain; MP (C) Chingford (majority 14,938); s of Gp Capt Wilfred George Gerald Duncan Smith, DSO, DFC (d 1996), and Pamela Duncan Smith; *b* 9 April 1954; *Educ* Conway, Univ of Perugia, RMA Sandhurst, Dunchurch Coll; *m* 1982, Hon Elizabeth Wynn, da of 5 Baron Cottesloe, *qv*; 2 s, 2 da; *Career* cmmnd Scots Gds 1975, ADC to Gen Sir John Acland and Cdr of Cwlth Monitoring Force in Zimbabwe 1979; with GEC Marconi 1981–88; dir: Bellwinch Property Ltd 1988–89, Jane's Information Group 1989–92; Parly candidate (C) Bradford W 1987, MP (C) Chingford 1992–; jt sec: Cons Back Bench Foreign and Cwlth Affrs Ctee, Cons Back Bench Def Ctee 1995; memb Select Ctee on Standards in Public Life (Standards and Privileges Ctee) 1995–; vice chm Fulham Cons Assoc 1991; Freeman City of London 1993; *Books* Who Benefits (Social Security), Game, Set and Match? (Maastricht), Facing the Future (Defence and Foreign and Commonwealth Affairs), 1994 and Beyond, A European Germany or A German Europe?; *Style*— Iain Duncan Smith, Esq, MP; ✉ House of Commons, London SW1A 0AA

DUNCANNON, Viscount; Myles Fitzhugh Longfield Ponsonby; s and ha of 11 Earl of Bessborough, *qv*; *b* 16 Feb 1941; *Educ* Harrow, Trin Coll Camb (BA 1962); *m* 1972, Alison Marjorie, 3 da of William Storey, OBE; 2 s (Hon Frederick Arthur William, b 9 Aug 1974, Hon Henry Shakerley b 1977), 1 da (Hon Chloë Patricia b 1975); *Career* banker; FCA; *Style*— Viscount Duncannon; ✉ 27 Wandsworth Bridge Road, Fulham, London SW6 2TA

DUNCANSON, Neil; s of Jack Duncanson (d 1994), and Olive, *née* Smith, of Saxmundham, Suffolk; *b* 14 Feb 1960; *Educ* Coopers' Co and Coborn Sch Upminster Essex, Harlow Tech Coll Essex, NCTJ (full cert), Nat Film and TV Sch (directors' course); *m* 1980, Julie, da of Reginald Green; 1 s (Sam b 7 Dec 1988), 1 da (Jessica b 12 Aug 1993); *Career* chief reporter Newham Recorder 1978–84, news journalist (on and off screen) Thames TV 1984–86, deviser/prodr Men on Earth series and others for Thames TV Sport 1986–88 (news ed ITV Olympics Seoul 1988), prodr/dir 2 Eyewitness series and 7–Sport for LWT 1988–90, freelance prodr 1990–91, with Chrysalis TV 1991–92, md Chrysalis Sport 1992–; credits incl: Italian Soccer (Channel 4), Rugby Special/Bowls (BBC), NBA (Channel 4), Graham Taylor: Cutting Edge (Channel 4), Formula 1 (ITV), Spanish Soccer, Baseball, Angling (BSkyB), Gazza's Coming Home (Channel 4); awards incl: Silver Shot (for The Fastest Men on Earth) Euro Film and TV Festival 1989, Gold Medal (for 7–Sport) NY Film and TV Festival 1990, Indie Award for Best Sports Programming (for Italian Football) 1993, Sports Video of the Yr Award 1994 and 1995, Sports Journalism Award (for Graham Taylor: Cutting Edge) RTS 1995; dir: Queen's Park Rangers FC, Wasps RUFC; memb RTS 1994; *Books* The Fastest Men on Earth (1988), Sports Technology (1991), The Olympic Games (1992), Tales of Gold (with Patrick Collins, 1992), Crown of Thorns (with Norman Giller, 1992); *Recreations* soccer, tennis, movies, writing, Egyptology, sports history, collecting sports memorabilia; *Style*— Neil Duncanson, Esq; ✉ Chrysalis Sport, 6 Church Studios, Camden Park Road, London NW1 9AY (☎ 0171 284 2288, fax 0171 284 1394, mobile 0385 261132)

DUNCOMBE, *see:* Pauncefort-Duncombe

DUNCUMB, Dr Peter; s of late William Duncumb, and Hilda Grace, *née* Coleman; *b* 26 Jan 1931; *Educ* Oundle, Clare Coll Cambridge; *m* 1955, Anne Leslie, *née* Taylor; 2 s, 1 da; *Career* dir and gen mangr TI Group Res Laboratories 1979–87, dir Res Centre in Superconductivity Univ of Cambridge 1988–89; hon prof Univ of Warwick 1990–; FRS; *Style*— Dr Peter Duncumb, FRS; ✉ 5A Woollards Lane, Great Shelford, Cambridge CB2 5LZ (☎ 01223 843064)

DUNDAS, (Robert) Alexander; sixteenth representative of the Robertsons of Auchleeks, who descend from Alexander of Struan (5th chief) in 1440; s of Ralph Dundas (d 1982), of Airds, Appin, Argyll, and Margaret Beryl, *née* Maclean of Ardgour; ggs of Ralph Dundas and Emily Bridget (d 1934), da of Robert Robertson, of Auchleeks; twelfth in male line descent from Sir William Dundas, 15 of Dundas (ka 1513 at Flodden Field); *b* 12 June 1947; *Educ* Harrow, Ch Ch Oxford; *m* 9 July 1977, Sarah Rosalind, da of (William) Simon Wilson, of Ballochmorrie, Barrhill, Girvan, Ayrshire, and Ann, da of Sir James Lithgow, Bt; 1 s (Ralph b 1988), 1 da (Catriona b 1985); *Career* portfolio mangr Far E Grieveson, Grant & Co stockbrokers 1974–79 (joined 1970), dir and investmt mangr Japan GT Management Asia Ltd 1980–95, dir GT Management plc 1984–96 (chm Investmt Ctee 1988–90); memb Queen's Body Guard for Scotland (Royal Co of Archers); *Recreations* Scottish history, art objects, wine, shooting, armchair cricket; *Clubs* Boodle's, Pratt's, Puffin's (Edinburgh), City of London, Beauchamp's Tap; *Style*— Alexander Dundas, Esq; ✉ 63 Victoria Road, London W8 5RH

DUNDEE, 12 Earl of (S 1660); Alexander Henry Scrymgeour of Dundee; also Viscount Dudhope (S 1641), Lord Scrymgeour (S 1641), Lord Inverkeithing (S 1660), Baron Glassary (UK 1954); Baron of Barony of Wedderburn; Hereditary Royal Standard Bearer for Scotland; s of 11 Earl of Dundee (d 1983), and Patricia, Countess of Dundee; *b* 5 June 1949; *Educ* Eton, Univ of St Andrews; *m* 1979, Siobhan Mary, da of David Llewellyn, of Sayers, Gt Somerford, Wilts; 1 s, 3 da (Lady Marina Patricia Siobhan b 21 Aug 1980, Lady Flora Hermione Vera b 30 Sept 1985, Lady Lavinia Rebecca Elizabeth b 5 Nov 1986); *Heir* s, Lord Scrymgeour, *qv*; *Career* contested (C) Hamilton by-election 1978; *Style*— The Rt Hon the Earl of Dundee; ✉ Farm Office, Birkhill, Cupar, Fife

DUNDERDALE, Sue; da of John Mason Dunderdale (d 1988), of Lytham St Anne's, and Dorothy, *née* Alderson; *b* 6 Sept 1947; *Educ* Morecombe GS, Univ of Manchester; *Career* director; fndr and first artistic dir Pentbus Theatre Co 1973–78; freelance theatre dir 1978–84; artistic dir: Solo Poly Theatre 1984–88, Greenwich Theatre 1988–89, BBC drama dirs course 1989; dir: Nativity Blues (BBC 2) 1988, Killing The Cat (by David Spencer, Royal Court Upstairs) 1990, EastEnders (BBC 1) 1991/92, Land of the Living (by David Soencer) 1993, Deborah's Daughter (BBC Radio 4), The Bill (LWT), Casualty (BBC 1), The Blood That's In You (BBC 2); co-chm Dirs' Guild of GB 1986–87; *Style*— Ms Sue Dunderdale; ✉ c/o Charles Walker, Peters Fraser and Dunlop, 503 The Chambers, Chelsea Harbour, Lots Road, London SW10 0XF (☎ 0171 352 4446, fax 0171 352 7356)

DUNDONALD, 15 Earl of (S 1669); (Iain Alexander) Douglas Blair; also Lord Cochrane of Dundonald (S 1647), Lord Cochrane of Dundonald, Paisley and Ochiltree (S 1669), and Marquis of Maranhão (Empire of Brazil 1823 by Dom Pedro I for 10 Earl); s (by 1 m) of 14 Earl of Dundonald (d 1986); *b* 17 Feb 1961; *Educ* Wellington, Royal Agric Coll (DipAg); *m* 4 July 1987, (M) Beatrice (L), da of Adolphus Russo, of Gibraltar; 2 s (Archie Iain Thomas Blair, Lord Cochrane b 14 March 1991, Hon James Douglas Richard b 10 May 1995), 1 da (Lady Marina Aphra Mariola b 26 Nov 1992); *Heir* s, Archie Iain Thomas Blair, Lord Cochrane b 14 March 1991; *Career* dir: Duneth Securities Ltd, Anglo Pacific Resources plc; hon Chilean consul to Scotland; *Recreations* skiing, sailing, shooting, fishing; *Style*— The Rt Hon the Earl of Dundonald; ✉ Lochnell Castle, Ledaig, Argyll PA37 1QT

DUNFORD, David John; s of Alfred George Dunford (d 1962), and Kate, *née* Spearman; *b* 30 Jan 1948; *Educ* Univ of Essex (BA); *m* 7 Sept 1978, Anne Wilson, da of James Fleming (d 1981); *Career* asst ed then dep chief sub ed Essex Co Newspapers 1973–78; BBC: joined 1978, successively sub ed, chief sub ed and duty ed BBC Radio News, fin journalist for BBC radio TV and World Service, currently ed BBC Regional News Serv providing comprehensive news and current affairs coverage to local and regnl stations and Br Forces Broadcasting; *Recreations* golf, trivial pursuit; *Clubs* Warren Golf (Maldon Essex); *Style*— David Dunford, Esq; ✉ 3 Avenue Road, Great Baddow, Chelmsford, Essex CM2 9TY (☎ 01245 356484); Room 233, BBC Broadcasting House, London W1A 1AA (☎ 0171 765 3422, fax 0171 580 6564)

DUNFORD, Neil Roy; s of Charles Roy Dunford, and Joyce Ellen Dunford; *b* 16 Jan 1947; *Educ* Edinburgh Acad, Sedbergh, Univ of St Andrews (MA); *m* 24 April 1976, Gillian; *Career* Deloitte & Co 1968–72, J Henry Schroder Wagg 1972–81, Scottish Widows Fund 1981–85, dir Morgan Grenfell Asset Management 1985–, chm Morgan Grenfell Investment Management Ltd 1992–; *Style*— Neil Dunford, Esq; ✉ 21 Ashley Drive, Walton-on-Thames, Surrey KT12 1JL (☎ 01932 246496); Morgan Grenfell Asset Management Ltd, 20 Finsbury Circus, London EC2M 1NB (☎ 0171 545 6000, fax 0171 545 0286)

DUNGARVAN, Viscount; John Richard Boyle; s & h of 14 Earl of Cork and Orrery, *qv*; *b* 3 Nov 1945; *Educ* Harrow, RNC Dartmouth; *m* 1973, Hon Rebecca Juliet Noble, yst da of Baron Glenkinglas (Life Peer; d 1984); 1 s (Hon Rory Jonathan Courtenay b 10 Dec 1978), 2 da (Hon Cara Mary Cecilia b 16 June 1976, Hon Davina Claire Theresa b (twin) 10 Dec 1978); *Career* Lt Cdr RN (ret); dir E D & F Man Sugar Ltd London; *Clubs* Boodle's; *Style*— Viscount Dungarvan; ✉ Lickfold House, Petworth, W Sussex GU28 9EY (☎ and fax 01798 861 266)

DUNHAM, Sir Kingsley Charles; kt (1972); s of Ernest Pedder Dunham, of Brancepeth, Co Durham (d 1974), and Edith Agnes, *née* Humphreys (d 1939); *b* 2 Jan 1910; *Educ* Durham Johnston Sch, Univ of Durham (DSc, PhD), Univ of Harvard (MS, SD); *m* 1936, Margaret, da of William Young, of Choppington, Northumberland; *Career* New Mexico Bureau of Mines 1935, geologist with HM Geological Survey of GB 1935–50, prof of geology Univ of Durham 1950–66, dir Inst of Geological Sciences 1967–75, consulting geologist 1976–, dir Weardale Minerals Ltd 1982–86; foreign sec Royal Soc 1971–76; hon doctorates from 11 UK and US univs; FRS, FRSE 1971, FEng 1976 (fndr fell), FIMM, FGS; *Recreations* music, gardening; *Clubs* Geological Soc, Probus (Durham); *Style*— Sir Kingsley Dunham, FRS, FRSE, FEng; ✉ Charleycroft, Quarryheads Lane, Durham DH1 3DY (☎ 0191 384 8977)

DUNHILL, Richard; s of Vernon Dunhill (d 1938), and Helen, *née* Field Moser (d 1984); Co Alfred Dunhill formed by gf 1907; *b* 27 Oct 1926; *Educ* Beaumont Coll; *m* 5 April 1952, Patricia Susannah, da of Henry B Rump (d 1965); 3 s (Christopher John b 1954, (Alfred) Mark b 1961, Jonathan Henry b 1962), 1 da (Susan Mary b 1953); *Career* army conscript 1944–48; Alfred Dunhill Ltd: joined 1948, dir 1961, dep chm 1967, chm 1977–; chm Dunhill Holdings plc 1981–89 (pres 1989–93); former Barker Variety Club of GB; Master Worshipful Co of Pipemakers and Tobacco Blenders 1987–88; *Recreations* gardening, backgammon; *Style*— Richard Dunhill, Esq; ✉ Alfred Dunhill Ltd, 27 Knightsbridge, London SW1X 7YB (☎ 0171 838 8000, fax 0171 838 8333)

DUNKEL, Arthur; *b* 28 Aug 1932; *Educ* Univ of Lausanne (BSc Econ); *m*; 2 children; *Career* Federal Office for Foreign and Econ Affrs: Dept of Public Economy Bern 1956–60, head of section for OECD Affrs 1960–64, head of section for Cooperation with Developing Countries 1964–71, head of section for World Trade Policy Min Plenipotentiary (appointed 1973) and permanent rep to GATT 1971–76; del and ambass Plenipotentiary for Trade Agreements of the Swiss Govt 1976–80; in charge of: world trade policy matters, multilateral econ and trade rels with developing countries industrialisation, trade in agriculture and primary products, bilateral trade rels with various trading ptnrs of Switzerland; head of the delegation of Switzerland 1976–80 to: GATT Multilateral Trade Negotiations (Tokyo Round), UNCTAD IV and V, UNIDO, commodity confs; dir gen GATT 1980–93, independent conslt 1993–; sr lectr Univs of Geneva and Fribourg; various studies, articles and reports published in econ reviews, winner Max Schmidheiny Fndn Freedom prize St Gallen Switzerland 1989 and Consumers for World Trade award (USA); vice chm and rapporteur UNCTAD Intergovernmental Gp on Supplementary Financing 1968, rapporteur UNCTAD Bd 1969, chm GATT Ctee of Balance of Payments Restrictions 1972–75, chm UN Conf on a New Wheat Agreement 1978; Hon Dr Univ of Fribourg 1980; *Style*— Arthur Dunkel, Esq; ✉ Boulevard de Theatre 6–4, CH 1204 Geneva, Switzerland

DUNKELD, Bishop (RC) of 1981–; Rt Rev Vincent Paul Logan; s of Joseph Logan (d 1975), and Elizabeth, *née* Flannigan; *b* 30 June 1941; *Educ* Blairs Coll Aberdeen, St Andrew's Coll Drygrange Melrose, CCC London (DipRE); *Career* ordained priest Edinburgh 1964; asst priest: St Margaret's Davidsons Mains Edinburgh 1964–66, CCC London 1966–67; chaplain St Joseph's Hosp Rosewell Midlothian 1967–77, advsr in religious educn Archdiocese of St Andrews and Edinburgh 1967–77, parish priest St Mary's Ratho Midlothian 1977–81, episcopal vicar for educn Archdiocese of St Andrews and Edinburgh 1978–81; *Style*— The Rt Rev the Bishop of Dunkeld; ✉ Bishop's House, 29 Roseangle, Dundee DD1 4LS (☎ 01382 224327)

DUNKELS, Paul Renton; QC (1993); s of George Antony Dunkels (d 1985), and Mollie, *née* Renton (d 1991); *b* 26 Nov 1947; *Educ* Harrow; *m* 2 Sept 1972, Melanie Gail, da of Lawrence Taverner; 2 da (Cynthia Leigh b 7 March 1975, Eleanor Claire b 6 Sept 1982), 1 s (Antony Lawrence Renton b 31 May 1977); *Career* called to the Bar Inner Temple 1972, in practice Western Circuit 1974–, recorder of the Crown Court 1988–; *Style*— Paul Dunkels, Esq, QC; ✉ Chambers: Walnut House, 63 St David's Hill, Exeter, Devon EX4 4DW (☎ 01392 279751, fax 01392 412080)

DUNKERLEY, Christopher; s of George William Dunkerley (d 1994), of Abbotskerswell, Devon, and Diana Margaret, *née* Lang; *b* 12 Dec 1951; *Educ* Charterhouse, Pembroke Coll Oxford (MA); *m* 16 Sept 1983, Kathleen Jane, *née* Hansen; 1 s (Jonathan b 18 Oct 1986), 1 da (Laura b 8 Sept 1988); *Career* graduate trainee William Brandts 1973–75, mangr Orion Bank 1975–76, asst gen mangr Saudi International Bank 1977–87, asst dir James Capel & Co 1987–89, chief exec Dartington & Co Group plc 1989–92, md Glen House Associates 1992–93, chief exec Swire Fraser Financial Management 1993–96, Latymer ptnr Coutts & Co Group 1996–; non-exec dir TR High Income Trust plc 1989–; *Recreations* ocean racing, golf; *Clubs* Royal Ocean Racing; *Style*— Christopher Dunkerley, Esq; ✉ Glen House, Sandy Lane, Abbots Leigh, Bristol BS8 3SE (☎ 01275 375510, fax 01275 375047)

DUNKLEY, Christopher; s of Robert Dunkley (d 1989), and Joyce Mary, *née* Turner (d 1993); *b* 22 Jan 1944; *Educ* Haberdashers' Aske's; *m* 1967, Carolyn Elizabeth, da of Lt-Col Arthur Philip Casey Lyons (d 1976), of Hampstead; 1 s (Damian b 1969), 1 da (Holly b 1971); *Career* journalist and broadcaster; feature writer and news ed UK Press Gazette 1965–68, reporter then specialist correspondent and critic The Times 1968–73, TV critic Financial Times 1973–, presenter of Feedback BBC Radio 4 1986–; occasional TV presenter: Man Alive, Panorama, This Week, Viewpoint etc; winner: Br Press Awards Critic of the Year 1976 and 1986, TV-am Broadcast Journalist of the Year 1989, Judges' Award 1990; *Books* Television Today and Tomorrow - Wall to Wall Dallas?; *Recreations* motorcycling, collecting, books, eating Italian food; *Style*— Christopher Dunkley, Esq; ✉ 38 Leverton St, London NW5 2PG (☎ and fax 0171 485 7101)

DUNLEATH, 5 Baron (UK 1892); Michael Henry Mulholland; 2 Bt (UK 1945), of Ballyscullion Park, Co Derry; s of Rt Hon Sir Henry George Hill Mulholland, 1 Bt (d 1971), of Ballyscullion Park, Bellaghy, NI; suc cousin 4 Baron Dunleath 1993; *b* 15 Oct 1915; *Educ* Eton, Pembroke Coll Cambridge (BA); *m* 1, 1942 (m dis 1949), Rosemary, o da of late Maj David Alfred William Ker, OBE; m 2, 1949, Elizabeth M (d 1989), da of Laurence B Hyde, of Bexhill-on-Sea; 1 s (Hon Brian Henry b 1950); *Heir* s, Hon Brian Henry Mulholland, *qv* b 25 Sept 1950; *Career* 2 Lt Oxford and Bucks LI 1936, served

WWII 1939–45, Maj 1946; joined Yorks & Flax Spinning Co Ltd Belfast as buyer in Belgium 1950, ret 1959; *Style—* The Rt Hon the Lord Dunleath; ✉ Storbrooke, 31 Massey Avenue, Belfast BT1 2JT (☎ 01232 763394)

DUNLOP, Rear Adm Colin Charles Harrison; CB (1972), CBE (1963), DL (Kent 1976); s of Rear Adm Samuel Harrison Dunlop, CB (d 1950), of Surrey, and Hilda Dunlop (d 1965); *b* 4 March 1918; *Educ* Marlborough; *m* 1, 1941, (Moyra) Patricia O'Brien (d 1991), da of John Albert Gorges (d 1968); 3 s (Angus, Robin (d 1946), Graham); m 2, 15 Dec 1995, Cmdt Elizabeth (Liz) Craig-McFeely, CB, WRNS, DL; *Career* RN 1935–74: served WWII HM Ships Kent, Valiant, Diadem and Orion in Far East, Med and Atlantic, cmd HMS Pembroke 1964–66, dir Def Policy 1968–69, Rear Adm 1969, cmd Br Naval Staff Washington 1969–71, Flag Offr Medway 1971–74, ret; dir gen Cable TV Assoc and Nat TV Rental Assoc 1974–83; *Recreations* cricket, country pursuits; *Clubs* Army and Navy, MCC, I Zingari, Free Foresters, Band of Bros; *Style—* Rear Adm C C H Dunlop, CB, CBE, DL; ✉ Moonrakers, Mockbeggar Lane, Biddenden, Ashford, Kent TN27 8ES (☎ 01580 291325)

DUNLOP, Eileen Rhona; da of James Dunlop (d 1982), and Grace, *née* Love (d 1977); *b* 13 Oct 1938; *Educ* Alloa Acad, Moray House Coll of Educn Edinburgh (dip, Steele prize); *m* 1979, Antony Kamm, s of George and Josephine Kamm; *Career* author; teacher Eastfield Sch Penicuik 1959–61, teacher Abercromby Sch Alloa 1961–63, dep head Sunnyside Sch Alloa 1963–79, headmistress Prep Sch of Dollar Acad 1980–90; memb: Pen Scottish Centre, Soc of Authors; *Books* Robinsheugh (1975), A Flute in Mayferry Street (1976), Fox Farm (1978), The Maze Stone (1982), Clementina (1985), The House on the Hill (1987), The Valley of Deer (1989), Finn's Island (1991), Green Willow's Secret (1993), Finn's Roman Fort (1994), Castle Gryffe (1995); ed with Antony Kamm: Scottish Verse to 1800 (1985), Scottish Traditional Rhymes (1985), A Book of Old Edinburgh (1983); *Recreations* reading, theatre, gardening; *Style—* Miss Eileen Dunlop; ✉ 46 Tarmangie Drive, Dollar, Clackmannanshire FK14 7BP (☎ 01259 742007)

DUNLOP, Frank; CBE (1977); s of Charles Norman Dunlop, and Mary, *née* Aarons; *b* 15 Feb 1927; *Educ* Kibworth Beauchamp GS, Univ Coll London (BA); *Career* National Theatre: assoc dir 1967–71, admin dir 1968–71; dir of prodns for NT at the Old Vic Theatre, W End of London, RSC, Royal Court, Young Vic, Edinburgh Festival and in Australia, Norway, Belgium, USA, France and Germany; Young Vic: fndr 1969, dir 1969–78 and 1980–83, conslt 1978–80; dir Edinburgh Int Festival 1984–91; hon fell UCL 1979, Hon Doctorate Philadelphia Coll of Performing Arts 1978; Hon DUniv: Heriot Watt 1989, Edinburgh 1990; Chev Order of Arts and Letters (France) 1987; *Style—* Frank Dunlop, Esq, CBE; ✉ c/o Piccolo Theatre Company, 6 Langley Street, London WC2H 9JA (☎ 0171 379 1084, fax 0171 379 1087); c/o E Nives, 157 W 57th St, Suite 1400, New York, NY 10019, USA (☎ 212 265 8787, fax 212 265 8873)

DUNLOP, Ian Charles Grant; s of James Andrew Merson Dunlop (d 1990), and Jean Margaret Dunlop; *b* 2 Jan 1950; *Educ* Tonbridge Sch, Univ of Leeds (BA); *m* 12 April 1990, Setsuko, da of Masahide Uematsu; 1 da (Emily Aya b 7 June 1990); *Career* gp product mangr Bass Charrington 1971–74, account mangr (Colgate-Palmolive account) D'Arcy McManus & Masius 1974–77, account mangr and account dir (accounts incl Cadbury Schweppes and Smiths Food Gp) Dorlands 1977–79, account dir (Sony and Zanussi accounts) BBDO 1979, bd dir Norman Craig & Kummel 1979–82, bd dir and client serv dir (accounts incl NatWest, Whitbread and Post Office) Owen Wade Delmonte (became Roose OWD 1987) 1982–90, dep md (accounts incl Twinings and British Coal) Alliance Advertising (formerly Alliance International) 1990–93, sr vice pres/gp div dir McCann-Erickson Inc Tokyo 1993–; memb Marketing Soc 1989; *Recreations* Rhododendrons and Azaleas, Art Nouveau, Far Eastern cuisine, travel; *Style—* Ian Dunlop, Esq; ✉ DDB Needham Japan Inc, 2nd Floor, Royal Building, 12–8 Niban-Cho, Chiyoda-Ku, Tokyo 102, Japan (☎ 00 81 3 3288 7551, fax 00 81 3 3288 7555)

DUNLOP, Dr James Montgomery; s of Gabriel Dunlop (d 1944), of Ormiston, Newburgh, Fife, and Margaret Louise, *née* Leiper (d 1991); *b* 25 Aug 1930; *Educ* Bell-Baxter Sch Cupar, Trinity Coll Dublin (MA, MB BCh, BAO), Univ of Glasgow (DPH, DPA); *m* 15 Sept 1960, Dr Joyce Lilian Dunlop, *qv*, da of William Strangman Hill (d 1968), of Ounavarra, Lucan, Co Dublin; 2 s (Jonathan b 1961, Douglas b 1966), 1 da (Joanne b 1964); *Career* RAF 1948–49; chief asst co MO N Riding of Yorks 1966–70, dep MOH Hull 1970–74, port MO Hull and Goole Port Health Authy 1970–95, dir of public health Hull Health Authy 1989–95 (dist community physician 1974–82, dist MO 1982–89); med referee Hull Crematorium 1970–; med advsr: Kingston upon Hull City Transport 1970–, Kingston Communications 1970–, Humber Bridge Bd 1981–, Univ of Humberside 1989–; author of numerous leading and other articles in professional jls; book reviews for: Medical Officer, Public Health, British Medical Journal; chm: Charitable Tsts BMA (fell 1978, memb 1959), Conjoint Ctee Epsom Coll 1990–92; memb Cncl: Soc of Public Health (pres 1992–93), Royal Inst Public Health and Hygiene 1992–, Epsom Coll 1992–; FFPHM (formerly Faculty of Community Med) 1978 (member 1972, treas 1990–95, FRMS 1953 (member 1949), FRCP 1992; *Recreations* stamp collecting, writing, travelling, reading; *Clubs* Rugby, Royal Philatelic Soc; *Style—* Dr James M Dunlop; ✉ Sungates, 136 Westella Rd, Kirkella, East Yorkshire HU10 7RR (☎ 01482 655680)

DUNLOP, John Leeper; OBE (1996); s of Dr John Leeper Dunlop (d 1959), and Margaret Frances Mary, *née* Fiffett (d 1972); *b* 10 July 1939; *Educ* Marlborough; *m* 22 June 1965, Susan Jennifer, da of Gerard Thorpe Page (d 1985), of Harpole, Northants; 3 s (Timothy b 1966 d 1987, Edward b 1968, Harry b 1976); *Career* Nat Serv 2 Lt Royal Ulster Rifles 1959–61; racehorse trainer 1964–, trained over 2,000 winners incl the Derby 1978 (Shirley Heights) and 1994 (Erhaab); memb Ctee: Nat Trainers Fedn, Stable Lads Welfare Tst, Br Racing Sch; memb Bd National Stud, dir Goodwood; *Recreations* breeding racehorses, owning show horses; *Clubs* Turf; *Style—* John Dunlop, Esq, OBE; ✉ House on the Hill, Arundel, W Sussex (☎ 01903 882106); Castle Stables, Arundel, W Sussex (☎ 01903 882194, fax 01903 884173, car tel 0860 339805, telex 87475 RACDEL)

DUNLOP, Dr Joyce Lilian; da of William Strangman Hill (d 1968), of Ounavarra, Lucan, Co Dublin, Ireland, and Doris Irene, *née* Odlum (d 1972); *b* 14 April 1933; *Educ* Glengara Park Sch Kingstown Co Dublin Ireland, Trinity Coll Dublin (MA, MB BCh, BAO); *m* 15 Sept 1960, Dr James Montgomery Dunlop, *qv*, s of Gabriel Dunlop (d 1944), of Ormiston, Newburgh, Fife, Scotland; 2 s (Jonathan b 1961, Douglas b 1966), 1 da (Joanne b 1964); *Career* sr house offr in anaesthetics Dumfries and Galloway Royal Infirmary 1959–61, sr registrar in psychiatry Kingston Gen Hosp Hull 1976–77, conslt psychiatrist De La Pole Hosp Hull 1978–; conslt advsr to Relate and Cruse Hull; pres E Yorks BMA 1991–92; FRCPsych 1996 (MRCPsych 1976), DObstRCOG; *Books* contribs incl: Practitioner (1978), British Journal of Psychiatry (1979 and 1988), British Medical Journal (1984 and 1994), When Doctors Get Sick (1988), British Journal of Sexual Medicine (1989); *Recreations* gardening, stamp collecting; *Style—* Dr Joyce Dunlop; ✉ Sungates, 136 Westella Rd, Kirkella, East Yorkshire HU10 7RR (☎ 01482 655680); De La Pole Hospital, Willerby, Hull HU10 6ED (☎ 01482 875875)

DUNLOP, Robert Fergus; AE (1956); s of Maj A Fergus Dunlop, OBE, TD (d 1980), and Gwendolen Elizabeth, *née* Coit; *b* 22 June 1929; *Educ* Marlborough, St John's Cambridge (MA), MIT (MSc); *m* 1966, Jane Clare, da of Lt-Col George Hervey McManus (d 1959), of Canada; 1 s, 2 da; *Career* cmmnd 2 Lt RA, later Flt Lt 501 (Co of Glos) Fighter Sqdn RAuxAF; Sloan fell 1960; Bristol Aeroplane Co Ltd and Br Aircraft Corp 1952–66, Westland Aircraft Ltd 1966–70, dep chm Lonrho plc 1992–94 (joined 1970, dir 1972–94), actg chm Observer Ltd 1992–93; CEng, MRAeS; *Recreations* diving, skiing, windsurfing; *Style—* Robert Dunlop, Esq, AE; ✉ 42 Woodsford Square, London W14 8DP (☎ 0171 602 2579); PO Box 3136, 8211 Paphos, Cyprus

DUNLOP, Thomas; s and h of Sir Thomas Dunlop, 3 Bt, *qv*; *b* 22 April 1951; *Educ* Rugby, Univ of Aberdeen (BSc); *m* 1984, Eileen, er da of Alexander Henry Stevenson (d 1990); 1 s (Thomas b 11 March 1990), 1 da (Nicola Mary b 1987); *Career* memb Inst of Chartered Foresters; ptnr Abbey Forestry, Pershore, Worcs; *Style—* Thomas Dunlop, Esq; ✉ Bredon Croft, Bredon's Norton, nr Tewkesbury, Glos GL20 7HB

DUNLOP, Sir Thomas; 3 Bt (UK 1916), of Woodbourne, Co Renfrew; s of Sir Thomas Dunlop, 2 Bt (d 1963); *b* 11 April 1912; *Educ* Shrewsbury, St John's Coll Cambridge; *m* 1947, (Adda Mary) Alison, da of Thomas Arthur Smith (d 1952), of Lindsaylands, Biggar; 1 s (Thomas b 1951), 1 da (Jennifer Margaret (Mrs David Johnson) b 1948); *Heir* s, Thomas Dunlop b 22 April 1951; *Career* ptnr Thomas Dunlop and Sons (Shipowners), former chm of Savings Bank of Glasgow, govr Hutchesons Sch 1957–80; CA; OStJ 1965; *Recreations* fishing, shooting and golf; *Clubs* Western Glasgow; *Style—* Sir Thomas Dunlop, Bt; ✉ The Corrie, Kilmacolm, Renfrewshire (☎ 01505 873239)

DUNLOP, Prof William; s of Alexander Morton Dunlop, and Annie Denham Rennie, *née* Ingram; *b* 18 Aug 1944; *Educ* Kilmarnock Acad, Univ of Glasgow (MB ChB), Univ of Newcastle upon Tyne (PhD); *m* 25 March 1968, Sylvia Louise, da of Dr Irwin Krauthamer; 1 s (Keith b 1972), 1 da (Emma b 1973); *Career* various jr posts in Obstetrics and Gynaecology Dept, Regius prof Univ of Glasgow 1969–74, seconded as lectr Univ of Nairobi 1972–73, MRC scientific staff Newcastle 1974–75, visiting assoc prof Med Univ of S Carolina 1980, prof and head of Dept Obstetrics and Gynaecology Univ of Newcastle upon Tyne 1982– (sr lectr 1975–82); hon sec RCOG 1992–; chm Blair-Bell Res Soc 1989–92; ed in chief Fetal and Maternal Med Review; FRCSEd 1971, FRCOG 1984 (MRCOG 1971); *Recreations* music, drama, literature; *Style—* Prof William Dunlop; ✉ Department of Obstetrics and Gynaecology, University of Newcastle upon Tyne, 4th Floor, Royal Victoria Infirmary, Newcastle upon Tyne NE1 4LP (☎ 0191 232 5131, fax 0191 222 5066)

DUNLUCE, Viscount Randal Alexander St John McDonnell; s and h of 9 Earl of Antrim, *qv*; *b* 2 July 1967; *Style—* Viscount Dunluce

DUNMORE, Helen; da of Maurice Ronald Dunmore, and Betty, *née* Smith; *b* 12 Dec 1952; *Educ* Nottingham HS for Girls, Univ of York (BA); *m* 24 Oct 1980, Francis Benedict Charnley; 1 s (Patrick Maurice b 28 July 1981), 1 da (Teresa Mary Benedicta b 11 Feb 1994), 1 step s (Oliver Benjamin b 13 Feb 1977); *Career* poet and novelist; external fell Univ of Glamorgan; *Poetry* incl: The Apple Fall (1983), The Sea Skater (1986, winner Poetry Soc's Alice Hunt Bartlett Award 1987), The Raw Garden (1988, Poetry Book Soc Choice winter 1988–89), Short Days, Long Nights, New and Selected Poems (1991), Recovering a Body (1994), Secrets (1994, The Signal Poetry Award 1995); *Children's Novels* Going to Egypt (1992), In the Money (1993), Amina's Blanket (1996), Go Fox (1996), Fatal Error (1996); *Fiction* Zennor in Darkness (1993, The McKitterick Prize 1994), Burning Bright (1994), A Spell of Winter (1995, winner inaugural Orange Prize for women fiction writers 1996), Talking to the Dead (1996); *Recreations* family life and friendships; *Style—* Ms Helen Dunmore; ✉ c/o Caradoc King, A P Watt Ltd, 20 John Street, London WC1N 2DR (☎ 0171 405 6774, fax 0171 831 2154)

DUNMORE, 12 Earl of (S 1686); Malcolm Kenneth Murray; also Viscount Fincastle, Lord Murray of Blair, Moulin and Tillimet (Tullimet; both S 1686); er s of 11 Earl of Dunmore (d 1995), and Margaret Joy, *née* Cousins (d 1976); *b* 17 Sept 1946; *Educ* Queechy HS, Launceston, Schools' Bd 'A' certificate; *m* 1970, Joy Anne, da of Arthur Partridge (d 1987), of Launceston, Tasmania; 1 s (Leigh Kenneth b 1977), 1 da (Elisa Anne b 1980) (both adopted); *Heir* bro, Hon Geoffrey Charles Murray b 1949; *Career* electrical tech offr Air Services Australia, licensed aircraft maintenance engr, pte pilot; patron: Scottish Australian Heritage Cncl's Annual Sydney Scottish Week, Murray Clan Socs of Victoria and Queensland, St Andrew Soc Tasmania. Tasmanian Caledonian Cncl, Launceston Caledonian Soc; *Recreations* flying, astronomy; *Clubs* Soaring Club of Tasmania; *Style—* The Rt Hon the Earl of Dunmore; ✉ PO Box 100E, E Devonport, Tas 7310, Australia

DUNN, Angus Henry; s of Col Henry George Mountfort Dunn (d 1969), and Catherine Mary (d 1986); *b* 30 Dec 1944; *Educ* Marlborough, King's Coll Cambridge (MA), Pennsylvania Univ; *m* 1973, Carolyn Jane, da of Alan Bartlett, of Cranbook, Kent; 2 s (Thomas b 1974, James b 1977), 1 da (Eliza b 1983); *Career* HM Diplomatic Service 1968–73 (FCO, Kuala Lumpur, Bonn); joined Morgan Grenfell & Co Ltd 1972 (dir 1978–88), exec deputy chm Morgan Grenfell (Asia) Ltd Singapore 1983–85; dir: Julianas Holdings plc 1983–85, Manufacturers Hanover Ltd 1988–91; independent conslt 1992–94, head Group Private Fin Unit Tarmac PLC 1994–96, Private Fin Unit DOE 1996–; *Books* Export Finance (co-author, 1983), Personal Accountant Tax Reckoner (software pubn, 1990–93); *Recreations* riding, sailing; *Clubs* Royal Thames Yacht, Royal Dart Yacht; *Style—* Angus Dunn, Esq; ✉ Dower House, Oxon Hoath, Tonbridge, Kent (☎ 01732 810330); Private Finance Unit, Department of the Environment, 2 Marsham Street, London SW1P 3EB (☎ 0171 276 3000)

DUNN, Prof Douglas Eaglesham; s of William Douglas Dunn (d 1980), and Margaret, *née* McGowan; *b* 23 Oct 1942; *Educ* Renfrew HS, Camphill Sch Paisley, Scottish Sch of Librarianship, Univ of Hull (BA); *m* 1, Lesley Balfour, *née* Wallace (d 1981); m 2, 10 Aug 1985, Lesley Jane, da of Robert Bathgate (d 1979); 1 s (William Robert Bathgate b 5 Jan 1987), 1 da (Lillias Ella Bathgate b 18 June 1990); *Career* writer; head Sch of English Univ of St Andrews 1995– (prof 1991–), St Andrews Scottish Studies Inst 1993– (fell in creative writing 1989–91); Somerset Maugham Award 1972, Geoffrey Faber Meml Prize 1975, Hawthornden Prize 1982, Whitbread Book of the Year Award for 1985 (1986), Cholmondeley Award 1989; Hon LLD Univ of Dundee 1987, Hon DLitt Univ of Hull 1995; hon prof Univ of Dundee 1987, hon fell Humberside Coll; FRSL 1981; *Books* books of poetry incl: Terry Street (1969), The Happier Life (1972), Love or Nothing (1974), Barbarians (1979), St Kilda's Parliament (1982), Elegies (1985), Selected Poems (1986), Northlight (1988), Dante's Drum-kit (1993); other books: Secret Villages (short stories, 1985), Andromache (translation, 1990), Poll Tax: The Fiscal Fake (1990), The Essential Browning (ed, 1990), Scotland: An Anthology (ed, 1991), Faber Book of Twentieth Century Scottish Poetry (ed, 1992), Boyfriends and Girlfriends (short stories, 1995), Oxford Book of Scottish Short Stories (ed, 1995); *Recreations* music, philately; *Style—* Prof Douglas Dunn, FRSL; ✉ School of English, Castle House, University of St Andrews, St Andrews, Fife KY16 9AL (☎ 01334 462666, fax 01334 462655)

DUNN, Geoffrey Richard; s of Kenneth Grayson Dunn, of Crawley, Sussex, and Nila Jane, *née* Griffiths; *b* 10 July 1949; *Educ* Ifield GS, Univ of Manchester (BSc, MSc), Manchester Business Sch (Dip); *m* 26 July 1973, Patricia Ann, da of John Thompson (d 1990), of Lightcliffe, nr Halifax, W Yorks; *Career* investmt controller ICFC Ltd 1975–78, corp fin exec SG Warburg & Co Ltd 1978–80, asst gp treas GKN plc 1980–83, head of fin and planning Midland Bank plc 1984–87, gp fin dir Exco International plc 1987–92, conslt 1993–94, chief fin offr Soc for Worldwide Interbank Fin Telecommunication SC Brussels 1994–; memb MCT 1982; *Recreations* mountaineering, skiing, opera and music; *Clubs* Alpine, London Mountaineering; *Style—* Geoffrey Dunn, Esq; ✉ Avenue de L'Echevinage, 16 Uccle, B-1180, Brussels, Belgium (☎ 00 32 2 375 9704); Croft House, Low Lorton, Cumbria CA13 9UW (☎ 01900 85014)

DUNN, His Hon Judge; (William) Hubert; QC (1982); s of William Patrick Millar Dunn (d 1964), of Tudor Hall, Holywood, Co Down, and Isobel, *née* Thompson (d 1954); *b* 8 July 1933; *Educ* Winchester, New Coll Oxford (BA); *m* 23 Sept 1971, Maria

Henriquetta Theresa D'Arouje Perestrello, da of George Hoffacker de Moser, 3 s of Count de Moser in the nobility of Portugal; 1 s (Sebastian b 29 Aug 1973), 1 da (Eugenia b 27 May 1972); *Career* 2 Lt The Life Gds 1956–57, Household Cavalry Reserve of Offrs 1957–64; called to the Bar Lincoln's Inn 1958; local govt cmmr 1963; recorder of the Crown Court 1980–93, circuit judge (SE Circuit) 1993–; chm Women Caring Tst 1995–; *Recreations* travel, literature; *Clubs* Boodle's; *Style*— His Hon Judge Dunn, QC; ✉ 19 Clarendon St, London SW1; Woolwich Crown Court, The Court House, Powis Street, London SE18 6JW

DUNN, John Churchill; s of John Barrett Jackson Dunn (d 1984), and Dorothy Dunn, *née* Hiscox; *b* 4 March 1934; *Educ* Christ Church Cathedral Choir Sch Oxford, The King's Sch Canterbury; *m* 19 April 1958, Margaret, da of Stanley Farrand Jennison (d 1982); 2 da (Joanna b 1960, Emma b 1963); *Career* broadcaster; BBC staff 1956–76, freelance (BBC Radio 2) 1976–; programmes incl: Breakfast Special, Late Night Extra, The John Dunn Show 1972–; TV and Radio Industs Club Personality of the Year 1971, 1984 and 1986, Variety Club of GB Radio Personality of the Year 1983, winner Daily Mail Silver Microphone 1988; *Recreations* working, skiing, sailing, wine; *Style*— John Dunn, Esq; ✉ BBC Radio 2, Broadcasting House, London W1A 1AA

DUNN, Prof John Montfort; s of Col Henry George Montfort Dunn (d 1970), and Catherine Mary, *née* Kinloch (d 1986); *b* 9 Sept 1940; *Educ* Winchester, Millfield, King's Coll Cambridge (BA); *m* 1, 1965 (m dis 1971), Susan Deborah, *née* Fyvel; m 2, 1973 (m dis 1987), Judith Frances Bernal; 2 s (Thomas William b 8 Dec 1989 d 1990, Charles Montfort b 11 Jan 1991); *Career* Univ of Cambridge: fell Jesus Coll 1965–66, fell King's Coll 1966–, lectr in political science 1972–77, reader in politics 1977–87, prof of political theory 1987–; visiting prof: Univ of Ghana, Univ of Br Columbia, Univ of Bombay, Tokyo Met Univ, Tulane Univ, Univ of Minnesota; Olmsted visiting prof Yale Univ 1991; foreign hon memb: American Acad of Arts and Sciences 1991, Bd of Conslts Kim Dae-Jung Fndn for the Asia-Pacific Region 1994; FBA 1989, FSA 1993; *Books* The Political Thought of John Locke (1969), Modern Revolutions (1972), Dependence and Opportunity (with A F Robertson, 1973), Western Political Theory in the Face of the Future (1979), Political Obligation in its Historical Context (1980), The Politics of Socialism (1984), Rethinking Modern Political Theory (1985), Interpreting Political Responsibility (1990), Democracy: the unfinished journey 508 BC - 1993 AD (ed, 1992), Contemporary Crisis of the Nation State? (ed, 1995), The History of Political Theory and Other Essays (1996); *Style*— Prof John Dunn, FBA, FSA; ✉ The Merchant's House, 31 Station Rd, Swavesey, Cambridge CB4 5QJ (☎ 01954 231451); King's College, Cambridge CB2 1ST (☎ 01223 331258)

DUNN, Baroness (Life Peer UK 1990), of Hong Kong Island in Hong Kong and of Knightsbridge in the Royal Borough of Kensington and Chelsea; Lydia Selina Dunn; DBE (1989, CBE 1983, OBE 1978), JP (1976); da of Yen Chuen Yih Dunn (d 1965), and Chen Yin-chu (d 1990); *b* 29 Feb 1940; *Educ* St Paul's Convent Sch Hong Kong, Univ of California at Berkeley (BS); *m* 1988, Michael David Thomas, CMG, QC, *qv*; *Career* dir: John Swire & Sons Ltd 1996–, Swire Pacific Ltd 1981–, John Swire & Sons (HK) Ltd 1978–, Cathay Pacific Airways Ltd 1985–; dep chm: Hongkong and Shanghai Banking Corporation 1992–96 (dir 1981–96), HSBC Holdings plc (formerly Hong Kong and Shanghai Banking Corporation Holdings (London)) 1992– (dir 1990–); memb Hong Kong Exec Cncl 1982–88 (sr memb 1988–95), memb Hong Kong Legislative Cncl 1976–85 (sr memb 1985–88); chm: Hong Kong Trade Devpt Cncl 1983–91, Hong Kong/Japan Business Co-operation Ctee 1988–95 (memb 1983–88), Lord Wilson Heritage Tst 1993–95; dir Volvo AB 1991–93 (memb Int Advsy Bd 1985–91), Lordemb Hong Kong/US Econ Co-operation Ctee 1984–93; Prime Minister of Japan's Trade Award 1987, US Sec of Commerce's Peace and Commerce Award 1988; Hon LLD: Chinese Univ of Hong Kong 1984, Univ of Hong Kong 1991, Univ of British Columbia 1991, Univ of Leeds 1994; Hon DSc Univ of Buckingham 1995; *Books* In the Kingdom of the Blind (1983); *Recreations* study of antiquities; *Clubs* Hong Kong, Hong Kong Jockey; *Style*— The Rt Hon the Baroness Dunn, DBE, JP; ✉ John Swire & Sons Ltd, Swire House, 59 Buckingham Gate, London SW1E 6AJ

DUNN, Martin; *b* 26 Jan 1955; *Educ* Dudley GS; *Career* journalist; Dudley Herald 1974–77; reporter: Birmingham Evening Mail 1977–78, Birmingham Post 1978–79, Daily Mail 1979–80; freelance journalist USA 1983, Bizarre ed The Sun 1984–88 (NY corr 1983–84); dep ed: News of the World 1988–89, The Sun 1989–91; ed: Today 1991–93, Boston Herald 1993; ed-in-chief New York Daily News 1993–96, ed Channel One Television 1996–, ed-in-chief Harmsworth New Media 1996–; *Recreations* squash, running; *Style*— Martin Dunn, Esq; ✉ Channel One Television, 60 Charlotte Street, London W1P 2AX (☎ 0171 209 1234)

DUNN, Air Marshal Sir Patrick Hunter; KBE (1965, CBE 1950), CB (1956), DFC (1941); s of late William Alexander Dunn, of Ardentinny, Argyllshire; *b* 31 Dec 1912; *Educ* Glasgow Acad, Loretto, Univ of Glasgow; *m* 1939, Diana Ledward Smith; 2 da (*see* Sir Nigel Marsden, Bt); *Career* cmmnd RAF 1933; served WWII Egypt, Libya, Sudan, Air Miny and Fighter Cmd; ADC to HM The Queen 1953–58, Cmdt RAF Flying Coll Manby 1956–58, Air Vice Marshal 1959, AOC No 1 Gp Bomber Cmd 1961–64, AOC-in-C Flying Training Cmd 1964–66, Air Marshal 1965, ret 1967; dir Mgmnt Servs British Steel Corp 1967–68, dep chm British Eagle International Airlines 1968, vice pres UK NATO Def Coll Assoc 1969, chm Eagle Aircraft Services Ltd 1969, dir Gloucester Cricklewood Kingston and Coventry Trading Estates Ltd 1969–81; tstee and govr Loretto Sch 1959–81; pres: Fettesian Lorettonian Club 1972–75, Lorettonian Society 1980–81; memb: Ctee Assoc of Governing Bodies of Public Schools 1976–79, Br Atlantic Ctee 1976–92; Liveryman Guild of Air Pilots and Air Navigators; FRAeS; *Clubs* RAF, RAF Yacht, Hurlingham; *Style*— Air Marshal Sir Patrick Dunn, KBE, CB, DFC; ✉ Little Hillbark, Cookham Dean, Berks SL6 9UF (☎ 01628 485625)

DUNN, Richard Johann; CBE (1995); s of Maj Edward Cadwalader Dunn, MBE, TD (d 1985), of Burgh, Suffolk, and Gudlaug, *née* Johannesdóttir; *b* 5 Sept 1943; *Educ* Forest Sch, St John's Coll Cambridge (MA); *m* 20 June 1972, Virginia Gregory, da of Norman Joseph Gaynor (d 1967), of Canton, Ohio; 2 s (Andrew Glover Gaynor b 1980, William Edward Gaynor b 1986), 1 da (Elizabeth Page Gaynor b 1987); *Career* writer and prodr Associated British Pathé 1967–72; chief exec Thames TV 1985–95 (dir 1982–95), md Pearson Television Holdings Ltd 1994–95; chm: Thames TV International 1985–95, ITV Assoc 1988–90 (dir 1985–92), ITN Ltd 1992–93 (dir 1985–93), Euston Films Ltd 1985–90, Cosgrove Hall Productions Ltd 1985–93, UK Living 1993–95, Financial Times TV 1993–95, BTA 1994–95, The Television Corporation 1996–; exec dir News International Television 1995–; dir: Swindon Viewpoint Ltd 1972–76, Starstream Ltd 1986–90, Independent Broadcasting Telethon Tst 1986–94, Thames Help Tst 1986–92, SES (Astra) 1987–95, Channel Four TV Co Ltd 1989–91, UK Gold 1992–95, Dorling Kindersley PLC 1994–; vice pres Royal TV Soc; govr Forest Sch; pres Battersea Arts Centre; winner Int Emmy (Founders') Award 1993; *Clubs* Garrick, Hawks' (Cambridge), RAC; *Style*— Richard Dunn, Esq, CBE; ✉ Lovel Dene, Woodside Road, Windsor Forest, Berks SL4 2DP; News International Television, 6 Centaurs Business Park, Grant Way, Isleworth, Middlesex TW7 5QD (☎ 0171 705 3667, fax 0171 705 3867)

DUNN, Robert John; MP (C) Dartford (majority 10,314); s of Robert Dunn (d 1986); *b* 14 July 1946; *Educ* State Schs; *m* 1976, Janet Elizabeth, da of Denis Wall (d 1983); 2 s; *Career* sr buyer J Sainsbury Ltd 1973–79; Parly candidate (C) Eccles 1974, MP (C) Dartford 1979–, jt sec Cons Backbench Educn Ctee 1980–82, advsr to Professional Assoc of Teachers 1982–83; PPS: to Parly Under-Sec of State Dept of Educn 1981–82, to Cecil Parkinson as Chm Cons Pty 1982–83; under sec of state Dept of Educn and Sci 1983–88; memb Select Ctee: on Selection 1991–, on Members' Interests 1992–94; chm Cons Backbench: Social Security Ctee 1988–89, Tport Ctee 1990–; memb Exec 1922 Ctee 1988–; pres Young Conservatives: Dartford 1976–, SE Area 1989; pres Eccles Cons Assoc 1995– (vice pres 1974–95); *Style*— Robert Dunn, Esq, MP; ✉ House of Commons, London SW1A 0AA (☎ 0171 219 5209)

DUNN, Rt Hon Sir Robin Horace Walford; kt (1969), MC (1944), PC (1980); s of Brig Keith Frederick William Dunn, CBE, DL (d 1985), and his 1 w, Ava, *née* Kays; *b* 16 Jan 1918; *Educ* Wellington, RMA Woolwich; *m* 1941, Judith Allan (d 1995), da of Sir Gonne St Clair Pilcher, MC (d 1966); 1 s, 1 da (and 1 da decd); *Career* cmmnd RA 1938, RHA 1941; served WWII France, Belgium, Libya, Normandy, NW Europe (despatches twice), Staff Coll 1946, ret Hon Maj 1948; Hon Col Cmdt RA 1981–1984, Hon Col 1984; called to the Bar Inner Temple 1948, jr counsel Registrar of Restrictive Trading Agreements 1959–62, memb Gen Cncl of the Bar 1959–63 (treas 1967–69), QC 1962, bencher Inner Temple 1969, judge High Ct of Justice Family Div 1969–80, presiding judge Western Circuit 1974–78, Lord Justice of Appeal 1980–84, ret; *Clubs* Cavalry and Guards'; *Style*— Rt Hon Sir Robin Dunn, MC; ✉ Lynch Mead, Allerford, Somerset TA24 8HJ (☎ 01643 862509)

DUNN, Stephen; s of William Thomas Corbett Dunn, of Newcastle upon Tyne, and Margaret, *née* Brennan; *b* 22 June 1960; *Educ* Heaton Comp Sch, Newcastle upon Tyne Coll of Art (HND DipAD); *Career* advertising art dir; Boase Massimi Pollitt 1979–82, Leagas Delaney 1982–93 (head art dir 1985, memb Bd 1988), joint creative dir Wieden and Kennedy Portland Oregon 1993–94, creative head of art Lowe Howard-Spink 1995– (freelance 1994–95); awards: 3 Design and Art Direction Silver awards, 3 Gold and 15 Silver Campaign Press awards, 4 Silver Campaign Poster awards, 4 Gold and 1 Silver One Show awards (US), 8 Gold and 6 Silver Creative Circle awards; memb Design and Art Directors Assoc; *Style*— Stephen Dunn, Esq; ✉ Lowe Howard-Spink Ltd, 3rd Floor West Wing, Bowater House, 68–114 Knightsbridge, London SW1X 7LT (☎ 0171 584 5033)

DUNN-MEYNELL, Hugo Arthur; s of Arthur James Dunn (d 1959), of London, and Mary Louise Maude, *née* Meynell (d 1945); *b* 4 April 1926; *Educ* John Fisher Sch Purley; *m* 1, 1952 (m dis 1980), Nadine Madeleine, da of late Percy Denson; 3 s, 1 da; m 2, 1980, Alice Wooledge, da of Dr Pierre Joseph Salmon, of Hillsborough, California; *Career* wine and food writer and conslt; pres Lonsdale Advertising International 1978–89; International Wine and Food Soc: chm 1978–80, exec dir 1983–; Liveryman Worshipful Co of Innholders; Grand-Officier Les Chevaliers du Tastevin; FRGS, FIPA; *Recreations* wine and travel; *Clubs* Athenaeum; *Style*— Hugo Dunn-Meynell, Esq; ✉ 14 Avenue Mansions, Sisters Avenue, London SW11 5SL (☎ 0171 223 2826); International Wine and Food Society, 9 Fitzmaurice Place, Berkeley Square, London W1X 6JD (☎ 0171 495 4191, fax 0171 495 4172)

DUNN-THOMAS, Paula; da of Paul Kenneth Dunn, and Louise, *née* Brissett; *b* 3 Dec 1964; *m* May 1990, Peter Thomas; 1 s (Kane-Paul b 1992); *Career* athlete (sprinter); UK champion 100m and 200m: 1986, 1987 and 1988; WAAA champion 100m and 200m: 1987, 1988 and 1989; Cwlth Games 1986: Silver medallist 100m, Gold medallist 4 x 100m relay; Olympic Games 1988: quarter-finalist 100m, semi-finalist 200m, semi-finalist 4 x 100m relay; Silver medallist Europa Cup 100m and 200m 1989; Silver medallist Cwlth Games 1990, Bronze medallist European Championship 1990; Cwlth Games 1994: Bronze medallist 100m, Bronze medallist 4x100m relay; athletic devpt offr and med clerical offr, also involved with local schs and sports clubs; Hon MA 1996; *Recreations* athletics, reading; *Clubs* Trafford AC; *Style*— Miss Paula Dunn-Thomas; ✉ 4 Salisbury Road, Chorlton-cum-Hardy, Manchester M21 1SL (☎ 0161 861 9319); Belle Vue Athletic Centre, Recreational Services, Pink Bank Lane, Longsight, Manchester M12 5GL

DUNNACHIE, James Francis (Jimmy); JP, MP (Lab) Glasgow Pollok (majority 7,883); s of late William Dunnachie, and late Mary, *née* Heaney; *b* 17 Nov 1930; *m* 27 Sept 1974, Marion Isobel, da of late Cyril Payne; *Career* formerly engr Rolls-Royce; formerly cncllr: Glasgow Corp (chm Clearance and Rehabilitation Ctee), Glasgow DC (chm Clearance and Rehabilitation Ctee), Strathclyde Regnl Cncl (vice chm Social Work Ctee); MP (Lab) Glasgow Pollok 1987–; *Recreations* reading, gardening, junior football; *Style*— Jimmy Dunnachie, Esq, JP, MP; ✉ 15 Loganswell Gardens, Glasgow G46 8HU (☎ 0141 638 9756); House of Commons, London SW1A 0AA

DUNNE, (W) Peter; s of William Joseph Dunne (d 1985), and Mary Anne, *née* Hynes (d 1958); *b* 6 Nov 1936; *Educ* Dublin; *m* 29 Nov 1969, Fionuala Anne, da of James Joseph Fox (d 1989), of Dublin; *Career* ret int civil servant; asst dir and head of Conference Unit Cwlth Secretariat (formerly Cwlth Econ Ctee) 1961–96; *Recreations* antiquarian books, music, cricket; *Clubs* MCC, Nat Lib, Royal Over-Seas League, RDS (Dublin); *Style*— W Peter Dunne, Esq; ✉ The Nuik, 55 Bodley Rd, New Malden, Surrey KT3 5QD (☎ and fax 0181 942 1434); 11 Martello Mews, Dublin 4

DUNNE, Sir Thomas Raymond; KCVO (1995), JP (Hereford and Worcester 1977); s of Philip Dunne, MC (d 1965), of East Clandon, Surrey, and his 1 wife Margaret Ann Willis, CBE, *née* Walker; *b* 24 Oct 1933; *Educ* Eton; *m* 17 July 1957, Henrietta Rose, da of Cosmo Stafford Crawley (d 1989); 2 s (Philip b 1958, Nicholas b 1970), 2 da (Camilla (Hon Mrs Rupert Soames) b 1960, Letitia b 1965); *Career* RMA Sandhurst 1951–53, cmmnd RHG 1953–58, farmer 1960–; Hon Col: 2 (volunteer) Bn Mercian Volunteers 1985–87, 4 (volunteer) Bn The Worcestershire and Sherwood Foresters Regt 1987–93 (formerly 2 Bn Mercian Volunteers), 5 (Shropshire and Herefordshire) Bn The Light Infantry (Volunteers); memb Hereford CC 1962–68; High Sheriff Herefordshire 1970, DL Hereford and Worcester 1974 (Herefordshire 1973), HM Lord Lieutenant Hereford and Worcester 1977–, Custos Rotularum 1977–; dir W Midland Regnl Bd Central TV, chm Tstees Worcester Museum of Porcelain 1985–, pres W Midlands TAVRA 1989–; KStJ 1977; *Style*— Sir Thomas Dunne, KCVO, JP; ✉ County Hall, Spetchley Road, Worcester

DUNNETT, Sir Alastair MacTavish; kt (1995); s of David Sinclair Dunnett, and Ishbel Crawford, *née* MacTavish; *b* 26 Dec 1908; *Educ* Hillhead HS Glasgow; *m* 1946, Dorothy, *née* Halliday (*see* Lady Dunnett, OBE); 2 s; *Career* Commercial Bank of Scotland Ltd 1925–33, The Claymore Press 1933–34 (co-fndr), Glasgow Weekly Herald 1935–36, The Bulletin 1936–37, Daily Record 1937–40, chief press offr to Sec of State for Scotland 1940–46; ed: Daily Record 1946–55, The Scotsman 1956–72; The Scotsman Publications Ltd: md 1962–70, chm 1970–74; memb Exec Bd The Thomson Organisation Ltd 1974–78; dir: Scottish Television Ltd 1975–79, Thomson Scottish Petroleum Ltd 1979–87 (chm 1972–79); memb: Scottish Tourist Bd 1956–69, Press Cncl 1959–62, Cncl Nat Tst for Scotland 1962–69, Cncl Cwth Press Union 1964–78, Ct Univ of Edinburgh 1964–66, Cncl Edinburgh Festival 1967–80; govr Pitlochry Festival Theatre 1958–64; Smith-Mundt scholarship to USA 1951; Hon LLD Univ of Strathclyde 1978; hon memb Saltire Soc 1991; *Books* Treasure at Sonnach (1935), Heard Tell (1946), Quest by Canoe (1950, reprinted as It's Too Late in the Year 1967, and as The Canoe Boys 1995), Highlands and Islands of Scotland (1951), The Donaldson Line (1952), The Land of Scotch (1953), The Duke's Day (as Alex Tavis, 1970), Alistair Maclean Introduces Scotland (ed, 1972), No Thanks to the Duke (1978), Among Friends (autobiog, 1984), The Scottish Highlands (with Dorothy Dunnett, 1988), End of Term (1989); *Plays* The Original John Mackay (Glasgow Citizens, 1956), Fit to Print (Duke of York's, 1962); *Clubs* Caledonian, New (Edinburgh), Puffin's (Edinburgh); *Style*— Sir Alastair Dunnett; ✉ 87 Colinton Road, Edinburgh EH10 5DF (☎ 0131 337 2107, fax 0131 346 4140)

DUNNETT, Anthony Gordon; s of Peter Sydney Dunnett (d 1988), and Margaret Eileen, *née* Johnson, of Wadhurst, East Sussex; *b* 17 June 1953; *Educ* St Dunstans Coll London, McGill Univ Montreal (Dip CS, BCom), Univ of Exeter (MA); *m* 1975, Ruth Elizabeth, da of Dennis Henry Barker; 1 s (Timothy b 1978), 2 da (Penelope b 1980, Emily b 1982); *Career* Nat Westminster Bank plc 1975–77; Royal Bank of Canada: Montreal 1977–80, Curacao 1980–82, Montreal 1982–86; corp banking dir Midland Bank 1986–88, corp dir Samuel Montagu 1988–89, corp dir Midland Bank 1990–91, fin dir Corp & Institutional Banking Midland Bank plc London 1991–94, on secondment as dir Industl Devpt Unit DTI 1994–96, chief exec English Partnerships 1996–; memb local church; FCIB 1981; *Recreations* gardening, theatre, opera, music; *Style—* Anthony Dunnett, Esq; ✉ English Partnerships, 16–18 Old Queen Street, London SW1H 9HP (☎ 0171 976 7070, fax 0171 976 8016)

DUNNETT, Lady; Dorothy; OBE (1992); da of late Alexander Halliday, and late Dorothy, *née* Millard; *b* 25 Aug 1923; *Educ* James Gillespie's HS for Girls Edinburgh; *m* 17 Sept 1946, Sir Alastair MacTavish Dunnett, *qv*; 2 s (Ninian b 1959, Mungo b 1964); *Career* Civil Service: asst press offr Scottish Govt Depts Edinburgh 1940–46, Scottish Economic Res Dept Bd of Trade Glasgow 1946–55; professional portrait painter 1950–, novelist 1960–; non-exec dir Scottish TV plc 1979–92; tstee: Scottish Nat War Meml 1962–96, Nat Library of Scotland 1986–95; memb Bd Edinburgh Book Festival 1988–; Flora Macdonald award (for Literature) from St Andrews Presbyterian Coll (N Carolina, USA) 1993; FRSA 1986; *Books* The Game of Kings (1961, republished 1992 and 1996), Queens' Play (1964, republished 1992 and 1996), The Disorderly Knights (1966, republished 1992 and 1997), Dolly and the Singing Bird (1968, republished as Rum Affair 1991), Pawn in Frankincense (1969, republished 1992 and 1997), Dolly and the Cookie Bird (1970, republished as Ibiza Surprise 1993), The Ringed Castle (1971, republished 1992 and 1997), Dolly and the Doctor Bird (1971, republished as Operation Nassau 1993), Scottish Short Stories (contrib, 1973), Dolly and the Starry Bird (1973, republished as Roman Nights 1993), Checkmate (1975, republished 1992 and 1997, Scottish Arts Cncl Award 1976), Dolly and the Nanny Bird (1976, republished as Split Code 1993), King Hereafter (1982, republished 1992), Dolly and the Bird of Paradise (1983, republished as Tropical Issue 1991), Niccolò Rising (1986, republished 1992), The Spring of the Ram (1987, republished 1993), The Scottish Highlands (with Alastair M Dunnett, 1988), Race of Scorpions (1989, republished 1993), Moroccan Traffic (1991, republished 1992), Scales of Gold (1991, republished 1993), The Unicorn Hunt (1993, republished 1994), To Lie with Lions (1995, republished 1996); *Recreations* travel, sailing, music, ballet, mediaeval history; *Clubs* New (Edinburgh), Caledonian; *Style—* Lady Dunnett, OBE; ✉ 87 Colinton Rd, Edinburgh EH10 5DF (☎ 0131 337 2107, fax 0131 346 4140)

DUNNETT, Jack; *b* 24 June 1922; *Educ* Whitgift Middle Sch Croydon, Downing Coll Cambridge; *m* 1951, Pamela Lucille; 2 s, 3 da; *Career* served WWII, Royal Fusiliers and Cheshire Regt (Capt); slr 1949; memb GLC 1964–67; MP (Lab): Nottingham Central 1964–74, Nottingham East 1974–83; PPS to: Sec of State for Defence and Min for Defence (Army) 1964–66, Min for Aviation 1966–67, Min for Transport 1969–70; Football Assoc: memb Cncl 1977–89, vice pres 1981–86 and 1988–89; Football League: memb Mgmnt Ctee 1977–89, pres Football League 1981–86 and 1988–89; memb Football Tst 1982–89; chm Notts County FC 1968–87, vice chm Portsmouth FC 1989–90; *Style—* Jack Dunnett, Esq; ✉ c/o Whitehall Court, London SW1A 2EP

DUNNETT, Sir (Ludovic) James; GCB (1969, KCB 1960, CB 1957), CMG (1948); s of Sir James Dunnett, KCIE (d 1953), bro of Sir George Sangster Dunnett; *b* 12 Feb 1914; *Educ* Edinburgh Acad, Univ Coll Oxford; *m* 1, 1944, Olga Adair (d 1980), m 2, 1983, Clarisse, Lady Dunnett; *Career* joined Air Miny 1936, transferred to Miny of Civil Aviation 1945 (asst sec 1945, under-sec 1948–51), under-sec (Air) Miny of Supply 1951–53 (dep sec 1953–58), dep sec Miny of Transport 1958 (permanent sec 1959–62), permanent sec Miny of Labour 1962–66, permanent under-sec of state MOD 1966–74; chm Int Maritime Industs Forum 1974–79; pres Institute of Manpower Studies 1977–80, memb SSRC 1977–83; visiting fell Nuffield Coll Oxford 1960–68; Liveryman Worshipful Co of Shipwrights; *Clubs* Reform; *Style—* Sir James Dunnett, GCB, CMG; ✉ 85 Bedford Gardens, London W8

DUNNILL, Dr Michael Simpson; s of Arthur Hoyle Dunnill (d 1958), of Bristol, and Florence Simpson, *née* Rollinson (d 1984); *b* 26 March 1928; *Educ* Bristol GS, Univ of Bristol (MB ChB, MD), Univ of Oxford (MA); *m* 30 Oct 1952, Hilda, da of H Eastman (d 1939), of Bristol; 2 s (Phillip Arthur Simpson b 1956, Michael Giles Simpson b 1964); *Career* Nat Serv MO RAMC Highland Light Infantry 1952–54; jr clinical pathologist Bristol Royal Infirmary 1954–55 (house physician and surgn 1951–52), demonstrator Univ of Bristol 1955–56; Univ of Oxford: joined 1956, lectr in pathology 1961, dir of clinical studies 1966–72, fell Merton Coll 1967–; res assoc Dept of Med Columbia Univ NY 1961–62, conslt pathologist Oxford 1961–93, examiner RCP 1972–80, memb Cncl RCPath 1977–80 (examiner 1977–93); FRCP 1971 (memb 1956), FRCPath 1972; *Books* Pathological Basis of Renal Disease (1976, 2 edn 1984), Pulmonary Pathology (1982, 2 edn), Morphometry (jtly, 1982); *Recreations* walking, fly fishing; *Clubs* Athenaeum, MCC; *Style—* Dr Michael Dunnill; ✉ Merton College, Oxford OX1 4JD

DUNNILL, Prof Peter; s of Eric Dunnill (d 1980), of Rustington, Sussex, and Majorie (d 1985); *b* 20 May 1938; *Educ* Willesden Tech Sch, UCL (BSc), Royal Inst (PhD); *m* 11 Aug 1962, Patricia Mary, da of Sidney Lievesley (d 1992), of Winchmore Hill, London; 1 s (Paul b 2 April 1971); *Career* staff MRC Royal Inst 1963–64; UCL: lectr 1964–79, reader 1976–84, prof of biochemical engrg 1984–91, dir BBSRC (formerly SERC) Interdisciplinary Research Centre for Biochemical Engineering 1991–95, dir BBSRC sponsored Advanced Centre for Biochemical Engrg 1996–; memb: SERC Biotechnology Directorate Management Ctee 1982–88 and 1993–94, Biotechnology Advsy Gp to the Heads of Res Councils 1987–90, Biotechnology Joint Advsy Bd 1989–92, Cncl BBSRC 1993–95; fell UCL 1991, FRSC 1979, FIChemE 1981, FEng 1985; *Books* Fermentation and Enzyme Technology (1979), Enzymic and Non-enzymic Catalysis (1980); *Recreations* music; *Style—* Prof Peter Dunnill, FEng; ✉ Advanced Centre for Biochemical Engineering, Department of Chemical & Biochemical Engineering, UCL, Torrington Place, London WC1E 7JE (☎ 0171 380 7031, fax 0171 388 0808, telex 29627 ENGG)

DUNNING, Prof Eric Geoffrey; s of Sydney Ernest Dunning (d 1981), and Florence Daisy, *née* Morton (d 1987); *b* 27 Dec 1936; *Educ* Acton Co GS for Boys, Univ of Leicester (BSc, MA); *m* 1, 12 July 1962 (m dis 1965), Ellen Adrienne, da of Col Nathaniel Sweets (d 1988), of St Louis, Missouri; m 2, 17 July 1969 (m dis 1986), (Ursula) Judith Clare Hibbert; 1 s (Michael James b 1976), 1 da (Rachel Clare b 1978); *Career* Univ of Leicester: asst lectr 1962, lectr 1963, sr lectr 1972, prof of sociology 1988–, dir Sir Norman Chester Centre for Football Res 1987–, res dir Centre for Research into Sport and Society 1992–; visiting lectureships: Univ of Warwick 1966–69, Univ of Nottingham 1974; visiting professorships: Brooklyn Coll NY 1964, Univ of Minnesota 1968, State Univ of NY 1970, Instituto Nacional de Educacion Fisica de Catalunya 1990, 1991 and 1992; assoc ed International Review for the Sociology of Sport; memb Br Sociological Assoc; *Books* The Sociology of Sport (1971), Barbarians Gentlemen and Players (1979), Hooligans Abroad (1984), Quest For Excitement (1986), The Roots of Football Hooliganism (1988), Football on Trial (1990), Sport and Leisure in the Civilizing Process (1992), The Sports Process (1993); *Recreations* music, theatre; *Style—* Prof Eric Dunning; ✉ Centre for Research into Sport and Society, University of Leicester, 14 Salisbury Road, Leicester LE1 7QR (direct ☎ 0116 252 5940)

DUNNING, Graham; s of Maj James Edwin Dunning, of Romsey Hants, and Jane Priscilla, *née* Hunt; *b* 13 March 1958; *Educ* King Edward VI Sch Southampton, Emmanuel Coll Cambridge (MA), Harvard Law Sch (LLM); *m* 26 July 1986, Claire Abigael, da of Dr W S C Williams, of Oxford; 2 s (William Nicholas, Thomas James b 1990); *Career* short serv cmmn 3 RTR 1977; called to the Bar Lincoln's Inn 1982, practising barrister; *Recreations* golf; *Style—* Graham Dunning, Esq; ✉ 50 Gibson Square, Islington, London N1 (☎ 0171 359 0777, fax 0171 226 1520); Essex Court Chambers, 24 Lincoln's Inn Fields, London WC2 (☎ 0171 813 8000, fax 0171 813 8080)

DUNNING, Prof John Harry; s of John Murray Dunning (d 1966), and Anne Florence, *née* Baker (d 1965); *b* 26 June 1927; *Educ* Lower Sch of John Lyons Harrow, City of Coll, UCL (BSc(Econ)), Univ of Southampton (PhD); *m* 1, (m dis 1975); 1 s (Philip John b 1957); m 2, 4 Aug 1975, Christine Mary, da of Ernest Stewart Brown (d 1992); *Career* Sub Lt RNVR 1945–48; lectr and sr lectr in economics Univ of Southampton 1952–64; Univ of Reading: fndn prof of economics 1964–75, Esmee Fairbairn prof of int investmt and business studies 1975–88; ICI res prof in int business 1988–92 (emeritus prof of int business 1992–); prof of int business Rutgers Univ 1989–; chm Economists Advisory Group Ltd; conslt to UK Govt depts, OECD and UNCTAD; memb: Royal Econ Soc, Acad of Int Business, Int Trade and Fin Assoc (pres 1994); AIB: pres 1987–88, dean of fellows 1994–96; Dr (hc) Universidad Autonome Madrid 1990, Hon PhD Uppsala Univ Sweden 1975, hon prof of int business Univ of Int Economics and Business Beijing 1985; *Books* incl: American Investment in British Manufacturing Industry (1958), British Industry - Change and Development in the Twentieth Century (with C J Thomas, 2 edn 1963), The Economics of Advertising (with D Lees and others, 1967), An Economic Study of the City of London (with E V Morgan, 1971), Readings in International Investment (1972), Economic Analysis and the Multinational Enterprise (1974), The World's Largest Industrial Enterprises 1962–77 (1981), International Capital Movements (with John Black, 1982), Multinational Enterprises, Economic Structure and International Competitiveness (1985), Japanese Participation in British Industry (1986), Explaining International Production (1988), Multinationals, Technology and Competitiveness (1988), Structural Change in the World Economy (with Allan Webster, 1990), Multinational Enterprises and the Global Economy (1993), The Globalization of Business (1993), Globalization and Developing Countries (with Khalil Hamdani, 1996), Foreign Direct Investment and Governments (with Rajneesh Narula, 1996), Alliance Capitalism and Global Business (1997), Governments, Globalization and International Business (1997); *Recreations* gardening, walking; *Clubs* Athenaeum; *Style—* Prof John H Dunning; ✉ c/o Department of Economics, University of Reading, Whiteknights, Reading, Berks RG6 2AA (☎ 0118 987 5123, fax 0118 931 0349)

DUNNING, Michael Anthony; s of Rolf Dunning, of Surrey, and Hanny, *née* Meyer; *b* 24 May 1952; *Educ* Purley GS, Hamble/BA Pilot Trg Coll, Univ of Sussex; *partner* Hilary Kay; *Career* photographer; asst to Graham Ford, Ray Massey and Barney Edwards London 1978–81, freelance asst NY 1981–82, in own studio (working for nat and int advtg agencies and design gps) London 1983–; Silver Award Assoc of Photographers 1995; memb Assoc of Photographers 1988; *Recreations* travel, scuba diving, skiing, flying, photography, sailing; *Style—* Michael Dunning, Esq

DUNNING, Sir Simon William Patrick; 3 Bt (UK 1930), of Beedinglee, Lower Beeding, Sussex; s of Sir William Leonard Dunning, 2 Bt (d 1961), and Kathleen Lawrie, *née* Cuthbert (d 1992); *b* 14 Dec 1939; *Educ* Eton; *m* 1975, Frances Deirdre Morton, da of Maj Patrick William Morton Lancaster, of Wapsbourne Manor, Sheffield Park, Sussex, and formerly w of Capt Nigel Edward Corbally Stourton; 1 da (Mariota Kathleen Masika b 1976); *Heir* none; *Career* insurance broker, underwriting memb Lloyd's until 1997; *Clubs* Turf, Western (Glasgow); *Style—* Sir Simon Dunning, Bt; ✉ Low Auchengillan, Blanefield, Glasgow G63 9AU

DUNNINGTON-JEFFERSON, Sir Mervyn Stewart; 2 Bt (UK 1958), of Thorganby Hall, East Riding of Yorkshire; s of Lt-Col Sir John Alexander Dunnington-Jefferson, 1 Bt, DSO (d 1979), and (Frances) Isobel, *née* Cape; *b* 5 Aug 1943; *Educ* Eton; *m* 1971, Caroline Anna, da of John Bayley, of Hillam Hall, Monk Fryston, Yorks; 1 s (John Alexander b 1980), 2 da (Annabelle Mary b 1973, Emma Elizabeth b 1978); *Heir* s, John Alexander Dunnington-Jefferson b 23 March 1980; *Career* ptnr Marldon; *Recreations* sport; *Clubs* MCC, Queen's; *Style—* Sir Mervyn Dunnington-Jefferson, Bt; ✉ 7 Bolingbroke Grove, London SW11 (☎ 0181 675 3395)

DUNPHIE, Maj-Gen Sir Charles Anderson Lane; kt (1959), CB (1948), CBE (1942), DSO (1943); s of Sir Alfred Dunphie, KCVO; *b* 20 April 1902; *Educ* RNCs Osborne and Dartmouth, RMA Woolwich; *m* 1, 1931, Eileen (d 1978), da of Lt-Gen Sir Walter Campbell, KCB, KCMG, DSO; 1 s, 1 da; m 2, 1981, Susan, widow of Col P L M Wright, of Roundhill, Wincanton; *Career* cmmnd RH and RFA 1921, served WWII (despatches) Brig RAC 1941, Cdr 26 Armoured Bde 1942–43, dep dir RAC WO 1943–45, dir gen Armoured Fighting Vehicles 1945–48, ret 1948; chm Vickers Ltd 1962–67; memb HM's Hon Corps Gentlemen-at-Arms 1952–62; Cdr Legion of Merit USA, Silver Star USA; *Clubs* Army and Navy; *Style—* Maj-Gen Sir Charles Dunphie, CB, CBE, DSO; ✉ Roundhill, Wincanton, Somerset BA9 8HH (☎ 01963 33278)

DUNPHIE, Brig Christopher Campbell; MC (1972); s of Maj-Gen Sir Charles Dunphie, CB, CBE, DSO, *qv*, of Roundhill, Wincanton, Somerset, and Eileen, *née* Campbell (d 1978); *b* 29 March 1935; *Educ* Eton, RMA Sandhurst; *m* 28 Sept 1963, Sonia Diana, da of Brig R C H Kirwan, DSO, OBE (d 1989); 1 s (Charles b 1970); *Career* cmmnd Rifle Bde 1955 (later Royal Green Jackets), Regtl Serv in Kenya, Malaya, BAOR and Cyprus 1955–67, Staff Coll 1968, MA to CGS 1969–71, 3 RGJ in UN Force Cyprus and NI 1971–73, instr Staff Coll 1973–76, CO 3 RGJ Berlin, UK and NI 1976–78, asst dir of def policy MOD 1979–82, COS to LANDEP C-in-C Fleet Falklands Op 1982, Cmdt Tactics Wing Sch of Inf 1983–85, Div Brig Light Div 1985–87, ret 1988; memb Queen's Body Guard for Scotland (The Royal Co of Archers); *Books* Brightly Shone the Dawn (with Garry Johnson, 1980); *Recreations* cricket, skiing, field sports, music; *Clubs* I Zingari, Free Foresters; *Style—* Brig Christopher Dunphie, MC; ✉ Wester Cloquhat, Bridge of Cally, Blairgowrie, Perthshire PH10 7JP (☎ 01250 886320)

DUNRAVEN AND MOUNT-EARL, 7 Earl of (I 1822); Sir Thady Windham Thomas Wyndham-Quin; 7 Bt (GB 1781); also Baron Adare (I 1800), Viscount Mount-Earl (I 1816), Viscount Adare (I 1822); s of 6 Earl of Dunraven and Mount-Earl, CB, CBE, MC (d 1965), and Nancy, *née* Yuille (d 1994); *b* 27 Oct 1939; *Educ* Ludgrove, Le Rosey Switzerland; *m* 1969, Geraldine, da of Air Cdre Gerard W McAleer, CBE; 1 da (Lady Ana b 1972); *Heir* none; *Career* farming and property devpt; *Clubs* Kildare Street (Dublin); *Style—* The Rt Hon The Earl of Dunraven and Mount-Earl; ✉ Kilcurly House, Adare, Co Limerick, Ireland (☎ 00 353 61 396201)

DUNROSSIL, 2 Viscount (UK 1959); John William Morrison; CMG (1981), JP; s of 1 Viscount, GCMG, MC, PC, QC (d 1961); *b* 22 May 1926; *Educ* Fettes, Oriel Coll Oxford; *m* 1, 1951 (m dis 1969), Mavis, da of A Llewellyn Spencer-Payne; 3 s, 1 da; m 2, 1969, Diana Mary Cunliffe, da of C M Vise; 2 da (Hon Joanna Catherine b 25 April 1971, Hon Mary Alison b 12 Dec 1972); *Heir* s, Hon Andrew William Reginald Morrison; *Career* served RAF 1945–48; CRO: entered 1951, private sec to Sec of State 1952–54, second sec Canberra Australia 1954–56, first sec and actg dep high cmmr E Pakistan 1958–60, first sec Pretoria Capetown 1961–64 (seconded to Foreign Service 1961), Diplomatic Service Admin Office 1965, on loan to Intergovernmental Maritime Consultative Orgn (IMCO) 1968–70, cnsllr and head of Chancery Ottawa 1970–75, cnsllr Brussels 1975–78, high cmmr Fiji, Republic of Nauru, and Tuvalu 1978–82, high cmmr

Barbados and (concurrently but non-resident) Antigua & Barbuda, St Vincent & The Grenadines, St Lucia, Cwlth of Dominica, Grenada and also Br Govt rep WI Assoc State of St Kitts-Nevis 1982–83, govr and C-in-C of Bermuda 1983–88, ret; conslt Bank of Bermuda Ltd, dir International Registries Inc; chm Bermuda Soc London; Lord Lt Western Isles 1993– (DL 1990); Liveryman Merchant Taylors' Co 1974; hon fell Oriel Coll Oxford 1994; KStJ 1983; *Clubs* RAF, Cwlth Tst; *Style*— The Rt Hon the Viscount Dunrossil, CMG, JP; ✉ Dunrossil House, Clachan Sands, by Lochmaddy, North Uist, Western Isles, Scotland HS6 5AY (☎ 01876 500213, fax 01876 500411)

DUNSANY, 19 Baron (I 1439); Lt-Col Randal Arthur Henry Plunkett; s of 18 Baron Dunsany, the author (d 1957), and Lady Beatrice (d 1970), *née* Child-Villiers, da of 7 Earl of Jersey; *b* 25 Aug 1906; *Educ* Eton; *m* 1, 1938 (m dis 1947), da of Senhor G De Sá Sottomaior, of São Paulo, Brazil; 1 s; m 2, 1947, Sheila Victoria Katrin, da of Sir Henry Philipps, 2 Bt, and widow of Maj John Frederick Foley, Baron de Rutzen, Welsh Gds; 1 da; *Heir* s, Hon Edward Plunkett; *Career* joined 16/5 Lancers (SR) 1926, transfd IA 1928, Guides Cavalry Indian Armoured Corps, ret 1947; *Style*— Lt-Col the Rt Hon the Lord Dunsany; ✉ Dunsany Castle, Co Meath, Ireland (☎ 00 353 46 25198)

DUNSDON, Graham Eric; s of Walter Eric Dunsdon (d 1985), of Horsham, W Sussex, and Dorothy Edith, *née* Hawkins (d 1975); *b* 13 Sept 1944; *Educ* Collyer's GS Horsham; *m* 18 Sept 1965, Mary, da of Joseph Nathaniel Bradley (d 1984); 1 s (Simon b 1967), 2 da (Helen b 1969, Lucy b 1973); *Career* insurance and banking, ACII, ret; currently change mgmnt conslt, stress cnsllr and exec mentor; asst gen mangr TSB Trust Co Ltd 1975–82; dir: TSB Insurance Services Ltd 1981–82, Household International (UK) Ltd 1984–95, HFC Bank plc 1989–; md: FIMS Ltd 1982–83, Hamilton Insurance Co Ltd 1983–90 (dir 1983–91), Hamilton Life Assurance Co Ltd 1983–90 (dir 1983–91); chm Hamilton Financial Planning Services Ltd 1986–95, managing ptnr Grahan Dunsdon Associates 1996–; memb Bd Ashridge Coll Assoc; *Recreations* church activities; *Style*— Graham Dunsdon, Esq; ✉ Southcroft, Fullerton Road, Wherwell, Andover, Hampshire SP11 7JS (☎ 01264 860228)

DUNSTAN, (Andrew Harold) Bernard; s of Dr Albert Ernest Dunstan (d 1963), and Louisa, *née* Cleaverley (d 1960); *b* 19 Jan 1920; *Educ* St Paul's, Byam Shaw Sch of Art, Slade Sch of Art (Slade scholar); *m* 1949, Diana Maxwell Armfield, RA, *qv*; 3 s (Andrew Joseph b 1950, David James b 1952, Robert Maxwell b 1955); *Career* painter; teacher W of England Sch of Art Bristol 1946–49, subseq teacher at Camberwell Sch of Art, Byam Shaw Sch of Art, and The City and Guilds London Art Sch; has exhibited regularly at London galleries, biennially at Roland Browse and Delbanco 1952–70 and regularly at Agnews 1973– (featured in British Painting 1900–75); work in public collections incl: London Museum, Arts Cncl, Royal West of England Acad, Royal Collection; tstee Royal Acad 1980–85; memb New English Art Club 1946 (hon memb 1992); RA 1968 (ARA 1956), RWA (pres 1976–82); *Books* incl: Pictures in Progress, Painting Methods of the Impressionists (1976, revised 1983), Ruskin's Elements of Drawing (ed, 1991), The Paintings of Bernard Dunstan (1993); *Recreations* music; *Clubs* Arts; *Style*— Bernard Dunstan, Esq, RA; ✉ 10 High Park Road, Kew, Richmond, Surrey TW9 4BH

DUNSTER, Francis Henry; s of Henry Frank Dunster (d 1960), and Elsie, *née* Whitehorn; *b* 24 Aug 1935; *Educ* Leighton Park Sch, Coll of Estate Mgmnt; *m* 19 Oct 1963, Maria Patricia, da of George Walsh (d 1983); 2 s (James b 1967, Charles b 1970), 1 da (Sarah b 1964); *Career* Healey & Baker: assoc ptnr 1965, equity ptnr 1969–, ptnr i/c Glasgow Office 1982–88; FRICS, ACIarb; *Recreations* tennis, golf, rugby; *Clubs* MCC, Royal Scottish Automobile, Reading Rugby, Maidenhead Golf; *Style*— Francis Dunster, Esq; ✉ Healey & Baker, 29 St George Street, Hanover Square, London W1A 3BG (☎ 0171 629 9292)

DUNTHORNE, John William Bayne; s of Philip Bayne Dunthorne, of Alton, Hants, and Ruth Mabelle, *née* Sturch; *b* 26 Aug 1946; *Educ* Abingdon Sch, Oxford Sch of Architecture (Dip Arch); *m* 16 Aug 1974, Maggie Alice, da of John Edgar Taylor (d 1988), of Blofield, Norfolk; 1 s (Oliver b 1983), 1 da (Joanna b 1981); *Career* assoc ptnr Chapman Lisle Assocs 1972–74, jt sr ptnr Dunthorne Parker Architects & Designers 1978–, dir DPSL 1985–; RIBA 1973, MCSD 1985; *Projects* incl: offices for BUPA, Brooke Bond and Swiss Life, industrial parks, historic shopping schemes in Oxford, Colchester, High Wycombe and Bury St Edmunds, restoration of Grade I listed buildings Golden Cross in Oxford, Red Lion in Colchester, Grade II offices in Clifton; *Awards* incl: Robertson Award, Ideas in Architecture Award, Oxford Preservation Tst Award, Royal Tunbridge Wells Civic Soc Conservation Award, Civic Tst Award; *Books* An Airport Interface (with M P Parker, 1971); *Recreations* cricket, golf, snow skiing; *Clubs* MCC, Chelsea Arts, Forty, Lord Gnome's CC; *Style*— J W B Dunthorne, Esq; ✉ 5 Aspley Rd, London SW18 2DB; Dunthorne Parker, Architects & Designers, 8 Seymour Place, London W1H 5WF (☎ 0171 258 0411)

DUNWICH, Viscount; Robert Keith Rous; s (by 1 m) and h of 6 Earl of Stradbroke, *qv*; *b* 17 Nov 1961; *Style*— Viscount Dunwich

DUNWOODY, Hon Mrs (Gwyneth Patricia); MP (Lab) Crewe and Nantwich (majority 2,695); o da of Baroness Phillips (Life Peer, d 1992), and Morgan Phillips (sometime Gen Sec of the Lab Pty, d 1963); *b* 12 Dec 1930; *Educ* Fulham County Secdy Sch, Convent of Notre Dame; *m* 1954 (m dis 1975), Dr John Elliot Orr Dunwoody; 2 s, 1 da; *Career* former journalist for Fulham local newspaper and writer for radio, also former memb Totnes Cncl; MP (Lab): Exeter 1966–70, Crewe 1974–83, Crewe and Nantwich 1983–; parly sec Bd of Trade 1967–70, UK memb of Euro Parl 1975–79, memb Lab NEC 1981–90, chm NEC Local Govt Sub-Committee Nov 1981–90, oppn front bench spokesman Health Service 1981, memb Lab Home Policy Ctee 1982–89; dir Film Prodn Assoc of GB 1970–74; responsibility for co-ordinating Lab Party campaigns 1983–89, memb Select Ctee Tport, life pres Lab Friends of Israel 1993–; *Style*— The Hon Mrs Dunwoody, MP; ✉ House of Commons, London SW1A 0AA (☎ 0171 219 3000)

DUNWOODY, (Thomas) Richard; MBE (1993); s of George Rutherford Dunwoody, of Clanfield, Oxon, and Gillian Margaret, *née* Thrale; *b* 18 Jan 1964; *Educ* Rendcomb Coll; *m* 16 July 1988, Carol Ann, da of Robert Ronald George Abraham, of Wantage, Oxon; *Career* nat hunt jockey; first winner 1983 (on Game Trust at Cheltenham), 3rd in Amateur Championship 1983–84; runner-up Jockeys Championship: 1989–90 (102 winners), 1990–91 (127 winners), 1991–92 (137 winners), 1992–93 Champion Jockey (173 winners), 1993–94 Champion Jockey (197 winners), 1994–95 Champion Jockey (163 winners); major wins: Grand National 1986 (West Tip), Cheltenham Gold Cup 1988 (Charter Party), King George VI Chase 1989 and 1990 (Desert Orchid) and 1996 (One Man), Champion Hurdle 1990 (Kribensis), Breeders Cup Chase 1989 and 1992 (Highland Bud), Grand National 1994 (Miinnehoma); jt pres Jockeys' Assoc of Great Britain; *Recreations* motor-sport, water-skiing, squash, fitness; *Style*— Richard Dunwoody, Esq, MBE; ✉ 1 Woodview, Faringdon, Oxon OX12 9PJ (☎ and fax 01367 243111)

DUPPLIN, Viscount; Charles William Harley Hay; s and h of 15 Earl of Kinnoull, Arthur William George Patrick Hay, and Countess of Kinnoull, Gay Ann Hay, *née* Lowson; *b* 20 Dec 1962; *Educ* Eton, Ch Ch Oxford (MA), City Univ, Inns of Court Sch of Law; *Career* called to the Bar Middle Temple 1990; investmt banker with Credit Suisse First Boston Ltd 1985–88, underwriter with Hiscox Group at Lloyd's 1990–; dir Hiscox Underwriting Ltd 1995–: tstee Royal Caledonian Ball 1992– (chm 1996–); memb Atholl Highlanders; *Recreations* skiing, squash, philately, motor cars, racing; *Clubs* White's, Turf, Royal Perth, MCC; *Style*— Viscount Dupplin; ✉ 59 Scarsdale Villas, London W8 (☎ 0171 938 4265); Pitkindie House, Abernyte, Perthshire (☎ 01828 686342)

DUPREE, Sir Peter; 5 Bt (UK 1921), of Craneswater, Portsmouth, Co Southampton; s of Capt Sir Victor Dupree, 4 Bt (d 1976); *b* 20 Feb 1924; *m* 1947, Joan, da of late Capt James Desborough Hunt; *Heir* kinsman, (Thomas William James) David Dupree b 5 Feb 1930; *Career* Liveryman Worshipful Co of Farriers; *Style*— Sir Peter Dupree, Bt; ✉ 15 Hayes Close, Chelmsford, Essex CM2 0RN

DURAND, Sir Edward Alan Christopher David Percy; 5 Bt (UK 1892), of Ruckley Grange, Salop; elder s of Rev Sir (Henry Mortimer) Dickon Marion St George Durand, 4 Bt (d 1992), and Stella Evelyn, *née* L'Estrange; *b* 21 Feb 1974; *Educ* St Columba's Coll Dublin, Milltown Inst Dublin, Univ of Ulster at Coleraine (currently studying philosophy); *Heir* bro, David Michael Dickon Percy Durand b 6 June 1978; *Career* writer of music reviews, poetry and articles for "Muse" fanzine; *Style*— Sir Edward Durand, Bt; ✉ Lisnalurg House, Sligo, Republic of Ireland

DURANT, Sir (Robert) Anthony Bevis; kt (1991), MP (C) Reading West (majority 13,928); s of Capt Robert Michael Durant (d 1962), of Woking, and Violet Dorothy, *née* Bevis; *b* 9 Jan 1928; *Educ* Bryanston; *m* 1958, Audrey Stoddart; 2 s, 1 da; *Career* agent Clapham Cons Office 1958–62, nat organiser Young Cons Movement, CCO 1962–67, dir Br Indust and Scientific Film Assoc 1967–70, dir AVCAS 1970–72, gen mangr and co sec Talking Pictures Ltd 1972–84, memb Woking Urban Cncl 1968–74 (chm Educn Ctee 1969–74), Parly candidate (C) Rother Valley 1970; MP (C): Reading North Feb 1974–83, Reading W 1983–; former memb Select Ctee Parly Cmmr for Admin; asst govt whip 1984–86, Lord Cmmr of the Treasy and govt whip 1986–90, Crown Estates Paving Cmmr 1987–90, vice chamberlain HM Household 1988–90; former memb Exec 1922 Ctee; chm: All-Pty Ctee on Inland Waterways, All-Pty Gp on the Film Indust, Br Delgn Cncl of Europe and WEU Parly Assembly; dir BFI; former conslt: Delta Electrical Ltd, Br Film Prodrs' Assoc; chm Cwlth Parly Assoc (UK Branch) 1987–90; *Recreations* boating, golf; *Clubs* Carlton; *Style*— Sir Anthony Durant, MP; ✉ House of Commons, Westminster, London SW1A 0AA

DURANTE, Viviana; da of Giulio Durante, and Anna Maria Durante; *b* 8 May 1967, Rome; *Educ* White Lodge, Royal Ballet School; *Career* ballet dancer; Royal Ballet Co: joined 1984, first artist 1986–87, soloist 1987–89, princ dancer 1989–96; regularly dances with Irek Mukhamedov (and has toured with his company), has also danced with Errol Pickford, Bruce Sansom and Tetsuya Kumakawa; subject (with Darcey Bussell) of South Bank Show profile and documentary (LWT) 1992; *Roles* debuts in 1988–89 season incl: Odette/Odile in Swan Lake (Australian tour 1988, London 1989), Princess Aurora in The Sleeping Beauty, title roles in Sir Frederick Ashton's Ondine and Cinderella, Juliet in Sir Kenneth MacMillan's Romeo and Juliet, leading roles in Natalia Makarova's La Bayadere, Ashton's Rhapsody and George Balanchine's Rubies; debuts in 1989–90 season incl: Lise in Ashton's La Fille mal Gardée, leading roles in MacMillan's The Prince of the Pagodas, Requiem and My Brother My Sisters; debuts in 1990–91 season incl: title role in MacMillan's Manon, the Golden Hours Girl in MacMillan's Elite Syncopations, Irina in MacMillan's Winter Dreams (created role), Sugar Plum Fairy in The Nutcracker, Roxane in David Bintley's Cyrano, Saturn Pas de Deux in The Planets, leading roles in MacMillan's Danses Concertantes, Balanchine's Stravinsky Violin Concerto (first Royal Ballet prodn of the work), Ashley Page's Bloodlines (created role), Ashton's Scenes de Ballet (USA tour), The Girl in Blue in Nijinska's Les Biches; debuts in 1991–92 season incl: title role in Giselle, Masha in Winter Dreams, Titania in Ashton's The Dream (Japan tour), The Woman in The Judas Tree (world première 1992, Sir Kenneth MacMillan's last one-act work), Ashton's Thais Pas de Deux, leading roles in Balanchine's Symphony in C, William Tuckett's Present Histories; 1996 season incl: Ashton's Rhapsody, Ashton's Symphonic Variations, title role in Sir Peter Wright's Giselle, Aurora in Anthony Dowell's Sleeping Beauty 1996; roles with Irek Mukhamedov and Company incl Diana and Actaeon Pas de Deux and Summer Pas de Deux from MacMillan's The Four Seasons; *Awards* incl: Time Out/01 For London Dance Award 1989, Dance & Dancers magazine Dancer of the Year 1989, Evening Standard Ballet Award 1989, Positano Prize (Italy) 1991; *Recreations* reading, swimming, tennis, relaxing; *Style*— Miss Viviana Durante

DURBIN, Leslie Gordon James; CBE (1976), MVO (1943); s of Harry Durbin (d 1918); *b* 21 Feb 1913; *Educ* Central Sch of Arts and Crafts; *m* 1940, Phyllis Ethel, da of Arthur James Ginger; 1 s, 1 da; *Career* silversmith; apprenticed to Omar Ramsden 1929–38, Worshipful Co of Goldsmiths' full-time and travelling scholarships 1938–40; served RAF 1940–45: Allied Central Interpration Unit making topographical target models, indefinite leave to make Stalingrad Sword (given by King George VI to Stalingrad) 1943; own workshop in partnership with Leonard Moss 1945–76; tutor: Central Sch 1945–50, Royal Coll of Art 1945–60; designed Silver Jubilee hallmark, Royal Mint accepted designs of four regions for new £1 coin 1983, designed Bank of England Tercentenary £2 coin 1994; 50 Years Silversmith Retrospective Exhibition (Goldsmiths' Hall) 1982; Liveryman Worshipful Co of Goldsmiths; Hon LLD Univ of Cambridge 1963; *Style*— Leslie Durbin; ✉ 298 Kew Rd, Richmond, Surrey TW9 3DU

DURBRIDGE, Francis Henry; *b* 25 Nov 1912; *Educ* Univ of Birmingham; *m*; 2 s; *Career* playwright and author; first play entitled Promotion; *Theatre* Suddenly at Home (first stage play, West End); other London plays incl: Murder with Love, The Gentle Hook, House Guest, Deadly Nightcap, A Touch of Danger; The Small Hours, Sweet Revenge (both Thorndike Theatre and nat tour); *Radio* created character Paul Temple (radio serials bdcast worldwide), LA Boutique (cmmnd by Euro Bdcasting Union, presented in over 15 countries); *Television* plays bdcast in numerous countries incl Germany, Switzerland, Austria, France and Italy; TV series incl: The World of Tim Frazer, The Doll, The Scarf, Melissa, A Game of Murder, A Man Called Harry Brent and Bat out of Hell; *Style*— Francis Durbridge, Esq; ✉ c/o The Agency, 24 Pottery Lane, London W11 4LZ (☎ 0171 727 1346, fax 0171 727 9037)

DURCAN, Paul; s of John James Durcan (d 1988), and Sheila MacBride; *b* 16 Oct 1944; *Educ* Gonzaga Coll Dublin, Univ Coll Cork (BA); *m* 1 Aug 1967 (sep), Nessa, *née* O'Neill; 2 da (Sarah O'Neill b 22 June 1969, Siabhra O'Neill b 20 July 1970); *Career* poet; Patrick Kavanagh Award 1974, Irish American Cultural Institute Poetry Award 1989, Heinemann Bequest Royal Soc of Lit 1995; memb Aosdána 1981; *Poetry* O Westport In The Light of Asia Minor (1975), Teresa's Bar (1976), Sam's Cross (1978), Selected Poems (1982), The Berlin Wall Café (Poetry Book Soc Choice, 1985), Going Home To Russia (1987), Jesus and Angela (1988), Daddy, Daddy (Whitbread Poetry award, 1990), Crazy About Women (1991), A Snail In My Prime (1993), Give Me Your Hand (1994), Christmas Day (Poetry Book Soc recommendation 1996); *Recreations* walking; *Style*— Paul Durcan, Esq; ✉ 14 Cambridge Avenue, Dublin 4

DURDEN-SMITH, Neil; OBE (1997); s of Anthony James Durden-Smith (d 1963), of Middx, and Grace Elizabeth, *née* Neill (d 1938); *b* 18 Aug 1933; *Educ* Aldenham, RNC; *m* 1964, Judith Chalmers, OBE, *qv*, da of David Norman Chalmers (d 1952), of Cheshire; 1 s (Mark b 1968), 1 da (Emma (Mrs Mark Bonnar) b 1967); *Career* RN 1952–63; ADC to Govr-Gen of NZ 1957–59; prodr BBC Outside Bdcasts Dept (special responsibility 1966 World Cup) 1963–66; radio and TV bdcasting incl: Test Match and Co Cricket, Olympic Games 1968 and 1972, Trooping the Colour, Royal Tournament, Money Matters, Sports Special; chm and md Durden-Smith Communications 1974–81, dir Ruben Sedgwick 1987–; chm: Sports Sponsorship Int 1982–87, The Altro Group 1982–94, Woodside Communications 1992–; conslt AON 1995–; dir BCM Grandstand 1993–, Children in Crisis 1993–95, The Anglo-American Sporting Clubs 1969–74; chm The Lord's Taverners 1980–82 (pres Middx Region 1993–); vice pres: Motor Neurone Disease

Assoc, Eng Schools Cricket Assoc, Eng Indoor Hockey Assoc, The Peter May Meml Appeal; chm The Brian Johnston Meml Tst 1994–; patron RAFT; Freeman City of London; memb Lloyd's 1983; *Books* Forward for England (1967), World Cup '66 (1967); *Recreations* theatre, current affairs, cricket, golf, reading the newspapers; *Clubs* MCC, Lord's Taverners, I Zingari, Wig & Pen, Free Foresters, Lords and Commons Cricket, County Cricketers Golf; *Style*— Neil Durden-Smith, Esq, OBE; ✉ 28 Hillway, Highgate, London N6 6HH (☎ 0181 348 2340, fax 0181 348 8224)

DURGAN, Graham Richard; *b* 7 Jan 1957; *Educ* BSc; *m* Jane; 2 s, 1 da; *Career* Coopers & Lybrand 1977–82, fin trg 1982–85, md BPP Accountancy Courses Ltd 1985–88, dir Esprit Ltd 1988–90; chief exec: Business Training Network 1990–92, Accountancy Tuition Centres 1992–; dir BNB Resources plc, chm Accountancy and Financial Publishing; memb Cncl ICAEW; ACA; *Recreations* sailing, skiing, tennis; *Style*— Graham Durgan, Esq; ✉ Accountancy Tuition Centre, 28 Farringdon Street, London EC4A 4EU (☎ 0171 634 1057, fax 0171 329 3117)

DURHAM, Earldom of (UK 1833) *see:* Lambton, (Lord) Antony Claud Frederick

DURHAM, David Edward; s of George Edward Durham (d 1981), and (Ethel Beatrice) Joy Durham, of Oxford; *b* 8 Aug 1936; *Educ* Magdalen Coll Sch Oxford, RMA Sandhurst, Medway Coll of Technol (DipCE), RMCS Shrivenham, Army Staff Coll Camberley, Open Univ (BA), South West London Coll (ACIS); *m* 8 Oct 1960, Valerie Susan, da of Harold John Wheeler (d 1994); 1 s (Mark Edward Andrew b 18 Jun 1965), 1 da (Suanne Belinda Clare b 7 Aug 1962); *Career* cmmnd 2 Lt Royal Engrs 1956, duties incl Helicopter Flt Cdr Thailand and Malaysia and OC Bomb Disposal Sqdn, ret as Lt-Col 1982; housing and environment mangr Rochester upon Medway City Cncl 1982–86; Parkside Health Authy London: unit gen mangr Community Servs 1986–88, unit gen mangr St Charles' Hosp 1988–90; Chief Exec and Registrar of Companies for England and Wales Companies House Executive Agency 1990–96; int corp advsr 1996–; MIMgt 1967, FCIS 1996 (ACIS 1982), MHSM 1989, FRSA 1991; *Recreations* golf, squash, playing the piano, DIY; *Style*— David Durham, Esq; ✉ Dickens, 26 Forrest Road, Penarth, Vale of Glamorgan CF64 5DP (☎ and fax 01222 707813)

DURHAM, Dean of; *see:* Arnold, Very Rev John Robert

DURHAM, Baron; Edward Richard Lambton; s and h of Lord Lambton; *b* 19 Oct 1961; *m* 1, 1983 (m dis), Christabel Mary, yst da of Rory McEwen (decd), of Bardrochat; 1 s (Fred b 23 Feb 1985); m 2, 19 Oct 1995, Catherine FitzGerald, eldest da of the Knight of Glin, *qv*; *Career* auditor James Bridle Meml Soc; *Recreations* watching cricket; *Style*— (known as) Lord Durham

DURHAM, Sir Kenneth; kt (1985); s of late George Durham, and Bertha, *née* Aspin; *b* 28 July 1924; *Educ* Queen Elizabeth GS Blackburn, Univ of Manchester (BSc); *m* 1946, Irene Markham; 1 s, 1 da; *Career* served WWII Flt Lt RAF; chm: BOCM Silcock Ltd 1971, Unilever Ltd 1982–86 (joined 1950, dir 1974, vice chm 1978), Kingfisher plc (formerly Woolworth Holdings plc) 1986–90 (non-exec chm 1985–86); non-exec dir Delta plc 1984–93, dir Morgan Grenfell Holdings 1986–90, vice chm British Aerospace 1986–90; chm: Food Drink and Packaging Machinery EDC NEDO 1981–86, Trade Policy Res Centre 1982–89, Industry and Commerce Liaison Ctee Royal Jubilee Tsts 1982–87, Econ and Fin Policy Ctee CBI 1983–86, Priorities Bd for Govt Agric Depts and AFRC 1984–87; memb: Cncl Policy Studies Inst 1978–85, British-N America Ctee 1982–87, British Shippers Cncl 1982–86, Bd British Exec Service Overseas 1982–86, Advsy Ctee CVCP 1984–, Cncl Royal Free Hosp Sch of Med 1984–, Governing Body ICC UK 1984–86, ACARD 1984–86, Euro Advsy Cncl NY Stock Exchange 1985–, Cncl for Industry and Higher Educn 1985–, Advsy Panel Sci Policy Res Unit Univ of Sussex 1985–, Advsy Bd Industl Res Labs Univ of Durham 1985–; vice pres: Liverpool Sch of Tropical Med 1982, Opportunities for the Disabled 1982–88, Help the Aged 1986; tstee: Leverhulme Tst 1974–, Civic Tst 1982; Hon LLD Univ of Manchester 1984; Hon DSc: Loughborough Univ 1984, Belfast 1987; CIMgt 1978, FIGD 1983; Cdr Order of Orange Nassau 1985; *Clubs* Athenaeum; *Style*— Sir Kenneth Durham

DURHAM, 93 Bishop of 1994–; Rt Rev (Anthony) Michael Arnold Turnbull; s of George Ernest Turnbull (d 1954), and Adeline Turnbull; *b* 27 Dec 1935; *Educ* Ilkley GS, Keble Coll Oxford (MA), St John's Coll Durham (DipTh); *m* 25 May 1963, Brenda Turnbull, JP, da of Leslie James Merchant; 1 s (Mark b 1966), 2 da (Rachel (Mrs Michael Duff) b 1964, Rebecca (Mrs Ian Francis) b 1970); *Career* curate Middleton and Luton 1960–65; chaplain: Archbishop of York 1965–69, Univ of York; rector of Heslington 1969–76, chief sec Church Army 1976–84, archdeacon of Rochester and canon residentiary Rochester Cathedral 1984–88, bishop of Rochester 1988–94; chm Archbishops' Cmmn on the Organisation of the C of E, chm College of Preachers, vice chm Central Bd of Fin C of E, memb Bd of Govrs Church Cmmrs, memb Archbishops' Cathedrals Cmmn; Hon DLitt Univ of Greenwich; *Books* God's Front Line (1978), Parish Evangelism (1980); *Recreations* cricket, books, walking; *Clubs* Athenaeum, MCC; *Style*— The Rt Rev the Bishop of Durham; ✉ Auckland Castle, Bishop Auckland, Co Durham DL14 7NR (☎ 01388 602576)

DURHAM HALL, Jonathan David; QC (1995); *b* 2 June 1952; *Educ* King Edward VII Sch Sheffield, Univ of Nottingham (LLB); *m* 1, Patricia Helen Bychowska; 1 da (Antonia b 14 July 1977), 1 s (Christian b 29 Oct 1980); m 2, 1996, Hilary Hart; *Career* called to the Bar Gray's Inn 1975, in practice NE Circuit, recorder 1995– (asst recorder 1991–95), head of chambers 1995–; memb Gen Cncl of the Bar 1994–95; memb Gray's Inn Barristers' Ctee; former memb Parochial Deanery and Diocesan Synod; served TA The Hallamshire Regt 1969–72; *Recreations* walking, skiing, all things countryside especially creation of rural woodland, plays of Shakespeare; *Clubs* Sheffield, Kandahar; *Style*— Jonathan Durham Hall, Esq, QC; ✉ Bank House Chambers, The Old Bank House, 3 Hartshead, Sheffield S1 2EL (☎ 0114 272 1223, fax 0114 276 8439)

DURIE, Sir Alexander Charles; kt (1977), CBE (1973); s of Charles Durie (d 1948); *b* 15 July 1915; *Educ* Queen's Coll Taunton; *m* 1941, Joyce May, da of late Lionel Richard Hargreaves; 1 s (Alistair b 1944, *qv*), 1 da (Juliet (Hon Mrs John Greville Napier) b 1942); *Career* serv WWII Lt-Col; dir: Shell Co (Aust) Ltd 1954–56, Shell-Mex and BP Ltd 1962–64 (joined 1933, md 1963–64), Mercantile Credit 1973–80, Thomas Cook Group 1974–79, Private Patients Plan Ltd 1977–87, H Clarkson Holdings 1978–85, Chelsea Building Soc 1979–87; vice pres: Br Assoc of Industl Eds 1959–71, Alliance Int de Tourisme 1965–71 (pres 1971–77), Ind Schs Careers Orgn 1973 (chm 1969–73), AA 1977– (DG 1964–77), Br Road Fedn 1978 (memb 1962–), Ashridge Coll 1978–93 (govr 1963–78), Surrey CCC 1980– (memb Ctee 1970–80, pres 1984–85); memb Govt Inquires into: Civilianisation of Armed Forces 1964, Cars for Cities 1964, Rd Haulage Operators' Licensing 1978; BIM: memb Cncl 1962–73, vice chm 1962–67, chm Exec Ctee 1962–65, chm Bd of Fells 1970–73; memb: Cncl Motor and Cycle Trades Benevolent Fund 1959–73, Nat Rd Safety Advsy Cncl 1965–68, Advsy Cncl on Road Res 1965–68, Mktg Ctee BTA 1970–77, Advsy Cncl Traffic and Safety Tport and Road Res Lab 1973–77, Int Road Fedn (London); gen cmmr of income tax 1960–85; memb Cncl Imperial Soc of Knights Bachelor 1978– (chm 1988); Freeman City of London, Liveryman Worshipful Co of Paviors; FCIT, Hon FInstHE, FIMgt; *Style*— Sir Alexander Durie, CBE; ✉ The Garden House, Windlesham, Surrey (☎ 01276 472035)

DURIE, Alistair John Lindsay; s of Sir Alexander Charles Durie, *qv*, of Windlesham, Surrey, and Joyce May, *née* Hargreaves; *b* 25 Nov 1944; *Educ* Rugby, Christ Church Oxford (MA); *m* 1, 19 July 1969 (m dis), Fiona Daphne, da of John Arden Franklyn; 1 s (Marcus Charles John b 21 Dec 1971), 1 da (Tanya Alexandra Franklyn b 17 Sept 1973); m 2, 14 April 1989, Linda Elizabeth, da of Michael Collopy; *Career* Binder Hamlyn: apprentice 1966, qualified CA 1969, mangr i/c Corp Fin Dept 1971–73, mangr i/c Nat Trg Prog 1973–77, audit ptnr 1977–, admin ptnr 1978–88, fin ptnr 1988–89, ptnr i/c Facilities Mgmnt 1989–95; ACA 1969; *Books* Weird Tales (1979); *Recreations* reading, travel, cricket; *Clubs* IOD (treas 1980–), Surrey County Cricket (treas 1994–); *Style*— Alistair Durie, Esq; ✉ Colnebrook, 4 Blois Road, Steeple Bumpstead, Suffolk CB9 7BN (☎ 01440 730349); Binder Hamlyn, 20 Old Bailey, London EC4M 7BH (☎ 0171 489 9000, fax 0171 489 6290)

DURIE, David Robert Campbell; CMG (1995); s of late Frederick Robert Edwin Durie (d 1995), of Ardrishaig, Argyll, and Joan Elizabeth Campbell, *née* Learoyd; *b* 21 Aug 1944; *Educ* Fettes, Christ Church Oxford (BA, MA); *m* 27 July 1966, Susan Frances, da of Arthur Leighton Hume Weller (d 1953); 3 da (Rosamund Clare b 1969, Madeleine Rachael b 1971, Eleanor Louise b 1975); *Career* asst princ Miny of Technol 1966, princ DTI 1971 (asst princ 1970), first sec UK Delgn to OECD Paris 1974; asst sec: DPCP 1978 (princ 1977), Dept of Trade 1980, Cabinet Office 1982, DTI 1984; under sec (Grade 3) DTI 1985, head of Investigations Div DTI 1989, dep sec (Grade 2) 1991, min and dep UK permanent rep to EC 1991–95, dep sec Regnl and Small Firms DTI 1995, currently dir gen Regnl and Smaller and Medium Enterprises DTI; *Recreations* moderately strenuous outdoor exercise, theatre, family, music; *Style*— David Durie, Esq, CMG; ✉ Department of Trade and Industry, 1 Victoria Street, London SW1H 0ET (☎ 0171 215 5000)

DURIE, Joanna Mary (Jo); da of John Durie (d 1984), of Bristol, and Diana Nell *née* Ford; *b* 27 July 1960; *Educ* Clifton HS; *Career* tennis player; winner under 12 and under 14 Nat Championships, won all three Nat Championships at age of 16, ranked 5 in the World 1984, ranked GB no 1 1983, 1984, 1985, 1987; semi-finalist US Open and French Championships 1983, winner of the Wimbledom mixed doubles title (with Jeremy Bates, *qv*) 1987; winner numerous tournaments worldwide; represented GB in Wightman Cup and Federation Cup; *Recreations* golf (handicap 20), skiing; *Style*— Miss Jo Durie

DURIE, (Thomas) Peter; MBE (Mil 1958), GM (1951), DL (Avon 1992–96, Somerset 1996–); s of Col Thomas Edwin Durie, DSO, MC (d 1963), and Madeleine Louise, *née* Walsh (d 1961); *b* 1 Jan 1926; *Educ* Fettes, Queen's Univ Belfast; *m* 1, 1952, Pamela Mary, *née* Bowlby (d 1982); 1 da (Jean Mary b 31 Aug 1954), 1 s (Thomas Michael b 9 Oct 1956); m 2, 4 June 1983, Mrs Constance Christina Mary Linton, *née* Whitehead; *Career* served Royal Horse Artillery and Airborne 1944–64, India, Egypt, Palestine, Tripoli, Germany, Cyprus and UK, latterly Lt-Col DS Staff Coll Camberley; Courage Ltd: joined 1964, gp asst md 1974, main bd dir 1974–86; chm Bristol and Weston Dist Health Authy 1986–90, chm Utd Bristol Healthcare NHS Tst 1991–94; Univ of Bristol: memb Ct and Cncl 1982–, vice chm Cncl 1995–, pro chllr 1994–; Freeman: City of Bristol 1979, City of London 1986; Liveryman: Worshipful Co of Brewers 1975, Soc of Merchant Venturers 1980 (Master 1988–89); *Recreations* gardening, birdwatching, music, sailing, skiing, tennis; *Clubs* Army & Navy; *Style*— Peter Durie, Esq, MBE, GM, DL; ✉ Gatesgarth, Wrington BS18 7QA (☎ 01934 862210)

DURKIN, Air Marshal Sir Herbert; KBE (1976), CB (1973); s of Herbert Durkin (d 1968), and Helen, *née* Shakeshaft (d 1974); *b* 31 March 1922; *Educ* Burnley GS, Emmanuel Coll Cambridge; *m* 1951, Dorothy Hope, da of Walter Taylor Johnson; 1 s, 2 da; *Career* joined RAF 1941, served WWII in Europe and India, Gp-Capt 1962, Air Cdre 1967, Air Vice Marshal 1971, Air Marshal 1976, controller of Engrg and Supply RAF, ret 1978; pres Inst of Electrical Engrs 1980–81, pres Assoc of Lancastrians in London 1988–89; *Recreations* golf; *Clubs* RAF, Moor Park Golf (capt 1988); *Style*— Air Marshal Sir Herbert Durkin, KBE, CB; ✉ Willowbank, Drakes Drive, Northwood, Middx HA6 2SL (☎ 01923 823167)

DURKIN, Dr Michael Anthony Patrick; s of John Durkin (d 1986), of Cheltenham and Wimbledon, and Philomena, *née* O'Shea; *b* 26 July 1950; *Educ* Whitefriars Sch Cheltenham, Middx Hosp Med Sch Univ of London (MB BS); *m* 19 July 1978, Susan Claire, da of Lawrence Paul Cotterell, of Cheltenham; 3 s (Luke b 1979, Jack b 1981, James b 1983), 1 da (Ellen b 1990); *Career* registrar in anaesthesia St Thomas' Hosp London 1976–79, res registrar Middx Hosp London 1980–81, sr registrar S Western RHA 1981–85; Gloucestershire Royal Hosp: conslt in anaesthesia and intensive care 1985–, clinical dir and chm Med Staff Ctee; visiting assoc faculty Yale Univ Sch of Med 1989 (asst prof 1982–84), med dir Gloucestershire Royal NHS Tst 1993–; articles in jls on anaesthesia, intensive care and monitoring, ed Anaesthesia Points West; referee: BMJ, Intensive Care Medicine, Critical Care Med, Br Jl of Hosp Medicine; ctee memb: Soc of Anaesthetists of S Western Region, Gloucester Dist Med Advsy Ctee, Regnl Ctee for Higher Specialist Trg (anaesthesia); tstee Intensive Care Charity; memb: Euro Intensive Care Soc, Int Anaesthesia Res Soc, Intensive Care Soc, Assoc of Anaesthetists GB; FRCA 1981, FCAnaes, memb BMA; *Books* Post Anaesthetic Recovery (2 edn, 1989); *Recreations* skiing, tennis, watching rugby; *Clubs* Lilleybrook; *Style*— Dr Michael Durkin; ✉ Medical Director, Gloucestershire Royal Hospital, Great Western Road, Gloucester GL1 3NN (☎ 01452 394736, fax 01452 394737)

DURLACHER, Nicholas John; CBE (1995); s of John Sydney Durlacher, MC; *b* 20 March 1946; *Educ* Stowe, Magdalene Coll Cambridge; *m* 1971, Mary Caroline, da of Maj Guy Lewis Ian McLaren (d 1978); 1 s (David Michael b 1976); *Career* memb London Stock Exchange, ptnr Wedd Durlacher Mordaunt & Co 1971–86, dir Barclays de Zoete Wedd Ltd 1986–; chm: LIFFE 1992–95, Securities and Futures Authy 1995–; *Recreations* skiing, tennis, golf, shooting; *Clubs* City of London, White's; *Style*— Nicholas Durlacher, Esq, CBE; ✉ BZW Ltd, Ebbgate House, 2 Swan Lane, London EC4R 3TS (☎ 0171 623 2323)

DURLACHER, Peter Laurence; s of Adm Sir Laurence Durlacher, KCB, OBE, DSC (d 1986), of Mas Tournamy, Mougins, France, and Rimma Durlacher, MBE, *née* Sass-Tissovsky; *b* 27 April 1935; *Educ* Winchester, Inst of Political Sci Paris, Magdalene Coll Cambridge; *m* 1, 14 March 1959 (m dis 1976), Jennifer Ann, da of Hugh Blauvelt (d 1967), of Drumnadrochit, Inverness; 2 s (Christopher b 1963, Julian b 1966), 2 da (Fenella b 1961, Sophie b 1968); m 2, Mary Cresswell-Turner, da of Richard Girouard (d 1989), of Colville Rd, London W11; *Career* Henry Ansbacher: joined 1957, dir 1966–72, an md 1970–72; i/c Overseas Dept Wedd Durlacher Mordaunt 1972–76, conslt to Stock Exchange and IMF 1976–80, ptnr Laurie Milbank Stockbrokers 1981–86, dir Parrish Stockbrokers 1986–90, chm Durlacher & Co (formerly Durlacher West Ltd) 1990–95, dir Nabarro Wells & Co Ltd 1995–; tstee Schoolmistresses and Governesses Benevolent Inst 1968–, hon treas Nat Youth Bureau 1977–89; Liveryman Worshipful Co of Cutlers; *Recreations* gardening, fox hunting; *Clubs* City of London, Beefsteak; *Style*— Peter Durlacher, Esq; ✉ 15 Moreton Terrace, London SW1V 2NS (☎ 0171 834 0655)

DURLING, David; *b* 15 Oct 1946; *Educ* Sir Philip Magnus Secdy Tech Sch London, Barnet Coll of FE (fndn course), Buckinghamshire Inst High Wycombe (BA), RCA (MA in industl design), Open Univ (PhD 1996); *m*; 1 child (b 1987); *Career* industl and furniture designer; design asst then sr designer and assoc i/c industl design team Graphics + Industrial Design Ltd Richmond Surrey 1971–75 (clients incl Royal Navy, Vickers Ship Engineering, ICI), freelance designer London 1975–76, sr designer Architect's Dept Notts CC 1976–83 (i/c interiors, furniture design and building graphics), sr lectr in industl design Sheffield City Poly 1983–84, fndr dir EDGE Ltd design and R & D conslts 1984– (pt/t dir 1984–89), course ldr and sr lectr in 3D design (furniture) Sch of Industl Design Leicester Poly 1986–89, md Lab Systems Ltd mfrs of laboratory furniture and equipment in UK 1991–93, dir of research and enterprise Sch of Design Staffs Univ 1996–; visiting lectr: Loughborough Coll of Art & Design, Leicester Poly,

Leeds Poly, Sheffield Poly, Univ of Teesside; registered inspr FE Funding Cncl 1992–; Chartered Soc of Designers: memb Nat Cncl 1987–91, local organiser Sheffield Area 1987–91, chm NE Regnl Cncl 1987–91, memb Design Educn Policy Gp; memb: Nat Cncl Design Res Soc 1993–, various tech ctees BSI; memb Ergonomics Soc 1981, FCSD 1987, FRSA; *Recreations* yacht cruising, sea fishing, cycling, serious music, the Arts, reading, electronic information systems; *Style*— Dr David Durling; ✉ School of Design, Staffordshire University, Stoke-on-Trent ST4 2DE (☎ 01782 294556, fax 01782 294873, e-mail d.durling@staffs.ac.uk)

DURMAN, David John; s of John Bloyd Durman, and Joan Winifred Durman; *b* 10 July 1948; *Educ* Sutton High Sch Plymouth, Univ of Leeds (BA); *m* 6 Jan 1973, Hilary Pamela Durman; *Career* IPC Magazines: ed Woman Magazine 1988–94, ed-in-chief Woman, Woman's Own and Chat Magazines 1994–, ed-in-chief IPC Woman's Group (overseeing launch of Now) 1996–; *Style*— David Durman, Esq; ✉ IPC Magazines, King's Reach Tower, Stamford St, London SE1 9LS (☎ 0171 261 5000)

DURRANCE, Philip Walter; s of Arthur Durrance (d 1960), of Ilkley, Yorkshire, and Marguerite Grace, *née* Rotheray (d 1966); *b* 30 June 1941; *Educ* Harrow, Oriel Coll Oxford (MA); *m* 16 Sept 1966 (m dis), Francoise Genevieve Jeanne, da of Marcel Tillier; 1 s (Christopher b 29 July 1968), 1 da (Genevieve b 8 Sept 1969); *Career* admitted slr 1965, ptnr Withers 1968–; dir: F Bender, Henkel, Leo Laboratories; FInstD, memb Law Soc; *Recreations* theatre, cinema, art, tennis, squash, cricket; *Style*— Philip Durrance, Esq; ✉ 34 Hamilton Gardens, London NW8 (☎ 0171 286 2428); Withers, 12 Gough Square, London EC4A 3DE (☎ 0171 936 1000, fax 0171 936 2589, telex 24213)

DURRANI, Prof Tariq Salim; s of Mohammed Salim Khan Durrani (d 1980), of London, and Bilquis Jamal; *b* 27 Oct 1943; *Educ* EPUET Dacca Bangladesh (BEng), Univ of Southampton (MSc, PhD); *m* 6 Aug 1972, Clare Elizabeth, da of late Howard Kellas; 1 s (Jamiel Tariq b 1986), 2 da (Monise Nadia b 1977, Sophia Jasmine b 1981); *Career* res fell Univ of Southampton 1970–76; Univ of Strathclyde: lectr 1976–79, sr lectr 1979–82, prof of signal processing 1982–, chm Dept of Electronic and Electrical Engrg 1986–90, dep princ (IT) 1990–91, special advsr (IT) 1991–94; former chm IEE Professional Gps on Signal Processing and Image Processing; chm: Centre for Parallel Signal Processing, Scottish Electronics Technol Gp, IEEE Periodicals Cncl 1996–97; pres IEEE Signal Processing Soc 1994–96; FIEE 1983, FIEEE 1989, FRSE 1994, FEng 1996; *Books* Laser Systems in Flow Measurements (with C Greated, 1977), Geophysical Signal Processing (with E A Robinson, 1986), Signal Processing (co-ed J L Lacoume and R Stora, 1987), Mathematics and Signal Processing (ed, 1987), Transputer Applications 3 (ed 1991); *Recreations* swimming; *Clubs* Ross Priory; *Style*— Prof Tariq Durrani, FRSE, FEng; ✉ 14 Duchess Park, Helensburgh, Dunbartonshire G84 9PY (☎ 01436 76590); University of Strathclyde, Department of Electronic and Electrical Engineering, 204 George St, Glasgow G1 1XW (☎ 0141 552 4400, ext 2540, fax 0141 552 2487)

DURRANT, His Hon Judge Anthony Harrisson; s of Frank Baston Durrant (d 1952), of London, and Irene Maude, *née* Drury (d 1985); *b* 3 Jan 1931; *Educ* Sir Joseph Williamson's Mathematical Sch Rochester Kent; *m* 30 June 1956, Jacqueline, da of John Ostroumoff (d 1945); 1 s (Max), 2 da (Caroline, Julia); *Career* admitted slr 1956; sr ptnr Horwood & James 1975, pres Bucks Berks and Oxon Incorporated Law Soc 1977–78, recorder 1987–91, circuit judge (SE Circuit) 1991–; dep chm Agric Land Tbnl (South Western Area) 1987–91; former hon slr: Br Paraplegic Sports Stadium Stoke Mandeville (memb Exec Ctee), Stoke Mandeville Hosp Post Grad Soc (memb Exec Cncl); memb Law Soc; *Recreations* reading, boating; *Clubs* Phyllis Court, Henley-on-Thames, Law Soc; *Style*— His Hon Judge Anthony Durrant; ✉ Isleworth Crown Court, 36 Ridgeway, Isleworth, Middlesex TW7 5LP

DURRANT, Hugh Russell; s of Derek Walter Durrant (d 1990), and Elsie Violet, *née* Russell (d 1980); *b* 12 July 1947; *Educ* Latymer Upper Sch, Magdalene Coll Cambridge (MA Fine Arts); *Career* costume, set and fashion designer; head of design: Birmingham Repertory 1973–76, Theatre Royal York 1976–78, Northcott Theatre Exeter 1979–81; assoc dir Nottingham Playhouse 1982–85; fashion posts held incl: Emanuel couture 1985, head of design Cojana Ltd London 1985–90, designer and couture designer Rafa Abu Dhabi 1991–92; estab own couture label 1988; design conslt (scenery) Holland America Westours Ltd 1993–97; visiting prof Nat Theater Inst Eugene O'Neill Center USA 1996; *Theatre* designed over 14 prodns Regent's Park Open Air Theatre, 12 pantomimes for Paul Elliott; costume design credits incl: Mystery of Irma Vep (Ambassadors) 1990, The Mikado (Cambridge and Prince of Wales), Barry Manilow's Copacabana (Prince of Wales 1994–95, UK tour 1995–96, Las Vegas 1996, South Africa 1996); set and costume credits incl: Sister Mary Ignatius (Ambassadors) 1984, The Hot Shoe Show (Palladium) 1984, Cinderella (Palladium) 1985, Babes in the Wood (Palladium) 1986–87, Lock Up Your Daughters (Chichester and Savoy Theatre London) 1996; UK tours incl: Amadeus, A Little Night Music, Company; Br premiere incl: Mack and Mabel, Lady in the Dark; *Dance* credits incl: Symphony in Waves (Dutch Nat Ballet), Frankenstein (Royal Ballet, La Scala Milan, Dutch National Ballet (sets only)), Footnotes (Nederland Dans), Window & Sleeping Birds (Rambert), Dash and Hot Shoe Show (for Wayne Sleep); *Other Credits* incl: Thomas Hardy's The Dynasts (Exeter Cathedral 900th anniversary (adapted and designed)), Voices from the Great War (Nottingham Playhouse (adapted, designed and directed)); *TV and Film* Ivanhoe (costumes), Future Soldiers (conceptual designer); *Style*— Hugh Durrant, Esq; ✉ 22 Alwyne Road, London N1 2HN (☎ 0171 354 4372); c/o Maxine Webster, 1st Framework, The Foundry, 156 Blackfriars Road, London SE1 8EN (☎ 0171 721 7158, fax 0171 721 7159)

DURRANT, John; s of Edward Henry Samual Stokes Durrant (d 1972), and Phyllis, *née* Howard-Spink (d 1988); *b* 6 July 1949; *Educ* N Paddington Sch, Oxford Poly (now Oxford Brookes Univ) (DMS); *m* June 1974, Susan, da of Thomas Clark, of Cliftonville, Kent; 3 s (Oliver Jon b 20 Nov 1975, Thomas Edward b 22 Sept 1978, William Jack b 3 Dec 1981); *Career* promotion mangr W B Saunders medical publishers London 1969–73, mktg dir European Bibliographical Centre Oxford 1973–78; Clio Press Ltd Oxford: jt md 1978–81, chm and md 1981–94, currently dir; chm and md Isis Publishing Ltd Oxford 1994–; *Books* Microcomputer Software Guide (1982), Microcomputer Software Guide Vol II (1982); *Style*— John Durrant, Esq; ✉ Isis Publishing Ltd, 7 Centremead, Osney Mead, Oxford OX2 0ES (☎ 01865 250333, fax 01865 790358)

DURRANT, Roy Turner; s of Francis Henry Durrant (d 1957), and Edna May, *née* Turner (d 1993); *Educ* Lavenham Sch Suffolk, Camberwell Art Sch (NDD); *m* 7 March 1959, Jean, da of Harold Malcolm Lyell (d 1982); 4 s (Francis b 11 Jan 1960, Timothy b 30 May 1962 (d 1964), John b 31 July 1964, Edward b 17 Feb 1966); *Career* Suffolk Regt 1944–47; admin post Vickers Ltd 1956–63; artist; dir Heffer Gallery Cambridge 1963–76; FRSA, FFPS, memb NEAC; *Exhibitions* incl: numerous RA Summer Exhbns 1950–, Beaux Arts Gallery London 1950, Roland Browse 1959, Artists Int Assoc Gallery 1953, 1957 and 1969, Loggia Gallery London 1973–, Gallerie of Br Art Lausanne Switzerland 1988, Patterson Gallery 1991, 1992, 1993, 1994 and 1995, City of Westminster Arts Cncl Open 1991, 1992, 1993, 1994 and 1995, Belgrave Gallery London 1991 (retrospective), 1994 and 1995 (post-war Br abstract paintings), Heffer Gallery Cambridge 1994, The Soc of Graphic Fine Art 1994, Chelsea Art Soc 1994, Ben Uri Gallery London 1994 and 1995, Impington Village Coll Cambridge 1994 and 1995, St Martins in the Fields Gallery London 1995, The Gallery London 1995, Mall Galleries London 1995 (Discerning Eye exhbn), Albany Gallery Cardiff 1995 (New English Art Club exhbn), Boscastle Gallery Cornwall (New English Art Club exhbn); *Work in Collections* works in numerous private collections at home and abroad incl HRH The Prince of Wales; public collections incl: The Tate, Dept of Biochemistry Univ of Cambridge, Usher Gallery Lincoln, Imperial War Museum, Bury St Edmunds Town Cncl, City of Bradford Art Gallery, Carlisle Art Gallery, Bertrand Russell Fndn Nottingham, Castle Museum Norwich, Univ of Adelaide Aust, WA Art Gallery Perth, Univ of Massachusetts Amherst USA, Worthing Art Gallery, RAF Museum Hendon, Hove Museum and Art Gallery, Sirrell Collection City of Westminster Arts Cncl; *Books* A Rag Book of Love (1960); *Recreations* reading, radio; *Style*— Roy Turner Durrant, Esq; ✉ 38 Hurst Park Avenue, Cambridge CB4 2AE (☎ 01223 61730)

DURRANT, Sir William Alexander Estridge; 8 Bt (GB 1784), of Scottow, Norfolk; JP (NSW); s of Sir William Henry Estridge Durrant, 7 Bt, JP (d 1994), and Georgina Beryl Gwendoline, *née* Purse (d 1968); *b* 26 Nov 1929; *m* 1953, Dorothy, da of Ronal Croker, of Quirindi, NSW; 1 s (David Alexander b 1960), 1 da (Susan Elizabeth b 1962); *Heir* s, David Alexander Durrant b 1 July 1960; *Career* farmer and grazier; Capt 12/16 Hunter River Lancers; *Style*— Sir William Durrant, Bt, JP; ✉ Red Hill, Nundle Road, Nemingha, NSW 2340, Australia

DURRELL, Prof Martin; s of Leslie Hay Durrell (d 1972), of Coltishall, Norfolk, and Audrey Lillian, *née* Easton; *b* 6 Nov 1943; *Educ* Manchester GS, Jesus Coll Cambridge (MA), Univ of Manchester (DipLing), Univ of Marburg (DPhil); *m* 30 Aug 1969, Ruth, da of Geoffrey Loy Barlow (d 1977), of Bury, Lancs; 1 s (John b 1975), 1 da (Ann b 1978); *Career* sr lectr (formerly lectr) Univ of Manchester 1970–86, guest prof Univ of Alberta 1983–84; prof of German: Univ of London 1986–90, Univ of Manchester 1990–; corresponding memb Academic Cncl Institut für Deutsche Sprache 1984–; Philogical Soc: memb Cncl 1989–, hon treas 1994–; *Recreations* music, theatre, ornithology; *Style*— Prof Martin Durrell; ✉ The German Department, University of Manchester, Manchester M13 9PL (☎ 0161 275 3182)

DURRINGTON, Prof Paul Nelson; s of Alec Edward Durrington, of Hurst Green, E Sussex, and May Ena, *née* Nelson; *b* 24 July 1947; *Educ* Chislehurst and Sidcup GS, Univ of Bristol (BSc, MB, ChB, MD); *m* 13 Dec 1969, Patricia Joyce, da of Capt Alfred Newton Gibbs, MC, of Barming, Kent; 1 s (Mark Christopher Newton b 1977), 2 da (Hannah Jane b 1975, Charlotte Lucy b 1987); *Career* house offr and sr house offr appts 1972–76 (Bristol Royal Infirmary, Bristol Royal Hosp for Sick Children, Frenchay Hosp Bristol); travelling fell: Br Heart Fndn, American Heart Assoc Univ of California San Diego 1979–80; Univ of Manchester: lectr in med 1976–82, sr lectr in med 1982–92, reader in med 1992–95, prof of med 1995–; hon conslt physician Manchester Royal Infirmary and Univ of South Manchester 1982–; memb Editorial Bd of Atherosclerosis and of Postgraduate Med Jl, chm Br Hyperlidaemia Assoc 1992–95, med dir Family Heart Assoc 1995–; FRCP 1987, FRCPath 1994; *Books* Hyperlipidaemia Diagnosis and Management (1989, 2 edn 1994), Preventive Cardiology (1993); *Recreations* angling; *Clubs* Prince Albert Angling Soc; *Style*— Prof Paul Durrington; ✉ University of Manchester, Department of Medicine, Manchester Royal Infirmary, Oxford Rd, Manchester M13 9WL (☎ 0161 276 4226)

DURSTON, Eur Ing Trevor David; s of David Stanley Durston, and Margery Winnifred, *née* Dalton; *b* 15 Feb 1948; *Educ* Univ of Leeds (BSc), Aston Univ (industl admin course); *m* 25 July 1970, Janet Teresa, *née* Field; 2 da (Hannah Frances b 23 June 1979, Ruth Aimee b 22 June 1981); *Career* graduate trainee Tube Investments Ltd 1969–71, devpt engr Churchill Gear Machines Ltd 1971–72, project ldr Leslie Hartridge Ltd 1978–81 (devpt engr 1972–78), plant engr Himal Hydro and General Construction Co Nepal 1982–84, office mangr Butwal Power Co Nepal 1982–84, prodn mangr Butwal Engineering Works Ltd Nepal 1984–85, dir of devpt and consulting servs Nepal 1985–88; United Mission to Nepal: asst dir Engrg and Industl Devpt Dept 1990–93, dir of personnel 1992–93; gen dir The Leprosy Mission Int 1993–; CEng 1978, MIMechE 1978, Eur Ing 1992, FIMgt 1995; *Style*— Eur Ing Trevor Durston; ✉ The Leprosy Mission International, 80 Windmill Road, Brentford, Middlesex TW8 0QH (☎ 0181 569 7292, fax 0181 569 7808)

DUSSEK, Julian Eric; s of Lt-Cdr Eric Albert Dussek, of Plaxtol, Kent, and Ivy Marion, *née* Wynne; *b* 12 April 1944; *Educ* St Lawrence Coll Ramsgate, Univ of London (MB BS); *m* 6 Sept 1969, (Margot) Vanessa Tryce, da of Lt-Cdr Edward Guy Tryce Morgan (d 1964); 1 s (John b 1976), 1 da (Nicola b 1973); *Career* conslt thoracic surgn: The Brook Regnl Cardiothoracic Unit 1981–89, Guy's Hosp 1981–, Brighton Health Authy 1981–, St Thomas' Hosp 1989–; author of contribs to books on cardiothoracic and oesophageal surgery; treas Soc of Cardiothoracic Surgns of GB & I, memb Cncl Euro Soc of Cardiothoracic Surgeons; FRCS 1974; *Recreations* cooking and the history of eating, motorcycling; *Style*— Julian Dussek, Esq; ✉ Tebolds, The Street, Plaxtol, Sevenoaks, Kent TN15 0QJ (☎ 01732 810489); The Cardiothoracic Unit, Guy's Hospital, London SE1 9RT (☎ 0171 955 4322)

DUTHIE, Prof Sir Herbert Livingston; kt (1987); s of Herbert William Duthie, and Margaret McFarlane, *née* Livingston; *b* 9 Oct 1929; *Educ* Whitehill Sch Glasgow, Univ of Glasgow (MB ChB, MD, ChM); *m* 1959, Maureen, *née* McCann; 3 s, 1 da; *Career* served RAMC 1954–56; Rockefeller travelling fell Mayo Clinic Rochester Minn 1959–60, subsequently academic appts Glasgow, Leeds and Sheffield (dean of med 1973–76), provost Univ of Wales Coll of Med 1979–94; memb: Surgical Res Soc (past pres), Assoc of Professors of Surgery (past chm), Assoc of Surgns of GB and I (pres 1989–90); chm Professional Conduct Ctee GMC (former treas); former chm Med Advsy Ctee Ctee of Vice-Chllrs and Princs (former rep France Ctee on Undergraduate Med and Dental Educn); Hon LLD: Univ of Sheffield 1990, Univ of Wales 1996; FRCS 1956; *Clubs* Army and Navy; *Style*— Prof Sir Herbert Duthie; ✉ St Curig, Windsor Road, Radyr, Cardiff CF4 8BQ (☎ 01228 43472)

DUTHIE, Prof Robert Buchan; CBE (1984); s of James Andrew Duthie (d 1964), and Elizabeth Jean, *née* Hunter (d 1967); *b* 4 May 1925; *Educ* Aberdeen GS, King Edward VI GS Chelmsford, Heriot-Watt Coll Edinburgh, Univ of Edinburgh Med Sch (MB ChB, ChM); *m* June 1956, Alison Ann Macpherson, da of Harold James Kittermaster; 2 s (Alasdair b 1960, Malcolm b 1966), 2 da (Catriona b 1959, Gillian b 1962); *Career* served Malaya RAMC 1949–51; house physician Western Gen Hosp Edinburgh 1949, registrar Royal Infirmary Edinburgh 1951–53 (house surgn 1948–49); res fell: Scottish Hosps Endowment Res Tst Edinburgh 1953–56, Nat Cancer Tst Bethesda USA 1956–57; external memb MRC and sr registrar Inst of Orthopaedics London 1957–58, prof of orthopaedic surgery Univ Sch of Med and Dentistry 1958–66, surgn-in-chief Univ of Rochester Med Centre USA 1958–66, Nuffield prof of orthopaedic surgery Oxford 1966–92, surgn Nuffield Orthopaedic Centre Oxford 1966–92, hon civil conslt in orthopaedic surgery to RN 1974–; emeritus fell Worcester Coll Oxford; govr Oxford Sch for Boys; Hon DSc Rochester NY 1982; FRCSEd, FRCS, Hon FACS 1987; Royal Sovereigns Order Malta; *Books* Management of Haemophilia (1994), Textbook of Orthopaedic Surgery (jtly, 1996); *Recreations* family; *Clubs* Oxford and Cambridge; *Style*— Prof Robert Duthie, CBE; ✉ Barna Brow, Harberton Mead, Headington, Oxford (☎ 01865 62745, fax 01865 62745); Nuffield Orthopaedic Centre, Windmill Rd, Headington, Oxford OX3 7LD (☎ 01865 227377, fax 01865 742348)

DUTHIE, Sir Robert Grieve (Robin); kt (1987), CBE (1978); s of George Duthie, and Mary, *née* Lyle; *b* 2 Oct 1928; *Educ* Greenock Acad; *m* 5 April 1955, (Violetta) Noel, da of Harry Maclean; 2 s (David b 1956, Peter b 1959), 1 da (Susan b 1962); *Career* Nat Serv 1946–49; apprentice CA Thomson Jackson Gourlay & Taylor 1946–51, qualified CA 1952; chm: Black & Edgington plc 1972–83 (md 1962–80), R G Duthie and Company Ltd 1983–, Bruntons (Musselburgh) plc 1984–86, Britoil plc 1988–90, Capital House plc

1988–92, Tay Residential Investments plc 1989–96, Neill Clerk Group plc 1994–; dir: British Asset Trust plc 1977–, Royal Bank of Scotland plc 1978–, Insight Group plc 1983–90 (formerly Black and Edgington), Investors Capital Trust plc 1985–95, Carclo Engineering Group plc 1986–, Royal Bank of Scotland Group plc 1986–, Sea Catch plc 1987–93, British Polythene Industries plc 1988–, Charterhouse plc 1991–93, Devol Engineering Ltd 1994–; chm: Made Up Textiles Assoc of Great Britain 1972, Clyde Port Authy 1978–81, Scottish Development Agency 1979–88; vice chm BP Advsy Bd Scotland 1990–; treas Nelson St EU Congregational Church Greenock 1970–, cmmr Scottish Congregational Ministers Pension Fund; memb: Scottish Telecommunications Bd 1972–78, Scottish Econ Cncl 1980–95, Ct Univ of Strathclyde 1988–94; Hon LLD Univ of Strathclyde 1984, Hon DTech Napier 1989; CIMgt 1975, FRSA 1983, FScotVEC 1988, FRIAS 1989; *Recreations* curling, golf; *Style—* Sir Robin Duthie, CBE; ✉ Fairhaven, 181 Finnart St, Greenock, Strathclyde (☎ 01475 722642)

DUTT, Trevor Peter; s of Dr Bishnu Pada Dutt (d 1970), of Mitcham, Surrey, and Phyllis Ida, *née* Roche; *b* 14 Sept 1943; *Educ* Dulwich, Bart's Med Coll (MB BS, MRCS, LRCP); *m* 27 May 1986, Pauline Deirdre, da of Walter Edward Chapman, of Chigwell, Essex; 1 s (Alexander Philip b 24 Feb 1991); 1 step s (Damien Nicholas Edward Caracatsanis b 2 May 1974); *Career* Surgn Cdr RNR (PMO London Div 1990–), SMO Royal Marines Res City of London 1988–90; jr med staff posts 1965–80 (Bart's, Whipps Cross, Royal Northern, City of London Maternity and Charing Cross Hosps), conslt in obstetrics and gynaecology Royal Northern and Whittington Hosps 1980–; hon conslt Hosp of St John and St Elizabeth; Freeman City of London 1967, Liveryman Worshipful Soc of Apothecaries 1967; FRCOG 1988 (MRCOG 1975), MAE 1994; *Recreations* flying, sailing, sub-aqua diving, horse riding; *Clubs* Athenaeum, Savage; *Style—* Trevor P Dutt, Esq; ✉ 129 Mount View Rd, London N4 4JH (☎ 0181 348 7054, fax 0181 340 1352); 28 Weymouth St, London WIN 3FA (☎ 0171 580 1723, fax 0171 580 1723, mobiles 0860 678980 and 0860 746868)

DUTTINE, John; s of Josef Duttine (d 1956), of Barnsley, Yorkshire, and Caroline Edith, *née* Hampton (d 1983), of Bradford, Yorkshire; *b* 15 March 1949; *Educ* Buttershaw Comprehensive Sch Bradford, Drama Centre London; *ptnr* common law wife, Carolyn Margaret, da of Donald Hutchinson; 1 s (Oscar James b 15 Sept 1980); *Career* actor; entered profession Glasgow Citizens Theatre 1970; *Theatre* incl: Hamlet 1984, Richard II 1987, The Browning Version 1988, The Woman in Black 1989; *Television* credits incl: A Pin to see the Peepshow 1973, Spend Spend Spend 1976, Saturday, Sunday, Monday 1977, People Like Us 1977, The Devils Crown 1978, The Mallens 1979, Wuthering Heights 1979, To Serve them all My Days 1980, Day of the Triffids 1981, The Outsider 1982, Woman of Substance 1983, Out of the Blue (BBC) 1995; *Films* incl: Zeffirelli's Jesus of Nazareth 1976, Who Dares Wins 1982; *Awards* winner of TV Times Best Actor Award 1980; *Style—* John Duttine, Esq; ✉ c/o Derek Webster, AIM, 5 Denmark Street, London WC2H 8LP (☎ 0171 836 2001, fax 0171 379 0848)

DUTTON, Maj-Gen Bryan Hawkins; CBE (1990, OBE 1984, MBE 1978); s of George Ralph Neale Dutton (d 1983), and Honor Badcoe, *née* Morris; *b* 1 March 1943; *Educ* Lord Weymouth Sch, RMA Sandhurst, Royal Military College of Science, Staff College Camberley; *m* 15 July 1972, Angela Margaret, da of Harold Keith Wilson (d 1970); 1 s (Charles b 1974), 1 da (Sophie b 1977); *Career* cmmnd Devonshire and Dorset Regt 1963, Regtl serv 1963–73 (NI, Germany, Libya, Br Guiana, UK, Belize); C-in-C's Mission to Soviet forces in E Germany 1976–78, Regtl duty NI and BAOR 1978–79, staff security co-ordinator NI 1979–81 (despatches 1979), instr Staff Coll Camberley 1981–82, mil asst to Adj-Gen 1982–84, CO 1 Bn Devonshire and Dorset Regt NI and Berlin 1984–87, UKLF overseas ops 1987, cmd 39 Infantry Brigade Ulster 1987–89, Dir Public Relations (Army) 1990–92, Dir of Infantry 1992–94, Cdr Br Forces Hong Kong 1994–; Col Cmdt The Prince of Wales's Div 1996–; *Recreations* offshore sailing, country pursuits, wildlife, music, history; *Clubs* Army & Navy; *Style—* Maj-Gen Bryan Dutton, CBE

DUTTON, Richard Odard Astley (Dickie); a cadet branch of the Duttons of Sherborne, Glos; s of William Astley Dutton (d 1959), of London, and Alice Margaret, *née* Halls; *b* 9 Sept 1935; *Educ* Lancing, RMA Sandhurst; *m* 2 Dec 1961 (sep 1991), Susan Kathleen, da of Maj J R O'B Warde, TD, JP, DL (d 1976), of Westerham, Kent; 1 s (Rodney Henry Odard Ralph b 1967), 2 da (Sarah b 1965, Harriet b 1972); *Career* cmmnd KOYLI 1956: Capt and Adj 1 Bn 1962–63, instr Mons Offr Cadet Sch 1963–65; sales mangr Ross Foods 1965–66, classified ad mangr The Times 1967–70, vice chm Marlar International 1972–89, dir The Butterfield Partnership 1989–90, md Dutton Executive Search 1990–; FRGS; *Recreations* long distance cycling, singing; *Clubs* Canada, Hurlingham; *Style—* Dickie Dutton, Esq; ✉ 27 Brecon Road, London W6 8PY; Dutton Executive Search, Hamilton House, 1 Temple Avenue, London EC4Y 0HA (☎ 0171 353 4212)

DUTTON, Timothy James; s of James Derek Dutton, JP, of Richmond, N Yorks, and Joan Rosemary, *née* Parsons; *b* 25 Feb 1957; *Educ* Repton, Keble Coll Oxford (BA); *m* 1 April 1987, Sappho, da of B Raschid, of Washington, USA; 1 da (Leila b 4 June 1988); *Career* called to the Bar Middle Temple 1979; jr SE circuit 1982, visiting faculty memb Nat Inst of Trial Advocacy USA 1987, memb Legal Aid Working Party Bar Cncl 1990; author of various articles on insurance law; *Recreations* French horn, sailing, Scottish gardens; *Clubs* Harbour; *Style—* Timothy Dutton, Esq; ✉ 28 Moreton Place, London SW1V 2NR (☎ 0171 821 9195); Farrar's Building, Temple, London EC4Y 7BD (☎ 0171 583 9241, fax 0171 583 0090)

DUVAL, Derrick Brian; s of Harold Smith (d 1985), and Florence Gertrude Smith, *née* Osborne (d 1960); *b* 1 Jan 1935; *Educ* Wednesbury Tech Coll, Birmingham and Portsmouth Schs of Architecture (DipArch); *m* 20 Aug 1960, Pauline, da of Horace Lockley; 1 s (Spencer Gavin b 1970); *Career* Nat Serv with RE (air reconnaissance intelligence); architect, princ Duval Brownhill Partnership (architects to the Close in Lichfield and conslts to English Heritage and numerous other heritage orgns), dir of property co; vice-chm Lichfield Cons Assoc, chm Staffordshire East and Derby Cons Euro Constituency Cncl; RIBA; *Recreations* political work; *Clubs* Rotary; *Style—* Derrick Duval; ✉ 23 Dam St, Lichfield, Staffs WS13 6AE (☎ 01543 264303); Duval Brownhill Partnership, Georgian House, 24 Bird St, Lichfield, Staffs WS13 6PT (☎ 01543 254257)

DUVAL, Robin Arthur Philip; s of Arthur Edward Bickersteth Duval (d 1976), of Exeter, Devon, and Jane Elizabeth, *née* Evans; *b* 28 April 1941; *Educ* King Edward's Sch Birmingham, UCL (BA), Univ of Michigan; *m* 20 Dec 1968, Lorna Eileen, da of Robert Watson, of Cardiff; 1 s (Sam b 1976, d 1978), 4 da (Polly b 1969, Sophie b 1971, Daisy b 1982, Martha b 1983); *Career* radio studio mangr BBC 1964–65, TV prodr J Walter Thompson 1965–68, princ Home Office 1981–83, head of UK prodn COI 1983–85 (TV prodr 1968–81), chief asst TV IBA 1985–90, dep dir of progs Independent Television Cmmn 1991–; memb RTS 1986; *Recreations* music, Aston Villa, theatre, food; *Style—* Robin Duval, Esq; ✉ Independent Television Commission, 33 Foley Street, London W1P 7LB (☎ 0171 255 3000)

DUVALL, Kenneth Edward; *b* 3 May 1941; *Educ* Liverpool Art HS, Liverpool Regnl Coll of Art, Central Sch of Art & Design London; *m* 5 April 1968, Anne-Marie, *née* Savage; *Career* chartered designer; asst gp industl designer Allied Ironfounders Ltd 1963–67; freelance designer 1967–79 for various clients incl: Plastics (Manchester) Ltd, Scot-waste (Manchester) Ltd, Barrett Industries and City of Manchester; asst to the Dean of the Faculty of Art and Design Manchester Poly 1974–79 (lectr then sr lectr in industl design when Manchester Coll of Art and Design 1967–74); chm Nat Jt Conf of CNAA Post-Grad Studies in Art and Design 1978–79, advsy offr for Art and Design, Technician Educn Cncl (DATEC) 1979–84; BTEC educn advsr for design and design bd offr 1984–92; project mangr for GNVQ 1992–95: Art and Design, The Built Environment, Manufacturing, Leisure and Tourism; freelance designer and art and design educn cnslt 1995–; SIAD: memb Cncl 1973–79, chm NW Region 1973–76, memb Info Bd 1974–76, vice pres 1976–79, chm Regnl Bd 1976–79, memb Mgmnt Ctee 1976–79, DATEC/BTEC observer on CSD Educn and Trg Bd 1979–90; CSD: memb Design Educn Gp 1983– (chm 1983–84), vice pres and memb Cncl 1991–94, memb Membership Ctee 1991–, chm 1996–; govr: Oldham Coll of Technol 1977–79, Bolton Tech Coll 1977–79, Barnet Coll Herts 1982–88; cncllr (Ind) Berkhamstead Town Cncl 1995–; memb Grand Union Canal Soc (hon treasurer 1993–94, hon sec 1994–); hon fell BIID, FCSD; *Style—* Kenneth Duvall, Esq; ✉ Bank Mill Cottage, Bank Mill Lane, Berkhamsted, Hertfordshire HP4 2NS (☎ 01442 872217)

DWEK, Joseph Claude (Joe); *b* 1 May 1940; *Educ* Carmel Coll, Univ of Manchester (BSc, BA); *m*; 2 c; *Career* chm Bodycote International plc and subsids in Germany, Netherlands, Sweden and USA; dir and memb Mgmnt Ctee Manchester Business Sch, memb Cncl CBI (vice chm NW Regnl Cncl); memb: Ct Univ of Manchester, Ct UMIST; FTI, AMCT; *Recreations* golf; *Style—* Joe Dwek, Esq; ✉ Bodycote International plc, 140 Kingsway, Manchester M19 1BB (☎ 0161 257 2345, fax 0161 257 2353, telex 667072)

DWEK, Prof Raymond Allen; s of Victor Joseph Dwek (d 1988), of Manchester, and Alice, *née* Liniado; *b* 10 Nov 1941; *Educ* Carmel Coll, Univ of Manchester (BSc, MSc), Lincoln Coll Oxford (DPhil), Exeter Coll Oxford (DSc); *m* 21 June 1964, Sandra, da of Dr David I Livingstone, of Manchester; 2 s (Robert b 14 July 1967, Joshua b 23 March 1978), 2 da (Juliet b 19 Dec 1965, Deborah b 3 Oct 1974); *Career* Univ of Oxford: res lectr in physical chemistry ChCh 1966–68, lectr in inorganic chemistry ChCh 1968–75, departmental demonstrator for Dept of Biochemistry 1969–74, res lectr in biochemistry ChCh 1975–76, lectr in biochemistry Trinity Coll Oxford 1976–84, fell Exeter Coll 1976–, prof of glycobiology and dir Glycobiology Inst Dept of Biochemistry until 1996, assoc head Dept of Biochemistry (with special responsibilities for postgrad and post doctoral trg) 1996–; visiting Royal Soc Res fell at Weizmann Inst Rehovot Israel 1969, Royal Soc Locke Res fell 1974–76; visiting professorships: Duke Univ N Carolina 1968 (seconded to Inst of Exploratory Res Fort Monmouth NJ), Univ of Trieste Italy 1974, Univ of Lund Sweden 1977, Inst of Enzymology Budapest Hungary 1980; author various articles in books and jls on physical chemistry, biochemistry and med; memb of various scientific ctees incl: Oxford Enzyme Gp 1971–88, Oxford Oligosaccharide Gp 1983–88, MRC AIDS Antiviral Steering Ctee 1987–92, dir and founding memb scientist Oxford GlycoScience Ltd (formerly Oxford GlycoSystems) 1988–; holder 27 patents; Wellcome Tst Award 1994, award for research in biochemisty related to med 1996; Doctor (hc) Katholieke Universitat Leuven Belgium 1996; *Books* Nuclear Magnetic Resonance in Biochemistry (1973), Principles and Problems in Physical Chemistry for Biochemists (jtly, 1975), Nuclear Magnetic Resonance in Biology (jtly 1977), Biological Spectroscopy (jtly, 1984); author over 300 scientific papers; *Style—* Prof Raymond Dwek; ✉ Ambleside, Vernon Avenue, N Hinksey, Oxford OX2 9AU (☎ 01865 242065); Glycobiology Institute, Department of Biochemistry, University of Oxford, South Parks Road, Oxford OX1 3QU (☎ 01865 275344 (direct), fax 01865 275216, telex 83681)

DWORKIN, Prof Ronald Myles; s of David Dworkin, and Madeline Talamo; *b* 11 Dec 1931; *Educ* Harvard Coll, Oxford Univ, Harvard Law Sch; *m* 1958, Betsy Celia Ross; 1 s, 1 da; *Career* Univ of Oxford: prof of jurisprudence 1969–, fell Univ Coll 1969–; FBA 1979; *Style—* Prof Ronald Dworkin, FBA; ✉ University College, Oxford OX1 4BH

DWYER, Joseph Anthony; *b* 20 June 1939; *Career* George Wimpey PLC: joined 1955, qualified as civil engr, main bd dir 1988–, gp chief exec 1991–, chm 1996–; co-chm Transmanche Link 1992–93; CEng, FICE, FCIOB; *Style—* Joseph Dwyer, Esq; ✉ George Wimpey PLC, 27 Hammersmith Grove, London W6 7EN (☎ 0181 846 2077, fax 0181 748 0076)

DWYER, Mark Peter; s of James Dwyer, and Philomena, *née* King; *b* 9 Aug 1963; *Educ* Christian Brothers; *m* 1990, Jane Mary Temple; 2 da (Emma Louise b 1991, Catherine Mary b 1996), 1 s (James Peter b 1992); *Career* national hunt jockey; apprentice with Liam Browne in Ireland; first winner on Cloneagh Emperor at Limerick Junction 1979; races won incl: Gold Cup 1985 and 1993, Scottish Grand Nat; highest number of winners ridden in a season (93) 1989–90; *Recreations* golf, tennis; *Style—* Mark Dwyer, Esq; ✉ Oaks Farm, West Knapton, Malton, North Yorkshire YO17 0RL (☎ 01944 758841, car 0860 502233)

DYER, Alan; QPM; s of William Arthur Butt (d 1949), of Doncaster, and Dorothy Ann, *née* Hunter; *b* 4 Jan 1934; *Educ* Henry Mellish GS Nottingham, Univ of Nottingham; *m* 31 Dec 1955, Penelope Jane, da of Capt Oswald Henry Peel Cox (d 1961), of Nottingham; 1 s (Jonathon Mark b 1959), 1 da (Sally Anne b 1957); *Career* able seaman RN 1952–54; Notts Constabulary 1954–80, Durham Constabulary 1980–82, Bedfordshire Police 1982–96 (latterly Chief Constable), ret; memb: Bedfordshire St John Cncl, Rotary Club of Kempston Bedford, Assoc of Chief Police Offrs 1980; OStJ; *Style—* Alan Dyer, Esq, QPM; ✉ c/o Police Headquarters, Woburn Road, Kempston, Bedford MK43 9AX

DYER, Charles; s of James Dyer (d 1980), and Florence, *née* Stretton (d 1975); *b* 7 July 1928; *Educ* Highlands Cncl Sch Ilford, Queen Elizabeth's GS Barnet; *m* 1960, Fiona, da of Elizabeth and Ernest Thomson; 3 s (John, Peter, Timothy); *Career* playwright, author, actor, director; Flying Offr RAFVR, navigator 512 Sqdn Europe and 243 Sqdn Pacific, demobbed 1948; actor in 250 plays and films, appeared at 120 theatres; made West End debut as Duke in Delderfield's Worm's Eye View (Whitehall) 1948; writer of plays for RSC; works, mostly duologues, are in constant prodn; latest prodns incl: Sottoscala (Satiri Theatre Rome 1987–88), Mother Adam (Rome Festival 1988), Lovers Dancing (Albery) 1983–84, L'Escalier (Lucernaire D'Art Theatre 1993–94), Staircase (trans-Germany Prodn) 1994–95; Loneliness Trilogy (Rattle of a Simple Man, Staircase, Mother Adam) translated into most languages; *Style—* Charles Dyer, Esq; ✉ Old Wob, Gerrards Cross, Bucks SL9 8SF

DYER, Dr James A T; s of Rev T J Dyer (d 1994), and Mary Watt, *née* Thomson; *b* 31 Dec 1946; *Educ* Robert Gordon's Coll, Univ of Aberdeen (MB, ChB, Ogston prize in surgery, Keith gold medal, Anderson gold medal and prize); *m* 1, 1969 (m dis 1994), Lorna, *née* Townson; 2 s (Paul b 1 Sept 1971, Euan b 22 Sept 1976), 1 da (Rowan b 11 Aug 1978); m 2, Suzanne, *née* Whitaker; 1 step s (Christopher b 4 April 1984), 2 step da (Sophie b 1 Sept 1989, Emily b 7 Nov 1990); *Career* various house jobs in Aberdeen Hosps 1970–71, trainee GP 1971–72; Royal Edinburgh Hosp: SHO and registrar posts in psychiatry 1972–75, sr registrar in psychiatry 1975–77; scientific offr MRC Unit for Epidemiological Studies in Psychiatry Edinburgh 1977–80, conslt in general and rehabilitation psychiatry Royal Edinburgh Hosp 1981–91, dir Mental Welfare Cmmn for Scotland 1993– (HM med cmmr 1991–); hon sr lectr in psychiatry Univ of Edinburgh 1981–; chm Section for social community and rehabilitation RCPsych 1994–; author of papers on parasuicide, schizophrenia, care of long term mentally ill and psychological aspects of nuclear war; FRCPsych; *Recreations* family, photography, reading, theatre, walking; *Style—* Dr James Dyer; ✉ 37 Lauder Road, Edinburgh EH9 1UE (☎ 0131 667 2479); Mental Welfare Commission for Scotland, 25 Drumsheugh Gardens, Edinburgh EH3 7RN (☎ 0131 225 7034, fax 0131 226 4027)

DYER, Lois Edith; OBE (1984); da of Richard Morgan Dyer (d 1961), and Emmeline Agnes Dyer, *née* Wells (d 1976); *b* 18 March 1925; *Educ* Richmond Co Sch, Middlesex Hosp Sch of Physiotherapy; *Career* physiotherapist Middlesex Hosp London 1945–47, sr physiotherapist Coronation Non-Euro Hosp Johannesburg SA 1948–51; supt physiotherapist: Johannesburg Gp of Hosps 1951–56, Westminster Hosp London 1958–61, Royal Nat Orthopaedic Hosp Stanmore Middlesex 1963–72; memb NHS Health Advsy Service teams 1972–76, physiotherapy offr DHSS London 1976–85; memb Hampstead Community Health Cncl 1996–; int freelance conslt physiotherapist; MCSP 1945, FCSP 1986; *Books* Care of the Orthopaedic Patient (Rowe and Dyer, 1977), Physiotherapy Theory and Practice Journal (co-ed, 1985–89); numerous publications in jls and books; *Recreations* country pursuits, music, bridge, animal welfare, conservation; *Style—* Miss Lois Dyer, OBE, FCSP; ✉ Garden Flat, 6 Belsize Grove, London NW3 4UN (☎ 0171 722 1794)

DYER, (Alexander) Patrick (Pat); s of John Alexander Dyer (d 1990), and Amie Moore Dyer (d 1956); *b* 30 Aug 1932; *Educ* US Military Acad (BS), Harvard Business Sch (MBA); *m* 1954; 1 s; *Career* various appts rising to exec vice pres and bd dir Air Products and Chemicals Inc USA 1963–89; The BOC Group plc: md Gases and main bd dir 1989–96, dep chm and chief exec offr 1993–96, chm Exec Ctee; non-exec dir and chm Bunzl plc 1993–; former chm: Int Oxygen Mfrs' Assoc, Compressed Gas Assoc; *Recreations* golf, skeet shooting; *Style—* Pat Dyer, Esq; ✉ BOC Group plc, Chertsey Road, Windlesham, Surrey GU20 6HJ (☎ 01276 477664)

DYER, Prof Sir (Henry) Peter Francis Swinnerton; 16 Bt (E 1678), of Tottenham, Middx; KBE (1987); s of Sir Leonard Schroeder Swinnerton Dyer, 15 Bt (d 1975), and Barbara, *née* Brackenbury (d 1990); *b* 2 Aug 1927; *Educ* Eton, Trinity Coll Cambridge; *m* 25 May 1983, Dr Harriet Crawford, er da of Rt Hon Sir Patrick Reginald Evelyn Browne, OBE, TD (d 1996); *Heir* kinsman, John Dyer-Bennet b 17 April 1915; *Career* Cwlth Fund fell Univ of Chicago 1954–55, res fell Trinity Coll Cambridge 1950–54 (fell 1955–73, dean 1963–73); master St Catharine's Coll Cambridge 1973–83; prof of mathematics Cambridge Univ 1971–88 (lectr 1960–71, univ lectr Cambridge Maths Lab 1960–67); vice chllr Cambridge Univ 1979–81; visiting prof Harvard 1971; chm: Ctee on Academic Orgn (London Univ) 1980–82, Steering Gp responsible for planning inst to replace New Univ of Ulster and Ulster Poly 1982–84; fellow Eton 1981–96, dir Prutec 1981–86, chm Univ Grants Ctee 1983–89, chief exec Univs Funding Cncl 1989–91, chm CODEST 1987–91 (memb 1984–91), memb Euro Science and Technol Assembly 1994–; Hon DSc Univs of: Bath 1981, Ulster 1991, Wales 1991, Birmingham 1992, Nottingham 1992, Warwick 1993; Hon LLD Univ of Aberdeen 1991; hon fell: Worcester Coll Oxford, Trinity Coll Cambridge, St Catharine's Coll Cambridge; fell Academia Europa, FRS; *Recreations* destructive gardening; *Style—* Prof Sir Peter Dyer, Bt, KBE, FRS; ✉ The Dower House, Thriplow, Cambs (☎ 01763 208220)

DYER, Dr Richard George; s of Cdr Charles William Dyer (d 1992), and Dorothy Patricia Victoria, *née* Vaughan-Hogan (d 1993); *b* 18 July 1943; *Educ* Churchers Coll Petersfield Hants, Univ of London (BSc), Univ of Birmingham (MSc), Univ of Bristol (PhD); *m* 14 Sept 1967 (m dis 1995), Shirley James Foulsham; 2 s (James William b 3 June 1970, Matthew Charles b 30 Dec 1971), 1 da (Emilie Kate b 13 Jan 1976); *Career* res assoc in anatomy Med Sch Univ of Bristol 1973–74 (res asst 1968–73); The Babraham Inst (formerly Inst of Animal Physiology and Inst of Animal Physiology and Genetics Res): princ sci offr 1974–82, sr princ sci offr 1982–89, head Dept of Neuroendocrinology 1985–90, head Cambridge Res Station 1989–93, assoc dir IAPGR 1991–93, dir The Babraham Inst 1994– (exec dir 1993–94); conslt WHO Geneva 1983–86; memb Editorial Bd: Experimental Brain Res 1978–90, Jl of Endocrinology 1983–89; memb: Animal Sci Ctee and Strategy Bd AFRC 1993–94, Animal Sci and Psychology Res Ctee BBSRC 1994–, Life and Environmental Sci Ctee Euro Sci Fndn 1995–; memb: Soc for Endocrinology 1969, Int Soc for Neuroendocrinology 1972, Physiological Soc 1973, Soc for the Study of Fertility 1973, Euro Soc for Comparative Endocrinology 1973, IBRO 1980, Br Neuroendocrine Gp 1985, Euro Neuroendocrine Assoc 1986, Soc for Neuroscience (USA) 1990; *Awards* Soc for Endocrinology Medal 1986, 50th Anniversary Medal of the Polish Physiological Soc 1987; *Books* Brain opioid systems in reproduction (ed with R J Bicknell, 1989); *Recreations* finding bargains, escaping to mountains and the sea, lively conversation with excellent food and wine; *Style—* Dr Richard Dyer; ✉ Babraham Institute, Babraham Hall, Babraham, Cambridge CB2 4AT (☎ 01223 832312, fax 01223 836122)

DYKE, *see:* Hart Dyke

DYKE-COOMES, Martin; s of Ernest Thomas Dyke-Coomes, and Gladys Dorothy, *née* Bignell (d 1995); *b* 14 Aug 1948; *Educ* Sarah Robinson Secdy Modern, Ifield GS, Architectural Assoc; *m* 24 June 1978, Maggie Pinhorn, *qv*, da of George Herbert Pinhorn (d 1996); 1 s (Ned Alexander b 1981), 1 da (Amy Elizabeth b 1983); 2 adopted s (Anthony b 1967, Claude b 1973); *Career* architect ARCUK 1973; fndr CGHP Architects in 1979; fndr Dyke Coomes Assocs 1989; principle works: Hoxton St London N1 Regeneration (Times/RIBA award 1985), Jubilee Hall Redevelopment 1984–87 (Times/RIBA award 1988), Holland and Thurstan Dwellings 1982–86; current works incl Care in the Community schemes, ecological housing devpt proposals and Stoke Newington Theatre; participant in 1986 RIBA 40 under 40's exhibition; RIBA; *Recreations* thinking, fishing, wishing, eating, sleeping, dreaming, loving; *Clubs* Manchester United; *Style—* Martin Dyke-Coomes, Esq; ✉ Dyke Coomes Associates Architects, 89–93 Shepperton Rd, London N1 3DF (☎ 0171 359 8230)

DYKER, Dr George Simpson; s of Alexander Dyker (d 1981), and Sarah Helen, *née* Simpson, of East Kilbride; *b* 6 July 1941; *Educ* Hutchesons' GS, Univ of Glasgow (MB ChB, MRCP(UK), MRCGP); *m* 1; 1 s (Alexander George b 1966), m 2, 1969, Dr Elspeth Jean Chalmers Smith, da of John Kilpatrick Smith; 2 da (Karen Elizabeth Simpson b 1971, Morven Jean Kilpatrick b 1978); *Career* house physician Stobhill Hosp Glasgow 1964–65, house surgn Royal Infirmary Glasgow Feb-Aug 1965, Faulds research fell Stobhill Hosp Glasgow 1965–66, princ in gen practice 1967–; dep regional advsr in gen practice 1989–96; memb BMA 1964, FRCGP 1987 (memb Cncl), FRCPGlas 1988; *Recreations* golf; *Style—* Dr George Dyker; ✉ 4 Old Coach Road, East Kilbride, Glasgow G74 4DP (☎ 013552 20045); Dyker, Dyker, Mackintosh, Ahmed & Young, Hunter Health Centre, Andrew Street, East Kilbride, Glasgow G74 1AD (☎ 013552 39111)

DYKES, Dr David Wilmer; s of Capt David Dykes, OBE (d 1978), and Jenny, *née* Thomas (d 1971); *b* 18 Dec 1933; *Educ* Swansea GS, CCC Oxford (MA), Univ of Wales (PhD); *m* 22 Sept 1967, Margaret Anne, da of Harvey Clifford George (d 1969); 2 da (Elizabeth Anne b 28 July 1972, Rosemary Louise b 29 July 1978); *Career* cmmnd RN and RNR 1955–62; civil servant Bd of Inland Revenue 1958–59, admin appts Univ of Bristol and Univ Coll of Swansea 1959–63, dep registrar Univ Coll of Swansea 1963–69, registrar Univ of Warwick 1969–72; Nat Museum of Wales: sec 1972–86, actg dir 1985–86, dir 1986–89; memb Cncl Royal Inst of South Wales 1962–69 and 1985–91, hon lectr in history Univ Coll Cardiff (later Univ of Wales Coll of Cardiff) 1975–, chllr Order of St John Priory for Wales 1991–, KStJ 1993; awarded Parkes-Weber prize and medal RNS 1954; fndn memb Welsh Livery Guild 1993; Freeman City of London 1985, Liveryman Worshipful Co of Tin Plate Workers 1985; FRNS 1958, FRHistS 1965, FSA 1973, FRSA 1990; *Books* Anglo-Saxon Coins in the National Museum of Wales (1977), Alan Sorrell: Early Wales Recreated (1980), Wales in Vanity Fair (1989), The University Coll of Swansea (1992); author of articles and reviews in numismatic, historical and other jls; *Recreations* numismatics, writing, gardening; *Clubs* Athenaeum, Cardiff & County (Cardiff), Bristol Channel Yacht (Swansea); *Style—* Dr David Dykes, FSA; ✉ Cherry Grove, Welsh St Donats, nr Cowbridge, South Glamorgan CF71 7SS

DYKES, Hugh John; MP (C) Harrow East (majority 11,098); s of Richard Dykes, of Weston-super-Mare, Somerset; *b* 17 May 1939; *Educ* Weston-super-Mare GS, Pembroke Coll Cambridge; *m* 1965, Susan Margaret, da of Elwand Smith of Wakefield, Yorks; 3 s; *Career* investment analyst and stockbroker: ptnr Simon & Coates 1968–78, assoc memb Quilter Goodison & Co (formerly Quilter, Hilton, Goodison) 1978–; dir Dixons plc Far Eastern Div 1985–; research sec Bow Group 1965–66, Parly candidate (C) Tottenham 1966, MP (C) Harrow E 1970–; PPS to: Parly under secs for Defence 1970–73, Parly under sec Civil Service Dept 1973; UK memb Euro Parl 1974, chm Cons Parly European Ctee 1979–80 (former sec, vice chm), vice pres Cons Gp for Europe 1982 (chm 1979–1980); Liveryman Worshipful Co of Farriers; *Clubs* Beefsteak, Garrick, Carlton; *Style—* Hugh Dykes, Esq, MP; ✉ House of Commons, London SW1A OAA

DYKES, Richard Thornton Booth; s of Alan Thornton Dykes (d 1979), and Myra McFie Booth (d 1991); *b* 7 April 1945; *Educ* Rossall Sch; *m* 1970 (m dis), Janet Rosemary, da of Cdr R J R Cundall; 1 s (Nicholas Thornton b 27 Oct 1972); *Career* articled clerk Dehn and Lauderdale slrs 1965–67, exec offr then higher exec offr Miny of Labour 1967–73, private sec to Sec of State for Employment 1973–76, princ Econ Policy Div Dept of Employment 1976–77, dir of industl relations British Shipbuilders 1977–80, non-exec dir Austin & Pickersgill Ltd Sunderland 1979–80; Dept of Employment: princ private sec to Sec of State for Employment 1980–82, head of Unemployment Benefit Serv 1982–85, sec Sr Mgmnt Gp 1985–86, head Inner Cities Central Unit 1986; Post Office Counters Ltd: gen mangr Greater London 1986–87, dir of ops 1987–92, md 1992–96; md Royal Mail 1996–; memb: Design Cncl, Forensic Sci Serv Advsy Bd, Economics Devpt Ctee Business in the Community; FRSA; *Style—* Richard Dykes, Esq; ✉ Royal Mail, Royal Mail House, 148–166 Old Street, London EC1V 9HQ (☎ 0171 250 2888)

DYMOKE, Lt-Col John Lindley Marmion; MBE (1960), DL (Lincs 1976); thirty-fourth Queen's Champion (in full: The Honourable the Queen's Champion and Standard Bearer of England); s of Lionel Marmion Dymoke (d 1963), and Rachel Isabel (d 1989), da of Hon Lennox Lindley (3 s of 1 Baron Lindley); *b* 1 Sept 1926; *Educ* Christ's Hosp; *m* 1953, Susan Cicely, eldest da of Lt Francis Fane, RN (himself ggggs of 8 Earl of Westmorland), of The Manor, Fulbeck, Lincs; 3 s (Francis, m 1982, Rosalie, da of Maj Anthony Goldingham; Philip, m 1982, Arabella, da of Sir Ralph Dodds, 2 Bt; Charles, m 1990, Kathryn, da of Rex Topham); *Career* Lt-Col Royal Anglian Regt, served Royal Lincolnshire Regt, instr RMA Sandhurst 1962, cmmnd 3 Bn Royal Anglian Regt 1966–69, ret 1972; landowner and farmer; memb E Lindsey Dist Cncl 1973–; High Sheriff of Lincs 1979; Vice-Lord Lt of Lincs 1991–; pres: Lincs Branch CLA 1995– (chm 1982–85), Lincs Agric Soc 1995; memb Ct of Assts Worshipful Co of Grocers (Master 1977); *Style—* Lt-Col John Dymoke, MBE, DL; ✉ The Estate Office, Scrivelsby Court, Horncastle, Lincs (☎ 01507 523325)

DYMOND, Dr Duncan Simon; s of Dr Sydney Cyril Dymond (d 1978), and Adele, *née* Spector (d 1977); *b* 25 Feb 1950; *Educ* St Paul's, Bart's Med Sch Univ of London (MB BS, MD); *m* 26 March 1977, Roberta Laura, da of Fiorenzo Bazzi, of Milan, Italy; 1 s (Daniel b 1982), 1 da (Francesca b 1979); *Career* asst prof of med and cardiology Mount Sinai Med Sch Univ of Wisconsin 1980–81, sr registrar in cardiology 1981–86, conslt cardiologist Bart's 1987–; fndr Br Nuclear Cardiology Gp, memb Cncl Br Cardiovascular Intervention Soc Scientific Ctee, hon sec Br Cardiac Soc 1990–94; memb: Br Nuclear Med Soc 1979, Br Cardiology Soc 1980, MRS 1981; fell American Coll of Cardiology 1983, fndr fell Euro Soc of Cardiology 1989; *Books* An Atlas of Myocardial Infarction (1994), The Jargon-Busters Guide to Heart Disease (1996); *Recreations* cricket, tennis, skiing, pianoforte, Italian opera, watercolours; *Clubs* MCC; *Style—* Dr Duncan Dymond; ✉ Cardiac Department, St Bartholomew's Hospital, London EC1A 7BE (☎ 0171 726 6233); 22 Upper Wimpole Street, London W1 (☎ 0171 935 6789, car 0836 297007)

DYNEVOR, 9 Baron (GB 1780); Richard Charles Uryan Rhys; s of 8 Baron Dynevor, CBE, MC (d 1962, fifth in descent from Baroness Dynevor, herself da of 1 and last Earl Talbot, of the same family as the Earls of Shrewsbury); *b* 19 June 1935; *Educ* Eton, Magdalene Coll Cambridge; *m* 1959 (m dis 1978), Lucy Catherine King, da of Sir John Rothenstein, CBE; 1 s, 3 da; *Heir* s, Hon Hugo Griffith Uryan Rhys b 19 Nov 1966; *Style—* The Rt Hon the Lord Dynevor; ✉ c/o House of Lords, London SW1A 0PW

DYSART, Countess of (eleventh holder of title, S 1643); Rosamund Agnes; also Lady Huntingtower (S 1643); da of Maj Owain Edward Whitehead Greaves, JP, DL (d 1941), and Countess of Dysart (tenth holder, d 1975); *b* 15 Feb 1914; *Heir* sister, Lady Katherine Grant; *Style—* The Rt Hon the Countess of Dysart; ✉ Bryn Garth, Grosmont, Abergavenny, Gwent

DYSON, Anthony Oakley; *b* 6 Oct 1935; *Educ* William Hulme's GS Manchester, Emmanuel Coll Cambridge (BA, MA), Exeter Coll Oxford (BD, DPhil), Ripon Hall Oxford, Marburg Univ Germany; *Career* cmmnd 2 Lt West Yorks Regt (Prince of Wales' Own) 1954–56; asst curate St Mary's Putney Diocese of Southwark 1961–63, princ Ripon Hall Oxford 1968–74 (chaplain and tutor 1963–68), memb Bd Faculty of Theology Univ of Oxford 1968–74 (memb 1963–68), canon St George's Chapel Windsor Castle 1974–77, lectr in theology Univ of Kent at Canterbury 1977–80 (dir Centre for the Study of Religion and Society); Univ of Manchester: Samuel Ferguson prof of social and pastoral theology 1980–, academic dir Centre for Social Ethics and Policy 1986–, dean Faculty of Theology 1985–87 and 1989–91; ed: The Teilhard Review 1966–72, The Modern Churchman 1981–93; memb Warnock Ctee on Fertilization and Embryology 1984, tstee Higher Educn Fndn; contrib to numerous academic and learned jls; Hon MTheol Univ of Manchester 1980; *Books* Who is Jesus Christ? (1969), The Immortality of the Past (1974), We Believe (1977), Transnational Corporations: Confronting the Issues (co ed Paul Brett, 1983), Experiments on Embryos (co ed with John Harris, 1989), Ethics and Biotechnology (co-ed with John Harris, 1993), The Ethics of IVF (1994); *Style—* Prof Anthony Dyson; ✉ 33 Danesmoor Road, West Didsbury, Manchester M20 3JT (☎ 0161 434 5410); Department of Religions and Theology, Faculty of Arts, University of Manchester, Manchester M13 9PL (☎ 0161 275 3597, 0161 275 3613)

DYSON, Hon Mr Justice; Hon Sir John Anthony; kt (1993); s of Richard Dyson (d 1988), of Leeds, and Gisella Elizabeth, *née* Kremsier; *b* 31 July 1943; *Educ* Leeds GS (fndn scholar), Wadham Coll Oxford (open classical scholar, MA); *m* 5 July 1970, Jacqueline Carmel, *née* Levy; 1 da (Michelle b 25 June 1971), 1 s (Steven b 21 May 1973); *Career* called to the Bar Middle Temple 1968 (Harmsworth scholar), QC 1982, recorder of the Crown Court 1986–93, judge of the High Court of Justice (Queen's Bench Div) 1993–; memb: Cncl of Legal Educn 1992–96, Judicial Studies Bd 1994– (chm Ethnic Minorities Advsy Ctee 1994–); *Recreations* music, walking, skiing, tennis; *Style—* The Hon Mr Justice Dyson; ✉ Royal Courts of Justice, Strand, London WC2A 2LL

DYSON, John Michael; s of Eric Dyson; *b* 9 Feb 1929; *Educ* Bradfield, CCC Oxford; *Career* admitted slr 1956; ptnr Field Roscoe & Co (subsequently Field Fisher & Co, then Field F Martineau) 1957–73; Chief Master of the Supreme Ct of Judicature (Chancery Div) 1992– (master 1973–92), a recorder 1994–; *Style—* J M Dyson Esq; ✉ 20 Keats Grove, London NW3 2RS (☎ 0171 794 3389)

DYSON, Prof Robert Graham; s of Jack Dyson (d 1970), of Saddleworth, Oldham, and Sylvia, *née* Schofield; *b* 6 Sept 1942; *Educ* Hulme GS Oldham, Univ of Liverpool (BSc), Univ of Lancaster (PhD); *m* 31 July 1965, Dorothy, da of Daniel Prestwich (d 1987), of Oldham; 1 s (Michael), 1 da (Joanne); *Career* sr systems technologist Pilkington Bros plc 1968–70 (res mathematician 1964–68); Univ of Warwick: lectr 1970–77, sr lectr 1977–84, prof of operational res and systems 1984–, pro-vice-chllr 1989–95; chm Warwick Business Sch 1978–81; memb: OR Panel SERC 1985–89, Operational Res Soc (former cncl memb and chm Educn Res Ctee); President's Medal Operational Res Soc,

Pergamon Prize for articles in Jl of Operational Res Soc; chm of Govrs Kenilworth Sch 1993–; *Books* Strategic Planning: Models and Analytical Techniques (1989); *Recreations* cricket (played for Uppermill, Southport & Birkdale and Leamington CC's), theatre; *Clubs* Warwickshire CCC, Coventry RFC; *Style*— Prof Robert Dyson; ✉ Warwick Business School, University of Warwick, Coventry CV4 7AL (☎ 01203 523775)

DYSON, Prof Roger Franklin; s of John Franklin Dyson (d 1969), of Oldham, Lancs, and Edith Mary, *née* Jobson (d 1981); *b* 30 Jan 1940; *Educ* Counthill GS Oldham, Univ of Keele (BA), Univ of Leeds (PhD); *m* 1, 1964 (m dis 1994), Anne Elizabeth, da of Travis Edward Greaves (d 1985), of Oldham; 1 s (Mark Franklin b 1965), 1 da (Miranda Jane b 1967); m 2, 1995, Dr Ann Frances Naylor, da of Albert Worsfold (d 1994), of Haslemere, Surrey; *Career* lectr in econ and industl rels Univ of Leeds 1966–74 (asst lectr 1963–66); Univ of Keele: sr lectr in industl rels and dep dir adult educn 1974–76, prof and dir of adult educn 1976–89, dir Clinical Mgmnt Unit Centre for Health Planning and Mgmnt 1989–; dir Mercia Publications Ltd 1984–, ed Health Servs Manpower Review 1975–86; conslt advsr to sec of state at DHSS 1979–81, chm North Staffs Health Authy 1982–86; RSM 1982; *Recreations* gardening, gastronomy; *Clubs* Carlton, Royal Soc of Med; *Style*— Prof Roger Dyson; ✉ 4 Huskards Fryerning, Ingatestone, Essex CM4 0HR (☎ 01227 354830); Centre for Health Planning and Management, Darwin Building, The Science Park, University of Keele, Staffs ST5 5BG (☎ 01782 621111, fax 01782 613847)

E

EABORN, Prof Colin; s of Tom Stanley Eaborn (d 1964), of Wrexham, Clwyd, and Caroline, *née* Cooper (d 1974); *b* 15 March 1923; *Educ* Ruabon GS, Univ Coll of N Wales Bangor (BSc, PhD, DSc); *m* 30 Aug 1949, Joyce, da of David Thomas, of Newcastle Emlyn, Dyfed; *Career* Univ of Leicester: asst lectr 1947, lectr 1950, reader in chemistry 1954; Univ of Sussex: prof of chemistry 1962, dean Sch of Molecular Scis 1964–68 and 1978–79, pro vice chllr sci 1968–72; res assoc Univ of Calif LA 1950–51, Robert Welch visiting scholar Rice Univ Texas 1961–62, Erskine fell Univ of Canterbury NZ 1965, distinguished prof New Mexico State Univ 1973, Canadian Cwlth fell and visiting prof Univ of Victoria BC 1976, Riccoboni lectr Univ of Padua 1977, Gilman lectr Iowa State Univ 1978; FS Kipping award of American Chem Soc 1964; Royal Soc Chemistry: Organometallic award 1975, Ingold medal 1976, Main Gp Element award 1989; hon sec Chem Soc 1964–71, chm Br Cmmn on Chem Educn 1967–69, vice pres Dalton Div Royal Soc of Chemistry 1971–75; memb: Italy UK Mixed Cultural Cmmn 1972–80, Cncl Royal Soc 1978–80 and 1988–89; contrib to Jl of Organometallic Chemistry (ed 1963–96) and Jl of Chemical Soc; Hon DSc Univ of Sussex 1990; FRSC, FRS 1970; *Books* Organosilicon Compounds (1960); *Style*— Prof Colin Eaborn, FRS; ✉ School of Chemistry Physics and Environmental Science, University of Sussex, Brighton BN1 9QJ (☎ 01273 606755, fax 01273 677196, e-mail C.Eaborn@sussex.ac.uk)

EADE, Robert Francis; s of Stanley Robert Eade (d 1994), of Hulverstone, Isle of Wight, and Kathleen Eade; *Educ* Bromsgrove, external BSc (London); *m* 1965, Mary Lindsay, da of Sidney John Coulson (d 1993), of Stratton-on-the-Fosse, Somerset; 2 s (Simon, James), 1 da (Jane); *Career* AEI (became GEC Group): sr design engr Industl Electronics Div 1963–65 (engr 1960–63), asst chief engr Devpt 1965–68; Thorn EMI plc: gen mangr then md Avo Ltd 1972–76 (tech dir 1970–72), md Measurement and Components Div 1976–79, md Thorn EMI Technology 1979–83, dir Commercial Technology 1983–85, md Int 1985–87; non-exec dir: Lloyd's Register Quality Assurance Ltd 1985–, Northern Engineering Centre 1992–95, Engineering Centre for Wales 1993–95, Sussex Careers Services 1995–; Crystalate Holdings plc: divnl dir 1987–88, gp chief exec 1988–90; conslt 1990–; dir Indust and Regions The Engrg Cncl 1992–95; memb Cncl: British Electrical and Allied Mfrs' Assoc (BEAMA) 1980–87, Standing Conf on Schs Science and Technol (SCSST) 1993–; pres: Scientific Instrument Mfrs' Assoc (SIMA) 1981–82, Assoc for the Instrumentation, Control and Automation Industry (GAMBICA) 1982–84; formerly memb: Cncl ERA Technol, Sec of State for Indust's Advsy Cncl on Calibration and Measurement, Sino Br Trade Cncl (and chm Electronics Ctee); CEng, FIEE, CIMgt, FRSA; *Style*— Robert Eade, Esq; ✉ Furnace Lodge, Furnace Farm Road, Felbridge, East Grinstead, W Sussex RH19 2PU (☎ 01342 713278)

EADES, Capt Geoffrey Alan; CBE (1989); s of Harry William Eades (d 1969), and Violet Eades (d 1985); *b* 14 Dec 1938; *Educ* Portsmouth GS, Britannia RNC; *m* 13 Aug 1966, Julia Marion, da of Richard Bastow (d 1978); 1 s (James b 1971), 1 da (Joanna b 1969); *Career* RN 1957–89: Cdr 1974, Capt 1979, Cdre RN Staff Coll 1984–86, SNO ME 1988; cmd of HM Ships: Greatford 1965, Russell 1972–74, Avenger 1977–79, Battleaxe 1983–84, Beaver and First Frigate Sqdn 1987–88; ADC to HM Queen 1987–89; naval and defence advsr: Ferranti International 1989–94, Westland Helicopters Ltd 1995–; nautical assessor to House of Lords 1991–96; memb VTS Ctee IALA 1992–; FNI 1995 (MNI 1977); *Recreations* sailing, genealogy, maritime history; *Clubs* Emsworth Sailing; *Style*— Capt Geoffrey Eades, CBE, RN; (☎ 01935 702211)

EADIE, Alastair Gordon; s of Col James Alister Eadie, DSO, TD, DL (d 1961), of Vernons Oak, Sudbury, Derbyshire; *b* 25 June 1940; *Educ* Eton; *m* 14 April 1966, Hon Jacqueline, da of 5 Baron Ashtown (d 1979); 3 s (James b 1967, Christopher b 1969, Edward b 1972); *Career* dir: Justerini & Brooks UK Ltd, Wine & Spirit Assoc of GB and NI (chm 1989–91), Wine & Spirit Benevolent Soc (chm 1987–88), The Benevolent Soc of the Licensed Trade of Scotland; pres FIVS (int wine and spirit fedn) 1996–98; tstee Grand Metropolitan Tst, memb Alcohol Educn & Research Cncl; Liveryman Worshipful Co of Distillers; *Recreations* shooting and stalking; *Clubs* Cavalry & Guards'; *Style*— Alastair Eadie, Esq; ✉ Bourne Orchard, Brickendon, Hertford SG13 8NU

EADIE, Craig Farquhar; *b* 22 April 1955; *Educ* Canford, Worcester Coll Oxford, Aix-Marseilles Univ France; *m* 3 Oct 1987, Deborah Ann, da of Leslie Burnett, of W Wycombe, Bucks; *Career* admitted slr 1980; ptnr Frere Cholmeley Bischoff 1986–; dir: Inst of Contemporary British History, Ercee (UK) Ltd, Watside Charities; legal advsr Kentish Town CAB; *Style*— Craig Eadie, Esq; ✉ 10 Denmark Road, Wimbledon, London SW19 4PG; Frere Cholmeley Bischoff, 4 John Carpenter Street, London EC4Y 0NH (☎ 0171 615 8000, fax 0171 615 8080)

EADIE, Douglas George Arnott; s of Herbert Arnott Eadie (d 1932), of Leeds, and Hannah Sophia, *née* Wingate (d 1974); *b* 16 June 1931; *Educ* Epsom Coll, The London Hosp Med Coll (MB BS, MS); *m* 7 May 1957, Gillian Carlyon, da of Maj Sydney Baron Coates, MC (d 1953); 2 s (Simon George Arnott b 1959, James Raymond b 1962), 2 da (Victoria Hannah Arnott b 1958, Lucy Jane Arnott b 1966); *Career* Capt Short Serv Cmmn RAMC 1957–60, served Far East Land Forces; Hugh Robertson exchange fell Presbyterian St Lukes Hosp Chicago USA 1963–64, conslt surgn King Edward VII Hosp of Offrs 1978–94, examiner in surgery Univ of London 1973–88; The London Hosp: surgical registrar 1963–67, sr lectr in surgery 1968–69, conslt surgn 1969–88, hon consltg surgn 1988; memb: Bd of Govrs Epsom Coll 1973–77, Cncl GMC 1983–88; treas Med Protection Soc 1986–90 (chm Cncl 1976–83), chm Med Advsy Bd The Cromwell Hosp 1990–93; Master Worshipful Soc of Apothecaries 1990–91 (memb Ct of Assts); memb Ct Univ of Bradford 1992–; memb Vascular Soc of GB & I (past hon sec); FRCS; *Recreations* country pursuits; *Clubs* MCC; *Style*— Douglas Eadie, Esq; ✉ Monks Lodge, Great Maplestead, Halstead, Essex CO9 2RN (☎ 017874 60440)

EADIE, Dugald McMillan; s of John Young Eadie (d 1984), of Aberdour, and Jean Huie Eadie; *b* 28 Oct 1944; *Educ* Kirkcaldy HS, Univ of Edinburgh (MA, Business Studies degree); *m* 3 Aug 1967, Eleanor, da of Hector Grant; 1 s (Douglas b 2 Feb 1969), 2 da (Alison b 4 Oct 1978, Heather b 18 March 1981); *Career* systems analyst Vickers Ltd 1967–68, ptnr Wood Mackenzie & Co Edinburgh 1973–84 (computer mangr 1968–73), chm and chief exec The WM Company 1984–94, gp md Henderson plc (formerly Henderson Administration Group plc) 1994–; chm Permanent Cmmn on Performance Measurement Euro Fedn of Fin Analysts Socs (EFFAS); AIIMR 1972; *Publications* Investment Analysis - A Practical Approach to Performance Measurement (1973); *Recreations* Scottish country dancing, hill walking, gardening; *Clubs* New (Edinburgh); *Style*— Dugald Eadie, Esq; ✉ Henderson Investors, 3 Finsbury Avenue, London EC2H 2PA (☎ 0171 410 4597, fax 0171 410 4414)

EADY, Anthony James; s of John James Eady (d 1995), and Doris Amy, *née* Langley (d 1988); *b* 9 July 1939; *Educ* Harrow, Hertford Coll Oxford (MA); *m* 23 June 1973, Carole June, da of Cyril Albert James Langley (d 1957); 2 s (Jeremy b 1974 d 1975, Nigel b 1976), 1 da (Joanna b 1978); *Career* Theodore Goddard and Co 1962–66, admitted slr 1966, J Henry Schroder Wagg and Co Ltd 1966–79, sec Lazard Bros and Co Ltd 1979–; Liveryman Worshipful Co of Slrs 1979; *Recreations* Hertford Soc (chm), road running; *Clubs* Thames Hare and Hounds, United Oxford and Cambridge University; *Style*— Anthony Eady, Esq; ✉ Lazard Bros and Co Ltd, 21 Moorfields, London EC2P 2HT (☎ 0171 588 2721, fax 0171 920 0670)

EADY, David; QC (1983); s of Thomas William Eady (d 1978), and Kate, *née* Day; *b* 24 March 1943; *Educ* Brentwood Sch, Trinity Coll Cambridge (MA, LLB); *m* 1974, Catherine, yr da of Joseph Thomas Wiltshire, of Bath; 1 s (James b 1977), 1 da (Caroline b 1975); *Career* called to the Bar Middle Temple 1966; recorder of the Crown Court 1986, memb Ctee on Privacy and Related Matters (The Calcutt Ctee) 1989–90; Bencher Middle Temple 1991; *Books* The Law of Contempt (jtly, with A J Arlidge, QC); *Style*— David Eady, Esq, QC; ✉ 1 Brick Ct, Temple, London EC4Y 9BY (☎ 0171 353 8845, fax 0171 583 9144)

EADY, David Max; s of Sir Wilfrid Eady, GCMG, KCB, KBE (d 1962), of Rodmell, Sussex, and Margaret Elisabeth, *née* Laistner (d 1969); *Educ* Westminster, Trinity Coll Cambridge (BA); *m* 28 Aug 1954, Gisèle Jeanne, da of Col Alfred Vacher (d 1966), of Gemozac, France; *Career* Capt Intelligence Corps 1943–45; writer and dir of: feature films, TV drama, commercials, documentaries; twice winner children's jury award Los Angeles Children's Film Festival; BISFA awards: gold, silver, bronze; winner Bronze Bear Berlin Film Festival, Acad Award nomination USA; memb: BAFTA 1955, Guild of Film Prodn Execs 1978; *Recreations* music, theatre, swimming; *Clubs* BAFTA; *Style*— David Eady, Esq; ✉ 14 Rue de la Liberation, Gemozac 17260, Charente Maritime, France (☎ 00 33 546 94 55 06)

EAGLE, Angela; MP (Lab) Wallasey (majority 3,809); da of André Eagle, and late Shirley Eagle; *b* 17 Feb 1961; *Educ* Formby HS, St John's Coll Oxford (BA); *Career* COHSE: joined as researcher 1984, later nat press offr, Parly liaison offr until 1992; MP (Lab, UNISON sponsored) Wallasey 1992–; various posts Crosby CLP 1978–80, chm Oxford Univ Fabian Club 1980–83, sec Peckham CLP 1989–91; memb Lab Pty NEC Women's Ctee 1989–92; former memb: Backbench Health Ctee and Treasy Ctee, Select Ctee on Members Interests, Select Ctee on Employment; currently oppn whip; chm Nat Conf of Lab Women 1991, chair Lab Backbench Employment Ctee; memb Exec Ctee: Socialist Health Assoc, Co-op Pty; memb NUJ, memb Br Film Inst; *Recreations* chess, cricket, cinema; *Style*— Ms Angela Eagle, MP; ✉ House of Commons, London SW1A 0AA

EAGLEN, Jane; da of Ronald Eaglen (d 1970), and Kathleen, *née* Kent; *Educ* South Park GS Lincoln, RNCM; *Career* soprano; princ memb ENO 1983–90; Peter Moores Fndn scholarship, Carl Rosa Tst award, Countess of Munster scholarship; *Performances* incl: Leonora in Il Trovatore (ENO), Elizabeth I in Mary Stuart (ENO), Eva in Die Meistersinger (ENO), Tosca (ENO, Perth Opera Aust, Buenos Aires, Cleveland Symphony Orch), Donna Anna in Don Giovanni (ENO, Scottish Opera, Vienna State Opera, Bologna Opera, Metropolitan Opera NY), Mimi in La Bohème (Scottish Opera), Fiordiligi in Cosi fan Tutte (Scottish Opera), Brunnhilde in Die Walküre (Scottish Opera, Costa Mesa USA, La Scala Milan and Vienna 1995), Brunnhilde in Siegried (Chicago), Madam Butterfly (Brisbane Opera Aust), Amelia in Un Ballo in Maschera (Bologna Opera, Opera Bastille Paris 1995), Mathilde in William Tell (Geneva Opera, Covent Garden), Norma (Scottish Opera, Seattle Opera, Ravenna Festival), recitals for Wagner Socs in London, NY and Argentina, Verdi's Requiem (gave performance for Lockerbie Disaster Appeal), Mahler's Eighth Symphony (bdcast live by Channel 4 TV); *Recordings* incl: Norma (EMI), Third Norn in Götterdämmerung (EMI), Die Flammen (Decca), Medea in Corinto (Opera Rara), Tosca (Chandos); *Style*— Miss Jane Eaglen; ✉ c/o AOR Management Ltd (Personal Management), Westwood, Lorraine Park, Harrow Weald, Middx HA3 6BX (☎ 0181 954 7646, fax 0181 420 7499)

EAGLES, Brian; s of David Eagles (d 1982), of London, and Anne, *née* Estrin (d 1994); *b* 4 Feb 1937; *Educ* Kilburn GS, Univ of London (LLB); *m* 30 May 1961, Marjorie, da of Leopold Weiss (d 1983), of London; 2 s (Simon b 1965, Paul b 1967), 1 da (Karen b 1963); *Career* slr; ptnr: J Sanson & Co 1960–67, Herbert Oppenheimer Nathan & Vandyk 1967–88, S J Berwin & Co 1988–94, Hammond Suddards 1994–; arbitrator; panel memb: World Intellectual Property Orgn (WIPO), American Arbitration Assoc, Law Soc, American Film Marketing Assoc; accredited CEDR mediator; panel mediator Central London County Ct and Patents Court; hon slr Celebrities Guild of GB 1983–; memb: Int Bar Assoc, Br Assoc of Lawyer Mediators (BALM), Int Assoc of Entertainment Lawyers, Law Soc 1960; regular contributor of articles to legal and entertainment industry publications; ACIArb; *Recreations* music, film, theatre, skiing, walking; *Style*— Brian Eagles, Esq; ✉ Montague House, 107 Frognal, Hampstead, London NW3 6XR; Hammond Suddards, Moor House, 119 London Wall, London EC2Y 5ET (☎ 0171 448 1000, fax 0171 448 1001)

EAGLES, Lt-Col (Charles Edward) James; LVO (1988); s of Maj Charles Edward Campbell Eagles, DSO, RMLI (ka 1918), and Esmé Beatrice, *née* Field (d 1965); *b* 14 May 1918; *Educ* Marlborough; *m* 1941, Priscilla May Nicolette, da of Brig Arthur Cottrell, DSO, OBE (d 1962), of Boughton Aluph Cottage, Ashford, Kent; 1 s (Anthony), 3 da (Susan, Jane, Mary); *Career* RM 1936–65; Civil Serv MOD 1965–83; HM Body Guard of Hon Corps of Gentlemen-at-Arms: memb 1967–88, Harbinger 1981–86, Standard Bearer 1986–88; *Recreations* shooting, genealogy; *Clubs* Army and Navy; *Style*— Lt-Col James Eagles, LVO; ✉ Fallowfield, Westwell, Ashford, Kent (☎ 01233 712552)

EAGLING, Wayne John; s of Eddie Eagling, and Thelma, *née* Dunsmore; *b* 27 Nov 1950; *Educ* Robert Louis Stevenson Sch Pebble Beach California, Royal Ballet Sch London; *Career* ballet dancer; Royal Ballet Co: joined 1969, soloist 1972–75, princ 1975–91; artistic dir Dutch National Ballet 1991–; created/choreographed new works incl: R B Sque (for Amnesty Int Gala 1983, Sadler's Wells Theatre 1984), Frankenstein - The Modern Prometheus (one act, for Royal Ballet 1985, La Scala Milan 1987, Dutch

Nat Ballet 1993), Beauty and the Beast (one act, for Royal Ballet 1986), Manfred (two acts), Senso (three acts), Nijinsky (two acts), Pas de Deuxs (Naples, Mantova, on RAI TV), The Queen of Spades (opera at La Scala Milan), The Wall Concert (with Roger Waters, Berlin), I Want to Break Free (video for pop group Queen), Alma (two act ballet on life of Alma Mahler, La Scala Milan) 1994; for Dutch National Ballet: Ruins of Times 1993, Symphony in Waves 1994, Duet 1995; co-choregraphed Nutcracker and Mouseking 1996 (with Toer van Schayk), Lost Touch (for Dancing for Duchenne, a Charity Gala Amsterdam) 1995, Holding a Balance (for opening of Vermeer exhbn, Mauritshuis The Hague) 1996; *Roles* classical incl: Prince Siegfried in Swan Lake, Prince Florimund in The Sleeping Beauty, The Prince in The Nutcracker, The Poet in Les Sylphides, Solor in La Bayadere, Albrecht in Giselle; by Sir Frederick Ashton incl: Colas in La Fille Mal Gardee, Tirrenio in Ondine, The Prince in Cinderella, The Young Man in The Two Pigeons, Tuesday and Friday's Child in Jazz Calendar; by Sir Kenneth MacMillan incl: The Brother in Triad (first created role), des Grieux in Manon Lescaut, Prince Rudolf in Mayerling, Edward Gordon Craig and Oskar Beregi in Isadora, Romeo and Mercutio in Romeo and Mercutio, The Messenger of Death in Song of the Earth, The Chosen One in The Rite of Spring, title role in Orpheus; by Jerome Robbins incl: Requiem Canticles, In the Night, Dances at a Gathering; by Balanchine incl: The Four Temperaments, Violin Concerto, Agon, Apollo, The Prodigal Son, Bugaku, Serenade; others incl: The Boy with Matted Hair in Tudor's Shadowplay, title role in Robert Helpmann's Hamlet, Jean de Brienne in Rudolf Nureyev's Raymonda Act III, created role of Ariel in Rudolph Nureyev's The Tempest; *Recreations* scuba diving, golf; *Style*— Wayne Eagling, Esq; ✉ Het Nationale Ballet, Het Muziektheater, Waterlooplein 22, 1011 PG Amsterdam, Netherlands (☎ 00 31 20 551 8138, fax 00 31 20 551 8071, telex 13572 MUZTH NL)

EAMES, Brian A A; *b* 12 June 1942; *Educ* Stamford Sch; *Children* 1 da (Jessica b 19 Sept 1985), 1 s (Sandy b 7 Aug 1987); *Career* trainee East Midland Allied Press 1958–64, sub-ed then chief sub-ed Berrows Newspapers 1964–68, press offr then sr press offr Imperial Group 1968–74, PR mangr Unigate Group (Foods) 1974–78, PR conslt 1978–85 (PPR Int, Y&R London, Sam Weller Associates London, Tibbenham PR of Norwich and Nottingham), PR mangr Sea Fish Indust Authy Edinburgh and London 1985–89, head of press and PR Scottish Enterprise/Scottish Devpt Agency 1989–91, sole proprietor Brian Eames Associates Edinburgh 1991–; former regnl chm: Br Assoc of Industl Eds, Inst of PR; lectr in PR strategy Univ of Stirling; Industl Writer of the Yr (Midlands) 1970, Best Newspaper (UK) 1988 and (Scotland) 1989; memb Br Assoc of Journalists, MCIM, FIPR, FAIE; *Clubs* Dalmahoy; *Style*— Brian Eames, Esq; ✉ Brian Eames Associates, 12 Liberton Drive, Edinburgh, Midlothian EH16 6NN (☎ and fax 0131 467 7048, mobile 0831 497 443)

EAMES, Baron (Life Peer UK 1995); Robert Henry Alexander; *see:* Armagh, Archbishop of

EARDLEY-WILMOT, Sir Michael John Assheton; 6 Bt (UK 1821), of Berkswell Hall, Warwickshire; s of Sir John Assheton Eardley-Wilmot, 5 Bt, LVO, DSC (d 1995), and Diana Elizabeth, *née* Moore; *b* 13 Jan 1941; *Educ* Clifton; *m* 1, 1971 (m dis 1985), Wendy, yr da of Anthony John Wolstenholme; 2 s (Benjamin John b 1974, Guy Assheton b 1979), 1 da (Holly Joanna b 1976); m 2, 1987, Diana Margaret, da of Robert Graham Wallis; 1 da (Poppy Clementine b 1987); *Heir* s, Benjamin John Eardley-Wilmot b 24 Jan 1974; *Career* md Famous Names Holdings 1974–86, md Beaufort Hotel; *Style*— Sir Michael Eardley-Wilmot, Bt; ✉ 26 Arundel Gardens, Holland Park, London W11 2LB (☎ 0171 221 6474)

EARL, Kimble David; s of late Leonard Arthur Earl, of Surrey, and Margaret Lucy, *née* Pulker; *b* 29 Nov 1951; *Educ* Caterham Sch Surrey; *Career* former: dep chief exec Argus Press Group, chief exec Newspaper Div and Consumer Publishing Div Argus Press Ltd; currently: chm and chief exec The Bull Nelson Ltd 1994–, md Landscape Holidays, md The Editorial Supplement Company, dir W A Cuthbertson Limited· former chm: Reading Newspaper Co Ltd, Windsor Newspaper Co Ltd, London and North Surrey Newspapers Ltd, West London and Surrey Newspapers Ltd, Surrey and South London Newspapers Ltd, South London Press Ltd, Argus Specialist Publications, Trident Press, Reading Newspaper Printing Co Ltd, Thames Valley Publishing, Argus Consumer Magazines Ltd, Argus Books, Argus Specialist Exhibitions, West London and Surrey Newspapers; former dir: SM Distribution Ltd, Argus Press Holdings Inc, Team Argus Inc, Argus Business Publications Ltd, Argus Retail Services Ltd; *Recreations* walking, motor coach driving, travel; *Style*— Kimble Earl, Esq; ✉ The Bull Nelson Ltd, 2/12 Whitchurch Road, Pangbourne, Reading, Berks RG8 7BP (☎ 0118 984 1394, fax 0118 984 5396)

EARL, Peter Richard Stephen; s of Peter Richard Walter Earl, and Patricia, *née* Lee; *b* 20 Jan 1955; *Educ* City of London Sch, Worcester Coll Oxford (open exhibitioner, MA, rowed for Univ), Harvard Univ (Kennedy scholar, rowed for univ); *m* Emma Elizabeth, *née* Saunders; 1 s (Peter Richard William John b 10 March 1987), 1 da (Amelia Rose Elizabeth b 8 July 1985); *Career* conslt Boston Consulting Group 1978–79, assoc Blyth Eastman Dillon Inc 1979–80, mangr Orion Bank 1980–82, dir ABC International Ltd 1982–85, vice-pres Arab Banking Corporation 1982–85, chm Tranwood Earl & Co Ltd (formerly Ifincorp Earl & Co Ltd) 1985–91, chief exec Tranwood plc 1988–91, chm and chief exec The Carter Organization Inc NYC 1990–, head of Euro corp fin Fieldstone Private Capital Group 1994–; fndr: Demerger Corporation plc 1985–, Analysis Corporation plc 1986–, The Independent Power Corporation plc 1995–; *Books* International Mergers & Acquisitions (1986); *Recreations* mountaineering (joint leader British 40th Anniversary Everest Expedition 1993), marathons, skiing; *Clubs* Vincent's, Brooks's; *Style*— Peter Earl, Esq; ✉ Prince Consort House, 27–29 Albert Embankment, London SE1 7TJ (☎ 0171 793 7676, fax 0171 793 7654)

EARL, Roger Lawrence; s of Lawrence William Earl (d 1994), of Hove, Sussex, and Doris Florence, *née* Copelin; *b* 4 Oct 1940; *Educ* St Christopher's Sch Kingswood Surrey, Hollingbury Ct Brighton Sussex, St Paul's Sch London; *m* 22 June 1968, Lynda Marion, da of late Harold Frederick Waldock, of Enfield, Middx; 2 da (Meredith Louise b 12 July 1970, Alexandra Kirsten b 20 June 1972); *Career* jr broker Arbon Langrish & Co (Lloyd's brokers) 1957–65; Bland Welch & Co/Bland Payne & Co (Lloyd's brokers): asst dir 1966–70, exec dir 1970–73, bd dir and md N American Div 1973–79; dep chm Fenchurch Group (Lloyd's brokers) 1996– (md and chief exec 1979–96), dir GPG plc 1987–89; memb: Kew Soc, Lloyd's 1970–95; *Recreations* motor sport, skiing, scuba diving, tennis; *Clubs* IOD, Hurlingham, BARC, BRSCC, HSCC, Ferrari Owners', Automobile Club de Monaco, Annabel's; *Style*— Roger Earl, Esq; ✉ 4 Cumberland Rd, Kew, Surrey TW9 3HQ (☎ 0181 948 1714, fax 0181 948 5737); Flouquet, Lacour de Visa, Tarn et Garonne, France; La Carabela, 28 Via Del Bosque, Canyamel, Mallorca, Spain; Fenchurch PLC, 136 Minories, London EC3N 1QN (☎ 0171 264 4125, fax 0171 264 4279, car 0831 283135/0836 201420, telex 8870047 LOQOTE G/884442 LOQOTE LONDON)

EARLAM, Richard John; s of Francis Earlam, MD (d 1959), of Mossley Hill, Liverpool, and Elspeth (Elsie) Noeline, *née* Skippers (d 1993); *b* 26 March 1934; *Educ* Liverpool Coll, Uppingham, Trinity Hall Cambridge (MA, MChir), Univ of Liverpool; *m* 6 Sept 1969, Roswitha, da of Alfons Teuber, playwright (d 1971), of Munich; 2 da (Melissa b 1976, Caroline b 1979); *Career* Capt RAMC 1960–62, surgical specialist Br Mil Hosp Hong Kong, TA MO 359 Field Regt RA; conslt gen surgn The London Hosp 1972, Fulbright scholar 1966, Alexander Von Humboldt fellowship W Germany 1968; chm: NE Thames Regnl Advsy Ctee in Gen Surgery, MRC Sub Ctee on Oesophageal Cancer; memb MRC: Cancer Therapy Ctee, Manpower Ctee; examiner RCS 1982–86, res asst Mayo Clinic USA 1966–67, clinical asst to Prof Zenker Munich 1968; memb RSM, FRCS; *Books* Clinical Tests of Oesophageal Function (1976), ABC of Major Trauma (co-ed, 1991, 2 edn 1996), Trauma Care (HEMS London, ed 1997); author of chapters and papers on abdominal surgery, oesophagus, stomach and gallbladder disease, epidemiology, surgical audit and coding; *Recreations* tennis, mountains summer and winter, beekeeping; *Clubs* Association of Surgeons, Collegium Internationale Chirurgiae Digestivae, Furniture History Soc, Bayerische Yacht, British Dragon Assoc; *Style*— Richard John Earlam, Esq; ✉ 4 Pembroke Gardens, London W8 6HS (☎ 0171 602 5255); 55 Harley St, London W1N 1DD (☎ 0171 637 4288)

EARLE, Sir (Hardman) George Algernon; 6 Bt (UK 1869), of Allerton Tower, Woolton, Lancs; s of Sir Hardman Alexander Mort Earle, 5 Bt (d 1979), and Maie, Lady Earle (d 1986); *b* 4 Feb 1932; *Educ* Eton; *m* 24 Jan 1967, Diana Gillian Bligh, da of Col Frederick Ferris Bligh St George, CVO (d 1970), ggs of Sir Richard Bligh St George, 2 Bt; 1 s (Robert George Bligh b 1970), 1 da (Katharine Susan b 1968); *Heir* s, Robert George Bligh Earle, b 24 Jan 1970; *Career* Nat Serv Ensign in Grenadier Gds; memb of London Metal Exchange 1962–73; *Recreations* fox hunting, sailing; *Clubs* Royal Yacht Sqdn; *Style*— Sir George Earle, Bt; ✉ Box 236, 2 Old Brompton Road, London SW7 3DQ (☎ 0171 413 9542)

EARLE, Dr James Henry Oliver; s of John James Earle (d 1942), of Worcester Park, Surrey, and Constance Mary, *née* Gardner; *b* 5 June 1920; *Educ* Tiffin GS Kingston-upon-Thames, King's Coll London, Westminster Med Sch (MD, BS); *m* 1, 26 Dec 1942 (m dis 1976), Jean Bessell, da of Edmund Bessell Whalley (d 1968), of Rogate, Sussex; 1 s (Nigel James b 1948), 1 da ((Mary) Jane b 1944); m 2, 7 Sept 1976, Lady Helen Norah, wid of Rt Hon Lord Runcorn, TD (d 1968), da of Sir Crosland Graham (d 1946), of Clwyd Hall, Ruthin, N Wales; *Career* lectr and sr lectr in clinical pathology Westminster Med Sch 1949–53, asst conslt pathologist Royal Marsden Hosp 1953–56, conslt pathologist and dir laboratories Royal Masonic Hosp 1956–63, conslt pathologist Teaching Gp Westminster Hosp 1963–85; vice pres Marie Curie Fndn (Cancer Care) 1993– (memb Cncl and Exec Ctee 1953–93); memb: Academic Bd Westminster Med Sch (subsequently Charing Cross Med Sch) 1970–85, Bd of Govrs Westminster Hosp 1972–74; rep Univ of London Kingston and Richmond Health Authy 1974–82 (vice chm 1978–82), chm DMT and Area Scientific Ctee Roehampton Health Dist 1974–82; Silver Jubilee medal 1977; Freeman City of London 1978, Liveryman Worshipful Soc of Apothecaries 1977; FRSM, FRCPath, MRCS, LRCP; *Recreations* fishing, gardening, opera, photography; *Style*— Dr James Earle; ✉ 18 Hillside, Wimbledon SW19 4NL (☎ and fax 0181 946 3507)

EARLE, Joel Vincent (Joe); s of James Basil Foster Earle (d 1989), of Kyle of Lochalsh, Ross-shire, and Mary Isabel Jessie, *née* Weeks (d 1992); *b* 1 Sept 1952; *Educ* Westminster, New Coll Oxford (BA); *m* 10 May 1980, Sophia Charlotte, da of Oliver Arbuthnot Knox, of London; 2 s (Leo b 1981, Martin b 1984); *Career* V&A Museum: keeper Far Eastern Dept 1983–87 (res asst 1974–77, asst keeper 1977–83), head of public servs 1987; exhibitions co-ordinator and head of public affairs Japan Festival 1991; ind arts conslt 1991–; maj exhibitions: Japan Style 1980, Gt Japan Exhibition 1981, Toshiba Gallery of Japanese Art 1986, Visions of Japan 1991, Songs of My People 1992; tstee The Design Museum; *Books* An Introduction to Netsuke (1980), An Introduction to Japanese Prints (1980), The Great Japan Exhibition (contrib, 1981), The Japanese Sword (translator, 1983), Japanese Art and Design (ed, 1987), Masterpieces by Shibata Zeshin (1995), The Index of Inro Artists (ed, 1995), The Khalili Collection of Japanese Art: Lacquer (ed, 1995), Flower Bronzes of Japan (1995); *Style*— Joe Earle, Esq; ✉ 123 Middleton Rd, London E8 4LL (☎ 0171 923 2662, fax 0171 923 2668, e-mail joe@bunkajin.demon.co.uk)

EARLE, Michael George; s of Henry George Earle (d 1984), of Hambleden, nr Henley-on-Thames, Oxon, and Elizabeth Mary, *née* Wheeler (d 1953); *b* 30 July 1944; *Educ* Sir William Borlase's Sch; *Career* dir Keene Game Products (UK) Ltd 1978–, md & dir British & General Tube Co Ltd 1977–84, dir Globelion Ltd 1984–, md Barnham Press Ltd 1985–95, dir Barfields Ltd 1990–, md Concept Response Ltd 1992–, md Barnham & Gurney Printers Ltd 1995–; *Recreations* shooting; *Style*— Michael Earle, Esq; ✉ 227 Marlow Bottom, Marlow, Bucks (☎ 01628 471618); Barnham Press Ltd, Marlborough Trading Estate, High Wycombe, Bucks HP11 2LB (☎ 01494 450631)

EARLE, Peter Desmond Noel; s of late Brigadier E G Earle, DSO, of Walton Hall, Bletchley, Bucks, and late Noel Fielding-Johnson, *née* Downs-Martin; *b* 20 Nov 1923; *Educ* Wellington, Ch Ch Oxford; *m* 6 Sept 1953, Hope, da of Wallace Sinclair Macgregor, of Vancouver, BC; 1 s (Robert b 1959), 2 da (Heather b 1960, Melanie b 1964); *Career* served RN 1942–47 home waters, South Atlantic, Indian Ocean and Pacific (Far East) Lt RNVR exec officer, navigator; company dir; pres The Country Gentlemen's Associations plc (chief exec 1972–86, chm 1983–86); editor CGA magazine and guide to country living (Hutchinson & David Charles); *Recreations* gardening, writing, swimming, tennis, skiing, yachting; *Clubs* Naval (vice pres), Dwits; *Style*— Peter Earle, Esq; ✉ 30 Hill Rise, Croxton, Thetford, Norfolk IP24 1LL (☎ 01842 763536)

EARLE, Richard Greville; DL (Dorset 1984); s of John Greville Earle, JP (d 1933), and Jacobina Reid, *née* Clark (d 1970); *b* 12 Nov 1925; *Educ* Winchester, Trinity Coll Cambridge (MA); *m* 19 Jan 1956, Joanna Mary Earle, JP, da of Cdr Henry Kelsall Beckford Mitchell, RN, CBE, JP, DL, of Sherborne, Dorset; 2 da (Elizabeth b 1957, Susan b 1959); *Career* RNVR 1943–47, Sub Lt (A); farmer and landowner; dir Wessex Grain Ltd 1985–; chm: Dorset NFU 1964, Dorset Small Industs Ctee (COSIRA) 1972–81, Standing Conf on Oil and Gas Exploration English Channel 1980–84, Leonard Cheshire Fndn Appeal in W Dorset 1985–88, W Dorset Family Support Serv 1987–93, Dorset CLA 1988–90; vice pres Community Cncl for Dorset 1990–; memb: Dorset CC 1967–85, Cncl CLA 1985–91; govr Kingston Maurward Collcd 1990–, hon treas Int Dendrology Soc 1994–, dir Dendrology Charitable Co 1994–; High Sheriff of Dorset 1983; *Recreations* countryside; *Clubs* Farmers'; *Style*— Richard Earle, Esq, DL; ✉ Frankham Farm, Ryme Intrinseca, Sherborne DT9 6JT (☎ 01935 872304)

EARLE, (Michael) Roderick; s of Rev Dennis Edward Joseph Earle (d 1971), and Fenella Ross Puddicombe (d 1966); *b* 29 Jan 1952; *Educ* King's Coll Taunton, St John's Coll Cambridge (choral scholar, MA), RCM (fndn scholar); *m* 29 July 1982, Angela Margaret Bostock; 1 s (Benjamin Michael Edward b 26 June 1983), 1 da (Fenella Therèse Mary Mima b 6 July 1990); *Career* bass-baritone; winner Gtr London Arts Assoc Musician of the Year Award 1976; worked with: L'Orchestre National du Capitole de Toulouse (under Michel Plasson), Royal Scottish Nat Orch (under Neeme Järve and Jansug Kakhidze), Philharmonia (under Charles Dutoit, Leonard Slatkin and James Levine), City of Birmingham Symphony Orch, Bournemouth Symphony, Polish Radio (under Anthony Witt), RPO, LSO (under Sir Colin Davis), LPO, London Sinfonietta, BBC Symphony Orch; recent concerts incl: Beethoven's Missa Solennis (for RAI Milano under Garry Bertini), Stravinsky's Les Noces (BBC Proms under Peter Eötvös); *Roles* with Royal Opera House: Antonio in Le Nozze di Figaro (debut 1980), Angelotti in Tosca, Masetto in Don Giovanni, Zuniga in Carmen, Hobson in Peter Grimes, Crespel in Les Côntes D'Hoffman, Schaunard in La Bohème, Abimélech in Samson et Dalila, the Bonze in Madama Butterly, Orestes in Elektra, Monterone in Rigoletto, Brander in La Damnation de Faust, Harasta in Cunning Little Vixen, Kothner in Die Meistersinger von Nurnberg, The Philospher in Chérubin, King Fisher in The Midsummer Marriage, Alberich in Siegfried and Götterdämmerung, Mandarin in Turandot (at Wembley Arena); King in Aida (ENO), Brander in La Damnation de Faust (ENO), Figaro in Le

Nozze di Figaro (Scottish Opera), Leporello in Don Giovanni, Giorgio in I Puritani and He-Ancient in The Midsummer Marriage (all for Opera North), Fafner in Rhinegold and Hunding in Die Walküre (both for Welsh Nat Opera), Angelotti in Tosca (Earls Court Arena) 1990, Kothner in Die Meistersinger (Teatro Regio Turin), Melchior in Amahl and the Night Visitors, Méhul's Uthal (Edinburgh Festival), Ariodante and Cavalli's Jason (Buxton Festival), Berlioz's Méphistophélès (Taormina Festival), Renard (Israel Festival), Jupiter in Castor et Pollux (Athens Festival), Leporello in Don Giovanni (Opera NI), Dolcamara in L'Elisir D'Amore (Opera Ireland); *Videos* La Fanciulla del West, Manon Lescaut, Andrea Chénier, Carmen, Salome, Otello, Traviata; Meeting Venus (sound track for film); *Television* Rossini's Stabat Mater (with BBC Welsh Symphony under Frühbeck de Burgos) 1991, Brander in Berlioz's Damnation de Faust (with L'Orchestre de Lyon under Emmanuel Krivine) Winter Olympics Festival 1992; *Recordings* Ferneyhough's Transit, Rossini's Stabat Mater (with Richard Hickox, nominated for Gramaphone Award 1990); *Recreations* family, gardening, architecture (particularly churches), reading, discovering new music; *Style*— Roderick Earle, Esq; ✉ Cotterstock, Crawley End, Chrishall, Nr Royston SG8 8QJ (☎ and fax 01763 838426; c/o Athole Still International Management, 25–27 Westow Street, London SE19 3RY (☎ 0181 771 5271, fax 0181 771 8172)

EARLES, Prof Stanley William Edward; s of William Edward Earles (d 1984), of Birmingham, and Winnifred Anne, *née* Cook (d 1959); *b* 18 Jan 1929; *Educ* King's Coll London (BSc, PhD, AKC), Univ of London (DSc); *m* 23 July 1955, Margaret Isabella, da of John Brown (d 1988), of Wormley, Hertfordshire; 2 da (Melanie Jane b 1962, Lucy Margaret b 1964); *Career* scientific offr Admiralty Engrg Laboratory 1953–55; Dept of Mechanical Engrg QMC: lectr 1955–69, reader 1969–75, prof 1975–76; King's Coll London: prof of mechanical engrg 1976–94, emeritus prof 1994–, head of Mechanical Engrg Dept 1976–90 and 1991–94, head of Sch of Physical Scis and Engrg 1990–91; dean of engrg Univ of London 1986–90; govr: Goff's Sch Hertfordshire 1964–88, Turnford Sch Hertfordshire 1970–87, Univ of Hertfordsire (formerly Hatfield Poly) 1989–93; FIMechE 1976, FEng 1992, FKC 1993; *Recreations* real tennis, gardening; *Style*— Prof Stanley Earles, FEng; ✉ Woodbury, Church Lane, Wormley, Broxbourne, Herts EN10 7QF (☎ 01992 464 616); Department of Mechanical Engineering, King's Coll, Strand, London WC2R 2LS (☎ 0171 873 2277, fax 0171 873 2437)

EARLS, Mark Benedict; s of Gerard Warmington Earls, of Harrow, Middx, and Kathleen Mary, *née* Orchard; *b* 12 July 1961; *Educ* John Lyon Sch Harrow, St Edmund Hall Oxford (BA); *Career* trainee Grey London (advtg agency) 1984–86, planner/sr planner Boase Massimi Pollit 1986–89, actg head of planning CDP Financial 1989–90; Ammirati and Puris/Lintas (formerly S P Lintas): sr planner/bd dir 1990–95, dir of planning Europe 1994–95; bd planning dir Bates Dorland 1995–; memb Ctee Account Planning Gp 1994–; memb Market Research Soc 1986; *Recreations* cricket (chm Wandsworth Gods CC), travel, walking, Italian cuisine, oysters; *Clubs* Vincent's; *Style*— Mark Earls, Esq; ✉ Bates Dorland Ltd, 121–141 Westbourne Terrace, London W2 6JR (☎ 0171 262 5077)

EARP, Denis Nigel Warriner; s of Fred Stanley Earp, and Ethel Marjorie, *née* Warriner; *b* 11 Oct 1929; *Educ* Bootham Sch York, King's Coll Cambridge (exhibitioner, state scholar, MA); *m* 1, 18 Sept 1954, Audrey Patricia, da of Arthur Percival Winsor; 2 s (Roger David b 20 Jan 1959, Michael John b 10 July 1960); m 2, 19 Dec 1975, Jean Mary Robbins, da of Gilbert George Francis Malpass; *Career* asst engr Binnie & Partners Consulting Engineers 1952–62, sr engr South Staffordshire Waterworks Co 1962–70, dep chief engr Colne Valley Water Co 1970–74, tech dir Welsh Water Authority 1984–86 (div mangr 1974–84), conslt Binnie & Partners 1986–94; panel AR engr DOE 1978–; former memb Ctee: Inst of Civil Engrs, Int Congress on Large Dams, Br Dam Soc, BSI, Nat Water Cncl, Water Authys Assoc, Inst of Water Engrs and Scientists, Inst of Mgmnt; elder United Reformed Church, former hon treas Cmmn of Covenanted Churches in Wales; FCIWEM 1970, FICE 1971 (MICE 1956), FEng 1988; *Recreations* travel, theatre, music, reading, voluntary work; *Style*— Denis Earp, Esq, FEng; ✉ 3 The Dell, Gower Rd, Killay, Swansea SA2 7DX (☎ 01792 204902)

EAST RIDING, Archdeacon of; *see:* Buckingham, Ven Hugh Fletcher

EASSON, Prof Angus; s of William Coleridge Easson (d 1987), and Olive Mary, *née* Hornfeck (d 1962); *b* 18 July 1940; *Educ* William Ellis GS, Univ of Nottingham (BA), Univ of Oxford (DPhil); *Career* lectr in English: Univ of Newcastle upon Tyne 1965–71, Royal Holloway Coll Univ of London 1971–77; Univ of Salford: prof of English 1977–, dean Faculty of Social Sciences and Arts 1986–89 and 1992–95, chm Modern Languages Dept 1989–92, chm English Dept 1992–; *Books* Elizabeth Gaskell (1979), Elizabeth Gaskell · Critical Heritage (1991); *Recreations* opera; *Style*— Prof Angus Easson; ✉ University of Salford, English Department, Salford, Greater Manchester M5 4WT (☎ 0161 745 5029)

EASSON, Malcolm Cameron Greig; s of Prof Eric Craig Easson (d 1983), of Cheshire, and Moira McKechnie, *née* Greig; *b* 7 April 1949; *Educ* Marple Hall GS, Univ of Manchester; *m* 6 July 1972, Gillian, da of Stanley Oakley, of Cheshire; 1 s (James b 1979), 1 da (Helen b 1982); *Career* princ of firm of CAs specialising in taxation and finance for doctors of med, regular contrib of fin articles to medical jls; FICA; *Recreations* golf, gardening, reading, music; *Style*— Malcolm C G Easson, Esq; ✉ Fieldhead, Macclesfield Road, Prestbury, Cheshire SK10 4BH; Rex Buildings, Wilmslow, Cheshire SK9 1HZ (☎ 01625 527351)

EAST, John Hilary Mortlock; s of Grahame Richard East, CMG (d 1993), and Cynthia Mildred, *née* Beck; *b* 6 March 1947; *Educ* St Paul's, BNC Oxford; *m* 22 Aug 1970, (Dorothy) Diane, da of Roy Cuthbert Tregidgo; 2 s (Richard b 1976, Jonathan b 1985), 2 da (Tamsyn b 1974, Emily b 1978); *Career* admitted slr 1972; Clifford Chance: ptnr 1976–, managing ptnr Singapore 1983–85, managing ptnr Hong Kong 1991–95; formerly govr Seaton House Sch Ltd Sutton Surrey; Freeman Worshipful Co of Slrs; memb Law Soc; *Recreations* rugby fives, real tennis, cricket, cinema, reading, theatre; *Clubs* Singapore Cricket, Hong Kong Cricket, Hong Kong, Jesters, The Royal Tennis Court (Hampton Court Palace); *Style*— John East, Esq; ✉ Clifford Chance, 200 Aldersgate Street, London EC1A 4JJ (☎ 0171 600 1000, fax 0171 600 5555)

EAST, John Richard Alan; s of Bertram David (Barry) East, of Eaton Square, London, and Gladys, *née* Stone (d 1957); *b* 14 May 1949; *Educ* Westminster; *m* 1, 14 May 1971 (m dis 1986), Judith Adrienne, da of Clive Hill, of Horshall, Surrey; 2 s (Robin b 1974, Christopher b 1978); m 2, 12 July 1986, Charlotte Sylvia, da of Lt Cdr Peter Gordon Merriman, DSC, RN (d 1965); *Career* Speechly Bircham (Slrs) 1967–70, Mitton Butler Priest & Co Ltd 1971–73, Panmure Gordon & Co 1973–77; Margetts & Addenbrooke (formerly Margetts & Addenbrooke East Newton, Kent East Newton & Co) 1977–86: sr ptnr 1977–80, managing ptnr 1980–86, sr ptnr 1983–86; dir: National Investment Group plc 1986–87, Guidehouse Group plc and subsids 1987–91; chm and chief exec John East & Partners Ltd (formerly Guidehouse Securities Ltd) 1987–; memb Stock Exchange 1974, MSI (dip) 1992; tstee and memb Ctee The Square Mile Charitable Tst; *Recreations* music, the playing and recording of electronic musical instruments, travel; *Clubs* Carlton, United & Cecil; *Style*— John East, Esq; ✉ Hermiston, 110 Victoria Drive, Wimbledon, London SW19 6PS (☎ 0181 789 4918); John East & Partners Ltd, Crystal Gate, 28–30 Worship Street, London EC2A 2AH (☎ 0171 628 2200, fax 0171 628 4473)

EAST, Prof Robin Alexander; s of Percy Alexander East (d 1981), of Romsey, Hants, and Winifred May, *née* Southwell (d 1993); *b* 11 Dec 1935; *Educ* Barton Peveril GS, Univ of Southampton (BSc, PhD); *m* 6 Oct 1962, June, da of George Henry Slingsby (d 1977), of Sheffield; 1 da (Jennifer Lynn b 1963); *Career* apprentice Vickers Supermarine 1953–57, visiting res fell Aust Nat Univ at Canberra 1973; Univ of Southampton: Sir Alan Cobham res fell 1960–63, lectr, sr lectr and reader in aeronautics 1963–85, head of Aeronautics Dept 1985–90, prof of aeronautics 1985–; memb various ctees and former chm Southampton Branch RAeS, chm Accreditation Ctee RAeS 1991–; memb Aviation Ctee DTI 1995–; assoc fell American Inst of Aeronautics and Astronautics 1991; CEng 1983, FRAeS 1985; *Books* Forty Years of the Spitfire (jt ed with I C Cheeseman, 1976), Spacecraft Systems Engineering (contrib, 1991); around 90 pubns on hypersonic aerodynamics and experimental facilities in int jls and conf proceedings; *Recreations* gardening, photography, ornithology, walking; *Style*— Prof Robin East; ✉ East Croft, North Common, Sherfield English, Romsey, Hants SO51 6JT (☎ 01794 340444); Dept of Aeronautics & Astronautics, Univ of Southampton, Southampton, Hants SO17 1BJ (☎ 01703 592324, fax 01703 593058)

EASTAWAY, Nigel Antony; s of Kenneth George Eastaway, and Muriel, *née* Angus; *b* 17 Nov 1943; *Educ* Chigwell Sch; *m* 17 Aug 1968, Ann, da of Cecil Douglas Geddes; 1 s (James Nigel Andrew b 18 May 1983), 1 da (Suzanne Emma Louise b 4 July 1980); *Career* CA; ptnr Moores Rowland; author of books on taxation: Moores Rowland's Yellow Tax Guide, Moores Rowland's Orange Tax Guide, Moores Rowland's Taxation of Farmers and Farming, Moores Rowland's A to Z of Tax Planning, Moores Rowland's Tax Planning for Recording Stars, Cousins Moores Rowland's Visiting Entertainers and Sportsmen, Handbook on the Capital Gains Tax 1979, Tax and Financial Planning for Medical Practitioners, Tax and Financial Planning for Professional Partnerships, Practical Share Valuation, Share Valuation Cases, Utilising Personal Tax Losses and Reliefs, Tax Aspects of Company Reorganisations, Utilising Company Tax Losses and Reliefs, Intellectual Property Law and Taxation, Allied Dunbar Expatriate Tax and Investment Guide, Taxation of Lloyd's Underwriters, Principles of Capital Transfer Tax, Hong Kong Stamp Duty, Tolley's Self-Assessment, Simons Taxes (contrib), ICAEW Taxation Service (contrib); tstee Russian Aviation Res Tst; memb: Taxation Ctee London C of C and Indust, Cncl Chartered Inst of Taxation (vice chm Tech Ctee); MBAE, FCA, FCCA, FCMA, FCIS, FTII, AIIT, fell Hong Kong Soc of Accountants, hon fell Hong Kong Inst of Taxation, fell Offshore Inst, memb Int Tax Planning Assoc; *Books* Soviet Aircraft Since 1918 (ed), Aircraft of the Soviet Union (contrib), Encyclopaedia of Russian Aircraft (contrib), Mikoyan MiG-21 (contrib), The Soviet Air Force (contrib), Janes All the World's Aircraft (contrib); *Recreations* Russian aircraft, playing with old cars, Bentleys, Jaguars and Morgans; *Clubs* Wig & Pen, Bentley Drivers', Vintage Sports Car, Morgan Sports Car, Air Britain; *Style*— Nigel Eastaway, Esq; ✉ Moores Rowland, Cliffords Inn, Fetter Lane, London EC4A 1AS (☎ 0171 831 2345, fax 0171 831 3004, mobile 0860 328500)

EASTEAL, Martin; s of Charles Owen Easteal (d 1994), of Seaton, Devon, and Iris Joan, *née* King; *b* 4 Nov 1947; *Educ* Buckhurst Hill Co HS, UC Oxford (MA), Harvard Univ (Knox fell); *m* 1972, Barbara Mary, *née* Clark; 2 da (Susanna b 1975, Sophie b 1980); *Career* asst princ then princ HM Treasy 1970–74, asst chief exec London Borough of Ealing 1974–79, general mangr Harlow Cncl 1979–83; dir: Public Policy PA Consulting Group 1983–88, Nat Audit Office 1988–92; chief exec: Local Govt Cmmn for England 1992–96, Chelmsford BC 1996–; memb: NE Thames Regnl Health Authy, Eastern Arts Assoc, Electricity Consumers Ctee, Harlow Theatre Trust, Essex Policy Authy, Princess Alexandra NHS Tst; fndr annual Redcliffe-Maud Meml Lecture; Freeman City of Norwalk California; FIMgt 1977, FIPM 1978, FRSA 1993, FRGS 1993; *Books* Nixon's Style of Government (1972), The Development of the General Manager (1985), Management Information Systems in Whitehall (1989); *Recreations* music, vintage cars; *Clubs* Reform; *Style*— Martin Easteal, Esq; ✉ Chelmsford Borough Council, Civic Centre, Duke Street, Chelmsford, Essex CM1 1JE (☎ 01245 490490)

EASTEN, Julian Maitland; s of George Maitland Easten (d 1961), of Newcastle-upon-Tyne, and Winifred, *née* Elliott (d 1987); *b* 14 Feb 1935; *Educ* Bedford Sch; *m* 1, 1957 (m dis 1989), Audrey, *née* Maris; 1 da (Linzi b 13 Jan 1957); m 2, Frances Penelope, da of Maurice Edward Cooke; 1 da (Alice Amelia b 13 Aug 1992); *Career* mgmnt trainee Rootes Group automobile mfrs Coventry 1952–53, asst mangr Competitions Dept Mintex Ltd responsibile for servs and PR for Grand Prix and Int Rally teams 1955–57, sales dir Rootes and Lotus Dealers (concurrently rally driver in nat and int events) 1958–61, zone, then regnl rising to nat sales mangr Volkswagen UK 1962–72, ind conslt to motor indust 1972–75, photography student Poly of Central London 1975–77, freelance advtg and editorial photographer 1977–; reg contrib various mags incl Country Life, music indust credits incl Kiri te Kanawa (Arabella), Jorge Bolet, Sophie Rolland, Christopher Hogwood, The Lindsay String and The Purcell Quartets; memb Assoc of Photographers 1979 (past vice chm, Northern chm, memb Judging Panel 11th Awards); *Books* Alexander Technique in Pregnancy (photographic contrib, 1993); *Recreations* motor sport; *Style*— Julian Easten, Esq; ✉ 10 Dover Road, Hunters Bar, Sheffield S11 8RH (☎ and fax 0114 268 7255)

EASTERLING, Prof Patricia Elizabeth; da of Edward Wilson Fairfax (d 1978), and Annie, *née* Smith (d 1989); *b* 11 March 1934; *Educ* Blackburn HS for Girls, Newnham Coll Cambridge (BA, MA); *m* 22 Dec 1956, (Henry) John Easterling, s of Rev Claude Easterling (d 1962); 1 s (Henry Thomas Fairfax b 1963); *Career* asst lectr Univ of Manchester 1957–58; Newnham Coll Cambridge: asst lectr 1958–60, fell and lectr 1960–87, vice princ 1981–86, hon fell 1987–94, professorial fell 1994–; univ lectr Univ of Cambridge 1969–87, prof of Greek UCL 1987–, Regius prof of Greek Univ of Cambridge 1994–; pres Classical Assoc 1988–89, pres Hellenic Soc 1996–; chm: Ctees of Jt Assoc of Classical Teachers, Cncl of Univ Classical Depts 1991–93; memb Academia Europaea 1995–; hon doctorate Univ of Athens 1996; *Books* Ovidiana Graeca (with E J Kenney, 1965), Sophocles Trachiniae (ed, 1982), Cambridge History of Classical Literature I (jt ed B M W Knox, 1985), Greek Religion and Society (jt ed J V Muir, 1985), The Cambridge Companion to Greek Tragedy (ed, 1997); *Recreations* walking; *Style*— Prof P E Easterling; ✉ Newnham College, Cambridge CB3 9DF (☎ 01223 335700, fax 01223 357898)

EASTERMAN, Nicholas Barrie; s of Cyril Saul Herman Easterman, of Lausanne, Switzerland, and Sheila, *née* Cope (d 1983); *b* 11 April 1950; *Educ* Millfield, UCL (LLB), Cncl of Legal Educn; *Career* called to the Bar Lincoln's Inn 1975; memb Lincoln's Inn 1969; *Recreations* photography, driving, good wine and cognac; *Clubs* RAC, Wig & Pen; *Style*— Nicholas Easterman, Esq; ✉ 4 Brick Court, Temple EC4Y 9AD (☎ 0171 797 8910)

EASTHAM, Kenneth; MP (Lab) Manchester Blackley; s of late James Eastham; *b* 11 Aug 1927; *Educ* Openshaw Tech Coll; *m* 1951, Doris, da of Albert Howarth; *Career* former planning engr GEC Trafford Park; cncllr Manchester City Cncl 1962–80 (sometime dep ldr, chm Educn Ctee), memb NW Econ Planning Cncl 1975–79; MP (Lab, AUEW sponsored) Manchester Blackley 1979–, memb Employment Select Ctee; *Style*— Kenneth Eastham, Esq, MP; ✉ House of Commons, London SW1A 0AA

EASTMAN, Brian Ralph; s of Leonard Eastman (d 1969), of Ashtead, Surrey, and Edith, *née* Beakhust (d 1983); *b* 31 May 1940; *Educ* Glyn Sch Epsom, Kingston Coll of Art (DArch); *m* 16 May 1964, (Dorothy) Mary, da of Arthur Randall (d 1973), of Ashtead, Surrey; 2 s (Andrew b 5 May 1965, Mark b 18 June 1966), 1 da (Ruth b 10 Aug 1972); *Career* Philip Goodhew Partnership chartered architects: assoc 1960–74, ptnr 1974–79, princ 1979–; conslt architect: Wandsworth Borough Cncl 1963–91, City of Westminster 1987–94; dir 54 Warwick Square Ltd; co sec: 52–53 Warwick Square Ltd, Tokenspin

Ltd, Warwick Square Co Ltd; chm Crawley Planning Gp 1975–78; churchwarden Ifield Team 1984–89, ldr Scout Assoc; RIBA 1965; *Clubs* IOD, Sloane, Crawley, S of England Agric Society; *Style—* Brian Eastman, Esq; ✉ 182 Buckswood Drive, Crawley RH11 8PS (☎ 01293 529414); Philip Goodhew Partnership, Chartered Architects, 54 Warwick Square, Westminster, London SW1V 2AJ (☎ 0171 828 1042, fax 0171 630 0270)

EASTMOND, Dr Clifford John; s of Charles John Henry Eastmond (d 1980), and Hilda, *née* Horrocks; *b* 19 Jan 1945; *Educ* Audenshaw GS, Univ of Edinburgh Med Sch (BSc, MB ChB, MD); *m* 25 March 1967, Margaret, da of Stanley Wadsworth (d 1976); 2 s (Nigel b 1970, Timothy b 1972), 1 da (Heather b 1975); *Career* house physician Northern Gen Hosp Edinburgh 1969, house surgn Royal Infirmary Edinburgh 1970, sr house offr Sefton Gen Hosp Liverpool 1970, registrar Liverpool Hosps 1971–74, res fell Univ of Liverpool Med Sch 1974–76, sr registrar Rheumatism Res Unit Leeds Univ and Gen Infirmary 1976–79, conslt rheumatologist Grampian Health Bd 1979–95, conslt rheumatologist Aberdeen Royal Hosps NHS Trust 1995– (clinical dir of med 1995–); clinical sr lectr Univ of Aberdeen 1979–; elder Skene Parish Church, memb and past pres Westhill and Dist Rotary Club 1989–90, memb Cairngorm Mountaineering Club; memb Br Soc of Rheumatology (cncl memb 1987–90), FRCPEd 1984, FRCP 1990; *Recreations* Scottish mountaineering, skiing, music; *Style—* Dr Clifford Eastmond; ✉ Whinmoor, 34 Leslie Crescent, Westhill, Skene, Aberdeenshire AB32 6UZ (☎ 01224 741009); Aberdeen Royal Hospitals NHS Trust, Foresterhill, Aberdeen AB9 2ZB (☎ 01224 681818)

EASTOE, Roger; *Career* working on women's magazines with D C Thomson 1968–70, IPC Women's Magazines 1970–74 (latterly advertisement mangr Young Magazine Section), mgmnt positions at Punch Publications working on Punch and High Life (British Airways in-flight magazine) 1974–76; Mirror Group Newspapers: joined as sales devpt exec 1976, advertisement dir 1982, bd dir 1984–, dep md 1990–; memb numerous industry ctees incl Audit Bureau of Circulations (former chm); *Style—* Roger Eastoe, Esq; ✉ Mirror Group plc, One Canada Square, Canary Wharf, London E14 5AP (☎ 0171 293 3844, fax 0171 293 3843)

EASTON, Anthony Miles; s of Peter Easton, of Dorset, and Bobbie Easton (d 1987); *b* 3 Oct 1963; *Educ* St Paul's, Chelsea Sch of Art, St Martin's Sch of Art; *m* Anna Claire, da of Richard Curtis; *Career* freelance graphic designer and TV prog maker 1983–87, bd dir Saatchi & Saatchi Advertising 1989–92 (art dir 1987–89), head of art Chiat/Day 1992–93; dir: with Howard Guard Productions 1993–95, with Stark Films 1995–; Best Press Campaign (Gold) Campaign Press Awards 1990, Best Magazine Ad and Best Campaign D&AD Awards 1990, Best Newspaper Ad D&AD Awards 1992; *Recreations* art, politics, media, sport; *Style—* Anthony Easton, Esq; ✉ Stark Films, 6–10 Lexington Street, London W1R 3HS (☎ 0171 287 3229)

EASTON, Ewan Reid; s of Norman Kidston Easton (d 1987), of Killearn, Stirlingshire, and Alison Gray, *née* Reid; *b* 10 May 1958; *Educ* Kelvinside Acad Glasgow, Sedbergh, Univ of Glasgow; *Career* Maclay Murray & Spens: apprentice 1980–82, slr 1982–84, seconded to Herbert Smith Slrs London 1984–85, ptnr Maclay Murray & Spens 1985–, head Litigation Dept 1992–; litigation advsr to various Scottish cos, slr to Edinburgh Festival 1990–; library curator and memb Cncl WS Soc 1994–; WS 1988; *Recreations* architecture, building restoration, Scottish paintings; *Clubs* New (Edinburgh); *Style—* Ewan Easton, Esq; ✉ 2 Upper Dean Terrace, Edinburgh (☎ 0131 332 4495); Maclay Murray & Spens, 3 Glenfinlas Street, Edinburgh EH3 6AQ (☎ 0131 226 5196, fax 0131 226 3174)

EASTON, Robert Alexander; s of Malcolm Edward George Easton (d 1981), and Violet May Liddell, *née* Taylor (d 1990); *b* 24 Oct 1948; *Educ* St Lawrence Coll, Univ of Manchester (BSc), Aston Univ (PhD); *m* 11 June 1983, Lynden Anne, *née* Welch; 2 da (Alexandra Anne b 17 Jan 1987, Robyn Mary b 17 Dec 1992); *Career* Delta plc: dir of planning 1980–84, md Industl Servs Div 1984–87, dep chief exec 1988–89, chief exec 1989–96; non-exec dir Harrisons & Crosfield plc 1991–; *Recreations* golf, tennis, medieval art, literature; *Style—* Robert Easton, Esq; ✉ c/o Harrisons & Crosfield plc, One Great Tower Street, London EC3R 5AH (☎ 0171 711 1400, fax 0171 711 1450)

EASTON, Sir Robert William Simpson; kt (1990), CBE (1980); s of James Easton and Helen Agnes, *née* Simpson; *Educ* Royal Technical Coll Glasgow; *m* 1948, Jean, da of H K Fraser; 1 s, 1 da; *Career* chm and md Yarrow Shipbuilders Ltd 1979–91; chm: Clyde Port Authority 1983–93, GEC Scotland Ltd 1989–, GEC-Marconi Naval Systems Ltd 1991–94, Clydeport Pension Trust 1993–; conslt GEC-Marconi Ltd 1994–96; dir: Glasgow Development Agency 1990–94, Merchants House of Glasgow 1993–, West of Scotland Water Authority 1995–; chllr Univ of Paisley 1993–; Liveryman Worshipful Co of Shipwrights; *Recreations* walking, sailing, golf, gardening; *Clubs* Caledonian, RNVR (Glasgow); *Style—* Sir Robert Easton, CBE

EASTON, Robin Gardner; OBE (1994); s of (Robert) Douglas Easton (d 1976), of Glasgow, (Agnes) Hope Scott, *née* Sloan (d 1992); *b* 6 Oct 1943; *Educ* Kelvinside Acad, Sedbergh Sch, Christ's Coll Cambridge (MA), Wadham Coll Oxford (dip of educn); *m* 23 Dec 1978, Eleanor Mary, da of Alexander McIlroy; 1 da (Fiona Mary b 8 April 1981), 1 s (Douglas Alexander b 9 Oct 1982); *Career* asst teacher Melville Coll Edinburgh 1966–72, housemaster and dep head of French Dept Daniel Stewart's and Melville Coll 1972–78, head of modern languages George Watson's Coll 1979–83, rector HS of Glasgow 1983–; memb: Headmasters' Conf, SHA, Headteachers' Assoc of Scotland, Assoc of Christian Teachers; elder Church of Scotland; *Recreations* hill-walking, visiting ancient monuments, watching rugby; *Style—* Robin Easton, Esq, OBE; ✉ 21 Stirling Drive, Bearsden, Glasgow G61 4NU (☎ 0141 943 0368); The High School of Glasgow, 637 Crow Road, Glasgow G13 1PL (☎ 0141 954 9628, fax 0141 959 0191)

EASTON, Timothy Nigel Dendy; s of Dendy Bryan Easton, of Tadworth, Surrey, and Iris Joan Easton; *b* 26 Aug 1943; *Educ* Mowden Sch, Christ Coll Brecon, Kingston Coll of Art, Scholarship Heatherley Sch of Art London; *m* 5 April 1967, Christine Margaret, da of Flt Lt James William Darling (d 1984); 2 da (Lucy Kathryn Rebecca b 1969, Isabella b 1971); *Career* artist/sculptor; works incl: mural Church of the Good Shepherd Tadworth 1969–71, mural Theological Coll Salisbury 1967–73 (drawings for Salisbury mural exhibited Chicago and Kansas USA 1968); first London exhibition Young Artists Upper Grosvenor Gallery 1970, began exhibiting sculptures in bronze 1971; various exhibitions of paintings and sculptures since 1970 in: England Germany, Luxembourg, America; Chris Beetles Gallery London 1990, Cadogan Gallery 1991; portraits incl: Dr Glyn Simon as Archbishop of Wales, Gen Sir Geoffrey Musson; cmmn for Surgeons of Queen Victoria Hosp E Grinstead 1989; Elizabeth Greensfields Meml Fndn Award Montreal Canada 1973; Winston Churchill Travelling fell 1996; lectr Cambridge and UEA Extra Mural Bds; *Books* An Historical Atlas of Suffolk (contributor, 1988); *Recreations* vernacular architecture in Suffolk; *Style—* Timothy Easton, Esq; ✉ Bedfield Hall, Bedfield, Woodbridge, Suffolk IP13 7JJ (☎ 01728 628380)

EASTWOOD, (Noel) Anthony Michael; s of Edward Norman Eastwood (d 1984), of Headingley, Yorks, and Irene, *née* Dawson (d 1979); *b* 7 Dec 1932; *Educ* The Leys Sch Cambridge, Christ's Coll Cambridge (MA); *m* 1965, Elizabeth Tania Gresham, da of Cdr Thomas Wilson Boyd, CBE, DSO, DL (d 1987); 3 s (Rupert b 1967, James b 1969, Alexander b 1972); *Career* Lt RA 1951–54, Pilot Offr RAFVR 1954–56; De Havilland Aircraft Co 1956–60, RTZ Group 1960–61, AEI Group 1961–64; dir: Charterhouse Japhet Ltd 1964–79, Daniel Doncaster & Sons Ltd 1971–81, The Barden Corporation 1971–81, Falcon Publishing (Bahrain) 1981–84, Caribbean Publishing Co 1981–84, Hawk Publishing Co (UAE) 1981–86, Oryx Publishing (Qatar) 1981–87, IDP Interdata (Aust) 1984–92 and 1995–, Spearhead Communications Ltd 1988–, European Public Policy Advisers Group SA 1987–96, Witte Boyd Holdings Ltd 1990–93, Seafish Falklands Ltd (Port Stanley) 1990–95, PGI Europe Ltd 1995–; chm: Burnett & Rolfe Ltd 1964–68, Wharton Crane & Hoist Ltd 1967–70, Interdata Group 1981–; pres Charterhouse Japhet Texas Inc 1974–77; memb: London Ctee Yorkshire and Humberside Devpt Assoc 1975–93, Mgmnt Ctee Offshore Europe Conf and Exhibition 1990–, S Atlantic Cncl 1991–, Exec Ctee CPRE 1995– (chm SE Regional Gp 1995–); memb Much Hadham PCC 1989–, Much Hadham PC cncllr 1995–; sec Royal Aeronautical Soc 1982–83, hon treas Herts Cons Soc 1992–; *Recreations* skiing, sailing ('Daydream'), desert travel, family; *Clubs* Royal Thames Yacht; *Style—* Anthony Eastwood, Esq; ✉ Palace House, Much Hadham, Herts SG10 6HW (☎ 01279 842409)

EASTWOOD, HE Basil Stephen Talbot; s of late Christopher Gilbert Eastwood, CMG, and Catherine Emma, *née* Peel; *b* 4 March 1944; *Educ* Eton, Merton Coll Oxford; *m* 1970, Alison Faith, *née* Hutchings; 4 da; *Career* HM Dip Serv: FO 1966–67, MECAS 1967–68, Jeddah 1968–69, Colombo 1969–72, Cairo 1972–76, seconded to Cabinet Office 1976–78, FCO 1978–80, Bonn 1980–84, Khartoum 1984–87, Athens 1987–91, dir Research and Analysis FCO 1991–96, HM ambass Syria 1996–; *Recreations* theatre; *Style—* HE Mr Basil Eastwood; ✉ c/o FCO (Damascus), King Charles Street, London SW1A 2AH

EASTWOOD, (Anne) Mairi; *née* Waddington; da of John Waddington (d 1979), and Helen Cowan, *née* MacPherson; *b* 11 July 1951; *Educ* St Leonards Sch, Imperial Coll Univ of London (BSc); *m* 10 Aug 1974 (m dis 1987), James William Eastwood, s of late Donald Smith Eastwood; 1 s (Donald James b 1983), 1 da (Joanna Elizabeth Irene b 1980); *Career* Arthur Young: chartered accountant 1976, ptnr in charge computer servs consultancy 1985–87, recruitment ptnr 1985–87, nat staff ptnr 1988–89; chief exec Eastwood Consulting Ltd 1989–; non-exec dir Kaisen Ltd 1992–95; memb Central Tport Consultative Ctee 1992–95; govr The Dragon Sch; FCA 1981; *Clubs* Reform, IOD; *Style—* Mrs Mairi Eastwood; ✉ Flexney's House, Stanton Harcourt, Oxford OX8 1RP; Eastwood Consulting Ltd, 22–25 Sackville St, London W1X 1DE (☎ 0171 287 3670)

EASTWOOD, Dr Wilfred; s of Wilfred Andrew Eastwood (d 1977), and Annice Gertrude, *née* Hartley (d 1985); *b* 15 Aug 1923; *Educ* Hemsworth GS, Sheffield Univ (BEng), Aberdeen Univ (PhD); *m* 1947, Dorothy Jean, da of Charles St George Gover, of 40 Grange Court, Totley, Sheffield; 1 s (Richard), 1 da (Janet d 1988); *Career* conslt engr; sr ptnr Eastwood and Ptnrs 1972–; prof of civil engrg Univ of Sheffield 1964–70, pres IStructE 1976–77; chm: Cncl of Engrg Insts 1983–84, Cwlth Engrg Cncl 1983–85; Hon DEng (Sheffield) 1984; FEng 1980; *Recreations* watching cricket from third man and gardening; *Clubs* Yorks CC; *Style—* Dr Wilfred Eastwood, FEng; ✉ 45 Whirlow Park Rd, Sheffield S11 9NN (☎ 0114 236 4645); office: St Andrew's House, 23 Kingfield Rd, Sheffield S11 9AS (☎ 0114 255 4554, fax 0114 255 4330)

EASTY, Prof David Leonello; s of Arthur Victor Easty, and Florence Margaret Easty; *b* 6 Aug 1933; *Educ* King's Sch Canterbury, Univ of Manchester (MD); *m* 14 Jan 1963, Božana, da of Milan Martinović (d 1968); 3 da (Valerie, Marina, Julia); *Career* Capt RAMC 1959–62; Moorfields Eye Hosp City Rd London 1966–72; currently: prof of ophthalmology Univ of Bristol and head of Dept of Ophthalmology, dir Corneal Transplant Serv Eye Bank; memb: BMA, Int Soc for Eye Res; FRSM, FRCS, FRCOphth; *Books* Virus Diseases of The Eye (1984), External Eye Disease (ed, 1985), Immediate Eye Care (1990), Current Ophthalmic Surgery (1990); *Recreations* squash, jogging, fishing; *Clubs* Army & Navy; *Style—* Prof David Easty; ✉ Department of Ophthalmology, Bristol University, Bristol Eye Hospital, Lower Maudlin St, Bristol BS1 2LX (☎ 0117 928 4827)

EASUN, William John; s of Michael John Easun, of Surrey, and Mary Patricia, *née* McKinstry; *b* 19 April 1955; *Educ* Haileybury, Guildford Coll of Law, Aix en Provence Univ (scholar); *m* 28 Sept 1991, Irene Ann, da of Bryce Luke; *Career* articled clerk Dale & Newbery Middx 1974–78, admitted slr 1979, Aix en Provence Univ 1979–80, asst slr Frere Cholmeley Paris and Monaco 1980–83, ptnr Frere Cholmeley Monaco 1983–89, ptnr i/c Monaco office Frere Cholmeley Bischoff 1989–; dir Christies Monaco 1991–; memb: Law Soc, Int Bar Assoc, Int Tax Planners' Assoc, STEP; *Recreations* wine and food, travel, cinema, game fishing, all leisure activities excluding sport of any kind which I consider harmful to my health; *Style—* William Easun, Esq; ✉ Frere Cholmeley Bischoff, Est-Ouest, 24 Boulevard Princesse Charlotte, MC 98000, Monaco (☎ 00 337 93 10 55 10, fax 00 337 93 10 55 11)

EATOCK TAYLOR, Prof (William) Rodney; s of William Taylor (d 1994), of Hadley Wood, Herts, and Norah O'Brien, *née* Ridgeway; *b* 10 Jan 1944; *Educ* Rugby, King's Coll Cambridge (BA, MA), Stanford Univ California (MS, PhD); *m* 16 Jan 1971, Jacqueline Lorraine Cannon, da of Desmond Cannon Brookes (d 1981); 2 s (Thomas b 1973, Henry b 1976); *Career* engr; Ove Arup and Partners 1968–70; UCL 1970–89: assoc res asst 1970–72, lectr 1972–80, reader 1980–84, prof of ocean engrg 1984–89, dean of engrg 1988–89; prof of mechanical engrg Univ of Oxford 1989– (fell St Hugh's Coll 1989–); author of numerous articles in jls; FRINA 1986 (MRINA 1979), FIMechE 1989, FEng 1990; *Recreations* music; *Clubs* Athenaeum; *Style—* Prof Rodney Eatock Taylor, FEng; ✉ University of Oxford, Department of Engineering Science, Parks Road, Oxford OX1 3PJ (☎ 01865 273144, fax 01865 273010)

EATON, Guy Ashley; s of Paul Eaton (d 1992), of Maidenhead, Berks, and Elizabeth Ann Eaton (d 1971); *b* 27 April 1951; *Educ* Oundle Sch, Univ of Bristol; *m* 21 Sept 1983, Ulker, da of Tarik Sagban, of Bursa, Turkey; 1 da (Natalia b 1987); *Career* CA; banker; FICA; *Recreations* music, photography; *Clubs* RAC; *Style—* Guy A Eaton, Esq; ✉ 212 Piccadilly, London W1 (☎ 0181 960 7037, fax 0181 960 7283)

EATON, Adm Sir Kenneth John; GBE (1994), KCB (1990); *b* 12 Aug 1934; *Educ* Fitzwilliam House Cambridge (BA); *m* 1959, Sheena; 2 s (Andrew b 1963, Richard b 1964), 1 da (Caroline b 1969); *Career* RN: asst dir communications planning 1979–81, asst dir command systems 1981–83, dir torpedoes 1983–85, DG Underwater Weapons (Navy) 1985–87, Naval Base Cdr Portsmouth 1987–89, Controller of the Navy 1989–94; dir Kenneth Eaton Associates Ltd 1994–; chm: Guy's & St Thomas' Hosps 1995–, National Remote Sensing Centre Ltd 1995–, UKAEA 1996–; exec tstee Mary Rose Tst; FIEE 1981, FEng 1994; *Recreations* countryside, theatre, opera, classical music; *Clubs* Army & Navy, IOD; *Style—* Adm Sir Kenneth Eaton, GBE, KCB, FEng; ✉ c/o United Kingdom Atomic Energy Authority, 521 Harwell, Didcot, Oxfordshire OX11 0RA (☎ 01235 436888, fax 01235 436886)

EATS, Richard John Drake; s of Thomas John Drake Eats (d 1978), of Effingham, Surrey, and Alma, *née* Holdham; *b* 11 Sept 1945; *Educ* Dulwich, Emmanuel Coll Cambridge (MA), Cranfield Sch of Mgmnt (MBA); *m* 1980, Hilary Martelli, da of Eric Vernon Dawson; 2 s (Thomas Martin Drake b 1981, Matthew James Drake b 1986); *Career* inspr of taxes Inland Revenue 1968–69, Save & Prosper Ltd 1969–71, Britannia Group 1971–74, mktg dir Chieftain Trust Managers 1976–84, md GT Unit Trust Managers 1989–92 (mktg dir 1984–89), md Henderson Touche Remnant Unit Trust Managers 1993–96, conslt Cadogan Financial 1996–; memb Exec Ctee Unit Tst Assoc 1990; *Recreations* golf, child rearing; *Clubs* Roehampton, Wellington Golf; *Style—* Richard Eats, Esq; ✉ 2 Muncaster Rd, London SW11 6NT (☎ 0181 265 4401); Cadogan Financial, 19 Buckingham Street, London WC2N 6EF (☎ 0171 976 2500, fax 0171 930 7402)

EATWELL, Baron (Life Peer UK 1992), of Stratton St Margaret in the County of Wiltshire; John Leonard Eatwell; s of Harold Jack Eatwell, of Swindon, Wilts, and Mary, *née* Tucker (d 1987); *b* 2 Feb 1945; *Educ* Headlands GS Swindon, Queens' Coll Cambridge (BA, MA), Harvard Univ (AM, PhD); *m* 24 April 1970, Hélène, da of Georges Seppain, of Marly-le-Roi, France; 2 s (Hon Nikolai b 1971, Hon Vladimir b 1973), 1 da (Hon Tatyana b 1978); *Career* teaching fell Harvard Univ 1968–69; Univ of Cambridge: res fell Queens' Coll 1969–70, fell and dir of studies in econs Trinity Coll 1970–96, univ lectr in econs 1977– (asst lectr 1975–77), pres Queens' Coll 1997–; visiting prof of econs New School for Social Research NY 1980–96; econ advsr to Rt Hon Neil Kinnock MP 1985–92; dir Anglia Television Group plc; memb: Cambridge Constituency Lab Pty, Royal Econ Soc, American Econ Assoc; *Books* An Introduction to Modern Economics (with Joan Robinson, 1973), Keynes's Economics and the Theory of Value and Distribution (with Murray Milgate, 1983), Whatever Happened to Britain? (1982), The New Palgrave Dictionary of Economics (with Murray Milgate and Peter Newman, 1987), The New Palgrave Dictionary of Money and Finance (with Murray Milgate and Peter Newman, 1992), Transformation and Integration: Shaping the Future of Central and Eastern Europe (1995), Global Unemployment (1996); *Recreations* watching ballet, modern dance and rugby football; *Style—* The Rt Hon Lord Eatwell; ✉ Queens' College, Cambridge CB3 9ET (☎ 01223 335556)

EBBSFLEET, Bishop of 1994–; Rt Rev John Richards; s of William Richards, of Exeter, and Ethel Mary Coates (d 1966); *b* 4 Oct 1933; *Educ* Reading Sch, Wyggeston GS Leicester, Sidney Sussex Coll Cambridge (MA), Ely Theological Coll; *m* 2 Sept 1958, Ruth, da of Wilfred Haynes (d 1985), of Heavitree, Exeter; 2 s (Peter b 1961, David b 1968), 3 da (Elizabeth b 1962, Rachel b 1964, Bridget b 1968); *Career* asst curate St Thomas Exeter 1959–64; rector: Holsworthy with Hollacombe and Cookebury 1964–74, Heavitree Exeter 1974–81; archdeacon of Exeter and canon of Exeter Cathedral 1981–94; church cmmr 1988–94 (memb Bd of Govrs 1993–94); memb: C of E Pensions Bd 1990–, Gen Synod 1985–94; *Recreations* gardening, walking, fishing; *Style—* The Rt Rev the Bishop of Ebbsfleet; ✉ The Rectory, Church Leigh, Stoke-on-Trent, Staffs ST10 4PT (☎ and fax 01889 512366)

EBDON, (Thomas) John; DL (West Sussex 1996); s of Thomas Dudley Ebdon (d 1992), of Rustington, W Sussex, and Hilda Minnie, *née* Hayward; *b* 3 April 1940; *Educ* Wallington GS, Brixton Sch of Building (HND); *m* 27 March 1965, Janet Wendy, da of Herbert Noel Cobley (d 1982); 1 s (Robert John b 1965), 1 da (Elizabeth Wendy b 1967); *Career* James Longley and Co Ltd: joined 1963, dir 1972, dep md 1987–94; dir: James Longley Holdings Ltd 1989–94 (building conslt 1994–), Heating & Ventilation Southern Ltd 1974–94, Fullers of Faversham 1992–94, James Longley Leisure Ltd 1992–94, Slinfold Golf and Country Club 1992–94; chm Pennthorpe Sch Trust Ltd 1979–89; St Catherine's Hospice Crawley: fndr memb 1979, chm 1989–94, vice pres 1994–; tstee and fndr memb Children's Hospice for SE 1995–; hon treas Ind Forum of Hospice Chairmen 1991–94, churchwarden Horsham (Diocese of Chichester) 1974–79; Freeman: City of London 1980, Worshipful Co of Paviors 1982; *Recreations* cricket, photography, philately, heraldry, calligraphy, walking; *Clubs* MCC, Sussex CCC; *Style—* John Ebdon, Esq, DL; ✉ Mullion, The Street, Slinfold, Horsham, West Sussex RH13 7RR (☎ and fax 01403 790609)

EBDON, Peter David; s of Michael George Ebdon, and Barbara, *née* Cheeseman; *b* 27 Aug 1970; *Educ* Highbury Grove Secdy Sch; *m* 18 July 1992, Deborah Karen, da of Garry Baldrey; *Career* professional snooker player 1991–; England rep at jr and sr level, world under 21 jr champion 1990, quarter-finalist Embassy World Championship 1992 (in first professional season); world record holder for most century breaks (4) in a 9–frame match Euro Open 1992 (also jt world record holder with 3 successive century breaks in same match), Skoda Grand Prix champion 1993, runner-up Dubai Duty Free 1994, Benson & Hedges Irish Masters snooker champion 1995; *Recreations* swimming, golf, cricket, chess, reading; *Style—* Peter Ebdon, Esq; ✉ c/o Ramsay McLellan Kowloon, 32 Staining Rise, Staining, Blackpool, Lancs FY3 0BU (☎ 01253 892998)

EBERLE, Adm Sir James Henry Fuller; GCB (1981, KCB 1979); s of Victor Fuller Eberle (d 1974), of Bristol, and Joyce Mary Eberle; *b* 31 May 1927; *Educ* Clifton, RNC Dartmouth; *m* 1950, Ann Patricia (d 1988), da of E Thompson, of Hong Kong; 1 s, 2 da; *Career* RN 1941–83; served WWII, Capt 1965, Rear-Adm 1971, asst chief of Fleet Support 1972–74; flag offr: Sea Training 1974–75, Aircraft Carriers and Amphibious Ships 1975–77; Chief of Fleet Support 1977–79, C-in-C Fleet and Allied C-in-C Channel and E Atlantic 1979–81, C-in-C Naval Home Cmd 1981–82, Flag ADC to HM The Queen 1981–82, Vice-Adm of the UK 1994; dir: Royal Inst of Int Affrs 1983–90, UK Japan 2000 Gp 1984; pres Assoc of Masters of Harriers and Beagles 1994, memb Bd BFSS; Hon LLD Univ of Bristol 1989, Hon DL Univ of Sussex 1990; Freeman City of London and Bristol; *Clubs* Farmers', All England Lawn Tennis, Society of Merchant Venturers (Bristol); *Style—* Adm Sir James Eberle, GCB

EBRAHIM, Sir (Mahomed) Currimbhoy; 4 Bt (UK 1910), of Bombay; s of Sir (Huseinali) Currimbhoy Ebrahim, 3 Bt (d 1952), and Alhaja Amina Khanum, *née* Jairazbhoy; *b* 24 June 1935; *m* 15 Nov 1958, Dur-e-Mariam, da of Minuchehir Ahmed Nurudin Ahmed Ghulam Ally Nana, of Karachi; 3 s (Zulfiqar Ali b 1960, Murtaza Ali b 1963, Raza Ali b 1964), 1 da (Durre Najaf b 1969); *Heir* s, Zulfiqar Ali Currimbhoy Ebrahim b 5 Aug 1960; *Career* memb Standing Council of Baronetage; *Style—* Sir Currimbhoy Ebrahim, Bt

EBRAHIM, Prof Shaheen Brian John (Shah); s of Donald William Ebrahim, and Marjorie Sybil, *née* Evans (d 1971); *b* 19 July 1952; *Educ* King Henry VIII GS Coventry, Univ of Nottingham Med Sch (BMedSci, BM BS, DM), London Sch of Hygiene and Tropical Med (MSc (Epidemiology), DCH (London); *m* 8 Dec 1984, Julia Lesley, *née* Shaw; *Career* Univ of Nottingham Med Sch: Wellcome Tst clinical epidemiology trg fellowship 1981–83, lectr in geriatric med Dept of Health Care of the Elderly 1983–85; Wellcome Tst lectr in epidemiology Dept of Social Med and Gen Practice St George's Hosp Med Sch London 1985–86, conslt physician and sr lectr Dept of Geriatric Med Royal Free Hosp Sch of Med London 1987–89, prof of geriatric med London Hosp Med Coll and Bart's Med Coll 1989–92, prof of clinical epidemiology Royal Free Hosp Sch of Med London 1992–; MRCGP 1981, FRCP 1993, FFPHM 1993; *Books* Clinical Epidemiology of Stroke (1990), The Health of Older Women (ed with J George, 1992), Essentials of Health Care in Old Age (with G Bennett, 1992, 2 edn 1995), Epidemiology in Old Age (1996); also author of scientific papers on clinical epidemiology and geriatric med; *Recreations* Capt Beefhart, Velvet Underground, coarse fishing; *Clubs* Royal Society of Medicine; *Style—* Prof Shah Ebrahim; ✉ University Department of Primary Care and Population Sciences, Royal Free Hospital School of Medicine, Rowland Hill Street, London NW3 2PF (☎ 0171 794 0500, fax 0171 794 1224, e-mail shah@rfhsm.ac.uk)

EBSWORTH, Hon Mrs Justice; Hon Dame Ann Marian; DBE (1992); da of late Arthur Ebsworth, OBE, BEM, and late Hilda Mary Ebsworth; *b* 1937; *Educ* Notre Dame Convent Worth, Portsmouth HS, Univ of London; *Career* called to the Bar Gray's Inn 1962, legal chm Mental Health Review Tbnls 1975–83 and 1984–89, recorder of the Crown Court 1978–83, circuit judge (Northern Circuit) 1983–92, judge of the High Court of Justice (Queen's Bench Div) 1992–; memb: Parole Bd 1989–92, Judicial Studies Bd 1991–92; *Style—* The Hon Mrs Justice Ebsworth, DBE; ✉ Royal Courts of Justice, Strand, London WC2A 2LL

EBSWORTH, Prof Evelyn Algernon Valentine; CBE (1996); s of Brig Wilfred Algernon Ebsworth, CB, CBE, (d 1978) of Cambridge, and Cynthia, *née* Blech (d 1975); *b* 14 Feb 1933; *Educ* Marlborough, Univ of Cambridge (BA, MA, PhD, ScD); *m* 20 Aug 1955, Mary (d 1987), da of Frank Reyner Salter, OBE; 1 s (Jonathan b 1962), 3 da (Nicolette b 1958, Rachel b 1960, Lucy b 1964); m 2 1990, Rose, *née* Stinson, wid of Prof J J Zuckerman; *Career* Univ of Cambridge: fell King's Coll 1957–59, fell Christ's Coll 1959–67, demonstrator 1959–64, lectr 1964–67, tutor Christ's Coll 1964–67; Crum Brown prof of chemistry Univ of Edinburgh 1967–90, Vice Chllr and Warden Univ of Durham 1990–; author of numerous papers published in learned jls; former memb Scot Examinations Bd, corresponding memb Acad of Sciences Göttingen; FRSC, FRSE 1969; *Books* Volatile Silicon Compounds (1963), Structural Methods in Inorganic Chemistry (jtly, 1988); *Recreations* opera, gardening; *Style—* Prof E A V Ebsworth, CBE, FRSE; ✉ University of Durham, Old Shire Hall, Durham DH1 3HP (☎ 0191 374 2000)

EBURY, 6 Baron (UK 1857); Francis Egerton Grosvenor; s of 5 Baron Ebury, DSO (d 1957, whose ggf, 1 Baron, was yr bro of 2 Marquess of Westminster and 2 Earl of Wilton; thus Lord Ebury is hp to 7 Earl of Wilton), by his 1 w, Anne, da of Herbert Acland-Troyte, MC (gn of Sir Thomas Acland, 10 Bt); *b* 8 Feb 1934; *Educ* Eton; *m* 1, 10 Dec 1957 (m dis 1962), Gillian Elfrida Astley, o da of Martin Roland Soames (d 1995), and Myra Drummond, niece of 16 Earl of Perth; 1 s; m 2, 8 March 1963 (m dis 1973), Kyra, o da of L L Aslin; m 3, 1974, Suzanne, da of Graham Suckling, of NZ; 1 da (Hon Georgina Lucy b 1973); *Heir* s, Hon Julian Grosvenor, *qv*; *Recreations* ornithology, horology, photography; *Clubs* Oriental, Hong Kong, Melbourne, Melbourne Savage; *Style—* The Rt Hon Lord Ebury; ✉ Moore Park, PO Box 53, Mount Macedon, Victoria 3441, Australia

ECCLES, 1 Viscount (UK 1964); David McAdam Eccles; CH (1984), KCVO (1953), PC (1951); also 1 Baron Eccles (UK 1962); s of William McAdam Eccles, FRCS (d 1946), and Anna Coralie, *née* Anstie (d 1932); *b* 18 Sept 1904; *Educ* Winchester, New Coll Oxford; *m* 1, 10 Oct 1928, Hon Sybil Frances Dawson (d 1977), eldest da of 1 & last Viscount Dawson of Penn, GCVO, KCB, KCMG, PC (d 1945); 2 s, 1 da; m 2, 26 Sept 1984, Mary, widow of Donald Hyde, of Four Oaks Farm, Somerville, NJ, USA; *Heir* s, Hon John Dawson Eccles CBE; *Career* sits as Conservative in House of Lords; MP (C) Chippenham Wilts 1943–62, min of Works 1951–54, min of Education 1954–57, pres Bd of Trade 1957–59, min of Educn 1959–62, chm of Tstees Br Museum 1966–70; Paymaster Gen 1970–73, chm Br Library Bd 1973–78, pres World Crafts Cncl 1974–78; *Style—* The Rt Hon Viscount Eccles, CH, KCVO, PC; ✉ Dean Farm, Chute, nr Andover, Hants (☎ 0126 470 210); 6 Barton Street, London SW1 (☎ 0171 222 1387)

ECCLES, George William; s of George Dunluce Eccles (d 1951), and Eileen Margaret Smith, *née* O'Neale; *b* 26 Dec 1950; *Educ* Downside, LSE (LLB); *m* 1986, Eve, *née* Wooler; 1 s (Dunluce b 1988), 1 da (Tabitha b 1991); *Career* Coopers & Lybrand (formerly Deloitte Haskins & Sells): trainee accountant 1974–77, worked in tech dept 1978–80, audit mangr 1980–87, ptnr UK 1987–94, ptnr Russia 1995–; chm Media Group 1982–94 (memb 1980–82); memb: RTS, Media Soc, Soc of Authors; MInstD, FCA; *Publications* Accounting for Research and Development (1978), EEC Fourth Directive: Company Accounts (1978), EEC Third Directive: Mergers (1979), The Sixth Directive: Prospectuses (1979), Unfair Dismissal (1979), The Seventh Directive: Group Accounts (1980), Employment Act (1980), Company's Act 1980 (1980), Company's Act 1981 (1982), Climate for Cable: Legislation, ATV and Marketing (1983), Television in Focus: Broadcasting in Europe (1990), Investing in UK Television (1991); *Recreations* horse racing, opera, Russian icons, France; *Clubs* Groucho, Special Forces, Academy, Berkshire Golf, Racehorse Owners' Assoc; *Style—* George Eccles, Esq; ✉ Skatertny Pereklok 22, Flat 37, Moscow Russia (☎ 00 7 095 290 5097, fax 00 7 095 232 2323)

ECCLES, Jack Fleming; CBE (1980); s of Thomas Eccles (d 1962), of Manchester; *b* 9 Feb 1922; *Educ* Chorlton HS Manchester, Univ of Manchester (BA); *m* 24 May 1952, Hon Milba Hartley; 1 s, 1 da; *Career* served Burma in ranks 1944–45; trade union official GMB 1948–86, chm and pres TUC 1984–85; dir Remploy Ltd 1976–90; memb English Estates (formerly English Industrial Estates Corporation) 1976–92, chm Plastics Processing Indust Trg Bd 1982–88, non-exec dir British Steel plc 1986–91; *Recreations* cine-photography; *Style—* Jack Eccles, Esq, CBE; ✉ Terange, 11 Sutton Rd, Alderley Edge, Cheshire SK9 7RB

ECCLES, Prof Sir John Carew; AC (1990), kt (1958); s of William James Eccles, of Melbourne, and Mary Eccles; *b* 27 Jan 1903; *Educ* Melbourne Univ, Magdalen Coll Oxford; *m* 1, 1928 (m dis 1968), Irene Frances, da of Herbert Miller, of Motueka, NZ; 4 s, 5 da; m 2, 1968, Dr Helena Táboříková; *Career* dir Kanematsu Inst Sydney Hosp 1937–43, prof of physiology Otago Univ NZ 1944–51, prof of physiology ANU Canberra 1951–66, Chicago Res Inst 1966–68, prof of neurobiology State Univ Buffalo New York 1968–75, emeritus 1975–; Hon Doctorate: Cambridge, Melbourne, Tasmania, British Columbia, Marquette, Loyola, Gustaphus Adelphus, Yeshiva, Prague, Oxford, Fribourg, Torino, Georgetown (Washington), Tsukuba (Japan), Basel, Madrid, Ulm; hon memb: Nat Acad of Sci, American Acad of Art and Scis, American Phylosophycal Soc, American Acad of Physicians, Academy dei Lincei, Pontifical Acad, Royal Belgian Acad, Indian Acad of Sci, Bavarian Acad, Academia Europea, and others; FRS, FAA, FRACP; *Awards* Baly Medal RCP 1961, Royal Medal Royal Society 1962, Cothenius Medal Deutsche Akademie der Naturforscher Leopoldina 1963, Nobel Prize for Medicine (jtly) 1963, Order of Rising Sun with Gold and Silver Stars (Japan) 1986, Cortina-Ulisse Literary Prize 1991, Golden Medal Charles Univ Prague Czech Republic 1993; *Books* incl: Physiology of Nerve Cells (1957), Physiology of Synapses (1964), The Inhibitory Pathways of the Central Nervous System (1969), Facing Reality (1970), The Understanding of the Brain (1973), The Self and its Brain (jtly, 1977), The Human Mystery (1979), The Human Psyche (1980), The Wonder of Being Human (jtly, 1984), Evolution of the Brain - Creation of the Self (1989), How the Self Controls its Brain (1993); *Style—* Prof Sir John Eccles, AC, FRS; ✉ Ca' a la Gra', CH 6646 Contra (TI), Ticino, Switzerland (☎ 00 41 91 7452931)

ECCLES, Hon John Dawson; CBE (1985); s and h of 1 Viscount Eccles, CH, KCVO, PC, and his 1 w Hon Sybil Frances Dawson (d 1977), da of 1 Viscount Dawson of Penn; *b* 20 April 1931; *Educ* Winchester, Magdalen Coll Oxford (BA); *m* 29 Jan 1955, Diana Catherine (Baroness Eccles of Moulton, *qv*), 2 da of late Raymond Wilson Sturge, of Ashmore, nr Salisbury; 1 s (Hon William David Eccles, *qv*), 3 da (one of whom (Hon) Catherine Sara Eccles); *Career* Capt TA; Head Wrightson & Co Ltd 1955–77; dir: Glynwed International plc 1972–96, Investors in Industry plc 1974–88, Davy International plc 1977–81, Courtaulds Textiles plc 1992– (non-exec chm 1995–); chm Chamberlain & Hill plc 1982–; memb: Monopolies & Mergers Cmmn 1976–85 (dep chm 1981–85), Cwlth Devpt Corp 1982–85 (chief exec 1985–94); chm: Bd of Tstees Royal Botanic Gdns Kew 1983–91, The Georgian Theatre Royal Richmond Yorks; Hon DSc Silsoe Coll Cranfield Inst of Technology 1989; *Recreations* gardening, theatre; *Clubs* Brooks's; *Style—* The Hon John Eccles, CBE; ✉ Moulton Hall, Richmond, Yorks (☎ 01325 377227); 6 Barton Street, London SW1P 3NG (☎ 0171 222 7559)

ECCLES, (Hugh William) Patrick; QC (1990); s of Gp Capt Hugh Haslett Eccles, of Esher, and Mary, *née* Cunnane; *b* 25 April 1946; *Educ* Stonyhurst, Exeter Coll Oxford (scholar, MA), Middle Temple London (Winston Churchill Pupillage prize); *m* 15 April 1972, (Rhoda) Ann, da of Patrick Brendan Moroney; 3 da (Katherine Ann b 15 July 1974, Clare b 18 Oct 1976, Fiona b 18 Oct 1980); *Career* called to the Bar Middle Temple 1968, head of Chambers 2 Harcourt Bldgs Temple 1985–, recorder of Crown Court 1987–; memb County Ct Rule Ctee 1987–91, asst Parly boundary cmmr 1993–; memb Hon Soc of the Middle Temple 1964; govr Sch of St Helen and St Katharine Abingdon Oxon 1991–; *Recreations* tennis, opera and P G Wodehouse; *Style—* Patrick Eccles, Esq, QC; ✉ Grapevine Cottage, High Street, Long Wittenham, Nr Abingdon, Oxon OX14 4QQ

(☎ 01865 407436); 2 Harcourt Buildings, Temple, London EC4Y 9DB (☎ 0171 353 6961); Harcourt Chambers, Churchill House, St Aldates Courtyard, 38 St Aldates, Oxford OX1 1BN (☎ 01865 791559)

ECCLES, Hon William David; o s of Hon John Dawson Eccles, CBE, *qv*, and Baroness Eccles of Moulton (Life Peer), *qv*; *b* 9 June 1960; *m* 1984, Claire Margaret Alison, da of Brian Seddon; 2 s (Peter b 1987, Tom b 1988), 1 da (Kate b 1991); *Career* dir: Foreign & Colonial Ventures Ltd, Foreign & Colonial Management Ltd; non-exec dir B Elliott plc; *Style—* The Hon William Eccles; ✉ Foreign & Colonial Ventures Ltd, 8th Floor, Exchange House, Primrose Street, London EC2A 2NY (☎ 0171 782 9829, fax 0171 782 9834)

ECCLES OF MOULTON, Baroness (Life Peer UK 1990), of Moulton in the Co of N Yorks; Diana Catherine Eccles; 2 da of late Raymond Wilson Sturge, of Lords Mead, Ashmore, Salisbury, Wilts, and Margaret Sturge; *b* 4 Oct 1933; *Educ* St James's Sch West Malvern, Open Univ (BA); *m* 29 Jan 1955, Hon John Dawson Eccles, CBE, *qv*, er s and h of 1 Viscount Eccles, CH, KCVO, PC; 1 s (Hon William David, *qv*, b 1960), 3 da (Hon Alice Belinda (Hon Mrs Ward) b 1958, (Hon) Catherine Sara Eccles (Hon Mrs Gannon), b 1963, Hon Emily Frances b 1970); *Career* chm: Ealing Dist Health Authy 1988–93, Ealing, Hammersmith & Hounslow Health Authy 1993–; dir: Tyne Tees Television 1986–94, J Sainsbury plc 1986–95, Yorkshire Electricity Group plc 1990–; memb: North Eastern Electricity Bd 1974–85, British Railways Eastern Bd 1986–92, Yorkshire Electricity Bd 1989–90, National & Provincial Building Society 1991–, Advsy Cncl for Energy Conservation 1982–84, Widdicombe Enquiry into Local Govt 1985–86, Home Office Advsy Panel on Licences for Experimental Community Radio 1985–86, Unrelated Live Transplant Regulatory Authy 1990–; vice-chm: Nat Cncl for Voluntary Organisations 1981–87, Durham Univ Cncl 1985– (lay memb 1981–85); Hon DCL 1995; chm Tyne Tees Television Programme Consultative Cncl 1982–84; tstee Charities Aid Fndn 1982–89; *Style—* The Rt Hon Lady Eccles of Moulton; ✉ Moulton Hall, Moulton, Richmond, N Yorks DL10 6QH; 6 Barton St, London SW1P 3NG

ECCLES-WILLIAMS, Hilary a'Beckett; CBE (1970); s of The Rev Cyril Archibald Eccles-Williams (d 1952), of Summer Fields, nr Oxford, and Hermione a'Beckett, *née* Terrell (d 1984); *b* 5 Oct 1917; *Educ* Eton, BNC Oxford (MA); *m* 21 Sept 1943, Jeanne Marjorie, da of W J Goodwin, of Solihull, W Mids; 2 s (Simon b 1955, Mark b 1959), 4 da (Virginia b 1946, Tamara b 1947, Sherry b 1949, Sophie b 1963); *Career* Nat Serv WWII Maj RA 1939–45, served Dunkirk and Normandy; consul: Cuba 1953–61, Nicaragua 1951–59, Bolivia 1965–82, Costa Rica 1964–94; chm and dir various cos; ldr govt trade missions Czechoslovakia and Canada 1965; chm: Br Export Houses Assoc 1958–60, Br Heart Fndn Midland Ctee 1973–76, Asian Christian Colls Assoc 1966–70, Guardians Birmingham Assay Office 1979–88, Birmingham Cons Assoc 1976–79 (pres 1979–84), W Midlands Met Ctee of Cons Party 1980–86, Latin American Forum Cons Foreign and Overseas Cncl 1985–88, Golden Jubilee Appeal Ctee Queen Elizabeth Hosp Birmingham 1987–89, W Midlands Macmillan Nurses Appeal 1991–94; pres: Birmingham C of C 1965–66, Assoc of Br Cs of C 1970–72, Birmingham Consular Assoc 1973–74, Birmingham E Euro Constituency 1984–94, Sparkbrook Constituency Cons Assoc 1988–92; vice pres W Mids Cons Cncl 1985–, memb Nat Union Exec Ctee Cons Pty 1975–85, gen cmmr Income Tax 1966–70, govr Univ of Birmingham 1967–, pres Cons Pty One Nation Forum W Mids Area 1990–; Hon Capt Bolivian Navy 1964–; Freeman: City of London, Worshipful Co of Goldsmiths; *Recreations* golf, walking; *Clubs* N Warwickshire Golf; *Style—* Hilary Eccles-Williams, Esq, CBE; ✉ 36 St Bernard's Road, Solihull, W Midlands B92 7BB (☎ 0121 706 0354)

ECCLESHARE, (Christopher) William; s of Colin Forster (d 1989), and Elizabeth, *née* Bennett; *b* 26 Oct 1955; *Educ* William Ellis Sch Highgate, Trinity Coll Cambridge (BA); *m* 1980, Carol Ann, da of Arnold W Seigel; 2 s (Thomas Christopher b 1984, Charles David b 1986), 1 da (Rose Judith b 1989); *Career* J Walter Thompson Company Ltd advtg agency: joined as graduate trainee 1978, assoc dir 1983, sr assoc dir 1985, main bd dir 1986, head of account mgmnt 1988, md 1990–92; chief exec PPGH/JWT Amsterdam 1992–95, dir of worldwide strategic planning J Walter Thompson Company Ltd 1995–96, chief exec Ammirati Puris Lintas Ltd 1996–; MIPA; *Recreations* politics, music, theatre; *Style—* William Eccleshare, Esq; ✉ Ammirati Puris Lintas Ltd, 84 Eccleston Square, Victoria, London SW1V 1PX (☎ 0171 932 8888)

ECCLESTON, Harry Norman; OBE (1979); s of Harry Norman Eccleston (d 1971), of Coseley, Staffs, and Kate, *née* Pritchard (d 1978); *b* 21 Jan 1923; *Educ* Bilston Sch of Art, Birmingham Coll of Art (Dip Painting, Art Teachers Dip), RCA Engraving Sch; *m* 5 Aug 1948, Betty Doreen (d 1995), da of Wilfrid Gripton (d 1954), of Bilston, Staffs; 2 da (Judith Elizabeth (Mrs Park) b 1950, Jennifer Margaret (Mrs Stanbridge) b 1954); *Career* RN 1942–46, temp cmmn RNVR 1943; artist, lectr in illustration and printmaking SE Essex Tech Coll 1951–58, artist designer Bank of England Printing Works 1958–83 (designer of series of banknotes with historical portraits: £1 Newton, £5 Wellington, £10 Nightingale, £20 Shakespeare, £50 Wren), conslt Bank of England Printing Works 1983–86; exhibited prints and watercolours home and abroad 1948–; ARE 1948, RE 1961 (pres 1975–89), RWS 1975, RWA 1991, memb Art Workers' Guild 1984, FRSA 1972, hon memb Royal Birmingham Soc of Artists 1989, hon memb New English Art Club 1995; *Clubs* Arts; *Style—* Harry Eccleston, Esq, OBE; ✉ 110 Priory Rd, Harold Hill, Romford, Essex RM3 9AL (☎ 01708 340275)

ECCLESTON, Simon Antony Sudell; JP (1977); s of James Thomas Eccleston (d 1995), of Shropshire, and Kathleen Mary, *née* Cryer (d 1964); *b* 4 April 1944; *Educ* Denstone Coll Staffs; *m* 4 Oct 1967, Angela Penelope Gail, da of Noel Harrison (d 1988), of Wolverhampton; 2 s (Piers Edward Dominic b 1971, Crispin Benedict Chad b 1982), 2 da (Cressida Sophie Heloise b 1974, Candida Annalee Gabriel b 1981); *Career* chief exec Conveyor Projects Ltd, exec chm Trans-Tech Industries Ltd; former chm: Conveyors Ltd, SAS Engineering Ltd; memb: Wolverhampton Health Authy 1987–89, Cncl (regnl and small firms) CBI, Staffs Shrops Euro Cons Exec, S Staffs Cons Assoc Exec 1972–, PCC, Black Country Steering Gp CBI, Cncl and Economic and Industrial Ctee Birmingham C of C, Bd Industl Devpt Bd DTI 1988–95, Bd Walsall Trg and Enterprise Cncl 1989– (chm Small Firms Gp), Exec Staffs and Shrops Magistrates Assoc, Ctee W Midlands Branch IOD 1988–, Bd Birmingham C of C 1995–; chm Cons Assoc Branch 1971–80, pres Walsall C of C and Indust 1986–87, chm Br Chambers of Commerce Nat Conf 1991–93; Freeman City of London 1989, Liveryman Worshipful Co of Loriners; FInstD; *Recreations* trout fishing, shooting, riding, ocean sailing, landscape gardening; *Clubs* City Livery; *Style—* Simon Eccleston, Esq, JP; ✉ Chatwell Court, Great Chatwell, Shropshire TF10 9BJ; Conveyor Projects Ltd, West Midlands House, Gipsy Lane, West Midlands WV12 2HZ (☎ 0121 609 7023, fax 0121 609 7025)

ECCLESTON, Prof William (Bill); s of Henry Eccleston, of Preston, Lancs, and Bertha Eccleston; *b* 3 March 1941; *Educ* Harris Coll Preston, Univ of London (BSc, MSc, PhD); *m* 12 April 1966, Catherine Yvonne, *née* Daley; 2 s (John b 25 Jan 1967, Daniel b 13 July 1969); *Career* sr princ sci Plessey Res Laboratories 1966–71; Univ of Liverpool: lectr 1971–81, sr lectr 1981–85, prof of electronics 1985–86, Robert Rankin prof of electronic engrg 1986–, head Dept of Electrical Engrg and Electronics 1986–91, dean of Faculty of Engrg 1992–95; numerous pubns in learned jls; chm: SERC/DTI VLSI Technology Sub-Ctee 1992–95, SERC/DTI IT Advsy Bd 1992–95; Freeman Borough of Preston; FIEE 1985, CEng 1985; *Recreations* music, football, walking, cricket; *Clubs* Lancashire Cricket, Preston North End; *Style—* Prof Bill Eccleston; ✉ Dept of Electrical Engineering & Electronics, University of Liverpool, Liverpool L69 3BX (☎ 0151 794 4502, e-mail beccle@liverpool.ac.uk)

ECHENIQUE, Prof Marcial Hernan; s of Marcial Echenique (d 1995), of Santiago, Chile, and Rosa, *née* Talavera; *b* 23 Feb 1943; *Educ* Catholic Univ Santiago Chile, Barcelona Univ Spain (DipArch, DArch), Univ of Cambridge (MA); *m* 23 Nov 1963, Maria Louisa, da of Ernesto Holzmann (d 1978), of Santiago, Chile; 2 s (Marcial Antonio b 16 July 1964, Martin Jose b 25 Nov 1965, d 13 July 1994), 1 da (Alejandra b 1 Aug 1969); *Career* asst lectr in urbanism Univ of Barcelona Spain 1963–65; Univ of Cambridge: lectr in architecture 1970–80, fell Churchill Coll 1972–, reader in architecture and urban studies 1980–93, prof of land use and tport studies 1993–; chm Marcial Echenique & Partners Ltd (architectural and planning conslts) 1990–; memb Bd: Banco de Bilbao y Vizcaya Spain 1988–94, Autopista Vasco Aragonesa Spain 1994–, Tecnologica SA Spain 1994–, Agroman Constructora Spain 1995–, Dockways Ltd Jersey 1996–; memb Civic Soc Huntingdon & Godmanchester 1979; FRSA 1986, ARCUK 1988, RTPI 1991; *Books* Urban Development Models (jtly, 1975), Modelos de la Estructura Espacial Urbana (1975), La Estructura Del Espacio Urbano (jtly, 1975); *Recreations* music; *Style—* Prof Marcial Echenique; ✉ Farm Hall, Godmanchester, Cambs; Marcial Echenique & Partners Ltd, 49–51 High Street, Trumpington, Cambridge CB2 2HZ (☎ 01223 840704, fax 01223 840384)

ECHLIN, Sir Norman David Fenton; 10 Bt (I 1721), of Dublin; s of Sir John Frederick Echlin, 9 Bt (d 1932); *b* 1 Dec 1925; *Educ* Masonic Boys' Sch Clonskeagh Co Dublin; *m* 8 Dec 1953, Mary Christine, o da of John Arthur, of Oswestry, Shropshire; *Heir* none; *Career* Capt (ret) IA; *Style—* Sir Norman Echlin, Bt; ✉ Nartopa, Marina Av, Appley, Ryde, Isle of Wight

ECKERSLEY, Thomas (Tom); OBE (1948); s of John Eckersley, and Eunice, *née* Hilton; *b* 30 Sept 1914; *Educ* Salford Coll of Art; *Career* graphic designer; in partnership with Eric Lombers 1934–39, graphic work for: London Transport, Shell Mex, General Post Office, BBC, Austin Reed; visiting lectr in graphic design Westminster Sch of Art 1937–39, RAF cartographer and designer of posters for General Post Office, Royal Soc for Prevention of Accidents and RAF 1940–45, head of Graphic Design Dept London Coll of Printing 1958–76; exhibitions: Shell Posters (Shell Mex House London) 1938, International Posters (Univ of Washington DC) 1940, Eight British Designers (National Museum Stockholm) 1952, Graphic Art from Britain (Amercian Inst of Graphic Arts New York) 1956, European Design (Univ of California) 1962, Documenta III (Kassel) 1964, Polish Poster Biennale (Warsaw) 1972–74, Homage to Tom (London Coll of Printing and Paperpoint Gallery) 1975, Brno Bienalle (Czechoslovakia) 1978, Thirties - British Art and Design Before the War (Hayward Gallery London) 1979, British Arts Centre Yale (USA) 1980, London Transport Museum 1985; regular exhibitions with Alliance Graphique Internationale; work in public collections: Museum of Modern Art (NY), Imperial War Museum, V & A Museum, London Transport Museum, Nat Gallery of Australia, Library of Congress (USA); awards: Royal Designer for Industry (RSA) 1963, Chartered Soc of Designers Medal for outstanding work over 60 years 1990; memb Alliance Graphique Internationale 1950; fell: Soc of Artists and Designers 1961, Soc of Typographic Designers 1961; hon fell: Manchester Coll of Art and Design 1961, Royal Coll of Art 1991, The London Inst 1996; RDI 1963; *Books* Poster Design (1954); *Style—* Tom Eckersley, Esq, OBE; ✉ 53 Belsize Park Gardens, London NW3 (☎ 0171 586 3586)

ECKERSLEY, Tobias William Hammersley (Toby); MBE (1989); s of Timothy Huxley Eckersley (d 1980), and Penelope Anne, *née* Hammersley; *b* 22 July 1941; *Educ* Charterhouse, St John's Coll Oxford (MA), LSE (MSc); *Career* HM Foreign Serv 1964–67, IMF 1967–71, Williams & Glyn's Bank 1971–75, ICI 1976–93; Parly candidate (C) Peckham 1983, chm Dulwich Cons Assoc 1988–90, memb Cons Pty Policy Gp for London 1983–86; London Borough of Southwark: ldr of oppn 1979–85, ldr Cons Gp 1990–, cncllr 1977–86 and 1990–, memb Ministerial Advsy Panel on Abolition of GLC and Met Counties 1984–86, fndr and sec London Assoc for Saving Homes 1974–77; chm of govrs Walworth Sch 1993–; *Recreations* painting; *Style—* Toby Eckersley, Esq, MBE; ✉ 30 Berryfield Road, London SE17 3QE (☎ 0171 701 3112)

ECKERSLEY-MASLIN, Rear Adm David Michael; CB (1984); eldest s of Cdr C E Eckersley-Maslin, OBE, RN, of Tasmania, and late Mrs L M Lightfoot, of Bedford; *b* 27 Sept 1929, Karachi; *Educ* RNC Dartmouth; *m* 1955, Shirley Ann, da of late Capt H A Martin, DSC, RN; 1 s, 1 da; *Career* Capt: HMS Eastbourne 1966–68, HMS Euryalus 1971–72, HMS Fife 1975, HMS Blake 1976, RCDS 1977; DOR RN 1978–80, ADC to HM The Queen 1979, flag offr Sea Trg 1980–82, ACNS (Falklands) 1982, ACDS (Signals) 1982, ACDS (CIS) 1983–84; asst dir: Cmd Control and Communications Systems, Int Mil Staff NATO HQ Brussels 1984–86, Dir Gen NATO Communications and Informations Systems Agency Brussels 1986–91; int vice pres AFCEA 1987–90 (awarded Leadership Gold medal 1991), memb Cncl Shipwreck Mariners Soc 1991–, chm AFCEA(UK) Educn Tst 1991–; *Recreations* tennis, golf; *Clubs* MCC; *Style—* Rear Adm David Eckersley-Maslin, CB; ✉ Dunningwell, Hall Court, Shedfield, Southampton, Hants SO32 2HL (☎ 01329 832350)

ECROYD, (Edward) Peter; s of William Edward Bedingfeld Ecroyd (d 1951), of Armathwaite, Cumberland, and Iris Bloxsome, *née* Day (d 1996); *b* 24 Nov 1932; *Educ* Harrow, Royal Agric Coll; *m* 25 April 1957, Felicity Anne Graham, er da of Frederick Graham Roberts, OBE (d 1981); 1 s (Edward Charles b 1959), 2 da (Emma Lucinda (Mrs Paul Dorahy) b 1961, Susanna Victoria b 1963); *Career* landowner; High Sheriff of Cumbria 1984–85; memb: Regnl Fisheries Ctee N W Water Authy 1974–89, Fisheries Ctee NW Area Nat Rivers Authy 1989–92; chm: Eden & District Fisheries Ctee 1974–80, N Area Fisheries Ctee 1980–83, Eden and District Fisheries' Assoc 1970–83 (pres 1984); vice chm Salmon and Trout Assoc 1988–91 (memb Cncl 1970–91), memb Salmon Advsy Ctee 1987–90, fndr and chm Eden Owners' Assoc 1986–, chm Cumberland Branch Country Landowners' Assoc 1988–90 (pres 1990–92); *Recreations* fishing, shooting; *Style—* Peter Ecroyd, Esq; ✉ Low House, Armathwaite, Carlisle, Cumbria CA4 9ST (☎ 016974 72242)

EDBROOKE, Dr David Louis; s of Edward John Edbrooke, of Skelton, York, and Doris Edbrooke (d 1984); *b* 29 Nov 1946; *Educ* St Peter's Sch York, Guy's Hosp Med Sch (MRCS, LRCP, FRCA 1976); *m* 22 March 1975, Judith Anne, da of Douglas Rex Whittaker (d 1956); 1 s (Nicholas Robert), 1 da (Claire Diane); *Career* conslt anaesthetist Rotherham Dist Gen Hosp 1979–82; Royal Hallamshire Hosp: dir Intensive Care Unit 1982–92, clinical dir of critical care 1990–, clinical dir Intensive Care Unit 1992–, sec Consultant Med Staff Ctee 1993–, dep chm Theatre Users Subctee of Med Staff Ctee, chm Disposables Subctee of Med Staff Ctee; chm Intensive Care Nat Audit and Research Centre Working Pty on Critical Care Costing Methodology, chm Southern Sector Div of Anaesthesia; dir Mercs (Medical Economics and Research Centre Sheffield), clinical dir Directorate of Critical Care; memb Trent Regnl Advsy Subctee of Anaesthesia, memb Trent Regnl Advsy Ctee on Performance Supplements for Assoc Specialists; approx 25 published papers; memb: BMA 1971, Intensive Care Soc 1982, Casualty Surgns Assoc 1984; *Books* Basic Concepts for Operating Room and Critical Care Personnel (with S J Mather and D L Edbrooke, 1982), Multiple Choice Questions for Operating Room and Critical Care Personnel (with S J Mather and D L Edbrooke, 1983), Prehospital Emergency Care (with S J Mather and D L Edbrooke, 1986); *Recreations* golf; *Clubs* Lindrick Golf Notts; *Style—* Dr David Edbrooke; ✉ Intensive Care Unit, Royal Hallamshire Hospital, Glossop Road, Sheffield S10 2JF (☎ 0114 276 6222)

EDDLESTON, Prof Adrian Leonard William Francis; s of Rev William Eddleston (d 1995), of Colyford, Colyton, Devon, and Kathleen Brenda, *née* Jarman; *b* 2 Feb 1940; *Educ* Queen Elizabeth's GS Blackburn, St Peter's Coll Oxford (MA, BM BCh, DM), Guy's Hosp; *m* 10 Sept 1966, Hilary Kay, da of Kenneth Radford (ka 1942); 3 s (Stephen b 1969, Andrew b 1972, Paul b 1974), 1 da (Carolyn b 1968); *Career* conslt physician King's Coll Hosp 1976–; Faculty of Clinical Med King's Coll Sch of Med and Dentistry: prof of liver immunology 1982–, sub dean curriculum 1984–89, vice dean 1987–92, dean 1992–; memb Camberwell Health Authy 1986–93; non-exec dir King's Healthcare Tst Bd 1993–; sec Euro Assoc Study of Liver 1982–84, Euro rep Cncl Int Assoc for Study of Liver 1984–88; FRCP 1974, memb Assoc of Physicians of GB and Ireland 1974; *Books* Immunology of Liver Disease (1979), Interferons in the treatment of chronic virus infections of the liver (1990); *Recreations* electronics, computing, model aircraft, music; *Clubs* Epsom Radio Flying; *Style*— Prof Adrian Eddleston; ✉ Institute of Liver Studies, King's College School of Medicine and Dentistry, Denmark Hill, London SE5 9RS (☎ 0171 346 3515, fax 0171 737 0447)

EDE, Ven Dennis; *b* 8 July 1931; *Educ* Univ of Nottingham (BA Theol), CSS, Barnett House Oxford, Ripon Hall Oxford, Univ of Birmingham (MSocSci); *m* 1956, Angela, *née* Horsman; 1 s, 2 da; *Career* Nat Serv Offr RAF 1950–52; curate St Giles Sheldon 1957–60; Hodge Hill Birmingham: curate St Philip and St James 1960–64, vicar 1964–70, team rector 1970–76; pt/t chaplain: E Birmingham Hosp 1960–76, Sandwell DGH; vicar All Saints Parish Church West Bromwich 1976–90, rural dean West Bromwich 1976–90, archdeacon of Stoke-upon-Trent 1990–; hon canon Lichfield Cathedral 1990– (prebendary 1982–90); memb Gen Synod 1975–76 and 1980–90; chm: Faith in Sandwell 1988–90, Communications Ctee Diocese of Lichfield 1983–, House of Clergy Diocese of Lichfield 1985–91, Shallowford Retreat House, Baracah House Chaplaincy Univ of Keele; co-ordinator for maj disasters with religous bodies in Staffordsire 1994–, co-ordinator for North Staffs Faith in Friendship, Bishop's spokesperson for Single Regeneration Funding/Euro Funding Lichfield Dio 1994–, chm Clergy Retirement/Widows Officers Lichfield Dio 1994–; *Recreations* walking, cycling, squash; *Style*— The Ven the Archdeacon of Stoke-upon-Trent; ✉ Archdeacon's House, 39 The Brackens, Clayton, Newcastle-under-Lyme, Staffs ST5 4JL (☎ 01782 663066, fax 01782 711165)

EDE, Maurice Gordon; s of William Gordon Ede, of Ashburton, Devon, and Phyllis Maud; *b* 12 Dec 1946; *Educ* Weymouth GS; *m* 1969, Margaret Anne, da of Robert Lockhart; 1 s (Simon Maurice b 1973), 1 da (Catherine Jane b 1976); *Career* articled clerk Butterworth Jones & Co Weymouth Dorset, CA Coopers & Lybrand, ptnr Finn-Kelcey and Chapman 1976–92, sole practitioner and co sec Hearn Engineering 1992–, chief exec Assoc of Br Independent Accounting Firms (ABIAF); memb: Ctee S Eastern Soc of CAs 1980– (pres 1987–88), Cncl ICAEW 1988–; FICE 1969; *Recreations* amateur dramatics, dancing; *Style*— Maurice Ede, Esq; ✉ Oakwood, Church Lane, Challock, Ashford, Kent TN25 4BU (☎ 01233 740381, fax 01233 740381)

EDELL, Stephen Bristow; s of Ivan James Edell (d 1958), and Hilda Pamela Edell (d 1976); *b* 1 Dec 1932; *Educ* Uppingham, Univ of London (LLB); *m* 20 Sept 1958, Shirley, da of Leslie Ross Collins (d 1984); 2 s (Philip b 1969, Nicholas b 1973), 1 da (Theresa b 1964); *Career* Nat Serv RA 2 Lt 1951–53; admitted slr 1958; ptnr: Knapp-Fishers 1959–75, Crossman Block & Keith 1984–87; law cmmr 1975–83, Building Societies ombudsman 1987–94, Personal Investment Authority ombudsman 1994–; *Books* Inside Information on The Family and The Law (1969), The Family's Guide To The Law (1974); *Recreations* family life, music, opera, theatre, golf, tennis; *Clubs* City Livery; *Style*— Stephen B Edell, Esq; ✉ Personal Investment Authority Ombudsman Bureau Ltd, Hertsmere House, Hertsmere Road, London E14 4AB (☎ 0171 216 0016)

EDELMAN, Colin Neil; QC (1995); s of Gerald Bertram Edelman (d 1955), and Lynn Queenie, *née* Tropp; *b* 2 March 1954; *Educ* Haberdashers' Aske's, Clare Coll Cambridge (MA); *m* 26 Oct 1978, Jacqueline Claire, da of Hardy Wolfgang Seidel, of London; 1 s (James Simon b 14 Jan 1984), 1 da (Rachel Laura b 17 Sept 1982); *Career* called to the Bar Middle Temple 1977, recorder 1996– (asst recorder 1993), in practice Midlands and Oxford Circuit; *Recreations* walking, badminton, skiing; *Style*— Colin Edelman, Esq, QC; ✉ Devereux Chambers, Devereux Court, London WC2R 3JJ (☎ 0171 353 7534, fax 0171 353 1724)

EDELMAN, David Laurence; s of Gerald Edelman (d 1955), and Lynn, *née* Tropp, JP; *b* 7 April 1948; *Educ* Haberdashers' Aske's, Univ of Leeds (BCom); *m* 4 July 1971, Sandra Marice, da of Ephraim Freeman; 1 s (Jonathan b 1984), 2 da (Emma b 1976, d 1979, Tanya b 1981); *Career* tax ptnr Edelman & Co (CAs) 1976–81, dir City Trust Ltd (bankers) 1981–86, dir Moorfield Estates plc 1983–94 (jt md 1986–92), md Northcliffe Properties Ltd 1992–, dir Moorfields Developments Ltd 1994–; chm London Borough of Hillingdon Wishing Well Appeal for Great Ormond St Hosp 1987–89; FCA 1972, MCT 1991; *Recreations* skiing, art, music; *Style*— David Edelman, Esq; ✉ 34 Links Way, Northwood, Middx HA6 2XB; Moorfield Developments Ltd, 1 Bennetthorpe, Doncaster, S Yorkshire (☎ 01302 320446, fax 01302 340125, mobile 0831 212004)

EDELMAN, Dr Jack; CBE (1987); s of Samuel Edelman (d 1971), and Netta, *née* Smith (d 1989); *b* 8 May 1927; *Educ* Sir George Monoux GS, Imperial Coll London (BSc), Univ of Sheffield (PhD), Univ of London (DSc); *m* 15 Aug 1958, Joyce Dorothy; 2 s (Alex b 1959, Daniel b 1961), 1 step s (Simon b 1954), 1 step da (Jane b 1950); *Career* reader in enzymology Imperial Coll London 1956–64, prof of botany Univ of London 1964–73, visiting prof Univs of Nottingham and London 1975–83; dir Ranks Hovis McDougall plc 1982–88, chm Marlow Foods 1987–90; chm Br Industl Biological Res Assoc 1978–83, chm The Latymer Fndn 1990– (govr 1983–), vice pres Inst of Biology 1984–86, chm Nutrition Ctee and tstee Rank Prize Funds 1984–, vice pres Br Nutrition Fndn 1989–; memb Cncl: Queen Elizabeth Coll London 1979–85, Univ of Kent at Canterbury 1983–91, King's Coll London 1985–95; memb of many industl and govt ctees, chm MAFF/DTI Link programme 1988–; author of various text books and children's science books; *Clubs* Athenaeum; *Style*— Dr Jack Edelman, CBE; ✉ 55 Black Lion Lane, London W6 9BG (☎ 0181 748 8299, fax 0181 563 0459)

EDELMAN, Keith Graeme; *b* 10 June 1950; *Educ* Haberdashers' Aske's, UMIST (BSc); *m* 29 June 1974, Susan Margaret; 2 s (Daniel b 3 April 1978, Nicholas b 1 July 1980); *Career* dir Ladbroke Group plc and chm Texas Homecare subsid 1986–91, md Carlton Communications plc 1991–93, group chief exec Storehouse plc (and subsid BhS Ltd) 1993–; non-exec dir Eurotunnel; *Recreations* skiing, tennis, collecting antiques, cooking; *Style*— Keith Edelman, Esq; ✉ Storehouse plc, Marylebone House, 129–137 Marylebone Road, London NW1 5QD (☎ 0171 262 3456)

EDELMANN, Anton; *b* 2 July 1952, Bubesheim, W Germany; *Educ* Volkschule; *m*; 3 da; *Career* apprentice chef Ulm Bundesbahn Hotel W Germany, commis saucier The Savoy London 1969–70, first commis saucier and gardemanger Hotel de la Paix Geneva 1970–71, chef de partie, chef gardemanger and chef de partie saucier Franziskauer Dusseldorf 1971–72; Mil Serv German Air Force 1972–74; chef saucier Bayrischer-Hof Munich 1974–75, successively chef de partie saucier, poissonier chaud, gardemanger then sr sous chef the Dorchester London 1975–79, premier sous chef and actg head chef Portman Intercontinental Hotel 1979–80, head chef Grosvenor House Hotel 1980–82 (oversaw opening of Ninety Park Lane), maître chef des cuisines and dir The Savoy London 1982– (recipient AA Rosette and The Ackerman Guide's Black Clover Award); Caterer & Hotelkeeper Chef of the Year Award 1985 and 1991; Christmas Cook (LBC Radio) since 1985, subject of profile in series The Real McCoy (Thames TV) 1990, regular appearances on Masterchef (BBC TV) since 1991, participant in Hot Chefs (BBC TV) 1992, subject of BBC Radio 4's Desert Island Discs prog 1993; memb British Branch Academie Culinaire; *Books* The Savoy Food and Drink Book (1989), Canapes and Frivolities (1991), Creative Cuisine (1993), Fast Feasts (1995), Christmas Feast (1996), Perfect Pastries (1996); *Style*— Anton Edelmann, Esq; ✉ Executive Chef, The Savoy, Strand, London WC2R 0EU

EDELSHAIN, Martin Bernard; s of Norman Israel Edelshain, of Israel, and Monna Annette Carlish; *b* 18 Dec 1948; *Educ* Clifton, Jesus Coll Cambridge (BA); *m* 1984, Yasuko, da of Yukitane Okada, of Japan; 1 s (Benjamin b 1986), 1 da (Deborah b 1987); *Career* dir: S G Warburg & Co Ltd 1983–86, S G Warburg, Akroyd, Rowe & Pitman, Mullens Securities Ltd 1986–88, S G Warburg & Co Ltd 1988–95, Chugai Pharma Europe Ltd 1995–; *Recreations* cricket, skiing; *Clubs* MCC, Oriental; *Style*— Martin B Edelshain, Esq; ✉ 8 Wellington Place, London NW8 9JA (☎ 0171 289 8733)

EDEN, Elizabeth Anne; da of John Reginald Ringrose-Voase (d 1956), of Ceylon, and Florence Marjorie, *née* Grandage (d 1970); *b* 4 April 1927; *Educ* Bedgebury Park Sch; *m* E A A Eden (d 1977), s of Lt-Col A G Eden; 1 s (Charles b 1959), 2 da (Isabel b 1961, Vanessa b 1964); *Career* first lady High Sheriff of Devon 1992–93; *Clubs* Naval & Military; *Style*— Mrs Elizabeth Eden

EDEN, Prof Richard John; OBE (1978); s of James Arthur Eden, and Dora M Eden; *b* 2 July 1922; *Educ* Hertford GS, Peterhouse Cambridge; *m* 1949, Mrs Elsie Jane Greaves, da of late Herbert Edwards; 1 s, 1 da, and 1 step da; *Career* Nat Serv WWII, Capt REME Airborne Forces Europe and India; Univ of Cambridge: lectr in maths 1957–64, reader in theoretical physics 1964–83, head High Energy Theoretical Physics Gp 1964–74, head Energy Res Gp 1974–89, prof of energy Cavendish Lab 1983–89, emeritus prof 1989–; Clare Hall Cambridge: fell 1966–89, emeritus fell 1989, vice pres 1987–89, hon fell 1993; visiting prof and scientist various univs in USA and Europe 1954–89; chm Caminus Energy Ltd 1985–91, memb Eastern Electricity Bd 1985–93; *Recreations* reading, painting; *Clubs* Army and Navy; *Style*— Prof Richard Eden, OBE; ✉ 6 Wootton Way, Cambridge CB3 9LX (☎ 01223 355591)

EDEN, Hon Robert Frederick Calvert; s (by 1 m) and h to baronetcies of Baron Eden of Winton, 9 and 7 Bt, PC; *b* 30 April 1964; *Style*— The Hon Robert Eden; ✉ c/o 41 Victoria Road, London W8 5RH

EDEN, Hon Robert Ian Burnard; s and h of 9 Baron Auckland, *qv*; *b* 25 July 1962; *Educ* Blundell's Sch Tiverton; *m* 24 May 1986, Geraldine Caroll, of Dublin; 1 da (Alanna Margaret b 2 Sept 1992); *Style*— The Hon Robert Eden; ✉ c/o Tudor Rose House, 30 Links Rd, Ashtead, Surrey KT21 2HF

EDEN OF WINTON, Baron (Life Peer UK 1983), of Rushyford, Co Durham; Rt Hon Sir John Benedict Eden; 9 Bt (E 1672), of West Auckland, Durham, and 7 Bt (GB 1776), of Maryland, America; PC (1972); s of Sir Timothy Calvert Eden, 8 and 6 Bt (d 1963), and Patricia Eden, *née* Prendergast (d 1990); *b* 15 Sept 1925; *Educ* Eton, St Paul's Sch USA; *m* 1, 28 Jan 1958 (m dis 1974), Belinda Jane, da of late Sir (Frederick) John Pascoe; 2 s, 2 da; m 2, 1977, Margaret Ann, da of late Robin Gordon, former w of Viscount Strathallan, *qv*; *Heir* (to baronetcies only) s, Hon Robert Frederick Calvert Eden; *Career* served WWII, Lt RB, 2 Gurkha Rifles, Adj The Gilgit Scouts 1943–47; MP (C) Bournemouth West Feb 1954–83; oppn front bench spokesman for Power 1968–70, min of state Miny of Technol June-Oct 1970, min for indust 1970–72, min of post and telecommunications 1972–74; memb Trade and Indust Sub-Ctee of Commons Expenditure Ctee 1974–76; chm: Select Ctee European Legislation 1976–79, Select Ctee Home Affrs 1979–83; pres: Ind Schs Assoc 1969–71, Wessex Area of Nat Union of Cons and Unionist Assocs 1974–77; hon life vice pres Assoc of Cons Clubs; chm: Lady Eden's Schools Ltd, WonderWorld plc 1982–, Gamlestaden plc 1987–92, The Bricom Group Ltd 1990–93, Bullers plc 1992–94; chm: Bd of Tstees Royal Armouries 1986–94, The British Lebanese Association Ltd 1989–; vice pres Int Tree Fndn; *Recreations* gardening, shooting; *Clubs* Boodle's, Pratt's; *Style*— The Rt Hon Lord Eden of Winton, PC; ✉ 41 Victoria Rd, London W8 5RH

EDER, Andrew Howard Eric; s of Hans Eder, of London, and Helga, *née* Fall; bro of Bernard Eder, QC, *qv*; *b* 21 April 1964; *Educ* St Paul's Sch London, King's Coll Sch of Med and Dentistry KCL, Eastman Dental Inst London (BDS, MSc, LDS RCS, MRD RCS RCPS, DGDP (UK)); *m* 31 July 1988, Rosina Jayne, da of Seymour and Shirley Saideman; 2 s (David Philip b 16 Dec 1990, Daniel Lewis b 12 Aug 1993); *Career* hon clinical asst Dept of Restorative Dentistry King's Coll Hosp Sch of Med and Dentistry 1988–89 (restorative house surgn Depts of Conservation, Periodontics and Prosthetics 1987–88), conslt (locum), assoc specialist and sr clinical lectr Dept of Conservative Dentistry Eastman Dental Hosp and Inst 1994– (registrar in conservative dentistry 1990–91, clinical lectr in conservative dentistry 1991–94), restorative dental practitioner Upper Wimpole St 1991–, recognised teacher in conservative dentistry Univ of London 1993–; Alpha Omega: memb 1984–, memb Cncl 1988–89 and 1995–98, treas 1989–93, tstee 1989–, chm 1994–95; Odontological Section RSM: jr fell 1991, Pres's award 1992, memb Cncl 1992–93, hon sec 1993–96, hon treas 1996–98; Br Soc for Restorative Dentistry: memb 1987–, meetings sec 1994–96, memb Cncl 1996–98; memb BDA 1984–, Med Defence Union 1987–, Faculty of Gen Dental Practitioners 1992–; Hon DGDP (UK) Faculty of Gen Dental Practitioners RCS 1992; *Publications* published articles in academic jls; *Recreations* tennis, swimming, skiing; *Style*— Andrew Eder, Esq; ✉ 34 Pangbourne Drive, Stanmore, Middx HA7 4QT (☎ 0181 958 8747); 25 Upper Wimpole Street, London W1M 7TA (☎ 0171 935 4525, fax 0171 486 8337); Conservation Department, Eastman Dental Hospital and Institute, 256 Gray's Inn Road, London WC1X 8LD (☎ 0171 915 1027, fax 0171 915 1028)

EDER, (Henry) Bernard; QC (1990); s of Hans Eder, and Helga Eder; bro of Andrew Eder, *qv*; *b* 16 Oct 1952; *Educ* Haberdashers' Aske's, BA (Cantab); *m* 11 July 1976, Diana; 4 s (Simon b 1979, Michael b 1981, James b 1983, Benjamin b 1991), 1 da (Hannah b 1988); *Career* called to the Bar Inner Temple 1975, asst recorder; *Recreations* tennis, skiing; *Style*— Bernard Eder, Esq, QC; ✉ Essex Court Chambers, 24 Lincoln's Inn Fields, London WC2A 3ED (☎ 0171 813 8000, fax 0171 813 8080, telex 888465)

EDES, (John) Michael; CMG (1981); s of late Lt-Col N H Edes, and Louise Edes; *b* 19 April 1930; *Educ* Blundell's, Clare Coll Cambridge (BA), Yale Univ (MA); *m* 1978, Angela Mermagen; 2 s; *Career* Diplomatic Serv, ret; ambass to Libya 1980–83, ambass and head UK Delegation to Conference on Security and Disarmament in Europe Stockholm 1983–86, visiting fell Int Inst for Strategic Studies 1987, ambass and head UK Delegation to Negotiations on Reductions in Conventional Armed Forces in Europe and on Confidence and Security Building Measures in Europe Vienna 1987–90; *Recreations* gardening, listening to music; *Clubs* Athenaeum, Hawks (Cambridge); *Style*— Michael Edes, Esq, CMG; ✉ c/o Foreign and Commonwealth Office, King Charles St, London SW1

EDEY, Prof Harold Cecil; s of Cecil Edey (d 1971), and Elsie Norah, *née* Walmsley (d 1965); *b* 23 Feb 1913; *Educ* HS for Boys Croydon, LSE (pt/t, BCom); *m* 1944, Dilys Mary Pakeman, da of Richard Idris Jones: 1 s (David Peter b 1949), 1 da (Nerys Elizabeth b 1946); *Career* cmmnd RNVR 1940–46; articled clerk John Baker Sons and Bell 1930–35; staff memb: Deloitte Plender Griffiths and Co 1935–36, S Pearson and Son Group 1936–40 and 1946–49; LSE: lectr in accounting and fin 1949–55, reader in accounting 1955–62, prof of accounting 1962–80, pro-dir 1967–70, emeritus prof 1980–, hon fell 1986; fndr govr London Business Sch 1965–71; memb: Cncl CNAA 1965–73, Senate Univ of London 1975–80; hon prof UCW 1980–95; laureate Chartered Accountants Founding Socs Centenary Award 1987, Silver Jubilee Medal 1977; Freeman City of

London 1986, Hon Liveryman Worshipful Co of Chartered Accountants in England and Wales 1986; Hon LLD CNAA 1972; ACA 1935 (memb Cncl 1969–80); *Books* National Income and Social Accounting (with A T Peacock, 1954), Business Budgets and Accounts (1959), Introduction to Accounting (1963), The Companies Act 1981 (with L H Leigh, 1981), Accounting Queries (1982); *Recreations* walking; *Style—* Prof Harold Edey

EDEY, Russell Philip; s of Lt-Col Anthony Russell Edey (d 1994), of Johannesburg, S Africa, and Barbara Stephanie Ann, *née* Rees-Jones; *b* 2 Aug 1942; *Educ* St Andrew's Coll Grahamstown S Africa; *m* 8 June 1968, Celia Ann Malcolm, da of James Bisdee Malcolm Green, of Colchester, Essex; 2 s (Philip b 1971, Anthony b 1975), 1 da (Kate b 1973); *Career* CA; N M Rothschild & Sons Ltd: dir 1981–, an md 1990–, currently head of corp fin; non-exec dir: Northern Foods plc 1988–, English China Clays plc 1995–, FKI plc 1996–; dir: The New Shakespeare Company Ltd 1990–, Shield Trust Ltd 1992–; memb Cncl of Mgmnt The Br Lung Fndn 1984–90, govr and memb Fin Ctee Anglia Poly Univ; UK tstee Euro Sch of Mgmnt; *Recreations* tennis, theatre, current affairs, wine; *Clubs* Australian, Melbourne; *Style—* Russell Edey, Esq; ✉ Starling Leeze, Coggeshall, Essex CO6 1SL; N M Rothschild & Sons Ltd, New Court, St Swithins Lane, London EC4P 4DU

EDGAR, David Burman; *b* 26 Feb 1948; *Educ* Univ of Manchester (BA); *m* 1979, Eve Brook; *Career* author and playwright; Univ of Birmingham: dir of playwriting studies 1989–, hon sr res fell 1988–, hon prof 1992–; hon assoc artist RSC 1989, hon fell Birmingham Poly 1991, Hon MA Univ of Bradford 1984, Hon DUniv of Surrey 1993; *TV and Radio* The Eagle Has Landed 1973, Sanctuary 1973, I Know What I Meant 1974, Ecclesiastes 1977, Vote For Them (with Neil Grant) 1989, A Movie Starring Me 1991, Buying A Landslide 1992, Citizen Locke 1994; *Film* Lady Jane 1986; *Awards* for Pentecost: Evening Standard Best Play Award 1995 and Olivier nomination for Best Play 1996; *Books* Destiny (1976), Wreckers (1977), The Jail Diary of Albie Sachs (1978), Teendreams (1979), Mary Barnes (1979), Maydays (1983), Entertaining Strangers (1985), Plays One (1987), That Summer (1987), The Second Time as Farce (1988), Vote For Them (1989), Heartlanders (1989), Edgar Shorts (1990), Plays Two (1990), The Shape of the Table (1990), Plays Three (1991), The Strange Case of Dr Jekyll and Mr Hyde (1992), Pentecost (1995); *Plays* The National Interest 1971, Excuses Excuses (Coventry) 1972, Death, Story (Birmingham Rep) 1972, Baby Love 1973, The Dunkirk Spirit 1974, Dick Deterred (Bush) 1974, O Fair Jerusalem (Birmingham Rep) 1975, Saigon Rose (Edinburgh) 1976, Blood Sports (Bush) 1976, Destiny (Aldwych 1977) 1976, Wreckers 1977, Our Own People 1977, The Jail Diary of Albie Sachs (adaptation, Warehouse Theatre) 1978, Mary Barnes (adaptation, Birmingham Rep then Royal Court) 1978–79, Teendreams (with Susan Todd) 1979, Nicholas Nickleby (adaptation, Aldwych then Plymouth Theatre NY) 1980–81, Maydays (Barbican) 1983, Entertaining Strangers (NT 1987) 1985, That Summer (Hampstead) 1987, Heartlanders (with Stephen Bill and Anne Devlin, Birmingham Rep) 1989, The Shape of the Table (NT) 1990, The Strange Case of Dr Jekyll and Mr Hyde (Barbican) 1991, Pentecost (RSC Other Place, then Young Vic) 1994; *Style—* David Edgar, Esq; ✉ c/o Michael Imison Playwrights Ltd, 28 Almeida Street, London N1 1TD (☎ 0171 354 3174, fax 0171 359 6273)

EDGAR, Prof (William) Michael; s of Benjamin Frederic Edgar (d 1987), of Hexham, Northumberland, and Marion, *née* Golightly (d 1979); *b* 10 June 1940; *Educ* Newcastle Royal GS, Univ of Newcastle (BDS, BSc, PhD, DDSc); *m* 4 Aug 1965, Christine Lesley, da of Alfred Leslie Tinwell (d 1983), of Tynemouth, Northumberland; 2 s (Thomas b 1970, James b 1974), 1 da (Abigail b 1967); *Career* sr lectr oral physiology Univ of Newcastle 1977–81 (lectr 1968–77); visiting scientist: Eastman Dental Centre Rochester NY 1972, Nat Inst Dental Res NIH Bethesda MD 1979; prof of dental sci Univ of Liverpool 1982–; hon sec Br Soc for Dental Res; FDSRCS; *Recreations* music, walking; *Style—* Prof Michael Edgar; ✉ Department of Clinical Dental Sciences, University of Liverpool, Liverpool L69 3BX (☎ 0151 706 5261/2); 14 Hougoumont Ave, Waterloo, Liverpool L22 0LL; Castley Bank, Grayrigg, nr Kendal, Cumbria LA8 9ET

EDGAR, Michael Alan; s of Alan Edgar (d 1992), of Christchurch, Hants, and Mary, *née* Robey; *b* 6 July 1937; *Educ* Univ of Cambridge (MA, MB BChir, MChir); *m* Hilary, da of Arthur (Plum) Warner; 3 da (Alison Jane b 7 July 1964, Jocelyn Ann b 15 April 1967, Claire Penelope b 6 Dec 1971); *Career* currently: sr conslt orthopaedic and spinal surgn The Middx and UCH, sr lectr in spinal deformities Inst of Orthopaedics and Royal Nat Orthopaedic Hosp London, hon conslt to Royal Nat Orthopaedic Hosp, Nat Hosp for Neurology and Neurosurgery and Nat Hosp for Sick Children Great Ormand St, civil consl advsr in orthopaedics to RAF, consl to King Edward VII Hosp for Offrs, pres Br Scoliosis Soc (1994–95), dean Inst of Sports Med; memb Editorial Bd: Neuro-Orthopaedics, Spine; dir Dept of Spinal Deformities Inst of Orthopaedics UCL 1980–88, referee in spinal surgery to RCS 1993, sec Br Orthopaedic Assoc 1989–92, memb Editorial Bd Jl of Bone & Joint Surgery 1982–86, examiner (MCH Orth) Liverpool 1989–92; tstee: Br Scoliosis Research Soc, Scoliosis Assoc of the UK, ARISE the Royal Nat Orthopaedic Hosp Scoliosis Research Tst; memb UK Exec: World Orthopaedic Concern, SICOT; memb: Clinical Servs Ctee Br Orthopaedic Assoc until 1993, Academic Cncl Inst of Sports Med, Awards Ctee NE Thames RHA; Awards: Br Orthopaedic Assoc Euro travelling fell 1972, Gold Medal lectr Robert Jones & Agnes Hunt Orthopaedic Hosp Oswestry 1983; corresponding memb Scoliosis Research Soc; memb Cncl RCS 1995–; memb: UK Inst Soc for Study of the Lumbar Spine, Euro Spinal Deformities Soc; fell Orthopaedic Section RSM, FRCS 1967, FBOA; *Publications* author of various papers and proceedings mainly concerning scoliosis and other spinal conditions; *Recreations* sailing, walking, antique restoration; *Clubs* Leander, Royal Thames Yacht, Royal Lymington Yacht; *Style—* Michael Edgar, Esq; ✉ 149 Harley Street, London W1N 2DE (☎ 0171 486 0027, fax 0171 487 5997); The Orthopaedic Department, The Middlesex Hospital, Mortimer Street, London W1N 8AA (☎ 0171 380 9037); The Royal National Orthopaedic Hospital, 45–51 Bolsover Street, London W1P 8AQ (☎ 0171 387 5070)

EDGCUMBE, Piers Valletorte; 2 surviving s of George Edgcumbe (d 1977), but er by his 2 w, Una Pamela, da of Edward Lewis George, of Perth, W Australia; hp to half-bro, 8 Earl of Mount Edgcumbe, *qv*; *b* 23 Oct 1946; *m* 1971 (m dis), Hilda Warn; 2 da (Prudence b 1972, Angela b 1975); *Style—* Piers Edgcumbe, Esq

EDGE, The; David Evans; s of Garvin Evans, of Dublin, and Gwenda; *b* 8 Aug 1961; *Educ* Mount Temple Sch; *Career* guitarist and fndr memb U2 1978– (with Bono, *qv*, Adam Clayton, *qv* and Larry Mullen, Jr, *qv*); first U2 release U23 (EP) 1979; *Albums* Boy 1980, October 1981, War 1983 (entered UK chart at no 1), Under A Blood Red Sky (live album) 1983, The Unforgettable Fire 1984 (entered UK charts at no 1), The Joshua Tree 1987 (entered UK charts at no 1, fastest selling album ever in UK), Rattle & Hum 1988 (entered UK charts at No 1), Achtung Baby 1991, Zooropa 1993 (No 1 in 18 countries); *Singles* incl: Fire 1981, New Year's Day (first UK Top Ten hit) 1983, Pride (In the Name of Love) 1984, Unforgettable Fire 1985, With or Without You 1987, I Still Haven't Found What I'm Looking For 1987, Where The Streets Have No Name 1987, Desire (first UK no 1 single) 1988, Angel of Harlem 1988, When Love Comes to Town 1989, All I Want Is You 1989, Night & Day (for AIDS benefit LP Red Hot & Blue) 1990, The Fly (entered UK charts at no 1) 1991, Stay 1993; *Film* Rattle & Hum 1988; *Tours* incl: UK, US, Belgium and Holland 1980, UK, US, Ireland and Europe 1981–83, Aust, NZ and Europe 1984, A Conspiracy of Hope (Amnesty International Tour) 1986, world Joshua Tree tour 1987, Rattle & Hum tour 1988, Zoo TV world tour (played to 5m people) 1992–93; also appeared at: Live Aid 1985 (Best Live Aid Performance Rolling Stone Readers' Poll 1986), Self Aid Dublin, Smile Jamaica (Dominion Theatre, in aid of hurricane disaster relief) 1988, New Year's Eve concert Dublin (broadcast live to Europe and USSR) 1989; performed at venues incl: Wembley Stadium, Madison Square Garden NY, Longest Day Festival Milton Keynes Bowl, Croke Park Dublin, Sun Devil Stadium Arizona; *Awards* Grammy awards: Album of the Year (The Joshua Tree) 1987, Best Rock Performance (Joshua Tree tour) 1987, Best Rock Performance (Desire) 1989, Best Video (Where The Streets Have No Name) 1989, Best Alternative Album (Zooropa) 1993; others incl: Best Band Rolling Stone Readers' Poll 1986 (also jt winner Critics' Poll), Band of the Year Rolling Stone Writers' Poll 1984, Best International Act BPI Awards 1989 and 1990, Best Live Act BPI Awards 1993; *Style—* The Edge; ✉ c/o Regine Moylett Publicity, First Floor, 145a Ladbroke Grove, London W10 6HJ (☎ 0171 221 0554, fax 0171 221 8532)

EDGE, Dr David Owen; s of Stephen Rathbone Holden Edge (d 1955), and Kathleen Edith, *née* Haines (d 1991); *b* 4 Sept 1932; *Educ* The Leys Sch Cambridge, Gonville and Caius Coll Cambridge (BA, MA, PhD); *m* 21 Feb 1959, Barbara, *née* Corsie; 2 s (Alastair Clouston b 23 Nov 1963, Gordon b 2 Oct 1966), 1 da (Aran Kathleen (Mrs Woodfin) b 23 June 1960); *Career* Nat Serv Corpl wireless instr RAF 1950–52; physics master Perse Sch Cambridge 1959, prodr Sci Talks BBC London 1959–66, dir Sci Studies Unit Univ of Edinburgh 1966–89 (reader 1979–92, reader emeritus 1992–), ed Social Studies of Science 1971–, pres Soc for Social Studies of Sci (4S) 1985–87; advsr HQ Scout Assoc Scot 1967–85, memb various ctees and panels CNAA 1972–89, pres Scout and Guide Graduate Assoc (former chm), chm Bd Science Policy Support Gp 1989–93; memb: ABRC Working Party on Peer Review 1990–91, DQA Auditing Team HEQC 1991–; winner J D Bernal Prize (4S) 1993; FRAS 1960, FRSA 1972, FAAAS 1989, FRSE 1992; *Books* Meaning and Control (ed with J N Wolfe, 1973), Astronomy Transformed: The Emergence of Radio Astronomy in Britain (with M Mulkay, 1976), Scientific Images and Their Social Uses (with I Cameron, 1979), Science in Context: Readings in the Sociology of Science (ed with B Barnes, 1982); *Recreations* hill walking, travel, enjoying music and sport; *Clubs* Baden-Powell House; *Style—* Dr David Edge, FRSE; ✉ 25 Gilmour Rd, Edinburgh EH16 5NS (☎ 0131 667 3497, fax 0131 668 4008, e-mail d.edge@ed.ac.uk); Science Studies Unit, Department of Sociology, University of Edinburgh, 21 Buccleuch Place, Edinburgh EH8 9LN (☎ 0131 650 4256, telex 727442 UNNED G, fax 0131 650 6886)

EDGE, Geoffrey; s of John Edge (d 1977), of Tividale, Warley, W Midlands, and Alice Edith, *née* Rimell (d 1986); *b* 26 May 1943; *Educ* Rowley Regis GS, LSE, Univ of Birmingham (BA); *Career* asst lectr in geography Univ of Leicester 1967–70, lectr in geography Open Univ 1970–74, res fell Birmingham Poly 1979–80, sr res fell Preston and NE London Polys 1980–84; New Initiatives co-ordinator Copec Housing Tst 1984–87, sr assoc PE International 1987–; chm Planning Ctee Bletchley UDC 1972–74, vice chm Planning Ctee Milton Keynes Borough Cncl 1973–76, MP (Lab) Aldridge Brownhills 1974–79 (Parly private sec, Dept Educn Science and Privy Cncl Office), chm Econ Devpt Ctee W Midlands CC 1981–86, chm W Midlands Enterprise Bd 1982–, leader Walsall Met Borough Cncl 1988–90 (chm Policy and Resources Ctee) 1988–90; memb: Regnl Studies Assoc, Geographical Assoc; FRGS; *Books* Regional Analysis & Development (jt ed, 1973); *Recreations* gardening, walking, travel, reading, listening to classical music; *Style—* Geoffrey Edge, Esq; ✉ West Midlands Enterprise Board, Wellington House, 31/34 Waterloo St, Birmingham B2 5JT (☎ 0121 236 8855, fax 0121 233 3942)

EDGE, Prof Gordon Malcolm; CBE (1992); *Educ* Bolton Inst Tech, Brunel Univ (DipEl, MIEE, CEng, DTech); *m* Nikki; 2 s (Tom, Matthew), 1 da (Lucy); *Career* md Cambridge Consultants Ltd 1961–69; PA Technology: fndr and chief exec 1970–86, memb Int Bd 1974–86, memb Bd Stockholm 1977–86; fndr Generics Holding Corporation 1986–; currently non-exec dir: Peek plc, Pharmacia BioSensor AB Sweden; speaker at seminars and conferences, contrib to books and jls; res visitor Dept of Zoology Univ of Cambridge 1982–83, visiting memb King's Coll London, visiting prof Brunel Univ 1985–; memb: Ericsson Sci Cncl Stockholm 1983–, ACARD 1984–86, Cncl BTG 1985–, Bd ADAS 1985–91, Ctee on Emerging Technols ACOST 1986–89 (chm Sub Gp on Advanced Mfrg 1988–91); advsr on R&D mgmnt to Volvo AB 1985–87; fell Royal Swedish Acad of Engrg Scis 1989, FBCS, FRSA; *Books* Technology Management (ed Wild, 1990); *Clubs* Athenaeum; *Style—* Prof Gordon Edge, CBE; ✉ Peek plc, 309 Reading Road, Henley-on-Thames, Oxon RG9 1EL (☎ 01491 415200, fax 01491 414404)

EDGE, Capt Sir (Philip) Malcolm; KCVO (1995); s of Stanley Weston Edge (d 1977), and Edith Harriet, *née* Liddell; *b* 15 July 1931; *Educ* Rock Ferry HS, HMS Conway, Liverpool Nautical Coll; *m* 18 Feb 1967, (Kathleen) Anne (d 1994), da of Richard Nelson Alfred Greenwood (d 1986); 1 s (David b 1977), 1 da (Caroline b 1974); *Career* i/c Shipping subsidiary BP 1969 (apprentice 1949, jr offr 1951); Corp of Trinity House: elder bro 1978–, dep master and chm Bd 1988–96; memb Port of London Authy 1980–, dir Standard Protection & Indemnity Assoc Ltd 1988– (chm 1992–); Freeman City of London 1980; Liveryman: Hon Co of Master Mariners 1980 (Hon Freeman 1988–96), Worshipful Co of Shipwrights 1990; Master Watermans Co of River Thames 1996 (Freeman 1983, jr warden 1993); hon memb Royal Yacht Squadron; FNI 1979; *Recreations* sailing, DIY; *Clubs* Royal Thames Yacht; *Style—* Capt Sir Malcolm Edge, KCVO; ✉ Hillside, Layters Way, Gerrards Cross, Bucks SL9 7QZ (☎ 01753 887937); Trinity House, Tower Hill, London (☎ 0171 480 6601, fax 0171 480 7662, telex 987526 NAVAID G)

EDGE, Stephen Martin; s of Harry Hurst Edge, of Bolton, Lancs, and Mary, *née* Rigg; *b* 29 Nov 1950; *Educ* Canon Slade GS Bolton, Univ of Exeter (LLB); *m* 6 Sept 1975, Melanie, da of Eric Stanley Lawler (d 1995), of Hassocks, Sussex; 2 da (Charlotte Louise b 1982, Katharine Sarah b 1987); *Career* admitted slr 1975; ptnr (specialising in corporate tax) Slaughter and May 1973–; various contribs to pubns and articles on tax; *Clubs* MCC; *Style—* Stephen Edge, Esq; ✉ Slaughter & May, 35 Basinghall Street, London EC2V 5DB (☎ 0171 600 1200, fax 0171 726 0038)

EDGLEY, Colin Ronald; s of late Andrew Charles Edgley, and Doreen, *née* Major; *b* 18 Dec 1945; *Educ* Haberdashers' Aske's; *m* 9 Aug 1969, Carole, da of Alexander Cornish (d 1981), of Wallington; 1 s (Simon Alexander Charles b 1972), 1 da (Alison Charlotte b 1975); *Career* various directorships Spillers Foods Ltd 1981–88 incl: Gland Supplies Ltd (chm), Manor Produce Ltd, Suir Endocrine Ltd 1982–84, Castlefield Foods Ltd (chm) 1986–88, Dalgety Foods 1988; chief exec Homepride Foods Ltd 1988–93; currently chm: Alphaquest Ltd, Thurlow Management Ltd; FCCA 1976; *Recreations* rugby, golf, opera; *Clubs* RAC; *Style—* Colin Edgley; ✉ Thurlow House, Long Thurlow, Suffolk IP31 3JA (☎ 01359 259539, fax 01359 258131)

EDGSON WRIGHT, Paul; s of Hugh Edgson Wright, MM (d 1979), of Folkestone, Kent, and Diana Christine, *née* Smith (d 1991); *b* 3 March 1935; *Educ* Marlborough; *m* 11 June 1960, Gillian Elspeth, da of Sidney Leonard Shaw, of Santiago, Chile; 2 s (Mark b 1963, (Andrew) Peter b 1967), 1 da (Kathryn b 1961); *Career* articled Barton Mayhew & Co CAs 1953–59, Riddell Stead Graham & Hutchinson CAs Montreal PQ Canada 1959–61, Stanhay (Ashford) Ltd Gp 1961–72 (taken over by Hestair plc 1971) (appointed fin dir and co sec 1970), chm Stanhay (Autos) Ltd 1972–76, gp chief accountant MacBlast gp of cos 1976–77, Rothman Pantall & Co CAs 1978–84, formed Shaws CAs (reg insolvency practitioner) specialising in insolvency and investigations 1985; MSPI, FCA; *Recreations* shooting, fishing, sailing, ornithology; *Style—* Paul Edgson Wright, Esq; ✉ Forstal Gate, Little Chart, Ashford, Kent TN27 0PU (☎ and fax 01233 840246);

Shaws, 12 Bourne Court, Southend Road, Woodford Green, Essex IG8 8HD (☎ 0181 550 7999, fax 0181 551 7999)

EDINBURGH, Dean of; *see:* Morris, Very Rev Timothy David

EDINBURGH, Bishop of 1986–; Most Rev Richard Frederick Holloway; s of Arthur Holloway (d 1987), and Mary, *née* Luke (d 1976); *b* 26 Nov 1933; *Educ* Kelham Theological Coll, Edinburgh Theological Coll, Union Theological Seminary New York (STM), BD London; *m* 20 April 1963, Jean Elizabeth, da of the Rev Edwin Oliver Kennedy, of Hackettstown, New Jersey; 1 s (Mark Ramsay b 16 May 1969), 2 da (Ann b 1964, Sara b 1966); *Career* Nat Serv RA 1952–54; priest i/c St Margaret and St Mungo's Glasgow 1963–68; rector: Old St Paul's Edinburgh 1968–80, The Church of the Advent Boston Mass 1980–84; vicar St Mary Magdalen Oxford 1984–86; Primus of Scottish Episcopal Church 1992–; memb Human Fertilisation and Embryology Authy 1990–; Hon: DUniv Strathclyde, DD Univ of Aberdeen; FRSA 1992, FRSE 1995; *Books* Let God Arise (1972), A New Vision of Glory (1974), A New Heaven (1979), Beyond Belief (1981), Signs of Glory (1982), The Killing (1984), The Anglican Tradition (ed, 1984), Paradoxes of Christian Faith and Life (1984), The Sidelong Glance (1985), The Way of the Cross (1986), Seven to Flee, Seven to Follow (1986), Crossfire: Faith and Doubt in an Age of Certainty (1988), When I Get to Heaven (1988), Another Country, Another King (1991), Anger, Sex, Doubt & Death (1992), The Stranger in the Wings (1994), Churches and How to Survive Them (with Bruce Avery, 1994), Behold Your King (1995), Limping Towards the Sunrise (1995); *Recreations* walking, reading, films, music; *Style—* The Most Rev the Bishop of Edinburgh, FRSE; ✉ 3 Eglinton Crescent, Edinburgh EH12 5DH (☎ 0131 226 5099); Diocesan Centre, 21A, Grosvenor Cresent, Edinburgh EH12 5EE (☎ 0131 538 7044, fax 0131 538 7088)

EDINGTON, (George) Gordon; s of George Adam Edington (d 1994), and Phyllis Mary, *née* Allen (d 1971); *b* 7 Sept 1945; *Educ* St Mary's Sch Kenya, St Lawrence Coll Kent; *m* 23 June 1973, Jane Mary, da of Jack Jesson Adie, CMG; 4 s (Daniel Jesson b 18 Jan 1975, Joel Adam b 7 Oct 1976, Sam Gordon b 31 July 1980, Jack Jesson b 1 June 1985); *Career* with Knight Frank & Rutley 1964–68, ptnr Anthony Lipton & Co 1968–72, dir Sterling Land Co Ltd 1972–73, dir Westwood Commercial Holdings Ltd 1973–75, conslt Amalgamated Investment and Property Co Ltd and Deloitte Haskins & Sells/Price Waterhouse 1975–76, jt md Summerbridge Investments Ltd 1976–81, md Lynton plc 1981–94 (now chm); BAA plc: joined following takeover of Lynton plc 1988, gp property dir (main bd appt) 1991–, chm BAA International 1992–, chm Airports UK Ltd 1991–92, Scottish Express Ltd 1991–93, BAA Hotels Ltd 1991–92 and Skycare Cargo Ltd 1991–94, BAA Art Prog 1994–; memb Gen Cncl Br Property Fedn; chm Michael Stuckey Tst (supporting young musicians), chm Public Art Devpt Tst; memb: Bd of Govrs The Wilson Centre Fitzwilliam Coll Cambridge, NCH Action for Children Millennium Devpt Cncl, Cncl of Advsrs Vision for London; chm Land and City Families Tst; Liveryman Worshipful Co of Chartered Surveyors; CEng, CIMgt, FRICS 1970, FRSA 1992, FICE; *Books* The Clowes Family of Chester Sporting Artists (Grosvenor Museum Chester, 1985); *Recreations* tennis, real tennis, golf, fishing, shooting, art, photography, opera, historic Thames rivercraft, hill walking; *Clubs* Arts, Riverside Racquet, Royal Wimbledon Golf, Flyfishers', Holyport, Real Tennis; *Style—* Gordon Edington, Esq; ✉ BAA plc, 130 Wilton Road, London SW1V 1LQ (☎ 0171 932 6806, fax 0171 932 6704)

EDINGTON, Paul Tellet; s of Dr Francis Cameron Edington, of Penrith, and Anella Jean, *née* Munro; *b* 24 April 1943; *Educ* Sedbergh, Selwyn Coll Cambridge (MA, MB BCh), St Mary's Hosp Med Sch London; *m* 3 March 1973, Jane Margaret, da of Dr Geoffrey Howard Bulow, of Wellington Heath; 2 s (James b 1976, David b 1978), 1 da (Katherine b 1982); *Career* registrar St Mary's Hosp London 1973–76, exchange registrar Univ of Cape Town 1975–76; sr registrar in rotation Newcastle upon Tyne: Newcastle Gen Hosp, Royal Victoria Hosp, Princess Mary Maternity Hosp, Queen Elizabeth Hosp Gateshead; conslt obstetrician and gynaecologist Univ Hosp Nottingham 1981–; LRCP, MRCS, FRCOG 1990 (MRCOG 1974); *Recreations* golf, cricket, squash, gardening, skiing, music; *Clubs* Hawks' (Cambridge), The Gynaecological Club; *Style—* Paul Edington, Esq; ✉ 1 Baildon Close, Wollaton Park, Nottingham NG8 1BS (☎ 0115 978 0187); University Hospital, Queen's Medical Centre, Nottingham NG7 2UH (☎ 0115 924 9924 ext 44106)

EDIS, HE Richard John Smale; CMG (1994); s of Denis Charles Edis, of Willand, Devon, and Sylvia Mary, *née* Smale; *b* 1 Sept 1943; *Educ* King Edward's Sch Birmingham, St Catharine's Coll Cambridge (MA); *m* 3 April 1971, Geneviève Nanette Suzanne, da of René Marcel Cérisoles, of Palm Beach and Nice; 3 s (Rupert b 1971, Oliver b 1972, Jamyn b 1975); *Career* HM Dip Serv 1966–; served: Nairobi, Lisbon, NY, Geneva; HM cmmr Br Indian Ocean Territory and head E African Dept FCO 1988, visiting fell in int studies Univ of Cambridge 1991–92; HM ambass: to Mozambique 1992–95, to Tunisia 1995–; awarded Special Constabulary Medal 1991; Knight Mil Order of Christ Portugal 1973; *Recreations* reading, writing on history and current affairs, sport; *Clubs* Travellers, Cambridge Union; *Style—* HE Mr Richard Edis, CMG; ✉ c/o Foreign and Commonwealth Office (Tunis), King Charles Street, London SW1A 2AH

EDKINS, George Joseph (John); s of George Henry John Edkins (d 1981), and Olympia, *née* Izzillo (d 1971); *b* 18 June 1930; *Educ* Mitcham GS, Oxted GS; *m* 17 July 1954, Audrey Joan, da of Arthur James Paul; 2 s (Paul Anthony b 1 Aug 1956, Peter David b 19 Sept 1962), 1 da (Sara-Jane b 15 June 1965); *Career* Served RAF Naval Fighter Intelligence 1948–50; Shell Int Petroleum 1950–55; chartered accountant: Frazer whiting 1955–60, Pike Russell & Co 1960–70; sr ptnr Russell Limebeer 1978–88, sr ptnr Fraser & Russell 1988–90 (ret 1990); chief exec Cystic Fibrosis Tst 1991–96; treas Int Cystic Fibrosis Assoc, memb Cncl Assoc of Med Res Charities 1992–96; Liveryman Worshipful Co of Butchers (memb Ct); FCA 1965; *Recreations* work, rugby, all sports; *Clubs* RAC, City of London, Marylebone Cricket; *Style—* John Edkins, Esq; ✉ Larks Meadow, Oxshott Rise, Cobham, Surrey KT11 2RW (☎ 01932 863017, fax 01932 860953)

EDLMANN, Stephen Raphael Reynolds; s of Capt Raphael Francis Reynolds (d 1975), and Waltraud Helga Mathilde, *née* Seveke (d 1984); *b* 13 March 1954; *Educ* Tonbridge, Trinity Hall Cambridge (MA); *m* 14 July 1979, Deborah Catherine, da of Roger John Nimmo Booth, of Co Durham; 5 s (Richard b 1980, Oliver b 1981, Nicholas b and d 1981, Lawrence b 1983, Joss b 1991); *Career* Linklaters & Paines: joined 1977, ptnr 1985–, currently head Int Finance Dept; memb Worshipful Co of Slrs 1985; memb: Law Soc 1979, Int Bar Assoc 1986; *Recreations* entertaining, racing, tennis, golf; *Clubs* Hawks', MCC, Roehampton, Harlequins; *Style—* Stephen Edlmann, Esq; ✉ Linklaters & Paines, Barrington House, 59–67 Gresham St, London EC2V 7JA (☎ 0171 606 7080, fax 0171 606 5113, telex 884349)

EDMISTON, Robert Norman; s of Vivian Randolph Edmiston and Norma Margaret Edmiston; *b* 6 Oct 1946; *Educ* Abbs Cross Tech Sch, Barking Regnl Coll of Technol; *m* 1967, Patricia Ann, da of Alfred Edward Talbot (d 1962); 1 s (Andrew b 1969), 2 da (Deborah b 1971, Angela b 1975); *Career* fin analyst Ford Motor Co, capital planning mangr Chrysler (mangr fin analysis), fin dir Jensen Motor Co, chm and chief exec IM Group Ltd; *Recreations* church activities, swimming, windsurfing, flying, shooting, skiing; *Style—* Robert Edmiston, Esq; ✉ IM Group Ltd, Ryder Street, West Bromwich, West Midlands B70 0EJ

EDMONDS, Dr Charles John; s of Charles John Edmonds, of Enfield, Middx, and Lilian, *née* Robertson; *b* 17 April 1929; *Educ* Latymer Sch Edmonton, Univ of London (MD, DSc); *m* 13 March 1965, Gillian Mary, da of Augustus Riggott (d 1988); 3 s (Nicholas, Christopher, Jonathan); *Career* Nat Serv Flt Lt RAF Inst of Aviation Med Farnborough Hants 1955–56; clinical scientist MRC 1967–94; conslt endocrinologist: UCH London 1967–91, Northwick Park Hosp Harrow Middx 1972–; author of many scientific pubns; FRCP, memb RSM; *Books* The Large Intestine (1981), Journal of Endocrinology (scientific ed); *Recreations* walking, cycling, gardening, reading; *Style—* Dr Charles Edmonds; ✉ Northwick Park Hospital, Watford Rd, Harrow, Middx HA1 3UJ

EDMONDS, David Albert; s of Albert Edmonds, of Kingsley, Cheshire, and Gladys Edmonds; *b* 6 March 1944; *Educ* Helsby GS Cheshire, Univ of Keele (BA); *m* 1966, Ruth, da of Eric Beech, of Christleton, Chester; 2 s (Jonathan, Benedict), 2 da (Jane, Elizabeth); *Career* asst princ Miny of Housing and Local Govt 1966–69 (private sec/Parly sec 1969–71), princ DOE 1971–73, observer Civil Serv Selection Bd 1973–74, visiting fell Johns Hopkins Univ Baltimore USA 1974–75; DOE: private sec/permanent sec 1975–77, asst sec 1977–79, private sec to Sec of State 1979–83, under sec Inner Cities Directorate 1983–84; chief exec The Housing Corp 1984–91, dep chm New Statesman and Society 1988–90; pres Int New Towns Assoc 1988–91, dir The Housing Fin Corp 1988–91, md Group Central Servs NatWest Group 1991–; tstee CRISIS 1994–, memb Cncl Univ of Keele 1996–; *Recreations* opera, golf, walking, films; *Clubs* Wimbledon Park Golf, Wimbledon Wanderers CC; *Style—* David Edmonds, Esq; ✉ 61 Cottenham Park Rd, Wimbledon, London SW20 0DR (☎ 0181 946 3729); NatWest Group, 41 Lothbury, London EC2P 2BP (☎ 0171 726 1424)

EDMONDS, John Christopher; CMG (1978), CVO (1971); s of Capt Archibald Charles Mackay Edmonds, OBE, RN (d 1961), of Bognor Regis, Sussex; *b* 23 June 1921; *Educ* Kelly Coll; *m* 1, 1948 (m dis 1965), Elena, da of Serge Tornow; 2 s; m 2, 1966, Armine, da of Clement Hilton Williams, MBE (d 1963), of Sonning, Berks; *Career* RN 1939–59, Cdr 1957; staff of: NATO Defence Coll 1953–55, C-in-C Home Fleet 1955–57, CDS 1958–59; Dip Serv 1959–81, cnsllr Br Embassy Ankara 1968–71, Paris 1972–74, head Arms Control and Disarmament Dept FCO 1974–77; leader UK delgn to comprehensive test ban treaty negotiations Geneva (with personal rank of ambassador) 1978–81; chm Cncl for Arms Control 1990–; *Clubs* Army and Navy; *Style—* John Edmonds, Esq, CMG, CVO; ✉ North Lodge, Sonning, Berkshire RG6 0ST

EDMONDS, John Walter; s of Walter Edgar Edmonds (d 1986), and Maude Rose, *née* Edwards; *b* 28 Jan 1944; *Educ* Christ's Hosp, Oriel Coll Oxford (MA); *m* 30 Sept 1967, (Janet) Linden, da of Franklin Arthur Callaby (d 1978); 2 da (Lucinda Jane b 1969, Nanette Sally b 1972); *Career* GMB (formerly GMWU): res asst 1965–67, dep res offr 1967–68, regnl organiser 1968–72, nat offr 1972–85, gen sec 1986–; visiting fell Nuffield Coll Oxford 1986–94; formerly: dir National Building Agency, memb Royal Cmmn on Environmental Pollution; govr LSE; dir Unity Bank, memb Nat Economic Devpt Cncl 1986–92; tstee Inst of Public Policy Res; memb: Cncl Consumers' Assoc, Gen Cncl TUC, Forestry Cmmn; Hon LLD Univ of Sussex 1993; FRSA 1989; *Recreations* cricket, carpentry; *Clubs* Wibbandune CC; *Style—* John Edmonds, Esq; ✉ 50 Graham Rd, Mitcham, Surrey CR4 2HA; GMB, 22–24 Worple Road, London SW19 4DD (☎ 0181 947 3131, fax 0181 944 6552)

EDMONDS, (Douglas) Keith; s of (Maxwell) John Edmonds, of Duffield, Derbyshire, and Margaret Agnes, *née* Morrison (d 1977); *b* 23 July 1949; *Educ* Ecclesbourne Sch Derbyshire, Univ of Sheffield Med Sch (MB ChB, capt Rugby Club); *m* 13 Oct 1990, Gillian Linda, da of Cyril Rose; 3 s (Alastair b 1991, Nicholas b 1992, Timothy b 1995); *Career* house physician Rotherham Hosp 1973–74, sr house offr Accident and Emergency Sheffield Hosp 1974–75 (house surgn 1974), lectr Dept of Anatomy Univ of Sheffield 1975, sr house offr Obstetrics and Gynaecology Jessop Hosp for Women Sheffield 1975–77, registrar in obstetrics and gynaecology Southampton Hosp 1977–78; sr registrar in obstetrics and gynaecology: Queen Elizabeth Hosp Aust 1979–80, Southampton and Winchester Hosps 1980–82; conslt obstetrician and gynaecologist to Queen Charlotte and Chelsea Hosp and Hosp for Sick Children 1982–; author of many scientific pubns; memb: Blair-Bell Res Soc, Ovarian Club, Br Fertility Soc (and American), World Cncl of Paediatric and Adolescent Gynaecology; FRSM, FRACOG 1982 (MRACOG 1979), FRCOG 1990 (MRCOG 1979); *Books* Practical Paediatric and Adolescent Gynaecology (1989); *Recreations* tennis, golf; *Clubs* Gynaecological Club of GB, Roehampton; *Style—* Keith Edmonds, Esq; ✉ 78 Harley St, London W1N 1AE (☎ 0171 636 4797)

EDMONDS, Noel; *b* 22 Dec 1948; *Educ* Brentwood Public Sch; *Career* television personality; newsreader and DJ Radio Luxembourg 1968–69, breakfast show presenter BBC Radio 1 1973–78 (joined 1969, Saturday morning show 1971–73); presenter for BBC TV: Top of the Pops (regular presenter while at Radio 1), Z Shed 1978, Multi-Coloured Swap Shop 1979–85, Lucky Numbers 1982–83, Juke Box Jury, Top Gear, Time of Your Life, Telly Addicts 1984–, The Late Late Breakfast Show 1986–91, Noel's House Party 1991–, Noel's Telly Years 1996–; dir: Unique Group, Unique Broadcasting Co, Unique Television, Unique Aviation Group; qualified helicopter pilot 1980, former saloon car racing driver (for Renault, Opel and Ford), former powerboat racer; fndr charity Airborne (helicopter flights for handicapped/underprivileged children) 1993; *Awards* numerous, most recently BAFTA Award for Best Light Entertainment Prodn (for Noel's House Party) 1993, Best BBC Presenter ITV Comedy Awards 1993 and 1995, BBC Personality of the Year TRIC Awards 1994; *Style—* Noel Edmonds, Esq; ✉ Unique Group Ltd, Broomford Estate, Jacobstowe, Devon EX20 3RH

EDMONDS, Richard Edward Howard; JP; s of late Eric Edmonds; *b* 7 July 1925; *Educ* Wellington, Oriel Coll Oxford; *m* 1958, Sarah Anne, da of Hugh Merriman, DSO, MC, TD, DL; 1 s (Charles b 1960), 2 da (Anna (Mrs Jamie Rankin) b 1959, Harriet b 1963); *Career* Lt Oxfordshire and Bucks LI, served Palestine 1945–47; chm: Clements (Watford) Ltd, Coln Gravel Ltd; High Sheriff Hertfordshire 1991; co dir and farmer; *Recreations* country sports; *Style—* Richard Edmonds, Esq, JP; ✉ Micklefield Hall, Rickmansworth, Herts WD3 6AQ (☎ 01923 774747)

EDMONDS, Robert Humphrey Gordon (Robin); CMG (1969), MBE (1944); s of Air Vice-Marshal Charles Humphrey Kingsman Edmonds, CBE, DSO (d 1954), and Lorna Karim Chadwick, *née* Osborn (d 1974); *b* 5 Oct 1920; *Educ* Ampleforth, Brasenose Coll Oxford (MA); *m* 1, 1951 (m dis 1975), Georgina, da of late Cdr Anthony Boyce Combe; 4 s (Charles d 1995, Dominic, Robert, James); m 2, 1976, Enid Flora (d 1994), widow of Dr Michael Balint; *Career* Army 1940–46, Maj (despatches); HM Foreign (later Diplomatic) Serv 1946–78; Kleinwort Benson Ltd: advsr 1978–83, conslt 1984–86; memb Cncl Royal Inst of Int Affairs 1986–92, Leverhulme research fell 1989–91; *Books* Soviet Foreign Policy - The Brezhnev Years (1983), Setting The Mould - The United States and Britain 1945–50 (1986), The Big Three: Churchill, Roosevelt and Stalin in peace and war (1991), Pushkin: The Man and His Age (1994); *Clubs* Turf; *Style—* Robin Edmonds, Esq, CMG, MBE; ✉ Raven House, Ramsbury, Wiltshire SN8 2PA

EDMONDSON, Prof Hugh Dunstan Christopher; s of Dr Dunstan Hugh Edmondson (d 1990), and Audrey Mary, *née* Burdon (d 1989); *b* 13 April 1936; *Educ* Stonyhurst, Univ of Birmingham (DDS, BDS, DA, MB ChB); *m* 13 May 1961, Eileen Margaret, da of William Burley; 1 s (Christopher Hugh b 1964), 2 da (Rowena Mary b 1962, Caroline Audrey b 1963); *Career* prof of oral surgery and oral med Univ of Birmingham 1983– (lectr 1971–75, sr lectr 1975–83); chm Dental Formulary Sub-Ctee BDA; memb: Advsy Ctee on NHS Drugs, Medicines Control Agency, Ctee on Safety of Medicines Advsy Panel; former memb Ctee on Dental and Surgical Materials; fell BAOMS, MRCS, LRCP, LDS RCS, FDS RCS; *Books* A Radiological Atlas of Diseases of the Teeth and Jaws (with R M Browne and P G J Rout, 1983), Atlas of Dental and

Maxillofacial Radiology and Imaging (with R M Browne and P G J Rout, 1995); *Recreations* shooting, fishing; *Style—* Prof Hugh Edmondson; ✉ Huddington Court, Huddington, Droitwich, Midlands WR9 7LJ (☎ 01905 69247); Dental School, St Chads, Queensway, Birmingham B4 6NN (☎ 0121 236 8611)

EDMONDSON, Dr Philip Charles; s of Dr Reginald Edmondson (d 1964), of Dunchurch, Rugby, and Phyllis Mary, *née* Elam (d 1996); *b* 30 April 1938; *Educ* Uppingham, Christ's Coll Cambridge (MA, MD, MB BChir, MRCP), St Bartholomew's Hosp London; *m* 7 Sept 1968, Margaret Lysbeth, da of Stanley Bayston, of Saxton, Tadcaster, Yorks; 3 da (Camilla b 25 April 1970, Claire b 12 May 1972, Cordelia b 5 Jan 1980); *Career* physician to: Westminster Abbey 1979, KLM (Royal Dutch Airlines) London, Australian High Cmmn London; conslt physician to many major industl cos; visiting med offr King Edward VII Hosp for Offrs London; Freeman City of London, Liveryman Worshipful Soc of Apothecaries; FRSM, fell Med Soc of London; *Recreations* fishing, country pursuits; *Clubs* Boodle's; *Style—* Dr Philip Edmondson; ✉ 18 Lennox Gardens, London SW1X 0DG (☎ 0171 584 5194); Hornton Lodge, Vicarage Lane, Dunchurch, Rugby (☎ 01788 810500); 99 Harley St, London W1N 1DF (☎ 0171 935 7501)

EDMONDSON, Dr Robert Somerville; s of William Edmondson (d 1974), and Eileen Edmondson (d 1971); *b* 11 Aug 1937; *Educ* Bradford GS, St Bartholomew's Hosp Univ of London (MB BS); *m* 20 July 1962, Brenda Sigrid, da of John Woodhead (d 1964); 2 s (Christopher Somerville b 1965, William Somerville b 1969), 2 da (Sarah Jane b 1964, Ann-Marie b 1967); *Career* conslt anaesthetist Leeds Gen Infirmary 1969– (chairman of faculty 1986–88), hon lectr Univ of Leeds 1969–; pres Yorkshire Soc of Anaesthetists 1991– (sec and treas 1975–85); FFARCS; *Books* Intensive Care (contrib, 1983), Contemporary Neurology (1984); *Recreations* rowing, sailing, squash, photography, travel; *Style—* Dr Robert Edmondson; ✉ Department of Anaesthesia, Leeds General Infirmary, Great George Street, Leeds LS1 3EX (☎ 0113 243 7172)

EDMONDSON, Stephen John; s of George Edmondson, of Scunthorpe, and Jean Mary, *née* Stanton; *b* 21 Aug 1950; *Educ* Scunthorpe GS, Middx Hosp Med Sch, Univ of London (BSc, MB BS); *m* 17 July 1976, Barbara Bridget Alison, da of Dr Malcolm Nugent Samuel Duncan, TD; 2 s (Adam George b 1984, John David b 1989); *Career* conslt cardiothoracic surgn Bart's 1984–; memb: Soc of Thoracic and Cardiovascular Surgns of GB and Ireland 1982, Br Cardiac Soc 1984, NE Thames Thoracic Soc, Euro Assoc of Cardiothoracic Surgery 1989; FRCS 1979, MRCP 1980; *Recreations* tennis, golf, squash, football; *Clubs* Vanderbilt Racquet, Ealing Golf, Ulysses FC; *Style—* Stephen Edmondson, Esq; ✉ 69 Harley St, London W1N 1DE (☎ 0171 935 6375, fax 0171 224 3823)

EDMONSTONE, Sir Archibald Bruce Charles; 7 Bt (GB 1774), of Duntreath, Stirlingshire; s of Sir Archibald Charles Edmonstone, 6 Bt (d 1954), and Gwendolyn Mary, *née* Field (d 1989); *b* 3 Aug 1934; *Educ* Stowe; *m* 1, 17 Jan 1957 (m dis 1967), Jane, er da of Maj-Gen Edward Charles Colville, CB, DSO (d 1982) (s of Adm Hon Sir Stanley Colville, GCB, GCMG, GCVO); 2 s (Archibald Edward Charles b 4 Feb 1961, Nicholas William Mark b 1964), 1 da (Philippa Carolyn b 1958); m 2, 12 June 1969, Juliet Elizabeth, o da of Maj-Gen Cecil Martin Fothergill Deakin, CB, CBE; 1 s (Dru Benjamin Marshall b 26 Oct 1971), 1 da (Elyssa Juliet b 11 Sept 1973); *Heir* s, Archibald Edward Charles Edmonstone, *qv*; *Career* 2 Lt Royal Scots Greys 1954–56; *Recreations* shooting, fishing; *Clubs* White's; *Style—* Sir Archibald Edmonstone, Bt; ✉ Duntreath Castle, Blanefield, by Glasgow (☎ 01360 70215)

EDMONSTONE, Archibald Edward Charles; s (by 1 m) and h of Sir Archibald Bruce Charles Edmonstone, 7 Bt, *qv*; *b* 4 Feb 1961; *Educ* Stowe, RMA Sandhurst; *m* 7 May 1988, Ursula, eldest da of Benjamin Worthington (d 1984); *Career* commissioned as 2 Lt Scots Gds 1982; *Style—* Archibald Edmonstone, Esq; ✉ 2a Rhodesia Road, London SW9 2EL

EDMONTON, Bishop of 1984–; Rt Rev Brian John Masters; s of Stanley William Masters (d 1965), and Grace Hannah, *née* Stevens (d 1993); *b* 17 Oct 1932; *Educ* Collyers Sch Horsham, Queens' Coll Cambridge (MA); *Career* insur broker Lloyd's 1955–62; asst curate St Dunstan and All Saints Stepney 1964–69, vicar Holy Trinity Hoxton 1969–82, bishop Fulham 1982–84; *Recreations* theatre; *Clubs* United Oxford and Cambridge Univ; *Style—* The Rt Rev the Bishop of Edmonton; ✉ 1 Regents Park Terrace, London NW1 7EE (☎ 0171 267 4455, fax 0171 267 4404)

EDMUND, John Humphrey; s of Charles Henry Humphrey Edmund (d 1995), of Swansea, and Vera May, *née* Warmington (d 1993); *b* 6 March 1935; *Educ* Swansea GS, Jesus Coll Oxford (MA); *m* 4 Sept 1965, (Elizabeth Ann) Myfanwy, da of William Lewis Williams, of Newport, Dyfed (d 1975); *Career* Nat Serv RN 1953–55; admitted slr 1961; ptnr Beor, Wilson & Lloyd Swansea 1963–95 (conslt 1995–); Under Sheriff W Glam 1983–, Clerk to Gen Cmmrs of Taxes (Swansea Div) 1986–; memb Law Soc 1962; *Clubs* Vincent's (Oxford), Bristol Channel Yacht; *Style—* John Edmund, Esq; ✉ 84 Pennard Rd, Pennard, Swansea, West Glamorgan SA3 2AA (☎ 01792 232526); Calvert House, Calvert Terrace, Swansea SA1 6AP (☎ 01792 655178, fax 01792 467002)

EDNAM, Viscount; William Humble David Jeremy Ward; s and h of 4 Earl of Dudley, *qv*; *b* 27 March 1947; *Educ* Eton, ChCh Oxford; *m* 1, 1972 (m dis 1976), Sarah Mary, da of Sir Alastair Francis Stuart Coats, 4 Bt; m 2, 1976 (m dis 1980), Debra Louise, da of George Robert Pinney; 1 da (Hon Bethany Rowena b 1977); *Style—* Viscount Ednam; ✉ Villa Montanet, Les Garrigues, 84220 Goult-Gordes, France

EDNEY, Dr Andrew Thomas Bailey; s of Sydney George Edney (d 1986), and Dorothy Mary, *née* Smith (d 1990); *b* 1 Aug 1932; *Educ* Borden Sch, Univ of London, RCVS (BVetMed), Open Univ (BA); *Career* Nat Serv 201 Sqdn RAF 1950–52; gen practice Odiham Hants 1958–65, MAFF 1966–67, vet advsr in industry Waltham Centre Leics 1968–85, vet consIt, author and ed 1985–, vet ed Butterworth Heinemann plc 1985–; 1985; chm Round Table; BSAVA: sec 1976–77, nat pres 1979–80; WSAVA: sec 1982–86, vice pres 1986–90, pres 1990–92, sr vice pres 1992–94; memb Bd of Govrs Blue Cross Animal Charity 1994–; MRCVS 1958, FRSM 1970; *Books* Dog and Cat Nutrition (1982, 1988), Pet Care (1984), Dog and Puppy Care (1985), Practical Animal Handling (with R S Anderson, 1990), Manual of Cat Care (1992); *Recreations* fine art related to animals, vintage aircraft, gardening; *Clubs* RSM, Kennel; *Style—* Dr Andrew Edney; ✉ 22 Crocket Lane, Empingham, Rutland, Leics LE15 8PW

EDRIC, Robert; s of E H Armitage, of Sheffield; *b* 14 April 1956; *Educ* Firth Park GS Sheffield, Univ of Hull (BA, PhD); *m* Helen Sara, *née* Jones; 1 s (Bruce Copley Jones); *Career* novelist; *Awards* James Tait Black Fiction Prize 1985, runner up Guardian Fiction Prize 1986, Arts Cncl Bursary 1995; *Books* Winter Garden (1985), A New Ice Age (1986), A Lunar Eclipse (1989), In The Days of The American Museum (1990), The Broken Lands (1992), The Earth Made of Glass (1994), Elysium (1995), In Desolate Heaven (1997); *Style—* Robert Edric, Esq

EDRIDGE, Olga; da of Col Bernard Alfred Edridge, OBE, of Athens, Greece, and Erica, *née* Mavrommati; *b* 22 March 1951; *Educ* Makris HS for Girls Athens Greece, London Film Sch (Dip in Film Making), Univ of Reading (BA); *Career* BBC: asst film ed and acting ed 1975–79, grad prodn trainee 1979–81, asst prodr and dir 1981–83, prodr of religious progs 1983–86, series ed Heart of the Matter 1986–91, exec prodr BBC Corporate Prodr Choice 1992–93, project mangr BBC Corporate Performance Review 1993–94, project dir BBC World Services Prodr Choice 1994–95, dir Special Projects BBC Worldwide TV 1995–; winner of Sandford St Martin Tst award 1985 and One World Bdcast Tst award 1987; *Recreations* walking the dogs, swimming, theatre, eating with friends; *Style—* Ms Olga Edridge; ✉ BBC Worldwide, Woodlands, 80 Wood Lane, London W12 0TT (☎ 0181 576 2089, e-mail olga.edridge@bbc.co.uk)

EDSON, Ven Michael; s of Joseph Pratt, of Clipstone, Notts, and Elsie, *née* Edson; assumed his mother's maiden name in lieu of his patronymic; *b* 2 Sept 1942; *Educ* Mansfield Secdy Tech GS, Univ of Birmingham (BSc), Univ of Leeds (BA); *m* 2 Sept 1968, Ann Frances, da of William John Tuffley; 1 da (Catherine Jane b 7 July 1971), 3 s (John Benedict b 8 June 1973, Samuel Francis b 28 Nov 1975, Thomas Michael Tuffley b 25 April 1978); *Career* trainee HM Inspectorate of Taxes 1964–66, mangr Procter & Gamble Ltd 1966–68, mgmnt conslt 1968–69, theol trg 1969–72, ordained 1972, team vicar St Peter and Holy Trinity Barnstaple 1976–82 (curate 1972–76), vicar of St Andrew Roxbourne Harrow 1982–89, area dean of Harrow 1985–89, priest-in-charge St Paul S Harrow 1987–89, warden of Lee Abbey Devon 1989–94, archdeacon of Leicester 1994–, diocesan evangelist 1997–; *Books* Renewal of the Mind (as Mike Pratt, 1987), Loved into Life (1993); *Recreations* walking, talking, interesting people, theatre; *Style—* The Ven the Archdeacon of Leicester; ✉ 13 Stoneygate Avenue, Leicester LE3 3HE (☎ 0116 270 4441, fax 0116 270 1091)

EDUR, Thomas; s of Enn Edur, of Estonia, and Liuda, *née* Mishustina, of Estonia; *b* 20 Jan 1969; *Educ* Tallinn Ballet Sch; *m* 1990, Agnes Oaks, *qv*, da of Juhan Oaks; *Career* ballet dancer; Estonia Ballet Theatre: Coppelia 1987, Giselle 1988, Paquita 1988, Sleeping Beauty 1989, Nostalgia 1989, Romeo and Juliet 1990, Swan Lake 1990, Estonian Ballads; English National Ballet: Coppelia 1990, The Nutcracker 1990, Les Sylphides 1990, 3 Preludes 1990, Our Waltzes 1990, Sanguine Fan 1990, Lucentsio in The Taming of the Shrew, Lenski in Eugene Onegin, Etudes, Four Last Songs, Apollo, Stranger I Came, Cinderella 1992, Swan Lake 1992, La Bayadere 1992, Spectre de la Rose 1992, Ashton Romeo and Juliet 1992, Sphinx 1993, Impromptu 1993, Sleeping Beauty 1993, Don Quixote (pas de deux) 1993, Seven Silences of Salome 1993 (winner Time Out Award), Derek Deane Paquita 1994, Derek Deane Giselle 1994, Romeo and Mercutio in Nuryev Romeo and Juliet 1995, Derek Deane Alice in Wonderland 1995, Encounters 1996, Cinderella 1996; joined Birmingham Royal Ballet 1996: Swan Lake 1996, Nutcracker Sweeties 1996, Sleeping Beauty 1996, Nutcracker 1996; *Recreations* nature lover; *Style—* Thomas Edur, Esq; ✉ Birmingham Royal Ballet, Thorpe Street, Birmingham B5 4AU

EDWARD, Judge David Alexander Ogilvy; CMG (1981), QC (Scot 1974); s of John Ogilvy Christie Edward (d 1960), of Perth, and Margaret Isabel, *née* MacArthur (d 1989); *b* 14 Nov 1934; *Educ* Sedbergh, Univ Coll Oxford (MA), Univ of Edinburgh (LLB); *m* 22 Dec 1962, Elizabeth Young, da of Terence McSherry, of Edinburgh; 2 s (Giles b 1965, John b 1968), 2 da (Anne b 1964, Katherine b 1971); *Career* Nat Serv Sub Lt RNVR 1955–57; advocate 1962, clerk and treas Faculty of Advocates 1967–77, pres Consultative Ctee of the Bars and Law Socs of the Euro Community 1978–80, Salvesen prof of European Instns Univ of Edinburgh 1985–89 (hon prof 1990–), judge of European Court of First Instance 1989–92, Judge of European Court of Justice 1992–; tstee: Nat Library of Scotland 1966–95, Industry and Parliament Trust, Carnegie Trust for the Universities of Scotland, Trier Acad of European Law; memb: Law Advsy Ctee British Cncl 1976–88, Panel of Arbitrators Int Centre for Settlement of Investmt Disputes 1979–89; pres Scottish Cncl for International Arbitration, tstee Hopetown House Preservation Tst (chm 1988–92); dir: Adam & Co Group plc 1983–89, The Harris Tweed Assoc Ltd 1984–89; chm Continental Assets Trust plc 1985–89; pres: Franco-Scottish Soc 1996, Johnson Soc Lichfield 1995; hon bencher Gray's Inn 1992; Hon LLD Univ of Edinburgh 1993, hon fell Univ Coll Oxford 1995; FRSE 1990; *Clubs* Athenaeum, New (Edinburgh); *Style—* Judge David Edward, CMG, QC, FRSE; ✉ 32 Heriot Row, Edinburgh EH3 6ES; European Court of Justice, L-2925 Luxembourg (☎ 00 352 4303 2203)

EDWARD, Ian; s of Charles Ewen Edward (d 1978), of Aberdeen, and Isobel Thomson, *née* Kynoch (d 1959); *b* 3 Sept 1935; *Educ* Robert Gordon's Coll Aberdeen, Univ of Aberdeen (MA, LLB), Fitzwilliam Coll Cambridge; *m* 20 Aug 1958, Marguerite Anne, *née* Leiper (d 1995); 1 da (Anne Isobel b 20 April 1960), 2 s (Timothy James b 12 March 1963, Robin Charles b 18 July 1968); *Career* admitted as slr in Scotland 1958, dist offr in N Rhodesia HM Oversea Civil Serv (Colonial Serv) 1958–62, ptnr C & P H Chalmers Aberdeen 1963, sr ptnr Ledingham Chalmers Aberdeen 1991–; memb: Law Soc of Scotland 1958–, Soc of Advocates in Aberdeen 1972–, Conveyancing Ctee Law Soc of Scotland 1990–93; govr Robert Gordon's Coll Aberdeen 1988–96, chm Scottish Motor Neurone Disease Assoc 1996–; *Recreations* golfing and gardening; *Clubs* Royal and Ancient (St Andrews), Royal Aberdeen Golf (archivist), Royal Northern and University (Aberdeen); *Style—* Ian Edward, Esq; ✉ 218 Queen's Road, Aberdeen, Scotland AB1 8DJ (☎ 01224 319585); Ledingham Chalmers, 17 Golden Square, Aberdeen AB9 8NY, Scotland (☎ 01224 638922, fax 01224 641009)

EDWARDES, Leonard Edward (Len); s of Charles James Henry Edwardes (d 1973), of 4 Grove Cottages, High St, Horsell, Woking, Surrey, and Emily, *née* Brown (d 1965); *b* 9 Oct 1931; *Educ* Goldsworth Co Secdy Sch Surrey; *m* 7 June 1954, Sheena, da of Robert George Gray (d 1968); 2 s (Simon b 7 April 1963, Richard b 15 May 1965); *Career* Nat Serv RAF 1950–52; chief engr Debenhams Ltd 1967–75, ptnr Cranage & Perkins consulting engrs 1975–80; sr ptnr: Edwardes Friedlander 1980–82, Edwardes Whittle Partnership 1982–; currently dir: Nationwide Maintenance Ltd, Falcon Mechanical Services Ltd, E & C Engineering Services Ltd; Freeman: City of London 1981, Worshipful Co of Fanmakers; FIMgt 1986; *Recreations* horse racing, golf; *Clubs* Ascot, Pyrford and Fernfell Golf; *Style—* Len Edwardes, Esq; ✉ Nationwide Maintenance Ltd, Falcon House, Catteshall Lane, Godalming, Surrey GU7 1JP (☎ 01483 428674, fax 01483 426987)

EDWARDES, Sir Michael Owen; kt (1979); s of Denys Owen Edwardes, and Audrey Noel, *née* Copeland; *b* 11 Oct 1930; *Educ* St Andrew's Coll Grahamstown S Africa, Rhodes Univ (BA); *m* 1, 1958 (m dis), Mary Margaret, *née* Finlay; 3 da; m 2, 1988, Sheila Ann, *née* Guy; *Career* formerly non-exec chm Chloride Group plc (dir 1969–77 and 1986); chm: BL Ltd 1977–82, Mercury Communications Ltd 1982–83, ICL plc 1984, Dunlop Holdings plc 1984–85, Tryhorn Investments Ltd 1987–, Charter plc (formerly Charter Consolidated plc) 1988–96, Porth Group plc 1991–95; dir: Hill Samuel Group 1980–87, Minorco SA 1984–93, Standard Securities plc 1985–87, Delta Motor Corporation (Pty) Ltd 1986–, Flying Pictures Ltd 1987–, Kaye Organisation 1987–88, Jet Press Holdings BV 1990–, ARC International Ltd (BVI) 1991, Strand Partners 1994, Syndicated Services Co Inc 1995–; dep chm R K Carvill (International Holdings) Ltd 1988; dir Int Mgmnt Devpt Inst Washington 1978–; memb: NEB 1975–77, President's Ctee CBI 1981; tstee Thrombosis Res Inst 1991–; pres Squash Rackets Assoc 1991–95; Hon LLD Rhodes Univ; Hon FIMechE 1981; CIMgt (vice-chm 1977–80); *Books* Back from the Brink (1983); *Clubs* Veterans Squash Club of GB, Royal Automobile, Jesters, Rand Club and Country Club (Johannesburg); *Style—* Sir Michael Edwardes

EDWARDES, Hon (William) Owen Alexander; s and h of 8 Baron Kensington, *qv*; *b* 21 July 1964; *m* 9 Aug 1991, (Marie Hélène Anne) Véronique, da of Jean-Alain Lalouette, of Vacoas, Mauritius; 1 s (William Francis Ivor b 23 March 1993); *Style—* The Hon Owen Edwardes; ✉ Friar Tuck, Mt West, PO Box 549, Mooi River 3300, Natal, S Africa (☎ 00 27 333 36355)

EDWARDS, Andrew John Cumming; CB (1994); s of John Edwards (d 1977), and Norah Hope, *née* Bevan (d 1992); *b* 3 Nov 1940; *Educ* Fettes, St John's Coll Oxford (MA), Harvard Univ (AM, MPA); *m* 1, 1969 (m dis 1987), Charlotte Anne, da of Arthur L Chilcot, MBE (d 1981); 1 s (Angus b 1974), 2 da (Hermia b 1972, Madeleine b 1978); m 2, 1994, Ursula Mary, da of Rev Matthew Richardson (d 1957); 1 s (Dominic b 1994);

Career asst master Malvern Coll 1962–63, asst princ HM Treasy 1963–67, private sec to Sir William Armstrong 1966–67, princ HM Treasy 1967–75, asst sec HM Treasy 1975–84, RCDS 1979, asst sec DES 1984–85, under sec HM Treasy 1985–89, dep sec (public servs) HM Treasy 1990–95; writer and conslt 1995–; Harkness fell Cambridge Mass 1971–73; conductor: Treasy Singers 1968–84, Acad of St Mary's Wimbledon 1980–; govr Br Inst of Recorded Sound 1975–79; sec Bd of Royal Opera House 1988–; *Books* Nuclear Weapons: The Balance of Terror, the Quest for Peace (1986); *Recreations* music, writing, reading, walking; *Style—* Andrew Edwards, Esq, CB; (☎ and fax 0181 944 6704)

EDWARDS, Prof Anthony Davies; s of Gwilym Morgan Edwards (d 1956), of Swansea, and Beryl Eileen, *née* Davies (d 1982); *b* 4 June 1936; *Educ* Bishop Gore GS Swansea, Corpus Christi Coll Cambridge (MA), Univ of London (MPhil), Univ of Exeter (PhD); *m* 16 April 1960, Ann Hopkins, da of William Henry Griffiths, of Penclawdd, Gower; 1 s (Ceri David b 1965), 2 da (Kathryn Jane b 1964, Megan Ruth b 1967); *Career* history teacher: Crown Woods Sch 1957–58, East Ham GS 1959–63, Latymer Upper Sch 1963–66; lectr in educn Univ of Exeter 1966–71, sr lectr Univ of Manchester 1976–79 (lectr in educn 1971–76), currently dean of educn Univ of Newcastle upon Tyne (prof of educn 1979–); memb City of Newcastle Educn Ctee, chm and co-chm Univs Cncl for Educn and Trg of Teachers 1991–95; memb Br Educnl Res Assoc; *Books* The Changing Sixth Form (1970), Language in Culture and Class (1976), The Language of Teaching (with V J Furlong, 1978), Investigating Classroom Talk (with D Westgate, 1987, 2 edn 1994), The State and Private Education: an Investigation of the Assisted Place Scheme (with J Fitz and G Whitty, 1989), Specialisation and Choice in Urban Education (with G Whitty and S Gewirtz, 1993); *Recreations* hill walking, travel, photography, cinema, music; *Style—* Prof Anthony Edwards; ✉ University Department of Education, St Thomas' St, Newcastle upon Tyne NE1 7RU (☎ 0191 222 6000, fax 0191 222 8170)

EDWARDS, Anthony William (Tony); s of William Bell Edwards (d 1989), and Lavinia Margaret, *née* Tyson (d 1991); *b* 3 June 1939; *Educ* Taunton Sch, Univ of St Andrews (MA Hons, George Cunningham Prize for Geography); *Career* asst brand mangr Procter and Gamble 1961–64, new products co-ordinator Johnson Wax International 1964–66; Spillers Ltd: gp mktg devpt mangr 1966–69, regnl mangr Overseas Div 1969–71, divnl dir Spillers Int 1971–74; Hartz Mountain Corporation (US): md UK ops 1974–80, chief exec Canadian and UK ops 1980–86, chm and chief exec UK ops 1986–90; chief exec: Association for International Cancer Research 1992–93, Royal Society for the Prevention of Accidents 1993–; dir and memb Exec Ctee Grocery Products Manufacturers of Canada 1982–86; fndr chm Grantham Assoc of Nat Tst 1990–92, memb Giving Clubs Advsy Bd Univ of St Andrews 1996–, life memb Woodland Tst; memb Royal Horticultural Soc, FIMgt 1980; *Recreations* 18th century British furniture and pictures, French wine and food, Scottish islands; *Clubs* Caledonian; *Style—* Tony Edwards, Esq; ✉ The Orchards, Old Somerby, Grantham, Lincs NG33 4AG (☎ 01476 565456); Royal Society for the Prevention of Accidents, Edgbaston Park, 353 Bristol Road, Birmingham B5 7ST (☎ 0121 248 2000, fax 0121 248 2001)

EDWARDS, (Lionel) Antony (Tony); *b* 4 Nov 1944; *Educ* Univ of Birmingham (BSc), Harvard Business Sch (MBA with Distinction); *married*; *Career* sr mgmnt positions with Rolls-Royce, General Electric (USA), Motorola and Canadair 1968–89, md Aerospace (subsequently gp md) Lucas Industries plc 1989–92, chief exec Dowty Aerospace and Main Bd dir TI Group plc 1992–, chm and chief exec Messier-Dowty International 1994–; former pres Soc of Br Aerospace Cos; chm Def & Aerospace Sector Panel UK Technol Foresight Prog, memb Aviation Ctee DTI, memb Nat Def Industs Cncl; memb Cncl: Air League, Royal Aeronautical Soc; *Recreations* classic car restoration, historic aircraft preservation; *Style—* Tony Edwards, Esq; ✉ Messier-Dowty International, Lambourn Court, Abingdon Business Park, Abingdon, Oxon OX14 1UH (☎ 01235 540164, fax 01235 520803)

EDWARDS, Arthur John; s of late Arthur James Edwards, and late Dorothy May, *née* Ward; *b* 12 Aug 1940; *Educ* St Bernard's RC GS Stepney London; *m* 16 Sept 1961, Ann Patricia, *née* Heaphy; 2 s (John Gerard b 7 April 1964, Paul Patrick b 26 Feb 1966), 1 da (Annmarie b 26 March 1971); *Career* press photographer; formerly freelance, with The Sun 1975–; *Recreations* walking, watching West Ham Utd; *Style—* Arthur Edwards, Esq; ✉ c/o The Picture Desk, The Sun, 1 Virginia St, London E1 9XP (☎ 0171 782 4110)

EDWARDS, (Ralph) Bernard; s of Henry Prytherch Edwards (d 1973), of London, and Anina, *née* Strömme; *b* 19 May 1951; *Educ* Springhead Sch, Univ of Manchester (BSc); *m* 9 Sept 1972, Pamela, da of William Ramsey; 2 s (Mark, John); *Career* psychotherapist NHS 1972–76, undergraduate 1976–79, Unisys Corporation 1979–90 (latterly dir of computer systems mktg), dir of mktg National & Provincial Building Society 1990–93; dir: Mood International, The Salamander Group, Innovation in Action; ind facilitator; MInstD 1992; *Recreations* theatre, golf, music, reading; *Style—* Bernard Edwards, Esq; ✉ Windy Ridge, Crowthorne, Berks RG45 6AR (☎ 01344 750711, fax 01344 780805)

EDWARDS, Prof Brian; CBE (1988); s of John Albert Edwards (d 1979), of Bebington, and (Ethel) Pat, *née* Davis (d 1980); *b* 19 Feb 1942; *Educ* Wirral GS; *m* 7 Nov 1964, Jean, da of William Cannon, of Neston; 2 s (Christopher b 28 April 1973, Jonathan (twin) b 28 April 1973), 2 da (Penny Adrienne b 27 May 1967, Paula Michelle b 14 Nov 1968); *Career* various hosp posts 1958–69, lectr in health serv studies Univ of Leeds 1969–71, dep gp sec Hull Hosp Mgmnt Ctee 1971–73, dist admin Leeds Dist Health Authy 1973–76, area admin Cheshire AHA 1976–81, regnl gen mangr Trent RHA 1984–93 (regnl admin 1981–83), chief exec W Midlands RHA 1993–96, regnl dir NHS Exec (West Midlands) 1994–96, prof of health care devpt and dean Sch of Health and Related Research Univ of Sheffield 1996–; visiting prof Univ of Keele 1989–, leader Patient's Charter Team 1992–, leader UK Delgn Hosp Ctee for Europe; pres Inst of Health Servs Mgmnt 1983; chm: Manpower Advsy Gp NHS 1983–85, Regnl Gen Mangrs Gp England 1986 and 1990–93, CPA (Ltd) 1991–; memb Standing Advsy Ctee on Audit RCP; conslt WHO in: India, Russia, Guyana, Czechoslovakia; ed Health Servs Manpower Review; Queen Elizabeth the Queen Mother Nuffield fell 1992; FHSM 1964, CIMgt 1988; *Books* Si Vis Pacem (1973), Planning the Child Health Services (1975), Manager and Industrial Relations (1979), Merit Awards for Doctors (1987), Controlling Doctors (1991), Managing the NHS (1992), A Manager's Tale (1993, 2 edn 1995); *Recreations* golf; *Clubs* Bakewell Golf (capt 1991); *Style—* Prof Brian Edwards, CBE; ✉ 3 Royal Croft Drive, Baslow, Derbyshire DE45 1SN (☎ 01246 583459, fax 01246 582583)

EDWARDS, (David) Cenwyn; s of Alwyn John Edwards (d 1986), of Pontarddulais, and Edwina Jane, *née* Thomas; *b* 27 Oct 1945; *Educ* Llanelli Boys GS, Univ of N Wales Bangor (BA); *m* 1, 17 April 1971 (m dis 1990), Margaret Eluned, da of Thomas Owen Davies (d 1977); 1 s (Gruffudd b 1979), 1 da (Lowri b 1977); m 2, Oct 1993, Meri Huws, da of Val and Gwynne Hughes; *Career* joined HTV 1969, asst head of news and current affrs 1978–82, head of current affrs 1982–85, asst prog controller and N Wales exec 1985–89, controller of factual and general progs 1989–91, commissioning ed of factual progs S4C 1991–; memb: Diplomatic and Cwlth Writers Assoc of Br, Nat Eisteddfod Court; *Recreations* drama, rugby, cricket; *Clubs* Llanelli RFC, Groucho; *Style—* Cenwyn Edwards, Esq; ✉ S4C, Parc ty Glas, Llanishen, Cardiff CF4 5DU (☎ 01222 747444)

EDWARDS, Sir Christopher John Churchill; 5 Bt (UK 1866), of Pye Nest, Yorkshire; s of Sir (Henry) Charles Serrell Priestley Edwards, 4 Bt (d 1963), and Daphne Marjory Hilda, *née* Birt; *b* 16 Aug 1941; *Educ* Frensham Heights Sch, Loughborough Coll; *m* 1972, Gladys Irene Vogelgesang; 2 s (David Charles Priestley b 22 Feb 1974, Ryan Matthew Churchill b 16 April 1979); *Heir* s, David Charles Priestley Edwards b 22 Feb 1974; *Career* gen mangr Kelsar Inc (American Home Products, San Diego, Calif) 1979–84, vice pres Valleylab Inc (Pfizer Inc, Boulder Colorado) 1984–89, dir Ohmeda (BOC Group, Louisville, Colorado) 1989–92, pres Intermed Consultants Westminster Colorado 1992–; vice pres Teledyne Water Pik Fort Collins Colorado 1994–95; exec vice pres and gen mangr RAM Electronics Corp Fort Collins Colorado 1995–; US Nat Certified Soccer Coach, fndr and vice-pres Westminster Wolves Youth Soccer Club; *Clubs* Ranch Country (Westminster, Colorado); *Style—* Sir Christopher Edwards, Bt; ✉ 11637 Country Club Drive, Westminster, Colorado 80234, USA (☎ 001 30346 93156, fax 001 30346 60310)

EDWARDS, Prof Christopher Richard Watkin; s of Wing Cdr Thomas Archibald Watkin Edwards (d 1986), and Beatrice Elizabeth Ruby, *née* Telfer (d 1993); *b* 12 Feb 1942; *Educ* Marlborough, Univ of Cambridge (MB BChir, MD); *m* 6 April 1968, Sally Amanda Le Blount, da of Sqdn Ldr Gerald Le Blount Kidd, OBE, of Westerham, Kent; 2 s (Adam b 1969, Crispin b 1974), 1 da (Kate b 1971); *Career* sr lectr in medicine and hon conslt physician St Bartholomew's Hosp London 1975, prof of clinical med Univ of Edinburgh and hon conslt physician to the Lothian Health Bd 1980–, chm Dept of Med Western Gen Hosp Edinburgh 1981–91, dean Faculty of Med 1991–95, provost Faculty Gp of Med and Vet Med 1992–95, princ Imperial Coll Sch of Med 1995–; memb MRC Cncl 1992–95, govr Wellcome Tst 1994–; FRCP 1979, FRCPE 1981, FRSE 1990; *Books* Essential Hypertension as an Endocrine Disease (co ed, 1985), Recent Advances in Endocrinology and Metabolism (co ed, 1992), Davidson's Principles and Practice of Medicine (co ed, 1995); *Recreations* golf, painting; *Clubs* Athenaeum; *Style—* Prof Christopher Edwards, FRSE; ✉ Imperial College of Science, Technology and Medicine, South Kensington, London SW7 2AZ (☎ 0171 594 8800, fax 0171 594 8802)

EDWARDS, Sir (John) Clive Leighton; 2 Bt (UK 1921), of Treforis, Co Glamorgan; s of Sir John Bryn Edwards, 1 Bt (d 1922), and Kathleen Ermyntrude, *née* Corfield (d 1975); *b* 11 Oct 1916; *Educ* Winchester; *Career* served WWII with RASC as Driver and as Capt Royal Pioneer Corps; memb: Brooklands Soc, Brooklands Museum; *Recreations* motoring, gardening; *Clubs* Bugatti Owners, Midland Automobile (hon life memb), RAC (hon life memb); *Style—* Sir Clive Edwards, Bt; ✉ Milntown, Lezayre, nr Ramsey, Isle of Man, IM7 2AB

EDWARDS, (John) Colin; s of John Henry Edwards (d 1985), of Penzance, and Gwendoline Doris, *née* Sara; *b* 27 Aug 1936; *Educ* Clifton Coll, Lincoln Coll Oxford (MA); *m* 22 Aug 1967, (Daphne) Paulette, da of (Herbert) Peter Bayley, of New Jersey, USA; 1 s (Gavin Perran b 30 March 1973), 1 da (Rebecca b 20 April 1971); *Career* slr 1960; attorney at law Jamaica 1971, dep coroner Truro Dist 1975–, chm Social Security Appeal Tbnl 1980–, dep dist judge High and Co Court Western Circuit 1985–; chm Jamaica Rugby Football Union 1972–74 (rep 28 times 1962–72), dep chm Truro Squash Club 1983–87 (Jamaican Champion 1962–72); memb: Law Soc 1960, Jamaica Law Reform Ctee; *Recreations* golf, surfing, reading, gardening; *Clubs* Truro Golf, Truro Squash; *Style—* Colin Edwards, Esq; ✉ 15 Nansavallon Road, Truro, Cornwall TR1 3JY (☎ 01872 77138); Carlyon & Son, 78 Lemon Street, Truro, Cornwall TR1 2PZ (☎ 01872 78641, fax 01872 72072)

EDWARDS, Very Rev Dr David Lawrence; OBE (1995); s of Lawrence Wright Edwards (d 1973), and Phyllis Swinburne, *née* Boardman (d 1981); *b* 20 Jan 1929; *Educ* The King's Sch Canterbury, Magdalen Coll Oxford (MA, Lothian Prize 1951); *m* (m dis 1983), Hilary Mary, *née* Phillips; 1 s (Martin David b 1970), 3 da (Helen Mary b 1961, Katharine Rachel b 1963, Clare Lucy b 1964); m 2, 1983, Sybil, *née* Falcoln; *Career* fell All Souls Coll Oxford 1952–59; ed and md SCM Press 1958–66; dean King's Coll Cambridge 1966–70, canon Westminster Abbey and rector St Margaret's Westminster 1970–78, chaplain to Speaker of House of Commons 1972–78, dean of Norwich 1978–82, provost of Southwark 1983–94; chm: Christian Aid 1971–78, Churches' Cncl on Gambling 1970–78; hon fell Southbank Univ 1990, DD (Lambeth) 1990; *Books* Religion and Change (1969), Leaders of the Church of England (1971), What Anglicans Believe (1974), A Key to the Old Testament (1976), A Reason to Hope (1978), Christian England (3 Vols, 1981–86), The Futures of Christianity (1987), Essentials: a Dialogue with John Stott (1988), Tradition and Truth (1989), Christians in a New Europe (1990), The Real Jesus (1992), What is Catholicism? (1994); *Recreations* walking; *Clubs* Athenaeum; *Style—* The Very Rev Dr David Edwards, OBE; ✉ 19 Cripstead Lane, Winchester SO23 9SF (☎ 01962 862597)

EDWARDS, David Manning; s of Maj Eric Arthur James Edwards, MC, OBE (d 1983), of Godalming, Surrey, and Sybil Manning, *née* Fenton; *b* 28 April 1947; *Educ* Guildford Sch of Art (BA); *m* 4 May 1974, Linda Jane, da of Norman Arthur Robert Winton, of Godalming, Surrey; 2 s (Adam Harry b 30 Nov 1979, Guy b 30 July 1982); *Career* cartoon film director and designer, creator Superted character for Siriol Productions/Sianel Pedwar Cymru (S4C); BAFTA Best Animated Cartoon Film 1986 (for Superted); *Recreations* motor racing; *Style—* David Edwards, Esq

EDWARDS, David Michael; CMG (1989); s of Ernest William Edwards (d 1991), and Thelma Irene, *née* Foxley; *b* 28 Feb 1940; *Educ* King's Sch Canterbury, Univ of Bristol (LLB); *m* 29 Jan 1966 (m dis), Veronica Margaret, da of Robert Postgate, of Cannes, France; 1 s (Lt Adrian David b 1969), 1 da (Vanessa Louise b 1967); *Career* admitted slr 1964, asst legal advsr FO 1967; legal advsr: Br Mil Govt Berlin 1972, Br Embassy Bonn 1974; legal cnsllr 1977, dir legal div IAEA Vienna (on secondment) 1977–79, legal cnsllr FCO 1979, agent of the UK Govt in cases before Euro Cmmn and Court of Human Rights 1979–82, cnsllr and legal advsr UK Mission to UN NY and HM Embassy Washington 1985–88, dep legal advsr FCO 1989–90, law offr (International Law) Hong Kong Govt 1990–95, sr counsel Bechtel Ltd 1995–; *Recreations* reading, travel, antique clocks, gardening; *Style—* David Edwards, Esq, CMG

EDWARDS, (Ronald) Derek Keep; JP (Hants 1978); s of Ronald Allan George Edwards (d 1981), of Hants, and Edith Vere, *née* Keep (d 1974); *b* 22 Nov 1934; *Educ* Winchester; *m* 1, 6 June 1958 (m dis 1984), Sally Anne, da of Patrick Boyle Lake Coghlan, of Fernhurst, W Sussex; 4 s (David b 1959, Simon b 1960, James b 1962, Charles b 1969); m 2, 3 March 1988, Julia Ann, *née* Knock; *Career* Kings Dragoon Gds 1953–55, Inns of Ct Regt (TA) 1955–61; memb Stock Exchange 1959; ptnr: R Edwards Chandler & Co 1960-69 (sr ptnr 1965–69), Brewin Dolphin & Co 1969–80, A H Cobbold & Co 1980–85; dir Cobbold Roach Ltd 1985–87, conslt Nielson, Cobbold Ltd 1991–; dir City Arts Trust Ltd 1994–; memb Advsy Bd Berliner Bank AG; govr Christ's Hosp Sch; memb Ctee Bassishaw Ward Club (chm 1971); vice chm: Sheriffs and Recorders' Fund, Greater London Fund for the Blind; chm Guildhall Sch of Music and Drama 1994–; memb Ct of Common Cncl 1978–, Sheriff of London 1989–90; Freeman City of London 1971, Liveryman Worshipful Co of Loriners; MSI, FIMgt, OStJ; *Recreations* field sports, riding, skiing; *Clubs* Cavalry and Guards'; *Style—* Derek Edwards, Esq, JP; ✉ Coneycroft House, Selborne, Hampshire; Neilson Cobbold, 5 North Pallant, Chichester, West Sussex (☎ 01243 775373)

EDWARDS, His Hon Judge (David) Elgan (Hugh); s of Howell Dan Edwards, JP (d 1986), of Rhyl, Clywyd, and Dilys, *née* Williams (d 1994); *b* 6 Dec 1943; *Educ* Rhyl GS, UCW Aberystwyth (LLB); *m* 1, 29 July 1967 (m dis 1981), Jane Elizabeth Hayward; 1 s (Daniel Richard Hugh b 1974), 1 da (Kathryn Sian Elizabeth b 1971); m 2, 31 July 1982, Carol Anne, da of Arthur Smalls, of Saughall, Chester; 1 s (Thomas Huw Elgan b 1984), 1 da (Nia Alexandra b 1991); *Career* called to the Bar Gray's Inn 1967, recorder (Wales and Chester Circuit) 1982–89, circuit judge (Wales and Chester Circuit) 1989–;

memb Chester City Cncl 1974–84, Sheriff City of Chester 1977–78; *Recreations* swimming; *Clubs* Chester City; *Style—* His Hon Judge Elgan Edwards; ✉ c/o Chester Crown Court, The Castle, Chester (☎ 01244 317606)

EDWARDS, Elizabeth Alice; OBE (1995); *b* 26 May 1937; *Educ* Coleraine HS NI, Univ of Edinburgh (BSc(SocSci)), SRN, SCM; *Career* staff nurse, midwife, ward sister and nurse mgmnt posts 1958–72 incl: Lt and Capt QARANC T & AVR 204 Gen Hosp RAMC (V) NI Cmd 1961–69, transferred 205 (Sc) Gen Hosp RAMC (V) 1969–72; princ nursing offr Edinburgh Northern Hosps Gp 1972–74, dist nursing offr N Lothian Dist Lothian Health Bd 1974–80; chief area nursing offr: Dumfries and Galloway Health Bd 1980–88, Tayside Health Bd 1988–94 (exec memb 1993–94); chm Dumfries and Galloway Community NHS Trust 1995–; conslt on nursing mgmnt WHO SE Asia Region 1975; memb: various gps Scottish Health Serv Planning Cncl 1981–84, Health Servs Res Ctee 1982–89, UK Central Cncl for Nursing, Midwifery and Health Visiting (memb Cncl), Bd of Govrs Dundee Inst of Technol 1988–94; dep chm: Nat Bd for Scotland 1985–93 (memb 1983–93), Abbeyfield Dumfries Society Ltd 1987–88 (memb Exec Ctee 1985–88); chm Dundee Hospital's Christmas Carol Concert Ctee in aid of Malcolm Sargent Cancer Fund for Children 1988–92; *Style—* Miss Elizabeth A Edwards, OBE; ✉ 19 Suffolkhill Avenue, Dumfries DG2 7PQ (☎ 01387 262384)

EDWARDS, Very Rev (Thomas) Erwyd Pryse; s of Richard Humphreys Edwards (d 1957), and Gwladys, *née* Morgan (d 1973); *b* 26 Jan 1933; *Educ* Machynlleth GS, St David's Univ Coll Lampeter (BA 1956), St Michael's Coll Llandaff; *m* 16 Sept 1961, Mair, da of William Thomas Roberts (d 1988); 2 s (Sion Erwyd b 6 Oct 1965, Huw Thomas b 25 Feb 1969); *Career* ordained deacon 1958, priest 1959, curate Caernarfon 1958–63, asst chaplain St George's Hosp London 1963–66, senior chaplain King's Coll Hospital London 1966–72; vicar: Penmon (Anglesey) 1972–75, Menai Bridge 1975–81, St David's Bangor 1981–86, St James 1986–88; canon Bangor 1988, dean of Bangor 1988–; chaplain St Davids Hospital Bangor 1981–83, memb of Chaplaincy team Ysbyty Gwynedd 1983–86, area chaplain (Wales) Butlins Holidays Ltd 1982–86, chm Provincial Readers Bd 1993–, Cathedral Cmmr (Wales) 1994; *Recreations* music, DIY, reading; *Style—* The Very Rev the Dean of Bangor; ✉ The Deanery, Cathedral Close, Bangor, Gwynedd LL57 1LH (☎ 01248 370693); Cathedral Office, Diocesan Centre, Cathedral Close, Bangor, Gwynedd LL57 1DS (☎ and fax 01248 370693)

EDWARDS, Dr Francis John (Frank); *b* 22 Oct 1941; *Educ* Humberstone Fndn Sch Cleethorpes, Univ of Nottingham (BSc, PhD); *m* 1967, Angela Margaret, *née* Middleton; 1 s (Richard J D b 1970), 1 da (Carolyn L b 1972); *Career* lectr Wye Coll 1966–69; British Council: Science Dept London 1969–71, science offr Buenos Aires 1971–74, science offr Rio de Janeiro and Brasilia 1974–78, science offr Paris 1978–83, dir Staff Trg Dept London 1983–86, dir Barcelona 1987–91, Americas, Pacific and Asia Div London 1991–93, regnl dir (Americas) London 1993–94, dir Mexico City 1994–; *Recreations* gardening/smallholding, bridge; *Style—* Dr Frank Edwards; ✉ The British Council, Maestro Antonio Caso 127, Col. San Rafael, Apartado postal 30–588, Mexico City 06470 DF, Mexico

EDWARDS, Frank Wallis; CBE (1984); s of Arthur Edwards (d 1962), of Ipswich, and Mabel Lily, *née* Hammond (d 1956); *b* 23 Dec 1922; *Educ* Royal Liberty Sch Essex, Univ of Bradford; *m* 1959, Valerie Ann, da of late Reginald Claude Hitch, of Balcombe; 2 da (Elena, Melinda); *Career* Capt REME 1944–47; Dorr-Oliver Co: project and sales engr 1953–59, dir 1959–70, md Euro ops 1966–69, divnl vice pres Int Div 1969–70; Humphreys & Glasgow International plc (formerly Humphreys & Glasgow Ltd) UK: joined 1970, dir 1971, md 1974, dep chm 1978–91; dir: Humphreys & Glasgow International Ltd 1973–91, Process & Energy Consultants Ltd 1974–91 (chm), MHG International Ltd 1975–83, Hydreq Ltd 1976–83 (chm 1982–83), Humphreys & Glasgow (Atlantic) Ltd 1976–91, Energy Industs Cncl 1976–88, Canatom Heavy Water Ltd 1978–91, Humphreys & Glasgow Inc 1981–91, Goldmace Ltd 1981–83, Project Evaluation & Implementation Ltd 1982–91, INITEC 1982–86, Humphreys & Glasgow (Overseas) Ltd 1982–91, Humphreys & Glasgow Pacific Pty Ltd 1984–91, Ebasco Humphreys & Glasgow 1984–86, BIMEC Industries plc 1991–92 (non-exec); memb Cncl: Br Chemical Engrg Contractors Assoc 1974–83 (chm 1982–83), process plant NEDO 1977–83, Latin America Trade Advsy Gp (BOTB) 1978–84 (chm 1982–84), China Britain Trade Gp (formerly Sino-Br Trade Cncl) (BOTB) 1977–93 (vice pres 1983–93); vice pres Woldingham Assoc 1980–; Liveryman Worshipful Co of Glass Sellers; CEng, FIChemE, MIMechE, FInstD, FRSA (1983); Ordre Du Mono Republic of Togo 1978; *Recreations* gardening, walking, theatre, woodland conservation; *Clubs* Army and Navy; *Style—* Frank Edwards, Esq, CBE; ✉ Spinney Corner, Church Road, Woldingham, Surrey CR3 7JH (☎ 01883 653360)

EDWARDS, His Hon Judge Gareth Owen; QC (1985); s of Arthur Wyn Edwards (d 1974), and Mair Eluned Jones; *b* 26 Feb 1940; *Educ* Herbert Strutt GS Derbyshire, Univ of Oxford (BA, BCL); *m* 1967, Katharine Pek Har, da of Goh Keng Swee, of Kuala Lumpur, Malaysia; 2 s (David b 1970, John b 1974), 1 da (Kim b 1968); *Career* called to the Bar Inner Temple 1963; Capt Army Legal Serv Germany 1963–65; asst legal advsr Cwlth Office 1965–67, practised Wales and Chester Circuit 1967–91, recorder of the Crown Court 1978–91, circuit judge (Wales and Chester Circuit) 1991–; asst cmmr Boundaries Cmmn 1975–80; *Recreations* chess, cricket, tennis, hill walking; *Clubs* Army & Navy; *Style—* His Hon Judge Gareth Edwards, QC

EDWARDS, Gareth Owen; MBE (1976); s of Thomas Granville Edwards, and Annie-Mary Edwards; *b* 12 July 1947; *Educ* Pontardawe Tech Sch, Millfield Sch, Cardiff Coll of Educn; *m* 6 July 1972, Maureen, da of Luther Edwards (d 1985); 2 s ((Geraint) Owen b 29 April 1974, (Dafydd) Rhys b 20 Oct 1975); *Career* co dir and former rugby union player; Welsh secdy schs rugby int 1965–66, English schs 200 yds hurdles champion 1966 (UK under 19 record holder); Wales: 53 caps 1967–78, capt 13 times, youngest capt aged 20 1968; Cardiff RFC 1966–78, Barbarians 1967–78, Br Lions 1968, 1971 and 1974; dir: Euro-Commercials (South Wales) Ltd 1982–, Players (UK) Ltd 1983–88; chm Hamdden Ltd 1991–; chm Regnl Fisheries Advsy Ctee Welsh Water Authy 1983–89; *Books* Gareth - an autobiography (1978), Rugby Skills (1979), Rugby Skills for Forwards (1980), Gareth Edwards on Fishing (1984), Gareth Edwards on Rugby (1986), Gareth Edwards' 100 Great Rugby Players (1987); *Recreations* fishing, golf; *Style—* Gareth Edwards, Esq, MBE; ✉ Hamdden Ltd, Plas y Ffynnon, Cambrian Way, Brecon, Powys LD3 7HP (☎ 01874 614657)

EDWARDS, Sir George Robert; OM (1971), kt (1957), CBE (1952, MBE 1945), DL (Surrey 1981); s of late Edwin George Edwards, of Highams Park, Essex; *b* 9 July 1908; *Educ* SW Essex Tech Coll, Univ of London (BSc); *m* 1935, Marjorie Annie (d 1904), da of John Lawrence Thurgood; 1 da; *Career* aeronautical engr; Vickers Aviation Ltd: joined design staff 1935, experimental mangr 1940, chief designer Weybridge Works 1945, dir Vickers Ltd 1955–67; chm BAC 1963–75; emeritus pro-chllr Univ of Surrey 1979 (pro-chllr 1964–79); Liveryman Guild of Air Pilots and Air Navigators; MRI 1971, FRS, FEng 1976 (fndr fell); *Style—* Sir George Edwards, OM, CBE, DL, FRS, FEng; ✉ Albury Heights, White Lane, Guildford, Surrey (☎ 01483 504488)

EDWARDS, Guy Richard Goronwy; QGM (1977), Austrian AC Gold Medal 1977; s of Sqdn Ldr Goronwy Edwards, DFC, RAF, of Liverpool, and Mary Christine Edwards; *b* 30 Dec 1942; *Educ* Liverpool Coll, Univ of Durham (BSc); *m* 26 April 1986, Daphne Caroline, da of William George McKinley, MRCVS, of Co Meath, Ireland; 1 s (Sean), 2 da (Natasha, Jade); *Career* professional racing driver 1965–85, winner 40 int races, drove as team mate to Graham Hill; Grand Prix Formula 1: Lola 1974, Lord Hesketh 1976, BRM 1977; drove Le Mans Twenty Four Hour 9 times for Porsche, BMW and Lola (fourth 1985); awarded QGM for helping rescue Niki Lauda from burning Ferrari at German Grand Prix 1976; chm Guy Edwards Racing Ltd (organising sponsorship for motor racing) 1985–, responsible for Jaguar Car Co's commercial sponsorship prog (resulted in their winning World Championship 1987, 1988 and 1991, and Le Mans 1988 and 1990), dir of mktg Lotus Formula 1 Team; Freeman: City of London, Worshipful Co of Coachmakers and Coach Harness Makers; *Books* Sponsorship and the World of Motor Racing; *Recreations* country pursuits, reading, water sports, fishing; *Clubs* British Racing Drivers, Club International des Anciens Pilotes de Grand Prix F1 BARC; *Style—* Guy Edwards, Esq, QGM; ✉ 46–47 Chancery Lane, London WC2A 1BA (☎ 0171 242 5052)

EDWARDS, Prof Gwynne; s of William Edwards (d 1964), of Clydach Vale, Mid Glamorgan, S Wales, and Rachel Mary Lamb (d 1986); *b* 14 April 1937; *Educ* Porth Co GS, Univ Coll Cardiff, King's Coll London (BA, PhD); *m* 1 Aug 1964, Gillian Marilyn Davies; 1 s (Gareth b 1971), 1 da (Eleri b 1968); *Career* lectr in Spanish Univ of Liverpool 1962–67; Dept of Euro Languages Univ of Wales Aberystwyth: lectr 1967–73, sr lectr 1973–80, reader 1980–83, prof 1983–, head of dept 1984–87; memb Assoc of Hispanists of England and Wales; professional theatre prodns: Lorca's Blood Wedding 1987 and 1992, Lorca's Women 1987–88, Mario Vargas Llosa's La Chunga 1988, Lorca's Doña Rosita 1989, Lorca's When Five Years Pass 1989 (winner of Scotsman Fringe First), Lorca's The Shoemaker's Wonderful Wife 1990 and 1991, Carlos Muñiz's The Ink-Well 1990, Lope de Vega's Punishment Without Revenge 1991, Calderón's Three Judgements in One 1991, Life is a Dream 1992, Egon Wolff's Paper Flowers 1993, Jose Triana's Medea in the Mirror 1996; *Books* The Prison and the Labyrinth: Studies in Calderonian Tragedy (1978), Lorca: The Theatre Beneath the Sand (1980), The Discreet Art of Luis Bunuel (1982), Dramatists in Perspective: Spanish Theatre in the Twentieth Century (1985), Lorca: Three Plays (1987), Lorca Plays: Two (1990), Calderón Plays: One (1991), Indecent Exposures: Buñuel, Saura, Erice, Almodóvar (1994), Lorca Plays: Three (1994), Burning the Curtain: Four Revolutionary Spanish Plays (1995); *Recreations* theatre, opera, music, sport, cinema, travel; *Style—* Prof Gwynne Edwards; ✉ 66 Maeshendre, Waun Fawr, Aberystwyth, Dyfed, Wales; Department of European Languages, University of Wales, Aberystwyth, Dyfed, Wales (☎ 01970 622558, fax 01970 622553)

EDWARDS, Dr Huw; s of Evan Dewi Edwards, of Carmarthen, and Doris Maud, *née* Evans; *b* 22 Dec 1938; *Educ* Queen Elizabeth GS Carmarthen, St Bart's Hosp Med Coll (MB BS, MRCS, LRCP, DPM); *m* 22 June 1963, Brenda Annie, da of Jack Burgess, of Carmarthen; 3 s (Siwan b 1965, Sioned b 1967, Manon b 1972); *Career* sr registrar Dept of Psychological Med Welsh Nat Sch of Med 1966–69; conslt psychiatrist 1969–: St David's Hosp, W Wales Gen Hosp, Bronglais Hosp; chm: Y Gymdeithas Feddygol (Welsh Med Soc) 1988–91, Welsh Psychiatric Soc 1995–96; memb: Plaid Cymru, Carmarthen Mind Assoc; FRCPsych 1984; *Books* Wynebu Bywyd (1979), Y Pryfyn Yn Yr Afal (1981), Cylch Cyflawn (1994); *Recreations* collecting old books, writing, fishing, gardening, botany and archaeology; *Style—* Dr Huw Edwards; ✉ Garth Martin, Ffordd Henfwlch, Caerfyrddin, Dyfed, Wales SA33 5EG (☎ 01267 211318); St David's Hospital, Carmarthen, Dyfed SA31 3HB (☎ 01267 237481)

EDWARDS, Jeffery; s of Walter Frederick (d 1983), and Hilda, *née* Fenemore; *b* 31 Aug 1945; *Educ* Orange Hill GS, Bushey GS, Leeds Coll of Art and Design (DipAD), RCA (MA, Printmaking prize); *m* 1969, Theresa, da of Cliff Tyrell; 1 s (Roland b 1970), 1 da (Chloë b 1972); *Career* artist; public collections incl: V & A, Tate Gallery, Br Cncl, Brooklyn Museum NY, Bradford City Art Gallery, Whitworth Art Gallery Manchester, Arts Cncl of Great Britain; sr lectr Chelsea Sch of Art 1982–; *Recreations* rhythm and blues, thoroughbred cars; *Clubs* Chelsea Arts; *Style—* Jeffery Edwards, Esq; ✉ Chelsea School of Art, Manresa Rd, London SW3 6LS (☎ 0171 351 3844)

EDWARDS, Jeremy John Cary; s of William Philip Neville Edwards, CBE, and The Hon Mrs Sheila Edwards, *née* Cary (d 1976); *b* 2 Jan 1937; *Educ* Ridley Coll Ontario Canada, Vinehall Sch Sussex, Haileybury and Imperial Serv Coll; *m* 1, 18 April 1963 (m dis), Jenifer (decd), da of late Capt Langton Mould; 1 s (Julian Peter Cary b 21 Jan 1967), 1 da (Venetia Hester b 16 Aug 1964); m 2, 1974, April Philippa Learmond, da of late Reginald Ernest Harding; 1 s (Benjamin Charles Cary b 17 Dec 1980); m 3, 1994, Amanda Mary Barber, da of Frank Rabone; *Career* Unilever Ltd 1955–57, Hobson Bates & Co Ltd 1957–59, Overseas Marketing & Advertising Ltd 1959–61, Courtaulds Ltd 1961–63, Vine Products Ltd 1963–66, Loewe SA 1966–68, Jessel Securities Ltd 1968–70, md Vavasseur Unit Trust Management 1970–74, gp md Henderson Administration Group plc 1974–95; currently non-exec dir: Vontobel Asset Management Zurich, Hakluyt & Co, College Hill Associates, Eurovest Limited; hon treas and tstee World Wide Fund for Nature UK, vice chm C of E Children's Soc, chm Business Supporters Gp Community Links; *Clubs* Boodle's, City of London, The Brook (NY); *Style—* Jeremy Edwards, Esq; ✉ 59 Dorothy Road, London SW11 2JJ (☎ 0171 228 6055)

EDWARDS, John; s of Joseph Edwards, CBE, and Lily, *née* Nager; *b* 6 Nov 1941; *Educ* Kantonsschule Zurich Switzerland, Trinity Coll Cambridge (MA); *m* 5 June 1980, Annemarie Alice Jessica, da of Claude Arpels, Légion D'Honneur, of Rye, NY; 1 s (Luke b 21 Nov 1980), 1 da (Kate b 5 Feb 1984); *Career* admitted slr 1969; currently ptnr Linklaters & Paines; sr visiting fell Queen Mary and Westfield Coll Univ of London; memb: Law Soc, Int Bar Assoc; *Recreations* swimming, skiing, music, literature, pictures; *Clubs* Annabel's, Mark's, RAC, City; *Style—* John Edwards, Esq; ✉ Linklaters & Paines, Barrington House, 59–67 Gresham St, London EC2V 7JA (☎ 0171 606 7080)

EDWARDS, John Andrew Child; s of Arnold Child Edwards (d 1989), and Cathleen Lilian, *née* Cooper; *b* 13 April 1946; *m* 2 c (Sophie Patricia b 20 Dec 1971, Timothy William Child b 14 Feb 1978); *Career* national hunt trainer; trainer's licence 1967; wins at Nat Hunt Festival Cheltenham incl: Queen Mother Champion Chase (twice), Kim Muir Chase (twice), Grand Annual Chase, Ritz Club Chase, Coral Hurdle, Sun Alliance Chase; other wins incl: Whitbread Trophy Liverpool, Scottish Grand National Ayr, Martel Cup Liverpool, Charterhouse Chase Ascot, Mackeson Gold Cup Cheltenham; *Recreations* hunting, shooting, fishing; *Clubs* Turf; *Style—* John Edwards, Esq; ✉ Caradoc Court, Sellack, Ross-on-Wye, Herefordshire HR9 6LS (☎ 01989 730259, fax 01989 730329)

EDWARDS, John Coates; CMG; s of Herbert John Edwards, and Doris May Edwards; *b* 25 Nov 1934; *Educ* Skinners' Sch Tunbridge Wells, BNC Oxford; *m* 1959, Mary, *née* Harris; 1 s, 1 da; *Career* HM Dip Serv: head British Devpt Div in the Caribbean 1978–81, head West Indian and Atlantic Dept FCO 1981–84, dep high cmmr Br High Cmmn Nairobi Kenya 1984–88, Br high cmmr Maserv Lesotho 1988–91, Br high cmmr Gaborone Botswana 1991–94; head UK Delgn EC Monitoring Mission in Former Yugoslavia 1995 and 1996; *Clubs* Royal Cwlth Soc, Muthaiga Country (Nairobi), Royal Over-Seas League; *Style—* John Edwards, Esq, CMG; ✉ Fairways, Back Lane, Ightham, Sevenoaks, Kent (☎ 01732 883556)

EDWARDS, John David; s of Rev T H D Edwards, of Tenbury Wells, Worcs, and Ann Gollan, *née* Adam; *b* 21 March 1959; *Educ* Haileybury, ISC, Leeds Poly (BA (Law)); *m* 25 March 1989, Louise Elisabeth, da of Raymond William Cooper, of Kidderminster, Worcs; *Career* called to the Bar Inner Temple, memb Gen of the Cncl Bar 1988–91, circuit jr Midland & Oxford Circuit 1993–94; *Recreations* tennis, squash, theatre; *Style—* John Edwards, Esq

EDWARDS, John Frederick; s of Fred Edwards, of Sheffield, and Lilian Ada Edwards; *b* 15 Oct 1948; *Educ* Henry Fanshaw GS Dronfield, Univ of Birmingham (BSc); *m* 1970, Linda; 1 s (Lewis Alexander James b 29 Sept 1974), 1 da (Frances Elizabeth b

8 March 1978); *Career* Massey Ferguson 1970, Chrysler UK 1971–75; Massey Ferguson: rejoined 1975, cost accountant, fin plans and control mangr then fin mangr Euro parts until 1979; fin dir: Jaguar Cars Ltd 1980–95, Northern Electric plc 1995–; FCMA 1984 (ACMA 1974); *Recreations* playing squash and tennis, keeping fit, watching rugby; *Clubs* Warwick Boat, Leicester FC, Northern FC; *Style—* John Edwards, Esq; ✉ Northern Electric plc, Carliol House, Market Street, Newcastle-upon-Tyne NE1 6NE (☎ 0191 210 2400)

EDWARDS, Prof John Hilton; s of Harold Clifford Edwards, CBE, of Cambridge (d 1989), and Ida Margaret, *née* Phillips (d 1981); *b* 26 March 1928; *Educ* Uppingham, Univ of Cambridge (MA, MB BChir); *m* 18 July 1953, Felicity Clare Edwards, OBE, da of Dr Charles Hugh Christie Toussaint (d 1985), of E Harling, Norfolk; 2 s (Conrad b 1959, Matthew b 1965), 2 da (Vanessa b 1956, Penelope b 1962); *Career* geneticist: unit of population genetics MRC Oxford 1958–59, Children's Hosp Philadelphia 1960; Univ of Birmingham 1961–79 (lectr, sr lectr, reader, prof), prof of genetics Univ of Oxford 1979–95, ret; conslt WHO 1972–95, med genetics NHS Oxford RHA 1979–95; memb Nat Radiological Protection Bd 1987–94; Liveryman Worshipful Soc of Apothecaries; FRCP 1972, FRS 1979; *Books* An Outline of Human Genetics (1978); *Recreations* gliding, skiing; *Clubs* Athenaeum; *Style—* Prof J H Edwards, FRS; ✉ 78 Old Rd, Headington, Oxford OX3 7LP (☎ 01865 60430)

EDWARDS, John Neill Thesen; s of Maj John Herbert Edwards (d 1984), of Pretoria, SA, and Aorea Georgina, *née* Thesen; *b* 2 May 1946; *Educ* St Andrew's Coll Grahamstown SA, Univ of Pretoria (MB ChB); *m* 1 May 1976, Katherine Martine, da of Stanley Douglas Abercrombie, of Poole, Dorset; 4 s (John Patrick Abercrombie b 1978, Charles Thomas Thesen b 1979, Andrew Neill Douglas b 1983, Harison Martin Ashdown b 1988); *Career* registrar in obstetrics and gynaecology John Radcliffe Hosp Oxford, sr registrar in obstetrics and gynaecology UCH, conslt in obstetrics and gynaecology Poole Gen Hosp 1986–; FRCOG (MRCOG 1981), FRCSEd 1986; *Recreations* sailing, fishing, shooting; *Clubs* Royal Motor Yacht (Poole), Bournemouth Constitutional; *Style—* John Edwards, Esq; ✉ Sarum House, 29 Forest Road, Branksome Park, Poole, Dorset BH13 6DQ (☎ 01202 765287)

EDWARDS, John Ralph; *b* 14 Jan 1950; *Educ* St Lawrence Coll Ramsgate, Univ of Bristol (BSc); *m* 13 May 1972, Susan Mary; 2 da (Rosalind b 3 Dec 1975, Jessica b 31 Oct 1983), 2 s (Tom b 13 Feb 1978, Will b 3 Oct 1981); *Career* articled clerk then CA Price Waterhouse London 1971–77, with Plantation Holdings 1977–79, Fairey Group 1979–89; TI Group plc: joined 1989, gp financial controller, fin dir Dowty Aerospace, dir corp fin 1994–; FCA 1980 (ACA 1974); *Style—* John Edwards, Esq; ✉ TI Group plc, Lambourn Court, Abingdon, Oxon OX14 1UH (☎ 01235 555570, fax 01235 540019, car 0850 602488)

EDWARDS, John Robert; s of John Ellis Edwards (d 1981), of London, and Lillian Hannah Hall (d 1983); *b* 3 March 1938; *Educ* Willesden Tech Coll, Hornsey Sch of Art, Leeds Inst of Educn, L'Ecole Nationale Superieure d'Architecture et d'Art Visuel Bruxelles (Br Cncl scholar); *m* 1960 (m dis 1973), Jeanette Christine Brown; 3 da (Chloe b 1966, Aphra b 1968, Cassandra b 1971); *Career* artist; sr lectr St Martin's Sch of Art London 1973; visiting artist: Syracuse Univ NY 1976, Sch of Visual Arts New York City 1980; head Dept of Painting and Sculpture St Martin's Sch of Art London 1986–88 (head of painting 1980–86); works in the collections of: Arts Cncl of GB, Br Cncl, Contemporary Art Soc London, Cncl for Nat Academic Awards, Govt Art Collection, Gulbenkian Fndn, Miny of Works Brussels, ICA, Solomon R Guggenheim Museum NY, Towner Art Gallery, Newcastle upon Tyne Poly; commissions: Northwick Park Hosp London 1984, John Hansard Gallery Univ of Southampton 1989; Winston Churchill Travel fell Netherlands and Germany 1989, Pollock-Krasner Fndn Grant 1996; memb London Group 1987; *Recreations* swimming, bicycle riding; *Style—* John Edwards, Esq; ✉ 52 Isledon Rd, London N7 7LD (☎ and fax 0171 609 7249)

EDWARDS, John Thomas; s of Jack Edwards (d 1953), and Gwendoline, *née* Davies (d 1982); *b* 16 Nov 1935; *Educ* Haverfordwest GS Dyfed; *m* Iris Mary; *Career* reporter: West Wales Guardian 1953–54, Liverpool Daily Post 1955–57; US corr Daily Mirror 1961–63 (staff corr London 1958–61); Daily Mail: feature writer 1969–71, SE Asia corr 1971–75, sr writer 1975–84, columnist 1984–; British Press Awards: Reporter of the Year 1975, commended feature writer 1977, commended foreign corr 1981; Reporter of the Year Granada TV Awards 1976; *Recreations* sailing, gardening; *Clubs* Cardiff and County, Hong Kong Press; *Style—* John Edwards, Esq; ✉ The Daily Mail, Northcliffe House, 2 Derry St, Kensington, London W8 5TT (☎ 0171 938 6000)

EDWARDS, Jonathan; MBE (1996); s of Andrew David Edwards, of Bearwood, and Jill, *née* Caulfield; *b* 10 May 1966; *Educ* West Buckland Sch; *m* 10 Nov 1990, Alison Joy, da of Ralph Briggs; 2 s (Samuel James b 10 Aug 1993, Nathan b May 1995); *Career* athlete (triple jump); English Schools Champion 1984, UK int 1988–; GB rep at Olympics 1988 and 1992; honours incl: Bronze medal World Cup 1989, Silver medal Commonwealth Games 1990 and 1994, Gold medal World Cup 1992, Bronze medal World Championships 1993, Gold medal World Championships Gothenburg 1995, Silver medal Olympic Games 1996; holder AAA National record (AAA Championships) 1994, UK Indoor All-Comers record, holder world record (18.29 metres) Gothenburg 1995; BBC Sports Personality of the Year 1995; *Recreations* chess, playing the guitar, reading; *Style—* Jonathan Edwards, Esq, MBE; ✉ c/o Annette Collins, Nova International Ltd, Newcastle House, Albany Court, Monarch Road, Newcastle upon Tyne NE4 7YB

EDWARDS, Joseph Robert; CBE (1963); yst s of Walter Smith Edwards; *b* 5 July 1908; *Educ* High Sch Gt Yarmouth; *m* 1, 1936, Frances Mabel Haddon Bourne (d 1975); 3 s, 1 da; m 2, 1976 (sep), Joan Constance Mary Tattersall; *Career* joined Austin Motor Co 1928, md British Motor Corp 1966–68; dep chm: Associated Engineering 1969–78, Martin Electrical Equipment (Theale) Ltd 1979–89, Theale Estates Ltd 1989–; chm: Harland & Wolff Ltd 1970, Penta Motors Ltd Reading 1978–87, Canewdon Consultants plc 1985–89 (conslt 1989–), Creative Industries Gp Inc (USA) 1985–; dir: Br Printing Corp 1973–81, CSE Aviation 1973–87; JP (Oxford 1964); *Style—* Joseph Edwards, Esq, CBE, JP; ✉ Flat 16, Shoreacres, Banks Rd, Sandbanks, nr Bournemouth, Dorset (☎ 01202 709315)

EDWARDS, (Alfred) Kenneth; CBE (1989, MBE 1963); s of Ernest Edwards (d 1959), of London, and Florence May Branch (d 1983); *b* 24 March 1926; *Educ* Latymer Upper Sch, Magdalene Coll Cambridge, Univ Coll London (BSc); *m* 17 Sept 1949, Jeannette Lilian, da of David Louis Speeks, MBE; 1 s (Vaughan b 1951), 2 da (Vivien b 1954, Deryn b 1960); *Career* Flying Offr RAF 1944–47 (RAF Coll Cranwell 1945); HM Overseas Civil Serv Nigeria 1952–63; gp mktg mangr Thorn Electrical Industries Ltd 1964, int dir Brookhirst Igranic Ltd (Thorn Gp) 1967, gp mktg dir Cutler Hammer Europa 1972, chief exec Br Electrical and Allied Manufacturers Associates Ltd (BEAMA) 1976–82; chm: FPM plc 1989–91, Business Services Europe 1989–95; memb Bd: Polar Electronics plc 1989–, Reliance Bank Ltd 1992–, Salvation Army Tstee Co; CBI: dep dir gen 1982–88, memb Cncl 1974 and 1976–82, memb Fin and Gen Purposes Ctee 1977–82, vice chm Eastern Regnl Cncl 1974, Pres's Ctee 1982– (memb 1979–82); memb: Exec Ctee Organisme de Liaison des Industries Metalliques Européennes (ORGALIME) 1976–82, Bd Br Standards Inst (BSI) 1978–82 and 1984–; chm: Br Electrotechnical Ctee and Electrotechnical Divnl Cncl 1981–82, BSI Quality Policy Ctee 1988–93; memb: BOTB 1982–88, Salvation Army Nat Advsy Bd 1982–, BBC Consultative Gp on Industrial and Business Affrs 1983–88; dir BTEC 1983–88; pres: European Ctee for Electrotechnical Standardisation (CENELEC) 1977–79 (memb Exec Ctee 1982–, chm Fin Ctee 1983–86), Union des Industries de la Communaute Europeenne (UNICE); memb Ct Cranfield Inst of Technol 1970–75; memb Bd and Exec Ctee Business in the Community 1987–89; FRSA 1985; *Recreations* music, books; *Clubs* Athenaeum, RAC, RAF; *Style—* Kenneth Edwards, Esq, CBE; ✉ 53 Bedford Road, Rushden, Northants NN10 OND

EDWARDS, Lyn; s of William David Edwards (d 1972), and Gwenllian, *née* Cox; *b* 28 Aug 1947; *Educ* Ogmore GS, Birmingham Sch of Architecture (DipArch), Univ of Aston (BSc), Univ of Reading (MSc); *m* 1971, Lynne, *née* Williams; 1 s (Nicholas Lloyd b 1978); 2 da (Philippa Louise b 1982, Rebecca Kathryn b 1985); *Career* asst: Malcolm H Peck & Partners 1969–71, Oxfordshire Co Architect's Dept 1971–72; GMW Partnership: project architect 1972, resident ptnr GMW International 1978, sr ptnr 1991– (ptnr 1980); *Projects* incl: Royal Opera House master plan and extension, King Saud Univ Riyadh, Inst of Ophthalmology, Royal Masonic Hosp, Ravenscourt Laboratories, Oxon CC Offices, Market Towers Nine Elms, Scottish Life House Surbiton, Townsend Car Ferries HQ Dover, BOC refurbishment, BOC Gp HQ Surrey, various BT refurbishments, City Gate Southwark, HQ Fisons PLC Ipswich, Pfizer (UK) Ltd Sandwich, Sun Life Bristol, New Covent Garden Market Nine Elms, Third Data Centre National Westminster Bank Staffs, bomb damage refurbishment NatWest Tower, Wharncliffe Gardens Devpt St John's Wood, sheltered housing projects in London, Bracknell and Watford, leisure centre projects Croydon, Plymouth and Newquay; memb Assoc of Project Mangrs 1988–; RIBA 1972; *Recreations* rugby-football (RFU Coaching Award), reading, music, family; *Clubs* East India; *Style—* Lyn Edwards, Esq; ✉ GMW Partnership, PO Box 1613, 239 Kensington High Street, London W8 6SL (☎ 0171 937 8020, fax 0171 937 5818)

EDWARDS, Malcolm John; CBE (1985); s of John James Edwards (d 1967), of London, and Edith Hannah, *née* Riley (d 1966); *b* 25 May 1934; *Educ* Alleyn's Sch Dulwich, Jesus Coll Cambridge (MA); *m* 2 Dec 1967, Yvonne Sylvia, da of J A W Daniels, of Port Lincoln, Australia; 2 s (Jonathan John b 1970, Mark b 1972); *Career* British Coal: dir of mktg 1973, commercial dir 1985, bd memb 1986, resigned 1992; fndr Edwards Energy Ltd 1992–; chm: Coal Investments plc 1993–96, Fin and Gen Purpose Ctee Southwark Diocesan Bd of Educn; Freeman City of London; CIMgt 1988; *Recreations* music, gardening, design 1860–1914; *Style—* Malcolm Edwards, Esq, CBE; ✉ Lodge Farm, Moot Lane, Downton, Salisbury, Wilts SP5 3LN (☎ 01725 511538)

EDWARDS, His Hon Judge; (Charles) Marcus; s of (John) Basil Edwards, CBE, JP (d 1996), and Molly Patricia, *née* Philips (d 1979); *b* 10 Aug 1937; *Educ* Dragon Sch, Rugby, BNC Oxford (BA); *m* 1, 1963, Anne Louise (d 1970), da of Sir Edmund Stockdale, of Hoddington House, nr Basingstoke; m 2, Sandra Edwards (formerly Mrs Wates), da of James Mouroutsos, of Mass, USA; 1 da (Alexandra b 1983); *Career* 2 Lt Intelligence Corps 1955–56; HM Dip Serv 1960–65; third sec: Spain, S Africa, Laos, Whitehall; called to the Bar 1962, practising 1965–86, circuit judge (SE Circuit) 1986–; chm Pavilion Opera 1986–; *Recreations* gardening, walking, travel; *Clubs* Beefsteak; *Style—* His Hon Judge Marcus Edwards; ✉ Melbourne House, South Parade, London W4 1JU; Brentford County Court, Alexandra Road, Brentford, Middlesex TW8 0JJ

EDWARDS, (Kenneth) Martin; s of late Kenneth Reginald Edwards, and Joan Isabel, *née* Bradley; *b* 7 July 1955; *Educ* Sir John Deane's GS Northwich, Balliol Coll Oxford (MA, Jenkyns Prize, Keasbey bursary, David Paton studentship, Winter Williams Award, Martin Wronker Award), Chester Coll of Law; *m* 30 April 1988, Helena Mary Caroline, da of late Michael James Shanks; 1 s (Jonathan Michael b 28 Dec 1990), 1 da (Catherine Juliet Ruth b 5 Jun 1993); *Career* writer and slr; articled clerk Booth and Co Solicitors Leeds 1978–80, admitted slr 1980, ptnr Mace and Jones Liverpool 1984– (slr 1980–84); memb editorial bd: Business Law Review, European Business Law Review; memb: Standing Ctee on Employment Law Law Soc, Crime Writers' Assoc, Soc of Authors; ACIArb; *Books* Understanding Computer Contracts (1983), Understanding Dismissal Law (1984, 2nd edn 1991), Managing Redundancies (1986), Executive Survival (1987, 2nd edn 1991), Northern Blood (editor, 1992), Careers in the Law (1995, 5 edns), Anglian Blood (co-editor, 1995), Northern Blood 2 (editor, 1995); *novels* All The Lonely People (1991), Suspicious Minds (1992), I Remember You (1993), Yesterday's Papers (1994), Eve of Destruction (1996); *Recreations* writing, music, cricket, travel, films; *Clubs* Athenaeum (Liverpool); *Style—* Martin Edwards, Esq; ✉ Watson Little Ltd, 12 Egbert Street, London

EDWARDS, (John) Michael; CBE (1986), QC (1981); er s of Dr James Thomas Edwards (d 1952), and Constance Amy (d 1985), yr da of Sir John McFadyean; *b* 16 Oct 1925; *Educ* Andover GS, Univ Coll Oxford (BA, BCL, MA); *m* 1, 1951 (m dis 1963), Morna Joyce, *née* Piper; 1 s (James b 1957), 1 da (Caroline (Mrs Martin Pearce) b 1955); m 2, 3 March 1964, Rosemary Ann, da of Douglas Kinley Moore (d 1982); 2 s (Tom b 1967, Owen b 1969); *Career* called to the Bar Middle Temple 1949 (bencher 1993), practising 1950–55 and 1993–, head of chambers; asst Parly counsel to the Treasy 1955–60; dep legal advsr and dir various subsid cos (exporting turn-key plants to E Europe) Courtaulds Ltd 1960–67; British Steel Corporation: joined 1967, dir of legal servs 1967–69, md Int 1968–81, chm and md Overseas Serv 1975–81; dir: Bell Group International Ltd (formerly Associated Communications Corp) 1982–89 (md 1988–89), Bell memb: Ctee Bar Assoc for Commerce Fin and Indust 1965–92 (chm 1972–78, vice pres 1980–82 and 1992–), Bar Cncl 1971–79 and 1980–83, E Euro Trade Cncl 1973–81, Overseas Project Bd 1973–81, Senate of Inns of Ct and the Bar 1974–79 and 1980–83 (memb Fin and Exec Ctees), Cncl Regnl Opera Tst (Kent Opera) 1981–88 (chm 1983–86), Academic Cncl Inst of Int Business Law and Practice of ICC Paris 1982–88, Disciplinary Appeal Ctee Chartered Assoc of Certified Accountants 1983–96 (chm 1987–90, dep chm 1990–96), Educnl Assets Bd 1989–; chm: Eastman Dental Hosp SHA 1983–96, Eastman Dental Inst (formerly Inst of Dental Surgery) Univ of London 1983–96; provost City of London Poly (now London Guildhall Univ) 1981–88; dep chm Ind Appeals Authy for Sch Examinations 1990–; govr Br Postgrad Med Fedn 1987–96; Freeman City of London 1979, memb Ct Worshipful Co of Ironmongers 1982 (Master 1994–95); CIMgt, FCIArb 1984; *Recreations* family and friends, driving old cars, making things work; *Clubs* Garrick; *Style—* Michael Edwards, Esq, CBE, QC; ✉ Verulam Chambers, Peer House, 8–14 Verulam Street, London WC1X 8LZ (☎ 0171 813 2400, fax 0171 405 3870, dx LDX436 CHANCERY LANE)

EDWARDS, Prof Michael; s of Frank Ernest Walter Edwards (d 1995), and Irene Louise Dalliston (d 1985); *b* 29 April 1938; *Educ* Kingston GS, Christ's Coll Cambridge (BA, MA, PhD); *m* 7 July 1964, Danielle, da of Jacques Bourdin, of Lamotte-Beuvron, France; 1 s (Paul), 1 da (Catherine); *Career* lectr in French Univ of Warwick 1965–73, sr lectr then reader in lit Univ of Essex 1973–87, prof of English Univ of Warwick 1987–; visiting prof Univ of Paris 1989–90; Medal Collège de France; *Books* La Tragédie Racinienne (1972), To Kindle The Starling (poems, 1972), Eliot/Language (1975), Where (poems, 1975), The Ballad of Mobb Conroy (poems, 1977), Towards a Christian Poetics (1984), The Magic, Unquiet Body (poems, 1985), Poetry and Possibility (1988), Of Making Many Books (1990), Raymond Mason (1994), Eloge de l'Attente (1996); *Recreations* walking; *Clubs* Cambridge Union; *Style—* Prof Michael Edwards; ✉ 4 Northumberland Rd, Leamington Spa, Warwickshire CV32 6HA (☎ 01926 312205); Department of English and Comparative Literary Studies, University of Warwick, Coventry, Warwickshire CV4 7AL (☎ 01203 523523)

EDWARDS, Dr Michael Frederick; OBE (1992); s of Henry Sandford Edwards (d 1965), and Jessie, *née* Wallwork; *b* 27 April 1941; *Educ* Tupton Hall GS, Univ Coll Swansea (BP scholarship, BSc, Harold Hartley Prize, PhD); *m* 30 Dec 1964, Margaret Roberta; 1 s (Peter Stephen b 22 April 1967), 1 da (Catherine Louise b 20 Aug 1969); *Career* lectr in engrg sci Univ of Warwick 1966–69, prof Chemical Engrg Dept Univ of

Bradford 1981–87 (lectr then sr lectr 1969–81), princ engr Unilever Research 1987–; visiting prof in chemical engrg UMIST; FIChemE, FEng 1992; *Books* Mixing in the Process Industries (ed, 1985, 2 edn 1992); *Recreations* walking, music; *Style—* Dr Michael Edwards, OBE, FEng; ✉ Unilever Research, Port Sunlight Laboratory, Quarry Road East, Bebbington, Wirral, Merseyside L63 3JW (☎ 0151 471 3137, fax 0151 471 1829)

EDWARDS, Patricia Anne (Mrs Roger Cox); da of late Maurice James Edwards, and Marion, *née* Lewis; *b* 29 May 1944; *Educ* Barry Co GS, Purley Co GS, King's Coll London (LLB); *m* 1970, His Hon Judge Roger Cox, s of late Reginald William Cox; *Career* called to the Bar Middle Temple 1967; Criminal Appeal Office 1965–74, Law Offrs' Dept 1974–77; Home Office: sr legal asst 1977–80, asst legal advsr 1980–88, princ asst legal advsr 1988–94, dep parly cmmr for admin 1994–; *Recreations* music, travel, reading, domestic pursuits; *Style—* Miss Patricia Edwards; ✉ Office of Parliamentary Commissioner for Administration, Church House, Great Smith Street, London SW1P 3BW

EDWARDS, Pauline; MBE (1991); *b* 23 April 1949; *Career* GB archery rep Olympic Games Munich 1972, Seoul 1988 (fifth place team event); honours incl Bronze medal World Championships 1973, Silver medals (individual and team) European Field Championships 1995; archery rep Nat Olympic Ctee 1992–96; vice pres Royal Toxophilite Soc; computer analyst; MBCS, CEng; *Clubs* Atkins Archers; *Style—* Miss Pauline Edwards, MBE; ✉ 11 Lewins Rd, Epsom, Surrey KT18 7TL

EDWARDS, Peter John; s of Alfred Edwards (d 1965), of Southend-on-Sea, Essex, and Hilda, *née* Lamb (d 1964); *b* 29 July 1936; *Educ* Thorpe Hall Sch; *m* 29 Aug 1964, Susan, *née* Scott; 1 s (Stuart b 1968), 1 da (Jacqueline b 1971); *Career* sports administrator; chartered sec: Drayton Group City of London 1953–67, Lifeguard Assurance 1967–76, John Laing 1976–79; sec and gen mangr Essex CCC 1979– (memb 1948–79); table tennis: chm Southend League 1964–72, chm Daventry League 1973–78, chm Northants County Assoc 1976–78 (also county umpire), represented Daventry and Southend Leagues as player; ACIS 1957; *Recreations* golf, foreign travel, music, theatre; *Clubs* MCC, Lord's Taverners, Thorpe Hall Golf; *Style—* Peter Edwards, Esq; ✉ Essex County Cricket Club, County Ground, New Writtle Street, Chelmsford, Essex CM2 0PG (☎ 01245 252420, fax 01245 491607)

EDWARDS, Prof Peter Philip; *b* 30 June 1949; *Educ* Univ of Salford (Chemistry Prize, BSc, PhD); *m* 4 Sept 1970, Patricia Anne, da of John Clancy; 2 s (Peter John b 23 April 1973, Karl b 17 March 1980), 1 da (Kerrie b 13 Dec 1971); *Career* Fulbright scholar and Nat Science fell Baker Lab of Chemistry Cornell Univ 1975–77, SERC/NATO fell and Ramsay Meml fell Inorganic Chemistry Lab Univ of Oxford 1977–79; Univ of Cambridge: lectr and dir of studies in chemistry 1979–90, Nuffield Science Research fell 1986–87, co-fndr and co-dir Interdisciplinary Research Centre in Superconductivity 1988, British Petroleum Venture Research fell 1988–90; prof of inorganic chemistry Univ of Birmingham 1991–; visiting prof Cornell Univ 1983–86, F S Kipping visitor Univ of Nottingham 1987; fell Jesus Coll Cambridge 1979–90; memb Materials Research Soc of India; Royal Soc of Chemistry: Corday-Morgan Medal 1987, Tilden Medal 1992, vice pres Dalton Div 1995; FRSC 1988, FRS 1996; *Books* The Metallic and Nonmetallic States of Matter (ed with C N R Rao, 1985), Metal-Insulator Transitions Revisited (1995); *Recreations* sporting activities; *Style—* Prof Peter Edwards, FRS; ✉ School of Chemistry, University of Birmingham, Edgbaston, Birmingham B15 2TT (☎ 0121 414 4379, fax 0121 414 4442)

EDWARDS, Peter Robert; s of Robert Edwards, of Worthing, West Sussex, and Doris Edith, *née* Cooper; *b* 30 Oct 1937; *Educ* Christ's Hosp; *m* 1, 1967, Jennefer Ann, da of Frederick Boys; m 2, 1970, Elizabeth Janet, da of Maitland Barrett; 1 s (Simon b 1970), 1 da (Sarah b 1971); *Career* Arthur Young 1955–90 (managing ptnr 1986–90), md Secretan plc 1990–92, ind memb Cncl FIMBRA 1990–94, public interest dir Personal Investment Authy, non-exec dir Blackwall Green Ltd 1993–96; Freeman City of London 1956, memb Worshipful Co of Merchant Taylors; ICAS 1960; *Recreations* ornithology; *Clubs* Caledonian; *Style—* Peter Edwards, Esq; ✉ Glebe Cottage, Church Lane, Bury, Pulborough, West Sussex RH20 1PB (☎ 01798 831774, fax 01798 831051); The Personal Investment Authority, 1 Canada Square, Canary Wharf, London E14 5AZ (☎ 0171 538 8860, fax 0171 418 9300)

EDWARDS, Prof Philip Walter; s of Robert Henry Edwards, MC (d 1950), and Bessie, *née* Pritchard (d 1972); *b* 7 Feb 1923; *Educ* King Edward's HS Birmingham, Univ of Birmingham (MA, PhD); *m* 1, 8 July 1947, Hazel Margaret (d 1950), da of late Prof C W Valentine, of Birmingham; m 2, 8 May 1952, Sheila Mary, da of Reginald Samuel Wilkes (d 1989), of Bloxwich, Staffs; 3 s (Matthew b 1953, Charles b 1956, Richard b 1958), 1 da (Catherine b 1967); *Career* sub Lt RNVR 1942–45; lectr in English Univ of Birmingham 1946–60, prof of English lit Trinity Coll Dublin 1960–66, prof of lit Univ of Essex 1966–74; Univ of Liverpool: King Alfred prof of English lit 1974–90, pro-vice-chllr 1980–83, emeritus prof of English lit 1990–; author of numerous articles; visiting prof: Univ of Michigan 1964–65, Williams Coll Mass 1969, Otago Univ NZ 1980, ICU Tokyo 1989; visiting fell: All Souls Coll Oxford 1970–71, Huntington Library California 1977 and 1983; FBA 1986; *Books* Sir Walter Raleigh (1953), Kyd's The Spanish Tragedy (ed, 1959), Shakespeare and the Confines of Art (1968), Shakespeare's Pericles (ed, 1976), Massinger Plays and Poems (co-ed C Gibson, 1976), Threshold of a Nation (1979), Shakespeare's Hamlet (ed, 1985), Shakespeare: A Writer's Progress (1986), Last Voyages (1988), The Story of the Voyage (1994), Sea-Mark (1997); *Recreations* walking, cycling, gardening; *Style—* Prof Philip Edwards; ✉ High Gillinggrove, Gillinggate, Kendal, Cumbria LA9 4JB (☎ 01539 721298)

EDWARDS, Rear Adm (John) Phillip; CB (1984), LVO (1971); s of Robert Edwards (d 1981), of Llanbedr, Ruthin, Clwyd, and Dilys Myfanwy, *née* Phillips (d 1947); *b* 13 Feb 1927; *Educ* Brynhyfryd Sch Ruthin, HMS Conway, RN Engrg Coll; *m* 1951, Gwen, da of John Lloyd Bonner (d 1982), of Llandyrnog, Denbigh, Clwyd; 3 da (Susan, Lynn, Siân); *Career* RN 1944–83; Rear Adm serving as DG Fleet Support Policy and Servs 1980–83; currently emeritus fell and devpt dir Wadham Coll Oxford (fell and bursar 1984–94), memb Welsh Health Policy Bd 1985–90; pres: Midland Naval Offrs' Assoc 1985–95, Oxford RN & RM Assoc; vice pres Oxfordshire SSAFA; tstee Oxford Preservation Tst; Freeman City of London, memb Worshipful Co of Engrs; CEng, FIMechE, FIMgt, FISTC; *Recreations* golf; *Clubs* Frilford Heath Golf; *Style—* Rear Adm Phillip Edwards, CB, LVO; ✉ Wadham College, Oxford OX1 3PN (☎ 01865 277970)

EDWARDS, (Ifan) Prys; s of Sir Ifan ab Owen Edwards (d 1971), of Aberystwyth, and Lady Eirys Mary, *née* Phillips; *b* 11 Feb 1942; *Educ* Leighton Park Sch Reading, Welsh Sch of Architecture Cardiff (Dip Arch (Wales)); *m* 1966, Catherine Edwards; 1 da (Lisa Mair b 1969), 1 s (Sion b 1971); *Career* chm S4C 1992–; memb: Devpt Bd for Rural Wales 1977–85, Wales and the Marches Postal Bd 1982–83; chm Wales Tourist Bd 1984–92, nat pres Urdd Gobaith Cymru (hon offr 1965–); RIBA; *Style—* Prys Edwards, Esq; ✉ Bryn Aberoedd, Cae Melyn, Aberystwyth, Dyfed (☎ 01970 623001); S4C, Parc Ty Glas, Llanishen, Cardiff CF4 5GG (☎ 01222 747444, fax 01222 754444)

EDWARDS, His Hon Judge Quentin Tytler; QC (1975); s of Herbert Jackson Edwards (d 1950), of Alexandria, Egypt and Burgess Hill, Sussex, and Juliet Hester, *née* Campbell (d 1940); *b* 16 Jan 1925; *Educ* Bradfield; *m* 18 Nov 1948, Barbara Marian, da of Lt-Col Alec Guthrie (d 1952), of Hampstead; 2 s (Adam b 1951, Simon b 1954), 1 da (Charlotte b 1949); *Career* WWII RN 1943–46; called to the Bar Middle Temple 1948, bencher 1972, circuit judge (SE Circuit) 1982–; chllr: diocese of Blackburn 1977–90, diocese of Chichester 1978; fndr memb Highgate Soc 1965–, chm Ecclesiastical Law Soc 1989–96 (vice chm 1987–89), pres Highgate Literary and Scientific Inst 1988–93; memb Bar Cncl 1958–60 and 1977–81, licensed as a reader in the diocese of London 1967–; memb: Legal Advsy Cmmn of Gen Synod C of E 1971–, Diocese Cmmn Gen Synod 1978–96; columnist Guardian Gazette 1975–82; Hon MA awarded by Archbishop of Canterbury 1961; *Books* Ecclesiastical Law (third edn), Halsbury's Law of England (with K Macmorran et al 1952); *Recreations* the open air, architecture; *Clubs* Athenaeum; *Style—* His Hon Judge Quentin Edwards, QC; ✉ Central London County Court, 13–14 Park Crescent, London W1N 3PD (☎ 0171 917 7830)

EDWARDS, Prof Richard Humphrey Tudor; s of Hywel Islwyn Edwards, of Llwyn Aeron, Llangollen, and Menna Tudor Edwards (d 1987); *b* 28 Jan 1939; *Educ* Llangollen GS, Middlesex Hosp Med Sch (BSc, MB BS); *m* 23 May 1964, Eleri Wyn, da of J Ernest Roberts; 1 s (Tomos Tudor, d 1982), 1 da (Rhiannon); *Career* resident appts at Middlesex Hosp London 1964, asst RMO Nat Heart Hosp 1965, house physician Hammersmith Hosp 1966, research fell Royal Postgrad Med Sch Hammersmith Hosp London 1966–69 (PhD 1969), Wellcome Swedish research fell Karolinska Inst Stockholm Sweden 1970–71, Wellcome sr research fell in clinical sci Royal Postgrad Med Sch 1971–76, hon conslt Hammersmith Hosp 1972–76, prof of human metabolism Univ Coll Hosp Med Sch 1976–84, head Dept of Med UCL 1982–84; Univ of Liverpool: prof of med and head of Dept of Med 1984–96, dir Magnetic Resonance Research Centre 1987–96, dir Muscle Research Centre 1988–96; prof and dir Office of Research and Devpt for Health and Social Care Univ of Wales Coll of Med 1996–; pres Euro Soc for Clinical Sci 1982–83, examiner for membership of RCP London; author of articles on muscle physiology in health and disease in scientific literature; Robert Bing Prize Swiss Acad of Med Sci 1977; FRCP 1976; *Recreations* land management for conservation, trees, mountain walking; *Style—* Prof Richard Edwards; ✉ Office of Research & Development for Health and Social Care, Hallinans House, 22 Newport Road, Cardiff CF2 1DB (☎ 01222 460015, fax 01222 492046)

EDWARDS, (John) Richard Martin; s of Arthur Crai Edwards (d 1989), of Stow on the Wold, and Barbara Leslee Mary, *née* Hart; *b* 2 Sept 1941; *Educ* Dulwich; *m* Rowena Gail, da of Cdr George McCracken Rutherford, MBE, DSC, VRD, RNR (ret); 1 s (James Lindsay b 3 Oct 1964), 1 da (Melanie Jane b 13 July 1963); *Career* various admin and mgmnt posts Trust House Forte Ltd 1961–76, md Chester Grosvenor Hotel (Prestige) 1982–86 (gen mangr 1976–82), dir Exclusive Div Trust House Forte 1986–87, md Forte Classic Hotels 1987–90, quality serv dir Trust House Forte UK Feb - Sept 1990, md Management Services International 1990–94; dir Grayshott Hall Health Fitness Retreat 1994–95, sec Phyllis Court Club 1995–; chm: Prestige Hotels 1981 and 1982, Master Innholders 1990–92, Thames & Chilterns Div BHRCA 1989–90; first Hotelier of the Year 1983, Master Innholder 1986; Freeman City of London 1986; Chevalier du Tastevin 1981, FHCIMA 1985, Conseiller Culinaire de Grande Bretagne, Confrerie de la Chaine des Rotisseurs 1989–95, chm Clubs Ctee BHA 1995–; *Recreations* tennis, painting, the South of France; *Clubs* Phyllis Court (Henley); *Style—* Richard Edwards, Esq; ✉ Phyllis Court Club, Marlow Road, Henley-on-Thames, Oxon RG9 2HT (☎ 01491 574366)

EDWARDS, Robert (Bob); *b* 4 June 1947; *Career* advtg exec; Colman Prentice & Varley 1965–67, Collett Dickenson Pearce 1967–73, TBWA 1973–84, Edwards Martin Thornton 1984–95, md Burkitt Edwards Martin 1995–96; MIPA, memb Mktg Soc; *Style—* Bob Edwards, Esq

EDWARDS, Robert Charlton (Rob); s of Lawrence Edwin Edwards (d 1977), and Muriel Eugénie, *née* Peel (d 1989); *b* 24 May 1949; *Educ* Worcester Royal GS, Pembroke Coll Oxford, Bristol Old Vic Theatre Sch; *Career* actor; *Theatre* RSC Stratford and the Aldwych 1980–81: Amintor in The Maid's Tragedy, Young Gobbo in The Merchant of Venice, Khomich in Lovegirl and the Innocent by Solzhenitsin, Charles Lamb in The Fool by Edward Bond; Young Vic 1986, 1989 and 1990: Lucio and The Duke in Measure for Measure, Mercutio in Romeo and Juliet; RSC Stratford and Barbican 1990–91: title role in Pericles (Barbican only), Pritikin in Barbarians by Maxim Gorky (Barbican only), First Citizen in Coriolanus; Apoo in Topakano's Martyrs' Day (Bush), Hamlet in Hamlet with the London Shakespeare Group (Far Eastern Tours for Br Cncl) 1985 and 1986, Max and Singer in Definitely the Bahamas by Martin Crimp and Angus in No More a-Roving by John Whiting (Orange Tree) 1987, Cassius in Julius Caesar (RSC) 1993; *Television* incl: Stephen Lovell in The Fourth Arm (BBC) 1981–82, John Fletcher in By the Sword Divided (BBC) 1983–84, Dr Chris Clarke in The Practice (Granada) 1985, Gilbert Whippet in Campion (BBC) 1988, Prince John in Henry IV Parts I & II and Henry V (BBC); *Recreations* scrambling, mountain walking; *Style—* Rob Edwards, Esq; ✉ c/o Marina Martin Associates, 12–13 Poland Street, London W1V 3DE (☎ 0171 734 4818, fax 0171 734 4832)

EDWARDS, Robert John; CBE (1986); s of William Gordon Edwards (d 1938); *b* 26 Oct 1925; *Educ* Ranelagh Sch Bracknell; *m* 1, 1952 (m dis 1972), Laura Ellwood; 2 s, 2 da; m 2, 1977, Brigid O'Neil Forsyth, *née* Segrave; *Career* ed: Tribune 1951–54, Sunday Express 1957–59 (dep), Daily Express 1961 (managing ed 1959–61), Evening Citizen Glasgow 1962–63, Daily Express 1963–65, Sunday People 1966–72, Sunday Mirror 1972–85; dep chm Mirror Group Newspapers 1985–86; ombudsman Today 1990–95; *Books* Goodbye Fleet Street (1988); *Recreations* reading, sailing; *Clubs* Garrick, Groucho's, Kennel, Reform; *Style—* Robert Edwards, Esq, CBE; ✉ Georgian Wing, Williamscot House, nr Banbury, Oxon OX17 1AE (☎ 01295 750809, fax 01295 750826)

EDWARDS, Robert Philip (Rob); s of Robert Aelwyn Edwards, of Abbots Langley, Herts, and Kathleen Isobel, *née* Brockbank; *b* 13 Oct 1953; *Educ* Watford Boys' GS, Jesus Coll Cambridge (MA); *m* 8 June 1977, Dr Fiona Grant Riddoch, da of Thomas Grant Riddoch; 2 da (Robyn Edwards Riddoch b 20 Feb 1990, Lindsay Edwards Riddoch b 1 Jan 1993); *Career* journalist and writer; organiser Scottish Campaign to Resist the Atomic Menace 1977–78, campaigns organiser Shelter (Scotland) 1978–80; work as Scottish corr Social Work Today 1981–83, res asst to Robin Cook MP 1980–83, co-ordinator of CND's case at Sizewell Inquiry 1982–85; Scottish corr: New Statesman 1983–89, The Guardian 1989–93; columnist Edinburgh Evening News 1989–94, environment ed Scotland on Sunday 1989–94, German corr New Scientist, Scotland on Sunday and The Scotsman 1994–96; prodr documentary Children Under Fire (Channel 4) 1993; Media Natura Regnl Journalist of the Year Br Environment and Media Awards 1989 (specially commended 1992), commended Industl Soc Environment Award 1993, commended UK Press Gazette Regnl Awards 1993; memb: NUJ, Soc of Authors; *Books* Fuelling the Nuclear Arms Race: the Links Between Nuclear Power and Nuclear Weapons (with Sheila Durie, 1982), Britain's Nuclear Nightmare (with James Cutler, 1988), Still Fighting for Gemma (with Susan D'Arcy, 1995); *Recreations* walking, opera, theatre, films and rock music; *Style—* Rob Edwards, Esq; ✉ 21 Cluny Terrace, Edinburgh EH10 4SW (☎ 0131 447 2796, fax 0131 447 0647, e-mail 100613.3411@compuserve.com)

EDWARDS, Roger John; s of late Flt Lt John Alfred Edwards, of Ewhurst, Surrey, and Melva Joyce, *née* Burrell; *b* 30 Nov 1941; *Educ* Isleworth GS, Univ of Hull; *m* 4 July 1964, Janet Amelia, da of Stanley Victor Holmes (d 1971); 2 s (Nicholas St John b 29 July 1966, Barnaby James b 20 Aug 1969); *Career* McCann Erickson 1964–67, Chesebrough Ponds 1967–70, Davidson Pearce Ltd 1970–77, chief exec offr Leo Burnett 1979–81, chm and chief exec Grey Communications Group 1982–, exec dir Grey Europe 1988–; FIPA 1983, FInstD; *Recreations* theatre, travel, walking, books, golf; *Clubs* Wisley Golf (dep chm); *Style—* Roger Edwards, Esq; ✉ Grey Communications Group Ltd, 215–227 Great Portland St, London W1N 5HD (☎ 0171 636 3399)

EDWARDS, Prof Ronald Walter (Ron); CBE (1992); s of Walter Henry Edwards (d 1975), of Birmingham, and Violet Ellen, *née* Groom; *b* 7 June 1930; *Educ* Solihull Sch, Univ of Birmingham (BSc, DSc); *Career* 2 Lt RAOC 1948–50; res scientist: Freshwater Biological Soc 1953–58, Water Pollution Res Laboratory 1958–68; prof and head dept Univ of Wales Inst Sci and Technol 1968–; memb NERC 1970–73 and 1981–84, memb and dep chm Welsh Water Authy 1974–89; Nat Rivers Authy: memb Advsy Ctee 1988–89, memb 1989–94, chm Wales; memb: Nat Ctee Euro Year of Environment 1987–88 (chm Wales), Prince of Wales's Ctee 1988–92, Cncl RSPB 1988–92 (chm Wales); chm: Nat Parks Review Panel 1989–91, Sea-Empress Environmental Evaluation Ctee 1996–; memb: Brecon Beacons Nat Parks Authy 1993–95, Environment Agency 1995– (memb Advsy Ctee 1995–); vice pres Cncl for Nat Parks 1993– hon prof Middlesex Univ 1994–96; FIBiol, FIWEM, FIFM; *Books* Ecology of the River Wye, Conservation and Productivity of Natural Waters, Pollution, Acid Waters; *Recreations* collecting 19 century Staffordshire pottery; *Style—* Prof Ron Edwards, CBE; ✉ Talybont-on-Usk, Brecon, Powys

EDWARDS, Ruth Dudley; da of Robert Walter Dudley Edwards (d 1988), and Sheila, *née* O'Sullivan (d 1985); *b* 24 May 1944; *Educ* Sacred Heart Convent Dublin, Sandymount HS Dublin, Univ Coll Dublin (BA, MA, DLitt), Girton and Univ Colls (now Wolfson Coll) Cambridge, City of London Poly (Dip in Business Studies); *m* 1, 31 July 1965 (m dis 1975), Patrick John Cosgrave, s of Patrick Joseph Cosgrave (d 1952); m 2, 10 Jan 1976 (m dis 1991), John Robert Mattock, s of John Leonard Mattock (d 1986); *Career* teacher 1965–67, mktg exec Post Office 1970–74, principal DOI 1975–79, freelance writer 1979–, company historian The Economist 1982–; memb Exec Ctee: Br Irish Assoc 1981–93, Crime Writers' Assoc 1995–; chm Br Assoc for Irish Studies 1986–93; *Books* An Atlas of Irish History (1973), Patrick Pearse: the triumph of failure (1977), James Connolly (1981), Corridors of Death (1981), Harold Macmillan: a life in pictures (1983), The Saint Valentine's Day Murders (1984), Victor Gollancz: a biography (1987), The School of English Murder (1990), Clubbed to Death (1992), The Pursuit of Reason: The Economist 1843–1993 (1993), The Best of Bagehot (1993), True Brits (1994), Matricide at St Martha's (1994), Ten Lords A-Leaping (1995), Murder in a Cathedral (1996); *Recreations* friends; *Clubs* Academy, Reform, Little House; *Style—* Miss Ruth Dudley Edwards; ✉ 40 Pope's Lane, Ealing, London W5 4NU (☎ 0181 579 1041, fax 0181 567 7989)

EDWARDS, Prof Sir Samuel Frederick (Sam); kt (1975); s of Richard Edwards, of Swansea, and Mary Jane Edwards; *b* 1 Feb 1928; *Educ* Swansea GS, Gonville and Caius Coll Cambridge (MA, PhD), Harvard Univ; *m* 1953, Merriell E M Bland; 1 s, 3 da; *Career* prof of theoretical physics Univ of Manchester 1963–72; Univ of Cambridge: fell Gonville and Caius Coll 1972 (pres 1993–), John Humphrey Plummer prof of physics 1972–84, Cavendish prof of physics 1984–95, pro vice chllr 1993–95; chm SRC 1973–77, UK del to Sci Ctee NATO 1974–79, memb Cncl Euro Res & Devpt (EEC) 1976–80; Inst of Mathematics and its Applications: memb Cncl 1976–, vice pres 1979, pres 1980–81; chm Def Scientific Advsy Cncl 1977–80 (memb 1973); non-exec dir: Lucas Industries plc 1981–93, Steetley plc 1985–92; sr scientific advsr Unilever and BP, chief scientific advsr Dept of Energy 1983–88 (memb Advsy Cncl on R&D 1974–77, chm 1983–88), pres BAAS 1988–89 (chm Cncl 1977–82); author of reports: Future of British Physics (HMSO) 1989, Evaluation of Science Programme EC 1990; memb Cncl AFRC 1990–94; Hon DSc (Bath, Birmingham, Edinburgh, Salford, Strasbourg, Wales, Sheffield, Dublin, Leeds, E Anglia), Hon DTech (Loughborough); hon fell Univ of Swansea; foreign memb: Academie des Sciences Paris, Nat Acad of Sciences Washington; FRS, FInstP, FRSC, FIMA; *Books* Technological Risk (1980), Theory of Polymer Dynamics (with M Doi, 1986), Networks of Rod Molecules (with S Aharoni, 1994); *Clubs* Athenaeum; *Style—* Prof Sir Sam Edwards, FRS; ✉ 7 Penarth Place, Cambridge CB3 9LU (☎ 01223 366610); Cavendish Laboratory, Cambridge (☎ 01223 337259, fax 01223 337000, e-mail sfell@phy.cam.ac.uk)

EDWARDS, Sandra Mouroutsos; da of James Mouroutsos, of USA, and Joanna, *née* Felopulos; *b* 14 July 1941; *Educ* Bennington HS, Mount Holyoke Coll (BA); *m* 1, 10 Jan 1965 (m dis 1975), Christopher Stephen Wates; 3 da (Melina b 1966, Georgina b 1967, Joanna b 1970); m 2, 21 Nov 1975, His Hon Judge (Charles) Marcus Edwards, *qv*; 1 da (Alexandra b 1983); *Career* ptnr Conspectus Project Management Consultants 1988–89 (conslt 1986–88); dir: The Fitzrovia Trust 1989–, J Hodgson Ltd 1993– (conslt 1992–93); assessor Nat Lottery Charities Bd 1995–; nat chm: Fair Play for Children 1972–77, Pre Sch Playgroups Assoc 1974–77; memb: Westminster City Cncl 1974–78, Ealing Borough Cncl 1978–82; chm: Paddington Churches Housing Assoc 1977–95, Sutherland Housing Assoc 1977–95, Knowles Tst 1980–96, Queen Charlotte's Special Tstees 1992–, Hillingdon Health Authy 1996–; Parly candidate Swansea East 1979; memb NW Thames RHA 1980–84, dep chm Hammersmith and Queen Charlotte's Special Health Authy 1986–94 (memb 1984–94), memb Hammersmith Hosp Tst 1994–96; Nat Fedn Housing Assocs Cncl: memb 1978–81 and 1987–95, dep chm 1989–91, chm 1991–94; *Recreations* indoor gardening; *Style—* Mrs Marcus Edwards; ✉ Melbourne House, South Parade, London W4 1JU (☎ 0181 995 9146)

EDWARDS, Shaun; OBE (1996); s of Jack Edwards, of Wigan, Lancs, and Phyllis, *née* Johnson; *b* 17 Oct 1966; *Educ* St John Fisher RC Secdy Sch Wigan, *Career* rugby league player; capt all levels under 11 to under 16 Wigan and Lancs, professional Wigan (currently capt) 1983– (world champions, winners Regal Trophy 1996); England schoolboys capt (rugby league and rugby union), 36 GB caps (full debut 1983, currently capt), Lions 1992; winner 17 major trophies incl playing in 6 Cup Finals, 30 major winners medals, winner Save & Prosper Sevens 1996; top try scorer in rugby league 1991–92, youngest player to appear in a Wembley Cup Final aged 17, youngest player at time to appear in a Test aged 18; Int of the Year award 1989, Man of Steel award for player of year 1990; memb Br Lions Orgn 1988–; *Recreations* golf, athletics (training), music; *Style—* Shaun Edwards, Esq, OBE; ✉ Wigan RLFC, Central Park, Wigan, Lancs

EDWARDS, Tracy Karen; MBE (1990); da of Antony Herbert Edwards (d 1973), of Purley-on-Thames, Berks, and Patricia Edwards; *b* 5 Sept 1962; *Educ* Highlands Tilehurst, Arts Educn Tring, Gowerton Comp Sch; *m* Nov 1994, Christopher M Cosslett; *Career* yachtswoman; Whitbread Round the World Race: crew memb Atlantic Privateer 1985–86, skipper, navigator and project leader Maiden Royal Jordanian (first all female challenge, first Br win in twelve years) 1989–90; co-presenter series of progs on the Whitbread Round the World Race (for Meridian TV) 1993–94; voted Yachtsman of the Year Yachting Journalists' Assoc of GB (first woman winner in the award's 35 year history), Daily Express Sportswoman of 1990; formerly employed with Insights Ltd (mgmnt devpt seminars), currently md Lady Endeavour Ltd (running first all female crew to race around the world non-stop in the Jules Verne Trophy), public speaking engagements through Park Associates Nottingham; *Books* Maiden (1990); *Recreations* horse riding; *Clubs* Royal Ocean Racing, Royal Southampton Yacht, RYA, Cape Horners; *Style—* Miss Tracy Edwards, MBE; ✉ Lady Endeavour Challenge, Saltmaker's House, Hamble Point Marina, School Lane, Hamble, Hants SO31 4NB (☎ 01703 457557, fax 01703 457657)

EDWARDS, Wilfred Thomas; s of Thomas Edwards (d 1965), of Caverswall, and Bessie Edith, *née* Rooke (d 1981); *b* 6 Jan 1926; *Educ* Newcastle HS, Univ of London (LLB, Dip HA); *Career* Nat Serv 1944–47; HM Inland Revenue 1948–86, tax conslt 1986–, lectr Adult Educn; memb Bd of Govrs English-Speaking Union Club 1972–78, chm Art Club 1974–; former chm Cncl Staffordshire Soc; Freeman City of London 1971; Liveryman: Worshipful Co Loriners 1981, Worshipful Co of Painter-Stainers 1992; FGS, FRSA; *Recreations* painting, landscape and portrait, voluntary assistant Westminster Abbey; *Clubs* Athenaeum, Hurlingham; *Style—* Wilfred T Edwards; ✉ Corner Cottage, Brancaster, Norfolk PE31 8AW; Friarswood, Cheltenham, Glos GL50 2SL; 18 North Lodge Close, London SW15 6QZ

EDWARDS-JONES, Diana Elizabeth; OBE; da of Dr John Cyril Edwards-Jones (d 1964), of Glyncollen House, Morriston, Swansea, and Nancy Gwenllian, *née* Davies (d 1937); *b* 13 Dec 1932; *Educ* Battle Abbey Sch Battle Sussex, Nat Coll of Music and Drama Cardiff, Bristol Old Vic Theatre Sch; *Career* stage mangr Swansea Repertory Co Grand Theatre; ITN 1955–89: prog dir American Election Results 1968–84 and General Election Results 1974–87, dir main news for ITV, helped create News at Ten, coverage of space exploration incl Apollos 14, 15, 16 and 17, prog dir numerous royal occasions, head of prog dirs 1980–89; Royal TV Soc award for General Election Results 1974; memb Ctee Wales in London; *Recreations* swimming, music, theatre, travel, reading, horse racing; *Style—* Miss Diana Edwards-Jones, OBE; ✉ 2 Park View, 87 Park Rd, Chiswick, London W4 3ER (☎ 0181 994 0904 or 01795 535297)

EDWARDS-STUART, Antony James Cobham; QC (1991); s of Lt-Col Ivor Arthur James Edwards-Stuart, of N Lodge, W Fleet, Weymouth, Dorset, and Elizabeth Aileen Le Mesurier, *née* Deck; *b* 2 Nov 1946; *Educ* Sherborne, RMA Sandhurst (RAC Young Officers Prize), St Catharine's Coll Cambridge (MA); *m* 11 May 1973, Fiona Ann, da of (Albert) Paul Weaver, OBE (d 1993), of London; 2 s (Luke b 29 Sept 1973, Thomas b 4 Sept 1980), 2 da (Anna b 26 March 1976, Rachel b 25 Feb 1982); *Career* cmmnd 1 Royal Tank Regt 1966, Adj 1973–75, Adj Kent & Sharpshooters Yeo 1975–77; called to the Bar Gray's Inn 1976, asst recorder 1991–; chm Home Office Advsy Ctee on Service Candidates 1995–; *Recreations* theatre, fishing, shooting, restoring property in France; *Style—* Antony Edwards-Stuart, Esq, QC; ✉ 2 Crown Office Row, Temple, London EC4Y 7HJ (☎ 0171 797 8100, fax 0171 797 8101)

EDZARD, Christine; da of Dietz Edzard (d 1961), of Paris, and Suzanne, *née* Eisendieck; *b* 15 Feb 1945; *Educ* Cours D'Hulst Paris, Institut D'Etudes Politiques Paris; *m* 23 Dec 1968, Richard Berry Goodwin, s of G Goodwin; 1 da (Sabine Eleanor b 23 Oct 1971); *Career* designer, writer, producer and director; former asst theatre designer to Lila de Nobili and Rotislav Doboujinsky; designed prodns for: Hamburg Opera, WNO, Camden Town Festival; fndr Sands Films 1976; designer and scripwriter (with Richard Goodwin) Tales of Beatrix Potter; writer and dir: Stories From a Flying Trunk (1979), The Nightingale (Channel 4, 1980), Biddy (1982), The Fool (also prodr, 1990); film adaptation of Little Dorrit (with Olivier Stockman) 1987, dir and prodr As You Like It 1991; BAFTA nomination for best screenplay Little Dorrit 1987, Oscar nomination for best screenplay based on material from another source Little Dorrit 1988; memb: ACTT, Directors Guild; *Style—* Ms Christine Edzard; ✉ c/o Sands Films Ltd, Grices Wharf, 119 Rotherhithe St, London SE16 4NF (☎ 0171 231 2209, fax 0171 231 2119)

EELEY, Nicholas John; s of Sqdn Ldr (Thomas) Ian Samuel Eeley (d 1979), of Lindfield, Sussex, and Muriel Evelyn, *née* Hockley (d 1994); *b* 16 April 1936; *Educ* Charterhouse; *m* 28 Sept 1963, Gillian Mary Francis, da of Cyril Joseph Cooke (d 1992), of Upminster, Essex; 1 da (Harriet Amelia Catherine b 6 Feb 1967); *Career* Nat Serv pilot RAF 1953–55; NM Rothschild & Sons Ltd 1956–83; dir: NM Rothschild Asset Management Ltd 1973–83, Global Asset Management Ltd 1984–; Freeman City of Oxford 1960; *Recreations* antique furniture; *Style—* Nicholas Eeley, Esq; ✉ 33 Chalcot Crescent, London NW1 8YG (☎ 0171 586 0366); Global Asset Management Ltd, 12 St James's Place, London SW1A 1NX (☎ 0171 493 9990, fax 0171 493 0715, telex 296099)

EFFINGHAM, 7 Earl of (UK 1837); David Mowbray Algernon Howard; also 17 Baron Howard of Effingham (E 1554); s of Hon John Anthony Frederick Charles Howard (d 1971, s of 5 Earl of Effingham); suc uncle 6 Earl of Effingham (d 1996); *b* 29 April 1939; *Educ* Fettes Coll, RNC Dartmouth; *m* 1, 1964 (m dis 1975), Anne Mary, da of Harrison Sayer (d 1980), of Cambridge; 1 s (Edward Mowbray Nicholas, Lord Howard of Effingham b 1971); m 2, 29 Dec 1992, Mrs Elizabeth Jane Turner, da of Dennis Eccleston (d 1990), of Great Saling, Essex, and formerly w of Peter Robert Easton Turner; *Heir* s, Edward Mowbray Nicholas, Lord Howard of Effingham b 11 May 1971; *Career* Cdr RN; The Royal British Legion County Field Offr for Essex; *Recreations* racing, shooting, fishing; *Clubs* Royal Navy; *Style—* Cdr the Rt Hon the Earl of Effingham, RN; ✉ Readings Farmhouse, Blackmore End, Essex CM7 4DH (☎ 01787 461182)

EFSTATHIOU, Prof George Petros; s of Petros Efstathiou, of London, and Christina, *née* Parperis; *b* 2 Sept 1955; *Educ* The Somerset Sch London, Keble Coll Oxford (BA), Univ of Durham (PhD); *m* 27 July 1976, Helena Jane (Janet), da of James Lewis Smart, of Poyntzpass, Newry, NI; 1 s (Peter b 1988), 1 da (Zoe b 1986); *Career* res asst Univ of California Berkley 1979–80, sr res fell King's Coll Cambridge 1984–88 (jr res fell 1980–84), asst dir of res Inst of Astronomy Cambridge 1984–88 (SERC res fell 1980–84), Savilian prof of astronomy Univ of Oxford 1988– (head of astrophysics 1988–94), fell New Coll Oxford 1988–, sr res fell Particle Physics and Astronomy Res Cncl 1994–; memb: various ctees SERC, IAU 1980; Maxwell Medal and Prize Inst of Physics 1990, Vainubappu Award Astronomical Soc of India 1988, Sherman Fairchild Distinguished Scholar Caltech 1991, Bodassaki Prize for Astrophysics 1994; FRAS 1977, FRS 1994; *Recreations* running, playing with my children; *Style—* Prof George Efstathiou, FRS; ✉ Department of Physics, Nuclear and Astrophysics Laboratory, Keble Rd, Oxford OX1 3RH (☎ 01865 273300, fax 01865 273390, telex 83295 NUCLOX G)

EGAN, Sir John Leopold; kt (1986), DL (Warwickshire 1989); s of James Edward Egan (d 1982); *b* 7 Nov 1939; *Educ* Imperial Coll London (BSc), London Business Sch (MSc); *m* 1963, Julia Emily, da of George Treble, of Leamington Spa; 2 da (Catherine (Mrs Jonathan Hart), Lydia); *Career* parts and service dir Leyland Cars 1971–76, corporate parts dir Massey Ferguson 1976–80, chm and chief exec Jaguar Cars Ltd 1980–90, chief exec BAA plc 1990–; chm London Tourist Bd and London First Visitors Cncl 1993–, bd memb Br Tourist Authy 1994–; non-exec dir: Legal & General Group plc 1987–, Foreign and Colonial Investment Trust Ltd; vice pres Chartered Inst of Mktg; fell Imperial Coll 1985, Hon Dr Cranfield Inst 1986, Hon Dr of Techonol Loughborough Univ 1987, hon fell London Business Sch 1987, Hon Dr of Business Admin Int Business Sch 1988, Hon LLD Univ of Bath 1988; hon fell: Chartered Inst of Mktg 1989 (fell 1987), Wolverhampton Poly 1989; hon prof: Dept of Engrg Univ of Warwick 1990–, Univ of Aston 1990–; Liveryman Worshipful Co of Coachmakers & Coach Harness Makers; Int Distinguished Entrepeneur Award Univ of Manitoba, RSA Bicentenary Medal 1995; *Recreations* skiing, squash, walking, music; *Clubs* Warwick Boat; *Style—* Sir John Egan, DL; ✉ BAA plc, 130 Wilton Road, London SW1V 1LQ (☎ 0171 932 6707)

EGAN, Patrick Valentine Martin; s of Eric Egan; *b* 17 July 1930; *Educ* Downside; *m* 1953, Mary Theresa, da of Frederick Hinds Coleman (d 1960); 3 da; *Career* signals instr RA Far E 1949–50; exec dir Unilever plc and Unilever NV 1978–May 1992; Fisons plc: non-exec dir 1985–92, chm 1992–Nov 1994; dir and chm: English Hops Ltd, English Hop Products Ltd; dir Kentish Garden Ltd; *Recreations* shooting, walking, gardening; *Style—* Patrick Egan, Esq; ✉ Whiteways, Sissinghurst, Cranbrook, Kent (☎ 01580 713201)

EGAN, Peter; *Educ* RADA; *m* Myra Frances, actress; 1 da (Rebecca); *Career* actor; *Theatre* roles with RSC incl: Valentine in Two Gentlemen of Verona, Osric in Hamlet, Richmond in Richard II, most recently Casanova in Camino Real 1996–97; Chichester Festival Theatre roles incl: Apollodorus in Caesar and Cleopatra (with Sir John Gielgud),

Jack Absolute in The Rivals (with Sir John Clements), Alexander in Dear Antoine; other stage credits incl: Stanhope in Journey's End (Cambridge, won Best Actor London Theatre Critics award) 1972, John Shand in What Every Woman Knows (Albery) 1973, Cheviot Hills in Engaged (NT) 1975, Charles Rolls in Rolls Hyphen Royce (Shaftesbury) 1977, Valentine in You Never Can Tell (Royal Gala opening Lyric) 1979, Sergius in Arms and the Man (Lyric) 1981, Rene Gallimard in M Butterfly (Shaftesbury) 1989, Sergei Nikolayich Tsyganov in RSC's Barbarians (Barbican) 1990, Astrov in Uncle Vanya (also dir, with Renaissance Theatre Co, Manchester Evening News Best Actor Award) 1991, Jimmy Porter in Déjàvu (Comedy Theatre) 1992, Three Hotels (Tricycle and West End) 1993; has also directed numerous plays at the Lyric and Savoy Theatres and at Mills Coll Oakland San Francisco; *Television* incl: Seth in Cold Comfort Farm 1967, the Earl of Southampton in Elizabeth R 1971, Millais in The Love School 1974, Oscar Wilde in Lillie Langtry 1978, title role in The Prince Regent 1978, Fothergill in Reilly Ace of Spies 1982, The Dark Side of the Sun 1983, Ever Decreasing Circles 1984, 1986, 1987 and 1989, A Woman of Substance, Pym in The Perfect Spy 1986, Joint Account 1988 and 1990, A Day in Summer 1988, The Price of the Bride 1989, Ruth Rendell's A New Lease Of Death 1991, MacGyver (Paramount) 1992, Vanity Dies Hard 1992, The Chief (YTV) 1993, Chiller (YTV) 1994, The Peacock Spring (BBC) 1995; *Films* incl: The Hireling (BAFTA Best Actor Award) 1972, Henessey 1973, Callan 1974, Chariots of Fire 1980, Henry Simcox in Paradise Postponed (Euston Films, winner TV Times Award 1986) 1985; *Style*— Peter Egan, Esq; ✉ ICM Ltd, Oxford House, 76 Oxford Street, London W1N 0AX (☎ 0171 636 6565, fax 0171 323 0101)

EGDELL, Dr (John) Duncan; s of John William Egdell, of Bristol (d 1990), and Nellie Egdell; *b* 5 March 1938; *Educ* Clifton Coll, Univ of Bristol (MB ChB), Univ of Edinburgh (Dip Soc Med); *m* 9 Aug 1963, Dr Linda Mary Flint, da of Edmund Harold Flint (d 1974), of Barnehurst, Kent; 2 s (Brian, Robin), 1 da (Ann); *Career* house physician and surgn Utd Bristol Hosps 1961–62, in gen practice 1962–65, asst sr med offr Newcastle Regnl Hosp Bd 1968–69 (admin med offr 1966–67), regnl specialist in community med SW RHA 1974–76 (asst sr med offr 1969–72, princ asst sr med offr 1972–74), regnl med offr Mersey RHA 1977–86, community physician and conslt in public health med Clwyd Health Authy 1986–93 (hon conslt 1993–); FFPHM (1990, FFCM 1979); *Recreations* nature conservation, delving into the past; *Style*— Dr Duncan Egdell; ✉ Gelli Gynan Lodge, Llanarmon-yn-Ial, nr Mold, Clwyd CH7 4QX (☎ 01824 780345)

EGEE, Dale Richardson; da of Wallace Caldwell Richardson (d 1979), of Vermont, USA, and Corinne Mitchell Richardson (d 1987); *b* 7 Feb 1934; *Educ* Sacred Heart Sch Greenwich Conn, Rosemont Coll Pennsylvania, Instituto D'Arte Florence; *m* 1, Peter H Lewis (d 1966); 2 s (Anthony b 1960, Adam b 1963), 1 da (Corinna b 1958); m 2, 4 Sept 1966, David Wayne Egee, s of Dr J Benton Egee, of Connecticut; 1 da (Eliza b 1968); *Career* tapestry designer Beirut Lebanon 1968–85; works purchased or cmmnd by: Lebanese Govt 1972, BCCI Bank 1973 and 1977, Hyatt Hotels 1977, Govt of Qatar 1979, US Govt 1985, 1986 and 1988; art conslt and gallery owner 1979– (specialising in Middle Eastern and African art), co-organiser first Contemporary Arab Graphics exhibition London 1981–83; recent gallery shows incl: Contemporary Islamic Calligraphy, Middle East Artists - Works on Paper; conslt to US State Dept for Art Collections for New Embassies 1985–93: Saudi Arabia, Bangladesh, N Yemen, Egypt, Jordan, Tel Aviv, Kuwait; guest curator for Contemporary North African Artists exhibition Rotterdam Museum of Ethnology 1994–95; assisted Br Museum and Jordan Nat Museum in acquisitions of contemporary Arab artists; articles in: Arts and the Islamic World 1988 and 1993, Eastern Art Report 1989; memb: Br-Lebanese Assoc, Saudi-Br Soc; FRGS 1987; *Recreations* reading, cookery; *Clubs* Chelsea Arts; *Style*— Ms Dale Egee; ✉ 72 Courtfield Gardens, London SW5 0NL (☎ 0171 370 3789); 9 Chelsea Manor Studios, Flood St, London SW3 5SR (☎ 0171 351 6818, fax 0171 376 3510)

EGERTON, Brian Balguy Le Belward; bro and hp of Sir (Philip) John Caledon Grey Egerton, 15 Bt, *qv*; *b* 5 Feb 1925; *Educ* Repton; *Style*— Brian Egerton, Esq; ✉ Regency Lodge, 56 Braidley Road, Bournemouth, Dorset BH2 6JY

EGERTON, Sir Stephen Loftus; KCMG (1988, CMG 1978); s of William le Belward Egerton, ICS (ggs of William Egerton, yr bro of Sir John and Rev Sir Philip Grey-Egerton, 8 and 9 Bts respectively) and Angela Doreen Loftus, *née* Bland; *b* 21 July 1932; *Educ* Eton, Trinity Coll Cambridge (MA); *m* 1958, Caroline, da of Maj Eustace Thomas Cary-Elwes, TD, of Albion House, Poringland, Norfolk; 1 s, 1 da; *Career* 2 Lt KRRC 1952–53; HM Dip Serv: joined 1956, consul gen Rio de Janeiro 1977–80, ambass Iraq 1980–82, asst under sec of state FCO 1982–86; ambass: Saudi Arabia 1986–89, Italy 1989–92 (also ambass (non-resident) Albania 1992); conslt to Enterprise Oil plc; dir St Andrew's Tst Lambeth Palace London SE1 7JU; *Clubs* Brooks's, Greenjackets, Nikaean; *Style*— Sir Stephen Egerton, KCMG; ✉ c/o Barclays Bank, Eton, Windsor SL4 6AU

EGERTON-WARBURTON, Peter; o s of Col Geoffrey Egerton-Warburton, DSO, TD, JP, DL (d 1961; ggs of Rowland Egerton, bro of Sir John Grey-Egerton, 8 Bt, and Rev Sir Philip Grey-Egerton, 9 Bt), and Hon Georgiana Mary Dormer, MBE (d 1955), eldest da of 14 Baron Dormer, CBE, DL; *b* 17 Jan 1933; *Educ* Eton, RMA Sandhurst; *m* 1, 29 Jan 1955 (m dis 1958), Belinda Vera, da of late James R A Young, of Cowdrays, East Hendred, Berks; m 2, 10 Nov 1960 (m dis 1967), Sarah Jessica, er da of Maj Willoughby Rollo Norman (2 s of Rt Hon Sir Henry Norman, 1 Bt); 2 s; m 3, 6 June 1969, Hon Marya Anne, 2 da of Baron Glenkinglas, PC; 1 s, 1 da (twin); *Career* cmmnd Coldstream Gds 1953, ret 1962 with rank of Capt; Maj Cheshire Yeo 1963; ptnr John D Wood Estate Agents 1966–86, fndr and chm Egerton Ltd Estate Agents 1986–; landowner; Lord of the Manor of Grafton, patron of the livings of Plemstall and Guilden Sutton; *Clubs* White's, Pratt's, Beefsteak; *Style*— Peter Egerton-Warburton, Esq; ✉ 54 Prince's Gate Mews, London SW7 2PR (☎ 0171 589 9254); Mulberry House, Bentworth, Alton, Hants GU34 5RB (☎ 01420 562360)

EGGAR, Timothy John Crommelin (Tim); PC (1995), MP (C) Enfield North (majority 9,430); s of John Drennan Eggar (d 1983), and Pamela Rosemary Eggar; *b* 19 Dec 1951; *Educ* Winchester, Magdalene Coll Cambridge, London Coll of Law; *m* 1977, Charmian Diana, da of Peter William Vincent Minoprio, CBE, late Capt Welsh Guards; 1 s, 1 da; *Career* barr, banker; PA to Rt Hon William Whitelaw 1974, MP (C) Enfield N 1979–, PPS to Min for Overseas Devpt 1982–85, Parly under-sec of state FCO 1985–89; min of state: Dept of Employment 1989–90, Dept of Educn and Science 1990–92, DTI 1992–96; dir Charterhouse Petroleum 1983–85, chm M W Kellogg Group Ltd 1996–; *Style*— The Rt Hon Tim Eggar, MP; ✉ House of Commons, London SW1 (☎ 0171 219 3544)

EGGINTON, Anthony Joseph; CBE (1991); s of Arthur Reginald Egginton (d 1952), and Margaret Anne, *née* Emslie (d 1951); *b* 18 July 1930; *Educ* Selhurst GS, UCL (BSc); *m* 30 Nov 1957, Janet Leta, da of Albert Herring (d 1966); 2 da (Katharine b 1960, Sarah b 1962); *Career* res assoc: UCL 1951–56, Gen Physics Div AERE Harwell 1956–61; head Beams Physics Gp, NIRNS Rutherford High Energy Laboratory 1961–65; head Machine Gp SRC Daresbury Nuclear Physics Laboratory 1965–88, Engrg Div SRC Central Office 1972–74, dir of engrg and nuclear physics 1974–78, dir of sci and engrg 1978–83, dir of engrg 1983–88; dir of progs and dep chm Sci and Engrg Res Cncl 1988–91; conslt, visiting prof and fell UCL 1991–; FRSA; *Publications* author of various papers and articles in jls and conf proceedings on particle accelerators; *Recreations* sport, cinema, music; *Clubs* Lansdowne; *Style*— Anthony Egginton, Esq, CBE; ✉ Witney House, West End, Witney OX8 6NQ (☎ 01993 703502)

EGGINTON, Prof Donald Albert (Don); s of Albert Edward Egginton (d 1943), and Ellen Egginton; *b* 14 March 1934; *Educ* Hamond's GS Swaffham Norfolk, LSE (BSc); *m* 5 Aug 1959, Angela Marion, da of Roy John Shirras; 1 s (David Christopher b 5 Sept 1964), 2 da (Jane Rebecca b 26 Dec 1966, Elizabeth Sarah b 29 May 1970); *Career* Nat Serv RAF 1952–54; Barclays Bank Norfolk 1950–57, Ross Group Westwick Norfolk 1957, articled clerk with Baker Sutton (chartered accountants) London (now merged with Ernst & Young) 1960–63; Univ of Bristol: lectr in accounting 1963–74, sr lectr 1975–80, reader 1980–86, personal professorship 1986–, head Dept of Economics 1990–93; visiting lectr Univ of Minnesota Minneapolis 1970–71; visiting prof: Univ of Newcastle NSW 1989, Univ of NSW 1994; Walter Taplin Prize for Accounting and Business Res: for paper on Distributable Profit and the Pursuit of Prudence 1982, for paper on Share Option Rewards and Management Performance 1990 (with J Forker and M Tippett); ACIB 1956, memb American Accounting Assoc 1964, FCA 1973 (ACA 1963); *Books* Management Accounting: A Conceptual Approach (with L R Amey, 1973), Accounting for the Banker (1977, 2 edn 1982); *Recreations* painting, swimming; *Style*— Prof Don Egginton; ✉ University of Bristol, Department of Economics, 8 Woodland Rd, Bristol BS8 1TN (☎ 0117 930 3030, fax 0117 928 8577)

EGGLESTON, Prof (Samuel) John; s of Edmund Eggleston (d 1959), and Josephine Eggleston (d 1985); *b* 11 Nov 1926; *Educ* Chippenham GS, Univ of London (MA, BSc, DLitt); *Career* prof of educn Univ of Keele 1967–84, prof of educn Univ of Warwick 1985–95 (emeritus prof 1995–), dir of res Multi Cultural Educn 1978–94; visiting prof of educational research Univ of Central England 1995–; memb Consultative Ctee Assessment of Performance Unit DES 1980–89; educn conslt: Arts Cncl 1987–, Crafts Cncl 1995–; chm Educn Ctee Central TV 1987–94, chm Technol Examinations Ctee RSA 1992–, vice chm and treas Design and Technol Assoc 1992–; chm of judges and tstees Young Electronics Designer Competition 1986–, govr Design Dimension Tst 1989–, academic advsr Routledge 1977–94, dir Trentham Books 1983–; ed: Sociological Review, Design and Technology Teaching, European Jl of Intercultural Studies; chm Editorial Bd Multicultural Teaching; lectr and examiner many home and overseas univs; Hon DUniv; FCP 1983; *Books* incl: The Ecology of the School (1977), Work Experience in Schools (1982), Education for Some (1986), The Challenge for Teachers (1992), Teaching Design & Technology (1992, revised 2 edn, 1995), Arts Education for a Multicultural Society (1995), Achieving Publication in Education (with G Klein, 1996); *Recreations* work in design and craft, skiing, riding, travel; *Style*— Prof John Eggleston; ✉ University of Warwick, Coventry, Warwickshire CV4 7AL (☎ 01203 524489, fax 01203 524110)

EGLETON, Lt-Col Clive Frederick William; s of Frederick Egleton (d 1964), of Ruislip, and Rose, *née* Wildman (d 1987); *b* 25 Nov 1927; *Educ* Haberdashers' Aske's; *m* 9 April 1949, Joan Evelyn (d 1996), da of Thomas Lane (d 1971), of Sandown, IOW; 2 s (Charles Barclay b 13 Aug 1953, Richard Wildman b 7 Jan 1958); *Career* Army Serv cmmnd Staffordshire Regt 1945, ret with rank Lt-Col 1975; author; memb: Crime Writers Assoc, Soc of Authors; *Novels* A Piece of Resistance (1970), Last Post For A Partisan (1971), The Judas Mandate (1972), Seven Days To A Killing (1973), The October Plot (1974), Skirmish (1975), State Visit (1976), The Mills Bomb (1978), Backfire (1979), The Winter Touch (1981), A Falcon For The Hawks (1982), The Russian Enigma (1982), A Conflict of Interests (1983), Troika (1984), A Different Drummer (1985), Picture of the Year (1987), Gone Missing (1988), Death of a Sahib (1989), In the Red (1990), Last Act (1991), A Double Deception (1992), Hostile Intent (1993), A Killing In Moscow (1994), Death Throes (1994), A Lethal Involvement (1995), Warning Shot (1996); under pseudonym John Tarrant: The Rommel Plot (1977), The Clauberg Trigger (1979), China Gold (1982); under pseudonym Patrick Blake: Escape to Athena (1979), Double Griffin (1981); *Non fiction* The Stealing of Muriel McKay (1978), The Baldau Touch (1982); *Recreations* gardening, travel; *Clubs* Army and Navy; *Style*— Lt-Col Clive Egleton; ✉ c/o Anthony Goff, David Higham Associates Ltd, 5–8 Lower John St, Golden Square, London W1R 5HA

EGLIN, Roger David; s of George Eglin (d 1968), of West Kirby, and Evelyn, *née* Sharrocks; *b* 29 June 1940, Bolton, Lancs; *Educ* Preston GS, Calday Grange GS, LSE (BSc Econ); *m* 5 Sept 1964, Judith Ann, da of Frederick Albert Kay; 2 da (Cordelia Jane b 26 Feb 1968, Penelope Lydia b 28 Jan 1970); *Career* journalist; res asst Financial Times 1960–61, economics corr Business Magazine 1962–66, business corr The Observer 1966–72; The Sunday Times: successively industl and business ed, then managing ed, currently assoc business ed; *Books* Fly Me I'm Freddie (1980); *Recreations* sailing, walking dog, reading; *Clubs* Island Sailing, Cowes Corinthian Yacht; *Style*— Roger Eglin, Esq; ✉ The Sunday Times, 1 Pennington Street, London E1 9XW (☎ 0171 782 5752, fax 0171 782 5100)

EGLINTON, Prof Geoffrey; s of Alfred Edward Eglinton, and Lilian Blackham; *b* 1 Nov 1927; *Educ* Sale GS, Univ of Manchester (BSc, PhD, DSc); *m* April 1955, Pamela Joan Coupland; 2 s (David Geoffrey, Timothy Ian), 1 da decd (Fiona Jayne); *Career* US Public Health fell Ohio State Univ 1951–52, ICI fell Univ of Liverpool 1952–54, reader in organic chemistry Univ of Glasgow 1964–67 (lectr 1954–64); Organic Geochemistry Unit Univ of Bristol: head 1967–93, sr lectr 1967–68, reader 1968–73, prof 1973–93, prof emeritus 1993; adjunct scientist Woods Hole Oceanographic Inst Mass USA 1990–, co-ordinator NERC Ancient Biomolecules Initiative 1993–; head Jt Honours Sch of Chemistry and Geology Univ of Bristol 1969–78, dir Biogeochemistry Research Centre Univ of Bristol 1991–; visiting prof Dept of Botany Univ of Texas Austin 1968, distinguished visiting prof Dept of Geology and Geophysics Univ of Oklahoma 1995; conslt: NASA Apollo Project 1969–71, Masspec Analytical Speciality Services Ltd 1975–78 (dir 1978–79); Hazelton Laboratories Europe Ltd 1979–84, Exploration Div BP plc 1981–; managing ed Chemical Geology 1984–89, assoc ed abroad Geochemical Jl Japan 1980–82, res assoc Univ of Calif Space Sciences Laboratory 1970–75, fndr memb Editorial Bd AOSTRA Jl of Res 1983–, chm Euro Assoc of Organic Geochemists 1990–95; memb: Cmmn of Organic Geochemistry of the Int Assoc of Geochemistry and Cosmochemistry 1971–73, Interdisciplinary Sci Reviews 1975–, Editorial Bd Origins of Life (D Reidel) 1983–, Sub-Ctee for Space Biology Royal Soc 1970–74, Gen Advsy Cncl of the BBC 1971–77, Planetology Ctee French Govt 1975–77, Sabrina Project Steering Gp Univ of Bristol 1969–80, Cncl Marine Biological Assoc of the UK 1981–84 and 1992–94, Nat Ctee on Oceanic Res Royal Soc 1981–87, Cncl NERC 1984–90, Steering Ctee Scientific Info Serv of CIBA Fndn 1984–96, Int Exchanges Ctee Royal Soc 1988–91, Marine Sci Ctee NERC 1984–90 (also Earth Sci Ctee 1995–96); dean graduate studies Univ of Bristol 1985–89; chm: Biomolecular Palaeontology Special Topic Steering Gp NERC 1989–94, ICPMS Ctee NERC 1990–94; memb: American Assoc for Advancement of Sci, Chemical Soc, Geochemical Soc, Geological Soc, Int Soc for Study of the Origins of Life, Academia Europaea, Euro Environmental Res Orgn; FRIC, FRS 1976; NASA Gold medal for Exceptional Scientific Achievement 1973, Alfred E Treibs Medal award (Organic Geochemistry Div Geochemical Soc) 1981, Major Edward D'Ewes Fitzgerald Coke medal (Geological Soc) 1986; *Books* Applications of Spectroscopy to Organic Chemistry (1965), Organic Geochemistry: Methods and Results (1969), Chemsyn (1972, 2 edn 1975); contrib to numerous learned jls; *Recreations* gardening, walking, sailing; *Clubs* Science (Bristol), Manchester Univ Mountaineering, Rucksack (Manchester); *Style*— Prof Geoffrey Eglinton, FRS; ✉ Oldwell, 7 Redhouse Lane, Bristol BS9 3RY (☎ 0117 968 3833, fax 0117 962 6065); Biogeochemistry Research Centre, Geology Department, University of Bristol BS8 1TH (☎ 0117 928 8858, fax 0117 925 8858)

EGLINTON AND WINTON, 18 Earl of (S 1507 and UK 1859); Archibald George Montgomerie; Lord Montgomerie (S 1449), Baron Seton and Tranent (UK

1859), Baron Ardrossan (UK 1806); Hereditary Sheriff of Renfrewshire; s of 17 Earl of Eglinton and Winton (d 1966), and Ursula (d 1987), da of Hon Ronald Bannatyne Watson, s of Baron Watson (Life Peer, d 1899); *b* 27 Aug 1939; *Educ* Eton; *m* 7 Feb 1964, Marion Carolina, da of John Henry Dunn-Yarker, of Le Château, La Tour de Peilz, Vaud, Switzerland; 4 s (Lord Montgomerie b 1966, Hon William b 1968, Hon James b 1972, Hon Robert b 1975); *Heir* s, Lord Montgomerie; *Career* ptnr Grieveson Grant Stockbrokers 1957–72, md Gerrard & National Holdings plc 1972–80 (dep chm 1980–92), chm Gerrard Vivian Gray Ltd 1992–95; chm Edinburgh Investment Tst plc; dir: Dunedin Income Growth Investment Tst plc, Dunedin Worldwide Investment Tst plc, Charities Investment Managers Ltd; chm Hong Kong Investment Tst plc; tstee: Charibond, Nat Assoc of Almshouses Common Investment Fund; past asst grand master United Grand Lodge of England; *Style*— The Rt Hon the Earl of Eglinton and Winton; ✉ Balhomie, Cargill, Perth PH2 6DS (☎ 01250 883222)

EGMONT, 11 Earl of (I 1733); Sir Frederick George Moore Perceval; 15 Bt (I 1661); also Baron Perceval (I 1715), Viscount Perceval (I 1722), Baron Lovel and Holland (GB 1762), Baron Arden (I 1770), Baron Arden (UK 1802); s of 10 Earl (d 1932 before establishing claim to Earldom), and Cecilia (d 1916), da of James Burns Moore; *b* 14 April 1914; *m* 31 Aug 1932, Ann Geraldine, da of Douglas Gerald Moodie, of Calgary, Alberta; 1 s (and 2 decd), 1 da; *Heir* s, Viscount Perceval; *Style*— The Rt Hon the Earl of Egmont; ✉ Two-dot Ranch, Nanton, Alberta, Canada

EGREMONT, 2 Baron (UK 1963) and 7 Baron Leconfield (UK 1859); (John) Max Henry Scawen Wyndham; DL (W Sussex); s of 6 Baron Leconfield and 1 Baron Egremont, MBE (d 1972; as John Wyndham was private sec to Rt Hon Harold Macmillan, when PM); *b* 21 April 1948; *Educ* Eton, Christ Church Coll Oxford; *m* 15 April 1978, Caroline, da of Alexander Ronan Nelson, and Hon Audrey Paget (da of 1 and last Baron Queenborough, s of Lord Alfred Paget, 5 s of 1 Marquess of Anglesey); 1 s (Hon George Ronan Valentine b 31 July 1983), 3 da (Hon Jessica Mary b 27 April 1979, Hon Constance Rose b 20 Dec 1980, Hon Mary Christian b 4 Oct 1985); *Heir* s, Hon George Wyndham; *Career* farmer and writer; memb Royal Cmmn on Historical Manuscripts 1989, chm The Friends of the Nat Libraries 1985–; tstee: The Wallace Collection, The Br Museum 1990–; Liveryman Worshipful Company of Drapers; *Books* The Cousins (1977), Balfour (1980), The Ladies Man (1983), Dear Shadows (1986), Painted Lives (1989), Second Spring (1993); *Style*— The Rt Hon Lord Egremont, DL; ✉ Petworth House, Petworth, W Sussex GU28 0AE (☎ 01798 342447, fax 01798 344331)

EHRHARDT, Marianne Luise (Mrs Nicholas Stacey); da of Wilhelm Alois Ehrhardt, of Friedrichshafen, Federal Republic of Germany, and Viktoria, *née* Hollenzer; *b* 2 May 1950; *Educ* Graf Zeppelin Gymnasium Friedrichshafen, Staatliche Hochschule fur Musik Freiburg; *m* 10 March 1987, Nicholas Anthony Howard Stacey, *qv*; *Career* flautist; fndr and musical dir Ondine Ensemble (19th and 20th century classical chamber music ensemble) 1979–, fndr Platform (charitable tst promoting young composers' unpublished works internationally) 1990–; cmmnd and premiered numerous major compositions, major tours and bdcasts in Germany and the USA; Cross of the Order of Merit (Germany); *Recreations* history, skiing; *Style*— Miss Marianne Ehrhardt; ✉ 35 Lennox Gardens, London SW1X 0DE

EHRMAN, John Patrick William; s of Albert Ehrman (d 1969), and Rina, *née* Bendit; *b* 17 March 1920; *Educ* Charterhouse, Trinity Coll Cambridge (MA); *m* 1 July 1948, Elizabeth Susan Anne, da of Vice Adm Sir Geoffrey Blake, KCB, DSO (d 1968); 4 s (William b 1950, Hugh b 1952, Richard b 1956, Thomas b 1959); *Career* fell Trinity Coll Cambridge 1947–52, historian Cabinet Office 1948–56, Lees Knowles lectr Univ of Cambridge 1957–58, James Ford special lectr Univ of Oxford 1976–77; hon treas Friends Nat Libraries 1960–77, vice pres Navy Records Soc 1968–70 and 1974–76, memb Reviewing Ctee on Export of Works of Art 1970–76, tstee Nat Portrait Gallery 1971–85, memb Royal Cmmn Historical Manuscripts 1973–94; chm: Advsy Ctee Br Library Reference Div (now Humanities and Social Sciences) 1975–84, Nat Manuscripts Conservation Tst 1989–94; FBA, FSA, FRHistS; *Books* The Navy in the War of William III (1953), Grand Strategy 1943–45, 2 vols (1956), Cabinet Government and War 1890–1940 (1958), The British Government and Commercial Negotiations with Europe (1962), The Younger Pitt (vol 1 1969, vol 2 1983, vol 3 1996); *Clubs* Army & Navy, Beefsteak, Garrick; *Style*— John Ehrman, Esq, FBA, FSA; ✉ The Mead Barns, Taynton, Burford, Oxfordshire OX18 4UH

EICHELBERGER, Alyce Faye; da of Albert Clinton McBride (d 1973), and Frances Fay, *née* Mitchell (d 1962); *b* 28 Oct 1944; *Educ* Oklahoma State Univ USA (BSc), Baylor Univ (MA, MSc), Univ of London Inst of Educn (DPMC); *m* 1, 22 Jan 1966, Martin Davis Eichelberger, Jr, s of Martin Davis Eichelberger; 2 s (Martin Davis III b 28 Sept 1969, Clinton Charles b 14 March 1973); *m* 2, 28 Dec 1992, John Marwood Cleese, *qv*; *Career* teacher secdy sch 1962–69, teaching asst to Dean of Special Educn Baylor Univ 1974–75, educnl psychologist Waco Ind Sch Dist Texas 1975–78, child psychotherapist Notre Dame Clinic 1981–87; teacher: in secdy sch for emotionally disturbed children 1980–83, of children with med and emotional problems ILEA 1983–84; child psychotherapist: Tavistock Clinic, Chalcot Sch; educnl psychologist Educn Records Bureau NY; psychotherapist and psychologist: American Sch of London, American Embassy, Tasis Sch Thorpe Park Surrey; in private practice: Holland Park, Kensington and Chelsea; memb: Republicans Abroad, Int Jr League Assoc of Child Psychotherapy 1986; co-fndr lunchtime lectures RGS (fndr memb and conslt); ABPS 1980, fell American Psychological Assoc 1980, fell American Med Psychotherapist Assoc 1987, memb RSM 1988, assoc fell Br Psychological Soc 1988; *Books* Comparative Education of Gifted Children in France (1979), Corporate Education of Gifted Children in the USSR (1979), A Case Study of Maladjusted Children in a London Day School (1983), Another Revolutionary - A Case Study of Psychotherapy With a Five Year Old Rastafarian Boy; *Recreations* yoga; *Style*— Mrs Alyce Faye Eichelberger or Mrs John Cleese

EILBECK, Prof (John) Christopher; *b* 8 April 1945; *Educ* The Queen's Coll Oxford (BSc), Univ of Lancaster (PhD); *Career* Royal Soc European fell ICTP Trieste 1969–70; Heriot-Watt Univ 1970–: head Dept of Mathematics 1984–89, prof of applied numerical analysis 1986–; visiting fell Los Alamos Nat Lab New Mexico 1983–84; FIMA 1985, FRSE 1987; *Books* Solitons and Nonlinear Wave Equations (jtly, 1982); also author of over 90 papers in learned jls; *Style*— Prof Chris Eilbeck, FRSE; ✉ Department of Mathematics, Heriot-Watt University, Riccarton, Edinburgh EH14 4AS (☎ 0131 451 3220, fax 0131 451 3249)

EILLEDGE, Elwyn Owen Morris; s of Owen Eilledge (d 1991), of Oswestry, Shropshire, and Mary Elizabeth Eilledge (d 1973); *b* 20 July 1935; *Educ* Oswestry Boys' HS, Merton Coll Oxford (BA, MA); *m* 30 March 1962; 1 s (Julian Alexander Stephen b 15 June 1970), 1 da (Amanda Gail Caroline b 20 Nov 1968); *Career* chartered accountant; Ernst and Young (formerly Ernst and Whinney): joined 1965, ptnr 1972–83, managing ptnr 1983–86, sr ptnr 1986–95, chm Ernst and Young International 1988–95; secondments: Govt of Liberia 1966–68, Hamburg 1968–71; chm BTR plc 1996– (dir 1995–); memb Financial Reporting Cncl 1991–95, chm Financial Reporting Advsy Bd to the Treasy 1996–; Liveryman Worshipful Co of Chartered Accountants; FCA (ACA 1963); *Recreations* opera, gardening, snooker; *Clubs* Brooks's; *Style*— Elwyn Eilledge, Esq; ✉ Whitethorn House, Long Grove, Seer Green, Beaconsfield, Bucks (☎ 01494 676 600); BTR plc, Silvertown House, Vincent Square, London SW1P 2PL (☎ 0171 821 3756, fax 0171 821 6536)

EILON, Prof Samuel (Sam); s of Abraham Joel (d 1974), and Rachel, *née* Deinard (d 1982); *b* 13 Oct 1923; *Educ* Reali Sch Haifa, Technion Haifa (BSc, Dip Ing), Imperial Coll London (PhD, DSc(Eng)); *m* 8 Aug 1946, Hannah Ruth, da of Max Samuel; 2 s (Amir, Daniel), 2 da (Romit, Carmel); *Career* engr in indust 1945–48; Maj Israel Defence Forces 1948–52; Imperial Coll London: res asst/lectr 1952–57, reader 1959–63, prof of mgmnt sci 1963–89 (head of section/dept 1955–87), emeritus prof and sr res fell 1989–; assoc prof Technion Haifa 1957–59, conslt to indust 1957–; former dir: ARC (formerly Amey Roadstone), Campari International, Spencer Stuart and Assoc; memb MMC 1990–97; Silver Medal The Operational Res Soc 1982; Hon FCGI 1978; FIMechE, FIEE, FEng 1976 (fndr fell); author of some 300 pubns (incl 15 books) on management; *Recreations* tennis, walking; *Style*— Prof Sam Eilon, FEng; ✉ 1 Meadway Close, London NW11 7BA (☎ 0181 458 6650, fax 0181 455 0561)

EINSIEDEL, Andreas Jean-Paul (GRAF von); s of Wittigo Graf von Einsiedel (d 1980), of Frankfurt am Main, Germany, and Walburga, *née* Graefin von Oberndorff; *b* 28 Jan 1953; *Educ* Marquartstein Bavaria, PCL (BA); *m* 2 June 1979 (m dis 1992), Harriet Angela Victoria, da of Henry George Austen de L'Etang Herbert Duckworth (d 1992); 3 s (Orlando Ernle Benedict b 19 Aug 1980, Evelyn b 26 Aug 1982, Robin b 12 April 1988), 1 da (Gwendolen b 24 Jan 1985); *Career* internationally renowned interiors photographer; work published regularly in many leading national and international interior magazines; *Style*— Andreas Graf von Einsiedel; ✉ 72–80 Leather Lane, London EC1N 7TR (☎ 0171 242 7674, fax 0171 831 3712)

EISLER, Hon Mrs (Jean Mary); 2 da of 1 Baron Layton, CH, CBE (d 1966), and Eleanor Dorothea, *née* Osmaston (d 1959); *b* 14 April 1916; *Educ* St Paul's Girls' Sch London, RCM (ARCM); *m* 12 June 1944, Paul Eisler (d 15 Aug 1966), yr s of Ernst Eisler (d 1951), of Prague; 2 s (John b 1946, Ivan b 1948); *Career* professional musician and music therapist; concert performer and teacher 1941–46; lived in Prague 1948–72, translator of Czech children's books, novels, belles lettres, modern vocal music incl 2 Janáček operas (Osud, Počátek Románu); Nordoff/Robbins Music Therapy Dip 1974; head Music Therapy Depts: Goldie Leigh 1976–90, Queen Mary's Hosp for Children Carshalton 1984–91; sr music therapist Nordoff/Robbins Music Therapy Centre London 1984–93 (fndr memb Mgmnt Ctee), conslt music therapist 1993–; RCM Tagore Gold Medal; *Style*— Hon Mrs Eisler; ✉ Syskon Cottage, 2 Millfield Lane, London N6 6JD (☎ 0181 348 0874)

EISNER, Hans Gunter; s of Ludwig Eisner (d 1972), of Chorlton-cum-Hardy, Manchester, and Hertha, *née* Buckwitz (d 1976); *b* 4 July 1929; *Educ* Manchester Central High GS, Univ of Manchester Sch of Architecture (BA); *m* 13 June 1953, (Doreen) Annette Elizabeth, da of Reginald Barker-Lambert (d 1992), and Doreen H Duffield (d 1963), of Exmouth, Devon; 2 s (Christopher Paul David b 20 Nov 1954, Andrew James Stephen b 27 May 1961); *Career* architect; assoc architect Fairhursts Manchester 1952–53, architect and gp leader Middlesbrough Educn Architects Dept 1954–56, architect i/c Drawing Office Borough of Watford 1956–57, sr assoc architect New School Section Derbyshire Co Architects Dept 1957–62, sr architect i/c R & D Gp Manchester City Housing Dept 1962–63, princ assoc architect SW Regnl Health Authy 1963–75, architect and area building offr Devon Area Health Authy 1975–83, in private practice 1983–; princ projects incl: Ladgate Primary Sch Middlesbrough, Devpt Project for Infant Educn Sawley Infants Sch Long Eaton Derbyshire, Royal United Hosp Bath Phase I; conslt project mangr Univ of Exeter 1987–; memb Cncl Assoc of Official Architects 1959–85 (chm 1972–82); RIBA: memb Public Relations TV and Bdcast Ctee 1965–69, memb Regnl Cncl 1975–78, memb Cncl 1975–78, memb Devon and Exeter Branch Exec 1984–89 and 1993–, memb SW Regnl Practice Ctee 1994–; memb Rotary Club Exeter (pres 1991–92); memb: ARCUK 1953, Assoc of Conslt Architects 1983; RIBA 1953, FRSA 1995, FRHS 1995; *Recreations* walking, music, sketching, travel, gardening; *Clubs* Rotary; *Style*— Hans G Eisner, Esq; ✉ Bickleigh House, Edginswell Lane, Kingskerswell, Devon TQ12 5LU (☎ 01803 873597)

EL NAHAS, Prof (Abdel) Meguid; s of Hassan Khalil El Nahas (d 1978), of Cairo, Egypt, and Fatma Galal Selim, *née* El Hegazy; *b* 1 Dec 1949; *Educ* Jesuits' Coll Cairo Egypt, Univ of Geneva Med Sch Switzerland, Univ of London (PhD); *m* 30 April 1983, Penelope Anne, da of Henry Denys Hanan, DSC, of Shrewsbury; 2 da (Gemma b 1983, Holly b 1985); *Career* res Mass Gen Hosp Boston USA 1977–78; res fell in nephrology: Paris 1978–79, Royal Postgrad Med Sch London 1979–82; renal registrar Royal Free Hospital London 1982–84, lectr in nephrology Univ of Wales Coll of Med Cardiff 1984–86, conslt renal physician Sheffield Kidney Inst Northern Gen Hosp Sheffield 1986–, prof of nephrology Sheffield Kidney Inst Univ of Sheffield 1996–; memb: Nat and Int Socs of Nephrology, Assoc of Physicians; FRCP; *Recreations* sports, history, theology, travelling; *Style*— Prof A Meguid El Nahas; ✉ Sheffield Kidney Institute, Northern General Hospital, Herries Rd, Sheffield S5 7AU (☎ 0114 271 4018, fax 0114 256 2514)

ELAM, (John) Nicholas; CMG (1994); s of John Frederick Elam, OBE, and Joan Barrington, *née* Lloyd; *b* 2 July 1939; *Educ* Colchester Royal GS, New Coll Oxford, Harvard Univ; *m* 14 Oct 1967, (Florence) Helen, da of Pieter Lentz; 2 s (Peter, Michael), 1 da (Alexandra); *Career* entered HM Dip Serv 1962, FO 1962–64, served Pretoria and Capetown 1964–68, Treasy Centre Admin Studies 1968–69, FCO 1969–71, first sec Bahrain 1971, commercial sec Brussels 1972–76, FCO 1976–79 (dep head News Dept 1978–79), cnsllr and Br Govt rep Salisbury 1979, dep high cmmr Salisbury (later Harare) 1980–83, consul gen Montreal 1984–87, head Cultural Relations Dept FCO 1987–94, chm Cncl for Cultural Cooperation Cncl of Europe 1993–94, ambass Luxembourg 1994–; *Recreations* travel, the arts; *Style*— Nicholas Elam, Esq, CMG; ✉ c/o Foreign and Commonwealth Office (Luxembourg), King Charles St, London SW1A 2AH

ELAND, Michael John; s of George Eland, and Betty, *née* Middleton-Walker; *b* 26 Sept 1952; *Educ* Worksop Coll Notts, Trinity Coll Oxford (MA); *m* Luned Rhiannon Wyn, *née* Jones; 1 da (Charlotte Sophie Fairbairn b 1986), 1 s (Thomas George Benjamin b 1988); *Career* called to the Bar Middle Temple 1975; HM Customs and Excise: admin trainee 1975, private sec to Chm 1979–81; Cabinet Office 1982–87, private sec to Lord Pres of the Cncl (Visc Whitelaw) 1987–88; HM Customs and Excise: asst sec 1988–92, cmmr 1992–; *Style*— Michael Eland, Esq; ✉ Commissioner, HM Customs and Excise, New King's Beam House, 22 Upper Ground, London SE1 9PJ (☎ 0171 865 5061, fax 0171 865 4051)

ELCOAT, Rev Canon (George) Alastair; s of George Thomas Elcoat (d 1955), of Wallsend-on-Tyne, and Hilda Gertrude, *née* Bee (d 1962); *b* 4 June 1922; *Educ* Tynemouth Sch, The Queen's Coll Birmingham; *Career* RAF 1941–46; ordained: deacon Newcastle 1951, priest 1952; asst curate Corbridge 1951–55; vicar: Spittal 1955–62, Chatton W Chillingham 1962–70, Sugley 1970–81, Tweedmouth 1987–91 (priest in charge 1981–87); rural dean: Newcastle West 1977–81, Norham 1982–91; chaplain to HM The Queen 1982–92; canon emeritus Newcastle Cathedral 1991; *Recreations* fell walking, music, photography; *Style*— Rev Canon Alastair Elcoat; ✉ 42 Windsor Crescent, Berwick-upon-Tweed, Northumberland TD15 1NT (☎ 01289 33 1936)

ELDEN, Jeremy Mark; s of Reginald Elden, and Sheilagh, *née* Carter; *b* 21 June 1958; *Educ* Northgate GS Ipswich, Hertford Coll (BA), Univ of Strathclyde (MSc); *m* 19 Sept 1987, Victoria Mary, *née* Bone; *Career* field engr Schlumberger Overseas SA 1980–82, reservoir engr Britoil 1982–83, oil analyst UBS Phillips & Drew 1984–90; dir oil res: BZW 1990–94, UBS Ltd 1994–; *Style*— Jeremy Elden, Esq; ✉ Snail Hall, Polstead,

Colchester CO6 5AU (☎ 01206 262526); UBS Ltd, 100 Liverpool Street, London EC2M 2RH (☎ 0171 901 3329, fax 0171 901 1997)

ELDER, Prof James Brown; s of David Elder (d 1988), of Linwood, Renfrewshire, Scotland, and Margaret Helen, *née* Cowan (d 1982); *b* 20 May 1938; *Educ* Shawlands Acad Glasgow, Univ of Glasgow (MB ChB, MD); *m* 12 Dec 1964, Sheena Jean Reid Fyfe, da of Colin McLay, of Paisley, Scotland; 3 da (Jacqueline b 1966, Karen b 1967, Alison b 1969); *Career* sr registrar in gen surgery Glasgow Western Infirmary 1968–71 (registrar 1965–68), reader in surgery Manchester Royal Infirmary Univ of Manchester 1976–83 (sr lectr and conslt surgn 1971–76), prof of surgery Univ of Keele Sch of Postgraduate Med 1983–, conslt surgn to N Staffs Hosp Centre 1983–; examiner in surgery Univs of: Manchester 1976–83, Glasgow 1981–83, Sheffield 1986–89, Nottingham 1985–89, Hong Kong 1994–; examiner: RCPS Glasgow, Univ of Manchester 1992–, Univ of Birmingham 1994–; chm W Midlands Regnl Research Awards Ctee memb: Nat Confidential Enquiry into Perioperative Death, Senate Univ of Keele, Surgical Res Soc, Br Soc of Gastroenterology, W Midlands Surgical Soc, Midlands Soc of Gastroenterology, The Prout Club; FRCSEd 1966, FRCS 1966, FRCS Glasgow 1981; *Recreations* hill walking, classical music, reading, photography; *Clubs* British Pottery Manufacturers' Federation (Stoke-on-Trent); *Style—* Prof James B Elder; ✉ Tara, 182 Seabridge Lane, Westlands, Newcastle-under-Lyme, Staffs ST5 3LS; Department of Surgery, University of Keele, School of Postgraduate Medicine, Thornburrow Drive, Hartshill, Stoke-on-Trent (☎ 01782 715444, fax 01782 747319)

ELDER, Mark Philip; CBE (1989); *b* 2 June 1947; *Educ* Bryanston, CCC Cambridge (music scholar, choral scholar, BA, MA); *m* 30 May 1980, Amanda Jane, *née* Stein; 1 da (Katherine Olivia b 13 April 1986); *Career* music dir: English National Opera 1979–93, Rochester Philharmonic Orchestra NY 1989–94; princ guest conductor City of Birmingham Orchestra 1992–95; other recent performances incl: Tristan und Isolde (ENO) 1996, BBC Symphony Orch BBC Proms 1996; *Style—* Mark Elder, Esq, CBE; ✉ c/o Ingpen and Williams Ltd, 14 Kensington Court, London W8 5DN (☎ 0171 937 5158, fax 0171 938 4175)

ELDER, Prof Murdoch George; s of Archibald James Elder (d 1992), of Biggar, Scot, and Lotta Annie Catherine, *née* Craig; *b* 4 Jan 1938; *Educ* Edinburgh Acad, Univ of Edinburgh (MB ChB, MD), Univ of London (DSc); *m* 3 Oct 1964, Margaret Adelaide, da of Dr James McVicker (d 1985), of Portrush, Co Antrim, Ireland; 2 s (James b 1968, Andrew b 1970); *Career* Nat Serv Captain RAMC (TA&VR) 1964; lectr Univ of Malta 1969–71, sr lectr and reader Univ of London (Charing Cross Hosp Med Sch) 1971–78, res fell WHO 1976, travelling fell RCOG 1977, prof and head Dept of Obstetrics and Gynaecology Royal Postgraduate Med Sch Univ of London 1978–; dir: Obstetrics and Gynaecology Service Hammersmith, Queen Charlotte's Special Health Authy, WHO Clinical Res Centre 1980–92; visiting prof Univs of: California (LA), Singapore, Natal; examiner Univs of: London, Oxford, Cambridge, Edinburgh, Glasgow, Leeds, Liverpool, Birmingham, Bristol, Dundee, Malta, Malaysia, Capetown, Singapore, Rotterdam, Helsinki; memb Hammersmith and Queen Charlotte's Special Health Authy 1982–90, chm Hosp Med Ctee 1980–85, sec Assoc of Profs (O and G) 1984–86; memb: WHO Steering Ctee on Contraception 1980–86, WHO Research and Ethics Group 1994–; author of over 200 scientific pubns; Silver medal Hellenic Obstetrical Soc 1983; FRCSEd 1968, FRCOG 1979; *Books* Current Fertility Control (1978), Pre Term Labour (1982), Reproduction, Obstetrics and Gynaecology (1988), Prematurity (1997); *Recreations* golf, travel; *Clubs* Roehampton, 1942; *Style—* Prof Murdoch Elder; ✉ 4 Stonehill Rd, London SW14 8RW (☎ 0181 876 4332); Hammersmith Hospital, Du Cane Rd, London W12 0HS (☎ 0181 743 7171)

ELDER, Air Vice-Marshal Ronald David (Ron); CBE (1991); *b* 27 May 1946; *Educ* RAF Coll Cranwell; *m* Sue; 1 s, 1 da; *Career* cmmnd pilot 1968, early experience as weapons instr in Ground Attack and Fighter Reconnaissance, staff appointment AAFCE NATO HQ, Jaguar pilot 1976–81, RAF Staff Coll 1981, Central Tactics and Trials Orgn 1981–86, converted to Tornado GR1 1986, subsequently cmd No 20 Sqdn RAF Laarbruch (first Tornado Laser Guided Bomb Unit), Gp Capt 1988, station cdr Tri-National Tornado Trg Estab RAF Cottesmore 1988–91, detached as RAF cdr to Tabuk Saudi Arabia (for early months of Operation Granby) 1990, RCDS 1991, Air Cdre 1991, Policy Area Central Staff MOD 1991–93, dir of Airspace Policy (responsible for strategy, planning and design of all arrangements for UK airspace) 1993–; *Recreations* real tennis, golf, skiing; *Clubs* RAF; *Style—* Air Vice-Marshal Ron Elder, CBE; ✉ Director of Airspace Policy, CAA House, 45–49 Kingsway, London WC2B 6TE

ELDERFIELD, Maurice; s of Henry Elderfield (d 1977), and Kathleen Maud, *née* James (d 1992); *b* 10 April 1926; *Educ* Southgate Co GS; *m* 22 Aug 1953, Audrey June, da of Sydney James Knight (d 1981); 1 s (Christopher b 10 March 1956), 3 da (Sallie b 15 May 1958, Carol (twin) b 15 May 1958, Jacqueline b 11 Oct 1961); *Career* WWII Fleet Air Arm RNVR 1944–47; memb Bd and fin dir Segas 1960–73, fin dir Southern Water Authority 1973–75, memb Bd of Fin PO 1975–76, fin dir Ferranti Ltd 1977, memb Bd of Fin British Shipbuilders 1977–80; chm: Throgmorton Trust 1972–84, Sheldon and Partners Ltd 1981–92, Sheldon Aviation Ltd 1980–90, Berfield Associates Ltd 1980–92; FCA 1949; *Recreations* golf, tennis; *Clubs* Gravetye Manor; *Style—* Maurice Elderfield, Esq; ✉ Hadleigh, Keeill Pharick Park, Glen Vine, Isle of Man

ELDERTON, Prof Richard John; s of Edward Fothergill Elderton (d 1986), and Hilda Mary Irene, *née* Thomas (d 1971); *b* 10 April 1942; *Educ* Lancing Coll Sussex, Univ of London (BDS, PhD); *m* 10 Sept 1966, Pamela Mary, da of Enslie Roy Bater Bolt (d 1987); 2 s (Charles b 1969, Edward b 1971), 1 da (Sophie b 1977); *Career* warrant offr in CCF; in gen dental practice 1965–66, res dental house surgn London Hosp 1966, clinical instr in operative dentistry State Univ of NY Buffalo USA 1966–68, sr lectr in conservative dentistry London Hosp Med Coll 1976–78 (lectr 1968–71, res fell experimental dental care project 1971–76), dir Dental Health Servs Res Unit Univ of Dundee 1979–85, prof of preventive and restorative dentistry Univ of Bristol 1985– (head Dept of Conservative Dentistry 1985–94); hon scientific advsr to the British Dental Journal 1984–, hon conslt in restorative dentistry to United Bristol Healthcare NHS Tst 1985–; memb: WHO Expert Advsy Panel on Oral Health 1987–, Jt Dental Ctee for MRC Health Depts and Serv 1987–92, Exec Bd Int Health Care Fndn 1994–; visiting prof McGill Univ and Dalhousie Univ, MRC distinguished visiting scientist Univs of Adelaide and Western Cape; LDS RCS 1965; memb: BDA, IADR, BSDR, BSRD, BASCD; *Books* Positive Dental Prevention (1987), Evolution in Dental Care (1990), The Dentition and Dental Care (1990), Professional Prevention in Dental Practice (1994); *Recreations* running, sailing, wood and metal work, painting, cartooning, philosophy; *Style—* Prof Richard Elderton; ✉ Department of Oral and Dental Science, Dental School, Lower Maudlin St, Bristol BS1 2LY (☎ 0117 929 1900, fax 0117 927 2298)

ELDON, 5 Earl of (UK 1821); John Joseph Nicholas Scott; Baron Eldon (GB 1799), Viscount Encombe (UK 1821); s of 4 Earl of Eldon, GCVO (d 1976, fifth in descent from the 1 Earl), and Hon Margaret Fraser, OBE (d 1969), da of 14 Lord Lovat; *b* 24 April 1937; *Educ* Ampleforth, Trinity Coll Oxford; *m* 1 July 1961, Countess Claudine, da of Count Franz von Montjoye-Vaufrey and de la Roche (originally a cr of Louis XV of France 1736, confirmed 1743 (also by Louis) and later by Emperor Franz Josef of Austria-Hungary 1888), of Vienna; 1 s, 2 da (Lady Tatiana b 1967, Lady Victoria b 1968); *Heir* s, John Francis Thomas Marie Joseph Columba Fidelis, Viscount Encombe b 9 July 1962; *Career* 2 Lt Scots Gds, Lt Army Emergency Reserve; *Style—* The Rt Hon The Earl of Eldon; ✉ c/o House of Lords, London SW1

ELDRED, Dr Vernon Walter; MBE (1970); s of Vernon Frank Eldred (d 1929), of Sutton Coldfield, and Dorothy, *née* Lyon (d 1968); *b* 14 March 1925; *Educ* Bishop Vesey's GS Sutton Coldfield, St Catharine's Coll Cambridge (MA, PhD); *m* 4 Aug 1951, Pamela Mary, da of Arthur Wood (d 1943), of Sutton Coldfield; 2 s (Andrew b 1952, John b 1958), 1 da (Sally b 1956); *Career* Dept of Scientific and Industl Res Fuel Res Station Greenwich 1945–47, AERE Harwell 1947–48, Dept of Metallurgy Univ of Cambridge 1948–53, Nelson Res Labs English Electric Co Stafford 1953–55; Windscale Laboratory UKAEA: princ scientific offr 1955–59, res mangr metallurgy 1959–76, head of Fuel Examination Div 1976–84, head of Fuel Performance Div and dep head of laboratory 1984–87, head of laboratory 1987–90; Royal Soc Esso award for Conservation of Energy 1979; memb Cncl Inst of Metallurgists 1966–69, chm Ctee Nat Certificates and Dips in Metallurgy 1967–73, memb Bd Br Nuclear Energy Soc 1974–77; fndr memb and first chm West Cumbria Metallurgic Soc; hon fell Inst of Nuclear Engrs 1988; pres: Gosforth Dist Agric Soc Cumbria 1990, Gosforth and Dist Probus Club 1992–93; FIM 1968, FEng 1984; *Recreations* beekeeping, fell walking, genealogy, gardening, computers; *Clubs* United Oxford and Cambridge Univ; *Style—* Dr Vernon Eldred, MBE, FEng; ✉ Fell Gate, Santon Bridge, Holmrook, Cumbria CA19 1UY (☎ 019467 26275)

ELDRIDGE, David John; s of Lt-Col Frederick George Eldridge (ret), of Haslemere, Surrey, and Irene Mary, *née* Buston; *b* 12 Jan 1935; *Educ* King's Coll Sch Wimbledon; *m* 1, 14 May 1960, Diana Mary (d 1981), da of Eric Copp, of Hartlepool, Cleveland; 1 s (Charles b 1961), 2 da (Catherine b 1964, Victoria b 1966); m 2, 15 Dec 1984, Anna Maria, da of Jerzy Kowalski, of Warsaw, Poland; *Career* admitted slr 1956; ptnr: Stanley Attenborough & Co 1958–74, Martin & Nicholson 1975–77, Amhurst Brown Colombotti 1977–, Amhurst Brown Warsaw Poland; tstee (since inception 1974) Musuem of Islamic Art Jerusalem; donation govr Christ's Hosp Horsham; Freeman City of London, Liveryman & memb Ct Worshipful Co of Fletchers (Master 1984–86), memb Ct of Assts Guild of Freemen (Master 1983–84); memb Law Soc 1957; *Recreations* fine arts, sport; *Clubs* Royal Automobile, City Livery; *Style—* David Eldridge, Esq; ✉ 13 Clonmel Road, London SW6 5BL (☎ 0171 731 2573); Warsaw, Poland; Amhurst Brown Colombotti, 2 Duke St, St James's, London SW1 (☎ 0171 930 2366, fax 0171 930 2250, telex 261857 Ambro)

ELDRIDGE, Mark; s of Bernard Derrick Eldridge, of Toronto, Canada (foster f George Hoare, of Liphook, Hants), and Anne May, *née* Murphy (foster mother Eileen Violet, *née* Luff); *b* 9 Aug 1954; *Educ* Churcher's Coll Petersfield Hants, Univ of Lancaster (BA), City Univ (Dip in Law), Inns of Court Sch of Law; *m* 3 July 1982, Alexandra Catherine, da of John Watling Illingworth, of Wellingborough, Northants; 1 s (Joseph b 10 July 1987), 3 da (Charlotte b 27 March 1983, Elizabeth b 27 Sept 1984, Catherine b 31 Jan 1986); *Career* practising barr; called to the Bar Gray's Inn 1982, memb Inner Temple 1985, elected memb Gen Cncl of the Bar 1986–91, chm Young Bar of England and Wales 1989; govr Thornhill Primary Sch 1986–88, chm Bd of Govrs Clerkenwell Parochial Sch 1993–96; Islington South and Finsbury Cons Assoc: vice chm 1986–89, chm 1989–92, vice pres 1992–; *Recreations* swimming, golf, tennis; *Clubs* Carlton, IOD; *Style—* Mark Eldridge, Esq; ✉ 114 Liverpool Rd, Islington, London N1 0RE (☎ 0171 226 9863); 10 King's Bench Walk, Temple, London EC4Y 7EB (☎ 0171 353 7742, fax 0171 583 0579)

ELEGANT, Robert Sampson; s of Louis Elegant (d 1965), and Lillie Rebecca, *née* Sampson (d 1984); *b* 7 March 1928; *Educ* Univ of Pennsylvania (BA), Yale, Columbia Univ (MA, MS); *m* 16 April 1956, Moira Clarissa Brady; 1 s (Simon David Brady b 1960), 1 da (Victoria Ann b 1958); *Career* Far East corr Overseas News Agency 1951–52, Int News Serv war corr Korea 1952–53; corr in Singapore and SE Asia for: Columbia Broadcasting Serv, McGraw-Hill News Serv and North American Newspaper Alliance 1954–55; S Asian corr & chief New Delhi Bureau Newsweek 1956–57, SE Asian corr & chief Hong Kong Bureau Newsweek 1958–61, chief Central Euro Bureau (Bonn-Berlin) Newsweek 1962–64, public lectr 1964–, chief Hong Kong Bureau Los Angeles Times 1965–69; foreign affrs columnist Los Angeles Times/Washington Post News Serv: Munich 1970–72, Hong Kong 1973–76; visiting prof of journalism and int affrs: Univ of South Carolina 1976, Boston Univ 1994–95; independent author and journalist 1977–; Pulitzer travelling fell 1951–52, fell Ford Fndn 1954–55, fell American Enterprise Inst 1976–78, sr fell Inst for Advanced Studies Berlin 1993–94, Edgar Allen Poe award Mystery Writers of America 1967, four Overseas Press Club awards; *Books* non-fiction: China's Red Leaders (1951), The Dragon's Seed (1959), The Centre of the World (1964), Mao's Great Revolution (1971), Mao vs Chiang: The Battle for China (1972), Pacific Destiny: Inside Asia Today (1990); novels: A Kind of Treason (1966), The Seeking (1969), Dynasty (1977), Manchu (1980), Mandarin (1983), White Sun, Red Star (1986), Bianca (1992), The Everlasting Sorrows (1994); *Recreations* sailing, raising Shih Tzu dogs; *Clubs* Hong Kong Foreign Correspondents, Royal Hong Kong Yacht; *Style—* Robert Elegant, Esq; ✉ The Manor House, Middle Green, Langley, Bucks SL3 6BS

ELEY, Dr Barry Michael; s of Horace Henry Eley (d 1971), and Ena Maud, *née* Cast (d 1975); *b* 6 March 1940; *Educ* St Olave's & St Saviour's GS, The London Hosp Dental Sch (BDS, LDS RCS); *m* 1 June 1963, Julie Christina, da of Arthur William Rumbold; 1 s (Peter John b 10 Dec 1965), 1 da (Esther Jane b 12 March 1968); *Career* house surgn London Hosp Med Sch 1963; King's Coll Hosp Dental Sch: asst lectr and registrar 1963–65, lectr in conservation dentistry 1965–74, sr lectr in periodontology 1974–80; King's Coll Sch of Med and Dentistry: sr lectr and conslt 1980–89, head of Periodontal Dept 1980–, dir Sch of Dental Hygiene 1980–, reader and conslt in periodontology; pres Br Soc of Periodontology 1993–94; author of over 90 scientific papers; FDS RCS 1972; memb: BDA, BSP, BSDR, RMS; *Books* Amalgam Tattoos (1982), Outline of Periodontics (with J D Mason, 2 edn 1989, reprint 1991, Japanese edn 1992, 3 edn 1993), Dental Amalgam: a review of Safety (1993); *Recreations* badminton, golf, listening to music, walking, astronomy; *Style—* Dr Barry Eley; ✉ 10 Grosvenor Road, Petts Wood, Orpington, Kent BR5 1QU

ELEY, Piers David Christopher; s of Sir Geoffrey Cecil Ryves Eley, CBE (d 1990), and Lady Eley, of East Bergholt, Suffolk; *b* 20 May 1941; *Educ* Sandroyds Sch, Eton, Trinity Coll Cambridge (MA), London Grad Sch of Business Admin (MSc); *m* 1 April 1967, Sarah Cloudesley, da of Lt-Col David E Long-Price, OBE (d 1992), of Fryerning, Ingatestone, Essex; 1 s (Damian Edward Piers b 24 Jan 1970), 1 da (Thalia Catherine b 9 Sept 1971); *Career* Norton Rose Botterell & Roche 1964, Hambros Bank Ltd 1964–73, dir Nordic Bank plc 1973–84, ptnr Coopers & Lybrand 1985–92; fin dir Prospect House Sch Putney Hill London 1990–; memb: Inner Temple 1961, London Business Sch Assoc 1969, Business Graduates Assoc 1969; Guildsman of St Brides Fleet St 1984, chm Friends of St Matthias Richmond 1986; *Recreations* painting, gardening, natural history, fishing, sailing, shooting, photography, music; *Clubs* Brooks's, Fox, Omar Khayyam, St Mawes Sailing; *Style—* Piers D C Eley, Esq; ✉ 35 Montague Rd, Richmond, Surrey TW10 6QJ (☎ 0181 940 0788, fax 0181 940 5007)

ELGIN AND KINCARDINE, 11 and 15 Earl of (S 1633 and 1647); Andrew Douglas Alexander Thomas Bruce; KT (1981), CD (1985) JP (Fife 1951); also Lord Bruce of Kinloss (S 1604), Lord Bruce of Torry (S 1647), Baron Elgin (UK 1849); 37 Chief of the Name of Bruce; s of 10 Earl of Elgin, KT, CMG, TD (ggs of the 7 Earl who removed to safety the statuary known as The Elgin Marbles from the Parthenon in Athens), and Hon Dame Katherine Elizabeth Cochrane, DBE, da of 1 Baron Cochrane of Cults; *b* 17 Feb 1924; *Educ* Eton, Balliol Coll Oxford (MA); *m* 27 April 1959, Victoria Mary, o da of Dudley George Usher, MBE, TD, of Gallowridge House, Dunfermline; 3

s (Lord Bruce, Hon Adam Robert, Hon Alexander Victor b 1971), 2 da; *Heir* s, Lord Bruce; *Career* served WWII (wounded); chm Nat Savings Ctee Scotland 1972–78; dir: Scottish Amicable Life Assurance Soc until 1994 (also former pres), Scottish Post Office Bd 1980–96; pres: Roy Caledonian Curling Club 1968–69, Royal Scottish Automobile Club; dir Royal Highland and Agric Soc 1973–76; Lord High Cmmr to Gen Assembly of Church of Scotland 1980–81; memb Ct of Regents Royal Coll of Surgns of Edinburgh; Grand Master Mason of Scotland 1961–65, Lieut Royal Co of Archers (Queen's Body Guard for Scotland); Lord-Lt Fife 1988– (DL 1955); Hon Col Elgin Regt of Canada (1969); Hon DLitt St Mary's NS 1976, Hon LLD Dundee 1977, Hon LLD Glasgow 1983; Order of Merit Norway 1994; *Style*— The Rt Hon the Earl of Elgin and Kincardine, KT, CD, JP; ✉ Broomhall, Dunfermline KY11 3DU (☎ 01383 872222, fax 01383 872904)

ELIAS, Brian David; s of Albert Murad Elias, and Julie Sophie, *née* Ephraim; *b* 30 Aug 1948; *Educ* St Christopher Sch, RCM, and with Elisabeth Lutyens; *Career* composer: La Chevelure 1969, Peroration 1973, Somnia 1979, L'Eylah (cmmnd for BBC Promenade Concerts) 1984, Geranos (cmmnd by Fires of London) 1985, Variations (for solo piano) 1987, Five Songs to Poems by Irina Ratushinskaya (cmmnd by the BBC) 1989, The Judas Tree (cmmnd by Royal Opera House) 1992; memb Assoc of Professional Composers; *Recreations* reading, gardening, theatre, art; *Style*— Brian Elias, Esq; ✉ Chester Music, 8/9 Frith St, London W1V 5TZ (0171 434 0066, fax 0171 439 2848, telex 21892 MSLDNG)

ELIAS, Dr Elwyn; s of Illtyd Elias (d 1965), and Rachel, *née* Jones; *b* 11 Jan 1943; *Educ* Ardwyn GS Aberystwyth, Guy's Hosp Med Sch (BSc, MB BS); *m* 3 April 1982, Irene Margaret, da of Rev Reginald Raymond Taylor (d 1977), of Nottingham; 3 s (Gareth b 15 Nov 1983, Joshua b 14 March 1986, Owen b 5 April 1991); *Career* registrar Hammersmith Hosp 1970–72, lectr and hon sr registrar Royal Free Hosp 1973–77, res fell Liver Study Unit of Chicago Hosp 1977–78, res assoc Univ of Yale Hosp 1978–79, conslt physician Queen Elizabeth Hosp Birmingham 1979–; *Books* Lecture Notes in Gastroenterology (1985); *Style*— Dr Elwyn Elias; ✉ Queen Elizabeth Hospital, Edgbaston, Birmingham (☎ 0121 472 1311)

ELIAS, Gerard; QC (1984); s of Leonard Elias, of Llandaff, Cardiff, and Patricia, *née* O'Neill; *b* 19 Nov 1944; *Educ* Cardiff HS, Univ of Exeter (LLB, capt cricket XI); *m* 14 March 1970, Elisabeth, o da of Sir George Henry Kenyon, JP, DL, *qv*, of Limefield House, Hyde, Cheshire; 3 s (David b 7 May 1971, Robert b 24 Feb 1973, James b 1 May 1976); *Career* called to the Bar Inner Temple 1968, bencher 1993, recorder of the Crown Court 1984–, asst boundary cmmr for Wales 1984–, ldr Wales and Chester Circuit 1993– (treas 1990–92), master of the Bench Inner Temple 1993; memb Bar Cncl 1986–89, dir Bar Mutual Insur Fund 1987–, govr and memb Cncl Malvern Coll 1988–; dep chm Glamorgan CCC 1993– (memb Exec Ctee 1985–93); Test and Co Cricket Bd: memb Registration Ctee 1993–, chm Disciplinary Sub-Ctee; *Recreations* sailing, cricket, music; *Clubs* Cardiff & County, Bristol Channel Yacht; *Style*— Gerard Elias, Esq, QC; ✉ Farrars Building, Temple, London EC4Y 7BD (☎ 0171 583 9241, fax 0171 583 0090)

ELIAS, Peter Raoul; s of Paul Elias, and Margarethe Rozenzweig; *b* 5 Feb 1933; *Educ* Kilburn GS; *m* 18 July 1953, Betty Ethel Kathleen, da of Joseph Kennedy; 1 s (Roger David b 1957), 1 da (Vivienne Zöe b 1955); *Career* RAF air wireless operator/mechanic; export sales mangr Lancashire Dynamo Electronic Products Ltd 1960–67, sales dir Training Systems International 1967–69, princ P R Elias and Assocs (financial advsrs) 1969–92; writer/reviewer 1992–; section offr Thames Valley Special Constabulary 1975–87, Special Constable Dyfed Powys Police 1987–90; Police Long Serv medal; *Recreations* golf, motorcycling, linguist, music lover, collecting and riding Harley-Davidsons; *Clubs* Carmarthen Golf, Lancia Motor, Vintage Motorcycle; *Style*— Peter R Elias, Esq; ✉ Bryn Cowin, Talog, Carmarthenshire SA33 6NY (☎ 01994 484214, fax 01994 484214)

ELIAS, Robin Pieter; s of Carel George Elias, of Dorking, and Nancy Elizabeth, *née* Harvey; *b* 11 Dec 1953; *Educ* Therfield Comp Leatherhead; *m* 24 June 1978, Sally Anne, da of Malcolm Alfred Henry Holder; 1 s (Samuel Jeremy b 19 March 1987), 1 da (Amy Grace b 10 Aug 1990); *Career* reporter Surrey Advertiser Guildford 1971–77, sub ed Press Association 1977–79, sub ed London Evening News 1979–80; ITN: joined as prodr 1980, prog ed Lunchtime News 1990–92, prog ed News at Ten 1992–, also head of Output 1996–; *Style*— Robin Elias, Esq; ✉ Norton, Reigate Road, Dorking, Surrey RH4 1QF; ITN Ltd, 200 Gray's Inn Road, London WC1X 8XZ (☎ 0171 833 3000)

ELIAS-JONES, Peter John; s of William Peter Jones (d 1973), of Llangefni, Anglesey, and Margaret, *née* Elias; *b* 29 May 1943; *Educ* Llangefni Ysgol Gyfun, Univ of Leeds (BA), Univ of Manchester (Dip); *m* 10 April 1971, Elinor Mair, da of Cyril Owens (d 1988), of Ammanford, Dyfed; 2 da (Elen b 1973, Mari Wyn b 1976); *Career* teacher of music and drama Wallasey GS Cheshire 1966, studio mangr TWW Ltd Cardiff 1967; HTV Ltd Cardiff: dir of news 1968, prodr and dir of children's progs 1971, head of children's progs 1974, asst prog controller 1981, prog controller entertainment 1988, dir of progs Agenda Television Ltd Cardiff and Swansea 1992–; publisher of books for young people and various articles; *Style*— Peter Elias-Jones, Esq; ✉ Agenda, Castell Close, Enterprise Park, Swansea, S Glam SA7 9FH (☎ 01792 470470, fax 01792 475878)

ELIBANK, 14 Lord (S 1643); Sir Alan D'Ardis Erskine-Murray; 14 Bt (NS 1628); s of Maj Robert Alan Erskine-Murray, OBE (d 1939), unc of 13 Lord; suc cous 1973; *b* 31 Dec 1923, Wynberg, SA; *Educ* Bedford, Peterhouse Cambridge; *m* 1962, Valerie Sylvia, o da of late Herbert William Dennis, of St Margaret's, Twickenham; 2 s; *Heir* s, Master of Elibank, *qv*; *Career* barr 1949–55, gen mangr and rep Shell Int Petroleum Co in Qatar 1977–80 (personnel 1955–77), personnel mangr Deminex Oil and Gas Ltd 1981–86; *Style*— The Rt Hon the Lord Elibank; ✉ The Coach House, Charters Road, Sunningdale, Ascot, Berks SL5 9QB

ELIBANK, Master of; Hon Robert Francis Alan Erskine-Murray; s and h of 14 Lord Elibank, *qv*; *b* 10 Oct 1964; *Educ* Harrow, Reading Univ (BA); *m* 20 Jan 1996, Antonia S W, yr da of Roger Carrington, of Rockbourne, Hants; *Recreations* soccer, tennis; *Style*— The Master of Elibank; ✉ 50 Reporton Road, Fulham, London SW6 7JR

ELIOT, Lord; Jago Nicholas Aldo Eliot; s and h of 10 Earl of St Germans, *qv*; *b* 24 March 1966; *Educ* Millfield; *Style*— Lord Eliot; ✉ Port Eliot, St Germans, Cornwall

ELIOTT OF STOBS, Sir Charles Joseph Alexander; 12 Bt (NS 1666), of Stobs, Roxburghshire; Chief of the Clan Elliott or Elliot; s of late Charles Rawdon Heathfield Eliott (himself s of half-bro of Sir Arthur Eliott of Stobs, 9 Bt), and Emma Elizabeth, *née* Harris; suc half second cousin, Sir Arthur Francis Augustus Boswell Eliott of Stobs, 11 Bt (d 1989); *b* 9 Jan 1937; *Educ* St Joseph's Christian Bros Rockhampton nr Brisbane; *m* 1959, Wendy Judith, da of Henry John Bailey, of Toowoomba, Queensland; 1 s (Rodney Gilbert Charles b 1966) and 1 s decd (Stephen John), 4 da (Elizabeth (Mrs Armanasco) b 1960, Jenny (Mrs Land) b 1961, Josephine (Mrs Grofski) b 1963, Clare Melinda b 1973); *Heir* s, Rodney Gilbert Charles Eliott b 1966; *Career* builder (C J & W J Eliott); *Style*— Sir Charles Eliott of Stobs, Bt; ✉ 27 Cohoe St, Toowoomba, Qld 4350, Australia (☎ 00 61 76 327390)

ELIS-THOMAS, Baron (Life Peer UK 1992), of Nant Conwy in the County of Gwynedd; Dafydd Elis Elis-Thomas; *b* 18 Oct 1946; *Educ* Ysgol Dyffryn Conwy, Univ Coll of North Wales; *m* 1, 1970, Elen M Williams; 3 s; m 2, 29 Dec 1993, Mair Parry Jones; *Career* tutor in Welsh studies Coleg Harlech 1971, subsequently taught at Univ Coll of N Wales Bangor, Aberystwyth, Cardiff and at the Open Univ; memb TGWU; Parly candidate (Plaid Cymru) Conway 1970; MP (Plaid Cymru): Merioneth Feb 1974–83, Meirionnydd Nant Conwy 1983–92; Plaid spokesman on: Educn and Social Policy 1975, Agric and Rural Devpt 1974; pres Plaid Cymru 1984–91 (vice pres 1979–81); memb Parly Select Ctee on Educn, Science and Arts 1979–83, served as memb of various other select ctees and standing ctees of House of Commons; hon sec: All Pty Mental Health Gp, Mind, Inst for Workers Control and Shelter; former broadcaster and prog presenter BBC Wales, HTV, S4C and Radio Wales; conslt to S4C, Welsh Devpt Agency, Rural Initiative Prog, Assembly of Euro Regions and Govt of Catalonia 1992–; memb Welsh Arts Cncl, chm Screen Wales, first chm Welsh Language Bd 1993–; *Style*— The Rt Hon Lord Elis-Thomas; ✉ Welsh Language Board, Market Chambers, 5–7 St Mary Street, Cardiff CF1 2AT (☎ 01222 224744, fax 01222 224577)

ELKAN, Prof Walter; s of Hans Septimus Elkan (d 1933), of Hamburg, and Maud Emily, *née* Barden (d 1957); *b* 1 March 1923; *Educ* Frensham Heights, LSE (BSc, PhD); *m* 28 Dec 1946 (m dis 1981), Susan Dorothea, da of Emanuel Jacobs (d 1965); 1 s (David b 1952), 2 da (Ruth b 1954, Jenny b 1955); *Career* served Pioneer Corps and RA 1942–47; sr res fell Makerere Inst Social Res Uganda 1953–60, lectr Univ of Durham 1960 (prof of econs 1965–79), visiting res prof Univ of Nairobi 1972–73, prof of econs Brunel Univ 1979–88 (emeritus prof 1988–); formerly: pres African Studies Assoc, memb Northern Econ Planning Cncl, memb Bd School of Hygiene and Tropical Med, Cncl Overseas Devpt Inst, Econ and Social Ctee for Overseas Res; currently memb Cncl Royal Econ Soc; *Books* An African Labour Force (1959), Economic Development of Uganda (1961), Migrants and Proletarians (1961), Introduction to Development Economics (1973 and 1995); *Recreations* music, art; *Style*— Prof Walter Elkan; ✉ 98 Boundary Rd, London NW8 0RH (☎ 0171 624 5102); Brunel University, Department of Economics, Uxbridge, Middx (☎ 01895 274000)

ELKELES, Dr Robert Samuel; s of Dr Arthur Elkeles (d 1978), of London, and Margaret, *née* Stein (d 1970); *b* 1 June 1942; *Educ* Highgate Sch, Middx Hosp Med Sch London (Ken Clifford scholar, Boldero scholar in med, MB BS, LRCP, FRCP, MD); *m* Jan 1971, Arran, *née* Miller; 1 s (Daniel Alexander b 4 May 1973), 1 da (Jennifer Margaret b 17 March 1976); *Career* house surgn in gen surgery Chase Farm Hosp Enfield 1965; house physician: Middx then Brompton Hosp 1966, Hammersmith Hosp 1967; asst to Sir George Pickering Radcliffe Infirmary Oxford 1967–68, registrar in endocrinology Hammersmith Hosp 1968–70, lectr in med Univ Hosp of Wales 1973–74 (registrar 1970–72), conslt physician Northwick Park Hosp and Clinical Res Centre Harrow 1974–78, conslt physician and sr lectr in med St Mary's Hosp Med Sch London 1978–, physician King Edward VII Hosp for Offrs London; chm Div of Med Paddington & N Kensington Health Dist 1982–85, chm NW Thames Regnl Physicians in Diabetes and Endocrinology 1990–; Br Diabetic Assoc: past memb Professional Advsy Ctee, chm Nutrition Sub-Ctee, memb Med and Scientific Assoc Ctee 1992–95; memb Ctee Br Hyperlipidaemia Assoc 1993–96; *Books* Biochemical Aspects of Human Disease (with A S Tavill, Blackwell Scientific Publications, 1983); *Recreations* tennis, cycling, sailing, walking; *Style*— Dr Robert Elkeles; ✉ 11 Askew Road, Moor Park, Northwood, Middx HA6 2JE (☎ 01923 827341); St Mary's Hosp, Praed Street, London W2 1NY (☎ 0171 725 6037)

ELKERTON, Iain Geoffrey William; s of William Harrison Elkerton (d 1963), and Elizabeth Hughes, *née* Smith; *b* 4 Jan 1942; *Educ* Merchant Taylors', Bournemouth GS; *m* 18 Oct 1969, Gretchen, da of Peter Tandy; 3 da (Lucy b 15 July 1971, Sophie b 2 March 1973, Chloe b 5 March 1976); *Career* articled clerk Chalmers Impey 1962–67; Touche Ross (now Deloitte & Touche): joined 1967, ptnr 1975–, currently audit ptnr specialising in insur and banking; ACA 1967; *Recreations* golf, travel; *Style*— Iain Elkerton, Esq; ✉ Deloitte & Touche, Stonecutter Court, 1 Stonecutter Street, London EC4A 4TR (☎ 0171 936 3000, fax 0171 583 1198)

ELKIN, Alexander; CMG (1976); o s of Boris Elkin (d 1972), and Anna Elkin (d 1973); *b* 2 Aug 1909, St Petersburg; *Educ* Grunewald Gymnasium and Russian Academic Sch Berlin, Univs of Berlin, Kiel and London (DJur, LLM); *m* 1937, Muriel, da of Edwin M Solomons (d 1964), of Dublin; *Career* wartime Govt Serv 1942–45 (BBC Monitoring Serv 1939–42); called to the Bar Middle Temple 1937, assoc chief Legal Serv UN Interim Secretariat 1945–46, asst dir UN Euro Office Geneva 1946–48, legal advsr to UNSCOB Salonica 1948, dep legal advsr and later legal advsr OEEC (OECD 1960–) 1949–61, UNECA legal conslt formation of African Devpt Bank 1962–64, acting gen counsel of ADB 1964–65, special advsr on Euro Communities Law FCO 1970–79; legal consultancies for: WHO 1948, IBRD 1966, UNDP 1967–68, W African Regnl Gp 1968, OECD 1975; lectured on Euro Payments System and OECD: Univ of the Saar 1957–60, Univ Inst of Euro Studies Turin 1957–65; lectr on drafting of treaties UNITAR Seminars The Hague, Geneva and NY for legal advsrs and diplomats 1967–84; lectr in language and law: Univ of Bradford 1979–83, Univ of Bath 1979–95; hon visiting prof Univ of Bradford 1982–84; memb RIIA; Ford Fndn Leadership Grant 1960; Hon Doctorate in Law Univ of Bath 1990; *Books* contrib: European Yearbook, Journal du Droit International, Revue Générale du Droit International Public, Survey of Int Affairs 1939–46, Travaux Pratiques de L'Institut de Droit Comparé de la Faculté de Droit de Paris; *Recreations* reading, visiting art collections, travel; *Clubs* Travellers; *Style*— Alexander Elkin, Esq, CMG; ✉ 70 Apsley House, Finchley Road, St John's Wood, London NW8 0NZ (☎ 0171 483 2475)

ELKIN, Sonia Irene Linda; OBE (1981, MBE 1966); da of Godfrey Albert Elkin (d 1947), and Irene Jessamine Archibald (d 1968); *b* 15 May 1932; *Educ* Beresford House Sch Eastbourne; *Career* overseas sec Assoc of Br C of C 1956, Overseas Dept Lloyds Bank 1966; CBI: head W Euro Dept 1967, head Regnl and Small Firms Dept 1972 (dep dir 1973), dir for Smaller Firms 1979–83, dir Regnl Orgn 1983, dir Regions & Smaller Firms 1985–92; non-exec dir: Kall Kwik Printing (UK) Ltd 1992–95, Greggs plc 1992–; cmmr Manpower Servs Cmmn 1981–85; *Books* What About Europe? (1967, updated 1971 as What About Europe Now?); *Recreations* music; *Clubs* United Oxford & Cambridge Univ (lady associate); *Style*— Miss Sonia Elkin, OBE

ELKINGTON, Robert John; s of late John David Rew Elkington, OBE; *b* 7 Oct 1949; *Educ* Eton, Univ of Exeter (BA); *m* 1, 1974 (m dis 1983), Penelope Josephine, da of late Lt-Col Richard Ian Griffith Taylor, DSO; 1 s; m 2, 1984, Mary Patricia, da of late Maj Hon Antony John Ashley Cooper; 2 da; *Career* banker; fin dir Gerrard and National Holdings plc; *Recreations* tennis, shooting, golf; *Clubs* Boodle's; *Style*— Robert Elkington, Esq; ✉ Cranbourne Grange, Sutton Scotney, Winchester, Hants SO21 3NA (☎ 01962 760494); Gerrard and National Holdings plc, Cannon Bridge, 25 Dowgate Hill, London EC4R 2GN (direct ☎ 0171 337 2806)

ELL, Prof Peter Josef; s of Josef Ell (d 1957), of Lisbon, Portugal, and Maria Karola Ell (d 1990); *b* 7 May 1944; *Educ* Univ of Lisbon (MD), Univ of London (MSc), Univ of Bern (PD); *m* 1980, Yvonne, da of Jan Brink; 2 s (Georg Mischa b 2 March 1981, Patrick Sascha b 8 Dec 1983); *Career* conslt physician Landes Unfallkrankenhaus Feldkirch 1974–76, conslt physician i/c nuclear med Middlesex Hosp 1976–, dir Inst of Nuclear Med Univ Coll Med Sch London 1986–, prof of nuclear med and established chair Univ of London 1987–; dep dir Inst of Nuclear Med 1984–, hon conslt physician Middlesex Hosp 1976–; visiting prof: Univ of Saskatchewan 1982, Kuwait 1983, Islamabad 1983, Cairo 1984, Univ of Lisbon 1986; UK del: Euro Nuclear Med Soc 1981–82, World Fedn of Nuclear Med and Biology 1984, 1988 and 1990; annual prize Soc of Med Sciences Portugal 1976, annual prize Soc of Medical Sciences Vorarlberg Austria 1979, first and third prize for best scientific oral presentation Br Nuclear Med Soc 1990; pres Euro Assoc of Nuclear Med 1994–; corresponding memb: Finnish Soc of Nuclear Med 1984, Swiss Soc of Nuclear Med 1993; fndr memb Euro Assoc of Nuclear Med 1985 (sec

1987–91 and 1991–93); Freeman City of Montpellier 1991; memb: American Soc of Nuclear Med 1974, Br Nuclear Med Soc 1974 (memb Cncl 1991–93, sec 1992–94), Br Inst of Radiology 1974 (memb Cncl 1984–87), NY Acad of Sciences 1976, Hosp Physicists Assoc 1977, RSM 1978, Br Cardiac Soc 1983, Assoc of Physicians of Great Br and Ireland 1994; FRCR 1984, FRCP 1990 (MRCP 1984); *Recreations* the study of languages, the arts in general, photography and cinema; *Style*— Prof Peter Ell; ✉ Institute of Nuclear Medicine, University College and Middlesex School of Medicine, Mortimer Street, London W1N 8AA (☎ 0171 631 1066, fax 0171 436 0603)

ELLARD, John Francis; s of (John) Edward Ellard, of Sidbury, Devon, and Marie, *née* Topping; *b* 5 April 1953; *Educ* John Fisher Sch Purley Surrey, King's Sch Chester, Trinity Hall Cambridge (MA); *m* 4 April 1987, Nicola Marigo, da of John David Pugh (d 1973); 2 s ((John) David b 12 Sept 1988, Robert Edward b 8 May 1990), 2 da (Caroline Francesca b 13 June 1992, (Sarah) Jane b 26 Dec 1993); *Career* admitted slr 1977; Linklaters & Paines: articled clerk 1975–77, asst slr 1977–83, ptnr 1983–, resident ptnr NY office 1986–89; memb Law Soc; *Recreations* music, reading, mountain walking, photography; *Clubs* Oxford & Cambridge; *Style*— John Ellard, Esq; ✉ 38 Shawfield St, London SW3 4BD; Linklaters & Paines, Barrington House, 59/67 Gresham St, London EC2V 7JA (☎ 0171 606 7080, fax 0171 606 5113, telex 884349/888167)

ELLEN, Eric Frank; QPM (1980); s of Robert Frank Ellen (d 1969), and Jane Lydia Ellen (d 1982); *b* 30 Aug 1930; *Educ* Univ of London (LLB); *m* 1949, Gwendoline Dorothy, da of John Thomas Perkins (d 1937); 1 s (Stephen), 1 da (Susan); *Career* Nat Serv; joined Port of London Police 1950, chief constable 1975, ret 1980; first dir ICC: Int Maritime Bureau 1981–, Counterfeiting Intelligence Bureau 1985–, Commercial Crime Bureau 1992–; chief exec ICC Commercial Crime Services (incorporating IMB, CIB and CCB) 1990–; conslt Commmercial Crime Unit, special advsr Int Assoc of Ports and Harbours on port security matters and maritime crime, pres Int Assoc of Airport and Seaport Police 1977–79, chm Euro Assoc of Airport and Seaport Police 1975–78 (now life memb, exec sec 1980–88); chm: Electronic Intelligence Ltd 1985–86, PEBs 1985, ICC Commercial Crime Services, Task Force on Commercial Crime 1996; memb: Hon Soc of the Middle Temple, Br Acad of Forensic Sciences, Ctee of Cons Lawyers examining Maritime Fraud, Inst of Shipbrokers Ctee on Maritime Fraud; presented or chaired seminars on int commercial fraud and product counterfeiting in over 50 countries, advised Barbados Govt on formation of a new police force for the Barbados Port Authy 1983, reviewed security at ports of Jeddah and Dammam in Saudi Arabia, chm Cambridge Symposia on Commercial Crime 1985–; frequent TV and radio appearances on the subject of marine fraud, terrorism, piracy and product counterfeiting; Freeman City of London; Police Long Serv and Good Conduct medal 1 class 1973, Repub of China Police medal 1 class 1979; CIMgt; *Books* International Maritime Fraud (co-author), Air and Seaport Security International Reference Book (conslt ed, 1987–89), Violence at Sea (ed, 1987), Piracy at Sea (ed, 1989), Ports at Risk (ed, 1994), published many articles on varied subjects including specialist policemen, marine sabotage, piracy and terrorism, product counterfeiting and fraud; *Recreations* golf; *Clubs* Wig and Pen; *Style*— Eric Ellen, Esq, QPM; ✉ International Maritime Bureau, Maritime House, 1 Linton Road, Barking, Essex IG11 8HG (☎ 0181 591 3000)

ELLEN, Susan Caroline; da of Albert John Davies, and Winifred ivy Caroline, *née* Emberton; *b* 14 Dec 1948; *Educ* Cardiff HS for Girls, Malvern Girls' Coll, Univ of Bristol (BSc); *m* 2 March 1974, Simon Tudor Ellen, s of Wing Cdr R A G Ellen, Rtd, OBE; 2 da (Katie Louise b 14 Feb 1980, Joanna Caroline b 14 April 1982); *Career* planning Westminster Hospital 1970–74, secondment to Kensington and Chelsea and Westminster Health Authy 1974–75, service planner Westminster and Chelsea Health Authy 1975–77; BUPA Hosps: exec dir 1977–80, devpt dir 1980–82, op dir 1982–87; BUPA Health Services: business devpt dir 1987–90, md 1990–95; govr BUPA 1990–95; md United Racecourses (Holdings) Ltd 1996–; non-exec dir Asda Group PLC 1992–; dep chm Independent Health Care Assoc 1990–95; memb: Fin Review Panel 1992–, Fin Reporting Cncl; MHSM 1972; *Recreations* national hunt racing, theatre, opera; *Style*— Mrs Susan Ellen; ✉ 47 Ennerdale Road, Kew, Richmond, Surrey TW9 2DN (☎ 0181 948 0858, fax 0181 332 6928); United Racecourses (Holdings) Ltd, Sandown Park Racecourse, Esher, Surrey KT10 8AJ (☎ 01372 463072)

ELLENBOROUGH, 8 Baron (UK 1802); Richard Edward Cecil Law; s of 7 Baron (d 1945); *b* 14 Jan 1926; *Educ* Eton, Magdalene Coll Cambridge; *m* 1, 9 Oct 1953, Rachel Mary (d 1986), da of late Maj Ivor Mathews Hedley, 17 Lancers; 3 s; m 2, 12 March 1994, Mrs Frances Kimberley; *Heir* s, Hon Rupert Law, *qv*; *Career* sits as Conservative Peer in House of Lords; former stockbroker, ptnr Parker McAnally Montgomery 1969–78, pres Nat Union of Rate Payers 1960–90; currently dir Towry Law & Co; Liveryman Worshipful Co of Gardeners; *Style*— The Rt Hon Lord Ellenborough; ✉ Withypool House, Observatory Close, Church Rd, Crowborough, East Sussex TN6 1BN (☎ 01892 663139)

ELLERAY, Anthony John; QC (1993); s of late Alexander John Elleray, of Waddington, Clitheroe, Lancs, and Sheila Mary, *née* Perkins; *b* 19 Aug 1954; *Educ* Bishop's Stortford Coll, Trinity Coll Cambridge (MA); *m* 17 July 1982, Alison Elizabeth, da of William Goring Potter, DFC, of Bollington, Cheshire; 1 s (Adam b 22 Sept 1989), 1 da (Harriet b 29 Aug 1985); *Career* called to the Bar Inner Temple 1977, barr Chancery Div Northern Circuit; memb: Chancery Bar Assoc, Northern Chancery Bar Assoc; *Recreations* bridge, theatre, pictures, wine; *Clubs* Manchester Tennis and Racquets; *Style*— Anthony Elleray, Esq, QC; ✉ St James' Chambers, 68 Quay St, Manchester M3 3EL (☎ 0161 834 7000, fax 0161 834 2341)

ELLERTON, Sir Geoffrey James; kt (1992), CMG (1963), MBE (1956); er s of Sir (Frederick) Cecil Ellerton (d 1962), and Dorothy Catherine, *née* Green (d 1991); *b* 25 April 1920; *Educ* Highgate Sch, Hertford Coll Oxford; *m* 1946, Peggy Eleanor, da of Frederick George Watson (d 1954); 3 s; *Career* Colonial Admin Serv Kenya 1945–63, sec to Cmmns on Mgmnt and Staffing in Local Govt 1964, chm Elder Dempster Lines 1972–74, exec dir Ocean Transport and Trading Ltd 1972–80, chm Electra Group Services 1980–83, dir Globe Investment Trust 1982–86, chm Local Govt Boundary Cmmn for England 1983–92; tstee Hakluyt Soc 1994– (hon treas 1986–94); chm Royal Over-Seas League 1995–; *Recreations* books and music; *Clubs* MCC, Brooks's; *Style*— Sir Geoffrey Ellerton, CMG, MBE; ✉ Briar Hill House, Broad Campden, Chipping Campden, Glos GL55 6XB (☎ 01386 841003)

ELLERY, Nina; *née* Petrova; da of Alexander Petrov (d 1968), of London, and Lubov Georgivna, *née* Nicholaeva (d 1978); *b* 9 June 1913; *Educ* St Dunstan's Abbey Rd Sch, Plymouth Sch, Carlyle Sch; *m* 31 July 1937, Maj (John) Edgar (Eggi) Ellery, s of James Ellery, OBE (d 1953); *Career* author (writes under name of Nina Petrova); recent broadcaster for BBC Overseas Serv; sec BRCS, memb Ctee Russian Refugee Relief Assoc (helped after war), sec local Leasehold Assoc 1970–71; memb Soc of Authors; *Books* Russian Cookery (1968), Best of Russian Cookery (1978); contrib Taste Magazine; *Recreations* reading, making clothes, garden; *Clubs* Britain-Russia Centre; *Style*— Mrs Edgar Ellery; ✉ 106 Edith Rd, London W14 9AP (☎ 0171 603 5106)

ELLES, Baroness (Life Peeress UK 1972), of the City of Westminster; Diana Louie Elles; da of Col Stewart Francis Newcombe, DSO (d 1956), and Elizabeth Chaki; *b* 19 July 1921; *Educ* Univ of London (BA); *m* 1945, Neil Patrick Moncrieff Elles, s of Edmund Hardie Elles, OBE; 1 s ((Hon) James Edmund Moncrieff Elles, MEP, *qv* b 1949), 1 da (Hon (Elizabeth) Rosamund (Hon Mrs Lockhart-Mummery) b 1947); *Career* Flight Offr WAAF 1942–45; called to the Bar 1956; memb Care Ctee Kennington 1956–72; UK delegate UN 1972, MEP 1973–75, memb UN Sub-Cmmn on Discrimination and Minorities 1974–75, oppn front bench spokesman on foreign and Euro affairs 1975–79, chm Cons Party Int Office 1973–78, MEP (EDG) Thames Valley 1979–89, vice pres European Parl 1982–87, chm Legal Affairs Ctee 1987–89; House of Lords: memb Euro Communities Select Ctee 1989–94, chm Sub-Ctee Law and Institutions 1992 (memb 1995); chm of Govrs Br Inst of Florence 1994–; Hon Bencher Lincoln's Inn 1993; *Style*— The Baroness Elles; ✉ 75 Ashley Gardens, London SW1 (☎ 0171 828 0175, fax 0171 931 0046)

ELLES, (Hon) James Edmund Moncrieff; MEP (EPP) Buckinghamshire and Oxfordshire East (majority 30,665); s of Neil Elles, of London, and Baroness Elles, *qv*; *b* 3 Sept 1949; *Educ* Eton, Univ of Edinburgh; *m* 1977, Françoise, da of François Le Bail; 1 s (Nicholas b 22 Aug 1982), 1 da (Victoria b 27 July 1980); *Career* admin external rels EC 1977–80, asst to Dep DG of Agric EC 1980–84; MEP (EPP): Oxford and Bucks 1984–94, Bucks and Oxon E 1994–; Euro Parl: memb Budget Ctee (EPP budgetary affairs spokesman), sub-memb Institutional Affairs Ctee, formerly sub-memb Foreign Affairs and Security Ctee, memb Delgn for Rels with US; co-fndr and patron Thames Action and Resource Gp for Educn and Trg (TARGET), fndr chm Transatlantic Policy Network (TPN); *Recreations* music, skiing, golf; *Clubs* Royal and Ancient Golf (St Andrews), Carlton; *Style*— James Elles, Esq, MEP; ✉ c/o Conservative Centre, 100 Walton Street, Aylesbury, Bucks HP21 7QP (☎ 01296 82102); 97–113 Rue Belliard, 1040 Bruxelles (☎ 00 32 2 84 59 51, fax 00 32 2 84 99 51)

ELLETSON, Harold Daniel Hope; MP (C) Blackpool North (majority 3,040); s of late Daniel Elletson, and Coral, *née* Peake-Cottam; *b* 8 Dec 1960; *Educ* Eton, Univ of Exeter, Univ of Voronezh USSR, Poly of Central London, Univ of Bradford; *m* 20 June 1987, Fiona Margaret, *née* Ferguson; 1 s; *Career* journalist and political researcher 1983–88, business devpt mangr (Russia) Illingworth Morris plc 1988–90, business conslt to cos trading in CIS and Eastern Europe 1990–, PR dir CBI Initiative 1992; Parly candidate (C) Burnley 1987, MP (C) Blackpool N 1992–; memb Select Ctee on Environment 1993–, sec Cons Backbench Ctee on Tourism, vice chm Future of Europe Tst; chm Exeter Univ Cons Assoc 1980–81, cncllr Lancs CC 1984–88; *Recreations* fell walking, opera, languages (fluent Russian speaker), agriculture; *Clubs* Carlton, Bispham Conservative, Wainwright Conservative; *Style*— Harold Elletson, Esq, MP; ✉ House of Commons, London SW1A 0AA

ELLICOCK, John Henry; *b* 17 June 1946; *Educ* Univ of Cambridge (MA), Univ of Loughborough (MSc); *m* Wendy; 1 s (Michael), 1 da (Clare); *Career* memb Bd Burmah Castrol plc 1987– (currently dir Lubricants Europe); Sword of Hon Sandhurst 1967; *Style*— John Ellicock, Esq; ✉ Burmah Castrol plc, Burmah Castrol House, Pipers Way, Swindon, Wilts SN3 1RE (☎ 01793 452231)

ELLINGTON, Marc Floyd; DL (Aberdeenshire 1984); Baron of Towie Barclay (Feudal Barony), Laird of Gardenstown and Crovie; s of Homer Frank Ellington (d 1984), of Memsie, Aberdeenshire, and Vancouver, and Harriette Hannah Kellas; *b* 16 Dec 1945; *m* 21 Dec 1967, Karen Leigh, da of Capt Warren Sydney Streater; 2 da (Iona Angeline Barclay of Gardenstown b 1979, Kirstie Naomi Barclay b 1983); *Career* memb: Nat Ctee Architectural Heritage Soc of Scotland, Historic Houses Assoc; vice pres Buchan Heritage Soc, tstee Scottish Historic Buildings Tst, chm Heritage Press (Scot); dir: Grampian Enterprise Ltd, Aberdeen Univ Research Ltd, Gardenstown Estates Ltd, Soundcraft Audio Guides, Grampian Highlands & Aberdeen Tourism Marketing Co; ptnr Heritage Sound Recordings; Saltire Award 1973, Civic Tst Award 1975, Euro Architectural Heritage Award 1975; contrib various architectural and historical jls and periodicals, composer and recording artiste, communications conslt, prodr of documentary films and TV progs; chm Grampian Region Tourism Task Force; memb: Br Heritage Ctee, Performing Rights Soc, Historic Building Cncl for Scotland 1980–, Convention of Baronage of Scotland; patron Banffshire Wildlife Rehabilitation Tst; serving brother Order of St John; FSA; *Recreations* sailing, historic architecture, art collecting, music; *Style*— Marc Ellington of Towie Barclay, DL; ✉ Towie Barclay Castle, Auchterless, Turriff, Aberdeenshire AB53 8EP (☎ 01888 511347)

ELLINGTON, Paul Robert; *b* 2 Aug 1937; *Educ* Dauntsey's Sch, Coll of Law; *m* 30 March 1960, Mireille; 2 s (James, Francis), 1 da (Nicole); *Career* slr, corp law and project fin and licensed insolvency practitioner; articled clerk: T Weldon Thomson & Co 1958–61, Marcan & Dean 1961–63; Clifford-Turner 1963–65, Allen & Overy 1965–68, ptnr McKenna & Co 1970– (slr 1968–70); memb: CBI Co Law Working Gp, Law Soc (assessor Post Qualification Casework Ctee), Int Bar Assoc Ctee on Insolvency and Creditors' Rights; chm Int Bar Assoc Ctee on Pubns and New Devpts; Freeman Worshipful Co of Slrs; *Recreations* reading, singing, theatre, concerts, walking; *Style*— Paul Ellington, Esq; ✉ McKenna & Co, Mitre House, 160 Aldesgate St, London EC1A 4DD (☎ 0171 606 9000, fax 0171 606 9100)

ELLIOT, Alan Christopher; s of Ian Frederick Lettsom Elliot (d 1981), of 142 Pavilion Rd, London, and Madeline Adelaide Mary, *née* Maclachlan (d 1977); *b* 9 March 1937; *Educ* Rugby, ChCh Oxford (MA); *m* 20 Jan 1967, Tara Louise Winifred, da of Sir Thomas Brian Weldon, 8 Bt (d 1979), and Countess Cathcart, of Moor Hatches, W Amesbury, Wilts; 1 s (Dominic b 1975), 3 da (Sacha b 1968, Larissa b 1970, Natalya b 1978); *Career* Nat Serv 1958–60: 2 Lt Welsh Guards cmmnd 1959, sr under offr Mons Offr Cadet Sch; PA to MD Metropole Industries 1960, md Dufay Ltd 1963 (dir 1962), chm Blick Time Recorders 1971– (organised mgmnt buyout from Dufay Ltd 1966), chm Blick plc 1986–, dir Foreign and Colonial High Income Trust plc 1993–; *Recreations* shooting, fishing, bridge, skiing; *Clubs* White's, Portland; *Style*— Alan Elliot, Esq; ✉ The Old Rectory, Chilton Foliat, Hungerford, Berks RG17 0TF (☎ 01488 682423, fax 01488 681139); 142 Pavilion Road, London SW1 (☎ 0171 235 3382); Blick plc, Bramble Rd, Swindon, Wilts (☎ 01793 692 401, fax 01793 618147, car 0831 171387, telex 44332)

ELLIOT, Sir Gerald Henry; kt (1986); s of Surgn Capt John Stephen Elliot, RN (d 1972), and Magda Virginia, *née* Salvesen (d 1985); *b* 24 Dec 1923; *Educ* Marlborough, New Coll Oxford (MA); *m* 1950, Margaret Ruth, da of Rev John Stephen Whale; 2 s, 1 da; *Career* served Indian Army 1942–46, Capt; consul for Finland in Edinburgh and Leith 1957–89, sec and chm Scottish Branch Royal Inst of Int Affrs 1963–77; chm: Forth Ports Authy 1973–79, Scottish Arts Cncl 1980–86, Christian Salvesen plc 1981–88 (dep chm and md 1973–81), Scottish Provident Instn 1983–89, Scottish Unit Managers Ltd 1984–88, Biotal 1987–90; memb Ct Univ of Edinburgh 1984–93; chm: Tstees David Hume Inst 1985–95, Prince's Scottish Youth Business Tst 1987–94, Scottish Opera 1987–92, Martin Currie Unit Trusts 1988–90, IOD (Scottish Div) 1989–92; pres: Univ of Edinburgh Devpt Tst 1990–94, Norwegian Scottish Assoc 1990–; vice chm Scottish Business in the Community 1986–89, tstee Nat Museums of Scotland 1987–91, vice pres RSE 1988–91, memb Ct of Regents Royal Coll of Surgns 1990–, pres UN 50 Scotland 1993–96, tstee Edinburgh Festival Theatre 1995–; Hon DUniv Edinburgh 1989, Hon LLD Univ of Aberdeen 1991; Knight First Class of the Order of the White Rose of Finland 1975; FRSE 1977; *Style*— Sir Gerald Elliot, FRSE; ✉ 8 Howe St, Edinburgh EH3 6TD

ELLIOT, Graeme Arthur; s of Ian Frederick Lettsom Elliot (d 1981), and Madeleine Adelaide Mary, *née* Maclachlan (d 1977); *b* 28 Aug 1942; *Educ* Rugby, Magdalene Coll Cambridge (MA); *m* 1, 1966, Hermione, da of Lt-Col John Delano-Osborne, of Hants; 2 da (Alexandra b 1968, Victoria b 1971); m 2, 1983, Nicola Nella Simpson, da of Keith Alexander Taylor, of Queensland; *Career* RTZ Corporation plc 1968–85, exec vice chm Slough Estates plc 1986–92; dir: Candover Investments plc 1988–94, Thames Valley

Enterprise Ltd 1990–92, Southern Regnl Advsy Bd National Westminster Bank plc 1991–92, The William Hill Group Ltd 1992–, Automated Securities (Holdings) plc 1993–96, American Endeavour Fund Ltd 1993–, Automotive Precision Holdings plc 1994–, Speciality Shops plc 1994–, NSM plc 1994–, Euro Sales Finance plc 1995–, Primary Health Properties PLC 1996–; advsy dir Samuel Montagu & Co Ltd 1994–; FCA; *Recreations* bridge, golf, tennis, skiing; *Clubs* White's, Queen's, Berks Golf, Royal Melbourne Golf, Sotogrande Golf; *Style*— Graeme A Elliot, Esq; ✉ Garden Flat, 1 Peterborough Villas, London SW6 2AT (☎ 0171 731 4870)

ELLIOT, Prof Harry; CBE (1975); s of Thomas Elliot (d 1961), of Mealsgate, Cumbria, and Hannah Elizabeth, *née* Littleton (d 1928); *b* 28 June 1920; *Educ* Allhallows Sch, Nelson Sch, Univ of Manchester (BSc, MSc, PhD); *m* 27 May 1943, Betty, da of Henry Leyman (d 1974), of Doddiscombsleigh, Devon; 1 s (Brian b 1944), 1 da (Jean b 1948); *Career* WWII 1941–46; PO Tech (SIGS) RAFVR, served Coastal Cmd incl liaison duties with USAAF and USN, demob Flt Lt 1946; lectr in physics Univ of Manchester 1948–53; Imperial Coll: sr lectr 1953–60, prof 1960–80, sr res fell 1981–90, emeritus prof; Holweck prize and medal Inst of Physics and French Physical Soc; author of numerous papers and articles in learned jls; ARCS Imperial Coll 1961; memb SRC; chm: Astronomy Space and Radio Bd 1971–77, Cncl Royal Soc 1978, various ctees Euro Space Agency; FRS 1973, FWAAS 1983, FRAS 1984; *Recreations* painting, gardening, military history; *Style*— Prof Harry Elliot, CBE, FRS; ✉ Broadwater Down, Tunbridge Wells TN2 5PE

ELLIOT, Virginia Helen Antoinette; MBE (1986); da of Col Ronald Morris Holgate (d 1980), and Heather Alice Mary, *née* Rice; *b* 1 Feb 1955; *Educ* abroad, Bedgebury Park Goudhurst Kent; *m* 1, 7 Dec 1985 (m dis 1989), Hamish Peter Leng, s of Gen Sir Peter John Hall Leng, KCB, MBE, MC, *qv*; m 2, 1 Oct 1993, Michael T Elliot, son of John Kerr Elliot, MC, of Park Street, Woodstock, Oxon; *Career* equestrian; Three Day Event wins incl: Jr Euro Champion 1974, Mini Olympics 1975, Euro Championships (team Gold) 1981, World Championships (team Gold) 1982, Euro Championships (team Silver) 1983, Olympic Games (team Silver) 1984, Euro Championships (team Gold) 1985, World Championships (team Gold) 1986, Olympic Games (team Silver) 1988; winner Burghley 1983, 1984, 1985, 1986 and 1989 (Euro Championship, horse Master Craftsman); winner Badminton 1985, 1989 (horse Master Craftsman) and 1993; individual Euro champion 1985, 1987 and 1989; World champion 1986; Olympics (individual Bronze 1984 and 1988); dir P and N Co; involved in Riding for the Disabled; Hon Freeman (Loriners) Worshipful Co of Saddlers 1990; *Novels* for children (Harper Collins): Winning (1994), Race Against Time (1995), The Final Hurdle (1996); *Recreations* skiing, sunning, sightseeing; *Style*— Mrs Michael Elliot, MBE; ✉ Holliers House, Middle Barton, Oxon OX5 3QH (☎ 01869 340453)

ELLIOT-MURRAY-KYNYNMOUND, Hon *see:* Minto, 6 Earl of

ELLIOTT, (Frank) Alan; CB; s of Frank Elliott, and Doreen, *née* Allen; *b* 28 March 1937; *Educ* Royal Belfast Academical Inst, Trinity Coll Dublin (BA); *m* 1964, Olive Lucy, *née* O'Brien; 1 s, 2 da; *Career* NI Civil Serv 1959–66; Miny of Health: princ 1966–71, asst sec 1971–75; DHSS: sr asst sec 1975–81, under sec 1981–87, perm sec 1987–; govr Sullivan Upper Sch 1982–; *Recreations* the arts, music, motoring; *Style*— Alan Elliott, Esq, CB; ✉ Department of Health and Social Services, Dundonald House, Upper Newtownards Road, Belfast BT4 3SF (☎ 01232 524790)

ELLIOTT, Chief Constable Alan George; QPM (1994); s of George Arthur Elliott (d 1942), and Eileen Jesse, *née* Pontin (d 1985); *b* 14 March 1942; *Educ* Redland Hill House Sch Bristol; *m* 15 June 1963, Eileen Elizabeth; 1 s (Clive b 24 June 1966); *Career* Avon & Somerset Constabulary: joined Bristol Constabulary 1963, various positions rising to rank of detective chief supt and head of CID; Sr Cmd Course Bramshill 1986; asst chief constable W Midlands Police 1986–88, dep chief constable Wiltshire Constabulary 1988–91, chief constable Cumbria Constabulary 1991–; memb ACPO 1986; CIMgt 1994, OStJ 1994; *Recreations* country walking, sport as a spectator, reading; *Style*— Chief Constable Alan G Elliott, QPM; ✉ Police Headquarters, Carleton Hall, Penrith, Cumbria CA10 2AU (☎ 01768 891999)

ELLIOTT, Prof Alexander Thomas; *b* 1 Feb 1949; *Educ* Trinity Acad Edinburgh, Univ of Stirling (BA), Univ of Glasgow (PhD, DSc); *m* Barbara, *née* Idle; 2 da (Fiona b 6 Jan 1979, Elspeth b 1 July 1980); *Career* temporary lectr Nuclear Med Unit Univ of Strathclyde 1974–75, lectr Dept of Nuclear Med Middlesex Hosp Med Sch and hon sr physicist Middlesex Hosp 1975–77, princ physicist Dept of Nuclear Med Bart's and hon lectr Bart's Med Coll 1977–81, top grade physicist Western Infirmary/Gartnavel General Unit, West of Scotland Health Bds, Dept of Clinical Physics and Bioengineering Univ of Glasgow 1981–90, dir West of Scotland Health Bds Dept of Clinical Physics and Bioengrg and prof of clinical physics Univ of Glasgow 1990–; chm Nat Consultative Ctee of Scientists in Med 1989– (memb 1982–); memb: Hosp Physicists' Assoc 1975 (memb Cncl 1984–86), American Soc of Nuclear Med 1978, British Nuclear Med Soc 1983 (memb Cncl 1987–90), Admin of Radioactive Substances Advsy Ctee 1988–, Editorial Bd Euro Jl of Nuclear Med 1989–, Acute Healthcare Res Ctee Scottish Office 1993–, American Soc of Nuclear Cardiology 1993; FInstP 1983 (MInstP 1978); author of over 200 papers, book chapters and presentations; *Style*— Prof Alexander Elliott; ✉ Department of Clinical Physics and Bioengineering, 22 Western Court, 100 University Place, Glasgow G12 8SQ (☎ 0141 211 2948, fax 0141 211 1772)

ELLIOTT, Ann Margaret; da of John Frederick Hildred (d 1976), and Evelyn Rose Collier; *b* 23 Feb 1945; *Educ* Shurnhold Sch Melksham (now George Ward Sch), Chippenham GS, Bath Acad of Art (Dip in Art and Design Graphics), Dept of Educn Univ of Bath (DipEd); *m* 1972, Robert Anthony Elliott; 2 s (b 1978 and 1983), 1 da (b 1980); *Career* art asst Cammell Hudson & Brownjohn Ltd (Films) 1967–68, curatorial asst Sheffield City Art Galleries 1969–72, gallery organiser Gardner Centre Gallery Univ of Sussex 1972–73, exhibition offr Fine Arts Dept Br Cncl 1973–77 and 1985–94 (temp offr 1972), head of sculpture The Hat Hill Sculpture Fndn (Sculpture at Goodwood) 1994–; pt/t res asst Aust Crafts Cncl 1977–78, advsr for S E Arts Visual Arts Bd, memb Bd Gardner Arts Centre Univ of Sussex; major projects incl: J M W Turner Exhibition (Moscow and Leningrad) 1975, Henry Moore Exhibitions (Hong Kong and Japan 1986, India 1988, Leningrad, Moscow and Helsinki 1991), Ben Nicholson Exhibitions (Madrid and Lisbon) 1987, Tony Cragg Venice Biennale 1988, Colours of the Earth (British ceramics, New Dehli, India and Malaysia) 1991–92, In Site (Oslo and as Made Strange in Budapest) 1993, Boyd and Evans Rainforest Paintings (Brunei and Singapore) 1993, Signs of the Times Paris and Sao Paulo Bienal 1994; *Recreations* art, running, King Charles Cavaliers; *Style*— Mrs Ann Elliott; ✉ Park Cottage, Wisborough Green, West Sussex RH14 0DF (☎ 01403 700211; Sculpture at Goodwood, Hat Hill Copse, Goodwood, Chichester, West Sussex PO18 0QP (☎ 01243 538449, fax 01243 531853)

ELLIOTT, Anthony Charles Raynor; s of Charles Edward Murray Elliott (d 1987), of London, and Lucy Eleanor, *née* Arthur (d 1982); *b* 28 Jan 1937; *Educ* Radley, Trinity Coll Cambridge (MA); *m* 1960, Christina, da of Capt William Theobald Hindson, RN (d 1992), of Surrey; 2 s (Nicholas Charles Raynor b 1964, Paul William Anthony b 1967); *Career* 2 Lt E Surrey Regt 1955–57; admitted slr 1963; Linklaters & Paines 1963–66; exec dir: RTZ Pillar Ltd (previously Pillar Holdings Ltd) 1966–76, S G Warburg & Co Ltd 1976–86; non exec-dir: Bridon plc, Norcros plc (dep chm); govr St Mary's Hall Brighton 1967–96 (chm 1989); *Recreations* classical music, arts, walking, wine; *Style*— Anthony Elliott, Esq

ELLIOTT, Anthony Michael Manton (Tony); s of Alan and Katherine Elliott; *b* 7 Jan 1947; *Educ* Stowe, Univ of Keele; *m* 1, Nov 1976 (m dis 1978), Janet Street-Porter, *qv*; m 2, June 1989, Jane Laetitia, *née* Coke; 3 s (Rufus George b 19 April 1988, Bruce Roland b 17 Oct 1990, Lawrence John (twin) b 17 Oct 1990); *Career* fndr and chm Time Out Group 1968–; *Recreations* travel, watching TV, cinema going, eating out with friends, newspapers and magazines, being with family in time left from working; *Style*— Tony Elliott, Esq; ✉ Time Out Group, Universal House, 251 Tottenham Court Road, London W1P 0AB (☎ 0171 813 3000, fax 0171 813 6001)

ELLIOTT, Dr Arnold; OBE (1977); *b* 27 Jan 1921; *Educ* Royal Belfast Academical Inst, Queen's Univ Belfast (MB BCh); *m* 8 June 1948, Lee; 2 s (Paul b 1955, Simon b 1957), 1 da (Louise b 1951); *Career* WWI Capt (later actg Maj) RAMC 1944–47; GP; BMA: memb 1948–, memb Gen Med Servs Ctee 1952–94, chm Practise Orgn Sub Ctee 1960–86, memb Cncl 1982–, chm Doctors and Social Work Ctee 1979–89, memb Mental Health Ctee until 1994, chm Community Care Ctee; Gen Med Cncl 1979–89: memb Exec, memb Educn Ctee, memb Health Ctee; pres Soc of Family Practitioner Ctees of England & Wales 1980; memb: Panel of Assessors Dist Nurse Trg 1972–82, Central Cncl for Educn and Trg in Social Work 1974–84, NHS Essex Exec Cncl until 1965, NHS Exec Cncl NE London 1965–74 (chm 1972–74), Redbridge and Waltham Forest Family Practitioner Ctee 1974–90 (chm 1974–77); sec Redbridge and Waltham Forest Local Med Ctee 1984–96, fndr and organiser Ilford and Dist Vocational Trg Scheme for Gen Practice 1977–87, provost NE London Faculty RCGP 1979–82; Freeman City of London 1971, Liveryman Worshipful Soc of Apothecaries 1968; FRCGP 1976, FRSM, FRSA; *Recreations* theatre, art, music; *Clubs* RSM; *Style*— Dr Arnold Elliott, OBE; ✉ 12 Ashburnham Close, London N2 0NH (☎ 0181 444 0131)

ELLIOTT, Rev Dr Charles Middleton; s of Joseph William Elliott (d 1982), and Mary Evelyn, *née* Jones (d 1958); *b* 9 Jan 1939; *Educ* Repton, Univ of Oxford (MA, DPhil); *m* 1962, Hilary Margaret, da of Harold Hambling, of Cockfosters, Barnet, Herts; 3 s (Jonathan, Francis, Giles); *Career* asst lectr (later lectr) in pure economics Univ of Nottingham 1963–65, sr res fell UN Res Inst of Social Devpt Geneva 1964–65, reader in economics and head of Dept Univ of Zambia 1965–69, asst sec and res dir Sodepax Geneva 1969–72, sr res assoc Overseas Devpt Gp Univ of E Anglia 1972–75, sr lectr in economics Sch of Devpt Studies Univ of E Anglia 1975–77, dir ODG and md ODG Co Ltd 1976–77, special advsr Parly Select Ctee on Overseas Aid and Devpt 1976–80, prof of Devpt Policy and Planning Univ of Wales 1977–82, dir Centre for Devpt Studies UC Swansea 1977–82, dir Christian Aid 1982–84, GEM Scott fell Univ of Melbourne Australia 1984–85, Benjamin Meaker prof Univ of Bristol 1985–86, prebendary of Lichfield Cathedral 1987–96, visiting prof King's Coll London 1987–88, dean Trinity Hall Cambridge 1990–; *Books* Praying the Kingdom (Collins Religious Book Prize, 1985), Comfortable Compassion (1987), Praying Through Paradox (1987), Sword and Spirit: Christianity in a Divided World (1989), Memory and Salvation (1995); *Recreations* fly-fishing, hill walking, sailing; *Style*— Rev Dr Charles Elliott; ✉ Trinity Hall, Cambridge CB2 1TJ

ELLIOTT, Sir Clive Christopher Hugh; 4 Bt (UK 1917), of Limpsfield, Surrey; s of Sir Hugh Francis Ivo Elliott, 3 Bt, OBE (d 1989), and Elizabeth Margaret, *née* Phillipson; *b* 12 Aug 1945; *Educ* Bryanston, Univ Coll Oxford (BA), Cape Town Univ (PhD); *m* 1975, Marie-Thérèse, da of Johann Rüttimann, of Hohenrain, Switzerland; 2 s (Ivo Antony Moritz b 1978, Nicolas Johann Clive b 1980); *Heir* s, Ivo Antony Moritz Elliott b 1978; *Career* ornithologist and international civil servant; research offr Cape Town Univ 1968–75; FAO/UN Regnl Quelea Project Tchad/Tanzania 1975–81; FAO project mangr: Arusha Tanzania 1982–86, Nairobi Kenya 1986–89; country projects offr AGO FAO Headquarters Rome 1989–95, sr migratory pest offr 1995–; *Books* Quelea Quelea - Africa's Bird Pest (ed with R L Bruggers, 1989); *Recreations* tennis; *Style*— Sir Clive Elliott, Bt; ✉ AGPP, FAO, via delle Terme di Caracalla, 00100 Rome, Italy

ELLIOTT, Sir David Murray; KCMG (1995), CB (1987); s of Alfred Elliott, ISM (d 1984), and Mabel Emily, *née* Murray (d 1960); *b* 8 Feb 1930; *Educ* Bishopshalt GS, LSE (Kitchener scholar, BScEcon); *m* 22 Sept 1956, Ruth Marjorie, da of Gilbert Ingram (d 1979); 1 s (b 1963 d 1963), 1 da (Rosalind Frances (Mrs Simon Pugsley) b 1968); *Career* Nat Serv RAF 1951–54; asst postal controller II Home Counties Region GPO 1954–57, training offr Fed Miny of Communications Enugu Nigeria 1958–62, asst postal controller I then princ HQ GPO 1962–69, asst sec Miny of Posts and Telecommunications (later part of DTI) 1969–75, cnsllr (external trade) UK Perm Representation to EC Brussels 1975–78, under sec Euro Secretariat Cabinet Office 1978–82, min and dep UK perm rep to EC Brussels 1982–91, dir-gen (internal market) Gen Secretariat Cncl of the EU Brussels 1991–95; memb Bd CARE International UK 1995–; *Clubs* Travellers'; *Style*— Sir David Elliott, KCMG, CB; ✉ 31 Ailsa Road, St Margarets, Twickenham, Middlesex TW1 1QJ

ELLIOTT, David Stuart; s of Arthur Elliott (d 1979), of East Leake, and May, *née* Wright (d 1989); *b* 29 April 1949; *Educ* Loughborough GS, Univ of Durham (BA), Courtauld Inst Univ of London (MA); *m* 23 Feb 1974, Julia Alison, da of Lt-Col John Debenham, MC, of Shrivenham, Wilts; 2 da (Joanna b 10 July 1977, Kate b 3 May 1979); *Career* regnl art offr Arts Cncl 1973–76, dir Museum of Modern Art Oxford 1976–96, dir Moderna Museet Stockholm 1996–; museum winner Sotheby's prize for excellence in the visual arts, Museum of the Year award 1983, winner Nat Art Collections Fund Collect award 1988; advsr VAAC Br Cncl 1979–96, Centre for Int Contemporary Arts NY 1986–92; memb: Cncl Great Britain-Russia Soc, London Cncl Central Sch of Speech and Drama 1994–96, Art Panel of Arts Cncl of GB 1992–95; visitor Ashmolean Museum; exec CIMAM (ICOM); *Books* Alexander Rodchenko (ed 1979), José Clemente Orozco (1981), Tradition and Renewal - Art in the GDR (1984), New Worlds - Art and Society in Russia (1986), Eisenstein at Ninety (ed 1988), 100 Years of Russian Art (1989), Alexander Rodchenko - Works on Paper 1914–1920 (1991), Photography in Russia 1840–1940 (1992), Art from Argentina 1920–1994 (ed 1994); *Recreations* collecting art books; *Style*— David Elliott, Esq; ✉ Moderna Museet, Box 16382, S-103 27, Stockholm, Sweden (☎ 00 46 8 666 4250, fax 00 46 8 611 8311)

ELLIOTT, Geoffrey Charles; s of Alfred Stanley Elliott (d 1985), of Coventry, and Elsie, *née* Wilday; *b* 10 May 1945; *Educ* Bablake Sch Coventry; *m* 5 April 1969, Lynda Barbara, da of John Arthur Williams (d 1980), of Shipston-on-Stour, Warwicks, and Bessie, *née* Parkinson; 1 s (Nicholas John b 1974), 1 da (Joanne Marie b 1971); *Career* Coventry Evening Telegraph: reporter, feature writer, chief feature writer 1962–72, dep ed 1973–79, ed 1981–90; ed Kent Messenger 1979–80, ed and dir The News Portsmouth 1990–; Guild of Br Newpaper Eds: chm Parly and Legal Ctee 1983–86, chm West Midlands 1987–88, chm Wessex 1993–94; memb: Press Cncl 1987–90, Press Complaints Cmmn 1995–; exec chm Common Purpose Coventry 1989–90; memb Portsmouth Common Purpose Cncl 1995–; memb Round Table: Rugby Webb Ellis (chm 1977–78), Bearsted Kent, Coventry Mercia; *Recreations* sport, gardening, music; *Style*— Geoffrey Elliott, Esq; ✉ Flint Barn, Pook Lane, East Lavant, Chichester, West Sussex (☎ 01243 532458); Portsmouth Publishing and Printing Ltd, Hilsea, Portsmouth, PO2 9SX (☎ 01705 664488, fax 01705 673363)

ELLIOTT, Grahame Nicholas; CBE (1991); s of Charles Morris William Elliott (d 1966); *b* 23 Dec 1938; *Educ* Mill Hill Sch; *m* 1968, Zita Catherine, *née* Jones; 2 s, 1 da; *Career* chartered accountant; former ptnr Elliott Templeton Sankey, later sr ptnr BDO Stoy Hayward Manchester (following merger), now conslt; currently chm Astral Finishes Ltd; *Clubs* Turf, Carlton, St James's (Manchester), Racquets (Manchester); *Style*— Grahame Elliott, Esq, CBE; ✉ c/o Astral Finishes Ltd, 29 First Avenue, Deeside Industrial Park, Deeside, Clwyd CH5 2NU (☎ 01244 280198)

ELLIOTT, Joe; *b* 1 Aug 1959; *Career* formerly storekeeper Osborn-Mushet Tools; currently singer; fndr memb Def Leppard 1977; Def Leppard tours: Pyromania 1983, Hysteria 1987, Adrenalize 1992; 1 UK top ten single (Animal 1987), 3 US top ten singles (Hysteria 1988, Pour Some Sugar On Me 1988, Armageddon 1989); albums with Def Leppard: On Through The Night (1980, UK no 15), High 'N' Dry (1981, UK no 26), Pyromania (1983, UK no 18, US no 2), Hysteria (1987, UK and US no 1), Adrenalize (1992), Retro-Active (1993), Slang (1996); awards incl: Favourite Heavy Metal Artist, Favourite Heavy Metal Album (for Hysteria) American Music Awards 1989; *Style*— Joe Elliott, Esq; ✉ c/o Bludgeon Riffola, Mercury, Chancellors House, 72 Chancellors Road, London W6 9QB (☎ 0181 910 5678, fax 0181 910 5896)

ELLIOTT, Prof John; s of Alfred George Lewis Elliott (d 1989), and Mary Dorothy, *née* Greason (d 1992); *b* 20 June 1938; *Educ* Ashford GS, Univ of London (MPhil, Dip in Phil of Educn); *m* 28 July 1967 (m dis 1993); 3 da (Dominique, Katherine, Jessica); *Career* sch teacher 1962–67, res offr Schs Cncl Humanities Project 1967–72, tutor Cambridge Inst of Educn 1976–84, prof of educn UEA 1987– (lectr 1972–76, reader in educn 1984–86, dean Sch of Educn 1992–95), memb Univ Cncl for the Educn of Teachers 1987–; tstee Keswick Hall Tst 1987–, pres Br Educnl Res Assoc 1989–90 (memb Cncl 1987–92, vice pres 1988–89); memb Philosophy Educn Soc of GB; FRSA; *Books* Issues in Teaching for Understanding (ed with D Ebbutt, 1985), Case Studies in Teaching for Understanding (ed with D Ebbutt, 1986), Rethinking Assessment and Appraisal (ed with H Simons, 1989), La Investigacion-Accion en Educacion (1989), Action-Research for Educational Change (1991), Reconstructing Teacher Education (ed, 1993); *Recreations* walking, golf, reading, travel; *Style*— Prof John Elliott; ✉ School of Education, University of East Anglia, Norwich NR4 7TJ (☎ 01603 56161)

ELLIOTT, John Charles Kennedy; s of Charles Morris William Elliott (d 1967), of Altrincham, Cheshire, and Lesley Margaret, *née* Bush; *b* 13 March 1937; *Educ* Merton House Sch Penmaenmawr, Mill Hill Sch London, Univ of Manchester; *m* 28 July 1962, Angela Mary, da of Col Geoffrey William Noakes OBE, JP, DL; 3 s (Charles Geoffrey b 3 Nov 1963, William James b 10 April 1965, Thomas Richard b 11 May 1969), 1 da (Vanessa Jane b 9 Feb 1967); *Career* admitted slr 1961; articled to Mr John Gorna 1956–61, James Chapman & Co 1961–62, Fentons Stansfield & Elliott 1962–68, fndr and sr ptnr Elliott & Co 1968–94 (conslt 1994–); dir: Northern Rock Building Society (Northern Bd) 1988–95, Bain Hogg Ltd UK Division; chm Young Slrs' Gp of Law Soc 1973–74, pres Manchester Law Soc 1980, chm Euro-American Lawyers' Gp 1992–95; NSPCC: chm Manchester and Salford Branch 1989–96, chm Gtr Manchester Area Ctee 1990–94, memb Central Exec Ctee 1980–87; Liveryman Worshipful Co of Horners; memb Law Soc; *Clubs* Carlton, The St James's (Manchester), Manchester Tennis and Racquets; *Style*— John C K Elliott, Esq; ✉ Bradwall House, Bradwall, Cheshire CW11 1RB (☎ 01270 765369); (business ☎ 01270 768074, fax 01270 768004, car tel 0860 619346)

ELLIOTT, Prof Sir John Huxtable; kt (1994); s of Thomas Charles Elliott (d 1969), and Janet Mary, *née* Payne (d 1991); *b* 23 June 1930; *Educ* Eton, Univ of Cambridge (MA, PhD); *m* 1958, Oonah Sophia, da of Sir Nevile Butler; *Career* lectr in history Univ of Cambridge 1962–67 (asst lectr 1957–62), prof of history KCL 1968–73, prof of history Inst for Advanced Study Princeton 1973–90, Regius prof of modern history Univ of Oxford 1990–97; fell: Trinity Coll Cambridge 1954–67 (hon fell 1991–), Oriel Coll Oxford 1990–; King Juan Carlos visiting prof New York Univ 1988; memb American Philosophical Soc 1982; corr memb: Hispanic Soc of America 1975, Real Academia Sevillana de Buenas Letras 1976; Wolfson Prize for History 1986, Gold Medal for the Fine Arts Spain 1990, Eloy Antonio de Nebrija Prize Spain 1993, Prince of Asturias Prize for Social Sciences Spain 1996; Visitante Ilustre de Madrid 1983, medal of honour Universidad Internacional Menéndez y Pelayo 1987; Cdr Order of Isabel la Católica 1987 (Grand Cross 1996), Grand Cross Order of Alfonso X El Sabio 1988; Hon Dr: Universidad Autónoma de Madrid 1983, Univ of Genoa 1992, Univ of Portsmouth 1993, Univ of Barcelona 1994, Univ of Warwick 1995; FBA 1972, FAAAS 1977; *Books* The Revolt of the Catalans (1963), Imperial Spain 1469–1716 (1963), Europe Divided 1559–1598 (1968), The Old World and the New 1492–1650 (1970), Memoriales y Cartas del Conde Duque de Olivares Vol I (1978), Vol II (1980), A Palace for King (with Jonathan Brown, 1980), Richelieu and Olivares (1984), The Count-Duke of Olivares (1986), Spain and Its World 1500–1700 (1989); *Recreations* looking at paintings; *Style*— Prof Sir John Elliott, FBA; ✉ 122 Church Way, Iffley, Oxford OX4 4EG (☎ 01865 71603); Oriel College, Oxford OX1 4EW (☎ 01865 277265)

ELLIOTT, (John) Malcolm; s of Jack Elliot, of 1 Prescott Rd, Wadsley, Sheffield, and Florence Patricia, *née* Hudson; *b* 1 July 1961; *Educ* Myers Grove Sch Sheffield; *Career* cyclist; champion: Nat Schoolboy 1977, RTTC Hillclimb 1980, Cwlth Team Time Trial and Individual Road Race 1982, Br professional Criterium 1984, Br Pursuit 1985, Kelloggs City Centre 1986, Milk Race 1987, Kelloggs Tour of Britain 1988, Tour of Spain 1989 (points), Nat Professional Road Race 1993; fifth place Moscow Olympics Team Pursuit 1980, race ldr Tour du Pont 1994 and 1995, memb Br Team Atlanta Olympics 1996; *Recreations* travel, motoring; *Style*— Malcolm Elliott, Esq; ✉ c/o Mr F Quinn, 4 Cumberland Street, Dun Laoghaire, Co Dublin, Ireland (☎ 01 2841067/01 2841145, fax 01 2804481)

ELLIOTT, Mark; CMG (1988); s of William Rowcliffe Elliott, CB (d 1996), of Farthinghoe, Northants, and Karin Tess, *née* Classen; *b* 16 May 1939; *Educ* Eton, New Coll Oxford (open scholar, BA); *m* 12 Sept 1964, Julian, da of Rev Matthew Richardson (d 1957); 2 s (Justin 1966, Giles b 1968); *Career* HM Dip Serv: joined FO 1963, third then second sec Tokyo 1965–69, first sec FCO 1969–73, private sec to Perm Under Sec FCO 1973–75, first sec Nicosia 1975–77, cnsllr Tokyo 1977–81, head Far Eastern Dept FCO 1981–85, under sec NI Office 1985–88, HM ambass Tel Aviv 1988–92, dep under sec FCO 1992–94, HM ambass Oslo 1994–; *Style*— HE Mr Mark Elliott, CMG; ✉ c/o Foreign & Commonwealth Office (Oslo), King Charles St, London SW1A 2AH

ELLIOTT, Martin John; s of John Elliott, MBE, of Sheffield, and Muriel, *née* Dyson; *b* 8 March 1951; *Educ* King Edward VII GS, Univ of Newcastle upon Tyne (MB BS, MD); *m* 15 Jan 1977, Lesley Rickard, da of Alan Rickard (d 1989), of Puddletown, Dorset; 2 s (Becan b 3 June 1981, Toby b 12 May 1983); *Career* sr registrar and first asst in cardiothoracic surgery Freeman Hosp Newcastle on Tyne 1978–83, conslt and sr lectr in cardiothoracic surgery Gt Ormond St 1985– (sr registrar 1984–85); visiting paediatric cardiac surgn: Malta 1989–, Tehran Heart Inst Iran 1991–, Sofia Bulgaria 1994–; hon conslt cardiothoracic surgeon: St Bartholomew's Hosp London, Harefield Hosp London 1994–; dir Euro Congenital Heart Defects Database; sec Euro Congenital Heart Surgeons Fndn; FRCS 1978; *Recreations* tennis, reading, cinema, music; *Style*— Martin Elliott; ✉ The Cardiac Wing, The Great Ormond Street Hospital for Children, Great Ormond Street, London WC1N 3JH (☎ 0171 405 9200, fax 0171 813 8262)

ELLIOTT, Martin John Henry; s of Patrick James Lawrence Elliott, of Blakesley Ave, Ealing, and Beryl Olivia Catherine, *née* Carroll; *b* 26 Aug 1955; *Educ* St Benedict's Sch Ealing, ChCh Oxford (BA); *m* 4 Aug 1984, Rosanna Lina, da of Capt William James Gorard, of Woodville Gardens, Ealing; 3 s (Benedict Edward Henry b 29 Nov 1988, Oliver James Ambrose b 16 Jan 1990, Edmund Giles Augustus b 4 Aug 1991), 2 da (Alice Clare Ianthe b 1 Aug 1993, Josephine Eleanor Naomi b 1 Sept 1995); *Career* admitted slr 1979; Linklaters & Paines: articled clerk 1977–79, slr 1979–85, ptnr 1985–; memb Law Soc; *Recreations* rugby, cricket, tennis, squash, golf, cycling, gardening; *Clubs* MCC; *Style*— Martin Elliott, Esq; ✉ Linklaters & Paines, Barrington House, 57–67 Gresham St, London EC2V 7JA (☎ 0171 606 7080, fax 0171 606 5113, telex 884349/888167)

ELLIOTT, Michael John; *b* 22 Aug 1953; *Educ* Manor Park GS Nuneaton, Sheffield City Coll of Educn (Univ of Sheffield Cert in Educn), Sheffield City Poly (Univ of Sheffield BEd); *Career* pt/t lectr Dept of Gen Studies Rotherham Coll of Technol 1978, res asst Dept of Educn Mgmnt Sheffield City Poly 1978–79, political advsr and res asst R G Caborn MEP 1979–82; Sheffield City Poly: gen mangr Union of Students 1982–84, asst to the princ 1984–86, head Publicity and Information Servs 1986; asst dir (resources) Yorkshire Arts Assoc 1987–88, dir West Midlands Arts Assoc 1989–91; chief exec: West Midlands Regnl Arts Bd 1992–96, Heart of England Tourist Bd 1996–; chair: Regnl Arts Bd Chief Execs' Gp 1990–94, RAB Services Ltd 1992, Aston Arts Advsy Bd 1995–; treas Euro Forum for Arts and Heritage 1995–96; memb: Cncl Univ of Birmingham 1990–96, Arts Liaison Ctee 1990–96, Governing Body Herefordshire Coll of Arts and Design 1990–, Governing Body Handsworth Coll 1995–, Chief Offrs' Gp 1991–96, Information Mgmnt Policy Gp Arts Funding System 1991–95, Mgmnt Ctee English Regnl Arts Bds 1993–95, Exec of the Chief Offrs' Gp Integrated Arts Funding System 1993–95, Convocation Tst for the Arts Univ of Sheffield 1994–96; memb Inst of Leisure and Amenities Mgmnt, FRSA; *Publications include* The Development of Consortia for Post 16 Provision in the Face of Falling Enrolments (with J A Mundy, 1978); *Recreations* walking, cycling, swimming, watching theatre, dance and football, listening to music, reading contemporary literature and keeping up to date with current affairs and good management practice, travel and continued learning through experience and practice; *Style*— Michael Elliott, Esq; ✉ The Heart of England Tourist Board, Woodside, Larkhill Road, Worcester WR5 2EF (☎ 01905 763436, fax 01905 763450)

ELLIOTT, Nicholas Blethyn; QC (1995); s of Col B W T Elliott, of Wilts, and Zara, *née* Codrington; *b* 11 Dec 1949; *Educ* Kelly Coll Tavistock Devon, Univ of Bristol (LLB); *m* Penelope Margaret Longbourne (Nemmy), da of Brig Hugh Browne; 2 s (Max Blethyn b 14 Aug 1982, George Hugh b 10 Feb 1984); *Career* pupillage chambers of Andrew Leggatt QC (now Lord Justice Leggatt), called to the Bar Gray's Inn 1972, currently in practice Gray's Inn; *Recreations* tennis, bridge, bicycling, swimming, rock and roll dancing; *Style*— Nicholas Elliott, Esq, QC; ✉ 3 Gray's Inn Place, Gray's Inn, London WC1R 5EA (☎ 0171 831 8441, fax 0171 831 8479)

ELLIOTT, Peter; MBE; *b* 9 Oct 1962; *Career* Athlete; memb Rotherham Athletics Club, England Schs int 1979 (jr 1977), jr UK int 1980–81, full UK int 1983–; achievements at 800m: AAA champion 1982 and 1987, UK champion 1983, 1984 and 1986, Bronze medal Euro Cup 1983, Silver medal Euro Indoor Championship 1983, Bronze medal Cwlth Games 1986, Silver medal World Championship 1987, fourth place Olympic Games Seoul 1988; achievements at 1500m: AAA champion 1984, Silver medal Olympic Games Seoul 1988, Gold medal Cwlth Games Auckland 1990, Gold medal Europa Cup 1991, UK all comers record holder; memb world record 4 x 800m team 1982, UK indoor records at 1500m and 1 mile; joiner 1979–90, now surveyor; Hon LLD Univ of Sheffield; *Recreations* golf, fishing, dog walking, movies, football, rugby league; *Clubs* Rotherham Harriers, Roundwood Golf; *Style*— Peter Elliott, Esq, MBE; ✉ Amateur Athletic Association, Edgbaston House, 3 Duchess Place, off Hagley Road, Edgbaston, Birmingham B16 8NM (☎ 0121 456 4050)

ELLIOTT, Ven Peter; s of James Reginald Elliott (d 1974), and Hilda, *née* Mowbray (d 1979); *b* 14 June 1941; *Educ* Queen Elizabeth's GS Horncastle, Hertford Coll Oxford (MA), Lincoln Theol Coll; *m* 1967, Evelyn, da of Robert Alban Embleton; 1 da (Ruth Catherine b 1968); *Career* curate: All Saints Gosforth 1965–68, St Peter Balkwell 1968–72; vicar: St Philip High Elswick 1972–80, N Gosforth 1980–87, Embleton with Rennington and Rock 1987–93; rural dean of Alnwick 1989–93, hon canon of Newcastle 1990–93, archdeacon of Northumberland and canon residentiary of Newcastle 1993–; *Style*— The Ven Peter Elliott; ✉ 80 Moorside North, Fenham, Newcastle upon Tyne NE4 9DU (☎ and fax 0191 273 8245); Church House, Grainger Park Road, Newcastle upon Tyne NE4 8SX (☎ 0191 273 0120, fax 0191 256 5900)

ELLIOTT, Prof Sir Roger James; kt (1987); s of James Elliott (d 1932), and Gladys, *née* Hill; *b* 8 Dec 1928; *Educ* Swanwick Hall Sch Derbys, New Coll Oxford (MA, DPhil); *m* 1952, Olga Lucy, da of Roy Atkinson (d 1940); 1 s (Martin James b 1962), 2 da (Jane Susan b 1955, Rosalind Kira b 1957); *Career* fell St John's Coll Oxford 1957–74, Wykeham prof of Physics Univ of Oxford 1974–88 (sr proctor 1969–70), fell New Coll Oxford 1974–96 (emeritus 1996–), sec to delegates and chief exec OUP 1988–93 (delegate 1971–88), prof of physics Oxford 1993–96 (emeritus 1996–); chm Computer Bd for Univs and Res Cncls 1983–87, physical sec and vice pres Royal Soc 1984–88, pt/t memb Bd UKAEA 1988–93; memb Bd British Cncl 1991–; pres Publishers' Assoc 1993–94; hon fell St John's Coll Oxford 1988; Hon DSc: Paris 1983, Bath 1991, Essex 1993; FRS 1976; *Clubs* Athenaeum; *Style*— Prof Sir Roger Elliott, FRS; ✉ 11 Crick Rd, Oxford OX2 6QL; Department of Theoretical Physics, 1 Keble Road, Oxford OX1 3NP (☎ 01865 273997)

ELLIOTT, Prof (Charles) Thomas; CBE (1994); s of Charles Thomas Elliott (d 1970), and Mary Jane, *née* Higgins (d 1991); *b* 16 Jan 1939; *Educ* Washington Alderman Smith GS, Univ of Manchester (BSc, PhD); *m* Brenda; 1 s (David b 1962), 2 da (Catherine Ann b 1963, Elizabeth Mary b 1966); *Career* asst lectr and lectr Electrical Engrg Dept Univ of Manchester 1963–67, visiting scientist MIT Lincoln Laboratory USA 1970–71; Defence Research Agency: sr scientific offr 1967–73, princ scientific offr 1973–79, sr princ scientific offr (individual merit) 1979–86, dep chief scientific offr (individual merit) 1986–91, distinguished visiting scientist Jet Propulsion Laboratory Calif 1987, chief scientific offr (individual merit) 1991–; visiting prof of physics Heriot-Watt Univ 1992–; Rank Prize for Optoelectronics 1982, The Churchill Medal for Engrg awarded by the Soc of Engrs 1986, MacRobert Award for Engrg (Royal Acad of Engrs) 1991; FRS 1988, FInstP 1990; *Recreations* reading, music, cycling, golf; *Style*— Prof Thomas Elliott, CBE, FRS; ✉ Defence Research Agency, St Andrews Rd, Malvern, Worcs WR14 3PS (☎ 01684 894820, fax 01684 896264)

ELLIOTT, Timothy Stanley; QC (1992); *b* 2 April 1950; *Educ* Marlborough Coll, Trinity Coll Oxford (exhibitioner, MA); *m* 1973, Katharine Barbara, *née* Lawrence; 1 s (b 1980), 1 da (b 1983); *Career* called to the Bar Middle Temple 1975; *Style*— Timothy Elliott, Esq, QC; ✉ 10 Essex Street, London WC2R 3AA (☎ 0171 240 6981, fax 0171 240 7722)

ELLIOTT, Hon Lord; Walter Archibald; MC (1943), QC (1960); s of Prof Thomas Renton Elliott, CBE, DSO, FRS (d 1961), of Broughton Place, Broughton, Peeblesshire, and Martha, *née* M'Cosh; *b* 6 Sept 1922; *Educ* Eton, Univ of Edinburgh; *m* 1954, Susan Isobel, da of late Phillip Mackenzie Ross; 2 s; *Career* Capt Scots Gds Italy, NW Europe WWII; barr and advocate 1950, pres Lands Tbnl for Scotland 1971–92, chm of Scottish Land Court with title Lord Elliott 1978–92; Brig Queen's Body Guard for Scotland (Royal Co of Archers); *Books* Us and Them, A Study of Group Consciousness (1986), Esprit de Corps (1996); *Recreations* gardening, travel; *Clubs* New (Edinburgh), Scottish Arts (Edinburgh); *Style*— The Hon Lord Elliott, MC; ✉ Morton House, Fairmilehead, Edinburgh EH10 (☎ 0131 445 2548)

ELLIOTT OF MORPETH, Baron (Life Peer UK 1985), of Morpeth in the Co of Northumberland and of the City of Newcastle-upon-Tyne; (Robert) William Elliott; kt (1974), DL (Northumbreland 1983); s of Richard Elliott (d 1957), of Low Heighley, Morpeth, Northumberland, and Mary Elizabeth, da of William Fulthorpe, of Morpeth; *b* 11 Dec 1920; *Educ* King Edward GS Morpeth; *m* 1956, (Catherine) Jane, da of Robert John Burton Morpeth, of Newcastle-upon-Tyne; 1 s (Hon Richard John b

1959), 4 da (Hon Alison Mary (Hon Mrs Campbell Adamson) b 1957, Hon Catherine Victoria (Hon Mrs Taylor) b 1962, Hon Sarah Ann (Hon Mrs Atkinson-Clark b (twin) 1962, Hon Louise Jane b 1967); *Career* farmer 1939–; chm, vice pres and pres Northern Area Young Conservatives 1948–55; contested (C) Morpeth 1954 and 1955; MP (C) Newcastle-upon-Tyne N 1957–83; PPS to: Jt Parly Secs Miny of Transport and Civil Aviation 1958–59, Parly Under Sec of State Home Office 1959–60, Min of State Home Office 1960–61, Min for Technical Co-operation 1961–63; asst govt whip 1963–64, opposition whip 1966–70; comptroller of HM Household June-Oct 1970; vice chm Conservative Party Organisation 1970–74; chm Select Ctee on Agriculture, Fisheries and Food 1980–83; chm United Artists Communications (North East); *Clubs* Northern Counties; *Style*— The Rt Hon Lord Elliott of Morpeth, DL; ✉ Lipwood Hall, Haydon Bridge, Northumberland (☎ 01434 684777); 19 Laxford House, Cundy Street, London SW1 (☎ 0171 730 7619)

ELLIS, Dr Adrian Foss; s of Henry James Ellis, of Swindon, Wilts (d 1976), and Marjorie Foss, *née* Smith (d 1975); *b* 15 Feb 1944; *Educ* Dean Close Sch Cheltenham, Univ of London (BSc(Eng)), Univ of Loughborough (PhD); *m* 1, Lesley Maxted, *née* Smith (d 1970); m 2, 1973, Hilary Jean, da of Alfred Miles; 2 da (Sarah Louise b 23 June 1974, Joanna Katherine b 22 Dec 1976), 1 s (Nicholas Edward James b 10 July 1983); *Career* student apprenticeship Richard Thomas and Baldwins 1962–67, sr res offr British Steel Corp 1969–71, district alkali inspr HM Alkali Inspectorate 1976–83 (alkali inspr 1971–76); HSE: head of Major Hazards Assessment Unit 1985–86 (dep head 1983–85), dep chief inspr (Chemicals) 1986–90, regnl dir Field Ops, dir Technol and Hazardous Installations Policy 1990–91, dir Technol and Health Sciences 1991–96, dir of field ops 1996–; ILO conslt on major hazards: India 1985, Pakistan 1988, Thailand 1989, Indonesia 1990, Soviet Union and Soviet States 1991, China 1994; visiting prof Cranfield Univ 1992–; fell Inst of Energy 1977, FIChemE 1977 (memb Cncl), FEng 1995; *Books* The International Labour Office Manual on Major Hazards Control (co-author); *Recreations* travel, Swindon Town FC, exploring car boot sales; *Clubs* Athenaeum; *Style*— Dr Adrian Ellis, FEng; ✉ Health and Safety Executive, Daniel House, Trinity Road, Bootle, Merseyside L20 7HE (☎ 0151 951 4702, fax 0151 951 4889)

ELLIS, Alice Thomas; *b* 9 Sept 1932; *see:* Haycraft, Anna Margaret

ELLIS, Andrew Steven; OBE (1984); s of Peter Vernon Ellis, and Kathleen, *née* Dawe; *b* 19 May 1952; *Educ* St Dunstan's Coll Catford, Trinity Coll Cambridge (BA), Univ of Newcastle (MSc), Newcastle Poly (BA); *m* 13 July 1975 (m dis 1987), Patricia Ann Stevens, da of William Skinner; m 2, 7 July 1990, Helen Prudence Drummond; *Career* proprietor Andrew Ellis (printing and duplicating services) 1973–81, election organiser 1981–85, sec gen Lib Pty 1985–88 (vice chm 1980–86), chief exec SLD 1988–89; conslt in public affrs, governmental relations and political organisation 1989–, dir Central and Eastern Europe GJW Government Relations Ltd 1990–; technical advsr to chm Palestine Central Election Cmmn 1994–96, trg advsr to Election Observation Mission Bosnia 1996; Parly candidate (Lib): Newcastle upon Tyne Central (1974, 1976 by-election, 1979), Boothferry (1983); ldr Lib Gp Tyne and Wear CC 1977–81; *Books* Algebraic Structure (with Terence Treeby, 1971), Let Every Englishman's Home be his Castle (1978); *Clubs* Nat Liberal; *Style*— Andrew Ellis, Esq, OBE; ✉ 56 drève du Tridge de la Bruyère, 1420 Braire L'Allend, Belgium (☎ and fax 00 322 351 4630)

ELLIS, Anthony John; s of Jack Ellis, of Scunthorpe, S Humberside, and Nancy Doreen, *née* Reed; *b* 15 June 1945; *Educ* Univ of London (BD, MA); *m* 1, 1966 (m dis), Maureen Jane Anne Twomey; 2 da (Kate b 14 Feb 1973, Seónaid b 19 May 1975); m 2, 4 Sept 1980, Alice Anne, da of late James Stanley Stewart Findlay, of Helmsdale, Sutherland; 1 da (Bridget b 7 May 1985); *Career* sr lectr Dept of Moral Philosophy Univ of St Andrews 1987–90 (lectr 1971–1987, chm 1985–89), prof of philosophy Virginia Cwlth Univ Richmond VA 1990– (visiting prof 1987–88); univ fell Univ of Wollongong 1989; ed and author of various pubns and books; *Recreations* music, hill walking; *Style*— Anthony Ellis, Esq; ✉ Dept of Philosophy, Virginia Commonwealth University, 915 W Franklin St, Richmond, Virginia 23284, USA (☎ 00 1 804 828 1224)

ELLIS, Brian William; s of Frank Albert Ernest Ellis (d 1988), and Beryl Christine, *née* Holdsworth (d 1955); *b* 28 Nov 1947; *Educ* Harrow, St Mary's Hosp Med Sch Univ of London (MB BS); *m* 10 July 1976, Loveday Ann, da of David Ernest Pusey (d 1952), of Coleshill, Amersham, Bucks; 1 s (David b 1981), 1 da (Rebecca b 1978); *Career* conslt surgn Ashford Hosp Middx 1983–, hon sr clinical res fell Academic Surgical Unit St Mary's Hosp Med Sch of London 1985–, hon clinical tutor to Charing Cross Med Sch, clinical advsr in surgery to British Airways, clinical advsr to Medical Systems Ltd, dir Medical Software Ltd; memb Cncl Br Assoc of Urological Surgns; author of various papers on clinical audit, computing, med and prostate surgery; referee for submissions to British Journal of Surgery and British Medical Journal; FRCS 1977; *Books* Hamilton Bailey's Emergency Surgery (ed, 12 edn), Journal of Managed Care (ed); *Recreations* wine, music, roses; *Style*— Brian W Ellis, Esq; ✉ Graylands, 124 Brox Road, Ottershaw, Surrey KT16 0LG (☎ and fax 01932 873254); Ashford Hospital, London Rd, Ashford, Middx TW15 3AA (☎ 01784 884429, fax 01784 884393)

ELLIS, Carol Jacqueline (Mrs Ralph Gilmore); CBE (1995), QC (1980), JP (West Central Div Inner London 1972); da of Ellis Wallace Ellis (d 1974), of London, and Flora, *née* Bernstein; *b* 6 May 1929; *Educ* Abbey Sch Reading, Univ of Lausanne, UCL (LLB); *m* 6 Jan 1957, (Cyril) Ralph Gilmore (d 1996); 2 s (Jeremy Charles b 1960, David Emanuel b 1962); *Career* called to the Bar Gray's Inn 1951; law reporter for The Times and legal jls 1952–69; Law Reports and Weekly Law Reports: law reporter 1954–69, asst ed 1969, managing ed 1970, ed Weekly Law Reports 1976–90 (now conslt), ed Law Reports 1976–96 (now conslt); memb Inner London Probation Ctee 1989–95; *Recreations* travel, music, theatre; *Style*— Miss Carol Ellis, CBE, QC, JP; ✉ 11 Old Square, Lincoln's Inn, London WC2A 3TS (☎ 0171 405 0238)

ELLIS, Carolyn Noeleen (stage name Carrie Ellis); da of Harold Ellis, of Lytham St Annes, Lancs, and Noeleen, *née* Balshaw; *b* 11 March 1960; *Educ* Witton Park HS Blackburn, Arts Educnl Sch London; *Career* actress; recently Miss Schmelling in Highly Sprung (BBC) 1995; *Theatre* Aladdin (Southport 1977, Watford 1978), Cinderella (Newcastle) 1979, Cabaret! (England and abroad) 1980–81, Annie (nat tour) 1981–84, Consuela in Westside Story (Her Majesty's) 1984–86, Liane in Gigi (Lyric) 1986, Pickwick (Exeter) 1986–87, Miss Silkworm in James and the Giant Peach (Queen's Hornchurch and nat tour) 1987, Ruth in Cheeky Chappie (Queen's Hornchurch) 1987, Gloria/Witch in Wizard of Oz (Exeter) 1987, King's Rhapsody (Churchill Bromley) 1988, Jane Asthon in Brigadoon (Victoria Palace) 1988–89, White Witch in Wizard of Oz (Chichester Festival) 1989–90, Lady Jaqueline in Me and My Girl (Adelphi) 1990–91, Kathy in Company (Exeter) 1991, Sybil Heston and Joan Collins' alter ego in Shadow Play (Tonight at 8:30, BBC) 1991, Joyce Horne in Teething Troubles 1992, princ in West End to Broadway (Babbacombe Theatre and Hippodrome Theatre Eastbourne 1993), Blue Fairy in Pinocchio (choreographer) 1992, Pirates of Penzance (tour) 1993, Jellylorum in Cats (New London Theatre) 1994; choreographer Showstoppers (tour) 1993, concert of Aspects of Love (Sydmonton Festival) 1988, charity performances of Hello Dolly, My One and Only and Cole Porter 1991; *Radio* Natasha Hapsburg in Taking It Up The Octave (Radio 3) 1996, Val in Chorus Line (Radio 2); *Recordings* Seven Brides for Seven Brothers, Singin' in the Rain, The Music Man 1996; *Recreations* walking, swimming, visiting historical places and homes, knitting, teaching dancing and choreography; *Style*— Ms Carolyn Ellis

ELLIS, David; *b* 13 Feb 1934; *Career* Nat Serv Army Special Investigations Branch 1952–55; Crusader Insurance Plc: mgmnt 1956–60, regnl mangr Nigeria 1960–63, city branch mangr 1963–66, PA to Investment and Admin Mangr 1966–69, secondment to US parent gp 1969–70, mangr admin 1971–76, dir and gen mangr 1976–85 (mktg and sales 1976–83, parent group 1983–84, life ops 1984–85); sr vice pres Cigna International Life Group and md Crusader 1986–89, chief exec Lane Clark & Peacock 1989–93, md Mast Organisation Ltd (int trg consultancy) 1993–, various directorships 1993–; memb Worshipful Co of Insurers 1987, Freeman City of London 1987; FCIS 1968 (two prizes), FCII 1972, FInstD 1986; *Recreations* golf, writing, reading, music; *Clubs* ESU; *Style*— David Ellis, Esq; ✉ The Old Playhouse, Cuckfield Lane, Warninglid, West Sussex RH17 5SP (☎ 01444 461619, fax 01444 461282)

ELLIS, His Hon Judge; David Raymond; s of Raymond Ellis (d 1986), of Charney Bassett, Nr Wantage, Oxon, and Ethel, *née* Gordon; *b* 4 Sept 1946; *Educ* St Edward's Sch Oxford, ChCh Oxford (MA); *m* 18 December 1974, Cathleen Margaret, da of late Dr Albert Joseph Hawe, CBE, of Accra, Ghana; 1 s (Thomas b 1978), 1 da (Caroline b 1979); *Career* called to the Bar Inner Temple 1970, recorder of the Crown Court 1991–95 (asst recorder 1986), circuit judge (SE Circuit) 1995–; *Clubs* Leander; *Style*— His Hon Judge Ellis; ✉ Lamb Building, Temple, London EC4Y 7AS

ELLIS, Diana Margaret; da of Robert Hall (d 1981), of Twickenham, and Mabel Helen, *née* Steadman (d 1990); *b* 11 April 1938; *Educ* Perivale Girls' Sch, Guildford Coll of Technol (MRSH); *m* 3 Sept 1966, John David Ellis, s of Frederick Henry Ellis (d 1994); 1 da (Claire Suzanne b 24 Aug 1969); *Career* dist mangr Surrey CC; competitive career: Middlesex 1954–57, joined St George's Ladies Rowing Club 1960, coxed winning crew Women's Eights Head of River Race 1969, 1971, 1972 and 1973 (stroked 1966–68), stroked GB eight Euro Championships 1966, coxed England 1972, Gold medal Nat Championships 1972 (Silver 1973); memb: Women's Rowing Ctee 1977–, Nat Championship Ctee 1977 (chm 1987–89), World Rowing Championship 1996 (vice pres), Ctee Women's Eights Head of River Race 1980–93; chm: Women's Rowing Cmmn 1984–87, Serpentine Regatta 1987–89, Exec Ctee Amateur Rowing Assoc 1989–; GB team mangr 1988; qualified umpire 1978; VAD BRCS; *Recreations* rowing; *Style*— Mrs Diana Ellis; ✉ Amateur Rowing Association, 6 Lower Mall, Hammersmith, London W6 9DJ (☎ 0181 748 3632, fax 0181 741 4658)

ELLIS, Geoffrey Albert; s of Albert Edward Ellis (d 1989), of Eaglescliffe, Cleveland, and Alice Isabel, *née* Bell; *b* 20 Sept 1937; *Educ* City of Leicester Boys' Sch, Univ of Manchester (Dip Arch); *m* 8 March 1969, Annette Ray Ellis; 2 da (Vanessa Claire b 1975, Verity Fiona b 1981); *Career* architect; asst then sr architect W S Hattrell & Ptnrs Manchester 1961–66, sr architect R Seifert & Ptnrs Manchester 1966–68; ptnr: Gelling Ellis Lomas & Ptnrs Douglas IOM 1968–78, Ellis Brown Ptnrship Douglas IOM 1978–; life memb Douglas Rugby Club, memb IOM Soc of Architects and Surveyors; RIBA 1966, FFAS 1984, FFB 1971; *Recreations* swimming, touring, camping; *Style*— Geoffrey Ellis, Esq; ✉ Longlast, Selborne Drive, Douglas, IOM; Ellis Brown, The Rechabite Hall, Allan St, Douglas, IOM (☎ 01624 621375/0624 622692, fax 01624 628465)

ELLIS, Geoffrey Gordon; s of Frederick Ellis (d 1966), of London, and Vera, *née* Clark; *b* 25 July 1940; *Educ* Gravesend GS, Isleworth GS; *m* 16 Sept 1961, Jean Heather, da of Ronald Coles (d 1978), of Bath; 1 da (Kate b 1971); *Career* public relations exec; journalist: Bath Evening Chronicle 1957–68, Thomson Regional 1968–71, The Guardian 1971–79, Now! Magazine 1979–81, The Times 1981–85; dir PR Broad Street Associates 1985–89, md Geoffrey Ellis Associates PR Ltd 1989–95, dir Tenet Public Relations 1995–96, md Metro Media Services Ltd 1996–; *Recreations* wine appreciation, aviation, jazz, books, cooking, France; *Style*— Geoffrey Ellis, Esq; ✉ Metro Media Services Ltd, Finsbury Business Centre, 40 Bowling Green Lane, London EC1R 0NE (☎ 0171 415 7005, e-mail metromedia@dial.pipex.com)

ELLIS, Prof Hadyn Douglas; s of Alfred Douglas Ellis, and Myrtle Lillian Ellis; *b* 25 Oct 1945; *Educ* Univ of Reading (BA, PhD), Univ of Aberdeen (DSc); *m* 17 Sept 1966, Diane Margaret, da of Denis Newton, of St Briavels, Glos; 3 s (Stephen David b 1967, Robert Huw b 1980, Jack Richard b 1983); *Career* Univ of Aberdeen: lectr 1970–79, sr lectr 1979–86; prof of applied psychology UWIST 1986–88; Univ of Wales Cardiff: prof of psychology 1988–, head Sch of Psychology 1989–, pro-vice-chllr 1995–97; FBPsS 1986; *Style*— Prof Hadyn Ellis; ✉ Llwynarthen House, Castleton, Cardiff CF3 8UN; School of Psychology, University of Wales College of Cardiff, Cardiff CF1 3YG (☎ 01222 874867)

ELLIS, Prof Harold; CBE; s of Samuel and Ada Ellis; *b* 13 Jan 1926; *Educ* Univ of Oxford (BM BCh, MCh, DM); *m* 20 April 1958, Wendy, da of Henry Levine; 1 s (Jonathan b 1959), 1 da (Suzanne b 1962); *Career* Capt RAMC 1950–51; res surgical appts 1948–60, sr lectr Univ of London 1960–62, prof of surgery Univ of London at Westminster Hosp 1962–88, univ clinical anatomist Univ of Cambridge 1989–93, clinical anatomist Guy's Hosp 1993–; former vice pres: RCS, RSM; pres Br Assoc of Surgical Oncology; FRCS, FRCOG; *Recreations* medical history; *Style*— Prof Harold Ellis, CBE; ✉ 16 Bancroft Ave, London, N2 0AS (☎ 0181 348 2720); Department of Anatomy, UMDS (Guy's Campus), London Bridge, London SE1 9RT

ELLIS, Dr (William) Herbert Baxter; AFC (1954); er s of William Baxter Ellis, and Georgina Isabella, *née* Waller; *b* 2 July 1921; *Educ* Oundle, Univ of Durham (MB BS, MD); *m* 1, 1948 (m dis), Margaret Mary, da of Frank Limb, OBE (d 1987), of Yorks; 1 s (Christopher b 1954), 1 da (Penny (Mrs Deakin) b 1952); m 2, 1978 (m dis), Molly Marguerite Clarke; m 3, 1994, Jean Stanley Stawell (wid of Ken Gross); *Career* Surgn Cdr RN 1945–59; qualified Naval Pilot appts incl: RN Hosp Malta 1945–47, RAF Inst of Aviation Med Farnborough 1950–56, US Navy Acceleration Laboratory Johnsville USA 1956–58, RN Air Med Sch Gosport 1958–59; mktg dir Appleyard Gp 1959–64, vice pres Schweppes (USA) 1964–65, dir Bewac 1965–71, dir gen Dr Barnardos 1971–73, med conslt DHSS 1973–91, Employment Med Advsy Serv 1973–81, med conslt Plesseys; St John Ambulance: Glos co surgn 1979–87, Glos co cdr 1987–89, chief cdr 1989–91; Freeman City of London, Freeman Worshipful Soc of Apothecaries 1993; OStJ 1979, CStJ 1987, KStJ 1989; Gilbert Blane Medal 1954; *Books* Hippocrates RN: Memoirs of a Naval Flying Doctor (1988), Why Not Live a Little Longer?; *Recreations* memories of walking, mending fences, writing; *Clubs* Army and Navy, Naval and Military, St John; *Style*— Dr Herbert Ellis, AFC; ✉ Little Dalling, Rocks Lane, High Hurstwood, E Sussex TN22 4BN (☎ and fax 01825 733139)

ELLIS, Herbert Douglas (Doug); s of Herbert Ellis; *b* 3 Jan 1924; *Educ* Chester Secdy Sch; *m* 1963, Heidi Marie, da of Rudolph Kroeger; 3 s; *Career* RN 1942–46; chm: Ellis Group of Cos (Ellmanton Construction Co Ltd, Ellmanton Investments Ltd), Aston Villa FC 1968–79 and 1982–, Aston Manor Brewery Co Ltd 1985–, Good Hope Hosp NHS Tst 1993–; memb Lloyd's; *Recreations* football, salmon fishing, foreign travel; *Style*— Doug Ellis, Esq; ✉ 2 Ladywood Road, Four Oaks, Sutton Coldfield, West Midlands B74 2SN (☎ 0121 308 1218)

ELLIS, Dr Ian Ogilvie; s of Philip Senior Ellis, of Cranford, Manchester, and Anna *née* Ure; *b* 24 Aug 1955; *Educ* Stockport GS, Univ of Nottingham Med Sch (BMed Sci, BM BS); *m* 20 Oct 1979 (sep), Jane Elisabeth, da of Dudley John Stevens, of Westbere House, Westbere, Kent; 1 s (James Ogilvie b 1987), 1 da (Sophie Hannah b 1989); *Career* lectr pathology Univ of Nottingham 1980–87, conslt histopathologist specialising in breast disease City Hosp Nottingham 1987–; author of numerous pubns on breast cancer pathology and prognostic factors; memb Working Gp Breast Cancer Screening RCPath, lectr UK Breast Screening Prog Nottingham Trg Centre; MRCPath 1985; *Recreations* game fishing, wine tasting; *Style*— Dr Ian Ellis; ✉ Yew Tree House, 2 Kenilworth Rd,

The Park, Nottingham (☎ 0115 947 2186); Department of Histopathology, City Hospital, Hucknall Rd, Nottingham N55 1PB (☎ 0115 969 1169, ext 46875)

ELLIS, (Thomas) James; s of Thomas James Ellis (d 1978), of Rotherham, and Emily Ford; *b* 9 May 1942; *Educ* Rotherham GS, Rotherham Coll of Technol, Administrative Staff Coll Henley; *m* 16 May 1964, Janet, da of Arthur Jarvis; 2 da (Deborah Janet b 14 Nov 1964, Joanne b 3 July 1967), 1 s (Neil James b 26 July 1966); *Career* student apprentice then various commercial engrg posts Yorkshire Electricity Bd 1958–67; South Eastern Electricity Board: asst commercial engr Commercial Dir's Dept 1967–69, sr asst engr Tariffs & Econs Commercial Dir's Dept 1969–72, dist commercial engr Tunbridge Wells 1972–73, dist commercial engr S E Sussex 1973–77, seconded asst commercial mangr Energy Mktg 1976, asst commercial mangr Tariffs and Economics 1977–81, mktg mangr 1981–85, commercial dir 1986–90; Seeboard plc: commercial dir 1990–91, chief exec 1992–96, chm and chief exec 1996–; chm Electricity Supply Industry's Domestic Energy Mktg Gp 1987–91; memb: Unipede Tariffs Gp of Experts 1977–92, CBI SE Regnl Cncl 1986–; CEng, FRSA 1996, FIEE, CIMgt; *Recreations* Downs walking, golf, racing (horse); *Style*— James Ellis, Esq; ✉ Seeboard plc, Forest Gate, Brighton Road, Crawley, West Sussex RH11 9BH (☎ 01293 565888, fax 01293 657320)

ELLIS, (Arthur) John; CBE (1986); s of Arthur Ellis, and Freda Jane Ellis; *b* 22 Aug 1932; *Educ* City of London Coll, SW Essex Tech Coll; *m* 1956, Rita Patricia; 2 s, 1 da; *Career* Fyffes Group Ltd: accountant 1954–64, mgmnt accountant 1964–65, chief fin offr 1965–67, fin dir 1967–69, chief exec 1969, chm 1984–; chm: National Seed Development Organisation Ltd 1982–87, Intervention Board for Agricultural Produce 1986–95; Liveryman Worshipful Co of Fruiterers; FCCA, MBCS, FCIMA, FICSA; *Recreations* golf, fishing, walking, reading; *Clubs* Reform, Farmers'; *Style*— John Ellis, Esq, CBE; ✉ Fyffes Group Ltd, 12 York Gate, Regent's Park, London NW1 4QJ (☎ 0171 487 4472, fax 0171 487 3644, telex 25392)

ELLIS, John Norman; OBE (1995); s of Albert Edward Ellis (d 1990), and Margaret, *née* Thompson (d 1986); *b* 22 Feb 1939; *Educ* Osmondthorpe Secdy Modern Leeds, Leeds Coll of Commerce; *m* 1 (m dis); *m* 2, 5 Oct 1985, Diane; 1 s (Martin John), 1 da (Karen Elizabeth (Mrs Landricumbe)), 2 step s (Graham Anderson, Robert James Anderson); *Career* messenger Post Office 1954–57, postman 1957–58, clerical offr Miny of Works 1958–67, exec offr MPBW 1967–68; Civil and Public Servs Assoc (CPSA): full time offr 1968–82, dep gen sec 1982–86, gen sec 1986–92; sec Council of Civil Service Unions 1992–95; industl relations conslt 1995–; vice chm Nat Whitley Cncl, sec Major Policy Ctee Cncl of Civil Service Unions; former memb: TUC Gen Cncl (memb Econ, Social Insur and Industl Welfare, Educn and Training, Equal Rights), TUC Public Services Ctee and Pension Special Ctee; memb: Exec Bd Civil Serv Housing Assoc (also dir), Exec Bd Inst of Employment Rights, Civil Serv Occupational Health Serv Advsy Bd, Industrial Tbnls London (S Region), Steering Ctee Centre for Public Sector Research, Inst of Employment Rights, Labour Party; *Recreations* politics, motoring, dog walking, reading, gardening; *Style*— John Norman Ellis, Esq, OBE; ✉ 26 Hareston Valley Road, Caterham, Surrey CR3 6HD (☎ 01883 380270, fax 01883 380271)

ELLIS, Sir John Rogers; kt (1980), MBE (1943); 3 s of late Frederick William Ellis, MD; *b* 15 June 1916; *Educ* Oundle, Trinity Hall Cambridge, London Hosp (MA, MD); *m* 1942, Joan, da of late C J C Davenport; 2 s, 2 da; *Career* Surgn-Lt RNVR 1942–46; dean London Hosp Med Coll 1968–81 (formerly sub dean then vice dean), physician to London Hosp 1951–81; pres Med Protection Soc 1986–89; chm Cncl of Govrs: Inst of Educn Univ of London 1983–93, Woodford Co HS for Girls; vice pres Assoc for the Study of Med Educn; hon MD Univ of Uppsala; hon fell: Queen Mary & Westfield Coll, London Hosp Med Coll, Inst of Educn Univ of London; Liveryman Worshipful Soc of Apothecaries; FRCP; *Recreations* painting, gardening; *Style*— Sir John Ellis, MBE; ✉ Little Monkhams, Monkhams Lane, Woodford Green, Essex IG8 0NP (☎ 0181 504 2292)

ELLIS, Dr Jonathan Richard (John); s of Richard Ellis, of Potters Bar, Herts, and Beryl Lilian, *née* Ranger (d 1985); *b* 1 July 1946; *Educ* Lochinver House Sch, Highgate Sch, King's Coll Cambridge (BA, PhD); *m* 11 July 1985, Maria Mercedes, da of Alfonso Martinez (d 1982), of Cali, Colombia and Miami Beach, Florida; 1 s (Sebastian b 19 July 1990), 1 da (Jennifer b 17 Jan 1988); *Career* res assoc Stanford Linear Accelerator Centre 1971–72, Richard Chase Tolman fell Calif Inst of Technol 1972–73, ldr Theoretical Studies Div Euro Orgn for Nuclear Res (CERN) Geneva 1988–94 (memb staff since 1973), Miller prof Univ of California Berkeley 1988; FRS 1984; FIOP 1991; *Recreations* reading, listening to music, hiking in mountains; *Style*— Dr John Ellis, FRS; ✉ 5 Chemin du Ruisseau, Tannay, 1295 Mies, Switzerland (☎ 00 41 22 776 48 58); Theoretical Studies Division, CERN, 1211–Geneva 23, Switzerland (☎ 00 41 22 767 4142, fax 00 41 22 767 3850)

ELLIS, Dr Julia Peregrine; da of Cecil Montague Jacomb Ellis (d 1942), of London, and Pamela Sage, *née* Unwin; *b* 25 March 1936; *Educ* North Foreland Lodge Sch, Middx Hosp Univ of London (MB BS, DCH, FRCP); *Career* St George's Hosp London 1966–69, sr registrar dermatology Oxford 1969–74, res dermatology Dept of Dermatology Univ of Miami Med Sch 1974; conslt dermatologist: Princess Margaret Hosp Swindon 1975–, Wessex Health Authy 1975–; former pres St John's Hosp Dermatological Soc London, former treas and pres Dowling Club; *Recreations* fishing; *Style*— Dr Julia P Ellis; ✉ Princess Margaret Hosp, Okus Rd, Swindon, Wilts SN1 4JU (☎ 01793 536231)

ELLIS, Nigel George; s of George Ellis, of Selsey, Sussex, and Ivy, *née* Howell; *b* 19 April 1939; *Educ* Farnborough GS; *m* 31 July 1965, Yvonne Meline Elizabeth, da of Norman Tracy (d 1976), of Crowborough, Sussex; 1 s (Timothy b 1971), 1 da (Victoria b 1968); *Career* co sec City of London Real Property Co 1967–74, dir Holland America UK Ltd 1974–79, dir Hammerson Property Development and Investment Corps 1979–88, fin dir BAA plc 1988–95, chm Quintain Estates & Development plc 1995–; FCA 1963, FCCA 1985; *Recreations* philately, chess; *Style*— Nigel Ellis, Esq; ✉ Willmead Farm, Bovey Tracey, Nr Newton Abbot, Devon TQ13 9NP (☎ 01647 277599, fax 01647 277598)

ELLIS, Dr Norman David; s of George Edward Ellis (d 1968), of London, and Annie Elsie, *née* Scarfe (d 1978); *b* 23 Nov 1943; *Educ* Minchenden Sch, Univ of Leeds (BA, PhD), Univ of Oxford (MA); *m* 1966, Valerie Ann, da of Haddon Fenn, of East Sussex; 1 s (Mark b 1975); *Career* res fell Nuffield Coll Oxford 1971–74; gen sec Assoc First Div Civil Servants 1974–78; under sec British Medical Assoc 1978–; *Recreations* reading, railways, local community affairs; *Style*— Dr Norman Ellis; ✉ British Medical Association, BMA House, Tavistock Square, London WC1H 9JP

ELLIS, Osian Gwynn; CBE (1971); s of Rev Thomas Griffith Ellis (d 1985), of Prestatyn, and Jennie, *née* Lewis (d 1976); *b* 8 Feb 1928; *Educ* Denbigh GS, RAM (Hovey scholar, Dr Joseph Parry prize, Vivian Dunn prize, Harriet Cohen award); *m* 5 Jan 1951, Irene Ellis, da of Richard Hugh Jones (d 1987), of Pwllheli; 2 s (Richard Llywarch b 1956, Tomos Llywelyn b 1959); *Career* concert harpist; played and recorded with: Melos Ensemble London 1954–, Lincoln Center Chamber Music Soc NY 1974–; prof of harp Royal Acad of Music 1959–89, princ harpist LSO 1960–94; has given concerts of poetry and music with Dame Peggy Ashcroft, Paul Robeson, Richard Burton, Lord David Cecil, Dorothy Tutin, Princess Grace and others; numerous recital tours with Sir Peter Pears Europe and USA; works written for him by Benjamin Britten: Harp Suite in C Maj 1969, Canticle V (for performance with Pears) 1974, Birthday Hansel 1975; harp concertos written for him by: Alun Hoddinott, William Mathias, Jorgen Jersild, Robin Holloway; solos and chamber music by: Malcolm Arnold, Elizabeth Maconchy, Colin Matthews, Menotti and William Schuman; awards: Grand Prix du Disque, French Radio Critics award; Hon DMus Univ of Wales 1970; FRAM 1960; *Style*— Osian Ellis, Esq, CBE; ✉ 90 Chandos Avenue, London N20 9DZ; Arfryn, Yr Ala, Pwllheli, Gwynedd LL53 5BN

ELLIS, Peter Johnson; s of Albert Goodall Ellis (d 1985), and Evelyn, *née* Johnson; *b* 24 Nov 1937; *Educ* Queen Elizabeth GS Wakefield, Trinity Coll Cambridge (MA); *m* 14 July 1960, Janet Margaret, da of Thomas Palmer, of Cambridge; 3 da (Jacqueline b 11 Oct 1961, Christine b 3 July 1964, Rosalind b 4 Jan 1967); *Career* Nat Serv RAF 1955–57; systems analyst IBM (UK) Ltd 1960–64, data processing mangr J & A Scrimgeour 1964–70, Grieveson Grant & Co 1970–86 (ptnr 1976–86, jt dep chief exec 1982–86), dep chm Kleinwort Benson Investment Management 1988– (jt chief exec 1986–88), dir Kleinwort Overseas Investment Tst PLC 1996–; chm Asset Mgmnt Ctee London Investment Banking Assoc 1996–; memb Soc of Investment Analysts 1970–92 (memb Cncl 1976–84); MSI 1992– (memb Stock Exchange 1973); *Recreations* theatre, reading, bridge; *Style*— Peter Ellis, Esq; ✉ La Barranca, Tyrrell's Wood, Leatherhead, Surrey (☎ 01372 372343); Kleinwort Benson Investment Management, 10 Fenchurch St, London EC3M 3LB (☎ 0171 956 7260, 0171 956 6600)

ELLIS, Prof (Francis) Richard; s of (Henry) Francis Ellis, of Halebarns, Cheshire, and Elsie May, *née* Pearson; *b* 3 March 1936; *Educ* Altrincham Co GS, Univ of Manchester (MB ChB), Univ of Leeds (PhD); *m* 9 June 1960, Maureen, da of (Francis) Syndey Statham (d 1983); 1 s ((Angus) Christian b 1963), 1 da (Charlotte (Rebecca) b 1965); *Career* res fell MRC 1966–68, prof of anaesthesia Univ of Leeds 1992– (reader in anaesthesia 1976–92, sr lectr 1971–76, lectr 1968–71); memb: Bd British Journal of Anesthesia; memb: BMA, RSM, Assoc of Anaesthetists; fell Royal Coll of Anaesthetists (memb Cncl and immediate past sr vice pres), DA, DObstRCOG; *Books* Inherited Disease and Anaesthesia, Essential Anaesthesia, Hyperthermic and Hypermetabolic Disorders; *Recreations* painting, playing jazz, wood turning; *Style*— Prof Richard Ellis; ✉ Academic Unit of Anaesthesia, Clinical Sciences Building, St James's University Hospital, Leeds LS9 7TF (☎ 0113 206 5274, fax 0113 206 4140)

ELLIS, Dr Richard Mackay; s of Valentine Herbert Ellis, FRCS (d 1953), of London, and Angela Peart, *née* Robinson (d 1991); *b* 9 July 1941; *Educ* Wellington Coll, Clare Coll Cambridge, St Thomas's Hosp; *m* 14 Aug 1976, Gillian Ann, da of Samuel Cole (d 1975), of Reading; 1 s (William b 1978), 1 da (Melissa b 1977); *Career* assoc prof of orthopaedics Univ of Rochester NY USA 1975–80, sr lectr in rehabilitation Univ of Southampton 1980, conslt in rheumatology and rehabilitation Salisbury Hosps 1980; ed jl of Orthopaedic Med, past pres Inst of Orthopaedic Med; FRCS 1971, FRCP 1989; *Style*— Dr Richard Ellis; ✉ 161 Bouverie Avenue South, Salisbury, Wilts SP2 8EB; Odstock District Hospital, Salisbury, Wilts SP5 8BJ (☎ 01722 336212)

ELLIS, Prof Richard Salisbury; s of late Capt Arthur Ellis, MBE, of Colwyn Bay, Wales, and Marion, *née* Davies; *b* 25 May 1950; *Educ* Ysgol Emrys ap Iwan, UCL (BSc), Wolfson Coll Oxford (DPhil); *m* 28 July 1972, Barbara; 1 s (Thomas Marc b 1978), 1 da (Hilary Rhona b 1976); *Career* princ res fell Royal Greenwich Observatory 1983–85, prof of astronomy Univ of Durham 1985–93 (lectr 1981–83), sr res fell SERC 1989–94 (chm Large Telescope Panel), Plumian prof of astronomy and experimental philosophy Univ of Cambridge 1993–, dir Inst of Astronomy Cambridge 1994–, professorial fell Magdalene Coll Cambridge 1994–; memb: American Astronomical Soc, Astronomical Soc of Pacific; FRAS, FRS 1995; *Books* The Epoch of Galaxy Formation (with C S Frenk, 1988), Observational Tests of Inflation (with T Shanks, 1991); *Recreations* travel; *Style*— Prof Richard Ellis, FRS; ✉ Institute of Astronomy, Madingley Road, Cambridge CB3 0HA (☎ 01223 330879, fax 01223 337523)

ELLIS, Richard Tunstall; OBE (1970), TD, DL (1967); s of Herbert Tunstall Ellis (d 1925), of Liverpool, and Mary Elizabeth Muriel, *née* Sellers (d 1929); *b* 6 Sept 1918; *Educ* Merchant Taylors' Crosby, Silcoates Sch Wakefield Yorkshire, Univ of Aberdeen (MA, LLB); *m* 2 Jan 1946, Jean Bruce Maitland, da of Maj Richard Reginald Maitland Porter, MC (d 1979), of Aberdeen; 2 s (Keith b 1949, Andrew b 1960), 2 da (Janet (Mrs Baldwin) b 1947, Katharine (Mrs Parker) b 1956); *Career* Royal Signals 51(H) Div 2 Lt 1939 (POW Germany 1940–45), Lt 1942, Capt 1945; sr ptnr Paull & Williamsons Advocates Aberdeen 1970–83 (ptnr 1949–70); chm: Trustee Savings Bank Scot 1983–86, TSB Scotland plc 1986–89; dir TSB Group plc 1986–89; memb: Scot Bd Norwich Union Insur Socs 1973–80, Aberdeen Bd Bank of Scot 1972–82, Ct Univ of Aberdeen 1984–93 (vice chm 1990–93), Cncl Nat Tst for Scot 1984–89; chm Scot Div IOD 1988–89; memb: Law Soc of Scot, Law Soc London; Hon LLD Aberdeen 1992; *Recreations* golf, hill walking, skiing; *Clubs* Army & Navy, Royal Northern (Aberdeen), New (Edinburgh), Royal Aberdeen Golf; *Style*— Richard Ellis, Esq, OBE, TD, DL; ✉ 18 Rubislaw Den North, Aberdeen AB15 4AN (☎ 01224 316680)

ELLIS, Ven Robin Gareth; s of Rev Joseph Walter Ellis, and Morva Phyllis, *née* Morgan-Jones; *b* 8 Dec 1935; *Educ* Oldham Hulme GS, Worksop Coll, Pembroke Coll Oxford (BCL, MA); *m* 1964, Anne, da of James Sydney Landers (d 1970); 3 s (Timothy b 1966, Simon b 1968, Dominic b 1971); *Career* asst curate St Peter's Swinton Manchester 1960–63, asst chaplain Worksop Coll 1963–66; vicar: Swaffham Prior with Reach Cambs 1966–74, St Augustine's Wisbech 1974–82, Yelverton 1982–86; archdeacon of Plymouth 1982–; *Recreations* cricket, theatre, prison reform; *Style*— The Ven the Archdeacon of Plymouth; ✉ 33 Leat Walk, Roborough, Plymouth PL6 7AT (☎ 01752 793397, fax 01752 774618)

ELLIS, Roger Henry; s of Francis Henry Ellis (d 1953), of Debdale Hall, Mansfield; *b* 9 June 1910; *Educ* Sedbergh, King's Coll Cambridge (MA); *m* 1939 (Audrey) Honor (d 1993), o da of late Arthur Baker, JP, DL; 2 da (Charlotte (Mrs Taylor), Susannah (Mrs Braithwaite)); *Career* WWII Private 1939, Maj 5 Fusiliers 1944, serv Italy and Germany, MFAA offr Italy and Germany 1944–45; Public Record Office: asst keeper 1934, princ asst keeper 1954, conslt ed Catalogue of Seals 1972–86; sec Royal Cmmn on Historical Manuscripts 1957–72, lectr in archive studies UCL 1947–57; Br Records Assoc: ed of Archives 1947–57, chm Cncl 1967–73, vice pres 1971–; pres Soc of Archivists 1964–73 (vice pres Business Archives Cncl 1958–); chm Br Standards Ctee for Drafting BS 5454 1967–72, memb and sec Jt Records Ctee Royal Soc and Royal Cmmn on Historical Manuscripts 1968–75; jt ed Rivista for Br Italian Soc 1946–49; author of articles in Br and foreign jls and collections on care and use of archives and manuscripts; memb: London Cncl Br Inst in Florence 1947–55, ICA Ctee on Sigillography 1962–77, Advsy Ctee on Export of Works of Art 1964–72, Exec Ctee Friends of the Nat Libraries 1965–88 (hon treas 1977–79); vice pres Royal Inst 1975–76 (mangr 1973–76); corresponding memb Indian Historical Records Cmmn, FSA, FRHistS; *Publications* The Principles of Archive Repair (1951), Ode on St Crispin's Day (1979), Catalogue of Seals in the Public Record Office, Personal Seals I and II (1979–81) Monastic Seals I (1986), Walking Backwards (1986); *Clubs* Athenaeum; *Style*— Roger H Ellis, Esq, FSA; ✉ 7 Straffan Lodge, Belsize Grove, London NW3 4XE

ELLIS, Roger Wykeham; CBE (1983); s of Cecil M J Ellis (d 1942), and Pamela Unwin (d 1994); *b* 3 Oct 1929; *Educ* Winchester, Trinity Coll Oxford (MA); *m* 25 July 1964, Margaret Jean, da of William H Stevenson (d 1972); 1 s (Alexander b 1967), 2 da (Katherine b 1965, Harriet (twin) b 1967); *Career* Nat Serv 1947–49; Harrow Sch: asst master 1952–61, housemaster 1961–67; headmaster Rossall Sch 1967–72, master Marlborough Coll 1972–86, mangr Graduate Recruitment Barclays Bank 1986–91; memb: Harrow Borough Educn Ctee 1956–60, Wiltshire Co Educn Ctee 1975–85; chm HMC 1983; govr: Harrow Sch, St Edward's Sch Oxford (chm), Campion Sch Athens; dir

Asquith Court Schools Ltd 1994–; *Recreations* golf, fishing; *Clubs* The East India; *Style*— Roger Ellis, Esq, CBE; ✉ 18 North Avenue, Ealing, London W13 8AP

ELLIS, Sir Ronald; kt (1978); s of William Ellis, and Besse Brownbill; *b* 12 Aug 1925; *Educ* Preston GS, Univ of Manchester (BScTech); *m* 1, 1956, Cherry Hazel, *née* Brown (d 1978); 1 s, 1 da; m 2, 1979 Myra Ann, *née* Lowdon; *Career* dir BL Motor Corporation 1970–76, chm Bus Manufacturers Holding Co 1972–76; head of def sales MOD 1976–81; dir: Wilkinson Sword Group 1981–86, Bull Thompson & Associates Ltd 1981–86; non-exec dir: Yarrow 1981–86, Redman Heenan International 1981–86; pres and md Allegheny International (Industl Div) 1982–85, chm EIDC Ltd 1981–93; govr and memb Cncl UMIST 1970–92 (vice pres 1983–92); FEng 1981, FIMechE, CIMgt, FRSA; *Recreations* fishing, reading; *Style*— Sir Ronald Ellis, FEng; ✉ Weavers Mill, Pincot Lane, Pitchcombe, Stroud, Glos GL6 6LY

ELLIS, Stephen; *b* 26 April 1955; *Educ* Quintin GS London, Univ of Sussex (BA); *Career* media researcher BMP Advertising 1977–78, prodn co-ordinator Encyclopaedia Britannica Audio Visual 1978–80, prodr/dir Straightline Video 1980–82; BBC TV: asst prodr BBC Presentation and Promotion 1982–84, prodr Breakfast Time 1984–85, prodr BBC Enterprises 1985–86; head of presentation and promotion Super Channel 1986–88 (also dep head of programming 1987–88), head of promotions Thames Television 1988–92, creative conslt UK Gold 1992, dir of bdcasting and new media Westcountry Television 1992–; *Style*— Stephen Ellis, Esq; ✉ Westcountry Television, Western Wood Way, Langage Science Park, Plymouth, Devon PL7 5BG (☎ 01752 333333, fax 01752 333444)

ELLIS, Susan Jacqueline; da of Michael John Irving Ellis, of Bridgwater, Somerset, and Juliette Wendy Scott, *née* Smith; *b* 30 April 1963; *Educ* Leamington Coll for Girls, City Univ Business Sch (BSc); *Career* Midland Bank International 1981–85, National Opinion Polls 1985–86, PR mangr Broad Street Associates 1987–88, jt md Square Mile Communications 1992– (jt fndr 1988); *Recreations* sport, cinema, theatre, literature; *Style*— Miss Susan Ellis; ✉ Square Mile Communications Limited, 11 Gough Square, London EC4A 3DE (☎ 0171 583 4567, fax 0171 583 0050)

ELLISON, Prof Arthur James; s of Lawrence Joseph Ellison, of Birmingham (d 1978), and Elsie Beatrice Ellison; *b* 15 Jan 1920; *Educ* Solihull Sch, Univ of London (BSc, DSc(Eng)); *m* 1, 1952, Marjorie (d 1955), da of Walter Cresswell, of Sheffield; m 2, 1963, Marian Elizabeth, da of John Gordon Gumbrell, of London (d 1976); 1 s, 1 da; *Career* design engr Higgs Motors Ltd 1938–43, tech asst Royal Aircraft Estab 1943–46, design engr British Thomson-Houston Co Ltd 1947–58 (graduate apprentice 1946); lectr and sr lectr Queen Mary Coll Univ of London 1958–72, hon prof Nat Univ of Engrg Lima Peru 1968, prof of electrical and electronic engrg and Head of Dept City Univ London 1972–85 (prof emeritus 1985–); conslt engr (retained by Thorburn Colquhoun Ltd); author of numerous papers and volumes on engrg and psychical res; fndr and chm Int Conf on Electrical Machines 1974–85 (pres of honour), pres Soc for Psychical Res 1976–79 and 1981–84; CEng, FIMechE, FIEE, Sr MIEEE; *Books* Electromechanical Energy Conversion (1965), Generalized Electric Machines (1967), Machinery Noise Measurement (with Yang, 1985), The Reality of the Paranormal (1988); *Recreations* reading, meditation, parapsychology and travel; *Clubs* Athenaeum; *Style*— Prof Arthur Ellison; ✉ 10 Foxgrove Avenue, Beckenham, Kent BR3 5BA (☎ 0181 402 3399); The City University, Northampton Square, London EC1V 0HB (☎ 0171 477 8000)

ELLISON, Prof (Ernest) Graham; s of Ernest Arthur Ellison (d 1987), of Evesham, and Phyllis May Ellison (d 1987); *b* 19 Feb 1932; *Educ* Prince Henry's GS Evesham, UCL (BSc, PhD); *m* 1, Aug 1955 (m dis), Jean, da of E J Williams (d 1988), of Kidwelly; 1 s (Huw Graham b 13 March 1959), 1 da (Karen Jane b 13 Aug 1961); m 2, April 1984, Barbara Janet, da of F Tremlin (d 1980), of Bristol; *Career* Gloster Aircraft Co 1955–57, Canadair Ltd Montreal Canada 1957–60, lectr QMC London 1960–62, sr res assoc Pratt & Whitney Aircraft Conn USA 1962–66, progressively lectr, reader then prof and head Dept of Mechanical Engrg Univ of Bristol 1966–96 (prof emeritus 1996–); author of numerous pubns on res; chm Engrg Profs Cncl; CEng, FIMechE; *Recreations* cricket, golf, lawn bowls, foreign travel; *Clubs* XL, Optimists Cricket (chm); *Style*— Prof Graham Ellison; ✉ 3 Uncombe Close, Backwell, Bristol BS19 3PU

ELLISON, Chllr His Hon John Harold; VRD (and clasp); s of Harold Thomas Ellison (d 1940), of Woodspeen Grange, nr Newbury, and Frances Amy, *née* Read (who m again and changed name to Swithinbank 1947 and d 1972), da of Robert John Read, of Norwich; *b* 20 March 1916; *Educ* Uppingham, King's Coll Cambridge (MA); *m* 1952, Margaret Dorothy Maud, da of Maynard Deedes McFarlane (d 1984), of Sun City, Arizona, USA; 3 s (John, Crispin, Francis), 1 da (Jane); *Career* res physicist and metallurgist then engrg mangr Thos Firth & John Brown Ltd Sheffield 1937–40 and 1946; Lt RE (49 W Riding Div TA) 1938–39; RNVR: Offr RNVR 1939–51, HMS Lorna and HMS St Day 1940, Gunnery Specialist HMS Excellent 1940, Gunnery Offr HMS Despatch and Sqdn Gunnery Offr 8 Cruiser Sqdn 1940–42, Staff Offr Trade Div Naval Staff 1942–44, Staff Offr Ops to Flag Offr Western Med 1944–45; called to the Bar Lincoln's Inn 1947, practised common law and criminal work Oxford Circuit 1947–71, circuit judge 1972–87; chllr Dios of Salisbury and Norwich 1955–, pres SW London Branch of Magistrates Assoc 1974–87, govr Forres Sch Tst Swanage 1974–88; fell Royal Astronomical Soc; *Books* Halsbury's Law of England (3 edn on Courts, 3 and 4 edns on Allotments and Small Holdings); *Recreations* organs and music, sailing, shooting, skiing, astronomy; *Clubs* Army and Navy, Bar Yacht, Kandahar Ski; *Style*— Chllr His Hon Judge Ellison, VRD; ✉ Goose Green House, Egham, Surrey TW20 8PE

ELLISON, Mark Christopher; s of Anthony Ellison (d 1959), and Arlette Maguire, *née* Blundell; *b* 8 Oct 1957; *Educ* Pocklington Sch, Skinners Sch, Univ of Wales (LLB), Inns of Ct Sch of Law; *m* 21 Nov 1981, Kate Augusta, da of Michael Humphrey Middleton, CBE; 2 s (Ned, Rollo), 2 da (Flora, Maudie); *Career* called to the Bar Gray's Inn 1979, in practice SE Circuit specialising in criminal law, jr Treasy counsel Central Criminal Ct; *Style*— Mark Ellison, Esq; ✉ Queen Elizabeth Building, Temple, London EC4Y 9BS (☎ 0171 583 5766)

ELLMANN, Lucy Elizabeth; da of Richard David Ellmann (d 1987), and Mary Joan, *née* Donahue (d 1989); *b* 18 Oct 1956; *Educ* Oxford HS for Girls, Falmouth Sch of Art, Canterbury Art Sch, Univ of Essex (BA), Courtauld Inst (MA); *m* 31 Dec 1982 (m dis 1988), Simon Gasquoine; 1 da (Emily Firefly b 1983); *Career* author; winner Guardian Fiction Prize 1987; *Books* Sweet Desserts (1987), Varying Degrees of Hopelessness (1991); *Recreations* cello; *Style*— Ms Lucy Ellmann; ✉ c/o Hamish Hamilton, 27 Wrights Lane, London W8 5TZ

ELLMANN, Dr Maud; da of Richard David Ellmann (d 1987), of Oxford, and Mary Joan Donahue Ellmann (d 1989); *b* 16 Jan 1954; *Educ* Oxford HS, Université de Paris Sorbonne, King's Coll Cambridge (MA, Rylands prize), St Anne's Coll Oxford (DPhil); *m* 16 Jan 1993, Christopher Giles Baldick; *Career* lectr Dept of English Univ of Southampton 1979–89, Andrew W Mellon faculty fell in humanities Harvard Univ 1989–90; Univ of Cambridge: univ lectr in English 1989–, fell and dir of studies King's Coll 1989–; visiting asst prof: Smith Coll Northampton Massachusetts 1984–85, Amherst Coll Massachusetts 1985–86; *Books* The Poetics of Impersonality: T S Eliot and Ezra Pound (1987), The Hunger Artists: Starving, Writing and Imprisonment (1993), Psychoanalytic Literary Criticism (1994); *Style*— Dr Maud Ellmann; ✉ King's College, Cambridge CB2 1ST (☎ 01223 331422)

ELLWOOD, Hugh Barton; s of Daniel Ellwood (d 1973), of Clayton-Le-Moors, Accrington, and Josephine, *née* Sharples; *b* 7 March 1938; *Educ* St Bede's Coll Manchester, Gregorian Univ Rome (PhL), Univ of Manchester (BArch); *m* 10 Aug 1966, Marie, da of Frederick Lawson; 2 s (Paul Andrew b 24 Sept 1969, Mark John b 4 Nov 1974), 2 da (Margaret Clare b 21 July 1967, Catherine Ann b 18 March 1980); *Career* architect; Building Design Partnership: architect Preston office 1966–70 (involved in public housing, student accommodation for Univ of Manchester, housing centre in Chorley), assoc Rome Office 1970–72 (involved in private housing in Rome, Lugano, Brussels, planning reports for areas of Calabria), assoc Preston Office 1972–76 (responsible for design and prodn info stages New Gen Infirmary Leeds, devpt plan for Provincial Maternity Hosp Milan), ptnr Preston Office (responsible for New Gen Infirmary at Leeds, Queen's Med Centre Nottingham, hosps in Southport Blackburn and Maghull), chm Preston office 1988–94, practice quality assur dir 1994–; memb ARCUK 1967, RIBA 1968; *Style*— Hugh B Ellwood, Esq; ✉ Building Design Partnership, Sunlight House, Quay Street, Manchester M60 3JA (☎ 0161 834 8441, fax 0161 832 4280)

ELLWOOD, Peter Brian; s of Isaac Ellwood (d 1986), of Bristol, and Edith Trotter (d 1981); *b* 15 May 1943; *Educ* King's Sch Macclesfield; *m* 14 Sept 1968, Judy Ann, da of Leonard George Windsor, of Bristol; 1 s (Richard b 23 Sept 1975), 2 da (Elizabeth b 21 April 1970, Rachel b 11 Jan 1973); *Career* Barclays Bank 1961–89: corp banker and gen mangr's asst to Sr Gen Mangr Head Office London, controller Barclaycard ops 1983–85, chief exec Barclaycard 1985–89; TSB Group plc: chief exec Retail Banking 1989–91, chief exec Retail Banking and Insurance 1991–92, gp main bd dir 1990–95, gp chief exec 1992–95, dep gp chief exec Lloyds TSB Group plc (following merger) 1995–, gp main bd dir Lloyds TSB 1995–; chm Visa International 1994–; non-exec dir: Sears plc 1994–, RPO 1996–; chm Gifts in Kind 1996–, tstee Royal Theatre Northampton, memb Ct Nene Coll Northampton; Hon LLD Univ of Leicester 1994, Hon DUniv Univ of Central England 1995; FCIB (memb Cncl), FRSA; *Recreations* theatre, music; *Style*— Peter Ellwood, Esq; ✉ Catesby House, Lower Catesby, Northants; TSB Group plc, 60 Lombard St, London EC3V 9DN (☎ 0171 398 3812)

ELLY, (Richard) Charles; s of Harold Elly, of Sherborne, Dorset, and Dora Ellen, *née* Luing (d 1988); *b* 20 March 1942; *Educ* Sir William Borlase's Sch Marlow, Hertford Coll Oxford (MA); *m* 7 Oct 1967, Marion Rose, da of Bernard Walter Blackwell (d 1987); 1 s (Mark b 1972), 1 da (Frances b 1975); *Career* admitted slr 1966, ptnr Reynolds Parry-Jones & Crawford 1968, recorder of the Crown Court 1995–; sec Southern Area Assoc of Law Socs 1975–82, pres Berks Bucks & Oxon Law Soc 1988–89 (sec 1975–82); Law Soc: memb 1966–, memb Cncl 1981–, chm Legal Aid Ctee 1984–87, chm Standards and Guidance Ctee 1987–90, chm Criminal Law Ctee 1991–92, dep vice pres 1992–93, vice pres 1993–94, pres 1994–95; chm Maidenhead Deanery Synod 1972–79, pres Cookham Soc 1987–, memb Berks CC 1980–81; Hon LLD Kingston Univ 1994; FRSA 1995; *Recreations* ornithology, theatre, walking, gardening; *Clubs* United Oxford and Cambridge Univ; *Style*— Charles Elly, Esq; ✉ Court Cottage, Dean Lane, Cookham Dean, Maidenhead, Berks SL6 9AF (☎ 01628 482637); 10 Easton St, High Wycombe, Bucks HP11 1NP (☎ 01494 525941, fax 01494 530701)

ELMES, Dr Peter Cardwell; s of Capt Florence Romaine Elmes (d 1965), of Hemyock, nr Cullompton, Devon, and Lilian Bryham Cardwell (d 1950); *b* 12 Oct 1921; *Educ* Rugby, ChCh Oxford (MA, BSc, BM BCh), Western Reserve Univ Cleveland USA (MD); *m* 19 Jan 1957, Margaret Elizabeth, da of Henry Sambell Staley (d 1960), of Jabalpur, India; 2 s (John Peter Henry b 1960, David Antony b 1964), 1 da (Ann Elizabeth b 1957); *Career* Capt RAMC 1946–49; Hammersmith Hosp 1950–57 (registrar, sr registrar and tutor in med); Dept of Therapeutics Queen's Univ Belfast 1958–76 (lectr, sr lectr, reader, prof); dir MRC Pneumoconiosis Unit 1976–82, conslt in occupational pulmonary disease 1982–; memb Poisons Bd NI, former chm Citizens Advice Bureaux NI, former memb Medicines Cmmn; chm: Dinas Powys Civic Tst and Mabon Club, S and Mid Glamorgan Branch Welsh Historic Gardens Tst; FRCP 1967, FFOM 1982; *Recreations* DIY, gardening; *Style*— Dr Peter Elmes; ✉ Dawros House, St Andrews Rd, Dinas Powys, S Glamorgan CF64 4HB (☎ 01222 512102, fax 01222 515975, e-mail elmes@celtic.co.uk)

ELMS, Michael Robert; s of Frederick James Elms, of Manchester, and Rosemary, *née* Groves; *b* 18 July 1954; *Educ* Gravesend GS Kent, Audenshaw GS Gtr Manchester; *m* 26 April 1975, Valerie Anne, da of Gordon Richards; 3 da (Georgina Elisabeth b 26 Nov 1980, Felicity Kathryn b 6 Jan 1983, Charlotte May b 5 Feb 1988); *Career* Ogilvy & Mather advtg agency: media trainee 1973–81, media dir 1981–89, md 1989–93; chief exec CIA (UK) Holdings 1993–; *Recreations* flying (PPL); *Style*— Michael Elms, Esq; ✉ CIA Group plc, 1 Paris Garden, London SE1 8NU (☎ 0171 633 9999, fax 0171 261 1226)

ELMS-ELEY, (Elizabeth) Susan; da of Ernest Frederick Butler, and Renée, *née* Dale; *b* 2 April 1962; *Educ* Brynteg Comp Sch, Bridgend Tech Coll, Kingston Poly (BA, Postgrad Mktg Dip); *m* (m dis); m 2, 1996; *Career* hairdresser 1978–81, student Kingston Poly 1981–85, research exec Leo Burnett advtg 1985–87, research mangr Lintas advtg 1987–89, bd dir Initiative Media London 1989–90, md Initiative Technologies Paris 1990–94, chief exec SP Consultants Worldwide 1994–95, int head of research Initiative Media International 1995–; former chm Media Research Group; memb European Society for Opinion Surveys and Mkt Research (ESOMAR), MRS; *Recreations* cinema, travel; *Style*— Mrs Susan Elms-Eley; ✉ Initiative Media International, 30 New Oxford Street, London WC1A 1AP (☎ 0171 636 3377, fax 0171 831 8054)

ELPHICK, Michael John; s of Herbert Frederick Elphick (d 1970), of Chichester, Sussex, and Joan, *née* Haddow; *b* 19 Sept 1946; *Educ* Lancastrian Sch Chichester, Central Sch of Speech and Drama (scholar); *children* 1 da (Kate Alexander Elphick); *Career* actor; *Theatre* incl: Hamlet (Royal Court, Round House, Broadway NY), Ticket of Leave Man (NT), Macbeth (Worcester, Tokyo, Manila, Hong Kong, Chichester Festival Theatre); *Television* incl: Holding On (LWT), Private Schultz (BBC), Blue Remembered Hills (BBC), This Year Next Year (Granada), Crown Court (Granada), Three Up Two Down (BBC), The Knowledge (Thames), Boon (Central); *Films* incl: Fraulein Doktor, Buttercup Chain, Cry of the Banshee, Hamlet, Quadrophenia, The Elephant Man, Trail of the Pink Panther, Memed My Hawk, The Krays, Privates on Parade, The First Great Train Robbery, Where's Jack, Withnail and I, Buddy's Song, I Bought a Vampire a Motorbike, The Antagonists, Let Him Have It; *Awards* Best Actor Rediffusion TV Awards 1986; *Recreations* boats; *Clubs* Groucho, Gerry's, Colony; *Style*— Michael Elphick, Esq; ✉ c/o ICM Ltd, Oxford House, 76 Oxford Street, London W1N 0AX (☎ 0171 636 6565, fax 0171 323 0101)

ELPHINSTON, Alexander; s and h of Sir John Elphinston of Glack, 11 Bt, *qv*; *b* 6 June 1955; *Educ* Repton, St John's Coll Durham; *m* 1986, Ruth Mary, er da of Rev Robert Curtis Dunnett, of Edgbaston, Warwickshire; 1 s (Daniel John b 24 Sept 1989), 1 da (Sarah Elisabeth b 21 Sept 1992); *Career* slr; ptnr Anstey Sargent & Probert; memb STEP (branch sec 1994–96), govr and tstee Emmanuel Sch Exeter 1994–; *Recreations* youth work, theatre, jigsaws, cricket; *Style*— Alexander Elphinston, Esq; ✉ High Banks, Sandy Lane, Brampford Speke, Exeter EX5 5HW (☎ 01392 841904)

ELPHINSTON OF GLACK, Sir John; 11 Bt (NS 1701), of Logie, Co Aberdeen; s of Thomas George Elphinston (d 1967; s of de jure 9 Bt), and Gladys Mary, *née* Congdon (d 1973); suc unc, Sir Alexander Logie Elphinstone of Glack, 10 Bt (d 1970); *b* 12 Aug 1924; *Educ* Repton, Emmanuel Coll Cambridge (BA); *m* 29 May 1953, Margaret Doreen, da of Edric Tasker (d 1968), of Cheltenham; 4 s (Alexander b 1955, Charles b 1958, Andrew James b 1961, William Robert b 1963); *Heir* s, Alexander Elphinston, *qv*; *Career* Lt RM 1942–47; chm Lancs, Cheshire and IOM Branches of RICS (Agric Div) 1975; pres

Cheshire Agric Valuers' Assoc 1967, memb Lancs River Authy 1969–74, former sch govr; estates mangr Mond Div ICI, ret; conslt land agent with Gandy & Son Northwich Cheshire 1983–88; FRICS, FAAV; *Recreations* church, country pursuits, cricket; *Style*— Sir John Elphinston of Glack, Bt; ✉ Pilgrims, Churchfields, Sandiway, Northwich, Cheshire CW8 2JS (☎ 01606 883327)

ELPHINSTONE, 19 Lord (S 1509); Alexander Mountstuart Elphinstone; also Baron Elphinstone (UK 1885); s of 18 Lord Elphinstone (d 1994), and Willa Mary Gabriel, *née* Chetwode; *b* 15 April 1980; *Heir* bro, Hon Angus John Elphinstone b 1982; *Style*— The Lord Elphinstone; ✉ Whitberry House, Tyninghame, Dunbar, East Lothian EH42 1XL

ELPHINSTONE, Sir John Howard Main; 6 Bt (UK 1816), of Sowerby, Cumberland; s of Sir (Maurice) Douglas Warburton Elphinstone, 5 Bt, TD (d 1995), and (Helen) Barbara, *née* Main; *b* 25 Feb 1949; *Educ* Loretto; *m* 20 Oct 1990, Diane Barbara Quilliam, da of Dr Brian Quilliam Callow (d 1973), of Johannesburg, S Africa; *Heir* unc, Rowland Henry Elphinstone b 1915; *Career* quality assurance and hygiene mgmnt in food processing cos, food hygiene advsr for Enviroguard (UK) Ltd (pest control co) 1988–; memb Soc of Food Hygiene Technology 1986; Dip Quality Assurance 1984, Advanced Food Hygiene Cert 1996; *Recreations* DIY, food, gardening; *Style*— Sir John Elphinstone, Bt; ✉ Garden Cottage, 6 Amherst Road, Sevenoaks, Kent TN13 3LS (☎ 01732 459077); Enviroguard (UK) Ltd, Unit 5, Penshurst Enterprise Centre, Penshurst, nr Tonbridge, Kent TN11 8BG (☎ 01892 870164, fax 01892 870062, e-mail john.elphinstone@envirogd.demon.co.uk)

ELRINGTON, Prof Christopher Robin; s of Brig Maxwell Elrington, DSO, OBE (ka 1945), and Beryl Joan, *née* Ommanney (d 1994); *b* 20 Jan 1930; *Educ* Wellington, Univ Coll Oxford (MA), Bedford Coll London (MA); *m* 1951, Jean Margaret, da of Col Robert Vernon Maynard Buchanan (d 1969), of Ferndown; 1 s (Giles), 1 da (Judy); *Career* ed Victoria History of the Counties of England 1977–94, prof of history Univ of London 1992–94 (prof emeritus 1994); FSA, FRHistS; *Style*— Prof Christopher Elrington, FSA; ✉ 34 Lloyd Baker St, London, WC1X 9AB (☎ 0171 837 4971); Institute of Historical Research, Univ of London WC1E 7HU (☎ 0171 636 0272)

ELSDALE, Robert (Bob); s of Henry Sefton Elsdale (d 1974), of Barbara Mary, *née* Henson; *b* 9 April 1947; *Educ* Brockenhurst GS, Univ of Loughborough (BSc); *m* 11 Feb 1978, Christine Susan, da of Cyril Charles Key; 1 da (Holly b 16 Aug 1979), 1 s (Robinson b 5 Sept 1981); *Career* asst to Phil Jude photographer 1972–75, freelance photographer 1975–; Association of Photographers Awards 1992, 1993 and 1994; *Recreations* fly fishing, travel; *Style*— Bob Elsdale, Esq; ✉ 10–11 Bishops Terrace, London SE11 4UE (☎ 0171 582 5287, fax 0171 582 5288)

ELSE, Martin Thomas; s of Richard Else (d 1992), and Lilian Margaret, *née* Stickells; *b* 21 May 1953; *Educ* Farnborough GS, Univ of Salford (BScEcon), Southampton Coll of Technol, London Business Sch (Sloan fell); *m* 1 July 1978, Jennifer Louise, da of Timithy George Bridges; 1 s (David Thomas b 20 May 1980), 1 da (Sharon Louise b 29 Jan 1982); *Career* fin trainee City and Hackney HA and City and E London AHA 1975–79; NE Thames RHA 1979–83: princ fin planning mangr 1979–82, princ asst treas 1982–83; Hampstead HA 1983–90: dep treas 1983–86, dir of fin, operational planning and supplies 1986–90, dep dist gen mangr 1986–90, memb Tavistock and Portman Special Mgmnt Ctee and hon treas to the Special Tstees 1986–90; Royal Free Hampstead NHS Tst 1990–: dir of fin, planning and supplies 1990–94, dep chief exec 1990–94, hon sec and treas to the Special Tstees 1990–94, chief exec 1994–, hon sec and treas to the Special Tstees Royal Free Hosp, tstee Appeal Tst for the Royal Free Hosp and chm Mgmnt Ctee Cancerkin charity 1994–; variously memb nat NHS ctees incl: Costing for Contracting Steering Gp 1992– (chm 1994–), Estate Info Review Ctee 1994–, Review of Financial Regime for NHS Tsts 1995–; variously memb NHS nat influence gps incl: NAHAT Contracting and Resource Gp 1991–, Tst Fedn Fin and Capital Standing Ctee 1994– (chm of Fin Dirs), Main Universities Teaching Hosps Tsts 1991–94 (fndr memb and former chm of Fin Dirs); CIPFA/Healthcare Fin Mangrs Assoc: memb Provider Mgmnt Gp 1993–94, memb Risk Mgmnt Review 1994; lectr to various orgns incl London Business Sch, City Univ, King's Fund, Audit Cmmn, Dept of Health Mgmnt Exec and CIPFA Conf and to professional health gps incl Coll of Radiographers and RCN; memb CIPFA 1979, MHSM 1994; *Style*— Martin Else, Esq; ✉ Chief Executive's Office, Royal Free Hampstead NHS Trust, Royal Free Hospital, Pond Street, London NW3 2QG (☎ 0171 830 2176)

ELSENER, Willi Josef; s of Martin Elsener, and Margrit, *née* Richter; *b* 16 Jan 1952, Rhäzüns, Switzerland; *Educ* Realschule Langnau Zürich Switzerland, Handelsschule Cressier NE Switzerland, Gewerbeschule Zürich (Swiss Federal Master Chef Diploma); *m* 26 July 1991, (Winsome) Jayne, da of Keith Francis Morrison; 3 c (Christof Hans and Marina Winsome (twins) b 9 Sept 1992, Talia Jayne b 16 April 1995); *Career* commis chef Hotel Ascot Zürich 1971–72 (apprenticeship 1969–71), chef Stadtspital Triemli Zürich (Nat Serv) 1972–73; Hotel Zürich: chef tournant 1974–75, larder chef 1975–77, sauce chef 1977–79; Hotel Beatus Merligen: roast chef (summer season) 1975, sous chef/sauce chef (summer season) 1977; sous-chef: Hotel Savoy Baur en Ville Zürich 1979–80, Hotel au Lac Zürich 1980–82; head chef Hotel Beatus Merligen 1982–85; The Dorchester Hotel London: exec sous-chef to Anton Mosimann, *qv* 1986–88, head chef rising to exec chef 1988–; stage 1989: Oriental Hotel Bangkok, Ritz Hotel Paris, Ecole Technique Hoteliere Tsuji Osaka Japan; special skills in ice carving and butter modelling; promotion with British Airways first class flights Sept-Nov 1991, jt promotion with Concorde Jan-Nov 1992; memb: Judging Panel of Chefs Hotelympia 1992–93, Grand Final Judging Panel Toque d'Or Competition 1992–93; weekly columnnist Daily Express 1992–93; *Awards* various awards at worldwide cooking competitions and exhibitions (22 Gold medals, 2 Silver medals, 3 special prizes), Caterer & Hotelkeeper Function Menu of the Month Sept 1991 and June 1992, Caterer & Hotelkeeper Chef of the Yr GB 1996; *Books* Daily Express All Colour Cookery Book (1994), A World of Flavours - Recipes from the Voyages of a Master Chef (1995), Music and Menus for Christmas (1996); *Style*— Willi Elsener, Esq; ✉ 9 Devenreux Road, Battersea, London SW11 6HX; The Dorchester Hotel, Park Lane, London W1A 2HJ (☎ 0171 629 8888, fax 0171 409 0114)

ELSTEIN, David Keith; s of Albert Elstein (d 1983), and Millie Cohen (d 1985); *b* 14 Nov 1944; *Educ* Haberdashers' Aske's, Gonville and Caius Coll Cambridge (BA, MA); *m* 16 July 1978, Jenny, da of Alfred Conway; 1 s (Daniel b 1981); *Career* asst prodr BBC 1964–68 (prodns incl The Money Programme, Panorama, Cause for Concern, People in Conflict), prodr Thames TV 1968–72 (prodns incl This Week, The Day Before Yesterday, The World at War), prodr Weekend World (LWT) 1972–73, ed This Week and exec prodr documentaries Thames Television 1973–82, exec prodr Goldcrest TV 1982–83 (prodns incl Concealed Enemies), md and exec prodr Brook Productions 1982–86 (prodns incl Almonds and Raisins, Low), md and exec prodr Primetime TV 1983–86 (prodns incl Seal Morning, Return to Treasure Island, The Deliberate Death of a Polish Priest, Double Image), dir of progs Thames Television 1986–93, chm Euston Films 1991–93, head of programming Sky TV 1993–96, chief exec Channel 5 1996–; James McTaggart Meml lectr Edinburgh Int Television Festival 1991; *Recreations* cinema, theatre, bridge, reading; *Style*— David Elstein, Esq; ✉ Channel 5 Broadcasting Ltd, 22 Long Acre, London WC2E 9LY (☎ 0171 911 0055)

ELSTOB, Eric Carl; s of Capt Eric Bramley Elstob, OBE, RN (d 1949), and Signe Mathilda, *née* Ohlsson (d 1968), RGCI (Sweden); *b* 5 April 1943; *Educ* Marlborough (scholar), Queen's Coll Oxford (exhibitioner, MA); *Career* dir: Foreign and Colonial Management Ltd 1969–95, GT Japan Investment Trust 1972, TR Smaller Companies Investment Trust 1973, Foreign and Colonial Investment Trust (joint mangr) 1973–95, S R Pan-European Investment Trust 1980, Bangkok Fund 1986, World Trust Fund 1991; dep chm: Foreign & Colonial Eurotrust 1972, Foreign & Colonial Pacific Investment Trust 1984, Foreign & Colonial German Investment Trust 1990, Saracen Value Trust 1994, Abtrust Asian Smaller Companies Investment Trust 1995; chm Friends of Christ Church Spitalfields; Brother Worshipful Co of Parish Clerks; *Books* Sweden - A Traveller's History (1978); *Recreations* fell walking, canoeing, architecture, history; *Clubs* Travellers, Brooks's; *Style*— Eric Elstob, Esq; ✉ 14 Fournier St, Spitalfields, London EC1 6QE (☎ 0171 247 5942, fax 0171 247 2822)

ELSTON, Christopher David (Chris); s of Herbert Cecil Elston (d 1962), and Ada Louisa Elston, *née* Paige (d 1978); *b* 1 Aug 1938; *Educ* Univ Coll Sch Hampstead, King's Coll Cambridge (BA), Yale Univ USA (MA); *m* 17 Oct 1964, Jennifer Isabel, da of Dr A E Rampling (d 1983), and Dr C M Rampling; 1 s (Peter b 1966), 2 da (Lucinda b 1968, Elizabeth b 1975); *Career* Bank of England: joined 1960, seconded to Bank for Int Settlements Basle Switzerland 1969–71, private sec to Govr Bank of England 1976–77, asst to Chief Cashier 1977–79, seconded HM Diplomatic Service as fin attaché Br Embassy Tokyo 1979–83, sr advsr (Asia and Australasia) 1983–94; chief exec London Bullion Market Assoc 1995–; advsr KorAm Bank London branch 1995–; *Recreations* music, photography, gardening, walking; *Style*— Chris Elston, Esq; ✉ Highfold, 23 Grasmere Avenue, Harpenden, Herts AL5 5PT (☎ and fax 01582 760147)

ELSTON, John David; s of Lt-Col John William Elston (d 1984), and Alwyn, *née* Fawbert; *b* 2 Aug 1946; *Educ* Norwich Sch, Richmond Sch Yorks, Univ of Newcastle upon Tyne (BA); *m* 27 Sept 1980, Victoria Ann Harding (Vicky), da of Victor William Brown, of Etobicoke, Toronto, Canada; 2 s (James b 1982, Henry b 1988), 1 da (Georgina b 1986); *Career* sr exec James Capel & Co 1985–94 (joined 1973), Panmure Gordon & Co 1995–; FCA 1979; *Recreations* squash, golf, tennis, bridge; *Style*— John Elston, Esq; ✉ Tara, Woodland Rise, Sevenoaks, Kent TN15 0HZ (☎ 01732 762162)

ELSTON, John Scorgie; s of Charles Henry Elston, of West Kirby, Merseyside, and Hilda Constance Mary Elston (d 1986); *b* 22 March 1949; *Educ* St Bees Sch Cumberland, St Thomas's Hosp Med Sch (BSc, MB BS); *partner* Frederika Estelle Smith; 1 s (Guy Scorgie b 11 Mar 1993), 1 da (Charlotte Rose Scorgie b 10 June 1990); *Career* med practitioner; house appts in gen med and surgery before specialising in ophthalmology; trg in ophthalmology: St Thomas's Hosp 1975–78, Moorfields Eye Hosp 1979–87, Hosp for Sick Children 1983–87; conslt ophthalmologist: Nat Hosp for Neurology and Neurosurgery 1987–91, St Mary's Hosp London 1987–91, Western Ophthalmic Hosp London 1987–91, Radcliffe Infirmary Oxford 1991–; FRCS 1982, FRSM 1988, FRCOphth 1989, MD 1990; *Books* Dystonia II (jtly, 1987), Pediatric Ophthalmology (jtly, 1990), Scientific Basis of Neurosurgery (jtly, 1991), Community Paediatrics (jtly, 1991); *Recreations* golf, tennis, walking, English literature; *Clubs* RSM; *Style*— John Elston, Esq; ✉ Radcliffe Infirmary, Oxford OX2 6AN (☎ 01865 224201, fax 01865 224739)

ELSWORTH, David Raymond Cecil; s of Violet Kathleen Elsworth; *b* 12 Dec 1939; *m* 20 Dec 1969, Jennifer Jane Kimber, da of J K R Macgregor; 2 s (Simon David b 30 May 1972, Iain Robert David b 6 June 1975), 1 da (Jessica Jane b 9 June 1984); *Career* nat hunt jockey 1957–72, racehorse trainer 1978–; nat hunt winners: Rhyme 'N' Reason (Grand National) 1988, Heighlin (Triumph Hurdle), Barnbrook Again (Queen Mother Champion Chase, twice), Desert Orchid (King George VI Rank Chase 1986 and 1988–90, Whitbread Gold Cup 1988, Cheltenham Gold Cup 1989, Jameson Irish Grand National 1990); trained on the flat: Mighty Flutter (third place, Derby) 1984, In the Groove (winner Goffs Irish One Thousand Guineas, first Classic and three further Group 1 races) 1990, Seattle Rhyme (Racing Post Trophy, Gp One Doncaster) 1991; champion Nat Hunt trainer 1987–88; *Recreations* shooting, golf; *Style*— David Elsworth, Esq; ✉ Whitsbury Manor Racing Stables Limited, Whitsbury, nr Fordingbridge, Hants (business ☎ 01725 518889, home 01725 518274)

ELTIS, Dr Walter Alfred; s of Rev Dr Martin Eltis (d 1968), and Mary, *née* Schnitzer (d 1977); *b* 23 May 1933; *Educ* Wycliffe Coll, Emmanuel Coll Cambridge (BA), Nuffield Coll Oxford (MA); *m* 5 Sept 1959, Shelagh Mary, da of Prebendary Douglas Aubrey Owen (d 1964); 1 s (David b 1963), 2 da (Sarah b 1966, Clare b 1968); *Career* PO navigator RAF 1951–53; fell and tutor in economics Exeter Coll Oxford 1963–88 (emeritus fell 1988–); visiting reader in economics Univ of W Aust 1970–71; visiting prof in economics: Univ of Toronto 1976–77, Euro Univ Florence 1979, Univ of Reading 1992–; Gresham prof of commerce 1993–96; gen ed Oxford Econ Papers 1975–81, dir gen Nat Econ Devpt Office 1988–92 (econ dir 1986–88), chief econ advsr to the Pres of the Bd of Trade 1992–95; memb: Cncl of Govrs Wycliffe Coll 1974–88, CNAA 1987–93 (chm Social Sci Ctee 1987–88), Cncl European Policy Forum 1992–, Fndn for Manufacturing and Indust 1993–; vice chm Cncl European Soc for History of Economic Thought 1996–; DLitt Univ of Oxford 1990; *Books* Economic Growth: Analysis and Policy (1965), Growth and Distribution (1973), Britain's Economic Problem: Too Few Producers (with Robert Bacon, 1976, 2 edn 1978, 3 edn as Britain's Economic Problem Revisited, 1996), The Classical Theory of Economic Growth (1984), Keynes & Economic Policy (with P Sinclair, 1988), Classical Economics, Public Expenditure and Growth (1993); *Recreations* chess, music; *Clubs* Reform (chm 1994–95), RAC; *Style*— Dr Walter Eltis; ✉ Danesway, Jarn Way, Boars Hill, Oxford OX1 5JF (☎ 01865 735440)

ELTON, Antony; s of Jack Elton Williams (d 1971), and Ena Frances Keeble (d 1967); *b* 3 July 1935; *Educ* Magdalen Coll Choir Oxford, RAM London (LRAM), Univ of Durham (BMus), Univ of Surrey (MMus); *m* 1 (m dis), Barbara Peni; 2 s (Conrad b 1966, Pearse b 1971), 1 da (Serena b 1963); m 2 (m dis), Jean Montanus; 1 da (Joy b 1977); *Career* composer, pianist, lectr, critic, poet, traveller, anti-cruelty activist; NZBC NZ Ballet and NZ Child Welfare 1957–62, ABC Australian Ballet and Victoria Educn Dept 1962–66, dir of music Durham Tech Coll 1968–73, sr lectr Univ of Nigeria Nsukka 1973–76 (chm Music Dept 1973–75), md Durham Theatre Co, critic Durham Advertiser 1978–85; tutor 1977–88: The Open Univ, Beamish Hall, Billingham Coll; SAGA music tutor 1991–; concert tours and events for: Amnesty Int, Red Cross, Cancer Research, NSPCC, RSPCA, WWF; fndr and hon sec The Cox Tst for Young Singers; memb: Performing Right Soc, Composers Guild, RSMGB, Charter 88; *Works* pre 1980 incl: Come Away Death, The Exile, Anne Frank, Trombone Quartets, Suite From Nigeria, Preludes to Midsummer, Scottish Sketchbook; post 1980 incl: Songs of Women, Polish Symphony, Hungarian Quartet, Balkan Journeys, Sonata for Lefthand, Gifts from Slovakia, Russian Impressions, Fate (dance drama), Heart of Albania, Bulgarian Excursion, Autumn, Decay Doom Delight, Summer Sky Sea, Memories of Portugal, Spain Then and Now, Finnish Suite, Italiano, Devon Suites, Songs of Life and Death, A Female Heart, Love Found and Lost, Woodwind Quartets, Birdsongs and Human Meditations, String Quartet; *Books* Music and Life (1985), The Kovac Letters (1989), Not Always Music (1993), Still Moving (1995), Man's Best Friend (1996); *Recreations* swimming, philosophy, history, cricket, dogs; *Style*— Antony Elton, Esq; ✉ Mole Cottage, 17 Prospect Terrace, New Brancepeth, Co Durham DH7 7EJ (☎ 0191 373 2893)

ELTON, Sir Arnold; kt (1987), CBE (1982); s of Max Elton (d 1953), and Ada, *née* Levy (d 1990); *b* 14 Feb 1920; *Educ* UCL (MS); *m* 9 Nov 1952, Billie Pamela, da of John Nathan Briggs; 1 s (Michael Jonathan b 1953); *Career* jr and sr Gold medal in surgery UCH, Gosse res scholarship Charing Cross Hosp 1951; formerly sr surgical registrar Charing Cross Hosp, house surgn, house physician and casualty offr UCH; conslt surgn: Mt

Vernon Hosp 1960–70, Harrow Hosp 1951–70, Northwick Park Hosp 1970–85; hon conslt surgn Northwick Park Hosp 1985–, conslt emeritus surgn Clementine Churchill Hosp, conslt surgn British Airways 1988–; memb: Ct of Patrons RCS, Cons Pty Central Cncl and Nat Exec Ctee, Br Assoc of Surgical Oncology (fndr memb), Govt Ctee on Screening for Breast Cancer, Hunterian Soc Assoc of Surgns; exec memb Int Med Parliamentarians Orgn 1995–, memb and chm Court of Examiners to RCS, previously examiner to Gen Nursing Cncl, surgical tutor RCS 1970–82, chm Cons Med Soc 1975–92 (pres 1992–); pres and Euro rep Cons Med Soc 1992–; ed CMS Euro Bulletin 1994–; dir Medical and Political Services (MPS) 1993–; Liveryman: Worshipful Soc of Apothecaries, Worshipful Co of Carmen; Jubilee Medal for Community Servs 1977; memb: Euro Soc of Surgical Oncology 1995, World Federation of Surgical Oncological Societies 1995–; FRCS, FICS; *Recreations* tennis; *Clubs* Carlton, RAC, MCC; *Style—* Sir Arnold Elton, CBE; ✉ Carlton Club, 69 St James's Street, London W1; The Consulting Rooms, Wellington Hospital, Wellington Place, London NW8 (☎ 0171 935 4101, fax 0171 483 0297)

ELTON, Sir Charles Abraham Grierson; 11 Bt (GB 1717), of Bristol; s of Sir Arthur Hallam Rice Elton, 10 Bt (d 1973), and Margaret Ann, *née* Bjornson (d 1995); *b* 23 May 1953; *Educ* Eton, Univ of Reading (BA); *m* 2 March 1990, Lucy Lauris, da of late Lukas Heller and Mrs Caroline Garnham; 1 da (Lotte Caroline b 15 Aug 1993); *Heir* kinsman, Charles Tierney Hallam Elton b 1898; *Career* with BBC Publications; *Style—* Sir Charles Elton, Bt; ✉ Clevedon Court, Clevedon, Somerset BS21 6QU; 34 Pembridge Villas, London W11

ELTON, Prof George Alfred Hugh; CB (1983); s of Horace William Elton (d 1980), and Violet Elton; *b* 27 Feb 1925; *Educ* Sutton County Sch, Univ of London (BSc, PhD, DSc); *m* 1951, Theodora Rose Edith, da of George Henry Theodore Kingham (d 1965); 2 da; *Career* under sec Miny of Agric Fisheries and Food 1974 (chief scientific advsr (food) 1971–85, dep chief scientist 1972), chm Nat Food Survey 1978–85; memb: Advsy Bd for Res Cncls 1981–85, Agric and Food Res Cncl 1981–85, Natural Environment Res Cncl 1981–85; vice chm EEC Scientific Ctee for Food 1985–92, dir Int Life Sciences Inst (Europe) Brussels 1987–, vice pres British Industrial Biological Research Assoc (BIBRA) 1996– (chm 1993–95); Europa Medal (EC) 1985; Hon DSc Univ of Reading 1984, Hon DUniv of Surrey 1991; FRSC 1951, FIBiol 1976, EurChem 1993; *Recreations* golf; *Clubs* MCC; *Style—* Prof George Elton, CB; ✉ Green Nook, Bridle Lane, Loudwater, Rickmansworth, Herts WD3 4JH

ELTON, Michael Anthony; s of Francis Herbert Norris Elton (d 1976), and Margaret Helen, *née* Gray; *b* 20 May 1932; *Educ* Peter Symonds Sch, Brasenose Coll Oxford (BCL, MA); *m* 16 July 1955, Isabel Clare, da of Thomas Gurney Ryott (d 1965); 2 s (Tim b 1965, Mark b 1970), 2 da (Caroline b 1960, Louise b 1969); *Career* articled 1954–57, admitted slr 1957; asst slr: Cumberland CC 1958–61, Surrey CC 1961–65; asst clerk Bucks CC 1965–70, dep clerk of the peace for Bucks 1967–70, chief exec ABTA 1970–86; dir gen: Euro Fedn for Retirement Provision 1987–91, Nat Assoc of Pension Funds 1987–95; former Hants Co squash player; CIMgt, FRSA; *Books* Future Perfect (with Gyles Brandreth, 1988), Travelling To Retirement (1989); *Recreations* music, tennis, bridge, gardening; *Clubs* Utd Oxford and Cambridge, Winchester Music, Winchester Lawn Tennis, South Winchester Golf; *Style—* Michael Elton, Esq

ELTON, Michael John; s of John Thomas Humphrey Elton (d 1981), and Kathleen Margaret, *née* Bird; *b* 20 Dec 1933; *Educ* SW Essex Tech Coll, Royal Naval Electrical Sch; *m* 26 March 1965, Carole Elizabeth, da of William Saunby, of Kettering, Northants; 2 s (James Robert b 1967, Charles Lindsey b 1969); *Career* Nat Serv Sub Lt RNVR 1955–57; serv: 108 Minesweeping Sqdn Malta, base electrical offr Cyprus; Lt RNR 1958–62; engrg and sales positions STC London 1957–63, staff of mktg dir ITT Europe Paris 1963–64, mktg mangr STC Data Systems London 1964–69, Control Data: mangr int data servs Minneapolis 1969–70 and Brussels 1970–71, md Stockholm 1971–74, chm and md Helsinki 1973–74, gen mangr Brussels 1974–79, gen mangr London 1979–81; Technitron: vice pres and gen mangr Technitron International Inc 1981–86, md and chief exec Technitron plc 1986–90; currently princ EMS Management Consultants and chm Travelcom International Ltd; CEng, FIEE, FBCS, FIMgt; *Recreations* golf, sailing, swimming; *Clubs* Naval, RNVR Yacht, Chobham Golf; *Style—* Michael Elton, Esq; ✉ 3 Oriel Hill, Camberley, Surrey GU15 2JW

ELTON, 2 Baron (UK 1934); Rodney Elton; TD (1970); s of 1 Baron Elton (d 1973), and Dedi (d 1977), da of Gustav Hartmann, of Oslo, Norway; *b* 2 March 1930; *Educ* Eton, New Coll Oxford; *m* 1, 18 Sept 1958 (m dis 1979), Anne Frances, da of late Brig Robert Adolphus George Tilney, CBE, DSO, TD, DL; 1 s, 3 da; m 2, 24 Aug 1979, (Susan) Richenda, yst da of late Sir Hugh Gurney, KCMG, MVO; *Heir* s, Hon Edward Paget Elton b 28 May 1966; *Career* formerly: farmer, teacher and lectr; contested (C) Loughborough Leics 1966 and 1970; oppn spokesman Educn and Welsh Affrs 1974–79, dep sec Int Affrs Ctee of Gen Synod of C of E 1976–78, dep chm Andry Montgomery Ltd 1977–79 and 1987–; memb Boyd Cmmn (South Rhodesia elections 1979); Parly under sec of state: NI Office 1979–81, DHSS 1981–82, Home Office 1982–84; min of state Home Office 1984–85, DOE 1985–86; memb Select Ctee on the Scrutiny of Delegated Powers; dep chm Assoc of Conservative Peers 1988–93; memb Panel on Takeovers and Mergers 1987–90; chm: FIMBRA 1987–90, Enquiry into Discipline in Schs 1988, Intermediate Treatment Fund 1990–93, Divert Tst 1993–; pres Bldg Conservation Tst 1990–95, tstee City Parochial Fndn & Tst for London 1991–97; hon life memb Cncl of City & Guilds of London Inst, hon vice pres Inst of Trading Standards Administration; *Clubs* Cavalry and Guards', Beefsteak, Pratt's; *Style—* The Rt Hon the Lord Elton, TD; ✉ House of Lords, London SW1A 0PW

ELVIDGE, John Allan; s of Allan Elvidge, and Edith *née* Dallman; *b* 19 March 1946; *Educ* Kingston GS, Downing Coll Cambridge (MA, LLB); *Career* called to the Bar Lincoln's Inn 1968, recorder of the Crown Court 1994–; ldr London Borough of Merton 1988–90; fell Downing Coll Cambridge 1969–75; *Recreations* golf, tennis; *Style—* John Elvidge, Esq; ✉ 1 Mitre Court Buildings, Temple, London EC4Y 7BS (☎ 0171 797 7070)

ELVIDGE, John William; s of late Herbert William Elvidge, and Irene Teresa, *née* Reynolds; *b* 9 Feb 1951; *Educ* Sir George Monoux Sch Walthamstow, St Catherine's Coll Oxford (BA); *partner* Maureen Margaret Ann McGinn; *Career* Scottish Office: joined as admin trainee 1973, various posts in educn, housing and tport, higher exec offr (A) 1976–78, princ 1978–84, asst sec and fin offr Scottish Economic Planning and Devpt Depts 1984, seconded as dir of implementation Scottish Homes 1988–89, asst sec 1989–93, under sec Industry and Devpt Dept 1993–; *Recreations* painting, film, theatre, modern novels, music, swimming, walking, food and drink; *Clubs* Peg's; *Style—* John Elvidge, Esq; ✉ The Scottish Office Development Department, Room 3–H07, Victoria Quay, Edinburgh EH6 6QQ (☎ 0131 244 0629)

ELWES, Henry William George; JP; s of Maj John Hargreaves Elwes, MC, Scots Gds (ka N Africa 1943), and Isabel Pamela Ivy, *née* Beckwith (later Mrs John Talbot, d 1993), gda of 7 Duke of Richmond and Gordon; a distant cous of Capt Jeremy Elwes, *qv*; *b* 24 Oct 1935; *Educ* Eton, RAC Cirencester; *m* 8 Sept 1962, Carolyn Dawn, da of Joseph William Wykeham Cripps (d 1958), of Ampney Crucis, Cirencester (3 cous of the post war chllr Sir Stafford Cripps); 3 s (John b 1964, Frederick b 1966, George b 1971, d 1993); *Career* late Lt Scots Gds; farmer and forester; chm Western Woodland Owners Ltd 1971–85 (pres 1981–), regnl dir Lloyds Bank plc 1985–91, dir Colebourne Estate Co; pres or memb of various Gloucestershire tsts and socs; memb: Prince's Youth Business Trust (Glos), Cirencester Rural Dist Cncl 1959–74, Glos CC 1971–91 (vice chm 1976–83 and 1991, chm 1983–85); High Sheriff Glos 1979–80; Lord-Lt Glos 1992– (DL 1982); *Clubs* Confrerie des Chevaliers du Tastevin; *Style—* H W G Elwes, Esq, JP; ✉ Colesbourne Park, nr Cheltenham, Glos GL53 9NP (☎ 01242 870262)

ELWES, Capt Jeremy Gervase Geoffrey Philip; DL (Lincs); s of Lt-Col Rudolph Philip Elwes, OBE, MC (d 1962; whose mother was Lady Winefride Feilding, da of 8 Earl of Denbigh, while his f, Gervase Elwes, was Privy Chamberlain to the Pope, and a celebrated tenor), and Helen Hermione, *née* Wright (d 1956); *b* 1 Sept 1921; *Educ* Ampleforth, Sandhurst; *m* 9 July 1955, Clare Mary, er da of Maj-Gen Arthur Joseph Beveridge, CB, OBE, MC; 4 s (Gervase, Giles, Robert, Hugh); *Career* served WWII Capt M East (despatches), KRRC and SAS; farmer in Lincs 1949–; pres Cncl Preservation Rural England (Lincs) 1979–89 (chm 1962–78); High Sheriff Lincs 1969; fndr Lincs and Humberside Arts Assoc 1964–91; fndr/chm: Shrievalty Assoc of GB 1971, Elwes Enterprises, Elsham Hall Country and Wildlife Park; DL: Lincs 1969, Humberside 1974; Vice Lord-Lt for Humberside 1983–96; vice chm Environmental Medicine Fndn 1987, co-fndr Scarbank Tst holidays for handicapped children; Knight SMOM; *Recreations* natural history, the Arts, handicapped people; *Clubs* Green Jackets, Royal Over-Seas League; *Style—* Capt Jeremy Elwes; ✉ Elsham Hall, nr Brigg, S Humberside DN20 0QZ (☎ 01652 688738)

ELWES, Sir Jeremy Vernon; kt (1994), CBE (1984); s of Eric Vincent Elwes (d 1985), of Sevenoaks, Kent, and Dorothea, *née* Bilton; *b* 29 May 1937; *Educ* Wirral GS, Bromley GS, City of London Coll; *m* 1963, Phyllis Marion, da of George Herbert Harding Relf, of Halstead, Sevenoaks, Kent; 1 s (Jonathan b 1969); *Career* chartered sec; dir Sevenoaks Constitutional Club Co Ltd 1977–; chm Cons Political Centre Nat Advsy Ctee 1981–84, personnel dir Reed Business Publishing Ltd 1982–93, human resources dir Reed Publishing Europe 1993–94; dir Sutton Enterprise Agency Ltd 1987–94 (chm 1987–90), chm SE Area Provincial Cncl 1986–90; Cons Pty Nat Union: memb Exec Ctee 1974–95, dep chm Euro Ctee 1991–95; Judge Int Wine and Spirits Competition Ltd 1983–; chm: St Helier NHS Tst 1991–, Walthamstow Hall 1984– (govr 1977–); govr Eltham Coll 1977–96, memb Exec Ctee Gen Cncl Cons Gp for Europe 1977–96; Liveryman Worshipful Co of Stationers and Newspapermakers; Chevalier Ordre des Chevaliers Bretvins (Bailliage de GB, Maitre des Ceremonies 1984–88, Chancelier 1986–92); ACIS, FRSA; *Recreations* wine, food, reading, golf; *Clubs* Carlton, Nizels Golf; *Style—* Sir Jeremy Elwes, CBE; ✉ Crispian Cottage, Weald Road, Sevenoaks, Kent TN13 1QQ (☎ 01732 454208, fax 01732 464153); The St Helier NHS Trust, Wrythe Lane, Carshalton, Surrey SM5 1AA (☎ 0181 296 3525, fax 0181 641 4717)

ELWES, Nigel Robert; s of late Maj Robert Philip Henry Elwes, MBE, MC, of Athry House, Ballinafad, Co Galway, Ireland, and his 1 wife, Vivien Elizabeth Fripp, *née* Martin-Smith; *b* 8 Aug 1941; *Educ* Eton; *m* 22 June 1965, Carolyn Peta, da of Sir Robin McAlpine, CBE, of Aylesfield, Alton, Hampshire; 1 s (Andrew b 1969), 2 da (Serena (Mrs Jeremy Bradbeer) b 1967, Melisa b 1973); *Career* CA, stockbroker, farmer and bloodstock breeder; ptnr Rowe & Pitman 1970–86, fin dir S G Warburg Securities 1986–91, chm Reyker Securities Ltd 1991–94; Stock Exchange: joined 1970, memb Cncl 1983–86 and 1988–91, chm Domestic Equity Market Ctee 1988–91, chm Special Ctee on Market Devpt (Elwes Ctee); dir Dorchester Hotel 1974–76; ptnr: Aylesfield Farms 1991–, Aylesfield Farms Stud 1993–; govr Lord Mayor Treloar Coll 1992–; vice chm: The Racing Welfare Charities 1992–, Stable Lads Welfare Tst 1993–; tstee Br Racing Sch 1992–; memb: Cncl Thoroughbred Breeders' Assoc 1996–, BHB Race Planning Ctee 1996–; FCA, MSI; *Recreations* hunting, shooting, racing; *Clubs* White's; *Style—* Nigel Elwes, Esq; ✉ Aylesfield, Alton, Hants GU34 4BY (☎ 01420 543248); Aylesfield Farms (☎ 01420 80825)

ELWES, Peter John Gervase; s of Lt-Col Simon Edmund Vincent Paul Elwes, RA (d 1975), of Amberley, Sussex, and Hon Gloria Elinor, *née* Rodd (d 1975); *b* 17 Oct 1929; *Educ* Eton, Miles Aircraft Tech Coll, Kingston and Gateshead Colls of Advanced Technol; *m* 7 May 1960, Hon Rosalie Ann, da of Brig James Brian George Hennessy, 2 Baron Windlesham (d 1962), of Askefield, Bray, Ireland; 3 s (Luke b 26 July 1961, Benedict b 4 May 1963, Marcus b 27 Nov 1964), 1 da (Harriet b 3 Dec 1968); *Career* 2 Lt Royal Scots Greys BAOR Germany 1950–52, Lt Northumberland Hussars 1953–56; Vickers Armstrong Ltd Weybridge and Newcastle 1948–53, Ransomes & Rapier Ltd Ipswich 1953–56, Rio Tinto-Zinc Corporation Ltd 1956–73, md Hamilton Bros Oil and Gas Ltd 1973–77, dir Kleinwort Benson Ltd 1977–89, chief exec Enterprise Oil plc 1983–84, md Renown Energy Ltd 1988–89; Hardy Oil & Gas plc: dep chm and chief exec 1989–94, exec dep chm 1995–96; chm Aminex 1996–; non-exec dir Energy Africa Limited 1996–; FInstPet; *Recreations* painting, gardening, music; *Clubs* Hurlingham; *Style—* Peter Elwes, Esq; ✉ 75 Murray Rd, Wimbledon, London SW19 4PF; Aminex plc, 10 Bedford Street, London WC2E 9HE (☎ 0171 240 1600, fax 0171 240 0295); 9 rue des Moulins, 37160 Abilly, France (☎ 00 33 47 92 90 69)

ELWORTHY, Air Cdre the Hon Timothy Charles; CVO (1995), CBE (1986); eldest s of Marshal of the RAF Baron Elworthy, KG, GCB, CBE, DSO, LVO, DFC, AFC (Life Peer, d 1993), and Audrey, *née* Hutchinson (d 1986); *b* 27 Jan 1938; *Educ* Radley, RAF Coll Cranwell; *m* 1, 1961 (m dis 1969), Victoria Ann, eldest da of Lt-Col H C W Bowring; 2 da (Katharine Emma Victoria b 1963, Lucinda Rose b 1965); m 2, 1971, Anabel, da of late Reginald Ernest Harding, OBE; 1 s (Edward Charles b 1974); *Career* RAF; Capt of The Queen's Flight 1989–94, Extra Equerry to HM the Queen 1991–, HM's Sr Air Equerry 1995–; Liveryman Guild of Air Pilots and Air Navigators; *Recreations* country pursuits, wine, travel; *Clubs* Boodle's; *Style—* Air Cdre the Hon Timothy Elworthy, CVO, CBE; ✉ The Office of Her Majesty's Senior Air Equerry, RAF Northolt, West End Road, Ruislip, Middx HA4 6NG

ELY, 8 Marquess of (I 1801); Sir Charles John Tottenham; 9 Bt (I 1780); sits as Baron Loftus (UK 1801); also Baron Loftus (I 1785), Viscount Loftus (I 1789); s of George Leonard Tottenham (d 1928), and gggs of Rt Rev Lord Robert Ponsonby Tottenham, Bp of Clogher, 2 s of 1 Marquess; suc kinsman 1969; *b* 30 May 1913; *Educ* Collège de Genève, Queen's Univ Kingston Ontario; *m* 1, 23 June 1938, Katherine Elizabeth (d 1975), da of Lt-Col W H Craig, of Kingston, Ontario; 3 s, 1 da; m 2, 1978, Elspeth Ann (d 1996), o da of late P T Hay, of Highgate; *Heir* s, Viscount Loftus, *qv*; *Career* headmaster Boulden House, Trinity Coll Sch, Port Hope, Ontario; *Style—* The Most Hon the Marquess of Ely; ✉ 20 Arundel Court, Jubilee Place, London SW3 (☎ 0171 352 9172); Trinity Coll School, Port Hope, Ontario, Canada L1A 3W2

ELY, Dean of; *see:* Higgins, Very Rev Michael John

ELY, Bishop of 1990–; Rt Rev Stephen Whitefield Sykes; *b* 1 Aug 1939; *Educ* Monkton Combe Sch Bath, St John's Coll Cambridge (MA, Carus Greek Testament prize), Harvard Univ (Joseph Hodges Choate Meml fell), Ripon Hall Oxford (Hulsean essay prize); *Career* St John's Coll Cambridge: fell, dean and dir of studies in theol 1964–74, asst lectr in divinity 1964–67, lectr in divinity 1967–74; van Mildert prof of divinity Univ of Durham and canon of Durham Cathedral 1974–85; Regius prof of divinity and fell St John's Coll Cambridge 1985–90; chm N of England Inst for Christian Educn 1980–85; pres Cncl St John's Coll Durham 1984–94; *Books* Friedrich Schleiermacher (1971), Christian Theology Today (1971), Christ, Faith and History (ed, 1972), The Integrity of Anglicanism (1978), Karl Barth: studies in his theological method (ed, 1980), New Studies in Theology (1980), England and Germany, Studies in Theological Diplomacy (ed, 1982), The Identity of Christianity (1984), Authority in the Anglican Communion (ed, 1987), The Study of Anglicanism (1988), Unashamed Anglicanism (1995); *Recreations* walking; *Style—* The Rt Rev the Bishop of Ely; ✉ The Bishop's House, Ely, Cambs CB7 4DW (☎ 01353 662749, fax 01353 669477)

ELYAN, David Asher Gremson; s of Max Elyan, of Castletown, IOM, and Freda, *née* Gremson; *b* 4 Oct 1940; *Educ* Cork GS, Trinity Coll Dublin (BA, BCom, MA); *Career* co sec Gordon & Gotch Holdings plc 1970–74, assoc dir AGB Research plc 1980–87 (co sec 1974–87); dir: Attwood Research of Ireland Ltd 1981–90, Irish TAM Ltd 1981–90, Corporate Lease Management Ltd 1984–93, Communication Investments Ltd 1987–, Langton Software Ltd 1987–, Elyan Estates Ltd 1987–93, CLM Fleet Management plc 1993–, The Bankside Gallery Ltd 1993–, Wigmore Investments Ltd 1994–; hon treas: Trinity Coll Dublin Dining Club 1968–94 (vice chm 1994–), Friends of Royal Watercolour Soc 1990–; memb: Senate Univ of Dublin 1966–, Corp of Lloyds 1983–, Post Office Advsy Ctee (POAC) 1991–, Cncl Royal Albert Hall 1996–; chm Friends of Royal Acad of Music 1993–; Freeman City of London, Liveryman Worshipful Co of Chartered Secs 1978; ACCS 1967, FCIS 1976 (ACIS 1969), FRSA 1972; *Recreations* collecting first editions, tennis, squash, art, music, bridge; *Clubs* MCC, Kildare St (Dublin), E Gloucestershire (Cheltenham), Union (Malta); *Style—* David Elyan, Esq; ✉ 49 Chester Ct, Regent's Pk, London NW1 4BU; 3 Coates Mill, Winchcombe, Glos GL54 5NH; Ground Floor, Queen's House, Holly Rd, Twickenham, Middx TW1 4EG

ELYAN, Prof Sir (Isadore) Victor; kt (1970); s of Jacob Elyan, PC, JP, and Olga Elyan; *b* 5 Sept 1909; *Educ* St Stephen's Green, Trinity Coll Dublin (BA, LLB, MA); *m* 1, 1939, Ivy Ethel Mabel Stuart-Weir (d 1965); m 2, 1966, Rosaleen Jeanette, da of William Andrew O'Shea; *Career* served WWII, GSO (2) Mil Sec's Branch (DAMS), Maj IA; admitted slr Ireland 1930; called to the Bar: King's Inn 1949, Middle Temple 1952; judge of appeal Ct of Appeal for Basutoland, Bechuanaland Protectorate and Swaziland 1955–66, chief justice Swaziland 1965–70; prof of law and dean Faculty of Law Durban-Westville Univ 1973–77; *Style—* Prof Sir Victor Elyan; ✉ PO Box 22001, Fish Hoek, Cape Province, South Africa

ELYSTAN-MORGAN, Baron (Life Peer UK 1981), of Aberteifi, Co Dyfed; (Dafydd) Elystan Elystan-Morgan; s of Dewi Morgan (d 1971), of Llandre, Aberystwyth, Cardiganshire, and Olwen Morgan; *b* 7 Dec 1932; *Educ* Ardwyn GS Aberystwyth, Univ Coll of Wales Aberystwyth; *m* 1959, Alwen, da of William E Roberts, of Carrog, Merioneth; 1 s (Hon Owain b 1962), 1 da (Hon Eleri (Hon Mrs Hurt) b 1960); *Career* sat as Lab Peer in House of Lords 1981–87, MP (Lab) Cardiganshire 1966–74, Parly under sec of state Home Office 1968–70, pres Welsh Local Authorities Assoc 1967–73, chm Welsh Parly Party 1967–68; called to Bar Gray's Inn 1971 (formerly a slr); recorder (Wales and Chester Circuit) 1983–87, circuit judge (Wales and Chester Circuit) 1987–; hon fell UCW Aberystwyth 1991; *Style—* His Hon Judge Lord Elystan-Morgan; ✉ Carreg-Afon, Dolau, Bow Street, Dyfed (☎ 01970 828408)

EMANUEL, David Leslie; s of John Lawrence Morris Emanuel, and Elizabeth Emanuel (decd); *b* 17 Nov 1952, Wales; *Educ* Cardiff Coll of Art (dip), Harrow Sch of Art (dip), RCA (MA); *m* 1975 (sep), Elizabeth Emanuel, *qv*; 1 s (Oliver), 1 da (Eloise); *Career* fashion designer; early career experience at Hardy Amies, Cojana and Marcel Fenez (with Roland Klein); fndr ptnr (with wife) Emanuel 1977–90 (designers of HRH The Princess of Wales' wedding dress), fndr David Emanuel Couture 1990–; finale spot: Night of 100 Stars Gala Fashion Show (Radio City Hall NY) 1984, Fashion Aid (with Bob Geldof, Royal Albert Hall) 1985, Fashion Aid Japan (Tokyo) 1986, 150th Anniversary Celebration of RCA Art Gala Fashion Show 1987; designs for ballet prodns incl Frankenstein, the Modern Prometheus (Royal Opera House Covent Garden 1985 and La Scala Milan 1987); FCSD; *Books* Style for All Seasons (1983); *Recreations* sport (horse-riding, tennis, jet/water skiing), the arts; *Clubs* Royal Ascot Tennis (Berks), White Elephant; *Style—* David Emanuel, Esq; ✉ Head Office, PO Box 40, Bracknell, Berkshire RH42 6YP; London (☎ 0171 482 6486, fax 0171 267 6627)

EMANUEL, Elizabeth Florence; da of Samuel Charles Weiner (Croix de Guerre), of Warfield, nr Bracknell, Berks, and Brahna Betty, *née* Charkham; *b* 5 July 1953; *Educ* City of London Sch for Girls, Harrow Coll of Art, Royal College of Art (MA); *m* 12 July 1975 (sep 1990), David Leslie Emanuel, *qv*, s of John Lawrence Morris Emanuel; 1 s (Oliver b 21 March 1978), 1 da (Eloise b 25 Dec 1979); *Career* fashion designer; opened London Salon 1978, designed wedding dress for HRH Princess of Wales 1981, launched new shop and design studio 1996; theatre designs incl: costumes for Andrew Lloyd Webber's Song and Dance 1982, sets and costumes for ballet Frankenstein - The Modern Prometheus (Royal Opera House Covent Garden, La Scala Milan) 1985, costumes for Stoll Moss prodn of Cinderella 1985; designed uniforms for: Virgin Atlantic Airlines 1990, Britannia Airways 1996; launched international fashion label under own name 1992, costumes for film The Changeling 1995, designed new range for Berkertex Brides 1994, launched new wedding lifestyle range in Japan 1994; active involvement with charities: WWF, Rainbow Tst; FCSD 1984; *Books* Style For All Seasons (with David Emanuel, 1983); *Recreations* music, ballet, cinema; *Style—* Mrs Elizabeth Emanuel; ✉ Elizabeth Emanuel PLC, 26 Chiltern Street, London W1M 1PF (☎ 0171 224 4995, fax 0171 224 4248)

EMANUEL, Dr Richard Wolff; s of Prof Joseph George Emanuel (d 1958), of Edgbaston, Birmingham, and Ethel Miriam Cecelia, *née* Wolff; *b* 13 Jan 1923; *Educ* Bradfield Coll, Oriel Coll Oxford (MA), Middx Hosp Med Sch (BM BCh, DM); *m* 2 Nov 1950, Lavinia, da of George Albert Hoffmann, of Old Bosham, W Sussex; 3 s (Richard b 8 Nov 1951, Tom b 21 March 1956, Mark b 18 Oct 1961); *Career* Capt RAMC 1948–50; res fell in med Vanderbilt Univ 1956–57, physician National Heart Hosp 1963–90 (asst dir Inst of Cardiology and hon physician 1961–63), physician Middx Hosp 1963–87, advsr in Cardiovascular Disease to Govt of Sudan; chm Med Ctee Nat Heart Hosp 1972–75, memb Academic Bd Middx Hosp Med Sch 1975–77, memb Cncl Middx Hosp Med Sch 1976–77, chm Dist Hosp Med Ctee Middx Hosp 1976–77, sec Working Pty of the RCP to examine the problem of Cardiovasular Fitness of Airline Pilots 1977, sec Working Pty of the RCP and RCS to revise the 1967 Report on A Combined Medical and Surgical Unit for Cardiac Surgery 1977; memb Cncl: Chest Heart and Stroke Assoc 1977–91, Br Heart Fndn 1979–92; chm Cardiology Ctee RCP 1979–85 (sec 1973–79); memb: Jt Liaison Ctee DHSS 1980–90, Chairs and Res Gps Ctee Br Heart Fndn, Res Funds Ctee, Br Heart Fndn 1982–85; chm: Physicians Ctee Nat Heart Hosp 1985–90, Cardiac Care Ctee Br Heart Fndn 1987–92; tstee Gordon Memorial Tst Fund 1987–; civilian conslt in Cardiology to the RAF 1979–89, advsr in Cardiology to the CAA 1981–91; contrib to over 90 publications on cardiovasular disease; memb: Br Acad of Forensic Sci 1960, Assoc of Physicians of GB and I; sec Br Cardiac Soc 1968–70 (memb 1961, asst sec 1966–68, memb Cncl 1981–85); hon memb: Assoc of Physicians of Sudan, Heart Assoc of Thailand; hon fell Phillippine Coll of Cardiology; Grand Commander of the Most Distinguished Order of The Crown of Pahang 1990; *Recreations* fishing, 18 Century glass and ceramics; *Clubs* Oriental; *Style—* Dr Richard Emanuel; ✉ 6 Lansdowne Walk, London W11 3LN

EMBER, Michael George; s of Dr George Leslie Ember (d 1972), and Margaret Ilona, *née* Ungar; *b* 13 May 1935; *Educ* The Gymnasium of Budapest Univ, Hungarian Acad of Drama, Univ of London (BA); *m* 1 April 1967, Elizabeth Ann, da of Sir Charles Sigmund Davis; 3 s (Nicholas Charles b 1969, Thomas Michael b 1972, Philip George b 1973); *Career* independent radio and TV prodr; formerly a chief prodr BBC Radio and originator of: Start the Week, Mid-Week, Stop the Week, In the Psychiatrist's Chair, All in the Mind (Radio 4), The Anthony Clare Interview (ITV); *Style—* Michael Ember, Esq; ✉ Michael Ember Associates, 2 Nightingale Road, Esher, Surrey KT10 8LL (☎ 01372 469825, fax 01372 469133)

EMBERY, Prof Graham; s of Joseph Henry Embery (d 1987), and Elizabeth Jane; *b* 20 Aug 1939; *Educ* King Edward VI GS Stourbridge Worcestershire; *m* 14 Jan 1967, Vivienne Lacey, da of William Horace Powell (d 1973); 2 s (Russell Geraint b 25 Nov 1971, James Toby William b 30 Dec 1973), 1 da (Philippa Jane b 24 June 1970); *Career* lectr Queen's Univ Belfast 1968–70, lectr Royal Dental Hosp 1970–73, reader Univ of Liverpool 1984–87 (lectr 1973–77, sr lectr 1977–84), prof of basic sci Univ of Wales Coll of Med Cardiff 1987–; sec gen Cncl of Euro Study Gp for Res on Surface and Colloidal Phenomena in the Oral Cavity; memb: Advsy Cncl of Int Soc for Fluoride Res, Int Assoc for Dental Res, Br Connective Tissue Soc, Biochemical Soc, Jt Dental Ctee MRC 1991–95, Sci and Engrg Res Cncl and Health Authys 1991–; pres Br Soc for Dental Res 1994–96, treas European Orgn for Caries Res 1994–96, Welsh Devpt Scheme for Health and Social Res 1995–99, Welsh NHS R & D Forum 1995–98; *Recreations* golf, oil painting, classic cars; *Style—* Prof Graham Embery; ✉ 16 Townfield Rd, West Kirby, Wirral, Merseyside L48 7EZ (☎ 0151 625 5954); Department of Basic Dental Science, Dental School, University of Wales College of Medicine, Heath Park, Cardiff, South Wales CF4 4XY (☎ 01222 744240, telex 498699 UniHos G, fax 01222 766343)

EMBIRICOS, Epaminondas George; s of George Epaminondas Embiricos (d 1980), of Athens, Greece, and Sophie, *née* Douma; *b* 15 July 1943; *Educ* Philips Exeter Acad New Hamps USA, MIT (BSc, MSc); *m* 19 March 1977, Angela, da of Nicholas Pittas, of London; 2 s (George Epaminondas b 8 May 1978, Nicholas Epaminondas b 8 June 1980); *Career* chm: Embiricos Shipping Agency Ltd 1969–91, Embiricos Shipbrokers Ltd 1991–; dir: Liberian Shipowners Cncl 1979–84, Baltic Exchange Ltd 1985–90, Chartering Brokers Mutual Insur Assoc 1986–; vice chm: Greek Shipping Co-op Ctee 1986–, Greek Ctee Det Norske Veritas 1986–; chm UK Freight Demurrage and Def Assoc 1993–96 (dir 1984–); Freeman City of London 1984, memb Ct of Assts Worshipful Co of Shipwrights 1994 (Liveryman 1985); *Recreations* sailing, reading; *Clubs* Royal Thames Yacht, Royal Yacht Club of Greece, Royal London Yacht, Island Sailing; *Style—* Epaminondas Embiricos, Esq; ✉ Commonwealth House, 1–19 New Oxford St, London WC1A 1NU (☎ 0171 404 0420, fax 0171 872 9387, telex 8812792)

EMBLIN, Roslyn Inglis; JP (City of London 1996); da of Norman Inglis Emblin (d 1973), of Halifax, W Yorkshire, and Christabel Gardner Emblin; *b* 13 Aug 1943; *Educ* Princess Mary HS Halifax, Univ of London, Kings Fund Coll London; *Career* student nurse St Thomas's Hosp 1963–67, pupil midwife Queen Charlotte's Maternity Hosp London 1967–68; St Thomas's Hosp: ward sister 1968–71, admin sister 1971–72, nursing offr 1972–76; int sec Royal Coll of Nursing 1976–83 (fndr Int Summer Sch 1977); Moorfields Eye Hosp: chief nursing offr 1983, chief nursing offr and dep chief exec 1985–, memb Govrs 1990–94, exec dir 1994–; memb: Victoria Health Authy 1982–84, Frink Award Ctee Greater London Fund for the Blind 1987–95, Health Servs Ctee RNIB 1990–95; chm Chief Nurses Gp of the Special Health Authys 1992–94; Sainsbury scholarship to study in USA and Canada 1981, Florence Nightingale scholarship to study in USA 1986; memb: RCN, American Socc for Ophthalmic Registered Nurses; *Books* Nursing Education and Practice in the European Community (RCN, 1980), Nursing in the EEC (Croom Helm, 1982); *Recreations* gardening, horse racing, travel; *Style—* Miss Roslyn Emblin, JP; ✉ Moorfields Eye Hospital, City Rd, London EC1V 2PD (☎ 0171 253 3411 ext 2427, fax 0171 253 4696)

EMBREY, Derek Morris; OBE (1986); s of Frederick Embrey (d 1972), and Ethel May, *née* Morris; *b* 11 March 1928; *Educ* Wolverhampton Poly; *m* 1951 (m dis 1996), Frances Margaret, da of Arthur Ewart Stephens (d 1971); 1 s (Stephen Adrian), 1 da (Fiona Jacquiline); *Career* Flight Lt RAFVR; group tech dir: AB Electronics Group plc 1973–91, AB Systems Ltd, AB Components Ltd, Voice Micro Systems Ltd; chm WAB 1987–90; conslt electrical engr 1991–; Univ of Loughborough: visiting prof 1977–86, external examiner 1984–88, visiting lectr 1988–; visiting lectr Univ of Birmingham 1989–; memb: Welsh Industries Bd 1982–85, Engrg Cncl 1982–86, Cncl UWIST 1983–89, NEC 1983–, USITT Bd Univ of Southampton 1988–96, Engrg Cncl EGC2 Ctee 1988–95; chm M&D Bd IEE 1993–94 (vice chm 1990–92), dir and memb Cncl BTEC 1993–96 (chm Engrg Advsy Ctee 1991–94); regnl chm for Wales ATC 1988–95, memb Air Cadet Cncl 1988–95; hon fell: Wolverhampton Univ 1987, Univ of Wales Inst - Cardiff 1992; Freeman City of London 1986, Liveryman Worshipful Co of Scientific Instrument Makers 1986, fndr memb Welsh Livery Guild 1992; CEng, FIEE, FIMechE; *Recreations* music, archaeology, piloting and navigating aircraft; *Clubs* RAF London; *Style—* Derek Embrey, Esq, OBE; ✉ 21 Rockfield Glade, Parc Seymour, Penhow, Newport, Gwent NP6 3JF (☎ and fax 01663 400995, e-mail DME235@AOL.COM)

EMBUREY, John Ernest; s of John Alfred Emburey (d 1984), and Rose Alice, *née* Roff; *b* 20 Aug 1952; *Educ* Peckham Manor Secondary Sch; *m* 1, 22 Sept 1974 (m dis 1980), Sandra Ann, *née* Ball; m 2, 20 Sept 1980, Susan Elizabeth Anne, da of John Michael Booth, of Melbourne, Aust; 2 da (Clare Elizabeth b 1 March 1983, Chloe Louise b 31 Oct 1985); *Career* cricketer; Middlesex CCC 1971–95: debut 1973, awarded county cap 1977, vice capt 1983–95, benefit 1986; chief coach Northamptonshire CCC 1996–; England: played in 64 test matches and 61 one day internationals, memb 8 overseas tours, capt to Sharjah 1987, capt in 2 tests v W Indies 1988, vice capt 1986–89; winner 7 County Championships Middlesex (1976, 1977, 1980, 1982, 1985, 1990 and 1993), memb unofficial England team touring S Africa 1989/90 (subsequently banned from test cricket until winter 1992), memb England team touring India and Sri Lanka 1992/93, memb squad Ashes series 1993; England A cricket mangr tour of Pakistan 1995; *Books* Emburey - A Biography (1987), Spinning in a Fast World (1989); *Recreations* golf, fishing; *Clubs* MCC, Harlequins RFC; *Style—* John Emburey, Esq; ✉ c/o Northamptonshire County Cricket Club, The County Ground, Wantage Road, Northampton NN1 4TJ

EMERSON, Michael Ronald; s of late James Emerson, of Wilmslow, Cheshire, and Priscilla Emerson; *b* 12 May 1940; *Educ* Hurstpierpoint Coll and Balliol Coll Oxford (MA in PPE); *m* 1966, Barbara Christine, da of late Harold Brierley; 1 s, 2 da; *Career* Price Waterhouse & Co London 1962–65; Orgn for Economic Cooperation and Devpt Paris: posts Devpt and Econs Depts, laterally head of General Economics Div 1966–73; EEC Brussels: head of Div for Budgetary Policy Directorate-Gen II 1973–76, econ advsr to President of the Commission 1977, dir for Nat Econs and Econ Trends 1978–81, dir Macroeconomic Analyses and Policy 1981–87, dir Econ Evaluation of Community Policies Directorate-Gen II EC Cmmn Brussels 1987–90, ambass and head of delgn of the EC to the Cwlth of Independent States 1991–96; fell Centre for Int Affairs Harvard Univ 1985–86; *Publications* Europe's Stagflation (ed, 1984), What Model for Europe (1987), The Economics of 1992 (1988), One Money, One Market (1990), The ECU Report (1991); contrib to various economic jls and ed of volumes on int and Euro economics; *Style—* Michael Emerson, Esq; ✉ c/o Diplomatic Bag, Delegation of the Commission of The European Communities Moscow, Rue de Genève 12, 1160 Brussels

EMERSON, Dr Peter Albert; s of Albert Richard Emerson (d 1979), of Epsom, Surrey, and Gwendoline Doris, *née* Davy (d 1968); *b* 7 Feb 1923; *Educ* Leys Sch, Clare Coll Cambridge (MA, MD), St George's Hosp Med Sch (MB BChir); *m* 22 Nov 1947, Ceris Hood, da of John Frederick Price (d 1943), of Stone, Staffs; 1 s (James Peter b 1949), 1 da (Sally (Mrs Stothard) b 1951); *Career* Sqdn Ldr med branch 1947–51; jr med posts 1947–48, registrar posts 1952–57, asst prof of med State Univ NY 1957–58, conslt physician Westminster Hosp 1958–88, hon conslt physician King Edward VII Hosp Midhurst 1969–88, hon conslt physician diseases of the chest to RN 1970–89, dean Westminster Med Sch 1981–84; vice pres and sr censor RCP 1985–86; conslt advsr on info technol Chelsea and Westminster Hosp; memb BMA, hon fell American Coll of Physicians, FRCP; *Books* Thoracic Medicine (1981); *Recreations* tennis, restoring old buildings; *Clubs* RAF; *Style*— Dr Peter Emerson; ✉ Kidlington Mill, Mill End, Kidlington, Oxon OX5 2EG (☎ 01865 372212); 3 Halkin Street, Belgrave Square, London SW1X 7DJ (☎ 0171 235 8529)

EMERSON, Ronald Victor; s of Albert Victor Emerson, and Doris, *née* Hird; *b* 22 Feb 1947; *Educ* W Hartlepool GS, Univ of Manchester (BSc), Univ of Durham (MSc); *m* 21 June 1969, Joan Margaret (d 1988), da of James Hubery Willis; 2 s (Christopher Mark b 28 May 1971, Simon Nicholas b 5 March 1975); *Career* De La Rue Group 1970–75, commercial devpt controller Formica International; Bank of America: joined 1975, head of London corp office and UK country mangr 1985–89, head of payment servs and fin insts Europe Middle East and Africa 1989; dir and gen mangr Nomura Bank International 1989–91, regnl gen mangr UK/Europe Standard Chartered Bank 1991–94; Standard Chartered Malaysia Berhad: chief exec offr 1994–95, gp head corp banking 1995–; FRSA; *Recreations* flying, sport, reading; *Style*— Ronald Emerson, Esq; ✉ The Reeds, Remenham Lane, Remenham, Henley-on-Thames, Oxon RG9 3DA

EMERSON, Timothy John Peter; s of Col (Thomas) John Emerson, OBE, TD, DL, JP, of Yelverton, and Rosemary Steeds, *née* White (d 1992); *b* 14 Feb 1942; *Educ* Kelly Coll Tavistock; *m* 9 June 1984, Susanna Jane, da of Sir Harry Evelyn Battie Rashleigh, 5 Bt (d 1984), of Stowford; 1 s (Tom b 2 Sept 1987), 1 da (Charlotte b 9 June 1985); *Career* admitted slr 1965 and Notary Public; Stafford Clark London 1965–67, Heppenstalls Lyndhurst 1967–73, ptnr Foot & Bowden Plymouth 1973–; slr to govrs Kelly Coll and St Michael's Sch Tavistock; tstee Lady Modiford Tst; memb Law Soc 1965; *Recreations* sailing, shooting, skiing, tennis; *Clubs* Royal Western Yacht; *Style*— Timothy Emerson, Esq; ✉ Coleraine, Yelverton, Devon PL20 6BN (☎ 01822 852070); Foot & Bowden, 21 Derry's Cross, Plymouth PL1 2SW (☎ 01752 675000, fax 01752 671802) and 17 St Helen's Place, London EC3A 6DE (☎ 0171 786 9310, fax 0171 786 9312)

EMERTON, Dame Audrey Caroline; DBE (1989), DL (Kent 1992); da of George William Emerton (d 1971), of Tunbridge Wells, and Lily Harriet, *née* Squirrell; *b* 10 Sept 1935; *Educ* Tunbridge Wells GS, Battersea Coll of Technol; *Career* SRN; sr tutor St George's Hosp London 1968, princ nursing offr teaching Bromley HMC 1968–70, chief nursing offr Tunbridge Wells and Leybourne HMC 1970–73, regnl nursing offr SE Thames RHA 1973–91; chief nursing offr St John Ambulance 1988–96 (co nursing offr 1970–84, Kent co cmmr 1984–88), chief offr Care in the Community 1996–; chm: Eng Nat Bd for Nurses Midwives and Health Visitors 1983–85, UK Central Cncl Nursing Midwives and Health Visitors 1985–93, Brighton Health Care NHS Trust Dec 1994–; Hon DCL Univ of Kent 1989; memb: RCN, RSM; FRSA; cr a life peer 1997; *Style*— Dame Audrey Emerton, DBE, DL; ✉ Carlton House, 3 Strettitt Gardens, East Peckham, Tonbridge, Kent TN12 5ES; St John Ambulance, 1 Grosvenor Crescent, London SW1X 7EF

EMERTON, Rev Prof John Adney; s of Adney Spencer Emerton (d 1969), of Southgate, and Helena Mary, *née* Quin (d 1964); *b* 5 June 1928; *Educ* Minchenden GS Southgate, Corpus Christi Coll Oxford, Wycliffe Hall Oxford (BA, MA), Univ of Cambridge (MA, BD, DD); *m* 14 Aug 1954, Norma Elizabeth, da of Norman Bennington (d 1986); 1 s (Mark Simon b 1961), 2 da (Caroline Mary b 1958, Lucy Anne b 1966); *Career* ordained: deacon 1952, priest 1953; curate Birmingham Cathedral 1952–53, asst lectr in theology Univ of Birmingham 1952–53, lectr in Hebrew and Aramaic Univ of Durham 1953–55, lectr in divinity Univ of Cambridge 1955–62, visiting prof of Old Testament and Near Eastern studies Trinity Coll Toronto 1960, reader in Semitic philology Univ of Oxford 1962–68, fell St Peter's Coll Oxford 1962–68, Regius prof of Hebrew Univ of Cambridge 1968–95 (emeritus prof 1995–), fell St John's Coll Cambridge 1970–; visiting fell Inst for Advanced Studies Hebrew Univ of Jerusalem 1983, visiting prof of Old Testament United Theol Coll Bangalore 1986, corresponding memb Göttingen Akademie der Wissenschaften 1990; ed Vetus Testamentum 1976–; pres: Soc for Old Testament Study 1979 (memb 1952–), Int Orgn for the Study of the Old Testament 1992–95 (sec 1971–89); hon canon St George's Cathedral Jerusalem 1984–; Hon DD Univ of Edinburgh 1977, Burkitt medal for Biblical Studies British Acad 1991; FBA 1979; *Books* The Peshitta of the Wisdom of Solomon (1959), The Old Testament in Syriac - the Song of Songs (1966); *Style*— The Rev Prof John Emerton; ✉ 34 Gough Way, Cambridge CB3 9LN; St John's College, Cambridge CB2 1TP

EMERTON, Philip John; s of Edward Alec Emerton (d 1987), of Springhill House, Goring-on-Thames, and Dorothy Evelyn, *née* East (d 1972); *b* 10 Feb 1935; *Educ* Abingdon Sch; *m* 25 July 1959, Mary Patricia, da of Harold Harvey Creedon (d 1970), of Petersfield; 2 s (Richard b 1960, Mark b 1963); *Career* served RA 1958–60, 2 Lt; ptnr Haines Watts Group 1963–94 (sr ptnr 1973–94); memb British Legion; FCA 1958; *Recreations* fishing, skiing, wine buying; *Style*— Philip Emerton, Esq; ✉ Herons Creek, Wargrave, Berks RG10 8EU (☎ 0118 940 2642, fax 0118 940 1468); Leysin, Switzerland; Cagnes-Sur-Mer and Meribel France

EMERY, Prof Alan Eglin Heathcote; s of Harold Heathcote-Emery (d 1977), and Alice, *née* Eglin (d 1972); *b* 21 Aug 1928; *Educ* Manchester GS, Chester Coll, Univ of Manchester (BSc, MSc, MB ChB, MD, DSc), Johns Hopkins Univ USA (PhD); *m* 13 Oct 1988, Marcia Lynn, da of John Miller (d 1986), of Cleveland, USA; *Career* Nat Serv 14/20 Kings Hussars 1945–47; conslt physician 1966–; emeritus prof and hon fell Univ of Edinburgh 1983– (prof of human genetics 1968–83), hon visiting fell Green Coll Oxford 1986–, res dir Euro Neuromuscular Center 1990–; foreign assoc RSS Africa, hon memb Gaetano Conte Acad (Italy); Hon MD: Univ of Naples, Univ of Würzburg; emeritus fell American Coll of Med Genetics; FRCPE 1970, FRSE 1972, FLS 1985, FRSM, memb Royal Soc of Lit; *Books* Modern Trends in Human Genetics (vol 1 1970, vol 2 1975), Antenatal Diagnosis of Genetic Disease (1973), Genetic Registers (1976), Psychological Aspects of Genetic Counselling (1984), Introduction to Recombinant DNA (1984, 2 edn 1995), Methodology in Medical Genetics (2 edn, 1986), Duchenne Muscular Dystrophy (2 edn 1993), Elements of Medical Genetics (8 edn, 1992), Principles & Practice of Medical Genetics (2 edn, 1990), Muscular Dystrophy - The Facts (1994), The History of a History of a Genetic Disease (1995), Diagnostic Criteria for Neuromuscular Disorders (1996); *Recreations* oil painting, marine biology; *Style*— Prof Alan Emery, FRSE; ✉ European Neuromuscular Center, Gen van Heutszlaan 6, Baarn, The Netherlands (☎ 00 31 35 5416093, fax 00 31 35 5421616, e-mail enmc@ib.com)

EMERY, Anthony Hayward; s of Thomas Frederick Emery; *b* 10 July 1930; *Educ* Bablake Sch Coventry, Univ of Bristol (BA), UCL; *Career* with Reed International until 1989 (former chm Reed Information Services Ltd and Industry Services International, dir Reed Business Publishing Group until 1989); former dep chm Heritage Educn Tst, fndr cmmr Historic Bldgs and Monuments Cmmn (England), chm Bath Archaeological Tst 1994– (tstee 1988–), memb Publications Ctee Cncl for Br Archaeology 1994–; *Publications* Dartington Hall (1970), Greater Medieval Houses of England and Wales: 1300–1500 (3 vols, 1996–99); *Recreations* architectural historian, independent travel, fine arts, nineteenth century piano music; *Style*— Anthony Emery, Esq; ✉ Willow House, The Green, Biddestone, Wilts SN14 7DG; Hightrees House, Nightingale Lane, London SW12 8AQ

EMERY, David John; s of John Emery, of Tolworth, Surrey, and Joan, *née* Bellenie; *b* 13 Oct 1946; *Educ* Tiffin Sch Kingston; *m* 13 April 1974, Irene Thelma, da of George Board, of Ealing; 2 s (Matthew David b 1979, Samuel Jack b 1984), 2 da (Alexandra Lillian b 1976, Georgia Lauren b 1987); *Career* journalist: Surrey Comet 1964–69, Hemel Hempstead Evening Post 1969–70, Daily Mail 1970–72, Daily Express 1972–78, Daily Star 1978–82; Daily Express: joined 1982, chief sports writer 1983–87, sports ed 1987–; highly commended in Sports Cncl Awards for Journalism 1987; chm Sports Writers Assoc of GB 1986–89, pres 26.2 Road Runners Club 1984; *Books* Lillian (1971), Waterskiing (with Paul Seaton, 1976), Who's Who of the 1984 Olympics, World Sporting Records (1986); *Recreations* squash, marathon running, cricket, golf; *Clubs* Mid Surrey Squash, 26.2 Road Runners, Claygate Cricket, Surbiton Golf; *Style*— David Emery, Esq; ✉ Daily Express, 245 Blackfriars Rd, London SE1 9UX (☎ 0171 928 8000, fax 0171 922 7974)

EMERY, Fred; s of Frederick G L Emery (d 1942), and Alice May, *née* Wright (d 1978); *b* 19 Oct 1933; *Educ* Bancroft's Sch, St John's Coll Cambridge (MA, Footlights); *m* 23 Aug 1958, Marianne, da of Nils Nyberg (d 1966); 2 s (Martin b 1960, Alex b 1963); *Career* Nat Serv Fighter Pilot 266 and 234 Sqdns RAF 1951–53 (cmmnd 1952); sch broadcasting Radio Bremen 1955–56; The Times: foreign corr (Paris and Algeria 1961–64, Tokyo, SE Asia and Vietnam 1964–67, SE Asia 1967–70, chief Washington corr 1970–77), political ed 1977–81, home ed 1981–82, exec ed 1982; presenter BBC TV: Panorama 1978–80, Platform 1, BBC specials 1980–82, Panorama 1982–92; reporter: Watergate series (BBC TV) 1994, Discovery Channel US special series 1994–95 (US Emmy 1995); broadcaster UK and US incl: BBC World Service (in French), CBC and French TV; *Books* Watergate, the Corruption and Fall of Richard Nixon (1994, paperback 1995); *Recreations* tennis, skiing, hill walking; *Clubs* Garrick, OBFC; *Style*— Fred Emery, Esq; ✉ 5 Woodsyre, London SE26 6SS

EMERY, John; s of John Emery (d 1981), of Carshalton, Surrey, and Florence Margaret, *née* Hankins (d 1991); *b* 2 Aug 1938; *Educ* Heath Clark GS, Regent St Poly, City & Guilds (final exam), Inst of Mgmnt Studies (cert in supervisory mgmnt studies); *m* Oct 14 1961, Heather, da of James Lamont; 1 s (Andrew John b 18 July 1977), 1 da (Lisa Jane b 6 July 1971); *Career* Nat Serv litho-camera operator 89 Field Survey Sqdn RE, later i/c Photographic Unit operating from The Survey of Kenya Govt offices; professional photographer; served apprenticeship with Fox Photos London, photographic printer Carlton Artists 1959–61, printer/photographer Streets Advertising 1961, chief photographer and mangr Streets Photographic Unit; photo-servs mangr Associated Newspapers Ltd (joined 1969 as dep darkroom mangr, ret 1993); FBIPP 1974; *Recreations* shooting, golf, swimming, archery; *Style*— John Emery, Esq; ✉ 12 Rutherwyke Close, Stoneleigh, Epsom, Surrey KT17 2NB (☎ 0181 393 5451); Associated Newspapers Ltd, Northcliffe House, 2 Derry St, Kensington W8 5TT (☎ 0171 938 6391, fax 0171 937 3073)

EMERY, Prof Paul; s of Lt Cdr Dr Leonard Lesley Emery RNVR, of Cardiff, and Beryl Olive, *née* Davis; *b* 30 Nov 1952; *Educ* Cardiff HS, Churchill Coll Cambridge (MB BChir, MA, MD), Guy's Hosp; *m* 19 July 1980, Shirley Macdonald, da of Sub Lt David Morton Bayne RNVR; 2 da (Lorna Megan b 25 Oct 1987, Joanna Louise b 17 March 1989); *Career* SHO Guy's Hosp Brompton, subsequently med registrar Guy's Hosp Lewisham 1980–83, sr registrar Guy's Hosp 1983–85, head of rheumatology Walter Eliza Hall and asst physician Royal Melbourne Hosp 1985–88, conslt and sr lectr Dept of Rheumatology Univ of Birmingham 1988–95, ARC prof of rheumatology Univ of Leeds 1995–; memb: Br Soc of Rheumatology, Br Soc of Immunology, BMA; FRCP 1992 (MRCP 1979); *Books* contrib: The Role of Cytokines in Rheumatological Inflammation Autoimmunregation and Autoimmune Disease (1987), Autoimmune Reactions to D-penicillamine, Autoimmun Toxicol (1989), Rheumatoid Arthritis, Oxford Textbook of Renal Medicine (1991); The Management of Early Arthritis (ed, 1992), Local Injection Therapy in Rheumatic Diseases (co-ed, 1992); *Recreations* golf, squash; *Clubs* Chapel Allerton Squash, Pannal Golf; *Style*— Prof Paul Emery; ✉ Rheumatology and Rheumatism Unit, University of Leeds, 36 Clarendon Road, Leeds LS2 9NZ (☎ 0113 233 4940, fax 0113 244 6066)

EMERY, Rt Hon Sir Peter Frank Hannibal; kt (1981), PC (1993), MP (C) Honiton (majority 16,511); s of Frank George Emery (d 1960), of Highgate; *b* 27 Feb 1926; *Educ* Scotch Plains NJ USA, Oriel Coll Oxford; *m* 1, 1954 (m dis), Elizabeth, da of Philip Nicholson, of Endsor, Derbys; 1 s, 1 da; m 2, 1972, Elizabeth, yst da of G J R Monnington, of Lewes, Sussex; 1 s, 1 da; *Career* MP (C): Reading 1959–66, Honiton 1967–; PPS to successive Mins of State for Foreign Affrs incl: Rt Hon David Ormsby-Gore (later Lord Harlech) 1960–61, Rt Hon Joseph Godber (later Lord Godber of Willington) 1961–63; oppn front bench spokesman Treasy Economics and Trade 1964–66, Parly under sec DTI 1972–74, Energy 1974; jt fndr and first sec Bow Gp, chm Select Ctee Procedure; chm: Winglaw Group, Nat Asthma Campaign 1986–; delegate to Cncl of Europe & WEU 1964–66 and 1970–72, memb North Atlantic Assembly 1983–, sr rapporteur and chm Science & Technical Ctee NAA 1986–; memb Assembly CSCE treas 1992–; capt House of Commons Bridge Team; FInstPS; *Recreations* skiing, tennis, golf, theatre, bridge, travel; *Clubs* Leander, Carlton, Portland; *Style*— The Rt Hon Sir Peter Emery, MP; ✉ 8 Ponsonby Terrace, London SW1P 4QA (☎ 0171 222 6666); Tytherleigh Manor, nr Axminster, Devon EX13 7BD (☎ 01460 20309); office: House of Commons (☎ 0171 219 4044, fax 0171 219 3021, sec's ☎ 0171 219 4497, fax 0171 219 2300)

EMERY, Ralph; OBE (1995); s of Frederick William Emery (d 1947), of Kingston-upon-Hull, and Beatrice Mary, *née* Linnett (d 1966); *b* 18 July 1907; *Educ* Hull GS, Christ's Coll Cambridge (MA), Toulouse Univ Bagnères-de-Bigorre; *m* Lina Madeleine Lalandi-Emery, OBE, *qv*, da of late Nikolas Kaloyeropoulos; *Career* Shell International Organisation 1929–64 (latterly gen mangr Shell Argentina Ltd 1950–53, gen mangr Shell Brazil Ltd 1953–56, co-ordinator for S America Shell International Petroleum Co Ltd 1956–64); advsr on Latin America and Spain to the Bd: Samuel Montagu & Co Ltd 1964–68, Wm Brandt's Sons & Co Ltd 1968–73; representative/gen mangr (later conslt) Banco de la Nación Argentina London 1973–86; fndr chm The English Bach Festival Tst (specialising in baroque opera and dance) 1962–; vice pres (formerly chm): The Hispanic and Luso-Brazilian Cncl (Canning House) 1978–, The Anglo-Argentine Soc and The Br-Uruguayan Soc 1980–; FRSA 1995; *Recreations* music, reading; *Clubs* Canning (chm 1970–95, pres 1995–); *Style*— Ralph Emery, Esq, OBE; ✉ 15 South Eaton Place, London SW1W 9ER (☎ 0171 730 5925, fax 0171 730 1456)

EMERY-WALLIS, Frederick Alfred John; DL; s of Frederick Henry Wallis (d 1949), and Lillian Grace Emery, *née* Coles (d 1963); *b* 11 May 1927; *Educ* Blake's Acad Portsmouth; *m* 22 Aug 1960, Solange, da of William Victor Randall (d 1957), of Mitcham, Surrey; 2 da (Selina b 4 April 1963, Jennette b 5 March 1971); *Career* SCU4 RCS Middle East Radio Security 1945–48; Portsmouth CC: cncllr 1961–74, Lord Mayor 1968–69, Alderman 1969–74; Hampshire CC: cncllr 1973–, vice chm 1975–76, ldr 1976–93; chm Southern Tourist Bd 1976–88 (vice pres 1988–); Assoc of CCs: memb Exec Ctee and Policy Ctee 1974–93, chm ACC Recreation Ctee 1982–85; memb Community Services Ctee 1990–93; govr Univ of Portsmouth (formerly Portsmouth Poly) 1962–95; chm Hampshire Archives Tst 1986–, chm of govrs Portsmouth HS for Girls 1962–92; chm Editorial Bd: Hampshire Record Series 1984–, Portsmouth Record Series 1990–, Hampshire Papers Series 1990–; tstee: New Theatre Royal Trust Portsmouth 1982–, Learning through Landscapes Tst 1990–91, Mary Rose Tst 1980–90; RN Museum Portsmouth 1991–; dir: Warrior Preservation Tst 1988–91, Bd of Welsh Nat Opera 1990–; chm Hampshire Sculpture Tst; memb: Cncl of the Br Records Assoc 1979–, Hampshire Gdns Tst 1984–, Hampshire Buildings Preservation Tst 1976–93, Victoria County History Ctee 1991–; pres of the Friends of Portsmouth City Records Office 1988–95; FSA, Hon FRIBA, Hon FLA; *Recreations* music, book collecting; *Style*—

Frederick Emery-Wallis, Esq, DL, FSA; ✉ Froddington, Craneswater Park, Portsmouth, Hampshire PO4 0NR (☎ 01705 731409); Hampshire County Council, The Castle, Winchester, Hampshire SO23 8UJ (☎ 01962 847943, fax 01962 867273, telex 477729)

EMLEY, Miles Lovelace Brereton; s of Col Derek Brereton Emley, OBE, of Sturminster Newton, Dorset, and Mary Georgina, *née* Lovelace (d 1996); *b* 23 July 1949; *Educ* St Edward's Sch Oxford, Balliol Coll Oxford (MA); *m* 26 June 1976, Tessa Marcia Radclyffe, da of Radclyffe Edward Crichton Powell, MBE (d 1985); 2 s (Oliver b 1978, Alexander b 1982), 1 da (Katherine b 1980); *Career* dir: N M Rothschild & Sons Ltd 1982–89 (joined 1972), Virago Press Ltd 1988–90; md UBS Phillips & Drew Securities Ltd 1989–92, chm St Ives plc 1993– (dep chm 1992–93); Liveryman Worshipful Co of Leathersellers 1979; FRSA 1991; *Style*— Miles Emley, Esq; ✉ Whitehall House, Ashford Hill, Thatcham, Berks RG19 8AZ (☎ 01635 268306); St Ives plc, St Ives House, Lavington Street, London SE1 0NX (☎ 0171 928 8844)

EMLY, John Richard Keith; s of Charles Richard Lewis Emly (d 1975), of London, and Lillian Villette, *née* Jenner (d 1971); *b* 15 Sept 1941; *Educ* St Dunstan's Coll Catford; *m* 26 July 1969, Maria Joan, da of Frederic Jozef Jan Gumosz (d 1964), of Catford; 2 s (Timothy b 1978, Benjamin b 1980), 2 da (Gillian b 1972, Sarah b 1974); *Career* jt investmt mangr The Law Debenture Corporation Ltd 1971–75 (joined 1960), dir Robert Fleming Investment Management Ltd 1978–88, main bd dir Robert Fleming Holdings Ltd 1985– (joined 1975); dir: Robert Fleming Asset Management Ltd 1988–90, Fleming Investment Management Ltd 1988–, Fleming Income and Capital Trust plc 1993–, Fleming Enterprise Investment Trust plc 1996–; non-exec dir Hemingway Properties plc 1995–; FRICS 1972, AIIMR, MSI; *Recreations* family life; *Style*— John Emly, Esq; ✉ Robert Fleming Holdings Ltd, 25 Copthall Avenue, London EC2R 7DR (☎ 0171 638 5858, fax 0171 382 8907, telex 297451)

EMMERSON, Ian Robert; OBE (1994); s of late Robert Leslie Emmerson, of Lincoln, and Ida Kathleen, *née* Marshall; *b* 18 Feb 1944; *Educ* City GS Lincoln; *m* 23 Nov 1968, Sheila Margaret, da of Ernest Raymond (Dick) Barber (d 1968); 2 s (Nathan Robert b 1972, Richard Ian b 1974); *Career* GPO 1960–83 (asst exec engr BT), currently dir Impsport (Lincoln) Ltd; pres Br Cycling Fedn 1985–95, chm Velo Club Lincoln 1964–95; vice chm Cwlth Games Cncl for Eng; memb: GB Nat Olympic Exec Ctee, Exec Ctee and vice pres Union Cycliste Internationale; dir Manchester 2002 Bid; Sheriff of Lincoln 1990–91; *Recreations* cycling, photography, travel; *Style*— Ian Emmerson, Esq, OBE; ✉ 5 Larkin Avenue, Cherry Willingham, Lincoln LN3 4AZ (☎ 01522 750000); Impsport (Lincoln) Ltd, Whisby Way, Lincoln LN6 3LQ (☎ 01522 500505, fax 01522 500455)

EMMERSON, John Corti; s of Sir Harold Corti Emmerson, GCB, KCVO (d 1984), and Lucy Kathleen, *née* Humphreys (d 1989); *b* 10 Sept 1937; *Educ* Merchant Taylors', Magdalen Coll Oxford; *m* 30 Oct 1970, Pamela Anne, da of Lt-Col James Shaw, TD (d 1970); 1 s (Dominic b 1973), 1 da (Kate b 1975); *Career* Nat Serv 2 Lt 4 Royal Tank Regt 1956–58, asst princ Air Ministry 1961–63; admitted slr 1967, ptnr McKenna & Co (head of Private Client Dept) 1983–91, currently ptnr Wilsons; dir Woodard Schs (Southern Div) Ltd, govr Ardingly Coll, tstee Wiltshire Community Fndn; *Recreations* fly-fishing; *Clubs* Brooks's; *Style*— John C Emmerson, Esq; ✉ Court Farm House, Wylye, Wilts; Wilsons, Steynings House, Fisherton St, Salisbury (☎ 01722 412412)

EMMERSON, Prof (Alfred) Michael; s of William Emmerson, and Elsie, *née* Barratt; *b* 17 Oct 1937; *Educ* UCH Med Sch (MB BS); *m* 30 April 1966, Elizabeth Barbara Mary, da of Dr John Lawn (decd), of Binbrook, Lincolnshire; 1 s (Mark b 29 Sept 1972), 1 da (Catherine b 8 Jan 1971); *Career* Nat Serv class 1 mechanical engr and decoder RN 1957–59; trainee microbiologist UCH London 1966–73 (house offr 1965–66), conslt microbiologist Whittington Hosp London 1973–84, prof of clinical microbiology Royal Victoria Hosp Queen's Univ Belfast 1984–89, prof and head of dept Univ of Leicester 1989–91, prof and head Dept of Microbiology Univ Hosp Nottingham 1991–; chm: Microbiology Advsy Ctee DHSS London, Br Standards Instn HCC/67 and CEN/TC 204, Specialist Advsy Ctee (microbiology) CPA (Accreditation) UK; memb Assoc of Professors in Med Microbiology; Liveryman Worshipful Soc of Apothecaries 1975; MRCS, LRCP, FRCPG, FRCPath, fell Hunterian Soc 1975, scientific fell Zoological Soc 1975; *Books* The Microbiology and Treatment of Life Threatening Infections (1982); *Recreations* rugby, athletics, London and Belfast marathons; *Clubs* Leicester Football; *Style*— Prof Michael Emmerson; ✉ Department of Microbiology, University Hospital, Queen's Medical Centre, Nottingham NG7 2UH (direct ☎ 0115 970 9162, fax 0115 970 9233)

EMMOTT, William (Bill); *b* 1956; *Educ* Magdalen Coll Oxford; *Career* The Economist: Brussels corr 1980–82, dep economics writer 1982–83, Tokyo corr 1983–86, fin ed 1986–89, business affairs ed 1989–93, ed 1993–; *Style*— Bill Emmott, Esq; ✉ The Economist, 25 St James Street, London SW1A 1HG

EMMS, David Acfield; OBE (1995); s of Archibald George Emms (d 1975), of Lowestoft, Suffolk, and Winifred Gladys, *née* Richards (d 1979); *b* 16 Feb 1925; *Educ* Tonbridge, BNC Oxford (MA); *m* 8 Sept 1950, Pamela Baker, da of Edwin Leslie Speed (d 1970), of Jesmond, Newcastle upon Tyne; 3 s (John b 1952, Richard b 1959, Christopher b 1969), 1 da (Victoria b 1954); *Career* Capt Royal Indian Airborne Artillery 1943, Hon Col 39 (City of London) Signal Regt 1988–91; asst master Uppingham Sch 1951–60; headmaster: Cranleigh Sch 1960–70, Sherborne Sch 1970–74; master Dulwich Coll 1975–86; chm: Headmasters' Conf 1984, Jt Educnl Tst 1987–90; dir London Goodenough Tst for Overseas Graduates 1987–95, vice pres Ind Sch Careers Orgn 1973–; dep chm ESU 1983–89; govr: Bickley Park Sch 1978–81, St Felix Sch Southwold 1983–88, Feltonfleet Sch Cobham 1968–87, Tonbridge Sch 1980 (exec chm 1988–91), Brambletye Sch East Grinstead 1982–88, Portsmouth GS 1987–, St George's Montreux 1989–, St Dunstan's Coll 1992–; dep pro chllr City Univ 1989–91; Freeman City of London 1950, memb Ct of Assts Worshipful Co of Skinners (Master 1987–88); FRSA 1988; *Publications* HMC Schools and British Industry (1981); *Recreations* radical gardening; *Clubs* Vincent's (Oxford), East India, Itchenor Sailing; *Style*— David Emms, Esq, OBE; ✉ Seaforth, Spinney Lane, Itchenor, nr Chichester, West Sussex PO20 7DJ

EMMS, Peter Anthony; s of Anthony Hubert Hamilton Emms, and Daphne, *née* Cooper-Lake; *b* 29 June 1949; *Educ* Stoneham GS Reading, City of London Poly (BA); *m* 6 Nov 1981, Susan Gwendolen, da of Harold Kemp; 1 s (Ben b 1975), 1 da (Joanna b 1977); *Career* exec dir mktg Allied Dunbar Assurance plc 1985–92, dir of sales and mktg M & G Group plc 1992–; FCII 1975; *Recreations* gardening, reading; *Style*— Peter Emms, Esq; ✉ M & G Group PLC, 7th Floor, 3 Minster Court, Great Tower Street, London EC3R 7XH (☎ 0171 626 4588, fax 0171 623 8615)

EMMS, Peter Fawcett; s of Reginald Ernest Emms (d 1977), and Hetty, *née* Fawcett; *b* 25 April 1935; *Educ* Derby Sch, Magdalen Coll Oxford (John Doncaster open scholar in modern languages, MA); *m* 17 Aug 1960, (Esther) Carola Graham, da of Prof Sir Edward Johnson Wayne (d 1990); 3 da (Helen Rachel b 1961, Katharine Margaret (Mrs Wilson) b 1963, Judith Ann (Mrs Shirley) b 1965); *Career* Nat Serv Jt Servs Russian Course Univ of Cambridge 1954–56; asst master of modern languages Abingdon Sch Berks 1959–62; Rugby Sch Warwicks: asst master of modern languages 1962–74 (seconded as visiting master Groton Sch Mass USA 1967–68), head of modern languages 1969–71, housemaster Town House 1971–74; princ (with posts in road safety, construction indust sponsorship and housing) Depts of the Environment and Tport 1974–79, asst sec (with posts in housing, higher and further educn and int tport) Depts of the Environment, Educn & Scis, and Tport 1979–89, grade 3 regnl dir Depts of the Environment and Tport Eastern Region 1989–94, Br Govt Know How Fund advsr to Ukrainian Cabinet of Mins 1994–; *Books* Social Housing - A European Dilemma? (1991); *Style*— Peter Emms, Esq; ✉ 2 Thorncroft, Leverstock Green, Hemel Hempstead, Herts HP3 8HP (☎ and fax 01442 252175); Les Theureaux, 71800 Vauban, France (☎ and fax 00 33 85 25 89 59)

EMPEY, Most Rev Walton Newcombe Frances; *see:* Dublin, Archbishop of

EMPSON, Adm Sir (Leslie) Derek; GBE (1975), KCB (1973, CB 1969); s of Frank Harold Empson (d 1960), of Four Oaks, Warwickshire, and Madeleine Norah, *née* Burge; *b* 29 Oct 1918; *Educ* Eastbourne Coll, Clare Coll Cambridge; *m* 1958, Diana Elizabeth, da of P J Kelly, of London; 1 s, 1 da; *Career* joined RNVR 1940, served WWII pilot Fleet Air Arm, Cdr 1952, Capt 1957, naval asst to First Sea Lord 1957–59, Rear Adm 1967, flag offr Aircraft Carriers 1967–68, asst Chief of Naval Staff (Ops and Air) 1968–69, Cdr Far East Fleet 1969–70, Vice Adm 1969, Second Sea Lord and Chief of Naval Personnel 1971–74, Adm 1972, C-in-C Naval Home Cmd and flag offr Portsmouth Area 1974–75, Flag ADC to HM The Queen 1974–75, ret 1976; Rear Adm of UK 1985–87, Vice Adm of UK 1987–89; conslt Thorn EMI Ltd 1976–86, chm Roymark Ltd 1983–92, conslt Astra Holdings plc 1987–90; chm of govrs Eastbourne Coll 1972–89, chm Fedn Against Copyright Theft 1983–88; *Style*— Adm Sir Derek Empson, GBE, KCB; ✉ Flat 21, Coral Beach Estate, PO Box 4929, Limassol, Cyprus

EMSLEY, Kenneth; s of Clifford Briggs Emsley, and Lily, *née* Goldsborough; *b* 7 Dec 1921; *Educ* Bingley GS, Loughborough Coll, St John's Coll Cambridge (MA), Univ of Newcastle upon Tyne (LLM); *m* 14 May 1959, Nancy Audrey, da of Alfred Ernest Slee; *Career* served WWII; chm Smith & Hardcastle Ltd 1955–65; painter of watercolour drawings and miniature paintings, author of books and articles, lectr in law, ret 1980; sr visiting scholar St Edmunds Coll Cambridge 1977–78, guest memb Law Faculty Univ of Newcastle-upon-Tyne 1978–79, hon research fell Univ of Bradford 1994–; pres: The Br Watercolour Soc, The Soc of Miniaturists, The Bradford Arts Club until 1985 (former chm); memb: Cncl Yorks Archaeological Soc Leeds, Brontë Soc, Soc of Authors; hon sec Wakefield Manorial Ct Rolls Series; FRSA 1945, ACIS 1970, MSEng 1948, FRHistS 1989, FRGS 1989; *Books* Tyneside (with C M Fraser, 1973), Northumbria (with C M Fraser, 1979, rewritten 1989), The Courts of the County Palatine of Durham (1984), Wakefield Manorial Court Rolls (with C M Fraser, vol 1 1979 and vol 5 1987), Historical Introduction of Durham Quarter Sessions Rolls 1471–1625 (Surtees Soc, Vol 199), Historic Howarth Today (1995); *Recreations* formerly cricket, rugby, tennis; now bowls, art and music; *Clubs* The Bradford, Bradford and Bingley Sports (fndr memb), Cambridge Union, Cambridge Univ Cricket; *Style*— Kenneth Emsley, Esq; ✉ 34 Nabwood Drive, Shipley, West Yorkshire BD18 4EL; The Yorkshire Archaeological Society, Claremont, Clarendon Road, Leeds LS2 9NZ

EMSLIE, Hon Derek Robert Alexander; QC (Scot 1987); 2 s of Baron Emslie, MBE, PC, QC (Life Peer), *qv*; *b* 21 June 1949; *Educ* Edinburgh Acad, Trinity Coll Glenalmond, Gonville and Caius Coll Cambridge (BA, history scholar), Univ of Edinburgh (LLB); *m* 1974, Elizabeth Jane Cameron, da of Andrew Maclaren Carstairs; 3 children; *Career* advocate; standing jr counsel DHSS 1979–87, standing jr counsel MDDUS 1980–87, advocate depute 1985–88, pt/t chm Pension Appeal Tbnl 1988–95, pt/t chm Medical Appeal Tbnl 1990–95; vice dean Faculty of Advocates 1995–; *Clubs* Hawks, Hon Co of Edinburgh Golfers; *Style*— The Hon Derek Emslie, QC; ✉ Faculty of Advocates, Parliament Square, Edinburgh EH1 1RF

EMSLIE, Baron (Life Peer UK 1979), of Potterton, in the District of Gordon; George Carlyle Emslie; MBE (1946), PC (1972); s of Alexander Emslie, and Jessie Blair Emslie; *b* 6 Dec 1919; *Educ* The HS of Glasgow, Univ of Glasgow (MA, LLB); *m* 1942, Lilias Ann Mailer, da of Robert Hannington, of Glasgow; 3 s (Hon Nigel, Hon Derek, Hon Richard, *qqv*); *Career* advocate Scot 1948, QC Scot 1957, sheriff of Perth and Angus 1963–66, dean of Faculty of Advocates 1965–70, senator of the Coll of Justice, a Lord of Session with title Lord Emslie 1970, Lord Justice Gen of Scotland and Lord Pres of the Ct of Session 1972–89; hon bencher Inner Temple and Inn of Ct of NI; Hon LLD Univ of Glasgow 1973; FRSE 1987; *Recreations* golf; *Clubs* New (Edinburgh); *Style*— The Rt Hon Lord Emslie, MBE, PC, FRSE; ✉ 47 Heriot Row, Edinburgh (☎ 0131 225 3657)

EMSLIE, Hon (George) Nigel Hannington; QC (Scot 1986); eldest s of Baron Emslie, MBE, PC (Life Peer), *qv*; *b* 1947; *Educ* Edinburgh Acad, Trinity Coll Glenalmond, Gonville and Caius Coll Cambridge (BA), Univ of Edinburgh (LLB); *m* 1973, Heather Ann, da of Arthur Frank Davis, of Bristol; has issue; *Career* barr; admitted Faculty of Advocates 1972; *Style*— The Hon Nigel Emslie, QC; ✉ c/o Advocates' Library, Parliament House, Edinburgh EH1 1RF

EMSLIE, Hon Richard Hannington; 3 and yst s of Baron Emslie, MBE, PC (Life Peer), *qv*; *b* 28 July 1957; *Educ* Edinburgh Acad, Trinity Coll Glenalmond, Gonville and Caius Coll Cambridge (MA); *Career* wildlife biologist, res into applied grazing ecology of Umfulozi and Hluhluwe Game Reserves Zululand; conslt ecologist incl conservation of the black and white rhino; scientific/prog offr IUCN/Species Survival Cmmn African Rhino Specialist Gp, memb IUCN Asian Rhino Specialist Gp, elected expert Southern African Rhino Mgmnt Gp; *Recreations* football, hockey, golf, skiing, squash, tennis, hypnosis, photography, bird-watching; *Clubs* Edinburgh Ski, Umfolozi Country; *Style*— The Hon Richard Emslie; ✉ PO Box 1212 Hilton, Kwa-Zulu Natal 3245, S Africa; 47 Heriot Row, Edinburgh EH3 6EX (☎ 0131 225 3657)

EMSLIE-SMITH, Dr Donald; s of Lt-Col Harry Emslie-Smith, IMS (d 1946), of Dunfermline, and Maribel, *née* Milne (d 1952); *b* 12 April 1922; *Educ* Trinity Coll, Glenalmond, Univ of Aberdeen (MD(Hons) ChB); *m* 19 Sept 1959, Ann Elizabeth, da of Col Thomas Milne, CB, DSO, Order of the Nile, of Milford-on-Sea, Hants; 1 s (Alistair b 1960), 1 da (Sophie b 1963); *Career* Flt Lt RAFVR (Med) UK, Egypt and Sudan 1946–48; registrar in cardiology Dundee Teaching Hosps 1953–54, E Wilson Meml res fell Baker Inst Melbourne 1955–56, tutor and sr registrar Royal Postgrad Med Sch and Hammersmith Hosp 1958–61; sr lectr in med: Univ of St Andrews 1961–67, Univ of Dundee 1967–71 (reader 1971–87, hon fell 1989); hon conslt cardiologist Tayside Health Bd 1961–87; extraordinary memb Br Cardiac Soc (chm 1987); sr memb: Assoc of Physicians of GB and Ireland (memb Exec Ctee 1977–80), Scottish Soc of Physicians; memb Harveian Soc of Edinburgh (pres 1986–87 and Harveian Orator), hon memb Scottish Cardiac Soc; OStJ; FRCP, FRCPE, FSA (Scot); *Books* Textbook of Physiology (8–11 edns, jt author and ed), Accidental Hypothermia (1977), chapters in med text books and papers in med jls mainly on cardiac electrophysiology and hypothermia; *Recreations* music, painting, fishing, sailing; *Clubs* Flyfishers', Royal Lymington Yacht; *Style*— Dr Donald Emslie-Smith; ✉ 48 Seafield Road, Broughty Ferry, Angus DD5 3AN; c/o Department of Medicine, The University, Dundee DD1 4HN

EMSON, Alan Leslie; *b* 25 Dec 1942; *Career* articled clerk Thornton Baker & Co 1959–65, sr mangr Coopers & Lybrand 1965–71; fin dir: Birmid Qualcast PLC 1971–89, Evans Halshaw Holdings plc 1989–92; fin dir (also responsible for properties, corp servs and human resources) IMI plc 1993–; FCA 1965, FCT 1979; *Recreations* sport, classical music; *Style*— A L Emson, Esq; ✉ 93 Fitz Roy Avenue, Harborne, Birmingham B17 8RG (☎ 0121 427 1977); IMI plc, PO Box 216, Witton, Birmingham B6 7BA (☎ 0121 356 4848, fax 0121 356 4831)

EMSON, Colin Jack; s of Alfred Jack Emson, of Ashford, Kent, and Rose Florence Jobson (d 1987); *b* 25 July 1941; *Educ* Maidstone GS; *m* 14 Sept 1974, Jennifer Claire, da of Lt-Col James Lynch, of Vancouver, Canada; 2 s (Alexander Chase b 1976, Henry James b 1980), 2 da (Annabel Christina b 1975, Camilla Rose b 1985); *Career* fndr ptnr

Emson & Dudley 1966–79, md Robert Fraser & Co Ltd (investment and finance gp) 1979–; chm Sterling Trust Ltd (investment holding company) 1988–; *Recreations* polo, skiing, tennis, tobogganing; *Clubs* Turf, Naval and Military, Cowdray Park Polo, St Moritz Tobogganing; *Style*— Colin Emson, Esq; ✉ Robert Fraser & Co Ltd, 29 Albemarle St, London W1X 3FA (☎ 0171 493 3211, fax 0171 408 1814)

EMSON, Brig James Bryce; CBE (1986); s of Capt Frederick James Emson, MC (d 1944), of Babraham, nr Cambridge; *b* 14 July 1938; *Educ* Felsted Sch, Nat Def Coll; *m* 24 Jan 1969, Suzanne Pauline, da of Frederick Anthony Evans, CVO, of Lower Froyle, Alton, Hants; 2 s (Benjamin b 1972, Rupert b 1974); *Career* Cmmnd Parachute Regt 1958, Cmd The Life Guards 1981–83, Cmdg Batus 1983–84, Cmdg Household Cavalry 1986–87; Dir Doctrine (Army) 1987–89, Asst Cmdt RMA Sandhurst 1990–92; md Int Art and Antiques Loss Register 1992–; dir: Royal Windsor Horse Show Club 1986–, Windsor Equestrian Promotions Ltd 1986–; govr Welbeck Coll 1987–89; *Books* Dinosaurs To Defence (1986); *Recreations* gardening, skiing, shooting, DIY poetry; *Clubs* Cavalry and Guards; *Style*— James Emson, Esq, CBE; ✉ Corscombe House, Corscombe, Dorset DT2 0NU

ENDACOTT, Charles George; s of John Kinsman Endacott, of London, and Rita, *née* Ellul; *b* 24 Sept 1950; *Educ* St John's Coll Southsea; *m* 1973 (m dis 1983), Hazel, *née* Short; 1 da (Natalie b 1 Aug 1979); *partner*, Barbara Joan Jacobs; *Career* messenger E Allan Cooper Advertising 1967–68, studio jr J L Lakings Studio 1968–69, jr designer SF & Partner Advertising 1969–70, freelance designer and visualiser 1970–71, sole proprietor RJB Associates (design and promotions conslts) 1976–83 (fndr ptnr 1971–76), chm RJB Manpower Ltd 1979–83, md Endacott RJB Ltd 1983–89; chm RJB Group Ltd (chm/md various subsids) 1989–; dir: Pristine Products Ltd 1991–, Computer Professionals (UK) Ltd 1992–; charity tstee Marketing Services UK - 'Promoting for Children' 1995; memb: Inst of Sales Promotion; *Recreations* tennis, classic cars, angling; *Clubs* David Lloyd; *Style*— Charles Endacott, Esq; ✉ Endacott RJB Marketing Ltd, 17–18 Great Pulteney St, London W1R 3DG (☎ 0171 439 8591, fax 0171 437 2447, car 0860 301011)

ENFIELD, Harry (*né* Henry); s of Edward Enfield and Deirdre Enfield; *b* 30 May 1961; *Educ* Worth Abbey, Univ of York; *Career* writer, actor and comedian; began performing whilst at York Univ, toured UK (incl London and Edinburgh Festival) with fringe show Dusty and Dick 1983, reg appearances on Saturday Night Live (Channel Four) creating characters incl Stavros and Loadsamoney, writer and actor Sir Norbert Smith... A Life? (Channel Four) 1989 (Silver Rose of Montreux, Gold Rockie Banff Awards, Int Emmy for Popular Arts Progs), own series Harry Enfield's Television Programme (BBC 2) 1991 and 1992, Gone to the Dogs (Central) 1991, Men Behaving Badly (Thames) 1992, Harry Enfield's Guide to Opera (Channel Four) 1993, Harry Enfield and Chums (BBC 1) 1994 and 1996, Radio FAB FM...The End of an Era (special for BBC 1); other TV appearances incl: Frocks on the Box, Girls on Top, Lenny Henry Show, Don't Miss Wax, The Tube, Filthy Rich and Catflap, French and Saunders; *Style*— Harry Enfield, Esq; ✉ c/o PBJ Management Ltd, 5 Soho Square, London W1V 5DE (☎ 0171 287 1112, fax 0171 287 1448)

ENFIELD, Viscount; William Robert Byng; s and h of 8 Earl of Strafford, *qv*, by his 1 wife, Jennifer Mary Denise, *née* May; *b* 10 May 1964; *Educ* Winchester, Univ of Durham; *m* 8 Oct 1994, Karen Elizabeth, *née* Lord; *Style*— Viscount Enfield

ENGEL, Matthew Lewis; s of Max David Engel, of Northampton, and Betty Ruth, *née* Lesser; *b* 11 June 1951; *Educ* Carmel Coll, Univ of Manchester (BA Econ); *m* 27 Oct 1990, Hilary, da of late Laurence Davies; 1 s (Laurence Gabriel b 28 May 1992); *Career* reporter; Northampton Chronicle and Echo 1972–75, Reuters 1977–79; The Guardian: joined 1979, cricket corr 1982–87, feature writer, sports columnist and occasional political, foreign and war corr 1987–; ed Wisden Cricketers' Almanack 1993–; awards: Granada Sportswriter of the Year 1985, Sports Journalist of the Year Br Press Awards 1992; *Books include* Ashes '85 (1985), The Guardian Book of Cricket (ed, 1986), Sportswriter's Eye (1989), The Sportspages Almanac (ed, 1989, 1990, 1991), Tickle The Public: a hundred years of popular newspapers (1996); *Recreations* not writing, not watching sport; *Clubs* Northamptonshire County Cricket (vice pres), Nothing Writers' Dining (ctee memb); *Style*— Matthew Engel, Esq; ✉ The Oaks, Newton St Margarets, Herefordshire HR2 0QN (☎ 01981 510250, fax 01981 510308); The Guardian, 119 Farringdon Road, London EC1R 3ER (☎ 0171 278 2332)

ENGEL, Susan; da of F Engel, and Anni, *née* Stefansky; *b* 25 March 1935; *Educ* Talbot Heath Sch Bournemouth, Sorbonne Paris, Univ of Bristol, Bristol Old Vic Sch; *m* Sylvester Morand; 1 da (Cathy b 16 March 1972); *Career* actress; Bristol Old Vic Theatre 1959, with RSC 1961 (playing lead roles incl Queen Elizabeth in War of the Roses); numerous appearances on TV and radio; *Theatre* incl: Olga in Three Sisters 1976, Gertrude in Hamlet, Watch on the Rhine (NT), A Kind of Alaska (Duchess Theatre), Brighton Beach Memoirs (Aldwych), Constance in King John (RSC Stratford and Barbican) 1988, Good Person of Sichuan (NT), Goneril in King Lear, Queen Margaret in Richard III (RNT, world tour) 1990–91, The Dybbuk (RSC at the Barbican), Hannah Pitt and Ethel Rosenburg in Angels in America (RNT) 1993, Mrs Heidelberg in The Clandestine Marriage (Queens), Mrs Sybil Birling in An Inspector Calls 1995; *Films* incl: Regan in King Lear (Peter Brook), Grand Duchess Olga in Anastasia, Charlie Bubbles, Butley, Damage 1993; *Style*— Ms Susan Engel; ✉ c/o Kate Feast Management, 10 Primrose Hill Studios, Fitzroy Road, London NW1 8TR (☎ 0171 586 5502, fax 0171 586 9817)

ENGESET, Jetmund; s of Arne Kaare Engeset (d 1973), and Marta, *née* Birkeland; *b* 22 July 1938; *Educ* Slemdal and Ris Skoler Oslo Norway, Univ of Aberdeen (MB ChB, ChM); *m* 3 June 1966, Anne Graeme, da of Allan Graeme Robertson (d 1946); 2 da (Anne-Marie, Nina Katrine); *Career* sr lectr Univ of Aberdeen 1974–87, surgn to HM The Queen in Scot 1985–, conslt surgn Grampian Health Bd 1987– (hon conslt surgn 1974–87); FRCSEd 1970, FRCS (Glas) 1982; *Recreations* skiing, squash, angling, gardening; *Style*— Jetmund Engeset, Esq; ✉ Pine Lodge, 315 North Deeside Rd, Milltimber, Aberdeen (☎ 01224 733753); Aberdeen Royal Infirmary, Foresterhill, Aberdeen (☎ 01224 681818)

ENGLAND, Christopher William (Chris); s of Alan William England, of Worksop, Notts, and Mary Winifred, *née* Blissett; *b* 20 Jan 1961; *Educ* Valley Comp Sch Worksop, Pembroke Coll Cambridge (exhibitioner, BA); *Career* writer and actor; toured UK and Aust with Cambridge Footlights Revue Hawaiian Cheese Party 1983–84, co-fndr Bad Lib Theatre Co 1984; co-writer and performer: Feeling the Benefit 1984, Get Your Coat, Dear, We're Leaving... 1984–85, The Preventers 1985, Weird and Wonderful's Big Top Summer Special 1987, The Return of the New Preventers 1988, The Fabulous Tony - A Life in Showbiz 1991; co-writer and performer (with Arthur Smith) An Evening With Gary Lineker (Edinburgh Festival then Duchess Theatre) 1991–92 (nominated Best Comedy Olivier Awards 1992) and film 1994 (nominated Best Comedy Prix Italia 1994); co-writer and performer in TV series: Revolting Animals 1987, Jellyneck 1989, All Change 1990, Murder Most Horrid 1994; *Books* An Evening With Gary Lineker (with Arthur Smith, 1992); *Recreations* football, supporting Oldham Athletic FC, cricket; *Clubs* Les Raymonds Celebres FC (fndr memb); *Style*— Chris England, Esq; ✉ c/o ICM Ltd, Oxford House, 76 Oxford Street, London W1N 0AX (☎ 0171 636 6565, fax 0171 323 0101)

ENGLAND, Glyn; JP; *b* 19 April 1921; *Educ* Penarth Co Sch, QMC, LSE; *m* 1942, Tania, *née* Reichenbach; 2 da; *Career* served WWII 1942–47; chief operations engr CEGB 1966–71, dir-gen SW Region 1971–73, chm SW Electricity Bd 1973–77, chm CEGB 1977–82 (p/t memb 1975–77); non-exec dir: F H Lloyd Holdings 1982–87, Triplex Lloyd plc 1987–90; conslt to World Bank, chm Cncl for Environmental Conservation 1983–88, dir UK Centre for Econ and Environmental Devpt 1984–; chm: Silvanus Tst (formerly Dartington Inst) 1985–94, Silvanus Services Ltd (formerly Woodlands Initiatives Ltd) 1989–94, Windcluster Ltd 1991–96; dir The Wind Fund plc 1994–; Freeman City of London; Hon DSc Univ of Bath; CIMgt, FEng 1981, FIEE, FIMechE; *Recreations* actively enjoying the countryside; *Style*— Glyn England, Esq, JP, FEng; ✉ Woodbridge Farm, Ubley, Bristol BS18 6PX (☎ 01761 462479)

ENGLANDER, Dr Peter David; s of Geoffrey Englander (d 1993), and Doris Ruth, *née* Levy; *b* 29 Nov 1951; *Educ* St Paul's, Univ of Manchester (BSc), MIT (Kennedy scholar, SM), Univ of London (PhD); *m* 1985, Leanda Abigail; 3 s (Simon Jonathan b 1990, Thomas Geoffrey b 1993, William Daniel b 1995); *Career* conslt Boston Consulting Gp 1977–80, dir Apax Partners & Co Ltd 1980–; non-exec dir: Asquith Court Holdings Ltd, Dr Solomon's Group plc, Virtuality Group plc; MSI; *Recreations* walking, cinema; *Style*— Dr Peter Englander; ✉ Apax Partners & Co Ltd, 15 Portland Place, London W1N 3AA (☎ 0171 872 6331, fax 0171 636 6475)

ENGLE, Sir George Lawrence Jose; KCB (1983, CB 1976), QC (1983); *b* 13 Sept 1926; *Educ* Charterhouse, ChCh Oxford; *m* 1956, Irene, da of late Heinz Lachmann; 3 da; *Career* called to the Bar Lincoln's Inn 1953, bencher 1988; entered Parly Counsel Office 1957, seconded as first Parly counsel to Fed Govt of Nigeria 1965–67, Parly counsel 1970–80, with Law Cmmn 1971–73, second Parly counsel 1980–81, first Parly counsel 1981–86; pres Cwlth Assoc of Legislative Cncl 1983–86; *Publications* Law for Landladies (1955), Ideas (contrib, 1954), O Rare Hoffnung (contrib, 1960), Oxford Companion to English Literature (contrib, 1985), Cross on Statutory Interpretation (co-ed 2 edn, 1987, 3 edn 1995); *Style*— Sir George Engle, KCB, QC; ✉ 32 Wood Lane, Highgate, London N6 5UB (☎ and fax 0181 340 9750)

ENGLEHART, Robert Michael; QC (1986); s of G A F Englehart (d 1969), of London, and of K P Englehart, *née* Harvey (d 1973); *b* 1 Oct 1943; *Educ* St Edward's Sch Oxford, Trinity Coll Oxford (MA), Harvard Law Sch (LLM), Bologna Centre; *m* 2 Jan 1971, Rosalind Mary Foster, *qv*, da of Ludovic Anthony Foster (d 1990), of Greatham Manor, Sussex; 1 s (Oliver b 1982), 2 da (Alice b 1976, Lucinda b 1978); *Career* assistente Univ of Florence 1967–68, called to the Bar Middle Temple 1969, recorder of the Crown Court 1987–, bencher 1995; chm London Common Law and Commercial Bar Assoc 1989–91; *Books* Il Controllo Giudiziario: a Comparative Study in Civil Procedure (contrib 1968); *Recreations* shooting, cricket, windsurfing; *Clubs* Garrick, MCC; *Style*— Robert Englehart, Esq, QC; ✉ 2 Hare Court, Temple, London EC4Y 7BH (☎ 0171 583 1770, fax 0171 583 9269)

ENGLEHEART, Henry Francis Arnold; DL (Suffolk 1988); s of Francis Henry Arnold Engleheart (d 1963), of Stoke by Nayland, Suffolk, and Filumena Mary, *née* Mayne (d 1983); *b* 18 March 1930; *Educ* Ampleforth, Downing Coll Cambridge (MA); *m* 9 June 1979, Victoria, da of Maj Ian Maitland Pelham Burn (d 1985), of Colgate, Horsham, Sussex; 1 s (John b 22 Oct 1981), 2 da (Lucy b 8 May 1980, Mary b 28 April 1985); *Career* land agent and chartered surveyor 1955–62, farmer 1957–; chm Suffolk Preservation Soc 1969–72; memb: Melford RDC 1964–74, Babergh DC 1973– (chm 1979–82), High Sheriff of Suffolk 1986; ARICS 1956; *Style*— Henry Engleheart, Esq, DL; ✉ The Priory, Stoke by Nayland, Suffolk CO6 4RL (☎ 01206 262 216)

ENGLISH, Cyril; s of Joseph English, and Mary Hannah English; *b* 18 Feb 1923; *Educ* Ashton-under-Lyne GS; *m* 1945, Mary Brockbank; 2 da; *Career* Nationwide Building Soc: asst sec 1961, asst gen mangr 1967, gen mangr 1971, dep chief gen mangr 1974, dir 1978–90, chief gen mangr 1981–85, dep chm 1989–90; pres Nationwide Housing Trust Ltd 1991– (chm 1987–90); memb Building Socs Investor Protection Bd 1987–95; *Recreations* golf, music; *Clubs* Calcot Park Golf, Reading; *Style*— Cyril English, Esq; ✉ Ashton Grange, Cedar Drive, Flowers Hill, Pangbourne, Berks RG8 7BH (☎ 0118 984 3841); Nationwide Housing Trust Ltd, Kings Park Road, Moulton Park, Northampton NN3 1NL (☎ 01604 794189)

ENGLISH, Sir Cyril Rupert; kt (1972); s of William James English; *b* 19 April 1913; *Educ* Northgate Sch Ipswich; *m* 1936, Eva Violet, da of George Alfred Moore; 2 s; *Career* served RN 1939–46; tech teacher 1935–39; HMI of Schools: inspr 1946–55, staff inspr 1955–58, chief inspr 1948–65, sr chief inspr 1965–68; dir gen City and Guilds of London Inst 1968–76; *Style*— Sir Cyril English; ✉ 12 Pineheath Rd, High Kelling, Holt, Norfolk

ENGLISH, Sir David; kt (1982); *b* 26 May 1931; *Educ* Bournemouth Sch; *m* 1954, Irene Mainwood; 1 s, 2 da; *Career* with Daily Mirror 1951–53, foreign corr Sunday Dispatch 1959–60; Daily Express: joined 1960, Washington corr 1961–63, chief US corr 1963–65, foreign ed 1965–67, assoc ed 1967–69; ed: Daily Sketch 1969–71 (feature ed 1956–59), Daily Mail 1971–92; took over editorial responsibility for Mail on Sunday July-Nov 1982; ed-in-chief and chm Associated Newspapers Ltd 1992–; pres Cmwlth Press Union 1994–; chm: Harmsworth Broadcasting 1992–, Channel 1 TV 1993–, Br Media Industry Gp 1993–, Teletext Ltd 1993–; govr Bournmouth Sch; memb PCC 1993–; *Style*— Sir David English; ✉ Associated Newspapers Ltd, Northcliffe House, 2 Derry St, London W8 5EE (☎ 0171 938 6000)

ENGLISH, Rev Dr Donald; CBE (1996); s of Robert and Ena Forster English; *b* 20 July 1930; *Educ* Univ of Leicester, Univ of London (BA, DipEd), Univ of Cambridge (MA); *m* 1962, Bertha; 2 s (Richard, Paul); *Career* Educn Offr promoted to Flying Offr RAF 1953–55; travelling sec Inter Varsity Fellowship 1955–58, asst tutor Wesley Coll Headingley 1960–62, ordained into Methodist Miny 1962, tutor in New Testament theology Trinity Coll Umuahia Eastern Nigeria 1962–66, circuit min Cullercoats Northumberland 1966–72, tutor in historical theology Hartley Victoria Coll Manchester (Lord Rank chair) 1972–73, tutor in practical theology and Methodism Wesley Coll Bristol 1973–82, gen sec Methodist Church Div Home Mission 1982–95, moderator Free Church Fedn Cncl 1986–87; memb: World Methodist Exec 1976–86, Central Religious Advsy Ctee 1987–93; pres Methodist Conf 1978–79 and 1990–91; vice chm World Methodist Cncl Exec 1986–91, chair World Methodism 1991–96; hon fell Roehampton Inst of Higher Educn (former chm and govr Southlands Coll); Hon DUniv Surrey 1990, Hon DD Asbury Theological Seminary Kentucky USA, Hon DLitt Univ of Leicester 1994; *Books* Evangelism and Worship (1971), God in the Gallery (1975), Christian Discipleship (1977), Windows on Passion (1978), Why Believe in Jesus? Evangelistic Reflections for Lent (1986), Everything in Christ (1988), The Meaning of the Warmed Heart (1988), The Message of Mark (1992), Windows on Salvation (ed, 1994), An Evangelical Theology of Preaching (1996); *Recreations* reading, gardening, spectator sports; *Style*— The Rev Dr Donald English, CBE

ENGLISH, Louise; da of Anthony Oswald English, of St John's Wood, London, and Elizabeth, *née* Reid, of Maida Vale, London; *b* 29 March 1962; *Educ* Stella Mann Sch of Dancing, Anne Sher Acting Sch; *m* 11 March 1995, Nigel Farmer; *Career* actress; *Theatre* Harlequinade (Richmond Fringe Co) 1981, You Ought to be in Pictures (Intima Theatre Sweden) 1983, Gypsy (Crucible Sheffield) 1986, Cider With Rosie 1986, Me and My Girl (Adelphi) 1987–88 and 1992–93, Tommy Boy (tour and Malvern Festival) 1988, My Dearest Ivor (Mill Theatre Sonning then tour) 1989, Tom Foolery (tour) 1990, Girl in My Soup (Mill Theatre Sonning) 1991, Sherlock Holmes (musical tour) 1993, Italian Idol (Oxford) 1993, The Belles of Notre Dame (Croydon Warehouse) 1993, Russ Abbot Tour 1994, Private Lives (Haymarket Basingstoke) 1995; *Pantomine* Aladdin: Southsea 1981, Lincoln 1983, Manchester 1984, Aberdeen 1985, Bournemouth 1986; Snow White:

Birmingham 1988, Bournemouth 1989, Strand Theatre London 1990; Dick Whittington: Guildford 1991; *Television* Thames: Benny Hill Show 1979–84, Don't Rock the Boat 1982, Full House 1982, Tom, Dick and Harriet 1982, Fresh Fields 1983, Chance in a Million 1984, Lytton's Diary 1984, Mike Yarwood Show 1986; Central: Saturday Royal 1983, Entertainment Express 1983, Elkie and Her Gang 1984; BBC: Brush Strokes 1990–91, Full Swing 1995; *Film* Bugsy Malone 1973, The House of the Long Shadows 1982; *Style*— Miss Louise English; ✉ c/o Creative Artists Management Ltd, 19 Denmark Street, London WC2H 8NA (☎ 0171 497 0448, fax 0171 240 7384)

ENGLISH, Sir Terence Alexander Hawthorne; KBE (1991), DL (Cambs 1996); s of Arthur Alexander English (d 1934), and Mavis Eleanor, *née* Lund (d 1959); *b* 3 Oct 1932; *Educ* Hilton Coll SA, Witwatersrand Univ SA (BSc), Guy's Hosp Med Sch (MB BS), Univ of Cambridge (MA); *m* 23 Nov 1963, Ann Margaret, da of Mordaunt Dicey (d 1964); 2 s (Arthur Alexander b 1968, William Andrew b 1971), 2 da (Katharine Ann b 1967, Mary Eleanor b 1970); *Career* sr surgical registrar Brompton and Nat Heart Hosps 1968–72, conslt cardiothoracic surgn Papworth and Addenbrooke's Hosps 1973–95, dir Heart Transplant Res Unit Br Heart Fndn 1980–88, conslt cardiac advsr Wellington Hosp London 1982–88, chief med advsr BUPA Hosps 1991–; pres: Int Soc for Heart Transplantation 1984 and 1985, BMA 1995/96; memb Cncl: RCS 1981–93, GMC 1983–89, Winston Churchill Meml Tst 1995–; memb Audit Cmmn 1993; hon fell: St Catharine's Coll Cambridge 1992 (master 1993–), Hughes Hall Cambridge 1993, UMDS Guy's and St Thomas's Hosp 1993; Hon Freeman Worshipful Co of Barbers 1993; Dr (hc) Nantes 1992, Hon DSc Univ of Sussex 1992, Hon MD Mahidol Univ Thailand 1993, Hon DSc Univ of Hull 1996; FRCS 1967 (pres 1989–92), FACC 1986, FRCP 1990; Hon: FRCP&S (Canada) 1990, FCS (S Africa) 1991, FRACS (Aust) 1991, FRCS (Thailand) 1991, FRCAnaes 1991, FRCSGlas 1991, CP&S (Pakistan) 1991, FDSRCS 1992, FACS 1992, FRCOphth 1993; *Recreations* tennis, walking, reading; *Clubs* Hawks (Cambridge), Athenaeum; *Style*— Sir Terence English, KBE, DL; ✉ The Master's Lodge, St Catharine's College, Cambridge CB2 1RL (☎ 01223 368744)

ENGLISH, Terence Michael; s of late John Robert English, of Edmonton, London, and Elsie Letitia, *née* Edwards; *b* 3 Feb 1944; *Educ* St Ignatius Coll Stamford Hill London, Univ of London (LLB external); *m* 23 July 1966, Ivy Joan, da of Charles William Weatherley (d 1959), of Wood Green, London; 1 s (Andrew b 1972), 1 da (Melanie b 1967); *Career* admitted slr Supreme Ct 1970; clerk to justices: Newbury Hungerford & Lambourn (now W Berks) 1977–85, Slough and Windsor 1985–86; met stipendiary magistrate 1986–; chm Panel Inner London Juvenile Ct 1989– (chm Family Panel 1991–93), recorder of the Crown Court 1994–; *Recreations* philately, golf, watching sport; *Style*— Terence M English, Esq; ✉ West London Magistrates Court, 181 Talgarth Road, London W6 8DN (☎ 0181 741 1234)

ENNIS, Catherine; da of Séamus Ennis (d 1982), of Dublin, and Margaret, *née* Glynn; *b* 20 Jan 1955; *Educ* Christ's Hosp Hertford, Kingsway Coll of FE, Guildhall Sch of Music and Drama, St Hugh's Coll Oxford; *m* 10 Dec 1988, John Arthur Higham, QC, *qv*, s of Frank Higham (d 1988); 2 s (Patrick b 14 Sept 1989, Edmund b 24 March 1992), 1 da (Cecily b 17 Jan 1994), 2 step da (Miranda, Charlotte), 1 step s (Christian); *Career* organist; organ scholar St Hugh's Coll Oxford 1973–76, dir of music St Marylebone Parish Church London NW1 1979–81, asst organist Christ Church Cathedral Oxford 1984–86, organist St Lawrence-Jewry-next-Guildhall London EC2 1985–; prof: RAM 1982–90, Guildhall Sch of Music 1986–88; has given numerous concerts throughout UK and Ireland, solo recitals at Royal Festival Hall 1985 and 1988, concert tours of USA (1985), Scandinavia (1989) and Eastern Europe (1990), given numerous recitals and concerto performances and presented various progs BBC Radio 3 1982–; various recordings (EMI); *Recreations* opera, cricket, children; *Style*— Ms Catherine Ennis

ENNISKILLEN, 7 Earl of (I 1789); Andrew John Galbraith Cole; also Baron Mountflorence (I 1760), Viscount Enniskillen (I 1776) and Baron Grinstead (UK 1815); s of 6 Earl of Enniskillen, MBE, JP (d 1989), and his 1 w, Sonia Mary, *née* Syers (d 1982); *b* 28 April 1942; *Educ* Eton; *m* 3 Oct 1964, Sarah Frances Caroline, o da of late Maj-Gen John Keith- Edwards, CBE, DSO, MC, of Nairobi; 3 da (Lady Amanda Mary b 4 May 1966, Lady Emma Frances b 14 Feb 1969, Lady Lucy Caroline b 8 Dec 1970); *Heir* uncle, Arthur Gerald Cole b 1920; *Career* late Capt Irish Guards; co dir; airline pilot; *Style*— The Rt Hon the Earl of Enniskillen; ✉ c/o Royal Bank of Scotland, 9 Pall Mall, London SW1

ENNISMORE, Viscount; Francis Michael Hare; s (by 3 m) and h of 5 Earl of Listowel, GCMG, PC, *qv*; *b* 28 June 1964; *Style*— Viscount Ennismore

ENNOR, George Patrick Francis; s of late Patrick George Albert Ennor, of Byfleet, Surrey, and Phyllis Mary Ennor, *née* Veitch; *b* 17 Dec 1940; *Educ* Malvern; *m* 30 April 1966 (m dis), Martha Bridget Liddell, da of Lewis Civval (d 1973), of Forest Green, Surrey; 2 s (Julian b 1970, Daniel b 1973), 1 da (Charlotte b 1968); *Career* racing journalist; The Sporting Life 1960–85 (sr corr 1984–85), chief reporter The Racing Post 1985–; pres Horserace Writers' and Reporters Assoc 1974–94; *Recreations* history, crime, politics, Portsmouth FC; *Style*— George P F Ennor, Esq; ✉ 59 Blenheim Rd, Horsham, Sussex (☎ 01403 260831); The Racing Post, 120 Coombe Lane, London SW20 (☎ 0181 879 3377)

ENO, Brian Peter George St John Baptiste de la Salle; s of William Arnold Eno (d 1988), of Woodbridge, Suffolk, and Maria Alphonsine, *née* Buslot; *b* 15 May 1948; *Educ* St Mary's Convent, St Joseph's Coll, Ipswich Sch of Art, Winchester Coll of Art; *m* 1, 11 March 1967, Sarah Grenville; 1 c (Hannah b 25 July 1967); m 2, 11 Jan 1988, Anthea Norman-Taylor; 2 c (Irial b 25 Jan 1990, Darla b 5 Aug 1991); *Career* musician and prodr; visiting prof RCA 1995–; numerous lectures worldwide on matters of culture; memb Global Business Network; Hon DTech Plymouth; *Music* The Maxwell Demon 1969, The Scratch Orchestra 1970, The Portsmouth Sinfonia 1971–73, Roxy Music 1971–73; solo records: Here Come The Warm Jets 1974, Taking Tiger Mountain (by Strategy) 1974, Another Green World 1975, Discreet Music 1975, Before and After Science 1977, Music For Films 1978, Music for Airports 1978, On Land 1981, Thursday Afternoon 1984, Nerve Net 1992, The Shutov Assembly 1992, Neroli 1993; collaborations: No Pussyfooting (with Robert Fripp) 1972, Evening Star (with Robert Fripp) 1975, Possible Musics (with Jon Hassell) 1980, Low, Heroes and Lodger (all with David Bowie) 1978–80, The Plateaux of Mirror (with Harold Budd) 1980, My Life in The Bush of Ghosts (with David Byrne) 1980, Apollo (with Daniel Lanois and Roger Eno) 1983, The Pearl (with Harold Budd) 1984, Wrong Way Up (with John Cale) 1990, Spinner (with Jan Wobble) 1995; selected prodns: Lucky Lief and the Longships (Bob Calvert) 1975, Are we not men? (Devo) 1978, More songs about buildings and food, Fear of Music and Remain in Light (all with Talking Heads) 1978–80, Unforgettable Fire, The Joshua Tree, Achtung Baby and Zooropa (all with U2) 1984–93, Bright Red (Laurie Anderson) 1995, Outside (David Bowie) 1995; *Visual* over 70 exhibitions of video artworks in museums and galleries worldwide incl: La Foret Museum (Tokyo) 1983, Stedelijk Museum (Amsterdam) 1984, Venice Biennale 1986, Centre D'Art (Barcelona) 1992, Circulo de Bellas Artes (Madrid) 1993, Permanent Inst Swarovski (nr Innsbruck, Austria) 1995; *Awards* Best Producer BRIT Awards 1994; *Publications* Oblique Strategies (with Peter Schmidt, 1975), A Year With Swollen Appendices (1996); *Recreations* perfumery, thinking, futurology; *Style*— Brian Eno, Esq; ✉ Opal Ltd, 3 Pembridge Mews, London W11 3EQ (☎ 0171 727 8656, fax 0171 221 4901)

ENRIGHT, Dennis Joseph; OBE (1991); s of George Roderick Enright (d 1934), of Leamington Spa, and Grace, *née* Cleaver (d 1986); *b* 11 March 1920; *Educ* Univ of Cambridge (MA), Univ of Alexandria Egypt (DLitt); *m* 3 Nov 1949, Madeleine; 1 da (Dominique b 1950); *Career* lectr Univ of Alexandria 1947–50, extra-mural tutor Univ of Birmingham 1950–53, visiting prof Kōnan Univ Japan 1953–56, visiting lectr Free Univ of Berlin 1956–57, Br Cncl prof Chulalongkorn Univ Bangkok 1957–59, prof of Eng Univ of Singapore 1960–70, co-ed Encounter magazine 1970–72, dir Chatto & Windus (publishers) 1974–82; Hon DLitt Univ of Warwick 1982, Hon DUniv Surrey 1985; Queen's Gold Medal for Poetry 1981; FRSL 1961; *Books* Academic Year (1955), Memoirs of a Mendicant Professor (1969), The Oxford Book of Death (ed, 1983), The Alluring Problem: An Essay on Irony (1986), Collected Poems 1987 (1987), Fields of Vision (1988), The Faber Book of Fevers and Frets (ed, 1989), The Oxford Book of Friendship (co-ed, 1991), Under the Circumstances: Poems and Proses (1991), The Way of the Cat (1992), Old Men and Comets: Poems (1993), The Oxford Book of the Supernatural (ed, 1994), Interplay: A Kind of Commonplace Book (1995), Poems of George Herbert (ed, 1996), The Sayings of Goethe (ed, 1996); *Recreations* work; *Style*— D J Enright, Esq, OBE

ENRIGHT, Leo Joseph; s of Laurence James Enright (d 1978), and Mary Elizabeth; *b* 18 March 1955; *Educ* St Fintan's HS Dublin, Univ Coll Dublin, MacAlester Coll Minnesota; *m* 1990, Lorraine, *née* Benson; 1 s (Robert Michael b 15 April 1992); *Career* reporter Meath Chronicle Co Meath 1976–77; Radio Telefís Éireann 1977–89: presenter News Features 1977–80, correspondent Middle East 1982–83 (N America 1980–81), head of News 1983–85, correspondent London 1986–89; BBC Dublin correspondent 1989–; princ commentator Spaceflight Irish Radio and TV 1972–; Nat Radio award Investigative Reporter of the Year 1978; fell: British Interplanetary Soc 1975, World Press Inst 1981, NUJ; *Books* Encyclopedia of Space Travel and Astronomy (1979); *Recreations* tennis, walking, swimming; *Clubs* United Arts (Dublin); *Style*— Leo Enright, Esq; ✉ c/o BBC Radio News and Current Affairs, Broadcasting House, London W1A 1AA; Ireland (☎ 00 353 1 679 5117, fax 00 353 1 679 5110)

ENSOR, His Hon Judge; George Anthony (Tony); s of George Ensor (d 1992), of Pwllheli, Gwynedd, and Phyllis, *née* Harrison; *b* 4 Nov 1936; *Educ* Malvern, Univ of Liverpool (LLB); *m* 14 Sept 1968, Jennifer Margaret (MB ChB), da of Dr Ronald Caile (d 1978), of Southport, Lancs; 2 da (Elizabeth b 1972, Jane b 1978); *Career* admitted slr 1961; Rutherfords (now Weightman Rutherfords): ptnr 1963–92, sr ptnr 1992–95; dep coroner (City of Liverpool) 1966–95; dep judge Crown Ct 1979–83, recorder of the Crown Court 1983–95, circuit judge (Northern Circuit) 1995–; pt/t chm Industl Tbnls 1975–95; dir Liverpool FC 1985–93, tstee Empire Theatre Liverpool 1986–; memb Judicial Studies Bd 1986–89; pres: Artists Club Liverpool 1976, Liverpool Law Soc 1982; govr Malvern Coll 1992–; *Recreations* golf, theatre; *Clubs* Artists (Liverpool), Formby Golf, Waterloo RUFC; *Style*— His Hon Judge Ensor; ✉ c/o Northern Circuit Office, 15 Quay Street, Manchester M60 9FD

ENTRECANALES de AZCARATE, Delfina; da of Jose Entrecanales Ibarra (d 1990), and Maria de Azcarate Florez, of Madrid; *b* 10 April 1927; *Educ* Convent of the Assumption Madrid; *m* 1, 1952 (m dis 1973), Paul Wansbrough; 3 s (Charles Jose b 1953, James Pablo b 1955, Edward Juan b 1957 d 1974), 1 da (Blanca Daphne b 1962); m 2, 1988, Digby Squires; *Career* fndr tstee Delfina Studios Trust 1987–, initiated Casa Manilva Festival of Opera and Classic Music Spain 1992; Hon FRCA; *Recreations* cycling, sailing, grandchildren and young people; *Clubs* Chelsea Arts; *Style*— Delfina Entrecanales; ✉ The Delfina Studios Trust, 50 Bermondsey Street, London SE1 3UD (☎ 0171 357 6600, fax 0171 357 7944)

ENTWISTLE, John Nicholas McAlpine; DL; s of Sir (John Nuttall) Maxwell Entwistle (d 1994), and Jean Cunliffe McAlpine, *née* Penman (d 1993); *b* 1941; *Educ* Uppingham; *m* 6 Sept 1968, Phillida Entwistle, *qv*; 1 s (Nicholas b 1970), 1 da (Louise b 1971); *Career* admitted slr 1963; asst attorney Shearman & Sterling New York 1963–64, UK rep Salzburg Seminar Scholarship 1966, ptnr Maxwell Entwistle & Byrne (solicitors) 1966–91; underwriting memb Lloyd's 1971–, conslt slr Davies Wallis Foyster 1992–, dir Rathbone Brothers Plc 1992–, pt/t chm Social Security Appeal Tbnls 1992–; memb Parole Bd 1994–; nat vice chm Bow Gp 1967–68, memb Liverpool City Cncl 1968–71, Parly candidate Huyton (opposed by Harold Wilson) 1970, memb Cncl Nat Fedn of Housing Assocs 1972–75, gen cmmr for Income Tax 1978–83, govr and dep treas Blue Coat Sch Liverpool 1971–85, Merseyside regnl chm NW Industl Cncl 1981–87, pres Friends of the Nat Museums & Galleries on Merseyside 1987–90 (chm and tstee 1984–87), Merseyside rep Nat Art-Collections Fund 1985–89, dir Merseyside TEC 1990–91; memb NW Regnl Ctee Nat Tst 1992–, tstee Nat Museums & Galleries on Merseyside 1990– (chm Devpt Tst 1991–); chm: Liverpool Chamber of Commerce and Industry 1992–94, NW Chambers of Commerce Assoc 1993–; a dep pres Br Chambers of Commerce 1996–; *Style*— John Entwistle, Esq, DL; ✉ Low Crag, Crook, Near Kendal, Cumbria LA8 8LE (☎ 015395 68268); Flat 6, 63 Mersey Road, Liverpool L17 6AQ (☎ 0151 427 2948); office: 5 Castle Street, Liverpool L2 4XE (☎ 0151 236 6226)

ENTWISTLE, Prof Kenneth Mercer; s of William Charles Entwistle, and Maude Elizabeth, *née* Hipkiss; *b* 3 Jan 1925; *Educ* Urmston GS, Univ of Manchester (BSc, MSc, PhD); *m* 9 July 1949, (Alice) Patricia Mary, da of Eric Maurice Johnson; 2 s (Martin Patrick b 1954, Peter Maurice b 1958), 2 da (Hilary Jane b 1953, Bridget Mary b 1965); *Career* Univ of Manchester: lectr 1948, sr lectr 1954, reader 1960, prof of metallurgy (UMIST) 1962–90, prof emeritus 1990, vice princ (UMIST) 1972–74, dean Faculty of Technol 1976–77, pro-vice chllr 1982–85; hon fell Sheffield Poly, companion UMIST 1991; chm Materials Ctee CNAA 1972–74, memb Educn Ctee Inst of Metallurgists 1977–79, memb Metallics Sub Ctee SRC 1979–81, chm Technol Sub Ctee UGC 1985–89, memb UGC 1985–89, advsr on engrg Univs Funding Cncl 1989–91; CEng, FIM; *Recreations* Scottish dancing, choral singing; *Clubs* Athenaeum; *Style*— Prof Kenneth Entwistle; ✉ Greenacre, Bridge End Lane, Prestbury, Macclesfield SK10 4DJ (☎ 01625 829269); Manchester Materials Science Centre, UMIST, Grosvenor St, Manchester M1 7HS (☎ 0161 200 3570, fax 0161 200 3586, telex 666 094)

ENTWISTLE, Phillida Gail Sinclair; JP (Liverpool 1980); da of Geoffrey Burgess, CMG, CIE, OBE (d 1972), and Jillian Margaret Eskens, *née* Hope; *b* 7 Jan 1944; *Educ* Cheltenham Ladies' Coll, Univ of London (BSc), Univ of Liverpool (PhD); *m* 6 Sept 1968, John Nicholas McAlpine Entwistle, *qv*, s of Sir (John Nuttall) Maxwell Entwistle (d 1994), of Stone Hall, Sedbergh, Cumbria; 1 s (Nicholas b 1970), 1 da (Louise b 1971); *Career* dir J Davey & Sons (Liverpool) Ltd 1983–88, gen cmmr of Inland Revenue 1985–92; memb: Mersey RHA 1987–90, Mental Health Act Cmmn 1989–94, Liverpool FHSA 1990–94; chm Furness Hosps NHS Tst 1994–, non-exec dir NW Water 1996–; memb Anchor Housing Assoc 1992–96, memb Rail Users' Consultative Ctee for the NW 1994–96; govr John Moores Univ of Liverpool (formerly Liverpool Poly) 1988–93; FRSA; *Style*— Mrs Phillida Entwistle, JP; ✉ Low Crag, Crook, Cumbria LA8 8LE (☎ and fax 01539 568268)

ENTWISTLE, Raymond Marvin; *b* 12 June 1944; *Educ* John Ruskin GS Surrey; *m* 23 March 1965, Barbara, *née* Hennessy; 2 s, 1 da; *Career* Lloyds Bank 1960–84 (latterly mangr Edinburgh); md Adam & Co plc 1991– (joined 1984), md Adam & Co Group plc 1993–, chm Adam & Co Investment Management Ltd; chm The FruitMarket Gallery 1990–, dir John Davidson Holdings and John Davidson (Pipes) Ltd 1990–96, govr Edinburgh Coll of Art 1989–, dir J W International plc 1995–; FCIB 1992; *Recreations* antiques, fishing, golfing, shooting, walking; *Clubs* New (Edinburgh), Caledonian (Edinburgh), Duddingston Golf; *Style*— Raymond Entwistle, Esq; ✉ The Glebe, Lauder,

Berwickshire TD2 6RW (☎ 01578 718751); Adam & Co Group plc, 22 Charlotte Square, Edinburgh EH2 4DF (☎ 0131 225 8484, fax 0131 225 5136)

ENZHU, HE Jiang; *see:* Jiang, Enzhu

EPERON, Alastair David Peter; s of Stanley Eperon, and Patricia, *née* Woodrow; *b* 17 Nov 1949; *Educ* Ramsden Sch for Boys Orpington Kent; *m* 1976, Ruth, *née* Tabbenor; 2 da (Veryan b 1983, Caroline b 1988); *Career* press offr Surrey CC 1972–74, head of public affrs The Housing Corporation 1974–78, sr conslt Shandwick PR 1978–80, dir then dep md Ogilvy & Mather PR 1980–84, chief exec Ogilvy & Mather Corporate Financial 1984–86, md McAvoy Wreford Bayley 1988–89 (dir 1986), dir Valin Pollen International plc 1989–90, chief exec McAvoy Bayley 1989–91, dir of corporate affrs The Boots Company PLC 1991–; chm CBI Distributive Trades Survey Panel 1995–, memb Bd British Retail Consortium 1995–; MIPR, FRSA 1993; *Recreations* countryside, gardening; *Style—* Alastair Eperon, Esq; ✉ The Boots Company plc, Group Head Office, Nottingham NG2 3AA (☎ 0115 968 7023, fax 0115 968 7161, London office 0171 495 8880)

EPPEL, Leonard Cedric; CBE (1992); s of Dr David Eppel (d 1963), of London, and Vera, *née* Diamond (d 1973); *b* 24 June 1928; *Educ* Highgate Sch; *m* 15 July 1954, Barbara Priscilla, da of Robert Silk, of London; 1 s (Stuart Neil b 26 March 1959), 1 da (Rochelle Eleanor b 7 Oct 1956); *Career* md Silks Estates Investments Ltd 1968 (dir 1954); chm: Arrowcroft Group plc 1969–, Albert Dock Co Ltd 1983; vice pres Br Red Cross Soc (Merseyside); dir: Millwall FC 1971 (chm 1979–83), Greater London Enterprise Ltd 1991, NW Tourist Bd; Freeman City of London, Liveryman Worshipful Co of Fletchers 1984; FVI 1962, FSVA 1968, FRSA, FInstD 1987; *Recreations* swimming, golf; *Clubs* Carlton; *Style—* Leonard Eppel, Esq, CBE; ✉ Arrowcroft Group plc, 24 Hanover Square, London W1R 9DD (☎ 0171 499 5432, fax 0171 493 0323, car 0860 422227)

EPSTEIN, Dr Owen; s of Dr Morris Epstein, and Nancy, *née* Frysh; *b* 12 May 1950; *Educ* Univ of Witwatersrand Johannesburg SA (MB BCh); *m* 10 Dec 1972, June, da of D David Armist; 2 s (Daniel b 4 Aug 1976, Marc b 14 June 1979); *Career* med registrar 1977–79, clinical res fell 1979–82, lectr in medicine 1982–85, conslt and clinical postgrad tutor Royal Free Hosp London 1985–; author of several scientific publications; chm gastroenterology Royal Free Hosp; FRCP 1989, (MRCP 1976); *Style—* Dr Owen Epstein; ✉ Royal Free Hampstead NHS Trust, Pond Street, Hampstead, London NW3 2QG (☎ 0171 794 0500, fax 0171 435 5342)

ERAUT, Prof Michael Ruarc; s of Lt-Col Ruarc Bertram Sorel Eraut (d 1987), and Frances Hurst (d 1972); *b* 15 Nov 1940; *Educ* Winchester, Trinity Hall Cambridge (BA, PhD); *m* 7 Aug 1964, (Mary) Cynthia, da of Michael William Wynne, of Great Shelford; 2 s (Patrick b 10 May 1968, Christopher b 27 Aug 1971); *Career* Univ of Sussex Centre for Educnl Technol: fell 1967, sr fell 1971, dir 1973–76, reader in educn 1976–86, prof of educn 1986–, dir Inst of Continuing and Professional Educn 1986–91; visiting prof of evaluation Univ of Illinois 1980–81 (educnl technol 1965–67); *Books* incl: Teaching and Learning: New Methods and Resources in Higher Education (1970), Analysis of Curriculum Materials (1975), Curriculum Development in Further Education (1985), Improving the Quality of YTS (1986), International Encyclopedia of Educational Technology (1989), Education and the Information Society (1991), Flexible Learning in Schools (1991), Developing Professional Knowledge and Competence (1994), Learning to Use Scientific Knowledge in Education and Practice Settings (1995); *Style—* Prof Michael Eraut; ✉ 49 St Annes Crescent, Lewes, E Sussex BN7 1SD (☎ 01273 475955); Education Development Building, University of Sussex, Falmer, Brighton (☎ 01273 606755)

ERDMAN, Edward Louis; s of Henry David Erdman (d 1945), and Pauline, *née* Jarvis (d 1950); *b* 4 July 1906; *Educ* Grocers' Co Sch; *m* 22 Dec 1949, Pamela, da of late John Howard Mason; 1 s (Timothy James b 1953); *Career* 1937 TA KRRC, Capt N Africa and Italy 1939–45; apprenticeship surveyors office 1923, fndr Edward Erdman surveyors (now Colliers Erdman Lewis) 1934 (ret and became conslt 1974), dir Chesterfield Properties 1960– (chm 1979–91), dir Warnford Investments plc 1962–; World of Property Housing Tst (now Sanctuary Housing Assoc): memb Central Cncl 1974, chm 1978, pres 1987; memb Property Advsy Panel to Treasy 1975–77; FSVA, FRSA; *Books* People and Property (1982); *Recreations* watching football, athletics; *Style—* Edward Erdman, Esq; ✉ 9 Marylebone Lane, London W1M 6HL (☎ 0171 629 8191, fax 0171 409 3124)

EREAUT, Sir (Herbert) Frank Cobbold; kt (1976); s of Herbert Parker Ereaut and May Julia, *née* Cobbold; *b* 6 May 1919; *Educ* Tormore Sch Upper Deal Kent, Cranleigh Sch, Exeter Coll Oxford; *m* 1942, Kathleen FitzGibbon; 1 da; *Career* served WWII RASC, N Africa, Italy, NW Europe; called to the Bar Inner Temple 1947; Jersey: slr gen 1958–62, attorney gen 1962–69, dep bailiff 1969–74, bailiff 1975–85; judge of the Ct of Appeal in Guernsey 1976–89; KStJ 1983 (CStJ 1978); *Recreations* music, gardening, travel; *Style—* Sir Frank Ereaut; ✉ Les Cypres, St John, Jersey, CI (☎ 01534 22317)

EREMIN, Prof Oleg; s of Theodore Eremin (d 1995), of Melbourne, Aust, and Maria, *née* Avramenko (d 1978); *b* 12 Nov 1938; *Educ* Christian Brothers Coll Melbourne Aust, Univ of Melbourne (MB BS, MD); *m* 17 Feb 1963, Jennifer Mary, da of Ellis Charles Ching (d 1972), of Melbourne, Aust; 2 s (Andrew b 1972, Nicholas b 1973), 1 da (Katherine b 1968); *Career* asst surgn Royal Melbourne Hosp Aust 1971–72 (house offr, sr house offr, registrar 1965–71), sr registrar Combined Norwich Hosps 1972–74, sr res assoc in immunology Dept of Pathology Univ of Cambridge 1977–80 (res asst 1974–77), sr lectr and conslt surgn Edinburgh Royal Infirmary 1981–85, prof of surgery and conslt surgn Aberdeen Royal Infirmary, hon professorial fell Rowett Research Inst Aberdeen 1992; memb: Assoc of Surgns of GB and I, Surgical Research Soc, Br Assoc of Surgical Oncology, James IV Assoc of Surgns, Int Surgical Gp; FRACS, FRCSE (memb Cncl 1994–98, examiner and chm Research Bd); *Recreations* classical music, literature, sport; *Clubs* Royal Northern and Univ; *Style—* Prof Oleg Eremin; ✉ 3 The Chanonry, Aberdeen AB24 1RP (☎ 01224 484065); Department of Surgery, University Medical Buildings, Foresterhill, Aberdeen AB9 2ZD (☎ 01224 681818 ext 53004, fax 01224 685157)

ERIAN, John; s of Dr Habib Erian (d 1976), of Cairo, and Aida, *née* Mitry; *b* 12 Aug 1948; *Educ* St George's Coll, Ain-Shams Med Univ Cairo (MB BCh); *m* 1, 7 July 1973, Jennifer, da of Norman Frank Felton, of Hanworth, Middx; 1 s (Michael b 1974), 2 da (Gehanne b 1976, Simonne b 1977); m 2; m 3, 25 Nov 1995, Hilary, da of George Walter Hutchings, of Leigh-on-Sea, Southend; *Career* conslt obstetrician and gynaecologist: W Cumberland Hosp 1975–79, St George's Hosp 1979–82, Queen Charlotte's Hosp and Chelsea Hosp for Women 1982–83, St Thomas' Hosp 1983, Guy's Hosp 1983–85, Farnborough Hosp Kent 1985–; fndr of Bromley Dist Colposcopy Serv and Endocrine Unit and Gift Treatment, pioneered YAG laser surgery in UK as an alternative to hysterectomy, preceptor in endoscopic surgery; author of various papers on endoscopic and laser surgery in gynaecology; memb: Br Endoscopy Soc, Int Menopause Soc, SE Gynaecological Soc, Egyptian Med Soc; MRCOG 1981, FRCOG 1993 (Merit Award 1995); *Recreations* tennis, table tennis, swimming, skiing, horse riding, travelling, theatre, music, food and wine; *Style—* John Erian, Esq; ✉ Aldwyn Lodge, Old London Road, Knockholt, Kent TN14 7JW (☎ 01959 533875); Farnborough Hospital, Farnborough Common, Locksbottom, Orpington, Kent (☎ 01689 814093)

ERICKSON, Prof Charlotte Joanne; da of Knut Eric Erickson (d 1965), of Rock Island, Illinois, and Lael Alberta Regina, *née* Johnson (d 1983); *b* 22 Oct 1923; *Educ* Augustana Coll Rock Island Illinois (BA), Cornell Univ NY (MA, PhD); *m* 19 July 1952, (Glen) Louis Watt, s of Thomas Watt (d 1941), of Dover; 2 s (Thomas b 1956, David b 1958); *Career* instr Vassar Coll Poughkeepsie NY 1950–52, res fell NIESR London 1952–55, LSE 1955–83 (asst lectr, lectr, sr lectr, reader, prof), Paul Mellon prof of American hist Univ of Cambridge 1983–90, MacArthur Prize fell 1990–95; FRHistS 1970; *Books* American Industry and the European Immigrant (1957), British Industrialists, Steel and Hosiery (1959), Invisible Immigrants (1974), Emigration from Europe, 1815–1914 (1976), Leaving England (1994); *Recreations* music, gardening; *Clubs* CCC Cambridge; *Style—* Prof Charlotte Erickson; ✉ 8 High Street, Chesterton, Cambridge CB4 1NG (☎ 01223 323184); History Faculty, West Road, Cambridge CB3 9EF (☎ 01223 335317)

ERICKSON, Prof John; s of Henry Erickson (d 1981), and Jessie, *née* Heys (d 1990); *b* 17 April 1929; *Educ* South Shields HS, St John's Coll Cambridge (BA); *m* 18 July 1957, Ljubica, da of Dr Branko Petrović (executed 1943), of Yugoslavia; 1 s (Ian Mark b 16 April 1964), 1 da (Amanda Jane b 20 Aug 1962); *Career* Nat Serv War Crimes Tbnl Army Intelligence (liaison with Red Army and Yugoslav Mil); res fell St Antony's Coll Oxford 1956–58, lectr Dept of History St Andrews Univ 1958–61, Dept of Govt Univ of Manchester 1961–67 (lectr, sr lectr, reader); Univ of Edinburgh: reader then lectr in higher def studies 1967, prof of politics (def studies) 1969–88, univ endowment fell 1988–93, dir Centre for Def Studies 1988–; visiting prof: Russian Res Centre Univ of Indiana 1967, Texas A & M Univ 1981, Dept of History Yale Univ 1987; pres Assoc of Civil Def and Emergency Planning Offrs 1981–; hon fell Aerospace Acad of Ukraine 1995; FRSE 1982, FBA 1985, FRSA 1991; *Books* incl: The Soviet High Command 1918–1941 (1962 and 1984), Soviet Military Power (1970), Stalin's War with Germany: Vol 1 - Road to Stalingrad (1975), Vol 2 - Road to Berlin (1983), Soviet Ground Forces - Operational Assessment (1985), Barbarossa: The Axis and the Allies (ed and contrib, 1994), The Road to Berlin (1996), The Soviet Armed Forces 1918–92: A Research Guide to Soviet Sources (with L Erickson, 1996); *Clubs* Scottish Arts; *Style—* Prof John Erickson, FRSE, FBA; ✉ 13 Ravelston House Road, Edinburgh EH4 3LP (☎ 0131 332 1787); Centre for Defence Studies, University of Edinburgh, 31 Buccleuch Place, Edinburgh EH8 9JT (☎ 0131 650 4263)

ERIKSEN, Gunn; *b* 28 Dec 1956; *Educ* Norway; *m* 9 Aug 1984, Fred Brown; *Career* worked as ceramicist and weaver in Norway and Scot until 1980; self taught chef and part owner Altnaharrie Inn 1980–; awards for cuisine incl: 5 out of 5 Good Food Guide, 3 Egon Ronay stars, 5 rosettes AA Restaurant Guide, 2 Michelin stars, one of top estabs in UK Ackerman Guide; *Recreations* reading, sailing, skiing, architectural drawing, music, creating things!; *Style—* Ms Gunn Eriksen; ✉ Altnaharrie Inn, Ullapool, Ross-shire, Scotland IV26 2SS (☎ 01854 633230)

ERITH, Robert Felix; TD (1977); eld s of Felix Henry Erith, FSA (d 1991), of Ardleigh, Essex, and Barbara Penelope, *née* Hawken; *b* 8 Aug 1938; *Educ* Ipswich Sch, Writtle Agric Coll; *m* 7 May 1966, Sara Kingsford Joan, da of Dr Christopher Frederick James Muller (d 1990); 3 s (Charles b 1967, James b 1970, Edward (twin) b 1970); *Career* 10 Hussars: 2 Lt Serv in Aqaba Jordan and Tidworth Hants 1957–58, AVR serv in Aden, Oman, Cyprus, Hong Kong, W Germany, Berlin, UK 1962–79, Maj 1973; builders merchants' salesman and mgmnt trainee 1960–64: Geo Wallis (London), Broad & Co (London), Hechinger Co (Washington DC), Simon Hardware Co (Oakland California), Bunnings Timber (Perth W Aust); EB Savory Milln & Co (Milln & Robinson until 1967): bldg specialist 1966, ptnr 1969–83, sr ptnr 1983–87; chm: SBCI Savory Milln Ltd 1987–89, Swiss Bank Corporation Equities Group 1989–93, conslt SBC Warburg (formerly Swiss Bank Corporation) 1993–; non-exec dir: Anglia Housing Association Group Ltd (chm), Graham Group plc, Crest Nicholson plc, Aspinwall & Co Ltd, The International Shakespeare Globe Centre Ltd; conslt: Secure Trust Group plc, CIGL Holdings Ltd (Canada), Royal London Mutual Insurance Society Ltd; churchwarden Holy Innocents Church Lamarsh; memb Ctee: Dedham Vale Soc, Colne-Stour Countryside Assoc; Parly candidate (C) Ipswich 1976–79; Liveryman Worshipful Co of Builders Merchants 1987, Freeman City of London 1987; AIIMR 1971, FInstD 1986, MSI 1993 (memb Stock Exchange 1969), FRPS 1994, FRSA 1995; *Books* Britain into Europe (jtly, 1962), The Role of the Monarchy (jtly, 1965), Savory Milln's Building Book (annual edns 1968–83); *Recreations* farming, environmental pursuits, village cricket, tennis, skiing, stamp collecting; *Clubs* Carlton, Cavalry and Guards', City of London, Pratt's, MCC, Royal Philatelic Soc; *Style—* Robert Erith, Esq, TD; ✉ Shrubs Farm, Lamarsh, Bures, Essex C08 5EA (☎ 01787 227520, fax 01787 227197); SBC Warburg, Swiss Bank House, 1 High Timber St, London EC4V 3SB (☎ 0171 711 4281, fax 0171 711 3333, telex 887434, car 0836 245536)

ERNE, 6 Earl of (I 1798); Henry George Victor John Crichton; JP; sits as Baron Fermanagh (UK 1876); also Baron Erne (I 1768) and Viscount Erne (I 1781); s of 5 Earl of Erne (ka 1940), and Lady Davidema (d 1995), da of 2 Earl of Lytton, KG, GCSI, GCIE, PC; *b* 9 July 1937; *Educ* Eton; *m* 1, 5 Nov 1958 (m dis 1980), Camilla Marguerite, da of late Wing Cdr Owen George Endicott Roberts; 1 s, 4 da; m 2, 1980, Mrs Anna Carin Hitchcock (*née* Bjorck); *Heir* s, Viscount Crichton; *Career* page of honour to HM King George VI 1952 and to HM The Queen 1952–54; Lt N Irish Horse 1960–68; Lord Lt Co Fermanagh; *Clubs* White's, Lough Erne Yacht; *Style—* The Rt Hon the Earl of Erne, JP; ✉ Crom Castle, Newtown Butler, Co Fermanagh (☎ 0136 573 8208)

ERRINGTON, Col Sir Geoffrey Frederick; 2 Bt (UK 1963), of Ness, in Co Palatine of Chester; s of Sir Eric Errington, 1 Bt (d 1973), and Marjorie, *née* Grant-Bennett (d 1973); *b* 15 Feb 1926; *Educ* Rugby, New Coll Oxford; *m* 24 Sept 1955, Diana Kathleen Forbes, da of late Edward Barry Davenport, of Edgbaston; 3 s (Robin Davenport b 1957, John Davenport b 1959, Andrew Davenport (twin) b 1959); *Heir* s, Robin Davenport Errington, *qv*; *Career* GSO 3 (Int) HQ 11 Armd Div 1950–52, GSO 3 MI 3 (b) WO 1955–57, Bde Maj 146 Inf Bde 1959–61, Co Cdr RMA Sandhurst 1963–65, mil asst to Adj-Gen 1965–67, CO 1 Bn King's Regt 1967–69, GSO 1 HQ 1 BR Corps 1969–71, Col GS HQ NW District 1971, AAG M1 (Army) MOD 1974–75, ret 1975; Col King's Regt 1975–86; dir personnel servs Br Shipbuilders 1977–78, employer bd memb Shipbuilding ITB 1977–78; chm: Executive Appointments Ltd 1982–90 (dir 1979), Harefield Hosp NHS Tst 1991–; chm Assoc for the Prevention of Addiction 1994– (vice chm 1991–94); Freeman City of London 1980, Liveryman Worshipful Co of Coachmakers and Coach Harness Makers; FRSA 1994; *Recreations* travelling and gardening; *Clubs* Boodle's, United Oxford and Cambridge, Woodroffes (chm 1987–95); *Style—* Sir Geoffrey Errington, Bt; ✉ 203a Gloucester Place, London NW1 6BU; Stone Hill Farm, Sellindge, Ashford, Kent TN25 6AJ

ERRINGTON, Sir Lancelot; KCB (1976, CB 1962); er s of Maj Lancelot Errington (d 1965), of Beeslack, Milton Bridge, Midlothian; *b* 14 Jan 1917; *Educ* Wellington, Trinity Coll Cambridge; *m* 1939, Katharine Reine, o da of T C Macaulay, MC, of Painswick, Glos; 2 s, 2 da; *Career* served WWII RNVR; entered Home Office 1939, Miny of Nat Insur 1945, asst sec 1953, under sec Miny of Pensions and Nat Insur 1957–65; seconded: Cabinet Office 1965, DHSS 1968; dep under sec of state 1971–73, 2 perm sec DHSS 1973–76; *Style—* Sir Lancelot Errington, KCB; ✉ St Mary's, Fasnacloich, Appin, Argyll (☎ 01631 730331)

ERRINGTON, Robin Davenport; s and h of Col Sir Geoffrey Frederick Errington, 2 Bt, *qv*; *b* 1 July 1957; *Educ* Eton; *Recreations* travel, flying, music; *Clubs* Queen's; *Style—* Robin Errington, Esq; ✉ 68 Orbain Road, London SW6 7JY

ERRINGTON, Stuart Grant; CBE (1994), JP (1970); s of Sir Eric Errington, Bt (d 1973), and Marjorie, *née* Grant Bennett (d 1973); *b* 23 June 1929; *Educ* Rugby, Trinity Coll Oxford (MA); *m* 19 June 1954, Anne, da of Eric Baedeker; 2 s (David, Charles), 1 da (Elizabeth (Mrs Corke)); *Career* Nat Serv, 2 Lt RA; mangr Ellerman Lines 1952–59, md

Astley Industl Tst 1959–70 (former mangr), chm Mercantile Credit 1977–89 (former exec dir 1970–77, chief exec), dir Barclays UK Ltd, Barclays Merchant Bank 1979–87, chair Nat Assoc of CABx 1989–94; non-exec dir: Nationwide Building Society, Northern Electric plc until 1997, Kleinwort Overseas Investment Trust plc; chm: Equipment Leasing Assoc 1976–78, European Leasing Assoc 1978–80, Finance Houses Assoc 1982–84, Sportsmatch Panel; vice chm Cncl Royal Holloway Univ of London, dep chm Berks and Oxon Magistrates' Cts' Ctee; Liveryman: Worshipful Co of Broderers (Warden), Worshipful Co of Coachmakers and Coach Harness Makers; CIMgt; *Recreations* fishing, golf, theatre; *Clubs* Boodle's; *Style*— Stuart Errington, Esq, CBE, JP; ✉ Earleywood Lodge, Ascot, Berks SL5 9JP (☎ 01344 25778, fax 01344 25778)

ERROLL, 24 Earl of (S 1452); Sir Merlin Sereld Victor Gilbert Hay of Erroll; 12 Bt (Baronetcy originally Moncreiffe of that Ilk, Perthshire, NS 1685); also 28 Hereditary Lord High Constable of Scotland (conferred as Great Constable of Scotland *ante* 1309 and made hereditary by charter of Robert I 1314), Lord Hay (S 1429) and Lord Slains (S 1452); Chief of the Hays; as Lord High Constable, has precedence in Scotland before all other hereditary honours after the Blood Royal; also maintains private officer-at-arms (Slains Pursuivant); s of Countess of Erroll (d 1978) by her 1 husb, Sir Iain Moncreiffe of that Ilk, 11 Bt (d 1985); his gggggf (the 18 Earl)'s w, Elizabeth FitzClarence, natural da of King William IV, whose arms he quarters debruised by a baton sinister; *b* 20 April 1948; *Educ* Eton, Trinty Coll Cambridge; *m* 8 May 1982, Isabelle, o da of Thomas Sidney Astell Hohler (d 1989), of Wolverton Park, Basingstoke; 2 s (Lord Hay, Hon Richard b 14 Dec 1990), 2 da (Lady Amelia b 23 Nov 1986, Lady Laline b 21 Dec 1987); *Heir* s, Harry Thomas William (Lord Hay) b 8 Aug 1984; *Career* computer conslt; chm CRC Ltd; memb Queen's Body Guard for Scotland (Royal Co of Archers); Lt Atholl Highlanders; memb Ct of Assts Worshipful Co of Fishmongers; OStJ, TEM; *Recreations* skiing, climbing; *Clubs* White's, Pratt's, Puffins; *Style*— The Rt Hon the Earl of Erroll; ✉ Woodbury Hall, Sandy, Beds SG19 2HR (☎ 01767 650251, fax 01767 651553)

ERROLL OF HALE, 1 Baron (UK 1964), of Kilmun, Co Argyll; Frederick James Erroll; PC (1960), TD; s of George Murison Erroll (d 1926; s of Bergmans Theodor John, of Rotterdam, by his w Margaret Murison (d 1924); he assumed the surname Erroll by deed poll 1914), and Kathleen Donovan Edington (d 1952); *b* 27 May 1914; *Educ* Oundle, Trinity Coll Cambridge; *m* 19 Dec 1950, Elizabeth, da of Richard Sowton Barrow, of Foxholes, Exmouth, Devon; *Career* MP (C) Altrincham and Sale 1945–64; Parly sec: Miny of Supply 1955–56, Bd of Trade 1956–58; economic sec to Treasury 1958–59, min of state Bd of Trade 1959–61 (pres 1961–63), min of power 1963–64, memb NEDC 1962–63; memb House of Lords Select Ctee on Sci and Technol 1985–91; chm: Bowater Corp 1973–84, Consolidated Gold Fields 1976–83 (pres 1983–), Whessoe plc 1970–86, Automobile Assoc 1973–86 (vice pres 1986–); *Style*— The Rt Hon Lord Erroll of Hale, PC, TD; ✉ House of Lords, London SW1A 0PW

ERSKINE, (Thomas) Adrian; s of Daniel Erskine, and Molly, *née* Balmer (d 1979); *b* 7 Aug 1934; *Educ* St Malachys Coll Belfast, Queen's Univ Belfast (BSc), Imperial Coll London (DIC); *Career* civil engr Dept of Highways Ontario Canada 1957–59, structural engr Ove Arup and Partners London 1960–62, head Ulster branch BRC Engineering Co Ltd 1964–69, assoc i/c civil and structural work Belfast office Building Design Partnership 1969–78, ptnr McGladdery & Partners (consltg, civil and structural engrs) Belfast 1978–; chm Jt Consultative Ctee for Bldg (N Ireland) 1990–93; CEng, FIStructE, MICE 1962; *Recreations* squash, golf, cricket; *Clubs* Belfast Boat, Belvoir Golf, Woodvale Cricket; *Style*— Adrian Erskine, Esq; ✉ 24 Sandhurst Drive, Belfast BT9 5AY (☎ 01232 668706); McGladdery and Partners, 64 Malone Ave, Belfast BT9 6ER (☎ 01232 660682)

ERSKINE, Barbara; da of Stuart Nigel Rose, of Hay-on-Wye, and Pamela Yvonne, *née* Anding (d 1988); *b* 10 Aug 1944; *Educ* St George's Harpenden, Univ of Edinburgh (MA); *m*; 2 s (Adrian James Earl, Jonathan Erskine Alexander); *Career* freelance editor and journalist, short story writer, novelist; memb: Soc of Authors, The Authors' Club; *Books* Lady of Hay (1986), Kingdom of Shadows (1988), Encounters (1990), Child of the Phoenix (1992), Midnight is a Lonely Place (1994), House of Echoes (1996), Distant Voices (1996); *Recreations* reading, growing and using herbs, exploring the past; *Style*— Mrs Barbara Erskine; ✉ Blake Friedmann Literary Agents, 37–41 Gower St, London WC1E 6HH (☎ 0171 631 4331)

ERSKINE, Sir (Thomas) David; 5 Bt (UK 1821), of Cambo, Fife; JP (Fife 1951), DL (1955); s of Lt-Col Sir Thomas Wilfrid Hargreaves John Erskine, 4 Bt, DSO, DL (d 1944, third in descent from Sir David Erskine, 1 Bt, natural gs of 9 Earl of Kellie) of Cambo, Kingsbarns, Fife, and Magdalen Janet, da of Sir Ralph Anstruther, 6 Bt of Balcaskie; *b* 31 July 1912; *Educ* Eton, Magdalene Coll Cambridge (BA); *m* 4 Oct 1947, Ann, da of Col Neil Fraser-Tytler, DSO, MC, TD, DL (d 1937), of Aldourie Castle, Inverness, and Mrs (C H) Fraser-Tytler, CBE (d 1995); 2 s (Thomas Peter Neil b 1950, William b 1952), 1 da (Caroline d 1976); *Heir* s, Thomas Peter Neil Erskine b 28 March 1950; *Career* served WWII, M East, India, Malaya as Maj Indian Corps Engrs; with Butterfield & Swire Hongkong & China 1935–41; landed proprietor (approx 1600 acres) & farmer 1946–; Fife CC: cncllr 1953–74, vice chm 1967–70, chm 1970–73; Fife regnl cncllr 1974–82; Vice Lord-Lt Fife 1982–87; *Recreations* gardening, shooting, travel; *Clubs* New (Edinburgh); *Style*— Sir David Erskine, Bt, JP; ✉ Westnewhall, Kingsbarns, St Andrews, Fife (☎ 01333 450228)

ERSKINE, Hon David Hervey; DL (Suffolk 1983); 3 s of John Francis Ashley, Lord Erskine, GCSI, GCIE (d 1953, himself s of 12 Earl of Mar and (14 Earl of) Kellie), and Lady Marjorie Hervey (d 1967), er da of 4 Marquess of Bristol; *b* 5 Nov 1924; *Educ* Eton, Trinity Coll Cambridge; *m* 1, 5 Dec 1953, Jean Violet (d 1983), da of Lt-Col Archibald Vivian Campbell Douglas of Mains; 3 da; m 2, 3 May 1985, Caroline Mary, widow of 2 Viscount Chandos (d 1980), and da of Rt Hon Sir Alan Frederick Lascelles, GCVO, KCB, CMG, MC (d 1981); *Career* War Serv Italy and Palestine 1944–47; called to Bar Inner Temple 1950, JP Suffolk 1971–86, late Capt Scots Gds; cncllr W Suffolk 1969–74 and Suffolk 1974–85; *Recreations* historical study, sightseeing; *Clubs* Brooks's; *Style*— The Hon David Erskine, DL; ✉ Felsham House, Felsham, Bury St Edmunds IP30 0QG (☎ 01449 736326); 17 Clareville Court, Clareville Grove, London SW7 5AT (☎ 0171 373 4734)

ERSKINE, (Thomas) Peter Neil; s and h of Sir David Erskine, 5 Bt, JP, DL, *qv*; *b* 28 March 1950; *Educ* Eton, Univ of Birmingham, Univ of Edinburgh (postgrad); *m* 1972, Catherine, da of Col G H K Hewlett; 2 s (Thomas Struan b 1977, James Dunbar b 1979), 2 da (Gillian Christian b 1983, Mary Caroline b 1986); *Career* worked hotel indust Brazil, returned home to estate; opened visitor centre on one of the farms 1982; currently converting the estate to organic farming; chm Scottish Organic Producer Assoc, chm Fife Rural Rural Training Gp; professional photographer; LBIPP; *Recreations* folk blues guitar; *Style*— Peter Erskine, Esq

ERSKINE, Hon Robert William Hervey; yst s of late John Francis Ashley, Lord Erskine, GCSI, GCIE (d 1953); *b* 13 Oct 1930; *Educ* Eton, King's Coll Cambridge; *m* 1, 21 May 1955 (m dis 1964), Jennifer Shirley, yr da of L J Cardew Wood, of Farnham Royal, Bucks; m 2, Oct 1969 (m dis 1975), Annemarie Alvarez de Toledo, da of Jean Lattes, of Paris; 1 s (Alistair Robert); m 3, 1977, Belinda, da of Raymond Blackburn, of London; 2 s (Thomas Gerald, Felix Benjamin); *Career* author, broadcaster; FSA 1990; *Style*— The Hon Robert Erskine, FSA; ✉ 100 Elgin Crescent, London W11 2JL

ERSKINE-HILL, Prof Howard Henry; s of Capt Henry Erskine-Hill (d 1989), of Malahide, Co Dublin, and Hannah Lilian, *née* Poppleton (d 1991); *b* 19 June 1936; *Educ* Ashville Coll, Univ of Nottingham (BA, PhD), Univ of Cambridge (LittD); *Career* tutor, asst lectr then lectr in English Univ Coll Swansea 1960–69; Univ of Cambridge: lectr in English 1969–83, reader in literary history 1984–, fell Jesus Coll 1969–80, fell Pembroke Coll 1980–94, prof of literary history 1994–; Olin fell Nat Humanities Center NC USA 1988–89; FBA 1985; *Books* Pope: Horatian Satires and Epistles (ed, 1964), Pope: The Dunciad (1972), The Social Milieu of Alexander Pope (1975), The Augustan Idea (1983), Swift: Gulliver's Travels (1993), Poetry and the Realm of Politics (1996), Poetry of Opposition and Revolution (1996); *Recreations* walking; *Clubs* Utd Oxford and Cambridge Univ; *Style*— Prof Howard Erskine-Hill, FBA; ✉ 194 Chesterton Road, Cambridge CB4 1NE; Pembroke College, Cambridge CB2 1RF (☎ 01223 338138)

ERSKINE-HILL, Sir (Alexander) Roger; 3 Bt (UK 1945), of Quothquhan, Co Lanark; er s of Sir Robert Erskine-Hill, 2 Bt (d 1989), and Christine Alison, *née* Johnstone; *b* 15 Aug 1949; *Educ* Eton, Univ of Aberdeen (LLB); *m* 6 Oct 1984 (m dis 1994), Sarah Anne Sydenham, da of Dr Richard John Sydenham Clarke (d 1970); 1 s (Robert Benjamin b 1986), 1 da (Kirsty Rose b 1985); *Heir* s, Robert Benjamin Erskine-Hill b 6 Aug 1986; *Career* dir: Salestrac Ltd, Map Marketing Ltd; *Style*— Sir Roger Erskine-Hill, Bt; ✉ Salestrac Ltd, Cowley Bridge Rd, Exeter EX4 5HQ (☎ 01392 429429)

ERVIN, Wilson; CBE (1986); s of Robert John Ervin (d 1966), of Belfast, and Jane, *née* McVeigh (d 1983); *b* 13 Dec 1923; *Educ* Royal Belfast Academical Inst; *m* Joan Catherine, da of John Mercer, of Belfast; *Career* served in Fleet Air Arm RN (non cmmnd) in Home Waters, Far East, India, Burma and Australia; former dir and chief exec Northern Bank Ltd; chm TBF Thompson (Garvagh) Ltd; former pres Inst of Bankers in Ireland, vice pres Royal Nat Lifeboat Inst; FIB; *Clubs* Ulster Reform, Belvoir Park Golf; *Style*— Wilson Ervin, CBE; ✉ 29 Broomhill Park, Old Stranmillis, Belfast BT9 5JB

ESCOTT COX, Brian Robert; QC (1974); s of George Robert Escott Cox, of Solihull; *b* 30 Sept 1932; *Educ* Rugby, Oriel Coll Oxford (BA); *m* 9 Aug 1969, Noelle, da of Dominique Gilormini, of Patrimonio, Corsica; 1 s (Richard b 10 Feb 1971), 1 da (Caroline b 8 Jan 1976); *Career* called to the Bar Lincoln's Inn 1954; in practice: Jr Bar 1954–74, Midland and Oxford Circuit 1954–; recorder of the Crown Court 1972–, Lord Chllr's list of Dep High Ct Judges 1979, bencher Lincoln's Inn 1985; *Style*— Brian Escott Cox, Esq, QC; ✉ 36 Bedford Row, London WC1R 4JH (☎ 0171 421 8000, fax 0171 421 8080)

ESHER, 4 Viscount (UK 1897); Lionel Gordon Baliol Brett; CBE (1970); also Baron Esher (UK 1885); s of 3 Viscount, GBE (d 1963); *b* 18 July 1913; *Educ* Eton, New Coll Oxford; *m* 22 Oct 1935, (Helena) Christian Olive, da of Ebenezer John Lecky Pike, CBE, MC, DL, of Ditcham Park, Petersfield, Hants; 5 s, 1 da; *Heir* s, Hon Christopher Brett; *Career* served WWII RA (despatches); architect and planner Hatfield New Town 1949–59; memb Royal Fine Art Cmmn 1951–69, pres RIBA 1965–67, memb Advsy Bd Victoria & Albert Museum 1967–72, govr London Museum 1970–77, rector and vice-provost Royal Coll of Art 1971–78; chm: Art Panel Arts Cncl of GB 1972–77, Advsy Bd for Redundant Churches until 1983; tstee Soane Museum 1976–93; chm Thames and Chilterns Nat Tst 1979–85; Hon DLitt Strathclyde 1967, Hon DUniv York 1970, Hon DSc Edinburgh 1981; *Books* (writes as Lionel Brett): Houses (1947), The World of Architecture (1963), Landscape in Distress (1965), York: a Study in Conservation (1969), Parameters and Images (1970), A Broken Wave: the Rebuilding of England 1940–80 (1981), The Continuing Heritage (1982), Our Selves Unknown (1984), The Glory of the English House (1991); *Clubs* Arts; *Style*— The Rt Hon Viscount Esher, CBE; ✉ Snowball Hill, Russell's Water, Henley on Thames, Oxon RG9 6EU

ESLER, Gavin William James; s of William John Esler, and Georgena, *née* Knight; *b* 27 Feb 1953; *Educ* George Heriot's Sch Edinburgh, Univ of Kent at Canterbury (BA), Univ of Leeds (MA); *m* 3 July 1979, Patricia Margaret, da of Bernard Cyril Warner; 1 da (Charlotte Virginia b 27 May 1992), 1 s (James Conor b 22 March 1994); *Career* Thompson Newspapers grad trainee then journalist Belfast Telegraph 1975–77, reporter/presenter Spotlight BBC Northern Ireland current affrs prog 1977–81; BBC: reporter/presenter Newsnight and TV News 1982–89, Washington corr 1989–, chief N America corr 1990–; freelance magazine and newspaper journalist; RTS Journalism Award for Newsnight Report 1987; memb White House Corrs' Assoc; *Books* Loyalties (novel, 1990), Deep Blue (novel, 1992), The Bloodbrother (novel, 1995); *Recreations* skiing, squash, hill walking, backwoods camping; *Style*— Gavin Esler, Esq; ✉ BBC Television, 2030 M Street NW, Room 607, Washington DC 20036, USA (☎ 00 1 202 223 2050, fax 00 1 202 775 1395)

ESMONDE, Sir Thomas Francis Grattan; 17 Bt (I 1629), of Ballynastragh, Wexford; s of His Hon Judge Sir John Henry Grattan Esmonde, 16 Bt (d 1987), and Pamela Mary, *née* Bourke; *b* 14 Oct 1960; *Educ* Sandford Park Sch, Trinity Coll Dublin (MD, MB BCh, BAO, MRCPI, MRCP); *m* 26 April 1986, Pauline Loretto, 2 da of James Vincent Kearns; 1 s (Sean Vincent Grattan b 1989), 2 da (Aisling Margaret Pamela Grattan b 17 Dec 1991, Niamh Pauline Grattan b 2 May 1996); *Heir* s, Sean Vincent Grattan Esmonde b 8 Jan 1989; *Style*— Sir Thomas Esmonde, Bt; ✉ 6 Nutley Avenue, Donnybrook, Dublin 4, Ireland

ESPENHAHN, Peter Ian; s of Edward William Espenhahn, of E Molesey, and Barbara Mary, *née* Winmill; *b* 14 March 1944; *Educ* Westminster, Sidney Sussex Coll Cambridge (MA); *m* 10 Feb 1968, Fiona Elizabeth, da of Air Vice Marshal Brian Pashley Young, of Didmarton, Glos; 2 d (Sarah b 1971, Caroline b 1975); *Career* Deloitte Plender Griffiths London 1965–72, dir Corp Fin Dept Morgan Grenfell & Co Ltd 1983– (joined 1973); FCA; *Recreations* sailing, rugby, opera; *Style*— Peter Espenhahn, Esq; ✉ 79 Mount Ararat Rd, Richmond, Surrey TW10 6PL; Morgan Grenfell & Co Ltd, 23 Great Winchester St, London EC2P 2AX (direct ☎ 0171 826 6255, fax 0171 826 6180)

ESPLEN, (Sir) John Graham; 3 Bt (UK 1921), of Hardres Court, Canterbury (but does not use title); o s of Sir (William) Graham Esplen, 2 Bt (d 1989), and Aline Octavia, *née* Hedley (d 1994); *b* 4 Aug 1932; *Educ* Harrow, St Catharine's Coll Cambridge (BA); *Heir* s, William John Harry Esplen b 24 Feb 1967; *Style*— Mr John Esplen; ✉ The Mill House, Moorlands Road, Merriott, Somerset TA16 5NF

ESSER, Robin Charles; s of Charles Esser (d 1982), and Winifred Eileen Esser (d 1972); *b* 6 May 1935; *Educ* Wheelwright GS Dewsbury, Wadham Coll Oxford (BA, MA); *m* 1, 5 Jan 1959, Irene Shirley, *née* Clough (d 1973); 2 s (Daniel b 1962, Toby b 1963), 2 da (Sarah Jane b 1961, Rebecca b 1965); m 2, 30 May 1981, Tui, *née* France; 2 s (Jacob b 1986, Samuel b 1990); *Career* cmmnd 2 Lt KOYLI 1955, transferred General Corps 1956, Capt acting ADPR BAOR 1957; freelance reporter 1956; Daily Express: staff reporter 1957–60, ed William Hickey Column 1962, features ed 1963, NY Bureau 1965, northern ed 1969, exec ed 1970; conslt ed Evening News 1977, exec ed Daily Express 1984–86, ed Sunday Express 1986–89, gp editorial conslt Express Newspapers 1989–90, ind editorial conslt 1990–; *Books* The Hot Potato (1969), The Paper Chase (1971); *Recreations* lunching, sailing, talking, reading; *Clubs* Garrick; *Style*— Robin Esser, Esq; ✉ 35 Elthiron Road, London SW6 4BW

ESSEX, David Albert; s of Albert Cook, of Romford, Essex, and Doris, *née* Kemp; *b* 23 July 1947; *Educ* Shipman Secdy Sch E London; *m* 12 March 1971, Maureen Annette, *née* Neal; 1 s (Daniel Lee), 1 da (Verity Leigh); *Career* actor, singer, composer, producer; given worldwide concerts for 17 years, winner many Gold and Silver Discs, numerous TV and radio appearances in UK, Europe, USA and Australia; with numerous charities incl Save the Children Fund, ambassador VSO 1990–92; made album of musicians from Third World countries (Under Different Skies); memb: Br Actors' Equity Assoc, Musicians' Union, American Fedn of TV and Radio Artists, Screen Actors' Guild; *Theatre* incl: Jesus in Godspell (Wyndhams, Variety Club Award) 1972–73, Che Guevara in Evita (Prince Edward, Variety Club Award) 1978, Lord Byron in Childe Byron (Young Vic) 1981, Fletcher Christian in own musical Mutiny (with Richard Crane, Piccadilly (recorded concept album with RPO)) 1985–86, She Stoops to Conquer (Queen's) 1993; wrote score for Beauty and the Beast (Russian All Stars Co on Ice) 1995–96; *Films* incl: That'll Be The Day 1973, Stardust 1974, Silver Dream Racer (also composed score) 1979–80, Shogun Mayeda 1990; *Recreations* cricket, flying helicopters (captain), squash; *Clubs* St James's, Lord's Taverners; *Style—* David Essex, Esq; ✉ c/o London Management, 2–4 Noel Street, London W1V 3RB (☎ 0171 287 9000, fax 0171 287 3036)

ESSEX, David Anthony Dampier; *b* 10 May 1946; *Educ* Lancing, City Univ Business Sch (MSc); *m* 29 April 1972, Virginia; 3 da (Harriet b 1974, Polly b 1976, Tiffany b 1978); *Career* CA; fin controller British Aerospace 1982–85 (chief internal auditor 1979–82); Ernst & Young: ptnr 1985–, ptnr i/c servs to mfrs 1987–94, aerospace & defence ptnr 1994–; FCA 1969; *Recreations* family, walking, the arts, gardening, France; *Style—* David Essex, Esq; ✉ 1 Lambeth Palace Rd, London SE1 7EU (☎ 0171 928 2000)

ESSEX, Francis; s of Harold Essex-Lopresti (d 1967; 5 in descent from Count Lopresti, of Sicily), and Beatrice Essex-Lopresti (d 1971); *b* 24 March 1929; *Educ* Cotton Coll N Staffs; *m* 13 Aug 1956, Jeanne, da of John Shires (d 1982); 2 s (Martin, Stephen d 1991); *Career* author, composer, prodr; prodr BBC TV (Light Entertainment) 1954–60, sr prodr ATV 1960–65, prog controller Scottish TV 1965–69, prodn controller ATV 1969–76 (dir 1974–81, dir of prodns 1976–81); wrote and presented The Bells of St Martins 1953, directed Six of One (Adelphi Theatre) 1964, musical Jolson (UK tour and West End) 1995; film scripts: Shillingbury Tales, The Silent Scream, The Night Wind, Cuffy (series), Gabrielle and the Doodleman; music scores: Luke's Kingdom, The Seas Must Live, The Lightning Tree, Maddie with Love, The Cedar Tree; writer of plays and songs; chm Conservatives Abroad Javea 1990 and 1991; FRTS; Br Acad Light Entertainment Award 1964, Leonard Brett Award 1964; *Books* Shillingbury Tales (1983), Skerrymor Bay (1984); *Recreations* blue water sailing, gardening, tennis; *Style—* Francis Essex, Esq; ✉ Punta Vista, Aldea de las Cuevas, Benidoleig, Alicante, Spain

ESSEX, 10 Earl of (E 1661); Robert Edward de Vere Capell; also Baron Capell of Hadham (E 1641), and Viscount Malden (E 1661); s of Arthur Algernon de Vere Capell (d 1924; gs of Capt Hon Algernon Capell, RN, bro of 6 Earl of Essex), and Alice Mabel, *née* Currie (d 1951); suc kinsman, 9 Earl, 1981, took seat in House of Lords 7 June 1989; *b* 13 Jan 1920; *m* 3 Jan 1942, Doris Margaret, da of George Tomlinson; 1 s; *Heir* s, Viscount Malden, *qv*; *Career* served WWII, Flt Sgt RAF; *Style—* The Rt Hon the Earl of Essex; ✉ 2 Novak Place, Torrisholme, Morecambe, Lancs

ESSEX, William Alexander Wells; s of Norman Arthur Essex, and Jane Rosemary Wells, *née* Tickler; *b* 13 Aug 1958; *Educ* Marlborough, UEA; *m* 24 Sept 1988, Penelope Anne, da of Lt Cdr David McKerrow Baird; 2 da (Clementine b 24 Oct 1990, Sophie b 13 March 1996), 1 s (Oliver b 17 Feb 1992); *Career* joined Financial Times Group 1982, ed Resident Abroad Magazine 1985–96, columnist Sunday Times 1996–; *Style—* William Essex, Esq; ✉ Potash Cottage, Strethall, Essex CB11 4XJ (☎ 01799 523507); The Sunday Times, 1 Pennington Street, London E1 9XW (☎ 0171 782 5000, fax 0171 782 5658)

ESSWOOD, Paul Lawrence Vincent; s of Alfred Walter Esswood, and Freda, *née* Garratt; *b* 6 June 1942; *Educ* West Bridgford GS Nottingham, Royal Coll of Music (Henry Blower singing prize); *m* 1, (m dis 1990); 2 s (Gabriel Peter b 1968, Michael William b 1971); m 2, 4 Aug 1990, Aimée Desirée; 1 da (Stella Jane b 1992), 1 s (Lawrence Galahad b 1993); *Career* opera, concert and recital singer (counter-tenor) specializing in Baroque period; operatic debut Univ of California Berkeley 1966; given performances at venues incl: Zurich, Cologne, Stuttgart, Chicago, La Scala Milan; prof of singing RCM 1977–80, prof of Baroque vocal interpretation RAM 1985–; lay vicar Westminster Abbey 1964–71; ARCM 1964, Hon RAM 1990; *Performances* incl: Monteverdi operas (Zürich), Britten's A Midsummer Night's Dream (Cologne), Penderecki's Paradise Lost (La Scala), Glass's Akhnaten (Stuttgart); solo recitals incl: Purcell's Music for a While, Schumann's Dichterliebe and Liederkreis Op39, English lute songs from Songs to My Lady; *Recordings* incl: all Bach Cantatas, St Matthew Passion, Christmas Oratorio, Purcell's Dido and Aeneas; recordings of Handel works incl: Brockes Passion, Jeptha, Saul, Belshazzar, Rinaldo, Xerxes, Messiah, Il Pastor Fido, Britten Folk Songs and Canticle II, Abraham & Isaac; *Recreations* gardening (organic); *Style—* Paul Esswood, Esq; ✉ c/o TransArt (UK), 8 Bristol Gardens, London W9 2JG (☎ 0171 286 7526, fax 0171 266 2687)

ESTALL, Prof Robert Charles; s of Estall John Thomas (d 1967), of London, and Hilda Lilian, *née* West (d 1976); *b* 28 Sept 1924; *Educ* St Mary's Coll Twickenham (Teacher's Certificate), LSE (BSc, PhD); *m* 2 April 1956, Mary, da of Frederick Willmott (d 1988), of Exeter; 3 s (Simon James b 1959, Martin Robert b 1961, Richard John b 1968), 1 da (Joanna Mary b 1957); *Career* Petty Offr RN 1942–46; visiting prof Clark Univ Mass USA 1958, res fell American Cncl of Learned Socs 1962–63, visiting prof Univ of Pittsburg PA USA 1967, prof of geography LSE 1988– (lectr in geography 1955–65, reader in econ geography of N America 1965–88); *Books* New England: A Study in Industrial Adjustment (1966), A Modern Geography of the United States (1976), Industrial Activity and Economic Geography (1980), Global Change and Challenge (ed with R Bennett, 1991); *Recreations* gardening, reading, walking, golf; *Style—* Prof Robert Estall; ✉ 48 The Ridings, Berrylands, Surbiton, Surrey KT5 8HQ (☎ 0181 399 0430); London School of Economics, Houghton St, London WC2A 2AE (☎ 0171 405 7686)

ESTEVE-COLL, Dame Elizabeth Anne Loosemore; DBE (1995); da of P W Kingdon and Nora Kingdon; *b* 14 Oct 1938; *Educ* Darlington Girls HS, Birkbeck Coll London (BA); *m* 1960, Jose Alexander Timothy Esteve-Coll; *Career* head of learning resources Kingston Poly 1977, univ librarian Univ of Surrey 1982, keeper Nat Art Library V & A Museum 1985, dir V & A Museum 1988–95, vice chllr Univ of E Anglia 1995–; *Recreations* reading, music, foreign travel; *Style—* Dame Elizabeth Esteve-Coll, DBE; ✉ University of East Anglia, Norwich, Norfolk NR4 7TJ (☎ 01603 456161, fax 01603 507753)

ETCHELLS, Dr (Dorothea) Ruth; da of Rev Walter Etchells (d 1961), of Lancs, and Ada, *née* Hawksworth (d 1981); *b* 17 April 1931; *Educ* Merchant Taylors' Sch for Girls Crosby Liverpool, Univ of Liverpool (BA, DipEd, MA), Univ of London (BD), DD (Lambeth); *Career* head English Dept Aigburth Vale HS 1959, sr lectr and res tutor Chester Coll of Educn 1965, sr lectr Univ of Durham 1973 (vice princ Trevelyan Coll 1972), princ St John's Coll with Cranmer Hall Univ of Durham 1979–88 (hon fell St John's Coll 1990); first woman princ of C of E Theological Coll; memb: Cncl CMS 1972–79, Governing Body Monkton Combe Sch 1979–90, Cncl Univ of Durham 1985–88, Gen Synod 1985–95 (memb Doctrine Cmmn 1985–91), Crown Appts Cmmn 1986–95, Cncl Ridley Hall Cambridge 1989–; conslt Lambeth Conf 1988, chm House of Laity Durham Diocese 1988–94 (memb Bishop's Cncl and Standing Ctee 1977–), memb Durham Family Practitioner Ctee (now Family Health Services Authy) 1988–96 (vice chm 1990–), chm Durham FSHA Med Servs Ctee 1990–96; tstee Greatham Hosp of God 1995–; memb Governing Body: Durham Sch 1993–95, Durham HS 1995–; *Books* Unafraid To Be (1969), The Man with the Trumpet (1970), A Model of Making (1983); Poets and Prophets: Robert Browning, John Milton, George Herbert, Early English Poets (ed, 1988), Praying with the English Poets (ed, 1990), Just as I am: personal prayers for every day (1994), Set My People Free: A Lay Challenge to The Churches (1995); *Recreations* friends, pets, country walking; *Style—* Dr Ruth Etchells; ✉ 12 Dunelm Court, South Street, Durham DH1 4QX (☎ 0191 384 1497)

ETHERINGTON, Stuart James; s of Ronald George Etherington, of Mudeford, Dorset, and Dorothy Lillian, *née* West; *b* 26 Feb 1955; *Educ* Sondes Place Sch Dorking, Brunel Univ (BSc), Univ of Essex (MA), London Business Sch (MBA); *Career* social worker 1977–79, researcher employed by housing tst 1980–83, policy advsr Br Assoc of Social Workers 1983–85, dir Good Practices in Mental Health 1985–87, chief exec RNID 1991–94 (dir of public affrs 1987–91), dir NCVO 1994–; *Books* Mental Health and Housing (1984), Emergency Duty Teams (1985), Social Work and Citizenship (1987), The Sensitive Bureaucracy (1986), Worlds Apart (1990), The Essential Manager (1993); *Recreations* collecting Nelsonian artefacts, watching cricket, reading, wine; *Clubs* Nat Liberal, Surrey CCC; *Style—* Stuart Etherington, Esq; ✉ 40 Walnut Tree Road, Greenwich, London SE10 9EU (☎ 0181 305 1379); National Council for Voluntary Organisations, Regent's Wharf, 8 All Saints St, London N1 9RL (☎ 0171 713 6161, fax 0171 713 6300)

ETHERINGTON, William (Bill); MP (Lab) Sunderland North (majority 17,004); *b* 17 July 1941; *Career* apprentice fitter Austin & Pickersgill Shipyard Southwick 1957–63, fitter Dawdon Colliery 1963–83; NUM: memb 1963–, branch delegate Durham Mechanics Branch 1973–83, full time official 1983–92, memb Nat Exec Ctee 1985–87, vice pres NE Area 1988–92; tstee Mineworkers' Pension Scheme 1985–87, NUM rep to Northern Regnl TUC 1985–92, NUM delegate to TUC 1990–91; MP (Lab) Sunderland N 1992–; former memb Exec Ctee Durham City CLP (treas Kelloe Ward 1983–88); *Recreations* fell walking, motorcycling, watching soccer, history, reading; *Style—* Bill Etherington, Esq, MP; ✉ House of Commons, London SW1A 0AA (☎ 0171 219 4603)

ETKIN, Dr Herbert; s of Jack and Helen Etkin, of South Africa; *Educ* Athlone HS, Univ of Witwatersrand SA (MB BCh, DPM); *m* 5 Jan 1965 (m dis 1981), Janet Rosemary; 3 da (Kerrith Anne b 1966, Laura Jane b 1969, Beverley Nan b 1970); *Career* conslt psychiatrist SE Thames and SW Thames RHAs 1974–95, clinical dir Young Person's Unit Ticehurst House Hosp E Sussex 1990–, med dir Ticehurst House Hosps 1995–; sch cnsllr Eton Coll 1993–; Freeman City of London 1987, Liveryman Worshipful Soc of Apothecaries; FRCPsych 1987; *Recreations* golf, squash, music; *Clubs* Lewes Golf, Southdown (Lewes); *Style—* Dr Herbert Etkin; ✉ 2 De Warrenne Rd, Lewes, E Sussex BN7 1BP (☎ 01273 471118); Ticehurst House Hospital, Ticehurst, nr Wadhurst, East Sussex TN5 7HU (☎ 01580 200391, fax 01580 201006)

EUGSTER, Christopher Anthony Alwyn Patrick; s of Gen Sir Basil Eugster, KCB, KCVO, CBE, DSO, MC and Bar, DL (d 1984), and Marcia Elaine Smyth-Osbourne (d 1983); *b* 17 March 1941; *Educ* Downside; *m* 12 Nov 1965, Carole Jane, da of Sqdn Ldr John Bouwens (ka 1941); 2 s (John b 1967, Rupert b 1969); *Career* former dir: Kleinwort Benson Ltd 1976, The Boddington Group plc; currently non-exec dir: Cardew & Co Ltd, Blick plc, Dares Estates plc, The Laurentian Financial Group plc, Mid-States PLC; former chm Sycamore Taverns Ltd; *Recreations* shooting, fishing; *Clubs* White's; *Style—* Christopher Eugster, Esq; ✉ Cardew & Co, 12 Suffolk Street, London SW1Y 4HQ (☎ 0171 930 0777); The Old Rectory, Little Bromley, Manningtree, Essex CO11 2TX

EUROPE, Suffragan Bishop in 1995–; Rt Rev Henry William Scriven; s of William Hamilton Scriven (d 1985), and Jeanne Mary, *née* Edwards, of Farnham, Surrey; *Educ* Repton Sch, Univ of Sheffield (BA Biblical Studies), St John's Coll Nottingham (Dip in Pastoral Studies); *m* 2 Aug 1975, Catherine Rose, da of Hoyt Nicholas Ware; 1 da (Anna Charis b 1 Nov 1979), 1 s (Joel Nicholas Hamilton b 3 Sept 1983); *Career* asst curate Holy Trinity Church Wealdstone Harrow 1975–79, missionary with S American Missionary Soc Salta Argentina 1980–82, asst rector Christ Episcopal Church Little Rock Arkansas USA 1982–83; missionary with S American Missionary Soc Spanish Episcopal Reformed Chruch: Salamanca Spain 1984–88, Madrid Spain 1988–90; chaplain Br Embassy Church of St George Madrid Spain (Dio in Europe) 1990–95; *Recreations* reading, tennis, music, walking; *Style—* The Rt Rev the Suffragan Bishop in Europe; ✉ 23 Carlton Road, Redhill, Surrey RH1 2BY (☎ and fax 01737 766617); Diocese in Europe, 14 Tufton Street, London SW1P 3QZ (☎ 0171 976 8001, fax 0171 976 8002, mobile 0468 662306, e-mail 100642.731@compuserve.com)

EUSTACE, Dudley Graham; s of Albert Eustace, MBE (d 1992), of Bristol, and Mary, *née* Manning; *b* 3 July 1936; *Educ* The Cathedral Sch Bristol, Univ of Bristol (BA Econs); *m* 30 May 1964, Diane, da of Karl Zakrajsek (d 1974), of Nova Racek, Yugoslavia; 2 da (Gabriella b 1965, Chantal b 1967); *Career* actg PO RAFVR 1955–58; CA 1962; appts Alcan Aluminium Ltd of Canada in: Canada, Argentina, Brazil, Spain, UK (treas Canada, dir of fin UK) 1964–87; dir of fin British Aerospace plc 1987–92, dir of fin and exec vice pres Philips Electronics NV Netherlands 1992–; memb: Advsy Bd Bayerische Landesbank, 100 Group of Fin Dirs, Bd Assoc for the Monetary Union of Europe; Freeman: City of London, Worshipful Co of Chartered Accountants; FCA; *Recreations* philately, gardening, reading; *Style—* Dudley G Eustace, Esq; ✉ Residence De Karpen 137, Javalaan, 5631 DB Eindhoven, Netherlands; Philips Electronics NV, Groenewoudseweg 1, 5621 BA Eindhoven, Netherlands; 28 Salisbury House, Bessborough Gardens, Pimlico, London

EUSTON, Earl of; James Oliver Charles FitzRoy; s and h of 11 Duke of Grafton, KG, *qv*; *b* 13 Dec 1947; *Educ* Eton, Magdalene Coll Cambridge (MA); *m* 1972, Lady Clare Amabel Margaret Kerr (appeal pres Elizabeth FitzRoy Homes), da of 12 Marquess of Lothian; 1 s (Henry Oliver Charles, Viscount Ipswich, b 1978), 4 da (Lady Louise Helen Mary b 1973, Lady Emily Clare b 1974, Lady Charlotte Rose b 1983, Lady Isobel Anne b 1985); *Heir* s, Viscount Ipswich; *Career* page of honour to HM The Queen 1962–63; asst dir J Henry Schroder Wagg & Co 1973–82; exec dir Enskilda Securities 1982–87; dir: Jamestown Investments Ltd 1987–91, Central Capital Holdings 1988–91, Capel-Cure Myers Capital Management 1988–; FCA; *Clubs* Turf (chm); *Style—* Earl of Euston; ✉ 6 Vicarage Gardens, London W8 4AH

EVANS, *see also:* Tudor Evans

EVANS, (Laurence) Adrian Waring; s of Laurence Ansdell Evans, and Barbara Alice Waring Blount, *née* Gibb; *b* 29 June 1941; *Educ* Stowe, Trinity Coll Cambridge (BA); *m* 1, 18 Aug 1962 (m dis 1981), Caroline Velleman, da of Antony Ireland Baron von Simunich; 1 s (Dominic b 11 Sept 1968, d 1989), 2 da (Kate b 26 Oct 1965, Laura b 23 July 1971); m 2, 25 Nov 1983, Ingela Brita Byng, da of Axel Berglund, of Stockholm; *Career* vice pres Citibank NA NY 1963–71, dir First National Finance Corp Ltd 1971–76, md Grindlays Bank plc 1976–85, gp md Benchmark Group plc 1986–90, dir TSB Commercial plc 1986–90, md Lazard Brothers & Co Ltd 1991–; chm Cncl of Mgmnt GAP Activity Projects, govr Stowe Sch; *Clubs* Brooks's, Tennis d'Orcier; *Style—* Adrian Evans, Esq; ✉ Lazard Brothers & Co Ltd, 21 Moorfields, London EC2P 2HT (☎ 0171 588 2721)

EVANS, Alan William; s of Harold Evans (d 1980), of London, and Dorothy, *née* Surry; *b* 21 Feb 1938; *Educ* Charterhouse, UCL (BA, PhD), Univ of Michigan; *m* 10 Aug 1964, Jill Alexandra, da of George Otto Brightwell (d 1961), of Vienna; 2 s (Christopher b 1969, Stephen b 1971); *Career* lectr Univ of Glasgow 1967–71, res offr Centre for Environmental Studies 1971–76, lectr LSE 1976–77; Univ of Reading: reader 1977–81, prof 1981–, pro-vice-chllr 1990–94, dep vice-chllr 1994–96; FCA 1961; *Books* The Economics of Residential Location (1973), Urban Economics (1985), No Room! No Room! (1988); *Recreations* theatre, cinema, reading, travel; *Style—* Alan Evans, Esq; ✉ Lianda, Hill Close, Harrow on the Hill, Middlesex HA1 3PQ (☎ 0181 423 0767); Department of Economics, Faculty of Urban and Regional Studies, University of Reading,

Whiteknights, Reading, Berks RG6 2AW (☎ 0118 931 8208, fax 0118 931 6533, telex 847813)

EVANS, Amanda Louise Elliot (Mrs Andrew Duncan); da of Brian Royston Elliot Evans, of Sevenoaks, Kent, and June Anabella, *née* Gilderdale; *b* 19 May 1958; *Educ* Tonbridge Girls' GS Kent; *m* 2 Sept 1989, Andrew Sinclair Duncan, s of Francis Duncan, of London; 1 s (Thomas Alexander Elliot b 24 Nov 1992), 1 da (Isobel Florence b 20 Oct 1990); *Career* features ed and writer The World of Interiors Magazine 1981–83, dep ed and conslt Mitchell Beazley Publishers 1983–84, ed Homes and Gardens Magazine 1986–96 (dep ed 1985–86); *Recreations* mountain climbing, vineyards, skiing; *Style—* Ms Amanda Evans; ✉ c/o IPC Magazines, King's Reach Tower, Stamford St, London SE1 9LS (☎ 0171 261 5678, fax 0171 261 6247)

EVANS, Anne Elizabeth Jane; da of David Evans (d 1965), of London, and Eleanor, *née* Lewis (d 1988); *b* 20 Aug 1941; *Educ* RCM, Conservatoire de Genève (Thomas Beecham operatic scholarship, Boise Fndn award); *m* 1, 1962 (m dis 1981), John Heulyn Jones; m 2, 1981, John Philip Lucas; *Career* soprano; Geneva debut as Annina in La Traviata 1967, UK debut as Mimi in La Bohème 1968; subseq roles incl: Brünnhilde in Der Ring (Bayreuth Festival 1989–92, Vienna Staatsoper, Deutsche Oper Berlin, Covent Garden, etc), Isolde in Tristan und Isolde (WNO, Brussels, Berlin, Dresden), Elisabeth in Tannhäuser (Metropolitan Opera NYC, Berlin), Elsa in Lohengrin (San Francisco, Buenos Aires), Leonore in Fidelio (Metropolitan Opera NYC), Chrysothemis in Elektra (Rome, Marseilles, Geneva); also numerous roles with English National Opera and Welsh National Opera incl: Marschallin in Der Rosenkavalier, Ariadne in Ariadne auf Naxos, Kundry in Parsifal, Donna Anna in Don Giovanni, Empress and Dyer's Wife in Die Frau ohne Schatten; Edinburgh Festival recital 1993; recordings: Brünnhilde in Der Ring 1991–92 (also video), Immolation Scene 1987; *Recreations* cooking, antiques; *Style—* Miss Anne Evans; ✉ c/o Ingpen and Williams, 14 Kensington Court, London W8 5DN

EVANS, Sir Anthony Adney; 2 Bt (UK 1920), of Wightwick, near Wolverhampton, Co Stafford; s of Sir Walter Harry Evans, 1 Bt (d 1954), and Margaret Mary, *née* Dickens (d 1969); *b* 5 Aug 1922; *Educ* Shrewsbury, Merton Coll Oxford; *m* 1, 1 May 1948 (m dis 1957), Rita Beatrice, da of late Alfred David Kettle, of Souldern, Oxon, and formerly w of Larry Rupert Kirsch; 2 s, 1 da; m 2, 1958, Sylvia Jean; *Heir* s; *Style—* Sir Anthony Evans, Bt

EVANS, Anthony David; s of William Price Evans, of Swansea, and Joan Furze, *née* Pitchford; *b* 14 Dec 1946; *Educ* Grove Park Sch Wrexham, Univ Coll Wales Aberystwyth (LLB); *m* 10 Jan 1987, Diane Janet, da of Bernard Pauls, of Leamington, Ontario, Canada; 2 da (Hannah b 30 May 1992, Amy b 15 Nov 1993); *Career* admitted slr 1971, ptnr Macfarlanes Slrs 1982–; *Clubs* Reform, Little Ship; *Style—* Anthony Evans, Esq; ✉ Macfarlanes, 10 Norwich St, London EC4A 1BD (☎ 0171 831 9222, fax 0171 831 9607, telex 296381 MACFAR G)

EVANS, Prof Anthony John; s of William John Evans (d 1965), and Marion Audrey, *née* Young (d 1988); *b* 1 April 1930; *Educ* Queen Elizabeth's Hosp Bristol, Sch of Pharmacy Univ of London (BPharm, PhD), UCL (PG Dip in Librarianship); *m* 21 Aug 1954, Anne, da of John Horwell (d 1960), of Grimsby; 2 da (Jane b 1957, Susan b 1960); *Career* lectr in pharmaceutical engrg sci Sch of Pharmacy Univ of London 1954–57, librarian Sch of Pharmacy Univ of London 1958–63; Loughborough Univ: librarian 1964–91, prof Dept of Info and Library Studies 1973–95 (emeritus prof 1996–), dean School of Educnl Studies 1973–76, dir Univ Alumni Office 1992–95; pres Cwlth Library Assoc 1994–; memb Exec Bd Int Fedn Library Assocs and Insts (IFLA) 1983–89 (treas 1985–89), hon life memb Int Assoc of Technol Univ Libraries (treas 1968–70, pres 1970–75), vice pres Assoc for Info Mgmnt (ASLIB) 1985–87; conslt: Br Cncl, ODA, UNESCO, UNIDO, World Bank in some 17 countries particularly Mexico, Kenya and China; FLA 1969 (Hon FLA 1990); IFLA medal 1989; *Recreations* canal cruising, model railways, 4 grandchildren; *Clubs* Cwlth Tst; *Style—* Professor Anthony Evans; ✉ 78 Valley Rd, Loughborough, Leicestershire LE11 3QA (☎ 01509 215670, e-mail a.j.evans@lboro.ac.uk)

EVANS, Prof Barry George; s of William Arthur Evans (d 1984), of Dartford, Kent, and Jean Ida, *née* Lipscombe; *b* 15 Oct 1944; *Educ* Univ of Leeds (BSc, PhD); *m* 1 (m dis 1983), Carol Ann, *née* Gillis; 1 s (Robert Iain Lawrie b 1971), 1 da (Lisa Jane b 1969); m 2, 10 March 1984, Rhian Elizabeth Marilyn, da of Russell Lewis Jones (d 1974), of Camarthen; 1 s (Rhys David Russell b 1984), 1 da (Cerian Elizabeth Lucy b 1985); *Career* lectr, sr lectr and reader in telecommunications Univ of Essex 1968–83, Satellite Systems Conslts C&W Ltd 1976–80, Alec Harley Reeves prof of info systems engrg Univ of Surrey 1983–, dir: Centre for Satellite Engineering 1990–, Satconsult, Speka Ltd; ed International Jl of Satellite Communications; author of over 150 papers on telecommunications and satellite systems published; vice chm URSI Cmmn C; memb: UK Foresight ITEC Panel, UK CCIR Ctees 5 and 8, DTI and EPSRC Link Mgmnt Ctee; CEng, FIEE, FEng 1991, FRSA; *Books* Telecommunications Systems Design (1974), Satellite Systems Design (1988, 2 edn 1991); *Recreations* travel, wine, sport; *Style—* Prof Barry Evans, FEng; ✉ Centre for Satellite Engineering Research, University of Surrey, Guildford GU2 5XH (☎ 01483 259131, fax 01483 259504, telex 859331)

EVANS, Hon Benedict Blackstone; o s of Thomas Charles Evans (d 1985), and Baroness Blackstone, *qv*; *b* 6 Sept 1963; *Educ* William Ellis Sch for Boys, Manchester Poly (BA), Royal Coll of Art (MA); *m* Suzanne, *née* Godson; 3 da; *Career* researcher to Mark Fisher, MP, as Shadow Min for Arts and Media 1989–92, lectr St Martin's Coll of Art and Design 1989–93, lectr Royal Coll of Art 1995–; advsr: to Chm and Chief Exec of English Heritage 1994–96, to Design Cncl 1994–95, to Sir David Puttnam 1995–; *Recreations* skiing, architecture and design; *Style—* The Hon Benedict Evans; ✉ 17 Princelet Street, Spitalfields, London E1 6QH (☎ 0171 247 1196, fax 0171 377 1197)

EVANS, Dr Christopher Charles; s of Robert Percy (d 1974), and Nora Carson, *née* Crowther (d 1992); *b* 2 Oct 1941; *Educ* Wade Deacon GS Widnes Cheshire, Univ of Liverpool (MB ChB, MD); *m* 5 Feb 1966, Dr Susan Evans, da of Dr Heinz Fuld, of Llanarmon Yn Ial, Mold, Clwyd; 1 s (Matthew b 1973), 2 da (Joanne b 1971, Sophie b 1975); *Career* sr lectr in med and hon conslt physician Univ of Liverpool 1974–78, conslt physician in gen and thoracic med Royal Liverpool Univ Hosp and Cardio-Thoracic Centre Liverpool 1978–, clinical sub-dean Royal Liverpool Hosp 1978–88; chief MO Swiss Pioneer, conslt MO Royal Life plc 1978, dir and memb Cncl Med Def Union; pres Liverpool Med Inst 1991–92; memb: Assoc of Physicians, Br Thoracic Soc; examiner and censor RCP London; FRCP 1979 (MRCP 1968); *Books* Chamberlain's Symptoms and Signs in Clinical Medicine (with C M Ogilvie, 1987); *Recreations* skiing, tennis, fell walking, watching theatre and Liverpool FC; *Clubs* XX Club; *Style—* Dr Christopher Evans; ✉ Lagom, Glendyke Rd, Liverpool L18 6JR (☎ 0151 724 5386); Royal Liverpool University Hosp, Prescot St, Liverpool L7 8XP (☎ 0151 706 3550); Cardio-Thoracic Centre, Liverpool L14 3PE (☎ 0151 228 1616)

EVANS, Clifford John; s of Wallace Evans (d 1971), and Elsie Evans (d 1975); *b* 9 Oct 1928; *Educ* Cardiff HS, Gonville and Caius Coll Cambridge (scholar, MA); *m* 4 April 1953, Sheila Margaret (Molly), da of James Walker, of Abergavenny, South Wales; 2 s (Christopher b 23 May 1957, Robert b 16 Sept 1959); *Career* chief engr Caribbean Construction Co Ltd Jamaica 1954–61, ptnr Wallace Evans and Partners (consltg engrs) and ptnr of assoc partnerships in Hong Kong and the Caribbean 1962–90 (sr ptnr 1971–90), chm Wallace Evans Ltd 1990–92 (life pres 1992–); chm Engrg Centre for Wales; pres IStructE 1982–83; memb: Cncl ACE 1980–82, Standing Ctee for Structural Safety 1983–89, Cncl ICE 1984–87 and 1989–92, Cncl CIArb 1987–93, Panel of Arbitrators ICE, CIArb and FIDIC, Advsy Ctee CADW (Historic Monuments Bd of Wales), Ct Univ of Wales Coll of Cardiff, Industl Advsy Bd Univ of Wales; convenor President's Ctee for Urban Environment 1987–90; attachè Welsh Team Cwlth Games Jamaica 1966; memb Penarth RNLI Ctee 1986–; pres Cardiff C of C and Indust 1993–94; Freeman City of London; Liveryman Worshipful Co of Engineers, Master Worshipful Co of Arbitrators 1995–96; FEng, FICE, FIStructE, FCIArb, FIHT, FIWEM, FHKIE, FASCE, MConsE; *Recreations* sailing, offshore yacht racing, skiing, swimming; *Clubs* Royal Thames Yacht, Royal Ocean Racing, Royal Jamaica Yacht, Hawks, Cardiff and County, Livery; *Style—* Clifford Evans, Esq, FEng; ✉ 6 Glynnetower, Bridgeman Road, Penarth, South Glamorgan CF64 3AW; Wallace Evans Ltd, Plymouth House, Penarth, South Glamorgan CF64 3BE (☎ 01222 705577, fax 01222 703889)

EVANS, Air Vice-Marshal Clive Ernest; CBE (1982); s of Leslie Roberts Evans (d 1987), and Mary Kathleen, *née* Butcher (d 1978); *b* 21 April 1937; *Educ* St Dunstan's Coll Catford; *m* 15 June 1963, Therese, da of Gp Capt Douglas Cecil Goodrich, CBE; 1 s (Guy b 1966), 1 da (Madeleine b 1970); *Career* RAF trg 1955–56, pilot, flying instr 1960; served on: Vampires, Hunters, Jet Provosts, Canberras, Lightnings, F111s; RAF Staff Coll 1972, PSO to Controller Aircraft 1973, OC 24 Sqdn (Hercules) 1974–76, NDC 1976–77, DS RAF Staff Coll 1977–79, head RAF Presentation Team 1979–81, OC RAF Lyneham 1981–83, RCDS 1984, COS and Dep Cdr Br Forces Falkland Is 1985, Dep Air Sec 1985–88, SDS (Air) at RCDS 1988–92; churchwarden St Mary's Sanderstead; hon pres Surrey Wing ATC, chm RO Selection Bds, govr Duke of York's Royal Mil Sch Dover; *Recreations* reading, cricket, golf, sailing, gardening; *Clubs* RAF; *Style—* Air Vice-Marshal Clive Evans, CBE; ✉ 43 Purley Bury Close, Purley, Surrey CR8 1HW

EVANS, David; CBE (1992); s of William Price Evans, and late Ella Mary Evans; *b* 7 Dec 1935; *Educ* Welwyn Garden City GS, UCL (BScEcon); *m* 1960, Susan Carter, da of late Dr John Connal; 1 s, 1 da; *Career* MAFF: joined 1959, private sec to Parly Sec (Lords) 1962–64, princ 1964, princ private sec to Mins 1970–71, asst sec 1971, seconded to Cabinet Office 1972–74, under sec 1976–80; Nat Farmers' Union: chief econ and policy advsr 1981–84, dep dir-gen 1984–85, dir-gen 1985–96; dir-gen Federation of Agricultural Co-operatives 1996–; *Style—* David Evans, Esq, CBE; ✉ Director General, Federation of Agricultural Co-operatives, 164 Shaftesbury Avenue, London WC2H 8HL (☎ 0171 331 7200, fax 0171 235 3526)

EVANS, David; *see:* Edge (The)

EVANS, Dr (William) David; s of William Harold Evans (d 1985), and Gladys Elizabeth Evans (d 1984); *b* 20 April 1949; *Educ* Haberdashers' Askes' Sch, St Catherine's Coll Oxford (BA, DPhil); *m* 1980, Elizabeth, *née* Crowe; 3 s (James William b 1982, Matthew David b 1984, Edward Michael b 1989), 1 da (Clare Elizabeth b 1986); *Career* civil servant; Dept of Energy 1974–80, first sec (sci and technol) Br Embassy Bonn 1980–83; Dept of Energy: asst sec 1984–89, chief scientist 1989–92; DTI: head Environment Div 1992–94, head Technol and Innovation Policy Div 1994–96, dir Technol and Standards 1996–; author scientific papers in professional jls; memb: NERC 1989–92, EPSRC 1994–, Particle Physics and Astronomy Research Cncl (PPARC) 1994–, Senate Engrg Cncl 1996–; FRAS 1975; *Recreations* music, reading, history of technology; *Style—* Dr David Evans; ✉ Department of Trade and Industry, 151 Buckingham Palace Road, London SW1W 9SS (☎ 0171 215 1659, fax 0171 215 4191)

EVANS, Prof David Alan Price; s of Owen Evans (d 1978), of Liverpool, and Ellen, *née* Jones (d 1975); *b* 6 March 1927; *Educ* Univ of Liverpool (BSc, MB ChB, MD, PhD, DSc, J Hill Abram prize for med, Sir Robert Kelly Meml medal for surgery, Henry Briggs Meml medal for obstetrics and gynaecology, Owen T Williams prize, N E Roberts prize, Samuels prize); *Career* Nat Serv Capt RAMC 1953–55 (active serv Japan, Singapore, Korea, Malaya); house physician and house surgn Liverpool Royal Infirmary 1951–52, Holt fell Univ of Liverpool 1952–53, sr house offr Broadgreen Hosp Liverpool 1955–56; med registrar: Stanley Hosp Liverpool 1956–58, Northern Hosp Liverpool 1959–60; res fell Johns Hopkins Univ Baltimore 1958–59, conslt physician Royal Hosp Liverpool (formerly Royal Infirmary) and Broadgreen Hosp Liverpool 1965–83, prof Dept of Med Univ of Liverpool 1968–72 (lectr 1960–62, sr lectr 1962–68), chm and prof Dept of Med and dir Nuffield Unit of Med Genetics Univ of Liverpool 1972–83, dir of med Riyadh Al Kharj Hosp Programme Riyadh Saudi Arabia 1983–; visiting prof: Karolinska Univ Stockholm, Helsinki Univ, Berne Univ, Ann Arbor Univ, Johns Hopkins Univ; emeritus prof Univ of Liverpool 1994–; sci ed Saudi Med Jl 1983–93, memb Editorial Advsy Bd Pharmacogenetics 1992–; memb Assoc of Physicians of GB and Ireland 1964, life memb Johns Hopkins Soc of Scholars 1972; FRCP 1968 (MRCP 1956); *Books* Genetic Factors in Drug Therapy (1993); author of numerous articles and chapters in books on pharmacogenetics; *Recreations* country pursuits; *Style—* Prof David A Price Evans; ✉ 28 Montclair Drive, Liverpool L18 0HA (☎ 0151 722 3112); Pen Yr Allt, Paradwys, Llangristiolus, Bodorgan, Anglesey, Gwynedd LL62 5PD (☎ 01407 840 346); C123 Riyadh Armed Forces Hospital, PO Box 7897, Riyadh 11159, Kingdom of Saudi Arabia (☎ 00 966 1 479 1000 ext 5282, fax 00 966 1 478 4057)

EVANS, Prof David Emrys; s of Evan Emrys Evans (d 1985), of Cross Hands, Dyfed, and Gwynneth Mair Eurfron, *née* Owen (d 1969); *b* 14 Oct 1950; *Educ* Ysgol Ramadeg Dyffryn Gwendraeth, Univ of Oxford (BA, MSc, DPhil); *m* 20 Oct 1984, Pornsawan; 2 s (Emrys Wyn b 12 June 1990, Arwyn Dafydd b 15 Mar 1993); *Career* Dublin Inst for Advanced Studies 1975–76, Oslo Univ 1976–77, Royal Soc exchange fell Copenhagen Univ 1978, SERC res fell Univ of Newcastle upon Tyne 1979, reader Univ of Warwick 1986–87 (lectr 1979–86), prof Univ of Wales Swansea 1987–, visiting prof Kyoto Univ Japan 1990–91; Jr Whitehead prize London Mathematical Soc 1989; memb: London Mathematical Soc, American Mathematical Soc; *Books* Dilations of Irreversible Evolutions in Algebraic Quantum Theory (with J T Lewis, 1977); *Style—* Prof David Evans; ✉ Department of Mathematics, University of Wales Swansea, Singleton Park, Swansea SA2 8PP (☎ 01792 295460, fax 01792 295843, e-mail david.e.evans@swansea.ac.uk)

EVANS, Prof (John) David Gemmill; s of John Desmond Evans (d 1977), and Babette Evans (d 1985); *b* 27 Aug 1942; *Educ* St Edward's Sch Oxford, Queens' Coll Cambridge (BA, MA, PHD); *m* 14 Sept 1974, Rosemary, da of Gweirydd Ellis, of Chippenham; *Career* fell Sidney Sussex Coll Cambridge 1964–78, dean of Faculty of Arts Queen's Univ Belfast 1986–89 (prof of logic and metaphysics 1978–); memb Exec Ctee Int Fedn of Philosophical Socs, memb Cncl Royal Inst of Philosophy, chm UK Nat Ctee for Philosophy; MRIA 1983; *Books* Aristotle's Concept of Dialectic (1977), Truth and Proof (1979), Aristotle (1987), Moral Philosophy and Contemporary Problems (1987); *Recreations* mountaineering, astronomy, poker; *Style—* Prof David Evans; ✉ Spinney View, Carryduff, Co Down, Northern Ireland BT8 8JD; Philosophy Department, Queen's University, Belfast BT7 1NN (☎ 01232 245133, fax 01232 247895)

EVANS, David Howard; QC (1991); s of David Hopkin Evans, of Stoneleigh, Warwicks, and Phoebe Dora, *née* Reading; *b* 27 July 1944; *Educ* The Woodlands Sch Coventry, LSE (BSc, MSc), Wadham Coll Oxford (BA); *m* 20 June 1973, Anne Celia, da of John Segall, of W London; 2 s (Oliver Anthony b 1977, Edward Alexander b 1980); *Career* called to the Bar Middle Temple 1972, practising barrister 1972–, recorder of the Crown Court 1992–; *Recreations* tennis, golf, reading, listening to music; *Clubs* Roehampton, Riviera Golf (Cannes); *Style—* David Evans, Esq, QC; ✉ 3rd Floor, Queen Elizabeth Buildings, Temple, London EC4Y 9BS (☎ 0171 583 5766, fax 0171 353 0359)

EVANS, David John; MP (C) Welwyn Hatfield (majority 8,465); *b* 23 April 1935; *Educ* Raglan Rd Sch, Tottenham Tech Coll; *m* Janice Hazel, *née* Masters; 2 s, 1 da; *Career*

MP (C) Welwyn Hatfield 1987–; PPS to Lord Hesketh as min for indust at DTI 1990–91; PPS to John Redwood: as Min for Corp Affrs at DTI 1991–92, as Min for Local Govt and Inner Cities DOE 1992–93, as Sec of State for Wales 1993–; elected to Exec 1922 Ctee 1993; sec Cons Backbench Sports Ctee 1987–90; memb Select Ctee on: Members' Interests 1990, Deregulation 1995–; currently treas Cons Pty; chm: Luton Town Football & Athletic Co Ltd 1984–89 (dir 1976–90), Broadreach Group Ltd 1990–, Bradnam Enterprises Ltd 1990–95; dir: Initial plc 1987–89, Trimoco plc 1987–89; fndr, chm and md Brengreen (Holdings) plc 1960–86; Freeman: City of London, Worshipful Co of Horners; *Style*— David Evans, Esq, MP; ✉ House of Commons, London SW1A 0AA

EVANS, Prof David John; s of Stanley Evans (d 1969), of Llanelli, Wales, and Margaret Ann, *née* King (d 1984); *b* 30 Sept 1928; *Educ* Llanelli GS, Univ Coll Wales Aberystwyth (BSc), Univ of Southampton (MSc), Univ of Manchester (PhD), Univ of Wales (DSc); *m* 6 Aug 1955, Naldera (Derry), da of Michael Owen (d 1983), of Bedford (late of Aberystwyth); 1 s (Neil Wyn b 1961), 2 da (Tracy Susanne b 1962 d 1990, Clare Joanne b 1963); *Career* Nat Serv RAF 1950–52; sr mathematician Rolls Royce Ltd Derby 1955–58, res fell Univ of Manchester 1958–64, dir Computing Laboratory Univ of Sheffield 1964–71; Loughborough Univ of Technol: prof of computing 1971–96 (emeritus prof 1996–), dir Parallel Algorithms Res Centre 1988–96; prof of computing Nottingham Trent Univ 1996–; FBCS, FIMA; *Books* Preconditioning Methods Theory and Applications (1983), Parallel Processing Systems (1983), Sparsity and its Applications (1985), Systolic Algorithms (1991); *Recreations* music; *Style*— Prof David Evans; ✉ Novel Architectures Research Group, Department of Computing, Nottingham Trent University, Burton Street, Nottingham, Notts NG1 4BU (☎ 0115 941 8418 ext 2255)

EVANS, David Julian; s of David Thomas Evans, of Chauncy Court, Hertford, and Brenda Muriel, *née* Bennett; *b* 12 May 1942; *Educ* Fosters Sch Sherborne, Queen Mary Coll Univ of London (BA); *m* 9 Sept 1967, Lorna Madeleine, da of Harry Jacques; 3 s (David Griffith b 29 July 1970, Gareth Owain b 29 Oct 1971, Rhodri James Meredith b 20 July 1976); *Career* VSO teacher Sainik Sch Chittorgarh India 1963–64, mgmnt trainee J Sainsbury Ltd 1964–65; British Council: seconded to VSO 1965–67, asst rep Sierra Leone 1967–70, dep rep Wales 1970–72, trg in educn and devpt Univ Coll Cardiff 1972–73, asst dir (Educn) Enugu Nigeria 1973–76, dir Istanbul 1976–80, dep dir Germany 1981–85, dir Exchanges Dept 1985, fndr dir Youth Exchange Centre 1985–88, dir Drama and Dance Dept 1988–89, dep dir Arts Div 1989–94, dir/cultural attaché USA 1994–; *Recreations* arts, especially theatre and cinema, museums, travel; *Style*— David Evans, Esq; ✉ Cultural Department/British Council, British Embassy, 3100 Massachusetts Avenue NW, Washington DC 20008–3600, USA (☎ 00 1 202 588 7843, fax 00 1 202 588 7918)

EVANS, David Lawrence; s of Arthur Henry Evans, OBE, FRCS (d 1950), of London, and Dorothy, *née* Briant (d 1983); *b* 21 Sept 1919; *Educ* Rugby, Gonville and Caius Coll Cambridge, Westminster Hosp Med Sch; *m* 14 Jan 1950, Betty Joan, da of Dr Hugh Moreland McCrea, OBE (d 1942), of London; 1 s (Timothy b 1955), 3 da (Joanna b 1950, Philippa b 1952, Gillian b 1957); *Career* Surgn Lt RNVR 1943–47; conslt orthopaedic surgn: Southend Gen Hosp 1957–59, Westminster Hosp 1959–85, St Stephen's Hosp Chelsea 1960–72, Queen Mary's Hosp Roehampton 1961–85; memb Sch Cncl Westminster Hosp Med Sch 1972–76 (chm Med Ctee 1972–75, memb Bd of Govrs 1972–74); chm Br Editorial Bd and Cncl of Mgmnt Journal of Bone and Joint Surgery 1975–92; pres Br Orthopaedic Assoc 1980 (travelling fell USA and Canada 1956, memb Exec Ctee 1964–69, hon sec 1966–67), hon fell Section of Orthopaedics RSM London 1987 (pres 1979); FRCS (memb Cncl 1983, vice pres 1989–91), FRCOG, Hon FDS RCS 1993, Hon DGDP (UK) RCS 1993; *Recreations* golf, fishing, bridge; *Clubs* Royal Wimbledon Golf (Captain 1981); *Style*— David Evans, Esq; ✉ Lane End, 12 The Drive, Wimbledon, London SW20 8TG (☎ 0181 946 4016)

EVANS, His Hon Judge David Marshall; QC (1981); s of Robert Trevor Evans (d 1991), and Bessie Estelle, *née* Thompson (d 1995); *b* 21 July 1937; *Educ* Liverpool Coll, Trinity Hall Cambridge (MA, LLM), Univ of Chicago (JD); *m* 1961, (Alice) Joyce, da of Ernest Rogers (d 1961); 2 s (Richard b 1967, James b 1969); *Career* teaching fell Stanford Univ Palo Alto California 1961–62, asst prof Univ of Chicago Illinois 1962–63, lectr UC of Wales Aberystwyth 1963–65; called to the Bar Gray's Inn 1964, in practice Northern circuit, recorder of Crown Ct 1984–87, circuit judge (Northern Circuit) 1987–; memb visiting ctee Univ of Chicago Illinois 1995–; *Recreations* walking, photography, visual arts, motorsport; *Clubs* Athenaeum (Liverpool), Artists (Liverpool); *Style*— His Hon Judge Marshall Evans, QC; ✉ Queen Elizabeth II Law Courts, Derby Square, Liverpool L2 1XA (☎ 0151 473 7373)

EVANS, David Mervyn; s of (Edward) Mervyn Evans, of Swansea, and Muriel Hawley, *née* Amison; *b* 18 Sept 1942; *Educ* Clifton, Middx Hosp Med Sch (MB BS); *m* 19 June 1971, Dr Elizabeth Cecily Evans, da of Frederick Hornung (d 1973); 1 s (Daniel b 1975), 1 da (Kate b 1976); *Career* conslt hand surgn: Royal Nat Orthopaedic Hosp London, St Thomas' Hosp, Queen Mary's Univ Hosp Roehampton; hon sec Br Soc for Surgery of the Hand 1986–88 (pres 1995), chm Med Commission on Accident Prevention 1991–94, ed Jl of Hand Surgery (Br vol) 1992–95; FRCS 1969; *Recreations* music, windsurfing; *Style*— David Evans, Esq; ✉ The Hand Clinic, Oakley Green, Windsor SL4 4LH (☎ 01753 831333, fax 01753 832109)

EVANS, David Morgan (Dai); s of David Morgan Evans (d 1966), and Elizabeth Margaret, *née* Massey (d 1993); *b* 1 March 1944; *Educ* King's Sch Chester, UCW (BA); *m* 1973, Sheena Gilfillan, da of James Wesley Milne; 3 da (Alexandra Elizabeth b 1976, Katherine Siân Morgan b 1978, Sarah Jane Massey b 1980); *Career* inspr Ancient Monuments (England) DOE and English Heritage 1977–92 (Wales 1969–77), general sec Soc of Antiquaries 1992–; MIFA; *Recreations* gardening, walking, opera, Montgomeryshire; *Style*— Dai Evans, Esq; ✉ Society of Antiquaries of London, Burlington House, Piccadilly, London W1V 0HS (☎ 0171 734 0193, fax 0171 287 6967)

EVANS, David Pugh; s of John David Charles Evans (d 1972), and Katherine Pugh (d 1947); *b* 20 Nov 1942; *Educ* Newbridge GS, Newport Coll of Art, Royal Coll of Art (RCA Silver Medal for Painting); *m* 1971 (m dis 1977), Patricia Ann, da of Kenneth Keay; *Career* artist; lectr Edinburgh Coll of Art 1965–68 and 1969–; Granada arts fell Univ of York 1968–69; ARCA, RSW 1974, RSA 1985 (ARSA 1974); *Solo Exhibitions* Univ of York 1969, Goosewell Gall 1969, Marjorie Parr Gall 1970, 1972 and 1974, Gilbert Parr Gall 1977 and 1980, Fruitmarket Gall (retrospective) 1982, Mercury Gall 1985, Open Eye Gall 1991; *Group Exhibitions* RA, RSA, Soc of Scottish Artists, Univ of Stirling, Univ of York, Aberdeen Art Gall, Dundee Art Gall, Fine Art Soc, Royal Glasgow Inst, Richard Demarco Gall, The Scottish Gall, Middlesbrough Art Gall, Open Eye Gall, Kirkcaldy Art Gall, Mercury Gall, Galerija Fakulteta Belgrade, Compass Gall, Royal West of England Gall, Bath Festival of Contemporary Arts, Basle Arts Fair; *Work in Collections* RA, City of Edinburgh, Royal Burgh of Arbroath, Hunterian Museum, Glasgow Art Galls and Museums, Carlisle Art Gall, Scottish Arts Cncl, Contemporary Arts Soc, Aberdeen Art Gall, St Catherine's Coll Oxford, Imperial Coll London, Scottish Television, Royal Bank of Scotland, Scottish and Newcastle Breweries; *Awards* Royal Burgh of Arbroath painting prize 1971, May Marshall Brown Award RSW 1978, W G Gillies Award RSW 1983, 1986 and 1989, W J Macaulay Award RSA 1984, Scottish Arts Club Award RSW 1993, Scottish Post Office Bd Award RSA 1994; *Style*— David Evans, Esq, RSA; ✉ 17 Inverleith Gardens, Edinburgh EH3 5PS (☎ 0131 552 2329)

EVANS, Rt Rev David Richard John; s of Maj William Henry Reginald Evans, of Seaford, Sussex, and Beatrix Catherine, *née* Mottram; *b* 5 June 1938; *Educ* Christ's Hospital, Gonville and Caius Coll Cambridge (MA); *m* 25 July 1964, Dorothy Evelyn, da of Rev Martin Parsons, of Weston-Super-Mare, Avon; 1 s (Peter b 16 Sept 1971), 2 da (Hilary b 4 Jan 1966, Caroline b 1 Oct 1967); *Career* 2 Lt Middx Regt 1957–59; ordained St Paul's Cathedral 1965, curate Christ Church Cockfosters 1965–68, asst priest Holy Trinity Lomas De Zamora Buenos Aires 1969–77, gen sec Asociacion Biblica Universitaria Argentina 1971–76, chaplain Good Shepherd Lima Peru 1977–83; bishop of: Peru 1978–88, Bolivia 1982–88; asst bishop of: Bradford 1988–93, Chichester 1993–, Rochester 1994–; gen sec S American Missionary Soc 1993–, memb Nat Cncl of Church Ministry to Jews, int coordinator of the Evangelical Fellowship of the Anglican Communion; coordinator: Latin American Forum Cncl of Churches for Britain and Ireland, S American Network of Partnership for World Mission of C of E; memb Bd of Mission of Gen Synod of C of E; *Books* En Dialogo Con Dios (1976); *Recreations* golf, ornithology, philately; *Style*— The Rt Rev David Evans; ✉ The Rectory, Maresfield, E Sussex (☎ and fax (home) 01825 763817, work 01892 38647)

EVANS, David Robert Howard; s of The Rev Denys Roberts Evans (d 1988), of Oxford, and Beryl Mary, *née* Toye; *b* 27 Feb 1950; *Educ* Magdalen Coll Sch Oxford, Univ of Exeter (LLB), King's Coll and LSE Univ of London (LLM), Brasenose Coll Oxford (DipLaw); *m* 1, 6 Jan 1979 (m dis 1988), Gillian Mary; 1 s (Matthew Charles b 1985); m 2, 7 May 1989, Janet Lea, formerly w of Amos Kollek, of Jerusalem, da of Nat T Kanarek, of New York; 1 da (Cordelia Moses Roberts b 1991); *Career* admitted slr 1976; slr: Freshfields 1975–77, British Railways Bd 1977–79, Linklaters & Paines 1980–82; ptnr: Berwin Leighton 1984–87 (slr 1982–83), D J Freeman & Co 1987–91; sr ptnr David Evans Slrs 1991–; md: Lox, Stock and Bagel Ltd 1992–, Anglo International Education Consultants Ltd 1992–, Janet's Bar 1996–; tstee Statute Law Tst; Freeman City of London 1981, Liveryman Worshipful Co of Slrs 1988; memb Law Soc 1976; *Recreations* playing clarinet, tennis, skiing, horse riding; *Clubs* Reform; *Style*— David Evans, Esq; ✉ David Evans Solicitors, 122 Temple Chambers, Temple Avenue, London EC4Y 0DA (☎ 0171 583 0381, fax 0171 583 0380)

EVANS, David Stanley; s of (Evan) Stanley Evans, CBE (d 1982), and Muriel Gordon, *née* Henderson (d 1983); *b* 12 May 1935; *Educ* Charterhouse, St Thomas' Hosp Univ of London (MB BS, MS); *m* 18 May 1968, Mary Agnes Christina, da of Dr John Tierney (d 1984); 1 s (James b 1973), 3 da (Katherine b 1972, Charlotte b 1980, Sarah b 1983); *Career* house surgn: St Thomas' Hosp 1960, Royal Post Grad Hosp Hammersmith 1962; sr house offr Hosp for Sick Children Great Ormond St 1963, sr surgical registrar St Thomas' Hosp 1970–74 (surgical registrar 1966–69), conslt surgn Royal Shrewsbury Hosp 1974–; Hunterian prof RCS 1971; author various papers on diagnosis of venous thrombosis and laparoscopic surgery; memb Shropshire Div BMA; pres W Midland Surgical Soc 1996–97; memb: RSM, BMA, Assoc of Surgns of GB and Ireland, Vascular Surgical Soc GB and Ireland, Assoc of Endoscopic Surgns of GB and Ireland; *Recreations* golf, shooting; *Style*— David Evans, Esq; ✉ Royal Shrewsbury Hospital, Mytton Oak Rd, Shrewsbury SY3 8XQ (☎ 01743 261190)

EVANS, David Vernon; s of Walter Evans (d 1976), of Osmotherley, N Yorks, and Florence Ethel, *née* Vernon (d 1995); *b* 8 March 1935; *Educ* Durham Sch, St Catharine's Coll Cambridge (MA, LLM); *m* 5 May 1962, Sonia Robinson Evans, JP; 1 s (Andrew b 1963), 2 da (Rachel b 1966, Judith b 1967); *Career* slr Crombie Wilkinson & Robinson York 1959–61; Simpson Curtis Leeds: joined 1961, ptnr 1963, managing ptnr 1982–92, sr ptnr 1992–95; ptnr Pinsent Curtis Leeds 1995–; govr Leeds GS, churchwarden Parish of Leeds City (tstee Leeds Parish Church appeal fund), former pres St Catharine's Soc, former chm Leeds Round Table; memb Law Soc; *Recreations* music, beekeeping; *Clubs* Leeds; *Style*— David Evans, Esq; ✉ Thorner Lodge, Thorner, Leeds LS14 3DE (☎ 0113 289 2517); Pinsent Curtis, 41 Park Square, Leeds LS1 2NS (☎ 0113 244 5000, fax 0113 244 8000, car 0860 227383, telex 55376)

EVANS, Prof (William) Desmond; s of Bryn Gwyn Evans (d 1993), and Evelyn Evans (d 1974); *b* 7 March 1940; *Educ* Ystalyfera GS, Univ of Swansea (BSc), Univ of Oxford (DPhil); *m* 26 Aug 1966, Mari, da of Murray Richards (d 1960); 2 s (Dyfed b 1969, Owain b 1973); *Career* Univ Coll Cardiff: lectr 1964–73, sr lectr 1973–75, reader 1975–77, prof 1977–; London Maths Soc: memb 1964, editorial advsr 1977–86, ed Proceedings 1986–92, memb Cncl 1989–91; *Publications* Spectral Theory and Differential Equations (with D E Edmunds, 1987), over 90 articles on differential equations in academic jls; *Recreations* walking, tennis, music; *Clubs* Icosahedron, Dinas Powys Tennis; *Style*— Prof Desmond Evans; ✉ Sch of Mathematics, Univ of Wales, Cardiff, Senghennydd Rd, Cardiff CF2 4AG (☎ 01222 874206, fax 01222 371921, telex 4998635)

EVANS, Prof (David) Ellis; yr s of David Evans (d 1948), and Sarah Jane, *née* Lewis; *b* 23 Sept 1930; *Educ* Llandeilo GS, UCW Aberystwyth, Univ Coll of Swansea, Jesus Coll Oxford; *m* 1957, Sheila Mary, er da of David Thomas Jeremy, of Swansea, Wales; 2 da; *Career* former lectr, reader and prof of Welsh language and literature Univ Coll Swansea, Jesus prof of Celtic Univ of Oxford and fell of Jesus Coll 1978–96 (prof and fell emeritus 1996–); Univ Coll Swansea: hon fell 1985, hon prof Dept of Welsh 1990–; hon fell UCW Aberystwyth 1992, hon foreign memb American Acad of Arts and Scis 1992; Hon DLitt Wales 1993; FBA 1983; *Recreations* music, walking; *Style*— Prof Ellis Evans, FBA; ✉ Jesus College, Oxford OX1 3DW (☎ 01865 279700/247184, fax 01865 279867)

EVANS, (William) Emrys; CBE (1981); s of Richard Evans (d 1965), of Bwlch-y-Pentre, Foel, Llangadfan, Welshpool, Powys, and Mary Elizabeth Evans (d 1956); *b* 4 April 1924; *Educ* Llanfair Caereinion Co Sch; *m* 26 May 1946, Mair, da of Evan Thomas (d 1953); 1 da (Ceridwen Eleri); *Career* WWII RN 1942–46 (despatches 1944); Midland Bank Ltd 1941–84: asst gen mangr 1967–72, regnl dir South Wales 1972–74, regnl dir Wales 1974–76, sr regnl dir Wales 1976–84; dir: Align-Rite Ltd 1984–, Floridan Ltd 1991–95; chm: CBI Wales 1979–81, Cncl Univ Coll of Wales Swansea 1982–, Welsh Ctee for Economic and Industl Affairs 1982–90, Midland Bank Advsy Cncl for Wales 1984–, Wishing Well Appeal in Wales 1987–89, Barnardos Centenary in Wales Appeal 1987–88, Menter a Busnes 1988–, Welsh Sports Aid Fndn 1988–94; vice chm Executive Secondment Ltd 1984–90; pres: Royal Nat Eisteddfod of Wales 1980–83, Welsh Congregational Church 1988–90, Welsh Sports Aid Fndn 1995–; vice pres: Royal Welsh Agric Soc 1972–, Tenovus Cancer Res Unit 1980–, Kidney Res Unit for Wales Fndn 1980–, Barnardos 1989–; dir: Devpt Corpn for Wales 1974–78, Wales Industl Devpt Advsy Bd 1975–86, Devpt Bd for Rural Wales 1976–89 (chm Fin and Mktg Ctee); sec Ebeneser Welsh Congregational Church Cardiff 1990–; treas: Welsh Congregational Church 1975–87, Mansfield Coll Oxford 1977–88; tstee: Catherine and Lady Grace James Fndn 1973–, John and Rhys Thomas James Fndn 1973–, Llandovery Coll 1980–93, Welsh Sports Aid Tst 1980–, Mansfield Coll Oxford 1988–; memb: Ct and Cncl Univ Coll Swansea 1972–, Cncl for the Welsh Language 1972–76, Ct and Cncl Univ of Wales 1973–, Prince of Wales Ctee 1975–87, Dairy Produce Quota Tbnl 1984–92; High Sheriff Co of S Glamorgan 1985–86; Hon LLD Univ of Wales 1983; FCIB; *Recreations* golf, gardening, music; *Clubs* Cardiff and County; *Style*— W Emrys Evans, Esq, CBE; ✉ Maesglas, Pen-y-turnpike, Dinas Powis, Vale of Glamorgan CF64 4HH (☎ 01222 512985)

EVANS, Ena Winifred; da of Frank Evans (d 1986), of Farndon, Cheshire, and Leonora, *née* Lewis (d 1994); *b* 19 June 1938; *Educ* The Queen's Sch Chester, Royal Holloway Coll Univ of London (BSc), Hughes Hall Cambridge (CertEd); *Career* Girls' Div Bolton Sch 1961–65, Bath HS GPDST 1965–72 (head of maths and second mistress 1970–72), dep head Friends' Sch Saffron Walden 1972–77, headmistress King Edward VI HS for Girls

Birmingham 1977–Sept 1996; pres: Girls' Sch Assoc 1987–88, W Midland Branch of Mathematical Assoc 1980–82; memb: Central Birmingham DHA 1988–90, Cncl Univ of Aston, Cncl Queen's Coll Birmingham; govr: Kingswood Sch Bath 1973–94, Bluecoat Sch Birmingham, St James's and The Abbey Sch Malvern, Derby HS, Woodhouse Grove Sch Yorkshire, Bedford HS; Hon DSc Univ of Aston; memb: SHA 1977, GSA 1977, Maths Assoc 1961; FRSA 1986; *Recreations* music; *Clubs* Univ Women's; *Style*— Miss Ena Evans; ✉ 26 Weoley Hill, Selly Oak, Birmingham B29 4AD (☎ 0121 472 0802)

EVANS, His Hon Judge Fabyan Peter Leaf; s of late Peter Fabyan Evans, and Catherine Elise Evans (d 1995); *b* 10 May 1943; *Educ* Clifton; *m* 12 Sept 1967, Karen Myrtle, da of Lionel Joachim Balfour; 2 s (Nigel Henley Fabyan b 26 April 1971, Alexander Peter Sommerville b 21 Feb 1976), 1 da (Jessica Ann b 30 May 1973); *Career* called to the Bar Inner Temple 1969, recorder of the Crown Court 1985–88, circuit judge (SE Circuit) 1988–; *Recreations* sailing, singing; *Clubs* Brooks's; *Style*— His Hon Judge Fabyan Evans; ✉ Middlesex Guildhall, Broad Sanctuary, London SW1P 3BB

EVANS, Frederick Anthony; CVO (1973); s of Herbert Anthony Evans, and Pauline, *née* Allen; *b* 17 Nov 1907; *Educ* Charterhouse, Corpus Christi Coll Cambridge (MA); *m* 1934, Nancy, da of H Meakin; 2 s (Peter, Richard), 1 da (Suzanne); *Career* HM Colonial Serv 1935–57: colonial sec and actg govr Bahamas 1947–51, perm sec Ghana 1951–57; gen sec Duke of Edinburgh's Award 1959–72; *Books* (nom de plume Deric) The State Apartments at Buckingham Palace - a Souvenir (1985), At St James's Palace (1991); *Style*— Frederick Evans, Esq, CVO; ✉ Bellsfield, Odiham, Hants

EVANS, Gareth Robert William; QC (1994); s of David Morris John Evans, of Pontllanfraith, Gwent, and Megan, *née* Hughes (d 1964); *b* 19 Jan 1947; *Educ* Caerfilli GS, Univ of London (external LLB); *m* 1971, Marion, *née* Green; 1 da (Judith Ann b 1 Nov 1978), 1 s (David Glyn b 18 April 1982); *Career* called to the Bar Gray's Inn 1973, recorder of the Crown Court 1993–; *Recreations* watching rugby, reading poetry, cooking, travelling and outdoor pursuits; *Style*— Gareth Evans, Esq, QC; ✉ 5 Fountain Court, Steelhouse Lane, Birmingham B4 6FR (☎ 0121 606 0500, fax 0121 606 1501)

EVANS, Garry Owen; s of Derek Alwyn Evans (d 1984), and Pamela, *née* Sladden; *b* 13 Feb 1961; *Educ* King's Sch Canterbury, Corpus Christi Coll Cambridge (MA), Kyoto Univ; *m* 15 Dec 1985, Michiko, da of Hisami Matsuda, of Miyazaki, Japan; 2 da (Anna Sian b 1 March 1991, Maya Emily b 16 April 1994); *Career* Euromoney Publications plc: joined 1986, ed Euromoney (Japanese edn) 1987–90, ed Euromoney 1990–; *Books* Memories of Silk and Straw (trans, by Junichi Saga, 1987); *Recreations* classical music, flying; *Style*— Garry Evans, Esq; ✉ 61 Swyncombe Avenue, London W5 4DR (☎ 0181 560 6470); Euromoney Publications plc, Nestor House, Playhouse Yard, London EC4V 5EX (☎ 0171 779 8888, fax 0171 779 8407)

EVANS, Garth; *Educ* Slade Sch of Art, UCL (Dip Fine Art), Manchester Regnl Coll of Art, Manchester Jr Coll of Art; *Career* artist and sculptor; visiting lectr: Central Sch of Art London 1960–65, Camberwell Sch of Art London 1960–69, St Martin's Sch of Art London 1965–79, Chelsea Sch of Art London 1978–79, Yale Sch of Art Yale Univ 1983, 1985 and 1986; visiting prof Minneapolis Coll of Art and Design 1973; visiting tutor Slade Sch of Fine Art UCL 1970–81, Goldsmiths' Coll London 1978–81; visiting artist: Sculpture Dept RCA London 1970–81, Mount Holyoke Coll S Hadley Mass 1979–81, Manchester Poly 1978–83, NY Studio Sch 1988–; assoc lectr in sculpture Camberwell Sch of Art London 1971–83, lectr Faculty of Sculpture Br Sch at Rome 1978–83; memb: Fine Art Advsy Panel S Glamorgan Inst of Higher Educn 1977–79, Fine Arts Award Policy Ctee Arts Cncl of GB 1977–79, Fine Art Bd Photography Bd CNAA 1976–79, Ctee for Art and Design CNAA 1976–79; *Solo exhibitions* Rowan Gallery London 1962, 1964, 1966, 1968, 1969, 1972, 1974, 1976, 1978 and 1980, Sch of Art and Design Gallery Sheffield 1971, Ferens Art Gallery Hull 1971, Faculty of Art and Design Gallery Leeds Poly 1971, Oriel Gallery of the Welsh Arts Cncl Cardiff 1976, Mount Holyoke Coll Art Museum S Hadley Mass 1980, Robert Elkon Gallery NY 1983, Tibor de Nagy Gallery NY 1984, HF Manes Gallery NY 1984, John Davis Gallery Akron Ohio 1986, Garth Evans Sculptures and Drawings 1979–87 (Yale Center for Br Art New Haven Conneticut) 1988, Charles Cowles Gallery NY 1988, Compass Rose Gallery Chicago 1989, Hill Gallery Birmingham Michigan 1990, Mayor Gallery London 1991, Wrexham Museum and Art Centre Wales 1991, Sheffield Poly Art Gallery 1991, Echoes: Sculpture from 1970 and Recent Works (Paul Mellon Gallery Choate Rosemary Hall Sch Wallingford Connecticut) 1993, Sulptural Metamorphosis (Freedman Gallery Reading Pennsylvania), Watercolours (Dana Arts Centre Colgate Univ USA) 1995, Phoenix Sculptures (Opera House Gallery Earlville USA) 1995, Sculptures and Works on Paper (Kora Gallery Drew Univ USA) 1996; *Group Exhibitions* incl: John Moores Exhibition (Liverpool) 1960, Reliefs Collages and Drawings (V & A) 1967, Drawings (Museum of Modern Art NYC) 1969, British Sculpture '72 (Royal Acad) 1972, The Condition of Sculpture (Hayward Gallery) 1975, David Leuerett Garth Evans and Dicter Rot (Tate Gallery) 1978, Sculpture Now 1 (Gallery Wintersburger Cologne) 1983, Three Sculptors (Wolff Gallery NY) 1984, Quest - Drawings by Faculty (NY Studio Sch) 1989, Before Sculpture - British Sculptors Drawings (NY Studio Sch) 1990, Evans Saunders Tribe Tucker Turnbull (Phillips Staib Gallery NY) 1990, Newer Sculpture (Charles Cowles Gallery NY) 1990, Discourse (NY Studio Sch) 1990, Physicality (Hunter Coll City Univ NY) 1990, Summer Group (Charles Cowles Gallery NY) 1991, Sculpture in the Yard (PMW Gallery Stamford) 1992, Set A/B (Tribeca 148 Gallery NY) 1992, Millfield British 20th Century Sculpture Exhib (Millfield Sch Somerset) 1992, Form, Shape and Vision (Schick Art Gallery NY) 1993, Summer Salon Show (Robert Morrison Gallery NY) 1993, French Ideals: French Idylls (NY Studio Sch of Drawing, Painting and Sculpture) 1993, American Academy Invitational Exhibition of Painting and Sculpture (American Acad of Arts and Letters New York) 1996; *Public collections* incl: Brooklyn Museum NYC, Gulbenkian Fndn Lisbon, Joseph H Hirshorn Museum and Sculpture Garden Washington DC, Metropolitan Museum of Art NYC, Museum of Modern Art NYC, Nat Museum of Modern Art Brazil, Power Gallery of Contemporary Art Sydney, Tate Gallery London, V&A; *Awards* Newcastle Cruddas Park Sculpture Competition 1961, Gulbenkian purchase award 1964, Arts Cncl of GB sabbatical 1966, BSC fellowship 1969, Oxford Gallery purchase prize 1972, Welsh Arts Cncl purchase prize 1974, Arts Cncl of GB maj award 1975, Gtr London Arts Assoc bursary 1978, Arts Cncl of GB film bursary 1979, Br Cncl exhibitions abroad grant 1979, Mount Holyoke Coll faculty award 1980, residency Yaddo Saratoga Springs NY 1982 and 1991, fell John Simon Guggenheim Meml Fndn 1986, The Marie Walsh Sharpe Art Fndn The Space Program 1992–93, Pollock-Krasner Fndn Award 1996; *Style*— Garth Evans; ✉ 106 North 6th St, Brooklyn, NY 11211, USA

EVANS, Gwilym; *see:* Evans, William Devenport

EVANS, Huw Prideaux; CB (1993); s of Richard Hubert Evans (d 1963), and Kathleen Annie, *née* Collins; *b* 21 Aug 1941; *Educ* Cardiff HS, King's Coll Cambridge (MA), LSE (MSc); *m* 1 April 1966, Anne, da of Prof Percival Thomas Bray (d 1988), of Cyncoed, Cardiff; 2 s (Richard b 1969, Lewis b 1971); *Career* dep sec HM Treasy Overseas Fin Gp 1989–94 (Econ Assessment Gp 1980–86), UK exec dir IMF and World Bank and min (economics) Br Embassy Washington 1994–; *Clubs* Oxford and Cambridge; *Style*— Huw P Evans, Esq, CB; ✉ IMF, 700 19th Street, NW, Washington DC, USA (☎ 00 1 202 623 4560)

EVANS, Iain Richard; *b* 17 May 1951; *Educ* Univ of Bristol (BSc), Harvard Business Sch (MBA); *Career* sr accountant Arthur Young McClelland Moores & Co 1975–76 (joined 1972); Bain & Co: conslt 1978–80, mangr 1980–82, ptnr 1982–83; Hyder plc (formerly Welsh Water plc): non-exec dir 1989–93, exec chm 1993–96, non-exec chm 1996–; chm The LEK Partnership 1991– (fndr ptnr 1983–); FCA 1981 (ACA 1975); *Recreations* golf, fishing, tennis; *Style*— Iain Evans, Esq; ✉ The LEK Partnership, The Adelphi, 1–11 John Adam St, London WC2N 6BW (☎ 0171 930 1244, fax 0171 839 3790, telex 8950994)

EVANS, Ieuan Cenydd; MBE; s of John Lewis Evans, of Carmarthen, and Margaret Eluned, *née* Davies; *b* 21 March 1964; *Educ* Queen Elizabeth GS Camarthen, Univ of Salford (BA); *Career* rugby union wing threequarter; clubs: Carmarthen Quins RFC, Llanelli RFC 1984– (currently capt, 201 appearances scoring 180 tries); Wales: B rep 1985, full debut v France 1987, memb World Cup squad 1987 (5 appearances) and 1995, tour NZ 1988 (2 test appearances), memb Triple Crown winning team 1988, 64 caps (Welsh record), capt 1991–95 (incl World Cup team 1991); jt record holder for most tries (4) in an int v Canada 1987, record number of times capt of Wales (28), record number of tries for Wales (27), record number of victories as capt (13); memb Br Lions tour Aust 1989 (3 test appearances scoring winning try in final test) and tour NZ 1993 (3 test appearances), 4 appearances Barbarians, represented Crawshays XV; formerly with PR Dept Nat Tst S Wales, currently business devpt exec Forthright Finance Ltd; with Masters International (mgmnt co); memb Bardic Circle; Hon MA Univ of Salford; *Recreations* American sports, travel, literature; *Style*— Ieuan Evans, Esq, MBE; ✉ Llanelli RFC, Stradey Park, Llanelli, Dyfed (☎ 01554 774060); Masters International (☎ 0118 934 4111)

EVANS, James; CBE (1995); s of Rex Powis Evans, and Louise Evans; *b* 27 Nov 1932; *Educ* Aldenham, St Catharine's Coll Cambridge (MA); *m* 1961, Jette Holmboe; 2 da; *Career* Thomson Group: chm and chief exec Times Newspapers Ltd 1980–81, chm and chief exec Thomson Regional Newspapers Ltd 1982–84, md and chief exec International Thomson Organisation plc 1985–86; chm The Press Association Ltd 1987–89 (dir 1983–90), dir Reuters Holdings plc 1984–92; memb Monopolies and Mergers Cmmn 1989–; *Style*— James Evans, Esq, CBE; ✉ Monopolies and Mergers Commission, New Court, Carey St, London WC2A 2JT (☎ 0171 324 1467)

EVANS, Capt James; MBE (1992), RD (1975), DL (1978); s of Thomas Evans (d 1966), and Hilda Margaret, *née* Atkinson (d 1976); *b* 9 May 1933; *Educ* Merchiston Castle Sch, Univ of Newcastle (BSc); *m* 12 July 1958, Patricia Alexena (Pat), da of Harry Kerr (d 1973); 1 s (Ian b 1963), 2 da (Lynn b 1961, Gwen b 1967); *Career* RNR 1956–80, Hon ADC 1979–80, ret 1980; apprenticeship: Wm Weatherhead & Sons 1950–52, Swan Hunter and Whigham Richardson 1952–56; engr Yarrow-Admiralty Res Dept 1958–63, nuclear engrg certificate 1960, engr UK Atomic Energy Authy 1963–68, md Eyemouth Boat Building Co Ltd 1968–90, conslt Naval Architect 1990–; tech advsr Scottish Fishermen's Fedn 1993–; chm Fishing Boat Builders' Assoc 1979–90, sec/treas Eyemouth and District Fishermen's Assoc 1993–; Nuclear Engrg Soc Silver Medal Award for a paper on Features of Interest in Small Pressurised Water Reactors 1963, author of East Coast Fishing Boat Building (1990), a tech paper of NE Coast Inst of Engrs and Shipbuilders; chm: Berwickshire Dist Co Cncl 1980–96; Freeman of Berwick-upon-Tweed; memb Court of Freemen of Eng and Wales, lord pres Court of Deans of Guilds of Scotland 1994–95; CEng, FRINA, MIMechE; *Style*— Capt James Evans, MBE, RD, DL; ✉ Makore, Northburn View, Eyemouth, Berwickshire TD14 5BG (☎ 01890 750701); Dundee House, Harbour Rd, Eyemouth, Berwickshire TD14 5JB (☎ 018907 750231, fax 01890 750701)

EVANS, Hon Jeffrey Richard; s of 2 Baron Mountevans (d 1974), and Deirdre, Lady Mountevans; hp of bro, 3 Baron Mountevans, *qv*; *b* 13 May 1948; *Educ* Nautical Coll Pangbourne, Pembroke Coll Cambridge (MA); *m* 1972, Hon Juliet, da of 2 Baron Moran, KCMG; 2 s (Alexander b 1975, Julian b 1977); *Career* shipbroker; dir H Clarkson & Co; memb Court of Assts Worshipful Co of Shipwrights; *Recreations* cross-country skiing, fishing, reading; *Style*— The Hon Jeffrey Evans

EVANS, John; MP (Lab) St Helens North (majority 16,244); s of James Evans (d 1937), and Margaret, *née* Robson (d 1987); *b* 19 Oct 1930; *Educ* Jarrow Central Sch; *m* 1959, Joan, da of Thomas Slater; 2 s, 1 da; *Career* former marine fitter and engr, memb Hebburn UDC 1962–74 (chm 1972–73, ldr 1969–74), memb S Tyneside Met Dist Cncl 1973–74, memb Euro Parl 1975–79 (chm Regnl Policy and Tport Ctee 1976–79); MP (Lab): Newton Feb 1974–83, St Helens N 1983–; asst govt whip 1978–79, oppn whip 1979–80, PPS to Rt Hon Michael Foot as ldr of oppn 1980–83, memb Lab Pty NEC 1982–, oppn front bench spokesman on employment 1983–87, chm National Lab Pty 1991–92; *Style*— John Evans, Esq, MP; ✉ House of Commons, London SW1

EVANS, Prof (Henry) John; CBE (1997); s of David Evans, DCM (d 1963), and Gladys May, *née* Jones; *b* 24 Dec 1930; *Educ* Llanelli GS, UCW Aberystwyth (BSc, PhD); *m* 1, 1 June 1957, Gwenda Rosalind, *née* Thomas (d 1974); 4 s (Paul b 16 Dec 1958, Hugh b 1 April 1960, John b 28 Dec 1961, Owen b 24 July 1963); m 2, 9 June 1976, Dr Roslyn Rose, da of Dr Leigh Angell, of Canberra, Aust; *Career* res scientist MRC Radiobiological Res Unit Harwell 1955–64, prof of genetics Univ of Aberdeen 1964–69, dir MRC Human Genetics Unit Edinburgh 1969–84, Boerhaave prof Univ of Leiden The Netherlands 1994–95; chm: Sci Ctee Cancer Research Campaign 1990–95, Beatson Inst Cancer Research 1993–; vice chm Caledonian Research Fndn 1994–; hon prof Univ of Edinburgh 1970, hon DSc Univ of Edinburgh 1996; FRSE 1968, FIBiol 1980, FRCPEd 1989, FRCSEd 1992; *Books* Human Radiation Cytogenetics (1967), Mutagen-Induced Chromosome Damage in Man (1978); *Recreations* golf, music; *Clubs* New (Edinburgh); *Style*— Prof John Evans, CBE, FRSE; ✉ 45 Lauder Rd, Edinburgh EH9 1UE (☎ 0131 667 2437)

EVANS, John Alfred Eaton; s of John Eaton Evans (d 1961), of Clifton, Bristol, and Millicent Jane, *née* Righton (d 1987); *b* 30 July 1933; *Educ* Bristol GS, Worcester Coll Oxford (MA, Univ Rugby first XV, half blue Rugby Fives); *m* 9 Aug 1958, Vyvyan Margaret, da of (Arthur) Henry Mainstone, of Bishopsworth, Bristol; 2 s (Stephen John Eaton b 1961, Hugh Jeffrey Eaton b 1963), 1 da (Susan Beverly Louise b 1965); *Career* Lt Nat Serv and AER RAOC 1952–58; asst master and house tutor: Old House Blundells 1958–63, Sch House Rugby 1963–73 (and housemaster Kilbracken 1973–81); classics tutor and housemaster Phillips Acad Mass USA 1968–69, headmaster Brentwood Sch 1981–93; chm London Div HMC 1993; govr and chm Crescent Sch Rugby 1968–78, govr Colfe's Sch 1994–, memb Cncl St Christopher's Sch Burnham-on-Sea 1994–; author of various articles on community serv in educn for HMC magazine (Conference); memb: Brentwood Music Soc 1981–93, CMS Selection 1983–90, Admty Interview Bd 1987–96, Army Scholarship Bd 1990–, Church of England Advsy Bd of Ministry 1993–; AMMA 1958, JACT 1970, FRSA 1983; *Recreations* rugger, rugby fives, cricket, walking, reading, composing, piano, singing; *Clubs* East India, Vincent's (Oxford), Oxford Union, Cryptics CC, Jesters; *Style*— John Evans, Esq; ✉ Manor Farm House, Easton, Wells, Somerset BA5 1ED (☎ and fax 01749 870270)

EVANS, Dr (Noel) John Bebbington; CB (1980); s of William John Evans, and Gladys Ellen, *née* Bebbington; *b* 26 Dec 1933; *Educ* Hymers Coll Hull, Christ's Coll Cambridge (MA, MB BChir), Univ of London (DPH); *m* 1, 1960 (m dis), Elizabeth Mary Garbutt; 2 s (David, Hugh), 1 da (Sarah); m 2, 1974, Eileen Jane, *née* McMullan; *Career* called to the Bar Gray's Inn 1965; dep CMO DHSS 1977–83, dep sec DHSS 1977–84, conslt in public health and health service mgmnt, Privy Cncl appointee on Royal Pharmaceutical Soc of GB Cncl; chm: Nat Biological Standards Bd, UK Transplant Support Serv; FFPHM, FRCP; *Style*— Dr John Evans, CB; ✉ Providence House, Wyre Lane, Long Marston, Stratford-upon-Avon, Warwickshire CV37 8RQ (☎ 01789 721509)

EVANS, John Noel Gleave; s of James Gleave Evans (d 1963), of Malaya, and Irene, *née* Schofield (d 1989); *b* 9 Dec 1934; *Educ* Cranbrook Sch Kent, St Thomas' Hosp London

(MB BS, DLO); *m* 23 July 1960, Elizabeth Violet, da of Rev Cuthbert Edward Guy Glascodine (d 1980); 1 s (Mark b 1966), 3 da (Philippa Macintyre b 1962, Charlotte Reid b 1963, Kate b 1971); *Career* SSC RAMC 1960–63, cmmn TA 1964–76, Maj RAMC (V); conslt ENT surgn: St Thomas' Hosp London 1971–94, Hosp for Sick Children London 1972; hon conslt ENT surgn: Queen Elizabeth Hosp Woolwich 1982, King Edward VII Hosp for Offrs 1988; hon conslt in otolaryngology to the Army 1989–; hon sec Br Assoc of Otolaryngologists 1980–88, hon treas Br Academic Conf in Otolaryngology 1984, ENT rep Euro Union of Med Specialists 1985–96; Freeman City of London 1979, elected Liveryman Worshipful Soc of Apothecaries of London 1979; FRCS 1965 (Edinburgh 1987), memb RSM 1972 (Cncl laryngology section 1975, vice pres 1985–86, pres 1993–94); corresponding memb American Laryngology Assoc 1984, int memb American Soc of Paediatric Otolaryngology 1989; *Books* Paediatric Otolaryngology Vol 6 Scott-Brown's Otolaryngology (1987); *Recreations* foreign travel, windsurfing; *Clubs* RSM; *Style*— John Evans, Esq; ✉ 55 Harley St, London W1N 1DD (☎ 0171 580 1481)

EVANS, John Russell; s of Henry Claude Evans, of Hamilton, Scotland; *b* 2 Aug 1945; *Educ* King James I GS Bishop Auckland, City Univ London (BSc); *m* (m dis); 1 s (Jonathan), 1 da (Nicola); *Career* apprentice Rolls Royce 1960–70, Ford 1970–72, General Motors 1972–77, gen mangr Butec Electrics (BL) 1977–78; md: Park Bros 1978–79, Bonser Engineering 1980–85, Lansing Henley 1979–85; mfrg dir Data Magnetics 1985–87; md: Renold Automotive 1988–90, Hamworthy Engineering 1990–93; Eur Ing, CEng, FIProdE; *Recreations* flying, rugby, sailing, squash; *Style*— John R Evans, Esq; ✉ Hamworthy Engineering Ltd, Fleet Corner, Poole, Dorset BH17 7LA (☎ 01202 665566)

EVANS, John Stanley; QPM (1990); s of William Stanley Evans (d 1970), and Doris, *née* Wooldridge (d 1994); *b* 6 Aug 1943; *Educ* Wade Deacon GS, Univ of Liverpool (LLB); *m* 25 Sept 1965, Beryl, da of Albert Smith (d 1976); 1 s (Mark 1967), 1 da (Lindsey 1971); *Career* Liverpool City then Merseyside Police 1960–80, asst chief constable Gtr Manchester Police 1980–84, dep chief constable Surrey Constabulary 1984–88, chief constable Devon & Cornwall Constabulary 1989–; chm Police Athletic Assoc 1989–; memb several ctees of Assoc of Chief Police Offrs incl: Terrorism (chm), Complaints and Discipline, Gen Purposes; FIMgt 1980; *Recreations* most sports (ran London Marathon in 1988 and 1989), service and charitable activities; *Style*— John S Evans, Esq, QPM; ✉ Devon and Cornwall Constabulary, Police Headquarters, Middlemoor, Exeter, Devon EX2 7HQ (☎ 01392 52101)

EVANS, John Walter; OBE (1988), JP (Staffordshire 1978–); s of Walter Evans (d 1957), of Birmingham, and Florence Beatrice, *née* Morton-Tooze (d 1978); *b* 10 July 1928; *Educ* George Dixon GS, Univ of Birmingham (BSc); *m* 18 Dec 1954, Barbara Anne Evans, da of Harry Atkins (d 1974), of Staffordshire; *Career* National Coal Board: chief mining engr Staffs Area 1972–74 (colliery gen mangr 1956–67, prodn mangr 1967–70, dep chief mining engr 1970–72), chief mining engr Western Area 1974–80; area dir Western Area Br Coal 1984–88 (dep area dir 1980–84), consulting mining engr 1988–; chm Panasonic Tst 1991–95, memb Royal Soc of St George, vice pres Staffs Soc; Freeman City of London 1984, memb Worshipful Co of Engrs 1984; FIMinE 1972, FEng 1988; *Recreations* music, travel; *Style*— John Evans, Esq, OBE, JP, FEng; ✉ Aincourt, 127 Allport Street, Cannock, Staffs WS11 1JZ (☎ 01543 504959)

EVANS, Jonathan Peter; MP (C) Brecon and Radnor (majority 130); s of David Evans, and Harriet Evans; *b* 2 June 1950; *Educ* Lewis Sch Pengam, Howardian HS Cardiff, Coll of Law Guildford and Lancaster Gate; *m* 24 Aug 1975, Margaret, *née* Thomas; 1 s, 2 da; *Career* slr, managing ptnr Leo Abse and Cohen slrs until 1992; Parly candidate (C): Ebbw Vale 1974 (both gen elections), Wolverhampton NE 1979, Brecon and Radnor 1987; MP (C) Brecon and Radnor 1992–; PPS: to Michael Mates, MP, Min of State NI Office 1992–93, to Rt Hon Sir John Wheeler, MP, Min of State 1993–94; Parly under sec DTI 1994–95 (min for corp affrs 1994–95, min for competition and consumer affrs 1995), Parly sec Lord Chancellor's Department 1995–96, Parly under sec of state Welsh Office 1996–; memb Welsh Affrs Select Ctee and Health Select Ctee; chm: Welsh Cons Parly Candidates 1985–90, Welsh Cons Policy Gp 1987–91; memb Nat Union of the Cons Pty 1991–; dep chm Tai Cymru (Housing Wales) 1988–92, dep chm Wales Cncl NSPCC 1991–; *Recreations* rugby, music, family, reading; *Clubs* Carlton, Cardiff and County; *Style*— Jonathan Evans, Esq, MP; ✉ House of Commons, London SW1A 0AA

EVANS, Kim; da of Jon Evans, and Gwendolen, *née* McLeod; *b* 3 Jan 1951; *Educ* Putney HS, Univ of Warwick (BA English and American Lit), Univ of Leicester (MA Victorian Studies); *partner* David Hucker; *Career* asst ed Crafts magazine 1974–76, sub-ed and restaurant critic Harpers & Queen magazine 1976–78, researcher The South Bank Show (LWT) 1978–82; prodr/dir: Hey Good Looking (Channel 4) 1982–83, The South Bank Show (LWT) 1983–88; BBC TV: prodr 1989–92, asst head of music and arts 1992–93, head of music and arts 1993–; Huw Wheldon (BAFTA) Award for Best Arts Documentary (for 'Angela Carter's Curious Room') 1993; memb Film, Broadcasting and Video Panel Arts Cncl; *Recreations* travelling, particularly in Africa, reading, dreaming; *Style*— Miss Kim Evans; ✉ BBC Television, Room EM06, BBC Television Centre, Wood Lane, London W12 7RJ (☎ 0181 895 6770, fax 0181 895 6586)

EVANS, Laurie; s of Hugh Evans, of Weston, Avon, and Greta, *née* Bryden (d 1989); *b* 10 July 1955; *Educ* Royal HS Edinburgh, Newcastle Poly, Bournemouth and Poole Coll of Art (DipAD); *m* March 1982, Lesley, da of Stanley Richardson, of Edinburgh; 2 s (James Ewan b 30 May 1983, Calum Thomas b 21 Sept 1986); *Career* photographer; Arts in Fife, freelance reportage photographer for Rock and Roll press (NME, Melody Maker), asst to Bryce Attwell, proprietor Laurie Evans Photographer 1982– (specialising in food and still life); clients incl: Boots, Sainsbury's, Nestlé, John West, Tesco; magazines incl: Good Housekeeping, Homes & Gardens; winner various awards incl: Silver award Assoc of Photographers 1986, 4 Clio awards USA 1986, 1988, 1989 and 1993, Award of Excellence Communication Arts Magazine, Silver award D&ADA 1990; columnist Image Magazine, contrib to over 30 cookery books; memb Assoc of Photographers (memb Cncl 1989, 1990 and 1991); *Recreations* very keen sailor, blues & jazz guitar; *Style*— Laurie Evans, Esq; ✉ Laurie Evans Photography, 11 Cameron House, 12 Castlehaven Road, London NW1 4QW (☎ 0171 284 2140, fax 0171 284 2130)

EVANS, Leslie Douglas; s of Leslie Edward Evans, of St Albans, and Violet Rosina, *née* Rogerson; *b* 24 June 1945; *Educ* St Albans GS for Boys, St Albans Sch of Art, Leeds Coll of Art (DipAD), Hornsey Coll of Art (Art Teachers' Certificate); *m* 4 Sept 1965, Fionnuala Boyd, *qv*, da of Joseph Douglas Allen Boyd (d 1990); 1 s (Jack Luis b 12 Sept 1969), 1 da (Ruby Rose b 2 Dec 1971); *Career* artist; began working with Fionnuala Boyd 1968, Bi-Centennial fell USA 1977–78; artist in residence: Milton Keynes Devpt Corp 1982–84, Brunei Rainforest Project 1991–92; *Solo Exhibitions* (with Fionnuala Boyd): Angela Flowers Gallery 1972, 1974, 1977, 1979, 1980, 1982, 1984, 1986 and 1988, Park Square Gallery Leeds 1972, Boyd and Evans 1970–75 (Turnpike Gallery, Leigh) 1976, Fendrick Gallery Washington DC 1978, Graves Art Gallery Sheffield 1979, Spectro Arts Workshop Newcastle 1980, Ton Peek Utrecht 1981, A Decade of Paintings (Milton Keynes Exhibition Gallery) 1982–83, Drumcroon Art Centre Wigan 1985, Bird (Flowers East, London) 1990, English Paintings (Brendan Walter Gallery, Santa Monica) 1990, Angela Flowers (Ireland) 1990, Flowers East London 1991, Brunei Rain Forest (Flowers East) 1993; *Gp Exhibitions* incl: Postcards (Angela Flowers Gallery) 1970, British Drawing 1952–72 (Angela Flowers Gallery) 1972, British Realist Show (Ikon Gallery) 1976, Aspects of Realism (Rothmans of Pall Mall, Canada) 1976–78, The Real British (Fischer Fine Art) 1981, Black and White Show (Angela Flowers Gallery) 1985, Sixteen (Angela Flowers Gallery) 1986, State of the Nation (Herbert Gallery, Coventry) 1987, Contemporary Portraits (Flowers East) 1988, The Thatcher Years (Flowers East) 1989, Picturing People - British Figurative Art since 1945 (touring exhibition Far East) 1989–90, Art '90 London (Business Design Centre) 1990; work in public collections of: Arts Cncl of GB, Br Cncl, Museum of Modern Art NY, Sheffield City Art Gallery, Wolverhampton City Art Gallery, Leeds City Art Gallery, Contemporary Art Soc, Leicester Educn Authy, Manchester City Art Gallery, Unilever plc, Tate Gallery, Williamson Art Gallery, Metropolitan Museum NY, Borough of Milton Keynes; *Awards* prizewinner Bradford Print Biennale, first prize 6 Festival Int de la Peinture Cagnes-sur-Mer; *Recreations* squash, films, friends, music, hill-walking; *Style*— Leslie Evans; ✉ Boyd and Evans, Flowers East, 199–205 Richmond Rd, London E8 3NJ (☎ 0181 985 3333, fax 0181 985 0067)

EVANS, Mark; QC (1995); s of Rev Clifford Evans (d 1968), of Cardiff, and Mary, *née* Jones; *b* 21 March 1946; *Educ* Christ Coll Brecon, King's Coll London (LLB); *m* (m dis); 1 s (John Clifford b 30 March 1974), 1 da (Claire Elizabeth b 1 April 1976); *Career* called to the Bar Gray's Inn 1971, currently recorder (Western Circuit); *Clubs* Bristol Savages; *Style*— Mark Evans, Esq, QC; ✉ 13 Ferrymans Quay, Queen Street, Bristol BS1 (☎ 0976 160880); All Saints Chambers, Broad Street, Bristol BS1 2HD (☎ 0117 921 1966, fax 0117 927 6493)

EVANS, Mark Armstrong; CVO (1994); s of Charles Tunstall Evans (d 1990), of Haywards Heath, Sussex, and Kathleen Armstrong; *b* 5 Aug 1940; *Educ* Marlborough, Clare Coll Cambridge (MA), Moscow State Univ, Univ of Bristol (PGCE); *m* 1965, Kate, da of Alfred Bastable; 1 da (Anneliese b 1970), 1 s (Alexander b 1979); *Career* head of German and Russian Chichester HS for Boys 1964–69, asst rep Br Cncl Bahrain 1969–71, asst dir Br Cncl Frankfurt 1971–73, Arabic language trg Mecas (Lebanon) 1974–75, dir Br Cncl UAE 1975–78, temp posting Kabul 1978, cultural attaché Br Embassy Paris 1979–85, head Office Servs Br Cncl London 1985–88, cultural cnsllr Br High Cmmn Ottawa 1988–92, cultural cnsllr Br Embassy Moscow and dir Br Cncl (Russia, Armenia, Belarus, Georgia, Kazakhstan, Kyrgyzstan, Moldova and Turkmenistan) 1992–96, dir Br Cncl Austria 1996–; memb Royal Asian Soc; *Recreations* model boats and domestic chores; *Style*— Mark Evans, Esq, CVO; ✉ The British Council, Schenkenstrasse 4, A1010 Vienna, Austria (☎ 00 43 1 533 26 16, fax 00 43 1 533 26 16 85)

EVANS, Mark Singleton; s of Arthur Singleton Evans (d 1954), and Constance Mary Jenkins (d 1980), da of late Walter Jenkins; *b* 27 Oct 1933; *Educ* Winchester, New Coll Oxford (MA); *m* 15 Dec 1962, Belinda Jane, da of Sir Kenelm Cayley, 10 Bt (d 1967); 2 s, 1 da; *Career* Nat Serv 2 Lt The Royal Dragoons 1952–54; pres: Scarborough Cons Assoc 1981, Kensington Cons Assoc 1989–95 (chm 1986–89), N Yorks CC 1993; ptnr Laing & Cruickshank 1964; dir: Mercantile House Holdings 1987, Credit Lyonnais Capital Markets 1987–93, Mercury European Privatisation Trust PLC, Heavitree Brewery PLC; *Clubs* White's, Swinley Forest Golf, Ganton Golf; *Style*— Mark Evans, Esq; ✉ 23 Bolingbroke Road, London W14 0AJ (☎ 0171 602 1262); Manor House, Brompton-by-Sawdon, nr Scarborough, North Yorkshire (☎ 01723 859233); Credit Lyonnais Laing, Broadwalk House, Appold St, London EC2A 2DA (☎ 0171 588 4000)

EVANS, Prof Michael Charles Whitmore; s of Allen Whitmore Evans, of London, and Doris, *née* Smith; *b* 24 Sept 1940; *Educ* King Edwards Sch Birmingham, Univ of Sheffield (BSc, PhD); *m* 28 Dec 1963, Christine Stella, da of John Marshall (d 1983); 2 s (Peter Whitmore b 1967, Nicholas John b 1969); *Career* assoc specialist Dept of Cell Physiology Univ of California Berkeley 1964–66, lectr in botany King's Coll London 1966–73, prof of plant chemistry UCL 1982– (reader 1973–82); contrib to numerous papers in scientific jls; chm Plant Sci and Microbiology Sub-Ctee 1987–90 (memb 1985–90), memb Ctee Biological Sci Ctee SERC 1987–90; *Recreations* birdwatching, gardening; *Style*— Prof Michael Evans; ✉ Department of Biology, Darwin Building, University College London, Gower St, London WC1E 6BT (☎ 0171 380 7312, fax 0171 380 7096)

EVANS, Michael John; s of Arthur Frank Evans (d 1990), and Flora Gertrude, *née* Burford; *b* 9 Feb 1939; *Educ* Handsworth GS Birmingham, Univ of Birmingham (MB ChB); *m* 10 July 1965, Dorothy Mavis, da of Gladstone Rule Osborn; 2 da (Susan Dorothy b 10 June 1966, Tania Michelle b 23 Oct 1974); *Career* registrar in orthopaedics Royal Free Hosp London, sr registrar in orthopaedics Middx and Royal Nat Orthopaedic Hosps 1972–78, conslt orthopaedic surgn Ealing and Hammersmith Hosps 1978–, hon sr lectr in orthopaedic surgy Royal Post Grad Med Sch 1978–; conslt orthopaedic surgn: Royal Masonic Hosp 1987–, Charing Cross Hosp 1996–; memb: Radio Soc of GB 1970, Medico-Legal Soc 1986, Soc of Shoulder and Elbow Surgns 1991; FRCSEd 1969, FRSM 1976, fell Br Orthopaedic Res Soc 1987; *Recreations* amateur radio, computing; *Clubs* RSM; *Style*— Michael Evans, Esq; ✉ White Lodge, Horton Road, Horton, Berkshire SL3 9NU (☎ 01753 685681); 144 Harley Street, London W1N 1AH (☎ 0181 967 5609, fax 0181 967 5630, mobile 0374 264404)

EVANS, Michael Murray; s of Harold Fisher Evans (d 1983), of Wigan, Lancs, and Constance, *née* Shannon (d 1984); *b* 6 July 1942; *Educ* Hesketh Fletcher HS Atherton Manchester; *Career* National Provincial Bank Ltd 1958–62, journalist Iliffe Press 1962–68, fndr and md Murray Evans Assocs PR Conslts (now Westminster Communications Group Ltd) 1968– (jt md 1989–), dir PRCA 1979–89; public affrs dir Motorcycle Indust Assoc 1974–93, DG Br Battery Mfrs' Assoc 1987–, dir Inst of Motorcycling 1974–94, memb RAC Motorcycle Ctee 1987–94; MIPR 1973; *Recreations* motorcycling, motoring, reading, swimming, travel; *Clubs* RAC; *Style*— Michael Evans, Esq; ✉ Westminster Communications Group Ltd, Cowley House, 9 Little College Street, London SW1P 3XS (☎ 0171 222 0666, fax 0171 233 0335)

EVANS, Michael Stephen James; s of William Henry Reginald Evans, of Seaford, Sussex, and Beatrix Catherine, *née* Mottram; *b* 5 Jan 1945; *Educ* Christ's Hospital, QMC London (BA); *m* 1971, Robyn Nicola, da of Samuel John Wilson Coles; 3 s (Samuel b 29 Nov 1974, Christopher b 6 July 1978, James b 1 July 1980); *Career* news ed Express & Independent Loughton Essex 1969–70 (reporter E London Office 1968); Daily Express: reporter Action Line consumer column 1970–72, gen news reporter 1972–77, home affairs corr 1977–82, def and dip corr 1982–86; def corr The Times 1987– (Whitehall corr 1986–87); vice pres and acting pres Dip and Cwlth Writers Assoc 1985–86; memb: Defence Correspondents Assoc, Assoc of Foreign Affrs Journalists; *Books* A Crack in the Dam (1978), False Arrest (1979), Great Disasters (1981), South Africa (1987), The Gulf Crisis (1988); *Recreations* cricket, tennis, golf, playing piano; *Style*— Michael Evans, Esq; ✉ The Times, 1 Pennington St, London E1 9XN (☎ 0171 782 5921, fax 0171 782 5988)

EVANS, (Arthur) Mostyn (Moss); s of Frederick Arthur Evans (d 1972), and Hannah Maria, *née* O'Brien (d 1960); *b* 13 July 1925; *Educ* Church Road Secdy Modern Sch Birmingham; *m* 22 Dec 1947, Laura Margaret, da of James Alfred Bigglestone; 2 s (Adrian Mostyn b 3 Aug 1948, Kevin b 2 May 1953 d 1979), 3 da (Yvonne b 2 Aug 1949, Vivienne Therese b 14 Aug 1957, Dianne b 31 Oct 1960); *Career* Transport & General Workers' Union: dist official Birmingham 1956–60, sec Regnl Engrg Gp 1960–66, nat sec Engrg Gp 1966–69, nat sec Chem Gp 1969, nat sec Engrg and Auto Gp 1969–73, nat organiser 1973–78, gen sec 1978–85; chm Ford Motor Company Negotiating Ctee 1969–79; memb: TUC Gen Cncl 1977–85 (chm Int Ctee), BOTB 1978–79, NEDC 1978–85, ACAS 1980–85, Exec Int Tport Workers' Fedn 1980–, NW Anglia Community Health Cncl 1992–; pres ICEF 1982–86 (vice pres 1980–82); Kings Lynn and W Norfolk: cncllr (Lab) BC 1991–, mayor 1996–97; *Recreations* music, horse racing;

Clubs Heacham Social; *Style—* Moss Evans, Esq; ✉ Cheney House, Cheney Hill, Heacham, Norfolk PE31 7BX (☎ 01485 70477)

EVANS, Nicholas; s of Anthony B Evans (d 1984), and Eileen, *née* Whitehouse, of Bromsgrove, Worcs; *b* 26 July 1950; *Educ* Bromsgrove Sch Worcs, St Edmund Hall Oxford (BA); *m* Jennifer, da of Ian Lyon; 2 s (Harry Hewland b 9 Jan 1980, Max b 3 Feb 1981), 1 da (Lauren b 31 March 1982); *Career* reporter Evening Chronicle Newcastle 1972–75, reporter then prodr Weekend World (LWT) 1975–79, ed The London Programme (LWT) 1979–82, exec prodr The South Bank Show (LWT) 1982–84, ind prodr and screenplay writer 1985–93, currently author; winner US ACE Award for best int movie on cable (Murder by the Book) 1991; *Books* The Horse Whisperer (1995); *Recreations* tennis, running, movies; *Style—* Nicholas Evans, Esq; ✉ c/o A P Watt, 20 John Street, London WC1N 2DR (☎ 0171 405 6774)

EVANS, Nigel Martin; MP (C) Ribble Valley (majority 6,542); s of late Albert Evans, of Swansea, and Betty Evans; *b* 10 Nov 1957; *Educ* Dynevor Sch Swansea, Univ Coll Swansea (BA); *Career* family newsagent business 1979–90; Parly candidate (C): Swansea W 1987, Pontypridd (by-election) 1989; MP (C) Ribble Valley 1992– (also contested by-election 1991); chm Cons Welsh Parly Candidates Policy Gp 1990, pres Cons North West Parly Candidates Gp 1991, sec North West Cons MPs 1992–, sec All Pty Tourism Gp 1992–, chm All Pty Music Gp 1992–; PPS to: Rt Hon David Hunt as Chllr of Duchy of Lancaster and Sec of State at Office of Public Service and Science 1993–95, Tony Baldry as Min of State MAFF 1995–96, Rt Hon William Hague as Sec of State for Wales 1996–; chm Central Lancs Marie Curie Cancer Centre; cncllr (C) Sketty Ward W Glamorgan CC 1985–91, former pres Swansea W Cons Assoc, former chm Swansea W Young Conservatives; campaigned for Republican Pty in US presidential elections 1980, 1984 and 1988 in NY, Florida and California; *Recreations* tennis, swimming, all spectator sports; *Clubs* Carlton; *Style—* Nigel Evans, Esq, MP; ✉ House of Commons, London SW1A 0AA (☎ 0171 219 3000)

EVANS, Ven Patrick Alexander Sidney; *b* 28 Jan 1943; *Educ* Clifton Coll Bristol, Lincoln Theol Coll; *m* 1969, Jane; 2 s, 1 da; *Career* curate: Holy Trinity Lyonsdown Barnet 1973–76, Royston 1976–78; vicar: Gt Gaddesden 1978–82, Tenterden 1982–89; rural dean West Charing 1988–89, archdeacon of Maidstone 1989–, dir of ordinands Diocese of Canterbury 1989–94, hon canon of Canterbury Cathedral 1989–; chm Pastoral Ctee, jt chm Dioceses of Canterbury and Rochester Cncl for Social Responsibility, memb Gen Synod; *Style—* The Ven the Archdeacon of Maidstone; ✉ Archdeacon's House, Charing, Ashford, Kent TN27 0LU

EVANS, Peter Michael; s of Michael Evans (d 1976), of Chesterfield, and Fiona Mary, *née* Cassidy; *b* 21 Sept 1952; *Educ* Uppingham, Univ of Oxford (MA); *m* 1, 1975 (m dis 1989), Mary-Ann, da of George Vere Howell; 1 s (Simon Michael b 9 May 1980), 1 da (Eloise Mary b 21 Sept 1981); m 2, 1992, Carol, da of Frank Longridge; 2 da (Holly Susannah and Sacha Fiona (twins) b 18 March 1995); *Career* IMI plc 1975–80 (personnel trainee, graduate recruitment offr, export mktg exec), regnl mangr West Africa Wellcome plc 1980–83, int personnel exec Booker plc 1983–85, MSL International (formerly Hay-MSL) 1985–91 (conslt, regnl dir, dir), dir Whitehead Mann Ltd 1991–; MIPD 1985, MInstD 1988; *Style—* Peter Evans, Esq; ✉ The Gables, Lower Rd, Cookham, Berks SL6 9EP (☎ 016285 20767); Whitehead Mann, 11 Hill Street, London W1X 8BB (☎ 0171 290 2000, fax 0171 290 2050)

EVANS, Dr (Ian) Philip; s of Joseph Emlyn Evans, of Ruthin, Clwyd, and Beryl, *née* Davies; *b* 2 May 1948; *Educ* Ruabon Boys' GS, Churchill Coll Cambridge (BA, MA), Imperial Coll London (PhD, DIC); *m* 15 Jan 1972, Sandra Veronica, da of Flying Offr Robert William Waggett, RAF (ret), of East Sheen, London; 2 s (Benjamin Joseph b 1976, Roland Mathonwy b 1978); *Career* post-doctoral fell Res Sch of Chemistry ANU 1973–75, asst master St Paul's Sch 1975–90 (head Chemistry Dept 1984–90), head master Bedford Sch 1990–; chief examiner A-level chemistry Univ of London Sch Examinations Bd 1987–90; memb: Royal Soc Sci Ctee 1990–93, School Examinations and Assessment Cncl 1991–93, School Curriculum and Assessment Authy 1993–, various ctees and working parties RSC; MRSC, CChem; *Publications* author of various papers in learned jls; *Recreations* music, cricket, poetry; *Style—* Dr Philip Evans; ✉ Bedford School, De Parys Avenue, Bedford MK40 2TU (☎ 01234 353436, fax 01234 340050)

EVANS, Dr Philip Rhys; *Educ* Shene Co GS, Guy's Hosp London (BA, MB BS, MRCS LRCP, DipObst RCOG, FRCGP), Open Univ; *Career* VSO Fiji Islands 1965–66; in gen practice: Dargaville NZ 1976–77, Leaf Rapids Canada 1977–78; princ in gen practice Bury St Edmunds Suffolk 1979–; postgrad trainer in gen practice 1981–89; RCGP: memb Int Ctee 1988–, sec 1991–94, chm 1994–, chm UK Euro Forum 1994–96; advsr to WHO in Romania, Hungary, Czech Repub and Turkey 1991–94; memb UK Delgn to Euro Union of Gen Practitioners (UEMO) 1988–, UK del Standing Ctee of Euro Doctors (CP) 1988–; UK rep: Int Soc of Gen Practice (SIMG) 1991–95, World Orgn of Family Doctors (WONCA) 1993–; hon sec Euro Soc of Gen Practice/Family Med 1995–; author of pubns on int gen practice and family med, jt ed Euro Jl of Gen Practice 1995–96; academic referee: Br Med Jl, Br Jl of Gen Practice; memb: VSO, BMA; *Recreations* cricket, golf, growing sweet peas; *Clubs* East India, Surrey CCC, Flempton Golf; *Style—* Dr Philip R Evans; ✉ The Guildhall Surgery, Lower Baxter Street, Bury St Edmunds, Suffolk IP33 1ET (☎ 01284 701601, fax 01284 702943)

EVANS, District Judge Rachel Anne; da of Benjamin Talwyn Evans (d 1992), and Clarice May, *née* Poley, of Cardiff; *b* 14 Jan 1943; *Educ* Neath Girls' GS, City of Cardiff HS, Westfield Coll London (BA), Coll of Law Guildford; *m* 9 June 1975, Robert David Chegwin; 1 da (Celia Louise b 23 May 1978); *Career* articled clerk 1965–67, admitted slr 1967, slr and ptnr Morgan Bruce Cardiff 1967–92, district judge 1992–; pt/t chm SSAT Tbnl and MAT Tbnl 1978–92; sometime: chm S Wales Marriage Guidance Cncl (now Relate), Legal Advr Guides Cymru; memb Law Soc 1965–; *Recreations* music, my family; *Style—* District Judge Rachel Evans; ✉ Olympia House (3rd Floor), Upper Dock Street, Newport, Gwent NP9 1PQ

EVANS, Prof Richard John; s of Ieuan Trefor Evans, and Evelyn, *née* Jones; *b* 29 Sept 1947; *Educ* Jesus Coll Oxford (MA), St Antony's Coll Oxford (DPhil), LittD (UEA) 1990; *m* 2 March 1976 (m dis 1993), Elín Hjaltadóttir, da of Hjalti Arnason; 1 step da (Sigridur Jónsdóttir b 1964); *partner* Christine L Corton; 1 s (Mathew b 1995); *Career* lectr in history Univ of Stirling 1972–76, prof of European history UEA 1983–89 (lectr 1976–83), prof of history Birkbeck Coll Univ of London 1989– (vice master 1993–); visiting assoc prof of European history Columbia Univ NY 1980; chair German History Soc 1989–92; Wolfson Literary Award for History 1988, William H Welch Medal of the American Assoc for the History of Med 1989, Hamburger Medaille für Kunst und Wissenschaft 1993, Fraenkel Prize for Contemporary History 1994; FRHistS 1978, FBA 1993; *Books* The Feminist Movement in Germany 1894–1933 (1976), The Feminists (1977), Society and Politics in Wilhelmine Germany (ed, 1978), Sozialdemokratie und Frauenemanzipation im Deutschen Kaiserreich (1979), The German Family (ed with W R Lee, 1981), The German Working Class (ed, 1982), The German Peasantry (ed with W R Lee, 1986), Rethinking German History (1987), Death in Hamburg (1987), Comrades and Sisters (1987), The German Unemployed (ed with D Geary, 1987), The German Underworld (ed, 1988), Kneipengespräche im Kaiserreich (1989), In Hitler's Shadow (1989), Proletarians and Politics (1990), The German Bourgeoisie (ed with D Blackbourn, 1991), Rituals of Retribution (1996); *Recreations* music (piano), cooking, gardening; *Style—* Prof Richard Evans, FBA; ✉ Department of History, Birkbeck College, University of London, Malet Street, London WC1E 7HX (☎ 0171 631 6268, fax 0171 631 6552)

EVANS, Sir Richard Mark; KCMG (1984, CMG 1978), KCVO (1986); s of Edward Walter Evans, CMG (d 1985), and Anna Margaret, *née* Young (d 1976); *b* 15 April 1928; *Educ* Repton, Magdalen Coll Oxford (MA); *m* 1, 1960 (m dis 1970), Margaret Elizabeth Sessinger; m 2, 1973, Rosemary Grania Glen, JP, o da of Brig (John) Brian Birkett, OBE, of West Tillingham House, Hartfield, E Sussex; 2 s (Mark, Peter); *Career* HM Dip Serv; served London, Peking, Berne, London; head of Near Eastern and subsequently Far Eastern Dept FCO 1970–74, commercial cnsllr Stockholm 1975–77, min (econ) Paris 1977–79, dep under sec of state FO 1982–83 (previously asst under sec), ambass Peking 1984–88; dir: China Investment Tst plc, Hong Kong Investment Trust plc; emeritus fell Wolfson Coll Oxford; memb Ct Worshipful Co of Ironmongers; *Books* Deng Xiaoping and The Making of Modern China (1993); *Style—* Sir Richard Evans, KCMG, KCVO; ✉ Sevenhampton House, Sevenhampton, Highworth, Wiltshire SN6 7QA

EVANS, Sir Robert; kt (1994), CBE (1987); s of Gwilym Evans, and Florence May Evans; *b* 28 May 1927; *Educ* Old Swan Coll Liverpool, City Tech Liverpool, Blackburn Tech; *m* 1950, Lilian May, *née* Ward; 1 s (David b 1954), 1 da (Vikki b 1959); *Career* mechanical engr 1943–50, gas exec 1950–56, exec Burmah Oil 1956–62, dir of engrg Southern Gas 1970–72 (exec engr 1962–70), dir of ops Gas Cncl and Br Gas Corp 1972–75, dep chm N Thames Gas 1975–77, chm E Midlands Region 1977–82; Br Gas Corp: md 1982–83, chief exec 1983–89, memb Bd 1983–; chm Br Gas plc 1989–93; past pres: Inst of Gas Engrs, Energy Industs Club, Inst of Energy 1991–92, Pipline Industs Guild 1990–92; chm Br Energy Assoc; Freeman: City of London 1976, Worshipful Co of Engrs 1984 (Liveryman 1985); Hon Freeman Worshipful Co of Tallow Chandlers; FEng, CIMgt, Hon FIGasE, FInstE, FIMechE; *Recreations* reading, DIY, golf; *Style—* Sir Robert Evans, CBE, FEng; ✉ Fourth Floor Suite, 16–18 Old Queen Street, London SW1H 9HP

EVANS, Robert John Emlyn; MEP (Lab) London NW (majority 17,442); s of Thomas Francis Evans, of Stone, Staffs, and Marjorie Gladys, *née* Macken (d 1986); *b* 23 Oct 1956; *Educ* County Sch Ashford Middx, Shoreditch Coll of Educn, Inst of Educn Univ of London (BEd, MA); *Career* teacher various middle schs Surrey 1978–89, headteacher Crane Jr Sch Hounslow 1990–94; MEP (Lab) London NW 1994–; chm Chertsey and Walton CLP 1987–89, memb London Regnl Exec Lab Pty 1992–93; contested (Lab): E Berks gen election 1987, London S and Surrey E Euro election 1989, Uxbridge gen election 1992; memb: NUT 1978, GMB 1988; *Recreations* hockey, cricket, cycling, theatre, travel; *Clubs* Ruskin House Labour Croydon, Ashford Cricket, Ashford Hockey, Middx CC; *Style—* Robert Evans, Esq, MEP; ✉ Labour Euro Office, The Pavitt Hall, Union Road, Wembley, Middlesex HA0 4AU (☎ 0181 900 0065, fax 0181 900 9412)

EVANS, Prof Robert John Weston; s of Thomas Frederic Evans (d 1992), of Cheltenham, and Margery, *née* Weston; *b* 7 Oct 1943; *Educ* Dean Close Sch Cheltenham, Jesus Coll Cambridge (BA, MA, PhD); *m* 10 May 1969, Catherine (Kati), da of Ferenc Róbert (d 1972), of Budapest; 1 s (David b 1973), 1 da (Margaret b 1979); *Career* res fell Brasenose Coll Oxford 1968–92, prof of Euro history Univ of Oxford 1992– (lectr 1969–90, reader 1990–92), jt ed English Historical Review 1986–95; FBA 1984; *Books* Rudolf II and his World (1984), The Making of the Habsburg Monarchy (1984); *Style—* Prof Robert Evans, FBA; ✉ Brasenose College, Oxford OX1 4AJ (☎ 01865 277890)

EVANS, Robin Hugh; s of Eben Evans, OBE, of Llanfairfechan, and Joan Margaret, *née* Howells; *b* 6 May 1947; *Educ* Bromsgrove Sch, Jesus Coll Oxford (MA); *m* 1973, Ana Lucia Galluzzi, da of Dr Sergio Araujo; 1 s (Andrew Julian b 1974); *Career* VSO teacher India 1965–66; British Council: trainee 1969–70, asst rep Rio de Janeiro 1970–73, regnl dir Recife 1974–76, asst regnl dir Oxford 1976–77, asst rep Cairo 1977–80, asst rep Lima 1980–82, head Cultural Affairs Unit New Delhi 1982–87, staff inspr London 1987–88, dir Mgmnt Servs Dept 1988–91, dir Chile 1991–; Medalha de Ouro Universidade Federal de Pernambuco 1976; *Recreations* theatre, reading; *Style—* Robin Evans, Esq; ✉ The British Council, Eliodoro Yañez 832, Casilla 115 Correo 55, Santiago, Chile (☎ 00 562 236 0193, fax 00 562 235 7375)

EVANS, His Hon Judge (David) Roderick; QC (1989); s of Thomas James Evans, of Morriston, Swansea, and Dorothy, *née* Carpenter; *b* 22 Oct 1946; *Educ* Bishop Gore GS Swansea, UCL (LLB, LLM); *m* 6 Nov 1971, Kathryn Rebecca, da of Leonard Thomas Lewis, of Morriston, Swansea; 3 s (Ioan b 1972, Gwion b 1974, Gruffudd b 1978), 1 da (Saran b 1976); *Career* called to the Bar Gray's Inn 1970; recorder of the Crown Ct attached to the Wales and Chester Circuit 1987–92, circuit judge (Wales and Chester Circuit) 1992–, resident judge Merthyr Tydfil Crown Court 1994–; *Style—* His Hon Judge D Roderick Evans, QC; ✉ c/o The Crown Court, Swansea, West Glamorgan

EVANS, Roderick Michael; s of Michael White Evans, of Monaco, and Helga Ingeborg, *née* Schneider; *b* 19 April 1962; *Educ* Millfield; *m* 7 April 1995, Ms Dawn Silver, er da of Geoffrey Richmond, of Alwoodley, Leeds; 1 s (Oliver William Roderick b 6 Nov 1996); *Career* dir of numerous companies incl: Evans of Leeds Plc 1990–, Astra House Ltd, Furnival Estates Ltd, Garpool Ltd, Mulgate Investments Ltd, Studfair Ltd, Lichfield Securities Ltd, Speylands Ltd, Evans Universal Ltd, Roando Holdings Ltd, Rowite Properties Ltd; *Recreations* motorcycling, shooting, flying; *Clubs* RAC, Royal Yorkshire Yacht; *Style—* Roderick Evans, Esq; ✉ Evans of Leeds plc, Millshaw, Ring Road, Beeston, Leeds LS11 8EG (☎ 0113 271 1888)

EVANS, Roger; s of Eric Evans (d 1947), of Bristol, and Celia Mavis, *née* Roe (d 1988); *b* 28 Oct 1945; *Educ* Lord Wandsworth Coll; *m* Julia Margaret, da of Arthur Horace Moore Household; 1 s (Rupert Alexander b 14 June 1981), 1 da (Rebecca Grace (twin) b 14 June 1981); *Career* various NHS mgmnt posts 1966–82, dep admin Wandsworth Health Authy 1982–85, gen mangr St George's Hosp 1985–90, gen mangr SW Thames RHA 1991–92, chief exec Mid Kent Healthcare Trust 1992–; memb Inst of Health Serv Mangrs 1971; FRSA; *Recreations* cricket, rugby union, fine arts, 18th century music, genealogy, Victorian novels; *Clubs* Sloane, Gloucestershire CCC, Wasps RFC; *Style—* Roger Evans, Esq; ✉ 36 Pepys Rd, Wimbledon, London SW20 8PF (☎ 0181 879 0729)

EVANS, Roger Kenneth; MP (C) Monmouth (majority 3,204); s of Gerald Raymond Evans, and late Dr Annie Margaret Evans; *b* 18 March 1947; *Educ* Bristol GS, Trinity Hall Cambridge (MA); *m* 6 Oct 1973, Worshipful (Doris) June Rodgers, *qv*, da of late James Rodgers, of Co Down, NI; 2 s (Edward Arthur, Henry William); *Career* called to the Bar Middle Temple 1970 (ad eundum Inner Temple 1979), Midland and Oxford Circuit until 1994; chm Cambridge Univ Cons Assoc 1969; Parly candidate (C): Warley West Oct 1974 and 1979, Ynys Môn (Anglesey) 1987, Monmouth by-election May 1991; MP (C) Monmouth 1992–, PPS to Jonathan Aitken March-July 1994, Parly under-sec of state Dept of Social Security 1994–; memb: Ecclesiastical Ctee of Parliament, Welsh Affairs Select Ctee 1992–94, pres: Cambridge Georgian Gp 1969, Cambridge Union 1970; memb Exec Ctee Friends of Friendless Churches 1983–; Freeman City of London 1976; *Recreations* gardening and architectural history; *Clubs* Carlton, Coningsby (chm 1976–77, treas 1983–87), Abergavenny Constitutional, Chepstow Cons, Monmouth Cons, Usk Cons; *Style—* Roger Evans, Esq, MP; ✉ House of Commons, London SW1A 0AA

EVANS, Ruth Elizabeth; *b* 12 Oct 1957; *Educ* Camden Sch for Girls, Girton Coll Cambridge (BA); *children* 1 da; *Career* co-ordinator Maternity Alliance 1981–86, dep dir then acting dir of MIND 1986–89, gen sec War on Want 1990, mgmnt conslt Dept of Health 1990–91, dir Nat Consumer Cncl 1992–; FRSA; *Style—* Ms Ruth Evans; ✉ National Consumer Council, 20 Grosvenor Gardens, London SW1W 0DH (☎ 0171 730 3469, fax 0171 730 0191)

EVANS, Sally Anne; da of Arthur Francis Gardiner Austin, and Joy, *née* Ravenor (d 1975); *b* 20 March 1948; *Educ* Darlington HS for Girls, Univ of Manchester (LLB); *m* July 1977, Richard Maurice Evans, s of late Maurice Evans; *Career* called to the Bar Gray's Inn 1971; Home Office: legal asst 1974–77, sr legal asst 1977–83, asst legal advsr 1983–95, dep legal advsr 1995–; *Recreations* theatre, cooking, summer gardening; *Style—* Mrs Sally Evans; ✉ Home Office, 50 Queen Anne's Gate, London SW1H 9AT (☎ 0171 273 2527, fax 0171 273 4075)

EVANS, Sarah Hauldys; da of Wyndham Bowen Evans, of Harrogate, Yorks, and Nancy Sarah, *née* Mills; *b* 4 March 1953; *Educ* King James' GS Knaresborough, Univ of Sussex (BA), Univ of Leicester (MA), Univ of Leeds (PGCE); *m* 1989, Andrew Romanis Fowler; 1 s (Kit Wyndam b 1993); *Career* asst teacher then head of English Leeds Girls' HS 1976–84, dep head Fulneck Girls' Sch Pudsey Yorks 1986–89; head: Friends' Sch Saffron Walden 1989–96, King Edward VI High Sch for Girls Birmingham 1996–; pres Guild of Friends in Educn 1991–92; memb Exec Ctee Boarding Schs' Assoc 1990–96 (vice chm 1995–96); SHMIS: memb Educn Ctee 1991–96, chair Educn Ctee 1992–96; non-exec dir Essex Ambulance Trust 1991–96; *Recreations* the arts; *Style—* Ms Sarah Evans; ✉ 38 Amesbury Road, Moseley, Birmingham B13 8LE (☎ 0121 449 4536); King Edward VI High School for Girls, Edgbaston, Park Road, Birmingham B15 2UB (☎ 0121 472 1834, fax 0121 471 3808)

EVANS, Siân Catherine; da of David Tudor Evans, of Nottington, Dorset, and Judith Anne, *née* Young; *b* 8 Jan 1963; *Educ* Weymouth GS, Bournemouth Sch of Art (Arts fndn dip), Cass Arts Faculty City of London Poly (BA); *m* Tara T Breen; *Career* jewellery designer; archaeological work experience Maiden Castle 1985, fndr Bell Lane Workshops 1986, first collection 1987 (subsequently twice annually), first exhbn (The British Designer Show) 1988 (seasonally since 1989), fndr memb London Works 1991– (exhbns at Janet Fitch Shop and The Smith Gallery Covent Garden 1992 and twice annually at Paris Fashion Week Premier Classe Exhibition), winter exhbn of works at The Barbican Centre 1992; various retail outlets throughout England (incl Harrods, Jess James and Whistles), and worldwide in USA, Canada, Japan, France, Spain, Germany, Holland and Belgium; *Style—* Ms Sian Evans; ✉ Sian Evans, 9 Bell Lane, Spitalfields, London E1 7LA (☎ 0171 377 6117)

EVANS, His Hon Judge Simon John; s of Dr Thomas Evans, of Bristol, and Dr Enid Allardice, *née* Taylour (d 1974); *b* 18 Jan 1937; *Educ* Diocesan Coll Cape Town S Africa, Inns of Ct Sch of Law; *m* 5 June 1968, Heather Wendy Champion, *née* Jones; 1 step da (Deborah Carol (Mrs Lahaise) b 4 Aug 1961), 1 s (Paul Michael b 29 July 1969); *Career* apprentice motor mechanic Public Works Dept N Rhodesia Govt Lusaka 1954, called to the Bar Middle Temple 1959, barr 4 Brick Ct Temple 1959–91, recorder (SE Circuit) 1989–91, circuit judge (SE Circuit) 1991–; memb: SE Circuit 1960–91, Surrey and S London Sessions Bar 1960–91, Criminal Bar Assoc 1973–91; *Recreations* Balinese cats, English footpaths, French studies; *Style—* His Hon Judge Simon Evans; ✉ Isleworth Crown Court, 36 Ridgeway Road, Isleworth, Middlesex TW7 5LP (☎ 0181 568 8811)

EVANS, Stephen Geoffrey; s of Eric Ward Evans (d 1984), and Madelane, *née* Cartledge (d 1982); *b* 23 Aug 1938; *Educ* Cheltenham Coll; *m* 2 June 1962, Valerie; 2 s (Nicholas b 1965, Christopher b 1967), 2 da (Harriet b 1969, Annabel b 1972); *Career* chartered surveyor; joined John Staite & Sons, sr ptnr until 1988 (when co sold to Prudential Property Services), ptnr Evans & Hardy Leamington Spa 1988–; High Sheriff of Warwickshire 1995–96; chm Warwicks Valuation Tbnl 1976, govr Kingsley Sch Leamington Spa 1980–, surveyor to Royal Agric Soc of Eng 1990–, memb Warwicks Probation Ctee 1992–, vice pres Leamington Spa RUFC; chm St Michael's PCC Weston-under-Wetherley, memb Deanery Synod, parish cncllr; past chm Leamington Round Table 1973; FRICS; *Recreations* sailing, fly fishing, tennis, gardening, golf, bridge; *Style—* Stephen Evans, Esq; ✉ The Glebe House, Weston under Wetherley, Leamington Spa, Warwickshire CV33 9BY (☎ 01926 632521); Evans & Hardy, Myton House, 40 Holly Walk, Leamington Spa, Warwickshire CV32 4HY (☎ 01926 888181, fax 01926 888018)

EVANS, Stephen Graham; s of William Campbell Evans, OBE, of Bradley Green, Redditch, Worcs, and Sarah Annie, *née* Duckworth; *b* 20 May 1944; *Educ* Northampton Town and Co GS, W Bromwich GS, Hall Green Tech Coll Birmingham, S Birmingham Tech Coll; *m* 11 May 1968, Gillian Kathleen, da of John Skidmore, and Winifred, *née* Felding; *Career* engr and sr engr Cooper MacDonald 1970–78, ptnr Peel and Fowler 1985– (sr engr and assoc 1979–85); FIStructE (former memb Cncl, chm CPD Forum, former chm Midland Co Branch), CEng, memb Assoc of Consulting Engrs 1986; *Recreations* sport, music, the arts, travel; *Style—* Stephen Evans, Esq; ✉ Peel and Fowler, Griffin House, Ludgate Hill, Birmingham B3 1DW (☎ 0121 236 7207, fax 0121 236 6918)

EVANS, Stuart John; s of John Redshaw Evans, and Mabel Elizabeth, *née* Brown (d 1974); *b* 31 Dec 1947; *Educ* Royal GS Newcastle upon Tyne, Univ of Leeds (LLB); *m* 2 Jan 1971, Margaret Elizabeth, da of Edgar John Evans (d 1966); 2 s (John Daniel b 1976, Thomas b 1977), 1 da (Elizabeth b 1983); *Career* articled clerk Stanley Brent & Co 1970–72, asst slr Slaughter and May 1972–79, ptnr Simmons & Simmons 1981– (asst slr 1979–80); memb Company Law Sub-Ctee City of London Law Soc; reader St Stephen's Church Canonbury; Freeman City of London Slrs' Co; *Books* A Practitioner's Guide to the Stock Exchange Yellow Book (contrib, 1996); *Recreations* squash, pictures; *Style—* Stuart Evans, Esq; ✉ Simmons & Simmons, 21 Wilson Street, London EC2M 2TX (☎ 0171 628 2020, fax 0171 628 2070, telex 888562 Simmon G)

EVANS, Prof Timothy William; s of Philip Charles Evans, of Endcliffe, Sheffield, and Mary Elizabeth, *née* Else; *b* 29 May 1954; *Educ* High Storrs GS Sheffield, Univ of Manchester (BSc, MB ChB), Univ of Sheffield (PhD), Univ of Calif San Francisco (MD), FRCP; *m* Dr Josephine Emir MacSweeney, da of Prof James MacSweeney (d 1972); 2 s (Charles James b 1990, Freddie William b 1993), 1 da (Verity Sarah Mary b 1995); *Career* Manchester Royal Infirmary 1980, Univ of Sheffield 1981, Royal Postgraduate Med Sch 1982, Nat Heart and Lung Inst 1982, Univ of Sheffield 1982–84, Univ of Calif San Francisco 1984–85, prof of intensive care med Imperial Coll Sch of Med Univ of London, conslt in intensive care/thoracic med Royal Brompton Hosp and Westminster London 1987–; *Publications* author of four books and over 150 chapters, invited articles and peer reviewed papers; *Recreations* flying and sailing; *Clubs* RSM; *Style—* Prof Timothy Evans; ✉ Department of Anaesthesia and Intensive Care, Royal Brompton Hospital NHS Trust, Sydney Street, London SW3 6NP (☎ 0171 351 8523, fax 0171 351 8524)

EVANS, Dr Trevor John; o s of Evan Alban (John) Evans, of Market Bosworth, Leics, and Margaret Alice, *née* Hilton; *b* 14 Feb 1947; *Educ* King's Sch Rochester, UCL (BSc, PhD); *m* 1973, Margaret Elizabeth, da of Felix Whitham, of Anlaby, Hull; 3 s (Thomas b 1979, Owen b 1984, Jacob b 1989), 1 da (Jessica b 1981); *Career* chem engr; chief exec Inst of Chem Engrs 1976–; jt sec-general Euro Fedn of Chem Engrg, former bd memb of Cncl of Sci and Technol Insts, memb Exec Ctee Cwlth Engrs Cncl; Kurnakov Meml Medal, Titanium ACHEMA Plaque; CEng, FIChemE, FIMgt; *Recreations* home renovation, travel; *Style—* Dr T J Evans; ✉ Davis Building, 165–189 Railway Terrace, Rugby, Warwickshire CV21 3HQ (☎ 01788 578214)

EVANS, Sir (William) Vincent John; GCMG (1976, KCMG 1970, CMG 1959), MBE (1945), QC (1973); s of Charles Herbert Evans (d 1978), and Elizabeth, *née* Jenkins (d 1965); *b* 20 Oct 1915; *Educ* Merchant Taylors' Northwood, Wadham Coll Oxford (BA, BCL, MA); *m* 4 Jan 1947, Joan Mary, da of Angus Bryant Symons (d 1964), of London; 1 s (David b 1950), 2 da (Marion b 1948, Jane b 1952); *Career* WWII Lt-Col GB and N Africa; called to the Bar Lincoln's Inn 1939 (hon bencher 1983); asst legal advsr FO 1947–54, legal cnsllr UK Perm Mission to UN NYC 1954–59, dep legal advsr FO 1960–68, legal advsr FCO 1968–75; chm Bryant Symons & Co 1964–85; UK rep: Cncl of Europe Ctee on Legal Co-operation 1965–75 (chm 1969–71), Steering Ctee on Human Rights 1976–80 (chm 1979–80); memb: Human Rights Ctee (set up under Int Covenant on Civil and Political Rights) 1976–84, Perm Ct of Arbitration 1987–; judge of Euro Ct of Human Rights 1980–91; hon fell Wadham Coll Oxford 1981, Hon DUniv Essex 1986; *Recreations* gardening; *Clubs* Athenaeum; *Style—* Sir Vincent Evans, GCMG, MBE, QC; ✉ 4 Bedford Road, Moor Park, Northwood, Middx HA6 2BB (☎ 01923 824085)

EVANS, William Anthony Lloyd (Bill); *b* 4 Feb 1924; *Educ* Aberdare Co Sch, Univ of Birmingham (BSc), Imperial Coll London, Univ of Wales (MSc, PhD); *m* 1949, Kathleen Evans, OBE, JP; 1 s (Wing Cdr C P A Evans b 1954); *Career* lectr and sr lectr in zoology 1946–86 and dean of sci UC Cardiff 1979–82, chief examiner in biology and zoology Welsh Jt Educn Ctee 1964–72, former memb Academic Bd and various Ctees Univ of Wales, former pres Cardiff Scientific Soc; athletics administrator; Cardiff Amateur Athletics Club: hon sec 1969–74, chm 1974–75, pres 1983–85; hon sec Welsh Amateur Athletics Assoc 1974–91, chm Br Amateur Athletics Bd 1980–84 (memb Cncl 1974–91); Amateur Athletics Assoc: memb Gen Ctee 1974–91, chm Sub Ctee on Amateur Status in Athletics 1980, chm Working Pty writing constitution for a Br Athletics Fedn 1988; chm Br Athletics Fedn 1991–93; memb Welsh Sports Cncl 1984–90 (memb Devpt Ctee 1981–84); chm: Ctee of Advsrs Welsh Sports Aid 1983–, Welsh Athletics Cncl 1987–89; hon sec Athletics Assoc of Wales 1989–91; Award of Honour for outstanding service to Welsh Amateur Athletics Assoc 1988; *Recreations* athletics; *Style—* Bill Evans, Esq; ✉ Winterbourne, 8 Greenway Close, Llandough, Penarth, South Glamorgan CF64 2LZ (☎ 01222 708102)

EVANS, William Devenport (Gwilym); s of William Owen Evans (d 1979), of Arafa Don, Benllech, and Cecily, *née* Devenport; *b* 18 April 1939; *Educ* Llangefni GS, Sunderland Tech Coll, Welsh Sch of Arch UWIST (DipArch); *m* 11 Aug 1962, Margaret; 2 s (Iwan Gwilym Devenport b 27 Nov 1964, Owain Devenport b 9 Jan 1973), 1 da (Gwenllian Devenport b 18 July 1966); *Career* architect; tech apprentice Richardson Westgarth Ltd Sunderland 1957–59, Architect's Dept Anglesey CC 1959–60, Welsh Sch of Arch Cardiff 1960–65, Ap Thomas Prydderch and Jones Architects 1965–70, ptnr Ap Thomas Partnership 1970–; pres: N Wales Soc of Architects 1987–89, Royal Soc of Architects in Wales 1993– (hon treas 1984–89); assoc Guild of Architects Schs, RIBA 1962, FRSA 1989; *Recreations* sailing, walking, choral singing, dry stone walling, travel in France; *Clubs* Llangefni Rotary; *Style—* Gwilym Evans, Esq; ✉ Bodhyfryd, Glanhwfa Road, Llangefni, Gwynedd LL77 7EU (☎ 01248 723002); Partneriaeth Ap Thomas Partnership, 42 Glanrafon, Bangor Gwynedd LL57 1LL (☎ 01248 362823, fax 01248 370203)

EVANS, Very Rev (John) Wyn; s of Ven David Eifion Evans, and Iris Elizabeth, *née* Gravelle (d 1973); *b* 4 Oct 1946; *Educ* Ardwyn GS Aberystwyth, UC Cardiff (BA), St Michael's Theol Coll Llandaff (BD), Jesus Coll Oxford; *Career* ordained deacon 1971, priest 1972; curate St Davids Dyfed 1971–72, minor canon St Davids Cathedral 1972–75, graduate student Jesus Coll Oxford 1975–77, permission to officiate Oxford Dio 1975–77, diocesan advsr on archives St Davids 1976–82, rector Llanfallteg with Castell Dwyran and Clunderwen with Henllan Amgoed and Llangan 1977–82, examining chaplain to Bishop of St Davids 1977, diocesan warden of ordinands 1978–83, diocesan dir of educn 1982–92; Trinity Coll Carmarthen: chaplain and lectr 1982–90, dean of chapel 1990–94, head Dept of Theology and Religious Studies 1991–94; St Davids Cathedral: hon canon 1988–90, canon (4th cursal) 1990–94, dean and precentor 1994–; FSA 1989, FRHistS 1994; *Publications* St Davids Cathedral 1181–1981 (with Roger Worsley, 1981), contrib to various jls incl Jl of Welsh Ecclesiastical History, Carmarthen Antiquary, Diwinyddiaeth; *Recreations* reading, music, antiquities; *Style—* The Very Rev J Wyn Evans, FSA; ✉ The Deanery, The Close, St Davids, Dyfed SA62 6RH (☎ 01437 720202, fax 01437 721885)

EVANS, Rev (Charles) Wyndham; s of late William Lloyd Evans, of Brookside Cottage, Corwen, and late Ada Henrietta, *née* Wright; *b* 16 Oct 1928; *Educ* Bala Church in Wales Sch, Bala GS, Univ Coll of N Wales (BA), St Catherine's Coll Oxford (BA, MA), St Stephen's House Oxford; *m* 2 Aug 1961, Sheila Huw, da of Hugh Jones, JP, MBE (d 1975), of Fern Bank, Llanfairfechan, Gwynedd; 1 s (Johnathan b 1966), 1 da (Helen b 1965); *Career* ordained: deacon 1952, priest 1953; curate Denbigh 1952–55, chaplain and housemaster Llandovery Coll 1955–67, chaplain and sr lectr in educn Trinity Coll Carmarthen 1967–79, vicar Llanrhaeadr YC 1979–, chaplain Ruthin Sch 1979–86, rural dean Denbigh 1984–, chaplain to the High Sheriff of Clwyd 1992–93; tstee St Mary's Tst, memb Welsh Nat Religious Educn Centre Bangor; *Books* Bible Families (1965); *Style—* The Rev Wyndham Evans; ✉ The Vicarage, Llanrhaeadr, Denbigh, Clwyd LL16 4NN (☎ 01745 890250); Parciau, 12 The Close, Llanfairfechan, Gwynedd (☎ 01248 681766)

EVANS, (John) Wynford; CBE; s of Gwilym Everton Evans, of Llanelli (d 1968), and Margaret Mary Elfreda, *née* Jones (d 1982); *b* 3 Nov 1934; *Educ* Llanelli GS, St John's Coll Cambridge (MA); *m* 20 April 1957, Sigrun, da of Gerhard Brethfeld; 3 s (Mark, Chris, Tim); *Career* dep chm London Electricity 1977–84; chm: South Wales Electricity plc (Swalec) 1984–95, The National Grid Holding plc 1994–95, Bank of Wales 1995– (dir 1989–); dir Welsh Nat Opera 1988–93; memb Welsh Language Bd 1988–89, dep chm Prince of Wales Ctee 1989–96; tstee and dep chm Cardiff Bay Opera House Tst 1994–; High Sheriff S Glamorgan 1995–96; Liveryman Worshipful Co of Tin Plate Workers; *Recreations* fly-fishing, cross-country skiing, golf; *Clubs* Fly-fishers, Cardiff & County, Wales Livery Guild, London Welsh; *Style—* Wynford Evans, Esq, CBE; ✉ Bank of Wales, Kingsway, Cardiff CF1 4YB

EVANS-BEVAN, David Gawain; s and h of Sir Martyn Evans-Bevan, 2 Bt, *qv*; *b* 16 Sept 1961; *m* 7 Nov 1987, Philippa Alice, yst da of Patrick Sweeney, of East Moors, Helmsley, N Yorks; 1 s (Patrick David b 9 Feb 1994), 1 da (Alice Laura b 14 Oct 1989); *Style—* David Evans-Bevan, Esq

EVANS-BEVAN, Sir Martyn Evan; 2 Bt (UK 1958), of Cadoxton-juxta-Neath, Co Glamorgan; s of Sir David Martyn Evans-Bevan, 1 Bt (d 1973), and Eira Winifred, *née* Glanley; *b* 1 April 1932; *Educ* Uppingham; *m* 12 Oct 1957, Jennifer Jane Marion, da of Robert Hugh Stevens, of Lady Arbour, Eardisley, Herefords; 4 s (David Gawain b 1961, Richard Martyn b 1963, Thomas Rhydian b 1966, Huw Evan b 1971); *Heir* s, David Gawain Evans-Bevan, *qv*; *Career* High Sheriff of Breconshire 1967–68, Freeman of City of London, Liveryman Worshipful Co of Farmers; company dir; *Clubs* Carlton; *Style—* Sir Martyn Evans-Bevan, Bt; ✉ Felinnewydd, Llandefalle, Brecon, Powys

EVANS-FREKE, Hon John Anthony; 2 s of 11 Baron Carbery, *qv*; *b* 9 May 1949; *Educ* Downside, RAC Cirencester; *m* 1972, Veronica Jane, yst da of Maj Eric Williams, of House of Lynturk, Alford, Aberdeenshire; 2 s (James Eric b 1976, Charles William Anthony b 1981), 1 da (Flora Mary b 1979); *Career* Cluttons Chartered Surveyors 1975–84 (ptnr 1980–), ptnr Humberts Chartered Surveyors 1984–88, head agent to Northumberland Estates 1988–92, managing ptnr Laxtons Chartered Surveyors; FRICS; *Style—* The Hon John Evans-Freke; ✉ Lynturk Home Farm, Alford, Aberdeenshire AB33 8DU (☎ 01975 562504); Blairs Estate Office, Aberdeen (☎ 01224 867626)

EVANS-FREKE, Hon Michael Peter; s and h of 11 Baron Carbery; *b* 11 Oct 1942; *Educ* Downside, Christ Church Oxford (MA), Strathclyde Univ (MBA), King's Coll London (PGCE); *m* 9 Sept 1967, Claudia Janet Elizabeth, o da of late Capt Percy Lionel

Cecil Gurney, of Little Chart, Penshurst, Kent; 1 s (Dominic Ralfe Cecil b 1969), 3 da (Richenda Clare b 1971, Isabel Lucy b 1973, Anna-Louise Rachel b 1979); *Style*— The Hon Michael Evans-Freke; ✉ 3 Westmead, Rock Road, Chilcompton, Bath BA3 4HX (☎ 01761 233062, fax 01761 233051)

EVANS-LOMBE, Hon Mr Justice; Hon Sir Edward Christopher; only s of Vice Adm Sir Edward Evans-Lombe, KCB, JP, DL (himself gs of Rev Henry Lombe, who took the name Lombe *vice* Evans 1862 under the terms of the will of his great-uncle, Sir John Lombe, 1 Bt. Sir John was bro of Mary, the Rev Henry's mother, who m Thomas Browne Evans). The surname of the Admiral's f, Alexander, became Evans Lombe following the marriage of his f with a cousin, Louisa Evans; *b* 10 April 1937; *Educ* Eton, Trinity Coll Cambridge; *m* 1964, Frances Marilyn, er da of Robert Ewen Mackenzie, of Lincoln; 1 s, 3 da; *Career* served Royal Norfolk Regt 1955–57, 2 Lt; called to the Bar Inner Temple 1963, standing counsel to Dept of Trade in Bankruptcy Matters 1971, QC 1978, recorder SE Circuit 1982–93, judge of the High Court of Justice (Chancery Div) 1993–; chm Agric Land Tbnl SE Area 1983; Master of the Bench Inner Temple 1985; *Style*— The Hon Mr Justice Evans-Lombe; ✉ Royal Courts of Justice, Strand, London WC2A 2LL

EVANS LOMBE, Capt Peter Michael; s of Maj John Michael Evans Lombe, MC (d 1938), and Patricia Routledge, *née* Gibson (d 1992); *b* 5 June 1933; *Educ* Wellington Coll, RMA Sandhurst; *m* 1964, Vera-Alexandra, da of Laurens Rijnhart Boissevain (d 1986), of Monte Carlo; 2 s (James Nicholas b 1967, Charles Patrick Laurens b 1971); *Career* Army 1951–60, cmmnd 3 Carabiniers Prince of Wales Dragon Gds 1953, 15/19 Kings Royal Hussars 1954, resigned 1960; ptnr Kitcat and Aitken Stockbrokers 1960–83, memb Stock Exchange (resigned 1983); dir: Hambros Bank 1983–93, Smith and Williamson Securities 1993–; Liveryman Worshipful Co of Skinners; *Recreations* fishing, shooting, sailing, golf; *Clubs* White's, Swinley Forest Golf, Royal West Norfolk GC; *Style*— Capt Peter Evans Lombe; ✉ 10 Child's St, London SW5 9RY (☎ 0171 370 5381); Roydon Lodge, Roydon, nr King's Lynn, Norfolk (☎ 01485 600215); Smith and Williamson Securities, 1 Riding House Street, London W1 (☎ 0171 637 5377, fax 0171 631 0741)

EVARISTI, Marcella Silvia; da of Louis Evaristi, and Marcella, *née* Visocchi; *b* 19 July 1953; *Educ* Notre Dame HS, Univ of Glasgow (MA); *m* 28 Jan 1982, (John) Michael Boyd, s of Dr John Truesdale Boyd; 1 s (Daniel b 25 Nov 1988), 1 da (Gabriella (twin) b 1988); *Career* playwright; plays incl: Dorothy and The Bitch 1976, Scotia's Darlings 1978, Hard to Get 1980 (Granada TV, 1983), Wedding Belles and Green Grasses 1981, Eve Set the Balls of Corruption Rolling 1982 (BBC Play for Today and winner of Pye Award for Best Writer New to TV 1982), Commedia 1982 (nominated Evening Standard Award Best Play by Newcomer 1982), Checking Out 1984, There's Something About A Convent Girl (1991); radio plays incl: The Works 1985, The Hat 1988, Terrestrial Extras 1985, The Theory and Practice of Rings 1992, Troilus and Cressida and Da di Da di Da 1992; playwright in residence: Univ of St Andrews 1979–80, Univ of Glasgow 1984–85, Univ of Strathclyde 1984–85; fell in creative writing Univ of Sheffield 1982–84; *Books* contrib: Delighting the Heart: A Notebook of Women Writers (1989), Plays without Wires (1989), There's Something about Convent School Girls (1991); *Style*— Marcella Evaristi

EVE, Trevor John; s of Stewart Frederick Eve, of Staffordshire, and Elsie, *née* Hamer; *b* 1 July 1951; *Educ* Bromsgrove Sch Worcs, Kingston Art Coll, RADA; *m* 1 March 1980, Sharon Patricia Maughan, da of Francis Maughan, of Holland Park, London; 1 da (Alice b 6 Feb 1982), 2 s ((James Jonathan) Jack b 23 Sept 1985, George Francis b 7 March 1994); *Career* actor; memb Ctee Br Deaf Assoc; *Theatre* incl: Children of a Lesser God (best actor) 1981, The Genius (Royal Court) 1983, High Society (NT) 1986, Man Beast and Virtue (NT) 1989, The Winter's Tale (Young Vic) 1991, Inadmissable Evidence (RNT) 1993, Uncle Vanya (Albery) 1996; *Television* incl: Shoestring (best actor) 1980, Jamaica Inn, A Sense of Guilt 1990, Parnell and the Englishwoman 1991, A Doll's House 1991, The Politician's Wife (Channel 4) 1995, Black Easter (Screen Two) 1995; *Film* incl: Hindle Wakes 1976, Dracula, A Wreath of Roses, The Corsican Brothers, Aspen Extreme, Psychotherapy, The Knight's Tale, The Tribe; *Recreations* polo, golf, tennis; *Clubs* Queen's, Hurlingham, St James's, Wentworth; *Style*— Trevor Eve, Esq; ✉ c/o ICM Ltd, Oxford House, 76 Oxford Street, London W1N 0AX (☎ 0171 636 6565, fax 0171 323 0101)

EVELEIGH, Rt Hon Sir Edward Walter; kt (1968), ERD, PC (1977); s of Walter William Eveleigh (d 1952), and Daisy Emily Eveleigh (d 1989); *b* 8 Oct 1917; *Educ* Peter Symonds Sch Winchester, BNC Oxford (MA); *m* 1, 1940, Vilma Bodnar; *m* 2, 1953, Patricia Helen Margaret (d 1990), da of Marcel and Doris Bury; 2 s (and 1 s decd); *Career* Cmmnd RA (SR) 1936, served WWII (despatches), Maj; called to the Bar Lincoln's Inn 1945, QC 1961, recorder Burton-upon-Trent 1961–64, recorder Gloucester 1964–68, bencher Lincoln's Inn 1968, judge High Court of Justice (Queen's Bench) 1968–77, presiding judge SE Circuit 1971–76, Lord Justice of Appeal 1977–85; memb Royal Cmmn on Criminal Procedure 1978–80; pres: Br-German Jurists' Assoc 1974–85, Bar Musical Soc 1980–89; chm Statute Law Soc 1985–90, treas Lincoln's Inn 1988; Liveryman Worshipful Co of Gunmakers; *Clubs* Garrick; *Style*— The Rt Hon Sir Edward Eveleigh, ERD

EVENNETT, David Anthony; MP (C) Erith and Crayford (majority 2,339); s of Norman Thomas Evennett, and Irene Evennett; *b* 3 June 1949; *Educ* Buckhurst Hill Co HS for Boys, LSE (MSc Econ); *m* 1975, Marilyn Anne, da of Ronald Stanley Smith; 2 s (Mark, Thomas); *Career* sch teacher 1972–74; Lloyds: broker 1974–81, memb 1976–92, dir Underwriting Agency 1982–91; memb Redbridge BC 1974–78, Parly candidate (C) Hackney S and Shoreditch 1979, MP (C) Erith and Crayford 1983–, memb Select Ctee on Educn, Sci and the Arts 1986–92; PPS: to Lady Blatch (Min of State at Dept of Educn) 1992–93, to John Redwood (Sec of State for Wales) 1993–95, to David Maclean and Lady Blatch (Mins of State at Home Office) 1995–96, to Rt Hon Gillian Shepherd (Sec of State for Education and Employment) 1996–; prospective Parly candidate (C) Bexleyheath and Crayford 1995; *Recreations* family, reading novels and biographies, cinema, going to theatre; *Clubs* Priory (Belvedere), Bexleyheath Cons; *Style*— David Evennett, Esq, MP; ✉ House of Commons, London SW1A 0AA

EVENS, Mark David; s of Ronald Clarence Evens, of Hawridge Common, Nr Chesham, Bucks and Rita Laura, *née* Meeks; *b* 13 Dec 1953; *Educ* Dr Challoners GS Amersham, Exeter Coll Oxford (exhibitioner, BA, MA); *m* 17 Sept 1977, Alison, da of George William Brown; 1 s (David Anthony b 17 June 1984), 1 da (Heather Frances b 6 May 1987); *Career* articled clerk Arthur Young McClelland Moores & Co 1975, qualified CA 1978, ptnr Arthur Young 1985 (mangr 1981), nat dir of information systems audit Ernst & Young (following merger) 1989–; FCA 1988 (ACA 1978); *Recreations* gliding, running, brewing; *Style*— Mark Evens, Esq; ✉ Ernst & Young, Rolls House, 7 Rolls Buildings, Fetter Lane, London EC4A 1NH (direct ☎ 0171 931 1388)

EVENS, Ven Robert John Scott; s of Reginald Evens, of Bristol, and Sheila, *née* Scott (d 1995); *b* 29 May 1947; *Educ* Maidstone GS, Trinity Coll Bristol (DipTh); *m* 1972, Susan, *née* Hayes; 1 s (Tom b 1979), 1 da (Claire b 1982); *Career* archdeacon of Bath 1995–; ACIB; *Recreations* swimming, caravanning; *Style*— The Ven the Archdeacon of Bath; ✉ 56 Grange Road, Saltford, Bristol BS18 3AG (☎ 01225 873609, fax 01225 874110)

EVERALL, Mark Andrew; QC (1994); s of John Dudley Everall, of London, and Pamela, *née* Odone; *b* 30 June 1950; *Educ* Ampleforth, Lincoln Coll Oxford (MA); *m* 16 Dec 1978, (Elizabeth) Anne, da of Thomas Hugh Richard Perkins; 2 da (Cecily Rose Frederika b 23 July 1990, Isobel Maria Constance b 25 Jan 1992); *Career* called to the Bar Inner Temple 1975; *Style*— Mark Everall, Esq, QC; ✉ 1 Mitre Court Buildings, Temple, London EC4 (☎ 0171 797 7070, fax 0171 797 7435)

EVERARD, John Vivian; s of William Ralph Everard, and Margaret Nora Jennifer, *née* Massey; *b* 24 Nov 1956; *Educ* King Edward VI Sch Lichfield, Emmanuel Coll Cambridge (William Turner Hunter bursary, MA), Peking Univ, Manchester Business Sch (MBA); *m* April 1990, Heather Ann, da of late William Starkey; *Career* HM Dip Serv; Far Eastern Dept FCO 1979–81, third sec Peking 1981–83, second sec Vienna 1983–84, Manchester Business Sch 1984–86, project conslt Metapraxis Ltd 1986–87, S America Dept FCO 1987–90, head Commercial Section Santiago 1990–93, chargé d'affaires then ambass Minsk 1993–95, OSCE Mission to Bosnia and Herzegovina 1995–96, Africa Dept (Equatorial) FCO 1996–; *Recreations* travel, cats; *Style*— John Vivian Everard, Esq; ✉ c/o Foreign & Commonwealth Office, King Charles Street, London SW1A 2AH

EVERARD, Richard Anthony Spencer; s of Maj Richard Peter Michael Spencer (d 1990), of Rotherby Grange, Melton Mowbray, Leicestershire, and Bettyne Ione, formerly Lady Newtown Butler (d 1989); *b* 31 March 1954; *Educ* Eton, RMA Sandhurst; *m* 9 May 1981, Caroline Anne, da of Reginald J Tower Hill, of Holfield Grange, Coggeshall, Essex; 1 s (Julian b 1989), 1 da (Charlotte b 1985); *Career* Royal Horse Guards 1st Dragoons (Blues and Royals) 1973–77, cmmnd 1973, Lt 1975; chm: Everards Brewery Ltd 1985– (dir 1983–), Leicester Promotions Ltd; pres Age Concern Leicestershire; Dip in Company Direction IOD; memb Ct of Assts Worshipful Co of Brewers; *Recreations* shooting, skiing, cricket, flying helicopters, motorcycling, golf; *Clubs* Eton Ramblers, Cavalry & Guards, Helicopter Club of GB, The Air Squadron, Leicestershire Golf; *Style*— Richard Everard, Esq; ✉ East Farndon Hall, Market Harborough, Leicestershire LE16 9SE; Everards Brewery Ltd, Castle Acres, Narborough, Leicestershire LE9 5BY (☎ 0116 281 4100, fax 0116 289 1970)

EVERARD, Sir Robin Charles; 4 Bt (UK 1911), of Randlestown, Co Meath; s of Lt-Col Sir Nugent Henry Everard, 3 Bt (d 1984), and Frances Audrey, *née* Jesson (d 1975); *b* 5 Oct 1939; *Educ* Harrow, Sandhurst; *m* 28 Sept 1963, Ariel Ingrid, eldest da of Col Peter Cleasby-Thompson, MBE, MC (d 1981), of Blackhill House, Little Cressingham, Norfolk; 1 s (Henry Peter Charles b 1970), 2 da (Catherine Mary b 1964, Victoria Frances b 1966); *Heir* s, Henry Peter Charles Everard b 6 Aug 1970; *Career* three year cmmn Duke of Wellington's Regt; md P Murray-Jones Ltd 1961–75, mgmnt conslt 1975–; *Style*— Sir Robin Everard, Bt; ✉ Church Farm, Shelton, Long Stratton, Norwich NR15 2SB

EVERARD, Simon; TD (1967), DL (Leics 1984); s of Charles Miskin Everard (d 1953), and Monica Mary Barford (d 1970), of Werrington Hall, Peterborough; *b* 30 Oct 1928; *Educ* Uppingham, Clare Coll Cambridge; *m* 1955, Joceline Margaret, da of Francis Jaime Wormold Holt (d 1985), of Seaview, IOW; 3 s (Nicholas b 1956, Mark b 1958, James b 1962), 1 da (Serena b 1967); *Career* Capt Leics and Derbys Yeo TA; chm Ellis & Everard plc (industl chemical distributor) 1980–90 and 1992–93 (hon pres 1994–), chm Alliance and Leicester Building Society (formerly Leicester Building Society) 1994– (vice chm 1982–94); non-exec dir Croda International PLC 1991–; *Recreations* shooting, gardening, tennis; *Clubs* Cavalry & Guards; *Style*— Simon Everard, Esq, TD, DL; ✉ Sludge Hall, Cold Newton, Billesdon, Leics LE7 9DA; Alliance & Leicester Building Society, 49 Park Lane, London W1Y 4EQ (☎ 0171 629 6661, fax 0171 408 1399)

EVERARD, Timothy John; CMG (1978); s of Charles Miskin Everard (d 1953), of Peterborough, and Monica Mary, *née* Barford (d 1970); *b* 22 Oct 1929; *Educ* Uppingham, Magdalen Coll Oxford (BA); *m* 23 July 1955, Josiane, da of Alexander Romano (d 1970), of Alexandria; 2 s (Timothy Charles b 1958, Alexander John b 1964), 2 da (Anne-Marie b 1956, Catherine Alison b 1960); *Career* Barclays Bank (Egypt, Sudan, Kenya, Zaire) 1952–62, dir Ellis & Everard Ltd 1966–67; HM Dip Serv: first sec FO 1962–64, first sec Bangkok 1964–66, FCO 1967–68, first sec Br Political Residency Bahrain 1969–72, consul gen and chargé d'affaires Hanoi 1972–73, cnsllr Athens 1974–78, cnsllr Paris 1978–81, min High Cmmn Lagos 1981–84, ambass E Berlin 1984–88, ret; sec gen Order of St John 1988–93, tstee Dresden Tst 1994–; Freeman City of London 1991; AIB; KStJ 1988; *Recreations* golf, tennis; *Clubs* Reform; *Style*— Timothy Everard, Esq, CMG; ✉ Leagues, Burnt Oak, Crowborough, E Sussex TN6 3SD (☎ 01892 653278)

EVERED, Dr David Charles; s of Thomas Charles Evered (d 1959), of Bannatyne, Furzefield Road, Beaconsfield, Bucks, and Enid Christian, *née* Frost; *b* 21 Jan 1940; *Educ* Cranleigh Sch, Middx Hosp Med Sch Univ of London (BSc, MB BS, MD); *m* 6 June 1964, Anne Elizabeth Massey (Kit), da of John Massey Lings (d 1944), of Bolton, Lancashire; 1 s (Alexander b 1975), 2 da (Elizabeth b 1966, Susanna b 1969); *Career* dir Ciba Fndn 1978–88, second sec MRC 1988–96, conslt physician Royal Victoria Infirmary Newcastle upon Tyne; memb: Assoc of Med Res Charities Ctee 1980–84 (vice chm 1987–88), St George's Hosp Med Sch Cncl 1983–91 (memb Fin Ctee 1984–91), Fndn Louis Jeantet de Médecine Geneva 1984–91 (vice pres Sci Ctee 1984–91), Zoological Soc of London (memb Cncl 1985–89), Scientists Inst for Public Info New York MRS Advsy Ctee 1985–, Governing Cncl Int Agency for Research on Cancer 1988–, Hammersmith and Queen Charlotte's Special Health Authy 1989–94; dir Hammersmith Hosps Tst 1995–; Freeman City of London 1983, Liveryman Worshipful Soc of Apothecaries; FRCP, FRSM (Med), FZS, FIBiol; *Books* Diseases of the Thyroid (1976), Atlas of Endocrinology (with R Hall 1979, 2 edn 1990), Collaboration in Medical Research in Europe (with M O'Connor, 1981); *Recreations* tennis, sailing, golf, reading, history; *Clubs* Oake Manor Golf; *Style*— Dr David Evered; ✉ Whitehall Cottage, Whitehall Lane, Checkendon, South Oxfordshire (☎ 01491 680737)

EVEREST, Dr David Anthony; s of George Charles Everest (d 1957), of Kenton, Middx, and Ada Bertha, *née* Wheddon (d 1950); *b* 18 Sept 1926; *Educ* Lower Sch of John Lyon Harrow, UCL (BSc, PhD); *m* 31 March 1956, Audrey Pauline, da of Reginald Holford Sheldrick, of Herts; 3 s (Peter Lindsey b 1958, Michael David b 1960, Richard Martin b 1966); *Career* environmental scientist; lectr in chemistry Battersea Poly 1949–56, princ sci offr Nat Chemical Laboratory 1958–64 (sr sci offr 1956–58), dep chief sci offr Nat Physical Laboratory 1970–77 (sr princ sci offr 1964–70), dep chief sci offr RTP Div Dept of Indust 1977–79, chief sci offr environmental pollution DOE 1979–86 (also dir of sci res policy 1983–86); visiting res fell Dept of Environmental Sciences Univ of East Anglia 1986–91, res assoc UK Centre for Econ and Environmental Devpt 1987–; ed Energy and Environment; *Publications* incl: The Chemistry of Beryllium (1964), chapter on beryllium in Comprehensive Inorganic Chemistry (1972), The Greenhouse Effect: Issues for Policy Makers (1988), The Provision of Expert Advice to Government on Environmental Matters: The Role of Advisory Committees (1990), chapter on Environmental and Natural Resources in Science and Technology in the United Kingdom (1991), The Government Sector in Environmental Dilemmas: Ethics and Decisions (1993); numerous papers and patents in inorganic chemistry, materials science, thermal plasmas energy conservation and the environment; *Recreations* walking; *Style*— Dr David Everest; ✉ Beech Boles, Quarry Wood, Cookham Dean, Berks SL6 9UA (☎ 01628 487390); Gazebo Cottage, High St, Porlock, Somerset TA24 8PS (☎ 01643 862393)

EVEREST, Richard Anthony; s of Cecil Carlyle Everest (d 1974), of Barton-on-Sea, and Dorothy Helen, *née* Soldan (d 1996); *b* 26 April 1938; *Educ* Highgate Sch, ChCh Oxford (MA); *m* 9 August 1969, Brenda Anne, da of Frederick John Ralph, of Westdene, Brighton; 2 s (Timothy b 1971, Philip b 1974); *Career* served RCS 1956–58; accountant; articled clerk Pridie Brewster and Gold 1962–66, audit sr Black Geoghegan and Till 1966–70, asst mangr Layton-Bennett Billingham and Co 1970–74, audit gp mangr Josolyne Layton-Bennett and Co 1974–79, princ mangr Arthur Young McClelland

Moores and Co 1979–82, dir and sec Henry G Nicholson (Underwriting) Ltd (Lloyd's membs' agents) 1986–91, dir Bell Nicholson Henderson Ltd (Lloyd's reinsurance brokers) 1987–93 (gp chief accountant 1982–93), dir (fin and admin) UIA (Insurance) Ltd 1994–; underwriting memb Lloyd's 1986–96; hon treas Friends of Herts County Youth Band 1987–95, govr Townsend C of E Sch 1993–; Freeman City of London 1959, memb Ct of Assts Worshipful Co of Cutlers (Freeman 1959, Master 1990); ACA 1966, FCA 1976; *Recreations* travel, swimming; *Style—* Richard Everest, Esq; ✉ 2 Palfrey Close, St Albans, Herts AL3 5RE (☎ 01727 835550)

EVERETT, HE Bernard Jonathan; s of late Arnold Edwin Everett, of Adderbury, Oxon, and Helene May, *née* Heine; *b* 17 Sept 1943; *Educ* King's Coll Sch Wimbledon, Lincoln Coll Oxford (BA); *m* 1 Oct 1970, (Maria) Olinda, *née* Goncalves de Albuquerque, da of Raul Correia de Albuquerque, of Faro, Portugal; 2 s (Christopher b 1980, Edward b 1981), 2 da (Caroline b 1974, Diana b 1976 d 1979); *Career* Dip Serv 1966–: third (later second) sec Lisbon 1967–71, consul Luanda 1975, first sec and head of chancery Lusaka 1978–80, consul (commercial) Rio de Janeiro 1980–83, asst head Information Dept FCO 1983–84, head Sub Saharan Africa Branch DTI 1984–87, ambass Guatemala 1987–91, consul gen Houston 1991–95, high cmmr Mozambique Jan 1996–; *Recreations* reading, the performing arts, tennis, horses; *Style—* HE Mr Bernard Everett; ✉ c/o FCO (Maputo), King Charles Street, London SW1A 2AH

EVERETT, Charles William Vogt; s of Dr Thomas Everett (d 1976), and Ingeborg, *née* Vogt (d 1971); *b* 15 Oct 1949; *Educ* Bryanston, Univ of Reading; *m* 1978, Elizabeth Vanessa, *née* Ellis; 3 s; *Career* Lord Chancellor's Dept: joined 1971, asst private sec to the Lord Chancellor 1974–76, seconded to Dept of Tport 1982–84, Legal Aid Bill Div 1987–88, sec to Legal Aid Bd 1988–89, Central Unit 1990–91, head Policy and Legal Services Gp 1991–95, dir of fin and admin The Court Service 1995–; *Style—* Charles Everett, Esq; ✉ The Court Service, Southside, 105 Victoria Street, London SW1E 6QT (☎ 0171 210 1696, fax 0171 210 1739, e-mail cc87@dial.pipex.com)

EVERETT, Christopher Harris Doyle; CBE (1988); s of late Alan Doyle Everett, MBE (d 1987), of Leatherhead, Surrey, and Annabel Dorothy Joan (Nancy), *née* Harris (d 1991); *b* 20 June 1933; *Educ* Winchester, New Coll Oxford (exhibitioner, BA); *m* 6 Aug 1955, Hilary Anne (Billy), da of Maj Raymond Gildea Robertson, DSO (two bars) (d 1954), of Ashtead and Farnham; 2 s (Charles b 7 May 1959, Nicholas b 31 May 1962), 2 da (Victoria b 30 Jan 1958, Alexandra b 2 Dec 1965); *Career* Nat Serv 2 Lt 1 Bn Grenadier Gds Windsor and London; HM Dip Serv: MECAS Lebanon 1957–59, Br Embassy Beirut 1959–61, Personnel Dept FO 1962–63, private sec to Ambass then first sec Chancery HM Embassy Washington 1963–67, planning staff FCO 1967–70; headmaster: Worksop Coll 1970–75, Tonbridge Sch 1975–89; dir-gen Daiwa Anglo-Japanese Foundation 1990–; JP: Nottinghamshire 1972–75, Kent 1976–89; chm HMC 1986; Liveryman Worshipful Co of Skinners; Hon FCP 1988; *Recreations* walking, current affairs; *Style—* Christopher Everett, Esq, CBE; ✉ Daiwa Anglo-Japanese Foundation, Daiwa Foundation Japan House, 13–14 Cornwall Terrace, London NW1 4QP (☎ 0171 486 4348, fax 0171 486 2914)

EVERETT, John; *b* 1947; *Educ* Univ of London (BSc Econ), ACMA; *Career* early career in fin planning with Fisons, British Steel and Bowater, latterly corp planning mangr British Leyland; currently ptnr i/c Deloitte & Touche Consulting Group (formerly Touche Ross) (joined 1978); *Style—* John Everett, Esq; ✉ Deloitte & Touche Consulting Group, Stonecutter Court, 1 Stonecutter Street, London EC4A 4TR (☎ 0171 936 3000, fax 0171 583 8517)

EVERETT, Martin Thomas; s of Dr Thomas Everett (d 1975), and Ingeborg Maria, *née* Vogt; *b* 24 Sept 1939; *Educ* Bryanston; *m* 14 Sept 1963, Susan Mary, da of John Peter Sworder, MC, TD (d 1987); 2 s (Oliver b 2 July 1965, George b 8 Sept 1967), 1 da (Daisy b 14 May 1975); *Career* Nat Serv 2 Lt 9/12 Royal Lancers 1959–61; Mayor Sworder and Co Ltd Wine Shippers: joined 1962, dir 1967, jt md 1974, md 1980; dir J T Davies & Sons 1995–; tstee St Olaves Southwark Church Act of 1918; Freeman City of London, Liveryman Worshipful Co of Glass Sellers (memb Ct of Assts), Liveryman Worshipful co of Vintners; memb Inst of Masters of Wine 1968; *Recreations* gardening, walking; *Style—* Martin Everett, Esq; ✉ Mayor Sworder & Co Ltd, 7 Aberdeen Road, Croydon, Surrey CR0 1EQ (☎ 0181 686 1155, fax 0181 686 2017)

EVERETT, Oliver William; CVO (1991, LVO 1980); s of Walter George Charles Everett, MC, DSO (d 1979), of Bognor Regis, and Gertrude Florence Rothwell, *née* Hellicar; *b* 28 Feb 1943; *Educ* Felsted Sch Essex, Western Res Acad Ohio USA, Christ's Coll Cambridge (MA), Fletcher Sch of Law & Diplomacy Tufts Univ Mass USA (MA), LSE; *m* 28 Aug 1965, Theffania, da of Lt Robert Vesey Stoney (d 1944), of Rosturk Castle, Co Mayo, Ireland; 2 s (Toby b 1979, William b 1982), 2 da (Kathleen b 1966, Grania b 1969); *Career* Dip Serv: first sec Br High Cmmn New Delhi 1969–73, first sec FCO 1973–78, asst private sec to HRH The Prince of Wales 1978–80, head Chancery Br Embassy Madrid 1980–81, private sec to HRH The Princess of Wales and comptroller to TRH The Prince and Princess of Wales 1981–83, asst librarian Windsor Castle 1984, librarian and asst keeper of the Queen's Archives Windsor Castle 1985–; *Recreations* skiing, rackets, windsurfing, baseball; *Clubs* Ski Club of GB; *Style—* Oliver Everett, Esq, CVO; ✉ Garden House, Windsor Castle, Berks SL4 1NG (☎ 01753 833711); The East Wing, Kirtlington Pk, Oxon OX5 3JN (☎ 01869 350589); The Royal Library, Windsor Castle, Berks SL4 1NJ (☎ 01753 868286, fax 01753 854910)

EVERETT, Peter; s of Henry Everett (d 1984), of Edinburgh, and Kathleen Isabel, *née* Cuddeford (d 1961); *b* 24 Sept 1931; *Educ* George Watson's Boys' Coll Edinburgh, Univ of Edinburgh; *m* 1 Oct 1955, Annette Patricia, da of George Edward Hyde (d 1988), of London; 1 da (Judith Anne b 1957), 3 s (David b 1959, Michael b 1962, John b 1964); *Career* Nat Serv RE 1953–55, 2 Lt 1954; Shell International Petroleum Co 1955–89: trainee engr The Hague 1955, petroleum engr Indonesia 1957–61, prodn engr Brunei 1961–64 (petroleum engr 1961–63), sr prodn engr Trinidad 1964–67, exploration and prodn economist Projects and Agreements Dept The Hague 1968–69, chief petroleum engr Brunei 1970–72, gen ops mangr Nigeria 1977–79 (petroleum engr mangr 1972–76, divnl mangr Western Div 1976–77), md Brunei 1979–84; md: Shell UK Ltd 1984–89, Shell UK Exploration and Prodn 1984–89; memb: Cncl UK Offshore Operators' Assoc, Dept of Energy's Offshore Energy Bd; memb Advsy Bd Petroleum Engrg Depts: Heriot-Watt Univ, Imperial Coll London; dir: Forth Ports plc 1989–, Scottish Hydro Electric plc 1990–, Ramco Energy Ltd 1993–, Edinburgh Java Trust 1994–; chm Pict Petroleum plc 1990–95; CIMgt 1985; Seri Paduka Mahkota (Brunei) 1984; *Recreations* golf, squash; *Clubs* Watsonian, Gleneagles, Auchterarder Golf; *Style—* Peter Everett, Esq

EVERITT, Anthony Michael; s of late Michael Anthony Hamill Everitt, and Simone Dolores Cathérine, *née* de Vergriette; *b* 31 Jan 1940; *Educ* Cheltenham Coll, Corpus Christi Coll Cambridge (MA); *Career* lectr at Nat Univ of Iran Tehran, SE London Coll of Further Educn, Birmingham Coll of Art and Trent Poly 1963–72; Birmingham Post: art critic 1970–75, drama critic 1974–79, features ed 1976–79; dir: Midland Gp Arts Centre 1979–80, E Midlands Art Assoc 1980–85; sec-gen Arts Cncl of GB 1990–94 (dep sec-gen 1985–90, memb Drama Panel 1974–78, memb Regnl Ctee 1979–80); visiting prof of performing and visual arts Nottingham Trent Univ 1996–; chm: Ikon Gallery Birmingham 1976–79, Birmingham Arts Lab 1977–79; vice-chm Cncl of Regnl Arts Assocs 1984–85; memb: Ctee for Arts and Humanities CNAA 1986–87, Performing Arts Ctee CNAA 1987–92, Gen Advsy Cncl IBA 1987–90; hon fell Dartington Coll of Arts 1995; *Books* Abstract Expressionism (1974); author of articles in papers and jls; *Style—* Prof Anthony Everitt; ✉ Westerlies, Anchor Hill, Wivenhoe, Essex CO7 9BL (☎ 01206 826718, fax 01206 827799, e-mail anthony@pentheus.demon.co.uk)

EVERITT, Michael Boswell; JP (1971); s of Ernest Skelton Everitt (d 1992), JP, of North Place, Lincoln, and Mary Gertrude, *née* Boswell; *b* 13 Dec 1933; *Educ* Gresham's Sch, Leicester Sch of Architecture (DipArch); *m* 18 Sept 1965, Bridgid Mary, da of Harold Thomas Ransley, of Little Abington, Cambridge; 2 s (Richard b 18 Feb 1971, William b 6 Feb 1973), 1 da (Mary b 30 Dec 1967); *Career* Nat Serv: served 1 Bn The Sherwood Foresters, Malaya 1958–59, cmmnd 2 Lt 1958; Sir Hugh Casson Neville Conder and Ptnrs 1959–61, ptnr Feilden & Mawson Architects 1966–93 (joined 1961, ret 1993); pres Norfolk & Norwich Art Circle 1989–92, chm Norfolk Art in Architecture Gp 1988–92; RIBA 1961, ACIArb 1975, FRSA 1990; *Recreations* the visual arts; *Style—* Michael Everitt, Esq, JP; ✉ 113 St Leonards Rd, Norwich NR1 4JF (☎ 01603 621020)

EVERITT, Prof (William) Norrie; s of Charles Ernest Everitt (d 1979), of Birmingham and Sidmouth, and Elizabeth Cloudsley, *née* Ross (d 1990); *b* 10 June 1924; *Educ* Kings Norton GS Birmingham, Univ of Birmingham, Balliol Coll Oxford; *m* 25 July 1953, Katharine Elizabeth, da of Rev Dr Arthur John Howison Gibson (d 1967), of Edinburgh; 2 s (Charles Kingston b 7 Jan 1956, Timothy Fraser b 25 March 1958); *Career* midshipman and Sub Lt RNVR 1944–47; Nelson Research Laboratories English Electric Co Ltd 1948–49; princ lectr in mathematics RMCS 1954–63; Baxter prof of mathematics: Univ of St Andrews 1963–67, Univ of Dundee 1967–82; emeritus prof Univ of Birmingham (Mason prof of mathematics 1982–89), visiting prof Univ of Surrey 1986–95, adjunct prof Northern Illinois Univ USA 1990–, hon prof Univ of Wales Coll of Cardiff 1994–; author of numerous pubns in mathematical periodicals; memb: Br Nat Ctee for Mathematics 1972–78, Cncl and Academic Advsy Cncl Univ of Buckingham 1973–94, Cncl London Mathematical Soc 1957–, Educn Ctee Royal Soc of London 1978–84; memb Cncl and pres Edinburgh Mathematical Soc 1963–, memb Cncl and vice pres RSE 1966–; awarded Mathematics medal Union of Czech Mathematicians and Physicists Prague 1990; memb: Royal Soc of Sciences Sweden 1973, Acad of Letters Sci and Arts Palermo Italy 1978; FIMA 1965, FRSE 1966; *Recreations* music, walking, Parson Woodforde Soc; *Style—* Prof W N Everitt, FRSE; ✉ 103 Oakfield Rd, Selly Park, Birmingham B29 7HW (☎ 0121 471 2437); School of Mathematics and Statistics, University of Birmingham, Edgbaston, Birmingham B15 2TT (☎ 0121 414 6601)

EVERITT, William Howard (Bill); s of Howard George Everitt (d 1978); *b* 27 Feb 1940; *Educ* Brentwood Sch, Univ of Leeds (BSc); *m* 1963, Anthea Cecilia, da of late William Nield; 2 c; *Career* dir AE plc 1978–86 (latterly md); T & N plc: joined on acquisition of AE plc 1986, dir 1987–, currently md Friction Products and Engrg Div; FEng 1988, FIMechE, FIEE; *Recreations* golf; *Style—* Bill Everitt, Esq, FEng; ✉ Horley House, Hornton Lane, Horley, nr Banbury, Oxon (☎ 01295 730603)

EVERITT-MATTHIAS, David Richard; s of Ronald Joseph Matthias (d 1996), and Kathleen Betty Matthias (d 1994); *b* 29 Oct 1960; *Educ* Sir Walter St Johns GS London, Ealing Coll of HE (City and Guilds); *m* 1 June 1985, Helen Mary, da of Peter Kingston Everitt; *Career* chef Inn on the Park London 1978–83, head chef Grand Cafe 1983–85, head chef Steamers Fish Restaurant 1985–86, head chef Fingals Restaurant Putney 1986–87, chef/proprietor Le Champignon Sauvage Cheltenham 1987–; taken part in: The Restaurant Show London 1994–96, Hotelolympia 1994 and 1996, Nat Restaurateurs Dinner 1995, Nat Chef of the Year Dinner 1996; memb Academie Culinaire de France; memb Sir Walter St Johns Old Boys Assoc; *Television appearances* Junior Masterchef 1996, Suprise Chefs 1996, This Morning TV 1996, Central TV 1996; *Awards* Acorn Award, Midland Chef of the Year 1995 and 1996, Egon Ronay Dessert Chef of the Year 1996, Nat Chef of the Year 1996 and 1997, Michelin Star 1995, AA Guide 4 Rosettes 1997, Roy Ackerman Guide Clover Leaf, Good Food Guide 3* out of 5, Egon Ronay Star; *Recreations* cricket, squash, art, jazz, reading; *Style—* David Everitt-Matthias, Esq; ✉ Le Champignon Sauvage, 24–26 Suffolk Road, Cheltenham, Gloucestershire GL50 2AQ (☎ and fax 01242 573449)

EVERS, Peter Lawson; s of John Henry Evers (d 1982), and Evelyn Jessica, *née* Hill; *b* 4 Jan 1938; *Educ* King Edward VI GS; *m* 5 Oct 1963, Margaret Elaine, da of William Edwin Homer; 3 s (Jonathan b 21 March 1971, Philip Alexander (twin) b 21 March 1971), 2 da (Elaine Louise b 14 Sept 1965, Alison Jane b 4 June 1967); *Career* press offr J Lucas Industries 1965–67 (press and publicity asst 1959–67), publicity mangr Fafnir Bearing Co Ltd 1967–68, gp press offr John Thompson Group 1968–71, conslt John Fowler Public Relations 1971–72, ptnr and co fndr Edson Evers Public Relations 1972–, dir and chief exec Edson Evers Communications Ltd 1980–95, UK dir PR Organisation International Ltd 1973– (pres 1985, 1991, 1992, 1993 and 1994); BAIE (renamed British Assoc of Communicators in Business 1995) newspaper award winner: 1985, 1988, 1989, 1990, 1991, 1992; MIPR 1969–93, FIPR 1993, memb BAIE (BACB) 1974, FRHS 1980; *Recreations* golf, tennis, gardening; *Clubs* Brocton Hall Golf; *Style—* Peter Evers, Esq; ✉ Edson Evers & Associates, Priory House, Friars Terrace, Stafford ST17 4AG (☎ 01785 255146, fax 01785 211518, mobile 0831 398322)

EVERSFIELD, Col John Claude; ERD (1967), TD (1979); s of Philip Claude Eversfield (d 1966), and Gladys Irene (d 1990), *née* Cottle; *b* 9 Dec 1932; *Educ* Norwich Sch; *m* 6 Sept 1958, Beryl Irene, da of Stanley Wymer (d 1940); 1 s (Geoffrey b 23 April 1964); *Career* Nat Serv 2 Lt RCS 1951, AER and TA Royal Signals 1953–86, cmd 31 Signal Regt TA 1973–75, Col TA 1976–86, ADC TA 1980–84; Nat Assistance Bd 1953–67 (exec offr 1953), DHSS 1967–88 (princ 1971), Dept of Social Security 1988–92 (asst sec 1989–92); conslt: Business in the Community 1992–, London First 1993–94, Prince's Tst 1994–95; community advsr Buckinghamshire CC; vice pres and tstee Middx Yeo Regtl Assoc; *Recreations* foreign travel, walking, theatre; *Clubs* Civil Serv; *Style—* Col John Eversfield, ERD, TD; ✉ 7 Home Farm Way, Stoke Poges, Slough SL3 6NZ (☎ 01753 662667)

EVERSHED, Ralph Jocelyn; s of Norman William Evershed (d 1983), and Jocelyn Slade, *née* Lyons; *b* 16 Nov 1944; *Educ* St Albans Boys GS, Univ of Strathclyde (BA); *m* 6 Sept 1968, Carol Ann, da of Jerry Esmond Cullum (d 1987); 3 s (Timothy b 1973, David b 1974, John b 1982 d 1994), 2 da (Ruth b 1977, Susannah b 1980); *Career* md Verulam Properties Ltd 1981–; chm: Eversheds Ltd, J E Properties Holdings Ltd 1987–; dir: Eversheds Group Ltd 1987–, Evershed Estates Ltd 1987–, Woodsilk Properties Ltd 1988–, Inter Varsity Press 1988–; MIOP, FInstD; *Style—* Ralph Evershed, Esq; ✉ Eversheds Ltd, Alma Rd, St Albans, Herts AL1 3AS (☎ 01727 854652, fax 01727 843908)

EVERSON, Sir Frederick Charles; KCMG (1968, CMG 1956); s of Frederick Percival Everson (d 1946); *b* 6 Sept 1910; *Educ* Tottenham Co Sch, London Univ; *m* 1937, Linda Mary (d 1984), da of Samuel Clark; 3 s (eldest of whom d 1984), 1 da; *Career* entered Foreign Serv 1934, ambass to El Salvador 1956–60, commercial counsellor Stockholm 1960–63, min (econ) Paris 1963–68; *Style—* Sir Frederick Everson, KCMG; ✉ Apartment 17, Aynhoe Park, Aynho, Banbury, Oxon OX17 3BQ

EVERSON, John Andrew; s of Harold Leslie Everson (d 1976), of Surrey, and Florence Jane, *née* Stone (d 1982); *b* 26 Oct 1933; *Educ* Tiffin Boys' Sch Kingston upon Thames, Christ's Coll Cambridge (MA), King's Coll London (PGCE); *m* 1961, Gilda, da of Osborne Ramsden (d 1956), of Manchester; 2 s (Simon John b 1965, Benedict David b 1967); *Career* 2 Lt RA 1952–54; schoolmaster: Haberdashers' Aske's Sch Elstree 1958–65, City of London Sch 1965–68; HM Inspectorate of Schs DES: joined 1968, sch cncl chief offr of Examination Unit 1973–76, staff inspr 1978–81, chief inspr for secdy educn 1981–89, seconded to Peat Marwick McLintock 1989–90, chief inspr for teacher educn 1990–92, educational conslt 1992–; *Recreations* opera, chess, walking; *Clubs* Athenaeum; *Style*— John Everson, Esq; ✉ c/o Athenaeum, 107 Pall Mall, London SW1

EVERSON, Noel Williams; s of Mervyn Cyril George Everson (d 1981), and Beryl Irene, *née* Williams; *b* 8 Dec 1944; *Educ* W Monmouth Sch, Middx Hosp Med Sch (MB BS), Univ of London (MS); *m* 1, 1969 (m dis 1982), Caroline Juliet Adams; 2 da (Juliet Claire b 1971, Katherine Frances Vivien b 1974); m 2, 27 June 1987, Elizabeth Mary, da of Donald Sellen; 2 da (Francesca Victoria Louise b 1990, Lucy Helen Jane b 1992); *Career* conslt surgn Leicester Royal Infirmary 1981–; memb: Br Assoc of Paediatric Surgns, Assoc of Surgns; FRSM, FRCS 1972; *Recreations* fly-fishing; *Style*— Noel Everson, Esq; ✉ 6 Meadowcourt Rd, Oadby, Leicester, Leicestershire LE2 2PB (☎ 0116 271 2512); The Leicester Royal Infirmary, Leicester, Leicestershire (☎ 0116 254 1414)

EVERTON, Clive Harold; s of Harold Brimley Everton, of Droitwich, Worcs, and Alma, *née* Pugh (d 1980); *b* 7 Sept 1937; *Educ* Kings's Sch Worcester, UCW Cardiff (BA); *m* Valerie, *née* Teasdale; 1 s (Daniel b 10 April 1974), 4 da (Jane b 7 Aug 1963, Julie b 2 Sept 1965, Kate b 22 Dec 1966, Lucy b 7 Oct 1969); *Career* journalist, author and broadcaster; freelance broadcaster and sports writer for various pubns 1962–, specialist in snooker and billiards 1973–; ed: Billiards and Snooker magazine 1966–70, Snooker Scene 1971–; billiards and snooker corr: Sunday Times 1967–, The Guardian 1977–; snooker commentator BBC TV 1978–; billiards player; Br under 16 champion 1952, Br under 19 champion 1955, Welsh amateur champion 5 times, semi-finalist World Amateur Billiards Championship 1975 and 1977, ranked 10 in world professional ratings 1991; 6 Welsh amateur snooker caps; memb Bd World Professional Billiards and Snooker Assoc 1990–91; *Publications* Embassy Book of World Snooker (1993); author of various snooker compendiums and instructional books, co-author various biographies; *Recreations* books, films, theatre; *Style*— Clive Everton, Esq; ✉ Everton's News Agency, Cavalier House, 202 Hagley Rd, Edgbaston, Birmingham B16 9PQ (☎ 0121 454 2931, fax 0121 452 1822)

EVERY, Sir Henry John Michael; 13 Bt (E 1641), of Egginton, Derbyshire; o s of Sir John Simon Every, 12 Bt (d 1988), and his 2 w Janet Marion, *née* Page; *b* 6 April 1947; *Educ* Malvern Coll; *m* 1974, Susan Mary, eldest da of Kenneth Beaton, JP, of Eastshotte, Hartford, Cambs; 3 s (Edward James Henry b 1975, Jonathan Charles Hugo b 1977, Nicholas John Simon b 1981); *Heir* s, Edward James Henry Every b 3 July 1975; *Career* ptnr Deloitte & Touche (formerly Deloitte & Touche) Birmingham; pres Birmingham and W Midlands Dist Soc of CAs 1995–96 (chm Dist Trg Bd 1989–92), parish cncllr; memb Ctee The Birmingham Lunar Soc 1991–; FCA 1970, FRSA; *Recreations* family, tennis, gardening, Nat Tst, supporting Nottingham Forest FC; *Style*— Sir Henry Every, Bt; ✉ Cothay, 26 Fishpond Lane, Egginton, nr Derby DE65 6HJ; Deloitte & Touche, Colmore Gate, 2 Colmore Row, Birmingham B3 1PA (☎ 0121 200 2211, fax 0121 695 5734)

EVES, David Charles Thomas; CB (1993); s of Harold Thomas Eves (d 1967), and Violet, *née* Edwards (d 1972); *b* 10 Jan 1942; *Educ* King's Sch Rochester, Univ of Durham (BA); *m* 1 Aug 1964, Valerie Ann, da of George Alexander Carter, of Pinner, Middx; 1 da (Catherine Alice b 1969); *Career* HM chief inspr of factories 1985–88, dep dir gen Health and Safety Exec 1989–; fell and hon vice pres Inst of Occupational Safety and Health; vice pres and sec gen Int Assoc of Labour Inspection; *Recreations* sailing, fishing, painting, gardening, reading, music; *Clubs* Athenaeum; *Style*— David Eves, Esq, CB; ✉ Health and Safety Executive, Rose Court, 2 Southwark Bridge, London SE1 9HS (☎ 0171 717 6450)

EVINGTON, John Charles; s of Malcolm F Evington, of Holmes Chapel, Cheshire, and Eve, *née* Slee (d 1989); *b* 28 Nov 1958; *Educ* Bramhall HS Sandbach Cheshire, King Edward VII GS Retford Notts, S Cheshire Coll, Portsmouth Poly (BA); *m* 4 Oct 1986 (m dis 1993), Sally Louise, da of Howard Latham, of Wistaston, Crewe; *Career* presenter and prodr Piccadilly Radio Manchester 1978–81, head of music Centre Radio Leicester 1981–83, presenter BBC Radio 2 1983, prog dir Signal Radio 1983–; bd dir: KFM Radio Stockport 1991–, North Staffordshire and South Cheshire Broadcasting 1992–; bdcast for Signal Radio from studios of NDR Frankfurt 1985 and CFTR Toronto 1988; *Style*— John Evington, Esq; ✉ North Staffordshire and South Cheshire Broadcasting Ltd, Stoke Road, Stoke-on-Trent, Staffs ST4 2SR (☎ 01782 747047, fax 01782 744110, car 0374 134018)

EWAN, Gordon Francis David; s of Albert Francis Ewan (d 1993), of Herts, and Rosemary, *née* Orchard (d 1988); *b* 9 Oct 1938; *Educ* St Audreys Hatfield, Poly of N London (DipArch); *m* 28 Nov 1959, Anne Freda, da of Norman McCard (d 1985), of Herts; 2 s (Simon b 1960, Mark b 1964), 1 da (Lesley b 1961); *Career* architect; chm Vincent and Gorbing Architects and Planners; RIBA; *Recreations* golf, fine wines, Rotary Int; *Style*— Gordon Ewan, Esq; ✉ 5 Long Ridge, Aston, Stevenage, Herts SG2 7EW (☎ 01438 880296); Vincent and Gorbing Ltd, Sterling Court, Norton Rd, Stevenage, Herts SG1 2JY (☎ 01438 316331, fax 01438 722035)

EWAN, Dr Pamela Wilson; da of Norman Wilson Ewan, of Cambridge, and Frances Patterson, *née* Sellars (d 1984); *b* 23 Sept 1945; *Educ* Forfar Acad, Royal Free Hosp Sch of Med (MB BS, DObstRCOG, FRCP, MRCPath); *m* 15 Sept 1979, Prof Sir (David) Keith Peters, s of Lionel Herbert Peters; 2 s (James b 1980, William b 1989), 1 da (Hannah b 1982); *Career* sr lectr in clinical immunology and dir Allergy Clinic St Mary's Hosp 1980–88, MRC clinical scientist and hon conslt in clinical immunology and allergy Univ of Cambridge Clinical Sch Addenbrooke's Hosp 1988–, dir of med studies Clare Hall Cambridge 1988–, assoc lectr Univ of Cambridge 1988–; hon sec RCP Ctee in Clinical Immunology; memb: Cncl Br Soc for Allergy and Clinical Immunology, Ctee Euro Acad of Allergy and Clinical Immunology; author of various chapters and papers in med books and scientific jls memb: Assoc of Physicians, BSACI, BSI, MRS; *Style*— Dr Pamela Ewan; ✉ 7 Chaucer Rd, Cambridge CB2 2EB; MRC Centre, Hills Rd, Cambridge CB2 2QH (☎ 01223 402422, fax 01223 243237)

EWANS, Sir Martin Kenneth; KCMG (1987, CMG 1980); s of John Ewans; *b* 14 Nov 1928; *Educ* St Paul's, Corpus Christi Coll Cambridge (MA); *m* 1953, Mary Tooke; 1 s, 1 da; *Career* HM Dip Serv: head E African Dept FCO 1973–78, min New Delhi 1978–82, high cmmr Zimbabwe 1983–85, high cmmr Nigeria 1986–88; chm Children's Aid Direct 1996–; *Publications* Bharatpur: Bird Paradise (1988), The Battle for the Broads (1992); *Recreations* ornithology, walking; *Style*— Sir Martin Ewans, KCMG; ✉ 24 Crockwell Street, Long Compton, Warwickshire CV36 5JN (☎ and fax 01608 684879)

EWARD, Paul Anthony; s of Rev Harvey Kennedy Eward (d 1969), and Delphine Eugenie Louise, *née* Pain; *b* 22 Dec 1942; *Educ* Radley; *m* 6 Sept 1966, Dene Kathleen, da of Geoffrey Louis Bartrip (d 1991), of Ross-on-Wye; 2 da (Sarah b 1969, Lucy b 1971); *Career* admitted slr 1967; ptnr: Slades (Newent), Orme Dykes & Yates (Ledbury); chm Newent Business & Professional Assoc 1981–83, sec PCC Ross-on-Wye 1972–88, lay co chm Ross and Archenfield Deanery Synod 1988–96 (hon treas (1980–88); memb Hereford Diocesan Synod 1988–96: Bd of Fin (and its Exec Ctee 1995–), Revenue Ctee, Vacancy in See Ctee 1985–, Patronage Ctee 1988–95; memb: Transport Users Consultative Ctee for W England 1990–94, Ctee Gloucestershire & Wiltshire Law Soc 1990–96, Rail Users' Consultative Ctee for W England 1994–; *Clubs* Gloucester Model Railway, EM Gauge Soc; *Style*— Paul Eward, Esq; ✉ Oakleigh, Gloucester Rd, Ross-on-Wye, Herefordshire HR9 5NA (☎ 01989 563845); Slades, 5 Broad St, Newent, Glos GL18 1AX (☎ 01531 820281)

EWART, John Walter Douglas; CBE (1995), DL (Northants 1993); s of Maxwell Douglas Ewart; *b* 27 Jan 1924; *Educ* Beaumont Coll Old Windsor Berks; *m* 1946, (Joan) Valerie, *née* Hoghton (d 1996); 1 da (Lavinia Anne (Mrs C G Perry) b 1947); *Career* Lt Royal Horse Gds 1942–46; md Paterson Ewart Group Ltd 1958–70; Carclo Engineering Group plc: md 1973–82, chm 1982–; memb: Northants CC 1970– (ldr 1991–93), Assoc of CCs 1973–93 (ldr 1992–93); High Sheriff Northants 1977–78; *Recreations* hunting, sailing; *Clubs* Cavalry and Guards', Royal Yacht Sqdn; *Style*— John Ewart, Esq, CBE, DL; ✉ Astrop, Banbury, Oxfordshire OX17 3QN (☎ 01295 811210, fax 01295 812034)

EWART, Sir (William) Michael; 7 Bt (UK 1887), of Glenmachan, Strandtown, Co Down, and of Glenbank, Belfast, Co Antrim; s of Sir (William) Ivan Cecil Ewart, 6 Bt, DSC (d 1995), and Pauline Chevallier, *née* Preston (d 1964); *b* 10 June 1953; *Educ* Radley; *Heir* none; *Style*— Sir Michael Ewart, Bt

EWART, Timothy John Pelham (Tim); s of John Terence Pelham Ewart, of Woodbridge, Suffolk, and Nancy, *née* Girling (d 1990); *b* 6 Feb 1949; *Educ* Gresham's, Ipswich Civic Coll; *m* 2, 8 Aug 1991, Penny, da of Alan Marshall; 2 c from prev m (Ben b 16 July 1977, Alice b 30 Nov 1980); *Career* newspapers 1967–74 (Bury Free Press, Leicester Mercury, Bermuda Sun), Radio 1974–77 (BBC World Service, Radio Orwell); reporter/presenter: BBC TV North (Leeds) 1977–80, Thames TV News 1980–81; ITN: Warsaw correspondent 1983–85, Washington correspondent 1986–90, Moscow correspondent 1990–92; chief correspondent GMTV 1992 (prior to start of franchise), rejoined ITN as weekend news presenter and reporter News at Ten Focus on Britain 1992, main presenter BBC Newsroom South East Sept 1993–96, rejoined ITN as sr reporter 1996–; *Recreations* golf, tennis; *Clubs* Woodbridge Golf; *Style*— Tim Ewart, Esq; ✉ Independent Television News Ltd, 200 Gray's Inn Road, London WC1X 8XZ (☎ 0171 833 3000)

EWBANK, Hon Sir Anthony Bruce; kt (1980); s of Rev Harold Ewbank, Rector of Windermere, and Gwendolen, *née* Bruce; *b* 30 July 1925; *Educ* St John's Sch Leatherhead, Trinity Coll Cambridge (MA); *m* 1958, Moya, da of Peter McGinn; 4 s, 1 da; *Career* RNVR 1945–47 and 1951–56; schoolmaster 1947–53, called to the Bar Gray's Inn 1954; jr counsel to the Treasy in probate matters 1969, QC 1972, recorder Crown Court 1975–80, bencher Gray's Inn 1980, a judge of the High Court of Justice (Family Div) 1980–95, ret; chm Family Law Bar Assoc 1978–80; *Style*— The Hon Sir Anthony Ewbank; ✉ 1 Chetwynd House, The Green, Hampton Court KT8 9BS

EWIN, *see:* Floyd Ewin

EWING, Kenneth Hugh Robert; s of Hugh Wands Ewing (d 1945), of Northwood, Middx, and Agnes Jack, *née* McCance (d 1968); *b* 5 Jan 1927; *Educ* Merchant Taylors Sch Herts, St John's Coll Oxford (MA); *Career* Nat Serv Flying Offr RAF 1948–50; writer and broadcaster BBC Euro Serv 1950–52; gen mangr Connaught Theatre Worthing 1952–59, md Fraser and Dunlop Scripts Ltd 1959–, pres Peters Fraser and Dunlop Group 1993– (jt chm 1988–93); currently dir: Oliver Moon Ltd; memb Personal Managers' Assoc; *Recreations* flying (PPL), theatre, dog-walking; *Clubs* Garrick; *Style*— Kenneth Ewing, Esq; ✉ 2 Crescent Grove, London SW4; 44 Sussex Square, Brighton, E Sussex; Peters Fraser and Dunlop Group, The Chambers, Chelsea Harbour, London SW10 (☎ 0171 344 1000, fax 0171 352 7356)

EWING, Margaret Anne; MP (SNP) Moray (majority 2,844); da of John McAdam (d 1984), of Biggar, and Margaret Jamieson Cuthbert, *née* Lamb; *b* 1 Sept 1945; *Educ* Univ of Glasgow (MA), Univ of Strathclyde (BA); *m* 1, 1968 (m dis 1980), Donald Bain; m 2, 30 Nov 1983, Fergus Stewart, s of Stewart Martin Ewing, of Glasgow; *Career* asst Eng and mathematics teacher Our Lady's High Cumbernauld 1968–71, princ teacher of remedial educn St Modans High Stirling 1971–74; MP (SNP): East Dunbartonshire 1974–79, Moray 1987–; freelance journalist 1979–81; coordinator W of Scot CSS Scheme 1981–87, SNP Parliamentary leader 1987– (contested Strathkelvin and Bearsden 1983); memb Bd of Govrs Westminster Fndn for Democracy; *Style*— Mrs Margaret Ewing, MP; ✉ Burns Cottage, Tulloch's Brae, Lossiemouth, Moray IV31 6QY (☎ 0134381 2222); House of Commons, London SW1A 0AA (☎ 0171 219 3494, fax 0171 219 6716)

EWING, Maria Louise; *b* 27 March 1950; *Career* soprano; Met Opera NY debut 1976 as Cherubino in The Marriage of Figaro 1976, European debut at La Scala Milan as Melisande in Pelleas et Melisande 1979, Covent Garden debut in title role in Salome 1988; worked with numerous conductors incl: James Levine, Bernard Haitink, Michael Tilson Thomas, Claudio Abbado, Semyon Bychkov, Pierre Boulez, Vladimir Askenazy, Richard Rodney Bennett, James Levine, Simon Rattle, Sir John Pritchard, Andrew Davis; given concert appearances and recitals with numerous orchs incl: City of Birmingham Symphony, Berlin Philharmonic, Bayerischer Rundfunk, Concertgebouw Orch, NY Philharmonic, Philharmonia Orch, Vienna Philharmonic, LSO, London Sinfonietta, BBC Symphony, Chicago Symphony, LA Philharmonic, Philadelphia Orch, Chamber Orch of Europe; appeared at numerous international venues incl: Lyric Opera Chicago, Washington Opera, Boston Opera, Houston Grand Opera, Barbican Hall, La Scala Milan, Le Chatalet Paris, Konzerthaus Vienna; *Roles* incl: Dorabella in Cosi fan Tutte, Susanna and Cherubino in the Marriage of Figaro, title roles in La Perichole and La Cenerentola, the Composer in Ariadne auf Naxos (Met Opera NY) 1985, title role in L'Incoronazione di Poppea (Glyndebourne) 1986, title role in Carmen (Met Opera 1986, Glyndebourne 1985, 1986 and 1987, Covent Garden 1988 and 1991, Earls Court 1988–89, Tokyo and Aust 1990, Oslo 1990), title role in Salome (LA Opera 1986, Covent Garden 1988 and 1992, Lyric Opera Chicago 1988–89, Washington Opera 1990, San Francisco Opera 1993), title role in The Merry Widow (Lyric Opera Chicago) 1986, Blanche in The Dialogues of the Carmelites (Met Opera) 1987, title role in Tosca (LA Opera 1989 and 1992, Covent Garden 1991, Seville with Placido Domingo 1991), Melisande in Pelleas et Melisande (Vienna State Opera 1991), title role in Madame Butterfly (LA Opera 1991), Dido in The Trojans (Met Opera) 1993; *Recordings* incl: Shéhérezade (with the CBSO and Simon Rattle) 1990, jazz album with the Royal Philharmonic Orch and Richard Rodney Bennett 1990, Pelleas et Melisande (with the Vienna Philharmonic Orch and Claudio Abbado) 1991, Lady Macbeth of Mtzensk (with the Bastille Opera) 1992; *Style*— Ms Maria Ewing; ✉ c/o Herbert Breslin, 119 West 57th Street, Room 1505, New York, NY 10019, USA FORIEGN

EWING, Dr Winifred Margaret; MEP (SNP) Highlands and Islands (majority 54,916); da of George Woodburn, and Christina Bell, *née* Anderson; *b* 10 July 1929; *Educ* Queen's Park Sr Secdy Sch, Univ of Glasgow (MA, LLB); *m* 1956, Stewart Martin Ewing; 2 s, 1 da; *Career* MP (SNP): Hamilton 1967–70, Moray and Nairn Feb 1974–79; MEP (SNP) Highlands and Islands 1979–; vice pres Euro Radical Alliance 1994; pres SNP 1987–; Hon DUniv Open Univ, Hon LLD Univ of Glasgow 1995; *Style*— Dr Winifred Ewing, MEP; ✉ Goodwill, Miltonduff, Elgin, Moray IV30 3TL

EWING OF KIRKFORD, Baron (Life Peer UK 1992), of Cowdenbeath in the District of Dunfermline; Harry Ewing; DL (Region of Fife 1995); s of William Ewing; *b* 20 Jan 1931; *Educ* Beath HS Cowdenbeath; *m* 1954, Margaret, da of John Greenhill, of Leven; 1 s (Hon Alan William John b 31 May 1961), 1 da (Hon Alison Margaret (Hon Mrs Binnie) b 26 July 1966); *Career* memb PO Workers' Union; contested (Lab) Fife E 1970; MP (Lab): Stirling and Falkirk 1971–74, Stirling Falkirk & Grangemouth 1974–83, Falkirk E 1983–92; sec Scottish Parly Lab Gp 1972–74, Parly under sec Scottish Office 1974–79, sr vice chm Trade Union Gp of Lab MPs 1979–87; oppn front bench spokesman on: Scottish Affrs 1981–83, Trade and Industry 1983–87; memb Cncl of Europe and Western Euro Union 1987–; specialist on Health Service matters; chm: Scottish Disability Fndn 1993–, Fife Health Care NHS Tst 1996–; *Style*— The Rt Hon Lord Ewing of Kirkford; ✉ 45 Glenlyon Rd, Leven, Fife KY8 4AA (☎ 01333 426123)

EWINS, Prof David John; s of Wilfred James Ewins, of Hemyock, Devon, and Patricia, *née* Goacher; *b* 25 March 1942; *Educ* Kingswood GS Bristol, Imperial Coll London (BSc, DSc), Trinity Coll Cambridge (PhD); *m* 1964, Brenda Rene, *née* Chalk; 3 da (Sally Ann b 1966, Sarah b 1968, Caroline Helene b 1971); *Career* research asst for Rolls-Royce Ltd at Univ of Cambridge 1966–67; Imperial Coll London: lectr then reader in mechanical engrg 1967–83, prof of vibration engrg 1983–, fndr Modal Testing Unit 1981, dir Centre of Vibration Engrg 1990–; sr lectr Chulalongkorn Univ Bangkok 1968–69, maitre de conf INSA Lyon France 1974–75; visiting prof: Virginia Poly and State Univ USA 1981, ETH Zurich 1986, Institut Nationale Polytechnique de Grenoble 1990, Nanyang Tech Univ Singapore 1994; Dynamic Testing Agency: fndr 1990, chm 1990–94, pres 1995–; ptnr ICATS; conslt to: Rolls-Royce 1969–, MOD 1977–, Boeing, Ford, NASA, Intevep, BMW, Mercedes, GM; MSEE 1970, MASME 1983, FIMechE 1982, FEng 1995; *Books* Modal Testing: Theory and Pratice (1984, 5 edn 1989); *Recreations* music, hill walking, travel, good food, French; *Clubs* Executive; *Style*— Prof David Ewins, FEng; ✉ Imperial College of Science, Technology and Medicine, Exhibition Rd, London SW7 2BX

EWINS, Peter David; *b* 20 March 1943; *Educ* Imperial Coll Univ of London (BSc), Cranfield Inst of Technol (MSc); *m* Barbara; 2 s (Mark, James), 1 da (Sarah); *Career* RAE MOD (PE) Farnborough: joined 1966, various research posts rising to princ scientific offr and section head Advanced Composite Materials 1975–80, responsible for extramural prog in structural R & D 1977–80; MOD (PE) Whitehall 1980–82, sr princ scientific offr and superintendent Helicopters Div RAF Farnborough 1982–84, asst sec and head Personnel Mgmnt Div Cabinet Office 1984–87, dir Nuclear Projects MOD 1987–88, dir Admiralty Research Establishment CERN Portsdown 1988–91; Defence Research Agency: md Maritime Div Portsdown April - Nov 1991, md Command and Maritime Systems Gp Farnborough 1991–93, md Operations 1993–94; chief scientist MOD Whitehall 1994–; FRAeS, FEng 1996; *Style*— Peter Ewins, Esq, FEng; ✉ Chief Scientist, Room 6311, Ministry of Defence, Main Building, Whitehall, London SW1A 2HB (☎ 0171 218 2848, fax 0171 218 6552)

EXETER, Dean of; *see:* Jones, Very Rev Keith Brynmor

EXETER, 69 Bishop of (cr 1050) 1985–; Rt Rev (Geoffrey) Hewlett Thompson; see consists of Devon (except seven parishes) and one parish in Somerset; s of Lt-Col Ralph Reakes Thompson, MC (late RAMC, d 1960), and Eanswythe Frances, *née* Donaldson (d 1993); *b* 14 Aug 1929; *Educ* Aldenham, Trinity Hall Cambridge (MA); *m* 29 Sept 1954, Elisabeth Joy, da of Col Geoffrey Fausitt Taylor, MBE (late IMS, d 1982), and Dr Frances Taylor; 2 s (Andrew b 1957, Benjamin b 1963), 2 da (Mary Clare b 1955, Louise b 1961); *Career* 2 Lt Royal West Kents 1948–49; curate St Matthew Northampton 1954–59; vicar: St Augustine Wisbech 1959–66, St Saviour Folkestone 1966–74; bishop of Willesden 1974–85; took seat in House of Lords 1990; chm Hosp Chaplaincies Cncl C of E 1991; *Clubs* United Oxford and Cambridge; *Style*— The Rt Rev the Lord Bishop of Exeter; ✉ The Palace, Exeter EX1 1HY (☎ 01392 272362, fax 01392 430923)

EXETER, 8 Marquess of (UK 1801; a previous Marquessate of Exeter was enjoyed by Henry Courtenay, Earl of Devon and gs of Edward IV, 1525–39); William Michael Anthony Cecil; also Baron Burghley (E 1571) and Earl of Exeter (E 1605; the de Reviers Earls of Devon, who enjoyed that title 1141–1262, were sometimes called Earls of Exeter), Hereditary Grand Almoner, and Lord Paramount of the Soke of Peterborough; s of 7 Marquess of Exeter (d 1988) (14 in descent from the Lord Burghley who was Elizabeth's I chief minister), and his 1 w Edith Lilian (d 1954), o da of Aurel Csanady de Telegd, of Budapest, Hungary; *b* 1 Sept 1935; *Educ* Eton; *m* 1967 (m dis 1993), Nancy Rose, da of Lloyd Arthur Meeker; 1 s, 1 da (Lady Angela Kathleen b 1975); *Heir* s, Lord Burghley, *qv*, b 1970; *Career* businessman and lecturer; *Books* The Rising Tide of Change (1986), Living at the Heart of Creation (1990); *Style*— The Most Hon the Marquess of Exeter; ✉ PO Box 8, 100 Mile House, Br Columbia V0K 2E0, Canada (☎ 00 1 604 395 2767, fax 00 1 604 395 2143)

EXMOUTH, 10 Viscount (UK 1816); Sir Paul Edward Pellew; 10 Bt (GB 1796); also Baron Exmouth (UK 1814); patron of one living; s of 9 Viscount (d 1970) and Maria Luisa, Marquesa de Olias (Sp cr of 1625) (d 1994), da of late Luis de Urquijo, Marques de Amurrio, of Madrid; *b* 8 Oct 1940; *Educ* Downside; *m* 1, 10 Dec 1964 (m dis 1974), Maria Krystina, o da of late Don Recaredo de Garay y Garay, of Madrid; 1 da (Hon Patricia b 1966); m 2, 1975, Rosemary Frances, da of Francis Harold Scoones, MRCS, LRCP, JP, and formerly w of Earl of Burford (now 14 Duke of St Albans, *qv*); 2 s (Hon Edward, Hon Alexander b (twins) 30 Oct 1978); *Heir* s, Hon Edward Francis Pellew b 30 Oct 1978; *Career* sits as Cross Bench Peer in House of Lords; MInstD; *Style*— The Rt Hon Viscount Exmouth; ✉ House of Lords, London SW1A 0PW

EXTON, Clive Jack Montague; s of Jack Ernest Brooks (d 1970), of Islington, London, and Marie, *née* Rolfe (d 1984); name changed by deed poll; *b* 11 April 1930; *Educ* Christ's Hosp; *m* 1, 1951 (m dis 1957), Patricia Fletcher, *née* Ferguson (d 1983); 2 da (Frances Brooks (Mrs N Morgan) b 1952, Sarah Brooks b 1954); m 2, 30 Aug 1957, Margaret Josephine (Mara); 2 da (Antigone (Mrs G White) b 1961, Plaxy (Mrs G Locatelli) b 1964), 1 s (Saul b 1965); *Career* actor 1951–59, writer 1959–; Nat Serv 1948–50; theatre prodn: Have You Any Dirty Washing Mother Dear? 1969; *Television* plays incl: No Fixed Abode 1959, Where I Live 1960, I'll Have You to Remember 1961, Hold My Hand Soldier 1961, The Trial of Doctor Fancy 1963, The Big Eat 1963, Land of My Dreams 1964, The Bone Yard 1965, The Close Prisoner 1965, The Boundary (with Tom Stoppard); series incl: The Crezz 1974, Agatha Christie's Poirot 1989–94, Jeeves and Wooster 1990–94 (Writers' Guild Award 1992), The Great British Murder 1995, Somethings Got to Give 1996; dramatizations of works by authors incl: Agatha Christie, Jean Cocteau, Ken Follett, Daphne du Maurier, Graham Greene, Somerset Maugham, Ruth Rendell, Georges Simenon, H G Wells, P G Wodehouse; *Films* incl: Night Must Fall, Isadora (with Melvyn Bragg), 10 Rillington Place, Entertaining Mr Sloane; *Recreations* panification; *Clubs* Groucho; *Style*— Clive Exton, Esq; ✉ c/o Rochelle Stevens & Co Ltd, 2 Terrett's Place, Upper Street, London N1 1QZ (☎ 0171 359 3900, fax 0171 354 5729)

EXTON, Rodney Noel; s of Maj Noel Exton (d 1969), and Winifred *née* Stokes (d 1963); *b* 28 Dec 1927; *Educ* Clifton Coll, Lincoln Coll Oxford (MA), Corpus Christi Coll Cambridge (PGCE); *m* 1961, Pamela Beresford, da of Alan Hardie, of Rose Bay, Sydney, NSW (d 1947), and wid of Ian Menzies Sinclair, of Glen Innes, NSW; 2 step s (Andrew, Colin), 2 step da (Virginia, Jane); *Career* Royal Hants Regt 1946–48; cricketer Hants CCC 1946; asst master Eton 1951–52, Int Res Fund scholarship to USA 1952, asst master then housemaster Mill Hill Sch 1952–63, State Educn Dept NSW 1959–60, headmaster Reed's Sch Cobham 1964–77; md Exton Hotels Co Ltd 1966–80, dir Purbeck Properties 1982–90, chm Kandic Ltd 1976–82; ed Johansens Hotel Guides 1992– (vice chm 1990–92); JP Surrey 1968–78; ESU/HMC Page scholar to USA 1971; memb: Nat Working Pty on Disadvantaged Children 1972, GAP Cncl of Mgmnt 1978–89; fell The Atlantic Cncl of the UK; dir: Ind Schs Careers Orgn (ISCO) 1978–88, Vocational Guidance Assoc 1989–90; govr Clifton Coll 1986–; vice pres Reed's Sch 1992–, pres Flycatchers CC 1989–; *Publications* Industrial Cadets (1972), Trouble with the Rules (1989); *Recreations* guitar; *Clubs* IOD, Royal Mid-Surrey Golf, Vincent's (Oxford); *Style*— Rodney Exton, Esq; ✉ 43 Temple Road, Kew Gardens, Richmond, TW9 2EB (☎ 0181 940 0305)

EYKYN, Dr Susannah Jane; (Viscountess Dilhorne); da of late Cdr W C Eykyn, RN; *Educ* Sherborne Sch for Girls, St Thomas's Hosp Med Sch (MB BS, FRCP, FRCS, FRCPath); *m* 1, 12 June 1962 (m dis 1980), Colin Gilchrist; 1 s (Mark b 1 June 1966), 1 da (Virginia b 18 Aug 1963); m 2, 17 Dec 1981, 2 Viscount Dilhorne, *qv*; *Career* sr lectr and hon conslt in clinical microbiology St Thomas' Hosp 1975–, reader and hon conslt 1982–; author of numerous papers on bacterial infection and antibiotics; memb Res and Med Advsy Ctee Cystic Fibrosis Research Tst 1985–90, memb Ctee on Safety of Med (CSM); *Recreations* skiing, mountain walking, riding, opera; *Style*— Dr Susannah Eykyn; ✉ Dept of Microbiology, St Thomas' Hospital, London SE1 7EH (☎ 0171 928 9292)

EYNON, (Richard) Mark; s of late Capt Melville Victor Eynon, of Caerleon, Gwent, and Phyllis Bertha, *née* Aitken-Smith, MBE; *b* 9 Nov 1953; *Educ* Monmouth, Univ of Manchester (BSc), Manchester Business Sch (MBA); *m* 18 Oct 1980, Susan Elspeth, da of Dr J T D Allen, of Liverpool; *Career* vice pres Bank of America 1982–86; dir S G Warburg Securities 1986–96, md Swiss Bank Corporation 1995–; chm S G Warburg Futures and Options 1992–96, dep chm LIFFE 1995– (dir 1984–); *Recreations* rugby, cricket; *Style*— Mark Eynon, Esq; ✉ Swiss Bank Corporation, Swiss Bank House, 1 High Timber Street, London EC4V 3SB (☎ 0171 329 0329)

EYRE, Dr Brian Leonard; CBE (1993); s of Leonard George Eyre (d 1988), and Mabel, *née* Rumsey (d 1984); *b* 29 Nov 1933; *Educ* Greenford GS, Univ of Surrey (BSc, DSc); *m* 5 June 1965, Elizabeth Caroline, da of Arthur Rackham (d 1954); 2 s (Peter John b 5 March 1966, Stephen Andrew b 22 Oct 1967); *Career* res offr CEGB 1959–62, prof of materials sci Univ of Liverpool 1979–84; UKAEA: various posts 1962–79, dir of fuel and engrg technol 1984–87, bd memb 1987–, dep chm 1989–, chief exec 1990–94; visiting prof: Univ of Liverpool 1984–, UCL 1995–; memb Cncl Univ of Salford 1986–; author of over 100 scientific papers, former chm Editorial Bd Jl of Nuclear Materials; CEng, CPhys, CIMgt, FIM, FInstP, FRSA, FEng 1992; *Recreations* walking, sailing, reading; *Clubs* Athenaeum; *Style*— Dr Brian Eyre, CBE, FEng; ✉ AEA Technology, Building 329, Harwell, Didcot, Oxfordshire OX11 0RA (☎ 01235 433206, fax 01235 433823)

EYRE, Sir Graham Newman; kt (1988), QC (1970); s of Cdr Newman Eyre, RNVR (d 1970); *b* 9 Jan 1931; *Educ* Marlborough, Trinity Coll Cambridge (MA, LLB); *m* 1954, Jean Dalrymple, da of late A D Walker; 1 s, 3 da; *Career* called to the Bar 1954 (Harmsworth Law scholar), bencher Middle Temple, recorder of the Crown Court 1975–; memb Lincoln's Inn, head of Chambers 1981–92; inspr Airport Inquiries (held at Quendon and Heathrow) 1981–83, Eyre Report on Airports submitted Nov 1984; justice of appeal British Indian Ocean Territory 1992; chm Walberton Parish Cncl 1971–76; *Clubs* Athenaeum; *Style*— Sir Graham Eyre, QC; ✉ Little Selham, Petworth GU28 0PS; Chambers, 2–3 Gray's Inn Square, Gray's Inn, London WC1R 5JH (☎ 0171 242 4986)

EYRE, Maj-Gen Sir James Ainsworth Campden Gabriel; KCVO (1986, CVO 1978), CBE (1980, OBE 1975); 2 s of Edward Joseph Eyre (d 1962), by his w, Hon Dorothy Elizabeth Anne Pelline Eyre, *née* Lyon-Dalberg-Acton, 2 da of 2 Baron Acton; *b* 2 Nov 1930; *Educ* Harvard (BA, LLB); *m* 1967, Monica Ruth Esther, da of Michael Joseph Smyth (d 1964), of Harley Street, London; 1 s (James b 1969), 1 da (Annabelle b 1970); *Career* RHG 1955 and RHG/D 1969; sec Chiefs of Staff Ctee MOD 1980–82, dir Def Prog Staff 1982–83; GOC London Dist and Maj-Gen Commanding Household Div 1983–86; dir Westminster Associates International Ltd 1989–; *Recreations* shooting, racing; *Clubs* Turf; *Style*— Maj-Gen Sir James Eyre, KCVO, CBE; ✉ Somerville House, East Garston, Berks RG17 7EX

EYRE, (Ethel) Mary; da of Cdr Charles Harding Drage (d 1983), and Enid Margaret, *née* Lomer; *b* 10 Sept 1931; *Educ* Elmhurst Ballet Sch, Rambert Sch, Royal Ballet Sch; *m* 1, 8 April 1958, Roderick Andrew (Rory) Fraser (d 1964), s of Maj the Hon Alastair Fraser, DSO (d 1949), of Moniack; 3 s (Anthony b 1959, Archibald b 1960, Thomas b 1964), 1 da (Eleanor b 1961); m 2, 7 July 1969, Edward (Ned) Eyre, s of Edward Eyre; 1 s (Robert b 1971), 3 da (Mathilda b 1970, Virginia b 1974, Constance b 1976); *Career* ballet dancer: Sadler's Wells Theatre Ballet 1948–50, Sadler's Wells Ballet (later the Royal Ballet) 1950–58 (soloist 1953, sr soloist 1956–58); teacher of classical Greek dance Royal Ballet Sch 1983–96; govr: Royal Ballet Sch 1984, Royal Ballet Co 1986; FISTD 1988; *Recreations* gardening, opera; *Clubs* Farmers'; *Style*— Mrs Edward Eyre; ✉ The Field House, Great Durnford, Salisbury, Wilts SP4 6AY (☎ 01722 782523)

EYRE, Peter Gervaise Joseph; s of Edward Joseph Eyre (d 1962), and Hon Dorothy Pelline, *née* Acton; *b* 11 March 1942; *Educ* Portsmouth Priory Sch Rhode Island USA, Downside; *Career* actor and director; contrib to numerous nat and int magazines; debut with Old Vic Co (Olympia Theatre Dublin, toured Russia and Poland) 1960, rep work in Harrogate, Glasgow, Nottingham, Liverpool, Leicester and Birmingham; *Theatre* incl: Alexeyev in Son of Oblomov (Comedy) 1964, title role in Benito Cereno (Mermaid) 1967, Prince Myshkin in The Idiot (Nottingham Playhouse Co) 1968–70, Konstantin in The Seagull (Chichester Festival) 1973, Oswald in Ghosts (Greenwich) 1974, title role in Hamlet (Greenwich) 1974, The Seagull (Greenwich) 1974, Tesman in Hedda Gabler (RSC, Aldwych, also toured Aust, Canada and USA) 1975, Baron Tuzenbach in The Three Sisters (Cambridge) 1976, The Man in Stevie (Vandeville) 1977, Raskolnikov in Crime and Punishment (Haymarket Leicester) 1978, Antiochus in Berenice (Lyric Hammersmith) 1982, Jacques in As You Like It (Chichester Festival) 1983, Tim in The Desert Air 1984–85, Toulon in Red Noses (RSC, Stratford, Barbican) 1984–85, Pyrrhus in Andromache (Old Vic) 1988, Edgar in King Lear (Old Vic) 1989, The Advocate in The Trial (Young Vic) 1993, Professor Brunelli in The Madman of the Balconies (Gate) 1993, Polonius in Hamlet (Almeida at Hackney, Belasco Theatre NY) 1995, Chere Maitre (Almeida and Melbourne Arts Festival) 1996; directed in theatre: Siblings (Lyric Hammersmith) 1989, Racine's Bajazet (Almeida) 1990; *Television* incl: A Misfortune, Platonov, The Birds Fall Down, Spyship, The Two Mrs Grenvilles, Memento Mori, Scarlett; *Films* incl: Mahler, Hedda, La Luna, Dragonslayer, Maurice, Just ask for Diamond, Mountains of the Moon, Let Him Have It, Orlando, The Remains of the Day, Princess Caraboo, Surviving Picasso, The Tango Lesson, The Honest Courtesan; *Publications* trans Klaus Mann's Siblings and The Children's Story (Marion Boyars); *Recreations* music; *Clubs* The Groucho, PEN, RAC; *Style*— Peter Eyre, Esq; ✉ ICM Ltd, Oxford House, 76 Oxford Street, London W1N 0AX (☎ 0171 636 6565, fax 0171 323 0101)

EYRE, Sir Reginald Edwin; kt (1984); s of Edwin Eyre, of Birmingham; *b* 28 May 1924; *Educ* King Edward's Camp Hill Sch Birmingham, Emmanuel Coll Cambridge (MA); *m* 1978, Anne Clements; 1 da Hermione Katharine (b 10 Nov 1979); *Career* RNVR 1942–45; slr 1950; sr ptnr Eyre & Co 1951–91; contested (C) Birmingham Northfield 1959; chm: W Midlands Area Cons Political Centre 1960–63, Nat Advsy Ctee 1964–66; MP (C) Birmingham Hall Green 1965–87; oppn whip 1966–70, Lord Cmmr Treasury 1970, comptroller of HM Household 1970–72, Parly under sec Environment (Housing and Construction) 1972–74, vice chm Conservative Party responsible for Urban Areas 1974–79; Parly under sec of state for: Trade (Corporate Affairs) 1979–82, Tport (Public Tport) 1982–83; chm: Birmingham Heartlands Ltd (East Birmingham Urban Devpt Agency) 1987–92, Birmingham Cable Ltd 1988–, Birmingham Heartlands Devpt Corp 1992–; dep chm Cmmn for the New Towns 1988–92; *Publications* Hope for our Towns and Cities (1977); *Clubs* Carlton; *Style*— Sir Reginald Eyre; ✉ 1041 Stratford Road, Birmingham B28 8AS; 7 Wallside, Monkwell Square, Barbican, London EC2Y 8BH (☎ 0171 374 2748)

EYRE, Richard Anthony; *b* 3 May 1954; *Educ* King's Coll Sch Wimbledon, Lincoln Coll Oxford (MA), Harvard Business Sch (AMP); *Career* airtime buyer Benton & Bowles 1972–76, sales gp head Scottish Television 1976–77, head of media planning Benton & Bowles 1980–84 (media planner 1977–80), media dir Aspect 1984–86, media dir Bartle Bogle Hegarty 1986–91 (Media Week Agency of the Year 1990 and 1991), md Capital

Radio plc 1991–; *Style*— Richard Eyre, Esq; ✉ Capital Radio plc, Euston Tower, London NW1 3DR (☎ 0171 608 6161, fax 0171 608 6184)

EYRE, Sir Richard Charles Hastings; kt (1997), CBE (1992); s of Cdr Richard Galfridus Hastings Giles Eyre, RN (d 1990), of Dorset, and Minna Mary Jessica (d 1992), o child of Vice Adm Sir Charles William Rawson Royds, KBE, CMG, antarctic explorer Scott's 1st Lt; *b* 28 March 1943; *Educ* Sherborne, Univ of Cambridge (BA); *m* 1973, Sue Elizabeth Birtwistle, *qv*; 1 da (Lucy b 1974); *Career* theatre, television and film dir; assoc dir Lyceum Theatre Edinburgh 1968–71, dir Nottingham Playhouse 1973–78, prodr Play For Today BBC TV 1978–80, dir Royal Nat Theatre 1988– (assoc dir 1980–86); Hon DLitt: Nottingham Trent Univ 1992, South Bank Univ 1994; hon fell Goldsmiths' Coll 1993, fell St Catherine's Coll 1997, Cameron MacKintosh Professorship 1997; hon memb Guildhall 1996; FKC 1994; *Theatre* incl: Comedians 1974, Hamlet 1980, Guys and Dolls 1982, Richard III 1990, Night of the Iguana 1992, David Hare Trilogy 1993, Skylight 1995, La Grande Magia 1995, The Prince's Play 1996, John Gabriel Borkman 1996; *Opera* incl La Traviata (Royal Opera House) 1994; *Films* The Ploughman's Lunch (Evening Standard Award for Best Film 1983), Laughterhouse (TV Prize Venice Film Festival 1984); *TV Films* incl: Suddenly Last Summer 1992, The Imitation Game, Pasmore 1980, Country 1981, The Insurance Man (Tokyo Prize) 1986, Past Caring 1986, v (RTS Award) 1988, Tumbledown (Italia RAI Prize 1988, BAFTA Award 1988), Absence of War 1995; *Awards* incl: SWET Dir of the Year 1982, Evening Standard Best Dir 1982, STV Awards for Best Production 1969, 1970 and 1971, Sorrento Film Festival De Sica Award 1986, The Patricia Rothermere Award 1995; many Olivier Award nominations for Best Director; *Books* Utopia and Other Places (autobiography, 1993); *Style*— Sir Richard Eyre, CBE; ✉ Royal National Theatre, South Bank, London SE1 9PX (☎ 0171 928 2033)

EYRE, Very Rev Richard Montague Stephens; s of Montague Henry Eyre (d 1974), and Ethel Mary, *née* Raw (d 1975); memb of Derbys branch of Eyre family; *b* 16 May 1929; *Educ* Charterhouse, Oriel Coll Oxford (MA); *m* 28 Dec 1963, Anne Mary, da of Canon G B Bentley, of 5 The Cloisters, Windsor Castle; 2 da (Chantal b 1966, Henrietta b 1972); *Career* asst curate St Mark Portsea 1956–59, tutor and chaplain Chichester Theol Coll 1959–62, chaplain Eastbourne Coll 1962–65; vicar: Arundel with Tortington and South Stoke 1965–73, Good Shepherd Brighton 1973–75; archdeacon of Chichester 1975–81, treas Chichester Cathedral 1978–81, dean of Exeter 1981–95, ret; *Recreations* golf, travel, wine, music; *Clubs* United Oxford and Cambridge Univ; *Style*— The Very Rev Richard Eyre; ✉ Hathersage, Enmore Road, Enmore, Bridgwater, Somerset TA5 2DP (☎ 01278 671790)

EYRE, Stephen John Arthur; s of Leslie James Eyre, of Solihull, and Joyce Mary, *née* Whitehouse; *b* 17 Oct 1957; *Educ* Solihull Sch, New Coll Oxford (MA, BCL); *m* 1 July 1989, Margaret Lynn, da of William John Goodman, of Coalville; *Career* called to the Bar Inner Temple 1981; lectr in law New Coll Oxford 1980–84; memb Solihull Met Borough Cncl 1983–91 and 1992–; Parly candidate (C): Birmingham (Hodge Hill) 1987, Strangford 1990; *Recreations* reading, theatre, bridge; *Style*— Stephen Eyre, Esq; ✉ 1 Fountain Court, Steelhouse Lane, Birmingham B4 6DR (☎ 0121 236 5721)

EYRE-TANNER, Peter Giles; *see:* Squire, Giles

EYSENCK, Prof Hans Jürgen; s of Eduard Anton Eysenck (d 1972), and Ruth, *née* Werner (d 1986); *b* 4 March 1916; *Educ* Bismarck Gymnasium Berlin, Friedrich Wilhelm Real-Gymnasium Berlin, Univ of London (BA, PhD, DSc); *m* 1, 1942 (m dis 1950), Margaret Davies; 1 s (Michael Eysenck, *qv*, b 1944); m 2, 30 Sept 1950, Sybil Bianca Guiletta, da of Max Rostal, OBE, of Berne, Switzerland; 3 s (Gary b 1953, Kevin b 1959, Darrin b 1966), 1 da (Connie b 1957); *Career* res psychologist Mill Hill Emergency Hosp 1942–49; Univ of London: reader in psychology 1949–55, prof 1955–83, emeritus prof 1983; visiting prof: Univ of Pennsylvania 1949–50, Univ of Calif Berkeley 1955; pres Int Soc for Study of Individual Differences 1983–85; fell: Br Psychological Soc, American Psychological Assoc, German Psychological Assoc; *Awards* Distinguished Sci Award American Psychological Assoc 1988, Distinguished Contributions Award Int Soc for the Study of Individual Differences 1991, William James Fellow Award American Psychological Soc 1994, Presidential Citation for Scientific Contribution American Psychological Assoc 1993, Fechner Empirical Aesthetics Award (for contribs to field of empirical aesthetics) Int Assoc of Empirical Aesthetics 1996, Centennial Award for Distinguished Contribs to Clinical Psychology American Psychological Assoc 1996, Fndn Medal Hans Juergen Eysenck Inst Winterthur Switzerland 1996; *Books* incl: Dimensions of Personality (1947), The Psychology of Politics (1954), Smoking, Health and Personality (1965), The Biological Basis of Personality (1967), Handbook of Abnormal Psychology (ed, 1973), Crime and Personality (1977), Structure and Measurement of Intelligence (1979), The Causes and Effects of Smoking (1980), Personality and Individual Differences (with M Eysenck, 1985), Decline and Fall of the Freudian Empire (1985), Genes, Culture and Personality (with L Eaves and N Martin, 1989); *Recreations* tennis, squash; *Style*— Prof Hans Eysenck; ✉ 10 Dorchester Drive, London SE24 (☎ 0171 733 8129); Institute of Psychiatry, De Crespigny Park, Denmark Hill, London SE5 8AF (☎ 0171 703 5411, fax 0171 703 5796)

EYSENCK, Prof Michael William; s of Hans Jürgen Eysenck, *qv*, of London, and Margaret Malcolm, *née* Davies (d 1986); *b* 8 Feb 1944; *Educ* Dulwich, UCL (BA, Rosa Morison Prize for outstanding arts graduate); *m* 22 March 1975, (Mary) Christine, da of Waldemar Kabyn, of London; 1 s (William James Thomas b 1983), 2 da (Fleur Davina Ruth b 1979, Juliet Margaret Maria Alexandra b 1985); *Career* reader in psychology Birkbeck Coll London 1981–87 (lectr 1965–80), prof of psychology and head of dept Royal Holloway and Bedford Coll Univ of London 1987–; chm Cognitive Psychology Section Br Psychological Soc 1982–87, memb Advsy Bd Euro Soc for Cognitive Psychology; MBPsS 1965; *Books* Human Memory - Theory, Research and Individual Differences (1977), Mindwatching (with H J Eysenck, 1981), Attention and Arousal - Cognition and Performance (1982), A Handbook of Cognitive Psychology (1984), Personality and Individual Differences (with H J Eysenck, 1985), Memory - A Cognitive Approach (with G Cohen and M E Levoi, 1986), Student Learning - Research in Education and Cognitive Psychology (with J T E Richardson and D W Piper, 1987), Mindwatching - Why We Behave the Way We Do (with H J Eysenck, 1989), Happiness - Facts and Myths (1990), Cognitive Psychology - An International Review (1990), Cognitive Psychology - A Student's Handbook (with M T Keane, 1990, 3 edn 1995), Blackwell's Dictionary of Cognitive Psychology (1990), Anxiety - The Cognitive Perspective (1992), Principles of Cognitive Psychology (1994), Perspectives on Psychology (1994), Individual Differences - Normal and Abnormal (1994), Simply Psychology (1996); *Recreations* tennis, travel, walking, golf, boules; *Style*— Prof Michael Eysenck; ✉ Royal Holloway, University of London, Department of Psychology, Egham Hill, Egham, Surrey TW20 0EX (☎ 01784 443530, fax 01784 434347)

EYTON, Anthony John Plowden; s of Capt John Seymour Eyton (d 1979), of Old Meadows, Silchester, nr Reading, and Phyllis Annie, *née* Tyser (d 1929); *b* 17 May 1923; *Educ* Canford, Univ of Reading, Camberwell Sch of Art (NDD); *m* 20 Aug 1960 (m dis 1986), (Frances) Mary Capell; 3 da (Jane Elizabeth Phyllis, Clare Alice, Sarah Mary); *Career* served Army 1942–47; artist; Abbey Maj scholarship 1951–53, John Moores prizewinner Liverpool 1972, Worshipful Co of Grocers fellowship 1973, first prize Second Br Int Drawing Biennale 1975, retrospective S London Art Gallery 1980, Charles Woolaston award Royal Acad 1981; exhibitions: Browse and Darby 1975, 1978, 1981, 1985, 1987, 1990, 1993 and 1996, Hong Kong Imperial War Museum 1983, Austin/Desmond Fine Art 1990; teacher Royal Acad Schs; RA 1986 (ARA 1976), RWS 1987, Royal Cambrian Acad 1993; memb: NEAC, RWA, hon memb Pastel Soc, Hon ROI; *Recreations* gardening; *Clubs* Arts; *Style*— Anthony Eyton, Esq, RA

EZRA, Baron (Life Peer UK 1982), of Horsham in the Co of West Sussex; Derek Ezra; kt (1974), MBE (1945); s of late David and Lillie Ezra; *b* 23 Feb 1919; *Educ* Monmouth Sch, Magdalene Coll Cambridge (MA); *m* 1950, Julia Elizabeth, da of Thomas Wilkins, of Portsmouth, Hants; *Career* Army Serv 1939–47; memb UK Delgn to Euro Coal and Steel Community 1952–56; Nat Coal Bd: joined 1947, regnl sales mangr 1958–60, dir gen Marketing 1960–65, memb Bd 1965–67, dep chm 1967–71, chm 1971–82; chm Br Iron & Steel Consumers' Cncl 1983–87; dir: Redland plc 1982–89, Solvay SA 1979–89; chm: Associated Heat Services PLC 1966–, Br Inst of Mgmnt 1976–78, Energy and Technical Services Group PLC 1990–; industl advsr to Morgan Grenfell 1982–87; pres: Coal Indust Soc 1981–86, Inst of Trading Standards Admin 1987–92; hon fell Magdalene Coll Cambridge; Liveryman Worshipful Co of Haberdashers; *Style*— The Rt Hon Lord Ezra, MBE; ✉ House of Lords, Westminster, London SW1A OPW

EZZAMEL, Prof Mahmoud Azmy; s of Mahmoud Mahmoud Ezzamel (d 1975), of Egypt, and Fatima, *née* El-Shirbini; *b* 24 Oct 1942; *Educ* Univ of Alexandria (BCom, MCom), Univ of Southampton (PhD); *m* 31 March 1979, Ann, da of Herbert Edgar Jackman, of Coventry; 1 s (Adam b 29 March 1983), 2 da (Nadia b 29 Jan 1985, Samia b 6 July 1988); *Career* lectr and sr lectr Univ of Southampton 1975–88, visiting assoc prof Queen's Univ Kingston Ontario Canada 1986–87, Ernst & Young prof of accounting Univ Coll Wales Aberystwyth 1988–90, Price Waterhouse prof of accounting and fin UMIST 1990–96, prof of accounting and fin Univ of Manchester 1996–; hon prof Univ Coll Wales Aberystwyth 1991–, visiting prof Massey Univ New Zealand March 1993, visiting Scholar Queen's Univ Canada July-Aug 1994; assoc ed Accounting and Business Research; *Books* Advanced Management Accounting: An Organisational Emphasis (1987), Perspectives on Financial Control (1992), Business Unit and Divisional Performance Measurement (1992, Italian edn 1995), Changing Managers and Managing Change (1996); *Recreations* volley-ball, tennis; *Clubs* UCW Aberystwyth, Aberystwyth Tennis; *Style*— Prof Mahmoud Ezzamel; ✉ Department of Accounting and Finance, University of Manchester, Oxford Road, Manchester M13 9PL (☎ (direct) 0161 275 4564, fax 0161 275 4023, e-mail Mahmoud.Ezzamel@man.ac.uk)

F

FABER, Lady (Ann) Caroline; *née* Macmillan; da of 1 Earl of Stockton (d 1986); *b* 1923; *m* 1944, Julian Tufnell Faber; 4 s (1 s d 1991), 1 da; *Style*— The Lady Caroline Faber; ✉ Fisher's Gate, Withyham, Hartfield, E Sussex TN7 4BB (☎ 01892 770 246)

FABER, David; MP (C) Westbury (majority 12,618); s of Julian Faber, and Lady Caroline Faber, *née* Macmillan, da of late 1 Earl of Stockton, OM, PC, FRS; *b* 7 July 1961; *Educ* Summer Fields, Eton, Balliol Coll Oxford (MA); *m* 1988, Sally, *née* Gilbert; 1 s; *Career* Cons res asst House of Commons 1984–85, in Campaigning Dept Cons Central Office 1985–87 (incl asst to Jeffrey Archer as dep chm), co-fndr and dir Sterling Marketing Ltd mktg consultancy 1987–; Parly candidate (C) Stockton N 1987, MP (C) Westbury 1992–; PPS to: Baroness Chalker of Wallasey 1994–96, Rt Hon Stephen Dorrell as Sec of State for Health 1996–; memb House of Commons Select Ctee on Social Security 1992–, sec Cons Backbench Educn Ctee 1992–94; memb Lloyd's; *Publications* Bearing the Standard - Themes for a Fourth Term (jtly with nine other Cons candidates, 1991); *Recreations* cricket, golf, squash, all things Spanish; *Clubs* Vincent's (Oxford), Royal St George's Golf, MCC, Queen's, White's; *Style*— David Faber, Esq, MP; ✉ House of Commons, London SW1A 0AA (☎ 0171 219 3000)

FABER, Sir Richard Stanley; KCVO (1980), CMG (1977); er s of Sir Geoffrey Cust Faber (d 1961), and Enid Eleanor (d 1995), da of Sir Henry Erle Richards, KCSI, KC; bro of Thomas Erle Faber, *qv*; *b* 6 Dec 1924; *Educ* Westminster, ChCh Oxford (MA); *Career* served RNVR 1943–46; entered HM Dip Serv 1950; served: Baghdad, Paris, Abidjan, Washington; cnsllr: The Hague 1969–73, Cairo 1973–75; asst under sec of state FCO 1975–77, ambass Algiers 1977–81, ret; Liveryman Worshipful Co of Goldsmiths; FRSL 1972; *Books* Beaconsfield and Bolingbroke (1961), The Vision and the Need: Late Victorian Imperialist Aims (1966), Proper Stations: Class in Victorian Fiction (1971), French and English (1975), The Brave Courtier (Sir William Temple) (1983), High Road to England (1985), Young England (1987), A Brother's Murder (1993); *Clubs* Travellers'; *Style*— Sir Richard Faber, KCVO, CMG, FRSL; ✉ Flat 2, 101 St Georges Drive, London SW1V 4DA

FABER, Thomas Erle; yr s of Sir Geoffrey Cust Faber (d 1961); bro of Sir Richard Faber, KCVO, CMG, *qv*; *b* 25 April 1927; *Educ* Oundle, Trinity Coll Cambridge (MA, PhD); *m* 1, 1959, Penelope Morton (d 1983); 2 s (Matthew b 1963, Tobias b 1965), 2 da (Henrietta b 1961, Polly b 1971); m 2, 1986, Elisabeth van Houts; 1 s (Benjamin b 1988), 1 da (Sophie b 1986); *Career* fell Corpus Christi Coll Cambridge 1953–, lectr in physics Univ of Cambridge 1959–93; chm Geoffrey Faber Holdings Ltd 1977– (dir 1969–); Liveryman Worshipful Co of Grocers; *Recreations* walking, local history; *Style*— Thomas Faber, Esq; ✉ The Old Vicarage, Thompson's Lane, Cambridge (☎ 01223 356685)

FABER, Thomas Henry; s of F S Faber (d 1954), of Romsey, Hants, and Amy, *née* Purcell-Gilpin (d 1957); *b* 5 Nov 1922; *Educ* Ampleforth, ChCh Oxford; *m* 28 July 1951, Jennifer Mary, da of A E L Hill, OBE, DL (d 1986), of Twyford, Winchester, Hants; 1 s (Robin H G Faber b 1955), 2 da (Caroline (Mrs Faber-Zini) b 1952, Juliet (Mrs Moore) b 1959); *Career* WWII Capt Grenadier Gds; served: N Africa, Italy (wounded 1944, despatches), Palestine, Egypt; chartered surveyor; ptnr James Harris Winchester (sr ptnr 1980), ret 1993; dir: Strong & Co 1967–73, Whitbread Wessex 1973–81, chm Hants Branch CLA 1976–79; FRICS 1956 (ARICS 1950); *Recreations* hunting, shooting; *Style*— Thomas Faber, Esq; ✉ Harewood Cottage, Chicksgrove, Tisbury, Salisbury, Wilts SP3 6NB (☎ 01722 714442)

FABER, Trevor Martyn; s of Harry Faber (d 1986), of Edgbaston, Birmingham, and Millicent, *née* Waxman (d 1988); *b* 9 Oct 1946; *Educ* Clifton, Merton Coll Oxford (MA, Capt OUABC and blue); *m* 16 Aug 1985, Katrina Sally, da of George James Clay, of Harborne, Birmingham; *Career* called to the Bar Gray's Inn 1970, in practice Midland and Oxford Circuit, recorder of the Crown Court 1994–; memb Tanworth-in-Arden Assoc for the Prosecution of Felons; *Recreations* theatre, literature, sport, music, food and wine; *Clubs* Vincent's (Oxford); *Style*— Trevor Faber, Esq; ✉ 3 Fountain Court, Steelhouse Lane, Birmingham B4 6DR (☎ 0121 236 5854, fax 0121 236 7008)

FABRICANT, Michael Louis David; MP (C) Staffordshire Mid (majority 6,236); s of late Isaac Nathan Fabricant, and Helen, *née* Freed; *b* 12 June 1950; *Educ* state schs, Loughborough Univ (BA), Univ of Sussex (MSc), Univ of London and Univ of Southern California LA (DPhil); *Career* former bdcaster BBC News and Current Affrs, co-fndr and dir int bdcast and communications gp until 1992, economist and advsr on bdcasting to Home Office and various foreign govts; Parly candidate (C) South Shields 1987, MP (C) Staffs Mid 1992–; PPS to Michael Jack as Fin Sec to the Treasy; vice chm Cons Pty Media Ctee, memb Nat Heritage Select Ctee 1993–, memb Euro Scrutiny Ctee B (Trade and Industry) 1993–, sec Cons Party Educn Ctee, treas All-Party Cable & Satellite Ctee; lawyer and chartered electronics engr; memb Cncl IEE; CEng, FIEE 1994; *Recreations* reading, music, fell walking, skiing, listening to the Archers; *Clubs* Rottingdean; *Style*— Michael Fabricant, Esq, MP; ✉ House of Commons, London SW1A 0AA

FACER, Roger Lawrence Lowe; CB (1992); s of John Ernest Facer (d 1983), of Epsom, and Phyllis, *née* Lowe (d 1979); *b* 28 June 1933; *Educ* Rugby, St John's Coll Oxford (MA); *m* 2 April 1960, Ruth Margaret, da of Herbert Mostyn Lewis, PhD (d 1985), of Gresford, Clwyd; 3 da (Sian b 1961, Lucinda b 1961, Emma b 1965); *Career* East Surrey Regt 2 Lt 1951–53; War Office 1957, asst private sec to Sec of State 1958, Cabinet Office 1966–68, private sec to Min of State (equipment) MOD 1970, Int Inst for Strategic Studies 1972–73, cnsllr UK Delegation MBFR Vienna 1973–75, private sec to Sec of State for Def 1976–79, asst under sec of state MOD 1979–81, under sec Cabinet Office 1981–83, Rand Corp Santa Monica USA 1984, asst under sec of state MOD 1984–87, dep under sec of state MOD 1988–93; DG Carroll Inst 1993–95; *Recreations* alpine gardening, hill walking, opera; *Style*— Roger Facer, Esq, CB; ✉ Kennett Lodge, Hambledon, Hants PO7 4SA

FAGAN, Mary; JP; da of Col and Mrs George Vere-Laurie, of Carlton Hall, Newark, Notts; *b* 11 Sept 1939; *Educ* St Elphins Sch Matlock, Southover Manor Sussex; *m* Capt Christopher Tarleton Feltrim Fagan, Grenadier Gds; 2 s (Capt Christopher Hugh Fagan (d 1987), Capt James Fagan); *Career* memb: Advsy Ctee Cancer Relief Macmillan Fund, Basingstoke and N Hants Industrial Mission; chm: Countess of Brecknock Hospice, Home Care Service Appeal; pres: Basingstoke Male Voice Choir, ESU, Hants Cncl of Community Service, Hants Co Scouts Cncl, Hants and Isle of Wight Youth Options, Hants Voluntary Housing Soc, Hants Appeal Ctee Prince's Tst and Prince's Youth Business Tst, Research Into Ageing (Hants), Hants Ctee Territorial Auxiliary and Volunteer Reserve Assoc, Winchester Assoc of Nat Tst Membs, Southern Region Ctee Winged Fellowship; vice pres: Hospital Saving Assoc, Southern Regnl Assoc for the Blind, Assoc for the Deaf, Enham Tst, Fortune Centre of Riding Therapy, Hants and Wight Tst for Maritime Archaeology, Mary Rose Tst; tstee: Edwina Mountbatten Tst, Whitchurch Silk Mill, Andover and District Med Fund, Hants Gardens Tst, Marwell Zoological Park, New Theatre Royal; patron: Basingstoke Ladies Choir, Bournemouth Orchestras' Centenary Appeal, Hants Branch Br Red Cross, Andover Branch Cruse, Hants Co Youth Band, Hants Music Tst, Helping Hand Campaign; govr King Edward VI Sch; Lord Lt for Co of Hants 1994–; memb Chapter Gen, memb Cncl King Edward VII Hosp; Freewoman Worshipful Co of Saddlers 1962; DStJ (pres Cncl for Hants 1994–); *Recreations* country sports; *Style*— Mrs Mary Fagan, JP; ✉ Deane Hill House, Deane, nr Basingstoke, Hants RG25 3AX (☎ 01256 780591, fax 01256 782627)

FAGAN, Neil John; s of Lt Cdr C H Fagan, of Bucks Horn Oak, nr Farnham, and Majorie Sadie-Jane, *née* Campbell-Bannerman; *b* 5 June 1947; *Educ* Cheam Sch Charterhouse, Univ of Southampton (LLB); *m* 21 June 1975, Catherine, da of R J Hewitt, of Hurtmore, Godalming, Surrey; 3 da (Caroline Louise b 31 Oct 1977, Felicity Clare b 1 May 1980, Emily Catherine b 20 June 1983); *Career* Lovell White Durrant (formerly Durrant Piesse, orginally Durrant Cooper and Hambling): articled clerk 1969–71, ptnr 1975–; memb Worshipful Co of Slrs; memb: Law Soc, Int Bar Assoc; *Books* Contracts of Employment (1990); *Recreations* family, swimming, sailing, gardening; *Clubs* Royal Lymington Yacht, MCC; *Style*— Neil Fagan, Esq; ✉ Little Orchard, Farm Lane, Crondall, Farnham, Surrey GU10 5QE; Lovell White Durrant, 65 Holborn Viaduct, London EC1 (☎ 071 236 0066)

FAGAN, Maj-Gen Patrick Feltrim; CB (1990), MBE (1966); s of Air Cdre Thomas Patrick (Paddy) Feltrim Fagan, RAF (d 1985), and Hon Isabel Mairi, *née* Arundell; *b* 8 Dec 1935; *Educ* Stonyhurst, RMA Sandhurst, UCL (MSc); *m* 29 July 1967, Veronica Eileen, da of Joseph Lorant (d 1990); 2 s (Daragh Patrick Feltrim b 1969, Rory Michael Feltrim b 1972); *Career* cmmnd RE 1955, served Gibraltar, Germany, Aden and Oman; int scientific expedition Karakoram 1961–62, UAE-Oman border survey 1964, jt servs expedition South Georgia 1964–65 (ldr surveying party, also made first ascent of an un-named peak, now offically known as Mount Fagan), 42 Survey Engr Regt 1965–68, Ordnance Survey 1969–73 (Maj 1969), Survey 4 MOD 1973–76 (Lt-Col 1974), cmd Tech Servs Gp 1976–79, geographic advsr HQ Allied Forces Central Europe (NATO) Netherlands 1979–83 (Col 1979), chief geographic offr Supreme HQ Allied Powers Europe (NATO) Belgium 1983–85, dir Survey Ops MOD 1985–87 (Brig 1985), dir gen Military Survey 1987–90 (Maj-Gen 1987), Col Cmdt RE 1991 (Representative Col Cmdt 1992); survey and mapping conslt 1990–; author of numerous articles on surveying and mapping in: Geographical Journal, Photogrammetric Record, Survey Review, Chartered Surveyor, RE Journal; author articles on ski mountaineering in subject journals; memb: Nat Ctee for Photogrammetry and Remote Sensing 1987–90, Cncl RICS (Land Survey) 1987–91, RICS Pres's Disciplinary & Appeals Tbnl 1989–95, Cncl RGS 1987–92 and 1993–95 (vice pres 1990–92), Ctee Royal Soc (Cartography) 1987–90, Cncl Br Schs Exploring Soc 1987–90, Advsy Bd Inst of Engrg Surveyors Univ of Nottingham 1988–91, Ctee of Mgmnt Mount Everest Fndn 1989–95 (dep chm 1990–92, chm 1992–94); dep pres Army Rugby Union 1989–91; FRGS 1966, FRICS 1981 (ARICS 1971), FIMgt 1981 (MIMgt 1971); *Recreations* mountain activities, cricket, boats, photography, music; *Clubs* MCC, Alpine, Alpine Ski (vice pres 1992–95, pres 1995–), Eagle Ski (pres 1988–91), Geographical, Royal Over-Seas League; *Style*— Maj-Gen Patrick Fagan, CB, MBE; ✉ c/o Royal Over-Seas League, Over-Seas House, Park Place, St James's Street, London SW1A 1LR

FAGGE, John Christopher; s and h of Sir John William Frederick Fagge, 11 Bt, *qv*; *b* 30 April 1942; *m* 13 April 1974, Evelyn Joy, *née* Golding; *Style*— John Fagge, Esq

FAGGE, Sir John William Frederick; 11 Bt (E 1660), of Wiston, Sussex; s of William Archibald Theodore Fagge (d 1924), 4 s of 8 Bt, and Nellie, *née* Wise (d 1924); suc unc, Sir John Harry Lee Fagge, 10 Bt, 1940; *b* 28 Sept 1910; *m* 11 May 1940, Ivy Gertrude (d 1992), da of William Edward Frier, of Newington, Kent; 1 s (John Christopher b 1942), 1 da (Pauline Joy b 1943); *Heir* s, John Christopher Fagge, *qv*; *Career* farmer; *Style*— Sir John Fagge, Bt; ✉ 11 Forbes Road, Faversham, Kent ME13 8QF

FAINT, John Anthony Leonard (Tony); s of Thomas Leonard Faint (d 1976), and Josephine Rosey, *née* Dunkerley; *b* 24 Nov 1942; *Educ* Chigwell Sch, Magdalen Coll Oxford (BA), Fletcher Sch Medford Mass (MA); *m* 24 June 1978, Elizabeth Theresa, da of Walter Winter (d 1960); *Career* Miny of Overseas Devpt (later Overseas Devpt Admin) 1965–71, 1974–80, 1983–86 and 1989–; study leave Cambridge Mass 1968–69, first sec (aid) Blantyre Malawi 1971–73, head SE Asia Devpt Div Bangkok 1980–83, UK alternate exec dir IBRD Washington 1986–89, head E Asia Dept ODA London 1989–90, under sec Int Div ODA 1990–91, under sec E Europe and UK exec dir European Bank for Reconstruction and Development 1991–92, under sec E Europe and Western Hemisphere 1993–; *Recreations* music, bridge, chess, squash, computers; *Style*— Tony Faint, Esq; ✉ Old Admiralty Building, Whitehall, London SW1A 2AF (☎ 0171 210 3809)

FAIR, Howard Russell; s of Donald Robert Russell Fair, of Folkstone, Kent, and Patricia Laurie, *née* Rudland; *b* 13 July 1943; *Educ* The King's Sch Canterbury; *m* 21 Aug 1971, Linda Frances, da of late Harold Richard Webber; 1 s (Nicholas Sebastian b 9 June 1974), 1 da (Catherine Jane b 11 Aug 1976); *Career* Coll of Air Trg Hamble 1961; Price Waterhouse CAs: articled clerk 1962–66, qualified sr 1966–67; chief accountant Spring Grove Services (part of Charterhouse Group) 1967–70, fin dir and co sec Henderson Kenton plc 1970–79, fin dir Home Charm plc 1979–81, fin dir Allen Brady & Marsh advtg agency 1982–84, UK gp fin dir Ted Bates Holdings advtg agency 1985–86, co-fndr and gp fin dir Woollams Moira Gaskin O'Malley 1986–90, gp chief fin offr and commercial dir SP Lintas Group 1990–94, chief fin offr Ammirati Puris Lintas Europe and Africa 1995–; Freeman City of London 1980, Liveryman Worshipful Co of Glass Sellers 1980; FCA, FIMgt, MIPA; *Recreations* deep sea sailing, golf, some distance running, jazz; *Clubs* Island Sailing, Southgate 41 (ex-Round Tablers); *Style*— Howard Fair, Esq; ✉ 29 Canons Close, Radlett, Herts WD7 7ER (☎ and fax 01923 853391); Ammirati Puris Lintas Worldwide, 84 Eccleston Square, Victoria, London SW1V 1PX (☎ 0171 932 8888, fax 0171 932 8577)

FAIR, Dr (James) Stuart; CBE (1997); s of late James S Fair, of Perth, and Margaret, *née* McCallum; *b* 30 Sept 1930; *Educ* Perth Acad, Univ of St Andrews (MA), Univ of Edinburgh (LLB); *m* 13 July 1957, Anne Lesley, da of late Rev Neil Cameron, of Monifieth; 2 s (Andrew Nigel b 1961, Donald James Cameron b 1965), 1 da (Hilary Anne b 1963); *Career* slr; formerly sr ptnr Thorntons WS Dundee (currently conslt); hon sheriff and temp sheriff; formerly: lectr in taxation and tutor in professional ethics Faculty of Law Univ of Dundee, clerk to Cmmrs of Inland Revenue Dundee Dist; dir of private investmt tst companies; chm Dundee Port Authy and Dundee Teaching Hosps NHS Tst until Dec 1996; tstee Caird's Travelling Scholarship Fund; formerly: memb Tayside Ctee on Med Research Ethics, chm Ct Univ of Dundee, pres Dundee and Tayside C of C & Indust, memb Tayside Health Bd, chm Review Ctee Perth Prison, memb Scot Slrs' Discipline Tbnl, memb Cncl Soc of Writers to Her Majesty's Signet, dean Faculty of Procurators Dundee, sec Tayside IOD, pres Dundee Choral Union; Hon LLD Univ of Dundee 1994; *Recreations* bridge, travel, opera-going; *Clubs* New (Edinburgh); *Style—* Dr J Stuart Fair, CBE, WS; ✉ Beechgrove House, 474 Perth Rd, Dundee DD2 1LL (☎ 01382 669783); Thorntons, Whitehall Chambers, 11 Whitehall St, Dundee DD1 4AE (☎ 01382 229111)

FAIRBAIRN, Sir (James) Brooke; 6 Bt (UK 1869), of Ardwick, Lancs; s of Sir William Albert Fairbairn, 5 Bt (d 1972), and Christine Renée Cotton, *née* Croft; *b* 10 Dec 1930; *Educ* Stowe; *m* 5 Nov 1960, Mary Russell (d 1992), o da of late William Russell Scott; 2 s (Robert William b 1965, George Edward b 1969), 1 da (Fiona Mary (Mrs James Gordon) b 1967); *Heir* s, Robert William Fairbairn, *qv*; *Career* proprietor of J Brooke Fairbairn & Co Newmarket (furnishing fabric converters); Upper Bailiff Worshipful Co of Weavers 1992–93; *Style—* Sir Brooke Fairbairn, Bt; ✉ Barkway House, Bury Rd, Newmarket, Suffolk CB8 7BT (☎ 01638 662733); The Railway Station, Newmarket, Suffolk CB8 9BA (☎ 01638 665766, fax 01638 665124)

FAIRBAIRN, David Ritchie; OBE (1990); s of George Forrester Fairbairn (d 1967), and Eileen Bartlett (d 1988); *b* 4 July 1934; *Educ* Mill Hill Sch, Gonville and Caius Coll Cambridge (MA); *m* 6 Sept 1958, Hon Susan, da of Baron Hill of Luton (Life Peer, d 1989); 1 s (Charles b 1963), 2 da (Carolyn b 1960, Heather b 1965); *Career* 2 Lt RA (Korea) 1952–54; overseas market mangr Arthur Guinness Son & Co Ltd 1960, mktg Guinness Overseas Ltd 1969, md ICC Dataset Ltd 1970, mangr Retail and Distribution Sector Int Computers Ltd 1975, co dir and md James Martin Assoc UK Ltd 1985–89, md James Martin Associates PLC 1989–91, gp md JMA Information Engineering Ltd 1991–94, md James Martin and Co Ltd 1991–93, vice chm James Martin Holdings Ltd 1993–, vice pres Texas Instruments Europe 1992–94; dir: The Nat Computing Centre 1980–86, Mkt EMI Medical Ltd 1976, British Standards Inst 1985; chm Automation and Information Technol Cncl 1985; has various other directorships; pres: Cambridge Union Soc 1958, Guinness Harp Corp NY 1964; vice chm Parly Info Technol Ctee 1982; memb: Focus Ctee on Standards 1982, Monopolies and Mergers Cmmn 1985–, Patent Office Steering Bd 1989–; Liveryman Worshipful Co of Information Technologists 1987; FIDPM; FBCS, FInstD, FRSA; *Recreations* sailing, skiing, water-skiing; *Clubs* Institute of Directors; *Style—* David Fairbairn, Esq, OBE

FAIRBAIRN, John Sydney; DL (1996); s of Sydney George Fairbairn, MC, and Angela Maude, *née* Fane; *b* 15 Jan 1934; *Educ* Eton, Trinity Coll Cambridge (MA); *m* 18 March 1968, Camilla, da of Geoffrey Norman Grinling, of Belmont, East Hoathly, Sussex; 1 s (John Harry b 1969), 2 da (Rose b (twin) 1969, Flora b 1972); 2 step s, 2 step da; *Career* Nat Serv 2 Lt 17/21 Lancers 1952–54; with Monkhouse Stoneham & Co 1957–60; M&G Group plc: joined 1961, dir 1974, dep chm 1979–89, non-exec dir 1989–; chm Esmée Fairbairn Charitable Tst 1988– (tstee 1965–); chm Central European Growth Fund PLC 1994–; dep chm LAUTRO Ltd 1986–89; chm Unit Tst Assoc 1989–91; hon treas and memb Cncl King's Coll London 1972–84 (also hon fell King's Coll), memb Cncl Univ of Buckingham 1987–95; memb Cncl Policy Studies Inst; tstee: Dulwich Picture Gallery, Monteverdi Tst, Friends of Royal Pavilion Art Gallery and Museums Brighton, Comeback; patron New Sussex Opera; Hon DUniv Buckingham; FCA; *Clubs* Brooks's, White's, MCC; *Style—* J S Fairbairn, Esq, DL; ✉ Harvest Hill, Cuckfield, W Sussex RH17 5AH

FAIRBAIRN, Robert William; s and h of Sir Brooke Fairbairn, 6 Bt, *qv*; *b* 10 April 1965; *Educ* King's Sch Ely, Univ of Durham (BA); *m* 10 Nov 1990, Sarah Frances Colleypriest, er da of Roger Griffin, of Malmesbury, Wilts; 1 da (Imogen Mary Colleypriest b 19 Aug 1993); *Career* investmt mangr: GT Management plc 1987–91, Lazard Investors 1991–94, Mercury Asset Management plc 1994–; *Clubs* The 91 Club; *Style—* Robert Fairbairn, Esq; ✉ Mercury Asset Management plc, 33 King William Street, London EC4R 9AS (☎ 0171 280 2800, fax 0171 280 2714)

FAIRBAIRNS, Zoë Ann; da of John Fairbairns, and Isabel Catherine, *née* Dippie; *b* 20 Dec 1948; *Educ* St Catherine's Convent Sch Twickenham, Univ of St Andrews (MA), Coll of William and Mary Williamsburg Virginia (exchange scholarship); *Career* writer; journalist; ed Sanity 1973–74, freelance journalist 1975–; contrib: The Guardian, TES, Times Higher Educational Supplement, The Leveller, Women's Studies International Quarterley, New African, New Scientist, New Society, New Behaviour, New Statesman, Spare Rib, Time Out; poetry ed Spare Rib 1978–82; occasional contrib 1982–: Women's Review, New Internationalist, New Statesman and New Society; fiction reviewer Everywoman 1990–, contrib Sunday Times and Independent 1991–; C Day Lewis Fellowship Rutherford Sch Paddington London 1977–78; creative writing tutor: City Lit Inst London 1978–82, Holloway Prison 1978–82, Wandsworth Prison 1987, Silver Moon Women's Bookshop London 1987–89, Morley Coll London 1988–89; various appts London Borough of Bromley under Writers in Schs Scheme 1981–; writer in residence: Deakin Univ Geelong Victoria Aust 1983, Sunderland Poly 1983–85, Surrey CC (working in schs and Brooklands Tech Coll) 1989; subtitler: BBC Television London 1992–93, Independent Television Facilities Centre London 1993–; Br Cncl travel grant to attend and give paper Women's Worlds - Realities and Choices Congress NY; memb Writers' Guild of GB 1985; *Publications* incl: Live as Family (1968), Down (1969), Benefits (1979, shortlisted for Hawthornden prize 1980, adapted for stage 1980), Stand We At Last (1983), Here Today (1984, winner Fawcett book prize 1985), Closing (1987), Daddy's Girls (1991), Tales I Tell My Mother (contrib, 1978), Despatches From the Frontiers of the Female Mind (contrib, 1985), Voices from Arts for Labour (contrib, 1985), More Tales I Tell My Mother (contrib, 1987), The Seven Deadly Sins (contrib, 1988), Finding Courage (contrib, 1989), The Seven Cardinal Virtues (contrib, 1990), Dialogue and Difference: English into the Nineties (contrib, 1989), By The Light of The Silvery Moon (contrib, 1994); *Recreations* walking, reading; *Style—* Ms Zoë Fairbairns; ✉ A M Heath & Co, 79 St Martins Lane, London WC2N 4AA (☎ 0171 836 4271, fax 0171 497 2561)

FAIRBANKS, Douglas Elton Jr; Hon KBE (1949), DSC (1944); s of Douglas Fairbanks Sr (d 1939), and his 1 wife, Anna Beth, *née* Sully (d 1967); *b* 9 Dec 1909, New York City; *Educ* Bovee Sch, Knickerbocker Greys Drill Sch, Collegiate Mil Sch, Harvard Mil Sch, Pasadena Poly; *m* 1, 3 June 1929 (m dis 1933), Joan Crawford (d 1977); m 2, 22 April 1939, Mary Lee Epling Hartford (d 1988), da of Dr Giles Epling, of Bluefield, W Virginia, and formerly w of George Huntington Hartford; 3 da; m 3, 30 May 1991, Vera Shelton; *Career* theatre, cinema and television actor, prodr, company dir, writer, sculptor and painter; former vice pres Franco-Br War Relief and nat vice pres Ctee Defend America by Aiding the Allies 1939–40, presidential envoy on special mission to Latin America 1940–41; Capt USNR, ret; chm: Douglas Fairbanks Ltd, Fairtel Inc (US), Boltons Trading Co Inc and dir other cos; currently memb: Bd of Tstees Edwina Mountbatten Tst, Bd of Dirs Mountbatten Meml Tst, Bd of Dirs American Friends of RSC and RSC Tst, Bd of Dirs Shakespeare Globe Theatre, Cncl American Museum in Britain, Utd World Colleges, Cncl on Foreign Relations (NY), Bd of Dirs Pilgrim Soc of US; govr Ditchley Fndn, visiting fell St Cross Coll Oxford, sr Churchill fell Westminster Coll Fulton MO, hon dep chllr American Friends of the Order of St John; KStJ 1950, Silver Star (US), Legion of Merit (US) with V (for Valor) Clasp, Officier Legion d'Honneur (France), Croix de Guerre avec Palme (France), Kt Cdr Order of George I (Greece), Cross of Mil Valour (Italy); *Theatre* numerous credits incl: Young Woodley, The Jest, Romeo and Juliet, Saturday's Children, My Fair Lady, The Pleasure of His Company, The Secretary Bird, Present Laughter, Out on a Limb, Sleuth; *Films* numerous credits incl: Stella Dallas, A Woman of Affairs (The Green Hat), The Dawn Patrol, Morning Glory, The Private Life of Catherine The Great, Mimi (La Boheme), The Prisoner of Zenda, Gunga Din, The Corsican Brothers, Sinbad the Sailor, The Exile, The Fighting O'Flynn, Little Caesar, State Secret (The Great Manhunt), Ghost Story, Rage of Paris, The Young in Heart; *Books* Knight Errant (Brian Connell), The Fairbanks Album (with Richard Schickel, 1975), Salad Days (1988), A Hell of a War (USA 1993, UK 1995); *Clubs* White's, RAC, Pall Mall, Puffins (Edinburgh), Brook (NY), Knickerbocker (NY), Century (NY), Metropolitan (Washington DC), Racquet (Chicago); *Style—* Capt Douglas Fairbanks Jr, KBE, DSC, USNR (ret); ✉ 575 Park Ave, New York, NY 10021, USA (☎ 00 1 212 838 4900); c/o Inverness Counsel, 545 Madison Ave, New York, NY 10022, USA (☎ 00 1 212 207 2135); c/o White's Club, St James's Street, London SW1

FAIRBROTHER, Neil Harvey; s of Leslie Robert Fairbrother, and Barbara, *née* Wakefield; *b* 9 Sept 1963; *Educ* Lymm GS; *m* 23 Sept 1988, (Margaret) Audrey, da of Robert Stewart Paul; *Career* professional cricketer; represented Cheshire Schs under 13 and under 19; Lancashire CCC: debut as amateur 1982, professional 1983–, scored 94 not out on professional debut, awarded county cap 1985, capt 1992; England: represented schs under 15 and under 19, 10 test matches (debut v Pakistan Old Trafford 1987), over 45 one day ints, memb tour NZ 1992, memb World Cup squad Aust 1992, memb tour India and Sri Lanka 1992/93, memb team touring Aust 1994/95, memb squad 7 match one day series v S Africa 1996; wins with Lancs: Benson & Hedges Cup 1984, 1990, 1995, and 1996, Refuge Cup 1988, Refuge League 1989, NatWest Trophy 1990; scored 366 v Surrey at the Oval 1990: highest score at the Oval, third highest score in England, twelfth highest score in the world, second highest score by a left hander, highest score by a player batting at number four; *Style—* Neil Fairbrother, Esq; ✉ c/o Lancashire CCC, Old Trafford, Manchester M16 0PX

FAIRBROTHER, Nicola Kim (Nik); MBE (1994); da of Leslie Ronald Fairbrother, of Sandhurst, and Lynda Mary, *née* Washer; *b* 1970; *Educ* Edgbarrow Comp Sch; *Career* judoka (under 56kg div 1988–); took up judo aged 8, memb Pinewood Judo Club Berks; honours incl: Euro jr featherweight champion Poland 1987, Bronze medal lightweight World Championships Spain 1991, Gold medal Euro Championships Paris 1992, Silver medal Olympic Games Barcelona 1992, Gold medal Euro Championships Athens 1993, Gold medal World Championships Canada 1993, Euro Fighter of the Year 1994, Gold medal Euro Championships Birmingham 1995; also currently sports journalist Reading Chronicle and Sunday Times; *Recreations* writing, movies, travel, golf, concerts and the arts; *Style—* Miss Nik Fairbrother, MBE; ✉ c/o Pinewood Judo Club, Pinewood Leisure Centre, Old Wokingham Rd, Crowthorne, Berks (☎ and fax 01344 775019)

FAIRCLOUGH, Anthony John; CMG (1990); s of Wilfrid Fairclough (d 1975), of 290 Hamstead Rd, Handsworth, Birmingham, and Lillian Anne, *née* Townsend (d 1967); *b* 30 Aug 1924; *Educ* St Philip's GS Birmingham, St Catharine's Coll Cambridge (BA, MA); *m* 3 Sept 1957, Patricia, da of Alexander Hamilton Monks (d 1967), of London; 2 s (Philip Simon b 19 Aug 1958, Andrew Joseph b 19 May 1962); *Career* researcher RAE Farnborough 1944–48; Colonial Office 1948–63, private sec to Min of State for Colonial and Cwlth Affrs Colonial Office 1963–64, head depts in Colonial Office and FCO 1964–70, transfd to DOE 1970, head of div responsible for Br new towns 1970–72, under sec i/c of a number of divs responsible for various environmental affrs 1973–74, dir Central Unit on Environmental Pollution 1974–78, dir int tport UK Dept of Tport 1978–81, dir for the environment with Cmmn EC 1981–85, acting dir gen for the environment, consumer protection and nuclear safety Cmmn EC 1985–86, dep dir gen for devpt Cmmn EC 1986–89, special advsr Cmmn EC 1989–94; dir: Environmental Resources Management UK (formerly Environmental Resources Ltd UK) 1989–, Groundwork Fndn UK 1989–95; chm Network for Environmental Technology Transfer (NETT) Brussels 1989–; FRSA 1980, companion ICE 1990–93; *Recreations* reading, gardening, travelling; *Style—* A J Fairclough, Esq, CMG; ✉ Director, Environmental Resources Management, 8 Cavendish Square, London W1M 0ER (☎ 0171 465 7353, fax 0171 465 7320)

FAIRCLOUGH, Geoffrey Charles; s of late John Holden Fairclough, and Kay, *née* Kear; *b* 16 Oct 1955; *Educ* Mount St Mary's Coll Derbyshire, Univ of London (BSc(Econ), external); *m* Sylvia, da of late Thomas Marshall Bird; 2 s (Alistair John b 20 April 1982, Richard Anthony b 6 Aug 1983); *Career* CA: Herring Conn Manchester 1976–80, Harry L Price Manchester 1980–83, Haines Watts 1983–, Haines Watts Ltd 1992–, Haines Watts Enterprises Ltd 1992–, H W Financial Services Ltd 1992–, Fort Belvedere Ltd 1996–; FCA 1990 (ACA 1980); *Recreations* cycling, walking; *Style—* Geoffrey Fairclough, Esq; ✉ White Hart House, Hampstead Norreys, Berks RG18 0TD; Haines Watts Ltd, Sterling House, 27 Couching Street, Watlington, Oxon OX9 5QF (☎ 01491 613611, fax 01491 613730)

FAIRCLOUGH, Ian Walter; s of Walter Amedee Fairclough (d 1978), of Effingham, and Ella Mildred, *née* Watson (d 1970); *b* 29 May 1938; *Educ* St Andrew's Sch Eastbourne, Malvern; *m* 2 Sept 1967, Patricia Margaret Anne, da of Brig Thomas Patrick Keene (d 1979); 1 s (William b 1977), 3 da (Annabel (Mrs Thomas Falcon) b 1968, Celia b 1970, Katharine b 1972); *Career* Nat Serv Lt 5 Royal Inniskilling Dragoon Gds 1957–59; rep Agent for Int SOS Assistance (med repatriation serv) 1981–; dir Fairclough Dodd & Jones (I & P) Ltd 1961–89; memb: Cncl Sail Trg Assoc 1980–, ISTA (Racing) Ctee 1977–, Cncl City & Guilds 1995–; govr St Andrew's Sch Eastbourne; memb Ct of Assts Worshipful Co of Girdlers (Master 1993), memb Livery Ctee City of London 1991–93; *Style—* Ian W Fairclough, Esq; ✉ Merrow Farm, Dunsfold, Godalming, Surrey GU8 4NX (☎ 01483 200215)

FAIRCLOUGH, Sir John Whitaker; kt (1990); *b* 23 Aug 1930, Thirsk, Yorkshire; *Educ* Univ of Manchester (BSc(Tech)); *m* Margaret Ann (d 1996); 2 s (Simon, Jeremy), 1 da (Sarah); *Career* Ferranti Ltd UK and Ferranti Electric USA 1954–57, project engr IBM Poughkeepsie 1957–59, lab dir IBM UK Laboratories Ltd 1964–68 (project mangr 1959–64), dir of data processing for mktg and serv IBM UK 1969–70, lab dir IBM Laboratory Raleigh NC 1970–72, vice pres Communications Systems IBM Corp 1972–74, chm IBM UK Laboratories Ltd 1974–82, dir Mfrg and Devpt and chm IBM UK Laboratories Ltd 1982–86, chief scientific advsr Cabinet Office 1986–90; chm: Rothschilds Venture Ltd 1990–, Centre for the Exploitation of Sci and Technol 1990–95, Group Technology Council Lucas Industries plc 1991–, Prince of Wales Innovation Initiative 1991–93; dir: NM Rothschilds and Sons Ltd 1990–, Oxford Instruments Group plc 1991–, UAPT Infolink 1991–93, Generic Group 1991–96, DSC (Europe) 1992–, DSC (Comp) 1992–; memb: Engrg Cncl 1982– (chm 1991–96), Advsy Cncl on Sci and Technol, Advsy Bd of the Res Cncl 1986–89, Advsy Cncl on Res and Devpt (Energy) 1986–89, Bd of Govrs Euro Jt Res Centre 1986–89, Ctee for Res on Sci & Technol (CREST) 1986–89, Bd Lucas Industries 1992–96, Bd LucasVarity plc 1996; author and co-author of over 20 pubns; Inst of Prodn Engrs Gold Medal 1989; Hon DSc: Univ of Southampton 1983, Univ of Cranfield 1987, Univ of Manchester 1988, Univ of Aston 1990, Univ of Westminster 1991, City Univ 1992; Hon DTech Univ of Loughborough 1990, hon fell Univ of Portsmouth (formerly Portsmouth Poly) 1991; FIEE 1975, FBCS 1975 (pres 1986), FEng 1987, fell Nat Acad of Engrg 1989, FIMechE, FICE 1996; *Style*— Sir John Fairclough, FEng; ✉ The Old Blue Boar, 25 St Johns Street, Winchester, Hants SO23 8HF

FAIREST, Paul Brant; s of Colin Banner Fairest (d 1975), and Marjorie Rosa, *née* Crutchley (d 1995); *b* 18 Jan 1940; *Educ* King Edward VII Sch Sheffield, Univ of Cambridge; *m* 1, 20 March 1965 (m dis 1987), Patricia Ann Rattee; 2 s (John Brant b 1966, David Nicholas b 1972), 1 da (Jane Alison b 1968); m 2, 15 April 1988, Hilary Christine, da of Leslie Edward Putman; *Career* lectr in law Univ of Cambridge 1969–74 (asst lectr 1964–69, fell Selwyn Coll 1964–74), prof of law Univ of Hull 1974–94; chm: NE Gas Consumers Cncl 1977–86, Transport Users' Consultative Ctee NE Eng 1987; memb Nat Consumer Cncl 1990–; *Books* Mortgages (1975), Consumer Protection Act (1987); *Recreations* walking, music, travel; *Style*— Paul Fairest, Esq; ✉ 8 Spring Walk, Brayton, Selby, N Yorks YO8 9DS (☎ 01757 704573)

FAIRFAX, Lady; Mary; *née* Wein; AM (1988), OBE (1975); o da of Kevin Wein; *Educ* Presbyterian Ladies Coll, Univ of Sydney; *m* 4 July 1959, Sir Warwick Oswald Fairfax (d 1987), o s of Sir James Oswald Fairfax, KBE (d 1928); 3 s, 1 da; *Career* hon consul of Monaco 1979; fndr, dir and life govr Opera Fndn Aust; opera scholarships to: Bayreuth (Germany), La Scala (Italy), Royal Opera (Covent Garden), Vienna State Opera 1993; chm Australian region Metropolitan Opera Auditions NY 1981, Opera Auditions in co-op Metropolitan Opera; founder and life pres Friends of the Ballet; dir Industrial Equity Ltd 1985–89; exec Australian Inst of Company Directors; memb Cultural Grants Ctee of Ministry for Culture, Sport and Recreation NSW, past pres Smith Family Summer Ctee, formerly exec Ladies Ctee Elizabethan Theatre Trust and Red Cross; memb: Int Ctee for the Ronald Reagan Presidential Fndn, Int Ctee US Information Agency, Int Ctee World Monuments Fund; fndr: Juilliard Scholarship Lincoln Center NY 1977, Lady James Fairfax Memorial Prize for Photography as Art-Portraiture for the Art Gallery of NSW, Lady James Fairfax Memorial Prize for Painting Australian Birds and Flowers for the Royal Agricultural Soc of NSW; *Recreations* working, the arts, writing, poetry, sculpture, fashion, entertaining, reading, swimming, walking, travel; *Clubs* Royal Yacht Squadron (Sydney), Assoc Union (Sydney), American National (Sydney), Lansdowne (London), Metropolitan (New York), Lyford Cay (Nassau); *Style*— Lady (Mary) Fairfax, AM, OBE; ✉ Fairwater, 560 New South Head Road, Double Bay, NSW 2028, Australia

FAIRFAX-LUCY, Duncan Cameron Ramsay; s of Capt Ewen Aymer Robert Ramsay-Fairfax-Lucy (d 1969), and Margaret Westall (d 1994), o da of Sir John Westall King, 2 Bt; *b* 18 Sept 1932; *Educ* Eton; *m* 26 Sept 1964, Janet Barclay, o da of P A B Niven and Mrs K Niven; 1 s (Spencer Angus Ramsay b 1966), 1 da (Anna Margaret Barclay b 1969); *Career* bursar Queen's Coll Birmingham 1981–93; FCA; *Clubs* Army and Navy; *Style*— D C R Fairfax-Lucy, Esq; ✉ The Malt House, Charlecote, Warwick CV35 9EW

FAIRFAX-LUCY, Sir Edmund John William Hugh Ramsay-; 6 Bt (UK 1836), of The Holmes, Roxburghshire; s of Maj Sir Brian Fulke Ramsay-Fairfax-Lucy, 5 Bt (d 1974), and Hon Alice Caroline Helen Buchan (d 1993), o da of 1 Baron Tweedsmuir, GCMG, GCVO, CH, PC; *b* 4 May 1945; *Educ* Eton, Royal Acad of Arts (Dip); *m* 1, 1974 (m dis), Sylvia, da of Graeme Ogden; m 2, 1986 (m dis 1989), Lady Lucinda Lambton, eldest da of Antony Claud Lambton (6 Earl of Durham until he disclaimed his peerage 1970); m 3, 1994, Erica, da of Warren Loane, of Crocknacrieve, Enniskillen; 1 s; *Heir* s, Patrick Samuel Thomas Fulke Fairfax-Lucy b 3 April 1995; *Career* painter, chiefly of still-life and interiors; *Recreations* landscape gardening, waterworks, building; *Style*— Edmund Fairfax-Lucy; ✉ Charlecote Park, Warwick

FAIRFAX OF CAMERON, 14 Lord (S 1627); Nicholas John Albert Fairfax; s of 13 Lord (d 1964; ninth in descent from the bro of the 2 Lord who defeated Prince Rupert at Marston Moor, and unc of the 3 Lord who, as C-in-C of the Parliamentarians, was the victor at Naseby, and who hired the poet, Andrew Marvell, as a tutor for his da Mary who m another poet, the 2 Duke of Buckingham); *b* 4 Jan 1956; *Educ* Eton, Downing Coll Cambridge; *m* 24 April 1982, Annabel, er da of late Nicholas Morriss, of Banstead Manor Stud, Newmarket; 3 s (Hon Edward Nicholas Thomas b 20 Sept 1984, Hon John Frederick Anthony b 27 June 1986, Hon Rory Henry Francis b 21 May 1991); *Heir* s, Hon Edward Nicholas Thomas b 20 Sept 1984; *Career* sits as Cons in House of Lords; dir Sedgwick Marine & Cargo Ltd 1995–96; *Recreations* sailing, motorcycling; *Style*— The Rt Hon the Lord Fairfax of Cameron; ✉ 10 Orlando Road, London SW4 0LF

FAIRFIELD, Ian McLeod; CBE (1982); s of late Geoffrey Fairfield, and Inez Helen Thorneycroft Fairfield (d 1977); *b* 5 Dec 1919; *Educ* Monkton House Sch Cardiff, Manchester Coll of Technol; *m* 1941, Joyce Ethel, da of Cdr Percy Fletcher, RN (d 1965); 2 s (Clive, Julian); *Career* cmmnd RNVR Electrical Branch 1940–45; engrg trainee Callenders Cables & Construction Co Ltd (now BICC plc), area sales mangr St Helens Cable & Rubber Co 1945–51; Chemring Group plc: sales dir 1951, md 1952, dep chm, chm and gp chief exec 1980, chm 1984, chm and gp chief exec 1985, gp chm 1985–91 (ret), dep chm 1991–, life pres 1994–; *Recreations* motor boat cruising; *Clubs* Athenaeum, Royal Naval Sailing Assoc; *Style*— Ian Fairfield, Esq, CBE; ✉ Chemring Group PLC, 1590 Parkway, Whiteley, Fareham, Hants PO15 7AG (☎ 01489 881880, fax 01489 881123, telex 86242)

FAIRGRIEVE, Sir (Thomas) Russell; kt (1981), CBE (1974), TD (1959), JP (Selkirkshire 1962); s of late Alexander Fairgrieve, OBE, MC, JP, of Galashiels, and Myma Margaret, *née* Crow; *b* 3 May 1924; *Educ* St Mary's Sch Melrose, Sedbergh, Scottish Coll of Textiles Galashiels; *m* 7 Dec 1952, Millie, da of Alexander Mitchell; 1 s (Sandy), 3 da (Patricia, Rosemary, Marjorie); *Career* cmmnd 8 Gurkha Rifles IA 1943, Co Cdr 1/8 Gurkha Rifles 1944–46, GSO (2) (Ops) 15 Indian Corps SE Asia 1964; TA, 4 KOSB 1947–63, Maj 2 i/c; pres Scottish Cons Assoc 1965–66, memb Exec Ctee Euro Movement (Scotland) 1970–74, MP (C) W Aberdeenshire 1974–83, chm Scottish Cons Gp for Europe 1974–78, Scottish Cons whip 1975, chm Scottish Cons Party 1975–80 (vice chm 1971), Parly under sec of state Scotland 1979–81; md Laidlaw & Fairgrieve Ltd 1958–68 (dir 1953–58); dir: Dawson Int plc 1961–73, William Baird & Co plc 1981–94; chm: Bain Hogg Ltd; *Style*— Sir Russell Fairgrieve, CBE, TD, JP; ✉ Pankalan, Boleside, Galashiels, Selkirkshire TD1 3NX (☎ 01896 752278)

FAIRHAVEN, 3 Baron (UK 1961); Ailwyn Henry George Broughton; JP (S Cambs 1975), DL (Cambridgeshire and Isle of Ely 1977); s of 2 Baron (d 1973), and Hon Diana (d 1937), da of Capt Hon Coulson Fellowes (s of 2 Baron De Ramsey, JP, DL, and Lady Rosamond Spencer-Churchill, da of 7 Duke of Marlborough, KG); *b* 16 Nov 1936; *Educ* Eton, RMA Sandhurst; *m* 23 Sept 1960, Kathleen Patricia, er da of Col James Henry Magill, OBE; 4 s (Hon James, Hon Huttleston Rupert b 1970, Hon Charles Leander b 1973, Hon Henry Robert b 1978), 2 da (Hon Diana Cara (who m Alan Brodie Henderson, *qv*), Hon Melanie Frances (Hon Mrs Edgar)); *Heir* s, Hon James Broughton b 25 May 1963; *Career* RHG 1957–71, Maj; Vice Lord-Lt Cambridgeshire 1977–85; Kt of the White Rose (Finland) 1970, KStJ 1992 (CStJ 1983); *Recreations* gardening, cooking; *Clubs* Jockey (sr steward 1985–89), White's; *Style*— The Rt Hon the Lord Fairhaven, JP, DL; ✉ Anglesey Abbey, Lode, Cambridge CB5 9EJ (☎ 01223 811746)

FAIRHURST, Harry Marshall; OBE (1993); s of Philip Garland Fairhurst (d 1987), and Janet Meikle, *née* Marshall; *b* 18 June 1925; *Educ* Clifton, Clare Coll Cambridge (MA), Northern Poly (Dip Arch); *m* 20 June 1959, Elizabeth Mary, da of Bernard Hudson Thorp, of Cheadle, Cheshire; 1 s (Timothy b 1968), 3 da (Katharine b 1960, Rachel b 1962, Philippa b 1964); *Career* architect in private practice; architect and surveyor to Fabric of Manchester Cathedral 1970–90, cmmnd architect for English Heritage 1978– (cathedrals survey 1991, bldgs for commerce, indust, educn, med and scientific res); memb and former pres Cathedral Architects Assoc; Hon MA Univ of Manchester, hon fell UMIST, FRIBA; *Recreations* forestry, contemporary art, design and crafts; *Clubs* St James's (Manchester), Manchester Literary & Philosophical Soc (former pres); *Style*— Harry M Fairhurst, Esq, OBE; ✉ 33 Macclesfield Road, Wilmslow, Cheshire SK9 2AF (☎ 01625 523784)

FAIRLIE, Andrew; s of James McGregor Fairlie, and Kay, *née* Sweeny; *b* 21 Nov 1963; *Educ* Perth Acad, Westminster Hotel Sch; *m* Ashley Gillian, da of William Laird; 1 da (Iiona b 15 Aug 1989); *Career* apprentice Station Hotel Perth 1980–82, commis de cuisine Charing Cross Hotel 1982–84, chef de partie Boodles Restaurant 1984–85, stagiare Chez Michel Guerard France June-Nov 1985, commis de cuisine tournant Hotel de Crillon Paris 1985–86, sous chef Chez Nanos Megeve 1986–87, chef de cuisine Royal Scotsman Edinburgh April-Nov 1987, stage sous chef Intercontinental Hotel Sydney 1987–88, chef de cuisine Royal Scotsman Edinburgh April-Nov 1988, chef conslt A & K Travel Kenya 1988–89, sous chef Ritz Club London 1989–90, sr sous chef Adare Manor Co Limerick 1990–91, chef de cuisine Disneyland Paris 1991–94, chef de cuisine One Devonshire Gardens Glasgow 1994–; team capt Ritz Club Olympia 1990 (9 silver medals, 8 bronze medals, 4 best exhibits); memb Academie Culinaire de France 1995; *Awards* third place Robert Carrier Nat Competition 1982, winner Michel Roux scholarship 1984, Scottish Chef of the Year 1996, Michelin Star 1996; *Recreations* hill walking, football; *Style*— Andrew Fairlie, Esq; ✉ One Devonshire Gardens, Glasgow G12 0UX (☎ 0141 339 2001, fax 0141 337 1663)

FAIRLIE-CUNINGHAME, Robert Henry; s and h of Sir William Henry Fairlie-Cuninghame, 16 Bt; *b* 19 July 1974; *Style*— Robert Fairlie-Cuninghame, Esq; ✉ 29A Orinoco St, Pymble, New South Wales 2073, Australia

FAIRLIE-CUNINGHAME, Sir William Henry; 16 Bt (NS 1630), of Robertland, Ayrshire; s of Sir William Fairlie-Cuninghame, 15 Bt, MC (d 1981), and Irene Alice (d 1970), da of Henry Margrave Terry; *b* 1 Oct 1930; *m* 1972, Janet Menzies, da of late Roy Menzies Saddington; 1 s ((William) Robert Henry b 1974); *Heir* s, (William) Robert Henry Fairlie-Cuninghame b 11 July 1974; *Style*— Sir William Fairlie-Cuninghame, Bt; ✉ 29A Orinoco Street, Pymble, New South Wales 2073, Australia

FAIRLIE OF MYRES, Capt David Ogilvy; MBE (1984), JP (Fife 1975), DL (Fife 1981); s of James Ogilvy Fairlie of Myres (d 1960), of Myres Castle, Auchtermuchty, Fife, and Constance Gertrude, *née* Lascelles (d 1982); *b* 1 Oct 1923; *Educ* Ampleforth, Oriel Coll Oxford; *m* 1, 19 April 1969, Ann Constance (d 1986) da of Dermot Francis Bolger (d 1974), of Quinta Avista Navios, Funchal, Madeira; m 2, 31 March 1995, Jane Elliot Bingham-Newland, *née* Low, wid of Capt Richard John Bingham-Newland (d 1989); *Career* Bde Signal Offr 32 Gds Bde UK 1943, PA to Maj-Gen C M F White France and Belgium 1944, Signal Offr HQ Allied Land Forces SE Asia Ceylon and Singapore 1945, Bde Signal Offr 37 Indian Bde Java and Malaya 1946, Signal Regt Scottish Cmd Edinburgh 1947–48, Signal Regt Northern Cmd Catterick 1949–50, Bde Signal Offr 29 Inf Bde Korea 1951–52, 2 i/c Signal Sqdn SHAPE 1953, Adj 51 Highland Divnl Signal Regt 1954–56, dist cmmr Cupar Scout dist 1960–65, co cmmr Fife Scouts 1966–85, pres Fife Area Scouts 1992–; chm E Fife branch Arthritis and Rheumatics Cncl 1986–; memb Queen's Body Guard for Scotland (The Royal Co of Archers) 1964–; Knight Cdr of the Equestrian Order of the Holy Sepulchre of Jerusalem, Lieutenant of Scot 1993–; *Books* Fairlie of that Ilk (history and genealogy of the family, 1987); *Recreations* gardening, bee keeping, photography, genealogy; *Clubs* Army and Navy, Royal Over-Seas League, Royal and Ancient Golf; *Style*— Capt David Fairlie of Myres, MBE, JP, DL; ✉ Myres Castle, Auchtermuchty, Fife KY14 7EW (☎ 01337 828350)

FAIRMAN, Dr Martin John; s of Henry Douglas Fairman, FRCS, of Bristol, and Stella Margaret, *née* Sheath; *b* 8 May 1945; *Educ* Monkton Combe Sch Bath, London Hosp Med Coll (MB BS); *m* 12 Aug 1967, Marianne Alison Louis, da of Sqdn Ldr Roland Ernest Burton, of Limousin, France; 2 s (James b 1969, Jack b 1978), 2 da (Jocelyn b 1971, Lydia b 1980); *Career* conslt physician S Lincolnshire Health Authy 1979–, hon sr lectr med Leicester Univ 1979–, fell in gastroenterology Cincinnati 1976–77, med dir Pilgrim Health NHS Tst 1993–; FRCP; *Recreations* golf, sailing; *Style*— Dr Martin J Fairman; ✉ Skirbeck Grange, Sibsey Rd, Boston, Lincs (☎ 01205 360743); Pilgrim Hosp, Boston, Lincs (☎ 01205 364801)

FAIRNEY, William; s of Thomas Fairney (d 1978), of Greenford, Middx, and Mary Evelyn, *née* Lambert; *b* 2 April 1941; *Educ* Latymer Upper Sch, Univ of Bristol (BSc); *m* 1, 1966 (m dis 1978), Barbara, *née* Wood; 2 da (Amelia Jane b 16 July 1969, Josephine Anne b 14 Jan 1972); m 2, 1981, Linda, da of Harold Thomas Gammage; 1 step s (Mark Harold Burrows b 6 Feb 1971), 1 step da (Sarah Alicia Burrows (Mrs Cook) b 20 Aug 1968); *Career* English Electric Co: graduate apprentice 1963–65, gen design engr 1965; CEGB: res offr 1965–74, gen design engr Generation Design and Construction Div 1974–77, electrical engrg mangr Midlands Region 1977–79, system tech engr 1979–85, dir of res 1985–86, dir of plant engrg 1986–89; National Power plc (formerly CEGB): dir of engrg and technol 1989–90, dir of engrg and project servs 1990–93, dir of projects devpt and construction 1993–95, dir of plant procurement and construction 1995–; visiting prof of engrg Univ of Durham 1985–, pres NW Area Assoc for Sci Educn 1988–, vice pres IEE 1993–96; chm: Power Divnl Bd IEE 1989, Professional Bd 1993–95, Centres Bd 1995–, Year of Engrg Success (YEARCO) 1995–; FIEE 1984 (MIEE 1977), FEng 1992; *Recreations* walking, mathematics, reading, flying, computing; *Style*— William Fairney, Esq, FEng; ✉ 2 The Tithe Barn, Hawkesbury Upton, Badminton, South Glos GL9 1AY (☎ 01454 238553); National Power plc, Windmill Hill Business Park, Whitehill Way, Swindon, Wilts SN5 9NX (☎ 01793 892200, fax 01793 892231, car 0860 891363)

FAIRTLOUGH, Gerard Howard; CBE (1989); s of Maj-Gen Eric Victor Howard Fairtlough, DSO, MC (d 1944), and Agatha Zoë, *née* Barker (d 1991); *b* 5 Sept 1930; *Educ* Marlborough, King's Coll Cambridge; *m* 1954, Elizabeth Ann, *née* Betambeau; 2 s, 2 da; *Career* Lt RA; md Shell UK Ltd 1974–78, div dir NEB 1978–80, chief exec Celltech Group plc 1980–90; chm The Coverdale Organisation plc 1984–93, dir Cantab Pharmaceuticals plc 1990–, chm Therexsys Ltd 1993–96, chm Landmark Information Group Ltd 1994–; memb Sci and Engrg Res Cncl 1989–94; Hon DSc: City Univ 1987, CNAA 1990; *Books* Creative Compartments: A Design for Future Organisation (1994); *Recreations* walking, theatre, yoga; *Style*— Gerard Fairtlough, Esq; ✉ 5 Belmont Grove, London SE13 (☎ 0181 852 3228)

FAIRWEATHER, Col Andrew Burton; OBE (1990), TD (1972 and 1980); s of Andrew Fairweather (d 1960), of Edinburgh, and Marion Ramsay, *née* Ritchie; *b* 26 Feb 1931; *Educ* Royal High Sch Edinburgh, Univ of Edinburgh, Open Univ (BA); *m* 16 July 1955, Elizabeth Fairbairn, da of James Brown (d 1982), of Edinburgh; 3 s (David Andrew b 1956, Alan James b 1958, Ian Cowper b 1961); *Career* Rifle Brigade and RAEC, Royal Scots (TA), and Royal Corps of Transport (TA), CO 495 Movement Control Liasion Unit BAOR 1977–81 (Col 1981); exec offr Dept of Health for Scotland 1951–54, sec Scot Med Practices Ctee 1954–58; Rent Assessment Panel for Scotland: higher exec offr 1958, sr exec offr 1965, sec 1965–67; Scottish Devpt Dept 1967–70, princ Civil Service Dept 1970, chief admin offr Civil Serv Coll 1970–72, princ Scot Economic Planning Dept 1972–74, sec Local Govt Staff and Property Cmmns 1974–77, princ Scot Devpt Dept 1977–81, princ Scot Office Central Servs 1981–82, sr princ Scot Office 1982–91; gen sec Abbeyfield Soc for Scot 1991–; MIMgt 1976; *Style—* Col Andrew Fairweather, OBE, TD; ✉ 127 Silverknowes Gardens, Edinburgh EH4 5NG (☎ 0131 336 4427)

FAIRWEATHER, Prof Denys Vivian Ivor; s of Albert James Ivor Fairweather (d 1935), and Gertrude Mary, *née* Forbes (d 1953); *b* 25 Oct 1927; *Educ* Forfar Acad, Websters Seminary Kirriemuir, Univ of St Andrews (MB ChB, MD); *m* 21 April 1956, (Gwendolen) Yvonne, da of John Phillips Hubbard, of Heckington, Lincs; 1 s (John b 1957), 2 da (Debbie b 1959, Sally b 1966); *Career* Sqdn Ldr Med Branch RAF 1950–55; registrar to Sir Dugald Baird Aberdeen 1955–59, sr lectr Univ of Newcastle upon Tyne 1959–66, vice provost for med UCL 1984–87 (prof and head Dept of Obstetrics and Gynaecology 1966–89, dean Faculty of Clinical Sci 1982–84), head UCH and Middx Sch of Med 1988–89, vice provost UCL 1988–90, pro vice chllr for med Univ of London 1989–92, prof emeritus of obstetrics and gynaecology Univ of London 1992–; memb Bloomsbury Health Authy 1983–90, vice pres Br FPA 1985–, sec gen Int Fedn of Gynaecology and Obstetrics 1985–94, memb Int Med Advsy Panel IPPF 1988–94 (pres Euro Regnl Cncl 1974–80, chm Mgmnt and Planning Ctee 1975–77); hon fell: American Assoc Reproductive Med 1969, UCL 1985, American Coll of Obstetrics and Gynaecology 1994; Freeman City of Krakow 1989; FRCOG 1967, FRSM 1968; *Books* Amniotic Fluid Research and Clinical Application (1973, 2 edn 1978), Labour Ward Manual (1985, 2 edn 1991); *Recreations* gardening, fishing, do-it-yourself; *Style—* Prof Denys Fairweather; ✉ 37 Lyndhurst Avenue, Mill Hill, London NW7 2AD (☎ 0181 959 4466)

FAIRWEATHER, Dr Frank Arthur; s of Frank Fairweather (d 1970), of Norwich, Norfolk, and Maud Harriet, *née* Jolly (d 1983); *b* 2 May 1928; *Educ* City of Norwich Sch, Middlesex Hosp Med Sch London (MB BS); *m* 18 July 1953, Christine Winifred, da of Frederick James Hobbs (d 1959), of Watford, Hertfordshire; 2 s (Martin Frank b 7 Feb 1957, Howard John b 21 May 1959); *Career* Mil Serv Surgn Lt HMS President RNR 1958–61; clinical house appts Ipswich Gp of Hosps 1955–56; pathologist 1956–60: Bland Sutton Inst of Pathology, Courtauld Inst of Biochemistry Middlesex Hosp and Soho Hosp for Women; jt sr registrar in pathology Middlesex and W Middlesex Hosps 1960–62, conslt pathologist Benger Laboratories 1961–62, chief pathologist and Nuffield Fndn scholar Br Industl Biological Res Assoc and hon sr lectr RCS 1962–65, assoc res dir Wyeth Laboratories Taplow 1965–69, SMO and PMO DHSS Ctee on Safety of Medicines 1969–72; 1972–82: sr PMO DHSS and head Chemical Contamination and Environmental Pollution Div, memb EEC Scientific Ctee on Food, chm EEC Scientific Ctee on Cosmetology, memb WHO Panels on Food Safety and Environmental Pollution; conslt advsr in toxicology to DHSS 1978–81, dir DHSS Toxicological Laboratory St Bartholomew's Hosp London 1978–82 (hon dir 1982–84), hon prof of toxicology Dept of Biochemistry Univ of Surrey 1978–84, hon prof of toxicology and comparative pathology Sch of Pharmacy Univ of London 1982–88, head of safety and environmental assurance Unilever plc 1982–93, currently conslt in toxicology and pathology; examiner RCPath 1979–, chm Br Industl Biological Res Assoc Toxicology Int 1987–93, chief examiner in toxicology Inst of Biology 1989–; FRCPath 1975 (MRCPath 1963), FIBiol 1972, memb Parly and Scientific Cmmn 1988–92, hon FFOM 1991; *Recreations* angling, gardening and water colours; *Style—* Dr Frank Fairweather; ✉ 394 London Rd, Langley, Slough, Berks SL3 7HX (☎ and fax 01753 544994)

FAIRWEATHER, Leslie Stephen; s of William Stephen Fairweather (d 1975), of Lewes, Sussex, and Ethel Mary Elizabeth, *née* Keen (d 1981); *b* 7 March 1929; *Educ* St Olave's GS, Dorking Co GS, Brighton Poly (ARIBA); *m* 26 Oct 1963, (Felicity) Anne, da of Henry Martin Williamson, MBE, of Balcombe, W Sussex; 3 s (David b 14 March 1966, Mark b 10 Oct 1968, Michael b 8 June 1971), 2 da (Ruth b 8 Sept 1964, Rachel b 11 Aug 1967); *Career* formerly architect in London and Sussex (work incl extensions and alterations to Glyndebourne Opera House), pt/t studio master Dept of Architecture Brighton Coll of Art and private tutor, lectr and res fell Dept of Architecture Univ of Bristol 1965–67, res fell Architects' Jl 1962–65; ed Info Library for Architects 1967–69, ed Architects' Jl 1973–84 (tech ed 1969–73); md Architectural Press 1984–89; chm MBC Architectural Press & Building Publications (div of Maxwell Business Communications) 1989–91, dir Clients' Advsy Serv RIBA 1991–95, prison research for Home Office and freelance writer and broadcaster 1995–; contrib: Architects' Jl, British Jl of Criminology, A Look Inside (BBC Radio 4) 1986; conslt: UNSDRI Rome, res into prison design with N London Poly and Home Office; chm RIBA Cmmn on Evidence to Lord Justice Woolf's Prison Enquiry 1990, initiator and sec prison Design Study Gp, dir Land Ltd, fndr memb Land Decade Educnl Cncl, external examiner at univ and poly depts of architecture, judge and assessor of nat and int awards and competitions; memb final year design thesis juries: AA, Barlett Sch of Architecture Univ of London; fndr and sec Conslt Contractor Barrier Gp, memb Panel of Church Surveyors Dio of Chichester, chm Balcombe Scout Gp Exec 1986–96 (awarded Chief Scout's Thanks Badge 1990), parent govr Haywards Heath Sixth Form Coll 1981–86, govr Balcombe Primary Sch 1990– (chm 1995–); cncllr: Mid Sussex DC 1991–, Parish of Balcombe 1991–; memb Action Aid; RIBA 1959 (Ashpital prizewinner 1957); *Books* The English Prisons (contrib, 1960), AJ Metric Handbook (1968), Prison Architecture (UN Social Def Res Inst, 1975), Balcombe - The Story of a Sussex Village (1981), Architecture of Incarceration (1994); *Recreations* family, music, writing, browsing, owl collecting; *Style—* Leslie Fairweather, Esq; ✉ Honeywood House, Deanland Road, Balcombe, W Sussex RH17 6LT (☎ 01444 811532)

FAIRWEATHER, (Cyril) Paul; s of James Armstead Fairweather, of St Nicholas, Glamorgan, and Marie Francis, *née* Esnouf; *b* 26 May 1952; *Educ* Westbourne House Penarth, Marlborough (exhibitioner Worshipful Co of Salters), Fitzwilliam Coll Univ of Cambridge (MA); *m* 9 May 1981, Angela Glen, da of Lt Col Donald Duncan Burns; 1 da (Charlotte Glen b 15 Feb 1982), 1 s (Ian Charles McIntyre b 15 Aug 1985); *Career* Price Waterhouse: London 1973–77, The Hague Netherlands 1977–78, London 1978–83, Windsor 1983–, tax ptnr 1984–, ptnr in charge Thames Valley 1992–, memb supervisory Ctee 1995–; memb ICAEW; FCA 1981 (ACA 1976); *Recreations* golf, skiing, shooting, rugby, sailing; *Clubs* Cardiff and County, Royal Porthcawl Golf, Phyllis Court; *Style—* Paul Fairweather, Esq; ✉ Price Waterhouse, Thames Court, 1 Victoria Street, Windsor, Berks SL4 1HB (☎ 01753 752000, fax 01753 864826, e-mail Paul_Fairweather@Europe.notes.pw.com)

FAITH, Dr Lesley; da of Norman Faith (d 1970), of Belfast, and Estelle, *née* Sharp; *b* 30 Aug 1955; *Educ* Methodist Coll Belfast, Univ of St Andrews (BSc), Univ of Manchester (MB ChB); *m* 13 June 1987, Ashwani Kumar, s of Krishan Kumar Korpal, of Manchester; 1 s (Aaron b 13 June 1991), 2 da (Natassha b 1988, Nicole b 1989); *Career* conslt psychiatrist: Bermuda 1986, Sydney Aust 1986–87, Stepping Hill Hosp Stockport Cheshire 1987–; Special Interest Devpt Serv for Drug Addiction and Alcohol Abuse; MRCPsych 1984; *Recreations* travel, reading; *Style—* Dr Lesley Faith; ✉ 27 Broomfield Rd, Heaton Moor, Stockport SK4 4NB (☎ 0161 432 0449); Stepping Hill Hospital, Stockport, Cheshire (☎ 0161 483 1010)

FALCON, Michael Gascoigne; CBE (1979), DL (Norfolk 1981); s of Michael Falcon, JP (d 1976), by his w Kathleen Isabel Frances, *née* Gascoigne (d 1985); *b* 28 Jan 1928; *Educ* Stowe, Heriot Watt Coll; *m* 1954, April Daphne Claire, *née* Lambert; 2 s (Michael b 1956, Andrew b 1958), 1 da (Claire b 1960); *Career* former head brewer and jt md E Lacon & Co Gt Yarmouth, tstee E Anglian Tstee Savings Bank 1963–75, exec dir Edgar Watts (Bungay Suffolk) 1968–73; dir: Securicor E Ltd 1969–72, Lloyds Bank (UK) Management Ltd 1979–85, Matthew Brown plc 1981–87, Greene King & Sons plc 1988–96, Br Rail Anglia Regional Bd 1988–92, chm: Nat Seed Devpt Orgn Ltd 1972–82, Pauls & Whites Ltd 1976–85 (dir 1973–85), Lloyds Bank Eastern Counties Regional Bd 1979–91 (dir 1972–91), Norwich Dist Health Authy 1988–94, Norfolk and Norwich Health Care NHS Tst 1994–; chm of tstees John Innes Fndn 1990–; Norwich Union Insurance Group: dir 1963, vice chm 1979, chm 1981–94; High Sheriff of Norfolk 1979–80, High Steward Borough Gt Yarmouth 1984–, JP Norfolk 1967; Hon LLD Univ of Nottingham 1988; CStJ 1986, OStJ 1968; *Recreations* country pursuits; *Clubs* Norfolk County, Royal Norfolk and Suffolk Yacht; *Style—* Michael G Falcon, Esq, CBE, DL; ✉ Keswick Old Hall, Norwich, Norfolk NR4 6TZ (☎ 01603 454348); Kirkgate, Loweswater, Cockermouth, Cumbria (☎ 01900 85271)

FALCON, Michael Geoffrey; s of Norman Leslie Falcon (d 1996), of Church Hanborough, Oxon, and Dorothy Muriel, *née* Freeman; *b* 15 Jan 1941; *Educ* Tonbridge, Trinity Coll Cambridge (exhibitioner, MA, MB BChir), Guy's Hosp Med Sch London (DO, MRCP); *m* 1969, Savithri, *née* Bhandary, of S India; *Career* jr hosp posts Guy's Hosp London and Royal Surrey Co Hosp Guildford 1967–70; Moorfields Eye Hosp London: resident surgical offr rising to sr resident surgical offr 1971–74, lectr Dept of Clinical Ophthalmology 1974–78; conslt ophthalmologist: Guy's Hosp 1978–81, St Thomas's Hosp London 1981–; Freeman City of London, Freeman Worshipful Co of Spectaclemakers; FRCS 1973, FRCOphth 1990 (examiner 1992–); *Publications* author of 3 chapters in ophthalmological textbooks 1982–94 and numerous pubns on herpetic keratitis, corneal surgery, cataract surgery and glaucoma; *Recreations* mountain walking, tennis, horticulture; *Style—* Michael Falcon, Esq; ✉ 25 Wimpole Street, London W1M 7AD (☎ 0171 580 7199, fax 0171 580 6855)

FALCONBRIDGE, Brian William; s of James Henry Falconbridge (d 1994), of Cromer, Norfolk, and Joyce Vera Lucy Spong (d 1995); *b* 1 May 1950; *Educ* Fakenham GS, Canterbury Coll of Art, Goldsmiths' Coll Sch of Art, Slade Sch of Fine Art; *m* 1970 (m dis 1989), Elizabeth Margaret, *née* Green; 1 s (Oliver William Merton b 9 Aug 1985), 1 da (Camilla Elizabeth Vita b 9 Sept 1982); *Career* sculptor; lectr: Eton 1977–81, Goldsmiths' Coll 1978–, Slade Sch of Fine Art 1979–86, Blackheath Sch of Art 1985–89; visiting prof Tamagawa Univ Tokyo 1994–95; pt/t and visiting lectr 1974: Brighton Museum, Brighton Poly, Bristol Poly, Camberwell Sch of Art, Colchester Inst Sch of Art, Falmouth Sch of Art, Maidstone Coll of Art, Morley Coll, Norwich Sch of Art, Portsmouth Poly, Ravensbourne Coll of Art and Design, The Royal Acad Schs, Sainsbury Centre for the Visual Arts Univ of E Anglia; memb Visual Art Panel Eastern Arts Assoc 1983–88, selector for post of Artist in Residence Lady Lodge Arts Centre Peterborough 1983, memb Exec Ctee for Tolly Cobbold/Eastern Arts 5th Nat Exhibition 1984–86, curator and selector A Spiritual Dimension 1986–90, Academic and Mgmnt Bds Blackheath Sch of Art 1987–89; RSBS: assoc memb 1994, memb Cncl 1995; work in several public collections; *Solo Exhibitions* House Gallery London 1977, Angela Flowers Gallery 1983, The Minories Colchester 1984, Newcastle Poly Art Gallery 1984, Arcade Gallery Harrogate 1984, Drawing Schs Gallery Eton Coll 1984, The Fermoy Centre Art Gallery King's Lynn 1986, Artist in Residence Kings' Lynn Festival (All Saints' Church with The Fermoy Centre) 1986, Artist in Residence Gaywood Park HS King's Lynn 1987, Great St Mary's Cambridge 1989, Jill George Gallery London 1990, Masterpiece Art Gallery Taipei Int Convention Centre Taiwan; *Group Exhibitions* incl: Goldsmiths' (S London Art Gallery) 1972, Royal Acad Summer Exhibition 1977, 1988, 1990, 1991, 1992, 1993, 1994 and 1996, Art for Today (Portsmouth Festival) 1979, Tolly Cobbold/Eastern Arts 3rd Nat Exhibition, Small is Beautiful (Angela Flowers Gallery) 1983, The Falconbridge Cross Highgate URC 1984, Art for Everywhere (Peterborough Museum and Art Gallery) 1985, A Spiritual Dimension touring exhibition 1989 and 1990, LA Art Fair (Thumb Gallery) 1989, New Icons touring exhibition 1989–90, Academicians' Choice (London Contemporary Arts and the Eye Gallery Bristol) 1990, London to Atlanta (Atlanta Thumb Gallery) 1990, Los Angeles Art Fair (Thumb Gallery) 1990, Drawing Show II (Thumb Gallery) 1990, Art 91 London (Thumb Gallery) 1990, Decouvertes - Grand Palais Paris (Jill George Gallery) 1991, Goldsmiths' Coll Centenary Exhibition 1991, Los Angeles Art Fair (Jill George Gallery) 1991, 1992 and 1993, ART 92 Business Design Centre (Jill George Gallery) 1992, ARCO 1992 Madrid (Jill George Gallery) 1992, Sumida Riverside Hall Gallery Tokyo 1993, Chelsea Harbour Sculpture 1993, Artists for Romanian Orphans at Bonhams 1994, The Language of Sculpture (Collyer-Bristow Gallery London) 1995; *Awards* Walter Newrath Art History award 1972, Arts Cncl minor award 1976, Eastern Arts Assoc award 1977, Tolly Cobbold E Arts regnl prize 1981, E Vincent Harris award for mural decoration 1984, prize winner 3 Int Exhibition of Miniature Art (Del Bello Gallery Toronto) 1988, Blackstone award Royal Acad Summer Exhibition 1991; *Style—* Brian Falconbridge, Esq; ✉ c/o Royal Society of British Sculptors, 108 Old Brompton Road, South Kensington, London SW7 3RA (☎ 0171 373 5554, fax 373 9202)

FALCONER, Alexander (Alex); MEP (Lab) Scotland Mid and Fife (majority 31,413); s of John Falconer, labourer, and Margaret, *née* McFarlane, canteen assistant; *b* 1 April 1940; *m* Margaret, *née* Aldridge; 1 s, 1 da; *Career* former foundry worker, served with RN 1959–68, insulator Rosyth Dockyard 1969–84, shop steward TGWU 1970–84; MEP (Lab): Mid Scotland and Fife 1984–94, Scotland Mid and Fife 1994–; memb: Euro Parl Ctees on Legal Affrs and Citizens' Rights and Regional Policy, CND; *Style—* Alex Falconer, Esq, MEP; ✉ c/o European Parliament, 93–113 Rue Belliard, 1040 Brussels, Belgium (☎ 00 32 2 383 419330, fax 00 32 2 383 417957)

FALCONER, Hon Sir Douglas William Falconer; MBE (1946); s of William Falconer (d 1956), of South Shields; *b* 20 Sept 1914; *Educ* Westoe S Shields, Univ of Durham; *m* 1941, Joan Beryl Argent (d 1989), da of late Archibald Samuel Bishop, of Hagley, Worcs (d 1961); 1 s (Ian), 1 da (Sally); *Career* called to the Bar Middle Temple 1950, QC 1967, appointed to exercise appellate jurisdiction of Bd of Trade under Trade Marks Act 1970, chm Patent Bar Assoc 1971–80, bencher Middle Temple 1973; memb Senate: Four Inns of Court 1973–74, Four Inns of Court and Bar 1974–77; memb Standing Advsy Ctee: on Patents 1975–79, on Trade Marks 1975–79; judge High Ct of Justice 1981–89; *Recreations* music, theatre; *Style—* The Hon Sir Douglas Falconer, MBE; ✉ Ridgewell House, West St, Reigate, Surrey RH2 9BZ

FALCONER, Peter Serrell; s of Thomas Falconer, FRIBA (eighth in descent from Patrick Falconer of Newton, unc of 1 Lord Falconer of Halkerton, S Lordship cr 1646, which was subsequently held by the Earls of Kintore, with the death of the tenth of whom in 1966 the Lordship became dormant; Peter is the presumed heir), and Florence Edith Falconer; *b* 7 March 1916; *Educ* Bloxham; *m* 1941, Mary, da of Rev C Hodson; 3 s, 1 da; *Career* architect; FRIBA; *Style—* Peter Falconer, Esq; ✉ St Francis, Minchinhampton, Glos (☎ 01453 882188, fax 01452 814044)

FALCONER OF HALKERTON, Lordship (S 1646) *see:* Falconer, Peter Serrell

FALDO, Nicholas Alexander (Nick); MBE (1988); s of George Arthur Faldo, of Welwyn Garden City, Herts, and Joyce, *née* Smalley; *b* 18 July 1957; *Educ* Sir Fredric Osborne Sch Welwyn Garden City; *m* 3 Jan 1986, Gillian, da of Gerald Bennett; 1 s (Matthew Alexander b 17 March 1989), 2 da (Natalie Lauren b 18 Sept 1986, Georgia Kate b 20 March 1993); *Career* professional golfer; amateur victories: Br Youths' Open 1975, English Championship 1975; tournament victories since turning professional 1976: Skol Lager 1977, Br PGA Championship 1978, 1980, 1981 and 1989, ICL Tournament

SA 1979, Haig Tournament Players' Championship 1982, French Open 1983, 1988 and 1989, Martini Int 1983, Car Care Plan Int 1983 and 1984, Lawrence Batley Int 1983, Ebel Swiss Masters 1983, Sea Pines Heritage Classic USA 1984, Spanish Open 1987, Br Open 1987, 1990 and 1992 (runner up 1993), Volvo Masters 1988, US Masters 1989, 1990 and 1996, Volvo PGA Championship 1989, Dunhill British Masters 1989, World Match-Play 1989 and 1992, Irish Open 1991, 1992 and 1993, Johnnie Walker Classic 1990 and 1993, Scandinavian Masters 1992, Euro Open 1992, Johnnie Walker World Championship 1992, Alfred Dunhill Open 1994; England Boys rep 1974, England int 1975–, with Br team 1975; memb Ryder Cup team: 1977, 1979, 1981, 1983, 1985 (winners), 1987 (winners), 1989 (winners), 1991, 1993 and 1995 (winners); memb England team Dunhill Cup 1985, 1986, 1987 (winners), 1988, 1991 and 1993; memb Hennessy Cup team: 1978, 1980, 1982 and 1984 (capt); Rookie of the Year 1977, finished top Order of Merit 1983 and 1992, BBC Sports Personality of the Year 1989; *Recreations* fly-fishing, woodwork, photography, helicopter flying; *Style*— Nick Faldo, Esq, MBE; ✉ c/o John Simpson, IMG, Pier House, Strand-on-the-Green, London W4 3NN (☎ 0181 233 5000, fax 0181 233 5001)

FALK, Brian Geoffrey; s of Lt Col Geoffrey Ferdinand Falk (d 1955), and Kathleen Falk (d 1982); *b* 8 Sept 1930; *Educ* Bryanston, Architectural Assoc (AADipl), Harvard Univ (MCP); *m* 7 Nov 1959, Gunilla Elisabet, da of Haåkon Wilhelm Abenius (d 1981), of Wasa Ordren; 3 s (Benedict b 1962, Magnus b 1963, Jasper b 1967); *Career* dir: Covell Matthews & Ptnrs and Covell Matthews Partnership International 1963–82, Falk Assocs Ltd 1983–, Moxley Jenner & Partners (London) Ltd 1988–91, Thames Estuary Airport Co Ltd 1992–94; chm Assoc Conslt Architects 1976–77, memb Haringey Borough Cncl 1968–78; Freeman of City of London 1975, Liveryman Worshipful Co of Architects 1990; RIBA 1955, MRTPI 1959, MUSA 1965, MAAK 1965, SADG 1954; *Recreations* gardening, travelling, sketching; *Style*— Brian Falk, Esq; ✉ High House, Bressingham, Diss IP22 2AP (☎ 01379 687388, fax 01379 687478); High House Studio, Bressingham, Diss IP22 2AP

FALK, Fergus Antony; TD (1979); s of Leonard Solomon Falk (d 1992), and Lucy, *née* Cohen (d 1970); *b* 30 Aug 1941; *Educ* Uppingham, Univ of London (BSc Econ); *m* 5 May 1973, Vivian Dundas, da of Leonard Cockburn Dundas Irvine (d 1968), Surgn Capt RNVR, of Hove; 2 da (Harriet b 1976, Annabel b 1979), 1 s (Sebastian b 1980); *Career* Maj HAC 1961–80; dept mangr: John Lewis and Co Ltd 1959–63, C Ulysses Williams Ltd 1964–65; Deloitte & Touche: joined 1965, ptnr 1975–, currently ptnr i/c forensic servs; treas Islington South and Finsbury Cons Assoc 1974–76 (Radwinter Branch 1976–79); memb: Ct of Assistants HAC 1975– (treas 1994–96, vice pres 1996–), Ct of Common Cncl 1984–95; candidate (C) Islington Borough Elections 1974; memb Worshipful Co of CAs; FCA 1973 (ACA 1969); *Recreations* family, gardening; *Clubs* HAC, MCC, Farringdon Ward, City Livery; *Style*— Fergus Falk, Esq, TD; ✉ Canfield Moat, Little Canfield, Gt Dunmow, Essex CM6 1TD (☎ 01371 872565, fax 01371 876264); Deloitte & Touche, Stonecutter Court, Stonecutter Street, London EC4A 4TR (direct ☎ 0171 303 5800, fax 0171 936 2638)

FALK, Sir Roger Salis; kt (1969), OBE (Mil 1945); s of Lionel David Falk (d 1949), of London; *b* 22 June 1910; *Educ* Haileybury, Univ of Geneva; *m* 1938, Margaret Helen (d 1958), da of Albert Stroud (d 1946); 1 s, 2 da; *Career* served WWII Wing Cdr RAFVR 1943; md D J Keymer & Co 1945–49 (dir 1935–49, vice chm 1950); chm: P E International Ltd 1973–76, London Board Provincial Insurance Co Ltd; dir gen BETRO 1950–52, dep chm Gaming Bd of GB 1978–81, vice pres Sadlers Wells Fndn 1986– (chm 1976–86); memb: Cncl of Industl Design 1958–67, Monopolies Cmmn 1965–79, Cncl RSA 1968–74, Cncl Imperial Soc of Kts Bachelor 1979–; life govr Haileybury 1971– (memb Cncl 1978–); Hon DLitt City Univ 1984; CIMgt; *Books* Business of Management (5 edns, 1961); *Recreations* music, writing, reading; *Clubs* Garrick, MCC; *Style*— Sir Roger Falk, OBE; ✉ 603 Beatty House, Dolphin Square, London SW1V 3PL (☎ 0171 828 3752)

FALKENDER, Baroness (Life Peeress UK 1974), of West Haddon, Co Northants; Marcia Matilda Falkender; *née* Field; CBE (1970); da of Harry Field; assumed by deed poll 1974 surname Falkender in lieu of Williams; *b* 10 March 1932; *Educ* Queen Mary Coll London (BA); *m* 1955 (m dis 1961), George Edmund Charles Williams; *Career* private sec Morgan Phillips (gen sec of Labour Pty) 1955–56; private and political sec to Rt Hon Lord Wilson of Rievaulx, formerly Rt Hon Sir Harold Wilson, KG, OBE, MP; political columnist Mail on Sunday 1983–88, memb British Screen Advisory Cncl and Film Ctee 1976–; dir Peckham Building Soc 1986–91, chm Canvasback Productions 1989–91; pres Tstees of UK Ctee of UNIFEM 1989–92, lay govr Queen Mary and Westfield Coll London 1988–93 (lay memb External Relations Ctee 1993–96), tstee The Silver Tst 1986–; *Books* Inside No 10 (1972), Perspective on Downing Street (1983); *Recreations* reading, film; *Clubs* Reform; *Style*— The Lady Falkender, CBE; ✉ 3 Wyndham Mews, Upper Montagu St, London W1

FALKINER, Benjamin Simon Patrick; s and h of Sir Edmond Charles Falkiner, 9 Bt, *qv*, and Janet Iris, *née* Darby; *b* 16 Jan 1962; *Educ* Queen Elizabeth's Boys' Sch Barnet; *children* 1 s (Samuel James Matthew b 30 Aug 1993), 1 da (Alice Katharine Sally b 19 Oct 1996); *Career* car parts wholesaler; *Recreations* rugby, cricket, music (drummer), youth work; *Clubs* Old Elizabethans Rugby Football, Old Elizabethans Cricket; *Style*— Benjamin Falkiner, Esq; ✉ 80 Crawford Rd, Hatfield, Herts (☎ 01707 266031); Godfrey Davis (St Albans) Ltd, Ashley Road, St Albans, Herts (☎ 01727 859155)

FALKINER, Sir Edmond Charles; 9 Bt (I 1778), of Annemount, Cork; s of Lt-Col Sir Terence Edmond Patrick Falkiner, 8 Bt (d 1987); *b* 24 June 1938; *Educ* Downside; *m* 8 Oct 1960, Janet Iris, da of Arthur Edward Bruce Darby, of The Park, Stoke Lacey, Bromyard, Herefords; 2 s (Benjamin Simon Patrick b 1962, Matthew Terence b 1964); *Heir* s, Benjamin Simon Patrick Falkiner, *qv*; *Career* pacifist; probation officer 1968–; *Clubs* Ronnie Scott's; *Style*— Sir Edmond Falkiner, Bt; ✉ 111 Wood St, Barnet, Herts EN5 4BX (☎ 0181 440 2426)

FALKLAND, The Master of; Hon Lucius Alexander Plantagenet Cary; s and h of 15 Viscount of Falkland, *qv*; *b* 1 Feb 1963; *Educ* Westminster, Loretto, RMA Sandhurst; *m* 1993, Linda, da of Raymond Purl, of Colorado Springs, USA; 1 s (b 6 Feb 1995); *Career* former Capt 2 Bn Scots Guards; screenwriter and film producer 1991–; *Recreations* drawing, skiing, tennis; *Clubs* Cavalry and Guards'; *Style*— The Master of Falkland; ✉ 10417 Ravenwood Court, Bel Air, CA 90077, USA

FALKLAND, 15 Viscount of (S 1620); Premier Viscount of Scotland; Lucius Edward William Plantagenet Cary; also 15 Lord Cary (S 1620); s of 14 Viscount (d 1984), and his 2 w Constance Mary, *née* Berry (d 1995); *b* 8 May 1935; *Educ* Wellington Coll; *m* 1, 26 April 1962 (m dis 1990), Caroline Anne, da of late Lt Cdr Gerald Butler, DSC, RN, of Ashton House, Ashton Keynes, Wilts; 1 s, 2 da (Hon Samantha b 1973, Hon Lucinda b 1974) (and 1 da decd); m 2, 12 Sept 1990, Nicole, da of late Milburn Mackey; 1 s (Hon Charles b 1992); *Heir* s, Master of Falkland, *qv*; *Career* 2 Lt 8 King's Royal Irish Hussars; journalist, theatrical agent and former chief exec C T Bowring Trading (Hldgs) Ltd; memb House of Lords Select Ctee on Overseas Trade 1984–85; dep whip Lib Democrats House of Lords 1988–, heritage spokesman 1995–; *Recreations* golf, motorcycling, cinema; *Clubs* Brooks's, Sunningdale Golf; *Style*— The Rt Hon Viscount of Falkland; ✉ House of Lords, London SW1

FALKNER, (Frederic Sherard) Neil; s of Francis Sherard Melville Falkner (d 1972), of Louth, Lincs, and Doris Mary, *née* Matthews (d 1990); *b* 28 Aug 1927; *Educ* Northampton Sch, Lincoln Coll Oxford (MA), Oberlin Coll Ohio USA (MA); *m* 27 June 1951, Maria Luisa, da of Max Aub (d 1974), of Mexico City; 1 s (Martin b 1959), 2 da (Elaine b 1954, Lynne b 1956); *Career* mktg exec Procter & Gamble 1951–56, mktg mangr Mars 1956–61, chief exec Chesebrough-Ponds 1961–66, ran own mfrg business 1966–77, chm and chief exec Development Capital Group 1977–89, dir Lazard Bros 1985–89, chm and chief exec Falkner Moller Partners Ltd 1989–; Liveryman Worshipful Co of Painter-Stainers 1971; *Recreations* shooting, fishing, music, medieval history; *Clubs* East India, City Livery; *Style*— Neil Falkner, Esq; ✉ 10 Emmanuel Road, Cambridge CB1 1JW (☎ 01223 461750, fax 01223 464718)

FALL, Sir Brian James Proetel; GCVO (1994), KCMG (1992, CMG 1984); s of John William Fall and Edith Juliet, *née* Proetel; *b* 13 Dec 1937; *Educ* St Paul's Sch, Magdalen Coll Oxford, Univ of Michigan Law Sch; *m* 1962, Delmar Alexandra Roos; 3 da; *Career* joined HM Dip Serv 1962, served in FO UN Dept 1963, Moscow 1965, Geneva 1968, Civil Serv Coll 1970, E Euro and Soviet Dept and Western Orgns Dept FO 1971, New York 1975, Harvard Univ Center for Int Affrs 1976, cnsllr Moscow 1977–79, head of Energy, Sci and Space Dept FCO 1979–80, head of E Euro and Soviet Dept FCO 1980–81, princ private sec to Sec of State for Foreign and Cwlth Affrs 1981–84; dir private office, sec gen NATO 1984–86, asst under sec (Def) FCO 1986–88, min Washington 1988–89, high cmmr Ottawa 1989–92, HM ambassador to Russian Federation 1992–95, ret; princ Lady Margaret Hall Oxford 1995–; *Style*— Sir Brian Fall, GCVO, KCMG; ✉ Lady Margaret Hall, Oxford OX2 6QA

FALLA, Paul Stephen; s of late Brig Norris Stephen Falla, CMG, DSO, of Wellington, New Zealand, and Audrey Frances, *née* Stock; *b* 25 Oct 1913; *Educ* Wellington Coll, Christ's Coll NZ, Balliol Coll Oxford; *m* 1958, Elizabeth Mary, *née* Shearer; 1 da; *Career* HM Foreign Service 1936–67, cnsllr (FO, FCO) 1950–67 (dep dir of Res 1958–67); editor Oxford English-Russian Dictionary published 1984; Scott Moncrieff Prize for translation from French 1972 and 1981, Schlegel-Tieck Prize for translation from German 1983; translated about 45 books from various languages on politics, history, art; FIL, fell Inst of Translation and Interpreting; *Recreations* reading (history, politics, philosophy, belles-lettres), studying languages; *Clubs* Travellers; *Style*— P S Falla, Esq; ✉ 63 Freelands Rd, Bromley, Kent BR1 3HZ (☎ 0181 460 4995)

FALLE, Sir Samuel (Sam); KCMG (1979, CMG 1964), KCVO (1972), DSC (1945); s of Theodore de Carteret Falle (d 1966), of Ickenham, Middx, and Hilda Falle (d 1979); *b* 19 Feb 1919; *Educ* Victoria Coll Jersey; *m* 1945, Merete, da of Paul Rosen, of Fredensborg, Denmark; 1 s, 3 da; *Career* RN 1937–48; HM Dip Serv: FO 1948, Shiraz and Tehran 1949–52, Beirut 1952–55, Baghdad 1957–61, consul-gen Gothenburg 1961–63, head UN Dept FO 1963; dep high cmmr: Kuala Lumpur Malaysia 1967, Aden 1967; ambass to Kuwait 1969–70, Br high cmmr in Singapore 1970–74, ambass to Sweden 1974–77, Br high cmmr to Nigeria 1977–78, ret; delegate Cmmn of the Euro Communities Algeria 1979–82, conslt chm of the Euro Communities Zambia 1983; *Publications* My Lucky Life (1996); *Recreations* swimming, skiing, languages; *Style*— Sir Sam Falle, KCMG, KCVO, DSC; ✉ Slattna, S 57030, Mariannelund, Sweden (☎ 00 46 496 50012)

FALLON, Ivan Gregory; s of Padraic Joseph Fallon (d 1974), and Dorothea, *née* Maher (d 1985); *b* 26 June 1944; *Educ* St Peter's Coll Wexford, Trinity Coll Dublin (BBS); *m* 14 Jan 1967, Susan Mary, da of Dr Robert Francis Lurring, of Kidderminster; 1 s (Padraic Robert b 1974), 2 da (Tania Helen b 1967, Lara Catherine b 1970); *Career* Irish Times 1964–66, Thomson Provincial Newspapers 1966–67, Daily Mirror 1967–68, Sunday Telegraph 1968–84, city ed Sunday Telegraph 1979–84, dep ed Sunday Times 1984–94, gp editorial dir Independent Group Newspapers Ltd 1994–; FRSA 1989; *Books* DeLorean: The Rise and Fall of a Dream Maker (with James Srodes, 1983), Takeovers (with James Srodes, 1987), The Brothers: The Rise of Saatchi and Saatchi (1988), Billionaire: The Life & Times of Sir James Goldsmith (1991), Paperchase (1993), The Player: The Life of Tony O'Reilly (1994); *Recreations* squash, tennis; *Clubs* Beefsteak, RAC, The Rand (Johannesburg); *Style*— Ivan Fallon, Esq; ✉ Independent Group Newspapers Ltd, 47 Sauer Street, PO Box 1014 Johannesburg 2000, South Africa

FALLON, Padraic Matthew; s of Padraic Joseph Fallon (d 1974), and Dorothea, *née* Maher (d 1985); *b* 21 Sept 1946; *Educ* St Peter's Coll Wexford, Blackrock Coll Co Dublin, Trinity Coll Dublin (BA); *m* 8 April 1972, Gillian Elizabeth, da of Graham Hellyer, of N Humberside; 1 s (Jolyon b 1975), 3 da (Nicola b 1977, Harriet b 1980, Annabel (twin) b 1980); *Career* fin reporter: Thomson City Office London 1969–70, Daily Mirror 1970–72; City pages Daily Mail 1972–74, seconded as managing ed ME Money Beirut 1974, ed Euromoney Magazine 1974–86; Euromoney Publications PLC (formerly Euromoney Publications Ltd): dir 1975, dep md 1982, md 1985, chief exec 1989, chm 1992; non-exec dir: Assoc Newspapers Holdings Ltd, Allied Irish Banks plc, Harmsworth Publishing Ltd; chm Latin American Financial Publications Inc, memb Creditanstalt International Advsy Bd; *Recreations* country sports; *Clubs* Kildare Street and Univ (overseas memb), Flyfishers'; *Style*— Padraic Fallon, Esq; ✉ 20 Lower Addison Gardens, London W14 8BQ (☎ 0171 602 1253); Euromoney Publications PLC, Nestor House, Playhouse Yard, London EC4V 5EX (☎ 0171 779 8888/8556, fax 0171 779 8656)

FALLOWELL, Duncan Richard; s of Thomas Edgar Fallowell, of Crowthorne, Berkshire, and La Croix Valmer, France, and Celia, *née* Waller; *b* 26 Sept 1948; *Educ* Palmer's Sch, St Paul's, Magdalen Coll Oxford; *Career* author; *Books* Drug Tales (1979), April Ashley's Odyssey (1982), Satyrday (1986), The Underbelly (1987), To Noto (1989), One Hot Summer in St Petersburg (1994), 20th Century Characters (1994); *Style*— Duncan Fallowell, Esq; ✉ 44 Leamington Road Villas, London W11 1HT

FALLOWFIELD, Richard Gordon; s of Capt Walter Herman Gordon Fallowfield, RN (d 1954), and Elizabeth Burnett, *née* Baker (d 1956); *b* 25 Jan 1935; *Educ* Marlborough; *m* 21 Sept 1963, Elfrida Charlotte, da of Sir Timothy Calvert Eden, 8 Bt (d 1963); 2 s (Timothy Gordon b 1965, Nicholas John b 1967), 1 da (Laura Louise b 1974); *Career* PR exec; Capt Argyll and Sutherland Highlanders 1952–54; dir: Young and Rubicam Inc 1973–80, McCann Erickson Ltd 1980–84, Grandfield Rork Collins (dep chm) 1985–91, Cardew & Co 1991–; memb IPA; *Recreations* squash, tennis, walking, reading biographies; *Style*— Richard Fallowfield, Esq; ✉ 78 West Side, Clapham Common, London SW4 9AY (☎ 0171 228 4428); Cardew & Co, 12 Suffolk St, London SW1Y 4HQ (☎ 0171 930 0777)

FANCOURT, Dr Graham John; s of Leonard Frank Fancourt (d 1982), of Gidea Park, Essex, and Iris, *née* Anscombe (d 1994); *b* 23 Feb 1953; *Educ* Brentwood Sch, Univ of London (MB BS); *m* 22 July 1978, Julie Valerie, da of Leslie Tyler, of Brentwood, Essex; 1 s (Russell Graham b 20 Jan 1992); *Career* conslt physician: Glenfield Gen Hosp, Loughborough Hospital; clinical tutor Univ of Leicester; pubns on respiratory med and physiology of ageing; memb BMA, MRCS 1977, FRCP 1984 (MRCP 1980); *Style*— Dr Graham Fancourt; ✉ Glenfield General Hosp, Groby Rd, Leicester LE3 9QD (☎ 0116 287 1471)

FANE, Hon Harry St Clair; yr s of 15 Earl of Westmorland, GCVO, DL (d 1993); hp to bro, 16 Earl of Westmorland, *qv*; *b* 19 March 1953; *Educ* Harrow; *m* 6 Jan 1984, Tessa, da of Capt Michael Philip Forsyth-Forrest; 1 s (Sam Michael David b 1989), 1 da (Sophie Jane b 1987); *Career* page of honour to HM The Queen 1966–68; *Style*— The Hon Harry Fane

FANE, Hon Julian Charles; s of 14 Earl of Westmorland (d 1948), and Diana (d 1983), da of 4 and last Baron Ribblesdale (d 1925); *b* 25 May 1927; *Educ* Harrow; *m* 1976, Gillian, yr da of John Kidston Swire (d 1983), and sis of Sir John Swire, CBE, *qv* and Sir Adrian Swire, DL, *qv*; *Career* author; FRSL 1974; *Books* incl: Morning, Best Friends, Cautionary Tales for Women, Hope Cottage, Eleanor, The Duchess of Castile, His Christmas Box, Memories of my Mother, Gentleman's Gentleman, Money Matters, The

Social Comedy, The Collected Works of Julian Fane Volume One; *Style*— The Hon Julian Fane, FRSL; ✉ Rotten Row House, Lewes, E Sussex BN7 1TN

FANE, Vere John Alexander; s of John Lionel Richards Fane (d 1945; whose gf Robert was 7 s of Hon Henry Fane, 2 s of 8 Earl of Westmorland), and Barbara, da of Falconer Wallace of Candacraig; *b* 21 April 1935; *Educ* Eton, Trinity Coll Cambridge; *m* 30 May 1964, Tessa Helen Murray, o da of John Murray Prain, DSO, OBE, DL, and Helen, *née* Skene, of Pitlour; 1 s (Rupert b 1967), 1 da (Miranda b 1968); *Career* former Lt Coldstream Gds; previously chm Wallace Brothers & Co (Holdings); currently chm Westminster Associates International Ltd; dir: Carter Holt Holdings NZ, North Borneo Timbers Malaysia, Ocean Leila Hong Kong, Flour Mills Fiji, Agricultural Investments Australia; *Recreations* shooting, golf; *Clubs* White's, Leander, Royal and Ancient; *Style*— Vere Fane, Esq; ✉ 18 Empire House, Thurloe Place, London SW7 2RU; Westminster Associates International Ltd, Regency House, 1–4 Warwick St, London W1R 5WB (☎ 0171 287 5788)

FANE TREFUSIS, Hon Charles Patrick Rolle; s and h of 22 Baron Clinton; *b* 21 March 1962; *m* 6 June 1992, Rosanna E, yr da of (Alexander) John Rennie Izat, JP, *qv*, of High Cocklaw, Berwick-upon-Tweed; 2 s (Edward Charles Rolle b 26 Feb 1994, James Henry Rolle b 16 July 1996); *Style*— Hon Charles Fane Trefusis

FANIBUNDA, Kersi; s of Burjor Fanibunda (d 1979), of Bombay, and Naja, *née* Lord; *b* 4 Nov 1936; *Educ* St Stanislaus HS Bombay, Univ of Bombay (BDS), Univ of Newcastle (MDS); *m* Mingi, da of Prof J J Chinoy; 1 s (Hector b 20 Jan 1973); *Career* Leeds Area Health Authy: house offr 1961–62, registrar 1962–65; Dept of Oral Surgery Dental Sch Univ of Newcastle: lectr 1965–78, sr lectr and hon conslt oral surgn 1978–, acting head 1989–; conslt in admin charge: Dept of Oral Surgery Newcastle Royal Victoria Infirmary 1989–90, Dept of Admissions Newcastle Dental Hosp 1989–; memb: Univ Teachers Oral and Maxillofacial Surgery Gp, BDA (former memb Cncl), British Assoc of Oral and Maxillofacial Surgns, North of England Odontological Soc (memb Cncl and pres), British Assoc of Dental and Maxillofacial Radiologists, General Dental Cncl 1991– (memb Professional Conduct Ctee); *Style*— Kersi Fanibunda, Esq; ✉ Department of Oral Surgery, The Dental School, University of Newcastle upon Tyne, Newcastle upon Tyne NE2 4BW (☎ 0191 222 6000, fax 0191 222 6137)

FANNER, His Hon Peter Duncan; s of Robert William Hodges Fanner (d 1945), slr, of Sheffield, and Doris Kitty, *née* Whiffin (d 1981); *b* 29 May 1926; *Educ* Pangbourne Coll; *m* 23 April 1949, Sheila Eveline, da of George England, of Bromley (d 1946); 1 s (Roger b 1953), 1 da (Elizabeth b 1957); *Career* pilot Fleet Air Arm, Lt (A) RNVR; admitted slr 1951, dep clerk to the Justices Gore Div 1952–56, clerk to Justices Bath 1956–72, memb Cncl of Justices Clerks Soc 1966–72, assessor memb Departmental Ctee on Liquor Licensing 1971–72, met stipendiary magistrate 1972–86, dep circuit judge 1974–80, recorder of the Crown Court 1980–86, circuit judge (Western Circuit) 1986–95, ret; *Style*— His Hon Peter Fanner

FANSHAWE OF RICHMOND, Baron (Life Peer UK 1983), of South Cerney, Co Glos; Sir Anthony Henry Fanshawe Royle; KCMG (1974); er s of Sir Lancelot Carrington Royle, KBE (d 1978), and Barbara Rachel, *née* Haldin (d 1977); *b* 27 March 1927; *Educ* Harrow, RMA Sandhurst; *m* 1957, Shirley, da of John Ramsay Worthington (d 1953); 2 da (Hon Susannah Caroline Fanshawe (Hon Mrs Lester) b 1960, Hon Lucinda Katherine Fanshawe Royle b 1962); *Career* served with The Life Gds in Germany, Egypt, Palestine and Transjordan 1945–48, 21 SAS Regt (TA) 1948–51; MP (C) Richmond (Surrey) 1959–83; PPS to: Under-Sec of State for the Colonies 1960, Sec of State for Air 1960–62, Min of Aviation 1962–64; memb Assembly Cncl of Europe and WEU 1965–67, oppn whip 1967–70, Parly under-sec of state for Foreign and Cwlth Affairs 1970–74, vice chm Cons Party Orgn and chm Cons Int Office 1979–84; chm Sedgwick Group plc 1993–; dir: Westland Group plc 1985–94, Rank Xerox UK Ltd 1988–, TI Group plc 1990–; memb European Advsy Cncl Pratt & Whitney 1993–; Most Esteemed Family Order of Brunei (1st class) 1974; *Clubs* Pratt's, White's, Brooks's; *Style*— The Rt Hon Lord Fanshawe of Richmond, KCMG; ✉ The Chapter Manor, South Cerney, Glos

FANTONI, Barry Ernest; s of late Peter Nello Secondo Fantoni, and Sarah Catherine, *née* Deverell; *b* 28 Feb 1940; *Educ* Archbishop Temple Sch, Camberwell Sch of Arts & Crafts; *m* 1972, Teresa Frances, da of Col Charles James Reidy, OBE; *Career* writer, artist, jazz musician and broadcaster; memb Editorial Staff Private Eye 1963; cartoonist: The Listener 1968, Times Diary 1983; dir: Barry Fantoni Merchandising Co Ltd 1985–91, Snartz 1989; *Clubs* Chelsea Arts, Arts; *Style*— Barry Fantoni, Esq; ✉ c/o Paul Marsh Agency, 138 Buckingham Palace Road, London SW1W 9SA (☎ 0171 730 1124, fax 0171 730 0037)

FARAJ, Mohammed; s of Faiq Faraj, of Baghadad, Iraq, and Hassiba Amin (d 1978); *b* 21 July 1947; *Educ* Coll of Engrg Univ of Baghdad Iraq (BSc), Inst of Planning Studies Univ of Nottingham (MA); *Career* architect; conslt firm Iraq 1968–70, James Cubitt & Ptnrs London 1973–80, conslt Design Works London 1980–; memb: ARCUK, RIBA 1982, RTPI 1984; *Recreations* tennis, keep fit, photography; *Style*— Mohammed Faraj, Esq; ✉ Designworks, 84 Cheviot Gardens, London NW2 1QA

FARINGDON, 3 Baron (UK 1916); Sir Charles Michael Henderson; 3 Bt (UK 1902); s of Lt-Col Hon Michael Thomas Henderson (16/5 Lancers, d 1953), 2 gs of 1 Baron; suc unc 1977; *b* 3 July 1937; *Educ* Eton, Trinity Coll Cambridge (BA); *m* 30 June 1959, Sarah Caroline, o da of Maj John Marjoribanks Eskdale Askew, CBE (d 1996), and Lady Susan Alice, *née* Egerton, da of 4 Earl of Ellesmere; 3 s (Hon James b 1961, Hon Thomas b 1966, Hon Angus b 1969), 1 da (Hon Susannah b 1963); *Heir* s, Hon James Henderson; *Career* ptnr Cazenove & Co 1968–96, chm Witan Investment plc 1980–; chm Bd of Govrs Royal Marsden Hosp 1980–85, hon treas Nat Art Collections Fund 1985–92, memb Bd of Mgmnt Inst of Cancer Res 1990–, chm Royal Cmmn on the Historical Monuments of England 1994–, chm Hardy Amies Ltd 1996–; Liveryman Worshipful Co of Plumbers; *Style*— The Rt Hon the Lord Faringdon; ✉ 28 Brompton Square, London SW3 2AD (fax 0171 589 0724); Buscot Park, Faringdon, Oxon SN7 8BU

FARIS, John Brian; s of William James Faris (d 1964), and Ivy Agnes, *née* Wheeler (d 1935); *b* 11 May 1934; *Educ* Eastbourne GS; *m* 20 June 1970, Patricia Millicent, *née* Bolongaro; 1 s (James Robert b 5 July 1972), 1 da (Alexandra Clare b 27 Aug 1974); *Career* Nat Serv RAEC 1952–54; chartered accountant Deloitte Plender Griffiths & Co 1960–73 (articled clerk 1954–60), ptnr Deloitte & Co 1973, tech ptnr Coopers & Lybrand (following successive mergers), ret 1994; pt/t lectr in accounting NW Poly London 1961–64; ICAEW: memb Tech Ctee 1986–90, chm Working Pty of Accounting Standards Ctee on Cash Flow Reporting 1989–90; non-exec dir The Royal Nat Orthopaedic Hosp Tst; memb: Fin Ctee Nat Assoc of Citizens Advice Bureaux, Welwyn Garden City Housing Assoc (memb Mgmnt Ctee, chm Fin Ctee), E London Panel The Prince's Youth Business Tst; tstee Northaw Charities; FCA (ACA 1960); *Recreations* talking and reading; *Style*— John Faris, Esq; ✉ 18 Tolmers Ave, Cuffley, Hertfordshire EN6 4QA (☎ 01707 873580)

FARISH, Stephen Graham; s of Peter Graham Farish, of Witchampton, Dorset, and Edna Winifred, *née* Bannerman; *b* 12 Dec 1961; *Educ* Canford Sch, Univ of Edinburgh (MA, univ 1st VIII rowing); *Career* editorial asst rising to news ed Medeconomics monthly med magazine 1985–88, freelance journalist and copywriter 1988–90; PR Week: joined as news ed 1990, dep ed 1991, ed 1992–; *Recreations* skiing, windsurfing, walking, photography, travel, creative writing; *Style*— Stephen Farish, Esq; ✉ PR Week, Haymarket Business Publications Ltd, 22 Lancaster Gate, London W2 3LP (☎ 0171 413 4166, fax 0171 413 4509)

FARLEY, Alastair Hugh; s of George Walker Farley (d 1970), of Bovinger, Ongar, Essex, and Phyllis Mary, *née* Davies (d 1977); *b* 2 Jan 1946; *Educ* Felsted Sch, Jesus Coll Cambridge (MA); *m* 1, 1971; 2 da (Claire Katharine b 26 Nov 1974, Joanna Helen b 22 June 1980), 1 s (Edward McMurdo b 20 Jan 1976); m 2, 1995; *Career* Norton Rose: articled clerk 1968–71, admitted slr 1971, asst slr 1971–73, ptnr 1974–82; fndr ptnr and sr ptnr Watson, Farley & Williams 1982–; non-exec dir Close Brothers Group plc 1993–, non-exec dir Stirling Shipping Company Limited 1996–; memb Law Soc 1971; Liveryman City of London Slrs' Co, memb Ct of Assistants Worshipful Co of Shipwrights 1990; *Recreations* shooting, tennis, country pursuits; *Clubs* RAC; *Style*— Alastair Farley, Esq; ✉ Watson, Farley & Williams, 15 Appold Street, London EC2A 2HB (☎ 0171 814 8000, fax 0171 814 8141)

FARLEY, Henry Edward (Rob); s of William Farley (d 1986), of Knutsford, Cheshire, and Frances Elizabeth Farley (d 1989); *b* 28 Sept 1930; *Educ* Harrow County Sch for Boys; *m* July 1955, Audrey Joyce, *née* Shelvey; 1 s (Sean b April 1967), 1 da (Sara b April 1969); *Career* Royal Bank of Scotland Group and subsids until 1990: joined National Bank 1947 (taken over by National Commercial Bank of Scotland, subeq merged with Royal Bank of Scotland), regnl dir North Williams & Glyn's Bank, head of domestic banking then chief gen mangr Royal Bank of Scotland, dep gp chief exec, dir Charterhouse Group plc, chm Williams & Glyn's (IOM) Ltd, chm Direct Line Insurance, chm Royscot Finance Group, ret 1990; former: chm Joint Credit Card Co (Access), dir Mastercard Inc USA, non-exec dir High Table Ltd; currently non-exec dir: Nationwide Building Society, Banque Rivaud Paris, Davenham Group plc, John Maunders Group plc; memb Ct and vice chm Cncl UMIST, dir Manchester Federal Sch of Business and Mgmnt; Freeman City of London, Liveryman Worshipful Co of Marketors; FCIB, FRSA; *Recreations* cricket, rugby, reading, writing; *Clubs* MCC, Middx CC, St James's Manchester, Pickwick Bicycle; *Style*— Rob Farley, Esq; ✉ c/o Nationwide Building Society, Nationwide House, Pipers Way, Swindon SN38 1HW

FARLEY, Prof Martyn Graham; s of Herbert Booth Farley (d 1985), of Bristol, and Hilda Gertrude, *née* Hendey (d 1963); *b* 27 Oct 1924; *Educ* Bristol Aeroplane Tech Coll, Merchant Venturers Tech Coll; *m* 20 March 1948, Freda, da of Fred Laugharne (d 1958), of Coventry; 2 s (Robin Laugharne b 1949 d 1984, Simon Laugharne b 1952), 1 da (Jane Elizabeth b 1958); *Career* Engine Div Bristol Aeroplane Co 1939–55: design apprentice, devpt engr, sr gas turbine designer; Bristol Siddeley Engines 1955–65: asst chief devpt engr, asst chief mechanical engr, chief devpt engr, chief engr (design and devpt); Rolls Royce Ltd 1965–75: chief engr, gen works mangr, mfrg and prodn dir, HQ exec to Vice Chm; RMCS and Cranfield Inst of Technol: prof of mgmnt sci 1975–86, vice chm Sch of Mgmnt and Mathematics 1984–86, emeritus prof 1986; chm: RC Ltd 1985–89, British Management Data Foundation Ltd 1979–, Aeronautical Trusts Ltd 1984–88 (dir 1975–88), Harwell Computer Power Ltd 1991– (dir 1986–); dir World Tech Ventures Ltd 1984–87, memb Advsy Cncl RNEC 1988–; memb Ct: Univ of Loughborough 1977–89, Cranfield Inst 1977–, Brunel Univ 1977–80, Univ of Bath 1983–; pres: RAeS 1983–84, CGIA Assoc 1984–, IProdE 1984–85; vice pres IIM 1979–; memb Sr Awards Ctee CGLI 1979, hon memb City & Guilds Cncl; hon fell: CGLI 1990, American IIM, American Soc of Mfrg Engrs (elected charter fell 1986), Aust IIM, Indian IProdE, Mfrg Mgmnt Fedn; hon CGIA; Freeman City of London, Liveryman Worshipful Co of Coachmakers and Harness Makers; CEng, FRAeS, FIProdE, FIEE, FIMechE, FIIM, CIMgt, MAIAA; *Recreations* gardening, walking, watching rowing and rugby; *Clubs* Athenaeum, Shrivenham, Ariel Rowing; *Style*— Prof Martyn Farley; ✉ Willow End, Vicarage Lane, Shrivenham, Swindon, Wilts SN6 8DT

FARMAN, Ian Glencairn Crisp; s of Stuart C Farman, of Chichester, W Sussex, and Joan G, *née* Wallace; *b* 27 Oct 1947; *Educ* Rugby, Univ of Southampton (LLB); *m* Susan Margaret, da of Maj-Gen P B Foster, RA; 4 da (Anna b 1975, Jenny b 1977, Christina b 1982, Isabel b 1984); *Career* Leslie & Godwin 1970–72; dir: MPA Ltd 1972–84, William M Mercer Ltd 1984–; slr Supreme Court 1975–; vice chm Int Bar Assoc 1993–; FRSA; *Recreations* sailing, tennis, wine, shooting; *Style*— Ian Farman, Esq; ✉ William M Mercer Ltd, Telford House, 14 Tothill St, London SW1H 9NB (☎ 0171 222 9121, fax 0171 222 6140); Little Meadow Cottage, Charlton, Chichester, W Sussex PO18 0HU

FARMBROUGH, Rt Rev David John; 2 s of late Charles Septimus Farmbrough, and Ida Mabel Farmbrough; *b* 4 May 1929; *Educ* Bedford, Lincoln Coll Oxford; *m* 1955, Angela Priscilla, da of Walter Adam Hill; 1 s, 3 da; *Career* ordained: deacon 1953, priest 1954; priest i/c St John's Hatfield 1957–63, vicar of Bishop's Stortford 1963–74, archdeacon of St Albans 1974–81, bishop of Bedford 1981–93; *Recreations* sailing, gardening; *Style*— The Rt Rev D J Farmbrough; ✉ 110 Village Road, Bromham, Bedford MK43 8HU (☎ 01234 825042)

FARMER, Dr (Edwin) Bruce; s of Edwin Bruce Farmer, and Doris, *née* Darby; *b* 18 Sept 1936; *Educ* King Edward's Birmingham, Univ of Birmingham (BSc, PhD); *m* 1962, Beryl Ann, da of late William Alfred Griffiths, of Birmingham; 1 s (Andrew b 1967), 1 da (Amanda b 1969); *Career* dir and gen mangr Brico Metals 1967–69; md: Brico Engineering 1970–76 (tech dir 1969–70), Wellworthy Ltd 1976–81; dir: The Morgan Crucible Co plc 1981– (gp md and chief exec 1983–), Morganite Aust Pty Ltd, Scapa Group plc 1993–; chm Allied Colloids 1996; Liveryman Worshipful Co of Scientific Instrument Makers; CEng, CIMgt, FRSA, FIM; *Recreations* squash, cricket, music; *Clubs* Carlton; *Style*— Dr Bruce Farmer; ✉ Weston House, Bracken Close, Wonersh, Surrey GU5 0QS (☎ 01483 898182); The Morgan Crucible Co plc, Morgan House, Madeira Walk, Windsor, Berks SL4 1EP (☎ 01753 837000, fax 01753 850872, telex 849025)

FARMER, Sir (Lovedin) George Thomas; kt (1968); s of Lovedin George Farmer (d 1952), of Droitwich Spa; *b* 13 May 1908; *Educ* Oxford HS, JDipMA; *m* 1, 1938, Editha Mary (d 1980), da of late F W Fisher, of Worcs; m 2, 1980, Muriel Gwendoline Mercer Pinfold, *née* Edwards; *Career* chm Rover Co Ltd 1963–73, dep chm British Leyland Ltd 1970–73, chm Zenith Carburetter Co Ltd 1973–77, dir Rea Bros (IOM) Ltd 1976–88; pres: Birmingham C of C 1960–61, Soc of Manufacturers and Traders 1962–64 (dep pres 1964–65, chm Exec 1968–72); past memb ECGD (Bd of Trade); govr, chm Fin Ctee and chm Exec Cncl Royal Shakespeare Theatre 1955–75, past chm Loft Theatre; pro-chllr Univ of Birmingham 1966–75; Liveryman Worshipful Co of Coachmakers & Coach Harness Makers; Hon LLD Birmingham 1975; FCA; *Recreations* theatre, golf, fishing; *Clubs* Royal and Ancient; *Style*— Sir George Farmer; ✉ Longridge, The Chase, Ballakillowey, Colby, Isle of Man (☎ 01624 832603)

FARMER, (Pryce) Michael; QC (1995); s of Sarah Jane Owen; *b* 20 May 1944; *Educ* Ysgol Dyffryn Nantlle Penygroes Gwynedd, King's Coll London (BA); *m* 31 March 1975, Olwen Mary, da of late Rev Griffith John Roberts, MA; 1 s (Siôn ap Mihangel b 17 July 1976), 1 da (Olwen Mair Mihangel b 1 Nov 1979); *Career* called to the Bar Gray's Inn 1972; in practice Wales and Chester Circuit 1972–, recorder of the Crown Court 1995– (jr 1991–93, asst recorder 1993–95), head of Chambers Sedan House Chester 1995–96, in main practice Goldsmith Building London 1995–; *Recreations* reading, gardening, music, watching rugby football; *Clubs* Reform, Clwb Rygbi yr Wyddgrug; *Style*— Michael Farmer, Esq, QC; ✉ Goldsmith Building, Temple, London EC4Y 7BL (☎ 0171 353 7881, fax 0171 353 5319); Sedan House, Stanley Place, Chester CH1 2LU (☎ 01244 348282, fax 01244 342336)

FARMER, Penelope Jane; da of Hugh Robert Macdonald Farmer, of Yping, Midhurst, Sussex, and Penelope Frances, *née* Boothby (d 1963); *b* 14 June 1939; *Educ* private sch,

St Anne's Coll Oxford (MA), Bedford Coll London (Dip in Sociology); *m* 1, 1962 (m dis), Michael John Mockridge; m 2, 1982, Simon David Shorvon, s of Dr H Shorvon; 1 da (Clare Penelope b 2 April 1964), 1 s (Thomas Michael Louis b 4 Dec 1965); *Career* author; runner-up Carnegie prize 1963; memb: Soc of Authors, PEN; *Children's Novels* The Summer Birds (1963), Emma in Winter (1965), Charlotte Sometimes (1969), Castle of Bone (1972), Year King (1976), Thicker Than Water (1989); *Adult Novels* Standing in the Shadow (1984), Eve: Her Story (1985), Away From Home (1987), Glasshouses (1988), Snakes and Ladders (1993), Penelope (1994), Two: Or the Book of Twins and Doubles (1996); *Recreations* exploring other people's cities; *Style—* Ms Penelope Farmer; ✉ c/o Deborah Owen Ltd, 78 Narrow St, London E14 8BP (☎ 0171 987 5119)

FARMER, Prof Richard Donald Trafford; s of Hereward Anderton Farmer (d 1987), and Kate Elizabeth Farmer (d 1986); *b* 14 Sept 1941; *Educ* Ashville Coll Harrogate, King's Coll London (MB BS), Univ of Leiden (PhD); *m* 20 Nov 1965, Teresa, da of Kenneth Roland Rimer, of Beckenham, Kent; 2 s (Dominic Michael Trafford b 5 Sept 1966, Christopher Kenneth Trafford b 24 June 1968); *Career* lectr Univ of Birmingham 1971–74, sr lectr Westminster Med Sch 1974–84, Boerhaave prof Univ of Leiden 1985, sr lectr Charing Cross and Westminster Med Sch 1986, prof of community med Univ of London 1986– (currently head Public Health & Primary Care Dept Charing Cross & Westminster Med Sch); memb Bd Int Soc for Pharmacoepidemiology; MRCS 1963, LRCP 1965, MRCGP 1968, MFCM 1979, FSS, FRSM; *Books* Lecture Notes on Epidemiology and Community Medicine (1977, 1983), The Suicide Syndrome (1979), Epidemiology of Diseases (1982); *Style—* Prof Richard Farmer; ✉ Department of Public Health & Primary Care, Chelsea & Wesminster Hospital, 369 Fulham Road, London SW10 9NH

FARMER, Robin Liempster; s of Alfred Victor Farmer (d 1977), of Bury St Edmunds, and Kathleen May, *née* Hand (d 1953); *b* 10 March 1933; *Educ* Radley, Christ Church Oxford (MA); *Career* Nat Serv 2/Lt 1st Bn Suffolk Regt, served Malaya 1951–52, Trieste 1953; Imperial Chemical Industries: ICI (India) 1956–57, various positions ICI UK 1957–78, gen mangr Mond Div 1978–87, ICI Chemicals & Polymers Ltd 1987–91, dir ICI (China) Ltd 1982–91, associated with 3 Queen's Awards for Export; chm: Aintree Hosps NHS Tst 1991–96, Mid Cheshire NHS Tst 1996–; *Recreations* reading, music, wines and food; *Style—* Robin L Farmer, Esq; ✉ Mid Cheshire NHS Trust, Leighton Hospital, Crewe CW1 4QJ

FARMER, Thomas (Tom); CBE (1990); s of John Farmer, and Margaret, *née* Mackie; *b* 10 July 1940; *Educ* Holy Cross Acad Edinburgh; *m* 10 Sept 1966, Anne Drury, da of James Scott; 1 s (John Philip b 14 June 1968), 1 da (Sally Anne (Mrs Nigel Swycher) b 4 July 1967); *Career* sales rep 1961–64, fndr Tyre and Accessory Supplies 1964–68, dir Albany Tyre Service 1968–70, fndr md Kwik-Fit Holdings Ltd 1971–84, chm and chief exec Kwik-Fit Holdings plc 1984–; memb Ct of Regents Royal Coll of Surgns of Edinburgh; *Recreations* swimming, tennis, skiing; *Style—* Tom Farmer, Esq, CBE; ✉ Kwik-Fit Holdings plc, 17 Corstorphine Road, Edinburgh EH12 6DD (☎ 0131 337 9200, fax 0131 337 0062, telex 727625)

FARMILOE, Timothy Miles; s of Miles Damer Bligh Farmiloe (d 1983), and Cynthia Joyce, *née* Holt (d 1990); *b* 22 Feb 1935; *Educ* Winchester, New College Oxford (MA); *Career* academic publishing dir Macmillan 1965– (ed 1957–65); *Style—* T M Farmiloe, Esq; ✉ The Macmillan Press Ltd, Houndmills, Basingstoke, Hants RG21 6XS (☎ 01256 29242, fax 01256 479476)

FARNCOMBE, Charles Frederick; CBE (1977); s of Harold Farncombe (d 1963), of London, and Eleanor Mary, *née* Driver (d 1965); *b* 29 July 1919; *Educ* Univ of London (BSc), Royal Sch Church Music, RAM (LRAM); *m* 20 May 1963, Sally Mae, da of Hugh Edgar Felps, MD (d 1976), of Riverside, California; 1 da (Eleanor b 8 May 1967); *Career* REME 1942–47 (Capt 21 Army Gp 1943); civil engr John Mowlem & Co 1940–42; musical dir Handel Opera Soc 1955–85, first conductor Royal Court Theatre Drottningholm Sweden 1970–79, chief conductor Annual Handel Festival Badisches Staats Theater Karlsruhe W Germany 1979–94; musical dir: London Chamber Opera 1984–93, Malcolm Sargent Festival Choir 1986–; guest conductor Komische Oper Berlin 1994–96; Hon Dr of Music: Columbus Univ Ohio 1959, Yankton Coll S Dakota 1959, City Univ 1988; AMICE 1945, FRAM 1963, hon fell Swedish Acad Music 1972; Gold medal: Drottningholm Sweden 1971, City of Karlsruhe 1992; Knight Cdr Order of North Star 1982; *Recreations* farm on Offa's Dyke; *Style—* Charles Farncombe, Esq, CBE; ✉ c/o Child and Co, 1 Fleet Street, London EC4Y 1BD

FARNDALE, Sir Martin Baker; KCB (1983, CB 1980); s of late Alfred Farndale, of Leyburn, N Yorks, and Margaret Louise, *née* Baker; *b* 6 Jan 1929, Alberta, Canada; *Educ* Yorebridge Sch Yorkshire, RMA Sandhurst; *m* 1955, Margaret Anne, da of late Percy Robert Buckingham, of Findon, Sussex; 1 s; *Career* cmmnd RA 1948, 1 Regt RHA 1949–54 (Egypt and Germany), HQ 7 Armd Div Germany 1955–56, 22 AD Regt UK 1957–58, Staff Coll 1959, HQ 17 Gurkha Div Malaya 1960–62, Mil Ops War Office 1962–64, cmd Chestnut Troop 1 Regt RHA South Arabia 1964–66, instr Staff Coll 1966–69, cmd 1 Regt RHA 1969–71 (UK, NI, Germany); sec def policy staff MOD 1971–73, Cdr 7 Armd Bde Germany 1973–75, dir PR (Army) MOD 1975–78, dir Mil Ops MOD 1978–80, GOC 2 Armd Div BAOR 1980–83, cmd 1 Br Corps 1983–85, C in C BAOR and Cmd Northern Army Gp Germany 1985–87, ret Jan 1988; Col Cmdt RA 1982–, Col Cmdt AAC 1980–88, Hon Col 3 Bn Yorks Volunteers 1983–89, Hon Col 1 Regt RHA 1982–89, Master Gunner St James's Park 1988–96, Col Cmdt RHA 1988–; pres: 2 Div Dinner Club 1983–, 7 Armd Div Dinner Club 1994–; dir Short Bros 1988–; def advsr: Deloitte Touche 1988–, Westland Helicopters 1989–96; vice pres Royal Patriotic Fund 1989–92, chm Royal United Servs Inst 1989–93; chm: Royal Artillery Historical Affairs Ctee 1987–95, English Heritage Battlefield Panel 1993–, RA Museums Ltd (pres 1989–96); pres Cncl Air League 1989–96; Freeman City of London 1996, Liveryman Worshipful Co of Wheelwrights 1996; Hon DLitt Univ of Greenwich 1996; *Books* History of Royal Artillery France 1914–18 (1987), History of Royal Artillery, The Forgotten Fronts 1914–18 (1988), History of Royal Artillery, The Years of Defeat 1939–41 (1996); *Recreations* gardening, military history; *Clubs* E India, Sports, Public Schs, Devonshire; *Style—* Sir Martin Farndale, KCB; ✉ c/o Lloyd's Bank, Cox & King's Branch, PO Box 1190, 7 Pall Mall, London SW1Y 5NA

FARNELL, Graeme; s of Wilson Elliot Farnell, of Nottingham, and Mary Montgomerie Wishart, *née* Crichton (d 1987); *b* 11 July 1947; *Educ* Loughborough GS, Univ of Edinburgh (MA), London Film Sch; *m* 19 July 1969, Jennifer Gerda, da of William Holroyd Huddlestone, of Nottingham; 1 s (Paul b 1983); *Career* asst keeper Museum of E Anglian Life Stowmarket 1973–76, curator Inverness Museum and Art Gallery 1976–79, dir Scot Museums Cncl 1979–86, dir gen Museums Assoc 1986–89; dir: Museum Devpt Co 1989–94, IMS Publications 1994–96, Heritage Development Ltd 1996–; FMA, MIMgt, FSA (Scot); *Recreations* Baroque opera; *Style—* Graeme Farnell, Esq; ✉ 8 Faraday Drive, Shenley Lodge, Milton Keynes MK5 7DA (☎ 01908 660 629); Heritage Development, Enterprise Way, Grovebury Road, Leighton Buzzard LU7 8S2 (☎ 01525 376110)

FARNHAM, 12 Baron (I 1756); Sir Barry Owen Somerset Maxwell; 14 Bt (NS 1627); s of Hon Somerset Arthur Maxwell, MP (died of wounds received in action 1942); suc gf 1957; *b* 7 July 1931; *Educ* Eton, Harvard Univ; *m* 19 Jan 1959, Diana Marion, er da of Nigel Eric Murray Gunnis; 2 da (adopted); *Heir* bro, Hon Simon Kenlis Maxwell; *Career* dir Brown Shipley & Co (merchant bankers) 1959–91; chm: Brown Shipley Holdings plc 1976–91, Avon Rubber plc 1978–97 (dir 1966–97), Provident Mutual Life Assurance Association 1989–95 (dir 1967–95), dir General Accident Life Assurance Ltd (following takeover of Provident Mutual Life Assurance Ass
United Grand Lodge of England 1991–; first pres the Tree C
Kildare Street and Univ (Dublin), City of London; *Style—* The
✉ 11 Earl's Court Gardens, London SW5 0TD; 25–31 Moorgate,

FARNSWORTH, Ian Ross; *b* 15 Feb 1938; *Educ* Nottingham
National Westminster Bank: joined 1954, dir National Westminster
1981–84, sr vice pres Exec Office National Westminster Bank USA 198
UK fin and mktg 1984–87, dir Euro businesses 1989–1990, gen mangr E
1990–91, gen mangr int businesses 1991–92, md Coutts & Co 1992–95 (a
1993–95), ret; ACIB; *Style—* Ian Farnsworth, Esq

FARQUHAR, Sir Michael FitzRoy Henry; 7 Bt (GB 1796), of Cadogan Middlesex; s of Lt-Col Sir Peter Walter Farquhar, 6 Bt, DSO, OBE (d 1986), and Eli Evelyn, *née* Hurt (d 1983); *b* 29 June 1938; *Educ* Eton, RAC Cirencester; *m* 29 June 1 Veronica Geraldine, er da of Patrick Rowan Hornidge (d 1983), of Helford Passage, Falmouth, Cornwall; 2 s (Charles Walter FitzRoy b 21 Feb 1964, Edward Peter Henry b 6 Dec 1966); *Heir* s, Charles Walter FitzRoy Farquhar b 21 Feb 1964; *Recreations* fishing, shooting, gardening; *Clubs* White's, Shikar; *Style—* Sir Michael Farquhar, Bt; ✉ Manor Farm, West Kington, Chippenham, Wilts SN14 7JG (☎ 01249 782671, fax 01249 782877)

FARQUHAR, Peter Guy Powlett; s of Guy Farquhar (d 1962), and Daphne Mary Christian, *née* Henry (d 1983); *b* 13 Feb 1936; *Educ* Eton; *m* 1, 1961, Rosemary Anne Eaton, da of Eaton Hammond, of Wroxham, Norfolk; 2 s (Richard Charles b 7 April 1962, James Edward b 6 Dec 1963); m 2, Carolyn, da of D Graham Robertson, of Sydney, Aust; 2 s (George Peter b 29 Feb 1980, Hugh Graham b 7 June 1984), 2 da (Jane Elizabeth b 12 Dec 1982 d 1983, Alice Rose Jane b 17 Nov 1987); *Career* 2 Lt KRRC (60th Rifles); stable lad 1954–59: St Albans Stables, Woodlands and Plantation Studs Newmarket, Sledmere Stud Yorkshire, Woodlands Stud NSW Aust; asst PR offr H J Heinz Company 1959–66, md Hill & Knowlton UK Ltd 1969–79 (sr exec 1967–69), fndr and dir Ludbrook Ltd 1979–, md Fleishman-Hillard Europe Ltd 1987–94, chm Fleishman-Hillard UK Ltd 1987–94, memb Int Advsy Bd Fleishman-Hillard Inc 1994–; MIPR, memb Int PR Assoc; *Recreations* racing, cartophily; *Clubs* MCC; *Style—* Peter Farquhar, Esq; ✉ 17 Netheravon Road, Chiswick, London W4 2NA (☎ 0181 747 1829, fax 0181 742 0896)

FARQUHAR, William John; s of John Catto Farquhar (d 1953), of Maud, Aberdeenshire, and Mary, *née* Whyte (d 1974); *b* 29 May 1935; *Educ* Peterhead Acad, Univ of Aberdeen (MA), Univ of Manchester (DSA); *m* 24 Feb 1962, Isabel Henderson, da of Rev Dr William Morgan Robertson Rusk (d 1965), of Aberdeen; 4 s (Callum, Tor, Gavin, Barry); *Career* admin trainee NHS 1958–61, hosp sec Whitehaven 1961–64, dep gp sec W Cumberland 1964–66, regnl staff offr SERHB Edinburgh 1966–69, dep sec Eastern RHB Dundee 1969–74, dist admin Lothian 1974–85, sec Planning Cncl Scottish Health Serv 1985–89, dir Planning Unit SHHD 1987–90, sec Advsy Cncl Scottish Health Serv 1989–93, sec Clinical Resource and Audit Group 1990–; elder Colinton Parish Church, convenor Health Care Advsy Gp Bd World Mission Church of Scotland, vice convener Bd of Nat Mission Church of Scotland 1991–94; memb: Exec Ctee Cross Roads Edinburgh, Cncl of Europe Med Fellowship 1988; FHSM 1963; *Recreations* walking, gardening, philately; *Style—* William Farquhar, Esq; ✉ Craigengar, 7 Harelaw Rd, Colinton, Edinburgh EH13 0DR (☎ 0131 441 2169); St Andrew's House, Edinburgh EH1 3DE (☎ 0131 244 2750)

FARQUHARSON, Rt Hon Sir Donald Henry; kt (1981), PC (1989); yr s of Charles Anderson Farquharson (d 1929), of Logie Coldstone, Aberdeenshire, and Florence Ellen, *née* Fox; *b* 26 Feb 1928; *Educ* Royal Commercial Travellers Schs, Keble Coll Oxford; *m* 1960, Helen Mary, er da of late Cdr H M Simpson, RN (ret), of Abbots Brow, Kirkby Lonsdale, Westmorland; 3 s, 1 da (decd); *Career* called to the Bar Inner Temple 1952, dep chm Essex QS 1970–72, QC 1972, recorder of Crown Cts 1972–81, legal assessor GMC and Gen Dental Cncl 1978–81, bencher Inner Temple 1979, High Ct judge (Queen's Bench) 1981–89, presiding judge SE circuit 1985–88, a Lord Justice of Appeal 1989–95, ret; chm: Judicial Studies Bd 1992–94, Criminal Justice Consultative Cncl 1992–94; hon fell Keble Coll Oxford 1990; *Recreations* opera going; *Style—* Rt Hon Sir Donald Farquharson; ✉ c/o Royal Courts of Justice, Strand, London WC2A 2LL

FARQUHARSON, Sir James Robbie; KBE (1960, CBE 1948, OBE 1944); s of Frank Farquharson, of Cortachy, Angus, and Agnes Jane, *née* Robbie; *b* 1 Nov 1903; *Educ* Royal Tech Coll Glasgow, Univ of Glasgow (BSc); *m* 1933, Agnes Binny (d 1992), da of James Graham, of Kirriemuir, Angus; 2 s; *Career* chief engr Tanganyika Railways 1941–45 (gen mangr 1945–48), chief engr and dep gen mangr E African Railways 1948–52; gen mangr: Sudan Railways 1952–57, E African Railways 1957–61; asst crown agent and engr-in-chief Crown Agents for Overseas Govts and Admins 1961–65, chm Millbank Technical Services Ordnance Ltd 1973–75; fell Scottish Cncl Devpt and Indust 1986; farmer; *Style—* Sir James Farquharson, KBE; ✉ Kinclune, by Kirriemuir, Angus, Scotland DD8 5HX (☎ 01575 574710)

FARQUHARSON, Robert Alexander (Robin); CMG (1975); s of Capt J P Farquharson, DSO, OBE, RN (d 1960), of Homington Manor, Salisbury, and Phyllis Ruth, *née* Prescott-Decie (d 1969); *b* 26 May 1925; *Educ* Harrow, King's Coll Cambridge (MA); *m* 4 Feb 1955, Joan Elizabeth, da of Sir Ivo Mallet, GBE, KCMG (d 1988); 3 s (John James b 1956, William b 1961, d 1984, Edward b 1962), 1 da (Charlotte b 1959); *Career* Sub Lt RNVR 1943–46; Dip Serv (formerly Foreign Serv): third sec Moscow 1950, second sec FO 1952, first sec Bonn 1955 (Panama 1958, Paris 1960), FO 1964, cnsllr and dir of Trade Devpt SA 1967, min Madrid 1971, consul gen San Francisco 1973, ambass Yugoslavia 1977; lay co-chm Deanery Synod; Lord of the Manor of Bockleton; *Recreations* country; *Clubs* Flyfishers'; *Style—* R A Farquharson, Esq, CMG; ✉ Tollard Royal, Salisbury SP5 5PS (☎ 01725 516 278)

FARQUHARSON OF FINZEAN, Angus Durie Miller; OBE (1995), DL (Aberdeenshire 1984); s of Dr Hugo Durie Newton Miller (d 1984), and Elsie Miller, *née* Duthie; *b* 27 March 1935; *Educ* Trinity Coll Glenalmond, Downing Coll Cambridge (MA); *m* 1 July 1961, Alison Mary Farquharson of Finzean, da of William Marshall Farquharson-Lang, CBE, 14 Laird of Finzean; 2 s (Donald b 1963, Andrew b 1967), 1 da (Jean b 1962); *Career* factor Finzean Estate; memb Cncl Scottish Landowners' Fedn 1980–88; memb Regnl Advsy Ctee Forestry Cmmn: E Scotland 1980–84, N Conservancy 1985–94 (chm 1993–94); memb: Red Deer Cmmn 1986–92, Nature Conservancy Cncl Ctee for Scotland 1986–91, NE Ctee SNH 1992–94; pres Kincardine/Deeside Scouts; elder and gen tstee Church of Scotland; dir Lathallan Sch; Vice Lord Lt of Aberdeenshire 1987–; FRICS; *Recreations* shooting, fishing, gardening, forestry, nature conservation; *Clubs* New (Edinburgh); *Style—* Angus Farquharson of Finzean, OBE, DL; ✉ Finzean House, Finzean, Aberdeenshire AB31 3NZ (☎ 01330 850229)

FARR, Dr Dennis Larry Ashwell; CBE (1991); s of Arthur William Farr (d 1961), and Helen Eva, *née* Ashwell; *b* 3 April 1929; *Educ* Luton GS, Univ of London, Courtauld Inst of Art; *m* 1959, Diana Farr, *qv*, da of Capt H J Pullein-Thompson, MC; 1 s, 1 da; *Career* asst keeper Tate Gallery 1954–64, curator Paul Mellon Collection Washington DC 1965–66, sr lectr and dep keeper Univ Art Collections Univ of Glasgow 1967–69, dir Birmingham City Museums Art Gallery 1969–80, memb UK Exec Bd Int Cncl of Museums 1976–84, pres Museums Assoc 1979–80 (vice pres 1978–79 and 1980–81), dir Courtauld Inst Galleries Univ of London 1980–93; tstee Birmingham City Museums and Art Gallery Appeal Fund 1980, chm Assoc of Art Historians 1983–86 (memb Exec Ctee 1981), memb Comité International d'Histoire de l'Art 1983–93 (membre honoraire 1994–), memb Registration Ctee Museums and Galleries Cmmn 1993–; JP Birmingham 1977–80; Hon DLitt Birmingham; FRSA, FMA; *Publications* William Etty (1958), Tate Gallery Modern British School Catalogue (2 vols, with Mary Chamot and Martin Butlin, 1964), English Art 1870–1940 (1978), Impressionist and Post-Impressionist Paintings from the Courtauld Collections (with William Bradford, 1984), The Northern Landscape (with William Bradford, 1986), Impressionist and Post Impressionist Masters: The Courtauld Collections (with John House and others, 1987), 100 Masterpieces from The Courtauld Collections (ed and contrib, 1987), Lynn Chadwick: Sculptor A Complete Catalogue (with Eva Chadwick, 1990), Thomas Gambier Parry as Artist and Collector (ed and contrib, 1993); *Recreations* reading, riding (hon sec Civil Service Riding Club London 1958–60), music, foreign travel; *Clubs* Athenaeum, Inst of Contemporary Arts; *Style—* Dr Dennis Farr, CBE; ✉ Orchard Hill, Swan Barn Road, Haslemere, Surrey GU27 2HY (☎ 01428 641880)

FARR, Diana; da of Capt Harold James Pullein-Thompson, MC (d 1957), and Joanna Maxwell, *née* Cannan; sis of Josephine Pullein-Thompson, *qv*, and Christine Popescu, *qv*; *b* 1 Oct 1930; *Educ* Wychwood Sch Oxford and privately; *m* 6 June 1959, Dennis Larry Ashwell Farr, *qv*, s of Arthur William Farr; 1 s (Benedict Edward b 7 March 1963), 1 da (Joanna Helen b 6 July 1964); *Career* professional author 1944–; dir Grove Riding Schs Peppard and Oxford 1946–52, PA to literary agent Rosica Colin 1953–55, memb Public Lending Right Ctee 1960–64, fndr memb Children's Writers Gp 1963–65, hon sec Save the Mere Campaign 1970–73; memb: Soc of Authors, International PEN; *Books* as Diana Pullein-Thompson books incl: I Wanted a Pony (1946), The Boy and The Donkey (1958), Cassidy In Danger (1979), Dear Pup, Letters To A Young Dog (1988), The Long Ride Home (1996), Fair Girls and Grey Horses (with her sisters, memoirs, 1996); as Diana Farr: Gilbert Cannan, A Georgian Prodigy (1978), Five at 10: Prime Ministers' Consorts Since 1957 (1985), Choosing (1988); *Recreations* walking, cinema, travel; *Style—* Mrs Dennis Farr; ✉ Orchard Hill, Swan Barn Road, Haslemere, Surrey GU27 2HY (☎ 01428 641880)

FARR, Sir John Arnold; kt (1984); 2 and er survg s of Capt John Farr, JP (d 1951), of Worksop Manor, Notts, and Margaret Anne, *née* Heath; *b* 25 Sept 1922; *Educ* Harrow; *m* 26 Aug 1960, Susan Ann, yr da of Sir Leonard John Milburn, 3 Bt (d 1957); 2 s (Jonathan b 1962, George b 1967); *Career* RN 1940–46, demobbed as Cdr RNVR; memb Lloyd's, landowner; dir Home Brewery Co Ltd 1950–55, pres Worksop Boys' Club 1951–55; Parly candidate (C) Ilkeston 1955, MP (C) Harborough 1959–92; sec Cons Agric Ctee 1970–74 (vice chm 1979–84), memb UK Delgn to WEU and Cncl of Europe 1973–78, vice chm Cons NI Ctee 1974–78; chm: Anglo-Irish Parly Gp 1977–80, Br Korea Parly Gp 1980–89, Br Zimbabwe Parly Gp 1980–89; memb Select Ctee on Standing Orders 1981–92, former sec All Pty Conservation Ctee, former chm All Pty Knitwear Group; *Clubs* Boodle's, Carlton; *Style—* Sir John Farr; ✉ 11 Vincent Square, London SW1; Shortwood House, Lamport, Northampton NN6 9HN (☎ 01604 686260, fax 01604 686628)

FARR, Richard Peter; s of Peter James Farr (d 1987), and Josephine Farr; *b* 8 July 1954; *Educ* Bedford Sch, Ecole de Commerce Neuchatel, Univ of Reading (BSc); *m* 1979, Susan Jane, *née* Fairburn; *Career* surveyor Knight Frank and Rutley 1977–80, sr surveyor Richard Ellis 1980–83, assoc dir Greycoat Group plc 1983–88, chief exec New Cavendish Estates plc 1988–90, chief exec Park Square Developments 1990–; FRICS (ARICS); *Recreations* skiing, vintage Bentleys, sailing; *Style—* Richard Farr, Esq; ✉ Park Square Developments, 40 Bedford Square, London WC1B 3DP (☎ 0171 209 3400, fax 0171 209 1850)

FARR, Prof Robert MacLaughlin (Rob); s of Robert James Farr (d 1984), of Clooneen, Marino, Holywood, Co Down, NI, and Henrietta Williamson, *née* MacLaughlin (d 1973); *b* 10 Dec 1935; *Educ* Sullivan Upper Sch Holywood, The Queen's Univ Belfast (BA, MA, DSc), Trinity Coll Dublin (Divinity Testimonium), Univ of London (PhD); *m* 3 Sept 1966 (m dis 1991), Ann-Marie, da of Henry James Wood (d 1964), of Udimore, nr Rye, Sussex; 1 s (Angus b 10 May 1971), 1 da (Fiona b 2 Nov 1973); *Career* asst lectr Queen's Univ Belfast 1962–64, res offr science 4 (RAF) MOD London 1964–66, lectr in social psychology UCL 1966–79; prof of psychology Univ of Glasgow 1979–83, prof of social psychology LSE 1983–; govr NE London Poly 1975–79; memb: Psychology Bd Cncl Nat Academic Awards 1980–84, Sr Scholars Ctee Fulbright Cmmn 1984–, Disciplinary Bd Br Psychological Soc 1991–94; pres Br Psychological Soc 1985–86 (hon gen sec 1970–75); chm: Library Ctee Br Library Political and Econ Sci 1987–90, Graduate Sch Ctee LSE 1993–96; memb: Academia Europaea 1991, Soc of Authors 1995; fell Br Psychological Soc (hon life memb 1992); CPsychol 1988; *Books* Social Representations (ed with S Moscovici, 1984 and 1989), Representations of Health, Illness and Handicap (ed with I Manhova, 1995), The Roots of Modern Social Psychology (1996); guest ed special issues: British Journal of Social Psychology on The History of Social Psychology (1983), Journal for the Theory of Social Behaviour on Social Representations (1987); *Recreations* walking, reading; *Style—* Prof Rob Farr; ✉ Apartment 8, 1 Avenue Elmers, Surbiton, Surrey KT6 4SP; Department of Social Psychology, LSE, Houghton St, The Aldwych, London WC2A 2AE (☎ 0171 955 7700, fax 0171 955 7565)

FARR, Sue; *b* 29 Feb 1956, Yorkshire; *Educ* Sheffield HS for Girls GPDST, Univ of Reading (BA); *m* 1979; *Career* graduate trainee rising to divnl mktg mangr Northern Foods plc 1977–79, sr conslt Kraushar And Eassie (KAE) Ltd (mktg consultancy) 1979–83, account dir BSB Dorland (advtg agency) 1983–85, new business devpt dir Wight Collins Rutherford Scott 1986–90, dir of corp communications Thames Television plc 1990–93 (seconded as launch mktg dir UK Gold 1992–93), head of mktg and publicity BBC Network Radio 1993–96, mktg controller BBC Broadcast 1996–; memb Bd Rajar (audience research bureau) 1996–; non-exec dir New Look plc 1994–96; memb Business in the Community; Mktg Soc: fell 1987, vice chm 1990, first woman chair 1991–93; memb Cncl Mktg Gp of GB, Forum UK, Women's Advtg Club of London; FRSA; *Style—* Mrs Sue Farr; ✉ 6 The Gables, 55 Netherhall Gardens, Hampstead, London NW3 5RH (☎ 0171 431 0381, fax 0171 431 1187)

FARRANCE, Roger Arthur; CBE; s of Ernest Thomas Farrance (d 1985), and Alexandra Hilda May, *née* Finch (d 1989); *b* 10 Nov 1933; *Educ* Trinity Sch of John Whitgift, LSE (BSc); *m* 8 Dec 1956, Kathleen Sheila, da of Henry Stephen Owen (d 1974); 1 da (Denise Lesley b 1957); *Career* HM inspr of factories Manchester, Doncaster and Walsall 1956–64, asst sec W of England Engrg Employers' Assoc Bristol 1964–67, industl rels and personnel mangr Foster Wheeler John Brown Boilers Ltd 1967–68, dep dir Coventry and Dist Engrg Employers' Assoc and Coventry Mgmnt Trg Centre 1968–75; Electricity Cncl: dep industl rels advsr 1975–76, industl rels advsr 1976–79, full time memb 1979–89, dep chm 1988–90; chief exec Electricity Association 1990–93, pres Inst of Personnel Mgmnt 1991–93; chm: Bd of Mgmnt Electrical and Electronics Industries Benevolent Assoc 1987–93, Devonshire House Mgmnt Club 1989–94; pres St John's 210 (London Electricity) Combined Div 1989–93; memb Cncl: ACAS 1983–89, CBI 1983–93; cncllr London Borough of Merton 1994–; OStJ; Liveryman Worshipful Co of Basketmakers; CIEE, CIMgt, CIPD; *Style—* Roger Farrance, Esq, CBE; ✉ 14 Bathgate Road, Wimbledon, London SW19 5PN (☎ 0181 879 7191, fax 0181 947 5292)

FARRAND, Dr Julian Thomas; Hon QC (1994); s of John Farrand, and E A Farrand; *b* 13 Aug 1935; *Educ* Portsmouth GS, Haberdashers' Aske's, UCL (Joseph Hume scholar, LLB, LLD); *m* 1, 1957 (m dis 1992), Winifred Joan, *née* Charles; 1 s, 2 da; m 2, 1992, Brenda Marjorie Hoggett (*see* Dame Brenda Hale); *Career* articled clerk to Lord Nathan at Herbert Oppenheimer, Nathan and Vandyk slrs 1957–60, slr of the Supreme Court 1960–, asst lectr then lectr King's Coll Univ of London 1960–63, lectr Univ of Sheffield 1963–65, reader in law Queen Mary Coll Univ of London 1965–68, prof of law Univ of Manchester 1968–88 (dean of the Faculty of Law 1970–72 and 1976–78); law cmmnr 1984–88, insur Ombudsman 1989–94, Pensions Ombudsman 1994–, chm: Govt Conveyancing Ctee 1984–85, Rent Assessment Panels Gtr Manchester and Lancs Area 1973–84 (vice pres 1977–84), Rent Assessment Panels London Area 1984–, Supp Benefit Appeals Tribunal 1977–80, Nat Insur Local Tbnl 1980–83, Social Security Appeal Tbnl 1983–88; memb appeals panel Consumer Credit Act 1974 and Estate Agents Act 1979 from licensing determinations of DG of Fair Trading; hon visiting prof of law UCL 1989–, Hon LLM Univ of Manchester 1972, 2on LLD Univ of Sheffield 1990; FCIArb; *Books* Contract and Conveyance (4 edn, 1983), Emmet On Title (ed, 1967–); author of numerous articles; *Recreations* bridge, chess, wine; *Style—* Dr Julian Farrand, QC; ✉ Pensions Ombudsman, 11 Belgrave Road, London SW1V 1RB (☎ 0171 834 9144, fax 0171 821 0065)

FARRANT, Peter William Stanley; s of His Hon Deemster Reginald Douglas Farrant, CP, JP (d 1952), of Douglas, IOM, and Marion Rose, *née* Barthelemy (d 1970); *b* 31 Oct 1924; *Educ* King William's Coll IOM, Shrewsbury Sch, Law Soc Sch of Law (IOM George Johnson Law prize 1948); *m* 27 Aug 1961, Daphne Rosemary Dorothy, da of late Joseph Egerton Leigh; 1 s (Robert Edward Leigh b 19 May 1965), 2 da (Katherine Veronica b 11 April 1963, Lucy Elizabeth (twin) b 19 May 1965); *Career* served WWII Rifle Bde and 1 KOYLI Italian Campaign Garigliano and Anzio 1943–44, cmmnd Green Howards Dec 1944, served with 2 Bn York and Lancaster Regt Calcutta 1945, demobbed 1947, Capt; called to the Bar Gray's Inn 1951, admitted advocate Manx Bar 1951, ptnr Kneale & Co Advocates & NPs 1955–69, sr ptnr Gelling Johnson Farrant & Co Advocates & NPs 1973–93 (conslt 1993–96), dir Rea Bros (IOM) Ltd 1987–; memb IOM War Pensions Ctee 1958–61; sec: Landlord & Tenant Cmmn 1953, Forces Help Soc and Lord Roberts Workshops 1958–70, IOM Branch St John's Emergency War Help Dept 1958–70; returning offr Castletown and N Douglas 1963–78; sec and treas: Dio of Sodor and Man Bd of Fin 1970–93, Church Cmmrs IOM 1970–93; Vicar Gen and Chllr Dio of Sodor and Man 1973–96, chm (ex-officio) House of Laity Diocesan Synod 1973–92 (elected lay memb Gen Synod 1987–90), ex-officio chm Clergy Compensation Tbnl (Pastoral measure) 1992–96; actg deemster Sept-Oct 1991 and May 1993–Feb 1994 chm Specially Constituted NHS (IOM) Med Tbnl 1991–92; chm Douglas 2000 1995; pres Douglas Branch Royal Br Legion 1980–; memb Isle of Man Law Soc 1951, FInstD 1987; *Recreations* shooting, swimming, walking; *Style—* Peter Farrant, Esq; ✉ 7 Mount Rule House, Braddan, Isle of Man (☎ 01624 852805)

FARRANT, Richard; *Career* chief exec The Securities and Futures Authy; *Style—* Richard Farrant, Esq; ✉ The Securities and Futures Authority Ltd, Cottons Centre, Cottons Lane, London SE1 2QB (☎ 0171 378 9000)

FARRAR, Austin Packard; s of Capt Alfred Farrar (d 1916), and Edith Celia, *née* Packard (d 1960); *b* 21 Feb 1913; *Educ* Imperial Serv Coll Windsor; *Career* tech offr Admiralty Dept of Torpedoes and Mining 1941–46; tech mangr Sussex Yacht Works Ltd 1939–41, md Woolverstone Shipyard Ltd 1946–62, memb Br Olympic Yachting Team 1948; dir: Seahorse Sails 1955–70, AusNin Farrar Sails Ltd 1970–82; Austin Farrar & Partners (conslts) 1980–; editorial conslt Ship and Boat; vice pres Amateur Yacht Res Soc; memb various Ctees: RYA, Soc for Nautical Res (hon vice pres), Small Craft Ctee RINA (awarded Small Craft Gp Medal 1988, IYRU Medal 1991); Br Sailmakers Award 1993; CEng 1980, FRINA 1970 (memb 1945); *Recreations* sailing, marine archaeology; *Clubs* Royal Ocean Racing, Royal Harwich Yacht; *Style—* Austin Farrar, Esq; ✉ Orchard House, Stutton, Ipswich, Suffolk IP9 2RY (☎ 01473 328236)

FARRAR, David James; s of James Farrar (d 1980), of Rawdon, Yorks, and Jessie, *née* Naylor; *b* 3 July 1942; *Educ* Leeds GS, St Thomas's Hosp Med Sch (MB BS, MS, FRCS); *m* 25 Jan 1969, Pamela Anne, da of Albert Sydney Allberry, MC, of Epsom, Surrey; 1 s (Nicholas b 19 Nov 1976), 1 da (Charlotte b 18 April 1970); *Career* conslt urological surgn: Selly Oak Hosp Birmingham 1978, Queen Elizabeth Hosp Birmingham 1993; hon clinical lectr Univ of Birmingham 1978; memb: Br Assoc Urological Surgns, Int Continence Soc, Royal Soc of Medicine; *Recreations* golf, sports history; *Style—* David Farrar, Esq; ✉ 36 Mirfield Rd, Solihull, West Midlands B91 1JD (☎ 0121 705 1710); 38 Harborne Road, Edgbaston, Birmingham (☎ 0121 454 1390); Queen Elizabeth Hospital, Edgbaston, Birmingham B15 2TH

FARRAR-HOCKLEY, Gen Sir Anthony Heritage; GBE (1981, MBE 1957), KCB (1977), DSO (1953, and bar 1964), MC (1944); s of Arthur Farrar-Hockley; *b* 8 April 1924; *Educ* Exeter Sch; *m* 1945, Margaret Bernadette Wells (d 1981); 2 s (and 1 s decd); m 2 1983, Linda Wood; *Career* Gloucestershire and Parachute Regt WW II; served: Med, Europe, Palestine, Korea 1950–53, later Cyprus, Port Said, Jordan, Aden; coll chief instr RMA Sandhurst 1959–61, CO 3 Para 1962–65, princ staff offr to Dir Borneo Ops 1965–66, Cdr 16 Parachute Bde 1966–68, defence fellowship Exeter Coll Oxford (BLitt) 1968–70, dir PR Army 1970, Cdr Land Forces NI 1970–71, GOC 4 Div 1971–73, dir Combat Devpt Army 1974–77, Lt-Gen 1977, GOC SE Dist 1977–79, Gen 1979, C-in-C Allied Forces N Europe 1979–82, ret 1983; def conslt and historian; cabinet office historian for Br Part in Korean War, ADC Gen to HM The Queen 1981–83, Col Cmdt Para Regt 1977–83, Col The Gloucestershire Regt 1978–84; pres Steering Ctee UK-Korea Forum 1992–; *Publications* The Edge of the Sword (1954), The Commander (ed 1957), The Somme (1964), Death of an Army (1968), Airborne Carpet (1969), War in the Desert (1969), General Student (1973), Goughie - The Life of General Sir Hubert Gough (1975), Opening Rounds (1988), British Part in the Korean War, Vol 1: A Distant Obligation (1990), Vol 2: An Honourable Discharge (1995), Army in the Air (1994), Oxford History of the British Army (contrib, 1995); assoc ed D-Day Encyclopaedia 1994; also author of numerous articles in newspapers, periodicals and journals as well as work for BBC and ITN news and features; *Style—* Gen Sir Anthony Farrar-Hockley, GBE, KCB, DSO, MC; ✉ Pye Barn, Moulsford, Oxon OX10 9JD

FARRELL, Anthony; s of Carlton Fredrick Farrell (d 1980), and Lurline Carmen, *née* Nelson; *b* 17 Jan 1969; *Educ* Fartown HS, Huddersfield Tech Coll (qualified chef); *partner* Ruth, da of Barrie Metcalfe; 1 da (Hanah Victoria b 9 Nov 1990), 1 s (Joel Cameron b 15 March 1994); *Career* professional rugby league second row; clubs: Fartown HS (capt) 1980–85, 64 1st team appearances Fartown RLFC 1986–89, 150 1st team appearances Sheffield Eagles 1989–; represented: Yorkshire Boys 1984–85, English Schs 1984–85, GB Colts 1987, GB U 21's (3 games) 1988 and 1989, England v Wales (1 full cap) 1995; memb 40 man squad World Cup 1995; dye operative Croda Colours 1989–; *Recreations* playing snooker, reading; *Style—* Anthony Farrell, Esq; ✉ Sheffield Eagles RLFC, Don Valley Stadium, Attercliffe Road, Sheffield, South Yorkshire

FARRELL, Sheriff, James Aloysius; Sheriff; s of James Stoddart Farrell, and Harriet Louise, *née* McDonnell; *b* 14 May 1943; *Educ* St Aloysius Coll, Univ of Glasgow (MA), Univ of Dundee (LLB); *m* 1, 2 Dec 1967 (m dis 1994), Jacqueline, da of Barnett Harvey Allen (d 1967); 2 da (Suzanne b 7 April 1970, Claire Louise b 16 Oct 1973); m 2, 11 May 1996, Patricia, da of Andrew Morgan McLaren; *Career* admitted to Faculty of Advocates 1974, advocate depute 1979–83; Sheriff: Glasgow and Strathkelvin 1984–85, Dumfries and Galloway 1985–86, Lothian and Borders at Edinburgh 1986–; *Recreations* sailing, cycling, hill walking; *Style—* Sheriff James Farrell

FARRELL, Shelagh; da of Delmege Frazer-Allen (d 1981), and Mildred Anne, *née* Grigg; *b* 12 Aug 1947; *Educ* Notting Hill and Ealing Girls' HS, Univ of Bristol Dental Sch (BDS), MGDS RCS, Eastman Dental Hosp Univ of London (MSc); *m* 1, 2 June 1973, John Hamilton-Farrell (d 1981), s of Robert Hamilton-Farrell, CB; m 2, 22 Sept 1990,

Christopher John Rutton May, s of Eric John Rutton May; 1 s (Jonathan Alexander Fraser b 15 July 1993); *Career* SHO Univ of Bristol Dental Sch 1972 (house offr 1971); in gen dental practice Frampton Cotterell nr Bristol 1973–95, in private dental practice Reigate Surrey 1995–; pt/t clinical lectr King's Coll Sch of Med and Dentistry 1987–95; memb: GDC 1986–91 and 1994–, Standing Dental Advsy Ctee 1988–91; Royal Coll of Surgns of England: memb Bd Dental Faculty 1987–91, memb Bd Gen Dental Practitioners (UK) since its inception 1992–; BDA: first woman memb Cncl 1987–90, pres Western Counties Branch 1994–95; first woman pres Br Soc for Gen Dental Surgery 1990–92; St John Ambulance Bde: dep cmmr for Avon 1986–89, memb Cncl for Surrey 1995–; memb Commanderie de Bordeaux (Bristol); memb: Br Soc for Gen Dental Surgery, Br Soc for Restorative Dentistry, Br Soc for the Study of Prosthetic Dentistry, Br Soc of Periodontology, Alpha Omega Fraternity, Bristol Medico-Legal Soc, Fédération Dentaire Internationale, Euro Prosthodontic Assoc; fell Int Coll of Dentists; *Recreations* opera, singing, cooking, travel; *Style*— Mrs Shelagh Farrell; ✉ Froghole Oast House, Crockham Hill, Edenbridge, Kent TN8 6TD; Ringley Park Dental Practice, 59 Reigate Road, Reigate, Surrey RH2 0QT (☎ 01737 240123, fax 01737 245704)

FARRELL, Terence (Terry); CBE (1996, OBE 1978); s of Thomas Farrell, and Molly, *née* Maguire; *b* 12 May 1938; *Educ* St Cuthbert's GS, Univ of Newcastle Sch of Architecture (BArch), Univ of Pennsylvania Sch of Fine Arts (MArch, Master of City Planning); *m* 1, 1960, Angela Rosemarie Mallam; 2 da; m 2, 1973, Susan Hilary Aplin; 2 s, 1 da; *Career* Planning Dept: Camden New Jersey USA, Colin Buchanan & Partners 1964–65; fndr ptnr Farrell Grimshaw Partnership 1965–80; currently chm Terry Farrell & Partners (formerly Terry Farrell Ltd); former teaching positions: Univ of Cambridge, Univ Coll London, Architectural Assoc London, Univ of Strathclyde Glasgow, Univ of Sheffield, Univ of Pennsylvania; English Heritage: cmmr 1980–96, memb London Advsy Ctee, memb Royal Parks Review Group 1991–96; former memb: Historic Areas Advsy Ctee, RIBA Clients Advsy Bd, RIBA Visiting Bd, RIBA Awards Panel; past pres Urban Design Gp, architectural assessor for Financial Times Architectural Awards 1983, external examiner RCA; representative projects: HQ Henley Regatta, Charing Cross devpt complex London, Edinburgh int fin and conf centre, Govt HQ bldg for PSA at Vauxhall Cross, redevelopment of The Peak Hong Kong, new Br Consulate-Gen bldg Hong Kong; numerous lectures in UK and abroad; MCP, ARIBA 1963, memb RTPI 1970, FCSD, FSIAD 1981, FRIAS 1996; *Publications* Urban Design Monograph (1993), The Master Architect Series: Terry Farrell (1994); articles in: Architectural Review, Architects' Journal, L'Architecture d'Aujourd'hui, Domus, Progressive Architecture, Baven und Wohnen, Abitare, Cree, Architectural Record, Interiors, British Architecture, RIBA Journal, Architectural Design, Architecture and Urbanism, Arkitektur DK, Decorative Arts (USSR), Architecture of the Soviet Union; *Style*— Terry Farrell, Esq, CBE; ✉ Terry Farrell & Partners, 17 Hatton Street, London NW8 8PL (☎ 258 3433, fax 0171 723 7059)

FARRELL, Thomas Henry (Tom); OBE; *b* 30 July 1925; *Educ* King's Coll Hosp London (LDS RCS, MGDS RCS); *m* 1, 8 Sept 1956, Joyce, da of Thomas Burgess; 2 s (Nicholas b 2 Oct 1958, Simon Henry b 17 Jan 1960); m 2, 6 Sept 1974, Anne Grieve, da of Dr Lawrence Dulake; *Career* SHO King's Coll Hosp 1955–56, gen dental practitioner 1956–95; pt/t lectr Royal London Hosp 1966–76, pt/t memb Bd Dental Estimates Bd for England and Wales 1974–85, pt/t chm Dental Practice Bd for England and Wales (formerly Dental Estimates Bd) 1986–92; BDA: memb Representative Bd 1978–85, memb Gen Dental Servs Ctee 1982–86; memb GDC 1981–96; pres Br Soc for Gen Dental Surgery 1986–88; memb Editorial Bd Dental Practice jl 1984–94; memb: BDA 1954 (life memb 1995), Soc for Gen Dental Surgery 1979, Faculty of Gen Dental Practitioners Royal Coll of Surgns 1991 (memb Bd 1991–92); FRSM; *Recreations* sport, gardening, wine, writing; *Style*— Tom Farrell, Esq, OBE; ✉ Vicars Haw, Trevereux Hill, Limpsfield Chart, nr Oxted, Surrey RH8 0TL (☎ 01883 723265)

FARRELL, Thomas Hugh Francis; CBE (1997), TD (1969), DL (E Riding Yorks 1971 and 1995, Humberside 1974); s of Hugh Farrell (d 1959); *b* 3 Feb 1930; *Educ* Ampleforth, Univ Coll Hull (LLB London); *m* 2 May 1964, Hon Clodagh Mary yr da of 2 Baron Morris; 1 da (Sophia Mary (Mrs Marco Betti-Berutto) b 1965), 1 s (James Thomas Hugh b 1966); *Career* admitted slr 1952; cmmnd The Queen's Bays 1953–55, Lt-Col cmdg Prince of Wales's Own Yorkshire Territorials 1967–69; Sheriff of Hull 1960–61; chm: Hull Cons Fedn 1963–68, Beverley Civic Soc 1970–74; Univ of Hull: treas 1976–80, pro-chllr and chm Cncl 1980–; Hon LLD (Hull) 1983; *Clubs* Cavalry and Guards'; *Style*— Thomas Farrell, Esq, CBE, TD, DL; ✉ 22 Wood Lane, Beverley, East Yorkshire HU17 8BS (☎ 01482 869367)

FARREN, Graham Richard; s of Dennis Henry Saunders Farren (d 1985), and Doris Margaret, *née* Francis; *b* 19 Jan 1947; *Educ* Hemel Hempstead GS, Churchill Coll Cambridge (MA); *m* 12 April 1975, Bridget Mary, da of late William Hardisty; 1 s (Richard), 1 da (Frances); *Career* Bacon Woodrow & De Souza 1973–77, ptnr Bacon & Woodrow 1977– (joined 1969); Freeman: City of London, Worshipful Co of Actuaries; FIA 1972, ASA 1974, APMI 1980; *Recreations* gardening, travelling, francophilia, beekeeping; *Style*— Graham Farren, Esq; ✉ Beltrees, Park Road, Stoke Poges, Bucks SL2 4PA (☎ 01753 522484); Bacon & Woodrow, Ivy House, 107 St Peters Street, St Albans, Herts AL1 3EW (☎ 01727 855566, fax 01727 814343)

FARREN, Peter Stefan; *b* 16 Oct 1944; *Educ* Mill Hill Sch, Université de Grenoble, King's Coll London (LLB); *m* 21 July 1973, Victoria Ann; 1 s (Ben b 11 April 1978), 2 da (Amy b 4 March 1980, Jessica b 30 Aug 1984); *Career* admitted slr 1969, William Brandt Son and Co Ltd 1973–76, Linklaters & Paines 1967–73 and 1976– (currently ptnr); memb Worshipful Co of Solicitors 1979, Freeman City of London 1979; memb Law Soc 1969; *Recreations* aviation, golf; *Clubs* Hadley Wood Golf; *Style*— Peter Farren, Esq; ✉ Linklaters & Paines, Barrington House, 59–67 Gresham St, London EC2 (☎ 0171 606 7080)

FARRER, His Hon Judge; Brian Ainsworth; QC (1978); s of Albert Ainsworth Farrer (d 1966), and Gertrude, *née* Hall (d 1985); *b* 7 April 1930; *Educ* King's Coll Taunton, UCL (LLB); *m* 1960, Gwendoline Valerie, JP, da of William Waddoup (d 1986), of Lichfield; 2 s, 1 da; *Career* called to the Bar Gray's Inn 1957, Midlands and Oxford Circuit 1958–85, recorder Crown Ct 1974–85, circuit judge (Midland and Oxford Circuit) 1985–; *Recreations* golf, bridge, chess; *Clubs* Aberdovey Golf; *Style*— His Honour Judge Farrer, QC; ✉ Shutt Cross House, Aldridge, West Midlands; Ardudwy Cottage, Ty Ardudwy, Aberdovey, Gwynedd

FARRER, (Arthur) Mark; DL (Essex 1996); s of Maj Hugh Frederick Francis Farrer, TD (d 1952), of Essex, and Elizabeth Mary; *b* 25 March 1941; *Educ* Eton; *m* 28 Oct 1969, Zara Jane, da of Donald Thesiger, of Essex; 1 da (Lucy Frances b 6 Aug 1971); *Career* ptnr Farrer & Co 1968–; chm: Essex Water Co 1992–94 (dep chm 1985–92), Suffolk Water Co 1992–94 (dep chm 1990–92), The Essex and Suffolk Water plc 1994–96, Timsbury Fishery plc 1995–; non-exec dir: Lyonnaise (Europe) Ltd 1988–96, Assoc of Lloyd's Members 1986– (chm 1991–92), Wellington Members Agency Ltd at Lloyd's 1993–96; external memb Cncl Lloyd's of London 1987–91; Liveryman Worshipful Co of Fishmongers, Liveryman Worshipful Co of Vintners; memb Law Soc; *Publications* author of various technical publications; *Recreations* gardening, salmon fishing, the steam railway; *Clubs* Brooks's, Essex; *Style*— Mark Farrer, Esq, DL; ✉ Farrer & Co, 66 Lincoln's Inn Fields, London WC2 (☎ 0171 242 2022, fax 0171 831 9748, telex 24318)

FARRER, Sir (Charles) Matthew; GCVO (1994, KCVO 1983, CVO 1973); s of Sir (Walter) Leslie Farrer, KCVO (d 1984), and Hon Lady (Marjorie Laura) Farrer (d 1981), da of 1 Viscount Hanworth, KBE, PC; *b* 3 Dec 1929; *Educ* Bryanston, Balliol Coll Oxford; *m* 1962, Johanna Creszentia Maria Dorothea, da of Prof Hans-Herman Bennhold, of Tübingen, Germany; 1 s, 1 da; *Career* admitted slr 1956; ptnr Messrs Farrer & Co 1959–93; private slr to HM The Queen 1965–94; tstee Br Museum 1989–, cmmr Royal Cmmn on Hist Manuscripts 1991–; memb British Library Bd 1994–; tstee Lambeth Palace Library 1991–; memb Ct of Assts Worshipful Co of Fishmongers; *Style*— Sir Matthew Farrer, GCVO; ✉ 6 Priory Ave, Bedford Park, London W4 1TX

FARRER, (John) Philip William; s of William Oliver Farrer, of Popmoor, Fernhurst, Haslemere, Surrey, and Margery Hope Farrer (d 1976); *b* 12 March 1958; *Educ* Eton, Sandhurst; *m* 19 July 1986, Maria Jane Margaret, da of Cuthbert Peter Ronald Bowlby, of Liphook, Hants; 4 da (Beatrice Hope b 27 July 1987, Katherine Isabella Caroline b 17 March 1989, Tara Georgina Hazel b 14 Feb 1991, Rosanna Maria Elizabeth b 16 Jan 1995); *Career* 2 Bn Coldstream Gds 1978–82; Grievson Grant & Co 1982–84, UBS Phillips & Drew 1985; dir Savory Milln/SBC Stockbroking 1986–89, md Merrill Lynch Pierce Fenner & Smith Ltd 1989–; MSI; *Recreations* skiing, golf, tennis; *Clubs* Liphook Golf; *Style*— J P W Farrer, Esq; ✉ Merrill Lynch, Pierce, Fenner & Smith Ltd, Ropemaker Place, 25 Ropemaker St, London EC2Y 9LY (☎ 0171 867 2000, fax 0171 867 2141, telex 8811047)

FARRER, Trevor Maurice; CBE (1991); s of (William) Maurice Farrer (d 1994), of Witherslack, Cumbria, and (Dorothy) Joyce Farrer; *b* 21 Dec 1931; *Educ* The Knoll Sch Woburn Sands, Dauntsey's Sch Devizes; *m* 2 April 1960 (m dis 1986), Eileen Mary; 2 s (Stewart William b March 1961, Noel Ecroyd b 25 Dec 1963), 1 da (Xanthe Rachel (twin) b 25 Dec 1963); m 2, 12 Aug 1992, Margaret Anne, *née* Hawken; *Career* Nat Serv KORR 1950–52; farmer 1952–82; memb Cncl NFU 1965–74 (co chm 1970–73); memb: Agric Land Tbnl 1974–, Cons Nat Union Exec 1988–90, S Westmorland RDC 1963–66, Lancs River Authy and NW Water Authy 1966–84, Cumbria CC 1977–89; memb Cncl Westmorland Cons 1963–, memb NW Area Cons Exec 1981–93; Freeman City of London 1986; *Recreations* music, travel, politics; *Clubs* Farmers; *Style*— Trevor Farrer, Esq, CBE; ✉ Whitbarrow Stables, Grange over Sands, Cumbria LA11 6SL (☎ 015395 52235)

FARRER, William Oliver; CVO (1991); s of John Oliver Farrer, MC (d 1942); *b* 23 June 1926; *Educ* Eton, Balliol Coll Oxford; *m* 1, 1955, Margery Hope (d 1976), da of William Yates (d 1931); 2 s, 1 da; m 2, 1979, Hazel Mary, da of Robert Clark Taylor (d 1963); *Career* Lt Coldstream Gds; slr; ptnr Farrer & Co 1955–91 (sr ptnr 1976–91); slr to the Duchy of Lancaster 1984–91, memb Slrs' Disciplinary Tbnl 1986–94; dir: Sotheby's London 1992–96, Bilton plc 1995–96; memb Cncl Inst of Cancer Research 1994–; Liveryman Worshipful Co of Fishmongers; *Recreations* golf, music; *Clubs* Brooks's, MCC, Royal and Ancient; *Style*— William Farrer, Esq, CVO; ✉ Popmoor, Fernhurst, Haslemere, Surrey GU27 3LL (☎ 01428 642564)

FARRINGTON, David; s of late Ellis Farrington, of Harrietsham, Kent, and Pauline Eleanor Miles, *née* Toyne; *b* 2 Dec 1948; *Educ* Balshaw's GS Leyland Lancs, UCL (LLB); *Career* called to the Bar Middle Temple 1972; tenant in Chambers of Louis Blom-Cooper QC Goldsmith Buildings Temple 1973–76, dep head of chambers of R Slowe 4 King's Bench Walk Temple 1976–85, head of chambers 2 Garden Court Temple 1985–91, dir Fleet Chambers Ltd 1991–94, Doughty Street Chambers 1994–96, 3 Gray's Inn Square 1996–; pt/t lectr in Law 1972–87, guest lectr 1987–; contrib on continuing educn for solicitors Select Television 1994; *Books* Know Your Rights (ed, 1976), Law for the Consumer (ed, 1978), A Practical Guide to the Criminal Justice Act 1988 (jtly, 1988); article DNA = Do Not Accept (New Law Jl, June 1993); *Recreations* theatre, films, tennis, travel; *Clubs* Cannons (Covent Garden); *Style*— David Farrington, Esq; ✉ 3 Gray's Inn Square, Gray's Inn, London WC1R 5AH (☎ 0171 831 2311, fax 0171 404 4939)

FARRINGTON, Prof David Philip; s of William Farrington (d 1967), of Ormskirk, Lancs, and Gladys Holden, *née* Spurr (d 1980); *b* 7 March 1944; *Educ* Ormskirk GS (state scholar), Clare Coll Cambridge (MA, PhD); *m* 30 July 1966, Sally, da of Frank Chamberlain (d 1977); 3 da (Lucy Clare b 14 April 1970, Katie Ruth b 28 March 1972, Alice Charlotte b 21 Feb 1975); *Career* research student Univ of Cambridge Psychological Lab 1966–69; Univ of Cambridge Inst of Criminology: research offr 1969–70, sr research offr 1970–74, asst dir of research 1974–76, lectr in criminology 1976–88, reader in psychological criminology 1988–92, prof of psychological criminology 1992–; visiting prof Dept of Sociology Univ of Akron 1977; visiting research worker Miny of the Solicitor Gen Ottawa 1978–79; visiting fell US Nat Inst of Justice Washington 1981; memb Parole Bd for England and Wales 1984–87; visiting scholar Nat Centre for Juvenile Justice Pittsburgh USA 1986; memb Advsy Bd: Nat Archive of Criminal Justice Data USA 1983–93, Nat Juvenile Court Data Archive USA 1987–; Nat Acad of Scis: memb Ctee on Law and Justice 1986–93, vice-chair Panel on Violence 1989–92; Br Psychological Soc: memb 1974, hon memb Div of Criminological and Legal Psychology (chm 1983–85), memb Scientific Affairs Bd 1977–78, memb Professional Affairs Bd 1983–85, memb Cncl 1983–85; Br Soc of Criminology: memb 1975, memb Organising Ctee 1978 and 1980–83, memb Cncl 1990–93, pres 1990–93, hon life memb 1996; American Soc of Criminology: fell 1983, memb Awards Ctee 1988–89, 1991–92 and 1993–94, memb Fells Ctee 1992–93, Sellin-Glueck Award for int contribs to criminology 1984; memb AUT 1979–; Euro Assoc of Psychology and Law: memb 1991–, memb Exec Bd 1991–, pres-elect 1994–96; memb Scientific Ctee Netherlands Inst for Study of Criminality and Law Enforcement 1995–; FBPsS, CPsychol; *Books* Who Becomes Delinquent? (co-author, 1973), The Delinquent Way of Life (co-author, 1977), Behaviour Modification with Offenders: A Criminological Symposium (co-ed, 1979), Psychology, Law and Legal Processes (co-ed, 1979), Abnormal Offenders, Delinquency and the Criminal Justice System (co-ed, 1982), Aggression and Dangerousness (co-ed, 1985), Reactions to Crime: The Public, The Police, Courts, and Prisons (co-ed, 1985), Prediction in Criminology (co-ed, 1985), Understanding and Controlling Crime: Toward a New Research Strategy (co-author, 1986, Prize for Distinguished Scholarship Criminology Section American Sociological Assoc 1988), Human Development and Criminal Behaviour: New Ways of Advancing Knowledge (co-author, 1991), Offenders and Victims: Theory and Policy (co-ed, 1992), Integrating Individual and Ecological Aspects of Crime (co-ed, 1993), Psychological Explanations of Crime (ed, 1994), Building a Safer Society: Strategic Approaches to Crime Prevention (co-ed, 1995); *Style*— Prof David P Farrington; ✉ Institute of Criminology, 7 West Road, Cambridge CB3 9DT (☎ 01223 335384, fax 01223 335356)

FARRINGTON, Col Sir Henry Francis Colden; 7 Bt (UK 1818), of Blackheath, Kent; s of Sir Henry Anthony Farrington, 6 Bt (d 1944); *b* 25 April 1914; *Educ* Haileybury; *m* 22 March 1947, Anne, eldest da of late Maj William Albert Gillam, DSO, Border Regt; 1 s (Henry William b 1951), 1 da (Susan Maria b 1949); *Heir* s, Henry William Farrington, *qv*; *Career* 2/Lt RA 1936, Maj 1942, ret 1960, Hon Col 1966; *Style*— Col Sir Henry Farrington, Bt; ✉ Higher Ford, Wiveliscombe, Taunton, Somerset TA4 2RL (☎ 01984 623219)

FARRINGTON, Henry William; s and h of Col Sir Henry Francis Colden Farrington, 7 Bt, *qv*; *b* 27 March 1951; *Educ* Haileybury, RAC Cirencester; *m* 1979, Diana Donne, yr da of Albert Geoffrey Broughton, of North Petherton, Somerset, 2 s (Henry John Albert b 1985, Charles George Donne b 1988); *Career* farmer, landowner; ARICS; *Style*— Henry Farrington, Esq; ✉ Castle, Wiveliscombe, Taunton, Somerset TA4 2TJ (☎ 01984 623606)

FARRINGTON, (William) Trevor; s of William Raymond Farrington, and Millicent, *née* Johnson; *b* 26 May 1941; *Educ* King's Coll Hosp Med Sch Univ of London (MB BS,

FRCS); *Career* currently conslt otolaryngologist and head and neck surgn Vict Univ of Manchester and conslt head and neck surgn Christie Hosp and Holt Radium Inst Manchester; pres: Section of Layrngology and Rhinology Royal Soc of Medicine, Manchester Surgical Soc; memb Court of Examiners Royal Coll of Surgns (England); *Recreations* country pursuits; *Clubs* St James's (Manchester), Carlton; *Style*— Trevor Farrington, Esq; ✉ Sandilands Farm, Crowley, Northwich, Cheshire CW9 6NX (☎ 01565 777462); Elm House, 2 Mauldeth Road, Withington, Manchester M20 9ND (☎ 0161 434 9715, fax 0161 448 0310)

FARROW, Christopher John (Kit); s of Thomas Farrow (d 1968), and Evangeline, *née* Kearney (d 1992); *b* 29 July 1937; *Educ* Cranleigh Sch, King's Coll Cambridge (BA, Adam Smith Prize), Stanford Univ (visiting scholar, Harkness Fell); *m* 1961, Alison, *née* Brown; 1 da, 1 s; *Career* with Bd of Trade/Dept of Trade and Indust 1961–83, Bank of England 1983–87, dir Kleinwort Benson Ltd 1987–92, dir gen London Investment Banking Assoc 1993–; non-exec dir: London Metal Exchange 1987–, Glynwed International plc 1993–; *Style*— Kit Farrow, Esq; ✉ London Investment Banking Association, 6 Frederick's Place, London EC2R 8BT (☎ 0171 796 3606, fax 0171 796 4345)

FARROW, Kenneth John; s of late Wing Cdr Cyril Arthur Farrow, of Harpenden, and Phyllis Mary, *née* Driver; *b* 31 Aug 1942; *Educ* Culford Sch Bury St Edmunds, Pembroke Coll Oxford (MA, BCL); *m* 15 April 1972, Jennifer Ann, da of late Ronald Lusby; 1 s (Robert b 1978), 1 da (Catherine b 1973); *Career* called to the Bar Gray's Inn 1966, chambers of Charles Sparrow, QC, *qv* 1967–, recorder of the Crown Court 1991– (asst recorder 1985), memb Legal Aid Bd 1988–92; *Style*— Kenneth Farrow, Esq; ✉ 13 Old Square, Lincoln's Inn, London WC2A 3UA (☎ 0171 242 6105, fax 0171 405 4004, telex 262207 ACT10)

FARROW, Nigel Alexander Emery; s of Arthur Hemsworth Farrow, of Bentley, Hants, and Estelle Frances, *née* Emery; *b* 24 March 1939; *Educ* Cheltenham, Queens' Coll Cambridge (MA); *m* 2 Dec 1961, Susan, da of Thomas Bertram Daltry (d 1974); 3 da (Miranda b 1965, Sarah b 1967, Imogen b 1970); *Career* publisher; ed Business Mgmnt 1964–67; chm: Xerox Publishing Group Ltd 1972–82, Ginn & Co Ltd 1972–78, University Microfilms Ltd 1972–82; dir and chm: Ashgate Publishing Ltd, Connaught Training Ltd, Dartmouth Publishing Co Ltd, Gower Publishing Co Ltd, Information Publications International Ltd, Information Publications, PTE Ltd Singapore; pres: Cheltonian Soc 1988–91, Cncl Cheltenham Coll 1992–; Hon DBA; FRSA; *Books* Gower Handbook of Management (ed), The English Library (ed); author of numerous articles on business and management; *Recreations* enjoying and supporting the arts, collecting 20th century British paintings; *Style*— Nigel Farrow, Esq; ✉ Dippenhall Gate, Dippenhall, Farnham, Surrey; Mecklenburgh House, 11 Mecklenburgh Square, London; Gower House, Croft Road, Aldershot, Hants

FARRY, James (Jim); s of James Farry (d 1972), and Helen Carlin (d 1992); *b* 1 July 1954; *Educ* Queen's Park Senior Secdy, Hunter HS, Claremont HS; *m* 17 June 1978, Elaine Margaret, da of William Alexander Campbell McInnes (d 1992), of Glasgow; 1 s (Ewan b 31 July 1984), 1 da (Alyson b 18 March 1982); *Career* sec Scottish Football League 1979–89; Scottish Football Assoc: admin asst 1972–77, asst sec 1977–79, sec elect 1989, chief exec 1990–; *Recreations* football spectating, fishing, reading; *Clubs* Royal Scottish Automobile, Caledonian, Cambuslang RFC; *Style*— Jim Farry, Esq; ✉ The Scottish Football Association Ltd, 6 Park Gardens, Glasgow G3 7YF (☎ 0141 332 6372, fax 0141 3327559, telex 778904)

FARTHING, (Richard) Bruce Crosby; s of Col Herbert Hadfield Farthing, RA (d 1978), and Marjorie Cora, *née* Fisher (d 1981); *b* 9 Feb 1926; *Educ* Alleyn's Sch, St Catharine's Coll Cambridge (BA, MA); *m* 1, 14 Feb 1959 (m dis 1986), (Anne) Brenda, da of Capt Thomas Williams (d 1961); 1 s (Richard Crosby b 24 July 1962), 1 da (Anne Crosby b 30 Nov 1959); m 2, 6 Nov 1986, Moira Jess Roupell, da of Lt-Col Curties, RA (d 1970); *Career* joined RA 1944, RA OCTU 1945–46, sr under offr 1946, served various field regts and 7 RHA in Europe, Egypt and Palestine 1946–47, demobbed as Lt 1948; called to the Bar Inner Temple 1954; govt legal serv 1954–59; Chamber of Shipping of the UK: legal advsr 1959, asst gen mangr 1966; sec Ctee of Euro Shipowners 1967–74, sec Ctee of Euro Nat Shipowners' Assocs 1967–74, sec gen Cncl of Euro and Japanese Nat Shipowners' Assoc (CENSA) 1974–76, dir Gen Cncl of Br Shipping 1976–80, dep dir-gen Gen Cncl of Br Sipping 1980–83; Rapporteur Sea Tport Cmmn (now Maritime and Surface Tport Cmmn) Int C of C 1976–95, conslt to ICC on maritime affrs 1983–93, conslt dir Int Assoc of Dry Cargo Shipowners 1983–; memb Ct of Common Cncl Corpn of London (Ward of Aldgate) 1982–, pres Aldgate Ward Club 1985 (vice pres 1984); City of London Sch: govr 1983–, dep chm Bd of Govrs 1988, chm 1990–93, dep chm 1993–94; govr Sch of Oriental and African Studies 1986–; memb Cncl City Univ 1993–; chm Reception Ctee for state banquet to King of Norway 1988, tstee Nautical Museums Tst 1983–; memb of Ct The Irish Soc 1992; Freeman City of London 1978, Liveryman Worshipful Co of Shipwrights 1982 (Freeman 1978); FIMgt 1983; Cdr Royal Norwegian Order of Merit 1988; *Books* Aspinalls Maritime Law Cases (ed vol 20, 1961), International Shipping - An Introduction to the Policies Politics and Institutions of the Maritime World (1987, 2 edn 1993, 3 edn 1997); *Recreations* sailing, gardening, music; *Clubs* Royal Ocean Racing, MCC, Incogniti Cricket, Rye Golf; *Style*— Bruce Farthing, Esq; ✉ Snaylham House, Icklesham, East Sussex TN36 4AJ (☎ 01424 812983, fax 01424 814746); 44 St George's Drive, London SW1V 4BT (☎ 0171 834 1211); Intercargo, 2 Floor, 4 London Wall Buildings, Blomfield Street, London EC2

FARTHING, Ramon; s of Clifford Ramon George Farthing (d 1983), and Patricia Carter, of 64 Rosebank, Parkeston Rd, Harwich, Essex; *b* 9 Feb 1961; *Educ* Sir Anthony Deane Secdy Sch, Colchester Inst of Higher Educn; *m* Karen Elaine, da of John Arundel; 1 s (Kai Ramon b 6 Dec 1990), 1 da (Leila Patricia b 20 June 1995); *Career* apprentice under Chris Oakley at The Pier Restaurant 1978–80, commis chef under Sam Chalmers at Le Talbooth Restaurant Dedham Essex 1980–83, personal chef to Lord and Lady Spencer Althorp House Northamptonshire 1983–84, second chef to Chris Oakes The Castle Hotel Taunton 1984–86, first head chef Calcot Manor Gloucestershire 1986–92 (Michelin Star Rating 1986–92, 1 AA Rosette for cooking 1987 rising to 3 AA Rosettes 1992, Akermann Guide Clover Leaf 1990–91, Catey Function Menu of the Year 1991), head chef and mgr Harveys Restaurant Bristol 1994– (head chef 1992–) (3 AA Rossettes, Ackermann Guide Clover Leaf, County Restaurant of the Year, 1 Michelin star 1994); rep chef of Br Food Festival Mandarin Hotel Jakarta Indonesia 1989; entries in Egon Ronay and The Good Food Guide; *Books* Great Fish Book (contrib), Great Pasta Book (contrib); *Recreations* music, reading cookery books; *Clubs* Caterer Acorn; *Style*— Ramon Farthing, Esq; ✉ 27 Sabrina Way, Stoke Bishop, Bristol (☎ 0117 968 5634); Harveys Restaurant, Denmark Street, Bristol BS1 5DQ (☎ 0117 927 5034, fax 0117 927 5003)

FARTHING, Stephen Frederick Godfrey; s of Dennis Jack Farthing (d 1985), of London, and Joan Margaret, *née* Godfrey; *b* 16 Sept 1950; *Educ* St Martin's Sch of Art, Royal Coll of Art, Br Sch Rome (Abbey Major scholar); *m* Joan Elizabeth, *née* Jackson; 1 da (Constance Beatrice); *Career* lectr in painting Canterbury Coll of Art 1977–79, tutor in painting Royal Coll of Art 1979–85, head Dept of Fine Art W Surrey Coll of Art and Design Farnham 1987–88 (head of painting 1985–87), artist in residence Hayward Gallery 1989; elected Ruskin master and professorial fell St Edmund Hall Oxford; tstee, memb Fine Art Faculty and Fin and Gen Purposes Ctee Br Sch at Rome 1994–; *Selected One Man Exhibitions* Town and Country (Edward Totah Gallery London) 1986, New Ashgate Gallery Farnham 1987, Edward Totah Gallery London 1987, Mute Accomplices (Museum of Modern Art Oxford (touring)) 1988, Stephen Farthing and the Leonardo Exhibition (Queen Elizabeth Hall London) 1989, Stephen Farthing at the Paco Imperial Rio De Janeiro, National Museum of Art Montevideo Uruguay, Museo de Monterray Mexico 1990, Museo de Gil Mexico 1990, The Knowledge (Nat Museum of Modern Art Kyoto) 1993; *Group Exhibitions* Now for the Future (Haywood Gallery London) 1990, RA Summer Exhibition 1990, 1992 and 1995; *Work in Collections* Leicester City Museum, Nat Museum of Wales, Bradford Art Galleries and Museums, Government Art Collection Fund, Br Cncl 1990; *Style*— Stephen Farthing, Esq; ✉ Ruskin School of Drawing, Oxford University, The High Street, Oxford OX1 4BG (☎ 01865 276940)

FARTHING, Thomas William; OBE (1983); s of late Thomas Farthing; *b* 19 Dec 1927; *Educ* Middlesbrough HS, Jesus Coll Cambridge (MA, PhD); *m* (m dis); 1 s, 1 da; *Career* metallurgist; IMI Res 1951–58, Beryllium project mangr IMI 1958–62, res mangr Traditional Metals IMI 1962–64, Euro res dir Int Copper Res Assoc 1964–66; md: Wolverhampton Metal Ltd 1966–74, IMI Titanium 1974–89 (additional responsibility for IMI corporate res and devpt 1983), ret 1989; currently: visiting prof Univ of Leeds, sr industl assoc Interdisciplinary Research Centre for Biomedical Materials Univ of London; former memb: Link Ctee Advanced Engrg Materials, former memb Aviation Ctee and Metals and Minerals Ctee DTI; memb Cncl and former pres Birmingham Metallurgical Assoc, former memb Cncl and vice pres Inst of Metals, former memb Cncl SBAC, chm SBAC Materials Gp Ctee; former memb England/Japan Scheme Royal Acad of Engrg, FEng 1984, FIMechE; *Recreations* walking, reading, music, gardening; *Style*— Thomas Farthing, Esq, OBE, FEng; ✉ 71 Sir Richard's Drive, Harborne, Birmingham B17 8SG

FARZANEH, Prof Farzin; *b* 19 Aug 1953, Teheran, Iran; *Educ* Brighton Coll of Technol (HND), Univ of Aberdeen (BSc, MSc), Univ of Sussex (SERC studentship, DPhil); *m* Lindsay Claire, *née* Stockley; 1 da (Leili Claire b 5 July 1987), 1 s (Benjamin Bijan b 18 Dec 1993); *Career* Beit meml fell Univ of Sussex 1979–82, EMBO fell Univ of Amsterdam 1982–83, MRC fell Univ of Sussex 1983–84; King's Coll Sch of Med and Dentistry: 'new blood' lectr Dept of Obstetrics and Gynaecology 1985–87, sr lectr Molecular Genetics Unit Dept of Obstetrics and Gynaecology 1987–90, dir Molecular Med Unit 1990–93, head Dept of Molecular Med 1993–, awarded personal chair in Molecular Med 1996; jt holder of patent (2244646B) on the prevention of viral infection by inhibitors of poly(ADP-ribose) polymerase; recognised teacher Univ of London, KCSMD rep Univ of London Bd of Biochemistry 1988–, KCSMD biological safety advsr and memb Health and Safety Ctee 1991–; external examiner Univs of Aberdeen, Bath, Brunel, Essex, Reading and Sussex; co-opted grad memb Ctee Br Soc for Developmental Biology 1977–79, memb Organising Ctee UK Molecular Biology of Cancer Network 1988–91; memb: Br Biochemical Soc, Cell Biology Soc, Genetics Soc, Developmental Biology Soc, American Assoc for the Advancement of Sci, American Soc for Microbiolgy; MRCPath 1990; *Publications* author of numerous original res papers in peer reviewed jls and of review articles and conf proceedings, also author of published books; *Style*— Prof Farzin Farzaneh; ✉ Department of Molecular Medicine, King's College School of Medicine and Dentistry, Denmark Hill, London SE5 8RX (☎ 0171 326 3126, fax 0171 733 3877)

FASHANU, John; s of Patrick Fashanu, of Nigeria, and Pearl Gopaul; *b* 18 Sept 1962; *Educ* Attleborough HS Norfolk; *children* 1 da (Amal); *Career* former professional footballer; jr player: Peterborough Utd, Cambridge Utd; Norwich City: signed professional 1979, debut v Shrewsbury Town 1982, 7 league appearances; 2 league appearances on loan Crystal Palace 1983, 36 league appearances Lincoln City 1983–84, 50 league appearances Millwall 1984–86, over 300 league appearances Wimbledon 1986–94 (107 goals), transferred to Aston Villa for fee of £1.35m 1994, ret as professional player 1995; 2 full England caps 1989; FA Cup winners medal Wimbledon 1988, Charity Shield medal Wimbledon 1988; former sch boy boxing county champion Norfolk; md of PR, sports and mgmnt companies; dir Kiss FM; presenter: Gladiators (co-presenter Ulrika Jonsson, *qv*, LWT) 1992–, Sssports (BBC) 1993; Lions Youth for int community work, Business Fedn Award Lloyds Bank 1990, Black Men and Women in Media Award World Sports Corp 1990, citation from pres UN Maj-Gen Joe Garba; appointed special rep of UNICEF; *Recreations* my businesses, tennis; *Style*— John Fashanu, Esq; ✉ Warm Seas House, 23 Wellington Road, St Johns Wood, London NW8 9SL (☎ 0171 586 0031, fax 0171 483 4372)

FASSETT, Kaffe; s of William Elliot Fassett, and Madeleine, *née* Ullman (d 1987); *b* 7 Dec 1937; *Educ* Museum of Fine Arts Sch Boston; *Career* author, textile designer and fine artist; retrospective at V & A (first exhibition of a living artist), subsequent world tour Kaffe Fassett's V & A Show; work incl in museum collections UK, USA, Norway, Canada and Aust, TV series Glorious Colour (Channel 4); *Books* Glorious Knitting (1985), Glorious Needlepoint (1987), Glorious Colour (1988), Family Album (1989), Glorious Inspiration (Century, 1991), Kaffe's Classics (1993), Glorious Interiors (1995); *Recreations* jogging, swimming, travelling; *Style*— Kaffe Fassett, Esq; ✉ c/o Ebury Press, 20 Vauxhall Bridge Rd, London SW1V 2SA (☎ 0171 973 9670, fax 0171 233 6127)

FATCHETT, Derek John; MP (Lab) Leeds Central (majority 15,020); s of Herbert and Irene Fatchett; *b* 8 Aug 1945; *Educ* Lincoln Sch, Univ of Birmingham, LSE; *m* 1969, Anita Bridgens, *née* Oakes; 2 s; *Career* formerly university lectr, cncllr Wakefield Met Borough Cncl; MP (Lab) Leeds Central 1983–; *Style*— Derek Fatchett, Esq, MP; ✉ House of Commons, London SW1A 0AA

FATHERS, Michael Allen; s of Walter Armstrong Fathers (d 1995), of Takapuna, New Zealand, and Joyce Alice, *née* Barwell (d 1975); *b* 7 July 1941; *Educ* King's Coll Auckland NZ, Victoria Univ Wellington NZ (BA); *m* 8 January 1972, Angela Lemoine, *née* Denman; 1 s (Thomas Benjamin b 31 July 1976), 1 da (Alexandra Frankie b 21 Sept 1974); *Career* journalist; NZ Press Assoc 1966–69, Reuters London office 1970–71, 1976–78 and 1984–85; foreign corr Reuters: Vietnam 1972–73, Tanzania 1974–75, Pakistan 1979–81, Thailand 1981–83, E Africa 1986; Asia ed The Independent 1986–89, writer The Independent on Sunday 1989–94, dir of information and public affairs Cwlth Secretariat 1994–; *Books* Tiananmen - The Rape of Peking (with Andrew Higgins, 1989); *Style*— Michael Fathers, Esq; ✉ Commonwealth Secretariat, Marlborough House, Pall Mall, London SW1Y 5HX (☎ 0171 747 6380, fax 0171 839 9081)

FAULDER, Carolyn Mary; da of Charles Clement Calburn (d 1977) (*see* Burke's Landed Gentry 18th Edn, vol 3), and Maria Clemencia, *née* Echeverria (d 1969); *b* 13 Feb 1934; *Educ* Bedford Coll London (BA Philosophy); *m* 2 June 1956 (m dis 1989), John Sewell Faulder; 1 s (Dominic b 1958), 2 da (Sarah b 1957, Clemencia b 1961); *Career* journalist, author and lectr; chairwoman Breast Cancer Care (formerly Breast Care and Mastectomy Assoc); *Books incl* Treat Yourself to Sex, The Women's Cancer Book, Whose Body is it?, A Special Gift, Always a Woman; *Recreations* many but specially the company of friends and family; *Style*— Ms Carolyn Faulder; ✉ 25 Belsize Park Gardens, London NW3 4JH (☎ 0171 916 6299)

FAULDER, John Sewell; s of Ronald Sewell Faulder (d 1982), and Ruth, *née* Huggins (d 1972); *b* 16 Jan 1930; *Educ* Marlborough, ChCh Oxford (MA), IMEDE Lausanne (Dip); *m* 2 June 1956 (m dis 1989), Carolyn Mary, da of Charles Clement Calburn (d 1977); 1 s (Dominic b 1958), 2 da (Sarah b 1957, Clemencia b 1961); *Career* Nat Serv 2 Lt Royal Dragoons 1951–53, Capt Inns of Court HQ 56 (London) Armoured Div TA 1953–62; controller Crosse & Blackwell The Nestlé Co Ltd 1958–69, Henry Ansbacher Ltd 1970–71, dir Charterhouse Development and chm subsidiaries Charterhouse Group plc 1971–82; dir: Sandell Perkins plc 1975–88, B T Batsford Ltd 1982–91; chm:

Electrothermal Engineering Ltd 1982–, Techgen International Ltd 1992–94, Centre for Analysis and Modelling 1994–; Freeman City of London, memb Ct of Assts Worshipful Co of Builders Merchants (Master 1986); govr Inst of Builders Merchants, memb Royal Inst of Int Affrs; FInstBM 1986; *Recreations* shooting, painting; *Clubs* Hurlingham; *Style—* John Faulder, Esq

FAULDS, Andrew Matthew William; MP (Lab) Warley E (majority 7,794); s of Rev Matthew Faulds, and Doris Faulds; *b* 1 March 1923; *Educ* George Watson's Coll Edinburgh, King Edward VI GS Louth, Daniel Stewart's Sch Edinburgh, Stirling HS, Univ of Glasgow; *m* 1945, Bunty Whitfield; 1 da; *Career* formerly actor with Shakespeare Meml Co Stratford, also TV, radio and films; MP (Lab): Smethwick 1966–74, Warley E 1974–; PPS to Min of State for Aviation Miny of Technol 1967–68, PMG 1968–69; oppn front bench spokesman on the arts 1970–73 and 1979–82 (sacked for opposing official Labour policy on Falklands crisis); chm: Parly Assoc for Euro-Arab Cooperation UK Branch 1974–, All-Party Heritage Gp, Br Delgn to Cncl of Europe and WEU 1975–80 and 1987–92, Exec Ctee IPU Br Section 1983–; offr of All-Pty Asean, Chinese, Egyptian, Jordanian, Omani, Saudi Arabian, Syrian and Thai Parly Gps, offr All-Party Parly Friends of Northern Cyprus; *Style—* Andrew Faulds, Esq, MP; ✉ 14 Albemarle St, London W1 (☎ 0171 499 7589); House of Commons, London SW1A 0AA (☎ 0171 219 3000)

FAULKNER, Amanda Jane; da of Richard George Butler Faulkner (d 1976), and Gillian Mary Josephine Hopkinson, *née* Park; *b* 5 Dec 1953; *Educ* St Anthony's Leweston, Canford Sch, Bournemouth Coll of Art, Ravensbourne Coll of Art, Chelsea Sch of Art; 1 s (Joseph b 21 March 1993); *Career* artist; *Solo Exhibitions* incl: Woodlands Art Gallery Blackheath London 1983, Angela Flowers Gallery 1985–86, Big Women (Metropole Arts Centre Folkestone) 1987, Seven Deadly Sins and Recent Drawings and Prints (Flowers East Gallery London) 1988, Breaking Water (Drumcroon Arts and Educn Centre Wigan) 1989, Flowers East London 1990 and 1992, Amanda Faulkner - Recent Drawings (Manchester City Art Galleries), Amanda Faulkner - Mares' Tails Flowers East at London Fields; *Gp Exhibitions* incl: The Print Show (Angela Flowers Gallery London) 1983; What's New in the Arts Council Collection (touring) 1984, Double Elephant (Concourse Gallery Barbican London) 1985, The Print Show - Woodcuts and Linocuts (Angela Flowers Gallery London) 1985, Identity/Desire - Representing the Body (Scot Arts Cncl touring) 1986, Print Biennale of Liège (Musée d'Art Moderne Belgium) 1987, Mother and Child (Lefevre Gallery London) 1988, Excavations (Galerie Hubert Winter Vienna and John Hansard Gallery Southampton) 1988, New Contemporary British Painting (The Contemporary Arts Centre Cincinatti Ohio and touring) 1988, Ljubljana Print Biennale (Yugoslavia) 1989, Barbican Concourse Gallery London 1989, Angela Flowers Gallery 1990, Flowers at Moos (Gallery Moos NY) 1990, Inaugural Exhibition (Cannon Cole Gallery Chicago) 1991, European Large Formant Printmaking (Guinness Hopstore Dublin) 1991, Postmodern Prints (V&A) 1991, Images of Hope and Disquiet - Expressionism in Britain in the Nineties (Castlefield Gallery Manchester) 1992, Myth, Dream and fable (Angel Row Gallery Nottingham) 1992; work in various public collections, selector for various awards; Sch of Fine Art Chelsea Coll of Art and Design London: princ lectr in printmaking 1991–93, sr lectr in combined media 1993–; *Clubs* Chelsea Arts; *Style—* Ms Amanda Faulkner; ✉ c/o Flowers East, 199–205 Richmond Rd, London E3 3NJ (☎ 0181 985 3333, fax 0181 985 0067)

FAULKNER, David Edwart Riley; CB (1985); s of Harold Ewart Faulkner (d 1968), of Manchester and London, and Mabel, *née* Riley (d 1960); *b* 23 Oct 1934; *Educ* Manchester GS, Merchant Taylors', St John's Coll Oxford (MA); *m* 16 Sept 1961, Sheila Jean, da of James Stevenson (d 1985), of Buckinghamshire; 1 s (Martin b 1962), 1 da (Rosemary b 1965); *Career* Nat Serv RA and Intelligence Corps, 2 Lt 1957–59; Home Office: asst princ 1959, princ 1963, asst sec 1969, private sec to the Home Sec 1969, Prison Dept 1970, Police Dept 1975, asst under sec of state 1976, seconded to the Cabinet Office 1978–79, dir of operational policy Prison Dept 1980, dep under sec of state Criminal and Res and Statistical Depts 1982, princ establishment offr 1990–92; fell St John's Coll Oxford and sr res assoc Oxford Centre for Criminological Res 1992–; memb: United Nations Ctee on Crime Prevention and Control 1984–91, Advsy Bd of Helsinki Inst for Crime Prevention and Control 1984–92; tstee: Gilbert Murray Tst, Divert, Fndn for Outdoor Adventure; memb Cncl: JUSTICE, Magistrates' Assoc, Howard League for Penal Reform; *Style—* David Faulkner, Esq, CB; ✉ St John's College, Oxford OX1 3JP (☎ 01865 274448, fax 01865 274445)

FAULKNER, Prof Douglas; s of Vincent Faulkner (d 1976), of Eastbourne, and Florence Emily, *née* Weller (d 1985); *b* 29 Dec 1929; *Educ* Royal Dockyard Coll Devonport (Naval Constructor Cadetship and Whitworth scholar), RNE and RN Colls, MIT Cambridge Mass (PhD); *m* 1 (m dis); 3 da (Wendy Ruth b 1956, Karelia Ann b 1958, Alison Claire b 1960); m 2, 11 Aug 1987, Isobel Parker, *née* Campbell; *Career* asst constructor (sea service, aircraft carrier structural design, prodn engrg) 1954–59, naval constructor and structural res (structural design of HMSM Dreadnought) 1959–63, asst prof RNC Greenwich 1963–68, constructor cdr Washington 1968–70, defence fell MIT Boston 1970–71, chief constructor Bath and Box Girder Bridge Enquiry 1971–73, head Dept of Naval Architecture and Ocean Engineering Univ of Glasgow 1973–95 (dean of engrg 1978–81, prof emeritus 1995–), conslt Conoco Inc Houston 1981–83, dir Veritec Limited 1985–88, visiting prof VPI Blacksburg Virginia 1986–87, ed Journal of Marine Structures 1987–; advsr Merison Box Girder Bridge Enquiry 1972; memb: American Ship Structures Ctee 1968–71, Defence Scientific Advsy Cncl Ctees 1975–86, Dept of Energy Advsy Gps on Offshore Structures 1976–81; UK rep Int Ship and Offshore Structures Congress 1976–85, chm Conoco-ABS Tension Leg Platform Design Ctee 1981–83, memb Bd of Govrs BMT Quality Assessors Ltd 1990–93; pres Instn of Engrs and Shipbuilders in Scotland 1995–97; winner David Taylor Medal 1991, William Froude Medal 1992, Peter the Great Medal 1993; Hon DSc Tech Univ of Gdansk 1993; memb: Whitworth Soc 1950 (pres-elect), Soc Naval Architects and Marine Engrs 1969; FRINA 1971, FIStructE 1972, FEng 1981, FSNAME 1991; *Books* Integrity of Offshore Structures (ed 1981, 1987, 1990 and 1993); *Recreations* hill walking, chess; *Style—* Prof Douglas Faulkner, FEng; ✉ 4 Murdoch Drive, Milngavie, Glasgow G62 6QZ (☎ 0141 956 5071)

FAULKNER, Hugh Branston; OBE (1980); s of Frank Faulkner (d 1964), and Ethel, *née* Branston (d 1968); *b* 8 June 1916; *Educ* Lutterworth GS; *m* 1954, Anne Carlton, *née* Milner; 1 s (Anthony), 1 da (Jane); *Career* admin asst City of Leicester Educn Ctee 1936–46, organising sec Fellowship of Reconciliation 1946–54, christian peace delegate USSR 1952, lectr in int affrs USA 1953; hon dir Voluntary and Christian Serv 1954–79 (a fndr tstee), dir Help the Aged (a fndr memb) 1961–83, del and speaker UN World Assembly on Ageing Vienna 1982, dir Asthma Res Cncl 1983–88; charity conslt 1988–; hon dir Persistent Virus Disease Research Fndn 1992–; tstee: Voluntary and Christian Serv, World in Need Tst, Lester Tst, Nat Asthma Training Centre; hon advsr Elderly Accommodation Counsel, memb Exec Ctee Cncl for Music in Hosps 1983–; memb Anchor Housing; FCIS; *Recreations* music, gardening; *Clubs* Nat Liberal; *Style—* Hugh Faulkner, Esq, OBE; ✉ Longfield, 4 One Tree Lane, Beaconsfield, Bucks HP9 2BU (☎ 01494 674769, fax 01494 680408)

FAULKNER, Cdr Hugh Douglas Younger; CVO (1996, LVO 1991); s of Rear Adm Hugh Webb Faulkner, CB, CBE, DSO, DL (d 1969), and Olave Mary, *née* Younger (d 1989); *b* 17 May 1931; *Educ* West Downs Winchester, RNC Dartmouth; *m* 28 July 1956, Fiona Naomi, da of Brig Dominick Andrew Sydney Browne, CBE (d 1981), of Breaghwy, Castlebar, Co Mayo; 2 s (Christopher Gerald b 15 Aug 1958, Anthony Dominick Hugh b 5 April 1961); *Career* Reg Cmmn RN 1949–78, ret; sec The Royal Warrant Holders' Assoc 1979–95; *Recreations* shooting, fishing, golf; *Clubs* Army and Navy; *Style—* Cdr Hugh Faulkner, CVO, RN; ✉ Currie Lee Crichton, Nr Pathhead, Midlothian EH37 5XB (☎ 01875 320563)

FAULKNER, John Richard Hayward; s of Capt Richard Hayward Ollerton (d 1943), and Lilian Elizabeth, *née* Carrigan; *b* 29 May 1941; *Educ* Archbishop Holgate's Sch, Keble Coll Oxford (BA); *m* 1970, Janet Gill (d 1994), da of Alfred George Herbert Cummings; 2 da (Abigail b 1976, Emma b 1984), 2 step da (Zoe b 1963, Amanda b 1966); *Career* worked with several theatre cos incl: Meadow Players, Century Theatre, Prospect Theatre Co (fndr memb), Cambridge Theatre Co, Sixty-Nine Theatre Co 1964–72; drama dir: Scottish Arts Cncl 1972–76, Arts Cncl of GB 1976–83; assoc prodr and later head of artistic planning Nat Theatre 1983–88; theatre and mgmnt conslt 1988–; assoc Theatre Futures, dir Vision Assocs; non-exec dir: Minotaur Films, The Arts for Nature Ltd; tstee: Arts Educnl Schs, Performing Arts Labs, Pleasance Theatre Tst; chm TNC/Writers Agreement Ctee; *Recreations* intricacies and wildernesses; *Style—* John Faulkner, Esq; ✉ 28 Ellesmere Road, Chiswick, London W4 4QH (☎ 0181 995 3041)

FAULKNER, Nicholas Odin; s of Sir Eric Odin Faulkner, MBE, TD (d 1994), of Ightham, Kent, and Joan Mary, *née* Webster (d 1991); *b* 30 Sept 1948; *Educ* St Ronan's Sch Kent, Millfield Somerset; *m* 20 May 1978, Rosalind Beatrice, da of the late Lt-Col A W N Cowper; 1 s (Jonathan Frederick Odin b 1980), 1 da (Freya Antonia Noelle b 1984); *Career* Hudson Bay Co Ltd Canada 1967–68, asst to md Firearms Co Ltd Somerset 1968–70; Roneo Vickers Ltd: various sales, sales mgmnt and mktg info posts 1970–75, overseas div exec 1975, gp business devpt exec 1976; head of market res and planning Vickers Dawson Ltd 1977–81, merchanting dir Morris Hanbury Jackson Le May Ltd (Hop Merchants and Factors) 1981–82, history project dir Allied-Lyons plc and Allied Breweries Ltd 1983–88, managing assoc Nicholas Faulkner Assocs 1983–; memb: IOD, Chartered Inst of Mktg, Business Archive Cncl; *Books* Allied Breweries - A Long Life (1988); contrib: Whatman 1740–1990 - 250 Years of Excellence (1989), Devenish - One Hundred Corporate Years (1990); *Recreations* shooting, sailing, music, fly fishing; *Style—* Nicholas Faulkner, Esq; ✉ Hecton House, Friday Street, East Sutton, Nr Maidstone, Kent ME17 3EA (☎ 01622 844744, business ☎ and fax 01622 844644)

FAULKNER, Richard Oliver; s of Harold Ewart Faulkner (d 1968), and Mabel, *née* Riley (d 1960); *b* 22 March 1946; *Educ* Merchant Taylors', Worcester Coll Oxford (MA); *m* 5 July 1968, Susan, da of Donald James Heyes (d 1978); 2 da (Julia b 1969, Tamsin b 1970); *Career* jt md Westminster Communications Group Ltd 1988–; communications advsr: Railway Trade Unions 1976–77, Bd BR 1977–, Littlewoods 1977–, Lloyds TSB Group (forerly TSB Group) 1987–, Interparly Union 1987–90, The Bishop at Lambeth 1990; vice chm Transport 2000 Ltd, dir Westminster Europe Ltd 1994–; Parly candidate (Lab): Devizes 1970 and Feb 1974, Monmouth Oct 1974, Huddersfield West 1979; memb Merton Borough Cncl 1971–78, communications advsr to oppn ldr and Lab Pty gen elections 1987 and 1992, co fndr Parly jl The House Magazine; Football Tst: fndr tstee 1979–83, sec 1983–86, dep chm 1986–90, first dep chm 1990–; chm: Women's FA 1988–91, Sports Grounds Initiative 1995–; memb Sports Cncl 1986–88; MIPR 1977; *Recreations* collecting Lloyd George memorabilia, tinplate trains, watching association football, travelling by railway; *Clubs* Reform; *Style—* Richard Faulkner, Esq; ✉ Westminster Communications Ltd, Cowley House, Little College Street, London SW1P 3XS (☎ 0171 222 0666, fax 0171 233 0335)

FAULKNER OF DOWNPATRICK, Baroness; Lucy Barbara Ethel; CBE; da of William John Harkness Forsythe (d 1960), of Bangor, and Jane Ethel, *née* Sewell; *b* 1 July 1925; *Educ* Trinity Coll Dublin; *m* 1951, Baron Faulkner of Downpatrick (Life Peer d 1977); 2 s, 1 da; *Career* nat govr BBC NI 1978–85; chm Bdcasting Cncl NI 1981–85; co dir; former journalist Belfast Telegraph; genealogist; tstee Ulster Hist Fndn 1980–, govr Belfast Linen Hall Library 1983–; memb NI Tourist Bd 1985–91; chm NI Advsy Bd Salvation Army; Hon LLD Queen's Univ Belfast 1994; *Recreations* hunting, dressage, book collecting; *Clubs* Royal Over-Seas League; *Style—* The Rt Hon Lady Faulkner of Downpatrick, CBE; ✉ Toberdoney, Seaforde, Downpatrick, Co Down, NI (☎ 013967 811712)

FAULKS, Edward Peter Lawless; QC (1996); s of His Hon Peter Faulks, MC, *qv*, and Pamela, *née* Lawless; bro of Sebastian Charles Faulks, *qv*; *b* 19 Aug 1950; *Educ* Wellington, Jesus Coll Oxford (MA); *m* 1990, Catherine Frances Turner; 2 s (Leo Alexander Lawless b 8 Aug 1992, Archie Dominic b 11 Nov 1994); *Career* called to the Bar Middle Temple 1973, in practice Midland and Oxford Circuit; FCIArb; *Recreations* cricket; *Clubs* Garrick; *Style—* Edward Faulks, Esq, QC; ✉ 62 Kensington Park Rd, London W11 3BJ (☎ 0171 727 7823); 1 Serjeants Inn, Fleet St, London EC4Y 1LL (☎ 0171 353 9901)

FAULKS, His Hon Judge; Esmond James; s of Sir Neville Major Ginner Faulks, MBE, TD (d 1985), and Bridget Marigold, *née* Bodley (d 1962); *b* 11 June 1946; *Educ* Uppingham, Sidney Sussex Coll Cambridge (MA); *m* 12 Sept 1972, Pamela Margaret, da of William Arthur and Margaret Ives, of Almora, Rockcliffe, Kircudbright; 1 s (Sam b 17 Oct 1973), 1 da (Nicola b 6 March 1976); *Career* barr; recorder Crown Court 1987–93; circuit judge (NE Circuit) 1993–; *Recreations* country pursuits; *Style—* His Honour Judge Faulks; ✉ Chesterwood, Haydon Bridge, Northumberland (☎ 01434 84 329)

FAULKS, His Hon Peter Ronald; MC (1943); s of late Maj James Faulks, of Reigate Heath, Surrey, and A M, *née* Ginner; *b* 24 Dec 1917; *Educ* Tonbridge, Sidney Sussex Coll Cambridge; *m* 1949, Pamela Brenda, da of late Philip Henry (Peter) Lawless; 2 s (Edward Peter Lawless Faulks, *qv* b 1950, Sebastian Charles Faulks, *qv* b 1953); *Career* slr 1949–80, recorder of the Crown Court 1972–80, dep chm Agric Land Tbnl (SE England) 1972–80, circuit judge 1980–90; *Recreations* country life; *Clubs* MCC, Farmers'; *Style—* His Hon Peter Faulks, MC; ✉ Downs Cottage, Boxford, Newbury, Berks RG20 8DJ (☎ 01488 608382)

FAULKS, Sebastian Charles; s of His Hon Peter Ronald Faulks, MC, *qv*, and Pamela, *née* Lawless; bro of Edward Peter Lawless Faulks, *qv*; *b* 20 April 1953; *Educ* Wellington Coll, Emmanuel Coll Cambridge (exhibitioner, BA); *m* 1989, Veronica, *née* Youlten; 2 s (William b 1990, Arthur b 1996), 1 da (Holly b 1992); *Career* writer; ed New Fiction Soc 1978–81, reporter Daily Telegraph 1978–82, feature writer Sunday Telegraph 1983–86, literary ed The Independent 1986–89; Independent on Sunday: dep ed 1989–90, assoc ed 1990–91; Author of the Year British Book Awards 1995; FRSL 1995; *Books* A Trick of the Light (1984), The Girl at the Lion d'Or (1989), A Fool's Alphabet (1992), Birdsong (1993), The Fatal Englishman: Three Short Lives (1996); *Recreations* cricket, cooking, drinking; *Clubs* Gaieties CC; *Style—* Sebastian Faulks, Esq, FRSL; ✉ c/o Aitken and Stone, 29 Fernshaw Road, London SW10 0TG

FAULL, Dr Margaret Lindsay; da of Norman Augustus Faull (d 1956), of Sydney, Australia, and Myra Beryl, *née* Smith; *b* 4 April 1946; *Educ* Fort St Girls' HS, Univ of Sydney (BA), Univ of Macquarie (MA), Univ of Sheffield (MA), Univ of Leeds (PhD); *Career* secdy sch teacher NSW Dept of Educn 1970–71, dep co archaeologist W Yorks CC 1984–85 (field archaeologist 1975–84), project mangr Thwaite Mills Industl Museum 1985–86, dir National Coal Mining Museum for England (formerly Yorkshire Mining Museum) Caphouse Colliery 1986–; ed Soc for Landscape Studies 1979–86, chm Yorkshire and Humberside Cncl for Br Archaeology 1982–84, sec Thwaite Mills Soc 1986–; MIFA 1983, MILAM 1986, assoc Inst of Mining Engrs 1988, MInstD 1990, FRSA 1996; *Books* Domesday Book: Yorkshire Chichester (jt ed, 1986); *Recreations* collecting

African carvings, opera, cricket; *Style*— Dr Margaret Faull; ✉ 39 Eldon Terrace, Leeds Road, Wakefield, West Yorks WF1 3JW (☎ 01924 379690), National Coal Mining Museum, Caphouse Colliery, New Rd, Overton, Wakefield, W Yorkshire WF4 4RH (☎ 01924 848806, fax 01924 840694)

FAURE, Hubert Rene Joseph; s of Frederic Faure (d 1978), and Jacqueline, *née* de Vendegies d'Hust (d 1957); *b* 5 Sept 1919; *Educ* Ecole Libre Sciences Politiques, Sorbonne Paris; *m* 1, 1948 (m dis 1957), Elizabeth de Cuevas; m 2, 1973, Genevieve Polonceau; 1 s (Adrien b 15 Jan 1975); *Career* attaché French Embassy Bogota Columbia 1947, mangr Ateliers Metallurgiques St Urbain 1949; pres: Ascinter-Otis 1961–72, Otis Europe Paris 1969–; Otis Elevator Company: pres and chief operating offr NYC 1975–77, chief exec 1977–79, chm, pres and chief exec 1979–81, chm and chief exec 1981–86; dir: Société Imetal until 1981, Grands Magasins Jones until 1979, United Technologies Corporation until 1987 (sr exec vice pres 1981–86), Danone Swiss Re (US), Sotheby's 1988–94, N M Rothschild (London) 1987–94; chm: Rothschild Espana 1988–, Rothschild Italia 1988–, Supervisory Bd Rothschild & Associes Banque 1987–96; memb Volvo Int Advsy Bd 1989–90; memb Conseil Economique et Social 1963 and 1964; Chevalier Légion d'Honneur France; *Clubs* Nouveau Cercle (Paris), Brook (NYC), White's (London); *Style*— Monsieur Hubert Faure; ✉ Albany, Piccadilly, London W1 (☎ 0171 439 4039); La Bruyere, Auvillars, 14340 Cambremer, France (☎ 00 33 23 165 0980); NM Rothschild & Sons Ltd, New Court, St Swithin's Lane, London EC4 (☎ 0171 280 5000)

FAURE WALKER, Henry John (Harry); s of Lt-Col Henry William Faure Walker (d 1990), and Elizabeth Alice Catherine, *née* Fordham (d 1993); *b* 25 July 1940; *Educ* Eton, Trinity Coll Cambridge (MA); *m* 5 Nov 1966, Elizabeth, da of Maj William Boyd Kennedy Shaw, OBE, of Elford, Staffordshire; 2 s (William b 1970, Henry b 1972), 1 da (Alice b 1968); *Career* fin conslt; regnl dir Barclays Bank plc (Cambridge Region) until 1996; chm H W Faure Walker Farms Ltd 1969–; tstee Papworth Tst, memb Appeals Ctee Children's Soc, chm E Anglian NELC, memb Cncl Eastern Regn CBI 1989–95; *Recreations* field sports, garden; *Style*— Harry Faure Walker, Esq; ✉ Mill House, Stoke Doyle, Oundle PE8 5TG

FAURE WALKER, Rupert Roderick; er s of Maj Roderick Edward Faure Walker, and his 1 w, Hon Mary Chaloner, da of 2 Baron Gisborough; *b* 9 Sept 1947; *Educ* Eton, Univ of Bristol (BSc); *m* 1975, Sally Anne Vivienne, da of Lt Cdr Francis John Sidebotham, RN (d 1995); 1 s (Nicholas b 1978), 2 da (Julia b 1980, Joanna b 1984); *Career* dir Samuel Montagu 1982–; FCA; *Style*— Rupert Faure Walker, Esq; ✉ Woodhill, Danbury, Essex CM3 4AN; c/o Samuel Montagu & Co Ltd, 10 Lower Thames St, London EC3R 6AE (☎ 0171 336 9000)

FAUROUX, Roger J L; *b* 21 Nov 1926; *Educ* Ecole Normale Paris, ENA (Nat Sch of Admin); *m* 16 Oct 1953, Marie Le Roy, *née* Ladurie; 6 c; *Career* various posts in French Civil Serv 1956–60 (latterly advsr to Min of Educn); Saint-Gobain Pont-àMousson: joined Compagnie Pont-à-Mousson as dir of admin 1960, financial mangr 1964, exec chm 1980–86; head of French Nat Sch for Public Admin (ENA) 1986; French Govt: min of industry and foreign trade 1988–89, min of industry and nat & regnl devpt 1989–91; chm emeritus Saint-Gobain 1991, dir Saint-Gobain Corp USA 1992–; also non-exec dir: Commercial Union plc 1992–, Siemens AG 1993; *Style*— Roger Fauroux, Esq; ✉ Commercial Union plc, St Helens, 1 Undershaft, London EC3P 3DQ (☎ 0171 283 7500)

FAUSET, Ian David; s of George William Fauset (d 1972), and Margaret, *née* Davies (d 1993); *b* 8 Dec 1943; *Educ* Chester City GS, King Edward VI Sch Lichfield, Univ of London (BSc), Univ of Aberystwyth (dip in statistics); *m* 1972, Susan, da of Donald George Best; 2 s (Richard George b 1975, James David b 1977), 1 da (Kate Margaret b 1984); *Career* Dept of Chief Scientist (RAF) MOD 1968–78, head of Air Studies Defence Operational Analysis Orgn in Germany 1978–82, Fast Jet Aircraft and Helicopter Projects MOD PE 1982–87, Civilian Mgmnt MOD 1987–89, dir Tornado Aircraft and EH101 Helicopter Projects MOD PE 1989–91, asst under sec of state (Civilian Mgmnt) Personnel 1991–; non-exec dir GEC Avery Ltd 1991–94; CEng, FRAeS; *Recreations* bridge, cricket, tennis, squash; *Clubs* Athenaeum; *Style*— Ian Fauset, Esq; ✉ MOD, Northumberland House, Northumberland Avenue, London WC2N 5BP (☎ 0171 218 4639)

FAUX, (James) Christopher; s of Dr Francis Reginald Faux (d 1974), of Bolton, Lancs, and Alison Mungo, *née* Park (d 1981); *b* 11 March 1940; *Educ* Fettes, Univ of Liverpool (MRCS, LRCP), Univ of Glasgow (FRCS); *m* 29 July 1967, Patricia Anne Lyon, da of Hugh Lyon Denson (d 1991), of Chester; 1 s (James), 2 da (Rachel, Charlotte); *Career* Liverpool Scottish TA 1960–65; conslt orthopaedic surgn Preston Health Authy 1977–; memb: Charnley Low Friction Soc, Liverpool Orthopaedic Circle, Sir John Charnley Trust, Liverpool Med Inst; FBOA; *Recreations* boating, rugby; *Style*— Christopher Faux, Esq; ✉ The Old Rectory, Whittington, via Carnforth, Lancs LA6 2NU (☎ 01524 272570); 7 Moor Park Ave, Preston, Lancs PR1 6AS (☎ 01772 204710, fax 01772 558705)

FAWCETT, Howard Antony; s of Frederick Albert Fawcett (d 1988), of Oxford, and May, *née* Smith (d 1986); *b* 8 July 1941; *Educ* Oxford GS, Oxford Sch of Architecture; *m* 27 Dec 1975, Jane, da of Patrick Bernard Brittain (d 1994), of Chalfont St Peter, Bucks; 2 da (Claire Jane b 1977, Zoe Natalie b 1980); *Career* architect; sr ptnr Howard Fawcett & Ptnrs 1977–, chm Howard Fawcett PM Ltd (Architects, Engineers, Surveyors); chm: Gt Missenden Cncl 1984–86, Bucks Soc of Architects 1977–79; RIBA 1970; *Recreations* boats; *Clubs* Grimms Hill Lawn Tennis Assoc; *Style*— Howard Fawcett, Esq; ✉ Brackenrigg, Moat Lane, Prestwood, Great Missenden, Bucks (☎ 01494 863600); Howard Fawcett & Partners, Chartered Architects, Chandos House, Back St, Wendover, Bucks (☎ 01296 625995, fax 01296 622817)

FAWCUS, Maj-Gen Graham Ben; CB (1991); s of Col Geoffrey Arthur Ross Fawcus, OBE (d 1972), of 39 St Catherine's Rd, Hayling Island, Hants, and Helen Sybil Graham, *née* Stronach; *b* 17 Dec 1937; *Educ* Wycliffe Coll Stonehouse Glos, RMA Sandhurst, King's Coll Cambridge (BA, MA); *m* 23 July 1966, Diana Valerie, da of Dr Patrick John Spencer-Phillips (d 1995), of Levells Hall, Bildeston, Suffolk; 2 s (Jeremy b 1967, Caspian b 1969), 1 da (Abigail b 1972); *Career* cmmnd RE 1958, 2 Lt (later Lt) troop cmd 33 Ind Field Sqdn RE Cyprus 1959–60, Lt (later Capt) troop cmd 25 Corps Engr Regt BAOR 1963–65, GSO3 (Ops) HQ 19 Inf Bde Borneo and UK (Colchester) 1965–68, Adj 35 Corps Engr Regt 1968, Capt (later Maj) RMCS Shrivenham and Staff Coll Camberley 1969–70, Maj GS02 (W) MG0 Sec 3 MOD 1971–72, OC 39 Field Sqdn RE BAOR 1973–75, DAAG AG7 MOD 1975–76, Lt-Col GSO1 (DS) Staff Coll Camberley 1977–78, CO 25 Engr Regt BAOR 1978–81, Col Cabinet Office 1981, Brig Cmdt RSME 1982–83, ACOS HQ 1 (Br) Corps BAOR 1984–85, Maj-Gen Chief Jt Servs Liaison Orgn 1986–89, Maj-Gen COS Live Oak Shape 1989–91; Representative Col Cmdt RE 1994; chm Cncl Royal Engrs Offrs' Widows Soc 1992–, proprietor Graham Fawcus at Flowton Hall (furniture restoration co) 1992–; *Recreations* skiing, tennis, furniture restoring, bird watching, Scottish dancing; *Style*— Maj-Gen G B Fawcus, CB; ✉ Flowton Hall, Flowton, Ipswich, Suffolk IP8 4LH

FAWCUS, Sir (Robert) Peter; KBE (1964), CMG (1960); s of Arthur Francis Fawcus, OBE, of Claygate, Surrey; *b* 30 Sept 1915; *Educ* Charterhouse, Clare Coll Cambridge; *m* 1943, Isabel Constance, da of late Simon Ethelston; 1 s (Simon William b 1945), 1 da (Isabel Jane b 1949); *Career* served WWII, Lt Cdr RNVR; barr 1941; Overseas Civil Serv: admin Basutoland 1946–54, govt sec Bechuanaland Protectorate 1954–59, resident cmmr 1959–63, Queen's cmmr 1963–65, ret; *Recreations* gardening; *Clubs* Royal Cwlth Soc, Royal Over-Seas League; *Style*— Sir Peter Fawcus, KBE, CMG; ✉ Dochart House, Killin, Perthshire (☎ 01567 820225)

FAWCUS, Prof Robert; s of Percival William Henry Fawcus (d 1984), of Harrow, Middlesex, and Helena, *née* Smith (d 1979); *b* 12 Dec 1936; *Educ* Acton Co GS, Kingdon Ward Sch of Speech Therapy, Birkbeck Coll Univ of London (BSc), Guy's Hosp Med Sch; *m* 21 Jan 1961, Margaret Ailsa, da of Leslie Charles Bingham Penwill, CBE; 2 s, 2 da; *Career* Nat Serv RAF 1955–57; tutor Kingdon Ward Sch of Speech Therapy 1960–62, speech therapist Middx Hosp 1960–68, dir of studies Kingdon Ward Sch 1962–70, sr speech therapist Guy's Hosp 1968–80, course dir human communication Guy's Hosp Med Sch 1970–82, sr lectr Sch for the Study of Human Communication 1970–82, prof and head of dept CCS City Univ 1982–95, specialist speech and language therapist Weald of Kent Community Tst 1995–; chm Computer Aid for Disabled People; memb: Advsy Ctee on Telecommunications for Elderly and Disabled People, Biological Engrg Soc, Br Psychological Soc; tstee: Kingdon Ward Speech Therapy Tst, Int Soc for Augmentative and Alternative Communication UK (exec vice pres Int Soc); fell Royal Coll of Speech Therapists 1972 (licentiate 1960); *Books* contrib to: Language Disability in Children, Voice Disorders and Their Management, Assistive Communication Aids, Handbook of Dentistry, Vulnerability and Resilience; *Recreations* cooking and eating, music, theatre, gardening; *Clubs* Friends of Greenwich Theatre, Goudhurst Amateur Dramatic Society; *Style*— Prof Robert Fawcus; ✉ Department of Speech and Language Therapy, Kent and Sussex Hospital, Mount Ephraim, Tunbridge Wells, Kent TN4 8AT (☎ 01892 526111, fax 01892 528381)

FAWCUS, His Hon Judge; Simon James David; s of Gp Capt Ernest Augustus Fawcus (d 1966), and Joan Shaw (Jill), *née* Stokes; *b* 12 July 1938; *Educ* Aldenham, Trinity Hall Cambridge (BA, MA); *m* 12 March 1966, Joan Mary, da of late William John Oliphant; 1 s (Adrian John Oliphant b 10 April 1974), 4 da (Juliet Jane b 11 March 1970, Meriel Ann b 13 Dec 1972, Madeline Clare b 22 Sept 1975, Annabel Barbara (twin) b 22 Sept 1975); *Career* called to the Bar Gray's Inn 1961, in practice Northern Circuit 1962–85, recorder of the Crown Ct 1981–85, circuit judge (Northern Circuit) 1985–; pres Cncl of Circuit Judges 1996; *Recreations* tennis, rackets, golf, music, bridge; *Clubs* MCC, Manchester Tennis and Racquet; *Style*— His Hon Judge Fawcus; ✉ Courts of Justice, Crown Square, Manchester

FAY, Charles Stewart; s of His Hon Edgar Stewart Fay, *qv*, of London and Ashdon, Essex, and Kathleen Margaret, *née* Buell (d 1970); *b* 16 May 1931; *Educ* Bradfield, Lincoln Coll Oxford (BA, MA); *m* 1, 16 July 1955, (Ann) Patricia Fay, OBE (d 1979), da of Lawrence Moore (d 1973), of Harrogate, Yorks; 2 da (Caroline b 1957, Rachel b 1959 (*see* Michael Lingens)); m 2, 24 March 1984, Audrey Augusta, da of Percy Joseph Semon (d 1963); *Career* Nat Serv RE 1950–51; called to the Bar Inner Temple 1955; memb: Western Circuit 1955–, Plymouth Legal Aid Ctee 1958–68; pt/t lectr in town planning law Dept of Town Planning Univ of London 1965–67, inspr holding Okehampton By-Pass Inquiry 1979–80; memb: Local Govt and Planning Bar Assoc, Parly Bar Mess, Soc of Cons Lawyers; memb: Amersham RDC 1961–64, Chenies Parish Cncl 1986–91 (vice chm 1989–91), Chorleywood Parish Cncl 1994–; chm Chenies Estate Res Assoc 1987–91 and 1996–; *Books* Hill's Town and Country Planning Acts (jt ed, 5 edn 1967); *Recreations* maps, stamp collecting, genealogy; *Clubs* Royal Ocean Racing; *Style*— Charles Fay, Esq; ✉ Roughwood Cottage, Chalfont Lane, Chorleywood, Herts WD3 5PP (☎ 01923 285410); 2 Mitre Court Buildings, The Temple, London EC4Y 7BX (☎ 0171 583 1380, fax 0171 353 7772)

FAY, His Hon Edgar Stewart; s of Sir Sam Fay (d 1953), of Romsey, Hants, and Beatrice Charlotte Scamell (d 1957); *b* 8 Oct 1908; *Educ* Courtenay Lodge Sch, McGill Univ (BA), Pembroke Coll Cambridge (MA); *m* 1, Kathleen Margaret, eld da of Charles Hewitt Buell, of Montreal, Quebec, and Brockville, Ontario; 3 s (Charles, *qv*, Peter, William); m 2, Jenny Julie Marie Henriette (d 1990), yr da of Dr William Roosegaarde Bisschop (d 1945), of Lincoln's Inn London; 1 s (Francis); m 3, Eugenia, yr da of Piero Berganzoli, of Milan, and wid of P W Bishop, of London and Washington DC; *Career* called to the Bar Inner Temple 1932, QC 1956, master of the bench Inner Temple 1962, practised at common law and Parly Bars 1932–71; rec: Andover 1956–61, Bournemouth 1961–64, Plymouth 1964–71; dep chm Hants Quarter Sessions 1960–71, official ref of the Supreme Ct and circuit judge 1971–80; memb: Bar Cncl 1955–59 and 1966–70, Senate of Four Inns of Court 1970–72, Compton Ctee on NI 1971; chm Inquiry into: Munich Air Disaster 1960 and 1969, Crown Agents 1975–77; FCIArb 1981; *Books* Life of Mr Justice Swift (1939), Official Referee's Business (1983); *Style*— His Hon Edgar Fay; ✉ Knox End, Ashdon, Saffron Walden, Essex CB10 2HR (☎ 01799 584275)

FAYLE, Michael John; s of Donald William Fayle, of the Isle of Man, and Patricia Josephine, *née* Briton; *b* 22 Nov 1953; *Educ* Wade Deacon GS Widnes, Douglas HS for Boys; *m* 12 Sept 1975, Vivien, da of late Clyde John Alexander Savage; 1 s (Thomas Edward b 1993); *Career* articled clerk to J G Fargher of B Sugden & Co Chartered Accts IOM 1972–77, qualified ACA 1977; ptnr: J G Fargher & Co 1982–86, KPMG 1986–; chm IOM Soc of CAs 1991; FCA 1983 (ACA 1977); *Recreations* fencing, collecting; *Style*— Michael J Fayle, Esq; ✉ Corleaa, Ballanard Road, Douglas, Isle of Man (☎ 01624 675725); KPMG, Heritage Court, 41 Athol Street, Douglas, Isle of Man (☎ 01624 681000, fax 01624 681097)

FAYRER, Sir John Lang Macpherson; 4 Bt (UK 1896), of Devonshire Street, St Marylebone, Co London; s of Lt-Cdr Sir Joseph Herbert Spens Fayrer, 3 Bt, DSC, RNVR (d 1976), and Helen Diana Scott, *née* Lang (d 1961); *b* 18 Oct 1944; *Educ* Edinburgh Acad, Univ of Strathclyde; *Heir* none; *Career* memb HCIMA; chief catering officer 1973–77, hotel night mangr 1977–80, clerical offr Univ of Edinburgh 1980–89, insurance broker 1989–90, research offr Heriot-Watt Univ 1991–; *Recreations* reading, walking, riding; *Style*— Sir John Fayrer, Bt; ✉ Overhailes, Haddington, E Lothian (☎ 0162 086 0444); 9 Westfield St, Edinburgh 11; Moray House College, Cramond Campus, Cramond Road North, Edinburgh EH4 7JD (☎ 0131 312 6001)

FAZEY, Ian Hamilton; OBE (1990); s of Albert Ronald Fazey (d 1959), of Birmingham, and Alice, *née* Livingston (d 1987); *b* 9 Aug 1942; *Educ* King's Norton GS Birmingham, Univ of Aston (BSc); *m* 1966, Dr Cindy Sylvia Joyce Fazey, da of Horace Joseph Brookes; *Career* asst engr W Midlands Gas Bd 1964–65; The Birmingham Post 1965–69, Liverpool Daily Post 1969–71, dep ed Liverpool Echo 1972–74, md Wirral Newspapers 1974–76, gen mangr Liverpool Daily Post & Echo 1977–80, freelance journalist 1980–, retained contrib Financial Times 1981–86, northern corr Financial Times 1986–; dir: Saxon Forlags Stockholm 1985–87 (non-exec), Data TV 1988–93; Glaxo award (sci writing) 1967, commended Provincial Journalist of the Year 1967; FIMgt 1977; *Books* Waterloo FC, 1882–1982, The How to of Small Business (1985), The Pathfinder: The Origins of the Enterprise Agency in Britain (1987); *Recreations* rugby union, visiting museums and galleries, gardening, cooking and eating, opera, books, mastering the 5-string banjo and fender Stratocaster; *Clubs* Waterloo Football (Rugby Union), British Field Sports Soc, National Trust; *Style*— Ian Hamilton Fazey, Esq, OBE; ✉ Financial Times, Alexandra Buildings, Queen St, Manchester M2 5LF (☎ 0161 834 9381, fax 0161 832 9248)

FEARN, Alan d'Arcy; s of Charles Henry Fearn, MM (d 1982), and Gladys Lily, *née* d'Arcy Jones (d 1983); bro of (Charles) Barry d'Arcy Fearn, *qv*; *b* 24 July 1924; *Educ* Bury GS, Terra Nova Sch Southport, Shrewsbury, Guy's Hosp Dental Sch; *m* 1, 1947 (m dis 1966), Kathleen, da of Frank Humphries (d 1955); 2 da (Gail b 1947, Cheryl b 1950); m 2, 19 Aug 1966, Doreen Barbara, da of Walter Milne (d 1989), of Rochdale;

Career RAF Air Gunner Sgt 1942–46; dental surgn, elected memb Gen Dental Cncl 1962–96 (longest serving elected memb, sr treas 1993–96); pres Gen Dental Practitioners' Assoc 1969, pres Br Dental Assoc 1986–87; Parly candidate (C): Ashton under Lyne 1970, Accrington 1974, Middleton & Prestwich 1974, Ashton under Lyne 1979, Rochdale 1983; generalist Tameside and Glossop AHA 1976–85, dep ldr Tameside MBC 1978–79; chm of tstees NGRC Greyhound Tst 1988–94, sr steward Nat Greyhound Racing Club 1988–94 (steward 1974–94); *Recreations* greyhound racing, gardening, theatre; *Clubs* Naval and Military, The Royal Soc of Medicine; *Style*— Alan Fearn, Esq; ✉ Tall Trees, Bentmeadows, Rochdale OL12 6LF (☎ 01706 45276)

FEARN, (Charles) Barry d'Arcy; TD (1993); s of Charles Henry Fearn (d 1982), and Gladys Lily, *née* d'Arcy Jones (d 1983); bro of Alan d'Arcy Fearn, *qv*; *b* 4 March 1934; *Educ* Shrewsbury, Gonville and Caius Coll Cambridge (MA, MB BChir), St Mary's Hosp Univ of London; *m* 21 April 1962, Gay Barbara Ann, da of Capt Edward Smythe (d 1940); 1 s (Giles b 1964), 3 da (Alexandra b 1967, Victoria b 1971, Jocasta b 1973); *Career* Nat Serv Capt RAMC, MO Royal Irish Fusiliers 1960, Capt RAMC (V) TAVR Regtl Surgn Kent and Co of London Yeo 1966, Maj RAMC (V) TA Regtl MO 71 YEO Signal Regt 1981; sr lectr and hon conslt orthopaedic surgn Khartoum Univ of Sudan 1969–70, sr registrar Nuffield Orthopaedic Centre Oxford 1970–72; conslt orthopaedic surgn 1972–: Royal Sussex Co Hosp Brighton, Princess Royal Hosp Haywards Heath, Sussex Nuffield Hosp, Ashdown Hosp; chm Higher Trg Ctee in Orthopaedic Surgery SE Thames Region 1990–95, regnl advsr in orthopaedics Royal Coll of Surgns; memb: Hove Civic Soc, Haywards Heath Amenity Soc; Freeman City of London, Liveryman Worshipful Soc of Apothecaries; exec tstee Sprint Fund; fell Br Orthopaedic Assoc; memb: Société Internationale de Chirurgie Ortopaedique et Traumatologie 1982–93, Regency Soc (Brighton), Trollope Soc; memb RSM, FRCS 1967, FRCSEd 1967; *Recreations* rowing coaching, opera, the theatre, TA, racing; *Clubs* Leander, RSM; *Style*— Barry Fearn, Esq, TD; ✉ Colwell House, Haywards Heath, West Sussex RH17 7TB

FEARN, Sir (Patrick) Robin; KCMG (1990, CMG 1983); s of Albert Cyprian Fearn (d 1968), and Hilary, *née* Harrison (d 1994); *Educ* Ratcliffe Coll Leicestershire, Univ Coll Oxford (MA); *m* 1961, Sorrel Mary, da of Benjamin Raymond Thomas; 3 s (Thomas Daniel b 16 Sept 1962, Matthew Robin b 23 Oct 1964, Richard Benjamin b 18 Oct 1967), 1 da (Alix Leah b 27 Aug 1975); *Career* overseas mktg Dunlop Rubber Co 1957–60, chemical export sales ICI 1960–61; HM Dip Serv: joined FCO 1961, second sec Caracas 1962–64, FCO 1964–66, first sec Budapest 1966–68, FCO 1968–72, head of Chancery Vientiane 1972–75, dep head of Sci and Technol Dept FCO 1975–76, cnsllr, head of Chancery and consul-gen Islamabad 1976–79, head of S American Dept FCO 1979–82, head of Falkland Islands Dept 1982, RCDS 1983, ambass Havana 1984–86, asst under-sec of state (Americas) FCO 1986–89, ambass Madrid 1989–94, ret; dir Oxford Univ Foreign Serv Prog 1995–, visiting fell UC Oxford 1995–; *Recreations* tennis, reading, walking, family life; *Clubs* United Oxford and Cambridge Univ; *Style*— Sir Robin Fearn, KCMG; ✉ c/o Barclay's Bank, 9 Portman Square, London W1A 3AL

FEARNLEY, Ian James; s of Dr Charles Fearnley, of Torrivieja, Spain, and Grace Muriel, *née* Askham; *b* 4 April 1959; *Educ* Stockport GS, Stockport Coll of Technol, Field Park Coll (HND); *Career* Media Solutions Ltd 1983–88, media dir Clark & Taylor (formerly Marketplace Communications) 1988–; memb Bd of Govrs Stockport Coll of Technol 1980; memb Inst of Sales Promotion 1990; MInstD 1993; *Recreations* badminton, football, cricket, softball; *Style*— Ian Fearnley, Esq; ✉ Clark & Taylor, 7 Holyrood St, London SE1 2EL (☎ 0171 717 7000, fax 0171 357 0839)

FEARNLEY, Stella Marie; da of Sydney Yates (d 1993), and Mary, *née* Prime, of Barrow on Soar, Leics; *b* 22 Jan 1946; *Educ* Astley GS, Univ of Leeds (BA); *m* 15 Sept 1973, Paul Douglas Fearnley, s of Raymond Fairfax Fearnley (d 1986); 2 da (Helen Mary b 31 Oct 1977, Rachel Florence b 12 Sept 1981); *Career* VSO 1968–69; Careers Res and Advsy Centre 1969–70; articled clerk Price Waterhouse 1970–73, Grant Thornton 1973–86 (audit sr rising to tech mangr), sr lectr Bournemouth Univ 1986–90 (asst to dir 1988–89), Grant Thornton lectr in accounting Univ of Southampton 1990–94, princ lectr in accounting Univ of Portsmouth 1994–; memb Nat Cncl ICAEW; past pres Southern Soc of Chartered Accountants; FCA 1978, FRSA 1993; *Recreations* music, swimming, fell walking; *Style* Mrs Stella Fearnley; ✉ Department of Accounting and Management Science, University of Portsmouth Business School, Locksway Road, Southsea, Hants PO4 8JF (☎ 01705 876543)

FEARON, Daniel; s of Henry Bridges Fearon (d 1995), of Maidenhead, Berks, and Alethea, *née* McKenna (d 1994); *b* 14 Oct 1944; *Educ* Canford; *m* 20 Feb 1971, Karen Dawn, da of Clifford M Wark, of Toronto, Canada; 1 s (James Adrian b 1978), 1 da (Letitia Jane b 1981); *Career* Sotheby & Co 1963–69, Parke Bernet NY 1969–70, Spink & Son 1970–86; md Glendining & Co 1986–93, head of coins and medals W & F C Bonham & Sons 1993–; memb Br Numismatic Soc 1960 (memb Cncl 1986); memb Worshipful Co of Drapers 1970; FRNS 1968; *Books* Catalogue of British Commemorative Medals (1984), Victorian Souvenir Medals (1986); *Style*— Daniel Fearon, Esq; ✉ Bonhams, Montpelier Street, Knightsbridge, London SW7 1HH (☎ 0171 393 3900, fax 0171 393 3905)

FEARON, Prof Douglas Thomas; s of Henry Dana Fearon (d 1987), and Frances Hudson, *née* Eubanks (d 1995); *b* 16 Oct 1942; *Educ* Williams Coll Williamstown Massachusetts (BA), Johns Hopkins Univ Sch of Med Baltimore Maryland (MD); *m* 26 May 1977, Clare MacIntyre, da of Burrows J Wheless; 1 da (Elizabeth MacIntyre b 5 Feb 1982), 1 s (Thomas Henry b 22 Oct 1984); *Career* residency (internal med) Johns Hopkins Hosp Baltimore 1968–70, Maj US Army Med Corps 1970–72 (Bronze Star); Harvard Med Sch Boston: research fell in med 1972–75, instr in med 1975–76, asst prof of med 1976–79, assoc prof of med 1979–84, prof of med 1984–87; prof of med Johns Hopkins Univ and dir Grad Immunology Prog 1987–93, Wellcome Tst research prof of med Univ of Cambridge Sch of Clinical Med and princ research fell Wellcome Tst 1993–; hon conslt in med Addenbrooke's Hosp Cambridge 1993–; Helen Hay Whitney Fndn research fellowship 1974–77, Merit Award Nat Insts of Health 1991, Lee C Howley Sr Prize for Arthritis Research Arthritis Fndn 1991; former memb Research Ctee: Arthritis Fndn, American Heart Fndn; currently memb Research Sub-ctee Arthritis and Rheumatism Cncl; author of numerous pubns in learned jls; memb Editorial Bd: Clinical and Experimental Immunology, Immunity, Science, Jl of Experimental Med; memb Exec Ctee Euro Jl of Immunology; memb: American Soc for Clinical Investigation 1979, Assoc of American Physicians 1984, Assoc of Physicians of GB and I 1994; FRCP 1994; *Recreations* tennis, golf; *Clubs* Country (Brookline, Massachusetts); *Style*— Prof Douglas Fearon; ✉ Wellcome Trust Immunology Unit, University of Cambridge School of Clinical Medicine, Hills Road, Cambridge CB2 2SP (☎ 01223 330528, fax 01223 336815, e-mail dtf 1000 @ cus.cam.ac.uk)

FEATES, Prof Francis Stanley (Frank); CB (1991); s of Stanley James Feates, and Dorothy Jenny, *née* Orford (d 1986); *b* 21 Feb 1932; *Educ* Poole GS Dorset, John Ruskin Sch Croydon, Birkbeck Coll London (BSc, PhD); *m* Gwenda Grace, da of Henry Victor Goodchild (d 1963); 1 s (Nigel Graham b 1959), 3 da (Lynda Jacqueline b 1958, Karen Frances b 1964, Ann Gwenda b 1967); *Career* chemist Wellcome Research Fndn Kent 1949–52, res scientist 1952–56 (Chester Beatty Res Inst, University of London), UK Atomic Energy Authy Oxford 1956–65; visiting scientist Argonne Nat Lab Univ of Chicago 1965–67; AERE Harwell 1967–78: head Hazardous Materials Serv, Nat Chem Emergency Centre and Environmental Safety Gp; chief radio chem inspr Dept of Environment 1978–87, dir HM Inspectorate of Pollution 1989–91 (chief inspr 1987–90), prof of environmental engrg UMIST 1991–95; dir Sir Alexander Gibb & Partners 1991–93; non-exec dir: Siemens Plessey Controls 1991–92, Grundon Waste Management 1991–92; CChem 1974, CEng 1991, FRIC 1972, FIChemE 1991; *Books* Handbook of Hazardous Material Spills (1982), Integrated Pollution Management (1994); *Recreations* cycling, walking, travelling; *Style*— Prof Frank Feates, CB; ✉ The Kilns, Beggarsbush Hill, Benson, Wallingford, Oxon OX10 6PL (☎ 01491 839276)

FEATHER, Prof John Pliny; s of Harold Renton Feather (d 1968), and Ethel May, *née* Barrett (d 1966); *b* 20 Dec 1947; *Educ* Heath Sch Halifax, Queen's Coll Oxford (Hastings scholar, BLitt, MA), Univ of Cambridge (MA), Univ of Loughborough (PhD); *m* 10 July 1971, Sarah, da of Rev Arthur Winnington Rees (d 1991), of Cardiff; *Career* ed Scolar Press 1970–71, asst librarian Bodleian Library Oxford 1972–79, fell Darwin Coll Cambridge 1977–78, Munby fell in bibliography Univ of Cambridge 1977–78; Univ of Loughborough: lectr 1979–84, sr lectr 1984–87, prof of library and info studies 1987–, head of Dept of Info and Library Studies 1989–94, dean of educn and humanities 1994–96, pro-vice-chllr 1996–; memb numerous nat and int professional ctees; *Books* English Book Prospectuses - An Illustrated History (1984), The Provincial Book Trade in Eighteenth-Century England (1985), A Dictionary of Book History (1986), A History of British Publishing (1988), Preservation and the Management of Library Collections (1991), The Information Society (1994), Publishing, Piracy and Politics (1994); *Recreations* cookery, photography; *Clubs* Athenaeum; *Style*— Prof John Feather; ✉ Department of Information and Library Studies, Loughborough University, Leics LE11 3TU (☎ 01509 223058, fax 01509 223053)

FEATHERBY, William Alan; s of Joseph Alan Featherby, of Cranleigh, Surrey, and Patricia Annie, *née* Davies; *b* 16 May 1956; *Educ* Haileybury, Trinity Coll Oxford (MA); *m* 12 April 1980, Clare Francis, da of Ian Richard Posgate, of Henley-on-Thames, Oxon; 5 s (Francis Alan b 1982, George Ian b 1986, John William b 1991, St John James Milton b 1993, William David b 1995), 5 da (Victoria Clare b 1985, Elizabeth Anne b 1988, Margaret Lucy b 1989, Eleanor Mary b 1990, Sarah Jane Webster b 1992); *Career* called to the Bar Middle Temple 1978; currently in private practice SE circuit; *Publication* A Yorkshire Furrow (1993); *Recreations* reading, writing, gardening, children; *Clubs* Carlton, Royal Motor Yacht; *Style*— William Featherby, Esq; ✉ Mansel House, 13 Mansel Road, Wimbledon, London SW19 4AA; 12 King's Bench Walk, Temple, London EC4Y 7EL (☎ 0171 583 0811, fax 0171 583 7228)

FEAVER, William Andrew; s of Douglas Russell Feaver, and Katherine Muriel Rose, *née* Stubbs (d 1987); *b* 1 Dec 1942; *Educ* St Albans Sch, Nottingham HS, Keble Coll Oxford; *m* 1, 1964–85, Anne Victoria Turton; m 2, 1985, Andrea Gillian Lester Rose; 6 c (Jane b 14 Oct 1964, Emily b 27 April 1966, Jessica b 20 Aug 1969, Silas b 1 Oct 1970, Dorothy b 11 May 1985, Alice b 21 Oct 1986); *Career* South Stanley Boys' Modern Sch Co Durham 1964–65, Royal GS Newcastle upon Tyne 1965–71, Univ of Newcastle (James Knott fell) 1971–73; art critic: Newcastle Jl 1968–73, London Magazine 1970–74, Art International 1970–74, Listener 1971–75, Sunday Times Magazine 1972–75, Vogue 1972–95, Financial Times 1974–75, Art News 1974–, The Observer 1975–, various other pubns, radio and TV; exhibition organiser; work incl: George Cruikshank (V&A) 1974, Thirties (Hayward Gallery 1979), Peter Moores Liverpool exhibitions 1984 and 1986; visiting prof Nottingham Trent Univ 1994–; memb: Art Panel Arts Cncl 1974–78, Art Ctee Nat Gallery of Wales 1991–; Critic of the Year Nat Press awards 1983 (commended 1986); *Books* The Art of John Martin (1975), Masters of Caricature (1980), Pitman Painters (1988); *Recreations* painting; *Style*— William Feaver, Esq; ✉ The Observer, 119 Farringdon Road, London EC1R 3ER (☎ 0171 278 2332); Rogers Coleridge and White (Agent)

FEDDEN, (Adye) Mary; da of Harry Vincent Fedden (d 1938), of Bristol, and late Ida Margaret, *née* Prichard; *b* 14 Aug 1915; *Educ* Badminton Sch Bristol, Slade Sch of Art (scholar); *m* 1951, Julian Otto Trevelyan (d 1988), s of Robert Trevelyan; *Career* artist; tutor: RCA 1956–64, Sir Yehudi Menuhin Sch 1964–74; *Solo Exhibitions* from 1948: Redfern Gallery London, Hamet Gallery London, New Grafton Gallery London, Christopher Hull Gallery London, Royal W of England Acad Bristol, Beaux Arts Gallery London and Bath, Bohun Gallery Henley and other provincial galleries; murals incl Charing Cross Hospital and Canberra (P&O liner); paintings in collections of HM The Queen, HRH Crown Prince Hassan of Jordan, Tate Gallery; pres Royal West of England Acad 1983–88; Hon DLitt Bath 1996; RA 1992; *Recreations* reading, cycling; *Style*— Ms Mary Fedden, RA; ✉ Durham Wharf, Hammersmith Terrace, London W6 9TS (☎ 0181 748 2749)

FEDER, Ami; s of Joseph Feder (d 1985), and Nicha, *née* Dornstein; *b* 17 Feb 1937; *Educ* Hebrew Univ of Jerusalem (Tel-Aviv Branch (LLB)); *m* 26 March 1970, Frances Annabel, da of late Michael August; 1 s (Ilan b 1974), 1 da (Shelley b 1972); *Career* Israeli Army 1956–58; called to the Bar Inner Temple 1965, currently in practice SE Circuit and Israeli Bar, advocate practising at the Israeli Bar; memb: Hon Soc of Inner Temple, Common Law and Commercial Bar Assoc, Criminal Bar Assoc, Bar European Gp; *Recreations* sport, music, theatre; *Style*— Ami Feder, Esq; ✉ 118 King Henry's Rd, London NW3 3SN (☎ 0171 586 4339); Chambers: The Chambers of Mr Ami Feder, Lamb Building, Temple, London EC4Y 7AS (☎ 0171 797 7788, fax 0171 353 0535); Office: 9 Yitzhak Rabin Square, Tel-Aviv 64163 (☎ 00 972 3 5243381, fax 00 972 3 5243387)

FEDORCIO, Richard Edward (Dick); s of Jan Adam Fedorcio, of East Tilbury, Essex, and Winifred Elsie, *née* Ambler; *b* 25 March 1953; *Educ* Campion GS Hornchurch Essex, London Coll of Printing; *m* June 1982, Helen Marie, da of William Stokoe (d 1987); 2 s (Alex b 11 June 1987, Leo b 3 May 1990), 1 da (Sarah b 31 July 1984); *Career* PR offr GLC 1974–83, co info offr W Sussex CC 1983–86, dir of corp communication Kent CC 1986–94, dir of communication Electricity Assoc 1994–; Inst of PR: chm Local Govt Gp 1985–87, Cncl memb on Educn Ctee 1988, chm Professional Practices Ctee 1989–90, pres 1992; tstee PR Educn Tst 1996–; MCB 1986, FIPR 1990 (MIPR 1984); *Recreations* soccer, cricket, sailing, photography; *Style*— Dick Fedorcio, Esq; ✉ Director of Communication, Electricity Association, 30 Millbank, London SW1P 4RD (☎ 0171 963 5735, fax 0171 963 5880)

FEELY, Terence John; s of Edward John Feely (d 1961), of Liverpool, and Mary Maude, *née* Glancy; *b* 20 July 1935; *Educ* St Francis Xavier Jesuit Coll Woolton Lancs, Univ of Liverpool (BA); *m* 15 Aug 1959, Elizabeth, da of Alphonsus William Adams (d 1963), of Southampton; *Career* screenwriter; Euro story chief: Paramount Films 1968–70, Warner Bros 1970–72; has written theatre plays, films, television and books; memb: Cncl of PDSA, Cncl of The Writers' Guild, Ctee 1900 Club; *Plays* Shout For Life (1963), Don't Let Summer Come (1965), Adam's Apple (1967), Who Killed Santa Claus? (1972), Murder in Mind (1982), The Team (1985); *Television* creator of: Callan (with James Mitchell), Arthur of The Britons (Writers' Guild Award), Affairs of The Heart (New York Literary Circle Award), Number Ten, The Gentle Touch, Cats' Eyes, Eureka (1989); *Films* Hazard of Hearts, The Lady and the Highwayman, A Ghost in Monte Carlo, Dangerous Love 1990, Cloche de Nuit 1992, Class Reunion 1992; *Books* Rich Little Poor Girl (1981), Limelight (1984), Number 10 (1982); *Recreations* travel, shooting, boxing (spectator), Shakespearian research; *Clubs* Garrick, Carlton; *Style*— Terence Feely, Esq; ✉ 55 Drayton Gardens, South Kensington, London SW10 9RU

FEESEY, Air Vice-Marshal John David Leonard; AFC (1977); *b* 11 Oct 1942; *Educ* Oldershaw GS; *m* 1968, Glen; 2 s (Sean and Colin); *Career* aircrew offr cadet 1961, cmmnd RAF 1962, flying trg 1962, Central Flying Sch 1963, flying instr (Jet Provosts)

Church Fenton 1964–66, pilot (Hunters and Harriers) West Raynham and Wittering then Flt Cdr and instr Harrier Operational Conversion Unit Wittering 1966–74, Wing Standards Offr Wildenrath then Gutersloh Germany 1974–78, RAF Staff Coll 1978, RAF Staff Offr MOD (Army Dept) 1979–80, student USAF Air War Coll Maxwell Alabama USA 1980–81, Chief Fighter Trg Div USAF Tactical Air Cmd HQ Langley Va 1981–83, OC No 1 (Harrier) Sqdn Wittering 1983–86, completed Air Warfare Course Cranwell 1986, Gp Capt 1986, station cdr Wittering 1986–89, Higher Cmmd and Staff Course Camberley 1989, exec offr to Cdr Allied Air Forces Central Europe 1989–91, dir airspace policy National Air Traffic Servs (NATS) 1991–93, Air Vice-Marshal 1993, DG policy and plans NATS 1993–96, Dep Cdr Interim Combined Air Ops Centre 4 (ICAOC 4) Germany 1996–; MRAeS 1987; *Recreations* maintaining a country cottage in Cornwall, hill walking, gardening, sailing, fishing and running; *Style—* Air Vice-Marshal John Feesey, AFC; ✉ Deputy Commander, ICAOC 4, Box 2005, BFPO 105

FEESEY, Mervyn Thomas; s of William Feesey (d 1926), of Bourne End, Bucks, and Grace Miriam, *née* Gilmore (d 1988); *b* 8 March 1926; *Educ* Queen Elizabeth Sch, Crediton and Barnstaple GS; *m* 1 Dec 1947, Doreen Esme, da of Edward James Norman (d 1989); 3 s (David Charles b 18 March 1949, John Graeme b 22 Nov 1954, James Andrew b 4 Dec 1955), 3 da (Susan Elizabeth b 22 Dec 1950, Jane Lavinia b 1 July 1953, Elizabeth Anne b 18 June 1958); *Career* RAF 1942–47; architect; Charles Ware & Sons 1942 and 1947–54; Oliver & Dyer Architects and Surveyors (later Dyer Feesey Wickham): joined 1954, ptnr 1964, princ 1974; memb Ctee: Exeter Branch RIBA, NCCPG Nat Plants Collection and Devon Br Nat Cncl Conservation of Plants and Gardens, Exeter Br Alpine Garden Soc, Devon Gdns Tst, Men of Trees; organiser Nat Gdns Scheme Devon, chm Barnstaple Conservation Advsy Ctee, memb Assoc Ancient Monuments Soc; RIBA, FIArb; *Books* Ornamental Grasses and Bamboos - Wisley Handbook (1983); *Recreations* horticulture, cricket, badminton, surfing; *Style—* Mervyn Feesey; ✉ Woodside, Higher Raleigh Rd, Barnstaple, N Devon EX31 4JA (☎ 01271 43095)

FEGGETTER, Jeremy George Weightman; TD (1986), QHS (1992); s of George Y Feggetter, of Newcastle upon Tyne, and Doris, *née* Weightman; *b* 5 May 1943; *Educ* Harrow, Univ of Newcastle upon Tyne (MB BS); *Career* sr res assoc Dept of Surgery Univ of Newcastle upon Tyne 1972–74, sr urological registrar Newcastle Gen Hosp 1975–76, sr surgical registrar Royal Victoria Infirmary Newcastle upon Tyne 1976–78 (house offr 1966–67, demonstrator in anatomy 1967–68, SHO 1968–69, registrar 1969–72), RSO St Paul's Hosp London 1978–79, conslt urologist Freeman Hosp and Wansbeck Hosp 1979–; FRCS, OStJ 1990; *Recreations* aviation, travel; *Clubs* RSM, Army and Navy; *Style—* Jeremy Feggetter, Esq; ✉ Department of Urology, Wansbeck General Hospital, Ashington, Northumberland NE63 (☎ 01670 529310)

FEHR, Basil Henry Frank; CBE (1979); s of Frank Emil Fehr, CBE (d 1948), and Jane Poulter (d 1961); *b* 11 July 1912; *Educ* Rugby, Ecole de Commerce Neuchatel Switzerland; *m* 1, 1936 (m dis 1951), Jane Marner, *née* Tallent; 2 s (Richard, James), 1 da (Ann); m 2, 1951 (m dis 1974), Greta Constance, *née* Bremner; 1 da (Olinda); m 3, 1974, Anne Norma, *née* Cadman; 1 da (Amanda); *Career* served WWII HAC, later instr Gunnery Sch of Anti-Aircraft RA, ret Maj; joined family firm Frank Fehr & Co 1934 (ptnr 1936), governing dir then chm Frank Fehr & Co Ltd London 1948–92 (now life pres), pres then chm Fehr Bros (Manufactures) Inc (later Fehr Bros Inc) NY 1949–91, currently chm Fehr Bros Industries Inc; chm: Cocoa Assoc of London 1952, London Commodity Exchange 1954, London Oil and Tallow Trades Assoc 1955, Copra Assoc London 1957, Inc Oilseed Assoc 1958, United Associates Ltd 1959, Colyer Fehr Pty Ltd Sydney 1984; elected to Baltic Exchange 1936, dir Baltic Mercantile and Shipping Exchange 1963–69 and 1970– (vice chm 1973–75, chm 1975–77, hon memb 1991); landowner; jurat of liberty of Romney Marsh 1979; Liveryman Worshipful Co of Horners; *Recreations* sports, farming; *Clubs* City Livery, MCC, RAC, West Kent CC, Littlestone Golf; *Style—* Basil H F Fehr, Esq, CBE; ✉ Slodden Farm, Dymchurch, Romney Marsh, Kent (☎ 01303 872241, 01303 872268, fax 01303 874669)

FEILDEN, Sir Bernard Melchior; kt (1985), CBE (1976, OBE 1969); s of Maj Robert Humphrey Feilden, MC, RHA (d 1925), of BC, Canada, and Olive, *née* Binyon (d 1971); *b* 11 Sept 1919; *Educ* Bedford Sch, Architectural Assoc (AADipl); *m* 1949, Ruth Mildred (d 1994), da of Robert John Bainbridge, of Gt Plumstead, Norfolk; 2 s (Henry, Francis), 2 da (Harriet, Mary); m 1995, Christina Matilda Beatrice Murdoch, *née* Tufnell; *Career* architect to Norwich Cathedral 1962–77; surveyor to: York Minster 1965–77, St Paul's Cathedral 1969–77; conslt architect to UEA 1968–77, dir ICCROM 1977–81 (emeritus 1983); Liveryman Worshipful Co of Carpenters; Aga Khan Award for Architecture 1986, ICOMOS/Gazzola Prize 1993; *Books* The Wonder of York Minster (1976), Introduction to Conservation (1979), Conservation of Historic Buildings (1982), Between Two Earthquakes (1987), Guidelines for Conservation: a Technical Manual (India, 1989), Guidelines for Management of World Cultural Heritage Sites (ICCROM, 1993); *Recreations* sketching, chess, sailing; *Clubs* Norfolk (Norwich); *Style—* Sir Bernard Feilden, CBE; ✉ Stiffkey Old Hall, Wells next the Sea, Norfolk NR23 1QJ (☎ and fax 01328 830585)

FEILDEN, Henry Rudyard; s and h of Sir Henry Wemyss Feilden, 6 Bt, and Ethel May, *née* Atkinson; *b* 26 Sept 1951; *Educ* Kent Coll Canterbury, Univ of Bristol (BVSc); *m* 1982, Anne, da of William Frank Bonner Shepperd (d 1985); 1 s (William Henry b 5 April 1983); *Career* veterinary surgn in small animal and equine practice 1975–84 and 1996–; Tuckett Gray and Partners Aylesbury Bucks 1976–78, Fraser and Smith Binfield Berks 1978–83, L A Gould Rossendale Lancs 1983–84, Riverside Veterinary Surgery Bishopstoke Eastleigh Hants 1996–; veterinary advsr Solvay-Duphar Veterinary Southampton 1984–96; MRCVS; memb: BVA, BSAVA, BEVA; *Recreations* DIY, natural history, military history, French travel, fine wine, antiques, good company; *Clubs* Old Canterburians; *Style—* Henry Feilden, Esq; ✉ 16 Surrey Close, West Totton, Southampton, Hants SO40 2QQ (☎ 01703 666050); Riverside Veterinary Surgery, Unit 2, Scotter Road, Bishopstoke, Eastleigh, Hants SO50 6AJ (☎ 01703 620607)

FEILDEN, Sir Henry Wemyss; 6 Bt (UK 1846), of Feniscowles, Lancashire; eld s of Col Wemyss Feilden, CMG (3 s of Sir William Feilden, 3 Bt, JP); suc 1 cous, Sir William Morton Buller Feilden, 5 Bt, MC, 1976; *b* 1 Dec 1916; *Educ* Canford Sch, King's Coll London; *m* 25 Aug 1943, Ethel May, da of late John Atkinson, of Annfield Plain, Co Durham; 1 s (Henry Rudyard b 26 Sept 1951), 2 da (Jennifer May (Mrs Graham Donald) b 1944, Anne Margaret (Mrs William Stokoe) b 1947); *Heir* s, Henry Rudyard Feilden, *qv*; *Career* served in RE WWII; civil servant (ret); memb Kipling Soc; *Recreations* gardening, watching cricket; *Clubs* MCC; *Style—* Sir Henry Feilden, Bt; ✉ Little Dene, Heathfield Rd, Burwash, Etchingham, E Sussex TN19 7HN (☎ 01435 882205)

FEILDEN, Dr (Geoffrey Bertram) Robert; CBE (1966); s of Maj Robert Humphrey Feilden, MC, RHA (d 1925), of Canada, and Olive, *née* Binyon (d 1971); *b* 20 Feb 1917; *Educ* Bedford Sch, King's Coll Cambridge (BA, MA); *m* 1, 1945, Elizabeth Ann, da of Rev J P Gorton (d 1952); 1 s (Richard b 1950), 2 da (Jane b 1948, Fiona b 1953); m 2, 1972, Elizabeth Diana, da of P C Lloyd (d 1961); *Career* chartered mechanical engr Lever Bros and Unilever Ltd 1939–40, Power Jets Ltd 1940–46; Ruston & Hornsby Ltd 1946–59: chief engr 1950, engrg dir 1954; md Hawker Siddeley Brush Turbines and dir Hawker Siddeley Industries 1959–61, gp technical dir (and dir of princ operating cos) Davy Ashmore Ltd 1961–68, dir gen Br Standards Inst 1970–81 (dep dir gen 1968–70), non-exec dir Avery's Ltd 1974–79, sr ptnr Feilden Associates 1981–, non-exec dir Plint & Ptnrs Ltd 1982–; Hon DTech Loughborough Univ 1970, Hon DSc Queen's Univ Belfast 1971; jt winner MacRobert Award for Engineering Innovation 1983; FRS 1959, FEng 1976 (fndr fell), Sr FRCA 1986; *Recreations* sailing, skiing, photography; *Clubs* Athenaeum; *Style—* Dr Robert Feilden, CBE, FEng, FRS; ✉ Feilden Associates, Verlands, Painswick, Glos GL6 6XP (☎ 01452 812112, fax 01452 812912)

FEINBERG, Peter Eric; QC (1992); s of Leon Feinberg (d 1976), of Bradford, and May, *née* Frais (d 1969); *b* 26 Oct 1949; *Educ* Bradford GS, UCL (LLB); *m* 13 Aug 1988, Tina, da of James Flannery, of Leeds; 2 s (Leon Jakob b 1991, Raphael Joseph b 1994); *Career* called to the Bar Inner Temple 1972, in practice SE Circuit, recorder of the Crown Court, pres Mental Health Tbnls; *Recreations* music, opera, running, The Czech Republic; *Style—* Peter Feinberg, Esq, QC; ✉ 1 Crown Office Row, Temple, London EC4 (☎ 0171 797 7111)

FEINSTEIN, Prof Charles Hilliard; s of Louis Feinstein, and Rose Feinstein; *b* 18 March 1932; *Educ* Univ of Witwatersrand SA (BComm), Univ of Cambridge (PhD), Univ of Oxford (MA); *m* 1, 1958, Ruth Loshak; 1 s, 3 da; m 2, 1980, Anne Digby; *Career* Univ of Cambridge: res offr Dept of Applied Economics 1958–63, lectr in economic history Faculty of Economics and Politics 1963–78, fell Clare Coll and dir of studies in economics 1963–78, sr tutor Clare Coll 1969–78, hon fell Clare Coll 1994; Univ of York: prof of economic and social history 1978–87, head Dept of Economics and Related Studies 1981–87; Univ of Oxford: reader in recent social and economic history and professorial fell Nuffield Coll 1987–89, currently fell All Souls Coll and Chichele prof of economic history; visiting appts incl: Fullbright and res fell Russian Res Center Harvard Univ 1967–68, visiting lectr in economic history Delhi Sch of Economics 1972, Fullbright fell and visiting scholar Dept of Economics Harvard Univ 1986–87 (Stanford Univ 1987), visiting fell Dept of Economic History Aust Nat Univ 1989, distinguished visitor Univ of Cape Town 1992–94, visiting prof Dept of Economics California Inst of Technol 1997; memb: Economic and Social History Ctee SSRC 1972–76, Economic Affairs Ctee ESRC 1982–86 (chm 1985–86), Cncl Royal Economic Soc 1979–93 (Exec Ctee 1980–91), Cncl Economic History Soc 1980–86 and 1988–; Br Acad: memb Overseas Policy Ctee 1988–91, memb Cncl 1990–93, vice-pres 1991–93; editorial memb Clare Gp 1976–91, ed ReFRESH 1985–94, ed Economic Journal 1980–86, memb Editorial Bd Twentieth Century British History 1988–; FBA 1983; *Books* Domestic Capital Formation in the United Kingdom (1965), Socialism Capitalism and Economic Growth - Essays presented to Maurice Dobb (ed, 1967), National Income Expenditure and Output of the United Kingdom 1855–1965 (1972), The Relevance of Economic Theories (ed with J Pajestka, 1980), York 1831–1981 (ed, 1981), British Economic Growth 1856–73 (with R C O Matthews and J C Odling-Smee, 1982), The Managed Economy - Essays in British Economic Policy and Performance since 1929 (ed, 1983), Studies in Capital Formation in the United Kingdom 1750–1920 (ed with S Pollard, 1988), New Directions in Economic and Social History (ed with A Digby, 1989), Banking, Currency and Finance in Europe Between the Wars (ed, 1995), The European Economy Between the Wars (with P Temin and G Toniolo, 1997), Chinese Technology Transfer in the 1990s (ed with C Howe, 1997); *Style—* Prof Charles Feinstein, FBA; ✉ Treetops, Harberton Mead, Headington, Oxford OX3 0DB

FEINSTEIN, Elaine Barbara; da of Isidore Cooklin (d 1974), and Fay, *née* Compton (d 1973); *b* 24 Oct 1930; *Educ* Wyggeston GS Leicester, Newnham Coll Cambridge; *m* 1956, Dr Arnold Feinstein; 3 s (Adam b Feb 1957, Martin b March 1959, Joel b June 1964); *Career* poet and novelist; judge Gregory Poetry Awards Soc of Authors 1986–91, judge Heinemann Awards Royal Soc of Literature 1990; winer Cholmondeley Award for Poetry 1990; memb Exec Ctee English Centre International PEN 1989–; chm of judges T S Eliot Award 1994; Hon DLitt Univ of Leicester 1990; FRSL 1980; *Novels* The Circle (1970), The Amberstone Exit (1972), The Glass Alembic (1973, US title The Crystal Garden), Children of the Rose (1975), The Ecstasy of Dr Miriam Garner (1976), The Shadow Master (1978), The Survivors (1982), The Border (1984), Mother's Girl (1988, shortlisted for LA Times Fiction Prize 1990), All You Need (1989), Loving Brecht (1992), Dreamers (1994), Lady Chatterley's Confession (1995); *Poetry* In a Green Eye (1966), The Magic Apple Tree (1971), At the Edge (1972), The Celebrants and Other Poems (1973), Some Unease and Angels - Selected Poems (1977), The Feast of Eurydice (1980), Badlands (1987), City Music (1990), Selected Poems (1994); trans: The Selected Poems of Marina Tsvetayeva (1971), Three Russian Poets - Margarite Aliger, Yunna Morits and Bella Akhmadulina (1976); ed: Selected Poems of John Clare (1968), New Poetry (1988); *Biographies* Bessie Smith (1986), A Captive Lion - The Life of Marina Tsvetayeva (1987), Lawrence's Women - The Intimate Life of D H Lawrence (1993); *Stories* Matters of Chance (1972), The Silent Areas (1980), New Stories (jt ed with Fay Weldon, 1979); *Television* Breath (BBC Play for Today, 1975), Lunch (dir Jon Amiel, 1981), 12–part series on The Edwardian Country Gentlewoman's Diary (1984), A Brave Face (BBC, 1985), A Passionate Woman (series on life of Marie Stopes, 1990), The Brecht Project (series on life of Bertolt Brecht); *Radio* plays: Echoes (1980), A Late Spring (1981), A Day Off (1983), Marina Tsvetayeva - A Life (1985), If I Ever Get On My Feet Again (1987), The Man in her Life (1990), Foreign Girls (1993), Winter Journey (1995), Women in Love (4 part adaptation, 1996); *Recreations* theatre, music, travel, the conversation of friends; *Style—* Ms Elaine Feinstein; ✉ c/o Gill Coleridge, Rogers Coleridge & White, 20 Powis Mews, London W11 (☎ 0171 221 3717, fax 0171 229 9084)

FELD, Robert Philip; s of Alfred Feld (d 1990), and Lily, *née* Green; *b* 3 Jan 1953; *Educ* Brighton & Hove Sussex GS, Imperial Coll of Sci and Technol; *m* 6 March 1987, Tara Louise, da of Edward Scannell (d 1996); 2 s (Daniel Mark Joseph b 1988, Joshua Alfred b 1991); *Career* md Resort Hotels plc 1983–94, chm Aubrey Business Group 1994–; non-exec dir Guide Dogs for the Blind Assoc Recreational Servs Ltd; Freeman City of London, Liveryman Worshipful Co of Loriners; FHCIMA, FInstD, MCFA, FRSA; *Recreations* private pilot, yachting; *Clubs* Carlton, City Livery, Sussex Motor Yacht; *Style—* Robert Feld, Esq; ✉ Aubrey House, The Green, Rottingdean, Brighton BN2 7HA (☎ 01273 300840, fax 01273 303884, e-mail rfeldabg@fastnet.co.uk)

FELDMAN, Baron (Life Peer UK 1995), of Frognal in the London Borough of Camden; Sir Basil Samuel Feldman; kt (1982); s of Philip Feldman, and Tilly Feldman; *b* 23 Sept 1926; *Educ* Grocers' Sch; *m* 1952, Gita, da of Albert Julius (d 1964); 2 s, 1 da; *Career* chm: Martlet Service Group Ltd 1973–81, Solport Ltd 1980–85, Watchpost Ltd 1983–; Gtr London area Nat Union of Cons and Unionist Assocs: dep chm 1975–78, chm 1978–81, pres 1981–85, vice pres 1985–; Nat Union of Cons and Unionist Assocs: dep chm 1982–85, chm 1985–86, vice pres 1986–, chm Exec Ctee 1991–96 (memb 1975–); chair Cons Conf Blackpool 1985; author of several party booklets and pamphlets; jt chm Cons Pty's Impact 80s Campaign 1982–; memb: Policy Gp for London 1975–81 and 1984–, Nat Campaign Ctee 1976 and 1978, Advsy Ctee on Policy 1981–, Ctee for London 1984–; vice pres Gtr London Young Cons 1975–77; pres: Richmond and Barnes Cons Assoc 1976–84, Hornsey Cons Assoc 1978–82; patron Hampstead Cons Assoc 1981–86, contested GLC elections Richmond 1973; memb: GLC Housing Mgmnt Ctee 1973–77, GLC Arts Ctee 1976–81; dir Young Entrepreneurs Fund 1985–, memb Free Enterprise Loan Soc 1977–84; chm: Better Made in Britain Campaign 1983–, The Quality Mark 1987–92, Shopping Hours Reform Cncl 1988–94, Better Business Opportunities 1990–, Festival of Arts and Culture 1994–95; membre consultatif Institutional Internat de Promotion et de Prestige Geneva (affiliated to UNESCO) 1978–93; memb: Post Office Users' Nat Cncl 1978–81, English Tourist Bd 1986–96; chm: Clothing EDC (NEDO) 1978–85, maker/user working party (NEDO) 1988–89, London Arts Season 1993–; FRSA 1987; *Books* Some Thoughts on Job Creation (for NEDO, 1984), Constituency Campaigning - a guide for Conservative Party workers; *Recreations* travel, golf, tennis, theatre, opera; *Clubs* Carlton; *Style—* The Rt Hon Lord Feldman; ✉ c/o National Union of Conservative & Unionist Associations, 32 Smith Square, London SW1P 3HH (☎ 0171 222 9000)

FELDMAN, Dr Keith Stuart; s of Reuben Feldman, of London, and Karola, *née* Landau (d 1977); *b* 29 July 1943; *Educ* Christ's Coll Finchley, Imp Coll of Sci and Technol (BSc, PhD); *m* 8 July 1971, Teresa Ann, da of Simon Wallace, of Elstree, Herts; 1 s (Alexander b 15 Dec 1981), 1 da (Cordelia b 15 May 1979); *Career* fndr Inter-Bond Services Ltd 1969–81, sr exec Datastream International Ltd 1979–81, dir Carr Kitcat & Aitken Ltd (formerly Galloway & Pearson) 1981–93, actuary Robert Fleming Securities Ltd 1993–; FIA 1976, MSI (Dip) 1992 (memb Int Stock Exchange 1984); *Publications* The Zilch in General Relativity (1965), Dispersion Theory Calculations for Nucleon-Nucleon Scattering (1965), A Model to Explain Investment Trust Prices and Discounts (1977), The Gilt Edged Market Reformulated (1977), AIBD Yield Book (1979), Report on the Wilkie Stochastic Investment Model (1992); *Recreations* chess, skiing; *Clubs* Argonauts; *Style—* Dr Keith Feldman; ✉ Skybreak, The Warren, Radlett, Hertfordshire WD7 7DU (☎ 01923 853777); Robert Fleming Securities Ltd, 25 Copthall Avenue, London EC2R 7DR (☎ 0171 638 5858, fax 0171 628 0053, telex 297451)

FELDMAN, Maurice Avrom; s of Lewis Feldman (d 1963), of Cardiff, and Leah, *née* Voloshen (d 1942); *b* 7 Aug 1927; *Educ* Cardiff HS for Boys, Univ of Bristol (MB ChB); *m* 22 Feb 1959, Vera, da of Armand Cohen (d 1973), of Bristol; 1 s (Adam b 1964), 1 da (Leah b 1960); *Career* Nat Serv RAMC Capt served in Singapore and Malaya 1953–55 (Malaya medal 1955), AER 1955–58; conslt surgn with special interests in vascular surgery, diabetic foot problems, leg ulcers and other raw areas Dudley Rd Hosp Birmingham 1967–93 (emeritus 1993), sr clinical lectr and examiner in surgery at Birmingham Med Sch 1975–93 (emeritus 1993); visiting conslt general surgn All Saints Psychiatric Hosp Birmingham 1967–93, visiting conslt surgn Winson Green Prison Birmingham 1970–93; memb: Medical Appeal Tbnl 1993–, Mgmnt Bd W Midlands Health Research Unit 1993–; Sir Ernest Finch Research Prize 1965; contrib to professional papers in various med and surgical jls; memb: Vascular Surgical Soc, W Midlands Surgical Soc, NHS Conslts Assoc, Assoc for Victims of Med Accidents; FRCSEd, FRCS; *Recreations* walking, gardening, toy making; *Style—* Maurice Feldman, Esq; ✉ 90 Knightlow Road, Harborne, Birmingham B17 8QA (☎ 0121 429 3357), Dudley Rd Hospital, Birmingham B18 7QH

FELDMAN, Dr Michael Morris; s of Louis Feldman (d 1975), and Shura Miller (d 1981); *b* 3 Dec 1938; *Educ* King Edward VII Sch Johannesberg, UCL (BA), UCH Univ of London (MPhil); *m* 7 Jan 1960, Wendy Bankes, da of Arthur Gerald Bankes Morgan (d 1975); 1 s (Matthew Richard Bankes b 1969), 2 da (Melanie Jane Bankes b 1960, Susan Rose b 1964); *Career* house officer UCH 1966, conslt psychotherapist Bethlem Royal and Maudsley Hosp 1975– (registrar 1969–72), sr lectr Inst of Psychiatry 1982– (lectr 1974–75), training analyst Inst of Psycho-Analysis 1983 (assoc member 1975, full member 1981); MRCP, FRCPsych; *Books* Psychic Equilibrium and Psychic Change: Selected Papers of Betty Joseph (co-ed, 1989), The Oedipus Complex Today: Clinical Implications (jtly, 1989); *Recreations* gardening, music, photography, inland waterways; *Style—* Dr Michael Feldman; ✉ Psychotherapy Unit, Maudsley Hosp, Denmark Hill, London SE5 8AZ (☎ 0171 703 6333); 32 Southwood Ave, London N6 5RZ

FELDWICK, Paul; s of Cyril Eric Feldwick, of Abergavenny, Gwent, and Ruby Marian, *née* Francis; *b* 25 April 1952; *Educ* Monmouth Sch, Trinity Coll Oxford (MA); *m* 9 May 1981, Karen Millicent, da of David Rolf Thesen; 3 s (Oliver Paul b 5 June 1985, Hereward David b 2 Aug 1987, Gregory William b 20 Feb 1989); *Career* BMP DDB (formerly Boase Massimi Pollitt): account planner 1974–86, dep head of planning 1986–88, head of planning 1988–91, exec planning dir 1992–; chm: Assoc of Qualitative Res Practitioners 1986–87, Account Planning Gp 1990–91; convenor of judges IPA Advertising Effectiveness Awards 1988–90; FIPA; full memb Market Res Soc; *Books* Advertising Works 5 (ed, 1990), Advertising Works 6 (ed, 1991); *Recreations* music, poetry; *Style—* Paul Feldwick, Esq; ✉ BMP DDB, 12 Bishops Bridge Road, London W2 (☎ 0171 258 3979)

FELL, Alison; da of Andrew Fell (d 1970), and Doris Johnstone; *b* 4 June 1944; *Educ* Kinloch Rannoch Sch, Lochmaben Sch, Lockerbie Acad, Dumfries Acad, Edinburgh Coll of Art (Dip Sculpture, post-dip scholarship and travelling scholarship); *m* 1964 (m dis), Roger Coleman, *qv*, s of Ronald Coleman; 1 s (Ivan b 1967); *Career* poet and novelist; co-fndr: The Welfare State Theatre Leeds 1969, The Women's Street Theatre Gp; journalist: Ink, Oz, Time Out; memb Spare Rib Editorial Collective 1975–79 (latterly fiction ed); writer in residence: C Day Lewis fell London Borough of Brent 1978, London Borough of Walthamstow 1981–82; tutor at writing workshops in arts centres across UK, writer in action SE Arts Kent 1985, tutor Arvon Fndn 1985–, writer in residence NSW Inst of Technol 1986, has recited at various arts venues throughout UK; Whispers in the Dark (BBC Scotland) 1995; awarded Alice Hunt Bartlett Prize (Nat Poetry Soc) for first collections 1985; memb Greater London Arts Lit Panel 1984–86; *Books* Hard Feelings (ed, 1979), The Grey Dancer (1981), Every Move You Make (1984), Truth, Dare or Promise (contrib, 1985), The Bad Box (1987), Close Company - Stories of Mothers and Daughters (contrib, 1988), The Seven Deadly Sins (ed and contrib, 1988), The Shining Mountain (1987, 2 edn 1988), Sex and the City (contrib, 1989) The Seven Cardinal Virtues (ed and contrib, 1990), Whose Cities? (contrib, 1991), Winters Tales (contrib, 1991), Mer de Glace (1991, Boardman Tasker award for mountain lit), The Pillow Boy of the Lady Onogoro (1994); *Poetry* Kisses for Mayakovsky (1984), The Crystal Owl (1988); *Anthologies* Serious Hysterics (ed and contrib, 1992); poetry in anthologies: Licking The Bed Clean (1978), Bread and Roses (1979), One Foot on the Mountain (1979) Smile Smile Smile Smile (1980), Angels of Fire, Apples and Snakes, The New British Poetry, Is That The New Moon?, Anthology of Scottish Women's Poetry (1991), The Faber Book of 20th Century Scottish Verse (1992), The Faber Book of Movie Verse (1993); stories in anthologies: Sex and the City (1992), Infidelity (1993), Bad Sex (1993), Shouting it Out (1996); publications in various magazines; *Style—* Ms Alison Fell; ✉ c/o Tony Peake, Peake Associates, 18 Grafton Crescent, London NW1 8SL (☎ 0171 485 6392, fax 0171 267 4241)

FELL, Sir Anthony; kt (1981); s of Cdr David Mark Fell, RN; *b* 18 May 1914; *Educ* Bedford Sch and in NZ; *m* 1938, June Warwick; 1 s, 1 da; *Career* contested (C): Brigg 1948, Hammersmith S 1949 and 1950; MP (C): Yarmouth 1951–66 (resigned party whip 1956 in protest at withdrawal from Suez), Yarmouth 1970–83; *Style—* Sir Anthony Fell; ✉ 11 Denny St, London SE11 4UX (☎ 0171 735 9021)

FELL, Sir David; KCB (1995, CB 1990); s of Ernest Fell (d 1964), of Belfast, NI, and Jessie, *née* McCreedy (d 1981); *b* 20 Jan 1943; *Educ* Royal Belfast Academical Inst, Queen's Univ Belfast (BSc); *m* 22 July 1967, Sandra Jesse, da of Hubert Moore (d 1982), of Co Fermanagh, NI; 1 s (Nicholas b 1976), 1 da (Victoria b 1972); *Career* sales mangr Rank Hovis McDougall 1965–66, teacher Belfast Model Sch 1966–67, res assoc Queen's Univ Belfast 1967–69; NI civil serv: asst princ Miny of Agric 1969–72, princ Miny of Commerce 1972–77, under sec Dept of Commerce 1981–82 (asst sec 1977–81), dep chief exec Industl Devpt Bd for NI 1982–84, perm sec Dept of Econ Devpt 1984–91; head NI Civil Serv and second perm under sec of state NI Office 1991–; CIMgt; *Recreations* golf, rugby, listening to and playing music; *Clubs* Belfast Old Instonians; *Style—* Sir David Fell, KCB; ✉ Stormont Castle, Belfast BT4 3ST (☎ 01232 528145/6)

FELL, John Arnold; s of Charles Arthur Fell (d 1994), and Susannah, *née* Arnold (d 1978); *b* 31 Aug 1928; *Educ* Merchant Taylors', Pembroke Coll Oxford (MA); *m* 10 Aug 1963, Janet Eva, da of Irvine Charles Parr, of Ottery St Mary, Devon; 2 da (Ruth Anne b 19 June 1966, Rachel Elizabeth b 18 May 1968); *Career* admitted slr 1955; articled clerk Kimbers 1952–56; asst slr: Conquest Clare & Binns 1956–58, Hatchett Jones & Co 1958–63; Wilde Sapte: asst slr 1963–64, ptnr 1964–91, conslt 1991–; dir: Portman Family Settled Estates Ltd, Portman Burtley Estate Co, Moor Park (1958) Ltd, Seymour Street Nominees Ltd; former chm: Broad St Ward Club, Queenhithe Ward Club; Common Councilman Corp of London 1982–; chm Tstees of Truro Fund; tstee: Royal Acad of Arts 1987–93, Housing Assoc Charitable Tst 1987–93, Lord Mayor's 800th Anniversary Awards Tst, Portman Family Settled Estates 1995; dep chm Bd of Govrs City of London Sch, govr of Christ's Hosp; Freeman City of London 1980, Liveryman Worshipful Co of Gardeners 1982; *Recreations* walking, gardening; *Clubs* Old Merchant Taylors' Soc Guildhall, City Livery; *Style—* John Fell, Esq; ✉ Dellfield, 43 Sandy Lodge Lane, Moor Park, Northwood, Middx HA6 2HX (☎ 01923 826508); Wilde Sapte, 1 Fleet Place, London EC4M 7WS (☎ 0171 246 7000, fax 0171 246 7777, telex 887793)

FELLOWES, Julian Alexander; s of Peregrine Edward Launcelot Fellowes, of Chipping Campden, and Olwen Mary, *née* Stuart-Jones (d 1980); *b* 17 Aug 1949; *Educ* Ampleforth, Magdalene Coll Cambridge (BA, MA); *m* 28 April 1990, Emma, da of Hon Charles Kitchener, ggniece of 1 Earl Kitchener of Khartoum, Lady-in-Waiting to HRH Princess Michael of Kent; 1 s (Peregrine Charles Morant Kitchener b 1991); *Career* actor, writer, lectr and prodr; *Theatre* West End appearances incl: Joking Apart (Globe), Present Laughter (Vaudeville), Futurists (NT); *Television* incl: The Greater Good (BBC), The Treaty (Central/RTE), A Very Open Prison (Hat Trick), Sharpe's Regiment (Sharpe Films), Killing me Softly (BBC); co-prodns as dir of Lionhead incl: Married Man (with LWT), Little Sir Nicholas (with BBC); as writer/adaptor: Little Lord Fauntleroy (BBC, winner of 1995 Int Emmy Award); as writer/prodr: The Prince and the Pauper (BBC); *Films* Baby, Fellow Traveller, Damage, Shadowlands, Savage Hearts; *Recreations* history, building; *Clubs* Boodle's; *Style—* Julian Fellowes, Esq; ✉ 15 Moore St, London SW3 2QN (☎ 0171 581 4071)

FELLOWES, Rt Hon Sir Robert; GCVO (1996, KCVO 1989, LVO 1982), KCB (1991, CB 1987), PC (1990); s of Sir William Albemarle Fellowes, KCVO (d 1986), agent to HM at Sandringham 1936–64, and Jane Charlotte (d 1986), da of Brig-Gen Algernon Francis Holford Ferguson; bro of Thomas Fellowes, *qv*; *b* 11 Dec 1941; *Educ* Eton; *m* 20 April 1978, Lady (Cynthia) Jane Spencer, da of 8 Earl Spencer; 1 s (Alexander Robert b 1983), 2 da (Laura Jane b 1980, Eleanor Ruth b 1985); *Career* Lt Scots Guards 1960–63; dir Allen Harvey & Ross (discount brokers and bankers) 1968–77, private sec to HM The Queen 1990– (asst private sec 1977–86, dep private sec 1986–90); Liveryman Worshipful Co of Goldsmiths; *Recreations* watching cricket, shooting, golf; *Clubs* White's, Pratt's, Athenaeum, MCC; *Style—* The Rt Hon Sir Robert Fellowes, GCVO, KCB

FELLOWES, Thomas William; s of Sir William Albemarle Fellowes, KCVO, DL (d 1986), and Jane Charlotte, *née* Ferguson (d 1986); bro of Sir Robert Fellowes, GCVO, KCB, PC, *qv*; *b* 3 Nov 1945; *Educ* Eton; *m* 1975, Rosamund Isobelle, da of Bernard van Cutsem (d 1975), and Lady Margaret Fortescue; 2 da (Catherine b 1977, Mary b 1978); *Career* dir Gerrard and National Discount Co Ltd 1973, dep chm Gerrard & National Holdings plc 1989–, non-exec dir: James Purdey & Sons Ltd 1991–, Plough Court Fund Mgmnt Ltd 1993–; chm London Discount Market Assoc 1995–97; memb Cncl Br Bankers Assoc 1995–97; Freeman Worshipful Co of Ironmongers; *Clubs* White's, Pratt's, RWNGC; *Style—* Thomas Fellowes; ✉ The Old Rectory, Barking, Ipswich, Suffolk IP6 8HH (☎ 01449 720734); c/o Gerrard & National Holdings, Cannon Bridge, 25 Dowgate Hill, EC4R 2GN (☎ 0171 337 2800)

FELLOWS, Derek Edward; s of Edward Frederick Fellows (d 1986), of Sussex, and Gladys Marguerite, *née* Parker (d 1989); *b* 23 Oct 1927; *Educ* Mercers' Sch; *m* 1948, Mary, da of William George Watkins (d 1977), of Surrey; 2 da (Angela b 1954, Nicola b 1959); *Career* chief actuary: Prudential Assurance Co Ltd 1981–88, Prudential Corporation plc 1985–88 (dir); vice pres Inst of Actuaries 1980–82; dir: Securities and Investmts Bd 1989–91, Hambro Assured plc 1992–; memb Occupational Pensions Bd 1974–78; church cmmr 1996–; FPMI, FIA; *Recreations* music, gardening, bridge, travel; *Clubs* Actuary's, Gallio; *Style—* Derek Fellows, Esq; ✉ 20 Fairbourne, Cobham, Surrey KT11 2BT (☎ 01932 865488)

FELLOWS, Derrick Charles; s of Charles Arthur Fellows (d 1988), and Peggy Irene, *née* Keeley (d 1989); *b* 28 Dec 1954; *Educ* Edmonton Co GS; *Career* area trg advsr Distributive Industry Trg Bd 1977–82, sole proprietor Consultancy and Training Servs 1982–; FCI 1978, MABE 1978, ACIS 1979, FIPD 1980, FSCA 1981, FFA 1986; *Books* Ready Made Activities for Financial Skills (1994); *Recreations* skiing; *Clubs* Mensa; *Style—* Derrick Fellows, Esq; ✉ 63 Wynndale Road, Woodford, London E18 1DY (☎ 0181 504 4639)

FELLOWS, Susannah Fitch; da of Donald Emory Fellows, of London, and Suzanne Knight, *née* Phillips; *b* 7 Oct 1956; *Educ* USA, Holland Park Comp London, Kingsway Coll London, LAMDA; partner, Teddy Kempner; *Career* actress; concert Some Enchanted Evening with LSO (Barbican Hall); organised and participated in many charity events and concerts for: Terence Higgins Tst and other AIDS charities, Children in Need, The Variety Club, Stage for Age; fndr dir Fitch's Ark (art gallery) Little Venice London 1994; *Theatre* incl: Evita (Prince Edward) 1978–79, RSC London season 1979–80 (Once In A Lifetime and The Greeks at the Aldwych), Me and My Girl (Adelphi) 1985–86, Lend Me A Tenor (Globe) 1986–87, Aspects of Love (Sydmonton Festival '88 Prince of Wales) 1989–90 and 1992, Chess (Manchester Opera House) 1990, City of Angels (Prince of Wales) 1993; *Television* incl: Separate Tables, Dempsey and Makepeace, Exiles (BBC Play of the Month); *Radio* incl: Summer Lightning and Pigs Have Wings (PG Wodehouse serialisations), Farewell My Lovely, Songs from the Shows, featured various plays; *Recreations* mosaic artwork, antiques, travelling, gardening, currently writing a book on performing in musical theatre; *Style—* Miss Susannah Fellows; ✉ c/o Barry Burnett Organisation Ltd, Suite 42–43, Grafton House, 2–3 Golden Square, London W1R 3AD (☎ 0171 437 7048/9, fax 0171 734 6118)

FELLS, Prof Ian; s of Dr Henry Alexander Fells, MBE (d 1975), of Sheffield, and Clarice, *née* Rowell; *b* 5 Sept 1932; *Educ* King Edward VII Sch Sheffield, Trinity Coll Cambridge (MA, PhD); *m* 17 Aug 1957, Hazel Denton, da of Donald Murgatroyd Scott, of Sheffield; 4 s (Nicholas Scott b 1959, Jonathan Wynne b 1961, Alastair Rowell b 1963, Crispin Denton b 1966); *Career* cmmnd RCS 1951, Chief Wireless Offr Br Troops in Austria 1952; lectr and dir of studies Dept of Fuel Technol and Chem Engrg Univ of Sheffield 1958–62, reader in fuel sci Univ of Durham 1962–75, prof of energy conversion Univ of Newcastle upon Tyne 1975– (public orator 1971–74), exec David Davies Inst of Int Affairs 1975–, pres Inst of Energy 1978–79; memb: Sci Consultative Gp BBC 1976–81, Electricity Supply Res Cncl 1979–89, Cncl for Nat Academic Awards 1988–92; Hatfield Meml medal and prize 1974, Beilby Meml medal and prize 1976, Sir Charles Parsons Meml medal and prize 1988, Royal Soc Faraday medal 1993; involved with various TV series incl: Young Scientist of the Year, The Great Egg Race, Earth Year 2050, Take Nobody's Word for It, Tomorrow Tonight, QED, Horizon; FEng 1979, FInstE, FRSC, FIChemE, FRSE 1996; *Books* UK Energy Policy Post-Privatisation (1991), Moving Ahead (1992), Energy for the Future (1995); *Recreations* sailing, cross-country skiing, energy conversation; *Clubs* Naval and Military; *Style—* Prof Ian Fells, FRSE, FEng; ✉ 29 Rectory Terrace, Newcastle upon Tyne NE3 1YB (☎ and fax 0191 285 5343); Department of Chemical & Process Engineering, University of Newcastle upon Tyne NE1 7RU (☎ 0191 222 7276, fax 0191 222 5292)

FELTWELL, Dr John Stewart Edmonds; s of Ray Parker Feltwell (d 1994), of Eastbourne, and Edna Mary, *née* Edmonds (d 1992); *b* 9 April 1948; *Educ* Sutton Valence, Royal Holloway Coll London (BSc, PhD), Univ of Kent at Canterbury (Dip in Adult and Further Educn 1984), King's Coll London (Dip in EC Law 1993); *m* 21 July 1979, Carol Lynn, da of Kenneth Thomas Mellor; 1 da (Zoë Ellen Victoria Feltwell b 16 March 1985), 1 s (Thomas Edgar Ray b 17 May 1989); *Career* entomologist; asst biology teacher Sutton Valence Sch 1973–78; proprietor: Wildlife Matters (consultancy and publisher) 1978–, Garden Matters 1993–, Garden Matters and Wildlife Matters Photographic Libraries; author of 30 books on entomology and natural history for children and adults, trans into 27 languages, also numerous scientific and popular articles and reviews; freelance lectr Univs of Kent, Sussex and Louisiana; Freeman: Worshipful Co of Poulters 1993, City of London 1994; FRES 1970, FLS 1970, CBiol 1970, FIBiol 1993; *Books* incl: Biology and Biochemistry of the Large White (1982), Butterflies and Other Insects of Britain (1984), Discovering Doorstep Wildlife (1985), Natural History of Butterflies (1986), Naturalist's Garden (1987), Animals and Where They Live (1988, published in 27 countries), A Guide to Countryside Conservation (1989), The Story of Silk (1990), Butterflies: A Practical Guide (1990), Beekeeping: A Practical Guide (1991), Slugs, Snails and Earthworms (1991), Recycling in the School Environment (1991), Meadows: A History and Natural History (1992), Pocket Guide to European Butterflies (1992), Butterflies and Moths (Dorling-Kindersley Eyewitness series, 1993), Encyclopaedia of Butterflies of the World (1993), Butterflies and Moths, Nature Facts (1993), Bugs, Beetles and Other Insects (1993), Live Oak Splendor, Gardens Along the Mississippi (1994), Pocket Guide to North American Butterflies (1994), Butterflies of North America Folio Edition (1994), Butterflies of Europe Folio Edition (1994), The Conservation of Butterflies in Britain, past and present (1995), A Creative Step by Step Guide to Climbers and Trellis Plants (1996), Wide World of Animals (1996), Spectacular Hanging Baskets (1996); *Recreations* observing nature; *Clubs* Farmers; *Style*— Dr John Feltwell; ✉ Marlham, Henley's Down, Battle, E Sussex TN33 9BN (☎ 01424 830566, fax 01424 830224, e-mail jfeltwell@aol.com, www http://wet.ftech.net/-gardens

FELTWELL, Robert Leslie (Bob); s of Ray Parker Feltwell (d 1994), of Eastbourne, and Edna Mary, *née* Edmonds (d 1992); *b* 15 Feb 1944; *Educ* King Edward VI Sch Norwich, Univ of London (BSc(Econ)); *m* 22 July 1967, Christine Renée, da of Richard Henry John Rees, of Horsham; 2 da (Alison Mary b 1970, Elizabeth Jane b 1972); *Career* family farm Hartfield Sussex 1962–67, graduate apprentice then prodn mangr Rolls-Royce Ltd Aero Engines 1967–70, telephone prodn mangr ITT UK and Belgium 1970–76, gen mangr Western Incubators Ltd 1976–78, overseas devpt mangr Pauls International Ltd 1978–79, prodn dir Eastern Counties Farmers Ltd 1979–90, chief exec and dir Suffolk Chamber of Commerce, Industry and Shipping 1990–; treas Br C of C Execs 1993–, regnl sec E Anglian Cs of C 1993–; dir Suffolk TEC 1993, fndr memb Univ for Suffolk Task Gp; ldr 9 UK Trade Missions to Far E, Malaysia, Singapore, Hong Kong, S Korea and Thailand 1993–96; regular bdcaster and writer on business and int trade; Freeman City of London 1993, Liveryman Worshipful Co of Poulters 1994; MIMgt 1979, MInstD 1994, MIEx 1995; *Recreations* travel, tennis; *Clubs* Farmers, Ipswich Rotary; *Style*— Bob Feltwell, Esq; ✉ Suffolk Chamber of Commerce, Industry and Shipping, Russell Road, Ipswich, Suffolk IP1 2DE (☎ 01473 210611, fax 01473 225488, e-mail 101505.2177@compuserve.com)

FENBY, Dr Eric William; OBE (1962); s of Herbert Henry Fenby (d 1954), of Scarborough, and Ada, *née* Brown (d 1974); *b* 22 April 1906; *Educ* Municipal Sch Scarborough, articled pupil to A C Keeton (BMus, FRCO); *m* 22 July 1944, Rowena Clara Teresa, da of Rev Percy Marshall (d 1950), of Scarborough; 1 s (Roger Delius), 1 da (Ruth); *Career* composer; amanuensis to Frederick Delius (A Song of Summer for orch, Songs of Farewell) 1928–34, lectr on Delius and his music 1935–82; composer film score Jamaica Inn 1939; prof of composition RAM 1964–77; memb: Composers' Guild of GB, Soc of Authors; hon memb Royal Philharmonic Soc; Hon DMus Jacksonville Univ Florida 1978; Hon DLitt: Univ of Bradford 1978, Univ of Warwick 1978; *Books* Delius As I Knew Him (1936), Menuhin's House of Music (1969), Delius (1971); *Style*— Dr Eric Fenby, OBE; ✉ 1 Raincliffe Ct, Stepney Rd, Scarborough, North Yorks (☎ 01723 372988)

FENBY, Jonathan Theodore Starmer; s of Charles Fenby (d 1974), and June, *née* Head; *b* 11 Nov 1942; *Educ* King Edward's Sch Birmingham, Westminster, New Coll Oxford (BA); *m* 1 July 1967, Renée; 1 s (Alexander b 1972), 1 da (Sara b 1970); *Career* corr bureau chief Reuters and ed Reuters World Serv 1963–77, corr The Economist France and West Germany 1982–86, home ed and asst ed The Independent 1986–88, dep ed The Guardian 1988–93 (dir 1990–); ed: The Observer 1993–95, South China Morning Post 1995–; *Books* The Fall of the House of Beaverbrook (1979), Piracy and the Public (1983), The International News Services (1986); *Style*— Jonathan Fenby, Esq; ✉ South China Morning Post, City Office, 29th Floor, Dorset House, 97 King's Road, Quarry Bay, Hong Kong

FENDALL, Prof (Neville) Rex Edwards; s of Francis Alan Fendall (d 1967), and Ruby, *née* Matthews (d 1975); *b* 9 July 1917; *Educ* Wallingbrook Devon, UCL and UCH (BSc, MB BS, MD, MRCS, LRCP), London Sch of Hygiene and Tropical Med (DPH); FFCM, FFPHM; *m* 11 July 1942, Margaret Doreen, da of William Beynon (d 1917), of Pontardawe, S Wales; *Career* HM Overseas Med Serv 1944–64: Nigeria, Malaya, Singapore, Br Mil Admin Malaya 1945–46, Kenya 1948–64, dir of med servs 1962–64; Rockefeller Fndn: travelling fell 1963, memb staff 1964–67; regnl dir Population Cncl NYC 1967–71, Middlemass Hunt prof of tropical community health Liverpool Sch of Tropical Med 1971–81, emeritus prof Univ of Liverpool 1982–; visiting lectr Harvard Univ 1965–71, visiting prof of public health Boston Univ USA 1982– (distinguished fell Centre for Int Health 1993), adjunct prof of community health sciences Univ of Calgary Canada 1983–88; Cwlth Fndn travelling fell S Pacific 1976; conslt and advsr to numerous nat and int orgns and especially developing countries 1961–; WHO: memb Panel of Experts 1957–, conslt SE Asia 1960; memb UK UNSCAT Delgn 1963; conslt: S Pacific Cmmn 1963, World Bank (investmt survey E Africa) 1970, UNFPA (family planning prog) Arab Repub of Egypt 1972, OEO (Office of Economic Opportunity) Alaska 1972–74, ODA (rural health care) Pakistan Govt 1974–76, UNFPA (manpower devpt) Pakistan Govt 1974–, Imperial Social Servs Iran (long term health planning) 1972–74, Int Devpt Res Cncl Canada (trg of health auxiliary teachers Nigeria, Malawi, Iran) 1973–75, Cwlth Secretariat (health manpower) Bangladesh 1976, UNFPA (manpower devpt) Bangladesh 1978, Br Cncl (health manpower) Bangladesh 1976 and 1987, Mauritius Govt (health planning) 1975, WHO (health and manpower devpt) Maldives 1984, Project Hope USA (primary health care planning for displaced persons) El Salvador 1986; lead speaker Cwlth Mins of Health Conf Colombo 1974, memb Econ Devpt Advsy Panel WHO Ochocerciasis 1976–77, UK project mangr CENTO (low cost rural health care) 1976–79, India-Br Univ collaboration scheme ODA 1978–; memb: UK Delgn WHO/UNICEF (primary health care ALMA ATA) 1978, Exec Bd Cwlth Human Ecology Cncl, USA Nat Cncl for Int Health (fndr memb) 1974–85; presentation to Cwlth Min of Health Conf (paper on community approaches to health promotion and disease prevention) Aust 1989; participant speaker jt symposium Planet Earth learned socs of Canada and Queen's Univ 1991; Gold medal Migrendra Med Tst Nepal 1983; memb: Cwlth Human Ecology Cncl, Soc of Public Health, Soc of Social Med, American Public Health Assoc, Acad of Med Physical and Natural Scis Guatemala 1986; memb BMA 1942, FFCM 1972; *Books* Auxiliaries in Health Care (1972), Use of Paramedicals for Primary Health Care in the Commonwealth (with J H Paxman and F M Shattock, 1979); some 150 plus publications on rural health centres, med educn, epidemiology, management primary health care, planning & orgn and ecology, with reference to developing countries; *Recreations* travel, gardening; *Clubs* Royal Cwlth Soc, Athenaeum (Liverpool); *Style*— Prof Rex Fendall; ✉ Berwyn, North Close, Bromborough, Wirral L62 2BU (☎ 0151 334 2193); The Coach House, Mill St, Ludlow, S Shropshire SY8 1BB (☎ 01584 877195)

FENHALLS, Richard Dorian; s of Roydon Myers and Maureen Fenhalls; *b* 14 July 1943; *Educ* Hilton Coll Univ of Natal (BA), Christ's Coll Cambridge (MA, LLM); *m* 1967, Angela Sarah, *née* Allen; 1 s, 1 da; *Career* Goodricke & Son, Attorney SA 1969–70, Citibank 1970–72; sr vice pres: Marine Midland Bank 1972–77, American Express Bank 1977–81; dep chm and chief exec Guinness Mahon & Co Ltd 1981–85, chm Henry Ansbacher & Co Ltd and chief exec Henry Ansbacher Holdings plc 1985–93, chief exec Strand Partners Ltd 1993–; *Recreations* sailing, skiing; *Clubs* Royal Ocean Racing, Royal Southern Yacht (Hamble), Royal Thames Yacht, Ski Club of Great Britain; *Style*— R D Fenhalls, Esq; ✉ 2nd Floor, 6 Pembridge Place, London W2 4XB; Strand Partners Limited, 110 Park Street, London W1Y 3RB (☎ 0171 409 3494, fax 0171 409 1761)

FENN, Sir Nicholas Maxted; GCMG (1995, KCMG 1989, CMG 1980); s of Rev Prof John Eric Fenn (d 1995), of Worcs, and Kathleen M, *née* Harrison; *b* 19 Feb 1936; *Educ* Downs Sch, Kingswood Sch, Peterhouse Cambridge (MA); *m* 1959, Susan Clare, da of Rev Dr G L Russell, of Dorset; 2 s (Robert b 1962, Charles b 1963), 1 da (Julia b 1974); *Career* Flying Offr RAF 1954–56; Burmese studies SOAS 1959–60, vice-consul Mandalay Burma 1960–61; third sec Br Embassy Rangoon Burma 1961–63; asst private sec to four successive Secs of State for Foreign and Cwlth Affrs 1963–67; first sec and head of Chancery Br Interests Section Swiss Embassy Algiers Algeria 1967–69; first sec for public affrs UK Mission to the UN NY 1969–72; dep head successively of Sci and Technol Dept and Energy Dept FCO 1972–75, counsellor head of Chancery and consul-gen Br Embassy Peking 1975–77; RCDS 1978; head of News Dept FCO, spokesman of the FCO and press sec successively to Lord Carrington and Francis Pym 1979–82 (press sec to Lord Soames, last Governor of S Rhodesia now Zimbabwe 1979–80); HM ambassador: Myanmar 1982–86, Republic of Ireland 1986–91; British high cmmr to Republic of India 1991–96, ret; chief exec Marie Curie Cancer Care 1996–; *Recreations* sailing; *Clubs* Utd Oxford & Cambridge Univ; *Style*— Sir Nicholas Fenn, GCMG; ✉ Applecroft, Chainhurst, Marden, Kent TN12 9SS

FENN-SMITH, Clive Antony Kemp; s of Gurth Kemp Fenn-Smith, MRCVS (d 1993), and Mary Esmée, da of Malcolm Watson (d 1977); *b* 13 March 1933; *Educ* Charterhouse, Univ of Cambridge (MA); *m* 29 April 1961, Jane Hester, da of Rt Rev Edward Barry Henderson (d 1986), formerly Bishop of Bath and Wells; 2 s (Oliver b 1965, Edward b 1974), 1 da (Emma b 1962); *Career* late 4/7 Royal Dragoon Gds, Lt 1952; slr: Messrs Letcher & Son Ringwood 1958–64, M & G Group Ltd 1968–80 (md 1977); dir: Barclays Bank Tst Co Ltd 1984–93, Barclays Financial Services Ltd 1986–93, Investors Compensation Scheme Ltd 1988–; *Recreations* sailing, gardening; *Clubs* Cavalry and Guards'; *Style*— Clive A K Fenn-Smith, Esq; ✉ 23 West End Terrace, Winchester, Hampshire SO22 5EN (☎ 01962 854341)

FENNELL, Hon Sir (John) Desmond Augustine; OBE (1982); s of Dr Augustine Joseph Fennell (d 1980), of Lincoln, and Maureen Eleanor, *née* Kidney (d 1995); *b* 17 Sept 1933; *Educ* Ampleforth, Corpus Christi Coll Cambridge (MA); *m* Feb 1966, Susan Primrose, da of John Marshall Trusted (d 1979); 1 s (Simon b 1969), 2 da (Alexandra b 1967, Charlotte b 1972); *Career* Lt Grenadier Gds 1956–58; called to the Bar Inner Temple 1959, dep chm Beds Quarter Sessions 1971–72, rec Crown Ct 1972–90, QC 1974, ldr Midland and Oxford Circuit 1983–88, master of the Bench Inner Temple 1983–, judge of the Court of Appeal Jersey and Court of Appeal Guernsey 1984–90, justice of The Queen's Bench Div of the High Court 1990–92, judge Employment Appeal Tbnl 1991–92; memb Gen Cncl of the Bar 1984 (vice chm 1988, chm 1989, memb Senate 1983), inspr King's Cross Underground Fire Investigation 1987–88 (reported 1988), chm WARA (formed to oppose siting of third London airport in Bucks) 1969–90, vice chm Wessex Area Cons 1978–80, pres Bucks Div Cons Assoc 1983–89 (chm 1976–79), chm Stoke Mandeville Burns and Reconstructive Surgery Res Tst 1994–; *Clubs* Boodle's, Pilgrims; *Style*— The Hon Sir Desmond Fennell, OBE

FENNER, John Ronald; OBE (1997); s of Louis Finkel, and Claire Lubkin (d 1975); *b* 7 Dec 1935; *Educ* Brunswick Sch Haywards Heath Sussex, Tonbridge, UCL (LLB); *m* 24 March 1963, Gillian Adelaide, da of Stanley Joshua Simmons; 2 s (Robert Matthew b 19 June 1965, Adam Edward b 28 Feb 1972), 1 da (Harriet Jane b 25 May 1967, d 1971); *Career* served articles Zeffertt Heard & Morley Lawson 1956–59, ptnr Lionel Leighton & Co 1962–70; Berwin Leighton: fndr ptnr 1970, managing ptnr 1980–84, chm 1984–90, sr ptnr 1990–94; fndr ptnr and sr ptnr Fenners 1994–; chm: Nat Cncl for Jews in the former Soviet Union 1989–93, of appeal Nightingale House 1986–93, BURA (British Urban Regeneration Assoc) 1991– (tstee BURA Charitable Tst 1993–), British Friends of Israel Philharmonic Orch Fndn 1993–96; memb Cncl: Housing Investment Group Ltd 1994–, Local Investment Fund 1995–; memb: Worshipful Co of Fletchers, City of London Slrs' Co (Grotius prize 1960); Freeman City of London; memb: Law Soc 1959, Southwestern Legal Fndn (USA) 1985, Int Bar Assoc 1985; *Recreations* tennis, skiing, opera, politics; *Clubs* City of London, Carlton, RAC; *Style*— John Fenner, Esq, OBE; ✉ Fenners, 180 Fleet Street, London EC4A 2HD (☎ 0171 430 2200, fax 0171 430 2218)

FENNER, Dame Peggy Edith; DBE (1986), DL (Kent 1992), MP (C) Medway (majority 8,786); *b* 12 Nov 1922; *Educ* LCC Sch Brockley, Ide Hill Sevenoaks; *m* 1940, Bernard S Fenner, s of F W Fenner, of Sevenoaks, Kent; 1 da; *Career* chm Sevenoaks UDC 1962 and 1963 (memb 1957–71), vice pres UDCs Assoc 1971, Parly candidate (Cons) Newcastle-under-Lyme 1966; MP (C): Rochester and Chatham 1970–74 and 1979–83, Medway 1983–; Parly sec MAFF 1972–74 and 1981–86, govt co chm Women's Nat Cmmn 1983–, chm All Pty Gp on the Retail Indust; memb: Br delgn to Euro Parl 1974, Cncl of Europe 1987, Western Euro Union (Def) 1987, Select Ctee on Accommodation and Works; *Style*— Dame Peggy Fenner, DBE, DL, MP; ✉ 12 Star Hill, Rochester, Kent (☎ 01634 42124); House of Commons, London SW1A 0AA (☎ 0171 219 3000)

FENNESSY, Sir Edward; kt (1975), CBE (1957, OBE Mil 1944); s of Edward Patrick Fennessy (d 1955), of London, and Eleanor, *née* Arkwright (d 1942); *b* 17 Jan 1912; *Educ* West Ham GS, Queen Mary College London (BSc); *m* 1, 1937, Marion (d 1983), da of late Albert Edwin Banks, of Sheffield; 1 s, 1 da; m 2, 1984, Leonora Patricia, wid of Trevor Birkett; *Career* WWII 60 Gp RAF (despatches); md: Decca Navigator 1946–50, Decca Radar 1950–65, Plessey Electronics 1965–69, PO Telecommunications 1969–77; dep chm: PO 1975–77, Muirhead until 1982, LKB Instruments Ltd 1978–87; chm: Biochrom 1978–87, British Medical Data Systems Ltd 1981–90; Hon Doctorate Univ of Surrey; FIEE, FRIN; *Recreations* gardening, sailing; *Clubs* RAF; *Style*— Sir Edward Fennessy, CBE; ✉ Northbrook, Littleford Lane, Shamley Green, Guildford, Surrey (☎ 01483 892444)

FENTIMAN, Prof Ian Stuart; s of Harold Latter Fentiman (d 1989), and Vida Frances, *née* Jones; *b* 23 June 1945; *Educ* Trinity Sch of John Whitgift, King's Coll Hosp London (MB BS, LRCP MRCS, FRCS, MD); *Career* conslt surgn Guy's Hosp 1982–, prof of surgical oncology Univ of London, hon dep dir Imperial Cancer Res Fund Clinical Oncology Unit Guy's Hosp; Arris and Gale lectr RCS 1978; FRCS, fell Assoc of Surgns; *Books* Detection and Treatment of Early Breast Cancer (1990), Prevention of Breast Cancer (1993), Breast Cancer (1994), Cancer in the Elderly: Research and Treatment

(1994); *Recreations* bookbinding; *Style—* Prof Ian Fentiman; ✉ Clinical Oncology Unit, Guy's Hosp, St Thomas Street, London SE1 9RT (☎ 0171 955 4540, fax 0171 403 8381)

FENTON, Prof Alexander; CBE (1986); s of Alexander Fenton (d 1960), and Annie Stirling Stronach; *b* 26 June 1929; *Educ* Turriff Acad, Univ of Aberdeen (MA), Univ of Cambridge (BA), Univ of Edinburgh (DLitt); *m* 1956, Evelyn Elizabeth, *née* Hunter; 2 da; *Career* ar asst ed Scottish National Dictionary 1955–59; Nat Museum of Antiquities of Scot: asst keeper 1959–75, dep keeper 1975–78, dir 1978–85; res dir Nat Museums of Scot 1985–89, dir Euro Ethnological Res Centre 1989–; chair of Scottish Ethnology and dir School of Scottish Studies Univ of Edinburgh 1990–94; author; Hon DLitt Univ of Aberdeen 1989; FRSE 1985, FRSGS 1992, HRSA 1996 (hon prof of antiquities); *Books* incl: The Various Names of Shetland, Scottish Country Life, The Island Blackhouse, The Northern Isles: Orkney and Shetland, The Rural Architecture of Scotland, The Shape of the Past (2 vol), Wirds an' Wark 'e Seasons Roon', Country Life in Scotland, The Turra' Coo, Craiters... or twenty Buchan tales; *Recreations* languages; *Clubs* New (Edinburgh); *Style—* Prof Alexander Fenton, CBE, FRSE; ✉ 132 Blackford Ave, Edinburgh EH9 3HH (☎ 0131 667 5456)

FENTON, Charles Miller; OBE (1982), JP; s of Sir William Charles Fenton, MC, JP (d 1976), of Fieldhead, Cleckheaton, W Yorks, and Margaret, *née* Hirst; *b* 24 Feb 1931; *Educ* Uppingham, Univ of Leeds (Dip Textile Industs); *m* 1963, Shirley Jane, da of George Arthur Windsor (d 1982), of Priestley Green, Halifax, W Yorks; 1 s, 1 da; *Career* chm Fenton Holdings Ltd, chm United Brake Ltd, non-exec chm British Mohair Holdings plc, non-exec dir Barr & Wallace Arnold Trust plc; High Sheriff W Yorks 1981; Hon FCGI, FTI; *Recreations* gardening, fishing; *Clubs* Carlton; *Style—* Charles Fenton, Esq, OBE, JP; ✉ Priestley Green, Norwood Green, Halifax, West Yorks HX3 8RQ (☎ 01422 202373)

FENTON, Rev Christopher Miles Tempest; s of Dr Victor Norman Fenton (d 1983), of Farnham, Surrey, and Doril, *née* Trewartha-James (d 1966), of Itchenor, W Sussex; descended from Sir Geoffrey Fenton, Princ Sec of State in Ireland for Elizabeth I; *b* 24 Jan 1928; *Educ* Bradfield, Queens' Coll Cambridge (BA, LLB, MA, LLM); *m* 1964, Elizabeth Christine, da of Robert Sutherland Macadie (d 1957), of Kington, Herefordshire; 2 s (Jonathan b 1968, Daniel b 1971); *Career* RAEC, Sergeant BAOR 1946–48; asst curate Welling Parish Church 1954–57, chaplain Malsis Sch W Yorks 1957–63, asst curate Bishop Hannington Church Hove 1963–65, vicar Christ Church Ramsgate 1965–71, priest-in-charge St Alban's Mottingham 1971–73; Westminster Pastoral Fndn London: staff psychotherapist 1971–72, supervisor and head of Dept of Gp Studies 1972–83; in private practice as an analytical psychotherapist; conslt: Assoc for Pastoral Care and Counselling, Cambridgeshire Consultancy in Counselling; dir St Anne's Centre Herefordshire 1984–, ed Foundation 1983–89; memb Gp Analytic Soc, founding memb Inst of Psychotherapy and Counselling, registered psychotherapist UK Cncl for Psychotherapy; *Recreations* design and typography, literature, walking, food and wine; *Clubs* East India and Sports; *Style—* The Rev Christopher Fenton; ✉ The Leys, Aston, Kingsland, Leominster, Herefordshire HR6 9PU (☎ 01568 708632)

FENTON, Derek Risian; MVO (1977), MBE (1973), DL (Greater London 1992); s of Arthur Fenton (d 1954), and Gladys, *née* Donaldson (d 1968); *b* 20 July 1921; *Educ* Clark's Coll; *m* 1943, Iris May, da of Sidney Francis Rendle Diamond (d 1958); 1 s (David), 1 da (Sheila); *Career* SBA RN 1940–42; Outra Belting & Rubber Ltd 1935–50, md Heston Codan Rubber Ltd 1978–86 (joined 1950, ret 1986); St John Ambulance: vol memb 1935–, every rank from cadet to cmmr 1975–83, cdr London (Prince of Wales's Dist) 1983–92, cdr Nat HQ 1992–96; head St Petersburg First Aid Project Team 1992–; memb Chapter Gen Order of St John 1982–; Freeman City of London 1977, Liveryman Worshipful Soc of Apothecaries 1984–; KStJ 1975; *Recreations* St John Ambulance and grandchildren; *Clubs* St John House; *Style—* Derek Fenton, Esq, MVO, MBE, DL; ✉ 11 Links Rd, West Acton, London W3 0ER (☎ 0181 993 4353, fax 0181 993 9898)

FENTON, Ernest John; s of Forbes Duncan Campbell Fenton (d 1970), of Angus, Scotland, and Janet Burnfield, *née* Easson (d 1978); *b* 14 Oct 1938; *Educ* Harris Acad Scot; *m* 2 March 1965, Ann Ishbel, da of Robert Ramsay; 1 s (Forbes b 1966), 2 da (Joanna b 1969, Elizabeth b 1976); *Career* ptnr W Greenwell & Co Stockbrokers 1968–81, dir Greenwell Montagu & Co 1986–87; chm and chief exec: Greenwell Montagu Stockbrokers 1988–92, Smith Keen Cutler Ltd 1988–92; DG Assoc of Investment Tst Companies 1993–; CA, AMIIMR, MSI, FRSA; *Recreations* shooting, curling; *Clubs* City; *Style—* Ernest Fenton, Esq; ✉ Dundale Farm, Tunbridge Wells, Kent (☎ 0189 282 2175); 519 Ben Jonson House, The Barbican, London; Association of Investment Trust Companies, Durrant House, 8–13 Chiswell Street, London EC1Y 4YY (☎ 0171 588 5347, fax 0171 638 1803)

FENTON, Lawrence Stanley; s of Charles Fenton (d 1974), of London, and Jochebed, *née* Leboff; *b* 3 Sept 1930; *Educ* The Kilburn GS; *m* 7 Oct 1956, Susan Fay, da of Bertram Barnet Defries (d 1985), of London; 1 s (David b 1965), 2 da (Alison b 1958, Danielle b 1961); *Career* chartered accountant; articled clerk F Rowland & Co 1947–52, sr Touche Ross 1952–54, mangr W A Browne & Co 1954–56; ptnr: Lawrence Fenton Masters & Co 1956–69, Stoy Hayward 1969–87; business and fin conslt 1988–, various non-exec directorships 1988–; tstee The Milly Apthorp Charitable Tst 1982–; former county treas Boy Scouts Assoc, former hon treas of various nat charities; FCA 1952; *Books* Hotel Accounts and Their Audit (1978, 1989, 1994), Charities and Voluntary Organisations, The Honorary Treasurer (1980); *Recreations* painting, golf, swimming, music; *Clubs* Grims Dyke Golf, Hartsbourne Golf & Country; *Style—* Lawrence Fenton, Esq

FENTON, Maria Elizabeth Josephine; *née* Neuman; da of Karol Kurt Neuman, of Surrey, and Betty Joan, *née* Hine; *b* 9 May 1956; *Educ* St Mary's Providence Convent, Kingston Poly, Coll of Law Guildford (BA); *m* 14 Nov 1981 (m dis 1990), William James Timothy Fenton, s of Wing Cdr William James Ferguson Fenton (ret), of Surrey; *Career* admitted slr of the Supreme Ct 1980; legal advsr HSBC (Holdings) plc; memb: Law Soc, Sussex Law Soc; *Style—* Mrs Maria Fenton; ✉ 13 Sceptre, Towergate, London Rd, Brighton BN1 6UF; Legal Adviser, HSBC (Holdings) plc, Group Legal, 10 Lower Thames Street, London EC3R 6AE (☎ 0171 260 4126)

FENTON, Dr Thomas William; s of Thomas William Fenton (d 1986), and Anne Elizabeth, *née* Pearson (d 1961); *b* 31 Aug 1931; *Educ* Gateshead GS, Univ of Edinburgh (MB ChB); *m* 18 Aug 1956, Wilma Favill Mackay; 1 s (Andrew Mackay b 21 Oct 1964), 2 da (Rachel Catherine b 26 Aug 1961, Laura Morrison b 24 July 1967); *Career* registrar in psychiatry Holloway Sanatorium Virginia Water Surrey 1959–62, sr registrar in psychiatry United Birmingham Hosp 1962–65, conslt psychiatrist Hollymoor Hosp Birmingham and E Birmingham Hosp 1965–90, med dir Hollymoor Hosp Birmingham 1970–90, ind conslt psychiatrist 1991–; DPM 1962, FRCPsych 1984; *Recreations* concerts, ballet, opera, wargaming, walking; *Style—* Dr T W Fenton; ✉ 79 May Lane, Hollywood, nr Birmingham B47 5PA (☎ 01564 822520)

FENWICK, (John) Andrew; s of John James Fenwick, of London, and Muriel Gillian, *née* Hodnett; *b* 8 Oct 1959; *Educ* Eton, Univ of Exeter (BA), Harvard Business Sch (PMD Program 1992); *m* 10 Sept 1994, (Fiona) Jane Morgan, da of Hubert John Watkins, of Presteigne, Powys; *Career* accountant Deloitte Haskins & Sells 1982–86, fin PR Broad St Assocs London 1986–87, fin dir and fin PR dir Brunswick Public Relations Ltd 1987–; Freeman City of London 1990, Liveryman Worshipful Co of Mercers 1992 (Freeman 1990); FCA 1995 (ACA 1985); *Recreations* travel, bridge, agriculture, horticulture; *Style—* Andrew Fenwick, Esq; ✉ Brunswick Public Relations Ltd, 15 Lincoln's Inn Fields, London WC2A 3ED (☎ 0171 404 5959, fax 0171 831 2823)

FENWICK, Maj Charles Xtafer Sebastian; LVO (1977); s of David Fenwick (d 1982); *b* 7 April 1946; *Educ* Ampleforth; *Career* Maj, Regt Offr Grenadier Guards 1965–78, tutor to Sheik Maktoum Bin Rashid Al Maktoum of Dubai 1968–69, equerry to HRH The Duke of Edinburgh 1975–77; dir: By Pass Nurseries Ltd 1978–, By Pass Nurseries (Seeds) Ltd 1978–; chm Int Garden Centre Assoc (Br Gp) Ltd 1984–; md The Chelsea Gardener 1984–; *Clubs* Turf; *Style—* Maj Charles Fenwick, LVO; ✉ Barhams Manor, Higham, nr Stoke by Nayland, Suffolk (☎ 01206 337231); 125 Sydney Street, Chelsea, London SW3

FENWICK, Rev Canon Jeffery Robert; s of Stanley Robert Fenwick, of West Clandon, Surrey, and Dorothy Evelyn, *née* Jeffery; *b* 8 April 1930; *Educ* Torquay and Selhurst GS, Pembroke Coll Cambridge (MA); *m* 12 April 1955, Pamela Frances, da of Rev Canon Leonard Galley (d 1979), of St Margarets, Foulsham, Norfolk; 1 s (Jeffery Francis b 1958), 2 da (Alison b 1956, Clare b 1960); *Career* priest: Dio of Liverpool 1955–58, Mashonaland 1958–75; examining chaplain to Bishops of Mashonaland 1966–75, rector Salisbury E Rhodesia and archdeacon of Charter 1970–75, dean and archdeacon of Bulawayo 1975–78, canon of Worcester 1978–88, dean of Guernsey and rector St Peter Port 1989–95, hon canon of Winchester 1989–; memb: Cncl USPG 1978–, Gen Synod 1989–91; chm: Cathedrals Finance Conf 1984–87 (memb 1978–88), Cathedrals Libraries Conf 1987–88 (memb 1978–88), govrs Elizabeth Coll Guernsey 1989–95; govr King's Sch Worcester 1979–88; *Books* A Pattern of History (1970), Chosen People (1971); *Recreations* walking, painting, gardening, music; *Style—* The Rev Canon Jeffery Fenwick; ✉ 4 Moffat Avenue, Hillside, Bulawayo, Zimbabwe

FENWICK, John James; DL (Tyne and Wear 1986); s of James Frederick Trevor Fenwick (d 1979), and Elizabeth Vere, *née* Meldrum; *b* 9 Aug 1932; *Educ* Rugby, Pembroke Coll Cambridge (MA); *m* 27 April 1957, (Muriel) Gillian, da of George Robert Hodnett (d 1978); 3 s (Andrew b 8 Oct 1959, Adam b 20 Oct 1960, Hugo b 29 Dec 1964); *Career* Fenwick Ltd: md 1972–82, dep chm 1972–79, chm 1979–; regnl dir Lloyds Bank plc 1982–86, dir Northern Rock Building Soc 1984–; tstee Civic Tst (North East) 1979–96; govr: Royal GS Newcastle upon Tyne 1975– (chm 1987–), St Paul's Girls' Sch 1988– (chm 1995–); master Worshipful Co of Mercers 1991–92 (memb 1979); *Recreations* travel, European history, shooting; *Clubs* Garrick, MCC; *Style—* J J Fenwick, Esq, DL; ✉ 63 New Bond Street, London W1A 3BS

FENWICK, Maj Justin Francis Quintus; QC (1993); s of David Fenwick (d 1982), of Barhams Manor, Higham, nr Colchester, Suffolk, and Maita Gwladys Joan, *née* Powys-Keck; *b* 11 Sept 1949; *Educ* Ampleforth, Clare Coll Cambridge (MA); *m* 21 June 1975, Marcia Mary, da of Archibald Dunn (d 1977), of Overbury Hall, Layham, Hadleigh, Suffolk; 1 s (Hubert George Francis b 3 Aug 1990), 3 da (Corisande Mary b 1983, Rosamund Xanthe b 1985, Madeleine Isobel b 1988); *Career* Grenadier Gds 1968–81: Maj and Adj 2 Bn 1977–79, Extra Equerry to HRH Duke of Edinburgh 1979–81; called to the Bar Inner Temple 1980; dir By Pass Nurseries Ltd 1982–; chm Soc of Chelsea Res Assoc 1988–; *Recreations* shooting, reading, wine; *Clubs* Garrick, Travellers'; *Style—* Maj Justin Fenwick, QC; ✉ 2 Crown Office Row, Temple, London EC4Y 7HJ (☎ 0171 797 8000)

FENWICK, Leonard Raymond; s of Leo Stanislaws Fenwick (d 1983), of Newcastle upon Tyne, and Hilda May, *née* Downey (d 1989); *b* 10 Aug 1947; *Educ* West Jesmond and John Harlay Schs Newcastle upon Tyne; *m* 1969, Jacqueline; 1 da (Kate b 1982); *Career* NHS: joined 1965, various posts in health serv mgmnt in NE Eng and Humbs 1966–74, admin then gen mangr Freeman Hosp since 1975, chief exec Freeman Gp of Hosps NHS Tst 1990–; cncllr Tyne and Wear CC 1981–86; Freeman City of Newcastle upon Tyne, memb Worshipful Co of Shipwrights 1968, chm Stewards Ctee of Incorporated Cos and Ct of Guild of City of Newcastle upon Tyne; memb Inst of Health Servs Mgmnt 1972; *Style—* Leonard Fenwick, Esq; ✉ The Freeman Group of Hospitals, High Heaton, Newcastle upon Tyne NE7 7DN (☎ 0191 284 3111, fax 0191 213 1968)

FENWICK, Mark Anthony; s of John Fenwick, of Newcastle upon Tyne, and Sheila E M, *née* Edwards; *b* 11 May 1948; *Educ* Millfield Sch; *m* 9 Nov 1972, Margaret Kathleen, da of Col Frederick Roger Hue-Williams (d 1987), of Newbury, Berks; 1 s (Leon b 26 Sept 1980), 1 da (Mia b 14 April 1978); *Career* vice chm Fenwick Ltd 1995–; *Recreations* music, outdoor activities; *Style—* Mark Fenwick, Esq; ✉ Fenwick Ltd, New Bond Street, London W1A 3BJ

FENWICK, Dr Peter Brooke Cadogan; s of Anthony Fenwick (d 1954), of Kenya, and Betty, *née* Darling (d 1983); *b* 25 May 1935; *Educ* Stowe, Trinity Coll Cambridge (MB BChir), St Thomas' Hosp Med Sch London (DPM); *m* 18 May 1963, Elizabeth Isobel, da of Harry Nicholas Roberts (d 1985), of Bracewell, Yorkshire; 1 s (Tristram Nicholas Cadogan b 2 Nov 1967), 2 da (Annabelle Sarah Cadogan b 9 March 1964, Natasha Jane Cadogan b 13 Nov 1965); *Career* sr lectr Institute of Psychiatry Univ of London 1972–, hon conslt research neurophysiologist Broadmoor Hosp 1973–; conslt neurophysiologist: Westminster Hosp 1974–77, St Thomas' Hosp 1974–89, Radcliffe Infirmary 1989–; conslt neuropsychiatrist Maudsley Hosp 1977–; author of numerous articles on epilepsy, neurophysiology, violence, automatic behaviour; FRCPsych; *Recreations* flying, music, hill walking, trout fishing; *Style—* Dr Peter Fenwick; ✉ Institute of Psychiatry, Denmark Hill, London SE5 8AZ (☎ 0171 703 6333)

FENWICK, Thomas Richard Featherstone; s of Edwin Arthur Featherstone Fenwick (d 1978), of Foresters Lodge, Wolsingham, Co Durham, and Marjorie Newton, *née* Weeks (d 1989); *b* 11 Dec 1926; *Educ* Charterhouse, Jesus Coll Cambridge; *m* 27 April 1957, Sarah Mary, da of Thomas Alexander Page (d 1970); 3 s, 1 s decd, 1 da; *Career* RA 1945; landowner, farmer, forester; JP Co Durham 1966–79, High Sheriff Co Palatine of Durham 1975–76; *Recreations* shooting; *Clubs* Farmers; *Style—* Thomas Fenwick, Esq; ✉ Bishop Oak, Wolsingham, Bishop Auckland, Co Durham DL13 3LT (☎ 01388 527 435)

FENWICK, Trevor James; s of Leslie Fenwick, of London, and Mabel Alice, *née* Lee; *b* 28 Feb 1954; *Educ* Highgate Sch, Univ of Essex (BA); *m* Jane Seton Hindley; 3 s (James b 1987, Edward b 1989, Charles b 1991); *Career* md Euromonitor plc 1988– (dir 1980–), pres Euromonitor International Inc 1993–; chm Directory Publishers Assoc 1993– (vice chm 1991–93); memb Bd Euro Assoc of Directory Publishers 1995–; memb New Media Gp and Copyright Gp Periodical Publishers Assoc; *Style—* Trevor Fenwick, Esq; ✉ 99 Richmond Avenue, London N1 0LT (☎ 0171 607 4757); Euromonitor plc, 60–61 Britton Street, London EC1M 5NA (☎ 0171 251 8024, fax 0171 608 3149, e-mail Trevor.Fenwick@Euromonitor.Com)

FERDINAND, Leslie (Les); *b* 8 Dec 1966; *Career* professional footballer; with Hayes FC until 1987, transferred to QPR (for £30,000) 1987–95 (on loan Brentford 1987–88 and Besiktas Turkey 1988–89), transferred to Newcastle United FC (for £6m) 1995–; England: 12 full caps and 5 goals (as at Jan 1997), memb squad Euro 96; voted PFA Player of the Year 1996; former painter and decorator; *Style—* Les Ferdinand, Esq; ✉ c/o Newcastle FC, St James's Park, Newcastle NE1 4ST

FERENS, (Charles) Richard; s of John Leslie Ferens (d 1987), of Harrogate, and Joan, *née* Mannington; *b* 23 Dec 1936; *Educ* The Leys Sch Cambridge, Trinity Hall Cambridge (MA); *m* 17 Sept 1960, Penelope Jane, da of Lt-Col Stuart Dewes Hayward (d 1983), of Suffolk; 3 da (Emma b 1962, Caroline b 1963, Sophie b 1965); *Career* Lt E Yorks Regt 1955–57; hon sec Land Agency and Agric Div RICS 1977–80 (chm E Anglian Branch); hon dir Royal Show 1982–87, vice pres Royal Agric Soc of England, chm Lincs Branch Br Food and Farming 1989; arbitrator to Lord Chllr; conslt surveyor to Strutt and Parker, valuer Agric Mortgage Corporation, chm Rural Devpt Cmmn (Lincolnshire);

Recreations shooting, fishing, gardening; *Clubs* Farmers'; *Style*— Richard Ferens, Esq; ✉ Casthorpe Lodge, Barrowby, Grantham, Lincs (☎ 01476 563559)

FERGUS, Jeffrey John (Jeff); s of George M Fergus (d 1979), of Glasgow, and Catherine, *née* Fellowes; *b* 23 March 1949; *Educ* Crookson Castle Sch Glasgow, Univ of Strathclyde (BA); *m* 18 March 1989, Emily, da of Leslie Kark; 2 s (Frederick George Arthur b 1 April 1991, Charles William Merry b 26 May 1993); *Career* Leo Burnett advtg agency: joined Account Mgmnt Dept 1969, appointed to bd 1975, head of dept 1979–83, dep md 1980–83; md Grandfield Rork Collins 1983–86; Leo Burnett: md and chief exec Europe and ME 1986–94, i/c Asia and the Pacific ops 1994–; MCIM 1980, MIPA 1982; *Clubs* RAC, Annabel's, Caledonian; *Style*— Jeff Fergus, Esq; ✉ c/o Leo Burnett Ltd, 60 Sloane Avenue, London SW3 3XB (☎ 0171 591 9111, fax 0171 591 9593)

FERGUS-THOMPSON, Gordon; s of George Leonard Thompson (d 1986), of Leeds, and Constance, *née* Webb; *b* 9 March 1952; *Educ* Temple Moor GS Leeds, Royal Manchester Coll of Music; *Career* concert pianist; debut Wigmore Hall 1976; performed as soloist with orchs incl: The Philharmonia, English Chamber Orch, City of Birmingham Symphony Orch, Royal Liverpool Philharmonic, Hallé Orch, Bournemouth Symphony Orch, BBC Symphony Orchs; regular bdcaster BBC Radio 3, toured extensively throughout Europe, Australia, Far East, South Africa and USA; awarded Calouste Gulbenkian fellowship 1978; prof of piano Royal Coll of Music 1996–; *Recordings* incl: Complete Works of Ravel (2 Vols) 1992, Complete Works of Debussy (5 vols, winner solo instrumental section Music Retailers Assoc awards 1991) 1989, Bach Transcriptions 1990, Complete Works of Scriabin (Vol 1 - Sonatas 4, 5, 9 and 10 and Studies Opus 42, winner Solo Instrumental Section MRA awards 1992) 1990, Rachmaninoff Etudes-Tableaux 1990, Bach transcriptions 1990, Two Rachmaninoff Sonatas 1987, Balakirev and Scriabin Sonatas 1987, Scriabin Vol 2 (Sonatas 2 and 3 and Studies Op 8) 1994, Scriabin Vol 3 (Preludes Op 2–17) 1994; *Recreations* art, chess, cooking, tennis, humour; *Style*— Gordon Fergus-Thompson, Esq; ✉ 150 Audley Rd, London NW4 3EG (☎ 0181 202 5861); c/o John Humphreys, Camerata Artists, 4 Margaret Rd, Birmingham B17 0EU (☎ 0121 426 6208)

FERGUSON, *see:* Johnson-Ferguson

FERGUSON, Alexander Chapman (Alex); CBE (1995, OBE 1984); s of Alexander Beaton Ferguson (d 1979), and Elizabeth, *née* Hardy (d 1986); *b* 31 Dec 1941; *Educ* Govan High Sr Secdy Sch; *m* 12 March 1966, Catherine Russell, da of Hugh Holding (d 1952); 3 s (Mark b 18 Sept 1968, Jason b 9 Feb 1972, Darren b (twin) 9 Feb 1972); *Career* professional football manager; player: Queen's Park 1958–60, St Johnstone 1960–64, Dumfermline Athletic 1964–67, Glasgow Rangers 1967–69, Falkirk 1969–73, Ayr Utd 1973–74, two Scot League caps; mangr: E Stirling 1974, St Mirren 1974–78 (First Div champions 1976–77), Aberdeen 1978–86 (winners Euro Cup Winners' Cup 1983, Super Cup winners 1983, Premier Div champions 1980, 1982 and 1984, 4 times Scot FA Cup winners, League Cup winners 1985), Scot Nat Team 1985–86 (asst mangr under Jock Stein 1985–86); Manchester Utd 1986–; honours with Manchester Utd: FA Cup winners 1990, winners Euro Cup Winners' Cup 1991, Super Cup winners 1991, Rumbelows Cup 1992, Charity Shield 1990, 1993, 1994 and 1996, winners inaugural FA Premier League Championship 1992/93, winners League and FA Cup double 1994 and 1996 (setting record); Manager of the Year Scotland 1983–85, Manager of the Year England 1993–94; Hon MA Univ of Salford 1996; *Books* A Light in the North (1985), Alex Ferguson - Six Years at United (1992), Just Champion (1994), A Year in the Life (1995); *Recreations* golf, snooker; *Style*— Alex Ferguson, Esq, CBE; ✉ Manchester Utd FC, Old Trafford, Manchester M16 0RA (☎ 0161 872 1661, fax 0161 873 7210, telex 666564 UNITED G)

FERGUSON, Prof Allister Ian; *b* 10 Dec 1951; *Educ* Univ of St Andrews (BSc, PhD), Univ of Oxford (MA); *Career* visiting scholar Stanford Univ 1977–79; postdoctoral fell: Univ of St Andrews 1979–80, Univ of Oxford 1980–83; sr lectr Univ of Southampton 1987–88 (lectr 1983–87); Univ of Strathclyde: prof of photonics 1989–, tech dir Inst of Photonics 1995–; Lindemann fell 1977–79, SERC postdoctoral fell 1981–86; Neil Arnott prize 1974, NPL Metrology award 1983; chm and md Microlase Optical Systems Ltd; memb: Int Steering Ctee Int Confs on Laser Spectroscopy, Editorial Bd Optical and Quantum Electronics; topical ed OSA Jl Applied Optics; FInstP 1990, FRSE 1993; author of numerous pubns and chapters in books; *Style*— Prof Allister I Ferguson, FRSE; ✉ Department of Physics and Applied Physics, University of Strathclyde, John Anderson Building, Glasgow G4 0NG (☎ 0141 552 4400, fax 0141 552 2891)

FERGUSON, Andrew James; s of K W E Ferguson, of Camberley, Surrey, and Sally, *née* Wragg (now Mrs Davis), of Cheltenham, Glos; *b* 22 Sept 1958; *Educ* St Chad's Cathedral Sch Lichfield Staffs, King's Sch Worcester, Br Sch of Osteopathy London (Dip); *m* May 1991, Louise, da of Nigel Mizen, of Dunsfold, Surrey; 2 c; *Career* in private osteopathic practice London 1980–, lectr Br Sch of Osteopathy 1982–86, osteopath to English Nat Ballet Sch 1992; memb Gen Cncl and Register of Osteopaths; *Books* Back and Neck Pain (1988); *Recreations* watching dance, gardening, writing; *Style*— Andrew Ferguson, Esq; ✉ 15 Pembridge Road, London W11 3HG (☎ 0171 937 2298)

FERGUSON, Andrew John Duncan; s of James Duncan Ferguson (d 1980), of Sutton, Surrey, and Kathleen Ann, *née* Kemp (d 1986); *b* 9 June 1940; *Educ* Epsom Coll, St John's Coll Cambridge (MA); *m* 25 March 1967, Elizabeth Mary, da of Cdr Leslie Edward Wright (d 1988), of Wisborough Green, W Sussex; 1 s (Ian Duncan b 5 April 1968), 3 da (Joanna Elizabeth b 12 Nov 1970, Kate Juliet b 30 Aug 1979, Gillian Mary b 1 Jan 1983); *Career* with Andrew W Barr & Co 1962–64, Standard Industrial Group 1964–67, Johnston Group plc 1967–87 (chief exec 1978–87); chm Blease Medical Equipment Ltd 1987–; Freeman City of London, Liveryman Worshipful Co of Coachmakers and Coach Harness Makers 1965 (Master 1992–93); FCA 1963; *Recreations* sailing, squash; *Clubs* RAC, Caledonian; *Style*— Andrew Ferguson, Esq; ✉ Mundys Hill, Shere Road, Ewhurst, Surrey GU6 7PQ (☎ 01483 277237)

FERGUSON, Anne; OBE; *Career* head of corp communications ICI plc until 1992, head of corp communications Zeneca plc (following demerger from ICI) 1992–93, conslt Spencer Stuart Associates Ltd recruitment conslts 1993–; non-exec dir: National Power plc 1992–, Capital Radio plc, Cornwell Parker plc; memb: Target Team, Opportunity 2000, Business in the Community; govr St Mary's Sch Calne; *Style*— Mrs Anne Ferguson, OBE; ✉ Spencer Stuart Associates Ltd, 16 Connaught Place, London W2 2ES (☎ 0171 493 1238)

FERGUSON, Christopher Mark; s of Maj Michael Frederick George Ferguson (d 1982), and Josephine Manners, *née* Ackland (d 1987); *b* 29 Nov 1957; *Educ* Sherborne; *m* 1 May 1982, Jacqueline, da of William Alexander Kirkwood, of Stamford, Lincs; 1 s (Robert b 1985), 2 da (Lucy b 1987, Alice b 1989); *Career* called to the Bar Middle Temple 1979; memb Middle Temple 1975–; *Recreations* various sports, music, theatre; *Style*— Christopher Ferguson, Esq; ✉ 7 The Glen, Westbury Park, Bristol BS6 7JH (☎ 0117 973 2283); Assize Court Chambers, 14 Small St, Bristol BS1 1DE (☎ 0117 926 4587, fax 0117 922 6835)

FERGUSON, Capt (Robert) Duncan; s of Lt-Col Robert Hunter Ferguson, ED (d 1966), of Glenlair, Knockvennie, Castle Douglas, Kirkcudbrightshire, and Jean Cooper, *née* Baxter; *b* 2 May 1940; *Educ* Fettes, Univ of London (BSc), Nato Defense Coll; *m* 2 Sept 1967, Henrietta MacDonald, da of Maj John Dunlop Williamson (KAR, ka Abyssinia 1942); 1 s (Angus b 1971), 2 da (Samantha b 1969, Emily b 1979); *Career* joined RN 1958, Weapon Engr Offr HMS Brighton 1965–67, Polaris Exec 1967–70, RNEC Maradon 1970–73, Weapon Engr Offr HMS Arrow 1974–77, Naval Sec 1977–78, Cdr 1977, BRNC Dartmouth 1978–80; Weapon Engr Offr: 4 Frigate Sqdn 1980–82 (despatches 1982), Dep Fleet Weapon Engr 1982–84; Capt 1983, Def advsr Wellington, Suva, Nuku' Alofa 1984–87, Flag Offr Scotland and NI as project co-ordinator Pitreavie Devpt Project 1987–90, Cdre 1990, Asst COS (CIS) AFSOUTH 1990–92, ret 1993; sr careers liaison offr (Navy) 1993–; chm RN Winter Sports Assoc 1988–90; pres Stewartry Sea Cadets 1994–; FIEE 1990, FIMgt 1993; *Recreations* offshore sailing, skiing, golf, fishing, shooting; *Clubs* Southerness Golf, RN and OF Golf Socs, RN Sailing Assoc, RN Winter Sports Assoc; *Style*— Capt Duncan Ferguson, RN (ret); ✉ Glenlair, Knockvennie, Castle Douglas, Kirkcudbrightshire DG7 3DF (☎ 01556 650209)

FERGUSON, George Robin Paget; s of Robert Spencer Ferguson, MVO, of Manningford Bruce House, Pewsey, Wilts, and Eve Mary, *née* Paget; *b* 22 March 1947; *Educ* Wellington, Univ of Bristol (BA, BArch); *m* 24 May 1969, (Aymée) Lavinia, da of Sir John Clerk, 10 Bt, of Penicuik House, Midlothian; 1 s (John b 1974), 2 da (Alice b 1971, Corinna b 1979); *Career* architect; fndr practice 1972; Ferguson Mann: ptnr 1979–87, md 1988–; fndr and dir Acanthus Associated Architectural Practices Ltd 1986–, ptnr Concept Planning Group 1991–; dir Bristol 97 1991–, chm Bristol Exploratory; govr Univ of West of England, memb Br Cathedral Fabric Ctee, tstee Gtr Bristol Fndn 1995–; Bristol City cncllr (Lib) 1973–79, Parly candidate (Alliance) Bristol West 1983–87; High Sheriff of Bristol 1996–97; memb Soc of Merchant Venturers 1995; RIBA 1972; *Books* Races Against Time (1983); *Recreations* writing, broadcasting, travel, photography, sketching, playing with science; *Style*— George Ferguson, Esq; ✉ Ferguson Mann Architects/Acanthus Bristol, Royal Colonnade, 18 Great George St, Bristol BS1 5RH (☎ 0117 929 9293, fax 0117 929 9295)

FERGUSON, Brig (John) Gordon Goddard de Poulton; OBE (1984), ADC (1995); s of Dr Stanley Fisher Ferguson, of Finchfield, Wolverhampton, W Mids, and Johanna Margaret McDougall, *née* Gordon (d 1952); *b* 5 March 1943; *Educ* Downside, RMA Sandhurst, Staff Coll Camberley, NATO Def Coll Rome; *m* 5 Jan 1968, Celia Mary, da of Cdr Claudius Alexander Herdman, DL, RN, (d 1993), of Sion Mills, Co Tyrone; 2 s (Edward Alexander de Poulton b 1978, Rory James de Poulton b 1980), 2 da (Clare Joanna de Poulton b 1968, Lucy Adelia de Poulton b 1970); *Career* cmmnd 1st The Queen's Dragoon Guards (QDG) 1962, helicopter pilot 1967–71, MA CinC North 1977–79, Dir Staff Army Staff Coll Camberley 1980–82, CO QDG 1982–85, Cdr Br Forces Lebanon 1983–84, ACOS G3 HQ 1 Br Corps 1985–87, Chief Policy SHAPE 1988–90, head Reinforcement Cell HQ NATO 1990–92, Dep Cmd and COS HQ S Dist Aldershot 1992–94, ACOS Ops HQ NORTH 1994–; FIMgt 1989; *Recreations* fishing, classical music, sailing and international politics; *Clubs* Army & Navy; *Style*— Brig Gordon Ferguson, OBE, ADC; ✉ ACOS Ops, HQ NORTH, BFPO 50, (☎ 00 47 5157 2550)

FERGUSON, Air Vice-Marshal Gordon MacArthur; CB (1993), CBE (1990); s of James Miller Ferguson, of Shirley, Southampton, and Elizabeth Thomson, *née* Barron (d 1996); *b* 15 April 1938; *Educ* King Edward VI Sch Southampton; *m* 16 July 1966, Alison Mary, da of Reginald Beaman Saxby (d 1977); 1 da (Alexandra Mary b 3 May 1967), 1 s (James Innes b 29 December 1969); *Career* cmmnd RAF 1960; Mobile Air Movements 1961–63, RAF Pergamos Cyprus 1963–65, RAF Nicosia Cyprus 1965–67, HQ 38 Gp 1967–69, RAF Stafford 1969–70, RAF Fylingdales 1970–73, MOD Supply Policy 1973–75, HQ 2 ATAF 1975–77, attended RAF Staff Coll 1977, OC Tactical Supply Wing 1977–79, MOD Supply Policy 1979–81, Air Warfare Course 1981, MOD Supply Policy 1981–85, Dir Supply Mgmnt 1987–89 (Dep Dir 1985–87), Dir Air Memb for Supply and Orgn Re-Organisation Implementation Team 1989–91, Air Offr Admin HQ Strike Command 1991–94, ret 1994; md Taylor Curnow Ltd mgmnt conslts 1994–; MInstD; *Recreations* golf, bridge, gardening; *Clubs* RAF; *Style*— Air Vice-Marshal G M Ferguson, CB, CBE; ✉ Lilley Cottage, Turnpike Hill, Withersfield, Suffolk CB9 7SA

FERGUSON, Dr Howard; s of Stanley Ferguson, of Belfast, NI, and Frances, *née* Carr; *b* 21 Oct 1908; *Educ* Westminster, RCM; *Career* composer, pianist and musicologist; compositions incl: Violin Sonatas 1 and 2 (1933 & 1949), Two Ballads (1934), Partita (1937), Piano Concerto (1952), Discovery Song-Cycle (1952), Amore Langueo (1956), The Dream of the Rood (1959); publications incl complete keyboard works of: Purcell (1963), Dagincour (1969), Croft (1974), Schubert (1978); asst organiser daily wartime Nat Gallery Concerts 1939–46; memb CCC; Hon DMus Queen's Univ Belfast 1959; *Books* Keyboard Interpretation (1975), Entertaining Solo, a Cookbook for the single host (privately printed, 1995), Keyboard Duets from the 16th to the 20th Century (OUP, 1995); *Recreations* reading, cooking; *Style*— Dr Howard Ferguson; ✉ 51 Barton Road, Cambridge CB3 9LG (☎ 01223 359206)

FERGUSON, Ian Cowan (Tim); *b* 3 July 1957; *Educ* Geelong GS Victoria Australia, Keio Gijuku Univ Tokyo, Univ Coll of Buckingham; *Career* with Hambros Bank Ltd 1979–81; County NatWest Ltd: md County NatWest Securities Japan 1983–89, chief exec County NatWest Securities Ltd 1989–91, dep chief exec County NatWest Ltd 1990–91; chief exec HSBC Asset Management Ltd 1991–; chm: HSBC Asset Management Hong Kong Ltd, HSBC Asset Management Bahamas Ltd, HSBC Life Ltd, HSBC Life International Ltd; also dir: HSBC Investment Bank Ltd, HSBC Asset Management Americas Inc, HSBC Private Equity Management Ltd, The Korea Asia Fund Ltd, The China Fund Inc, Private Equity Management BVI Ltd; *Style*— Tim Ferguson, Esq; ✉ HSBC Asset Management Ltd, 6 Bevis Marks, London EC3A 7QP (☎ 0171 336 5838, fax 0171 929 0524)

FERGUSON, James Gordon Dickson; s of Col James Dickson Ferguson, OBE, ERD, DL (d 1979), of Banbridge, Co Down, and Jean, *née* Gordon; *b* 12 Nov 1947; *Educ* Cargilfield Sch Edinburgh, Winchester Coll, Trinity Coll Dublin (BA); *m* 20 June 1970, Nicola Hilland, da of Walter G H Stewart; 2 s (Jim, William), 1 da (Jessica); *Career* Stewart Ivory & Co Ltd (formerly Stewart Fund Managers Ltd): joined 1970, dir 1974–, chm 1989–; dir: Value & Income Trust plc, Olim Convertible Trust plc; dep chm Assoc of Investment Trust Cos; govr Gordonstoun Sch; *Recreations* country pursuits; *Clubs* New (Edinburgh); *Style*— James Ferguson, Esq; ✉ 25 Heriot Row, Edinburgh, EH3 6EN; Stewart Ivory & Co Ltd, 45 Charlotte Square, Edinburgh EH2 4HW (☎ 0131 226 3271, fax 0131 226 5120, telex 72500)

FERGUSON, Col James Henderson; s of John Ferguson (d 1953), and Esther Isobel Ferguson (d 1981); *b* 26 July 1928; *Educ* Dunoon GS, Staff Coll Camberley, NATO Defence Coll Rome; *m* 16 Nov 1957; 1 s (John Stuart b 20 Feb 1960), 2 da (Catherine Mary Esther b 6 Sept 1958, Jennifer Mary Anne b 1 Aug 1964); *Career* CO 22 Air Def Regt 1969–72, GSO1 Ops/Plans SHAPE 1972–74, Chief Military Personnel SHAPE 1978–81, Chief Public Relations AFCENT 1981–83; dir Salmon and Trout Assoc 1985–92, sec Salmon and Trout Assoc Charitable Tst 1990–; clerk River Ruel District Salmon Fishery Bd 1994–; memb: Salmon Advsy Ctee 1987–, Regnl Fisheries Advsy Ctee Southern EA 1991–; gen sec Fédération Internationale de la Pêche Sportive à la Mouche 1991–; *Recreations* golf, skiing, fishing; *Clubs* Army and Navy, Rye Golf; *Style*— Col James Ferguson; ✉ 6 The Strand, Rye, E Sussex TN31 7DB (☎ and fax 01797 222601)

FERGUSON, Jeremy John; s of Archibald John Lindo Ferguson (d 1975), of Great Missenden, Bucks, and Ann Meryl, *née* Thomas; *b* 12 Nov 1935; *Educ* Stowe; *m* 19 July 1958, Josephine Mary (d 1995), da of Arthur William John Hitchcock (d 1969), of Northam, Bideford, Devon; 1 s (Paul b 1962), 1 da (Elizabeth b 1966); *Career* ptnr: Seldon Ward & Nuttall 1960–74, Jeremy Ferguson & Co 1974–91, Chanters Barnstaple 1986–91, Chanter Ferguson Bideford & Barnstaple 1991–; dep coroner N Devon 1964–74, memb N Devon Manufacturers Assoc, hon slr (memb and past pres) Bideford C of C, fndr and sec Bideford Devpt Project, pres Law Soc Motor Club, memb: Legal Aid Area Ctee,

Devon and Exeter Law Soc; *Recreations* motor racing, flying (PPL), video photography; *Style—* Jeremy Ferguson, Esq; ✉ Langleys, 25 Bay View Rd, Northam, Bideford, Devon EX39 1BH (☎ 01237 474855); 17 The Quay, Bideford, North Devon EX39 2EN (☎ 01237 478751, fax 01237 470893); Bridge Chambers, Barnstaple, North Devon EX31 1HF (☎ 01271 42268)

FERGUSON, Kenneth Gordon; OBE (1990); s of James Ferguson, of Aberdour, Fife, and Blanche Stockdale, *née* MacDonald; *b* 17 Feb 1944; *Educ* Leith Acad, Heriot Watt Univ, Napier Coll; *m* 21 Aug 1970, Jennifer Day, da of late Hugh MacTaggart Love, and Margaret, *née* Anderson; 2 da (Amanda b 11 Aug 1971, Rebecca b 19 June 1975); *Career* chartered quantity surveyor; trainee Robert T B Gilray 1962–67; asst: Boyden and Cockrane 1967–69, City of Edinburgh Architect's Dept 1969–71, Todd and Ledson 1972–79; sr ptnr Kenneth Ferguson and Partners 1979–; vice pres SCUA 1985–87, memb Edinburgh DC 1977–92, chm Advsy Bd Commercial Unit Cardonald Coll Glasgow 1992–; tstee dir Castles of Scotland Building Preservation Tst 1994–; FRICS 1979 (ARICS 1969), ACIOB 1991; *Clubs* Scottish Arts; *Style—* Kenneth G Ferguson, Esq, OBE; ✉ 68 Hill View Terrace, Edinburgh EH12 8RG (☎ 0131 334 3400)

FERGUSON, Prof Mark William James; s of late James Ferguson, of Marple Bridge, Cheshire, and Elanor Gwendoline, *née* McCoubrey; *b* 11 Oct 1955; *Educ* Coleraine Academical Inst, Queen's Univ Belfast (BSc, BDS, PhD); *m* (m dis); 2 da (Fleur Marcia b 9 Sept 1987, Astrid Olivia b 8 May 1991); *Career* Winston Churchill fell 1978, lectr in anatomy Queen's Univ Belfast 1979–84, prof of basic dental sci and head Dept of Cell and Structural Biol Univ of Manchester 1984–, dean Sch of Biological Sciences Univ of Manchester 1994–; Colyer prize RSM 1980, Alan J Davis Achievement award American Dental Assoc 1981, Conway medal Royal Acad of Med in Ireland 1985, Darwin lectr Br Assoc for the Advancement of Sci 1987, distinguished scientist award Int Assoc for Dental Res Washington 1988, President's medal Br Assoc of Oral and Maxillofacial Surgeons 1990, John Tomes prize RCS 1990, hon fell RCS (Ireland) 1990, Steager lecture New York Univ 1992, faculty day lectr and visiting prof Univ of Witwatersrand Johannesburg 1994, Teale lecture RCP London 1994, 86th Kelvin lecture IEE London 1995, J J Pindborg int prize for research in oral biology 1996, Sheldon Friel medal and lecture Euro Orthodontic Soc 1996, Broadhurst lecture Harvard Med Sch 1996; chm Health and Life Scis Panel UK Govt Technol Foresight Prog, memb Cncl Euro Res Gp on Oral Biology, sec and treas Euro Tissue Repair Soc, govr Research into Ageing, pres Med Section Br Assoc for the Advancement of Scis, pres Craniofacial Soc, memb Life Sciences Ctee European Space Agency, memb Higher Educn Cncl for England Basic Med and Dental Scis Panel 1996–; author of over 200 papers and books on: palate devpt, wound healing, sex determination, alligators and crocodiles; *Books* The Structure, Development & Evolution of Reptiles (1984), Crocodiles & Alligators: an Illustrated Encyclopaedic Survey by International Experts (1989), Cleft Lip & Palate: Long Term Results & Future Prospects (1990), Egg Incubation, Its Effects on Embryonic Development in Birds & Reptiles (1991), Gray's Anatomy (38th ed); *Recreations* scientific research, biology, travel, wildlife, reading, antiques; *Style—* Prof Mark Ferguson; ✉ School of Biological Sciences, University of Manchester, 3.239 Stopford Building, Manchester M13 9PT (☎ 0161 275 6775, fax 0161 275 5945)

FERGUSON, Nicholas Eustace Haddon; s of Capt Derrick Ferguson, RN (d 1992), of Craigard, Tighnabruaich, Argyll, and Betsy, *née* Eustace; *b* 14 Oct 1948; *Educ* Winchester Coll, Univ of Edinburgh (BSc Econ), Harvard Business Sch (MBA, Baker scholar); *m* 18 Dec 1976, (Margaret) Jane Dura, da of Robert Collin, of Wheatsheaf House, Hook Norton, Oxon; 2 s (Alexander b 1978, Thomas b 1985), 1 da (Cornelia b 1979); *Career* venture capitalist; chm Schroder Ventures Ltd, dir J Henry Schroder Wagg and Co Ltd; also dir: Singapore International Merchant Bankers Ltd, Schroder Real Estate Investment Inc, Schroder Venture Mangrs (Guernsey) Ltd, Schroder Securities (Japan) Ltd, Schroder PTV Ptnrs KK, Int Students Club (C of E) Ltd; *Recreations* sailing, skiing; *Clubs* Brooks's; *Style—* Nicholas Ferguson, Esq; ✉ 18 Queensdale Rd, London W11 4QB (☎ 0171 229 0503); Schroder Ventures, 120 Cheapside, London EC2V 6DS (direct ☎ 0171 382 6613, telex 885029, fax 0171 382 6878)

FERGUSON, Richard; QC (NI 1973, UK 1986); s of Wesley Ferguson (d 1972), of Derrygonnelly, Co Fermanagh, and Edith, *née* Hewitt (d 1995); *b* 22 Aug 1935; *Educ* Methodist Coll, Queen's Univ Belfast (LLB), Trinity Coll Dublin (BA); *m* 1 (m dis), Janet, da of Irvine Magowan, CB (d 1978), of Mount Norris, Co Armagh; 3 s (Richard b 1964, William b 1966, James b 1968), 1 da (Kathrine b 1962); m 2, Roma Felicity, da of J A Whelan, ERD, of Antrim Rd, Belfast; 1 s (Patrick b 1987); *Career* Lt Royal Irish Fus TA 1958–61; called to the Bar Gray's Inn 1956, head of chambers, sr counsel Republic of Ireland 1983; chm: Criminal Bar Assoc of England and Wales, Bar Cncl of England and Wales 1990–95, Mental Health Review Tbnl (NI); bencher Gray's Inn 1994; MP S Antrim 1986–88; FRGS; *Recreations* swimming; *Clubs* Kildare St (Dublin); *Style—* Richard Ferguson, Esq, QC; ✉ Sandhill House, Derrygonnelly, Fermanagh, NI; 61 Highbury Hill, London N5; 1 Crown Office Row, Temple, London EC4Y 7HH (☎ 0171 797 7111, fax 0171 353 3923)

FERGUSON, Dr Roger; s of Dr Alan Hudspeth Ferguson (d 1967), and Betty Fielding, *née* Willatt; *b* 23 Aug 1946; *Educ* City Sch Lincoln, Univ of Birmingham (MB ChB, MD); *m* 12 Jan 1974, Ruth Elizabeth, da of Prof Harold Spencer, of Willaston, Cheshire; 3 da (Sarah Helen b 1975, Jean Alison b 1976, Fiona Jane b 1978); *Career* med registrar Worcester Royal Infirmary 1970–73, res registrar Birmingham Gen Hosp 1973–75, sr med registrar Nottingham Gen Hosp and Derby Royal Infirmary 1975–79; conslt physician and gastroenterologist: Arrowe Park Hosp Wirral 1979–, BUPA Murrayfield Hosp Wirral 1980–; memb: Midland Gastroenterological Soc, Northern Gastroenterological Soc, Br Soc of Gastroenterology; former chm Wirral Wine Soc; FRCP 1987 (MRCP 1972); *Books* Text Book of Gastroenterology (contrib, 1990 and 1993); *Recreations* swimming, golf, music, reading; *Clubs* Caldy Golf; *Style—* Dr Roger Ferguson; ✉ 89 Bidston Rd, Oxton, Birkenhead, Wirral, Merseyside L43 6TS (☎ 0151 652 3722); Arrowe Park Hospital, Arrowe Park Rd, Upton, Wirral L4G 5LM (☎ 0151 678 5111)

FERGUSON, William James; OBE (1997), DL (Aberdeen); s of William Adam Fergsuon (d 1955), and Violet, *née* Wiseman; *b* 3 April 1933; *Educ* Turriff Acad, N of Scotland Coll of Agric; *m* 27 June 1961, Carroll Isobella, da of Robert Shaw McDonald Milne, of Kincardineshire; 1 s (William b 27 April 1962), 3 da (Kim b 29 May 1963, Nicola b 17 Aug 1965, Emma b 5 Aug 1968); *Career* 1 Bn Gordon Highlanders 1952–54; farmer 1954–; vice chm Aberdeen and Dist Milk Mktg Bd 1984–94; chm: Aberdeen Milk Co Ltd 1994–95, Aberdeen Milk Servs 1995–; memb Scottish Co Life Museums Tst Ltd, dir Hannah Research Inst 1995–; vice chm: Scottish Agric Coll until 1996, Rowet Res Inst; FRAgS; *Recreations* golf, skiing, field sports; *Style—* William J Ferguson, Esq, OBE, DL; ✉ Rothiebrisbane, Fyvie, Turriff, Aberdeenshire AB53 8LE (☎ 01651 891213, fax 0161 891214)

FERGUSON DAVIE, Sir Antony Francis; 6 Bt (UK 1847), of Creedy, Devonshire; s of Rev Sir (Arthur) Patrick Ferguson Davie, 5 Bt, TD (d 1988), and Iris Dawn, *née* Cable-Buller (d 1992); *b* 23 March 1952; *Educ* Stanbridge Earls Sch, Birkbeck Coll London; *Heir* kinsman, John Ferguson Davie b 1 May 1906; *Style—* Sir Antony Ferguson Davie, Bt; ✉ c/o First Direct, Millshaw Park Lane, Leeds LS11 0LT

FERGUSON-SMITH, Prof Malcolm Andrew; s of Dr John Ferguson-Smith (d 1978), of Strathay, Perthshire, and Ethel May, *née* Thorne (d 1993); *b* 5 Sept 1931; *Educ* Stowe, Univ of Glasgow (MB ChB); *m* 11 July 1960, Marie Eve, da of Stanislaw Franciszek Gzowski (d 1981), of Baltimore, USA; 1 s (John b 1970), 3 da (Anne b 1961, Nicola b 1965, Julia b 1976); *Career* prof of med genetics Univ of Glasgow 1973–87, dir West of Scot Regnl Genetics Serv 1973–87, ed in chief Prenatal Diagnosis 1980–, prof of pathology Univ of Cambridge 1987–, hon conslt in med genetics Addenbrooke's Hosp 1987–, dir E Anglian Regnl Genetics Serv 1987–95, fell Peterhouse Cambridge 1987–; Makdougall-Brisbane Prize Royal Soc of Edinburgh 1988; memb Neurology Bd MRC 1974–76, vice pres Genetical Soc 1978–81, pres Clinical Genetics Soc 1979–81, memb Cncl RCPath 1983–86, pres Perm Ctee Int Congress of Human Genetics 1986–91, fndr memb Exec Ctee Human Genome Orgn 1988–92, WHO advsr in human genetics 1988–, memb Cell Bd MRC 1989–93, pres elect European Soc of Human Genetics 1996; Hon DSc Strathclyde 1992; FRCP(Glas) 1974, FRCPath 1978, FRSE 1978, FRS 1983, foreign memb Polish Acad of Sci 1988, FRCOG 1993; *Books* Early Prenatal Diagnosis (1983), Prenatal Diagnosis & Screening (1992), Essential Medical Genetics (4 edn, 1993); *Recreations* sailing, swimming, fishing; *Style—* Prof Malcolm Ferguson-Smith, FRS, FRSE; ✉ 16 Rustat Rd, Cambridge CB1 3QT (☎ 01223 246277); Dept of Pathology, University of Cambridge, Tennis Court Rd, Cambridge CB2 3QP (☎ 01223 333691, fax 01223 339067, telex 81240 C)

FERGUSSON, Sir Ewen Alastair John; GCMG (1993, KCMG 1987), GCVO (1992); s of Sir Ewen MacGregor Field Fergusson (d 1974), and Winifred Evelyn Fergusson; *b* 28 Oct 1932; *Educ* Rugby, Oriel Coll Oxford (MA); *m* 19 Dec 1959, Sara Carolyn, da of late Brig-Gen Lord Esmé Gordon-Lennox KCVO, CMG, DSO; 1 s (Ewen b 30 Nov 1965), 2 da (Anna b 15 June 1961, Iona b 7 May 1967); *Career* 2 Lt 60 Rifles KRRC 1954–56; Dip Serv 1956, asst private sec MOD 1957–59, Br Embassy Addis Ababa 1960, FO 1963, Br Trade Devpt Office NYC 1967, cnsllr and head of Chancery Office UK Perm Rep to Euro Communities 1972–75, private sec to Foreign and Cwlth Sec 1975–78, asst under sec state FCO 1978–82, ambass South Africa 1982–84, dep under sec state FCO 1984–87, ambass France 1987–92; chm: Coutts and Co 1993–, Savoy Hotel Group 1994– (non-exec dir 1993–); non-exec dir: British Telecommunications plc 1993–, Sun Alliance Group plc 1993–96; chm of govrs Rugby 1995– (govr 1985–); tstee Nat Gallery 1995–; King of Arms of the Order of St Michael and St George 1996–; grand officier Légion d'Honneur 1992; hon fell Oriel Coll Oxford 1987, Hon LLD Univ of Aberdeen 1995; FCIB 1994; *Clubs* RAC, Beefsteak, Jockey (Paris); *Style—* Sir Ewen Fergusson, GCMG, GCVO; ✉ 111 Iverna Court, London W8 6TX

FERGUSSON, George Duncan Raukawa; s of Baron Ballantrae (Life Peer), KT, GCMG, GCVO, DSO, OBE (d 1980), 3 s of Sir Charles Fergusson, 7 Bt, of Kilkerran, by his w Laura Margaret Grenfell (d 1979) (*see* Peerage Baron Grenfell 1976); *b* 30 Sept 1955; *Educ* Hereworth Sch NZ, Eton, Magdalen Coll Oxford (BA); *m* 10 Jan 1981, Margaret Sheila, da of Michael John Wookey, of Camberley, Surrey; 1 s (Alexander b 1984), 3 da (Laura b 1982, Alice b 1986, Elizabeth b 1991); *Career* civil servant 1978– (Home Civil Serv 1978–90), seconded to NI Dept of Commerce 1979–80, first sec Br Embassy Dublin 1988–91 (transferred to Dip Serv 1990), FCO London 1991–93, first sec Br Embassy Seoul 1994–96; *Style—* George Fergusson, Esq; ✉ c/o Foreign and Commonwealth Office, King Charles Street, London SW1 (☎ and fax 0171 582 2505)

FERGUSSON, Ian Lewis Campbell; s of John Douglas Fergusson (d 1978), of London W1, and Alice Aleyn, *née* Maartewsz (d 1968); *b* 11 April 1942; *Educ* Rugby, Univ of Cambridge (MA, MB BChir); *m* 16 Dec 1972, Marylin Susan, da of Lt-Col Guy Philip Arthur Shelley, OBE (d 1988), of Turleigh, Wiltshire; 1 s (Jamie b 4 Sept 1974), 3 da (Katie b 28 April 1976, Sally b 20 Feb 1980, Molly b 25 July 1982); *Career* RNR Lt-Cdr and surgn (ret 1980); conslt obstetrician and gynaecologist St Thomas' Hosp 1979, conslt gynaecologist Chelsea Hosp for Women 1980–89, sr civilian gynaecologist to the RN 1982–, hon gynaecologist to St Luke's Hosp for the Clergy; jt chm St Thomas' Hosp Baby Fund; Freeman: City of London, Worshipful Soc of Apothecaries; FRCS 1971, FRCSEd 1971, memb BMA; *Books* Records and Curiosities in Obstetrics and Gynaecology (1980); *Recreations* fishing, watercolour painting; *Clubs* Army and Navy, MCC, West Surrey Golf; *Style—* Ian Fergusson, Esq; ✉ 112 Fentiman Rd, London SW8 1QA (☎ 0171 735 3867); 10 Upper Wimpole St, London W1 (☎ 0171 935 8273)

FERGUSSON, (Frederick) James; s of Frederick Peter Fergusson, of Hythe, Kent, and Oenone Barbara, *née* Wicks; *b* 28 March 1943; *Educ* Haileybury, ISC, Univ Coll Oxford (BA); *m* 11 Nov 1966, Diane Frances (Sophie), da of Leslie Eric Duncan Darley (d 1986), of Rochester, Kent; 2 s (William b 1975, Edward b 1984), 2 da (Polly b 1973, Isobel b 1982); *Career* James Capel and Co: joined 1969, ptnr 1976, dir 1984, dep chm 1987–93; chm Stephens International Ltd 1993–, owner Canon Gallery (fine art) Petworth; *Recreations* skiing, tennis, music, reading; *Style—* James Fergusson, Esq

FERGUSSON, James; s of Adam Dugdale Fergusson, of London, and Elizabeth Catherine Penelope, *née* Hughes; *b* 2 Nov 1966; *Educ* Eton, Brasenose Coll Oxford (Oppidan scholar, BA); *Career* freelance journalist with various newspapers (incl The Independent, The Daily Telegraph) 1989–92, five month internship DG X Euro Cmmn Brussels 1989–90, dep ed The Indy 1990, asst news ed The European 1991, freelance corr Algeria, Cuba, and Haiti 1992, features ed The European 1992–95; *Recreations* motorcycling, scuba diving, narrow boating; *Style—* James Fergusson, Esq; ✉ Barge Serenity, Lower Mall, Hammersmith, London W6 (☎ 0181 748 1534)

FERMAN, James Alan; *b* 11 April 1930; *Educ* Great Neck HS NY, Cornell Univ (BA), King's Coll Cambridge (MA); *m* 1956, Monica Sophie, *née* Robinson; 1 s, 1 da; *Career* actor and lectr until 1957; TV dir: ABC 1957–59, ATV 1959–65; freelance 1965–75, dir British Board of Film Classification 1975–; dir: The Planemakers (BAFTA Award 1964), Miss Hanago (ITV entry Monte Carlo Festival 1964/65), The Pistol (BAFTA nomination for Best Dir), Who's A Good Boy Then? I Am, Kafka's Amerika (Critics' Circle Award 1966), Death of a Private, Before the Party (BAFTA Award 1970), When the Bough Breaks, Chariot of Fire, Terrible Jim Fitch, Three Sisters, Mooney and His Caravans, This Space Is Mine; pt/t lectr in community studies Central London Poly 1973–76, educn advsr Standing Conf on Drug Abuse, vice pres Assoc for the Prevention of Addiction; *Style—* James Ferman, Esq; ✉ British Board of Film Classification, 3 Soho Square, London W1V 6HD (☎ 0171 439 7961, fax 0171 287 0141)

FERMONT, Dr David Calvin; s of David Andre Fermont, of Esher, Surrey, and Edith Mary, *née* Kew; *b* 31 Oct 1946; *Educ* Cheltenham, Middx Hosp Med Sch (MB, BS); *m* 28 Sept 1974, Linda Jane, da of Maj Geoffrey Noel Marks, of Hove, Sussex; 1 s (James Alexander b 29 July 1983), 1 da (Sara Louise b 7 June 1980); *Career* conslt oncologist and dir Cancer Centre Mount Vernon Hosp, Northwick Park and St Marks Hosps 1983–; tstee Barnet Cancer Care Appeal, chm Hillingdon Health Authy District Med Ctee, memb Hillingdon DHA Mgmnt Bd, med exec dir Mount Vernon Hosp Tst; FRCS (Eng), FRSM, FRCR, memb Br Inst of Radiology; *Books* numerous med pubns; *Recreations* cricket; *Style—* Dr David Fermont; ✉ Great Sarratt Hall Cottage, Sarratt, Herts WD3 4PD; Cancer Centre, Mount Vernon Hospital, Northwood, Middlesex HA6 2RN (☎ 01923 844231, fax 01923 844138)

FERMOR, Patrick Michael Leigh; *see:* Leigh Fermor, Patrick Michael

FERMOR-HESKETH, Hon John; 3 s of 2 Baron Hesketh (d 1955); *b* 15 March 1953; *Educ* Ampleforth; *m* 1, 2 Dec 1980 (m dis), Anna, o da of Hamish Wallace, of Old Corrimony, Glen Urquhart, Inverness; m 2, 14 July 1986, Helena Marian, o da of Robert Hunt, of Petropolis, Brazil; 1 da (Alice Mary Louisa b 5 March 1987); *Clubs* White's, Beefsteak, Pratt's; *Style—* The Hon John Fermor-Hesketh

FERMOY, 6 Baron (I 1856); (Patrick) Maurice Burke Roche; s of 5 Baron Fermoy (d 1984), and Lavinia, *née* Pitman (who m 2, 1995, Nigel E Corbally Stourton);

b 11 Oct 1967; *Educ* Eton; *Heir* bro, Hon (Edmund) Hugh Burke Roche b 5 Feb 1972; *Career* Page of Honour to HM Queen Elizabeth The Queen Mother 1982–85, former Capt The Blues and Royals; with Bass Taverns 1995–; *Recreations* horses, scuba diving; *Clubs* Turf; *Style*— The Rt Hon Lord Fermoy

FERN, Prof Dan; s of George Fern (d 1967), of Gainsborough, and Gwen Fern (d 1981); *b* 1 July 1945; *Educ* Queen Elizabeth GS Gainsborough, Manchester Coll of Art and Design, RCA; *m* 1969, Kate Fern; 1 s (Hugo b 1985), 2 da (Zoë b 1976, Ella b 1979); *Career* illustrator; Royal Coll of Art: head of illustration 1986–, prof of illustration 1989–, head Sch of Communication Design 1993–, prof of graphic art and design 1994–; *Solo Exhibitions* Print and Collage Constructions (Curwen Gallery London) 1982, Collage, Print and Type Constructions (Curwen Gallery) 1985, Recent Work (Entrepotdok Amsterdam) 1986, Mapworks (Pentagram Gallery) 1994, Box Set (Pentagram Gallery) 1994; *Gp Exhibitions* incl: Art/Work (Nat Theatre) 1979, Homage to Herge (Joan Miro Fndn Barcelona) 1984, Art Meets Science (Smiths Gallery London) 1988, Image and Object (Nat Museum of Modern Art Kyoto Japan) 1990, Gate 14 (RCA) 1993, Collage (England & Co) 1993, Permanent Collection V&A; clients incl: Sunday Times Magazine, Radio Times, New Scientist, Penguin Books, Pan Books, J Walter Thompson, Young and Rubicam, Conran Design, Michael Peters Group, Pentagram, Thames Television, Assoc of Illustrators, The Royal Court Theatre, Royal Acad London; cmmnd work incl: video on drawing (for Faber-Castell) 1993, film on Deutsche Romantik theme (for South Bank Centre and Goethe Inst) 1994, film for Harrison Birtwhistle Festival (premiered South Bank) 1996; lectr and speaker various conferences and workshops; head Educn Ctee Assoc of Illustrators 1977–79, memb various jury panels; twice winner of both Gold & Silver D & AD awards; FRCA, FCSD, FRSA; *Books* Works with Paper (1990); *Recreations* opera and other performing arts, mountaineering, cycling, collecting (books, stamps, printed ephemera); *Style*— Prof Dan Fern; ✉ 58 Muswell Rd, London N10 2BE (☎ 0181 883 5604); Communication Design, Royal College of Art, Kensington Gore, London SW7 (☎ 0171 584 5020, fax 0171 225 1487)

FERNANDO, Oswald Nihal; s of Cyril Philip Neri Fernando, and Louise, *née* Edline; *b* 22 Oct 1934; *Educ* Ceylon (MB BS); *m* 8 April 1961, (Susan Dulcie) Tallulah, da of Dr Charles Talbot; 3 s (Dr Hiran Chrishantha b 16 Jan 1962, Rohan Prashantha b 1 April 1963, Bimbi Shiran b 27 Feb 1967); *Career* conslt surgn Royal Free Hosp 1976– (res fell in renal transplantation 1969–70, lectr in surgery 1971–76); hon sr lectr Royal Free Hosp Sch of Med 1976–; hon conslt surgn 1976–: Hosp of St John and St Elizabeth, Hosp for Sick Children Gt Ormond St; memb: Br Transplant Soc, RSM, Br Assoc of Urological Surgns; FRCS, FRCSEd; *Recreations* swimming, squash; *Style*— Oswald N Fernando, Esq; ✉ Renal Transplant Unit, Royal Free Hospital, Pond St, London NW3 2QG (☎ 0171 794 0500, fax 0171 830 2125, car 0860 323 002)

FERNEYHOUGH, Prof Brian John Peter; s of Frederick George Ferneyhough (d 1982), and Emily May, *née* Hopwood (d 1992); *b* 16 Jan 1943; *Educ* Birmingham Sch of Music, Royal Acad of Music, Royal Conservatory Amsterdam, Musikakademie Basel; *m* 19 May 1990, Stephanie Jan, *née* Hurtik; *Career* prof of composition Musikhochschule Freiburg Germany 1973–86, composition lectr Darmstadt Summer Sch 1976–, leader composition master class Civica Scuola di Musica di Milano 1984–87, composition teacher Royal Conservatory of The Hague Netherlands 1986–87, ldr composition master class Fndn Royaumont 1990–, prof of music Univ of Calif at San Diego 1987–, chair of poetics Mozarteum Salzburg 1995–; memb: Jury Gaudeamus Int Composition Competition 1984 (Netherlands), Int Jury for World Music Days of Int Soc for Contemporary Music (Finland 1978, Hong Kong 1989); ARAM 1990; Chev dans L'Ordre des Arts et des Lettres Paris 1984, Koussevitsky prize 1978; *Compositions* incl: Sonatas for String Quartet 1967, Transit 1975, Time and Motion Studies I-III 1974–77, La Terre est un Homme 1979, Carceri d'Invenzione 1981–86, La Chute d'Icare 1988, Fourth String Quartet 1990, Bone Alphabet, Allgebrah 1991, Terrain 1992, On Stellar Magnitudes 1994, String Trio 1995; *Recreations* reading, wine, cats; *Style*— Prof Brian Ferneyhough; ✉ Music B-0326, University of California at San Diego, La Jolla, CA 92093–0326, USA (☎ 00 1 619 534 3230, fax 00 1 619 534 8502)

FERNIE, Prof Eric Campbell; CBE (1995); s of Sidney Robert Fernie (d 1988), of Johannesburg, SA, and Catherine Reid, *née* Forrest (d 1959); *b* 9 June 1939, Edinburgh; *Educ* Marist Brothers Coll Johannesburg, Univ of Witwatersrand (BA); *m* 28 Nov 1964, (Margaret) Lorraine, da of John Henry French, of Norfolk; 1 s (Ivan b 1969), 2 da (Lyndall b 1965, Jessica b 1969); *Career* sr lectr Univ of East Anglia 1974–84; Univ of Edinburgh: Watson Gordon prof of fine art 1984–95, dean Faculty of Arts 1989–92; dir Courtauld Inst of Art 1995–; cmmr English Heritage; chm: Ancient Monuments Bd Scotland 1989–95, Durham Cathedral Fabric Ctee; vice pres Soc of Antiquaries of London 1992–95; tstee: National Galleries of Scotland, Heasher Tst for the Arts; memb Br Acad Corpus of Romanesque Sculpture Ctee; FSA 1973, FRSE 1993; *Books* The Communar and Pitancer Rolls of Norwich Cathedral Priory (1972), The Architecture of the Anglo Saxons (1983), Medieval Architecture and its Intellectual Context (1990), An Architectural History of Norwich Cathedral (1993), Art and it's Methods (1995); *Style*— Prof Eric Fernie, CBE, FSA, FRSE; ✉ The Courtauld Institute of Art, Somerset House, Strand, London WC2R 0RN (☎ 0171 872 0220)

FEROZE, Sir Rustam; kt (1983); s of Dr Jehangir Moolan-Feroze (d 1962), and Diana Lester Feather (d 1993); *b* 4 Aug 1920; *Educ* Sutton Valence, Univ of London (MB BS, MD); *m* 1947, Margaret, da of Harry Dowsett (d 1975); 3 s, 1 da; *Career* Surgn Lt RNVR Atlantic and Far E 1943–46; conslt obstetrician Queen Charlotte's Hosp London 1962–73, conslt gynaecologist Chelsea Hosp for Women 1952–73, conslt obstetrician and gynaecologist KCH London 1952–85, dean Inst of Obstetrics and Gynaecology Univ of London 1954–67; now ret; contrib to med books 1981–84; pres RCOG 1981–84, currently hon pres Euro Assoc of Gynaecologists and Obstetricians (first pres 1985–88); FRCS, FRCOG, Hon FRCSI 1984, Hon FRACOG 1985, Hon FACOG 1986; *Recreations* swimming, gardening; *Clubs* RAC; *Style*— Sir Rustam Feroze; ✉ 21 Kenwood Drive, Beckenham, Kent BR3 6QX (☎ 0181 650 2972)

FERRAN, Brian; *b* 1940; *Educ* Courtauld Inst Univ of London (BA), Queen's Univ Belfast (Dip Business Admin); *Career* artist and administrator; art teacher 1963–66; Arts Council of NI: on staff 1966–, now chief exec; cmmr for NI Biennale Paris 1980, cmmr for Ireland Bienal São Paulo 1985, organiser exhbn Houston Int Festival Texas 1990, editorial advsr Irish Arts Review; at Brera Acad of Fine Art Milan 1970–71; *Works* cmmns incl: 3 stained glass windows St Patrick's Coll Maghera Co Derry 1989, mural St Columb's Coll Derry 1990; *Exhibitions* recent solo exhbns: Salve Regina Coll Rhode Island 1990, Gallery Green Lexington 1991, Aisling Gallery Hingham Mass 1991, Museum of Art Univ of Wisconsin 1992, Ib Jorgensen Gallery Dublin 1993, Utd First Parish Church Quincy Mass 1993, Emily Lowe Gallery Hofstra Univ Long Island 1996; numerous gp exhbns incl: Irish Art 1943–73 Cork 1980, Belfast Artists Mexico City 1984, Northern Irish Artists Hong Kong 1985, Sense of Ireland Festival - Contemporary Works on Paper Singapore 1986, the Best of British Boston 1991, Curators' and Critics Exhbn (Boat House Gallery Co Cork) 1994; *Collections* work in numerous incl: Arts Council of NI, Belfast Education and Library Board, Great Southern Hotels, Inst of Public Administration Dublin, Kilkenny Design Centre, Northern Bank Finance Group, Dept of Commerce NI, Ulster Museum, Crawford Municipal Art Gallery Cork, Allied Irish Bank; *Awards* Douglas Hyde Gold Medal Oireachtas Exhbn 1965, Leverhulme European 1969, Irish Arts Council Oireachtas Exhbn 1978, Conor Prize Royal Ulster Academy 1979, Pittsburg Creative Arts Fellowship Italy 1983, Ulster Watercolour Soc Haughton Award 1995; *Publications* Ireland: A Cultural Encyclopaedia (1983), Four Irish Artists at the São Paulo Bienal (1985), Belfast's Cultural Environment 1957–97, Belfast and It's Region (for Province City and People, 1987), The Visual Arts in Northern Ireland (for Irish Banker Quarterly, 1989), Basil Blackshaw - Painter (monograph, 1995), review of Tony O'Malley's Monograph (Irish Times, 1996); *Style*— Brian Ferran, Esq; ✉ Arts Council of Northern Ireland, 185 Stranmillis Road, Belfast BT9 5DU (☎ 01232 381591, fax 01232 661715)

FERRELL, Dr William Russell; *b* 5 March 1949, St Louis, Missouri; *Educ* St Aloysius Coll Glasgow, Univ of Glasgow (MB ChB, PhD, MRCP); *Career* jr house offr posts in surgery (Southern Gen Hosp Glasgow) and med (Stirling Royal Infirmary) 1973–74, sessional clinical work 1974–, visiting res fell Dept of Orthopaedic Surgery Univ of Western Aust May-Aug 1984; Univ of Glasgow: lectr in physiology 1977–89, sr lectr 1989–91, reader 1991–93, head of physiology 1993–94, head of biomedical scis 1994–; expert referee: Jl of Physiology, Experimental Physiology, Jl of Rheumatology, Br Jl of Pharmacology, Clinical Sciences, Brain, Brain Research, Annals of the Rheumatic Diseases; memb: Physiological Soc 1981, BMA, Br Soc of Med and Dental Hypnosis, Euro Neuropeptide Club; MRCPGlas 1994; *Recreations* classical music, reading, electronics, keeping fit, DIY; *Style*— Dr William Ferrell; ✉ Institute of Biomedical & Life Sciences, West Medical Building, The University, Glasgow G12 8QQ (☎ 0141 330 5860, fax 0141 330 4100)

FERRERS, 13 Earl (GB 1711); Sir Robert Washington Shirley; 19 Bt (E 1611), PC (1982), DL (Norfolk 1983); also Viscount Tamworth (GB 1711); s of 12 Earl Ferrers (d 1954, 17 in descent from Sir Hugh Shirley, Grand Falconer to Henry IV and victim of mistaken identity at the Battle of Shrewsbury through being accoutred as the King); 16 in descent from Sir Ralph Shirley, one of the principal commanders at Agincourt; 9 in descent from Dorothy, da of Elizabeth I's favourite, Essex, through whom Lord Ferrers descends from Edward III, hence the quartering of the arms of Fr and Eng on the Shirley escutcheon; 5 in descent from Hon Walter Shirley, yr bro of 4 Earl, the last Lord to be tried for homicide by his Peers; *b* 8 June 1929; *Educ* Winchester (fell 1988–), Magdalene Coll Cambridge (MA); *m* 21 July 1951, Annabel Mary, da of Brig William Greenwood Carr, CVO, DSO, JP, DL (d 1982), of Ditchingham Hall, Norfolk; 2 s (Viscount Tamworth b 1952, Hon Andrew b 1965), 3 da (Lady Angela Ellis b 1954, Lady Sallyanne b 1957, Lady Selina Chenevière b 1958); *Heir* s, Viscount Tamworth, *qv*; *Career* sits as (C) Peer in the House of Lords; served Coldstream Gds, Lt, Malaya; Lord-in-Waiting and govt whip Lords 1962–64 and 1971–74, oppn whip Lords 1964–67, jt-dep ldr of oppn Lords 1976–79, Parly sec Agric, Fisheries and Food 1974, min of state Agric, Fisheries and Food 1979–83, dep ldr Lords 1979–83 and 1988–; min of state: Home Office 1988–94, DTI 1994–95, Dept of Environment 1995–; memb: Cncl Food from Britain 1985–88, Armitage Ctee on Political Activities of Civil Servants 1976, Central Bd TSB 1977–79; tstee: E Anglian TSB 1957–75 (vice-chm 1971–75), TSB of E England 1975–79 (chm 1977–79), Central TSB Ltd 1978–79, TSB Trustcard 1978–79; dir: Economic Forestry Group plc 1985–88, Norwich Union Insurance Group 1975–79 and 1983–88, Chatham Historic Dockyard Tst 1984–88, Governing Body of Rothamstead Agric Station 1984–88; chm British Agric Export Cncl 1984–88; High Steward Norwich Cathedral 1979–; chm Royal Cmmn on Historical Monuments (England) 1984–88; *Recreations* shooting, music, travel; *Clubs* Beefsteak; *Style*— The Rt Hon Earl Ferrers, PC, DL; ✉ Ditchingham Hall, Bungay, Suffolk NR35 2LE (☎ 01508 482250, fax 01508 482332)

FERRERS-WALKER, Thomas Weaving; s of Thomas Ferrers (d 1970), and Undine Ferrers, *née* Weaving (d 1962); *b* 24 Sept 1925; *Educ* Bradfield; *m* 1, 1948, late Pamela Mary Beer; 2 s (Richard b 1949, John b 1952); m 2, 1956, Shirley, wid of Edward Kenneth Dunlop, and da of Herbert Cordingley (d 1950); 1 s (Edward b 1961), 1 da (Undine b 1965); *Career* WWII served RNVR combined ops Europe and Pacific 1942–46; RNVSR 1947–65, Lieut RNR 1965–71; chm Thomas Walker plc 1994– (chm and chief exec 1971–94); tstee: Shakespeare Birthplace Tst 1985– (Exec Ctee 1986–), RN Museum 1987–; pres: Stratford-on-Avon Nat Tst Assoc 1985–, Solihull Nat Tst Centre 1994– (vice pres 1980–94); patron of the living of Baddesley Clinton (achieved transfer of Baddesley Clinton to Nat Tst 1980); memb Regnl Ctee Historic Houses Assoc Heart of England Region 1975–88; memb Cncl Order of St John for the County of W Midlands 1973–96 (OStJ 1985, CStJ 1996); *Recreations* gardening, photography for recording purposes, historical and naval research and preservation, conservation of historic and natural landscape and buildings; *Clubs* Naval; *Style*— T W Ferrers-Walker, Esq; ✉ Westfield, 30 Fiery Hill Rd, Barnt Green, Worcestershire B45 8LG (☎ 0121 445 1785); Thomas Walker plc, 39 St Paul's Square, Birmingham B3 1QY (☎ 0121 236 5565, fax 0121 236 6725)

FERRIER, Prof Robert Patton; s of William McFarlane Ferrier (d 1963), and Gwendoline Melita, *née* Edward (d 1976); *b* 4 Jan 1934; *Educ* Glebelands Sch, Morgan Acad, Univ of St Andrews (BSc, PhD), Univ of Cambridge (MA); *m* 2 Sept 1961, Valerie Jane, da of Samuel George Duncan (d 1986); 2 s (Hamish b 1965, Alan b 1969), 1 da (Elizabeth b 1967); *Career* sci offr UKAERE Harwell 1959–61, res assoc Mass Inst of Technol USA 1961–62, asst dir of res Cavendish Lab Univ of Camb 1966–73 (sr asst 1962–66), guest scientist IBM Res Div San Jose Calif USA 1972–73, prof of nat philosophy Univ of Glasgow 1973–; memb: local Episcopal Church, various ctees of Sci and Engrg Res Cncl 1970–85 (former chm); FInstP 1964, FRSE 1977; *Recreations* tennis, gardening, reading crime novels; *Style*— Prof Robert Ferrier; ✉ Glencoe, 31 Thorn Road, Bearsden, Glasgow G61 4BS (☎ 0141 570 0769); Department of Physics and Astronomy, The University, Glasgow G12 8QQ (☎ 0141 330 5388, 0141 339 8855, fax 0141 330 4464, telex 777070 UNIGLA)

FERRIS, Dr Elizabeth Anne Esther; da of Roy Ferris (d 1975), and Dorothy Philomena, *née* Roth (d 1990); *b* 19 Nov 1940; *Educ* Francis Holland Sch Clarence Gate, Middlesex Hosp Med Sch Univ of London (MB BS); *m* Julian Melzack; 1 da (Sophie b 1978); *Career* doctor and former int springboard diver; achievements as diver: represented GB 1957–64, Bronze medal Cwlth Games Cardiff 1958, Bronze medal Olympic Games Rome 1960, Gold medals springboard and highboard World Student Games Sofia 1961, Silver medal Cwlth Games Perth Aust 1962; freelance journalist, writer and broadcaster on sport, women and sport, sports medicine, alternative medicine, health fitness 1968–; doctor specialising in: acupuncture 1972–86, autogenic trg 1980–, sports psychology 1980–; therapist cnsllr 1989–; chm The Olympians, vice pres World Olympians Assoc; memb: Int Olympic Ctee Cmmn on Women and Sport, IAAF Workshop on Gender Verification in Sport 1990–, Research Ctee Int Cncl of Sport Science and Physical Educn UNESCO, Editorial Advsy Bd Annals of Sports Medicine USA, Scientific Section Int Fedn of Physical Educn; awarded Medal of the Olympic Order by Int Olympic Ctee for work with women in sport 1980; *Books* Forty Plus (1992); *Videos* Bodyplan (1992); *Style*— Dr Elizabeth Ferris; ✉ c/o The Olympians, 1 Wandsworth Plain, London SW18 1EH

FERRIS, Neil Jeremy; s of Oscar Ferris, and Benita, *née* Lewis; *b* 5 April 1955; *Educ* Brighton Hove and Sussex GS; *m* 25 Jan 1980, Jill Denise, da of William Charles Anderson, of London; 1 s (Daniel Mark); *Career* jr PR Dept EMI Records 1974; PR Dept: NEMS Records 1976, CBS Records 1977; formed The Ferret Plugging Co 1980 representing: UB40, Erasure, Depeche Mode and other major recording artists; produced TV special about Erasure for BBC 2 1988 and a documentary on Depeche Mode for BBC TV 1989; md Ferret and Spanner PR 1985–95, md Brilliant PR Ltd 1995–, md

Ferret Music and chm The Brilliant Recording Co Ltd; speaker on various subjects relating to the music indust and the media; *Recreations* helicopter flying (R22 and Jetranger), Thames slipper launches, photography, antiques (early oak furniture), 16/17th Century paintings (British); *Style*— Neil Ferris, Esq; ✉ Chairman, Brilliant! Group of Companies, 76 Stanley Gardens, London W3 7BL (☎ 0181 746 1818, fax 0181 746 1011)

FERRIS, Paul Fredrick; s of Frederick Morgan Ferris (d 1965), and Olga, *née* Boulton (d 1992); *b* 15 Feb 1929; *Educ* Swansea GS; *m* 1, 1953 (m dis 1995), Gloria Moreton; 1 s (Jonathan b 1955), 1 da (Virginia Ann b 1960); m 2, 1996, Mary Turnbull; *Career* journalist and author; S Wales Evening Post 1949–52, Woman's Own 1953, Observer Foreign News Serv 1953–54; *Books* incl: The City (1960), The House of Northcliffe (1971), The Detective (1976), Dylan Thomas (1977), Talk to Me About England (1979), Children of Dust (1988), Sir Huge - The Life of Huw Wheldon (1990), Sex and the British - a 20th Century History (1993), Caitlin - The Life of Caitlin Thomas (1993), The Divining Heart (1995); *Style*— Paul Ferris, Esq; ✉ c/o Curtis Brown Ltd, 4th Floor, Haymarket House, 28–29 Haymarket, London SW1Y 4SP (☎ 0171 396 6600)

FERRY, Bryan; s of Frederick Charles Ferry (d 1984), and Mary Ann, *née* Armstrong (d 1991); *b* 26 Sept 1945; *Educ* Washington GS, Univ of Newcastle; *m* 26 June 1982, Lucy Margaret Mary, da of Patrick Helmore; 4 c (Otis b 1 Nov 1982, Isaac b 16 May 1985, Tara b 6 Jan 1990, Merlin b 5 Dec 1990); *Career* vocalist and fndr memb Roxy Music 1971, solo recording artist; recordings with Roxy Music: Roxy Music (1972), For Your Pleasure (1973), Stranded (1973), Country Life (1974), Siren (1975), Viva (1976), Manifesto (1979), Flesh & Blood (1980), Avalon (1982), The High Road (1983), Streetlife (1986); solo recordings: These Foolish Things (1973), Another Time Another Place (1974), Let's Stick Together (1976), In Your Mind (1977), The Bride Stripped Bare (1978), Boys and Girls (1985), Bête Noire (1987), Taxi (1993), Mamouna (1994); Bryan Ferry and Roxy Music Video Collection (Virgin, 1996); *Style*— Bryan Ferry, Esq; ✉ c/o Christopher Scott, Virgin Records, Kensal House, Harrow Road, London W10 4RH (☎ 0181 968 6688)

FERSHT, Prof Alan Roy; s of Philip Joseph Fersht (d 1970), and Betty, *née* Mattleson; *b* 21 April 1943; *Educ* Sir George Monoux GS, Gonville & Caius Coll Cambridge (MA, PhD); *m* 18 Aug 1966, Marilyn, da of Montague Persell (d 1973); 1 s (Philip b 1972), 1 da (Naomi b 1970); *Career* memb scientific staff MRC Laboratory of Molecular Biology Cambridge 1969–77, Wolfson res prof Royal Soc and prof of chemistry Imperial Coll 1978–, Herchel Smith prof of organic chemistry Univ of Cambridge 1988–, dir Cambridge Interdisciplinary Res Centre for Protein Engrg 1989; memb: EMBO 1980, Academia Europaea 1989; hon foreign memb American Acad of Arts and Scis 1988, foreign assoc Nat Acad of Sci USA; Gabor Medal of the Royal Soc 1991; FRS 1983, FRSC 1986; *Books* Enzyme Structure and Mechanism (1978, 1985); *Recreations* chess, horology; *Style*— Prof Alan Fersht; ✉ 2 Barrow Close, Cambridge CB2 2AT (☎ 01223 352 963); University Chemical Laboratory, Lensfield Rd, Cambridge CB2 1EW (☎ 01223 336 341, fax 01223 336 445)

FESTING, Andrew Thomas; s of Field-Marshal Sir Francis Festing, GCB, DSO, DL (d 1971), of Birks, Northumberland, and Mary Cecilia, *née* Riddell (d 1992); *b* 30 Nov 1941; *Educ* Ampleforth, RMA Sandhurst; *m* 1968, Virginia Mary, da of Lt-Gen Sir Richard Fyffe, CBE, DSO; 1 da (Charlotte b 1975); *Career* cmmnd Rifle Bde until 1968; head English Picture Dept Sotheby & Co 1977–81, full time portrait painter 1981–; commissions incl: HM The Queen, HM Queen Elizabeth The Queen Mother, Cardinal Hume, Prince and Princess Fürstenberg, The Duke of Northumberland, The Duke of Wellington; RP 1992; *Recreations* hunting, shooting, fishing, gardening; *Style*— Andrew Festing, Esq, RP; ✉ c/o Royal Society of Portrait Painters, 17 Carlton House Terrace, London SW1Y 5AH

FETHERSTON-DILKE, Lt Cdr (John) Timothy; CBE (1986); y s of Dr Beaumont Albany Fetherston-Dilke, MBE (d 1968), of Maxstoke Castle, Warwicks, and Phoebe Stella, *née* Bedford (d 1968); *b* 4 Feb 1926; *Educ* RNC Dartmouth; *m* 1, 1956 (m dis 1965), Idonea, er da of Sir Hugh Chance, CBE, DL (d 1981), of Worcs; 1 s (Timothy b 9 June 1958), 1 da (Miranda (Mrs William Lindsay) b 6 May 1956); m 2, 19 July 1966, Olivia, da of Dr E C Turton (d 1983), of Hants; 1 s (Edmund b 9 June 1969), 1 da (Natalia b 11 Aug 1967); *Career* RN 1939–59 (navigation specialist): sea serv during WWII (Atlantic and East Indies) and Korean War, ret 1959 Lt Cdr; patent agency 1959–65, HM Coastguard Serv 1966–86 (HM Chief Coastguard 1978–86), int marine conslt 1986–93; advsr to Govt of People's Republic of Mozambique 1986–90; *Recreations* gardening, carpentry, family and music; *Style*— Lt Cdr Timothy Fetherston-Dilke, CBE; ✉ 85 Christchurch Rd, Winchester, Hants SO23 9QY (☎ and fax 01962 868661)

FEUCHTWANGER, Antonia Mary (Mrs Simon Cox); da of Dr Edgar Joseph Feuchtwanger, of Sparsholt, nr Winchester, Hampshire, and Primrose Mary, *née* Essame; *b* 12 Nov 1963; *Educ* St Swithun's Sch Winchester, Jesus Coll Cambridge (exhibitioner, MA, Gray prize for Latin Reading, Fencing half blue); *m* 24 June 1989, Simon Cox, s of Prof Antony Dawson Cox, *qv*; 2 s; *Career* graduate trainee Morgan Grenfell 1985–87, corporate fin analyst C J Lawrence Morgan Grenfell Inc (New York) 1987–89, banking corr Daily Telegraph 1989–94 (city reporter 1989), freelance 1994–; *Style*— Ms Antonia Feuchtwanger; ✉ c/o The Daily Telegraph, City Office, Salters' Hall, 4 Fore Street, London EC2Y 5DT (☎ 0171 538 5000, fax 0171 628 0343)

FEVERSHAM, 6 Baron (UK 1826; the full designation is 'Feversham of Duncombe Park'); Charles Antony Peter Duncombe; s of Col Antony John Duncombe-Anderson, TD (d 1949; gggs of 1 Baron Feversham), and Gloranna Georgina Valerie, *née* McNalty (d 1989); suc to Barony of kinsman, 3 Earl of Feversham and Viscount Helmsley (which titles became extinct 1963); *b* 3 Jan 1945; *Educ* Eton; *m* 1, 12 Sept 1966, Shannon (d 1976), da of late Sir Thomas Foy, CSI, CIE; 2 s (Hon Jasper b 1968, Hon Jake b 1972), 1 da (Hon Melissa b 1973); m 2, 6 Oct 1979, Pauline, da of John Aldridge, of Newark, Notts; 1 s (Hon Patrick b 1981); *Heir* s, Hon Jasper; *Career* journalist and author; chm: Yorks Arts Assoc 1969–80, Standing Ctee of Regional Arts Assocs 1969–76, Tstees Yorks Sculpture Park 1982–; co pres Arvon Foundation 1976–86; pres: Yorks Parish Cncls Assoc 1977–, Yorks Arts Assoc 1986–91, Nat Assoc Local Cncls 1986–; *Books* A Wolf in Tooth (1967), Great Yachts (1970); *Style*— The Rt Hon the Lord Feversham; ✉ Duncombe Park, Helmsley, York YO6 5EB (☎ 01439 770213)

FEWSON, Prof Charles Arthur; s of Arthur Fewson (d 1985), and Brenda Margaret, *née* Consitt; *b* 8 Sept 1937; *Educ* Hymers Coll Hull, Univ of Nottingham (BSc), Univ of Bristol (PhD); *m* 1965, Margaret Christina Rose, *née* Moir; 2 da (Margaret Claire b 14 Jan 1972, Catriona Ann b 27 Dec 1976); *Career* res fell Cornell Univ 1961–63; Dept of Biochemistry Univ of Glasgow: asst lectr 1963–64, lectr 1964–68, sr lectr 1968–79, reader 1979–82, prof 1982–94; dir Inst of Biomedical and Life Sciences Univ of Glasgow 1994–; pubns mangr Fedn of Euro Microbiological Soc 1990; memb: Biochemical Soc, Soc for General Microbiology; author of nearly 200 scientific articles; FIBiol, FRSE; *Recreations* watching cricket; *Style*— Prof Charles Fewson, FRSE; ✉ 39 Falkland Street, Glasgow G12 9QZ (☎ 0141 339 1304); West Medical Building, University of Glasgow, Glasgow G12 8QQ (☎ 0141 339 8855, fax 0141 330 4750)

FEWTRELL, Nicholas Austin; s of Austin Alexander Fewtrell (d 1994), of Abergele, Wales, and Marjorie Edna, *née* Kimberlin (d 1996); *b* 1 July 1955; *Educ* Bramcote Hills GS, Queen Mary's Coll Univ of London (LLB); *m* 26 Nov 1983, Mahshid, da of Kazem Pouladdej, of Tehran, Iran; 1 s (Alexander Darius b 7 June 1991), 1 da (Stephanie Roxanne b 6 June 1989); *Career* called to the Bar Inner Temple 1977; memb The Honourable Soc of the Inner Temple 1975; *Recreations* golf, football, squash, travel; *Clubs* Ringway Golf; *Style*— Nicholas Fewtrell, Esq; ✉ Shiraz, Brooks Drive, Hale Barns, Cheshire WA15 8TR (☎ 0161 904 8990); 18 St John Street, Manchester M3 4EA (☎ 0161 834 9843, fax 0161 835 2051)

FFOLKES, Sir Robert Francis Alexander; 7 Bt (GB 1774), of Hillington, Norfolk; OBE (1990); s of Sir (Edward John) Patrick Boschetti ffolkes, 6 Bt (d 1960); *b* 2 Dec 1943; *Educ* Stowe, Ch Ch Oxford; *Heir* none; *Career* with Save The Children Fund 1974–; *Clubs* Turf; *Style*— Sir Robert ffolkes, Bt, OBE; ✉ Coastguard House, Morston, Holt, Norfolk NR25 7BH

FFORDE, (Arthur) John Brownlow; *b* 18 April 1927; *Educ* Rugby, Trinity Coll Oxford (MA); *Career* Linklaters & Paines: articled clerk 1951–54, slr 1954–56, ptnr 1956–87; Woolwich Building Society: dir 1986–96, dep chm 1991–96, chm Woolwich Life Assurance Co 1990–93; dir London Life Association Ltd 1960–89; tstee Lord Wandsworth Fndn 1969–96; Liveryman Worshipful Co of Fishmongers 1974; *Style*— John fforde, Esq; ✉ c/o Woolwich Building Society, Corporate Headquarters, Watling Street, Bexleyheath, Kent DA6 7RR (☎ 0181 298 5000)

FFOWCS WILLIAMS, Prof John Eirwyn; s of Rev Abel Ffowcs Williams (d 1989), and Elizabeth, *née* Davies; *b* 25 May 1935; *Educ* Friends' Sch Gt Ayton, Derby Tech Coll, Univ of Southampton (BSc, PhD), Univ of Cambridge (MA, ScD); *m* 10 Oct 1959, Anne Beatrice, da of Percy Cecil Mason (d 1984); 2 s (Aled Ceiriog b 1969, Gareth Idris b 1980), 1 da (Awena Lynn (Mrs Andrew Sanders) b 1966); *Career* Rolls Royce prof of applied mathematics Imperial Coll London 1969–72, Rank prof of engrg Univ of Cambridge 1972–, Master Emmanuel Coll Cambridge 1996–; dir VSEL plc 1988–95; FEng 1988; *Recreations* friends and cigars; *Clubs* Athenaeum, Danish; *Style*— Prof John Ffowcs Williams, FEng; ✉ Emmanuel College, Cambridge CB2 3AP (☎ 01223 332629)

FFRENCH, 8 Baron (I 1798); Sir Robuck John Peter Charles Mario ffrench; also Bt (I 1779); s of 7 Baron ffrench (d 1986), and Katherine Sonia, da of Maj Digby Coddington Cayley (d 1965); *b* 14 March 1956; *m* 20 June 1987, Dörthe Marie-Louise Schauer-Lixfeld, da of Capt Wilhelm Schauer, of Zürich, Switzerland, and Mrs Marie-Louise Schauer-Lixfeld, of Attymon House, Co Galway; 1 da (Hon Tara Elise Sofia Eleonora b 1993); *Style*— The Rt Hon Lord ffrench; ✉ Castle ffrench, Ballinasloe, Co Galway, Ireland

FFRENCH BLAKE, Col Robert John William; s of Lt-Col Desmond O'Brien Evelyn ffrench Blake (d 1943), of Hants, and Elizabeth Iris Hogg, *née* Cardale; *b* 21 June 1940; *Educ* Eton, RMA Sandhurst; *m* 21 Sept 1976, Ilynne Sabina Mary, da of Michael Charles Eyston, of Oxon; 3 da (Nicola b 1977, Alice b 1980, Emily b 1983); *Career* 13/18 Royal Hussars (QMO): cmmnd 1960, CO 1981–83, Hon Col 1990–93; Hon Col The Light Dragoons 1993–95; asst mil attaché Washington DC 1985–88, ret 1989; chief exec Gds Polo Club 1989–91; agent Belvedere Farm 1992–94; conslt polo promotions and marketing 1994–; memb HM Body Gd of The Hon Corps of Gentlemen at Arms 1990–; *Recreations* farming, skiing, shooting, polo, travel, gardening; *Clubs* Cavalry and Guards; *Style*— Col Robert J W ffrench Blake; ✉ c/o Hoares Bank, 37 Fleet Street, London EC4P 4DQ

FFYTCHE, Timothy John; s of Louis E S ffytche (d 1987), of Wilbraham Place, London, and Margaret Law (d 1996); *b* 11 Sept 1936; *Educ* Lancing, King's Coll London, St George's Hosp London (MB BS, DO); *m* 13 May 1961, Bärbl, da of Günther Fischer, of W Germany; 2 s (Dominic b 1962, Mattias b 1965); *Career* conslt ophthalmic surgeon: St Thomas's Hosp London, Moorfields Hosp, King Edward VII Hosp London, Hosp for Tropical Diseases; surgeon oculist to Royal Household; chm Ophthalmic Aid to Eastern Europe (OAEE); author of articles and papers on retinal disease and ocular leprosy; Liveryman Worshipful Soc of Apothecaries; FRCS, FRCOphth; *Recreations* fishing, occasional cricket; *Style*— Timothy ffytche, Esq; ✉ 1 Wellington Square, London SW3 4NJ; 149 Harley Street, London W1N 2DE

FIALKOWSKA, Janina; da of Jerzy Fialkowski, formerly of Lwow, Poland, now of Montreal, Canada, and Bridget, *née* Todd; *b* 7 May 1951; *Educ* Ecole Vincent d'Indy Montreal, private study with Yvonne Lefebure Paris, Juillard Sch NY; *Career* pianist; debut with Montreal Symphony Orch 1962, London debut with London Philharmonic Orch Royal Albert Hall 1976, Paris debut with Orchestre National de France Theatre des Champs Elysee 1976, London recital debut Queen Elizabeth Hall 1980, performed world première of newly rediscovered Liszt Piano Concerto (opus posthumous) with Chicago Symphony Orch Chicago 1990; performed with orchs incl: Royal Philharmonic, Philharmonia, Hallé, BBC Philharmonic, BBC Scottish, Scot Nat, Amsterdam Concertgebouw, Warsaw Philharmonic, Israel Philharmonic, Hong Kong Philharmonic, London Mozart Players, all major Canadian orchs, orchs of Philadelphia, Cleveland, LA, Minneapolis, Detroit, Washington DC and Chicago; *Recreations* ice hockey, tennis, skiing, dog walking, the Brontës, ancient Greece; *Style*— Ms Janina Fialkowska; ✉ c/o Ingpen & Williams Ltd, 14 Kensington Court, London W8 5DN (☎ 0171 937 5158, fax 0171 938 4175)

FIBBENS, Michael (Mike); s of Donald Fibbens, and Margaret, *née* Odell; *b* 31 May 1968; *Educ* Richard Hale Sch, Kelly Coll Devon; *Career* swimmer; 108 int caps, winner 89 Gold medals at int meetings, 43 nat titles; honours incl: finalist 4 x 100m freestyle Olympic Games Seoul 1988, Barcelona 1992 and Atlanta 1996, Br 50m and 100m freestyle champion 1989, Bronze medal 100m freestyle Cwlth Games Auckland 1990 (also Silver medals 4 x 100m freestyle and 4 x 100m individual medley), Bronze medal 50m freestyle Euro Championships 1991, World Grand Prix Series freestyle sprint champion 1992, Bronze medal Euro medley relay 1993, Nat 50m and 100m freestyle champion 1993, Bronze medallist World Championships 1993, medallist Cwlth Games 1994, two times nat champion 1994; holder English, Br and Cwlth 100m freestyle record; Br Swimming Coaches Assoc award for outstanding achievement of 1991, Southern Cos Male Swimmer of the Year 1991, reporter GB Swimmer 1994; memb Ctee for Devpt Sports Aid Fndn 1994–; *Style*— Mike Fibbens, Esq; ✉ 19 Millers Lane, Stanstead Abbotts, Ware, Herts SG12 8AF (☎ 01902 870797, mobile 0973 501908)

FIDGEN, Roger Stewart; s of Eric Frank Fidgen, and Vera, *née* Clark; *b* 14 May 1946; *Educ* Sherborne; *m* 1, 10 Nov 1971 (m dis 1988), Sarah Dorothy, da of William Nevill Dashwood Lang (d 1988); 2 s (Patrick b 1973, Robert b 1976), 1 da (Joanna b 1979); m 2, 20 May 1988, Jennifer Godesen, da of Stanley Angold; *Career* Sub Lt RNR 1969–72; chartered quantity surveyor; ptnr Gardiner and Theobald 1975–; Liveryman: Worshipful Co of Barbers 1973, Worshipful Co of Chartered Surveyors 1980; FRICS; *Recreations* fishing, shooting, sailing, skiing; *Clubs* Royal Thames Yacht, Flyfishers; *Style*— Roger Fidgen, Esq; ✉ Wield House Farm, Upper Wield, Alresford, Hants SO24 9RS (☎ 01420 564292); 32 Bedford Sq, London WC1B 3EG (☎ 0171 209 3000)

FIDLER, Peter John Michael; s of Dr Harry Fidler, of Bramhall, nr Stockport, Cheshire, and Lilian, *née* Kahn; *b* 16 March 1942; *Educ* Bradford GS, St John's Coll Oxford (MA); *m* 19 July 1984, Barbara Julia Gottlieb, da of Harold Pinto, of Wembley, Middx; 1 s (David Robert b 1985), 1 step s (Richard Charles b 1979), 2 step da (Clare Rachel b 1973, Katherine Anna b 1977); *Career* admitted slr 1967; articled clerk Peacock Fisher & Finch (now Field Fisher Waterhouse) 1964–67, Coward Chance 1967–72, DJ Freeman 1972–84, ptnr Stephenson Harwood 1984–; rep GB at croquet 1974; memb: City of London Solicitors Co, Law Soc, City of London Law Soc; *Books* Sheldon's Practice and Law of Banking (now Sheldon and Fidler's, asst ed 1972, ed 1982); *Recreations* music, theatre; *Style*— Peter Fidler, Esq; ✉ 237 West Heath Rd, London NW3 7UB (☎ 0181 455 2247); Stephenson Harwood, One St Paul's Churchyard, London EC4M 8SH (☎ 0171 329 4422, fax 0171 606 0822, telex 886789)

FIELD, Brig Anne; CB (1980), CBE (1996); da of Capt Harold Derwent and Annie Helena, *née* Hodgson; *b* 4 April 1926; *Educ* Keswick Sch, St George's Harpenden, LSE; *Career* joined ATS 1947, cmmnd 1948; WRAC 1949–92: Lt-Col 1968, Col 1971, Brig 1977–82, Dep Controller Cmdt 1984–92; Dep Col Cmdt Adj Gen's Corps 1992–93; special cmmr The Duke of York's Royal Military Sch; Hon ADC to HM The Queen 1977–82; regional dir Lloyds Bank plc London Regions 1982–91; Freeman City of London 1981, Liveryman Worshipful Co of Spectacle Makers 1990; *Style*— Brig Anne Field, CB, CBE; ✉ c/o The Duke of York's Royal Military School, Dover, Kent CT15 5EQ

FIELD, Arnold; OBE (1965); s of Wilfred Field (d 1933); *b* 19 May 1917; *Educ* Sutton Coldfield Royal Sch, Erdington C of E Sch, Birmingham Tech Coll; *m* 1943, Kathleen Dulcie, da of Albert Bennett (d 1930); 1 s, 1 da; *Career* served RAF WWII, Sqdn Ldr Coastal Cmd and Air Miny Special Duty List 1940–46; air traffic control offr 1946–61, divnl air traffic control offr 1961–65, supt London Air Traffic Control Centre 1965–71, dir Civil Air Traffic Ops 1971–74, dir gen Nat Air Traffic Serv 1974–77; aviation conslt and technical journalist 1977–; memb Aviation/Space Writers' Assoc; gp ed: International Defence Newsletter, Law Enforcement International Industry Digest; *Books* The Control of Air Traffic (1980), International Air Traffic Control Management of the World's Airspace (1985), International Directory of Military Simulation and Training Aids (1988); *Recreations* vintage motor cars, flying; *Clubs* Bentley Drivers'; *Style*— Arnold Field, Esq, OBE; ✉ Footprints, Stoke Wood, Stoke Poges, Bucks SL2 4AU (☎ 01753 64 2710)

FIELD, Barry John Anthony; TD (1984), MP (C) Isle of Wight (majority 1,827); s of Edward Ernest Field, of Crawley, Sussex, and Marguerite Eugenie, *née* Bateman (d 1979); *b* 4 July 1946; *Educ* Collingwood Boys' Sch, Mitcham GS, Bembridge Sch, Victoria Street Coll; *m* 11 Oct 1969, Jacqueline Anne, da of Cdr Alfred Edward Joseph Miller, RN, of Emsworth, Hants; 1 s (Jason b 1977), 1 da (Penny b 1978); *Career* dir: Gt Southern Cemetery and Crematoria Co Ltd 1969–86, J D Field and Sons 1981–84; cncllr Horsham Dist Cncl 1983–86 (chm Housing Ctee 1984–85), memb IOW CC 1986–89, MP (C) Isle of Wight 1987–; chm Select Ctee: on the Environment 1994–95 (memb 1991–94), on Deregulation 1995–; vice chm All Pty Maritime Gp, chm Cons Backbench Shipping and Shipbuilding Ctee, vice chm Tourism Ctee; memb Ct of Assts Worshipful Co of Turners; *Recreations* sailing, skiing, theatre; *Clubs* Island Sailing, House of Commons Yacht (Cdre); *Style*— Barry Field, Esq, TD, MP; ✉ House of Commons, London SW1A 0AA (☎ 0171 219 3000)

FIELD, Frank; MP (Lab) Birkenhead (majority 17,613); s of late Walter Field, and Annie Field; *b* 16 July 1942; *Educ* St Clement Danes GS, Univ of Hull; *Career* former lobbyist, memb TGWU, cncllr Hounslow 1964–68, Parly candidate (Lab) S Bucks 1966; dir Child Poverty Action Gp 1969–79, fndr and dir Low Pay Unit 1974–80; MP (Lab) Birkenhead 1979–, oppn spokesman on educn 1979–81, Parly conslt to Civil and Public Servs Assoc, front bench oppn spokesman on health and social security 1983–, chm Select Ctee on Social Servs 1987–; *Books* Unequal Britain (1974); Inequality In Britain: Freedom, Welfare and The State (1981); Poverty and Politics (1982); The Minimum Wage: Its Potential And Dangers (1984); Freedom And Wealth In A Socialist Future (1987), The Politics of Paradise (1987); Losing Out: The Emergence of Britain's Underclass (1989); co author To Him Who Hath: A Study of Poverty And Taxation (1976); ed: 20th Century State Education (co-ed, 1971), Black Britons (co-ed, 1971), Low Pay (1973), Are Low Wages Inevitable? (1976), Education And The Urban Crisis (1976); The Conscript Army: A Study of Britain's Unemployed (1976); The Wealth Report (1979, 2 edn 1983); Policies Against Low Pay: An International Perspective (1984); *Style*— Frank Field, Esq, MP; ✉ House of Commons, London SW1A 0AA (☎ 0171 219 3000)

FIELD, Dr Ian Trevor; CBE (1994); s of Major George Edward Field, MBE and Bertha Cecilia, *née* Davies; *b* 31 Oct 1933; *Educ* Shri Shivaji Sch Poona, Bournemouth Sch, Royal Sch of Military Engrg, Guy's Hosp Med Sch London (MB BS); *m* 14 May 1960, Christine Mary Field, JP, da of Roland Reginald Osman; 3 s (Hugh Michael b 1962, Giles Edmund b 1964, Clive Robert b 1965), 1 da (Clare b and d 1961); *Career* Nat Serv RE 1952–54; house posts 1960–62, in gen practice 1962–64 (asst then princ), BMA 1964–75 (asst sec then under sec), sr princ med offr/under sec DHSS 1978–85 (sr med offr 1975–78), chief med and health services advsr ODA of FCO 1978–83, sec BMA 1989–93 (dep sec 1985–89); sec-gen World Med Assoc 1994–; memb: Cncl Liverpool Sch of Tropical Med 1979–83 and 1993–, Bd of Mgmnt London Sch of Hygiene & Tropical Med 1979–83 (memb Cncl 1979–83 and 1993–), Cncl RVC London 1982–88, Upper Norwood Cncl of Churches 1970–92 (chm 1984–89), Southwark RC Diocesan Ecumenical Cmmn for SE London 1984–93, Camberwell Deanery Pastoral Cncl 1986–92; Freeman City of London, memb Ct of Assts Worshipful Soc of Apothecaries 1986– (Liveryman 1971); FFPHM 1979 (memb 1975), FFOM 1991, CIMgt 1993; *Recreations* opera, military history, watching rugby & cricket; *Clubs* Athenaeum; *Style*— Dr Ian Field, CBE; ✉ 10 Rockwells Gardens, Dulwich Wood Park, London SE19 1HW

FIELD, (Edward) John; CMG (1991); s of Lt-Col Arthur Field, OBE, MC, TD, of 4 Fox Hill, Northam, nr Bideford, N Devon, and Dorothy Agnes, *née* Strouts (d 1943); *b* 11 June 1936; *Educ* Highgate, Corpus Christi Coll Oxford (MA), Univ of Virginia (ESU scholar); *m* 16 July 1960, Irene du Pont (Renny), da of Colgate Whitehead Darden Jr (d 1981), former Govr of Virginia; 1 s (Edward du Pont Darden b 12 July 1968), 1 da (Dorothy Agnes Justine b 24 March 1964); *Career* Nat Serv 2 Lt RA then Intelligence Corps 1954–56; Courtaulds Ltd 1960–63; FCO: Br Embassy Tokyo 1963–68, American Dept London 1968–70, 1 sec (cultural) Br Embassy Moscow 1970–72, 1 sec (commercial) Br Embassy Tokyo 1973–76; asst head: South Asian Dept 1976–77, Exports to Japan Unit DTI London 1977–79; cnsllr Br Embassy Seoul 1980–83; Centre for Int Affrs Harvard Univ 1983–84; cnsllr (economic and social) UK Mission to UN New York 1984–87, min Tokyo 1988–91, high cmmr Sri Lanka (Colombo) 1991–96, ret; *Recreations* tennis, golf; *Clubs* Tokyo, Travellers'; *Style*— John Field, Esq, CMG; ✉ c/o Foreign & Commonwealth Office, King Charles Street, London SW1A 2AH

FIELD, Sir Malcolm David; kt (1991); s of Maj Stanley Herbert Raynor Field (d 1970), of Selsey, Sussex, and Constance Frances, *née* Watson; *b* 25 Aug 1937; *Educ* Highgate Sch, London Business Sch; *m* 1, 1963 (m dis 1970), Jane, da of James Barrie; 2, 1974 (m dis 1982), Anne Carolyn, *née* Churchill; 1 da (Joanna Clare b 1974); *Career* 2 Lt WG 1956–58; dir WH Smith & Son Ltd 1970; W H Smith Group plc: dir 1974, md wholesale 1978, md retail 1978, gp md 1982–94, gp chief exec 1994–96, chm W H Smith Group (USA) Inc 1988; chm Civil Aviation Authority 1996–; NAAFI (non-exec): dir 1973, dep chm 1985, chm 1986–93; non-exec dir: MEPC plc 1988–, Scottish & Newcastle plc 1993–, The Stationery Office 1996–; non-exec memb Advsy Bd Phoenix Fund Mangrs 1992–; CIMgt 1988; *Recreations* tennis, cricket, golf, collecting watercolours, civil aviation; *Clubs* Garrick, MCC, Vanderbilt; *Style*— Sir Malcolm Field; ✉ Civil Aviation Authority, 45–59 Kingsway, London WC2B 6TE (☎ 0171 379 7311, fax 0171 240 1153)

FIELD, Marshall Hayward; CBE (1985); s of Maj Harold Hayward Field (d 1973), and Hilda Maud, *née* Siggers (d 1983); *b* 19 April 1930; *Educ* Dulwich; *m* 9 July 1960, Barbara Evelyn, da of Douglas Richard Harris (d 1950); 2 da (Alexandra b 1962, Katherine b 1964); *Career* Nat Serv Intelligence Corps 1955–57, served Cyprus; Phoenix Assurance: joined 1958, actuary 1964, gen mangr and actuary 1972–85, dir 1980–85; chm Life Offices Assoc 1983–85, memb Fowler Enquiry into Provision for Retirement 1984, conslt Securities and Investments Board 1985–86, conslt Bacon Woodrow 1986–; non-exec dir: TSB Trust Co 1985–89, TSB Group plc 1990–95, Ark Life Assurance Co Dublin 1991–; chm Dulwich Estates 1988–91 (govr 1973–95); govr: Dulwich Coll 1987–, James Allen's Girls' Sch 1981–96; memb Ctee Dulwich Picture Gallery 1985– (tstee 1994–); Freeman City of London 1980, Liveryman Worshipful Co of Actuaries 1984 (Court asst 1989, Master 1996); FIA 1957 (memb Cncl 1966, hon sec 1975–77, vice pres 1979–82, pres 1986–88); *Recreations* theatre, art generally; *Style*— Marshall Field, Esq, CBE; ✉ 12 Gainsborough Court, College Road, London SE21 7LT (☎ 0181 693 1704); Bembridge, IOW; Bacon & Woodrow, St Olaf House, London Bridge, London SE1 2PE (☎ 0171 357 7171)

FIELD, Richard Alan; QC (1987); s of Robert Henry Field, and Ivy May, *née* Dicketts; *b* 17 April 1947; *Educ* Ottershaw Sch, Univ of Bristol (LLB), LSE (LLM); *m* 31 Aug 1968, Lynne, da of Ismay Hauskind; 2 s (Matthew Ismay b 15 Feb 1978, Thomas Richard b 26 Nov 1988), 2 da (Rachel Eva b 3 June 1974, Beatrice Jasmine b 17 June 1981); *Career* asst prof Faculty of Law Univ BC 1969–71, lectr Hong Kong Univ 1971–73, assoc prof Faculty of Law McGill Univ Montreal Canada 1973–77, called to the Bar Inner Temple 1977; memb Honourable Soc of The Inner Temple; *Recreations* opera, theatre, cricket, rugby football (as a spectator); *Clubs* Garrick, Roehampton; *Style*— Richard Field, Esq, QC; ✉ 11 King's Bench Walk, Temple, London EC4Y 7EQ (☎ 0171 583 0610, fax 0171 583 9123/3690)

FIELD, Richard David; OBE (1987); s of Lt-Col G W H Field, of Austwick, North Yorks, and Pepita Mary Field; *b* 7 April 1945; *Educ* Malvern; *m* 15 July 1967, Shirley Philippa (Pippa), da of F P Mountford (d 1968), of Sheffield; 2 da (Catherine b 1969, Elizabeth b 1971); *Career* CA 1968; fin dir Bridon Wire 1975–78 (chief accountant 1973–75), Manchester Business Sch 1978, dir Bamford Business Servs 1980–91 (conslt 1978–80); chm: J & J Dyson plc; dir The Organisation for Cooperation & Trust Ltd; chm: Sheffield TEC 1991–93, Bd of Govrs Queen Margaret's Sch Escrick York 1986–93; pres: C of C 1986–93, ABCC Cncl 1988–90, Exec Ctee Industl Soc 1991–92; Master Co of Cutlers in Hallamshire, Liveryman Worshipful Co of Marketors; FCA, CIMgt, FCIM, FIPD, FRSA; *Recreations* tai chi, shiatsu, martial arts (black belt in ju-jitsu 2 Dan), running, walking, reading, total quality management, developing others to their full potential; *Style*— Richard D Field, Esq, OBE; ✉ 134 Townsend Road, Dore, Sheffield S17 3AQ; J & J Dyson plc, The Griffs, Stannington, Sheffield S6 6BW (☎ 0114 232 5655, fax 0114 232 0710)

FIELD, Robin Shaun; s of Harold Ivor Field (d 1988), of Highworth, Wilts, and Margaret Gleaves, *née* Doyle (d 1993); *b* 10 May 1938; *Educ* Cheltenham, Corpus Christi Coll Cambridge (MA); *m* 23 July 1960, Wendy, da of Joseph Addison Brace (d 1963); 2 s (Mark b 28 Dec 1961, Michael b 9 Dec 1964), 1 da (Alison b 3 Nov 1973); *Career* Shell International Petroleum Co 1960–66, mgmnt servs mangr John Waddington Ltd 1967–69, commercial dir (later dir and gen mangr) Plastona (John Waddington) 1969–76; Touche Ross Management Consultants: joined 1976, ptnr 1980–93, fndr Health Group 1983; non-exec chm SEL Laboratory Products, chm Royal National Orthopaedic Hospital Tst; CEng, MIEE, FCMA; *Recreations* sailing, skiing, opera, gardening; *Style*— Robin Field, Esq; ✉ 26 Gordon Avenue, Stanmore, Middlesex HA7 3QD (☎ 0181 954 0079)

FIELD, Roy William; s of William Laurie Field, and Cicely May, *née* Holland; *b* 19 Aug 1934; *Educ* Eton Coll Choir Sch, Buckingham Coll Harrow; *m* 13 Sept 1958, Patricia Ann, da of William Muston; 2 s (Timothy William b 1961, Peter Michael b 1962), 1 da (Alison Louise b 1965); *Career* GAOC 1952–54, NCO Austria; Br Film Indust 1952–, Rank Organisation 1956–71; md: Field Films Ltd 1971–, Optical Film Effects Ltd 1981–; Hollywood Oscar for achievement in visual effects Superman the Movie, Br Acad Award Sir Michael Balcon Award for outstanding achievement in Br cinema Superman, nomination BAFTA Award for visual effects Dark Crystal, nomination BAFTA Award for visual effects Labyrinth; FRKSTS; memb: Br Soc of Cameramen, Guild of Br Camera Technicians, BAFTA; *Style*— Roy Field, Esq; ✉ Optical Film Effects Ltd, Pinewood Studios, Iver Heath, Bucks SL0 0NH (☎ 01753 655486, fax 01753 656844, telex 847505 PINEW G)

FIELD-FISHER, Thomas Gilbert; TD (1949), QC (1969); s of Caryl Hillyard Field-Fisher (d 1953), of Torquay, Devon, and Dora Kate, *née* Purvis (d 1946); *b* 16 May 1915; *Educ* King's Sch Bruton, Peterhouse Cambridge (MA); *m* 8 Sept 1945, Ebba, da of Max Larsen, of Linwood, Utah, USA; *Career* QVR KRRC WWII 1939–47, BEF 1940 (POW, despatches), Maj i/c War Crimes Dept DJAG CMF (Italy) 1945–47; called to the Bar Middle Temple 1942 (bencher 1976, reader 1991); joined Western Circuit 1947, recorder of the Crown Ct 1972–86; acting deemster Isle of Man 1990–91, memb Bar Cncl 1962–66, chm Maria Colwell Inquiry 1973–74; dep chm: SW Agric Claims Tbnl 1962–82, Cornwall QS 1967–72; vice chm London Cncl of Social Serv 1966–79, vice pres London Vol Serv Cncl 1979–, memb Home Office Ctee on Animal Experiments 1980–87 (memb Animal Pro Ctee 1987–89), chm Battersea Dogs Home 1982–95 (vice pres 1995–), chm and fndr Assoc of Br Dogs Homes 1985–, vice pres Universities Fedn for Animal Welfare 1993–; pres Cornwall Magistrates Assoc 1985–; *Books* Animals and the Law (1964), Rent Regulation and Control (1967), contribs to Halsbury's Laws of England (3, 4 and revised edns) and other legal publications; *Recreations* dogs, collecting watercolours, gardening, MG cars, lawn tennis; *Clubs* Hurlingham, Int Lawn Tennis of GB; *Style*— Thomas Field-Fisher Esq, TD, QC; ✉ 38 Hurlingham Court, London SW6 3UW (☎ 0171 736 4627); 2 Kings Bench Walk, Temple, London EC4Y 7DE (☎ 0171 353 1746)

FIELD-JOHNSON, Nicholas Anthony; s of Henry Anthony Field-Johnson (d 1988), and Magdalena, *née* von Evert (d 1971); *b* 28 March 1951; *Educ* Harrow, Univ of Oxford (MA, treas Oxford Union Soc), Harvard Business Sch (MBA); *m* Sarah Katherine, *née* Landale; 3 s (Anthony Russell b Oct 1984, Ben Sebastian b May 1986, Oliver Nicholas b Dec 1988); *Career* corporate financier Citibank NA London 1974–78, investmt advsr Atlantic Richfield Co Los Angeles Calif 1979–82, gen mangr World Trade Bank Los Angeles 1983–85, head of M&A Dresdner Bank AG London 1986–90, dir NM Rothschild & Sons Ltd 1990–91, chief exec offr Case International Holdings Ltd 1992–; *Recreations* fishing, sailing, shooting, tennis, food and bridge; *Clubs* Carlton, Annabel's; *Style*— Nicholas Field-Johnson, Esq; ✉ 28 Ashchurch Park Villas, London W12 9SP (☎ 0181 743 4097)

FIELDEN, (John) Anthony Haigh; s of late Lt-Col John Haigh Fielden, TD, and late Jean, *née* Turnbull; *b* 18 March 1937; *Educ* Rossall, Keble Coll Oxford (MA); *m* 29 Sept 1962, Deryl Anne, da of Arthur Leonard Collinson, of Bury, Lancs; 1 s (Nicholas b 30 May 1964), 1 da (Tiffany b 23 Nov 1965); *Career* admitted slr 1961; ptnr: Emerson & Fielden 1962–68, Whitworths 1968–70; sr ptnr: Leak Almond & Parkinson 1985–87 (ptnr 1970–85), Cobbett Leak Almond (now Cobbetts) 1987–; clerk to tstees Manchester Guardian Soc Charitable Tst, memb Bd of Mgmnt Wood St Mission, vice chm Manchester Fin and Professional Forum; memb Law Soc; *Recreations* cricket and real tennis; *Clubs* MCC, Manchester Tennis and Racquet; *Style*— Anthony Fielden, Esq; ✉ Rosehill, Rostherne, Knutsford, Cheshire WA16 6RT (☎ 01565 830 430); The Wool Barn, Westington, Chipping Campden, Glos; Cobbetts, Ship Canal House, King St, Manchester M2 4WB (☎ 0161 833 3333, fax 0161 833 3030)

FIELDEN, Dr Christa Maria; *née* Peix; da of Ludwig Robert Peix (d 1974), and Margaret Freer-Hewish, *née* von Neumann; *b* 28 June 1943; *Educ* Hamps Co HS for Girls, Univ of London (BSc, MSc, PhD); *m* 29 Jan 1964 (m dis 1983), Christopher James Fielden; 2 s (James b 15 July 1966, William b 4 Oct 1968, d 1989); *Career* with Civil Serv 1970–74, head Computer Dept CNAA 1974–75, called to the Bar Lincoln's Inn 1982, in practice SE Circuit; FSS 1982; *Recreations* skiing, psychology, dogs; *Style*— Dr Christa Fielden;

✉ 9 Woburn Ct, Bernard St, London WC1 (☎ 0171 837 8752); 3 Paper Buildings, Temple, London EC4 (☎ 0171 353 6208)

FIELDEN, Christopher Thomas; s of Wilfred Fielden, of Nottingham (d 1968), and Nellie, *née* Shaw (d 1994); *b* 22 Nov 1942; *Educ* Nottingham HS, Downing Coll Cambridge (MA, LLB); *m* 30 March 1964, Pauline Mary, da of Joseph Frederick Hoult, of Nottingham (d 1982); 2 s (Henry b 1964, Timothy b 1968); *Career* admitted slr 1967; dir: Gallaher Ltd 1987–91 (gp legal advsr 1972), Gallaher Tobacco Ltd 1986–91, Forbuoys plc 1984–95, The Whyte & Mackay Distillers Group plc 1990–, Dollond & Aitchison Group plc 1992–94, The Prestige Group plc 1993–95; *Recreations* golf; *Style*— Christopher Fielden, Esq; ✉ Evergreens, Elstead Rd, Tilford, Farnham, Surrey GU10 2AJ (☎ 01252 782407); Gallaher Ltd, Members Hill, Brooklands Rd, Weybridge, Surrey KT13 0QU (☎ 01932 859777, fax 01932 857829)

FIELDHOUSE, (James) Richard; s of Sir Harold Fieldhouse, KBE, CB (d 1991), of Dormy House, Sunningdale, Surrey, and Mabel Elaine, *née* Elliot; bro of Adm of the Fleet Lord Fieldhouse, GCB, GBE (d 1992); *b* 4 May 1933; *Educ* Merchant Taylors', Guy's Med Sch (BDS, LDS, Golf purple), RCS (Dip in Orthodontics); *m* 1957, Lily Guillemina, da of late Carlos Auqusto Lopez; 2 da (Laura Catherine b 23 Oct 1958, Katherine Anne Clare b 9 Sept 1961); *Career* short serv cmmn Surgn Lt (D) RN in Malta HMS Ranpura and Ausonia 1957–61; gen dental practice Epsom Surrey 1962–72, lectr in children's dentistry Royal Dental Hosp of London 1972–75; specialist orthodontic practice: High Wycombe Bucks 1975–, Cavendish Square London 1975–87, Harley St London 1987–; Liveryman Worshipful Co of Clockmakers, Freeman City of London; memb: BDA, Br Assoc of Orthodontics, Br Soc for the Study of Orthodontics; *Recreations* tennis, golf, bridge, gardening, friends; *Clubs* West Hill Golf (Surrey, hon life memb); *Style*— Richard Fieldhouse, Esq

FIELDING, Claude Eric; s of Frederick Fischl (d 1943), and Elisabeth, *née* Meldola (d 1937); *b* 29 June 1926; *Educ* King's Sch Canterbury; *m* 8 Feb 1953, Olga Rachel, da of Dr Jacob Michael Raphael (d 1972); 2 da (Rachel b 1956, Jenny b 1959); *Career* clerk Stephens and Scown Solicitors St Austell 1941–43, managing clerk in articles Crawley & de Reya London 1943–50, admitted slr 1950; ptnr Crawley & de Reya (film, entertainment and media law) 1950–78, head entertainments and communications Law Dept Bartletts de Reya (now Michon de Reya) 1978–92 (conslt 1992–95), conslt Entertainment & Communication Gp Theodore Goddard 1996–; bd dir: British and American Investment Tst plc, Richard Attenborough Productions Ltd; dir: SE Arts Bd 1992–, Br Film Cmmn 1992–93; hon clerk Oxshott Heath Conservators 1971–91; Liveryman Worshipful Co of Solicitors 1960; memb: Law Soc 1950, Int Bar Assoc 1976; Commendatore Republic of Italy; *Recreations* sailing, skiing; *Clubs* Bosham Sailing, Downhill Only, Royal Over-Seas League; *Style*— Claude Fielding, Esq; ✉ Windfalls, 29 Prince's Drive, Oxshott, Surrey KT22 0UL (☎ 01372 842926, fax 01372 844208); Theodore Goddard, 150 Aldersgate Street, London EC1A 4EJ (☎ 0171 606 8855, fax 0171 606 4390, e-mail tg@link.org)

FIELDING, Hon Mrs (Daphne Winifred Louise); da of 4 Baron Vivian, DSO (d 1940); *b* 11 July 1904; *m* 1, 27 Oct 1926 (m dis 1953), 6 Marquess of Bath (d 1992); 2 s (7 Marquess of Bath, Lord Christopher Thynne, *qqv*) and 2 s decd, 1 da (Duchess of Beaufort, d 1995); m 2, 11 July 1953 (m dis 1978), Major Alexander Wallace (Xan) Fielding, DSO (d 1991), s of Alexander Lumsden Wallace Fielding (d 1966), of Kirkcaldy; *Career* writer; *Books* Mercury Presides (autobiography), The Nearest Way Home (autobiography), The Duchess of Jermyn Street (biography of Rosa Lewis), Emerald and Nancy (biography of Emerald and Nancy Cunard), The Rainbow Picnic (biography of Iris Tree), The Face on the Sphinx (biography of Gladys Deacon, Duchess of Marlborough), The Adonis Garden (fiction), History of Longleat, Before the Sunset Fades (both guides to Longleat); *Style*— The Hon Mrs Fielding; ✉ Old Laundry, Badminton GL9 1DD

FIELDING, David Ian; s of William Fielding and Nora, *née* Kershaw; *b* 8 Sept 1948; *Educ* Central Sch of Art and Design; *Career* theatre director and designer; designer for Pet Shop Boys World Tour 1991 and the album Very; *Theatre* as dir prodns incl: Britannicus (Crucible Sheffield), The Intelligence Park (Almeida Festival), The Hypochondriacs (Citizens Glasgow), Elisabeth II (Gate), The New Menoza (Gate), Betrayal (Citizens Glasgow), The Park (RSC, The Pit) 1995; design cmmns RSC incl: The Tempest, The Plain Dealer, Restoration, King Lear; other design credits incl: Scenes from an Execution (Almeida), Mother Courage (RNT) 1995; *Opera* as dir prodns for Garsington Opera incl: Capriccio, Daphne, Idomeneo, Die Ägyptische Helena; other credits incl: Elisa E Claudio (Wexford Festival Opera), Soundbites (ENO), Tannhäuser (Opera North); UK design cmmns: Wexford Festival Opera incl: Medea in Corinto, Giovanna D'Arco, Hans Heiling, La Legenda Di Sakuntala, The Turn of the Screw; for Scottish Opera incl: Seraglio, Die Fledermaus, Rigoletto, Wozzeck, The Rise and Fall of the City of Mahagonny; for Welsh Nat Opera incl: The Turn of the Screw, Il Trovatore, Elektra; Kent Opera incl: Ruddigore, The Marriage of Figaro, King Priam (also filmed); ENO incl: Rienzi, Mazeppa, Xerxes, Simon Boccanegra, Clarissa, A Masked Ball, Don Carlos, Street Scene (co-prod Scottish Opera); other prodns incl: Der Fliegende Hollander (Royal Opera House), La Clemenza Di Tito (Glyndebourne); cmmns abroad incl: The Rake's Progress (Netherlands Opera), Werther (Nancy Opera), Iolanthe (Komisch Oper Berlin), Don Carlos (San Jose Symphony), Idomeneo (Vienna State Opera), Jules Cesar (Paris Opera); *Recreations* bridge, crosswords, Central American archaeology, gardening; *Style*— David Fielding, Esq; ✉ c/o Harriet Cruickshank, 97 Old South Lambeth Road, London SW8 1XU (☎ 0171 735 2933, fax 0171 820 1081)

FIELDING, Sir Leslie; KCMG (1987); o s of Percy Archer Fielding (d 1963), and Margaret, *née* Calder Horry; *b* 29 July 1932; *Educ* Queen Elizabeth's Sch Barnet, Emmanuel Coll Cambridge (MA, hon fell), SOAS London, St Antony's Coll Oxford (MA); *m* 1978, Dr Sally Patricia Joyce Fielding, da of late Robert Stanley Thomas Stibbs Harvey; 1 s, 1 da; *Career* joined Foreign Serv 1956, Tehran 1957–60, FO 1960–64, Singapore 1964, chargé d'affaires Phnom Penh 1964–66, Paris 1966–70, FCO 1970–73; transferred to European Cmmn in Brussels 1973, head of delgn Cmmn of Euro Communities in Japan 1978–82, DG for external rels Euro Cmmn in Brussels 1982–87; vice chllr Univ of Sussex 1987–92, memb High Cncl Euro Univ Inst Florence 1988–92, chm UK Nat Curriculum Working Gp for Geography 1989–90, memb House of Laity of the General Synod of the C of E 1990–92; hon pres Univ Assoc for Contemporary Euro Studies 1990–; memb: Japan-Euro Community Assoc 1988–, UK-Japan 2000 Gp 1993–, Cons Gp for Europe 1993, European Movement 1996–; supporter Action Centre for Europe 1994–; reader C of E 1981–; hon fell Sussex European Inst 1993–; Hon LLD Univ of Sussex 1992; Grand Offr of the Order of St Agatha (San Marino) 1987, Knight Cdr of the Order of the White Rose (Finland) 1988, Silver Order of Merit with Star (Austria) 1989; FRSA 1989, FRGS 1991; *Recreations* living in the country, articles and broadcasts on international and religious affairs; *Clubs* Brooks's, Travellers'; *Style*— Sir Leslie Fielding, KCMG; ✉ Sutton Court, Stanton Lacy, Ludlow, Shropshire SY8 2AJ

FIELDING, Richard Walter; s of Walter Harrison Fielding, MBE (d 1988), of New Milton, Hants, and Marjorie Octavia Adair, *née* Roberts; *b* 9 July 1933; *Educ* Clifton; *m* 1, 27 April 1961, Felicity Ann (d 1981), da of the late Dr V D Jones; 1 s (Timothy b 1965), 3 da (Vanessa b 1962, Anabel b 1968, Lucinda (twin) b 1968); m 2, 1983, Mrs Jacqueline Winifred Digby, *née* Hussey, formerly w of late Henry Berkeley Digby; *Career* Nat Serv Lt RE 1951–53; broker rising to dir Bland Welch & Co Ltd 1954–68, dir and md C E Heath & Co Ltd 1968–75, fndr chm and chief exec offr Fielding and Ptnrs 1975–86, fndr and chm Charter Reinsurance Co Ltd 1986–; C E Heath plc: chief exec 1986, chm & chief exec offr 1987–90, chm 1990–92; fndr and dir: Syndicate Capital Trust PLC, Insurance Analysis Ltd; *Style*— Richard Fielding, Esq; ✉ Syndicate Capital Trust plc, 114 Middlesex Street, London E1 7HY (☎ 0171 247 6373)

FIELDS, Gordon Ivan Jr (Gifi); s of Gordon Ivan Fields, of Los Angeles, Calif, USA, and Dr Nancy Gayer, *née* Davidson, of London and Santa Monica, California, USA; *b* 29 June 1951, Santa Monica, California, USA; *Educ* Shrewsbury, William Ellis Sch London; *m* 11 Jan 1985, Catherine, da of Fredrick Henry Aldham, and Mary Aldham; 1 s (Jacob Harry Samual b 29 March 1987), 1 da (Elisha b 26 Jan 1986); *Career* memb staff: International Times 1967–68, UFO Club 1967–68, Middle Earth Club 1968–69; travelled to Afghanistan 1969–70; fashion entrepreneur: Trotsky International Ragfreak Clothing Co 1970–71, Gingernut Clothing Co 1971–75, Snob Shops 1983–87, Coppernob Group 1976–; garment designs sold worldwide 1970–; past and present retail customers incl: Harvey Nichols, Harrods, Bloomingdales, Fiorucci, Henri Bendel, I Magnin, Galleries Lafayette, Karstadt, JC Penny, Sears Group, Burton Group, GUS, Otto Group, BHS; fndr first retail and mfrg co USSR (jt venture with Leningrad State Bank and Nevski Zori Liliaw Co-op); reg conf speaker; fndr memb BFC (chair Mid-Season and London Shows 1983–89); nominee Br Fashion Awards 1990; FCIM 1989; *Recreations* golf, travel, wine and family, an interest in politics (memb Labour Party), history, literature, writing, wine and all sports; *Clubs* Coombe Hill Golf (Kingston Surrey); *Style*— Gifi Fields; ✉ Chief Executive, Coppernob Group, 12 Great Portland Street, London W1N 6LD (☎ 0171 436 3600, fax 0171 637 3232)

FIELDSEND, John Charles Rowell; s of Charles Edward Fieldsend, MC (d 1962), of Kirmond, Lincoln, and Phyllis Mary, *née* Brucesmith (d 1963); *b* 13 Sept 1921; *Educ* Michaelhouse Natal, Rhodes Univ Coll Grahamstown SA (BA, LLB); *m* 4 Dec 1945, Muriel, da of Oswald Gedling (d 1959), of Ripon, Yorks; 1 s (Peter Charles Rowell b 1949), 1 da (Catherine Margaret Ann b 1953); *Career* Lt RA 1941–45; called to the Bar Rhodesia 1947, advocate 1947–63, QC Rhodesia 1959; pres Special Income Tax Ct Fedn Rhodesia and Nyasaland 1958–63, judge High Ct S Rhodesia 1963–68 (resigned); sec Law Cmmn for England and Wales 1979–80 (asst slr 1968–79), chief justice Zimbabwe 1980–83; chief justice (non-resident): Turks and Caicos Is 1985–87, British Indian Ocean Territory 1987– (princ legal advsr 1984–87); memb Ct of Appeal: St Helena 1985–, Falklands and Antarctic Dependencies 1985–, Gibraltar 1986– (pres 1991–); *Style*— John Fieldsend, Esq; ✉ Great Dewes, Ardingly, W Sussex RH17 6UP (☎ 01444 892343)

FIENNES, Very Rev the Hon Oliver William TWISLETON-WYKEHAM-; s of 20 Baron Saye and Sele, OBE, MC (d 1968), and Hersey Cecilia Hester (d 1968), da of Capt Sir Thomas Dacres Butler, KCVO; *b* 17 May 1926; *Educ* Eton, New Coll Oxford (MA); *m* 26 June 1956, Juliet, yr da of Dr Trevor Braby Heaton, OBE; 2 s, 2 da; *Career* Lt Rifle Bde; ordained 1954, rector of Lambeth 1963–68, dean of Lincoln 1968–89, dean emeritus 1989; chm St Matthew Soc 1994–; chm Advsy Cncl BBC Radio Lincolnshire 1992–94; world fell Thanksgiving Square Dallas 1980–; KStJ; *Style*— The Very Rev the Hon Oliver Fiennes; ✉ Home Farm House, Colsterworth, nr Grantham, Lincs NG33 5HZ (☎ 01476 860811)

FIENNES, Ralph Nathanial; s of Mark Fiennes, of London, and Jennifer, *née* Lash (d 1993); *b* 22 Dec 1962; *Educ* St Kieran's Coll Kilkenny Ireland, Bishop Wordsworth Sch Salisbury, Chelsea Sch of Art, RADA (Kendal Award, Forbes-Robertson Award, Emile Littler Award); *Career* actor; memb Br Actors' Equity Assoc; *Theatre* The Open Air Theatre 1985: Twelfth Night, A Midsummer Night's Dream, Ring Round The Moon; Theatre Clwyd: Night and Day, See How They Run; The Oldham Coliseum 1986: Me Mam Sez, Don Quixote, Cloud Nine; The Open Air Theatre 1986: Romeo in Romeo & Juliet, Lysander in A Midsummer Night's Dream; Nat Theatre 1987–88: Six Characters in Search of an Author, Fathers and Sons, Ting Tang Mine; RSC 1988–91: Henry VI in The Plantagenets, Claudio in Much Ado about Nothing, Lewis the Dauphin in King John, Bert Jefferson in The Man Who Came to Dinner, Gant in Playing with Trains, Troilus in Troilus and Cressida, Edmund in King Lear, Berowne in Love's Labours Lost; title role in Hamlet (Hackney Empire and Broadway, Best Actor Tony Award) 1995; *Films* T E Lawrence in A Dangerous Man: Lawrence After Arabia (ATV), Heathcliff in Wuthering Heights (Paramount), the Son in The Baby of Macon (dir Peter Greenaway), John in The Cormorant (BBC), Amon Goeth in Schindler's List (dir Steven Spielberg, BAFTA Best Supporting Actor Award 1994, London Film Critics' British Actor of the Year Award 1995), Charles van Doren in Quiz Show (dir Robert Redford), Lenny Nero in Strange Days (dir Kathryn Bigelow), The English Patient (dir Anthony Minghella), Oscar and Lucinda (dir Gillian Armstrong); *Recreations* reading, swimming, music; *Style*— Ralph Fiennes, Esq; ✉ c/o Larry Dalzell Associates, 91 Regent Street, London W1R 7TB (☎ 0171 287 5131, fax 0171 287 5161)

FIENNES, Sir Ranulph (TWISLETON-WYKEHAM-); 3 Bt (UK 1916), of Banbury, Co Oxford; OBE (1993); s of Lt-Col Sir Ranulph Twisleton-Wykeham-Fiennes, 2 Bt, DSO (d 1943, gs of 17 Baron Saye and Sele), and Audrey Joan, *née* Newson (d 1995); *b* 7 March 1944, (posthumously); *Educ* Eton, Mons Offr Cadet Sch; *m* 11 Sept 1970, Virginia Frances, da of Thomas Pepper (d 1985); *Career* Capt Royal Scots Greys, Capt 22 SAS Regt 1966, Capt Sultan of Oman's Armed Forces 1968–70; exec conslt for Western Europe to Chm Occidental Petroleum Corp 1984–90; author and explorer; leader of first polar circumnavigation of earth (The Transglobe Expedition) that arrived back in UK in Sept 1982 after 3 years non-stop travel, first man (with colleague) to reach both Poles by surface travel, achieved world record for unsupported northerly travel reaching 88 degrees and 28 minutes Siberian Arctic 1990, leader of Ubar Expedition which discovered the lost city of Ubar 1992, record unsupported Polar trek of 1,272 miles in 96 days 1992–93 (also first unsupported crossing of Antarctic Continent); *Awards* French Parachute Wings 1968, Dhofar Campaign Medal 1968, Sultan of Oman's Bravery Medal 1970, Man of the Year Award 1982, Livingstone Gold Medal Royal Scottish Geographical Soc 1983, Gold Medal NY Explorers Club 1984, Fndr's Medal RGS 1984, The Polar Medal 1984 with Bar 1995 by HM the Queen (first recipient, wife was first first female recipient), ITV Award for the event of the decade 1990; Hon DSc Loughborough Univ; *Books* Talent for Trouble (1968), Icefall in Norway (1971), The Headless Valley (1972), Where Soldiers Fear to Tread (1975), Hell on Ice (1978), To the Ends of the Earth: Transglobe Expedition 1979–82 (1983), Bothie The Polar Dog (jtly with wife, 1984), Living Dangerously (1987), The Feather Men (1991), Atlantis of the Sands - The Search for the Lost City of Ubar (1992), Mind Over Matter (1993), The Sett (1996); *Recreations* skiing, photography; *Clubs* Guild of Vintners, Garrick; *Style*— Sir Ranulph Fiennes, Bt, OBE

FIENNES, Hon Richard Ingel; s and h of 21 Baron Saye and Sele, *qv*; *b* 19 Aug 1959; *Style*— The Hon Richard Fiennes; ✉ Broughton Castle, Banbury, Oxon

FIENNES-CLINTON, Hon Edward Gordon; o s and h of 18 Earl of Lincoln, *qv*; *b* 7 Feb 1943; *m* 1970 (m dis 1989), Julia, da of William Howson, of Armadale, Perth, W Australia; 2 s (Robert Edward b 1972, William Roy b 1980), 1 da (Marian Dawn b 1973); *Style*— The Hon Edward Fiennes-Clinton; ✉ 6 Jasminum Place, Carcoola Estate, Pinjarra, W Australia 6208, Australia

FIFE, Eugene Vawter (Gene); s of Clark E Fife, and Margaret Ellen, *née* Morton; *b* 23 Sept 1940; *Educ* Virginia Poly Inst (BS), Univ of Southern California (MBA); *m* 1, 4 June 1966, Susan Schucker (d 1981); 1 s (David b 1971), 1 da (Amy b 1974); m 2, 16 June 1984, Anne, da of Waldo Leisy; 1 s (Alexander b 1985), 1 da (Elizabeth b 1988); *Career* Lt US Air Force 1962–65; assoc Blyth & Co Inc 1968–70, Goldman Sachs & Co NY,

Los Angeles and San Francisco 1970–86, chm and md Goldman Sachs International 1986–Nov 1995; *Clubs* Union (NY), Pilgrim's; *Style*— Gene Fife, Esq; ✉ c/o Goldman Sachs International, Peterborough Court, 133 Fleet Street, London EC4A 2BB (☎ 0171 774 1000, fax 0171 774 4001)

FIFE, 3 Duke of (UK 1900); James George Alexander Bannerman Carnegie; 9 Bt (NS 1663); also 12 Earl of Southesk (S 1633), Earl of Macduff (UK 1900), Lord Carnegie of Kinnaird and Leuchars (S 1616), and Baron Balinhard (UK 1869); o s of 11 Earl of Southesk, KCVO, DL (d 1992), and his 1 w, HH Princess Maud Alexandra Victoria Georgina Bertha (d 1945; granted title of Princess, style of Highness, and special precedence immediately after all members of Royal Family bearing style of Royal Highness 1905), 2 da of 1 Duke of Fife and HRH Princess Louise (The Princess Royal), eldest da of HM King Edward VII; suc his maternal aunt, HRH Princess Arthur of Connaught, Duchess of Fife 1959; *b* 23 Sept 1929; *Educ* Ludgrove, Gordonstoun, Royal Agric Coll Cirencester; *m* 11 Sept 1956 (m dis 1966), Hon Caroline Cecily Dewar, da of 3 Baron Forteviot, MBE, DL (d 1993) (she m 2 Gen Sir Richard Worsley, *qv*); 1 s (Earl of Southesk b 1961), 1 da (Lady Alexandra Carnegie b 1959); *Heir* s, Earl of Southesk, *qv*; *Career* served in Malaya Campaign Scots Guards 1948–50; landowner, farmer and co dir; Freeman City of London 1954, Sr Liveryman of Clothworkers' Co 1954; pres Amateur Boxing Assoc 1959–73, vice patron 1973; a vice patron of Braemar Royal Highland Soc; a vice pres British Olympic Assoc; ships pres HMS Fife 1967–87; *Clubs* Turf; *Style*— His Grace the Duke of Fife; ✉ Elsick House, Stonehaven, Kincardineshire AB39 3NT; Kinnaird Castle, Brechin, Angus

FIGES, Eva; da of Emil Eduard Unger (d 1973), and Irma Alice, *née* Cohen (d 1991); *b* 15 April 1932; *Educ* Kingsbury Co GS, Queen Mary Coll London (BA); *m* John G Figes (m dis); 1 da (Catherine Jane b 1957), 1 s (Orlando Guy b 1959); *Career* writer; Guardian Fiction Prize 1967; fell Queen Mary Coll London 1990–; memb Writers' Guild of Gt Britain; *Novels* Equinox (1966), Winter Journey (1967), Konek Landing (1969), B (1972), Days (1974), Nelly's Version (1977), Waking (1981), Light (1983), The Seven Ages (1986), Ghosts (1988), The Tree of Knowledge (1990), The Tenancy (1993), The Knot (1996); *Non-fiction* Patriarchal Attitudes (1970), Tragedy and Social Evolution (1976), Little Eden (1978), Sex and Subterfuge - Women Writers to 1850 (1982); *Recreations* music, theatre, cinema, my grand-daughters; *Style*— Ms Eva Figes; ✉ Rogers, Coleridge & White Ltd, 20 Powis Mews, London W11 1JN (☎ 0171 221 3717, fax 0171 229 9084)

FIGG, Sir Leonard Clifford William; KCMG (1981, CMG 1974); s of Sir Clifford Figg (d 1947), of Gt Missenden, Bucks, and Eileen Maud, *née* Crabb (d 1968); *b* 17 Aug 1923; *Educ* Charterhouse, Trinity Coll Oxford; *m* 1955, Jane, eldest da of late Judge Harold Brown; 3 s; *Career* Dip Serv: joined 1947, consul gen and min Milan 1973–77, asst under sec of state 1977–80, ambass to Republic of Ireland 1980–83; vice chm Br Red Cross Soc 1983–88; pres: Aylesbury Divnl Cons Assoc 1985–95, Bucks Assoc of Youth Clubs 1987–; Chiltern Soc 1990–; chm Bucks Farming & Wildlife Advsy Gp 1990–; *Clubs* Brooks's; *Style*— Sir Leonard Figg, KCMG; ✉ Court Field House, Little Hampden, Great Missenden, Bucks

FIGGESS, Sir John George; KBE (1969, OBE 1949), CMG (1960); eldest s of Percival Watts Figgess, and Leonora, *née* McCanlis; *b* 15 Nov 1909; *Educ* Whitgift Sch; *m* 1948, Alette, da of Dr P J A Idenburg, of The Hague; 2 da; *Career* cmmnd Intelligence Corps 1939, Japanese linguist, liaison offr with C-in-C Eastern Fleet WWII (India, Burma), Maj 1942, Temp Lt-Col 1943, Temp Col 1956; Mil Attaché Tokyo 1956–61, cnsllr (info) Br Embassy Tokyo 1961–68, cmmr gen for Britain at Expo '70 Osaka 1968–70, dir Christie Manson and Woods Ltd 1973–82; *Style*— Sir John Figgess, KBE, CMG; ✉ The Manor House, Burghfield, Berks RG3 3TG

FIGGIS, Sir Anthony St John Howard; KCVO (1996), CMG (1993); s of R R Figgis (d 1984), and Philippa Maria, *née* Young (d 1988); *b* 12 Oct 1940; *Educ* Rugby, King's Coll Cambridge; *m* 6 June 1964, Miriam Ellen (Mayella), da of Dr F C Hardt (d 1954); 2 s (Benedict b 1968, Oliver b 1972), 1 da (Sophie b 1966); *Career* HM Dip Serv: joined 1962, Belgrade 1963–65 and 1982–85, Bahrain 1968–70, Madrid 1971–74 and 1979–82, Bonn 1988–89, dir of res and analysis FCO 1989–91, Vice-Marshal of the Diplomatic Corps and an asst under sec FCO 1991–96, ambass Austria 1996–; *Recreations* fly-fishing, tennis, music (piano); *Style*— Sir Anthony Figgis, KCVO, CMG; ✉ c/o Foreign & Commonwealth Office (Vienna), King Charles Street, London SW1A 2AH

FIGURES, Sir Colin Frederick; KCMG (1983, CMG 1978), OBE (1969); s of Frederick and Muriel Figures; *b* 1 July 1925; *Educ* King Edward's Sch Birmingham, Pembroke Coll Cambridge (MA); *m* 1956, Pamela Ann Timmis; 1 s, 2 da; *Career* joined FO 1951, first sec Vienna 1966, FCO 1969–85, dep sec Cabinet Office 1985–89; *Style*— Sir Colin Figures, KCMG, OBE; ✉ c/o Midland Bank, 130 New Street, Birmingham B2 4JU

FILBY, Ven William Charles Leonard; s of William Richard Filby (d 1946), of Middx, and Dorothy, *née* Evans (d 1980); *b* 21 Jan 1933; *Educ* Ashford Co Sch Middx, London Univ (BA); *m* 1958, Marion Erica, da of Prof T W Hutchison, of Birmingham; 4 s (Jonathan b 1959, Andrew b 1961, Christopher b 1963, William b 1968), 1 da (Rebecca b 1966); *Career* vicar: Holy Trinity Richmond 1965–71, Bishop Hannington Hove 1971–79; rector Broadwater 1979–83, rural dean Worthing 1980–83, canon Chichester Cathedral 1981–83, archdeacon of Horsham 1983–; dir Diocesan Industrial Mission Advsy Panel 1988–; chm: Redcliffe Missionary Training Coll 1970–92, Sussex Churches Broadcasting Ctee 1984–95; govr: St Mary's Hall Brighton 1984–, Pennthorpe Sch 1984–95, W Sussex Inst of High Educn 1985–; memb Keswick Convention Cncl 1973–93; bishop's advsr for hosp chaplains 1986–; *Recreations* sport, music; *Style*— The Ven the Archdeacon of Horsham; ✉ The Archdeaconry, Itchingfield, Horsham, N Sussex RH13 7NX (☎ 01403 790315, fax 01403 791153)

FILER, Denis Edwin; CBE (1992), TD (1962 and 1974); s of Edwin Francis Filer (d 1951), of Manchester, and Sarah Ann, *née* Stannard (d 1984); *b* 19 May 1932; *Educ* Manchester Central GS, Univ of Manchester (BSc), Open Univ (BA); *m* 17 Aug 1957, Pamela, da of Sam Armitage, of Manchester; 1 s (Nigel John Denis b 1967), 2 da (Fiona Anne b 1962, Katharine Helen b 1964); *Career* Nat Serv 2 Lt REME served BAOR 1953–55; TA serv culminating: Lt-Col ADEME 1970–75, Col 1975–78, Hon Col REME(V) West 1978–87; ICI: project mangr and maintenance engineer (Holland, Grangemouth and Hillhouse) 1955–73, asst works mangr Wilton Works 1973–76, engrg mangr Welwyn 1976–78, engrg and prodn dir Welwyn 1978–81, dir of engrg 1981–88, non-exec dir Innvotec Corporate Ventures Ltd (formerly Electra Corporate Ventures Ltd) 1989–, chm Adwest Group plc 1994– (non-exec dir 1991–94); DG The Engrg Cncl 1988–95 (formerly memb Cncl); Hon DSc Univ of Hertfordshire; FEng 1985, FIMechE, FIChemE, CIMgt; *Recreations* tennis; *Clubs* Army and Navy; *Style*— Denis E Filer, Esq, CBE, TD, FEng; ✉ Brambles, Watton Green, Watton-at-Stone, Hertford SG14 3RB (☎ 01920 830207); Adwest Group plc (☎ 0118 969 7171)

FILER, Michael Harold; s of Horace Filer (d 1994), and Raie, *née* Behrman (d 1978); *b* 11 Aug 1939; *Educ* Clifton, Inst of Taxation (ATII); *m* 5 Dec 1965, Anne Brenda, da of Peter Packer; 1 s (Samuel b 1978), 3 da (Lucy b 1967, Katy b 1970, Sadie b 1981); *Career* CA 1963; currently sr ptnr Filer Knapper; memb Bournemouth CC 1969–79 and 1983–87; Mayor of Bournemouth 1984–85; memb numerous charitable ctees; FCA; *Recreations* cricket (played in 1957 Clifton Coll Cricket Team at Lord's, player mangr UK Cricket Team in Maccabiah Games Israel 1974), tennis; *Style*— Michael H Filer, Esq; ✉ 8 Boscombe Cliff Rd, Bournemouth, Dorset BH5 1JL (☎ 01202 304464); Filer Knapper, Chartered Accountants, 10 Bridge Street, Christchurch, Dorset BH23 1EF (☎ 01202 483341, fax 01202 483550)

FILKIN, David Shenstone; s of Brian Shenstone Filkin, of Birmingham, and Lilian Winifred, *née* Franklin; *b* 22 Nov 1942; *Educ* King Edward's Sch Birmingham, Univ Coll Oxford (BA); *m* 31 Aug 1968, Angela Elizabeth, da of Geoffrey Callam (d 1970), of Woking, Surrey; 3 s (Neil b 1973, Jonathan b 1975, Matthew b 1978); *Career* BBC TV: prodr Man Alive 1964–79, exec prodr Holiday 74 1974, deviser and ed Brass Tacks 1978, ed Tomorrow's World 1979–84, ed QED 1984–91, deviser and ed Body Matters 1985–90, head of science and features 1991–94; md David Filkin Enterprises 1994–; pres BBC RFC 1979–86, memb Surrey Met Rugby Football Referees Soc; *Books* Tomorrow's World Today (1982), Bodymatters (1987); *Recreations* rugby union football coaching and refereeing, sea angling, golf, wine tasting; *Clubs* BBC RFC, The Home Park Golf, Bisley & District Sea, Anglers, The Wine Soc; *Style*— David Filkin, Esq; ✉ 29 Bloomfield Rd, Kingston upon Thames, Surrey KT1 2SF (☎ 0181 549 3204, fax 0181 549 3204, e-mail 100670,1477@compuserve.com)

FILKIN, Elizabeth Jill; da of John Tompkins, and Frances Trollope; *b* 24 Nov 1940; *Educ* Univ of Birmingham (BSocSci), Brunel Univ; *m* 1, 1974 (m dis 1994), Geoffrey Filkin, CBE, *qv*; 3 da; m 2, 1996, Michael John Honey; *Career* organiser Sparkbrook Association Birmingham 1961–64, res fell Anglo-Israel Association London and Israel 1964, lectr and researcher Univ of Birmingham 1964–68, lectr National Institute for Social Work London 1968–71 (also community worker North Southwark), community work services offr London Borough of Brent Social Services Dept 1971–75, lectr in social studies Univ of Liverpool 1975–83, chief exec National Association CAB 1983–88, asst chief exec London Docklands Development Corporation 1991–92 (dir Community Servs 1988–91), The Adjudicator 1993–; dir: Britannia Building Society 1992–, Hay Management Consultants 1992–, Logica plc 1995–; chm Advsy Cncl Centre for Socio-Legal Studies Wolfson Coll Oxford 1995–; memb: Advertising Standards Authy, Cncl Royal Holloway Univ of London 1995–; *Books* The New Villagers (1969), What Community Worker Needs to Know (1974), Community Work & Caring for Children (1979), Caring for Children (1979), Women and Children First (1984); *Recreations* swimming, walking; *Style*— Elizabeth Filkin; ✉ The Adjudicator's Office, 28 Haymarket, London SW1Y 4SP (☎ 0171 930 3965)

FILKIN, (David) Geoffrey Nigel; CBE (1997); s of Donald Geoffrey Filkin (d 1994), and Winifred, *née* Underwood; *b* 1 July 1944; *Educ* King Edward VI GS Birmingham, Clare Coll Cambridge (MA), Univ of Manchester (DipTP); *m* (m dis), Elizabeth Filkin, *qv*; 3 da (Fiona, Victoria, Beatrice); *Career* town planner Redditch Development Corporation 1969–72, mangr Housing Aid Centre Brent 1972–75, dir of housing and dep chief exec Merseyside Improved Housing 1975–79, dir of housing Ellesmere Port 1979–82, dir of housing Greenwich 1982–88, chief exec Reading Borough Council 1988–91, sec Assoc of District Councils 1991–; memb Dept of Environment Advsy Panel on Sponsored Bodies; hon memb Soc of Local Authy Chief Execs, hon fell Inst of Local Govt Univ of Birmingham; MIH, MRTPI; *Recreations* walking, opera, music, bird watching; *Style*— Geoffrey Filkin, CBE; ✉ Association of District Councils, 26 Chapter Street, London SW1P 4ND (☎ 0171 233 6868, fax 0171 976 5693)

FILOCHOWSKI, (Edward) Jan; *Educ* BA, MA; *m* Sheila Mary, *née* Bell; 1 s (Tom), 1 da (Kate); *Career* chief exec Poole Hosp NHS Tst; MHSM; *Style*— Jan Filochowski, Esq; ✉ Poole Hospital NHS Trust, Longfleet Road, Poole, Dorset BH15 2JB (☎ 01202 442624, fax 01202 442743, car 0831 148008)

FILOCHOWSKI, Julian; s of Tadeusz Filochowski, of Normanton, W Yorks, and Jean, *née* Royce; *b* 9 Dec 1947; *Educ* St Michael's Coll Leeds, Churchill Coll Cambridge (BA, MA); *Career* Central America coordinator Br Volunteer Programme Guatemala City 1969–73, educn sec Catholic Inst for Int Rels (CIIR) 1973–82, dir Catholic Fund for Overseas Devpt (CAFOD) 1982–; *Books* Reflections on Puebla (jtly, 1980), Archbishop Romero - Ten Years On (1990); *Style*— Julian Filochowski, Esq; ✉ Catholic Fund for Overseas Development, Romero Close, Stockwell Road, London SW9 9TY (☎ 0171 733 7900, fax 0171 274 9630, e-mail jfilocho@cafod.attmail.com)

FINAN, John Charles; *b* 2 May 1938; *m* Denise Mary; 3 c; *Career* Pearl Assurance: joined as insurance agent 1959, various field mgmnt and head office mgmnt appts until 1987, dir Pearl Assurance plc 1987–88, also dir Pearl Assurance Unit Funds Ltd, Pearl Assurance Marketing Services Ltd, Pearl Trust Managers Ltd and Pearl Assurance Unit Linked Pensions Ltd until 1988; chief exec and dep chm NEL Britannia (insurance arm of INVESCO MIM plc, formerly Britannia Arrow) 1989–92, dir numerous subsid cos (incl MIM Britannia Unit Trust Managers Ltd and MIM Ltd), NEL acquired by UNUM Corporation 1990; md Provident Life Association Ltd 1992–; chm Winterthur Life Ltd 1995–; rep on Home Service Ctee Assoc of Br Insurers, former chm UK and rep of Ireland Advsy Ctee LIMRA International, fndr chm Euro Educn Ctee LIMRA; *Recreations* golf, squash; *Style*— John Finan, Esq; ✉ Winterthur Life UK Ltd, Basingstoke, Hants RG21 6SZ (direct ☎ 01256 798474, fax 01256 814399)

FINBOW, Roger John; s of Frederick Walter Finbow, of Sudbourne, Woodbridge, Suffolk, and Olivia Francis, *née* Smith; *b* 13 May 1952; *Educ* Woodbridge Sch Suffolk, Mansfield Coll Oxford (MA); *m* 23 May 1984, Janina Fiona (Nina), da of John Doull, of Shorne, Kent; 3 da (Romy b 1985, Georgina b 1987, Isobel b 1989); *Career* Ashurst Morris Crisp London: articled clerk 1975–77, asst 1977–83 (Paris 1978–79), assoc 1983–85, ptnr 1985–; former pres: Old Woodbridgian Soc, Mansfield Assoc; tstee Adfam (Suffolk), memb Fin and Gen Purposes Ctee Seckford Fndn, dir Ipswich Town Football Club Co Ltd; *Books* UK Merger Control: Law and Practice (jtly, 1995); *Recreations* cars, collecting model cars, keeping fit, badminton, football spectating, ballet; *Style*— Roger Finbow, Esq; ✉ Yew Tree House, Higham, Colchester, Essex CO7 6JZ (☎ 01206 337378); Ashurst Morris Crisp, Broadwalk House, 5 Appold St, London EC2A 2HA (☎ 0171 638 1111, fax 0171 972 7990)

FINCH, Prof Janet Valerie; da of Robert Bleauley Finch (d 1975), of Liverpool, and Evelyn Muriel, *née* Smith; *b* 13 Feb 1946; *Educ* Merchant Taylors' Sch for Girls Crosby, Bedford Coll Univ of London (BA), Univ of Bradford (PhD); *m* 1, 1967 (m dis 1981), Geoffrey O Spedding; m 2, 1994, David H J Morgan; *Career* research asst Dept of Anthropology Univ of Cambridge 1969–70, postgraduate research student Univ of Bradford 1970–73, lectr in sociology Endsleigh Coll of Educn Hull 1974–76; Univ of Lancaster: lectr in social admin 1976–84, sr lectr 1984–88, prof of social relations 1988–, head Dept of Applied Social Science 1988–91, memb Senate 1984–87 and 1989–91, memb Academic Planning Ctee 1989–, chair Equal Opportunities Ctee 1990–93, memb Staffing Ctee 1991–93, pro-vice-chllr 1992–95; vice-chllr Univ of Keele 1995–; CVCP: memb The Sutherland Ctee (Academic Standards Gp) 1988–92, pt/t secondment to the Academic Audit Unit 1990–91, memb Jt Working Party with the Br Acad on postgraduate studentships in the humanities 1991–92; Br Sociological Assoc: memb Nat Exec 1980–84, chair Exec 1983–84; memb ESRC: Research Centres Bd 1992–93, Cncl 1993–97, chair Research Grants Bd; memb Advsy Gps 1990–92: Nursing Research Unit King's Coll London, Home Office project on Imprisonment and Family Ties Univ of Cambridge, Rowntree project on Young People and Housing Univ of Kent; memb: various Ctees CNAA 1982–92, Professoriate Standing Ctee Sheffield Poly (now Sheffield Hallam Univ) 1989–92, External Panel of Experts in Social Admin Univ of London 1990–93; govr: Edge Hill Coll 1990–92, Sheffield Hallam Univ 1992–95; chair Preston Cncl for Racial Equality 1982–86 (exec memb 1977–86); memb N Western RHA 1992–; *Books* Married to the Job: Wives' Incorporation in Men's Work (1983), Education as Social Policy (1984), Research and Policy: the Uses of Qualitative Methods in Social and Educational Research (1986), Family Obligations and Social Change (1989), Negotiating Family

Responsibilities (with J Mason, 1993), Will Inheritance and Families (contrib, 1996); also author of numerous book chapters and of articles in refereed jls; *Style*— Prof Janet Finch; ✉ Vice-Chancellor's Office, Keele University, Keele, Staffordshire ST5 5BG

FINCH, Martin Anthony; s of Francis James William Finch, and Margaret Helen, *née* Simmons (d 1967); *b* 24 Feb 1938; *Educ* Tech Sch Kent, Art Sch Kent (NDD); *Career* Nat Serv 1958–60; jr visualiser Smees Advertising 1960–61, graphic designer ICT (now ICL) 1961–63; publicity mangr: A B Dick Co 1963–64, Letraset 1964–68; dir Matthew Finch Design Consultants Ltd 1968–; MCIM 1967, FCSD 1971, FInstD 1975; *Recreations* antiquarian books (speciality cookery), fine arts, painting, ceramics; *Style*— Martin Finch, Esq; ✉ Fernwood House, High St, Farningham, Kent DA4 ODT (☎ 01322 862140); Matthew Finch Design Consultants Ltd, The Courtyard Studio, Fernwood House, High St, Farningham, Kent DA4 0DT (☎ 01322 860292)

FINCH, Michael James; s of Reginald James Finch, of Chadwell Heath, Essex, and Florence Anne, *née* Selby; *b* 6 July 1957; *Educ* Redbridge Tech Coll, Ravensbourne Coll of Art (BA), Royal Coll of Art (MA); *partner* Bridget, da of John Strevens; 1 da (Ella); *Career* painter; chair Fndn Parsons Sch of Design Paris 1996– (prof 1992–); one man shows: Peterborough City Museum and Art Gallery 1983, Groucho Club 1987 and 1988, Pomeroy Purdy Gallery 1990 and 1992 (curator 1988–91), Purdy Hicks Gallery 1994; included in various gp shows; paintings in collections: Peterborough City, Unilever, Burston, County NatWest, BDO Binder Hamlyn, Colas, Deutsch Bank; Unilever award 1985, Burston award 1985, Ile de France FRAC; *Recreations* jazz; *Clubs* Groucho; *Style*— Michael Finch, Esq; ✉ 59 Rue de Meaux, Senlis 60300, France (☎ 00 33 44 60 94 20, fax 00 33 44 60 00 00); c/o Purdy Hicks Gallery (☎ 0171 237 6062, fax 0171 237 3049)

FINCH, Robert Gerard; JP (1992); s of Brig J R G Finch, OBE, and Patricia Hope, *née* Ferrar, now of Freemantle, W Australia; *b* 20 Aug 1944; *Educ* Felsted; *m* Patricia Ann; 2 da (Alexandra b 8 May 1975, Isabel b 8 June 1978); *Career* articled clerk Monro Pennefather & Co 1963–68, ptnr Linklaters & Paines 1974– (slr Property Dept 1969–); Blundell Memorial lectr; Alderman City of London; Assistant Worshipful Co of Slrs, Liveryman Worshipful Co of Innholders; govr: Christ's Hosp, Witley Sch; memb Law Soc 1969; *Recreations* sailing, hill walking, skiing, ski mountaineering; *Clubs* Itchenor Sailing, Alpine Ski, Ski Club of Great Britain; *Style*— Robert G Finch, Esq, JP; ✉ Linklaters & Paines, Barrington House, 59–67 Gresham St, London EC2V 7JA (☎ 0171 606 7080, fax 0171 600 2885)

FINCH, Stephen Clark; OBE (1989); s of Frank Finch (d 1955), of Haywards Heath, and Doris, *née* Lloyd (d 1958); *b* 7 March 1929; *Educ* Ardingly, RMCS, Sch of Signals; *m* 26 April 1975, Sarah Rosemary Ann, da of Adm Sir Anthony Templer Frederick Griffith Griffin, GCB (d 1996), of Bosham; 2 da (Clare b 1977, Alice b 1980); *Career* cmmnd Royal Signals 1948, Troop Cdr BAOR 1949–50, Troop Cdr Korea 1951–52, RMCS 1953–56, Instr Sch of Signals 1956–59, Troop Cdr BAOR 1959–62, seconded Miny of Aviation 1962–64, Sqdn Cdr BAOR 1964–66, Staff Offr BAOR 1966–68, ret as Maj 1968; BP: mangr Communications Div 1968–71, gp communications mangr 1971–81, sr advsr regulatory affairs 1981–84, asst coordinator info systems 1984–89; ind conslt in info tech 1989–; chm Telecommunications Mangrs Assoc 1981–84 (memb 1968–, memb Exec Ctee 1971–91), chm Int Telecommunications Users Gp 1987–89 (memb Cncl 1981–94); memb: MMC 1985–, Sec of State's Advsy Panel on Licensing Value Added Network Servs 1982–87, City of London Deanery Synod 1981– (lay chm 1994–), London Area Synod 1989–, London Diocesan Synod 1994–; Freeman City of London 1975; FInstAM (memb Cncl 1981–84, medallist 1985), FIMgt, FTMA; *Recreations* sailing, skiing, swimming, music; *Clubs* National; *Style*— Stephen Finch, Esq, OBE; ✉ 97 Englefield Rd, Canonbury, London N1 3LJ

FINCHER, Jayne; da of Terence (Terry) Edgar Fincher, *qv*, and June, *née* Smith; *b* 24 April 1958; *Educ* Tillingbourne Secdy Sch, Godalming GS; *m* 31 July 1982, Alan Barlow; *Career* photographer; trained at Photographers International as darkroom printer/jr photographer 1975–77; specialist photographer of Royal family 1977–; official portraits Prince of Wales' 40th birthday photographs 1988; *Awards* Martini Royal Photographer of the Year 1982, 1984 and 1992 (Royal Photographer of the Decade 1987), Nikon Royal Photographer of the Year 1992; *Books* Debrett's Illustrated Fashion Guide to the Princess of Wales (co-author, 1989), My Young Friends (photographer, 1989), Travels with a Princess (1990); *Recreations* skiing, gardening, horse riding; *Style*— Ms Jayne Fincher; ✉ Photographers International, Sandilands, Blackheath, Nr Guildford, Surrey GU4 8RB (home ☎ 01483 893646, business ☎ 01483 898695, fax 01483 894874, mobile 0831 403416)

FINCHER, Terence Edgar (Terry); s of Leonard Edgar Fincher (d 1979), and Ruth, *née* Walker (d 1961); *b* 8 July 1931; *Educ* C of E Sch Bucks; *m* 19 March 1955, June, da of William Smith; 3 da (Jayne, *qv*, b 24 April 1958, Sally b 18 March 1960, Lucy b 29 April 1964); *Career* Nat Serv; messenger boy Keystone Press 1945–49, freelance photographer 1949–51, staff photographer Keystone Press 1951–57; news photographer: Daily Herald 1957–62, Daily Express 1962–69, freelance 1969–70, The Sun 1970; fndr Photographers International 1971, numerous commissions for various newspapers and magazines; FRPS; *Awards* Photographer of the Year (1957, 1959, 1964 and 1967), third prize World Photo Contest; *Books* Creative Techniques in Photo-Journalism (1980), The Fincher File (co-author, 1981), Debrett's Illustrated Fashion Guide of The Princess of Wales (co-author, 1989); *Recreations* walking, photography; *Style*— Terry Fincher, Esq; ✉ Photographers International Ltd, Sandilands, Blackheath, nr Guildford, Surrey GU4 8RB

FINDLATER, Richard Napier; s of George Richard Park Findlater (d 1963), and Rita Margaret, *née* Wade (d 1981); *b* 27 May 1947; *Educ* Pangbourne Coll, Harvard Business Sch; *m* 18 Aug 1972, Susan, da of Ronald Edmund Charlton; 2 s (Timothy Richard Park b 4 March 1975, Simon Ian Alexander b 25 May 1978), 1 da (Harriet Leila Alexandra b 11 Sept 1987); *Career* Harry Price & Co CAs Eastbourne 1964–70; ptnr Ernst & Young 1976–, currently vice-chm Ernst & Young International; ATII 1968, FCA 1970, FIMgt 1982; *Recreations* golf, paintings, food and wine; *Style*— Richard Findlater, Esq; ✉ Ernst & Young, Becket House, 1 Lambeth Palace Road, London SE1 7EU (☎ 0171 928 2000)

FINDLAY, Brig (William Francis) Allan; OBE (1973); s of James Arthur Findlay (d 1966), of London, and Gladys Anna, *née* Ker (d 1971); *b* 30 Nov 1929; *Educ* Eagle House Sch, Wellington Coll, RMA Sandhurst; *m* 21 April 1956, Bridget Gay, da of Air Vice Marshal Augustus Henry Orlebar, CBE, AFC (d 1943), of Sandy, Beds; 2 s (Giles b 1959, Oliver b 1962); *Career* CO Queen's Own Yeo 1971–73, Brig 1977, Col 5 Royal Inniskilling Dragoon Gds 1981–86, ADC to HM The Queen 1982; mktg exec MEL Defence Electronics 1982–89; memb Chichester DHA 1989–90, memb W Sussex CC 1993–; master Catterick Beagles 1955–56; *Recreations* gardening, field sports; *Clubs* Cavalry and Guards'; *Style*— Brig Allan Findlay, OBE; ✉ Upmeadow Lodge, Graffham, Petworth, West Sussex (☎ 01798 867236)

FINDLAY, Donald Russell; QC (Scot 1988); s of James Findlay (d 1980), of Edinburgh, and Mabel, *née* Muirhead (d 1985); *b* 17 March 1951; *Educ* Harris Acad Dundee, Univ of Dundee (LLB), Univ of Glasgow (MPhil); *m* 28 Aug 1982, Jennifer Edith, *née* Borrowman; *Career* lectr in law Heriot Watt Univ Edinburgh 1975–76, advocate 1975–; past chm Advocates Criminal Law Gp, past chm Faculty of Advocates Criminal Practices Ctee; Lord Rector of St Andrews Univ; vice chm Glasgow Rangers FC; memb: Lothian Health Bd 1987–91, Faculty of Advocates 1975; FRSA; *Recreations* Glasgow Rangers FC, Egyptology, The Middle East, wine, malt whisky, travel, ethics, American football, Sumo; *Clubs* Royal Burgess Golfing Soc, Glasgow Rangers Bond, RAC (Glasgow); *Style*— Donald R Findlay, Esq, QC; ✉ 20 Kelvinside Gardens, Glasgow G20 6BB (☎ 0141 946 2660); Advocates' Library, Parliament House, Edinburgh EH1 1RF (☎ 0131 226 2881, fax 0131 225 3642, car tel 0860 410749, telex 727856 FACADV G)

FINDLAY, Gordon Francis George; s of Francis Gordon Findlay (d 1975), of Edinburgh, and Muriel Arras Maitland; *b* 9 Feb 1950; *Educ* George Watson's Coll Edinburgh, Univ of Edinburgh (BSc, MB ChB); *m* 5 April 1975, Andrea May, da of Lt Ewart Leslie Cooper, of Buxted, Surrey; 1 s (Iain b 5 Jan 1978), 2 da (Claire b 10 Oct 1980, Emma b 27 Dec 1985); *Career* conslt neurosurgn with special interest in spinal disease Walton Hosp Liverpool 1983–; extensive pubns in jls and textbooks on spinal disease; memb Br Soc of Neurosurgns; fndr memb: Br Cevical Spine Soc, Euro Spine Soc; FRCS 1978; *Recreations* family, golf, music; *Style*— Gordon Findlay, Esq; ✉ Walton Hospital, Department of Neurosciences, Rice Lane, Liverpool L9 1AR (☎ 0151 525 3611)

FINDLAY, Martin Charles; s of Cdr Noel Charles Mansfeldt Findlay, RN (d 1976), of Hastingleigh, Kent, and Lady Mary Cecilia, da of 7 Earl Dartmouth, GCVO, JP, DL; *b* 27 June 1935; *Educ* Marlborough, St John's Coll Cambridge (MA); *m* 26 May 1966, Davina Margaret da of Sir Thomas Dundas Bt, MBE (d 1970), of Slaugham, Sussex; 2 s (Mark b 1967, Adam b 1969); *Career* Nat Serv 2 Lt Royal Dragoons 1953–55; Whitbread & Co plc: personnel dir 1976–86, vice chm 1982–92; non-exec dir: Provident Mutual Life Assurance Assoc 1989–95, Checkmate International plc 1996–; vice chm Business in the Community 1990–96, memb Cncl RSA 1991–96, tstee Baring Fndn 1992–, dir Ground Work Fndn 1995–, memb Nat Lottery Regnl Advsy Panel 1996–; Freeman: City of London 1986, Worshipful Co of Brewers; MInstD, FRSA 1988; *Style*— Martin Findlay, Esq; ✉ Ledburn Manor, Leighton Buzzards, Bedfordshire LU7 0PX (☎ 01525 373110 fax 01525 850286)

FINDLAY, Paul Hudson Douglas; s of Prof John Niemeyer Findlay (d 1987), and Aileen May, *née* Davidson (d 1993); *b* 26 Sept 1943; *Educ* Univ Coll Sch London, Balliol Coll Oxford (BA), London Opera Centre; *m* 9 Sept 1966, Francoise Christiane, da of Albert Victor Willmott (d 1987); 1 s (Anthony b 4 May 1968), 1 da (Lucy b 4 June 1972); *Career* prodn and tech mangr New Opera Co 1967, dir London Sinfonietta 1967–, stage mangr Glyndebourne Touring Opera and English Opera Gp 1968, chm Opera 80 1987; Royal Opera House Covent Garden: asst press offr 1968–72, PA to Gen Dir 1972–76, asst dir 1976–87, opera dir 1987–93; md Royal Philharmonic Orch 1993–Dec 1995; Cavaliere Ufficiale del Ordine al Merito della Repubblica Italiana, Chev des Arts et des Lettres 1991; *Recreations* tennis, gardening, walking; *Style*— Paul Findlay, Esq

FINDLAY, Richard; *Educ* Royal Scottish Acad of Music and Dramatic Art Glasgow; *m*; 3 c; *Career* work in radio and TV, English language radio station Govt of Saudi Arabia, ed English language newspaper Saudi Arabia, Central Office of Information London, commercial radio London then Scotland; dep chm Radio Forth Group plc, chief exec Scottish Radio Holdings plc (parent co of Radio Forth) 1996–; chm: Radio Tay Ltd, Radio Borders Ltd; dir: Carlisle Radio Ltd, Moray Firth Radio Ltd, Central FM (Holdings) Ltd, Scottish and Irish Radio Sales Ltd, Score Press Ltd, Morton Newspapers Ltd, Scottish Radio Network Sales Ltd; chm Iatros Ltd; dir Lothian Health Bd, chm Royal Lyceum Theatre Co Ltd Edinburgh; *Recreations* sailing, golf; *Style*— Richard Findlay, Esq; ✉ Scottish Radio Holdings plc, Clydebank Business Park, Clydebank, Glasgow G81 2RX (☎ 0141 306 2202, fax 0141 306 2322)

FINDLAY, Sheila Anne Macfarlane; da of William Ramsay Findlay (d 1976), of Kirriemuir, Angus, and Mary, *née* Seaton (d 1970); *b* 22 April 1928; *Educ* Webster's Seminary Angus, Edinburgh Coll of Art (scholarship to travel in France, Italy, Sweden); *m* 1958, Alfred Hackney, s of John Thomas Hackney; 2 da (Fiona Anne Seaton b 23 Nov 1959, Isla Katrina b 6 June 1962); *Career* artist; early career as freelance designer and illustrator London 1950s; work in numerous public and private collections; House & Garden Award for best interior RA Summer Exhbn 1993; RWS 1969; *Exhibitions* gp exhbns: RA, RWS Bankside Gallery, Young Contemporaries, Int Art Fair (Olympia), World of Watercolours (Park Lane), Bourne Gallery Reigate, RWS Harrods Exhbn, Metropole Arts Centre Folkestone, The Medici Soc London, 20/20 Vision (Bankside Gallery) 1989, Anthony Dawson Fine Art (Barbican), Anthony Dawson Artists on tour 1989–90, Coach House Gallery Guernsey 1991, A Room with a View (Wherry Quay Gallery Ipswich) 1992, exhbn of women artists Guildford Festival, Singer and Friedlander Watercolour Competition, also touring exhbns in USA, Europe and Australia; solo exhbn Catto Gallery Hampstead 1990; *Recreations* gardening, golf, swimming; *Clubs* Rochester and Cobham Park Golf; *Style*— Miss Sheila Findlay; ✉ Barnside, Lodge Lane, Cobham, Kent DA12 3BS (☎ 01474 814676)

FINE, Anne; da of Brian Laker (d 1989), and Mary Baker; *b* 7 Dec 1947; *Educ* Northampton HS for Girls, Univ of Warwick (BA); *m* 3 Aug 1968 (m dis 1990), Kit Fine, s of Maurice Fine; 2 da (Ione b 3 Aug 1971, Cordelia b 26 Feb 1975); *Career* writer; memb Soc of Authors; *Awards* Scot Arts Cncl Book Award 1986, Smarties Award 1990, Guardian Children's Fiction Award 1990, Carnegie medal 1990 and 1993, Childrens Author of the Year Award Br Book Awards 1990 and 1993, Whitbread Award for a children's book 1993; children's books incl: The Summer House Loon (1978), The Other Darker Ned (1979), The Stone Menagerie (1980), Round Behind the Icehouse (1981), The Granny Project (1983), Scaredy-Cat (1985), Anneli the Art Hater (1986), Madame Doubtfire (1987, filmed 1993), Crummy Mummy and Me (1988), A Pack of Liars (1988), Stranger Danger? (1989), The Country Pancake (1989), A Sudden Puff of Glittering Smoke (1989), Goggle-Eyes (1989, adapted for BBC), Bill's New Frock (1989), Only a Show (1990), A Sudden Swirl of Icy Wind (1990), Flour Babies (1993) Step by Wicked Step (1995); books for adults: The Killjoy (1986), Taking the Devil's Advice (1990), In Cold Domain (1994); *Recreations* walking, reading; *Style*— Mrs Anne Fine; ✉ c/o David Higham Associates, 5–8 Lower John Street, Golden Square, London W1R 4HA (☎ 0171 437 7888, fax 0171 437 1072)

FINE, Dr Jeffrey Howard; s of Nathan Fine, of Penylan, Cardiff, and Rebecca, *née* Levi; *b* 5 Oct 1955; *Educ* The Howardian HS Cardiff, Med Coll of St Bartholomew's (MB BS); *m* 1 May 1993, Kirsty Elizabeth, da of Adolf Knul, of London; 1 s (Alexander David b 27 June 1990), 1 da (Charlotte Anne b 19 May 1992); *Career* professorial registrar Acad Unit of Psychiatry Royal Free Hosp London 1981, registrar in psychological med Nat Hosp for Nervous Diseases London 1982–83, MO Home Office 1981–89, gen med practice London 1985, Euro neuroendocrine advsr Eli Lilly Pharmaceuticals Co 1986–87, private med psychiatric practice 1987–; completed London marathon 1983; freedom and key Kansas City Missouri USA 1976; MRCPsych 1984, FRSM 1987; memb: BMA 1980, Euro Assoc and Int Coll of Neuropsychopharmacology, Br Assoc of Neuropsychiatry 1988, Assoc of Independent Drs 1989; *Publications* author of papers on depression, light and obesity (Jl of Affective Disorder, 1987); *Recreations* jazz, tennis, painting; *Clubs* Ronnie Scott's, West Heath Lawn Tennis; *Style*— Dr Jeffrey H Fine; ✉ 16 Gayton Road, Hampstead, London NW3 1TX; 68 Harley Street, London W1N 1AE (☎ 0171 935 3980, fax 0171 636 6262)

FINE, Prof Leon Gerald; s of Matthew Fine (d 1964), of Cape Town, SA, and Jeannette, *née* Lipshitz; *b* 16 July 1943; *Educ* Univ of Cape Town (Myer Levinson scholar, Crasnow scholar, MB BS, medals in chemistry, physiology and med, Univ Gold medal); *m* 1966, Brenda, da of Nico Sakinovsky; 2 da (Michele b 1968, Dana b 1970); *Career* Mil Serv 1971–72; asst prof of med Albert Einstein Coll of Med NY 1975–76 (fell in nephrology 1972–74, instr in med 1974–75), asst prof of med Univ of Miami 1976–78, prof of med

Univ of California 1982–91 (assoc prof 1978–82), prof of med and head Dept of Med UCL 1991–94, head Jt Dept of Med UCL and Royal Free Schs of Med 1994–; visiting prof: Univ of Heidelberg 1988, Univ of Colorado 1989, Univ of Sheffield 1989, Univ of Minnesota 1990, Stanford Univ 1991, Univ of Manchester 1992, Univ Coll Dublin 1993; Lance Lipton visiting prof Univ of Toronto 1992; visiting res scientist: Imperial Cancer Research Fund 1982, Univ of Nice 1984, Univ Coll and Middx Sch of Med 1988, MRC Mammalian Devpt Unit 1989; numerous invited lectures at nat and int meetings, author of numerous research papers and book chapters in scientific pubns; memb: Exec Ctee MRS 1991–, Res Ctee RCP 1993–; ed Experimental Nephrology, co-ed Int Yearbook of Nephrology; memb numerous professional socs incl: American Soc of Nephrology, Int Soc of Nephrology, American Fedn for Clinical Research, Soc for Experimental Biology and Med, American Physiological Soc, American Heart Assoc, American Assoc for the History of Med, NY Acad of Sciences, American Soc of Cell Biology, Renal Assoc, Euro Renal Assoc, Euro Dialysis and Transplantation Assoc, Assoc of Physicians of GB and Ireland (pres 1993), Assoc of American Physicians, American Soc for Clinical Investigation; fell American Coll of Physicians 1978, FRCP 1986 (MRCP 1971), FRCP(Glas) 1993; *Recreations* book collecting, tennis, book binding; *Clubs* Athenaeum; *Style*— Prof Leon Fine; ✉ University College London Medical School and Royal Free Hospital School of Medicine, Rayne Institute, 5 University Street, London WC1E 6JJ (☎ 0171 209 6186, fax 0171 209 6211)

FINER, Alexander; s of Sir Morris Finer (d 1974), of London, and Lady Finer, *née* Edith Rubner; *b* 12 March 1947; *Educ* Mill Hill Sch, LSE (LLB), Univ of California Berkeley (LLM); *m* 13 Sept 1974, Linda Anne, da of John and Dorothy Barnard, of California; 1 da (Jasmine Liliane b 21 Feb 1993); *Career* journalist; called to the Bar Gray's Inn 1970; journalist Sunday Times 1970–78, Evening Standard 1978–79, Illustrated London News 1982–88, Daily Telegraph 1988–90 (asst ed special projects); ed: Esquire 1990–92, Hot Air (Virgin Atlantic) 1992–, Sunday Express London Section 1993–94; editorial dir John Brown Publishing 1994–; *Books* Deepwater (1983); *Clubs* Garrick; *Style*— Alexander Finer, Esq; ✉ John Brown Publishing, The Boat House, Crabtree Lane, Fulham, London SW6 8NJ

FINER, Dr Elliot Geoffrey; s of Rueben Finer (d 1958), and Pauline Finer; *b* 30 March 1944; *Educ* Royal GS High Wycombe, Cheadle Hulme Sch, East Barnet GS, St Catharine's Coll Cambridge (maj open scholarship, BA), UEA (MSc, PhD); *m* 1970, Viviane; 2 s (Robin b 1973, Stephen b 1975); *Career* res scientist Unilever 1968–75; Dept of Energy: joined 1975, under sec and DG Energy Efficiency Office 1988–90; dir Spiller Foods Ltd 1989–92, head Mgmnt Devpt Gp Cabinet Office 1990–92; DTI: head Enterprise Initiative Div 1992, head Chemicals and Biotechnology Div 1992–95; dir-gen Chemical Industries Association 1996–; author of various scientific papers and articles; companion Inst of Energy; FRCS; *Recreations* home and family, reading, DIY, gardening, music; *Style*— Dr Elliot G Finer; ✉ Chemicals Industries Association, King's Buildings, Smith Square, London SW1P 3JJ (☎ 0171 834 3399, fax 0171 834 4470)

FINER, Dr Nicholas; s of Sir Morris Finer (d 1974), and Edith, *née* Rubner; *b* 24 Dec 1949; *Educ* The Hall Sch Hampstead, Mill Hill Sch, UCL (BSc, MB BS); *m* 1 March 1975, Susan, da of Prof Charles Dent, CBE (d 1975); 3 da (Emily b 30 Nov 1976, Sarah b 2 Aug 1978, Louise (twin) b 2 Aug 1978); *Career* conslt physician and dir Research and Devpt Luton and Dunstable Hosp 1988–, visiting prof Univ of Luton 1996–, visiting specialist Addenbrooke's Hosp 1996–; hon conslt physician Guy's Hosp, hon sr lectr United Med and Dental Schs of Guy's and St Thomas' Hosp 1988 (lectr 1981–88); chm Assoc for The Study of Obesity 1993–96, assoc ed Drugs and Therapeutics Bulletin; FRCP 1994 (MRCP 1977); *Books* contrib: Health Consequences of Obesity (1988), Progress in Sweeteners (1989), Handbook of Sweeteners (1991); *Style*— Dr Nicholas Finer

FINESTEIN, His Hon Israel; QC (1970); yst s of Jeremiah Finestein (d 1957), of Hull, Yorks; *b* 29 April 1921; *Educ* Kingston HS Hull, Trinity College Cambridge (MA); *m* 1946, Marion Phyllis, er da of Simon Oster, of Hendon, Middx; *Career* formerly major scholar and prizeman of Trinity Coll Cambridge; called to the Bar Lincoln's Inn 1953, circuit judge 1972–89; author; memb Cncl Utd Synagogue; pres: Cncl Jewish Historical Soc of England, Bd of Deps of Br Jews 1991–94; *Books* Short History of the Jews of England, Sir George Jessel; *Style*— His Hon Israel Finestein, QC

FINGLAND, Sir Stanley James Gunn; KCMG (1979, CMG 1966); s of Samuel Gunn Fingland (d 1969), of Edinburgh, and Agnes Christina, *née* Watson; *b* 19 Dec 1919; *Educ* Royal HS Edinburgh; *m* 1946, Nell, da of late Charles Lister; 1 s, 1 da; *Career* Maj RS (despatches Italy) 1939–47; HM Dip Serv: dep high cmmr Port of Spain 1962, Salisbury Rhodesia 1964, high cmmr Freetown 1966–69, asst under sec of state FO 1969–71, ambass Havana 1972–75, high cmmr Nairobi and Br rep to the UN Environmental Prog and to UN Habitat HQ in Nairobi 1975–79; *Recreations* fishing; *Style*— Sir Stanley Fingland, KCMG

FINGLETON, David Melvin; s of Lawrence Arthur Fingleton, and Norma Phillips, *née* Spiro; *b* 2 Sept 1941; *Educ* Stowe Sch, UC Oxford (MA); *m* 1975, Clare, yr da of Ian Colvin (d 1975); *Career* barr 1965–80, met stipendiary magistrate 1980–95; music critic Daily Express, stage design corr Arts Review; *Books* Kiri (biography of Dame Kiri Te Kanawa, 1982); *Recreations* music, travel; *Clubs* Garrick, MCC; *Style*— David Fingleton, Esq; ✉ c/o John Johnson Agency, Clerkenwell House, 45–47 Clerkenwell Green, London EC1R 0HT

FINGRET, His Hon Judge; Peter; s of Iser Fingret (d 1975), and Irene, *née* Jacobs (d 1979); *b* 13 Sept 1934; *Educ* Leeds Modern Sch, Univ of Leeds (LLB), Open Univ (BA); *m* 1, 11 Dec 1960 (m dis), June Gertrude; 1 s (Andrew b 1963), 1 da (Kathryn b 1966); m 2, 14 March 1980, Ann Lilian Mary; *Career* slr 1960–82; stipendiary magistrate: County of Humberside 1982–85, metropolitan 1985–92; recorder Crown Court 1987–92, circuit judge (SE Circuit) 1992–; chm Lord Chllr's Advsy Ctee on JPs (Inner London cmmn area) 1996–; *Recreations* golf, music, theatre; *Clubs* Reform, Garrick; *Style*— His Hon Judge Fingret; ✉ Southwark Crown Court, 1 English Grounds, off Battlebridge Lane, London SE1 2HU

FINIGAN, John Patrick; s of John Joseph Finigan (d 1991), of Sale, Cheshire, and Mary Matilda Finigan (d 1983); *b* 12 Nov 1949; *Educ* Ushaw Coll Univ of Durham, St Bede's Coll Manchester, Cncl of Legal Educn London, Univ of Manchester, Harvard Law Sch; *m* 6 Dec 1976, Elizabeth, da of Joseph Liew, of Bandar Seri Begawan, Brunei; 1 s (Damien b 1980), 1 da (Emily Jane b 1982); *Career* slr; Standard Chartered Bank 1967–78, National Bank of Abu Dhabi 1978–82; gen mangr The National Bank of Kuwait SAK 1982–95, chief exec Qatar National Bank Doha 1995–; memb Hon Soc of Lincoln's Inn; FRSA, AIB 1970, ACIS 1973, FCIB 1980, MSI 1994; *Recreations* tennis, squash, music, literature; *Clubs* Oriental, Overseas Bankers'; *Style*— John Finigan, Esq; ✉ Barton Hse, Middle Barton, Oxon; Qatar National Bank SAQ, Government House Road, Doha, State of Qatar (☎ 00 974 430240, fax 00 974 438349)

FINK, Prof George; s of John H Fink (d 1965), and Therese, *née* Weiss; *b* 13 Nov 1936; *Educ* Melbourne HS, Univ of Melbourne (MB BS, MD), Hertford Coll Oxford (DPhil),; *m* 1959, Ann Elizabeth, da of Mark Langsam; 1 da (Naomi b 1961), 1 s (Jerome b 1965); *Career* jr and sr house offr Royal Melbourne and Alfred Hospitals Victoria Australia 1961–62, demonstrator in anatomy Monash Univ Victoria 1963–64, Nuffield Dominions demonstrator Univ of Oxford 1965–67, sr lectr in anatomy Monash Univ Victoria 1968–71, lectr Univ of Oxford 1971–80, offical fell in physiology and medicine Brasenose Coll Oxford 1974–80, dir MRC Brain Metabolism Unit 1980–, hon prof Univ of Edinburgh 1984–; prosector in anatomy Univ of Melbourne 1956; Wolfson lectr Univ of Oxford 1982, first G W Harris lectr Physiological Soc Cambridge 1987, Arthur M Fishberg visiting prof The Mt Sinai Med Sch NYC 1988; memb: Cncl of the Euro Neuroscience Assoc 1980–82 and 1994–, Mental Health Panel Wellcome Tst 1984–89, Steering Ctee Br Neuroendocrine Gp 1984–88 (tstee 1990–), Co-ordinating Ctee ESF Network on Neuroimmunomodulation 1990–92; chm External Monitoring Panel and 5 Year Review Ctee EU Biomedicine Prog; memb: The Physiological Soc, Anatomical Soc of GB and Ireland, Soc for Endocrinology (UK), The Endocrine Soc (USA), The Soc for Neuroscience (USA), Euro Neuroscience Assoc (pres 1991–), Int Brain Res Orgn, Int Soc for Neuroendocrinology, Euro Neuroendocrine Assoc, Soc for the Study of Fertility, BMA; Royal Soc and Israel Acad exchange fell Weizmann Inst 1979, Walter Cottman fell and visiting prof Monash univ 1985 and 1989; FRSE 1989; *Books* Neuropepides - Basic and Critical Aspects (ed with L J Whalley, 1982), Neuroendocrine Molecular Biology (ed with A J Harmar and K W McKerns, 1986), Neuropeptides - A Methodology (ed with A J Harmar, 1989); author of over 300 scientific pubns, mainly on neuroendocrinology, neuroendocrine molecular biology and psychoneuroendecrinology; *Recreations* skiing; *Style*— Prof George Fink, FRSE; ✉ Medical Research Council, Brain Metabolism Unit, University Department of Pharmacology, 1 George Square, Edinburgh EH8 9JZ (☎ 0131 650 3548, fax 0131 662 0240)

FINK, Graham Michael; s of Horace Bertram Fink, of Oxford, and Margaret May, *née* Betts; *b* 7 Sept 1959; *Educ* Wood Green Comp Sch Oxford, Banbury Sch of Art, Univ of Reading; *Career* French Gold Abbott advertising agency 1980–81, Collett Dickenson Pearce 1981–87, head of art WCRS 1987, gp head Saatchi & Saatchi 1987–90, dep creative dir Gold Greenless Trott 1990–94, commercials dir Paul Weiland Film Co 1994–; winner various advtg awards for: Hamlet, Land Rover, Benson & Hedges, Metropolitan Police, British Airways (Global commercial), Silk Cut and more recently Red Rock Cider, Ariston, Persil; memb: Creative Circle, Exec Ctee D&AD (pres 1996); *Style*— Graham Fink, Esq; ✉ c/o Paul Weiland Film Co, 14 Newburgh Street, London W1 (☎ 0171 287 6900, e-mail grah@mfink.cityscope.co.uk)

FINKELSTEIN, Prof Ludwik; OBE (1990); s of Adolf Finkelstein (d 1950), of London, and Amalia, *née* Diamantstein (d 1980); *b* 6 Dec 1929; *Educ* Univ of London (BSc, MSc), City Univ (DSc), Leo Baeck Coll (MA); *m* 1957, Mirjam Emma, da of Dr Alfred Wiener (d 1964), of London; 2 s (Anthony b 1959, Daniel b 1962), 1 da (Tamara b 1967); *Career* physicist Electronic Tubes Ltd 1951–52, scientist Instrument Branch Mining Res Estab NCB 1952–59; Northampton Coll London and City Univ 1959–: prof of instrument and control engrg 1970–80, prof of measurement and instrumentation 1980–, dean Sch of Electrical Engrg and Applied Physics 1983–88, head Dept of Physics 1980–88, head Dept of Systems Sci 1974–79, co-dir Measurement and Instrumentation Centre 1970–, dean Sch of Engrg 1988–93, pro vice chllr 1991–94; vice pres Int Measurement Confedn; Queen's Silver Jubilee Medal 1977, Hon DUniv St Petersburg Univ of Technol; Liveryman Worshipful Co Scientific Instrument Makers; FEng 1986, FIEE, Hon FInstMC (Sir Harold Hartley Silver medal 1981), CPhys, FInstP; *Recreations* books, conversation, Jewish studies; *Style*— Prof Ludwik Finkelstein, OBE, FEng; ✉ 9 Cheyne Walk, Hendon, London NW4 3QH (☎ 0181 202 6966, fax 0181 203 4735); City University, Northampton Square, London EC1V 0HB (☎ 0171 477 8139, fax 0171 477 8568)

FINLAY, Sir David Ronald James Bell; 2 Bt (UK 1964), of Epping, Co Essex; s of Sir Graeme Bell Finlay, 1 Bt, ERD (d 1987), and June Evangeline, *née* Drake; *b* 16 Nov 1963; *Educ* Marlborough, Univ of Grenoble, Univ of Bristol; *Heir* none; *Career* KPMG Peat Marwick McLintock 1986–91, Hill Samuel Financial Services 1992–94, Gerrard Vivian Gray 1994–; Freeman City of London 1991; *Recreations* skiing, shooting, travel; *Style*— Sir David Finlay, Bt

FINLAY, (Robert) Derek; s of William Templeton Finlay (d 1972), and Phyllis, *née* Jefferies (d 1948); *b* 16 May 1932; *Educ* Kingston GS, Emmanuel Coll Cambridge (BA, MA); *m* 1956, Una Ann, da of late David Smith Grant; 2 s (Rory, James), 1 da (Fiona); *Career* Lt Gordon Highlanders Malaya 1950–52, Capt Gordon Highlanders TA 1952–61; Mobil Oil Co UK 1955–61; McKinsey & Co Inc: assoc 1961–67, princ 1967–71, dir 1971–79; H J Heinz Co: md H J Heinz Co Ltd UK 1979–81, sr vice pres corp devpt World HQ H J Heinz Co Pittsburgh Pa 1981–93, also chief fin offr 1989–92, area vice pres 1992–93; chm Dawson International 1995–; *Recreations* tennis, rowing, walking, music, theatre; *Clubs* Caledonian, Highland Brigade, Leander, Annabel's; *Style*— Derek Finlay, Esq; ✉ Grantully Castle, by Aberfeldy, Perthshire PH15 2EG

FINLAY, Frank; CBE (1984); *b* 6 Aug 1926; *Educ* St Gregory the Great Sch Farnworth Lancs, Bolton Tech Coll, RADA; *m* Doreen, *née* Shepherd; 2 s (Stephen Francis, Daniel Joseph Laurence), 1 da (Anna Catherine (Cathy)); *Career* actor; professional debut in rep Halifax 1952; hon fell Bolton Inst 1992; Freeman City of Baltimore Maryland USA 1979; *Theatre* roles incl: The Queen and the Welshman (Edinburgh Festival, Lyric Hammersmith, two tours) 1957, Harry Kahn in Arnold Wesker's Chicken Soup with Barley (Belgrade Coventry, Royal Court), Percy Elliott in John Osborne's Epitaph for George Dillon (John Golden Theatre NY), Corporal Hill in Wesker's Chips with Everything (Royal Court and Vaudeville), Iago in Othello (with Laurence Olivier, Chichester Festival) 1963, Jesus in Dennis Potter's Son of Man (Phoenix Leicester and The Roundhouse), Bernard Link in David Mercer's After Haggerty (with RSC, Aldwych and Criterion), Peppino in Saturday Sunday Monday (Nat Theatre, Old Vic and Queen's), Freddy Malone in Plunder (first prodn at new NT South Bank), Henry VIII in Kings and Clowns (Phoenix) 1978, Filumena (Lyric and USA tour) 1978–79, Salieri in Amadeus (Her Majesty's) 1981–82, The Cherry Orchard (Haymarket) 1983, Capt Bligh in Mutiny (Piccadilly) 1985, Sir David Metcalfe QC in Jeffrey Archer's Beyond Reasonable Doubt (Queen's, Aust tour, UK tour) 1987–90, Sir Lewis Messenger in Ian Ogilvy's A Slight Hangover (Bromley and nat tour) 1991, Dr Sloper in The Heiress (Bromley and nat tour) 1992, The Woman in Black (nat tour) 1993, Captain Hook/Mr Darling in Peter Pan (Chichester Festival Theatre, Norwich and nat tour) 1994–95, Gaslight (UK tour) 1995; *Television* roles incl: Brutus in Julius Caesar, Jean Val Jean in Les Miserables, Andrew Firth in Ingmar Bergman's The Lie, title role in Dennis Potter's Casanova, title role in The Death of Adolf Hitler, Sancho Panza in Don Quixote, Voltaire in Candide, Shylock in The Merchant of Venice, Bouquet of Barbed Wire series and sequel Another Bouquet, Frank Doel in 84 Charing Cross Road, Peppino in Lord Olivier's prodn of Saturday Sunday Monday, Bridie in Dear Brutus, Arc de Triomphe, In The Secret State, The Verdict on Erebus (4 part series), Sir Arthur Conan Doyle in Encounters - The Other Side, Stalin (with Robert Duval for HBO), Mountain of Diamonds (series, 1990), Charlemagne, Lovejoy, Heartbeat, Dalgliesh; *Films* incl: The Longest Day, The Loneliness of the Long Distance Runner, The Comedy Man, The Sandwich Man, A Study in Terror, Othello (with Laurence Olivier, Oscar, Golden Globe and BAFTA nominations) I'll Never Forget What's 'is Name, The Deadly Bees, Inspector Clouseau, Gumshoe, Shaft in Africa, three Van der Valk films, The Three Musketeers and two sequels, The Wild Geese, Neither the Sea nor the Sand, The Thief of Baghdad, Sherlock Holmes - Murder by Decree, The Return of the Soldier, The Key (in Italy, Positano Award for Best Film, Golden Cinema Ticket Award), Jacob Marley in A Christmas Carol, Life Force, Sigmund Freud in 1919, Cthulhu Mansion, The Sparrow 1993, Limited Edition 1995; *Awards* Man of the Year 1981; for Best Actor incl: Clarence Derwent Award (for Wesker's Chips with Everything), BAFTA Award (for The Death of Adolf Hitler and Don Quixote), TV Times Award (for Bouquet of Barbed Wire), San Sebastian Film Festival Award (for Othello); nominations for Best Actor incl: five BAFTA's and an Oscar; *Style*— Frank Finlay, Esq, CBE; ✉ c/o Ken McReddie Ltd, 91 Regent Street, London W1R 7TB (☎ 0171 439 1456, fax 0171 734 6530)

FINLAY, Ian Gardner; s of John Gardner Finlay, of Ladybank, Fife, and Margaret Finlay, of Lothian; *Educ* St Andrew's Univ (BSc), Univ of Manchester (MB ChB); *m* 21 March 1981, Patricia Mary, *née* Whiston; 1 da (Nicola b 24 March 1984), 1 s (Euan b 21 Feb 1986); *Career* jr surgical trainee Royal Infirmary Manchester 1976–78, registrar in surgery W of Scotland Registrar Rotational Trg Scheme 1978–83, sr surgical registrar Glasgow Royal Infirmary 1983–87, clinical asst Univ of Minnesota 1985, sr registrar in colorectal surgery St Mark's Hosp London 1986, conslt colorectal surgn Dept of Coloproctology Royal Infirmary Glasgow (organised and developed dept as first unit of its type in UK) and hon sr lectr Univ of Glasgow 1987–; Patey Prize Surgical Research Soc 1982, Research Award American Soc of Colon and Rectal Surgns 1987, Audiovisual Prize Assoc of Surgns 1990, Moynihan Prize (jtly) Assoc of Surgns of GB and I 1995; memb Cncl Br Assoc of Coloproctology RSM 1991–; author of over 100 pubns incl book chapters, editorials and original articles relating to topics in coloproctology; FRCSGlas (hon treas and memb Cncl), FRCSEd 1993; *Recreations* rugby referee, sailing, skiing, ornithology and antique furniture; *Clubs* Queen's Park Rugby Football (Glasgow), Glasgow Cricket, Scottish Royal Automobile; *Style*— Ian Finlay, Esq; ✉ Department of Coloproctology, Ward 61, Royal Infirmary, Glasgow G31 2ER (☎ 0141 552 3535 ext 4084, fax 0141 304 4991)

FINLAY, Ronald Adrian; s of Harry Finlay, of London NW3, and Tess, *née* Matz; *b* 4 Dec 1956; *Educ* Univ Coll Sch London, St John's Coll Cambridge (BA, MA); *m* 1992, Jennifer, *née* Strauss; 1 da; *Career* Br Market Res Bureau 1979–81, Merrill Lynch 1982–83; dir: Valin Pollen Ltd 1986–90 (joined 1983), Fishburn Hedges 1991–; sec SDP Hendon S 1984–85; memb Market Res Soc 1996 (assoc 1980); *Recreations* bridge, hill-walking, tennis; *Style*— Ron Finlay, Esq; ✉ 12 Grey Close, London NW11 6QG (☎ 0181 455 1367, fax 0181 455 1367); Fishburn Hedges Ltd, 1 Northumberland Avenue, London WC2N 5BW (☎ 0171 839 4321, fax 0171 839 2858)

FINLAY-MAXWELL, Dr David Campbell; MBE (1994); s of Luke Greenwood Maxwell (d 1937), and Lillias Maule Finlay (d 1955); *b* 2 March 1923; *Educ* St Paul's, Heriot-Watt Univ Edinburgh (CEng, MIEE), Univ of Leeds (PhD); *m* 1954, Constance Shirley, da of James Douglas Hood, CBE (d 1981); 1 s (Douglas), 1 da (Carol); *Career* Maj Royal Signals SOE Operations 1939–45, served in Europe, India and Malaysia; dir and chm John Gladstone & Co Ltd and John Gladstone & Co (Engrg) 1948–89 (dir and pres 1989–91, tech dir 1992–); co-fndr and dir Maxwell-Schofield 1958–65, owner D F Maxwell Co 1991–; chm: Manpower Working Party NEDO 1970–73, Wool Industs Research Assoc 1974–77, Textile Research Cncl 1977–82, Wool Textile EDC 1977–79; cncllr and dir Br Textile Cncl 1977–84; UK rep Consultative Ctee for R & D Brussels 1979–84; memb: Cncl Textile Inst 1972–74 (granted fellowship), Textile Industry Advsy Ctee, Leeds Univ Cncl 1974– (hon lectr), Soc of Dyers & Colourists 1950– (granted fellowship), Scientific Devpt Sub Ctee, CBI Science & Research Ctee 1980–87; dir The Wool Fndn (IWS) 1985–, pres Comitextil Sci and Res Ctee Brussels 1979–85, EEC reviewer ESPRIT prog 1986–, memb RNIB; hon organizer UK Technical Volunteer Helpers for Blind 1947–; MIEE, CEng, FTI, FSDC; *Recreations* radio propagation, satellite tracking; *Clubs* RSAC, Special Forces; *Style*— Dr David Finlay-Maxwell, MBE; ✉ D F Maxwell Co, Prospect House, Prospect Street, Huddersfield HD1 2NU (☎ 01484 450982, fax 01484 450703)

FINLAYSON, Dr Niall Diarmid Campbell; s of Dr Duncan Iain Campbell Finlayson, of Edinburgh, and Helen Rita, *née* Blackney; *b* 21 April 1939; *Educ* Loretto, Univ of Edinburgh (BSc, MB ChB, PhD); *m* 12 Aug 1972, Dale Kristin, da of Dr Richmond Karl Anderson, of Chapel Hill, North Carolina, USA; 1 s (Iain b 1977), 1 da (Catriona b 1973); *Career* asst prof of med Cornell Univ Med Coll NY 1970–72, conslt physician Royal Infirmary Edinburgh 1973–, hon sr lectr in med Univ of Edinburgh Med Sch 1973–; memb: American Assoc for the Study of Liver Diseases, BMA, Br Soc of Gastroenterology; FRCP, FRCPEd; *Books* Diseases of the Gastro Intestinal Tract and Liver (jtly, 2 edn 1989); *Recreations* music; *Style*— Dr Niall Finlayson; ✉ Centre for Liver and Digestive Disorders, Royal Infirmary, Lauriston Place, Edinburgh EH3 9YW (☎ 0131 536 1000)

FINLAYSON, Robert William (Robin); s of William Francis Finlayson (d 1988), and Isabella Forrester, *née* Knox (d 1982); *b* 16 Dec 1949; *Educ* Glasgow Acad, Univ of Edinburgh (LLB, BCom); *m* 22 March 1975, Jennifer Catherine, da of Thomas Nicol Dickson; 2 s (Colin Stuart b 11 Feb 1977, Andrew Graham b 17 Nov 1979), 1 da (Louise Catherine b 22 Nov 1983); *Career* apprentice Touche Ross & Co Glasgow 1972–75; Ernst & Young (formerly Arthur Young McClelland Moores): tax sr 1976–77, tax supervisor/asst mangr Glasgow 1977–79, tax ptnr Birmingham 1981–82 (tax mangr 1979–81), dir Ernst & Young Financial Management Ltd 1989–, office managing ptnr Edinburgh 1991– (head of tax 1982–91); ICAS: memb 1975, convenor Ethics Ctee and Professional Standards Bd 1991–92; AInstT (1977); *Recreations* golf, sailing, skiing, hillwalking; *Clubs* Murrayfield Golf, Royal Forth Yacht, Royal Northern Clyde Yacht, Edinburgh Sports; *Style*— Robin Finlayson, Esq; ✉ Ernst & Young, 10 George Street, Edinburgh EH2 2DZ (☎ 0131 226 6400, fax 0131 247 5224)

FINLEY, Michael John; s of Walter Finley (d 1940), and Grace Marie Butler, *née* Sykes; *b* 22 Sept 1932; *Educ* King Edward VII Sch Sheffield; *m* 19 March 1955, Sheila Elizabeth (d 1992), da of late Harold Cole, of Osbournby, Lincs; 4 s (Nicholas b 1955, Andrew b 1959, Jonathan b 1967, Robert b 1968); *Career* ed Sheffield Telegraph 1964–69, gen mangr and dir Kent Messenger Group 1979–82 (editorial dir 1969–79), exec dir Periodical Publishers' Assoc 1982–88, dir Fedn Int de la Presse Periodique 1989–92; memb Advsy Cncl BBC 1975–80, govr Int Press Fndn 1988–; chm Kent IOD 1980–82, govr Cranbrook Sch 1977–; hon memb Guild of Br Newspaper Eds 1979–, memb Assoc of European Journalists 1990–; *Books* Advertising And The Community (contrib, 1969); *Recreations* tennis, golf, snooker, watching rugby, walking; *Style*— Michael Finley, Esq; ✉ Sorrento, Staplehurst, Kent TN12 0PZ (☎ 01580 893160)

FINN, Johanna Elizabeth; da of Bartholomew Anthony Finn, of London, and Anna Maria, *née* Kreuth; *b* 30 Aug 1951; *Educ* Convent of the Sacred Heart London, UCL (BSc); *m* (m dis); 2 s (Benedict Daniel Siddle b 20 Jan 1982, Leo Dominic Siddle b 1 Oct 1984), 1 da (Chloe Anneliese Siddle b 22 June 1990); *Career* King's Coll Hosp London 1972–73, nat admin trainee NHS Nat Training Scheme SE Thames RHA 1973–75, asst admin Northwick Park Hosp Harrow Middx 1975–77, dep sector admin Withington Hosp S Manchester 1977–79, sector admin W Middx Univ Hosp Isleworth 1979–82, unit admin St Mary's Hosp Paddington 1982–85, acting dep dist admin Paddington & North Kensington Health Authy London 1985–86; unit gen mangr: Mile End Hosp and Bethnal Green Hosp Tower Hamlets London 1986–89, Community & Priority Services Tower Hamlets London 1989–90; acting chief exec The Royal London and Assoc Community Services NHS Trust 1990–91, regnl dir of corp affairs NW Thames RHA 1991–93, chief exec The West Suffolk Hosps Tst 1993–; dir Suffolk Trg and Enterprise Cncl 1994–; assoc memb Inst of Health Service Mangrs 1975; *Recreations* music, theatre, reading; *Clubs* October, Hospital Officers'; *Style*— Miss Johanna Finn; ✉ Chief Executive, West Suffolk Hospitals Trust, Hardwick Lane, Bury St Edmunds, Suffolk IP33 2QZ (☎ 01284 713013)

FINN, Paul Howard; s of Thomas Finn (d 1982), of Heaton, Bradford, West Yorkshire, and Mary, *née* Wheatcroft; *b* 10 July 1939; *Educ* St Bede's GS Heaton Bradford; *m* 3 Oct 1964, Jill, da of John France; 3 s (James Alexander b 14 May 1969, Robert Adam b 2 March 1972, Charles Edward b 26 March 1974); *Career* articled clerk Clifford Long & Son Bradford 1959–63, qualified chartered accountant 1963, Trevelyan & Co Leeds 1965, Chalmers Impey & Co 1981 (following merger), nat dir of corp reconstruction and insolvency servs Hodgson Impey 1989 (merged 1985), head of insolvency Kidsons Impey 1990–93 (following merger), sr ptnr Finn Associates 1993–; md Jamie Group 1970–78; FCA 1974 (ACA 1964), FFB 1974; memb: Insolvency Practitioners' Assoc, Soc of Practitioners in Insolvency; Freeman City of London 1995; *Books* Insolvency in Business - How to Avoid It, How to Deal With It (1988, 1990), A General Practitioner's Guide to Insolvency (1993); *Recreations* music, writing, golf; *Clubs* Wig & Pen, City Livery; *Style*— Paul Finn, Esq; ✉ Tong Hall, Tong Village, West Yorkshire BD4 0RR; Finn Associates, Temple Chambers, Temple Avenue, London (☎ 0171 353 2082, fax 0171 353 2083)

FINNEGAN, Prof Ruth Hilary; da of Prof Tom Finnegan (d 1964), and (Lucy) Agnes, *née* Campbell (d 1995); *b* 31 Dec 1933; *Educ* The Mount Sch York, Somerville Coll Oxford (BA, Dip in Anthropology, BLitt), Nuffield Coll Oxford (DPhil); *m* 1963, David John Murray, s of Jowett Murray; 3 da (Rachel Clare b 1965, Kathleen Anne b 1967, Brigid Aileen b 1969); *Career* teacher Malvern Girls Coll 1956–58, lectr in social anthropology Univ Coll of Rhodesia and Nyasaland 1963–64, sr lectr in sociology Univ of Ibadan Nigeria 1967–69 (lectr 1965–67), sr lectr in comparative social instns Open Univ 1972–75 (lectr in sociology 1969–72); Univ of the South Pacific Suva Fiji: reader in sociology 1975–78, head sociology discpline 1976–78; Open Univ: sr lectr 1978–82, reader 1982–88, prof of comparative social instns 1988–; visiting prof of anthropology Univ of Texas at Austin 1989; memb SSRC/ESRC Social Anthropology and Social Affrs Standing Ctees 1978–86 (vice chm Social Affrs Ctee 1985–86); hon ed Man (jl of Royal Anthropological Inst) 1987–89; assoc memb Finnish Literature Soc 1989, Folklore fell 1991; FBA 1996; *Books* Survey of the Limba people of northern Sierra Leone (1965), Limba stories and story-telling (1967), Oral literature in Africa (1970, 1976), Modes of thought. Essays on thinking in Western and non-Western societies (co-ed, 1973), Oral poetry: its nature, significance and social context (1 edn 1977, 2 edn 1992), The Penguin book of oral poetry (ed, 1978, published as A World treasury of oral poetry, 1982), Essays on Pacific literature (co-ed, 1978), Concepts of Inquiry (ed jtly, 1981), New approaches to economic life (ed jtly, 1985), Information Technology: social issues (ed jtly, 1987), Literacy and orality: studies in the technology of communication (1988), The hidden musicians: music-making in an English town (1989), Oral traditions and the verbal arts: a guide to research practices (1992), From family tree to family history (co-ed, 1994), Sources and methods for family and community historians: a handbook (co-ed, 1994), South Pacific oral traditions (co-ed, 1995), Project reports in family and community history (CD-ROM, co-ed, 1996); also author of articles in learned jls; *Recreations* singing in local choirs, walking; *Style*— Prof Ruth Finnegan, FBA; ✉ Faculty of Social Sciences, The Open University, Walton Hall, Milton Keynes MK7 6AA (☎ 01908 654458, fax 01908 654488, e-mail r.h.finnegan@open.ac.uk)

FINNEY, His Hon Judge; Jarlath John; s of Victor Harold Finney (d 1970), (Lib MP for Hexham 1923–24, subsequently sec gen Lloyd George's Cncl of Action for Peace and Reconstruction) of Dorking, Surrey, and Aileen Rose Finney, *née* Gallagher; *b* 1 July 1930; *Educ* Wimbledon Coll; *m* 27 April 1957, Daisy Emöke, da of Dr Matyas Veszy, formerly of Budapest (d 1959); 2 s (Mark b 1960, Gavin b 1963), 2 da (Patricia Finney, *qv*, b 1958, Victoria b 1965); *Career* Nat Serv 1953–55, 2 Lt 8 RTR 1953–55 (Lt 1955); called to the Bar Gray's Inn 1953; recorder of the Crown Ct 1980–86, circuit judge (SE Circuit) 1986–; *Books* Gaming, Lotteries, Fundraising and The Law (1982), Sales Promotion Law (jtly, 1986); *Recreations* books, wild flowers (FLS), walking in the country; *Clubs* Wig and Pen; *Style*— His Hon Judge Finney; ✉ The Crown Court, Lordship Lane, Wood Green, London N22 5LF

FINNEY, Rt Rev John Thornley; *see:* Pontefract, Bishop of

FINNEY, Malcolm James; s of Alfred James Finney (d 1983), and Audrey, *née* Saynor; *b* 19 March 1948; *Educ* Univ of Hull, Univ of Sheffield and Univ of Bradford (BSc, MSc); *m* (sep); 2 s (Matthew b 1977, Nicholas b 1980); *Career* Spear and Jackson Int 1970–72, Duncan C Fraser and Co 1972–73, J Henry Schroder Wagg and Co Ltd 1973–76, J F Chown and Co Ltd 1976–79, Grant Thornton 1979–89, Malcolm J Finney & Ptnrs 1989–92, Nabarro Nathanson 1992– (currently head of Tax Dept); MIMgt 1975, AFIMA 1972; *Books* Captive Insurance Companies - Tax Strategy (1979), Business Tax Handbook (1978), Companies Operating Overseas and Tax Strategy (1983), Captives - A Tax Analysis (1991), Tolleys International Tax Planning; *Recreations* photography, cars, cycling, reading; *Style*— Malcolm Finney, Esq; ✉ Nabarro Nathanson, 50 Stratton Street, London W1X 6NX (☎ 0171 493 9933, fax 0171 629 7900)

FINNEY, Patricia Deirdre Emöke; da of His Hon Judge Finney, *qv*, and Daisy Gizella Emöke, *née* Veszy; *b* 12 May 1958; *Educ* Henrietta Barnett Sch London, Wadham Coll Oxford (BA); *m* 28 Feb 1981, Christopher Alan Perry, s of William J Perry; 1 da (Alexandra b 18 Dec 1987), 1 s (William b 2 Dec 1989); *Career* incl: TV reviewing The Evening Standard, sub-editing, running a medical jl, sec, freelance journalism, pt/t work in social servs, corp entertaining, selling advtg; four time runner-up Katherine Pakenham Award; memb NUJ; also writes under pseudonym P F Chisholm; *Radio plays* The Flood (R3, 1977), A Room Full of Mirrors (R4, 1988, first prize Radio Times Drama Awards); *TV plays* Biology Lessons (1986, second prize Radio Times Drama Awards); *Novels* A Shadow of Gulls (1977, David Higham Award for Best First Novel), The Crow Goddess (1978), Firedrake's Eye (1992), as P F Chisholm: A Famine of Horses (1994), A Season of Knives (1995); *Recreations* history, making things, science, martial arts, live role-playing; *Style*— Ms Patricia Finney; ✉ c/o Jennifer Kavanagh, 44 Langham Street, London W1N 5RG (☎ 0171 636 2477)

FINNIS, Prof John Mitchell; s of Maurice Meredith Steriker Finnis (d 1995), of Adelaide, and Margaret McKellar, *née* Stewart; *b* 28 July 1940; *Educ* St Peter's Coll, St Mark's Coll Adelaide (LLB), Univ of Oxford (DPhil); *m* 20 June 1964, Marie Carmel, *née* McNally; 3 s (John-Paul b 1967, Jerome b 1977, Edmund b 1984), 3 da (Rachel b 1965, Catherine b 1971, Maria b 1974); *Career* assoc in law Univ of California Berkeley 1965–66; Univ of Oxford: fell and praelector in jurisprudence Univ Coll 1966–, Rhodes reader in laws of Br Cwlth and US 1972–89, prof of law and legal philosophy 1989–; prof and head Law Dept Univ of Malawi 1976–78, Huber distinguished visiting prof Boston Coll 1993–94; Biolchini prof of law Univ of Notre Dame Indiana USA 1995–; called to the Bar Gray's Inn 1970; special advsr to Foreign Affrs Ctee of House of Commons on the role of UK Parliament in Canadian Constitution 1980–82; memb Int Theological Cmmn Vatican 1986–92; FBA 1990; *Books* Natural Law and Natural Rights (1980), Fundamentals of Ethics (1983), Nuclear Deterrence, Morality and Realism (1987), Commonwealth and Dependencies Halsbury's Laws of England (vol 6 1971, 1990), Moral Absolutes (1991); *Style*— Prof John Finnis, FBA; ✉ 12 Staverton Rd, Oxford OX2 6XJ; University College, Oxford OX1 4BH (☎ 01865 276602)

FIONDA, Andrew; *Educ* Trent Poly Nottingham (BA Fashion), Royal Coll of Art (MDes); *Career* fashion designer; former experience with established Br design houses incl Marks & Spencer and Alexon Internation, fndr ptnr own label Pearce Fionda (with Ren Pearce, *qv*) 1984–; New Generation Designers of the Yr (Br Fashion Awards) 1995, Newcomers Award for Export (Br Knitting and Clothing Export Cncl/Fashion Weekly) 1995, World Young Designers Award (Int Apparel Fedn Istanbul) 1996; worldwide stockists incl: Liberty, Harrods, Harvey Nichols and Selfridges (UK), Saks 5th Avenue and Bergdorf Goodman (USA), Lidia Shopping (Italy), CRC (Thailand), Brown Thomas

(Ireland); gp exhbns incl: Design of the Times (RCA) 1996, The Cutting Edge of British Fashion 1947–1997 (V&A) 1997; *Style—* Andrew Fionda; ✉ Pearce Fionda, 27 Horsell Road, Highbury, London N5 1XL (☎ and fax 0171 609 6470)

FIREMAN, Bruce Anthony; s of Michael Fireman (d 1982), of Vinnitsa, Ukraine; *b* 14 Feb 1944; *Educ* Kilburn GS, Jesus Coll Cambridge (open scholar); *m* 1968, Barbara, *née* Mollett; *Career* slr 1970; chm Fireman Rose Ltd 1986–, conslt on media and communications Guinness Mahon & Co Ltd 1991–93, seconded as md London News Radio Ltd 1993–94 (non-exec dir 1994–), returned to Guinness Mahon & Co as md media and communications 1994–; dir: Newspaper Publishing plc (The Independent) 1986–93, D G Durham Group plc 1988–93, Culver Holdings plc 1991–; *Clubs* City of London; *Style—* Bruce Fireman, Esq; ✉ 1 Wood Lane, London N6 5UE (☎ 0171 444 7125); Guinness Mahon & Co Ltd, 32 St Mary at Hill, London EC3P 3AJ (☎ 0171 772 7111, fax 0171 772 7772)

FIRMAN, Clive Edward; s of John Edward Firman (d 1984), of Rustington, Sussex, and Rosaline Mary, *née* Smith (d 1995); *b* 22 May 1951; *Educ* Cranleigh Sch Surrey, Univ of London (BA); *m* 1974, Wendy, da of John Gill Burrell; 1 s (Duncan Mark Edward b 4 Jan 1981), 1 da (Carolyn Mary b 16 Oct 1982); *Career* NHS: trainee admin 1973–74, personnel mangr Harrow Health Authy 1974–76, admin St George's Hosp London 1976–78, dep sector admin rising to sector admin Waltham Forest 1979–81, admin Tooting Bec Hosp 1981–86, gen mangr All Saints' Hosp Birmingham 1986–94, mgmnt conslt 1994–; memb Inst of Health Serv Mgmnt 1976, AIPM 1978, MIMgt 1986; *Recreations* voluntary work, badminton, swimming, weight-training, mainly family; *Style—* Clive Firman, Esq; ✉ 49 Alderbrook Road, Solihull B91 1NR

FIRMSTON-WILLIAMS, Peter; CBE (1987, OBE 1979); s of Geoffrey Firmston-Williams (d 1964), and Muriel Firmston-Williams; *b* 30 Aug 1918; *Educ* Harrow; *m* 1945, Margaret, da of Wilfred Butters Beaulah (d 1967); 1 s, 1 da; *Career* Capt (mil) N Africa, Low Countries and Germany; md: Cooper and Co's Stores Ltd 1958–62, Key Markets Ltd 1962–71, Asda Stores Ltd 1971–81; dir: Associated Dairies Ltd 1973–81, BAT Stores 1981–82; dep chm Woolworth Holdings 1982–; chm: Covent Garden Market Authy 1982–, British Retail Consortium 1984–, Flowers and Plants Assoc 1985–; *Recreations* golf, water skiing, wind surfing; *Style—* Peter Firmston-Williams, Esq, CBE; ✉ Oak House, 12 Pembroke Road, Moor Park, Northwood, Middx

FIRTH, Colin; s of David Firth and Shirley Firth; *b* 10 Sept 1960; *Educ* Montgomery of Alamein Sch, Winchester, Drama Centre London; *Career* actor; *Theatre* roles incl: Bennett in Another Country (Queens) 1983, Dubedat in Doctor's Dilemma (Bromley and Guildford) 1984, Felix in The Lonely Road (Old Vic) 1985, Eben in Desire Under The Elms (Greenwich) 1987, Aston in The Caretaker 1991, Chatsky (Almeida) 1993; *Television* Truelove in Dutch Girls (LWT) 1984, Herncastle in Lost Empires (Granada) 1985–86, Robert Lawrence in Tumbledown (BBC) 1987, Alan in Out Of The Blue (BBC) 1990, Hostages (Granada) 1992, Master of the Moor (Meridian) 1993, The Deep Blue Sea (BBC) 1994, Mr Darcy in Pride and Prejudice (BBC) 1994; *Radio* Richard II in Two Planks and a Passion (BBC) 1986, Rupert Brooke in The One Before The Last (BBC) 1987; *Film* Judd in Another Country 1983, Camille 1984, Birkin in A Month in the Country 1986, Adrian in Apartment Zero 1988, title role in Valmont 1988, Smith in Wings of Fame 1989, Femme Fetale 1990, The Hour of the Pig 1992, Good Girls 1994, Circle of Friends 1995; *Awards* winner RTS Best Actor Award (and BAFTA nomination) for Tumbledown, The Broadcasting Press Guild Award for Best Actor for Pride and Prejudice 1996; *Style—* Colin Firth, Esq; ✉ c/o ICM Ltd, Oxford House, 76 Oxford Street, London W1N 0AX (☎ 0171 636 6565, fax 0171 323 0101)

FIRTH, David; s of Ivor Firth Coleman (d 1991), of Bedford, and Beatrice, *née* Jenkins (d 1990); *b* 15 March 1945; *Educ* Bedford Modern Sch, Univ of Sussex (BA), Guildhall Sch of Music and Drama; *m* 2 Jan 1969, Julia Elizabeth, da of Albert Gould; 2 s (Matthew b 24 Sept 1973, Ben b 3 March 1980); *Career* actor, writer and singer; *Theatre* incl: Notes from Underground (Garrick) 1967, RSC 1967–70, The Courier-1776 (New Theatre) 1970 (nominated Most Promising Actor in Plays and Players Awards), Gawain and the Green Knight (Phoenix Leicester) 1972; NT 1973 incl: Macbeth, The Cherry Orchard, Measure for Measure; Hedda (Roundhouse) 1980, Hamlet (Piccadilly) 1982, Marilyn (Adelphi) 1983, The Importance of Being Earnest (Ambassadors) 1984, The Ratepayers Iolanthe (Phoenix) 1984, Canary Blunt (Latchmere) 1985, The Metropolitan Mikado (Queen Elizabeth Hall) 1985, The Phantom of the Opera (Her Majesty's) 1986, King Lear (Old Vic) 1988, The Hunting of the Snark 1991, A Tree Grows in Brooklyn (Barbican) 1992, Jubilee (Barbican) 1992, Assassins (Donmar) 1992, Knickerbocker Holiday (Barbican) 1993, Follies (Brighton) 1993, Forty Years On (West Yorkshire Playhouse) 1994, Love Life (Barbican) 1995, Passion (Queens) 1996; *Television* incl: Search for the Nile, Eyeless in Gaza, Love Story, Armchair Theatre, Village Hall, Terra Firma, Love for Lydia, Wings, Raffles, Saint Joan, The Gondoliers, Nanny's Boy, Troilus and Cressida, Sorry I'm A Stranger Here Myself, Lucky Jim, Yes Minister, Drummonds, Cardtrick, Singles, One Way Out, Stay Lucky, Murder East Murder West, Poirot, Between the Lines, The Late Show; *Film* Out on a Limb 1985; *Writing* for TV and theatre incl: Sorry I'm A Stranger Here Myself (Thames) 1980, The Live Rail (Thames) 1982, Canary Blunt (Latchmere) 1985, Cause for Complaint 1986, Oblique Encounter and Sod's Law (Thames) 1987, Home James (Thames) 1989, Shelley (Thames) 1990, Otherwise You'd Cry (Hat Trick Prodns) 1992; *Style—* David Firth, Esq; ✉ c/o Conway van Gelder Robinson Ltd, 18–21 Jermyn Street, London SW1Y 6HP (☎ 0171 287 0077, fax 0171 287 1940)

FIRTH, Mary Flora MacKinnon; OBE (1993), JP (Greater Manchester 1971), DL (Greater Manchester 1991); da of Dr Thomas Downie Hunter (d 1964), of Grasscroft, Oldham, and Catherine MacPhail, *née* Johnstone (d 1983); *b* 13 Oct 1929; *Educ* Oldham Hulme GS for Girls; *m* 1, 1949, Dr Gilbert Hamilton Campbell (d 1982); 2 da (Dr Catherine Hamilton Campbell b 23 Sept 1956, Dr Margaret Stewart Duper b 17 Feb 1964), 1 s (Dr James Hunter Campbell b 26 Feb 1958); m 2, 27 Dec 1985, Lees Firth, s of Lees Firth; *Career* chm Oldham Dist Health Authy 1986–91, chm Oldham NHS Tst 1992–; pres Greater Manchester Branch Br Red Cross Soc 1988–94, hon vice chm Littleborough and Saddleworth Cons Assoc (former pres); memb: Exec Ctee Guides Assoc 1951–79, Ctee Oldham Ladies' Luncheon Club 1961–82 (former pres), Saddleworth Guide Dogs for the Blind 1965–71 (fndr memb), Bd of Visitors Buckley Hall Detention Centre 1978–86, Friends of the Hallé Orch 1983–, Manchester Friends of Glyndebourne, Special Events Ctee Royal Exchange; High Sheriff of Greater Manchester 1996–97; *Style—* Mrs Mary F M Firth, OBE, JP, DL; ✉ Oldham NHS Trust, Trust Headquarters, Westhulme Avenue, Oldham, Lancs OL1 2PN (direct ☎ 0161 627 8714, fax 0161 627 3130)

FIRTH, Peter; s of Eric Macintosh Firth, of Yorkshire, and Mavis, *née* Hudson; *b* 27 Oct 1953; *Educ* Hanson Boys Sch Bradford; *m* 1990, Lindsey, da of William George Readman, of Cleveland; 1 da (Amy Mary b 1991), 1 s (Alexander William b 1993); *Career* actor; *Theatre* Mozart in Amadeus (Broadhurst NY); National Theatre incl: Alan Strang in Equus (also NY), Melchior in Spring Awakening, Romeo in Romeo and Juliet; *Television* BBC incl: Potter in Murder in Eden, Steve in The Laughter of God, Joe Hillier in Children Crossing, Henry Tilney in Northanger Abbey, Roy in Aerodrome, Dominic Hide in Another Flip for Dominic and The Flipside of Dominic Hide, Dorian Gray in The Picture of Dorian Gray, Armand Duval in The Lady of the Camellias, Ben Bagot in The Ballad of Ben Bagot, Arsenic in Her Majesty's Pleasure, Cis Farrington in The Magistrate; Granada incl: Roger in The Simple Life, Tommy in The Sullens Sisters; other roles incl: Michael in The Way, The Truth, The Video (Regent Prodns), Hardy in The Man at the Top (Anglia); *Films* incl: Rusticello in Marco Polo (Gilgamesh Prodns), Jenson in Seasick, Dr Craig in Shadowlands, Lesley Steckler in the White Angel (Living Spirit Pictures), Franz in The Perfect Husband (Portman Entertainment), Major Henry in Prisoner of Honour (HBO), Wilhelm in The Incident, Putin in Hunt for Red October, Terence in Tree of Hands (Greenpoint Films), Clive in Prisoner of Rio (Dis Irmaos Prodns), Paul Bergson in The Master Musician (Dehlavi Films), Ken Parrish in Chain Reaction (Morning Star Prodns), Yuri in Letter to Brezhnev (Year Dream Prodns), Caine in Lifeforce (London Canon Films), Angel Clare in Tess (Burill Renn Prodns), Stephen in Red Ryder, Alan Strang in Equus, title role in Joseph Andrews (both United Artists), Croft in Aces High (EMI), Friar Elia in Brother Son and Sister Moon; *Awards* nominations for Equus: Academy Award Best Supporting Actor and Tony Award; also for Equus: winner of Golden Globe Award as Best Supporting Actor, Theatre World Award, Plays and Players Award for Best Young Actor; also Evening Standard Award Most Promising Newcomer (for Aces High); *Recreations* sailing, cookery; *Style—* Peter Firth, Esq; ✉ c/o Markham & Froggatt Ltd, Julian House, 4 Windmill Street, London W1P 1HF (☎ 0171 636 4412, fax 0171 637 5233)

FIRTH, Rt Rev Peter James; s of Atkinson Vernon Firth (d 1952), of Stockport, Cheshire, and Edith, *née* Pepper (d 1967); *b* 12 July 1929; *Educ* Stockport GS, Emmanuel Coll Cambridge (BA, MA, DipEd), St Stephen's House Oxford; *m* 27 Aug 1955; Felicity Mary, da of late Longworth Allan Wilding, of Oxford; 2 s (Julian b 8 Jan 1961, Matthew b 10 Aug 1966), 3 da (Gabriel 23 Oct 1958, Susannah b 12 Nov 1962, Linda Hennessy (fostered since 1974) b 17 Feb 1967); *Career* asst curate St Stephen's Barbourne Worcs 1955–58, priest i/c Ascension Church Malvern Link 1958–62, rector St George's Abbey Hey Gorton Manchester 1962–66, asst prodr Religious Progs BBC Manchester 1966–67, sr prodr and organiser Religious Progs BBC Bristol Network Centre 1967–83, last Bishop of Malmesbury (Bristol Dio) 1983–94, ret 1994; winner Int Radio Award Seville Festival 1975; chm Public Enquiry into Swindon Rail Closure 1985 (with John Garnett and Lord Scanlon); *Books* Lord of the Seasons (1978), The Love that moves the Sun (1996); *Recreations* photography, music, R S Thomas and T S Eliot, Manchester Utd; *Style—* The Rt Rev Peter Firth; ✉ 7 Ivywell Rd, Bristol BS9 1NX (☎ 0117 968 5931)

FIRTH, Prof Sir Raymond William; kt (1973); s of Wesley Hugh Bourne Firth (d 1977), and Marie Elizabeth Jane, *née* Cartmill (d 1962); *b* 25 March 1901; *Educ* Auckland GS NZ, Auckland Univ Coll (MA), LSE (PhD); *m* 1936, Rosemary, da of Sir Gilbert Upcott, KCB (d 1967); 1 s; *Career* lectr and acting prof of anthropology Univ of Sydney 1930–32, reader in anthropology LSE 1936–44 (lectr 1933–35), prof of anthropology Univ of London 1944–68 (now emeritus); visiting prof various USA univs, research in Tikopia Solomon Islands and Kelantan Malaysia; author of numerous pubns on anthropological subjects; life pres Assoc Social Anthropologists; hon degrees: Oslo, Michigan, Exeter, E Anglia, Br Columbia, Chicago, Australian NU, Auckland, Cracow, London; hon fell LSE 1970; FBA; *Recreations* Romanesque painting and sculpture, early music; *Clubs* Athenaeum; *Style—* Prof Sir Raymond Firth, FBA; ✉ 33 Southwood Ave, London N6 (☎ 0181 348 0768)

FIRTH, Prof William James; s of William John Flett Firth (d 1993), and Christina May Coltart, *née* Craig (d 1994); *b* 23 Feb 1945; *Educ* Perth Acad, Univ of Edinburgh (BSc, capt Univ hockey team), Heriot-Watt Univ (PhD); *m* 15 July 1967, Mary MacDonald, da of Charles Ramsay Anderson (d 1972); 2 s (Michael John Charles b 11 Feb 1973, Jonathan William b 25 Aug 1975); *Career* reader Dept of Physics Heriot-Watt Univ 1984–85 (asst lect 1967–69, lectr 1969–82, sr lectr 1982–84), prof of experimental physics Dept of Physics and Applied Physics Univ of Strathclyde 1985– (head of dept 1990–93); visiting prof Arizona Center for Mathematical Sciences Tucson USA 1989–; Royal Soc euro fell Univ of Heidelberg 1978–79; chm Ctee of Scottish Professors of Physics 1992–96; ed: Progress in Quantum Electronics 1984–89, Cambridge Studies in Modern Optics 1986–92; MInstP 1972, FRSE 1989, fell Optical Soc of America 1996 (memb 1986); *Publications* author of over 150 scientific articles; *Recreations* golf, the universe and everything; *Style—* Prof William Firth, FRSE; ✉ 21 Dalhousie Terrace, Edinburgh EH10 5NE (☎ 0131 447 7277); Department of Physics and Applied Physics, University of Strathclyde, John Anderson Building, 107 Rottenrow, Glasgow G4 0NG (☎ 0141 552 4400 ext 3269, fax 0141 552 2891)

FISCHEL, David Andrew; *b* 1 April 1958; *Career* md Liberty International Holdings plc; ACA 1983; *Style—* David Fischel, Esq; ✉ Liberty International Holdings plc, 40 Broadway, London SW1H 0BT (☎ 0171 222 5496, fax 0171 222 5554)

FISCHEL, John Roy; s of late Roy Fischel, MC; *b* 2 Sept 1924; *Educ* Cheltenham and RN; *m* 1952, Anita, da of late Capt Maximilian Despard, DSC, RN; 2 s, 3 da; *Career* commodity merchant; L M Fischel & Co Ltd: dir 1960–, chm 1966–, non-exec dir 1984–90; Baltic Mercantile & Shipping Exchange 1975–80; underwriting memb Lloyd's; Liveryman Worshipful Co of Tallow Chandlers; *Recreations* shooting; *Clubs* Castaways, RCC, RNSA, MCC, Kent CCC; *Style—* John Fischel, Esq; ✉ The Mount, Shoreham, nr Sevenoaks, Kent (☎ 01959 522071)

FISH, Anthony William (Tony); s of George Fish (d 1952), of Weybridge, Surrey, and Edith Eliza, *née* Donaldson; *b* 16 April 1951; *Educ* Kingston GS Kingston Surrey; *m* (m dis); 2 da (Jo b 1975, Sarah b 1983); *Career* BBC Radio: radio presenter London 1975–81, radio trainer local radio trg unit 1981–83, prog organiser York 1983–88, station mangr Newcastle 1988–; memb Radio Acad; *Recreations* microlight aviation, music; *Clubs* Eshott Flying; *Style—* Tony Fish, Esq; ✉ BBC Radio Newcastle, Broadcasting Centre, Newcastle upon Tyne NE99 1RN (☎ 0191 232 4141)

FISH, Prof Francis (Frank); OBE (1989); s of William Fish (d 1980), of Houghton-le-Spring, Tyne and Wear, and Phyllis Fish, *née* Griffiths (d 1983); *b* 20 April 1924; *Educ* Houghton-le-Spring GS, Sunderland Tech Coll (BPharm, external London Univ), Univ of Glasgow (PhD); *m* 10 Aug 1949, Hilda Mary, da of James Percy Brown (d 1980), of Houghton-le-Spring; 2 s (David James, Andrew William); *Career* Univ of Strathclyde (formerly The Royal Coll of Sci and Tech Glasgow): asst lectr and lectr 1946–62, sr lectr 1962–69, reader in pharmacognosy and forensic sci 1969–76, prof and head Forensic Sci Unit 1976–78, dean Sch of Pharmaceutical Sci 1977–78 (vice dean 1974–77); Univ of London: dean Sch of Pharmacy 1978–88, prof of pharmacy 1988, emeritus prof 1989, hon fell Sch of Pharmacy 1992–; author of res papers in pharmaceutical and forensic jls; formerly: memb Chemistry Pharmacy and Standards Sub-Ctee of Ctee on Safety of Medicines, memb UGC Med Sub Ctee, chm UGC panel on studies allied to medicine, memb Ctee on Safety of Medicines, memb Ctee on Review of Medicines, Br Pharmacopoeia Cmmn, chm Post Qualification Educn Bd for Health Serv Pharmacists in Scot; memb Nuffield Fndn Ctee of Inquiry into Pharmacy, vice chm DHSS Standing Pharmaceutical Advsy Ctee, vice pres Cncl of Forensic Sci Soc; FRPharmS 1946; *Recreations* gardening, golf; *Style—* Prof Frank Fish, OBE; ✉ Grianan, Hazel Avenue, Crieff, Perthshire

FISH, George Marshall; OBE (1996), JP, DL (Notts 1995); s of George Frederick Fish (d 1940), of Hamilton House, and Dorothy, *née* Creswell (d 1984); *b* 26 June 1928; *Educ* Sedbergh Sch Yorks; *m* 9 Feb 1952, Josephine Lilian, da of Joseph Sydney Plant Lowater (d 1991); 3 s (William, James, Charles); *Career* Capt RA 1946–48, Capt S Notts Hussars, 350 Heavy Regt RA (TA) 1948–52; chartered builder; chm Thomas Fish & Sons Ltd; currently chm Notts Magistrates Cts Ctee, chm Nottingham PSD, chm and tstee Nottingham Bldg Fndn, tstee Nottingham Almshouse Charities; FCIOB, FFB; *Recreations* cricket, walking, golf, gardening; *Clubs* Nottingham and Notts United

Services; *Style*— George Fish, Esq, OBE, JP, DL; ✉ The Manor House, Old Main Rd, Bulcote, Notts NG14 5GU (☎ 0115 931 3159); Office: Little Tennis St, Nottingham (☎ 0115 958 7000, fax 0115 958 6385)

FISH, Michael John; s of Aubrey John Richard Fish (d 1970), of Eastbourne, and Dora, *née* Amos (d 1970); *b* 27 April 1944; *Educ* Eastbourne Coll, City Univ; *m* 21 Sept 1968, Susan Mary, *née* Page; 2 da (Alison Elizabeth b 9 May 1971, Nicola Katherine b 25 Nov 1975); *Career* meteorologist and television weatherman; Meteorological Office Gatwick Airport 1962–65, posted to Bracknell as scientific offr 1965–67; BBC Weather Centre (London Weather Centre until 1991): joined 1967, higher scientific offr 1971–89, sr scientific offr 1989–; first radio bdcasts 1971 (BBC), first TV bdcasts 1974; numerous other appearances on TV and radio in various light entertainment and factual progs; also co-ordinator training courses for TV weather crews in Africa; Hon DSc City Univ 1996; FRMetS 1965; *Recreations* travel, DIY, genealogy, after dinner speaking; *Style*— Michael Fish, Esq; ✉ c/o Weather Unit, Room 2050, BBC Television Centre, Wood Lane, London W12 7RJ (☎ 0181 743 8000, fax 0181 749 2864)

FISH, His Hon Judge; (Peter) Stuart; s of Geoffrey Chadwick Fish (d 1987), of Preston, and Emma, *née* Wood (1995); *b* 18 Dec 1938; *Educ* Rydal Sch Colwyn Bay, Trinity Hall Cambridge (MA); *m* 1963, Nola Ann, da of Joseph William Worrall; 2 s (Jonathan David William b 3 Aug 1965, Daniel Giles Henry b 9 April 1973), 2 da (Anna Mary Rachel b 14 July 1970, d 1972, Rosemary Rebecca Josephine b 3 June 1974); *Career* admitted slr 1963, dist registrar (subsequently dist judge) Manchester 1987, recorder 1991, circuit judge (Northern Circuit) 1994–; *Recreations* golf, music, gardening; *Clubs* Royal Birkdale Golf; *Style*— His Hon Judge Fish; ✉ c/o Northern Circuit Office, 15 Quay Street, Manchester M60 9FD

FISH, William Francis (Frank); s of William Francis Fish, of Lancs, and Marie, *née* Williams (d 1942); *b* 26 Feb 1940; *Educ* St Joseph's Coll Darjeeling, Xaverian Coll, Univ of Manchester (LLB, Dountesey jr and sr scholarships); *m* 6 Jan 1967, Mary Rosetta Hughes, da of Dr Peter Esmond Cosgrove, of NI; 1 s (Kevin b 1969), 3 da (Paula b 1968, Anne-Marie b 1971, Helen b 1980); *Career* slr (Stephen Healis Gold Medal); pt/t lectr in law Univ of Manchester 1967–96; sometime dep dist registrar of the High Court and dep County Court registrar 1974–76; sometime asst dep coroner of the High Peak Derbys 1978; memb area ctee No 10 Legal Aid Area; *Books* Butterworths Family Law Service (ed); *Recreations* walking, swimming, angling, gardening; *Style*— William F Fish, Esq; ✉ Mount Delphi, 11 Melia Close, Rossendale, Lancashire BB4 6RQ (☎ 01706 220487); 61 Mosley Street, Manchester M2 3HZ (☎ 0161 236 0321)

FISHBURN, (John) Dudley; MP (Cons) Kensington (majority 3,548); s of late Eskdale Fishburn and Bunting Fishburn; *b* 8 June 1946; *Educ* Eton, Harvard; *m* 1981, Victoria, da of Sir Jack Boles and step da of Lady Anne Boles (da of 12 Earl Waldegrave); 2 da (Alice b 1982, Honor b 1984), 2 s (Jack b 1985, Marcus b 1987); *Career* journalist; exec ed The Economist 1979–88; MP (C) Kensington 1988–, PPS at the Foreign and Commonwealth Office 1989–90 and the DTI 1990–93; non-exec dir: Household International (Chicago), Business Post plc, Euclidian plc, Cordiant plc; memb Bd of Overseers Harvard Univ, chm Open Univ Foundation, tstee Prison Reform Tst, govr Exec Ctee The National Trust; *Publications* World in 1996 (The Econimst, ed); *Clubs* Brooks's; *Style*— Dudley Fishburn, Esq, MP; ✉ 7 Gayfere Street, London SW1; The Old Rectory, Englefield, Berkshire

FISHER, Charles Murray; s of Kenneth John Fisher (d 1996), of Cheltenham, and Beryl Dorothy, *née* Pearman; *b* 24 Dec 1949; *Educ* Cheltenham Coll, St Edmund Hall Oxford, Harvard Business Sch; *m* 29 Sept 1984, Denise Ellen, *née* Williams; 2 da (Louisa Dora b 13 Dec 1985, Jasmine Diana b 24 June 1987); *Career* int trainee Petrofina SA in Bussels and Paris 1971–76, md Sandfords Ltd 1980–84 (dir 1976–84), chm Sharpe & Fisher plc 1989– (dir 1980–, chief exec 1985–89); non-exec dir: South West Electricity plc 1990–95, John Mowlem & Co plc 1993–; Freeman of City of London, Liveryman Worshipful Co of Builders Merchants; *Recreations* tennis, travel, reading; *Clubs* MCC, Turf, Annabel's; *Style*— Charles Fisher, Esq; ✉ Warneford House, Sudgrove, nr Miserden, Glos GL6 7JD; Sharpe & Fisher plc, Gloucester Road, Cheltenham, Glos (☎ 01242 224833)

FISHER, David Paul; QC (1996); s of Percy Laurence Fisher (d 1964), and Doris Mary, *née* Western; *b* 30 April 1949; *Educ* Felsted, Coll of Law, Inns of Court Sch of Law; *m* 1, 18 Sept 1971, Cary Maria Cicely (d 1977), da of Charles Egan Lamberton; 1 da (Clair Helen Maria b 14 Dec 1976); m 2, 7 July 1979, Diana Elizabeth, da of John Harold Dolby (d 1962); *Career* called to the Bar Gray's Inn 1973, recorder of the Crown Court 1991– (asst recorder 1987); memb Gen Cncl of the Bar 1997; *Recreations* travel, sport, gardening, cinema; *Style*— David Fisher, Esq, QC; ✉ 6 King's Bench Walk, Temple, London EC4Y 7DR (☎ 0171 583 0410, fax 0171 353 8791)

FISHER, David Richard; s of William Horace Fisher (d 1976), and Margaret Catherine, *née* Dashper (d 1993); *b* 13 May 1947; *Educ* Reading Sch, St John's Coll Oxford (BA); *m* Sophia Josephine, da of Prof George Hibbard; 2 da (Caroline b 1979, Diana b 1982); *Career* MOD: private sec to successive RAF Mins 1973–74, on staff Naval Prog and Budget 1976–79, Defence Budget 1981–83, seconded as visiting res fell Nuffield Coll Oxford 1983–84, head of resources and progs (Air) 1984–88, seconded to FCO as defence cnsllr UK Delgn to NATO 1988–92, asst under sec of state (Systems) 1992–; memb: Mgmnt Ctee Cncl on Christian Approaches to Defence and Disarmament, Aristotelian Soc; *Books* Morality and the Bomb (1985), Ethics and European Security (contrib, 1986), Just Deterrence (contrib, 1990); contrib to numerous jls on defence and ethical issues; *Recreations* philosophy and gardening; *Clubs* Nat Liberal, Commonwealth Soc; *Style*— David Fisher, Esq; ✉ Ministry of Defence, Main Building, Whitehall, London SW1A 2HB (☎ 0171 218 2217)

FISHER, Dudley Henry; CBE (1990), DL (South Glamorgan, 1991); s of Arthur Fisher (d 1926), and Mary Eliza, *née* Greenacre (d 1965); *b* 22 Aug 1922; *Educ* City of Norwich Sch; *m* 1, 1946, Barbara Lilian Sexton (d 1984); 1 s (Christopher), 2 da (Pamela, Angela); m 2, 1985, Jean Mary Livingstone Miller, da of late Dr and Mrs R B Miller, of Cowbridge, S Glamorgan; *Career* Flt Lt RAF 1941–46; chm Wales Region British Gas Corporation 1974–87 (fin dir 1968–70, dep chm 1970–74); memb: Audit Cmmn for Local Authorities in Eng and Wales 1983–88, Bdcasting Cncl for Wales 1985–90, Admin Ctee WEC 1986–89, Cncl Univ of Wales Coll of Cardiff 1988–; chm CBI Cncl for Wales 1987–89 (memb 1974–77); hon treas Br Nat Ctee World Energy Conference 1977–89, nat tstee Help the Aged 1987–, govr United World Coll of the Atlantic 1987–96, High Sheriff South Glamorgan 1988–89, dep chm Help Age Int 1990–, dep chm Inst of Welsh Affairs 1991–96, chm Wales Festival of Remembrance Ctee 1995–; memb Cncl Univ of Wales Coll of Medicine 1994–; Liveryman Welsh Livery Guild; memb CIPFA; *Recreations* golf, music, reading; *Clubs* Cardiff & County, RAF; *Style*— Dudley Fisher, Esq, CBE, DL; ✉ Norwood Edge, 8 Cyncoed Ave, Cardiff CF2 6SU (☎ 01222 757958)

FISHER, Gillian Elizabeth; da of Norman James Fisher, of Oadby, Leics, and Patricia Jean, *née* Warrington; *b* 12 March 1955; *Educ* Beauchamp Coll Oadby, Univ of Warwick (LLB), Royal College of Music (ARCM); *m* 11 Feb 1983, Brian Christopher Kay, *qv*, s of Noel Bancroft Kay; *Career* soprano; concert singer, mainly Baroque and Classical repertoire; professional debut Queen Elizabeth Hall 1979; has sung at numerous major venues and festivals worldwide incl: Royal Opera House Covent Garden (debut 1981), Royal Festival Hall, Barbican Hall, Edinburgh Festival (debut 1984), BBC Proms (regular soloist since debut 1985), Three Choirs Festival, Bath and York Festivals, Paris, Monte Carlo, Madrid, Vienna, Milan, Venice, Cologne, Frankfurt, Concertgebouw Amsterdam, Brussels, Oslo, New York (debut Lincoln Centre 1983, further tours 1988 and 1989), Japan and Far East (debut 1987, further tours 1989 and 1992), Australia (debut Sydney Opera House 1992); has worked with numerous major conductors incl: John Eliot Gardiner, Trevor Pinnock, Christopher Hogwood, Robert King, Roger Norrington, Ton Koopman; *Recordings* numerous incl: Purcell Complete Odes and Welcome Songs (with King's Consort under Robert King, Hyperion, 8 CDs), Pergolesi Stabat Mater (with King's Consort and Michael Chance under Robert King, Hyperion, Gramophone Critics' Choice 1988), Great Baroque Arias (with King's Consort, Pickwick, in US classical top ten for several months 1988), Handel Duets (with James Bowman and King's Consort), Purcell's The Fairy Queen (with The Sixteen under Harry Christophers, Collins Classics), Purcell's King Arthur (with Monteverdi Choir under John Eliot Gardiner, Erato), Purcell's Dioclesian and Timon of Athens (with Monteverdi Choir under Gardiner, Erato), various Handel works with London Handel Orch under Denys Darlow, Bach Cantatas (with The Sixteen under Harry Christophers), Monteverdi Vespers (with Kammerchor Stuttgart, Deutsche Harmonia Mundi); *Recreations* reading, gardening, watching cricket; *Style*— Ms Gillian Fisher; ✉ c/o Magenta Music International, 4 Highgate High St, London N6 5JL (☎ 0181 340 8321, fax 0181 340 7823)

FISHER, Hon Sir Henry Arthur Pears; kt (1968); eld s of Most Rev and Rt Hon Baron Fisher of Lambeth, GCVO, PC (d 1972), formerly 99 Archbishop of Canterbury, and Rosamond (d 1986), da of Rev Arthur Forman; *b* 20 Jan 1918; *Educ* Marlborough, Ch Ch Oxford; *m* 18 Dec 1948, Felicity, da of late Eric Sutton, of Cheyne Place, Chelsea; 1 s (Thomas Henry Sutton b 1958), 3 da (Emma b 1949, Lucy b 1951, Francesca b 1955); *Career* served WWII Leics Regt and Staff Coll Quetta, also as Staff Offr (GSO 14th Army 1945, rank of Hon Lt-Col 1946); called to the Bar 1947, QC 1960, recorder Canterbury 1962–68, High Ct Judge (Queen's Bench) 1968–70, chm Gen Cncl Bar 1966–68 (vice-chm 1965–66, memb 1959–63 & 1964–68); vice pres: Senate of Inns of Court 1966–68, Bar Assoc for Commerce Finance & Industry 1973–; chm Appeal Ctee of Panel on Takeovers and Mergers 1981–86; pres Wolfson Coll Oxford 1975–85, fell All Souls Coll Oxford 1946–73 and 1991– (sub-warden 1965–67, emeritus fell 1976–91), memb Cncl Marlborough Coll 1965–82 (chm 1977–81), chm Governing Body Imperial Coll 1974–88, tstee Pilgrim Tst (chm 1979–83 and 1989–91); chm various ctees of inquiry (most recently 1979–80 into self-regulation at Lloyd's); chm Jt Lib/Soc Democrat Cmmn on Constitutional Reform; former memb Cncl on Tbnls and Law Reform Ctee; memb BBC Programmes Complaints Cmmn 1972–79; *Style*— The Hon Sir Henry Fisher

FISHER, Prof John Robert; s of John Robert Fisher, of Barrow-in-Furness, Cumbria, and Eleanor, *née* Parker; *b* 6 Jan 1943; *Educ* Barrow GS, UCL (BA, MPhil), Univ of Liverpool (PhD); *m* 1 Aug 1966, (Elizabeth) Ann, da of Stephen Gerard Postlethwaite, of Barrow-in-Furness; 3 s (David John b 27 Sept 1967, Nicholas Stephen b 10 Dec 1970, Martin Joseph b 27 Aug 1973); *Career* Univ of Liverpool: lectr 1966–75, sr lectr 1975–81, dir Inst of Latin American Studies 1983–, dean Faculty of Arts 1986–92, prof 1987–93, pro-vice-chllr 1995–; chm Soc of Latin American Studies 1986–88, gen sec Euro Assoc of Historians of Latin America 1987–93; FRHistS 1975; *Books* Government and Society in Colonial Peru (1970), Silver Mines and Silver Miners in Colonial Peru (1976), Commercial Relations between Spain and Spanish America 1778–1797 (1985), Peru (1989), Reform and Insurrection in Bourbon, New Granada and Peru (1990), Trade, War and Revolution (1992); *Recreations* theatre, music, walking, gardening, travel; *Style*— Prof John Fisher; ✉ University of Liverpool, PO Box 147, Liverpool L69 3BY (☎ 0151 794 3078, fax 0151 794 3080, telex 627095 G)

FISHER, 3 Baron (UK 1909); John Vavasseur Fisher; DSC (1944), JP (Norfolk 1970); s of 2 Baron (d 1955, himself s of Adm of the Fleet, 1 Baron (Sir John) Fisher, GCB, OM, GCVO); *b* 24 July 1921; *Educ* Stowe, Trinity Coll Cambridge; *m* 1, 25 July 1949 (m dis 1969), Elizabeth Ann Penelope, yr da of late Maj Herbert P Holt, MC; 2 s (Hon Patrick, *qv*, Hon Benjamin b 1958), 2 da (Hon Frances b 1951, Hon Bridget b 1956); m 2, 1970, Hon Rosamund Anne, da of 12 Baron Clifford of Chudleigh and formerly w of Geoffrey Forrester Fairbairn; *Heir* s, Hon Patrick Fisher b 14 June 1953; *Career* sometime Lt RNVR WWII; dir Kilverstone Latin American Zoo 1973–91; memb: Eastern Gas Bd 1961–70, E Anglian Economic Planning Cncl 1969–77; DL Norfolk 1968–82; *Style*— The Rt Hon the Lord Fisher, DSC, JP; ✉ Marklye, Rushlake Green, nr Heathfield, E Sussex (☎ 01435 830270)

FISHER, Jonathan Simon; s of Aubrey Fisher; *b* 24 Feb 1958; *Educ* St Dunstan's Coll, N London Poly (BA), St Catharine's Coll Cambridge (LLB); *m* 21 Dec 1980, Paula Yvonne, da of Rev Louis Goldberg (d 1988); 2 s (Benjamin b 1984, David b 1990), 2 da (Hannah b 1986, Leah b 1995); *Career* called to the Bar Gray's Inn 1980, ad eundem Inner Temple 1985; second standing counsel to Inland Revenue (Central Criminal Ct and London Crown Cts); visiting fell City Univ, UK case corr Jl of Int Banking Law; *Style*— Jonathan Fisher, Esq; ✉ 5 King's Bench Walk, Temple, London EC4 (☎ 0171 797 7600, fax 0171 797 7648)

FISHER, Julie Kay; da of Brian James Brennan Fisher, of Newark, Notts, and Rita Adelaide, *née* Byfield; *b* 9 Sept 1958; *Educ* Stamford HS for Girls; *partner* Kiran Master; 1 s (Maximilian b 23 Oct 1992); *Career* photographer 1980–; Assoc of Photographers: Merit Award 1987, 1988 and 1991, Silver Award 1995; *Style*— Ms Julie Fisher; ✉ The Terrace, 149 Green Lanes, London N16 9DB (☎ 0171 359 0108, fax 0171 359 0132, mobile 0973 172749)

FISHER, Lady Karen Jean; *née* Carnegie; er da of 13 Earl of Northesk (d 1994); *b* 22 Dec 1951; *Educ* Queen's Coll London; *m* 1977, Hon Patrick Vavasseur Fisher, *qv*; 3 s (John b 1979, Benjamin b 1986, Robin b (twin) 1996), 4 da (Juliet b 1978, Penelope b 1982, Suzannah b 1984, Liberty Jean b 1996); *Career* dir Macrae Farms Ltd 1981–, non-exec dir Mid Anglia Community Health Tst 1992–; memb for Risby Ward on St Edmundsbury Borough Cncl 1989–, vice pres Suffolk Red Cross (former chm Appeals); memb Bd of Govrs Riddlesworth Hall Sch Norfolk; *Style*— The Lady Karen Fisher; ✉ Kilverstone Hall, Thetford, Norfolk

FISHER, Keith Plunket; s of Francis St George Fisher (d 1990), of Cragg, and Patricia, *née* Lyon (d 1955); *b* 28 Oct 1935; *Educ* Harrow; *m* 1 (m dis), Anne, da of Percy Collingwood Charleton; 1 s (Kiwa b 1966); m 2, 1986, Julia, da of Derek Pattinson, OBE; 2 s (Jeremy b 1987 d 1987, Alexander b 1989), 3 da (Poppy Frances b 1991, Xara b 1994, Kitty b (twin) 1994); *Career* ptnr Overton Shirley & Barry 1981–95; landowner Higham Estate 1990–; *Style*— Keith Fisher, Esq; ✉ Cragg, Cockermouth, Cumbria CA13 9YB (☎ 01768 776277, fax 01768 776067)

FISHER, Kenneth John; s of Stanley Joseph Fisher (d 1983), of Dalton-in-Furness, Cumbria, and Gertrude Isabel, *née* Ridding (d 1980); *b* 26 June 1927; *Educ* Uppingham, St John's Coll Cambridge (MA, LLM, Sir Joseph Larmer award); *m* 8 May 1954, Mary Florence, da of William Isaac Towers, JP (d 1971), of Barrow-in-Furness, Cumbria; 1 s ((Stephen) John b 6 Oct 1957), 1 da (Anne Rosemary b 24 April 1956); *Career* Sub-Lt RNVR 1945–48; admitted slr 1953, sr ptnr Kendall & Fisher; clerk to the Gen Cmmrs of Taxes Lonsdale North; chm: Agric Land Tbnl (Northern Area), Social Security Appeal Tbnl, Dalton and Dist Recreational Charity Tst, Furness Probation Support Gp; memb: S Cumbria Healthcare Tst (chm Med Servs Ctee), Cumbria Family Health Servs Authy; memb Furness Hosp NHS Tst 1994–95, chm Area Ctee The Legal Aid Bd, clerk to Billincoat Charities, pres Dalton Town Band; past pres: N Lonsdale Law Assoc, N Lonsdale, Lowick and Cartmel Agric Soc, Barrow-in-Furness Branch Royal Soc of St George; life govr Imperial Cancer Research Fund; hon slr to St Mary's Hospice; chm Govrs of Chetwynde Sch; life memb: Lancs RFC, Furness RFC; *Recreations* rugby, cricket, skiing, gardening; *Clubs* Hawks', Cambridge LX, Uppingham Rovers, Cambridge

Union; *Style—* Kenneth J Fisher, Esq; ✉ Glenside House, Springfield Rd, Ulverston, Cumbria LA12 OEJ (☎ 01229 583437); Kendall & Fisher, 68 Market St, Dalton-in-Furness, Cumbria LA15 8AD (☎ 01229 462126, fax 01229 62083)

FISHER, Mark; MP (Lab) Stoke-on-Trent Central (majority 13,420); s of Sir Nigel Thomas Loveridge Fisher, MC (d 1996), by his 1 w, Lady Gloria Vaughan, da of 7 Earl of Lisburne; *b* 29 Oct 1944; *Educ* Eton, Trinity Coll Cambridge; *m* 1971, Ghilly (Mrs Ingrid Hunt), da of late James Hoyle Geach; 2 s, 2 da; *Career* former principal Tattenhall Educn Centre; former documentary writer and film producer; Parly candidate (Lab) Leek 1979, MP (Lab) Stoke-on-Trent Central 1983–; memb: Staffs CC 1981–85, Treasy and Civil Service Select Ctee 1983–86, BBC Gen Advsy Cncl 1987–, Cncl Policy Studies Inst 1989–; dep pro-chllr Univ of Keele 1989–; opposition whip 1985–86, shadow min for arts and media 1987–92, oppn spokesman on Citizens' Charter and Open Government 1992–93, shadow min for the Arts 1993–; Hon FRIBA, Hon FRCA; *Books* City Centres, City Cultures (1988), Whose Cities? (ed, 1991), A New London (1992); *Style—* Mark Fisher, Esq, MP; ✉ House of Commons, London SW1A 0AA

FISHER, Hon Patrick Vavasseur; s (by 1 m) and h of 3 Baron Fisher, *qv*; *b* 14 June 1953; *m* 1977, Lady Karen Jean Carnegie, *qv*, da of 13 Earl of Northesk (d 1994); 3 s (John Carnegie Vavasseur b 1979, Benjamin Carnegie Vavasseur b 1986, Robin Carnegie Vavasseur b (twin) 1996), 4 da (Juliet Elizabeth b 1978, Penelope Mary-Jean b 1981, Suzannah Jane b 1984, Liberty Jean b 1996); *Style—* The Hon Patrick Fisher; ✉ Kilverstone Hall, Thetford, Norfolk IP24 2RL

FISHER, Rev Peter Timothy; s of Rev Canon James Atherton Fisher, of Charfield, Glos, and Joan Gardiner, *née* Budden; *b* 7 July 1944; *Educ* City of London Sch, Univ of Durham (BA, MA), Cuddesdon Coll Oxford; *m* 6 Sept 1968, Elizabeth, da of late Charles Lacey; 2 s (Andrew Richmond b 28 Oct 1971, David Geoffrey b 5 July 1973); *Career* vol serv Calcutta 1964; asst curate St Andrew's Bedford 1970–74, chaplain Univ of Surrey 1974–78, sub-warden Lincoln Theol Coll 1978–83, rector Houghton-le-Spring, St Michael and All Angels 1983–94, princ Queen's Coll Birmingham 1994–; *Recreations* piano, watercolouring; *Style—* The Rev Peter Fisher; ✉ The Queen's College Birmingham, Somerset Road, Edgbaston, Birmingham B15 2QH (☎ 0121 454 1527, fax 0121 454 1817)

FISHER, Rick; s of Samuel M Fisher, of Philadelphia, and Helene, *née* Korn (d 1973); *b* 19 Oct 1954; *Educ* Haverford HS Philadelphia, Dickinson Coll Carlisle Pennsylvania; *Career* lighting designer; chm Assoc of Lighting Designers; *Theatre* RNT: Black Snow, Peer Gynt, The Coup, An Inspector Calls (Tony Award 1994, Drama Desk Award 1994, Olivier Award nomination 1993), Pericles (Olivier Award nomination 1995), Machinal (Olivier Award 1994), What the Butler Saw, Under Milk Wood, Blinded by the Sun, The Designated Mourner; Royal Court: Three Birds, Alighting in a Field, King Lear, Hysteria (Olivier Award 1994), Six Degrees of Separation, Bloody Poetry, Serious Money; RSC: Temptation, Restoration, Some Americans Abroad (also Lincoln Centre NYC), Two Shakespearean Actors, The Virtuoso, 'Tis Pity She's a Whore, Artists and Admirers, All's Well That Ends Well, The Gift of the Gorgon, Elgar's Rondo, The Broken Heart; other prodns incl: Moonlight (Almeida), Much Ado About Nothing (Queen's), The Cryptogram (Ambassador's), A Walk in the Woods (Comedy Theatre), The Life of Stuff and Threepenny Opera (Donmar Warehouse), A Picture of Dorian Gray (Lyric Hammersmith), Rat in the Skull (Duke of York's), The Changing Room (Duke of York's); *Opera* incl: Gloriana, La Bohème, L'Étoile, Peter Grimes (Opera North), The Magic Flute (Teatro Regio, Parma), Cosi Fan Tutte (WNO), The Fairy Queen (ENO), Musica Nel Chiostro (3 seasons, Batignano Italy); numerous dance pieces for The Kosh and Swan Lake for Adventures in Motion Pictures; *Recreations* cycling, travel, camping; *Style—* Rick Fisher, Esq; ✉ c/o Denis Lyne Agency, 108 Leonard Street, London EC2A 4RH (☎ 0171 739 6200, fax 0171 739 4101)

FISHER, Dr Ronald Albert; JP; s of Albert Edward Fisher (d 1963), and Hannah Jackson, *née* Byrom (d 1986); *b* 3 June 1917; *Educ* Heversham Sch Cumbria, Downing Coll Cambridge (MA), Middx Hosp London; *m* 23 Feb 1952, Gwyneth Ena, da of Harold Arthur Mackinnon (d 1983); 2 da (Deborah Anne b 22 March 1956, Teresa b 2 Dec 1963); *Career* Surgn Lt RNVR 1943–46, convoy duties 1943–45 (Western Approaches, Russia, Gibraltar), landing in Java and MO Port Souabaya 1945–46; Bournemouth and E Dorset Gp of Hosps: conslt anaesthetist and admin 1953–73, memb Hosp Mgmnt Ctee 1960–71, chm Med Exec Ctee 1965–71 (memb Med Advsy Ctee to Wessex Regnl Health Bd), dir postgrad educn 1963–67; fndr then conslt physician to the Macmillan Unit at Christchurch Hosp Dorset (pioneering hospice care in the NHS) 1974–82, started first home-care serv (McMillan Serv) in the NHS 1975, started first day-care unit in the NHS 1977, conslt advsr and memb Bd of Mgmnt Lewis Manning Cancer Care Serv Poole 1992–; chm Select Ctee of Experts on Problems Relating to Death Cncl of Europe Strasbourg 1977–80, opened new hospice Riverside Hosp Columbus Ohio and gave first Libby Bradford Meml Lecture 1989, formerly hon conslt in continuing cancer care and tstee Cancer Relief; chm bd of dirs Palace Ct Theatre Bournemouth; formerly: chm Bournemouth Little Theatre Club, dir LM Theatres Ltd; President's medal Cancer Relief; MRCS, LRCP, FRCA; memb: BMA, Nat Soc for Cancer Relief; *Books* Palliative Care for People with Cancer (ed, 1991, 2 edn 1995), Palliative Day Care (ed, 1996); *Recreations* philosophy, theatre, literature, family; *Style—* Dr Ronald Fisher, JP; ✉ Waders, 6 Lagoon Rd, Lilliput, Poole, Dorset BH14 8JT (☎ 01202 708 867)

FISHER, Baroness; Hon Rosamund Anne; *née* Clifford; da of 12 Baron Clifford of Chudleigh (d 1964); *b* 22 May 1924; *Educ* St Mary's Convent Ascot; *m* 1, 21 July 1945 (m dis 1965), Geoffrey Forrester Fairbairn (decd); 2 s (James b 1950, Charles b 1956), 1 da (Katrina b 1947); m 2, 1970, 3 Baron Fisher, DSC, *qv*; *Career* zoo dir and author; *Style—* The Rt Hon Lady Fisher; ✉ Marklye, Rushlake Green, Heathfield, E Sussex (☎ 01435 830270)

FISHER, Roy; s of Walter Fisher (d 1959), of Birmingham, and Emma, *née* Jones (d 1965); *b* 11 June 1930; *Educ* Handsworth GS, Univ of Birmingham (BA, MA); *m* 1, 1953 (m dis 1987), Barbara, da of Harold Davenport Venables; 2 s (Joel b 1957, Benjamin b 1963); m 2, 1987, Joyce, da of Arthur Holliday; *Career* lectr rising to sr lectr in Eng Dudley Coll of Educn 1958–63, head of Dept of Eng and Drama Bordesley Coll of Educn Birmingham 1963–71, lectr rising to sr lectr Univ of Keele 1971–82; freelance writer, broadcaster and jazz pianist 1982–; Birmingham is What I Think With (film, 1991); Andrew Kelus Poetry prize 1969, Cholmondeley award 1980; memb: Musicians' Union 1957–, Soc of Authors 1980–; *Books* City (1961), The Ship's Orchestra (1966), Collected Poems 1968 (1968), Matrix (1971), The Cut Pages (1971), The Thing About Joe Sullivan (1978), Poems 1955–1980 (1980), A Furnace (1986), Poems 1955–1987 (1988), Birmingham River (1994), The Dow Low Drop (1996); *Style—* Roy Fisher

FISHER OF REDNAL, Baroness (Life Peeress UK 1974), of Rednal in the City of Birmingham; Doris Mary Gertrude Fisher; JP (Birmingham 1961); da of late Frederick James Satchwell, BEM; *b* 13 Sept 1919; *Educ* Tinker's Farm Girls' Sch, Fircroft Coll, Bournville Day Continuation Coll; *m* 1939, Joseph Fisher (d 1978); 2 da (Hon Pauline Mary (Hon Mrs Platt) b 1940, Hon Veronica Mary (Hon Mrs Pickering) b 1945); *Career* sits as Labour peer in House of Lords; joined Lab Pty 1945, memb Birmingham City Cncl 1952–74, MP (Lab) Birmingham (Ladywood) 1970–74, MEP 1975–79; hon alderman Birmingham 1974, memb Warrington New Town Devpt Corp 1974–81; memb GMC 1974–79, govr Hunter's Hill Sch Bromsgrove 1988–94; vice pres: Assoc of Municipal Authorities, Assoc of District Cncls, Guardian Birmingham Assay Office 1982–89, Inst of Trading Standards Admin 1988, Hallmarking Cncl 1989–94; pres Birmingham Royal Instn for the Blind 1983–; Midland County chm: NSPCC 1994–, Macmillan Fund Appeal 1994–; patron St Basil's Birmingham Working With Young Homeless; *Style—* The Rt Hon Lady Fisher of Rednal, JP; ✉ 60 Jacoby Place, Priory Road, Birmingham B5 7UW

FISHER-SMITH, Richard James; s of Derrick William Smith, of Stevenage, Herts, and Patricia, *née* Cheek; *b* 10 Oct 1964; *Educ* Alleyne's Boys' Sch, Stevenage Coll of Art & Design (DATEC), Berkshire Coll of Art & Design (BTEC); *m* 6 Sept 1986, Sally Josephine, da of Edward Terrence Fisher (d 1982); 1 da (Elizanell Jessica Ellen b 5 Sept 1988), 2 s (Oscar Arthur Edward James b 26 June 1991, Moses Blue Edward James b 14 Oct 1995); *Career* designer; freelance designer 1985–86; KB Design: designer 1987–89, sr designer 1989–90, sr designer Pentagram Design Ltd 1990–92; assoc dir Crescent Lodge Design Ltd 1994– (sr designer 1992–94); Communication Arts America Award of Excellence 1988, Int Logo and Trademark Assoc NYC Award of Excellence 1989, Art Directors' Club Award of Merit 1992; work featured in numerous jls and annuals; *Recreations* native American tradition, alternative life style, cinema, travel; *Style—* Richard Fisher-Smith, Esq; ✉ Wilbury Hill Farmhouse, Wilbury Hills Road, Letchworth, Herts SG6 4LB (☎ 01462 485128, e-mail fishers@dircon.co.uk); Crescent Lodge Design Ltd, 51 1/2 Barnsbury Street, London N1 1TP (☎ 0171 607 6733, fax 0171 609 6069)

FISHLOCK, Dr David Jocelyn; OBE (1983); s of William Charles Fishlock (d 1958), of Bath, and late Dorothy Mary Fishlock; *b* 9 Aug 1932; *Educ* City of Bath Boys' Sch (now Beechen Cliff Sch), Bristol Coll of Technol (now Univ of Bath); *m* 21 Dec 1959, Mary Millicent, *née* Cosgrove; 1 s (William David b 12 June 1960); *Career* assoc ed McGraw-Hill Publishing Co 1959–62, technol ed New Scientist 1962–67, science ed Financial Times 1967–91, ed and publisher R & D Efficiency 1991–; editorial conslt Pharmaceutical Forum 1993–96; Glaxo Travelling Fellowship for science writing 1977; Hon DLitt Royal Univ of Salford 1982, Hon DSc Univ of Bath 1993; FIBiol 1988, companion Inst of Energy 1987; *Books* author or ed of twelve books incl: The Business of Science (1975), Biotechnology - Strategies for Life (with Elizabeth Antebi, 1987); *Clubs* Athenaeum, Beaconsfield Golf; *Style—* Dr David Fishlock, OBE; ✉ Traveller's Joy, Copse Lane, Jordans, Bucks HP9 2TA (☎ and fax 01494 873242)

FISHMAN, Prof William Jack; *b* 1 April 1921; *Educ* Central Fndn GS for Boys London, LSE (BSc Econ), Univ of London (DSc Econ); *m* 1 June 1947, Doris; 2 s (Barrie Paul b 26 June 1948, Michael Ian b 8 March 1953); *Career* Home Serv and Far East Br Army 1940–46; princ Tower Hamlets Coll of Further Educn 1954–69; visiting fell Balliol Coll Oxford 1965; visiting prof: Columbia Univ NY 1967, Univ of Wisconsin Madison 1969–70; Action Tst major res fell in History 1970–72, prof QMC London 1986– (Barnet Shine sr res fell 1972); conslt and participant BBC radio and TV and ITV progs relating to the East End (US, W German and Finnish TV), memb Ctee Toynbee Hall 1991, govr Raines Fndn Sch, former academic advsr Museum of Labour History, founding govr East End Jewish Museum; *Books* The Insurrectionists (1970), East End Jewish Radicals (1975), The Streets of East London (1979), East End 1888 (1988), East End and Docklands (with John Hall and Nicholas Breach, 1990); *Recreations* travel, reading and conducting local history tours; *Style—* Prof William Fishman; ✉ 42 Willowcourt Avenue, Kenton, Harrow, Middlesex (☎ 0181 907 5166); Department of Political Studies, Queen Mary and Westfield College, Mile End Rd, London E1 (☎ 0171 975 5555)

FISHWICK, Avril; DL (Gtr Manchester 1982); da of Frank Platt Hindley (d 1966), and Charlotte Winifred, *née* Young (d 1940); *b* 30 March 1924; *Educ* Woodfield Sch, Wigan HS for Girls, Univ of Liverpool (LLB, LLM); *m* 4 Feb 1950, Thomas William Fishwick, s of William Fishwick, of Rainford; 2 da (Lizbeth Joanna b 1951, Hilary Alean b 1953); *Career* FO Bletchley Park 1942–45; admitted slr 1949; ptnr Frank Platt & Fishwick 1958–94; High Sheriff Gtr Manchester 1983–84, Vice Lord-Lt Gtr Manchester 1988–; memb Wigan and Leigh Hosp Mgmnt Ctee 1960–73, chm Wigan AHA 1973–82, memb N W Regnl Health Authy 1984–88; hon memb Soroptimist Int, pres Wigan Branch RSPCA 1974–, dir N Advsy Bd Nat West Bank 1984–92; memb Ct Univ of Manchester 1984–; pres: Wigan Civic Tst 1975–88, Wigan Little Theatre 1985–91, Friends of Drumcroon Arts Centre; Countryside Cmmn rep Groundwork Tst 1985–94, chm Environmental Research and Consultancy Unit Tidy Britain (ERCU Ltd); vice pres Gtr Manchester Co Scout Cncl; tstee: Skelton Bounty, Gtr Manchester Police Community Charity, Friends of Rosie; HM The Queen Mother's Birthday Award for Environmental Improvement 1996; Hon MA Univ of Manchester; memb Law Soc, Paul Harris fell Rotary Int; *Recreations* countryside, natural history; *Style—* Mrs Avril Fishwick, DL; ✉ Haighlands, Haigh Country Park, Haigh, Wigan (☎ 01942 831291, fax 01942 831291)

FISK, David John; s of late John Howard Fisk, and Rebecca Elizabeth, *née* Haynes; *b* 9 Jan 1947; *Educ* Stationers' Company's Sch Hornsey, St John's Coll Cambridge (BA, MA, ScD), Univ of Manchester (PhD); *m* 1972, Anne Thoday; 1 s, 1 da; *Career* DOE: Building Res Estab 1972, higher sci offr 1972–73, sr sci offr 1973–75, princ sci offr 1975–78, sr princ sci offr and head Mechanical and Electrical Engrg Div 1978–84, asst sec Central Directorate of Environmental Protection 1984–87, dep chief scientist 1987–88, under sec and chief scientist 1988–, dir Environment and Int 1995–; visiting prof Univ of Liverpool 1988–; FCIBSE 1983, CEng 1983; *Books* Thermal Control of Buildings (1981); author of numerous papers on building science, systems theory and economics; *Style—* David Fisk, Esq; ✉ Department of the Environment, 43 Marsham St, London SW1

FISK, Dr Peter Geoffrey; s of Sydney Harold Fisk (d 1990), and Mrs Fisk, *née* Gawan (d 1981); *b* 4 Feb 1945; *Educ* Raynes Park Co GS, Queen Elizabeth Coll, London Hosp Med Coll (BSc, MB BS, LRCP, MRCS); *m* 20 Oct 1973, Ann Prentice, da of Graeme Smith (d 1979); 1 s (Christopher Jeffrey b 1 Aug 1979), 1 da (Emily Mary b 6 Oct 1976); *Career* registrar St Thomas' Hosp 1976–79, sr registrar and hon lectr Middx Hosp 1979–83, conslt in genitourinary med Leicester Royal Infirmary 1983–; memb: Assurance Med Soc, Med Soc for the Study of Venereal Disease, AGUM, BMA; MRCP 1980, FRCP 1992; *Books* Pocket Guide to Cystitis (1982), Learning Genitourinary Medicine and HIV Disease Through MCQ (1990); *Recreations* art, sport; *Style—* Dr Peter Fisk; ✉ 6 Holt Drive, Kirby Muxloe, Leicester LE9 2EX (☎ 0116 238 6057); Department of Genitourinary Medicine, Leicester Royal Infirmary, Leicester (☎ 0116 254 1414)

FISKE, Alison Mary; da of Roger Elwyn Fiske (d 1987), of Ambleside, Cumbria, and Elizabeth Margaret, *née* Sadler; *Educ* Assoc Arts Sch Wimbledon, Central Sch of Speech and Drama, The Drama Centre; *m* 1967, Stephen Fagan; 1 da (Harriet b 1974), 1 s (Tom b 1981); *Career* actress; seasons at Perth and Liverpool Everyman; *Theatre* incl: Donkey's Years, Hobson's Choice, The Marriage of Figaro (Crucible Sheffield), The Lady from the Sea (Watford), The Cherry Orchard (Oxford Playhouse, Roundhouse), Hamlet (Manchester Royal Exchange, Barbican), Woman in Mind (Leicester Haymarket), Rumours (Chichester Festival), The Two Gentleman of Verona, The Merchant of Venice (Regent's Park), Post Mortem (Soho Poly), Dusa Fish Stas and Vi (Hampstead Mayfair, SWET Award for Best Actress), Incident at Tulse Hill (Hampstead), When She Danced (Globe), Relative Values (Savoy, Chichester Theatre, TMA Award for Best Supporting Actress); RSC: The Merchant of Venice, Much Ado About Nothing, The Lower Depths, Les Liaisons Dangereuses; RNT: For Services Rendered, Brighton Beach Memoirs, The Magistrate, Three Men on a Horse (also Vaudeville), The Night of The Iguana, Pygmalion, Sweet Bird of Youth, The Children's Hour, Absolute Hell, La Grande Magia; *Television* incl: The Roads to Freedom, Helen - A Woman of Today, 'Tis Pity She's A Whore, Tales of the Unexpected, For Services Rendered, The Detective, David Copperfield, Tales from Hollywood, Dr Finlay, Mansfield Park; *Radio* incl: Alceste, The Years, Persuasion; *Recreations* reading, fell walking; *Style—* Miss Alison Fiske; ✉ c/o

Ginette Chalmers, Peters Fraser & Dunlop Ltd, 503 The Chambers, Chelsea Harbour, Lots Road, London SW10 0XF (☎ 0171 344 1010, fax 0171 352 8135)

FISON, Sir (Richard) Guy; 4 Bt (UK 1905), of Greenholme, Burley-in-Wharfedale, West Riding of Yorkshire, DSC (1944); s of Capt Sir (William) Guy Fison, 3 Bt, MC (d 1964); *b* 9 Jan 1917; *Educ* Eton, New Coll Oxford; *m* 28 Feb 1952, Elyn (d 1987), da of Mogens Hartmann, of Bordeaux, and formerly wife of Count Renaud Doria; 1 s (Charles William b 1954), 1 da (Isabelle Frances b 1957); *Heir* s, Charles William Fison b 6 Feb 1954; *Career* Lt RNVR, served Atlantic, N Sea and Channel; dir Saccone and Speed International 1952–83 (sometime chm), non-exec dir Whitehead Mann 1982–84, chm Fine Vintage Wines plc 1986–95; pres Wine and Spirit Assoc of GB 1976–77, chm Wine Devpt Bd 1982–83, dir Wine Standards Bd 1984–87; memb Ct of Assts Worshipful Co of Vintners (Upper Warden 1982–83, Master 1983–84); Master of Wine 1954; *Clubs* MCC; *Style*— Sir Guy Fison, Bt, DSC; ✉ Medwins, Odiham, Hants RG29 1NE (☎ 01256 704075)

FITCH, Adrian Hill; s of Brian Hill Fitch, of Gerrards Cross, Bucks, and Susan Margeret, *née* Edwards; *b* 2 March 1959; *Educ* Merchant Taylors'; *Career* former money broker Tullett & Tokyo Forex International Ltd, currently dir Red Squirrel Company Ltd; *Recreations* squash, shooting, wind surfing, motor cycling, classic car collecting; *Clubs* MG Owners', Jaguar Drivers', RAC; *Style*— Adrian H Fitch, Esq; ✉ 3 King's Avenue, London N10 1PA (☎ 0181 442 0889)

FITCH, Brian Hill; s of Stanley Hill Fitch (d 1961), of Hampstead, and Marjorie Winifred, *née* Browne (d 1988); *b* 19 May 1930; *Educ* Haileybury; *m* 1955, Susan Margaret, da of Rex Edwards, LDS (d 1935), of Scarborough; 1 s (Adrian Hill), 1 da (Judy Susan); *Career* Lloyd's broker 1950–65, md The London & Westminster Property Co Ltd 1965–93 (dir 1956), chm Caledonian Municipal Investments Ltd 1970–80, chm and md The London & Westminster (Sterling Brokers) Ltd 1972–80, licensed dealer in securities 1974–87, md London Finance Agency Ltd 1980–93, underwriting memb Lloyd's 1982–91; memb: Royal Agric Soc of England, Br Assoc for Shooting and Conservation; FInstD; *Recreations* curio and antique collector, vintage and classic motor cars, shooting, swimming; *Clubs* Rolls Royce Enthusiasts'; *Style*— Brian Fitch, Esq; ✉ Grayleigh, St Hubert's Lane, Gerrards Cross, Bucks SL9 7BW (☎ 01753 884702, fax 01753 888302)

FITCH, Colin Digby Thomas; s of Thomas Charles Fitch (d 1993), of Hayling Is, Hampshire, and Grace Leila Fitch; *b* 2 Jan 1934; *Educ* St Paul's, St Catharine's Coll Cambridge (MA, LLM); *m* 15 Dec 1956, Wendy Ann, da of Edward Davis (d 1961); 4 s (Alaric b 1959, Quentin b 1960, Joshua b 1971, Felix b 1972), 1 da (Cressida b 1964); *Career* Nat Serv 1951–53, cmmnd into The Queens Own Royal W Kent Regt 1952; TA 1953–58; called to the Bar Inner Temple 1970, ptnr Rowe and Pitman 1968–76, md Wardley ME Ltd 1976–80, ptnr Grieveson Grant and Co 1980–86, dir Kleinwort Benson Securities Ltd 1986–94; non-exec dir Manders plc 1993–, non-exec dep chm Merrydown plc 1994–; memb Stock Exchange 1968–94, FCIS 1970, FRSA 1987; *Clubs* Brooks's; *Style*— Colin Fitch, Esq; ✉ The Coach House, Royston, Hertfordshire SG8 7DB (☎ 01763 242072); Bouyou, Mayrinhac-Lentour, Gramat, 46500 Lot, France (☎ 00 33 65 38 15 57)

FITCH, (John) Derek; s of John Dowson Fitch (d 1979), and Nora Fitch (d 1984); *b* 22 Sept 1937; *Educ* Rutherford GS Newcastle upon Tyne, Univ of Durham (BA); *m* 22 June 1963, Maureen Rose; 1 s (John Stephen b 1968); *Career* mgmnt conslt; dep chief exec Lombard North Central plc (subsid of National Westminster Bank) 1991–; chm Rover Finance Ltd; dir: Lombard Bank, Lombard Tricity Finance; *Recreations* golf, swimming (ex British record holder); *Style*— Derek Fitch, Esq; ✉ Douglas Cottage, Coombe End, Kingston, Surrey KT2 7DQ (☎ 0181 942 8009); Lombard House, 3 Princess Way, Redhill, Surrey RH1 1NP

FITCH, Douglas Bernard Stocker; s of William Kenneth Fitch (d 1970), and Hilda Alice, *née* Barrington (d 1953); *b* 16 April 1927; *Educ* St Albans Sch, Abbey Gateway St Albans, RAC Cirencester; *m* 1952, Joyce Vera, da of Arthur Robert Griffiths-Cirencester (d 1941), of Glos; 3 s (Christopher b 1958, Simon b 1961, Adrian b 1964); *Career* RE 1944–48; chartered surveyor; dir Land and Water Serv MAFF 1980–87 (ret); RICS: memb Gen Cncl 1980–86, pres Land Agency and Agric Divnl Cncl 1985–86, memb Standing Conf on Marine Resources 1985–91; RAC: memb Bd of Govrs (with responsibility for int liaison) 1986–; prof rural planning and natural resources mgmnt Euro Faculty for Land Use 1988; FRICS, FAAV, MRAC; *Clubs* Farmers, Civil Service; *Style*— Douglas Fitch, Esq; ✉ 71 Oasthouse Crescent, Hale, Farnham, Surrey GU9 0NP (☎ 01252 716742)

FITCH, Rodney Arthur; CBE (1990); s of Arthur Francis Fitch (d 1982), of Wilts, and Ivy Fitch; *b* 19 Aug 1938; *Educ* Willesdon Poly, Sch of Architecture, Central Sch of Arts & Crafts, Hornsey Sch of Art; *m* 28 Aug 1965, Janet Elizabeth, da of Sir Walter Stansfield, CBE, QPM (d 1984); 1 s (Edward b 18 Aug 1978), 4 da (Polly Jane b 27 May 1967, Emily Kate b 18 June 1968, Louisa Claire b 7 Nov 1971, Tessa Grace b 29 Oct 1974); *Career* Nat Serv Pay Corps RA 1958–60; trainee designer Hickman Ltd 1956–58, Charles Kenrick Assoc 1960–62, Conran Design Group Ltd 1962–69, CDG (design conslts) Ltd 1969–71, fndr chm Fitch plc (formerly Fitch RS plc) 1971–94, fndr Rodney Fitch 1994; clients incl Virgin; memb: Design Cncl 1988–94, Governing Cncl RCA 1988–94; dep chm Ct of Govrs London Inst 1989; CSD (formerly SIAD): vice pres 1982–86, hon treas 1984–87, pres 1988–90; pres D&AD Assoc 1983; FRSA 1976; *Recreations* cricket, tennis, opera, theatre, family; *Style*— Rodney Fitch, Esq, CBE; ✉ Rodney Fitch, Northumberland House, 155 Great Portland Street, London W1N 5FB (☎ 0171 580 1331)

FITCHEW, Geoffrey Edward; CMG (1993); s of Stanley Edward Fitchew (d 1976), and Elizabeth, *née* Scott (d 1971); *b* 22 Dec 1939; *Educ* Uppingham, Magdalen Coll Oxford (MA), LSE (MSc); *m* 17 Sept 1966, Mary Theresa, da of Dr Joseph Patrick Spillane (d 1989); 2 s (William Owain b 1971, Benedict Wyndham b 1975); *Career* asst princ HM Treasy 1964, private sec to Perm Sec Dept of Economic Affairs 1966–67; HM Treasy: private sec to Econ Sec 1967–68, asst sec 1975, cnsllr (econ and fin) UK Perm Representation to EC 1978–80, under sec (Euro Communities Gp) 1983–85, under sec (Int Fin Gp) 1985–86; dir gen Directorate-General XV (Fin Instn and Company Law) EC 1986–93, dep sec Cabinet Office 1993–94; chm Building Societies Cmmn 1994–; FRSA; *Recreations* tennis, golf, reading, theatre; *Style*— Geoffrey Fitchew, Esq, CMG; ✉ Building Societies Commission, 15 Great Marlborough Street, London W1V 2LL

FITT, Baron (Life Peer UK 1983), of Bell's Hill, Co Down; Gerard Fitt; s of George Patrick and Mary Ann Fitt; *b* 9 April 1926; *Educ* Christian Brothers Sch Belfast; *m* 1947, Susan Gertrude (Anne), *née* Doherty (d 1996); 5 da (Hon Joan, Hon Eileen, Hon Patsy, Hon Betty, Hon Geraldine) (and 1 da decd); *Career* merchant seaman 1941–53; cncllr Belfast Corp (alderman) 1958–61; MP (Eire Lab) NI for Dock Div of Belfast 1962–72; MP (Repub Lab) Belfast W 1966; dep chief exec NI Exec 1974; fndr and ldr Social Democratic and Lab Pty NI, MP (SDLP) 1970–79, MP (Socialist) Belfast W 1979–83; *Style*— The Rt Hon Lord Fitt; ✉ House of Lords, London SW1A 0PW

FITTALL, William Robert; s of Arthur Fittall (d 1987), and Elsie, *née* Cole; *b* 26 July 1953; *Educ* Dover GS for Boys, ChCh Oxford (MA); *m* 1978, Barbara Staples; 2 s (Jonathan b 1982, Matthew b 1984); *Career* Home Office: joined 1975, private sec to Timothy Raison as Min of State 1979–80, princ 1980; Ecole Nationale d'Administration Paris 1980–81; Broadcasting Dept Home Office 1981–85, private sec to Home Secs Sir Leon Brittan then Douglas Hurd 1985–87, asst sec 1987, sec to Review of Parole System 1987–88, Prison Service HQ 1988–91, princ private sec to Secs of State for NI Peter Brooke then Sir Patrick Mayhew 1992–93, Police Dept Home Office 1993–95, asst under sec of state Cabinet Office 1995–; lay reader C of E 1976–, church organist; *Recreations* playing church organs, watching sport, reading; *Style*— William Fittall, Esq; ✉ Cabinet Office, 70 Whitehall, London SW1A 2AS (☎ 0171 270 0370, fax 0171 930 1419)

FITTER, Richard Sidney Richmond; s of Sidney H Fitter (d 1962), of Banstead, Surrey, and Dorothy Isacke, *née* Pound (d 1926); *b* 1 March 1913; *Educ* Eastbourne Coll, LSE (BSc); *m* 19 April 1938, Alice Mary Stewart (Maisie) (d 1996), da of Dr R Stewart Park (d 1945), of Huddersfield, Yorks; 1 da (Jenny Elizabeth (Mrs Graham) b 1942), 2 s (Julian Richmond b 1944, Alastair Hugh b 1948); *Career* res staff: PEP 1936–40, Mass Observation 1940–42; RAF Ops Res Section Coastal Cmd 1942–45; sec Wild Life Conservation Special Ctee, Miny of Town & Country Planning 1945–46, asst ed The Countryman 1946–59, open air corr The Observer 1958–66, dir Intelligence Unit Cncl for Nature 1959–63; Fauna & Flora International (formerly Fauna Preservation Soc): hon sec 1964–81, vice chm 1981–84, chm 1984–87, vice pres 1987–; Berks Bucks & Oxon Naturalists Tst 1959– (hon sec, vice chm, chm, vice-pres, pres), memb Survival Serv Cmmn Int Union for Conservation of Nature 1963– (chm Steering Ctee 1975–88), tstee and memb Cncl World Wildlife Fund UK 1977–85, memb Falklands Conservation 1972– (hon sec 1979–88, vice chm 1988–92), vice pres Galapagos Conservation Quest 1995–; sometime memb: Cncl RSPB, Royal Soc for Nature Conservation; sci FZS; *Books* London's Natural History (1945), Wildlife for Man (1986), Field Guide to the Countryside in Winter (with Alastair Fitter, 1988), and 28 other books on wildlife (mainly field guides on birds and wild flowers); *Recreations* bird watching, botanising, reading; *Clubs* Athenaeum; *Style*— Richard Fitter; ✉ Drifts, Chinnor Hill, Chinnor, Oxon OX9 4BS (☎ 01844 351223)

FITZ, (Cheryl) Jane; da of Cyril Albert Berwick (d 1987), and Grace, *née* Wagner; *b* 23 Feb 1947; *Educ* Launceston HS Tasmania, Univ of Tasmania (BSc, DipEd), Birkbeck Coll London (BSc, Alexander Silberfield Prize); *m* 26 Aug 1967, Dr John Fitz; 1 da (Emily Rose b 12 Aug 1988); *Career* teacher Sacred Heart Convent Sch Hobart Tasmania 1967–69, supply teacher Surrey CC 1970, computer programmer William Cory & Sons London 1970–71; head of Chemistry: Bromley HS for Girls GPDST 1971–73, S Hampstead HS GPDST (second mistress, third mistress); headmistress: Notting Hill & Ealing HS GPDST 1983–91, Howell's Sch Llandaff Cardiff GPDST 1991–; memb Assoc of Science Educn 1975; FRSA 1988; *Recreations* tennis, theatre, opera, gardening; *Style*— Mrs Jane Fitz; ✉ Howell's School, Cardiff Road, Llandaff, Cardiff (☎ 01222 562019, fax 01222 578879)

FITZALAN HOWARD, Lord Mark; OBE (1994); 4 and yst s of 3 Baron Howard of Glossop, MBE (d 1972), and Baroness Beaumont, OBE (d 1971); bro of 17 Duke of Norfolk, KG, GCVO, CB, CBE, MC, EM; *b* 28 March 1934; *Educ* Ampleforth; *m* 17 Nov 1961, Jacynth Rosemary, o da of Sir Martin Alexander Lindsay of Dowhill, 1 Bt, CBE, DSO; 2 da (Amelia b 1963, Eliza b 1964, m 1987 Timothy Bell); *Career* late Coldstream Gds; dir: Robert Fleming Holdings Ltd 1971–94, Universities Superannuation Scheme Ltd; non-exec dir: several investment tsts, National Mutual Life Assurance Society 1972–; chm Assoc of Investment Trust Cos 1981–83; *Clubs* Brooks's; *Style*— The Lord Mark Fitzalan Howard, OBE; ✉ 13 Campden Hill Square, London W8 7LB (☎ 0171 727 0996, fax 0171 727 0492); Long Leys House, Leys Road, Cumnor, Oxford OX2 9QF (☎ 01865 862687)

FITZALAN HOWARD, Lord Martin; JP (N Riding of Yorks 1966), DL (N Yorks 1982); 3 s of 3 Baron Howard of Glossop, MBE (d 1972), and Baroness Beaumont, OBE; bro of 17 Duke of Norfolk, KG, GCVO, CB, CBE, MC; *b* 22 Oct 1922; *Educ* Ampleforth, Trinity Coll Cambridge; *m* 5 Oct 1948, Bridget Anne, da of late Lt-Col Arnold Ramsay Keppel (fourth in descent from Hon Frederick Keppel, sometime Bishop of Exeter and 4 s of 2 Earl of Albemarle, KG, KB); 1 s, 4 da; *Career* served WWII (wounded), Palestine 1945–46, Capt Gren Gds; High Sheriff N Yorks 1979–80; *Style*— Lord Martin Fitzalan Howard, JP, DL; ✉ 3/E Whittingstall Rd, SW6 (☎ 0171 736 0520); Brockfield Hall, Warthill, York YO3 9XJ (☎ 01904 489298)

FITZALAN HOWARD, Maj-Gen Lord Michael; GCVO (1981, KCVO 1971, MVO 4 Class 1952), kt SMO Malta, CB (1968), CBE (1962, MBE 1949), MC (1944), DL (Wilts 1974); 2 s of 3 Baron Howard of Glossop, MBE, and Baroness Beaumont, OBE (Barony called out of abeyance in her favour 1896); bro of 17 Duke of Norfolk, KG, GCVO, CB, CBE, MC; granted rank of Duke's s 1975; *b* 22 Oct 1916; *Educ* Ampleforth, Trinity Coll Cambridge (MA); *m* 1, 4 March 1946, Jean Marion (d 1947), da of Sir Hew Hamilton-Dalrymple, 9 Bt; 1 da; m 2, 20 April 1950, Jane Margaret (d 1995), yr da of Capt William Patrick Meade Newman; 4 s, 1 da; *Career* served WWII, Scots Gds, Europe and Palestine, subsequently Egypt, Malaya, Germany, GOC London Dist and Maj-Gen cmdg Household Div 1968–71, Marshal Dip Corps 1972–82; Col Life Gds 1979–, Gold Stick to HM The Queen 1979–; pres Cncl TAVR Assocs 1981–84 (chm 1973–81); Freeman City of London 1985; hon recorder Br Cwlth Ex Service League 1992–; *Clubs* Pratt's, Buck's; *Style*— Maj-Gen Lord Michael Fitzalan Howard, GCVO, CB, CBE, MC, DL; ✉ Fovant House, Fovant, Salisbury, Wilts SP3 5LA (☎ 01722 714617)

FITZGERALD, Adrian James Andrew Denis; s and h of Sir George FitzGerald, 5 Bt, MC, 23 Knight of Kerry, *qv*; *b* 24 June 1940; *Educ* Harrow; *Career* hotelier 1983–90; cncllr Royal Borough of Kensington and Chelsea 1974– (mayor 1984–85); chm Educ and Libraries Ctee 1995–; dep ldr London Fire and Civil Def Authy 1989–90, chm Anglo Polish Soc 1989–92, vice chm London Chapter Irish Georgian Soc 1990–; Knight of Honour and Devotion SMOM; *Clubs* Pratt's; *Style*— Adrian FitzGerald, Esq; ✉ 16 Clareville St, London SW7 5AW; Lackaneask, Valentia Island, Co Kerry

FITZGERALD, Christopher Francis; s of Lt Cdr Michael Francis FitzGerald, RN (ret), of Hove, E Sussex, and Anne Lise, *née* Winther; *b* 17 Nov 1945; *Educ* Downside, Lincoln Coll Oxford (MA); *m* 1, 1968 (m dis 1984); 1 s (Matthew b 1973), 2 da (Francesca b 1975, Julia b 1978); m 2, 31 Oct 1986, Jill, da of late Dr Douglas Gordon Freshwater, of Upton-on-Severn, Worcs; 2 step da (Joanna b 1978, Victoria b 1979); *Career* admitted slr 1971; Slaughter and May: ptnr 1976–95, Hong Kong Office 1981–84, exec ptnr fin 1986–90, head of banking 1990–95; gen counsel National Westminster Bank Plc 1995–; *Recreations* travelling, music, reading; *Style*— Christopher FitzGerald, Esq; ✉ 21 Palace Gardens Terrace, London W8 4SA; National Westminster Bank Plc, 41 Lothbury, London EC2P 2BP (☎ 0171 726 1222, fax 0171 726 1846)

FITZGERALD, Rev (Sir) Daniel Patrick; 4 Bt (UK 1903), of Geraldine Place, St Finn Barr, Co Cork, but does not use the title; s of Sir John FitzGerald, 2 Bt, suc bro, Rev (Sir) Edward Thomas FitzGerald (3 Bt) (d 1988); *b* 28 June 1916; *Heir* cousin, John Finnbarr FitzGerald b 1918; *Career* Roman Catholic priest; *Style*— The Rev Daniel FitzGerald; ✉ c/o J F FitzGerald, Esq, Meadowlands, Wilton Road, Cork, Ireland

FITZGERALD, Desmond John Villiers; *see:* Glin, Knight of

FITZGERALD, Dr Frank; CBE (1989); s of George Arthur Fitzgerald (d 1970), and Sarah Ann Brook (d 1974); *b* 11 Nov 1929; *Educ* Barnsley Holgate GS, Univ of Sheffield (BSc (Tech), PhD); *m* 25 Aug 1956, Dorothy Eileen, da of Frederic David Unwin (decd); 2 s, 1 da; *Career* scientific offr Rocket Propulsion Dept Royal Aircraft Estab Westcott Bucks 1955–58, lectr Birmingham Coll of Advanced Technol 1958–60; United Steel Cos (later British Steel Corp, now British Steel plc) 1960–92: head Fuel and Furnace Res Section 1965–70, process res mangr Special Steels Div 1970–72, head Corporate Advanced Process Laboratory 1972–77, dir res and devpt 1977–81, chm BSC (Overseas Servs) Ltd 1981–89, md tech 1981–92, dir British Steel 1986–92, chm British Steel

Stainless 1989–91; currently consulting engr, dir Sheffield Forgemasters Ltd; chm Tech Ctee Int Iron and Steel Inst 1987–90, memb Advsy Cncl on Res Devpt Dept of Trade and Indust 1990–94; Hadfield Medal (Iron and Steel Inst) 1972, Melchett Medal (Inst of Energy) 1988, Bessemer Gold Medal (Inst of Metals) 1991, Esso Energy Award (Royal Soc) 1991, Frank Scott Russell Meml Lecture (Refractories Assoc) 1983, Hatfield Meml Lecture (Univ of Sheffield) 1990; Hon DEng Univ of Sheffield 1993; FEng 1977, FIChemE, FInstE; *Recreations* music, rock climbing, mountaineering; *Clubs* Alpine, Climbers'; *Style—* Dr Frank Fitzgerald, CBE, FEng

FITZGERALD, Dr Garret; s of Desmond FitzGerald (Min of External Affairs Irish Free State 1922–27, Min of Defence 1927–32), and Mabel, *née* McConnell; *b* 9 Feb 1926; *Educ* St Brigid's Sch Bray, Colaiste na Rinne Waterford, Belvedere Coll Dublin, Univ Coll Dublin (BA, PhD), King's Inns Dublin; *m* 1947, Joan, da of late Charles O'Farrell; 2 s, 1 da; *Career* called to the Bar 1946, res and schedules mangr Aer Lingus 1947–58; Rockefeller res asst Trinity Coll Dublin 1958–59, lectr in political economics Univ Coll Dublin 1959–73; memb: Seanad Eireann 1965–69, Dail Eireann 1969–92; min for Foreign Affrs 1973–77, ldr and pres Fine Gael 1977–87, Taoiseach (PM) 1981–82 and 1982–87; pres: Cncl of Mins of EEC Jan-June 1975, Euro Cncl July-Dec 1984, Irish Cncl of Euro Movement 1977–81 and 1982; formerly vice pres Euro People's Pty Euro Parl; formerly Irish corr: BBC, Financial Times, Economist and other overseas papers; formerly econ corr Irish Times; formerly md Economist Intelligence Unit of I; dir: Trade Development Institute, Point International Systems; former dir: Comer International Ireland, GPA; memb: Cncl of State, Royal Irish Acad, Senate National University of Ireland, Action Ctee for Europe, Advsy Bd Centre for Economic Policy Res, Bd Int Peace Acad NY, Radio Telefis Eireann Authy; chm Bd of Patrons Saferworld London; Hon LLD: NY Univ, St Louis Univ, St Mary's Univ of Halifax Canada, Univ of Keele, Boston Coll Mass, Westfield Coll Mass, Univ of Oxford, Nat Univ of Ireland; hon bencher King's Inns Dublin; *Publications* State-Sponsored Bodies (1959), Planning in Ireland (1968), Towards a New Ireland (1972), Unequal Partners (UNCTAD 1979), Estimates for Baronies of Minimum Level of Irish Speaking Amongst Successive Decennial Cohorts 1771–1781 to 1861–1871 (1984), All In A Life (autobiog, 1991); *Style—* Dr Garret FitzGerald; ✉ 30 Palmerston Road, Dublin 6, Ireland (☎ 00 353 1 496 2600, fax 00 353 1 496 2126)

FITZGERALD, Sir George Peter Maurice; 5 Bt (UK 1880), of Valencia, Co Kerry; MC (1944); The 23rd Knight of Kerry (first recorded use of title 1468; The Green Knight); 2, but only surviving s of Capt Sir Arthur Henry Brinsley Fitzgerald, 4 Bt (The 22nd Knight of Kerry) (d 1967), and Mary, *née* Forester; *b* 27 Feb 1917; *Educ* Harrow, RMC Sandhurst; *m* 1939, Angela Dora, da of late Capt James Rankin Mitchell, of 2 Mansfield Street, London W1; 1 s (Adrian James Andrew Denis b 1940), 1 da (Rosanna (Countess Gurowska) b 1945); *Heir* s, Adrian James Andrew Denis Fitzgerald b 24 June 1940; *Career* 2 i/c 1 and 2 Bn Irish Gds, cmmnd 1937, served Palestine 1938 (despatches), served WWII Norway, N Africa, Italy, Maj 1943, ret 1948; *Style—* Sir George Fitzgerald, Bt, MC, The Knight of Kerry; ✉ Colin's Farm House, 55 High Street, Durrington, Salisbury, Wilts SP4 8AQ

FITZGERALD, James Gerard; s of John Fitzgerald (d 1974), and Josephine, *née* Murphy (d 1952); *b* 22 May 1935; *m* 1; 1 s (Timothy John b 1962), 1 da (Lisa Siobhan b 1964); m 2, 22 March 1978, Jane Latta, da of A C Leggat, of Lindsaylands, Biggar, Lanarks; 1 da (Kirsty Isobel b 1985); *Career* racehorse trainer; major races won include: Tote Cheltenham Gold Cup, Power Gold Cup, Vincent O'Brien Irish Gold Cup, Arkle Challenge Trophy Cheltenham, Princess of Wales's Stakes Newmarket, Hennessy Cognac Gold Cup, Tote-Ebor Handicap, Tote Cesarewitch (twice), NBA Northumberland Plate, Sun Alliance Chase Cheltenham, Timeform Chase Haydock (twice), Philip Cornes Saddle of Gold Final Newbury, Wm Hill Scottish Nat Ayr (twice), SGB Chase Ascot, Hermitage Chase Newbury, Coral Golden Hurdle Final Cheltenham, Coral Cup Cheltenham, Victor Chandler Handicap Chase Ascot (twice); best horses trained include: Androma, Barbaroja, Brave Fellow, Bucko, Canny Danny, Danish Flight, Fairy King, Forgive 'n' Forget, Galway Blaze, Kayudee, Meikleour, Sapience, Sybillin, Tickite Boo, Trainglot, Treasure Hunter, Uncle Ernie; *Recreations* shooting; *Style—* James Fitzgerald, Esq; ✉ Norton Grange, Norton, Malton, N Yorkshire YO17 9EA (☎ 01653 692718, fax 01653 600214)

FITZGERALD, Lord John; 2 s of 8 Duke of Leinster by his 2 w Anne, yr da of late Lt-Col Philip Eustace Smith, MC; *b* 3 March 1952; *Educ* Millfield, RMA Sandhurst; *m* 11 Dec 1982, Barbara, eldest da of late Andreas Zindel, of St Moritz, Switzerland; 1 s (Edward b 27 Oct 1988), 1 da (Hermione b 11 Oct 1985); *Career* Capt 5 Royal Inniskilling Dragoon Gds; racehorse trainer, racing admin; *Recreations* shooting, fishing, golf; *Clubs* Turf; *Style—* Lord John FitzGerald; ✉ PO Box 1178, Dubai, United Arab Emirates (☎ 00 971 4 313311, fax 00 971 4 313322)

FITZGERALD, Kate; da of Mark Walsh, of Liverpool, and Eileen, *née* Collins; *Educ* Notre Dame Collegiate Sch Liverpool, The Drama Centre; *Career* actress; worked extensively on the fringe in various theatre cos incl: Women's Theatre Gp, 7.84; fndr Lighthouse Theatre Co; *Theatre* RSC incl: Children of the Sun, Wild Oats, Once in a Lifetime, Men's Beano, Captain Swing; Liverpool Playhouse incl: Ladies in Waiting, April 1st Show, Blood on the Dole, Stags and Hens, Skirmishes, Educating Rita; Nottingham Playhouse incl: Lady Macbeth in Macbeth, Raymonde in A Flea in her Ear, Dunyasha in The Cherry Orchard; Maggie in Dancing at Lughnasa (Garrick and nat tour), Linda in Blood Brothers (Lyric), Shirley Valentine (Duke of Yorks and tour); most recently incl: Doris in Same Time Next Year (nat tour), Two (Liverpool Everyman), Confusions (nat tour); *Television* incl: Daughters of Albion, The Tempest, Call Collect, Casualty, The Bill, Doreen Corkhill in Brookside; *Recreations* swimming, travelling, reading, films, theatre, concerts; *Clubs* Portobello Green; *Style—* Kate Fitzgerald; ✉ c/o Saraband Associates, 265 Liverpool Road, London N1 1LX (☎ 0171 609 5313, fax 0171 609 2370)

FITZGERALD, Michael Frederick Clive; QC (1980); s of late Sir William James FitzGerald MC, QC, and late Erica Critchley, *née* Clarke; *b* 9 June 1936; *Educ* Downside, Christ's Coll Cambridge (MA); *m* 1966 (m dis 1992), Virginia Grace, da of Col William Sturmy Cave, DSO, TD (d 1953); 1 s (Hamilton b 14 March 1971), 3 da (Emma Grace b 2 Feb 1967, Charlot Grace b 7 June 1968, Harriet Grace b 11 Aug 1969); *Career* 2 Lt 9 Queen's Royal Lancers 1954–56, called to the Bar Middle Temple 1961, Master of the Bench 1987, head of chambers; *Recreations* opera, fishing, shooting; *Clubs* Athenaeum, Boodle's; *Style—* Michael FitzGerald, Esq, QC; ✉ 2 Mitre Court Buildings, Temple, London EC4Y 7BX (☎ 0171 583 1380, fax 0171 353 7772)

FITZGERALD, Michael John; s of Albert William Fitzgerald (d 1980), of Dynerth, Heather Lane, West Chiltington, and Florence Margaret Fitzgerald, *née* Stannard (d 1981); *b* 14 May 1935; *Educ* Caterham Sch; *m* 9 June 1962, Judith-Ann, da of Dr A C Boyle, of The Barn, Iping; 2 s (Alistair b 1964, Malcolm b 1966), 1 da (Aimee-Louise b 1970); *Career* CA; vice pres and gen mangr Occidental International (Libya) Inc 1985, exec vice pres Occidental International Oil Inc 1987; dir: Canadian Occidental North Sea Petroleum Ltd, Langham Publishing Ltd; md OVP Associates Ltd 1996–; dir Arundale Sch Tst; MInstPet, MInstD; *Recreations* golf, gardening, cricket, opera; *Clubs* West Sussex Golf, Travellers'; *Style—* Michael J Fitzgerald, Esq; ✉ Fir Tops, Grove Lane, West Chiltington, W Sussex RH20 2RD (☎ 01798 812258); OVP Associates Ltd, 3 Beeston Place, London SW1W 0JJ (☎ 0171 828 5700)

FITZGERALD, Dr Michael Richard (Mike); s of Richard Michael Fitzgerald, and Janet Kilpatrick Costine Fitzgerald; *b* 4 May 1951; *Educ* St Mary's Coll Crosby Liverpool, Selwyn Coll Cambridge (MA), Univ of Leicester (PhD); *m* 2 s (Paul Kumar b 6 March 1973, Daniel Arthur Lentell b 19 July 1983); *Career* tutorial asst Univ of Leicester 1973–75, sr lectr then dean and dir of studies Social Sciences Open Univ 1975–87, dep dir Coventry Poly 1987–91, vice-chllr Thames Valley Univ 1991–; FRSA 1991; *Books* author of eight books on criminology and penology; *Recreations* football, cricket, golf, sleeping, rock music; *Clubs* Reform, Chelsea Arts; *Style—* Dr Mike Fitzgerald; ✉ Thames Valley University, St Mary's Road, Ealing, London W5 5RF (☎ 0181 231 2204, fax 0181 231 2937)

FITZGERALD, Niall William Arthur; s of William FitzGerald (d 1972), and Doreen, *née* Chambers; *b* 13 Sept 1945; *Educ* St Munchins Coll Limerick, Univ Coll Dublin (MCom); *m* 2 March 1970, Monica Mary, da of John Cusack (d 1985); 2 s (Colin b 30 Jan 1976, Aaron b 24 March 1982), 1 da (Tara b 5 Dec 1973); *Career* Unilever plc: joined Unilever Ireland as accountant 1967, various positions with subsids Paul & Vincent, Lever Bros Ireland and W & C McDonnell, Unilever Head Office London 1972–76 (PA to fin dir 1974–76), overseas commercial offr 1976–78, commercial offr N American ops 1978–80, fin dir Unilever South Africa (Pty) Ltd 1980–92, md Van den Bergh & Jurgens (Pty) Ltd S Africa 1982–85, gp treas London 1985–86, fin dir 1986–89, main bd dir Unilever plc and Unilever NV 1987–, edible fats and dairy co-ordinator 1989–90, detergents co-ordinator 1991–95, vice chm 1994–95, exec chm 1996–; non-exec dir: Prudential Corporation plc 1993–, Bank of Ireland; former memb: Cncl of Assoc of Corp Treasurers, Accounting Standards Review Ctee, Fin and Industry Ctee NEDC, Int Policy Cncl for Agriculture and Trade; memb Cncl Co-operation Ireland; FCT 1986, FRSA; *Recreations* opera, running, golf, and an active family; *Clubs* RAC, Wisley Golf; *Style—* Niall FitzGerald, Esq; ✉ Unilever plc, PO Box 68, Unilever House, Blackfriars, London EC4P 4BQ (☎ 0171 822 5252)

FITZGERALD, Penelope Mary; da of Edmund Valpy George Knox (poet and ed of Punch, d 1971), and Christina Frances, *née* Hicks (d 1934); *b* 17 Dec 1916; *Educ* Wycombe Abbey, Somerville Coll Oxford (BA 1938); *m* 15 Aug 1942, Desmond John Lyon Fitzgerald, MC, s of Thomas Fitzgerald (d 1960); 1 s ((Edmund) Valpy b 1947), 2 da (Christina Rose b 1950, Maria b 1953); *Career* writer; winner Heywood Hill Literary Award 1996; FRSL 1989; *Biography* Edward Burne-Jones (1975), The Knox Brothers (1977), Charlotte Mew and her Friends (1984, Br Acad Mary Rose Crawshay award); *Fiction* The Golden Child (1977), The Bookshop (1978), Offshore (1979, Booker McConnell Award for Fiction), Human Voices (1980), At Freddies (1982), Innocence (1986), The Beginning of Spring (1988), The Gate of Angels (1990), The Blue Flower (1996); *Style—* Mrs Penelope Fitzgerald, FRSL; ✉ c/o HarperCollins, 77–85 Fulham Palace Rd, Hammersmith, London W6 8JB

FITZGERALD, Peter Gilbert; OBE (1993); s of P H FitzGerald (d 1995), and Hilda Elizabeth, *née* Clark; *b* 13 Feb 1946; *Educ* Harvey GS Folkestone; *m* 5 Dec 1970, Elizabeth Thora, da of F L Harris (d 1970), of Cornwall; 1 s (Timothy b 24 Oct 1973); *Career* CA; dir Valor Vanguard Ltd 1965–66, md FitzGerald Lighting Ltd 1980– (dir 1973–80); dir Bodmin & Wenford Railway plc 1985–; chm: E Cornwall Business Link, Cornwall Economic Forum 1992–; FCA 1972; *Recreations* cycling, walking, transport; *Style—* Peter G FitzGerald, Esq, OBE; ✉ FitzGerald Lighting Ltd, Normandy Way, Bodmin, Cornwall (☎ 01208 75611, fax 01208 74893)

FITZGERALD, Dr Richard; s of Dr Patrick Fitzgerald, of Cork, Eire, and Mary, *née* O'Donnell; *b* 14 May 1955; *Educ* Christian Brothers' Coll Cork Eire, Univ Coll Cork NUI (MB BCh, BAO); *Career* house offr Cork Regnl Hosp 1979–81, registrar then sr registrar West Midlands Radiology Trg Scheme Birmingham 1981–86, conslt radiologist to Wolverhampton Hosps 1986–; FRCR 1985, memb BIR; *Recreations* swimming, hillwalking, cinema; *Clubs* Shifnal Squash and Swimming; *Style—* Dr Richard Fitzgerald; ✉ 10 Meadway, Silvermere Park, Shifnal, Shropshire TF11 9QB (☎ 01952 461729); X-Ray Department, New Cross Hospital, Wolverhampton WV10 0QP (☎ 01902 307999)

FITZGERALD, Tara Anne Cassandra; da of Michael Callaby (d 1979), and Sarah Geraldine Fitzgerald; *b* 18 Sept 1967; *Educ* Walsingham Girls' Sch, The Drama Centre London; *Career* actress; *Theatre* incl: Angela Caxton in Our Song (Apollo and Bath Theatre Royal) 1992/93, Ophelia in Hamlet (Hackney Empire and Belasco Theatre NY); *Television* incl: Victoria Mordaunt in The Black Candle (Tyne Tees), Polly Cuthbertson in The Camomile Lawn (Channel 4) 1992, Dolly Stokesay in Anglo-Saxon Attitudes (Thames), The Step-daughter in Six Characters in Search of An Author (BBC 2), Catherine Pradier in Fall from Grace (SkyTV) 1994, Poppy Carew in The Vacillations of Poppy Carew (Carlton) 1994; *Film* incl: Nancy Doyle in Hear My Song 1992, Estella Campion in Sirens 1993, Adele Rice in A Man of no Importance 1994, Betty from Cardiff in The Englishman Who Went Up a Hill But Came Down a Mountain 1994; *Awards* Drama Desk Award for outstanding featured actress in a play (for Hamlet); *Recreations* music, cinema, painting, friends, restaurants; *Clubs* The Soho House; *Style—* Ms Tara Fitzgerald; ✉ Caroline Dawson Associates, Apartment 9, 47 Courtfield Road, London SW7 4DB (☎ 0171 370 0708, fax 0171 835 1403)

FITZGIBBON, Louis Theobald Dillon; Comte Dillon in France; s of Lt Cdr Robert Francis Dillon FitzGibbon, RN (d 1954), and Kathleen Clare, *née* Atcheson (d 1950); *b* 6 Jan 1925; *Educ* St Augustine's Abbey Sch Ramsgate, RNC Dartmouth, Univ of London Sch of Eastern European and Slavonic Studies (for Nav Polish Interpreters' Course); *m* 1, 1950 (m dis 1962), Josephine Miriam Maud Webb; m 2, 15 Aug 1962, Madeleine Sally Hayward-Surry (d 1980); 1 s (James b 7 Nov 1963), 2 da (Simone b 16 Nov 1962, Michèle b 24 April 1965); m 3, 12 Sept 1980 (m dis 1994), Joan Elizabeth Jevons; *Career* Midshipman RN 1942, Sub Lt 1944, Lt 1946, Lt Cdr (ret) 1954; dir De Leon Properties Ltd 1954–72; hon sec Jt Ctee for Preservation of Historic Portsmouth 1959–61; slrs' articled clerk 1960–63; Anglo-Polish Conf Warsaw 1963; PA to Rt Hon Duncan Sandys, MP (later Lord Duncan-Sandys) 1967–68; gen sec Br Cncl for Aid to Refugees 1968–72; UN Mission to S Sudan 1972–73; dir of a med charity 1974–76; exec offr Nat Assoc for Freedom 1977–78; gen sec of a trade assoc 1978–80; memb several missions to: Somalia 1978–85, Sudan and Egypt 1982, Sudan, German Parl, Euro Parl 1984, UN 1984, 1986, 1987, 1988, 1989 and 1995, Sudan and Libya 1991–92, Sudan 1995; author of reports and contribs to int and nat jls, contrib reports to Br and other govts, EC and UN; memb: RIIA 1982 and 1988, Anglo-Somali Soc; hon sec Katyn Meml Fund 1971–77; hon sec Br Horn of Africa Cncl 1984–92; elected guest memb Sudan People's Int Friendship Cncl 1991; won first Airey Neave Meml scholarship 1981; area pres St John Ambulance Bde (Hants East) 1974–76; Sovereign Mil and Hospitaller Order of Malta: Kt of Honour and Devotion 1972, Officer of Merit 1985; Polish Gold Cross of Merit 1969; Order of Polonia Restituta (Polish govt in exile): Offr 1971, Cdr 1972, Kt Cdr 1976; Katyn Meml medal Bronze (USA) 1977, Laureate van de Arbeid (Netherlands) 1982, Officer Order of Merit (Germany) 1990; *Books* Katyn - A Crime without Parallel (1971), The Katyn Cover-up (1972), Unpitied and Unknown (1975), Katyn - Triumph of Evil (Ireland 1975), The Katyn Memorial (1976), Katyn Massacre (paper 1977, 3rd edn 1989) Katyn (USA 1979), Katyn (in German 1979), The Betrayal of the Somalis (1982), Straits and Strategic Waterways in the Red Sea (1984), Ethiopia Hijacks the Hijack (1985), The Evaded Duty (1985); *Recreations* travel, politics, writing, reading, history, languages, refugee problems, Horn of Africa affairs, Islamic matters; *Style—* Louis FitzGibbon, Esq; ✉ 8 Portland Place, Brighton BN2 1DG (☎ and fax 01273 685661)

FITZHARRIS, Viscount; James Carleton Harris; s and h of 6 Earl of Malmesbury; *b* 19 June 1946; *Educ* Eton, Queen's Coll Univ of St Andrews (MA); *m* 14 June 1969, Sally Ann, da of Sir Richard Newton Rycroft, 7 Bt; 3 s (Hon James, Hon Edward b 1972, Hon Guy b 1975), 2 da (Hon Frances b 1979, Hon Daisy b 1981); *Heir* s, Hon James Hugh Carleton Harris b 29 April 1970; *Style—* Viscount FitzHarris; ✉ Greywell Hill, Greywell, Hook, Hampshire RG29 1DB (☎ 01256 703565, fax 01256 701658)

FITZHERBERT, Giles Eden; CMG (1985); er s of Capt Henry Charles Hugh FitzHerbert, Irish Gds, and Sheelah, *née* Murphy; *b* 8 March 1935; *Educ* Ampleforth, ChCh Oxford; *m* 1, 1962, Margaret (d 1986), da of Evelyn Waugh; 2 s, 3 da; m 2, 1988, Alexandra, *née* Eyre; 3 s, 1 da; *Career* 2 Lt 8 King's Royal Irish Hussars; with Vickers da Costa & Co 1962; fought Fermanagh and S Tyrone in Lib interest 1964; HM Dip Serv: first sec Rome 1968–71, cnsllr Kuwait 1975–77 and Nicosia 1977–78, head Euro Community Dept (External) FCO 1978–81, sabbatical year 1982, inspr 1983, min Rome 1983–87, ambass Caracas 1988–93, ret 1993; *Clubs* Beefsteak, Kildare St and Univ (Dublin); *Style—* Giles FitzHerbert, Esq, CMG; ✉ Fenagh Rectory, Co Carlow, Ireland

FITZHERBERT, Sir Richard Ranulph; 9 Bt (GB 1784), of Tissington, Derbyshire; o s of Rev David Henry FitzHerbert, MC (d 1976), and Charmian Hyacinthe, da of late Samuel Ranulph Allsopp, CBE, DL; suc his uncle, Sir John Richard Frederick FitzHerbert, 8 Bt 1989; *b* 2 Nov 1963; *Educ* Eton; *m* 17 April 1993, Caroline Louise, da of Maj Patrick Shuter, of Grangefield House, Tetbury, Glos; 1 s (Frederick David b 23 March 1995); *Heir* s, Frederick David FitzHerbert b 23 March 1995; *Career* pres: Derbyshire Community Fndn 1995–, Derbyshire Rural Community Cncl 1995–, Ashbourne Heritage Soc 1995–; *Clubs* Bachelor's, MCC, White's, Stansted Hall CC, Parwich RBLCC; *Style—* Sir Richard FitzHerbert, Bt; ✉ Tissington Hall, Ashbourne, Derbyshire DE6 1RA

FITZHERBERT-BROCKHOLES, Francis Joseph; eldest s of Michael John Fitzherbert-Brockholes, *qv*; *b* 18 Sept 1951; *Educ* Oratory Sch, CCC Oxford (MA); *m* 7 May 1983, Jennifer, da of Geoffrey George Watts, of Grassdale, Wandering, W Aust; 2 s (Thomas Antony b 8 Nov 1985, George Frederick b 1 March 1988), 1 da (Susannah Louise b 23 Feb 1984); *Career* called to the Bar 1975; in chambers Manchester 1976–77; assoc: Cadwalader Wickersham & Taft 1977–78, White & Case 1978–85 (ptnr 1985–); admitted New York Bar 1978; *Style—* Francis Fitzherbert-Brockholes, Esq; ✉ White & Case, 7–11 Moorgate, London EC2R 6HH (☎ 0171 726 6361, fax 0171 726 8558, telex 884757)

FITZHERBERT-BROCKHOLES, Michael John; OBE (1989), JP (Lancashire 1960), DL (1975); s of John William Fitzherbert-Brockholes, CBE, MC, JP, DL (d 1963), sometime Privy Chamberlain of Sword and Cape to Pope Pius XI, and Hon Eileen French, da of 4 Baron de Freyne; the Brockholes have been seated at Claughton since the 14 century and the estate passed through female descent to the Hesketh s in 1751 and from them to the Fitzherberts in 1783, when William Fitzherbert assumed the additional surname and arms of Brockholes (*see* Burke's Landed Gentry, 18 edn, vol II, 1969); *b* 12 June 1920; *Educ* Oratory Sch, New Coll Oxford; *m* 28 Sept 1950, Mary Edith, da of Capt Charles Joseph Henry O'Hara Moore, CVO, MC, late Irish Guards (d 1965), of Mooresfort, Co Tipperary, by his w Lady Dorothie Feilding, da of 9 Earl of Denbigh, GCVO; 4 s (Francis Joseph b 18 Sept 1951, *qv*, Antony John b 23 Nov 1952, Simon Peter b 15 March 1955, William Andrew Charles b 1 Dec 1958); *Career* Maj Scots Gds (Italy and N W Europe) 1940–46; memb Lancashire CC 1967–89 (chm Education Ctee 1977–81); Vice Lord-Lieut Lancs 1977–95; Constable of Lancaster Castle 1995–; Knight of St Gregory 1978, OStJ; *Recreations* gardening; *Style—* Michael Fitzherbert-Brockholes, Esq, OBE, JP, DL; ✉ Claughton Hall, Garstang, nr Preston, Lancashire (☎ 01995 640286)

FITZHUGH, (Edmund Francis) Lloyd; OBE (1995), JP (Wrexham) 1990, DL (Clwyd) 1994; s of Godfrey Edmund FitzHugh (d 1985), of Plas Power, Wrexham, and Burness Grace, *née* Clemson; *b* 2 Feb 1951; *Educ* Eton, Shuttleworth Agricultural Coll; *m* 13 Sept 1975, Pauline, *née* Davison; 2 s (Tristam Edmund b 20 March 1978, Benjamin Lloyd b 24 Jan 1981); *Career* farmer and landowner; chm Bd of Mgmnt Royal Welsh Agricultural Soc 1991–, vice chm Local Govt Boundary Cmmn for Wales 1995–, chm Gofal Cymuned Clwydian Community Care NHS Tst; *Recreations* church music; *Style—* Lloyd FitzHugh, Esq, OBE, JP, DL; ✉ Plas Power, Ruthin Road, Wrexham LL11 3BS (☎ 01978 263522, fax 01978 263522, mobile 0468 531909)

FITZPATRICK, Anthony James; s of James Matthew Fitzpatrick, of London, and Ornella, *née* Corti (d 1992); *b* 9 June 1951; *Educ* St Bonaventure's GS, Univ of Leeds (Holst prize, BSc); *m* 1972, Janet, da of Willian Turnbull; 3 da (Sarah Helen b 1982, Kristina Matthea b 1984, Alexandra Jessica b 1986), 1 s (Nicholas James b 1990); *Career* Ove Arup and Partners: London 1972–73, Newcastle 1973–75, Tehran 1975–79, assoc London 1979–82, project dir Hong Kong 1982–86 (sr structural engr 1985–86), dir London 1986–, involved in estab New York office 1988–90; buildings incl: Hong Kong and Shanghai Bank 1982–85, Century Tower Tokyo 1986–87, Barcelona Tower 1987–88, Tour Sans Fins Paris 1989–; Telford medal ICE 1988; MIStructE 1979, memb Hong Kong Inst of Engrs 1982, FEng 1993; *Recreations* children, food, rough bicycling (sometimes all 3 together); *Style—* Anthony Fitzpatrick, Esq, FEng; ✉ Ove Arup & Partners, 13 Fitzroy Street, London W1P 6BQ (☎ 0171 636 1531, fax 0171 465 3675)

FITZPATRICK, (Gen) Sir (Geoffrey Richard) Desmond; GCB (1971, KCB 1965, CB 1961), GCVO (1997), DSO (1945), MBE (1942), MC (1940); o s of Brig-Gen Sir (Ernest) Richard Fitzpatrick, CBE, DSO (d 1949), and Georgina Ethel, *née* Robison; *b* 14 Dec 1912; *Educ* Eton, RMC Sandhurst; *m* 22 April 1944, Mary Sara (d 1996), o da of Sir Charles Campbell, 12 Bt, of Auchinbreck (d 1948); 1 s (Brian Richard Charles b 1950), 1 da (Sara Georgina (Mrs R Stewart Whittington) b 1948); *Career* Royal Dragoons 1932, served Palestine 1938–40 (MC), Middle E, Italy and NW Europe 1941–45 (despatches, DSO, MBE), Brevet Lt-Col 1951, Col 1953, ADC to HM the Queen 1959, Asst Chief of Def Staff (Maj-Gen) 1959–61, Dir of Mil Ops, WO 1962–63, COS BAOR 1964–65, GOCIC NI Cmd 1965–66, Lt-Gen 1965, Vice CGS 1966–68, C in C BAOR and Cdr NAG 1968–70, Gen 1968, Dep Supreme Cdr Allied Forces Europe 1970–74; Lt-Govr and C-in-C Jersey 1974–79; Dep Col Blues and Royals 1969–74, Col 1979–, Gold Stick to the Queen 1979–; Col Cmdt RAC 1971–74; *Recreations* sailing, shooting; *Clubs* RYS, Cavalry and Guards', Bucks; *Style—* Sir Desmond Fitzpatrick, GCB, GCVO, DSO, MBE, MC; ✉ Belmont, Otley, Ipswich, Suffolk IP6 9PF (☎ 01473 890 206)

FITZPATRICK, James Bernard; CBE (1983), DL (1985), JP (1977); s of Bernard Arthur Fitzpatrick (d 1963), and Jessie Emma, *née* Blunt; *b* 21 April 1930; *Educ* Bootle GS, Univ of London (LLB); *m* 2 Sept 1965, Rosemary, da of Capt Edward Burling Clark, RD, RNR, of Glust Hendre, N Wales; 1 s (Simon b 1967), 1 da (Susan b 1970); *Career* chm: Mersey Docks and Harbour Co 1984–87 (md 1977–84), Liverpool Health Authy 1986–91, Royal Liverpool Univ Hosp NHS Tst 1991–; dir: Plan Invest plc 1984–91, Teeside Holdings 1992–95; *Recreations* fell walking, gardening; *Clubs* Oriental, Pilgrims; *Style—* James Fitzpatrick, Esq, CBE, DL, JP; ✉ 57 Hilbre Road, West Kirby, Wirral L48 3HB (☎ 0151 625 9612); Royal Liverpool Hospital, Prescot Street, Liverpool L7 8XP (☎ 0151 706 2000)

FITZPATRICK, Air Marshal Sir John Bernard; KBE (1984), CB (1982); s of Joseph Fitzpatrick (d 1946), and Bridget Fitzpatrick (d 1985); *b* 15 Dec 1929; *Educ* RAF App Sch Halton, RAF Coll Cranwell; *m* 1954, Gwendoline Mary, da of Edwin Abbott; 2 s, 1 da; *Career* RAF offr: SASO HQ Strike Cmd 1980–82, Air Marshal 1983, AOC No 18 Gp 1983–86; independent inspr Dept of Tport and DOE 1986–; *Recreations* reading, popular music, DIY; *Clubs* RAF; *Style—* Sir John Fitzpatrick, KBE, CB

FITZPATRICK, Dr Kieran Thomas Joseph; s of Kieran Gerard Fitzpatrick (d 1966), of Strabane, Co Tyrone, and Margaret, *née* Ohle; *b* 23 March 1954; *Educ* Christian Brothers' GS, Omagh and St Coleman's HS Strabane, Queen's Univ Belfast (MB BCh, BAO); *m* 24 Feb 1986, Elizabeth Maureen, da of Robert McKee; 2 da (Laura Jane b 25 Feb 1987, Lucy Claire b 11 May 1990), 1 s (Andrew Kieran b 24 April 1989); *Career* jr house offr Belfast City Hosp 1979–80, SHO (anaesthetics) Belfast City Hosp 1980–81; registrar (anaesthetics): Ulster Hosp Dundonald 1981–82, Belfast City Hosp 1982–83, Coleraine Hosp 1983–85; sr registrar (anaesthetics) Royal Victoria Hosp Belfast 1985–86, sr tutor Dept of Anaesthetics Queen's Univ Belfast 1986–87, res fell Royal Belfast Hosp for Sick Children 1987–88, conslt anaesthetist Belfast City Hosp 1988–; memb: BMA 1980, Assoc of Anaesthetists of GB and I 1980, NI Soc of Anaesthetists, Anaesthetic Research Soc 1986, Obstetric Anaesthetists Assoc 1986; FFARCSI 1983; *Recreations* gardening, walking and my family; *Style—* Dr Kieran Fitzpatrick; ✉ 171 Killinchy Road, Comber, Co Down, BT23 5NE (☎ 01238 542357); Department of Clinical Anaesthesia, Belfast City Hospital, 97 Lisburn Road, Belfast BT9 7AB (☎ 01232 329241 ext 3084)

FITZPATRICK, (Francis) Michael John; s of Francis Latimer FitzPatrick (d 1982), of E Bergholt, Suffolk, and Kathleen Margaret, *née* Gray; *b* 14 July 1938; *Educ* Brentwood Sch; *m* 4 April 1964, Patricia Hilbery, OBE, da of Sir George Frederick Chaplin, CBE, DL, JP (d 1975), of Great Warley, Essex; 1 s (Richard b 1965), 1 da (Kathryn b 1967); *Career* chartered surveyor, conslt Messrs Hilbery Chaplin; Freeman City of London, Liveryman Worshipful Co of Chartered Surveyors; FRICS; *Recreations* music, travel, wine, gardening; *Clubs* Royal Over-Seas League; *Style—* Michael FitzPatrick, Esq; ✉ Wood House, Stratford St Mary, Suffolk CO7 6LU; 19 Eastern Rd, Romford, Essex (☎ 01708 745004)

FITZPATRICK, Nicholas David; s of Prof Reginald Jack Fitzpatrick, of Norwoods, Rectory Lane, Heswall, Wirral, Merseyside, and Ruth, *née* Holmes; *b* 23 Jan 1947; *Educ* Bristol GS, Nottingham Univ (BA); *m* 23 Aug 1969, (Patricia) Jill, da of Peter Conway Brotherton; 1 s (Daniel b 12 Jan 1976), 1 da (Paula b 14 Dec 1973); *Career* trainee analyst Friends Provident 1969–72, equity mangr Abbey Life 1972–76, equity mangr then investmt mangr BR Pension Fund 1976–86, ptnr and investmt specialist Bacon & Woodrow 1986–; AMIIMR 1972, FIA 1974; *Recreations* rugby, woodwork; *Style—* Nicholas Fitzpatrick, Esq; ✉ Sommarlek, Woodhurst Park, Oxted, Surrey (☎ 01883 717927); Bacon & Woodrow, St Olafs House, London Bridge City, London SE1 2PE (☎ 0171 357 7171)

FITZROY, Lord Edward Anthony Charles; DL (Norfolk 1986); s of 10 Duke of Grafton (d 1970), and his 2 wife Lucy Eleanor, *née* Barnes (d 1943); *b* 26 Aug 1928; *Educ* Eton, RMA Sandhurst; *m* 26 April 1956, Veronica Mary, da of Maj Robert Francis Ruttledge, MC, of Doon, Newcastle Greystones, Co Wicklow; 1 s (Michael b 1958), 2 da (Joanna b 1957, Shauna b 1963); *Career* joined Coldstream Gds 1948, Capt 1954, ret 1955; chm Ross Poultry Ltd 1969–75, chm and md Imperial Foods International Technical Services 1975–82; dir: Imperial Foods Ltd 1969–82, Ross Breeders Ltd 1982–95; promoter DTI 1993–95; chm Caledonian Cartridge Co 1987–; High Sheriff of Norfolk 1987; chm of govrs Wymondham Coll, tstee TSB Charitable Fndn; *Recreations* shooting, fishing, gardening, travel; *Clubs* Norfolk (Norwich); *Style—* The Lord Edward FitzRoy, DL; ✉ Norton House, Norwich, Norfolk NR14 6RY (☎ 01508 548303, fax 01508 548553)

FITZROY, Hon Edward Charles; o surviving s and h of 6 Baron Southampton, *qv*; *b* 8 July 1955; *Educ* Gresham's Sch Holt, RAC Cirencester; *m* 30 March 1978, Rachel Caroline Vincent, 2 da of Peter John Curnow Millett, of West Underdown, Drewsteignton, Devon; 1 s (Charles Edward Millett b 18 Jan 1983), 3 da (Fiona Joan Margaret b 24 Nov 1979, Sarah Barbara Sibell b 12 April 1981, Julia Rachel Caroline b 6 Nov 1984); *Recreations* painting, books, tennis, golf, riding, shooting, fishing; *Style—* The Hon Edward FitzRoy; ✉ Venn Farm, Morchard Bishop, Crediton, Devon EX17 6SQ

FITZROY NEWDEGATE, Hon James Edward; s and h of 3 Viscount Daventry, JP, DL; *b* 27 July 1960; *Educ* Milton Abbey, RAC Cirencester; *m* 10 Sept 1994, Georgia, yr da of John Stuart Lodge, of Daglingworth Place, Cirencester, Glos; 1 s (Humphrey John b 23 Nov 1995); *Career* dir Penrose Forbes Ltd; *Recreations* shooting, fishing, racing, golf, farming, occasional gardening; *Clubs* White's, Turf, Royal Automobile; *Style—* The Hon James FitzRoy Newdegate; ✉ 17 Rosenau Road, London SW11 4QN

FITZSIMONS, Prof James Thomas; s of Robert Allen Fitzsimons, FRCS, and Dr Mary Patricia Fitzsimons, *née* McKelvey; *b* 8 July 1928; *Educ* St Edmund's Coll Ware, Gonville and Caius Coll Cambridge (MB BChir, MA, PhD, MD, ScD); *m* 1961, Aude Irène Jeanne, da of Gén Jean Etienne Valluy, DSO; 2 s, 1 da; *Career* house appts Leicester Gen and Charing Cross Hosps 1954–55; Flight Lt RAF Inst of Aviation Med 1955–57; Univ of Cambridge: MRC scholar Physiological Lab 1957–59, demonstrator in physiology 1959–64, lectr 1964–76, reader 1976–90, prof of med physiology 1990–95, emeritus prof 1995; Gonville and Caius Coll Cambridge: fell 1961–, tutor 1964–72, lectr in physiology 1964–93, dir of studies in med 1978–93; memb: Physiological Soc Ctee 1972–76 (chm 1975–76), IUPS Cmmn on Physiology of Food and Fluid Intake 1973–80 (chm 1979–80); Royal Soc rep British Nat Ctee for Physiological Scis 1976–80; ed Biological Reviews 1984–; Hon MD Lausanne 1978; FRS 1988; *Books* The Physiology of Thirst and Sodium Appetite (1979), author of scientific papers in professional jls; *Style—* Prof James Fitzsimons, FRS; ✉ Physiological Laboratory, Downing Street, Cambridge CB2 3EG (☎ 01223 333836)

FITZSIMONS, Patrick Anthony (Tony); *b* 16 March 1946; *Educ* St Phillips GS Birmingham, LSE (BSc); *m* Ruth; 2 s; *Career* formerly with Esso, Chrysler then Perkins Engines Ltd; Rank Xerox: joined 1970, in Australia 1972–75, Southern Europe 1975–76, Middle East 1976–79, regnl control dir London 1979–81; Grand Metropolitan plc: financial, systems and strategy dir Brewing and Retail Div 1981–83, md Host Group (under Chef & Brewer and Open House identities) 1983–85; md personal banking Citibank London 1985–89, md and chief exec Bristol & West Building Society 1989–93, conslt 1993–; memb Diary Ctee Duke of Edinburgh's Award Scheme; CIMgt, FRSA; *Recreations* squash, polo, antiques, music, sailing; *Clubs* Lord's Taverners; *Style—* Tony FitzSimons, Esq

FITZWALTER, 21 Baron (E 1295); (Fitzwalter) Brook Plumptre; JP (Kent 1949); s of George Beresford Plumptre (d 1934), yr bro of 20 Baron (d 1932, but the present Lord FitzWalter was not summoned to Parl till 1953); Lord FitzWalter is eleventh in descent from Frances, w of Sir Thomas Mildmay and half sis of 3 Earl of Sussex (whose 2 w Frances, da of Sir William Sydney, of Penshurst, left £5,000 to establish a Cambridge Coll to be called 'Sydney Sussex'); Frances was twelfth in descent from Robert FitzWalter, the leading enforcer among the Barons of Magna Carta; by his w (and 1st cousin) Mary Augusta, *née* Plumptre (d 1953); *b* 15 Jan 1914; *Educ* Diocesan Coll Cape Town, Jesus Coll Cambridge; *m* 29 Sept 1951, Margaret Melesina, 3 da of Herbert William Deedes, JP (d 1966), and sis of Baron Deedes, *qv*, sometime ed of the Daily Telegraph; 5 s (Julian, Henry, George, William, Francis); *Heir* s, Hon Julian Plumptre; *Career* served WWII Capt; landowner and farmer (2,500 acres); *Recreations* shooting, gardening; *Style—* The Rt Hon the Lord FitzWalter; ✉ Goodnestone Park, Canterbury, Kent CT3 1PL (☎ 01304 840218)

FITZWALTER, Raymond Alan; s of Robert Fitzwalter, of Bury, Lancs, and Lucy, *née* Fox; *b* 21 Feb 1944; *Educ* Derby Sch, LSE (BScEcon); *m* 1, 6 Aug 1966 (m dis 1993), Mary, da of Richard Towman (d 1989), of Bury, Lancs; 2 s (Stephen Anthony b 24 Nov

1968, Matthew Paul b 11 Aug 1970), 1 da (Kathryn Anne b 16 Dec 1974); m 2, 7 May 1994, Ann Luise Nandy, *qv*, da of Lord Byers (Life Peer; d 1984); *Career* Bradford Telegraph and Argus: trainee journalist 1965–67, feature writer 1967–68, dep news ed 1968–70; Granada TV: exec prodr World in Action 1986–93 (researcher 1970–75, prodr 1975–76, ed 1976–86), commissioning exec news and current affrs 1987–89, head of current affrs 1989–93, exec prodr What The Papers Say and drama documentaries 1989–93; independent prodr Ray Fitzwalter Associates Ltd 1993–; visiting fell Univ of Salford 1993–; northern rep and memb Cncl PACT 1994–, chm Campaign for Qualitiy Television 1995–; CPU scholar to Pakistan 1969, Young Journalist of the Year IPC Awards 1970 (commended 1968), BAFTA award best factual series for World in Action 1987, RTS awards for World in Action 1981, 1983 and 1985, BAFTA Desmond Davis award for outstanding creative contrib to TV 1991; FRTS 1993; *Books* Web of Corruption: The Story of John Poulson and T Dan Smith (with David Taylor, 1981); *Recreations* chess, naval history, a garden; *Style*— Raymond Fitzwalter, Esq; ✉ Ray Fitzwalter Associates, Lloyds House, 22 Lloyd Street, Manchester M2 5WA (☎ 0161 832 3337, fax 0161 832 5535)

FITZWILLIAMS, Duncan John Lloyd; s of Charles Collinsplat Lloyd Fitzwilliams, (d 1984), of Cilgwyn, Newcastle Emlyn, Dyfed, and Rosamond Muriel, *née* Hill; *b* 24 May 1943; *Educ* Harrow, St Edmund Hall Oxford (MA); *m* 1, 1968, Hon Sarah Samuel, da of 4 Viscount Bearsted; m 2, 1978, Anna, da of Gp Capt Rex Williams, of Newton Ferrers, Devon; 2 da (Angharad, Victoria), 1 s (Logie); *Career* chm and jt fndr CASE plc 1969–88; dir: Foreign and Colonial Investment Trust plc 1973–91, Foreign and Colonial Pacific Investment Trust plc 1975–89, Anvil Petroleum plc 1975–85, Flextech Holdings plc 1976–86, Walker Greenbank plc 1977–88, Venture Link Ltd (chm) 1978–87, Henry Venture Fund II Inc (USA) 1985–, Lazard Leisure Fund 1986–, Bespak plc 1986–, Oakes Fitzwilliams & Co Ltd 1987–; co chm Quadrant Healthcare plc 1992–; memb Bd City Friends of Templeton Coll Oxford, former memb Info Technol Panel LSE; coracle champion of River Teifi 1956; MIIMR 1974; *Recreations* fishing, golf; *Clubs* White's, MCC, Berkshire Golf; *Style*— Duncan Fitzwilliams, Esq; ✉ Fishers Copse House, Bradfield, nr Reading, Berkshire RG7 6LN (☎ 0118 974 4527); Oakes Fitzwilliams & Co Ltd, 7/9 St James's Street, London SW1A 1EE (☎ 0171 925 1125, fax 0171 925 1026)

FITZWILLIAMS, Richard Brathwaite Lloyd; s of Maj Robert Campbell Lloyd Fitzwilliams, TD, and Natalie Jura Stratford, *née* Mardall (d 1965); the family has four registered Royal Descents from Ethelred II (Ethelred the Unready), Edward I (through the Howards), Edward III and Malcolm II, King of Scots, all through Richard Fitzwilliams' ggg grandmother Jane Maria, da and co-heir of Adm Richard Brathwaite; *b* 14 Oct 1949; *Educ* Univ of Cape Town (BA, three Lestrade scholarships); *m* 16 Nov 1981 (m dis 1995), Gillian, da of Frederick William Savill, of Blaby, Leicestershire; *Career* worked on project for Shadow Min of Educn United Party SA 1972, Europa Publications London 1972–, ed Int Who's Who 1975–; contrib numerous political articles and film reviews to SA newspapers; memb: Bow Gp, Hampstead and Highgate Cons Assoc (memb Town and Frognal Ward Ctee, former memb Exec Cncl); *Recreations* entertaining, cinema, shooting, travel, swimming, theatre; *Clubs* Naval and Military; *Style*— Richard B L Fitzwilliams, Esq; ✉ 84 North End Rd, London NW11 7SY (☎ 0181 455 7393); Europa Publications Ltd, 18 Bedford Square, London WC1B 3JN (☎ 0171 580 8236, 0171 636 1664, fax 0171 636 1664, telex 21540 EUROPA G)

FIVET, Edmond Charles Paul; *b* 12 Feb 1947; *Educ* St Marks Sch London, RCM (ARCM), Coll of St Mark & St John London (CertEd), Open Univ (pt/t BA), City Univ (pt/t MA); *m*; 1 step s; 2 c from previous m; *Career* professional freelance teacher and performer 1965–71, head of brass Surrey CC 1971–73, dir Jr Dept RCM 1983–89 (registrar 1973–82), princ Welsh Coll of Music and Drama 1989–; external examiner for BMus Birmingham Conservatoire 1995–; Assoc Bd of the Royal Schs of Music: examiner 1977–92, memb Consultative Ctee 1984–86, memb Examinations Bd 1986–89; music dir Audi Jr Musician (nat competition for 12–16 year olds) 1986–; memb: Nat Assoc of Youth Orchs 1983–84, Working Party Nat Fndn for Educnl Research LEA Instrumental Provision 1986–88, Ctee Welsh Colls of HE 1989–, Assoc of Euro Conservatoires 1989–, Ctee Princs of Conservatoires 1990–, Ctee Nat Centre for Dance and Choreography 1994–, Heads of HE Wales 1996–; vice pres Arts Cncl Richmond upon Thames (memb Exec Ctee 1982–86, vice chm 1984–86), chm Richmond Music Festival 1985–94; memb: Music Ctee Welsh Arts Cncl 1991–94, Music Ctee Cardiff Int Festival 1992–95, Steering Ctee Nat Youth Orch of Wales 1991–, Arts Strategy Task Force Cardiff CC 1996–; FRCM 1988, FRSA; *Recreations* golf, reading, theatre, music, current affairs; *Clubs* Parc Golf; *Style*— Edmond Fivet, Esq; ✉ Welsh College of Music and Drama, Castle Grounds, Cathays Park, Cardiff CF1 3ER (☎ 01222 390666, fax 01222 239462)

FLACH, Timothy Irvine; s of Robert Thomas Francis Flach, and Mary, Lady Crofton; *b* 16 April 1958; *Educ* Launceston Coll, North East London Poly (BA), St Martin's Sch of Art; *m* 2 (m dis); *Career* photographer; gp exhibitions incl: Assoc Gallery New Members Show 1989, Assoc of Photographers Awards Show 1990–93 and 1995 (Merit 1993), RPS 1990–93, PANL Amsterdam 1990–93, Journal De L'Image Professional 1990–93; gp exhibitions of painting: Art International 1978, RSBA 1978, 1980 and 1981, RSMA 1979, New English Art Club 1979 and 1980, RSPP 1982; memb Assoc of Photographers; UK French Jive Champion 1994; running coach to World Runners Club 1983–; *Recreations* rock & roll, lindy hop dancing, running; *Clubs* World Runners; *Style*— Timothy Flach, Esq; ✉ 17 Willow Street, London EC2A 4QH (☎ 0171 613 1894, fax 0171 613 5802)

FLACK, Rt Rev John Robert; *see:* Huntingdon, Bishop of

FLACK, Mervyn Charles; s of Maj Henry George Flack (d 1978), and Marjorie, *née* Lofthouse (d 1991); *b* 30 June 1942; *Educ* Raynes Park Co GS, Northampton Coll of Advanced Technol; *m* 5 Oct 1963, Margaret Elizabeth, da of George Robert Cumnock (d 1983); 1 s (James b 3 Nov 1969), 1 da (Emma b 2 Oct 1975); *Career* asst statistician, res analyst Gillette Industries Ltd 1962–67, co statistician Marplan Ltd 1967–69, chief statistician Attwood Statistics Ltd 1969–70, dir Opinion Research Centre 1971–79, dep md Louis Harris International 1978–79 (res dir 1973–78), dir Travel & Tourism Research Ltd 1981–83; chm: City Research Associates Ltd 1980–, Applied Research & Communications Ltd 1995–; chm and chief exec City Research Group plc 1990–; memb: Cncl Assoc of Br Market Research Cos 1981–84, Market Research Soc, Euro Soc for Opinion & Marketing Research; author various articles on mkt res; FSS 1963, FIS 1978 (MIS 1964); *Recreations* private pilot, food, wine; *Style*— Mervyn Flack, Esq; ✉ Crossrigg, Pondfield Road, Kenley, Surrey; City Research Group plc, Lector Court, 151–153 Farringdon Rd, London EC1R 3AD (☎ 0171 833 1681, fax 0171 278 5981)

FLAGG, Rt Rev John William Hawkins (Bill); s of Wilfred John Flagg (d 1974), and Emily, *née* Hawkins (d 1989); *b* 16 April 1929; *Educ* Wolsey Hall, All Nations' Christian Coll, Clifton Theological Coll; *m* 4 May 1954, Marjorie, da of Norman Lund (d 1968); 2 s (Andrew, Timothy), 4 da (Richenda, Rachel, Rosalind, Patricia); *Career* agric missionary in Southern Chile 1951–58, anglican chaplain and mission supt Paraguay 1959–64, archdeacon Northern Argentina 1964–69; bishop of: Paraguay and Northern Argentina 1969–73, Peru 1977 (asst 1973–77); asst bishop: Peru and Bolivia 1973–77, Liverpool 1978–86; vicar St Cyprians' with Christ Church 1978–85, priest i/c Christ Church Waterloo 1985–86, gen sec S American Missionary Soc 1986–93, hon asst bishop of Rochester 1986–92, asst bishop of Southwell 1992–, diocesan advsr in healing, stewardship and rural min 1992–97; presiding bishop Anglican Cncl of S America 1974–77; memb: Anglican Consultative Cncl 1974–79, S Atlantic Cncl 1984–93, Mission Issues and Strategy Gp (Anglican Cmmn) 1988–93; Cross of St Augustine (awarded by Archbishop of Canterbury) 1996; *Recreations* walking, chess; *Style*— The Rt Rev Bill Flagg; ✉ 8 Ransome Close, Beacon Heights, Newark NG1 2IQ (☎ and fax 01636 74889)

FLANAGAN, Andrew Henry; s of Francis Andrew Desmond Flanagan, of Glasgow, and Martha Gilmour White, *née* Donaldson; *b* 15 March 1956; *Educ* Hillhead HS Glasgow, Univ of Glasgow (Bachelor of Accountancy); *m* 21 March 1992, Virginia Annette, da of James Richard Alastair Walker; *Career* articled clerk Touche Ross 1976–79, audit sr Price Waterhouse 1979–81, fin mangr ITT Europe Inc 1981–86, dir of fin Europe PA Consulting Group 1986–91, gp fin dir The BIS Group Ltd 1991–93; Scottish Television plc: gp fin dir 1994–96, md 1996–; MICAS; *Recreations* golf, jogging, skiing, cinema, reading, television; *Clubs* RAC; *Style*— Andrew Flanagan, Esq; ✉ Scottish Television plc, Cowcaddens, Glasgow G2 3PR (☎ 0141 300 3000, fax 0141 300 3030)

FLANAGAN, Mary; da of Martin James Flanagan (d 1981), and Mary, *née* Nesbitt (d 1977); *b* 20 May 1943; *Educ* Brandeis Univ Waltham Mass (BA); *Career* writer; began writing 1979; works to date: Bad Girls (collection of short stories, 1984), Trust (1987), Rose Reason (1991), The Blue Woman (collection of short stories, 1994); critic for: Sunday Times, Evening Standard, New Statesman, Observer, The New York Times Book Review; reviewer for Kaleidoscope (Radio 4); teacher of creative writing UEA Sept-Dec 1995; memb: Soc of Authors 1986, Authors' Guild (USA) 1986, PEN (Eng and American) 1990; *Recreations* gardening, music, environmental activist; *Style*— Ms Mary Flanagan; ✉ c/o Bloomsbury Publishing Ltd, 2 Soho Square, London W1V 5DE

FLANAGAN, Prof Terence Patrick (Terry); OBE (1987); s of Thomas Flanagan (d 1934), of Dudley, Worcs, and Harriet Selina, *née* Beard (d 1979); *b* 25 Sept 1924; *Educ* St Joseph's Sch Dudley, Queen Mary Coll London (BSc, MSc); *m* 1, 9 July 1949 (m dis 1980), Marian Margaret, da of Horace Riddleston (d 1954), of Chesterfield, Derbys; 3 da (Helen (Mrs Russell) b 6 Feb 1955, Jane b 19 Jan 1957, Margaret b 19 Sept 1959); m 2, 31 Jan 1981, Sheila Mary, da of John Wallace McDonald, of Bromley, Kent; *Career* Flt Sgt RAF Aircrew 1943–47; electronics designer Marconi Instruments 1950–57; SIRA Ltd: head Nucleonics Dept 1957–63, head Indust Measurement Div 1963–74, exec dir 1974–79, md 1979–87, chief exec SIRA Certification Service 1992–; conslt UKAEA 1964–88, indust conslt 1987–, conslt National Physical Laboratory 1988–94; non-exec dir: Ometron Ltd 1987– (chm 1981–87), SIRA Safety Services Ltd 1987–90 (chm 1981–87); ed Measurement and Control Series 1987–92; visiting prof City Univ London; memb Metrology & Standards Requirements Bd DTI 1980–87, chm Sch of Engrg Advsy Ctee City Univ 1980–93, pres Inst of Measurement and Control 1983, govr Ravensbourne Coll of Design & Communication 1984–88, lectr Kent Area Understanding Industry Campaign; chm: Bromley NSPCC Centenary Ctee 1990–91, Kent Centre Inst of Electrical Engrg 1994–, Tenterden Residents' Assoc 1994–; vice chm: Tenterden Age Concern 1993–, Tenterden Day Centre 1994–; Freeman City of London 1982, Liveryman Worshipful Co of Scientific Instrument Makers 1982; Hon DSc City Univ 1990; FIEE, FInstP, FInstMC; *Recreations* cricket, music, DIY, local affairs; *Style*— Prof Terry Flanagan, OBE; ✉ 11 Eastgate Rd, Tenterden, Kent (☎ and fax 01580 764070)

FLATHER, Gary Denis; QC (1984); s of Joan Ada, *née* Walker; *b* 4 Oct 1937; *Educ* Oundle, Pembroke Coll Oxford; *m* Shreela (*see* Baroness Flather), da of Aftab Rai; *Career* 2 Lt 1 Bn York and Lancaster Regt 1956–58, Hallamshire Bn TA 1958–61; called to the Inner Temple Bar 1962, recorder of the Crown Court 1986– (asst recorder 1983–86), bencher Inner Temple 1995; memb Panel of Chairmen ILEA Disciplinary Tbnl 1974–90, asst Parly boundary cmmr 1982–, inspr DTI for enquiries under Fin Servs Act 1987–88; regular chm: Police Disciplinary Appeal Tbnl 1987–, MOD Police Disciplinary Appeal Tbnl 1991–; legal memb Mental Health Review Tbnl 1987–; legal assessor: GMC 1987–, Gen Dental Cncl 1987–; chm: Statutory Ctee Royal Pharmaceutical Soc of GB 1990–, Disciplinary Ctee CIM; dir Fearnehough (Bakewell) Ltd; escort to Mayor Royal Borough of Windsor and Maidenhead 1986–87, vice pres Community Cncl for Berkshire 1987–; pres Maidenhead Rotary 1990–91; chm Bar Cncl Panel for the Disabled; *Recreations* travel, music, coping with Multiple Sclerosis; *Style*— Gary Flather, Esq, QC; ✉ 4–5 Gray's Inn Square, Gray's Inn, London WC1R 5AY (☎ 0171 404 5252, fax 01628 75355, car 0860 875832)

FLATHER, Baroness (Life Peer UK 1990), of Windsor and Maidenhead in the Royal County of Berkshire; Shreela Flather; JP (1971), DL (Berks 1994); da of Rai Bahadur Aftab Rai (d 1972), of New Delhi, and Krishna Rai (d 1989); *Educ* UCL (LLB); *m* Gary Denis Flather, QC, *qv*; 2 s (Hon Paul, Hon Marcus); *Career* infant teacher ILEA 1965–67; teacher of English as foreign language: Altwood Comp Sch Maidenhead 1968–74, Broadmoor Hosp 1974–78; cncllr Royal Borough of Windsor and Maidenhead 1976–91, UK del to Econ and Social Ctee EC 1987–90, pres Cambs Chilterns and Thames Rent Assessment Panel, vice pres Building Socs Assoc 1976–91; vice chm and fndr memb Maidenhead Community Rels Cncl, vice chm Maidenhead Volunteer Centre, sec and organiser Maidenhead Ladies' Asian Club 1968–78, fndr New Star Boys' Club for Asian boys, fndr summer sch project for Asian children in Maidenhead, vice chm and memb Mgmnt Ctee CAB, vice chm Estates and Amenities and Leisure Ctees Royal Borough of Windsor and Maidenhead, sec Windsor and Maidenhead Cons Gp, exec ctee memb Anglo-Asian Cons Soc, memb Thames and Chilterns Tourist Bd, memb Dist Youth and Community Ctee, community rels advsr Berks Girl Guides, race rels tutor for sr police offrs' courses, govr Slough Coll of Higher Educn 1983–89; memb: Berks FPC, Spoore Merry and Rixman Fndn, Poole's Charity, Ring's Charity; dir Daytime TV Ltd; memb: Lord Chllr's Legal Aid Advsy Ctee 1958–88, Broadmoor Hosp Bd, BBC South and East Regnl Advsy Ctee, W Met Conciliation Ctee of Race Rels Bd 1973–78, Bd of Visitors Holloway Prison, Police Complaints Bd 1982–85, Swann Ctee (enquiry into educn of children from ethnic minority gps) 1979–85, HRH Duke of Edinburgh's Ctee of Enquiry into Br Housing 1984–85, Commission for Racial Equality 1980–86; Mayor Royal Borough of Windsor and Maidenhead 1986–87 (Dep Mayor 1985–86); memb: Social Security Advsy Ctee 1987–90, Servite Houses Ctee of Management, Nat Union Exec Ctee Cons Pty 1989, Cons Women's Nat Ctee 1975–89, exec ctees of Br sections Int Unions of Local Authys, LWT Programme Advsy Bd, Hillingdon Hosp Tst; dir: Thames Valley Training and Enterprise 1990–93, Meridian Broadcasting (MAI) Ltd; chm: STARFM 101.6, Local Independent Radio Slough, Windsor and Maidenhad, Ethics Ctee Broadmoor Hosp; treas Indo-Br Parly Gp, tstee Sir William Borlase Sch Marlow; pres: Broadmoor League of Friends, Berkshire Community Cncl; vice pres Assoc of District Cncls; chm Maidenhead Community Consultative Cncl; vice chm: Police Consultative Ctee, The Refugee Cncl; tstee Berks Community Tst; UK rep on EU Advsry Cmmn on Racism and Xenophobia 1995; govr Cwlth Inst 1993–; tstee Rajiv Gandhi (UK) Fndn 1993–; *Recreations* travel, cinema; *Clubs* Oriental; *Style*— The Baroness Flather, JP, DL; ✉ The House of Lords, London SW1A 0PW; (fax 01628 75355)

FLAUX, Julian Martin; QC (1994); s of Louis Michael Flaux, of Malvern, Worcs, and Maureen Elizabeth Brenda, *née* Coleman; *b* 11 May 1955; *Educ* King's Sch Worcester, Worcester Coll Oxford (BCL, MA); *m* 24 Sept 1983, Matilda Christian, da of Michael Hansard Gabb, of Canterbury, Kent; 3 s; *Career* called to the Bar Inner Temple 1978, in practice Temple 1979–; *Recreations* walking, reading, opera; *Style*— Julian Flaux, Esq, QC; ✉ 7 King's Bench Walk, Temple, London EC4 (☎ 0171 583 0404, fax 0171 583 0950, telex 887491 KBLAW)

FLAXEN, David William; s of William Henry Flaxen (d 1963), of Tyldesley, and Beatrice, *née* Laidlow (d 1984); *b* 20 April 1941; *Educ* Manchester GS, BNC Oxford (MA),

UCL (DipStat); *m* 22 Feb 1969, Eleanor Marie, da of Stewart Ferguson Easton (d 1975), of Andover, Massachusetts; 2 da (Sophia b 1970, Clare b 1974); *Career* statistician; Miny of Lab 1967–71, UN advsr Swaziland 1971–72, Dept of Employment 1973–76, Inland Revenue 1977–81, asst dir Central Statistical Office 1983–89 (also 1964–67, 1976–77 and 1981–83), dir of statistics Dept of Tport 1989–; *Recreations* bridge, wine, books, music, cooking; *Style*— David Flaxen, Esq; ✉ Department of Transport, Romney House, 43 Marsham Street, London SW1P 3PY (☎ 0171 276 8030)

FLAXMAN, Charles; s of William Henry Flaxman, and Amy, *née* Williams; *b* 12 April 1926; *Educ* Owen's Sch London; *m* 7 April 1947, (Muriel) Jane, *née* Colbear; 2 s (Roger b 1951, Jeremy b 1954), 1 da (Sara b 1953); *Career* Nat Serv 1944–48, cmmnd Royal Fusiliers 1945 (Capt 1947); worked for various Lloyd's Brokers 1942–61, underwriter Frank Barber & Ors Lloyd's 1982–86 (dep underwriter 1962–81), ptnr Morgan Fentiman & Barber Lloyd's 1982–, conslt Bowring Professional Indemnity Fund Ltd 1987–90, tech dir Solicitors Indemnity Fund Ltd 1987–91 (non-exec 1991–95), chm ADR Net Ltd 1992–94; memb Saffron Walden Town Cncl 1979–87; memb Worshipful Co of Insurers 1984; ACII 1952, MBAE 1992, FRSA, memb Br Insur Legal Assoc; *Recreations* music, walking, reading, work; *Style*— Charles Flaxman, Esq; ✉ Yeoman's Hempstead, Saffron Walden, Essex (☎ 01799 599345)

FLECK, Prof Adam; s of Adam Fleck (d 1981), of Glasgow, Scotland, and Beatrice Ada Stirton, *née* Goldie; *b* 19 Oct 1932; *Educ* Hillhead HS, Allan Glens Sch Glasgow, Univ of Glasgow (BSc, MB ChB, PhD); *m* 12 July 1960, Elizabeth, da of Alexander MacLean, of Glasgow; 1 s (Adam b 1962), 2 da (Barbara Anne b 1965, Isabel Beatrice b 1968); *Career* conslt biochemist Glasgow Royal Infirmary 1966–74, sr lectr in pathological biochemistry Univ of Glasgow 1974–79 (lectr 1961–65), hon conslt W Infirmary Glasgow 1974–79; prof of chemical pathology Charing Cross and Westminster Med Sch 1979–, hon conslt chem pathologist Hammersmith Hospitals Tst London; pres Assoc of Clinical Biochemists 1991–94, chm Joint Examining Bd For The Mastership In Clinical Biochemistry (1988–91); Burgess of the City of Glasgow, memb Incorporation of Bakers of Glasgow 1988; FRSC 1971, FRSE 1973, FRCPath 1979, FRCPG 1979, FRSM 1980, FIBiol 1988; *Recreations* golf and walking (time and energy permitting); *Clubs* Roehampton; *Style*— Prof Adam Fleck, FRSE; ✉ Department of Chemical Pathology, Charing Cross & Westminster Medical School, St Dunstan's Rd, London W6 8RP (☎ 0181 846 7075, fax 0181 846 7007)

FLECK, Richard John Hugo; s of Peter Hugo Fleck (d 1975), and Fiona Charis Elizabeth, *née* Miller; *b* 30 March 1949; *Educ* Marlborough, Univ of Southampton (LLB); *m* 1983, Mary, da of Wing Cdr Frederick Thomas Gardiner, DFC; 1 da (Sara Katherine Victoria b 10 May 1987), 1 s (Peter Frederick Hugo b 3 March 1990); *Career* ptnr Herbert Smith 1980– (joined 1971); memb: Auditing Practices Ctee 1986–91, Auditing Practices Bd 1991–; Freeman City of London, Liveryman Tallow Chandlers Co; memb Law Soc; *Recreations* sailing, real tennis, golf, rackets; *Clubs* MCC, Royal Ocean Racing, City Law, Jesters, Itchenor Sailing, Petworth House Tennis; *Style*— Richard Fleck, Esq; ✉ Slinfold Manor, Slinfold, nr Horsham, West Sussex (☎ 01403 791085, fax 01403 791086); Herbert Smith, Exchange House, Primrose St, London EC2A 2HS (☎ 0171 374 8000)

FLECKER, James William; s of Henry Lael Oswald, CBE (d 1958), and Mary Patricia, *née* Hessey; *b* 15 Aug 1939; *Educ* Marlborough, BNC Oxford (MA); *m* 22 July 1967, Mary Rose, da of Noel Jeremy Firth, of Sandal, Yorks; 3 da (Rachel b 1969, Lara b 1970, Brontë b 1974); *Career* asst master: Sydney GS NSW 1962–63, Latymer Upper Sch Hammersmith 1964–67; housemaster Marlborough 1975–80 (asst master 1967–80), headmaster Ardingly Coll 1980–; *Recreations* hockey, flute playing, writing children's operas; *Style*— James Flecker, Esq; ✉ Headmaster's House, Ardingly College, Haywards Heath, W Sussex RH17 6SQ (☎ 01444 892330)

FLEET, Kenneth George; s of Fred Major Fleet, and Elizabeth Doris, *née* Brassey; *b* 12 Sept 1929; *Educ* Calday Grange GS Cheshire, LSE (BSc); *m* 1953, Alice Brenda, da of Capt H R Wilkinson, RD; 3 s (Ian b 1957, Malcolm b 1959, Graham b 1964), 1 da (Elizabeth b 1962); *Career* Jl of Commerce Liverpool 1950–52; Sunday Times 1955–56, dep city ed Birmingham Post 1956–58, dep fin ed the Guardian 1958–63; city ed: Sunday Telegraph 1963–66, Daily Telegraph 1966–77 (dep city ed 1963); ed business news Sunday Times 1977–78, city ed Sunday Express 1978–82, city ed i/c Express Newspapers plc 1982–83, exec ed (fin and indust) The Times 1983–87, dir TVS Entertainment plc 1990–93; dir Young Vic 1976–83, chm Chichester Festival Theatre 1985– (dir 1984), govr LSE 1989; Wincott award 1974; *Recreations* theatre, books, sport; *Clubs* MCC, Lord's Taverners', Piltdown Golf; *Style*— Kenneth Fleet, Esq

FLEET, Dr Stephen George; s of George Fleet (d 1976), and Elsie Fleet, of Lewes, Sussex; *b* 28 Sept 1936; *Educ* Brentwood Sch, Lewes County GS, St John's Coll Cambridge (MA, PhD); *Career* Univ of Cambridge: demonstrator in mineralogy 1962–67, univ lectr in mineralogy 1967–83, registrary 1983–; Downing Coll Cambridge: fell 1974–, bursar 1974–83, pres 1983–85, vice master 1985–88 and 1991–94; chm: Bd of Examinations 1974–83, Bursars' Ctee 1980–83; tstee Fndn of Edward Storey 1977–; memb: Cncl of Senate Univ of Cambridge 1975–82, Fin Bd Univ of Cambridge 1979–83, Ctee of Mgmnt of Charities Property Unit Tst 1983–88, Fin Ctee Int Union of Crystallography 1987–; tstee Mineralogical Soc of GB 1977–87, treas Cambridge Cwlth Tst 1983–, Cambridge Overseas Tst 1989–; fell: Fitzwilliam House Cambridge 1963–66; fndn fell Fitzwilliam Coll 1966–73; pres: Fitzwilliam Soc 1977, Downing Assoc 1991; FInstP, FRSA; *Recreations* books, music, history of Sussex; *Clubs* Athenaeum, Royal Over-Seas League; *Style*— Dr Stephen Fleet; ✉ Downing College, Cambridge CB2 1DQ (☎ 01223 334843); University Registry, Old Schools, Cambridge (☎ 01223 332294)

FLEMING, Alistair; s of James Anderson Fleming, of Glasgow, and Elizabeth Brown Davies; *b* 31 March 1944; *Educ* Univ of Strathclyde (BSc 1st Class Hons); *m* 9 July 1966, Sandra Rosemary, da of William Gillies; 2 da (Lorraine Rosalynne b 19 June 1970, Melissa Caroline b 30 April 1975), 1 s (Stuart Alexander b 4 Feb 1985); *Career* project mgmnt and engrg roles ICI Petrochemical Div UK and Aust 1965–75, project mangr Corpus Christi Petrochemicals then asst dir of engrg ICI America 1975–80, regnl mangr Western Europe Britoil Clyde Field Project 1987–87, gen mangr of project BP Exploration 1987–89, md of construction Eurotunnel 1990–91, dir The Weir Group plc (and subsids) 1991–96, gp chief exec Forth Ports plc 1996–; memb Scottish Cncl CBI, chm Scottish Cncl for Educn Technol; CEng, FIMechE, MInstPet, FEng 1993; *Recreations* golf; *Style*— Alistair Fleming, Esq, FEng; ✉ Forth Ports plc, Tower Place, Leith, Edinburgh EH6 7DB (☎ 0131 554 6473, fax 0131 553 7462)

FLEMING, Prof Christopher Alexander; s of Brian Alexander Fleming (d 1984), and Marguerite Grace, *née* Allingham; *b* 14 Aug 1948; *Educ* Alleyn's Sch Dulwich, Univ of Aberdeen (BSc), Univ of Reading (PhD); *m* 17 July 1970, Christeen, da of John Louis MacLean; 1 s (Lewis Alexander b 12 Feb 1977), 1 da (Kazia Anne b 26 Sept 1980); *Career* Sir William Halcrow & Partners Ltd: graduate engr UK 1970–72, site engr Port Victoria 1972, asst engr Marine Dept UK 1972–73; Univ of Reading (PhD) 1973–75, rejoined Sir William Halcrow & Partners Ltd: engr Marine Dept 1975–77, section engr Mina Jebel Ali Dubai 1977–79, resident engr Jebel Ali Hotel Marine Works Dubai 1978–79, project engr Mina Jebel Ali Dubai Halcrow International Partnership 1979–80, head Maritime Computer Applications Unit UK 1980–82, conslt to KPCL Toronto 1982–84, dir of Halcrow MOE and of Halcrow-Ewbank 1983–84, dir Sir William Halcrow & Partners Ltd and dir Halcrow Offshore 1984–, UK dir Water and Maritime Div 1984–; visiting prof of coastal engrg Univ of Plymouth 1994–; former advsr to House of Commons Environment Ctee on Coastal Zone Protection and Planning, chm Nat Coastal Impact Modelling Ctee, chm Steering Ctee Beach Mgmnt Manual CIRIA, memb Advsy Bd Engrg Dept Univ of Aberdeen; govr Ridgeway Sch Wroughton Wilts; author of numerous publications in various learned jls; memb: Permanent Int Assoc of Navigation Congresses (PIANC), Int Assoc of Hydraulic Research; CEng, memb Fédération Européene d'Associations Nationales d'Ingénieurs, FICE 1991 (1979), FRGS 1991, FEng 1996; *Recreations* sailing, skiing, golf, tennis; *Clubs* The Wiltshire; *Style*— Prof Christopher Fleming, FEng; ✉ Woodham House West, Bakers Road, Wroughton, Wiltshire SN4 0RP (☎ 01793 813543); Sir William Halcrow & Partners Ltd, Burderop Park, Swindon, Wilts SN4 0QD (☎ 01793 812479, fax 01793 812089, mobile 0836 387761, e-mail 100113.1142@compuserve.com)

FLEMING, Ven David; s of John Frederick Fleming, BEM (d 1976), of Norfolk, and Emma Fleming (d 1996); *b* 8 June 1937; *Educ* Hunstanton Co Primary, King Edward VII GS King's Lynn, Kelham Theol Coll; *m* 1966, Elizabeth Anne Marguerite, da of Bernard Bayleys Hughes (d 1947), of Birmingham; 3 s (Christopher b 1967, Nicholas b 1968, Matthew b 1972), 1 da (Fiona b 1970); *Career* curate St Margaret Walton on the Hill 1963–67, chaplain HM Gaynes Hall, vicar Great Staughton 1968–76, rural dean St Neots 1972–76, vicar Whittlesey 1976–85, rural dean March 1977–82, hon canon Ely Cathedral 1982–, archdeacon of Wisbech 1984–93, vicar Wisbech St Mary 1985–88, chaplain gen of HM prisons 1993–; chaplain to HM The Queen 1995–; *Recreations* television, tennis, extolling Hunstanton; *Clubs* Whittlesey Rotary; *Style*— The Ven the Archdeacon of Prisons; ✉ Fair Haven, 123 Wisbech Road, Littleport, Cambridgeshire CB6 1JJ (☎ 01353 862498)

FLEMING, Prof George; *b* 16 Aug 1944, Glasgow; *Educ* Univ of Strathclyde (BSc), Univ of Strathclyde/Stanford Univ (PhD); *Career* vice pres/dir Hydrocomp International California and Glasgow 1969–77, conslt Watson Hawksley High Wycombe 1980–92; Univ of Strathclyde: lectr 1971–76, sr lectr 1976–82, reader 1982–85, vice dean Faculty of Engrg 1984–87, personal prof 1985–86, chair prof Dept of Civil Engrg 1986–, dir Water and Environmental Mgmnt Unit 1986– (Better Environment Award for Industry RSA 1987), head Div of Water Engrg and Environmental Mgmnt 1989–, head Dept of Civil Engrg 1991–93, chm Mgmnt Gp David Livingstone Inst 1992–, md Centre for Environmental Mgmnt Studies Ltd 1993–; visiting prof Padova Univ Italy 1980–88; conslt Clydeport Ltd (formerly Clyde Port Authy) 1987–, dir Scottish Consultants International 1987–; memb Overseas Projects Bd DTI 1991–95; chm: Glasgow and W of Scotland Assoc of Civil Engrs 1984–85, Cncl ICE 1985–89, Environment Ctee SERC 1985–89, Engrg Ctee Royal Acad of Engrg 1988–91; conslt to numerous nat and int orgns incl: UN Food and Agriculture Orgn, ILO, World Meteorological Orgn; conslt to govt agencies incl: Scottish Devpt Agency, S of Scotland Electricity Bd, Central Electricity Generating Bd; conslt to private companies incl: Babtie Shaw and Morton, Binnie and Partners, Mott MacDonald, Bovis, Wimpey Waste; significant projects incl: dams in Kenya Labuan and Brunei, Strathclyde Park Reservoir, Dinorwig Power Station Project, reservoir mgmnt in the Alps, flood control in California, Chicago and Brazil; MIWM, MIWEM, FICE, FEng 1987, FRSE 1992; *Books and Publications* research pubns incl contribs to 11 books and over 200 pubns in jls; has produced 4 video documentaries and a perm exhbn; *Style*— Prof George Fleming, FRSE, FEng; ✉ Department of Civil Engineering, University of Strathclyde, John Anderson Building, 107 Rottonrow, Glasgow G4 0NG (☎ 0141 553 4169, fax 0141 553 2066, e-mail g.fleming@strath.ac.uk)

FLEMING, Grahame Ritchie; QC (Scot, 1990); s of Ian Erskine Fleming, of Forfar, and Helen, *née* Wallace; *b* 13 Feb 1949; *Educ* Forfar Acad, Univ of Edinburgh (MA, LLB); *m* 23 June 1984, Mopsa Dorcas, eld da of Gerald Neil Robbins; 1 da (Leahna Damaris Robbins b 23 Aug 1985); *Career* called to the Scottish Bar 1976, standing jr counsel to the Home Office in Scotland 1986–89, sheriff of the Lothians and Borders at Linlithgow 1993–; *Recreations* travel, food, rugby; *Style*— Sheriff Grahame Fleming, QC; ✉ Advocates' Library, Parliament House, Edinburgh EH1 1RF

FLEMING, Dr Ian; s of David Alexander Fleming (d 1988), and Olwen Lloyd, *née* Jones (d 1996); *b* 4 Aug 1935; *Educ* King Edward VI Sch Stourbridge, Pembroke Coll Cambridge (MA, PhD, ScD); *m* 1, 3 Aug 1959 (m dis 1962), Joan, *née* Irving; m 2, 12 Nov 1965, Mary Lord, *née* Bernard; *Career* res fell Pembroke Coll Cambridge 1962–64, postdoctoral res Harvard Univ 1963–64; Univ of Cambridge: fell Pembroke Coll 1964–, demonstrator 1964–65, asst dir of res 1965–80, lectr 1980–86, reader in organic chemistry 1986–; RSC: memb 1962, Tilden lectr 1981, prize for organic synthesis 1983; memb American Chemical Soc 1964; FRS 1993; *Books* Spectroscopic Methods in Organic Chemistry (1966, 5 edn 1995), Selected Organic Syntheses (1973), Frontier Orbitals and Organic Chemical Reactions (1976), Comprehensive Organic Synthesis (jt ed, 1991); *Recreations* watching films, reading, music; *Style*— Dr Ian Fleming, FRS; ✉ Department of Chemistry, University of Cambridge, Lensfield Road, Cambridge CB2 1EW (☎ 01223 336372, e-mail if10000@cam.ac.uk)

FLEMING, Robert Atholl; s of Atholl Fleming, MBE (d 1972), and Phyllis Wallace, *née* Best (d 1983); *b* 19 July 1933; *Educ* Cranbrook Sch, Sydney; *m* 15 Sept 1982, Marion Heather, da of Maurice Leigh (d 1969); *Career* TV documentary prodr, dir and writer; md Argo Productions Ltd; hon sec Primary Club 1996; Freeman City of London; JP 1983–84; *Books* Scotland Yard; *Clubs* Garrick, MCC, Royal Sydney Golf; *Style*— Robert Fleming, Esq; ✉ 5 South Villas, Camden Square, London NW1 9BS (☎ 0171 267 3316, fax 0171 485 6808)

FLEMING, Robert (Robin); DL (Oxfordshire 1989); s of Maj Philip Fleming (d 1971), of Barton Abbey, Oxfordshire, and Joan Cecil, *née* Hunloke (d 1991); *b* 18 Sept 1932; *Educ* Eton, RMA Sandhurst; *m* 28 April 1962, Victoria Margaret, da of Frederic Howard Aykroyd (d 1978); 2 s (Philip b 15 April 1965, Rory David b 5 June 1968), 1 da (Joanna Kate b 19 Nov 1963); *Career* serv Royal Scots Greys 1951–58; joined Robert Fleming 1958, dir Robert Fleming Trustee Co Ltd 1961– (chm 1985–91), dir Robert Fleming Investment Trust Ltd 1968–, chm Robert Fleming Holdings Ltd 1990–97 (dir 1974–, dep chm 1986–90), dir Glenshee Chairlift Co Ltd 1995–; tstee BFSS 1975–; High Sheriff Oxfordshire 1980; *Recreations* most country pursuits especially stalking and fishing, music especially Scottish traditional; *Style*— Robin Fleming, Esq, DL; ✉ Robert Fleming Holdings Ltd, 25 Copthall Avenue, London EC2R 7DR (☎ 0171 638 5858, fax 0171 588 7219, car 0831 214 509)

FLEMING, (Ronald) Stewart; s of Norman Fleming, and Laurena Fleming; *b* 14 Aug 1943; *Educ* Wallesey GS, Horace Mann Sch NY, Emmanuel Coll Cambridge; *m* Jennifer Mary, da of Gordon McQuie; 2 s (Sam Jonathan b 8 Feb 1973, Joshua James b 17 Nov 1975); *Career* journalist; Bootle Times 1963–65, Prudential Assurance 1965–68, The Guardian 1968–74; Financial Times: joined 1974, NY corr 1976–80, Frankfurt corr 1980–83, US economics corr Washington 1983–86, US ed Washington 1986–89, fin ed 1989–92; corr New Statesman 1996; *Recreations* reading, swimming; *Style*— Stewart Fleming, Esq

FLEMING, (Dr) Thomas Kelman (Tom); OBE (1980); s of Rev Peter Fleming (d 1939); *b* 29 June 1927; *Educ* Daniel Stewart's Coll Edinburgh; *Career* actor, writer, producer and broadcaster; co-fndr Edinburgh Gateway Co 1953–65, RSC 1962–64 (roles incl Prospero, Cymbeline, Brutus, Kent and Buckingham), fndr and dir Royal Lyceum Theatre Co 1965–66, govr Scottish Theatre Tst 1980–82, dir Scottish Theatre Company 1982–87; Edinburgh Festival prodns of: Molière, Aristophanes, Sir David Lyndsay, Sidney Goodsir Smith; The Thrie Estaites STC Warsaw 1986 (Roman Szydlowski Award); films incl: King Lear, Mary Queen of Scots, Meetings with Remarkable Men; numerous TV incl: title role Jesus of Nazareth, Henry IV (parts 1 & 2), Weir of

Hermiston, Reith; over 2000 broadcasts since 1944; BBC Radio commentator (royal events) 1950–; BBC TV commentator on over 300 national and state occasions incl: Silver Wedding 1972, Princess Anne's Wedding 1973, Prince of Wales's Wedding 1981, State visits to USA and Japan, Silver Jubilee 1977, The Queen Mother's 80th Birthday Celebrations 1980, The Queen's 60th Birthday 1986, Queen's Birthday Parade 1970–88, Cenotaph Service of Remembrance 1961, 1965–88 and 1994–, Installations of Archbishop of Canterbury 1975 and 1980, two Papal Inaugurations 1978, Falklands Meml Serv St Paul's 1982, Gulf Meml Serv Glasgow Cathedral 1991, 50th Anniversary Battle of Alamein 1992, D Day +50 Serv Normandy 1994, VE +50 Serv St Paul's 1995, VJ +50 The Final Tribute 1995; also commentator on funeral of: Duke of Gloucester, Duke of Windsor, Montgomery of Alamein, Mountbatten of Burma, King Frederick of Denmark, Marshal Tito, Princess Grace, King Olav, Cardinal Heenan, Pope John Paul I; Hon DUniv Heriot-Watt 1984; FRSAMD 1986; *Books* So That Was Spring (poems), Miracle at Midnight (play), Voices Out of the Air, BBC Book of Memories (contrib); *Recreations* hill walking, music; *Clubs* Royal Cwlth Soc, Scottish Arts (Hon), Royal Scottish Pipers' Soc (Hon); *Style*— Tom Fleming, Esq, OBE; ✉ 56 Murrayfield Gardens, Edinburgh; Tomfarclas, Ballindalloch, Banffshire

FLEMMING, John Stanton; s of Sir Gilbert Nicolson Flemming, KCB (d 1981), and Virginia, *née* Coit (d 1992); *b* 6 Feb 1941; *Educ* Rugby, Trinity Coll Oxford (BA, MA), Nuffield Coll Oxford; *m* 1963, Jean Elizabeth, da of George Briggs (d 1982); 3 s (Edward b 1968, Thomas b 1970, William b 1973), 1 da (Rebecca b 1966); *Career* economist; lectr and fell Oriel Coll Oxford 1963–65, offical fell and bursar Nuffield Coll Oxford 1965–80 (emeritus fell 1980), ed Economic Journal 1976–80; chief advsr Bank of England 1980–83, econ advsr to the Govr Bank of England 1983–88, exec dir Bank of England 1988–91, chief economist European Bank of Reconstruction and Development 1991–93, warden Wadham Coll Oxford Oct 1993–; dir Kleinwort's Emerging Markets Investment Tst 1993–; chm: NIESR 1996–, Nat Academics Policy Advsy Gp on Energy and the Environment, Hansard Soc/EU Policy forum Cmmn on Regulation of Privatised Utilities 1996; memb: Cncl and Exec Ctee Royal Econ Soc 1980– (treas 1992–), Advsy Bd on Res Cncls 1986–91, Cncl Brunel Univ 1989–91 and 1993–, Royal Cmmn on Environmental Pollution 1995–; hon fell: Oriel Coll Oxford 1993, Trinity Coll Oxford 1993; FBA 1991 (memb Cncl 1993–, hon treas 1995–); *Style*— John Flemming, Esq, FBA; ✉ Wadham College, Oxford OX1 3PN (☎ 01865 277904, fax 01865 277937)

FLESCH, Michael Charles; QC (1983); s of Carl Franz Flesch, and Ruth, *née* Seligsohn (d 1987); *b* 11 March 1940; *Educ* Gordonstoun, UCL (LLB, 1st XV rugby, 1st VI tennis); *m* 2 Aug 1972, Gail, *née* Schrire; 1 s (Daniel b 1976), 1 da (Dina b 1973); *Career* called to the Bar Gray's Inn 1963 (Lord Justice Halker sr scholarship), bencher 1993; Bigelow teaching fell Univ of Chicago 1963–64, pt/t lectr in revenue law UCL 1965–82, practice at Revenue Bar 1966– (chm Revenue Bar Assoc 1993–95), chm Taxation and Retirement Benefits Ctee of Bar Cncl 1985–93; govr Gordonstoun Sch 1976–96; *Recreations* all forms of sport; *Clubs* Arsenal FC, Middx CCC, Brondesbury Lawn Tennis and Cricket; *Style*— Michael Flesch, Esq, QC; ✉ Gray's Inn Chambers, Gray's Inn, London WC1R 5JA (☎ 0171 242 2642, fax 0171 831 9017)

FLESHER, Peter; s of Ernest Flesher (d 1966), of Bradford, and Hilda, *née* Binns; *b* 21 March 1935; *Educ* Belle Vue GS Bradford, Bradford Tech Coll (ARIC external), Univ of Leeds (MSc); *m* 29 March 1958, Audrey, da of Harold Mark Foster; *Career* Allied Colloids plc: joined 1951, res dir 1973–80, dep md 1980–82, md 1982–95, ret; non-exec dir Yorkshire Water plc 1989–; memb: Cncl Univ of Leeds 1987–, Bd of Govrs Bradford CTC 1990–, Yorks, Humberside and E Mids Regnl Industl Devpt Bd 1991–, DTI Environmental Technol Advsy Gp 1991–; patron Soc of Dyers and Colourists 1989–90 (vice pres 1990–91); pres: Heaton Amateur Operatic and Dramatic Soc 1989–, Belle Vue Old Boys' Assoc 1992–93; Hon DSc Univ of Bradford 1992; ARIC, CIMgt; *Recreations* reading, bridge, watercolour painting, fell walking; *Style*— Peter Flesher, Esq

FLESHER, Peter Stewart; s of William Owen Flesher (d 1981), of Shelf, Halifax, and Edith Alice, *née* Asquith (d 1969); *b* 20 Nov 1942; *Educ* Hipperholme GS; *m* Carol Lesley, da of Lesley Taylor; 1 s (David Gregory b 2 May 1976), 1 da (Adele Suzanne b 15 March 1974); *Career* Williamson Butterfield Roberts (now Grant Thornton): articled clerk 1958–64, qualified chartered accountant 1964, audit and tax 1964–73, fndr ptnr i/c insolvency Leeds/Bradford 1974, ptnr i/c London and SE Regn insolvency 1992–95, regnl insolvency ptnr NE Region 1995–, memb Insolvency Panel, managing ptnr Bradford Office 1988–90; memb Cncl: Insolvency Practitioners' Assoc 1989–93 (chm Ethics Ctee 1989–93), Soc of Practitioners of Insolvency 1990–; memb Assoc Européene des Practiciens de Procedures Collectives (AEPPC) 1992; FCA 1977 (ACA 1964), FIPA 1983, MICM 1980; *Recreations* cricket, golf, watching rugby & soccer, music, travel, reading; *Clubs* Bradford, Shipley Golf, Old Brodleians Rugby, Shelf Cricket; *Style*— Peter Flesher, Esq; ✉ Grant Thornton, St Johns Centre, 110 Albion Street, Leeds LS2 8LA (☎ 0113 245 5514, fax 0113 246 0828, car 0860 659429)

FLESHER, Timothy James; s of James Amos Flesher (d 1994), of Haywards Heath, and Evelyn May Flesher; *b* 25 July 1949; *Educ* Haywards Heath GS, Hertford Coll Oxford (BA); *m* 1986, Margaret, da of John McCormack; 1 da (Siobhan Rachel b 30 June 1991); *Career* civil servant; lectr Cambs Coll of Arts and Technol 1972–74; Home Office: joined 1974, private sec to Min of State 1977–79, sec to Prisons Bd 1979–82, private sec to PM 1982–86, head of div Immigration Dept 1981–89, head Personnel Div 1989–91, head Probation Servs Div 1991–92, dir Admin Office for Standards in Educn 1992–94, dep dir gen Immigration and Nationality Directorate 1994–; *Recreations* psephology, American football; *Style*— Timothy Flesher, Esq; ✉ Immigration and Nationality Directorate, The Home Office, Apollo House, 36 Wellesley Road, Croydon CR9 3RR (☎ 0181 760 8526, fax 0181 760 8529)

FLETCHER, Alan Gerard; s of Bernard Fletcher, and Dorothy, *née* Murphy; *b* 27 Sept 1931; *Educ* Christ's Hosp Sch, Central Sch of Arts and Crafts, RCA, Sch of Architecture & Design Yale Univ (MFA); *m* 5 July 1956, Paola Biagi; 1 da (Raffaella b 1961); *Career* designer Fortune Magazine NY 1958–59, freelance practice London 1959–62; ptnr: Fletcher Forbes Gill 1962–65, Crosby Fletcher Forbes 1965–72; fndr ptnr Pentagram Design 1972–92; pres Designers & Art Dirs' Assoc 1973, int pres Alliance Graphique Int 1982–85; awards: One Show Gold award NY 1974, Gold award 1974 and President's award Designers' and Art Dirs' Assoc London 1977, medal Soc of Industl Artists and Designers 1982, Prince Philip prize for Designer of the Year 1993, memb NY Art Dirs Club Hall of Fame 1994; FSIAD 1964, ARCA, memb AGI, RDI 1972, sr fell RCA 1989; *Books* Graphic Design: Visual Comparisons (with Colin Forbes and Bob Gill, 1963), Was Ich Sah (1967), A Sign Systems Manual (with Theo Crosby and Colin Forbes, 1970), Identity Kits: A Pictorial Survey of Visual Arts (with Germano Facetti, 1971); with Pentagram ptnrs: Pentagram: The Work of Five Designers (1972), Living by Design (1978), Ideas on Design (1986), Pentagram, The Compendium (1993), Beware Wet Paint (1996); *Style*— Alan Fletcher, Esq; ✉ 12 Pembridge Mews, London W11 3EQ (☎ 0171 229 7095, fax 0171 229 8120)

FLETCHER, Andrew Fitzroy Stephen; s of (Maj) Fitzroy Fletcher, of Ansford, Castle Cary, Somerset, and Brygid, *née* Mahon; *b* 20 Dec 1957; *Educ* Eton, Magdalene Coll Cambridge (MA); *m* 1 Sept 1984, Felicia, da of Maj John Philip Pagan Taylor (d 1986), of nr Honiton, Devon; 2 s (Thomas b 1987, James b 1989); *Career* 2 Lt Welsh Gds 1976; called to the Bar Inner Temple 1980; Freeman City of London 1986, Liveryman Worshipful Co of Grocers 1994 (Freeman 1986); *Recreations* travel, fishing, reading; *Clubs* Boodle's, Pratt's, MCC; *Style*— Andrew Fletcher, Esq; ✉ 4 Pump Court, Temple, London EC4Y 7AN (☎ 0171 353 2656, fax 0171 583 2036)

FLETCHER, Prof Anthony John; s of John Molyneux Fletcher (d 1986), and Isabel Clare (Delle), *née* Chenevix-Trench; *b* 24 April 1941; *Educ* Wellington, Merton Coll Oxford (MA); *m* 29 July 1967, Tresna Dawn, da of Charles Henry Railton Russell; 2 s (Crispin b 1970, Dickon b 1972); *Career* history teacher King's Coll Sch Wimbledon 1964–67, successively lectr, sr lectr then reader Dept of History Univ of Sheffield, subsequently prof Dept of History Univ of Durham, currently prof Dept of History Univ of Essex; pres Ecclesiastical History Soc 1996–97; FRHistS; *Books* Tudor Rebellions (1967), A County Community in Peace and War: Sussex 1600–1660 (1975), The Outbreak of the English Civil War (1981), Reform in the Provinces (1986), Gender, Sex and Subordination in England 1500–1800 (1995); *Recreations* theatre, music, opera, walking, gardening; *Style*— Prof Anthony Fletcher; ✉ 4 The Tennis, Cassington, Witney, Oxon OX8 1EL; Department of History, University of Essex, Wivenhoe Park, Colchester CO4 3SQ (☎ 01206 872305, answerphone 01206 872302, fax 01206 873757)

FLETCHER, Giles; s of Thomas Simons Fletcher (d 1985; nephew of 1 Earl Attlee, KG, OM, CH, PC), of Nunton Cottage, Nunton, Salisbury, and Janet, *née* Bigg (d 1987); *b* 12 Aug 1936; *Educ* Marlborough; *m* 18 Jan 1964, Jennifer Marion Edith, da of Sir Eric Cecil Heygate Salmon, MC, DL (d 1946), of The Vale House, Old Church St, London SW3; 2 s (James b 1965, Timothy b 1974), 1 da (Alice b 1967); *Career* Fletcher and Partners: ptnr 1964–76, senior ptnr 1977–; govr Godolphin Sch; treas: Southern Cathedrals Festival, Salisbury Cathedral Girl Choristers' Fund; tstee Charitable Tsts; churchwarden; FCA 1961; *Recreations* hill walking, English and French Cathedrals and Churches; *Style*— Giles Fletcher, Esq; ✉ Apple Tree House, Middle Woodford, Salisbury SP4 6NG (☎ 01722 782329); Fletcher and Partners, Crown Chambers, Bridge St, Salisbury SP1 2LZ (☎ 01722 327801, fax 01722 323839)

FLETCHER, Ian Macmillan; s of John Malcolm Fletcher, JP, of Gourock, Scotland, and Jane Ann Cochran Fletcher (d 1980); *b* 16 Feb 1948; *Educ* Greenock Acad, Univ of Glasgow (LLB); *m* 15 Jan 1977, Jennifer Margaret, da of Capt John Brown William Daly, MN (d 1972), of Glasgow; 1 s (Richard John Malcolm b 13 Jan 1980), 2 da (Elizabeth Jane b 4 Aug 1978, Eleanor Kathleen b 21 Aug 1985); *Career* admitted slr: Scotland 1971, England 1978; asst slr Richards Butler 1977–79; ptnr: MacRoberts 1980–87, Richards Butler 1987–; authorised insolvency practitioner; former co sec Chilton Brothers Ltd; memb Cncl: Insolvency Lawyers Assoc Ltd (past pres), Law Soc of Scotland (currently convener Insolvency Slrs' Ctee), Soc of Practitioners of Insolvency (memb Int Ctee); memb: Law Soc, Law Soc of Scotland, Soc WS, Int Bar Assoc (memb Ctee J Section on Business Law), Soc of Scottish Lawyers London (past pres); WS, LTCL, LRAM, ARCO, MInstD, MIPA, FSPI; *Books* The Law and Practice of Receivership in Scotland (jtly, 1987, 2nd edn 1992), Insolvency and Finance in the Transportation Industry (jtly, 1993), The Law and Practice of Corporate Administrations (jtly, 1994); *Recreations* music, golf, swimming; *Clubs* Caledonian, Western (Glasgow), Gog Magog Golf (Cambridge); *Style*— Ian Fletcher, Esq, WS; ✉ Beaufort House, 15 St Botolph St, London EC3A 7EE (☎ 0171 247 6555, fax 0171 247 5091, telex 949494 RBLAW)

FLETCHER, Prof James Pearse; s of Harold Stanton Fletcher (d 1985), of Clifton, Bristol, and Bessie Florence, *née* Pearse (d 1976); *b* 25 Oct 1928; *Educ* King's Coll Taunton, Univ of Bristol (BDS); *m* 8 Sept 1962, Judith Mary, da of John Abbott (d 1982), of Caerleon, Gwent; 1 s (Anthony b 1963), 1 da (Suzanne b 1967); *Career* Nat Serv RADC 1953–55, Lt, Capt; NHS Hosp appts and private practice 1952–57, lectr in paradontal diseases Univ of Liverpool 1957–58; Univ of Bristol: lectr in dental surgery 1959, lectr in dental med 1959–63, conslt sr lectr in dental med 1963–80; Univ of Liverpool: prof of dental surgery 1980–82, Louis Cohen prof of dental surgery 1982–90, sr fell 1990–93, emeritus prof 1990–; memb Liverpool Health Authy 1981–87 (conslt 1980–91, emeritus conslt 1991–); alternate advsr Mersey Region RCS Faculty of Dental Surgery 1981–87, pres Br Soc of Periodontology 1981–82 (vice pres 1980–81 and 1982–83), memb Cncl Br Soc for Oral Med 1982–85, chm Post Grad Advsy Panel for Hosp Dental Surgery Mersey Region 1989–90, hon treas Liverpool Odontological Soc 1991–94 (pres 1996–97); BDA: chm Mersey Region Hosps Gp 1986–87, pres elect W Lancs, W Cheshire and N Wales branch 1992–93, pres 1993–94, life memb 1995–; memb: Int Assoc for Dental Res (life memb 1993–), Br Soc for Dental Res, Br Soc for Oral Pathology, Br Soc for Oral Med, Int Assoc of Oral Pathologists; FRSM, LDSRCS, FDSRCS (Eng); *Books* Human Disease for Dental Students (jtly, 1981), Elementi di Patologia Generale e di Patologia Umana (Medica e Chirurgica) Per Studenti di Odontoiatria (jtly, 1983); *Recreations* music, watercolour painting, photography; *Style*— Prof James Fletcher; ✉ 65 Salisbury Road, Cressington Park, Liverpool, Merseyside L19 0PH (☎ 0151 427 3379)

FLETCHER, Janis Richardson (Jan); da of Stuart Richardson Smith, of Hopeman, nr Elgin, and Ruby, *née* MacIntosh; *b* 11 May 1954; *Educ* Colne Valley HS, Knightsbridge Univ (MBA); *m* Edward Peter Fletcher; 2 da (Charlotte Richardson b 7 Oct 1975, Helena Elizabeth b 21 Oct 1976); *Career* md Manchester Commercials 1974–83, chm The Fletcher Group 1983–, chm Bryans of Headingley 1984–, non-exec dir Skipton Building Soc 1995–, dir Bee Health Group 1995–, chm M S F Motor Group 1995–; Veuve Cliquot Business Woman of the Year 1994, Yorkshire Woman of the Year 1995, BusinessAge Top 40 under 40 Award 1995; memb: Retail Motor Industry (RMI) 1983–, Nat Franchise Dealer's Assoc (NFDA) 1983–, Women's Network 1985–, Motor Industry Management (MIM); *Recreations* flying (PPL holder), skiing, swimming, keep fit, water skiing, entertaining, business; *Clubs* Westminster Dining; *Style*— Ms Jan Fletcher; ✉ The Fletcher Group, Meadow Road, Leeds LS11 9BX (☎ 0113 280 0200, fax 0113 280 0201)

FLETCHER, Jo(anna) Louise (GOULD-); da of Colin Adrian Gould-Fletcher, of London, and Edwina Charlotte, *née* Dean; *Educ* Queen Elizabeth's Sch Faversham Kent, Harlow Tech Coll; *Career* The Whitstable Times & Kentish Observer 1978–81 (jr reporter, sr reporter, film critic); sr reporter: The Hillingdon Mirror 1981–82, The Middlesex Advertiser & Gazette 1982–83, The Ealing Gazette 1983; freelance journalist 1983–88, film critic and columnist News of the World 1991–93 (joined 1988); conslt ed: Headline Book Publishing plc 1986–88, Mandarin Books 1988–91, Pan Books 1991–94; science fiction publisher Victor Gollancz Ltd 1994–, contributing ed Science Fiction Chronicle NY 1982–; sometime guest lectr UCLA and Loyola USA, specialist tutor DipHE Univ of E London; memb: Bd World Fantasy Convention 1979–, World Horror Convention 1989–; tstee: Horror Writers' Assoc 1989–, Tony Godwin Memorial Tst; memb: NUJ 1979, Science Fiction & Fantasy Writers of America 1987; *Books* Gaslight & Ghosts (ed, 1988), Horror At Hallowe'en (ed, 1995); *Recreations* science fiction, fantasy and horror, book collecting; *Style*— Ms Jo Fletcher; ✉ 24 Pearl Road, Walthamstow, London E17 4Q2 (☎ 0181 521 3034, fax 0181 923 4870)

FLETCHER, Dr (Timothy) John; s of George Spencer Fletcher (d 1981), of Silsden, W Yorks, and Pattie Margaret, *née* Beaver; *b* 12 Sept 1946; *Educ* The Leys Sch Cambridge, Univ of Glasgow (BVMS), Magdalene Coll Cambridge (PhD); *m* 8 July 1972, Nichola Rosemary, da of Hubert Henry Ormerod Chalk (d 1981); 2 da (Stella b 1978, Martha b 1979); *Career* fndr first British deer farm 1973 (awarded Queen's Award for Export Achievement 1990), dir British Deer Producers' Society Ltd 1983–91; chm British Deer Farmers' Assoc 1982–84, pres Veterinary Deer Soc, dir Scot Deer Centre 1987–90, memb Cncl RZS (Scotland); appointed first RCVS specialist in deer mgmnt 1995; *Recreations* food, wine, travel, collecting deer literature and ephemera, gardening; *Clubs*

Farmers'; *Style—* Dr John Fletcher; ✉ Reediehill Farm, Auchtermuchty, Fife KY14 7HS (☎ 01337 828369, fax 01337 827001)

FLETCHER, John W S; *Educ* Uppingham, Teeside Poly (H Dip in Civil and Structural Engrg); *m* 1964, Jacqueline; 2 s, 1 da; *Career* Cleveland Bridge and Engineering Company (acquired by Cementation 1968, pt of Trafalgar House 1970): joined as trainee civil engr 1959, dir 1968–75, md 1975–82, divnl md 1982; currently mktg and business devpt dir Kvaerner ASA (acquired Trafalgar House Plc 1996) and dir various subsid cos, memb Mgmnt Bd Kvaerner ASA and chm and md Kvaerner Corporate Development Ltd; chm: GEI International plc, Gammon Construction Ltd, Heavylift Aviation Holdings Ltd, Trafalgar House Construction (India) Ltd; currently dir: The Cementation Company (Africa) Ltd, Arboyne NL, AUSI Steel Ltd, Kvaerner Davy Ltd, Kvaerner John Brown Ltd, Lusoponte - Concessionaria para a Travessia do Tejo SA, PT Citra Ganesha Marga Nusantara; *Recreations* sailing; *Style—* John W S Fletcher, CBE; ✉ Kvaerner Corporate Development Ltd, Suite 5506–7, 55th Floor, Central Plaza, 18 Harbour Road, Wanchai, Hong Kong (☎ 00 852 2868 1100, fax 00 852 2868 1522)

FLETCHER, Prof John Walter James; s of Roy Arthur Walter Fletcher, MBE (d 1994), of Sherborne, Dorset, and Eileen Alice, *née* Beane; *b* 23 June 1937; *Educ* Yeovil Sch Somerset, Trinity Hall Cambridge (BA, MA), Univ of Toulouse (MPhil, PhD); *m* 14 Sept 1961, Beryl Sibley, da of William Stanley Connop (d 1963), of Beckenham, Kent; 2 s (Hilary b 1976, Edmund b 1978), 1 da (Harriet b 1972); *Career* lectr in English Univ of Toulouse 1961–64, lectr in French Univ of Durham 1964–66, prof of European literature Univ of E Anglia 1989– (French lectr 1966–68, reader in French 1968–69, prof of comparative lit 1969–89, pro vice chllr 1974–79); memb: Soc of Authors, Translators' Assoc; *Books* The Novels of Samuel Beckett (1964), Claude Simon and Fiction Now (1975), Novel and Reader (1980), The Georgics (by Claude Simon, trans 1989, Scott Moncrieff prize for translation from French, 1990); *Recreations* listening to Monteverdi and Schubert; *Style—* Prof John Fletcher; ✉ School of Modern Languages and European Studies, University of East Anglia, Norwich, Norfolk NR4 7TJ (☎ 01603 592743, fax 01603 250599, telex 975197)

FLETCHER, Kim Thomas; s of Jack Fletcher, and Agnes, *née* Coulthwaite; *b* 17 Sept 1956; *Educ* Heversham GS, Hertford Coll Oxford (BA jurisprudence); *m* May 1991, Sarah Sands; 1 s (Rafe b 1992), 1 da (Matilda b 1994), 1 step s (Henry Sands b 1985); *Career* journalist; The Star Sheffield 1978–81, The Sunday Times 1981–86 (Home Affairs corr, Labour corr), The Daily Telegraph 1986–87, freelance feature writer 1987–88; The Sunday Telegraph: joined 1988, news ed 1991–94, dep ed (News) 1994–95, dep ed 1995–; jt Reporter of the Yr 1982; *Recreations* football, theatre; *Clubs* Groucho; *Style—* Kim Fletcher, Esq; ✉ The Sunday Telegraph (☎ 0171 538 7331)

FLETCHER, Malcolm Stanley; MBE (1982); s of Harold Fletcher, and Clarice Fletcher; *b* 25 Feb 1936; *Educ* Manchester GS, Univ of Manchester (BSc), Univ of London (MSc), Imperial Coll London (DIC); *m* 21 Aug 1965, Rhona Christina; 2 da (Sarah b 1966, Rachael b 1972), 1 s (Lawrence b 1968); *Career* asst site engr (Dokan Dam Iraq) Binnie, Deacon & Gourley 1957–60, site engr (Thelwall Viaduct M6) Raymond International 1960–61, engr and site mangr G Dew & Co Contractors 1961–65, resident engr (New Jhelum Bridge Pakistan) Donovan Lee & Partners 1965–67, chm Sir William Halcrow & Partners Ltd 1991– (joined 1968); memb: Structural Ctee CIRIA 1979–82, Prestressed Concrete Ctee Concrete Soc 1980–84; chm Structures Steering Gp Civil Engrg Science and Engrg Res Cncl 1984–89, memb Cncl Assoc of Consulting Engrs 1988– (chm Highways Panel 1988–91); author of numerous articles in various pubns; FEng 1993, FICE, FGS; *Projects with Sir William Halcrow & Partners* chief asst engr Giuliana Bridge Libya 1968–70, resident engr Benghazi Corniche Project Libya 1970–72, sr rep Libya 1972–74; project engr: based UK 1974–77 (work incl Al Garhoud Bridge UAE, Sharjah Airport Interchange Bridge UAE and Wayaya Bridge Oman), River Orwell Bridge 1977–82, Al Kadan Bridge Yemen 1978–79, Malaysia 1980–85, Monnow Bridge Monmouth 1983–84; team ldr: Karnali Bridge Nepal 1984–85, Dartford Bridge 1986–91; project dir: Constantius Bridge Hexham 1986–87, Town Ham Viaduct Glos 1986–87, Blue Nile Bridge Ethiopia 1988–90, Thames Bridge 1988–, second Severn Bridge 1990–; memb Technical Advsy Bd Lantau Fixed Crossing Hong Kong 1991–; *Recreations* cycling; *Style—* Malcolm Fletcher, Esq, MBE, FEng; ✉ Sir William Halcrow & Partners Ltd, Burderop Park, Swindon SN4 0QD (☎ 01793 812479, fax 01793 812089)

FLETCHER, Mandie Elizabeth; da of Sqdn-Ldr C W Fletcher (ret), of Homefield, Lodsworth, Midhurst, Sussex, and Shirley, *née* Hull; *b* 27 Dec 1954; *Educ* Guildford HS Surrey; *Career* producer and director; dir Fletcher Sanderson Films; *Television* Blackadder II 1988 (ACE Award for Best Comedy Series), Blackadder the Third 1988 (BAFTA Award for Best Comedy Series), Shalom Joan Collins 1989, Born Kicking 1991, various commercials; *Films* Deadly Advice 1993; *Style—* Miss Mandie Fletcher; ✉ Fletcher Sanderson Films, 1 Marshall Street, London W1B 1LQ (☎ 0171 734 5678)

FLETCHER, Marjorie Helen Kelsey; CBE (1988); da of late Norman Farler Fletcher, and late Marie Amelie, *née* Adams; *b* 21 Sept 1932; *Educ* Avondale HS, Sutton Coldfield HS for Girls; *Career* slr's clerk 1948–53; WRNS: telegraphist 1953, Third Offr 1956, Second Offr 1960, First Offr 1969, Chief Offr 1976; NDC 1979, directing staff RN Staff Coll 1980–81, psc 1981, Supt 1981, Int Mil Staff NATO HQ 1981–84, asst dir Naval Staff Duties 1984–85, Cmdt 1986, dir WRNS 1986–88; ADC to HM the Queen 1986–88; CIM 1987; *Books* The WRNS; *Recreations* reading, collecting pictures, needlework, painting, natural and English history; *Style—* Miss Marjorie Fletcher, CBE; ✉ Room 44, Nenthorn House, Kelso, Roxburghshire TD5 7RY

FLETCHER, Mark Walter; s of Prof Charles Montague Fletcher (d 1995), and Hon Mrs Louisa Mary, *née* Seely; *b* 3 Oct 1942; *Educ* Eton, Trinity Coll Cambridge (MA); *m* 1, 9 Nov 1968 (m dis 1982), Amelia Henrietta Rose, da of Richard Tyler; 1 s (Benjamin Charles b 14 July 1971), 1 da (Ellen Maisie Madeleine b 21 March 1973); m 2, 5 Nov 1988, Lindy, da of Brig Michael Neal Harbottle; *Career* asst slr Coward Chance 1968–77 (articled clerk 1966–68); Taylor Joynson Garrett (formerly Taylor Garrett, Taylor Humbert): asst 1978, ptnr 1979–; memb Law Soc; *Recreations* gardening, skiing, windsurfing; *Style—* Mark Fletcher, Esq; ✉ 30 Musgrave Crescent, London SW6 4QE (☎ 0171 736 5216); Taylor Joynson Garrett, Carmelite, 50 Victoria Embankment, London EC4Y 0DX (☎ 0171 353 1234, fax 0171 936 2666, mobile 0374 800739)

FLETCHER, Martin Anthony; s of Anthony Travers Nethersole Fletcher, of Brandeston, Suffolk, and Nancy Evelyn, *née* Scott (d 1994); *b* 7 July 1956; *Educ* Uppingham, Univ of Edinburgh, Univ of Pennsylvania (MA); *m* 10 Oct 1981, Catherine Jane, *née* Beney; 1 s (Barnaby Martin b 12 April 1986), 2 da (Hannah Catherine b 2 June 1984, Imogen Nancy b 26 April 1989); *Career* journalist; North Herts Gazette 1980–82, Daily Telegraph 1982–83; The Times: lobby corr 1986–89, Washington corr 1989–92, US ed 1992–; *Books* The Good Caff Guide (1980); *Recreations* tennis, squash, skiing, children; *Style—* Martin Fletcher, Esq; ✉ 3236 Juniper Lane, Falls Church, VA 22044, USA (☎ 00 1 703 534 2953); The Times of London, 529 14th St, NW, Suite 1040, Washington DC 20045 (☎ 00 1 202 347 7659)

FLETCHER, Michael; s of Richard Fletcher (d 1990), of Cardiff, and Catherin, *née* Thomas (d 1981); *b* 11 March 1945; *Educ* Whitchurch GS Cardiff, The Architectural Assoc Sch of Arch (AADipl); *m* 1, 1969 (m dis 1982), Lesley Saunders; 1 s (Luke Fletcher b 1973), 1 da (Daisy Fletcher b 1977); m 2, 1990, Malory Massey; 1 da (Vita Massey Fletcher b 1992); *Career* architect; Farrell Grimshaw Architects 1970–72, assoc Wolff Olins design consultancy 1972–78, fndr ptnr Fletcher Priest Architects 1978–, fndr Fletcher Priest Bösl (German office) 1993–; RIBA: memb Cncl 1993–, chm Clients Advsy Serv 1994–, vice chm London Region 1996; RIBA 1972, FIMgt 1973; *Awards* Civic Tst commendation (for Babmaes St offices) 1989, Br Cncl of Offices Bldg of the Yr Award and Br Inst of Facilities Mgmnt Bldg of the Yr Award (for Powergen offices) 1996; *Recreations* water sports; *Style—* Michael Fletcher, Esq; ✉ Fletcher Priest Architects, 23–27 Heddon Street, London W1R 8RA (☎ 0171 439 8621, fax 0171 439 8526, e-mail fparch@demon.co.uk)

FLETCHER, Sheriff Michael John; s of Walter Fletcher (d 1992), and Elizabeth, *née* Pringle (d 1986); *b* 5 Dec 1945; *Educ* Dundee HS, Univ of St Andrews (LLB); *m* 19 Oct 1968, Kathryn Mary, da of John Bain; 2 s (Christopher Michael b 13 Sept 1971, Mark Richard b 11 March 1977); *Career* apprentice slr Kirk Mackie and Elliot Edinburgh 1966–68; slr: Ross Strachan & Co Dundee 1968–88, Hendry & Fenton Dundee 1988–92, Miller Hendry Dundee 1992–94; sheriff S Strathclyde Dumfries and Galloway (at Dumfries) 1994–; *Recreations* golf, gardening; *Style—* Sheriff Michael Fletcher; ✉ Sheriff Chambers, Buccleuch Street, Dumfries DG1 2AN

FLETCHER, (Peter) Neil; s of Alan Fletcher, of Thurnby, Leicester, and Ruth Fletcher (d 1961); *b* 5 May 1944; *Educ* Wyggeston Boys' GS Leicester, City of Leeds Coll of Educn, Univ of London (BA), London Business Sch (MBA 1994); *m* 9 Sept 1967, Margaret Mary, da of Anthony Gerald Monaghan (d 1967); 2 s (Ben b 25 May 1971, Sam b 18 July 1974); *Career* teacher Leeds 1966–68; lectr in further educn: Leeds 1969–70, Harrow 1970–73, Merton 1973–76; educn offr (and head Educn Dept) NALGO 1991–93 (princ admin offr 1976–91), dir strategic projects UNISON 1994–95 (educn offr 1993–94), mgmnt consit 1995–; cncllr London Borough of Camden 1978–86 (dep ldr 1982–84); ILEA: memb 1979–90, chm Further and Higher Educn Sub-Ctee 1981–87, leader 1987–90; chm: Assoc of Metropolitan Authorities Educn Ctee 1987–90 (memb 1981–90), Cncl of Local Educn Authorities 1987–90; govr: Penn Sch Bucks 1985–, London Inst 1985–, LSE 1990–, City Literary Inst 1996–; FRSA 1989; hon fell Coll of Preceptors 1990; *Recreations* cooking, walking, theatre, cricket, football; *Clubs* Royal Over-Seas League; *Style—* Neil Fletcher, Esq; ✉ 42 Narcissus Road, London NW6 1TH (☎ and fax 0171 435 5306)

FLETCHER, Paul Thomas; CBE (1959); s of Stephen Baldwin Fletcher (d 1971), of Maidstone, and Jessie Carrie, *née* Rumsby (d 1963); *b* 30 Sept 1912; *Educ* Nicholson Inst Isle of Lewis, Maidstone GS, Medway Tech Coll (BSc); *m* 12 April 1941, Mary Elizabeth, da of Percy Howard King (d 1936), of Maidstone; 3 s (John b 1947, David b 1949, Peter b 1952); *Career* chartered engr; chief engr Miny of Works 1951–54 (joined 1939), engrg dir UKAEA Industrial Group 1954–61, dir United Power Co 1961–65, md GEC Process Engineering Ltd 1965–70, dep chm Atomic Power Construction Ltd 1976–80 (md 1970–75), consit NNC Ltd 1980–; dep pres Br Standards Inst 1981–89 (chm 1979–81), hon fell IMechE 1989 (pres 1975–76); FEng 1978, FICE, FIMechE, FIEE; *Recreations* motoring, photography; *Style—* Paul Fletcher, Esq, CBE, FEng

FLETCHER, Dr (Archibald) Peter; s of Walter Archibald Fletcher (d 1970), and Dorothy Mabel Fletcher; *b* 24 Dec 1930; *Educ* Kingswood Sch Bath, London Hosp Med Coll, UCL, St Mary's Hosp Med Sch; *m* 1972, Patricia Elizabeth Samson, *née* Marr; 3 s, 2 da; *Career* sr lectr in chemical pathology St Mary's Hosp London 1967–70, head of biochemistry American Nat Red Cross 1970–73, princ med offr and med assessor to Ctee on Safety of Medicines 1977, chief scientific offr and sr princ med offr DHSS 1978, res physician Upjohn Int 1978–80, sr med offr DHSS 1978–79; currently: ptnr Documenta Biomedica, med dir IMS International, dir PMS International Ltd; *Publications* numerous papers in scientific and med jls on: glycoproteins, physical chemistry, metabolism of blood cells, safety evaluation of new drugs; *Recreations* gardening, cooking; *Clubs* Wig and Pen, Royal Society of Medicine; *Style—* Dr Peter Fletcher; ✉ Hall Corner Cottage, Little Maplestead, Halstead, Essex CO9 2RU (☎ 01787 475465)

FLETCHER, Air Chief Marshal Sir Peter Carteret; KCB (1968), OBE (1944), DFC (1942), AFC (1952); s of Frederick Wheeler Trevor Fletcher (d 1964), of Norton, S Rhodesia, and Dora, *née* Clulee; *b* 7 Oct 1916; *Educ* St George's Coll S Rhodesia, Rhodes Univ; *m* 1940, (Marjorie) Isobel, da of Gilbert Percival Kotzé (d 1953), of Grahamstown, SA; 2 da (Anne, Elizabeth); *Career* transferred from S Rhodesian Air Force to RAF 1941, CO 135 Fighter Sqdn and 258 Fighter Sqdn 1940–42, CO 25 Elementary Flying Training Sch 1942–43; memb directing staff: RAF Staff Coll 1943–44, Jt Services Staff Coll 1945–46, IDC 1956–57; CO RAF Abingdon 1958–60, dir Operational Requirements (B) Air Miny 1961–63, Air Cdre 1961, Air Vice-Marshal 1964, Asst Chief of Air Staff (Policy and Planning) 1964–66, AOC 38 Gp, Transport Cmd 1966–67, Air Marshal 1967, Vice-Chief of Air Staff 1967–70, Controller of Aircraft Miny of Aviation Supply 1970, Air Systems Controller Def Procurement Exec 1971–73; dir: Hawker Siddeley Aviation Ltd 1974–77, corp strategy and planning British Aerospace 1977–82, Airbus Industry Supervisory Bd 1979–82; aerospace consit 1983–91; FRAeS 1986; *Recreations* books, travel; *Clubs* RAF; *Style—* Air Chief Marshal Sir Peter Fletcher, KCB, OBE, DFC, AFC; ✉ 85A Campden Hill Court, Holland St, Kensington, London W8 7HW (☎ 0171 937 1982)

FLETCHER, Philip John; s of Alan Philip Fletcher, QC, of Royston, Herts, and Annette Grace, *née* Wright; *b* 2 May 1946; *Educ* Marlborough, Trinity Coll Oxford (MA); *m* 12 Feb 1977, Margaret Anne, da of J E Boys, of Witley, Surrey; 2 da (Helen b 1978 d 1989, Sarah b 1982); *Career* teacher VSO 1967–68; MPBW then Dept of the Environment: joined 1968, asst princ 1968, W Midlands Regnl Office 1973–76, asst sec private sector housebuilding 1980, local govt expenditure 1982–85, under sec fin 1986–90, land use planning 1990–93, dep sec and chief exec PSA and Property Holdings 1993–94, dep sec cities and countryside 1994–95; receiver for the Met Police Dist 1996–; lay reader St Michael's Stockwell; *Style—* Philip Fletcher, Esq; ✉ New Scotland Yard, Broadway, London SW1H 0BG (☎ 0171 230 1212, fax 0171 230 0742)

FLETCHER, Piers Michael William; s of Col Michael James Rex Fletcher, MBE, of Folkestone, Kent, and Mary Anita, *née* Williams; *b* 10 Aug 1956; *Educ* Wellington Coll, Christ Church Oxford (MA); *m* 8 Aug 1986, Paula Harvey Anne, da of John Levey, and Jacqueline Levey; *Career* 2 Lt 6 QEO Gurkha Rifles 1975; dir: GNI Ltd 1984–, Baltic Futures Exchange 1988–91, London Commodity Exchange 1991–96; MSI; *Recreations* polo, cooking, photography; *Style—* Piers Fletcher, Esq; ✉ Blackberry Farm, Winterslow, Salisbury SP5 1QP (☎ 01980 862104); GNI Ltd, Cannon Bridge, 25 Dowgate Hill, London EC4R 2GN (☎ 0171 337 3500, car 0836 600869)

FLETCHER, Dr Robin Anthony; OBE (1984), DSC (1944); s of Maj P C Fletcher, MC, TD (d 1961), of Hinton Priory, Hinton Charterhouse, Bath, and Edith Maud, *née* Okell, JP (d 1978); *b* 30 May 1922; *Educ* Marlborough, Trinity Coll Oxford (MA, DPhil); *m* 9 Dec 1950, Jinny May; 2 s (Clive b 1951, Denys b 1954); *Career* ordinary seaman RN HMS Gambia 1941–42, Sub Lt (later Lt) RNVR 1943–46 (Levant Schooner Flotilla Med, minesweeping trawlers UK); Univ of Oxford: lectr in Modern Greek 1949–79, domestic bursar Trinity Coll 1950–74, sr proctor 1966–67, memb Hebdomedal Cncl 1967–74; sec Rhodes Tst and warden Rhodes House 1980–89, former tstee Oxford Preservation Tst; former memb Bd of Govrs: Kelly Coll, Cheltenham Coll, Marlborough Coll, Radley Coll, Sherborne Sch; bronze medallist GB hockey team Olympic Games 1952, hockey player for England 1949–55, pres Hockey Assoc 1972–83; *Books* Kostes Palamas (1984); *Recreations* golf, listening to music; *Clubs* Naval, Vincent's (Oxford); *Style—* Dr Robin Fletcher, OBE, DSC; ✉ Binglea, Quoyloo, Stromness, Orkney KW16 3LU (☎ 01856 841532)

FLETCHER, Robin Charles; s of Brian and Elaine Fletcher; *b* 11 Feb 1966; *Educ* Rugby, South Glamorgan Inst (NCTJ); *Career* reporter Birmingham Post and Mail

1984–89, sr ed Midland Weekly Newspapers and ed Solihull News 1990–92; ed: Northampton Chronicle and Echo 1992–94, West Lancashire Evening Gazette 1994–95, Wales on Sunday 1996–; dir: Northampton Mercury Co Ltd 1994, Blackpool Gazette & Herald Ltd 1994–95; Guild of Editors: memb 1993–, vice-chm Gen Purposes Ctee 1996, hon sec S Wales region 1996; memb Employment Support Ctee Blackpool Fylde & Wyre Soc for the Blind 1995–; memb and newsletter ed Cardiff Inst for the Blind 1996–; highly commended Regional Ed of the Year Newspaper Focus Awards 1994; *Recreations* squash, reading, writing, country walking, piano composition; *Style*— Robin Fletcher, Esq; ✉ Wales on Sunday, Western Mail and Echo Ltd, Havelock Street, Cardiff CF1 1XR (☎ 01222 583583, fax 01222 583125)

FLETCHER, Prof Roger; s of Harry Fletcher (d 1942), and Alice, *née* Emms (d 1996); *b* 29 Jan 1939; *Educ* Huddersfield Coll, Univ of Cambridge (MA), Univ of Leeds (PhD); *m* 23 Sept 1963, Mary Marjorie, da of Charlie Taylor (d 1970), of Harrogate; 2 da (Jane Elizabeth b 17 Nov 1968, Sarah Anne b 13 Sept 1970); *Career* lectr Univ of Leeds 1963–69, princ scientific offr AERE Harwell 1969–73, prof Univ of Dundee 1984– (sr lectr and reader 1973–84); FIMA, FRSE 1988; *Books* Practical Methods of Optimization Vol I (1980), Vol 2 (1981); *Recreations* hillwalking, bridge; *Style*— Prof Roger Fletcher, FRSE; ✉ Department of Mathematics and Computer Science, University of Dundee, Dundee DD1 4HN (☎ 01382 23181, telex 76293)

FLETCHER, Dr Ronald Frank; s of Capt Roland Fletcher, OBE (d 1973), and Lizzie May, *née* Furniss (d 1970); *b* 30 Jan 1927; *Educ* King Edward VI HS Birmingham, Univ of Birmingham (BSc, MB ChB, PhD, MD); *m* 22 April 1954, June Margaret, da of Ephraim Preston Astill (d 1971); 3 s (Martin b 12 May 1956, Preston b 29 Dec 1958, Stephen b 29 March 1962); *Career* Nat Serv Capt RAMC 1952–54; sr house offr Metabolic Res Unit E Birmingham Hosp 1954–59, Eli Lilly res fell Sinai and Johns Hopkins Hosps Baltimore USA 1959–60, conslt physician Dudley Rd Hosp Birmingham 1965–91, ret; hon fell Univ of Birmingham 1995– (lectr in med 1960–65); vice chm Birmingham City Hosp NHS Tst; FRCP 1972; *Books* Lecture Notes on Endocrinology (1967, 1978, 1982 and 1987); *Recreations* mountaineering, travel; *Clubs* Midland Assoc of Mountaineers, Birmingham Med Res Expeditionary Soc; *Style*— Dr Ronald Fletcher; ✉ 11 St Mary's Rd, Harborne, Birmingham B17 0EY (☎ 0121 427 4043); City Hospital, Dudley Rd, Birmingham B18 7QH (☎ 0121 554 3801)

FLETCHER, Susan Jane; da of Prof Leonard Fletcher, of Bakewell, Derbys, and Joan, *née* Edmunds; *b* 3 March 1950; *m* Nicholas W Stuart, CB, *qv*; 1 da (Emily Fletcher b 12 Sept 1983), 1 s (Alexander Fletcher b 1 Feb 1989); *Career* managing ed Sphere Books Ltd 1979–83, publishing dir MacDonald & Co 1983–87, jt dep md Headline Book Publishing PLC 1987–93, dep md Hodder & Stoughton 1993–; *Style*— Ms Susan Fletcher; ✉ 181 Chevening Road, Queen's Park, London NW6 6DT; Hodder & Stoughton, Hodder Headline PLC, 338 Euston Road, London NW1 3BH (☎ 0171 873 6000, fax 0171 873 6024)

FLETCHER, Winston; s of Albert Fletcher (d 1963), of London, and Bessie, *née* Miller (d 1955); *b* 15 July 1937; *Educ* Westminster City Sch, St John's Coll Cambridge (MA); *m* 14 June 1963, Jean, da of Alfred Brownston (d 1968), of Bristol; 1 da (Amelia b 1 Jan 1966); *Career* dir Sharps Advertising 1964–69 (joined as trainee 1959), md MCR Advertising 1970; Fletcher Shelton Delaney: fndr 1974, md 1974–81, chm 1981–83; chm and chief exec Ted Bates UK 1983–85; chm: Delaney Fletcher Delaney 1985–89, Delaney Fletcher Bozell 1989–96, Bozell Europe 1989–; regular author for nat business and advertising trade press; visiting prof Lancaster Univ Mgmnt Sch; memb Cncl Advertising Standards Authy 1986–93, chm The Advertising Assoc 1993–97; tstee Open Coll of the Arts 1990–, dep chm Central London Training and Enterprise Cncl 1991–95; FIPA (pres 1989–91), FRSA; *Books* The Admakers (1972), Teach Yourself Advertising (1978), Meetings, Meetings (1983), Commercial Breaks (1984), Superefficiency (1986), The Manipulators (1988), Creative People (1990), A Glittering Haze (1992), How to Capture the Advertising High Ground (1994); *Recreations* reading, writing, arithmetic; *Clubs* Reform, Royal Institution, Annabel's, Thirty, Harry's, Groucho; *Style*— Winston Fletcher, Esq; ✉ Chapman's Farm, Dunsden Green, Oxon RG4 9PP (☎ 0118 947 8819); 12 Bourdon Street, Berkeley Square, London W1 (☎ 0171 629 4844); c/o Delaney Fletcher Bozell, 25 Wellington Street, London WC2E 7DA (☎ 0171 836 3474)

FLETCHER-COOKE, Sir Charles; kt (1981), QC (1958); yr s of Capt Charles Arthur Fletcher-Cooke (d 1924), and Gwendolen May Fletcher-Cooke; *b* 1914; *Educ* Malvern, Peterhouse Cambridge; *m* 1959 (m dis 1967), Diana Mary Margaret Westcott (d 1993), yr da of Capt Edward Westcott King, RA, and formerly wife of 3 Baron Avebury; *Career* barrister 1938; MP (C) Darwen 1951–83, jt parly under-sec of state Home Office 1961–63, MEP 1977–79; Dato of the Kingdom of Brunei 1978; *Clubs* Garrick, Pratt's; *Style*— Sir Charles Fletcher-Cooke, QC; ✉ The Red House, Clifton Hampden, Oxon OX14 3EW (☎ 01865 407754)

FLETCHER ROGERS, Helen Susan; da of Peter Alexander Stewart (d 1995), and Jessie Mary, *née* Sykes (d 1978); *b* 24 Sept 1941; *Educ* Greenhead HS Huddersfield, Univ Coll London; *m* 28 Sept 1972, David Geoffrey Fletcher Rogers, s of Murray Rowland Fletcher Rogers (d 1991); 2 s (Anthony, Jonathan); *Career* called to the Bar Gray's Inn 1965; PA Thomas & Co 1964–67; Kodak Ltd: joined 1967, currently co sec, dir 1990–, Euro legal dir 1995–; vice chm Northwick Park and St Mark's Hosp NHS Trust 1992–; *Books* Butterworths Encyclopaedia of Forms and Precedents Vol 16a (contrib on patents and designs), Microfilm and the Law; *Recreations* walking, working, theatre, music; *Style*— Mrs Helen Susan Fletcher Rogers; ✉ Kodak Ltd, PO Box 66, Hemel Hempstead, Herts HP1 1JU (☎ 01442 844413, fax 01442 844807)

FLETCHER-VANE, *see:* Vane

FLEW, Prof Antony Garrard Newton; o s of Rev Dr R Newton Flew (d 1962); *b* 11 Feb 1923; *Educ* Kingswood Sch Bath, SOAS, St John's Coll Oxford (John Locke scholar, MA); *m* 1952, Annis Ruth Harty, da of Col Frank Donnison; 2 da; *Career* prof of philosophy: Univ of Keele 1954–71, Calgary Univ 1972–73, Univ of Reading 1973–82, York Univ Toronto 1983–85; distinguished research fell Social Philosophy and Policy Centre Bowling Green State Univ 1986–91; fndr memb: Cncl of Freedom Assoc, Academic Cncl Adam Smith Inst, Educn Gp of the Centre for Policy Studies; *Books incl* Hume's Philosophy of Belief (1961), God and Philosophy (1967), Crime or Disease (1973), Sociology, Equality and Education (1976), The Presumption of Atheism (1976), A Rational Animal (1978), The Politics of Procrustes (1981), Darwinian Evolution (1984), Thinking about Social Thinking (1985), David Hume: Philosopher of Moral Science (1986), The Logic of Mortality (1987), Power to the Parents (1987), Equality in Liberty and Justice (1989), Atheistic Humanism (1993), Shephard's Warning (1994); *Recreations* walking, house maintenance; *Style*— Prof Antony Flew; ✉ 26 Alexandra Road, Reading, Berks RG1 5PD (☎ 0118 926 1848)

FLIGHT, Howard Emerson; s of Bernard Thomas Flight (d 1990), of Devon, and Doris Mildred Emerson, *née* Parker; *b* 16 June 1948; *Educ* Brentwood Essex, Magdalene Coll Cambridge (MA), Univ of Michigan Business Sch (MBA); *m* 1973, Christabel Diana Beatrice, da of Christopher Paget Norbury (d 1975), of Worcestershire; 1 s (Thomas b 1978), 3 da (Catherine b 1975, Josephine b 1986, Mary Anne b 1988); *Career* jt md Guinness Flight Global Asset Management (formerly Investmt Div of Guinness Mahon); dir: Guinness Flight International Fund Ltd, Guinness Flight Global Strategy Fund Ltd; Parly candidate (Cons) Bermondsey and Southwark both elections 1974, prospective Parly candidate (Cons) Arundel and S Downs 1996; govr Brentwood Sch, tstee The Elgar Fndn, pres Magdalene Coll Assoc; *Books* All You Need to Know About Exchange Rates (jtly, 1988); *Recreations* skiing, classical music, fruit farming; *Clubs* Carlton, Winchester House; *Style*— Howard Flight, Esq; ✉ 6 Ruvigny Gardens, Putney, London SW15 1JR (☎ 0181 789 0923); The Norrest, Leigh Sinton, Worcestershire; Guinness Flight Global Asset Management Ltd, Lighterman's Court, 5 Gainsford St, London SE1 2NE (☎ 0171 522 2100, fax 0171 403 3597)

FLINDALL, Jacqueline; JP (Oxford and Salisbury 1982); da of Henry Flindall (d 1940), and Lilian, *née* Evans (d 1940), brought up by unc Alfred Thomas Evans, OBE, late Chief Constable of Pembrokeshire; *b* 12 Oct 1932; *Educ* St David's Sch Ashford, Middlesex; *Career* RGN Univ Coll Hosp; SCM: St Luke's Hosp Guildford, Watford Maternity Hosp; asst matron Wexham Park Hosp 1957–63, dep supt of Nursing Prince of Wales Hosp 1964–66; chief nursing offr: Northwick Park Hosp 1969–73, Oxfordshire Health Authy 1973–83; regnl nursing offr Wessex RHA 1983–85, nursing conslt 1985–; Hon FRCN 1983; *Recreations* painting; *Style*— Jacqueline Flindall; ✉ 4 Mill Lane, Romsey, Hants SO51 8EU (☎ 01794 513926)

FLINT, Prof Anthony Patrick Fielding; *b* 31 Aug 1943; *m* 1967 (m dis 1996), Chan Mun Kwun; 2 s; *Career* res fell Depts of Physiology and Obstetrics and Gynaecology Univ of Western Ontario 1969–72, sr res biochemist Dept of Obstetrics and Gynaecology Welsh Nat Sch of Med 1972–73, lectr Nuffield Dept of Obstetrics and Gynaecology Univ of Oxford 1973–77; AFRC: sr scientific offr 1977–79, princ scientific offr 1979–85, sr princ scientific offr 1985–87, visiting scientist 1987–95; dir Inst of Zoology Univ of London 1987–93, dir of sci Zoological Soc 1987–93; prof of animal physiology Univ of Nottingham 1993–; memb numerous ctees and ed bds; author of over 240 publications in scientific journals; medal Soc for Endocrinology 1985, medal of Polish Physiological Soc 1990; memb: Physiological Soc 1979, Blair-Bell Res Soc 1974, Soc for the Study of Fertility 1973, Soc for Endocrinology 1973, Biochemical Soc 1967; FIBiol 1982; *Clubs* Zoological; *Style*— Prof Anthony Flint; ✉ Department of Physiology and Environmental Science, University of Nottingham, Sutton Bonington, Loughborough, Leics LE12 5RD

FLINT, Charles John Raffles; QC (1995); *Career* called to the Bar 1975, jr counsel to the Crown 1991–95; *Style*— Charles Flint, Esq, QC; ✉ 2 Hare Court, Ground Floor, Temple, London EC4Y 7BH (☎ 0171 583 1770)

FLINT, Prof Colin David; s of Oswald George Flint (d 1981), of London, and Maud Elisabeth, *née* Hayes; *b* 3 May 1943; *Educ* Leyton HS, Imperial Coll London (BSc, DIC, PhD, DSc); *m* 3 Aug 1968, Florence Edna, da of Charles Cowin (d 1969), of Isle of Man; 2 s (Richard Charles b 6 March 1972, Peter David b 25 July 1974); *Career* NATO postdoctoral fell Univ of Copenhagen Denmark 1967–69, prof of chemistry Birkbeck Coll London 1981– (lectr 1969–76, reader chemical spectroscopy 1976–81, head of dept 1979–86); visiting prof: Univ of Virginia USA 1982, Univ of Chile 1985, 1987, 1991 and 1994, Tech Univ of Graz Austria 1986 and 1989, Univ of Copenhagen 1988, Univ of Padova 1991; author of about 160 pubns in learned jls; ARCS, FRSC, CChem; *Books* Vibronic Processes in Inorganic Chemistry (ed, 1989); *Recreations* swimming, travel; *Style*— Prof Colin Flint; ✉ Laser Laboratory, Birkbeck College, Gordon House, 29 Gordon Square, London WC1H 0PP (☎ 0171 380 7466, 0171 380 7467, fax 0171 380 7464)

FLINT, Douglas Jardine; s of Prof David Flint, and Dorothy, *née* Jardine; *b* 8 July 1955; *Educ* Univ of Glasgow (BAcc), Harvard Business Sch (PMD); *m* 25 May 1984, Fiona Isobel Livingstone, *née* McMillan; 2 s (Jamie Livingstone b 3 May 1989, Stuart David b 19 Jan 1991), 1 da (Catriona Lindsey b 13 Aug 1992); *Career* KPMG (formerly Peat Marwick Mitchell & Co): articled clerk 1977–80, accountant 1980–88, ptnr 1988–95; gp fin dir HSBC Holdings plc 1995–; ACA 1980, memb ACT 1996; *Recreations* golf, tennis; *Clubs* Caledonian, Sloane, Denham Golf, Cooden Beach Golf; *Style*— Douglas Flint, Esq; ✉ HSBC Holdings plc, 10 Lower Thames Street, London EC3R 6AE (☎ 0171 260 7360, fax 0171 260 6686)

FLINT, Helen Sarah; da of Prof John Edgar Flint, of Nova Scotia, and Shiela Doreen, *née* Curran (d 1979); *b* 7 June 1952; *Educ* Dalhousie Univ Canada (BA), St Anne's Coll Oxford (BA, Postgrad CertEd, Univ Entrance scholarship, Univ Prize for English literature); *m* 1977, John Christopher Lawlor, s of Prof John James Lawlor, *qv*; 1 da (Alice Rachel b 1979), 1 s (John Maxwell b 1981); *Career* writer; Sch Library Assoc Oxford 1974, reviews and advertising for The School Librarian 1976–78, English, drama, classical studies and Russian teacher Sch of St Helen & St Katharine Abingdon 1979–81, abstracting/translating Art Bibliographies Clio Press Oxford 1979–86, home tutor sch refusers and delinquents 1990, teacher residential course for writers Arvon Fndn 1990; Betty Trask Award 1987, K Blundell Award 1989, Southern Arts Literary Award 1991; memb Soc of Authors; *Books* Return Journey (1987), In Full Possession (1989), Making the Angels Weep (1992), Not Just Dancing (1993); *Recreations* driving cars, Humanism and avoiding poor substitutes; *Style*— Ms Helen Flint; ✉ 36 Grand Avenue, Bournemouth BH6 3TA (☎ 01202 248531); Agent: Rosemary Sandberg Ltd, 6 Bayley Street, London WC1B 3HB (☎ 0171 304 4110, fax 0171 304 4109)

FLINT, Michael Frederick; s of Gp Capt Frederick Nelson La Fargue Flint (d 1972), and Nell Dixon, *née* Smith (d 1965); *b* 7 May 1932; *Educ* St Peter's Sch York, Kingswood Sch Bath, Law Soc Sch of Law; *m* 1, (m dis 1984), Susan Kate Rhodes; 2 s (Jonathan Frederic Rest b 22 Jan 1958, Anthony Michael Rest b 30 Oct 1962), 1 da (Sarah Rest b 19 Feb 1960); m 2, 6 April 1984, Phyllida Margaret Medwyn, da of Dr Trevor Hughes, of Ruthin, Clwyd; *Career* ptnr Denton Hall and Burgin 1961–66 (asst slr 1956–60), vice-pres Paramount Pictures Corpn 1967–70, chm London Screen Enterprises 1970–72, ptnr Denton Hall Burgin and Warrens (now Denton Hall) 1972–94 (chm 1988–93); exec prodr Glastonbury Fayre, Can I Help You?; dep chm Br Screen Advsy Cncl; vice-pres Br Archaeological Assoc 1988, chm Cncl Inst of Intellectual Property; memb BAFTA, FSA 1965; *Books* A User's Guide to Copyright (Butterworths, 3 edn, 1990), Television by Satellite: Legal Aspects (1987), Intellectual Property: The New Law (jtly, 1989); *Recreations* tennis, sailing, painting; *Clubs* Savile, Wig and Pen, Lord's Taverners, Orford Sailing; *Style*— Michael Flint, Esq, FSA; ✉ c/o Denton Hall, Five Chancery Lane, Clifford's Inn, London EC4A 1BU (☎ 0171 242 1212, fax 0171 404 0087)

FLITCROFT, Gary; *b* 6 Nov 1972; *Career* professional footballer (midfielder); with Manchester City 1991–96, transferred to Blackburn Rovers 1996–; memb England under-21 team; *Style*— Gary Flitcroft; ✉ Blackburn Rovers Football Club, Ewood Park, Blackburn BB2 4JF (☎ 01254 55432, fax 01254 671042)

FLÖCKINGER, Gerda; CBE (1991); da of Karl Flöckinger (d 1950), of Austria, and Anna, *née* Frankl (d 1985); *b* 8 Dec 1927; *Educ* Maidstone Girls' GS, Dorchester Co HS, S Hampstead HS, St Martin's Sch of Art (painting, NDD), Central Sch of Art (etching, jewellery and enamelling); *m* 1954 (m dis 1962); *Career* jewellery designer and lectr; Goldsmiths' Hall travel award 1956; fndr course in modern jewellery Hornsey Coll of Art 1962–68; *Solo Exhibitions* Br Crafts Centre London 1968, V&A 1971, City of Bristol Mus and Art Gall 1971, Dartington Cider Press Gall 1977, V&A 1986, Solo Showcase Exhbn Crafts Cncl Shop at V & A 1991, British Jewellery Mainz 1995; *Group Exhibitions* incl: ICA 1954–64, Arnolfini Gall Bristol 1962–73, The Observer Jewellery Exhbn Welsh Arts Cncl touring 1973–74, Treasures of London (Goldsmiths' Hall London 1976–77, Diamond Story Electrum Gall 1977, Objects The V&A Collects V&A 1978, British Women's Art House of Commons 1981, Sotheby's Craft Exhbn Sotheby's London 1988, British Jewellery Crafts Cncl London 1989, Christie's Amsterdam 1990, 20th Anniversary Exhbn Electrum Gall 1991, What Is Jewellery? Crafts Cncl 1994; *Public Collections* City of Bristol Mus and Art Gall, Royal Mus of Scotland Edinburgh, The Worshipful Co of

Goldsmiths Goldsmiths' Hall London, Crafts Cncl London, V&A, Castle Mus Nottingham, Schmuckmuseum Pforzheim Germany; work also in many private collections and featured in numerous publications, books, articles, leaflets and catalogues, public lecture in series Pioneers of Modern Craft Crafts Cncl 1995; *Recreations* gardening (hybridising Iris Germanica), growing camellias, poetry, Siamese cats, pistol shooting, sewing, photography; *Clubs* Siamese Cat, Tabby Pointed Siamese Cat, British Iris Soc, Int Camellia Soc; *Style*— Ms Gerda Flöckinger, CBE; ✉ c/o Clare Beck, Crafts Shop at the V & A, Victoria & Albert Museum, Exhibition Rd, London SW7 (☎ 0171 581 0614, fax 0171 589 5070)

FLOOD, David Andrew; s of Frederick Joseph Alfred Flood, of Selsey, W Sussex, and June Kathleen, *née* Alexander; *b* 10 Nov 1955; *Educ* Royal GS Guildford, St John's Coll Oxford (MA), Clare Coll Cambridge (PGCE); *m* 26 June 1976, Alayne Priscilla, da of Maurice Ewart Nicholas, of Farnborough, Hants; 2 s (Christopher Nicholas b 1982, Joshua Samuel b 1986), 2 da (Olivia Kathryn b 1979, Annalisa Harriet b 1989); *Career* asst organist Canterbury Cathedral 1978–86, music master King's Sch Canterbury 1978–86; organist and master of choristers: Lincoln Cathedral 1986–88, Canterbury Cathedral 1988–; organist for enthronement of Archbishop Runcie 1980, organist for visit of Pope John Paul II 1982; asst dir Canterbury Choral Soc 1978–85, fndr and dir Canterbury Cantata Choir 1985–86; musical dir: Lincoln Choral Soc 1986–88, Canterbury Music Club 1984–86 and 1988–, musical dir for enthronement of Archbishop Carey 1991; hon sr memb Darwin Coll Univ of Kent; FRCO 1976 (chm 1975); *Recreations* travel, motoring, DIY; *Style*— David Flood, Esq; ✉ 6 The Precincts, Canterbury, Kent CT1 2EE (☎ 01227 765 219, office 01227 762 862, fax 01227 762789)

FLOOD, Prof John Edward; OBE (1986); s of Sydney Edward Flood (d 1983), of London, and Elsie Gladys Flood (d 1967); *b* 2 June 1925; *Educ* City of London Sch, QMC London (BSc, PhD, DSc); *m* 23 April 1949, Phyllis Mary, da of John Charles Groocock (d 1978), of Worthing; 2 s (Nicholas John b 20 Oct 1951, Stephen Charles b 25 May 1954); *Career* experimental offr Admiralty Signals Estab 1944–46, devpt engr Standard Telephones and Cables Ltd 1946–47, exec engr PO Research Station 1947–52, chief engr advanced devpt laboratories Telecommunications Div Associated Electrical Industries Ltd 1952–65; Aston Univ: prof of electrical engrg 1965–90, head of dept 1967–81 and 1983–89, dean Faculty of Engrg 1971–74, sr pro-vice-chancellor 1981–83, emeritus prof 1990–; chm: IEE Professional Gp on Telecommunications Systems & Networks 1974–77, Univs Ctee on Integrated Sandwich Courses 1981–82, Br Standards Ctee on Telecommunications 1981–92, S Midland Centre IEE 1978–79; memb MMC 1985–; memb Cncl Selly Oak Colls 1966–85, pres Birmingham Electrical Club 1989–90; Freeman City of London 1957; CGIA 1954, FIEE 1959, FInstP 1987, FCGI 1991; *Books* Telecommunication Networks (1975), Transmission Systems (1991), Telecommunications Switching, Traffic and Networks (1995); *Recreations* swimming, writing, winemaking; *Clubs* Royal Over-Seas League; *Style*— Prof John Flood, OBE; ✉ 60 Widney Manor Rd, Solihull, West Midlands B91 3JQ (☎ 0121 705 3604); Aston University, Aston Triangle, Birmingham B4 7ET (☎ 0121 359 3611, fax 0121 359 0156, telex 336 997)

FLOOD, Michael Donovan (Mik); s of Gp Capt Donovan John Flood, DFC, AFC, of Brampton, Huntingdon, Cambs, and Vivien Ruth, *née* Allison; *b* 7 May 1949; *Educ* St George's Coll Weybridge Surrey, Llangefni County Sch Anglesey; *m* 1975 (m dis 1989), Julie, da of Paul Ward; 1 da (Amy Louise b 8 April 1976); *Career* fndr and artistic dir Chapter Arts Centre Cardiff 1970–81, devpt dir Baltimore Theater Project USA 1981–82, administrator Pip Simmons Theatre Group 1982–83, freelance prodr and conslt 1983–85; dir: Watermans Arts Centre Brentford 1985–90, Inst of Contemporary Arts 1990–; prodr: Woyzeck (open air prodn with Pip Simmons Theatre Group) 1976, Deadwood (open air prodn with Son et Lumiere Theatre Group, Time Out award winner) 1986, Offshore Rig (open air prodn with Bow Gamelan Ensemble) 1987; awarded HRH Queen Elizabeth II Silver Jubilee Medal for outstanding services to the arts and community in Wales 1977; dir Pip Simmons Theatre Group Ltd 1977–81, co-fndr Nat Assoc of Arts Centres 1976; memb: West Midlands Arts Assoc Assessment Ctee 1976, Welsh Arts Cncl Film Ctee 1976–80, SE Wales Arts Assoc Exec Ctee 1980–81, Ct Royal Coll of Art 1990–; *Recreations* sailing, ichthyology; *Style*— Mik Flood, Esq; ✉ Institute of Contemporary Arts, The Mall, London SW1Y 5AH (☎ 0171 930 0493, fax 0171 873 0051)

FLOOD, Thomas Oliver (Tom); s of Thomas Flood (d 1988), of Dublin, and Elizabeth, *née* O'Byrne; *b* 21 May 1947; *Educ* Dominican Coll Newbridge, Univ Coll Dublin (BA); *Career* A E Herbert Ltd (machine tools) 1969–70, W S Atkins (consulting engrs) 1970–72; 3M United Kingdom PLC: Market Research Dept 1972–73, mktg Industl Products 1973–75, mktg Packaging Systems Gp 1975–77, sales mangr Strapping Systems 1977–79, sales and mktg mangr Decorative Packing 1979–82, gp mktg mangr Packaging Systems 1982–86; British Trust for Conservation Volunteers: mktg dir 1986–90, dep chief exec 1990–92, chief exec 1992–; chm The Red Admiral (counselling charity), tstee Age Resource, memb Bd Tree Cncl; FRSA 1996, FIMgt 1996; *Recreations* gardening, cooking, opera, theatre, walking; *Style*— Tom Flood, Esq; ✉ British Trust for Conservation Volunteers, 36 St Mary's Street, Wallingford, Oxfordshire OX10 0EU (☎ 01491 839766, fax 01491 839646, e-mail t.flood@dial.pipex.com)

FLORENCE, Prof Alexander Taylor; CBE (1994); s of Alexander Charles Gerrard Florence (d 1985), and Margaret, *née* Taylor; *b* 9 Sept 1940; *Educ* Queen's Park Sch Glasgow, Univ of Glasgow (BSc, PhD), Royal Coll of Sci and Technol, Univ of Strathclyde (DSc); *m* 6 June 1964, Elizabeth Catherine, da of James McRae (d 1969); 2 s (Graham b 1966, Alastair b 1969), 1 da (Gillian b 1972); *Career* prof of pharmacy Univ of Strathclyde 1976–88 (lectr in pharmaceutical chemistry 1966–72, sr lectr 1972–76), dean Sch of Pharmacy Univ of London 1989–; memb Ctee on Safety of Meds (chm Sub Ctee on Chemistry Pharmacy and Standards), memb Standing Pharmaceutical Advsy Ctee; FRSC 1977, FRSE 1987, FRPharmS 1987, FRSA 1989; *Books* Solubilization by Surface Active Agents (with P H Elworthy and C B Macfarlane, 1968), Surfactant Systems (with D Attwood, 1983), Physicochemical Principles of Pharmacy (with D Attwood, 1988); *Recreations* music, painting, writing; *Style*— Prof Alexander Florence, CBE, FRSE; ✉ 29 Torrington Square, London WC1E 7JL (☎ 0171 637 2695); The School of Pharmacy, University of London, 29–39 Brunswick Square, London WC1N 1AX (☎ 0171 753 5819, fax 0171 837 5092)

FLOREY, Prof Charles du Vé; s of Baron Florey, OM, FRS, MD (Life Peer, d 1968), and his 1 w Mary Ethel, *née* Reed (d 1966); *b* 11 Sept 1934; *Educ* Rugby, Univ of Cambridge (MD), Yale Univ (MPH); *m* 14 April 1966, Susan Jill, da of Cecil Hopkins, of Tuttle Hill, Nuneaton, Warwicks; 1 s, 1 da; *Career* prof Dept of Epidemiology and Public Health Ninewells Hosp and Medical Sch; FFCM; FRCPE; *Style*— Prof Charles Florey; ✉ Ninewells Hospital and Medical Sch, Dundee DD1 9SY (☎ 01382 632124)

FLOUD, Jean Esther; CBE; da of Ernest Walter McDonald (d 1957), and Annie Louisa, *née* Watson (d 1958); *b* 3 Nov 1915; *Educ* LSE (BSc Econ); *m* 2 April 1938, Peter Castle Floud, CBE (d 1960), s of late Sir Francis Floud, KCB, KCSI, KCMG; 1 s (Andrew Thomas b 27 Nov 1948, d 1981), 2 da (Frances Ellen (Mrs Little) b 11 May 1952, Esther Mary (Mrs Bagenal) b 27 Dec 1955); *Career* asst dir of educn City of Oxford 1940–46, teacher of sociology LSE and Inst of Educn Univ of London 1947–62, official fell Nuffield Coll Oxford 1963–72, princ Newnham Coll Cambridge 1972–83; hon fell: LSE 1972, Nuffield Coll 1983, Newnham Coll 1983, Darwin Coll Cambridge 1986; memb: Franks Cmmn of Inquiry into the Univ of Oxford 1964–66, Univ Grants Ctee 1969–74, Social Sci Res Cncl 1970–73, Exec Ctee PEP 1975–77, Advsy Bd for the Res Cncls 1976–81, Cncl Policy Studies Inst 1979–83; Hon LittD Univ of Leeds 1973, Hon DLitt City Univ 1978; *Books* Social Class and Educational Opportunity (with A H Halsey and F M Martin, 1956), Dangerousness and Criminal Justice (with Warren Young, 1981); *Style*— Mrs Jean Floud, CBE; ✉ Elderwick House, The Ridings, Shotover, Oxford (☎ 01865 62860)

FLOUD, Prof Roderick Castle; s of Bernard Francis Castle Floud (d 1967), and Ailsa, *née* Craig (d 1967); *b* 1 April 1942; *Educ* Brentwood Sch, Wadham Coll Oxford (BA, MA), Nuffield Coll Oxford (DPhil); *m* 6 Aug 1964, Cynthia Anne, da of Col Leslie Harold Smith, OBE, of Leicester; 2 da (Lydia b 1969, Sarah b 1971); *Career* lectr in econ history: UCL 1966–69, Univ of Cambridge 1969–75; fell and tutor Emmanuel Coll Cambridge 1969–75, prof of modern history Birkbeck Coll London 1975–88, visiting prof Stanford Univ 1980–81, provost and prof London Guildhall Univ (formerly City of London Poly) 1988–; fell Birkbeck Coll 1995; memb ESRC 1993–; Freeman Co of Information Technologists 1996; FRHistS 1980, FRSA 1989; *Books* An Introduction to Quantitative Methods for Historians (1973, 1979), Essays in Quantitative Economic History (ed, 1974), The British Machine Tool Industry 1850–1914 (1976), The Economic History of Britain since 1700 (co-ed, 1981, 2 edn 1994), The Power of the Past: Essays in Honour of Eric Hobsbawm (co-ed, 1984), Height, Health and History: Nutritional Status in the United Kingdom 1750–1980 (with K Wachter and A Gregory, 1990), The People and the British Economy 1830–1914 (1997); also author of numerous articles and reviews incl Words, Not Numbers: John Harold Clapham - Historians in their Times (in History Today, 1989); *Recreations* walking, skiing, theatre; *Clubs* Athenaeum; *Style*— Prof Roderick Floud; ✉ 21 Savernake Rd, London NW3 2JT (☎ 0171 267 2197); London Guildhall University, 31 Jewry Street, London EC3N 2EX (☎ 0171 320 1310, fax 0171 320 1390, e-mail FLOUD@LGU.AC.UK)

FLOWER, Dr Antony John Frank (Tony); s of Frank Robert Edward Flower (d 1977), of Clyst Hydon, Devon, and Dorothy Elizabeth, *née* Williams; *b* 2 Feb 1951; *Educ* Chipping Sodbury GS, Univ of Exeter (BA, MA), Univ of Leicester (PhD); *Career* graphic designer 1973–76, first gen sec Tawney Soc 1982–88, co-ordinator Argo Venture 1984–; fndr memb SDP 1981, memb Cncl for Soc Democracy 1982–83; dir: Res Inst for Econ and Social Affrs 1982–92, Argo Tst 1986–, Healthline Health Info Serv 1986–88, Health Info Tst 1987–88 (tstee 1988–90), Centre for Educnl Choice 1988–90, Environmental Concern Centre in Europe 1990–92; dir of devpt Green Alliance 1991–92; sec Ecological Studies Inst 1991–92, conslt mangr Construction Industry Environmental Forum 1992–96; dep dir: Inst of Community Studies 1994– (tstee 1993–), Mutual Aid Centre 1994– (tstee 1990–); conslt: Joseph Rowntree Reform Tst Ltd 1993–, Family Covenant Assoc 1994–; GAIA: memb Cncl 1988–, ed Tawney Journal 1982–88; co-fndr and managing ed Samizdat magazine 1988–91; assoc: Open Coll of the Arts 1988–, Redesign Ltd 1989–94, Nicholas Lacey Jobst and Partners (architects) 1989–, Inst for Public Policy Res 1989–95, Rocklabs (Geological Analysts) 1993–; memb Advsy Bd The Earth Centre 1990–, tstee Tower Hamlets Summer Univ 1995–; FRSA; *Books* Starting to Write (with Graham Mort, 1990), The Alternative (with Ben Pimlott and Anthony Wright, 1990), Young at Eighty (ed with Geoff Dench and Kate Gavrom, 1995), Guide to Pressure Groups (consultant ed, PMS, 1995); *Recreations* boats, making and restoring musical instruments; *Style*— Dr Tony Flower; ✉ 18 Victoria Park Square, London E2 9PF (☎ 0181 980 6263, fax 0181 981 6719)

FLOWER, Dr Christopher Dennis Robin; s of William Grosvenor Flower (d 1942), and Molly, *née* Jacobs; *b* 3 Aug 1939; *Educ* Royal Masonic Sch, King's Coll Cambridge, St Bartholomew's Hosp (MA, MB BChir); *m* 21 Jan 1963, Diana Mary, da of Charles Patrick Crane (d 1988); 1 s (Paul b 1965), 1 da (Emma b 1967); *Career* house physician St Bartholomew's Hosp 1964, resident Toronto Western Hosp 1968, dir radiology Addenbrooke's Hosp Cambridge 1973–, ed Clinical Radiology 1987–90, warden Royal Coll of Radiologists 1990–94; co-author of books and articles on radiology and thoracic med; FRCR, FRCP(Canada); *Recreations* travel, golf, ornithology; *Style*— Dr Christopher Flower; ✉ Addenbrooke's Hospital, Hills Road, Cambridge CB2 2QQ (☎ 01223 216203)

FLOWER, Keith David; s of Frank Leslie Flower (d 1976), of 20 St Ursula Grove, Pinner, Middx, and Catherine Elizabeth, *née* Millo (d 1981); *b* 20 Jan 1945; *Educ* Merchant Taylors; *m* 11 May 1973, Jennifer, da of Edward Arthur Howick; 1 da (Melanie b 1976); *Career* admitted slr 1969; HJ Heinz Ltd 1970–73, John Laing Properties Ltd 1973–76, sr ptnr Keith Flower & Co 1976–; memb Rotary Club Pinner; memb Law Soc; *Clubs* Durrants; *Style*— Keith Flower, Esq; ✉ 103a The Drive, Rickmansworth, Herts WD3 4DY (☎ and fax 01923 772622); 25/27 Pinner Green, Pinner, Middx HA5 2AF (☎ 0181 868 1277, fax 0181 868 1356)

FLOWER, Prof Roderick John; s of Gp Capt Leslie Ralph Flower MBE, MM (d 1994), of Stubbington, Hants, and Audrey Ellen, *née* Eckett (d 1991); *b* 29 Nov 1945; *Educ* Kingwell Court Sch Wiltshire, Woodbridge Sch Suffolk, Univ of Sheffield (BSc, Thomas Woodcock physiology prize), Univ of London (PhD, DSc); *m* 1994, Lindsay Joyce, da of Henry Arthur Joseph Riddell; *Career* sr scientist Dept of Prostaglandin Res Wellcome Research Labs Kent 1975–84 (memb of staff 1973–75); head Sch of Pharmacy and Pharmacology Univ of Bath 1987–89 (prof of pharmacology 1984–89); prof of biochemical pharmacology Bart's Med Coll 1989–; Br Pharmacological Soc: memb 1974, chm Ctee 1989–92, Sandoz prize 1978, Gaddum Meml lecture and medal 1986; memb Biochemical Soc 1985; *Recreations* light aviation, scuba diving, photography, the history of pharmacology; *Style*— Prof Roderick Flower; ✉ Department of Biochemical Pharmacology, The William Harvey Research Institute, The Medical College of St Bartholomew's Hospital, Charterhouse Square, London EC1M 6BQ (☎ 0171 982 6072, fax 0171 982 6076)

FLOWERS, Adrian John; s of Col Edward Flowers, JP (d 1948), of Southsea, Hants, and Kathleen Mary, *née* West (d 1972); *b* 11 July 1926; *Educ* Sherborne, Univ of London, RAF Sch of Photography, London Sch of Photography; *m* 1, 1952 (m dis 1973), Angela Mary Flowers, *qv*, da of Charles Geoffrey Holland; 3 s (Adam b 1953, Matthew, *qv*, b 1956, Daniel b 1959), 1 da (Francesca b 1965); m 2, 1985, Francoise Marguerite, da of Jean-Baptiste Lina; *Career* advertising photographer; freelance photographer 1949–, asst to Zoltan Glass 1954–55; in own studio: Dover Street Mayfair (began specialising in advtg photography) 1955–59, Tite Street Chelsea 1959–89, St Paul's Studios Hammersmith 1989–; cmmns incl: Australian Fruit campaign (competition winner) 1958, Brooke Bond campaign (Kenya, Tansania and India) 1962, Benson and Hedges campaign 1970's, DEC, Le Creuset, Knorr, Visions and Tesco campaigns 1980's, Peninsula Hotels campaign (Hong Kong, Beijing, Bangkok, NY and Los Angeles) 1991; exhibitions: perm exhibits Photography Hall of Fame (Photographic Arts & Sci Fndn) Santa Barbara Calif 1973, large prints Economist Building 1993, small prints Flowers East 1994 and 1995, Canvas and Camera II (Assoc of Photographers); recipient various Layton, D&AD and Assoc of Photographers awards, sole photographer to be chosen as Artist of the Week (Channel 4's Watching Brief) 1989; selected as participant Newschool-91 Bangalore (one week seminar addressing over 400 professional Indian photographers on advtg photography), participant and moderator Newschool-93 New Delhi (introduced other expert photographers as key speakers from London), advsr Newschool-95 Bombay, lectr for other orgns incl RPS, Assoc of Photographers and Ilford's Focus; memb: RPS, RGS, D&AD, Assoc of Photographers, AIPA (India); *Recreations* music, art, epistemology, eclectic collecting; *Clubs* Chelsea Arts; *Style*— Adrian Flowers, Esq; ✉ 147 Talgarth Road, London W14 (☎ 0181 846 8566, fax 0181 846 9015)

FLOWERS, Angela Mary; da of Charles Geoffrey Holland (d 1974), of Ashford, Kent, and Olive Alexandra, *née* Stiby (d 1987); *b* 19 Dec 1932; *Educ* Westonbirt Sch Glos, Wychwood Sch Oxford, Webber Douglas Sch of Singing & Dramatic Art (Dip); *m* 1, 1952 (m dis 1973) Adrian Flowers, *qv*; 3 s (Adam b 1953, Matthew, *qv*, b 1956, Daniel b 1959), 1 da (Francesca b 1965); *partner* Robert Heller, *qv*; 1 da (Rachel Pearl b 1973); *Career* worked in stage, film and advtg until 1967, fndr Angela Flowers Gallery Lisle St 1970 (Portland Mews W1 1971–78, Tottenham Mews W1 1978–88, Richmond Rd E8 1988–), chm Angela Flowers Gall PLC 1989–, promotes encourages and shows the work of young emerging and established artists; memb Bd Nat Youth Jazz Orchestra 1988; tstee John Kobal Fndn 1992; sr fell RCA 1994; *Recreations* singing, piano, cooking; *Style*— Mrs Angela Flowers; ✉ Flowers East, 199–205 Richmond Road, London E8 3NJ (☎ 0181 985 3333, fax 0181 985 0067)

FLOWERS, Baron (Life Peer UK 1979); Brian Hilton Flowers; kt (1969); o s of late Rev Harold Joseph Flowers, of Swansea; *b* 13 Sept 1924; *Educ* Bishop Gore GS Swansea, Gonville and Caius Coll Cambridge, Univ of Birmingham; *m* 1951, Mary Frances, er da of Sir Leonard Frederick Behrens, CBE (d 1978); 2 step s; *Career* physicist; head Theoretical Physics Div AERE Harwell 1952–58, prof of theoretical physics Univ of Manchester 1958–61, Langworthy prof of physics Univ of Manchester 1961–72, chm SRC 1967–73, rector Imperial Coll of Sci and Technol 1973–85 (fell 1972); chm: Royal Cmmn on Environmental Pollution 1973–76, Standing Cmmn on Energy and Environment 1978–81; managing tstee Nuffield Fndn 1982– (chm 1987–); chm Ctee of Vice Chllrs and Princs 1983–85; vice chllr Univ of London 1985–90, chllr Victoria University of Manchester 1995–; chm Select Ctee on Science and Technol House of Lords 1989–93; awarded: Rutherford medal and prize IPPS 1968, Glazebrook medal IPPS 1987, Chalmers medal Sweden 1980; MA Oxon 1956; Hon DSc: Sussex 1968, Wales 1972, Manchester 1973, Leicester 1973, Liverpool 1974, Bristol 1982, Oxford 1986 NUI 1990, Reading 1996, London 1996; Hon DEng Nova Scotia 1983, Hon ScD Dublin; Hon LLD: Dundee, Glasgow 1987, Manchester 1995; Hon FCGI 1975, Hon FIEE 1975, Hon MRIA 1976; sr fell RCA 1983, fell Goldsmiths' Coll 1991, hon fell Royal Holloway 1996, hon fell Univ of Wales Swansea 1996; Offr de la Légion d'Honneur 1981; Hon FRCP 1992, FRS 1961; *Style*— The Rt Hon Lord Flowers, FRS; ✉ 53 Athenaeum Road, London N20 9AL (☎ and fax 0181 446 5993)

FLOWERS, Matthew Dominic; s of Adrian John Flowers, *qv*, of 147 Talgarth Rd, London, and Angela Mary Flowers, *qv*; *b* 8 Oct 1956; *Educ* William Ellis GS; *m* 1, 17 Feb 1985, Lindy, da of Arthur James Wesley-Smith; 1 s (Patrick b 30 Jan 1987); m 2, 19 July 1992, Huei Chjuin, da of late Et Ping Hong; 1 s (Jackson Hong Fu b 15 Jan 1995); *Career* asst Angela Flowers Gallery 1975–78, mangr and keyboard player for pop group Sore Throat 1975–81, played in various other bands including Blue Zoo (Cry Boy Cry Top Twenty hit 1982, led to two appearances on Top of the Pops) 1981–83; Angela Flowers Gallery (became a plc 1989): pt/t asst 1981–83, mangr 1983–88, md 1988–; memb: Cncl Mgmnt of Art Servs Grants 1987–92, Organising Ctee of London Art Fair 1989–95, Bradford Print Biennale Ctee 1989, govr of Byam Shaw Sch of Art 1990–, Exec Soc of London Art Dealers 1993–96, Organising Ctee Miami Art Fair 1995, Patrons of New Art (Tate Gallery) 1995–; *Recreations* playing football for Singer United, chess; *Style*— Matthew Flowers, Esq; ✉ Flowers East, 199–205 Richmond Road, Hackney, London E8 3NJ (☎ 0181 985 3333, fax 0181 985 0067)

FLOWERS, Timothy David (Tim); s of Kenneth Alfred Flowers, of Kenilworth, Warwicks, and Mary Bryan, *née* Garlick; *b* 3 Feb 1967; *Educ* Abbey Hall Secdy Sch; *m* 11 June 1988, Jane Louise, da of Brian Alan Everett; 2 da (Emma Jane b 24 Dec 1989, Katie Louise b 2 March 1992); *Career* professional footballer (goalkeeper); 63 league appearances Wolverhampton Wanderers (debut v Sheffield Utd) 1984–86, over 210 appearances Southampton 1986–93, 7 appearances on loan Swindon Town 1987; Blackburn Rovers FC: joined 1993, winners FA Premier League 1994/95; England: 3 youth caps v Scotland (twice) and Yugoslavia, 3 under 21 caps (v Morocco, France, W Germany) 1987–88, 8 full caps, first full cap (v Brazil) 1993, memb squad Euro 96; Zenith Data Systems Cup runners-up medal Southampton 1991; Player of the Year Wolverhampton Wanderers 1984, Young Player of the Year Midland Sportswriters 1984, Away Player of the Year Southampton 1990/91, 1991/92 and 1992/93, Southampton Player of the Year 1991/92 and 1992/93; *Recreations* fishing, music, walking; *Style*— Tim Flowers, Esq; ✉ Blackburn Rovers Football Club, Ewood Park, Nuttall Street, Blackburn, Lancs BB2 4JF (☎ 01254 698888)

FLOYD, Christopher David; QC (1992); s of David Floyd, journalist, and Hana, *née* Goldman; *b* 20 Dec 1951; *Educ* Westminster, Trinity Coll Cambridge (MA); *m* 1974, Rosalind Jane, *née* Arscott; 1 s, 2 da; *Career* called to the Bar Inner Temple 1975, head intellectual property chambers at 11 South Square Gray's Inn 1994–, asst recorder Patents Co Ct 1994–, a dep chm Copyright Tbnl 1996–; memb Irish Bar 1989; writer of various articles in jls; *Recreations* cycling, walking, tennis, watching cricket, Austin Sevens; *Clubs* Garrick, Austin 7 Owners, 750 Motor; *Style*— Christopher Floyd, Esq, QC; ✉ 11 South Square, Second Floor, Gray's Inn, London WC1R 5EU

FLOYD, David Henry Cecil; s and h of Sir Giles Henry Charles Floyd, 7 Bt, *qv*, and The Lady Gillian Kertesz, *née* Cecil; *b* 2 April 1956; *Educ* Eton; *m* 20 June 1981, Caroline Ann, da of John Henry Beckly, of Manor Farm Cottage, Bowerchalke, Wilts; 2 da (Suzanna b 1983, Claire b 1986); *Career* Lt 15/19 The King's Royal Hussars; merchant banker; FCA 1993 (ACA 1982); *Clubs* Cavalry & Guards'; *Style*— David Floyd, Esq; ✉ Manor Farm, Bowerchalke, Nr Salisbury, Wiltshire SP5 5BU

FLOYD, Sir Giles Henry Charles; 7 Bt (UK 1816); s of Lt-Col Sir John Duckett Floyd, 6 Bt, TD (d 1975); *b* 27 Feb 1932; *Educ* Eton; *m* 1, 23 Nov 1954 (m dis 1978), Lady Gillian Moyra Katherine Cecil, da of 6 Marquess of Exeter, KCMG; 2 s (David Henry Cecil b 1956, Henry Edward Cecil b 1958); m 2, 1985, Judy Sophia, er da of late William Leonard Tregoning, CBE, of Landue, Launceston, Cornwall, and formerly w of Thomas Ernest Lane, of Tickencote Hall, Stamford; *Heir* s David Henry Cecil Floyd, *qv*, b 2 April 1956; *Career* farmer; dir Burghley Estate Farms 1958–; High Sheriff of Rutland 1968; Liveryman Worshipful Co of Skinners; *Recreations* fishing; *Clubs* Turf, Farmers'; *Style*— Sir Giles Floyd, Bt; ✉ Tinwell Manor, Stamford, Lincs PE9 3UD (☎ 01780 62676)

FLOYD, John Anthony; s of Lt-Col Arthur Bowen Floyd, DSO, OBE (d 1965, himself grandson of Major-General Sir Henry Floyd, 2 Bt), and Iris Clare, *née* Belding; *b* 12 May 1923; *Educ* Eton; *m* 5 Oct 1948, Margaret Louise, o da of late Major Hugo Rosselli, of Worlington Old Hall, Suffolk; 2 da (Elizabeth b 1951, Caroline b 1953); *Career* served WWII in KRRC; chm: Christie Manson & Woods Ltd 1974–85, Christie's International plc 1976–88; *Clubs* Boodle's, White's, MCC; *Style*— John Floyd, Esq; ✉ Ecchinswell House, Newbury, Berkshire (☎ 01635 298237)

FLOYD, Richard Eaglesfield; s of Harold Bailey Floyd, of Purley, Surrey, and (Edith) Margeret, *née* Griffith (d 1954); *b* 9 June 1938; *Educ* Dean Close Sch Cheltenham; *m* 1995, Linda Ann Robinson, *née* Newnham; *Career* articled clerk Fincham Vallance & Co 1956–61 (sr clerk 1961–62 and 1964–65), insolvency administrator Cork Gully 1965–70, ptnr Floyd Nash & Co (now Floyd Harris) 1971– (held appointments as administrative receiver, administrator, liquidator and tstee); author of numerous articles on insolvency matters in specialised jls; memb Editorial Advsy Bd of Insolvency Law and Practice; Freeman City of London 1985; memb: Association Européenne des Practiciens des Procédures Collectives, Soc of Practitioners of Insolvency; FCA, fell Insolvency Practitioners' Assoc; *Books* with I S Grier: Voluntary Liquidation and Receivership (3 edn, 1991), Personal Insolvency - A Practical Guide (1987, 2 edn 1993), Corporate Recovery: Administration Orders and Voluntary Arrangements (1995); *Recreations* writing, lecturing, mountain walking; *Style*— Richard Floyd, Esq; ✉ 9 Beaufort Rd, Kingston-upon-Thames, Surrey KT1 2TH (☎ 0181 546 5833); Floyd Harris, 44–46 Fleet St, London EC4Y 1BN (☎ 0171 583 7108, fax 0171 583 2921)

FLOYD EWIN, Sir David Ernest Thomas; kt (1974), LVO (1954), OBE (1965); 7 s of Frederick P Ewin (d 1929), and Ellen, *née* Floyd, of Blackheath; *b* 17 Feb 1911; *Educ* Eltham; *m* 1948, Marion Irene, da of William Robert Lewis, of Paignton, S Devon; 1 da; *Career* NP; St Paul's Cathedral: lay admin 1939–43, registrar and receiver 1944–78, conslt to the Dean and Chapter 1978–; chm: Tubular Edgington Group plc 1978–90, memb of Ct Common Cncl for Ward of Castle Baynard 1964–95 (dep 1972–95), vice pres Castle Baynard Ward Club (chm 1962 and 1988); chm Corp of London: Gresham Ctee 1975–76, Benevolent Assoc 1991–95; memb: Lord Mayor and Sheriffs Ctee 1976 and 1978 (chm 1988), Ct of Assts Hon Irish Soc 1976–79; surrogate for Province of Canterbury; tstee: City Parochial Fndn 1967–89 (chm Pensions Ctee 1978–89), St Paul's Cathedral Tst 1978–96, Temple Bar Tst 1979–96, City of London Endowment Tst for St Paul's Cathedral (dep chm 1982–), Allchurches Tst; hon dir Br Humane Assoc; govr: Sons of the Clergy Corp, St Gabriel's Coll Camberwell 1946–72; Past Master Worshipful Co of Scriveners, Liveryman Worshipful Co of Wax Chandlers, Freeman City of London, Sr Past Master Guild of Freemen of City of London; MA (Lambeth); gold staff offr at Coronation of HM 1953; KStJ 1970 (OStJ 1965); *Books* A Pictorial History of St Paul's Cathedral (1970), The Splendour of St Paul's (1973); *Recreations* tennis, fishing, gardening; *Clubs* City Livery, Guildhall; *Style*— Sir David Floyd Ewin, LVO, OBE; ✉ 13 Seaborne Court, Alta Vista Road, Paignton, Devon (☎ 01803 523993); Chapter House, St Paul's Churchyard, London EC4M 8AD (☎ 0171 248 2705)

FLOYER, Prof Michael Antony; s of Cdr William Antony Floyer, RN, Chev Legion of Honour (d 1943), of Inglewood, Camberley, Surrey, and Alice Rosalie, *née* Whitehead (d 1979); *b* 28 April 1920; *Educ* Sherborne, Trinity Hall Cambridge (MB ChB, MD), The London Hosp Med Coll; *m* 8 June 1946, Lily Louise Frances, da of H P Burns (d 1940); 2 s (David b 1947, Christopher b 1951), 1 da (Jennifer b 1948); *Career* Sqdn Ldr RAF 1946–48, med specialist RAF Hosps at Karachi and Cawnpore; London Hosp Med Coll 1948–86: clinical tutor 1948–, lectr 1948, sr lectr 1951–67, asst dir of Med Unit 1953–86, reader 1967–74, prof of medicine 1974–86, dean 1982–86, fell 1988–; The London Hosp: hon conslt physician 1958–86, conslt i/c Emergency and Accident Dept 1976–86, consltg physician 1986–, locum consultant 1987–89; seconded as prof of med to Nairobi Univ 1973–75 (external examiner in med 1978–93); sec Med Res Soc 1962–67 (memb 1949–), memb Tower Hamlets Dist Health Authy 1982–86; pres and treas The London Hosp Clubs Union; pres: RFC, Climbing and Backpacking Club, History Soc; MD 1952, FRCP 1963; *Recreations* wild things and wild places, music, rugby football; *Style*— Prof Mike Floyer; ✉ 40 Free Trade Wharf, 340 The Highway, London E1 9ET (☎ 0171 702 7577); The London Hosp Med Coll, London E1 2AD (☎ 0171 377 7602)

FLYNN, Barbara (née Barbara Joy McMurray); da of James McMurray (d 1994), latterly of Hastings, and Joyce (Joy) Crawford Hurst; *b* 5 Aug 1948; *Educ* St Mary's Sch Baldslow, Guildhall Sch of Music and Drama (Gold medalist 1966–68); *m* 27 Feb 1982, Jeremy George Taylor; 1 s (Linus James Hallam b 26 Aug 1990); *Career* actress; *Theatre* NT incl: Helen Schwartz in Tales from Hollywood, title role in Antigone, Gloria in Early Days, Sylvia Craven in The Philanderer, Prudence Malone in Plunder; other credits incl: Millamant in The Way of the World (Lyric Hammersmith), Andromache in Women of Troy (Gate), Epifania Ognisanti in The Millionairess (Greenwich), Barbara in The Perfectionist (Hampstead), Ursula in Short List (Hampstead), Annie in Norman Conquests (Birmingham Rep), Kate in Sorry (Sheffield Crucible), Iphigeneia in Agamemnon's Children (Gate Nottinghill), Mary Queen of Scots in Vivat Vivat Regina (Mermaid); *Television* BBC incl: Eleanor Goodchild in The Justice Game, Jane in The Benefactors, Belinda in Seasons Greetings, Rose Marie in A Very Peculiar Practice (series 1 and 2), Milkwoman in Open All Hours, Mary Bold in Barchester Chronicles, Jill in Where Angels Fear, Joanna Lassiter in Lucky Jim, Shirley in The Last Song, Margaret Hanson in No Visible Scar, Dorothy Kemp in Maybury, Monica in Love on a Gunboat, Sue in Bagthorpes, Heather in Standing in for Henry, Murder Most English, A Flight Fund; other credits incl: Dee in Chandler and Co (BBC/SKREBA), Judith in Cracker (series I, II & III, Granada), Madame Maigret in Maigret II (Granada), Sheila Green in Boon (Central), Jill Swinburne in The Beiderbecke Connection, The Beiderbecke Affair and The Beiderbecke Tapes (YTV), Monica Height in Inspector Morse (Channel 4/Zenith), Judy in Day to Remember (TVS), The Daughter in Afternoon Dancing (ATV), Freda Ashton in Family At War (Granada), Sarah Fletcher in Second Chance (YTV), Marlene in Keep it in the Family (Thames), Sandy Whitman in The Gentle Touch (LWT); *Film* Nurse Green in Britannia Hospital; *Style*— Ms Barbara Flynn; ✉ c/o Markham & Froggatt Ltd, 4 Windmill Street, London W1P 1HF (☎ 0171 636 4412, fax 0171 637 5233)

FLYNN, John Gerrard; CMG (1992); s of Thomas Flynn (d 1985), of Glasgow, and Mary Chisholm (d 1963); *b* 23 April 1937; *Educ* Univ of Glasgow (MA); *m* 10 Aug 1973, Drina Anne Coates, da of Lt Herbert Percival Coates (d 1971), of Montevideo, Uruguay; 1 s (Andrew b 1984), 1 da (Alexandra b 1985); *Career* FO: joined 1965, second sec Lusaka 1966, first sec FCO 1968, asst dir gen Canning House 1970, head of Chancery Montevideo 1971, FO 1976, chargé d'affaires Luanda 1978, cnsllr (political) Brasilia 1979, cnsllr (economic and commercial) Madrid 1982, high cmmr Mbabane 1987–90; HM ambass: Luanda 1990–93, Caracas 1993–97 (concurrently non-resident ambass Dominican Repub 1993–95); *Recreations* walking, golf; *Clubs* Travellers'; *Style*— John Flynn, Esq, CMG; ✉ c/o Foreign & Commonwealth Office, King Charles Street, London SW1A 2AH

FLYNN, Dr Patricia Josephine; da of Michael Joseph Flynn, of Nutley Lane, Dublin, and Mary Josephine, *née* O'Dwyer; *b* 1 April 1947; *Educ* Convent of the Sacred Heart Dublin, Univ Coll Dublin (MB BCh, BAO, DCH, DObst, DA FFARCSI, FRCA); *m* 26 Sept 1987, Anthony William Goode, s of William Henry Goode, of Tynemouth, Northumberland; *Career* sr lectr in anaesthesia London Hosp Med Coll 1982–, dep dir Anaesthetics Unit; sec gen Br Acad of Forensic Scis; memb: Assoc of Anaesthetists of GB and Ireland, Anaesthetic Res Soc, Euro Acad of Anaesthesiology, RSM, BMA; *Recreations* antiquarian books, art, music; *Style*— Dr Patricia Flynn; ✉ Anaesthetics Unit, St Bartholomew's and The Royal London School of Medicine and Dentistry, The Royal London Hospital, London E1 1BB (☎ 0171 377 7119)

FLYNN, Paul Phillip; MP (Lab) Newport West (majority 7,779); s of James Flynn (d 1939), and Kathleen Rosien, *née* Williams (d 1988); *b* 9 Feb 1935; *Educ* St Illtyd's Coll Cardiff, Univ Coll Cardiff; *m* 1, 6 Feb 1962, Ann Patricia; 1 s (James Patrick b 1965), 1 da (Rachel Sarah b 1963 d 1979); m 2, 31 Jan 1985, Lynne Samantha; *Career* chemist in steel indust 1955–81; since worked in local radio and as research asst to Euro MP Llewellyn Smith; MP (Lab) Newport W 1987–, front bench spokesman on Welsh affrs May 1988–, front bench spokesman on social security Nov 1988–90; *Clubs* Ringland Labour, Pill Labour; *Style*— Paul Flynn, Esq, MP; ✉ House of Commons, London SW1A 0AA (☎ 0171 219 3478)

FLYTE, Ellis Ashley; da of Thomas Hynd Duncan, and Anne Margaret Paterson Little Duncan; *Educ* The Mary Erskine Sch for Young Ladies Edinburgh, London Coll of Fashion (Dip in Art and Fashion Design); *m* Nov 1990, Brian David Henson, *qv*; *Career* fashion and costume designer (former bunny girl Dorchester Hotel and former ballet dancer); costume designs for RSC, Royal Opera House and Thames TV and for films incl Dark Crystal, Out of Africa, Labyrinth and The Tall Guy; fndr Ellis Flyte Fashion Design Showroom London 1984, fndr designer (with Richard Ostell, *qv*) Flyte Ostell Ltd 1990; winner New Generation Best Designer Award (British Fashion Awards) 1992; memb BECTU; *Recreations* travel, photography, film, dance, jacuzzis, music, art, dressing up; *Clubs* Le Petit Opportune Paris, The Groucho, Salon des Arts (fndr memb); *Style*— Ms Ellis Flyte; ✉ business: 30 Oval Road, Camden, London NW1 7DE (☎ 0171 284 2273)

FOAKES, Prof Reginald Anthony; s of William Warren Foakes, and Frances, *née* Poate; *b* 18 Oct 1923; *Educ* West Bromwich GS, Univ of Birmingham (MA, PhD); *m* 1, 1951, Barbara (d 1988), da of Harry Garratt, OBE; 2 s, 2 da; m 2, 1993, Mary, da of Albert White; *Career* sr lectr in English Univ of Durham 1963–64 (lectr 1954–62), Cwlth Fund (Harkness) fell Yale Univ 1955–56; Univ of Kent at Canterbury: prof of English lit 1964–82, dean Faculty of Humanities 1974–77, currently emeritus prof of Eng and American lit; visiting prof: Univ of Toronto 1960–62, Univ of Calif Santa Barbara 1968–69, UCLA 1981; prof of English UCLA 1983; *Books* Shakespeare's King Henry VIII (ed 1957), The Romantic Assertion (1958, 1972), Henslowe's Diary (ed with R T Rickert, 1961), Coleridge on Shakespeare (1971), Marston and Tourneur (1978), Illustrations of the English Stage 1980–1642 (1985), Coleridge's Lectures 1808–1819, On Literature (ed 2 Vols, 1987), Hamlet versus Lear: Cultural Politics and Shakespeare's Art (1993); *Style*— Prof Reginald Foakes; ✉ Department of English, University of California at Los Angeles, 405 Hilgard Avenue, Los Angeles, Calif 90024, USA

FOALE, Air Cdre Colin Henry; s of William Henry Foale (d 1979), of Galmpton, Devon, and Frances Margaret, *née* Muse (d 1969); *b* 10 June 1930; *Educ* Wolverton GS, RAF Coll Cranwell, RAF Staff Coll Bracknell, Jt Servs Staff Coll Latimer, RCDS Belgrave Sq; *m* 19 Sept 1954, Mary Katherine, da of Prof Samuel Bannister Harding (d 1925), of Minneapolis, USA; 2 s (Michael b 6 Jan 1957, Christopher b 13 March 1958, d 1979), 1 da (Susan b 2 May 1962); *Career* pilot 13 photo recce sqdn (Meteor) Kabrit Egypt 1952–53, Flt Cdr 32 Fighter Sqdn (Vampire), Deversoir Egypt 1953–54, RAF Flying Coll Manby (fighter instr Hunters) 1954–57, instr in selection techniques Offr Selection Centre RAF Hornchurch 1958–60, Sqdn Cdr 73 light Bomber Sqdn Akrotiri Cyprus 1960–63, organiser Biggin Hill Battle of Br display 1963, chm Cockpit Ctee TSR2 MOD (PE) 1965, Wing Cdr Air Plans HQ RAF Germany 1965–68, Sqdn Cdr 39 photo recce sqdn (Canberras) Luqa Malta 1969–71, Gp Capt SO flying MOD (PE) 1971–74, station cdr RAF Luqa Malta 1974–76, dir RAF PR 1977–79, ret at own request 1979; aviation advsr Yorks TV Drama 1979–80, trg advsr to Chm Cons Pty Central Office 1980–81, pilot to Ctee for Aerial Photography Univ of Cambridge 1981–90; memb: St Catherine's Coll Cambridge, Univ Air Sqdn, Selwyn Coll Cambridge, RAF Historical Soc, Air League, National Tst, Woodland Tst, RSPB, RYA, Cormorants, RCDS; FIMgt 1980, FIWM 1981; *Recreations* flying, sailing, world, travel, theatre, music, writing; *Clubs* RAF; *Style*— Air Cdre Colin H Foale; ✉ 37 Pretoria Rd, Cambridge CB4 1HD; St Catharine's College, University of Cambridge

FOALE, Graham Douglas Kenneth; JP (1981); s of Hubert Douglas Foale (d 1985), of Essex, and Lilian Kate, *née* Tolchard (d 1985); *b* 27 May 1938; *Educ* Clifton Coll Bristol; *m* 30 May 1964, Jean Barbara, da of Frederick Kershaw Sunderland (d 1949), of Rochdale; 2 s (Robin b 1967, Matthew b 1969); *Career* ptnr Bishop Fleming CAs Plymouth 1969–; memb S W Regnl Ind Devpt Bd 1977–83; chm: Plymouth Round Table 1974–75, Cornwall & Plymouth Branch of CAs 1979–80; memb: Small Practitioners' Ctee, Inst of CAs 1982–86; FCA; *Recreations* walking, toy collecting; *Style*— Graham D K Foale, JP; ✉ 8 Blue Haze Close, Plymbridge Road, Glenholt, Plymouth PL6 7HR (☎ 01752 695188); 2 Marlborough Rd, North Hill, Plymouth PL4 8LP (☎ 01752 262611)

FOALE, Marion Ann; da of Stuart Donald Foale (d 1972), and Gertrude Lillian Maud, *née* Rayner; *b* 13 March 1939; *Educ* SW Essex Tech and Sch of Art, Sch of Fashion Design RCA (DesRCA, designed Queen's Mantle for OBE); *children* 1 da (Polly Jones b 14 Dec 1972), 1 s (Charley Jones b 25 Jan 1977); *Career* fashion designer; fndr ptnr (with Sally Tuffin) Foale and Tuffin Ltd Carnaby Street 1961–72, signed with Puritan Fashions NY for 'Youth Quake' 1965; clothes designer for films: Kaleidoscope (with Susannah York) 1966, Two for the Road (with Audrey Hepburn) 1966; fndr own label Marion Foale (predominately producing hand knitwear) 1982–; *Books* Marion Foale's Classic Knitwear (1987); *Style*— Ms Marion Foale; ✉ Foale Ltd, Church Farm, Orton on the Hill, nr Atherstone, Warwickshire CV9 3NG (☎ 01827 880348, fax 01827 880807)

FOALE, Dr Rodney Alan; s of Maurice Spencer Foale, of Melbourne, Australia, and Lyle Gwendolin, *née* Wallace; *b* 11 Sept 1946; *Educ* Scotch Coll Melbourne, Univ of Melbourne Med Sch; *m* 1980, Lady Emma Cecile Gordon, er da of the Marquis of Aberdeen and Temair; 2 s (Archie Alexander b 17 Sept 1984, Jamie Alexander b 1 April 1986); *Career* St Vincent's Hosp Univ of Melbourne 1972–73, med offr Australian Himalayan Expdn through Indonesia India and Kashmir 1974–75, registrar Nat Heart Hosp 1975–79, clinical res fell Harvard Univ and MIT, Massachusetts Gen Hosp 1980–82, sr registrar in cardiology Hammersmith Hosp 1982–85, conslt cardiologist and clinical dir of cardiovascular science St Mary's Hosp 1985–; hon sr lectr Hammersmith Hosp 1985–, recognised teacher Univ of London 1985–; FACC 1986, FESC 1988, FRCP 1994 (MRCP 1976); *Recreations* various; *Clubs* Flyfishers', Chelsea Arts; *Style*— Dr Rodney Foale; ✉ 66 Harley St, London W1N 1AE (☎ 0171 323 4687, fax 0171 631 5341)

FOCKE, Paul Everard Justus; QC (1982); s of Frederick Justus Focke (d 1959), and Muriel Focke (d 1995); *b* 14 May 1937; *Educ* Downside, Exeter Coll Oxford, Trinity Coll Dublin; *m* 13 Dec 1973, Lady Tana Focke, da of late 6 Earl of Caledon; 2 da 2 da (Diana Natasha b 1974, Victoria Justine b 1976); *Career* Nat Serv 1955–57; Capt Cheshire Yeo TA 1957–65; called to the Bar: Gray's Inn 1964, NZ 1982; QC NSW 1984; recorder of the Crown Court 1986–, bencher 1992, head of chambers; *Recreations* travelling, aeroplanes; *Clubs* Turf, Beefsteak, Pratt's, Cavalry and Guards', St Botolph (Boston, Mass); *Style*— Paul Focke, Esq, QC; ✉ 7 Cheyne Walk, London SW3 5QZ (☎ 0171 351 0299); 1 Mitre Court Buildings, Temple, London EC4Y 7BS (☎ 0171 797 7070, fax 0171 797 7435, car 0836 215504)

FODEN, Edwin Peter; CBE (1993); s of Edwin Richard Foden (d 1950), and Mary, *née* Cooke; *b* 24 Feb 1930; *Educ* Rossall, N Staffs Tech Coll; *m* 1957, Judith, da of James Harding Baxter, of Nantwich, Cheshire; 3 s; *Career* Lt REME (UK and Germany); chm and chief exec ERF (Holdings) plc; chm: ERF Ltd (family firm), ERF S Africa (Pty) Ltd; vice pres: SMMT 1971–83, Inst of Motor Industry 1981–; Liveryman Worshipful Co of Carmen; FRSA, FIMI; *Recreations* golf, shooting, motor racing; *Clubs* REME Officers', Annabel's; *Style*— Edwin Peter Foden, Esq, CBE; ✉ Oak Farm, The Heath, Sandbach, Cheshire (☎ 01270 762732); ERF Ltd, Sun Works, Sandbach, Cheshire (☎ 01270 763223, fax 01270 766068, telex 36152)

FOGDEN, Michael Ernest George (Mike); CB (1994); s of George Charles Arthur Fogden (d 1970), of Worthing, Sussex, and Margaret May Fogden; *b* 30 May 1936; *Educ* Worthing HS Sussex, Lycee du Garcons Le Mans France; *m* 1 June 1957, (Rose) Ann, da of James Arthur Diamond (d 1983), of Morpeth, Northumberland; 3 s, 1 da; *Career* Nat Serv RAF 1956–58; Miny of Social Security 1959–67, private sec of state for Social Services 1968–70, DHSS 1971–82, Dept of Employment 1982–87; chief exec British Employment Service 1987–; chm: First Division Assoc 1979–82, Public Mgmnt Forum; FRSA; *Recreations* music, gardening, snooker; *Clubs* IOD; *Style*— Mike Fogden, Esq, CB; ✉ Employment Service, St Vincent House, 30 Orange St, London WC2H 7HT (☎ 0171 389 1497, fax 0171 389 1457)

FOGEL, Steven Anthony; s of Joseph Gerald Fogel, JP, and Benita Rose Fogel; *b* 16 Oct 1951; *Educ* Carmel Coll, King's Coll London (LLB, LLM); *m* 2 Jan 1977, Joan Selma, da of Curtis Holder (d 1972); 1 da (Frances Leah), 2 s (George Curtis, Jonathan Raphael); *Career* admitted slr 1976; ptnr and head Property Dept Titmuss Sainer Dechert; memb: Editorial Bd Jl of Property Finance, Br Cncl of Shopping Centres, Br Cncl of Offices, Anglo American Real Property Inst, 1954 Act Arbitration Sub Ctee RICS, Commercial Property Policy Panel RICS; dir Spiro Inst; tstee Motivation; Freeman: City of London, Worshipful Co of Slrs; ACIArb; *Books* Rent Reviews (1986), The Landlord and Tenant Factbook (jtly, 1992), Rental Inducements (jtly, 1994), Privity of Contract, A Practitioner's Guide (jtly, 1995); *Recreations* jazz, skiing, writing; *Style*— Steven Fogel, Esq; ✉ Titmuss Sainer Dechert, 2 Serjeants' Inn, London EC4Y 1LT (☎ 0171 583 5353, fax 0171 353 3683/2830)

FOGELMAN, Dr Ignac; s of Richard Fogelman (d 1975), and Ruth, *née* Tyras (d 1995); *b* 4 Sept 1948; *Educ* HS of Glasgow, Univ of Glasgow (BSc, MB ChB, MD); *m* 18 March 1974, Coral Niman, da of Harvey Norton (d 1980); 1 s (Richard b 1982), 1 da (Gayle b 1974); *Career* dir Osteoporosis Screening and Res Unit Guy's Hosp 1988– (conslt physician 1983–, dir Nuclear Med Dept 1988–); memb Cncl Nat Osteoporosis Soc; memb Int Skeletal Soc 1988; FRCP 1987; *Books* Bone Scanning in Clinical Practice (1987), An Atlas of Clinical Nuclear Medicine (with M Maisey, 1988), An Atlas of Planar and Spect Bone Scans (with D Collier, 1988); *Recreations* bridge, theatre, opera, music, tennis, books; *Style*— Dr Ignac Fogelman; ✉ Department of Nuclear Medicine, Guy's Hospital, St Thomas St, London SE1 9RT (☎ 0171 955 4593, fax 0171 955 4657)

FOGELMAN, Prof Kenneth Robert (Ken); s of Joseph Alfred Fogelman (d 1987), and Vera May, *née* Corrie; *b* 29 Jan 1945; *Educ* Ifield GS Crawley Sussex, Univ of Keele (BA); *m* 26 Aug 1967, Audrey Elaine, da of Angus Corkan, of Douglas, IOM; *Career* secdy maths teacher 1966–67, res offr Sch to Univ Res Unit Nat Fndn for Educnl Res 1969–72 (res asst Section for Mathematical and Conceptual Studies 1967–69), asst dir Nat Children's Bureau 1981–85 (princ res offr 1972–81), dep dir Social Statistics Res Unit City Univ 1985–88, prof of educn Univ of Leicester 1988–; fndr memb: Br Educnl Res Assoc, Social Res Assoc; memb Assoc of Child Psychiatrists and Psychologists; FBPsS 1988; *Books* Piagetian Tests for the Primary School (1970), Leaving the Sixth Form (1972), Britain's Sixteen Year Olds (1976), Growing Up in Great Britain (1983), Putting Children First (ed with I Vallender, 1988), Citizenship in Schools (1991), Developing Citizenship in the Curriculum (ed with J Edwards, 1993), Going Comprehensive in England and Wales (with A Kerckhoff, D Crook and D Reeder, 1996); *Recreations* badminton, music, travel, photography; *Style*— Prof Ken Fogelman; ✉ The Red House, Main Street, Belton-in-Rutland, Leics LE15 9LB; School of Education, University of Leicester, 21 University Rd, Leicester LE1 7RF (☎ 0116 252 3588, fax 0116 252 3653)

FOGG, Prof Gordon Elliott (Tony); CBE (1983); s of Rev Leslie Charles Fogg (d 1951), of Ranmoor, Sheffield, and Doris Mary, *née* Elliott (d 1976); *b* 26 April 1919; *Educ* Dulwich, Queen Mary Coll London (BSc), St John's Coll Cambridge (PhD, ScD); *m* 7 July 1945, Elizabeth Beryl, da of Rev Thomas Llechid Jones (d 1946), of Old Colwyn, Clwyd; 1 s (Timothy b 1951), 1 da (Helen b 1947); *Career* seaweed survey of Br Isles Miny of Supply 1942, plant physiologist Pest Control Ltd Cambridge 1943–45, Dept of Botany UCL 1945–60 (asst lectr, lectr, reader), prof of botany Westfield Coll Univ of London 1960–71, prof of marine biology Univ Coll of N Wales 1971–85 (prof emeritus 1985); govr Marine Biol Assoc 1973–, pres Section K Br Assoc 1973 (biological gen sec 1967–72), chm Cncl Freshwater Biological Assoc 1974–85, pres Inst of Biology 1976–77, tstee Br Museum (Natural History) 1976–85, memb Royal Cmmn on Environmental Pollution 1979–85, tstee Royal Botanic Gardens Kew 1983–89; Hon LLD Univ of Dundee 1974; FIBiol 1960, FRS 1965; *Books* The Metabolism of Algae (1953), The Growth of Plants (1963), Photosynthesis (1968), The Bluegreen Algae (with WDP Stewart, P Fay and AE Walsby, 1973), Algal Cultures and Phytoplankton Ecology (with B Thake, 1987), The Explorations of Antarctica (with D Smith, 1990), A History of Antarctic Science (1992); *Recreations* walking, Antarctic history, listening to music; *Clubs* Athenaeum; *Style*— Prof Tony Fogg, CBE, FRS; ✉ Bodolben, Llandegfan, Isle of Anglesey LL59 5TA (☎ 01248 712 916); School of Ocean Sciences, Marine Science Laboratories, Menai Bridge, Isle of Anglesey LL59 5EY (☎ 01248 351 151, fax 01248 716 367)

FOLDES, Prof Lucien Paul; s of Egon Foldes (d 1935), of Marta, *née* Landau (d 1961); *b* 19 Nov 1930; *Educ* Bunce Court Sch, Monkton Wyld Sch, Regent St Poly, LSE (BCom, DBA, MSc); *Career* Nat Serv Private OC then 2 Lt 1952–54, later Lt TA; LSE: asst and asst lectr in economics 1951–52 and 1954–55, lectr 1955–61, reader 1961–79, prof of economics 1979–96, emeritus prof 1996; memberships incl: Royal Economic Soc, London Mathematical Soc; *Publications* author of numerous articles in learned jls; *Recreations* mathematics, literature; *Style*— Prof Lucien Foldes; ✉ London School of Economics, Houghton St, London WC2A 2AE (☎ 0171 405 7686, fax 0171 831 1840, telex 24655 LSELON G)

FOLEY, 8 Baron (GB 1776); Adrian Gerald Foley; s of 7 Baron Foley (d 1927), and Minoru, *née* Greenstone (d 1968); *b* 9 Aug 1923; *m* 1, 23 Dec 1958 (m dis 1971), Patricia, da of Joseph Zoellner III, of Pasadena, California, and formerly w of Minor de Uribe Meek; 1 s, 1 da (Hon Alexandra Mary); m 2, 1972, Ghislaine, da of Cornelius Willem Dresselhuys, of The Hague, Holland, and formerly w of (1) Maj Denis James Alexander, later 6 Earl of Caledon, and (2) 4 Baron Ashcombe, *qv*; *Heir* s, Hon Thomas Henry Foley; *Career* composer and pianist; *Clubs* White's; *Style*— The Rt Hon Lord Foley; ✉ c/o Marbella Club, Marbella, Malaga, Spain

FOLEY, Rt Rev Graham Gregory; s of Theodore Gregory Foley (d 1940), and Florence Cassan, *née* Page (d 1967); *b* 13 June 1923; *Educ* Wade Deacon GS Widnes, Queen Elizabeth GS Wakefield, King Edward's GS Aston Birmingham, King's Coll London, St John's Coll Univ of Durham (BA, DipTheol); *m* 14 June 1944, Florence, da of late Charles Frederick Redman; 2 s (Mark Gregory b 1954, Simon John b 1957), 2 da (Alison Moyra b 1948, Sheelagh Mary b 1951); *Career* ordained priest 1951, curate of Holy Trinity South Shore Blackpool 1950–54, vicar of St Luke Blackburn 1954–60, dir of educn Diocese of Durham 1960–71, rector of Brancepeth Co Durham 1960–71, vicar of Leeds 1971–82, chaplain to HM The Queen 1977–82, bishop of Reading 1982–89, assistant bishop Diocese of York 1989–; ret hon canon: Durham Cathedral 1965–71, Ripon Cathedral 1971–82; *Books* Religion in Approved Schools (1965); *Recreations* walking on the moors, reading detective stories, watching other people mow lawns; *Clubs* Royal Commonwealth; *Style*— The Right Rev Graham Foley; ✉ Ramsey Cottage, 3 Poplar Avenue, Kirkbymoorside, York YO6 6ES (☎ 01751 432439)

FOLEY, Hugh Smith; s of John Walker Foley (d 1970), and Mary Hogg, *née* Smith; *b* 9 April 1939; *Educ* Dalkeith HS; *m* 7 Sept 1966, Isobel King, da of James Halliday (d 1970); 2 s (Mark b 31 May 1970, Paul b 28 Jan 1974); *Career* Nat Serv RAF 1959–61; student actuary Standard Life Assurance Co 1956–59, entered Scot Ct Serv (Ct of Session Branch) 1962, asst clerk of session 1962–71, depute clerk of session 1972–80, seconded to Sheriff Ct Edinburgh 1980–81, princ sheriff clerk depute Glasgow 1981–82, sheriff clerk Linlithgow 1982, dep princ clerk of session 1982–86, sr dep princ clerk 1986–89, princ clerk of session and justiciary 1989–; *Recreations* walking, painting, reading, listening to music; *Style*— Hugh Foley, Esq; ✉ Supreme Courts, Parliament House, Edinburgh EH1 1RQ (☎ 0131 225 2595, fax 0131 225 8213)

FOLEY, His Hon Judge; John Dominic; s of Cyril Patrick Foley (d 1972), of Bristol, and Winifred Hannah, *née* McAweeny (d 1980); *b* 17 Jan 1944; *Educ* St Brendan's Coll

Bristol, Univ of Exeter (LLB); *m* 1978 (m dis 1986), Helena Frances, da of Dr Kemp McGowan; 2 da (Jessica Rosalind b 23 Sept 1978, Helena Rachel b 25 Nov 1980); *Career* called to the Bar Inner Temple 1968, in practice Western Circuit 1969–, recorder of the Crown Court 1990–94 (asst recorder 1986–90), circuit judge (Western Circuit) 1994–; *Recreations* cricket, rugby, travel, theatre; *Clubs* Somerset CCC, Bristol RFC, Clifton RFC; *Style*— His Hon Judge Foley; ✉ c/o Western Circuit Office, Bridge House, Sion Place, Clifton, Bristol BS8 4BN

FOLEY, Lt-Gen Sir John Paul; KCB (1994, CB 1991), OBE (1979), MC (1976); s of Maj Henry Thomas Hamilton Foley, MBE (d 1959), of Stoke Edith, Hereford, and Helen Constance Margaret, *née* Pearson (d 1985); *b* 22 April 1939; *Educ* Bradfield Coll (Mons OCS), Army Staff Coll; *m* 3 June 1972, Ann Rosamund, da of Maj John William Humphries; 2 da (Annabel b 11 July 1973, Joanna b 8 May 1976); *Career* Royal Green Jackets: Lt 1959–60, Capt 1961–69; Maj RMCS 1970–71; Cmdg Offr 3 Bn 1978–80; Brigade Maj, 51 Inf Bde Hong Kong 1974–76; Camberley: army staff course 1972–74, Lt Col dir staff 1976–78; Cmdt jr div Staff Coll Warminster 1981–82; Brig: arms dir MOD 1983–85, student RCDS 1986; chief Br mission to Soviet forces Berlin 1987–89; Maj Gen central staffs MOD 1989–92, Cdr Br Forces Hong Kong 1992–94, Col Cmdt The Lt Div 1994, Lt-Gen central staffs MOD 1994–; Freeman City of London 1970, memb Ct of Assts Worshipful Co of Skinners 1996 (Freeman 1965, Liveryman 1972); *Recreations* tennis, walking, shooting, reading; *Clubs* Boodle's; *Style*— Lt-Gen Sir John Foley, KCB, OBE, MC; ✉ Ministry of Defence, Room 204, Old War Office Building, Whitehall SW1A 2EU

FOLEY, Martin John; s of Bernard Francis Foley (d 1987), and Bridget Doreen Foley; *b* 7 March 1947; *Educ* Univ of Manchester (BA); *m* 25 March 1970, Joyce, da of L Kenneth Dixon; 2 s (Daniel John b 16 Nov 1979, Alexander William b 17 Feb 1984); *Career* Watney Mann 1969–72; Price Waterhouse: joined 1972, ptnr 1984–, head Corp Fin London 1991–95, head Corp Fin India 1995–; FCA; *Style*— Martin Foley, Esq; ✉ Price Waterhouse, 1 London Bridge, London SE1 9QL (☎ 0171 939 5414, fax 0171 403 2283, mobile 0831 318037)

FOLEY, Sheila; da of Leslie Crossley (d 1970), of Hebden Bridge, W Yorkshire, and Agnes, *née* Mitchell (d 1976); *b* 5 July 1944; *Educ* Calder HS Mytholmroyd, Mabel Fletcher Tech Coll Liverpool; *m* 5 March 1966 (m dis), John Kevin Foley, s of Robert Foley; 1 s (Sean Michael b 16 Feb 1968), 1 da (Siobhain Clare b 25 Jan 1967); *Career* registered mental nurse St John's Hosp Lincoln 1974–78, registered general nurse Luton Dunstable Hosp 1978–84, nurse mangr Charing Cross Hosp London 1984–85, dir of nursing servs West Lambeth Health Authy 1985–86; unit gen mangr and chief nurse advsr: Mental Health Unit 1986–89, Priority Care Servs 1989–92, Chester Health Authy; chief exec Learning Disabilities Unit Kidderminster & District Health Authy 1992–93, unit general mangr Rampton Hosp 1993–; gen sec Psychiatric Nurses Assoc 1986; memb: Health Advsy Serv 1986–, Wirral Health Authy 1987–90, Rampton Review Team 1989; memb Royal Coll of Nursing 1971; *Recreations* walking, reading; *Style*— Mrs Sheila Foley; ✉ Wheelwright's Hub, Lincoln Road, Holton cum Beckering, Lincoln LN3 5NG (☎ 01673 857424); Rampton Hospital, Retford, Notts DN22 0PD (☎ 01777 247301)

FOLKESTONE, Viscount; William Pleydell-Bouverie; s (by 1 m) and h of 8 Earl of Radnor; *b* 5 Jan 1955; *Educ* Harrow, RAC Cirencester; *m* 11 May 1996, A Melissa, o da of James Keith Edward Stanford, of Grange Farm, Spratton, Northants; *Style*— Viscount Folkestone; ✉ Alward House, Alderbury, Salisbury, Wiltshire SP5 3DJ

FOLLETT, Prof Sir Brian Keith; kt (1992); s of Albert James Follett (d 1961), of Bournemouth, and Edith Annie, *née* Taylor (d 1981); *b* 22 Feb 1939; *Educ* Bournemouth Sch, Univ of Bristol (BSc, PhD), Univ of Wales (DSc); *m* Lady Deb Follett; 1 da (Karen Tracy Williams b 4 June 1965), 1 s (Richard James b 1 May 1968); *Career* NIH res fell Washington State Univ 1964–65, lectr in zoology Univ of Leeds 1965–69, lectr, reader then prof of zoology Univ of Wales Bangor 1969–78, prof of zoology Univ of Bristol 1978–93, vice-chllr Univ of Warwick 1993–; memb: Univs Funding Cncl 1988–91, Higher Educn Funding Cncl 1991–96, AFRC 1982–88, BBSRC (formerly AFRC) 1994– (chm Sci and Engrg Bd); tstee British Museum (Natural History) 1988–; author of over 250 scientific papers published in fields of reproductive physiology and biological clocks; Hon LLD Univ of Wales 1992; FRS 1984 (biological sec and vice-pres 1987–93); *Recreations* history; *Style*— Prof Sir Brian Follett, FRS; ✉ Vice-Chancellor's Lodge, Cryfield Old Farmhouse, Gibbet Hill Road, Coventry CV4 7AJ (☎ 01203 692078, fax 01203 690293); Office of the Vice-Chancellor, University of Warwick, Coventry CV4 7AL (☎ 01203 523630)

FOLLETT, James; s of late James Follett, and late Yvonne, *née* Mills; *b* 27 July 1939; *m* 13 Aug 1960, Christine Marie, *née* Panichelli; 1 s (Richard b 3 Aug 1966), 1 da (Joanna Samantha b 16 Nov 1968); *Career* writer; trained as marine engr, worked as tech dir MOD, full-time writer 1976–; designer of computer games; *Radio* wrote first radio play for BBC 1973, subsequently numerous plays and drama documentaries for BBC Radio 4; *Television* incl episodes for: Crown Court, Blake's Seven, The Squad, Today and Tomorrow, BBC Children's TV; *Novels* The Doomsday Ultimatum (1976, 2 edn 1991), Crown Court (1977), Ice (1979), Churchill's Gold (1980), Earthsearch (1981), Tiptoe Boys (1982, filmed as Who Dares Wins), Earthsearch II: Deathship (1982), Dominator (1984), Swift (1985), Mirage (1988), U-700 (1989), A Cage of Eagles (1990), Torus (1990), Trojan (1991), Savant (1992), Those in Peril (1993), Mindwarp (1993); *Recreations* Radio 'Ham' (Callsign G1LXP), collecting boring postcards; *Style*— James Follett, Esq; ✉ c/o Jacqui Lyons, Marjacq Scripts Ltd, 161 Bickenhall Mansions, Bickenhall Street, London W1H 3DF (☎ 0171 935 9499, fax 0171 935 9115)

FOLLETT, Kenneth Martin (Ken); s of Martin Dunsford Follett, of Yatton, Somerset, and Lavinia Cynthia, *née* Evans; *b* 5 June 1949; *Educ* Harrow Weald GS, Poole Tech Coll, UCL (BA); *m* 1, 5 Jan 1968 (m dis 1985), Mary Emma Ruth, da of Horace Henry Elson (d 1988), of Kinson, Bournemouth; 1 s (Emanuele b 13 July 1968), 1 da (Marie-Claire b 11 May 1973); m 2, 8 Nov 1985 (Daphne) Barbara, *née* Hubbard; *Career* journalist: S Wales Echo 1970–73, London Evening News 1973–74; dep md Everest Books 1976–77 (editorial dir 1974–76); author 1977–; memb: Stevenage Lab Party, Arts for Lab, Liberty, Amnesty, American Cncl on Civil Liberties, Authors' Guild USA 1979, Cncl Nat Literary Tst; fell UCL 1995; *Books* Eye of the Needle (1978), Triple (1979), The Key to Rebecca (1980), The Man from St Petersburg (1982), On Wings of Eagles (1983), Lie Down With Lions (1986), The Pillars of the Earth (1989), Night over Water (1991), A Dangerous Fortune (1993), A Place Called Freedom (1995), The Third Twin (1996); *Recreations* bass guitarist of Damn Right I Got the Blues; *Clubs* Groucho; *Style*— Ken Follett, Esq; ✉ PO Box 708, London SW10 ODH

FOLLEY, Malcolm John; s of John Trevail Folley, of Peacehaven, Sussex, and Rosina, *née* O'Hara (d 1975); *b* 24 April 1952; *Educ* Lewes Co GS for Boys; *m* 5 June 1976, Rachel, da of Peter Ivan Kingman; 2 da (Siân Trevail b 27 July 1987, Megan Trevail b 19 Dec 1988); *Career* sports writer; indentured Sussex Express and County Herald 1968–72; news ed: Wimpey News 1972–73, Hayter's Sports Agency 1973; sports reporter: United Newspapers (London-based) 1973–75, Daily Express 1975–82, Mail on Sunday 1982–83; tennis corr Daily Mail 1984–86, dep ed Sportsweek 1986–87, sr sports writer Daily Express 1987–92, dep sports ed Mail on Sunday 1992 (chief sports reporter 1992–); highly commended Magazine Sports Writer of the Year 1986, Sports Reporter of the Year 1991; *Books* Hana: the Autobiography of Hana Mandlikova (co-author, 1989); *Recreations* golf, skiing, tennis; *Clubs* Drift Golf (Surrey); *Style*— Malcolm Folley, Esq; ✉ Mail on Sunday, Northcliffe House, 2 Derry St, London W8 5TS (☎ 0171 938 7069, fax 0171 937 4115)

FOLLIE, Robert Pierre; s of Robert Maurice Follie (d 1983), and Marie-Rose, *née* Bossard; *b* 3 Dec 1951; *Educ* Institut Etudes Politiques Paris, Université de Droit de Rouen; *m* 1978, Anne-Michelle Seronie-Vivien; 3 c (Robert Jean b 16 Oct 1979, Anne-Laure b 13 Oct 1982, Pierre b 9 Oct 1986); *Career* in-house counsel Exxon Corp (France and USA) 1978–86, avocat White & Case (law firm) Paris 1986–90, co-ordinating ptnr Paris office Lovell White Durrant 1992– (opened office 1990); legal advsr to various major multi-national cos in USA, UK and France; *Clubs* Anglo Belgian, Yacht Club de France (Paris); *Style*— Robert Follie, Esq; ✉ Lovell White Durrant, 37 Avenue Pierre 1er de Serbie, 75008 Paris, France (☎ 00 33 49 52 04 26, fax 00 33 47 23 96 12)

FOLWELL, Nicholas David; s of Alfred Thomas Folwell (d 1975), and Irmgard Seefeld, of Market Drayton; *b* 11 July 1953; *Educ* Spring Grove GS, Middx Royal Acad of Music, London Opera Centre; *m* 31 Jan 1981, Anne-Marie, da of George Ives; 1 s (Alexander Thomas b 22 July 1981), 1 step s (Adrian Marshal Matheson-Bruce b 15 Aug 1974); *Career* baritone; joined Welsh Nat Opera 1978, first professional role The Bosun in Billy Budd 1978; later WNO roles incl: Marchese in La Traviata 1979, Melot in Triston Und Isolde 1979, Ottone in The Coronation of Poppea 1980, Figaro in The Marriage of Figaro 1981 and 1987, Melitone in La Forza del Destino 1981, Leporello in Don Giovanni 1982, Klingsor in Parsifal 1983, Pizarro in Fidelio 1983, Alberich in Das Rheingold 1983, Schaunard in La Bohème 1984, Alberich in Siegfried and Götterdämmerung 1985; other roles incl: Beckmesser in The Mastersingers of Nuremberg (Opera North) 1985, Leporello in Don Giovanni (Opera North) 1986, The Four Villians in The Tales of Hoffmann (Scottish Opera) 1986, Tonio in Pagliacci (ENO) 1986, Alberich in Der Ring (WNO at Covent Garden) 1986, The Poacher in The Cunning Little Vixen (WNO) 1987, Father in The Seven Deadly Sins (Royal Festival Hall) 1988, Figaro in The Marriage of Figaro (Scottish Opera) 1987, Papageno in The Magic Flute (ENO) 1988, Marullo in Rigoletto (Frankfurt Opera) 1988, Alberich in Das Rheingold (Scottish Opera) 1989, Koroviev in Der Meister und Margarita (world premiere, Paris Opera) 1989, Creon and The Messenger in Oedipus Rex (Scottish Opera) 1990, Melitone in La Forza del Destino (Scottish Opera) 1990, The Poacher in The Cunning Little Vixen (Royal Opera) 1990, Pizarro in Fidelio (Glyndebourne) 1990, Figaro in Le Nozze di Figaro (Opera Zuid Holland) 1991, Count in The Marriage of Figaro (Opera NI) 1996; also numerous classical concerts in UK and abroad; ARAM; *Recordings* incl: Tristan und Isolde (as Melot), Jailer in Tosca, Klingsor in Parsifal, Rimsky-Korsakov Christmas Eve, Tchaikovsky Vakula The Smith, The Cunning Little Vixen (as the Poacher), Der Zwerg (as the Haushofmeister); *Recreations* golf; *Style*— Nicholas Folwell, Esq; ✉ c/o Robert Gilder & Co, Enterprise House, 59–65 Upper Ground, London SE1 9PQ (☎ 0171 928 9008)

FONE, Michael; s of Lawrence Fone, of Chipperfield, Herts, and late Mabel Edith Fone; *b* 21 Feb 1933; *Educ* Hemel Hempstead GS, QMC London; *Career* md Rea Bros Group PLC 1972–88 (dir 1969–72), dir Jupiter Asset Management Ltd 1988–; hon treas and dir St Peter's Res Tst 1975–; AIIMR; *Recreations* gardening, the arts; *Clubs* Garrick; *Style*— Michael Fone, Esq; ✉ 29 Huguenot House, 19 Oxendon St, London SW1Y 4EH (☎ 0171 839 3978); Marshfield Chippenham, Wilts SN14 8NU (☎ 01225 891752); Jupiter Asset Management Ltd, Knightsbridge House, 197 Knightsbridge, London SW7 1RB (☎ 0171 412 0703)

FONSECA, Jose Maria; da of Amador Francis Gabriel Fonseca (d 1984), of Abergavenny, Gwent, and Kathleen, *née* Jones; *b* 9 Jan 1944; *Educ* Sacred Heart Convent Highgate, Ursuline Convent San Sebastian Spain, Ursuline Convent St Pol de Leon Brittany, St Godric's Secretarial Coll Hampstead; *m* 1, 1975 (m dis 1982); m 2, 1985, Dick Kries; *Career* secretary, waitress, mangr of boutique, worked in model agency English Boy 1966–68, fndr Models One 1968–; *Style*— Mrs Jose Fonseca; ✉ Models One, Omega House, 471–473 Kings Road, London SW10 0LU (☎ 0171 351 1195 and 0171 351 6033, fax 0171 376 5821)

FOOKES, Dame Janet Evelyn; DBE (1989), MP (Cons) Plymouth Drake (majority 2,013); da of Lewis Aylmer Fookes (d 1978), and Evelyn Margery, *née* Holmes (d 1996); *b* 21 Feb 1936; *Educ* Hastings and St Leonards Ladies' Coll, Hastings HS for Girls, Royal Holloway Coll Univ of London (BA); *Career* teacher 1958–70, chm Educn Ctee Hastings County Borough Cncl 1967–70 (memb 1960–61 and 1963–70); MP (C): Merton and Morden 1970–74, Plymouth Drake 1974–; chm: Educn, Arts and Home Office Sub-Ctees of Expenditure Ctee 1975–79, Parly Animal Welfare Gp 1985–92; vice chm All Pty Mental Health Gp 1985–92 (sec 1979–85); memb: Select Ctee on Home Affrs 1983–92, Cwlth War Graves Cmmn 1987–; dep speaker and second dep chm of Ways and Means 1992– (thus ex-officio memb Speaker's Panel of Chairmen); fell Indust and Parl Tst; memb: Cncl RSPCA 1973–92 (chm 1979–81), Cncl Stonham Housing Assoc 1980–92, Cncl SSAFA 1980–, Cncl of Mgmnt Coll of St Mark and St John 1989–; *Recreations* keep-fit exercises, swimming, theatre, gardening; *Style*— Dame Janet Fookes, DBE, MP; ✉ House of Commons, London SW1A 0AA (Message Bureau ☎ 0171 219 4343)

FOOKES, Prof Peter George; s of George Ernest James Fookes (d 1980), of Reigate, Surrey, and Ida Corina, *née* Wellby (d 1988); *b* 31 May 1933; *Educ* Reigate Sch, Queen Mary and Imperial Colls London (BSc, PhD, DSc(Eng)); *m* 1, 4 Dec 1962, Gwyneth Margaret, da of Harry William Jones, of Stratford upon Avon; 2 s (Gregory Peter Gwyn b 20 Oct 1964, Timothy David b 17 July 1968), 3 da (Jennifer Marjorie b 7 Sept 1963, Anita Janet b 19 Dec 1971, Rosemary Eleanor (twin) b 19 Dec 1971); m 2, 25 July 1987, Edna May, da of John Arthur Nix, of Surbiton, Surrey; *Career* formerly chemical/soils lab technician, co engrg geologist Binnie & Ptnrs 1960–65, lectr in engrg geology Imperial Coll London 1966–71, conslt engrg geologist in private practice 1971–; visiting prof: of geomaterials QMC London 1979–96, of geology City Univ 1991–96, of engrg geology Univ of Newcastle 1993–; Br Geotechnical Soc Prize 1981, William Smith Medal Geological Soc 1985; ICE: Telford Premium 1981, Overseas Premium 1982, George Stephenson Gold Medal 1990, Webb Prize 1990, Coopers Hill War Meml Medal and Prize 1992, Overseas Premium 1982 and 1992; author of over 130 published professional papers and books; memb: Geologists Assoc 1956, Br Geotechnical Soc 1963, Br Acad of Experts 1989; FGS 1960, companion ICE 1966, FIMM 1977, CEng 1977, FIGeol 1986, CGeol 1991, FEng 1991, FRSA 1994; *Recreations* industrial archaeology, narrow boating (life memb Kennet & Avon Canal Tst), steam railways (life memb Mid-Hants Railway Preservation Soc); *Style*— Prof Peter Fookes, FEng; (☎ 01962 863029, fax 01962 842317)

FOOKS, John Anthony; JP; s of William John Fooks; *b* 24 Aug 1933; *Educ* Shrewsbury, Trinity Coll Cambridge; *m* 1959, (Maureen) Heather, da of Percival Charles Jones, sometime High Sheriff of Gwent; 3 s, 1 da; *Career* chm: Fooks Property Co Ltd, East Surrey Holdings plc, The Water Companies (Pension Fund) Trustee Co; dir: Pittards plc, The Bradford Property Trust plc, Delyn Group plc, Warner Estates Holdings plc; gen cmmr Inland Revenue; memb Lloyd's 1975; High Sheriff of East Sussex 1996–97; Freeman City of London 1976, memb Ct of Assts Worshipful Co of Broderers; FCA; *Recreations* golf, shooting, music, bridge; *Clubs* Cardiff & County, Royal & Ancient Golf, Rye Golf, Golf Match, MCC, Lloyd's Yacht, Royal Thames Yacht; *Style*— John Fooks, Esq, JP; ✉ 52 Trinity Church Square, London SE1 4HT; Woodgate House, Beckley, Rye, E Sussex TN31 6UH (☎ 01797 260472, fax 01797 260334)

FOOT, Cedric Charles Gainsborough (Ric); OBE (1990); s of Charles Gainsborough Foot (d 1965), and Mary Letitia, *née* Basnett (d 1993); *b* 12 Jan 1930; *Educ* St Paul's, Worcester Coll Oxford (MA); *m* 1977, Pauline Mary (d 1995), da of William Stoner;

Career Philips Electronics UK Ltd 1954–91: joined Lighting Div as mgmnt trainee 1954, various sales roles 1955–67, commercial mangr Philips Lighting Div 1967–72, nat sales mangr 1972–74, divnl dir Philips Lighting 1974–77, divnl dir Philips Consumer Electronics 1977–81, seconded to DTI as special advsr to manage and promote the growth of teletext 1981–84, dir of UK corp relations Philips Electronics 1984–91; in own mktg and PR consultancy RF Associates 1991–; Electrical Indust Personality of the Yr 1982; memb Cncl: Lighting Indust Fedn 1973–77, Br Radio and Electrical Indust Mfrs Assoc 1978–80 and 1984–90, ISBA 1984–90, IPR 1991–93 (fndr Home Counties South regnl gp 1991, winner Best Gp Award 1992); memb Advtg Advsy Ctee IBA 1988–90; fndn govr The King's Sch Grantham 1993–95, vice pres City branch Red Cross 1990; memb: City of London Historical Soc, Royal Soc of St George, Batti-Wallahs Soc 1996; Freeman: City of London 1984, Worshipful Co of Wax Chandlers 1996; Master: Worshipful Co of Lightmongers 1986–87, Worshipful Co of Information Technologists 1995–96 (Dep Master 1996–97); fell Order of the Lampmaker (only Br person to receive accolade) 1979; FCIBSE 1976, FRSA 1977, FIPR 1992; *Recreations* exploring latest computer, landscape gardening, building design, philology, jigsaws and crosswords, classical music and opera, wine and food; *Clubs* City Livery; *Style*— Ric Foot, Esq, OBE; ✉ West Wing, Limpsfield Court, Ice House Wood, Oxted, Surrey RH8 9DW (☎ 01883 712675, fax 01883 730196, mobile 0860 923282)

FOOT, Baron (Life Peer UK 1967), of Buckland Monachorum, Co Devon; John Mackintosh Foot; 3 s of Rt Hon Isaac Foot, PC (d 1960), and his 1 w Eva, *née* Mackintosh (d 1946); bro of Lord Caradon (d 1990) and Rt Hon Michael Foot, *qv*; *b* 17 Feb 1909; *Educ* Bembridge Sch, Balliol Coll Oxford (BA); *m* 25 June 1936, Anne Bailey, da of Dr Clifford Bailey Farr, of Bryn Mawr, Pa, USA; 1 s (Hon John Winslow b 1939), 1 da (Hon Katherine Elliott (Hon Mrs Illingworth) b 1937); *Career* Maj RASC WWII; slr 1934–95 (sr ptnr Foot & Bowden of Plymouth), chm UK Immigrants Advsy Serv 1970–78; Parly candidate (Lib): Basingstoke 1934 and 1935, Bodmin 1945 and 1950; pres Dartmoor Preservation Assoc 1976–95; chm Cncl of Justice 1983–89; *Recreations* chess, crosswords; *Style*— The Rt Hon Lord Foot; ✉ Yew Tree, Crapstone, Yelverton, Devon PL20 7PJ (☎ 01822 853417)

FOOT, Michael David Kenneth Willoughby; s of Kenneth Willoughby Foot (d 1980), and Ruth Joan, *née* Cornah; *b* 16 Dec 1946; *Educ* Latymer Upper Sch, Pembroke Coll Cambridge (BA, MA), Yale Univ (MA); *m* 16 Dec 1972, Michele Annette Cynthia, da of Michael Stanley Macdonald, of Kingsgate, Kent; 1 s (Anthony b 5 June 1978), 2 da (Helen b 28 Oct 1980, Joanna b 22 July 1985); *Career* Bank of England 1969–: mangr Gilt-Edged Div 1981, mangr Money Market Div 1983, head Foreign Exchange Div 1988–90, head Euro Div 1990–93, head of banking supervision 1993–94, dep dir supervision and surveillance 1994–96, dir of banking supervision 1996–; UK alternate dir to IMF 1985–87; AIB 1973; *Recreations* church singing, chess, youth work; *Style*— Michael Foot, Esq; ✉ Bank of England, Threadneedle St, London EC2R 8AU (☎ 0171 601 4862, fax 0171 601 3629, telex 885001)

FOOT, Rt Hon Michael Mackintosh; PC (1974); 4 s of Rt Hon Isaac Foot, PC (d 1960), MP (Lib) for Bodmin 1922–24 and 1929–35, pres Lib Party Orgn 1947, and his 1 w Eva, *née* Mackintosh (d 1946); bro of Lord Caradon (d 1990) and Lord Foot, *qv*; *b* 23 July 1913; *Educ* Forres Sch, Leighton Park, Wadham Coll Oxford; *m* 21 Oct 1949, Jill, *née* Craigie, former w of Jeffrey Dell; *Career* pres Oxford Union 1933, ed Tribune 1948–52 and 1955–60 (md 1945–74), actg ed Evening Standard 1942, subsequently book critic, column for Daily Herald 1944–64; Parly candidate (Lab) Monmouthshire 1935; MP (Lab): Devonport 1945–55 (Parly candidate 1959), Ebbw Vale 1960–83, Blaenau Gwent 1983–92; oppn spokesman on Power and Steel Industries 1970–71, shadow ldr of House 1971–72, spokesman EEC Affairs 1972–74, sec of state Employment 1974–76, Lord Pres of the Cncl and leader House of Commons 1976–79, succeeded Rt Hon James Callaghan as ldr of Oppn 1980–Oct 1983; Freeman: City of Plymouth 1982, Borough of Blaenau Gwent 1983; hon fellow Wadham Coll Oxford; Hon LLD: Univ of Exeter 1990, Univ of Nottingham 1990; *Books* Guilty Men (with Frank Owen and Peter Howard, 1940), Armistice 1918–39 (1940), Trial of Mussolini (1943), Brendan and Beverley (1944), Still at Large (1950), Full Speed Ahead (1950), Guilty Men (with Mervyn Jones, 1957), The Pen and the Sword (1957), Parliament in Danger (1959), Aneurin Bevan Vol I 1897–1945 (1962), Vol II 1945–60 (1973), Debts of Honour (1980), Another Heart and Other Pulses (1984), Politics of Paradise (1988), The History of Mr Wells (1995); *Style*— The Rt Hon Michael Foot

FOOT, Michael Richard Daniell; s of Richard Cunningham Foot (d 1969), of Clareville Beach, NSW, and Nina, *née* Raymond (d 1970); *b* 14 Dec 1919; *Educ* Winchester, New Coll Oxford (MA, BLitt); *m* 1, Philippa Ruth, da of William Sydney Bence Bosanquet, DSO; m 2, Elizabeth Mary Irvine, da of Thomas Irvine King; 1 s (Richard Jeffery b 1963), 1 da (Sarah Rosamund Irvine (Mrs G M K Schrecker) b 1961); m 3, Mirjam Michaela, da of Prof Carl Paul Maria Romme; *Career* WWII RA rose to rank of Maj (despatches twice); taught at Univ of Oxford 1947–59, prof of modern history Univ of Manchester 1967–73, dep warden European Discussion Centre 1973–75; historian; Croix de Guerre 1945, offr Order of Orange-Nassau 1990; memb: Royal Hist Soc 1958, Soc of Authors 1960; *Publications* Gladstone and Liberalism (with J L Hammond, 1952), British Foreign Policy since 1898 (1956), Men in Uniform (1961), SOE in France (1966), The Gladstone Diaries (volumes I and II, ed, 1968, volumes III and IV, ed with H C G Matthew, 1974), War and Society (ed, 1973), Resistance (1976), Six Faces of Courage (1978), MI9 Escape and Evasion 1939–45 (with J M Langley, 1979), SOE: An Outline History (1984, 3 edn 1995), Holland at War against Hitler (1990), Art and War (1990), Oxford Companion to the Second World War (ed with I C B Dear, 1995); *Recreations* reading; *Clubs* Savile, Special Forces; *Style*— M R D Foot, Esq; ✉ Martins Cottage, Bell Lane, Nuthampstead, Herts SG8 8ND; agent: Michael Sissons, Messrs Peters, Fraser & Dunlop, 503/4 The Chambers, Chelsea Harbour, Lots Rd, London SW10 0XF (☎ 0171 344 1000, fax 0171 352 7356)

FOOT, (Hon) Paul Mackintosh; eldest s of Baron Caradon, GCMG, KCVO, OBE, PC (Life Peer, d 1990), and Florence Sylvia, *née* Tod (d 1985); *b* 8 Nov 1937; *Educ* Univ Coll Oxford; *m* 1, 23 June 1962 (m dis 1970), Monica, da of Dr Robert P Beckinsale; 2 s (John Mackintosh b 1964, Matthew Isaac b 1966); m 2, 27 July 1971 (m dis 1995), Roseanne, da of Robert Harvey; 1 s (Tom b 1979); *Career* journalist; reporter Socialist Worker 1972–78; columnist: The Daily Mirror 1979–93 (constructively dismissed), Private Eye 1993–; Journalist of the Year (Granada What the Papers Say Awards) 1972 and 1989, Campaigning Journalist of the Year (Br Press Awards) 1980, Orwell Prize for Journalism (jtly) 1994; *Books* Immigration and Race in British Politics (1965), The Politics of Harold Wilson (1968), The Rise of Enoch Powell (1969), Who Killed Hanratty? (1971), Why You Should Be a Socialist (1977), Red Shelley (1981), The Helen Smith Story (1983), Murder at the Farm: Who Killed Carl Bridgewater? (1986), Who Framed Colin Wallace? (1989); *Style*— Paul Foot

FOOT, Dr Rosemary June; da of Leslie William Foot, MBE (d 1993), and Margaret Lily Frances, *née* Fidler (d 1986); *b* 4 June 1948; *m* 27 Aug 1996, Timothy Kennedy; *Career* lectr in int relations Univ of Sussex 1978–90, John Swire sr research fell in the int relations of East Asia St Antony's Coll Oxford 1990–; Fulbright/American Cncl of Learned Societies scholar Columbia Univ New York 1981–82; FBA 1996; *Books* The Wrong War: American Policy and the Dimensions of the Korean Conflict 1950–53 (1985), A Substitute for Victory: The Politics of Peace Making at the Korean Armistice Talks (1990), Migration: The Asian Experience (ed with Prof Judith M Brown, *qv*, 1994), The Practice of Power: US Relations with China since 1949 (1995), Hong Kong's Transitions, 1842–1997 (ed with Prof Judith M Brown, *qv*, 1997); *Recreations* walking, music, sailing; *Style*— Dr Rosemary Foot, FBA; ✉ St Antony's College, Oxford OX2 6JF (☎ 01865 284754, fax 01865 274559, e-mail rosemary.foot@sant.ox.ac.uk)

FOOTMAN, John William; s of Harold Footman (d 1982), and Mary, *née* Jones; *b* 23 Aug 1937; *Educ* Kings Norton GS; *m* 26 Nov 1960, Maureen Dorothy, da of William Ernest Band, of Worcs; 1 s (Stephen b 1969), 2 da (Debra b 1962, Sharon b 1965); *Career* Nat Serv RAF 1956–58; joined NU Way 1954; Plumb Center (formerly OBC Ltd): buyer 1958, purchasing dir 1968, md 1979; currently chief exec UK building distribution Wolseley plc (parent co of Plumb Center); *Recreations* golf, gardening; *Clubs* Knaresborough Golf; *Style*— John Footman, Esq; ✉ Holber Hill, Burton Leonard, Harrogate, North Yorkshire HG3 3SQ (☎ 01765 677075); Wolseley Centers Ltd, PO Box 21, Boroughbridge Rd, Ripon, North Yorks HG4 1SL (☎ 01765 690690, fax 01765 690100)

FOOTTIT, Ven Anthony Charles; s of Percival Frederick Foottit (d 1961), and Mildred, *née* Norris (d 1977); *b* 28 June 1935; *Educ* Lancing, King's Coll Cambridge (MA); *m* 10 Dec 1977, Rosamond Mary Alyson, da of Robert James Buxton (d 1968); 1 s (James b 1978), 2 da (Caroline b 1980, Georgina b 1983); *Career* asst curate Wymondham Abbey 1961, team vicar Blakeney Gp 1964, team rector Camelot Parishes 1971, rural dean Cary 1979, St Hugh's missioner Lincolnshire 1981, archdeacon of Lynn 1987–; *Recreations* gardening, botany, conservation; *Style*— The Ven the Archdeacon of Lynn; ✉ Ivy House, Whitwell Street, Reepham, Norwich NR10 4RA (☎ 01603 870340)

FOPP, Dr Michael Anton; s of Sqdn-Ldr Desmond Fopp, AFC, AE, and Edna Meryl, *née* Dodd; *b* 28 Oct 1947; *Educ* Reading Blue Coat Sch, City Univ (MA, PhD); *m* 5 Oct 1968, Rosemary Ann, da of V G Hodgetts, of Ashford, Kent; 1 s (Christopher Michael b 5 April 1973); *Career* keeper Battle of Britain Museum 1982–85 (dep keeper 1979–81), co sec Hendon Museums Trading Co Ltd 1981–85, visiting lectr City Univ 1984–93; dir: London Tport Museum 1985–87, RAF Museum 1988–; chm London Tport Flying Club Ltd; vice pres Friends of RAF Museum, London Underground Railway Soc; Freeman: City of London 1980, Guild of Air Pilots and Navigators 1987; FIMgt 1990 (MIMgt 1980), FMA 1990; *Books* The Battle of Britain Museum (1981), The Bomber Command Museum (1982), Washington File (1983), The Royal Air Force Museum (1984), RAF Museum Children's Activity Book (ed, 1985), The RAF Museum (1992), High Flyers (ed, 1993), Managing the Museum (1997); *Recreations* flying and building light aircraft, Chinese cookery, writing; *Clubs* RAF; *Style*— Dr Michael A Fopp; ✉ Royal Air Force Museum, Hendon, London NW9 5LL (☎ 0181 205 2266)

FORBES, *see:* Stuart-Forbes

FORBES, The Hon Sir Alastair Granville; kt (1960); s of Granville Forbes (d 1943), and Constance Margaret, *née* Davis; *b* 3 Jan 1908; *Educ* Blundell's, Clare Coll Cambridge; *m* 11 Jan 1936, Constance Irene Mary (d 1995), da of late Capt Charles Everard Hughes White, DSO, DSC, RN; 2 da (Anne Margaret b 1936, Elizabeth Mary b 1938); *Career* called to the Bar Gray's Inn 1932; HM Colonial Serv 1936, HM Overseas Judiciary 1956, puisne judge Kenya 1956, justice of appeal Ct of Appeal for Eastern Africa 1957 (vice pres of the Ct 1958), federal justice Federal Supreme Ct of Rhodesia and Nyasaland 1963; pres Cts of Appeal: Seychelles 1965–76, St Helena, Falkland Is, Br Antarctic Territories 1965–88, Gibraltar 1970–83 and Br Indian Ocean Territory 1986–88; pres Pensions Appeal Tbnl for England and Wales 1973–80; *Recreations* gardening, fishing; *Clubs* Royal Cwlth Soc; *Style*— The Hon Sir Alastair Forbes; ✉ Badgers Holt, Church Lane, Sturminster Newton, Dorset DT10 1DH

FORBES, (John) Alistair Ponsonby; s of Col Courtenay Fergus Ochoncar Grey Forbes (late Coldstream Gds, d 1971), and Dorothea, *née* Staveley-Hill, of Langport, Somerset; *b* 22 April 1937; *Educ* St Peter's Seaford, Eton, Millfield Sch Somerset; *m* 1965, Mary Dorothea, da of Sir William Macnamara Goodenough, 1 Bt (former chm Barclays Bank, d 1951); 1 s (James William Courtenay b 1970), 1 da (Sophie Louisa Dorothea b 1968); *Career* Offr Coldstream Gds, ret 1966; md Wilson & Co 1984–86 (mktg dir 1970–84), dir Hogg Robinson 1984–86, DG British United Industries 1986–92, dep dir Aims of Industry 1989–92, chm Design Bridge Ltd 1986–; Liveryman Worshipful Co of Broderers; *Recreations* shooting, fishing, gardening, politics; *Clubs* Boodle's, Pratt's, IOD; *Style*— Alastair Forbes, Esq; ✉ Design Bridge Ltd, 18 Clerkenwell Close, London EC1R 0AA (☎ 0171 814 9922, fax 0171 814 9024)

FORBES, Anthony David Arnold William; s of Lt-Col David Walter Arthur William Forbes, MC, Coldstream Guards (ka 1943), and Diana Mary, *née* Henderson (who m 2, 6 Marquess of Exeter; he d 1981, she d 1982); *b* 15 Jan 1938; *Educ* Eton; *m* 1, 14 June 1962 (m dis 1973), Virginia June, yr da of Sir Leonard Ropner, 1 Bt, MC, TD (d 1977); 1 s (Jonathan David b 1964), 1 da (Susanna Jane b 1966); m 2, 1973, Belinda Mary, da of Sir Hardman Earle, 5 Bt (d 1979); *Career* Lt Coldstream Gds 1956–59; memb Stock Exchange 1965, jt sr ptnr Cazenove & Co stockbrokers 1980–94; non-exec dir: Carlton Communications plc 1994–, Royal Insurance Holdings plc 1994–, Merchants Trust plc, Phoenix Group, Watmoughs (Holdings) PLC; chm: Hosp and Homes of St Giles, Royal Choral Soc; tstee Botanic Gardens Conservation International; Hon DBA De Montfort Univ 1994; FRSA; *Recreations* music, shooting, gardening; *Style*— Anthony Forbes, Esq; ✉ Wakerley Manor, nr Oakham, Leics LE15 8PA (☎ 01572 747549)

FORBES, Bryan; *b* 22 July 1926; *Educ* West Ham Secdy Sch, RADA; *m* 1955, Nanette Newman, *qv*; 2 da (Emma Forbes, *qv*, Sarah, m John Standing, *qv*); *Career* writer, director and producer; actor 1942–60; formed Beaver Films with Richard (now Lord) Attenborough 1959; md and head of prodn ABPC Studios 1969–71, md and chief exec EMI-MGM Elstree Studios 1970–71, dir Capital Radio Ltd 1973–96; memb: Gen Advsy Cncl BBC 1966–69, BBC Schs Cncl 1971–73; pres: Beatrix Potter Soc 1982–94, Nat Youth Theatre 1984–, Writers Guild of GB 1988–91; Hon DLit London 1987; *Theatre* theatre dir incl: Macbeth (Old Vic) 1980, Star Quality (Theatre Royal Bath) 1984, Killing Jessica (Savoy) 1986, The Living Room 1987 (Royalty Theatre); *Television* dir/prodr incl: Edith Evans I Caught Acting Like the Measles (Yorkshire TV) 1973, Elton John Goodbye Norma Jean and other Things (ATV) 1973, Jessie (BBC) 1980, The Endless Game 1988; acted in: December Flower (Granada) 1984, First Among Equals (Granada) 1986; *Films* writer, dir and prodr of numerous films incl: The Angry Silence, The League of Gentlemen, Only Two Can Play, Whistle down the Wind 1961, The L Shaped Room 1962, Seance on a Wet Afternoon 1963, King Rat 1964, The Wrong Box 1965, The Whisperers 1966, Deadfall 1967, The Madwoman of Chaillot 1968, The Raging Moon 1970, The Stepford Wives 1974, The Slipper and the Rose 1975, International Velvet 1978, The Sunday Lovers 1980, Better Late than Never 1981, The Naked Face 1983; *Awards* winner of: Br Academy Award 1960, writers Guild Award (twice), numerous int awards; *Books* Truth Lies Sleeping (1950), The Distant Laughter (1972), Notes for a Life (autobiography, 1974), The Slipper and the Rose (1976), Ned's Girl (biography of Dame Edith Evans, 1977), International Velvet (1978), Familiar Strangers (1979), That Despicable Race (1980), The Rewrite Man (1983), The Endless Game (1986), A Song At Twilight (1989), A Divided Life (autobiography, 1992), The Twisted Playground (1993), Partly Cloudy (1995), Quicksand (1996); *Recreations* running a bookshop, reading, photography, landscape gardening; *Style*— Bryan Forbes, Esq; ✉ Bryan Forbes Ltd (fax 01344 845174)

FORBES, Prof Charles Douglas; s of John Forbes (d 1985), and Annie Robertson, *née* Stuart (d 1982); *b* 9 Oct 1938; *Educ* HS of Glasgow, Univ of Glasgow (MB ChB, MD, DSc); *m* 6 March 1965, Janette MacDonald, da of Ewan Robertson (d 1980); 2 s (John

Stuart b 20 Dec 1967, Donald Alexander Ewan b 20 Sept 1971); *Career* lectr med Univ of E Africa Nairobi 1965–66, Fulbright fell American Heart Assoc 1968–70, sr lectr then reader in med Univ of Glasgow 1972–86 (lectr in therapeutics 1962–65), prof of med Univ of Dundee 1986–; author of specialist books on blood coagulation and thrombosis; FRCPG 1974, FRCPE 1976, FRCP 1978, FRSA 1990, FRSE 1992; *Recreations* gardening, walking; *Style*— Prof Charles Forbes, FRSE; ✉ East Chattan, 108 Hepburn Gdns, St Andrews, Fife KY16 9LT (☎ 01334 472428); Department of Medicine, Ninewells Hospital and Medical School, Dundee DD1 9SY (☎ 01382 660111, fax 01382 660675)

FORBES, Colin Ames; s of John Cumming Forbes, and Kathleen Ethel Ames Forbes; *b* 6 March 1928; *Educ* Central Sch of Art and Crafts London (BA); *m* 1 (m dis), Elizabeth Hopkins; 1 da (Christine Coppe); m 2, Wendy Maria Schneider; 1 s (Aaron Forbes), 1 da (Jessica Forbes Russo); *Career* graphic design asst Herbert Spencer Studio London 1952–53, freelance graphic designer/lectr Central Sch London 1953–57, art dir Stuart Advertising London 1957–58, head Graphic Design Dept Central Sch 1958–60, freelance graphic designer 1960–62; ptnr: Fletcher Forbes Gill 1962–65, Crosby Fletcher Forbes 1965–72, Pentagram Design Ltd 1972–78, Pentagram Design Inc NY 1978–93; consulting ptnr Pentagram Design AG 1993–; chm Stanford Design Forum Stanford Calif 1988, sr critic (graphic design) Yale Sch of Art New Haven Connecticut 1989; memb: American Inst of Graphic Arts (pres 1983–84), Alliance Graphique Internationale (pres 1976–79); hon memb American Center for Design 1993; RDI 1974; *Major Design Projects* British Petroleum corp identity 1968–71, Lucas Industries corp identity 1972–79, Kodak International forms 1974, Drexel Burnham Lambert corp pubns 1979–89, ITM logo 1981, American Standard corp identity 1982, Columbia-Presbyterian Medical Center identity 1982, Nissan Motor Co logo 1982, Met Transit Authy subway station design 1982–85, Hilton International Hotels literature 1982–86, IBM corp pubns 1985 and 1990–91, 'Toray' identity 1986, Neiman Marcus identity study 1987–88, Hallmark Cards design consultancy 1989–90, Kubota Corporation identity 1989, Airco Gases retail design consultancy 1989–90, Hotel Hankyu International identity 1990; *Awards* Silver Award 4th Biennale Int Art Book Prize 1975, Pres's Award D&AD 1977, AIGA Medal American Inst of Graphic Arts 1992; *Books* Graphic Design: Visual Comparisons (jtly, 1963), A Sign Systems Manual (jtly, 1970), New Alphabets A-Z (jtly, 1973), Living by Design (jtly, 1978), Pentagram: The Compendium (jtly, 1993); *Recreations* horseback riding; *Style*— Colin Forbes; ✉ 403a Route 2, Westfield, NC 27053, USA (☎ 00 1 910 351 3941, fax 00 1 910 351 3949)

FORBES, Derek Francis Kemball; s of Flt Lt Francis William Forbes (d 1972), of E Finchley, and Vera Maud Rosalind Forbes (d 1994); *b* 2 Feb 1943; *Educ* City of London Sch, Law Soc Sch of Law; *m* 1 Aug 1972, Carol Ann, da of Colin Robert Knight (d 1985), of Highgate, London; *Career* sr assoc Abbey Life 1971–79 (advertising mangr 1968–71), sr branch mangr Crown Life 1979–84, asst head of sales Sun Alliance 1984–88, agency mangr Sun Life 1988–91; proprietor Forbes Marketing and Forbes Management; writer, lectr and management conslt; Life Insur Assoc: chm Nat Ctee of Mangrs Forum 1984–87, hon sec 1985, treas 1986; dir Guild of Licensed Estate Planning Lawyers 1995; memb: Sales Qualifications Bd for NVQs, Nat Cncl Soc of Will-Writers (hon memb Soc of Will-Writers 1994, hon chllr 1996); Hon Freeman City of London 1964, Liveryman Worshipful Co of Gold and Silver Wyre Drawers; memb Million Dollar Round Table 1976; FLIA 1971, CInstSMM 1990 (sr sales mgmnt trainer); *Books* The Save and Prosper Book of Money (jtly, 1968), The Secrets of Success in Selling (1991); *Style*— Derek Forbes, Esq; ✉ 22 Cherry Tree Rd, East Finchley, London N2 9QL (☎ 0181 883 2985)

FORBES, Emma; da of Bryan Forbes, *qv*, and Nanette Newman, *qv*; *b* 14 May 1965; *Educ* Hurst Lodge Sunningdale, Urdang Acad of Ballet and Performing Arts; *m* 5 Sept 1987, Graham Clempson; *Career* television presenter; press officer Next 1985–87, freelance stylist and journalist 1987–90; tv credits incl: Going Live (cookery slot, BBC) 1990–93, Live and Kicking (BBC) 1993–1996, Talking Telephone Numbers (Carlton) 1993–96, Speakeasy (LWT) 1993–95, What's My Line (Meridian) 1993–96; *Publications* Entertaining (1988), Emma Forbes Going Live Cook Book (1992), Emma Entertains (1994), Take 3 Cooks (1996); *Style*— Ms Emma Forbes; ✉ c/o James Grant Media Group Ltd, Syon Lodge, London Road, Syon Park, Middlesex TW7 5BH (☎ 0181 232 4100, fax 0181 232 4101, e-mail jgrant.ftec.co.uk)

FORBES, Very Rev Graham John Thomson; s of John Thomson Forbes (d 1986), of Edinburgh, and Doris, *née* Smith; *b* 10 June 1951; *Educ* George Heriots Sch Edinburgh, Univ of Aberdeen (MA), Univ of Edinburgh (BD), Edinburgh Theol Coll; *m* 25 Aug 1973, Jane, da of John Tennant Miller, of Edinburgh; 3 s (Duncan, Andrew, Hamish); *Career* curate Old St Paul's Edinburgh 1976–82; provost: St Ninian's Cathedral Perth 1982–90, St Mary's Cathedral Edinburgh 1990–; non-exec dir Radio Tay 1986–90; fndr Canongate Youth Project Edinburgh, pres Lothian Assoc of Youth Clubs 1986–, HM (lay) Inspr of Constabulary for Scotland 1995–; memb: Scottish Community Educn Cncl 1981–87, Children's Panel Advsy Ctee Tayside 1986–90, Parole Bd 1990–95, Scottish Consumer Cncl 1995–, Gen Med Cncl 1996–; *Recreations* discovering dry rot, fly-fishing, running, visiting Russia; *Style*— The Very Rev the Provost of St Mary's Cathedral Edinburgh; ✉ 8 Lansdowne Crescent, Edinburgh EH12 5EQ (☎ 0131 225 2978); St Mary's Cathedral, Palmerston Place, Edinburgh EH12 5AW (☎ 0131 225 6293, fax 0131 225 3181)

FORBES, Maj Sir Hamish Stewart; 7 Bt (UK 1823), of Newe and Edinglassie, Aberdeenshire, MBE (Mil 1945), MC; s of Lt-Col James Stewart Forbes (d 1957, gs of 3 Bt), and Féridah Frances, da of Hugh Lewis Taylor; suc cousin, Col Sir John Stewart Forbes, 6 Bt, DSO, JP, DL (d 1984); *b* 15 Feb 1916; *Educ* Eton, Lawrenceville USA (Abbott scholarship), SOAS London; *m* 1, 2 June 1945 (m dis 1981), Jacynthe Elizabeth Mary, o da of late Eric Gordon Underwood; 1 s (James Thomas Stewart b 1957), 3 da (Caroline Serena (Mrs Nicholas Herbert) b 1947, Jane Henrietta Mary (Mrs T R B Leslie-King) b 1950, Christian Clare (Mrs B V S Scrimgeour) b 1961); m 2, 1981, Mary Christine, MBE, da of late Ernest William Rigby; *Heir* s, James Thomas Stewart Forbes, *qv*, b 28 May 1957; *Career* Maj (ret) WG, served WWII (POW) France, Germany, Turkey; KJStJ 1983; patron Lonach Highland and Friendly Society 1984–; hon dir: Br Humane Assoc 1988–, Chapter-General OStJ 1990–96, Inc Soc The Church Lads' and Girls' Bde 1978–92; life pres CLB and CGB Assoc; *Recreations* shooting, sculpture; *Clubs* Turf, Chelsea Arts, Pilgrims, Royal Asian Soc; *Style*— Maj Sir Hamish Forbes, Bt, MBE, MC; ✉ Newe, Strathdon, Aberdeenshire AB36 8TY (☎ 019756 51431)

FORBES, James; s of Maj Donald Forbes (d 1963), of Edinburgh, and Rona Ritchie, *née* Yeats (d 1963); *b* 2 Jan 1923; *Educ* Christ's Hosp, Offrs Trg Sch Bangalore S India; *m* 14 Aug 1948, Alison Mary Fletcher, da of Maj George K Moffat (d 1979), of Dunblane, Perthshire; 2 s (Lindsay b 11 Oct 1953, Moray b 29 June 1962); *Career* WWII cmmnd 15 Punjab Regt 1942, qualified as Inspecting Ordnance Offr 1943, CO (Capt) Mobile Ammunition Inspection Unit 1943–44, Maj DADOS Amm GHQ (1) 1945–46, released as Hon Maj 1947; Peat Marwick Mitchell 1952–58; Schweppes plc 1958–69: ops res mangr 1960–63, gp chief accountant and dir of subsid cos 1963–69; gp fin dir Cadbury Schweppes 1970–78 (fin advsr on formation 1969–70); non-exec dir: British Transport Hotels 1978–83, British Rail Investments 1980–84, Steetley plc 1984–89, Compass Hotels Ltd 1984–, Lautro Ltd 1986–90; vice chm Tate & Lyle 1980–84 (sr exec dir 1978–80, chm Pension Fund 1978–85); Forestry cmmr 1982–88, treas and chm Cncl of Almoners Christs Hosp 1987–96 (chm Resources Ctee 1985–87); memb Highland Soc of London; Worshipful Co of CAs in England and Wales; FCA 1966 (memb Cncl 1971–88, treas 1984–86); *Recreations* golf; *Clubs* Caledonian, Chiddingfold Golf; *Style*— James Forbes, Esq; ✉ Lower Ridge, Courts Mount Rd, Haslemere, Surrey GU27 2PP (☎ 01428 652461)

FORBES, James Thomas Stewart; s and h of Sir Hamish Stewart Forbes, 7 Bt, MBE, MC, *qv*; *b* 28 May 1957; *Educ* Eton, Univ of Bristol (BA); *m* 1986, Kerry Lynne, o da of Rev Lee Toms, of Sacramento, Calif, USA; 2 da (Theodora Christine b 23 Jan 1989, Katherine Elizabeth b 16 Nov 1990); *Career* Forbes Mount Veeder Vineyards Napa Valley Calif; creator TV show This Is Your Fridge (shown Germany, Sweden, Denmark and The Netherlands); *Clubs* Pratt's, Lonach Highland and Friendly Soc (hon vice pres); *Style*— James Forbes, Esq; ✉ 3550 Mount Seeder Road, Napa, California 94558, USA (☎ 00 1 707 259 1767); The Cottage, Hambleden, nr Henley-on-Thames, Oxon RG9 6RT (☎ 01491 575914)

FORBES, Vice Adm Sir John Morrison; KCB (1978); s of Lt-Col Robert Hogg Forbes, OBE (d 1976), and Gladys M, *née* Pollock; *b* 16 Aug 1925; *Educ* RNC Dartmouth; *m* 1950, Joyce Newenham, da of late Addison Perrit Hadden, of Ireland; 2 s, 2 da; *Career* 2 i/c and Operational Cdr Royal Malaysian Navy 1966–68, directorate of Naval Plans 1969–71, Capt HMS Triumph 1971–72, Capt RNC Dartmouth 1972–74, naval sec 1974–76, Vice Adm 1977, flag offr Plymouth 1977–79, Cdr Central Sub Area Eastern Atlantic and Cdr Plymouth Sub Area Channel 1977–79; chm Civil Serv Cmmrs Interview Panel 1980–93; Naval ADC to HM The Queen 1974; awarded Kesatria Manku Negara 1968; *Recreations* country pursuits; *Clubs* Army & Navy, RNSA; *Style*— Vice Adm Sir John Forbes, KCB; ✉ c/o National Westminster Bank, 93 London Rd, Waterlooville, Portsmouth, Hants PO7 7EG

FORBES, Master of; Hon Malcolm Nigel Forbes; DL (Aberdeenshire 1996); s and h of 23 Lord Forbes, KBE, *qv*; *b* 6 May 1946; *Educ* Eton, Univ of Aberdeen; *m* 1, 30 Jan 1969 (m dis 1982), Carole Jennifer Andrée, da of Norman Stanley Whitehead (d 1981), of Aberdeen; 1 s (Neil Malcolm Ross b 10 March 1970), 1 da (Joanne Carole b 23 April 1972); m 2, 15 Feb 1988, Mrs Jennifer Mary Gribbon, da of Ian Peter Whittington (d 1991), of Tunbridge Wells, Kent; *Heir* s, Neil Malcolm Ross Forbes b 1970; *Career* dir Instock Disposables Ltd, dir Castle Forbes Collection Ltd; farmer and landowner; sec Donside Ball; *Recreations* skiing, cricket, croquet; *Clubs* Royal Northern & Univ (Aberdeen), Eton Ramblers, XL Club; *Style*— The Master of Forbes, DL; ✉ Castle Forbes, Alford, Aberdeenshire AB33 8BL (☎ 019755 62524, fax 019755 62898)

FORBES, 22 Lord (Premier S Lordship before July 1445); Sir Nigel Ivan Forbes; KBE (1960), JP (Aberdeenshire 1955), DL (1958); s of 21 Lord Forbes (d 1953), and Lady Mabel Anson (d 1972), da of 3 Earl of Lichfield; *b* 19 Feb 1918; *Educ* Harrow, RMC Sandhurst; *m* 23 May 1942, Hon Rosemary Katharine Hamilton-Russell, da of 9 Viscount Boyne; 2 s, 1 da; *Heir* s, Master of Forbes, *qv*; *Career* served WWII, France and Belgium (wounded), N Africa, Sicily, NW Europe Adjt Grenadier Gds, Staff Coll 1945–46, mil asst high cmmr Palestine 1947–48, Maj Grenadier Gds; representative peer for Scotland 1955–63; pres Royal Highland and Agric Soc for Scot 1958–59; memb Inter-Parly Union Delgn to: Denmark 1956, Hungary 1965, Ethiopia 1971; memb Cwlth Parly Assoc Delgn to: Canada 1961, Pakistan 1962; min of state Scottish Office 1958–59; chm Rolawn Ltd 1975–; chm Don Dist River Bd 1961–73; bd memb: Scottish Nature Conservancy 1961–67, Aberdeen Milk Mktg Bd 1962–72; memb Sports Cncl for Scot 1966–71; dep chm Tennant Caledonian Breweries Ltd 1964–74; dir: Blenheim Travel Ltd 1981–88, Grampian TV 1960–88; pres Scottish Scouts Assoc 1970–88, chm Scottish Branch Nat Playing Fields Assoc 1965–80; *Recreations* wildlife, conservation, photography, travel; *Clubs* Army and Navy; *Style*— The Rt Hon the Lord Forbes, KBE, JP, DL; ✉ Balforbes, Alford, Aberdeenshire AB33 8DR (☎ 019755 62516, office 019755 62574, fax 019755 62898)

FORBES, Prof Sebastian; s of Dr Watson Forbes, and Mary Henderson, *née* Hunt; *b* 22 May 1941; *Educ* Univ Coll Sch Hampstead, RAM, Univ of Cambridge (MA, MusD); *m* 1, 1968 (m dis 1977); 2 da (Joanna b 1971, Emily b 1974); m 2, 24 Sept 1983, Tessa Mary, da of John Brady (d 1967); 1 s (Alistair b 1984), 1 da (Nicola b 1986); *Career* prodr BBC (sound) 1964–67; lectr Univ Coll of N Wales Bangor 1968–72; Univ of Surrey: lectr 1972–, prof of music 1981–; conductor Horniman Singers 1981–90; compositions incl: String Quartet no 1 (Radcliffe award 1969), Essay for Clarinet and Orchestra (1970), Death's Dominion (1971), Symphony in Two Movements (1972), Sinfonias 1 (1967, rev 1989), 2 (1978) and 3 (1990), Sonata for 21 (1975), Voices of Autumn, 8 Japanese Tanka for choir and piano (1975), Sonata for 8 (1978), Violin Fantasy no 2 (1979), Evening Canticles (Aedis Christi 1 (1980), Aedis Christi 2 (1984)), String Quartet no 3 (1981), Sonata for 17 (1987), Bristol Mass (1990), Hymn to St Etheldreda (1995); memb: Performing Rights Soc, Composers Guild of GB; LRAM, ARCM, ARCO, ARAM; *Style*— Prof Sebastian Forbes; ✉ Octave House, Boughton Hall Avenue, Send, Woking, Surrey GU23 7DF; Department of Music, University of Surrey, Guildford, Surrey GU2 5XH (☎ 01483 259317)

FORBES ADAM, Sir Christopher Eric; 3 Bt (UK 1917), of Hankelow Court, Co Chester; s of Eric Forbes Adam, CMG (2 s of Sir Frank Forbes Adam, 1 Bt, CB, CIE, JP, DL), by his w Agatha, widow of Sidney Spooner and eldest da of Reginald Walter Macan, sometime Master Univ Coll, Oxford; suc unc, Gen Sir Ronald Forbes Adam, 2 Bt, GCB, DSO, OBE, 1982; *b* 12 Feb 1920; *Educ* Abinger Hill Sch Surrey, privately; *m* 17 Sept 1957, Patricia Anne Wreford, yr da of John Neville Wreford Brown, of Maltings, Abberton, Colchester, Essex; 1 adopted da (Sarah Anne (Mrs Allen) b 1960); *Heir* 1 cous, Rev (Stephen) Timothy Beilby Forbes Adam, *qv*; *Career* sometime journalist with Yorkshire Post; *Style*— Sir Christopher Forbes Adam, Bt; ✉ 46 Rawlings St, London SW3 2LS

FORBES ADAM, Rev (Stephen) Timothy Beilby; er s of Colin Gurdon Forbes Adam, CSI, JP, DL (d 1982, 3 s of Sir Frank Forbes Adam, 1 Bt, CB, CIE, JP, DL), by his w Hon Mrs (Irene Constance) Forbes Adam (d 1976); hp to 1 cous, Sir Christopher Forbes Adam, 3 Bt, *qv*; *b* 19 Nov 1923; *Educ* Eton, Balliol Coll Oxford, RADA, Chichester Theol Coll; *m* 28 Sept 1954, Penelope, da of George Campbell Munday, MC, of Leverington Hall, Wisbech, Cambs; 4 da; *Career* served Rifle Bde 1942–47 in France and Far East; ordained 1962, rector of Barton-in-Fabis with Thrumpton, Southwell, Notts 1964–70, priest-in-charge: Southstoke 1974–84, Bath & Wells 1984–; non-stipendiary priest Tadmarton UB Dio of Oxford; *Style*— Rev Timothy Forbes Adam; ✉ Woodhouse Farm, Escrick, N Yorks YO4 6HT (☎ 01904 728827)

FORBES-LEITH, George Ian David; s and h of Sir Andrew George Forbes-Leith of Fyvie, 3 Bt; *b* 26 May 1967; *m* 3 June 1995, Camilla Frances, eldest da of Philip Ely, of Crawley, Hants; *Clubs* Royal and Northern University (Aberdeen); *Style*— George Forbes-Leith Esq; ✉ Estate Office, Fyvie, Turriff, Aberdeenshire AB53 8JS (☎ 0165 1 891 246)

FORBES-LEITH OF FYVIE, Sir Andrew George; 3 Bt (UK 1923), of Jessfield, Co Midlothian; s of Sir (Robert) Ian Algernon Forbes-Leith of Fyvie, 2 Bt, KT, MBE (d 1973), and Ruth Avis, *née* Barnett (d 1973); *b* 20 Oct 1929; *Educ* Eton; *m* 1962, Jane Kate (d 1969), o da of late David McCall-McCowan, of Dalwhat, Moniaive, Dumfries; 2 s (George Ian David b 1967, John Charles b 1969), 2 da (Miranda Jane (Mrs Julian N W McHardy) b 1963, Louisa Mary (Mrs Thomas W Leader) b 1965); *Heir* s, George Ian David Forbes-Leith b 26 May 1967; *Style*— Sir Andrew Forbes-Leith of Fyvie, Bt; ✉ Dunachton, Kingussie, Inverness-shire (☎ 0154 04 651226)

FORBES OF CRAIGIEVAR, Sir John Alexander Cumnock; 12 Bt (NS 1630), of Craigievar, Aberdeenshire; JP (Wigtownshire 1978); s of Rear Adm Hon Arthur Lionel Ochoncar Forbes-Sempill (d 1962, yst s of 17 Lord Sempill), and his 3 w, Mary Cutting

Holland, *née* Cumnock (d 1940); suc kinsman, Hon Sir Ewan Forbes of Craigievar, 11 Bt (d 1991); *b* 29 Aug 1927; *Educ* Stowe, Sandhurst; *m* 1, 26 June 1956 (m dis 1963), Penelope Margaret Ann, da of Arthur Gordon Grey-Pennington; m 2, 1966, Jane Carolyn, da of C Gordon Evans, of Portpatrick, Wigtownshire; *Heir* kinsman, Andrew Iain Ochoncar Forbes b 28 Nov 1945; *Career* former Capt Seaforth Highlanders; dir: Garrick Theatre London 1951–64, Ace Equestrian Centre Newton Stewart 1972–94; freelance photojournalist; memb: Scottish Cncl, Br Show Jumping Assoc; *Clubs* Naval and Military; *Style*— Sir John Forbes of Craigievar, Bt, JP; ✉ Benevean, Kendoon, St John's Town of Dalry, Castle Douglas, Kircudbrightshire DG7 3UB (☎ and fax 01644 460626)

FORD, *see:* St Clair-Ford

FORD, Rev Adam; s of Rev John Ford, and Jean Beattie, *née* Winstanley; *b* 15 Sept 1940; *Educ* Minehead GS, King's Coll London (BD, AKC), Univ of Lancaster (MA); *m* 2 Aug 1969 (m dis 1993), Veronica Rosemary Lucia, da of David Cecil Wynter Verey (Capt Royal Fus, d 1984), of Barnsley House, Cirencester, Glos; 2 s (Nathaniel b 1972, Joshua b 1977), 2 da (Imogen b 1970, Natasha b 1973); *Career* asst Ecumenical Inst of World Cncl of Churches Geneva 1964, curate Cirencester Parish Church Glos 1965–69, vicar Hebden Bridge W Yorks 1969–76, chaplain St Paul's Girls' Sch London 1976– (head Lower Sch 1986–92), regular contrib to Prayer for the Day (BBC Radio 4) 1978–, priest in ordinary to HM The Queen Chapel Royal 1984–90; author of several articles in The Times and science jls on the relationship between science and religion; Star Gazers Guide to the Night Sky (audio guide to astronomy, 1982), Whose World? (6 video progs for TV, 1988) FRAS 1960; *Books* Spaceship Earth (1981), Weather Watch (1982), Universe: God, Man and Science (1986), The Cuckoo Plant (1991), Mr Hi Tech (1993); *Recreations* astronomy, dry stone walling, field walking; *Style*— The Rev Adam Ford; ✉ 55 Bolingbroke Rd, Hammersmith, London W14 0AH (☎ 0171 602 5902); St Paul's Girls' School, Brook Green, London W6 (☎ 0171 603 2288)

FORD, Prof Alec George; s of George Thomas Ford (d 1958), of Leicester, and Alice Ann, *née* Agar (d 1954); *b* 22 June 1926; *Educ* Wyggeston Sch Leicester, Wadham Coll Oxford (BA, MA, DPhil); *m* 1, 17 Sept 1952, Peggy (d 1972), da of John Peck (d 1955), of Coventry; 2 s (Mark b 1955, Alan b 1958), 1 da (Sara b 1953); m 2, 28 May 1983, Angela, da of E Needham, of Gerrards Cross; *Career* Sgt RA WWII 1944–47; sr lectr in economics Univ of Leicester 1963–65 (lectr 1953–63), pro vice chllr Univ of Warwick 1977–89 (reader in economics 1965, prof of economics 1970–89, emeritus prof 1989); memb: Royal Econ Soc, Econ Hist Soc; Hon DLitt Univ of Warwick 1990; *Books* The Gold Standard 1880–1914: Britain and Argentina (1962), Planning and Growth in Rich and Poor Countries (ed, 1965), Income Spending and the Price Level (1971); *Recreations* photography, steam railways, church architecture; *Style*— Prof Alec Ford; ✉ 26 Church Hill, Leamington Spa, Warwickshire CV32 5AY (☎ 01926 426596); c/o Department of Economics, University of Warwick, Coventry CV4 7AL (☎ 01203 523523)

FORD, Sir Andrew Russell; 3 Bt (UK 1929), of Westerdunes, Co of East Lothian; s of Sir Henry Russell Ford, 2 Bt, TD, JP (d 1989), and Mary Elizabeth, *née* Wright; *b* 29 June 1943; *Educ* Winchester, New Coll Oxford, Loughborough Coll of Education (DLC), London (BA external), Birmingham (MA external); *m* 8 Aug 1968, Penelope Anne, o da of Harold Edmund Relph (d 1995), of West Kirby, Wirral; 2 s (Toby Russell b 1973, David Andrew b 1984), 1 da (Julia Mary b 1970); *Heir* s, Toby Russell Ford b 11 Jan 1973; *Career* schoolmaster: Blairmore Sch Aberdeenshire 1967–71, St Peter's Sch Cambridge NZ 1971–74; lectr Chippenham Tech Coll 1974–, currently lectr in English; *Style*— Sir Andrew Ford, Bt; ✉ 20 Coniston Road, Chippenham, Wilts SN14 OPX

FORD, (John) Anthony; s of Frank Everatt Ford, of Banstead, Surrey, and Dorothy Mary, *née* Hearn; *b* 28 April 1938; *Educ* Epsom Coll, St Edmunds Hall Oxford; *m* 1, 1963 (m dis), Caroline Rosemary Wharrad; 1 da (Joanna); m 2, 1984, Sandra Edith, *née* Millar; *Career* admitted slr 1964; dir: Arts Services Grants 1974–79, Crafts Cncl 1988– (joined 1979); vice pres for Europe World Crafts Cncl 1987–93; memb: Working Party Calouste Gulbenkian Fndn Craft Initiative 1985–89, Visual Arts Advsy Ctee The British Cncl 1988–, Fabric Ctee Rochester Cathedral 1989–, Court RCA 1989–, Ct of Govrs The London Inst 1993–; FRSA 1989; *Style*— Anthony Ford, Esq; ✉ Crafts Council, 44a Pentonville Road, London N1 9BY (☎ 0171 278 7700, fax 0171 837 6891)

FORD, Sir (Richard) Brinsley; kt (1984), CBE (1978); eld s of Capt Richard Ford (d 1940), and Rosamund Isabel (d 1911), da of Sir John Ramsden, 5 Bt (and gggda of Richard Brinsley Sheridan, the orator and dramatist); ggs of Richard Ford, author of Handbook for Spain; *b* 10 June 1908; *Educ* Eton, Trinity Coll Oxford; *m* 1937, Joan Mary, da of Capt Geoffrey Vyvyan, Royal Welch Fus (ka 1914); 2 s (Francis, Augustine), 1 da (Marianne); *Career* joined TA 1939; served for one year as Troop Sgt Maj RA, cmmnd 1941, and transferred to Intelligence Corps, Maj (1945); Nat Art Collections Fund: memb 1927–, memb Exec Ctee 1960–88, vice chm 1974–75, chm 1975–80; tstee: Nat Gallery 1954–61, Watts Gallery Compton 1955–95 (chm 1974–84); fndr Richard Ford Award (administered by RA) 1976; sec of Soc of Dilettanti 1972–88, jt hon advsr on paintings to the Nat Tst 1980–95, chm Nat Tst Fndn for Art Ctee 1986–90, pres Walpole Soc 1986–; contrib to Burlington Magazine and Apollo, owner Ford Collection of works by Richard Wilson; hon fell Royal Academy 1981, companion NEAC 1983; Hon LLD Univ of Exeter 1990; FSA 1973; Belgian Order of Leopold II (1945), US Bronze Star (1946), Médaille d'Argent de la Reconaissance, Française (1947), Order of Isabel la Catolica of Spain (First Class A 1986); *Publications* The Drawings of Richard Wilson (1951); *Clubs* Brooks's; *Style*— Sir Brinsley Ford, CBE, FSA; ✉ 14 Wyndham Place, Bryanston Square, London W1H 1AQ (☎ 0171 723 0826)

FORD, Colin John; CBE (1993); s of John William Ford, of London, and Hélène Martha, *née* Richardson; *b* 13 May 1934; *Educ* Enfield GS, Univ Coll Oxford (MA); *m* 1, 12 Aug 1961 (m dis 1980), Margaret Elizabeth, da of Ernest Cordwell; 1 s (Richard John b 22 Nov 1970), 1 da (Clare Michaela Elizabeth b 5 Dec 1972); m 2, 7 Sept 1984, Susan Joan Frances Grayson; 1 s (Thomas Grayson b 29 May 1985); *Career* mangr and prodr Kidderminster Playhouse 1958–60, gen mangr Western Theatre Ballet 1960–62, visiting lectr in English and drama California State Univ at Long Beach 1962–64, dep curator Nat Film Archive 1965–72, organiser Thirtieth Anniversary Congress of Int Fedn of Film Archive London 1968, dir Cinema City exhibition 1970, prog dir London Shakespeare Film Festival 1972, keeper of film and photography Nat Portrait Gallery 1972–81, head Nat Museum of Photography, Film and TV 1982–93, dir Nat Museums and Galleries of Wales 1993–; film: Masks and Faces 1966 (BBC TV version Omnibus 1968); Hon MA Univ of Bradford 1989; *Books* An Early Victorian Album (with Roy Strong, 1974, 2 edn 1977), The Cameron Collection (1975), Happy and Glorious: Six Reigns of Royal Photography (ed, 1977), Rediscovering Mrs Cameron (1979), People in Camera (1979), A Hundred Years Ago (with Brian Harrison, 1983), Portraits (Gallery World of Photography, 1983), Oxford Companion to Film (princ contrib), André Kértesz: The Manchester Collection (contrib, 1984), The Story of Popular Photography (ed, 1989), You Press the Button, We do the Rest (with Karl Steinorth, 1989), Lewis Carroll, Photographers (with Karl Steinoven, 1991); *Recreations* travel, music, small boats; *Style*— Colin Ford, Esq, CBE; ✉ National Museum and Gallery, Cathays Park, Cardiff CF1 3NP (☎ 01222 397951)

FORD, Prof David Frank; s of George Ford (d 1960), of Dublin, and Phyllis Mary Elizabeth, *née* Woodman; *b* 23 Jan 1948; *Educ* The High Sch Dublin, Trinity Coll Dublin (fndn scholar, BA Classics, Berkeley gold medal), St John's Coll Cambridge (scholar, MA Theol, Naden research student, PhD), Yale Univ (Henry fell, STM); *m* 1982, Deborah Perrin, da of Rev Prof Daniel Wayne Hardy; 3 da (Rebecca Perrin b 1985, Grace b and d 1988, Rachel Mary b 1989), 1 s (Daniel George b 1991); *Career* research Tübingen Univ 1975; Univ of Birmingham: lectr in theol 1976–90, sr lectr 1990–91; Univ of Cambridge: regius prof of divinity 1991–, fell Selwyn Coll 1991–, fndn memb Trinity Coll 1991–, chm Faculty Bd of Divinity 1993–95, memb Syndicate Cambridge Univ Press 1993–, chm Center for Advanced Religious and Theol Studies 1995–; pres Soc for the Study of Theol 1997–99; memb Centre of Theol Inquiry Princeton Univ 1993–; visiting fell Yale Univ 1982, Donnellan lectr Trinity Coll Dublin 1984; church warden St Luke's Church Bristol St Birmingham 1979–84; memb: Faith and Order Advsy Gp C of E 1988–90, Bishop's Cncl Birmingham Dio 1989–91, Theol Working Gp on C of E Urban Policy 1989, Archbishop of Canterbury's Urban Theol Gp 1991–95, Cncl Ridley Hall Theol Coll 1991–; chm Westcott House Theol Coll 1991–; memb Mgmnt Ctee Newhaven Housing Assoc 1978–84, govr Lea Mason Sch 1984–91, tstee Henry Martyn Tst 1991–; memb American Acad of Religion; *Books* Barth and God's Story: Biblical Narrative and the Theological Method of Karl Barth in the Church Dogmatics (1981), Jubilate: Theology in Praise (with Daniel W Hardy, 1984), Meaning and Truth in 2 Corinthians (with F M Young, 1988), The Modern Theologians (ed, vols I and II, 1989), A Long Rumour of Wisdom: Redescribing Theology (1992); *Recreations* family life, swimming, ball games, gardening, poetry, drama, walking; *Style*— Prof David Ford; ✉ Faculty of Divinity, University of Cambridge, St John's Street, Cambridge CB2 1TW (☎ 01223 332590, fax 01223 332582)

FORD, Sir David Robert; KBE (1988, OBE 1976), LVO (1975); s of William Ewart, and Edna Ford; *b* 22 Feb 1935; *Educ* Tauntons Sch; *m* 1, 1958 (m dis 1987), Elspeth Anne, *née* Muckart; 2 s, 2 da; m 2, 1987, Gillian Petersen, *née* Monsarrat; *Career* Nat Serv 1953–55, reg cmmn RA 1955; regimental duty Malta 1953–58, Lt UK 1958–62, Capt Commando Regt 1962–66; active serv: Borneo 1964, Aden 1966; Staff Coll Quetta 1967, seconded to Govt of Hong Kong 1967, ret from Army as Maj 1972; dir Govt of Hong Kong Information Serv 1974–76 (dep dir 1972–74), dep sec Govt Secretariat Hong Kong 1976, under sec NI Office 1977–79, sec for information Govt of Hong Kong 1979–80, Hong Kong cmmr in London 1980–81, RCDS 1982, sec for housing Govt of Hong Kong 1985 (dir of housing 1983–84), sec for the Civil Serv 1985–86, chief sec Hong Kong 1986–93, Hong Kong cmmr London 1994–; *Recreations* tennis, fishing, photography, theatre; *Style*— Sir David Ford, KBE, LVO; ✉ Hong Kong Government Office, 6 Grafton Street, London W1

FORD, Sir Edward William Spencer; KCB (1967, CB 1952), KCVO (1957, MVO 1949), ERD (1987), DL; 4 s (twin) of Very Rev Lionel George Bridges Justice Ford, Dean of York (d 1932), and Mary Catherine, *née* Talbot; *b* 24 July 1910; *Educ* Eton, New Coll Oxford; *m* 1 Dec 1949, Hon Virginia (d 1995), da of 1 and last Baron Brand; 2 s; *Career* WWII Lt-Col Grenadier Gds; called to the Bar 1937, in practice 1937–39; asst private sec to HM King George VI 1946–52 and to HM The Queen 1952–67 (extra equerry 1955–); dir: Eydon Hall Estates Ltd 1963–83, London Life Assoc Ltd 1970–83; sec Pilgrim Tst 1967–75, sec and registrar Order of Merit 1975–; pres St Christopher's Hospice Sydenham 1991–; High Sheriff Northants 1970; OStJ 1976; hon fell New Coll Oxford 1982; memb Ct of Assts Worshipful Co of Goldsmiths 1970– (Prime Warden 1979); *Clubs* White's, MCC, Beefsteak, Pratt's; *Style*— Sir Edward Ford, KCB, KCVO, ERD, DL; ✉ Canal House, 23 Blomfield Rd, London W9 1AD (☎ 0171 286 0028)

FORD, Air Marshal Sir Geoffrey Harold; KBE (1979), CB (1974); s of Harold Alfred Ford (d 1961), of Lewes; *b* 6 Aug 1923; *Educ* Lewes GS, Univ of Bristol; *m* 1951, Valerie, da of late Douglas Hart Finn, of Salisbury; 2 s; *Career* served RAF WWII, cmmnd (Tech Branch) 1942, air offr Engrg Strike Cmd 1973–76, DG Engrg and Supply 1976–78, chief engr 1978–81; dir Metals Soc 1981–84, sec Inst of Metals 1985–88; FEng 1987; *Clubs* RAF; *Style*— Air Marshal Sir Geoffrey Ford, KBE, CB, FEng; ✉ c/o Barclays Bank plc, The Old Bank, Lewes, E Sussex

FORD, (James) Glyn; MEP (Lab) Gtr Manchester East (majority 55,986); s of Ernest Benjamin Ford (d 1990), of Glos, and Matilda Alberta James (d 1986); *b* 28 Jan 1950; *Educ* Marling Sch Stroud, Univ of Reading (BSc), UCL (MSc); *m* 1, 1973 (m dis), Hazel Nancy, da of Hedley John Mahy (d 1969), of Guernsey; 1 da (Elise Jane b 1981); m 2, 1992, Daniella Zanelli; 1 s (Alessandro Aled b 1996); *Career* undergraduate apprentice BAC 1967–68, course tutor in oceanography Open Univ 1976–78, teaching asst UMIST 1977–78; res fell Univ of Sussex 1978–79; Univ of Manchester: res fell 1976–79, lectr 1979–80, sr res fell Prog of Policy Res in Engrg Sci and Technol 1980–84, hon visiting res fell 1984–; visiting prof Univ of Tokyo 1983; Parly candidate (Lab) Hazel Grove Gen Election 1987, chm Ctee of Inquiry into Growth of Racism and Fascism in Europe for Euro Parl 1984–86, vice chm Security and Disarmament Sub Ctee of Euro Parl 1987–89, rapporteur Ford Report Ctee of Inquiry into Racism and Xenophobia 1989–90, ldr European Parly Labour Party 1989–93 (dep ldr 1993–94), first vice chm Socialist Gp Euro Parl 1989–93, pres Euro Parl Chapter; memb: Nat Exec Ctee Lab Party 1989–93, TU Liaison Review Gp into Trade Union links, Consultative Ctee on Racism and Xenophobia 1994–, nat treas Anti-Nazi League; *Publications* The Future of Ocean Technology (1987), Fascist Europe (1992), Evolution of a European (1993), Changing States (1996); author of various articles in jls of sci and technol; *Clubs* Groucho, Manchester Literary and Philosophical Society; *Style*— Glyn Ford, Esq, MEP; ✉ 46 Stamford Rd, Mossley, Lancs OL5 0BE (☎ 01457 836276, fax 01457 834927, e-mail glynford.euromp@zen.co.uk)

FORD, Graham; s of James Ford, GM, of Tunbridge Wells, and Muriel Betty, *née* Whitfield; *b* 8 May 1950; *Educ* St Dunstan's Coll Catford, Medway Coll of Design; *m* 4 June 1977, Rachel Anne, da of Prof H W F Saggs; 2 s (Joseph b 1 March 1978, Oscar b 8 Feb 1989), 2 da (Charlotte b 14 May 1980, Florence b 30 Nov 1986); *Career* photographer; asst to David Davies, Bob Croxford and David Thorpe 1968–76, freelance 1977–; clients incl: Volvo, Parker Pens, Sainsbury's, Levis, BMW, Whitbread, Absolut Vodka, Land Rover, Oxfam, NSPCC, RSPCA, COI; various awards from: D&AD, Campaign, Assoc of Photographers, NY One Show, Cannes, Art Dirs' Club of Italy, Art Dirs' Club of Europe; memb: D&AD 1979, Assoc of Photographers 1979; *Recreations* family, sailing, photography, wine; *Style*— Graham Ford, Esq; ✉ Unit 3, Perseverance Works, 38 Kingsland Road, London E2 8DD (☎ 0171 739 6898)

FORD, Prof Sir Hugh; kt (1975); s of Arthur Ford (d 1969), of Welwyn Garden City, Herts, and Constance Ford; *b* 16 July 1913; *Educ* Northampton Sch, Imperial Coll London (DSc, PhD); *m* 1, 1942, Wynyard Scholfield (d 1991); 2 da (Clare, Vanessa); m 2, Nov 1993, Thelma Alys Jensen; *Career* res engr ICI 1939–42, chief engr Br Iron & Steel Fedn 1942–48; Imperial Coll London: reader and then prof of applied mechanics 1948–69, prof of mechanical engrg 1969–82 (now emeritus), head of dept 1965–78, pro rector 1978–80; memb Agric Res Cncl 1976–81, pres Inst of Mechanical Engrs 1976–77; chm: Engrs Bd SERC 1970–74, Sir Hugh Ford & Associates Ltd 1982– (formerly of Ford & Dain Ptnrs Ltd); dir: Air Liquide UK 1970–95, International Dynamics Ltd 1982–91 (formerly RD Projects Ltd); vice pres Royal Acad of Engrg 1981–84; pres: Welding Inst 1983–85, Inst of Metals 1985–87; fell Imperial Coll 1983; Hon DUniv Sheffield 1984; Hon DSc: Univ of Salford, Queen's Univ Belfast, Aston Univ, Univ of Bath, Univ of Sussex; James Watt Int Gold medal 1985; Freeman: City of London, Worshipful Co of Blacksmiths, Worshipful Co of Engineers; FRS 1967, FEng 1976 (fndr fell), Hon MASME, FCGI, FICE, Hon FIMechE, Hon FIChemE, FIM; *Recreations* gardening, music, model engineering; *Clubs* Athenaeum; *Style*— Prof Sir Hugh Ford, FRS, FEng; ✉ 18 Shrewsbury House, Cheyne Walk, London SW3 5LN (☎ 0171 352 4948, fax 0171 352 5320); Shamley Cottage, Shamley Green, Surrey GU5 0ST (☎ 01483 898012)

FORD, James Allan; CB (1978), MC (1946); 2 s of Douglas Ford (d 1948), and Margaret Duncan, *née* Allan; *b* 10 June 1920; *Educ* Royal HS Edinburgh, Univ of Edinburgh; *m* 1948, Isobel, *née* Dunnett; 1 s, 1 da; *Career* WWII Capt 2 Bn The Royal Scots Hong Kong; civil servant: registrar gen for Scotland 1966–69, princ estab offr SO 1969–79, ret 1979; tstee Nat Library of Scotland 1981–91; novelist; *Books* The Brave White Flag (1961), Season of Escape (1963, Frederick Niven Award 1965), A Statue for a Public Place (1965), A Judge of Men (1968, Scottish Arts Cncl Award 1968), The Mouth of Truth (1971); *Clubs* Scottish Arts, Royal Scots; *Style*— James Ford, Esq, CB, MC; ✉ 6 Hillpark Court, Edinburgh EH4 7BE

FORD, Dr (Sydney) John; s of Sidney James Ford (d 1982), and Barbara Essenhigh (d 1982); *b* 23 Aug 1936; *Educ* Bromsgrove HS, Bishop Gore Sch Swansea (state scholar), Univ of Wales (BSc, PhD, Dip in Math Statistics); *m* 1, 1960 (m dis 1990), Beryl, da of Albert G Owen; 2 s (Gareth b 1966, Rhodri b 1969); m 2, 1990, Morag, da of late Finlay J Munro; *Career* various positions rising to md British Aluminium Corporation 1966–82, dep md British Alcan Aluminium PLC 1982–85, UK ops dir Williams Holdings PLC 1985–88, dir CS European Distribution Christian Salvesen PLC 1988–93, chief exec Driving Standards Agency 1993–94, chief exec DVLA 1995–; memb North Midlands Rugby Referees Soc; *Recreations* rugby referee and coach, art, photography; *Style*— Dr S John Ford; ✉ Chief Executive, Driver & Vehicle Licensing Agency, Longview Road, Morriston, Swansea SA6 7JL (☎ 01792 782363, fax 01792 783003)

FORD, John Anthony (Tony); s of Frank Everatt Ford (d 1993), of Banstead, Surrey, and Dorothy Mary, *née* Hearn; *b* 28 April 1938; *Educ* Epsom Coll, St Edmund Hall Oxford (MA Eng Lit); *m* 1, 1963 (m dis), Caroline Rosemary Wharrad; 1 da (Joanna); m 2, 1984, Sandra Edith Williams; *Career* admitted slr 1964; slr and lectr in law 1964–76, dir Arts Services Grants (artists' charity) 1976–79; Crafts Council: head of mktg and grants then dep dir 1979–88, dir 1988–; memb: Working Party for Calouste Gulbenkian Tst Craft Initiative 1985–89, Visual Arts Advsy Ctee Br Cncl 1988–; Euro pres and memb Exec Bd World Crafts Cncl (WCC) 1987–93 (advsr WCC Europe 1993–); memb: Court Royal Coll of Art 1989–, Fabric Ctee Rochester Cathedral 1989–, Advsy Cncl Centre for Tapestry Arts New York, Court of Govrs London Inst 1993–; FRSA 1989; *Style*— Tony Ford, Esq; ✉ Director, Crafts Council, 44a Pentonville Road, London N1 9BY (☎ 0171 278 7700, fax 0171 837 6891)

FORD, Sir John Archibald; KCMG (1977, CMG 1967), MC (1945); s of Ronald Mylne Ford (d 1963), of Newcastle-under-Lyme, Staffs, and Margaret Jesse Coghill (d 1977); *b* 19 Feb 1922; *Educ* Sedbergh, Oriel Coll Oxford; *m* 1956, Emaline, da of Mahlon Burnette (d 1989), of Leesville, Virginia; 2 da; *Career* served WWII as Maj RA Field Regt; HM Dip Serv: consul gen NY, DG Br Trade Devpt in USA 1971–75, Br ambass Jakarta 1975–78, high cmmr Ottawa 1978–81, ret; lay admin Guildford Cathedral 1982–84; chm: Voluntary and Christian Serv 1985–88, Aids Care Educn and Trg 1989–93; tstee Opportunity Tst: UK 1992–96, USA 1994–95; *Books* Honest to Christ (1988), The Answer is the Christ of AD 2000 (1996); *Recreations* walking, writing, sailing; *Clubs* Farmers', RHS; *Style*— Sir John Ford, KCMG, MC; ✉ Loquats, Guildown, Guildford, Surrey GU2 5EN

FORD, Leslie John; s of Sidney George Frederick Ford (d 1971), and Doris Irene, *née* Davies; *b* 16 March 1936; *Educ* Sir Walter St John Sch, Univ of London (BSc); *m* 24 Sept 1960, Janet Loraine, da of Max Gilbert Frost (d 1972); 1 s (Samuel b 1964), 1 da (Madeleine b 1966); *Career* chem engr with ICI plc 1959–86 (conslt chem engr 1986–), co-ordinator for the Sci and Engrg Res Cncl prog in particulate technol 1984–92; vice chm: Hitchin UDC 1974–75, Bd of Dirs IFPRI 1979–85; pres Int Fine Particle Res Inst Inc 1985–, dir Deeside House Educnl Tst 1991–; CEng, FIChemE, ACMA; *Recreations* squash, badminton, politics; *Clubs* Naval; *Style*— Leslie Ford, Esq; ✉ 2 High View, Helsby, Cheshire WA6 9LP (☎ 01928 723886); G1, Waterloo Centre, Waterloo Rd, Widnes, Cheshire WA8 0PR (☎ 0151 420 1850, fax 0151 424 1495)

FORD, (John) Peter; CBE (1969); s of late Ernest Ford, of Westminster, and Muriel Ford; *b* 20 Feb 1912; *Educ* Wrekin Coll, Gonville and Caius Coll Cambridge; *m* 1939, Phoebe Seys, da of Herbert and Gwendolen McGregor Wood, of Hampstead; 1 s, 2 da; *Career* md: Brush Export, Assoc Brit Oil Engines Export Ltd 1949–58, Coventry Climax International Ltd 1958–63; dir Plessey Overseas Ltd 1963–70, chm Inst of Export 1954–56 and 1965–67, vice pres London C of C 1972–; chm Br Shippers Cncl 1972–75, chm and md International Jt Ventures Ltd 1974–, chm Metra Martech Ltd 1988–; Master Worshipful Co of Ironmongers 1981 (memb Ct of Assts); *Recreations* athletics (Cambridge Univ and Int teams); *Clubs* United Oxford & Cambridge Univ, City Livery, MCC, Hawks (Cambridge); *Style*— Peter Ford, Esq, CBE; ✉ 40 Fairacres, Roehampton Lane, London SW15 5LX (☎ 0181 876 2146, office 0181 563 0666)

FORD, Peter John; s of John Frederick Arthur Ford (d 1984), of Guildford, Surrey, and Hazel Mary Ford; *b* 21 Nov 1938; *Educ* King's Sch Canterbury, Chrish Church Oxford (BA Chemistry), Harvard Business Sch (MBA Distinction); *m* 1966, Olivia Mary, *née* Temple; 2 s (Adrian b 1971, Gregory b 1984), 2 da (Alice b 1974, Maxine b 1975); *Career* research chemist/salesman Shell Chemical Co 1961–65, McKinsey & Co New York 1967–70, exec dir Sterling Guarantee Trust 1970–93, exec dir P & O Steam Navigation Co and chm P & O European Ferries 1970–93, chm London Transport 1994–; pres Sheffield C of C 1985–86, chm Chris Fund Sheffield Children's Hosp 1983–90, chm Sheffield Business Sch 1986–92, govr Kingston Univ 1993–; *Recreations* walking, music, tennis, family pursuits; *Clubs* RAC; *Style*— Peter Ford, Esq; ✉ 16 The Drive, London SW20 8TG (☎ 0181 944 7207, 0181 944 5325); London Transport, 55 Broadway, London SW1H 0BD (☎ 0171 918 3157, fax 0171 918 3458, mobile 0374 192867)

FORD, Richard James Cameron; s of Bernard Thomas Ford (d 1967), of Little Estcotts, Burbage, Wilts, and Eveline Saumarez Ford (d 1952); *b* 1 Feb 1938; *Educ* Marlborough; *m* 27 Sept 1975, Mary Elizabeth, da of James Arthur Keevil; 3 s (James Richard Keevil b 26 July 1976, Charles John Cameron b 26 July 1978, William Bernard Saumarez b 29 May 1980); *Career* admitted slr 1961, ptnr Ford and Ford 1965, sr ptnr Ford Gunningham and Co 1970–; dir: Ramsbury Building Society 1984–86, West of England Building Society 1986–89, Regency and West of England Building Society 1989–90, Portman Building Society 1990; tstee Glos and Wilts Law Soc 1983– (pres 1982–83); memb Salisbury Diocesan Synod 1985–93, lay chm Pewsey Synod 1987–93; memb: Wyvern Hosp Mgmnt Ctee 1967–70, Swindon Hosp Mgmnt Ctee 1970–74, Wiltshire Area Health Authy 1974–82; vice chm Swindon Health Authy 1982–87; memb Cncl Law Soc 1992–; clerk to Cncl Marlborough Coll 1994–; *Recreations* riding, sailing; *Clubs* Royal Solent Yacht, East India and Sports; *Style*— Richard Ford, Esq; ✉ Little Estcotts, Burbage, Wilts SN8 3AQ; Ford Gunningham & Co, Kingsbury House, Marlborough, Wilts SN8 1HU (☎ 01672 512265, 01672 514891)

FORD, Richard John; s of Arthur William Ford (d 1992), of Christchurch, Dorset, and Violet, *née* Banbury; *b* 10 April 1949; *Educ* Hove Co GS for Boys, Portsmouth Poly Sch of Architecture (BA), Poly of Central London (DipArch); *m* Janet Kathleen; 1 s (Edward Richard b 5 Feb 1984); *Career* student Portsmouth Poly and Poly of Central London 1976–80; exec creative dir responsible for all creative product Landor Associates 1984–; cmmns incl identity and environmental design for: British Airways 1984, Chase Manhattan Bank Europe 1985, Royal Jordanian Airline and Alfred Dunhill 1986, BAe and Abbey National 1987, Cepsa Petroleum Spain, Depaso Convenience Stores Spain and Ballantyne Cashmere 1988, Emlak Bank Turkey 1989, Deutsche Shell 1990, Egnatia Bank Greece 1991, Seville Expo and Neste Petroleum Finland 1992, Lincoln Mercury USA, Telia (Swedish Telecom) and Cathay Pacific Airline 1993, Royal Mail and Delta Air Lines USA 1994, Montell (Worldwide) and KF (Swedish Co-op) 1995, Reuters (Worldwide) and Air 2000 (UK) 1996; RIBA 1983; *Style*— Richard Ford, Esq; ✉ Landor Associates, Klamath House, 18 Clerkenwell Green, London EC1R 0DP (☎ 0171 880 8000)

FORD, Gen Sir Robert Cyril; GCB (1981, KCB 1977, CB 1973), CBE (1971, MBE 1958); s of John Stranger Ford (d 1970), and Gladys Ford (d 1986), of Yealmpton, Devon; *b* 29 Dec 1923; *Educ* Musgrave's Coll; *m* 1949, Jean Claudia, da of Gp Capt Claude Luther Pendlebury, MC, TD (d 1961), of Yelverton; 1 s; *Career* served WWII 4/7 Royal Dragoon Gds NW Europe (despatches), Egypt and Palestine 1947–48 (despatches); instr Mons OCS 1949–50, trg offr Scottish Horse (TA) 1952–54, Staff Coll Camberley 1955, GSO2 Mil Ops WO 1956–57, GSO1 to Adm of Fleet Earl Mountbatten 1964–65, CO 4/7 Royal Dragoon Guards 1966–67, Cdr 7 Armd Bde 1968–69, Princ Staff Offr to CDS 1970–71, Maj-Gen 1971, Cdr Land Forces NI 1971–73, Cmdt RMA Sandhurst 1973–76, Lt-Gen 1976, Mil Sec MOD 1976–78, Gen 1978, Adj-Gen 1978–81 and ADC Gen to HM The Queen 1980–81, ret 1981; Col Cmdt RAC 1980–82 and SAS 1980–85, Col 4/7 Royal Dragoon Gds 1984–88; govr: Royal Hosp Chelsea 1981–87, Corps of Commissionaires 1981–; chm: Army Benevolent Fund 1981–87 (pres 1986–), Royal Cambridge Home for Soldiers' Widows 1981–87; nat pres Forces Help and Lord Roberts Workshops 1981–91, cmmr Cwlth War Graves Cmmn 1981–88 (vice chm 1989–93); CBIM; *Recreations* tennis, cricket, war studies; *Clubs* Cavalry and Guards', MCC; *Style*— Gen Sir Robert Ford, GCB, CBE; ✉ c/o National Westminster Bank, 45 Park St, Camberley, Surrey GU15 3PA

FORD, Robert Webster; CBE (1982); s of Robert Ford, and Beatrice, *née* Webster; *b* 27 March 1923; *Educ* Alleyne's Sch; *m* 2 June 1956, Monica Florence, da of Ernest George Tebbett; 2 s (Martin b 1957, Giles b 1964); *Career* WWII RAF 1939–45; radio offr 1945; Br Mission Lhasa Tibet, Political Agency Sikkin and Bhutan, Tibetan Govt Serv, political prisoner communist China 1950–55, freelance writer and broadcaster Tibetan and Chinese affrs 1955–56; HM Dip Serv 1956–83: Saigon 1957–58, Djakarta 1959, Washington 1960–62, FO 1962–67, Tangier 1967–70, Luanda 1970–74, Bordeaux 1974–78, Gothenburg 1978–80, Geneva 1980–83; memb Cncl Tibet Soc; FRGS 1956, FRComs 1956; *Books* Captured in Tibet (1956, 2 edn 1990); *Recreations* skiing, gardening, travelling; *Style*— Robert Ford, Esq, CBE; ✉ Cedar Garth, Latimer Rd, Monken Hadley, Barnet, Herts EN5 5NU

FORD, Timothy Graham; s of John Hamilton Ford (d 1974), of Charleston, Cornwall, and Dorothy Joyce Ford (d 1989); *b* 27 Jan 1945; *Educ* Bancrofts Sch Woodford Green Essex, Coll of Law Lancaster Gate; *m* 4 March 1972, Marian Evelyn, da of Charles Frederick Bernard Hayward, MBE, of Wye, Kent; 2 s (Paul b 1973, Simon b 1977); *Career* Inns of Ct and City Yeo 1965–67, cmmnd RCS TA 1967, 36 Eastern Signal Regt V; admitted slr 1969, managing ptnr Park Nelson slrs (ptnr 1971–); dir Guy's and Lewisham NHS Tst 1991–93, dep chm Guy's and St Thomas's Hosps NHS Tst 1993–, special tstee Guy's Hosp 1993–, special tstee St Thomas's Hosp 1995–; chm Industrial Tribunal 1992–94 (memb 1989–92); sec gen Nat Pawnbrokers' Assoc 1988–; contrib to professional press, particularly in architectural press on business and planning law matters; dir Blackheath Preservation Trust, Parly candidate (Alliance) Greenwich Gen Election 1983; Freeman: City of London 1978, City of London Slrs' Co, Liveryman Worshipful Co of Painter Stainers; memb: Law Soc 1969, IOD 1987; FRSA; *Books* practice manual on procedures under the Consumer Credit Act 1974 for Lending Insts; *Recreations* golf, fly fishing, cricket, music, reading Charles Dickens; *Clubs* Royal Blackheath Golf, East India, MCC, City Livery; *Style*— Timothy Ford, Esq; ✉ The Pavilion, Manorbrook, Blackheath, London SE3 9AW (☎ 0181 297 2575, fax 0181 318 0031); Park Nelson, 1 Bell Yard, London WC2A 2JP (☎ 0171 404 4191, fax 0171 405 4266)

FORD DAVIES, Oliver Robert; s of Robert Cyril Davies (d 1974), of Ealing, and Cicely Mary, *née* Ford (d 1990); *b* 12 Aug 1939; *Educ* King's Sch Canterbury, Merton Coll Oxford (DPhil, pres OUDS); *m* Jenifer Armitage, da of Edward Armitage; 1 da (Miranda Katherine b 1975); *Career* actor; lectr in history Univ of Edinburgh 1964–66; seasons at: Birmingham, Cambridge, Leicester, Oxford, Nottingham; *Theatre* incl: played Bishop Talacryn in Hadrian VII (Mermaid, Haymarket) 1968–69, Tonight at Eight (Hampstead, Fortune) 1971–72, Mary Rose 1972, 1975–87; 25 prodns with RSC incl: Henry IV, Henry V, Henry VI, Henry VIII, As You Like It, Coriolanus, Love's Labours Lost, The Greeks, Troilus and Cressida, The Love Girl and The Innocent, The Forest, Measure for Measure, Waste (also Lyric 1985), The Danton Affair, Principia Scriptoriae, Merry Wives of Windsor, Jekyll and Hyde; RNT 1988–91: The Shaughraun, Hamlet, Lionel Espy in Racing Demon (Olivier Award for Actor of the Year), The Shape of the Table, The Absence of War 1993; Heartbreak House (Yvonne Arnaud Guildford and Haymarket) 1992; *Television* incl: Cause Célèbre, A Taste for Death, Death of a Son, A Very British Coup, Inspector Morse, The Police, The Cloning of Joanna May, Anglo-Saxon Attitudes, The Absence of War, Truth or Dare, A Royal Scandal, A Dance to the Music of Time, Kavanagh QC; *Films* incl: Luther, Defence of the Realm, Scandal, Paper Mask, Sense and Sensibility; *Books* God Keep Lead out of Me - Shakespeare on War and Peace (jtly) 1985; has also written plays produced by Orange Tree Theatre, ATV and BBC Radio; *Recreations* music, history, carpentry; *Style*— Oliver Ford Davies, Esq; ✉ c/o Caroline Dawson Associates, Apartment 9, 47 Courtfield Road, London SW7 4DB (☎ 0171 370 0708, fax 0171 835 1403)

FORD-HUTCHINSON, Sally Mary Ann (Mrs Anthony Yeshin); da of Peter William Scott Ford-Hutchinson (d 1961), and Giuseppina Adele, *née* Leva; *b* 20 Aug 1950; *Educ* Holy Trinity Convent Kent, Bristol Poly (HND, Dip in Mktg); *m* 2 June 1977, Anthony David Yeshin; 2 s (Mark b 26 Dec 1979, Paul b 31 May 1983); *Career* res exec Leo Burnett Advertising Agency 1972–74, Benton & Bowles 1974–77; res mangr H J Heinz Ltd 1977–79, head Res Dept Wasey Campbell Ewald 1979–83, memb Planning Dept Grandfield Rork Collins 1983–86; DMB&B 1986–: dir, head Planning Dept and memb Mgmnt Ctee until 1996, a global planning dir 1996–; winner commendation IPA Advtg Effectivenes award; memb MRS, assoc MInstM; *Recreations* opera, walking in the country, reading, playing games with my children; *Style*— Ms Sally Ford-Hutchinson; ✉ D'Arcy Masius Benton & Bowles, 123 Buckingham Palace Road, London SW1W 9DZ (☎ 0171 630 0000, fax 0171 630 0033)

FORDE, Dr the Hon Harold McDonald; CHB; s of William McDonald Forde (d 1978), of Bridgetown, Barbados, and Gertrude, *née* Williams (d 1920); *b* 10 Jan 1916; *Educ* Harrison Coll Barbados, Univ Coll Hosp London (MD); *m* 1949, Alice Elaine, da of William Leslie, of Belize City; 1 s (William d 1987), 2 da (Stella, Ann); *Career* MO Govt of Belize 1947–52, lectr in med Univ of WI 1952–57, conslt physician Miny of Health Govt of Barbados 1957–84, sr lectr in med Univ of WI 1967–78, chief med offr Belize 1978–79, memb Privy Cncl Barbados 1980–85, high cmmr for Barbados to UK 1984–86; conslt physician in private practice 1986–; former ambass to: Norway, Sweden, Denmark, Finland, Iceland, Holy See; memb: NY Academic Sciences, Lions Clubs Int (life memb and past dist govr, Melvin Jones fell); FRCP (Edinburgh), Hon FACP, DPH, DTM & H (London); *Recreations* cricket, soccer, bridge; *Clubs* Surrey CCC; *Style*— Dr the Hon Harold Forde, CHB; ✉ Bethesda Medical Centre, Black Rock, St Michael, Barbados, W1 (☎ home 00 809 424 9580, office 00 809 436 5862)

FORDHAM, His Hon Judge; (John) Jeremy; s of (John Hampden Fordham, CBE, and Rowena, *née* May; *b* 18 April 1933; *Educ* Gresham's Sch, Univ of New Zealand (LLB NZ); *m* 1962, Rose Anita, *née* Brandon, of Wellington NZ; 1 s, 1 da; *Career* Merchant Navy 1950–55; labourer, fireman etc 1955–60; barrister and slr New Zealand

1960–64, called to the Bar Inner Temple 1965, in practice 1965–71 and 1976–78, sr magistrate Gilbert and Ellice Is 1971–76, met stipendiary magistrate 1978–86, recorder 1986, circuit judge (SE Circuit) 1986–; *Recreations* boats, games; *Clubs* Garrick; *Style*— His Hon Judge Fordham; ✉ Inner London Crown Court, Sessions House, Newington Causeway, London SE1 6AZ

FORDHAM, John Anthony; s of Lt Cdr J H Fordham, CBE (d 1967), and Ebba Fordham; *b* 11 June 1948; *Educ* Gresham's Sch Holt Norfolk; *m* 25 June 1974, Lynda Patricia, da of Bernard Green, of Weston-Super-Mare; 2 s (Michael b 28 Dec 1979, Timothy b 3 Aug 1983); *Career* with Bowater Corporation Ltd 1973–81, head of mergers and acquisitions Hill Samuel Bank Ltd 1986–90 (joined 1981, dir 1985), md Lloyds Merchant Bank Ltd 1991–93, dir European Investment Banking Alex Brown & Sons Ltd 1993–; *Recreations* squash, running, golf, gardening; *Clubs* Royal Wimbledon Golf, Rye Golf, The Jesters, The Escorts; *Style*— John Fordham, Esq; ✉ Sandgate, 81 Thurleigh Road, London SW12 8TY (☎ 0181 675 7950); Alex Brown & Sons Ltd, Austin Friars House, 2–6 Austin Friars, London EC2N 2HE (☎ 0171 786 7444)

FORDHAM, John Michael; s of John William Fordham, and Kathleen Mary; *b* 15 Dec 1948; *Educ* Dulwich, Gonville and Caius Coll Cambridge (MA); *m* 28 Oct 1972, Sarah Anne, da of Denis Victor Burt; 1 s (Benjamin John b 1979), 1 da (Rebecca Kate b 1977); *Career* admitted slr 1974, ptnr Stephenson Harwood 1979–, hd of litigation 1995; vice pres Sutton CC; Liveryman Worshipful Co of Solicitors, memb Law Soc; *Recreations* cricket (player), abstract art, jazz, twentieth century literature, pasta and chianti (consumer); *Style*— John Fordham, Esq; ✉ High Trees, 31 Shirley Avenue, South Cheam, Surrey SM2 7QS (☎ 0181 642 1517); Stephenson Harwood, One St Paul's Churchyard, London EC2M 8SH (☎ 0171 329 4422, fax 0171 606 0822, telex 886789 SHSPC G)

FORDHAM, Julia; da of Royston Fordham, of Hayling Island, and Muriel Fordham; *b* 10 Aug 1962; *Educ* The Hayling Sch; *Career* singer; sang own material at local folk clubs, moved to London as backing vocalist; signed recording contract as soloist 1987; album releases: Julia Fordham 1988 (Silver and Gold disc 1988, Gold Japan 1992), Porcelain 1989 (Gold disc 1990, Gold Japan 1992), Swept 1991 (Gold disc Japan 1992), Falling Forward 1994 (Gold disc Japan); tours: UK/Europe 1988, 1989, 1991 and 1994, USA 1990, Japan 1989, 1990, 1992 and 1994; winner Silver prize Tokyo Music Festival 1989; *Style*— Ms Julia Fordham; ✉ c/o JFD Management, 106 Dalling Road, London W6 0JA (☎ 0181 748 0244, fax 0181 748 0759)

FORDHAM, Prof (Sigurd) Max; OBE (1994); s of Dr Michael Scott Montague Fordham (d 1995), of Jordans, Bucks, and Molly, *née* Swabey (d 1941); *b* 17 June 1933; *Educ* De Carteret Sch Jamaica, Dartington Hall Sch Totnes Devon, Trinity Coll Cambridge (MA), Nat Coll of Heating Ventilation Refrigeration and Fan Engrg (William Nelson Haden scholar); *m* 24 Sept 1960, Thalia Aubrey, da of late Dr Reginald John Dyson; 3 s (Jason Christopher Lyle b 26 Sept 1962, Cato Michael Sigurd b 17 Nov 1964, Finn William Montague b 12 Nov 1967); *Career* Nat Serv Pilot Fleet Air Arm RN 1952–54; devpt engr Weatherfoil Heating Systems Ltd 1958–61, Ove Arup & Ptnrs Building Gp (later Arup Assocs) 1961–66, fndr Max Fordham & Ptnrs 1966– (constituted as co-op practice 1974), fndr ptnr Max Fordham Assocs 1984–; dir: Nestar Ltd 1987–, Panopus Printing Ltd 1987–, National Engineering Specification 1987–; visiting prof in building and design Univ of Bath 1990–; external examiner: Architectural Assoc 1991–, Univ of Edinburgh 1992–; chm Working Gp for Communications for Building IT 2000, accreditation panelist CIBSE 1989– (memb Cncl 1993–96), chm Res Sub Ctee for Intelligent Façades for the Centre for Window & Cladding Technol 1993–; FCIBSE 1971 (MCIBSE 1964), MConsE 1974, FRSA 1982, CEng 1987, Hon FRIBA 1992, FEng 1992; *Publications* A Global Strategy for Housing in the Third Milleneum - The Envelope of the House in Temperate Climates (Royal Soc, 1992), also numerous tech papers and articles; *Style*— Professor Max Fordham, OBE, FEng; ✉ Max Fordham & Partners, 42/43 Gloucester Crescent, London NW1 7PE (☎ 0171 267 5161, fax 0171 482 0329)

FORDY, (George) Malcolm; OBE (1997); s of George Laurence Fordy (d 1970), and Louise, *née* Birdsall; *b* 27 Aug 1934; *Educ* Durham Sch; *m* 7 June 1957, Pauline, da of William Stanley Thompson, of Northallerton, North Yorks; 1 s (Nicholas b 1960), 2 da (Susan b 1958, Sarah b 1965); *Career* chm and chief exec: FT Construction Group (Holdings) Ltd (George Fordy & Son Ltd/Walter Thompson (Contractors) Ltd and associated companies), Fordy Holdings Ltd; chm BEC Pension Tstee Ltd, dir Bldg & Civil Engrg Holidays Scheme Mgmnt Ltd; pres Nat Fedn Bldg Trades Employers 1982–83, ldr Employers' Side Nat Jt Cncl for the Building Indust, memb Bd Construction Indust Trg Bd 1976–82 and 1985–96, chm Vocational Trg Cmmn of the Fedn de L'Industrie Européene de la Construction 1985–94, chm Employers Gp of Building Civil Engrg and Public Works Ctee Int Labour Organisation Geneva 1992; FCIOB 1978, FIMgt 1978; *Recreations* the countryside, travel; *Clubs* Cleveland (Middlesbrough), YCCC, ACdeM; *Style*— Malcolm Fordy, Esq, OBE; ✉ High Farm House, Ingleby Greenhow, Great Ayton, North Yorks TS9 6RG; FT Construction Group, Construction House, Northallerton, North Yorks DL7 8ED (☎ 01609 780700, fax 01609 777236)

FORECAST, Trevor Cecil; s of Cecil Arthur Forecast (d 1989), of St Albans, Herts, and Daisy Edith, *née* Lovell; *Educ* St Albans Sch; *m* 29 June 1963, Christine Kay, da of Keith Lionel Stephens (d 1978); 2 da (Katie Jane b 1967, Emma Kay b 1969); *Career* RAF 1956–58; mktg mangr Polymer Corp (UK) Ltd 1968–72; md and proprietor: Crown Hotel Downham Market Ltd 1972–82, Congham Hall Country House Hotel Kings Lynn Norfolk 1982–; dir Norfolk & Waveney TEC 1990–94, dir Pride of Britain Ltd 1988–, chm Pride of Britain Hotels 1994–; former pres Kings Lynn Hotels & Catering Assoc, dep chm Nat Cncl BHA, memb Ctee West Norfolk Tourism Forum, former pres Downham Market Chamber of Trade, fndr pres Downham Market RC, pres Grimston CC; Master Innholders' award 1991; Freedom City of London 1991; MIPE 1955, CEng 1956, MInstM 1968, FHCIMA; *Recreations* shooting; *Clubs* Old Albanian, IOD; *Style*— Trevor Forecast, Esq; ✉ Congham Hall, Country House Hotel & Restaurant, Grimston, Kings Lynn, Norfolk PE32 1AH (☎ 01485 600 250, fax 01485 601191)

FOREMAN, Michael; s of Walter Foreman (d 1938), of Lowestoft, Suffolk, and Gladys, *née* Goddard (d 1982); *b* 21 March 1938; *Educ* Notley Road Secdy Modern, Lowestoft Sch of Art, RCA (USA scholar, MA, Silver medal); *m* 22 Dec 1980, Louise Amanda, da of Basil Gordon Phillips; 3 s (Mark b 1961, Ben b 1982, Jack b 1986); *Career* illustrator; former: art dir Playboy, King and Ambit magazines, prodr animated films in Scandinavia and for BBC; writer and illustrator of over 100 books (incl children's and travel books), reg contrib American and Euro magazines, held exhibitions Euro, America and Japan; awards: Aigle d'Argent at Festival International du Livre France 1972, Francis Williams Prize V & A Museum and Nat Book League 1972 and 1977, Graphic Prize Bologna, Kurt Maschler Award, Kate Greenaway Medal 1982 and 1989, Smarties Grand Prix 1984; memb: AGI 1972, RDI 1986, hon fell RCA 1989; *Clubs* Chelsea Arts; *Style*— Michael Foreman, Esq

FOREMAN, Sir Philip Frank; kt (1981), CBE (1972), DL (Belfast 1975); s of late Frank Foreman, and Mary Foreman; *b* 16 March 1923; *Educ* Soham GS, Loughborough Coll; *m* 1971, Margaret, da of John Petrie Cooke, of Belfast; 1 s; *Career* with RN Scientific Serv 1943–58; chm, chief exec and md Short Brothers Ltd (aerospace mfrs) 1983–88 (joined 1958, md 1967); chm: BSI 1988–91, Progressive Building Society 1990–, Ricardo International plc 1992–; dep chm Simon Engineering plc 1993–94; conslt Foreman Assoc; pres Inst of Mechanical Engrs 1982; memb Senate Queen's Univ Belfast 1993–; Freeman City of London; Hon DSc Queen's Univ Belfast 1976, Hon DTech Loughborough Univ 1983, Hon DUniv Open Univ 1985; Hon FRAeS, Hon FIEI, FEng 1982, FIMechE, FRSA, CIMgt; *Clubs* Athenaeum; *Style*— Sir Philip Foreman, CBE, DL, FEng; ✉ Ashtree House, 26 Ballymenoch Rd, Holywood, Co Down BT18 0HH (☎ 01232 425767, fax 01232 427841)

FOREMAN-PECK, Dr James Stanley; s of John Foreman-Peck (d 1984), and Muriel Joan Foreman-Peck; *b* 19 June 1948; *Educ* Alleyns Sch, Univ of Essex (BA), LSE (MSc, PhD); *m* 22 June 1968, Lorraine, da of Walter Alexander McGimpsey; 1 s (Alexander b 1978), 1 da (Eleanor b 1985); *Career* economist Electricity Cncl 1971–72, lectr in econs Thames Poly 1972–79, visiting lectr Univ of Reading 1974–75, lectr in econs Univ of Newcastle upon Tyne 1979–88, visiting assoc prof Univ of California 1981–82, prof of econ history Univ of Hull 1988–90, Hallsworth fell in political econ Univ of Manchester 1990–91, fell St Antony's Coll Oxford and univ lectr in econ history 1990–; cncllr London Borough of Greenwich 1978–79; memb: Amnesty Int, Nat Tst, Royal Econ Soc, Econ History Soc; *Books* A History of the World Economy: International Economic Relations since 1850 (1983, 2 edn 1994), European Telecommunications Organisations (ed, 1988), New Perspectives on the Late Victorian Economy (ed, 1991), Public and Private Ownership of Industry in Britain 1820–1990 (1994), The British Motor Industry (1995), Smith and Nephew on the Healthcare Industry (1995); *Recreations* squash, sailing, literature, piano; *Style*— Dr James Foreman-Peck; ✉ St Antony's College, University of Oxford, Oxford OX2 6JF (☎ 01865 274465, fax 01865 274478)

FORESTER, 8 Baron (UK 1821); (George Cecil) Brooke Weld-Forester; DL (Shropshire 1995); s of 7 Baron Forester (d 1977), and Marie Louise Priscilla (d 1988), da of Col Sir Herbert Perrott, 6 and last Bt, CH, CB; *b* 20 Feb 1938; *Educ* Eton, RAC Cirencester; *m* 14 Jan 1967, Hon Catherine Elizabeth Lyttelton, 2 da of 10 Viscount Cobham, KG, GCMG, GCVO, TD, PC; 1 s (Hon George b 1975), 3 da (Hon Selina b 1968, Hon Alice b 1969, Hon Alexandra b 1973); *Heir* s, Hon (Charles Richard) George Forester b 8 July 1975; *Career* Patron of 3 livings; dir: Linley Farms 1974–, Sipolilo Estates 1977–, Lady Forester Hospital Trust Ltd 1994–, Callkilo Ltd 1996–; former chm: Shropshire Tree Cncl, Regnl Advsy Ctee Forestry Cmmn; pres: The Greenwood Tst 1990–, Shropshire FWAG 1991–; CLA: memb Minerals Working Pty 1980–, memb Cncl 1987–96, memb Exec 1990–95, chm Shropshire branch 1990–93; memb W Midland Cncl for Sport and Recreation 1991–95; this nobleman has in his possession a licence of the time of Henry VIII, giving to John Forester of Watling St, Co Salop, the privilege of wearing his hat in the Royal presence; *Recreations* fishing, silviculture, fine arts, the environment; *Style*— The Rt Hon Lord Forester, DL; ✉ Willey Park, Broseley, Shropshire (☎ 01952 882146 and (London) 0171 589 8543)

FORESTIER-WALKER, Sir Michael Leolin; 6 Bt (UK 1835); s of Lt-Col Alan Ivor Forestier-Walker, MBE, 7 Gurkha Rifles (ka Malaya 1954, s of Ivor Forestier-Walker, 5 s of 2 Bt) and Margaret Joan, da of Maj Henry Bennet Marcoolyn, MBE; suc kinsman, Sir Clive Radzivill Forestier-Walker, 5 Bt, 1983; *b* 24 April 1949; *Educ* Wellington, Royal Holloway Coll London (BA); *m* 16 July 1988, Elizabeth, da of Joseph Hedley, of Bellingham, Northumberland; 1 s (Joseph Alan b 2 May 1992), 1 da (Chloë b 15 Jan 1990); *Heir* s, Joseph Alan Forestier-Walker b 2 May 1992; *Career* teacher Feltonfleet Sch Cobham; *Recreations* sailing, electronics, computing; *Style*— Sir Michael Forestier-Walker, Bt; ✉ Bibury, 116 Hogshill Lane, Cobham, Surrey

FORFAR, Dr (John) Colin; s of Prof J O Forfar, MC, of Edinburgh, and Isobel Mary Langlands, *née* Fernback; *b* 22 Nov 1951; *Educ* Edinburgh Acad, Univ of Edinburgh (BSc, MD, PhD), Univ of Oxford (MA); *m* (m dis); 1 da (Katriana Louise b 1981); *Career* reader in cardiovascular med Univ of Oxford 1985–86, physician and conslt cardiologist Oxford RHA 1986–; author of numerous med pubns; memb: Br Cardiac Soc (former local sec), MRS, Oxford Med Soc; FRCPE 1987, FRCP 1991; *Recreations* walking, squash; *Style*— Dr Colin Forfar; ✉ 6 Church Road, Ickford, Aylesbury, Bucks HP18 9HZ (☎ 01844 339626); Department of Cardiology, John Radcliffe Hospital, Oxford OX3 9DU (☎ 01865 220326)

FORGE, Gilly Rosamund; da of John Bliss Forge, of Cirencester, Glos, and Margaret, *née* Whitwell (d 1966); *b* 27 Feb 1956; *Educ* The Abbey Malvern Worcs, New Hall Boreham Essex, Trinity Coll Dublin (LLB); *Career* milliner; former journalist, estab millinery business 1989; designers worked with incl: Jean Muir, Anouska Hempel, Caroline Charles, Amanda Wakeley; model hat range sold exclusively, diffusion range sold in major retailers throughout UK, Europe and USA; designer to Chester Jeffries glove mfrs 1992–; *Style*— Miss Gilly Forge; ✉ 14 Addison Avenue, London W11 4QR (☎ 0171 603 3833, fax 0171 603 2032)

FORKER, Rev Dr William George (Wilbert); s of William Forker, of Portadown, Co Armagh, and Esther Forker; *b* 15 July 1935; *Educ* Shaftesbury House Belfast, Edgehill Coll Belfast, GFT Indiana (MBA), DMin; *m* 29 June 1959, Maureen, *née* McMullan; 1 s (Christopher Michael b 17 May 1960), 1 da (Kathryn Esther b 2 March 1963); *Career* ordained minister Methodist Church in Ireland 1961; minister Methodist Missionary Soc: Guyana 1959–62, St Vincent 1964–66, Barbados 1966–68; memb Exec Staff World Cncl of Churches 1968–72, currently exec vice pres Templeton Fndn Nassau Bahamas (exec dir 1972–); Templeton Theological Seminary Nassau Bahamas: fndr 1985, pres 1987, chm Bd of Tstees 1989–; admin Templeton Prize for Progress in Religion 1972–; fndr and chm Tournament with a Heart Charity Golf Tournament Bahamas, memb Advsy Bd Int Cncl of Christians and Jews 1991–, memb Harvard Univ Bd Centre for the Study of World Religions 1993–; treas Lyford Cay Property Owners Assoc 1985–88; dir: Lismore Ltd Cayman Is, North Atlantic Management Company Ltd, The Compass Fund 1994–; FRSA 1995; *Books* The Templeton Prize (vol 1 1977, vol 2 1988, vol 3 1992), The Future Agenda (1992); *Recreations* golf, reading, philately; *Clubs* Arts, Athenaeum, Lyford Cay (Nassau); *Style*— The Rev Dr Wilbert Forker; ✉ PO Box N-7776, Nassau, Bahamas (☎ 00 1 242 362 4904)

FORMAN, Sir (John) Denis; kt (1976), OBE (1956); s of Rev Adam Forman, CBE (d 1977), of Dumcrieff, Moffatt, Scot, and Flora, *née* Smith; *b* 13 Oct 1917; *Educ* Loretto, Pembroke Coll Cambridge; *m* 1, 1948, Helen Blondel de Moulpied (d 1987); 2 s; m 2, 1990, Moni Cameron; *Career* Lt-Col (OSDEF Battle Sch, N Africa, Italy); chief prodn offr COI Films 1947; chm: Bd of Govrs Br Film Inst 1971–73 (dir 1948–55), Novello and Co 1971–88, Granada Television 1974–87 (dir 1955–87); dep chm Granada Group 1984–90 (dir 1964–90); Royal Opera House: dir 1980, dep chm 1984, chm Opera Bd 1988; memb Cncl Royal Northern Coll of Music 1977–84; Hon Doctorate: Univ of Stirling 1982, Univ of Essex 1986; Hon LLD: Manchester 1983, Lancaster 1989, Keele 1992, Bourgogne 1993; companion RCM 1993; *Publications* Mozart's Piano Concertos (1971), Son of Adam (autobiog, 1990), To Reason Why (autobiog, 1991), Good Opera Guide (1994); *Recreations* music; *Clubs* Garrick, Savile; *Style*— Sir Denis Forman, OBE; ✉ The Mill House, Howe St, Chelmsford, Essex CM3 1BG

FORMAN, (Francis) Nigel; MP (Cons) Carshalton and Wallington (majority 9,943); s of late Brig J F R Forman; *b* 25 March 1943; *Educ* Shrewsbury, New College Oxford, Coll of Europe Bruges, Harvard Univ, Univ of Sussex; *Career* former asst dir CRD, Parly candidate (C) Coventry NE Feb 1974; MP (C): Sutton Carshalton 1976–83, Carshalton and Wallington 1983–; memb Select Ctee on Sci and Technol 1976–79; sec Cons ctees: Educn 1976–79, Energy 1977–79; PPS to Douglas Hurd as Min of State FCO 1979–1983, vice chm Cons Fin Ctee 1983–87, PPS to Rt Hon Nigel Lawson as Chllr of the Exchequer 1987–89, under sec of state DES 1992; memb: Foreign Affairs Select Ctee 1990–92, Exec 1922 Ctee 1990–92, Treasy Select Ctee 1993–; chm GB-East Europe Centre 1990–92; *Style*— Nigel Forman, Esq, MP; ✉ House of Commons, London SW1A 0AA

FORMAN, Roy; s of Edwin Leslie Forman (d 1988), and Wilhelmina Mowbray, *née* Donkin (d 1964); *b* 28 Dec 1931; *Educ* Nunthorpe GS, Univ of Nottingham (BA); *m* 24 July 1954, Mary, da of Kenneth Francis Nelson (d 1961); 3 s (Ian b 1957, Nicholas b 1960, Simon b 1962), 1 da (Sally b 1964); *Career* Flying Offr RAF 1953–56; commercial dir S Wales Electricity Bd 1972–76, commercial advsr The Electricity Cncl 1976–80; Private Patients Plan Ltd: gen mangr mktg and sales 1980–81, mktg dir 1981–85, md and chief exec 1985–94, chm Principal Investment Management Ltd (PPP subsid) 1987–94, chm PPP Lifetime Ltd 1991–94; non-exec dir General Healthcare Group plc 1994–, dep chm Age Concern Enterprises 1994–; memb Cncl and chm Kent Branch IOD 1982–85, chm Tunbridge Wells CAB 1988–92; CIMgt, FRSA; *Recreations* music, walking; *Style*— Roy Forman, Esq; ✉ The Beacon Cottage, Staplecross, nr Robertsbridge, East Sussex TN32 5QR (☎ and fax 01580 830034)

FORMARTINE, Viscount; George Ian Alastair; s and h of Earl of Haddo, *qv* (himself s and h of 6 Marquess of Aberdeen and Temair, *qv*), and Joanna Clodagh, da of late Maj Ian George Henry Houldsworth; *b* 4 May 1983; *Style*— Viscount Formartine

FORMBY, Roger Myles; s of Myles Landseer Formby, CBE (d 1994), of Storrington, W Sussex, and his 1 w, Dorothy Hussey, *née* Essex (d 1991); *b* 15 March 1938; *Educ* Winchester, Univ of Oxford (MA); *m* 15 Sept 1962, (Alice) Jane, da of Herbert Victor Woof (d 1950), of Bedford; 2 da (Kate b 1965, Emily b 1967); *Career* Nat Serv 2 Lt Oxford and Bucks LI 1957; admitted slr 1965; managing ptnr Macfarlanes 1987– (ptnr 1967–, head of property 1970–86); *Recreations* golf, skiing, travel; *Clubs* City of London; *Style*— Roger M Formby, Esq; ✉ Macfarlanes, 10 Norwich Street, London EC4A 1BD (☎ 0171 831 9222, fax 0171 831 9607, telex 296381)

FORRES, 4 Baron (UK 1922); Sir Alastair Stephen Grant Williamson; 4 Bt (UK 1909); s of 3 Baron Forres (d 1978), by his 1 w, Gillian Ann Maclean, *née* Grant; *b* 16 May 1946; *Educ* Eton; *m* 2 May 1969, Margaret Ann, da of late George John Mallam, of Mullumbimby, NSW; 2 s (Hon George, Hon Guthrie b 1975); *Heir* s, Hon George Archibald Mallam Williamson b 16 Aug 1972; *Career* chm Agriscot Pty Ltd; dir Jaga Trading Pty Ltd; Australian rep Tattersalls; *Clubs* Australian Jockey, Tattersalls (Sydney), Sydney Turf; *Style*— The Rt Hon the Lord Forres; ✉ Kenso Park, Forest Road, Orange, NSW 2800, Australia

FORREST, Prof (William) George Grieve; s of William Downie Forrest, of London, and Christina (Ina) Mitchell Grieve *née* Welsh; *b* 24 Sept 1925; *Educ* LCC Merton Park, UCS Hampstead, New Coll Oxford (BA, MA); *m* 14 July 1956, Margaret Elizabeth Mary, da of Frederick Drummond Hall (d 1955); 2 da (Catherine b 1957, Alison b 1959); *Career* Meteorological Serv RAF 1943–47, ret Actg Corpl; fell and tutor Wadham Coll Oxford 1951–76 (fell emeritus 1992), Wykeham prof of ancient history Univ of Oxford and fell New Coll Oxford 1976–92 (fell emeritus 1992), prof emeritus Univ of Oxford 1992; visiting prof: Univ and Trinity Colls Toronto 1961, Yale 1968; visiting fell Br Sch at Athens 1986; Univ memb Oxford City Cncl 1962–64; fell Parmiter's Sch 1986; Hon DPhil Athens 1991; *Books* Emergence of Greek Democracy (1966), History of Sparta (1968); *Recreations* socialism; *Style*— Prof George Forrest; ✉ 9 Fyfield Rd, Oxford, OX2 6QE (☎ 01865 556187); New Coll, Oxford OX1 3BN (☎ 01865 279555)

FORREST, Dr John Richard; s of Prof John Samuel Forrest, and Ivy May Ellen, *née* Olding; *b* 21 April 1943; *Educ* King's Coll Sch Wimbledon, Sidney Sussex Coll Univ of Cambridge (BA, MA), Keble Coll Univ of Oxford (DPhil); *m* 8 Sept 1973, Jane Patricia Robey, da of John Robey Leech, of Little Hockham Hall, Great Hockham, Norfolk; 2 s (Nicholas John b 1975, Alexander Iain b 1980), 1 da (Katharine Elizabeth b 1977); *Career* UCL: lectr 1970–79, reader 1979–82, prof 1982–84; tech dir Marconi Defence Systems Ltd 1984–86, dir of engrg IBA 1986–90, chief exec National Transcommunications Ltd 1991–94, dep chm NTL Group Ltd 1994–94, chm Brewton Group Ltd 1994–; dir: Egan International Ltd 1994–, News Digital Systems Ltd 1996–, Loughborough Sound Images plc 1996–, Drake Automation Ltd 1996–; hon sec (electrical engrg) Royal Acad of Engrg 1995–; memb Cncl Brunel Univ 1996–; FIEE 1980, FEng 1985, FRSA 1987, FRTS 1990, Hon FBKSTS 1990, FInstD 1991; Chevalier de l'Ordre des Arts et des Lettres 1990; Hon DSc City Univ London 1992, Hon DTech Brunel Univ 1995; *Recreations* theatre, music, reading, sailing, mountain walking; *Clubs* Athenaeum; *Style*— Dr John Forrest, FEng; ✉ The Old Town House, Balmer Lawn Road, Brockenhurst, Hants SO42 7TS (☎ and fax 01590 624294); 15 Carlyle Court, Chelsea Harbour, London SW10 0UQ (☎ and fax 0171 376 5731, mobile 0385 251734)

FORREST, Nigel; s of Wing Cdr Gerald Vere Forrest, of Sydney, New South Wales, Aust, and Elizabeth, *née* Burnett (d 1991); *b* 12 Sept 1946; *Educ* Harrow, Oriel Coll Oxford (MA), INSEAD (MBA); *m* 22 Nov 1980, Julia Mary, da of Philip Nash (d 1970), of Dorking, Surrey; 1 s (Dominic b 18 April 1982), 1 da (Harriet b 9 Feb 1984); *Career* commercial technol sales mangr Rolls Royce Ltd 1972 (graduate trainee 1969), mangr Lazard Bros & Co Ltd 1978 (exec 1973), dep md Nomura International plc 1989–96 (assoc md 1986, exec dir 1983, mangr 1981), sr conslt NatWest Markets 1996–; chm Fundraising Ctee Highbury Roundhouse 1978–81; *Publications* The Channel Tunnel - Before The Decision (1973), also author of five financial training books (1996); *Style*— Nigel Forrest, Esq; ✉ NatWest Markets, 135 Bishopsgate, London, EC2M 3UR (☎ 0171 648 3003, fax 01372 460176)

FORREST, Prof Sir (Andrew) Patrick McEwen; s of Rev Andrew James Forrest, BD (d 1962), and Isabella, *née* Pearson (d 1962); *b* 25 March 1923; *Educ* Dundee HS, Univ of St Andrews (BSc, MB ChB, ChM, MD); *m* 1, 1955, Margaret Beryl (d 1961), da of Capt Frederick Hall, MBE; 1 s (Andrew David b 27 Sept 1961), 1 da (Susan Catriona b 9 May 1959); m 2, 1964, Margaret Anne, da of Harold E Steward (d 1980); 1 da (Anne Elizabeth); *Career* Surgn Lt RNVR 1946–48; civilian conslt to RN (surgery res) 1977–88; prof of surgery Welsh Nat Sch of Med 1962–71, Regius prof of clinical surgery Univ of Edinburgh 1971–88 (prof emeritus and hon fell 1989–); visiting scientist Nat Institutes of Health (Bethesda) 1989–90, assoc dean (clinical studies) Int Med Coll Kuala Lumpur 1993–95, visiting prof Univ of Malaya 1995; memb: MRC 1976–80, Advsy Bd for Res Cncls 1982–85, Cncl RCSEd 1974–84; chief scientist Scottish Home and Health Dept (pt/t) 1981–87; pres: Surgical Res Soc 1974–76, Assoc of Surgns GB and I 1988–89; chm Govt Working Gp on breast cancer screening 1985–86; Lister Medal RCSEng 1987, Gold Medal Netherlands Assoc of Surgeons 1988, McKenzie-Davidson Medal Br Inst of Radiology 1988; Hon DSc: Univ of Wales, Chinese Univ of Hong Kong; Hon LLD Univ of Dundee; FRCS, FRCSEd, FRCSGlas, FIBiol, FRSE 1976, Hon FACS, FRACS, FRCSCan, FRCR; *Books* Prognostic Factors in Breast Cancer (jt ed 1968), Principles and Practice of Surgery (jtly 1985, 1990), Breast Cancer: The Decision to Screen (1990); *Recreations* golf, sailing; *Clubs* New (Edinburgh); *Style*— Prof Sir Patrick Forrest, FRSE; ✉ 19 St Thomas Road, Edinburgh EH9 2LR (☎ 0131 667 3203)

FORREST, Paul Esme Acton; s of Richard Acton Forrest (d 1994), of Ashcott, Somerset, and Lucille Muriel, *née* Knott; *b* 1 Jan 1943; *Educ* Dr Morgans GS, Univ of Southampton; *m* 29 April 1967, Josephine Anne, da of Gp Capt John Enfield Kirk, OBE, of Winscombe, N Somerset; 2 s (Richard b 1975, James b 1977), 1 da (Charlotte b 1980); *Career* admitted slr 1971, called to the Bar Gray's Inn 1979; HM Coroner Dist of Avon; *Recreations* golf, fishing, jazz; *Clubs* Burnham and Berrow Golf, The Clifton, The County; *Style*— Paul Forrest, Esq; ✉ Springhead Farm, Upper Langford BS18 7DN; The Coroner's Court, Backfields, Bristol BS2 8QP

FORREST, Dr (Alexander) Robert Walker; s of Alexander Muir Forrest, of Boston, Lincolnshire, and Rose Ellen, *née* Ringham (d 1976); *b* 5 July 1947; *Educ* Stamford Sch, Univ of Edinburgh (BSc, MB ChB); *m* (sep), Teresa Anne, da of Albert E Booth, of Sheffield; 2 s (Michael b 1981, David b 1984); *Career* conslt chem pathologist Royal Hallamshire Hosp 1981–, hon lectr in forensic toxicology Univ of Sheffield 1985– (clinical lectr in human metabolism and clinical biochemistry 1981–), asst dep coroner South Yorkshire (West) 1988–91 and 1993– (dep coroner 1991–93); visiting prof in forensic toxicology Univ of Bradford 1996–; hon sec Cncl Forensic Science Soc; FRSC 1985, FRCPE 1989, FRCPath 1992 (MRCPath 1980), FRCP 1992; LLM 1993; *Recreations* computers, books; *Style*— Dr Robert Forrest; ✉ 3 Betjeman Gardens, Sheffield S10 3FW (☎ 0114 266 9769, e-mail aF45@Dial.pipex.com); Royal Hallamshire Hospital, Sheffield S10 2JF (☎ 0114 271 2199)

FORREST, Prof (Archibald) Robin; s of Samuel Forrest (d 1982), of Edinburgh, and Agnes Dollar, *née* Robin; *b* 13 May 1943; *Educ* Daniel Stewart's Coll Edinburgh, Univ of Edinburgh (BSc), Trinity Coll Cambridge (PhD); *m* 7 April 1973, Rosemary Ann, da of Ralph Kenneth Foster (d 1983), of Grantham, Lincs; 1 s (Matthew b 1975), 1 da (Susanna b 1977); *Career* asst dir res Computer Laboratory Cambridge Univ 1971–74 (tech offr Engrg Dept 1968–71); visiting prof: Syracuse Univ NY 1971–72, Univ of Utah 1979, Univ of São Paulo 1996; visiting expert Beijing Inst of Aeronautics and Astronautics 1979, prof of computing sci UEA 1980– (reader in computing studies 1974–80), visiting scientist Xerox Palo Alto Res Centre 1982–83; CEng, CMath, FBCS, FIMA 1978; *Recreations* collecting wine, reading maps; *Style*— Prof Robin Forrest; ✉ 3 Highlands, Folgate Lane, Old Costessey, Norwich, Norfolk NR8 5EA (☎ 01603 742315); University of East Anglia, School of Information Systems, University Plain, Norwich, Norfolk NR4 7TJ (☎ 01603 592605, fax 01603 593344)

FORREST, Rear Adm Sir Ronald Stephen; KCVO (1975), JP (Honiton 1978), DL (Devon 1985); s of Dr Stephen Forrest (d 1957), of Edinburgh, and Maud M McKinstry; *b* 11 Jan 1923; *Educ* Belhaven Hill, RNC Dartmouth; *m* 1, 1947, Patricia (d 1966), da of Dr E N Russell, of Alexandria, Egypt; 2 s, 1 da; m 2, 1967, June, wid of Lt G Perks, RN, and da of L W Weaver (d 1945), of Budleigh Salterton; 1 step s, 1 step da; *Career* RN: serv at sea 1940–72, dir Seamen Offrs Appts 1968, CO HMS London 1970, Def Serv sec 1972–75, Rear Adm 1972; co cmmr St John Ambulance Bde Devon 1976–81, cdr St John Ambulance Devon 1981–87, pres Devon Co Agric Assoc 1990; KStJ; *Clubs* Naval, Army & Navy; *Style*— Rear Adm Sir Ronald Forrest, KCVO, JP, DL; ✉ Higher Seavington, Stockland, Honiton, Devon EX14 9DE

FORRESTER, David Michael; s of Reginald Grant Forrester (d 1970), of London, and Minnie, *née* Chaytow (d 1985); *b* 22 June 1944; *Educ* St Paul's Sch, King's Coll Cambridge (MA), Kennedy Sch of Govt Harvard Univ (Kennedy Meml scholar); *m* 1, Diana, *née* Douglas; m 2, Helen Mary Williams, *née* Myatt; 1 s (James b 1983), 1 da (Natasha b 1986); *Career* DES (now DFEE): joined as asst princ 1967, various positions incl private sec to Parly Under Sec of State Lord Belstead and princ 1967–76; princ HM Treasy 1976–78, asst sec DES 1979–85, asst sec DTI 1985–87, under sec DFEE 1988–95, dir Further Educn and Youth Trg DFEE 1995–; *Clubs* Pretenders; *Style*— David Forrester, Esq; ✉ Department for Education and Employment, Sanctuary Buildings, Great Smith Street, London SW1P 3BT (☎ 0171 925 5800, fax 0171 925 5379)

FORRESTER, Rev Prof Duncan Baillie; s of William Roxburgh Forrester, MC, and Isobel Margaret Stewart, *née* McColl; *b* 10 Nov 1933; *Educ* Madras Coll St Andrews, Univ of St Andrews (MA), Univ of Chicago, Univ of Edinburgh (BD), Univ of Sussex (DPhil); *m* 9 June 1964, Rev Margaret Rae, da of William R McDonald; 1 s (Donald McColl b 1966), 1 da (Catriona McAskill b 1968); *Career* pt/t asst in politics Univ of Edinburgh 1957–58, asst min Hillside Church Edinburgh and leader St James Mission 1960–61, Church of Scotland missionary, lectr and then prof of politics Madras Christian Coll Tambaram S India 1962–70; ordained presbyter Church of S India 1962; pt/t lectr in politics Univ of Edinburgh 1966–67, chaplain and lectr in politics Univ of Sussex 1970–78; Univ of Edinburgh: prof of christian ethics and practical theol 1978–, princ New Coll 1986–96, dean Faculty of Divinity 1996–; chm Edinburgh Cncl of Social Serv 1983–86; memb: World Cncl of Churches Faith and Order Cmmn 1983–, Policy Ctee Scottish Cncl of Voluntary Orgns 1986–89; dir Centre for Theology and Public Issues 1984–; pres: Soc for the Study of Theology 1991–93, Soc for the Study of Christian Ethics 1991–94; *Books* Caste & Christianity (1980), Encounter with God (co-author, 1983), Studies in the History of Worship in Scotland (co-ed, 1984), Christianity and the Future of Welfare (1985), Theology and Politics (1988), Just Sharing (co-author, 1988), Beliefs, Values and Policies (1989), Worship Now Book II (co-ed, 1989), Theology and Practice (1990), Christian Justice and Public Policy (1997); *Recreations* hill walking, reading, listening to music; *Style*— The Rev Prof Duncan Forrester; ✉ 25 Kingsburgh Road, Edinburgh EH12 6DZ (☎ 0131 337 5646); University of Edinburgh, New College, The Mound, Edinburgh EH1 2LX (☎ 0131 650 8951)

FORRESTER, His Hon Judge; Giles Charles Fielding; s of Basil Thomas Charles Forrester (d 1981), and Diana Florence, *née* Sandeman; *b* 18 Dec 1939; *Educ* Rugby, Trinity Coll Oxford (MA); *m* 29 Oct 1966, Georgina Elizabeth, *née* Garnett; 1 s (Edward Charles b 7 Feb 1969), 1 da (Emily Rachel b 31 Aug 1971); *Career* account exec Pritchard Wood and Partners (advtg agents) 1962–66, memb HAC Inf Bn 1963–67 (veteran 1994–), called to the Bar Inner Temple 1966, in practice SE Circuit, recorder 1986, circuit judge (SE Circuit) 1986–; pres HAC RFC 1994–; *Clubs* Roehampton, Royal Western Yacht, St Enedoc Golf, New Zealand Golf (Weybridge); *Style*— His Hon Judge Forrester; ✉ c/o Central Criminal Court, Old Bailey, London EC4M 7EH

FORRESTER, Helen; *b* 6 June 1919, Hoylake, Cheshire; *Educ* privately, Liverpool Evening Schs; *Career* Canadian citizen, resident Canada 1953–, freelance writer 1955–; writer-in-residence: Lethbridge Community Coll 1980, Edmonton Public Library 1990; contrib: Government of Alberta Heritage Magazine, book reviews Canadian Author & Bookman and Edmonton Jl; patron Chester Literature Festival (UK); Hudson's Bay Beaver Award 1970 and 1977, honoured for distinguished contrib to lit and to the life of The City of Edmonton 1977, Govt of Alberta Award for Lit 1979, YWCA Woman of the Arts 1987; Hon DLitt: Univ of Liverpool 1988, Univ of Alberta 1993; memb: Writers' Union of Canada, Soc of Authors London, Canadian Assoc of Children's Authors, Illustrators and Performers (CANSCAIP), The Authors' Lending and Copyrights Soc Ltd London; *Books* Alien There Is None (novel, 1959, republished as Thursday's Child, 1985), The Latchkey Kid (novel, 1971), Twopence To Cross The Mersey (autobiography, 1974), Most Precious Employee (as June Edwards, novel, 1976), Minerva's Stepchild (autobiography, 1979, retitled Liverpool Miss 1982), Liverpool Daisy (novel, 1979), Anthology 80 (collection of Alberta writings as fiction ed, 1979), By The Waters of Liverpool (autobiography, 1981), The Suicide Tower (short story, 1981), Three Women of Liverpool (novel, 1984), Lime Street At Two (autobiography, 1985, Alberta Culture's Literary Award 1986), A Matter of Friendship (short story, 1986), The Moneylenders of Shahpur (novel, 1987), Yes, Mama (novel, 1987, Writers' Guild Fiction Award 1989), The Lemon Tree (novel, 1990), The Liverpool Basque (novel, 1993), Mourning Doves (novel, 1996); *Recreations* reading, travel; *Clubs* Univ of Alberta Faculty; *Style*— Ms Helen Forrester; ✉ c/o Ms Vivien Green, Sheil Land Associates Ltd, 43 Doughty St, London WC1N 2LF (☎ 0171 405 9351, fax 0171 831 2127)

FORRESTER, Ian Stewart; QC (Scot 1988); s of Alexander Roxburgh Forrester (d 1976), of Glasgow, and Elizabeth Richardson, *née* Stewart (d 1947); *b* 13 Jan 1945; *Educ* Kelvinside Acad Glasgow, Univ of Glasgow (MA, LLB), Tulane Univ of Louisiana New Orleans (MCL); *m* 7 March 1981, Sandra Anne Thérèse, da of M C Keegan, of Jefferson, Louisiana; 2 s (Alexander Stewart Daigle b 24 Sept 1982, James Roxburgh b 29 May 1985); *Career* with Maclay Murray & Spens 1968–69, Davis Polk & Wardwell 1969–72 (admitted Faculty of Advocates 1972), Cleary Gottlieb Steen & Hamilton 1972–81 (admitted Bar State of NY 1977), estab ind chambers Brussels (with Christopher Norall) 1981 (now known as Forrester Norall & Sutton), practising before Euro Cmmn and Court; chm: Br Cons Assoc in Belgium 1982–86, Euro Trade Law Assoc 1987–; hon visiting prof in Euro law Univ of Glasgow 1991–; memb: Euro Advsy Bd Tulane Univ Law Sch, UK Assoc for Euro Law, American Bar Assoc, Int Bar Assoc, The Stair Soc; *Publications* The German Civil Code (1975), The German Commercial Code (1979), author of numerous articles and chapters on EEC law and policy in The Oxford Yearbook of European Law, International Antitrust Law, The European Law Review, The Common Market Law Review; *Recreations* politics, wine, cooking, restoring old houses; *Clubs* Athenaeum, International Château Sainte-Anne (Brussels), Royal Yacht of Belgium; *Style—* Ian Forrester, Esq, QC; ✉ 73 Square Marie-Louise, 1000 Brussels, Belgium; 1 Place Madou, Box 34, 1210 Brussels, Belgium (☎ 00 32 2 2191620, fax 00 32 2 2191626, telex 23190)

FORRESTER, Prof Peter Garnett; CBE (1981); s of Arthur Forrester (d 1949), of Cheshire, and Emma, *née* Garnett (d 1962); *b* 7 June 1917; *Educ* Manchester GS, Univ of Manchester (BSc, MSc); *m* 1942, Marjorie Hewitt, da of Robert Berks (d 1940), of Staffs; 2 da (Patricia b 1945, Claire b 1954); *Career* metallurgist; Royal Aircraft Estab Farnborough, Tin Research Inst; chief metallurgist Glacier Metal Co 1948–63; conslt John Tyzack & Ptnrs 1963–66; dir Cranfield Sch of Mgmnt 1967–82; Cranfield Inst of Technol: prof of industl mgmnt 1966–82, pro-vice chllr, emeritus prof 1983–; dir: Jackson Taylor International Group Ltd 1984–88, Faculties Partnership Ltd; chm Rye and Winchelsea Nat Tst Centre 1991–93; Hon DSc Cranfield 1983; Burnham medal 1979; FIM, CIMgt, FRSA; *Recreations* research, writing, gardening, walking, sailing; *Style—* Prof Peter Forrester, CBE; ✉ Strawberry Hole Cottage, Ewhurst Lane, Northiam, nr Rye, E Sussex TN31 6HJ (☎ 01797 252255)

FORSTER, Alan Roger; s of Harold Edgar Forster (d 1979), and Annie Dorothy, *née* Wenham; *b* 27 Oct 1933; *Educ* Eastbourne GS; *m* 1, 1956, Diana, da of Herbert Raymond Love; 1 s (Paul b 1957), 1 da (Emma b 1966); m 2, 1979, Valerie, da of James Fisk; *Career* chm: Booker Overseas Trading Ltd, Bookers Sugar Co Ltd; *Recreations* watching football and cricket; *Clubs* MCC; *Style—* Alan R Forster, Esq; ✉ Little Ridge, Chislehurst Rd, Chislehurst, Kent BR7 5LD (☎ 0181 467 1094, 0181 467 3684); Bookers Sugar Co Ltd, 21/24 Chiswell Street, London EC1Y 4SH (☎ 0171 628 1511, fax 0171 628 1535)

FORSTER, Sir Archibald William; kt (1987); s of William Henry Forster (d 1955), and Matilda (d 1969); *b* 11 Feb 1928; *Educ* Tottenham GS, Univ of Birmingham (BSc); *m* 1954, Betty Margaret, da of Edgar Norman Channing (d 1984); 3 da (Nicola b 1959, Jacqueline b 1961, Amanda b 1967); *Career* RAF (FO) 1949–51; chm Esso Pension Trust 1980–93, chief exec Esso Petroleum Co Ltd 1980–93; chm and chief exec: Esso UK plc 1983–93, Esso Exploration and Production UK Ltd 1983–93; non-exec dir: Midland Bank plc 1986–, Rover Group plc 1986–88, Trafalgar House plc 1992–96, United News & Media plc (formerly United Newspapers) 1993–96; exec memb Bd Lloyd's Register of Shipping 1981–94, memb Monopolies and Mergers Cmmn; FEng 1983; *Recreations* work; *Style—* Sir Archibald Forster, FEng; ✉ Grasmere, Easton, Winchester SO21 1EG (☎ 01962 779267, fax 01962 779902)

FORSTER, John Henry Knight; s of Henry Knight Forster, MBE, of Salcombe, Devon, and Margaret Rutherford, *née* Metcalf (decd); bro of Robert Anthony Forster, *qv*; *b* 14 Feb 1941; *Educ* Dean Close Cheltenham; *m* 1, 1965 (m dis 1985), Hilary; 1 s (Gregory b 9 April 1969), 2 da (Heidi b 7 April 1966, Hayley b 12 July 1967); m 2, 1986, Carol Ann, da of Arthur Lamond (decd); *Career* dir: Bonser Engineering Ltd 1984–89, Lansing Bagnall Ltd 1981–89, Hart Ventures plc 1989–, Precoat International plc 1995–, Color Steels Ltd 1978–, Elvetham Hall Ltd 1981–, Kaye Enterprises Ltd 1989–, Pegasus Holdings plc 1986–, Pegasus Retirement Homes plc 1979–, Kaye Office Supplies Ltd 1989–, Kingfield Wholesale Office Supplies Ltd 1983–, Industrial Modernisation Ltd 1982–, Pegasus Court Management Ltd 1992–, Planmatics plc 1991–, 25 St James's Place Management Ltd 1992–; chm: Pool & Sons (Hartley Wintney) Ltd 1979–, St Michael's Hospice (North Hampshire) 1993–; FCA 1976 (ACA 1965), FCT 1981; *Recreations* country pursuits, mycology; *Style—* John H K Forster, Esq; ✉ The Lady Calthorpe Room, Elvetham, Hampshire RG27 8BB (☎ 01252 842381); Precoat International plc, Hart House, Hartley Wintney, Hampshire RG27 8PE (☎ 01252 843811, fax 01252 845266)

FORSTER, Margaret; da of Arthur Gordon Forster, and Lilian, *née* Hind; *b* 25 May 1938; *Educ* Somerville Coll Oxford; *m* 1960, (Edward) Hunter Davies, *qv*; 1 s, 2 da; *Career* author; *Books* incl: Dames's Delight (1964), Georgy Girl (1965), Elizabeth Barrett Browning (1988), Have the Men Had Enough? (1989), Daphne du Maurier (1993), Hidden Lives (1995), Shadow Baby (1996); *Style—* Miss Margaret Forster; ✉ 11 Boscastle Rd, London NW5

FORSTER, Neil Milward; s of Norman Milward Forster, and Olive Christina, *née* Cockrell; bro of Sir Oliver Forster, KCMG, LVO, *qv*; *b* 29 May 1927; *Educ* Hurstpierpoint, Pembroke Coll Cambridge (BA); *m* 1954, Barbara Elizabeth Smith; 1 s, 2 da; *Career* dir: Clan Line Steamers 1967 (joined 1952), British & Commonwealth Shipping Co 1974–78, British and Commonwealth Holdings plc 1974–88 (gp md 1982–86); chm Air UK Group Ltd 1982–; chm: Calcutta Liners Conf 1962–66, Europe/SA Shipping Confs 1977–87, UK/SA Trade Assoc 1985–87; *Style—* Neil Forster, Esq; ✉ The Orchard, Upper Slaughter, Cheltenham, Glos GL54 2JB

FORSTER, Sir Oliver Grantham; KCMG (1983, CMG 1976), LVO (1961); 2 s of Norman Milward Forster, and Olive Christina, *née* Cockrell; bro of Neil Milward Forster, *qv*; *b* 2 Sept 1925; *Educ* Hurstpierpoint, King's Coll Cambridge; *m* 1953; 2 da; *Career* HM Dip Serv: Cwlth Rels Office 1951, 1 sec Madras 1959, and Washington 1962, min Br High Cmmn New Delhi 1975, asst under sec of state and dep chief clerk FCO 1975–79, ambass Pakistan 1979–84; *Style—* Sir Oliver Forster, KCMG, LVO; ✉ The White House, 71 Raglan Road, Reigate, Surrey

FORSTER, (A) Paul; s of Alfred Forster (d 1965), of Reading, and Dorothy Forster (d 1984); *b* 19 Feb 1942; *Educ* Stoneham Sch Reading, Univ of Nottingham (BA); *m* 1965, Patricia, *née* Hammond; 2 da (Simone b 19 Sept 1968, Eleanor b 1 Oct 1971); *Career* mktg exec; Cadbury Schweppes Plc 1962–72: gen mangr Retail CTN Stores, mktg mangr confectionary Count Line Market; ptnr Lippa Newton Ltd (advtg agency) 1972–74, KMPH Group Plc 1974–77 (md PLN Partners Ltd), Saatchi & Saatchi Group Plc 1977–79 (md Roe Downton Ltd); Euro RSCG (formerly Colman RSCG Group) 1979–94: md until 1988, chief exec and chm communications group of companies 1988–94; non-exec dir N Brown Group plc 1993–, chm and chief exec Lifetime Business Group 1994–, non-exec dir Int Performance Textiles Group Ltd 1996–; visiting prof Nottingham Business Sch and memb Bd of Govrs Nottingham Trent Univ 1993–; MIPA, MInstM; *Recreations* tennis; *Clubs* Reform, Vanderbilt; *Style—* Prof Paul Forster; (☎ 01494 793326, fax 01494 783804)

FORSTER, Rt Rev Peter Robert; *see:* Chester, Bishop of

FORSTER, Robert Anthony; s of Capt Henry Knight Forster, MBE, of Salcombe, S Devon, and late Margaret Rutherford, *née* Metcalf; bro of John Henry Knight Forster, *qv*; *b* 26 July 1945; *Educ* Llandaff Cathedral Sch Llandaff, Dean Close Sch Cheltenham; *m* 12 Sept 1970, Christine Elizabeth, da of Frederick William Milward, of Cardiff; 1 da (Annabel b 16 May 1973); *Career* accountant 1964–74: EM Manufacturing Co Ltd, Western Mail & Echo Ltd, Standard Telephone & Cables Ltd, Aeroquip UK Ltd; md Biomet Ltd 1974–; memb Cncl Cardiff C of C (former pres); memb Ctee: IOD Wales Div (former sec), CIMA S Wales Branch (former sec, chm, pres); chm ETEOP (Enterprise Agency); dir S Glamorgan TEC, govr Barry Coll; FCMA 1973, FInstD 1977; *Recreations* travel, gardening, fine arts, flying (PPL); *Style—* Robert Forster, Esq; ✉ 7 Duffryn Crescent, Peterston Super Ely, South Glamorgan CF5 6NF (☎ 01446 760162); BIOMET Ltd, Waterton Industrial Estate, Bridgend CF31 3XA (☎ 01656 655221, fax 01656 645454, telex 497920)

FORSYTH, Alastair Elliott; s of Maj Henry Russell Forsyth (d 1941), and Marie Elaine, *née* Greensmith (d 1958); *b* 23 Oct 1932; *Educ* Christ's Hosp, Keble Coll Oxford (MA); *m* 21 July 1973, Margaret Christine, da of Maj Royston Ivor Vallance, of Weasenham St Peter, nr King's Lynn Norfolk; 4 s (Angus b 1963, Jamie b 1966, Alexander b 1975, John b 1978); 1 da (Arethusa b 1980); *Career* banker; dir J Henry Schroder Wagg & Co Ltd 1982–92, advsr Latin America 1992–, dir CASA Consultores Asociados Sur Americanos; Orden del Libertador Venezuela 1996; *Recreations* Colombian and Venezuelan history; *Clubs* Sloane; *Style—* Alastair Forsyth, Esq; ✉ The Gardens, Hoxne, Eye, Suffolk AP21 5AP

FORSYTH, Dr Angela; da of James Robert Forsyth, of Abbeyfield House, Malmesbury, Wilts, and Mary, *née* Fennell (d 1994); *b* 5 Feb 1945; *Educ* St Anne's Convent GS Southampton, Univ of Glasgow (MB ChB); *m* 24 June 1975, Robert Andrew Marshall, s of Andrew Gardner Marshall (d 1995), of Dalbeattie, Kirkudbrightshire; 1 s (Alasdair b July 1980), 2 da (Jane b June 1977, Ruth b Dec 1982); *Career* conslt dermatologist Gtr Glasgow Health Bd 1979, hon clinical sr lectr Univ of Glasgow 1980; author of pubns on methods of measurement of skin reactions by instruments; memb Ctee Br Contact Dermatitis Gp; FRCPG 1985; *Recreations* music, gardening, cooking, needlework; *Style—* Dr Angela Forsyth; ✉ Contact Dermatitis Investigation Unit, Glasgow Royal Infirmary University NHS Trust, Glasgow G4 0SF (☎ 0141 211 4510)

FORSYTH, Bruce Joseph (né Forsyth-Johnson); s of John Frederick Forsyth-Johnson (d 1961), and Florence Ada Forsyth-Johnson (d 1957); *b* 22 Feb 1928; *Educ* Latimer Sch Edmonton; *m* 1, 1951, Olivia, da of Calvert, of NI; 3 da (Debbie b 1955, Julie b 1958, Laura b 1964); m 2, 24 Dec 1973, Anthea, da of Bernard Redfern, of Torquay; 2 da (Charlotte b 1976, Louisa b 1977); m 3, 15 Jan 1983, Wilnelia, da of Enrique Merced, of Puerto Rico; 1 s (Jonathan Joseph b 1986); *Career* entertainer and television host; *Theatre* Little Me (original Br prodn) 1964, Travelling Music Show 1978, One Man Show (Winter Garden NY 1979, Huntington Hartford Los Angeles 1979, London Palladium); numerous extensive tours UK, NZ and Aust; *Television* incl: Sunday Night at the London Palladium 1958–63, Piccadilly Spectaculars, Bruce Forsyth Show (ATV), The Generation Game (BBC, 1971–77 and 1990–94), Bruce's Big Night (LWT) 1978, Play Your Cards Right 1980–87 (ten series) and 1994–, Slingers Day (Thames) 1985–86, Hollywood or Bust 1984, You Bet! (LWT) 1987–89, Takeover Bid (BBC) 1990–91, Bruce's Guest Night (BBC) 1992–93, Bruce's Price is Right 1996; numerous specials incl: Bring on the Girls (Thames) 1976, Bruce and More Girls (Thames) 1977, Bruce Meets the Girls, The Forsyth Follies, Sammy and Bruce (with Sammy Davis Jr), The Entertainers (with Rita Moreno), The Muppet Show, The Mating Season, The Canterville Ghost; *Films* Star 1968, Can Heironymous Merkin Ever Forgive Mercy Humppe and Find True Happiness 1969, Bedknobs and Broomsticks 1971, The Seven Deadly Sins 1971, Pavlova 1984; *Awards* Daily Mirror National TV Award 1961, Variety Club Showbusiness Personality of the Year 1975, The Sun TV Personality of the Year 1976 and 1977, TV Times Favourite Male TV Personality 1975, 1976 and 1977, TV Times Favourite Game Show Host 1984, BBC TV Personality of the Year 1991, Lifetime Achievement Award for Variety 1995; *Recreations* golf, tennis; *Clubs* Tramp, Crockfords; *Style—* Bruce Forsyth, Esq; ✉ Bruce Forsyth Enterprises Ltd, Straidarran, Wentworth Drive, Virginia Water, Surrey GU25 4NY (☎ and fax 01344 84 4056)

FORSYTH, James Law; s of Richard Forsyth (d 1970), of Glasgow, and Jessie, *née* Law (d 1967); *b* 5 March 1913; *Educ* HS of Glasgow, The Glasgow Art Sch (Dip); *m* 1, 1938 (m dis 1945), Helen Stewart; 2 s (Antony b 1940, Richard b 1948); m 2, 5 Aug 1955, Dorothy Louise Tibble (d 1983); *Career* Mil Serv 1940–46: trained Scots Gds Chelsea, cmmnd 2 Monmouthshire Regt S Wales Borderers, Capt Signals Inf (serv Normandy, NW Euro Theatre), Adj Italy (decorated for gallantry 1946); artist; exhibitions 1934–35, designer GPO film unit 1936–40, illustrator Basic Eng Project 1936–40, Sussex annual exhibitions 1981–96; playwright, active serv and writing 1940–46; resident playwright Old Vic Theatre 1946–49; poetry incl: Poetry in Wartime (1942), The War Poets (1945); collections of poems: On the Sussex Days - On Such A Day As This (1989), From Time to Time (1990), A Woman There Will Be (love poems, 1991); stage plays incl: The Medicine Man 1950, Heloise 1951, The Other Heart 1952, The Pier 1958, Trog 1959, Emmanuel 1960, Defiant Island 1961, Dear Wormwood 1965, If My Wings Heal 1966, Lobsterback 1975, One Candle 1994, The Bridge Between 1994; TV plays incl: The English Boy 1969, Four Triumphant 1969, The Last Journey 1972, The Old Man's Mountain 1972; radio plays incl: The Bronze Horse 1948, Christophe 1958, Every Pebble on the Beach 1962, When the Snow Lay Round About 1978, Fifteen Strings of Cash 1979, The Threshing Floor 1982; also author of Back to the Barn (a history of barn theatre) 1986; visiting prof of drama: Howard 1962, Tufts Univ 1963, Florida State Univ 1964; memb: Exec Ctee League of Dramatists 1950–75, Theatres Advsy Cncl 1962–67, Soc of Sussex Authors 1970–96 (chm 1988–92); dir Tufts in London, overseas drama programme Tufts Univ Mass 1967–71; artistic dir Forsyth's Barn Theatre Sussex 1971–83; awarded Civil List Pension for Servs to Lit 1984; memb Soc of Authors 1946; Bronze Cross Netherlands 1946; *Recreations* walking, gardening, music, reading; *Style—* James Forsyth, Esq; ✉ Grainloft, Ansty, West Sussex RH17 5AG (☎ 01444 413 345)

FORSYTH, John Howard; s of George Howard Forsyth, MBE (d 1980), of Cartmel, Cumbria, and Marjorie Christine, *née* Cook; *b* 23 Aug 1945; *Educ* Oundle, St John's Coll Cambridge; *m* 19 Sept 1968, Barbara, da of Major C G G Cook, of Ockbrook, Derbyshire; 2 s (Mark b 1977, James b 1980), 1 da (Alicia b 1975); *Career* chief economist Morgan Grenfell & Co Ltd 1973, gp dir Morgan Grenfell & Co Ltd 1988–91 (dir 1979–88); affiliated lectr Univ of Cambridge 1992–; *Recreations* books, country pursuits; *Style—* John Forsyth, Esq; ✉ 38 Well Walk, London NW3 1BX (☎ 0171 794 3523)

FORSYTH, Michael Bruce; PC (1995), MP (C) Stirling (majority 703); s of John Tawse Forsyth, and Mary Watson; *b* 16 Oct 1954; *Educ* Arbroath HS, Univ of St Andrews (MA); *m* 1977, Susan Jane, da of John Bryan Clough; 1 s, 2 da; *Career* nat chm Fedn of Cons Students 1976, memb Westminster City Cncl 1978–83, MP (C) Stirling 1983–; PPS to Foreign Sec 1986–87, Parly under sec of state Scottish Office 1987–90; min of state: Scottish Office 1990–92, Dept of Employment 1992–94, Home Office 1994–95; sec of state for Scotland 1995–; chm Scottish Cons Pty 1989–90; *Recreations* mountaineering, gardening, photography, astronomy; *Style—* The Rt Hon Michael Forsyth, MP; ✉ House of Commons, London SW1A 0AA

FORSYTH, Dr Michael Graham de Jong; s of Eric Forsyth, of Wallasey, Merseyside, and Lucy Rebecca, *née* de Jong; *b* 26 Nov 1951; *Educ* Univ of Liverpool Sch of Architecture (BA, BArch), British School at Rome, Univ of Bristol (PhD); *m* 18 Sept 1985, Vera, da of Nicos Papaxanthou, of Nicosia, Cyprus; 1 s (James b 28 Sept 1983), 2 da (Antonia b 18 Dec 1985, Henrietta b 18 March 1988); *Career* architectural practice Toronto Canada 1976–79, res fell Univ of Bristol 1984–90 (lectr 1979–84), dir Plato Consortium Ltd Bath 1985–, ptnr Forsyth Chartered Architects Bath 1987–, sr visiting lectr Univ of Bath 1996–; awarded: Rome Scholarship in Architecture 1975, nineteenth annual ASCAP Deems Taylor award for books on music; many articles reviews and radio bdcasts; memb: Selection Board British School at Rome 1987–93, Renovations Ctee Bath Preservation Tst 1989–, Exec Ctee Friends of Bristol Art Gallery 1985–90, Exec Ctee Friends of Victoria Art Gallery Bath 1994– (chm 1995–); hon sec Soc of Rome Scholars 1984–89; RIBA 1979, ARCUK 1979; *Books* Buildings for Music: The Architect, the Musician, and the Listener from the Seventeenth Century to the Present Day (1985), Auditoria: Designing for the Performing Arts (1987); *Recreations* the violin, cross-country running; *Clubs* Chelsea Arts; *Style*— Dr Michael Forsyth; ✉ Oakwood, Bathwick Hill, Bath BA2 6EQ

FORSYTH OF THAT ILK, Alistair Charles William; JP (Angus); Chief of the Name and Clan of Forsyth, Baron of Ethie (territorial); s of Capt Charles Forsyth of Strathendry, FCA (d 1981), and Ella Millicent Hopkins (d 1983); *b* 7 Dec 1929; *Educ* St Paul's Sch; *m* 1958, Ann, OStJ, da of Col Percy Arthur Hughes, IA (d 1950); 4 s; *Career* cmmnd The Queen's Bays (2 Dragoon Gds) 1948–50; dir and chm of cos; Freeman of the City of London, Liveryman Worshipful Co of Scriveners; CStJ, Kt of the Equestrian Order of the Holy Sepulchre 1992; *Recreations* hill walking, Scottish antiquities; *Clubs* Cavalry and Guards', New (Edinburgh); *Style*— Alistair Forsyth of that Ilk, JP; ✉ Ethie Castle, by Arbroath, Angus

FORSYTHE, Clifford James; MP (UUP) Antrim South (majority 24,559); *b* 1929; *Career* former professional footballer Linfield and Derry City, plumbing and heating contractor, Mayor of Newtownabbey 1982–83, memb NI Assembly 1982–86; MP (UUP) Antrim S 1983–, vice-chm Health & Social Servs Ctee, memb Select Ctee on Social Security 1991–, Parly spokesman on tport, communications and local govt; fell Indust and Parly Tst, pres NI section of Inst of Plumbing, chm Chest, Heart and Stroke Assoc Glengormley branch; *Style*— Clifford Forsythe Esq, MP; ✉ House of Commons, London SW1A 0AA (☎ 0171 219 4144); constituency office: 19 Fountain St, Antrim BT41 4BG (☎ 018494 60776)

FORSYTHE, Prof (John) Malcolm; s of Dr John Walter Joseph Forsythe (d 1988), and Dr Charlotte Constance Forsythe, *née* Beatty (d 1981); *b* 11 July 1936; *Educ* Repton, Guy's Med Sch London Univ (BSc, MB BS, MRCS, DObstRCOG), Univ of N Carolina, London Sch Hygiene and Tropical Med Univ of London (MSc); *m* 1, 28 Oct 1961 (m dis 1984), Delia Kathleen, da of late Dr J K Moore; 1 s (Marcus John Malcolm b 30 Sept 1965), 3 da (Suzanne Delia b 9 July 1962, Nicola Kathleen (twin) b 9 July 1962, Sarah Louise b 16 May 1969); m 2, 27 Jan 1985, Patricia Mary Murden, *née* Barnes; *Career* house surgn Guy's 1961–62, house offr Farnborough 1962, house physician Lewisham 1962–63, GP Beckenham 1963–65, MO Birmingham Regnl Hosp Bd 1965–68, princ asst sr admin med offr Wessex RHB 1968–72, dep sr admin offr SE Met RHB 1972–73 (acting sr admin offr 1973–74), area MO Kent AHA 1974–78; regnl MO SE Thames RHA 1978–89 (dir of planning 1983–89), regnl MO and dir of Public Health and Serv Devpt SE Thames RHA 1989–92; memb: Bd Public Health Laboratory Serv 1985–95, Bd of Mgmnt Horder Centre for Arthritis 1993–96, BUPA Ltd 1993–, Charitable Tst; dir Inst of Public Health 1990–91, prof of public health Univ of Kent Canterbury 1992–, sr lectr King's Coll Hosp Med Sch London 1992–; chm: GMC Working Party on assessment in public health med 1995–, Horder Centre for Arthritis 1996–; hon conslt in public health med Camberwell Health Authy 1992–; FFPHM, FRCP; *Recreations* tennis, ornithology; *Clubs* RSM, New Chasers; *Style*— Prof Malcolm Forsythe; ✉ Buckingham House, 1 Royal Chase, Tunbridge Wells TN4 8AX; Centre for Health Service Studies, George Allen Wing, The University, Canterbury, Kent CT2 7NF (☎ 01227 823681, fax 01227 827868, e-mail j.m.forsythe-2@ukc.ac.uk); Department of Public Health and Epidemiology, King's College School of Medicine and Dentistry, Bessemer Road, London SE5 9PJ (☎ 0171 346 4694, fax 0171 737 3556)

FORSYTHE, Max; *b* 2 May 1944, Staffordshire; *Educ* Newry GS NI, Belfast Coll of Art, London Coll of Printing; *m* Jane; 2 c; *Career* early career experience as art dir working at various advtg agencies incl Collett Dickenson Pearce; dir of various TV commercials and photographer (specialising in location and reportage photography for advtg indust) since 1972; campaign work for int accounts incl: Nike, Parker Pens, Bacardi, Teachers Whisky, P&O Cruises, Club Mediterranee, Bergasol, Hawaiin Tropic, Heineken, Iford, and car mfrs Audi, Mercedes, Citroen, Range Rover, Vauxhall, BMW, Rolls Royce; numerous awards for photography in UK, USA and Europe incl: 5 Silvers (D&AD), Bronze Lion for direction (Cannes); first one-man exhbn Hamiltons Gallery London 1984; work in the collections of RPS and Nat Museum of Photography; chm Assoc of Photographers 1994; *Style*— Max Forsythe, Esq; ✉ 120 Richmond Hill, Richmond, Surrey TW10 6RJ (☎ 0181 948 6888, fax 0181 332 1047)

FORT, HE Maeve Geraldine; CMG (1990); da of Frank Leslie Fort (d 1969), of Worleston, Nantwich, Cheshire, and Ruby Elizabeth, *née* Galbraith (d 1982); *b* 19 Nov 1940; *Educ* Nantwich and Acton GS, Trinity Coll Dublin (MA), Sorbonne Paris; *Career* joined Foreign Serv London 1963, UK Mission to UN NYC 1964–65, Cwlth Relations Office 1965–66, SEATO Bangkok 1966–68, Bonn 1968–71, Lagos 1971–73, second later first sec FCO 1973–78, UK Mission to UN NYC 1978–82, FCO 1982–83, RCDS 1983–84, head of Chancery and consul-gen Santiago Chile 1984–86, FCO and later additionally HM ambass (non-residential) Chad 1986–89, HM ambass Mozambique 1989–92, Lebanon 1992–Nov 1996, Br high cmmr South Africa Nov 1996–; *Style*— HE Miss Maeve Fort, CMG; ✉ c/o FCO (Cape Town), King Charles Street, London SW1A 2AH

FORTE, Baron (Life Peer UK 1982), of Ripley, Co Surrey; Sir Charles Forte; kt (1970); s of Rocco (Giovanni) Forte, of Monforte, Casalattico, Italy; *b* 26 Nov 1908; *Educ* Alloa Acad, Dumfries Coll, Mamiani Rome; *m* 1943, Irene Mary, da of Giovanni and Olga Chierico, of Venice; 1 s (Hon Rocco Forte, *qv*), 5 da (Hon Olga Polizzi, *qv* (who m 2, William Shawcross, *qv*), Hon Marie Louise (Hon Mrs Burness), Hon Irene (Hon Mrs Danilovich), Hon Giancarla (Hon Mrs Alen-Buckley), Hon Portia b 7 Feb 1964); *Career* Forte plc (formerly Trusthouse Forte plc, began as milk bar in Regent Street 1935): dep chm 1970–78, chief exec 1971–78, exec chm 1978–81, chm 1982–92, pres and non-exec dir 1993, ret 1996; hon consul-gen for San Marino; Hon DUniv Strathclyde 1992; Liveryman Worshipful Co of Horners; FRSA, FIMgt; *Books* Forte (autobiography, 1986); *Recreations* music, fencing, golf, fishing, shooting; *Clubs* Carlton, Caledonian, Royal Thames Yacht; *Style*— The Lord Forte; ✉ Lowndes House, Lowndes Place, London SW1X 8DB (☎ 0171 235 6244)

FORTE, Hon Sir Rocco John Vincent; kt (1995); o s of Baron Forte (Life Peer), *qv*; *b* 18 Jan 1945; *Educ* Downside, Pembroke Coll Oxford (MA); *m* 15 Feb 1986, Aliai, da of Prof Giovanni Ricci, of Rome; 1 s (Charles Giovanni b 6 Dec 1991), 2 da (Lydia Irene b 1987, Irene Alisea b 1988); *Career* former chm and chief exec Forte plc (formerly Trusthouse Forte plc) 1983–96 (chm 1993–96), subsequently estab Rocco Forte Associates; memb: Br Tourist Authy, Grand Cncl Hotel & Catering Benevolent Assoc; memb Worshipful Co of Bakers; FHCIMA, FCA, FInstD; Cavaliere Ufficiale of Order of Merit of the Italian Republic 1988; *Recreations* golf, fishing, shooting, running; *Style*— The Hon Sir Rocco Forte; ✉ office: 16 Lincoln's Inn Fields, London WC2A 3ED (☎ 0171 396 7474, fax 0171 396 7475)

FORTE DELLE MANDRIOLE, Marchese (Marquis of Mandriole, creation of the Republic of San Marino 1963, AD, and in year 1663 of the Republic) Olimpio; s of Francesco Forte (d 1940) and Maria Ciaraldi. Original founder of family: Angelo Forte di Lecce who was granted the title of Baron by Charles VIII, King of France, on 1st April 1485, in Naples. Giovanni Forte was among the first fifty people to be made a Knight of Justice of the Order of Constantine St George 19 March 1834; *b* 8 March 1918, Casalattico, Frosinone, Italy; *Educ* Casalattico; *m* 1948, Iolanda Dese (b in Scotland), da of Silviano Forte (d 1956); 1 s (heir, Francesco Pietro, m 1984, Rosalin Good; 1 s, Gino Olimpio b 1985), 1 da (Sandra Francesca Maria); *Career* Italian Army 1940–46, memb Allied Resistance Force Underground Movement, First Lt Italian Army 1945, Lt-Col Allied Resistance Forces IMOS 1947, DSC, IMOS (first class), Monte Cassino Cross, Combatant Partisan War Cross, isolated on Cassino Front, Knight Grand Cross Holy Sepulchure of Jerusalem, Grand Cordon of the Order of Polonia Restituta, Grand Cross Ordre of Merit Legion de Honor de la Republica de Cuba, Grand Croix de l'Ordre de l'Encouragement Public Français, Knight Sov Mil Order of Constantine of St George, Medaille d'Honneur d'Or de Société d'Encouragement au Progress, Knight Cdr Ordre du Merite Francais D'Outre Mer, Knight Cdr Royal Order of St Sava, Knight Sov Mil Order of Malta, Knight Cdr Italian Republic, Grand Cordon Sov Order of St Stanislas, Knight Order of St Gregory the Great, Grand Offr Royal Crown of Yugoslavia, (late King Peter of Yugoslavia) War Cross of the Royal Yugoslav Army 1941–45 and Sword of Honour, Mil Cross Virtuti Military (silver) Commemorative War Medal Dwight D Eisenhower 1939–45, Commemorative War Medal Gen George Patton 1944–45, Cert of Gratitude from Field Marshal Alexander 1939–45, Grand Cross of the Fed of Partisan 1939–45, Euro Cross, DDL Nat Univ of Canada 1947; financier; Institute des Relations Diplomatiques: Ordre du Merite Diplomatique; Medaille d'Or of Association Nationale Franco-Britannique, Etoile du Mérite Franco-Allié (of Union of Mérite Franco Alliés) 1939–45; landowner and dir of various cos; *Recreations* golf; *Style*— Marchese Forte delle Mandriole; ✉ Montforte, Cassalattico, Frosinone, Italy; Balsorano, 207 Cooden Drive, Bexhill On Sea, E Sussex TN40 1RE (☎ 01424 845306)

FORTESCUE, (John) Adrian; LVO (1972); s of Trevor Victor Norman Fortescue, CBE, and Margery Stratford Fortescue; *b* 16 June 1941; *Educ* Uppingham, King's Coll Cambridge (MA), LSE (Dip in Business Admin); *m* 1 (m dis 1988), Jillian, *née* Valpy; 1 s (James b 1966); m 2, 26 May 1989, Marie, *née* Wolfcarius; *Career* HM Dip Serv 1964–94; Lebanon 1964–65, Amman Jordan 1966–68, Paris 1968–72, Brussels 1973–75, Washington 1979–81, FCO London 1976–79 and 1981–82, Budapest 1983–84, on secondment to Euro Cmmn 1985–94; dep dir gen Euro Cmmn 1994–; Ordre du Mérite France 1972; *Style*— Adrian Fortescue, Esq; ✉ 44 Avenue Beau-Séjour, 1180 Brussels, Belgium (☎ 00 322 374 3810); Commission of the European Communities, 200 Rue De La Loi, 1049 Brussels, Belgium (☎ 00 322 295 5727)

FORTESCUE, 8 Earl (GB 1789); Charles Hugh Richard Fortescue; o s of 7 Earl Fortescue (d 1993), and his 1 w, Penelope Jane, *née* Henderson (d 1959); *b* 10 May 1951; *Educ* Eton; *m* 1974, Julia, er da of Air Cdre John Adam Sowrey; 3 da (Lady Alice Penelope b 8 June 1978, Lady Kate Eleanor b 25 Oct 1979, Lady Lucy Beatrice b 29 April 1983); *Heir* unc, Hon Martin Denzil Fortescue, *qv*; *Style*— The Rt Hon Earl Fortescue; ✉ House of Lords, London SW1A 0PW

FORTESCUE, Hon Martin Denzil; yr s of 6 Earl Fortescue, MC, TD (d 1977), and his 1 wife Marjorie Ellinor, OBE, *née* Trotter (d 1964); hp of nephew 8 Earl Fortescue; *b* 5 Jan 1924; *Educ* Eton; *m* 1, 23 April 1954, Prudence Louisa (d 1992), yr da of Sir Charles Samuel Rowley, 6 Bt, TD; 2 s, 2 da; m 2, 18 Nov 1994, Mrs Caroline Loftie, widow of W H P Loftie; *Career* Lt RN (Emergency List); FRICS; *Style*— The Hon Martin Fortescue; ✉ Wincombe Park, Shaftesbury, Dorset

FORTESCUE, The Hon Seymour Henry; s of 6 Earl Fortescue, MC, TD (d 1977), and his 2 w Hon Sybil Mary (d 1985), da of 3rd Viscount Hardinge; *b* 28 May 1942; *Educ* Eton, Trinity Coll Cambridge (MA), London Graduate Sch of Business Studies (MSc); *m* 1, 25 July 1966 (m dis 1990), Julia, o da of Sir John Arthur Pilcher GCMG (d 1990); 1 s (James Adrian b 10 April 1978), 1 da (Marissa Clare b 20 Oct 1973); m 2, 23 Aug 1990, Jennifer Ann Simon; 1 da (Alexandra Kate b 10 July 1991); *Career* chief exec Barclaycard 1982–85, dir UK Retail Servs Barclays Bank plc 1987–91 (gen mangr 1985–87), dir of finance and fundraising Imperial Cancer Research Fund 1991–96, chief exec Health Educn Authy 1996–; currently Second Warden Worshipful Co of Grocers; *Style*— The Hon Seymour Fortescue; ✉ 22 Clarendon St, London SW1V 4RF (☎ 0171 834 2146, fax 0171 413 2618)

FORTEVIOT, 4 Baron (UK 1917); Sir John James Evelyn Dewar; 4 Bt (UK 1907); er s of 3 Baron Forteviot, MBE, DL (d 1993), and Cynthia Monica, *née* Starkie (d 1986); *b* 5 April 1938; *Educ* Eton; *m* 17 Oct 1963, Lady Elisabeth Jeronima Waldegrave, 3 da of 12 Earl Waldegrave, KG, GCVO, TD, DL (d 1995); 1 s (Hon Alexander John Edward b 4 March 1971), 3 da (Hon Mary-Emma Jeroniima (Hon Mrs Adam Drummond) b 1 June 1965, Hon Miranda Phoebe b 1 March 1968, Hon Henrietta Cynthia b 27 Jan 1970); *Heir* s, Hon Alexander John Edward Dewar b 4 March 1971; *Clubs* Boodle's, Royal Perth Golfing Society; *Style*— The Rt Hon Lord Forteviot; ✉ Aberdalgie House, Perth PH2 0QD

FORTH, Rt Hon Eric; PC (1997), MP (C) Worcestershire Mid (majority 9,870); s of late William Forth, and Aileen Forth; *b* 9 Sept 1944; *Educ* Jordanhill Coll Sch Glasgow, Univ of Glasgow; *m* 1967 (m dis 1994), Linda St Clair; 2 da; m 2, 1994, Carroll Goff; *Career* memb Brentwood UDC 1968–72, Parly candidate (C) Barking Feb and Oct 1974, MEP (EDG) Birmingham N 1979–84, MP (C) Worcestershire Mid 1983–; chm EDG Backbench Ctee 1979–83, chm Euro Affrs Backbench Ctee House of Commons 1986–87 (vice chm 1983–86), PPS to Min of State Dep of Educn and Sci 1986–87; Parly under-sec of state: for indust and consumer affrs DTI 1988–90, Dept of Employment 1990–92, DES 1992–94; min of state: Dept for Educn 1994–95, Dept for Educn and Employment 1995–; *Style*— The Rt Hon Eric Forth, MP; ✉ House of Commons, London SW1A 0AA

FORTH, Dr Michael William; s of William Henry Forth (d 1990), and Gwendoline Forth (d 1994); *b* 17 Aug 1938; *Educ* King's Coll London and King's Coll Hosp Med Sch (MB BS, MRCS LRCP, AKC, DPM, MRCPsych); *m* 21 Feb 1970, Margaret Foster, da of Lt Col R T Robertson, of Cape Town; 1 s (Robert William b 17 Feb 1974); *Career* conslt psychiatrist and sr lectr Royal Liverpool Hosp 1977–; Mental Health Act cmmr 1984–86, regnl advsr in psychiatry Mersey Region 1987–91, med dir N Mersey Community Tst 1991–95; RCPsych: chm NW Div 1990–94, memb Cncl and Ct of Electors 1994–; FRCPsych 1986; *Recreations* golf, music, crosswords; *Clubs* Eaton Golf (Chester); *Style*— Dr Michael Forth; ✉ University Department of Psychiatry, Royal Liverpool Hospital, PO Box 147, Liverpool L69 3BX (☎ 0151 706 4147)

FORTIN, Richard Chalmers Gordon; s of Gordon Chalmers Fortin (d 1995), of Lavenham, Suffolk, and Nancy Avant, *née* Chivers (d 1969); *b* 12 April 1941; *Educ* Wellington Coll, CCC Oxford (Trevelyan scholarship); *m* 12 July 1969, Jane Elizabeth, da of C L Copeland; 3 da (Abigail Sarah Jane b 16 Feb 1973, Elizabeth Ruth Alice b 1 May 1975, Katharine Mary Anne b 6 May 1977); *Career* Lever Brothers Limited 1964–72, London Sloan fellowship 1972–73, asst dir Morgan Grenfell & Co Limited 1973–79, head of corp fin Lloyds Bank International Limited 1979–85; md: Lloyds Merchant Bank Limited 1985–91, Ealing Health Authy 1992–93; former dir: Lord Rayleigh's Dairies Ltd, Bridge Farm Dairies Ltd 1992–93, The Spring Ram Corporation plc 1993–96; currently dir: Heywood Williams Group plc, Britannic Assurance plc, Adwest Group plc; tstee Royal Armouries; *Recreations* sailing, cricket, walking, beekeeping, theatre; *Clubs* MCC, Vincents' (Oxford); *Style*— Richard Fortin, Esq; ✉ 5 Dealtry Road, Putney, London SW15 6NL (☎ 0181 788 6514 fax 0181 785 6008)

FORTNUM, Rebecca; da of John Fortnum, and Eve, *née* Lomas, of London; *b* 19 Sept 1963; *Educ* Camden Sch for Girls London, Camberwell Sch of Arts and Crafts London, Corpus Christi Coll Oxford (BA), Univ of Newcastle upon Tyne (MA); *Career* artist; fell in painting Exeter Faculty of Art Poly SW 1989–90, fell Skowhegan Sch of Painting and Sculpture Maine USA 1991, visiting fell in painting Winchester Sch of Art 1992–93, sr lectr Painting Dept Norwich Sch of Art 1993–; visiting lectr at numerous art colls and univs; author of numerous articles in art jls and nat press; *Solo Exhibitions incl* Positions of Silence (Collective Gallery Edinburgh) 1989, Wounds of Difference (Spacex Gallery Exeter and Southwark Coll Gallery London) 1990, Contra Diction (Winchester Gallery) 1993, Smith-Jariwala Gallery London 1994, Third Person (Kapil Jariwala Gallery London) 1996; *Gp Exhibitions incl* South Bank Picture Show 1991/92, (Dis)Parities (Mappin Art Gallery Sheffield, Pomeroy Purdy Gallery London and Herbert Art Gallery Coventry) 1992–93, Somatic States: The Body Abstract (Middx Univ Gallery and Norwich Gallery) 1992, Art 93 London Contemporary Art Fair 1993, Lead and Follow, the Continuity of Abstraction (Bede Gallery Jarrow and Atlantis Gallery London), Join the Dots (Galerie Solzo Salsburg Austria), Certain Events (Gasworks London); *Awards incl* The Clothworkers Fndn 1987, Nuffield Fndn 1987, Northern Arts Travel award to USA 1988, Pollock-Krasner Fndn NYC 1991, British Cncl travel award to Botswana 1993, Abbey scholarship Br Sch in Rome 1997; *Style*— Ms Rebecca Fortnum; ✉ Gasworks Studios, 155 Vauxhall Street, London SE11 (☎ 0171 735 3445)

FORTY, Prof (Arthur) John; CBE (1991); s of Alfred Louis Forty (d 1947), and Elizabeth, *née* East (d 1938); *b* 4 Nov 1928; *Educ* Univ of Bristol (BSc, PhD, DSc); *m* 8 Aug 1950, (Alicia) Blanche Hart, da of William Gough (d 1943); 1 s (Jonathan b 1957); *Career* Short Serv Cmmn RAF 1953–56; sr scientist TI Res Laboratories 1956–58, lectr in physics Univ of Bristol 1958–65, Univ of Warwick 1965–86 (a prof of physics, head Physics Dept, pro-vice chllr), princ and vice chllr Univ of Stirling 1986–94; hon fell Univ of Edinburgh 1994–, chm Edinburgh Parallel Computing Centre 1994–; author of various pubns in learned jls; memb and vice chm UGC 1982–86; chm: Computer Bd Univs and Res Cncls 1988–91, Jt Policy Ctee for Advanced Res Computing 1988–91, Ctee of Scottish Univ Principals 1990–92, Information Systems Ctee of Univ Funding Cncl 1991–92; memb Bd British Library 1987–94, tstee Nat Library of Scotland 1995–; Hon LLD Univ of St Andrews 1989, Hon DUniv Stirling 1995; FRSE 1988; *Recreations* sailing, gardening; *Clubs* Royal Over-Seas League; *Style*— Prof John Forty, CBE, FRSE; ✉ Port Mor, St Fillans, Crieff PH6 2NF

FORWELL, Prof George Dick; OBE (1993); s of Harold Cecil Forwell (d 1955), and Isabella L Christie; *b* 6 July 1928; *Educ* George Watson's Coll, Univ of Edinburgh (MB ChB, PhD); *m* 1957, Catherine Forsyth Campbell, *née* Cousland; 2 da; *Career* lectr Dept of Public Health & Social Med, asst dean Faculty of Med Univ of Edinburgh 1959–63, sr admin med offr Eastern Regnl Hospital Bd 1963–67, princ med offr Scot Home & Health Dept 1967–73, chief admin offr and dir of public health Greater Glasgow Health Bd 1973–93; visiting prof Univ of Glasgow, hon prof Univ of St Andrews 1993–; QHP 1980–83; memb GMC 1984–89; *Recreations* running; *Clubs* RAF; *Style*— Prof George Forwell, OBE; ✉ 20 Irvine Crescent, St Andrews, Fife KY16 8LG (☎ 01334 472943)

FORWOOD, Sir Dudley Richard; 3 Bt (UK 1895), of The Priory, Gateacre, Childwall, Co Palatine of Lancaster; s of Lt-Col Sir Dudley Baines Forwood, 2 Bt, CMG (d 1961), and Norah Isabel, *née* Lockett (d 1961); gs of Rt Hon Sir Arthur Bower Forwood, 1 Bt, Lord Mayor of Liverpool, PC, MP; *b* 6 June 1912; *Educ* Stowe; *m* 27 May 1952, Mary Gwendoline, da of Basil S Foster (she m 1, Inigo Brassey Freeman-Thomas, Viscount Ratendone (later 2 Marquess of Willingdon); m 2, Frederick Robert Cullingford; m 3, Brig Donald Croft-Wilcock); 1 adopted s (Rodney Simon Dudley); *Heir* cous, Peter Noel Forwood b 15 Oct 1925; *Career* Scots Guards (Capt); hon attaché British Legation Vienna 1934–37; equerry to HRH the Duke of Windsor 1937–39; underwriting memb of Lloyd's; master New Forest Buckhounds 1957–65; vice pres Royal Agric Soc of England (hon dir 1972–77); chm: New Forest Agric Soc 1964–82 (pres 1983–), New Forest Consultative Panel 1970–82, Crufts Dog Show 1970–87; official verderer New Forest 1974–82; vice pres: The Kennel Club, The Tree Cncl 1992; vice pres British Deer Soc (chm 1984–87); *Recreations* hunting, wildlife conservation; *Style*— Sir Dudley Forwood, Bt; ✉ Uppacott, Bagnum, nr Ringwood, Hants BH24 3BZ (☎ 01425 471480)

FORWOOD, Margaret Elizabeth Louise; da of Christopher Warren Forwood (d 1975), and Mona Blanche, *née* Williams (d 1978); *b* 25 March 1943; *Educ* Oswestry Girls' HS Shropshire, Univ of Manchester; *Career* reporter Wolverhampton Express & Star 1964–70, TV ed and critic The Sun 1970–84; TV columnist: The People 1984–89, Daily Express 1989–; chm Bdcasting Press Guild 1981–83; *Books* The Real Benny Hill (1992); *Style*— Ms Margaret Forwood; (fax 0181 241 8820)

FORWOOD, Nicholas James; QC (1987); s of Lt-Col Harry Forwood, RA, of Cobham, Surrey, and Wendy, *née* French-Smith; *b* 22 June 1948; *Educ* Stowe, St John's Coll Cambridge (BA, MA); *m* 4 Dec 1971, Sally Diane, da of His Hon Judge Basil Gerrard (decd), of Knutsford, Cheshire; 3 da (Victoria b 1974, Genevra b 1976, Suzanna b 1979), 1 s (Thomas b 1990); *Career* called to the Bar Middle Temple 1970, called to the Irish Bar 1982; hon vice pres British Assoc for Shooting and Conservation 1991–; *Recreations* golf, opera, skiing, sailing, shooting; *Clubs* United Oxford and Cambridge, Ski Club of GB; *Style*— Nicholas Forwood, Esq, QC; ✉ 11 Avenue Juliette, 1180, Brussels, Belgium (☎ 00 32 2 375 2542); 15–19 Devereux Ct, Temple, London WC2R 3JJ (☎ 0171 583 0777, fax 0171 583 9401)

FORWOOD, Peter Noel; s of Arthur Noel Forwood (d 1959, 3 s of 1 Bt), and his 2 w, Hyacinth, *née* Pollard; hp to cousin, Sir Dudley Richard Forwood, 3 Bt; *b* 15 Oct 1925; *Educ* Radley; *m* 1950, Roy, da of James Murphy, MBE, FRCS, LRCP, of Horsham, Sussex; 6 da; *Career* Welsh Gds WWII; *Style*— Peter Forwood, Esq; ✉ Newhouse Farm, Shillinglee, Chiddingfold, Surrey

FOSKETT, David Robert; QC (1991); s of Robert Frederick Foskett, of Devon, and Ruth, *née* Waddington; *b* 19 March 1949; *Educ* Warwick Sch, King's Coll London (LLB, Jelf Medal, Graveson Cup for Mooting, pres Union); *m* 11 Jan 1975, Angela Bridget, da of Maj Gordon Jacobs, MBE; 2 da (Rosanna Marie b 14 Dec 1984, Marianne Claire b 1 Dec 1991); *Career* called to the Bar Gray's Inn 1972, in practice Common Law Bar 1972–, asst recorder 1992–95, recorder 1995–; FCIArb; *Books* The Law and Practice of Compromise (1980, 4 edn 1996); *Recreations* theatre, reading poetry and composing verse, birdwatching, cricket, golf; *Clubs* Athenaeum, MCC, Woking Golf; *Style*— David Foskett, Esq, QC; ✉ 1 Crown Office Row, Temple, London EC4Y 7HH (☎ 0171 797 7500, fax 0171 797 7550)

FOSS, Kate; *née* Arden; da of George Arden (d 1958), and May Elizabeth Arden (d 1959); *b* 17 May 1925; *Educ* Northampton HS, Whitelands Coll; *m* 1951, Robert Foss, s of Laurence Foss (d 1957); 1 s (Jonathan b 1959); *Career* chm: Insur Ombudsman Bureau 1985–91, chm Direct Mail Servs Standards Bd 1989–96 (memb 1983–96); memb: Cncl Licensed Conveyancers 1985–88, Standing Ctee Licensed Conveyancing 1985–88, Data Protection Tribunal 1986–, Nat Consumer Cncl 1981–84; *Recreations* golf; *Style*— Mrs Kate Foss; ✉ Merston, 61 Back Lane, Knapton, York (☎ 01904 782549)

FOSTER, (David) Alan; s of Wilfred John Foster (d 1971), of Esher, Surrey, and Edith Mary, *née* Rowling (d 1990); *b* 13 April 1935; *Educ* Oundle, ChCh Oxford; *m* 17 Sept 1960, Jacqueline Marie, da of Charles Edward Fredrick Stowell (d 1976), of Langstone, Hants; 2 s (Mark b 1961, Richard b 1962), 2 da (Nicola b 1964, Susannah b 1971); *Career* cmmnd RA 1953–55; ptnr De Zoete & Gorton (later De Zoete & Bevan) 1963, dep chm Barclays De Zoete Wedd Asset Management Ltd 1986–88; govr Christ's Hospital; Freeman City of London 1959, Master Worshipful Co of Needlemakers 1991 (Freeman 1959, Memb Ct 1982, Sr Warden 1990); FPMI 1988 (APMI 1976), FRSA 1992; *Recreations* sailing; *Clubs* City of London, RAC; *Style*— Alan Foster, Esq; ✉ Torrington, 10 Fairmile Lane, Cobham, Surrey KT11 2DJ (☎ 01932 864249, fax 01932 867897)

FOSTER, Andrew William; s of George William Foster, and Gladys Maria Foster; *b* 29 Dec 1944; *Educ* Abingdon Sch, Newcastle Poly (BSc), LSE (Post Grad Dip in Social Studies); *Children* 1 s, 1 da; *Career* social worker 1966–71, asst dir of social servs Haringey 1971–75; dir of social servs: Greenwich 1979–82, N Yorks 1982–87; regnl gen mangr Yorks RHA 1987–91, dep chief exec NHS Mgmnt Exec 1991–92, controller Audit Commission 1992–; *Recreations* golf, walking, travel, theatre, food, wine; *Style*— Andrew Foster, Esq; ✉ The Audit Commission, 1 Vincent Square, London SW1P 2PN (☎ 0171 828 1212, fax 0171 976 6187)

FOSTER, Ann Fyffe; da of John Fyffe Sibbald, and Irene, *née* Strickland; *b* 28 Sept 1949; *Educ* Hutchesons' GS, Univ of St Andrews (MA), Univ of Reading (MA(Educ)); *m* (m dis); *Career* with Harrods Ltd Knightsbridge 1970–72, sr lectr in mgmnt studies ILEA Coll for the Distributive Trades 1972–78, researcher then food policy advsr Nat Consumer Cncl 1978–91, dir Scottish Consumer Cncl 1991–; memb Govt ctees: Ctee on Med Aspects of Food Policy, Nutrition Task Force, Scottish Diet Action Gp, Advsy Gp on Sustainable Devpt (Scotland), Nat Disability Cncl, Ownership Bd Meat and Hygiene Service; non-exec dir Scottish Ambulance Serv NHS Tst 1995–; FRSA; *Books* The Retail Handbook (with W H Thomas, 1982); *Recreations* skiing, golf, gardening, opera, music; *Clubs* Western (Glasgow), Farmers' (London); *Style*— Ms Ann Foster; ✉ Scottish Consumer Council, Royal Exchange House, 100 Queen Street, Glasgow G1 3DN (☎ 0141 226 5261, fax 0141 221 0731)

FOSTER, Anthony; s of Rufus Foster (d 1971), of Gravesend, Kent, and Margery Beatrice, *née* Dace (d 1978); *b* 11 April 1926; *Educ* private; piano: Anne Collins, Arthur Tracy Robson; organ: John Cook, John Webster; orchestration: Richard Arnell, Dr Gordon Jacob, CBE; LRAM, ARCO; *m* 26 July 1952, Barbara (d 1991), da of Capt Frederick William Humphreys (d 1967), of Gravesend; 1 da (Charlotte b 1958); *Career* composer; published compositions incl: Slow Waltz and Calypso (instrumental, 1968), Dona Nobis Pacem (vocal and instrumental, 1973), Jonah and the Whale (vocal and instrumental, 1974), The St Richard Evening Service (vocal, 1981), Christ The Lord is Risen Again (Easter Carol, 1982), A Child is Born (vocal, 1983), Jubilate Deo (for organ, 1985), Three Sketches for Guitar (1989), Classical Suite (for organ, 1990), The Sailor and the Maid (musical, libretto by Barbara Foster, 1991), The Blessed Virgin Mary Evening Service (vocal, 1993), Prelude - Interlude - Postlude for Organ (first performance by Jeremy Suter Carlisle Cathedral), O Jesu, King Most Wonderful (anthem), The BVM Evening Service (1993, first performance Carlisle Cathedral); organ accompaniments of various hymn tunes (1992–94); incidental music for BBC prodns: Monty Python's Flying Circus (1970), The Wizard of Oz (1970); hon vice pres Brighton Schs Music and Drama Assoc 1977–; memb: Composers' Guild of GB 1961, Performing Rights Soc 1982; *Recreations* cinematography; *Style*— Anthony Foster, Esq; ✉ 1 Cawley Road, Chichester, West Sussex PO19 1UZ (☎ 01243 780134)

FOSTER, Barry; *Career* actor; *Theatre* West End prodns incl: The Night of the Ball, The Desperate Hours, The Balcony, Fairy Tales of New York, My Place, Judith, Brecht on Brecht, Next Time I'll Sing to You, Let's Get a Divorce, The Tea Party and The Basement, After Haggerty, Getting Away With Murder, The Rear Column, Born in the Gardens, The Trojan War Will Not Take Place, Passion Play, The Mysteries, A Slight Ache, The Quartered Man, Timon of Athens, Grand Hotel, Mischa's Party (RSC), An Inspector Calls (Aldwych, Aust and Vienna); other credits incl: King John (Nottingham Playhouse), Macbeth (Nottingham Playhouse), Lord Arthur Savile's Crime (Royal Exchange), Master Builder (Cambridge), Scribes (Newcastle), The Crucible (Royal Exchange), Dancing Attendance (Bush), Party Time/Mountain Language (Almeida), The Gigli Concert (Almeida), The Private Ear and the Public Eye (Broadway, USA tour); *Musical* incl: The Hostage (Bristol Old Vic) 1960, The Soldier's Tale (with Yehudi Menuhin at Bath Festival) 1968, Time Out? - Not A Ghost Of A Chance (Sadler's Wells) 1973, Oedipus Rex (with Norman Del Mar) 1975, Ode To Lincoln (with Bournemouth Symphony Orchestra on New Year's morning) 1976, A Midsummer Night's Dream (by Mendelsshon, Festival Hall) 1976, Lelio (with Simon Rattle, Brighton Festival) 1989; *Television* incl: Hamlet, Ghosts (with Katina Paxinou), Jack's Horrible Luck, Where the Difference Begins, Dan Dan the Charity Man, Mogul, The Soldier's Tale (with Yehudi Menuhin), Taste of Honey, Van Der Valk, Divorce His/Hers (with Richard Burton and Elizabeth Taylor), Fall of Eagles, Old Times, Under Western Eyes, Wingate, The Three Hostages, A Family Affair, Random Moments in a May Garden, Rabbit-Pie Day, Smiley's People, The Rear Column, A Woman Called Golda, How Many Miles To Babylon, Death of an Expert Witness, Woyzeck, After Pilkington, Hotel Du Lac, Born in the Gardens, Inspector Morse, A Curious Suicide (with Nicol Williams and Jane Lapotaire), King Of The Wind, The Free Frenchman, Van Der Valk Series 1 (4 films), Van Der Valk Series 2 (3 Films), Party Time; *Films* Sea of Sand, King and Country, The Family Way, Twisted Nerve, The Guru, Battle of Britain, Ryan's Daughter, Frenzy (lead for Alfred Hitchcock), A Quiet Day in Belfast, Der Letzie Schrei (co-starred with Delphine Seyrig), The Sweeney, The Wild Geese, Heat and Dust, To Catch a King, The Whistleblower, Three Kinds of Heat, Succubus, Maurice; *Style*— Barry Foster, Esq; ✉ c/o Ken McReddie Ltd, 91 Regent Street, London W1 7TB (☎ 0171 439 1456, fax 0171 734 6530)

FOSTER, Brendan; MBE (1976); s of Francis Foster, and Margaret Foster; *b* 12 Jan 1948; *Educ* St Joseph's GS Co Durham, Univ of Sussex (BSc), Carnegie Coll Leeds (DipEd); *m* 1972, Susan Margaret, da of Kenneth Frank Alston, of Clacton, Essex; 1 s (Paul b 1977), 1 da (Catherine b 1979); *Career* sch teacher St Joseph's GS Hebburn 1970–74, recreation mangr Gateshead Metropolitan Borough Cncl 1974–81, chm Nike (UK) Ltd 1981–87 (md Nike Europe), md Nova International Ltd 1987–; former athlete; Cwlth Games medals incl: Bronze 1500m 1970, Silver 5000m 1974, Silver 5000m 1978, Gold 10,000m 1978; Euro Championships medals incl: Bronze 1500m 1971, Gold 5000m 1974; Olympic Games Bronze medal 10,000m 1976; world record holder: 2 miles 1973, 3000m 1974; UK record holder: 10,000m 1978, 1500m, 3000m, 2 miles, 5000m; BBC commentator on athletics 1980–; Hon MEd Univ of Newcastle, Hon DLitt Univ of Sussex, fell Sunderland Poly; *Style*— Brendan Foster, Esq, MBE; ✉ Whitegates, 31 Meadowfield Rd, Stocksfield, Northumberland NE43 7PY

FOSTER, Bryan Hayward; s of William R Foster (d 1974), and Gladys, *née* Hayward (d 1982); *b* 24 Dec 1928; *Educ* Clifton Coll (scholar); *m* Susan, *née* Colborne Mackrell; *Career* served RN 1946–68; stockbroker Argenti & Christopherson 1968–72; Westlake & Co stockbrokers: joined 1972, ptnr 1973–80, sr ptnr 1980–86, chm (following incorporation) 1986–87; dir Allied Provincial plc 1986–93; chm: Provincial Unit Stock Exchange 1984–87, Sutton Harbour Holdings plc (formerly Sutton Harbour Co) 1991– (non-exec dir 1986–91); MSI (memb Stock Exchange 1972); *Recreations* relaxing at home; *Clubs* MCC, Army & Navy; *Style*— Bryan Foster, Esq; ✉ Sutton Harbour Holdings plc, Harbour Offices, Guys Quay, Plymouth, Devon (☎ 01752 264000)

FOSTER, Sir Christopher David; kt (1986); s of Capt George Cecil Foster (d 1978), and Phyllis Joan, *née* Mappin (d 1964); *b* 30 Oct 1930; *Educ* Merchant Taylors', King's Coll Cambridge (MA); *m* 26 July 1958, Kay Sheridan, da of Hubert Percy Bullock (d 1987), of Horsehay, Shropshire; 2 s (Oliver Drummond b 1960, Sebastian Luke b 1968), 3 da (Henrietta Sheridan Jane b 1959, Cressida Imogen Dakeyne b 1963, Melissa Catherine Mappin b 1964); *Career* RAOC 1949, cmmnd 1 Bn The Seaforth Highlanders Malaya 1949–50, 1 Bn The London Scottish TA 1950–53, General Service Medal Malaya 1950; res fellowship 1954–64: Univ of Pennsylvania, King's Coll Cambridge, Univ of Manchester, Jesus Coll Oxford (hon fell 1992–); official fell and tutor in econs Jesus Coll

Oxford 1964–66, dir gen of econ planning Miny of Tport 1966–69, visiting prof of econs and urban studies MIT 1969–70, visiting fell Dept of City Planning Univ of California Berkeley 1970; LSE: head of Centre for Urban Econs 1970–75, prof of econs and urban studies 1975–78, visiting prof of econs 1978–85; dir Centre for Environmental Studies 1976–78; Coopers and Lybrand Associates: ptnr 1978–85 and 1988–93, head of Econs and Public Policy Div 1978–84, head of business devpt 1984–85, memb Mgmnt Ctee and MCS Mgmnt Ctee (econs practice ldr) 1988–91 (advsr to chm 1991–); commercial advsr to the Bd British Telecom 1986–88; memb Smeed Ctee on Road Pricing 1962–63, pt/t econ advsr to DOE 1974–77, chm Ctee of Inquiry on Roads Goods Licensing 1978–79, memb Ctee of Inquiry into Civil Serv Pay 1981–82, memb Audit Cmmn 1983–88, econ assessor Sizewell B Inquiry 1982–86, special advsr to the Sec of State for Transport on British Rail Privatisation 1992–93; memb: ESRC 1985–89, London Docklands Devpt Cmmn 1987–96, Railtrack; chm: NEDO Construction Industry Sector Group 1988–92, Construction Round Table 1993–; hon fell Jesus Coll Oxford 1992; *Books* The Transport Problem (1963), Politics, Finance and the Role of Economics (1972), Local Government Finance (with R Jackson and M Perlman, 1980), Privatisation, Public Ownership and the Regulation of Natural Monopoly (1992), The State under Stress (1996); *Recreations* opera, theatre; *Clubs* Reform, RAC; *Style*— Sir Christopher Foster; ✉ 6 Holland Park Avenue, London W11 2QU (☎ 0171 727 4757); Coopers and Lybrand, Plumtree Court, London EC4A 4HT (☎ 0171 213 4795, telex 887470)

FOSTER, Christopher Kenneth; s of Kenneth John Foster (d 1982), of Sunningdale, and Christina Dorothy, *née* Clark; *b* 5 Nov 1949; *Educ* Harrow HS; *Career* chm and dir Springwood Books Ltd 1975–; dir: Chase Corporation plc 1985–88, Wiggins Group plc 1993–, Tomorrow's Leisure plc; Lord of the Manor of Little Hale; *Recreations* golf, music, art; *Clubs* Sunningdale Golf; *Style*— Christopher Foster, Esq; ✉ Springwood House, The Avenue, Ascot, Berks SL5 7LR (☎ 01344 28753); The Wiggins Group plc, 39 Upper Brook Street, London W1Y 1PE (☎ 0171 495 8686, fax 0171 493 0189)

FOSTER, Rt Hon Derek; MP (Lab) Bishop Auckland (majority 10,087), PC (1993); s of Joseph Foster (d 1959), and Ethel, *née* Ragg (d 1982); *b* 25 June 1937; *Educ* Bede GS Sunderland, St Catherine's Coll Oxford; *m* 1972, (Florence) Anne, da of Thomas Bulmer, of Sunderland; *Career* youth and community worker 1970–73, further educn organiser 1973–74, asst dir of educn Sunderland Cncl 1974–79, chm N of England Devpt Cncl 1974–76, memb Tyne & Wear CC and Sunderland Borough Cncl; MP (Lab) Bishop Auckland 1979–, additional oppn spokesman Social Security 1982, oppn whip 1982, PPS to Neil Kinnock 1983–85, oppn chief whip 1985–95, shadow chllr of the Duchy of Lancaster 1995–; vice chm Youthaid 1979–85; *Recreations* brass bands, male voice choirs; *Style*— The Rt Hon Derek Foster, MP; ✉ 3 Linburn, Rickleton, Washington, Tyne and Wear NE38 9EB (☎ 0191 417 1580)

FOSTER, Donald (Don); MP (Lib Dem) Bath (majority 3,768); s of late Rev J A Foster, and late I E Foster; *b* 31 March 1947; *Educ* Lancaster Royal GS, Univ of Keele (BSc, CertEd), Univ of Bath (MEd); *m* 31 Dec 1968, Victoria Jane Dorcas, *née* Pettegree; 1 s, 1 da; *Career* science teacher Sevenoaks Sch 1969–75, science project dir Resources for Learning Devpt Unit Avon Educn Authy 1975–80, lectr in educn Univ of Bristol 1980–89, mgmnt conslt Pannell Kerr Forster 1989–92; cncllr Cabot Ward Avon CC 1981–89 (chm Educn Ctee 1987–89), Parly candidate (Alliance) Bristol E 1987, MP (Lib Dem) Bath 1992–; Lib Dem spokesman on: educn and trg 1992–94, educn and employment 1994–; memb Parly Office of Sci and Technol 1992–94, memb Educn and Employment Select Ctee 1996–; vice chm: Nat Campaign for Nursery Educn 1993–, Br Assoc for Central and Eastern Europe 1994–; hon pres Br Youth Cncl 1993–; CPhys, MInstP; *Recreations* classical music, modern ballet, travel, sport; *Clubs* National Liberal; *Style*— Don Foster, Esq, MP; ✉ House of Commons, London SW1A 0AA

FOSTER, Giles Henry; s of Stanley William Foster (d 1986), and Gladys Maude, *née* Moon; *b* 30 June 1948; *Educ* Monkton Combe Sch, Univ of York (BA), Royal Coll of Art (MA); *m* 28 Sept 1974, Nicole Anne, da of Alan Coates, of London; 2 s (George b 1982, William b 1987); *Career* film and Television director; *Television* incl: Oliver's Travels, The Rector's Wife, Adam Bede, The Lilac Bus, Monster Maker, Northanger Abbey, Hotel du Lac (BAFTA Award), Silas Marner (BAFTA nomination), Dutch Girls, The Aerodrome, Last Summers Child, The Obelisk, five scripts by Alan Bennett (incl Talking Heads: A Lady of Letters, BAFTA nomination); *Films* incl: Devices and Desires (Grierson Award), Consuming Passions, Tree of Hands; *Clubs* Groucho's; *Style*— Giles Foster, Esq; ✉ c/o Anthony Jones, Peters Fraser & Dunlop Ltd, 503 The Chambers, Chelsea Harbour, Lots Road, London SW10 0XF (☎ 0171 344 1000, fax 0171 352 7356)

FOSTER, Dr James Michael Gerard; s of Dr Robert Marius Foster, and Margaret Rhona, *née* Holland; *b* 19 Dec 1949; *Educ* King's Sch Canterbury and St Bartholomew's Hosp Med Coll, Univ of London (Crawford exhibitioner), MB BS, MRCS LRCP; *m* 22 Nov 1986, Felicity Patricia, da of Dr Charles Mathurin Vaillant; 2 s (Charles James Vaillant b 2 March 1989, Simon James Holland b 16 Nov 1991); *Career* sr house offr St Bartholomew's Hosp London: in neurosurgery and cardiothoracic surgery 1976–77, in anaesthesia 1977–79; registrar in anaesthesia St George's Hosp London 1979–81; sr registrar in anaesthesia Guy's Hosp London 1981–84; sr registrar in pain relief Sir Charles Gairdner Hosp Perth West Australia 1984 (King's Fund travelling fellowship bursary); conslt in anaesthesia and pain relief St Bartholomew's Hosp London 1985–; hon sr lectr St Bartholomew's Hosp Med Coll; recognised teacher in anaesthetics Univ of London; memb: Euro Soc of Regnl Anaesthesia, Int Assoc for the Study of Pain; FRCA, DA; *Sporting Achievements incl* Kenya Coast Open jr tennis championship 1968, ascent of Mt Kilimanjaro Tanzania 1969, completing West Australia Marathon 1984; *Books* Terminal Care Support Teams (contrib, 1990), Coloproctology and the Pelvic Floor (contrib, 1992); *Recreations* golf, running, photography; *Clubs* RSM, Berkshire Golf (Ascot), Royal Cinque Ports Golf (Deal), Royal Berkshire Racquets and Health; *Style*— Dr James Foster; ✉ Heathend Lodge, Windsor Road, Ascot, Berks SL5 7LQ (☎ 01344 21549); Private Consulting Rooms, The Princess Grace Hospital, 42–52 Nottingham Place, London W1M 3FD (☎ 0171 486 1234, fax 0171 487 4476)

FOSTER, Jerome; s of Cecil William Foster, of Islip, Oxon, and Rosaleen, *née* Game (d 1988); *b* 3 Aug 1936; *Educ* Wellington, Univ of Grenoble; *m* 27 May 1961, Joanna Foster, *qv*, da of Michael Mead, OBE; 1 s (Hugo b 1969), 1 da (Kate b 1972); *Career* Nat Serv 2 Lt Oxfordshire & Bucks LI (now 1 Green Jackets) 1954–56; advertisement mangr Benn Brothers Ltd 1957–61, mangr TLS Times Newspapers Ltd 1961–67, dir Euro Offices Benn Group 1967–72, dir Continuing Educn INSEAD 1972–79; assoc dean: for exec educn Carnegie-Mellon Univ Pittsburgh 1979–82, Templeton Coll Oxford 1982–84, for exec educn INSEAD 1984–87; chief exec Ambrosetti Europe (mgmnt conslts) 1987–89, dean exec educn London Business Sch 1990–94; founding princ Oxford Development Associates; FRSA; *Recreations* family, Europe, singing, sailing; *Style*— Jerome Foster; ✉ Confessor's Gate, Islip, Oxford OX5 2SN (☎ 01865 841121, fax 01865 841277)

FOSTER, Joanna; *née* Mead; da of Michael Mead, OBE, and Lesley Mead; *b* 5 May 1939; *Educ* Benenden Sch Kent, Grenoble Univ France (Dip); *m* 27 May 1961, Jerome Foster, *qv*, s of Cecil William Foster; 1 s (Hugo b 1969), 1 da (Kate b 1972); *Career* sec Vogue magazine, press attachée INSEAD Fontainebleau 1975–79, dir of educn corp servs Western Psychiatric Inst and Clinic Univ of Pittsburgh 1979–81, head Youth Trg Industl Soc London 1983–85, head Pepperell Unit Industl Soc 1985–88, chair Equal Opportunities Cmmn 1988–93, pres Euro Cmmn's Advsy Ctee on Equal Opportunities 1992; dir: Welsh Nat Opera 1990–94, BT Forum (British Telecommunications plc) 1995–; dep chair TSB Fndn 1992–, chair UK Cncl UN International Year of the Family 1993–94, govr Oxford Brookes Univ 1993–, pres Relate Marriage Guidance Cncl 1993–96 (resigned); memb Exec Ctee Nat Advsy Cncl for Careers and Educnl Guidance; hon fell St Hilda's Coll Oxford; Hon Doctorate: Kingston Univ 1992, Oxford Brookes Univ, Univ of Essex, Univ of the West of England 1993, Univ of Strathclyde 1994, Univ of Salford 1994, Univ of Bristol 1996; *Recreations* family, food, friends; *Clubs* Reform; *Style*— Mrs Joanna Foster; ✉ Confessor's Gate, Islip, Oxford OX5 2SN

FOSTER, Sir John Gregory; 3 Bt (UK 1930), of Bloomsbury, Co London; o s of Sir Thomas Saxby Gregory Foster, 2 Bt (d 1957), and Beryl, *née* Ireland; *b* 26 Feb 1927; *Educ* Michaelhouse Coll Natal, Witwatersrand Univ (MB, BCh), FRCP Edinburgh, DIH London; *m* 24 Nov 1956, Jean Millicent, eldest da of late Elwin Watts, FRCSE, of Germiston, S Africa; 1 s (Saxby Gregory b 1957), 3 da (Deborah Jean Gregory b 1959, Carolyn Gregory b 1962, Rosemary Gregory b 1963); *Heir* s, Saxby Gregory Foster b 3 Sept 1957; *Career* med registrar 1955–56, med offr 1957–61, physician 1961–; *Style*— Sir John Foster, Bt; ✉ 7 Caledon Street, PO Box 1325, George 6530, Cape Province, S Africa (☎ 00 27 441 743333, fax 00 27 441 732507)

FOSTER, John Stewart; s of Dr Donald Stewart Foster, of Kenilworth, Warwickshire, and Rosemary Margaret Kate, *née* Weber; *b* 16 June 1947; *Educ* The King's Sch Canterbury, Univ of Lancaster (BA); *m* 14 Nov 1970, Alethea Valentine Mary, da of Prof Roberto Weiss (d 1969), of Henley on Thames, Oxfordshire; 2 s (Julien b 1971, William b 1973); *Career* reporter then sr reporter and specialist feature writer Coventry Evening Telegraph 1969–74 (special award winner Midlands Journalist of the Year Competition 1974); BBC: regnl journalist TV Birmingham 1974–78, parly journalist Radio News 1978–82, TV reporter and radio and TV presenter of assorted progs on current affrs Scotland 1982–85, home affrs corr TV Scotland 1985, chief parly journalist Corporate News 1985–88, chief parly corr News and Current Affrs 1988–89, chief parly corr and parly ed regnl TV News and Current Affrs 1989–90, parly ed BBC TV Scotland 1991–; presenter BBC TV incl: Scottish Lobby, Scottish Question Time, Conference Live; memb House of Commons: Press Lobby 1985–, Press Gallery Ctee 1989; *Recreations* Home duty, Away Days; *Clubs* Belle Toute (Lancaster); *Style*— John Stewart Foster, Esq; ✉ BBC Westminster, 4 Millbank, London SW1P 3JQ

FOSTER, Jonathan Rowe; QC (1989); s of Donald Foster (d 1980), and Hilda Eaton, *née* Rowe; *b* 20 July 1947; *Educ* Oundle, Keble Coll Oxford; *m* 1978, Sarah; 4 s; *Career* called to the Bar Gray's Inn 1970, recorder of the Crown Court 1988–, treas Northern Circuit 1992–, dep judge of the High Ct (Family) 1994–; memb Criminal Injuries Compensation Bd 1995–; govr Ryley's Sch 1990–; *Recreations* outdoor activities, golf, bridge; *Clubs* St James Manchester, Hale Golf, Bowdon Lawn Tennis; *Style*— Jonathan Foster, Esq, QC; ✉ 18 St John Street, Manchester (☎ 0161 834 9843)

FOSTER, Michael Robert; s of Robert O Foster (d 1996), and Nannette, *née* Howat; *b* 6 July 1941; *Educ* Felsted Sch Essex, Woodberry Forest Sch Virginia USA (ESU exchange scholar), AA Sch of Arch (AADipl), Univ of Essex (MA History and Theory of Arch); *m* 17 Sept 1971, Susan Rose, *née* Bolson; 3 s (Jamie b 15 Sept 1973, Tom b 15 April 1976, Marcus b 11 July 1978); *Career* architect; asst Stillman & Eastwick-Field London and Skidmore Owings & Merrill Chicago 1965–66, asst and job architect YRM Architects and Planners 1966–69, student Univ of Essex 1969–70, full-time teacher Dept of Arch Poly of Central London 1970–71 (pt/t 1968–70), ptnr The Tooley & Foster Partnership (architects, engrs and designers) 1971–; pt/t teacher: Environmental Design Dept Wimbledon Sch of Art and in history and contextual studies Dept of Arch Poly of Central London 1971–73, Sch of Environmental Design RCA 1973–76, Schs of Arch and 3 Dimensional Design Kingston Poly 1975–79; pt/t lectr in history of design Middx Poly fndn course 1977–79; external examiner: interior design course Sch of 3 Dimensional Design Kingston Poly 1982–84, degree course in arch South Bank Univ 1989–93; Architectural Assoc: unit master Sch of Arch 1979–83, memb Cncl 1986–93, pres 1989–91; ARCUK: memb Educn Grants Panel Bd of Educn 1975–82, memb Cncl 1992–93; sec Standing Conf of Heads of Schs of Arch 1995–; tstee Geffrye Museum 1990– (chm Friends of Geffrye Museum 1981–90); RIBA 1968, MCSD 1981, memb L'Ordre des Architectes (France) 1991; *Books* The Principles of Architecture: Style, Structure and Design (1983); occasional contrib: AA Quarterly, Architect's Jl, Town and Country Planning, The Architect, Building Design; *Recreations* golf, painting and drawing; *Style*— Michael Foster; ✉ The Tooley & Foster Partnership, Warwick House, Palmerston Road, Buckhurst Hill, Essex IG9 5LQ (☎ 0181 504 9711, fax 0181 506 1779)

FOSTER, Murray Egerton; s of Maurice Foster, OBE, of Grindleford, Derbyshire, and Mary, *née* Davies; *b* 17 Dec 1946; *Educ* Carliol Carlisle, Welsh Nat Sch of Med (BDS, MB BCh, MScD); *m* 13 July 1974, Margaret Elizabeth, da of Glynmore Jones, of Chester; 2 s (Lawrence b 1981, Richard b 1983), 1 da (Catherine b 1984); *Career* sr registrar St George's Hosp and St Thomas' Hosp 1977–80, conslt in oral maxillo-facial surgery NW Region and postgrad tutor Univ of Manchester; memb: RSM, BMA, BDA, BAOMS; FDS, FFD, FRCSEd; *Books* Dental, Oral and Maxillo-facial Surgery (jtly, 1986); *Recreations* walking, photography; *Clubs* Oral Surgery (sec); *Style*— Murray Foster; ✉ 7 Higher Lydgate Park, Grasscroft, Saddleworth OL4 4EF (☎ 01457 874196); 2 St John St, Manchester (☎ 0161 835 1149)

FOSTER, Neil William Derick; s of William Robert Brudenell Foster (d 1992), and Jean Leslie, *née* Urquhart (d 1986); bro of Richard Francis Foster, *qv*; *b* 13 March 1943; *Educ* Harrow, Aix en Provence Univ; *m* 2 Sept 1989, Anthea Caroline, da of Ian Gibson Macpherson, MC, of The Old Hall, Blofield, Norwich, Norfolk; 1 da (b 21 Nov 1992); *Career* underwriting memb Lloyd's 1971–, dir John Foster & Sons plc 1975–93, dir and past chm Norfolk Churches Tst 1976–, dir Norfolk Marketing Ltd 1985–95; memb Ctee HHA East Anglia, gen cmmr of income tax 1992– (vice chm Dereham Div 1996); past chm: East Anglia Div Royal Forestry Soc, The Game Conservancy Norfolk, East Anglia region Timber Growers Assoc, CLA Norfolk; chm Upper Nar Internal Drainage Bd 1993– (memb 1992–); Liveryman Worshipful Co of Clothworkers 1965 (4th Warden 1995, 2nd Warden 1996); *Recreations* shooting, forestry, gardening; *Clubs* Boodle's, Norfolk; *Style*— Neil Foster, Esq; ✉ Lexham Hall, King's Lynn, Norfolk PE32 2QJ (☎ 01328 701 341); The Estate Office, Lexham Hall, King's Lynn, Norfolk PE32 2QJ (☎ 01328 701 288, fax 01328 700 053)

FOSTER, Nigel Pearson; s of Gordon Pearson Foster (d 1985), of Wilmslow, Cheshire, and Margaret Elizabeth, *née* Bettison (d 1989); *b* 18 Feb 1952; *Educ* Oswestry Sch Shropshire; *m* 20 May 1988, Mary Elizabeth, da of Edward Bangs; 1 da (Elizabeth Margaret b 9 June 1990), 1 s (Charlie Edward b 13 Oct 1994); *Career* Rowlinson-Broughton 1969–72, Clough Howard Richards Manchester 1972–74, prodn asst Royds Manchester 1974–76, account exec The Advertising and Marketing Organisation 1976–79, TV prodr Wasey Campbell Ewald 1980–82 (account exec 1979–80), TV prodr Foote Cone Belding 1982–84; head of TV KMP 1984–86; J Walter Thompson: TV prodr 1986–89, head of TV UK 1989–96, exec dir of TV prodn Europe 1996–; FIPA; *Style*— Nigel Foster, Esq; ✉ J Walter Thompson Ltd, 40 Berkeley Square, London W1X 6AD (☎ 0171 499 4040)

FOSTER, Sir Norman Robert; kt (1990); s of Lilian and Robert Foster, of Manchester; *b* 1 June 1935; *Educ* Univ of Manchester Sch of Art (DipArch 1961, CertTP), Yale Univ Sch of Architecture; *Career* Nat Serv RAF 1953–55; architect; fndr Foster Assocs 1967, became Sir Norman Foster & Partners 1992 then Foster & Partners 1996 (chm); winner of 25 national and international competitions 1979–95 for projects incl: Al Faisaliah Complex Riyadh, British Museum Redevelopment London, New German Parliament Reichstag Berlin, New Airport Terminal at Chek Lap Kok Hong Kong, Duisburg

Harbour, Lycée Fréjus France, Rennes Viaduct, Hongkong and Shanghai Bank HQ Hong Kong, BBC Radio Centre, Nat German Athletics Centre Frankfurt, Carré d'Art Nîmes, Collserola Tower Barcelona, Bilbao Metro System, King's Cross Masterplan; current projects incl: new wing Joslyn Arts Museum Nebraska, Univ of Cambridge Law Faculty, Musée de la Préhistoire Verdon, new HQ Commerzbank Frankfurt, Congress Hall for city of Valencia; other projects incl: Masterplans Rotterdam, Barcelona, Mallorca, Berlin, Nîmes, Cannes, Greenwich, Micro-electronic Park Duisburg, Stansted Airport Terminal Zone, Century Tower Tokyo, The Sackler Galleries at the Royal Acad (RIBA Building of the Year Award 1993), ITN Headquarters London, Crescent Wing and Sainsbury Centre Norwich, Renault Centre Swindon, Willis Faber and Dumas Ipswich; conslt architect Univ of East Anglia 1978–87; teacher 1967–77: London Poly, Bath Acad of Arts, Univ of Pennsylvania, Architectural Assoc; over 125 major national and international awards incl: Fin Times Industl Architecture Award 1967, 1970, 1971, 1974 and 1981, RIBA Awards 1969, 1972, 1977, 1978, 1981, 1992 and 1993, Structural Steel Award 1972, 1980, 1984, 1986 and 1992, RS Reynolds Award 1976, 1979 and 1986, International Prize for Architecture 1976 and 1980, Br Tourist Bd Award 1979, Ambrose Congreve Award 1980, Royal Gold Medal for Architecture 1983, Civic Tst Award 1984 and 1992, Premio Compasso d'Oro Award 1987, PA Innovations Award 1988, Kunstpreis Berlin Award 1989, RIBA Tstees Medal 1990, Mies van der Rohe Pavilion Award 1991, Gold medal French Academie de Paris, Arnold W Brunner Memorial Prize NY 1992, RFAC & Sunday Times Best Building of the Year Award 1992, ICE Merit Award 1992, ISE Special Award 1992, Concrete Soc Award 1992 and 1993, Interiors USA Award 1988, 1992 and 1993, BCO Award 1992 and 1993, BCIA Award 1991, 1992 and 1993, Benedictus Award, Gold medal American Inst of Architects 1994, BBC Design Award finalist 1994, Bund Deutsche Architekten Award 1994, Queen's Award for Export Achievement 1995; TV documentaries incl: BBC Omnibus 1981 and 1995, Anglia Enterprise 1983, BBC Late Show 1990 and 1991, Building Sites 1991; featured in international publications and jls; exhibitions of work held in: London, New York, Paris, Bordeaux, Lyon, Nîmes, Tokyo, Berlin, Madrid, Barcelona, Milan, Venice, Florence, Hong Kong, Antwerp; work in permanent collections of Museum of Modern Art New York and Centre Pompidou Paris; vice-pres AA 1974 (memb Cncl 1973), memb RIBA Visiting Bd of Educn 1971 (external examiner 1971–73); memb Cncl RCA 1981; assoc Academie Royale de Belgique, memb Ordre Français des Architectes, hon memb Bund Deutsche Architekten 1983, hon fell American Inst of Architects 1980, foreign memb Royal Acad of Fine Arts Sweden; IBM fell 1980, hon fell Kent Inst of Art and Design 1994; Hon LittD East Anglia 1980, Hon DSc Bath 1986; hon doctorate: RCA 1991, Univ of Valencia 1992, Univ of Humberside 1992; Hon LLD: Univ of Manchester 1993, Technical Univ of Eindhoven 1996, Univ of Oxford 1996; RIBA 1965, FCSD 1975, ARA 1983, RDI 1988, Hon FEng 1995; *Books* The Work of Foster Associates (1978), Norman Foster, Buildings and Projects, Vols 1, 2 & 3 (1989–90), Foster Associates (1991), Norman Foster Sketches (1991), Recent Works Foster Associates (1992), Architecture As Building (1993); *Recreations* flying, skiing, running; *Style*— Sir Norman Foster; ✉ Foster & Partners, Riverside Three, 22 Hester Rd, London SW11 4AN (☎ 0171 738 0455, fax 0171 738 1107/1108)

FOSTER, (John) Peter; OBE (1990); s of Francis Edward Foster (d 1953), of Newe Strathdon, and Evelyn Marjorie Forbes (d 1953); *b* 2 May 1919; *Educ* Eton, Trinity Hall Cambridge (MA); *m* 1944, Margaret Elizabeth, da of George John Skipper (d 1948); 1 s (Edward Philip John b 1949), 1 da (Elizabeth Anne b 1946); *Career* cmmnd RE 1941, served Norfolk Div, joined Gds Armd Div 1943, served France and Germany, Capt (SORE2) 30 Corps 1945, discharged 1946; architect; Marshall Sisson: joined 1948, later ptnr, sole ptnr 1971; ptnr (with John Peters) Vine Press Hemingford Grey 1957–63; surveyor Royal Acad of Arts 1965–80, surveyor of the fabric Westminster Abbey 1973–88 (surveyor emeritus 1989); memb Fabric Ctee: Canterbury Cathedral 1987– (chm 1990–91), Ely Cathedral 1990–; chm Cathedral Architects' Assoc 1987–90; memb: Tech Panel Soc for Protection of Ancient Bldgs 1976–91, Historic Bldgs Cncl for Eng 1977–84, Advsy Bd Redundant Churches 1979–91, Exec Ctee Georgian Gp 1983–91; pres Surveyors Club 1980, govr Suttons Hosp Charterhouse 1982, tstee Art Workers' Guild 1985 (memb 1971, master 1980); ARIBA 1949, FSA 1973, FRSA 1994; Commander Brother OStJ 1988; *Recreations* painting, books; *Clubs* Athenaeum; *Style*— Peter Foster, Esq, OBE, FSA; ✉ Harcourt, Hemingford Grey, Huntingdon, Cambs PE18 9BJ (☎ 01480 461101, fax 01480 492188)

FOSTER, Peter George; s of Thomas Alfred Foster (d 1945), and Eileen Agnes, *née* Moore (d 1980); *b* 1 Oct 1936; *Educ* Merchant Taylors', CCC Oxford (MA, hon memb Greyhound RFC); *m* 26 Oct 1968, Hilary Anne Foster, da of Thomas Frederick Barton; 2 da (Katrina Jane b 27 June 1969, Jessica Sophie b 4 March 1971); *Career* Baileys Shaw & Gillett: articled clerk, asst slr 1963, ptnr 1964, sr ptnr 1988–; pres Legalliance EEIG 1990–92; Freeman City of London 1976; memb Law Soc 1964; *Recreations* walking, music, watching sport, archaeology; *Style*— Peter Foster, Esq; ✉ Baileys Shaw & Gillett, 17 Queen Square, London WC1N 3RH (☎ 0171 837 5455, fax 0171 837 0071)

FOSTER, Peter James; s of James Milton Foster (d 1995), and Doris May Foster; *b* 18 Aug 1946; *Educ* Bromley Tech HS; *m* Vivien Helen; 3 s (David b 1974, Julian b 1984, John b 1987), 1 da (Suzanne b 1978); *Career* Commercial Union plc: gp fin controller 1985–91, gen mangr (Finance) 1991–94, gp fin dir 1994–; memb 100 Gp of Finance Directors, tstee Trade Indemnity Pension Fund; fell Chartered Inst of Certified Accountants 1980; *Recreations* sports (playing and spectating), fishing; *Style*— Peter Foster, Esq; ✉ Commercial Union plc, St Helens, 1 Undershaft, London EC3P 3DQ (☎ 0171 662 2955, fax 0171 662 2755)

FOSTER, Peter Martin; CMG (1975); s of Capt Frederick Arthur Peace Foster, RN (d 1948), and Marjorie Kathleen, *née* Sandford (d 1988); *b* 25 May 1924; *Educ* Sherborne, Corpus Christi Coll Cambridge; *m* 1947, Angela Hope, *née* Cross; 1 s, 1 da; *Career* WWII Maj Royal Horse Gds; joined HM Dip Serv 1948, HM Embassy Vienna 1948–52, FO 1952–54, Warsaw 1954–56, FO 1956–59, SA 1959–61, FO 1961–64, Bonn 1964–66, dep high cmmr Kampala 1966–68, IDC 1969, cnsllr Tel Aviv 1970–72, head of Central and S Africa Dept FCO 1972–74, ambass and UK perm rep to Cncl of Europe Strasbourg 1974–78, ambass GDR 1978–81, ret 1981; dir Cncl for Arms Control 1984–86; chm Int Social Serv (GB) 1985–90; *Style*— Peter Foster, Esq, CMG; ✉ Rew Cottage, Abinger Common, Dorking, Surrey (☎ 01306 730114)

FOSTER, Prof Peter William; s of Percy William Foster (d 1966), and Florence Harriet, *née* Bedford (d 1976); *b* 6 Dec 1930; *Educ* UCL (BSc, PhD); *m* 16 Aug 1952, Elizabeth, da of Walter Goldstern, of Altrincham; 2 s (Anthony P b 1958, Andrew P b 1960), 2 da (Frances M b 1956, Theresa K b 1962); *Career* tech offr Nobel Div ICI 1954–57, assoc prof Univ of Nebraska 1957–58, res chemist E I du Pont de Nemours Inc 1958–63, mangr Du Pont International SA Geneva 1963–66, md and dir Heathcoat Yarns and Fibres and John Heathcoat 1966–82, chm Steam Storage Co Ltd 1975–, md Universal Carbon Fibres Ltd 1982–85, prof Dept of Textiles UMIST 1986–, vice princ UMIST 1991–94; memb: Textile Inst, Chem Soc; FTI, FRSA; *Recreations* chess, theatre; *Clubs* Rotary; *Style*— Prof Peter Foster; ✉ Department of Textiles, UMIST, PO Box 88, Sackville St, Manchester M60 1QD (☎ 0161 200 4142, fax 0161 228 7040, telex 666094)

FOSTER, Richard Anthony; s of Eric Kenneth Foster (d 1945), of Bournemouth, and Sylvia Renee, *née* France (now Mrs Westerman); *b* 3 Oct 1941; *Educ* Kingswood Sch Bath, LSE (BSc), Univ of Manchester (MA); *m* 31 Aug 1964, Mary Browning, da of Arthur Leslie James, OBE (d 1990), of Saltburn, Cleveland; 2 s (James b 28 May 1970, William b 27 May 1973), 1 da (Polly b 12 Aug 1979); *Career* student asst Leicester Museum 1964–66, museum asst Bowes Museum 1967–68, keeper i/c Durham LI Museum and Arts Centre 1968–70; dir: Oxford City and Co Museum 1970–74, Oxfordshire Co Museums 1974–78, Merseyside Co Museums 1978–86, Nat Museums and Galleries on Merseyside 1986–; cmmr Museum and Galleries Cmmn, pres Int Congress of Maritime Museums 1993–96; tstee Horniman Museum and Gardens 1994; hon fell Liverpool John Moores Univ; FSA 1976, FMA 1980; *Recreations* sailing, watching football; *Style*— Richard Foster, Esq, FSA; ✉ National Museums and Galleries on Merseyside, Liverpool Museum, William Brown St, Liverpool, L3 8EN (☎ 0151 207 0001, fax 0151 478 4321)

FOSTER, Richard Anthony (Tony); s of Donald and Jean Foster, of Bishops Stortford; *b* 2 April 1946; *Educ* King Edward VI GS Chelmsford, St Peter's Coll Birmingham, Cardiff Coll of Art; *m* 1968, Ann Margaret, da of Donald Partington (d 1987), and Joan Partington (d 1985); *Career* artist; art teacher Leicester, Cayman Is and Cornwall 1968–75, visual arts co-ordinator S Hill Park Arts Centre Bracknell 1976–78, visual arts offr South West Arts 1978–84, professional artist 1984–; co-fndr with Jonathan Harvey and James Lingwood of TSWA; winner Yosemite Renaissance Prize 1988; FRGS 1993; *Solo Exhibitions* incl: Royal Watercolour Soc London 1985, Yale Center for British Art New Haven Conn 1985, Francesca Anderson Gallery Boston Mass 1985 and 1988, City of Edinburgh Art Centre 1987, Ecology Centre London 1987, Calif Acad of Sciences San Francisco 1987, Smithsonian Inst Washington DC 1989, Plymouth Arts Centre Devon 1990, Newlyn Orion Penzance 1990, Montgomery Gallery San Francisco 1990, 1993 and 1995, Bruton Gallery Bath 1992, Royal Albert Museum Exeter 1993, Harewood House Yorks 1993, Royal Botanic Gardens Kew 1995; *Art Projects* incl: Travels Without a Donkey in the Cevennes (with James Ravilious) 1982, Thoreau's Country (walks and canoe journeys in New England) 1985, John Muir's High Sierra 1986–87, Exploring the Grand Canyon 1988–89, Rainforest Diaries (Costa Rica) 1991–93, Arid Lands (walks across deserts) 1993–95, Rim of Fire (series of paintings about volcanoes of Pacific Rim) 1996–; *Recreations* snooker, walking, writing to my MP; *Style*— Tony Foster, Esq; ✉ 1 Well Street, Tywardreath Par, Cornwall PL24 2QH (☎ 01726 815300)

FOSTER, Richard Francis; s of William Robert Brudenell Foster (d 1992), of Lexham Hall, King's Lynn, and Jean Leslie, *née* Urqhuart (d 1986); bro of Neil Foster, *qv*; *b* 6 June 1945; *Educ* Harrow, Trinity Coll Oxford, Studio Simi Florence, City & Guilds of London Art Sch; *m* 1970 (m dis 1984), the Hon Sarah Rachel Jane Kay-Shuttleworth (now the Hon Mrs Figgins), da of 4 Baron Shuttleworth (d 1975); 1 s (Edward William Thomas b 7 March 1978), 2 da (Henrietta Victoria b 10 Aug 1973, Georgiana Pamela b 2 May 1975); *Career* landscape and portrait painter; numerous public and private portrait cmmns; *Exhibitions* solo incl: Jocelyn Feilding Fine Art 1974, Spink & Son Venice 1978, Spink & Son India 1982 and 1991, Spink & Son Egypt 1984; group incl: Royal Soc of Portrait Painters (annually) 1969–, Royal Acad (most years) 1972–; Lord Mayor's Award for London Landscapes 1972; Liveryman Worshipful Co of Clothworkers, Brother Art Workers' Guild; RP (vice pres 1991–94); *Recreations* travel, country sports, family life; *Clubs* Chelsea Arts, Pratt's; *Style*— Richard Foster, Esq; ✉ Manor House, Colkirk, Fakenham, Norfolk NR21 7JE (☎ 01328 864276); 5a Clareville Grove, London SW7 5AU (☎ 0171 244 7164)

FOSTER, Robert; s of David Foster, of Ascot, and Amelia, *née* Morris; *b* 12 May 1943; *Educ* Oundle, Corpus Christi Coll Cambridge (MA); *m* 1967, Judy, *née* Welsh; 1 s (Alan b 30 March 1976), 1 da (Joanna b 2 April 1978); *Career* research and devpt engr: Parkinson Cowan Ltd 1964–66, Automation Ltd 1966–71; DTI: princ 1977–84, asst sec 1984–91, under sec and head Aerospace Div 1992–; CEng, FIEE; *Recreations* music, squash, tennis, reading and theatre; *Style*— Robert Foster, Esq; ✉ Department of Trade and Industry, 151 Buckingham Palace Road, London SW1W 9SS (☎ 0171 215 1159, fax 0171 215 1319)

FOSTER, Sir Robert Sidney; GCMG (1970, KCMG 1964, CMG 1961), KCVO (1970); s of late Sidney Charles Foster, and late Jessie Edith, *née* Fry; *b* 11 Aug 1913; *Educ* Eastbourne Coll, Peterhouse Cambridge; *m* 1947, Margaret (d 1991), da of Joseph Charles Walker; *Career* Serv 2 Bn N Rhodesian Regt (Africa and Madagascar) 1940–43; entered Colonial Serv N Rhodesia 1936, sr dist offr 1953, prov cmmr 1957, sec to Min of Native Affairs 1960, chief sec Nyasaland 1961–63, dep govr 1963–64, high cmmr for Western Pacific 1964–68, govr and C-in-C Fiji 1968–70, govr-gen Fiji 1970–73; Offr Légion d'Honneur, KStJ 1968; *Clubs* Leander (Henley on Thames), Royal Over-Seas League, Hawks; *Style*— Sir Robert Foster, GCMG, KCVO; ✉ 18 Windmill Lane, Histon, Cambridge CB4 4JF (☎ 01223 234295)

FOSTER, Rosalind Mary (Mrs R M Englehart); da of Ludovic Anthony Foster (d 1990), of Greatham Manor, Pulborough, Sussex, and Pamela Margaret, *née* Wilberforce; *b* 7 Aug 1947; *Educ* Cranborne Chase Sch Tisbury Wiltshire, Lady Margaret Hall Oxford (BA); *m* 2 Jan 1971, Robert Michael Englehart, QC, *qv*, s of Gustav Axel Englehart (d 1969), of London; 1 s (Oliver b 1982), 2 da (Alice b 1976, Lucinda b 1978); *Career* called to the Bar Middle Temple 1969, bencher 1996, recorder of the Crown Court 1987–; *Recreations* singing, theatre, travel; *Style*— Miss Rosalind Foster; ✉ 2 Temple Gardens, The Temple, London EC47 9AY (☎ 0171 583 6041, fax 0171 583 2094)

FOSTER, Roy William John; s of Francis Edwin Foster, of Axminster, Devon, and Marjorie Florence Mary, *née* Chapman (d 1944); *b* 25 May 1930; *Educ* Rutlish Sch Merton; *m* 6 Sept 1957, Christine Margaret, da of Albert Victor Toler (d 1972); 2 s (Nicholas Charles Roy b 23 April 1960 d 1969, Richard James b 25 March 1964); *Career* Nat Serv RAF 1953–54, cmmnd PO 1953; qualified CA 1955, ptnr Coopers & Lybrand 1960–90; dir J Bibby & Sons plc; memb Cncl: CBI 1986–96, Roedean Sch, Imperial Cancer Research Fund; Freeman City of London; Liveryman: Worshipful Co of Painter Stainers (treas), Worshipful Co of CAs; ATII 1964, FCA 1965; *Recreations* rugby and cricket watching, music, theatre, food and wines; *Clubs* RAF, HAC, MCC, City Livery; *Style*— Roy Foster, Esq; ✉ Cuddington, 28 Downs Side, Cheam, Surrey SM2 7EQ (☎ and fax 0181 642 3965)

FOSTER, Saxby Gregory; s and h of Sir John Gregory Foster, 3 Bt; *b* 3 Sept 1957; *m* 1 July 1989, Rowan Audrey, da of Reginald Archibald Ford (d 1984); 2 s (Thomas James Gregory b 1 May 1991, Robert John Gregory b 10 Dec 1992); *children* 1 s (Thomas James Gregory Foster b 1 May 1991); *Style*— Saxby Foster, Esq

FOSTER, Stephen Anthony; s of Peter Earnest Foster, of Gloucester, and Freda Joan, *née* Howell; *b* 20 March 1952; *Educ* Sir Thomas Rich's GS Glos, Univ of Nottingham (BEd), Univ of London (MA); *m* 1973, Jane Elizabeth Foster; 1 da (Jessica b 4 March 1980), 1 s (William Thomas b 1 March 1990); *Career* teacher Nottingham 1975–80, dir Axiom Gallery Cheltenham 1980–87, dir John Hansard Gallery Univ of Southampton 1987–; FRSA; *Style*— Stephen Foster, Esq; ✉ 33 Cedar Avenue, Shirley, Southampton SO15 5GX (☎ 01703 778363); John Hansard Gallery, The University, Southampton SO17 1BT (☎ 01703 592158, fax 01703 593939)

FOSTER-THOMPSON, Dr Foster; s of F Foster Thompson (d 1965), of Sunderland, Co Durham, and Maude Ann, *née* Quénet; *b* 18 June 1929; *Educ* Durham Sch, Univ of Durham (MB BS); *m* 1 (m dis 1972), Shirley Margaret Creighton, *née* Nuttal; m 2, Sonja Fredrikke, da of Olav Poppe; 1 s (Andrew Iain Thompson), 1 da (Abigail Margaret Sargent); *Career* Intelligence Corps 1946–48, Capt RAMC (TA) 1954–57; conslt physician 1964–94, hon conslt physician Walsgrave NHS Tst 1994– md: John Thompson & Sons Ltd Sunderland 1968–70, Air Commuter Ltd 1970–72; chm Coventry Airport Users'

Assoc 1970–72; civil aviation med examiner: CAA 1970–, Dept of Transportation Federal Aviation Admin of USA 1988–, Transport Health and Welfare Canada 1992; owner Newlands Nursing Home 1972–89; immediate past pres Hosp Consltѕ' and Specialists' Assoc 1994– (hon treas 1987–91, pres 1992–94, tstee 1994–); memb Br Nuclear Med Soc 1989; MRCP 1964; *Recreations* aviation, golf; *Style—* Dr Foster Foster-Thompson; ✉ 1 Clarendon Crescent, Leamington Spa, Warwickshire CV32 5NR (☎ 01926 335487, fax 01926 470852)

FOUCAR, Antony Emile; s of Emile Charles Victor Foucar, MC (d 1963), of Devon, and Mabel Emma, *née* Harris (d 1956); *b* 3 Aug 1926; *m* 1959, Anne, da of Arthur Otway Gosden (d 1950), of Sussex; 2 s (Adam b 1960, James b 1961), 1 da (Charlotte b 1964); *Career* called to the Bar Middle Temple 1949; *Clubs* Oriental, Royal Wimbledon Golf; *Style—* Antony Foucar, Esq; ✉ Greystock, 5 Peek Crescent, London SW19 5ER (☎ 0181 946 8973, fax 0181 944 0853)

FOULDS, Neal Robert; s of Geoff Foulds, of Perivale, Middx, and Patricia, *née* Williams; *b* 13 July 1963; *Educ* Dormers Wells HS Southall; *m* (m dis); 1 s (Darren Michael); *Career* professional snooker player; British jr champion 1981; turned professional 1983; winner: BCE Int 1986, Dubai Masters 1988, Regal Masters 1992, Pot Black 1992; runner-up: English Championship 1986 and 1988, UK Open 1986, British Open 1987, Irish Masters 1988, Hong Kong Masters 1988; semi-finalist World Championships 1987; 3 int appearances England; *Recreations* cricket, golf, greyhound racing; *Style—* Neal Foulds, Esq; ✉ 22 Torrington Gardens, Perivale, Middlesex UB6 7EN (☎ 0181 723 1794)

FOULDS, Roy; s of Franklin Foulds (d 1964), of Long Eaton, and Agnes, *née* Merriman; *b* 30 Jan 1947; *Educ* Nottingham HS; *m* 2 Aug 1969, Christine, da of late Rev Ronald E Thorne; 1 s (Simon b 2 May 1972), 1 da (Rachel b 19 Aug 1975); *Career* Barclays Bank plc: joined 1963, accountant Gallowtree Gate Leicester 1973–75, office mangr Loughborough 1975–78, asst mangr Carlisle 1978–80, mangr Business Advsy Serv 1980–81, mangr Old Market Square Nottingham 1981–82; admin St John's Coll Nottingham 1982–89, co-ordinating sec Central Servs Unit Methodist Church 1996– (gen sec Fin Div 1989–96); chm Methodist Ministers' Housing Soc; sec Central Fin Bd Methodist Church; memb various Methodist bds and ctees; ACIB 1969; *Recreations* music, theatre, reading; *Style—* Roy Foulds, Esq; ✉ The Methodist Church, 25 Marylebone Road, London NW1 5JR (☎ 0171 486 5502, fax 0171 224 1520)

FOULDS, Prof Wallace Stewart; CBE (1988); s of James Foulds (d 1977), of Renfrewshire, and Nellie Margach, *née* Stewart; *b* 26 April 1924; *Educ* George Watson's Coll Edinburgh, Paisley GS, Univ of Glasgow (MB ChB, MD, ChM); *m* 20 Dec 1947, Margaret Holmes, da of Albert Daniel Walls (d 1952), of Ealing; 1 s (Iain Stewart b 1950), 2 da (Margaret Elizabeth (Mrs Rudd) b 1951, Alison Sutherland (Mrs Tambling) b 1958); *Career* RAF Med Branch 1947–49; house surgn to Sir Charles Illingworth Glasgow 1946–47, res surgn Moorfields Eye Hosp London 1950–52, sr registrar UCH 1953–58, res fell and hon sr lectr Inst of Ophthalmology 1953–64, conslt ophthalmologist Addenbrooke's Hosp Cambridge 1958–64, hon lectr Univ of Cambridge 1960–64, prof of ophthalmology Univ of Glasgow 1964–89, conslt ophthalmologist Gtr Glasgow Health Bd 1964–89, visiting prof Nat Univ Singapore and Singapore Nat Eye Centre 1990–; hon fell (and founding pres) Royal Coll of Ophthalmologists, hon fell Royal Soc of Med; hon memb: NZ Ophthalmological Soc, Egyptian Ophthalmological Soc, Portuguese Ophthalmological Soc, Jules Gonin Soc (former vice pres); memb and former chm Assoc Eye Research; memb: American Acad of Ophthalmology, American Macula Soc, Oxford Ophthalmological Congress; Hon DSc Strathclyde; Hon FRCOphth (former pres), Hon FCMSA, Hon FRACO, FRCS (England and Glasgow); *Publications* various relating to ophthalmology; *Recreations* sailing, gardening, natural history; *Clubs* Royal Scot Automobile; *Style—* Prof Wallace Foulds, CBE; ✉ 68 Dowanside Rd, Glasgow G12 9DL (☎ 0141 334 2463, fax 0141 357 4297, e-mail wallace@w.s.foulds.demon.co.uk)

FOULIS, Sir Iain Primrose Liston; 13 Bt (NS 1634), of Colinton, Edinburgh; s of Lt-Col James Alastair Liston Foulis (d 1942, s of Lt-Col Archibald Primrose Liston-Foulis (ka 1917), 4 s of 9 Bt), and Kathleen, da of Lt-Col John Moran and Countess Olga de la Hogue, yr da of Marquis de la Hogue (Isle of Mauritius); suc kinsman, Sir Archibald Charles Liston-Foulis, 12 Bt (d 1961); Sir James Foulis, 2 Bt, was actively engaged in the wars of Scotland after the death of Charles I and was knighted during his f's lifetime; distant cous of Sir Archibald Primrose, 2 Bt of Ravelston who took arms and name of Primrose, fought with Hussars at Culloden, beheaded at Carlisle 1746, title of Ravelston and Estates forfeited; ggggs of Sir Charles Ochterlony, 2 Bt, fndr of The Gurkhas; *b* 9 Aug 1937; *Educ* Hodder, St Mary's Hall, Stonyhurst, Cannington Farm Inst Bridgewater; *Career* practical farming Somerset 1955; Nat Serv Argyll and Sutherland Highlanders 1957–59, Cyprus 1958; language tutor Madrid 1959–61 and 1966–83, ret; trainee exec Bank of London and S America 1962, Bank of London and Montreal Ltd Bahamas, Guatemala and Nicaragua 1963–65, sales Toronto Canada 1966; landowner 1962–; *Recreations* mountain walking, country pursuits (hunting wild boar), swimming, camping, travelling, car racing and rallies, looking across the plains of Castille to the mountains; *Clubs* ADA, Friends of the Castles, Friends of the St James' Way (all in Spain); *Style—* Sir Iain Foulis, Bt; ✉ Residencial Cuzco, Calle Soledad 11, Portal 5–2–C, San Agustin de Guadalix, 28750 Madrid, Spain (☎ and fax 00 34 91 841 8978, mobile 908 829347/907 716845); Calle Universidad 28, Escalera 2, 5–D Jaca (Huesca), Spain

FOULKES, HE Arthur Alexander; *b* 11 May 1928, Mathew Town, Inagua; *Educ* public schs Mathew Town Inagua and Nassau Bahamas; *m* Joan Eleanor, *née* Bullard; 10 c (from previous m); *Career* Nassau Guardian 1945–48, progressively linotype op, reporter then news ed The Tribune 1948–62, ed Bahamian Times 1962–67, fndr chm Diversified Services (PR firm) 1967–70, dir of PR Free Nat Movement 1970–92 (concurrently ed several edns of The Bahamas Handbook and columnist The Nassau Guardian and The Tribune); Bahamian diplomat; memb Bahamian Parl: Progressive Lib Pty 1967–71, Free Nat Movement 1971–92 (co-fndr 1971); appointed: chm Bahamas Telecommunications Corp (Govt-owned) 1967, min of communications 1968, min of tourism 1969; re-appointed to Senate 1977; Bahamas high cmmr to UK and non-resident ambass to EC, Belgium, France, Germany and Italy 1992–; drafted (and memb delegn to UN) Oppn's petition on majority rule 1965, drafted (and memb delgn to conf) Oppn's memorandum for Independent Constitution Conf London 1972; *Recreations* literature, classical and jazz music, theatre; *Style—* HE Mr Arthur A Foulkes; ✉ Bahamas High Commission, Bahamas House, 10 Chesterfield Street, London W1X 8AH (☎ 0171 408 4488, fax 0171 499 9937)

FOULKES, George; JP (Edinburgh 1975), MP (Lab & Co-op) Carrick, Cumnock and Doon Valley (majority 16,626); s of late George Foulkes, and Jessie M A W Foulkes; *b* 21 Jan 1942; *Educ* Keith GS, Haberdashers' Aske's, Univ of Edinburgh; *m* 1970, Elizabeth Anna, da of William Hope; 2 s, 1 da; *Career* pres: Univ of Edinburgh Students Rep Cncl 1963–64, Scottish Union of Students 1965–67; rector's assessor at Univ of Edinburgh; dir: Enterprise Youth 1968–73, Age Concern Scotland 1973–79; cncllr and bailie Edinburgh City Cncl 1970–75, chm Lothian Region Educn Ctee 1974–79, cncllr Lothian Regnl Cncl 1974–79; chm: Educn Ctee Convention of Scot Local Authys 1976–79, Scottish Adult Literacy Agency 1977–79; MP (Lab): S Ayrshire 1979–83, Carrick, Cumnock and Doon Valley 1983–; memb Commons Select Ctee on Foreign Affrs 1981–83, jt chm Commons All-Party Pensioners' Ctee 1983–; front bench oppn spokesman: Euro and Community Affrs 1983–85, Foreign Affrs 1985–92, Defence 1992–93, Overseas Devpt 1994–; memb: Exec Cwlth Parly Assoc (UK), Inter Parly Union (GB); dir Cooperative Press Ltd 1990–, chm John Wheatley Centre 1991–; treasurer Parliamentarians for Global Action (International) 1993–; *Recreations* boating, supporting Heart of Midlothian FC; *Clubs* Edinburgh Univ Staff; *Style—* George Foulkes, Esq, JP, MP; ✉ 18A Ewenfield Rd, Ayr, Scotland (☎ 01292 265776, fax 01292 287914); House of Commons, London SW1A 0AA (☎ 0171 219 3474, fax 0171 219 2407)

FOULKES, Sir Nigel Gordon; kt (1980); s of Louis Augustine Foulkes, and Winifred Foulkes; *b* 29 Aug 1919; *Educ* Gresham's, Balliol Coll Oxford (MA); *m* 1; 1 s, 1 da; m 2, 1948, Elisabeth (d 1995), da of Ewart B Walker, of Toronto; *Career* WWII Sqdn Ldr RAF; formerly with: H P Bulmer, P E Management Group, International Nickel, Rank Xerox (dep md 1964–67, md 1967–70); dir: Charterhouse Group 1972–83, Bekaert Group 1973–85, Stone-Platt Industries 1975–80; chm: British Airports Authy 1972–77, CAA 1977–82, Equity Capital for Industry 1983–86 (vice chm 1982–83), ECI Management Jersey 1986–91, ECI International Management Ltd 1987–91, Equity Capital Trustee Ltd 1983–90; ret; CIMgt; *Clubs* RAF; *Style—* Sir Nigel Foulkes; ✉ Westway House, West Adderbury, nr Banbury, Oxon OX17 3EU (☎ 01295 810220)

FOULKES, Prof (Albert) Peter; s of Henry Foulkes (d 1990), of Yorks, and Edith Cavell, *née* O'Mara (d 1989); *b* 17 Oct 1936; *Educ* Univ of Sheffield (BA), Univ of Cologne, Univ of Tulane (PhD); *m* 1959, (Barbara) Joy, da of William Joseph French (d 1981); 2 da (Imogen b 21 May 1960, Juliet b 26 Nov 1961); *Career* prof Stanford Univ California 1965–75, prof of German Univ of Wales 1977–; Alexander Von Humboldt fell 1972; Inst of Linguists: memb Cncl 1982–89, chm Examinations Bd 1985–90, tstee 1986–90, vice pres 1990–; FIL 1982; *Books* The Reluctant Pessimist, Franz Kafka (1967), The Search for Literary Meaning (1975), Literature and Propaganda (1983); *Recreations* gardening, rambling, theatre, conjuring, photography; *Style—* Prof Peter Foulkes; ✉ Clara, Prades, 66500 France (☎ 00 33 68 96 42 88)

FOUNTAIN, Eric Dudley; OBE (1986); s of William Arthur Fountain (d 1957), of Markyate, Herts, and Lily Eva, *née* Severn; *b* 15 March 1929; *m* 18 May 1957, Yvonne Ruby, da of Edward Blacknell (d 1967); 2 s (Roderic Mark, Gregory Richard), 1 da (Lynn Janette); *Career* dir: Becenta (Beds Enterprise Agency), Beds TEC; chm: Luton Crime Reduction, Beds County Regeneration Gp, Westoning House Ltd, Luton and Dunstable Hosp Tst; tstee Luton and S Beds Hospice, dir Research into Ageing Beds, county vice pres St John Ambulance; High Sheriff for County of Bedfordshire 1993–94; FIMI (memb Cncl), FInstD; *Recreations* golf, football, tennis; *Style—* Eric Fountain, Esq, OBE; ✉ 41 Church Road, Westoning, Bedfordshire MK45 5LP (☎ 01525 712352)

FOURMAN, Prof Michael Paul; s of Prof Lucien Paul Rollings Fourman (d 1968), of Leeds, and Dr Julia Mary, *née* Hunton (d 1981); *b* 12 Sept 1950; *Educ* Allerton Grange Sch Leeds, Univ of Bristol (BSc), Univ of Oxford (MSc, DPhil); *m* 12 Nov 1982, Jennifer Robin, da of Hector Grainger Head (d 1970), of Sydney, Aust; 2 s (Maximillian b 1987, Robin b 1992), 1 da (Paula b 1984); *Career* jr res fell Wolfson Coll Oxford 1974–78, JF Ritt asst prof of mathematics Columbia Univ NY 1976–82; Dept of Electrical and Electronic Engrg Brunel Univ: res fell 1983–86, Hirst reader in integrated circuit design 1986, prof of formal systems 1986–88; Univ of Edinburgh: prof of computer systems 1988–, head of informatics 1994–, head of computer sci 1995–; *Recreations* cooking, sailing; *Clubs* Royal Forth Yacht, Cruising Assoc; *Style—* Prof Michael Fourman; ✉ Department of Computer Science, University of Edinburgh, James Clerk Maxwell Building, The King's Buildings, Edinburgh EH9 3JZ (☎ 0131 650 5197, fax 0131 667 7209)

FOWDEN, Sir Leslie; kt (1982); s of Herbert Fowden, and Amy D Fowden; *b* 13 Oct 1925; *Educ* UCL (PhD); *m* 1949, Margaret Oakes; 1 s, 1 da; *Career* UCL: lectr in plant chemistry 1950–55, reader 1956–64, prof 1964–73, dean Faculty of Sci 1970–73; dir: Rothamsted Experimental Station 1973–86, AFRC Inst of Arable Crops Res 1986–88; chm Agric Vet Advsy Ctee Br Cncl 1987–95; memb: Cncl Royal Soc 1970–72, Scientific Advsy Panel Royal Botanic Gardens Kew 1977–83 (Bd of Tstees 1983–93); tstee Bentham-Moxon Tst 1994; Hon DSc Univ of Westminster 1993; FRS; *Style—* Sir Leslie Fowden, FRS; ✉ 31 Southdown Rd, Harpenden, Herts AL5 1PF

FOWKE, Sir David Frederick Gustavus; 5 Bt (UK 1814), of Lowesby, Leicestershire; s of late Lt-Col Gerrard Fowke, 2 s of 3 Bt; suc unc, Sir Frederick Fowke, 4 Bt (d 1987); *b* 28 Aug 1950; *Educ* Cranbrook Sch Sydney, Sydney Univ (BA); *Heir* none; *Style—* Sir David Fowke, Bt

FOWKE, Philip Francis; s of Francis Henry Villiers (d 1974), of Volos, Greece, and Florence, *née* Clutton; *b* 28 June 1950; *Educ* Downside, began piano studies with Marjorie Withers, RAM (studied piano with Gordon Green, OBE); *Career* concert pianist; Wigmore Hall debut 1974, Royal Festival Hall debut 1977, Proms debut 1979, US debut 1982; performs regularly with all leading Br orchs and for BBC Radio, toured extensively in Europe; contrib to Times Literary Supplement, music magazines and obituaries for nat press; prof of piano RAM 1981–91, prof of piano Welsh Coll of Music and Drama 1994–95, dir of Keyboard Studies Trinity Coll of Music London 1995–; first prize Nat Fedn of Music Socs Award 1973, BBC Piano Competition 1974; Churchill Fellowship 1976; FRAM; *Recordings* incl: Virtuoso Piano Transcriptions, Complete Chopin Waltzes, Chopin Sonatas Nos 2 and 3, Bliss Piano Recital, Bliss Piano Concerto (with Liverpool Philharmonic and David Atherton), Britten Scottish Ballad (with City of Birmingham Orch and Simon Rattle), Finzi Grand Fantasia and Toccata (with Liverpool Philharmonic and Richard Hickox), Rachmaninoff Piano Concerto No 2 and Rhapsody on a Theme from Paganini (with Royal Philharmonic and Yuri Temirkanov), Ravel Piano Concertos (with London Philharmonic and Serge Baudo), Saint-Saëns Carnival of Animals (with Scot Nat Orch and Sir Alexander Gibson), Tchaikovsky Piano Concertos Nos 1 and 2 (with London Philharmonic and Wilfried Boettcher), Delius Piano Concerto (with Royal Philharmonic and Norman del Mar), Hoddinott Piano Concerto No 1 (with Royal Philharmonic and Barry Wordsworth); *Recreations* architecture, monasticism; *Clubs* Royal Over-Seas League, Savage; *Style—* Philip Fowke, Esq; ✉ c/o Patrick Garvey Management, 59 Lansdowne Place, Hove, E Sussex BN3 1FL (☎ 01273 206623, fax 01273 208484)

FOWLDS, Derek James; s of James Witney Fowlds (d 1941), and Ketha Muriel, *née* Treacher (d 1993); *b* 2 Sept 1937; *Educ* Ashlyn's Sch, Watford Tech Coll, RADA; *m* 1, 1964 (m dis 1973), Wendy, *née* Tory; 2 s (James b 14 Oct 1964, Jeremy b 7 Jan 1968); m 2, 1974 (m dis 1978), Leslie, *née* Judd; *Career* actor; *Theatre* incl: The Miracle Worker, How are you Johnnie?, Spring Awakening, Chips with Everything, Child's Play, A Private Matter, Confusions, No Sex Please We're British, Run for your Wife, Billy Liar, Look Homeward Angel, Hamlet, Macbeth, Rattle of a Simple Man; *Television* incl: Play for Today, Dr Finlay's Casebook, The Villains, The Basil Brush Show, Yes Minister, Yes Prime Minister, Rules of Engagement, Die Kinder, Van der Valk, Perfect Scoundrels, Darling Buds of May, Firm Friends, Casualty, Heartbeat, The Detectives; *Films* incl: We Joined the Navy, Tamahine, Doctor in Distress, Hot Enough for June, Tower of Evil, Hotel Paradiso, Frankenstein Created Woman, Mistress Pamela, East of Sudan, Over the Hill; *Recreations* golf, swimming; *Clubs* Stage Golfing Soc, Holmes Place Health; *Style—* Derek Fowlds, Esq; ✉ c/o Caroline Dawson Associates, Apartment 9, 47 Courtfield Road, London SW7 4DB (☎ 0171 370 0708, fax 0171 835 1403)

FOWLE, (William) Michael Thomas; s of William Thomas Fowle (d 1968), of Salisbury, and Nancy, *née* Williams (d 1971); *b* 8 Jan 1940; *Educ* Rugby, Clare Coll Cambridge (MA); *m* 1, (m dis), Judith Anderson; m 2, Margaret Dawes; 1 da (Emma Curtis), 1 s (John); *Career* KPMG: ptnr 1976–, sr UK banking and fin ptnr 1986–90, chm KPMG Banking & Finance Group 1989–93, sr UK audit ptnr 1990–93, sr ptnr London office and SE Region 1993–; Liveryman Worshipful Co of Chartered Accountants; FCA (ACA 1965); *Recreations* collecting; *Clubs* Athenaeum; *Style—* Michael Fowle, Esq; ✉ KPMG, 8 Salisbury Square, London EC4Y 8bb (☎ 0171 311 8492)

FOWLER, Prof Alastair David Shaw; s of David Fowler (d 1939), and Maggie, *née* Shaw (d 1978); *b* 17 Aug 1930; *Educ* Queens Park Sch Glasgow, Univ of Glasgow, Univ of Edinburgh (MA), Pembroke Coll Oxford, Queen's Coll Oxford (MA, DPhil, DLitt); *m* 23 Dec 1950, Jenny Catherine, da of Ian James Simpson (d 1981), of Giffnock House, Helensburgh; 1 s (David b 1960), 1 da (Alison b 1954); *Career* jr res fell Queen's Coll Oxford 1955–59, visiting instr Univ of Indiana 1957–58, lectr Univ Coll Swansea 1959–61, fell and tutor of Eng lit BNC Oxford 1962–71, Regius prof of rhetoric and Eng lit Univ of Edinburgh 1972–84 (univ fell 1984–87); Univ of Virginia: visiting prof 1969, 1979 and 1985–90, prof of English 1990–; visiting prof Univ of Columbia 1964, memb Inst for Advanced Study Princeton 1966 and 1980, visiting fell Cncl of Humanities Univ of Princeton 1974, fell of humanities Res Centre Canberra 1980, visiting fell All Souls Coll Oxford 1984; external assessor Open Univ 1972–77; advsy ed: New Literary History, English Literary Renaissance, Word and Image, Swansea Review, The Seventeenth Century, Connotations, Translation and Literature; memb: Harrap Academic Advsy Ctee 1983–89, Scottish Arts Cncl 1972–74, Nat Printed Books Panel 1977–79, Carlyle Soc (hon vice pres 1972), Eng Union Edinburgh (pres 1972), Renaissance Soc, Renaissance Eng Text Soc, Soc Emblem Studies, Spenser Soc, Bibliographical Soc Virginia; memb AUT 1971–84; FBA 1974; *Books* Spenser and the Numbers of Time (1964), The Poems of John Milton (with John Carey, 1968), Triumphal Forms (1970), Conceitful Thought (1975), Catacomb Suburb (1976), From the Domain of Arnheim (1982), Kinds of Literature (1982), A History of English Literature (1987), The New Oxford Book of Seventeenth Century Verse (1991), The Country House Poem (1994), Time's Purpled Masquers (1996); *Recreations* swimming; *Clubs* United Oxford and Cambridge; *Style—* Prof Alastair Fowler, FBA; ✉ August to December: Department of English, University of Virginia, Bryan Hall, Charlottesville, Virginia 22903, USA (☎ 00 1 804 924 6621, 00 1 804 979 9119); January to July: Department of English, University of Edinburgh, George Square, Edinburgh EH8 9JX (☎ 0131 650 3620)

FOWLER, Christopher Gordon; s of Gordon Fowler, of Cardiff, and Elizabeth Aled, *née* Biggs; *b* 19 March 1950; *Educ* King Alfred's GS Wantage, Middx Hosp Med Sch, Univ of London (BSc, MB BS); *m* 15 Dec 1973 (m dis 1996), Dr Clare Juliet Fowler, *qv*, da of Peter Amyas Wright, of Horton-on-Studley, Oxon; 1 s (William b 9 Aug 1980), 1 da (Alice b 28 June 1977); *Career* sr lectr in urology London Hosp Med Sch 1988– (lectr 1982), conslt urologist The London Hosp and Newham Health Dist 1988–; author of articles and chapters on fibreoscopy, laser surgery and uro-neurology; MRCP, FRCS (Urol); *Recreations* horse riding, jogging, family; *Clubs* Y; *Style—* Christopher Fowler, Esq; ✉ Department of Urology, The Royal London Hospital, London E1 1BB (☎ 0171 377 7327)

FOWLER, Dr Clare Juliet; da of Peter Wright, of Oxford, and Dr Jean Crum; *b* 1 July 1950; *Educ* Wycombe Abbey Sch, Middx Hosp Med Sch (MB BS, MSc); *m* 1973 (m dis 1996); 1 s (William Gordon Peter b 9 Aug 1980), 1 da (Alice Clare b 28 June 1977); *Career* sr registrar in clinical neurophysiology Middx Hosp and Nat Hosp 1984–86; conslt in clinical neurophysiology: Bart's 1987–89, Middx and UCH 1987–; conslt in uro-neurology Nat Hosp for Neurology and Neurosurgery 1987–, sr lectr Inst of Neurology 1996–; memb: Cncl EEG Soc 1987–91, Cncl Neurology Section Standing Ctee RSM; chm: Clinical Autonomic Res Soc 1990–92 (hon sec 1986–89), SUBDIMS; hon sec Br Soc of Clinical Neurophysiology 1992–95, memb Scientific Ctee Int Continence Soc 1995–97; FRCP; *Style—* Dr Clare Fowler; ✉ Department of Uro-Neurology, The National Hospital for Neurology and Neurosurgery, Queen Square, London WC1N 3BG (☎ 0171 837 3611, fax 0181 749 8913, e-amil cfowler@ion.ucl.ac.uk)

FOWLER, Prof Godfrey Heath; OBE (1989); s of Donald Heath Fowler (d 1985), of Wolverley, Worcs, and Dorothy, *née* Bealey (d 1987); *b* 1 Oct 1931; *Educ* Sebright Sch, University Coll Oxford (MA, BM BCh); *m* 15 Sept 1962, Sissel, da of Arnfred Vidnes (d 1983), of Oslo, Norway; 2 s (Jeremy Kristen b 1964, Adrian Dag b 1965 d 1995); *Career* GP Oxford 1959–, professorial fell Balliol Coll 1978–, prof of gen practice Univ of Oxford 1996– (reader 1978–96); hon dir ICRF Gen Practice Res Unit 1988–; *Books* Preventive Medicine in General Practice (1983), Essentials of Preventive Medicine (1984), Prevention in General Practice (1993), Prevention of Cardiovascular Disease (1996); *Recreations* skiing, mountaineering, photography; *Style—* Prof Godfrey Fowler, OBE; ✉ Orchard House, Squitchey Lane, Oxford OX2 7LD (☎ 01865 58331); University Department of Public Health and Primary Care, Radcliffe Infirmary, Oxford OX2 6HE (☎ 01865 319111, fax 01865 511635)

FOWLER, Ian; OBE (1993); s of Norman William Frederick Fowler, OBE, QPM, of Herne Bay, Kent, and late Alice May, *née* Wakelin; *b* 20 Sept 1932; *Educ* The King's Sch Canterbury, St Edmund Hall Oxford (MA); *m* 3 April 1961, Gillian Cecily Fowler, JP, da of late Desmond Allchin; 2 s (Aidan Lewis b 12 May 1966, Edmund Ian Carloss b 18 March 1970), 1 da (Sarah May b 1964); *Career* Nat Serv 2 Lt (Lt TA) 2 Bn The Green Howards 1951–53; called to the Bar Gray's Inn 1957; princ chief clerk and clerk to Ctee of Magistrates Inner London Magistrates' Courts Serv 1979–94 (joined 1959), dep traffic cmmr Eastern Traffic Area 1987–; cncllr: Herne Bay UDC 1961–74, Canterbury City Cncl 1974–83; Mayor of Canterbury 1976–77; memb Ct Univ of Kent 1976–; *Recreations* reading; *Style—* Ian Fowler, Esq, OBE; ✉ 6 Dence Park, Herne Bay, Kent (☎ 01227 375530)

FOWLER, Jennifer Joan; da of Russell Aubrey Fowler (d 1971), and Lucy, *née* Tobitt; *b* 14 April 1939; *Educ* Bunbury HS, Univ of W Aust (BA, BMus, DipEd); *m* 18 Dec 1971, John Bruce, s of Maj Frederick Paterson (d 1983); 2 s (Martin b 1973, Adrian b 1976); *Career* composer; major works: Hours of the Day (for 4 singers, 2 oboes and 2 clarinets) 1968, Ravelation (for string quintet) 1971, Veni Sancte Spiritus (for 12 solo singers) 1971, Chant with Garlands (for orchestra) 1974, Voice of the Shades (for soprano, oboe, violin) 1977, Tell Out My Soul (for soprano, cello, piano) 1980, When David Heard (for choir and piano) 1982, Echoes from an Antique Land (for ensemble) 1983, Lament (for baroque oboe, viol) 1988, And Ever Shall Be (for mezzo and ensemble) 1989, Reeds, Reflections (for oboe and string trio) 1990, Plainsong for Strings (for string orchestra) 1992, Lament for Dunblane (for 4 solo voices) 1996, Singing the Lost Places (for large ensemble) 1996; int prizes: Acad of the Arts Berlin, Radcliffe award of GB, Gedok prize Mannheim; memb: Composers' Guild of GB, Women in Music, Sonic Arts Network, SPNM, Int Alliance for Women in Music; *Recreations* literature, gardening; *Style—* Ms Jennifer Fowler; ✉ 21 Deodar Road, Putney, London SW15 2NP

FOWLER, Keith Harrison; s of late Lancelot Harrison Fowler; *b* 20 May 1934; *Educ* Aldenham; *m* 1961, Vicki Belinda, *née* Pertwee; 3 c; *Career* Lt Army Suez Canal; exec chm Edman Communications Group plc 1977–88, chief exec Cresta Corporate Services Ltd 1988–89, dir Cresta Holdings Ltd 1988–89, chief exec Euro RSCG Marketing Group Ltd 1990–95, chm Scholefield Turnbull & Partners Ltd; memb Cncl Nat Advertising Benevolent Soc 1978–, chm Winchester House School Trust Ltd 1968–, dir Pertwee Holdings 1982–; ACIS; *Recreations* riding, tennis, classic cars, pictures; *Clubs* Arts, Lansdowne, Solus; *Style—* Keith Fowler, Esq; ✉ Corfield Cottage, Arrewig Lane, Chartridge, nr Chesham, Bucks (☎ 01494 837089; 21 Cedar Drive, The Causeway, London N2 0RS (☎ 0181 883 1688)

FOWLER, Maurice Anthony; s of Benjamin Arthur Fowler (d 1975), of Broadstairs, Kent, and Dorothy Fowler (d 1970); *b* 17 July 1937; *Educ* Whitgift Sch Croydon; *m* 9 Sept 1961, Evelyn Jessica, da of Joseph Sidney Currell (d 1961), of Croydon, Surrey; 1 s (Russell b 1967), 1 da (Louise b 1964); *Career* CA Hartley Fowler 1971–; cnllr London Borough of Croydon, past pres Croydon C of C, past mayor London Borough of Croydon; govr Whitgift Fndn; Freeman City of London, Liveryman Worshipful Co of Carmen; FCA 1961, FCIArb 1965; *Recreations* politics, cricket, sport, bridge; *Clubs* Surrey CCC; *Style—* Maurice Fowler, Esq; ✉ Nelson House, 58 Wimbledon Hill Road, London SW19 7PA (☎ 0181 946 1212, fax 0181 947 0998)

FOWLER, Neil Douglas; s of Arthur Vincent Fowler, of Hockley, Essex, and Helen Pauline, *née* Douglas (d 1990); *b* 18 April 1956; *Educ* Southend HS for Boys, Univ of Leicester (BA); *m* 9 June 1989, Carol Susan, da of Kenneth Sydney Eric Cherry; 1 da (Helen Christine b 28 Jan 1993), 1 step s (Maurice Christopher John Volans b 13 March 1976); *Career* trainee (later sr reporter) Leicester Mercury 1978–81, dep news ed (later asst chief sub ed) Derby Evening Telegraph 1981–84, asst to the ed (later asst ed) Lincolnshire Echo 1984–85; ed: Lincolnshire Echo 1985–87, Derby Evening Telegraph 1987–91, The Journal Newcastle-upon-Tyne 1991–94 (Newspaper Indust Awards: North East Newspaper of the Year 1992, Regnl Newspaper of the Year 1994), The Western Mail Cardiff 1994–; Newspaper Industry Awards 1993: winner Best Use of Photography, highly commended Best Use of Colour, highly commended Regnl Ed of the Year; Newspaper Industry Awards 1994: Regnl Newspaper Ed of the Year, highly commended Best Use of Colour; *Recreations* cricket, cinema, music of Frank Zappa; *Clubs* Essex CCC; *Style—* Neil Fowler, Esq; ✉ Western Mail and Echo Ltd, Thomson House, Havelock Street, Cardiff CF1 1WR (☎ 01222 583650, fax 01222 583416)

FOWLER, Rt Hon Sir (Peter) Norman; PC (1979), MP (C) Sutton Coldfield (majority 26,036); s of N F Fowler (d 1964), of Chelmsford, and Katherine Fowler; *b* 2 Feb 1938; *Educ* King Edward VI Sch Chelmsford, Trinity Hall Cambridge; *m* 1, 1968 (m dis 1976), Linda Christmas; m 2, 1979, Fiona Poole, da of John Donald; 2 da (Kate Genevieve b Nov 1981, Isobel Geraldine b July 1984); *Career* with The Times 1961–70 (special corr 1962–66, home affrs 1966–70), memb Editorial Bd Crossbow 1962–69; MP (C): Nottingham S 1970–74, Sutton Coldfield Feb 1974–; PPS NI Office 1972–74, oppn spokesman Home Affrs 1974–75; chief oppn spokesman: Social Servs 1975–76, Tport 1976–79; min Tport 1979–81; sec of state: Tport Jan-Sept 1981, Social Servs 1981–87, Employment 1987–90; special advsr to Prime Minister 1992 general election; chm Conservative Party 1992–94; chm: Midland Independent Newspapers, National Housebuilding Cncl; non-exec dir: NFC plc, Bardon plc; *Style—* The Rt Hon Sir Norman Fowler, MP; ✉ House of Commons, London SW1A 0AA

FOWLER, Peter James; CMG (1990); *b* 26 Aug 1936; *Educ* Nunthorpe GS York, Trinity Coll Oxford (BA); *m* 1962, Audrey June, *née* Smith; 3 da, 1 s; *Career* Army Serv 1954–56; HM Dip Serv: Foreign Office 1962–64, third sec Budapest 1964–65, second later first sec Lisbon 1965–67, first sec and head of Chancery Calcutta 1968–71, FCO 1971–75, first sec and head of Chancery E Berlin 1975–77, cnsllr on loan to Cabinet Office 1977–80, cnsllr Geneva (Comprehensive Test Ban Delgn) 1980, cnsllr (Bonn Gp) Bonn 1981–85, cnsllr FCO 1985–88, min and dep high cmmr New Delhi 1988–93, high cmmr to Bangladesh 1993–96, ret; non-exec dir Cairn Energy plc 1996–; *Recreations* reading, opera, life in South Asia; *Style—* Peter Fowler, Esq, CMG; ✉ 110 Kenilworth Avenue, London SW19 7LR; Cairn Energy plc, Cairn House, 61 Dublin Street, Edinburgh EH3 6NL (☎ 0131 557 2299, fax 0131 557 2220)

FOWLER, Richard Nicholas; QC (1989); s of Ronald Hugh Fowler (d 1971), and Winifred Mary, *née* Hull; *b* 12 Oct 1946; *Educ* Bedford Sch, Brasenose Coll Oxford (BA); *Career* called to the Bar Middle Temple 1969; Liveryman Worshipful Co of Goldsmiths 1989 (Freeman 1980); *Recreations* walking, opera, dogs; *Style—* Richard Fowler, Esq, QC; ✉ 93 Cheyne Walk, London SW10 0DQ (☎ 0171 352 4966); 4 Raymond Buildings, Gray's Inn, London WC1R 5BP (☎ 0171 405 7211, fax 0171 405 2084)

FOWLER, Richard Thomas; s of Arthur Fowler (d 1984), of Huddersfield, and Joan Eileen Fowler; *b* 8 Sept 1950; *Educ* Holme Valley GS, Loughborough Coll of Art & Design, Ravensbourne Coll of Art & Design (BA); *m* 11 Aug 1984, Jane Lesley, da of Col W P Fletcher; 1 s (Daniel John Fletcher b 6 Sept 1987), 1 da (Bryony Anne b 29 July 1990); *Career* memb design staff British Museum then display offr International Harvester Company of GB Ltd 1974–80; exhibit designer Science Museum 1980–83 (designed Concorde exhbn at Yeovilton 1980 and the Nuclear Physics and Nuclear Power Gallery S Kensington 1982), head of design National Museum of Photography, Film and Television Bradford 1983–89 (estab new displays TV Galleries 1986 and Kodak Museum 1989), visiting designer Computer Museum Boston (memb design and prodn team of the Giant Walk-through Computer) 1989–90, head of design Eureka! (educnl museum for children) 1990–93, fndr/designer Richard Fowler Associates 1993–; recent projects incl: More Than a Game exhbn of football culture for Euro '96 Championships, Naturequest Interactive Natural Sci Centre for Wollaton Hall, Darwin Initiative/Bio-diversity exhbn for Nat History Museum; current work incl: Wigan Pier second stage (display of the Robert Opie Collection), Creepy Crawlies/Arthropods Gallery for Nat History Museum, Interactive Natural Sci Centre for Harewood House, Ceramica exhbn Celebration of Pottery Indust for Burslem Community Devpt Tst; external assessor Museum and Exhbn Design degree course Univ of Humberside; chm Museum and Exhbn Design Gp 1992–95; memb: Museums Assoc, NAME; MCSD 1983; *Recreations* drawing, fly fishing, watching sport; *Style—* Richard Fowler, Esq; ✉ 53 Lower Mill Bank Road, Mill Bank, Sowerby Bridge, Yorkshire HX6 3ED (☎ 01422 823171); Richard Fowler Associates, 4 Crown Yard, Southgate, Elland, Yorkshire HX5 0DQ (☎ 01422 375680, fax 01422 374157)

FOWLER, Sheila Patricia; da of George William Spurs (d 1975), of Sunderland, and Lillian Bean, *née* Callum (d 1986); *b* 22 April 1946; *Educ* St Anthony's GS Sunderland, Monkwearmouth Coll Sunderland, Univ of Sunderland (HNC business studies); *m* 1 March 1976, Richard Fowler, s of Richard Fowler; *Career* local govt offr Sunderland BC 1962–65, industl market res offr rising to PRO Corning Glass Co Sunderland 1965–71; PRO: Washington Devpt Corp 1971–72, N of England Devpt Cncl (Promotions) 1972–74; industl devpt offr Cleveland CC 1974–79, PR dir Sweetman Marketing Ltd Middlesbrough 1979–82, princ Sheila P Fowler Associates 1982–, chm Fowler Advertising Ltd 1982–; ICP Promotional Achievement Award USA 1984, 1986 and 1987; FIPR 1987 (MIPR 1971); *Recreations* golf, reading, travelling, Spanish culture; *Clubs* Hartlepool Golf, Castle Eden Golf; *Style—* Mrs Sheila Fowler; ✉ Sheila P Fowler Associates, 10 Holyrood Crescent, Hart Village, Hartlepool TS27 3BB (☎ 01429 272553, fax 01429 223442, mobile 0831 331242)

FOWLER, Dr Timothy John; s of Eric Fowler (d 1978), of Crowborough, E Sussex, and Agatha Clare, *née* Turner (d 1985); *b* 10 Dec 1937; *Educ* Downside, Oriel Coll Oxford (BA, MA, BM BCh, DM), MRCP 1965, FRCP 1979, St Bartholomew's Hosp Med Sch London; *m* 6 Sept 1975, Sheila Barbara, da of Harrison Parkin (d 1977); 1 s (Thomas Gregory b 3 July 1979), 2 da (Clare Judith b 10 Nov 1976, Emma Jane b 23 Feb 1978); *Career* house physician St Bartholomew's Hosp, registrar in neurology Queen Elizabeth Hosp Birmingham, registrar and sr registrar in neurology Nat Hosp for Nervous Diseases, sr registrar in neurology St Mary's Hosp London; conslt neurologist 1974–: King's Coll Hosp London, Kent and Sussex Weald Trust Tunbridge Wells; memb Assoc of Br Neurologists; *Books* Clinical Neurology for House Physicians in the Neurological Unit (1982), Neurology (jtly, 1985), Headache (ed, 1987), Clinical Neurology (jtly, 1990); *Style—* Dr Timothy Fowler; ✉ Kent and Sussex Hospital, Mount Ephraim, Tunbridge Wells TN4 8AT

FOWLES, John; OBE (1986), JP (1972); s of Harold Fowles (d 1983), and Helen Fowles (d 1983); *b* 28 June 1932; *Educ* Reading Collegiate Sch, Harvard Business Course; *m* 22 April 1961, Diana Mary, da of Victor Urrey Oldland; 2 s (Charles b 1962, James b 1964), 1 da (Jayne b 1963); *Career* RAF Tech Trg Cmd, Fighter Cmd 90 Gp 1949–53; chm Gowring Group (joined 1953); CBI: memb Southern Regn Cncl 1979–89 (chm 1983–85, vice chm 1981–83), memb Nat Cncl (Chm's Ctee and Pres Ctee 1981–86); dir: Newbury Racecourse plc 1983–89, Southern Advsy Bd National Westminster plc 1990–92; chm: Berkshire Indust Year 1986, HM gen cmmn for Inland Revenue 1981–; Freeman City of London, Liveryman Worshipful Co of Basketmakers; FRSA; *Recreations* fishing, shooting, golf; *Clubs* MCC, Guild of Freemen, City Livery; *Style*— John Fowles, Esq, OBE, JP; ✉ Burghclere Manor, nr Newbury, Berks RG20 9NS; Gowrings plc, 245 Finchampstead Road, Wokingham, Berks RG40 3JS (☎ 0118 977 0101)

FOWLES, John; *b* 31 March 1926; *Educ* New Coll Oxford; *Career* writer; PEN Silver Pen Award 1969, W H Smith Award 1970; judge NCR Book Award 1992; *Books* The Collector (1963), The Aristos (1965), The Magus (1966, revised edn 1977), The French Lieutenant's Woman (1969), Poems (1973), The Ebony Tower (1974, televised 1984), Shipwreck (1975), Daniel Martin (1977), Islands (1978), The Tree (with Frank Horvat, 1978), John Aubrey's Monumenta parts 1 and 2 (ed, 1980) part 3 and Index (ed, 1982), The Enigma of Stonehenge (1980), Mantissa (1982), Thomas Hardy's England (1984), Land (1985), A Maggot (1985); *Recreations* mainly Sabine; *Style*— John Fowles, Esq; ✉ c/o Sheil Land Associates Ltd, 43 Doughty Street, London WC1N 2LF

FOWLIE, Dr Hector Chalmers; OBE (1989); s of Hector McIntosh Fowlie (d 1954), and Agnes Blue, *née* Turner (d 1966); *b* 21 June 1929; *Educ* Harris Acad Dundee, Univ of St Andrews (MB ChB); *m* Christina Napier Morrison, da of Peter Walker (d 1967); 2 s (Stephen b 1956, Peter b 1962), 1 da (Kay b 1958); *Career* psychiatrist; formerly physician supt Royal Dundee Liff and Strathmartine Hosps Dundee, conslt psychiatrist Tayside Health Bd Dundee, chm Dundee Healthcare NHS Tst; vice chm: Mental Welfare Cmmn for Scotland, Parole Bd for Scotland; memb Ct Univ of Abertay Dundee; FRCPE, FRCPsych; *Style*— Dr Hector Fowlie, OBE; ✉ 21 Clepington Road, Dundee DD4 7EL (☎ 01382 456926)

FOX, Dr Alan Martin; s of Sidney Nathan Fox (d 1987), and Clarice, *née* Solov; *b* 5 July 1938; *Educ* Bancrofts Sch Woodford, Queen Mary Coll London (BSc, PhD, Pres of Union); *m* 20 June 1965, Sheila Naomi, da of Lazarus Pollard, of Bournemouth; 1 s (James Henry Paul b 1974), 2 da (Victoria Charlotte b 1968, Louise Rachel b 1971); *Career* Miny of Aviation and Technol 1963–72 (private sec to John Stonehouse MP and Julian Snow MP 1965–67), first sec Aviation and Def Br Embassy Paris 1973–75; MOD: operational analysis studies Fin of Def Nuclear Weapons Prog 1975–78, RCDS 1979, fin control of RAF Material Requirements 1980–84, Def Intelligence Staff 1984–88, asst under sec (Ordnance) 1988–92, visiting fell Centre for Int Affrs Harvard Univ 1992–93, asst under sec (Quartermaster) 1994–95, asst under sec (Export Policy and Finance) 1995–; *Recreations* bridge, chess, watching rugby and cricket; *Clubs* Surrey County Cricket; *Style*— Dr Alan Fox; ✉ c/o Ministry of Defence, Whitehall, London SW1

FOX, Brian Michael; s of Walter Fredrick Fox (d 1969), and Audrey May Fox; *b* 21 Sept 1944; *Educ* East Ham GS for Boys; *m* 1966, Maureen Ann; 1 da (Joanne Clare b 1973); *Career* HM Treasy: private sec to Fin Sec 1967–69, seconded to 3i Group 1980–82, dep establishment offr 1983–87, head Defence Policy Div 1987–89, princ establishment and fin offr 1989–94; head of sr and public appointments gp and dir of public appointments Cabinet Office 1994–95, dir of Senior Civil Serv Gp 1995–; *Recreations* table tennis, soccer, badminton; *Style*— Brian Fox, Esq; ✉ Cabinet Office, Horse Guards Road, London SW1P 3AL (☎ 0171 270 6220, fax 0171 270 6116)

FOX, Edward Charles Morice; eld s of Maj Robin Fox, MC, RA (d 1971), of Cuckfield, Sussex, and Angela Muriel Darita, *née* Worthington; bro of James Fox and Robert Michael John Fox, *qqv*; *b* 13 April 1937; *Educ* Harrow, RADA; *m* 1958 (m dis), Tracy Reed, da of late Anthony Pelissier, of Sussex; 1 da (Lucy Arabella (Mrs David Grenfell) b 1960); *ptnr* (since 1972), Joanna David, *qv*; 1 s (Frederick Samson Robert Morice b 5 April 1989), 1 da (Emilia Rose Elizabeth b 31 July 1974); *Career* stage, screen and television actor 1958–; late Coldstream Gds, 2 Lt Loyal N Lancs Regt; *Theatre* incl: Knuckle (Comedy) 1973, The Family Reunion (Vaudeville) 1979, Anyone for Denis (Whitehall) 1981, Quartermaine's Terms (Queen's) 1981, Hamlet (Young Vic) 1982, Interpreters (Queen's) 1985, Let Us Go Then You and I (Lyric) 1987, The Dance of Death (Manchester) 1987, The Admirable Crichton (Haymarket) 1988, Another Love Story (also dir, Leicester Haymarket) 1990, The Philanthropist (West End), My Fair Lady (tour) 1992, Quartermaine's Terms 1993, The Father 1995; *Television* incl: Hard Times 1977, Edward and Mrs Simpson 1978 (BAFTA Award for Best Actor 1978, TV Times Top Ten Award for Best Actor 1978–79, Br Broadcasting Press Guild TV Award for Best Actor 1978, Royal TV Soc Performance Award 1978–79), Gulliver's Travels 1995; *Films* incl: The Go-Between 1971 (Soc of Film and TV Arts Award for Best Supporting Actor, 1971), The Day of the Jackal 1973, A Doll's House 1973, Galileo 1976, The Squeeze 1977, A Bridge Too Far 1977 (BAFTA Award for Best Supporting Actor), The Duellists 1977, The Cat and the Canary 1977, Force Ten from Navarone 1978, The Mirror Crack'd 1980, Gandhi 1982, Never Say Never Again 1983, The Dresser 1983, The Bounty 1984, The Shooting Party 1985, A Month by the Lake 1996; *Recreations* music, gardening; *Clubs* Savile; *Style*— Edward Fox, Esq; ✉ c/o Michael Whitehall Ltd, 125 Gloucester Road, London SW7 4TE (☎ 0171 244 8466, fax 0171 244 9060)

FOX, Frederick Donald; s of Lesley James Fox (d 1950), of Urana, NSW, Aust, and Ruby Mansfield, *née* Elliott (d 1965); *b* 2 April 1931; *Educ* St Joseph's Convent Sch Jerilderie NSW Aust; *Career* milliner, started in business 1962, currently designer for the Royal Family; pres Millinery Trades Benevolent Assoc; granted Royal Warrant to HM The Queen 1974; Freeman City of London 1989, Liveryman Worshipful Co of Feltmakers 1989; *Recreations* gardening, photography; *Style*— Frederick Fox, Esq; ✉ Model Hats, 87–91 New Bond St, London W1Y 9LA (☎ 0171 629 5705, 5706, fax 0171 629 3048)

FOX, Lady; Hazel Mary; da of John Matthew Blackwood Stuart, CIE (d 1941), and Lady (Joan Daria) Denning, *née* Elliot Taylor; *b* 22 Oct 1928; *Educ* Roedean, Somerville Coll Oxford (MA); *m* 1954, Rt Hon Sir Michael John Fox, *qv*; 3 s, 1 da; *Career* called to the Bar 1950; Somerville Coll Oxford: lectr in law 1951–58, fell and tutor in law 1977–82, hon fell 1989–; chm: London Rent Assessment Panel 1977–, London Leasehold Valuation Tbnl 1981–; dir Br Inst of International and Comparative Law 1982–89, gen ed Int and Comparative Law Quarterly 1987–, memb Home Office Departmental Ctee on Jury Serv 1963–65, chm Tower Hamlets Juvenile Ct 1968–76; JP London 1956–77; additional Bencher Lincoln's Inn 1989; assoc tenant 4/5 Gray's Inn Square WC1 1994–; memb Cncl of Legal Educn (for England and Wales) 1990–94; govr Summer Fields Sch 1968–; QC (Honoris Causa) 1993; *Books* International Arbitration (with J L Simpson 1959), International Economic Law and Developing States (ed, 1988 and 1992), Joint Development of Offshore Oil and Gas Vol I and II (ed, 1989 and 1990), Effecting Compliance (ed with Michael A Meyer, 1993); *Style*— Lady Fox, QC; ✉ British Institute of International and Comparative Law, Charles Clore House, 17 Russell Square, London WC1B 5DR (☎ 0171 636 5802, fax 0171 323 2016)

FOX, James; s of Maj Robin Fox, MC, RA (d 1971), of Cuckfield, Sussex, and Angela Muriel Darita, *née* Worthington; bro of Edward Charles Morice Fox, *qv*, and Robert Michael John Fox, *qv*; *b* 19 May 1939; *Educ* Harrow; *m* 15 Sept 1973, Mary Elizabeth, da of Maj Allan Piper, of Wadhurst, Sussex; 4 s (Thomas b 1975, Robin b 1976, Laurence b 1978, Jack b 1985), 1 da (Lydia b 1979); *Career* actor; *Television* incl: A Question of Attribution 1991, Headhunters 1993, The Choir (BBC) 1994, The Old Curiosity Shop (Disney Channel, Cable TV) 1994, Gullivers Travels (Channel 4) 1995, Elgars 10th Muse (Channel 4) 1995; *Film* The Servant 1963, King Rat 1964, Thoroughly Modern Millie 1966, Performance 1969, A Passage to India 1984, The Russia House 1990, Patriot Games 1992, The Remains of the Day 1993; *Books* Comeback An Actors Direction (1983); *Recreations* tennis, windsurfing; *Style*— James Fox, Esq; ✉ Michael Whitehall Ltd, 125 Gloucester Road, London SW7 4TE (☎ 0171 244 8466, fax 0171 244 9060)

FOX, James George; s of George Romney Fox (d 1968), of Falmouth, Cornwall, and Barbara Muriel, *née* Twite (d 1994); *b* 14 May 1943; *Educ* Eton, Univ of Newcastle upon Tyne (BA), Univ of Pennsylvania (MBA); *m* 4 May 1974, Rebecca Jane, da of Charles Wright, of Canyon, Texas; 2 s (Francis b 1977, Romney b 1981), 2 da (Rachel b 1975, Sarah b 1979); *Career* dir: Hill Samuel Investment Management 1968–78, Warburg Investment Management 1982–85, Falmouth Hotel plc 1981–92; md: Morgan Grenfell Trust Managers 1985–, Morgan Grenfell Equity Income Trust plc 1991–, Anglo & Overseas Tst plc 1992–, Morgan Grenfell Latin American Companies Tst plc 1994–; *Recreations* sailing; *Clubs* Athenaeum; *Style*— James Fox; ✉ Trewardreva, Constantine, Falmouth, Cornwall (☎ 01326 340207); 57 Andrewes House, Barbican, London EC2 (☎ 0171 638 9103); Morgan Grenfell, 20 Finsbury Circus, London EC2M 1NB (☎ 0171 256 7500)

FOX, Dr (Anthony) John; s of Freddie Fox, OBE, and Gertrude, *née* Preis; *b* 25 April 1946; *Educ* Dauntseys Sch, UCL (BSc), Imperial Coll London (PhD, DIC); *m* 9 Sept 1971, Annemarie, da of Ladislas Revesz, of Frankfurt; 1 s (Sebastian Stefan b 3 Dec 1982), 2 da (Simone Nikki b 11 Oct 1973, Zoe Valerie b 31 Jan 1977); *Career* statistician Health and Safety Exec; Office of Population Censuses and Surveys: statistician, chief med statistician, dep dir; currently gp dir of census, population and health Office for National Statistics; prof of social statistics City Univ 1980–88; FSS 1970; *Books* Socio-Demographic Mortality Differentials (1982), Health Inequalities in European Countries (1989), Health and Class: the early years (with Power and Manor, 1991); *Recreations* tennis, bridge, family; *Clubs* RSM; *Style*— Dr John Fox; ✉ Office for National Statistics, St Catherine's House, 10 Kingsway, London WC2B 6JP (☎ 0171 396 2160)

FOX, Dr Kim Michael; s of Lt-Col Michael Allen Fox (d 1980), of Edinburgh, and Veronica Venetia Fox, *née* Sweeney; *b* 17 June 1948; *Educ* Fort Augustus Abbey Sch, Univ of St Andrews (MB ChB, MD); *children* 1 s (Michael James b 6 March 1978); *Career* conslt cardiologist at The Royal Brompton Hosp; ed and author of textbooks in cardiology, ed Euro Heart Jl; FRCP 1988, fell Euro Soc of Cardiology; *Books* Diseases of the Heart (ed 1988, 2 edn 1996), Wolfe Atlases of Cardiology; *Style*— Dr Kim Fox; ✉ Chuffs House, Hollyport, Berks SL6 2NA; The Royal Brompton Hospital, Sydney Street, London SW3 6NP (☎ 0171 352 8121); 81 Harley Street, London W1 (☎ 0171 486 4617)

FOX, Dr Levi; OBE (1964), DL (1967 Warwickshire); s of John William Fox (d 1952), of Coleorton, Leics, and Julia Sophia, *née* Stinson (d 1938); *b* 28 Aug 1914; *Educ* Ashby de La Zouch Boys' GS, Oriel Coll Oxford (MA), Univ of Manchester (MA); *m* 1938, Jane Richards; 1 s, 2 da; *Career* dir and sec: Incorporated Tst, Shakespeare Birthplace Tst 1945–89 (dir emeritus 1990); author of books on Shakespeare Stratford-upon-Avon and Warwickshire; hon vice pres Int Shakespeare Assoc (formerly dep chm); Hon LHD George Washington Univ, Hon DLitt Birmingham Univ; medallist New York Univ; FSA, FRHistS, FRSL; *Books* Coventry's Heritage (1945), The Borough Town of Stratford-upon-Avon (1953), Shakespeare's England (1972), A Country Grammar School (1967), In Honour of Shakespeare (1972), Stratford-upon-Avon: an appreciation (1976); *Recreations* country life, gardening; *Style*— Dr Levi Fox, OBE, DL, FSA, FRSL; ✉ Silver Birches, 27 Welcombe Rd, Stratford-upon-Avon, Warwickshire CV37 6UJ (☎ 01789 292648); The Shakespeare Centre, Stratford-upon-Avon, Warwickshire (☎ 01789 204016)

FOX, Dr Liam; MP (C) Woodspring (majority 17,509); s of William Fox, and Catherine Fox; *b* 22 Sept 1961; *Educ* St Brides HS E Kilbride, Univ of Glasgow (MB ChB, MRCGP); *Career* gen practitioner, also Army MO (civilian) RAEC and divnl surgn St John Ambulance; nat vice chm Scottish YCs 1983–84, sabbatical as guest of US State Dept studying drug abuse and Republican campaigning techniques 1985; individual speaking prize World Debating Competition Toronto 1982, best speaker's trophy Univ of Glasgow 1983; Parly candidate (C) Roxburgh and Berwickshire 1987, MP (C) Woodspring 1992–; memb Scottish Select Ctee 1992–93, sec Cons Backbench Health Ctee 1992–93, sec Cons West Country Members Ctee 1992–93, PPS to Rt Hon Michael Howard as Home Sec 1993–94, asst govt whip 1994–95, Lord Cmmr HM Treasy (sr Govt whip) 1995–96, Parly under-sec of state FCO 1996–; *Style*— Dr Liam Fox, MP; ✉ House of Commons, London SW1A 0AA

FOX, Rt Hon Sir (John) Marcus; PC (1996), kt (1986), MBE (1963), MP (C) Shipley (majority 12,382); s of late Alfred Hirst Fox; *b* 11 June 1927; *Educ* Wheelwright GS Dewsbury; *m* 1954, Ann, da of F W J Tindall; 1 s, 1 da; *Career* served Duke of Wellington's Regt and The Green Howards 1945–48; memb Dewsbury Borough Cncl 1956–65; contested (C): Dewsbury 1959, Huddersfield W 1966; MP (C) Shipley 1970–, memb Race Relations and Immigration Select Ctee 1970–72, asst govt whip 1972–73, Lord Cmmr of the Treasy 1973–74; oppn front bench spokesman: Environment 1974, Housing 1974–75, Tport 1975–76; vice-chm Cons Pty (responsible for candidates) 1976–79, Parly under-sec state DOE 1979–81, memb Select Ctee on Members' Salaries 1981–82, chm 1922 Ctee 1992– (vice-chm 1983–92), chm Ctee of Selection 1984–92; nat chm Assoc of Cons Clubs 1988–; Liveryman Worshipful Co of Gold & Silver Wyre Drawers; *Style*— The Rt Hon Sir Marcus Fox, MBE, MP; ✉ House of Commons, London SW1A 0AA

FOX, Rt Hon Lord Justice; Rt Hon Sir Michael John; kt (1975), PC (1981), QC (1968); s of Michael Fox; *b* 8 Oct 1921; *Educ* Drayton Manor Sch Hanwell, Magdalen Coll Oxford; *m* 1954, Hazel Mary, *qv*, da of John Matthew Blackwood Stuart, CIE; 3 s, 1 da; *Career* served Admty 1942–45; called to the Bar Lincoln's Inn 1949, judge High Ct (Chancery) 1975–81, a Lord Justice of Appeal 1981–92; *Style*— The Rt Hon Sir Michael Fox; ✉ c/o Royal Courts of Justice, The Strand, London WC2A 2LL

FOX, Ven Michael John; *b* 28 April 1942; *Educ* Barking Abbey GS, Univ of Hull (BSc), Coll of the Resurrection Mirfield; *Career* ordained deacon 1966, priested 1967; curate: St Elizabeth Beacontree 1966–70, Holy Trinity S Woodford 1970–72; vicar: Church of Ascension Victoria Docks 1972–76, All Saints Chelmsford 1976–88; priest-in-charge Church of Ascension Chelmsford 1985–88, rural dean of Chelmsford 1986–88, rector of St James' Colchester 1988–93, archdeacon of Harlow 1993–95, archdeacon of West Ham 1995–; *Style*— The Ven the Archdeacon of West Ham; ✉ 86 Aldersbrook Road, Manor Park, London E12 5DH

FOX, Miles; s of Victor Fox (d 1950), and Marie Fox (d 1988); *b* 22 Feb 1927; *Educ* Univ of Manchester (MB ChB, MD, ChM), FRCS 1955; *m* Valerie Jean; 5 da (Helena b 1957, Mary Jane b 1959, Candida b 1965, Emily Susan b 1978, Anna Victoria (twin) b 1978); *Career* MRC res fell in transplantation Dept of Surgery Univ of Edinburgh 1959–60; sr registrar in urology: St Peter's Hosp London 1959–60, Gen Infirmary and St James' Hosp Leeds 1962–66; conslt urological surgn: Sheffield Health Authy 1966–92, Claremont Hosp Sheffield 1966–; hon clinical teacher Univ of Sheffield 1966–92, surgical res fell in tranplantation Harvard Med Sch and Peter Bent Brigham Hosp Boston USA 1966, dir Renal Transplant Unit Royal Hallamshire Hosp Sheffield 1970–83, Hunterian prof RCS 1976, Br Cncl travelling fell Turkey 1977; memb: Br Assoc of Urological Surgns, Int Soc of Urology, Br Transplantation Soc, Int Transplantation Soc, Finnish Med Soc, Br Microsurgical Soc; *Books* numerous pubns incl: Prostatectomy in Patients of 70 years and Over (1980), Vasectomy Reversal - Microsurgery for Best Results (1994); *Recreations* skiing, stamp collecting, walking, classical music, gardening, computers; *Clubs* Sheffield Doctors; *Style*— Miles Fox, Esq; ✉ 54 Stumperlowe Crescent Road, Sheffield S10 3PR; 27 Wilkinson St, Sheffield S10 2GB (☎ 0114 272 3711, fax 0114 230 3613); Claremont Hospital, Sandygate Road, Sheffield S10 5UB (☎ 0114 263 0330)

FOX, Sir (Henry) Murray; GBE (1974); s of Sidney Joseph Fox (d 1962), of London, and Molly Button; *b* 7 June 1912; *Educ* Malvern, Emmanuel Coll Cambridge; *m* 1941, Helen Isabella Margaret (d 1986), da of late J B Crichton; 1 s, 2 da; *Career* Alderman Ward of Bread St 1966–82, Sheriff City of London 1971–72, Lord Mayor of London 1974–75, one of HM Lts City of London 1976–82; pres City & Metropolitan Building Soc 1985–91 (chm 1976–85), chm Trehaven Holdings Ltd; dir: Municipal Mutual Insurance Ltd 1977–91, Toye Kenning & Spencer Ltd 1976–91; tstee Morden Coll 1976–; Hon Asst Worshipful Co of Coopers, Past Master Worshipful Co of Wheelwrights; *Style*— Sir Murray Fox, GBE; ✉ 7 Aldford St, London W1Y 5PQ (☎ 0171 408 2454)

FOX, Neil; MBE (1983); s of Thomas Fox (d 1986), of Sharlston, West Yorks, and Stella, *née* Schofield; *b* 4 May 1939; *Educ* Sharlston Sch West Yorks; *m* 3 June 1961, Molly, da of Hubert Bentley; 1 s (Jonathan Neil b 20 March 1965), 1 da (Amanda Jayne b 16 Feb 1963); *Career* former rugby league player; capt Yorkshire Schs 1954, 574 appearances Wakefield Trinity 1956–74 (professional debut aged 16); various clubs 1974–79: 70 appearances Bradford Northern, 59 appearances Hull Kingston Rovers, 13 appearances York, 23 appearances Bramley, 21 appearances Huddersfield, last professional match Aug 1979; 17 Yorkshire Co caps, 29 GB caps; holder of various records with Wakefield Trinity: most goals in a season 183, most goals in a career 1836, most points in a match 33, most points in a career 4,488; world record points scorer 6,220 between 1956–79; Lance Todd Trophy winner v Huddersfield 1962, entered Rugby League Hall of Fame 1989; former: apprentice fitter NCB, fitter CEGB, proprietor chain of betting shops; jt proprietor: two retail sports shops, mail order sportswear company; *Style*— Neil Fox, Esq, MBE

FOX, 'Doctor' Neil Andrew Howe; s of Kenneth Roy Fox, of Thames Ditton, Surrey, and Florence Lillian, *née* Buckley; *b* 12 June 1961; *Educ* Kingston GS, Univ of Bath (BSc); *Career* Radio Wyvern Worcester 1986–87, Radio Luxembourg 1987, presenter Pepsi Network Chart Capital FM 1993– (joined 1987), host of Dr Fox's Jukebox LWT 1995–96; *Awards* Smash Hits Award Sony DJ 1991, Sony Award 1993, 3 Sony Awards 1994, Sony Gold Award Broadcaster of the Year 1995, 2 World Radio Awards New York 1995; *Recreations* skydiving, waveboarding, motorcycling, tennis; *Style*— Doctor Fox; ✉ Capital Radio PLC, PO Box 958, Euston Tower, London NW1 3DR (☎ 0171 608 6132, fax 0171 962 6044)

FOX, Norman Alfred; s of Rupert Alfred Fox (d 1972), of Whitstable, and Evelyn Clare, *née* Earle; *b* 28 April 1942; *Educ* Sir William Nottidge Sch Whitstable, Canterbury Tech Coll; *m* 3 Oct 1964, Gillian, da of late Archie Lawrance, MBE; 2 da (Anneliese b 14 Aug 1969, Melanie b 5 June 1971); *Career* apprentice Whitstable Times and Kentish Observer 1959–62, chief reporter Mitcham News 1962–63, dep sports ed Kentish Times 1963, sub ed and writer World Sports Magazine 1963–66; The Times 1966–89: sub ed and reporter 1966–76, football corr 1976–80, athletics and gen sports corr 1980–82, sports ed 1982–86, dep managing ed 1986–89 (covered: Cwlth Games 1970 and 1974, Olympic Games 1972, 1976 and 1980, World Cup 1978 and 1982); The Independent On Sunday 1990–96 (covered World Cup 1990, Cwlth Games 1994, Olympic Games 1996), freelance 1996–; memb Sports Writers' Assoc; *Books* World Cup '82; *Recreations* walking, golf, motorcycling; *Style*— Norman Fox, Esq; ✉ 23 Wood End Road, Harpenden, Hertfordshire AL5 3EE

FOX, Peter Gerald; s of Thomas Fox (d 1985), and Stella, *née* Schofield; *Educ* Wakefield Jr Tech Coll; *m* 30 Nov 1957, Joan Margaret, da of late Arthur Nicholson; 2 da (Karen Beverley b 19 Sept 1958, Susan Elizabeth b 30 Nov 1961); *Career* professional rugby league coach; player: Yorks Schs 1948, Featherstone Rovers 1953–56, Batley 1956–62 and 1964–67, Hull Kingston Rovers 1962–64, Wakefield Trinity 1967 (ret through injury); coach: Featherstone Rovers 1971–74 and 1987–91, Wakefield Trinity 1974–76, Bramley 1976–77, Bradford Northern 1977–85 (team mangr 1991–95), Leeds 1985–86, England 1977 (v Wales and France), GB 1978 (3 Tests v Aust), Yorkshire 1985–92 (unbeaten); honours as coach incl: Challenge Cup winners Featherstone Rovers 1973 (runners up 1974), promotion to Div 1 Bramley 1977 and Featherstone Rovers 1988, Premiership Cup winners Bradford Northern 1978 (runners up 1979 and 1980), Yorkshire Cup winners Bradford Northern 1979 (various runners up), Div 1 champions Bradford Northern 1980 and 1981, John Player Cup winners Bradford Northern 1980, Div 2 Premiership Cup runners up Featherstone Rovers 1988; Bradford Northern first team to retain Div 1 title 1981; rugby league coach of the year 1980; draughtsman British Jeffrey Diamond Wakefield 1953–59 (apprentice engr 1948–53), design draughtsman Yorkshire Imperial metals Leeds 1960–77, trg and safety offr IMI Yorkshire Alloys Leeds 1977–91, ptnr Impact Sports Consultancy 1995–, rugby league summariser BBC Radio 5 Live 1996–; *Recreations* rugby, golf, boxing, most other sports; *Style*— Peter Fox, Esq; ✉ 7 Woodlands, East Ardsley, nr Wakefield, West Yorkshire WF3 2JG (☎ 01924 824314); Impact Sports Consultancy, 66 Walton Lane, Sandal, Wakefield WF2 6EU (☎ 01924 253828/862177/824314)

FOX, Rachel; *see:* Crosbee, Rachel

FOX, Richard John; s of Dennis William Fox (d 1956), of Bristol, and Winifred Joan Fox; *b* 23 Dec 1943; *Educ* Cotham GS, Bristol, Univ of Wales Cardiff (BSc(Econ)); *m* Sandra Wynne; 2 c (Mark Douglas b 1970, Helen Victoria b 1971); *Career* CA; Grace Darbyshire & Todd Bristol 1965–71 (articled clerk 1965–68), Coopers & Lybrand 1971–78; ptnr: Neville Russell 1982–87 (joined 1978), KPMG Peat Marwick 1987–93, Business Improvement Partnership and The Learning Corporation 1993–; dir: British Approvals Bd for Telecommunications, EMRAD Ltd; chm Guildford Business Forum 1992–; fndr memb Guildford Chamber Choir, memb St Saviour's Church Guildford; ACA 1968; *Recreations* trekking, music especially choral, the countryside, reading; *Clubs* Wentworth; *Style*— Richard J Fox, Esq; ✉ 7 Mountside, Guildford, Surrey GU2 5JD (☎ and fax 01483 63523)

FOX, Richard Munro; MBE (1986); s of Roger Henry Fox, of Ingoldsby, Lincs, and Jennifer Jean Munro, *née* Betten; bro of Rachel Crosbee, *qv*; *b* 5 June 1960; *Educ* St Albans Grammar Verulam Sch, Univ of Birmingham (BA); *m* 30 Sept 1990, Myriam, da of Victor Jerusalmi, of Marseilles; 2 da (Jessica and Esther (twins) b 11 June 1994); *Career* canoeist; world canoe slalom champion 1981, 1983, 1985, 1989 and 1993, winner Europa Cup 1982, 1984, 1986 and 1988, winner World Cup 1988, 1989 and 1991, 8 times Br champion; appointed Sports Cncl 1988–92; Freeman City of Wausau Wisconsin USA 1988; *Recreations* skiing, travel; *Clubs* Nottingham Kayak, Royal Canoe; *Style*— Richard Fox, Esq, MBE; ✉ Marseille, France

FOX, Prof Robert; s of Donald Fox (d 1972), and Audrey Hilda, *née* Ramsell (d 1993); *b* 7 Oct 1938; *Educ* Doncaster GS, Oriel Coll Oxford (BA, MA, DPhil); *m* 20 May 1964, Catherine Mary Lilian, da of Dr Edmund Roper Power (d 1990); 3 da (Tessa b 1967, Emily b 1969, Hannah b 1972); *Career* asst master Tonbridge 1961–63, Clifford Norton jr research fell The Queen's Coll Oxford 1965–66, prof of history of science Univ of Lancaster 1987–88 (lectr 1966–72, sr lectr 1972–75, reader 1975–87), dir Centre de Recherche en Histoire des Sciences et des Techniques Cité des Sciences et de l'Industrie CNRS Paris 1986–88, asst dir Science Museum 1988, prof of history of science Univ of Oxford and fell Linacre Coll Oxford 1988–; pres: Br Soc of the History of Science 1980–82, Int Union for the History and Philosophy of Science 1995–97 (first vice pres Div of History of Sci 1989–93, pres Div of History of Sci 1993–); FRHistS 1974, FSA 1989; *Books* The Caloric Theory of Gases from Lavoisier to Regnault (1971), Sadi Carnot. Réflexions sur la Puissance Motrice du Feu (1978, 1986, 1988 and 1992), The Organization of Science and Technology in France 1808–1914 (ed with G Weisz, 1980), The Culture of Science in France 1700–1900 (1992), Education, Technology and Industrial Performance in Europe 1850–1939 (ed with A Guagnini, 1993), Science, Industry and the Social Order in Post-Revolutionary France (1995), Technological Change (1996); *Clubs* Athenaeum; *Style*— Prof Robert Fox, FSA; ✉ Modern History Faculty, Broad St, Oxford OX1 3BD (☎ 01865 277268, fax 01865 250704)

FOX, Dr Robert McDougall (Robin); s of Sir Theodore Fortescue Fox (d 1989), and Margaret Evelyn, *née* McDougall (d 1970); *Educ* Leighton Park Sch, Univ of Edinburgh (MB ChB); *m* 1969, Susan Gertrude Standerwick, da of James Clark; 1 da (Katharine b 1970), 2 s (Duncan b 1970, James b 1975); *Career* various hosp posts 1965–68; The Lancet: asst ed 1968–75, dep ed 1975–90, ed 1990–95; Euro assoc ed Circulation 1995–, ed Jl of the Royal Soc of Med 1996–; FRCPE 1991, FRCP Lond 1996 (MRCP 1993); *Recreations* the hoe and the bassoon; *Style*— Dr Robin Fox; ✉ Green House, Rotherfield, Crowborough, E Sussex TN6 3QU (☎ and fax 01892 853520)

FOX, Robert Michael John; s of Maj Robin Fox, MC, RA (d 1971), of Cuckfield, Sussex, and Angela Muriel Darita, *née* Worthington; bro of Edward Charles Morice Fox and James Fox, *qqv*; *b* 25 March 1952; *Educ* Harrow; *m* 1, 26 Feb 1974 (m dis 1990), Celestia, da of Henry Nathan Sporborg, CMG (d 1985); 1 s (Sam Henry b 24 June 1978), 2 da (Chloe Victoria b 24 May 1976, Louisa Mary b 18 July 1983); m 2, 16 Dec 1990 (m dis), Natasha Jane (actress Natasha Richardson), da of Tony Richardson (d 1991) and Vanessa Redgrave, *qv*; m 3, 31 Jan 1996, Fiona, o da of late John Golfar; *Career* producer; actor When Did You Last See My Mother? (Royal Court) 1970, asst dir Royal Court Theatre 1971–73, PA to Michael White (Michael White Ltd) 1973–80, fndr Robert Fox Ltd 1980–; prodns incl: Goose Pimples (Evening Standard Drama Desk Award for Best Comedy) 1981, Anyone for Denis?, exec prodr Another Country (Olivier Award for Best Play) 1982, Crystal Clear, The Seagull, Torch Song Trilogy, Interpreters, Orphans, J J Farr, Chess, Lettice & Lovage (Evening Standard Drama Desk Award for Best Comedy), Anything Goes, A Madhouse in Goa, Burn This, The Big Love, When She Danced, The Ride Down Mt Morgan, Vita and Virginia, Three Tall Women (Evening Standard Best Play Award) 1994, Skylight 1995, Who's Afraid of Virgina Wolf 1996; Month by the Lake (film), Oscar's Orchestra (BBC TV childrens animation series); *Recreations* tennis; *Clubs* Bucks; *Style*— Robert Fox, Esq; ✉ Robert Fox Ltd, 6 Beauchamp Place, London SW3 (☎ 0171 584 6855, fax 0171 225 1638)

FOX, Robert Trench (Robin); CBE (1993); s of Waldo Trench Fox (d 1953), of Penjerrick, Falmouth, Cornwall; *b* 1 Jan 1937; *Educ* Winchester, Univ Coll Oxford (MA); *m* 1962, Lindsay Garrett, da of Sir Donald Forsyth Anderson (d 1973); 2 s (Barclay Trench b 27 April 1971, Caspar Lloyd b 6 Oct 1972), 2 da (Fenella Garrett (Mrs John Dernie) b 23 Oct 1964, Tamara Forsyth (Mrs Robert Onslow) b 24 June 1967); *Career* dir Kleinwort Benson Ltd 1972–85, vice chm Kleinwort Benson Group 1986–; chm: Export Guarantees Advsy Cncl, Centro Internationale Handelsbank, The China Investment & Development Fund Ltd; dir Whiteaway Laidlaw Bank Ltd; memb: Deposit Protection Bd and Overseas Projects Bd; chm Cncl City Univ Business Sch; *Recreations* shooting, walking, sailing; *Clubs* Brooks's, Royal Cornwall Yacht; *Style*— Robin Fox, Esq, CBE; ✉ Cheriton House, Cheriton, Alresford, Hampshire SO24 0QA (☎ 01962 771230); Kleinwort Benson Ltd, 20 Fenchurch Street, London EC3P 3DB (☎ 0171 623 8000, fax 0171 956 8160)

FOX, Ronald David; s of Walter Fox (d 1985), of London, and Eva, *née* Covo; *b* 27 Sept 1946; *Educ* Mercers Sch, City of London Sch, Lincoln Coll Oxford (MA); *m* 11 Feb 1973, Sonya Claudine, da of Shalom Birshan; 1 s (Michael b 31 Jan 1979), 1 da (Susan b 8 July 1976); *Career* admitted slr 1972; ptnr Oppenheimers 1974–88, ptnr Denton Hall 1988–89, sr ptnr Fox Williams 1989–; nominated Star of Year 2000 by Legal Business Magazine 1990, Distinguished Serv award City of London Slr's Co 1989; hon slr Br-Israel C of C 1974– (memb Exec Ctee 1988–), memb Int Bar Assoc 1984– (chm Practice Mgmnt Sub Ctee 1995–), memb Br-German Jurists' Assoc 1979–; Law Soc: co-opted memb of Completion Cheque Scheme Working Pty 1981–82, memb Standing Ctee on Co Law 1985–89, memb Cncl Membership Ctee 1990–; City of London Law Soc: memb Problems of Practice Sub Ctee 1985–93, Working Pty (preparing evidence of City Slrs to Lady Marre's Ctee on the future of the legal profession) 1986, co-ordinator Survey on City Slrs' Attitudes to Multi-Disciplinary Practices 1987 (co-opted memb Ctee 1988, elected memb of Ctee 1988, Court rep 1994–); chm Working Party (preparing the response of City Slrs to the Govt Green Paper on the Work and Organisation of the Legal Profession) 1989; Liveryman Worshipful Co of Slrs 1984 (Asst 1991, Warden 1996); hon memb Assoc of Fells and Legal Scholars of the Centre for Int Legal Studies, FRSA; *Books* Due Diligence, Disclosures and Warranties in Corporate Acquistion Practice - the United Kingdom (1988, 2 edn 1992), International Business Transactions-Service Agreements for Multinational Corporate Executives in the United Kingdom (1988), Payments on Termination of Employment (1981, 3 edn 1990), Legal Aspects of Doing Business in England & Wales (1984, 2 edn 1990), International Professional Practice - England and Wales (1992), Product Tampering in the United Kingdom (1993); also author of numerous articles on legal topics; *Recreations* opera, theatre, cinema, swimming, skin diving, and scuba diving, motoring and other forms of transport, management studies; *Clubs* RAC; *Style*— Ronald Fox, Esq; ✉ Fox Williams, City Gate House, 39–45 Finsbury Square, London EC2A 1UU (☎ 0171 628 2000, fax 0171 628 2100, car 0836 238436)

FOX, Ruel; *b* 14 Jan 1968; *Career* professional footballer; clubs: Norwich City 1985–93 (over 140 appearances, 15 goals), Newcastle Utd 1993–95, Tottenham Hotspur FC (for transfer fee of £4.2m) 1995–; memb England B team 1994; *Style*— Ruel Fox, Esq; ✉ c/o Tottenham Hotspur FC, 748 High Road, Tottenham, London N17 0AP

FOX, Stephen Howard; s of Louis Fox, and Augusta Fox; *b* 8 Oct 1948; *Educ* Manchester GS, Coll of Law; *Career* admitted slr 1973, sr ptnr Betesh Fox & Co slrs (specialising in defence of serious fraud actions); memb Law Soc; *Recreations* writing, raconteur; *Style*— Stephen Fox, Esq; ✉ Betesh Fox & Co, 17 Ralli Court, West Riverside, Manchester M3 5FT (☎ 0161 832 6131)

FOX-ANDREWS, His Hon James Roland Blake; QC (1968); *b* 24 March 1922; *Educ* Stowe, Pembroke Coll Cambridge (BA); *m* 7 Oct 1950, Angela Bridget (d 1991), da of Brig Charles Swift, OBE, MC; 2 s (Jonathan Mark Piers b 7 May 1952, Piers Norman James b 11 Aug 1954); *Career* served RNVR 1940–45; called to the Bar Gray's Inn 1949, dep chm Devon QS 1970–71, recorder of Winchester 1971 (hon recorder 1972–), recorder of the Crown Ct 1972–85, ldr W Circuit 1982–84, circuit judge (Official Referees' Ct) 1985–94 (dep official referee 1994–); bencher Gray's Inn 1974, memb Gen Cncl of the Bar 1968–72, memb Senate of Inns of Ct and the Bar 1976–79; author and contrib to numerous legal pubns; FCIArb; *Style*— His Hon James Fox Andrews, QC; ✉ 20 Cheyne Gardens, London SW3 5QT (☎ 0171 352 9484); Official Referees' Court, St Dunstan's House, 133/137 Fetter Lane, London EC4A 1HD (☎ 0171 936 6457/8, fax 0171 936 7428)

FOX-ANDREWS, (Jonathan) Mark Piers; s of His Hon Judge James Roland Blake Fox-Andrews, QC, and (Angela) Bridget, *née* Swift (d 1991); *b* 7 May 1952; *Educ* Eton,

Trinity Hall Cambridge (BA, MA); *m* 22 Sept 1984, Rosemary Anne, da of Dennis Jenks; 2 s (Maximillian George b 28 March 1987, Alfred James b 3 Dec 1993), 2 da (Florence Rose b 14 July 1989, Constance Augusta b 26 Jan 1992); *Career* Drexel Burnham Lambert: trader 1977–80, mangr Singapore Office 1980–83, mangr Sydney Office 1984, md (Futures Ltd) London Office 1984–90; dir Sabre Fund Management Ltd 1990–93, md Mees Pierson Derivatives Ltd 1993–; *Books* Futures Fund Management (1991), Derivatives Markets and Investment Management (1995); *Clubs* Garrick, Queen's, Hurlingham; *Style*— J M P Fox-Andrews, Esq; ✉ 62 Redcliffe Road, London SW10 9NQ; Mees Pierson Derivatives Ltd (☎ 0171 444 8324)

FOX BASSETT, Nigel; s of Thomas Fox Bassett (d 1960), of London, and Catherine Adriana, *née* Wiffen (d 1960); *b* 1 Nov 1929; *Educ* Taunton Sch, Trinity Coll Cambridge (MA); *m* 9 Sept 1961, Patricia Anne, da of Stanley William Lambourne (d 1986), of E Horsley, Surrey; 1 s (Jonathan b 30 July 1966), 1 da (Emma (Mrs Lines) b 19 Jan 1964); *Career* Nat Serv 2 Lt RA 1949–50 (served Canal Zone Egypt with Mauritian Gds), Capt 264 (7 London) Field Regt RA TA 1950–60; admitted slr 1956, sr ptnr Clifford Chance (formerly Coward Chance) 1990–93 (articled clerk 1953, ptnr 1960); cmmr Building Societies Cmmn 1993–; dir London First 1993–; chm Exec Ctee Br Inst of Int and Comparative Law 1986– (memb Cncl 1977–); memb Cncl: London C of C and Indust 1993–, Int Assoc for the Protection of Industl Property (Br Gp) 1984–89, Int Law Assoc (Br Branch) 1974–86; chm Ctee Int Regulation of Fin Markets 1989–93; memb UK Govt Know How Fund Banking and Fin Mission to Poland 1989–90; chm Intellectual Property Sub Ctee City of London Slrs' Co 1982–87 (memb Sub Ctee 1969–87); memb Ctee Business Section IBA (Anti Tst, Patents and Trademarks, Securities Ctees) 1969–93; memb: Law Soc Euro Gp 1969–93, American Bar Assoc (Futures Regulation Ctee) 1979–93, Assoc Europeenne d'Etudes Juridiques et Fiscales (UK memb) 1969–; pres Cncl Taunton Sch 1994–; memb: Glyndebourne Festival Opera Soc and Kent Opera, The Pilgrims of GB 1988–; vice pres Dulwich Hockey Club, chm Old Tauntonians Sports Club until 1989, pres Kemsing Cricket Club 1994–, memb Ctee Seaview Yacht Club 1995–; Freeman Worshipful Co of Slrs 1960; memb Law Soc; *Books* English Sections of: Branches and Subsidiaries in the European Common Market (1976), Business Law in Europe (1982 and 1990); *Recreations* shooting, beagling, cricket, art, opera; *Clubs* Garrick, City of London, MCC, Seaview Yacht; *Style*— Nigel Fox Bassett, Esq; ✉ c/o Clifford Chance, 200 Aldersgate Street, London EC1A 4JJ (☎ 0171 600 1000, fax 0171 282 6477, telex 887847)

FOX-STRANGWAYS, Hon Raymond George; 2 s of 8 Earl of Ilchester (d 1970), and hp of bro, 9 Earl; *b* 11 Nov 1921; *Educ* Exeter Sch, Seale Hayne Agric Coll; *m* 15 Nov 1941, Margaret Vera, da of late James Force, of North Surrey, BC, Canada; 2 s; *Career* served RAF WWII; Civil Serv 1949–76, ret; *Recreations* walking, riding, ornithology; *Style*— The Hon Raymond Fox-Strangways; ✉ 4 Trull Green Drive, Trull, Taunton, Somerset TA3 7JL (☎ 01823 282879)

FOXALL, Colin; CBE (1995); s of Alfred George Foxall, of Chatham, Kent, and Ethel Margaret, *née* Hall; *b* 6 Feb 1947; *Educ* Gillingham GS; *m* 2 Feb 1980, Diana Gail, da of John Edward Bewick; 2 s (Ian b 1981, Neil b 1984); *Career* Dept of Trade 1974–75; NCM Credit Insurance Ltd (formerly ECGD until privatisation 1991): joined 1966, asst sec 1982–86, gp dir/under sec of insur servs 1986–91, chief exec and md 1991–; chief exec and md NCM Holdings (UK) Ltd, memb Managing Bd NCM NV; MIEx, MICM; *Recreations* clay pigeon shooting, cycling; *Style*— Colin Foxall, Esq, CBE; ✉ NCM Credit Insurance Ltd, 3 Harbour Drive, Capital Waterside, Cardiff CF1 6TZ (☎ 01222 824664, fax 01222 824101)

FOXALL, Prof Gordon Robert; s of Gordon William Foxall (d 1978), of Birmingham, and Marion, *née* Radford; *b* 16 July 1949; *Educ* Holly Lodge Sch Worcs, Univ of Salford (BSc, MSc), Univ of Birmingham (PhD, DSocSc), Univ of Strathclyde (PhD); *m* 26 June 1971, Jean, da of William Morris, of Birmingham; 1 da (Helen b 1977); *Career* Univ of Newcastle upon Tyne 1972–79, Univ of Birmingham 1980–83, reader Cranfield Inst of Technol 1983–86; prof: Univ of Strathclyde 1987–90, Univ of Birmingham 1990–; Maynard Phelps distinguished lectr Univ of Michigan 1988–91, sabbatical visitor Balliol Coll Oxford 1993–94, visiting prof Univ of Guelph Ontario 1994, visiting prof Univ of S Australia 1994; AFBPsS 1987, CPsychol 1988, Fell Br Acad of Mgmnt; *Books* Consumer Behaviour (1980), Marketing Behaviour (1981), Strategic Marketing Management (1981), Consumer Choice (1983), Corporate Innovation (1984), Consumer Psychology (1990), Consumer Psychology for Marketing (1994), Consumers in Context (1996); *Recreations* reading, walking; *Clubs* Reform; *Style*— Prof Gordon Foxall; ✉ 4 Ridgewood Drive, Four Oaks, Sutton Coldfield B75 6TR; University of Birmingham, Department of Commerce, Edgbaston, Birmingham B15 2TT (☎ 0121 414 3344)

FOXELL, Clive Arthur Peirson; CBE; s of Arthur Turner Foxell (d 1955), and Lillian, *née* Ellerman (d 1979); *b* 27 Feb 1930; *Educ* Harrow HS, Univ of London (BSc); *m* 1956, Shirley Ann Patey, da of Idwal Morris; 1 da (Elizabeth); *Career* mangr GEC Semiconductor Labs 1968, md GEC Semiconductors Ltd 1971; dep dir: of res PO 1975, PO Procurement Exec 1978–79; dir: of purchasing PO 1980, of procurement BT (chief exec 1983–85), BT Systems Ltd 1982–89, chm: Fulcrum Communications Ltd 1985–86, Phonepoint Ltd 1989–92; memb Bd BT 1986–89; pres Mobile Radio Trg Tst 1991–94; author of numerous articles and papers on electronics; memb Bulgin Premium IERE 1964; IEE: memb Cncl 1975–78, 1982–85 and 1987–91, vice chm Electronics Div 1980–81, dep chm 1982–83, chm 1983–84, vice pres 1996–; Engrg Bd SRC 1977–80, ACARD Working Pty on Info Tech 1981, DTI CS Ctee 1985–88, Cncl SERC 1986–90, EEA Bd 1987–92, Cncl Fndn of Sci & Technol 1995–; dir CSTI 1992–94; treas Nat Electronics Cncl 1995–; Hon DSc Southampton 1994; Liveryman Worshipful Co of Engrs; FEng 1985, FIEE, FInstP (pres 1992–94), FCIPS; *Books* Low Noise Microwave Amplifiers (1968), Chesham Shuttle (1996); *Recreations* photography, railways; *Style*— Clive Foxell, Esq, CBE, FEng; ✉ 4 Meades Lane, Chesham, Bucks (☎ 01494 785737)

FOXLEY-NORRIS, Air Chief Marshal Sir Christopher Neil; GCB (1973, KCB 1968, CB 1966), DSO (1945), OBE (1956); s of Maj John Perceval Foxley-Norris, Cheshire Regt (d 1922), and Dorothy Brabant Smith; *b* 16 March 1917; *Educ* Winchester (scholar), Trinity Coll Oxford, Middle Temple; *m* 1948, Joan Lovell, da of Maj Percy H Hughes (d 1953), of Crondall, Hants; *Career* Air Chief Marshal 1970, chief of personnel and logistics MOD 1971–74, ret; chm: Battle of Britain Fighter Assoc 1978–, Gardening for the Disabled Tst 1980–, Ex-RAF and Dependents Severely Disabled Holiday Tst 1984–; chm emeritus Leonard Cheshire Fndn 1982– (chm 1974–82); Liveryman Worshipful Co of Insurers; CIMgt; *Recreations* golf, cricket, writing, bridge; *Clubs* RAF, Huntercombe Golf, MCC, Phyllis Court Henley; *Style*— Air Chief Marshal Sir Christopher Foxley-Norris, GCB, DSO, OBE; ✉ Tumble Wood, Northend Common, Henley-on-Thames, Oxon (☎ 01491 638457)

FOXWOOD, Philip Anthony; o s of Maj Ibrahim Fazil, RA (d 1978), and his w Kate (d 1973), o da of (Calvin) Amory Stevens; *b* 5 Sept 1935, Upper Woodford; *Educ* Harrow, RMA Sandhurst; *m* 12 July 1971, (Rose) Mary, o da of Clifford Mansel Reece, QC (d 1973), and sis of His Hon Judge Paynter Reece, *qv*; 1 s (Hugo b 2 Feb 1973); *Career* cmmnd Coldstream Gds 1955, Capt Parachute Regt 1961, served Cyprus and Aden (invalided 1966); fndr memb Royal Assoc for Disability and Rehabilitation (RADAR) 1977–; memb: Oxon War Pensions Ctee 1986–90, Beds, Bucks, Herts and Oxon War Pensions Ctee 1991–95, Chilterns War Pensions Ctee 1996–; *Recreations* gardening, genealogy; *Clubs* Boodle's, Pratt's, Tent XII; *Style*— Philip Foxwood, Esq; ✉ Ann's Cottage, Ramsden, Chipping Norton, Oxon OX7 3AZ (☎ 01993 868592, fax 01993 868250)

FOYLE, Christina Agnes Lilian; da of William Alfred Foyle (d 1963), and Christina Tulloch (d 1976); *b* 30 Jan 1911; *Educ* Aux Villas Unspunnen, Interlaken Switzerland; *m* 1938, Ronald Frederick James Batty (d 1994); *Career* began Foyle's Literary Luncheons, where distinguished writers and artists meet the reading public 1930; memb Ctee Univ of Essex, memb Cncl Royal Soc of Arts 1963–69 (chm E Anglican Region 1978); landowner (1000 acres); *Recreations* book collecting, reading; *Style*— Miss Christina Foyle; ✉ Beeleigh Abbey, Maldon, Essex; Foyles, Charing Cross Rd, London WC2

FOYLE, (William Richard) Christopher; s of (William) Richard Foyle (d 1957), and Alice (later Mrs Harrap), da of Eugen Kun, of Vienna; the Foyles are an ancient W Country family (*see* Burke's Landed Gentry, 18 Edn, vol 3); *b* 20 Jan 1943; *Educ* Radley; *m* 27 July 1983, Catherine Mary, da of Rev David William Forrester Jelleyman, of Melbourn, Cambs; 3 da (Charlotte b 1984, Annabel b 1985, Christine b 1987); *Career* trained in publishing and bookselling in London, Tuebingen, Berlin, Helsinki and Paris; mangr W & G Foyle Ltd 1965–72, ptnr Emson & Dudley and dir Emson & Dudley Securities Ltd 1972–78, proprietor Christopher Foyle Aviation (Leasing) Co 1977–; md: Air Foyle Ltd 1978–, Air Foyle Executive Ltd 1988–, Charters Ltd 1994–, Air Foyle Charter Airlines Ltd 1994–, Air Foyle Holding Co Ltd 1996–; tstee and memb Bd International Air Cargo Assoc 1992– (pres 1997–), vice pres Guild of Aviation Artists; Liveryman Guild of Air Pilots and Air Navigators, Freeman City of London; *Recreations* travel, skiing, flying, reading non-fiction, wine and food; *Clubs* White's, Air Squadron, Annabel's; *Style*— Christopher Foyle, Esq; ✉ c/o Lloyds Bank plc, 8–10 Waterloo Place, London SW1Y 4BE; Air Foyle Ltd, Halcyon House, Luton Airport, Luton, Beds LU2 9LU (☎ 01582 419792, telex 825538 AFOYLE G, fax 01582 453736)

FOYLE, John Lewis; s of Roland Bernard Foyle (d 1996), of Portsmouth, Hants, and Rose Vera, *née* Taylor; *b* 7 June 1948; *Educ* Portsmouth Northern GS, St John's Coll Cambridge (MA); *m* 19 Feb 1972, Patricia Mary, da of John Victor Ketteringham (d 1986), of Ruthin, Clwyd; 3 s (James b 1972, Thomas d 1978, William b 1980); *Career* sec: Inflation Accounting Steering Gp 1976–78, Jt Exchanges Ctee 1982–96, ECOFEX 1988–96; dep chief exec London Int Fin Futures Exchange; dir Assoc of Futures Brokers and Dealers 1985–91; FCA 1973; *Recreations* sport, music; *Style*— John Foyle, Esq; ✉ Brookmead, Moat Farm Chase, Chipping Hill, Witham, Essex CM8 2DE; LIFFE, Cannon Bridge, London EC4R 3XX (☎ 0171 623 0444, fax 0171 588 3624)

FRACKOWIAK, Prof Richard Stanislaus Joseph; s of Capt Joseph Frackowiak, of London, and Wanda, *née* Majewska; *b* 26 March 1950; *Educ* Latymer Upper Sch, Peterhouse Cambridge (MB BChir, MA, MD); *m* 19 Feb 1972, Christine Jeanne Françoise, da of Louis Thepot, of St Cloud, France; 1 s (Matthew), 2 da (Stephanie, Annabelle); *Career* sr lectr and hon conslt Hammersmith Hosp and Nat Hosp for Neurology and Neurosurgery 1984–94, asst dir MRC Cyclotron Unit 1988–94, prof of clinical neurology Univ of London 1991–94, currently prof and head Wellcome Dept of Cognitive Neurology, dir Leopold Muller Functional Imaging Lab and Wellcome princ research fell Inst of Neurology 1994–; adjunct prof of neurology Cornell Univ Med Sch NY 1992–, visiting prof UCL 1994–; memb Academia Europaea, hon foreign memb Société Française de Neurologie, corresponding memb American Neurological Assoc; memb: Belgian Neurological Soc, Academie Royale de Medecine Belge; FRCP 1987; *Recreations* motorcycling, travel; *Clubs* Hurlingham, Athenaeum; *Style*— Prof Richard Frackowiak; ✉ Wellcome Department of Cognitive Neurology, Institute of Neurology, 12 Queen Square, London WC1N 3BG (☎ 0171 833 7456, fax 0171 813 1445)

FRADD, Dr Simon Oakley; s of Frederick Ronald Fradd, of Otford, Kent, and Beryl Grace, *née* Milledge; *b* 20 April 1950; *Educ* Sevenoaks Sch Kent, W Kent Coll Tunbrige Wells, KCL (BSc), Westminster Med Sch London, FRCS (England); *m* 1 May 1976, Elizabeth Harriett, da of Norman Allen Birtwhistle; *Career* house surgn Westminster Med Sch 1977; SHO: in paediatrics Queen Mary's Roehampton 1978, in neonatology Whittington Hosp London 1979, in A/E then orthopaedics St George's Tooting 1980–81; registrar: in surgery Burton Gen Hosp Burton-on-Trent 1981–84, in urology Univ Hosp of Wales Cardiff 1984–85; GP trainee: Burton-on-Trent 1985–86, under Dr Saunders Nottingham 1986–87, Castle Donington Leics 1987; GP princ Saunders & Fradd Nottingham 1988–; chm: Hosp Doctors' Assoc 1979–82, Negotiators' Hosp Jr Staff Ctee 1986–87 (dep chm 1984–86), Jr Membs' Forum BMA 1990; memb Med Practices Ctee 1989–93, Gen Med Servs Ctee negotiator 1993–; memb GMC 1989–; Freeman City of London 1976, Liveryman Worshipful Co of Needlemakers 1976, Yeoman Worshipful Soc of Apothecaries 1993–; *Books* Hospital Doctors' Association Guide to Your Rights (jtly, 1981), Making Sense of Partnerships (jtly, 1994), Nottingham Non-Fundholder Project, Members Reference Book RCGP (1995); *Recreations* DIY, gardening, skiing, gliding; *Style*— Dr Simon Fradd; ✉ 147 Tollerton Lane, Nottingham NG12 4FT (☎ 0115 937 5038); Greenwood and Sneinton Family Medical Centre, 249 Sneinton Dale, Sneinton, Nottingham NG3 7DQ (☎ 0115 948 4999, mobile 0860 693315)

FRAENKEL, Peter Maurice; s of Ernest Fraenkel, and Luise, *née* Tessmann; *b* 5 July 1915; *Educ* Battersea Poly, Imperial Coll London (BSc); *m* 1946, Hilda Muriel, da of William Norman; 2 da; *Career* sr ptnr Peter Fraenkel & Ptnrs (consulting engrs); chm Peter Fraenkel Maritime Ltd; dir British Maritime Technology Ltd 1991–96; Queen's Award for Export 1982; FEng 1984, FICE, FIStructE, FIHT; *Clubs* Athenaeum; *Style*— P M Fraenkel, Esq, FEng; ✉ Little Paddock, Rockfield Road, Oxted, Surrey RH8 0EL

FRAKER, Ford McKinstry; s of Harrison Shedd Fraker, and Marjorie Tomlinson Fraker (d 1987); *b* 15 July 1948; *Educ* Phillips Acad Andover Mass, Harvard Univ (BA); *m* 24 Dec 1984, Linda Margaret, da of T Hanson; 1 da (Antonia b 21 Jan 1986), 2 s (Jonathan b 2 May 1987, Charles b 29 Jan 1990); *Career* vice pres and regnl mangr Chemical Bank (NY) Bahrain Arabian Gulf 1977–79; Saudi International Bank London: mangr Middle East 1979–82, asst gen mangr, head of gen banking 1982–85, head of credit 1985–90, head of client devpt and mktg 1990–91; dir Saudi International Bank Nassau 1987–90, princ Fraker & Co 1991–93, md Mees Pierson Investment Finance (UK) Ltd 1993–96; *Recreations* tennis, art, travel; *Clubs* Nantucket Yacht, Harvard Club of NYC, Harvard Varsity, Owl; *Style*— Ford M Fraker; ✉ Fieldgrove House, Bitton BS15 6HU (☎ 0117 932 2264); 12 Mt Vernon Street, Nantucket, Mass 02554, USA (☎ 00 1 508 228 8682)

FRAME, Frank Riddell; *b* 15 Feb 1930; *Educ* Univ of Glasgow (MA, LLB); *m* 1958, Maureen Milligan; 1 s, 1 da; *Career* admitted slr 1954; North of Scotland Hydro-Electric Board 1955–60, UK Atomic Energy Authy (UKAEA) 1960–68, The Weir Group plc 1968–76 (dir 1971–76); The Hongkong and Shanghai Banking Corporation Limited: joined as gp legal advsr 1977, exec dir 1985, dep chm 1986–1990; advsr to the board HSBC Holdings plc 1990–; chm Wallem Group Ltd 1992–; dir: Baxter International Inc 1992–, Edinburgh Dragon Trust plc 1994–, The British Investment Trust plc 1995–; former chm: South China Morning Post Limited, Far Eastern Economic Review Ltd; former dir: Marine Midland Banks Inc, Swire Pacific Limited, The British Bank of the Middle East, Consolidated Press International Ltd, Securities and Futures Commission Hong Kong; *Publications* The Law relating to Nuclear Energy (with Prof Harry Street); *Clubs* Brooks's; *Style*— Frank Frame, Esq; ✉ 43 Shrewsbury House, Cheyne Walk, London SW3 5LW (☎ 0171 352 3968)

FRAME, Roger Campbell Crosbie; s of Andrew Crosbie Frame, of Giffnock, Glasgow, and Jessie Caldwell, *née* Campbell; *b* 7 June 1949; *Educ* Glasgow Acad; *m* 10 Sept 1973,

Angela Maria, da of Louis Evaristi, of Giffnock, Glasgow; 2 s (Nicholas Roger b 1976, Mark Christopher b 1980), 1 da (Lorenza Charlotte b 1988); *Career* chartered accountant; sr ptnr Frame & Co; dir: Camos Ltd, Frame & Co Management Services Ltd; treas Glasgow Gp of Artists 1983–89; sec: Glasgow Eastern Merchants and Tradesman Soc, Royal Scottish Soc of Painters in Watercolour (RSW) 1986–; chm James Cusator Wards Fund (Univ of Glasgow) 1984–, offr Incorporation of Weavers of Glasgow; Freeman: City of Glasgow, City of London; *Recreations* clay pigeon shooting, art; *Clubs* Glasgow Art; *Style*— Roger C C Frame, Esq; ✉ Dunglass, 56 Manse Rd, Bearsden, Glasgow G61 3PN; Frame & Co Chartered Accountants, 29 Waterloo St, Glasgow G2 6BZ (☎ 0141 226 3838)

FRAME, Ronald William Sutherland; s of Alexander Frame, and Isobel, *née* Sutherland; *b* 23 May 1953; *Educ* The High Sch of Glasgow, Univ of Glasgow (Foulis scholarship, MA (1st Class), Bradley Medal), Jesus Coll Oxford (BLitt); *Career* writer 1981–; various radio and television plays; *Awards* jt winner Betty Trask Prize 1984, Samuel Beckett Prize 1986, TV Industries Panel Most Promising Writer New to TV 1986; *TV scripts* Paris (1985), Out of Time (1987), Ghost City (1994), A Modern Man (1996); *Radio scripts* incl: The Lantern Bearers (1997), The Hydro (1997); *Novels and short story collections* Winter Journey (1984, 3 Sony Radio Award nominations 1985), Watching Mrs Gordon (1985), A Long Weekend with Marcel Proust (1986), Sandmouth People (1987), A Woman of Judah (1987), Paris: A Television Play (1987), Penelope's Hat (1989), Bluette (1990), Underwood and After (1991), Walking My Mistress in Deauville (1992), The Sun on the Wall (1994); *Recreations* swimming, walking; *Style*— Ronald Frame, Esq; ✉ c/o Curtis Brown Ltd, 4th Floor, Haymarket House, 28–29 Haymarket, London SW1Y 4SP (☎ 0171 396 6600, fax 0171 396 0110)

FRANCE, Sir Arnold William; GCB (1972, KCB 1965, CB 1957); s of William Ernest France (d 1939), of Knutsford, Cheshire and Southport, Lancs; *b* 20 April 1911; *Educ* Bishop's Stortford Coll; *m* 1940, Frances Margaret Linton, da of Dr Charles John Linton Palmer (d 1926), of Gosport; 4 da; *Career* served WWII Capt ME; dep econ advsr Min of State Office ME, civil servant; HM Treasy 1945–63, dep sec Miny of Health 1963–64, perm sec Miny of Health 1964–68, chm Bd Inland Revenue 1968–73, ret; *Recreations* reading; *Clubs* Reform; *Style*— Sir Arnold France, GCB; ✉ Thornton Cottage, 38 Mount Pleasant Road, Lingfield, Surrey RH7 6BS (☎ 01342 832278)

FRANCE, Elizabeth Irene; da of Ralph Salem, of Leicester, and Elizabeth Joan, *née* Bryan; *b* 1 Feb 1950; *Educ* Kibworth Beauchamp GS, Univ Coll of Wales Aberystwyth (BSc(Econ)); *m* 24 July 1971, Dr Michael William France, s of Bert France (d 1976); 2 s, 1 da; *Career* Home Office: admin trainee 1971–77, princ (grade 7) 1977–86, grade 5 1986–94; The Data Protection Registrar 1994–; DSc (hc) Univ Coll of Wales Aberystwyth 1996; FRSA; *Recreations* skiing, squash, cooking, the family; *Style*— Mrs Elizabeth France; ✉ Office of the Data Protection Registrar, Wycliffe House, Water Lane, Wilmslow, Cheshire SK9 5AF (☎ 01625 545700, fax 01625 524510)

FRANCE, Prof Peter; s of Edgar France, of Haslemere, and Doris Woosnam, *née* Morgan (d 1984); *b* 19 Oct 1935; *Educ* Bridlington Sch, Bradford GS, Magdalen Coll Oxford (MA, DPhil); *m* 30 Sept 1961, Siân Reynolds; 3 da (Katharine b 18 Aug 1962, Rose Mair and Siriol Jane (twins) b 7 Dec 1966); *Career* research fell Magdalen Coll Oxford 1960–63, successively asst lectr, lectr then reader Sch of Euro Studies Univ of Sussex 1963–80; Univ of Edinburgh: prof of French 1980–90, endowment fell 1990–; pres: Int Soc for the History of Rhetoric 1993–95, British Comparative Literature Assoc 1993–; French ed Modern Languages Review 1979–85; Dr (hc) Chuvash State Univ 1996; Officier de l'Ordre des Palmes Académiques 1992; FBA 1989; *Books* Racine's Rhetoric (1965), Rhetoric and Truth in France (1972), Racine: Andromaque (1977), Diderot (1982), Poets of Modern Russia (1982), Rousseau: Confessions (1987), An Anthology of Chuvash Poetry (trans, 1991), Poetry in France (ed with K Aspley, 1992), Politeness and its Discontents (1992), New Oxford Companion to Literature in French (1995); also translator of works by Rousseau, Diderot, Blok, Pasternak, Etkind, and Aygi; *Style*— Prof Peter France, FBA; ✉ 10 Dryden Place, Edinburgh EH9 1RP (☎ 0131 667 1177); Department of French, University of Edinburgh, 60 George Square, Edinburgh EH8 8JU (☎ 0131 650 8417)

FRANCE, Rev Canon Dr Richard Thomas; s of Edgar France, of Haslemere, Surrey, and Doris Woosnam, *née* Morgan (d 1984); *b* 2 April 1938; *Educ* Bradford GS, Balliol Coll Oxford (MA), Univ of London (BD), Univ of Bristol (PhD); *m* 30 July 1965, Barbara, da of Ernest Wilding (d 1972), of Stockport, Cheshire; 1 s (David Martyn b 22 May 1968), 1 da (Susan Janet b 10 Jan 1971); *Career* lectr Univ of Ife Nigeria 1969–73, sr lectr Univ of Ahmadu Bello Zaria Nigeria 1976–77, warden Tyndale House Cambridge 1978–81 (librarian 1973–76), vice princ London Bible Coll 1981–88, princ Wycliffe Hall Oxford 1989–95, rector of Wentnor with Ratlinghope, Myndtown, Norbury, More, Lydham and Snead (Dio of Hereford) 1995–; hon canon Ibadan Cathedral Nigeria 1994–; SNTS 1977; *Books* Jesus and the Old Testament (1971), Gospel Perspectives Vols 1–3 (ed, 1980–83), The Gospel of Matthew (1985), The Evidence for Jesus (1986), Jesus the Radical (1989), Matthew: Evangelist and Teacher (1989), Divine Government (1990), Evangelical Anglicans (ed, 1993), Women in the Church's Ministry (1995); *Recreations* wild life, travel, mountain walking, theatre; *Style*— Rev Canon Dr Richard France; ✉ The Rectory, Wentnor, Bishop's Castle, Shropshire SY9 5EE (☎ and fax 01588 650244)

FRANCE-HAYHURST, Jean; da of William Smith (d 1950), of Banffshire, and Mair, *née* Davies (d 1979); *b* 20 Jan 1950; *Educ* Towyn GS, Univ of Wales, Inns of Court Sch of Law; *m* 1, 1978 Anthony Jamieson; 1 s (Charles b 1979); m 2, James France-Hayhurst, s of late Robert France Hayhurst; 2 da (Lucinda b 1984, Serena b 1986); *Career* called to the Bar Gray's Inn 1972, pupillage and practice 1974–78, lectr in law 1972–78, slr 1980–86, recalled to the Bar 1987, recommenced practice 1992; Parly candidate (Cons) Montgomery 1992; chair Women's Enterprise Network 1989–90, vice chair Chester Cathedral Devpt Tst; *Recreations* family, friends, the countryside, music, antiques; *Clubs* Mensa, Westminster Dining; *Style*— Ms Jean France-Hayhurst; ✉ Mayfield, Bunbury, Cheshire (☎ 01829 261427); Chambers of David Harris, QC, Peel House, Harrington Street, Liverpool L2 9XN (☎ 0151 236 0718)

FRANCÈS, Philippe; *Career* with Schneider-Laden GmbH (subsid of Philips Group) until 1973, chief exec Financière Darty SA 1986– (joined 1973), chief exec Kingfisher Electrical Retailing Ltd (KERL) and main bd dir Kingfisher plc 1993– (following merger with Darty); *Style*— Philippe Francès, Esq; ✉ Kingfisher plc, North West House, 119 Marylebone Road, London NW1 5PX (☎ 0171 724 7749)

FRANCIES, Duncan; s of Joseph Standish Noel Francies (d 1988), and Jeanne Zoe, *née* Dordan-Pyke; *b* 5 June 1945; *Educ* Sutton Valence; *m* 1, 1983 (m dis), Patricia Mary, da of Samuel Field, of Brisbane, Aust; 1 s (Edward), 1 da (Olivia); m 2, 29 Feb 1992, Gillian Jane, da of Donald James Graham, of Cheshire; 1 da (Sophia); *Career* admitted slr 1968; ptnr Richards Butler; Freeman: Worshipful Co of Slrs 1976, City of London 1978; memb: Law Soc 1963, Slrs' Benevolent Assoc 1976; *Recreations* gardening, swimming; *Clubs* Broadgate, Wig and Pen; *Style*— Duncan Francies, Esq; ✉ Richards Butler, Beaufort House, 15 St Botolph Street, London EC3A 7EE (☎ 0171 247 6555, fax 0171 247 5091)

FRANCIS, Andrew James; s of Frank Sidney Francis, DFC (d 1971), of Ashtead, Surrey, and Ann, *née* Velody (d 1994); *b* 1 Nov 1953; *Educ* City of London Freeman's Sch, Univ of Oxford (BA); *m* 18 Dec 1982, Victoria Louise, da of Francis Henry Gillum-Webb (d 1972), of Weybridge, Surrey; 1 s (Hugo b 27 March 1993), 3 da (Amelia, Alexandra, Charlotte (twin with Hugo)); *Career* called to the Bar Lincoln's Inn 1977, in practice at Chancery Bar 1979–; memb Hon Soc Lincoln's Inn; *Style*— Andrew Francis, Esq; ✉ 11 New Square, Lincoln's Inn, London WC2A 3QB (☎ 0171 831 0081, fax 0171 405 2560)

FRANCIS, Clare Mary; MBE (1978); da of Owen Francis, CB, and Joan St Leger, *née* Norman; *b* 17 April 1946; *Educ* Royal Ballet Sch, UCL (BSc Econ); *m* 1977 (m dis 1985), Jacques Robert Redon; 1 s (Thomas Robert Jean b 1978); *Career* transatlantic singlehanded crossing 1973, first woman home Observer Singlehanded Transatlantic Race and holder women's record 1976, first woman skipper Whitbread Round The World Race 1977–78; hon fell: UCL 1979, UMIST 1981; *Books* non-fiction: Come Hell or High Water (1977), Come Wind or Weather (1978), The Commanding Sea (1981); fiction: Night Sky (1983), Red Crystal (1985), Wolf Winter (1987), Requiem (1991), Deceit (1993), Betrayal (1995); *Recreations* opera, theatre; *Style*— Miss Clare Francis, MBE

FRANCIS, Clive; s of Raymond Francis (d 1987), of Brighton, and Margaret, *née* Towner; *b* 26 June 1946; *Educ* Ratton Secdy Modern Sch Sussex, RADA; *m* May 1989, Natalie, da of Martin Ogle, OBE; 1 da (Lucinda b Dec 1989), 1 s (Harry b Feb 1992); *Career* actor; caricaturist 1983–; five solo exhibitions; designer various theatre posters and book covers; *Theatre* West End incl: The Servant of Two Masters, Three, The Mating Game, Bloomsbury, The Return of A J Raffles, The Rear Column, The School for Scandal, Benefactors, The Importance of Being Earnest, Single Spies, A Small Family Business and 'Tis Pity She's A Whore (RNT), What The Butler Saw, An Absolute Turkey; for RSC incl: A Christmas Carol, Three Hours After Marriage, Troilus and Cressida; Chichester Festival Theatre incl: Monsieur Perichon's Travels, The Circle, Look After Lulu; *Television* incl: Poldark, Entertaining Mr Sloane, As You Like It, Masada, The Critic, A Married Man, The Far Pavilions, Yes Prime Minister, Oedipus, Adventures of Sherlock Holmes, After The War, The Rear Column, Quartermain's Terms, Old Flames, Lipstick on your Collar; *Books* Laughlines (1989), Sir John, The Many Faces of Gielgud (1994); *Recreations* walking, exploring England, twentieth century first editions; *Clubs* Garrick; *Style*— Clive Francis, Esq; ✉ c/o Peters Fraser & Dunlop Ltd, 503 The Chambers, Chelsea Harbour, Lots Road, London SW10 0XF (☎ 0171 352 4446, fax 0171 352 7356)

FRANCIS, Dick; *see:* Francis, Richard Stanley (Dick)

FRANCIS, Ven Edward Reginald; s of Alfred John Francis (d 1978), of 43 Monins Rd, Dover, Kent, and Elsie Hilda, *née* Hiscock (d 1991); *b* 31 Jan 1929; *Educ* Monmouth, Dover GS, Rochester Theol Coll; *m* 21 Oct 1950, Joyce Noreen, da of George James Atkins (d 1935); 3 s (Paul, Nigel, Jonathan); *Career* ordained 1961, chaplain Training Ship Arethusa and asst curate All Saints' Frindsbury Rochester 1961–64, vicar St William's Chatham 1964–73, vicar and rural dean Rochester 1973–79, archdeacon of Bromley 1979–94, archdeacon emeritus 1994–; memb Gen Synod 1981–90, jt chm Canterbury and Rochester Diocesan Cncl for Social Responsibility 1983–88; ACII 1958; *Recreations* ornithology, walking, rugby football, poetry; *Style*— The Ven Edward Francis; ✉ 71 Ash Tree Drive, West Kingsdown, Sevenoaks, Kent TN15 6LW (☎ 01474 853202)

FRANCIS, George Carwardine; s of Guy Lancelot Brereton Francis (d 1962), and Mabel Edith Mary, *née* Clay (d 1957); *b* 15 April 1929; *Educ* Malvern; *m* 1960, Barbara Peggy, da of John Francis Brooke (d 1977), of W Chiltington; 2 da; *Career* admitted slr 1956; md The Chepstow Racecourse plc 1963–, vice chm Racecourse Assoc Ltd 1986–; *Recreations* cricket, racquets, real tennis, squash, shooting; *Clubs* MCC, Free Foresters, I Zingari; *Style*— George Francis, Esq; ✉ The Chepstow Racecourse PLC, 17 Welsh Street, Chepstow, Gwent MP6 5YH

FRANCIS, Gerald Charles James (Gerry); s of Royston Albert Francis, and Pauline Elsie Francis; *b* 6 Dec 1951; *Educ* Stavely Secdy Modern Sch Chiswick; *partner* Julie; 1 s (Adam b 1993), 1 da (Chloe b 1995); *Career* professional football manager; player Queens Park Rangers 1968–79 and 1981–82: debut v Liverpool as apprentice 1968, 352 appearances, 65 goals; other clubs as player: 66 appearances Crystal Palace 1979–81 (9 goals), 54 appearances Coventry City 1982–83 (2 goals), 7 appearances Swansea City 1984–85, 5 appearances Portsmouth 1985; Exeter City 1983–84: player-mangr, 31 appearances, 3 goals; Bristol Rovers: joined 1985, 39 appearances, 1 goal, mangr 1987–91; manager Queens Park Rangers 1991–94, Tottenham Hotspur 1994–; England: 6 under 23 caps (capt 1973–75), 12 full caps (capt 1975–76), 3 goals; honours as player Queens Park Rangers: promotion to Div 1 1972–73, runners up League Championship 1976; honours as mangr Bristol Rovers: Div 3 Championship 1990, runners up Leyland Daf Cup 1990; winner Goal of the Season (BBC TV) 1975/76, Barclays Div 3 mangr of the year 1990, winner Sports Personality of the West 1990, mangr of the month March 1988, March 1990, March 1992 and Dec 1994; *Recreations* racing pigeons, squash, Winston Churchill; *Style*— Gerry Francis, Esq; ✉ Tottenham Hotspur Football Club, 748 High Road, Tottenham, London N17 0AP (☎ 0181 808 6666, fax 0181 885 1951)

FRANCIS, Graham John; s of Clarence William Francis, and Barbara Jean, *née* Henstridge; *b* 10 Nov 1945; *Educ* Univ of Manchester (BA, BArch); *m* Irene Frances, *née* Aykroyd; 1 da (Anna b 31 Oct 1980), 1 s (William b 6 Nov 1983); *Career* project architect: GLC Housing Div 1970–72 (asst architect GLC Town Devpt 1968–69), Ahrends Burton and Koralek 1973–80; Sheppard Robson (architects, planners and interior designers) London: joined 1980, assoc 1982, ptnr i/c tech matters and managing ptnr for Commercial Gp 1984–; recent projects incl: master planning of offices and associated activities Euston Centre London 1988–, BP's architect for Britannic Tower redevpt 1988–94, subsequently appointed exec architect for City Point (following name change) 1996–, The Helicon Project (store and commercial premises in S Islington for London and Manchester Properties) 1992–96, major refurbishment of teaching site in Regent St for Univ of Westminster 1993, master plan/design for mfrg/office facility for Motorola 1995–; RIBA; *Recreations* tennis, squash, walking; *Clubs* Hampstead Cricket, Stormont; *Style*— Graham Francis, Esq; ✉ Sheppard Robson, 77 Parkway, London NW1 7PU (☎ 0171 485 4161, fax 0171 267 3861, e-mail 100436.315@compuserv.com)

FRANCIS, Prof Hazel; da of Harry Wright (d 1961), of Brownhills, Staffs, and Ethel Vera, *née* Bedson (d 1965); *b* 12 April 1929; *Educ* Queen Mary's HS for Girls Walsall, Girton Coll Cambridge (MA), Univ of Leeds (MA, PhD); *m* 23 May 1953, Dr Huw Wesley Stephen Francis, s of Rev Matthew Francis (d 1954), of Walsall; 2 s (Andrew Martin b 1958, Jonathan Mark b 1962), 3 da (Susan Margaret b 1954, Keren Mary b 1956, Hilary Ann b 1960); *Career* teacher Handsworth GS for Girls Birmingham 1950–53; lectr and sr lectr Sch of Educn Univ of Leeds 1973–78 (p/t lectr Dept of Psychology 1969–73), pro-dir Inst of Educn Univ of London 1985–90, prof of educnl psychology Univ of London 1978–94 (prof emeritus 1994–); author of numerous articles in relevant scientific jls; memb: Br Educnl Research Assoc, Univs Cncl for the Educn of Teachers 1978–92, Br Psychological Soc, American Research Assoc, Euro Assoc for Research on Learning and Instruction; Hon PhD Univ of Linköping Sweden 1996; CPsychol 1988, FBPSsS 1980 (memb Cncl 1979–85), FRSA 1996; *Books* include: Language in Childhood (1975), Language in Teaching and Learning (1977), Learning to Read - Literate Behaviour and Orthographic Knowledge (1982), Minds of Their Own (1984), Learning to Teach: Psychology in Teacher Training (ed, 1985), The British Journal of Educational Psychology (ed, 1985–89); *Recreations* mountain walking, swimming, tennis; *Style*— Prof Hazel Francis; ✉ Institute of Education, University of London, 20 Bedford Way, London WC1H 0AL (☎ 0171 580 1122)

FRANCIS, Jan; *Career* actress; previously worked with Cheltenham Repertory Co, Bristol Old Vic Co, Royal Court and Bromley Theatre; *Theatre* incl: Lend me a Tenor (Globe Theatre), Hay Fever (Chichester Festival Theatre); *Television* incl: The Long

Chase, Anne of Green Gables, The Lonely Man's Lover, Raffles, Country Matters, Fall of Eagles, Duchess of Duke Street, London Assurance, The Magistrate, The Party of the First Part, The Good Companions (YTV), A Chance to Sit Down (BBC), Secret Army, Ripping Yarns, Death Can Add (Anglia TV), The Plot to Murder LLoyd George (BBC), Just Good Friends (3 series, BBC), Aladdin and the Forty Thieves (BBC), Minder (Euston Films), Stay Lucky (3 series, YTV), Under the Hammer (New Penny Prodns); *Films* incl: Dracula, Champions, The Corvini Inheritance; *Style*— Ms Jan Francis; ✉ c/o Julian Belfrage Associates, 46 Albemarle Street, London W1X 4PP (☎ 0171 491 4400, fax 0171 493 5460)

FRANCIS, Jeremy Inglesby; s of Gordon Cedric Francis (d 1963), and Marguerite June, *née* Smith; *b* 7 Jan 1951; *Educ* Wrekin Coll, Queens' Coll Cambridge (MA); *m* 30 June 1973, Susan Jane, da of late John Clark; 2 s (Matthew b 23 Aug 1978, Thomas b 10 Feb 1982), 1 da (Ellen b 7 Dec 1987); *Career* Robson Rhodes: articled clerk 1972, CA 1975, ptnr 1982–, involved in estab of Cambridge office 1985, ptnr in charge 1987–95, memb Mgmnt Bd 1989–, nat head of tax 1993–; ACA 1975, ATII 1989 (John Wood medal); *Recreations* bridge, piano playing, listening to classical music, reading; *Style*— Jeremy Francis, Esq; ✉ Robson Rhodes, Daedalus House, Station Road, Cambridge CB1 2RE (☎ 01223 368020, fax 01223 365436, mobile 0860 293739)

FRANCIS, Dr John Michael; s of William Winston Francis (d 1939), of Haverfordwest, Pembrokeshire, and Beryl Margaret, *née* Savage; *b* 1 May 1939; *Educ* Gowerton GS, Royal Coll of Science, Imperial Coll Univ of London (BSc, ARCS, PhD, DIC); *m* 14 Sept 1963, Eileen, da of Hugh Foster Sykes (d 1977), of Whitley Bay, Northumberland; 2 da (Sarah Katherine b 1966, Rachel Victoria b 1968); *Career* R & D Dept CEGB 1963–70, first dir Soc Religion and Technol Project Church of Scot 1970–74, sr res fell in energy studies Heriot-Watt Univ 1974–76, asst sec Scot Office 1981– (princ 1976–80); chief exec Nature Conservancy Cncl for Scot 1991–92 (memb Advsy Ctee 1974–76, dir Scot NCC 1984–91); visiting fell Inst for Advanced Studies in the Humanities Univ of Edinburgh 1988, visiting fell Centre for Values and Social Policy Univ of Colorado at Boulder 1991; contribs to numerous professional and scientific jls; conslt (science, technol and social ethics) World Cncl of Churches Geneva 1971–83, rep UN Environment Conf Stockholm 1972; chm: Ctee on Society Religion and Technol Church of Scot 1980–94, Edinburgh Forum 1986–92; memb: Oil Devpt Cncl for Scot 1973–76, Ind Cmmn on Tport 1974, Cncl Nat Tst for Scot 1984–92, Crown Estate Cmmn Advsy Ctee on Marine Fish Farming 1989–92; memb St Giles' Cathedral Edinburgh; assoc memb Scot Inst of Human Rels; chm Francis Group conslts (Europersona (trade mark)) 1991–, professional memb World Futures Soc Washington DC 1991–, memb Reference Gp Millenium Project UN Univ Washington DC 1992–, memb John Muir Tst; FRIC 1969, FRSGS 1990, FRSE 1991, FRZSScot 1992; *Books* Scotland in Turmoil (1973), Changing Directions (jtly, 1974), The Future as an Academic Discipline (jtly, 1975), Facing up to Nuclear Power (1976), The Future of Scotland (jtly, 1977), North Sea Oil and the Environment (jtly, 1992); also author of a review paper - Nature Conservation and the Voluntary Principle (1994); *Recreations* ecumenical travels, hill walking, theatre, writing on environmental conservation, values and ethics; *Style*— Dr John M Francis, FRSE; ✉ 49 Gilmour Rd, Newington, Edinburgh EH16 5NU (☎ and fax 0131 667 3996); The Scottish Office Environment Department, St Andrew's House, Edinburgh EH1 3DE (☎ 0131 244 2033)

FRANCIS, Mark Robert; s of Cecil Francis, and Lilian Louisa, *née* Richards; *b* 6 Sept 1962; *Educ* Scabo HS Newtownards, Regent House GS Newtownards, St Martin's Sch of Art (BA), Chelsea Sch of Art (MA); *Career* artist; *Exhibitions* incl: Summer Show (Tom Caldwell Gallery Dublin) 1983, New Contemporaries (The Mall Gallery) 1983, Stowells Trophy (Royal Acad) 1984, Summer Gp Show (Tom Caldwell Gallery Belfast) 1984, Another View of Ireland (Irish Artists in London) 1985, Athena Int Awards (Mall Galleries) 1985, Riverside Open (Riverside Studios) 1985, 4 New Painters (Paton Gallery) 1986, ILEA Class of 86 (Royal Festival Hall) 1986, On The Wall Gallery Belfast 1986, Contemporary Art Soc Market (Smith's Gallery) 1987, 1989, Art' 89 (Business Centre London) 1989, Christie's New Contemporaries (RCA) 1989, 5 Abstract Painters (Thumb Gallery) 1989, 4th Int Contemporary Art Fair LA, USA (Thumb Gallery) 1989, Four Painters (New Acad Gallery London) 1990, Art '90 London (Thumb Gallery) 1990, Bonhams Contemporary Auction (London) 1990, London to Atlanta (Atlanta, USA) 1990, 5th Int Contemporary Art Fair LA, USA (Thumb Gallery) 1990, solo exhibition (Thumb Gallery) 1990, Decouvertes (Paris) 1991, ARCO '92 (Madrid) 1992, solo exhibition (Jill George Gallery) 1992, Whitechapel Open 1992, British Art comes to St Helena (St Helena) 1992, New Displays (Tate Gallery) 1992, Euro Parl touring exhibition (Belfast, Edinburgh, Zürich, Brussells, London) 1992–93, Another Country (Rebecca Hossack Gallery) 1993, Snap Shots (Eagle Gallery) 1993, Ikon touring exhibition 1993, Machida Tokyo int print exhibition (winner grand prize) 1993, Contemporary Art at the Courtauld Inst 1993, Interim (solo show London) 1994, East 94 (Norfolk Inst of Art and Technol) 1994, Paintmarks (Kettles Yard Gallery) 1994, Unveiled (Cornerhouse Gallery) 1994, Recent British Art (Richard Salmon Fine Art) 1994, Anthony Reynolds: The Curators Egg (London) 1994, Europa 94 (Munich) 1994, Mark Francis/Brad Lahore (Herve Mikaeloff Gallery Paris) 1994, solo exhibition (Manchester City Art Gallery) 1994, solo exhibition (Kerlin Gallery Dublin) 1995, solo exhibition (Galerie Thieme & Pohl Darmstadt Germany) 1995, solo exhibition (Maureen Paley/Interim Art London) 1995, Testing the Water (Tate Gallery Liverpool) 1995, Voyage Anglais (Rheimes and touring) 1995, From Here (Karsten Schubert/Waddington Galleries London) 1995, Painters' Opinion (Bloom Gallery Amsterdam) 1995, Absolut Vision - New British Paintings in the 1990s (MOMA Oxford) 1996, Scattering Matrix (Richard Heller Gallery Santa Monica) 1996, Black Grey & White (Galerie Bugdahn und Kaimer Düsseldorf) 1996, British Abstract Art III (Flowers East Gallery London) 1996, Terra Nova - New Territories (solo exhibition, Harewood House Leeds) 1996, solo exhibition Mary Boone Gallery NY 1997; *Work in Collections* incl Unilever plc, British Credit Trust Co, Heytesbury Holdings Ltd, Arthur Andersen, Leicester Educn Authy, Chelmsford Borough Cncl, Metropolitan Museum NY, Stanhope PLC, Tate Gallery, Euro Parl, Manchester City Art Gallery, Simmons & Simmons, Contemporary Art Soc, V&A, Machida City Museum of Graphic Art Tokyo, St Peter's Coll Oxford, de Young Memorial Museum San Francisco, Mead Gallery Univ of Warwick, Irish Museum of Modern Art Dublin, St Louis Museum USA, Ulster Museum, Saatchi Collection London, Caldic Collection Amsterdam, NatWest Gp Art Collection London, Lambert Collection Zürich, Deutsche Morgan Grenfell London, Deutsche Bank Germany; *Style*— Mark Francis, Esq; ✉ Paragon Centre, Searles Rd, London SE1; c/o Maureen Paley, Interim Art, 21 Beck Road, London E8 (☎ 0171 254 9607)

FRANCIS, Matthew (*né* Francis Edwin Matthews); s of Ronald Leslie Matthews, OBE, and Dorothy Olive Alice, *née* Mitchell; *b* 10 Jan 1953; *Educ* Harrow County Sch for Boys, Univ Coll Oxford; *Career* assoc dir Chichester Festival Theatre 1983–87, fndr dir Cut & Thrust Theatre Co 1987–89, artistic dir Greenwich Theatre 1990–; visiting dir Univ of South Florida; memb: Brit Actors' Equity (1975), Nat Youth Theatre Assoc, Laban Centre, London Library; *Theatre* prodns for Greenwich incl: The Corn is Green (with Patricia Routledge), Cyrano de Bergerac (with Edward Petherbridge), The Government Inspector (with Timothy Spall), Caesar and Cleopatra (with Alec McCowen); other credits incl: Rosencrantz and Guildenstern are Dead (RNT), Fidelio (NI Opera); *Publications* adaptations incl: The Prisoner of Zenda (Samuel French, 1994), A Tale of Two Cities (Samuel French, 1995); *Recreations* French Pyrenees, gardening, cooking, theatre, films; *Clubs* Broadgate; *Style*— Matthew Francis, Esq; ✉ The Greenwich Theatre, Crooms Hill, Greenwich, London SE10 8ES (☎ 0181 858 4447, fax 0181 858 8042)

FRANCIS, Penelope Julia Louise; da of Vincent Robert Paul Palmer, of Pont Royal, France, and Cynthia Ann Palmer; *b* 9 Nov 1959; *Educ* St Anne's Coll Sanderstead, Univ of Bristol (LLB); *m* 8 June 1985, Barry Hugh Francis, s of Stanley Francis; *Career* asst slr Beachcroft Stanleys 1984–89 (articled clerk 1982–84); Lawrence Graham: asst slr 1989–91, ptnr 1991–94, equity ptnr 1994–, currently head Property Litigation Dept; memb Law Soc 1984; *Recreations* Middle and Far East travel, ballet, eating; *Clubs* Reform, Property Litigation; *Style*— Mrs Penelope Francis; ✉ Lawrence Graham, 190 Strand, London WC2R 1JN (☎ 0171 379 0000, fax 0171 379 6854)

FRANCIS, Richard Mark; s of Ralph Lawrence Francis, of Oakham, Leicestershire, and Eileen Nellie, *née* Jenkins (d 1993); *b* 20 Nov 1947; *Educ* Oakham Sch Rutland, Selwyn Coll Cambridge (BA), Courtauld Inst of Art (MA); *m* 7 Oct 1976, Tamar Janine Helen, da of Donald Beazley Burchill (d 1972); 1 da (Jasmine Helen b 1979); *Career* Walker Art Gallery Liverpool 1971–72, exhibition offr Arts Cncl of GB 1973–80, asst keeper of modern collection The Tate Gallery 1980–86, curator Tate Gallery Liverpool 1986–90, independent curator and assoc curator Tate Gallery 1990–92, chief curator Museum of Contemporary Art Chicago USA 1992–; *Books* Jasper Johns (1984); *Recreations* buying books; *Style*— Richard Francis; ✉ 237 East Ontario Street, Chicago, Illinois 60611, USA

FRANCIS, Richard Maurice; s of Hugh Elvet Francis, QC (d 1986), and Emma Frances Wienholt, *née* Bowen; *b* 28 June 1946; *Educ* Mill Hill, Univ of Durham (BA); *m* 2 Oct 1993, Victoria Adzoa, da of Godslove C Acolatse, of Accra, Ghana; 1 step da; *Career* called to the Bar Gray's Inn 1974, in practice Wales and Chester Circuit 1976–, in practice as a mediator 1996–; chm The Montgomeryshire Soc 1994–, sec Cardiff Christian Educn Centre 1993–; Golden Cross of the Polish Republic 1985; memb RIIA; *Books* The British Withdrawal from the Baghdad Railway Project (1973), A History of Oakley Park Church (1976); *Recreations* family, church work, listening to BBC Radios 3 and 4; *Clubs* Cardiff and County; *Style*— Richard Francis, Esq; ✉ 9 Park Place, Cardiff, South Glamorgan CF1 3DP (☎ 01222 382731, fax 01222 222542, dx 50751 CARDIFF 2); The Mediation Centre, Penarth CF64 3BH (☎ 01222 700131)

FRANCIS, Richard Stanley (Dick); OBE (1984); s of George Vincent Francis (d 1960), of Embrook, Wokingham, Berks, and Catherine Mary, *née* Thomas (d 1970); *b* 31 Oct 1920; *Educ* Maidenhead Co Boys' Sch; *m* Mary Margaret, *née* Brenchley; 2 s (Merrick Ewen Douglas b 1950, Felix Richard Roger b 1953); *Career* flying offr RAF 1940–45; steeplechase jockey 1946–57 (champion jockey 1953–54, first jockey to be retained by Her Majesty Queen Elizabeth The Queen Mother under National Hunt rules 1953–57), racing corr Sunday Express 1957–73, author 1962– (over 30 novels, translated into 23 languages); memb: Crime Writers' Assoc of GB, Mystery Writers' Assoc of America; Hon LHD Tufts Univ Boston 1991; *Books* The Sport of Queens (autobiography, 1957), Dead Cert (1962), Nerve (1964), For Kicks (Crime Writers' Assoc of GB Silver Dagger award, 1965), Odds Against (1965), Flying Finish (1966), Blood Sport (1967), Forfeit (Mystery Writers' of America award, 1969), Enquiry (1969), Rat Race (1970) Bonecrack (1971), Smoke Screen (1972), Slay-Ride (1973), Knock Down (1974), High Stakes (1975), In the Frame (1976), Risk (1977), Trial Run (1978), Reflex (1980) Whip Hand (Crime Writers' Assoc Gold Dagger award, Mystery Writers' of America award, 1980), Twice Shy (1981), Banker (1982), The Danger (1983), Proof (1984), Break In (1985), Lester - the official biography (1986), Bolt (1986), Hot Money (1987), The Edge (1988), Straight (1989), Great Racing Stories (jt ed, 1989), Longshot (1990), Comeback (1991), Driving Force (1992), Decider (1993), Wild Horses (1994), Come to Grief (1995), To the Hilt (1996); *Recreations* boating, travel; *Clubs* Tower (Fort Lauderdale); *Style*— Dick Francis, Esq, OBE; ✉ c/o Andrew Hewson, John Johnson (Authors' Agent) Ltd, Clerkenwell House, 45/47 Clerkenwell Green, London EC1R 0HT (☎ 0171 251 0125, fax 0171 251 2172)

FRANCIS, Robert Anthony; QC (1992); s of John Grimwade Francis, and Jean Isobel, *née* Wilson; *b* 4 April 1950; *Educ* Uppingham Sch, Univ of Exeter (LLB, pres Guild of Students 1971–72); *m* 1976, Catherine, da of John Georgievsky; 2 da (Anna Elizabeth b 1979, Helen Alexandra b 1981), 1 s (Nicholas John b 1985); *Career* called to the Bar 1973, tenant in chambers of Mr Philip Naughton QC at 3 Serjeants Inn 1973–; *Recreations* cricket; *Style*— Robert Francis, Esq, QC; ✉ 3 Serjeants Inn, London EC4Y 1BQ (☎ 0171 353 5537, fax 0171 353 0425)

FRANCIS, Stewart; s of Elgar Francis Thompson, of Rudgwick, Sussex, and Cathleen Winifred, *née* Allwood; *b* 7 March 1951; *Educ* Warlingham Co Sch; *m* 1, 16 May 1970 (m dis 1995), Stephanie Jane, da of Richard Stanley Butler, of Sanderstead, Surrey; 2 s (Matthew b 20 Dec 1973, Nicholas Peter b 7 Feb 1978); m 2, 5 Oct 1996, Jaki Marilyn, da of Bernard George Fox, of Kings Lynn, Norfolk; *Career* freelance disc-jockey 1968–72, presenter LBC 1973–75, dep prog controller Pennine Radio 1975–79, md Hereward Radio plc 1984–87 (prog controller 1980–83), md Mid Anglia Radio plc 1988–95 (chm 1995–); dir Assoc of Ind Radio Contractors until 1995 (chm 1991–94); chief exec Greater Peterborough Business Link 1995–96, tstee Mid Anglia Radio Appeal for the Disabled, vice chm Peterborough Creative Partnership; *Recreations* cricket, football; *Style*— Stewart Francis, Esq; ✉ 24 Thorpe Meadows, Peterborough PE3 6GA (☎ and fax 01733 341528)

FRANCIS, Trevor; *b* 19 April 1954; *Career* former professional football player and manager; clubs as player: joined Birmingham City 1971 (317 appearances, 127 goals), transferred Nottingham Forest (first Br £1m transfer) 1979 (87 appearances, 37 goals, Euro Cup winners 1979 and 1980, runners up League Cup 1980), transferred Manchester City 1981 (29 appearances, 14 goals), joined Sampdoria Italy 1982 (68 appearances, 17 goals), joined Atalanta Italy 1986 (21 appearances, 1 goal), transferred Glasgow Rangers 1987 (22 appearances, Scottish League Cup winners 1987); player/manager: Queens Park Rangers as player 1988, also mangr 1989–90 (32 appearances, 15 goals), Sheffield Wednesday as player 1990, also mangr 1991–95 (winners League Cup 1991, runners up FA Cup 1993, runners up Coca-Cola Cup 1993); mangr Birmingham City 1996–; England: 5 under 23 caps, 52 full caps 1977–86; *Style*— Trevor Francis, Esq; ✉ c/o Birmingham City FC, St Andrews, Birmingham B9 4NH

FRANCIS, Sir (Horace) William Alexander; kt (1989), CBE (1976); s of Horace Fairie Francis, and Jane McMinn Murray; *b* 31 Aug 1926; *Educ* Dumbarton Acad, Royal Tech Coll Glasgow, Battersea Poly London; *m* 9 July 1949, Gwendoline Maud, da of Walter Dorricott; 2 da (Susan Jane b 8 Dec 1950, Dorcas Gwendoline b 3 Oct 1961), 2 s (Peter Alexander b 13 March 1954, Maxwell Stuart b 17 Feb 1957); *Career* Babtie Shaw & Morton Glasgow 1943–45, Binnie Deacon & Gourlay London 1945–49, Shrewsbury Corporation 1949–53; Tarmac 1953–77: dir Tarmac Civil Engineering Ltd 1960, md Tarmac Construction Ltd 1963, dir Tarmac plc 1964, chm construction related subsids 1968–77, vice chm Tarmac plc 1973–77: Trafalgar House 1978–88: dir Trafalgar House plc 1978–86 (chm Cementation International, chm Cementation Construction, chm Cleveland Bridge and Engineering, dep chm Trollope & Colls), dir Trafalgar House Oil & Gas 1986–88; chm Black Country Development Corporation 1987–94; dir Mining (Scotland) Ltd 1994–, bd memb British Rail 1994–, dir Barr Holdings Ltd 1995–; memb Advsy Bd ECGD 1974–80, vice chm Construction Exports Advsy Bd 1975–78, memb BOTB 1977–80, chm Overseas Project Bd 1977–80 (memb 1973–80); pres ICE 1987–88 (vice pres 1984–87), memb Engrg Cncl 1995–96; tstee Birmingham Children's Hosp 1995–; memb: Worshipful Co of Paviors 1967, Worshipful Co of Constructors 1983, Worshipful Co of Engrs 1984; Hon LLD Univ of Strathclyde 1988, Hon DSc Aston Univ

1990; fell Inst of Highway Engrs 1963, FICE 1964 (MICE 1952), FEng 1977; *Recreations* golf, fishing, shooting, conservation, construction; *Clubs* Livery, Royal Over-Seas League; *Style—* Sir William Francis, CBE, FEng; ✉ The Firs, Cruckton, Shrewsbury SY5 8PW; British Railways Board, Euston House, 24 Eversholt Street, London NW1 1DZ (☎ 0171 922 6310, fax 0171 922 6927)

FRANCOME, John; MBE (1986); s of Norman John Francome, and Lillian Maud Francome; *b* 13 Dec 1952; *Educ* Park Sr HS Swindon; *m* 1976, Miriam, da of Andrew Strigner, of London; *Career* champion jockey seven times, 1138 wins (nat hunt record); racehorse trainer and commentator; *Books* Born Lucky (autobiography, 1985), Eavesdropper (1986), Riding High (1987), Declared Dead (1988), Bloodstock (1989); *Recreations* tennis, music; *Style—* John Francome, Esq, MBE; ✉ c/o Channel Four Racing, Channel Four Television Corporation, 124 Horseferry Road, London SW1P 2TX

FRANK, Sir (Robert) Andrew; 4 Bt (UK 1920), of Withyham, Co Sussex; s of Sir Robert John Frank, 3 Bt (d 1987), and his 2 w Margaret Joyce, *née* Truesdale (d 1995); *b* 16 May 1964; *Educ* Ludgrove, Eton; *m* 23 June 1990, Zoë Alia, er da of S A Hasan, of Windsor, Berks, and Pauline, *née* Davidson; *Heir* none; *Career* retailer/prodr 1986–; *Recreations* theatre, croquet, travel; *Style—* Sir Andrew Frank, Bt; ✉ Ruscombe End, Waltham St Lawrence, nr Reading, Berks RG10 0HE

FRANK, Dr Andrew Oliver; s of Ernest Oliver Frank (d 1993), of Haywards Heath, Sussex, and Doris Helen, *née* McBean (d 1985); *b* 4 Sept 1944; *Educ* Kingswood Sch Bath, Middx Hosp Med Sch (MB BS, MRCP); *m* 23 June 1973, Cynthia Mary, da of James Siviter, of Lugwardine, Hereford; 1 s (Anthony b 1979), 2 da (Christina b 1982, Julia b 1986); *Career* lectr in med Univ of Malaya 1974–76, sr registrar in med rheumatology and rehabilitation Salisbury Health Dist 1977–80; Northwick Park Hosp and Inst of Med Res: conslt physician in rehabilitation med and rheumatology 1980–, clinical dir of orthopaedics, rheumatology and rehabilitation 1990–95; Med Disability Soc (now Br Soc of Rehab Med): fndr and hon sec 1984–87, regional co-ordinator 1995–, chm Educn Ctee 1996–; memb Disability Ctee RCP 1979–87, chm NW Thames Physical Disability Advsy Gp 1992–94; memb: Soc of Research into Rehabilitation 1982 (memb Cncl 1995–), RSM; FRCP 1990; *Books* Disabling Diseases: Physical, Environmental and Psychosocial Management (with G P Maguire, 1989); *Recreations* family, music; *Style—* Dr Andrew Frank; ✉ Northwick Park Hospital, Watford Rd, Harrow, Middlesex HA1 3UJ (☎ 0181 869 2102, fax 0181 869 2803)

FRANK, Sir (Frederick) Charles; kt (1977), OBE (1946); eld s of Frederick Frank (d 1971), and Medora Frank; *b* 6 March 1911; *Educ* Thetford GS, Ipswich Sch, Lincoln Coll Oxford; *m* 1940, Maia Maita, yst da of Prof Boris Michaelovich Asché (d 1943); 1 c (d at birth); *Career* scientist; Air Scientific Intelligence 1940–46; Bristol Univ Dept of Physics 1946–76: prof 1954, head of dept 1969–76; vice pres Royal Soc 1967–69, Royal medallist 1979, Copley medallist 1994; holder of numerous hon degrees from Br and foreign univs; FRS 1954; *Recreations* gardening; *Clubs* Athenaeum; *Style—* Sir Charles Frank, OBE, FRS; ✉ Orchard Cottage, Grove Rd, Coombe Dingle, Bristol BS9 2RL (☎ 0117 968 1708)

FRANK, David Thomas; s of Thomas Frank (d 1984), of Robertsford, Shrewsbury, and Margaret McCrea, *née* Cowan; *b* 29 April 1954; *Educ* Shrewsbury, Univ of Bristol (LLB); *m* 10 July 1982, Diane Lillian, da of Stephen Nash Abbott, of Farnham Common, Bucks; 1 s (Charles b 1988), 1 da (Lucinda b 1986); *Career* admitted slr 1979; Slaughter and May: asst slr 1979–86, ptnr 1986–, head of Capital Markets 1993–; *Recreations* the turf, lawn tennis, cars; *Style—* David Frank, Esq; ✉ Slaughter and May, 35 Basinghall St, London EC2V 5DB (☎ 0171 600 1200, fax 0171 726 0038, telex 883486)

FRANK, Sir Douglas George Horace; kt (1976), QC (1964); s of late George Maurice Frank, of Osterley, and Agnes Winifred Frank; *b* 16 April 1916; *Educ* City of London Sch and privately; *m* 1, 1939, late Margaret Clara, da of Alfred William Shaw, OBE; 1 s, 2 da; m 2, 1963, late Sheila Frances, da of late Cdre Lawrence King Beauchamp, RN; 2 da; m 3, 1979, Audrey, yr da of Charles Leslie Thomas, of Neath, Glamorgan; *Career* served Lt RA TA 1936–43; called to the Bar Gray's Inn 1946, bencher 1970, dep judge of the High Ct 1975–89; memb Ctee for Public Participation in Planning 1968, pres Lands Tbnl 1973–88, hon pres Anglo-American Real Property Inst 1980–89; sometime dep boundary cmmr for England and Wales; *Style—* Sir Douglas Frank, QC; ✉ c/o 4/5 Gray's Inn Chambers, London WC1 (☎ 0171 404 5252); La Mayne Longue Haute, Sauveterre-La-Lemance, 47500 Fumel, France (☎ 00 33 53 40 68 98)

FRANK, Simon; s of Maj Godfrey Noel Frank, of Highcliffe, Dorset, and Dorothy Louise, *née* Underwood; *b* 17 May 1959; *Educ* Bryanston, Univ of Exeter (BA(Hons) Political Sci); *m* 24 April 1984, Barbara May Christine, da of Mervyn Alexander Hadden; 1 s (Daniel Alexander b 21 Sept 1987), 1 da (Erin Barbara b 11 Feb 1990); *Career* advtg exec; writer Finsbury Data Services 1980–83 (helped launch Textline News Serv now owned by Reuters), bd dir/copywriter Ogilvy & Mather 1994 (joined as trainee copywriter 1983), sr copywriter Euro RSCG 1984–95, creative dir Lansdown Conquest 1995–; recipient numerous advtg awards (British TV, Independent London Radio, Campaign Press and Poster, Clio and Creative Circle Awards); *Recreations* currently feature film scriptwriting; *Style—* Simon Frank, Esq; ✉ Lansdown Conquest Ltd, 4 Flitcroft Street, London WC2H 8DJ (☎ 0171 240 4949, fax 0171 240 9094)

FRANKEL, William; CBE (1971); s of Isaac Frankel (d 1963), of London, and Anna, *née* Lecker (d 1946); *b* 3 Feb 1917; *Educ* Poly Secdy Sch Regent St London, Univ of London (LLB); *m* 1, 1939 (m dis 1972), Gertrude Freda, da of Louis Reed, of London; 1 s (John), 1 da (Anne); m 2, 1973, Mrs Claire Neuman, da of Herold J Schwab, of Birmingham, Alabama, USA; *Career* barr; chm Jewish Chronicle 1991–94 (ed 1958–77); chm: Social Security Appeal Tbnl 1977–89, Mental Health Review Tbnl 1978–89; special advsr to The Times 1977–81, London corr Statesman (Calcutta and Delhi); *Books* Israel Observed: an anatomy of the State (1981); *Clubs* Athenaeum, MCC; *Style—* William Frankel, Esq, CBE; ✉ 30 Montagu Sq, London W1H 1RJ

FRANKLAND, Christopher John (Chris); s of Leonard Frankland (d 1958), and Kathleen Mary, *née* Burningham (d 1996); *b* 7 Nov 1942; *Educ* Forest Sch London; *m* 18 June 1966, Eve Marie, da of Lt Cdr Victor J Chown, of Feniton, Devon; 1 s (Philip Thomas b 16 Aug 1969), 2 da (Angela Tara (twin) b 16 Aug 1969, Gail Marie b 4 Dec 1972); *Career* chartered accountant; articled clerk Hereward Scott Davies & Co 1959–65; Ernst & Young: joined Bristol office 1966, mangr 1968, transferred to London office 1972, ptnr 1978, currently ptnr Tech Servs Dept; Freeman City of London 1980, Liveryman Worshipful Co of Needlemakers; FCA; *Recreations* hill and beach walking; *Style—* Chris Frankland, Esq; ✉ 29 Montalt Rd, Woodford Green, Essex IG8 9RS (☎ 0181 504 2106); 14c Cliff Parade, Hunstanton, Norfolk PE36 6DP (☎ 01485 534531); Ernst & Young, Rolls House, Fetter Lane, London EC4A 1NL (☎ 0171 928 2000)

FRANKLAND, (Frederick) Mark; s of The Hon Roger Nathaniel Frankland (d 1989), and Elizabeth Cecil, *née* Sanday (d 1968); *b* 19 April 1934; *Educ* Charterhouse, Pembroke Coll Cambridge (BA), Brown Univ USA; *Career* FO 1958–59; dep ed Time & Tide 1960–61; The Observer: Moscow corr 1962–64, Indochina corr (also for The Economist) 1967–73, Toyko corr 1973–75, Washington corr 1975–78, Moscow corr 1982–85, East Euro corr 1987–90; winner David Holden award (Br Press Awards) 1984 and 1986; memb Soc of Authors; *Books* Khrushchev (1966), The Mother-of-Pearl Men (1985), Richard Robertovich (1987), The Sixth Continent (1987), The Patriots' Revolution (1990), Freddie the Weaver (1995); *Recreations* travel; *Style—* Mark Frankland, Esq

FRANKLAND, Dr (Anthony) Noble; CB (1983), CBE (1976), DFC (1944); s of Edward Percy Frankland (d 1958), of Westmorland, and Maud, *née* Metcalfe-Gibson (d 1979); *b* 4 July 1922; *Educ* Sedbergh, Trinity Coll Oxford (open scholar, MA, DPhil); *m* 1, 28 Feb 1944, Diana Madeline Forvargue (d 1981), da of George Victor Tavernor (k 1928); 1 s (Arnold Edward Roger b 1951), 1 da (Linda Helga Elizabeth (Mrs Michael O'Hanlon) b 1953); m 2, 7 May 1982, Sarah Katharine, da of His Hon the late Sir David Davies, QC, and the late Lady Davies (the novelist Margaret Kennedy); *Career* RAF: joined 1941, navigator Bomber Cmd 1943–45, Flt Lt 1945; narrator Air Hist Branch Air Miny 1948–51, official mil historian Cabinet Office 1951–60; dep dir of studies RIIA 1956–60, dir Imperial War Museum 1960–82 (Duxford 1976–82, HMS Belfast 1978–82); Rockefeller fell 1953, Lees Knowles lectr Trinity Coll Cambridge 1963, hist advsr Thames TV Series The World at War 1971–74; vice chm Br Nat Ctee of Int Ctee for the Study of WWII 1976–82; memb: Cncl Morley Coll 1962–66, HMS Belfast Tst 1971–78 (vice chm 1972–78), HMS Belfast Bd 1978–82; *Books* Crown of Tragedy, Nicholas II (1960), The Strategic Air Offensive Against Germany 1939–45 (4 Volumes with Sir Charles Webster, 1961), The Bombing Offensive Against Germany, Outlines and Perspectives (1965), Bomber Offensive, The Devastation of Europe (1970), Prince Henry, Duke of Gloucester (1980), The Politics and Strategy of the Second World War (jt ed series, 1974–), Decisive Battles of the Twentieth Century, Land, Sea and Air (jt ed, 1976), The Encyclopedia of Twentieth Century Warfare (gen ed, 1989), Witness of a Century, Prince Arthur, Duke of Connaught (1993); *Clubs* Royal Over-Seas League; *Style—* Dr Noble Frankland, CB, CBE, DFC; ✉ Thames House, Oxford Road, Eynsham, Witney, Oxon OX8 1DA (☎ 01865 881327)

FRANKLAND, Timothy Cecil; s of Hon Roger Nathaniel Frankland (d 1989, yr s of Mary Cecil, Baroness Zouche), and his 1 w Elizabeth Cecil, *née* Sanday (d 1968); *b* 4 Oct 1931; *Educ* Charterhouse; *Career* Lt 15/19 Hussars 1950–52; Binder Hamlyn & Co CAs 1952–67; dir: Hill Samuel & Co 1967–, Newman Tonks Gp; non-exec dep chm: Refuge Group plc, Jarvis Porter Group plc; govr Charterhouse Sch; FCA 1957; *Clubs* MCC, Berkshire, Royal Mid Surrey; *Style—* Timothy Frankland, Esq; ✉ Hill Samuel Bank Ltd, 100 Wood St, London EC2 (☎ 0171 600 6000)

FRANKLAND-PAYNE-GALLWEY, Sir Philip; 6 Bt (UK 1812); o s of Lt-Col Lowry Philip Payne-Gallwey, OBE, MC (d 1958, ggs of 1 Bt), and Janet, *née* Payne-Gallwey; suc kinsman, Sir Reginald Frankland-Payne-Gallwey, 5 Bt, 1964; assumed by Royal Licence 1966 the additional surname of Frankland before that of Payne and Gallwey; *b* 15 March 1935; *Educ* Eton; *Heir* none; *Career* late Lt 11 Hussars; dir British Bloodstock Agency Ltd; *Style—* Sir Philip Frankland-Payne-Gallwey, Bt; ✉ 29 Cadogan Street, London SW3 2PP

FRANKLIN, Daniel John (Dan); s of Michael Howard Franklin, of Manningtree, Essex, and Suzanne Mary, *née* Cooper (d 1992); *b* 2 May 1949; *Educ* Bradfield, UEA (BA); *m* 29 June 1985, Lucy, da of Michael Hughes-Hallett, of Barton-on-the-Heath, Glos; 2 da (Lettice b 1 March 1990, Mary (twin) b 1 March 1990); *Career* editorial dir William Heinemann 1987, publisher Secker & Warburg 1988, publishing dir Jonathan Cape 1993–; *Style—* Dan Franklin, Esq; ✉ Jonathan Cape, 20 Vauxhall Bridge Road, London SW1V 2SA (☎ 0171 973 9730, fax 0171 233 6117)

FRANKLIN, George Henry; s of George Edward Franklin (d 1975), and Annie Franklin (d 1991); *b* 15 June 1923; *Educ* Hastings GS, Hastings Sch of Art, Architectural Assoc Sch of Architecture (AADipl), Sch of Planning and Res for Regnl Devpt London (SPDip); *m* 1950, Sylvia Daisy, *née* Allen; 3 s, 1 da; *Career* WWII Capt RE, served Europe Parachute Sqdn RE, SE Asia, Bengal Sappers and Miners Royal Indian Engrs; architect planner Finchley Borough Cncl 1952–54, architect Christian Med Coll Ludhiana Punjab India 1954–57; physical planning advsr (Colombo Plan): Republic of Indonesia 1958–62, Govt of Malaysia 1963–64; Miny of Overseas Devpt later Overseas Devpt Admin FCO 1966–83, conslt on Third World planning and devpt, hon prof Dept of Town Planning UWIST 1982–88, sr advsr Devpt Planning Unit UCL 1983–, memb Int Advsy Bd Centre for Devpt and Environmental Planning Oxford Poly 1985–, chm overseas sch Town and Country Planning Summer Sch 1970–75; Cwlth Assoc of Planners: memb Exec Ctee 1970–80, pres 1980–84, hon sec 1984–88; memb Exec Ctee Cwlth Human Ecology Cncl 1970–91; papers to int conferences and professional jls concerning physical planning, development, building and housing in the Third World; memb Editorial Bd: Third World Planning Review 1979–91, Cities 1983–91; memb World Service Ctee United Bible Socs 1968–77, chm Warminster Bible Soc Action Gp 1991–; Leonard Cheshire Care At Home Service (formerly Family Support): chm Warminster and Westbury Dist 1990–94, vice chm W Wilts 1994–96; coordinator Christian Aid Warminster Dist 1990–; assoc: Indian Inst of Architects 1955, Inst of Town Planners India 1956; RIBA, FRTPI, FRSA; *Recreations* the family, Christian, Third World and environmental interests and activities, fly fishing; *Clubs* Cwlth Trust, Victory Services; *Style—* George Franklin, Esq; ✉ The Manse, Sutton Veny, Warminster, Wiltshire BA12 7AW (☎ and fax 01985 840072)

FRANKLIN, Prof Ian Maxwell; s of Edwin William Franklin, of London, and Elizabeth Joyce, *née* Kessler; *b* 6 Sept 1949; *Educ* Owen's Boys Sch Islington London, Univ of Leeds (BSc, MB ChB), UCH Med Sch (PhD); *m* 19 July 1975, Anne Christine, da of Harry Norman Bush, of Leeds; 1 s (Matthew Charles Maxwell b 1988), 1 da (Sophie Rose b 1991); *Career* MRC res fell UCH Med Sch 1977–80, sr registrar haematology UCH and Hosp for Sick Children Gt Ormond St 1980–82, conslt haematologist Queen Elizabeth Hosp Birmingham 1982–92, dir of haematology Central Birmingham Health Authy 1989–91, dir Bone Marrow Transplant Unit and conslt haematologist Royal Infirmary Glasgow 1992–96; scientific sec Br Soc for Haematology 1995–; memb: American Soc of Hematology, Assoc of Physicians of GB & Ireland; FRCP (London) 1990 (MRCP 1977), FRCPGlas 1994, FRCPEd 1996; *Recreations* sailing, cycling; *Clubs* Royal Gourock Yacht, Clyde Cruising, Royal Over-Seas League; *Style—* Prof Ian Franklin; ✉ Department of Medicine, Royal Infirmary, 10 Alexandra Parade, Glasgow G31 2ER (☎ 0141 211 4680, fax 0141 552 2953, e-mail imf1c@clinmed.gla.ac.uk)

FRANKLIN, John Andrew; s of Bernard Franklin (d 1979); *b* 21 Nov 1943; *Educ* Rugby, Pembroke Coll Cambridge (MA); *m* 1976, Elizabeth Anthea, da of Samuel John Noel Bartley, of Constantine Bay, Cornwall; 2 s; *Career* slr Slaughter and May 1968–72, dir Morgan Grenfell & Co Ltd 1979–91 (joined 1972, conslt 1991–94), dir Fox-Pitt Kelton Ltd 1994–; govr Utd World Coll of the Atlantic; *Recreations* skiing, sailing, wine, golf, shooting; *Clubs* Boodle's, Hurlingham, HAC, The Leash, (New York), Hunstanton Golf; *Style—* John Franklin, Esq; ✉ 76 Lansdowne Road, London W11 2LS (☎ 0171 727 1659)

FRANKLIN, Sir Michael David Milroy; KCB (1983, CB 1979), CMG (1972); s of Milroy Llewellyn Capon Franklin, of Trowbridge; *b* 24 Aug 1927; *Educ* Taunton Sch, Peterhouse Cambridge; *m* 1951, Dorothy Joan, da of James Stuart Fraser, of Wallasey, Cheshire; 2 s, 1 da; *Career* joined MAFF 1950, UK delgn to OEEC (now OECD) 1959–61, private sec to Min 1961–64, under sec MAFF 1968–73; dep dir gen Directorate-Gen of Agric EEC 1973–77, head Euro Secretariat Cabinet Office 1977–82; perm sec: Dept of Trade 1982–83, MAFF 1983–87; dir: Barclays plc 1988–93, Agricultural Mortgage Corporation 1987–93, Whessoe plc 1988–, Whitbread plc 1991–; chm British Invisibles European Ctee; memb: Int Policy Cncl on Agric and Trade, Cncl RIIA 1988–95; pres W India Ctee 1988–95; *Clubs* Oxford and Cambridge; *Style—* Sir Michael Franklin, KCB, CMG; ✉ 15 Galley Lane, Barnet, Herts EN5 4AR (fax 0181 440 8513)

FRANKLIN, Peter; s of William Sydney Franklin (d 1987), of Winchester, Hants, and Mary Elizabeth, *née* Todd; *b* 11 May 1952; *Educ* Peter Symonds' Sch Winchester, UCL (LLB); *m* 1976, Susan Ann, da of John Goslett Edwards; 3 s (Daniel Thomas b 19 March

1982, Nicholas Stephen b 14 June 1984, Edward Mark b 12 Feb 1987); *Career* sr auditor Thomas McLintock 1973–77, fin controller BFI Line 1977–79, treasy mangr FMI Ltd 1979–81, mangr of int control Salomon Brothers International 1981–84, asst vice pres Bache Securities (UK) Ltd 1984–86, dir of capital market operations County Natwest 1986–89, dir of fin and admin Rea Brothers Ltd 1989–94, head of ops Fin Dept European Bank for Reconstruction and Development 1994–; non-exec chm Menhir Ltd 1994–; FRSA 1990, FCA 1981 (ACA 1978), MCT 1992; *Recreations* cinema, music, a great fondness for all sports; *Style*— Peter Franklin, Esq; ✉ European Bank for Reconstruction and Development, One Exchange Square, London EC2A 2EH (☎ 0171 338 6153)

FRANKLIN, Prof Raoul Norman; CBE (1995); s of Norman George Franklin, JP (d 1977), of Auckland, NZ, and Thelma Brinley, *née* Davis; *b* 3 June 1935; *Educ* Howick DHS NZ, Auckland GS NZ, Auckland Univ (BE, BSc, ME, MSc), Univ of Oxford (DPhil, MA, DSc); *m* 29 July 1961, Faith, da of Lt-Col Harold Thomason Carew Ivens (d 1951), of Beaconsfield; 2 s (Robert b 1965, Nicholas b 1967); *Career* Capt NZ Def Scientific Corps 1957–63, sr res fell RMCS Shrivenham 1961–63, lectr in engrg sci Univ of Oxford 1966–78, vice-chllr The City Univ 1978–; dir City Technol Ltd 1978–93, chm Gen Bd of Faculties Univ of Oxford 1971–74; memb: Hebdomadal Cncl 1971–74 and 1976–78, Cncl Gresham Coll 1981–, Sci Bd SERC 1982–85, Governing Body Ashridge Mgmnt Coll 1986–, London Pension Fund Authy 1989–95, Associated Examining Bd 1993– (chm 1994–); hon fell Keble Coll Oxford 1980– (fell 1963–78); govr Ashridge Mgmnt Coll 1987–; Liveryman Worshipful Co of Curriers; Cdr Order of Merit (Poland) 1995; FEng 1990; *Books* Plasma Phenomena in Gas Discharges (1976), Physical Kinetics (ed 1981), Interaction of Intense Electromagnetic Fields with Plasma (ed 1981); *Recreations* walking, gardening, tennis; *Clubs* Athenaeum; *Style*— Prof Raoul Franklin, CBE, FEng; ✉ 20 Myddelton Square, London EC1R 1YE; The City University, Northampton Square, London EC1V 0HB (☎ 0171 477 8002, fax 0171 477 8561)

FRANKLIN, Victoria Anne; da of William George Bott, and Dorothea Florence, *née* Bleasby; *b* 19 April 1954; *Educ* Redland HS Bristol, St Hugh's Coll Oxford (MA); *m* 8 Nov 1982, Andrew Vernon Franklin, s of John Vernon Henry Franklin; 2 s (Samuel Andrew b 19 March 1985, Toby Thomas b 20 Dec 1989); *Career* press office asst RNT 1976–77, Arts Cncl scholarship for trg in arts admin 1977–78, head of PR i/c launch Opera North Co 1978–80, head of press/publicity Old Vic Theatre Co 1980–81, sr TV press offr LWT and launch offr LWT International 1981–85, freelance PR conslt 1985–87, fndr dir Premier Relations (incl PR/mktg consultancy); former memb: NUJ, ACTT; memb: PRCA (independent memb), NFSB; *Recreations* swimming, keep fit, yoga, horse riding, opera and theatre going, walking; *Clubs* Sandown Health and Fitness; *Style*— Ms Victoria Franklin; ✉ Premier Relations, 1 Meadway, Oxshott, Surrey KT22 0LZ (☎ 01372 842446, fax 01372 843819, mobile 0973 512077, e-mail 106226.251@compuserve.com)

FRANKLIN, Rt Rev William Alfred; OBE (1965); s of George Amos Franklin (d 1956), and Mary Ann Catherine, *née* Scott (d 1980); *b* 16 July 1916; *Educ* Church Sch in London, Kelham Theol Coll Nottingham; *m* 1945, Winifred Agnes, *née* Jarvis; 1 s, 1 da; *Career* ordained: deacon 1940, priest 1941; curate: St John Bethnal Green 1940–43, St John's Palmers Green 1943–45; asst chaplain St Saviour's Anglican Church Buenos Aires 1945–48, rector Holy Trinity Lomas De Zamora Buenos Aires 1948–58, rector canon and sub dean St Andrew's Santiago Chile 1958–65, rector St Alban's Anglican Church Bogota and archdeacon of Colombia (Episcopal church of USA) 1965–71, consecrated Lord bishop of Colombia 1972, resigned 1978; full-time asst bishop Diocese Peterborough and hon canon Peterborough Cathedral 1978–86; hon canon emeritus of Peterborough Cathedral 1987, hon asst bishop of Canterbury 1985–92; *Recreations* fishing, writing, study of Church growth; *Style*— The Rt Rev William Franklin, OBE

FRANKLIN, William John; DL (Mid Glamorgan 1989); s of William Thomas Franklin (d 1958), and Edith Hannah Franklin (d 1954); *b* 8 March 1927; *Educ* Monkton House Sch Cardiff; *m* 1951, Sally, da of David Roderick Davies (d 1967); 1 da (Ann Elizabeth b 1952); *Career* chief exec Powell Duffryn plc 1976–85, dep chm Chartered Tst plc 1986–; chm: Powell Duffryn Wagon Ltd 1986–89, Howells Motors Ltd 1986–89; treas Univ Coll of Swansea 1989–92; FCA until 1993 (resigned); *Recreations* Royal Porthcawl Golf; *Style*— John Franklin, Esq, DL; ✉ 80 South Road, Porthcawl, Mid Glamorgan CF36 3DA (☎ 01656 785194)

FRANKLYN, William Leo; s of Leo Franklyn (d 1975), of London, and Mary Victoria, *née* Rigby; *b* 22 Sept 1925; *Educ* Wesley Coll Melbourne, Haileybury Coll Melbourne, Leas House Sch London; *m* 1969, Susanna Jane, da of Edmund Jupp (d 1943), of Hong Kong; 3 da (Sabina, Francesca, Melissa); *Career* actor and director; *Theatre* roles incl: The Tunnel of Love, There's a Girl in my Soup, Deathtrap, Dead Ringer, A Touch of Danger, Noel Coward in Two Keys, The Man Most Likely To, The Greenhouse Effect, Veronica's Room, The Trouble With Old Lovers; as dir incl: There's a Girl in my Soup, Tunnel of Love, Subway in the Sky, Later Leonardo, That's No Lady (re-titled The Bedwinner), Castle in the Air, Rope, Same Time Next Year; *Television* BBC serials incl: The Makepeace Story, No Wreath for the General, No Cloak, No Dagger, Moon and Son, Lovejoy; ITV series incl: Top Secret, What's On Next, Paradise Island, Masterspy, The Steam Video Company, GBH, Diana, her True Story, Young Indy; TV film series incl: The Scarlet Pimpernel, Charlie Chan, The Avengers, The Saracens, Troubleshooters, Public Eye; *Radio* Speaking Franklyn (London News Radio); *Films* incl: The Snorkel, The Flesh is Weak, Danger Within, Fury at Smuggler's Bay, Pit of Darkness, The Legend of Young Dick Turpin, The Intelligence Men, Cul-de-Sac, The Satanic Rites of Dracula, Splitting Heirs, Robert Ryland's Last Journey; *Recreations* cricket, squash, tennis, Italy; *Clubs* MCC, Hurlingham; *Style*— William Franklyn, Esq; ✉ c/o William Morris Agency (UK) Ltd, 31/32 Soho Square, London W1V 6DG (☎ 0171 434 2191, fax 0171 437 0238)

FRANKOPAN, Princess; (Thyra) Ingrid Hildegard, Countess Doimi de Lupis; da of Nils Andreas Detter (d 1961), and Thyra Carin, *née* Hellberg (d 1995); *b* 24 Nov 1939; *Educ* Lyceum Stockholm, Mon Fertile Lausanne, Univ of Oxford (DPhil), Univ of Stockholm (Jur Kand, Jur Lic, Jur Dr), Univ of Paris (Lic en droit), Univ of Turin (CHEE, Dip Euro Law); *m* 2 April 1968, Prince Louis Frankopan Šubić-Zrinski, Count Doimi de Lupis, s of Prince Peter Frankopan Šubić-Zrinski (d 1964); 3 s (Prince Peter b 1971, Prince Nicholas b 1975, Prince Lawrence b 1977), 2 da (Princess Paola b 1969, Princess Christina b 1973); *Career* asst judge Stockholm Central and Civil and Criminal Court 1962–63, barr Middle Temple and Lincoln's Inn 1977–; Univ of Oxford: fell St Antony's Coll 1963–64 (sr assoc memb 1982–88), tutor Merton Coll 1963–64, fell Lady Margaret Hall 1964–68, lectr 1964; res prof of law of Euro communities Swedish State Cncl 1968–72, prof of int law Univ of Uppsala 1974–76, visiting prof LSE 1980– (lectr 1972–74), advsr on int law to the Holy See 1984–, prof of int law Univ of Stockholm 1988–97, DG Inst for Studies in Environmental Law 1989–; dep MP (Cons) Stockholm 1991–92; judge Swedish Immigration Tbnl 1990–93, advsr to Croatian Govt 1990– (official spokesman 1990–94); memb: Br Inst of Int Comparative Law 1965–, Royal Inst Int Affrs 1976–, Nat Exec Stockholm Int Law Assoc 1976– (memb Exec Bd London 1976–96), Int Inst for Strategic Studies 1985–, Union Int des Avocats 1986–, Energy Ctee Int Bar Assoc 1987–, Int Inst for Space Law Paris 1989–, Euro Space Agency Law Centre Paris 1989– (fndr), State Cncl for Natural Resources Stockholm 1989–94, Issues Ctee Catholic Union 1991–; chm Ctee Maritime Neutrality 1989–93, fell Int Acad of Astronautics 1990–; *Books* incl: Law Making by International Organisations (1965), Essays on the Law of Treaties, The East African Community and the Common Market (1971), International Law and the Independent State (1973, 2 edn, 1987), Finance and Protection of Investment in Developing Countries (1974, 2 edn 1987), The Law of Economic Integration (1976), The Law of War (1987), The Concept of International Law (1988, 2 edn 1993), International Law (1993), The International Legal Order (1995), Early Croatian Kings (ed, 1996); *Recreations* music, skiing; *Clubs* Hurlingham; *Style*— Princess Frankopan; ✉ 10 Wellington Court, 116 Knightsbridge, London SW1X 7PL (☎ 0171 589 0413, fax 0171 225 2929); 1 Hare Court, Temple, London EC4 (☎ 0171 351 3171, fax 0171 583 9127)

FRANKS, Anthony Kenric Stapleton; s of Maurice Kenric Franks (d 1955); *b* 13 June 1928; *Educ* Nautical Coll Pangbourne; *m* 1960, Sarah Georgina Cochrane, *née* Watson; 3 s; *Career* Phicom plc (previously Plantation Holdings Ltd): md 1971–84, chm and chief exec 1984–86; chm: Beck Electronics Ltd 1986–, Datek International Ltd 1991–92, Royal Hosp for Neuro-Disability 1988–; dep chm RNLI 1996– (former memb Exec Ctee); Liveryman: Worshipful Co of Gunmakers, Worshipful Co of Scientific Instrument Makers; *Recreations* shooting, sailing; *Clubs* Boodle's, Royal Yacht Sqdn; *Style*— Anthony Franks, Esq; ✉ Becketts Grove, Matfield, Tonbridge, Kent TN12 7LH (☎ 01892 722175)

FRANKS, Sir Arthur Temple (Dick); KCMG (1979, CMG 1967); s of late Arthur Franks, of Hove, Sussex; *b* 13 July 1920; *Educ* Rugby, Queen's Coll Oxford; *m* 1945, Rachel Marianne, da of Rev A E S Ward, of Thame, Oxon; 1 s, 2 da; *Career* serv WWII (despatches); entered Foreign Serv 1949, Br ME Office 1952, Tehran 1953, Bonn 1962, FCO 1966–81, ret; *Clubs* Travellers', Army and Navy, Aldeburgh Golf; *Style*— Sir Dick Franks, KCMG; ✉ Roefield, Alde Lane, Aldeburgh, Suffolk

FRANKS, His Hon; Desmond Gerald Fergus; s of late Frederick Franks, MC; *b* 24 Jan 1928; *Educ* Cathedral Choir Sch Canterbury, Manchester GS, UCL; *m* 1952, Margaret Leigh, da of late Clarence Daniel; 1 da; *Career* called to the Bar Middle Temple 1952, in practice N Circuit, asst rec Salford 1966, dep recorder Salford 1971, recorder of Crown Ct 1972, circuit judge 1972–93, pres SW Pennine Magistates' Assoc, liaison judge to Oldham Magistrates (ret 1992); *Recreations* music, photography; *Style*— His Hon D G F Franks; ✉ 4 Beathwaite Drive, Bramhall, Cheshire SK7 3NY

FRANKS, John Alexander; s of Morris Franks, JP, and Jennie, *née* Alexander; *b* 10 Dec 1928; *Educ* Shaftesbury GS, Univ Coll London (LLB), Inst of Advanced Legal Studies (LLM); *m* 1, 1952, Golda Yacha (d 1976), da of Michael Lawrence (d 1950); 2 s (Michael b 1954, Gerald b 1958), 1 da (Jane b 1961); m 2, 1983, Sheila, da of William J Clark (d 1969); 1 da (Sara b 1954); *Career* admitted slr 1952; chm: Sunlight Service Group 1974–87 (dep chm on merger Godfrey Davis Group plc 1987), Disciplinary Ctee of Architects Registration Cncl 1981–88, Appeal Ctee of Nat House Builders' Registration Cncl; memb Cncl Law Soc 1974–, complaints cmmr Assoc of Authorised Public Accountants 1992–; FCIArb, FInstD; *Books* Company Director and the Law (edn 1986); *Recreations* collecting Vanity Fair caricatures and English Cottage Glass; *Clubs* City Livery, MCC; *Style*— John Franks, Esq; ✉ Chethams, 84 Baker St, London W1M 1DL (☎ 0171 935 7360, fax 0171 935 4068)

FRANKS, Michael John Alan; s of Jacob Franks, MD (d 1976); *b* 6 May 1928; *Educ* Epsom Coll, Merton Coll Oxford (MA); *m* 1, 3 Nov 1962 (m dis 1978), Anne, yr da of Sir David George Home, 13 Bt; 2 da (Lucinda b 1964, Miranda b 1966); m 2, 1980, Nicola Stewart, da of Col George Harcourt Stewart Balmain (d 1962); *Career* called to the Bar Gray's Inn 1953, in practice Chancery Bar 1953–59; Royal Dutch/Shell 1959–69; dir Beaverbrook Newspapers 1969–73; chm: Clyde Paper Co 1971–76, Schwarzkopf UK 1981–86; dep chm Goodhead Group plc 1985–91; chm: Innsite Hotel Services 1987–90, Silicon Bridge 1989–96; dir: Select Appointments plc 1987– (chm 1991–92), Van Diemen 1993–, Nortec Production 1993– (chm 1993–96); *Recreations* sailing, skiing, travel; *Clubs* Royal Thames Yacht; *Style*— Michael Franks, Esq; ✉ Field House, Mapledurwell, Basingstoke, Hants RG25 2LU (☎ 01256 464861)

FRANKS, Prof Stephen; *b* 14 Sept 1947; *Educ* Woodhouse GS Finchley, UCL (MB BS 1970, MRCP 1972, MD 1978, FRCP 1988); *m* 31 Aug 1972, Victoria Elizabeth, *née* Nunn; 2 s (Benjamin Paul b 8 May 1975, Joshua Jeremy b 17 Nov 1980), 1 da (Sarah Anne b 21 Jan 1977); *Career* postdoctoral res fell in endocrinology McGill Univ Montreal Canada (MRC travelling res fell, JB Collip fell) 1977–79, lectr in med Univ of Birmingham 1979–82, prof of reproductive endocrinology St Mary's Hosp Med Sch 1988– (sr lectr 1982–88); Carl Gemzell lectr Univ of Uppsala Sweden 1990, Plenary lectr Fertility Soc of Aust Adelaide 1992; ed Clinical Endocrinology; memb: Soc for Endocrinology (memb Ctee 1989–92, ed Newsletter 1992–), BMA; Hon MD Univ of Uppsala Sweden 1995; *Publications* author of original papers and articles in refereed jls; *Recreations* music, theatre, tennis; *Style*— Prof Stephen Franks; ✉ Department of Obstetrics and Gynaecology, St Mary's Hospital Medical School (Imperial College of Science, Technology and Medicine), Norfolk Place, London W2 1PG (☎ 0171 725 1050/1869)

FRANKS, Stephen George; s of Geoffrey Raymond Franks (d 1988), and Jean Margaret, *née* Macaree; *b* 18 Sept 1955; *Educ* De-Burgh Sch Epsom; *m* Sarah, da of Tony Bagnall Smith; 3 s (Archie (George) b 4 Oct 1986, Henry (James) b 14 Sept 1989, Fergus (William) b 25 Feb 1992); *Career* designer Lock and Petersen 1979–82; sr designer: Tayburn London 1982–83, Landsdown Euro 1983–84; ptnr and design dir Coley Porter Bell 1984–95, in own co Franks and Franks 1995–; memb D & AD 1980; FRSA 1994; *Style*— Stephen Franks, Esq; ✉ Franks and Franks, Church Farm House, Upper Wolvercote, Oxford OX2 8AH (☎ 01865 310893)

FRANSMAN, Laurens Francois (Laurie); s of Henri Albert Fransman, of Johannesburg, SA, and Stanmore, London, and Hannah Lena, *née* Bernstein; *b* 4 July 1956; *Educ* King David HS, Linksfield Johannesburg South Africa, Univ of Leeds (LLB); *m* 1, 7 Aug 1977 (m dis 1985), Claire Frances, da of Prof Colin Howard Ludlow Goodman (d 1990), of Mill Hill, London; 1 s (Piers b 1980); m 2, 9 July 1994, Helena Mary, da of Leonard George Cook, of Caterham, Surrey; *Career* barr, author, lectr, broadcaster and advsr; called to the Bar Middle Temple 1979, barr-at-law 2 Garden Ct Temple 1987–; UK contrib ed Immigration Law and Practice Reporter NY 1985, memb Editorial Bd Immigration and Nationality Law and Practice 1987–, conslt in Nationality Law to Halsbury's Laws of England (4 edn) 1991; numerous lectures in UK and USA; numerous radio and TV broadcasts in UK 1982–; fndr Immigration Law Practitioners' Assoc 1983 (chm, memb Exec Ctee); memb Cncl of Europe/Commission Internationale de l'Etat Civil ad hoc Ctee of Experts on Citizenship 1992; *Books* British Nationality Law and the 1981 Act (1982), Tribunals Practice and Procedure (jtly, 1985), Immigration Emergency Procedures (jtly, 1986, 2 edn 1994), Fransman's British Nationality Law (1989), The Constitution of the United Kingdom (contrib, 1991), Strangers and Citizens (contrib, 1994), Citizenship and Nationality Status in the New Europe (contrib, 1997); *Recreations* guitar playing, history, geology, food, music, theatre; *Style*— Laurie Fransman, Esq; ✉ 2 Garden Court, Temple, London EC4Y 9BL (☎ 0171 353 1633, fax 0171 353 4621)

FRANZ, Very Rev Dr Kevin Gerhard; s of Karl Gerhard Franz, of Cupar, Fife, and Anne, *née* Todd; *b* 16 June 1953; *Educ* Univ of Edinburgh (MA, BD, Foubister Prize, PhD), Edinburgh Theol Coll (Luscombe scholar); *m* 1 May 1976, Veda, *née* Fairley; 1 da (Joanna b 20 Oct 1986), 1 s (Peter b 22 Oct 1989); *Career* asst curate St Martin's and St Luke's Edinburgh 1979–83, rector St John's Selkirk 1983–90, provost St Ninian's Cathedral Perth 1990–; chair: Wester Hailes Youth Opportunity Prog 1981–83, Perth and Kinross Assoc of Vol Serv 1994–; *Recreations* hill-walking, travel in Eastern Europe; *Style*— The Very Rev Dr Kevin Gerhard Franz; ✉ St Ninian's House, 40 Hay Street,

Perth PH1 5HS (☎ 01738 626874); St Ninian's Cathedral, North Methven Street, Perth (☎ 01738 627982)

FRASE, (Antony) Richard Grenville; s of Flt Lt Stanislaw Frase (d 1957), and Joy, *née* Thompson; *b* 8 July 1954; *Educ* Repton, Trinity Coll Cambridge (MA); *m* 26 May 1990, Sarah-Louise, da of John Gregor Walker, of Chateau de Thury, Burgundy; 1 s (James Grenville b 8 April 1992), 1 da (Amelia b 28 Feb 1995); *Career* 2 Lt TAVR 1976–78; admitted slr 1981, asst slr Allen & Overy 1981–83 (articled clerk 1978–80), ptnr Denton Hall Burgin & Warrens 1988–93 (asst slr 1983–87); general counsel MeesPierson ICS Ltd 1993–95, head of litigation Personal Investment Authy 1995–; seconded to The Securities and Futures Authy 1989–91; memb: SFA Derivatives Ctee 1991–92, SFA Arbitration Panel 1992–, Arbitration Panel London Metal Exchange 1993–, Law Soc; ACIArb 1993; *Publications* The Euromoney Guide to World Equity Markets (contrib, 1991–97), Futures Trading, Law and Regulation (contrib, 1993), various articles on fin servs law; *Recreations* financial history, art, France; *Clubs* United Oxford and Cambridge Univ, Cavalry and Guards'; *Style*— Richard Frase, Esq; ✉ Wykeham, Portsmouth Road, Milford, Surrey GU8 5DP (☎ 01483 415281)

FRASER, Alasdair Andrew; s of John Paterson Fraser (d 1993), of Edinburgh, and Muriel, *née* Robertson; *b* 18 June 1957; *Educ* George Watson's Coll Edinburgh, Univ of Edinburgh (BSc); *m* 2 Sept 1988, Linda Anne, da of Bernard Joseph Stockton; 2 s (James Matthew b 20 March 1989, Timothy Patrick b 28 March 1991), 1 da (Amy Rae b 14 June 1993); *Career* BMP/Omnicom advtg: grad trainee 1979–80, account planner 1980–81, account mangr 1982; WCRS advtg: account mangr 1982–83, account dir 1983–84, assoc dir 1985–86, bd dir 1987–88; bd dir Aspect Hill Holliday advtg 1988–89, fndr ptnr Laing Henry advtg agency & mktg conslts 1990 (after MBO of Aspect Hill Holliday 1990), strategic dir/new business dir Laing Henry 1990–95 (merged with Saatchi & Saatchi Advertising 1995), planning dir Saatchi & Saatchi Advertising 1995–; MIPA; *Recreations* sport (tennis, golf, squash, ex-rugby), charity (Samaritan volunteer); *Clubs* London Scottish Rugby; *Style*— Alasdair Fraser, Esq; ✉ Saatchi & Saatchi Advertising Ltd, 80 Charlotte Street, London W1A 1AQ (☎ 0171 636 5060)

FRASER, Alasdair Campbell; *b* 5 Oct 1930; *Educ* St Mary's Hosp Med Sch London (MB BS, MRCS, LRCP); *m* Ann Elaine; 4 c; *Career* dir of clinical studies St Mary's Hosp Med Sch 1973–78; consIt obstetrican and gynaecologist St Mary's Hosp and Samaritan Hosp for Women London 1966–94, hon consIt St Lukes Nursing Home for the Clergy London, regnl advsr in maternal deaths Dept of Health, med advsr Family Div High Ct of Justice; examiner: final MB examiner to Univs of London Manchester Liverpool and Glasgow, Diploma and membership of RCOG; memb: Bd of Govrs St Mary's Hosp 1971, Fellowship Selection Ctee RCOG; pres Section of Obstetrics RSM 1991–92, chm and memb numerous hosp and med sch ctees; FRCOG; *Books* Handbook for Obstetric House Officers (with Miss M Anderson, 1968), author of numerous articles in med jls; *Clubs* Flyfishers; *Style*— Alasdair Fraser, Esq; ✉ 9 The Common, London W5 3TR

FRASER, Alasdair MacLeod; CB (1992), QC (1989); s of Rev Dr Donald Fraser (d 1993), and Ellen Hart McAllister (d 1986); *b* 29 Sept 1946; *Educ* Sullivan Upper Sch, Trinity Coll Dublin (BA, LLB), Queen's Univ Belfast (Dip in Laws); *m* 8 Aug 1975, Margaret Mary, da of Dr Brian Patrick Glancy; 2 s (Andrew Ian b 1979, James Michael b 1986), 1 da (Katy Margaret b 1983); *Career* called to the Bar NI 1970; Dept of Dir of Public Prosecutions NI: court prosecutor 1973, asst dir 1974, sr asst dir 1982, dep dir 1988, dir 1989–; *Style*— Alasdair Fraser, Esq, CB, QC; ✉ Royal Courts of Justice, Belfast, NI BT1 3NX (☎ 01232 546160)

FRASER, Andrew John; s of John A Fraser; *b* 23 Oct 1950; *Educ* Denstone Coll, Harvard Sch Los Angeles (ESU scholar), Univ of Sussex (BA), UCLA; *m* 1, 1976 (m dis 1987), Julia; 2 da (Sarah Alice b 12 Dec 1977, Emily Clare b 11 Nov 1979); m 2, June 1996, Jane; *Career* Young & Rubicam 1972–76, md Thailand McCann Erickson 1976–80, worldwide dir of devpt (London, HK, NY) and exec vice pres Saatchi & Saatchi Advertising 1980–92, md cdpDentsu Europe 1992–94, chief exec Invest in Britain Bureau DTI 1994–; *Recreations* theatre, sports, conversation, food and wine; *Clubs* MCC, RAC; *Style*— Andrew Fraser, Esq; ✉ Invest in Britain Bureau, DTI, 1 Victoria Street, London SW1H OET (☎ 0171 215 5684, fax 0171 215 5616)

FRASER, Dr Andrew Kerr; s of Sir William Kerr Fraser, GCB, FRSE, *qv*, and Marion, *née* Forbes, LT; *Educ* George Watson's Coll Edinburgh, Univ of Aberdeen, Univ of Glasgow; *m* 20 April 1985, Geraldine, da of Brendan Martin, of Dublin; 3 s (Alasdair b 29 Sept 1988, Colum b 17 Feb 1990, Moray b 20 Jan 1995), 1 da (Roseanne b 25 Feb 1992); *Career* med dir Nat Servs Div Common Servs Agency NHS in Scotland Edinburh 1993–94, dir of public health/chief admin med offr Highland Health Bd Inverness 1994–; MRCP 1987, MFPHM 1993; *Recreations* music, mountain walking; *Style*— Dr Andrew Fraser; ✉ Highland Health Board, Beechwood Park, Inverness IV2 3HG (☎ 01463 717123)

FRASER, Sir Angus McKay; KCB (1985, CB 1981), TD (1965); s of late Thomas Douglas Fraser; *b* 10 March 1928; *Educ* Falkirk HS, Univ of Glasgow (MA, DLitt), Bordeaux Univ; *m* 1, 1955 (m dis 1968), Margaret Neilson; 1 s (Simon), 1 da (Caroline Mary d 1996); m 2, 3 July 1991, Mrs Gillian T Fenwick; 1 step da (Virginia); *Career* RA 1950–52, 44 Para Bde (TA) 1953–66; HM Customs and Excise 1952–61, 1965–73, 1976–80 and 1983–87 (dep chm 1978, chm Bd 1983–87), Treasy 1961–64, CSD 1973–76 and 1980–83 (first Civil Serv cmmr 1981–83); advsr to PM on efficiency in public serv 1988–92; Liveryman Worshipful Co of Distillers; FRSA 1985, FSA 1991; *Clubs* Reform, Caledonian, Norfolk (Norwich); *Style*— Sir Angus Fraser, KCB, TD, FSA; ✉ 84 Ennerdale Rd, Kew, Richmond, Surrey TW9 2DL (☎ 0181 940 9913)

FRASER, Angus Robert Charles; s of Donald Fraser, and Irene, *née* Tonge; *b* 8 Aug 1965; *Educ* Gayton HS Harrow, Orange Hill Senior HS; *Career* professional cricketer; Middlesex CCC 1984– (awarded county cap 1988); England: 32 test matches 1989–, and over 30 one day ints, memb tour Aust and NZ 1990–91, memb team touring W Indies 1993/94, Australia 1994/95 (replacing Martin McCague) and S Africa 1995/96; honours with Middlesex: County Championship 1985 and 1990, Nat West Trophy 1988, Benson & Hedges Cup 1986, Nixdorf Computers Middlesex Player of the Year 1988 and 1989, one of Wisdens 5 Cricketers of the Year 1996; qualified cricket coach; *Recreations* golf, watching Liverpool FC and rugby internationals, anything in sport but racing; *Style*— Angus Fraser, Esq; ✉ c/o Middlesex CCC, Lord's Cricket Ground, London NW8 8QN (☎ 0171 289 1300)

FRASER, Air Cdre Anthony Walkinshaw; s of Robert Walkinshaw Fraser (d 1956), and Evelyn Elisabeth, *née* Watts (d 1955); *b* 15 March 1934; *Educ* Stowe; *m* 1, 1955 (m dis 1990), Angela Mary Graham, da of George Richard Shaw (d 1983), of Darlington, Co Durham; 1 s (Robert), 3 da (Amanda (Hon Mrs Timothy Buxton), Antonia, Alexandra); m 2, Grania Eleanor Ruth, da of Ean Stewart-Smith, MBE, of Stanley Hall, Halstead, Essex; *Career* RAF Pilot, Instr and Staff Offr, Air Cdre 1977, Cmdt Central Flying Sch, ret 1979; ADC to HM The Queen 1977–79; dir: Society of Motor Manufacturers & Traders Ltd 1980–88, Goddard Kay Rogers (Northern) Ltd 1988–89, Nissan UK Ltd 1989–91; chm and chief exec offr: Personal Guard Sarl 1992–94, IntaNet Commercial Services Ltd 1993–95, Chlorella Products Ltd 1995–; pres Organisation Internationale des Constructeurs d'Automobiles 1983–87; Liveryman Worshipful Co of Coachmakers & Coach Harness Makers; *Recreations* golf, shooting, fishing, languages; *Clubs* Boodle's, RAF, Sunningdale; *Style*— Air Cdre Anthony Fraser; ✉ 31 Grove End Rd, London NW8 9LY; Chlorella Products Ltd (☎ 01793 791111)

FRASER, Lady Antonia; *née* Pakenham; da of 7 Earl of Longford, PC, *qv*, and Countess of Longford, CBE, *qv*; *b* 27 Aug 1932; *Educ* Dragon Sch Oxford, St Mary's Convent Ascot, LMH Oxford; *m* 1, 25 Sept 1956 (m dis 1977), Rt Hon Sir Hugh Fraser, MBE, PC, MP (d 1984), s of 16 Lord Lovat; 3 s (Benjamin b 1961, Damian b 1964, Orlando b 1967), 3 da (Rebecca (Mrs Edward Fitzgerald) b 1957, Flora (Mrs Peter Soros) b 1958, Natasha b 1963); m 2, 27 Nov 1980, Harold Pinter, CBE, *qv*; *Career* writer; chm: Soc of Authors 1974–75, Crimewriters' Assoc 1985–86; co-tstee Authors' Fndn 1984–; pres English PEN 1988–89; *Books* incl: Mary Queen of Scots (James Tait Black Memorial Prize 1969), Cromwell our chief of Men (1973), James I & VI of England and Scotland (1974), Kings and Queens of England (ed, 1975), King Charles II (1979), The Weaker Vessel (Wolfson History Award 1984), Boadicea's Chariot: The Warrior Queens (1988), Quiet as a Nun (1977), Cool Repentance (1980), The Wild Island (1978), Oxford Blood (1985), Your Royal Hostage (1987), A Splash of Red (1981, basis TV series Jemima Shore 1983), Jemima Shore's First Case (1986), The Cavalier Case (1990), Jemima Shore at the Sunny Grave (1991), The Six Wives of Henry VIII (1992), The Pleasure of Reading (ed, 1992), The Gunpowder Plot (1996, CWA Non-Fiction Dagger 1996, published in US as Faith and Treason: the story of the Gunpowder Plot, St Louis Literary Award 1996); *Recreations* gardening (watched by cats), grandchildren; *Style*— The Lady Antonia Fraser; ✉ c/o Curtis Brown Group Ltd, 28–29 Haymarket, London SW1Y 4SP (☎ 0171 396 6600, fax 0171 396 0110)

FRASER, Bruce William; s of Douglas Edward Fraser, of Tayport, and Isobel, *née* Lambie; *b* 21 Oct 1947; *Educ* Madras Coll St Andrews, Royal Scot Acad of Music, Guildhall Sch of Music (DRSAM); *m* 20 Sept 1969, Patricia Martha; *Career* composer; Scottish Opera Orch 1971–79, first work Suite for 4 Trombones 1978, numerous cmmns for both amateur and professional gps, prizewinner Worshipful Co of Musicians Competition 1984, world prizewinner Corciano Int Competition 1985, fndr Lomond Music; former memb: Ctee BASBWE, Fife Sinfonia Ctee; conductor: Tayport Instrumental Band, Lochgelly Band, Anstruther Philharmonic Soc; memb: Composers' Guild of GB, Scottish Soc of Composers, memb Performing Rights Soc; publishers: Chester Music, R Smith & Co, Studio Music, Bandleader Publications, Kirklees Music, Fortune Music; MCPS, MPA; *Recreations* swimming, walking; *Style*— Bruce Fraser, Esq; ✉ Heston Bank, 32 Bankton Park, Kingskettle, Fife KY15 7PY (☎ 01337 830974)

FRASER, Sir (James) Campbell; kt (1978); s of Alexander Ross Fraser, and Annie McGregor Fraser; *b* 2 May 1923; *Educ* Univ of Glasgow, McMaster Univ Hamilton Canada, Dundee Sch of Economics (BCom 1950); *m* 1950, Maria Harvey, *née* McLaren, JP (d 1995); 2 da; *Career* pres CBI 1982–84 (former chm CBI Industrial Policy Ctee); chm: Scottish Television plc 1975–91, Dunlop Holdings 1978–83, Tandem Computers 1985–, Pauline Hyde and Associates 1991–93, Arlen plc 1992–95; non-exec dir: BP 1978–92, BAT Industries plc until 1993, Bridgewater Paper Co 1984–, Alexander Proudfoot plc 1987–95, Barkers Communications Scotland; tstee The Economist 1978–, chm Int Advsy Bd Wells Fargo; memb NEDC 1982–84; pres Soc of Business Economists 1972–84; visiting prof: Univ of Strathclyde 1980–85, Univ of Stirling 1980–88; FRSE 1978, CBIM, FPRI, Hon LLD Univ of Strathclyde, Hon DUniv Stirling, Hon DCL Bishops; *Recreations* sport, cinema, reading; *Clubs* Caledonian; *Style*— Sir Campbell Fraser, FRSE; ✉ Tandem Computers, Tandem House, 7 Roundwood Avenue, Stockley Park, Uxbridge, Middx UB11 1AU (☎ 0181 564 6000)

FRASER, Sir Charles Annand; KCVO (1989, CVO 1985, LVO 1968), DL (1985), WS (1956); s of Very Rev Dr John Annand Fraser, MBE, TD (d 1985), and Leila, *née* Campbell (d 1989); *b* 16 Oct 1928; *Educ* Hamilton Acad Lanarkshire, Univ of Edinburgh (MA, LLB); *m* 1957, Ann, da of William Francis Scott-Kerr (d 1976), of Sunlaws Roxburghshire; 4 s (Simon, Ian, James, Robert); *Career* WS; ptnr W & J Burness Slrs 1956–93; purse bearer to Lord High Cmmr to Gen Assembly of Church of Scot 1969–88; directorships incl: Signetics (UK) Ltd 1969–, British Assets Trust plc 1972–, Scottish Widows Fund and Life Assurance Soc 1976–94, United Biscuits (Holdings) plc 1977–95 (vice chm 1986–95), Scottish TV plc 1979–, Walter Alexander plc 1981–90, Grosvenor Developments Ltd 1981–92, Selective Assets Trust plc 1988–95 (chm), Scottish Business in the Community 1982–, Adam and Co plc 1983– (chm), The Patrons of the Nat Galleries of Scot 1984–; chm Lothian & Edinburgh Enterprise Ltd 1990–94; memb Cncl Law Soc of Scotland 1966–72, memb Ct Heriot-Watt Univ 1972–78, govr Fettes Coll 1976–86, tstee Scottish Civic Tst 1978–92, chm Scot Div IOD 1978–81, tstee Univ of Edinburgh Fndn Fund 1989–, memb Ct of Regents Royal Coll of Surgns of Edinburgh; Hon Doctorate: Univ of Edinburgh 1991, Napier Univ Edinburgh 1992; FRSE 1993; *Clubs* New (Edinburgh); *Style*— Sir Charles Fraser, KCVO, FRSE, DL, WS; ✉ Shepherd House, Inveresk, Midlothian (☎ 0131 665 2570)

FRASER, Colin Gall; TD (1966), GSM (with Malaya Clasp) 1953; s of Douglas Fraser (d 1978), and Annie Louise (Nancy), *née* Gall (d 1994); *b* 18 Feb 1934; *Educ* Cottesmore Sch, Aldenham, Trinity Hall Cambridge (MA); *m* 14 Dec 1963, Gabrielle Genista (Gay), da of Brig-General Sir Eric Edward Boketon Holt-Wilson, CMG, DSO (d 1950); 1 s (Andrew b 1967), 1 da (Fiona b 1964); *Career* Nat Serv rifleman RB 1952, Queen's Own Royal W Kent Regt 1953; served as subaltern: 1 Bn Malaya 1953–54, BAOR 1954; served in 4/5 Bn (TA) 1954–68, ret as Maj; admitted slr 1960, ptnr Joynson-Hicks 1964–89 (articled clerk 1957–60), ptnr Taylor Joynson Garrett 1989–95 (consIt 1995–96, ret); speaker at seminars, contrib articles on copyright; dep to Under Sheriff of Surrey 1966–79, chm Dorking Gp Home Sub Ctee Surrey Fedn Housing Assoc 1980–94, tstee Old Cottesmorian Educn Tst 1981–95; chm: Dorking Cncl of Churches (first lay chm) 1981–84, Dorking Christian Centre Mgmnt Policy Ctee 1985–95; memb Br Literary and Artistic Copyright Assoc (sec 1993–96); *Recreations* golf, watching cricket, reading history; *Clubs* United Oxford and Cambridge, Aula; *Style*— Colin Fraser, Esq, TD; ✉ High Trees, South Drive, Dorking, Surrey RH5 4AG (☎ 01306 883423)

FRASER, David Richard; *b* 11 Nov 1955; *Educ* Denstone Coll Staffs, St Christopher's Sch Richmond Virginia (ESU scholar), Sidney Sussex Coll Cambridge (open exhibitioner, MA); *m*; 3 c; *Career* admin trainee Dept of Employment 1976, private sec to Min of State for Employment 1980–82; gen mangr The Duke's Playhouse Lancaster 1982–84; Granada Television Ltd: mangr of regnl progs 1984–88, head of programme servs 1988, head of business affrs 1992, subsequently controller of programme servs and personnel, appointed to Bd 1995, md 1996–; *Recreations* theatre, books, food, travel; *Style*— David Fraser, Esq; ✉ Granada Television Ltd, Television Centre, Quay St, Manchester M60 9EA (☎ 0161 832 7211)

FRASER, Gen Sir David William; GCB (1980, KCB 1973), OBE (1962), DL (Hants 1982); er s of Brig Hon William Fraser, DSO, MC (d 1964, yst s of 18 Lord Saltoun), and Pamela Cynthia, *née* Maude (d 1975); *b* 30 Dec 1920; *Educ* Eton, ChCh Oxford; *m* 1, 26 Sept 1947 (m dis 1952), Anne, yr da of Brig Edward William Sturgis Balfour, CVO, DSO, OBE, MC; 1 da (Antonia Isabella (Mrs Timothy Hanbury) b 1949); m 2, 11 Oct 1957, Julia Frances, yr da of Maj Cyril James Oldridge de la Hey; 2 s (Alexander James b 1960, Simon b 1963), 2 da (Arabella (Mrs Gordon Birdwood) b 1958, Lucy (Hon Mrs Alexander Baring) b 1965); *Career* WWII cmmnd Grenadier Gds 1941; served: UK and NW Europe 1939–45, Malaya 1948, Egypt 1952–54, Cyprus 1958, British Cameroons 1961, Borneo 1965; GOC 4 Div 1969–71, ACDS (Policy) MOD 1971–73, vice CGS 1973–75, Br mil rep to NATO Brussels 1975–77, Cmdt RCDS 1977–80, ADC Gen to HM The Queen 1977–80, Col The Royal Hampshire Regt 1981–87; pres Soc for Army Historical Res 1980–93; chm Treloar Tst and Governing Body Lord Mayor Treloar Coll 1982–93; Hon DLitt Univ of Reading; *Books* Alanbrooke (1982), And We Shall Shock Them (1983),

The Christian Watt Papers (1983), August 1988 (1983), A Kiss for the Enemy (1985), The Killing Times (1986), The Dragon's Teeth (1987), The Seizure (1988), A Candle for Judas (1989), In Good Company (1990), Adam Hardrow (1990), Codename Mercury (1991), Adam in the Breach (1993), Knights Cross (1993), The Pain of Winning (1993), Will - a Portrait of William Douglas Home (1995); *Recreations* shooting; *Clubs* Turf, Pratt's; *Style—* Gen Sir David Fraser, GCB, OBE, DL; ✉ Vallenders, Isington, Alton, Hants GU34 4PP (☎ 01420 23166)

FRASER, Prof Derek; s of Jacob Fraser, of Birmingham, and Dorothy, *née* Hayes; *b* 24 July 1940; *Educ* King Edward's Camp Hill Sch Birmingham, Univ of Leeds (BA, MA, PhD); *m* 1962, Ruth, *née* Spector; 2 s (Philip Neal b 1963, Adam Jason b 1970), 1 da (Clio Lynn b 1965); *Career* sch teacher Birmingham 1962–65; sr lectr, reader then prof of modern history Univ of Bradford 1965–83, prof of English history UCLA 1982–84, HM's Inspector of Schs history and higher educn 1984–88, staff inspector for higher educn DES 1988–90; Sheffield City Poly: asst princ (on secondment), dep princ 1991–92; vice-chllr Univ of Teesside 1992–; Andrew W Mellon distinguished visiting prof Franklin and Marshall Coll Penn 1979; visiting prof: Univ of Vermont 1980, Stanford Univ 1981; FRHistS 1980; *Books* The Evolution of the British Welfare State (1984), Urban Politics in Victorian England - The Structure of Politics in Victorian Cities (1976), Power and Authority in the Victorian City (1979); *Recreations* music, bridge, film, squash; *Style—* Prof Derek Fraser; ✉ Vice-Chancellor, University of Teesside, Middlesbrough, Cleveland TS1 3BA (☎ 01642 342002, fax 01642 342000, e-mail derek.fraser@tees.ac.uk)

FRASER, Donald David (Don); s of David Sydney Fraser (d 1975), of Broadstairs, Kent, and Ellen Louise, *née* Grogan (d 1957); *b* 4 June 1941; *Educ* Holy Trinity Sch Broadstairs Kent, St Georges Sch Ramsgate Kent (awarded 1st year top place prize by Archbishop of Canterbury in July 1953 for Academic Achievement); *m* 1, 23 July 1960 (m dis 1970), Jennifer Carol, da of Sidney Palmer; 2 da (Rebecca Jane b 11 Aug 1961, Deborah Ann b 11 Oct 1962); m 2, 11 Sept 1971 (m dis 1982), Anne, da of Kenneth William Whyatt; 1 s (Mark Simon Lovat b 2 March 1972); *Career* internationally recognised image mangr, corporate photographer, art dir; apprentice Industl/Advtg Photography Dept of Sunbeam Photos Thanet 1957–60, photographer Valerie Lilley Studios Surbiton 1960, in-plant photographer Carrier Engineering London 1961, sr photographer Kingston Photographic Ltd 1963, fndr dir Academy Studios Ltd Surrey 1964 (md 1965–91), fndr Academy Design Ltd and Academy Communications Gp 1976 (chm 1977–91); fndr and md: Don Fraser Image Management (formerly Don Fraser Associates (UK)) 1991, Don Fraser Image Management Pty Ltd (Aust) 1991, The Original Stiff Picture Company Pty Ltd (t/a Stiff Displays) (Aust); mktg dir Elephant Pool Ltd 1992; nat pres BIPP 1982–83; awards incl: numerous Ilford awards, Industl Photographer of The Year FT 1971 and 1974, Export Trophy FT 1972, Best Monochrome Industl Photograph FT 1973, BIPP Citation and Presidential Award for outstanding contrib to professional photography 1983, Fame Award Norway 1989, Skyline Displays Inc USA General's Award 1991, Hon FBIPP in recognition of dedication and success in raising the profile of the professional image maker within the wider worlds of business and commerce 1995; Fell Master Photographers Assoc 1964, FBIPP 1974, FRPS 1974; *Style—* Don Fraser, Esq; ✉ c/o Don Fraser Image Management, Allied House, Unit 4, Business Park 1, Kingston Road, Leatherhead, Surrey KT22 7LA (☎ 01372 379933, fax 01372 372867); Don Fraser Image Management Pty Ltd, Suite 3902, Floor Level 39, Northpoint Tower, 100 Miller Street, North Sydney, NSW 2060, Australia (☎ 00 61 2 9923 2878, fax 00 61 2 9923 2088); Lakeside Lodge Plantation, Wollombi, Hunter Valley, NSW, Australia

FRASER, Donald Hamilton; s of Donald Fraser (d 1964), and Dorothy Christiana, *née* Lang (d 1973); *b* 30 July 1929; *Educ* Maidenhead GS, St Martin's Sch of Art London, Paris (French Govt scholarship); *m* 6 July 1954, Judith, da of Francis William Wentworth-Sheilds (d 1969); 1 da (Catherine Jane b 1955); *Career* artist; over 60 one-man exhibitions in Br, Euro, Japan and North America; work in public collections includes: Boston Museum of Fine Arts, Albright-Knox Gallery Buffalo, Carnegie Inst Pittsburgh, Yale Univ Art Gallery, City Art Museum St Louis, Wadsworth Atheneum Hartford, Desert Art Museum Palm Springs, Smithsonian Inst Washington DC, Nat Gallery Canada, Nat Gallery Victoria Melbourne, many corp collections and Br galleries, Arts Cncl, Govt Art collection; designed Cwlth issue postage stamps 1983; tutor RCA 1958–83; vice pres: Artists' Gen Benevolent Inst 1981– (chm 1981–86), Royal Over-Seas League 1986–; cmmr Royal Fine Art Cmmn 1986–; hon fell RCA, hon curator RA 1992–; tstee Royal Academy 1993–; RA 1985 (ARA 1975); *Books* Gauguin's Vision after the Sermon (1969), Dancers (1989); *Clubs* Arts; *Style—* Donald Hamilton Fraser, Esq, RA; ✉ c/o Royal Academy of Arts, Burlington House, Piccadilly, London W1V 0DS

FRASER, Elizabeth (Liz); da of Kenneth Essex, of London, and Joan, *née* White; *b* 14 July 1951; *Educ* St Michael's Convent Grammar, Queen Elizabeth Coll London (now KCL) (BSc); *m* 3 April 1976, Ian Fraser; 2 s (Alastair b 10 May 1984, Duncan b 17 March 1987); *Career* PR exec: London Co-op 1972–73, TI Domestic Appliances 1973–74, RHM 1974–76; account exec rising to account dir Burson Marsteller 1976–80, fndr dir Granard Communications 1980–88 (acquired by Saatchi and Saatchi 1986), md Granard Rowland 1988–90, jt md The Rowland Company 1990, fndr md The Tenet Group plc 1990–94, md London office Key Communications 1994–; Br Assoc of Industl Editors Editing for Industry Award 1982 and 1983, PR Week Award for Staff Devpt 1988 and 1989; lectr to int PR Dip students Watford Coll; author of PRCA guidance paper on Evaluating Public Relations; MIPR, MInstD; *Recreations* gardening, walking, family, entertaining; *Style—* Ms Liz Fraser; ✉ Key Communications Ltd, Mimet House, 5a Praed Street, London W2 1NJ (☎ 0171 724 3246, fax 0171 724 2458)

FRASER, Hon Mrs (Elizabeth Penelope); *née* Methuen; o da of 5 Baron Methuen (d 1975); *b* 4 July 1928; *Educ* Downe House Newbury; *m* 8 Dec 1956, Malcolm Henry Alastair Fraser, er s of (Hugh) Alastair Hamilton Fraser, JP (d 1987), of Mill Place, Stanton Drew, Somerset; 2 da (Elizabeth b 1957, Anne b 1961); *Career* Nat Fedn of Young Farmers' Clubs: past county pres for Somerset, SW Area pres 1987–90, nat dep pres 1988–94, life vice pres 1994–; area vice pres St John Ambulance Wilts 1993–; ESU: former vice chm Bath and Dist Branch, vice pres Bristol Branch 1991–; *Recreations* travel, the arts; *Clubs* ESU Dartmouth House, The GB-China Centre, Lansdowne; *Style—* The Hon Mrs Fraser; ✉ South Bank House, Lacock Road, Corsham, Wiltshire SN13 9HS (☎ 01249 714958)

FRASER, Dr Ewan John Stanley; s of Maj I M Fraser MC (d 1988), of Chipstead, Surrey, and Mary Stanley (d 1964); *b* 15 May 1947; *Educ* Eton, Christ Church Oxford (MA, DPhil); *Career* investmt analyst James Capel and Co (Stockbrokers) 1975 - (sr exec 1985); memb (Cons) Oxford City Cncl 1969–70 and 1971–72; MSI 1984; *Recreations* fly fishing, cricket, reading, ballet; *Style—* Dr Ewan Fraser; ✉ James Capel & Co, PO Box 551, 6 Bevis Marks, London EC3A 7JQ (☎ 0171 621 0011, fax 0171 621 0496, telex 888866)

FRASER, George MacDonald; s of William Fraser, of Carlisle, and Anne Struth, *née* Donaldson; *b* 2 April 1925; *Educ* Carlisle GS, Glasgow Acad; *m* 1949, Kathleen Margarette, da of George Hetherington, of Carlisle; 2 s (Simon, Nicholas), 1 da (Caroline); *Career* served Br Army 1943–47, infantryman Border Regt Burma, Lt Gordon Highlanders; journalist 1947–69, dep ed Glasgow Herald; author; *Film Screenplays* incl: The Three Musketeers (1973), The Four Musketeers (1974), Royal Flash (1975), The Prince and the Pauper (1977), Octopussy (1983), Casanova (1987), The Return of the Musketeers (1989); *Books* the Flashman novels and various other books; *Recreations* writing, history, talking to wife; *Style—* George Fraser, Esq; ✉ Baldrine, Isle of Man

FRASER, Glendon John (Glen); s of John Stewart Fraser, of Waldren, E Sussex, and Diane Louise, *née* Witt; *b* 1 April 1962, Melbourne, Australia; *Educ* Chigwell Sch for Boys; *m* 2 Dec 1989, Fiona Jane, da of Thomas Edmund Butcher; 1 s (Alexander Thomas Anthony b 11 Aug 1993), 1 da (Lucy Florence Ellen b 12 May 1991); *Career* fund mangr Lloyds Life Assurance 1979–81, prodn then account mangr J Walter Thompson advtg agency 1981–86; Gold Greenlees Trott Advertising: account mangr 1986–88, account dir 1988–90, bd account dir 1990–June 1992, business devpt dir June 1992–94; bd account dir rising to client servs dir K Advertising (formerly KHBB) 1994–96, business devpt dir Griffin Bacal 1996–; *Recreations* shooting, golf; *Clubs* Melbourne Cricket (Australia); *Style—* Glen Fraser, Esq; ✉ Griffin Bacal Advertising, 20–22 Stukeley Street, London WC2B 5LR (☎ 0171 831 4555)

FRASER, Graham; *Career* fndr ptnr Workers For Freedom (with Richard Nott, *qv*); initial trg in accountancy, subsequent experience in fashion becoming fashion merchandise mangr Liberty Regent Street, opened own menswear shop Soho 1985, expanded to incl womenswear exporting to NY, LA, Tokyo, Paris and Milan, first collection shown London 1987, currently shows regularly in London and Paris; BFC Designer of the Year Award 1989; *Style—* Graham Fraser, Esq; ✉ Workers for Freedom, 6 Spice Court, London SW11 3UE

FRASER, Helen Jean Sutherland; da of George Sutherland Fraser (d 1980), and Eileen Lucy, *née* Andrew; *b* 8 June 1949; *Educ* Collegiate Girls' Sch Leics, St Anne's Coll Oxford (MA); *m* 16 April 1982, Grant James McIntyre, s of Atholl McIntyre, of Cornwall; 2 da (Blanche b 1980, Marina b 1983); *Career* editorial dir William Collins 1977–87, publisher William Heinemann 1987–91, publisher Heinemann/Mandarin 1991–92, md Reed Trade Books 1996– (publishing dir 1992–96); *Style—* Miss Helen Fraser; ✉ William Heinemann, Michelin House, 81 Fulham Rd, London SW3 6RB (☎ 0171 225 9524, fax 0171 225 9109)

FRASER, Brig Sir Ian; kt (1963), DSO (1944), OBE (1941), DL (Belfast 1955); s of Robert Moore Fraser, MD, of Knock, Belfast, and Margaret Boal, *née* Ferguson; *Educ* Royal Belfast Academical Inst, Queen's Univ Belfast (MB BCh, MD, MCh); *m* 2 Sept 1931, Eleanor Margaret (d 1992), da of Marcus Adolphus Mitchell, of Quarry House, Belfast; 1 s (Mark), 1 da (Mary Alice); *Career* served WWII RAMC W Africa, N Africa, France and India, Brig 1945; Hon Col: 143 Field Ambulance 1948–71, 204 Gen Hosp TA 1961–71; sr surgn Royal Victoria Hosp Belfast and Royal Belfast Hosp for Children 1955–66; currently conslt surgn; surgn in ordinary to the Govr of NI, hon conslt surgn to the Army in NI; chm Police Authy RUC 1970–76; former pres: BMA, Assoc of Surgns of GB and I; GCStJ 1974, Ordre de la Couronne (Belgium) 1963, Ordre des Palmes Académiques (France) 1964, Order of Orange Nassau (Netherlands) 1969, Chevalier de la Légion d'Honneur (France) 1981, Knight Cdr Commandery of Ards (Ulster); Hon DSc: Oxon, New Univ of Ulster; Hon LLD Queen's Univ Belfast; FRCSI, FRCS Eng, FACS, FRSE 1939, Hon FRCSEd, Hon FRCSGlas, Hon FRCPI; *Books* Blood, Sweat and Cheers (autobiography); *Style—* Brig Sir Ian Fraser, DSO, OBE, DL, FRSE; ✉ 19 Upper Malone Rd, Belfast, N Ireland (☎ 01232 668235)

FRASER, Lt Cdr Ian Edward; VC (1945), DSC (1943), RD (and Bar 1948), JP (Wirral 1957); s of Sydney Fraser (d 1976), of Bourne End, Bucks; *b* 18 Dec 1920; *Educ* Royal GS High Wycombe, HMS Conway; *m* 1943, Melba Estelle, da of late Stanley Hughes; 4 s, 2 da; *Career* Lt Cdr RNR Atlantic, Pacific, N Africa, N Sea; dir Star Offshore Services Ltd 1975–82, chm Nordive (W Africa) Ltd, md North Sea Diving Services Ltd 1965–77, Universal Divers Ltd 1946–; younger brethren Trinity House 1980; Hon Freeman Metropolitan Borough of Wirral 1993; *Books* Frogman VC (1952); *Recreations* golf, model ships; *Clubs* Hoylake Sailing, New Brighton Rugby, Leasowe Golf (capt 1975); *Style—* Lt Cdr Ian Fraser, VC, DSC, RD, JP; ✉ Sigyn, 1 Lyndhurst Rd, Wallasey, Merseyside L45 6XA

FRASER, Sir Ian James; kt (1986), CBE (1972), MC (1945); s of Hon Alastair Thomas Joseph Fraser, DSO, Lovat Scouts (d 1949, s of 13 Lord Lovat), and Lady Sibyl, *née* Grimston (d 1968), da of 3 Earl of Verulam; *b* 7 Aug 1923; *Educ* Ampleforth, Magdalen Coll Oxford; *m* 1, 25 Oct 1958, (Evelyn Elizabeth) Anne (d 1984), yr da of Maj Alastair Edward George Grant, DSO, 9 Lancers, of Nutcombe Manor, Clayhanger, Tiverton; 2 s, 2 da; m 2, 25 June 1993, Mrs Fiona Margaret Douglas-Home, da of Maj the Hon Henry Montagu Douglas-Home, MBE (d 1980), and former w of Gregory Martin; 2 step da; *Career* Lt Scots Gds WWII (despatches); former Reuters corr; dir S G Warburg & Co 1963–69, DG City Panel on Take-overs and Mergers; dir: Davy International, BOC International, S Pearson & Son, Pearson Longman, EMI; chm: Rolls Royce Motors 1971–80, Datastream 1976–77, Lazard Bros 1980–85; dep chm: Vickers 1980–89, TSB Gp plc 1985–90; chm Accepting Houses Ctee 1981–85; FRSA, CIMgt; Kt of Honour and Devotion SMOM 1971; *Style—* Sir Ian Fraser, CBE, MC; ✉ South Haddon, Skilgate, Taunton, Somerset TA4 2DR (☎ 013983 31247); Lazard Brothers, 21 Moorfields, London EC2P 2HT (☎ 0171 588 2721)

FRASER, Prof Sir James David; 2 Bt (UK 1943), of Tain, Co Ross; o s of Sir John Fraser, 1 Bt, KCVO, MC (d 1947), and Agnes Govane, *née* Herald (d 1983); *b* 19 July 1924; *Educ* Edinburgh Acad, Magdalen Coll Oxford (BA), Univ of Edinburgh (MB ChB, ChM); *m* 16 Sept 1950, Edith Maureen, da of late Rev John Reay, MC, of Bingham Rectory, Notts; 2 s (Iain Michael b 1951, Christopher John b 1954); *Heir* s, Iain Michael Fraser b 27 June 1951; *Career* late Maj RAMC, served Far East 1949–51; sr lectr in clinical surgery Univ of Edinburgh and hon conslt surgn Royal Infirmary 1963–70, prof of surgery Univ of Southampton 1970–80, hon conslt surgn Univ of Southampton Hosp Gp 1970–80, postgrad dean Univ of Edinburgh Med Sch 1981–89; pres RCS Edinburgh 1982–85 (currently memb Ct of Regents); *Recreations* golf, gardening; *Style—* Prof Sir James Fraser, Bt; ✉ 2 Lennox St, Edinburgh (☎ 0131 332 3205)

FRASER, James Edward; CB (1990); s of Dr James Fowler Fraser, TD (d 1979), of Aberdeen, and Dr Kathleen Nevill Blomfield (d 1974); *b* 16 Dec 1931; *Educ* Aberdeen GS, Univ of Aberdeen (MA), Christ's Coll Cambridge (BA); *m* 10 Oct 1959, Patricia Louise, da of John Henry Stewart (d 1970), of Perth; 2 s (Paul Anthony b 1960, Mark Edward b 1962); *Career* Capt RA HQ Tel-el-Kebir Garrison 1954–55; civil servant; private sec to: Perm Under Sec Scot Office 1960–62, Parly under sec Scot Office 1962; Cabinet Office 1964–66, HM Treasy 1966–68, under sec Scot Office Local Govt Fin Gp 1976–81, Scot Home and Health Dept 1981–91, sec of Cmmns for Scot 1992–94; pres Scot Hellenic Soc of Edinburgh and Eastern Scotland 1987–93; FSA (Scot); *Recreations* reading, music, walking, Greece (ancient and modern); *Clubs* Scottish Arts (Edinburgh); *Style—* J Edward Fraser, Esq, CB; ✉ 59 Murrayfield Gardens, Edinburgh EH12 6DH (☎ 0131 337 2274)

FRASER, John Denis; MP (Lab) Norwood (majority 7,216); s of Archibald Fraser (d 1976), and Frances, *née* Benedict; *b* 30 June 1934; *Educ* Sloane GS Chelsea, Loughborough Co-Op Coll, Law Soc Sch of Law; *m* 1960, Ann, da of George Oswald Hathaway; 2 s (Mark b 26 July 1961, Andrew John Fitzgerald b 5 Aug 1964), 1 da (Sarah Ann b 22 July 1962); *Career* bank official 1950–52; Sgt RAEC 1952–54; admitted slr 1960, subsequently sr ptnr Lewis Silkin; memb Lambeth BC 1962–68, MP (Lab) Norwood 1966– (Parly candidate 1964), PPS to Barbara Castle as Employment and Productivity Sec 1968–70, oppn front bench spokesman on Home Affrs 1972–74, Parly under sec Employment 1974–76, min of state Dept of Prices and Consumer Protection 1976–79; front bench oppn spokesman: on Trade Prices and Consumer Protection

1979–83, on Housing and Construction 1983–87; shadow law officer 1987–94; memb Law Soc 1960; *Recreations* athletics, music, football; *Style*— John Fraser, Esq, MP; ✉ House of Commons, London SW1A 0AA (☎ 0171 219 5128)

FRASER, John Stewart; s of Donald Stewart Fraser, of Beaumaris, Melbourne, Aust; *b* 18 July 1931; *m* 1955, Diane Louise, da of late William Frederick Witt; 3 c; *Career* mktg mangr Ilford (Aust) Pty Ltd 1968–73, head of mktg Ilford 1973–78, md and chief exec Ilford Ltd 1978–84, md CIBA-GEIGY (plastics and additives) 1982–84; chm: The Clayton Aniline Co, Ciba-Geigy Chemicals Ltd; Ciba-Geigy PLC: gp md 1984–87, gp md and chief exec 1987–90, chm and chief exec 1990–; non-exec dir Westminster Health Care Holdings PLC 1992–; pres Chemical Industries Assoc 1995 (vice pres 1990–95); *Recreations* golf; *Style*— John Fraser, Esq; ✉ Ciba-Geigy PLC, Hulley Rd, Macclesfield, Cheshire SK10 2NX (☎ 01625 421933, fax 01625 619637, telex 667336); 2 Kennerleys Court, 39 Hawthorn Lane, Wilmslow, Cheshire SK9 5EQ (☎ 01625 537361)

FRASER, June (Mrs Allen Cull); da of Donald Stuart Denholm Fraser (d 1986), of Dorset, and Myrtle Josephine, *née* Ward; *b* 30 Aug 1930; *Educ* Talbot Heath Sch Bournemouth, Beckenham Coll of Art, RCA; *m* 7 Oct 1963, Allen Hans Cull, s of Ernest Albert Cull, of Burridge, Southampton, Hants; 1 da (Zoë Gail b 27 July 1970); *Career* dir Design Res Unit 1968 (ptnr 1963), head of graphic design John Lewis Partnership 1980–84, head of the Industl Design Div The Design Cncl 1984–88, own design practice 1988; pres Chartered Soc of Designers 1983–85; memb: Ct RCA 1986, Bd ICSID 1987–93; chm Sign Design Soc 1995–; govr: Kent Inst, Talbot Heath Sch; ARCA 1957, FCSD, MInstP 1968; *Recreations* travel, horticulture, design, tennis, piano, films, theatre; *Style*— Miss June Fraser; ✉ 5 Combemartin Rd, London SW18 5PP (☎ and fax 0181 788 2353)

FRASER, Nicholas Andrew; s of W Lionel Fraser, CMG (d 1965), of London, and Cynthia Elizabeth Fraser, OBE, *née* Walter (d 1992); *b* 2 March 1935; *Educ* Eton, King's Coll Cambridge (MA); *m* 1, 1964 (m dis 1979), Jill (d 1985), da of Roy Butterfield, of Yorkshire; 1 s (Tom b 1968), 2 da (Kate b 1960, Emily b 1966); m 2, 1981, Charlotte Ann, da of John Warren-Davis, of Dyfed, Wales; *Career* Helbert Wagg & Co Ltd 1957–62, Doubleday Inc and William Heineman 1963–65, Bank of London & S America 1965–67; James Capel & Co 1967–93: head of institutional equity sales 1977, head of investmt mgmnt 1983, dir 1986; currently dep chm Matheson Securities Ltd and dir SCI Perches (owner of vineyard in SW France, Domaine de Perches); tstee Whitechapel Art Gallery Fndn; Liveryman Worshipful Co of Fishmongers; *Style*— Nicholas Fraser, Esq; ✉ Longmeadow, Chiswick Mall, London W4 2PR (☎ 0181 995 3385, fax 0181 742 8399); Domaine de Perches, 81600 Gaillac, France (☎ 00 33 63 33 16 05, fax 00 33 63 33 17 11)

FRASER, Air Marshal Rev Sir (Henry) Paterson; KBE (1961, CBE 1945), CB (1953), AFC (1937); s of late Harry Paterson Fraser, MBE (d 1956), of Johannesburg, and Edith May, *née* Coxhead; *b* 15 July 1907; *Educ* St Andrew's Coll Grahamstown S Africa, Pembroke Coll Cambridge (MA); *m* 1933, Avis Gertrude, da of Hugh Charles Haswell, of Johannesburg (d 1962); 2 s; *Career* joined RAF 1929, directorate War Organization 1938–40, CO Experimental Flying Section (Royal Aircraft Estab) 1940–42, Gp Capt 1941, memb RAF element Combined Chiefs of Staff Washington 1942, sr admin plans 2 TAF D Day 1943, dep AOA 2 TAF 1944, Air Cdre cmdg Aircraft and Armament Experimental Estab 1945, Imperial Defence Coll 1951, SASO Fighter Cmd 1952–54, Air Vice-Marshal 1953, COS AAFCE (actg Air Marshal) 1954–56, AOC 12 Gp Fighter Command 1956–58, Air Marshal 1959, dir RAF Exercise Planning 1959, UK rep on Perm Military Deputies Gp Central Treaty Orgn Ankara 1960–62, Inspr-Gen RAF 1962–64, ret; chm Barclays Unicorn Int (IOM) Ltd 1972–82, dir Barclays Unicorn Gp 1976–82; concrete conslt (former technologist with Readymix (IOM) Ltd); ordained deacon 1977, priest 1978; CEng, FRAeS; *Style*— Air Marshal The Rev Sir Paterson Fraser, KBE, CB, AFC; ✉ 803 King's Court, Ramsey, Isle of Man IM8 1LP (☎ 01624 813069)

FRASER, Prof Ronald Strathearn Smith (Ron); s of Allan Fraser (d 1965), and Elizabeth, *née* Smith; *b* 10 July 1944; *Educ* Univ of Edinburgh (BSc, PhD, DSc); *m* 11 April 1987, Hilary Margaret, *née* Haigh; 2 da (Rosalind Jane Strathearn b 4 Feb 1989, Eleanor Mary Haigh b 28 Aug 1990); *Career* res scientist Max-Planck Inst für Biologie Tübingen 1968–70, res fell Medical Res Cncl Dept of Zoology Univ of Edinburgh 1970–77, princ scientific offr and head Biochemistry Section Nat Vegetable Res Station Wellesbourne 1977–87; Inst of Horticultural Research: head Plant Science Div 1987–90, head of Station IHR Littlehampton 1987–, dir of res in crop protection 1990–; hon lectr: Sch of Pure and Applied Biology Univ of Wales 1980–94, Dept of Microbiology Univ of Birmingham 1981–; currently hon prof Sch of Biological Scis Univ of Birmingham; memb: Soc for Gen Microbiology, Assoc of Applied Biologists, British Soc for Plant Pathology; FIHort 1989; *Books* Mechanisms Of Resistance To Plant Diseases (1985), The Biochemistry Of Virus-Infected Plants (1987), Recognition and Response In Plant Virus Interactions (1990); *Recreations* hill walking, music; *Style*— Prof Ron Fraser; ✉ Crop Protection, Institute of Horticultural Research, Worthing Road, Littlehampton, West Sussex BN17 6LP

FRASER, Sheriff Simon William Hetherington; s of George MacDonald Fraser, of Baldrine, IOM, and Kathleen Margarette, *née* Hetherington; *b* 2 April 1951; *Educ* Glasgow Acad, Univ of Glasgow (LLB); *m* 7 Sept 1979, Sheena Janet, *née* Fraser; 1 da (Julie Katyana b 10 Dec 1981); *Career* apprentice slr Kerr Barrie & Duncan Slrs Glasgow 1971–73, asst slr McGrigor Donald Slrs Glasgow 1973–75, ptnr Flowers & Co Slrs Glasgow 1976–89 (asst slr 1975–76), temp sheriff 1987–89, sheriff of N Strathclyde at Dumbarton 1989–; pres Glasgow Bar Assoc 1981–82; *Recreations* cricket; *Clubs* Avizandum; *Style*— Sheriff Simon Fraser; ✉ Sheriff's Chambers, Sheriff Court, Church Street, Dumbarton G82 1QR (☎ 01389 763266)

FRASER, Susan (Sue); *b* 15 July 1966; *Educ* Peterhead Acad, Northern Coll of Educn; *Career* int hockey player; former memb Glasgow Western Ladies Hockey Club, currently memb Bonagrass Grove Ladies Hockey Club; 99 Scottish caps, 75 GB caps 1991–; top Scottish scorer (6 goals) at Euro Championships 1991, memb GB squad Olympic Games: Barcelona 1992 (Bronze medal), Atlanta 1996 (fourth place); primary sch teacher; *Recreations* golf, squash, films, music, walking, cooking, eating good food; *Style*— Miss Sue Fraser; ✉ c/o Scottish Hockey Union, The Pleasance, Edinburgh

FRASER, Veronica Mary; da of Archibald Fraser (d 1966), of London, and Eleanor Fairfield, *née* Chinn (d 1976); *b* 19 April 1933; *Educ* Richmond County Sch for Girls, St Hugh's Coll Oxford (MA); *Career* headmistress Godolphin Sch Salisbury 1968–80, diocesan dir of educn Worcester Diocese 1985–93; chm Diocesan Dirs 1990–91; pres Assoc of Sr Membs St Hugh's Coll Oxford 1994–, memb Governing Body SPCK 1994–, tstee All Saints Educational Tst 1995–; *Recreations* choral singing, painting, bargello; *Style*— Miss Veronica Fraser; ✉ Timbers, Upper Churchfields, Cradley, Malvern, Worcs WR13 5LJ

FRASER, Wendy; *b* 23 April 1963; *Educ* Bellahouston Acad, Dunfermline Coll (BEd); *Career* int hockey player; memb Western Klick Photopoint (Glasgow Western) Ladies Hockey Club (Silver medal Euro Club Championships 1990–92); 100 GB caps 1985–92, 103 Scot caps; Bronze medal Olympic Games Barcelona 1992; Player of the Year Scot Hockey Union 1990 and 1992; PE teacher Hutchesons' GS Glasgow, Scottish Under-18 (Girls) coach 1993–96, Scottish Under-21 (Girls) coach 1996–; *Recreations* coaching hockey, hill walking, skiing; *Style*— Miss Wendy Fraser; ✉ c/o Scottish Hockey Union, 48 Pleasance, Edinburgh EH8 9TJ (☎ 0131 650 8170)

FRASER, Prof William Irvine; s of Duncan Fraser (d 1979), and Muriel, *née* Macrae (d 1977); *b* 3 Feb 1940; *Educ* Greenock Acad, Univ of Glasgow (MB ChB, MD, DPM); *m* 1 Oct 1964, Joyce Carroll, da of Douglas Gilchrist (d 1978); 2 s (Ewen Duncan b 31 May 1966, Alan Douglas b 1 Sept 1968); *Career* physician supt and dir Fife Mental Handicap Servs 1974–78, hon sr lectr in psychology Univ of St Andrews 1973–89, pt/t sr lectr Univ of Edinburgh 1974–89, conslt psychiatrist Royal Edinburgh Hosp 1978–79, ed Journal of Intellectual Disability Research 1982–, prof of learning disability Univ of Wales Coll of Med 1988–; Burden Neurological Inst Prize medallist for res into mental handicap 1989, Int Assoc for Sci Study of Intellectual Disabilities Distinguished Achievement Award for Scientific Literature 1996; memb Gen Projects Ctee Mental Health Fndn 1981–87, co-dir Welsh Centre for Learning Disability 1994–; FRCPsych 1978 (chm Welsh Div); *Books* Communicating with Normal and Retarded Children (with R Grieve, 1981), Caring for People with Mental Handicaps (with A Green R McGillray, 1991); *Recreations* sailing; *Clubs* RSM; *Style*— Prof William Fraser; ✉ 146 Wenallt Rd, Rhiwbina, Cardiff CF4 6TQ (☎ 01222 628644); Welsh Centre for Learning Disabilities, Meridian Court, North Road, Cardiff (☎ 01222 562323)

FRASER, Sir William Kerr; GCB (1984, KCB 1979, CB 1978); s of late Alexander Macmillan Fraser, and Rachel, *née* Kerr; *b* 18 March 1929; *Educ* Eastwood Sch, Glasgow Univ (MA, LLB); *m* 1956, Marion Anne, *née* Forbes, LT (1996), chm Christian Aid; 3 s (1 of whom Dr Andrew Fraser, *qv*), 1 da; *Career* joined Scot Home Dept 1955, perm under sec of state Scot Office 1978–88 (dep sec 1975–78); princ and vice chllr Univ of Glasgow 1988–95, chm Royal Cmmn on the Ancient and Historical Monuments of Scotland 1995–; chllr Univ of Glasgow 1996–; Hon LLD Univs of Aberdeen, Edinburgh, Glasgow and Strathclyde; Hon FRCP (Glasgow), FRSE 1985, Hon FRSAMD 1995; *Clubs* New (Edinburgh); *Style*— Sir William Fraser, GCB, FRSE; ✉ Broadwood, Edinburgh Road, Gifford, East Lothian EH41 4JE (☎ and fax 01620 810319)

FRASER OF CARMYLLIE, Baron (Life Peer UK 1989), of Carmyllie in the District of Angus; Peter Lovat Fraser; PC (1989), QC (Scot 1982); s of Rev George Robson Fraser, of Corrennie, Edinburgh, and Helen Jean, *née* Meiklejohn; *b* 29 May 1945; *Educ* Loretto, Gonville and Caius Coll Cambridge, Univ of Edinburgh; *m* 1969, Fiona Macdonald, da of Hugh Murray Mair, of Lanark; 1 s (Hon James Murray b 1974), 2 da (Hon Jane Helen Anne b 1972, Hon Catriona Elizabeth b 1981); *Career* advocate (Scotland) 1969–; lectr in constitutional law Heriot-Watt Univ 1972–74; standing jr counsel (Scotland) to FCO 1979; contested (C) Aberdeen North Oct 1974; MP (C): Angus South 1979–83, Angus East 1983–87; PPS to George Younger (sec state Scotland) 1981–82, slr gen for Scotland 1982–89, Lord Advocate 1989–92; min of state Scottish Office 1992–95, min of state DTI 1995–; hon bencher of Lincoln's Inn 1989; hon visiting prof of Law Univ of Dundee 1985; *Style*— The Rt Hon Lord Fraser of Carmyllie, PC, QC; ✉ Slade House, Carmyllie by Arbroath, Angus (☎ 01241 860215)

FRATER, Alexander Russell; s of Dr Alexander Smail Frater (d 1972), and Lorna Rosie, *née* Fray (d 1986); *b* 3 Jan 1937; *Educ* Scotch Coll Melbourne, Univ of Melbourne, Univ of Durham, Univ of Perugia; *m* 1963, Marlis, da of Erwin Pfund; 1 s (Alexander John b 1969), 1 da (Tania Elisabeth b 1964); *Career* asst ed Punch 1963–66, retained writer The New Yorker 1964–68, staff writer Daily Telegraph Magazine 1979–84, asst ed Radio Times 1977–79; The Observer: asst ed magazine 1979–84, dep ed magazine 1984–86, chief travel corr 1986–; TV presenter: The Last African Flying Boat (BBC) 1990 (BAFTA award for Best Single Documentary), Monsoon (BBC) 1991, In the Footsteps of Buddha (BBC) 1993; Br Press Award commendations 1982 and 1989, Br Press Award Travel Writer of the Year 1990, 1991 and 1992; *Books* Stopping-Train Britain (1983), Great Rivers Of The World (ed, 1984), Beyond The Blue Horizon (1986), Chasing The Monsoon (1990); *Recreations* books, walking; *Style*— Alexander Frater, Esq; ✉ The Observer, 119 Farringdon Road, London EC1R 3ER (☎ 0171 278 2332)

FRATER, Iain Grant; s of John Robert Frater (d 1979), of Melrose, Roxburghshire, and Williamina Mary, *née* Whitehead (d 1975); *b* 11 Jan 1946; *Educ* Melrose GS, Hawick HS, Univ of Edinburgh (MA), Univ of Clermont-Ferrand, KCL (MA); *Career* teacher Univ of Central America 1969–71, int mktg trainee Burmah Oil Trading Co 1972–74, exec sec Christian Concern for Southern Africa 1974–75; British Council: asst dir Lagos 1975–76, exchanges offr London 1976–78, asst dir Singapore 1978–80; seconded as trg advsr DG for Devpt Cmmn of the EC 1981–84, educn attaché Br Embassy Washington DC 1985–89, cultural attaché Br Embassy E Berlin 1989–90, dir British Council Netherlands 1994– (E Germany 1990–93); *Recreations* walking, travelling, reading, listening to music; *Style*— Iain Frater, Esq; ✉ The British Council, Keizersgracht 343, 1016 EH Amsterdam, Netherlands

FRAY, Prof Derek John; s of Arthur Joseph Fray, of London, and Doris Lilian Wilson (d 1981); *b* 26 Dec 1939; *Educ* Emanuel Sch, Imperial Coll London (BSc Eng, ARSM, PhD, DIC, state scholar, royal scholar), Univ of Cambridge (MA); *m* 14 Aug 1965, Mirella Christine Kathleen, da of Leslie Honey, of Thames Ditton, Surrey; 1 s (Shelton Lanning b 1972), 1 da (Justine Chloe b 1974); *Career* asst prof of metallurgy MIT Cambridge Mass USA 1965–68, gp ldr Res Dept Imperial Smelting Corp Ltd Avonmouth Bristol 1968–71, univ lectr Dept of Materials Sci and Metallurgy Univ of Cambridge 1971–90; Fitzwilliam Coll Cambridge: fell 1972–90, librarian 1973–74, tutorial and estates bursar 1974–86, bursar 1986–88; prof of mineral engrg and head Dept of Mining and Mineral Engrg Univ of Leeds 1991–96; prof of materials chemistry Dept of Materials Sci and Metallurgy Univ of Cambridge 1996–; visiting prof Univ of Leeds 1996–; hon prof of science and technology Beijing 1995–; dir: Ion Science Ltd, Ion Science Messtechnik, Cambridge Advanced Materials Ltd; *Awards* Matthey prize 1967, AIME Extractive Metallurgy Technol award 1980, Sir George Beilby medal 1981, Nuffield SERC visiting fellowship 1981, Bd of Review AIME 1985, Kroll medal and prize Inst of Metals 1987, John Phillips medal 1991; memb: Inst of Materials, Soc of Chemical Industry, AIME; MIM 1966, FIMM 1988 (memb Organizing Ctee for extraction metallurgy 1981–85 and 1987, and for pyrometallurgy 1987, memb Editorial Bd, memb Cncl), FEng 1989; *Books* Worked Examples in Mass and Heat Transfer in Materials Technology (1983); author of over 180 papers and 35 published patents; *Recreations* sailing, reading; *Style*— Prof Derek Fray, FEng; ✉ Evergreen Cottage, Kirk Deighton, N Yorks LS22 4DZ (☎ 01937 588273); Department of Materials Science and Metallurgy, University of Cambridge, Pembroke Street, Cambridge CB2 0QZ

FRAYLING, Prof Christopher John; s of Maj Arthur Frederick Frayling, OBE (d 1993), and Barbara Kathleen, *née* Imhof; *b* 25 Dec 1946; *Educ* Repton, Churchill Coll Cambridge (scholar, MA, PhD); *m* 1981, Helen Ann Snowdon; *Career* lectr in history Univ of Exeter 1971–72, film archivist Imperial War Museum 1972–73, lectr in history of ideas Univ of Bath 1973–79; Royal Coll of Art: prof of cultural history and head of dept 1979–, pro-rector 1992–96, rector 1996–; visiting prof Shanghai Univ of Technol E China 1991; tstee: Victoria & Albert Museum 1983– (memb Educn and chm Bethnal Green Museum Ctee, memb Advsy Bd 1981–83), Holburne of Menstrie Museum Bath 1983–; govr Br Film Inst 1982–86 (chm Educn Ctee 1983–86); memb Crafts Cncl 1982–85 (and chm Educn and Pubns Ctees); Arts Council of GB: memb Photography Panel 1983–85, chm Art Projects Ctee 1985–88, memb Cncl 1987–, chm Visual Arts Panel 1987–94 (dep chm 1984–87), chm Film, Video and Broadcasting Panel 1994–, chm Educn and Trg Panel 1996–; chm: Crafts Study Centre Bath 1981–, Free Form Arts Trust 1984–89; memb Nat Advsy Body Working Party on Higher Educn in the Arts 1985–88, patron Parnham House Crafts Courses; writer and presenter of numerous TV series incl: The Art of Persuasion (Channel 4) 1984, Busting the Block (Channel 4) 1986, Cinema

Profiles (BBC 2) 1984–90, The Face of Tutankhamun (BBC 2) 1993, Strange Landscape - the illumination of the Middle Ages (BBC 2) 1994–95, Nightmare - the birth of horror (BBC 1) 1996–97; memb: Advsy Bd Inst of Contemporary Art, ARTEC (educn and technol gp); hon fell Humberside Poly 1991; FRSA 1984, FCSD 1994; *Books* Napoleon Wrote Fiction (1972), The Vampyre - Lord Ruthven to Count Dracula (ed, 1977), The Schoolmaster and the Wheelwrights (1980), Spaghetti Westerns - Cowboys and Europeans from Karl May to Sergio Leone (1981), The Royal College of Art: one hundred and fifty years of art and design (1987), Vampyres - Lord Byron to Count Dracula (1991), Beyond the Dovetail - crafts, skill and imagination (ed 1991), Clint Eastwood - a critical biography (1992), The Face of Tutankhamun (1992), The Art Pack (with Helen Frayling, 1992), Strange Landscape (1994), Things to Come - a film classic (1995), Design of the times (with Claire Catterall, 1996), Nightmare - the birth of horror (1996); numerous articles in learned and rather less learned journals and exhbn catalogues on aspects of Euro and American cultural history; *Recreations* finding time; *Style*— Prof Christopher Frayling; ✉ Royal College of Art, Kensington Gore, London SW7 2EU (☎ 0171 584 5020)

FRAYLING, Rev Canon Nicholas Arthur; s of Arthur Frederick Frayling, OBE (d 1993), and Barbara Kathleen, *née* Imhof; *b* 29 Feb 1944; *Educ* Repton, Univ of Exeter (BA), Cuddesdon Coll Oxford; *Career* mgmnt trg retail trade 1962–64, temp probation offr (prison welfare) Inner London Probation and After-care Serv 1965–66 (pt/t 1966–71), ordained Southwark Cathedral 1971, asst curate St John's Peckham 1971–74, vicar All Saints Tooting Graveney 1974–83, chm Diocesan Advsy Ctee for Care of Churches 1980–83, canon residentiary and precentor Liverpool Cathedral 1983–87, rector of Liverpool 1987–; chaplain: Huyton Coll 1987–91, St Paul's Eye Hosp Liverpool 1987–90, to the High Sheriff of Merseyside 1992–93; hon canon Liverpool Cathedral 1989–; chm Religious Advsy Panel BBC Radio Merseyside 1988–, chair Welfare Organisations Ctee Liverpool Cncl of Voluntary Service 1992–; memb Worshipful Co of Skinners 1980; *Books* Pardon and Peace - a reflection on the making of peace in Ireland (1996); *Recreations* music, friends; *Clubs* Cwlth Tst, Athenaeum (Liverpool), Artists (hon memb), Liverpool Racquet (hon memb); *Style*— The Rev Canon Nicholas Frayling; ✉ 25 Princes Park Mansions, Sefton Park Road, Liverpool L8 3SA (☎ 0151 727 4692); Liverpool Parish Church, Old Churchyard, Liverpool L2 8TZ (☎ 0151 236 5287, fax 0151 236 4118)

FRAYN, Michael; s of late Thomas Allen Frayn, and late Violet Alice, *née* Lawson; *b* 8 Sept 1933; *Educ* Kingston GS, Emmanuel Coll Cambridge; *m* 1, 1960 (m dis 1989), Gillian, *née* Palmer; 3 da; m 2, 5 June 1993, Claire Tomalin, *qv*; *Career* author and playwright; columnist: The Guardian 1959–62 (reporter 1957–59), Observer 1962–68; recipient of numerous drama awards; hon fell Emmanuel Coll Cambridge 1985; *Stage plays* The Two of Us 1970, The Sandboy 1971, Alphabetical Order 1975, Donkeys' Years 1976, Clouds 1976, Balmoral 1978 (new version Liberty Hall 1980), Make and Break 1980, Noises Off 1982 (film 1991), Benefactors 1984, Look Look 1990, Here 1993, Now You Know 1995, La Belle Vivette (opera) 1995; *TV plays and films* incl: Jamie, On a Flying Visit 1968, Birthday 1969, Clockwise 1986, First and Last 1989, A Landing on the Sun 1994; *TV documentaries* incl: Second City Reports 1964, Beyond a Joke 1972, Making Faces (series) 1975, One Pair of Eyes 1968, Laurence Sterne Lived Here 1973, Imagine a City Called Berlin 1975, Vienna: The Mask of Gold 1977, Three Streets in the Country 1979, The Long Straight (Great Railway Journeys of the World) 1980, Jerusalem 1984, Prague: the Magic Lantern 1994, Budapest: Written in Water 1996; *Translations of plays* incl: The Cherry Orchard, Three Sisters, The Seagull, Uncle Vanya, Wild Honey (all Chekhov), The Fruits of Enlightment (Tolstoy), Exchange (Trifonov), Number One (Anouilh), The Sneeze (adaption of Chekhov Short Stories); *Novels* incl: The Tin Men (1965, Somerset Maugham Award), The Russian Interpreter (1966, Hawthornden Prize), Towards the End of the Morning (1967), A Very Private Life (1968), Sweet Dreams (1973), The Trick of It (1989), A Landing On The Sun (1991, Sunday Express Book of the Year Award), Now You Know (1992); *Non-fiction* incl: Constructions (philosophy, 1974), several volumes of collected writings and translations; *Style*— Michael Frayn; ✉ c/o Elaine Green Ltd, 37 Goldhawk Road, London W12 9PU (☎ 0181 749 0315)

FRAYNE, Very Rev David; s of Philip John Frayne, of Stratford upon Avon, and Daisy Morris, *née* Eade; *b* 19 Oct 1934; *Educ* Reigate GS, St Edmund Hall Oxford (MA), Univ of Birmingham and Queen's Coll Birmingham (dip in theol); *m* 8 April 1961, Elizabeth Ann, da of John Douglas Grant; 2 da (Clare Frances b 6 Sept 1962, Hilary Ann b 24 Sept 1964), 1 s (Mark Edmund b 23 May 1971); *Career* Pilot Offr RAF 1954–55; asst curate E Wickham (Dio of Southwark) 1960–63, priest-in-charge St Barnabas Downham 1963–67, vicar of N Sheen 1967–73, rector of Caterham 1973–83, rural dean of Caterham 1981–83, hon canon Southwark Cathedral 1982–83 (emeritus 1983), vicar of St Mary Redcliffe with Temple and St John the Baptiste Bedminster (Dio of Bristol) 1983–92, rural dean of Bedminster 1986–92, proctor in convocation (Gen Synod) 1987–90, hon canon Bristol Cathedral 1991–92, provost of Blackburn (Dio of Blackburn) 1992–; *Recreations* music, walking, camping; *Clubs* Oxford Society; *Style*— The Very Rev David Frayne; ✉ Provost's House, Preston New Road, Blackburn, Lancs BB2 6PS (☎ 01254 52502); Cathedral Offices, Cathedral Close, Blackburn, Lancs BB1 5AA (☎ 01254 51491, fax 01254 667309)

FRAZER, Christopher Mark; s of Michael Leslie Frazer, of Twickenham, Middx, and Pamela Mary, *née* Stoakes; *b* 17 June 1960; *Educ* King's Coll Sch Wimbledon, St John's Coll Cambridge (exhibitioner, Macaulay scholar, McMahon law student, MA, LLM, College prizeman); *m* 20 May 1989, Victoria Margaret, da of John Peter Hess, of Chorlton-by-Backford, Chester; 1 s (Thomas Michael John b 19 June 1994), 1 da (Laura Charlotte Mary b 31 Aug 1996); *Career* called to the Bar Middle Temple 1983, ad eundem Inner Temple; practises on Midland and Oxford, Western and Wales and Chester circuits; memb Gen Cncl of the Bar 1989–94, chm Bar Conf 1994; chm Editorial Bd Counsel magazine 1995–; chm Young Barristers' Ctee of England and Wales 1991; vice chm and treas Twickenham Cons Assoc 1985–89, common councilman Corporation of London 1986–95 (memb City of London Police and Health Ctees), Parly candidate (C) Peckham Gen Election 1992, chm and fndr Cons Young Lawyers 1984, sec Soc of Cons Lawyers 1988–89; Freeman City of London 1986; *Books* Thoughts for a Third Term (1987), Privatise the Prosecutors (1993); *Recreations* dinghy sailing, Classic FM, amusing my children; *Clubs* Guildhall, West Wittering Sailing; *Style*— Christopher Frazer, Esq; ✉ 2 Harcourt Buildings, Temple, London EC4Y 9DB (☎ 0171 353 6961, fax 0171 353 6968)

FRAZER, Ian William; s of William George Frazer (d 1982), of Hutton, Essex, and Grace Marjorie, *née* Willis (d 1979); *b* 26 Jan 1933; *Educ* Framlingham Coll; *m* 3 March 1964, Priscilla, da of Capt John Daniell (ka 1943), of Kimpton, Herts; 3 da (Annabel b 1965, Katharine (Mrs James Fenwick) b 1966, Henrietta b 1970); *Career* Nat Serv cmmnd The Queen's Bays (2 Dragoon Gds) 1955–57; Army Emergency Reserve 1957–64, ret Lt 1 Queen's Dragoon Gds; qualified CA 1955, sr ptnr (formerly ptnr) Littlejohn Frazer (formerly Frazer Whiting & Co) 1971–; govr: Morpeth Sch Tower Hamlets 1967–, St Mary's Sch Wantage 1984–; cncl memb Chelsea Soc 1972–, tstee Chelsea Festival 1992–; FCA 1955; *Recreations* music, reading, shooting, skiing; *Clubs* Cavalry and Guards', City of London; *Style*— Ian Frazer, Esq; ✉ 6 Edith Terrace, Chelsea, London SW10 0TQ (☎ 0171 352 3310); Irish Hill Cottage, Hamstead Marshall, Newbury, Berks RG20 0JB; Littlejohn Frazer, 1 Park Place, Canary Wharf, London E14 4HJ (☎ 0171 987 5030)

FRAZER, Rupert Peter; s of Simon Frazer, of Powys, and Dawn, *née* Gwynne-Howell (d 1992); *b* 12 March 1947; *Educ* Wellington Coll Berks, Drama Centre London; *m* 1975, Janie Alison, da of Col David Cattermull; 1 s (Hugo b 25 Dec 1975), 2 da (Liberty b 18 March 1982, Jessamy b 13 Nov 1985); *Career* actor; *Theatre* incl: Royal Hunt of the Sun, War Music, The Tempest, Dracula, Ring Round the Moon, Torch Song Trilogy, The White Devil, Blithe Spirit, Rosmersholm, Lady Windermere's Fan; *Television* incl: Testament of Youth, Penmarric, Cover Her Face, The Far Pavillions, The Importance of Being Earnest, The House of Elliot; *Films* incl: The Shooting Party, Empire of the Sun, The Girl in a Swing; *Recreations* reading, swimming, tennis, riding; *Clubs* 2 Brydges; *Style*— Rupert Frazer; ✉ c/o Markham & Froggatt, 4 Windmill Street, London W1P 1HF (☎ 0171 636 4412)

FREARS, Stephen Arthur; s of Dr Russell E Frears (d 1977), of Nottingham, and Ruth M Frears (d 1971); *b* 20 June 1941; *Educ* Gresham's, Trinity Coll Cambridge (BA); *m* 1967 (m dis 1973), Mary K, *née* Wilmers; 2 s (Sam b 1972, William b 1973); *ptnr* Anne Rothenstein; 1 s (Francis Frears b 1983), 1 da (Lola Frears b 1985); *Career* film director; *Films* Gumshoe 1971, Bloody Kids 1980, The Hit 1984, My Beautiful Launderette 1985, Prick up Your Ears 1986, Sammy and Rosie Get Laid 1987, Dangerous Liaisons 1988, The Grifters 1989, Accidental Hero 1992, The Snapper 1994, Mary Reilly 1995, The Van 1996; *Style*— Stephen Frears, Esq; ✉ c/o Casarotto Ramsay Ltd, National House, 4th Floor, 60–66 Wardour Street, Londo W1V 3HP (☎ 0171 287 4450, fax 0171 287 9128)

FRECKLETON, Fiona Mary Emma; da of Stanley Freckleton, of Braishfield, Hants, and Frances Alice, *née* Ladd; *b* 6 Nov 1960; *Educ* Westgate Sch Winchester, Peter Symond's Coll Winchester, Somerville Coll Oxford; *Career* amateur rower; stroke Oxford Univ women's boat race eight 1982 and 1983; achievements in coxless pairs: English club champions (with Sarah Talbot) 1983, Scottish champions (with Morag Simpson) 1986, Scotland rep Cwlth Games (with Morag Simpson) 1986, Bronze medal World Championships Vienna (with Miriam Batten, *qv*) 1991; ninth place GB coxless four World Championships Tasmania 1990, seventh place in eights Olympic Games Barcelona 1992, eigth place in coxless fours World Championships Roudnice 1993, Bronze medal for Scotland single sculls Cwlth Regatta London Ontario 1994; first Br women's crew to win World Championship medal, Sunday Times Sports Woman of the Year team award 1991, Times/Minet supreme award 1991; mathematics teacher: Cherwell Sch Oxford 1983–86, Westminster Sch (also rowing coach) 1986– (first woman housemaster 1996); *Recreations* expeditions, travel, skiing, mountaineering, cycling; *Style*— Miss Fiona Freckleton

FREDERICK, Sir Charles Boscawen; 10 Bt (GB 1723), of Burwood House, Surrey; s of Lt-Col Sir Edward Boscawen Frederick, 9 Bt, CVO (d 1956), and Edith Katherine (Kathleen) Cortlandt, *née* Mulloy (d 1970); *b* 11 April 1919; *Educ* Eton; *m* 8 Oct 1949, Rosemary, er da of late Lt-Col Robert John Halkett Baddeley, MC, of Home Close, Donhead St Mary, Shaftesbury, Dorset; 2 s (Christopher St John b 1950, James Boscawen b 1963), 2 da (Anne Rosemary (Mrs M French) b 1952, Jill Elizabeth (Mrs Stephen Douglas) b 1956); *Heir* s, Christopher St John Frederick b 28 June 1950; *Career* Maj (ret) Grenadier Gds; memb London Stock Exchange 1954–62, gen cmmr Income Tax 1966, memb Stock Exchange Cncl 1973–75, chm Provincial Unit of Stock Exchange 1973–75; *Style*— Sir Charles Frederick Bt, JP; ✉ Virginia Cottage, Stoke Trister, Wincanton, Somerset BA9 9PQ

FREDERICK, Christopher St John; s and h of Sir Charles Boscawen Frederick, 10 Bt, *qv*; *b* 28 June 1950; *m* 1990, Camilla Elizabeth, only da of Sir (Walter) Derek Gilbey, 3 Bt; 1 s (Benjamin St John b 29 Dec 1991), 1 da (Amy Rose b 11 July 1994); *Style*— Christopher Frederick, Esq

FREDJOHN, Dennis; MBE (1990); s of late Maurice Fredjohn; *b* 22 Feb 1925; *Educ* Westminster City Sch, St John's Coll Cambridge; *m* 1947, Pamela Jill, *née* Samms; 1 s, 2 da; *Career* Flying Offr RAF served WWII, Lt RN; exec dir Rio Tinto Zinc 1970–73, dir Arbuthnot Latham Holdings 1973–76, md Alusuisse (UK) Ltd 1976–80, dir BPB Industries plc 1980–96; memb: Doctors' and Dentists' Review Body 1989–95, Cncl Lloyd's of London 1982–84; *Recreations* squash, farming, bridge; *Style*— Dennis Fredjohn, Esq, MBE; ✉ Laurentides, Redmarley, Glos GL19 3JT (☎ 0153 1650477)

FREEBORN, David Michael; s of Herbert Aubury Freeborn (d 1976), of Whetstone, London, and May Beatrice, *née* Inwards; *b* 15 May 1950; *Educ* Christ Church Secondary Sch London, Tottenham Tech Coll, St Albans Coll of Further Educn; *m* 25 Feb 1983, Janis, da of Roy James Lambert, of Maidstone; 1 da (Claire b 27 June 1983); *Career* dir Jarvis plc, md J Jarvis & Sons plc; MCIOB 1972, FRICS 1983; *Recreations* golf; *Clubs* RAC; *Style*— David M Freeborn, Esq; ✉ c/o Jarvis plc, Construction House, Southend Arterial Road, Romford, Essex RM3 0NU (☎ 01708 718000, fax 01708 347690)

FREEBOROUGH, Nicholas Geoffrey; s of Geoffrey Freeborough (d 1978), and Cynthia Lena Douglas Cox (d 1970); *b* 13 Aug 1947; *Educ* Canford Sch; *m* 24 July 1971, Josephine, da of Dr Selwyn Graham de Clive Lowe; 3 s (James Alexander b 23 Nov 1974, David Anthony b 15 June 1977, Luke Geoffrey b 14 May 1983); *Career* articled to A R Drummond of A R Drummond & Co Epsom 1964–69, admitted as slr 1970, ptnr Freeborough Slack & Co London 1971–80 (asst slr 1970–71), ptnr A R Drummond & Co 1981–91 (asst slr 1980–81), dep Co Ct registrar 1983–91, district judge Willesden Co Ct 1991–93, Croydon County Ct 1993–; memb: Law Soc 1964– (full memb 1970–), Assoc of District Judges 1991–; govr Wallace Fields Middle Sch 1990–; Freedom of the City of London 1986; *Recreations* skiing, fine wines, visiting France, archery; *Style*— District Judge Nicholas Freeborough; ✉ Croydon Combined Courts Centre, Altyre Road, Croydon (☎ 0181 681 2533)

FREEDLAND, Michael Rodney; s of David Freedland, and Lily, *née* Mindel; *b* 18 Dec 1934; *Educ* Luton GS; *m* 3 July 1960, Sara, da of Abram Hockerman; 1 s (Jonathan Saul b 1967), 2 da (Fiona Anne b 1963, Daniela Ruth b 1964); *Career* journalist for local newspapers 1951–60, Daily Sketch 1960–61; freelance journalist 1961–; contrib: The Times, Sunday Telegraph, The Guardian, Economist, Spectator, etc; broadcaster 1962– (progs incl You don't have to be Jewish (BBC and LBC) 1971–94); *Books* 30 books including studies of: Al Jolson (1971), Irving Berlin (1973), Fred Astaire (1976), Gregory Peck (1979), The Warner Brothers (1982), Danny Kaye (1987), Leonard Bernstein (1987), Jane Fonda (1988), Dustin Hoffman (1989), Kenneth Williams (1990), André Previn (1991), Music Man (1994), Sean Connery, A Biography (1994), All The Way, The Sinatra Biography (1997); also: Jolson (music show, opened London 1995); *Recreations* reading, being with my wife and family; *Style*— Michael Freedland, Esq; ✉ Bays Hill Lodge, Barnet Lane, Elstree, Herts WD6 3QU (☎ 0181 953 3000)

FREEDMAN, Cyril Winston; s of Sydney Freedman (d 1951), and Irene Rosalind, *née* Anekstein; *b* 31 Aug 1945; *Educ* Brighton Coll, Brighton Coll of Art and Design (Dip Graphic Art and Design); *m* 25 March 1970, Christine Mary, da of Cecil Shipman, of Swanwick, Derbys; 1 s (Mark b 1973), 1 da (Anna b 1977); *Career* chm: CWF Advertising Ltd 1971–74, Halls Homes and Gardens 1978–80 (md 1977–78, dir 1974–81); dir Pentos plc and subsidiaries 1979–81, chm Serco Ryan Ltd 1982–87, chief exec WBH Group Ltd (subsidiary of Lopex plc) 1985–88, dir Armour Automotive Products Group (subsidiary of Armour Trust plc) 1985–91; chm: Deeko plc 1988–90 (dir 1986–90), Hennell plc 1988–94, Worth Fine Fragrances plc 1992–; dir Apax Partners & Co Ventures Ltd (formerly known as Alan Patricof Associates Ltd) 1988–95; dep chm and chief exec S Daniels plc 1995–; dir: New Covent Garden Soup Co 1989–, Stead & Simpson Group 1992–; FInstD, MCIM; *Recreations* painting, collecting fine art; *Style*— Cyril Freedman, Esq; ✉ S Daniels plc, 1 Duchess Street, London W1N 6DE (☎ 0171 436 2007)

FREEDMAN, Dr Danielle Beverley; *b* 28 Aug 1953; *Educ* Woodhouse GS London, Royal Free Hosp Sch of Med London (Winifred Ladd scholar, MB BS, Edith Peachy

Phipson prize, MRCPath); *m* (m dis); 1 s; *Career* Royal Free Hosp London: house physician and house surgn posts 1977–78, SHO in clinical pathology 1978–79, registrar Dept of Chemical Pathology 1979–81; clinical lectr (sr registrar) Dept of Chemical Pathology Courtauld Inst of Biochemistry Middx Hosp Med Sch London 1981–84; Luton and Dunstable Hosp NHS Tst: conslt chemical pathologist and assoc physician in clinical endocrinology and metabolism 1985–, clinical dir of pathology 1990–, clinical dir of pathology and pharmacy 1993–; regnl postgraduate dean rep Univ of London and Univ of Cambridge; nat surveyor King's Fund Organisational Audit (Accreditation UK), nat inspr Clinical Pathology Accreditation (CPA) UK Ltd, memb Nat Working Pty for implementation of clinical guidelines; past chm Clinical Biochemistry Sub-Ctee NW Thames RHA; RCPath: memb Cncl, memb Standing Ctee for Chemical Pathology, memb Nat Clinical Audit Ctee, RCPath rep Assoc of Clinical Biochemists Cncl, memb Standing Ctee on RCPath Academic Activities, memb Pubns Ctee, RCPath rep NHS Mgmnt Exec working with professions to develop service specifications, E Anglia rep for chemical pathology; Assoc of Clinical Biochemists: memb Scientific Ctee, sr ed Venture Pubns Gp, chm Jt Working Gp looking at near patient testing, chm Clinical Investigations Sub-Ctee, Nat Ames Award and Medal for Research 1981, Prize for Clinical Audit 1992; FRCPath 1995; *Books* A Short Textbook of Chemical Pathology (ed), Clinical Chemistry (ed); numerous pubns in academic jls; *Style*— Dr Danielle Freeman; ✉ The Luton and Dunstable Hospital NHS Trust, Lewsey Road, Luton LU4 0DZ (☎ 01582 491122, fax 01582 598990)

FREEDMAN, Prof Lawrence David; CBE (1996); s of Lt Cdr Julius Freedman, RN (d 1987), and Myra, *née* Robinson (d 1995); *b* 7 Dec 1948; *Educ* Whitley Bay GS, Univ of Manchester (BA), Univ of York (BPhil), Univ of Oxford (PhD); *m* 1974, Judith Anne, da of Harry Hill; 1 s (Samuel b 1981), 1 da (Ruth b 1984); *Career* teaching asst Dept of Politics Univ of York 1971–72, res (prize) fell Nuffield Coll Oxford 1974–75, lectr in politics (pt/t) Balliol Coll Oxford 1975, res assoc Int Inst for Strategic Studies 1975–76, res fell on British foreign policy Royal Inst of Int Affairs 1976–78, head of policy studies Royal Inst of Int Affairs 1978–82, prof of war studies King's Coll London 1982–; columnist: Independent 1987–93, Times 1993–; specialist advsr House of Commons Defence Ctee 1980–; memb: Current Affairs Advsy Gp Channel 4 1986–87, Govt and Law Ctee Economic and Social Res Cncl 1982–87, Cncl Int Inst for Strategic Studies 1984–92 and 1993–, Cncl David Davies Meml Inst 1990–95, Cncl Sch of Slavonic and E European Studies; memb Editorial Bds: Foreign Policy, Int Security, Political Quarterly, Intelligence and National Security; fell King's Coll London 1992; FBA 1995; *Books* US Intelligence and the Soviet Strategic Threat (1977, reprinted with new foreword 1986), Britain and Nuclear Weapons (1980), The Evolution of Nuclear Strategy (1981, 2 edn 1989), The Atlas of Global Strategy (1985), The Price of Peace: Living with the Nuclear Dilemma (1986), Britain and the Falklands War (1988), The Troubled Alliance: Atlantic Relations in the 1980s (ed, 1983), Nuclear War and Nuclear Peace (jtly 1983, 2 edn 1988), US Nuclear Strategy: A Reader (co-ed, 1989), Military Power in Europe: Essays in Memory of Jonathan Alford (ed, 1990), Signals of War: The Falklands Conflict of 1982 (jtly, 1990), Britain in the World (jtly, 1991), The Gulf Conflict 1990–91 (jtly, 1993), Military Intervention in European Conflicts (ed, 1994), War: A Reader (ed, 1994); *Recreations* political cartoons, tennis; *Style*— Prof Lawrence Freedman, CBE, FBA; ✉ Department of War Studies, King's College, The Strand, London WC2R 2LS (☎ 0171 873 2025/2200, fax 0171 873 2026)

FREEDMAN, Lisa Diane; da of Bernard William Freedman, of London, and late Toby Robins Freedman; *b* 21 July 1955; *Educ* Queen's Coll Harley Street London, Univ of London (BA); *m* 1994, Andrew John Martin, s of John Martin; 1 s (Nathaniel James Martin b 11 Aug 1994); *Career* sub-ed Vogue magazine 1978–80, fashion ed Sunday Express magazine 1980–86 (sub-ed 1980), ed ES magazine London Evening Standard 1989–91, features ed The Sunday Telegraph 1993, currently freelance; *Style*— Ms Lisa Freedman

FREEDMAN, Michael John; s of late Joseph Leopold Freedman, of London, and late Rosa Annie, *née* Bosman (d 1987); *b* 4 July 1946; *Educ* Clifton, Christ's Coll Cambridge; *m* 1973, Pamela Dawn, da of late Cyril Kay, and late Hilda Kay; 1 s (Jonathan Leonard b 13 April 1979), 1 da (Natalie Kay b 31 Jan 1976); *Career* mktg mangr Royal Angus Hotels 1965–69; mktg dir: Securadet Ltd 1969–72, Paul Kaye Studio Ltd 1972–; chm Cover Shots International 1990–; memb Cncl BIPP 1989–93; FBIPP, FMPA; *Recreations* tennis, swimming, reading, walking; *Style*— Michael Freedman, Esq; ✉ Paul Kaye Studio Ltd, 20 Park Road, London NW1 4SH (☎ 0171 723 2444, fax 0171 262 5966)

FREELAND, James Gourlay; s of James Gourlay Freeland (d 1989), and Jessie McRobie, *née* Brown (d 1995); *b* 3 Aug 1936; *Educ* Haileybury & ISC, Trinity Hall Cambridge (MA); *m* 27 May 1961, Diana, da of Bryce Graham Dewsbury (d 1971); 1 s (Jeremy b 1963), 2 da (Joanna (Mrs Henry B Lloyd) b 1965, Stephanie b 1971); *Career* Nat Serv RM Malta 1955–57; shipbroker and dir H Clarkson & Co Ltd London 1966–91, investmt banker (shipping) and dep chm First International Capital Ltd 1991–92, dir Braemar Shipbrokers Ltd London 1993–; Warden Worshipful Co of Shipwrights 1995– (Liveryman 1963–); *Recreations* golf, shooting; *Clubs* Brooks's, Caledonian, MCC, Jesters; *Style*— James G Freeland, Esq; ✉ 122 Rivermead Court, Ranelagh Gardens, London SW6 3SD (☎ 0171 736 1511); Grenna House, Chilson, Oxfordshire OX7 3HU (☎ 01608 676349); Braemar Shipbrokers Ltd, Windsor House, 50 Victoria Street, London SW1H 0NW (☎ 0171 233 2400)

FREELAND, Sir John Redvers; KCMG (1984, CMG 1973), QC (1987); o s of Clarence Redvers Freeland, and Freda, *née* Walker; *b* 16 July 1927; *Educ* Stowe, Corpus Christi Coll Cambridge; *m* 1952, Sarah Mary, er da of late Sidney Pascoe Hayward, QC; 1 s (Nicholas b 1956), 1 da (Petra b 1959); *Career* RN 1945 and 1948–51; called to the Bar Lincoln's Inn 1952, bencher 1985; HM Dip Serv: asst legal advsr FO 1954–63 and 1965–67, legal advsr HM Embassy Bonn 1963–65, legal cnsllr FCO 1967–70 and 1973–76, cnsllr (legal advsr) UK Mission to UN NY 1970–73, second legal advsr FCO 1976–84, legal advsr FCO 1984–87, ret; judge Arbitral Tbnl and Mixed Cmmn for the Agreement on German External Debts 1988–, judge Euro Court of Human Rights 1991–; memb US-Chile Int Cmmn of Investigation 1989–; memb: Exec Ctee David Davies Meml Inst of Int Studies 1974–, Cncl of Mgmnt British Inst of Int and Comparative Law 1984–87, Ctee of Mgmnt Inst of Advanced Legal Studies 1984–87, Bd of Govrs Br Inst of Human Rights 1992–; *Clubs* Travellers'; *Style*— Sir John Freeland, KCMG, QC

FREELAND, Rowan Charles Bayfield; s of Col Paul Rowan Bayfield Freeland, of Lacock, Wilts, and Susanna Brigitta Elizabeth, *née* Burch; *b* 13 Dec 1956; *Educ* Wellington, St Catherine's Coll Oxford (BA); *m* 12 Dec 1987, Davina Alexandra Claire, da of Maj Dennis Edward Salisbury (d 1964); 3 da (Marigold Claire Salisbury b 31 Oct 1990, Constance Margaret Alexandra b 12 Nov 1992, Beatrix Emily Faith b 1 June 1995); *Career* admitted slr 1982; ptnr Simmons & Simmons 1988–; sec The Haydn-Mozart Soc 1984–; *Recreations* family, opera, gardening, reading; *Style*— Rowan Freeland, Esq; ✉ Simmons & Simmons, 21 Wilson Street, London EC2M 2TX (☎ 0171 628 2020, fax 0171 628 2070)

FREELING, Nicolas; *b* 3 March 1927; *Educ* some scraps of education in too many schools in England, Ireland and France; *m* 1954, Cornelia; 4 s, 1 da; *Career* Nat Serv RAF 1947–49; various jobs in kitchens, hotels and restaurants throughout Europe 1950–62; writer 1960–; *Books* incl: Love in Amsterdam (1961), Because of the Cats (1963), Gun before Butter (1963), Valparaiso (1964), Double Barrel (1964), Criminal Conversation (1965), The King of the Rainy Country (1966), The Dresden Green (1966), Strike out Where Not Applicable (1967), This is the Castle (1968), Tsing-Boum (1969), Kitchen Book (1970), Over the High Side (1971), Cook Book (1972), A Long Silence (1972), Dressing of Diamond (1974), What Are the Bugles Blowing For (1975), Lake Isle (1976), Gadget (1977), The Night Lords (1978), The Widow (1979), Castang's City (1980), One Damned Thing After Another (1981), Wolfnight (1982), The Back of the North Wind (1983), No Part in Your Death (1984), A City Solitary (1985), Cold Iron (1986), Lady Macbeth (1988), Not as far as Velma (1989), Sandcastles (1989), Those in Peril (1990), A Pretty How Town (1992), You Who Know (1994), The Seacoast of Bohemia (1994), Criminal Convictions: Essays (1994), A Dwarf Kingdom (1995); *Recreations* environment, gardening, treeplanting; *Style*— Nicolas Freeling, Esq; ✉ Grandfontaine, 67130 Schirmeck, France

FREEMAN, Alan Leslie; s of Edward Ernest Freeman (d 1980), and Annie Leer, *née* Bowers (d 1965); *b* 6 July 1927; *Career* announcer: 7LA Lanceston Tasmania 1952–53, 3KZ Melbourne 1953–57; Radio Luxembourg 1958–68; BBC Radio: joined Light Prog 1960, Pick of the Pops 1961, Saturday Rock Show 1973–78; Capital Radio 1978–89; presenter BBC Radio 1: Pick of the Pops 1989–92, Saturday Rock Show 1989–94; rejoined Capital Radio 1994 (currently presenter Pick of the Pops Take 3 Saturdays and Pick of the Pops Take 3 Special Sundays); memb: British Actors Equity, Radio Acad; *Television* incl: Top of the Pops, All Systems Freeman; *Films* incl: Absolute Beginners, Just for Fun, Dr Terrors House of Horrors; *Awards* Radio Personality of the Year Sony Award 1987, Outstanding Contrib to Music Radio Radio Acad Award 1988, Top Radio Show (for The Saturday Rock Show 1974–78), Best Radio Show (for Pick of the Pops) 1971; *Recreations* opera, tennis; *Clubs* Grand Order of Water Rats; *Style*— Alan Freeman, Esq; ✉ Capital Radio plc, Euston Tower, London NW1 3DR (☎ 0171 608 6080, fax 0171 387 2345)

FREEMAN, Andrew Lawrence D; s of Richard D Freeman, and Diana L, *née* Cranwell; *b* 4 March 1963; *Educ* Balliol Coll Oxford (BA), Merton Coll Oxford (sr scholar); *m* Hazel Mary Mills; 2 s (Luke Edward Freeman-Mills b 1991, Maximilian James Downing Freeman-Mills b 1993); *Career* asst ed Global Investor Euromoney Publications 1988 (staff writer 1987); Financial Times: stockmarket reporter 1988, Euromarket reporter 1989, Lex Column 1990–92; The Economist: banking corr 1992–94, American finance ed 1995–; Silver Award Amex Bank Review annual essay competition (for The Future of Finance: capitalism without owners); *Publications* Managing Global Portfolios (co-ed C Stoakes, 1989), The Armoire de Fer and the French Revolution (1990), International Securities Lending (IBC Publications, 1991), New Tricks to Learn; a survey of international banking (The Economist, 1993), Other People's Money; a Survey of Wall Street (The Economist, 1995); *Style*— Andrew Freeman, Esq; ✉ The Economist, Editorial Department, 111 West 57th Street, New York NY 10019, USA

FREEMAN, Catherine; da of Harold Dove (d 1966), and Eileen, *née* Carroll (d 1982); *b* 10 Aug 1931; *Educ* Convent of the Assumption, St Anne's Coll Oxford (BA, MA); *m* 1, 1958 (m dis 1961), Charles Wheeler; m 2, 1962 (m dis 1976), Rt Hon John Freeman, *qv*; 2 s (Matthew b 1961, Tom b 1963), 1 da (Lucy b 1966); *Career* prodr/dir BBC TV 1954–58; Thames Television: joined as sr prodr 1976, ed daytime programmes 1976–82, controller of documentaries, features and religion 1982–86, controller of features and religion 1986–89; originator and series prodr Citizen 2000 1982–; fndr dir Dove Productions 1989–, dir One World Broadcasting Trust 1990–95; memb Devlin Ctee on Identification Procedures 1974–76, dir ICA 1983–93, memb: Lit Panel Arts Cncl 1981–84, Broadcasting, Film and Video Panel Arts Cncl 1986–88; *Style*— Mrs Catherine Freeman; ✉ 2 Chalcot Crescent, London NW1 8YD (☎ 0171 586 0448); Dove Productions, 93 Ashmill Street, London NW1 6RA (☎ 0171 262 0063, fax 0171 724 1233)

FREEMAN, Colin James; s of Albert Ernest Freeman, of Streatham, London, and Ivy Kathleen, *née* James; *b* 8 Aug 1940; *Educ* Bec GS; *m* 25 Jan 1964, Margaret Anne, da of Capt Robert Robinson (d 1983); 2 s (James b 30 Oct 1968, David b 22 March 1972); *Career* TAVR, RAMC, Lt RARO 1980; LWT: mangr of drama 1968–69, head of prog fin 1971, controller of prog fin and resources 1984, controller of transmission fin 1989–; *Recreations* walking, travelling and reading; *Style*— Colin Freeman, Esq; ✉ c/o LWT (Holdings) Ltd, The London Television Centre, Upper Ground, London SE1 9LT (☎ 0171 261 3262, fax 0171 928 0396)

FREEMAN, David Charles; s of Howard Wilfred Freeman, of Sydney, and Ruth Adair, *née* Nott; *b* 1 May 1952; *Educ* Sydney GS, Sydney Univ (BA); *m* 1 May 1985, Marie Louise, da of (Francis) John Angel (d 1968), of Pinnaroo, Australia; 1 da (Catherine Elinor b 13 May 1989), 1 s (Lachlan John b 28 Feb 1993); *Career* opera prodr; fndr and dir: Opera Factory Sydney 1973–76, Opera Factory Zurich 1976–, Opera Factory London 1981–, Opera Factory Films Ltd 1991–; assoc artist ENO 1981–; prodns incl: Monteverdi's Orfeo (ENO) 1981, Birtwistle's Punch and Judy (OFL 1981) and The Mask of Orpheus (ENO) 1986, Cosi Fan Tutte (OFL) 1986, Glass's Akhnaten (Houston, NY and London), Prokofiev's The Fiery Angel (St Petersburg, Covent Garden, Metropolitan NYC) 1992, Marschner's Der Vampyr (Zurich Opera Factory) 1993, Zimmermann's Die Soldaten (ENO) 1996; theatre: Goethe's Faust I and II (Lyric Hammersmith) 1988, adapted and directed Malory's Le Morte d'Arthur I and II (Lyric Hammersmith) 1990, The Bacchae (Xenakis' music for play) 1993; 8 TV prodns incl: all three Mozart/da Ponte operas (viz Cosi fan Tutte, Don Giovanni and The Marriage of Figaro) for Channel Four 1989–91, Punch and Judy (Channel Four) 1992; Chevalier dans L'Ordre des Arts et Lettres France 1985; *Style*— David Freeman, Esq; ✉ Opera Factory London, 9 The Leather Market, Weston Street, London SE1 3ER

FREEMAN, David John; s of Meyer Henry Freeman (d 1984), of London, and Rebecca, *née* Lubinsky (d 1980); *b* 25 Feb 1928; *Educ* Christ's Coll Finchley; *m* 19 March 1950, Iris Margaret, da of Cyril Henry Alberge (d 1980), of London; 2 s (Michael Ian b 1951, Peter Geoffrey b 1955), 1 da (Jill Barbara b 1953); *Career* Army Lt 1946–48; admitted slr 1952; fndr and sr ptnr D J Freeman 1952–92, currently conslt; Dept of Trade inspr into affairs of AEG Telefunken (UK) Ltd and Credit Collections Ltd 1977; govr Royal Shakespeare Theatre 1979–96; memb Law Soc; *Recreations* reading, theatre, gardening, golf; *Clubs* Athenaeum, Huntercombe Golf; *Style*— David J Freeman, Esq; ✉ 6 Hyde Park Gardens, London W2 (☎ 0171 262 0895); Old Greenfield House, Christmas Common, Watlington, Oxon; c/o D J Freeman, 43 Fetter Lane, London EC4A 1NA (☎ 0171 583 4055, fax 0171 353 7377, telex 894579)

FREEMAN, Dr Ernest Allan; s of William Freeman, and Margaret, *née* Sinclair; *b* 16 Jan 1932; *Educ* Sunderland Poly, King's Coll Univ of Durham (BSc, PhD), Univ of Oxford (MA), Univ of Newcastle-upon-Tyne (DSc); *m* 1954, Mary Jane Peterson; 2 da; *Career* The Sunderland Forge and Engineering Co Ltd 1948–55, The English Electric Company 1957–58, Ferranti Ltd Edinburgh 1958–59, research dir in applied electronics for Sunderland Tech Coll 1959–61, head Dept of Control Engineering Sunderland Poly 1965–72, dir Low Cost Automation Centre 1967, fell and tutor in engrg St Edmund Hall Oxford 1972–76, rector Sunderland Poly 1976–80, dir Trent Poly 1981–83; consultancy and secondment to numerous cos; referee to IEE and American IEE for papers submitted for pubn; former memb: Ctee of IEE for Control Theory, CNAA Systems and Instrumentation Bd, Electronics Divnl Bd of IEE London Ctee, Advsy Ctee to Dept of Mathematics and Statistics Thames Poly, Br Cncl Ctee for Academic Interchange with Europe, Control Theory Centre Advsy Bd Univ of Warwick, Science Bd of Science and Engrg Res Cncl, Cncl Inter Univs and Polys Cncl Higher Educn Overseas; vice chm: N Eastern Centre Ctee of IEE for Electronic and Control, Sci Res Cncl Ctee for Control Engrg (memb Educn Panel, chm Inter-Univ Inst of Engrg Control Panel); Ctee of Dirs of Polys: memb, chm Advsy Ctee on Computing, Acad Affairs Ctee, memb Technician Educn Liaison Gp, memb Fin and Planning Ctee; external examiner various Univ and Polys; author of many contribs to the Proceedings IEE and other scientific jls; Mather Scholarship 1955–57, Heaviside Prize 1974; CEng, CMath; FIEE 1968, FIMA 1969, FRSA 1980; *Recreations* photography, swimming, bridge, browsing around antiques; *Style—* Dr Ernest Allan Freeman; ✉ 12 Rolfe Place, Headington, Oxford OX3 0DS

FREEMAN, Prof George Kenneth; s of Cdr John Kenneth Herbert Freeman, RN (ret), of Brighton, E Sussex, and Jean Forbes, *née* Irving; *b* 4 Aug 1944; *Educ* Kingswood Sch Bath Avon, Trinity Coll Cambridge (BChir), St Thomas' Hosp Med Sch London (MRCP, MRCGP, FRCGP), MD (Cantab); *m* 1, 1968 (m dis 1980), Marjorie Rose, *née* Downing; 1 da (Anna b 1971), 1 s (Thomas b 1973); m 2, 1982 (sep 1993), Dr Jennifer Field; 2 s (Michael b 1983, Timothy b 1986); *partner* Dr Alison Hill; *Career* house offr St Thomas's Hosp then Southampton Gen Hosp 1968–69, SHO Portsmouth Hosp, Wessex Neuro Centre Southampton, Southampton Gen Hosp then Knowle Hosp Fareham 1969–71, GP trainee Southampton 1971–72, GP Aldermoor Health Centre Southampton 1972–93, lectr then sr lectr in primary med care Univ of Southampton 1972–93 (actg head of dept 1991–93), prof of gen practice Charing Cross and Westminster Med Sch 1993–, pt/t GP London 1993–; Br Cncl exchange visit Univs of Utrecht and Nijmegen 1978, Janet Nash visiting fell Univ of Cincinatti Ohio 1989; sec Assoc of Univ Depts of Gen Practice 1985–91; *Recreations* steam railways, classical organs and their music, DIY in Victorian houses, foreign travel, child raising and support; *Style—* Prof George Freeman; ✉ Charing Cross and Westminster Medical School, 4th Floor, Department of Public Health and Primary Care, Chelsea and Westminster Hospital, 369 Fulham Road, London SW10 9NH (☎ 0181 746 8078, fax 0181 746 8151)

FREEMAN, Gillian; da of Jack Freeman (d 1981), of London and Henley on Thames, and Freda, *née* Davids; *b* 5 Dec 1929; *Educ* Francis Holland, Lynton House Maidenhead, Univ of Reading (BA); *m* 12 Sept 1955, Edward Thorpe, s of Ronald Thorpe (d 1986), of Hythe, Hants; 2 da (Harriet Amelia b 1957, Matilda Helen Rachel b 1960); *Career* author; *Plays* incl: Pursuit (NT 1969), Mayerling-Scenario (Royal Ballet 1978); *Films* incl: The Leather Boys (1963), That Cold Day in the Park (1969), Day After the Fair (1987); *Books* 12 novels incl: The Liberty Man (1955), The Leather Boys (1961), The Marriage Machine (1975), An Easter Egg Hunt (1981), Termination Rock (1989); non-fiction incl: The Undergrowth of Literature (1967), The Schoolgirl Ethic: The Life and Work of Angela Brazil (1976), Ballet Genius (with Edward Thorpe, 1988); *Style—* Ms Gillian Freeman; ✉ c/o Rochelle Stevens & Co, 2 Terretts Place, Upper Street, London N1 1QZ

FREEMAN, Prof Hugh Lionel; s of the late Bernard Freeman, and Dora Doris, *née* Kahn; *b* 4 Aug 1929; *Educ* Altrincham GS, St John's Coll Oxford (DM, MA); *m* 1957, (Sally) Joan, da of Philip Casket; 3 s, 1 da; *Career* Capt RAMC 1956–58; house surgn Manchester Royal Infirmary 1955, registrar Bethlem Royal and Maudsley Hosps 1958–60, sr registrar Littlemore Hosp Oxford 1960–61; conslt psychiatrist: Salford Royal Hosp 1961–70, Hope Hosp 1961–88; hon conslt: Salford Mental Health Trust, Univ of Manchester Sch of Med 1988–; WHO conslt: Grenada 1970, Chile 1978, Philippines 1979, Bangladesh 1981, Greece 1985; rapporteur: WHO Conf on Mental Health Servs Trieste 1984, WHO Ruanda 1985, Cncl of Europe Conf on Health in Cities 1985; ed: Br Jl of Psychiatry 1983–93 (asst ed 1978–83), Current Opinion in Psychiatry 1986–93; lectr worldwide; vice chm MIND 1983–87; hon prof Univ of Salford, hon visiting fell Green Coll Oxford; memb: Mercian Regnl Ctee Nat Tst 1986–92, Mental Health Cmmn 1983, Mental Health Review Tbnls, City of Manchester Bldgs Panel, Home Sec's Ctee on Fear of Crime 1989; vice chm Manchester Heritage Tst; corresponding fell American Psychiatric Assoc; hon memb: Chilean Soc of Psychiatry Neurology and Neurosurgery, Egyptian Psychiatric Assoc, Polish Psychiatric Assoc, Hungarian Psychiatric Assoc, Bulgarian Soc for Neurosciences; Freeman City of London, Liveryman Worshipful Soc of Apothecaries; FRCPsych, FFPHM; *Publications* Trends in Mental Health Services (1963), New Aspects of the Mental Health Service (jt ed, 1968), La Malattie del Potere (1984), Mental Health Services in Europe (1985), Mental Health and the Environment (ed, 1985), 150 Years of British Psychiatry (jt ed, Vol I 1991, Vol II 1996), Community Psychiatry (jt ed, 1991); *Recreations* architecture, travel, music; *Clubs* United Oxford & Cambridge Univ; *Style—* Prof Hugh Freeman; ✉ 21 Montagu Square, London W1H 1RE (☎ 0171 486 2604)

FREEMAN, Sir James Robin; 3 Bt (UK 1945), of Murtle, Co Aberdeen; s of Sir (John) Keith Noel Freeman, 2 Bt (d 1981), and Patricia Denison, *née* Thomas; *b* 21 July 1955; *Heir* none; *Style—* Sir James Freeman, Bt; ✉ c/o Midland Bank, 192 Hoe St, Walthamstow, London E17 4QN

FREEMAN, Rt Hon John; MBE (1943), PC (1966); eldest s of Horace Freeman, barrister-at-law (d 1954); *b* 19 Feb 1915; *Educ* Westminster, BNC Oxford; *m* 1, 1938 (m dis 1948), Elizabeth Allen, *née* Johnston; m 2, 1948, Margaret Ista Mabel, *née* Kerr (d 1957); 1 adopted da; m 3, 1962 (m dis 1976), Catherine, *qv*, da of Harold Dove and formerly wife of Charles Wheeler; 2 s, 1 da; m 4, 1976, Judith, *née* Mitchell; 2 da; *Career* served WWII; MP (Lab): Watford Div of Herts 1945–50, Borough of Watford 1950–55; New Statesman: asst ed 1951–58, dep ed 1958–60, ed 1961–65; Br high cmmr in India 1965–68, ambass in Washington 1969–71; chm: LWT 1971–84, ITN 1976–81, LWT (Hldgs) 1976–84, Hutchinson Ltd 1978–83, Page & Moy (Hldgs) 1979–84; vice pres RTS 1975–84 (winner Gold medal for distinguished service to the broadcasting industry 1981), chm BFI 1976–82; visiting prof of int rels Univ of Calif at Davis 1985–90, hon fell Brasenose Coll Oxford 1968; Hon LLD Univ of S Carolina; *Style—* The Rt Hon John Freeman, MBE

FREEMAN, Michael Alexander Reykers; s of Donald George Freeman (d 1937), of Ockley, Surrey, and Florence Julia, *née* Elms (d 1962); *b* 17 Nov 1931; *Educ* Stowe, Corpus Christi Coll Cambridge (Open scholar, BA, MB BCh, MD, Bacon Prize), London Hosp Med Coll (FRCS(Eng)); *m* 1, 1951 (m dis), Elizabeth Jean; 1 s (Jonathan b 29 May 1954), 1 da (Julianne b 5 June 1952); m 2, 1959 (m dis), Janet Edith; 1 s (Dominic b 3 April 1965), 1 da (Emma b 18 May 1962); m 3, 26 Sept 1968, Patricia, da of Leslie Gill (d 1976), of Bristol; 1 s (James b 14 April 1971 d 1971), 1 da (Clare b 31 Dec 1972); *Career* clinical trg in med surgery and orthopaedic surgery London Hosp, Westminster Hosp and Middx Hosp; awarded Copeman medal, Robert Jones Gold medal, co-fndr and dir Biomechanics Unit Dept of Med Engrg Imperial Coll 1966–79, sr lectr in orthopaedic surgery London Hosp Med Coll 1968–95, conslt orthopaedic surgn London Hosp 1968–95, hon conslt orthopaedic surgn Royal Hospitals Tst 1996–; co-dir Bone and Joint Res Unit London Hosp Med Coll 1975; past pres: European Fedn of Nat Societies of Orthopaedics and Traumatology, Br Orthopaedic Soc, Br Hip Soc, Int Hip Soc; past memb: Bd of Govrs London Hosp, Clinical Res Bd MRC; Yeoman Worshipful Soc of Apothecaries; AAOS, BOA, RSM, BES, ORS, IHS, SICOT; *Books* Adult Articular Cartilage (ed, 1973), The Scientific Basis of Joint Replacement (ed with S A V Swanson, 1977), Arthritis of the Knee (ed, 1980), Osteoarthritis in the Young Adult Hip (ed with D Reynolds, 1984); *Style—* Mr Michael Freeman; ✉ 79 Albert St, London NW1 (☎ 0171 387 0817, fax 0171 388 5731); 149 Harley St, London W1 (☎ 0171 935 4444 ext 4201, fax 0171 935 7780)

FREEMAN, Prof Michael David Alan; s of Raphael Freeman, of London, and Florence, *née* Wax; *b* 25 Nov 1943; *Educ* Hasmonean GS Hendon, UCL (LLB, LLM); *m* 23 July 1967, Vivien Ruth, da of Sidney Brook, of Leeds; 1 s (Jeremy Simon Richard b 1973), 1 da (Hilary Rachel b 1971); *Career* called to the Bar Gray's Inn 1969; lectr in law: E London Coll of Commerce 1965–66, Univ of Leeds 1967–69 (asst lectr 1966–67); reader in law UCL 1979–84 (lectr 1969–79), prof of English law Univ of London (tenable at UCL) 1984–; ed: Annual Survey of Family Law 1983–, Current Legal Problems 1992–, Int Jl of Children's Rights 1992–; dir of trg Nicholson Graham and Jones 1989–91; formerly govr S Hampstead HS; *Books* incl: Introduction To Jurisprudence (1 edn 1972, 4 edn 1994), The Children Act 1975 (1976), Violence In The Home (1979), Cohabitation Outside Marriage (1983), The Rights and Wrongs of Children (1983), Essays In Family Law (1986), Dealing With Domestic Violence (1987), Medicine Ethics And The Law (1988), Children, their Families and the Law (1992), The Ideologies of Children's Rights (1992); *Recreations* opera, theatre, cricket, literature; *Clubs* Middlesex CCC; *Style—* Prof Michael Freeman; ✉ University College London, Gower Street, London WC1E 6BT (☎ 0171 391 1443, fax 0171 387 9597)

FREEMAN, Dr Paul Illife; CB (1992); s of late John Percy Freeman, and Hilda Freeman; *Educ* Univ of Manchester (BSc, PhD); *m* 1959, Enid Ivy May Freeman; 1 s, 1 da; *Career* post doctoral fell Nat Res Cncl of Canada 1959–61, res scientist Dupont De Nemours Co Ltd USA 1961–64; princ sci offr Nat Physical Laboratory 1970–74 (sr sci offr 1964–70), exec offr Res Requirements Bds DTI 1973–77; dir: Computor Aided Design Centre 1977–83, Nat Engrg Laboratory 1980–83, Central Computer and Telecommunications Agency HM Treasy 1983–88; controller and chief exec HM Stationery Office and The Queen's printer of acts of Parliament 1989–95, ret; author of various scientific papers; memb: Advsy Cncl Civil Serv Coll 1983–88, Bd Nat Computer Centre 1983–88, Cncl Univ of E Anglia 1994–; visiting prof Univ of Strathclyde 1981–86; CIMgt 1995; *Recreations* reading, walking, gardening; *Style—* Dr Paul Freeman, CB

FREEMAN, Peter John; s of Cdr John Kenneth Herbert Freeman, MVO, RN (ret), of Brighton, and Jean Forbes, *née* Irving; *b* 2 Oct 1948; *Educ* Kingswood Sch Bath (scholarship), Goethe Inst Berlin, Trinity Coll Cambridge (exhibitioner, MA), Inns of Court Sch of Law, Université Libre de Bruxelles (Licence Spéciale en Droit Européen); *m* 1972, Elizabeth Mary, da of Frank and Barbara Rogers; 2 da (Catharine b 1 Nov 1977, Sarah b 20 July 1988), 2 s (Christopher b 29 May 1979, Henry b 22 March 1983); *Career* called to the Bar 1972, requalified as slr 1977; Simmons & Simmons: joined 1973, ptnr 1978–, head EC and Competition Law Gp 1987–, managing ptnr Commercial and Trade Law Devpt 1994–; advsr to UK and int cos and trade assocs on EC law (especially competition and trade law) and UK competition law; fndr memb (and currently vice chm) Regulatory Policy Inst Oxford (Hertford Coll), memb Jt Working Party of Bar and Law Socs on Competition Law; *Publications* Butterworths Competition Law (jt gen ed), UK Competition Law Reform - a practitioner's view (RPI, 1993); *Style—* Peter Freeman, Esq; ✉ Simmons & Simmons, 21 Wilson Street, London EC2M 2TX (☎ 0171 628 2020, fax 0171 628 2070)

FREEMAN, Sir Ralph; kt (1970), CVO (1964), CBE (1952, MBE (mil) 1945); s of Sir Ralph Freeman (d 1950), and Mary, *née* Lines (d 1958); *b* 3 Feb 1911; *Educ* Uppingham, Worcester Coll Oxford (MA); *m* 19 May 1939, Joan Elizabeth, da of Col John George Rose, DSO, VD (d 1973), of Wynberg, Cape Town, SA; 2 s (Anthony b 29 March 1946, Hugh b 16 Feb 1949), 1 da (Elizabeth b 10 May 1942); *Career* Civilian Serv, Admty and other war work 1939–42, cmmnd 2 Lt RE 1943, served RE 1943–45 at Experimental Bridging Estab, seconded as bridging advsr to CE 21 Army Gp HQ NW Europe campaign 1944, Maj 1945; Col Engr and Tport Staff Corps RE (TA), Col Cmdg 1969–74, ret 1976; chartered engr; construction engr: Dorman Long & Co (SA, Rhodesia, Denmark) 1932–36 and 1937–39, Braithwaite & Co 1936–37; Freeman Fox and Ptnrs: staff 1939–43 and 1946, ptnr 1947–79, sr ptnr 1963–79, conslt 1979–88; pres Inst Civil Engrs 1966–67, chm ACE 1974–75, pres Welding Inst 1974–76; consltg engr Sandringham Estate 1949–76, memb Royal Fine Art Cmmn 1968–85; chm Limpsfield Common Mgmnt Ctee 1957–82 (memb 1954–82, under Nat Trust from 1972); hon fell Worcester Coll Oxford 1980, Hon Doctorate Univ Surrey, Hon MConsE, Hon MIRoyE, Hon FIMechE, hon fell Zimbabwe Inst of Engrs, emeritus memb Smeatonian Soc, FEng 1976 (fndr fell), FICE, FWeldI, FRSA, FASCE; kt (4th class) Order of Orange Nassau 1945; *Recreations* carpentry, metalwork, writing letters; *Clubs* Army and Navy, Leander; *Style—* Sir Ralph Freeman, CVO, CBE, FEng; ✉ Ballards Shaw, Ballards Lane, Limpsfield, Oxted, Surrey RH8 0SN (☎ and fax 01883 723284)

FREEMAN, Prof Raymond (Ray); s of Albert Freeman (d 1940), and Hilda Frances, *née* Bush (d 1983); *b* 6 Jan 1932; *Educ* Nottingham HS, Lincoln Coll Oxford (MA, DPhil, DSc); *m* 19 April 1958, Anne-Marie Cathérine, da of Philippe Périnet-Marquet (d 1969); 2 s (Jean-Marc b 1964, Lawrence b 1969), 3 da (Dominique b 1959, Anne b 1960, Louise b 1962); *Career* ingénieur Centre D'Études Nucléaires de Saclay France 1957–59, sr sci offr Nat Physical Laboratory Teddington Middx 1959–63, mangr Nuclear Magnetic Resonance Res Varian Assoc Palo Alto California 1963–73; Univ of Oxford: lectr in physical chemistry 1973–87, fell Magdalen Coll 1973–87, Aldrichian praelector in chemistry 1982–87; Univ of Cambridge: John Humphrey Plummer prof of magnetic resonance 1987–, fell Jesus Coll 1987–; pres Int Soc of Magnetic Resonance 1989–92; Leverhulme medal Royal Soc 1990; FRS 1979; *Books* A Handbook of Nuclear Magnetic Resonance (1987), Spin Choreography: Basic Steps in High Resolution NMR (1997); *Style—* Prof Ray Freeman, FRS; ✉ 29 Bentley Rd, Cambridge CB2 2AW (☎ 01223 323958); Department of Chemistry, University of Cambridge, Lensfied Rd, Cambridge CB2 1EW (☎ 01223 336450)

FREEMAN, Richard Downing; OBE (1936); s of John Lawrence Freeman (d 1989), of Victoria, Australia, and Phyllis Jean, *née* Walker (d 1984); *b* 28 Sept 1936; *Educ* Trinity GS Melbourne, Univ of Melbourne (BComm, MComm, Lacrosse blue); *m* 21 May 1960, Diana Lynne, da of Harold Thomas Cranwell; 3 s (Christopher Thomas b 7 Aug 1961, Andrew Lawrence Downing b 4 March 1963), Timothy David b 4 Dec 1965); *Career* economist; British Petroleum: joined group as jr exec BP Australia 1955, Cooper trainee BP London then BP Germany, asst aviation mangr BP Australia until 1963; lectr then sr lectr and actg prof Univ of Melbourne 1963–70, econ advsr then sr econ advsr HM Treasury London 1971–73, head of division OECD Paris 1973–84, corporate chief economist ICI plc 1984–; econ advsr Ctee for Econ Devpt of Australia 1963–70, review and assoc ed Economic Record 1965–70, ed OECD Economic Outlook 1976–78; chm: Econ Appraisal Ctee Chemical Industries Assoc 1984–, Econ Ctee CEFIC 1989–92, CBI Working Gp on Environmental Econ Instruments 1990–, Research Centres Bd ESRC 1994–96, Research Priorities Bd ESRC 1996–; memb: CBI Econ Situation Ctee 1984–92, Croham Ctee on Exchange Rates 1985–86, Chemical Trade Ctee NEDO 1985–86, Cncl Soc of Business Economists 1985–, Res Ctee Royal Inst of International Affrs 1988–91, Econ Ctee ESRC 1985–88, Industry Economy and Environment Ctee ESRC 1988–92, City and Industry Finance Ctee NEDO 1988–90, Cncl Royal Economic Soc 1989–94, Business and Trade Bd Chemical Industries Assoc 1989–, Cncl Inst of Fiscal Studies, Innovation Advsy Bd Action Gp on Industry-City Communications 1990–91, CBI Working Gps on Inflation and on Economic and Monetary Union 1990, Environmental Policy Gp ICAEW 1991–92, Innovation Advsy Bd DTI 1991–93, Research Centres Bd ESRC 1992–93, Econ Affrs Ctee CBI 1992–, Sub-Ctee on Monetary Policy CBI 1992–93, Cncl ESRC 1993–; fell Soc of Business Economists; *Publications* author of various articles in jls and chapters in books, incl Environmental Costs and International Competitiveness (in Green Futures for Economic Growth, ed Terry Barker and David Cope 1991), The Future of UK Manufacturing (in jl The Business Economist Spring 1991), How the UK Economy Should Be Run in the 1990s (editorial of The Business Economist Winter 1992); *Style—* Richard Freeman, Esq, OBE; ✉ Cranford, Coley Avenue, Woking, Surrey

GU22 7BS (☎ 01483 772247); ICI plc, 9 Millbank, London SW1P 3JF (☎ 0171 798 5428, fax 0171 798 5170)

FREEMAN, Roger John; s of Lt Cdr Harold Cecil Freeman, MBE, VRD (d 1984), of Much Hadham, Herts, and Jacqueline Mary Freeman; *b* 21 June 1944; *Educ* Wellington, Exeter Univ (BA), Wharton Sch Univ of Pennsylvania (MBA); *m* 12 May 1971, Kitty, da of Juan Carlos Yegros (d 1966), of Asuncion, Paraguay; 2 s (Jonathan b 1981, Christopher b 1989); *Career* Bank of London and S America 1968–72, Harris Tst 1974–79, Libra Bank 1979–90 (gen mangr 1985–90), dir Morgan Grenfell & Co Ltd 1990–96; *Recreations* sport; *Clubs* MCC; *Style—* Roger Freeman, Esq; ✉ 108 Highgate West Hill, London N6 6AP (☎ 0181 340 1227, fax 0181 341 1890)

FREEMAN, Rt Hon Roger Norman; PC (1993), MP (C) Kettering (majority 11,154); s of Norman and Marjorie Freeman; *b* 27 May 1942; *Educ* Whitgift Sch, Balliol Coll Oxford (MA); *m* 1969, Jennifer Margaret, *née* Watson; 1 s, 1 da; *Career* pres Oxford Univ Cons Assoc 1964, md Bow Publications 1968 (former memb Cncl and treas Bow Group), md Lehman Brothers 1972–83 (joined Lehman Bros US 1969, first Englishman invited to join US ptnrship); Parly candidate (C) Don Valley 1979, MP (C) 1983–; Parly under sec of state: armed forces MOD 1986–88, Dept of Health 1988–90; min of state: Dept of Tport 1990–92, for public transport Dept of Tport 1992–94, for defence procurement MOD 1994–95; chllr of the Duchy of Lancaster and cabinet min for the public serv 1995–; non-exec dir: Martini & Rossi Ltd, McCormick International Investments Ltd; fndr memb Hundred Gp of UK CA Fin Dirs; FCA 1978; *Publications* incl: Pensions Policy, Professional Practice, A Fair Deal for Water; *Recreations* travel; *Clubs* Carlton, Kennel; *Style—* The Rt Hon Roger Freeman, MP; ✉ House of Commons, London SW1A 0AA (☎ 0171 219 6436)

FREEMAN, Roland John Michael; JP (1972); s of Cornelius Alexander Freeman (d 1972), of London, and Marjorie Dolores Kathleen Freeman (d 1974); *b* 7 May 1927; *Educ* Chippenham GS, St Joseph's Coll Beulah Hill, Coll of St Mark and St John, LSE; *m* 18 Dec 1976, Marian, da of John Kilroy, of Rugby; *Career* sch master 1947–53, Cons Res Dept 1958–59, dir London Municipal Soc 1959–61, campaign mangr Aims of Indust 1961–65; md: PR (Indust) Ltd 1965–69, Welbeck City Ltd 1969–76, Roland Freeman Ltd 1976–94; dir LWT Ltd 1981–89, memb LWT Prog Advsy Bd 1989–93; currently studying composition at Univ of Southampton; composer Requiem in B minor for soloists, chorus and organ; Wandsworth Borough Cncl 1949–65 (ldr and chm Fin Ctee), GLC 1967–70 and 1975–81 (chm Fin Ctee 1967–69); Parly candidate: (Cons) Nuneaton 1974, (SDP/Alliance) Tonbridge and Malling 1983; memb Alliance Central Ctee Gen Election 1987; joined Labour Pty 1989; Liveryman Worshipful Co of Tallow Chandlers 1970; FCIS 1962, MIPR 1986; *Books* Becoming a Councillor (2 edn, 1975); *Recreations* music, mountain walking, gardening; *Clubs* Reform; *Style—* Roland Freeman, Esq, JP; ✉ Brockswood, Canal Lane, Alderbury, Wiltshire SP5 3NY (☎ 01722 710190)

FREEMAN, Simon David; s of Alfred Freeman (d 1976), of Hove, Sussex, and Doris Freeman; *b* 16 Aug 1952; *Educ* Hove GS for Boys' Sussex, Worcester Coll Oxford (BA); *Career* graduate training scheme Mirror Group Plymouth 1974–76, reporter Evening Standard London 1976–79, Sunday Times 1979–89 (rep, co ed (Insight), special writer, foreign corr), chief foreign corr Sunday Correspondent 1989–90, news ed The European London 1990–91, freelance writer 1992– (The Sunday Telegraph, Esquire, Scotland on Sunday, Vanity Fair, The Observer), special writer The Guardian 1992–; NCTJ proficiency certificate; runner up Inst of Journalists Young Journalist of the Year 1975, commended Reporter of the Year Br Press Awards 1980, commended Argos Press Awards 1982; memb NUJ; *Style—* Simon Freeman, Esq; ✉ c/o Levy Gee, 66 Wigmore Street, London W1H 0HQ (☎ 0171 467 4000)

FREEMAN-GRENVILLE, Dr Greville Stewart Parker; s of Rev Ernest Charles Freeman (d 1936), of Shipton-under-Wychwood, Oxon, and Agnes Mary Gibson, *née* Parker (d 1966); surname changed from Freeman to Freeman-Grenville by Decree of the Lord Lyon King of Arms 1950; *b* 29 June 1918; *Educ* Eastbourne Coll, Worcester Coll Oxford (BA, BLitt, MA, DPhil); *m* 29 Aug 1950, Beatrice Mary Grenville, Lady Kinloss, *qv*, da of Rev the Hon Luis Francis Chandos Temple Morgan-Grenville, Master of Kinloss (d 1944); 1 s (Bevil David Stewart Chandos, Master of Kinloss b 1953), 2 da (Teresa Mary Nugent b 1957, Hester Josephine Anne b 1960); *Career* WWII Capt Royal Berks Regt, Personnel Selection Staff 1939–46; HM Overseas Civil Service Tanganyika 1951–60; educnl advsr Aden Protectorate 1961–64; sr res fell: Univ of Ghana 1964–66, Univ of York 1966–69; hon fell Univ of York 1969–, prof of history State Univ of NY 1969–74; visiting fell Dept of Archaeology Univ of York 1995–; author and writer; memb: Ctee on Fontes Historiae Africanae British Acad 1972–95, Cncl The Hakluyt Soc 1986–90, Cncl Royal Asiatic Soc 1992–, Exec Ctee Palestine Exploration Fund 1992–; contrib to: Encyclopaedia Britannica, Encyclopaedia of Islam, various journals; Papal Cross Pro Ecclesia et Pontifice 1984, Kt of the Holy Sepulchre 1982; fell Royal Numismatic Soc 1956–95, FSA 1961, FRAS 1966; *Books* The Medieval History of the Coast of Tanganyika (1962), The East African Coast: Select Documents (1962), The Muslim and Christian Calendars (1963 and 1977), Chronology of African History (1973), Chronology of World History (1976), Modern Atlas of African History (1976), The Queen's Lineage: from AD 495 to HM The Queen Elizabeth II (1977), Atlas of British History (1977), The Mombasa Rising of 1631 (1980), The Beauty of Cairo (1981), The Beauty of Jerusalem (2 edn, 1988), The Beauty of Rome (1988), The Swahili Coast 2nd to 19th Centuries (1988), A New Atlas of African History (1991), Memoirs of an Arabian Princess (by Emily Said-Ruete, ed, 1982 and 1995), Historical Atlas of the Middle East (1993), The Basilica of the Annunciation Nazareth (1993), The Basilica of the Holy Sepulchre Jerusalem (1993), The Basilica of the Nativity Bethlehem (1993), The Islamic and Christian Calendars, AD 622–2222 (AH 1–1650) (1995), The Holy Land: a Pilgrim's Guide to Israel, Jordan and the Sinai (1996); *Recreations* travel; *Clubs* Civil Service; *Style—* Dr G S P Freeman-Grenville, FSA; ✉ North View House, Sheriff Hutton, York YO6 1PT (☎ 01347 878447)

FREEMANTLE, Brian Harry; s of Harold Freemantle, and Violet, *née* Street; *b* 10 June 1936; *Educ* Bitterne Park Secdy Modern Sch Bitterne Park Southampton; *m* 1956, Maureen Hazel, *née* Tipney; 3 da (Victoria b 13 June 1957, Emma b 2 Aug 1973, Charlotte b 13 July 1975); *Career* reporter: New Milton Advertiser 1953–58, Bristol Evening World 1958, London Evening News 1959–61; reporter and asst foreign ed Daily Express 1961–68; foreign ed: Daily Sketch 1969–71, Daily Mail 1971–75; author; nominee Mystery Writers of America Edgar Allan Poe award 1985; *Books* non fiction incl: KGB, CIA, The Fix (int drug trade), The Steal (industl espionage); novels incl: The Factory, The Bearpit, The Run Around, The Kremlin Kiss, The Man Who Wanted Tomorrow, 10 books in The Charlie Muffin series; *Recreations* reading, driving; *Clubs* Lord's Taverners; *Style—* Brian Freemantle, Esq; ✉ 4 Great Minster St, Winchester, Hampshire SO23 9HA (☎ 01962 861212); Jonathan Clowes Ltd, 10 Iron Bridge House, Bridge Approach, London NW1 8BD (☎ 0171 722 7674, fax 0171 722 7677)

FREER, (Joan Marian) Penelope (Mrs Terence Fuller); da of Frederick George Sinderby Freer, of Bromley, Kent, and Doris Florence, *née* Wynne; *b* 6 Feb 1950; *Educ* Bromley HS for Girls, Lady Margaret Hall Oxford (exhibitioner, BA, MA); *m* 1975, Terence Ronald Fuller, s of Cecil Ronald Fuller; 1 s (Timothy b 17 Dec 1980), 1 da (Emily b 17 July 1983); *Career* articled clerk Lee & Pembertons 1971–73, asst slr Nabarro Nathanson 1973–75, ptnr Freshfields 1979–96 (asst slr 1975–79); memb The City of London Slrs' Co; memb Law Soc; *Clubs* Reform; *Style—* Ms Penelope Freer; (☎ 0181 693 3739, fax 0181 333 2151)

FREER, Air Chief Marshal Sir Robert William George; GBE (1981, CBE 1966), KCB (1977); s of William Freer (d 1979), of Stretton, Cirencester, Glos, and Margaret Jane, *née* Clements (d 1957); *b* 1 Sept 1923; *Educ* Gosport GS; *m* 1950, Margaret Tinkler, 2 da of late John William Elkington, of Ruskington Manor, nr Sleaford, Lincs; 1 s (Adrian), 1 da (Anna); *Career* flying instr 1944–47, RAF Coll Cranwell 1947–50; 54 and 614 Fighter Sgdns 1950–52, Queen's Commendation 1955; cmd 92 Fighter Sqdn 1955–57, USAF Acad 1958–60, staff of CDS 1961–63, station cdr RAF Seletar 1963–66, DD Def Plans 1966–67, Air ADC to HM The Queen 1969–71, dep cmdt RAF Staff Coll 1969–71, SASO HQ Near East Air Force 1971–72, AOC 11 Gp 1972–75, dir gen orgn MOD Air 1975, AOC 18 Gp 1975–78, dep C-in-C RAF Strike Cmd 1979–80, Air Chief Marshal, cmdt RCDS 1980–82, ret; dir: Rediffusion 1982–88, Rediffusion Simulation Ltd 1985–88, British Manufacture and Research Co Ltd 1982–88, Pilatus Britten-Norman 1988–96; pres: RAF LTA 1975–81, Sports Cncl 1980–82; chm: BM Pension Tstees Ltd 1985–88; CIMgt, FRAeS; *Recreations* tennis, golf, hill-walking; *Clubs* RAF, Hankley Common Golf, All England Lawn Tennis; *Style—* Air Chief Marshal Sir Robert Freer, GBE, KCB; ✉ c/o Lloyds Bank, 75 Castle St, Farnham, Surrey

FREESON, Rt Hon Reginald Yarnitz; PC (1976); *b* 24 Feb 1926; *Educ* Jewish Orphanage W Norwood; *m*; 1 s, 1 da; *Career* served in Army 1944–48; journalist 1948–64; memb: Willesden Cncl 1952–65 (ldr 1958–65), Brent Cncl 1964–68 (chm 1964–65); MP (Lab) Willesden E and Brent E 1964–87, PPS to Min Transport 1964–67; Parly sec: Miny Power 1967–69, Miny Housing and Local Govt 1969–70; oppn front bench spokesman Housing, Construction and Urban Affairs 1970–74, min of Housing and Construction (responsible for inner cities, planning, land and local govt) 1974–79, oppn front bench spokesman Social Security 1979–80; memb: Select Ctee on the Environment 1980–83 (chm 1982–83), Cncl of Europe Parly Assembly 1983–87, Western Euro Assembly 1983–87; memb: Jewish Welfare Bd 1971–74 (memb Exec 1973–74), Housing Centre Tst 1987–, Cwlth Parly Assoc, Int Voluntary Service, UNA Int Serv, Town and Country Planning Assoc, Nat Tst, YHA; fndr chm Willesden/Brent Community Rels Cncl and Cncl of Voluntary Service 1959; fndr memb: War on Want, CND, Campaign for Democracy in Ulster 1964; fndr ed Searchlight (against facism and anti-semitism) 1964–66; dir J B G Housing Soc 1982–83, fndr Reg Freeson & Associates (Urban Renewal Conslts) 1986–, chm Poale Zion 1981–85 (political sec 1987–94), ed Jewish Vanguard 1988–94, dir Lab Friends of Israel 1992–93; memb: Lab Party 1948, Co-operative Party 1958, Fabian Soc 1958, Poale Zion-Labour Zionists 1964, Int Centre for Peace in the ME 1982, Lab Finance and Industry Gp 1991, Socialist Environment Resources Assoc; *Recreations* gardening, reading, theatre, music, country walking, town and country planning, environment, urban regeneration and governance, constitutional reform, int devpt and serv; *Style—* The Rt Hon Reginald Freeson; ✉ 159 Chevening Rd, London NW6 6DZ (☎ and fax 0181 969 7407)

FREESTONE, Susan Mathilda (Sue); da of Charles Anthony Freestone, of Canada, and June Freestone (d 1991); *b* 27 March 1948; *Educ* Westdale Collegiate Sch Canada, North London Poly (BA(Eng)); *m* 1, 1966 (m dis 1978), Anthony Ashley Frank Meyer; 1 da (Sophie Mathilda Barbadee b 1972); partner, 1978–85, Donald John Macintyre,*qv*; 1 s (James Kenneth Freestone Macintyre b 1979); m 2, 1989, Vivian Louis White; *Career* bookseller 1966–69, business forecaster IBM 1969–72, ed William Heinemann 1984–1990, ed dir: Mandarin Books 1990–91, Jonathan Cape 1991; publishing dir Hutchinson 1992–; *Recreations* smoking and lunching; *Clubs* Groucho; *Style—* Ms Sue Freestone; ✉ Hutchinson, Random House, 20 Vauxhall Bridge Road, London SW1V 2SA (☎ 0171 973 9000, fax 0171 233 7870)

FREETH, Peter Stewart; s of Alfred William Freeth, of Fovant, Wilts; *b* 15 April 1938; *Educ* King Edward's GS Aston Birmingham, Slade Sch of Fine Art, Br Sch of Rome; *m* 5 August 1967, Mariolina, da of Prof Leonardo Meliadò, of Rome; 2 s (Dylan b 5 July 1969, Paul b 1 July 1972); *Career* artist; tutor in printmaking Royal Acad Schs 1967–; pt/t posts: Colchester Sch of Art, Camden Inst, Kingsway Coll; RE 1987, RA 1992 (ARA 1990); *Solo Exhibitions* Christopher Mendez Gallery London 1987 and 1989, Royal Acad 1991; *Public Collections* Br Museum, V&A, Arts Cncl, Fitzwilliam Museum, Metropolitan Museum NYC, Nat Gallery Washington DC, Harvard Univ; *Awards* Prix de Rome 1960, Royal Acad Best Print Prize 1986, Wakayama Biennale Print Prize 1989; *Recreations* music, reading; *Style—* Peter Freeth, Esq, RA, RE; ✉ c/o The Royal Academy, London W1V 0DS

FREI, Matt; s of Peter Frei, of Baden-Baden, and Anita Frei; *b* 26 Nov 1963; *Educ* Westminster Sch, St Peter's Coll Oxford (MA); *partner* Penelope Quested; *Career* BBC Radio: disc jockey German Service 1986–87, prodr Current Affairs World Service 1987–88, reporter Jerusalem 1988–89, corr Bonn 1989–91, corr Foreign Affairs 1991–92, corr S Europe Rome 1992–; regular contrib: The Spectator, London Review of Books, Wall Street Journal; *Clubs* Gridiron (Oxford), Travellers' (assoc memb); *Style—* Matt Frei, Esq; ✉ BBC Rome Bureau, la Piazza Colegio Romano, 00186 Rome, Italy

FREMLIN, Celia Margaret (Mrs Leslie Minchin); da of Heaver Stuart Fremlin (d 1953), of Heavers, Ryarsh, nr Maidstone, Kent, and Margaret, *née* Addiscott (d 1932); *b* 20 June 1914; *Educ* Berkhamsted Sch for Girls, Somerville Coll Oxford (open scholar, BA, BLitt, Canon Gamble prize for poetry); *m* 1, 1942, Dr Elia Sidney Goller, s of Dr Simon Goller; 1 s (Nicholas b 20 Jan 1943), 2 da (Geraldine b 14 March 1947, Sylvia b 10 May 1949); m 2, 1984, Leslie Minchin; *Career* author; formerly: waitress, counter-hand, charwoman, domestic help, shop asst, factory worker (unskilled); with Mass-Observation and pt/t raid warden WWII; Edgar Award Mystery Writers of America 1959, runner-up Gold Dagger Award Crime Writers' Assoc 1990; memb: PEN, Crime Writers' Assoc; *Books* author of: 17 suspense novels 1959–94, 3 vols of short stories; non-fiction: The Seven Chars of Chelsea (1939), War Factory (1943); *Recreations* reading other people's novels, listening to other people's life stories; *Style—* Ms Celia Fremlin; ✉ 11 Parkhill Road, London NW3 2YH (☎ 0171 722 8022); c/o Lisanne Radice, 3 Barb Mews, London W6 2PA (☎ 0171 610 4676, fax 0171 610 4686)

FRENCH, Dr Cecil Charles John; s of late Ernest French, of Harlow, Essex, and late Edith Hannah, *née* Norris; *b* 16 April 1926; *Educ* Newport Essex Sch, King's Coll London (MSc, DSc), Columbia Univ NY; *m* 1, 14 July 1956, (Olive) Joyce (d 1969), da of late Arthur James Edwards, of Lancing, Sussex; 2 da (Alison b 1957, Hilary b 1961); m 2, 23 Oct 1971, Shirley Frances, da of late Montague Charles Outten, of Colchester, Essex; 1 s (Matthew b 1975), 1 da (Elizabeth b 1973); *Career* Ricardo Consulting Engineers Ltd 1952–90: dir 1969, vice chm 1982; chm G Cussons Ltd 1985–87, dir and conslt Ricardo International plc 1991–92 (gp tech dir 1990–91), ret 1992; visiting prof in mechanical engrg King's Coll London 1983–89; author of numerous papers on internal combustion engrg; pres: IMechE 1988–89 (vice pres 1982–86, dep pres 1986–88), Int Cncl on Combustion Engines (CIMAC) 1983–85; Freeman City of London 1986, Liveryman Worshipful Co of Engrs 1986; FEng 1982, FIMechE, FIMgt, MASME, FSAE, FIMarE; *Recreations* folk dancing, photography; *Clubs* Shoreham and Southwick Rotary; *Style—* Dr Cecil French, FEng; ✉ 303 Upper Shoreham Rd, Shoreham-by-Sea, W Sussex BN43 5QA (☎ 01273 452050)

FRENCH, (Edward Frank) Christopher; s of Frank Charles French, of W Malling, Kent, and Mary, *née* Parish; *b* 28 July 1950; *Educ* Roan GS for Boys; *m* 29 March 1969, Rita Margaret, da of Brian Stuart; 1 s (James b 1983), 1 da (Sally b 1977); *Career* Nationwide Building Society: trainee mangr 1971, branch mangr 1978, sec 1985; Nationwide Anglia Building Society: asst gen mangr 1988, gen mangr 1990, divnl dir 1991–92; chief operating offr National Home Loans plc 1992–95, chief exec Norland

Capital Ltd 1995–; chm: Nationwide Building Society Staff Assoc 1980–82, Fedn of Bldg Soc Staff Assocs 1980–81; FCIB 1978, DMS 1985, FRSA 1993; *Recreations* music, history; *Style*— Christopher French, Esq; ✉ Norland Capital Limited, 96 Kensington High Street, London W8 4SG

FRENCH, Hon Mr Justice; Hon Sir Christopher James Saunders; kt (1979); s of Rev Reginald French, MC (d 1961, hon chaplain to HM The Queen and to the late King George VI), and Gertrude Emily Mary, *née* Haworth; *b* 14 Oct 1925; *Educ* Denstone Coll (scholar), Brasenose Coll Oxford (scholar); *m* 1957, Philippa, da of Philip Godfrey Price, of Abergavenny, Monmouthshire; 1 s, 1 da; *Career* called to the Bar Inner Temple 1950 (bencher 1977), QC 1966, dep chm Bucks QS 1966–71, recorder Coventry 1971, recorder and hon recorder Coventry 1972–79, judge of the High Court of Justice (Queen's Bench Div) 1982– (Family Div 1979–82), presiding judge SE Circuit 1982–86; memb Lord Chllr's Advsy Ctee on Trg Magistrates 1974–80; *Publications* contrib Agency in Halsbury's Laws of England (4 edn); *Recreations* walking, music, painting; *Clubs* Garrick, Pilgrims'; *Style*— The Hon Mr Justice French; ✉ Royal Courts of Justice, Strand, London WC2

FRENCH, David; s of Capt Godfrey Alexander French, CBE, RN (d 1988), of Stoke Abbott, Dorset, and Margaret Annis, *née* Best; *b* 20 June 1947; *Educ* Sherborne, St John's Coll Durham (BA); *m* 3 Aug 1974, Sarah Anne, da of Rt Rev Henry David Halsey, former Bishop of Carlisle; 4 s (Thomas b 1978, Alexander b 1980, William b 1983, Henry Kenneth Robert b 1993); *Career* with Nat Cncl of Social Serv 1971–74, head Social Servs Dept RNID 1974–78, dir of serv C of E Children's Soc 1978–87, dir RELATE Nat Marriage Guidance 1987–95; chm: London Corrymeela Venture 1974–76, St Alban's Int Organ Festival 1985–87; memb: Cncl UK Assoc for Int Year of the Family 1993–95, Governing Cncl Family Policy Studies Centre 1988–; tstee Charity Appointments 1984–91; Liveryman Worshipful Co of Glaziers 1990; MIPD, MRSM, FRSA; *Recreations* children and boats; *Style*— David French, Esq; ✉ 21 Prospect Rd, St Albans, Herts AL1 2AT

FRENCH, Douglas Charles; MP (C) Gloucester (majority 6,058); s of Frederick Emil French, of Surrey, and late Charlotte Vera, *née* Russell; *b* 20 March 1944; *Educ* Glyn GS Epsom, St Catharine's Coll Cambridge (MA), Inns of Court Sch of Law; *m* 1978, Sue, da of late Philip Arthur Phillips; 2 s (Paul b 1982, David b 1985), 1 da (Louise b 1983); *Career* dir PW Merkle Ltd 1972–87 (exec 1966–71), called to the Bar Inner Temple 1975, Parly candidate Sheffield Attercliffe 1979, md Westminster & City Programmes 1979–87, MP (C) Gloucester 1987–, special advsr to Chllr of Exchequer 1982–83 (asst to Rt Hon Sir Geoffrey Howe QC, MP 1976–79); PPS to the Min of State: FCO 1988–89, ODA 1989–90, MAFF 1992–93, Local Govt and Planning 1993–94; PPS to Sec of State for Environment 1994–; chm Bow Group 1978–79; chm All Party Building Socs Gp, vice chm All Party Occupational Pensions Gp, sec All Party Insur & Financial Servs Gp, vice chm All Party Central Asia Gp; *Recreations* skiing, gardening, squash; *Clubs* RAC, Coningsby; *Style*— Douglas French, Esq, MP; ✉ House of Commons, London SW1A 0AA (☎ 0171 219 4564)

FRENCH, Prof Edward Alexander; s of Edward Francis French (d 1967), and Clara French (d 1982); *b* 17 Oct 1935; *Educ* Bemrose Sch Derby, LSE (BSc (Econ), LLB, PhD); *m* 11 Aug 1967, Lillias Margaret, da of Walter Riddoch (d 1972); 3 s (Daniel b 1974, Gregory b 1976, Steven b 1979); *Career* Nat Serv RAF 1955–57; called to the Bar Lincoln's Inn; audit examiner Dist Audit Serv 1955–59, princ (former asst princ) Home Civil Serv GPO 1963–67, lectr in accounting LSE 1967–77, prof and head of Dept of Accounting and Fin Control Univ Coll Cardiff 1977–87, prof Univ of Wales Coll of Cardiff 1987–95 (prof emeritus 1996–); pres S Wales Soc of Certified Accountants 1982–83, memb Nat Cncl Chartered Soc of Certified Accountants 1983–86; appointed by Privy Cncl to Academic Advsy Cncl Univ of Buckingham 1992– FCCA, FRSA; *Recreations* golf, gardening, swimming, reading; *Clubs* Radyr Golf, Cullen Golf; *Style*— Prof Edward French; ✉ 112 Pencisely Rd, Llandaff, Cardiff CF5 1DQ (☎ 01222 562599)

FRENCH, Philip Neville; s of John Wakefield French (d 1971), and Bessie, *née* Funston (d 1978); *b* 28 Aug 1933; *Educ* Merchant Taylors' Sch Crosby, Bristol GS, Exeter Coll Oxford (BA), Indiana Univ; *m* 31 Dec 1957, Kersti Elisabet, da of Dr Mauritz Molin, of Karlstad, Sweden; 3 s (Sean, Patrick, Karl); *Career* Nat Serv cmmnd 2 Lt Duke of Cornwall's Light Inf, seconded to The Parachute Regt 1952–54; drama critic New Statesman 1957–58, film critic London Magazine 1957–58; BBC: prodr N American Serv 1959–61, sr prodr talks and documentaries 1961–90; film critic The Observer 1978–; *Books* Age of Austerity 1945–51 (jt ed, 1963), The Novelist As Innovator (ed, 1965), The Movie Moguls (1969), Westerns (1974), Three Honest Men: Edmund Wilson, Lionel Trilling, F R Leavis (1981), The Third Dimension (ed, 1983), The Press: Observed and Projected (jt ed, 1991), Malle on Malle (ed, 1992), The Faber Book of Movie Verse (jt ed, 1993), Wild Strawberries (jtly with Kersti French, 1995); *Style*— Philip French, Esq; ✉ 62 Dartmouth Park Rd, London NW5 1SN (☎ 0171 485 1711); Kärne 35, 65593 Karlstad, Sweden

FRENCH, Ralph John; OBE; s of Alfred William French (d 1965), and Flora Regan (d 1972); *b* 22 June 1935; *Educ* Haberdashers' Aske's, Waldschulheim Breuer Aachen, Coll of Law London, Inns at Ct Sch of Law, Manchester Business Sch, Ashridge Coll Bucks; *m* 1, 1964 (m dis 1982); m 2, 1982, Rosemary Joan (Rosie), da of John Frederick Wearing (d 1974); 1 s (Rupert John Wolfe b 6 Nov 1967), 2 da (Charlotte Elizabeth b 25 Jan 1966, Juliette Louise b 22 July 1970), 2 step da; *Career* Royal Welch Fusiliers 2 Lt 1954–56, HMOCS 1957–62; called to the Bar Lincoln's Inn 1964; ICI: asst sec Plastics Div 1965–71, div sec and business res mangr Plastics Div 1971–75, head East Euro Dept Corp HQ 1975–85, dir East Euro Rels and ICI (Export) 1985–89; memb Bar Assoc for Fin Commerce and Indust 1965–, E Euro Trade Cncl BOTB 1980–89; pres Welwyn/Hatfield YMCA 1996– (fndr memb 1965, chm 1967–75), chm BSCC 1980–89 (memb Cncl 1975); ldr first and second Br Trade Missions to Mongolia 1987 and 1988; treas Britain-Russia Centre 1992–; Freeman City of London 1972, Freeman and Liveryman Worshipful Co of Masons 1972 (master 1995–96); 1300th Anniversary of Fndn of Bulgarian State medal 1981 (for servs Bulgaria), NY 1988 (for services to export); *Recreations* climbing, sailing, water sports, wine; *Clubs* Athenaeum; *Style*— Ralph French, Esq, OBE; ✉ 30 Addison Grove, London W4 1ER (☎ and fax 0181 995 7959)

FRENCH, Raymond James (Ray); s of James Owen French (d 1988), of St Helens, and Ellen, *née* Fairhurst; *b* 23 Dec 1939; *Educ* Cowley Sch St Helens, Univ of Leeds (BA, CertEd); *m* 1 June 1963, Helen, da of Eric Bromilow; 1 s (Gary James b 2 Dec 1967), 1 da (Susan Anne b 14 May 1965); *Career* rugby league commentator and correspondent; schoolmaster: Fairfield Sch Widnes 1962–65, Cowley Sch St Helens 1965–94; rugby league commentator BBC TV 1981–, corr Rugby Leaguer magazine 1981–, corr/commentator BBC Radio Merseyside 1982–, corr Today newspaper 1984–; rugby player: St Helens, Lancs, England (4 caps) and Barbarians rugby union 1958–61, St Helens, Widnes, Lancs and GB rugby league 1961–72; honours (rugby league): Challenge Cup winners 1966, Championship winners 1966 (runners-up 1965 and 1967), Lancs Cup winners 1961–68; *Books* My Kind of Rugby (1979), Running Rugby (1980), Coaching Rugby League (1982), Rugby League Lions (1984), Ray French's 100 Great Rugby League Players (1989), More Kinds of Rugby (1989), The Match of My Life (1994); *Recreations* rugby, cricket, walking, swimming, theatre; *Style*— Ray French, Esq

FREND, Rev Prof William Hugh Clifford; TD (clasp); s of Rev Edwin George Clifford Frend (d 1937), of Tyneham Rectory, Dorset, and Edith Bacon (d 1966); *b* 11 Jan 1916; *Educ* Haileybury, Keble Coll Oxford (BA, DPhil, MA, DD), Univ of Cambridge (BD), Berlin Univ, Sorbonne; *m* 2 June 1951, Mary Grace, da of E A Crook (d 1984); 1 s (Simon William Clifford b 1957), 1 da (Sarah Anne b 1952); *Career* Craven fell Oxford 1937–40; WWII asst princ WO 1940–41, Cabinet Offices 1941–42, PWE Intelligence Offr 1942–45, mil govt Austria 1945–46, 2 Lt S Queen's Regt TA 1947; TA 1.0. Bde, 131 Bde; liaison offr vol serv Cambridge 1962–67; full time memb Editorial Bd German Foreign Miny Project 1947–51, res fell Univ of Nottingham 1951–52, asst lectr then lectr in church history and doctrine Univ of Cambridge 1954–69, dir of studies in archaeology and anthropology Gonville and Caius Coll Cambridge 1961–69 (Bye fell 1952–54, fell of Gonville and Caius 1956, jr proctor 1957, Birkbeck lectr 1968), dean of divinity Univ of Glasgow 1972–75 (prof of ecclesiastical history 1969–84); visiting prof: Rhodes Univ 1964, Univ of SA 1976, John Carroll Univ Ohio 1981; sr fell Dumbarton Oaks 1984; ordained: deacon 1982, priest 1983; non stipendary minister St Mary's Aberfoyle 1983–84, priest i/c Barnwell Benefice 1984–90; hon asst priest Fulbourn parish; chm AUT Scotland 1976–78, pres Cmmn International d'Histoire Ecclésiastique Comparée 1980–83; Hon DD Edinburgh 1974; FSA 1952 (Cncl 1992), FRHistSoc 1954, FRSE 1979, FBA 1983; Gold Cross of Merit with Swords Polish govt in exile 1950; *Books* Martyrdom and Persecution in the Early Church (1965), Religion Popular and Unpopular in the Early Christian Centuries (1976), Rise of the Monophysite Movement (2 edn, 1979), Town and Country in the Early Christian Centuries (1980), Rise of Christianity (1984), The Donatist Church (3 edn, 1985), The Early Church (4 edn, 1991), Saints and Sinners in the Early Church (3 edn, 1987), Archaeology and History in the Study of Early Christianity (1988), The Archaeology of Early Christianity: a history (1996); *Recreations* romano-british archaeology, gardening; *Clubs* Authors; *Style*— Rev Prof William Frend, TD, FBA, FRSE, FSA; ✉ The Clerks Cottage, Little Wilbraham, Cambridge CB1 5LB (☎ 01223 811731)

FRENDO, Paul Anthony (Tony); *b* 2 Nov 1947; *Career* Argyll Group plc: joined group 1973, dir 1989–94, md fin and admin Safeway plc until 1994; non-exec chm Dawsongroup plc 1994–; non-exec dir: Cathedral Tableware Ltd 1994–, Colleagues Group plc, Marten Gibbon Associates Ltd; FCA; *Style*— Tony Frendo, Esq; ✉ Dawsongroup plc, Delaware Drive, Tongwell, Milton Keynes, Bucks MK15 8JH (☎ 01908 218111, fax 01908 218444)

FRERE, Vice Adm Sir Richard Tobias (Toby); KCB; s of Alexander Stewart Frere, CBE (d 1984), and Patricia Marion Caldecott, *née* Wallace (d 1995); *b* 4 June 1938; *Educ* Eton, Britannia Royal Naval Coll; *m* 27 July 1968, Jane, da of Sir Kenneth Barraclough; 2 da (Susannah b 1971, Kate b 1974); *Career* Nat Serv 1955–56, cmmnd RN 1958, served Canada and Aust 1960–66; cmd submarines: HMS Andrew 1968, HMS Odin 1971, HMS Revenge 1978; cmd frigate HMS Brazen 1984; RCDS 1982, formerly DG Fleet Support and Flag Offr Submarines, currently Chief of Fleet Support on the Admiralty Bd; Freeman City of London 1970, Liveryman Grocers Co 1989; FIMgt; *Recreations* sailing, walking; *Clubs* Garrick, MCC; *Style*— Vice Adm Sir Toby Frere, KCB; ✉ c/o Ministry of Defence, Quay House, The Ambury, Bath BA1 5AB (☎ 01225 472087)

FRERIS, Marika; da of Leonard Freris, of Herts, and Delphine, *née* Squire; *b* 24 July 1962; *Educ* Loreto Coll Sch for Girls St Albans, Imperial Coll London (BSc Microbiology); *Career* sr research asst Dept of Molecular Biology The Wellcome Research Labs Beckenham 1983–85, clinical research scientist Dept of Clinical Immunology and Chemotherapy The Wellcome Fndn Beckenham 1985–89; Hill & Knowlton (UK) Ltd: account dir Eurosciences 1989–91, assoc dir Eurosciences 1991–94, dir Healthcare 1994–96; dir Professional Rels Churchill Communications Europe 1996–; memb: ActionAid, Oxfam, Nat Trust, Friends of the Earth, Action on Addiction; *Style*— Ms Marika Freris; ✉ Churchill Communications Europe, Maple House, 149 Tottenham Court Road, London W1P 9LL (☎ 0171 896 2115, fax 0171 896 2112, mobile 0836 378992)

FRESHWATER, Timothy George (Tim); s of George John Freshwater (d 1986), and Rosalie, *née* MacLauchlan (d 1987); *b* 21 Oct 1944; *Educ* Eastbourne Coll, Emmanuel Coll Cambridge (MA, LLB); *m* Judy, *née* Lam; *Career* Slaughter and May: joined 1967, ptnr 1975, seconded to Hong Kong office 1979–85, ptnr London (corp fin) 1985–; pres Law Soc Hong Kong 1984–85, co-chm Jt Working Party on China of Law Soc and the Bar, memb Int Ctee Law Soc; *Books* The Practitioner's Guide to the City Code on Take-Overs and Mergers (contrib); *Style*— Tim Freshwater; ✉ Slaughter and May, 35 Basinghall St, London EC2V 5DB (☎ 0171 600 1200, fax 0171 726 0038)

FRESKO, Adrienne Sheila; da of Mendel Marcus (d 1982), and Esther Marcus, of Manchester; *b* 22 Feb 1957; *Educ* Manchester HS for Girls, St Anne's Coll Oxford (MA Experimental Psychology); *m* 24 June 1979, Marc Fresko; 2 da (Madeleine Xenia b 14 April 1989, Nadine Sarah b 9 July 1992); *Career* Citibank 1978–89 (vice pres Human Resourses Citicorp Diners Club USA 1984–86, divnl personnel head Europe, ME and Africa Citibank Private Banking Gp 1986–89), princ Adrienne Fresko Human Resourses Consulting 1989–; non-exec dir London Ambulance Serv 1990–92, chm Croydon DHA 1992–96, lead chm Croydon Health Commissioning Agency 1994–96, chm Croydon HA 1996–, memb Audit Cmmn 1996–; former memb Human Resources Advsy Gp NAHAT; memb: S Thames NHS R&D Liaison Gp, Dept of Health Nat Working Gp on Long Term Devpt Needs of HAs; MIPD 1990; *Recreations* family, travel, cookery, theatre, house restoration; *Style*— Mrs Adrienne Fresko; ✉ Croydon Health Authority, Knollys House, 17 Addiscombe Road, Croydon CR0 6SR (☎ 0181 401 3969, fax 0181 680 3893)

FRETER, Michael Charles Franklin; s of Leslie Charles Freter, of Sidmouth, Devon, and Myra, *née* Wilkinson; *b* 29 Oct 1947; *Educ* Whitgift Sch, St Edmund Hall Oxford (BA); *m* 2 June 1979, Jan, da of Brian Wilson, of Ealing, London; *Career* sr brand mangr Elida Gibbs Ltd 1970–76, account dir BBDO Advertising Ltd 1976–78, exec dir McCann-Erickson Advertising Ltd 1988–94 (joined 1978), managing ptnr The Imagination Brokers 1994–96, gp business dir Summerfield Wilmot Keene 1996–; *Style*— Michael Freter, Esq; ✉ 16 Molasses House, Clove Hitch Quay, Plantation Wharf, London SW11 3TN

FRETWELL, Clive; s of Derek Ernest Fretwell, of Yorkshire, and Doris Jean, *née* Mitchell; *b* 16 Sept 1961; *m* 18 Sept 1982, Julie, da of late Richard Sharrock; 2 da (Selina-Jane b 10 Oct 1984, Claire Louise b 14 Jan 1986); *Career* head chef Le Manoir aux Quat' Saisons 1986– (commis chef 1982–86); dir Le Petit Blanc Ecole de Cuisine 1991–96; memb Academie Culinaire de France; winner Boccuse d'Or Individual Gold Medal 1991 and 1993; *Recreations* cycling, windsurfing, squash; *Style*— Clive Fretwell, Esq; ✉ Le Manoir aux Quat' Saisons, Church Road, Great Milton, Oxfordshire OX44 7PD (☎ 01844 278881, fax 01844 278846)

FRETWELL, Sir (Major) John Emsley; GCMG (1987, KCMG 1982, CMG 1975); s of Francis Thomas Fretwell, of Chesterfield; *b* 15 June 1930; *Educ* Chesterfield GS, Univ of Lausanne, King's Coll Cambridge; *m* 1959, Mary Ellen Eugenie, da of Frederick Charles Dubois; 1 s, 1 da; *Career* joined FO 1953, served Hong Kong and Peking, first sec Moscow 1959–62, FO 1962–67, first sec (commercial) Washington 1967–70, cnsllr (commercial) Warsaw 1971–73, head EID 1973–76, asst under sec FCO 1976–79, min Washington 1980–81, ambass France 1982–87, political dir FCO 1987–90; memb Cncl of Lloyd's 1991–92; specialist advsr House of Lords 1992–93, specialist assessor Higher Educn Funding Cncl 1995–96; chm Franco-British Soc 1995–, conslt Eurofleet 2000 1995–; *Recreations* hill walking, skiing, travel, wine; *Clubs* Brooks's; *Style*— Sir John Fretwell, GCMG; ✉ c/o Brooks's, St James's Street, London SW1A 1LN

FREUD, Anthony Peter; s of Joseph Freud, of London, and Katalin, *née* Löwe (d 1990); *b* 30 Oct 1957; *Educ* King's Coll Sch Wimbledon, King's Coll London (LLB), Inns of Court Sch of Law; *Career* pupillage as barr 1979–80; theatre mangr Sadler's Wells

Theatre 1980–84, co sec and dir of opera planning Welsh Nat Opera 1984–92, exec prodr (opera) Philips Classics Productions (The Netherlands) 1992–94, gen dir Welsh Nat Opera 1994–; memb Hon Soc of Gray's Inn 1979; *Recreations* the Arts, cooking, travel; *Style*— Anthony Freud, Esq; ✉ General Director, Welsh National Opera Ltd, John Street, Cardiff CF1 4SP (☎ 01222 464666, fax 01222 483050)

FREUD, Bella; da of Lucian Freud, OM, the painter, and Bernardine Coverley; *b* 1961; *Educ* Michael Hall Sch E Sussex, Academia di Costuma e di Moda Rome, Institutto Mariotti Rome; *Career* fashion designer; asst to Vivienne Westwood, *qv* 1986–89 (formerly shop asst Seditionaries Kings Road 1978), own label since 1990; winner Innovative Design - The New Generation category Br Fashion Awards 1991; *Style*— Ms Bella Freud; ✉ 48 Rawstorne Street, London EC1V 7ND (☎ 0171 713 6466)

FREUD, Sir Clement Raphael; kt (1987); s of Ernst L Freud (d 1970), and Lucie, *née* Brasch (d 1989); bro of Lucian Freud, CH (gs of Prof Sigmund Freud); *b* 24 April 1924; *Educ* Dartington Hall, St Paul's; *m* Sept 1950, June Beatrice (Jill), 2 da of H W Flewett, MA; 2 s (Dominic Martin b 11 Nov 1958, Matthew Rupert b 2 Nov 1963), 2 da (Nicola Mary b 24 Oct 1951, Emma Vallencey, *qv*, b 25 Jan 1962); *Career* Royal Ulster Rifles 1942–47, liaison offr Int Mil Tribunal Nüremberg 1946–47; writer, broadcaster, cook, nightclub owner; rector Dundee Univ 1974–80; MP (Lib): Isle of Ely 1973–1983, NE Cambs 1983–87; sponsor Official Info Bill 1978–79; MUniv Open Univ 1989; *Books* Grimble (1968), Grimble at Christmas (1973), Freud on Food (1978), Book of Hangovers (1981), Below the Belt (1983), No-One Else Has Complained (1988), The Gourmet's Tour of Great Britain and Ireland (1989); *Clubs* MCC, British Rail Staff Assoc, March, Groucho; *Style*— Sir Clement Freud; ✉ 22 Wimpole St, London W1M 7AD (☎ 0171 580 2222)

FREUD, Emma Vallencey; da of Sir Clement Freud, *qv*, and Lady Freud; *b* 25 Jan 1962; *Educ* St Mary's Convent, Queen's Coll London, Univ of Bristol, Univ of London (BA); *children* 1 da (Scarlett b 21 June 1995); *Career* backing singer to Mike Oldfield 1979–81, musical dir regnl theatres 1984–86, co-dir Open Air Theatre Regent's Park 1986–87; freelance journalist: The Guardian, The Independent; memb band The Girls 1988–91, tstee Comic Relief 1993 (conslt 1990–); host: BAFTA awards BBC 2, The Turner Prize Channel 4; film script ed Four Weddings and a Funeral 1994; *Television* incl: reporter Six O'Clock Show (LWT) 1986–88; host: Pillowtalk (LWT) 1987–89, Plunder (BBC) 1990–91; presenter: The Media Show (C4) 1990–91, The Big Picture Show (C4) 1991–92, The Pulse (C4) 1993, Everyman (BBC1) 1994, Edinburgh Nights (BBC2) 1994–, Theatreland (LWT) 1996–; *Radio* incl: reporter Loose Ends (BBC Radio 4) 1987–, presenter Daily Sequence (GLR) 1989–90, The Lunchtime Programme (BBC Radio 1) 1994; *Clubs* Groucho; *Style*— Ms Emma Freud; ✉ c/o ICM Ltd, Oxford House, 76 Oxford Street, London W1N 0AX (☎ 0171 636 6565, fax 0171 323 0101)

FREUD, Esther Lea; da of Lucian Freud, OM, and Bernardine Coverley; *b* 2 May 1963; *Educ* Michael Hall Sch, Drama Centre London; *Career* writer; actress 1983–91; *Books* Hideous Kinky (1992), Peerless Flats (1993); *Style*— Miss Esther Freud; ✉ c/o Toby Eady Associates, 9 Orme Court, London W2

FREUD, Matthew; s of Sir Clement Freud, *qv*, and June, *née* Flewitt; *b* 2 Nov 1963; *Educ* Westminster, Pimlico; *m* Caroline Victoria, da of Rupert Hutton, of Algarve, Portugal; 1 s (George Rupert b 3 Oct 1995); *Career* press offr RCA Records 1983–85, chm Freud Communications (formerly Matthew Freud Associates) 1985– (acquired by Abbott Mead Vickers plc Dec 1994); clients incl: Planet Hollywood, BT, Pepsi, Volvo, Channel 4 and BBC Radio 1; *Clubs* Groucho's; *Style*— Matthew Freud, Esq; ✉ Freud Communications Ltd, 93 Newman Street, London W1P 4HQ (☎ 0171 580 2626, fax 0171 637 2626)

FREWER, Prof Richard John Barrett; s of Dr Edward George Frewer (d 1972), and Bridget Audrey Christina Pennefather, *née* Ford (d 1994); *b* 24 Jan 1942; *Educ* Shrewsbury, Gonville and Caius Coll Cambridge (MA), AA (Dip Arch); *m* 19 July 1969, Carolyn Mary, da of Thomas Arthur Butler (d 1969); 1 da (Emelye b 1971); *Career* architect Arup Assocs 1966– (ptnr 1977–92, cnslt 1992–); major works incl: Sir Thomas White Bldg, St John's Coll Oxford (with Sir Philip Dowson), Theatre Royal Glasgow, Liverpool Gardon Festival Hall, Baburgh DC Offs Suffolk, Stockley Park Arena Heathrow; prof of architecture Univ of Bath; pt/t professional tenor soloist, Bach Specialist, Lieder and Oratorio repertoire; memb Cncl: Royal Sch of Church Music, Construction Indust Cncl (chm Educn and Trg); dir Bath Festivals Tst, tstee Holburne of Menstrie Museum Bath; RIBA, FRSA; *Recreations* painting, gardening; *Style*— Prof Richard Frewer; ✉ Arup Associates, 37 Fitzroy Square, London W1 (☎ 0171 465 5555); Department of Architecture and Civil Engineering, University of Bath, Claverton Down, Bath BA2 7AY (☎ 01225 826296, fax 01225 826691)

FREYBERG, 3 Baron (UK 1951); Valerian Bernard Freyberg; o s of 2 Baron Freyberg, OBE, MC (d 1993), and Ivry Perronelle Katharine, *née* Guild; *b* 15 Dec 1970; *Style*— The Rt Hon the Lord Freyberg; ✉ Munstead House, Godalming, Surrey GU8 4AR

FREYD, Michael; s of Cecil Freyd (d 1971), and Joan, *née* Woodhead (d 1960); *b* 5 June 1948; *Educ* Burnage GS Manchester, Univ of Hull (BSc); *m* 21 March 1971, Marilyn Sharon (Lyn), da of Ivor Paul Levinson (d 1960); 1 s (Mark b 29 Aug 1979), 2 da (Danielle b 14 June 1972, Elana b 7 May 1976); *Career* dep md UBS (formerly Phillips & Drew) (joined 1969, ptnr 1980–94, memb Option Ctee 1986–92), dir (with responsibility for mktg and business devpt) Objective Asset Management Ltd 1994–; memb Soc of Investmt Analysts; MSI; *Recreations* golf, skiing, bridge, chess; *Style*— Michael Freyd, Esq; ✉ Objective Asset Management Ltd, Austin Friars House, 2–6 Austin Friars, London EC2N 2HE (☎ 0171 628 3717)

FRICKER, Brenda; *Career* actress; *Theatre* RSC: Macbeth, Outskirts, TV Times, The Accrington Pals, The Irish Play; RNT: The Plough and the Stars, Lavender Blue, Lost Worlds; Nuffield Theatre Southampton: Just a Kick in the Grass, Romeo and Juliet; other roles incl: The Saxon Shore (Almeida), title role in Big Maggie (Abbey Theatre Dublin), title role in Typhoid Mary (Bristol Old Vic), Flesh and Blood (nat tour), Skirmishes (Salisbury Playhouse); *Television* incl: Lottie in Journey (Hallmark Hall of Fame USA TV Film), Mother Steed in A Woman of Independent Means (Robert Greenwald Films), Stella in Seekers (Central TV), Eliza Graham Bell in The Sound and the Silence (mini-series, South Pacific Pictures), Sister Agnes in Brides of Christ (mini-series, ABC Australia) Megan Roache in Casualty (5 series, BBC), Licking Hitler (BAFTA Best Play Award), Just Like Eddie (HTV), Your Man from the Six Counties, The Ballroom of Romance (BAFTA Award and the New York Silver Award Best Play), To Have and to Hold (LWT), The Picnic (BBC), Helen: A Woman of Today (LWT), Eh Brian, It's a Whopper (Central), The Practice (Granada), The Sinners (Granada), Mein Kampf (BBC), Stephen D (BBC), The Man Outside (BBC), The Gathering Seed (BBC); *Films* incl: Mrs Mazzawatti in Moll Flanders (Trilogy Productions for MGM), Lily Byrne in A Man of No Importance (Littlebird Films), Maggie in Angels in the Outfield (Disney), Iris in Deadly Advice (Zenith Films), May MacKenzie in So I Married an Ax Murderer (Tri-Star), Pigeon Lady in Home Alone II (20th Century Fox), Marta in UTZ (Viva Pictures), Vinnie Moore in Lethal Innocence (Turtleback Productions), Maggie McCane in The Field (PBS), My Left Foot (Academy Award for Best Supporting Actress), Our Exploits at West Poley, The Woman who Married Clark Cable, Sinful Davy, Of Human Bondage, Rose in Swann (Greenpoint Films), Ethel Twitty in A Time to Kill (Warner Bros); *Style*— Ms Brenda Fricker; ✉ c/o Mayer & Eden Ltd, 34 Kingly Court, London W1R 5LE (☎ 0171 434 1242, fax 0171 287 5834)

FRICKER, Colin Frank; s of Frank Charles Fricker (d 1989), and Hilda Emily, *née* Ingle (d 1955); *b* 9 April 1936; *Educ* Dulwich, Univ of London (LLB); *m* 20 June 1964, Elizabeth Ann Brooke, da of John Douglas Skinner, of Eastleigh, Hants; 2 s (Henry b and d 1975, Robert), 1 da (Annabel); *Career* Nat Serv RAF 1954–56; asst dir C E Heath Home Ltd 1968–70, dir Assoc of Br Launderers & Cleaners 1979–84, ldr employers' side of Laundry Wages Cncl 1979–84, dir gen Br Direct Mktg Assoc 1985–92; dir legal affrs DMA (UK) 1992–; memb Cncl CBI 1979–84 and 1994–; Freeman: City of London, Worshipful Co of Launderers 1979; FCII 1960; *Recreations* cricket, rugby, genealogy; *Clubs* MCC, Lord's Taverners; *Style*— Colin Fricker, Esq; ✉ c/o DMA (UK), Haymarket House, 1 Oxendon Street, London SW1Y 4EE (☎ 0171 321 2525, fax 0171 321 0191)

FRICKER, His Hon Judge; (Anthony) Nigel; QC (1977); s of late Dr William Shapland Fricker, and Margaret, *née* Skinner; *b* 7 July 1937; *Educ* King's Sch Chester, Univ of Liverpool (LLB); *m* 1960, Marilynn Ann, da of late August L Martin, of Pennsylvania, USA; 1 s (Joseph b 1969), 2 da (Deborah b 1962, Susan b 1964); *Career* called to the Bar Gray's Inn 1960; prosecuting counsel to DHSS Wales and Chester Circuit (North) 1975–77, recorder Crown Court 1975–84, asst cmmr Boundary Cmmn Wales 1981–84, circuit judge (NE Circuit) 1984–; pres Cncl of HM Circuit Judges 1997; *Books* Emergency Remedies in the Family Courts (gen ed and jt author, 1990, 2 edn 1993, 3 edn 1996), Enforcement of Injunctions and Undertakings (with David Bean, 1991), The Family Court Practice (consulting ed, 1993–); *Style*— His Honour Judge Fricker, QC; ✉ c/o North Eastern Circuit Office, 17th Floor, West Riding House, Albion Street, Leeds LS1 5AA (☎ 0113 244 1841)

FRICKERS, Gordon Stuart Allen; s of Capt Alan Frickers (d 1988), and Winnifred Anne Frickers; *b* 25 May 1949; *Educ* Broomham, South Bromley Coll, Maidstone Coll of Art, Medway Coll of Art (Dip Visual Communications), Falmouth Tech Coll, Painting Sch of Montmiral France; *m* 26 Nov 1983, Patricia Eileen, da of George Winterburn, of Brentwood, Old Swan, Liverpool; 1 s (Aaron b 9 June 1987), 1 da (Hannah b 24 Aug 1985); *Career* photographer advertising and press 1971–74, md SE Boatbuilders Ltd 1975–79; currently dir: Blue Ribband (Fine Art) Ltd, Victory 2005 Ltd; artist (painter); exhibited: onboard Cutty Sark, Buckingham Palace, London International Boatshow, RSMA, Chester City Hall, Ville de Brest; patrons incl: Yamaha, Corum (Admirals Cup Team), Cunard, British Telecom (Marine) Ltd, Sir Robin Knox-Johnstone, Peter de Savary, Richard Branson, Sail Training Assoc, Maiden GB (Tracy Edwards); limited editions: The Schooner Vagrant 1988, Atlantic Repair 1991, Ice Maiden 1991, Royal Yacht Britannia (1893) 1993, Cunard Express Steamer 1993, Port of Chester (1863) 1993, The Clipper Way 1996; reg contribs to magazines; memb: Nat Scorpion Assoc 1973–79, Soc Nautical Res, World Ship Soc, Nat Maritime Historical Soc of USA, WWF; *Recreations* life drawing, sailing, travel; *Clubs* Royal Plymouth Corinthian Yacht; *Style*— Gordon Frickers, Esq; ✉ Drakeside Studio, 94 Radford Park Rd, Plymouth PL9 9DX (☎ and fax 01752 403344)

FRIDD, Nicholas Timothy; s of Norman Sidney Fridd, and Beryl Rosamond, *née* Phillips; *b* 21 Sept 1953; *Educ* Wells Blue Sch, ChCh Oxford (MA); *m* 14 Sept 1985, Fiona Bridgnell, da of Dr Keir Mackessack-Leitch, of Chart House, Bloxham, Oxon; 1 s (John Bridgnell b 2 Nov 1989), 1 da (Charlotte Mary b 11 Jan 1988); *Career* called to the Bar Inner Temple 1975; *Books* Basic Practice in Courts, Tribunals and Inquiries (1989, 2 edn 1993); *Recreations* carpentry, walking disused railways; *Style*— Nicholas Fridd, Esq; ✉ Manor Farm, East Horrington, Wells, Somerset BA5 3DP (☎ 01749 679832, fax 01749 679849); All Saints Chambers, Holbeck House, 9–11 Broad Street, Bristol BS1 2HP (☎ 0117 921 1966, fax 0117 927 6493)

FRIEBE, John Percy; s of Charles Friebe (d 1962); *b* 9 May 1931; *Educ* Glasgow HS, Univ of Glasgow; *m* 1966, Laura Mary, da of Archibald Fleming (d 1961); *Career* fin dir Smith and MacLaurin Ltd 1958–64, mktg dir Millard Brothers Ltd 1964–70; gp md Stoddard Holdings plc 1970–83, md Carpets International (UK) 1984–85 (mktg dir 1983–84); dir: Carpets International plc 1984–85, John Crowther Group plc 1985–86; chm Koninklijke Vereenigde Tapijtfabrieken NV 1989–90; chm Fleming Friebe Assoc 1986–95; vice chm Intersport GB Ltd 1986–95; MICAS, FICMA; *Recreations* golf, gardening, rugby; *Style*— John P Friebe, Esq; ✉ Hunters Heights, Uphampton, Ombersley, Worcs (☎ and fax 01905 620 854)

FRIEDBERGER, Maj-Gen John Peter William; CB (1991), CBE (1986, MBE 1975); s of Brig John Cameron Friedberger, DSO (d 1971), and Phyllis, *née* Daniels (d 1971); *b* 27 May 1937; *Educ* Wellington, Sandhurst; *m* 13 Aug 1966, Joanna Mary, da of Andrew Thorne, ERD; 1 s (Richard b 1973), 2 da (Rosanna b 1967, Lucinda b 1970); *Career* cmmnd 10 Royal Hussars (PWO) 1956; served: Jordan, Germany, S Arabia; seconded Northern Frontier Regt Sultan's Armed Forces Oman 1961–63, RMCS Shrivenham 1968, Aust Army Staff Coll 1969, MOD 1970–72, Brig Major 8 Brig 1973–75, CO Royal Hussars (PWO) 1975–78, Royal Coll of Def Studies 1978–79, seconded Cdr Royal Brunei Armed Forces 1982–86, Administrator Sovereign Base Areas and Cdr Br Forces Cyprus 1988–90; chief exec British Helicopter Advsy Bd 1992–; Hon Col The King's Royal Hussars 1992–; DPKT (Brunei) 1984; FRGS; *Recreations* travel; *Clubs* Cavalry and Guards'; *Style*— Maj-Gen John Friedberger, CB, CBE

FRIEDLANDER, Rabbi Prof Albert Hoschander; s of Alex Friedlander (d 1956), of Memphis, Tennessee, and Sali Friedlander (d 1966); *b* 10 May 1927, Berlin; *Educ* Univ of Chicago (PhB), Hebrew Union Coll Cincinnati Ohio (BHL, MA), Columbia Univ NYC (PhD); *m* 9 July 1961, Evelyn, da of Walter Philipp; 3 da (Ariel Judith b 1963, Michal Sali b 1965, Noam Ilana Alexandra b 1973); *Career* ordained rabbi 1952; rabbi: Utd Hebrew Congregation Fort Smith Arkansas 1952–56, Temple B'nai Brith Wilkes Barre Pa 1956–61; chaplain/cnsllr Columbia Univ NYC 1961–66, fndr rabbi Jewish Center of the Hamptons E Hampton NY 1961–66, rabbi Wembley Liberal Synagogue Harrow Middx 1966–71, sr rabbi Westminster Synagogue London 1971–; Leo Baeck Coll London: lectr 1967–71, dir 1971–82, dean 1982–; visiting prof (and lectr): Emory Univ Atlanta Georgia 1975, Univ of Berlin 1981 and 1982; visiting prof: Kirchliche Hochschule Wuppertal Germany April-July 1988, Univ of Basel (Theol Faculty) March-July 1993; Martin Buber guest prof of theology Frankfurt Univ 1996; guest lectr Univs of: Berlin, Heidelberg, Cambridge, Oxford, London, etc; regular bdcaster: BBC World Service (Meditations, Words of Faith, etc) 1970–, BBC Radio 3 and 4; occasional bdcasts: Spectrum Radio, Capital Radio; TV appearances on Ch4 (Heart of the Matter, Open Window, After Dark) and for various interviews and religious progs (incl Judas Iscariot prog 1993); conslt on various film scripts, religious advsr and script-writer for Franco Zeffirelli's Jesus of Nazareth; contrib (religious articles/obituaries): The Times 1970–, The Independent, The Guardian; ed: Littman Library (OUP) 1989–93, European Judaism Magazine 1982– (on staff 1967–); memb: Central Conf of American Rabbis 1952–, Rabbinic Conf, Union of Liberal and Progressive Synagogues Cncl of Reform Rabbis 1966–; vice pres World Union for Progressive Judaism 1975–95; pres World Conf for Religions for Peace UK 1993 (chm 1992, hon int pres 1995–); Hon DD Hebrew Union Coll 1977, Gold medal (Sir Sigmund Sternberg Award of the Conf of Jews and Christians) presented by Cardinal Hume 1990; Offr's Cross Order of Merit (FRG) 1993; memb Athenaeum Club 1975–85, fell PEN 1986 (memb 1970); *Books* Early Reform Judaism: A Serial History (1955), Leo Baeck: Teacher of Theresienstadt (1968, 2 edn 1992), Leo Baeck: Leben und Lehre (1973, revised 1991), Never Trust a God over Thirty (1967), Out of the Whirlwind (1968), The Six Days of Destruction (with E Wiesel, 1988 and 1989), A Thread of Gold (1991), Riders Towards the Dawn: From Pessimism to Tempered Optimism (1993), The Gate of Perfection (with W Homolka, 1994); ed/trans: Leo Baeck's This People Israel (1965), The Five Megillot (1983), The Writings of Leo Baeck (ed-in-chief, Vol I, 1996); author of over over 100 articles in academic jls; *Libretti*

The Five Scrolls (music by Donald Swann, 1975), Terezin Kaddish (music by Ronald Senator, 1985), Wedding Song (music by Malcolm Williamson, 1981); *Style*— Rabbi Professor A H Friedlander; ✉ Westminster Synagogue, Knightsbridge, Rutland Gardens, London SW7 1BX; Leo Baeck College, 80 East End Road, Finchley, London N3 3SY (☎ 0181 349 4525, fax 0181 343 2558)

FRIEDMAN, Brian Sydney; s of Roy Friedman, of London, and Denise Adele, *née* Salter; *b* 25 Feb 1957; *Educ* Highgate Sch, St John's Coll Cambridge (MA); *m* 1983, Frances Patricia, *née* Davey; 1 da (Emma b 24 April 1987), 1 s (Jonathan b 1 March 1989); *Career* chartered accountant; Coopers & Lybrand 1978–84, Stoy Benefit Consulting 1985–94, ptnr and head of Employee Compensation and Benefits Arthur Andersen 1994–; pres Soc of Share Scheme Practitioners 1995–; ACA 1981, FTII 1988, MIPM 1990; *Books* Effective Staff Incentives (1991), Company Car Taxation (1993), Pay and Benefits Handbook (1994); *Recreations* children, travel, reading; *Clubs* RSA; *Style*— Brian Friedman, Esq; ✉ Arthur Andersen, 1 Surrey Street, London WC2R 2PS (☎ 0171 438 2238)

FRIEDMAN, David Peter; QC (1990); s of Wilfred Emanuel Friedman (d 1973), and Rosa, *née* Lees (d 1972); *b* 1 June 1944; *Educ* Tiffin Boy's Sch, Lincoln Coll Oxford (BCL, MA); *m* 29 Oct 1972, Sara Geraldine, da of Dr Sidney Linton; *Career* called to the Bar 1968, asst recorder 1990–; *Recreations* good food (cooked by others), reading; *Clubs* Landsdowne; *Style*— David P Friedman, Esq, QC; ✉ 4 Pump Court, Temple, London EC4Y 7AN (☎ 0171 353 2656, fax 0171 583 2036)

FRIEDMAN, Maria; da of Leonard Matthew Friedman (d 1994), of Edinburgh, and Clair Llewellyn Friedman; *b* 19 March 1960; *Educ* E Barnet Comp Sch, Arts Educnl Sch Golden Lane London; *children* 1 s (Toby Oliver Sams-Friedman b 26 Nov 1994); *Career* actress and singer; *Theatre* RNT incl: Ghetto (Evening Standard Award for Best Play 1990), Sunday in the Park with George (Olivier Award for Best Musical 1991), Square Rounds; other prodns incl: Blues in the Night (Donmar Warehouse, Piccadilly), April in Paris (Ambassadors) 1994, The Break of Day (Royal Court) 1995, Passion (Queen's) 1996; *Concerts* venues incl: Barbican, Royal Festival Hall, Palladium, Drury Lane, Albert Hall and St David's Hall; By Special Arrangement (Donmar Warehouse, Olivier Awards Best Entertainment 1995), By Extra Special Arrangement (Whitehall) 1995; *Television* incl: Me and the Girls, Blues in the Night, Red Dwarf, Casualty, Frank Stubbs Promotes; *Clubs* Barbican Health and Fitness Centre; *Style*— Ms Maria Friedman; ✉ c/o Michael Foster, ICM Ltd, Oxford House, 76 Oxford Street, London W1N 0AX (☎ 0171 636 6565, fax 0171 323 0101)

FRIEND, Carol Anne; da of Leslie George Friend, of London, and Ida Margaret, *née* Earl; *b* 11 Sept 1949; *Educ* Tiffins Girls GS Kingston upon Thames, St Johns Coll of Further Educn Manchester (HND, DipCAM PR); *Career* dir Wyndham Public Relations 1977–80, md Pielle + Co Ltd 1980–; chm Orbit Cromwell Housing Assoc 1984–86; CAM Fndn: govr 1985–92, chm 1992–94, dep chm 1994–95, vice pres 1995–; pres The Inst of Public Relations 1986, memb PO Users Nat Cncl 1987–90; chm London W End PO and Telecommunications Advsy Ctees 1987–; tstee PR Educn Tst 1989–95; memb: London Region Cncl CBI 1990–, Gtr London Regnl Ctee Further Educn Funding Cncl 1995–, Nat Cncl CBI 1995–; awarded Sir Stephen Tallents Medal of Inst of PR for outstanding contrib to PR educn and professional standards 1993; FIPR 1987, FCAM 1992; *Style*— Miss Carol Friend; ✉ Pielle + Company Limited, Museum House, 25 Museum St, London WC1A 1PL (☎ 0171 323 1587, fax 0171 631 0029)

FRIEND, Lionel; s of Norman Alfred Child Friend (d 1991), and Moya Lilian, *née* Dicks; *b* 13 March 1945; *Educ* Royal GS High Wycombe, RCM, London Opera Centre; *m* 1969, Jane, da of Norman Edward Hyland; 1 s (Toby Thomas b 1984), 2 da (Clea Deborah b 1972, Corinne Jane b 1977); *Career* conductor WNO 1969–72, Glyndebourne Festival and Touring Opera 1969–72; 2 Kapellmeister Staatstheater Kassel Germany 1972–75; staff conductor ENO 1976–89; music dir: Nexus Opera 1981–, New Sussex Opera 1989–96; guest conductor: Philharmonia, City of Birmingham Symphony Orch, BBC Symphony Orch, Royal Ballet, Orchestre National de France, Nouvel Orchestre Philharmonique, Austrian Radio Symphony Orch, Swedish Radio Symphony Orch, Hungarian State Symphony Orch, Budapest Symphony Orch, Scot Chamber Orch, London Sinfonietta, Nash Ensemble, Opera Omaha, and other orchs and ensembles abroad; recordings incl: The World's Winter (Payne), Songs (Bliss), Le Bal Masqué, Chansons de Bilitis, The Great Journey (Matthews), Variations, Symphony 1 (Milner), Violin Concerto, Symphony 18, Symphony 3 (Brian), L'histoire du Soldat, Sinfonietta (Durkó), Sonata (Souster), Ode to Napoleon (Schönberg), Mary of Egypt (Tavener), Phaedra, Sinfonietta (Britten); *Recreations* reading, theatre; *Style*— Lionel Friend, Esq; ✉ 136 Rosendale Road, London SE21 8LG (☎ and fax 0181 761 7845); Allied Artists, 42 Montpelier Square, London SW7 1JZ (☎ 0171 589 6243, fax 0171 581 5269)

FRIEND, Mark; *b* 23 Nov 1957; *Educ* Gonville & Caius Coll Cambridge (BA), Institut D'Etudes Européennes Brussels (Licence Spéciale en Droit Européenne); *Career* admitted slr 1982, ptnr (specialising in competition law and regulation) Allen & Overy 1990–; author of numerous contributions to legal periodicals on competition law; *Style*— Mark Friend, Esq; ✉ Allen & Overy, One New Change, London EC4M 9QQ (☎ 0171 330 3000, fax 0171 330 9999)

FRIEND, Martyn Patrick; s of Philip Wyndham Friend (d 1987), and Eileen Marion Adams, *née* Erskine; *b* 23 Nov 1942; *Educ* Steyning GS, Hertford Coll Oxford (BA); *m* 1, 1968 (m dis 1980), Nicole June Hamilton-Fletcher; 2 da (Cassandra Maria b 28 May 1973, Emily Alice Louisa b 24 Nov 1977); m 2, 1982 (m dis 1988), Marianne Maskell; *Career* freelance television and film director; ITV and BBC: researcher and writer 1964, formerly floor mangr, prodn mangr and asst dir; dir BBC 1973–76 (incl Onedin Line, Softly Softly), freelance TV video and film dir 1976–; memb: BAFTA 1980, Dirs' Guild of GB 1987; *Film and Television* credits incl: The Voyage of Charles Darwin 1978, Sweet Nothings 1980, first episode of Bergerac 1980, Fair Stood The Wind for France 1981, Shackleton 1982, Anna of the Five Towns 1984, The Daughter-in-Law 1985, The Daily Woman 1985, All Passion Spent 1986, 4.50 from Paddington 1987, first episode of Campion 1988, Summer's Lease 1989, Survival of the Fittest 1990, Titmuss Regained 1991, Inspector Alleyn Mysteries 1992–93, Love on a Branch Line 1993, Seaforth 1994, Cuts 1995; *Awards* incl: BAFTA Award 1978, Press Guild Award 1978, RTS Award 1986; 3 BAFTA nominations; *Recreations* theatre, film, walking, photography, music, travelling; *Style*— Martyn Friend, Esq; ✉ c/o Peters Fraser & Dunlop, The Chambers, Chelsea Harbour, Lots Road, London SW10 OXF (☎ 0171 376 7676, fax 0171 352 7356)

FRIEND, Dame Phyllis Muriel; DBE (1980, CBE 1972); da of Richard Edward Friend; *b* 28 Sept 1922; *Educ* Herts & Essex HS Bishop's Stortford, London Hosp (SRN), Royal Coll of Nursing (RNT); *Career* dep matron St George's Hosp 1956–59; chief nursing offr: London Hosp 1969–72 (matron 1961–68, dep matron 1959–61), DHSS 1972–82; *Style*— Dame Phyllis Friend, DBE; ✉ Barnmead, Start Hill, Bishop's Stortford, Herts (☎ 01279 654873)

FRIEND, Prof Richard Henry; s of John Henry Friend, and Dorothy Jean, *née* Brown; *b* 18 Jan 1953; *Educ* Rugby, Trinity Coll Cambridge (MA, PhD); *m* 1979, Carol Anne Maxwell, *née* Beales; 2 da (Rachel Frances b 31 July 1981, Lucy Alexandra 14 Feb 1984); *Career* res fell St John's Coll Cambridge 1977–80; Univ of Cambridge: demonstrator in physics 1980–85, lectr 1985–93, reader 1993–95, Cavendish prof of Physics 1995–; visiting prof Univ of California Santa Barbara 1986–87; visiting fell Royal Instn London 1992–; Nuffield Sci res fell 1992–93; J V Boys prize Inst of Physics 1988, interdisciplinary award RSC 1991, Hewlett-Packard Prize European Physical Soc 1996; MInstP 1988, FRS 1993; *Publications* author of numerous papers on solid state and chemical physics in scientific journals; *Style*— Prof Richard Friend, FRS; ✉ University of Cambridge, Cavendish Laboratory, Madingley Road, Cambridge CB3 OHE (☎ 01223 337218, fax 01223 353397, e-mail rhf10@cam.ac.uk)

FRIER, Dr Brian Murray; s of William Murray Frier, of Edinburgh, and Christina Roper, *née* Anderson; *b* 28 July 1947; *Educ* George Heriot's Sch Edinburgh, Univ of Edinburgh (BSc(Hons), MB ChB, MD); *m* 25 Oct 1985, Isobel Margaret, da of Dr Henry Donald Wilson (d 1991), of Edinburgh; 1 da (Emily Margaret b 15 Nov 1989); *Career* jr med appts Edinburgh and Dundee 1972–76, research fell in diabetes and metabolism Cornell Univ NY USA 1976–77, sr med registrar Edinburgh 1978–82; conslt physician: W Infirmary and Gartnavel Gen Hosp Glasgow 1982–87, Royal Infirmary Edinburgh 1987–; currently pt/t reader in medicine Univ of Edinburgh; author of numerous papers on diabetes and hypoglycaemia; former govr George Heriot's Tst Edinburgh; memb: Br Diabetic Assoc (R D Lawrence lectr 1986), Assoc of Physicians GB and I, Euro Assoc for the Study of Diabetes; FRCPE 1984, FRCPG 1986; *Books* Hypoglycaemia and Diabetes: Clinical and Physiological Aspects (jt ed with B M Fisher, 1993); *Recreations* history (ancient and modern), appreciation of the arts; *Style*— Dr Brian M Frier; ✉ 100 Morningside Drive, Edinburgh EH10 5NT (☎ 0131 447 1653); Royal Infirmary of Edinburgh, Lauriston Place, Edinburgh EH3 9YW (☎ 0131 536 2074, fax 0131 536 2075)

FRIER, (Gavin Austin) Garry; s of Gavin Walter Rae Frier (d 1985), and Isabel Fraser, *née* Austin (d 1981); *b* 18 May 1953; *Educ* Hutchesons' Boys Glasgow, Univ of Strathclyde (BA); *m* 1978, Jane Carolyn, da of John Keith Burton, of Glasgow; 1 s (Stuart Austin b 1981); *Career* CA; dir County Bank Ltd (renamed County Natwest Ltd) 1985–87; chief exec: Ferrum Holdings plc 1987–94, Williams De Broë plc Edinburgh 1995–; dir A R Brown McFarlane Ltd 1993–; MICAS 1978; *Recreations* tennis, shooting, skiing; *Clubs* Western (Glasgow); *Style*— Garry Frier, Esq; ✉ Cedar Grove House, Dirleton, North Berwick, East Lothian EH39 5DR; Williams De Broë plc, 7 Forres Street, Edinburgh EH3 6BJ (☎ 0131 220 3686)

FRIES, Richard James; s of Felix Theodore Fries (d 1942), Joan Mary, *née* Hickling; *b* 7 July 1940; *Educ* Kingston GS, King's Coll Cambridge; *m* 1970, Carole Anne, da of Henry Wilson Buick; 2 da (Hannah Jane b 21 Oct 1971, Jessica Marion b 26 May 1974), 1 s (James Wilson b 31 March 1978); *Career* various positions Home Office 1965–92, Chief Charity Cmmr 1992–; *Recreations* music, chess, walking; *Style*— Richard Fries, Esq; ✉ The Charity Commission, St Alban's House, 57–60 Haymarket, London SW1Y 4QX (☎ 0171 210 4465)

FRISBY, Roger Harry Kilbourne; QC (1969); *Educ* Univ of Oxford (MA), Univ of London (LLB); *Career* called to the Bar Lincoln's Inn 1950, recorder; *Clubs* Hurlingham; *Style*— Roger Frisby, Esq, QC; ✉ Queen Elizabeth Building, Temple, London EC4Y 9BS (☎ 0171 583 5766)

FRISBY, Simon Rollo; s of Lt-Col Lionel Claud Frisby, DSO, MC (d 1936), of Farleigh Wallop, Basingstoke, Hants, and Angela Beryl, *née* Hoare (d 1990); *b* 23 Oct 1933; *Educ* Ludgrove Sch, Eton; *m* 29 Sept 1959, (Sara) Belinda, da of Capt William Herbert Fox (ka 1940), of Adbury Park, Newbury, Berks, and Marjorie Ellen, *née* Ayscough (d 1992); 1 s (Richard b 1961), 2 da (Angela (Mrs Wolrige Gordon) b 1963, Caroline (Mrs Henson) (twin) b 1963); *Career* Lt short serv cmmn Coldstream Guards 1952–56; C Hoare & Co Bankers 1956–57; ptnr: David A Bevan Simpson & Co 1968 (joined 1957), De Zoete & Bevan 1970–86, Barclays de Zoete Wedd 1986–90; memb London Stock Exchange 1963–93; *Recreations* fishing, gardening; *Clubs* Cavalry and Guards', MCC, Worplesdon Golf; *Style*— Simon Frisby, Esq; ✉ The Field House, Longstock, Stockbridge, Hants SO20 6DZ; 59 Rosaville Rd, London SW6 (☎ 0171 381 0918)

FRISBY, Terence Peter Michael; s of William Alfred Frisby (d 1967), of Borough Green, Kent, and Kathleen Campbell Day, *née* Caseley (d 1994); *b* 28 Nov 1932; *Educ* Dartford GS, Central Sch of Speech Trg and Dramatic Art; *m* 28 Aug 1963 (m dis 1971), Christine, da of Luigi Vecchione; 1 s (Dominic b 9 Sept 1969); *Career* playwright, actor, dir, prodr (over 200 acting and directing roles in theatre, TV, film, West End and rep for over 36 years); most notable prodn Woza Albert (Criterion) 1983–84; published plays: The Subtopians (1962), There's A Girl In My Soup (1966, filmed 1971 starring Peter Sellers and Goldie Hawn, winner Writers' Guild of GB award for Best Br Comedy 1970), The Bandwagon (1969), It's All Right If I Do It (1977), Seaside Postcard (1978), Rough Justice (1994); radio play Just Remember Two Things - It's Not Fair And Don't Be Late (1988, winner Giles Cooper award); many TV plays incl: Blackmail, Guilty, Don't Forget The Basics; two TV series: Lucky Feller (LWT 1976), That's Love (TVS 1988–92, winner Houston Int Film Festival Gold Award 1991); acting roles in theatre incl: A Christmas Carol (1978), Rookery Nook (1979), The Real Inspector Hound (1983–84), The Entertainer (1984), Hay Fever (1985), Once A Catholic (1981–86); TV roles incl: Two Townsmen, When The Boys Come Out To Play, The Brothers, A Strike Out of Time; memb: Writers' Guild of GB, Equity; *Style*— Terence Frisby

FRISCHMANN, Dr Wilem William; CBE; s of Lajos Frischmann (d 1944), of Hungary, and Nelly Frischmann (d 1945); *Educ* Hammersmith Coll of Art and Building, Imperial Coll of Sci and Technol (DIC), City Univ of London (PhD); *m* 1 Sept 1957, Sylvia, da of Maurice Elvey (d 1980), of Glasgow; 1 s (Richard Sandor), 1 da (Justine Elinor); *Career* CJ Pell & Partners 1956–68 (ptnr 1961–68), sr ptnr Pell Frischmann & Ptnrs 1968–, chm Pell Frischmann Group 1984–; chm Conseco International Ltd; FEng 1985, FCGI, FIStructE, MConsE, MASCE; MSISdeFr; *Recreations* tennis, swimming, skiing; *Clubs* Arts; *Style*— Dr Wilem Frischmann, CBE, FEng; ✉ Pell Frischmann, 5 Manchester Square, London W1A 1AU (☎ 0171 486 3661, fax 0171 487 4153, telex 21536 Consec G)

FRITCHIE, Dame Irene Tordoff (Rennie); DBE (1996); da of Charles Fredrick Fennell (d 1975), and Eva, *née* Tordoff; *b* 29 April 1942; *Educ* Ribston Hall GS for Girls; *m* 21 Oct 1960, Don Jamie Fritchie (d 1992), s of Frederick Fritchie; 2 s (Charles Eric b 14 March 1962 d 1991, Andrew Peel b 30 Sept 1965); *Career* early career experience in family hotel Royal George Birdlip, admin offr Endsleigh Insurance Brokers 1970–73, sales trg offr Trident Insurance Ltd 1973–76, head of trg confs and specialist trg advsr on women's devpt Food and Drink Industl Trg Bd 1976–80, conslt Social Ecology Associates 1980–81, dir Transform Ltd conslts on organisational change 1981–85, The Rennie Fritchie Consultancy 1985–89, md Working Choices Ltd 1989–91, Mainstream Development Consultancy 1991–; chair: Gloucester Health Authy 1988–92, S Western RHA 1992–94, S and W RHA 1994–96; hon visiting prof (with chair in creative leadership) Univ of York 1996–; non-exec dir Stroud and Swindon Building Society 1995–96; memb NHS Policy Bd 1994–96, Home Sec's rep on Selection Panel for Independent Membs of Police Authorities; visiting faculty memb HSMU Univ of Manchester 1994–; non-exec bd memb Br Quality Fndn; pres Winston's Wish 1996–; patron: Headway Glos, Art in Health; chair Nat Advsy Gp on Nursing; memb Working Parties: on women in NHS, examining non-exec bd membership for the public sector; formerly: bd memb Nat Centre for Mental Health, non-exec dir Inst of Health Servs Mgmnt Consultancy, bd memb Int Outward Bound Sch, visiting faculty memb Ashridge Mgmnt Coll (specialising in leadership devpt), cncl memb Cheltenham and Gloucester Coll of HE; memb: Assoc of Mgmnt Educn and Devpt 1981–93, Forum UK 1993, GMC 1996–; Hon DPhil Univ of Southampton 1996; *Books* Working Choices (1988), The Business of Assertiveness (1991); *Recreations* family, reading, gardening, swimming, theatre, cooking, The Archers and Coronation Street; *Style*— Dame Rennie Fritchie, DBE; ✉ The Stream, Ashleworth, Gloucestershire GL19 4JH (☎ 01452 700777); Centre for Leadership & Management, Department of Health Studies, University of York, Innovation Centre, York Science Park, York YO1 5DG

FRITH, David Edward John; s of Edward Frith (d 1989), of Sydney, and Patricia Frith (d 1971); *b* 16 March 1937; *Educ* Canterbury HS Sydney; *m* 11 May 1957, Debbie Oriel Christina, da of Reuben Henry Pennell, of Ipswich, Queensland; 2 s (Peter James David b 1958, John Michael Denis b 1961), 1 da (Julianne Edie b 1962); *Career* Daily Mirror Sydney 1954, Overseas Shipping Assoc 1955–60, Alan Davis Advertising 1960–62, Abrahams Packaging 1962–64, Servowarm Central Heating 1964–72, ed The Cricketer 1972–78, fndg ed Wisden Cricket Monthly 1979–96; *Awards* Cricket Soc Jubilee Literary Awards 1970 and 1987, Wombwell Cricket Lovers' Soc Cricket Writer of the Year 1984, Br Sportswriter (Magazines) of the Year 1988 (highly commended 1992); memb: Cricket Writers' Club 1968– (memb Ctee 1978–), Assoc of Cricket Statisticians, The Cricket Soc, Cricket Memorabilia Soc (vice pres); *Publications* author of 20 books incl: The Fast Men, The Slow Men, England v Australia Test Records, The Golden Age of Cricket 1890–1914, Cricket Gallery, England v Australia - A Pictorial History of the Test Matches Since 1877, Pageant of Cricket, By His Own Hand, Stoddy's Mission; also compiler two cricket videos: Benson & Hedges Golden Greats (Batsmen and Bowlers); *Recreations* playing cricket, walking through Queensland rainforest; *Clubs* MCC; *Style—* David Frith, Esq; ✉ 6 Beech Lane, Guildford, Surrey GU2 5ES

FRITH, Mark; *b* 22 May 1970; *Educ* Gleadless Valley Sch Sheffield, Univ of East London; *Career* ed coll magazine 'Overdraft' 1989–90 (writer 1988–89); Smash Hits: writer 1990–93, features ed 1993–94, ed 1994–96; ed Sky Magazine 1996–; runner-up Student Journalist of the Year The Guardian/NUS Student Media Awards 1990; *Style—* Mark Frith, Esq; ✉ c/o Sky Magazine, Mappin House, 4 Winsley Street, London W1N 7AR (☎ 0171 436 1515)

FRITH, Ven Richard Michael Cokayne; s of Canon Roger Cokayne Frith (d 1989), and Joan Agnes, *née* Pearson; *b* 8 April 1949; *Educ* Marlborough, Fitzwilliam Coll Cambridge (MA), St John's Coll Nottingham; *m* 1975, Jill, da of Norman Richardson; 2 s (James b 1977, Timothy b 1982), 2 da (Rachel b 1979, Elizabeth b 1985); *Career* ordained: deacon 1974, priest 1975; curate Mortlake with E Sheen (Dio of Southwark) 1974–78, team vicar Thamesmead (Dio of Southwark) 1978–83, team rector Keynsham (Dio of Bath and Wells) 1983–92, archdeacon of Taunton 1992–; *Recreations* cricket, theatre; *Clubs* MCC; *Style—* The Ven the Archdeacon of Taunton; ✉ 4 Westerkirk Gate, Staplegrove, Taunton, Somerset TA2 6BQ (☎ 01823 323838, fax 01823 325420)

FRITH, Hon Royce Herbert; QC (Canada); s of George Harry Frith, and Annie Beatrice, *née* Royce (decd); *b* 12 Nov 1923, Montréal, Québec; *Educ* Lachine Québec HS, Parkdale Collegiate Inst Toronto Ontario, Victoria Coll Univ of Toronto (BA), Osgoode Hall Law Sch Toronto (LLB), Univ of Ottawa (Diplôme d'études supérieures, DES); *m* Elizabeth Mary Davison (decd); 1 da (Valerie Elizabeth), 1 s (Gregory Royce (decd)); *Career* Canadian diplomat; ret lawyer, ret Canadian senator; pres Ontario Lib Assoc 1961–62, cmmr Royal Cmmn on Bilingualism and Biculturalism 1963–70; Senate of Canada: summoned 1977, dep govt ldr 1980–84, dep ldr of the oppn 1984–91, ldr of the oppn 1991–93, memb Govt Front Bench 1993–94; high cmmr to Ct of St James's 1994–96; practised law Toronto and Perth Ontario 1949–89; former legal advsr to the Cmmr of Offical Languages, ret memb Law Soc of Upper Canada; conslt Ladner Downs Barristers & Slrs Vancouver BC Canada 1996–; *Recreations* music, amateur theatre, golf, tennis, squash; *Style—* The Hon Royce Frith, QC; ✉ Ladner Downs, 1200 Waterfront Centre, 200 Burrard Street, PO Box 48600, Vancouver, BC, V7X 1T2, Canada

FRIZZELL, Colin Frazer; s of Thomas Norman Frizzell (d 1976), of Grosvenor House Hotel, London, and Susanna Alice Clogh, *née* Boyd (d 1979); *b* 8 April 1939; *Educ* Oundle; *m* 9 June 1962, Anna Georgina, da of Thomas Stewart-Johnstone (d 1986); 2 da (Nicola (Mrs Johnny Gayner) b 1963, Sarah (Mrs Simon Gore) b 1965); *Career* Lt Royal Fusiliers 1958–59; chm The Frizzell Group Ltd insurance and financial servs until 1981–96 (joined 1957); Liveryman: Worshipful Co of Insurers, Woshipful Co of Coachmakers & Coach Harness Makers; *Recreations* fly-fishing, golf, music; *Clubs* Royal and Ancient Golf (St Andrews), Grimersta Estate (Isle of Lewis); *Style—* Colin Frizzell, Esq; ✉ Smewins Barn, Smewins Road, White Waltham, Maidenhead, Berks SL6 3SR (☎ 0118 934 3062, fax 0118 934 3063)

FRIZZELL, Edward William; s of Edward Frizzell (d 1987), of Bridge of Allan, and Mary McArthur, *née* Russell (d 1996); *b* 4 May 1946; *Educ* Paisley GS, Univ of Glasgow (MA); *m* 4 April 1969, Moira, da of late Alexander Calderwood; 3 s (Gregor Edward b 6 March 1973, Euan Alexander b 23 May 1980), 1 da (Karen Elizabeth b 9 Aug 1975); *Career* Scottish Milk Mktg Bd 1968–73, SCWS Ltd 1973, Scottish Cncl Devpt and Indust 1973–76, princ Dept of Agric and Fisheries for Scotland Scottish Office 1976–78, first sec Office of the UK Perm Rep to the EC FCO 1978–82; Scottish Office: asst sec Scottish Educn Dept 1982–86, Fin Div 1986–89, dir Indust Dept/Scottish Devpt Agency 1989–91, chief exec (grade 3) Scottish Prison Serv 1991–; *Recreations* running, mountain biking, hill walking; *Clubs* Mortonhall Golf (Edinburgh); *Style—* Edward Frizzell, Esq; ✉ Chief Executive, Scottish Prison Service, Calton House, 5 Redheughs Rigg, Edinburgh EH12 9HW (☎ 0131 244 8522, fax 0131 244 8774)

FRODSHAM, Anthony Freer; CBE (1978); s of George William Frodsham (d 1929), and (Constance) Violet, *née* Neild (d 1949); descendant of Charles Frodsham (1810–71), the London clockmaker; *b* 8 Sept 1919, in Peking, China; *Educ* Ecole Lacordaire Paris, Faraday House Engrg Coll London (DFH); *m* 1953, Patricia Myfanwy, da of Cdr A H Wynne-Edwards, DSC, RN (d 1971); 2 s (Simon, David); *Career* Lt (E) RN 1940–46, served in China, E Indies and Med (despatches); retired mgmnt conslt, chartered engr and co dir; chief exec P-E Consulting Group 1963–72; dir: Tace plc 1973–75, UDT Industries Ltd 1973–75, F Pratt Engineering Corporation 1982–85, Greyfriars Ltd 1984–87; conducted study for MOD on the provision of Engr Offrs for the Armed Forces 1983; dir gen Engrg Employers' Fedn 1975–82, ind chm Int Compressed Air and Allied Machinery Ctee 1977–96, vice chm Br Export Fin Advsy Cncl 1982–87; chm: Mgmnt Consits Assoc 1968–70, Machine Tools EDC 1973–79, Advsy Ctee Euro Business Inst 1982–; pres: Inst of Mgmnt Consits 1966–68, Inst of Linguists 1986–89; memb: Engrg Indust Trg Bd 1975–79, CBI Employment Policy Ctee 1975–82, CBI Grand Cncl 1975–82, CBI President's Ctee 1979–82; gen cmmr of taxes 1975–94, chm Cncl Euro Business Sch 1983–90, memb Advsy Cncl Royal Naval Engrg Coll 1988–94, DTI Enterprise cnsllr 1988–91; Hon Dr Business Admin 1991; Hon FIL 1986; *Clubs* Carlton, RAC; *Style—* Anthony Frodsham, Esq, CBE; ✉ 36 Fairacres, Roehampton Lane, London SW15 5LX (☎ 0181 878 9551)

FROGGATT, Anthony Grant (Tony); *b* 9 June 1948; *Educ* Queen Mary Coll London (LLB), Columbia Univ NYC (MBA); *Career* with Gillette Co (USA, Asia and Aust) 1974–78, H J Heinz Aust 1978–83, md Swift & Moore Aust (drinks distributor) 1983–88, dir gen Cinzano Switzerland 1988–92; pres: IDV Asia Pacific 1992–95, IDV Europe 1995–; *Style—* Tony Froggatt, Esq; ✉ International Distillers & Vintners Ltd, 8 Henrietta Place, London W1M 9AG (☎ 0171 518 5455, fax 0171 518 4626, mobile 0802 271003)

FROGGATT, Sir Peter; kt (1985); s of Albert Victor Froggatt (d 1964), of Belfast, and Edith, *née* Curran (d 1949); *b* 12 June 1928; *Educ* Royal Belfast Acad Inst, Royal Sch Armagh, Trinity Coll Dublin (MB, MA, MD, LLD), Queen's Univ Belfast (DPH, PhD, LLD); *m* 1958, Norma Alexandra Irene, da of Robert Alexander Cochrane (d 1976), of Belfast; 4 s (Mark b 1961, Richard b 1964, Ian b 1968, Keith b 1970); *Career* med conslt 1963–86; Queen's Univ Belfast: prof of epidemiology 1968–76, dean Sch of Med 1971–76, vice-chllr and pres 1976–86; non-exec dir: Allied Irish Banks plc, First Trust Bank plc, Mater Hosp Med Tst; Freeman City of London 1990; Hon DSc NUI 1982; FRCP 1979, FFCM, FRCP (Ire), FFCM (Ire), FFOM (Ire), FRCS (Ire, hc), MRIA, CIMgt; *Recreations* golf, music, travel; *Style—* Sir Peter Froggatt; ✉ c/o First Trust Bank, 4 Queens Square, Belfast BT1 3DJ (☎ 01232 325559)

FROSSARD, Sir Charles Keith; KBE (1992), kt (1983); s of Rev Edward Louis Frossard, CBE (d 1968), formerly Dean of Guernsey, and Margery Smith, *née* Latta (d 1958); *b* 18 Feb 1922; *Educ* Elizabeth Coll Guernsey, Univ of Caen (Bachelier en Droit); *m* 10 April 1950, Elizabeth Marguerite, da of John Edmund Leopold Martel, OBE (d 1973), of Grange Court, Guernsey; 2 da (Marguerite, Jeanne); *Career* WWII: enlisted Gordon Highlanders 1940, cmmnd IA 1941, Capt 17 Dogra Regt, seconded Tochi Scouts and Chitral Scouts, NW Frontier India 1942–46; called to the Bar Gray's Inn 1949, advocate of the Royal Ct of Guernsey 1949; People's Dep States of Guernsey 1958, conseiller States of Guernsey 1967, slr gen 1969, attorney gen 1973, dep bailiff 1977, bailiff of Guernsey 1982–92, judge of Cts of Appeal of Guernsey and Jersey 1992–95; pres Indian Army Assoc 1993–; Docteur de L'Université (Honoris Causa) Caen 1990; KGStJ 1987; Médaille de Vermeil Ville de Paris 1984; *Recreations* golf; *Clubs* Naval and Military; *Style—* Sir Charles Frossard, KBE; ✉ Les Lierres, Rohais, St Peter Port, Guernsey GY1 1YW, Channel Islands (☎ 01481 22076)

FROST, Alan John; s of Edward George Frost (d 1981), and Ellen Lucy, *née* Jamieson (d 1979); *b* 6 Oct 1944; *Educ* Stratford Co GS, Univ of Manchester (BSc); *m* 15 Dec 1973, Valerie Jean, da of Francis David Bennett; 2 s (Christopher, Patrick); *Career* investmt dir Abbey Life Group 1986–89, md Abbey Life Assurance Co Ltd 1989–, dir Lloyds Abbey Life plc 1989–; dir Dorset TEC, chm S Wessex Industrial Project Duke of Edinburgh's Award; Freeman City of London 1986, Liveryman Worshipful Co of Actuaries 1986; FIA 1970, FIMgt 1990; *Books* A General Introduction to Institutional Investment (with D P Hager, 1986), Debt Securities (with D P Hager, 1990); *Recreations* opera, genealogy; *Style—* Alan Frost, Esq; ✉ Abbey Life House, PO Box 33, 80 Holdenhurst Rd, Bournemouth, Dorset BN8 8AL (☎ 01202 407278, fax 01202 401940)

FROST, Sir David Paradine; kt (1993), OBE (1970); s of Rev Wilfred John Paradine Frost (d 1967), of Tenterden, Kent, and Maud (Monna) Evelyn, *née* Aldrich (d 1991); *b* 7 April 1939; *Educ* Gillingham GS, Wellingborough GS, Gonville and Caius Coll Cambridge (MA); *m* 1, 1981 (m dis 1982), Lynne Frederick (d 1994), widow of Peter Sellers; m 2, 19 March 1983, Lady Carina Mary Anne Gabrielle, da of 17 Duke of Norfolk, KG, GCVO, CB, CBE, MC, *qv*; 3 s (Miles Paradine b 1984, Wilfred Paradine b 1985, George Paradine b 1987); *Career* TV presenter, producer, author; chm and chief exec The David Paradine Gp of Cos 1966–, jt fndr London Weekend Television, jt fndr and dir TV-am plc 1981–93; pres Lord's Taverners 1985, memb Cncl Wellbeing 1989–; Freeman of Louisville (Kentucky, USA) 1971; Hon LLB Emerson Coll Boston Mass USA 1970; *Television* BBC progs incl: That Was The Week That Was 1962–63, A Degree of Frost 1963 and 1973, Not So Much a Programme More a Way of Life 1964–65, The Frost Report 1966–67, Frost Over England 1967, Frost Over America 1970, Frost's Weekly 1973, The Frost Interview 1974, We British 1975–76, Forty Years of Television 1976, The Frost Programme 1977, The Guinness Book of Records Hall of Fame 1986, 1987, 1988, Breakfast With Frost 1993–; ITV series and progs incl: The Frost Programme 1966–67 and 1967–68, Frost on Friday 1968–69 and 1969–70, The Sir Harold Wilson Interviews 1976, The Nixon Interviews 1976–77, Frost on Sunday (TV-am) 1983–92, Through the Keyhole (ITV until 1995, Sky One 1996–) 1987–, The Frost Programme 1993–; Frost's Century (NBC Super Channel) 1995; subjects of PBS TV series Talking with David Frost incl: George and Barbara Bush, Andrew Lloyd Webber, Gen Norman Schwarzkopf, John Major, Robin Williams, Margaret Thatcher, Ted Turner, Elton John, Norman Mailer, Warren Beatty, Bill Clinton, Ross Perot, Sir John Gielgud, Dan Quayle, Al Gore, Isaac Stern, John Sununu, Sally Quinn, Peter Stone, Calvin Trillin, Clint Eastwood, F W de Klerk, Nelson Mandela, Mangosuthu Buthelezi, Boutros Boutros-Ghali, Salmon Rushdie, Lord Owen, Vladimir Zhirinovsky; *Films* prodns incl: The Rise and Rise of Michael Rimmer 1970, Charley-One-Eye 1972, Leadbelly 1974, The Slipper and the Rose 1975, James A Michener's Dynasty 1975, The Ordeal of Patty Hearst 1978, The Remarkable Mrs Sanger 1979; *Awards* Montreux Golden Rose for Frost over England 1967, RTS Silver Medal 1967, Richard Dimbleby Award 1967, Emmy Awards 1970 and 1971, Religious Heritage of America Award 1970, Albert Einstein Award Communication Arts 1971; *Books* That Was The Week That Was (1963), How to Live under Labour (1964), Talking with Frost (1967), To England With Love (1967), The Presidential Debate 1968 (1968), The Americans (1970), Whitlam and Frost (1974), I Gave them a Sword (1978), I Could Have Kicked Myself - David Frost's Book of the World's Worst Decisions (1982), Who Wants to be a Millionaire (jtly, 1983), The Mid-Atlantic Companion (jtly, 1986), The Rich Tide (jtly, 1986), The World's Shortest Books (1987), David Frost: An Autobiography Part One; *Recreations* cricket, soccer, tennis, food, wine; *Clubs* Queen's, MCC, Mark's, Annabel's, Harry's Bar, Mosimann's; *Style—* Sir David Frost, OBE; ✉ The David Paradine Group of Companies, 5 St Mary Abbots Place, Kensington, London W8 6LS (☎ 0171 371 3111, fax 0171 602 0411)

FROST, Derek Norton; s of John Norton Frost, of Nutley, E Sussex, and Elizabeth, *née* Gibson; *b* 24 April 1952; *Educ* Tonbridge; *partner* since 1978, Jeremy Gordon Norman, *qv*; *Career* designer; trained under David Hicks; dir of interior design Mary Fox Linton Ltd; formed own co Derek Frost Associates Ltd 1984; int practice specialising in interior design/furniture design; projects include: Heaven (night club), The Kobler Centre, many residential installations; solo exhibition of furniture Leighton House 1988; ISID; *Recreations* gardening, music, contemporary arts, craft, scuba diving; *Style—* Derek Frost, Esq; ✉ Derek Frost Associates, Moreton Yard, Moreton Terrace Mews North, London SW1V 2NT (☎ 0171 828 6270, fax 0171 976 5059)

FROST, Gerard Bernard John; s of Reginald John Frost (d 1971), and Patricia Martha, *née* Stanley (d 1990); *b* 22 Jan 1935; *Educ* Douai Abbey Sch, Salesian Coll Farnborough; *m* 21 May 1964, Priscilla Mary Frances, da of Patrick Bell; 2 da (Caroline Mary Frances b 11 Dec 1965, Angela Patricia Charlotte b 7 May 1967); *Career* Nat Serv RAF 1953–56; with Gardiner Hunter & Co (chartered accountants) until 1966 (joined as articled clerk 1956), accountant Singleton Fabian & Co London 1966–67, chief accountant Printing Div Oxford University Press 1967–86, sec and chief exec St Dunstan's London 1994– (chief accountant 1986–94); AInstT 1965, FCA 1975 (ACA 1965); *Recreations* music, heraldry, local history, foreign travel; *Style—* Gerard Frost, Esq; ✉ 27 Ditchley Road, Charlbury, Chipping Norton, Oxfordshire OX7 3QS (☎ 01608 810578); Secretary, St Dunstan's, PO Box 4XB, 12–14 Harcourt Street, London W1A 4XB (☎ 0171 723 5021, fax 0171 262 6199)

FROST, James Douglas (Jim); s of Richard George Frost, and Glynn Valirie, *née* Middlemass; *b* 31 July 1958; *Educ* Ashburton Secdy Sch; *m* 29 July 1986, Nicola, da of Antony Hornby; 2 s (Daniel George b 24 Sept 1987, Hadden James b 19 July 1990), 1 da (Bryony Mae b 13 April 1995); *Career* national hunt jockey; first ride as amateur 1972, turned professional 1982, ridden over 400 winners; major wins: Grand National 1989 (Little Polvier), Breeder's Cup Steeplechase 1990–91 (Morely Street), Sandeman Hurdle and Supreme Novice Hurdle (Forest Sun) Cheltenham Festival 1990, Bishop Cleve Hurdle 1991 (Crystal Spirit); youngest rider to win a 3 mile steeplechase aged 13; farmer; *Recreations* skiing, playing with the kids; *Style—* Jim Frost, Esq; ✉ Hawson Court, Buckfastleigh, South Devon TQ11 0HP (☎ 01364 642267)

FROST, (Cecil) John William (Jack); s of Benjamin John Frost (d 1963), and Gladys, *née* Raynes (d 1979); *b* 27 May 1942; *Educ* Royal Liberty GS; *m* 1 Sept 1962, Janice Rhoda, da of Herbert Cook (d 1971); 2 s (Stephen John, Jeremy William); *Career* md Cater Allen Ltd 1977–, dir Cater Allen Holdings plc 1983–; FCIB 1965; *Recreations* sailing, opera, jazz; *Style—* Jack Frost, Esq; ✉ Redwalls, Friars Close, Shenfield, Brentwood, Essex CM15 8HX; Cater Allen Ltd, 20 Birchin Lane, London EC3V 9DJ (☎ 0171 623 2070)

FROST, Michael Eric; s of Donald Jack Frost, MBE, and Marion Cecily, *née* Lines; *b* 26 Aug 1934; *Educ* Ipswich Sch; *m* 6 Sept 1967, Elsie Jean, da of Walter Whitehead; *Career* photographer; studio mangr Desmond Groves Ltd London and Wilmslow 1963–66, fndr The Michael Frost Studio York 1966, lectr on portraiture and wedding photography in Britain and abroad at professional photographic seminars; memb Qualifications Bd BIPP; awards: BIPP Wedding Photographer of the Year 1977, BIPP Portrait Photographer of the Year 1978 and 1981, Kodak Gold award for Portraiture 1985, 1988 and 1989; FBIPP, FRPS, FRSA, FMPA, CrPho (USA) 1992; memb Professional Photographers of America; *Books* Saleable Portraits - The Style and Technique (1989); *Recreations* travel, music, art; *Style—* Michael Frost, Esq; ✉ The Michael Frost Studio, The Shambles, York YO1 2LZ (☎ 01904 623895)

FROST, Ronald Edwin; s of Charles Henry Frost, and Doris, *née* Foggin; *b* 19 March 1936; *m* 19 Sept 1959, Beryl, da of Leonard Ward (d 1964), of Windsor; 1 s (Stephen Charles b 1962), 2 da (Jane Samantha b 1965, Louise Karen b 1966); *Career* chm and chief exec Hays Group Ltd 1986–89, exec chm Hays plc 1989–; dir: Hays Marine Services Ltd 1983–, Hays Distribution Services Ltd 1983–, Hays Holdings Ltd 1985–, Hays Personnel Services (Australia) Ltd 1987–, Hays Chemical Distribution Ltd 1988–, Hays Fril SA 1992–, Hays Commercial Services Ltd 1992–, Hays Marine Holdings Ltd 1992–, Hays Overseas Holdings Ltd 1992–, Hays Personnel Services Holdings Ltd 1992–, Dairy Crest Ltd 1993–, Hays Italia SpA 1995–; *Recreations* game shooting, sailing; *Clubs* RAC, Royal Thames Yacht, IOD, Carlton; *Style—* Ronald Frost, Esq; ✉ Hays plc, Hays House, Millmead, Guildford, Surrey GU2 5HJ (☎ 01483 302203, fax 01483 300388, car tel 0836 222159)

FROST, Terence Ernest Manitou (Terry); *b* 13 Oct 1915; *Educ* Central Sch Leamington Spa, Camberwell Sch of Art; *m* 11 Aug 1945, Kathleen May, *née* Clarke; 5 s (Adrian Dudley b 14 July 1947, Anthony b 4 May 1951, Matthew James b 24 Sept 1954, Stephen George b 28 Dec 1955, Simon Arnold b 13 Feb 1958), 1 da (Mary Charlotte Kate b 9 June 1961); *Career* WWII Serv 1939–45, Warwicks Yeo Army, served France and Palestine, transferred Commandos 1941, served Sudan, Abyssinia, Egypt and Crete, POW Poland then Bavaria 1941–45; formerly employed in non-artistic professions 1930–39; artist; visiting lectr Bath Acad of Art Corsham 1952–54, Gregory fell in painting Univ of Leeds 1954–56; pt/t teacher: Leeds Coll of Art 1956–67, Coventry Sch of Art 1963–64; fell in painting Univ of Newcastle 1965; Univ of Reading: pt/t then full time lectr Dept of Fine Art 1964–70, reader 1970–77, prof of painting 1977–81, prof emeritus 1981–; Hon LLD CNAA 1978; hon fell RCA 1990; RA; *Exhibitions* solo incl: Leamington Public Library 1944, Leicester Galleries London 1952, 1956 and 1958, Waddington Galleries 1959–80, Bertha Schaeffer Gallery NY 1960 and 1962, Retrospective Exhibition (Laing Gallery Newcastle upon Tyne and tour to York, Hull and Bradford, San Francisco, Santa Barbara and San Joes Art Galleries) 1964, Museum of Modern Art Oxford 1969, Arnolfini Gallery Bristol 1972, Retrospective Exhibition (Serpentine Gallery London) 1977, New Art Centre London 1981, Terry Frost - Painting in the 1980's (Univ of Reading and tour to Lincoln, Ayr, Plymouth and Newlyn) 1987–88, The Belgrave Gallery London and Austin Desmond Fine Art London 1989, The Mayor Gallery London 1990 and 1994, Adelson Gallery NY 1994, Coram Gallery London 1994, Belgrave Gallery London 1994, Green on Red Gallery Dublin 1995, The McGeary Gallery Brussels 1995, Newlyn Art Gallery Cornwall 1995, Flowers East London 1995; *Works in Public Collections* incl: Aberdeen Art Gallery, Art Gallery of South Aust Adelaide, Arts Cncl of GB, Birmingham City Art Gallery, Bristol City Art Gallery, Christchurch Art Gallery NZ, Contemporary Art Soc London, Dept of Environment, Fitzwilliam Museum Cambridge, Univ of Glasgow, Nat Gallery of Canada Ottowa, Nat Gallery of NSW Sydney, Nat Portrait Gallery, Scot Nat Gallery of Modern Art Edinbrugh, Tate Gallery, Tel Aviv Museum, Ulster Museum Belfast, V N A; *Clubs* Chelsea Arts; *Style—* Terry Frost, Esq, RA; ✉ Gernick Field Studio, Tredavoe Lane, Newlyn, Penzance TR18 5DL (☎ 01736 65902)

FROSTICK, Raymond Charles; DL (Norfolk 1979); s of Harry Frostick, of Hoveton, Norfolk (d 1965), and Ethel Marion, *née* Preston (d 1983); *b* 18 May 1931; *Educ* Norwich Sch, CCC Cambridge (MA, LLM); *m* 27 July 1957, (Rosemary) Claire, da of Sir George Harold Banwell, of Lincoln (d 1982); 2 s (Richard b 1960, Andrew b 1963), 2 da (Marion b 1958, Elizabeth b 1961); *Career* Nat Serv RAF 1949–51; admitted slr 1957; conslt Eversheds 1994–; vice chm R G Carter Holdings Ltd 1975–; dir: East Anglian University Residences plc 1991–; Univ of East Anglia: memb Cncl 1972–, treas 1985–90, pro chllr and chm Cncl 1990–; chm: Norfolk AHA 1978–82, Norwich Health Authy 1982–85; pres Norwich and Norfolk C of C and Indust 1985–88; cncllr: Norwich City Cncl 1966–79, Norfolk CC 1973–85 (chm 1983–84); Lord Mayor of Norwich 1976–77, vice pres RELATE Nat Marriage Guidance 1990– (chm 1986–90), pres RELATE Norfolk and Norwich 1990–; memb Law Soc 1957; Hon DCL UEA 1991; FRSA 1985; *Books* The Dutch Connection: Some Norfolk Maps and Their Makers (1988); *Recreations* cartography, travel; *Clubs* Royal Cwlth Soc; *Style—* Raymond Frostick, Esq, DL; ✉ 425 Unthank Rd, Norwich, Norfolk NR4 7QB (☎ 01603 452937); Eversheds, Holland Court, The Close, Norwich, Norfolk NR1 4DX (☎ 01603 272727, fax 01603 610535)

FROWEN, Prof Stephen Francis; s of Adolf Frowein (d 1964), and Anna, *née* Bauer (d 1968); *b* 22 May 1923; *Educ* Univs of Cologne, Würzburg, Bonn and London (BSc, MSc); *m* 21 March 1949, Irina, da of Dr Sam Minskers; 1 s (Michael b 17 Jan 1950 d 1989), 1 da (Tatiana Hosburn b 20 Sept 1955); *Career* ed The Bankers' Magazine (now The Chartered Banker) 1954–60, econ advsr Indust and Commercial Fin Corp (now 3i) 1960–61, res offr Nat Inst of Econ and Social Res London 1961–62; sr lectr: Univ of Greenwich 1962–67, Univ of Surrey 1967–87; prof of economics Univ of Frankfurt 1987, Bundesbank prof of monetary economics Free Univ of Berlin 1987–89, hon res fell UCL 1989–, sr res assoc Von Hügel Inst St Edmund's Coll Cambridge 1991–, external professorial res assoc Inst for German Studies Univ of Birmingham 1995–; special advsr UNIDO Vienna 1980–81, visiting prof Würzburg Univ 1983; Commander's Cross of the Order of Merit of the Federal Republic of Germany 1993, KSG 1996; *Books* ed: Economic Issues (jtly, 1957), Monetary Policy and Economic Activity in West Germany (jtly, 1977), A Framework of International Banking (1979), Controlling Industrial Economies - Essays in Honour of Christopher Thomas Saunders (1983), Business, Time and Thought - Selected Papers of G L S Shackle (1988), Unknowledge and Choice in Economics (1990), Monetary Policy and Financial Innovations in Five Industrial Countries - the UK, the USA, Germany, France and Japan (jtly, 1992), Monetary Theory and Monetary Policy - New Tracks for the 1990s (1993), Financial Decision-Making and Moral Responsibility (jtly, 1995), The German Currency Union of 1990 - A Critical Assessment (jtly, 1996), Hayek: Economist and Social Philosopher - A Critical Retrospect (1996), Welfare and Values (jtly, 1997); author of numerous articles in learned jls and chapters in books, ed of several conf transactions in the field of economics; *Recreations* numismatics, painting, music, reading; *Clubs* Reform, International PEN; *Style—* Prof Stephen Francis Frowen; ✉ 40 Gurney Drive, London N2 0DE (☎ and fax 0181 458 0159); Von Hügel Institute, St Edmund's College, Cambridge CB3 0BN (☎ 01223 336090, fax 01223 62590)

FROY, Prof Martin; s of late William Alan Froy, and Helen Elizabeth, *née* Spencer; *b* 9 Feb 1926; *Educ* St Paul's, Magdalene Coll Cambridge, Slade Sch of Fine Art UCL (Dip Fine Art); *Career* Gregory fell in painting Univ of Leeds 1951–54; teacher: engraving Slade Sch of Fine Art 1952–55, Bath Acad of Art 1954–65 (latterly head of fine art); head Painting Sch Chelsea Sch of Art 1965–72, prof of fine art Univ of Reading 1972–91 (emeritus prof 1991); commissions incl: mosaic decoration Belgrade Theatre Coventry 1957–58, mural panels Morley Coll Concert Hall 1958–59; public collections: Tate Gallery London, Museum of Modern Art New York, Museum of Art Santa Barbara, Chicago Art Inst, The Arts Council of GB, Contemporary Art Society, Royal W of England Acad, Univ of Leeds, Univ Coll London, The Slade Collection, City Art Galleries (Bristol, Carlisle, Leeds, Reading, Southampton, Wakefield); solo exhibitions: Hanover Gallery London 1952 and 1969, Univ of Leeds 1951 and 1953, Wakefield City Art Gallery 1953, Belgrade Theatre Coventry 1958, Leicester Galleries London 1961, Royal W England Acad Bristol 1964, Univ of Sussex 1968, Arnolfini Gallery Bristol 1970, Park Square Gallery Leeds 1970, Seven Paintings (City Art Gallery Bristol) 1972, Univ of Reading 1979, New Ashgate Gallery Farnham 1979, Serpentine Gallery London (Arts Cncl) 1983; group exhibitions incl: Int Abstract Artists (Riverside Museum New York and ICA London) 1950, Figures in Their Setting (Tate Gallery London), Beaux Arts Gallery London 1953, Br Painting and Sculpture (Whitechapel Gallery London) 1954, Le Congres pour la Liberte de la Culture Rome Paris Brussels 1955, Pittsburgh Int 1955, Six Young Painters (Arts Cncl touring the UK) 1956, ICA Gregory Memorial (Bradford City Art Gallery) 1960, Corsham Painters and Sculptors (Arts Cncl touring UK) 1965, Three Painters (Bath Festival) 1970, Park Square Gallery Leeds and The Ruskin Sch Univ of Oxford 1978, Newcastle Connection (Newcastle Poly) 1980, Six Painters (Univ of Reading Art Gallery) 1984, Homage to Herbert Read (Canterbury Coll) 1984, Public Property (Reading Museum and Art Gallery) 1987, Corsham a Celebration (Victoria Art Gallery Bath and touring); memb: Fine Art Panel Nat Cncl for Dips in Art and Design 1962–71, Nat Cncl for Dips in Art and Design 1969–71, Panel of Advisors Cwlth Scholarships Cmmn 1974–78, Standing Conf Univ Entrance, Cncl Museum of Modern Art Oxford 1974–79, Cncl Nat Tst 1976–79, Faculty of Painting British Sch at Rome 1978–81, Consortium for Art Design and Architecture Hants 1983–86, Bd Studies in Fine Art Univ of London, Ctee Slade Sch Univ Coll London 1966–92; tstee: Nat Gallery 1972–79, Tate Gallery 1975–79; Leverhulme Res award 1963, Sabbatical award Arts Council of GB 1965; *Style—* Prof Martin Froy; ✉ Department of Fine Art, University of Reading, Earley Gate, Reading, Berkshire RG1 5AQ

FROY, Robert Anthony Douglas; s of Hienz Louis Froy (d 1981), and Gisela Anna, *née* Salomon; *b* 23 Aug 1936; *Educ* Clarks Coll; *m* 8 July 1960, (Diana) Wendy, *née* Likeman; 2 s (Stephen b 4 April 1963, Nicholas b 21 Feb 1965); *Career* md: Montagu Loebl Stanley 1969–87, Lloyds Bank Stockbrokers 1987–, The Otford Group 1987 (chm), Hanover Property Unit Trust 1987, McLeod Russel Holdings plc 1994–; dir Lloyds Private Banking Ltd 1993–; Liveryman Worshipful Co of Pattenmakers; MSI; *Recreations* sport, walking, gardening; *Clubs* City of London; *Style—* Robert Froy, Esq; ✉ 171 Defoe House, Barbican, London EC2Y 8ND (☎ 0171 628 0083); Lloyds Bank Stockbrokers Ltd, 48 Chiswell Street, London EC1Y 4XX (☎ 0171 562 6000, fax 0171 562 6261, telex 888301)

FRY, Dr Anthony Harold; s of Henry Fry (d 1976), and Marjorie, *née* Davies; *b* 9 Nov 1942; *Educ* Highgate Sch, King's Coll Hosp (MB BS, LRCP, MRCS, MPhil, DPM); *m* 16 Nov 1974, Lynda Mary, da of Leslie Reginald Devenish, of Sussex; 3 s (Alexander b 4 June 1976, Nick b 28 April 1978, Robert b 6 Aug 1980); *Career* conslt psychiatrist; formerly recognised teacher psychiatry United Med Sch of Guy's and St Thomas' Univ of London, sr conslt physician in psychological med Guy's Hosp 1977–90, med dir Stress Mgmnt Unit London Bridge Hosp 1988–, conslt Charter Nightingale Hosp 1990–; ed Holistic Med 1984–88, med advsr Nat Marriage Guidance Cncl (Relate) 1979–90; chm and md Corporate Stress Therapy 1991–; memb Exec Ctee Ind Doctors' Forum 1994–; memb Royal Soc of Med Colloquium on Traditional and Complementary Med 1989; MRCPsych 1972, memb BMA 1980; *Books* Safe Space (1987); *Recreations* travel, squash, walking, poetry; *Clubs* RAC; *Style—* Dr Anthony Fry; ✉ 129 Hemingford Road, Barnsbury, Islington, London N1 1BZ (☎ 0171 609 0000); Suite 207, London Bridge Hospital, 27 Tooley Street, London SE1 (☎ 0171 607 3937, fax 0171 607 3815)

FRY, Anthony Michael; s of Denis Seymour Fry, of Worthing, Sussex, and Trixie, *née* Barter; *b* 20 June 1955; *Educ* Stonyhurst, Univ of Florence, Magdalen Coll Oxford (BA, Atkinson prize, treas Oxford Union Soc); *m* 27 July 1985, Anne Elizabeth, da of Harry Birrell; 1 s (Edward Harry Seymour b 21 Jan 1993), 1 da (Sophie Alexandra b 27 April 1991); *Career* N M Rothschild & Sons Ltd: joined 1977, mangr International Pacific Corporation Melbourne Australia (renamed Rothschild Australia 1983) 1980–85, exec dir corp fin 1985–96; md Barclays de Zoete Wedd 1996–; non-exec dir Southern Water plc 1994–96; chm Opera at the Garden, vice chm British Lung Fndn, tstee National History Museum Development Tst, memb Guild of Bonnetmakers Glasgow; FRSA; *Recreations* opera, theatre, cricket; *Clubs* Carlton, Australian, Armadillos CC, Incogniti CC, The Blake; *Style—* Anthony Fry, Esq

FRY, Dr Christopher; *b* 18 Dec 1907; *Educ* Bedford Modern Sch; *m* 1936, Phyllis Marjorie, *née* Hart; *Career* dramatist; actor Citizen House Bath 1927, teacher Hazelwood Prep Sch Limpsfield Surrey 1928–31; dir: Tunbridge Wells Repertory Players 1932–35, Oxford Repertory Players 1940 and 1944–46; staff dramatist Arts Theatre London 1947 (dir 1945); Queen's Gold Medal for Poetry 1962; DLitt Lambeth 1988; Hon DLitt: Sussex 1994, De Montfort Univ 1994; hon fell Manchester Metropolitan Univ 1988; FRSL; *Plays* A Phoenix Too Frequent (Mercury 1946, St Georges 1983), The Lady's Not for Burning (Arts 1948, Globe 1949, Chichester 1972, subsequent revival Old Vic), The Firstborn (Edinburgh Festival 1948, Winter Garden Theatre London 1952), Thor with Angels (Canterbury Festival) 1948, Venus Observed (St James's) 1950, The Boy with a Cart (Lyric) 1950, Ring Round the Moon (trans from French of Jean Anouilh, Globe) 1950, A Sleep of Prisoners (St Thomas's Regent St) 1951, The Dark is Light Enough (Aldwych) 1954, The Lark (trans from French of Jean Anouilh, Lyric) 1955, Tiger at the Gates (trans from French of Jean Giraudoux, Apollo) 1955, Duel of Angels (trans from Pour Lucrece of Jean Giraudoux, Apollo) 1958, Curtmantle (RSC) 1962, Judith (trans from Giraudoux, Her Majesty's) 1962, A Yard of Sun (National) 1970, Peer Gynt (trans, Chichester) 1970, Cyrano de Bergerac (trans, Chichester) 1975, One Thing More or Caedmon Construed (Chelmsford Cathedral) 1986; *Television* The Brontës of Haworth (four plays) 1973, Sister Dora 1977, The Best of Enemies 1977; film commentary for The Queen is Crowned (Coronation film, 1953); *Film Scripts* contrib to Ben Hur, The Bible, The Beggars Opera, Barabbas; *Publications* The Boy with a Cart (1939), The First Born (1946), A Phoenix too Frequent (1946), The Lady's Not for Burning (1949), Thor with Angels (1949), Venus Observed (1950), A Sleep of Prisoners (1951), The Dark is Light Enough (1954), The Lark (trans, 1955), Tiger at the Gates (1955), Duel of Angels (trans, 1958), Curtmantle (1961, Heinemann award RSL), Judith (trans, 1962), A Yard of Sun (1970), Peer Gynt (trans, 1970), Cyrano de Bergerac (trans, 1975), Can You Find Me: A Family History (1978), One Thing More (1986); published lectures: Death is a Kind of Love (The Tidal Press, 1979), Genius, Talent & Failure (King's Coll London, 1990), Looking for a Language (King's College, 1992); *Clubs* Garrick; *Style—* Christopher Fry, Esq, FRSL, DLitt; ✉ The Toft, East Dean, Chichester, West Sussex

FRY, Dominic Lawrence Charlesworth; s of Richard Noël Fry, of Lyme Regis, Dorset, and Jean Marianne, *née* Brunskill-Davies; *b* 28 Aug 1959; *Educ* Christ's Hosp, Faculté des Lettres Université Paul Valéry III Montpellier, Univ of North Carolina (Morehead scholar, BA); *m* 5 April 1993, Ann-Marie, *née* Finn; *Career* UK communications dir AT&T UK 1990–95; gp communications dir: Eurotunnel plc 1995–96, J Sainsbury plc 1996–; PRO Award for Excellence in Public Relations (AT&T) 1993; co-ordinator of arts sponsorship for the Almeida Theatre London 1990–95, business advsr Comité Europeene pour le Rapprochement de l'Economie et de la Culture (CEREC) 1994–; memb: ABSA, Business in the Arts Initiative; MIPR 1983; *Recreations* sailing, tennis, reading, rugby football; *Clubs* Wig and Pen; *Style*— Dominic Fry, Esq; ✉ J Sainsbury plc, Stamford House, Stamford Street, London SE1 9LL (☎ 0171 921 6000)

FRY, Jeremy Joseph; s of Roderick Fry (d 1952), of Grove House, Frenchay, Bristol, and Olave Kate, *née* Anderson (d 1950); *b* 19 May 1924; *Educ* Gordonstoun, The Architectural Assoc Sch of Architecture, RAF pilot trg; *m* 1955 (m dis 1967), Camilla, da of Geoffrey Grinling; 2 s (Francis Penrose b 1956, Cosmo Joseph b 1957), 2 da (Polly Elizabeth b 1960, Minna b 1965); *Career* product designer Frenchay Products Ltd 1954–57; fndr Rotork Engineering Co Ltd 1957 (now Rotork plc), with Rotork subsids in France Germany Italy USA Canada Spain and Holland 1960–70, fndr Rotork Marine Ltd 1967, ret 1984; pres Theatre Royal Bath (bought 1979, formed tst/restored theatre, chm 1979–84), chm Arnolfini Gallery Ltd Bristol (rebuilt interior) 1985–93, dir Eaton Hall Product Development 1985–93; chm: Green Park Station Ltd (a co to further arts in Bath) 1986–93, Northern Ballet Theatre (restructured co and moved to Halifax) 1989–94; fndr and pres Nelliyampathi Hills Conservation Soc India 1994–; RSA Bicentenary Medal 1992; *Recreations* arts in general; *Style*— Jeremy Fry, Esq; ✉ Magali Estates, Padagiri 678509, Palghat District, Kerala, India (fax 00 91 484 222066)

FRY, John Marshall; s of Montague Philip Fry, and Margery Maud, *née* Marshall; *b* 3 March 1936; *Educ* Tonbridge, Trinity Hall Cambridge (MA); *m* 12 Aug 1967, Diana Margaret, da of John Wybert Nowell Clark; 2 da (Amanda b 1969, Susannah b 1971); *Career* Royal Dragoons 1954–56; mgmnt trainee Marshall Cambridge (Ltd) 1959–61; Abbey National Building Society: mangr personnel and trg 1965–72, divnl mangr 1972–79, gen mangr 1979, dir 1984, mangr gp servs 1988; Abbey National plc: gp servs dir 1989–94, md Insurance 1994–95, dep chm 1995–96; pres Chartered Bldg Socs Inst 1986–87 (memb Cncl 1979), memb Cncl Chartered Inst of Bankers; chm of govrs Queenswood Sch Herts; FCIS 1972; *Recreations* gardening, equestrian activities; *Clubs* Cavalry and Guards'; *Style*— John Fry, Esq; ✉ Clonmel, Flaunden, nr Hemel Hempstead, Herts HP3 0PP (☎ 01442 832204)

FRY, Jonathan Michael; s of Stephen Fry (d 1979), of London, and Gladys Yvonne, *née* Blunt; *b* 9 Aug 1937; *Educ* Repton, Trinity Coll Oxford (MA); *m* 21 Feb 1970, Caroline Mary, da of Col Vincent Ashforth Blundell Dunkerly, DSO, JP (d 1968); 4 da (Lucy b 1971, Camilla b 1973, Victoria b 1977, Sophie b 1979); *Career* account exec Pritchard Wood & Ptnrs 1961–65, account supervisor Norman Craig & Kummel 1965–66, engagement mangr McKinsey & Co 1966–72, dir and chief exec Foods Div Unigate Ltd 1972–77, chief exec Burmah Castrol plc 1993– (joined 1978, md 1990–93); dep chm: Northern Foods plc 1996–, Christian Salvesen plc 1996–; chm: Woodborough Cons Assoc 1976–83, Beechingstoke Parish Cncl 1978–91, St Francis Sch Pewsey 1984–92; *Recreations* cricket, skiing, archaeology; *Clubs* MCC, Vincent's (Oxford); *Style*— Jonathan Fry, Esq; ✉ Beechingstoke Manor, Pewsey, Wilts; Burmah Castrol plc, Burmah Castrol House, Piper's Way, Swindon, Wilts SN3 1RE (☎ 01793 512712, fax 01793 513419, car 0831 887885)

FRY, Dr Lionel; s of Dr Ancel Fry (d 1972), and Barbara, *née* Mintzman (d 1979); *b* 19 March 1933; *Educ* King's Coll London (BSc, MD, BS); *m* 27 Nov 1955, Minnè, da of Dr Jack Sidney Zidel; 1 s (Michael b 1959), 2 da (Tessa Joanne b 1961, Kathrine b 1963); *Career* conslt dermatologist St Mary's Hosp London; author: Dermatology - An Illustrated Guide, Immunological Aspects of Skin Disease; *Recreations* tennis, walking, music, theatre; *Style*— Dr Lionel Fry; ✉ 16 Caroline Place, London W2 4AN (☎ 0171 229 7790); St Mary's Hosp, London W2 1NY; 96 Harley St, London W1 (☎ 0171 935 2421)

FRY, Dame Margaret Louise; DBE (1989, OBE 1982); da of Richard Reed Dawe, of Tavistock, and Ruth Dora, *née* Every (d 1968); *b* 10 March 1931; *Educ* Tavistock GS; *m* 11 April 1955, (Walter William) John Fry, s of Walter William Fry (d 1972), of Launceston; 3 s (Jeremy b 24 March 1957, Patrick b 17 March 1960, Robert b 12 May 1966); *Career* former Devon hockey player; memb: Cons Party 1947– (pres Torridge and W Devon Cons Assoc 1992–), Rail Users' Consultative Ctee 1984–96, Union of Cons and Unionist Assocs (pres Western Area 1995–), S and W Regnl Health Authy 1990–96, local church warden; chm: Western Area Women's Advsy Ctee 1978–81 (former memb and vice chm 1975–78), Cons Women's Advsy Ctee 1984–87 (vice chm 1981–82), Torridge and W Devon Cons Assoc, Nat Union of Conservative and Unionist Assocs 1990–91 (vice chm 1987–90); former memb: Tavistock Cons Assoc, Tavistock Young Cons, Nat Fedn of Young Farmers Clubs; *Recreations* farming and conservation, sport; *Style*— Dame Margaret Fry, DBE; ✉ Thorne Farm, Launceston, Cornwall PL15 9SN (☎ 01566 784308)

FRY, Michael Edward (Mike); s of Stanley Edmund Fry, of Preston, Lancs, and Margaret, *née* Hunt; *b* 16 Jan 1958; *Educ* Lostock Hall Co Secdy Sch, W R Tuson Coll Preston, Univ of Newcastle upon Tyne (BA), Univ of Leeds (MA); *m* Sept 1986, Dr Lindsay Margaret Herrington, da of Rodney Herrington, of Godalming, Surrey; *Career* graduate NHS admin job placements in Bath, Winchester, Newport IOW and Alton Hampshire 1980–82, admin St Martin's and Claverton Downs Hosps Bath 1982–84, dep admin and subsequent head of admin Freeman Gp of Hosps Newcastle upon Tyne 1984–88, unit gen mangr Christie Hosp S Manchester Heath Authy 1988–91, first chief exec Christie Hosp NHS Tst 1991–; hon fell Univ of Manchester 1992; MIHSM; *Recreations* motor sport, tennis; *Style*— Mike Fry, Esq; ✉ Christie Hospital NHS Trust, Wilmslow Rd, Withington, Manchester M20 9BX (☎ 0161 446 3000, fax 0161 446 3977)

FRY, Nicholas Rodney Lowther; s of Rodney William Lowther Fry (d 1993), of Derby, and Mary Winifred Rosalind, *née* Ellis; *b* 28 April 1947; *Educ* Malvern, Christ's Coll Cambridge (MA); *m* 1972, Christine Sarah, da of Edmund De Chazal Rogers (d 1967), of London; 1 s (Jonathan b 1976), 2 da (Emma b 1974, Lucy b 1981); *Career* investment banker; dir S G Warburg & Co Ltd 1983–95, dir SBC Warburg 1995–96, md NatWest Markets 1996–; memb Cncl Trinity Hospice Clapham; FICA; *Recreations* music, gardening, recreational sport; *Style*— Nicholas Fry, Esq; ✉ 38 Lyford Rd, London SW18 3LS (☎ 0181 874 7608); NatWest Markets Corporate Finance Limited, 135 Bishopsgate, London EC2M 3UR (☎ 0171 375 5000, fax 0171 648 3191)

FRY, Sir Peter Derek; kt (1994), MP (C) Wellingborough (majority 11,816); s of Harry Walter Fry, of High Wycombe, Bucks, and late Edith Fry; *b* 26 May 1931; *Educ* Royal GS High Wycombe, Worcester Coll Oxford (MA); *m* 1, 1958 (m dis 1982), Edna, da of John Roberts, of Liverpool; 1 s, 1 da; m 2, 1982, Helen Claire Mitchell, da of late James Gregson; *Career* memb Bucks CC 1961–67, insur broker 1963–69, London area political educn offr CCO 1961–63; contested (C): Nottingham N 1964, Willesden E 1966; MP (C) Wellingborough 1969–, memb Transport Select Ctee 1979–92, memb Br Delgn to Cncl of Europe Western Euro Union 1992–; chm Political Research & Communications International Ltd 1982–87, dir Countryside Political Communications Ltd 1987–91; vice pres British Yugoslav Soc; *Clubs* RAC; *Style*— Sir Peter Fry, MP; ✉ House of Commons, London SW1 (☎ 0171 219 3443)

FRY, Stephen John; s of Alan John Fry, ARCS (Lieut REME), of Booton, Norfolk, and Marianne Eve, *née* Newman; *b* 24 Aug 1957; *Educ* Uppingham, Queens' Coll Cambridge (MA); *Career* actor and writer; weekly Fry on Friday column in The Daily Telegraph 1989–91; patron: Studio 3 (arts for young people), Freeze (nuclear disarmament charity), Norwich Play House, Prisoners Abroad; memb: Amnesty Int, Comic Relief, Hysteria Tst; rector Univ of Dundee; *Theatre* appeared with Cambridge Footlights in revue The Cellar Tapes at Edinburgh Festival 1981 (Perrier award, televised BBC 1982); Latin (Scotsman Fringe First award 1980 and Lyric Hammersmith 1983), Forty Years On (Chichester Festival and Queen's Theatre London) 1984, The Common Pursuit (Phoenix Theatre London) 1988, Look Look (Aldwych) 1990; re-wrote script for musical Me and My Girl 1984 (London, Broadway, Sydney), Homesick (West End) 1995; *Television* Alfresco (Granada) 1982–84, The Young Ones (BBC) 1983, Happy Families (BBC) 1984, Saturday Night Live (Channel 4) 1986–87, Blackadder's Christmas Carol (BBC) 1988, Blackadder Goes Forth (BBC) 1989, A Bit of Fry and Laurie (4 series, BBC) 1989–94, Jeeves and Wooster (Granada) 1991–93, Stalagluft (Yorkshire) 1993, Cold Comfort Farm (BBC) 1994; *Radio* Loose Ends 1986–87, Whose Line Is It Anyway? 1987, Saturday Night Fry 1987; *Films* The Good Father, A Fish Called Wanda 1988, A Handful of Dust, Peter in Peter's Friends 1992, IQ (with Meg Ryan and Walter Matthau) 1995; *Books* The Liar (Heinemann, 1991), Paperweight (1992), The Hippopotamus (1994), Making History (1996); *Recreations* chess, computing, dining out, light alcoholic refreshments; *Clubs* Oxford and Cambridge, Chelsea Arts, Groucho, Freds, Savile, Dorchester, Browns; *Style*— Stephen Fry, Esq; ✉ c/o Hamilton Asper Management, Ground Floor, 24 Hanway Street, London W1P 9DD (☎ 0171 636 1221, fax 0171 636 1226)

FRYDENSON, Henry; s of Samuel Frydenson, and Barbara Frydenson; *b* 9 Nov 1954; *Educ* Hasmonean GS for Boys, UCL (LLB); *m* Aug 1980, Sarah, da of Samuel Reifer; 6 s (Alan, Jonathan, Martin, Sheldon, Andrew, Simon), 1 da (Deborah); *Career* admitted slr 1981; ptnr Paisner and Co 1984– (joined 1979); memb Soc of Tst and Estate Practitioners (STEP); Freeman City of London 1984; *Recreations* swimming, climbing, football, cricket, first aid, computers; *Style*— Henry Frydenson, Esq; ✉ Paisner & Co, Bouverie House, 154 Fleet St, London EC4A 2DQ (☎ 0171 353 0299, fax 0171 583 8621, telex 263189 pailex g)

FRYER, John Beresford; s of Reginald Arthur Fryer (d 1966), and Joyce Edith Fryer (d 1986); *b* 18 Feb 1945; *Educ* Chigwell Sch Essex; *m* 1, 3 April 1971, Jennifer Margaret Glew (d 1995); 2 da (Polly Jane b 12 Dec 1976, Sally Ann b 31 March 1980); m 2, 3 Aug 1996, Gillian Holmes; *Career* sub-ed and reporter: local newspapers in East London and Essex 1963–67, Daily Sketch 1967–68, London Evening Standard 1968–69; labour corr then labour ed Sunday Times 1969–82, industl corr (formerly labour corr) BBC News 1982–; regular contribs to all TV news and BBC Radio progs incl the Money Programme, Newsnight and Today; Parly candidate (Lab): Harwich 1974 (Feb and Oct), Buckingham 1979; *Recreations* tennis, watching West Ham United FC; *Clubs* Grays, Buckhurst Hill Lawn Tennis (Essex); *Style*— John Fryer, Esq; ✉ BBC News, BBC Television Centre, Wood Lane, London W12 7RJ (☎ 0181 576 7485)

FRYER, Martin John; s of David Ivor Fryer (d 1971), and June Laurie, *née* Bradley; *b* 3 Sept 1956; *Educ* Christ Church Cathedral Sch Oxford, Radley, Corpus Christi Coll Cambridge (MA); *Career* VSO teacher Lawas Sarawak 1978–80, sponsorship asst Jacob de Vries Ltd 1981–82, VSO field co-ordinator Bangkok 1982–85; British Council: regnl offr E Europe and N Asia Dept 1986–87, asst regnl dir São Paulo 1987–90, corp planning offr London 1990–93, dir Istanbul 1993–; *Recreations* music, reading, travel; *Style*— Martin Fryer, Esq; ✉ British Consulate General, Office of the Consul for British Council and Cultural Affairs, PK436 Beyoglu, 80060 Istanbul, Turkey

FRYER, Noel; s of John Fryer (d 1985), of Alsager, Cheshire, and Norah, *née* Leeson; *b* 15 Dec 1943; *Educ* Repton; *m* Anne Katherine, da of John William Walton; 1 s (James Christian Walton b 26 July 1976); *Career* articled clerk Peat Marwick Mitchell 1961–66, self employed chartered accountant 1966–89 and 1993–, exec ptnr Pannell Kerr Forster 1989–93; pres Rotary Int 1995–96 (dist govr 1986–87, hon treas 1990–93, vice pres 1994–95); FCA 1974 (ACA 1966); *Recreations* shooting, fishing, farming; *Clubs* East India, Lancashire CCC; *Style*— Noel Fryer, Esq; ✉ Little Moss Farm, Oakhanger, nr Crewe, Cheshire (☎ 01270 874012)

FRYER-SPEDDING, John Henry Fryer; OBE, DL; s of Lt-Col James Eustace Spedding, OBE (d 1969), of Windebrowe, Keswick, Cumbria, and Mary Catherine, *née* Fryer; *b* 23 Jan 1937; *Educ* Harrow, Trinity Coll Cambridge (MA); *m* 15 Aug 1968, Clare Caroline, da of Ven Walter Frederick Ewbank, of Carlisle, Cumbria; 2 s (James b 1970, Jack b 1972); *Career* Royal Green Jackets 1958–68; serv: Germany, Cyprus, Borneo; ret Maj 1968; DLI (TA) 1969–78, CO 7 Bn LI (TA) 1976–78, ret Lt-Col 1978; called to the Bar Gray's Inn 1970, practising Newcastle upon Tyne; recorder of the Crown Court; asst Parly Boundary Cmmn, chm VAT and Duties Tbnls; tstee: Wordsworth Tst, Calvert Tst for Disabled People; vice pres Tennyson Soc; High Sheriff of Cumbria 1997; *Recreations* forestry, beekeeping; *Style*— John Fryer-Spedding, Esq, OBE, DL; ✉ Mirehouse, Keswick, Cumbria CA12 4QE (☎ 017687 72287); Trinity Chambers, 12 Trinity Chare, Quayside, Newcastle NE1 3DF (☎ 0191 232 1927, fax 0191 232 7975)

FUCHS, Sir Vivian Ernest; kt (1958); s of Ernest Fuchs (d 1957), of Heatherdene, Tilford, Surrey, and Annie Violet, *née* Watson; *b* 11 Feb 1908; *Educ* Brighton Coll, St John's Coll Cambridge (MA, PhD); *m* 1, 1933, Joyce (d 1990), 2 da of John Alexander Connell (d 1914), of Langley, Putney; 1 s (Peter), 2 da (Rosalind (decd), Hilary); m 2, 8 Aug 1991, Mrs Eleanor Honnywill, da of Sir Hugh Vincent Biscoe (d 1932), of the Indian Political Service; *Career* WWII served W Africa and NW Europe, Maj; geologist and author; expeditions include: Greenland 1929, E Africa 1930–31, 1934 and 1937–38; field cdr Falkland Islands Dependencies Survey 1947–50, dir FIDS Scientific Bureau 1950–55, dir Br Antarctic Survey 1958–73; leader Commonwealth Trans-Antarctic Expedition 1955–58; pres: Int Glaciological Soc 1963–66, British Assoc for the Advancement of Science 1972, Royal Geographical Soc 1981–83; FRS; *Books* Crossing of Antarctica (1958), Antarctic Adventure (1959), Forces of Nature (ed, 1977), Of Ice and Men (1982), A Time to Speak (1990); *Recreations* gardening; *Clubs* Athenaeum; *Style*— Sir Vivian Fuchs, FRS; ✉ 106 Barton Rd, Cambridge CB3 9LH (☎ 01223 359238)

FUGARD, Michael Teape; CB (1990); s of Rev Theodore Charles William Cooper Teape Fugard (d 1984), rural dean of Malton, Yorks, and Lilian Rhodes, *née* Freeman Baker (d 1954); *b* 27 March 1933; *Educ* Sherborne; *m* 22 Dec 1961, Theresia, da of Anton Hollensteiner (d 1952), of Leiben, Lower Austria; 2 s (Robert b 1963, William b 1970), 2 da (Alison b 1962, Berenice b 1966); *Career* admitted slr 1957; cmmnd Army Legal Servs (subseq Army Legal Corps) 1958, Maj CO Army Legal Aid FARELF 1960–64, Lt-Col asst dir BAOR 1971, Col Legal Staff HQUKLF 1979–82, Brig Cdr Army Legal Gp UK 1983–86, dir of army legal servs 1986–90, Maj-Gen; hon legal advsr Kingston upon Thames CAB 1965–66; memb Law Soc's Salaried Slrs' Ctee 1973–78, chm UK Gp Int Soc for Military Law of War 1988–90; govr Royal Sch Bath 1984–92 (vice chm 1990–92), memb Spire Appeal Ctee Salisbury Cathedral 1985–86, chm Bd of Govrs Leadenhall Sch Salisbury 1988–95, memb Lord Chllr's Panel of Ind Insprs 1990–91, adjudicator Immigration Appeals in London 1991–95 (pt/t 1990–91), recorder of the Crown Court 1992–95 (asst recorder 1986–92), ret 1995; *Clubs* Lansdowne; *Style*— Michael Fugard, Esq, CB; ✉ 5 Elm Grove, Salisbury, Wiltshire SP1 1NQ

FUJII, HE Hiroaki; *b* 1933, Tokyo; *Educ* Faculty of Liberal Arts Tokyo Univ, Amherst Coll USA (grad); *m* Kiyoko; 3 da; *Career* Japanese diplomat; entered Miny of Foreign Affrs 1956, subsequently student Amherst Coll until 1958; Miny of Foreign Affrs: dir Economic Affrs Div UN Bureau 1971–72, private sec to Min for Foreign Affrs 1972–74, dir Second Economic Cooperation Div Economic Cooperation Bureau 1974–75; fell Center for Int Affrs Harvard Univ 1976–77, cnsllr Washington DC 1977–79; Miny of Foreign Affrs: dir Personnel Div 1979–81, dep DG Asian Affrs Bureau 1981–83; consul-gen Hong Kong 1983–85; Miny of Foreign Affrs: DG N American Affrs Bureau 1985–88, dep vice-min 1988–89; Japanese ambass: to OECD Paris 1989–92, to Thailand 1992–94, to the Ct of St James's 1994–; *Style*— HE Mr Hiroaki Fujii; ✉ Embassy of Japan, 101–104 Piccadilly, London W1V 9FN (☎ 0171 465 6500)

FUKE, Roberta Jane; da of Leslie Clifford Fuke, of Clifton, Bristol, and Sheila Kathleen, *née* Speller; *b* 1 Sept 1962; *Educ* Henbury Comp Sch Bristol, Univ of Bristol (BA), Bath Coll (PA Dip); *Career* sales exec Bass Mitchells & Butlers 1984–85, account exec Shipway Communications PR consultancy 1985–86; Hall Harrison Cowley PR Birmingham: account exec 1986–87, accounts mangr 1987–88, account dir 1988–90, bd dir 1990–91; md: Bonham Public Relations 1991–93, Leedex Public Relations 1993–95; sr conslt Countrywide Porter Novelli Ltd 1995–; MIPR; *Style*— Miss Roberta Fuke; ✉ Countrywide Porter Novelli Ltd, 51 The Green, South Bar, Banbury, Oxon OX16 9AB (☎ 01295 272288)

FULANI, Dan; *see:* Hare, John Neville

FULFORD, Adrian Bruce; QC (1994); s of Gerald John Fulford, and Marie Bettine, *née* Stevens; *b* 8 Jan 1953; *Educ* Elizabeth Coll Guernsey, Univ of Southampton (BA); *Career* housing advsr Housing Aid Centre Shelter 1974–76, called to the Bar Middle Temple 1978, in practice 1978–; *Recreations* tennis, golf, riding; *Clubs* Reform; *Style*— Adrian Fulford, Esq, QC; ✉ Barrister's Chambers, 14 Tooks Court, Cursitor Street, London EC4A 1LB (☎ 0171 405 8828, fax 0171 405 6680)

FULFORD, Robert Ian; s of (Howard) Bruce Fulford, of Colchester, Essex, and Mary Elizabeth, *née* Frost; *b* 26 Aug 1969; *Educ* Colchester Royal GS, St Aidan's Coll Durham, Univ of Essex; *Career* croquet player; memb Colchester Croquet Club, competitive debut 1986; achievements incl: Br under 19 champion 1986 and 1987, Br Masters champion 1989, Br men's champion 1990, Br Open doubles champion (with C Clarke) 1990, 1991, 1992, 1993 and 1996, world champion 1990, 1992 and 1994, Br Open champion 1991, 1992 and 1996, NZ Open champion 1993, Canadian Open champion 1993 and 1994, French Open champion 1993, Australian Open champion 1994; GB Test matches: USA 1989, 1990, 1991, 1992, 1994 and 1996, Aust 1990, 1993 and 1996, NZ 1990, 1993 and 1996; *Recreations* bridge, chess, snooker, most other sports and games; *Style*— Robert Fulford, Esq; ✉ Ramparts Farm, Bakers Lane, Colchester, Essex CO4 5BB (☎ 01206 852635)

FULFORD, Ronald S; *Career* chm Imperial Tobacco Ltd, sr assoc dir Hanson plc; *Style*— Ronald Fulford, Esq; ✉ Imperial Tobacco Ltd, PO Box 244, Southville, Bristol BS99 7UJ (☎ 0117 963 6636, fax 0117 966 7405)

FULFORD-DOBSON, Capt Michael; s of Lt Col Cyril Fulford-Dobson (d 1974), of Laleham-on-Thames, and Betty Bertha, *née* Bendelack-Hudson-Barmby (d 1982); *b* 6 April 1931; *Educ* Pangbourne Coll, Royal Naval Colls Dartmouth and Greenwich; *m* 17 Dec 1966, (Elizabeth) Barbara Mary Rose, da of Maj Oswald James Tate (d 1980); 3 da (Jemima Nancy Grace b 16 Jan 1968, Jessica Barbara Eliza b 29 April 1969, Rachel Eleanor Jane b 7 Sept 1971); *Career* midshipman Korean War, Co HMS Dark Avenger 1956–57, Flag Lt Suez Operation 1956, Flag Lt to Flag offr 2 i/c Mediterranean Fleet 1956–59, ops offr HMS Hogue first Cod War 1959, qualified Signal Offr 1960, HMS Jaguar S Atlantic 1964–65, Cdr 1969, Br nat rep Turkish Miny of Defence 1969–71, ops offr UK Strategic Worldwide Communications Network 1972–74, exec offr RNAS Yeovilton 1976–81, Capt 1981, sr Br naval offr, Asst Chief of Staff and Asst Chief Signals Offr Allied Forces N Europe; gentleman usher to HM The Queen 1985–; chm W Dorset General Hosps NHS Tst 1990–; dir: W Dorset Cncl on Alcohol 1986–91, In and Out Ltd 1993–96; pres Dorset Branch Cncl for the Protection of Rural England 1995–, chm Dorset Tst 1991–; High Sheriff for Co of Dorset 1994–95; *Recreations* restoring historic buildings, field sports, cross country skiing; *Clubs* White's, Naval and Military; *Style*— Capt Michael Fulford-Dobson, RN; ✉ Cerne Abbey, Dorset DT2 7JQ (☎ 01300 341284); West Dorset General Hospitals NHS Trust, Trust Headquarters, Damers Road, Dorchester, Dorset DT1 2JY (☎ 01305 254647, fax 01305 254185)

FULHAM, Suffragan Bishop of 1996–; Rt Rev John Charles Broadhurst; s of Charles Harold Broadhurst (d 1992), of St Albans, Herts, and Dorothy Sylvia, *née* Prince; *b* 20 July 1942; *Educ* Owens Sch Islington, KCL (AKC), St Boniface Coll Warminster, STh Lambeth (by thesis); *m* 9 Oct 1965, Judith Margaret, *née* Randell; 2 s (Mark John b 27 Feb 1970, Benedict Peter b 12 March 1979), 2 da (Jane Elizabeth (Mrs Sanders) b 5 Oct 1967, Sarah Helena (Mrs Panteli) b 27 June 1973); *Career* ordained deacon 1966, priest 1967; asst curate St Michael-at-Bowes 1966–70, vicar St Augstine Wembley Park 1975–85 (priest-in-charge 1970–75), team rector Wood Green 1985–96; area dean: Brent 1982–85, E Haringey 1985–91; memb Gen Synod 1972–96 (memb Standing Ctee 1988–96), pro-prolocutor Convocation of Canterbury 1990–96; memb: 7th Assembly WCC Canberra 1990, Anglican Consultative Cncl 1991–96; nat chm Forward in Faith 1992–, exec memb The Church Union; *Publications* Quo Vaditis (ed and contrib); numerous articles; *Recreations* gardening, history, travel; *Style*— The Rt Rev the Bishop of Fulham; ✉ c/o London Diocesan Office, 26 Canonbury Park South, London N1 2FN (☎ 0171 932 1100)

FULLENWIDER, Fran; da of Dale Fullenwider (d 1975), and Kelsey La Verrier-Stuart Fullenwider (d 1963); *b* 16 Nov 1945; *Educ* Univ of Maryland (BA), NY Univ (Graduate Study in Film, TV and Radio), RADA (Stage Mgmnt Diploma); *Career* actress, starring in romantic film comedies in Italy 1976–, dir Pilgrim Prodns 1987–; *Recreations* writing, interior decoration, food; *Clubs* Groucho, The Arts, The Polite Society; *Style*— Miss Fran Fullenwider; ✉ c/o Susan James Personal Management, 22 Westbeer Rd, London NW2 3SR (☎ 0171 794 1286)

FULLER, Anthony Gerard Fleetwood; CBE (1990); 2 s of Maj Sir Gerard Fuller, 2 Bt, JP (d 1981), and his 1 w, Lady Fiona Pratt (later Countess of Normanton, d 1985), yr da of 4 Marquess Camden; *b* 4 June 1940; *Educ* Eton; *m* 19 Nov 1964, Julia Mary, er da of Lt-Col Eric Astley Cooper-Key, MBE, MC; 1 s (William Gerard Fleetwood b 13 July 1968), 1 da (Camilla Fleetwood (Mrs Allan Christensen) b 16 Feb 1966); *Career* Lt Life Gds 1959–62; Lloyd's underwriter; Fuller Smith & Turner plc (brewers): dir 1967–, md 1978–92, and chm 1982–92, chm 1992–; non-exec dir Mentzendorff & Co Ltd 1992–; chm London region CBI 1995–; Freeman, Liveryman and past Master Brewers' Co; chm Brewers Soc 1986–89; *Recreations* shooting, gardening; *Style*— Anthony Fuller, Esq, CBE; ✉ Griffin Brewery, Chiswick, London W4 2QB (☎ 0181 996 2000); Little Chalfield Manor, Melksham, Wilts SN12 8NN (☎ 01225 865934)

FULLER, Brian Leslie; CBE (1989), QFSM (1981); s of Walter Leslie Victor Fuller, and Eliza May Fuller; *b* 18 April 1936; *Educ* St Albans Co GS for Boys; *m* 1957, Linda, *née* Peters; 3 s; *Career* fireman rising to station offr Herts Fire Brigade 1960–66, station offr Warwicks Fire Brigade 1966–68, asst divnl offr Notts Fire Brigade 1968–69, divnl cdr Essex Fire Brigade 1969–72; chief fire offr: Glamorgan Fire Brigade 1973–74 (dep chief offr 1972–73), Mid Glamorgan Fire Brigade 1974–80, Notts Fire Brigade 1980–81, W Mids Fire Serv 1981–90; cmdt Fire Serv Coll 1990–94; past chm Fedn of Br Fire Orgns, past pres Chief and Asst Chief Fire Offrs' Assoc, vice pres Comité Technique Int de Prevention et d'Extinction du Feu (CTIF); FIFireE; *Recreations* cricket, squash, music, reading; *Style*— Brian Fuller, Esq, CBE, QFSM

FULLER, John Leopold; s of Roy Broadbent Fuller (d 1991), and Kathleen, *née* Smith (d 1993); *b* 1 Jan 1937; *Educ* St Paul's Sch, New Coll Oxford (MA, BLitt, Newdigate prize); *m* 1960, Cicely Prudence, da of Christopher Martin; 3 da (Sophie b 1961, Louisa b 1964, Emily b 1968); *Career* poet and writer; visiting lectr SUNY Buffalo NY 1962–63, asst lectr in English Univ of Manchester 1963–66, fell and tutor in English Magdalen Coll Oxford 1966–; Geoffrey Faber Award 1974, Cholmondely Award, Whitbread Prize 1983, Forward Prize 1996; FRSL 1980; *Poetry* Fairground Music (1961), The Tree That Walked (1967), Cannibals and Missionaries (1972), Epistles to Several Persons (1973), The Mountain in the Sea (1975), Lies and Secrets (1979), The Illusionists (1980), Waiting for the Music (1982), The Beautiful Inventions (1983), Partingtime Hall (with James Fenton, 1987), The Grey Among the Green (1988), The Mechanical Body (1991), Stones and Fires (1996), Collected Poems (1997); *Fiction* Flying to Nowhere (1983), The Adventures of Speedfall (1985), Tell It Me Again (1988), The Burning Boys (1989), Look Twice (1991), The Worm and the Star (1993); *Criticism* Dramatic Works of John Gay (ed, 1983), A Reader's Guide to W H Auden (1970), The Sonnet (1972); *Recreations* printing, music, chess; *Style*— John Fuller, Esq, FRSL; ✉ 4 Benson Place, Oxford OX2 6QH (☎ and fax 01865 556154); Peters, Fraser & Dunlop, 503/4 The Chambers, Chelsea Harbour, London SW10 0XF (☎ 0171 376 7676, fax 0171 352 7356)

FULLER, Maj Sir John William Fleetwood; 3 Bt (UK 1910), of Neston Park, Corsham, Wiltshire; s of Maj Sir (John) Gerard Henry Fleetwood Fuller, 2 Bt (d 1981), and his 1 w, Lady Fiona Pratt, yr da of 4 Marquess Camden; *b* 18 Dec 1936; *Educ* Bradfield; *m* 9 Jan 1968, Lorna Marian, o da of F Richard Kemp-Potter, of Findon, Sussex; 3 s (James, Andrew William Fleetwood b 1972, Edward Richard Fleetwood b 1977); *Heir* s, James Henry Fleetwood Fuller b 1 Nov 1970; *Career* Maj (ret) Life Gds; *Style*— Major Sir John Fuller, Bt; ✉ Neston Park, Corsham, Wilts SN13 9TG (☎ 01225 810211)

FULLER, Keith Lewis; s of Charles Fuller (d 1964), of Cheam, Surrey, and Marie, *née* Varndell (d 1968); *b* 27 Oct 1932; *Educ* Epsom Coll, Univ of London (BSc); *m* 1973, Patricia, da of F Bernard Humphreys; 2 da (Rowena b 6 Dec 1975, Cassandra b 1 Oct 1977); *Career* Mullard (now Philips) Research Laboratories 1956–81, gp tech dir Racal-Decca 1981–85, md Philips Research Laboratories 1985–91, chm Philips Research Laboratories 1992, conslt 1992–; chm Electronics Div IEE 1989–90; FIEE 1975 (AMIEE 1956), FEng 1987; *Recreations* cars, music, photography; *Clubs* Aston Martin Owners'; *Style*— Keith Fuller, Esq, FEng; ✉ Almondwood, The Way, Reigate, Surrey RH2 0LD (☎ and fax 01737 240500)

FULLER, Martin Elliott; *b* 9 Feb 1943; *Educ* Mid-Warwickshire Coll of Art, Hornsey Coll of Art; *Career* artist; awarded Guggenheim-McKinsley scholarship (American Art Workshop Italy) 1964, formerly worked in Italy and America, now in London; winner Discerning Eye Award Modern Painters Magazine 1996; *Solo Exhibitions* incl: Arnolfini Gallery Bristol 1968, Midland Art Centre Birmingham 1968, Centaur Gallery Bath 1969, Bristol Art Gallery 1970, Arnolfini Gallery Bristol 1971, Bear Lane Gallery Oxford 1971, Camden Art Centre London 1971, Bear Lane Gallery Oxford 1973, Festival Gallery Bath 1973, Grabowski Gallery London 1973, Thumb Gallery London 1976 and 1979, Oxford Gallery 1983, RZA Galerie Dusseldorf 1983, Austin Desmond Fine Art 1985, On The Wall Gallery Belfast 1987, Hendriks Gallery Dublin 1987, Austin Desmond Fine Art 1990; *Commissions* incl: New Mexico USA Feb/Oct 1990, Murel New York 1992/93, collections for Peregrine Securities London 1994, Rowland Worldwide NY 1994, Times Mirror International Publishers Ltd London 1995, Dubai UAE 1996; *Clubs* Chelsea Arts, Groucho, Garrick; *Style*— Martin Fuller, Esq; ✉ c/o Chelsea Arts Club, 143 Old Church St, London SW3 6EB (fax 0181 678 6008)

FULLER, Michael John; s of Thomas Frederick Fuller, of Great Bookham, and Irene Emily, *née* Pope; *b* 20 July 1935; *Educ* Wallington GS; *m* 1, 26 March 1955 (m dis 1989), (Maureen) Rita, da of Frederick Slade; 2 s (Nicholas b 1960, Richard b 1962), 2 da (Laura b 1966, Jacqueline (twin) b 1966); m 2, 2 June 1990, Elizabeth Marion, da of Terence Townsend; *Career* Midland Bank plc: various positions 1952–77, gp public affairs advsr 1977–79, regnl dir Southampton 1979–81, gen mangr 1981–83, gen mangr business devpt 1983–85, UK ops dir 1985–87, dep chief exec UK banking sector 1987–89, chief exec UK banking sector 1989–90; gen mangr National Bank of Abu Dhabi 1991–92, chief exec Al-Ahli Commercial Bank BSC Bahrain 1992–; FCIB, FRSA; *Recreations* reading, travelling, rough golf; *Clubs* RAF; *Style*— Michael Fuller, Esq; ✉ Al Ahli Commercial Bank BSC, PO Box 5941, Manama, State of Bahrain (☎ 00 973 209101)

FULLER, Paul Malcolm; s of John Taylor Fuller, of Billericay, Essex; *b* 4 Nov 1946; *Educ* Southend HS for Boys; *m* 1969, Jenifer Mary Elizabeth, da of Percy Beere (d 1955); 1 s, 2 da; *Career* accountant; fin dir: Lacrinoid Products Ltd 1973–78, TKM Foods Ltd 1978–83; ptnr Deloitte & Touche (formerly Touche Ross) 1983– (consulting gp ptnr 1987); memb IOD; fell Chartered Inst of Mgmnt Accountants, FIMgt, FCCA; *Recreations* walking, the arts; *Style*— Paul Fuller, Esq; ✉ Pen-Y-Bryn House, 1 Buckingham Rd, Hockley, Essex SS5 4UE (☎ (office) 0171 936 3000, fax 0171 583 1198)

FULLER, Simon William John; CMG (1994); s of Rowland William Bevis Fuller (d 1993), of Ham Common, Richmond, and Madeline, *née* Bailey (d 1963); *b* 27 Nov 1943; *Educ* Wellington Coll, Emmanuel Coll Cambridge (BA); *m* 15 Sept 1984, Eleanor Mary, da of Peter and Ruth Breedon, of Crookham Village, Hants; 3 s (Edward William b 5 Sept 1986, James Francis b 13 June 1988, Peter John b 12 April 1991); *Career* HM Dip Serv 1968–; FCO 1968, second sec Br High Cmmn Singapore 1969–71, second sec Br Embassy Kinshasa 1971–73; first sec: Cabinet Office 1973–75, FCO 1975–77, UK Mission to UN NY 1977–80, FCO 1980–84; counsellor and dep head Personnel Ops Dept 1984–86, dep head Mission Br Embassy Tel Aviv 1986–90, head of Near East and N Africa Dept FCO 1990–93, ambass and head of UK delgn to Orgn for Security and Co-operation in Europe Vienna 1993–; *Recreations* cricket, golf; *Clubs* Brooks's, MCC, Berkshire Golf; *Style*— Simon Fuller, Esq, CMG; ✉ c/o Foreign and Commonwealth Office (Vienna), King Charles Street, London SW1A 2AH (☎ 0171 270 3000)

FULLER, Prof Watson; s of Edward Fuller (d 1983), of Haslingden, Lancashire, and Alice, *née* Worrall (d 1991); *b* 25 Feb 1935; *Educ* Haslingden GS, King's Coll London (BSc, AKC, PhD); *m* 9 Sept 1961, Shirley Ann, da of Cedric Pollack (d 1934), of London, and Vera Winifred, *née* Bowes (d 1982); 1 s (Laurence b 17 Dec 1965), 1 da (Catherine b 13 Nov 1967); *Career* scientific staff MRC 1960–63, reader in biophysics King's Coll London 1967–73 (lectr 1963–67); Keele Univ: prof of physics 1973–, head Physics Dept 1973–96, dep vice chllr 1980–83, 1984–85 and 1988–94; dir R & D for Health N Staffs 1994–; FInstP 1974; *Style*— Prof Watson Fuller; ✉ Oaklands, 50 Station Rd, Keele, Staffs ST5 5AH (☎ 01782 627220); Department of Physics, Keele University, Staffs ST5 5BG (☎ 01782 583320, telex 36113 UNKLIB G, fax 01782 711093, e-mail pha40@cc.keele.ac.uk, 100102.163@compuserve.com)

FULLERTON, Fiona Elizabeth; da of Brig B V H Fullerton, CBE, ADC, RAPC (ret), and Pamela, *née* Crook; *b* 10 Oct 1956; *Educ* Elmhurst Ballet Sch; *m* 1976 (m dis 1982), Simon MacCorkindale, *qv*; 2 m 1994, Neil Shackell; 1 da (Lucy b 16 October 1995); *Career* actress; dir Savoy Theatre Ltd; *Theatre* incl: title role in Cinderella (Palladium) 1976–77, Sally Bowles in I am A Camera 1979, Polly Peachum in The Beggar's Opera (Lyric Hammersmith) 1980, Gypsy Rose Lee in Gypsy 1981, The Boyfriend 1982, Queen Guinevere in Camelot (Apollo) 1982–83, The Royal Baccarat Scandal (Theatre Royal Haymarket) 1988–89, Revenge (Redgrave Theatre Farnham) 1991, Shakespeares's Henry

VIII and Valentine's Day (Chichester) 1991, Revenge tour 1992, Paulina in Death and the Maiden (Northcott Exeter) 1994, Eliza in Pygmalion (Chichester) 1994, Constance in The Constant Wife (Royal Theatre Northampton and tour) 1994–95; *Television* incl: Angels 1975–76, Gaugin, The Savage 1979, Leo Tolstoy: A Question of Faith 1979, Shaka Zulu 1985, Hold the Dream 1986, The Charmer 1986, Hazard of Hearts 1987, The Life of Hemingway 1987, A Taste for Death 1988, A Ghost in Monte Carlo 1989, Secret Life of Ian Fleming 1989, To Be The Best 1990, The Bogie Man (BBC) 1992; *Films* incl: Run Wild Run Free 1968, Anastasia in Nicholas and Alexandra 1970, title role in Alice's Adventures in Wonderland 1972, The Human Factor 1979, The Ibiza Connection 1984, A View to a Kill 1984, A Girl Called Harry 1990; *Style—* Miss Fiona Fullerton; ✉ c/o Jean Diamond, London Management, 2–4 Noel Street, London W1V 3RB (☎ 0171 287 9000, fax 0171 287 3036)

FULLERTON, John Charles Mark; s of Capt John Robert Rankin Fullerton (d 1966), by his 2 wife Evelyn Mary (d 1960), 2 da of Sir Alfred Molyneux Palmer, 3 Bt; *b* 21 Dec 1924; *Educ* Eton; *m* 1, 1955, Pamela Blanche Gwynedd (d 1982), da of Robert Crespigny Gwynedd Vivian (d 1982), of Jersey; 2 s (John, David), 1 da (Carolin); m 2, 1984, Philippa Nancy Le Marchant, *née* Denby; *Career* Staff Capt 60 Rifles KRRC; writer; former advertising exec; md Ogilvy & Mather Ltd Hong Kong 1978–79 (dir 1967), chm Assoc of Accredited Advertising Agents (Hong Kong) 1979; MIPA; *Novels* incl: If Chance is a Stranger, Beloved Enemy, The Man Who Spoke Dog; *Recreations* writing, sailing; *Style—* John Fullerton, Esq; ✉ Cwmirfon Lodge, Llanwrtyd Wells, Powys LD5 4TN (☎ and fax 01591 610849)

FULLERTON, HE William Hugh; CMG (1990); s of Maj Arthur Hugh Theodore Francis Fullerton, RAMC (d 1950), and Mary, *née* Parker; *b* 11 Feb 1939; *Educ* Cheltenham, Queens' Coll Cambridge (MA); *m* 1968, Arlene, da of late Dr J Jacobowitz; 1 da (Elizabeth b 1970); *Career* Shell Int Petroleum Co Uganda 1963–65; HM Dip Serv: joined FO 1965, MECAS Lebanon 1965–66, info offr Jedda 1966–67, UK Mission to UN (NYC) 1967, FCO 1968–70, head of Chancery Kingston Jamaica 1970–73, head of Chancery Ankara 1973–77, FCO 1977–80, cnsllr (econ and commercial) 1980–83, consul gen Islamabad 1981–83, ambass to Somalia 1983–87, on loan to MOD London 1987–88, govr of the Falkland Islands 1988–92, high cmmr British Antarctic Territory 1988–89, cmmr South Georgia and South Sandwich Islands 1988–92; ambass: to Kuwait 1992–96, to Morocco (concurrently non-resident ambass to Mauritania) 1996–; Medallion (First Class) Kuwait; *Recreations* travelling in remote areas, sailing, reading, walking; *Clubs* Travellers'; *Style—* HE Mr William Fullerton, CMG; ✉ c/o FCO (Rabat), King Charles Street, London SW1A 2AH

FULTHORPE, Jonathan Mark; s of Henry Joseph Fulthorpe, and Betty May, *née* Forshew; *b* 21 March 1949; *Educ* Sir Joseph Williamson's Mathematical Sch Rochester, UCL (LLB), Univ of London (LLM); *m* 1, 1973 (m dis 1978), Clare Elizabeth, *née* Stephenson; m 2, 1979, Carol Margaret, da of late Stanley Gordon Greenfield, of Brantford, Ontario, Canada; 1 s (James Mark Charles b 1981), 3 step da (Sarah Lynne b 1970, Jennifer Anne b 1972, Alison Claire b 1975); *Career* called to the Bar Inner Temple 1970, in practice Western circuit 1973–; fndr tstee Br Vascular Fndn 1992–; FRGS 1972; *Recreations* watching cricket, the study of geography, architecture, travel to rare places; *Clubs* Hampshire (Winchester), Hampshire CCC, Bentham, Flyfishers, Malaysian Cricket Supporters (Kuala Lumpur); *Style—* Jonathan Fulthorpe, Esq; ✉ 16 Abbotts Way, Southampton, Hants SO2 1QT (☎ 01703 584 879); chambers: 17 Carlton Crescent, Southampton SO1 2ES (☎ 01703 320320, fax 01703 320321)

FULTON, Rev John Oswald; s of Robert Fulton (d 1994), of Clydebank, and Margaret, *née* Wright; *b* 9 July 1953; *Educ* Clydebank HS, Univ of Glasgow (BSc, BD(Hons)); *m* 1989, Margaret Paterson, da of Robert Wilson (d 1981), of Glasgow; 1 da (Ruth Janet b 6 Sept 1991); *Career* United Free Church of Scotland: ordained 1977, min Croftfoot Glasgow 1977–94, gen sec 1994–; convener Ctee on Trg for the Miny 1984–89, moderator Presbytery of Glasgow and The West 1987–88, convener Ctee on Miny and Home Affrs 1989–93; *Recreations* gardening, photography, music, reading; *Style—* The Rev John Fulton; ✉ 12 Peveril Avenue, Burnside, Rutherglen, Glasgow G73 4RD (☎ 0141 630 0068); United Free Church of Scotland, 11 Newton Place, Glasgow G3 7PR (☎ and fax 0141 332 3435)

FULTON, Robert Andrew; s of late Rev Robert Morton Fulton, of Isle of Bute, Scotland, and Janet White, *née* Mackenzie; *b* 6 Feb 1944; *Educ* Rothesay Acad, Univ of Glasgow (MA, LLB); *m* 29 Aug 1970, Patricia Mary Crowley; 2 s (Daniel Robert b 8 Oct 1972, Edward Patrick b 8 Sept 1974), 1 da (Joanna Mary b 9 May 1979); *Career* HM Dip Serv; third sec FCO 1968, third then second sec Saigon 1968–72; first sec: Rome 1973–77, E Berlin 1978–81, FCO 1981–84; cnsllr: Oslo 1984–87, FCO 1987–89, UK Mission to UN NY 1989–92, FCO 1993–94, Washington 1995–; *Recreations* golf, national hunt racing, reading, cinema; *Clubs* The University Club (Washington DC); *Style—* R A Fulton, Esq; ✉ c/o Foreign and Commonwealth Office, King Charles Street, London SW1A 2AH

FUNG-ON, Eton Gregory; s of Leslie Rupert Fung-On, of Kent, and Avis Christabel, *née* Woon-Shing; *b* 14 Oct 1947; *Educ* Beckenham and Penge GS; *m* 3 July 1971, Patricia Helen, da of late Frederick Ernest Dodd, of Sussex; 2 s (Richard b 1973, Neil b 1974); *Career* CA, mgmnt conslt; various sr fin and mgmnt positions in public, commercial and industl orgns 1966–86, fin and investmt advsr Ficci Investments Ltd 1986–92; dir and treas Worldwide News Inc (t/a UPI) 1993–94, dir and treas ANA Holdings Inc (ANA Television and Radio Networks) 1993–94, vice pres ARA Group International 1994–96; FCA; *Recreations* church activities, gardening, sports; *Style—* Eton G Fung-On, Esq; ✉ 412 Upper Shoreham Rd, Shoreham-by-Sea, W Sussex BN43 5NE (☎ and fax 01273 462656)

FUNNELL, (Robert) Simon; s of Kenneth James Funnell (d 1987), of West Malling, Kent, and Morwenna Gladys, *née* Foster; *b* 17 Oct 1944; *Educ* King's Sch Rochester, Trinity Coll Cambridge (MA) King's Coll London (PGCE); *m* 6 July 1968, Sheila Ann, da of Desmond James Kibblewhite; 2 da (Rosalind Sophy b 16 Jan 1970, Isabel Ann b 12 July 1979), 1 s (Edward James b 7 Jan 1973); *Career* mgmnt training scheme 1966–68, publishing mangr 1968–70, head of English Eastbourne Coll 1973–76 (asst master English 1971–76); Shrewsbury Sch: head of English 1976–81, housemaster 1981–88; headmaster King's Coll Taunton 1988–; *Recreations* golf, tennis, picture-framing, walking; *Style—* Simon Funnell, Esq; ✉ The Headmaster's House, King's College, Taunton, Somerset TA1 3DX (☎ 01823 272708)

FURBER, (Robert) John; QC (1995); s of Frank Robert Furber, of Blackheath, London, and Anne Wilson, *née* McArthur; *b* 13 Oct 1949; *Educ* Westminster, Gonville and Caius Coll Cambridge (MA); *m* 16 April 1977, (Amanda) Cherry, da of Frederick Colbran Burgoyne Varney, OBE, of Blackheath, London; 1 s (Thomas b 1980), 2 da (Sophia b 1983, Olivia b 1989); *Career* called to the Bar Inner Temple 1973; *Books* jt ed: Halsbury's Laws of England (Landlord and Tenant) (1981), Hill and Redman's Law of Landlord and Tenant (1981–96), Halsbury's Laws of England (Compulsory Acquisitions) (1996); *Recreations* wine, literature, music, cricket; *Clubs* Buck's, Beefsteak; *Style—* John Furber, Esq, QC; ✉ 52 Southbrook Rd, Lee, London SE12 (☎ 0181 852 5770); 4 Breams Buildings, London EC4 (☎ 0171 353 5835)

FURLONG, Monica; da of Alfred Gordon Furlong (d 1972), of Co Cork, and Bessie Winifred Esther, *née* Simpson (d 1985); *b* 17 Jan 1930; *Educ* Harrow Co Girls Sch, UCL; *m* 12 Aug 1953 (m dis 1977), William John Knights; 1 s (Alexander William b 1961), 1 da (Charlotte Ann b 1957); *Career* Daily Mail 1961–68, prodr BBC 1974–78; moderator Movement for the Ordination of Women 1982–85, co fndr St Hilda Community 1987; DD Gen Theol Seminary NY 1986, Hon DLitt Univ of Bristol (1995); *Books* With Love To The Church (1964), Travelling In (1974), The Cat's Eye (1976), Merton (1980), Cousins (1983), Genuine Fake (1986), Thérèse of Lisieux (1987), Wise Child (1987), A Year and a Day (1990), A Dangerous Delight (1991), Robin's Country (1994), Bird of Paradise (1995); *Clubs* Soc of Authors; *Style—* Mrs Monica Furlong; ✉ c/o Sheil Land Associates, 43 Doughty Street, London WC1N 2LF (☎ 0171 405 9351, fax 0171 831 2127)

FURMANOVSKY, Jill; *b* 1953, Rhodesia; *Educ* Claremont Sch Kenton, Harrow Sch of Art, Central Sch of Art; *m*; 1 da; *Career* photographer; in-house photographer Rainbow Theatre 1972–79, freelance photo journalist 1970s and 1980s (contrib Sounds, Melody Maker, NME, Smash Hits and The Face); fndr JFA Studio 1982 (extending photography coverage to incl advtg and fashion); work featured in Sunday Times, The Observer, The Guardian, Q Magazine and others; stills photographer on films: Sister My Sister 1992, Institute Benjamenta 1993, Carrington 1994, Secret Agent 1995; official photographer to pop group Oasis; author of articles published in Photography Magazine 1987 and Br Journal of Photography 1990–91; *Awards* incl: Nikon Honourable Award 1984, Diamond Euro Music Photographer of the Year 1987, Ilford Award 1990, The Observer Portrait Award 1992, Kodak Gold Award 1994; *Books* The Moment - 25 Years of Rock Photography (1995); *Style—* Ms Jill Furmanovsky; ✉ Jill Furmanovsky & Associates, 8 Fitzroy Road, London NW1 8TY (☎ 0171 722 4716, fax 0171 916 4930, e-mail jfa@netcomuk.co.uk)

FURMSTON, Prof Michael Philip; TD; s of Joseph Philip Furmston (d 1987), of Chipstead, Surrey, and Phyllis, *née* Clowes; *b* 1 May 1933; *Educ* Wellington, Exeter Coll Oxford (BA, BCL, MA), Univ of Birmingham (LLM); *m* 26 Sept 1964, Ashley Sandra Maria, da of Edward Cope, of Cumnor, Oxon; 3 s (Simon b 1977, Thomas b 1981, Timothy b 1983), 7 da (Rebecca b 1967, Rachel b 1969, Charlotte b 1971, Clare b 1973, Alexandra b 1975, Antonia b 1978, Olivia b 1979); *Career* Nat Serv RA 1951–53, cmmnd 2 Lt 1952, TA serv 1953–78 (Maj 1966); lectr in law: Univ of Birmingham 1957–62, Queen's Univ Belfast 1962–63; fell Lincoln Coll Oxford and lectr in law 1964–78; Univ of Bristol: prof of law 1978–, dean Faculty of Law 1980–84 and 1995–, pro vice-chllr 1986–89; bencher Gray's Inn 1989; Freeman Worshipful Co of Arbitrators; *Books* Cheshire Fifoot and Furmston's Law of Contract (ed 8 to 13 edns, 1972–96), A Building Contract Casebook (with V Powell-Smith, 1984, 2 edn 1990), The Law of Tort: Policies and Trends in Liability for Damage to Property and Economic Loss (ed, 1986), You and the Law (ed with V Powell-Smith, 1987), Sale and Supply of Goods (2 edn 1995); *Recreations* chess (rep British team in 2 correspondence olympiads), dogs, Austin A35s, watching cricket; *Clubs* Reform, Naval and Military; *Style—* Prof Michael Furmston, TD; ✉ The Old Post Office, Shipham, Winscombe BS25 1TQ (☎ 0193 484 2253); Faculty of Law, University of Bristol, Wills Memorial Building, Queens Rd, Bristol BS8 1RJ (☎ 0117 928 7441, fax 0117 922 5136)

FURNEAUX, Paul; s of James Furneaux, of Aberdeen, and Nora Mavis, *née* Davidson; *b* 2 March 1962; *Educ* Aberdeen GS, Edinburgh Coll of Art (BA, postgrad Dip); *Career* artist; pt/t lectr in drawing and painting Edinburgh Coll of Art and Watercolour Workshop Aberdeen Art Gallery, visiting artist Cheltenham Coll of Art, teacher Summer Sch Edinburgh Coll of Art; *Solo Exhibitions* Todd Gallery London 1989 and 1991, Compass Gallery Glasgow 1989, Gordonstoun Sch 1990, Yamaquchi City Japan 1990, Wild Boar Gallery Aberdeen 1992, New Works (369 Gallery Edinburgh) 1994, Colores De Un Extrano Otono (Inst of Anglo-Mexico Culture) 1995; *Group Exhibitions* incl: Edinburgh Scene (City Art Centre) 1986, Christmas Show (Mercury Gallery) 1986, New Generation (Compass Gallery Glasgow) 1987, On a Small Scale (Open Eye Gallery) 1987, New Works (Backroom Gallery) 1987, The Chosen Few (Open Eye Gallery Edinburgh) 1988, Figure Form and Fantasy (Todd Gallery) 1988, Prints from the Four Colleges (Printmakers Workshop Edinburgh) 1988, Dozen Full of Talent (Kingfisher Gallery Edinburgh) 1989, Royal Scottish Acad Annual Show 1989 and 1990, Idylls of 89 (Todd Gallery) 1989, Aberdeen Against the Poll Tax (Arts Centre) 1989, Aberdeen Artists Annual Show 1990, Surrealist Tendencies in Contemporary Scottish Art (Open Circle Gallery Glasgow) 1990, Royal Soc of Painters in Watercolour Edinburgh 1991, Aberdeen Artists 57 (Aberdeen Art Gallery) 1991, Royal Scottish Acad Annual Show Edinburgh 1991, Largo Award Winners Exhibition (Loomshop Gallery Lower Largo Fyfe) 1991, The Spectator/Adam & Co Fourth Annual Award for Professional Young Artists (Edinburgh and The William Jackson Gallery London) 1991, Prints from Peacock (Gulausy Gallery Budapest) 1991, Made in Japan (Aberdeen Art Gallery) 1991, Soc of Scottish Artists Centenary Exhibition 1991, The Spectator Adam & Company Fifty Annual Award for Professional Artists (The Fruitmarket Gallery Edinburgh and The Barbican Centre London) 1992, The Inverclyde Biannual (Greenock) 1992, The Society of Scottish Artists (Edinburgh Royal Acad) 1992, Art for a Fairer World (organised by Oxfam for their 50th Anniversary Art Gallery and Museum Kelvingrove Glasgow, St David's Hall Cardiff and Smiths Galleries Covent Garden London) 1992, Back from Paris (an exhbn of works of the Miller Award Winners, Gallery of the Institut Francais d'Ecosse Edinburgh) 1992, An Artist's Choice (June Redfern Selects, Bohn Gallery Henley on Thames) 1993, Thursday's Child (Robert Billcliffe Fine Art Glasgow) 1994, Royal Scottish Academy Annual Exhibition Edinburgh) 1994, Times Ten (Gracefield Arts Centre Dumfries and Galloway Arts Festival Exhibition) 1994, Gathering (Galerie Beeldspraak Amsterdam) 1995, Edinburgh Coll of Art Staff Exhibition (Castillo De Soutomajor Arcade Ponte Vedra Spain) 1995; *Work in Collections* City Art Centre Edinburgh, Jean F Watson Bequest Purchase, Aberdeen Art Gallery, Heriot-Watt Univ, Edinburgh Coll of Art, Royal Scottish Acad, BBC Scotland, Cornhill Hosp Aberdeen, Eastern Gen Hosp Edinburgh, Aberdeen City Library, Forester Hill Hosp Aberdeen; *Awards* Royal Scottish Acad Keith Prize 1986, Edinburgh DC Spring Fling first prize for painting 1986, Young Scottish Artist of the Year 1987, Clason-Harie Bursary for Postgrad Exhibition 1987, Print Prize 1987, Largo Award Edinburgh Coll of Art, Sunday Times Scotland Mayfest Award for Visual Art 1989, Royal Over-Seas League Prize 1989, Alister E Salvesen Art scholar 1990, Royal Scottish Acad Meyer Openheim Prize 1991, Soc of Scottish Artists J F M Purchase Prize 1991, Royal Scottish Acad Ireland Alloys Award 1994, Br Cncl travel grant to travel and exhibit in Mexico 1994; memb Cncl Soc of Scottish Artists, professional memb Aberdeen Artists Soc 1994; *Recreations* hill walking in Scotland; *Style—* Paul Furneaux, Esq; ✉ Jenny Todd, Todd Gallery, 1–5 Needham Rd, London W11 2RP (☎ 0171 792 1404); 369 Gallery (Studio 2), 233 Cowgate, Edinburgh EH1 1NQ (☎ and fax 0131 220 3339)

FURNELL, Prof James Rupert Gawayne; s of Percy Gawayne Furnell (d 1986), of London, and Margaret Katherine Aslett, *née* Wray (d 1979); *b* 20 Feb 1946; *Educ* Leighton Park Soc of Friends Sch Reading, Univ of Aberdeen (MA), Univ of Glasgow (DCP), Univ of Stirling (PhD), Univ of Dundee (LLB, Dip LP); *m* 14 Sept 1974, Lesley Anne, da of John Ross, of Glasgow; 1 s (Alistair b 1976), 1 da (Rachael b 1978); *Career* clinical psychologist Royal Hosp for Sick Children Glasgow 1970–72, conslt clinical psychologist (child health) Forth Valley Health Bd 1980– (sr clinical psychologist 1972–80), memb Forth Valley Health Bd 1984–87; admitted Faculty of Advocates and called to Scottish Bar Parliament House Edinburgh 1993; visiting prof Caledonian Univ of Glasgow 1996–; memb Nat Consultative Ctee in Professions Allied to Med 1984–87, chm Div of Clinical Psychology Br Psychological Soc 1988–89; assoc ed Criminological and Legal Psychology; hon fell Univ of Edinburgh 1987–; FBPsS; *Recreations* flying, cross country skiing; *Clubs* Gleneagles; *Style—* Prof James Furnell; ✉ Glensherup

House, Glendevon, Perthshire (☎ 01259 781234); Advocates Library, Parliament House, Edinbugh EH1 1RF (☎ 0131 226 5071); Department of Child Clinical Psychology, Stirling Royal Infirmary, 1 Randolph Rd, Stirling (☎ 01786 434000)

FURNELL, Stephen George; s of George Edward Furnell (d 1971), of Kettering, Northants, and Norah Delia, *née* Barritt (d 1995); *b* 30 June 1945; *Educ* Kettering GS, Cambridgeshire HS, Leicester Poly (Dip); *m* 12 Feb 1972, Maxine, da of Harry Smith (d 1989), of Edmonton, London; 2 s (Thomas b 1972, Henry b 1982); *Career* Architects Dept Leicester CC 1967, ptnr TP Bennett 1987–93 (joined 1969), fndr Furnell Associates 1993–; ARIBA 1970, MCSD 1987, FRSA 1987; *Recreations* cricket, badminton, photography, painting; *Style*— Stephen Furnell, Esq; ✉ Furnell Associates, 20 Broadlands Avenue, London SW16 1NA (☎ 0181 769 4150, fax 0181 677 1431)

FURNESS, Alan Edwin; CMG (1991); s of Edwin Furness (d 1985), and Marion *née* Senton (d 1988); *b* 6 June 1937; *Educ* Eltham Coll, Jesus Coll Cambridge (BA, MA); *m* 27 Nov 1971, (Aline) Elizabeth Janine, da of Cdr R Barrett, RN (d 1972); 2 s (Roderick b 1972, Christian b 1975); *Career* CRO 1961, private sec to Parly Under Sec of State, CRO (Duke of Devonshire) 1961–62, third then second sec Br High Cmmn New Delhi 1962–66, DSAO 1966–69; first sec: UK Delegation to Euro Communities Brussels 1967–72, Br Embassy Dakar 1972–75; FCO 1975–78; cnsllr Br Embassy: Jakarta 1978–81, Warsaw 1982–85; head of S Pacific Dept FCO 1985–89, Br dep high cmmr Bombay 1989–93, ambass Senegal and non-resident ambass Mali Cape Verde and Guinée-Bissau 1993–97, concurrently non-resident ambass Guinea 1994–97; *Clubs* United Oxford and Cambridge Univ; *Style*— Alan Furness, Esq, CMG; ✉ 40 Brunswick Court, 89 Regency Street, London SW1P 4AE (☎ 0171 821 5063)

FURNESS, Michael Fitzroy Roberts; s and h of Sir Stephen Roberts Furness, 3 Bt, *qv*; *b* 12 Oct 1962; *Educ* Sedbergh, Askham Bryan Coll of Agric and Hort (HND); *Career* farmer; *Recreations* rugby, shooting, sculpture, travelling, contemplation, music; *Style*— Michael Furness, Esq; ✉ Glebe Farm, South Otterington, Northallerton, N Yorks (☎ 01609 780654)

FURNESS, Prof Raymond Stephen; s of Albert Victor Furness (d 1965), of Hatfield, Herts, and Margaret Anne, *née* O'Neil (d 1977); *b* 25 Oct 1933; *Educ* Univ of Wales (BA, MA), Univ of Munich, Univ of Berlin, Univ of Manchester (PhD); *m* 28 Aug 1965, Janice Clare, da of Norman Frank Fairey, of Sutton Coldfield, W Midlands; 1 s (Rupert William b 1967), 2 da (Cordelia Jane b 1969, Rosalind Lydia b 1974); *Career* Artillery and Intelligence Corps 1955–57; Univ of Manchester: lectr, sr lectr, reader 1959–84; prof Dept of Germany Univ of St Andrews 1984–; *Books* Expressionism (1973), A Literary History of Germany 1890–1945 (1978), Wagner and Literature (1982), A Companion to Twentieth Century German Literature (with M E Humble, 1991), An Introduction to German Literature 1871–1990 (with M E Humble, 1993), The Dedalus Book of German Decadence (1994); *Recreations* sleeping; *Style*— Prof Raymond Furness; ✉ The Dirdale, Boarhills, Fife KY16 8PP (☎ 01334 880469); The University, St Andrews, Fife KY16 9PH (☎ 01334 476161)

FURNESS, Col Simon John; DL (Berwickshire 1984); s of Sir Christopher Furness, 2 Bt (d 1974), of Netherbyres, Eyemouth, Berwickshire, and Violet Flower Chipchase, *née* Roberts (d 1988); *b* 18 Aug 1936; *Educ* Charterhouse, RMA Sandhurst; *Career* cmmnd Durham LI 1956, cmd 5 Bn 1976–78, ret Lt-Col 1978, Hon Col 1993; Dep Col Durham LI 1989–93; memb Exec Ctee Nat Tst for Scotland; Vice Lord Lt Berwickshire 1990; *Recreations* gardening, field sports; *Clubs* Army and Navy; *Style*— Col Simon Furness, DL; ✉ The Garden House, Netherbyres, Eyemouth, Berwickshire TD14 5SE (☎ 018907 50337)

FURNESS, Sir Stephen Roberts; 3 Bt (UK 1913), of Tunstall Grange, W Hartlepool; s of Sir Christopher Furness, 2 Bt (d 1974, 2 cous of 2 Viscount Furness), and Violet Flower Chipchase, *née* Roberts; *b* 10 Oct 1933; *Educ* Charterhouse; *m* 6 April 1961, Mary, er da of Jack Fitzroy Cann, of Newland, Cullompton, S Devon; 1 s (Michael Fitzroy Roberts, *qv* b 1962), 1 da (Serena Mary (Mrs Mark Searight) b 1964); *Heir* s, Michael Fitzroy Roberts Furness b 12 Oct 1962; *Career* late Lt RN, ret 1962; farmer and sporting artist (as Robin Furness); jt MFH Bedale Foxhounds 1979–87; *Recreations* hunting, racing, looking at paintings; *Style*— Sir Stephen Furness, Bt; ✉ Stanhow, Northallerton, North Yorkshire DL7 0TJ (☎ 01609 748614)

FURNISS, Air Vice-Marshal Peter; DFC (1944), TD (1964); s of John Furniss (d 1930), and Mary Furniss; *b* 16 July 1919; *Educ* Sedbergh; *m* 1954, Denise Andrée Gisèle, da of Charles Cotet, of S France; 1 s (Anthony Charles b 1965), 2 da (Caroline b 1959, Diana b 1960); *Career* cmmnd Liverpool Scottish TA, Queen's Own Cameron Highlanders 1939, seconded to RAF 1942, served in Med theatre of ops, cmd 73 Fighter Sqdn, demob 1946; admitted slr 1948, cmmnd in Legal Branch RAF 1950, dir Legal Servs HQ Air Forces M East, Aden 1961–63, HQ Far E AF Singapore 1969–71, HQ RAF Germany 1973–74, dir Legal Servs RAF 1978–82 (dep 1975–78); pres: Maidstone Branch RAFA, 40 (F) Maidstone Sqdn ATC; *Recreations* country pursuits; *Clubs* RAF; *Style*— Air Vice-Marshal Peter Furniss, DFC, TD; ✉ 18 Sevington Park, Loose, Maidstone, Kent ME15 9SB (☎ 01622 744620)

FURNIVAL JONES, Sir (Edward) Martin; kt (1967), CBE (1957); s of Edward Furnival Jones (d 1946); *b* 7 May 1912; *Educ* Highgate Sch, Gonville and Caius Coll Cambridge (MA); *m* 1955, Elizabeth Margaret, da of Bartholomew Snowball, AMIEE; 1 da; *Career* served WWII GSO SHAEF and War Office (despatches); slr 1937; attached to MOD; chm Bd Frensham Heights 1973–76 (pres 1977–96); *Style*— Sir Martin Furnival Jones, CBE

FURSDON, (Edward) David; o s of Maj-Gen (Francis William) Edward Fursdon, CB, MBE, *qv*, and Joan Rosemary, *née* Worssam; succeeded uncle as owner of 700 year old Fursdon family estate in Devon 1981; *b* 20 Dec 1952; *Educ* Sherborne, St John's Coll Oxford (scholar, BA, MA, cricket blue); *m* 7 Oct 1978, Catriona Margaret, da of Geoffrey Crichton McCreath, of Berwick-upon-Tweed; 3 s (Oliver b 1980, Thomas b 1982, Charles b 1986); *Career* 6 QEO Gurkha Rifles 1972; MOD (Whitehall and UN Geneva) 1975–79, ptnr Stags auctioneers 1994–; govr Blundell's Sch 1984–; lord of the manors of Cadbury and South Zeal; ARICS 1988, FAAV 1988; *Recreations* sport, travel; *Clubs* MCC, Vincent's (Oxford); *Style*— David Fursdon, Esq; ✉ Fursdon, Cadbury, Exeter, Devon; c/o Stags, 21 Southernhay West, Exeter, Devon (☎ 01392 55202)

FURSDON, Maj-Gen (Francis William) Edward; CB (1980), MBE (1958); s of George Ellsworth Sydenham Fursdon (d 1936), and Aline Lucinda, *née* Gastrell (d 1982); family resident at Fursdon in Devon since 1251; *b* 10 May 1925; *Educ* Westminster, Aberdeen (MLitt), Leiden (DLitt); *m* 1950, Joan Rosemary, da of Charles Archie Worssam, OBE (d 1971); 1 s ((Edward) David, *qv*), 1 da (Sabina b 1956); *Career* RE 1942; Cmd 25 Engr Regt BAOR 1967–69; AA & QMG HQ Land Forces Gulf 1970–71, Dep Cmd and COS Land Forces Gulf 1971, Col Qtg HQ BAOR 1972–73; dir Def Policy MOD (Euro and NATO) 1974–77 and Mil Asst Off MOD 1977–80; advsr to Govr of Rhodesia and sr Br offr Zimbabwe 1980; ret Maj-Gen 1980; def and mil corr Daily Telegraph 1980–86; ind def conslt and corr 1986–; UK corr Salut, special affairs corr Army Quarterly and Defence Jl; dir of Ceremonies Order of St John 1980–94; Freeman City of London; KStJ 1980; *Books* Grains of Sand (1971), There are no Frontiers (1973), The European Defence Community - a History (1980), Falklands Aftermath (1988); *Recreations* travel, writing, gardening; *Clubs* St John House; *Style*— Maj-Gen Edward Fursdon, CB, MBE; ✉ c/o St John House, 50 Eaton Place, London SW1 8AP

FURST, Stephen Andrew; QC (1991); *Career* called to the Bar Middle Temple 1975; *Style*— Stephen Furst, Esq, QC; ✉ Keating Chambers, 10 Essex Street, Outer Temple, London WC2R 3AA (☎ 0171 240 6981)

FUSSEY, Dr David Eric; s of (Frank) Eric Fussey, of Bridlington, N Humberside, and Edna May, *née* Rowntree; *b* 5 Sept 1943; *Educ* Hymers Coll Hull, Corpus Christi Coll Cambridge (MA Mech Scis), Univ of Warwick (PhD); *m* 1966, Beryl Kathleen, da of David Bruce and Kathleen Stella Taylor; 2 s (Peter Michael b 1970, Richard Paul b 1971); *Career* res offr CEGB Marchwood Engrg Laboratories 1964–69, lectr in mech engrg Univ of Nottingham 1969–78, prof and head mech engrg Univ of Technol Lae Papua New Guinea 1978–82, prof and head mech engrg (then dean of technol) Plymouth Poly 1982–89, dep dir Coventry Poly/Univ 1989–93, vice chllr Univ of Greenwich 1993–; memb: Senate Engrg Cncl 1990–, Jt Info Systems Ctee 1993–96, Cwlth Scholarships Cmmn 1995–, HEFCE 1996–; *Recreations* choral and keyboard music, long distance walking; *Style*— Dr David Fussey; ✉ Vice Chancellor, University of Greenwich, Southwood House, Avery Hill Road, Eltham, London SE9 2HB (☎ 0181 331 8880, fax 0181 331 8875)

FYFE, Brig Alastair Ian Hayward; DL (Somerset 1995); s of Archibald Graham Fyfe (d 1979), of Misterton, Somerset, and Alison Amy, *née* Hayward (d 1982); *b* 21 Oct 1937; *Educ* Lancing, RMA Sandhurst, Staff Coll Camberley; *m* 15 Aug 1964, Deirdre Bettina, da of Air Cdre James Maitland Nicholson Pike, CB, DSO, DFC, of Watlington, Oxford; 1 s (Andrew b 31 Aug 1967), 1 da (Nicola b 22 June 1966); *Career* cmmnd Duke of Cornwall's LI 1958, cmd 1 Bn LI 1980–82 (Adj 1968–69), mil attaché Moscow 1988–91, hon ADC to HM The Queen 1989–91, regimental sec LI (Somerset) 1991–, Hon Col Somerset ACF 1995–; fell Western Div Woodard Schs; govr: King's Coll Taunton, King's Hall Sch 1992; memb Nat Tst; *Recreations* music, walking, cricket; *Clubs* Army and Navy; *Style*— Brig Alastair Fyfe, DL

FYFE, Cameron Stuart; s of James Fyfe, of Dumfries, and Kathleen, *née* Hardman (d 1976); *b* 27 July 1954; *Educ* Dumfries Acad, Univ of Edinburgh (LLB); *m* 12 June 1995, Nuala McGrory; 1 step s (Mark b 17 Jan 1988); 1 da (Caitlin b 14 June 1996); *Career* apprentice then asst slr Cornillon Craig & Co Edinburgh 1976–80; Ross Harper: asst slr Edinburgh 1980–81, ptnr Court Dept East Kilbride 1981–89, in charge head office 1989–94, managing ptnr Ross Harper 1994–; winner first Scottish case for annulment of arranged marriage; *Books* Layman's Guide to Scotland's Law (1995); *Recreations* golf, tennis, fishing, hill climbing, painting, writing, guitar; *Clubs* Hilton Park Golf, Univ of Glasgow Tennis; *Style*— Cameron Fyfe, Esq; ✉ Ross Harper & Murphy, 163 Ingram Street, Glasgow G1 1DW (☎ 0141 552 6343, fax 0141 552 8150)

FYFE, Maria; MP (Lab) Glasgow Maryhill (majority 13,419); da of James O'Neill (d 1972), and Margaret, *née* Lacey (d 1980); *b* 25 Nov 1938; *Educ* Notre Dame High Glasgow, Univ of Strathclyde (BA); *m* 4 April 1964, James Joseph Fyfe (d 1986), s of James Fyfe (d 1974); 2 s (Stephen James b 1965, Christopher Paul b 1966); *Career* lectr 1976–87, MP (Lab) Glasgow Maryhill 1987–; convener Scottish Group of Labour MPs 1991–92, shadow spokesperson on Scottish affairs 1992–95, convener Scot All-Pty Gp on Children 1996–; memb: Glasgow Dist Cncl 1980–87, T&GWU, CND, Anti-Apartheid, Campaign for Scottish Assembly; *Recreations* reading, walking, cooking, eating, dancing; *Style*— Ms Maria Fyfe, MP; ✉ c/o House of Commons, London SW1A 0AA (☎ 0171 219 4430); Constituency Office, 1508 Maryhill Rd, Glasgow G20 (☎ and fax 0141 945 1495)

FYFE, William Stevenson; CBE (1992, OBE 1987); *b* 10 June 1935; *Educ* Dollar Acad, Scottish Coll of Commerce; *m* Margaret, *née* Auld; 1 s, 1 da; *Career* co dir and co mgmnt conslt; cncllr: Prestwick Town Cncl 1967–73, Ayr CC 1970–73; chm: Ayrshire and Arran Health Bd 1981–93, Gtr Glasgow Health Bd 1993, ret; chm Scottish Health Serv Advsy Cncl 1989–93, memb Gen Whitley Cncl 1989–93; dir Glagow Ayrshire Soc 1986– (chm 1988–89); fell Inst of Industl Managers 1985; *Recreations* relaxing; *Style*— William Fyfe, Esq, CBE; ✉ Ford House, Pennyglen, Culzean, Scotland KA19 8JW

G

GABATHULER, Prof Erwin; s of Hans Gabathuler (d 1972), of NI, and Anne Lena Gabathuler, *née* Graham (d 1970); *b* 16 Nov 1933; *Educ* Queen's Univ of Belfast (BSc, MSc), Univ of Glasgow (PhD); *m* 27 July 1962, Susan Dorothy, da of Charles Powell Jones (d 1988), of Essex; 2 s (John b 1966, David b 1970), 1 da (Helen b 1964); *Career* res fell Cornell Univ USA 1961–64, gp leader in res for SERC, Daresbury Laboratory UK 1964–74; CERN Geneva: visiting scientist 1974–77 and 1991–92, head Experimental Physics Div 1978–80, dir of research; Univ of Liverpool: prof of physics 1983–91, Sir James Chadwick prof of physics 1991–, head of Physics Dept 1986–91 and 1996–; author of various articles in res jls; chm Particle Physics Ctee SERC 1985–88; memb: Extended Scientific Cncl of Desy Hamburg W Germany, CNRS (IN2P3), France, Euro Physical Soc; Doctoris Honoris Causa Uppsala Univ of Sweden 1982, Rutherford Medal and Prize Inst of Physics 1992; CPhys, FInstP, FRS 1990; *Recreations* swimming, walking; *Style—* Prof Erwin Gabathuler, FRS; ✉ 3 Danebank Rd, Lymm, Cheshire WA13 9DQ; Physics Dept, Oliver Lodge Laboratory, Oxford St, University of Liverpool, PO Box 147, Liverpool L69 3BX (☎ 0151 7943350, fax 0151 7943444, telex 627095 UNIPL G)

GABLE, Christopher Michael; CBE (1996); *Educ* Sadler's Wells Ballet Sch; *Career* formerly ballet dancer with Sadler's Wells Opera and Theatre Ballets, Covent Garden Opera Ballet and Royal Ballet (princ dancer); cr numerous roles, danced all major classical roles, ptnr to all ballerinas of the Royal Ballet (notably Lynn Seymour); ret as dancer after ten years at Royal Opera House, became actor; worked with RSC (Lysander in Peter Brook's prodn of A Midsummer Night's Dream) and at Royal Exchange Theatre Manchester; fndr and artistic dir Central Sch of Ballet London 1982–, artistic dir Northern Ballet Theatre 1987–; award-winning prodns incl: Giselle (Manchester Evening News Award for Dance 1990), Romeo & Juliet (Manchester Evening News Award for Dance, SWET nomination 1991); Horniman Award for Outstanding Servs to Theatre 1989; hon memb RNCM; *Roles* as dancer incl: male leads in The Invitation, The Two Pigeons, Jeu de Cartes and House of Birds, Romeo in Kenneth MacMillan's Romeo and Juliet, L S Lowry in Gillian Lynne's A Simple Man (Northern Ballet Theatre); film and TV incl: Bassanio in The Merchant of Venice, Trofimov in The Cherry Orchard, Eric Fenby in Ken Russell's Delius, male leads in Ken Russell's The Boyfriend and The Rainbow; *Style—* Christopher Gable, Esq, CBE; ✉ Northern Ballet Theatre, West Park Centre, Spen Lane, Leeds LS16 5BE 0AQ (☎ 0113 274 5355, fax 0113 274 5381)

GABRIEL, Peter; *b* 13 Feb 1950; *Educ* Charterhouse; *Career* singer and songwriter; formed band The Garden Wall whilst at Charterhouse, merged with another sch band The Anon to form Genesis 1966 (with Tony Banks, *qv* and Mike Rutherford, *qv*); albums with Genesis: From Genesis to Revelation (1969), Trespass (1970), Nursery Cryme (1971), Foxtrot (1972), Genesis Live (1973), Selling England by the Pound (1973), The Lamb Lies Down on Broadway (1974); left gp to pursue solo career 1975; solo albums: Peter Gabriel I (1977), II (1978), III (1980) and IV (1982), Peter Gabriel Plays Live (1983), So (1986), Shaking the Tree (compilation, 1990), Us (1992); soundtrack albums: Birdy, Passion (for Last Temptation of Christ); musical collaborations with: Youssou N'Dour, Laurie Anderson, Tom Robinson, Robert Fripp, Joni Mitchell, Robbie Robertson, Cat Stevens, Charlie Drake, Colin Scot, Johnny Warman, Jimmy Pursey, Phil Collins, The Call, Nona Hendryx; fndr: World of Music Arts and Dance (featuring music from around the world) 1982, Real World Group (developing projects in arts and technol) 1985, Real World Studios 1986, Real World Records (world music record label) 1989, Real World Multimedia 1994; launched Witness (human rights prog) 1992; Hon DMus Univ of Bath 1996; *Style—* Peter Gabriel, Esq; ✉ c/o Real World, Box Mill, Box, Wiltshire SN14 9PL

GABRIELLE, *née* (Louise) Gabrielle Bobb; *Career* singer; signed recording contract with GO! Discs Ltd 1993; singles: Dreams (1993, UK no 1, highest chart entry for a debut artist), Going Nowhere (1993, UK no 6), I Wish (1993), Give Me A Little More Time (1996), If You Ever (with East 17, 1996); debut album Find Your Way (1993), Gabrielle (1996); Best British Newcomer BRIT Awards 1994; *Style—* Gabrielle; ✉ c/o GO! Discs Ltd, 72 Black Lion Lane, Hammersmith, London W6 9BE (☎ 0181 748 7973, fax 0181 741 5936)

GADD, (John) Staffan; s of late John Gadd, and Ulla, *née* Olivecrona; *b* 30 Sept 1934; *Educ* Stockholm Sch of Economics (MBA); *m* 1958, Margaretha, da of Gösta Löfborg; 1 s, 1 da; m 2, 1990, Kay McGreeghan; *Career* sec Confedn of Swedish Industs 1958–61, Skandinaviska Banken 1961–69 (London rep 1964–67); Scandinavian Bank Ltd: dep md 1969–71, London 1969–80, chief exec and md 1971–80; chm and chief exec Samuel Montagu & Co 1982–84 (chief exec 1980–82), chm Montagu & Co AB Stockholm 1982–85, dir Guyerzeller Zurmont Bank AG Switzerland 1983–84; chm: Saga Securities Ltd 1985–, J S Gadd & Cie SA Geneva 1989–; hon vice pres Swedish C of C for UK 1996– (chm 1993–96); *Recreations* skiing, shooting, the arts, travel; *Style—* Staffan Gadd, Esq; ✉ Locks Manor, Hurstpierpoint, W Sussex BN6 9JZ

GADDUM, Anthony Henry; s of Peter William Gaddum (d 1986), of Mobberley, Cheshire, and Josephine Margaret Ferguson Wynne, *née* Roberts (d 1983); *b* 16 Feb 1939; *Educ* Rugby, Univ of Grenoble; *m* 7 June 1968, Hilda McIntosh, da of Rev James McIntosh Scott (d 1991); 3 s (Toby b 1971, Giles b 1973, Benedict b 1975); *Career* Nat Serv 2 Lt 13/18 Royal Hussars 1959–61; chm: H T Gaddum & Co Ltd 1984– (dir 1964–), Gaddum & Wood Holdings Ltd 1991–; dir British Crepe Ltd 1976–; nat delegate Int Silk Assoc 1979–91, delegate Euro Commission for the Promotion of Silk; dep vice pres Int Silk Assoc 1991–, chm Silk Assoc 1995–; author of articles on silk and genealogy; chm Clarkes & Marshalls Charity Manchester, hon treas Boys and Girls' Welfare Soc; Freeman Worshipful Co of Weavers; *Recreations* genealogy, gardening, fishing; *Clubs* Institute of Directors; *Style—* Anthony Gaddum, Esq; ✉ Lane Ends House, Sutton Lane Ends, nr Macclesfield, Cheshire (☎ 01260 252456); H T Gaddum & Co Ltd, 3 Jordangate, Macclesfield, Cheshire (☎ 01625 427666, fax 01625 511331, telex 667139)

GADSBY, (Gordon) Neville; CB (1972); s of William George Gadsby (d 1978), and Margaret Sarah Gadsby; *b* 29 Jan 1914; *Educ* King Edward VI Sch Stratford upon Avon, Univ of Birmingham (BSc, DipEd, Cadbury prize); *m* 1938, Jeanne, *née* Harris; 2 s, 1 da; *Career* dir: Army Operational Res Estab 1961–64, Biological and Chemical Def MOD 1965–67; dep chief scientist (Army) MOD 1967–68, dir Chemical Def Estab 1968–72, min and head of Def Res and Devpt Staff Br Embassy Washington 1972–75; gp ldr The MITRE Corporation USA 1976–80, conslt NUS Corporation USA 1980–91; CChem, FRSC; *Recreations* oil painting; *Style—* G Neville Gadsby, Esq, CB; ✉ Ruan House, Cliff Rd, Sidmouth, Devon EX10 8JN (☎ 01395 577842)

GADSBY, Dr Roger; s of Frank William Gadsby, and Nellie Irene Gadsby; *b* 2 March 1950; *Educ* King Henry VIII Sch Coventry, Univ of Birmingham Med Sch (BSc, MB ChB, MRCGP); *m* 19 Oct 1974, Pamela Joy, da of Clifford Raine; 1 da (Emma Elizabeth b 1 Nov 1978), 1 s (Andrew David b 6 Sept 1981); *Career* postgraduate med trg Birmingham and Stoke on Trent 1974–77, trainee in gen practice 1977–79, ptnr in gen practice Nuneaton 1979–; pt/t sr lectr in gen practice Sch of Postgraduate Med Educn Univ of Warwick 1992–; memb various ctees Br Diabetic Assoc; memb Cncl RCGP 1994– (vice chm Midland Faculty 1993–); FRCGP 1992; *Recreations* jogging, gardening; *Style—* Dr Roger Gadsby; ✉ Redroofs Practitioners, Redroofs, 31 Coton Road, Nuneaton, Warwickshire CV11 5TW (☎ 01203 346047, fax 01203 642036)

GADSDEN, Sir Peter Drury Haggerston; GBE (1979), AC (1988); er s of Rev Basil Claude Gadsden, ACT, ThL (d 1958), of Whitney-on-Wye, Hereford, and Mabel Florence, *née* Drury (d 1964); *b* 28 June 1929; *Educ* Wrekin Coll, Jesus Coll Cambridge (MA); *m* 16 April 1955, Belinda Ann de Marie, eld da of Capt Sir (Hugh) Carnaby de Marie Haggerston, 11 Bt (d 1971); 4 da (Juliet Mary (Mrs Cartwright) b 4 March 1956, Caroline Mabel (Mrs Simpson) b 4 Aug 1957, Clare Louise (Mrs McWhirter) b 29 June 1960, Elizabeth Ann b 28 Feb 1962); *Career* served as 2 Lt King's Shropshire LI 1948–49, Hon Col 5 Bn Shropshire and Hereford LI Volunteers 1988–93; Lord Mayor City of London 1979–80 (Alderman (Farringdon Without) 1971–, HM Lt 1979–); chm Private Patients Plan Ltd 1984–96, pres PPP Healthcare Group 1996–; dep chm W Canning plc 1991–; mineral mktg conslt, memb London Metal Exchange; chm: City of London Branch IOD, The Britain-Australia Bicentennial Tst 1984–, The Britain-Australia Soc 1989–92 (vice pres 1992–); pres Australian-Br C of C 1993–; pt/t memb: Crown Agents for Overseas Govts and Admin 1981–87, Crown Agents' Holding & Realisation Bd 1981–87; pres: Metropolitan Soc for Blind, Ironbridge Gorge Museum Devpt Trust; vice pres Robert Jones and Agnes Hunt Orthopaedic Hosp; tstee: Chichester Festival Theatre, Bermuda Maritime Tst; fndr chm Bermuda Soc; dir Clothworkers' Fndn 1978–; memb Ct of Assts Worshipful Co of Clothworkers (Sr Warden 1982–83, Master 1989–90); memb: Guild of Freemen City of London 1963– (Master 1984–85), Co of World Traders in London 1985– (Master 1987–88); fndr Master Worshipful Co of Engineers 1983–85; Hon Liveryman: Worshipful Co of Plaisterers, Worshipful Co of Marketers; Hon Freeman Worshipful Co of Actuaries; Hon DSc City Univ 1980; KStJ (1980, OStJ 1977); Officier de l'Etoile Equatoriale de la Republique Gabonaise 1970; CEng, FInstM 1976, CEng 1979, FEng 1980, FIMM 1979, FRCA, FRSH; *Recreations* fishing, walking, photography, gardening; *Clubs* City Livery, City of London, Guildhall, Royal London Yacht, Pilgrims'; *Style—* Sir Peter Gadsden, GBE, AC, FEng; ✉ Private Patients Plan Ltd, 2nd Floor, Tavistock House South, Tavistock Square, London WC1H 9RA (☎ 0171 391 4281, fax 0171 391 4286)

GADSDEN, Peter John; s of Lt-Col George Edward Graham Gadsden, DSO, OBE, TD (d 1981), and Doris Lillian, *née* Benson; *b* 28 May 1929; *Educ* Eton, Worcester Coll Oxford (MA); *m* 19 Dec 1953, Yvonne, da of Issa Khalil Shousha (d 1964); 3 s (Paul Martin b 1954, Mark Jeremy b 1956, James Michael b 1964 d 1983), 2 da (Mary Anne (Mrs Hansell) b 1958, Jane Christine (Mrs Phillips) b 1963); *Career* slr; clerk Stroud RDC 1965–73, dep asst coroner 1965–68, superintendent registrar 1965–91; chm Stroud and Swindon Building Society 1991–96 (vice chm 1986–91); dir Co of the Proprietors of the Stroudwater Navigation 1993– (chm 1980–93); pres Glos and Wilts Inc Law Soc 1993–94 (vice pres 1992–93), vice pres Cotswold Canals Tst 1993–; memb Law Soc, life memb Slrs' Benevolent Soc; *Recreations* travel, sailing, reading; *Clubs* Leander; *Style—* Peter Gadsden, Esq; ✉ Bournestream, Wotton-under-Edge, Glos GL12 7PA (☎ 01453 842202)

GAFFNEY, Thomas Francis; s of Thomas F Gaffney (d 1954), and Margaret, *née* Carroll; *b* 2 April 1932; *Educ* St John's Univ NY (BA), St John's Law Sch, American Inst of Foreign Trade Phoenix Arizona; *m* 30 Oct 1954, Carmen, da of Benito Vega Luna, of Bucaramanga, Colombia; 2 s (Thomas b 30 Dec 1957, Peter b 21 Sept 1968), 1 da (Elisa b 14 Jan 1960); *Career* Chase Manhattan Bank NY 1954–87, seconded to several Latin-American Banks (incl period as chief exec Banco Continental Lima) 1962–72, chief exec Libra Bank plc London 1972–84, pres Chase Investment Bank London 1984–87, chief exec and md West LB UK Ltd 1988–91, chm The Plus 500 Income Fund Ltd 1992–, chm Latinvesst Holdings Ltd 1992–, DFA Trustee Services Limited 1994–; mangr: Bank Gesellschaft Berlin, LandisBank Berlin 1992–95; dir: CTI Holdings SA 1996–, Bankgesellschaft Berlin (UK) PLC 1995–, Raffaello Fund 1995–; author numerous articles on econ and fin matters in professional magazines; registered rep SFA; *Recreations* art appreciation, music, theatre; *Clubs* Overseas Bankers, Ends of the Earth, Oriental; *Style—* Thomas F Gaffney, Esq; ✉ Marvells, Five Ashes, Mayfield, East Sussex TN20 6NL (☎ 01435 873030)

GAGE, Deborah Pamela; da of Quentin Henry Moreton Gage, and Hazel Olive, *née* Swinton-Home; *b* 26 March 1950; *Educ* Moira House Eastbourne, Study Centre of the Fine & Decorative Arts London (dip); *Career* running Antique Porcelain Co/Antique Co of New York Inc NYC 1971–78, ind dealer 17th/18th c Euro decorative arts and paintings and late 19th/early 20th c French & British pictures 1981–; treas Nat Antique & Art Dealers Assoc of America NYC 1974–78; fndr and tstee The Charleston Trust 1979–88 (opened Charleston Farmhouse Sussex, home of the artists Vanessa Bell and Duncan Grant, to public 1985); *Books* Tobacco Containers and Accessories - Their Place in Eighteenth Century European Social History (with Madeleine Marsh, 1988); *Recreations* travel, photography, riding, scuba diving, tennis; *Style—* Miss Deborah Gage; ✉ Deborah Gage (Works of Art) Ltd, 38 Old Bond Street, London W1X 3AE (☎ 0171 493 3249, fax 0171 495 1352, e-mail 106255,2041@compuserve.com)

GAGE, 8 Viscount (I 1720); Sir (Henry) Nicolas Gage; 15 Bt (E 1622); also Baron Gage of Castlebar (I 1720), and Baron Gage (GB 1790), of High Meadow, Co Gloucester; yr s of 6 Viscount Gage, KCVO (d 1982), and his 1 w, Hon Alexandra Imogen Clair Grenfell (d 1969), da of 1 Baron Desborough; suc his bro, 7 Viscount Gage (d 1993); *b* 9 April 1934; *Educ* Eton, Ch Ch Oxford; *m* 1974, Lady Diana Adrienne Beatty, da of 2 Earl Beatty (d 1972); 2 s (Hon Henry William b 1975, Hon David Benedict b 1977); *Heir* s, Hon Henry William Gage b 25 June 1975; *Career* 2 Lt Coldstream Gds 1953; dir Firle Estate Co; tstee: Smith's Charity, HACT; *Style—* The Rt Hon the Viscount Gage; ✉ Firle Place, Lewes, E Sussex BN8 6LP (☎ 01273 858256, fax 01273 858043); The Cottage, Charwelton, Daventry, Warwickshire (☎ 01327 60205)

GAGE, Hon Mr Justice; Hon Sir William Marcus; kt (1993); s of His Honour Conolly Hugh Gage, (former circuit judge d 1984), and Elinor Nancy, *née* Martyn; *b* 22 April 1938; *Educ* Repton, Sidney Sussex Coll Cambridge (MA); *m* 16 June 1962, Penelope Mary, da of Lt-Col James Jocelyn Douglas Groves, MC (d 1985); 3 s (Marcus b 1964, Timothy b 1966, Hugh b 1970); *Career* Nat Serv 1956–58, 2 Lt Irish Gds; called to the Bar Inner Temple 1963, chllr Diocese of Coventry 1980–, QC 1982, recorder of the Crown Court 1985–93, judge of the High Court of Justice (Queen's Bench Div) 1993–, presiding judge SE Circuit 1997–; chllr Diocese of Ely 1989–; memb Criminal Injuries Compensation Bd 1987–93, bencher Inner Temple 1991; *Recreations* shooting, fishing, travel; *Clubs* Beefsteak; *Style*— The Hon Mr Justice Gage; ✉ Royal Courts of Justice, Strand, London WC2A 2LL

GAGGERO, Charles Germain; CBE (1992, OBE 1970), JP; s of Charles Gaggero, OBE, JP (d 1987), and Eugenie, *née* Rugeroni (d 1981); *b* 28 May 1930; *Educ* Downside, Magdalene Coll Cambridge (MA); *m* July 1957, Jean, da of Col John Lawrance; 3 da (Katherine b 26 April 1958, Susan b 10 March 1960, Alexandra b 31 Aug 1963); *Career* cmmnd Gibraltar Defence Force 1957; dir Saccone & Speed (Gibraltar) Ltd 1968–95 (chm 1992–93) and subsid cos, chm Amalgamated Builders' Merchants Ltd and subsid cos, dir Hambros Bank (Gibraltar) Ltd; hon consul gen for Greece 1967, doyen of Consular Corps Gibraltar; chm: John Mackintosh Tst, John Mackintosh Educnl Tst, Pyrmont Ltd, Gibraltar Tport Assoc 1962–68, Gibraltar Museum 1965–68, St John Cncl for Gibraltar 1966–77; dir C of C 1953–62; pres: Societa Dante Alighieri 1968–75, Lottery Ctee 1956–68, Social Welfare Ctee 1960–68, Econ Advsy Ctee 1963–66, Prison Bd 1964–68, Bd of Mgmnt Med & Health Servs 1965–68, Bd of Visitors St Joseph's Hosp 1965–68, Labour Planning and Productivity Ctee 1966–68; Knight Order of St John (UK), Knight Order Star of Italian Solidarity (Italy), Knight Order of St Gregory the Great (Holy See), Knight of Magistral Grace SMO of Malta (Br Assoc), Knight of Merit Constantinian Order of St George, Officer of Merit SMO of Malta; Freeman: City of London 1990, Worshipful Co of Builders Merchants 1990; *Recreations* numismatics; *Clubs* United Oxford & Cambridge University, Royal Gibraltar Yacht; *Style*— Charles Gaggero, Esq, CBE, JP; ✉ 4 College Lane, Gibraltar (☎ 00 350 77410)

GAGGERO, John George; OBE (1981), JP (1972); s of Sir George Gaggero, OBE, JP (d 1978), of Gibraltar, and Lady Mabel, *née* Andrews-Speed (d 1986); *b* 3 March 1934; *Educ* Downside; *m* 1961, Valerie, da of John Malin, OBE, JP, of Gibraltar; 2 s (John b 12 Nov 1962, George b 4 Sept 1965), 2 da (Katrina b 23 Oct 1966, Amanda b 22 Feb 1970); *Career* Lt 12 Royal Lancers Malaya; dep chm Bland Group of Companies (incl Gibraltar Airways, Rock Hotel and Cadogan Travel) 1970–86; chm: M H Bland & Co Ltd 1986–, M H Bland Stevedores Ltd 1990–96; hon consul for Denmark in Gibraltar 1964–; chm Gibraltar Shipping Assoc 1993–; CEng, MRINA; Knight of the Royal Order of the Dannebrog; *Recreations* boating; *Clubs* Royal Gibraltar Yacht; *Style*— John Gaggero, Esq, OBE, JP; ✉ Cloister Building, Gibraltar (☎ 00 350 72735)

GAGGERO, Joseph James; CBE (1989); s of Sir George Gaggero, OBE, JP (d 1978), of Gibraltar, and Lady Mabel, *née* Andrews-Speed (d 1986); bro of John Gaggero, OBE, JP, *qv*; *Educ* Downside; *m* 1, Nov 1958, Marilys Healing; 1 s (James b 1 Aug 1959), 1 da (Rosanne b 27 Dec 1960); m 2, July 1994, Christina Russo; *Career* chm and md of Bland Group of Companies (incl GB Airways, Gibraltar Airways, Rock Hotel, Bland Travel, Cadogan Travel, House of Bellingham and assoc cos); dir: Hovertravel, Credit Suisse (Gibraltar) Ltd; hon consul gen for Sweden in Gibraltar until Dec 1995; dir Gibraltar C of C 1951–56, head Gibraltar Govt Tourist Dept 1955–59, memb Cncl of Br Travel Assoc 1958–69; chm: Hotel Assoc 1962–75, 1978 and 1986–90, Gibraltar Shipping Assoc 1970–79; pres: Gibraltar Rotarians 1973–74, Gibraltar Branch for Maritime League 1983–84; former chm Gibraltar Soc for Handicapped Children, Gibraltar Branch of Royal Life Saving Soc; Cdr Order of North Star (Sweden), Knight of the Holy Sepulchre (Vatican); *Recreations* painting; *Clubs* Travellers', Royal Gibraltar Yacht; *Style*— Joseph Gaggero, Esq, CBE; ✉ Cloister Building, Gibraltar (☎ 00 350 78456, fax 00 350 76189)

GAHAGAN, Michael; *Career* civil servant; former chartered surveyor Manchester; various jobs within DOE, with Inner Cities Directorate (ICD) 1979, regnl controller (planning) London until 1988, dir Inner Cities Unit DTI 1988–91, head Regeneration Directorate DOE 1991– (projects incl Single Regeneration Budget, City Challenge, Rural Devpt); *Style*— Michael Gahagan, Esq; ✉ Room P2/117 Regeneration Directorate, DOE, 2 Marsham Street, London SW1P 3EB (☎ 0171 276 4473, telex 3004)

GAIND, Dr Raghunandan; s of Meher Chand Gaind (d 1972), of Jammu, Kashmir, and Gian Devi, *née* Bawa (d 1976); *b* 1 Oct 1934; *Educ* Haddow Meml Sch Srinagar Kashmir, Punjab Univ (MB BS, Gold medal), Univ of London (DPM); *m* 1, 1959 (m dis 1989), June Florence Beddoe; 2 s (Anil b 5 April 1963, Ranjit Meher Chand b 19 March 1977), 4 da (Mrs Sushilla Cooke b 21 April 1960, Mrs Gita Connors b 30 Nov 1961, Mrs Tripta Dawson b 23 June 1964, Shobha Savitri Devi b 1974); m 2, 7 July 1989, Dr Susan Lesley Davenport; *Career* jr hosp appts 1957–69 (Addenbrooke's Hosp Cambridge, Nat Hosp London, Maudsley Hosp London), physician in psychological med Guy's Hosp London 1969–86 (chm Dept of Psychological Med 1979–85); clinical tutor Br Postgrad Med Fedn and recognized teacher in psychiatry Univ of London 1970–86, advsr in mental health Kingdom of Saudi Arabia 1973–83, pres Indian Med Assoc of GB 1977–82; chm: SE Thames Regnl Psychiatry Speciality Sub-Ctee 1980–85, Inst of Social Psychiatry 1982–; sec World Assoc for Social Psychiatry Jl 1988–90, ed Current Themes in Psychiatry and Int Jl of Social Psychiatry; visiting prof in psychiatry Univ of Jamaica, Univ of West Indies and UCLA, external examiner Univs of West Indies, Malta and Hong Kong; Hon MD Punjab Univ 1986, Distinguished Citizen of India 1993; memb: BMA 1957, RSM 1963, Medico-Legal Soc of London; FRCP, FRCPE, FRCPsych; *Books* Current Themes in Psychiatry (1978, 4 vol 1987); *Recreations* sailing, bridge, travel, gardening; *Clubs* Oriental, Gymkhana (New Delhi); *Style*— Dr Raghunandan Gaind; ✉ Milgate House, Bearsted, Kent ME14 4NN (☎ 01622 739911, fax 01622 630544, mobile 0860 836015); Keat's House, Guy's Hospital, 24–26 St Thomas Street, London SE1 9RT (☎ 0171 955 4290)

GAINFORD, 3 Baron (UK 1917); Joseph Edward Pease; s of 2 Baron Gainford, TD (d 1971), and Veronica Margaret, *née* Noble (d 1995); *b* 25 Dec 1921; *Educ* Eton, Gordonstoun, Open Univ Dip in Euro Humanities 1995; *m* 21 March 1953, Margaret Theophila Radcliffe, da of Henry Edmund Guise Tyndale (d 1948), of Winchester Coll, and Ruth Isabel Walcott, da of Alexander Radcliffe, of Bag Park, S Devon; 2 da (Joanna Ruth Miriam b 22 Aug 1959, Virginia Claire Margaret b 13 Oct 1960); *Heir* bro, Hon George Pease; *Career* serv WWII as Sgt RAFVR 1941–46; with: Hunting Aerosurveys Ltd 1947, Directorate of Colonial Surveys 1951, Soil Mechanics Ltd 1953, LCC 1958, GLC 1965; UK delegate to UN 1973; memb Coll Guardians Nat Shrine of Our Lady of Walsingham 1979–; memb Plaisterers' Co 1976; FRGS, MSST; *Clubs* MCC, Pathfinder; *Style*— The Rt Hon the Lord Gainford; ✉ Swallowfield, 1 Dedmere Court, Marlow, Bucks SL7 1PL (☎ 01628 484679)

GAINHAM, Sarah Rachel (Mrs Rachel Ames); da of Tom Stainer and May Genevieve Gainham; *b* 1 Oct 1922; *Educ* Newbury HS for Girls; *m* 1, 1947 (m dis 1962), Antony Terry; m 2, 1964, Kenneth Ames (d 1975); *Career* Central Europe corr The Spectator 1956–66; author; contribs incl: Encounter, Atlantic Monthly, BBC; FRSL 1984; *Books* Time Right Deadly (1956), Cold Dark Night (1957), The Mythmaker (1957), Stone Roses (1959), Silent Hostage (1960), Night Falls on the City (1967), A Place in the Country (1968), Takeover Bid (1970), Private Worlds (1971), Maculan's Daughter (1973), To the Opera Ball (1975), The Habsburg Twilight (1979), The Tiger Life (1983); *Recreations* theatre, opera, European history; *Style*— Ms Sarah Gainham, FRSL; ✉ Altes Forsthaus, Schlosspark, A2404 Petronell, Austria

GAINSBOROUGH, 5 Earl of (UK 1841); Sir Anthony Gerard Edward Noel; 7 Bt (GB 1781), JP (Leics 1974, formerly Rutland 1957); also Baron Barham (UK 1805), Viscount Campden and Baron Noel (both UK 1841); patron of two livings (but being a Roman Catholic cannot present); s of 4 Earl of Gainsborough, OBE, TD, JP (d 1927), sometime Private Chamberlain to Popes Benedict XV and Pius XI; *b* 24 Oct 1923; *Educ* Worth Sussex, Georgetown Maryland USA; *m* 23 July 1947, Mary, er da of Hon John Joseph Stourton, TD, of Miniature Hall, Wadhurst, 2 s of (24) Baron Mowbray, (25 Baron) Segrave, and (21 Baron) Stourton; 4 s, 3 da (and 1 da decd); *Heir* s, Viscount Campden, *qv*; *Career* pres Caravan Club; chm Rutland CC 1970–73, pres Assoc of Dist Cncls 1974–80; memb: House of Lords All Party London Gp, House of Lords Horse Racing Advsy Ctee; Bailiff Grand Cross SMO Malta (pres Br Assoc 1968–74); Sr Past Master Worshipful Co of Gardners; Hon FICE, KStJ; *Clubs* Brooks's, Bembridge Sailing, Pratts, Royal Yacht Squadron; *Style*— The Rt Hon the Earl of Gainsborough, JP; ✉ Horn House, Exton Park, Oakham, Leics LE15 7QU

GAINSFORD, Sir Ian Derek; kt (1995); s of Rabbi Dr Morris Ginsberg (d 1969), and Anne Freda, *née* Aucken (d 1950); *b* 24 June 1930; *Educ* Thames Valley GS, King's Coll London (BDS, LDS, FDS, MGDS RCSEng), Toronto Univ (DDS); *m* 13 June 1957, Carmel, da of Dr Lionel Bertram Liebster; 1 s (Jeremy Charles b 1961), 2 da (Ann Marietta b 1959, Deborah Jane b 1965); *Career* jr staff King's Coll Hosp 1955–57, lectr (later sr lectr) London Hosp Med Coll 1957–70; King's Coll Hosp Med Sch 1970: sr lectr (hon conslt) Conservative Dentistry Dept, dep dean of dental studies 1973–77, dean of dental studies 1977–87, dean of med and dentistry 1988–; vice princ KCL 1994–; memb Univ of London Ctees: Senate, Academic Cncl, Standing Ctee in Med; chm Educn Ctee Gen Dental Cncl 1990–94; FKC 1984; hon memb American Dental Assoc; FICD, FACD; *Books* Silver Amalgam in Clinical Practise; *Recreations* canal cruising, theatre; *Clubs* Carlton, Athenaeum; *Style*— Sir Ian Gainsford; ✉ 31 York Terrace East, London NW1 4PT (☎ 0171 935 8659); 16 Sloane Square, London SW1; School of Medicine and Dentistry, King's College London, Bessemer Road, London SE5 9PJ (☎ 0171 346 3000)

GAISFORD, Rt Rev John Scott; *see:* Beverley, Bishop of

GAISMAN, Jonathan Nicholas Crispin; QC (1995); o s of Peter Gaisman, of Kirdford, W Sussex; *b* 10 Aug 1956; *Educ* Eton, Worcester Coll Oxford (BCL, MA); *m* 24 April 1982, Teresa Mignon (Tessa), MBE (1991), eldest da of Sir John Jardine Paterson, of Norton Bavant, Wilts; 1 s (Nicholas b 1989), 2 da (Clementine b 1986, Imogen b 1987); *Career* called to the Bar Inner Temple 1979; memb Panel of Arbitrators Lloyd's Arbitration Scheme 1993–; a dir: English Chamber Orchestra and Music Soc 1992–, Int Musicians' Seminar 1994–; *Recreations* the arts, travel, country pursuits; *Clubs* I Zingari, Brooks's; *Style*— Jonathan Gaisman, Esq, QC; ✉ 7 King's Bench Walk, Temple, London EC4Y 7DS (☎ 0171 583 0404)

GAIT, (Robert) Charles Campbell; s of Robert William Gait (d 1986), of Pembroke, and Jean, *née* Campbell (d 1981); *b* 16 July 1955; *Educ* Pembroke GS, Jesus Coll Cambridge (MA); *m* 9 Sept 1978, Anne Rose, da of Edward Nicholson, of Pembroke; 3 s (Michael Huw b 30 Sept 1984, Jonathan Edward b 25 June 1986, Nicholas Matthew b 27 July 1988); *Career* admitted slr 1980; ptnr McKenna & Co 1985 (articled clerk 1978–80), specialising in property devpt and investment work; memb: Law Soc, UK Chapter of FIABCI; *Recreations* golf, rugby football, enthusiastic but incompetent skier; *Style*— Charles Gait, Esq; ✉ McKenna & Co, Mitre House, 160 Aldersgate St, London EC1A 4DD (☎ 0171 606 9000, fax 0171 606 9100)

GAITSKELL, Robert; QC (1994); s of Stanley Gaitskell (d 1967), and Thelma Phyllis, *née* Holmes (d 1987); *b* 19 April 1948; *Educ* Hamilton HS Zimbabwe, Univ of Cape Town (BSc(Eng)); *m* 1974, Dr Deborah Lyndall Bates; 1 da (Kezia Lyndall b 2 Nov 1983); *Career* graduate trainee Reyrolle Parsons 1971–73, engr Electricty Dept Bulawayo Zimbabwe 1973–75, electrical engr GEC (SA) 1975–76; called to the Bar Gray's Inn 1978, in practice 1979–; lectr Centre of Construction Law & Mgmnt King's Coll London; chm: Mgmnt Div IEE, Professional Gp on Engrg and the Law; memb Ctee London Common Law and Commercial Bar Assoc; FIEE, CEng, FCIArb; *Recreations* Methodist local preacher, theatre, walking; *Style*— Robert Gaitskell, Esq, QC; ✉ Keating Chambers, 10 Essex Street, London WC2R 3AA (☎ 0171 240 6981, fax 0171 240 7722)

GALASKO, Prof Charles Samuel Bernard; s of David Isaac Galasko (d 1951), and Rose, *née* Shames (d 1996); *b* 29 June 1939; *Educ* King Edward VII Sch Johannesburg, Univ of Johannesburg (MB BCh, ChM); *m* 29 Oct 1967, Carol Freyda, da of Michael Lapinsky; 1 s (Gavin b 1972), 1 da (Deborah b 1970); *Career* med trg Johannesburg Gen Hosp 1963–66, lectr Univ of Witwatersrand 1964–66; registrar: Hammersmith Hosp 1967–69, Royal Postgrad Med Sch 1967–69; sr registrar Radcliffe Infirmary and Nuffield Orthopaedic Centre Oxford 1970–73; conslt orthopaedic surgn Hammersmith Hosp 1973–76 (former dir of orthopaedic surgery), asst dir Div of Surgery Royal Postgrad Med Sch 1973–76 (former dir orthopaedic surgery), prof of orthopaedic surgery Univ of Manchester 1976–, hon conslt orthopaedic surgn Salford Royal Hosps NHS Tst and Manchester Children's Hosp Tst 1976–; contrib over 200 published articles; temp advsr World Health Authy 1981, pres SIROT 1990–93 (memb Exec Ctee 1981–96, memb Prog Ctee 1981–84, prog chm 1984–87, chm Membership Ctee 1987–90), chm Award Ctee SICOT 1984–87 and 1990–93, treas Int Assoc Olympic Med Offrs 1988–, vice chm English Olympic Wrestling Assoc, chm Br Amateur Wrestling Assoc 1992–96 (vice pres 1996–); chm Assoc of Profs of Orthopaedic Surgery 1983–86, vice pres Section of Oncology RSM 1987 (memb Cncl 1980–87); memb: Cncl Br Orthopaedic Assoc 1988–91, Med Sub Ctee British Olympic Assoc 1988–, Cncl RCS 1991– (chm Trg Bd 1995–); fndr memb: Int Orthopaedic Res Soc, Metastatis Res Soc, S African Surgical Res Soc; Hon MSc Univ of Manchester 1980; memb Br Orthopaedic Res Soc; fell Br Orthopaedic Assoc, FRCS (London), FRCSEd; *Books* Radionuclide Scintigraphy in Orthopaedics (jt ed, 1984), Principles of Fracture Management (ed, 1984), Skeletal Metastases (1986), Neuromuscular Problems in Orthopaedics (ed, 1987), Recent Developments in Orthopaedic Surgery (jt ed, 1987), Current Trends in Orthopaedic Surgery (jt ed, 1988), Imaging Techniques in Orthopaedics (jt ed, 1989); *Recreations* sport, music, theatre; *Style*— Prof Charles Galasko; ✉ Department of Orthopaedic Surgery, Clinical Sciences Building, Hope Hospital, Eccles Old Road, Salford M6 8HD (☎ 0161 787 4291, fax 0161 787 4706)

GALATOPOULOS, Stelios Emille; s of John Galatopoulos (d 1978), of Nicosia, Cyprus and Athens, and Maria, *née* Stylianaki (d 1948); *b* 2 Aug 1932; *Educ* The English Sch Nicosia, Univ of Southampton (BSc(Eng)); *Career* civil and structural engr; designer: T C Jones 1954–55, Kellogg Int Corp 1956–60; designer and head of Civil and Structural Dept Tripe and Wakeham (chartered architects) London and Cyprus for Akrotiri Strategic Base 1960–66, freelance engr 1967–72, designer Pell Frischmann 1972–75, freelance engr 1975–, lectr, concert presenter and compere; opera and music critic-journalist: Music and Musicians, Records and Recordings, Lirica nel Mondo (Italy), Opera, Musical America; broadcaster: BBC, CBC (Cyprus), RTE (Dublin) America; memb Soc of Authors 1971–, vice pres Opera Italiana 1985; *Books* Callas La Divina (1966), Italian Opera (1971), Callas Prima Donna Assoluta (1976); *Recreations* opera, theatre, ballet, concerts, tennis, swimming, skiing; *Style*— Stelios Galatopoulos, Esq; ✉ Flat 2, 38 Shalstone Road, London SW14 7HR (☎ 0181 878 9731)

GALBRAITH, Anne; *b* 1940; *Educ* Univ of Durham (LLB); *m* 1965, John Galbraith; 1 s (b 1970), 1 da (b 1971); *Career* chm Newcastle CAB 1982–87, memb Northern RHA

1988–91, chm Royal Victoria Infirmary and Associated Hosps NHS Tst 1991–, special tstee Newcastle Univ Hosps 1992–, tstee Rothley Tst 1994–, PM's advsr Citizens' Charter Advsy Panel 1994–; govr Prudhoe HS 1984–87; *Recreations* gardening; *Style*— Mrs Anne Galbraith; ✉ Royal Victoria Infirmary and Associated Hospitals NHS Trust, Queen Victoria Road, Newcastle upon Tyne NE1 4LP (☎ 0191 227 5162)

GALBRAITH, Hon James Muir Galloway; CBE (1984); 3 but eldest surviving s of 1 Baron Strathclyde, PC (d 1985); *b* 27 Sept 1920; *Educ* RNC Dartmouth, ChCh Oxford, RAC Cirencester; *m* 27 Sept 1945, Anne, er da of late Maj Kenneth Paget; 3 s, 1 da; *Career* served with RN WW II (wounded); dir Buccleuch Estates Ltd; chm: Timber Growers UK 1980–85, Forestry Indust Ctee GB 1985–89, Scottish Forestry Tst 1989–95, Roxburgh & Berwickshire Cons and Unionist Assoc 1992–95; JP Inverness-shire 1953–54; FRICS; *Clubs* Army & Navy, New (Edinburgh); *Style*— Hon James Galbraith, CBE; ✉ Rawflat, Ancrum, Roxburghshire (☎ 01835 830302)

GALBRAITH, Jeremy; *b* 14 Aug 1966; *Educ* King's Sch Worcester, Univ of Leeds Faculty of Law (LLB); *Career* researcher to Dr Keith Hampson, MP 1988–89, conslt Market Access International 1989–95 (dep md 1994–95); md: Burson-Marsteller Government and Public Affairs London 1995–, Burson-Marsteller Europe Government Relations 1996–; Parly candidate (Cons) Newham NE 1992; nat vice chm Cons Friends of Israel 1990–; *Recreations* tennis, running, opera, film and restaurants; *Clubs* Carlton; *Style*— Jeremy Galbraith, Esq; ✉ Burson-Marsteller Government and Public Affairs, 24–28 Bloomsbury Way, London WC1A 2PX (☎ 0171 831 6262, fax 0171 404 2360, e-mail jeremy_galbraith@bm.com)

GALBRAITH, Samuel Laird (Sam); MP (Lab) Strathkelvin and Bearsden (majority 3,162); s of late Sam Galbraith, and Cathie Galbraith; *b* 18 Oct 1945; *Educ* Univ of Glasgow (BSc, MB ChB, MD, FRCS); *m* 1987; 3 da; *Career* conslt in neurosurgery Gtr Glasgow Health Bd 1978–87, MP (Lab) Strathkelvin and Bearsden 1987–, oppn spokesman on Scottish affrs and on health 1988–92, oppn spokesman on employment 1992–93; hon sr res fell Univ of Glasgow; *Style*— Sam Galbraith, Esq, MP; ✉ House of Commons, London SW1A 0AA

GALE, Prof Edwin Albert Merwood; s of Dr (George) Edwin Gale, CBE (d 1994), of Southsea, Hants, and Carole, *née* Waldron; *b* 21 March 1945; *Educ* Sevenoaks Sch, Univ of Cambridge (MA, MB BChir); *m* 26 June 1982, Lone Anita Brogaard, da of Jens Christian Pedersen; 1 s (John b 1986), 2 da (Emily b 1982, Rebecca b 1984); *Career* sr lectr med 1984–, hon conslt physician, head Dept Diabetes and Metabolism St Bartholomew's Hosp, prof of diabetes 1992–, dir Barts-Oxford Family Study of Childhood Diabetes; memb: Br Diabetic Assoc, American Diabetic Assoc, Euro Assoc for Study of Diabetes; FRCP (1987); *Books* Diabetes - Clinical Management (with R B Tattersall, 1989); *Recreations* collecting fossils; *Style*— Dr Edwin Gale; ✉ 76 Linthorpe Rd, Stamford Hill, London N16 5RF (☎ 0181 802 6061); Department of Diabetes and Metabolism, St Bartholomew's Hosp, London EC1 (☎ 0171 606 2032)

GALE, (Thomas Henry) John; OBE (1986); s of Frank Haith Gale (d 1970), and Martha Edith Gale; *b* 2 Aug 1929; *Educ* Christ's Hosp, Webber Douglas Sch of Drama; *m* 24 Nov 1950, Liselotte Ann, da of Ian Dennis Wratten, CBE (d 1988); 2 s (Timothy Simon b 1956, Matthew Ian b 1959); *Career* 2 Lt RASC 1948; former actor; dir: Gale Enterprises Ltd 1960–, John Gale Productions Ltd 1960–, West End Managers Ltd 1972–89, Lisden Productions Ltd 1975–82; dir Chichester Festival Theatre 1985–89 (exec prodr 1983–84); prodr and co prodr of over eighty plays around the world incl: Candida 1960, On The Brighter Side 1961, Boeing-Boeing, Devil May Care 1963, Windfall 1963, Where Angels Fear to Tread 1963, The Wings of the Dove 1963, Amber for Anna 1964, Present Laughter 1964 and 1981, Maigret and the Lady 1965, The Platinum Cat 1965, The Sacred Flame 1966, An Evening With GBS 1966, A Woman of No Importance 1967, The Secretary Bird 1968, Dear Charles 1968, Highly Confidential 1969, The Young Churchill 1969, The Lionel Touch 1969, Abelard and Heloise 1970, No Sex Please - We're British 1971 (the longest running comedy in Br theatre history), Lloyd George Knew My Father 1972, The Mating Game 1972, Parents Day 1972, At the End of the Day 1973, Birds of Paradise 1974, A Touch of Spring 1975, Separate Tables 1977, The Kingfisher 1977, Sextet 1977, Cause Celebre 1977, Shut Your Eyes and Think of England 1977, Can You Hear Me At The Back? 1979, Middle Age Spread 1979, Private Lives 1980, A Personal Affair 1982; pres Soc of London Theatre (formerly SWET) 1972–75, govr Almoner Christ's Hosp 1978–96, chm of govrs Guildford Sch of Acting 1991–, chm Theatres Nat Ctee 1979–85, memb Amicable Soc Blues 1981–; Liveryman Worshipful Co of Gold and Silver Wyredrawers 1974–; FRSA 1991; *Recreations* travel, rugby; *Clubs* Garrick, London Welsh RF; *Style*— John Gale, Esq, OBE; ✉ East Dean Hill, Cottage East Dean, nr Chichester, W Sussex PO18 0JA (☎ 01243 811407)

GALE, Michael; QC (1979); s of Joseph and Blossom Gale; *b* 12 Aug 1932; *Educ* Cheltenham GS, Grocers Sch, King's Coll Cambridge (exhibitioner); *m* 1963, Joanna Stephanie Bloom; 1 s, 2 d; *Career* Royal Fus 1956–58; called to the Bar Middle Temple 1957 (Harmsworth scholar), bencher, recorder of the Crown Court 1977–; legal assessor to GMC; memb Gen Cncl of the Bar 1986–94; *Recreations* arts, country pursuits; *Clubs* United Oxford & Cambridge, MCC; *Style*— Michael Gale, Esq, QC; ✉ 6 Pump Court, Temple EC4 (☎ 0171 797 8400)

GALE, Roger James; MP (C) Thanet North (majority 18,210); s of Richard Byrne Gale, and Phyllis Mary, *née* Rowell (d 1948); *b* 20 Aug 1943; *Educ* Hardye's Sch Dorchester, Guildhall Sch of Music and Drama; *m* 1, 1964 (m dis 1967), Wendy Dawn Bowman; m 2, 1971 (m dis), Susan Sampson; 1 da (Misty); m 3, 1980, Suzy Gabrielle, da of Thomas Leopold Marks (d 1972); 2 s (Jasper, Thomas); *Career* formerly: reporter BBC Radio, prodr BBC Radio 4 Today Show, dir BBC Children's TV, prodr and dir Thames Children's TV, editor Teenage Unit Thames; Parly candidate (C) Birmingham Northfield (by-election) 1982, MP (C) Thanet N 1983–; PPS to Min of State for the Armed Forces 1992–94; currently chm: Cons Banckbench Media Ctee, All-Pty Animal Welfare Gp; fell: Indust and Parl Tst, Parl and Armed Forces Fellowship, Parl and Police Fellowship; *Recreations* swimming, sailing; *Clubs* Kent CCC, Farmers'; *Style*— Roger Gale, Esq, MP; ✉ House of Commons, London SW1A 0AA (☎ 01227 722366)

GALGANI, Franco; s of Piero Galgani, of Leghorn and Vilia Galgani; *b* 28 March 1949; *Educ* Saffi Secdy Sch Florence Italy, Florence Hotel Sch Florence (Nat Dip), Open Univ UK (BA); *m* 1, 1967 (m dis 1977), Mary Ellen, *née* McElhone; 3 s (Lorenzo b 1968, Riccardo b 1969, Giancarlo b 1971); m 2, 1981, Lynne, *née* MacDonald; 1 da (Daniela b 1983); *Career* restaurateur; industl trg 1963–68: Alberg Ristorante L'Elba nr Grosseto Italy, Grand Hotel Florence, Hotel Iselba Island of Elba, Hotel de la Plage St Raphael France, Hotel Baglioni Florence, Grand Hotel Florence, George Hotel Keswick Eng, Hotel Parco Rimini Italy; food and beverage supervisory and mgmnt appts 1968–76: Granville Restaurant Glasgow, MacDonald Hotel (Thistle) Giffnock Glasgow, Stuart Hotel (Thistle) and Bruce Hotel (Swallow) E Kilbride Strathclyde; mangr and ptnr Balcary Bay Hotel Scot 1976–82; gen mangr: Buchanan Arms Hotel Loch Lomond Scot 1982–85, Stakis Dunkeld House Perthshire Scot 1985–86, Marine Highland Hotel Troon Ayrshire Scot 1986–91, Carlton Highland Hotel 1991–; mktg dir Scottish Highland Hotels 1996–; former memb: Bd of Dirs Ayrshire Tourist Bd, Cncl Ayr Coll of Further Educn, Glasgow Coll of Food Technol; former chm Edinburgh Principal Hotels Assoc; bd dir Edinburgh and Lothians Tourist Bd; Master Innholders Award 1989, Scottish Highland Hotels Group Mangr of the Year 1990; FHCIMA 1989; *Recreations* travel, theatre and classical music, outdoor pursuits with family; *Style*— Franco Galgani, Esq; ✉ Carlton Highland Hotel, Edinburgh, Scotland EH1 1SD (☎ 0131 556 7277, fax 0131 556 2691)

GALITZINE, Prince Yuri (Yurka) Nikolaievitch; o s of Prince Nicolas Alexandrovitch Galitzine (d 1963), and Emma Lilian, *née* Hodgson (d 1948); *b* 5 Feb 1919, Yokohama, Japan; *Educ* Stowe; *m* 1, 22 Nov 1944 (m dis 1951), Constance Irene, da of John Higginson; 1 da (Alexandra b 13 Nov 1946); m 2, 6 Oct 1952 (m dis 1962), Shelaigh, da of Col Benjamin Sanford-Johnson; 1 s (Gregoriy b 10 July 1955), 1 da (Sophia b 5 March 1958); m 3, 30 Nov 1965 (m dis 1974), Elizabeth Gwynneth, da of Charles Herbert Tighe; 1 s (Nikolai b 30 Dec 1968), 1 da (Amalia b 3 Feb d 5 Feb 1970); m 4, 19 Nov 1976, Dr Jean Mary Shanks, *qv*, da of Peter Shanks; *Career* shop floor French leather and British aircraft industs until 1939; WWII Serv: cmmnd Royal Northumberland Fusiliers, posted to Political Warfare Exec 1943, subsequently served as Psychological Warfare Staff Offr SE France, Holland and Western Germany; Hunting Group (shipping, oil and aviation cos) 1945–54 (asst md Hunting Air Travel Ltd 1949–51); chm Galitzine and Partners Ltd (PR consultancy) 1954–86 (acted for Federal Govt of Nigeria in Civil War of 1966–69, PR advsr to P&O Group 1954–74), vice pres International Public Relations Group of Companies Inc 1960–86, currently chm Specialised International Service Ltd; chm Br Soc of Ind PR Consultants 1957–61, fndr memb Exec Cncl PRCA, memb UK Cncl IPRA, first accredited Euro memb PR Soc of America; FIPR 1963 (MIPR 1951); *Style*— Prince Yuri Galitzine; ✉ Specialised International Service Ltd, 8 South Eaton Place, London SW1W 9JA (☎ 0171 730 3931, fax 0171 824 8174)

GALL, Henderson Alexander (Sandy); CBE (1988); s of Henderson Gall (d 1963), of Banchory, Scotland, and Jean, *née* Begg (d 1970); *b* 1 Oct 1927; *Educ* Glenalmond Perthshire, Univ of Aberdeen (MA); *m* 11 Aug 1958, Eleanor Mary Patricia Anne, da of Michael Joseph Smyth (d 1964), of London; 1 s (Alexander Patrick Henderson b 17 June 1960), 3 da (Fiona Deirdre b 7 May 1959, Carlotta Maire Jean b 2 Nov 1961, Michaela Monica b 27 March 1965); *Career* Nat Serv RAF 1945–48; foreign corr Reuters 1953–63 (Berlin, Nairobi, Suez, Geneva, Bonn, Budapest, Johannesburg, Congo); ITN: foreign corr 1963–92 (ME, Africa, Vietnam, Far East, China, Afghanistan, Pakistan, Gulf War), newscaster 1968–90 (News at Ten 1970–90), prodr/presenter/writer of 9 documentaries (subjects incl Cresta Run 1970 and 1985, King Hussein 1972, Afghanistan 1982, 1984 and 1986, George Adamson 1989, Richard Leakey 1995, Empty Quarter 1996); freelance writer; independent TV prodr 1993–; rector Univ of Aberdeen 1978–81; Sitara-i-Pakistan 1985, Lawrence of Arabia Medal RSAA 1987; Hon LLD Univ of Aberdeen 1981; *Books* Gold Scoop (1977), Chasing the Dragon (1981), Don't Worry About the Money Now (1983), Behind Russian Lines, an Afghan Journal (1983), Afghanistan: Agony of a Nation (1987), Salang (1989), George Adamson: Lord of the Lions (1991), A Year in Kuwait (1992), News from the Front (1994); *Recreations* golf, Cresta Run; *Clubs* Turf, Special Forces, Rye Golf, Royal St George's Golf, St Moritz Tobogganing; *Style*— Sandy Gall, Esq, CBE; ✉ Doubleton Oast House, Penshurst, Tonbridge, Kent TN11 8JA (☎ 01892 870576, fax 01892 870977)

GALLACHER, Bernard; OBE (1996); s of Bernard Gallacher Sr, of Bathgate, Scotland, and Matilda Gallacher; *b* 9 Feb 1949; *Educ* St Marys Acad Bathgate Scotland; *m* Lesley; 1 s (Jamie b 22 May 1977), 2 da (Kirsty Jane b 20 Jan 1976, Laura Kate b 28 June 1987); *Career* professional golfer; club professional Wentworth 1975–; amateur: boys int 1965 and 1966, full int 1967, Scot Open Amateur Stroke Play Champion 1967; professional wins: Schweppes PGA 1969, Westward Ho Wills Open 1969, Martini Int 1971 and 1982, Young Professionals 1973, Carrolls Int 1974, Dunlop Masters 1974 and 1975, Spanish Open 1977, French Open 1979, Tournament Players 1980, Manchester Open 1981, Jersey Open 1982 and 1984; Ryder Cup: memb team 1969, 1971, 1973, 1975, 1977, 1979, 1981, 1983, capt 1991, 1993 and 1995; Hennessy Cognac Cup 1974, 1978, 1982, 1984, World Cup 1969, 1971, 1974, 1982, 1983, Scot Professional Champion 1971, 1973, 1974, 1977, 1984; rookie of the year 1968, Harry Vardon Trophy winner 1969; *Recreations* reading, walking dogs, keeping fit; *Style*— Bernard Gallacher, Esq, OBE; ✉ Professional Shop, Wentworth Club, Virginia Water, Surrey GU25 4LS (☎ 01344 843353, fax 01344 842122)

GALLACHER, Dr Stephen John; *b* 29 May 1961; *Educ* St Aloysius' Coll Glasgow, Univ of Glasgow (MB ChB, MRCP, MD); *Career* jr house offr: (med) Univ Dept of Med Glasgow Royal Infirmary 1983–84, (surgery) Dept of Surgery Duke Street Hosp Glasgow 1984; SHO/registrar (med rotation) Southern Gen Hosp Glasgow 1984–87, lectr in med Univ Dept of Med Glasgow Royal Infirmary 1990–95 (registrar in med 1987–90), conslt physician with an interest in diabetes and endocrinology Southern Gen Hosp NHS Tst 1995–; memb Cncl RCPSGlas 1993–95; *Publications* author of over 50 pubns in the field of metabolic bone diseases; *Style*— Dr Stephen Gallacher; ✉ Southern General Hospital NHS Trust, 1345 Govan Road, Glasgow G51 4TF (☎ 0141 201 1100, fax 0141 201 2399)

GALLAGHER, Edward Patrick; s of Charles Henry Gallagher (d 1977), and Lucy Georgina, *née* Gardiner (d 1996); *b* 4 Aug 1944; *Educ* Univ of Sheffield (BEng, Dip Business Studies, Mappin medal, John Brown award); *m* 3 April 1969, Helen, da of Ronald George Wilkinson; 2 s (James Edward b 16 Feb 1975, Robert Daniel b 28 July 1977); *Career* systems analyst Vauxhall Motors 1963–68, corp planning mangr Sandoz Products Ltd 1968–70, computer servs mangr Robinson Willey Ltd 1970–71; Black and Decker: fin mangr 1970–73, production mangr 1973–78, dir Mktg Servs 1978–79, dir Serv and Distribution 1979–81, dir Business Analysis based USA 1981–83, dir Market and Product Devpt 1983–86; Amersham International: dir Corp Devpt 1986–88, divnl chief exec 1988–90, mfrg dir 1990–92; chief exec: Nat Rivers Authy 1992–95, Environment Agency 1995–; memb Cncl Univ of Bristol 1994– (memb Fin Advsy Gp); Middlesex Univ: visiting prof Business Sch and Faculty of Technology, memb Faculty of Technology Advsy Gp, govr and chm Audit Ctee; tstee Living Again Tst; Hon DEng Univ of Sheffield 1996; CEng, FIEE 1990, MRI 1992, FIWEM 1994, FRSA 1995, CIMgt 1996; *Recreations* the countryside, golf, tennis, theatre, playing the guitar; *Style*— Edward Gallagher, Esq; ✉ Chief Executive, Environment Agency, Rio House, Aztec West, Almondsbury, Bristol BS12 4UD (☎ 01454 624401)

GALLAGHER, Eileen; *Educ* Queen Margaret's Acad Ayr, Univ of Glasgow (MA), Univ of Wales Coll of Cardiff (NCTJ Cert); *Career* freelance journalist 1980–84 (for newspapers incl Glasgow Herald and Daily Record); Scottish Television: joined as press offr 1984, hd of prog planning 1987–91, hd of Bdcasting Div 1991–92, concurrently i/c scheduling Children's ITV for ITV Network 1991–92, dir of bdcasting and main bd dir Scottish Television plc 1992–94; md Broadcasting Granada/LWT 1994–96, md LWT and dep md Granada UK Broadcasting 1996–; *Style*— Ms Eileen Gallagher; ✉ LWT, The London Television Centre, Upper Ground, London SE1 9LT (☎ 0171 620 1620)

GALLAGHER, Jock James Young; s of Joseph Gallagher (d 1938), and Margaret, *née* Young (d 1984); *b* 31 March 1938; *Educ* Greenock HS; *m* 31 Dec 1970, Sheenagh Glenn, da of Richard Jones (d 1958); *Career* journalist with various newspapers 1958–66; BBC: news prodr 1966–70, head network radio 1980–89 (ed 1970–80), head special projects 1989–90; md BroadVision; chm: Metro Television, Georgina Von Etzdorf Ltd; dep chm The European Journal plc; dir: BroadStaff, News Fact Ltd; exec dir Assoc of Br Eds, ed British Editor, past pres Radio and TV Industs Club (Midlands), vice pres Birmingham Press Club, patron Bewdley Festival, vice chm Stars Orgn for Spastics, govr RASE; pres Wyre Forest Lib Dems, vice chm W Midland Lib Dems; Euro Parly candidate (Lib Dem) for Hereford and Shropshire 1994, Parly candidate (Lib Dem) Birmingham Edgbaston 1997; memb: Euro Lib Dem and Reform Gp, Chartered Inst of Journalists, Radio Acad, Assoc of Euro Journalists; *Books* History of the Archers (1975), Portrait of A Lady - biography of Lady Isobel Barnett (1980), The Life And Death of Doris Archer - biography of Gwen Berryman (1981), To The Victor The Spoils (1986),

Return to Ambridge (1987), Borchester Echoes (1988), The Archers Omnibus (1990), Europress (1992); *Recreations* golf, reading, politics; *Clubs* National Liberal, Chelsea Arts, Kidderminster Golf; *Style*— Jock Gallagher, Esq; ✉ Rock House, Bewdley, Worcs DY12 1BY (☎ 01299 403110); BroadVision, 49 Frederick Road, Birmingham B15 1HN (☎ 0121 455 7949, fax 0121 454 6187)

GALLAGHER, Sister Maire Teresa; CBE (1992, OBE 1987); da of Owen Gallagher (d 1952), of Glasgow, and Annie, *née* McVeigh; *b* 27 May 1933; *Educ* Notre Dame Coll of Educn Glasgow (DCE), Univ of Glasgow (MA); *Career* memb Sisters of Notre Dame de Namur 1959–, princ teacher of history Notre Dame HS Glasgow 1965–72, lectr in secondary educn Notre Dame Coll Glasgow 1972–74, headteacher Notre Dame HS Dumbarton 1974–87, Sister Superior Convent of Notre Dame Dumbarton 1987–93; memb: Consultative Ctee on the Curriculum 1976–91, Ctee of Enquiry into Salary and Conditions of Service of Teachers 1986; chm: Ctee on Secondary Educn 1983–87, Consultative Ctee 1987–88, Scottish Consultative Cncl on the Curriculum 1988–91, Cmmn on Mission Evangelism and Educn ACTS 1989–93 and 1995–, Central Cncl ACTS 1995–; fell Scottish Vocational Educn Cncl 1989; Hon MEd CNAA 1992; *Recreations* reading, birdwatching; *Style*— Sister Maire Teresa Gallagher, CBE, SND; ✉ 67 Moorpark Avenue, Glasgow G52 4ET (☎ 0141 810 4214)

GALLAGHER, Paul; CBE (1996); s of Joseph Gallagher (d 1965), and Ann Hesmondhalgh; *b* 16 Oct 1944; *Educ* St Anne's Sch Droylesden; *m* 6 Feb 1974, Madeleine; *Career* EETPU: elected full time official 1966, memb Exec Cncl 1978–95 (initially with responsibility for membership in Manchester and N Wales Area), pres 1986–91, gen sec 1992–May 1994, gen sec Amalgamated Engrg and Electrical Union (AEEU) following merger with AEU May 1992–95, ret; *Recreations* reading, gardening, music; *Style*— Paul Gallagher, Esq, CBE

GALLAGHER, (Arthur) Robin; s of Hon James Albert Gallagher (d 1965), of York, and Winifred Mary, *née* Dill (d 1994); *b* 7 April 1941; *Educ* St Bedes Coll Manchester; *m* 1969 (m dis 1992), 2 da (Kirsten b 8 March 1974, Kate b 1 Dec 1977); *partner* Christine Lloyd; *Career* Lt RNR 1960–66; Touche Ross and Co Manchester and Leeds 1966–74, Ladyship International Group 1974–80, Whitecroft plc 1980–81, dir Antler Property Corporation plc 1981–94, md Wellholme Ltd 1988–95; dir: Towngate plc 1990–, Brigdale Ltd 1990–, Data Protection Ltd 1995–, Towngate Homes Ltd 1996–; chm Oakland Securities Ltd 1991–96; jt fndr Save Baguley Hall Campaign 1966; vice pres Leeds Jr C of C 1973–75; FCA; *Recreations* old buildings, antiques, riding; *Clubs* St James; *Style*— Robin Gallagher, Esq; ✉ Oakwood House, Bowling Alley, Rastrick, West Yorkshire HD6 3ET (☎ and fax 01484 715576, mobile 0802 279410)

GALLAGHER, Stephen; *b* 13 Oct 1954; *Career* writer; res Documentaries Dept Yorkshire TV, Presentation Dept Granada TV 1975, freelance writer 1980–; Northern chair Writers' Guild of GB 1994–96; novels incl: Chimera (1982), Follower (1984), Valley of Lights (1987), Oktober (1988), Down River (1989), Rain (1990), The Boat House (1991), Nightmare, With Angel (1992), Red, Red Robin (1995); radio plays incl: The Last Rose of Summer 1977, Hunter's Moon 1978, The Babylon Run 1979, A Resistance to Pressure 1980, The Kingston File 1987, By The River, Fontainebleau 1988, The Horn 1989, Life Line 1992; TV: Warriors' Gate (BBC) 1981, Terminus (BBC) 1984, Moving Targets (BBC) 1988, Chimera (Zenith/Anglia) 1991, Here Comes The Mirror Man (YTV) 1995; writings also incl short fiction and criticism; *Style*— Stephen Gallagher, Esq; ✉ c/o A P Watt Ltd, 20 John Street, London WC1N 2DR

GALLAND, Robert Brian; s of Raymond Harry Galland, and Olwyn Lilian Gladys, *née* Aston; *b* 26 Dec 1947; *Educ* Halesowen GS Univ of Manchester (MB ChB, MD); *m* 21 May 1977, Janet Carmichael, da of Edward Yates (d 1982); 3 da (Emma Louise b 30 March 1979, Joanne Laura b 20 June 1980, Rebecca Jamie b 26 Dec 1985); *Career* conslt surgn Royal Berkshire Hosp Reading 1988–; memb Ct of Examiners RCS 1992–; author of pubns on: vascular surgery, gastroenterology, surgical infection; FRCS 1976; *Books* Radiation Enteritis (ed with J Spencer, 1990), Clinical Problems in Vascular Surgery (ed with C A C Clyne, 1994); *Recreations* philately, reading; *Style*— Robert Galland, Esq; ✉ Little Orchard, Gardener's Lane, Upper Basildon, Berks RG8 8NN (☎ 01491 671852); Department of Surgery, Royal Berkshire Hospital, London Rd, Reading, Berks (☎ 0118 987 5111)

GALLEMORE, Michael; s of Ronald Gallemore (d 1988), of Chapel-en-le-Frith, Derbys, and Mary, *née* Slater, of Rhos-on-Sea, Colwyn Bay; *b* 3 Nov 1944; *Educ* Manchester Central GS; *m* 7 July 1967, Janetta Florence, da of Frank and Ada Reeves (d 1985); 1 s (Alexander Michael b 3 Nov 1974); *Career* interviewer Nat Rheumatism Survey 1961, joined Steward & Hartleys news agency Manchester as reporter 1962, contrib various series to nat newspapers on subjects incl drugs, crime and the judicial system; Mirror Group Newspapers 1964–93: joined staff of Daily and Sunday Mirror 1964, worked as reporter, art ed, sub-ed, led attempted mgmnt buyout of MGN, managing ed (North) MGN 1985–88, ed The Sporting Life 1989–93 (managing ed 1988), responsible for editorial launch of The European and Racing Times (NY), left MGN 1993; joined Barkers Trident Communications corp publishers 1993, commercial dir/ed Action Line magazine, Racing International and various other racing magazines; memb Br Field Sports Soc; *Books* ed: All Such Fun (by Michael Pope, 1992), A Year in Red Shirts (by Jack Berry); *Recreations* hunting, point-to-point riding, race riding, golf, rugby, soccer, cricket, tennis, squash, former semi-professional soccer and rugby league player; *Clubs* Shrigley Hall Country, Racehorse Owners' Assoc, Point-to-Point Owners' Assoc; *Style*— Michael Gallemore, Esq; ✉ Browside Farm, Stoneheads, Whaley Bridge, Derbyshire SK12 7BT (☎ 01663 732841)

GALLETLY, Eur Ing Prof Gerard Duncan; s of John Edward Galletly (d 1972), and Marion, *née* Musker (d 1973); *b* 17 March 1928; *Educ* Bootle GS, Univ of Liverpool (BEng, MEng, DEng), MIT Cambridge USA (SM, ScD); *m* 17 Oct 1953, Marjorie, da of Leonard Archer (d 1973); 1 da (Diana b 1974); *Career* airfield construction serv RAF 1947–49, Flying Offr Germany; head Plates and Shells Section David Taylor Model Basin US Navy Washington DC 1952–55, specialist in structural mechanics Shell Development Co Emeryville California 1955–61, asst dir Advanced Materials R&D Laboratory Pratt & Whitney Aircraft North Haven Connecticut 1961–64; Univ of Liverpool: prof of applied mechanics 1964–95 (Alexander Elder prof 1987–95), dean of engrg 1980–83, emeritus prof 1995–; author of over 100 tech papers in various journals; memb Tech Ctees Br Standards Instn, govr Birkenhead HS for Girls (GPDST) 1986–94; Best Res Paper of the Year (in Jl of Pressure Vessels and Piping) ASME 1979; IMechE: Thomas Bernard Hall Prize 1985, Ernest William Moss Prize 1986, Donald Julius Groen Prize 1990, Water Arbitration Prize 1990, Special Medal Int Conference on Shell Buckling Lyons 1991; Dr (hc) Cracow Univ of Technol 1995; FICE 1976, FIMechE 1977, FEng 1989, Eur Ing 1989; *Recreations* sport, music; *Clubs* RAF; *Style*— Eur Ing Prof Gerard Galletly, FEng; ✉ Department of Mechanical Engineering, The University, PO Box 147, Liverpool, Merseyside L69 3BX (☎ 0151 794 4812, fax 0151 794 4848, telex 627095)

GALLEWAY, William Henry; s of Major Harold Galleway, JP (d 1963), and Marjorie, *née* Frankland; *b* 30 July 1931; *Educ* Whitby GS, Univ of Leeds (BCom); *Career* articled to M Wasley Chapman 1949; ptnr: Carlill Burkinshaw Ferguson 1963–, Hodgson Impey (formerly Hodgson Harris) 1970, Price Waterhouse 1990–95; dir William Jackson & Son plc 1995; pres Humberside and Dist Soc CA's 1982–83; memb Cncl ICEAW 1982–95; memb Worshipful Co of CAs 1988; FCA 1966 (ACA 1955); *Recreations* antique collecting, philately; *Clubs* Lansdowne; *Style*— William H Galleway, Esq; ✉ Streonshalh, 1 North Promenade, Whitby, North Yorkshire YO21 3JX (☎ 01947 602280)

GALLEY, Roy; s of Kenneth Haslam Galley, and Letitia Mary, *née* Chapman; *b* 8 Dec 1947; *Educ* King Edward VII GS Sheffield, Worcester Coll Oxford; *m* 1976, Helen Margaret Butcher; 1 s, 1 da; *Career* PO mangr; contested (C) Dewsbury 1979, MP (C) Halifax 1983–87; memb Social Services Select Ctee 1983–87, sec Cons Backbench Health Ctee 1983–87; memb Calderdale Met Borough Cncl 1980–83; chm: Kingston and Esher Health Authy 1989–93, Kingston and Richmond Health Authy 1993–, Kingston and St George's NHS Coll of Health Studies 1993–96; Royal Mail London: dir of facilities 1992–94, dir of restructuring 1994–96, of operations programmes 1996–; *Style*— Roy Galley, Esq

GALLIAN, Jason Edward Riche; *b* 25 June 1971; *Career* professional cricketer; Lancashire CCC: debut 1990, awarded county cap 1994; played for Aust under 19 (capt v England) 1989–90, Oxford Univ 1992–93 (capt 1993); memb England touring team S Africa 1995/96; *Style*— Jason Gallian, Esq; ✉ c/o Lancashire CCC, Old Trafford, Manchester M16 0PX (☎ 0161 848 7021)

GALLIANO, John Charles; s of John Joseph Galliano, of Gibraltar, and Anita, *née* Guillen; *b* 28 Nov 1960; *Educ* Wilsons GS, St Martins Sch of Art; *Career* fashion designer; chief designer: Givenchy (Paris) 1995–96, Dior (Paris) 1996–; work on permanent display The Museum of Costume Bath 1987; Designer of the Year (Br Fashion Awards) 1987, 1994 and 1995, award (Telva Magazine's T Awards Spain) 1995; *Style*— John Galliano, Esq; ✉ Dior Couture, 11 rue François I, 75008 Paris, France (☎ 00 33 1 40 73 54 44)

GALLIE, Philip Roy (Phil); MP (C) Ayr (majority 85); s of George Gallie, and Ivy Gallie; *b* 3 June 1939; *Educ* Dunfermline HS, Kirkcaldy Tech Coll (HNC); *m* 5 Sept 1964, Marion, da of William Whyte; 1 s (Craig), 1 da (Kristeen); *Career* apprentice electrical fitter HM Dockyard Rosyth 1955–60, seagoing electrical engr Ben Line 1960–64, various posts in electricity supply industry 1964–92 rising from maintenance electrician through various maintenance engrg posts to mangr Galloway and Lanark Hydros and Inverkip Power Stn; Parly candidate (C): Cunninghame S 1983, Dunfermline W 1987; MP (C) Ayr 1992–, sec Scottish Cons Members Ctee 1992–, vice chm Scottish All Party Housing Ctee; chm: Bute and N Ayrshire Cons Assoc 1978–80, Cunninghame North Cons Assoc 1986–87, Strathclyde W Cons Euro-constituency Cncl 1987–89, W of Scotland Area Cons Cncl 1990–91; vice chm Scottish Cons and Unionist Pty 1995–; cncllr Cunninghame DC 1980–84; elder Church of Scotland; MIPlantE; *Recreations* hill walking, sport, politics; *Clubs* Scottish Royal Automobile, Ayr RFC; *Style*— Phil Gallie, Esq, MP; ✉ House of Commons, London SW1A 0AA (☎ (sec) 0171 219 6927); 1 Wellington Square, Ayr, Strathclyde (☎ 01292 263991, fax 01292 280480)

GALLIERS-PRATT, Rupert Anthony; s of Anthony Malcolm Galliers-Pratt, CBE, and Angela, 2 da of Sir Charles Cayzer, 3 Bt; bro of Nigel Cayzer, *qv*; *b* 9 April 1951; *Educ* Eton; *m* 1973, Alexandra Mary, da of Maj Hugh Rose; 2 s (George b 1979, Frederick b 1980), 2 da (Isabella b 1985, Alexandra b 1988); *Career* chm: Princess Resources Ltd, Optical Care plc; dir Oriel Group plc, former dir various other cos; *Clubs* White's, Turf, The Brook; *Style*— Rupert Galliers-Pratt, Esq; ✉ Mawley Hall, Cleobury Mortimer, Worcs; 26 Eaton Terrace, London SW1

GALLIFORD, Rt Rev David George; s of late Alfred Edward Bruce Galliford, of Withycombe Raleigh, Exmouth, Devon, and late Amy Doris, *née* Pawley; *b* 20 June 1925; *Educ* Bede Coll Sunderland, Clare Coll Cambridge (MA); *m* 1, 27 May 1954, Enid May (d 1983), da of late Arthur Drax, of Bridlington; 1 da (Clare Frances Hope b 1956); m 2, 21 April 1987, Mrs Claire Margaret Phoenix, da of late Alfred Henry Smalley, of Stretford, Manchester; *Career* curate St John's Newland Hull 1951–54, minor canon Windsor 1954–56, vicar St Oswald's Middlesbrough 1956–61, rector Bolton Percy and diocesan trg offr 1961–71, canon of York 1965–69, residentiary canon and treas of York Minster 1969–75, bishop of Hulme 1975–84, bishop of Bolton 1984–91, asst bishop of York 1991–; SBStJ 1992; *Recreations* music, painting, gardening; *Style*— The Rt Rev D G Galliford; ✉ Bishopsgarth, Maltongate, Thornton-le-Dale, N Yorks YO18 7SA (☎ 01751 474605)

GALLIFORD, Peter; CBE (1992, OBE 1981); s of T J Galliford; *b* 21 Oct 1928; *Educ* King Edward VI Sch Nuneaton; *m* 1963, Rona, *née* Pearson; 3 s (Marcus, Miles, Bruce); *Career* fndr dir Galliford & Sons Ltd 1952, md Galliford Group of Cos 1952–73, chm Galliford plc (Wolvey Leics) 1973–93 (non-exec dir 1993–); dir Birmingham Regeneration Ltd (urban renewal agency), non-exec chm Rugby NHS Tst; chm Fedn of Civil Engrg Contractors 1978 (pres 1993–96); past pres: Construction Indust Res and Info Assoc, Fédération de l'Industrie Européenne de la Construction, Confedn of Int Contractors Assocs; memb: Warwicks CC 1964–70, Severn Trent Water Authy 1973–76, Civil Engrg Ctee NEDO 1978–84; vice pres Warwicks Rural Community Cncl; FIHT, FICE; *Style*— Peter Galliford, Esq, CBE; ✉ Hunters Gap, Ashlawn Rd, Rugby CV22 5QE (☎ 01788 543835)

GALLIGAN, Prof Denis James; s of John Felix Galligan (d 1973), and Muriel Maud, *née* Johnson; *b* 4 June 1947; *Educ* Downlands Coll Toowoomba Aust, Univ of Queensland (B of Law), Univ of Oxford (MA, BCL); *m* 20 June 1972, Martha Louise, da of Alfred Lewis Martinuzzi, of Innisfail, Queensland, Aust; 1 s (Finbar John b 10 Sept 1977), 1 da (Francesca Louise b 22 Feb 1975); *Career* lectr Faculty of Law UCL 1974–76, pt/t lectr Magdalen Coll Oxford 1975, fell Jesus Coll Oxford and CUF lectr Univ of Oxford 1976–81, sr lectr Faculty of Law Univ of Melbourne 1982–84, dean of the Faculty of Law Univ of Southampton 1987–90 (prof 1985–93), prof of socio-legal studies and dir Centre for Socio-Legal Studies Univ of Oxford 1993–; fell Wolfson Coll Oxford; pres UK Assoc for Legal and Social Philosophy 1989–91, memb Socio-Legal Studies Assoc; barrister of the Supreme Ct Queensland and Gray's Inn; *Books* Essays in Legal Theory (1984), Law, Rights and the Welfare State (1986), Discretionary Powers: A Legal Study of Official Discretion (1986), Procedure (1992), Administrative Law (1992), Australian Administrative Law (1993), Socio-Legal Readings in Administrative Law (1995), Due Process and Procedural Fairness (1995), Socio-Legal Studies in Context (1995); *Recreations* reading, gardening; *Style*— Prof Denis Galligan; ✉ The Rosery, Beckley, Oxford OX3 9UU (☎ and fax 01865 351281); Centre for Socio-Legal Studies, Wolfson College, Linton Road, Oxford OX2 6UD (☎ 01865 284220, fax 01865 284221)

GALLIMORE, Michael; s of John Gallimore, of Surbiton, Surrey, and Rita Ida Doreen, *née* Clarke; *b* 8 March 1958; *Educ* Kingston GS, St Catharine's Coll Cambridge (MA, capt Hockey Club, Hockey blue); *m* 29 July 1983, Jane Frances, da of Alfred Aspinall, of Southport, Merseyside; 1 s (William Mark b 1990), 1 da (Claire Edith b 1994); *Career* admitted slr 1983, ptnr Lovell White Durrant 1988–; England Hockey international; memb: Law Soc 1983, City of London Slrs' Co 1983; *Recreations* golf, hockey, theatre; *Clubs* Porters Park Golf, Ladykillers Hockey, Hawks' (Cambridge); *Style*— Michael Gallimore, Esq; ✉ Lovell White Durrant, 65 Holborn Viaduct, London EC1A 2DY (☎ 0171 236 0066, fax 0171 248 4212, telex 887122)

GALLIMORE, Patricia Mary; da of Capt Charles Philip Gallimore, RN (d 1988), and Elizabeth St John, *née* Benn (d 1977); *b* 7 Aug 1944; *Educ* Hermitage House Sch Bath, Westbourne Sch Glasgow, St Margaret's Sch Sutton Coldfield, Birmingham Sch of Speech & Drama; *m* 7 April 1973, Charles Gardner, s of John Gardner; 1 s (Thomas Charles b 27 May 1977), 1 da (Harriet Mary Elizabeth b 26 July 1982); *Career* radio actress 1965–; twice memb BBC Radio Drama Co; leading roles in plays and serials incl: War and Peace, The Forsyte Saga, Wuthering Heights, Cold Comfort Farm, Waggoners Walk (BBC Radio 2) 1969–71, Pat Archer in The Archers (BBC Radio 4) 1974–; TV appearances incl: Spy-Ship (BBC), Aliens in the Family (BBC), Kinsey (BBC),

Jupiter Moon (BSB); continues work on projects incl voice overs, audio cassette books, commentaries and poetry recitals; winner BBC Student Radio Drama Prize (now Carleton Hobbs Award) 1965; *Recreations* swimming, reading, walking, enjoying time with friends and family; *Clubs* BBC; *Style—* Patricia Gallimore; ✉ c/o The Archers, BBC Pebble Mill, Birmingham (☎ 0121 414 8400, fax 0121 414 8873)

GALLINER, Peter; s of Dr Moritz Galliner, and Hedwig Isaac; *b* 19 Sept 1920; *Educ* Berlin and London; *m* 1, 1948, Edith Marguerite Goldschmidt; 1 da; m 2, 1990, Helga Stenschke; *Career* Reuters 1942–47, foreign mangr Financial Times 1947–60, chm and md Ullstein Publishing Group (Berlin) 1960–64, vice chm and md British Printing Corporation Publishing Group 1965–70, int publishing conslt 1965–67 and 1970–75, chm Peter Galliner Associates 1970–; dir International Press Institute 1975–93, currently dir International Encounters (consultancy for int conference and seminar projects); Federal Cross of Merit (first class, FGR), Ecomienda Orden de Isabel la Catolica (Spain), Cdr's Cross Order of Merit (FRG); *Recreations* music, reading; *Style—* Peter Galliner, Esq; ✉ Untere Zäune 9, Zürich 8001, Switzerland (☎ 01 251 8664); 27 Walsingham, St John's Wood Park, London NW8 6RH (☎ 0171 722 5502, fax 0171 722 5217)

GALLOWAY, George; MP (Lab) Glasgow Hillhead (majority 4,826); s of George Galloway, of Dundee, and Sheila Reilly; *b* 16 Aug 1954; *Educ* Harris Acad; *m* 1979 (sep 1987), Elaine, da of James Fyffe, of Dundee; 1 da (Lucy b 1982); *Career* labourer jute & flax indust 1973, prodn worker Michelin Tyres 1973, organiser Dundee Lab Pty 1977, dir War on Want 1983, MP (Lab) Glasgow Hillhead 1987–; Hilal-i-Quaid-i-Azzam decoration for servs to the movement for the restoration of democracy in Pakistan 1990, Hilal-i-Pakistan decoration for work on self-determination for Jammu and Kashmir 1996; *Books* Downfall - The Ceausescus and the Romanian Revolution (jtly, 1991); *Recreations* sport, films, music; *Style—* George Galloway, MP; ✉ House of Commons, London SW1

GALLOWAY, Janice; da of late James Galloway, and Janet Clark McBride (d 1982); *b* 2 Dec 1956; *Educ* Ardrossan Acad, Univ of Glasgow; *children* 1 s (James b 21 Feb 1992); *Career* writer, sometime English teacher; E M Forster Award 1994; *Books* The Trick is to Keep Breathing (1990, winner SAC Award, MIND/Allan Lane award), Blood (1991, winner SAC Award), Foreign Parts (1994, winner McVitie's prize for Scottish Writer of the Year 1994, SAC Award), Where You Find It (1996); *Style—* Ms Janice Galloway; ✉ c/o Jonathan Cape, 20 Vauxhall Bridge Road, London SW1V 2SA; c/o Derek Johns, AP Watt Agency, 20 St John Street, London WC1N 2DR (☎ 0171 405 6774, fax 0171 831 2154)

GALLOWAY, Bishop of (RC) 1981–; Rt Rev Maurice Taylor; s of Maurice Taylor (d 1967), of Hamilton, and Lucy, *née* McLaughlin (d 1975); *b* 5 May 1926; *Educ* Our Lady's HS Motherwell, Pontifical Scots Coll Rome, Pontifical Gregorian Univ Rome (DTheol); *Career* Nat Serv RAMC 1944–47, served in UK, India, Egypt; lectr in theology St Peter's Coll Cardross Scotland 1960–65 (lectr in philosphy 1955–60), rector Royal Scots Coll Valladolid Spain 1965–74, parish priest Our Lady of Lourdes East Kilbride 1974–81; episcopal sec Bishops' Conf, vice pres Catholic Inst for Int Rels London, vice chm Episcopal Bd Int Cmmn on English in the Liturgy; *Books* The Scots College in Spain (1971), Guatemala: A Bishop's Journey - A Story of Brutality, Survival and Faith (1991), El Salvador: Portrait of a Parish (1992), Opening our Lives to the Saviour (with Ellen Hawkes, 1995), Listening at the Foot of the Cross (with Ellen Hawkes, 1996); *Style—* The Rt Rev the Bishop of Galloway; ✉ Candida Casa, 8 Corsehill Rd, Ayr KA7 2ST (☎ and fax 01292 266750)

GALLOWAY, Nicholas Robert; s of Norman Patrick Robert Galloway, and Eileen, *née* Thompson; *b* 12 May 1935; *Educ* Shrewsbury, Univ of Cambridge, Univ of Edinburgh (BA, MB ChB, DO, MD); *m* 28 July 1962, Jennifer, *née* Shell; 2 s (Peter b 10 March 1969, James b 15 Jan 1978), 1 da (Sarah b 15 Oct 1967); *Career* house surgn Western Gen Hosp Edinburgh 1959–60, sr registrar Moorfields Eye Hosp 1963–65, conslt ophthalmic surgn and clinical teacher Nottingham Univ Hosp 1967–; master Oxford Ophthalmological Congress 1988–90, pres Nottingham Medico Chirurgical Soc 1993–94, memb Bd Int Soc for Clinical Electrophysiology of Vision; FRCS, FRCOphth; memb: BMA, Johnian Soc; *Books* Ophthalmic Electrodiagnosis (1981), Common Eye Diseases and their Management (1985), Ophthalmology (1988); *Recreations* gardening, photography; *Clubs* Royal Soc of Med; *Style—* Nicholas Galloway, Esq; ✉ Queen's Medical Centre, Clifton Boulevard, Nottingham NG7 2UH

GALLOWAY, Rev Dr Peter John; OBE (1996), JP (City of London 1989); s of Henry John Galloway (d 1986), and Mary Selina, *née* Beshaw; *b* 19 July 1954; *Educ* Westminster City School, Univ of London (BA, PhD); *Career* ordained: deacon 1983, priest 1984; curate: St John's Wood London 1983–86, St Giles-in-the-Fields London 1986–90; vicar Emmanuel West End Hampstead London 1995– (priest-in-charge 1990–95); chm of govrs Emmanuel Sch 1990–, tstee Grant Maintained Schs Fndn 1991–; St John Ambulance: asst DG 1985–91, dep DG 1991–, chm Nat Publications Ctee 1988–95; vice chm The Goldsmiths' Soc 1991–, memb Goldsmiths' Coll Cncl Univ of London 1993–; Freeman City of London 1995; FRSA 1988; OStJ 1986, ChStJ 1992; *Books* The Order of St Patrick 1783–1983 (1983), Henry F B Mackay (1983), Good and Faithful Servants (1988), The Cathedrals of Ireland (1992), The Order of the British Empire (1996), Royal Service: The Royal Victorian Order (1996); *Recreations* reading, writing, book collecting, solitude; *Clubs* Athenaeum; *Style—* The Rev Dr Peter Galloway, OBE, JP; ✉ The Vicarage, Lyncroft Gardens, London NW6 1JU (☎ 0171 435 1911, fax 0171 431 5521)

GALLOWAY, 13 Earl of (S 1623); Sir Randolph Keith Reginald Stewart; 12 Bt (of Corsewell S 1627 and 10 Bt of Burray S 1687); also Lord Garlies (S 1607) and Baron Stewart of Garlies (GB 1796); s of 12 Earl of Galloway, JP (d 1978); *b* 14 Oct 1928; *Educ* Harrow; *m* 1975, Mrs May Lily Budge, yst da of late Andrew Miller, of Duns, Berwickshire; *Heir* kinsman, Andrew Stewart; *Style—* The Rt Hon the Earl of Galloway; ✉ Senwick House, Brighouse Bay, Borgue, Kircudbrightshire, Scotland DG6 4TP (☎ 0155 77 236)

GALLWEY, *see:* Frankland-Payne-Gallwey

GALPIN, Rodney Desmond; s of Sir Albert James Galpin, KCVO, CBE (d 1984), and Vera Alice, *née* Tiller (d 1980); *b* 5 Feb 1932; *Educ* Haileybury and Imperial Serv Coll; *m* 1956, Sylvia, da of Godfrey Craven (d 1981); 1 s (Paul), 1 da (Fenella); *Career* exec dir Bank of England 1984–88, chm Johnson Matthey Bankers 1984–85, chm Standard Chartered plc 1988–93, dir Cater Allen Holdings plc 1993–, chm Alpha Airports Group plc 1994–; dir: Capital Shopping Centres plc 1994–, Ascot Holdings plc 1994–; non-exec dir Peninsular & Oriental Steam Navigation Co plc Jan 1996–; chm: Look Ahead Housing Assoc 1994–, Code of Banking Practice Review Ctee 1994–; OStJ; *Style—* Rodney Galpin, Esq; ✉ Aldermans Cottage, Lutmans Haven, Knowl Hill, Reading RG10 9YN

GALSWORTHY, Anthony Charles; CMG (1985); s of Sir Arthur Norman Galsworthy, KCMG (d 1986), and Margaret Agnes, *née* Hiscocks (d 1973); *b* 20 Dec 1944; *Educ* St Paul's, Corpus Christi Coll Cambridge (MA); *m* 30 May 1970, Jan, da of Dr A W Dawson-Grove; 1 s (Andrew b 1974), 1 da (Carolyn b 1975); *Career* Dip Serv; Far East Dept FCO 1966–67, language student Hong Kong 1967–69, third sec (later second sec) Peking 1970–72, Rhodesia Dept FCO 1972–74, private sec Min of State 1974–77, first sec Rome 1977–81, first sec (later cnsllr and head of Chancery) Peking 1982–84, head Hong Kong Dept FCO 1984–86, princ private sec to Sec of State for Foreign and Cwlth Affrs 1986–88; visiting res fell Royal Inst of Int Affrs 1988–89; sr Br rep Sino-Br Jt Liason Gp on Hong Kong 1989–93; chief of assessments staff Cabinet Office 1993–95; dep under sec of state FCO 1995–; Order of the Lion of Finland 1975, Order of Adolph of Nassau Luxembourg 1976; *Recreations* ornithology, wildlife; *Clubs* Oxford and Cambridge; *Style—* Anthony Galsworthy, Esq, CMG; ✉ c/o FCO, King Charles St, London SW1A 2AH

GALSWORTHY, (Arthur) Michael Johnstone; DL (Cornwall 1993); s of Sir John Edgar Galsworthy, KCVO, CMG (d 1992), of Lanzeague, St Just-in-Roseland, Truro, Cornwall, and Jennifer Ruth, *née* Johnstone; *b* 10 April 1944; *Educ* Radley, Univ of St Andrews (MA); *m* 1, 20 June 1972, Charlotte Helena Prudence (d 1989), da of Col S M Roberts (d 1958), of Soranks Manor, Fairseat, Kent; 1 s (Stamford Timothy John b 20 May 1976), 2 da (Olivia Victoria Jane b 4 Aug 1974, Susannah Catherine Rose b 14 Nov 1979); m 2, 26 Oct 1991, Sarah Christian, da of Cdr Rev Peter Durnford, of St Mawes, Cornwall; 1 s (William Jack Heywood b 8 Aug 1994), 1 da (Imogen Rosdew Claire b 5 March 1996); *Career* International Harvester Corp (UK) 1967–69, English China Clays International PLC 1970–81, md Hawkins Wright Associates 1981–87, dir Woodard Corporation 1983–87; chm: Trewithen Estates Management Co Ltd 1984–, Probus Garden Estate Co Ltd 1984–; local advsy dir Barclays Bank plc 1988–; dir Westcountry Development Corporation 1993–; chm: Royal Cornwall Hospitals NHS Tst 1991–93, Cornwall County Playing Fields Assoc 1984–, Cornwall Rural Housing Assoc 1985–96; memb Prince of Wales' Cncl 1985–, dir Cncl for Small Industs in Rural Areas 1985–88, tstee Rural Housing Tst 1986–91, rural devpt cmmr 1987–91, vice pres Royal Cornwall Agric Assoc, chm Cncl Order of St John Cornwall 1995–; High Sheriff of Cornwall 1994–95; Freeman City of London 1973, Liveryman Worshipful Co of Goldsmiths 1991 (Freeman 1973); FZS 1981; *Publications* In Pursuit of Excellence - a Testimony of Current Business Achievements in Cornwall (1994), The Business Journal for Cornwall (1995); *Recreations* gardening, fishing, shooting; *Clubs* Brooks's, Farmers'; *Style—* Michael Galsworthy, DL; ✉ Trewithen, Grampound Rd, nr Truro, Cornwall TR2 4DD (☎ 01726 882418); Trewithen Estates Management Company, Estate Office, Grampound Road, Truro, Cornwall (☎ 01726 882763, fax 01726 882301)

GALTON, Prof David Jeremy; s of Maj Ernest Manuel Galton, and Cecilia, *née* Leyburn; *b* 2 May 1937; *Educ* Highgate School, Univ of London (MD, DSc); *m* 11 April 1967, (Gwynne) Merle; 1 s ((James) Seth b 1970), 1 da (Clare Judith b 1968); *Career* conslt physician St Bartholomew's Hosp 1971–, conslt physician i/c Moorfields Eye Hosp 1974–, prof Univ of London 1987–; chm Clinical Science 1979–81, sec Euro Atherosclerosis Soc; memb: Med Res Soc 1971, Assoc Physicians UK 1975, RSM; *Books* The Human Adipose Cell (1971), Molecular Genetics of Common Metabolic Disease (1985), Hyperlipidaemia in Practice (1991); *Recreations* skiing, sailing, music; *Style—* Prof David Galton; ✉ St Bartholomew's Hospital, West Smithfield, London EC1 (☎ 0171 601 8432, fax 0171 601 8042)

GALTON, Prof Maurice James; s of James Galton (d 1948), and Olive, *née* Prendergast (d 1987); *Educ* Salesian Coll Oxford, Univ of Durham (BSc), Univ of Newcastle (MSc), Univ of Leeds (MEd), Univ of Leicester (PhD); *m* 19 March 1960, Pamela Jean, da of Rev Canon Albert John Bennitt (d 1985); 3 s (Simon b 1960, Giles b 1963, Matthew b 1964), 3 da (Philippa b 1968, Bridget b 1969, Su b 1977); *Career* asst master St Paul's Sch 1960–65, instr Univ of Leeds 1965–70; Univ of Leicester: lectr 1970–82, prof 1982–, dean Faculty of Educn and Continuing Studies 1995–; Parly candidate (Lib) Bosworth 1974–75; conslt Cncl of Europe Primary Project 1982–88, memb Primary Ctee Nat Curriculum Cncl (NCC) 1988–; memb Leicester Theatre Tst 1975–81; FRSA 1986; *Books* Inside The Primary Classroom (1980), Moving From The Primary Classroom (1984), Primary Teaching (1988), Handbook of European Primary Education (1989), Group Work in the Primary Classroom (1992), Crisis in the Primary Classroom (1994); *Recreations* golf, cricket, walking, theatre; *Style—* Prof Maurice Galton; ✉ Brookside House, Main St, Tilton on the Hill, Leics LE7 9RF (☎ 0116 259 7268); School of Education, 21 University Road, Leics LE1 7RF (☎ 0116 252 3680, e-mail MJG5@ Leicester.UK.AC)

GALTON, Raymond Percy (Ray); s of Herbert Galton, and Christina Galton; *b* 17 July 1930; *Educ* Garth Sch Morden; *m* 1956, Tonia Phillips (d 1995); 1 s, 2 da; *Career* scriptwriter and author (in collaboration with Alan Simpson, *qv*); *Theatre* incl: Way Out In Piccadilly 1966–67, The Wind in the Sassafras Trees 1968, Albert och Herbert (Sweden) 1981; with John Antrobus: When Did You Last See Your Trousers 1987–88 (nat tour 1994); *Radio* incl: Hancock's Half Hour 1954–59, The Frankie Howerd Show, Back with Braden, Steptoe and Son 1966–73; *Television* incl: Hancock's Half Hour 1956–61, Citizen James 1961, BBC Comedy Playhouse, Steptoe and Son 1962–74, Galton and Simpson Comedy 1969, Milligan's Wake, Frankie Howerd, Clochemerle 1971, Casanova 1973, Dawson's Weekly 1975, The Galton and Simpson Playhouse 1976–77, Camilo e Filho (Portugal Steptoe) 1995, Paul Merton In Galton & Simpson's... (series) 1996; with Johnny Speight: Spooner's Patch 1977–81; with John Antrobus: Room at the Bottom 1986–87; *Films* incl: The Rebel 1960, The Bargee 1963, The Wrong Arm of the Law 1964, The Spy with the Cold Nose 1966, Loot 1970, Steptoe and Son 1971, Steptoe and Son Ride Again 1973, Den Siste Fleksnes (Norway) 1974, Le Petomane 1977; with Andrew Galton: Camping (Denmark) 1990; *Awards* John Logie Baird award for outstanding contribution to TV, Writers' Guild award (twice), Guild of TV Producers and Directors 1959 Merit Awards for Scriptwriters of the Year, Screenwriters' Guild Best TV Comedy Series (for Steptoe and Son) annually 1962–65, Dutch TV Best Comedy Series (for Steptoe and Son) 1966, Screenwriters' Guild Best Comedy Screenplay (for Steptoe and Son) 1972, Banff Festival Best TV Comedy (for Room at the Bottom) 1987; *Books* Hancock (1961), Steptoe and Son (1963), The Reunion and Other Plays (1966), Hancock Scripts (1974), The Best of Hancock (1986), Hancock - The Classic Years (1987), The Best of Steptoe and Son (1988); *Style—* Ray Galton, Esq; ✉ The Ivy House, Hampton Court, Middx (☎ 0181 977 1236)

GALVIN, Guglielmo Patrizio; s of William Joseph Galvin (d 1976), and Rosina, *née* Gabriele; *b* 15 March 1939; *Educ* St Michael's Sch Dublin, Bolton St Tech Coll Dublin, City of Westminster Coll London; *m* 18 July 1970, Patricia, da of John Dennis Reardon; 1 s (Liam b 20 Dec 1972), 1 da (Roisin Amy b 15 Oct 1974); *Career* professional photographer; photographic colour printer, pt/t lectr London Coll of Printing, freelance photographer for Sunday Times, Observer and numerous other pubns; *Style—* Guglielmo Galvin, Esq; ✉ 26 Curzon Road, Muswell Hill, London N10 2RA (☎ 0181 883 6131)

GALVIN, Patrick Derek Thomas; s of Maj Thomas Derek Galvin (d 1952), and Teresa Christina, *née* Innes; *b* 20 March 1939; *Educ* Downside, Christ's Coll Cambridge (BA); *m* 23 Jan 1982, Juliana Mary, da of Sir Conrad Marshall Swan, KCVO, *qv*, former Garter Princ King of Arms; 5 s (Thomas b 23 Jan 1984, Edward b 9 June 1985, Nicholas b 3 Dec 1986, Alexander b 8 Sept 1988, Frederick b 5 March 1990), 1 da (Elizabeth b 12 Nov 1982); *Career* investmt analyst Equity and Law Life 1960–62, property ed Investors Chronicle 1963–68, assoc Rowe Rudd and Co 1971 (joined 1968), ptnr de Zoete & Bevan 1982, dir Barclays de Zoete Wedd International Equities 1986–93 (conslt 1993–94), assoc Charles Stanley & Co 1993–94, South-East Asia strategist Nikko Europe 1994–96; memb Cncl Soc of Investmt Analysts 1979–84 (treas 1982–83); MSI (memb Stock Exchange 1971), AIIMR (AMSIA 1970); *Recreations* gardening, wine, opera, skiing, sailing, travel; *Clubs* Royal Harwich Yacht; *Style—* Patrick Galvin, Esq; ✉ Longwood House, Nayland, nr Colchester, Essex (☎ 01206 262482)

GALWAY, 12 Viscount (I 1727); George Rupert Monckton-Arundell; CD; also Baron Killard (I 1727); s of Philip Marmaduke Monckton (d 1965), and Lavender, *née* O'Hara; suc 1 cous once removed, 11 Viscount, 1980; *b* 13 Oct 1922; *Educ* Victoria Coll;

m 1944, Fiona Margaret, da of Capt W de P Taylor (d 1979), of Sooke, Br Columbia; 1 s, 3 da; *Heir* s, Hon (John) Philip Monckton, *qv*; *Career* Lt-Cdr RCN 1941–67; stockbroker 1967–83, ret; *Recreations* painting, 'birding', golfing, travelling; *Style*— The Rt Hon the Viscount Galway, CD; ✉ 787 Berkshire Drive, London, Ontario N6J 3S5, Canada

GALWAY, James; OBE (1977); s of James Galway; *b* 8 Dec 1939; *Educ* RCM, Guildhall Sch of Music, Conservatoire National Supérieur de Musique (Paris); *m* 1; 1 s; m 2; 1 s, 2 da (twins); m 3, 1984, Jeanne Cinnante; *Career* flute-player; princ flute: London Symphony Orch 1966, Royal Philharmonic Orch 1967–69, Berlin Philharmonic Orch 1969–75; solo career 1975–; records for BMG Classics; Hon MA Open Univ 1979; Hon DMus: Queen's Univ Belfast 1979, New England Conservatory of Music 1980; *Publications* Flute (Yehudi Menuhin Music Guide Series, 1982), James Galway - An Autobiography (1978); *Recreations* music, swimming, walking, theatre, films, TV, chess, backgammon, talking to people; *Style*— James Galway, Esq, OBE; ✉ c/o Kathryn Enticott, IMG Artists, Media House, 3 Burlington Lane, London W4 2TH (☎ 0181 233 5800, fax 0181 233 5801)

GAMBACCINI, Paul Matthew; s of Mario Matthew Gambaccini, of Westport, Connecticut, and Dorothy, *née* Kiebrick; *b* 2 April 1949; *Educ* Staples HS, Dartmouth Coll (BA), Univ Coll Oxford (MA); *Career* disc jockey and music journalist; Rolling Stone Magazine 1970–77, Radio One 1973–86 and 1991–93, Kaleidoscope Radio Four 1976–, ILR 1986–88, Capital Radio 1988–91, Classic FM 1992–95, BBC Radio Three 1995–96; TV incl: Omnibus (BBC 1), Pebble Mill at One (BBC 1), Summer Festivals (BBC 2), The Other Side of the Tracks (C4) 1983–85, TV-am 1983–92, Television's Greatest Hits (BBC 1), GMTV 1993–; fundraiser: Amnesty International, Terrence Higgins Tst; *Books* Guinness Book of British Hit Singles (co-ed 10 edns), Guinness Book of British Hit Albums (co-ed 7 edns), Radio Boy (1986), Top 100 Albums (1987), Television's Greatest Hits (1993), Love Letters (1996); *Recreations* gym, films, theatre, music, comic books; *Clubs* RAC; *Style*— Paul Gambaccini, Esq; ✉ 2 Hungerford Road, London N7 9LX (☎ 0171 609 8278, fax 0171 607 1275)

GAMBLE, Prof Andrew Michael; s of Marcus Elkington Gamble, of Sevenoaks, Kent, and Joan, *née* Westall; *b* 15 Aug 1947; *Educ* Brighton Coll, Queens' Coll Cambridge (BA), Univ of Durham (MA), Gonville and Caius Coll Cambridge (PhD); *m* 15 June 1974, Christine Jennifer, da of Allan Edwin Rodway; 1 s (Thomas Simon b 7 March 1977), 2 da (Corinna Lucy b 25 Feb 1980, Sarah Eleanor b 3 August 1983); *Career* Univ of Sheffield: lectr in politics 1973–82, reader 1982–86, prof 1986–, pro-vice-chllr 1994–; visiting prof: Univ of Kobe 1990, Univ of Hitotsubashi 1992, Univ of Chuo 1994; Isaac Deutscher Meml Prize 1972, Mitchell Prize 1977; memb Political Studies Assoc; *Books* The Conservative Nation (1974), Britain in Decline (1981), The Free Economy and the Strong State (1988), Hayek: The Iron Cage of Liberty (1996); *Recreations* music, books, walking; *Style*— Prof Andrew Gamble; ✉ Department of Politics, University of Sheffield, Sheffield S10 2TN (☎ 0114 282 4596, fax 0114 273 9769, e-mail a.m.gamble@sheffield.ac.uk)

GAMBLE, Sir David Hugh Norman; 6 Bt (UK 1897), of Windlehurst, St Helens, Co Palatine of Lancashire; s of Sir David Gamble, 5 Bt (d 1984), and Dawn Adrienne, da of late David Hugh Gittins; *b* 1 July 1966; *Heir* kinsman, Hugh Robert George Gamble b 3 March 1946; *Style*— Sir David Gamble, Bt; ✉ c/o Keinton House, Keinton Mandeville, Somerton, Somerset TA11 4DX

GAMBLE, David Martin; s of Rev Alfred Edward Gamble, of Scotland, and Yvonne, *née* Cornforth (d 1973); *b* 10 March 1953; *Educ* Soham Village Coll, Ealing Sch of Photography; *Career* photographer Observer Magazine 1984–; other magazines incl: Independent, Sunday Times, Telegraph, Life (NY), Fortune (NY), Time (NY), Elle, Paris Match, El Mundo, The New Yorker Magazine, Newsweek (NY); photographic subjects incl: Margaret Thatcher, The Dalai Lama, The King of Redonda, José Carreras, Lord (Jacob) Rothschild, Sir George Solti, Alastair Cooke, The Duke of Gloucester, Karsh of Ottowa; exhibitions incl: Arles 1987 (jtly), Assoc of Photographers Gallery 1987, Kodak Euro Exhibition 1988, World Press Awards 1989, Les Portes d'Europe (Provence) 1992; winner Kodak Grande Prix Euro Award France 1987; film documentary: Faces 1989, Groucho, Portraits Exhibition London 1996; memb AFAEP; painter; pt/t artist in residence Ecole National de la Photographie; *Recreations* watching cricket, jazz, photography; *Clubs* Groucho's; *Style*— David Gamble, Esq; (☎ 0181 694 1945)

GAMBLE, Neil Walton; s of Sydney Joseph Gamble (d 1983), of Manchester, and Florence Mildred, *née* Walton (d 1989); *b* 17 Jan 1943; *Educ* Stockport GS, Univ of Manchester (BA), St Edmund Hall Oxford (DipEd, cricket blue, lacrosse half blue), Univ of Nottingham (MEd); *m* 16 Aug 1967, Susan Elizabeth, da of Thomas Ernest Allott Vardey; 2 da (Helen Sarah b 8 Sept 1970, Angela Claire b 12 Jan 1973), 1 s (Ian Peter b 4 Sept 1979); *Career* mgmnt trainee Turner and Newall plc 1965–66, asst master Moseley Co GS 1966–67, head of economics and politics Repton Sch 1967–81, dep head Kirkham GS 1981–84, headmaster King Edward VI Aston Sch Birmingham 1985–92, headmaster Exeter Sch 1992–; Birmingham exec SHA 1986–92 (memb 1984–), memb Economics Assoc 1970–, memb Headmasters Conference 1992–; played cricket Derbyshire 2 XI and Cheshire; played lacrosse: British Univs, Lancashire, South of England and England trial; *Recreations* classical music, fine art, rugby, cricket, golf, theatre; *Clubs* Vincent's (Oxford), Sutton Coldfield CC, Aston Old Edwardians Rugby (pres 1985–92), Devon CC (memb Ctee); *Style*— Neil Gamble, Esq; ✉ Exeter School, Exeter EX2 4NS (☎ 01392 73679)

GAMBLE, Richard Arthur; s of Arthur Gamble (d 1985), of New Malden, Surrey, and Grace Emily, *née* Little; *b* 19 Sept 1939; *Educ* Raynes Park County GS; *m* 26 April 1966, Elizabeth Ann, da of Edward Godwin Atkyns; 2 s (Simon b 1967, James b 1970); *Career* articled clerk W J Gilbert & Co CAs London 1957–62, asst mangr Turquand Youngs & Co CAs 1962–66, dir and co sec Lee Davy Group Ltd 1966–68, dir and sec Hamilton Smith Lloyd's Brokers 1968–70, fin dir Lowndes Lambert International Lloyd's Brokers 1970–76, European fin dir Data 100/Northern Telecom Systems 1976–80, fin dir McDonnell Douglas Information Systems and dir McDonnell Douglas UK 1980–84, dep chief fin offr British Airways 1984–89; Royal Insurance Holdings plc: gp fin dir 1989–91, gp chief operating offr 1991, gp chief exec 1992–96; gp chief exec Royal & Sun Alliance Insurance Group plc 1996–; chm The Policyholders' Protection Bd, memb Advsy Ctee on Business and the Environment (ACBE) (chm Fin Sector Working Gp 1993–96), dir Assoc of Br Insurers; tstee Crimestoppers; FCA, CIMgt; *Recreations* sport, theatre; *Style*— Richard Gamble, Esq; ✉ Chart Hall Farm, Green Lane, Chart Sutton, Kent ME17 3ES (☎ 01622 842526); Royal & Sun Alliance Insurance Group plc, 1 Cornhill, London EC3V 3QR (☎ 0171 283 4300, fax 0171 283 4841)

GAMBLE, Thomas (Tom); s of Thomas Gamble (d 1987), of Stockton-on-Tees, and Dorothy, *née* Naylor (d 1986); *b* 6 Feb 1924; *Career* artist; served RN 1942–46; formerly sr lectr Loughborough Coll of Art and Design; Freeman City of London, Liveryman Worshipful Co of Painter-Stainers; memb Artworkers' Guild, fell Royal Watercolour Soc; *Exhibitions* incl: Royal Acad, Royal Watercolour Soc, Bankside Gallery, Royal Festival Hall, The Arts Club, Painters Hall, Paterson's Gallery Albermarle St London, Brian Sinfield, Milne and Moller, American Watercolour Soc, Canadian Watercolour Soc, Exposicion Internacional de Acuarela Barcelona; *Work in Collections* incl: Lloyd's of London, Middlesbrough Art Gallery, Loughborough Univ of Technol, Leics CC, Notts CC; *Style*— Tom Gamble, Esq, RWS; ✉ 10 Blythe Green, East Perry, Huntingdon, Cambs PE18 0BJ (☎ 01480 810468)

GAMBLING, Prof William Alexander; s of late George Alexander Gambling, of Port Talbot, and late Muriel Clara, *née* Bray; *b* 11 Oct 1926; *Educ* Univ of Bristol (BSc, DSc), Univ of Liverpool (PhD); *m* 1, 1952 (m dis 1994), Margaret Pooley; 1 s (Paul b 1956), 2 da (Alison b 1960, Vivien b 1962); m 2, 1994, Colleen O'Neil; *Career* lectr in electric power engrg Univ of Liverpool 1950–55, NRC fell Univ of BC 1955–57; Univ of Southampton: lectr, sr lectr and reader 1957–64, dean of Engrg & Applied Sci 1972–75, prof of electronics 1964–80 (head of dept 1974–79), prof of optical communication 1980–95, dir Optoelectronics Res Centre 1989–95; Royal Soc Kan Tong Po visiting prof and dir Optoelectronics Centre City Univ of HK 1996–; industl conslt and co dir; visiting prof: Univ of Colorado 1966–67, Bhabha Atomic Res Centre India 1970, Univ of Osaka Japan 1977; hon prof: Huazhung Univ of Sci and Technol Wuhan China 1986–, Beijing Inst of Posts and Telecommunications 1987–, Shanghai Univ of Sci and Technol 1990–; hon dir Beijing Optical Fibres Inst 1987–; pres IERE 1977–78 (hon fell 1983); memb: Electronic Res Cncl 1977–80 (memb Optics and Infra-Red Ctee 1965–69 and 1974–80), Bd Cncl of Engrg Instns 1974–79, Nat Electronics Cncl 1977–78 and 1984–95, Technol Sub-Ctee of UGC 1973–83, British Nat Ctee for Radio Sci 1978–87, Engrg Working Gp Nat Advsy Bd for Local Authy HE 1982–84, Engrg Cncl 1983–88, British Nat Ctee for Int Engrg Affrs 1984–88; chm Cmmn D Int Union of Radio Sci 1984–87 (vice chm 1981–84); Selby fell Aust Acad of Sci 1982, foreign memb Polish Acad of Sci 1985; Freeman City of London 1988, Liveryman Worshipful Co of Engrs 1988; Hon Dr Universidad Politéchnica de Madrid 1994, Hon DSc Aston Univ 1995; FIERE 1964, CEng, Hon FIEE 1967, FEng 1979, FRS 1983; *Awards* Bulgin Premium IERE 1961, Rutherford Premium IERE 1964, Electronics Div Premium IEE 1976 and 1978, Oliver Lodge Premium IEE 1981, Heinrich Hertz Premium IERE 1981, J J Thomson Medal IEE 1982, Faraday Medal IEE 1983, Churchill Medal Soc of Engrs 1984 (Simms Medal 1989), Academic Enterprise Award 1982, Int Micro-Optics Award Japan 1989, Dennis Gabor Award Int Soc for Optical Engrg USA 1990, Rank Prize for Opto-Electronics UK 1991, Fndn for C & C Promotion Medal and Prize Japan 1993, Mountbatten Medal NEC 1993; *Publications* various papers on electronics and optical fibre communications; *Recreations* music, reading; *Style*— Prof W A Gambling, FRS, FEng; ✉ Royal Society Kan Tong Po Visiting Professor and Director, Optoelectronics Centre, City University of Hong Kong, Tat Chee Avenue, Kowloon, Hong Kong (☎ 00 852 2788 7828, fax 00 852 2788 7791)

GAMBON, Michael John; CBE (1990); s of Edward Gambon, and Mary Gambon; *b* 19 Oct 1940; *Educ* St Aloysius Sch for Boys London; *m* 1962, Anne Miller; *Career* actor; formerly engrg apprentice; Liveryman Worshipful Co of Gunmakers; *Theatre* incl: first stage appearance Edwards/Mac Liammoir Dublin 1962, Nat Theatre, Old Vic 1963–67, RSC Aldwych 1970–72, Norman Conquests (Globe) 1974, Otherwise Engaged (Queen's) 1976, Just Between Ourselves (Queen's) 1977, Alice's Boys (Savoy) 1978; National Theatre: Galileo 1980 (London Theatre Critics' Best Actor Award), Betrayal 1980, Tales From Hollywood 1980, A Chorus of Disapproval 1985 (Olivier Best Comedy Performance Award), Tons of Money 1986, A View from the Bridge 1987 (Evening Standard Best Actor Award, Olivier Award, Plays and Players London Theatre Critics' Award, Variety Club Best Stage Actor Award), A Small Family Business 1987, Mountain Language 1988, Skylight (Olivier Award nomination for Best Actor 1996) 1995, Volpone (Evening Standard Best Actor Award) 1995; King Lear and Cleopatra (RSC Stratford and Barbican) 1982–83, Old Times (Haymarket) 1985, Uncle Vanya (Vaudeville) 1988, Veterans' Day (Haymarket) 1989, title role in Othello 1990, Taking Steps 1990, Man of the Moment (Globe) 1990; *Television* incl: The Singing Detective 1986 (BAFTA Best Actor Award 1987), Maigret (Granada) 1991, The Entertainer (BBC) 1993, Faith (Central) 1994; *Films* incl: The Cook, The Thief, His Wife and Her Lover (dir Peter Greenaway) 1989, The Heat of the Day 1989, Paris by Night 1989, A Dry White Season 1990, Mobsters 1990, Toys 1991, Clean Slate 1992, Indian Warrior 1993, Browning Version 1993, Two Deaths 1994, Man Of No Importance 1994, Bullet To Beijing 1994, Midnight In Moscow 1994, The Innocent Sleep 1995, Mary Reilly 1996; *Recreations* flying, gun collecting, clock making; *Style*— Michael Gambon, Esq, CBE; ✉ Conway van Gelder Robinson Ltd, 18–21 Jermyn Street, London SW1Y 6HP (☎ 0171 287 0077, fax 0171 287 1940)

GAMES, Prof David Edgar; s of Alfred William Games (d 1956), and Frances Elizabeth Bell, *née* Evans; *b* 7 April 1938; *Educ* Lewis Sch Pengam, King's Coll London (BSc, PhD), Univ of Wales (DSc); *m* 28 Dec 1961, Marguerite Patricia, da of John Lee, of 21 Enville Rd, Newport, Gwent; 2 s (Gwilym John b 1971, Evan William b 1972); *Career* successively lectr in chemistry, sr lectr, reader then personal chair Univ of Wales Coll of Cardiff 1965–89; Univ of Wales Swansea: prof of mass spectrometry and dir of Mass Spectrometry Res Unit 1989–, head of chemistry 1996–; FRSC, CChem; *Recreations* swimming, walking; *Style*— Prof David Games; ✉ Mass Spectrometry Research Unit, Department of Chemistry, University of Wales Swansea, Singleton Park, Swansea SA2 8PP (☎ 01792 295298, 01792 295506, fax 01792 295717)

GAMMAGE, Antony Marshall (Tony); s of Thomas Marshall Gammage (d 1986), of Deal, Kent, and Cicely May, *née* Coates (d 1980); *b* 22 Aug 1934; *Educ* Dover Coll; *m* 25 July 1959, Janet, da of Dr John Colin Dixon Carothers, of Havant, Hants; 3 s (Derek b 1963, Mark b 1965, Thomas b 1967); *Career* dir and sec French Kier Holdings plc 1973–86; conslt Fitzpatrick plc 1986–; dir: Beazer plc 1986, Dunton Group plc 1986–92, Jarvis plc 1987–94; asst dist cmmr Essex Co Scout Assoc; Freeman City of London 1973; FCA 1957, FCMA 1962; *Recreations* sailing, genealogy; *Style*— Tony Gammage, Esq; ✉ Fitzpatrick plc, Hertford Road, Hoddesdon, Herts EN11 9BX (☎ 01992 445757, fax 01992 446882)

GAMMIE, Gordon Edward; CB (1981), QC (1989); eld s of late Dr Alexander Edward Gammie, and Ethel Mary, *née* Miller; *b* 9 Feb 1922; *Educ* St Paul's, The Queen's Coll Oxford (MA); *m* 1949, Joyce, da of late Arthur Arnold Rust; 2 s (David, Peter); *Career* WWII Capt 1 Bn Argyll and Sutherland Highlanders served Western Desert and Italy; under sec Cabinet Office 1975–77, dep slr Treasy 1977–79, legal advsr and slr to MAFF 1979–83, counsel to the Speaker (Euro legislation) 1983–93; ret 1993; *Recreations* music, dog walking; *Clubs* Athenaeum; *Style*— Gordon Gammie, Esq, CB, QC; ✉ 52 Sutton Lane, Banstead, Surrey SM7 3RB (☎ 01737 355287)

GAMMIE, Malcolm James; s of Maj James Ian Gammie, MC (d 1987), of Bickley, Kent, and Florence Mary, *née* Wiggs; *b* 18 Feb 1951; *Educ* Edge Grove Sch Aldenham, Merchant Taylors' Sch Northwood, Sidney Sussex Coll Cambridge (MA); *m* 21 Dec 1974, Rosalind Anne, da of William James Rowe, of Bromley, Kent; 1 s (Christopher James b 18 May 1981), 3 da (Helen Victoria b 10 Feb 1979, Isabel Margaret Ruth b 19 Feb 1985, Catharine Alice Louise b 17 Feb 1988); *Career* Linklaters & Paines: articled clerk 1973–75, slr Tax Dept 1975–78 and 1985–87, ptnr 1987–; dep head of Tax Dept CBI 1978–79; dir: Nat Tax Office Thomson McLintock & Co 1979–84, Nat Tax Servs KMG Thomson McLintock 1984–85; ed Law and Tax Review 1982–88, contrib to Financial Times on tax matters 1983–87; sr visiting fell Centre for Commercial Law Studies Queen Mary and Westfield Coll London; memb: Special Ctee of Tax Law Consultative Bodies, Taxation Ctee IOD, City of London Slrs Co; chm Law Soc's Revenue Law Ctee, vice chm Br Branch Ctee Int Fiscal Assoc; chm Exec Ctee, memb Cncl and chm Capital Taxes Working Pty Inst for Fiscal Studies; Chartered Inst of Taxation: memb Cncl 1983–96, chm Tech Ctee 1990–92 and 1994–95, pres 1993–94; memb Cabinet Office: Taxation Deregulation Gp 1993–, Fiscal Studies Working Pty Advsy Cncl on Sci & Technology 1993; London C of C and Indust: memb 1976–, memb Cncl 1989–92, chm

Taxation Ctee 1989–92; sec and memb Cncl Assoc of Taxation Technicians 1989–91; FRSA 1993; *Books* Taxation Publishing, Tax on Company Reorganisations (with Susan Ball, 1980 and 1982), Tax Strategy for Companies (1981, 1983 and 1986), Stock Relief (with D Williams, 1981), Tax Focus on Interest and Discounts (with D Williams, 1983), Tax Strategy for Directors, Executives and Employees (1983 and 1985), Land Taxation (ed, 1985–), Whiteman on Capital Gains Tax (with P Whiteman, QC, and Mark Herbert, 1988), The Process of Tax Reform in the United Kingdom (Law Soc, 1990); Butterworths Tax Handbooks (conslt ed, 1994–); *Recreations* playing recorder, church architecture, cycling; *Style*— Malcolm Gammie, Esq; ✉ Linklaters & Paines, Barrington House, 59–67 Gresham St, London EC2V 7JA (☎ 0171 606 7080, fax 0171 606 5113, tlx 884349 888167)

GAMMON, Philip Greenway; s of Stanley Arthur John Gammon (d 1979), of Chippenham, Wilts, and Phyllis Joyce, *née* Paul; *b* 17 May 1940; *Educ* Chippenham GS, RAM (scholar), Badische Müsikhochschule Karlsruhe Germany; *m* 1963, Floretta, da of Konstantin Volovinis; 2 s (Paul Christopher b 1968, Anthony John b 1970); *Career* pianist; dep piano teacher RAM and RSAM 1964, pianist Royal Ballet Covent Garden 1964–68; princ pianist: Ballet For All 1968–71, Royal Ballet 1971–; solo pianist and conductor London Contemporary Dance 1979; tours of many countries incl Brazil, USSR, Aust, China, Japan, S Korea, Argentina and Israel; first orchestral arrangement of La Chatte Metamorphosée en Femme by Offenbach (Staatsoper Vienna, Royal Opera House Covent Garden) 1985, arrangement of MacMillan's Winter Dreams by Tchaikovsky 1991; ARCM 1968, ARAM 1991; *Performances* major solo performances with Royal Ballet incl: The Four Temperaments 1973, Elite Syncopations 1974, A Month in the Country 1976, La Fin du Jour 1979, Rhapsody 1980, Return to the Strange Land 1984, Rubies 1989, Winter Dreams 1991, Ballet Imperial 1994, Duo Concertant 1995, Mr Worldly Wise 1996; other performances as solo pianist incl: concert for 50th Anniversary of Royal Ballet (with Royal Liverpool Philharmonic Orchestra, Philharmonic Hall Liverpool) 1981, gala performance celebrating 100 years of Performing Arts (Metropolitan Opera House NY) 1984, meml serv for Sir Frederick Ashton Westminster Abbey 1988, meml serv for Dame Margot Fonteyn 1991 and for Sir Kenneth MacMillan 1993 Westminster Abbey; as conductor incl: Coppelia (Ballet for All, debut, Theatre on the Green Richmond) 1970, Royal Ballet Touring Company 1976, Sleeping Beauty (Royal Ballet, Royal Opera House debut) 1978, Royal Ballet Sch performances (Royal Opera House) 1987, 1989, 1990 and 1992; recent conducting assignments with Royal Ballet incl: Ondine 1989, The Planets 1990, The Prince of the Pagodas 1990; *Awards* Assoc Bd Gold medal Grade 8 1954, Recital Diploma 1960, Walter MacFarren Gold medal 1961, Karlsruhe Culture prize 1962, Performer's Dip Badische Musikhochschule Karlsruhe 1963 *Recordings* incl: Elite Syncopations (Continental Record Distributors), A Month in the Country (EMI Int Classical Div), Winter Dreams (NVC Arts, Teldec Video); presenter Music and Reminiscence (memoirs with Royal Ballet and music); *Recreations* walking, reading, holidaying in Greece; *Style*— Philip Gammon, Esq; ✉ 19 Downs Avenue, Pinner, Middlesex HA5 5AQ (☎ 0181 866 3260)

GAMON, Hugh Wynell; CBE (1979), MC (1944); s of His Hon Judge Hugh Reece Percival Gamon (d 1953), of Acomb, York, and Eleanor Margaret, *née* Lloyd (d 1992, aged 100); *b* 31 March 1921; *Educ* St Edward's Sch Oxford, Exeter Coll Oxford (MA); *m* 17 Dec 1949, June Elizabeth, da of William Temple (d 1986), and Florence, *née* Helmore (d 1989), of Underriver, Sevenoaks, Kent; 1 s (Charles b 1956), 3 da (Mary-Anne b 1952, Sarah b 1954, Jane b 1959); *Career* Maj 1 Div Signals WWII 1940–46, served N Africa, Italy and Palestine; slr and Parly agent (HM Govt agent 1970–93); sr ptnr Sherwood & Co (part of Messrs Winckworth & Pemberton) 1972–95, ret; *Recreations* gardening, walking; *Clubs* St Stephen's Constitutional, Westminster; *Style*— Hugh W Gamon, CBE, MC; ✉ Black Charles, Underriver, Sevenoaks, Kent TN15 0RY (☎ 01732 833036)

GANDER, Dr Derek Reginald; s of Owen Douglas Gander (d 1965), of Farringleys, Shortlands, Kent, and Annie Neil (d 1985); *b* 20 Sept 1928; *Educ* Cathedral Sch Shanghai China, prisoner Japanese camp 1942–45, Worcester GS, Middx Hosp Med Sch Univ of London (MB BS, DPM, Inorganic Chemistry prize, Walter Butcher prize); *m* 1, 1955, Phyllis Marian (d 1974), da of Joseph C Williams; 1 s (Timothy Paul b 7 July 1960), 3 da (Alison Jane b 22 Sept 1957, Sarah Elizabeth b 23 July 1962, Jill Fiona b 2 July 1964); m 2, 1979, Barbara Ann, da of Thomas L Hewitt; 1 da (Kate Eliza b 6 Feb 1981); *Career* Middx Hosp: house physician 1953, house surgn 1954, casualty offr 1955; house surgn Queen Alexandra Hosp for Children Brighton 1955, asst in gen practice London 1956, med registrar Mt Vernon Hosp 1956–59, registrar Bethlehem Royal and Maudsley Hosp 1959–62, chief asst Dept of Psychological Med St Thomas Hosp 1962–66, sr conslt psychiatrist Queen Elizabeth II Hosp 1966–87 (sec then vice chm, then chm Med Staff Ctee and memb E Dist Med Ctee), jtly estab Drug Addiction Clinic 1968, Br Postgrad Med Fedn tutor in psychiatry with jt responsibility for Postgrad Centre Queen Elizabeth II Hosp (lectr to student midwives), lectr N W Thames Royal Health Authy, psychiatric conslt Hertfordshire Marriage Guidance Counselling Serv, currently conslt psychiatrist in private practice; memb UK Register of Expert Witnesses in Medico Legal Work; MRCP 1959 (memb Educn Sub Ctee and clinical tutor), FRCPsych 1977 (MRCPsych 1971, memb RCPsych Visiting Accreditation Teams); *Recreations* travel, swimming, shooting, gardening; *Style*— Dr Derek Gander; ✉ 8 St Peters Close, St Albans, Herts AL1 3ES (☎ 01727 850584, fax 01727 850584); 7 Wimpole Street, London W1M 7AB (☎ 0171 580 1584)

GANDERTON, Prof David; OBE (1995); *b* 28 Aug 1935; *Educ* Northampton GS, Brighton Tech Coll (external BPharm Sch of Pharmacy Univ of London, PhD); *Career* asst lectr Dept of Pharmaceutics Sch of Pharmacy Univ of London 1961–63, sr lectr Sch of Pharmacy Sunderland Poly 1963–66, lectr in pharmaceutical processes Dept of Pharmacy Univ of Strathclyde 1966–70; ICI: joined as section mangr Pharmaceuticals Div, mangr Pharmaceutical Res Dept 1975–77, mangr Dept of Product and Analytical Devpt 1977–85; chm: British Pharmaceutical Conf 1979, Chelsea Dept of Pharmacy KCL 1985, British Pharmacoepia Cmmn 1990; memb: Standing Advsy Ctee for Pharmacy to the Min for Health 1981, Advsy Ctee on NHS Drugs DHSS 1985, Chemistry Pharmacy and Standards Sub-ctee for Ctee on Safety of Meds 1989; ldr UK Delgn to Euro Pharmacoepia Cmmn 1990; hon lectr Dept of Pharmacy Univ of Manchester; FRPharmS 1981; *Style*— Prof David Ganderton, OBE; ✉ Crooked Chimneys, Cheriton Bishop, Devon EX6 6JL (☎ 01647 24318, fax 01647 24010); British Pharmacopoeia Commission, Market Towers, 1 Nine Elms Lane, London SW8 5NQ

GANDHI, Ramesh Govindlal; JP (1991), DL (Lancs 1994); s of Govindlal Jivanlal Gandhi (d 1973), of Ahmedabad, India, and Kamladevi Shah (d 1987); *b* 2 Sept 1935; *Educ* B J Med Coll Gujarat Univ India (MB BS); *m* 1, 1961 (m dis 1975); 1 s (Mayur Ramesh b 7 May 1966); m 2, 16 July 1975, Frances May, da of Francis Mark Fletcher, of Barnsley, S Yorks; 2 s (Neil Ramesh b 28 June 1978, Mark Ramesh b 18 Feb 1980); *Career* registrar in cardio-thoracic surgery: Killingbeck Hosp Leeds 1969–72, Leeds Gen Infirmary 1972–74; sr registrar in cardio-thoracic surgery Univ Hosp of Wales Cariff and Llandough Hosp Penarth 1974–78, conslt cardio-thoracic surgn 1978–94; dir of fundraising Blackpool Victoria Hosp NHS Tst 1994–; memb GMC 1994–; vice pres Overseas Dirs Assoc UK Ltd 1987–93, pres Br Heart Fndn Wyre Ctee 1985–93, vice chm Blackpool Musical Festival, divnl surgn St John Ambulance Brigade Poulton-le-Fylde, memb Blackpool Palatine Rotary Club, govr Baines Sch Poulton 1991; hon fell Int Coll of Angiology USA 1988; memb: Manchester Med Assoc, Soc of Cardio-thoracic Surgns of UK and I, Hosp Specialist Conslt Assoc; FRCSEd 1973, FRCS 1974, fell Overseas Dirs Assoc in the UK Ltd 1988, MICFM 1995; *Recreations* listening to music, swimming, bridge playing; *Style*— Ramesh Gandhi, Esq, JP, DL; ✉ April Cottage, Hardhorn, Poulton-Le-Fylde, Blackpool FY6 8DJ (☎ 01253 899075); Blackpool Victoria Hospital NHS Trust, Furness Drive, Poulton-le-Fylde, Lancashire FY6 8JT (☎ 01253 303142, fax 01253 303106)

GANDON, Christopher Martin; s of late Norman Gandon, of Chiddingstone Hoath, nr Penshurst, Kent, and Sadie, *née* Evans; *b* 13 Nov 1945; *Educ* Penarth Co GS, Leamington Coll for Boys; *m* 6 July 1974, Christine Margaret, da of Harry Wharton; 2 s (Simon William b 10 Dec 1975, Nicholas Robert b 10 Oct 1977), 1 da (Joanna Elizabeth Edith b 19 Oct 1980); *Career* articled clerk Leech Peirson Evans & Co Coventry, chartered accountant Whinney Murray (now Ernst & Young) 1970, Rowland & Co 1971, ptnr Rowland Nevill (after merger with Nevill Hovey Gardiner) 1975– (firm now known as Moores Rowland following merger with Edward Moore & Sons); Freeman City of Coventry 1969; FCA 1979 (ACA 1969), MAE; *Recreations* sailing, rugby football, tennis, gardening, DIY; *Clubs* Wig & Pen, Sevenoaks RFC; *Style*— Christopher Gandon, Esq; ✉ Moores Rowland, 7 St Botolph's Rd, Sevenoaks, Kent TN13 3AJ (☎ 01732 460808)

GANE, Barrie Charles; CMG (1988), OBE (1978); s of Charles Ernest Gane, and Margaret, *née* Price; *b* 19 Sept 1935; *Educ* King Edward's Sch Birmingham, CCC Cambridge (MA); *m* 1, (m dis 1974); 2 da (Christine Anne b 1963, Nicola Vanessa b 1966); m 2, 5 July 1974, Jennifer Anne, da of Lt Cdr George Pitt; *Career* Nat Serv RN 1955–57, Sub Lt RNVR; FO 1960, third sec Vientiane 1961–63, seconded staff HM Govr Sarawak 1963, second sec Kuching 1963–66, FO 1966–67, second sec (commercial) Warsaw 1967, first sec Kampala 1967–70, FCO 1970–77, on loan to HQ Br Forces Hong Kong 1977–82, FCO 1982–93; dir of gp res Group 4 Securitas (International) BV 1993–; *Recreations* reading, walking; *Clubs* Brooks's; *Style*— Barrie Gane, Esq, CMG, OBE; ✉ c/o Group 4 Securitas (International) BV, 7 Carlos Place, Mayfair, London W1Y 5AE

GANELLIN, Prof (Charon) Robin; s of Leon Ganellin (d 1969), and Beila, *née* Cluer (d 1972); *b* 25 Jan 1934; *Educ* Harrow Co GS, QMC London (BSc, PhD), Univ of London (DSc); *m* 27 Dec 1956, Tamara, da of Jacob Greene (d 1988); 1 s (Mark b 1963), 1 da (Nicole b 1960); *Career* res chemist Smith Kline & French Labs Ltd 1958–59, res assoc MIT 1960, vice pres Smith Kline & French Research Ltd 1984–86 (vice pres res 1980–84, dir 1978–86, head of chemistry 1962–78, medicinal chemist 1961–62); Smith Kline & French prof of medicinal chemistry UCL 1986–, dir Upjohn Euro Discovery Unit UCL 1987–93; hon prof Univ of Kent 1979–; chm Soc for Drug Res 1985–87; Prix Charles Mentzer 1978; Royal Soc of Chemistry: Medicinal Chemistry Medal 1977, Tilden Medal 1982; Div of Medicinal Chemistry Award American Chemical Soc 1980, Soc Chemistry Indust Messel Medal 1988, Soc for Drug Res Award for Drug Discovery 1989, USA Nat Inventors Hall of Fame 1990; fell Queen Mary & Westfield Coll London 1992; Hon DSc Aston Univ 1995; FRSC 1968, FRS 1986; *Books* Pharmacology of Histamine Receptors (1982), Frontiers in Histamine Research (1985), Dictionary of Drugs (1990), Medicinal Chemistry (1993); *Recreations* music, sailing, walking; *Style*— Prof Robin Ganellin, FRS; ✉ Department of Chemistry, University College London, 20 Gordon St, London WC1H OAJ (☎ 0171 387 7050)

GANS-LARTEY, Joseph Kojo; s of Charles Botway Lartey (d 1977), of Ghana, and Felicia Adoley, *née* Gans-Boye (d 1995); *b* 28 Aug 1951; *Educ* Presbyterian Secdy Sch X'Borg Accra Ghana, Croydon Coll Surrey (HNC), Ealing Coll of Higher Educn (LLB), LSE (LLM); *m* 28 Oct 1978, Rosmarie, da of Harold Ramrattan (d 1987), of Trinidad and Tobago; 1 da (Josephine Annmarie Laatele b 11 Sept 1985), 1 s (Charles Andrew b 10 April 1990); *Career* sr enrolled psychiatric nurse 1978–82 (trainee 1974–76, enrolled 1976–78), sr legal asst RAC 1985–86, crown prosecutor 1986–, sr crown prosecutor 1989–, princ crown prosecutor 1990–, princ team ldr 1995; voluntary legal advsr Croydon Race Rels Cncl; memb: Hon Soc of Lincoln's Inn 1983, Bar of Trinidad and Tobago 1984; *Recreations* sports, international relations, reading, writing, parenting; *Style*— Joseph Gans-Lartey, Esq; ✉ Crown Prosecution Service, Prospect West, 81 Station Road, Croydon CR6 2RD (☎ 0181 251 5479/5400, fax 0181 251 5454)

GANZONI, Hon (Mary) Jill; DL (Suffolk 1988); only da of 1 Baron Belstead (d 1958); *b* 27 March 1931; *Educ* Crofton Grange Sch, Eastbourne Sch of Domestic Economy, House of Citizenship; *Career* memb Gen Synod of Church of England 1970–95, church cmmr 1978–93; *Recreations* bridge; *Style*— The Hon Jill Ganzoni, DL; ✉ Rivendell, Spring Meadow, Playford, nr Ipswich (☎ 01473 624062)

GAPES, Michael John (Mike); MP (Lab) Ilford South (majority 402); s of Frank Gapes, and Emily Gapes; *b* 4 Sept 1952; *Educ* Buckhurst Hill County HS, Fitzwilliam Coll Cambridge (MA), Middx Poly; *m* 1992, Frances Smith; 1 da, 2 step da; *Career* VSO teacher Swaziland 1971–72, sec Cambridge Students' Union 1973–74, chm Nat Orgn of Lab Students 1976 (vice chm 1975); Lab Pty: nat student organiser 1977–80, res offr International Dept 1980–88, sr international offr 1988–92; Parly candidate (Lab) Ilford N 1983, MP (Lab and Co-op Pty sponsored) Ilford S 1992–, memb Foreign Affairs Select Ctee; vice chair PLP Defence Ctee 1992–94 and 1996–; chair PLP Children and Families Ctee 1993–94; memb: Co-op Pty, TGWU; vice pres Ilford Football Club; *Recreations* watching football, blues and jazz music; *Clubs* West Ham Supporters'; *Style*— Mike Gapes, Esq, MP; ✉ House of Commons, London SW1A 0AA (☎ 0171 219 6485, fax 0171 219 3911); constituency (☎ 0181 514 8261, fax 0181 478 8549)

GARBUTT, Nicholas Martin Antony; s of Anthony Joseph Garbutt, of Manchester, and Norah, *née* Payne; *b* 21 June 1959; *Educ* Xaverian Coll Manchester, Oriel Coll Oxford (BA, Judo half blue); *m* 3 Sept 1988, Frances, da of Francis Burscough, of Preston; *Career* journalist; reporter: Ashton-under-Lyme Reporter 1980–83, Chester Evening Leader 1983–84, Telegraph and Argus Bradford 1984; mgmnt trainee Liverpool Echo 1987–88 (reporter 1984–87), news ed Daily Post Liverpool 1988–89, asst ed Sunday Tribune Dublin 1989–90, ed The Irish News Belfast 1990–94, dep ed Belfast Telegraph 1994–96, dir of business devpt Belfast Telegraph Newspapers 1996–; *Recreations* study of Irish History and Culture, martial arts; *Style*— Nicholas Garbutt, Esq; ✉ Belfast Telegraph, Royal Avenue, Belfast (☎ 01232 264167)

GARDAM, David Hill; QC (1968); s of Harry Hill Gardam (d 1929), and Cecilia Clara, *née* Winkworth (d 1972); *b* 14 Aug 1922; *Educ* Oundle, Univ of Oxford (BA, MA); *m* 20 April 1954, Jane Mary, da of William Pearson (d 1989); 2 s (Timothy David b 1956, Thomas Hugh b 1965), 1 da (Catharine Mary Louise b 1958); *Career* served RNVR 1941–46 (temp Lt 1945); called to the Bar Inner Temple 1949, bencher 1978–; *Recreations* painting, printmaking, gardening; *Clubs* Arts; *Style*— David Gardam, Esq, QC; ✉ 1 Atkin Chambers, Gray's Inn, London WC1R 5BQ (☎ 0171 404 0102, fax 0171 405 7456)

GARDAM, Jane Mary; da of William Pearson (d 1988), of Coatham, N Yorkshire, and Kathleen Mary, *née* Helm (d 1988); *b* 11 July 1928; *Educ* Saltburn HS for Girls, Bedford Coll London; *m* 20 April 1954, David Hill Gardam, QC, s of Harry Hill Gardam; 2 s (Tim b 1956, Thomas b 1965), 1 da (Catharine b 1958); *Career* novelist; travelling librarian Red Cross Hospital Libraries 1951, sub ed Weldon's Ladies Jl 1952, asst literary ed Time and Tide 1952–54; memb Ctee: NSPCC, PEN; FRSL 1973; *Novels* A Long Way from Verona (1971), The Summer After the Funeral (1973), Bilgewater (1977), God on the Rocks (1978), The Hollow Land (1981, Whitbread Award), Bridget and William (1981), Horse (1982), Kit (1983), Crusoe's Daughter (1985), Kit in Boots (1986), Swan (1987), Through The Doll's House Door (1987), Faith Fox (1996); short stories: A Few Fair Days (1971), Black Faces, White Faces (1975, David Highams Award, Winifred Holtby Award), The Sidmouth Letters (1980), The Pangs of Love (1983, Katherine

Mansfield Award 1984), Showing The Flag (1989), The Queen of the Tambourine (1991, Whitbread Award), Going to a Dark House (1994, PEN Silver Pen Award); *Non-Fiction* The Iron Coast (1994); *Recreations* botanical; *Clubs* Arts, PEN, University Women's; *Style*— Jane Gardam, FRSL; ✉ Haven House, Sandwich, Kent (☎ office 01304 612680)

GARDAM, Timothy David; s of David Hill Gardam, QC, of Sandwich, and Jane, *née* Pearson; *b* 14 Jan 1956; *Educ* Westminster, Gonville and Caius Coll Cambridge (BA); *m* Kim Scott, da of Capt Gordon Walwyn, RN, CVO, of Warblington; 1 da; *Career* BBC: trainee 1977, prodr Newsnight 1979–82, exec prodr Timewatch 1982–85, exec prodr Bookmark 1984–85, output ed Newsnight 1985–86, dep ed Gen Election 1987, ed Panorama 1987–90, ed Newsnight 1990–93, head of weekly progs BBC News & Current Affairs 1994–96; controller of news, current affairs and documentaries Channel 5 Broadcasting 1996–; *Recreations* gardening, ruins; *Style*— Timothy Gardam, Esq; ✉ Channel 5 Broadcasting Ltd, 22 Long Acre, London WC2E 9LY (☎ 0171 421 7123)

GARDEN, Dr (David) Graeme; s of Robert Symon Garden (d 1982), of Preston, Lancs, and Janet Anne, *née* McHardy; *b* 18 Feb 1943; *Educ* Repton, Emmanuel Coll Cambridge (BA), King's Coll Hosp (MB BChir); *m* 1, 16 March 1968 (m dis 1981), (Mary) Elizabeth, da of Clive Wheatley Grice (d 1979); 1 s (John b 9 June 1975), 1 da (Sally b 2 April 1971); m 2, 12 Feb 1983, Emma, da of John David Valentine Williams; 1 s (Thomas b 2 Dec 1984); *Career* actor and writer; writer and performer: I'm Sorry I'll Read That Again (radio), I'm Sorry I Haven't A Clue (radio), The Goodies (TV); writer for TV with Bill Oddie: Doctor In The House, Doctor At Large, The Astronauts; presenter Bodymatters BBC TV; theatre: Nat Theatre, Royal Ct, Royal Exchange Manchester, Cambridge Theatre Co; author The Magic Olympical Games Nat Theatre, writer and dir trg films Video Arts; *Books* The Seventh Man (1981), The Skylighters (1987); *Recreations* TV, fishing; *Style*— Dr Graeme Garden; ✉ Roger Hancock Ltd, 4 Water Lane, London NW1 8NZ (☎ 0171 267 4418)

GARDEN, (Olivier) James; s of late James Garden, OBE, of Lanark, and Marguerite Marie Jeanne, *née* Vourc'h; *b* 13 Nov 1953; *Educ* Lanark GS, Univ of Edinburgh (BSc, MB ChB, MD), FRCPSGlas, FRCS(Ed); *m* 15 July 1977, Amanda Gillian, da of Austin Merrills, OBE, of Dunbar, Lothian; 1 s (Stephen James b 21 July 1988), 1 da (Katherine Laura b 13 Aug 1991); *Career* lectr in surgery Univ Dept of Surgery Glasgow Royal Infirmary 1985–88, chef de clinique Unit de Chrurgie Hepatobiliare Hôpital Paul Brousse Villejuif France 1986–87, sr lectr in surgery and hon conslt surgn Univ Dept of Surgery and Scottish Liver Transplant Unit Royal Infirmary Edinburgh 1988–; FRCSGlas 1981; *Recreations* golf, skiing; *Style*— James Garden, Esq; ✉ University Department of Surgery, The Royal Infirmary, Edinburgh EH3 9YW (☎ 0131 536 3813, fax 0131 228 2661)

GARDEN, Air Marshal Sir Timothy; KCB (1994, CB 1992); s of Joseph Garden (d 1979), and Winifred Mary, *née* Mayes (d 1991); *b* 23 April 1944; *Educ* King's Sch Worcester, St Catherine's Coll Oxford (MA), Magdalene Coll Cambridge (MPhil); *m* 13 Nov 1965, Susan Elizabeth, da of Henry George Button, of Cambridge; 2 da (Alexandra Sarah b 1970, Antonia (Mrs Jonathan Rolph) b 1971); *Career* joined RAF 1963, pilot 1967–71, flying instr 1972–75, Army Staff Coll 1976, staff offr MOD 1977–79, OC 50 Sqdn 1979–81, dir Def Studies 1982–85, station cdr RAF Odiham 1985–87, asst dir Def Progs 1987–88, dir Air Force Staff Duties MOD 1988–90, Asst Chief of the Air Staff MOD 1991–92, Asst Chief of the Def Staff (Progs) 1992–94, Cmdt RCDS 1994–95, ret RAF 1996; dir Royal Institute of International Affairs Jan 1997–; hon fell St Catherine's Coll Oxford; memb: Cncl RUSI 1984–87, IISS, RIIA, Cncl for Arms Control, Guild of Air Pilots and Air Navigators, IOD, Air League, Devpt Cncl St Catherine's Coll Oxford, Sr Advsy Bd Univ of Hull Centre for Security Studies, Advsy Bd NATO Def Coll Rome, Advsy Bd Centre for Int Studies Univ of Cambridge, Advsy Bd Assoc of Pathfinders, Cncl Academic Study Gp on Israel and the ME; tstee World Humanity Action Tst; FRAeS, FRUSI; *Books* Can Deterrence Last? (1984), The Technology Trap (1989); *Recreations* writing, bridge, photography, computing, exploring the Internet; *Clubs* RAF, National Liberal; *Style*— Air Marshal Sir Timothy Garden, KCB; ✉ Royal Institute of International Affairs, Chatham House, 10 St James's Square, London SW1Y 4LE (☎ 0171 957 5700, fax 0171 957 5710, e-mail tg@tgarden.demon.co.uk, internet http://www.tgarden.demon.co.uk)

GARDHOUSE, Ian Robert; s of Robert Gardhouse (d 1976), of Newcastle upon Tyne, and Mildred Roper, *née* Dorward (d 1984); *b* 5 Sept 1945; *Educ* Royal GS Newcastle upon Tyne, Univ of Bristol (BA); *m* 24 Aug 1967, Kathleen; 2 da (Lisa b 3 April 1971, Chloë b 7 March 1973); *Career* formerly: actor, milkman, teacher, lectr; BBC Newcastle 1970–76; BBC London 1976–, currently ed Factual Entertainment in Magazine Progs (incl Desert Island Discs, Start The Week, Midweek, Loose Ends, Relative Values, The Treatment and various ad hoc progs and series); *Style*— Ian Gardhouse, Esq; ✉ BBC Broadcasting House, Portland Place, London W1A 1AA (☎ 0171 765 4390, fax 0171 580 4125)

GARDINER, Dr Austen James Sutherland; s of James Martin Gardiner, CBE, of The Firs, Dalmunzie Road, Aberdeen, and Nellie Wallace, *née* Sutherland (d 1979); *b* 27 Jan 1934; *Educ* Aberdeen GS Strathallan, Univ of Aberdeen (MA, ChB, MD); *m* 27 July 1961, Ruth, da of Leslie Duncan, of Costorphine, Edinburgh; 2 s (Nicholas b 1962, Peter b 1966), 1 da (Julia b 1964); *Career* sr registrar internal med Royal Infirmary Aberdeen 1968, res fell Dept of Med McGill Univ of Montreal 1967–69, conslt physician (specializing in respiratory disease) and postgrad tutor Monklands Hosp Lanarkshire 1975–; author of numerous pubns on respiratory physiology and respiratory disease; MRCP 1966, FRCPE 1978, FRCPG 1979; *Recreations* reading, classical music, golf, fishing, shooting; *Clubs* Dunblane, Gleneagles; *Style*— Dr Austen Gardiner; ✉ Farringford, St Margaret's Drive, Dunblane, Perthshire (☎ 01786 822124); Medical Unit, Monklands Hosp, Airdrie, Lanarkshire (☎ 01236 748748)

GARDINER, David Alfred William; DL (Berks 1992); s of Neil William Gardiner (d 1973), of Burghfield Common, Berks, and Norah, *née* Clegg (d 1963); *b* 11 April 1935; *Educ* Winchester, Imperial Coll London, Harvard Business Sch; *m* 1963, Carolyn Georgina, da of Thomas Humphrey Naylor (d 1966), of Ashton, Chester; 2 s (James b 1965, Andrew b 1971), 1 da (Georgina (Mrs Charles Mullins) b 1968); *Career* Lt Grenadier Gds 1953–55; dir Huntley & Palmers Ltd and associated cos 1961–83; farmer and landowner; High Sheriff of Berkshire 1988–89; chm Berks CLA 1989–92, pres Newbury & Royal Co of Berks Show 1993; *Recreations* field sports; *Style*— David Gardiner, Esq, DL; ✉ The Old Rectory, Lilley, Newbury, Berks RG20 7HH (☎ and fax 01488 638227)

GARDINER, Gavin Thomas; s of George Gardiner (d 1965), of Wellington, NZ, and Constance Gardiner (d 1991); *b* 1 Oct 1941; *Educ* Wellington Coll Wellington NZ, Univ of Otago NZ, St Bartholomew's Hosp London; *Career* sr registrar oral surgery: Royal Dental Hosp, St George's Hosp, Royal Surrey Co Hosp Guildford; conslt oral and maxillofacial surgn 1979–: Mt Vernon Hosp, Hillingdon Hosp, Northwick Park Hosp; fell: RSM, Br Assoc of Oral and Maxillofacial Surgns; *Recreations* golf; *Style*— Gavin Gardiner, Esq; ✉ Kelburn House, Mount Park Avenue, Harrow on the Hill HA1 3JW (☎ 0181 423 9474); Department of Oral and Maxillofacial Surgery, Mount Vernon Hospital, Northwood, Middx

GARDINER, Sir George Arthur; kt (1990), MP (C) Reigate (majority 17,664); s of Stanley Gardiner (d 1958), of Maldon, Essex, and Emma Gardiner (d 1987); *b* 3 March 1935; *Educ* Harvey GS Folkestone, Balliol Coll Oxford; *m* 1, 1961 (m dis 1980), Juliet Wells; 2 s, 1 da; m 2, 1980, Helen, *née* Hackett; *Career* dep political corr The Sunday Times 1966–70, chief political corr Thomson Regional Newspapers 1964–74; Parly candidate (C) Coventry S 1970, MP (C) Reigate 1974–; ed Cons News 1972–79, memb Exec 1922 Ctee 1987–93; chm Cons Euro Affrs Ctee 1980–87 (sec 1976–79, vice chm 1979–80), vice chm Cons Foreign and Cwlth Affrs Ctee 1988–, memb Home Affrs Select Ctee and Immigration and Race Rels Sub Ctee 1979–82; *Books* The Changing Life of London (1972), Margaret Thatcher - From Childhood to Leadership (1975); *Recreations* cooking, gardening; *Style*— Sir George Gardiner, MP; ✉ House of Commons, London SW1A 0AA (☎ 0171 219 5177)

GARDINER, Ian David; s of Maj David Gardiner, MC (d 1939), and Dorothea, *née* Caswell (d 1985); *b* 14 April 1928; *Educ* Harlow Coll, Univ of London (BSc); *m* 12 Aug 1950, Dorothy Anderson, da of Frank Arnold Onians (d 1985); 2 s (David b 1954, Andrew b 1969), 2 da (Elizabeth b 1951, Anne b 1958); *Career* TA RE 1972, Col 1984; The English Electric Co 1948–70: mangr Bombay 1957, mangr Calcutta 1959, mangr Victoria Aust 1960–65, commercial mangr Diesel Div 1965–70; BR Engineering Ltd 1970–81: commercial dir 1970–73, engrg dir 1973–76, md 1976–81; dir of engrg BR 1981–85; memb Cncl City Univ 1982–94 (chm Convocation 1978–81), memb Cncl and chm Prodn Ctee CBI 1980–84, memb Bd BSI 1982–84, vice pres IMechE 1984–90; Freeman City of London 1982, Liveryman Worshipful Co of Engrs 1984; FIMechE 1970, FIEE 1971, FRSA 1975, FEng 1982; *Recreations* gardening, swimming, fishing, choral singing; *Style*— Ian Gardiner, Esq, FEng; ✉ Cottesloe, 8 Barrs Ave, New Milton, Hants BH25 5HJ (☎ 01425 638039)

GARDINER, John Eliot; CBE (1990); s of Rolf Gardiner, and Marabel, *née* Hodgkin; *b* 20 April 1943; *Educ* Bryanston, King's Coll Cambridge (MA), King's Coll London; *m* 1981, Elizabeth Suzanne, *née* Wilcock; 3 da; *Career* conductor; studied with Nadia Boulanger in Paris 1967–68; fndr and artistic dir: Monteverdi Choir 1964, Monteverdi Orchestra 1968, English Baroque Soloists 1978, L'Orchestre Révolutionnaire et Romantique 1990; youngest conductor Henry Wood Promenade concert Royal Albert Hall 1968; debut: Sadler's Wells Opera London Coliseum 1969, Royal Festival Hall 1972, Royal Opera House 1973; guest conductor with maj orchestras in: Paris, Brussels, Geneva, Frankfurt, Dresden, Leipzig, London; US/Canadian debuts: Dallas Symphony 1981, San Francisco Symphony 1982, Carnegie Hall NY 1988, Toronto Symphony 1988, Boston Symphony 1991, Cleveland Orch 1992; Euro music festivals incl: Aix-en-Provence, Aldeburgh, Bath, Berlin, Edinburgh, Flanders, Holland, City of London, Salzburg, BBC Proms; revived works of Purcell, Handel, Rameau (world première stage of opera Les Boréades in Aix-en-Provence 1982), and Berlioz (world première The Berlioz Mass Westminster Cathedral 1993); princ conductor CBC Vancouver Orchestra 1980–83; Opéra de Lyon: musical dir 1983–88, chef fondateur 1988–; artistic dir: Göttingen Handel Festival 1981–90, Veneto Music Festival 1986; princ conductor NDR Symphony Orchestra Hamburg 1991–; has made over 100 records; Grand Prix du Disque 1978, 1979 and 1980, Prix Caecilia 1982, 1983 and 1985, 13 Gramophone awards incl Record of the Year 1991; other awards: Edison award 1982, 1986, 1987, 1988 and 1989, Arturo Toscanini Music Critics award 1985 and 1986, IRCA prize Helsinki 1987, Deutscher Schallplatten preis 1986 and 1994, Nat Acad of Recording Arts and Sciences nominations 1986, 1987 and 1989; Hon DUniv Lumière de Lyon 1987; Officier dans l'Ordre des Arts et des Lettres 1988; fell King's Coll London 1992, FRSA 1992; *Recreations* forestry, organic farming; *Style*— John Eliot Gardiner, Esq, CBE; ✉ IMG Artists Europe, Media House, 3 Burlington Lane, London W4 2TH (☎ 0181 747 9977, fax 0181 747 9131)

GARDINER, Prof John Graham; s of William Clement Gardiner, of Ilkley, and Ellen, *née* Adey (d 1976); *b* 24 May 1939; *Educ* King Edward VI GS Birmingham, Univ of Birmingham (BSc, PhD); *m* 29 Dec 1962, Sheila Joyce, da of Cecil Walter Andrews (d 1958); 2 da (Tabitha Jane b 19 July 1966, Emily Josephine 12 Dec 1972), 1 s (Benjamin John b 21 Oct 1967); *Career* pre-univ apprenticeship GEC Coventry 1957–58, Racal post doctoral res fell Univ of Birmingham 1964–66, software engr Racal Research Ltd Tewkesbury 1966–68, sr engr Racal (Slough) Ltd 1968; Univ of Bradford: lectr 1968–72, sr lectr 1972–78, reader in electronic engrg 1978–86, chm Postgrad Sch of Info Systems Engrg 1984–88, prof of electronic engrg 1986–, head Dept of Electronic and Electrical Engrg 1993–96, dean of engrg and physical scis 1996–; dir: Aerial Facilities Ltd 1974–90, Aerial Group Ltd 1990–, Nortel (Communications) Ltd 1976–96; conslt: Telecommunications Div DTI 1987–, EC DG XIII 1988–91 and 1994; nat coordinator Link Personal Communications Programme 1987–93, chm Professional Gp E8 IEE 1990–93; CEng 1971, MIERE 1971, FIEE 1984 (MIEE 1971), FEng 1994; *Books* Mobile Communication Systems (with J D Parsons, 1989), Personal Communication Systems (with B West, 1995); *Recreations* music - occasionally performing, but mostly, these days, listening; *Style*— Prof John Gardiner, FEng; ✉ 1 Queen's Drive Lane, Ilkley, West Yorkshire LS29 9QS (☎ 01943 609581); Department of Electronic & Electrical Engineering, University of Bradford, Richmond Road, Bradford BD7 1DP (☎ 01274 384003, fax 01274 384054, mobile 0468 248243)

GARDINER, Prof John Macdonald; s of Kenneth Macdonald Gardiner (d 1977), and Alice Marjorie, *née* Taylor (d 1975); *b* 15 Sept 1941; *Educ* Wycliffe Coll, Bognor Regis Coll of Educn, Univ of London (BSc, PhD); *Career* primary sch teacher 1964–69; City Univ London: lectr 1972, sr lectr 1978, reader 1981, prof of psychology 1986–; consulting ed Br Jl of Psychology 1981–83; consulting ed Jl of Experimental Psychology: Learning, Memory, and Cognition 1985–, Memory 1993–, Psychonomic Bulletin and Review 1994–; consulting ed European Journal of Cognitive Psychology 1995–; memb: American Psychological Soc, Experimental Psychology Soc, Euro Soc for Cognitive Psychology, Psychonomic Soc; FBPsS; *Recreations* jaunts, walks, the occasional lunch; *Style*— Prof John Gardiner; ✉ Memory & Cognition Research Group, Psychology Dept, City University, Northampton Square, London EC1V 0HB

GARDINER, Dr Julie Patricia; da of Norman Arthur Gardiner, of Knaresborough, Yorks, and Jean Margaret, *née* Driver; *b* 9 March 1958; *Educ* High Wycombe HS for Girls, Univ of Reading (BA, PhD); *m* 1981 (m dis 1994), John Arthur Davies; *Career* freelance archaeologist (projects incl E Hants field survey, Cranborne Chase project, Hengistbury Head) 1983–84, asst then managing ed E Anglian Archaeology Norfolk Archaeological Unit 1984–89, managing ed Cncl for British Archaeology 1989–91, reports mangr Wessex Archaeology 1991–; author and ed of numerous articles and monographs incl definitive account of excavations of Stonehenge (1995); dir Prehistoric Society Ltd 1991–; Prehistoric Soc: memb Cncl, ed PAST newsletter 1991–94, ed Proceedings 1994– (asst ed 1993); memb Inst of Field Archaeologists 1986 (ed Occasional Papers series 1991–93); FSA, MIFA; *Recreations* gardening, art, cinema, walking; *Style*— Dr Julie Gardiner, FSA; ✉ Trust for Wessex Archaeology Ltd, Portway House, Old Sarum Park, Salisbury, Wilts SP4 6EB (☎ 01722 326867, fax 01722 337562)

GARDINER, Patrick Lancaster; s of Clive Gardiner (d 1960), and Lilian, *née* Lancaster (d 1973); *b* 17 March 1922; *Educ* Westminster, Christ Church Oxford (MA); *m* 7 July 1955, (Kathleen) Susan, da of Herbert Booth (d 1984); 2 da (Josephine b 1956, Vanessa b 1960); *Career* Army 1942–45: Lt 1943, Capt 1945, serv N Africa and Italy; visiting prof Columbia Univ NY 1955; Univ of Oxford: lectr in philosophy Wadham Coll 1949–52, fell in philosophy St Antony's Coll 1952–58, fell and tutor in philosophy Magdalen Coll 1958–89 (emeritus fell 1989–); FBA 1985; *Books* The Nature of Historical Explanation (1952), Schopenhauer (1963), Kierkegaard (1988); ed: Theories of History (1959), Nineteenth-Century Philosophy (1969), The Philosophy of History (1974); *Style*— Patrick Gardiner, Esq; ✉ The Dower House, Wytham, Oxford (☎ 01865 242205); Magdalen College, Oxford (☎ 01865 276000)

GARDINER, (John) Ronald; s of John Ritchie Gardiner, OBE, GM (d 1990), of Millstonford, West Kilbride, Ayrshire, and Mary Winifred, *née* Breckenridge (d 1994); *b* 25 Oct 1938; *Educ* St Mary's Sch Melrose, Fettes, Univ of Edinburgh (BL); *m* 4 Dec 1965, Aileen Mary, da of late William Montgomery; 2 s (Alastair Montgomery b 21 Oct 1966 d 5 Oct 1991, Douglas Ritchie b 1 Feb 1972), 1 da (Fiona Mary b 24 Jan 1969); *Career* slr; Nat Serv 2 Lt Cameronians (Scottish Rifles) 1957–59; apprentice slr John C Brodie Cuthbertson & Watson WS 1960–63, admitted slr 1963; Brodies WS (formerly Brodie Cuthbertson & Watson WS): asst slr 1963, ptnr 1964–, sr ptnr 1992–; memb: Revenue Ctee Law Soc of Scotland 1966–78, Rent Assessment Panel for Scotland 1973–, Cncl WS Soc 1978–81; govr The Fettes Tst 1986–96; hon sec: Standing Cncl of Scottish Chiefs 1970–72, Salmon & Trout Assoc (Scottish Branch) 1971–84; WS 1964, NP 1966; *Recreations* fishing, shooting, golf, gardening; *Clubs* New (Edinburgh), Hon Co of Edinburgh Golfers (Muirfield); *Style*— Ronald Gardiner, Esq, WS; ✉ 55 Fountainhall Road, Edinburgh EH9 2LH; Brodies WS, 15 Atholl Crescent, Edinburgh EH3 8HA (☎ 0131 228 3777, fax 0131 228 3878)

GARDINER, Terence; s of William Gardiner (d 1990), and Winifred Audrey Elizabeth, *née* Iles (d 1984); *b* 5 March 1937; *Educ* Gillingham GS, RNC Dartmouth/Greenwich, Harvard Business Sch; *m* 18 Dec 1957, Shirley Anne, da of Walter Windsor (d 1962); 2 da (Nicola Anne (Mrs Kenneth Russell) b 24 Dec 1964, Alison Claire (Mrs Mark Merrington) b 18 Jan 1967); *Career* Naval Offr 1955–61; Rowntree & Co (now Rowntree Mackintosh and Nestlé): with UK Sales Dept 1961–63, export sales exec 1963–69, memb Bd Export Div (sales dir, mktg dir then dep chm) 1969–81, memb Bd Rowntree Mackintosh Ltd (sales dir and dep md) 1981–91, memb Mgmnt Ctee Nestle-Rowntree 1992–93, ret 1995; fndr H G Consultants York 1995–; memb Co of Merchant Adventurers of York; *Style*— Terence Gardiner, Esq; ✉ H G Consultants, York YO3 3JG (☎ and fax 01904 760725)

GARDINER, William Griffiths; s of James Gardiner (d 1962), of Glasgow, and Muriel, *née* Griffiths; *b* 8 March 1938; *Educ* Glasgow HS; *m* 7 July 1967, Una, da of David Anderson (d 1945); 2 s (David b 1969, Ian b 1971); *Career* CA 1960, co sec Stenhouse Holdings plc 1970–84, head fin investmt small business div Scottish Devpt Agency 1984–87, fin dir Glasgow Investmt Mangrs Ltd 1987–; *Recreations* golf, curling, music; *Clubs* Glasgow HS (pres 1990–91), Glasgow Golf; *Style*— William Gardiner, Esq; ✉ 5 Ardoch Rd, Bearsden, Glasgow G61 2BB (☎ 0141 942 7338); Glasgow Investment Managers Ltd, 29 St Vincent Place, Glasgow G1 2DR (☎ 0141 226 4585, fax 0141 226 3632)

GARDINER-HILL, Peter Farquhar; s of Dr Harold Gardiner-Hill (d 1982), and Margaret Helen, *née* Buzzard (d 1984); *b* 22 Oct 1926; *Educ* Eton, ChCh Oxford; *m* 1955, Susan Mary, da of John Harold Strachan; 2 s (David b 1958, Edward b 1974), 2 da (Jane (Mrs Holmes-Smith) b 1955, Alice (Mrs Yeates) b 1960); *Career* Lt Scots Gds 1945–48; British Celanese/Courtaulds 1951–58, EMI Ltd 1958–64, Roland Berger Technics Ltd 1964–81, co-fndr and chm GHN Ltd career mgmnt consultancy 1981–, dir Penna plc 1994–; memb Cncl Industry Churches Forum; FRSA; *Clubs* Utd Oxford and Cambridge Univ, Royal & Ancient Golf (capt 1982–83), Rye Golf, Trevose Golf, Oxfordshire Golf, Pine Valley Golf (Philadelphia); *Style*— Peter Gardiner-Hill, Esq; ✉ Flat 6, 14 Onslow Square, London SW7 3NP (☎ 0171 584 2752); Uprising, Rye Hill, Rye, E Sussex TN31 7NH (☎ 01797 222306); GHN Ltd, 16 Hanover Square, London W1R 9AJ (☎ 0171 493 5239, fax 0171 629 9245)

GARDNER, *see:* Bruce-Gardner

GARDNER, Brenda Ann Ellen; da of Michael Sweedish, of Canada, and Flora, *née* Gibb; *b* 1 June 1947; *Educ* Univ of Saskatchewan (BA), Washington Univ; *m* 1968, (James) Douglas Gardner (d 1986), s of James Gardner (d 1966); *Career* teacher USA and UK 1968–72, asst ed Penguin Books 1972–77; ed: W H Allen 1977–79, E J Arnold 1979–81, Evans 1981–83; md and chair Piccadilly Press 1983–; chair Children's Book Circle 1981–82; *Recreations* reading, aerobics, swimming, tennis, theatre, films; *Clubs* Groucho; *Style*— Ms Brenda Gardner; ✉ Piccadilly Press, 5 Castle Road, London NW1 8PR (☎ 0171 267 4492, fax 0171 267 4493, telex 295441)

GARDNER, Brian Patrick; s of T C Gardner, CBE, of Hill Court, Station Rd, Whittlesford, Cambs, and B T Gardner; *b* 17 July 1948; *Educ* St George's Coll Harare Zimbabwe, Beaumont Coll Old Windsor, Univ of Oxford (MA, BM BCh); *m* 18 Oct 1980, Stephanie Catherine Mary, da of Dr Faller (d 1980); 4 s (Paul b 1983, Martin b 1988, Benedict b 1994, Liam b 1996), 4 da (Catherine b 1982, Laura b 1984, Annabelle b 1989, Edel b 1991); *Career* various jr med posts 1974–79, registrar in neurosurgery Royal Victoria Hosp Belfast 1980–82, sr registrar in spinal injuries Mersey Regnl Spinal Cord Injuries Centre Southport 1982–85, conslt surgn in spinal injuries Nat Spinal Injuries Centre 1985–; memb BMA; MRCP 1978, FRCS 1980, elected FRCP (London) 1995, FRCPEd 1996; *Recreations* tennis, family, walking; *Style*— Brian Gardner, Esq; ✉ 2 Northumberland Ave, Aylesbury, Bucks HP21 7HG (☎ 01296 23420, fax 01296 24627); National Spinal Injuries Centre, Stoke Mandeville Hospital, Aylesbury, Bucks HP21 8AL

GARDNER, Brigid Catherine; da of John Henthorn Cantrell Brennan, of Shalbourne, Wilts, and Rosamond Harriet, *née* Gardner; *b* 5 May 1941; *Educ* The Alice Ottley Sch Worcester, Girton Coll Cambridge (MA, lacrosse half blue); *m* July 1963 (m dis 1980), Michael Henry Davies; 3 da (Rosamund Frances b 1967, Eleanor Mary b 1970, Hilary Julia b 1972); *Career* asst English and History teacher Harrogate HS 1963–66, English language teacher Hong Kong 1967–69, pt/t A level coaching 1969–76; James Allen's Girls Sch: head of history 1976–83, dep head 1981–83, headmistress 1984–94; princ St George's Sch Rome 1994–; govr: Oundle Sch, Whitgift Fndn, Oxford and Cambridge Examinations Board; ran London Marathon 1986; *Recreations* gardening, house restoration, reading, sailing; *Style*— Mrs Brigid Gardner; ✉ via Euclide Turba 18, Roma 00195, Italy (☎ and fax 00 39 6 3701964)

GARDNER, Christopher James Ellis; QC (1994); s of James Charles Gardner (d 1984), of Dartmouth, and Phillis May, *née* Wilkinson; *b* 6 April 1945; *Educ* Rossall Sch Lancs, Fitzwilliam Coll Cambridge (MA); *m* 1972, Arlene Sellers; 1 s (Simon James b 19 Feb 1973), 1 da (Sophie Ruth b 16 Aug 1978); *Career* called to the Bar Gray's Inn (Lord Justice Holker sr exhibitioner) 1968, legal assessor to GMC and GDC, recorder of the Crown Court 1993–; specialist in personal injury and professional negligence litigation; memb Common Law, Professional Negligence and Inter-Pacific Bar Assocs; *Recreations* open air theatre, bell ringing, golf, cooking curries; *Style*— Christopher Gardner, Esq, QC; ✉ Lamb Chambers, Lamb Building, Temple, London EC4Y 7AS (☎ 0171 797 8300, fax 0171 797 8308)

GARDNER, Prof David; OBE (1995); s of Fred Gardner (d 1990), of Kirkham, nr Preston, and Mary, *née* Anderson (d 1978); *b* 11 July 1941; *Educ* St Joseph's Coll Blackpool, Loughborough Univ of Technol (BTech, DLC, cricket colours); *m* April 1964, Hazel, da of late Harold Bailey; 1 s (Anthony Paul b 6 Sept 1974), 1 da (Sarah Louise b 7 april 1977); *Career* English Electric (became BAC, British Aerospace plc since 1986): joined as apprentice 1959, asst engr rising to engr Aerodynamics Dept 1965 (res into wing design of Jaguar aircraft), sr engr 1968 (leading work into afterbody/engine installation aspects of MRCA), princ devpt engr 1974 (leading Aerodynamic Team on Tornado and for devpt of air defence variant), asst chief aerodynamicist then chief flight test project engr Tornado ADV 1979, project mangr Tornado 1981, exec dir Tornado 1983, exec dir aircraft projects 1984, tech dir (Warton) Mil Aircraft Div 1986; Mil Aircraft Div British Aerospace Defence Ltd: tech dir 1992–94, dep md and dir Euro Progs 1994–; systems engrg dir Panavia GmbH Munich 1986–94, bd dir Eurofighter Jagdflugzeug GmbH, Panavia Aircraft GmbH and SEPECAT (managing Eurofighter, Tornado and Jaguar collaborative projects); author of numerous papers on tech subjects and on int collaborations; industl prof Dept of Tport Technol Loughborough Univ of Technol 1991–, memb Weapon System Bd Def Scientific Advsy Cncl 1992–, pres Preston Branch RAeS; FRAeS, FEng 1992, FRSA 1995; *Recreations* golf, gardening, theatre; *Clubs* Warton Cricket (pres); *Style*— Prof David Gardner, OBE, FEng; ✉ British Aerospace Defence Ltd, Military Aircraft Division, Warton Aerodrome, Lytham Road, Warton, Preston PR4 1AX (☎ 01772 852760, fax 01772 679370)

GARDNER, Dr David Alan; s of John Lawrence Gardner, of Hadley Wood, Herts, and Alice Winifred, *née* Cattermole; *b* 29 April 1938; *Educ* Minchenden Sch Southgate, Univ of Leeds; *m* 17 Sept 1966, Gillian Ann, da of Capt Edmund Patrick Flowers, of Bangor, N Wales; 3 s (Leon b 1977, Oliver b 1980, Joshua b 1985), 4 da (Philippa b 1967, Amanda b 1969, Samantha b 1971, Jemima b 1974); *Career* registrar Guy's Hosp London 1968–70, conslt pathologist Kensington Chelsea and Westminster Hosp 1973–74, conslt pathologist UCH 1974– (sr registrar 1971–73, sr lectr 1974–); chm: S Camden Pathology Ctee, NE Thames Regnl Biochemistry Ctee; memb NE Thames Regnl Scientific Ctee; FRCPath 1984 (MRCPath 1971), MRCS, LRCP; *Recreations* British campaign medals, Baptist Historical Soc; *Style*— Dr David Gardner; ✉ 18 Jennings Road, St Albans, Herts AL1 4NT (☎ 01727 862019); Department of Chemical Pathology, Windeyer Building, Cleveland St, London W1P 6DB (☎ 0171 636 8333, fax 0171 380 9496)

GARDNER, Cdr Derek George Montague; VRD; s of Alfred Charles Gardner, FRSE (d 1952), and Florence Mary, *née* Johnson (d 1955); *b* 13 Feb 1914; *Educ* Oundle; *m* 14 July 1951, Mary, da of Joseph Harry Dalton; 1 s (Charles Henry Penn b 11 May 1954), 1 da (Angela Mary b 2 June 1952); *Career* Midshipman RNVR (Clyde Div) 1934, mobilised HMS Proserpine 1939, HM (trawler) Ocean Fisher 1939–41, HMS Osprey 1941, HMS Broke (despatches 1942), HMS Highlander 1942–43, Lt Cdr Staff of C-in-C Western Approaches HMS Eaglet 1943–45, Cdr Asst CSO to Flag Offr Ceylon HMS Lanka 1945–46, Cdr RNVR 1946, ret 1947; chartered civil engr Miny of Works Kenya HMOCS 1947–63, regnl engr Kenya 1953–63, ret HMOCS 1963; elected memb RSMA 1966 (hon life vice pres); works in: Nat Maritime Museums Greenwich and Bermuda, RNC Dartmouth; one man shows Polak Gallery London: 1972, 1975, 1979, 1982, 1987, 1990 and 1995; lay vice patron of the Missions to Seamen 1983; RSMA, CEng, FICE; *Clubs* Naval; *Style*— Cdr Derek Gardner, VRD; ✉ High Thatch, Corfe Mullen, Wimborne, Dorset BH21 3HJ (☎ 01202 693211)

GARDNER, Douglas Frank; s of Lt Ernest Frank Gardner (decd), and Mary, *née* Chattington (decd); *b* 20 Dec 1943; *Educ* Woolverstone Hall, Coll of Estate Mgmnt, Univ of London (BSc); *m* 5 Sept 1978, Adèle, da of Maj Charles Macmillan Alexander, 1 s (Mark b 1972), 2 da (Teresa b 1971, Amy b 1979); *Career* chief exec Properties Div Tarmac plc 1976–83, chm Brixton Estate plc 1993– (md 1983–93); chm: Brixton Investments Ltd, Brixton France SA; *Recreations* tennis; *Style*— Douglas Gardner, Esq; ✉ Brixton Estate plc, 22/24 Ely Place, London EC1 (☎ 0171 400 4400, fax 0171 405 1630)

GARDNER, Sir Edward Lucas; kt (1982), QC (1960); s of late Edward Walker Gardner, of Fulwood, Preston, Lancs; *b* 10 May 1912; *Educ* Hutton GS; *m* 1, 1950 (m dis 1962), Noreen Margaret, da of late John Collins, of Moseley, Birmingham; 1 s, 1 da; *m* 2, 1963, Joan Elizabeth, da of late B B Belcher, of Bedford; 1 s, 1 da; *Career* served WWII Cdr RNVR; former journalist; called to the Bar Gray's Inn 1947; dep chm QS: E Kent 1961–71, Kent 1962–71, Essex 1968–71; bencher Gray's Inn 1968, recorder Crown Ct 1972–85; Soc of Cons Lawyers: chm 1975–85, vice-pres 1985–, chm Exec Ctee 1969–75; contested (C) Erith & Crayford 1955; MP (C): Billericay 1959–66, South Fylde 1970–87; PPS to Attorney-Gen 1962–63, cmmr Cwlth War Graves Cmmn 1971–87, chm House of Commons Home Affrs Select Ctee 1984–87; govr Thomas Coram Fndn for Children 1962–96, steward British Boxing Bd of Control 1975–84; *Clubs* Pratt's, Garrick; *Style*— Sir Edward Gardner, QC; ✉ Sparrows, Hatfield Broad Oak, Bishop's Stortford, Herts CM22 7HN (☎ 01279 718265)

GARDNER, James Jesse; CVO (1995), CBE (1986), DL; s of James Gardner (d 1987), and Elizabeth Rubina Gardner (d 1993); *b* 7 April 1932; *Educ* Kirkham GS, Univ of Manchester (LLB); *m* 14 Nov 1955, Diana, da of Arthur William Sotheran; 3 s (James Howard b 1957, Jeremy Peter b 1959, Christopher John b 1964), 1 da (Emma Jane b 1968); *Career* town clerk Stockton-on-Tees BC 1966–68, assoc town clerk and slr London Borough of Greenwich 1968–69, town clerk and chief exec Co Borough of Sunderland 1970–73, chief exec Tyne & Wear CC 1973–86, chief exec Northern Development Co Ltd 1986–87, sec Northern Regnl Cncls Assoc 1987; chm: Tyne & Wear PTE 1983–86, The Prince's Tst 1986–94 (formerly chm Northumbria Ctee), Prince's Tst Events Ltd 1987–93, Park Estates 1987–90, Sunderland DHA 1988–90, Mgmnt Bd The Princes & Royal Jubilee Trusts 1986–93, Northumbria OFWAT Customer Servs Ctee 1990–, North East Television Ltd 1991–92, Threshold Ltd (formerly Prince's Trust Trg and Employment) 1992–95, OFWAT Nat Customer Cncl 1993–, St Benedict's Hospice 1993–, Century Radio Ltd (formerly Radio North East Ltd) 1993–; tstee: Tyne Tees TV Tst 1988–91, NE Civic Tst (also dir 1986–92); hon fell Sunderland Univ 1986; FRSA 1976, CIMgt 1987; *Recreations* golf, music, theatre, food and drink; *Style*— James Gardner, Esq, CVO, CBE, DL; ✉ Wayside, 121 Queen Alexandra Road, Sunderland, Tyne & Wear SR2 9HR (☎ 0191 528 2525)

GARDNER, John Linton; CBE (1976); s of Capt Alfred Linton Gardner, RAMC (ka 1918), of Ilfracombe, and Muriel, *née* Pullein-Thompson; *b* 2 March 1917; *Educ* Wellington, Exeter Coll Oxford; *m* 1955, Jane Margaret Mary, da of late Nigel James Abercrombie, of Ringmer, Lewes, E Sussex; 1 s, 2 da; *Career* composer; chief music master Repton 1939–40, on music staff Royal Opera House 1946–52, prof of harmony and composition RAM 1956–86; dir of music: St Paul's Girls' Sch 1962–75, Morley Coll 1965–69; dep chm Performing Rights Soc 1983–88; *Compositions incl* the opera The Moon and Sixpence, three symphonies, three string quartets, concertos for piano, oboe, trumpet, flute and organ, many large-scale choral works; *Recreations* tesseraphily; *Style*— John Gardner, Esq, CBE; ✉ 20 Firswood Avenue, Ewell, Epsom, Surrey KT19 0PR

GARDNER, Prof Julian; *b* 6 May 1940; *Educ* Balliol Coll Oxford (BA), Courtauld Inst of Art (Dip in History of Art, PhD 1969), British Sch at Rome (Rivoira Scholar); *Career* lectr Courtauld Inst of Art 1966–74; Univ of Warwick: fndn prof in the history of art 1974–, pro-vice-chllr 1987–91 and 1995–, sometime memb numerous ctees and policy gps; visiting research prof Max-Planck-Gesellschaft Bibliotheca Hertziana Rome 1983–85 and 1992, Kuratorium Kunsthistorisches Institut Florence 1993; British Library: chm Standing Ctee on Art Documentation, memb Advsy Bd Humanities and Social Scis; Assoc of Art Historians: exec memb, chm Libraries Sub-Ctee, chm Universities Sub-Ctee; membre titulaire Comité Internationale d'Histoire del'Art; memb Editorial Bd: Burlington Magazine, Arte Cristiana, Italian Mediaeval & Renaissance Studies; FSA 1977; *Books* The Tomb and the Tiara. Curial tomb sculpture in Italy & Avignon 1200–1400 (1992), Patrons, Painters and Saints (1993); *Style*— Prof Julian Gardner, FSA; ✉ History of Art Department, University of Warwick, Coventry, Warwickshire CV4 7AL (☎ 01203 523459, fax 01203 523006)

GARDNER, Capt Nicolas Charles Eric; s of Maj Laurie Gardner (d 1969), and Erica Sylva Margareta Herta, *née* Steinmann (d 1976); *b* 23 July 1946; *Educ* Eton, Keble Coll Oxford (MA); *m* 3 Oct 1974, Roseanne Serena, da of Charles Douglas Neville Walker, MM, of Verteillac, France; *Career* cmmnd Irish Gds 1966, Capt 1971, ADC to C-in-C

UKLF 1972–74, ret 1974; Queen's Messenger 1987–; Liveryman Worshipful Co of Drapers 1983; *Recreations* shooting, gardening; *Style*— Capt Nicolas Gardner; ✉ Breamore Cottage, Breamore, Fordingbridge, Hampshire SP6 2DB (☎ 01725 512265); Foreign & Commonwealth Office, King Charles St, London SW1

GARDNER, Prof Richard Lavenham; s of Allan Constant Gardner (d 1943), of Beare Green, Surrey, and Eileen May Alexander, *née* Clarke (d 1961); *b* 10 June 1943; *Educ* St John's Leatherhead, St Catharine's Coll Cambridge (BSc); *m* 14 Dec 1968, Wendy Joy, da of Charles Hampton Trevelyan Cresswell (d 1989), of Cobham, Surrey; 1 s (Matthew Thomas b 18 April 1985); *Career* res asst Physiological Laboratory Univ of Cambridge 1969–73, lectr Dept of Zoology Univ of Oxford 1973–77, student ChCh Oxford 1974–, Henry Dale res prof Royal Soc 1978–, hon dir Developmental Biology Unit Imperial Cancer Res Fund 1985–96; memb Academia Europaea 1989, ind memb Advsy Bd for the Res Cncl 1990–93; FRS 1979; *Recreations* sailing, painting, ornithology, gardening; *Style*— Prof Richard Gardner, FRS; ✉ Department of Zoology, South Parks Rd, Oxford OX1 3PS (☎ 01865 281312, fax 01865 281310)

GARDNER, Trevelyan Codrington; CBE (1960); s of Lt Cdr Thomas Gardner, DSC, RN (d 1928); *b* 3 Aug 1917; *Educ* Taunton's Sch, Queen's Coll Oxford (MA); *m* 1944, Briege Theresa, da of Patrick Feehan, of Castle Carra, Dundalk; 2 s, 3 da; *Career* Maj Royal Hampshire Regt 1939–45, served Italy; Colonial Serv 1946–64, sec for fin N Rhodesia 1958–60, min of fin N Rhodesia 1960–64; treas Univ of Cambridge until 1983 (emeritus 1983–); administrator: American Friends of Cambridge Univ 1983–87, Friends of the Oxford and Cambridge Boat Race 1988–95; md Cambridge Capital Services Ltd 1991–, dir United World Colleges (International) Ltd; emeritus fell Wolfson Coll Cambridge; hon fell: Robinson Coll Cambridge, Darwin Coll Cambridge; *Recreations* golf, gardening; *Clubs* Army and Navy, Gog Magog Golf; *Style*— Trevelyan Gardner, Esq, CBE; ✉ Hill Court, Station Rd, Whittlesford, Cambridge (☎ 01223 832483); Cambridge Capital Services Ltd, 13 Station Road, Cambridge CB1 2JB (fax 01223 65704)

GARDNER, Dr William Norman; s of Norman Charles Gardner (d 1979), of Sydney, NSW, Australia, and Ngaire Jean, *née* Dawson (d 1995); *b* 24 Jan 1943; *Educ* Penrith HS NSW Australia, Sydney Univ (MB, BS), Univ of Oxford (DPhil); *m* 1, 1971 (m dis 1974), Lydia, *née* Sinclair; m 2, 1981, Jane Elizabeth, da of Alan Maurice Stainer (d 1990), of 2 St Mary's Close, Kidlington, Oxon; 3 s (Timothy b 1981, Nicholas b 1985, Joseph b 1988); *Career* med house appts Sydney and Royal Adelaide Hosps 1966–68, sr house appt Brompton, London Chest and Westminster Hosps 1969–71, Wellcome grad student then MRC res offr Dept of Physiology and then Nuffield Inst Oxford 1971–80, memb Wolfson Coll Oxford until 1983, sr lectr and hon conslt physician King's Coll Sch of Med 1987– (lectr in med Dept of Thoracic Med 1981–87); Euro Respiratory Soc: chm Control of Breathing Gp 1993–95, head Clinical Physiology Assembly 1995–; memb Br Thoracic Soc 1981; author of various articles on respiratory and foetal physiology, respiratory med and hyperventilation syndromes; FRCP 1991 (MRCP 1971); *Recreations* windsurfing, jazz piano; *Style*— Dr William Gardner; ✉ Dept of Thoracic Medicine, King's Coll Sch of Med and Dentistry, Bessemer Rd, London SE5 9PJ (☎ 0171 346 3165, fax 0171 346 3589)

GARDNER OF PARKES, Baroness (Life Peer UK 1981), of Southgate, Greater London, and of Parkes in the State of New South Wales and Commonwealth of Australia; (Rachel) Trixie Anne Gardner; JP (N Westminster Inner London 1971); da of Hon (John Joseph) Gregory McGirr (d 1949; MLA, NSW State Govt), and late Rachel, *née* Miller; *b* 17 July 1927; *Educ* Monte Sant Angelo Coll N Sydney, Sydney Univ (BDS); *m* 1956, Kevin Anthony Gardner (Lord Mayor of Westminster 1987–88), s of late George Gardner, of Sydney, Australia; 3 da (Hon Sarah Louise (Hon Mrs Joiner) b 1960, Hon Rachel Trixie (Hon Mrs Pope) b 1961, Hon Joanna Mary b 1964); *Career* dental surgeon; memb: Westminster City Cncl 1968–78, GLC Havering 1970–73, Enfield-Southgate 1977–86; Parly candidate (C): Blackburn 1970, N Cornwall 1974; govr National Heart Hosp 1974–90, memb Industrial Tbnl Panel for London 1974–, British chm European Union of Women 1978–82, national women's vice chm Cons Party 1978–82, UK rep on UN Status of Women Cmmn 1982–88, memb LEB 1984–90; dir: Gateway Building Society 1987–88, Woolwich Building Society 1988–93; vice pres: Bldg Socs Assoc 1985–90, Nat House Building Cncl 1990–; vice chm NE Thames RHA 1990–94, UK chm Plan International 1989–, chm Suzy Lamplugh Tst 1993–96, chm Royal Free Hampstead NHS Tst 1994–; tstee Parly Advsy Cncl on Tport Safety 1992–; *Recreations* gardening, cooking, travel, historic buildings, family life; *Style*— The Rt Hon Baroness Gardner of Parkes; ✉ House of Lords, London SW1A 0PW

GARDNER-THORPE, Dr Christopher; s of Col Sir Ronald Gardner-Thorpe, GBE, TD, JP (d 1991), and Hazel Mary St George, *née* Dees; *b* 22 Aug 1941; *Educ* St Philip's Sch London, Beaumont Coll Old Windsor Berks, St Thomas' Hosp Med Sch London (MB BS), Univ of London (MD); *m* 1 April 1967 (m dis 1988), Sheelah, da of Dr Edward Irvine (d 1993), of Exeter; 2 s (Damian, James), 3 da (Catherine, Anne, Helen); *Career* registrar in neurology: Wessex Neurological Centre Southampton Gen Hosp 1967–69, Gen Infirmary Leeds 1969–71, Special Centre for Epilepsy Bootham Park Hosp York 1969–71; sr registrar in neurology Newcastle Gen Hosp and Royal Victoria Infirmary Newcastle upon Tyne 1971–74, conslt neurologist SW Regnl Health Authy (duties principally Exeter and N Devon) 1974–, hon tutor in neurology Post Grad Med Sch Univ of Exeter 1983–; ed various books and papers on epilepsy and other neurological topics; memb Int League Against Epilepsy 1969–, fndr memb and hon tres SW Eng Neurosciences Assoc 1981, fndr memb S Eng Neurosciences Assoc; memb: Harveian Soc 1966–, SW Physicians Club 1974–, Devon and Exeter Med Soc 1974– (hon asst sec 1978–81, hon sec 1981–85, hon reporting sec 1989–), Advsy Ctee Northcott Devon Med Fndn; fndr hon med advsr Devon Sports Assoc for the Disabled 1976–, memb Northumbrian Pipers Soc 1976–; Order OStJ 1980, HM Lieut City of London 1981; Freeman City of London 1978, Liveryman Worshipful Co of Barbers 1980; FRSM 1968, FRCP 1985; *Books* Antiepileptic Dry Monitoring (chief ed, 1977), James Parkinson 1755–1824 (1987); author of various papers on epilepsy and other neurological topics; *Recreations* music, travel, reading, photography, sailing, gardening, walking; *Clubs* Starcross Yacht; *Style*— Dr Christopher Gardner-Thorpe; ✉ The Coach House, 1A College Rd, Exeter EX1 1TE (☎ 01392 433941)

GAREL-JONES, Rt Hon (William Armand Thomas) Tristan; PC (1992), MP (C) Watford (majority 9,590); s of Bernard Garel-Jones, of Madrid, and Meriel, *née* Williams; *b* 28 Feb 1941; *Educ* King's Sch Canterbury; *m* 1966, Catalina, da of Mariano Garrigues, of Madrid; 4 s, 1 da; *Career* MP (C) Watford 1979–; PPS to Barney Hayhoe 1981–82, asst Govt whip 1982–83, a Lord Cmmr of the Treasy 1983–86; HM Household: vice chamberlain 1986–87, comptroller 1987–89, treas (dep chief whip) 1989–90; min of state for Europe FCO 1990–93; *Recreations* collecting books; *Clubs* Beefsteak; *Style*— The Rt Hon Tristan Garel-Jones, MP; ✉ House of Commons, London SW1A 0AA

GAREY, Prof Laurence John; *b* 18 July 1941, Peterborough; *Educ* Deacon's Sch Peterborough, Univ of Nottingham (state scholarship to read modern languages), Worcester Coll Oxford (Theodore Williams scholar in anatomy, MA), Dept of Human Anatomy Oxford (MRC trg scholar, DPhil, Rolleston meml prize), St Thomas' Hosp London (clinical scholar, BM BCh (Oxon)); *m*; 2 c; *Career* Reserve Offr (Pilot) Nottingham and Oxford Univ Air Sqdns RAF 1959–63; house offr in gen med Memorial Hosp Watford 1968; Univ of Oxford: departmental demonstrator Dept of Human Anatomy 1968–71, lectr Balliol and Merton Colls 1968–72, Schorstein research fell in med sci 1970–72; Sir Henry Wellcome travelling fell and visiting prof Dept of Physiology Univ of Calif Berkeley 1972–73; Univ of Lausanne: professeur asst Inst of Anatomy 1973–76, professeur associé Inst of Anatomy 1976–87, lectr Sch of Ergotherapy 1976–87; assoc prof Dept of Anatomy Nat Univ of Singapore 1987–90; Univ of London: prof and head Dept of Anatomy Charing Cross and Westminster Med Sch 1990–, vice pres Bd of Studies in Human Anatomy and Morphology 1993–, dep convenor Subject Panel in Human Anatomy and Morphology 1993–; memb Ctee of Admin Neurobiology Research Gp Nat Cncl for Scientific Research Marseille 1979; Inst of Neurophysiology and Psychophysiology Marseille: memb Ctee of Admin 1977–81, scientific dir Dept of Cellular Neurobiology 1982–84; visiting fell Aust Nat Univ Canberra 1982; memb: London Ctee of Licensed Teachers of Anatomy 1990– (chm 1993–), Ct of Examiners RCS 1992–; hon memb Centre for Neuroscience UC London; memb: Acad of Med of Singapore, Afro-Asia Oceania Assoc of Anatomists (memb Int Ctee 1988–), Anatomical Soc of GB and I (vice pres 1994–), Assoc of Profs of the Univ of Lausanne (memb Ctee 1983–87), Aust Neuroscience Soc, Br Neuropathological Soc, Child Vision Research Soc, Euro Biomedical Research Assoc (fndr memb), Euro Brain and Behaviour Soc, Euro Neuroscience Assoc, Hong Kong Soc of Neurosciences, Int Brain Research Orgn (treas 1983–85), Nat Postgraduate Med Coll of Nigeria, NY Acad of Scis, Physiological Soc, RSM, Singapore Neuroscience Assoc (pres 1988–90), Soc for Neuroscience, Swiss Soc of Anatomists, Histologists and Embryologists, Swiss Soc of Cellular and Molecular Biology (vice pres 1980–82), Union of Swiss Socs of Experimental Biology; *Books* Plastic and Reconstructive Surgery of the Orbitopalpebral Region (jtly, 1990); translations: Neuronal Man - The Biology of Mind (1985, 2 edn 1986), The Population Alternative (1986), Localisation in the Cerebral Cortex (1994); author of various scientific articles on neuroanatomy; *Style*— Prof Laurence J Garey; ✉ Department of Anatomy, Charing Cross and Westminster Medical School, London W6 8RF (☎ 0181 846 7036, fax 0181 846 7025, e-mail l.garey@cxwms.ac.uk)

GARFIELD, John Samuel; s of Montagu Garfield (d 1976), of Hove, and Marguerite, *née* Elman (d 1983); *b* 13 Feb 1930; *Educ* Bradfield Coll, Emmanuel Coll Cambridge (MA, MB MChir); *m* 6 Oct 1962, Agnes Clara Teleki, da of Count Joseph Teleki de Szek (d 1985), of Pomaz, Hungary; 3 da (Stephanie b 1963, Johanna Francoise b 1965, Marie-Claire b 1969); *Career* jr specialist med RAMC 1956–58, conslt neurosurgeon 1968, hon emeritus Univ of Southampton Trust Hosps 1992–; numerous pubns on neurosurgical topics; former pres Soc of Br Neurological Surgns, memb Cncl Med Def Union, former chm Wessex Regnl Med Advsy Ctee; FRCS 1961, FRCP 1971; photographer; exhibitions in London, Winchester Southampton, Brussels and Ypres 1980–95; *Photographic Publications* The Fallen (1990), The Eye, the Brain and the Camera (1993), History of EANS (1995); *Recreations* photography (exhibitions Winchester, London, Brussels, Ypres and Southampton 1980–90); *Clubs* Athenaeum; *Style*— John Garfield, Esq; ✉ Keyhaven, Hadrian Way, Chilworth, Southampton SO16 7HY (☎ 01703 767674)

GARFIELD, Simon Frank; s of Herbert Sidney Garfield (d 1973), and Hella Helene, *née* Meyer (d 1979); *b* 19 March 1960; *Educ* UCS Hampstead, LSE (BSc Econ); *m* 1987, Diane, da of Rubin Samuels; 2 c; *Career* sub ed Radio Times 1981, scriptwriter radio documentaries BBC 1981–82, ed Time Out magazine 1988–89 (writer 1982–88), news feature writer Independent and Independent on Sunday newspapers 1990–; winner: Guardian/NUS Student Journalist of the Year 1981, Br Soc of Magazine Editors' Ed of the Year (Time Out) 1989; *Books* Expensive Habits: The Dark Side of the Music Industry (1986), The End of Innocence: Britain in the time of AIDS (1994, Somerset Maugham Prize 1995), The Wrestling (1996); *Recreations* painting, music, poker, cricket; *Clubs* Two Brydges Place; *Style*— Simon Garfield, Esq; ✉ c/o Peters Fraser & Dunlop Ltd, 503 The Chambers, Chelsea Harbour, Lots Road, London SW10 0XF (☎ 0171 352 4446, fax 0171 352 7356)

GARFITT, His Hon Alan; s of Rush Garfitt, and Florence Garfitt; *b* 20 Dec 1920; *Educ* King Edward VII GS King's Lynn, Metropolitan Coll, Inns of Court Sch of Law (LLB); *m* 1, 1941, Muriel Ada Jaggers; 1 s, 1 da; m 2, 1973, Ivie Maud Hudson; m 3, 1978, Rosemary Lazell; 1 s, 1 da; *Career* Metropolitan Police 1938–41, served RAF 1941–46; called to the Bar Lincoln's Inn 1948, circuit judge 1977–92, judge Cambridge County Court and Wisbech Crown Court 1978–92; memb Assoc of British Riding Schs 1960– (pres 1977–93, fell 1989); hon fell Faculty of Law Univ of Cambridge 1978; *Recreations* dinghy sailing; *Clubs* Ely Sailing; *Style*— His Hon Alan Garfitt; ✉ Leap House, Barcham Road, Soham, Ely, Cambs CB7 5TU (☎ 01353 720925)

GARLAND, Nicholas Withycombe; s of Thomas Ownsworth Garland, and Margaret, *née* Withycombe; *b* 1 Sept 1935; *Educ* Rongotai Coll NZ, Slade Sch of Fine Art; *m* 1, 1964 (m dis 1968), Harriet Crittall; m 2, 19 Dec 1969, Caroline Beatrice, da of Sir Peter Medawar; 3 s (Timothy William b 1957, Alexander Medawar b 1970, Theodore Nicholas b 1972), 1 da (Emily b 1964); *Career* political cartoonist: Daily Telegraph 1966–86 and 1991–, The Independent 1986–91; *Style*— Nicholas Garland, Esq; ✉ The Daily Telegraph, 1 Canada Square, Canary Wharf, London E14 5DT (☎ 0171 538 5000)

GARLAND, Patrick; s of Capt Ewart Garland, DFC, RFC (d 1985), of Brockenhurst, Hants, and Rosalind (d 1984), da of Herbert Granville Fell; *b* 10 April 1935; *Educ* St Mary's Coll Southampton, St Edmund Hall Oxford (MA); *m* 1980, Alexandra Bastedo; *Career* artistic dir Festival Theatre Chichester 1981–85 and 1990–94; prodr: Fanfare for Europe at Covent Garden 1975, Fanfare for Elizabeth (for HM the Queen's 60th birthday) 1986, Celebration of a Broadcaster Westminster Abbey 1987, cantata The Plague and the Moonflower for Inter-Parly Union St Paul's Cathedral; dir: Brief Lives, Forty Years On, Billy, Snow Goose (film), The Doll's House (film), The Secret of Sherlock Holmes (Wyndhams Theatre) 1989, Tovarich (Piccadilly) 1991, Handel's opera Ottone (for King's Consort, Royal Festival Hall London, Tokyo and Osaka Japan) 1992, Pickwick - the musical (Chichester Festival Theatre and Sadler's Wells) 1993, Vita and Virginia (The Minerva Chichester and Ambassadors) 1993, The Tempest (Regent's Park) 1996; writer and dir A Room of One's Own (with Eileen Atkins as Virginia Woolf, Playhouse, Broadway and Thames TV) 1992; TV interviews: Rex Harrison 1987, Laurence Olivier 1987; organised Thanksgiving Serv for Lord Olivier (with Dean of Westminster) at Westminster Abbey 1989; Hon DLitt Univ of Southampton 1994, pres Dramatists Club 1995; *Books* Wings of the Morning (1988), Angels in the Sussex Air (1995); *Recreations* idling in Corsica; *Clubs* Garrick; *Style*— Patrick Garland, Esq; ✉ 47 Cadogan Square, London SW1X 0HX

GARLAND, Hon Mr Justice; Hon Sir Patrick Neville; kt (1985); s of Frank Neville Garland (d 1984), and Marjorie, *née* Lewis (d 1972); *b* 22 July 1929; *Educ* Uppingham, Sidney Sussex Coll Cambridge (MA, LLM); *m* 1955, Jane Elizabeth, da of Harold John Bird, JP (d 1970), of Troston, Suffolk; 2 s, 1 da; *Career* called to the Bar Middle Temple 1953; asst recorder Norwich 1971, recorder of the Crown Court 1972, QC 1972, bencher Middle Temple 1979, dep High Ct judge 1981, judge of the High Court of Justice (Queen's Bench Div) 1985–; pres: Official Referees' Bar Assoc 1985– (chm 1982–85), Central Cncl of Probation Ctees 1986–; vice chm Parole Bd 1989–90 (memb 1988–90); presiding judge S Eastern Circuit 1989–94; hon fell Sidney Sussex Coll Cambridge 1991; *Recreations* gardening, shooting, industl archaeology; *Clubs* Cumberland Lawn Tennis; *Style*— Hon Mr Justice Garland; ✉ c/o Royal Courts of Justice, Strand, London WC2A 2LL

GARLAND, Prof Peter Bryan; s of Frederick George Garland (d 1978), and Molly Kate, *née* Jones; *b* 31 Jan 1934; *Educ* Hardye's Sch Dorchester, Downing Coll Cambridge (Athletics blue), King's Coll Hosp London (MA, MB BChir, PhD); *m* 7 Feb 1959, Ann, da of Arthur Apseley Bathurst (d 1951); 1 s (James b 1964), 2 da (Joanna b 1961, Clare b 1962); *Career* reader in biochemistry Univ of Bristol 1969–70 (lectr 1964–68), prof of biochemistry Univ of Dundee 1970–84, visiting fell Aust Nat Univ Canberra 1983, princ scientist and head of biosciences Unilever Res Colworth House Laboratory 1984–87, dir of res Amersham Int 1987–89, chief exec Inst of Cancer Research London 1989–, prof of biochemistry Univ of London 1992–; author of numerous original articles on biochemistry and biophysics; visiting prof Johnson Res Fndn Philadelphia 1967–69, memb MRC 1980–84 (chm Cell Biology Disorders Bd 1980–82), memb Scientific Ctee Cancer Res Campaign 1983–92, chm Cancer Res Campaign Technology Ltd 1988–91 (dep chm 1991–), chm Bd Cambridge Antibody Technology Ltd 1995– (memb 1990–); Colworth Medal Biochemical Society 1970; LLD (hc) Univ of Dundee 1990; FRSE 1977, memb EMBO 1981; *Recreations* sport, skiing, windsurfing, sailing, theatre; *Clubs* Athenaeum, Bosham Sailing; *Style*— Prof Peter B Garland, FRSE; ✉ Institute of Cancer Research, Chester Beatty Laboratories, Fulham Road, London SW3 6JB (☎ 0171 352 8133)

GARLAND, Peter Leslie; s of Leslie Garland, and Stella, *née* Haskins; *b* 21 Sept 1946; *Educ* Bristol Cathedral Sch, Univ of Manchester (BA); *m* 25 May 1979, Janet Rosemary, da of Harold Prescott; 3 da (Alice b 13 Aug 1981, Harriet b 29 May 1983, Grace b 10 March 1986); *Career* DHSS: joined 1974, asst sec 1989–93, under sec 1993, currently dep dir of fin and performance NHS Executive; *Recreations* family, gardening; *Style*— Peter Garland, Esq; ✉ NHS Executive, Quarry House, Quarry Hill, Leeds LS2 7UE (☎ 0113 254 5174)

GARLAND, Hon Sir Victor; KBE (1981); s of Idris Victor Garland; *b* 5 May 1934; *Educ* Hale Sch, W Aust Univ (BA); *m* 1960, Lynette May Jamieson; 2 s, 1 da; *Career* RAAF 1952; practised as CA 1958–69; memb for Curtin (Lib) Aust Fed House of Reps 1969–81; Parly and ministerial positions: min assisting the Treas 1972 and 1975–76, min for Supply 1971–72, opposition chief whip 1974–75, chm Expenditure Ctee 1976–77, min for Special Trade Representations 1977–79 (incl GATT negotiations), min for Business and Consumer Affrs 1979–80; high cmmr for Aust in the UK 1981–83; non-exec dir Prudential Corporation plc 1984–93; dir: TR Far East Income Trust 1984– (chm) Throgmorton Trust plc 1985–, Govett Funds Inc 1991–, Nelson Hurst 1993–, Glenchewton plc 1993– (chm), other public companies; vice chm: South Bank Bd 1986–, Royal Cwlth Soc for the Blind; Freeman City of London 1982, Liveryman Worshipful Co of Tallow Chandlers, Hon Freeman Worshipful Co of Butchers; FCA; *Clubs* White's, Weld (Australia); *Style*— Hon Sir Victor Garland, KBE; ✉ Wilton Place, Knightsbridge, London SW1

GARLICK, Sir John; KCB (1976, CB 1973); s of late Charles Garlick; *b* 17 May 1921; *Educ* Westcliff HS Essex, Univ of London (BSc); *m* 1945, Frances Esther (d 1992), da of late Edward Stanley Munday; 3 da (Marion, Pamela, Susan); *Career* entered Miny of Tport 1948, private sec to Ernest Marples 1959–60, second perm sec Cabinet Office 1974–77, perm sec Dept of Environment 1978–81, dir Abbey National Building Soc (now Abbey National plc) 1981–92; memb London Docklands Devpt Corpn 1981–92, chm Alcohol Concern 1986–96; *Style*— Sir John Garlick, KCB; ✉ 16 Astons Rd, Moor Park, Northwood, Middx HA6 2LD (☎ 01923 824628)

GARLICK, Paul Richard; QC (1996); s of Arthur Garlick (d 1978), and Dorothy Sylvia, *née* Allan; *b* 14 Aug 1952; *Educ* Scarisbrick Hall Sch Lancs, Univ of Liverpool (LLB); *m* 1976, Helen Mary, da of John Douglas Keep; 1 da (Harriet Elizabeth b 1984); *Career* called to the Bar Middle Temple 1974, standing counsel to HM Customs & Excise 1990–96; memb Hon Soc of Middle Temple 1972; *Recreations* music, cooking, walking, skiing, athletics; *Style*— Paul Garlick, Esq, QC; ✉ 3 Pump Court, Upper Ground, Temple, London EC4Y 7AJ (☎ 0171 353 0711, fax 0171 353 3319)

GARLING, Dr David John Haldane (Ben); s of Leslie Ernest Garling, and Frances Margaret, *née* Hannah; *b* 26 July 1937; *Educ* Highgate Sch, St John's Coll Cambridge (BA, MA, PhD, ScD); *m* 30 Aug 1963, Anthea Mary Eileen (Ann), da of George Richard Septimus Dixon, MBE (d 1983); 2 s (Hugh b 1969, Owen b 1974), 1 da (Julia b 1972); *Career* Nat Serv RA 1955–57; Univ of Cambridge: fell St John's Coll 1963– (tutor 1971–78, pres 1987–91), asst lectr 1963–64, lectr 1964–78 reader in mathematical analysis 1978–, head Dept of Pure Maths and Mathematical Statistics 1984–91, pro-proctor 1995–96, sr proctor 1996–97; memb: Maths Ctee SERC 1981–84, London Mathematical Soc 1963– (memb Cncl 1984–87 and 1995–, meetings and memb sec 1995–), Cambridge Philosophical Soc 1963–; *Books* Galois Theory (1986); *Style*— Dr Ben Garling; ✉ St John's College, Cambridge (☎ 01223 338600, fax 01223 337920, e-mail d.j.h.garling@pmms.cam.ac.uk)

GARMOYLE, Viscount; Hugh Sebastian Frederick Cairns; s and h of 6 Earl Cairns, CBE; *b* 26 March 1965; *Educ* Eton, Univ of Edinburgh, London Coll of Law; *m* 19 Dec 1991, Juliet, o da of Andrew Eustace Palmer, CMG, CVO (*qv*), of Little Missenden, Bucks; 1 s (Hon Oliver David Andrew b 7 March 1993), 1 da (Hon Tara Davina Amanda b 3 April 1995); *Career* Freshfields Slrs 1990–94, Cazenove & Co 1994–; Liveryman Worshipful Co of Fishmongers; *Style*— Lord Garmoyle; ✉ 11 Lonsdale Road, London W11 2BY

GARNER, Alan; s of Colin Garner (d 1983), of Cheshire, and Marjorie, *née* Greenwood Stuart; *b* 17 Oct 1934; *Educ* Manchester GS, Magdalen Coll Oxford; *m* 1, 1956, Ann, da of Harry Cook (d 1976), of Oxford; 1 s (Adam), 2 da (Ellen, Katharine); m 2, 1972, Griselda, da of Paul Greaves (d 1986), of St Petersburg, Russia; 1 s (Joseph b 1973), 1 da (Elizabeth b 1975); *Career* author; Mil Serv Lt RA; memb Editorial Bd Detskaya Literatura Publishers Moscow; *Plays* Holly from the Bongs (1965), Lamaload (1978), Lurga Lom (1980), To Kill a King (1980), Sally Water (1982), The Keeper (1983); *Dance Drama* The Green Mist (1970); *Libretti* The Bellybag (1971), Potter Thompson (1972), Lord Fame (1996); *Films* The Owl Service (1969), Red Shift (1978), Places and Things (1978), Images (1981, First Prize Chicago Int Film Festival), Strandloper (1992); *Books* The Weirdstone of Brisingamen (1960), The Moon of Gomrath (1963), Elidor (1965), Holly from the Bongs (1966), The Old Man of Mow (1967), The Owl Service (1967, Library Assoc Carnegie Medal 1967, Guardian Award 1968), The Hamish Hamilton Book of Goblins (1969), Red Shift (1973), The Breadhorse (1975), The Guizer (1975), The Stone Book (1976, Phoenix Award Children's Book Assoc of US 1996), Tom Fobble's Day (1977), Granny Reardun (1977), The Aimer Gate (1978), Fairy Tales of Gold (1979), The Lad of the Gad (1980), A Book of British Fairy Tales (1984), A Bag of Moonshine (1986), Jack and the Beanstalk (1992), Once Upon a Time (1993), Strandloper (first adult book 1996); *Recreations* work; *Clubs* The Portico Library; *Style*— Alan Garner, Esq; ✉ Blackden, Holmes Chapel, Cheshire CW4 8BY

GARNER, Sir Anthony Stuart; kt (1984); s of Edward Henry Garner, MC, FIAS (1953), and Dorothy May Garner (d 1985); *b* 28 Jan 1927; *Educ* Liverpool Coll; *m* 1967, Shirley, da of William Henry Taylor (d 1963), of East Grinstead; 2 s; *Career* Grenadier Gds 1945–48; Cons agent Halifax 1951–56, nat organising sec of Young Cons Movement 1956–61; Cons Central Office agent: London area 1961–64, Western area 1964–66, NW area 1966–76; dir of orgn Cons Central Office 1976–88, Parly conslt 1988–; dir Clifton Court Residents Ltd; life govr Liverpool Coll, pres Oldlerpoolian Soc 1995–; memb Ctee Royal Liverpool Sch for the Blind; *Recreations* boating, theatre; *Clubs* Carlton, St Stephen's; *Style*— Sir Anthony Garner; ✉ The Beeches, Bottom Lane, Seer Green, Beaconsfield, Bucks HP9 2UH (☎ 01494 678445)

GARNER, His Hon Judge Michael Scott; s of William Garner (d 1968), of Huddersfield, and Doris Mary, *née* Scott (d 1958); *b* 10 April 1939; *Educ* Huddersfield Coll, Univ of Manchester (LLB); *m* 1, 30 July 1964, Sheila Margaret (d 1981), da of Edward Frederick Garland (d 1972); 1 s (John William Scott b 1968), 1 da (Caroline Louise b 1966); m 2, 12 Aug 1982, Margaret Anne, da of Philip Senior (d 1985); *Career* admitted slr 1965; asst recorder 1978–85, recorder 1985–88, circuit judge (NE Circuit) 1988–; pres Huddersfield Inc Law Soc 1985–86; *Recreations* motoring, walking, watching opera; *Style*— His Hon Judge Michael Garner; ✉ c/o Circuit Administrator, West Riding House, Albion St, Leeds, W Yorks

GARNETT, Ven David Christopher; s of Douglas Garnett, of Elland, W Yorks, and Audrey, *née* Cragg; *b* 26 Sept 1945; *Educ* Giggleswick Sch, Univ of Nottingham (BA), Fitzwilliam Coll Cambridge (BLitt, MA), Westcott House Cambridge; *m* 1974, Susanne, *née* Crawford; 2 s (Christopher b 1977, Timothy b 1978); *Career* curate of Cottingham E Yorks 1969–72, chaplain, fell and tutor Selwyn Coll Cambridge and pastoral advsr Newnham Coll Cambridge 1972–77, rector of Patterdale and diocesan dir of ordinands Dio of Carlisle 1977–80, vicar of Heald Green and chaplain St Ann's Hospice Dio of Chester 1980–87, rector of Christleton and Bishop's theol advsr 1987–92, team rector of Ellesmere Port Dio of Chester 1992–96, archdeacon of Chesterfield 1996–; supporter Christian Aid; *Recreations* part time farming, poultry breeding and genetics (memb Laced Wyandotte Club), clarinet, natural history; *Style*— The Ven the Archdeacon of Chesterfield; ✉ The Old Parsonage, Taddington, Buxton, Derbyshire (☎ 01298 85607, fax 01298 85583)

GARNETT, Gerald Archer; s of Leslie Pearson Garnett (d 1985), of Westcliff-on-Sea, Essex, and Betty Gladys, *née* Archer; *b* 1 March 1937; *Educ* Framlingham Coll Suffolk, INSEAD Fontainebleau; *m* 24 Feb 1973, Sheila Mary, da of Col David Bruce Ronald, CBE, of West Byfleet, Surrey; 1 s (Rupert b 13 Feb 1978), 1 da (Clare b 20 May 1980); *Career* RAF 1955–57; sec Ranks Hovis McDougall plc 1979–93; dep sec Rexam PLC 1995–; dir CDB Merger Services Ltd; Freeman City of London, memb Ct of Assts Worshipful Co of Armourers and Brasiers; FCIS; *Recreations* squash, tennis, theatre; *Clubs* Naval and Military; *Style*— Gerald Garnett, Esq; ✉ Southbury Farmhouse, Ruscombe, Berks (☎ 0118 934 0132); Rexam PLC, 114 Knightsbridge, London SW1X 7NN (☎ 0171 590 7043, fax 0171 590 7110)

GARNETT, (William) John Poulton Maxwell; CBE (1970); s of Dr (James Clerk) Maxwell Garnett, CBE (d 1958), and Margaret Lucy Poulton; *b* 6 Aug 1921; *Educ* Rugby, Kent Sch (USA), Trinity Coll Cambridge; *m* 1, 1943 (m dis), Barbara, da of Dr Rex Rutherford-Smith; 2 s, 2 da (*see* Rt Hon Virginia Bottomley, PC, MP); m 2, 3 April 1985, Julia Charity Cleverdon, CBE,, *qv*; 2 da (Charity b 1982, Victoria b 1987); *Career* with ICI 1947–62, the dir of The Industrial Society 1962–86, dir Spencer Stuart and Associates mgmnt conslts (chm 1979–81); dep chm UNA 1954–56, chm West Lambeth Health Authy 1986–90; *Style*— John Garnett, Esq, CBE; ✉ 8 Alwyne Rd, London N1 2HH (☎ 0171 359 2423)

GARNETT, Richard Duncan Carey; s of David Garnett (d 1981), of Hilton, Cambs, and Rachel Alice, *née* Marshall (d 1940); *b* 8 Jan 1923; *Educ* Beacon Hill, Beltane, King's Coll Cambridge (MA); *m* 15 April 1954, (Mary Letitia) Jane, da of Bruce Dickins; 2 s (Oliver William Grierson b 17 March 1956, Edward Alexander b 11 March 1959); *Career* dir Rupert Hart-Davis Ltd 1954–66 (prodn mangr 1951–59), dir Adlard Coles Ltd 1963–66, dir Macmillan London Ltd (in charge of The New Grove Dictionary of Music) 1972–82 (ed 1966–82), dir Macmillan Publishers Ltd 1982–87; writer; *Books* Constance Garnett - A Heroic Life (1991), Goldsmith - Selected Works (ed, 1950), Joyce (ed with Reggie Grenfell, 1980), Sylvia and David - The Townsend Warner/Garnett Letters (ed, 1994); trans: The Art of the Aqualung (Robert Gruss, 1953), On the Track of Unknown Animals (Bernard Heuvelmans, 1958), In the Wake of the Sea-Serpents (Bernard Heuvelmans, 1968); *Children's Books* The Silver Kingdom (1956), The White Dragon (1963), Jack of Dover (1966); *Recreations* glass engraving, letter cutting, light verse; *Clubs* Cranium, Double Crown; *Style*— Richard Garnett, Esq; ✉ Hilton Hall, Hilton, Huntingdon, Cambs PE18 9NE (☎ 01480 830417); c/o A P Watt Ltd, 20 John Street, London WC1N 2DR (☎ 0171 405 6774)

GARNHAM, Caroline Xania; da of Edward Hatch (d 1981), of Guildford, and Elisabeth Houtman; *b* 10 Oct 1955; *Educ* George Abbott Sch for Girls Guildford, Univ of Exeter (BSc); *m* 1, 30 Dec 1977 (m dis 1984), Hugh Laurence Garnham, s of Jack Garnham; m 2, 9 Aug 1991, Michael Robert Little, *qv*; 1 s (Edward Charles Frank b 21 Nov 1992), 1 da (Georgia Elizabeth Medina b 10 Nov 1995); *Career* tax and tst ptnr Simmons and Simmons; writer: Saturday Financial Times (family and fin page); memb Law Soc; *Recreations* hunting, skiing, writing; *Style*— Mrs Michael Little; ✉ 51 Connaught St, London W2 2BB (☎ 0171 706 4320); The Lydes, Toddington, nr Cheltenham, Glos (☎ 01242 621419); Simmons and Simmons, 21 Wilson St, London EC2M 2TX (☎ 0171 628 2020, fax 0171 588 4129, telex 888562 SIMMON G)

GARNHAM, Dr John Claude; s of Prof (Percy) Cyril Claude Garnham, CMG, FRS (d 1994), of Southernwood, Farnham Common, Bucks, and Esther, *née* Long-Price (d 1995); *b* 7 May 1932; *Educ* Merchant Taylors', Univ of Paris (Dip de CF), Univ of London (MB BS), Bart's Med Coll London; *m* 11 Dec 1954, Frances Joan, da of Frank Kirkup (d 1951); 3 s (Timothy Claude b 1956, Frank Jasper b 1959, Simon Philip b 1960), 1 da (Francesca b 1971); *Career* med practice 1957–65, clinical res 1965–, vice pres med affrs Abbott Laboratories USA 1970–71, private med practice 1980–; chm Chiltern International Ltd, med dir Havenfern Laboratories Ltd; Freeman City of London, Master Worshipful Co of Farriers 1994–95; fell American Soc of Clinical Pharmacology & Therapeutics; memb: BMA, Br Soc of Pharmacology; MRCS, LRCP, FRSM, FRSTM&H, FFPM RCP 1989; *Recreations* fishing, clay pigeon shooting, bridge, golf, tennis, riding; *Clubs* Guards Polo, IOD, Stoke Poges Golf; *Style*— Dr John Claude Garnham; ✉ Kynance, Manor Rd, Penn, Bucks HP10 8JB (☎ 01494 812177, fax 01494 816281); Chiltern International plc, Chiltern Place, Upton Road, Slough, Berks SL1 2AD (☎ 01753 512000, fax 01753 511116)

GARNIER, Edward Henry; QC (1995), MP (C) Harborough (majority 13,543); s of William d'Arcy Garnier (Col RA, d 1989), and Hon Mrs Garnier (*née* Hon Lavender Hyacinth de Grey); *b* 26 Oct 1952; *Educ* Wellington, Jesus Coll Oxford (MA); *m* 17 April 1982, Anna Caroline, da of Michael James Mellows (d 1974), of Belton House, Rutland; 2 s (George Edward b 20 July 1986, James William b 21 Jan 1991), 1 da (Eleanor Katharine Rose b 21 Sept 1983); *Career* called to the Bar Middle Temple 1976; vice pres Hemsworth Cons Assoc; contested: Wandsworth Borough Cncl by-election 1984, Tooting ILEA election 1986; Parly candidate (C) Hemsworth W Yorks 1987, MP (C) Harborough 1992–; PPS to Mins of State for Foreign and Cwlth Affrs: Rt Hon Alastair Goodlad 1994–95, David Davis 1994–95; PPS to Rt Hon Sir Nicholas Lyell as Attorney Gen and to Sir Derek Spencer as Slr Gen 1995–; memb Home Affrs Select Ctee 1992–95, sec Cons Backbench Foreign Affrs Ctee 1992–94, jt chm All-Pty Parly Knitwear and Textile Indust Gp 1992–94; UK election observer: Kenya 1992, Bosnia 1996; Parly fell St Anthony's Coll Oxford 1996–97; *Books* Halsbury's Laws of England (contrib, 4 edn), Bearing the Standard (jtly, 1991), Facing the Future (jtly, 1993); *Recreations* cricket, shooting, opera; *Style*— Edward Garnier, Esq, QC, MP; ✉ 1 Brick Ct, Temple, London EC4Y 9BY (☎ 0171 353 8845, fax 0171 583 9144); House of Commons, London SW1A 0AA (☎ 0171 219 3000)

GARNIER, Rear Adm Sir John; KCVO (1990, LVO 1965), CBE (1982); s of Rev Thomas Vernon Garnier (d 1939), and Helen Davis, *née* Stenhouse (d 1993); *b* 10 March 1934; *Educ* Berkhamsted Sch, Britannia Royal Naval Coll; *m* 31 Dec 1966, Joanna Jane (Dodie), da of Alan Cadbury (d 1994), and Jane Cadbury, *née* Walker, of Haffield, Ledbury, Herefordshire; 2 s (Thomas b 1968, William b 1970), 1 da (Louisa b 1972); *Career* joined RN 1950, served in HMY Britannia 1956–57, HMS Tyne 1956, qualified navigation specialist 1959, Naval Equerry to HM The Queen 1962–65, cmd HMS Dundas 1968–69, Directorate of Naval Ops and Trade 1969–71, cmd HMS Minerva 1972–73, Def Policy Staff 1973–75, exec offr HMS Intrepid 1976, Asst Dir Naval Manpower Planning 1976–78, RCDS 1979, cmd HMS London 1980–81, Dir Naval Ops and Trade 1982–84, Cdre Amphibious Warfare 1985, Flag Offr Royal Yachts 1985–90, Extra Equerry to HM The Queen 1988, Private Sec and Comptroller to HRH Princess Alexandra 1991–95; govr Sherborne Sch for Girls 1985–; memb Cncl Shipwrecked Fishermen and Mariners' Royal Benevolent Soc 1996–; Younger Bro of Trinity House 1974, Freeman City of London 1982; *Recreations* sailing, gardening, opera, golf, computers; *Style*— Rear Adm Sir John Garnier, KCVO, CBE; ✉ Bembury Farm, Thornford, Sherborne, Dorset DT9 6QF

GARNIER, Thomas Stenhouse (Tom); s of Rev Thomas Vernon Garnier, OBE (d 1939), and Helen, *née* Stenhouse (later Mrs Davis, d 1993); *b* 26 Oct 1932; *Educ* Berkhamsted Sch, Trinity Coll Oxford (MA), London Business Sch; *m* 11 Feb 1961, Heather Colquhoun (d 1995), da of James Grant (d 1981); 2 s (Edward b 20 May 1966, James b 27 March 1981), 2 da (Rachel b 8 March 1968, Elisabeth b 7 Dec 1977); *Career* Kalamazoo plc: asst overseas sales mangr 1956–63, asst to md 1963–66, personnel divnl mangr 1966–68, dir i/c personnel and printing 1968–72, dir i/c sales and personnel 1972–74, dep md 1974–77, gp md 1977–87, gp chm 1985–89; chm: Kalamazoo Finance Ltd 1978–89, MBM Systems & Equipment Ltd Hong Kong 1982–89, K3 Software Services Ltd 1984–87, Alfred Gilbert & Sons Ltd 1984–86; administrateur Société Anonyme des Etablissements Kalamazoo 1974–86; independent conslt trading as consultsgarnier 1990–; dir: Birmingham Chamber Training Ltd 1987–, Kalamazoo (NZ) Ltd 1987–89; Birmingham Chamber of Indust & Commerce: memb Educn and Trg Ctee 1973–91, ctee chm 1979–85, memb Working Pty on Industl Democracy 1977, memb Cncl 1980–, memb Gen Purposes Ctee 1981–95, memb Mgmnt Ctee 1987–91, vice pres 1987–89, chm Overseas Trade Policy Ctee 1987–89, pres 1989; Inst of Mgmnt: memb Working Pty on Indust Educn and Mgmnt 1976–77, memb Mgmnt Devpt Servs and Educn Ctee 1978–89, memb Cncl 1979–85, memb New Business Panel 1982–83, memb West Midlands Regnl Bd 1982–90; tstee Middlemore Homes 1968–89, memb Bd Mgmnt Res Groups 1977–94, memb West Midlands Economic Planning Cncl 1978–79, memb Bd Co-Operative Devpt Agency 1981–90, memb West Midland Regnl Cncl CBI 1983–89; tstee RALI Fndn 1985–, chm Midlands Area Employer Advsy Cncl APEX Tst 1989, memb Bd Birmingham Trg and Enterprise Cncl 1989, cncl memb Aston Univ 1990–93; CIMgt 1982; *Recreations* languages, bridge, reading, riding, swimming; *Style*— Tom Garnier, Esq; ✉ Woodfold, Down Hatherley Lane, Down Hatherley, Gloucester GL2 9QB (☎ 01452 730378, business ☎ 01452 731354/730378, fax 01452 731354)

GARNONS WILLIAMS, Dorothea Margaret; OBE (1982), JP (1963), DL Powys (1987); da of Maj-Gen Sir Geoffrey Raikes, CB, DSO (d 1975), and Dorothy Amabel Wilson, *née* Fox (d 1952); *b* 2 Jan 1925; *Educ* Overstone Sch; *m* 1, 1948, Maj Robin Duncan Raikes (d 1984); 1 s (David Geoffrey b 1949), 2 da (Susan Elizabeth b 1952, Gillian Rosalind b 1958); m 2, 1990, Lt-Col David Penry Garnons Williams; *Career* WRNS 1943–46; Board of Welsh Water Authy 1974–82, cmmr Countryside Cmmn 1981–87, vice chm Ctee for Wales 1983–87, vice pres Campaign for the Protection of Rural Wales (chm 1990–94); memb: Regnl Forestry Advsy Ctee 1989–94, Prince of Wales Ctee 1989–96; *Recreations* gardening, painting in watercolours, walking; *Style*— Mrs D Garnons Williams, OBE, JP, DL; ✉ Treberfydd, Bwlch, Brecon, Powys LD3 7PX (☎ 01874 730205)

GARRATT, Colin Dennis; s of Sqdn Ldr Dennis Herbert Garratt, of Uppingham, Leics, and Margaret Alice, *née* Clarke; *b* 16 April 1940; *Educ* Mill Hill Leicester; *m* 1, 1975 (m dis); m 2 (m dis), Margaret Elizabeth, *née* Grzyb; 1 s (James Daniel b 2 Aug 1987); m 3, Carol Lesley, *née* Cardwell; 1 da (Marie-Louise b 3 June 1993); *Career* photographer, author, publisher, audio visual producer and presenter; engaged in professionally documenting the last steam locomotives of the world 1969–; writer and illustrator of 45 books incl Around the World in Search of Steam (autobiography, David & Charles, 1987); regular contrib to TV and radio, tours multi-image audio visual theatre shows based on global expeditions and on behalf of the railway industry; tstee Railworld (international show-case for rail); *Recreations* ornithology, politics, music, art, the appreciation of fine cigars; *Style*— Colin Garratt, Esq; ✉ Milepost, 92 1/2 Newton Harcourt, Leicester LE8 9FH (☎ 0116 259 2068)

GARRATT, Sheryl; da of Frank Stephen Garratt, of Birmingham, and June Valerie, *née* Fray; *b* 29 March 1961; *Educ* Barr Beacon Comp Birmingham, UCL (BA); *m* 22 March 1994, Mark McGuire; 1 s (Liam James McGuire b 12 Feb 1996); *Career* freelance writer New Musical Express 1980–83, music ed City Limits 1983–86, freelance writer The Observer, The Sunday Telegraph, Honey, New York Rocker, The Face, News on Sunday, Looks 1986–88, ed The Face 1990–95 (music/prodn ed 1988–90), freelance writer The Sunday Times, The Independent, The Guardian and New Statesman 1995–; The Face winner International Magazine of the Year (PPA Awards) 1994; *Books* Signed Sealed and Delivered (1984); *Recreations* drinking, dancing, reading, talking; *Clubs* Chuff Chuff, Velvet Underground, Riki Tik; *Style*— Ms Sheryl Garratt; ✉ 56c St Thomas's Road, London N4 2QW (☎ 0171 266 8836, fax 0171 503 6748)

GARRATT, Timothy George; s of George Herbert Garratt (d 1976), of Chichester, Sussex, and Hylda Joyce, *née* Spalton (d 1958); *b* 7 Sept 1942; *Educ* Stowe; *m* 24 April 1965, Vanessa Ann, da of Charles Albert Wright (d 1980), of Chichester, Sussex; 2 s (Alastair b 1969, James b 1973); *Career* chartered surveyor; ptnr Rendells Auctioneers Valuers & Estate Agents S Devon 1976–; memb Gen Cncl RICS 1969–73; chm: Devon and Cornwall Branch RICS 1989–90, Western Counties Agric Valuers' Assoc 1993–94; memb Cncl Livestock Auctioneers' Assoc 1992–95; pres Chagford and Dist Lions Club 1984–85 and 1992–93, zone chm Lions Club Int Zone 1985–86; FAAV 1968, FRICS 1975; *Recreations* farming, sporting shooting, gardening, country wine making, home butchery; *Clubs* Lions Int, RICS 1913; *Style*— Timothy Garratt, Esq; ✉ Baileys Hey, Chagford, Devon TQ13 8AW (☎ 01647 433396); Rock House, Chagford, Devon TQ13 8AX (01647 432277)

GARRETT, Anthony David (Tony); CBE (1993); s of Sir William Garrett (d 1977), of Eastbourne, Sussex, and Lady Marion, *née* Houghton (d 1967); *b* 26 Aug 1928; *Educ* Ellesmere Coll, Clare Coll Cambridge (MA); *m* 17 May 1952, Monica, da of Richard V Harris (d 1976), of Sidmouth, Devon; 3 s (Nicholas b 1954, David b 1959, Mark b 1962), 1 da (Jennifer b 1956); *Career* Nat Serv 4 Queen's Own Hussars 1946–48; md Proctor & Gamble UK & Italy 1969–73, vice pres int The Procter & Gamble Co 1973–82; memb Bd The Post Office 1983–87, dep master and chief exec The Royal Mint 1988–93; non-exec dir NPI (formerly National Provident Institution) 1988–95; FRSA 1991; *Recreations* golf, bridge, chess, mountain walking, gardening; *Style*— Tony Garrett, Esq, CBE; ✉ Cammock House, Goldsmith Avenue, Crowborough, East Sussex TN6 1RH

GARRETT, Dr Daniel James (Dan); s of Jennie Sinclair, *née* Garrett; *b* 29 April 1941; *Educ* The Judd Sch Tonbridge, Fitzwilliam Coll Cambridge (BA), Univ of Hull (PhD); *m*; 2 da (Tess b 1968, Leoni b 1971), 1 s (Reuben b 1974); *Career* head of drama Furzedown Coll 1972–75, chief prodr BBC Radio 1975–91, freelance prodr, writer, bdcaster 1991–; memb: CND, Gauge O Guild; *Books* Drama Workshop Plays (4 vols, 1984), Family Frictions (1987), Girls (1988), Taking Issue (1988), Kids' Oz (with Warrill Grindrod, 1988), World in View: Australia (with Warrill Grindrod, 1989), World in View: Scandinavia (1990), World in View: Germany (with Charlotte Drews-Bernstein, 1990); *Recreations* gardening, model railways, railway history; *Clubs* Lewisham Labour; *Style*— Dr Dan Garrett; ✉ 20 Weald Close, Weald, Sevenoaks, Kent TN14 6QH (☎ 01732 463496, fax 01732 741151)

GARRETT, Godfrey John; OBE (1982); s of Thomas Garrett (d 1978), and May Louisa, *née* Botten; *b* 24 July 1937; *Educ* Dulwich, Sidney Sussex Coll Cambridge (MA); *m* 23 March 1963, Elisabeth Margaret, *née* Hall; 4 s (Mark b 1964, Edward b 1967, William b 1968, Richard b 1970), 1 da (Anna b 1974); *Career* FO: joined 1961, third sec Kinshasa (formerly Leopoldville) 1963–65, second sec Prague 1965–68, first sec Buenos Aires 1971–73, first sec (later cnsllr) Stockholm 1981–83, cnsllr Bonn 1983–88, cnsllr E Berlin 1990, cnsllr Prague 1990–92, head UK Delgn to EC Monitoring Mission Zagreb 1994, ambass Orgn for Security and Cooperation in Europe (OSCE) Mission to Ukraine 1995; *Recreations* skiing, mountain walking, gardening, languages; *Style*— Godfrey J Garrett, Esq, OBE; ✉ White Cottage, Henley, Haslemere, Surrey GU27 3HQ (☎ 01428 652172)

GARRETT, John Francis; s of Dr George Garrett (d 1970), of Liverpool, and Louise Mary, *née* Harrison; *b* 1 Feb 1945; *Educ* Ampleforth, Liverpool Coll of Building, Harvard Business Sch (AMP); *m* Sept 1966, Patricia Margaret, da of John M Pinnington (d 1994), of Scorton, Lancs; 1 s (Patrick b 1968), 3 da (Joanne b 1967, Kimberley b 1971, Jenni b 1974); *Career* md Gillette Australia 1980, regnl dir Gillette Australia N Zealand Pacific Basin 1983, pres Gillette Personal Care Europe 1986, non-exec dir Harrison and Jones 1985–; dir: Gillette Industries Ltd 1986–91, Gillette Personal Care UK Ltd 1986–91; md Recreation Div The Rank Organisation plc 1991–; *Recreations* rugby, cricket, golf, shooting; *Clubs* Stoke Poges Golf, Peninsula CGC (Aust), Harvard; *Style*— John Garrett, Esq; ✉ The Rank Organisation plc, 6 Connaught Place, London W2 2EZ (☎ 0171 706 1111, fax 0171 262 035)

GARRETT, John Laurence; MP (Lab) Norwich South (majority 6,181); s of Laurence Garrett, and Rosina Garrett; *b* 8 Sept 1931; *Educ* Sir George Monoux GS London, Univ of Oxford, UCLA Business Sch; *m* 1959, Wendy Ady; 2 da; *Career* former: lab offr in chem indust, head of market res in car indust, public serv mgmnt conslt; dir int mgmnt consultancy practice; MP (Lab) Norwich South 1974–83 and 1987– (also contested 1983); PPS to: Civil Serv Min 1974, Social Security Min 1977–79; oppn spokesman: Treasy 1979–80, Indust 1980–83, Energy 1987, Indust 1988–89, Civil Service 1993–95; memb House of Commons Cmmn 1995–; campaign co-ordinator for S England 1989–92; *Style*— John Garrett, Esq, MP; ✉ c/o House of Commons, London SW1A 0AA

GARRETT, Prof John Raymond; s of Charles Raymond Garrett, MM (d 1976), of Winchester, and Irene Lily, *née* Rogers (d 1978); *b* 28 March 1928; *Educ* Peter Symonds Sch, King's Coll Hosp Dental Sch (LDS RCS), King's Coll (BSc), King's Coll Hosp Med Sch (MB BS, PhD); *m* 28 April 1958, Daphne Anne, da of Edwin Owen Parr (d 1953); 1 s (Malcolm b 1964), 1 da (Claire b 1963); *Career* RADC Lt 1950–51, Capt 1951–52, Nat Serv active parachutist in Airbourne Servs in 23 Para Field Ambulance; res fell Nuffield 1961–64, sr lectr pathology King's Coll Hosp Med Sch 1964, prof and head of Dept of Oral Pathology King's Coll Hosp Dental Sch 1971–93 (reader 1968), emeritus prof 1993, research into Secretory mechanisms; former pres Int Fedn of Socs of Histochemistry and Cytochemistry, former pres Royal Microscopical Soc; Freeman City of London 1971, memb Worshipful Soc of Apothecaries; Hon MD Univ of Lund 1985; MRCPath 1965, FRCPath 1977; *Books* Histochemistry of Secretory Processes (1976); *Recreations* med history; *Style*— Prof John Garrett; ✉ 15 Deepdene Rd, London SE5 8EG (☎ 0171 274 6488); The Rayne Inst, King's Coll Med Dental Sch, 123 Coadharbour Lane, London SE5 9NU (☎ 0171 346 3019)

GARRETT, Maj-Gen (Henry Edmund Melvill) Lennox; CBE (1975); s of John Edmund Garrett (d 1978), and Mary, *née* Jamieson; *b* 31 Jan 1924; *Educ* Wellington, Clare Coll Cambridge (MA); *m* 1973, Rachel Ann; 1 step s (Richard Beadon b 1961), 1 step da (Sarah Beadon b 1961); *Career* cmmnd 1944, Staff Coll 1956, US Armed Forces Staff Coll 1960, OC 7 Field Sqdn 1960, CO 35 Engr Regt 1965, Col GS, MOD 1968, Cdr 12 Engr Bde 1969, RCDS 1972, COS NI 1972, Maj-Gen i/c admin UKLF 1975, Vice Adj-Gen 1976, dir Army Security 1978–89; chm: Royal Engineers Assoc 1989–93, Forces Help Soc and Lord Roberts Workshop 1991; vice pres SSAFA 1991; *Recreations* walking, reading; *Clubs* Army and Navy; *Style*— Maj-Gen Lennox Garrett, CBE; ✉ c/o National Westminster Bank Ltd, 7 Hustlergate, Bradford, West Yorkshire BD1 1PP

GARRETT, Lesley; *b* 10 April 1955; *Educ* RAM (Countess of Munster Award, Decca-Kathleen Ferrier Memorial Prize), Nat Opera Studio; *m* 1991; 1 s, 1 da; *Career* soprano; studies with Joy Mammen; princ ENO 1984–; previous engagements incl: Wexford Festival, Welsh Nat Opera, Opera North, Buxton Festival, Glyndebourne; Gramaphone Award for best selling classical artist of the year 1996; FRAM; *Roles* incl: title role in Mozart's Zaide, Susanna in The Marriage of Figaro, Despina in Cosi fan Tutte, Carolina in Cimarosa's The Secret Marriage, Atalanta in Xerxes, Eurydice in Orpheus in the Underworld, Bella in Tippet's Midsummer Marriage, Musetta in La Bohème, Adele in Die Fledermaus, Rose in Kurt Weill's Street Scene, Zelrina in Don Giovanni, Dalinda in Ariodante, title role in The Cunning Little Vixen, Jenny in Kurt Weill's The Rise and Fall of the City of Mahagonny, title role in La Belle Vivette; *Television* Jobs for the Girls (BBC 1, with Pauline Quirke and Linda Robson), Viva La Diva (BBC 2); *Recordings* DIVA! A Soprano at the Movies (silver disc), PriMadonna, Simple Gifts, Soprano in Red 1995 (silver disc, No 1 Classical Charts 1995), Soprano in Hollywood 1996; *Recreations* watching cricket; *Style*— Ms Lesley Garrett; ✉ c/o Patrick Voullaire, PV Productions, Park Offices, 121 Dora Road, London SW19 7JT (☎ 0181 946 8848, fax 0181 944 1317)

GARRETT, Malcolm Leslie; s of Edmund Garrett, of Northwich, Cheshire, and Edna, *née* Mullin; *b* 2 June 1956; *Educ* St Ambrose Coll Altrincham Cheshire, Univ of Reading, Manchester Poly (BA); *Career* fndr and design dir Assorted Images graphic design consultancy 1977–94, fndr and multimedia prodr AMXdigital 1994–, conslt art dir Radar Records 1978–79, art dir Today's Length magazine 1981; contributing designer: i-D magazine 1981, New York Rocker magazine 1981; design dir New Sounds New Styles magazine 1981–82, conslt art dir Sky magazine 1986–87, art dir The Independent Catalogue 1993–94, conslt art dir 10–15 magazine 1995–; visiting lectr/teacher numerous univs in UK, Denmark and USA; work exhibited in Liverpool, London, Manchester, Edinburgh, Holland, Austria, France, Denmark, Sweden, USA and Japan 1981–; work in permanent collection Dept of Prints and Drawings V&A; memb Jury: Graphic Front (11th Nippon graphic exhibition, Tokyo) 1990, D & AD Annual Awards 1988–90, Proctor & Stevenson Awards 1992–95, TIA 25th Anniversary Awards 1993, Design Week Awards 1993 and 1995; memb: Design Sub-Ctee D&AD 1989–90, Graphic Design Subject Review Steering Ctee CNAA 1989–90; fndr memb Assoc of Music Indust Designers 1990; *Books* Duran Duran - Their Story (with Kasper de Graaf, 1982), When Cameras Go Crazy - Culture Club (with Kasper de Graaf, 1983), Interference (with Nick Rhodes, 1984), Duran Duran - The Book of Words (ed with Kasper de Graaf, 1985), More Dark Than Shark (with Brian Eno, Russell Mills and Rick Poynor, 1986), New British Graphic Designers (with Neville Brody and Peter Saville, 1991), System Error (1991), Malcolm Garrett - Ulterior Motifs (graphic devices 1977–91) (1991), The Graphic Beat Vol 1 (1992), Sublime (1992), Designing for Music (1992); *Recreations* collecting and driving classic American cars; *Clubs* Classic Camaro; *Style*— Malcolm Garrett, Esq; ✉ AMXdigital, 124 Curtain Road, London EC2A 3PS (☎ 0171 613 5300, fax 0171 613 5333, compuserve 100345,1053, applelink amx.uk, internet amxdigital@eworld.com)

GARRETT, Richard Anthony (Tony); CBE (1986); s of Charles Victor Garrett (d 1945), and Blanche, *née* Michell (d 1968); *b* 4 July 1918; *Educ* Kings Sch Worcester; *m* 5 Jan 1946, Marie Louise, da of Rear Adm Robin Campsie Dalglish (d 1937); 1 s (Rupert

Charles Anthony b 8 July 1961), 2 da (Anne b 8 Jan 1947, Amanda b 2 Feb 1955); *Career* Royal Glos Hussars TA 1938, RMC Sandhurst 1940, WWII 22 Dragoons 1941–46; chm and md Imperial Tobacco Ltd 1971–79 (joined 1936), dep chm HTV Group plc 1976–83, dir Standard Commercial Corporation USA 1981–95; chm NABC 1980–87, tstee Glynebourne Arts Tst 1976–88; Freeman Worshipful Co of Tobacco Pipe Makers; CIMgt, FInstD; *Recreations* golf, gardening, music; *Clubs* Naval & Military, MCC; *Style*— Tony Garrett, Esq, CBE; ✉ Marlwood Grange, Thornbury, Bristol BS12 2JB (☎ 01454 412630)

GARRETT, Stephen James; s of James Leslie Michael Peter Garrett, of Sussex, and Margot, *née* Fleischner; *b* 16 April 1957; *Educ* Westminster, Merton Coll Oxford (BA); *m* 22 June 1989, Layla Alla, da of Feodor Andreyev, of Tashkent, USSR; *Career* Granada TV Manchester 1978–81, BBC TV 1982–83; freelance dir and ind prodr 1984–87, commissioning ed youth progs Channel 4 TV 1988–92, md Kudos Productions 1992–, dir Rapture (cable channel) 1995–; exec prodr: Rory Bremner - Who Else? (Channel 4, BAFTA Award 1994) 1994–, The Complete Guide to Relationships, Cultural Rabies, Screaming Reels (RTS Award 1995), Good Ideas of the 20th Century, Come On Down and Out, The Bad Government Awards, Desperately Seeking Something; *Recreations* tennis, photography, learning Russian; *Style*— Stephen Garrett, Esq; ✉ Kudos Productions, 12–14 Argyll Street, London W1V 1AB (☎ 0171 287 0097, fax 0171 734 9204)

GARRETT, Terence; CMG (1990), CBE (1967); s of Percy Herbert Garrett (d 1972), and Gladys Annie, *née* Budd (d 1972); *b* 27 Sept 1929; *Educ* Alleyn's Sch, Gonville and Caius Coll Cambridge (MA); *m* 1960, Grace Elizabeth Bridgeman, yr da of Rev Basil Kelly Braund (d 1981); 2 s (Andrew b 1960, Charles b 1963) 3 da (Bridget b 1966, Katharine b 1969, Ruth (twin) b 1969); *Career* instr Lt RN 1952–55; lectr Ewell County Tech Coll 1955–56, sr lectr RMC of Sci Shrivenham 1957–62, Programmes Analysis Unit Miny of Technol 1967–70, scientific cnsllr Br Embassy Moscow 1962–66 and 1970–74, Int Technol Collaboration Unit Dept of Trade 1974–76, sec to Bd Govrs and Gen Conf IAEA Vienna 1976–78, sci and tech cnsllr Br Embassy Bonn 1978–82, dep chief scientific offr Res and Technol Policy Div DTI 1982–87, sci and tech cnsllr Br Embassy Moscow 1987–91, asst sec (int affrs) Royal Society 1991–94; *Recreations* travel; *Clubs* Hawks; *Style*— Terence Garrett, Esq, CMG, CBE; ✉ Lime Tree Farmhouse, Chilton, Didcot, Oxon OX11 0SW

GARRICK, Sir Ronald; kt (1994), CBE; s of Thomas Garrick and Anne, *née* MacKay; *b* 21 Aug 1940; *Educ* Royal Coll of Science and Technology Glasgow, Univ of Glasgow (BSc); *m* 1965, Janet Elizabeth Taylor Lind; 2 s, 1 da; *Career* chief exec and md Weir Group plc, chm Weir Pumps Ltd; non-exec dir: Scottish Power plc 1992–, Shell UK Ltd; dir Devonport Management Ltd, dep chm Scottish Enterprise; memb Restrictive Practices Court; hon sec for Mechanical Engrg Royal Acad of Engrg 1991–94; FEng 1984, FRSE 1992, FIMechE; *Style*— Sir Ronald Garrick, CBE, FRSE, FEng; ✉ The Weir Group plc, 149 Newlands Road, Cathcart, Glasgow G44 4EX (☎ 0141 637 7111, fax 0141 637 0215)

GARROD, Lt-Gen Sir (John) Martin Carruthers; KCB (1988), OBE (1980), DL (Kent, 1992); s of late Rev William Francis Garrod, and late Isobel Agnes, *née* Carruthers; *b* 29 May 1935; *Educ* Sherborne; *m* 1963, Gillian Mary, da of Lt-Col Robert Granville Parks-Smith, RM (ka 1942); 2 da (Catherine, Fenella (Mrs Mikhail Ignatiev)); *Career* Lt-Gen RM, cdr 3 Commando Bde RM 1983–84 (despatches NI 1974); ADC to HM The Queen 1983–84, COS to Cmdt Gen RM 1984–87, Cmdt Gen RM 1987–90; dep dir Maastricht Referendum Campaign 1993, memb EC Monitor Mission in Bosnia 1993–94, chief of staff to EU Administrator of Mostar 1994–96, EU special envoy Mostar 1996–; Liveryman Worshipful Co of Plaisterers 1990; *Recreations* portrait photography; *Clubs* East India; *Style*— Lt-Gen Sir Martin Garrod, KCB, OBE, DL; ✉ c/o Lloyds Bank, Petersfield, Hants GU32 3HL

GARROD, Norman John; CBE (1992); s of Frank Albert Garrod (d 1965); *b* 10 July 1924; *Educ* Alleyn's Sch Dulwich; *m* 1945, Beryl Portia Betty, *née* Bastow; 2 c; *Career* served WWII, Flt Lt RAF, UK, Middle East and Far East; master printer; chm: Garrod and Lofthouse Ltd 1952–86, Theatreprint Ltd 1970–, Video Business Publications Ltd 1983–, Garrod Properties Ltd 1987–; pres Printers Charitable Corporation 1994–95 (chm 1981–94), vice pres Variety Club of Great Britain (chief barker 1984–85); Liveryman Worshipful Co of Stationers & Newspaper Makers; *Recreations* dogs, fishing; *Clubs* Garrick, RAF; *Style*— Norman Garrod, Esq, CBE; ✉ Great Common, Big Common Lane, Bletchingley, Surrey RH1 4QE (☎ 01883 743375); Garrod Properties Ltd, Strandgate, 18–20 York Buildings, London WC2N 6JU (☎ 0171 839 5355)

GARSIDE, Charles Alexander; *b* 9 April 1951; *Educ* Queen Elizabeth GS Blackburn Lancs; *m* Carole; 1 s (James), 1 da (Victoria); *Career* reporter with news agency in NW 1970–73, fndr own news agency Ellesmere Port Cheshire 1973–74, ptnr Mercury Press Agency Liverpool (and own PR agency) 1974–76, sr dist journalist and dep to Northern News Ed The Sun Manchester 1976–79, asst news ed Daily Star Manchester 1979, news ed London Evening News 1979–80, assoc news ed The Sun 1980–81, news ed The London Standard 1981–85 (asst ed 1986), dep news ed The Times 1987, dep ed The Sunday Express 1988–89, asst ed The Times 1990–91; The European: dep ed 1991, ed and gen mangr 1992–93, ed-in-chief June 1994–; *Recreations* fly fishing, cricket, snooker, reading, theatre; *Clubs* Travellers'; *Style*— Charles Garside, Esq; ✉ Editor-in-Chief, The European, 200 Gray's Inn Road, London WC1X 8NE (☎ 0171 418 7777)

GARSIDE, Gill; da of Roy Garside, of Huddersfield, West Yorkshire, and Mavis, *née* Holdsworth; *b* 23 March 1954; *Educ* Greenhead HS Huddersfield, Univ of Liverpool (BSc); *Career* editorial asst: Heyden Publishing 1976, Good Housekeeping Magazine 1977–79; press offr Tesco Stores 1979–81; account exec: VandenBurg Associates PR 1981–83, Leslie Bishop Company PR 1983–84; currently md Darwall Smith Associates Ltd PR consultancy (joined 1984); memb Mktg Soc 1988, MInstD; *Recreations* horse riding, cycling, swimming, walking, cinema; *Style*— Ms Gill Garside; ✉ Darwall Smith Associates Ltd, Smoke House Yard, 44/46 St John St, London EC1M 4DT (☎ 0171 490 1100, fax 0171 253 0342, car 0831 382809)

GARSIDE, Prof John; *b* 9 Oct 1941; *Educ* Christ's Coll Finchley, UCL (state scholar, Salters' scholar, BSc(Eng), PhD, DSc(Eng)); *Career* pt/t lectr Dept of Chemical Engrg Borough Poly London 1964–66, tech offr Res and Devpt Dept Imperial Chemical Industries Ltd Agric Div Billingham Teesside 1966–69, Fulbright sr scholar and visiting prof Dept of Chemical Engrg Iowa State Univ USA 1976–77, reader in chemical engrg UCL 1981 (lectr 1969–81); UMIST: prof of chemical engrg 1982–, head of dept 1983–88 and 1990–92, vice princ for academic devpt and external affrs 1985–87, dep princ 1986–87; Monbusho/BC visiting prof Dept of Chemical Engrg Tokyo Univ of Agric and Technol Japan Sept-Dec 1992; memb: Engrg and Materials Sci Panel Res Corp Tst 1985–88, Engrg Bd SERC 1990–93, Cncl IChemE 1992– (pres 1994–95), Senate Engrg Cncl; UK del Euro Fedn of Chemical Engrg Working Pty on Crystallization 1990– (chm 1994–); assoc ed Chemical Engrg Communications 1985–; fell UCL 1994; CEng 1969, FRSA 1985, FIChemE 1986, FEng 1988; *Style*— Prof John Garside, FEng; ✉ Chemical Engineering Department, UMIST, PO Box 88, Manchester M60 1QD (☎ 0161 200 4360, fax 0161 200 4399)

GARSIDE, Roger Ramsay; s of Capt Frederick Rodney Garside, CBE, RN, and Margaret Ada Beatrice, *née* Ramsay; *b* 29 March 1938; *Educ* Eton, Clare Coll Cambridge (MA), Sloan Sch of Mgmnt (MIT, MSc), Univ of Hong Kong (CSC Mandarin Chinese); *m* 11 Oct 1969, Evelyne Madeleine Pierrette, da of André René Émile Guérin (d 1982); 3 da (Juliette b 1972, Alice b 1974, Rebecca b 1978); *Career* Nat Serv cmmnd offr 1/6 Queen Elizabeth's Own Gurkha Rifles; Dip Serv 1962–71: London, Rangoon, Hong Kong, Peking; World Bank Washington 1972–74; Dip Serv 1975–87: London, Peking, Paris; London Stock Exchange 1987–90, dir of public affrs and advsr on int relations, chm GMA Capital Markets Ltd (formerly Garside Miller Associates Ltd) advsrs to emerging financial markets 1990–; memb RIIA; *Books* Coming Alive: China After Mao (1981); *Recreations* walking, writing; *Clubs* Reform; *Style*— Roger Garside, Esq; ✉ 36 Groveway, London SW9 0AR (☎ 0171 582 1577); GMA Capital Markets Ltd, 113 Warnford Court, 29 Throgmorton Street, London EC2N 2AT (☎ 0171 920 0555, fax 0171 628 3854)

GARSON, Capt Robin William; CBE (1975); s of Peter James Garson (d 1922), and Ada Frances, *née* Newton (d 1965); *b* 13 Nov 1921; *Educ* SOAS (Japanese interpreter); *m* 1946, Joy Ligertwood Taylor, *née* Hickman; 1 s (Simon), 1 da (Nicola); *Career* entered RN 1937, served WWII 1939–45; HM Ships: Resolution, Nigeria, Cyclops; HM Submarines: Seawolf, H33, Spark; CO HM submarines 1945–54: Universal, Uther, Seraph, Saga, Sanguine, Springer, Thule, Astute; Chief Staff Offr Intelligence Far East 1966–68, Sr Polaris UK Rep Washington 1969–71, Capt 1 Submarine Sqdn 1971–73, Cdre HMS Drake 1973–75; ADC to HM The Queen 1974; advsr to AMA on Arts and Recreation 1976–85, memb Library Advsy Cncl (Eng) 1977–81, dir of Leisure Services London Borough of Hillingdon 1975–85, advsr Sports Cncl 1979–85, patron Submarine Museum Gosport; *Recreations* golf, skiing, tennis; *Clubs* Moor Park, Army & Navy, Hunstanton Golf; *Style*— Capt Robin Garson, CBE; ✉ Gateways, Hamilton Rd West, Old Hunstanton, Norfolk, PE36 6JB

GARSTON, Clive Richard; s of Henry Leslie Garston (d 1978), of Manchester, and Sheila Esther, *née* Cohen; *b* 25 April 1945; *Educ* Manchester GS, Univ of Leeds (LLB), Coll of Law; *m* 25 Feb 1973, Racheline Raymonde, da of Jacques Sultan; 1 s (Nicholas Nathan b 15 July 1974), 1 da (Louise Anne b 22 May 1978); *Career* slr; Hall Brydon Manchester: articled clerk 1966–68, asst slr 1968–71, ptnr 1971–78; sr ptnr Halliwell Landau Manchester 1989–95 (ptnr 1978–89 and 1995–); non-exec dir The Inter Care Group plc 1990–; memb Law Soc 1968; *Recreations* swimming, skiing, watching Manchester United and Lancashire County Cricket; *Clubs* RAC, Lancashire CC, Mere Golf and Country, IOD; *Style*— Clive R Garston, Esq; ✉ Sandy Ridge, Bollinway, Hale, Cheshire WA15 0NZ (☎ 0161 904 9822); Halliwell Landau, St James's Court, Brown St, Manchester M2 2JF (☎ 0161 835 3003, fax 0161 835 2994, car 0802 356614)

GARSTON, (Eric) Michael; s of Dr Maurice Kopelowitz (d 1971), of Newcastle upon Tyne, and Mabel, *née* Garston (d 1949); *b* 23 May 1931; *Educ* Malvern, Univ of Durham (LLB); *m* 20 Nov 1960 (m dis 1976), Jill Rosemary, da of Jack Kleeman (d 1983), of Regents Park, London; 1 s (Jeremy b 1963), 1 da (Annabel b 1966); *Career* slr; sr ptnr Reynolds Porter Chamberlain 1988–91, currently conslt Boodle Hatfield; non-exec dir numerous private cos; memb: Chllr's Ct of Benefactors Univ of Oxford, Exec Ctee Anglo Austrian Soc, Legal Gp Friends of Hebrew Univ; chm Bd of Tstees The World Resource Fndn; tstee and memb Exec Ctees of several UK charities incl: Fndn and Friends of Royal Botanic Gardens Kew, The National Maritime Museum, Cystic Fibrosis Tst, Weald & Downland Open Air Museum, Restoration of Appearance and Function Tst Mount Vernon Hosp; govr Oxford Centre for Hebrew/Jewish Studies; hon fell The Royal Free Hosp Med Sch; Liveryman Worshipful Co of Glaziers 1986; memb: Law Soc 1954, Int Bar Assoc 1966; *Recreations* swimming, walking, theatre; *Clubs* MCC, RAC; *Style*— Michael Garston, Esq; ✉ 97 Abbotsbury Rd, Holland Park, London W14 8EP (☎ 0171 603 2903, fax 0171 602 0881); 61 Brook Street, London W1Y 2BL (☎ 0171 491 9576, fax 0171 499 3941)

GARTON, Dr (George) Alan; s of William Edgar Garton, DCM (d 1966), and Frances Mary Elizabeth, *née* Atkinson (d 1967); *b* 4 June 1922; *Educ* Scarborough HS, Univ of Liverpool (BSc, PhD, DSc); *m* 21 Aug 1951, Gladys Frances, da of Francis James Davison (d 1978), of Glasgow; 2 da (Dr Alison Frances b 7 Sept 1952, Dr Fiona Mary b 19 May 1955); *Career* WWII serv Miny of Supply; Johnston res and teaching fell Univ of Liverpool 1949–50; Rowett Res Inst: biochemist 1950–63, head Lipid Biochemistry Dept 1963–83, dep dir 1968–83, hon res assoc 1984–92, hon professorial fell 1992–; hon res fell Univ of Aberdeen 1987–; visiting prof of biochemistry Univ of North Carolina 1967, memb Cncl Br Nutrition Fndn 1982–, pres Int Conferences on Biochemistry of Lipids 1982–89, chm Br Nat Ctee for Nutritional and Food Sciences 1985–87; FRSE 1966, FRS 1978; SBStJ 1986; *Books* contributor to several multi author books on ruminant physiology and lipid biochemistry; *Recreations* gardening, golf, philately, foreign travel; *Clubs* Farmers, Deeside Golf; *Style*— Dr Alan Garton, FRSE, FRS; ✉ Ellerburn, 1 St Devenick Crescent, Cults, Aberdeen AB15 9LL (☎ 01224 867012)

GARTON, John Leslie; CBE (1974, MBE 1946); er s of Charles Leslie Garton (d 1940), and Madeline Laurence; *b* 1 April 1916; *Educ* Eton, Magdalen Coll Oxford (MA); *m* 1939, Elizabeth Frances, da of Sir Walter Erskine Crum, OBE (d 1923); 1 s (and 2 s decd); *Career* Maj TA 1938–51; chm: Coca-Cola Bottling Co (Oxford) Ltd 1951–65, Coca-Cola Western Bottlers Ltd 1966–71; Thames Conservator 1970–74; pres: Oxford Univ Boat Club 1939, Amateur Rowing Assoc 1969–77 (hon life vice pres 1978–), Henley Royal Regatta 1978– (chm 1966–77), Leander Club 1980–83 (capt 1946, chm 1958–59); memb Fin and Gen Purposes Ctee Br Olympic Assoc 1969–77, chm World Rowing Championships 1975; High Sheriff Bucks 1977; Liveryman Worshipful Co of Grocers; *Recreations* shooting, fishing, supporting the sport of rowing; *Clubs* Leander; *Style*— John L Garton, Esq, CBE; ✉ Mill Green House, Church St, Wargrave, Berks RG10 8EP (☎ 0118 940 2944)

GARTON ASH, Timothy John; s of John Garton Ash, and Lorna Garton Ash; *b* 12 July 1955; *Educ* Sherborne, Exeter Coll Oxford (BA), St Antony's Coll Oxford (MA); *m* 1982, Danuta; 2 s (Thomas b 1984, Alexander b 1986); *Career* editorial writer on Central Euro affrs The Times 1984–86, foreign ed The Spectator 1984–90, columnist The Independent 1988–90, regular contrib to The Times and New York Review of Books; fell: Woodrow Wilson Int Center for Scholars Washington 1986–87, St Antony's Coll Oxford 1990–; David Watt meml prize 1989, Commentator of the Year in Granada TV What the Papers Say Awards 1990; Order of Merit (Poland) 1992, memb Berlin-Brandenburg Acad of Sci 1994, Order of Merit (Germany) 1995, Imre Nagy Meml Plaque (Hungary) 1995, Premio Napoli 1995; *Books* Und Willst Du Nicht Mein Bruder Sein... Die DDR heute (1981), We The People (1990), The Polish Revolution: Solidarity (2 edn 1991, Somerset Maugham award 1984), The Uses of Adversity (2 edn 1991, Prix Européen de l'Essai 1989), In Europe's Name (1993); *Recreations* literature, architecture, travel; *Clubs* Institut für die Wissenschaften vom Menschen (Vienna); *Style*— Timothy Garton Ash, Esq; ✉ St Antony's College, Oxford OX2 6JF

GARTSIDE, Edmund Travis; TD (1968), DL (Greater Manchester 1990); s of Col J B Gartside, DSO, MC, TD, JP, DL (d 1964), and Cora Maude, *née* Baker; *b* 11 Nov 1933; *Educ* Winchester, Trinity Coll Cambridge (MA); *m* 1, 29 Aug 1959 (m dis 1982), Margaret Claire, *née* Nicholls; 1 s (Michael Travis b 1961), 1 da (Vanessa Perry Anne (Mrs Anderson) b 1962); m 2, 5 May 1983, Valerie Cox, da of Cyril Vowels, of Instow, N Devon; *Career* Nat Serv 2 Lt RE and Lancs Fusiliers 1952–54; TA: Lancs Fusiliers (Maj) 1954–67, E Lancs Regt 1967–68; chm and md Shiloh plc (formerly Shiloh Spinners Ltd) 1966– (mgmnt trainee 1957, dir 1960, gen mangr Roy Mill 1961–65, dep chm 1963–66, md 1965), chm Amberguard Ltd 1977–; dir Oldham & Rochdale Textile Employers' Assoc 1965– (pres 1971–75), memb Central Ctee Br Textile Employers' Assoc 1969–89 (pres 1976–78); pres: Eurocoton 1985–87, Cncl of Br Cotton Textiles

1989–; High Sheriff Greater Manchester 1995–96; memb Ct Univ of Manchester 1979–94, govr Manchester GS 1984–; CIMgt, FInstD; *Clubs* Army & Navy; *Style*— Edmund Gartside, Esq, TD, DL; ✉ Shiloh plc, Holden Fold, Royton, Oldham, Lancs OL2 5ET (☎ 0161 624 8161, fax 0161 627 3840)

GARVAGH, 5 Baron (I 1818); (Alexander Leopold Ivor) George Canning; s of 4 Baron Garvagh (d 1956) by his 2 w, Gladys Dora May (d 1982), da of William Bayley Parker, of Edgbaston, and widow of Lt-Col D M Dimmer, VC; *b* 6 Oct 1920; *Educ* Eton, Christ Church Oxford; *m* 1, 12 July 1947 (m dis 1973), Edith Christine, da of Jack H Cooper, of Worplesdon, Surrey; 1 s, 2 da; m 2, 1974, Cynthia Valerie Mary, da of Eric Ernest Falk Pretty, CMG (d 1967), of Kingswood, Surrey; *Heir* s, Hon Spencer George Stratford de Redcliffe Canning; *Career* served Indian Army WW II in Burma (despatches); accredited rep trade and industry Cayman Islands 1981–, past memb Court Worshipful Co of Painter and Stainers; MIMgt, FInstD, MIEx; *Style*— The Rt Hon the Lord Garvagh

GARVIE, (Fiona) Jane; *b* 19 May 1956; *Educ* Westbourne Sch for Girls Glasgow, Univ of Glasgow (MA, LLB); *Career* Maclay Murray & Spens: legal apprentice 1979–81, asst slr 1981–84, seconded to Bristows, Cooke & Carpmael London 1984–85, litigation ptnr 1985–, also currently head Employment Law Unit; vice chm Discrimination and Gender Equality Ctee Int Bar Assoc 1996–, memb Educn and Trg Ctee Law Soc of Scotland; memb: Law Soc of Scotland 1981, Law Soc 1992; *Publications* Indirect Discrimination in Managing a Legal Practice (Int Legal Practitioner, Sept 1995); *Recreations* music, reading, gardening, walking, exploring cities; *Clubs* Royal Scottish Automobile; *Style*— Miss Jane Garvie; ✉ Maclay Murray & Spens, 151 St Vincent Street, Glasgow G2 5NJ (☎ 0141 248 5011, fax 0141 248 5819)

GARVIN, Michael John Moore; s of Stephen Garvin, MBE, of Sussex, and Gilda Constance, *née* Moore (d 1955); *b* 12 Sept 1943; *Educ* Rugby; *m* 22 Sept 1976, Bridget, da of Thomas A Tolhurst (d 1969); 2 s (Patrick b 1978, Fergus b 1983), 1 da (Melissa b 1981); *Career* CA 1966; dir: Barclay Securities 1972–73, Hampton Areas 1973–79, Trident Television 1979–83, Condé Nast 1983–; *Clubs* Travellers', Hurlingham; *Style*— Michael Garvin, Esq

GASCOIGNE, (Arthur) Bamber; s of Derick (Ernest Frederick) Orby Gascoigne, TD (of the old Yorks family dating back to the 14 century, and gggs of Gen Isaac Gascoigne, whose er bro's da Frances was the Gascoigne heiress who m 2 Marquess of Salisbury, whence also the Salisbury family name of Gascoyne-Cecil) and Hon Mary (Midi) Louisa Hermione O'Neill (d 1991), sis of 3 Baron O'Neill; *b* 24 Jan 1935; *Educ* Eton, Magdalene Coll Cambridge; *m* 1965, Christina Mary, da of late Alfred Henry Ditchburn, CBE; *Career* author, broadcaster and publisher; Cwlth fund fellow Yale 1958–59; theatre critic: Spectator 1961–63, Observer 1963–64; co-ed Theatre Notebook 1968–74, fndr St Helena Press 1977–, chm Ackermann Publishing 1981–85, tstee Nat Gall 1988–95, memb Bd of Dirs Royal Opera House 1988–95, memb Cncl Nat Tst 1989–94, tstee Tate Gall 1993–95; TV presenter: University Challenge 1962–87, Cinema 1964; presenter and author: The Christians 1977, Victorian Values 1987, Man and Music 1987, The Great Moghuls 1990, Connoisseur 1988; Liveryman Worshipful Co of Grocers; FRSL 1976; *Publications* incl: Twentieth Century Drama (1962), World Theatre (1968), The Great Moghuls (1971), The Treasures and Dynasties of China (1973), The Christians (1977), Quest for the Golden Hare (1983), How to Identify Prints (1986), Encyclopedia of Britain (1993); *Style*— Bamber Gascoigne, Esq, FRSL; ✉ St Helena Terrace, Richmond, Surrey TW9 1NR

GASCOIGNE, Keith; *b* 14 Sept 1926; *Educ* Coleshill GS, Univ of Birmingham (BA); *m* Arún (d 1994); 3 da (Caroline, Charlotte, Clare); *Career* PR exec; journalist: Sheffield Telegraph 1949–54, Daily Express 1954–55, The Birmingham Post 1955–60, The Guardian 1960–63; business ed The Birmingham Post 1963–69, PR mangr IMI plc (formerly IMI Ltd and Imperial Metal Industries Ltd) 1969–84, md Gascoigne Moody Associates Ltd 1984–90; GMA Public Relations Ltd: md 1990–94, chm 1994–95; conslt The Warman Group Ltd (after takeover) 1995–; pres Inst of Journalists 1968–69; chm: Birmingham Press Club 1979, Midlands region PRCA 1989–94; memb Inst of PR, fell Inst of Journalists; *Recreations* theatre, music, walking, reading; *Clubs* Birmingham Press, Birmingham Chamber; *Style*— Keith Gascoigne, Esq; ✉ The Warman Group Ltd, 8 The Wharf, Bridge Street, Birmingham B1 2JS (☎ 0121 605 1111)

GASCOIGNE, Paul John; s of John Gascoigne, and Carol, *née* Harold; *b* 27 May 1967; *Educ* Brighton Avenue Jr HS, Heathfield Sr Sch; *children* 1 s (Regan b 18 Feb 1996); *Career* professional footballer; Newcastle Utd 1985–88: apprentice then professional, 106 appearances, 22 goals; transferred for £2m to Tottenham Hotspur 1988 (FA Cup winners' medal 1991), transferred to Lazio Italy 1992, transferred for £4.3m to Glasgow Rangers 1995 (champions Bell's Scottish Premier League 1995–96); England: 13 under 21 caps, 46 full caps and 9 goals (as at Jan 1997), played in World Cup Italy 1990 and Euro 96; PFA Young Player of the Year 1988, Scottish Professional Footballers' Assoc Player of the Year 1996; *Recreations* football, fishing, tennis, swimming, table tennis, tenpin bowling; *Style*— Paul Gascoigne, Esq; ✉ c/o Arram Berlyn Gardner, Holborn Hall, 100 Gray's Inn Road, London WC1X 8BY (☎ 0171 753 5511, fax 0171 404 0109)

GASCOYNE, David Emery; s of Leslie Noel Gascoyne (d 1968), and Winifred Isobel Emery Gascoyne (d 1970); *b* 10 Oct 1916; *Educ* Salisbury Cathedral Choir Sch, Regent St Poly Secdy Sch; *m* 17 May 1975, Mrs (Lorna) Judith Lewis, da of Capt Guy Tyler, MC (d 1966), of Upper Redpits, Marlow, Bucks; 4 stepchildren; *Career* writer, poet and translator; contrib to TLS, The Independent and various int reviews and jls; Chevalier of the Order of Arts and Letters (France); FRSL 1951; *Books* A Short Survey of Surrealism (1935, USA edn 1982), Holderlin's Madness (1938), Poems 1937–42 (1943, illustrated by Graham Sutherland), A Vagrant and Other Poems (1950), Night Thoughts (1956), Collected Poems (1965), Paris Journal 1937–39 (1978), Journal 1936–37 (1980), La Mano del Poeta (selected poems with Italian translation, 1982, Biella Prize for Euro Poetry 1982), Journal de Paris et d'Ailleurs (1984), Collected Poems (1988), Miserère (poems 1937–42 with French translation, 1989), Collected Journals 1936–42 (1991); *Style*— David Gascoyne, Esq, FRSL

GASCOYNE-CECIL, *see:* Cecil

GASELEE, Nicholas Auriol Digby Charles (Nick); s of Lt-Col Auriol Stephen Gaselee, OBE (d 1987), of Tonbridge; *b* 30 Jan 1939; *Educ* Charterhouse; *m* 1966, Judith Mary, da of Dr Gilmer; 1 s (James b 1968), 1 da (Sarah b 1970); *Career* Life Gds 1958–63; racing trainer to HRH The Prince of Wales, trained Grand National winner Party Politics 1992; *Recreations* coursing; *Clubs* Turf; *Style*— Nick Gaselee, Esq; ✉ Saxon Cottage, Upper Lambourn, Berks RG16 7QN (☎ 01488 71503)

GASH, Michael Alfred; s of Benjamin Thomas Gash (d 1969), of Solihull, and Brenda Aileen, *née* Crockett; *b* 24 Oct 1943; *Educ* Sharmans Cross HS for Boys; *m* 24 Oct 1967, Sandra Ruth, da of Albert Ernest Wright (d 1977), of Kidderminster; 1 da (Kate b 1 April 1972); *Career* CA; articled Cox & Furse Birmingham 1962–67, sr supervisor and mangr Coopers & Lybrand London 1967–72, ptnr Kidsons Impey Birmingham 1974–94 (mangr 1972–74), gp fin dir Hampson Industries plc 1994–; memb Rotary Club of Edgbaston Convention; FCA 1967, ATII 1970; *Recreations* golf, bridge, reading, theatre, cooking; *Clubs* The Edgbaston Priory, Harborne Golf; *Style*— Michael Gash, Esq; ✉ Charnwood, 54 Richmond Hill Rd, Edgbaston, Birmingham B15 3RZ (☎ 0121 455 8440); Hampson Industries PLC, 7 Harbour Buildings, Waterfront West, Dudley Road, Brierley Hill, W Midlands DY5 1LN (☎ 01384 485345, fax 01384 485346)

GASH, Prof Norman; CBE (1988); s of Frederick Gash, MM, and Kate, *née* Hunt; *b* 16 Jan 1912; *Educ* Reading Sch, St John's Coll Oxford (MA, MLitt); *m* 1 Aug 1935, (Ivy) Dorothy (d 1995), da of Edward Whitehorn, of Reading, Berks; 2 da (Harriet b 3 March 1944, Sarah b 30 Jan 1946); *Career* asst lectr UCL 1936–40; Army 1940–46, Maj GS 1945; prof of modern history Univ of Leeds 1953–55, Hinkley visiting prof Johns Hopkins Univ 1962, Fords lectr Univ of Oxford 1963–64, dean Faculty of Arts Univ of St Andrews 1978–80 (lectr St Salvators Coll 1946–53, prof of history 1955–70, vice princ 1967–71), Sir John Neale lectr UCL 1981, Swinton lectr 1989; hon fell St John's Coll Oxford 1987; Hon DLitt: Univ of Strathclyde 1984, Univ of St Andrews 1985, Univ of Southampton 1988; FRHistS 1953, FBA 1963, FRSL 1973, FRSE 1977; *Books* Politics in the Age of Peel (1953), Mr Secretary Peel (1961), Reaction and Reconstruction in English Politics 1832–1852 (1965), Sir Robert Peel (1972), Aristocracy and People 1815–1865 (1979), Lord Liverpool (1984), Pillars of Government (1986), Robert Surtees and Early Victorian Society (1993); *Recreations* gardening, swimming; *Style*— Prof Norman Gash, CBE, FRSE, FRSL, FBA; ✉ Old Gatehouse, Portway, Langport, Somerset TA10 0NQ (☎ 01458 250334)

GASKELL, (Richard) Carl; s of (Henry) Brian Gaskell (d 1982), and Doris Winnifred, *née* Taylor; *b* 23 March 1948; *Educ* Gateway Sch Leicester, Univ of Newcastle upon Tyne (LLB); *m* 29 Dec 1973, Margaret Annette, da of Stanley Walter Humber; 1 s (Philip b 1975), 3 da (Victoria b 1976, Elizabeth b 1979, Gillian b 1983); *Career* called to Bar Lincoln's Inn 1971, Midland and Oxford circuit, asst recorder of the Crown Ct 1989–; chm Desford Branch Bosworth Cons Assoc; *Style*— Carl Gaskell, Esq; ✉ 65–67 King Street, Leicester LE1 6RP (☎ 0116 254 7710)

GASKELL, Dr Colin Simister; CBE (1987); s of James Gaskell (d 1987), of Dukinfield, Cheshire, and Carrie, *née* Simister (d 1968); *b* 19 May 1937; *Educ* Manchester GS, Univ of Manchester (BSc), St Edmund Hall Oxford (DPhil); *m* Aug 1961, Jill, da of A Travers Haward (d 1980), of Torquay, Devon; 1 s (John b 1970), 1 da (Sarah b 1974); *Career* tech dir Herbert Controls 1971–74, md Marconi Instruments Ltd 1979–90 (dir 1977–79), gp md The 600 Group plc 1990–; chm The Coda Group plc; dir: Telemetrix plc, St Albans Enterprise Agency; FEng 1989, FIElecIE (vice pres), FIEE (hon treas), CIMgt, FRSA; *Recreations* reading, theatre, walking; *Style*— Dr Colin Gaskell, CBE, FEng; ✉ The 600 Group plc, Witan Court, 284 Witan Gate, Milton Keynes MK9 1EJ (☎ 01908 2346000, fax 01908 235600)

GASKELL, Dr (John) Philip Wellesley; s of John Wellesley Gaskell, and Olive Elizabeth, *née* Baker; *b* 6 Jan 1926; *Educ* Dragon Sch Oxford, Oundle, King's Coll Cambridge (MA, PhD, LittD); *m* 1, 1948 (m dis) Margaret, da of late H S Bennett; 2 s, 1 da; m 2, 1984 Annette Ursula Beighton; 1 da; *Career* served WWII; Lance-Bombadier RA 1943–47 (BLA 1944–45); King's Coll Cambridge: fell 1953–60, dean 1954–56, tutor 1956–58; head of English Dept and librarian Oundle Sch 1960–62; Glasgow Univ: keeper of Special Collections of University Library 1962–66, warden Maclay Hall 1962–64 and Wolfson Hall 1964–66; Trinity Coll Cambridge: fell 1967–, librarian 1967–86, tutor 1973–83, life fell 1986; Sandars reader in bibliography Univ of Cambridge 1978–79; pt/t prof of literature CIT 1983–88; *Books* The First Editions of William Mason (1951), John Baskerville a bibliography (1959, revised edn 1973), Caught! (1960), A Bibliography of The Foulis Press (1964, revised edn 1986), Morvern Transformed (1968, revised edn 1980), The Library of Trinity College Cambridge (with R Robson, 1971), A New Introduction to Bibliography (1972, revised edns 1974, 1979 and 1985), From Writer to Reader (1978), Trinity College Library - the first 150 years (1980), Ulysses - a Review of Three Texts (jtly, 1989), The Orthotypographia of Hieronymus Hornschuch (ed and translator with P Bradford, 1972); *Style*— Dr Philip Gaskell; ✉ Primrose Cottage, Mawgan, Helston, Cornwall TR12 6AB (☎ 01326 221314)

GASKELL, Sir Richard Kennedy Harvey; kt (1989); s of Dr Kenneth Harvey Gaskell (d 1990), of Bristol, and Jean Winsome, *née* Beaven; *b* 17 Sept 1936; *Educ* Marlborough; *m* 1965, Judith (Judy), da of Roy Douglas Poland (d 1963), of Hedgerley, Bucks; 1 s (Simon Poland Harvey b 1966), 1 da (Susanna Jane b 1968); *Career* admitted slr 1960; articled to Burges Salmon Bristol 1955–60, ptnr Tucketts 1963–85 (asst slr 1960–63), sr ptnr Lawrence Tucketts Bristol 1989– (ptnr 1985–); legal advsr The Laura Ashley Fndn 1988– (tstee 1990–); memb: Crown Ct Rules Ctee 1977–83, Lord Justice Watkins Working Pty on Criminal Trials 1981–83, Lord Chllr's Efficiency Cmmn 1986–88 and 1989–92, Marre Ctee on Future of Legal Profession 1986–88; Law Soc: nat chm Young Slrs' Gp 1964–65, memb Cncl 1969–92; chm Contentious Business Ctee 1979–82, memb Advocacy Trg Team 1968–87 (chm 1974–87); dir Law Soc Tstees 1974–92 (chm 1982–92); Law Soc Servs Ltd 1987–89: dep vice pres 1986–87, vice pres 1987–88, pres 1988–89; memb: Cncl Bristol Law Soc 1965–92 (pres 1978–79), Ctee Somerset Law Soc 1969–92, Criminal Justice Consultative Cncl 1991–94, Criminal Injuries Compensation Bd 1992–; pres Assoc of S Western Law Socs 1980–81; memb: Security Service Tbnl 1989–, Intelligence Serv Tbnl 1994–; tstee Frenchay and Southmead Med Tst 1968–; Wildfowl and Wetlands Tst: memb Cncl 1980–92, memb Exec Ctee 1982–89, chm 1983–87, vice pres 1992–; memb Mgmnt Ctee Bristol 5 Boys' Club 1960–66, hon cases sec Bristol branch NSPCC 1966–76, memb Ct Univ of Bristol 1973– (convocation 1989–); memb Cncl: Bristol Zoo 1988–, SS Great Britain Project 1990– (also Exec Ctee) chm 1992–; memb Advsy Cncl Prince's Youth Business Tst 1988–; Hon LLD Univ of Bristol 1989, Hon LLM Bristol Poly 1989; *Style*— Sir Richard Gaskell; ✉ Bush House, Prince Street, Bristol BS99 7JZ (☎ 0117 929 5295, fax 0117 929 8313)

GASKIN, Catherine Majella Sinclair; da of James Gaskin (d 1980), and Mary Harrington (d 1952); *b* 2 April 1929; *Educ* Holy Cross Coll Aust, Conservatorium of Music Sydney; *m* 1955, Sol Cornberg, s of Joseph Cornberg (d 1928); *Career* author; memb: Soc of Authors, Authors' Guild of America; *Books* This Other Eden (1946), With Every Year (1947), Dust in Sunlight (1950), All Else is Folly (1951), Daughter of the House (1952), Sara Dane (1955), Blake's Reach (1958), Corporation Wife (1960), I Know My Love (1962), The Tilsit Inheritance (1963), The File On Devlin (1965), Edge of Glass (1967), Fiona (1970), A Falcon For A Queen (1972), The Property of A Gentleman (1974), The Lynmara Legacy (1975), The Summer of The Spanish Woman (1977), Family Affairs (1980), Promises (1982), The Ambassador's Women (1985), The Charmed Circle (1988); *Recreations* music, reading; *Style*— Miss Catherine Gaskin; ✉ White Rigg, E Ballaterson, Maughold, IOM IM7 1AR (☎ 01624 812145)

GASKIN, James Joseph; s of James Joseph Gaskin (d 1979), of Berks, and Caroline, *née* Myers (d 1988); *b* 23 April 1945; *Educ* Wembley Co GS; *m* 26 Oct 1968, Linda, da of Thomas William Arundel, of Middx; 1 s (Matthew b 1972), 1 da (Sarah b 1974); *Career* dir 1976–84: Hull Blyth & Co Ltd, Oakwool Gp Ltd, Seatronics (UK) Ltd, Wm Jacks (UK) Ltd, Suttons Gp Ltd; fin dir: Ocean Cory Investment 1979–80, Ocean Cory Energy 1980–82; md Repcon (UK and Ireland) Ltd 1982–84, dep chief exec FIMBRA 1985–94, md Countrywide Independent Advisers Ltd 1994–; FCA; *Recreations* riding, classical music; *Style*— James Gaskin, Esq; ✉ Altura, Brook Street, Kingston Blount, Oxon

GASKIN, Prof John Charles Addison; s of Harry James Gaskin, of Mixbury, Oxfordshire, and Evelyn Mary Addison Gaskin, *née* Taylor, of Aberdeen; *b* 4 April 1936; *Educ* City of Oxford Sch, Univ of Oxford (MA, BLitt); *m* 20 May 1972, Diana Katherine, da of Maurice Dobbin (d 1969); 1 s (Rupert John Addison b 1974), 1 da (Suzette Jane Addison b 1975); *Career* Royal Bank of Scotland 1959–61, prof of naturalistic philosophy Trinity Coll Dublin 1994– (previously jr dean, lectr and prof); FTCD; *Books* incl: Hume's Philosophy of Religion (1978, 1988), The Quest for Eternity (1984), Varieties of Unbelief (1989), The Epicurean Philosophers (1994); *Recreations* eating and dreaming, writing ghost stories, old wine, gardening, walking; *Clubs* Kildare St and University (Dublin);

Style— Prof John C A Gaskin; ✉ Trinity College Dublin, Dublin 2, Ireland (☎ 00 353 1 6081529); Crook Crossing, Netherwitton, Morpeth, Northumberland

GASKIN, Malcolm Graeme Charles; s of Charles Augustus Gaskin (d 1981), of Blyth, Northumberland, and Jean, *née* Denton; *b* 27 Feb 1951; *Educ* Blyth GS, Manchester Poly, Sch of Art and Design; *m* Deborah Ann, da of Michael Loftus, of Osterley, Middx; 2 s (Jack Alexander b 1983, Lewis Ross (twin) b 1983), 1 da (Francesca Vita b 1985); *Career* art dir Leo Burnett 1973–77 (created 'Eau' campaign for Perrier); creative dir: TBWA 1977–81, Woollams Moira Gaskin O'Malley 1987–95, Osprey Park Agency 1995–96; advertising awards for Lego, Land Rover, CIGA, Nursing Recruitment and AIDS; pres Advertising Creative Circle; memb: Creative Circle, D&AD 1975; *Books* Design and Art Direction (1975); *Recreations* gardening, angling, hiking, art; *Clubs* Soho House; *Style*— Malcolm Gaskin, Esq

GASKIN, Prof Maxwell; DFC (1944, Bar 1945); s of Albert Gaskin (d 1960), and Beatrice Ada, *née* Boughey (d 1967); *b* 18 Nov 1921; *Educ* Quarry Bank Sch, Univ of Liverpool (BA, MA); *m* 24 July 1952, Brenda Patricia Rachel, da of Rev William Dale Stewart (d 1954), of Crieff, Perthshire; 1 s (Richard b 1960), 3 da (Rosemary b 1953, Hilary b 1957, Fiona b 1962); *Career* WWII Flt Engr RAF Bomber Cmd 1941–46, 161 Sqdn, 7 (PFF) Sqdn; sr lectr (formerly lectr) in economics Univ of Glasgow 1951–65, Jaffrey prof of political economy Univ of Aberdeen 1965–85 (emeritus prof 1985–); econ conslt to Sec of State for Scotland 1965–87; chm: Bd of Mgmnt Foresterhill and assoc hosps 1972–74, Retail Bespoke Tailoring Wages Cncl 1978–93, Section F Br Assoc 1978–79; memb: Scot Agric Wages Bd 1972–90, Civil Engrg EDC 1978–84, Royal Econ Soc 1951, Scot Econ Soc 1951 (pres 1981–84); *Books* Scottish Banking (1965), North East Scotland - A Survey of its Development Potential (jtly 1969), The Economic Impact of North Sea Oil on Scotland (jtly 1978), The Political Economy of Tolerable Survival (jtly 1981); *Recreations* music, tree planting; *Style*— Prof Maxwell Gaskin, DFC; ✉ Westfield, Ancrum, Roxburghshire TD8 6XA (☎ 01835 830237)

GASS, Lady; Elizabeth Periam Acland Hood; JP (Somerset 1996), DL (Somerset 1995); da of Hon (Arthur) John Palmer Acland-Hood, barrister (d 1964; s of 1 Baron St Audries, Barony extinct 1971), and Dr Phyllis Acland-Hood, *née* Hallett; *b* 2 March 1940; *Educ* Cheltenham Ladies' Coll, Girton Coll Cambridge; *m* 1975, Sir Michael David Irving Gass, KCMG (d 1983, sometime HM Overseas Civil Serv in W Africa, colonial sec Hong Kong, high cmmr for W Pacific, British high cmmr for New Hebrides); *Career* memb Somerset County Cncl 1985–, chm Exmoor National Park Ctee 1989–93, memb Cncl Cheltenham Ladies' Coll 1992–, dir Avalon NHS Tst 1993–96, memb Wessex Regnl Ctee Nat Tst 1994–, cmmr English Heritage 1995–; High Sheriff of Somerset 1994, Vice Lord Lt of Somerset 1996–; *Style*— Lady Gass, JP, DL; ✉ Fairfield, Stogursey, Bridgwater, Somerset TA5 (☎ 01278 732251, fax 01278 732277)

GASSON, Andrew Peter; s of Sidney Samuel Gasson and Elsie Gasson; *b* 18 July 1943; *Educ* Dulwich, Henry Thornton GS, City Univ; *Career* in private practice (specialising in contact lenses) 1972–; pres Contact Lens Soc 1974–75; examiner: Spectacle Makers' Co, Br Coll of Optometrists 1975–84; memb: Cncl Br Contact Lens Assoc 1986, Contact Lens Ctee BSI 1980–82; lectr at numerous sci meetings; chm Wilkie Collins Soc 1981–; Freeman City of London, Liveryman Worshipful Co of Spectacle Makers; FRGS, FRSM, FBOA, FSMC, FBCO, DCLP, GFell American Acad of Optometry; ARPS; *Books* The Contact Lens Manual (jtly, 1991), The Good Cat Food Guide (jtly, 1992), The Good Dog Food Guide (jtly, 1993); *Recreations* antiquarian books, travel, photography, cricket, motoring; *Clubs* MCC; *Style*— Andrew Gasson, Esq; ✉ 6 De Walden St, London W1M 7PH (☎ 0171 224 5959)

GATEHOUSE, Hon Sir Robert Alexander Gatehouse; kt (1985); s of Maj-Gen Alexander Hugh Gatehouse, DSO, MC (d 1964), and Helen Grace, *née* Williams (d 1969); *b* 30 Jan 1924; *Educ* Wellington Coll, Trinity Hall Cambridge (BA); *m* 1, Oct 1950, Henrietta, da of Air Vice-Marshal Sir Oliver Swann (d 1948); m 2, 18 Aug 1966, Pamela Riley, da of late Frederick Fawcett; *Career* served WWII, cmmnd Royal Dragoons, NW Europe 1944; called to the Bar Lincoln's Inn 1950, bencher 1977, QC 1969, judge of the High Court of Justice (Queen's Bench Div) 1985–96; govr Wellington Coll 1970–94; *Style*— The Hon Sir Robert Gatehouse; ✉ Cross Farm, Frimley Green, Camberley, Surrey GU16 6LS

GATENBY, David; s of Robert Richley Gatenby (d 1991), of Shipley, W Yorks, and Catherine Maria, *née* O'Hara (d 1988); *b* 10 Dec 1942; *Educ* Sir Titus Salt HS Shipley; *m* 3 April 1965, Margaret, *née* Tyler; 3 s (Martin Paul b 21 May 1966, Neil Christopher b 23 May 1968, Simon David b 31 May 1975); *Career* civil servant; joined Nat Assistance Bd as exec offr 1961, various mgmnt and specialist positions incl mangr Hull West Office and regnl personnel mangr and area dir Benefits Agency, dir of Info Servs and Business Planning Contributions Agency 1992–95, chief exec UK Passport Agency 1995–; *Recreations* family, motor sport, jogging, travel; *Style*— David Gatenby, Esq; ✉ Chief Executive, United Kingdom Passport Agency, Clive House, 70–78 Petty France, London SW1H 9HD (☎ 0171 271 8500, fax 0171 271 8824)

GATENBY, Ian Cheyne; s of Lt-Col William Gatenby (d 1971), of Esher, Surrey, and Frances Alice, *née* Davies (d 1982); *b* 30 June 1942; *Educ* Royal GS Newcastle-upon-Tyne, Exeter Coll Oxford (MA); *m* 1, Jan 1973 (m dis 1989); 1 s (Piers b 5 Aug 1975), 1 da (Catherine b 9 April 1977); m 2, 30 April 1994, Anne Margaret, *née* Storrs; *Career* admitted slr 1968, assoc ptnr Lovell White & King 1973–77 (articled clerk then asst slr 1966–73), ptnr McKenna & Co 1977– (joined 1975, currently head Planning and Rating Gp); former co-ed Law Soc Gazette business issues, ed property section Kluwer-Harrap on business law, author of numerous articles on planning and rating; memb Law Soc 1988 (memb Planning Panel 1993); legal assoc RTPI 1993; *Recreations* skiing, sailing, English National Opera, gardening; *Clubs* Ski of GB, Ranelagh Sailing; *Style*— Ian Gatenby, Esq; ✉ 54 Southdean Gardens, London SW19 6NU; McKenna & Co, Mitre House, 160 Aldersgate St, London EC1A 4DD (☎ 0171 606 9000)

GATENBY, John Keirl; s of Walter Edmund Gatenby, of Hartlepool, Cleveland, and Mary, *née* Keirl; *b* 26 April 1950; *Educ* Hartlepool GS, Trinity Hall Cambridge (MA, LLM); *m* 20 Sept 1975, (Thelma) Eunice, da of George Edmund Holmes, of The Hyde, London; 2 da (Amy b 1980, Joanna b 1982); *Career* admitted slr 1975; slr Linklaters & Paines 1975–82 (articled clerk 1973–75), admitted barrister and slr NZ 1980, head Litigation Dept Withers 1983–84; Addleshaw Sons & Latham: assoc 1984–85, ptnr 1985–, head Litigation and Dispute Resolution Dept 1991–; occasional speaker on civil procedure and arbitration law, memb Bd Centre for Dispute Resolution, co-opted memb Sub-Ctee of Independent Working Pty of Gen Cncl of the Bar and the Law Soc on Civil Justice; elder Poynton Baptist Church; memb: Amnesty International, Evangelical Alliance, Nat Tst, RSPB, Hallé Concerts Soc, Law Soc, Manchester Law Soc, London Slrs' Litigation Assoc, Int Bar Assoc; MICM 1990, FCIArb 1991; *Books* Notes on Discovery and Inspection of Documents (2 edn 1975), Recovery of Money (4 edn 1976, 7 edn 1989, gen ed 8 edn 1993); *Recreations* music (play piano, organ, clarinet), gardening, photography, computers and walking the dog; *Style*— John Gatenby, Esq; ✉ Addleshaw Sons & Latham, Dennis House, Marsden St, Manchester M2 1JD (☎ 0161 832 5994, fax 0161 832 2250, telex 668886)

GATES, Martin Douglas Clift; s of Douglas Hansford Ellis Gates (d 1980), and Lily Madeline, *née* Pook; *b* 30 March 1934; *Educ* Epsom Coll; *m* 26 Sept 1964, Margaret Florence, da of William Albert George Smith; 2 s (Richard b 4 May 1966, d 7 Feb 1996, Andrew b 5 March 1968); *Career* Nat Serv RAF 1955–57; articled clerk EC Brown & Batts 1951–55 and 1958–59, qualified chartered accountant 1960; audit sr: Finnie Ross Welch & Co 1961–64, Peat Marwick Cassleton Elliott & Co Nigeria 1965–66, Woolley & Waldron 1966–68; ptnr: Woolley & Waldron 1969–77, Whinney Murray & Co 1977–79, Ernst & Whinney 1979–89, Ernst & Young 1989–91 (all following mergers), conslt 1991–; hon treas: Hampshire Remembers D-Day 1993–96, Rhododendron Gp RHS 1995–; FCA 1971; *Recreations* golf, walking, gardening; *Style*— Martin Gates, Esq; ✉ 12 Marlborough Road, Chandlers Ford, Eastleigh, Hampshire SO53 5DH (☎ 01703 252843)

GATES, Paul Christopher Thomas; s of Geoffrey Robert Gates (d 1968), and Marie-Irene, *née* Hardy du Bignon (d 1973); *b* 5 Sept 1936; *Educ* Crosby Hall Acocks Green Birmingham, Regent Street Poly London (City and Guilds Final, 1 Class Photography), Inst of Incorporated Photographers (intermediate); *m* 1, 16 Aug 1962, Dorothy Jean, da of Arthur Magnall (d 1985); 3 da (Alyson Sarah b 14 Nov 1964, Helan Irene Elizabeth b 13 Oct 1967, Celia Wendie b 28 Sept 1969); m 2, 26 April 1995, Vera Anne, da of Ernest Thomas Robey (d 1981); *Career* apprentice/asst photographer to Walden Hammond (Leamington Spa) 1952–53, student Regent Street Poly 1953–54; Nat Serv photographer RAF 1955–57; portait studio photographer Ellistons' Store studio then colour printer Ancor Colour Labs London 1957–58, asst photographer/printer to James Hewitt Buddle (T E Howe Ltd Chatham) 1958–61; Kodak Ltd 1961–93: tech correspondent 1961–67, gen sales asst 1967–68, mktg devpt specialist 1968–79, mktg devpt coordinator 1979–85, assignment Advtg Dept 1985–86, mktg support mangr 1986–93; visiting lectr Medway Coll of Art 1958–69; ed Professional magazine (Kodak) 1988–93; first hon life memb Assoc of Photographers 1994; *Books* The Snapshot Photograph (with Brian Coe, 1977); *Recreations* photography, collecting vintage photographica and books, pastel drawing, French furniture; *Style*— Paul Gates, Esq; ✉ 3 rue des Pres, 50220 Ducey, France (☎ 00 33 33 58 23 46)

GATFIELD, Stephen John; s of Dennis Edward Gatfield, of Barnard Castle, Yorks, and Hilary Marie Gatfield; *b* 2 Sept 1958; *Educ* Churchers Coll Petersfield Hants, City of London Freemans' Sch Ashtead Surrey, Univ of Bristol (BSc), IMD PED (Business Sch Mgmnt Dip); *m* 31 May 1992, Eliza, da of Dr Ronald Tepper; *Career* account planner Leo Burnett advtg 1981–84, account dir Grandfield Rork Collins 1984–85, gp account planner Saatchi & Saatchi 1985–86; Leo Burnett: bd dir 1987–, head of account mgmnt 1988–90, dep md 1990–91, md 1991–96, chief exec 1992–; memb: IPA, IDM, MRS 1981, Strategic Planning Soc 1990; *Recreations* tennis, golf, theatre, jazz, modern art; *Clubs* RAC, Riverside Racquet, IMD Alumni; *Style*— Stephen Gatfield, Esq; ✉ Leo Burnett Ltd, The Leo Burnett Building, 60 Sloane Avenue, London SW3 3XB (☎ 0171 591 9111, fax 0171 591 9126/7)

GATFORD, Ven Ian; s of Frederick Ernest Gatford (d 1952), and Chrissie Lilian, *née* McKeown (d 1993); *b* 15 June 1940; *Educ* Drayton Manor GS Hanwell London, KCL (AKC), St Boniface Coll Warminster Wilts; *m* 31 July 1965, Anne Maire, da of Peter Whitehead (d 1986); 3 da (Sarah b 24 July 1967, Delphis Charlotte b 18 Oct 1973, (Chloe) Tamsin b 5 April 1978), 1 s (Andrew b 30 Aug 1970); *Career* commercial apprentice Taylor Woodrow Ltd 1959–62, KCL 1962–67; ordained 1967, curate St Mary's Clifton Nottingham 1967–71, team vicar Holy Trinity Clifton Nottingham 1971–75, vicar St Martin's Sherwood Nottingham 1975–84, canon residentiary Derby Cathedral 1984– (precentor 1984–93, sub-provost 1990–93), archdeacon of Derby 1993–; community care progs presenter BBC Radio Nottingham 1975–84, religious affrs presenter BBC Radio Derby 1984–93; *Recreations* playing piano, hill walking, music, theatre, reading and speaking German, cycling; *Style*— The Ven the Archdeacon of Derby; ✉ Derby Church House, Full Street, Derby, DE1 3DR (☎ 01332 382233, fax 01332 292969)

GATH, Prof Ann Mary Gethin; da of Sqdn Ldr Henry Gethin Lewis (d 1986), of Penarth, Glamorgan, and Gwendolen Joan, *née* David (d 1989); *b* 4 July 1934; *Educ* Westonbirt Sch, St Hugh's Coll Oxford (DM, MA), St Thomas's Hosp (BM, BCH); *m* 3 Dec 1960 (m dis 1978), Dennis Hanson; 1 s (Alexander b 1964), 2 da (Charlotte (Mrs Miller) b 1962, Victoria (Mrs Echlin) b 1963); *Career* conslt psychiatrist Borocourt Hosp Oxfordshire 1976–79, conslt child and adolescent psychiatrist W Suffolk Hosp 1980–87, conslt in the psychiatry of mental handicap in childhood and adolescence Maudsley and Bethlem Royal Hosps 1987–91, prof of developmental psychiatry UCL 1991–94, conslt in child and adolescent psychiatry (with special interest in developmental disability) Mid Anglian Community NHS Tst 1994–; registrar of the RCPsych 1988–; MRCPsych 1972, FRCPsych; *Books* Down's Syndrome and the Family - The Early Years (1978); *Recreations* carriage driving, Connemara ponies, opera; *Style*— Prof Ann Gath; ✉ Child Health Centre, Hospital Road, Bury St Edmunds

GATHERCOLE, Ven John Robert; s of Robert Gathercole (d 1976), of Turvey, Bedfordshire, and Winifred Mary, *née* Price (d 1982); *b* 23 April 1937; *Educ* Judd Sch Tonbridge, Fitzwilliam Coll Cambridge (BA, MA), Ridley Hall Theol Coll; *m* 6 July 1963, (Joan) Claire, da of Eric Horton London, MBE, of Bexhill-on-Sea; 1 s (Andrew John b 1967), 1 da (Katharine Claire (Kate) b 1965); *Career* curate: St Nicholas Durham City 1962–66, St Bartholomew's Croxdale 1966–70; social and industl advsr to Bishop of Durham 1967–70, industl chaplain Redditch, Diocese of Worcester 1970–87, rural dean Bromsgrove 1978–85, hon canon Worcester Cathedral 1980–, team ldr Worcestershire Industl Mission 1985–91, archdeacon of Dudley 1987–; memb Industl Mission Assoc, sec The Malvern Conf 1991, memb Gen Synod of the Church of England 1995–; *Recreations* vintage cars, motor sport, music; *Clubs* The Vintage Sports Car; *Style*— The Ven The Archdeacon of Dudley; ✉ Diocese of Worcester, The Old Palace, Deansway, Worcester WR1 2JE (☎ and fax 01905 773301)

GATHERCOLE, Richard Benjamin David; s of late Evan Frederick James Gathercole, and Kathleen Mary, *née* Burrows; *b* 28 Sept 1956; *Educ* Salesian Coll, Univ of Leicester (BSc), UCL (MSc); *Career* dir and head of govt sales Hoare Govett Ltd 1981–88, dir of UK govt sales Banque Nationale de Paris 1988–; *Recreations* golf, motorcycle riding; *Style*— Richard Gathercole, Esq; ✉ 71 Vineyard Hill Road, London SW19 7JL; Banque Nationale de Paris, 8–13 King William Street, London EC4N 7DN (☎ 0171 398 9808)

GATLEY, Dr Malcolm Stanley; *b* 3 June 1933; *Educ* Univ of Liverpool (MB ChB, MRCS, LRCP, DLO, DIH); *m* 1, 10 July 1959, Marcia (d 1975); 1 s (Stephen b 22 Sept 1959), 1 da (Denise b 18 Dec 1962); m 2, 9 Sept 1976, Clelia; *Career* conslt occupational physician N Manchester NHS Healthcare Tst 1983–; fndr memb Assoc NHS Occupational Physicians; memb: Manchester District Medicological Soc, BMA; FFOM 1985 (AFOM 1975, MFOM 1982); *Recreations* music, skiing, European languages, travel; *Style*— Dr Malcolm Gatley; ✉ 125 Manchester Rd, Wilmslow, Cheshire SK9 2JN (☎ 01625 524760); N Manchester General Hospital, Occupational Health Dept, Delaunays Rd, Manchester M8 6RB (☎ 0161 720 2727, fax 0161 720 2728); 16 St John St, Manchester M3 4EA (☎ 0161 835 1144, fax 0161 835 1465)

GATTEY, Charles Neilson; s of Francis William Gattey (d 1931), and Victoria Adele De Bücher Neilson (d 1970); *b* 3 Sept 1921; *Educ* St John's Sch Battersea, Univ of London; *Career* playwright, author, broadcaster and lecturer; pres Soc of Civil Serv Authors 1980–; contrib to About the House (jl of Friends of Covent Garden); over 1,000 lectures on subjects incl theatre, opera, remarkable women, the paranormal and the Royal Family, numerous radio and TV bdcasts; *Books* The Bloomer Girls (1968), Gauguin's Astonishing Grandmother (Flora Tristan biography, 1970), A Bird of Curious Plumage (Princess Cristina di Belgiojoso biography, 1971), The Incredible Mrs Van der Elst (1973), They Saw Tomorrow (1977), Queens of Song (1979), The Elephant that Swallowed a Nightingale (1981), Peacocks on the Podium (1982), Great Dining Disasters (1983), Foie Gras and Trumpets (1984), Farmer George's Black Sheep (1986), Excess in

Food and Drink (1987), Visionaries and Seers (1988), In Bed With An Elephant (1989), A Tiger At The Tailor's (1989), Prophecy and Prediction in the Twentieth Century (1990), The Florentine Nightingale (Luisa Tetrazzini biography, 1995); *Plays* The White Falcon 1951, The King Who Could Not Stay The Tide (winner Hampstead Festival of Br Playwrighting Competition); with Zelma Bramley-Moore: The Eleventh Hour, A Spell of Virtue, Man in a Million, By a Hand Unknown, True Love or the Bloomer, The Colour of Anger; numerous radio plays bdcast in UK and abroad, 14 one act plays; co-author: La Nuit des Reines (Radio Paris play) 1953, The White Falcon (BBC TV play) 1956; *Film* co-author The Love Lottery 1954; *Clubs* Garrick; *Style*— Charles Neilson Gattey, Esq; ✉ 15 St Lawrence Drive, Pinner, Middlesex HA5 2RL (☎ 0181 868 4746)

GATTI, Daniele; *b* 6 Nov 1961; *Educ* Artisit Liceo; *m* Silvia Chiesa; *Career* conductor; fndr and musical dir Stradivari (orchestra da camera) 1986–92, res conductor Pomeriffi Musicali Orchestra Milan 1986, AsLi Co 1988–89, conductor Teatro Comunale Bologna 1990–92, res conductor Accademia Nazionale di Santa Cecilia Orchestra 1993–, princ guest conductor Royal Opera House, music dir Royal Philharmonic Orch 1996–; conductor: Teatro alla Scala 1988, Rossini Opera Festival 1988, Carnegie Hall NY 1990, Toronto Symphony Orch 1991, Los Angeles Philharmonic 1991, Orchestre Symphonique de Montréal 1993, Bayerische Runddfunk 1993, LSO 1993, Philadelphia Orch 1993, Cincinnati Symphony Orch 1994, Nat Symphony Orch Washington 1994, Chicago Symphony Orch 1994, San Francisco Symphony 1994, LPO 1994, White Nights Festival St Petersburg 1994, BBC Proms 1995, New York Philharmonic 1996, Berlin Philharmoniker 1997; Opera: Madama Butterfly (Lyric Opera Chicago) 1991, Un Ballo in Maschera (Lyric Opera Chicago) 1992, Puritani and Capuleti e Montecchi (Covent Garden) 1992, Rigoletto (Staatsoper Berlin) 1993, Tancredi (La Scala) 1993, Turandot (Covent Garden) 1994, Madama Butterfly (début Metropolitan Opera NY) 1994, Aida (Covent Garden) 1995; recordings on Decca and Sony Classical labels; winner Int Prize Le Muse Florence 1996; *Recreations* reading, walking, football, chess; *Style*— Daniele Gatti, Esq; ✉ The Royal Philharmonic Orchestra, 16 Clerkenwell Green, London EC1R 0DP (☎ 0171 608 2381, fax 0171 608 1226)

GATTING, Michael William (Mike); OBE (1987); s of William Alfred Gatting, and Vera Mavis, *née* Lucas; *b* 6 June 1957; *Educ* John Kelly Boys' HS; *m* 9 Sept 1980, Elaine Elizabeth, da of late Bernard and Jean Mabbott; 2 s (Andrew Michael Bernard b 21 Jan 1983, James Ian William b 11 July 1986; *Career* professional cricketer; Middlesex CCC: debut 1975, awarded county cap 1977, capt 1983–, benefit 1988; former rep Young England under 15, 17 and 19; England: 74 test matches 1977–93, capt 1986–88 (23 tests), 85 one day ints, memb 9 overseas tours; capt unofficial England team touring S Africa 1989/90 (subsequently banned from test cricket until winter 1992), memb England team touring India and Sri Lanka 1992/93 and Aust 1994/95; Young Cricketer of the Year 1981; *Books* Limited Overs (1986), 1986–87 Triumph in Australia, Leading from the Front (autobiography, 1988); *Recreations* reading science fiction thrillers, listening to music; *Style*— Mike Gatting, Esq, OBE; ✉ Middlesex CCC, Lord's Cricket Ground, London NW8 8QN (☎ 0171 289 1300)

GAU, John Glen Mackay; CBE (1989); s of Cullis William Gau (d 1944), and Nan, *née* Munro (d 1992); *b* 25 March 1940; *Educ* Haileybury and ISC, Trinity Hall Cambridge (BA), Univ of Wisconsin USA; *m* 2 Sept 1966, Susan, da of John William Tebbs (d 1976); 2 s (William Merlin b 17 Aug 1972, Christopher Wilkie b 1 July 1978); *Career* BBC TV: prodr current affairs 1966–72, dep ed Midweek 1973–74, ed Nationwide 1975–78, head of current affairs 1978–81; independent and chief exec John Gau Productions 1981–88, dep chief exec and dir progs British Satellite Broadcasting 1988–90, jt chief exec John Gau Productions 1991–; chm: Ind Prog Prodrs Assoc 1984–86, RTS 1986–89; dir Channel 4 Bd 1985–88; fell RTS 1985; *Books* Soldiers (with John Keegan and Dr Richard Holmes, 1985), Lights, Camera, Action! (with Tony Bilbow, 1995); *Style*— John Gau, Esq, CBE; ✉ John Gau Productions, Burston House, 1 Burston Rd, London SW15 6AR (☎ 0181 788 8811)

GAULTER, Andrew Martin; s of Derek Vivian Gaulter, of Chorleywood, Herts, and Edith Irene, *née* Shackleton (d 1996); *b* 4 April 1951; *Educ* Merchant Taylors', Peterhouse Cambridge (exhibitioner, BA); *m* 30 Sept 1978, Susan Jane Wright; 2 da; *Career* articled clerk Messrs Beachcrofts London, admitted slr 1976; co sec: J Henry Schroder & Co Ltd 1990– (joined 1976), Schroders plc (holding co of Schroder Group) 1990–; memb: Law Soc, Law Soc Commerce and Industry Gp; *Recreations* golf; *Style*— Andrew Gaulter, Esq; ✉ Schroders plc, 120 Cheapside, London EC2V 6DS (☎ 0171 382 6329, fax 0171 382 3977)

GAULTER, Derek Vivian; CBE (1978); s of Jack Rudolph Gaulter, MC (d 1967), of Cleveleys, nr Blackpool, and Muriel, *née* Westworth (d 1982); *b* 10 Dec 1924; *Educ* Denstone Coll, Peterhouse Cambridge; *m* 1 Jan 1949, Edith Irene (d 1996), da of Frederick Norman Shackleton (d 1964), of Hunstanton, Norfolk; 1 s (Andrew b 1951), 3 da (Briony b 1953, Catherine b 1959, Deborah b 1964); *Career* Sub Lt RNVR 1943–46 (serv MTBs in N Sea and minesweepers in Far East); called to the Bar Gray's Inn 1949, practising Common Law Bar (Manchester) 1949–54; Fedn of Civil Engrg Contractors: successively legal sec, gen sec, dep DG, DG 1967; chm Construction Indust Trg Bd 1985–90; former memb Cncl and President's Ctee CBI; former memb Civil Engrg Econ Devpt Ctee; tstee The Woodland Tst 1995–; companion Inst of Civil Engrs 1983; *Recreations* gardening, travel, photography; *Style*— Derek Gaulter, Esq, CBE; ✉ Philips Hill, Old Shire Lane, Chorleywood, Herfordshire WD3 5PW

GAUME, Bernard Jean; s of Marie Henri Robert (d 1974), of Diou Allier, France, and Eugenie Francoise, *née* Prunier (d 1974); *b* 14 Oct 1934; *Educ* College Amede Gasquet Clermont Ferrand, Chambre des Metiers du Loiret France (Certificat de Compagnon); *m* 20 Dec 1962, Daphne Elizabeth, da of Frederick Arthur Perry; 1 s (Jean-Pierre Louis b 26 March 1967), 1 da (Helene Elizabeth b 1 May 1963); *Career* chef; apprentice under Marconet Louis Hotel de l'Allier Moulins France 1951–53, chef poissonier The Savoy Hotel London 1959–60, sous chef Hotel de l'Abbaye Talloires June-Oct 1960, chef de cuisine Restaurant Meunier Autun 1960–61; chef saucier: Les Bergues Geneva 1961–62, Gleneagles Hotel Perthshire March-Sept 1962, Americana of New York 1962–63, Regency Hotel New York March-Oct 1963; sous chef Hotel Intercontinental Geneva 1964–65; exec chef: Hotel Intercontinental Dublin 1965–68, Hyatt Carlton Tower London 1968–; Maitrise Escoffier 1972, Maitre Cuisinier de France 1982, Medaille des Operations de Securite et de l'Ordre en AFN Chevalier du Merite Agricole, Catey Chef of the Year Award 1992; memb: Mutuelle des Cuisiniers de France, Academie Culinaire de France; *Recreations* fishing; *Style*— Bernard Gaume, Esq; ✉ Hyatt Carlton Tower Hotel, Cadogan Place, London SW1X 9PY (☎ 0171 235 5411)

GAUNT, Jonathan Robert; QC (1991); s of Dr Brian Gaunt, and Dr Mary Joyce Gaunt, *née* Hudson; *b* 3 Nov 1947; *Educ* St Peter's Coll, Radley (exhibitioner), Univ Coll Oxford (scholar, BA), Lincoln's Inn (Mansfield scholar); *m* 18 Jan 1975, Lynn Adele, da of Terence Arthur John Dennis; 1 da (Arabella b 10 April 1985); *Career* called to the Bar Lincoln's Inn 1972, jt head of chambers; *Books* Halsbury's Law of England vol 27 Landlord and Tenant (ed 1981 and 1984 edns), Gale on Easements (16 edn, 1996); *Recreations* golf, sailing; *Clubs* North Middx Golf; *Style*— Jonathan Gaunt, Esq, QC; ✉ Falcon Chambers, Falcon Court, London EC4Y 1AA (☎ 0171 353 2484, fax 0171 353 1261)

GAUNT, Dr Lawrence Michael; s of Robert Gaunt (d 1972), of London, and Lily, *née* Phillips; *b* 2 Oct 1934; *Educ* Ilford Co HS, The London Hosp (BDS, LDS, Harold Final prize Clinical Dental Surgery); *m* 31 March 1957, Ruth Margarette, da of late William Trackman; 3 s (Colin Murry b 25 Sept 1959, Peter Tony b 6 Nov 1961, David Ramon b 26 April 1964); *Career* house surgn The London Hosp 1957, in gen dental practice 1958–70, registrar Guy's Hosp 1960, in private practice Harley St 1970–; ptnr Lawrence Antiques (Victorian & Georgian jewellery), computer software specialist LMG Random Data; memb RCS; *Recreations* bridge, computing; *Clubs* New Amersham Bridge; *Style*— Dr Lawrence M Gaunt; ✉ 92 Harley St, London W1N 1AF (☎ 0171 935 4392, 0171 486 9359, fax 0181 958 9699)

GAUNT, William Charles Anthony; s of William Ivor Gaunt, of N Yorks, and Helen, *née* Bushell; *b* 3 April 1937; *Educ* Fulneck Sch Pudsey, Giggleswick Sch N Yorks, RADA, Waco Univ Texas USA; *m* 7 Sept 1974, Carolyn Joan, da of Charles Lyster; 1 s (William Albert (Albie) b 28 Nov 1978), 1 da (Matilda (Tilly) b 15 June 1977); *Career* actor; former artistic dir Liverpool Playhouse; *Theatre* incl: The Flip Side (Apollo), The Boys in the Band (Wyndhams), When Did You Last See Your Trousers (Garrick), Run For Your Wife! (Whitehall), Having a Ball (Comedy), Murder by Misadventure (Vaudeville and Whitehall), Travels with My Aunt (Wyndhams and Whitehall), The Miracle Worker (Comedy and Wyndhams); as dir: Macbeth (Open Air Theatre Regent's Park), One for the Road (Lyric), Here's a Funny Thing (Fortune); also numerous credits as actor/dir overseas; *Television* series incl: Sergeant Cork, The Champions, No Place Like Home, Gentleman's Club, Capstick's Law, GBH, Next of Kin (BBC) 1995; *Recreations* reading, walking, music, theatre, films; *Style*— William Gaunt, Esq; ✉ c/o London Management, 2–4 Noel Street, London W1V 3RB (☎ 0171 287 9000, fax 0171 287 3036)

GAUNTLETT, (Malcolm) Victor; s of Michael Errington Gauntlett (d 1971), and Adele Sylvia Dolores, *née* Montgomerie; *b* 20 May 1942; *Educ* St Marylebone GS; *m* 22 Oct 1966, Jean, da of James Brazier, of Burwarton, Shropshire; 3 s (Michael b 1971, Mark b 1981, Richard b 1982), 1 da (Sarah b 1969); *Career* exec chm: Pace Petroleum Ltd 1972–83, Aston Martin Lagonda Ltd 1981–91; chm: Aston Martin Lagonda Group Ltd 1984–91, Proteus Petroleum Ltd 1988–; vice chm The Air League; FRSA, FIMI, FInstPet; *Recreations* motoring, music, aviation; *Clubs* Carlton, Cavalry and Guards', RAC, MCC; *Style*— Victor Gauntlett, Esq; ✉ 1 Eastgate House, East Street, Andover, Hampshire SP10 1EP (☎ 01264 334440, fax 01264 334442)

GAUTREY, Peter; CMG (1972), CVO (1961); s of Robert Harry Gautrey (d 1961), of Surrey, and Hilda Morris (d 1972); *b* 17 Sept 1918; *Educ* Abbotsholme Sch Derbyshire; *m* 1947, Marguerite Etta, da of Horace Ewart Uncles (d 1963); 1 s (Christopher b 1948), 1 da (Sarah Jennifer b 1951); *Career* WWII Army Capt 1939–46; Home Office 1936, CRO 1948; first sec: Br Embassy Dublin 1950–53, New Delhi 1955–57; cnsllr New Delhi 1960–63, dep high cmmr Bombay 1963–65, inspr Corps of Dip Serv 1965–68; high cmmr: Swaziland 1968–72, Brunei 1972–75, Guyana (concurrently ambass Surinam) 1975–78; DK (Brunei) 1972; *Recreations* walking, music; *Style*— Peter Gautrey, CMG, CVO; ✉ 24 Fort Rd, Guildford, Surrey GU1 3TE (☎ 01483 568407)

GAVIN, Maj-Gen James Merricks Lewis; CB (1967), CBE (1963, OBE 1953); s of Joseph Merricks Gavin (d 1945), of Antofagasta, Chile, and Frances Edith, *née* Lewis (d 1955); *b* 28 July 1911; *Educ* Uppingham, Univ of Cambridge (MA); *m* 1942, Barbara Anne Elizabeth (d 1994), da of Gp Capt Charles Geoffrey Murray, CBE (d 1962), of Hayling Island, Hants; 1 s (Angus), 2 da (Lindy, Janine); *Career* cmmnd 2 Lt RE 1931, served WWII Far East, ME, Italy and France, also post-war in USA, Germany and France, Maj-Gen at SHAPE 1964–67; dir (Technical) British Standards Institution 1967–76; memb Everest Expedition 1936; *Recreations* yachting (Corruna), skiing, climbing; *Clubs* Royal Yacht Sqdn, Royal Cruising, Royal Ocean Racing, Alpine; *Style*— Maj-Gen James Gavin, CB, CBE; ✉ Maysleith, Milland, Liphook, Hants GU30 7JN

GAVIN, Kenneth George (Kent); s of George Henry Gavin (d 1970), of London, and Norah Sylvia, *née* Vine (d 1993); *b* 11 Aug 1939; *Educ* Tollington Park London; *m* (m dis), Thelma, *née* Diggins; 2 da (Stephanie Kim b 22 Dec 1961, Tracy June b 8 March 1963); *Career* Nat Serv RAF 1959–61; apprentice then freelance photographer Keystone Press Agency, currently chief photographer Daily Mirror (joined 1965); FRPS; *Awards* winner of over 135 incl: Br Press Photographer of the Year (four times), Royal Photographer of the Year (nine) times, Royal Photographer of the Decade (twice), World Press News Feature Photographer of the Year, Ilford News Picture of the Age 25th Anniversary Photographic Awards 1992; *Books* Flash Bang Wallop - Inside Stories of Fleet Street's Top Press Photographers, Princely Marriage (with Anthony Holden); *Recreations* football, gardening, reading, Koi carp; *Clubs* Tramp; *Style*— Kent Gavin, Esq; ✉ Daily Mirror, 1 Canada Square, Canary Wharf, London E14 5NU

GAWKRODGER, Dr David John; s of Walter Robert Gawkroger, of Keynsham, Bristol, and Elma Jean, *née* Chalmers; *b* 14 Nov 1953; *Educ* King Edward's Sch Bath, Univ of Birmingham (MB ChB, MD); *Career* house physician and surgn Queen Elizabeth Hosp Birmingham 1976–77, med sr house offr and registrar N Staffordshire Hosp Centre Stoke-on-Trent 1977–81, registrar and sr registrar in dermatology Royal Infirmary Edinburgh 1981–85, lectr in dermatology Univ of Edinburgh 1985–88, conslt dermatologist Royal Hallamshire Hosp Sheffield and clinical lectr in dermatology Univ of Sheffield 1988–; ed-elect Br Jl of Dermatology 1996– (co-ed 1994–96); hon sec Dowling Club 1987–88, referee Med Res Cncl NZ; memb Br Assoc of Dermatologists; MRCP, FRCPEd, FRCP; *Books* Skin Disorders in the Elderly (contrib, 1988), Immunology (contrib, 2 edn, 1989), Dermatology - An Illustrated Colour Text (1992); *Recreations* painting, drawing; *Style*— Dr David Gawkrodger; ✉ Department of Dermatology, Royal Hallamshire Hospital, Glossop Rd, Sheffield S10 2JF (☎ 0114 271 2203)

GAWLER, Dr Jeffrey; *b* 17 July 1945; *Educ* St Olave's GS London, Med Coll St Bartholomew's Hosp Univ of London (MB BS); *m* 19 Dec 1970, Janet Mary; 1 s (Robert b 12 March 1973), 3 da (Ruth b 23 Sept 1975, Susan b 4 April 1978, Sarah b 6 Oct 1980); *Career* head conslt Dept of Neurology Royal London and St Bartholomew's Hosps 1995– (conslt neurologist 1976–); memb: BMA, Assoc Br Neurologists; FRCP; *Books* Neurology and Computed Tomography; *Recreations* literature, oenology, hill-walking; *Style*— Dr Jeffrey Gawler; ✉ 149 Harley St, London W1N 2DE (☎ 0171 224 0640, fax 0171 935 7245); Royal London Hospital, London E1 1BB (☎ 0171 377 7214)

GAY, Bramwell Clifford (Bram); s of Clifford Gay, of Rhondda, and Effield, *née* Brown; *b* 19 Sept 1930; *Educ* Porth County Sch, Birmingham Sch of Music, Guildhall Sch of Music; *m* 9 Jan 1954, Margaret Ivy, da of late Augustus Bywater; 3 s (Peter John Noel b 1956, David b 1957, Jonathan Michael b 1958); *Career* served Scots Guards 1949–53; princ trumpet: City of Birmingham Symphony Orch 1953–60, Hallé Orch 1960–69, Royal Opera House Covent Garden 1969–74; orchestral dir Royal Opera House 1974–95; fndr: CBSO Brass Ensemble, Hallé Brass Consort, Granada Brass Band Festival 1971–87; ed Brass Music (Novello & Co) 1967–; LRAM 1950; Liveryman Worshipful Co of Musicians; *Recreations* music, boating; *Style*— Bram Gay, Esq; ✉ 46 Victoria Crescent, Wyton, Huntingdon PE17 2AL (☎ and fax 01480 469636)

GAY, Rear Adm George Wilsmore; CB (1969), MBE (1946), DSC (1943), JP (Plymouth 1970); s of George Murch Gay, Engr Cdr RN (d 1933), and Olive Trounsell, *née* Allen (d 1971); *b* 2 Oct 1913; *Educ* Eastmans Sch Southsea, The Nautical Coll Pangbourne, RN Engrg Coll Keyham; *m* 15 Feb 1941, Nancy Agnes, da of Robert John Hinton Clark, MBE (d 1976), of Plymouth, Devon; 2 s (John b 1943, Paul b 1945), 1 da (Jane b 1948); *Career* RN 1930–69; WWII submarines, Cdr 1947, Capt 1958; CO HMS Sultan 1960–63; Chief Staff Offr material to Flag Offr Submarines 1963–66; Rear Adm 1967; dir gen Naval Trg 1967–69; ret 1969; FIMechE; *Recreations* fishing, gardening; *Style*— Rear Adm George Gay, CB, MBE, DSC, JP; ✉ 29 Whiteford Rd, Mannamead, Plymouth, Devon PL3 5LU (☎ 01752 664486)

GAY, John Edward; s of Edward John Clement Gay (d 1980), and Florence Ellen, *née* Coombs; *b* 5 May 1934; *Educ* Bishop Wordsworth Sch Salisbury; *m* 15 Sept 1962, Sharon, da of Fred Duke, of Bromley, Kent; 1 s (Richard James Clement b 1967), 3 da (Katharine (Mrs Harrison) b 1963, Mary Louise (Mrs Navey) b 1964, Margaret Elizabeth b 1969); *Career* Nat Serv 1957–59: 2 Lt Loyal NL Regt, active serv Malaya and Hong Kong (GSM with Malaya Bar); articled clerk Fawcett Brown & Pinnegar Salisbury 1951–56, personal asst to Tax Ptnr Champness & Co 1959–62; ptnr: Dawson & Gordon 1966–78 (mangr 1962–66), Miles Dawson & Co (following merger) 1978–81; sr ptnr Spicer & Oppenheim International (following merger) 1987–90 (managing ptnr 1981–87), sr ptnr Touche Ross & Co 1990–91; ret; ICAEW: chm Bournemouth Students Gp 1967–68, chm Bournemouth Local Membs Gp 1972–73 (sec 1968–71), careers advsr Bournemouth CA 1971–79, memb SOSCA Soc Ctee 1971–81 (pres 1979–80); hon auditor Bournemouth Private Hotel & Guest House Assoc 1965–91, hon treas Bournemouth Speakers Club 1968–95, memb Ctee Fisheads Club 1975–, pres Rotary Club of Bournemouth 1990–91; St Saviour's Church Iford: hon treas 1973–80, warden 1980–86, vice chm 1988–91, reader 1995–; chm CAB Bournemouth 1991–; Neighbourhood Watch: treas 1993–, vice chair 1995–; FCA 1968 (ACA 1957); *Recreations* computers, books, crosswords, music, opera, glass etching, oil painting, sailing, walking, discovering France; *Clubs* Bournemouth Constitutional, Rotary Club of Bournemouth, Fishheads, 3/4d Luncheon; *Style*— John Gay, Esq; ✉ Sandown, 76 Durrington Rd, Bournemouth, Dorset BH7 6PZ (☎ 01202 428474)

GAY, Richard; s of Roy Gay, of Hull, and Carol, *née* Butler; *b* 9 March 1969; *Educ* Eastfield JHS, Sydney Smith SHS; *m* Feb 1996, Kathleen, da of Ben Streater; *Career* rugby league full back; played for various school, colts and under 19 teams and also Charters Towers in N Queensland Australia; formerly with Hull FC: debut v Castleford 1989, 224 appearances, 61 tries; currently with Castleford Tigers RLFC; England: memb team v Wales 1995 (scored 1 try), v France 1995; non sporting career: welder, lifeguard, swimming, teacher, swimming pool supervisor, circuit training instr; *Recreations* all sports in general; *Style*— Richard Gay, Esq; ✉ c/o Castleford Tigers RLFC, Wheldon Road, Castleford, West Yorkshire WF10 2SD

GAYA, Dr Harold; s of Ralph Gaya (d 1994), and Anne, *née* Salamon (d 1964); *b* 15 Oct 1940; *Educ* Glasgow HS, Univ of Glasgow (MB ChB); *m* 1 June 1969, Celia, da of Ronald Mark Jeffries (d 1964); 3 s (Andrew b 1970, David b 1972, Richard b 1974); *Career* lectr in microbiology St Bartholomew's Hosp Med Coll London 1968–71, conslt bacteriologist and lectr Royal Postgrad Med Sch Hammersmith Hosp London 1971–74, reader in bacteriology Wright-Fleming Inst St Mary's Hosp Med Sch and hon conslt bacteriologist St Mary's Hosp 1974–80; conslt microbiologist: Nat Heart Hosp 1980–89, London Chest Hosp 1980–95, Royal Brompton Hosp 1980–, The London Clinic 1983–; hon sr lectr Nat Heart and Lung Inst 1980–; treas Int Anti-Microbial Therapy Co-op Gp of the Euro Orgn for Res and Treatment of Cancer 1987– (fndr chm 1973–78, co-ordinating sec and treas 1978–87); author of numerous pubns on prevention and treatment of infection; FRSM 1969, FRCPath 1982 (MRCPath 1970), corresponding fell Infectious Diseases Soc of America 1983; *Recreations* bridge, travel, music, photography; *Clubs* Royal Soc Med; *Style*— Dr Harold Gaya; ✉ 10 Mowbray Rd, Edgware, Middx HA8 8JQ; Royal Brompton Hospital, Sydney Street, London SW3 6NP (☎ 0171 351 8440, fax 0171 351 8443)

GAYLER, Paul Michael; s of Stanley Joseph Gayler, of Clacton-on-Sea, and Lilian May, *née* Hall (d 1993); *b* 7 July 1955; *Educ* Priory Comp Sch Dagenham Essex, Grays Thurrock Tech Coll; *m* 30 June 1979, Anita Pauline, da of Alan Blackburn; 2 s (Lee Daniel b 24 July 1983, Ryan James b 25 April 1985), 2 da (Lauren Marie b 21 April 1987, Rosie Adele b 11 Feb 1992); *Career* chef; apprenticeship Palace Hotel Torquay 1974–75, trg Royal Garden Hotel London 1975–80, sous chef Dorchester Hotel London 1980–82; head chef: Inigo Jones Restaurant London 1982–89 (dir 1985–89), Halkin Hotel Belgravia 1990–91; exec chef Lanesborough Hotel London 1991–; winner Mouton Cadet competition 1979–82, finalist Pierre Tattinger competition Paris (later Br judge), various Gold & Silver medals Germany, Switzerland, Austria and Britain, judge Roux Scholarship 1989, 1990 and 1991; Master Craftsman Cookery and Food Assoc, Palmes Culinaire Assoc Culinaire Française; memb: Académie Culinaire de France, Chefs and Cooks Circle, Guild de Fromagers de France, Craft Guild of Chefs, Master Chefs of GB; *Style*— Paul Gayler, Esq; ✉ The Lanesborough Hotel, Hyde Park Corner, London SW1X 7TA (chef's office ☎ 0171 333 7009, fax 0171 259 5606)

GAYMER, Janet Marion; da of Ronald Frank Craddock (d 1994), of Nuneaton, Warks, and Marion Clara, *née* Stringer (d 1988); *b* 11 July 1947; *Educ* Nuneaton HS for Girls, St Hilda's Coll Oxford (MA), LSE (LLM); *m* 4 Sept 1971, John Michael Gaymer, s of Kenneth John Gaymer, of Great Bookham, Surrey; 2 da (Helen b 1977, Natalie b 1979); *Career* admitted slr 1973; ptnr and head Employment and Immigration Law Dept Simmons & Simmons 1977–; chm Employment Law Ctee Law Soc 1993–96 (memb 1987), former chm Employment Law Sub Ctee City of London Law Soc 1987, fndr chm Employment Lawyers Assoc 1993; memb Editorial Advsy Bd: Sweet & Maxwell's Encyclopaedia of Employment Law 1987, Tolley's Health and Safety at Work 1995; memb: Justice Ctee Industl Tbnls 1987, Cncl ACAS 1995–, Cncl Justice 1995–; Freeman Worshipful Co of Slrs 1977; affiliate IPD, memb Law Soc; *Recreations* learning to play the flute, swimming, theatre, music; *Clubs* RAF; *Style*— Mrs Janet Gaymer; ✉ Simmons & Simmons, 21 Wilson Street, London EC2M 2TQ (☎ 0171 628 2020, fax 0171 628 2070, telex 888562 SIMMON G)

GAYMER, Vivien Murray; *née* Gall; da of Dr Louis Adrian Murray Gall (d 1973), of Spalding, Lincs and Patricia Violet, *née* Boothby, JP (d 1989); *Educ* Felixstowe Coll, Northfield Sch Mass USA (ESU scholar), Univ of Sheffield (LLB); *Career* called to the Bar Middle Temple 1971; counsel Mobil Oil London and NY 1975–84, co sec Enterprise Oil plc 1991– (head of legal affrs 1984–); tstee Petroleum and Mineral Law Educn Tst; memb: Editorial Advsy Bd International Co and Commercial Law Review, Bd of Tstees Parentline UK Ltd; *Recreations* opera, theatre and village life; *Style*— Mrs Vivien Gaymer; ✉ Enterprise Oil plc, Grand Buildings, Trafalgar Square, London WC2N 5EJ (☎ 0171 925 4000, fax 0171 925 4321, telex 8950611 EPRISE G)

GAYTON, Alan William; OBE (1994), JP (Leicester 1963); s of Frank Gayton (d 1961), of Leicester, and Susannah Edith Anne Drackley (d 1975); *b* 21 June 1923; *Educ* Wyggeston GS Leicester, LSE, Sandhurst; *m* 1, Dec 1948 (m dis), Jean Urquhart; 1 s (John Charles b 1956), 1 da (Susan Mary b 1953); m 2, Feb 1974, Jean Frances, da of Frank Kelly (d 1976), of Leicester; *Career* WWII served N Africa and Italy, Capt 17/21 Lancers; chm Gayton Graham Advertising Ltd Leicester; chm Leicester City Bench 1987–92; FIPA; *Recreations* golf, theatre; *Style*— Alan W Gayton, Esq, OBE, JP; ✉ Gayton Graham Ltd, 94 London Road, Leicester LE2 0QS (☎ 0116 233 7711)

GAZDAR, Prof Gerald James Michael; s of John Gazdar (d 1966), of Hatfield, and Kathleen, *née* Cooper (d 1993); *b* 24 Feb 1950; *Educ* Heath Mount Sch, Bradfield Coll, UEA (BA), Univ of Reading (MA, PhD); *Career* Univ of Sussex: lectr in linguistics 1975–80, reader in linguistics 1980–84, reader in artificial intelligence and linguistics 1984–85, prof of computational linguistics 1985–, dean Sch of Cognitive and Computing Scis 1988–93; fell Center for Advanced Study in the Behavioral Scis Stanford Univ 1984–85; memb: ACL, ASL, LAGB, AAAI, ACM; FBA 1988; *Books* Pragmatics (1979), Order, Concord and Constituency (with Klein and Pullum, 1983), Generalized Phrase Structure Grammar (with Klein, Pullum and Sag, 1985), New Horizons in Linguistics II (with Lyons, Coates and Deuchar, 1987), Natural Language Processing in the 1980s (with Franz, Osborne, Evans, 1987), Natural Language Processing in Prolog/Lisp/Pop-11 (with Mellish, 1989); *Style*— Prof Gerald Gazdar, FBA; ✉ School of Cognitive and Computing Sciences, University of Sussex, Brighton BN1 9QH (☎ 01273 678029, fax 01273 671320)

GAZE, Dr Mark Nicholas; s of John Owen Gaze (d 1987), and May Susan, *née* Skelton; *b* 6 Feb 1958; *Educ* Med Coll of St Bartholomew's Hosp Univ of London (MB BS MD); *m* 22 June 1987, Dr Janet Ann Wilson, da of Dr Henry Donald Wilson (d 1991); 1 s (Donald John b 1991); *Career* house surgn Southend Hosp Essex 1981–82, house physician St Bartholomew's Hosp London 1982; sr house offr in med: Severalls Hosp Colchester 1983, St Mary's Hosp Portsmouth 1983–85; registrar in radiation oncology Royal Infirmary and Western Gen Hosp Edinburgh 1985–87; lectr in radiation oncology: Univ of Edinburgh 1987–89, Univ of Glasgow 1989–92, sr registrar in clinical oncology Beatson Oncology Centre Glasgow 1992–93, conslt oncologist UCL Hosps and Great Ormond Street Hosp for Children 1993–, hon sr lectr UCL and Inst of Child Health Univ of London 1993–; chm Collegiate Membs Ctee RCPE 1989–90 (memb Cncl 1988–90); MRCP 1984, FRCR 1988, FRCPEd 1995; *Books* Stell and Maran's Head and Neck Surgery (3 edn, 1993); *Style*— Dr Mark Gaze; ✉ Meyerstein Institute of Oncology, The Middlesex Hospital, Mortimer Street, London W1N 8AA (☎ 0171 636 8333, fax 0171 436 0160)

GAZE, Dr (Raymond) Michael; s of William Mercer Gaze (d 1959), of Blue Mills, Wickham Bishops, Essex, and Kathleen Grace, *née* Bowhill (d 1974); *b* 22 June 1927; *Educ* Sch of Med of the Royal Colls Edinburgh, Univ of Oxford (BA, DPhil); *m* 20 March 1957, Robinetta Mary, da of Prof Roger Noel Armfelt (d 1955), of Woodlea, Shadwell Lane, Leeds; 2 da (Harriet Carlin b 1958, Hannah Mary b 1959), 1 s (Julian Mercer (twin) b 1959); *Career* MO RAMC 1953–55; house physician Chelmsford and Essex Hosp 1949, lectr in physiology Univ of Edinburgh 1955–62, Alan Johnston Lawrence and Moseley res fell of the Royal Soc 1962–66, reader in physiology Univ of Edinburgh 1966–70, head Div of Developmental Biology Nat Inst Med Res London 1970–83, head MRC Neural Devpt and Regeneration Gp Dept of Zoology Univ of Edinburgh 1984–92; FRSE 1964, FRS 1972; *Books* The Formation of Nerve Connections (1970); author of numerous scientific papers; *Recreations* hill walking, drawing, music; *Style*— Dr Michael Gaze, FRS, FRSE; ✉ 37 Sciennes Road, Edinburgh EH9 1NS

GAZE, Nigel Raymond; s of Raymond Ernest Gaze, of Knutsford Cheshire, and Beatrice Maud, *née* Caswell; *b* 11 Feb 1943; *Educ* Prescot GS, Univ of Liverpool (MB ChB), Univ of London (BMus); *m* 6 Aug 1966, Heather Winifred, da of Ronald Douglas Richardson, of Oakley House, Leeswood, Mold, Clwyd; 3 s (Richard b 8 April 1972, Thomas b 27 Aug 1974, Harry b 29 March 1985), 3 da (Julia b 4 Aug 1967, Celia b 23 March 1970, Mary b 7 Jan 1979); *Career* conslt plastic surgn Royal Preston and Blackpool Victoria Hosps 1980–; contrib various articles on med subjects in jls; organist, accompanist and composer; musical dir Elizabethan Singers, accompanied Hutton GS Chamber Choir on the record And My Heart Shall Be There, organist Clitheroe Assoc of Church Choirs and Fishergate Baptist Church, several published compositions for organ and choir; memb: Victorian Soc, RSCM, Preston Select Vestry, CPRE, Nat Tst, Br Inst of Organ Studies, Cncl Br Assoc of Aesthetic Plastic Surgns; memb: BMA, Br Assoc Plastic Surgns, Hospital Consultants and Specialists Assoc; FRCS, FRCSEd, FRCO, FTCL, FVCM, LRAM, MBAE; *Books* Year Book of Plastic Surgery (contrib, 1981); *Recreations* collecting books and interesting junk, architecture, DIY; *Style*— Nigel Gaze, Esq; ✉ Priory House, 35 Priory Lane, Penwortham, Preston, Lancs PR1 0AR (☎ 01772 743821); Royal Preston Hospital, Sharoe Green Lane, Fulwood, Preston, Lancs PR2 9HT (☎ 01772 716565); Fulwood Hall Hospital, Midgery Lane, Fulwood, Preston, Lancs PR2 5SX

GAZZARD, Dr Brian George; s of Edward George Gazzard, and Elizabeth, *née* Hill; *b* 4 April 1946; *Educ* Cambridge Univ (MA, MD); *m* 21 June 1969, Joanna Alice, da of Thomas Binson Koeller; 3 s (Simon, Nicholas, Luke); *Career* sr registrar Liver Unit KCH 1974–76, St Bartholomew's Hosp 1976–78; conslt physician and AIDS dir Westminster and St Stephen's Hosps 1978–; memb various ctees organising res and fin for AIDS patients; FRCP; *Books* Peptic Ulcer (1988), Gastroenterological Manifestations of AIDS, Clinics in Gastroenterology (1988); *Recreations* gardening; *Style*— Dr Brian Gazzard; ✉ Old Blew House, Dulwich Common, London SE21 (☎ 0171 693 1151); 138 Harley St, London W1 (☎ 0181 746 8239, fax 0181 834 4240, telex 919263 VHAG)

GAZZARD, Michael John (Mike); s of Kenneth Howard Gazzard, of Littlehaven, Sunbury on Thames, Middx, and Nancy Campbell, *née* Lawrence; *b* 20 June 1949; *Educ* Oakham Sch Oakham Rutland, Enfield Coll of Technol Enfield Middx (BA), City Univ London (MSc); *m* Brenda, *née* Porth; 1 da (Hannah Sascha Louise b 9 July 1991), 1 s (George Alexander Howard b 5 March 1993); *Career* Student Trg Prog Simca Cars Paris 1969–70, market analyst Chrysler International SA London 1972–73; VAG United Kingdom (formerly VW GB Ltd): Volkswagen product mangr (cars) 1973–76, area sales mangr 1976–79, Audi product mangr 1979–83); Toyota (GB) Ltd: advtg and sales promotion mangr 1983–91, mktg ops mangr 1991–93, dir of mktg ops 1993–94, dir of corp affrs and external communications 1994–96; marketing mangr Rolls-Royce Motor Cars Ltd 1996–; memb Inst of Mktg 1976, FIMI 1987; *Recreations* golf, hockey, swimming, tennis, squash, skiing; *Clubs* RAC (London and Epsom), Effingham Golf, Horsley Sports, Clandon Regis Golf; *Style*— Mike Gazzard, Esq; ✉ Rolls-Royce Motor Cars Ltd, Crewe, Cheshire CW1 3PL (☎ 01270 255155, fax 01270 500620)

GAZZARD, Roy James Albert; s of James Henry Gazzard, MBE (d 1976), of New Milton, Hants, and Ada Gwendoline, *née* Willis (d 1973); *b* 19 July 1923; *Educ* Stationers' Company's Sch Hornsey Middx, Architectural Assoc Sch of Architecture (Dip), Sch of Planning & Res for Regnl Devpt (Dip); *m* 6 Jan 1947, (Muriel) Joy, da of Frederick William Morgan (d 1952), of Higher Odcombe, Somerset; 2 s (Paul b and d 1948, Mark b 1953), 2 da (Sarah (twin) b 1953, Naomi b 1958); *Career* cmmnd Middx Regt 1942, Glider Pilot Regt 1943, Support Capt HQ 6 Airlanding Bde 6 Airborne Div 1944, demobbed Maj 1947; govt town planner Uganda 1949–54 (devpt plans for Jinja 1954), staff architect Barclays Bank 1953–60, chief architect planner Peterlee New Town Devpt Corp 1960–62; dir: devpt Northumberland CC 1962–70, postgrad studies urban geography and planning Univ of Durham 1970–76; under sec DOE 1976–79, dir Centre for Middle Eastern and Islamic studies Univ of Durham 1984; advsr: Sultanate of Oman 1973, Republic of Vanuatu 1989, Republic of Seychelles 1990; memb Sec of State's Working Party preparing UK evidence for UN conf on the environment 1972, chief professional advsr Sec of State's Environmental Bd 1976–79; chm Northern Region RIBA 1970, vice chm BBC NE Advsy Cncl 1970–73, govr Sunderland Poly 1972–76, memb Cncl Northern Arts 1970–76, chm BBC Radio Newcastle Advsy Cncl 1980–83, tstee City of Durham Tst 1970–94; Liveryman Worshipful Co of Stationers 1970 (Renter Warden 1985–86); hon fell Centre for Middle Eastern and Islamic Studies Univ of Durham 1988; FRTPI 1957, FRIBA 1967; *Books* Durham: Portrait of a Cathedral City (1983); *Recreations* independent travel in remote locations, esp Arabia, dry stone walling, castles and castle towns; *Clubs* City Livery; *Style*— Roy Gazzard, Esq; ✉ 13 Dunelm Court, South Street, Durham City DH1 4QX (☎ and fax 0191 386 4067)

GEAR, William; s of Porteous Gordon Gear (d 1965), of Fife, Scotland, and Janet, *née* Inglis (d 1955); *b* 2 Aug 1915; *Educ* Edinburgh Coll of Art, Univ of Edinburgh, Academie Fernand Leger Paris; *m* 7 July 1949, Charlotte (d 1988), da of Moses Chertok (d 1962), of New York; 2 s (David Alexander b 1949, Robert Gordon b 1951); *Career* RCS, Middle East, Italy, Germany 1940–47, cmmnd 1941, staff off MFA and A control cmmn for

Germany 1946–47; painter; head of fine art Birmingham Coll of Art and Poly 1964–75; worked in Paris 1947–50, Arts Cncl Purchase prize Festival of Britain 1951, David Cargill award 1967, Lorne fellowship 1976; memb: Cncl NCDAD, Fine Art Ctee CNAA; Hon DUniv Univ of Central England in Birmingham 1994; RBSA 1966, RA 1995; *Solo Exhibitions incl* London Gimpel Fils Gallery 1948–, S London Art Gallery (retrospective) 1954, Edinburgh Fest 1966, Arts Cncl N Ireland 1969, Scottish Arts Cncl (retrospective) 1969, Univ of Sussex 1975, RBSA Birmingham (retrospective) 1976, Talbot Rice Art Centre, Univ of Edinburgh and Ikon Gallery 1982, Spacex Gallery Exeter 1983, Kirkcaldy Art Gallery 1985, Netherbow Art Centre 1985, Cobra Malmo 1986, Redfern Gallery London 1987, Taipeh 1987, Stockholm 1987, Odense Denmark 1988, Galerie 1900–2000 Paris 1988, Karl & Faber Munich 1989, Gabriele von Loeper Hamburg 1989, Kunsthandel Leeman Amsterdam 1990 and 1992, Redfern Gallery London 1990 and 1992, Galerie Wullkopf Darmstadt 1992, Gabriele von Loeper 1992, Cobra Liege 1993, The Colourist Legacy Edinburgh 1994, City Art Gallery Birmingham 1995, Galerie Scheffel Bad Homburg 1996, Galerie Zellermayer Berlin 1996; *Public Collections incl* Tate Gallery, Arts Cncl, Contemporary Art Soc, Scottish Nat Gallery of Modern Art, Scottish Arts Cncl, V & A Museum, Laing Art Gallery, Inst of Contemporary Art Lima, Towner Gallery Eastbourne, Nat Gallery of Aust, Br Museum, Nat Gallery of Canada, Musée d'Art Moderne Liège, City Art Gallery Birmingham, City Art Gallery Glasgow, Hunterian Art Gallery Glasgow, Museum of Art Tel Aviv, Museum of Art Fort Lauderdale Florida, City Art Centre Edinburgh, Univ of Birmingham, Univ of Central England, Cobra Museum Amstelveen; *Recreations* travel, music, sport; *Clubs* Royal Over-Seas League, Scottish Arts, The Lunar Soc; *Style—* William Gear, Esq, RA; ✉ 46 George Road, Birmingham B15 1PL (☎ 0121 454 1602)

GEAREY, John Marchant; s of Reginald George Gearey (d 1973), of St Albans, and Dorothy May, *née* Townsend (d 1982); *b* 27 March 1938; *Educ* St Albans Sch; *m* 11 Feb 1961, Margaret Isobel, da of Ronald George Reek; 3 s (Michael b 5 Dec 1961, David b 7 Oct 1964, Ian b 27 Feb 1967), 1 da (Carolyn b 26 June 1963); *Career* CA; articled clerk Hartleys Wilkins & Flew 1955, ptnr Peat Marwick Uganda 1964–67 (mangr 1962–64); Mann Judd: joined 1967, ptnr 1969–79, ptnr in charge Midlands practice 1969–79 memb Mgmnt Bd 1975–79, memb Policy Bd 1978–79, chm Computer Steering Ctee 1978–79 (co merged with Touche Ross 1979), ptnr 1979–92, internal auditor 1983–84, regnl mktg ptnr 1984–87, ptnr in charge Midland region mgmnt consultancy practice 1986–88 (seconded as dir of fin Cerestar SA/NV Brussels 1988–89); ptnr Gearey Smith & Windle 1992–; author of various professional books; memb of Cncl Birmingham Chamber of Commerce and Indust 1986–94; FCA 1972 (ACA 1961); *Recreations* church treasurer, travelling, walking, music, light opera, grandchildren; *Style—* John M Gearey, Esq; ✉ The Manor House, Hadzor, Droitwich, Worcs WR9 7DR (☎ 01905 772588); Gearey Smith & Windle, One Waterloo Street, Birmingham B2 5PG (☎ 0121 633 0633, fax 0121 632 5433)

GEARY, Kevin; s of Frank Geary (d 1992), and Hilda, *née* Stott; *b* 3 Nov 1951; *Educ* Manchester GS, Univ of Kent at Canterbury (BA, MA); *children* 2 da (Kerry b 11 March 1977, Rachel b 9 June 1982); *Career* successively: ODI fell Miny of Finance Swaziland 1974–76, ptnr Coopers & Lybrand 1978–94, md Cigamon Ltd, currently head of business devpt Clifford Chance; author of numerous pubns; *Recreations* tennis, squash, theatre, cinema; *Style—* Kevin Geary, Esq; ✉ Clifford Chance, 200 Aldersgate Street, London EC1A 4JJ (☎ 0171 600 1000, fax 0171 600 5555)

GEARY, Michael John; s of John Geary (d 1980), of Hemel Hempstead, Herts, and Joyce Nellie, *née* Lee; *b* 18 June 1950; *Educ* Apsley GS Hemel Hempstead, Worcester Coll Oxford (MA); *m* 4 Jan 1975 (m dis 1992), Susan Mary, da of Henry Spilman Wood (d 1989), of Turweston, Northants; 2 s (John b and d 1979, Malcolm b 1980), 1 da (Hazel b 1982); *Career* exec engr PO Telecommunications (now British Telecommunications plc) 1971–74, controller Industrial and Commercial Finance Corporation Ltd (now 3i plc) 1974–79, investmt exec Charterhouse Development Ltd 1979–82, md Munford White plc 1982–85; dir: Tunstall Development Ltd 1985–86, Prudential Venture Managers Ltd 1986–92; chief exec offr Euroventures BV 1992–; chm-elect Euro Venture Capital Assoc; *Recreations* sailing, skiing; *Clubs* Royal Southern Yacht, Ski Club of GB; *Style—* Michael Geary, Esq; ✉ Gresham House, Lower Plantation, Loudwater, Rickmansworth, Herts WD3 4PQ (☎ 01923 721250); Euroventures BV, Julianaplein 10, 5211 BC s'-Hertogenbosch, Netherlands (☎ 00 31 73 613 7800)

GEAVES, Fiona Jane; da of Robert William Geaves (d 1974), and Janet Hillary; *b* 6 Dec 1967; *Educ* Brockworth Comp Sch; *Career* squash player; represented England at under 16, under 19 and sr level, memb team under 19 World Jr Open Winners 1985; tournaments won incl: British Open under 23's 1989, Stockholm Grays Open 1989, Dutch Open 1989, Mikkeli Open Finland 1990, Boston Open 1993, New York Open 1993; world ranking 6 1994, British ranking 3, nat champion 1995; *Style—* Miss Fiona Geaves

GEBBETT, Stephen Henry; s of Albert Gebbett, of Hundon, Suffolk, and Elsie Mary, *née* Kettle; *b* 24 Jan 1949; *Educ* Raynes Park CGS, Univ of Wales (BSc); *m* 22 Dec 1973, Linda Margaret; 1 s (Timothy Giles b 5 Oct 1976), 1 da (Kimberley Sarah b 13 May 1981); *Career* graduate trainee and assoc dir F J Lyons PR Consultancy 1970–76; Marketing Div Charles Barker (formerly Charles Baker Lyons): assoc dir 1976–79, dir 1979–86, md 1986–88, chief exec 1988–91, chm and chief exec 1991–92; dir Charles Barker plc 1992–, md Charles Barker Marketing 1996–; MIPR 1976; *Recreations* squash, gardening, humour; *Style—* Stephen Gebbett, Esq; ✉ Charles Barker plc, 56 Dean St, London W1V 5HX (☎ 0171 494 1331)

GÉBLER, Carlo Ernest; s of Ernest Gébler, of Dalkey, Co Dublin, and Edna, *née* O'Brien; *b* 21 Aug 1954; *Educ* Bedales Sch, Univ of York (BA), Nat Film and TV Sch; *m* Tyga; 2 da (India Rose b 1981, Georgia Madeleine b 1994), 2 s (Jack Redmond b 1987, Finn b 1990); *Career* author, script writer, film director; memb Aosdána (Eire) 1990; tutor of creative writing HMP Maze 1995; *Publications* The Eleventh Summer (1985), August In July (1986), Work and Play (1987), Driving through Cuba: An East-West Journey (1988), The TV Genie (1989), Malachy and his Family (1989), Life of a Drum (1990), The Witch That Wasn't (1991), The Glass Curtain: Inside an Ulster Community (1991), The Cure (1994); *Plays* How to Murder a Man (1995); author of reviews, articles, short stories, travel pieces; contrib to short story collections: Travellers Tales, London Tales, 20 under 35, Winter's Tales 6, New Writing Two; *Films* writer and dir: Croagh Patrick (1977), The Beneficiary (1979), Over Here (1980), Rating Notman (1981), Country & Irish (1982), Two Lives: A Portrait of Francis Stuart (1985), George Barker (1987), August in July (writer, 1990), Plain Tales from Northern Ireland (1993), Life After Death (1994), The Widow's Daughter (writer, 1995), A Little Local Difficulty (1995); *Recreations* walking, travelling; *Style—* Carlo Gébler, Esq; ✉ c/o Virginia Bonham Carter, 1 Kingswood Avenue, London NW6 6LA (☎ 0181 969 0476)

GEDDES, His Hon Judge Andrew Campbell; s of Hon Alexander Geddes, OBE, MC, TD (d 1974), and Hon Margaret, *née* Addis, of London; *b* 10 June 1943; *Educ* Stowe, Christ Church Oxford (MA); *m* 1, 1974, Jacqueline Tan Bunzl, da of Emil Bunzl; 2 s (Nicholas Campbell b 1975, Dominic Campbell b 1978); m 2, Bridget Bowring; 1 s (Leo Patrick b 1981), 1 da (Katharine Arabella b 1986); *Career* fndr Building Product Index 1968; called to the Bar Inner Temple 1972, recorder 1990–94, circuit judge (Midland & Oxford Circuit) 1994–, authorised to sit as High Ct judge Aug 1995; *Books* Product and Service Liability in the EEC (1992), Protection of Individual Rights in EC Law (1995), Public and Utility Procurement (1996); *Recreations* writing, walking, music, gardening; *Style—* His Hon Judge Andrew Geddes; ✉ c/o Courts Administrators Office, 33 Bull Street, Birmingham B4 6DW

GEDDES, Prof Duncan Mackay; s of Sir Reay Geddes, KBE, *qv*, of London, and Imogen, *née* Matthey; *b* 6 Jan 1942; *Educ* Eton, Magdalene Coll Cambridge (MA), Westminster Med Sch (MB BS), Univ of London (MD); *m* 16 April 1968, Donatella Flaccomio Nardi Dei, da of Marchesa A Roselli del Turco Medici Tornaquinci; 2 s (Gavin b 27 Feb 1971, Acland b 3 March 1981), 1 da (Gaia b 5 April 1973); *Career* jr hosp appts Westminster, Hammersmith, Middx and Brompton Hosps 1971–78; conslt physician: London Chest Hosp 1978–87, Brompton Hosp 1978–; civilian conslt in diseases of the chest to: the Army 1988–, the Navy 1991–; hon sec Br Thoracic Soc 1981–84; FRCP 1982; *Books* Practical Medicine (1976), Airways Obstruction (1981), Respiratory Medicine (1990), Cystic Fibrosis (1994); author of over 200 scientific articles and invited chapters; *Recreations* tennis, painting; *Clubs* Queen's; *Style—* Prof Duncan Geddes; ✉ Royal Brompton Hospital, Fulham Rd, London SW3 (☎ 0171 352 8121, fax 0171 351 8999)

GEDDES, 3 Baron (UK 1942), of Rolvenden; Euan Michael Ross Geddes; s of 2 Baron, KBE (d 1975), and Enid, *née* Butler; *b* 3 Sept 1937; *Educ* Rugby, Gonville and Caius Coll Cambridge (MA), Harvard Business Sch; *m* 1, 7 May 1966, Gillian (d 1995), yr da of late William Arthur Butler, of Henley-on-Thames; 1 s (Hon James b 1969), 1 da (Hon Clair b 1967); m 2, 7 Sept 1996, Susan Margaret, da of late George Harold Carter, of Kingswood, Surrey; *Heir* s, Hon James George Neil Geddes; *Career* Lt Cdr RNR (ret); chm: Geddes & Co Ltd 1985–, Port Directories (CI) Ltd 1992–; dir: John Broadwood & Sons Ltd 1986–, Stewart Consultants & Offshore Technology Services Ltd 1986–, Parasol Portrait Photography Ltd 1988–, Regional Airports Ltd 1990–, AES Electric Ltd 1993–; chm Trinity Coll London 1992–, dir Trinity Coll of Music; chm House of Lords Euro Sub Ctee B (Energy, Tport and Technol) 1995–; *Recreations* golf, music, skiing, bridge, gardening; *Clubs* Brooks's, Aldeburgh Golf, Hong Kong, Royal Hong Kong Golf, Noble and Gentlemen's Catch; *Style—* The Rt Hon the Lord Geddes; ✉ The House of Lords, London SW1A 0PW (home ☎ 01256 862105, fax 01256 862029)

GEDDES, Michael Dawson; s of David Geddes, and Audrey Clinton, *née* Phillips; *b* 9 March 1944; *Educ* Sherborne, Univ of British Columbia (Goldsmiths' exhibitioner, BA); *m* 1966, Leslie Rose, *née* Webb; 2 s (b 1969 and 1971); *Career* Cranfield Inst of Technol: admin asst 1968–71, planning offr 1971–76, devpt and estates offr 1976–83, fin controller (RMCS) 1983–84; sec Ashridge (Bonar Law Meml) Trust; dir: Admin Ashridge Mgmnt Coll, Ashridge Strategic Mgmnt Centre, Ashridge Mgmnt Devpt Servs, Ashridge Mgmnt Res Gp 1984–90; chief exec: Recruitment and Assessment Servs 1990–95, Civil Serv Cmmn 1990–; dir Milton Keynes Economic Partnership 1995–; *Books* Project Leadership (1990); author of numerous articles in various jls; *Recreations* golf, gardening; *Style—* Michael Geddes, Esq; ✉ 11 Main Street, Mursley, Milton Keynes, Bucks MK17 0RT (☎ 01296 720601)

GEDDES, Philip Clinton; s of David Geddes, and Audrey Clinton, *née* Phillips; *b* 26 Aug 1947; *Educ* Sherborne, Queens' Coll Cambridge; *m* 27 Oct 1984, Selina Valerie, da of Capt Derek Head, RNR; 3 s (David b 1985, James b 1989, Thomas Christian b 1991), 1 da (Emily Anne b 1993); *Career* gen trainee BBC 1970, prodr BBC features 1973–80, exec prodr TVS and head of sci and indust progs 1981–88; currently: ed Special Reports Financial Times TV, chm Chevron Presentation Training Ltd, writer and conslt to business; *Books* In the Mouth of the Dragon (1981), Inside the Bank of England (1988); *Recreations* cricket; *Clubs* Ooty; *Style—* Philip Geddes, Esq; ✉ Manor Farm, Upper Wield, Alresford, Hants (☎ 01420 562361)

GEDDES, Sir (Anthony) Reay Mackay; KBE (1968, OBE 1943); s of Rt Hon Sir Eric Campbell Geddes, GCB, GBE (bro of 1 Baron Geddes, d 1937), and Ada Gwendolen, *née* Stokes (d 1945); *b* 7 May 1912; *Educ* Rugby, Magdalene Coll Cambridge; *m* 14 April 1938, Imogen, da of Capt Hay Matthey; 2 s (Prof Duncan Geddes, *qv*, Piers), 3 da (Alison, Lindsay, Candida); *Career* chm Dunlop Holdings 1968–78, dep chm Midland Bank 1978–83 (dir 1967–83); dir: Shell Transport of Trading 1968–82, Rank Organization 1975–84; pres: The Abbeyfield Soc 1985–89, Charities Aid Fndn 1990–93; tstee Volunteer Centre UK 1989–95, dir Salzburg Seminar 1992–95; *Style—* Sir Reay Geddes, KBE; ✉ 49 Eaton Place, London SW1X 8DE (☎ 0171 235 5179)

GEDYE, Robin Eric Bernard; s of George Eric Rowe Gedye (d 1971), and Alice, *née* Mehler; *b* 17 Aug 1949; *Educ* Clifton Coll, Portsmouth Poly (BA), Univ of Cardiff; *m* 20 July 1985, Rowena Elizabeth, da of Stephen Hugh Sharp; 1 s (Benedict Robin Stephen b 15 Aug 1992), 1 da (Melita Alice Rachel b 1 Nov 1989); *Career* journalist; Reuters (corr Vienna for 18 months) 1974–79; Daily Telegraph: joined 1979, Warsaw corr 1980, Eastern Europe corr 1982 and 1985, Moscow corr 1985, Germany corr 1989–; *Recreations* dry fly-fishing, skiing; *Style—* Robin Gedye, Esq; ✉ Daily Telegraph, ZR19 Pressehaus 1, Heussallee 2–10, Bonn 53, Germany (☎ 00 49 228 215 631)

GEE, His Hon Judge; David Stephenson; s of William Gee (d 1969), of Warrington, and Marianne, *née* Bogie; *b* 16 Dec 1944; *Educ* William Hulmes GS, Univ of Leeds (LLB); *m* 14 Oct 1972, Susan Margaret, da of John Hiley; 2 da (Catherine Tracey b 26 Nov 1974, Rachel Helen b 30 March 1978), 2 s (Richard Michael b 25 Nov 1976, Christopher Phillip b 12 Feb 1980); *Career* admitted slr 1970, registrar and latterly district judge Northern Circuit 1982, recorder 1990, circuit judge (Northern Circuit) 1992–; memb Law Soc, chm Selcare Tst 1989–95; advsy ed Atkins Court Forms; *Recreations* music, reading, walking; *Clubs* Commonwealth; *Style—* His Hon Judge Gee; ✉ c/o Northern Circuit Office, 15 Quay Street, Manchester M60 9FD

GEE, Ian Ernest; s of William Alan Gee (d 1986), of Cheltenham Gloucestershire, and Anne Mary Duncan, *née* Walton (d 1987); *b* 19 Oct 1936; *Educ* The Manchester GS, Manchester Coll of Science and Technol; *m* 1964, Anne Rosemary, *née* Thorpe; 2 s (Nicholas Ian b 10 March 1969, Andrew Nigel b 11 July 1975); *Career* Nat Serv photographer RAF 1957–59, industl photographer AV Roe & Co Ltd 1959–60, commercial photographer and colour printer Stagshead Studios Manchester 1960–63, self employed industl photographer then specialist portrait photographer in exec portraits of authors, artists and politicians 1963–, currently lectr on professional techniques for Fuji Photo Film Company; co-fndr The Guild of Wedding Photographers 1988, author of various articles in specialist photographic press; winner of numerous awards incl: Photographic Craftsman award (Professional Photographers of America) 1988, BIPP President's award 1988, BIPP Brides' Choice Album award Wedding Photographer of the Year 1990; BIPP: memb Admissions and Qualifications Panel 1975–, memb Cncl 1976–88, pres 1980–81; memb Professional Photographers of America 1961, FBIPP 1974 (MBIPP 1957); *Books* Wedding Photography Today (the Manual of Professional Wedding Photograpy); *Recreations* cricket, theatre, reading political biography, walking; *Clubs* RPS; *Style—* Ian Gee, Esq; ✉ 54 The Downs, Altrincham, Cheshire WA14 2QJ (☎ 0161 928 3716, fax 0161 929 1786)

GEE, Kathryn Olive Perry (Kathy); da of Dr Eric Arthur Gee, FSA (d 1989), of York, and Olive Mary, *née* Deer (d 1992); *b* 2 July 1951; *Educ* Mill Mount GS York, Univ of Exeter (BA), Univ of Leicester (postgrad cert in mus studies); *m* 1975 (sep 1989), Julian Elsworth Tanner; *Career* museum service dir; curator Cookworthy mus Devon and Wheal Martyn Mus Cornwall English China Clays 1973–84, freelance conslt 1983–90: Torquay Museum, Nat Trust, N Devon Dist Cncl, Victor Cox Museum Cleveland, Tiverton Museum, Area Museum Cncl for the SW; dir W Midlands Regnl Museums Cncl 1990–; external examiner UCL 1994–96; memb: Ctee Area Museum Cncls 1990–, Midlands Fedn of Museums 1990–, W Midlands Regnl Heritage & Leisure Agencies Gp

1991–, Prison Servs Museum Ctee 1990–95, Assoc of Ind Museums (memb Cncl 1988–96), Exec Bd Ironbridge Gorge Museum 1994– (memb Academic and Cultural Ctee 1991–94), Women in Mgmnt 1994–, Ctee of Industry '96 (Standards & Qualifications Ctee of MTI) 1993–96, Working Pty on Criteria for Designation Museums & Galleries Cmmn 1996–; memb Bd, Exec and Staffing Sub-Ctee SW Area Museum Cncl 1987–90, pres SW Fedn of Museums 1987–89 memb Ctee until 1990), fndr and co-convenor Devon Fedn of Museums 1986–90; sec Feckenham Forest Local History Soc 1990–94; memb Vernacular Architecture Gp 1991–; parish cncllr 1995–, tstee Feckenham Village Amenity Tst 1995–, vice-chm Village Green Mgmnt Ctee 1995–; author of numerous articles in jls and pamphlets; FMA 1986 (AMA 1976); *Publications* five local history leaflets for Cookworthy Museum, two guide books for Wheal Martyn Museum, four leaflets for Nat Trust, two book on local history, book of photos of Kingsbridge area (1988), Museum Projects - a handbook for volunteers (1989), The Heritage Web - structures and relationships (1993), First Principles - a framework for museum development in the West Midlands (1996); *Recreations* local history, restoring a 17th century cottage, walking the dog; *Style—* Ms Kathy Gee; ✉ West Midlands Regional Museum Council, Hanbury Road, Stoke Prior, Bromsgrove, Worcs (☎ 01527 872258)

GEE, Prof Kenneth Philip; s of Philip Gee (d 1984), of Bramhall, and Nancy, *née* Green (d 1992); *b* 27 Dec 1946; *Educ* Cheadle Hulme Sch, Univ of Bristol (BSc), Univ of Manchester (PhD), Univ of Salford (DLitt); *m* 31 July 1971, Hilary, da of Gerald James Carmichael (d 1989), of Sale; 1 da (Freya b 9 Oct 1973); *Career* lectr Dept of Mgmnt Sciences UMIST 1972–74, sr lectr Dept of Accounting and Fin Univ of Lancaster 1974–79, prof of accountancy Univ of Salford 1979– (dean of Social Sciences and Arts 1989–92); chm British Accounting Assoc 1991 (vice chm 1990); *Books* Management Control and Information (1973), Management Planning and Control in Inflation (1977), Advanced Management Accounting Problems (1986); *Recreations* reading; *Style—* Prof Kenneth Gee; ✉ 50 Broad Rd, Sale, Cheshire M33 2BN (☎ 0161 973 4034); Department of Business Studies, University of Salford, The Crescent, Salford M5 4WT (☎ 0161 745 5581, fax 0161 745 5556, e-mail k.p.gee@business.salford.ac.uk)

GEE, Dr Maggie Mary; da of Victor Gee, of Holt, Norfolk, and Aileen, *née* Church; *b* 2 Nov 1948; *Educ* Horsham HS for Girls Sussex, Somerville Coll Oxford (major open scholar, MA, BLitt), Wolverhampton Poly (PhD); *m* 1983, Nicholas Rankin; 1 da (Rosa b 1986); *Career* writer 1982–; judge Booker Prize 1989; writing fell Univ of E Anglia 1982, hon visiting fell Univ of Sussex 1986–; Hawthornden fell 1989, Northern Arts fell 1996; memb Mgmnt Ctee Soc of Authors 1991–94; FRSL 1994; *Books* Dying In Other Words (1981), The Burning Book (1983), Light Years (1985), Grace (1988), Where are the Snows (1991), Lost Children (1994); *Recreations* film, visual arts, walking, swimming; *Style—* Dr Maggie Gee, FRSL; ✉ c/o Gillon Aitken, Aitken Stone & Wylie, 29 Fernshaw Road, London SW10 0TG (☎ 0171 351 7561, fax 0171 376 3594)

GEE, His Hon Judge Richard; s of John Gee, and Marie, *née* Cohen; *b* 25 July 1942; *Educ* Kilburn GS, UCL (LLB); *m* 3 s (Simon b 1967, Matthew b 1970, Alexander b 1973); *Career* articled Goodman Derrick & Co London, admitted slr 1964, sr ptnr J B Wheatley & Co London, recorder 1988–91 (asst recorder 1983–88), circuit judge (SE Circuit) 1991–; Judicial Studies Bd: memb Main Bd 1988–93, memb Criminal Sub-Ctee 1988–91, memb Ethnic Minorities Advsy Ctee 1991–93; *Recreations* poetry and music, golf and tennis; *Clubs* Hampstead Golf; *Style—* His Hon Judge Gee; ✉ Middlesex Guildhall, Broad Sanctuary, London SW1P 3BB

GEE, Stephen; s of Norman and Barbara Gee; *b* 18 Feb 1944; *Educ* Ardingly Coll; *Career* Price Waterhouse CAs 1962–68, Forte plc 1968–70, Samuel Montagu & Co Ltd 1970–75, md Waterbrook Ltd 1975–82, fin dir and dep chm My Kinda Town plc 1982–; FCA; *Recreations* tennis, sailing, shooting; *Style—* Stephen Gee, Esq; ✉ My Kinda Town plc, 195–197 Kings Road, London SW3 5ED (☎ 0171 351 6996, fax 0171 376 5076)

GEE, Steven Mark; QC (1993); s of Dr Sidney Gee, of Regent's Park, London, and Dr Hilda Gee, *née* Elman; *b* 24 Aug 1953; *Educ* Tonbridge, Brasenose Coll Oxford (open scholar, MA, Gibbs prize for law); *Career* called to the Bar Middle Temple (Harmsworth scholar, Senate of Inns of Court prizeman in Bar Finals) 1975; in commercial practice, standing jr counsel in export credit guarantee matters DTI; *Books* The Law and Practice of Mareva Injunctions (1987), Mareva Injunctions and Anton Piller Relief (1990, 2 edn 1995); *Recreations* marathon running; *Clubs* Serpentine Running, MCC; *Style—* Steven Gee, Esq, QC; ✉ 38 Eaton Terrace, London SW1W 8TS (☎ 0171 823 4660); 1 Essex Court, Temple, London EC4 (☎ 0171 583 2000, fax 0171 583 0118)

GEE, Timothy Edward Daniel (Tim); s of Archibald Geoffrey Gee, of Northampton, and Rosemary Noel, *née* Foster; *b* 26 May 1962; *Educ* Bedford Sch, Worcester Coll Oxford (Simmons & Simmons open scholar, BA Jurisprudence); *m* 3 July 1993, Anita Kau Heung; *Career* Baker & McKenzie: articled clerk 1984–86, based London 1986–88, Hong Kong 1989–90, Budapest 1991, ptnr (based London) 1992–, currently head Securities Dept; memb Law Soc 1986, admitted slr Hong Kong 1989; *Recreations* rugby, flyfishing, wine; *Clubs* East India, Old Bedfordians, Hong Kong Football; *Style—* Tim Gee, Esq; ✉ Baker & McKenzie, 100 New Bridge Street, London EC4V 6JA (☎ 0171 919 1000, fax 0171 919 1999)

GEERING, Ian Walter; QC (1991); s of Wilfrid Robert Geering (d 1969), and Barbara Pearce, *née* James; *b* 19 July 1947; *Educ* Bedford Sch, Univ of Edinburgh (BVMS); *m* 2 Aug 1975, Alison Diana, da of David Sinclair Burne; 2 s (Nicholas Redman b 16 April 1980, Christopher Robert b 6 Feb 1984), 2 da (Caroline Evelyn b 5 Feb 1979, Philippa Amelia b 25 Feb 1982); *Career* called to the Bar Inner Temple 1974, recorder of the Crown Court 1995– (asst recorder 1990–95); *Recreations* sailing, reading, photography, walking, shooting; *Style—* Ian Geering, Esq, QC; ✉ 3 Veyulam Buildings, Gray's Inn, London WC1R 5NT (☎ 0171 831 8441, fax 0171 831 8479)

GEERING, Michael William; s of John George William Geering, of London, and Winifred, *née* Green; *b* 5 Aug 1944; *Educ* Stationers' Company's Sch, Univ of Southampton (BSc); *m* 19 Sept 1970, Jean Mavis, da of Samuel Frederick George Fletcher, of Cardiff; 1 s (Jonathan b 3 July 1974), 1 da (Nicola b 4 Aug 1972); *Career* CA 1965; articled clerk Binder Hamlyn 1965–68, trainee analyst Laing & Cruickshank Stockbrokers 1968–69, audit sr Ernst & Whinney 1969–72; James Capel & Co 1973–92: joined as investmt analyst 1973, head of UK equity res 1985–92, main bd dir i/c UK Equity Div 1986–92; dir UK Institutional Div Mercury Asset Management plc 1993–94, dir of institutional mktg James Capel & Co 1994–; FCA, AIIMR, MSI(Dip); *Recreations* golf, swimming, tennis, horse racing; *Clubs* Gnomes, Wisley Golf, St George's Hill Golf; *Style—* Michael W Geering, Esq; ✉ Lion Hill, West Rd, St George's Hill, Weybridge, Surrey KT13 OLZ; James Capel & Co Ltd, Thames Exchange, 10 Queen Street Place, London EC4R 1BL (☎ 0171 621 0011, fax 0171 621 0496, telex 888866)

GELARDI, Geoffrey Alan David; s of Albert Charles Gelardi, and Noreen, *née* Eagles; *b* 28 July 1953; *Educ* St George's Coll Weybridge Surrey; *m* 4 May 1984, Eileen Mary, da of William Sheridan; 2 da (Piera Maria b 27 Oct 1985, Georgina Maria b 28 Jan 1987); *Career* hotelier; various positions: Carlton Tower London 1970–71, Grand Hotel et Tivollier Toulouse 1971–72, London Hilton Hotel 1972–74; grad trainee prog Waldorf Astoria NYC 1974, co-ordinator of hotel opening and mangr Terrace Coffee Shop Hilton Hotel of Philadelphia 1975, asst to Food & Beverage Dir Waldorf Astoria 1976; dir of food & beverage ops: New York Statler Hilton NYC 1977, Arlington Park Hilton Chicago 1978, Resorts International Casino Hotel Atlantic City New Jersey 1979–81; resident mangr Plaza of the Americas Dallas 1981, mangr Remington Hotel Houston 1982; md Bel Air Hotel Los Angeles 1983–85, md/ptnr Sorrento Hotel Seattle 1985–90, md The Lanesborough London 1990–; memb: London C of C, St George's Hosp Charity Ctee, Queen Charlotte's Ball Ctee, Preferred Hotels and Resorts Worldwide, Waldorf Alumni; *Recreations* squash, tennis, horseriding; *Clubs* RAC, Annabel's; *Style—* Geoffrey Gelardi, Esq; ✉ The Lanesborough, 1 Lanesborough Place, London SW1X 7TA (☎ 0171 259 5599, fax 0171 333 7026, car 0831 155500)

GELARDI, Peter Anthony; s of Albert Charles Gelardi, of Weybridge, Surrey, and Noreen Annis, *née* Eagles; *b* 5 April 1946; *Educ* Stonyhurst, RAF Coll Cranwell, Univ of Aston Business Sch (MBA); *m* Jane Rosemary, da of Charles Kenneth Bell; 2 s (Nicholas b 10 Jan 1975, Jonathan b 15 April 1977), 1 da (Annabel b 13 Sept 1983); *Career* pilot RAF 1968–70; mangr Hobbs Pagett & Co 1970–73, mangr Midland Northern Trust 1973–75, md E Africa Chloride Group plc 1976–80, md Amalgamated Alloys Ltd 1980–88, chm and md Amroth Ltd (developers of hotels and country clubs) 1988–91, dir London Jazz Radio plc (operators of Jazz FM) 1989–91 (md 1989–90), currently md World Telecom plc (telecommunications); MIMgt 1974, MRSA 1994; *Recreations* tennis, golf, running, bridge; *Clubs* RAF, Harbour, Foxhills Country (Surrey); *Style—* Peter Gelardi, Esq; ✉ Amroth, Woburn Hill, Weybridge, Surrey KT15 2QE (☎ 01932 848597); World Telecom plc, Quayside Lodge, London SW6 2UZ (☎ 0171 384 5000, fax 0171 384 5002)

GELBER, David; s of Edward Gelber (d 1970), of Toronto, and Anna, *née* David (d 1974); *b* 10 Nov 1947; *Educ* Whittinghame Coll Brighton, Hebrew Univ Jerusalem (BSc), Univ of London (MSc); *m* 1, 1969 (m dis 1979), Laura Beare; 1 s (Jeremy Edward b 1973), 1 da (Amy b 1975); *m* 2, 1982, Vivienne, da of Harry Cohen, of Weybridge; *Career* Morgan Guaranty Tst 1975–76, vice pres Citibank/Citicorp 1976–85, md (head of global swaps and foreign exchange options) Chemical Bank 1985–89, global mangr (head of swaps and options) HongkongBank 1989–92, jt md James Capel Gilts Ltd 1992–94, chief operating offr Midland Global Markets, gp managing dir Intercapital Ltd 1994–; *Recreations* tennis, squash; *Clubs* RAC Cumberland Lt; *Style—* David Gelber, Esq; ✉ 6 Clorane Gardens, London NW3 7PR (☎ 0171 794 1352); Intercapital Ltd, Park House, 16 Finsbury Circus, London EC2M 7DJ (☎ 0171 3742084, fax 0171 638 2911)

GELDARD, Robin John; CBE (1996); s of Cyril John Geldard (d 1984), of Thornton Dene, South Glam, and Gertrude Nellie Lawrence (d 1971); *b* 9 Aug 1935; *Educ* Aldenham, Coll of Law; *m* 4 Sept 1965, Susan Elizabeth, da of Sir Martin Llewellyn Edwards (d 1987), of Pentwyn Farm, Lisvane, nr Cardiff; 2 s (Bruce b 1967, Michael b 1972), 1 da (Anna b 1972); *Career* recruit RM 1958, Mons Offr Cadet Sch, cmmnd RM 1959, 2 Lt Commando Trg Unit, RM rugby team 1958–60; slr, ptnr then sr ptnr Edwards Geldard 1962–95; asst registrar 1980–85; dir various cos 1980–95, currently dir Minories Underwriting Agencies Ltd; pres: Cardiff Incorporated C of C and Indust 1987–89, Cardiff Incorporated Law Soc 1988–89 (vice pres 1987–88), Federated Welsh C of C 1988–94 (vice pres 1987–88), Assoc British Chambers of Commerce 1994–96 (dep pres 1992–94); hon consul for Japan at Cardiff 1993 and 1996; memb Lloyd's 1986; *Recreations* sailing, flyfishing, music, photography; *Clubs* Flyfishers', Naval, Cardiff and Co, RYA; *Style—* Robin Geldard, Esq, CBE; ✉ Mole End, Pillory Hill, Noss Mayo, Plymouth PL8 1ED (☎ 01752 873094)

GELDER, Prof Michael Graham; s of Philip Graham Gelder (d 1972), and Alice Margaret, *née* Graham (d 1985); *b* 2 July 1929; *Educ* Bradford GS, Queen's Coll Oxford, Univ Coll Hosp Med Sch; *m* 21 Aug 1954, Margaret Constance, da of Lt-Col John William Smith Anderson (d 1984); 1 s (Colin b 31 May 1960), 2 da (Fiona (Mrs Timothy Harry) b 12 Jan 1963, Nicola (Mrs Zeno Poggi) b 9 May 1964); *Career* Capt RAMC 1955–57; sr house physician Univ Coll Hosp 1957 (house physician 1955), registrar Bethlem Royal and Maudsley Hosps 1958–61, MRC fell in clinical res 1962–63; Inst of Psychiatry: lectr 1964–65, sr lectr 1965–67, vice dean 1967–68; prof of psychiatry Univ of Oxford 1969–96 (emeritus prof 1996–), fell Merton Coll Oxford 1969– (subwarden 1992–94); chm: Neurosciences Bd MRC 1978–79 (memb 1976–78 and 1988 91), Neurosciences Ctee Wellcome Tst 1990–95; vice pres RCPsych 1982–84; FRCP 1970, FRCPsych 1973; *Books* Psychological Aspects of Medical Practice (ed 1973), Agoraphobia: Nature and Treatment (jtly 1981), Oxford Textbook of Psychiatry (jtly 1983, 3 edn 1996), Concise Oxford Textbook of Psychiatry (jtly, 1994); *Recreations* real tennis, reading, photography; *Style—* Prof Michael Gelder; ✉ Merton College, Oxford OX1 4JD

GELFAND, Jennifer; da of Jeffrey A Gelfand, and Janet V Gelfand; *b* 14 Oct 1971; *Educ* Buckingham Browne & Nichols Sch Cambridge MA, Boston Ballet Sch; *Career* ballet dancer; studied under David Howard; awarded scholarships from David Howard Fndn, Boston Ballet Sch, Rebekah Harkness Fndn; professional debut Sugar Plum Fairy in The Nutcracker (Eglevsky Ballet) 1985; toured with Joffrey II Dancers 1988–89, Boston Ballet 1989–95 (princ 1990), princ Birmingham Royal Ballet 1995–96; subject of television documentary Children With Wings; *Roles* with Joffrey II Dancers: Columbine and Unicorn in Richard England's Beauty and the Beast, Mark Chaim's Gardens of Boboli, Matthew Wrights' Visitations, Monica Levy's Amnesia Variations, Edward Stierle's Pyrogen, Flower Festival at Genzano pas de deux; princ roles with Boston Ballet incl: Juliet in Choo San Goh's Romeo and Juliet, Irma in Bournonville's Abdallah, Odette/Odile in Swan Lake, Kitri in Ann-Marie Holmes's Don Quixote, Olga in John Cranko's Eugene Onegin, title role in Giselle and Coppelia, Ben Stevenson's Cinderella, title role in Fernando Bujones's Raymonda Act III, Sanguinic variation in George Balanchine's The Four Temperaments, Ballerina in Harald Lander's Etudes, Twyla Tharp's A Brief Fling and Waterbaby Bagatelles, Monica Levy's Sky Beneath the Waves, Rick McCullough's Others Because, Paul Taylor's Company B, cr role in Jill Bahr's The Wild Swans and Richard Colton's Before Ever After; Birmingham Royal Ballet: Frederick Ashton's Birthday Offering, La Fille Mal Gardee, Sir Peter Wright's Swan Lake and Coppelia; guest artist: Rudolph Nureyev & Friends Farewell Tour Boston, Aurora (debut) in The Sleeping Beauty (ptnr Fernando Bujones) for Indianapolis Ballet Theater 1991, The Nutcracker for Ballet Mississippi, Esmeralda for Pittsburgh Ballet, World Ballet Festival Japan 1994; performed at Le Don des Etoiles Gala Canada annually since 1990, opening gala Int Ballet Competition 1990, Noche de Danza Centro Cultural de la Villa Madrid; *Awards* Gold Medal Int Ballet Competition Mississippi 1986, American Acad of Achievement Award 1988, Nat Fndn for Advancement in the Arts Award 1988, presidential scholar and medal awarded in ceremony at White House 1989; *Style—* Ms Jennifer Gelfand; ✉ The Birmingham Royal Ballet, Birmingham Hippodrome, Thorp Street, Birmingham B5 4AU (☎ 0121 622 2555)

GELL, Peter Donald Marriott; s of Harold Marriot Gell, MC, of Chipping Campden, Glos; *b* 17 March 1929; *Educ* Sherborne, Worcester Coll Oxford (MA); *m* 1960, Jean, da of Lt-Col David Livingstone Graham, of Crowborough; 1 s, 3 da; *Career* former dir Bunzl plc, chm Bucks FHSA; currently chm Iain Rennie Hospice at Home; Liveryman Worshipful Co of Stationers & Newspaper Makers, memb Ct of Assts Worshipful Co of Paviors; FCA, FCIS; *Recreations* music, country pursuits; *Clubs* East India; *Style—* Peter Gell, Esq; ✉ Shearings, Witheridge Lane, Penn, Bucks HP10 8PQ (☎ 01494 813243, fax 01494 814486)

GELLHORN, Peter; s of Dr Alfred Gellhorn (d 1972), and Else Agathe, *née* Fischer (d 1950); *b* 24 Oct 1912; *Educ* Schiller Real Gymnasium Charlottenburg, Univ of Berlin, Berlin Acad of Music (passed with distinction final exams as pianist 1932 and conductor 1934); *m* 18 May 1943, Olive Shirley, 3 da of 1 Baron Layton of Danehill, CH, CBE (d 1966); 2 s (Martin b 1945, Philip b 1951), 2 da (Mary b 1959, Barbara b 1960); *Career* musical dir Toynbee Hall London 1935–39, asst conductor Sadler's Wells Opera 1941–43, indust war serv 1943–45, conductor Royal Carl Rosa Opera 1945–46, conductor and head music staff Royal Opera House Covent Garden 1946–53, conductor and chorus master Glyndebourne Festival Opera 1954–61, dir BBC chorus (incl conducting Promenade Concerts) 1961–72, rejoined Glyndebourne 1974–75, co fndr and musical dir Opera Barga Italy 1967–69; conductor: The Elizabethan Singers 1976–80, Morley Coll Opera Gp 1973–79, Barnes Choir 1973–; music dir London Opera Players 1950–, memb opera sch staff RCM 1980–88, prof Guildhall Sch of Music and Drama 1981–92, lectr and adjudicator GB and overseas; compositions incl: music for the silhouette and puppet films of Lotte Reiniger, Aucassin and Nicolette (Festival of London 1972); memb Royal Philharmonic Soc, ISM, FGSM; *Recreations* swimming, walking, going to plays; *Style*— Peter Gellhorn; ✉ 33 Leinster Ave, East Sheen, London SW14 7JW (☎ 0181 876 3949)

GEMMELL, Gavin John Norman; s of late Gilbert Anderson Sloan Gemmell, of Gullane, E Lothian, and Dorothy Maud, *née* Mackay; *b* 7 Sept 1941; *Educ* George Watson's Coll; *m* 18 March 1967, Kathleen Fiona (Kate), da of Alexander Drysdale, of Edinburgh; 1 s (John Gilbert b 9 Sept 1971), 2 da (Alison Fiona b 22 Aug 1969, Lynsey Jane b 4 April 1975); *Career* CA 1964; Baillie Gifford & Co: investmt trainee 1964, ptnr 1967, ptnr i/c pension fund clients 1973, sr ptnr 1989–; chm: Toyo Trust Baillie Gifford Ltd 1990–, Baillie Gifford & Co Ltd 1995–; dep chm Scottish Widows Fund & Life Assurance Society 1984–; dir: Baillie Gifford Overseas Ltd 1983–, Baillie Gifford Shin Nippon plc 1985–, Guardian Baillie Gifford 1991–, TSB Bank Scotland plc 1991–; pres Watsonian Club 1993–94; memb: Ct Heriot-Watt Univ, Scottish Episcopal Church Educn Bd; *Recreations* golf, squash, travel; *Clubs* Gullane Golf, Hon Co of Edinburgh Golfers; *Style*— Gavin Gemmell, Esq; ✉ 14 Midmar Gardens, Edinburgh EH10 6DZ (☎ 0131 447 8135); Baillie Gifford & Co, 1 Rutland Court, Edinburgh EH3 8EY (☎ 0131 222 4000, fax 0131 222 4099, telex 72310 BGCO G)

GEMMELL, James Henry Fife; s of James Walter Shanks Gemmell (d 1962), and Vera McKenzie, *née* Scott (d 1990); *b* 17 May 1943; *Educ* Dunfermline HS, Univ of Edinburgh; *m* 27 Dec 1972, (Catherine) Morna Davidson, da of John Wilson Gammie, of Elgin, Morayshire; 2 da (Caroline b 1974, Catriona b 1976); *Career* CA 1965; ptnr: Fryer Whitehill and Co 1975–82, Clark Whitehill 1982–; chm: Clark Whitehill Associates Ltd 1985–, Clark Kenneth Leventhal 1992–94 (vice chm 1990–92), Bridford Career Mgmnt plc 1990–; memb Disciplinary Ctee Insur Brokers Registration Cncl 1985–; ICAS: memb Cncl 1988–94, chm Fin and Gen Purposes Ctee 1990–94, Eng and Wales Area Ctee 1989–92, memb Discipline Ctee 1994–; chm Flexlands Sch Educnl Tst Ltd 1988–, memb Cncl Horwath International 1994–; FRSA; *Books* RICS Accounts Rules (1978), Insurance Brokers Accounts and Business Requirement Rules (1979), How to Value Stock (1983); *Recreations* gardening; *Clubs* Caledonian; *Style*— James Gemmell, Esq; ✉ Clark Whitehill, 25 New St Square, London EC4A 3LN (☎ 0171 353 1577, fax 0171 583 1720)

GEMMILL, (Alexander) David; s of William Gemmill (d 1961), and Kathleen Gertrude Stoney, *née* Archer (d 1992); *b* 11 April 1941; *Educ* Univ of Oxford (MA); *m* 30 Sept 1967, Jacqueline Gaye, da of Denis Benjamin Conoley (d 1969); 1 s (Mark William), 1 da (Lucy); *Career* Nat Serv 2 Lt Rhodesia 1965–67; Lazard Bros and Co Ltd 1967–85 (md 1983–85), vice chm West Merchant Bank Ltd 1996– (dep chief exec 1986–96); non-exec dir Amey plc 1996–; *Recreations* tennis, gardening, bee keeping; *Clubs* Brooks's; *Style*— David Gemmill, Esq; ✉ West Merchant Bank Ltd, 33–36 Gracechurch St, London EC3V 0AX (☎ 0171 623 8711, telex 884689 WMB G, fax 0171 626 1610)

GEMMILL, Scot; s of Archie Gemmill (the football coach), of Allestree, Derby, and Elizabeth Travers, *née* Maitland; *b* 2 Jan 1971; *Educ* Ecclesbourne Comp Sch Duffield Derbyshire; *Career* professional footballer; Nottingham Forest: YTS apprentice April 1988–Jan 1990, professional Jan 1990–; honours: Zenith Data Systems Cup winners 1992 (scored 2 goals in final v Southampton), Rumbelows Cup runners-up 1992; Scotland: capped under 21s Euro Championship, first full cap (v Japan) June 1995; Young Player of the Month award Sept 1990; *Recreations* music, golf, tennis; *Style*— Scot Gemmill, Esq; ✉ Nottingham Forest FC, City Ground, West Bridgford, Nottingham NG2 5FJ (☎ 0115 982 2202)

GEMS, Iris Pamela (Pam); da of Jim Price (d 1930), of Christchurch, Dorset, and Elsa Mabel Annetts (d 1989); *Educ* Christchurch Priory Sch, Brockenhurst GS, Univ of Manchester; *m* Sept 1949, Keith Leopold Gems, s of Leopold Frederick Gems; 2 s (Jonathan b 1952, David b 1960), 2 da (Sara b 1954, Elizabeth (Lalla) b 1965); *Career* playwright; author of: Dusa, Fish, Stas and Vi (1976), Queen Christina (1977), Piaf (1978) Franz into April (1978), The Treat (1979), Pasionaria (1981), Camille (1985), The Danton Affair (1986), The Blue Angel (1991), Deborah's Daughter (1994), I Wish You Love (1995), Stanley (1995 (Evening Standard Award for Best Play 1996)); novels: Mrs Frampton (1989), Bon Voyage, Mrs Frampton (1990), memb: Theatre Writers' Union, Dramatists' Guild (US), Writers' Guild; *Recreations* gardening; *Style*— Mrs Pam Gems; ✉ Sebastian Born, c/o The Agency, 24 Pottery Lane, Holland Park, London W11 4LZ (☎ 0171 727 1346)

GENNARD, Prof John; s of Arthur Gennard (d 1962), of Manchester, and Vera Edith, *née* Stone (d 1980); *b* 26 April 1944; *Educ* Univ of Sheffield (BA), Univ of Manchester (MA); *m* 8 May 1976, Florence Anne, da of Daniel Russell (d 1973), of Iver Heath; 1 s (John Cooper), 1 da (Julie Anne); *Career* lectr LSE 1970–81 (res offr 1968–70), prof of industl rels Univ of Strathclyde 1981–, dean Strathclyde Business Sch 1987–93; memb Panel of Arbitrators ACAS; FIPD (memb Membership and Educn Ctee, nat chief examiner Employee Rels); *Books* The Reluctant Militants (1972), Financing Strikers (1977), Closed Shop in British Industry (1983), A History of the National Graphical Association (1990), A History of the Society of Graphical and Allied Trades (1995); *Recreations* football, politics, food and drink; *Clubs* Carluke Rotary; *Style*— Prof John Gennard; ✉ 4 South Avenue, Carluke, Lanarkshire ML8 5TW (☎ 01555 751361); Department of Human Resource Management, University of Strathclyde, Hills Building, Richmond Street, Glasgow G4 0GE (☎ 0141 5524400 ext 3999, telex UNSLIB 77472)

GENT, Christopher Charles; s of Charles Arthur Gent (d 1967), and Kathleen Dorothy Gent, of Beckenham; *b* 10 May 1948; *Educ* Archbishop Tennison GS; *m* Lynda Marion, da of William David Tobin; 2 da (Felicity Sarah b 1978, Clarissa Naome b 1981); *Career* National Westminster Bank 1967, various posts in operations mgmnt, customer service and mktg Schroder Computer Services 1971–79, market devpt mangr rising to md Baric Computing Services (ICL/Barclays Bank joint venture) 1979–84, dir Network Servs Div ICL 1983–84; Vodafone: joined as md when part of Racal plc 1985, dir Racal Telecom plc (name changed following partial flotation) 1988–91, md Vodafone Ltd and dir Vodafone Group plc (following full demerger from Racal) 1991–97, chief exec Vodafone Group plc 1997–, chm Vodafone Australasia, chm Panafon and Panavox (Greece), chm numerous other gp companies in UK, dir Supervisory Bd Libertec (Netherlands); nat chm Young Conservatives 1977–79, vice pres Computer Services Assoc Cncl 1984; *Recreations* family, cricket, politics, horse racing; *Clubs* Carlton, Ancient Britons, Goodwood; *Style*— Christopher Gent, Esq; ✉ Vodafone Group plc, The Courtyard, 2–4 London Road, Newbury, Berkshire RG14 1JX (☎ 01635 33251, fax 01635 35237, Vodafone 0836 200001)

GENT, (John) David Wright; s of Pilot Offr Reginald Philip Gent, RAFVR (d 1942), and Stella Eva Wright (d 1988); *b* 25 April 1935; *Educ* Lancing; *m* 19 Aug 1970, Anne Elaine, da of John Leslie Hanson (d 1988), of Ilkley, Yorks; *Career* admitted slr 1959; dep dir SMMT 1971–80 (legal advsr 1961–63, asst sec 1964, sec 1965–70), gen mangr Lucas Service UK Ltd 1980–82, gp PR mangr Lucas Industries plc 1982–83; dir Br Rd Fedn 1983–85, dir gen Retail Motor Indust Fedn (formerly Motor Agents Assoc) 1985–95, chm Motor Industry Pensions Ltd 1985–95, specialist conslt 1995–, dir D C Cook Holdings plc 1995–; memb Rd Tport Indust Trg Bd 1985–91; Freeman City of London 1985, Liveryman Worshipful Co of Coach Makers and Coach Harness Makers 1985; FIMI 1985, FRSA 1995; *Recreations* gardening, golf; *Clubs* RAC; *Style*— David W Gent, Esq; ✉ 44 Ursula St, London SW11 3DW (☎ 0171 228 8126); 219 High St, Henley-in-Arden, Warwickshire B95 5BG (☎ and fax 01564 793922)

GENTLE, Mary; da of George William Gentle, of Dorset, and late Amy Mary, *née* Champion; *Educ* Bournemouth Univ (BA), Goldsmiths' Coll London (MA), King's Coll London (MA); *Career* author; computer game script and voice direction ZombieVille (1996); *Books Books* A Hawk in Silver (1977), Golden Witchbreed (1983), Ancient Light (1987), Scholars and Soldiers (1989), Rats and Gargoyles (1990), The Architecture of Desire (1991), Grunts! (1992), Left to His Own Devices (1994), Dares (as Roxanne Morgan, 1995), Ash (1997); *Recreations* sword fighting, live role-play games; *Style*— Ms Mary Gentle; ✉ c/o The Maggie Noach Literary Agency, 21 Redan St, London W14 0AB (☎ 0171 602 2451)

GENTLEMAN, David William; s of Tom Gentleman (d 1966), and Winifred Murgatroyd (d 1966); *b* 11 March 1930; *Educ* Hertford GS, St Albans Sch of Art, Royal Coll of Art (ARCA); *m* 1, 1953 (m dis 1966), Rosalind Dease; 1 da (Fenella); m 2, 1968, Susan, da of George Ewart Evans (d 1988), of Brooke, Norfolk; 1 s (Tom), 2 da (Sarah, Amelia); *Career* painter and designer; work incl: painting in watercolour, lithography, wood engraving, illustration, graphic design, posters, postage stamps, Eleanor Cross mural designs for Charing Cross Underground Station 1979; Master of Faculty RDI 1989–91; memb Alliance Graphique Internationale, memb Cncl AGBI (Artists' Gen Benevolent Inst), memb Properties' Ctee Nat Tst; RDI 1970; hon dr of design Kingston Univ; Hon FRIBA, Hon FRCA; *Solo Exhibitions* Watercolours Mercury Gallery 1970–97; *Work in Collections* Tate Gallery, V&A, British Museum, various private collections; *Books* Design in Miniature (1972), David Gentleman's Britain (1982), David Gentleman's London (1985), A Special Relationship (1987), David Gentleman's Coastline (1988), David Gentleman's Paris (1991), David Gentleman's India (1994), David Gentleman's Italy (1997); edns of lithographs (1967–96); *Style*— David Gentleman; ✉ 25 Gloucester Crescent, London NW1 7DL (☎ and fax 0171 485 8824)

GENTLEMAN, Douglas de Regnéville; s of James Gentleman (d 1990), of Glasgow, and Jeanne Lucie Emma, *née* Leneveu; *b* 2 Jan 1954; *Educ* Hutchesons' Boys' GS Glasgow, Univ of Glasgow (BSc, MB ChB, Brunton meml prize, pres Glasgow Univ Medico-Chirurgical Soc 1977–78); *m* 1984, Marjorie, da of George Armstrong; 1 da (Emma b 12 April 1987), 1 s (Philip b 22 July 1989); *Career* jr surgical trg posts Glasgow and Manchester 1978–82, registrar then sr registrar in neurosurgery Inst of Neurological Scis Glasgow 1982–92, conslt neurosurgn Dundee Teaching Hosps NHS Tst 1992–96, head Dept of Surgical Neurology Univ of Dundee 1995–96, conslt in charge Brain Injury Rehabilitation Unit Dundee Healthcare NHS Tst 1996–; memb: GMC 1984– (chm Scottish Cncl 1993–), Dept of Health Standing Advsy Ctee on Med Manpower (Campbell Ctee) 1991–, Advsy Ctee on Med Estabs (advising Sec of State for Scotland) 1993–, Scottish Cncl for Postgrad Med and Dental Educn 1983–91 (observer 1993–); sec-gen Perm Working Gp of Euro Jr Hosp Doctors 1984–88, vice chm Hosp Doctors Ctee Standing Ctee of Doctors of the Euro Community 1985–88, memb Jt Ctee on Higher Surgical Trg 1988–90; memb: Soc of Br Neurological Surgns, Br Trauma Soc, Int Neurotrauma Soc, Scottish Head Injury Forum; FRCS 1982, FRCPS 1982; *Publications* author of pubns on head injury, brain injury rehabilitation and other neurosurgical subjects; *Style*— Douglas de R Gentleman, Esq; ✉ 49 Clepington Road, Stobsmuir, Dundee DD4 7EL (☎ 01382 462496); Brain Injury Rehabilitation Unit, Royal Victoria Hospital, Dundee (☎ 01382 566246, fax 01382 667685)

GEOFFREY, Iqbal (Sayyid Mohammed Jawaid Iqbal Jafree of Slarpore); eldest s of Syed Iqbal Hussain, and Shahzadi Mumtazjehan Shah; *b* 1 Jan 1939; *Educ* Govt Coll Lahore (BA), Punjab Univ (LLB, Gold Medal in Jurisprudence), Harvard Univ (LLM), Read Coll (PhD), Sangamon State Univ (MA); *m* 1, 1967 (m dis 1978), Regina Wai-Ling Cheng; 1 s (Syed Hussain Haider), 1 da (Shahzadi Zohra Elinoi); m 2, March 3 1988, Sayyeda Farzawna Nuccwe; *Career* conceptual artist and public interest advocate; called to the Bar Pakistan 1959 (pupillage under Malik Mohammed Akram, later Chief Justice of Pakistan), called to the Bar USA 1972; ptnr and sr counsel Geoffrey & Khitran Int Lawyers 1960–; grad ed Harvard Art Review 1965–66; human rights offr UN 1966–67, chief accountant British Lion Films London 1968–69, gen counsel Pakistan Inst of Human Rights 1971–, chief accountant Kuwaiti Embassy London 1974–75, special advsr to pres of Pakistan 1980–84 (author of the Estab of the Office of the Ombudsman Order 1983); prof of fine arts: St Mary's Coll Indiana, Central Washington State Univ, Cleveland State Univ Ohio, The Read Univ; external examiner Punjab Univ 1967–70; fell: Huntington Hartford II 1962–65, John D Rockefeller III Fund Creative Painting, Fay B Kent/Alpha Chi Omega, Univ of Bradford Mgmnt Centre 1975–76; memb Bd of Regents S M Jahan Tst 1972–; Hon LLD Read Univ; FRSA 1962; *Solo Exhibitions* incl: Arts Cncl of NI Queen's Univ Belfast 1962, Univ of Hull 1962, Univ of Birmingham 1963, Los Angeles Municipal Art Gallery, Pasadena Art Museum 1963, Seton-Hall Univ 1964, Santa Barbara Museum of Art 1965, UN NYC 1967, Johnson Museum Cornell Univ NY 1972, Everson Museum of Art 1973, liquid sculpture Adoration of Maggie outside Nat Gallery London 1984, Arts Cncl of Pakistan Karachi and Lahore 1985, Indus Gallery Karachi 1989, Hayward Gallery London 1989–90, Embassy of France Pakistan 1992, H W Janson Gallery of Modern Art 1992, Hayward Gallery 1992, Sua Sponte Shows incl Victoria Mirio and Love Here 1993, Nat Art Gallery Islamabad 1993, Lahore Gallery of Art 1995; *Public Collections* Tate Gallery, British Museum, Arts Cncl of GB, Lord Baden-Powell House, St James's Palace, Pasadena Art Museum Calif, Worcester Art Museum, Johnson Art Museum Cornell Univ, The Phillips Collection Washington DC, Boston Museum of Fine Arts, Chase Manhattan Bank NYC, Boston Safe Deposit and Trust Co; *Awards* Central Model Sch's Al Bairuni Prize 1953, Paris Biennial Award 1965, Arts Cncl of GB Award 1968, Gold Shield for Servs to Art & Human Rights Chicago Met Cncl 1979, Sir Herbert Read Silver Medal 1992, Iqbal Geoffrey Day (20 Jan 1992) proclaimed by Govr of Illinois; *Books* Qose-Qizah (1957), Justice is the Absence of Dictatorial Prerogative (1965), Human Rights in Pakistan (1966), A Critical Study of Moral Dilemmas, Iconographical Confusions and Complicated Politics of XXth Century Art (1967), The Concept of Human Rights in Islam (1981), International Recognition and Enforcement of Judgements (American Bar Assoc, 1994); *Style*— Iqbal Geoffrey; ✉ 66 Hall Tower, Hall Place, London W2 1LW; Sül-Sabeil, Gulberg, 54660 Lahore, Pakistan (☎ 00 92 42 878544, 00 92 42 636 2036, 00 92 42 724 8518, fax 00 92 42 636 9430)

GEORGALA, Prof Douglas Lindley; CBE; s of John Michael Georgala (d 1966), and Izetta Iris, *née* Smith; *b* 2 Feb 1934; *Educ* S African Coll Sch, Univ of Stellenbosch (BSc), Univ of Aberdeen (PhD); *m* 18 Dec 1959, Eulalia Catherina, da of George Philip Lochner (d 1962); 1 s (David b 12 May 1963), 1 da (Jeanette b 5 March 1961); *Career* res microbiologist Fishing Res Inst Univ of Cape Town SA 1957–60, tech memb Unilever Coordination 1973–77, head Unilever Res Colworth Laboratory 1977–86 (res microbiologist and div mangr 1960–72), industrial conslt DTI 1987–88; dir of food res Inst of Food Res AFRC 1988–94 (memb Strategy Bd); memb Food Advsy Ctee 1989–95, chm Advsy Ctee on Microbiological Safety of Food 1996– (memb 1991–); external prof Univ of Leeds 1993–; FIFST 1988; *Recreations* gardening, music, cycling; *Style*— Prof Douglas Georgala, CBE; ✉ Institute of Food Research, Earley Gate, Whiteknights Road, Reading RG6 2BZ

GEORGE, Anthony Frank (Tony); *b* 15 March 1936; *Educ* The Leys Sch Cambridge, Christ's Coll Cambridge (MA, LLM), Birkbeck Coll London (BSc); *Career* GKN plc 1969–96 (co sec 1987–96), ret; chm: Bd Central England TEC, NE Worcs Coll Corp; vice pres Inst of Royal Engrs; former Col TA; *Recreations* flying; *Style*— Tony George, Esq; ✉ 39 Frederick Road, Edgbaston, Birmingham B15 1JN (☎ 0121 454 3968, fax 0121 456 4794)

GEORGE, Rear Adm Anthony Sanderson; CB (1983); s of Sandys Parker, and Winifred Marie George; *b* 8 Nov 1928; *Educ* RNC Dartmouth, RN Engrg Coll Manadon; *m* 1953, Mary Veronica Frances Bell; 2 da; *Career* Captain 1972 (served aboard HMS Nelson), Rear Adm 1981; dir Dockyard Production & Support 1981–82, chief exec Royal Dockyards 1983–86, chief exec World Energy Business 1986, port mangr Portsmouth 1987–95; *Style*— Rear Adm Anthony George, CB

GEORGE, Sir Arthur Thomas; kt (1972), AO (1987); s of Thomas George; *b* 17 Jan 1915; *Educ* Sydney Boys' HS, Slrs' Admission Bd Course; *m* 1939, Renée, da of Anthony Freeleagus; 1 da; *Career* slr and co dir; chm and md The Sir Arthur George Family Trust Group 1943–; chm and govr Arthur T George Foundation Ltd 1972–; chm Assoc of Classical Archaeology Univ of Sydney (endowed chair of classic archaeology) 1966–; pres Aust Soccer Fedn 1969–88, exec memb FIFA 1980–94 (Gold Order of Merit 1994, hon memb 1996); hon pres Ctee Oceania Football Confedn; Queen's Silver Jubilee Medal, Elizabethan Medal, Gold Cross Order of Phoenix (Greece), Grand Cdr and Keeper Cross of Mt Athos (Greek Orthodox Church); hon fell Senate Univ of Sydney 1985, fell Confedn of Aust Sport 1985; *Recreations* swimming, theatre; *Clubs* American Nat; *Style*— Sir Arthur George, AO; ✉ 1 Little Queen's Lane, Vaucluse, NSW 2030, Australia (☎ 00 61 2 9371 4030, fax 00 61 2 9327 7738)

GEORGE, Brian Victor; CBE (1995); s of Victor George, of Bournemouth, and Agnes Amelia, *née* Sweet; *b* 5 Feb 1936; *Educ* Southall GS, Southall Tech Coll, Brunel Coll of Advanced Technology (BTech); *m* 19 May 1962, Joan Valerie, da of John Keith Bingham; 2 s (Graham Michael b 2 Dec 1965, David Brian b 10 April 1968); *Career* welding and sheet metal worker APV (Aust) Pty Ltd 1952–54, trade and student apprentice D Napier & Sons Ltd 1954–60; NPC (W) Ltd Whetstone: engr 1960–63, section leader 1963–66, office head Boilers and Gas Circuits 1966–69, asst chief engr Mech Plant 1969–70, asst chief engr Future Systems 1970–75, chief engr Mech Plant & Systems Dept 1975–76, mangr Fast Reactors 1976–77, engr mangr designate PWR; head Nuclear Plant Design Branch CEGB GD & CD 1979–81, dir PWR CEGB GD & CD 1981–89, project and tech dir Project Mgmnt Bd PWR 1984–89; Nuclear Electric plc: chief exec PWR Project Gp 1989–92, exec dir of planning and construction 1992–94, exec dir of engrg 1994–95; chief exec GEC-Marine (comprising VSEL, YSL and NNC) and assoc dir GEC 1995–; DTech (hc); FEng 1989, FIMechE, Hon FINucE; *Recreations* golf, bowls, DIY; *Style*— Brian George, Esq, CBE, FEng; ✉ Wethersfield, Wood Street, Bushley Green, Tewkesbury GL20 6JA (☎ 01684 275880); GEC-Marine, VSEL, Barrow-in-Furness, Cumbria LA14 1AF

GEORGE, (William Norman) Bruce; s of Norman Macdonald George (d 1922), and Isobella Elizabeth Dunn (d 1964); *b* 3 Dec 1915; *Educ* Liverpool Univ Sch of Architecture (BArch), Sch of Planning and Res for Regnl Devpt; *Career* WWII Lt RA 1940–46 (POW 1942); architect; formerly sr ptnr George/Trew/Dunn/Beckles Willson/Bowes, ret 1984; served: Practice Ctee and Panel of Arbitrators RIBA, CNAA; princ buildings: The Guards' Chapel 1963, Wellington Barracks London 1984, Huddersfield Royal Infirmary 1966, Aberdeen Royal Infirmary 1967 and 1976; other works at: King's Coll Hosp London, King's Coll Hosp Med Sch, Halifax Gen Hosp, New Cross Hosp Wolverhampton; ARIBA, AMTPI, FRSA; *Books* The Architect in Practice; *Recreations* sculpture, portrait painting, music, cricket; *Style*— Bruce George, Esq; ✉ 1 Copley Dene, Wilderness Rd, Chislehurst, Kent BR7 5EY (☎ 0181 467 5809)

GEORGE, Bruce Thomas; MP (Lab) Walsall South (majority 3,178); s of Edgar Lewis George, of Mountain Ash, Glam; *b* 1 June 1942; *Educ* Mountain Ash GS; Univ Coll of Wales Swansea (BA), Univ of Warwick (MA); *m* 1992, Lisa Carolyn Toelle; *Career* asst lectr in politics Glamorgan Coll of Technol 1964–66, lectr in politics Manchester Poly 1968–70, sr lectr politics Birmingham Poly and pt/t tutor Open Univ 1971–74, pt/t lectr Dept of Government Univ of Essex (hon fell), ed Jane's NATO Handbook 1989–92; Parly candidate (Lab) Southport 1970, MP (Lab) Walsall S 1974–, memb Select Ctee on Defence 1979–, sr oppn memb Defence Ctee House of Commons, gen rapporteur Political Ctee North Atlantic Assembly; vice pres: The Atlantic Cncl of the UK, Assoc of Euro-Atlantic Cooperation (Moscow); *Recreations* football; *Style*— Bruce George, Esq, MP; ✉ 42 Wood End Road, Walsall, W Midlands (☎ 01922 27898); House of Commons, London SW1A 0AA (☎ 0171 219 3000)

GEORGE, Prof Charles Frederick; s of William Hubert George (d 1957), and Evelyn Margaret, *née* Pryce, of Ringwood, Hants; *b* 3 April 1941; *Educ* Oundle, Univ of Birmingham (BSc, MB ChB, MD); *m* 17 May 1969 (m dis 1973), Rosemary, da of late Edward Moore, JP; *Career* med registrar: Birmingham Gen Hosp 1968–69, Hammersmith Hosp London 1969–71; tutor in med and clinical pharmacology Royal Postgraduate Med Sch London 1971–73; Univ of Southampton: sr lectr in med 1974–75, prof of clinical pharmacology 1975–, dean of med 1986–90 and 1993–; memb GMC (chm Educn Ctee); chm: Jt Formulary Ctee of Br Nat Formulary; hon fell Faculty of Pharmaceutical Med RCP 1989; FRCP 1978; *Books* Topics in Clinical Pharmacology (1978), Presystemic Drug Metabolism (with Renwick & Shand, 1982); *Recreations* windsurfing; *Style*— Prof Charles George; ✉ 15 Westgate St, Southampton SO14 2AY (☎ 01703 229100); Clinical Pharmacology Group, University of Southampton, Medical Biosciences Building, Bassett Crescent East, Southampton SO16 7PX (☎ 01703 594263, fax 01703 594262)

GEORGE, Charles Richard; QC (1992); s of Hugh Shaw George, CIE, IFS (d 1967), and Joan, *née* Stokes; *b* 8 June 1945; *Educ* Bradfield Coll, Magdalen Coll Oxford (MA), Corpus Christi Coll Cambridge; *m* Joyce Tehmina, da of Rev Robert James Barnard; 2 da (Tara Sophie b 1978, Eva Jane b 1981); *Career* asst master Eton Coll 1967–72; called to the Bar: Inner Temple 1974, Irish Bar King's Inns 1995; in planning, admin and Parly law practice 1975–, asst recorder of the Crown Ct 1994–; memb Ctee of Admin Law Bar Assoc 1987–; *Books* The Stuarts - An Age of Experiment (1973); *Recreations* tennis, history and travel; *Style*— Charles George, Esq, QC; ✉ Ashgrove Farm, Ashgrove Road, Sevenoaks, Kent TN13 1SU; 2 Harcourt Buildings, Temple, London EC4Y 9DB (☎ 0171 353 8415)

GEORGE, Edward Alan John (Eddie); s of Alan, and Olive Elizabeth George; *b* 11 Sept 1938; *Educ* Dulwich, Emmanuel Coll Cambridge (BA, MA); *m* 1962, Clarice Vanessa, *née* Williams; 1 s, 2 da; *Career* Bank of England 1962–: seconded to Bank for Int Settlements 1966–69, Int Monetary Fund 1972–74, dep chief cashier 1977–80, asst dir Gilt-Edged Div 1980–82, exec dir 1982–90, dep govr 1990–93, govr 1993–; hon degree London Guildhall Univ 1996; Liveryman Worshipful Co of Mercers; *Recreations* bridge, sailing; *Style*— Eddie George, Esq; ✉ Bank of England, Threadneedle St, London EC2R 8AH (☎ 0171 601 4444)

GEORGE, Jill Findlay; da of Ronald Francis George (d 1987), and Joan Findlay, *née* Brooks (d 1987); *b* 12 Sept 1954; *Educ* St Margaret's Sch Bushey, Univ of Florence, Sheffield Coll of Art (BA); *Career* PR Dept V&A Museum 1972–74, antique shop N Devon 1976–77; Jill George Gallery (Thumb Gallery until 1991): joined 1978, dir 1981, co dir 1983, sole owner and dir 1986–; represented Herts in jr tennis; memb Ctee Art Business Design Centre 1989–92; *Recreations* theatre going, films, music, tennis, classic car shows, croquet; *Clubs* Groucho, Chelsea Arts; *Style*— Ms Jill George; ✉ 7 West Common Way, Harpenden, Herts (☎ 01582 460383); 16 Gillingham Rd, London NW2 (☎ 0181 450 1867); Jill George Gallery, 38 Lexington St, Soho, London W1R 3HR (☎ 0171 439 7343/7319, fax 0171 287 0478)

GEORGE, John Charles Grossmith; er s of Col Edward Harry George, OBE, WS (d 1957), and Rosa Mary, Papal Medal Benemerenti (d 1988), da of George Grossmith, OStJ, Chev de la Legion d'Honneur, Gold Cross of the Order of the Redeemer, Cross Pro Ecclesia et Pontefice; *b* 15 Dec 1930; *Educ* Ampleforth; *m* 1972, Margaret Mary Maria Mercedes (late sec to Garter King of Arms), Dame of Honour and Devotion SMO Malta, Offr of Order Pro Merito Melitense, da of Maj Edric Humphrey Weld, TD, JP (d 1969), and Maria Mercedes, da of Henry Scrope, of Danby; *Career* Lt Hertfordshire Yeo (RA, TA); College of Arms 1963–72: Earl Marshal's liaison offr with Churchill family State Funeral of Sir Winston Churchill 1965, Green Staff Offr Investiture of HRH The Prince of Wales 1969; Garioch Pursuivant to the Countess of Mar 1976–86, Kintyre Pursuivant in the Ct of the Lord Lyon 1986–; Genealogist for Scotland 1995–; memb Cncl: The Heraldry Soc 1976–84, The Heraldry Soc of Scotland 1986–89; co-designer Royal Wedding Stamp (Crown Agents Issue) 1981; vice pres BBC Mastermind Club 1979–81; Col and Hon ADC to the Govr State of Kentucky USA 1991; FSA (Scot) 1975, FHS 1983; Freedom of Loudon County of Virginia USA 1968; Kt of Obedience SMO Malta 1975 (dir of ceremonies Br Assoc 1976–80), Kt of Grace and Devotion 1971, Kt of Grace Constantian Order of St George (Naples) 1982, Cdr of Order Pro Merito Melitense 1983 (Offr 1980); *Books* The Puffin Book of Flags; *Recreations* nineteenth century English operetta, musical comedy, hagiography, watching sport principally racing, rugby and golf; *Clubs* New (Edinburgh); *Style*— J C G George, Esq, Kintyre Pursuivant of Arms; ✉ 115 Henderson Row, Edinburgh EH3 5BB (☎ and fax 0131 557 1605); Court of the Lord Lyon, HM New Register House, Edinburgh EH1 3YT (☎ 0131 556 7255, fax 0131 557 2148)

GEORGE, Prof Kenneth Desmond; s of Horace Avory George (d 1962), of Craig-Cefn-Parc, nr Swansea, and Dorothy Margaret, *née* Hughes; *b* 11 Jan 1937; *Educ* Ystalyfera GS, Univ Coll of Wales Aberystwyth; *m* 18 July 1959, Elizabeth Vida, *née* Harries; 2 s (Alun Michael b 30 Nov 1962, David Keith b 16 Feb 1964), 1 da (Alison Elizabeth b 5 March 1969); *Career* lectr in economics: Univ of Western Australia 1960–63, Univ Coll N Wales 1963–64; Univ of Cambridge: res fell Dept of Applied Economics 1964–66, lectr in economics 1966–73, fell Sidney Sussex Coll 1965–73; prof of economics and head dept Univ Coll Cardiff 1973–88; Univ of Wales Swansea: prof of economics and head dept 1988–95, dean Faculty of Econ and Social Science 1992–93, vice-princ 1993–95, pro vice-chllr 1995–; pt/t memb MMC 1978–86; memb Cncl Royal Econ Soc 1987–92, EC advsr to Poland's Anti-Monopoly Office 1992–94; *Books* The Allocation of Resources (with J Shorey, 1978), Industrial Organization (with C Joll, 1981, 4th edn with C Joll and E L Lynk, 1992), The Welsh Economy (ed with Dr L Mainwaring, 1988); *Recreations* walking, photography, music; *Style*— Prof Kenneth George; ✉ Department of Economics, Universty of Wales Swansea, Singleton Park, Swansea (☎ 01792 295168, fax 01792 295872, telex 48358)

GEORGE, Llewellyn Norman Havard; s of late Cdr Benjamin William George, DSO, RNR, and late Annie Jane George; *b* 13 Nov 1925; *Educ* Cardiff HS, Fishguard GS; *m* 30 Aug 1950, Mary Patricia Morgan, da of late David Morgan Davies, of Fishguard; 1 da (Sarah b 1957); *Career* slr; HM coroner 1965–80, recorder Wales and Chester Circuit 1980–; pres: West Wales Law Soc 1973–74, Pembs Law Soc 1982–3; chm (no5) S Wales Law Soc Legal Aid Ctee 1979, chm Agric Land Tbnl Wales 1990– (dep chm 1985–90); memb Farrand Ctee on Conveyancing 1985–86; *Recreations* golf, reading, chess; *Clubs* Newport Pembs Golf, Pembs County; *Style*— Llewellyn George, Esq; ✉ Goodwick House Chambers, West Street, Fishguard, Dyfed (☎ 01348 873691)

GEORGE, Martin Francis; s of William Anthony George (d 1984), and Margot, *née* Cooper; *b* 1 Nov 1942; *Educ* Repton; *m*; 1 s (Michael David b 1973), 1 da (Alison Mary Rachel b 1975); *Career* Whitworths Holdings Ltd: mangr Animal Feeds 1964–1970, dir Flour Mills 1970–80, bd dir 1980–84, jt md 1984–85, chm 1985–87, gp md 1992–; pres UK Agric Supply Trade Assoc 1981–82; chm Leicester FC plc, former chm Mid Anglia Radio plc; *Style*— Martin George, Esq; ✉ Fotheringhay Manor, Peterborough, Cambs PE8 5HZ; Whitworths Holdings Ltd, Victoria Mills, London Road, Wellingborough, Northants NN8 2DT (☎ 01933 443444, fax 01933 443346)

GEORGE, Michael; s of John James George (d 1964), of Thorpe St, Andrew, Norwich, Norfolk, and Elizabeth, *née* Holmes; *b* 10 Aug 1950; *Educ* King's Coll Cambridge Choir Sch, Oakham Sch, RCM; *m* 15 July 1972, Julie Elizabeth Kennard (soprano), da of Stanley Kennard; 1 s (Nicholas James Stanley b 19 Aug 1980), 2 da (Lucy Elizabeth Sullivan b 27 May 1975, Emilie Jane b 1 Aug 1978); *Career* bass baritone; ranges from twelfth century to present day; has appeared at all maj festivals throughout Britain incl The Proms 1990 (4 separate concerts performing Bach, Janacek, Arvo Part and Renaissance music), The Three Choirs Festival and elswhere with City of Birmingham Symphony, Scot Chamber and BBC Symphony Orchs; performed abroad 1990: Messiah (Italy, Spain, Poland and France), Mozart's Requiem (with Trevor Pinnock, Ottawa), Handel (California and Boston), Haydn's Creation (under Hogwood, Holland, Germany and Italy) *Recordings* incl: Carmina Burana (4 vols), Acis and Galatea, Haydn's Creation, Beethoven's Ninth Symphony, Missa Solemnis (with Hanover Band), Handel's Messiah, St John Passion (with The Sixteen), Handel's Joshua, Stravinsky's Le Rossignol (with BBC Symphony Orch), Holst's At the Boar's Head (under David Atherton), 8 vols of Purcell Odes (with The King's Consort, Hyperion); *Recreations* tennis, golf, food; *Clubs* Riverside, Concert Golfing; *Style*— Michael George, Esq; ✉ c/o IMG Artists, Media House, 3 Burlington Lane, London W4 2TH (☎ 0181 747 9977, fax 0181 747 9131)

GEORGE, Nicholas; s of Wallace Yewdall Evelyn George, and Joy Isabel Gilbert, *née* Hickey; *b* 1 Feb 1954; *Educ* Radley; *Career* articled clerk Edward Moore & Sons 1973–77, Joseph Sebag & Co 1977–79, Rowe & Pitman; dir: WI Carr Sons & Co 1981–86, BZW Securities 1986–93, BZW Asia 1991–93, Drayton Asia Trust plc 1989–93; dir and head of SE Asian equities and emerging market securities Robert Fleming Ltd 1993–; FCA 1978, AIIMR 1980; *Recreations* shooting, fishing, travelling; *Style*— Nicholas George, Esq; ✉ Robert Fleming Ltd, 25 Copthall Avenue, London EC2R 7DR (☎ 0171 638 5858); 108 Elgin Crescent, London W11 2JL

GEORGE, Patrick Herbert; s of Alfred Herbert George, and Nora, *née* Richards; *b* 28 July 1923; *Educ* The Downs Sch, Bryanston, Edinburgh Coll of Art (scholar), Camberwell Sch of Art; *m* 1, July 1953 (m dis 1980), June, da of Dr A Griffith; 4 da (Kate, Victoria, Alice, Nancy); m 2, 1981, Susan Jean Elizabeth, da of Philip Ward; *Career* artist; RNVR 1942–46; lectr: Slade Sch UCL 1949–58 and 1961–82, Nigerian Coll of Art Zaria 1959–60; Univ of London: reader, prof 1983–86, Slade prof 1986–89, emeritus prof 1989; exhibitions incl: One Man Exhibition Gainsborough's House Sudbury 1975, Retrospective Serpentine Gallery London 1980; dealer Browse & Darby; works in public collections in GB and USA; *Style*— Patrick George, Esq; ✉ 33 Moreton Terrace, London SW1V 2NS (☎ 0171 828 3302); Grandfather's, Great Saxham, Bury St Edmunds, Suffolk IP29 5JW (☎ 01284 810997)

GEORGE, Susan Melody; da of Norman Alfred George, of Wraysbury, Berks, and Eileen, *née* Percival; *b* 26 July 1950; *Educ* Corona Acad; *m* 1984, Simon MacCorkindale, *qv*; *Career* actress and producer; dir AMY International Productions; *Films* as actress incl: Billion Dollar Brain 1965, The Sorcerers 1966, The Strange Affair 1967, Eye Witness 1969, Fright 1970, Straw Dogs 1971, Dirty Mary, Crazy Larry 1972, Dr Jekyll and Mr Hyde 1972, Mandingo 1973, Tiger Shark 1975, Tomorrow Never Comes 1977,

Venom 1980, A Texas Legend 1980, Enter The Ninja 1981, The House Where Evil Dwells 1982, The Jigsaw Man 1984, Czech Mate 1985, The White Stallion 1986, White Roses 1988/89, The House That Mary Bought 1994; as exec prodr: Stealing Heaven 1987–88, White Roses 1988–89, The House That Mary Bought 1994; *Awards* Valentino Award for Best Actress, Virgin Islands Film Festival Award for Best Actress, Anthony Asquith Award for Best New Composer (film theme That Summer of White Roses); *Books* Songs to Bedroom Walls (limited edn, 1987); *Style*— Ms Susan George; ✉ c/o Amy International Productions, PO Box 17, Towcester, Northants NN12 8YJ (☎ 01295 760256, fax 01295 760889)

GEORGE, Terence Paul (Ted); s of Harold Dennis George (d 1988), and Olive Maud, *née* Swann; *b* 1 June 1948; *Educ* Gt Yarmouth GS, Churchill Coll Cambridge (BA, MA); *m* 15 July 1972, Diana, da of Prof Edward O'Farrell Walsh (d 1972), of Hong Kong; 2 s (Richard b 1976, William b 1984), 1 da (Joanna b 1979); *Career* engr Sir Alexander Gibb & Ptnrs 1971–74, co-ordinator Severn Trent Water Authy 1974–79, conslt PA Mgmnt Consits 1979–82; HTV Ltd: tech controller 1982–87, dir of engrg 1987–88; md HTV West Ltd 1991–92; HTV Group plc: dir 1988–, dep chief exec 1993–, dir of broadcasting 1994–; dir Cardiff ITEC Ltd; MICE 1974, AMIMC 1982; *Recreations* sailing, tennis, hill walking; *Style*— Ted George, Esq; ✉ HTV Group, Television Centre, Culverhouse Cross, Cardiff, Wales CF5 6XJ (☎ 01222 590617)

GEORGE, Timothy John Burr; CMG (1991); s of Brig John Burr George (d 1990), and Margaret Brenda, *née* Harrison (d 1989); *b* 14 July 1937; *Educ* Aldenham Sch, Christ's Coll Cambridge (BA, scholar); *m* 21 July 1962, Richenda Mary, da of late Alan Reed, FRIBA, and Ann *née* Rowntree; 1 s (Andrew John Timothy b 1963), 2 da (Rebecca Caroline Ann b 1965, Natasha Mary Jane b 1967); *Career* Mil Serv 2 Lt RA 1956–58; HM Dip Serv: entered FCO 1961, third sec Hong Kong 1962–63, second sec Peking 1963–66, second then first sec FCO 1966–68, first sec (econ) New Delhi 1969–72, asst political advsr Hong Kong 1972–74, first sec FCO 1974–78, cnsllr and head of chancery Peking 1978–80, res assoc Int Inst for Strategic Studies London 1980–81, cnsllr UK Perm Delgn to OECD Paris 1982–86, head Repub of Ireland Dept FCO 1986–90, ambass Kathmandu 1990–95; *Books* Security in Southern Asia (co author 1984); *Style*— Timothy George, Esq, CMG; ✉ Martlets, Ogbourne St George, Marlborough, Wilts SN8 1SL

GEORGE, His Hon Judge; William; s of William Henry George (d 1979), of Alderwasley, Derbyshire, and Elizabeth, *née* Ashley; *b* 28 Sept 1944; *Educ* Herbert Strutt GS Belper, Victoria Univ of Manchester (LLB, LLM); *m* Susan Isabel, *née* Pennington; 2 da (Elizabeth Barbara b 20 July 1977, Francesca Gordon b 18 Nov 1979); *Career* called to the Bar Lincoln's Inn (Mansfield scholar) 1968, in practice Chancery Bar 1969–95, head of chambers 1985–95, standing counsel to Treasy in charity matters in Liverpool 1984–95, recorder of the Crown Court 1993–95 (asst recorder 1990), circuit judge (Northern Circuit) 1995–; chm Northern Chancery Bar Assoc 1992–94; *Recreations* contemporary English artists, military history (the American Civil War), English history, gardening, flying kites (memb Kite Society); *Clubs* Athenaeum (Liverpool); *Style*— His Hon Judge George; ✉ c/o Northern Circuit Office, 15 Quay Street, Manchester M60 9FD

GEORGE, Dr William Richard Philip; CBE (1996); s of William George (d 1967), and Anita Williams (d 1943); *b* 20 Oct 1912; *Educ* Friars Sch Bangor Gwynedd, Wrekin Coll, Wellington; *m* 19 Dec 1953, Margarete, da of Leonhard Bogner (d 1956), of Nurnberg; 1 s (Philip b 1956), 3 da (Anita b 1959, Elizabeth b 1961, Gwen b 1966); *Career* slr 1934, pt/t clerk to Justices Barmouth 1948–75, dep circuit judge 1975–80; co cncllr rep Criccieth Ward Gwynedd CC 1967–96 (chm Cncl 1982–83, currently chm Parly Ctee), memb ACC 1982–96, chm Assembly of Welsh Counties 1991–93; chm: Criccieth Meml Hall Ctee, Criccieth Town Cncl 1967–; hon sec Criccieth Welsh Baptist Church 1958–; winner Poetry Crown Royal Nat Eisteddfod of Wales 1974, hon slr Royal Nat Eisteddfod 1979–; Archdderwydd Cymru (Archdruid of Wales) 1990–93; Hon DLitt Univ of Wales 1988; memb Law Soc 1934; *Books* 5 vols Welsh verse (1947, 1969, 1974, 1979, 1989), The Making of Lloyd George (1976), Lloyd George: Backbencher (1983), Gyfaill Hoff (the letters of Welsh Patagonian authoress Eluned Morgan, ed 1972); *Recreations* golf, currently writing autobiography; *Clubs* Criccieth Golf; *Style*— Dr William George, CBE; ✉ Garthcelyn, Criccieth, Gwynedd LL52 0AH (☎ 01766 522625); office: 103 High St, Porthmadog, Gwynedd (☎ 01766 512011 and 01766 512474, fax 01766 514363)

GEORGIADIS, Philip Andrew; s of Jack Constantine Georgiadis, and Jean Alison, *née* Tytler; *b* 6 May 1962; *Educ* Kings Coll Sch Wimbledon, Univ of York (BA); *m* 23 Dec 1991, Penelope, da of John Granville Brenchley; 1 da (Olivia Florence b 13 June 1992); *Career* media exec Benton & Bowles advtg agency 1984–85 (joined as trainee media buyer 1983), media exec Ray Morgan & Partners Sept-Nov 1985; WCRS: media planner/buyer 1985–87, media mangr/assoc dir 1987–89, bd dir 1989–91, media dir Esprit Media 1990–91, exec media dir 1991–94, vice chm 1994–95; chief exec Initiative Media 1995–; MIPA; *Recreations* travelling, eating, golf, squash; *Clubs* Lambton Place; *Style*— Philip Georgiadis, Esq; ✉ 2 Cleveland Square, London W2 (☎ 0171 467 6723); Initiative Media London Ltd, The Courtyard, 30 New Oxford Street, London WC1A 1AP (☎ 0171 636 3377)

GERAGHTY, Billy; s of William Thomas Geraghty, of Galway, and Catherine Lansbury; *b* 12 March 1963; *Educ* Woodroffe Sch Lyme Regis, East 15 Acting Sch; *Career* actor; *Theatre* incl: Road, Midnight Hour (Bolton Octagon), A Lie of the Mind (Royal Court), How I got to Spain (one man show, Foundry), Gentleman Jim (Nottingham Playhouse), Buddy Holly in Buddy (Victoria Palace Theatre, Her Majestey's Theatre Sydney) 1989–92; most recently Heathcliff in Wuthering Heights (Good Co, dir Sue Pommeray); *Television* incl: The Ritz, Hard Cases, Split Enz, Aufwiedersehen Pet, Chancer, The Bill, Criss Cross, Soldier Soldier, The Riff Raff Element, Hale and Pace, Peak Practice, Heartbeat; *Films* incl: Wilt, Closing Ranks, The Nose; *Recreations* football, tennis, cricket, athletics, baseball, swimming, rally cross, motor bike racing, hang gliding, scuba diving, playing drums, percussion, electric and acoustic guitar, piano, synthesiser and harmonica, singing in musical shows and rock bands; *Style*— Billy Geraghty, Esq; ✉ c/o Creative Artists Management Ltd, 19 Denmark Street, London WC2H 8NA (☎ 0171 497 0448, fax 0171 240 7384)

GERAINT, Baron (Life Peer UK 1992), of Ponterwyd in the County of Dyfed; Geraint Wyn Howells; s of David John and Mary Blodwen Howells; *b* 15 April 1925; *Educ* Ardwyn GS; *m* 1957, Mary Olwen Hughes, da of Margaret Ann Griffiths, of Tregaron; 2 da (Hon Gaenor Wyn b 14 Aug 1960, Hon Mari Wyn b 8 Sept 1964); *Career* vice-chm Brit Wool Marketing Bd 1971–83, chm Wool Producers of Wales Ltd 1977–87; MP (Lib) Cardigan 1974–83, (Lib 1983–88, then Lib Dem) Ceredigion and Pembroke North 1983–92; *Style*— The Rt Hon the Lord Geraint; ✉ c/o House of Lords, London SW1A OPW

GERARD, 5 Baron (UK 1876); Sir Anthony Robert Hugo Gerard; 17 Bt (E) 1611; s of Maj Rupert Gerard, MBE (d 1978, great nephew of 2 Baron); suc 2 cous once removed, 4 Baron Gerard (d 1992); *b* 3 Dec 1949; *Educ* Harvard; *m* 1976, Kathleen, eldest da of Dr Bernard Ryan, of New York; 2 s (Hon Rupert Bernard Charles b 17 Dec 1981, Hon John Frederick William b 1986); *Heir* s, Hon Rupert Bernard Charles Gerard b 17 Dec 1981; *Style*— The Rt Hon the Lord Gerard; ✉ PO Box 2308, East Hampton, NY 11937, USA

GERARD LEIGH, Col William Henry; CVO (1983), CBE (1981); s of Lt-Col J C Gerard Leigh (d 1965), of Thorpe Satchville Hall, Melton Mowbray, Leics, and Helen, *née* Goudy (d 1964); *b* 5 Aug 1915; *Educ* Eton, Univ of Cambridge; *m* 29 Oct 1946, (Nancy) Jean, da of Wing Cdr Sir Norman Leslie 8 Bt, CMG, CBE (d 1937); 2 s (John b 24 Jan 1949, David b 28 Aug 1958), 2 da (Carolyn (Mrs Charles Benson) b 12 Nov 1947, Camilla (Mrs Hugh Seymour) b 4 July 1952); *Career* LG: joined 1937, served ME Italy and Germany 1939–45, Lt-Col Cmdg 1953–56, Col Cmdg Household Cavalry and Silver Stick in Waiting to HM The Queen 1956–59, Gentleman Usher to HM The Queen 1967–85; chm Nat Cncl YMCA's 1974–81; *Clubs* White's; *Style*— Col W H Gerard Leigh, CVO, CBE; ✉ Hayes, East Woodhay, Newbury, Berks RG20 0AN (☎ 01488 668228)

GERHARD, Dr Derek James (Jeremy); CB (1986); s of Frederick James Gerhard (d 1983), of Banstead, Surrey, and Lily Muriel, *née* Hubbard (d 1984); *b* 16 Dec 1927; *Educ* Highgate, Fitzwilliam Coll Cambridge (MA), Univ of Reading (PhD); *m* 5 April 1952, Dr Sheila Decima Gerhard, da of Dr Gerald Kempster Cooper (d 1979); 3 s (Timothy b 1955, Mark b 1961, Christopher b 1965), 2 da (Jane b 1957, Julia b 1963); *Career* civil servant 1951–88 (various positions Air Miny, Dept of Scientific and Industl Res, Br Embassy in Washington, BOT and DTI rising to dep master and comptroller (chief exec) Royal Mint 1978–88); business conslt 1988–; churchwarden St John's Belmont 1988–92, hon treas Cncl for Churches of Britain and Ireland 1993–; hon fell Fitzwilliam Coll Cambridge; *Recreations* genealogy, woodwork, gardening; *Style*— Dr Jeremy Gerhard, CB; ✉ Little Dowding, Walton Heath, Surrey KT20 7TJ (☎ 01737 813045, fax 01737 814335, compuserve 100415,415)

GERKEN, Vice Adm Sir Robert William Frank; KCB (1986), CBE (1975), DL (Devon 1995); s of Francis Sydney Gerken, and Gladys Gerken; *b* 11 June 1932; *Educ* Chigwell Sch, RNCs Dartmouth and Greenwich; *m* 1, 1966, Christine Stephenson (d 1981); 2 da (Charlotte b 1967, Victoria b 1970); m 2, 1983, Mrs Ann Fermor, widow of Graham Fermor, née Blythe; *Career* Royal Navy 1948–87; Capt of the Fleet (C-in-C Fleet's Staff at Northwood Middx) 1978–81, Rear Adm and Flag Offr 2 Flotilla 1981–83, dir gen Naval Manpower and Trg 1983–84, Vice Adm 1984–87, Flag Offr Plymouth and Port Adm Devonport 1985–87, placed on Retired List April 1987; chm Plymouth Development Corporation 1993–96; chm Corps of Commissionaires Management Ltd 1992; govr Chigwell Sch, pres Port of Plymouth Lifeboat (RNLI) 1988, chm of tstees China Fleet Club (UK) 1987; Hon DSc Univ of Plymouth 1993; *Recreations* sailing; *Clubs* Royal Western Yacht Club of England (Cdre 1993–97); *Style*— Vice Adm Sir Robert Gerken, KCB, CBE, DL; ✉ 22 Custom House Lane, Millbay, Plymouth PL1 3TG (☎ 01752 665104)

GERLIS, Dr Laurence; s of Toby Gerlis, of Herts, and Sylvia, *née* Sussman; *b* 17 May 1950; *Educ* City of London Sch (scholar), Clare Coll Cambridge (scholar, MA, MB BCh, William Butler prize in med), London Hosp (scholar, DipPharmMed, MRCP, paediatrics & pathology prize); *m* 1971, Pauline Benveniste; 1 s (Adam b 1982), 2 da (Melanie b 1974, Sarah b 1977); *Career* Med Unit London Hosp 1974–76, med dir Novo Laboratories 1976–82, dir of clinical res Biogen Geneva 1982–85; formerly radio doctor LBC Radio; currently: int lectr on clinical res MCRC Ltd, registered specialist in diabetes care; conslt physician Kuwait Med Centre, visiting conslt King Edward VII Hosp Port Stanley; appearances on radio and TV med progs incl: LBC, BBC, Thames, C4, Br Med TV; memb Faculty Pharmaceutical Physicians 1990; *Books* Good Clinical Practice (1987, 2 edn 1989), Biotechnology Made Simple (1989), Consumer's Guide to Prescription Medicines (1990), Thomas Cook Health Passport (1990), Consumer's Guide to Non-Prescription Medicines (1991); *Style*— Dr Laurence Gerlis; ✉ 21 Devonshire Place, London W1N 1PD (☎ 0171 935 0113)

GERMAIN, (Dennis) Richard; s of Capt Dennis George Alfred Germain (d 1956), and Catherine Emily Violet, *née* Tickner; *b* 26 Dec 1945; *Educ* Mayfield Coll; *m* 7 Sept 1968, (Jadwiga) Anne Teresa, da of Zygfryd Nowinski (d 1988); 1 s (Richard b 1973), 1 da (Suzanne b 1976); *Career* called to the Bar Inner Temple 1968; memb Criminal Bar Assoc; *Recreations* cinema, photography, stamp collecting, antiques; *Style*— Richard Germain, Esq; ✉ Mander Lara, Oxford Road, Gerrards Cross, Bucks SL9 8TB (☎ and fax 01753 885775); 4 Brick Court, Temple, London EC4Y 9AD (☎ 0171 583 8455, fax 0171 353 1699, DX 453 LON/CH'RY LN)

GERMAN, (Frank) Clifford; s of Reginald Frank German, of Northampton, and Jessie, *née* Henson; *b* 13 March 1934; *Educ* Northampton GS, St John's Coll Cambridge (open exhibitioner, BA, pres Liberal Club); *m* 1967, Muriel Mary Norton, da of Stanislaus Norton; 2 c (Catherine Victoria b 1970, Richard George b 1972); *Career* Nat Serv RN 1952–54, Lt RNVR; Fulbright scholar, teaching fell Univ of Michigan Ann Arbor 1957–58, lectr in geography Wayne State Univ Detroit 1959–61, Financial Times 1961–63, The Times 1963–66; Daily Telegraph: joined 1966, fin correspondent 1968–86, dep city ed 1972–76, assoc city ed 1976–86; city ed: Today 1986–87, The Scotsman 1987–94; personal fin ed: Independent on Sunday 1995, Independent 1995–; FRGS 1959; *Books* Geography of the Soviet Union (with J P Cole, 1961), Guide to Mortgage Finance (1988); *Recreations* cricket, old cars; *Clubs* MCC; *Style*— Clifford German, Esq; ✉ 25 Rollscourt Ave, London SE24 0EA (☎ 0171 274 7126); The Independent, 1 Canada Square, Canary Wharf, London E14 5DL (☎ 0171 293 2116)

GEROSA, Peter Norman; s of Enrico Cecil Gerosa (d 1944), and Olive Doris Minnie, *née* Harry (d 1931); *b* 1 Nov 1928; *Educ* Whitgift Sch, Birkbeck Coll London (BA); *m* 1955, Dorothy Eleanor, da of Newton Cunningham Griffin; 2 da (Susan, Catherine); *Career* Civil Serv 1945–82; served in: FO, Home Office, Customs & Excise, Dept of Tport; under sec DOE 1972–82; sec Tree Cncl 1983–91, vice pres RoSPA 1984–, chm Nat Automobile Safety Belt Assoc 1986–; *Recreations* languages, numismatics, singing, enjoying architecture and the countryside; *Style*— Peter Gerosa, Esq; ✉ 17 Friths Drive, Reigate, Surrey RH2 0DS (☎ 01737 243771)

GERRARD, The Ven David Keith Robin; s of Eric Henry Gerrard, and Doris Jane, *née* Dance; *b* 15 June 1939; *Educ* Royal GS Guildford, St Edmund Hall Oxford (BA); *m* 12 Oct 1963, Jennifer Mary, da of John Stell Hartley (d 1981); 2 s (Stephen John b 1967, Jacob b 1972), 2 da (Ruth b 1965, Rachel b 1969); *Career* ordained: deacon 1963, priest 1964; curate: St Olave Woodberry Down 1963–66, St Mary Primrose Hill 1966–69; vicar: St Paul Lorrimore Square 1969–79, St Andrew and St Mark Surbiton 1979–89; rural dean Kingston 1983–88, hon canon Southwark Cathedral 1985, archdeacon of Wandsworth 1989–; *Books* Urban Ghetto (1976); *Recreations* family, Yorkshire, embroidery, Proust; *Style*— The Ven The Archdeacon of Wandsworth; ✉ 68 North Side, Wandsworth Common, London SW18 2QX (☎ 0181 574 5766); Kingston Episcopal Area Office, Whitelands College, West Hill, London SW15 3SN (☎ 0181 780 2308)

GERRARD, David Lester; *b* 13 Dec 1942; *Educ* King Edward VI Sch Birmingham, Birmingham Coll of Art; *m* 6 April 1974, Catherine Robin; 2 da (Sophia Elizabeth b 22 March 1978, Charlotte Mary b 16 Oct 1980); *Career* industl designer Robert Matthew Johnson-Marshall & Partners Edinburgh 1967–72, prod designer Pakistan Design Inst Karachi 1974–76, princ Gerrard & Medd (product, interior and furniture design consltancy) 1977–; external assessor Nat Coll of Art Lahore Pakistan 1976, visiting design lectr Dept of Architecture Nova Scotia Tech Coll Halifax 1977, internal assessor Design Sch Glasgow Sch of Art 1991 (visiting lectr 1978–90), currently external assessor South Bank Univ; memb Bd Heritage Unit Robert Gordon's Univ Aberdeen 1993–; vice pres CSD 1990–93 (chm Scottish Regn 1986–88); awards: Scottish Designer of the Year 1980, Civic Trust award 1985, Oscar for a domestic sink design for Carron Phoenix, Bureau du Syndicat National des Architectes d'Interieur Paris 1990; ASTD 1969, FCSD 1978; *Recreations* gardening, skiing, travelling, worrying; *Style*— David Gerrard, Esq; ✉ Gerrard and Medd, Quadrant, 17 Bernard St, Edinburgh EH6 6PW (☎ 0131 555 0670, fax 0131 554 1850)

GERRARD, Neil; MP (Lab) Walthamstow (majority 3,022); s of late Francis Gerrard, and Emma Gerrard; *b* 3 July 1942; *Educ* Manchester Grammar, Wadham Coll Oxford; *m* 1968 (m dis 1983); 2 s; *Career* teacher Queen Elizabeth's Sch Barnet 1965–68, lectr Hackney Coll 1968–92; Parly candidate (Lab) Chingford 1979, MP (Lab) Walthamstow 1992–; London Borough of Waltham Forest: cncllr 1973–90, ldr Lab Gp 1983–90, ldr of Cncl 1986–90; bd memb: Theatre Royal Stratford E London; memb: NATFHE, GMB; *Recreations* theatre, cinema, reading, music, sport; *Style*— Neil Gerrard, Esq, MP; ✉ House of Commons, London SW1A 0AA

GERRARD, Peter Noël; CBE (1991); s of Sir Denis Gerrard (d 1965), of Fulbourn, Cambs, and Hilda Goodwin, *née* Jones (who m 2, Sir Joseph Cantley and d 1995); *b* 19 May 1930; *Educ* Rugby, ChCh Oxford (MA); *m* 15 June 1957, Prudence, da of Herbert Lipson-Ward (d 1937), of Shanghai; 1 s (Hugo b 1963), 2 da (Phyllida b 1958, Deborah b 1960); *Career* Nat Serv 2 Lt XII Royal Lancers Malaya; admitted slr 1959, sr ptnr Lovell White & King 1980–88 (ptnr 1960–80), sr ptnr Lovell White Durrant 1988–91, gen counsel London Stock Exchange 1991–94; memb: Bd of Banking Supervision 1990–, City Capital Markets Ctee 1974–91, Cncl of St George's Hosp Med Sch 1982–94, Bd of Inst of Advanced Legal Studies 1985–96, Cncl of the Law Soc 1972–82; *Recreations* walking, music; *Clubs* Athenaeum, City of London; *Style*— Peter Gerrard, Esq, CBE; ✉ Pightle Cottage, Ashdon, Saffron Walden, Essex CB10 2HG (☎ 01799 584374)

GERRARD-WRIGHT, Maj-Gen Richard Eustace John; CB (1985), CBE (1977, OBE 1971, MBE 1965), DL (1993 Cambs); s of Rev R L Gerrard-Wright; cous of Maj (Arthur) Alexander Greenwood, *qv*; *b* 9 May 1930; *Educ* Christ's Hosp, RMA Sandhurst; *m* 1960, Susan Kathleen Young; 2 s, 2 da (1 decd); *Career* Dep Col Royal Anglian Regt 1975–80, Col Cmdt The Queen's Div 1981–84, GOC Eastern Dist 1980–82, Dir TA & Cadets MOD 1982–85, ret; *Style*— Maj-Gen R E J Gerrard-Wright, CB, CBE, DL; ✉ c/o Lloyds Bank, Minster Place, Ely, Cambs CB7 4EN

GERRETSEN, Wob; *b* 18 Feb 1942; *Educ* Univ of The Hague (BSc); *Career* gen surveyor and bill of quantities engr Port Authy Rotterdam 1964–65, dredge supt/surveyor Blok BV (civil engrg and dredging contractors) 1965–66; Costain Group plc: joined 1966, dredge supt Middlesbrough 1966–69, site mangr irrigation project Iraq 1969–70, asst site mangr airport reclamation project Seychelles 1970–72, site mangr port devpt contract Mauritius 1972–74, area mangr responsible for dredging ops ME (based Dubai) 1974–76, contracts mangr Holland 1976–81, dir/gen mangr 1981–86, chm Costain Mining Dredging and Concrete Div 1986–89, md Costain Engineering & Construction Ltd 1989–90, main bd dir and chm Costain Engineering & Construction Ltd 1991–95; exec dir responsible for Business Devpt, Energy Settlements and Information Services Ltd National Grid Group plc 1995–; *Recreations* sailing, horseriding, music, history; *Clubs* Royal Thames Yacht, Royal Society of Arts; *Style*— Wob Gerretsen, Esq; ✉ National Grid Group plc, National Grid House, Kirby Corner Road, Coventry CV4 8JY (☎ 01203 537777)

GERSON, Michael Joseph; s of Maj John Leslie Gerson, TD (d 1980), and Jeanne Ida, *née* Marx (d 1981); *b* 2 Nov 1937; *Educ* Gresham's Sch Holt; *m* 28 Oct 1962, Shirley Esther, da of Alfred Simons; 3 s (Anthony, Peter, Simon); *Career* RNVR 1952–58; chm Michael Gerson Ltd 1980– (md 1961–80); chm Inst of Furniture Warehousing and Removal Indust, pres Fedn Int Brussels 1982–83, dir N London TEC; Freeman City of London 1984, Liveryman Worshipful Co of Carmen 1984; MCIT, FIFF, FMI; *Recreations* sailing; *Clubs* City Livery; *Style*— Michael Gerson, Esq; ✉ Downland Close, Whetstone, London N20 9LB (☎ 0181 446 1300, fax 0181 446 5088)

GERSTENBERG, Frank Eric; s of Eric Gerstenberg (d 1982), and Janie, *née* Thomas (d 1989); *b* 23 Feb 1941; *Educ* Glenalmond Coll Perthshire, Clare Coll Cambridge (MA), London Inst of Educn (PGCE); *m* 30 July 1966, Valerie Myra, da of Dr Peter Desmond MacLellan, of Westerham, Kent; 1 s (Neil John b 1968), 2 da (Anna Myra b 1971, Wendy Jane b 1971); *Career* asst master Kelly Coll Devon 1963–67, housemaster and head of history Millfield Sch Somerset 1967–74, headmaster Owestry Sch Shropshire 1974–85, princ George Watson's Coll Edinburgh 1985–; memb: Headmasters Conf 1985, Secdy Heads Assoc 1974; *Recreations* golf, skiing, travel; *Clubs* New (Edinburgh); *Style*— Frank Gerstenberg, Esq; ✉ George Watson's College, Colinton Rd, Edinburgh EH10 5EG (☎ 0131 447 7931, fax 0131 452 8594)

GETHIN, Maj Sir Richard Joseph St Lawrence; 10 Bt (I 1665), of Gethinsgrott, Cork; s of Lt-Col Sir Richard Patrick St Lawrence Gethin, 9 Bt (d 1988), and Fara, *née* Bartlett; *b* 29 Sept 1949; *Educ* Oratory, RMA Sandhurst, RMCS Shrivenham (BSc), Cranfield Inst of Technol (MSc); *m* 1974, Jacqueline Torfrida, da of Cdr David Cox, RN; 3 da (Katherine Torfrida b 1976, Rosanna Clare b 1979, Belinda Jacqueline b 1981); *Heir* uncle, Lt-Col William Allan Tristram Gethin, MC, RA b 13 Oct 1913; *Career* serv HM Forces, Maj; distribution mangr Beck and Pollitzer, consultation mangr Union Railways; MILog; *Recreations* tennis, carpentry; *Style*— Maj Sir Richard Gethin, Bt

GETHING, Brian Constantine Peter; s of Lt-Col Burton William Eills Gething, of 5 Royal Northumberland Fus (d 1936), and Lady Donatia Faith Mary, *née* Wentworth-Fitzwilliam (d 1943, 3 da of 7 Earl Fitzwilliam, KCVO, CBE, DSO); *b* 11 June 1926; *Educ* RNC Dartmouth; *m* 6 Jan 1954, (Ann) Sigrid (d 1991), da of Sir John Musker (d 1992), of Shadwell Park, Thetford, Norfolk; 1 s (William b 1959), 1 da (Caroline b 1957); *Career* served RN 1943–52, Lt 1948, ADC to HE Govr of Trinidad and Tobago 1950–52; dir: Hurst Park Club Syndicate Ltd 1957–63, British Bloodstock Agency plc 1964–91 (conslt 1991–); *Recreations* shooting; *Clubs* White's, Pratt's, MCC, Jockey Club Rooms (Newmarket), Hon Soc of Knights of the Round Table; *Style*— Brian Gething, Esq; ✉ British Bloodstock Agency plc, Queensberry House, High Street, Newmarket, Suffolk CB8 9BD (☎ 01638 665021)

GETHING, Air Cdre Richard Templeton; CB (1960), OBE (1945), AFC (1939); s of George A Gething, of Wilmslow, Cheshire; *b* 11 Aug 1911; *Educ* Malvern, Sydney Sussex Cambridge; *m* 1940, Margaret Helen, da of Sir Herbert William Gepp (d 1954), of Melbourne, Australia; 1 s, 1 da; *Career* RAF 1933–60; served WWII Canada, UK, Burma, India; acting gp capt 1943, gp capt 1950, acting air cdre 1956, dir ops Maritime, Navigation and Air Traffic Air Ministry 1956–60, ret; navigator and co-pilot of Vickers Wellesley which set world straight-line distance record (flying Egypt to Darwin non-stop) 1938; *Style*— Air Cdre Richard Gething, CB, OBE, AFC; ✉ Garden Hill, Kangaroo Ground, Vic 3097, Australia

GETTY, (John) Paul; Hon KBE (1986); s of J Paul Getty (d 1976), and his 4 w Helen Ann, *née* Rork (d 1988); *b* 7 Sept 1932; *Educ* Univ of San Francisco; *m* 1, Jan 1956 (m dis 1964), Gail, da of Judge George Harris, of California; 2 s (Paul b 4 July 1956, Mark b 9 July 1960), 2 da (Aileen (Mrs Christopher Wilding) b 14 July 1957, Ariadne b 23 July 1962); m 2, 10 Dec 1966, Talitha Dina (d 1971), da of Willem Pol, painter; 1 s (Tara Gabriel Galaxy Gramaphone b 30 May 1968); m 3, 29 Dec 1994, Victoria Holdsworth; *Career* served US Army Korea 1952–53; md Getty Oil Italiana 1959–68; *Recreations* bibliophilia, early gramophone recordings, films, watching cricket; *Clubs* MCC, Pratt's; *Style*— J Paul Getty, KBE

GEWANTER, Henry Leonard; s of Sidney Martin Lester Gewanter, of North Carolina, USA, and Louise Davida, *née* Pearlman; *b* 4 Jan 1954; *Educ* Bronx HS of Sci NY City, Univ of Lausanne Switzerland, King's Coll Cambridge (BA, MA); *m* 14 Sept 1991, Susan Carolyn, da of A W Thompson (d 1986); 2 s (William Anthony Benjamin b 17 March 1993, Alexander Nicholas Adam b 3 Feb 1996); *Career* National Westminster Bank plc: Domestic Banking Div Foreign Dept Head Office 1978–79, International Banking Div Corporate Financial Services 1979–82, Business Devpt Div Advertising Dept 1983–86, tutor Investmt Revision Course NatWest Training Centre 1983–87; dep head PR County NatWest Ltd 1986–88, dir First Financial Advertising Ltd 1988–93, dir Financial Dynamics Ltd 1993–; lectr 1987–: Hammersmith and West London Coll, London Guildhall Univ, Chartered Inst of Bankers (asst examiner in investmt); Real Estate Bd Examination NY State 1977; memb: Assoc for Consumer Research, Consultancy Panel Assoc of Banking Teachers 1982, City & Financial Group IPR; FRSA 1985, MIPR 1989, FCIB 1992; *Recreations* collecting comic books and ancient Roman coins; *Style*— Henry L Gewanter, Esq; ✉ Financial Dynamics Ltd, 30 Furnival St, London EC4A 1JE (☎ 0171 831 3113, fax 0171 831 7961)

GHAFFARI, Dr Kamran; s of Mir Jalil Ghaffari, of Milan, Italy, and Aschraf Ghaffari; *b* 17 July 1948; *Educ* King's Sch Ely, Univ of Milan (MD); *m* 8 Nov 1986, Farnaz, da of Mir Jafar Ghaffari-Tabrizi; *Career* sr registrar and lectr in psychiatry St Thomas's Hosp 1984–86, md and conslt psychiatrist Psychiatric and Psychological Consultant Services Ltd 1987–91, conslt psychotherapist W Middx Univ Hosp and Ashford Hosp 1992–; conslt psychiatrist and psychoanalyst in private practice, conslt i/c Eating Disorders Unit Huntercombe Manor Hosp 1991–93; memb: Br Psycho-analytic Soc, Assoc of Psycho-analytic Psychotherapy in the NHS; MRCPsych; *Recreations* theatre, bridge, chess, computer sciences; *Style*— Dr Kamran Ghaffari; ✉ 14 Devonshire Place, London W1N 1PB (☎ 0171 935 0640)

GHILÈS, Francis Christopher; s of Marcel Francois Ghiles, of Grenoble, France, and Margaret Esme Hyman; *b* 13 Nov 1944; *Educ* Lycée Francois de Londres, Lycée Champollion Grenoble, Institut d'Etudes Politiques Grenoble France, St Antony's Coll Oxford (BLitt); *Career* political scientist; research asst to Pierre Mendes France MP 1966–68; reporter: City Press 1974–76, Euromoney 1976–77, The Financial Times 1977–94; currently independent conslt specialising in political, economic, fin and energy analysis of the N African region; freelance assignments for: The International Herald Tribune, The New York Times, Institutional Investor, Euromoney, Le Monde, Liberation, El Pais, Political Exterior, CBC, BBC World Service, BBC TV, CNN; lectr at numerous univs and research insts throughout UK and overseas; co-fndr annual Mediterranean Gas Conf 1992; *Recreations* skiing, theatre; *Style*— Francis Ghilès, Esq; ✉ 43a Glenmore Road, London NW3 4DA (☎ 0171 586 5622, fax 0171 722 5479)

GHODSE, Prof Abdol-Hamid (Hamid); s of Abdol Rahim Ghods, of Iran, and Batool, *née* Daneshmand; *b* 30 April 1938; *Educ* Univ of Iran (MD), Univ of London (PhD, DPM); *m* 30 June 1973, Barbara, da of Capt of William Bailin, of Tring; 2 s (Amir-Hossein b 1975, Ali-Reza b 1979), 1 da (Nassrin b 1977); *Career* Lt Iranian Health Corps 1965; subsequent postgrad trg/research psychiatrist and lectr Morgannwg Hosp Wales, Bart's and Maudsley Hosps London, conslt St George's and St Thomas' Hosp 1978–87, prof of psychiatry of addictive behaviour St George's Hosp Med Sch 1987–; dir S Thames Regnl Drug and Alcohol Problem Team; RCPsych: chm Substance Misuse Section, memb Cncl 1990–94, memb Ct of Electors 1993–; memb: Expert Advsy Panel WHO 1979–, UN Int Narcotics Control Bd 1992– (pres 1993–95), Cncl St George's Med Sch 1993–, Subject Panel and i/c higher degrees in psychiatry Univ of London 1993–; FRCP 1992 (MRCP 1988), FRCPsych 1985 (MRCPsych 1980), MFPHM 1996; *Publications* approx 200 incl: Psychoactive Drugs - Improving Prescribing Practices (1988), Drugs and Addictive Behaviour - A Guide to Treatment (1989, 2 edn 1995), Misuse of Drugs (3 edn, with P Bucknell, 1996); *Recreations* cycling, reading; *Clubs* Athenaeum; *Style*— Prof Hamid Ghodse; ✉ St George's Hospital Medical School, Cranmer Terrace, London SW17 0RE (☎ 0181 672 9516)

GHOSH, Dr Chandra; da of Prof Bhupendranath Ghosh (d 1988), and Dr Sati Ghosh (d 1992); *b* 15 June 1944; *Educ* St John's Diocesan Girls HS, Univ of Calcutta (MB BS), Univ of London (DPM), MRCPsych (Eng) 1975; *m* 22 May 1983, Dr Norman Alexander Hindson, s of John Savage Hindson; *Career* sr house offr, registrar and sr registrar Univ of Liverpool, conslt psychiatrist Broadmoor Special Hosp 1988– (Park Lane Special Hosp 1977–87); memb: Mental Health Assoc, Trans-Cultural Soc; *Style*— Dr Chandra Ghosh; ✉ Broadmoor Hospital, Crowthorne, Berks RG11 7EG (☎ 01344 773111)

GHOSH, Dr Mrinal Kanti; s of Dr Jitendra Nath Ghosh (d 1981), of India, and Lalita, *née* Ghosh (d 1947); *b* 17 Jan 1938; *Educ* Calcutta Univ India (MB BS), Delhi Univ India (DTCD); *m* 12 Dec 1963, (Chitralekha) Roma, da of Sudhir Chandra Konar, of Burdwan, W Bengal, India; 1 s (Neil b 6 Aug 1973), 1 da (Mita b 23 Nov 1966); *Career* sr house offr geriatric med and neurology 1972–74, asst physician Amersham Gen Hosp Bucks 1974–76, conslt physician geriatric med Rotherham DHA 1976–, clinical tutor Rotherham Postgrad Med Educn Rotherham Dist Gen Hosp 1985–92, currently hon clinical lectr Univ of Sheffield, trainer GP Vocational Trg Scheme Rotherham; former memb Regnl Higher Educn Sub-Ctee, memb Ethical Ctee Rotherham Dist Gen Hosp, chm Calcutta Med Coll Ex-Students Assoc (UK) 1990–92, past treas BMA; MRCP, FRCPG 1987, FRCP 1988; *Recreations* sporting activities; *Clubs* Rotherham Sitwell Rotary; *Style*— Dr Mrinal Ghosh; ✉ District General Hospital, Rotherham, S Yorks S65 2UD (☎ 01709 820000 ext 5939)

GIACHARDI, Dr David John; *b* 17 May 1948; *Educ* Watford Boys' GS, Merton Coll Oxford (Open postmaster, BA (1st Class) Chemistry), St John's Coll Oxford (DPhil); *m*; 1 da; *Career* research asst contracted to Concorde Div DTI Physical Research Laboratory Univ of Oxford 1973–74, Boston Consulting Group Ltd 1974–79; Courtaulds PLC: joined 1979, head Policy & Planning Unit and memb Divnl Bd National Plastics Ltd 1981–82, dir Courtaulds Fibres Ltd 1982–87, chm Courtaulds Chemicals 1986–89, dir of research and technol 1982–94, memb Main Bd 1987– (currently responsible for Human Resources, Health, Safety and Environment), memb Gp Exec 1988–, chm Mgmnt Ctee Courtaulds Pension Fund 1991; memb EPSRC, chm Sci Educn & Technol Ctee UK Chemical Industries Assoc; FRSC; *Style*— Dr David Giachardi; ✉ Courtaulds plc, 50 George Street, London W1A 2BB (☎ 0171 612 1000, fax 0171 612 1500)

GIARDELLI, (Vincent Charles) Arthur; MBE (1973); s of Vincent Ausonio Elvezio Giardelli (d 1953), of Broadway Mansion, Laugharne, Dyfed, and Annie Alice Sophia, *née* Lutman (d 1972); *b* 11 April 1911; *Educ* Hertford Coll Oxford (MA); *m* 1, 10 April 1937 (m dis 1980), Phillis Evelyn, da of Lt Cdr John Berry; 1 s (Lawrence b 1942), 1 da (Judith b 1940); m 2, 21 May 1976, Beryl Mary, da of George Trotter (d 1952), of Croydon, Surrey; *Career* fireman 1939–45, tutor then sr tutor Univ Coll of Wales Aberystwyth 1958–78, artist attached to Grosvenor Gallery London 1962–; one man exhibitions incl: Nat Library of Wales 1963, Manchester Coll of Art 1964, Welsh Arts Cncl 1975, Univ of Wales 1977 and 1978, Gallerie Convergence Nantes 1980, Grosvenor Gallery 1987 and 1994; collections incl: Nat Library of Wales, Nat Museum of Wales, Gallery of Modern Art Dublin, Arts Cncl of GB, Welsh Arts Cncl, Musée des Beaux Arts Nantes, Nat Gallery Slovakia, Nat Gallery Prague, Tate Gallery; winner of Br Cncl award 1979, chm 56 Gp Wales 1958–95, nat chm Assoc of Tutors in Adult Educn 1964–67, memb Calouste Gulbenkian Enquiry into economic situation of the visual artist 1977; hon fell Univ Coll Wales 1979–85; memb Assoc of Visual Artists Wales; Silver Medal Czechoslovak Soc for International Relations 1985; *Books* Up with the Lark (1939), The Delight of Painting (1976), The Grosvenor Gallery 1960–71 (1988); *Recreations* viola, foreign travel; *Style*— Arthur Giardelli, Esq, MBE; ✉ The Golden Plover, Warren, Pembroke, Dyfed SA71 5HR (☎ 01646 661201)

GIBB, Prof (Arthur) Allan; OBE (1987); s of Arthur Gibb (d 1975), and Hilda, *née* Coleman (d 1977); *b* 20 Nov 1939; *Educ* Monkwearmouth GS Sunderland, Univ of Manchester (BA), Univ of Durham (PhD); *m* 12 Aug 1961, Joan, da of Eric Waterhouse (d 1964); 1 s (Stephen b 21 Sept 1962), 1 da (Jennie b 23 March 1965); *Career* res assoc and conslt Economist Intelligence Unit 1961–65, res fell Univ of Durham 1965–70, mangr Craven Bros 1970–71, chm small business centre Durham Univ Business Sch 1992– (dir 1971–91); chm Steering Gp, memb UK Enterprise and mgmnt Assoc; *Recreations* fell walking, tennis, watching football, travel; *Style*— Prof Allan Gibb, OBE; ✉ Kendonville, Crossgate Peth, Nevilles Cross, Durham (☎ 0191 386 4061); Durham University Business School, Mill Hill Lane, Durham DH1 3LB (☎ 0191 374 2234, fax 0191 374 3748, telex 537351 DURUBG)

GIBB, Frances Rebecca; da of Matthew Gibb, of Islington, London, and Bettina Mary, *née* Dawson; *b* 24 Feb 1951; *Educ* St Margaret's Sch Bushey Herts, Univ of East Anglia Norwich (BA); *m* 5 Aug 1978, Joseph Cahill, s of Col E J Cahill; 3 s (Thomas b 3 Aug 1983, James b 19 April 1985, Patrick b 8 April 1989); *Career* news res asst Visnews 1973, trainee reporter Times Higher Education Supplement 1974–78, art sales corr Daily Telegraph 1978–80; The Times: reporter 1980–82, legal affairs corr 1982–; *Style*— Ms Frances Gibb; ✉ The Times, 1 Pennington St, London E1 9XN (☎ 0171 782 5931)

GIBB, Sir Francis Ross (Frank); kt (1987), CBE (1982); s of Robert Gibb (d 1932), and Violet Mary Gibb; *b* 29 June 1927; *Educ* Loughborough Coll (BSc); *m* 1950, Wendy Marjorie, da of Bernard Fowler (d 1957); 1 s, 2 da; *Career* with Taylor Woodrow plc 1948–, dir Taylor Woodrow Int 1969–85; chm: Taywood Santa Fe 1975–85, chm and chief exec Taylor Woodrow plc 1985–89 (jt md 1979–85, jt dep chm 1983–85), pres Taylor Woodrow Construction Ltd 1985– (chm 1978–85, jt md 1979–84); non-exec dir: Babcock International Group plc 1990–, Steetley plc 1990–92, Nuclear Electric 1990–94, Energy Saving Tst Ltd 1992– (chm 1995–); pres Fedn of Civil Engrg Contractors 1984–87 (chm 1979–80, vice pres 1980–84); dir: Holiday Pay Scheme 1980–83, Tstees Benefits Scheme 1980–83, Bldg and Civil Engrg Tstees 1980–83; chm: Agreement Bd 1980–82, Nat Nuclear Corp 1981–88; dir Br Nuclear Assocs 1980–88; memb: Cncl CBI, Governing Body London Business Sch 1985–89; vice pres Inst Civil Engrs 1988–90; Hon DTech 1989, Hon FCGI, FEng 1980, FICE; *Recreations* ornithology, gardening, walking, music; *Clubs* Arts; *Style*— Sir Frank Gibb, CBE, FEng; ✉ Ross Gibb Consultants, 18 Latchmoor Avenue, Gerrards Cross, Bucks

GIBB, James Robertson; RD (1983); s of David Craig Gibb (d 1971), and Mina, *née* Speirs (d 1981); *b* 19 April 1934; *Educ* Paisley GS, Univ of Glasgow (MA); *m* 21 March 1973, Elizabeth Milford, da of James Herries Henderson; 1 s (Donald James Hepburn), 1 da (Audrey Hepburn); *Career* investmt mangr Scottish Amicable Life Assurance Society 1962–67 (apprentice actuary 1956–62), dir Speirs & Jeffrey Ltd 1967–; Lt Cdr RNR (ret), FFA 1962; *Recreations* yachting, curling, skiing; *Clubs* Mudhook Yacht, R Gourock Yacht, Scottish Ski, Partick Curling; *Style*— James Gibb, Esq; ✉ Speirs & Jeffrey Ltd, 36 Renfield St, Glasgow G2 1NA (☎ 0141 248 4311, fax 0141 221 4764)

GIBB, Walter Frame; DSO (1945), DFC (1943); s of Robert Gibb, and Mary Florence, *née* Davies; *b* 26 March 1919; *Educ* St Peter's Weston-super-Mare, Clifton; *m* 26 Feb 1944, (Pauline) Sylvia, da of Edward Baines Reed (d 1972); 3 da (Philippa Jane b 1947, Alison Mary b 1950, Anne Charlotte b 1956); *Career* RAFVR 1940, Night Fighter Mosquitos 264, 6O5, 515, 239 Sqdns, Wing Cdr 1944, CO 239 Sqdn, Wing Cdr Flying TFU 1945, RAF Defford, demobbed 1946; Bristol Aeroplane Co: apprentice Engine Div 1937–40, war service until 1946, test pilot, chief test pilot 1956; achieved World Altitude Record in Olympus Canberra WD 952 1953 (63, 668 feet) and 1955 (65, 890 feet), flew Brabazon and Britannia Aircraft; sales and service mangr British Aircraft Corporation (now British Aerospace plc) 1961, chm and md British Aerospace Australia Ltd 1978, ret 1984; JP Bristol 1974; *Recreations* sailing, swimming; *Clubs* RAF, Royal Sydney Yacht Sqdn, Thornbury Sailing; *Style*— Walter Gibb, Esq, DSO, DFC; ✉ Merlin Haven Lodge, 21 Merlin Haven, Wotton-under-Edge, Glos GL12 7BA (☎ 01453 844889)

GIBBENS, Barnaby John (Barney); OBE (1989); s of Dr Gerald Hartley Gibbens (d 1989), of Sidmouth, Devon, and Deirdre Mary, *née* Wolfe (d 1972); *b* 17 April 1935; *Educ* Winchester; *m* 1, 30 June 1960 (m dis 1990), Sally Mary, da of Geoffrey Harland Stephenson (d 1961), of Guildford; 1 s (Nicolas b 1974), 2 da (Penelope b 1962, Virginia b 1967); m 2, 26 Feb 1990, Kristina, da of Romulo de Zabala (d 1966); *Career* fndr CAP Gp (later SEMA Gp) 1962; pres Computing Servs Assoc 1975; chm: Computing Servs Industry Trg Cncl 1984–94, Info Technol Industry Lead Body 1987–; dir Nat Computing Centre 1987–90, memb Nat Cncl for Vocational Qualifications 1989–92, chm Tstees Skin Treatment and Research Tst 1990–; chm: Callhaven plc 1990–92, Enterprise Systems Group Ltd 1990–96; dir and co sec UK Skills 1990–; dir Info Technol Indust Trg Orgn (ITITO) 1991–96, memb Nat Cncl for Educnl Technol (NCET) 1991–94; chm: Info Technol Trg Accreditation Cncl (ITTAC) 1991–96, The Royal Tennis Court Hampton Court Palace 1994–; Freeman City of London 1987; fndr master Worshipful Co of Info Technologists 1987; hon memb City & Guilds of London Inst 1993; FBCS 1970, FCA 1972; FRSA 1993; *Recreations* golf, real tennis, photography, gardening; *Clubs* Savile, Wisley Golf; *Style*— Barney Gibbens, Esq, OBE; ✉ 12 Kings Rd, Wimbledon, London SW19 8QN (☎ 0181 542 3878)

GIBBERD, Dr (Frederick) Brian; s of Dr George Frederick Gibberd, CBE (d 1976), and Margaret Erica, *née* Taffs (d 1976); *b* 7 July 1931; *Educ* Aldenham, Univ of Cambridge (MA, MB BChir, MD), Westminster Med Sch; *m* 3 Sept 1960, Margaret Clare, da of David James Sidey (d 1939); 4 da (Ruth b 1962, Judith b 1965, Lucy b 1966, Penelope b 1968); *Career* conslt physician and neurologist Westminster Hosp (now Chelsea and Westminster Hosp) 1965–, neurologist Queen Mary's Hosp Roehampton 1965–96; chm Med Ctee: Westminster Hosp 1983–86, Riverside DHA 1985–87 (conslt memb 1987); RSM: memb Cncl 1971 and 1975–79, pres Clinical Section 1972–74, hon librarian 1975–79; RCP: chm Standing Ctee of Membs 1970–72, examiner 1973–, memb Cncl 1989–, censor 1990–92; memb GMC 1992–; Freeman City of London 1968; Worshipful Soc of Apothecaries: Liveryman 1968, memb Ct 1986–, Master 1996; memb Harveian Soc of London 1982 (pres 1995); Hon FFOM, FRCP (London) 1972, FRCPEd 1993; *Style*— Dr Brian Gibberd; ✉ Chelsea and Westminster Hospital, 369 Fulham Road, London SW10 9NH (☎ 0181 746 8316/8320/8599)

GIBBERD, Lady; Patricia; *née* Spielman; *b* 17 Oct 1926; *m* 1, Gerald Fox-Edwards; 1 da; m 2, 1972, as his 2 w, Sir Frederick Gibberd, CBE, RA, FRIBA, FRTPI, FILA (d 1984, architect of Liverpool Met Cathedral, Inter-Continental Hotel London, London Airport Terminal Buildings and Chapel); *Career* memb Eastern Arts Bd 1991–96 (chm Visual Arts Panel 1984–90), chm Harlow Art Tst (fndr memb 1952), chm Commissions East; memb Mgmnt Ctees 1984–90: Yorkshire Sculputre Park, Kettle's Yard; patron: Art & Architecture, Landscape & Art Network; tstee: Copped Hall Tst, Human Rights Sculpture Tst; memb Bd Gainsborough's House Sudbury; chm Harlow Health Centres Tst; FRSA; *Style*— Lady Gibberd; ✉ Marsh Lane, Harlow, Essex CM17 0NA (☎ 01279 427131)

GIBBINGS, Sir Peter Walter; kt (1989); s of Walter White Gibbings (d 1963), of London, and Margaret Russell, *née* Torrance (d 1963); *b* 25 March 1929; *Educ* Rugby, Wadham Coll Oxford (MA); *m* 1, Sept 1953 (m dis 1974), Elspeth Felicia, da of Cedric Macintosh; 2 da (Sarah b 1957, Jane b 1959); m 2, March 1975, Hon Louise Barbara Lambert, da of 2 Viscount Lambert; 1 s (Dominic b 1976); *Career* 2 Lt 9 Queen's Royal Lancers 1951–52; called to the Bar Middle Temple 1953, dep legal advsr Trinidad Oil Co Ltd 1955–56, Associated Newspapers Ltd 1956–60, The Observer 1960–67 (dep mangr and dir 1965–67), md Guardian Newspapers Ltd 1967–73, chm Guardian and Manchester Evening News 1973–88 (dir 1967–73), dir Reuters Holdings plc 1984–88, chm Press Association Ltd 1986–87 (dir 1982–88), dir The Economist 1987–, chm Anglia TV Group plc 1988–94 (dir 1981, dep chm 1986–88); memb Press Cncl 1970–74, pres CPU 1989–92, chm Radio Authy 1995–; dir Rothschild Trust Corp 1989–, memb Cncl Univ East Anglia 1989–95; Liveryman Worshipful Co of Stationers & Newspaper Makers; *Recreations* tennis; *Style*— Sir Peter Gibbings; ✉ The Radio Authority, Holbrook House, Great Queen Street, London WC2B 5DG

GIBBON, Gen Sir John Houghton; GCB (1977, KCB 1972, CB 1970), OBE (1945, MBE 1944); er s of Brig John Houghton Gibbon, DSO (d 1960), of The Manor House, Little Stretton, Salop, and Jessie Willoughby, *née* Campbell; *b* 21 Sept 1917; *Educ* Eton, Trinity Coll Cambridge; *m* 1951, Brigid Rosamund, da of Dr David Armitage Bannerman, OBE, of London; 1 s; *Career* cmmnd RA 1939, served France, Western Desert, Sicily and Europe WWII, 6 Airborne Div Palestine 1945–47, instr and chief instr RMA Sandhurst 1947–51, AQMG WO 1955–58, Co Field Regt 1959–60, Bde Cdr Cyprus 1962, Dir Def Plans MOD 1962–65, Maj-Gen 1966, Sec Chiefs of Staff Ctee and Dir Def Ops Staff MOD 1966–68, DASD (Army) 1969–71, Lt-Gen 1971, Vice-Chief of Def Staff 1971–74, Gen 1974, Master Gen of the Ordnance 1974–77, ADC Gen to HM the Queen 1976–77, Col Cmdt RA 1972–82; chm Regular Forces Employment Assoc 1982–88 (vice chm 1977–82); hon memb of Ct and Liveryman Worshipful Co of Glass Sellers; *Recreations* fishing, shooting, rowing; *Clubs* Naval and Military, Leander; *Style*— Gen Sir John Gibbon, GCB, OBE; ✉ Beech House, Northbrook Close, Winchester, Hants SO23 0JR (☎ 01962 866155)

GIBBON, Lindsay Harwin Ward (Lin); da of James Ferguson Gibbon, and Joyce Harwin, *née* Ellis; *b* 29 Nov 1949; *Educ* Glasgow Sch of Art; *m* 30 June 1973 (m dis 1996); 1 da (Katherine Jane Harwin Gibbon McGregor b 1985); *Career* dir Randak Design Consultants Ltd 1978– (graphic designer specialising in corp literature and packaging design); vice pres and chm Nat Bd CSD 1996– (memb Cncl 1993–95), chm CSD Scotland 1993–95, memb Bd of Dirs Scottish Design 1994–, fndr chm Scottish Design Res Forum 1994–; FCSD 1994; *Recreations* horses and roses; *Style*— Lin Gibbon; ✉ Sorisdale, by Lanark; Randak Design Consultants Ltd, Gordon Chambers, 90 Mitchell Street, Glasgow G1 3NQ (☎ 0141 221 2142, fax 0141 226 5096)

GIBBON, Maggie; da of Peter Lewin Gibbon, of Le Bourg, Taillecavat, 33580 Monségur, France, and Alice Louise, *née* Hall; *b* 6 July 1949; *Educ* Fareham Girls' GS Fareham Hants, Univ of Essex (BA); *Career* advertisement sales exec on Radio Times for BBC Publications 1974–76, media planning exec with two advertising agencies (BBDO and CDP) 1976–80, advertisement sales exec The Observer 1980–81, memb Launch Team World of Interiors Magazine then Tatler for Condé Nast Publications 1980–84, advertisement mangr then publisher Over 21 Magazine 1984–88, publisher New Woman Magazine 1988–92, advertisement dir Private Eye 1992–93, gp advertisement dir Decanter 1994–; *Recreations* swimming, sailing, cooking, theatre; *Clubs* Groucho's; *Style*— Miss Maggie Gibbon; ✉ Decanter Magazine Ltd, Priory House, The Cloisters Business Centre, 8 Battersea Park Road, London SW8 4BG (☎ 0171 627 8181, fax 0171 738 8688)

GIBBON, His Hon Judge; Michael; QC (1974); s of Frank Oswald Gibbon (d 1959), of Ty-Draw Rd, Cardiff, and Jenny Muriel, *née* Leake (d 1958); *b* 15 Sept 1930; *Educ* Brightlands, Charterhouse, Pembroke Coll Oxford (MA); *m* 15 Feb 1956, Malveen Elliot, da of Capt John Elliot Seager, MC, DL, JP, OStJ (d 1955); 2 s (Nigel Elliot b 1958, David Frank b 1960), 1 da (Juliet Rebecca b 1963); *Career* RA 1949–50, Lt TA 1950–58; called to Bar 1954, recorder of the Crown Ct 1972–79, circuit judge (Wales and Chester Circuit) 1979, sr circuit judge Cardiff 1993–; chm Advsy Ctee to Home Sec 1972, Local Govt Boundary Cmmn for Wales 1978–79 (dep chm 1974–79); memb Parole Bd for England and Wales 1986–88, chm Lord Chllr's Advsy Ctee for S Glam 1990–, chm Criminal Justice Liaison Ctee for Counties of Glamorgan and Gwent 1992–; hon recorder of the City of Cardiff 1986–; *Recreations* music, golf; *Clubs* Cardiff and County, Royal Porthcawl Golf; *Style*— His Hon Judge Gibbon, QC; ✉ Cardiff Crown Court, The Law Courts, Cathays Park, Cardiff CF1 3PG (☎ 01222 345931)

GIBBON, Ronald Bryan; s of Robert Robinson Gibbon (d 1967), and Ethel Winifred Gibbon (d 1978); *b* 23 Sept 1928; *Educ* Kings Coll Durham (BSc); *m* 19 April 1958, Brenda Eunice, da of Sidney Walter Nicholls; 2 s (David Keith Christopher b 6 July 1960, Andrew Neil Michael b 3 Oct 1962); *Career* graduate apprentice CA Parsons 1952–54, AERE 1954–56, head Materials Technology International Research and Development Co 1957–66; Gas Council: design advsr Engineering Research Centre 1966–68, quality control engr then engrg servs mangr HQ 1968–75; British Gas: central controller Prodn and Supply Div 1975–87, HQ dir construction 1987–90, dir The National Transmission System 1990–; chm Bd QUASCO; dir: Port Greenwich Ltd, Methane Services Ltd; memb UK Offshore Operators Assoc 1980– (chm Engrg and Devpt Ctee 1984–87); awarded H Jones medal 1987; MInstM 1963, FIQA 1969, FIGasE 1970, FEng 1988; *Recreations* wine tasting, gardening, church work; *Style*— Ronald Gibbon, Esq, OBE, FEng; ✉ Suoluno, Curls Lane, Maidenhead, Berks SL6 2QF

GIBBON-WILLIAMS, Andrew; s of Ivor James Williams (d 1990), of Barry, S Glamorgan, and Grace Mary, *née* Thomas; *b* 6 March 1954; *Educ* Barry Boys' GS, Edinburgh Coll of Art Univ of Edinburgh (Huntly-MacDonald Sinclair travelling scholarship, MA); *Career* artist and art critic; art critic The Sunday Times Scotland 1988–, regnl art critic The Times 1988–, regular contrib to BBC Arts progs; winner: Young Artist bursary Scottish Arts Cncl 1982, Warwick Arts Tst Artist award 1989; *Solo Exhibitions* 369 Gallery Edinburgh 1979, 1980, 1982 and 1986; *Group Exhibitions* incl: Scottish Painters (Chenil Gallery, London) 1978, The Royal Scottish Academy 1980, Scottish Painting (Watts Gallery, Phoenix, Arizona) 1981, Best of 369 (St Andrews Festival) 1983, The Scottish Expression: 1983 (Freidus Ordover Gallery, NY) 1983, Peintres Contemporains Ecossais (Galerie Peinture Fraiche, Paris) 1983, New Directions - British Art (Puck Bldg, NYC) 1983, Chicago Int Art Exposition 1983–89, Int Contemporary Art Fair (London) 1984, Contemporary Scottish Art (Clare Hall, Cambridge) 1984, Scottish Painting (Linda Durham Gallery, Sante Fe) 1985, Scottish Art Since 1900 (Scottish Nat Gallery of Modern Art, Edinburgh and The Barbican Gallery, London 1989–90); *Work in Public Collections* incl: The Scottish Arts Cncl Dundee Art Gallery, Glasgow Museums and Art Galleries, IBM UK Ltd, Philips Petroleum, Scottish Nat Gallery of Modern Art, City of Edinburgh Public collection, The Warwick Arts Tst collection, L&M Moneybrokers Ltd, NatWest Bank, The McDonald Corporation (USA); *Books* The Bigger Picture (1993), An American Passion (1995), Craigie: The Art of Aitchison (1996); *Recreations* travel, music; *Style*— Andrew Gibbon-Williams, Esq; ✉ Merlindale Lodge, Broughton, Lanarks ML12 6JD (☎ and fax 0141 552 8462)

GIBBONS, Christopher Adney Walter; s of Adney Walter Gibbons (d 1941), of London, and Lady Taylor, *née* Constance Ada Shotter (d 1989); *b* 14 May 1930; *Educ* Charterhouse, Trinity Coll Cambridge; *m* 1, Jan 1953 (m dis 1964), Gillian Elizabeth Sugden Temperley; 1 da (Virginia b 10 March 1954); m 2, Sept 1964, Charlotte Sophia, da of Sir George Bull, Bt (d 1986); 2 da (Jemima b 31 Aug 1965, Loveday b 8 Nov 1967); *Career* 2 Lt Grenadier Gds 1949–50; called to the Bar Middle Temple 1954, practised at Bar 1954–60, admitted slr 1961, asst slr Linklater and Paines 1961–66, ptnr Stephenson Harwood 1966–95; conslt 1995–96: Stephenson Harwood, The Law Cmmn, Jt Disciplinary Scheme; memb IMRO Disciplinary Tbnl Panel 1995–; non-exec dir: The Throgmorton Trust plc, The New Throgmorton Trust plc, The Throgmorton Dual Trust plc 1984–91, TT Finance plc 1986–91, The Fifth Throgmorton Co plc 1988–91, Liberty Mutual Insurance Company (UK) Ltd 1994–, Liberty (Europe) Ltd 1995–, Liberty Syndicate Management Ltd 1995–; City of London Slrs' Co: dep chm Professional Business Ctee 1982–84 (memb 1976–84), chm Banking Law Sub-Ctee 1980–84, memb

Co Law Sub Ctee 1968–86; memb Law Soc Standing Ctee on Co Law 1978–96 (leader Accounting Matters Gp 1987–92), cncllr Hammersmith Met Borough 1968–71 (vice chm Fin Ctee); memb Mgmnt Ctee: Hammersmith Cncl of Community Rels 1968–74, Fulham Legal Advice Centre 1968–74, Shepherds Bush Housing Assoc 1968–80; Freeman City of London 1978, Liveryman City of London Slrs' Co; memb Law Soc; *Recreations* racing, walking, swimming; *Clubs* City of London; *Style—* Christopher Gibbons, Esq; ✉ Stephenson Harwood, 1 St Paul's Churchyard, London EC4M 8SH (☎ 0171 329 4422, fax 0171 606 0822, telex 886789 SHSPC G)

GIBBONS, Christopher Peter; s of William Frederick Gibbons, of Holmes Chapel, Cheshire, and Hazel Doreen, *née* Flint; *b* 10 March 1949; *Educ* Manchester GS, Keble and Wolfson Coll Oxford (MA, DPhil, BM BCh, MCh); *m* 4 July 1970, Ann Lawrence, da of George Robert White Dalgleish; 3 da (Kate b 1975, Rachel b 1978, Susannah b 1982); *Career* surgical registrar Univ Hosp of Wales 1979–82, surgical registrar Royal Hallamshire Hosp Sheffield 1982–83, clinical res fell Univ of Sheffield 1984–85, sr surgical registrar Cardiff and Swansea 1985–89, conslt gen surgn Morriston Hosp Swansea 1989– (clinical dir of surgery 1992–96), surgical tutor 1992–96; author of pubns on aspects of physiology and surgery; memb: BMA, Br Transplantation Soc 1985, Assoc of Surgns 1988, Vascular Surgical Soc of GB and I 1990, Euro Soc for Vascular Surgery 1990; FRCS 1980; *Recreations* sketching, classical guitar; *Style—* Christopher Gibbons, Esq; ✉ Morriston Hospital, Swansea (☎ 01792 702222)

GIBBONS, Hon Sir (John) David; KBE (1985), JP (Bermuda 1974); s of Edmund Graham Gibbons, CBE (d 1972), and Winifred Gladys Gibbons, MBE, *née* Robinson (d 1972), of Palm Grove, Devonshire, Bermuda; *b* 15 June 1927; *Educ* Saltus GS Bermuda, Hotchkiss Sch Conn, Harvard Univ (BA); *m* 1958, Lully, da of Johannes Jorgen Lorentzen, of Oslo; 3 s (William, John, James), 1 da by former marriage (Edith); *Career* MP (Utd Bermuda Pty) 1972–75, min for health and social servs 1974–75, min for fin 1975–84 (post held concurrently with premiership), premier of Bermuda 1977–82; chm: Bermuda Monetary Authy 1984–86, Bank of N T Butterfield & Son Ltd 1986–; Liveryman Worshipful Co of Distillers; *Recreations* tennis, golf, skiing, swimming; *Clubs* Lyford Cay (Bahamas), Royal Bermuda Yacht, Royal Hamilton Dinghy, Mid Ocean, Riddells Bay, Harvard (New York); *Style—* Hon Sir David Gibbons, KBE, JP; ✉ Leeward, 5 Leeside Drive, Point Shares, Pembroke, Bermuda HM 05 (☎ 00 44 1 29 5 2396); Apartment 7A 3 East 71 St, NY 10021, USA; 29 Montpelier Walk, London SW7 1JF; Bank of N T Butterfield & Son Ltd, Hamilton, Bermuda (☎ 00 44 1 295 8154)

GIBBONS, Jeremy Stewart; QC (1995); s of Geoffrey Seed Gibbons, of Bighton, Hants, and Rosemary Marion, *née* Stewart (d 1978); *b* 15 July 1949; *Educ* St Edward's Sch Oxford, Coll of Law Guildford; *m* 1974, Mary Mercia, da of Rev Kenneth Sutton Bradley; 2 s (Edward b 16 April 1977, Tim b 13 Dec 1983), 2 da (Harriet b 21 Oct 1979 (decd), Polly b 27 March 1981); *Career* articled clerk 1967–71, called to the Bar Gray's Inn 1973, head of Chambers 1991–, recorder of the Crown Court 1993– (asst recorder 1989–93); *Recreations* skiing, cooking, gardening, carpentry; *Style—* Jeremy Gibbons, Esq, QC; ✉ 17 Carlton Crescent, Southampton, Hants SO15 2XR (☎ 01703 320320, fax 01703 320321)

GIBBONS, Dr John Ernest; s of John Howard Gibbons (d 1979), and Lilian Alice, *née* Shale (d 1982); *b* 20 April 1940; *Educ* Oldbury GS, Birmingham Sch of Architecture (DipArch, DipTP), Univ of Edinburgh (PhD); *m* 3 Nov 1962, Patricia, da of Eric John Mitchell, of Albany, WA; 1 s (Mark b 16 March 1963), 2 da (Carey b 20 May 1964, Ruth b 29 July 1967); *Career* lectr: Aston Univ 1964–66, Univ of Edinburgh 1969–72; Scot Devpt Dept: princ architect 1972–74 and 1976–78, superintending architect 1978–82; res scientist CSIRO Melbourne Aust 1975; SO: dep dir bldg directorate 1982–84, dir of bldg 1984–, chief architect 1984–; memb: Cncl Edinburgh Architectural Assoc 1977–80, Cncl Royal Incorporation of Architects in Scot 1977–80, Cncl Architects Registration Cncl of UK 1984–, Design Cncl 1984–88; RIBA 1964, ARIAS 1967, FSA (Scot) 1984, FRSA 1987; *Clubs* New Club Edinburgh; *Style—* Dr John Gibbons; ✉ Crichton Ho, Pathhead, Midlothian EH37 5UX (☎ 01875 320 085); The Scottish Office, Victoria Quay, Edinburgh EH6 6QQ (☎ 0131 244 4149)

GIBBONS, John Robert Pelham; MBE (1970), TD (1968); s of Leonard Norman Gibbons (d 1948), of Solihull, Warwickshire, and Gladys Elizabeth, *née* Smith (d 1989); *b* 26 Nov 1926; *Educ* Moseley GS, Pates Sch Cheltenham, Univ of Leeds (MB ChB); *m* 7 Nov 1952, (Elizabeth) Marie-Jeanne Morwenna, da of Maj Philip Brookes, TD, of Kirkstall House, Kirkstall, Leeds, Yorks; 4 s (Robert b 1954, Maxime b 1958, Paul b 1966, Charles b 1967), 2 da (Anne-Marie b 1956, Marie-Lucie b 1960); *Career* Lt Royal Warwickshire Regt, Maj Parachute Regt; conslt Royal Free Hosp London 1976, conslt surgn Royal Victoria Hosp Belfast 1977–, hon consulting surgn Military Wing Musgave Park Hosp Belfast, conslt thoracic surgn Cambridge Military Hosp Aldershot 1989–; Hunterian prof RCS 1984; memb: Forces Help Soc and SSAFA, Lord Roberts Workshops, Br Legion, Parachute Regt Assoc; FRCS 1960, FRCSEd 1960, FRCSI 1988, fell American Coll of Chest Physicians 1988, FICS 1992; *Recreations* watching rugby football; *Clubs* Ulster Reform; *Style—* John Gibbons, Esq, MBE, TD; ✉ Jenkins Barn, 70 Horsham Road, Cranleigh, Surrey GU6 8DU (☎ 01483 276558); Royal Victoria Hospital, Belfast BT12 6BA (☎ 01232 894772, fax 01232 240899); Cambridge Military Hospital, Aldershot, Hampshire GU11 2AN (☎ 01252 350432)

GIBBONS, Ven Kenneth Harry; s of Harry Gibbons (d 1968), and Phyllis, *née* Priday (d 1963); *b* 24 Dec 1931; *Educ* Blackpool GS, Chesterfield GS, Univ of Manchester (BSc), Cuddesdon Coll Oxford; *m* 2 June 1962, Margaret Ann, da of Bertie Tomlinson (d 1962), of Billinghay, Lincoln; 2 s (David Austen b 1963, Andrew Kenneth b 1964); *Career* RAF 1952–54; ordained 1956, asst curate of Fleetwood 1956–60, sec Student Christian Movement in Schs 1960–62, sr curate St Martin-in-the-Fields Westminster 1962–65; vicar: St Edward New Addington 1965–70, St Mary Portsea 1970–81, Weeton 1981–85, St Michaels-on-Wyre 1985–; archdeacon of Lancaster 1981–; acting chaplain to the Forces at Weeton Barracks 1981–85, diocesan dir of Ordination Candidates 1982–90; *Recreations* gardening, cinema; *Clubs* Reform; *Style—* The Ven the Archdeacon of Lancaster; ✉ The Vicarage, Hall Lane, St Michael's-on-Wyre, nr Preston, Lancs PR3 0TQ (☎ 01995 679242)

GIBBONS, (Ronald) Peter; s of Lt Arthur James Gibbons (d 1935), of Bombay, and Mary Christina, *née* Kiernan; *b* 7 Nov 1929; *Educ* Abbey Sch Fort Augustus, Univ of Glasgow (MA), Balliol Coll Oxford (BA); *m* 2 Dec 1957 (m dis 1980), Jill Rosemary, da of Arthur Holden Lowe (d 1958), of Kensington, London; 1 s (Nicholas b 1960), 4 da (Caroline b 1958, Lucy b 1961, Julia b 1963, Mary Jane b 1967); *Career* Slrs Office Inland Revenue, called to the Bar Gray's Inn 1958, chm Social Security Appeal Tbnl Central London 1981–; head of Chambers 1988–; contrib reference books on revenue law; *Recreations* swimming; *Style—* Peter Gibbons, Esq; ✉ 54 Fleet Street, London EC4Y 1JV (☎ 0171 583 3354)

GIBBONS, Stephen John; s of John Gibbons, of Luton, and Wendy Patricia, *née* Luery; *b* 8 Oct 1956; *Educ* Bedford Modern Sch, Luton Sixth Form Coll, Dunstable Coll of FE, RCA (MA); *m* Valerie Anne, da of Michael Mercer; 1 da (Francesca Louisa b 29 Dec 1990), 1 s (Frederick Jim b 27 July 1993); *Career* graphic designer Minale Tattersfield 1982–84, ptnr The Partners 1985–96 (joined 1984); clients incl: Asda Group, Black & Decker, BA, Vauxhall, Harrods, Procter & Gamble, Shimizu Corp, Unilever, Vidal Sassoon, Woolworths; recipient 2 Silver D&AD awards for environmental graphics and signing schemes, various others from CSD/Minerva Awards, XYZ Magazine Awards, Communication Awards in the Building Indust, Donside Graphic Design and Print Awards and DBA Design Effectiveness Awards; work selected for various int awards/pubns incl: Art Dirs' Club of NY, PDC Gold Awards USA, Creativity USA, Communication Arts USA, Graphis Switzerland, Int Poster Biennale Poland; memb Exec Ctee and occasional design juror D&AD, lectr at various UK univs and seminars/confs on graphic design; memb Sign Design Soc UK; *Style—* Stephen Gibbons, Esq

GIBBONS, Sir William Edward Doran; 9 Bt (GB 1752), of Stanwell Place, Middlesex; JP (Inner London 1994); s of Sir John Edward Gibbons, 8 Bt (d 1982), and Mersa Wentworth, *née* Foster; *b* 13 Jan 1948; *Educ* Pangbourne Sch, RNC Dartmouth, Univ of Bristol (BSc); *m* 1972, Patricia Geraldine Archer, da of Roland Archer Howse; 1 s (Charles William Edwin b 1983), 1 da (Joan b 1980); *Heir* s, Charles William Edwin Gibbons b 28 Jan 1983; *Career* Sealink UK: asst shipping and port mangr Parkeston Quay 1979–82, serv mangr Anglo-Dutch 1982–85, mangr Harwich-Hook 1985–87, gen mangr Isle of Wight Servs 1987–90; tport and mgmnt conslt 1990–94, dir Passenger Shipping Assoc 1994–; chm Manningtree Parish Cncl 1985–87, non-exec memb IOW Dist Health Authy 1990–94; JP Portsmouth 1990–94; MCIT, DipBA; *Style—* Sir William Gibbons, Bt, JP; ✉ 5 Yarborough Road, Southsea, Hants PO5 3DZ

GIBBS, Maj Andrew Antony; MBE (1945), TD (1945); s of The Ven the Hon Kenneth Francis Gibbs, Archdeacon of St Albans (d 1935, 5 s of 1 Baron Aldenham), and Mabel Alice, *née* Barnett (d 1953); *b* 31 March 1914; *Educ* Winchester, ChCh Oxford (MA); *m* 9 May 1947, Elizabeth Joan (d 1993), wid of Capt Peter George William Savile Foljambe (ka 1944), and da of Maj Eric Charles Montagu Flint, DSO (d 1962); 2 s (John, Alan), 1 step-s (Earl of Liverpool, *qv*), 1 step-da (Jane); *Career* served WWII, Maj Herts Regt; dir: Barclays Bank 1962–84, Barclays UK Management Ltd 1971–79, Barclays Insurance Services Co Ltd 1970–75, York Waterworks Co 1969–89; memb: York Minster Fund (memb High Steward's Ctee) 1967–89, York Diocesan Bd of Fin 1964–85; chm Fin Ctee Dean and Chapter of York 1969–96; govr St Edward's Sch Oxford 1948–88, chm Sch Cncl Worksop Coll 1962–84; hon life memb BRCS, fell Midland Div of Woodard Corp 1959–84 (hon fell 1985); *Recreations* shooting; *Clubs* Travellers', Pratt's; *Style—* Maj Andrew Gibbs, MBE, TD; ✉ Kilvington Hall, Thirsk, N Yorkshire YO7 2NS (☎ 01845 537213)

GIBBS, Antony Richard; s of Dr Antony James Gibbs (d 1993), of Mercers Cottage, The Common, Cranleigh, Surrey, and Helen Margaret, *née* Leuchars; *b* 25 May 1939; *Educ* Bradfield, Byam Shaw Sch of Drawing & Painting (scholar), Kingston Sch of Art (NDD); *m* Sept 1965, Mary Jane (Janie), da of Frank Day; 1 s (Rupert Nicolas Antony b 28 April 1968), 1 da (Emily Jo b 26 July 1970); *Career* formerly: designer David Ogle Associates, prod designer STC Consumer Product Div, chief stylist Radfords (Coachbuilders) Ltd, assoc TEE Design; dir Murdoch & Gibbs 1975–80; Hop Studios 1980–92 (fndr ptnr, co sec, dir), fndr Gibbs Design Partnership 1992–; awarded: Design Cncl award for outstanding design 1977, BIO Industrial Design award Yugoslavia 1977; memb: Design Cncl, Design Cncl Awards Ctee, Bursaries Judging Panel RSA; moderator BA Assessment Panel Central Sch of Art; *Books* Industrial Design in Engineering (jtly); FCSD, FRSA; *Recreations* music compositions; *Style—* Antony Gibbs, Esq; ✉ Gibbs Design Partnership, 6 Tarleton Gardens, Forest Hill, London SE23 3XN (☎ 0181 699 8917)

GIBBS, Capt Beresford Norman (Bobby); DL (1990); s of The Rev Canon John Stanley Gibbs, MC (d 1952), of Badminton, Glos, and Mary Rosamond, *née* McCorquodale (d 1966); *b* 27 Feb 1925; *Educ* Eton, RAC; *m* 22 Aug 1956, (Mary) Jane, da of William Arthur Norman Thatcher (d 1965), of Middle Barton, Oxon; 2 s (Jack b 1957, David b 1965), 2 da (Cecily (Mrs Illingworth) b 1960, Alice (Mrs Kerr) b 1963); *Career* Nat Serv Capt RHG 1943–47, RHG RARO 1949–75 (The Blues and Royals 1969–); in gen practice as land agent; asst to GC Laws of Westcote Barton Oxon 1952–58, own account managing properties since 1958 incl: Gloucestershire, Wilts, Oxon, Staffs, Eire; High Sheriff Wilts 1989–90; memb: Land Agents' Soc 1957, Malmesbury DC 1958–64, Oaksey Parish Cncl 1961–66; churchwarden Oaksey 1968–88, vice chm CPRE N Wilts Gp 1979–93, chm Oaksey CC 1985–93, vice pres Youth Action Wilts 1990–, chm Action for Play (NPFA) Wilts 1991–; MRAC, FRICS 1958; *Recreations* lawn tennis, history, cricket, genealogy, forestry; *Clubs* MCC; *Style—* Capt Bobby Gibbs, DL; ✉ Willow Tree, Tuners Lane, Malmesbury, Wiltshire SN16 9EL (☎ 01666 577282)

GIBBS, Christopher Henry; 5 and yst s of Hon Sir Geoffrey Cokayne Gibbs, KCMG (d 1975; 2 s of 1 Baron Hunsdon of Hunsdon, 4 s of 1 Baron Aldenham, JP), and Helen Margaret Gibbs, CBE, JP, *née* Leslie (d 1979); *b* 29 July 1938; *Educ* Eton, Stanbridge, Université de Poitiers; *Career* art dealer; dir Christopher Gibbs Ltd; tstee: Edward James Fndn, J Paul Getty Jr Charitable Tst, American Friends of the National Gallery, American Sch of Tangier Morocco; chm Dorchester Abbey Preservation Tst; *Recreations* antiquarian pursuits, gardening; *Clubs* Beefsteak; *Style—* Christopher Gibbs, Esq; ✉ Manor House, Clifton Hampden, Abingdon, Oxon; L6 Albany, Piccadilly; Christopher Gibbs Ltd 8 Vigo St, London W1 (☎ 0171 439 4557)

GIBBS, David Charles Leslie; AM; eldest s of Hon Sir Geoffrey Cokayne Gibbs, KCMG (d 1975; 2 s of 1 Baron Hunsdon of Hunsdon, JP, himself 4 s of 1 Baron Aldenham, JP), and Helen Margaret Gibbs, CBE, JP, *née* Leslie; *b* 15 Aug 1927; *Educ* Eton, ChCh Oxford; *m* 20 March 1965, (Charmian) Fleur, da of Dalzell Pulteney Mein, of Toolang, Coleraine, Victoria, Aust; 2 s, 2 da; *Career* Antony Gibbs Group in Eng and Aust 1949–80 (dir Antony Gibbs & Sons, chm Gibbs Bright & Co); chm: C T Bowring Reinsurance Australia Pty Ltd 1981–91, Marsh & McLennan Pty Ltd and predecessors 1977–87, B G J Holdings Ltd 1982–86, Folkestone Ltd 1983– (dir 1976–), ANZ Executors & Trustee Co Ltd 1990– (dir 1985–); dir: Australia & NZ Banking Group 1979–91, ANZ Life Assurance Co Ltd 1991–, ANZ Managed Investments Ltd 1991–, John Swire & Sons Pty Ltd 1983–, Parbury Ltd 1984–94, Marsh and McLennan Pty Ltd 1987–89, Victoria State Opera Co Ltd 1985–; pres: World Wide Fund for Nature Aust 1988–92 (memb Cncl 1983–92), Victoria State Opera Fndn 1986–91 (memb Cncl 1982–92); memb Cncl: Museum of Victoria 1979–85, Victoria Cncl, Aust Bicentennial Authy 1984–88; Liveryman Worshipful Co of Grocers; *Recreations* fishing, opera, ornithology, farming, old master drawings; *Clubs* White's, Pratt's, Melbourne, Australian (Melbourne), Australia (Sydney); *Style—* David Gibbs, Esq, AM; ✉ 21 William St, S Yarra, Melbourne, Vic 3141, Australia

GIBBS, David Phillip; s of William Charles Gibbs (d 1961); *b* 6 May 1941; *Educ* Cranleigh Sch; *m* 1, 1964 (m dis 1981), Gillian; 2 s, 1 da; m 2, 1982, Vanessa Susan Jane; *Career* exec dir Hambros Bank Ltd 1985– (dir 1973–85); dir City of Oxford Investment Trust; MSI; *Recreations* golf, skiing, gardening; *Style—* David Gibbs, Esq; ✉ Hill Farm House, Slaugham Lane, Plummers Plain, Sussex; Hambros Bank, 41 Tower Hill, London EC3N 4HA (☎ 0171 480 5000)

GIBBS, Hon Sir Eustace Hubert Beilby; KCVO (1986), CMG (1982); 4 s of 1 Baron Wraxall, TD, PC, JP, DL (d 1931), yr s by his 2 w (Hon Ursula Mary Lawley, OBE, er da of 6 and last Baron Wenlock); hp to bro, 2 Baron; *b* 3 July 1929; *Educ* Eton, Ch Ch Oxford; *m* 23 Oct 1957, Veronica, o da of Sydney Keith Scott, of Reydon Grove Farm, Southwold; 3 s (Hubert b 1958, Andrew b 1965, Jonathan b 1969), 2 da (Miranda b 1961, Alexandra b 1971); *Career* entered Foreign Serv 1954, ret 1986; HM The Queen's Vice-Marshal of the Dip Corps 1982–86; RCDS 1974–75, served Bangkok, Rio de Janeiro, Berlin, Caracas, Vienna & Paris, ret 1986; *Recreations* music, golf; *Clubs* Pratt's, Beefsteak; *Style—* Hon Sir Eustace Gibbs, KCVO, CMG; ✉ Coddenham House, Coddenham, Ipswich, Suffolk (☎ and fax 01449 760332)

GIBBS, Jeremy Herbert; s of Rt Hon Sir Humphrey Gibbs, GCVO, KCMG, OBE (d 1990, 3 s of 1 Baron Hunsdon of Hunsdon), and Dame Molly Gibbs, DBE, *qv*; *b* 26 May 1935; *Educ* Bishops Sch Cape Town, Christ Church Oxford (MA); *m* 8 April 1958, Alison Douglas, da of Col Douglas McCrone Martin, of Dunchattan, Troon, Ayrshire; 4 da; *Career* insur broker; govr: St Mary's Sch Wantage, London House for Overseas Students; *Recreations* fishing; *Clubs* Bulawayo (Zimbabwe); *Style*— Jeremy Gibbs, Esq; ✉ Upper Kennards, Leigh, Kent TN11 8RE (☎ 01732 832160; office: 01732 771818)

GIBBS, Julian Herbert; 3 s of Hon Sir Geoffrey Cokayne Gibbs, KCMG (d 1975; 2 s of 1 Baron Hunsdon of Hunsdon, JP, himself 4 s of 1 Baron Aldenham, JP), and Helen Margaret, CBE, *née* Leslie (d 1977); *b* 26 Nov 1932; *Educ* Eton; *Career* 2 Lt KRRC 1951–53, Lt Queen's Westminsters (TA) 1953–56; with Antony Gibbs & Sons Ltd (merchant bankers) 1953–74; chm Antony Gibbs Personal Fin Planning Ltd, Julian Gibbs Associates Ltd 1975–82, First Market Intelligence Ltd 1983–90, freelance journalist, currently columnist Money Marketing; former vice chm London Fedn of Boys' Clubs, former chm P M Club; former memb ctee: Distressed Gentlefolks' Assoc, Queen's Inst of Dist Nursing; Freeman City of London, Liveryman Worshipful Co of Grocers 1961; FCII (vice pres); *Books* Living with Inflation, A Simple Guide to Lump Sum Investment; *Recreations* travel, theatre, opera, France; *Clubs* Carlton, MCC; *Style*— Julian Gibbs, Esq; ✉ 35A Colville Terrace, London W11 2BU (☎ 0171 221 8034, fax 0171 460 1234)

GIBBS, Michael John; s of Harold Percy Gibbs (d 1980), of Solihull, and Alice, *née* Groom (d 1974); *b* 8 April 1931; *Educ* Solihull Sch, Univ of Bristol (BA); *m* 22 June 1957, Pamela Jessie, da of Jesse Pane, of Bristol; 1 s (Alexander b 22 April 1964); *Career* sec Leicester Permanent Building Society 1968–71; Gateway Building Society: asst gen mangr 1971–75, dep chief exec 1975–81, md 1981–88; exec vice chm Woolwich Building Society 1988–91; dir: Woolwich Building Society 1988–96, Woolwich Life Assurance Company Ltd 1990–96, Woolwich (Guernsey) Ltd 1990–92; chm: Woolwich Property Services Ltd 1991–95, Woolwich Financial Advisory Services Ltd 1989; chm Met Assoc of Bldg Socs 1984–85, cncl memb Bldg Socs Assoc 1982–88; *Recreations* golf, cricket, horse racing; *Clubs* MCC, British Sportsmen's, Lord's Taverners'; *Style*— Michael Gibbs, Esq

GIBBS, Dame Molly Peel; *née* Nelson; DBE (1969); (The Hon Lady Gibbs); 2 da of John Peel Nelson, of Bulawayo; *b* 13 July 1912; *Educ* Girls' HS Barnato Park Johannesburg; *m* 17 Jan 1934, Rt Hon Sir Humphrey Vicary Gibbs, GCVO, KCMG, OBE (d 1990), 3 s of 1 Baron Hunsdon of Hunsdon; 5 s (*see* Jeremy Herbert Gibbs); *Style*— Dame Molly Gibbs, DBE; ✉ 22 Dornie Road, Borrowdale, Harare, Zimbabwe

GIBBS, His Hon Judge; Richard John Hedley; QC (1984); s of Brian Conaway Gibbs (d 1946), Asst Dist Cmmr Colonial Admin Serv, and Mabel Joan, *née* Gatford; *b* 2 Sept 1941; *Educ* Oundle, Trinity Hall Cambridge (MA); *m* 26 June 1965, Janet, da of Francis Herbert Whittall, of Reigate, Surrey; 1 s (Christopher b 1979), 3 da (Sarah b 1966 d 1991, Susannah b 1968, Julia b 1971); *Career* barr Inner Temple 1965, recorder Crown Ct 1981–90, circuit judge (Midland and Oxford Circuit) 1990–; *Style*— His Hon Judge Gibbs, QC; ✉ The Court Service, Wolverhampton Combined Court, Centre Pipers Row, Wolverhampton WV1 3LQ

GIBBS, Sir Roger Geoffrey; kt (1994); 4 s of Hon Sir Geoffrey Cokayne Gibbs, KCMG (2 s of 1 Baron Hunsdon of Hunsdon, JP, who himself was 4 s of 1 Baron Aldenham) and Hon Lady Gibbs, CBE, JP; *b* 13 Oct 1934; *Educ* Eton, Millfield; *Career* The Wellcome Trust 1983– (chm 1989–); dir: Gerrard and National Holdings plc 1971–94 (chm 1975–89), Arsenal FC plc 1980–, Howard de Walden Estates Ltd 1989– (chm 1993–), The Colville Estate Ltd 1989–; chm Arundel Castle Cricket Fndn 1986–; memb: Cncl Royal Nat Pension Fund for Nurses 1975–, Ct of Advsrs St Paul's Cathedral 1989–, Ctee MCC 1991–94; Liveryman Worshipful Co of Merchant Taylors; *Recreations* sport, travel; *Clubs* Boodle's, Pratt's, Swinley; *Style*— Sir Roger Gibbs; ✉ The Wellcome Trust, 183 Euston Road, London NW1 2BE (☎ 0171 611 8888)

GIBBS, Field Marshal Sir Roland Christopher; GCB (1976, KCB 1972), CBE (1968), DSO (1945), MC (1943), JP; yr s of Maj Guy Melvil Gibbs, TD (d 1959), of Parkleaze, Ewen, Cirencester (yr bro of Col William Otter Gibbs, *see* Gibbs, Martin Antony), and Margaret, *née* St John (d 1964); bro of Col Sir Martin Gibbs, KCVO, CB, DSO, TD, Lord-Lt Glos (d 1992); *b* 22 June 1921; *Educ* Eton, Sandhurst; *m* 1955, Davina, da of Lt-Col Eion Merry, MC (d 1966), of Lucknam Park, Chippenham, and Jean (da of Hon Arthur Crichton, 3 s of 4 Earl of Erne, KP, PC, sometime MP Enniskillen); 2 s, 1 da; *Career* served WWII: N Africa, Italy, NW Europe, 2 Lt 60 Rifles 1940; Lt-Col 1960, Brig 1963, cmd 16 Parachute Bde 1963–66, COS Middle East Cmd 1966, IDC 1968, Cdr Br Forces Gulf 1969, Maj-Gen 1969, Lt-Gen 1971, GOC1 (Br) Corps 1971–74, GOC-in-C UKLF 1974, Gen 1974, Chief of Gen Staff 1976–79, ADC Gen to HM The Queen 1976–79, Field Marshal; Col Cmdt: 2 Bn Royal Green Jackets 1971–78, Parachute Regt 1973–77; Lord-Lt Wilts 1989–96 (Vice Lord-Lt 1982–89, DL 1980–82); constable HM Tower of London 1985–90; *Recreations* outdoor recreations, painting; *Clubs* Turf, Cavalry & Guards'; *Style*— Field Marshal Sir Roland Gibbs, GCB, CBE, DSO, MC, JP; ✉ Patney Rectory, Devizes, Wilts (☎ 01380 840733)

GIBBS, Stephen Cokayne; 2 s of Hon Sir Geoffrey Gibbs, KCMG (d 1975, 2 s of 1 Baron Hunsdon of Hunsdon, JP, himself 4 s of 1 Baron Aldenham, JP), and Hon Lady Gibbs, CBE, JP; *b* 18 July 1929; *Educ* Eton; *m* 1972, Lavinia Winifred, 2 da of Sir Edmund Bacon, 13 Bt, KG, KBE, TD (d 1982); 2 s, 1 da; *Career* 2 Lt KRRC, Maj QVR (TA) 1960–63 and Royal Green Jackets; dir: Charles Barker plc 1962–87, Vaux Group plc 1971–; Nat Tst for Scotland: memb Exec Ctee 1987–, memb Cncl 1991–96; memb: RUCC for Scotland 1992–, Red Deer Cmmn 1993–; chm Assoc of Deer Mgmnt Gps 1994–; *Recreations* shooting, gardening; *Clubs* Pratt's; *Style*— Stephen Gibbs, Esq; ✉ Dougarie, Isle of Arran KA27 8EB (☎ 01770 840229/840259, fax 01770 840266)

GIBBS-KENNET, Peter Adrian; s of Reginald Ernest Gibbs Gibbs-Kennet, DLI (ka WWII), and Ruth, *née* Wyatt (d 1991); *Educ* Plymouth and Mannamead Coll Devon, Oriel Coll Oxford (MA, Dip Ed, Coll VIII); *m* 12 July 1968, Anna Eleanor, da of Gp Capt Hugh Llewellyn Jenkins, MD, OStJ, and Vivienne, *née* Pawson; 1 s (Swithun Aurelian Wyatt b 6 July 1972); *Career* asst sec UCCA until 1971, academic registrar Lanchester Poly (now Univ of Coventry) 1971–80, dir of educn and practice standards RIBA 1980–95; sec Editorial Bd Jl of Architecture 1995–; Freeman City of London 1994; FIMgt 1981, FRSA 1982; *Recreations* inertia; *Clubs* Oxford and Cambridge; *Style*— Peter Gibbs-Kennet, Esq; ✉ Norwich Cottage, Bisley, Gloucestershire GL6 7AD (☎ 01452 770462)

GIBRALTAR, Dean of; *see:* Horlock, Very Rev Brian William

GIBRALTAR IN EUROPE, Bishop of 1993–; Rt Rev John William Hind; s of Harold Hind, and Joan Mary, *née* Kemp (d 1976); *b* 19 June 1945; *Educ* Watford GS, Univ of Leeds (BA); *m* 16 April 1966, Janet Helen, da of David Hamilton Burns McLintock; 3 s (Dominic b 1967, Jonathan b 1969, Philip b 1971); *Career* asst master Leeds Modern Sch 1966–69, asst lectr King Alfred's Coll Winchester 1969–70, student Cuddesdon Theol Coll Oxford 1970–72; asst curate: St John the Baptist Church Catford Southend, Downham Team Ministry Dio of Southwark 1972–76; vicar Christ Church Forest Hill Dio of Southwark 1976–82, priest i/c St Paul's Forest Hill 1981–82, princ Chichester Theol Coll 1982–91, Bursalis prebendary and residentiary canon Chichester Cathedral 1982–91, bishop of Horsham 1991–93; chm: Faith and Order Advsy Gp 1991–, Chichester Dio Ctee for Social Responsibility 1991–93; *Books* contrib to: Stepping Stones (1987), Church, Kingdom, World (1986), Working for the Kingdom (1986); *Recreations* judo, languages; *Style*— The Rt Rev the Bishop of Gibraltar in Europe; ✉ Bishop's Lodge, Worth, Crawley, W Sussex RH10 7RT (☎ 01293 883051, fax 01293 884479, e-mail 101741.3160@compuserve.com)

GIBRIL, Hassan Alieu; *b* 10 June 1951; *Educ* Gambia HS Banjul, Univ of Lovanium Zaire, Univ of Nice (BA), Int Inst of Public Admin Paris (MA); *m*; 1 c; *Career* Gambian diplomat; asst sec Office of the Pres and Miny of External Affrs Banjul 1978, second sec/consul Dakar Senegal 1979, first sec/head of Chancery Lagos Nigeria 1980–82, first sec/head of Chancery and actg cnsllr London 1982–83; cnsllr/head of Chancery: Dakar 1983–86, Washington DC 1986–87; actg dep perm rep to United Nations NY 1988–90, cnsllr/head of Chancery Paris 1991–93, high cmmr to the Ct of St James's 1994–96 (dep high cmmr 1993–94), concurrently ambass to Ireland, Sweden, Norway, Denmark, Finland, Austria, Israel, The Vatican, UNIDO and Cwlth Secretariat 1994–96; *Style*— Mr Hassan Gibril

GIBSON, Anne; da of Harry Tasker (d 1967), of Lincolnshire, and Jessie, *née* Roberts; *b* 10 Dec 1940; *Educ* Caistor GS, Chelmsford Coll of Further Educn, Univ of Essex (BA); *m* 1, 1962 (m dis 1985), John Donald Gibson; 1 da (Rebecca Bridgid b 1964); m 2, 8 Oct 1988, John Bartell, s of Henry Bartell (d 1983), of Liverpool; *Career* full-time organiser Lab Pty (Saffron Walden) 1965–70, researcher House Magazine (jl of Houses of Parliament) 1975–77, Party candidate (Lab) Bury St Edmunds 1979, asst/asst sec and dep head Orgn and Industl Rels Dept TUC (with special responsibility for equal rights area of work) 1977–87; nat offr MSF with special responsibility for: voluntary sector and equal rights section 1987–96, policy and political work 1996–; memb: Gen Cncl TUC 1989–, Lab Pty NEC Women's Ctee 1990–, Dept of Employment Advsy Gp on Older Workers 1993; Equal Opportunities cmmr 1991–, Health and Safety cmmr 1996–; *Books* author numerous TUC and MSF Equal Opportunities Booklets incl latest Charter of Equal Opportunities For 1990s (1990), Disability and Employer - A Trade union Guide (1989), Lesbian and Gay Rights in Employment (1990), Recruitment of Women Workers (1990), Part time Workers Rights (1991), Sexual Harassment at Work (1993), Caring - A Union Issue (1993), Women in MSF (1991); *Recreations* reading, theatre, knitting, embroidery; *Style*— Ms Anne Gibson; ✉ M S F, M S F Centre, 33/37 Moreland Street, London EC1V 8BB (☎ 0171 505 3000, fax 0171 505 3200)

GIBSON, Anthony Gair; TD (1971); s of Wilfrid Humble (Tim) Gibson (d 1993), of Linnel Hill, Hexham, Northumberland, and Joan Margaret, *née* Gair; *b* 10 Nov 1937; *Educ* Ampleforth, Lincoln Coll Oxford (BA); *m* 23 July 1966, (Jennifer) Bryony, da of Maj Timothy Basil Ellis, of Trinity Hall, Bungay; 4 s (Benjamin Timothy b 7 Jan 1968, Toby James b 12 Sept 1969, Richard Gair (twin) b 12 Sept 1969, Anthony Daniel b 30 April 1975); *Career* King's Dragoon Gds 1956–58 (despatches), Northumberland Hussars & Queen's Own Yeo 1958–77; admitted slr 1965; memb Slrs' Disciplinary Tbnl 1980–, pres Newcastle upon Tyne Incorp Law Soc 1989–90; chm Hexham Steeplechase Co Ltd; memb Law Soc; *Recreations* shooting, fishing, forestry; *Clubs* Cavalry & Guards', Northern Counties; *Style*— Anthony G Gibson, Esq, TD; ✉ Newbiggin, Hexham (☎ 01434 602 649); Barclays Bank Chambers, Denton Burn, Newcastle-upon-Tyne (☎ 0191 274 1241, fax 0191 274 2164)

GIBSON, Cdr Bryan Donald; s of Donald Gibson (d 1983), of Barnston, Wirral, Cheshire, and Inez Margaret, *née* Lawrence (d 1983); *b* 21 Jan 1937; *Educ* Birkenhead Park GS Victoria, Univ of Manchester (BSc, MSc); *m* 1 Jan 1966, (Frances) Mary, da of Reginald Herbert Greenhalgh (d 1982), of Swinton, Lancashire; 1 s (James b 1968), 1 da (Helen b 1970); *Career* cmmnd RN 1962, lectr RN Engrg Coll 1963–66; served: HMS Bulwark 1967, HMS Sultan (Nuclear Propulsion Sch) 1968–70; sr lectr Dept of Nuclear Sci and Technol RNC Greenwich 1970–72, head of materials technol RN Engrg Coll Manadon Plymouth 1973–78, ret 1978; academic sec Chartered Assoc of Certified Accountants 1978–82, sec Inst of Metallurgists 1982–84, dep sec Inst of Metals 1985–91, dir Inst of Materials 1992–96; formerly memb Ctee: CNAA, RSA, Engrg Cncl, CSTI; vice pres Inst of Nuclear Engrs 1976–78; Freeman City of London 1984, Liveryman Worshipful Co of Engrs 1984 (Clerk 1986–); hon memb CGLI; FIM 1975, CEng 1977, FRSA 1996; *Recreations* gardening, DIY; *Clubs* Anglo Belgian, City Livery; *Style*— Cdr Bryan Gibson, RN; ✉ Worshipful Company of Engineers, c/o Kiln Bank, Bodle St Green, nr Hailsham, E Sussex BN27 4UA (☎ 01323 833554, fax 01323 833979)

GIBSON, His Hon Judge; Charles Andrew Hamilton; s of Rev Prebendary Leslie Andrew Gibson (d 1963), of Colwall, Herefordshire, and Kathleen Anne Frances, *née* Hamilton (d 1991); *b* 9 July 1941; *Educ* Sherborne, Hertford Coll Oxford (MA); *m* 9 Aug 1969, Susan Judith, er da of Geoffrey Christopher Rowntree; 2 da (Catherine Sarah b 7 Aug 1970, Rachel Caroline b 11 Jan 1974); *Career* called to the Bar Lincoln's Inn 1966, in practice 1966–96, recorder 1991–96 (asst recorder 1987), circuit judge (SE Circuit) 1996–; chm Southwark Diocesan Pastoral Ctee 1993–; *Books* Surveying Buildings (with Prof M R A Hollis 1983, 3 edn 1991); *Recreations* music, theatre, wine; *Clubs* United Oxford and Cambridge University; *Style*— His Hon Judge Gibson; ✉ c/o Woolwich Crown Court, 2 Belmarsh Road, London SE28 0EY (☎ 0181 312 7000)

GIBSON, Christopher Allen Wood; QC (1995); s of Sir Ralph Brian Gibson, of London, and Ann Chapman, *née* Reuther; *b* 5 July 1953; *Educ* St Paul's, BNC Oxford (BA); *m* 4 Aug 1984, Alarys Mary Calvert, da of David Eaton, of Emsworth, Hants; 2 da (Harriet b 10 Dec 1984, Julia b 24 May 1987); *Career* called to the Bar Middle Temple 1976; memb Hon Soc of Middle Temple, FCIArb 1992; *Recreations* sailing, motorcycles, photography; *Clubs* Vincent's, BSA Owners'; *Style*— Christopher Gibson; ✉ 2 Crown Office Row, Temple, London EC4Y 7HJ (☎ 0171 797 8000, fax 0171 797 8001)

GIBSON, Rev Sir Christopher Herbert; 4 Bt (UK 1931), of Linconia, and of Faccombe, Co Southampton; o s of Sir Christopher Herbert Gibson, 3 Bt (d 1994), and Lilian Lake, *née* Young; *b* 17 July 1948; *Heir* kinsman, Robert Herbert Gibson b 1966; *Career* ordained a Roman Catholic priest 1975; CP; *Style*— The Rev Sir Christopher Gibson, Bt, CP; ✉ Holy Cross, Buenos Aires, Argentina

GIBSON, Hon Clive Patrick; 2 s of Baron Gibson (Life Peer), and Elizabeth, da of Hon Clive Pearson (2 s of 1 Viscount Cowdray, GCVO, PC, DL), and Hon Alicia Knatchbull-Hugessen, da of 1 Baron Brabourne; *b* 24 Jan 1948; *Educ* Eton, Magdalen Coll Oxford (BA); *m* 1974, Anne Marie Jeanne, da of late Comte Jacques de Chauvigny de Blot; 1 s (Patrick Clive b 1975), 1 da (Beatrice Dione Elizabeth b 1978); *Career* Cmmn of the Euro Communities 1973–74, Pearson Gp 1974–83; dir: Château Latour (chm), Pearson Longman 1979–82, Financial Times 1978–83, The Economist 1978–83, Penguin Books 1978–82, Longman Gp 1978–82, J Rothschild Group 1985–96, Cordiant plc 1991–, Perseus Investment Group 1996–; *Recreations* music, shooting, skiing; *Clubs* Brooks's; *Style*— The Hon Clive Gibson; ✉ 27 St James's Place, London SW1A 1NR (☎ 0171 493 8111)

GIBSON, Colin Raymond; s of Raymond Gibson, and Muriel, *née* Power (d 1992); *b* 9 Feb 1957; *Educ* William Hulmes GS Manchester, Nat Cncl for Trg of Journalists Coll Preston (Dip); *m* 6 June 1987, Patricia Mary, da of David Coxon; 1 da (Emma Catherine b 19 Aug 1989), 1 s (Michael Peter b 3 Aug 1993); *Career* sports writer; St Regis Newspapers Bolton (Stretford & Urmiston Jl) 1976–79, sports ed Messenger Newspapers Stockport 1979–80; sports corr: Daily Telegraph 1984 (joined 1980), Daily Mail 1984–86; chief sports writer Daily Telegraph 1986–93, sports ed Sunday Telegraph 1993–; memb: Sports Writers' Assoc of GB 1984, Football Writers' Assoc 1982; *Books* Glory, Glory Nights (1986), Football Association Publications (1990–); *Recreations* golf, travel; *Clubs* Assoc of Lancastrians, Lancashire CCC, Hawarden Golf; *Style*— Colin Gibson, Esq; ✉ 1 St Paul's Close, Hawarden, Clwyd (☎ 01244 538893); Sunday Telegraph, 1 Canada

Square, Canary Wharf, London E14 5DT (☎ 0171 538 5000, fax 0171 538 7896, car 0836 256704)

GIBSON, Maj (William) David; s of George Cock Gibson, OBE (d 1989), of Landwade Hall, Exning, Newmarket, Suffolk, and Angela Madeleine, *née* Llewellin-Evans (d 1993); *b* 26 Feb 1925; *Educ* Harrow, Trinity Coll Cambridge; *m* 1, 16 Jan 1959, Charlotte Henrietta (d 1973), da of Norman Selwyn Pryor, JP, DL (d 1982), of Manuden House, Bishops Stortford, Herts; 3 s (Martin, George, Edward), 1 da (Anna); m 2, 1975, Jane Marion, da of Brig Ladas L Hassell, DSO, MC (d 1963); *Career* serv Welsh Guards 1944–57 (Palestine 1947, Egypt 1953–56, Maj); dir: W J Tatem Ltd 1957 (chm 1970–96), Atlantic Shipping & Trading Co Ltd 1957 (chm 1970–77), West of England Ship Owners Mutual Protection & Indemnity Assoc London 1959–86 (Luxembourg 1970–83), Int Shipowners Investmt Co 1970–83 (chm 1977–83); chm: Tatem Ltd 1990–94 (dir 1994–), Waverley Components and Products Ltd 1990–94; steward Nat Hunt Ctee 1963–66 (sr steward 1966), dep sr steward Jockey Club 1969–71; memb: Tattersalls Ctee 1963–69 (chm 1967–69), Farriers Registration Cncl; Master Worshipful Co of Farriers 1979 (memb Ct of Assts); *Recreations* racing, sailing (Klaxton); *Clubs* Jockey, Royal Yacht Squadron, Royal Thames Yacht, Cavalry and Guards'; *Style—* Maj David Gibson; ✉ Bishopswood Grange, nr Ross on Wye, Herefordshire HR9 5QX (☎ 01594 860444)

GIBSON, David; s of Frank Edward Gibson (d 1973), of Retford, Notts, and Nora Jessie, *née* Gurnhill (d 1989); *b* 8 Sept 1939; *Educ* King Edward VI GS Retford; *m* 6 Sept 1963, Roberta Alexandra, da of James Henry McMaster (d 1963); 1 s (Peter), 2 da (Catherine, Sarah); *Career* exec offr: GPO 1958–63, MAFF 1963–68; various posts Belfast City Cncl 1968–72, princ offr Dept of Commerce 1973–81; Dept of Econ Devpt: dir Accounting Servs 1982–85, asst sec 1985–87, under sec 1987–; memb and pres Chartered Assoc of Certified Accountants Irish Region 1982–83, FCCA 1969; *Recreations* reading, music, walking; *Style—* David Gibson, Esq; ✉ Department of Economic Development, Netherleigh, Massey Ave, Belfast BT4 2JP (☎ 01232 529470, fax 01232 529556)

GIBSON, David; s of John Love Gibson (d 1984), and Patricia Ann, *née* Cowcill (d 1984); *b* 19 May 1962; *Educ* Truro Boys' Sch, Univ of Kent at Canterbury (BA), Coll of Law; *m* Marishelle, da of Donald Booth; 2 s (Angus Edmund b 16 Dec 1993, Alasdair Theodore b 9 May 1996); *Career* Alsop Wilkinson 1985–89, co sec and dir of legal affrs Rexam plc (formerly Bowater plc) 1989–; involved with: Richmond Legal Advice, Harrow Environment Fund, A Faith for the Future; memb Law Soc 1987; *Style—* David Gibson, Esq; ✉ Rexam plc, 114 Knightsbridge, London SW1X 7NN (☎ 0171 584 7070, fax 0171 590 7042)

GIBSON, Rev Father (Sir) David Ackroyd; 4 Bt (UK 1926), of Great Warley, Co Essex; discontinued use of title 1996; s of Sir Ackroyd Herbert Gibson, 3 Bt (d 1975); *b* 18 July 1922; *Educ* Cathedral GS Wells, Warfleet Trg Coll Dartmouth, Greenwich Coll, Oscott Coll; *Career* Lt RNVR 1939–46: N Sea and N Atlantic 1940–41, Med 1941–43, Indian and Pacific Oceans 1944–45; Roman Catholic priest: Plymouth 1956–60, Weymouth 1960–66; fndr Societas Navigatorum Catholica (Catholic Mariner's YC) 1958; Capt RA chaplain: Germany 1967–69, NI 1969–70; RC priest: Helston 1971–75, Liskeard 1975–85; *Books* A Series of Circles (autobiog), Battle in the Irish Sea, The Life and Death of HMS Manners; *Clubs* Societas Navigatorum Catholica; *Style—* Rev Father David Gibson; ✉ St Therese's Court, 138 Raglan Road, Devonport, South Devon PL1 4NQ (☎ 01752 559541)

GIBSON, David Frank; s of Reginald James Gibson, of Warrington, Cheshire, and Emily, *née* Tanner; *b* 4 Dec 1946; *Educ* Boteler GS Warrington, UCL (BSc, DipArch); *m* 2 Sept 1969, Mary, da of John Greaves, of Warrington, Cheshire; 1 s (Timothy Edward Phillip b 1984), 1 da (Helen Emily Mary b 1988); *Career* architectural asst James Stirling and Ptnr 1968–70, assoc Colin St John Wilson and Ptnrs 1978–79 (architect 1971–79), studio tutor Bartlett Sch of Architecture 1979–88, Julian Harrap Architects 1981–84, assoc Alex Gordon and Partners 1985–87 (architect 1979–80), princ David Gibson Architects 1987–; RIBA 1979; *Recreations* architecture, bicycle maintenance, flying; *Clubs* Reform; *Style—* David Gibson, Esq; ✉ 22 St George's Ave, London N7 0HD (☎ 0171 607 8193); David Gibson Architects, 131 Upper St, London N1 1QP (☎ 0171 226 2207, fax 0171 226 6920)

GIBSON, David Reginald Ernest; s of Reginald Gibson (d 1970), of Northallerton, and Betty, *née* Hewitt (d 1963); *b* 9 May 1946; *Educ* HS for Boys Scarborough, Northern Poly; *m* 3 Oct 1970, Marion Elaine, da of William Alexander McLeish, of Melrose, Roxburghshire; 2 da (Julia Amanda b 20 Sept 1972, Rowena Anne b 27 Oct 1975); *Career* chief architect Loughborough Recreation Planning Conslts 1971–79, dir Consarc partnership 1979–84, ptnr The Gibson Hamilton Partnership 1984–; pres Leicestershire and Rutland Soc of Architects 1987–89 (chm Environment Ctee 1979–84), chm Loughborough Civic Tst 1989–; memb Worshipful Co of Chartered Architects; RIBA 1971, FRSA; *Recreations* walking, fishing, reading, travel; *Style—* David Gibson, Esq; ✉ Unit 19 Loughborough Technology Centre, Epinal Way, Loughborough, Leicestershire LE11 0QE (☎ 01509 610510, fax 01509 211510)

GIBSON, Lt-Col Edgar Matheson; MBE (1986), TD (1975), DL (1976); s of James Edgar Gibson (d 1976), and Margaret Johnston, *née* Matheson; *b* 1 Nov 1934; *Educ* Kirkwall GS, Gray's Coll of Art; *m* 1960, Jean, *née* McCarrick; 2 s (Edgar James b 10 Oct 1962, Sigurd Matheson b 3 Nov 1970), 2 da (Laura Margaret b 18 April 1961, Ingrid Mary b 7 Dec 1965); *Career* Lt-Col, Nat Serv 1958–60, TA & TAVR Lovat Scouts 1961–, Cadet Cmdt Orkney 1979–86, JSLO Orkney 1980–85; asst headmaster Kirkwall GS until 1990; ind artist 1990–; Hon Col Orkney Lovat Scouts ACF 1986, Hon Sheriff Grampian Highlands and Islands 1992; chm: St Magnus Cathedral Fair 1982–, Northern Area Highland TA&VR Assoc 1987–93, Orkney Branch SSAFA and FHS 1990–; vice chm Italian POW Chapel Preservation Ctee 1994–; memb Orkney Health Bd 1991–; hon pres Soc of Friends of St Magnus Cathedral 1994–; *Recreations* BA playing (old Norse game), whisky tasting; *Clubs* Highland Brigade; *Style—* Lt-Col Edgar M Gibson, MBE, TD, DL; ✉ Transcona, New Scapa Rd, Kirkwall, Orkney (☎ 01856 872849)

GIBSON, Ven (George) Granville; s of George Henry Gibson (d 1987), and Jessie, *née* Farrand; *b* 28 May 1936; *Educ* Queen Elizabeth GS Wakefield, Barnsley Coll of Technol, Cuddesdon Coll Oxford; *m* 20 Dec 1958, Edna, da of late James Reginald Jackson; 3 s (Julian Andrew b 8 June 1960, Paul Quentin b 25 Feb 1966, Christopher James b 11 Dec 1968), 1 da (Cathryn Ann (twin) b 11 Dec 1968); *Career* ordained deacon 1971, priest 1972; team vicar Cramlington Northumberland 1973–77, vicar Newton Aycliffe Co Durham 1977–85, rector Bishopmearmouth and rural dean Sunderland 1985–93, hon canon Durham Cathedral 1988–, archdeacon of Auckland 1993–; memb Gen Synod 1980–, church cmmr and memb Bd of Govrs 1993–, tstee Church Urban Fund 1993–; *Recreations* gardening, grandchildren, cactus plants; *Style—* The Ven the Archdeacon of Auckland; ✉ Glebe House, Sunderland Bridge, Durham DH6 5HB (☎ 0191 378 0273, fax 0191 378 3885, e-mail vergg@gibven.demon.co.uk)

GIBSON, Hon Hugh Marcus Thornely; DL; eldest s of Baron Gibson (Life Peer), *qv*; *b* 23 June 1946; *Educ* Eton, Magdalen Coll Oxford (BA); *m* 31 March 1967, Hon Frances Towneley, da of Hon Anthony Strachey (d 1955); 1 s (Jasper Tallentyre b 1975), 2 da (Effie Dione b 1970, Amelia Mary b 1973); *Career* md Royal Crown Derby and Minton, dir Royal Doulton Ltd; *Recreations* Nat Tst, book collecting, wine, fishing; *Clubs* Reform; *Style—* Hon Hugh Gibson, DL; ✉ The Fold, Parwich, Ashbourne, Derbys DE6 1QL

GIBSON, Ian; CBE (1990); s of Charles Gibson (d 1991), and Kate, *née* Hare (d 1971); *b* 1 Feb 1947; *Educ* Burnage GS, Univ of Manchester (BSc, vice pres Union), London Business Sch; *m* 1969 (m dis 1985), Joy Dorothy, da of Geoffrey Musker; 2 da (Janine Victoria b 17 June 1972, Sarah Rachel b 15 Feb 1975); m 2, 1988, Susan Margaret, da of John Lawrence Wilson; 1 s (Daniel Lancelot b 2 Nov 1989); *Career* research asst ICI 1968, various industl relations and mfrg mgmnt positions Ford Motor Co Ltd and Ford Werke AG Germany 1969–84; Nissan Motor Manufacturing: dir purchasing and prodn control 1984–87, dep md 1987–89, chief exec 1989–; chm Nissan Yamato Engineering 1989–, dir Nissan European Technology Centre 1990–, dir Nissan Motor GB 1992–, vice pres Nissan Europe NV 1994–, dir Nissan Motor Iberica SA 1996–; Asda Group plc: non-exec dir 1993–96, dep chm 1996–; chm Ctee NEDO, vice pres SMMT 1995–; memb Governing Body London Business Sch, bd memb Tyne & Wear Development Corp; Hon DBA Univ of Sunderland 1993; FRSA 1990, CIMgt 1990; *Recreations* sailing, skiing, hill walking; *Clubs* RAC; *Style—* Ian Gibson, Esq, CBE; ✉ Nissan Motor Manufacturing UK Ltd, Washington Road, Sunderland, Tyne & Wear SR5 3NS (☎ 0191 415 2301)

GIBSON, Ian Robert; s of John Wilfred Gibson (d 1971), of Bridlington, and Eileen Margaret, *née* Pudsey (d 1965); *b* 19 Aug 1948; *Educ* St Peter's York, The Queen's Coll Oxford (BA); *m* 9 Sept 1972, Valerie Ann, da of Capt Frederick Alfred Armitage, MBE, GM, SGM (d 1968); 2 da (Alison b 1975, Anna b 1978), 1 s (Edward b 1984); *Career* admitted slr 1972; ptnr Frere Cholmeley Bischoff 1978–; non-exec dir G Maunsell & Partners International Ltd; memb: Law Soc, Int Fiscal Assoc; *Recreations* music, walking; *Style—* Ian Gibson, Esq; ✉ Parkgate, Aldwickbury, Harpenden, Herts AL5 1AB; 4 John Carpenter Street, London EC4Y 0NH (☎ 0171 615 8000, fax 0171 615 8080, telex 27623)

GIBSON, Rev Prof John Clark Love; s of Rev Herbert Booth Gibson (d 1968) of Manse of Whifflet, Coatbridge, Lanarkshire, and Margaret Harvey, *née* Marshall (d 1975); *b* 28 May 1930; *Educ* Coatbridge HS, Univ of Glasgow (MA, BD), Magdalen College Oxford (DPhil); *m* 25 Dec 1956, Agnes Gilmour, da of Robert Russell, of Bellshill, Lanarkshire; 4 s (Ian b 1957, Robin b 1961, Peter b 1964, Guy b 1965), 1 da (Jane (Mrs Weatherly) b 1960); *Career* min of New Machar Aberdeenshire 1959–62; Univ of Edinburgh: lectr in Hebrew and Semitic languages 1962–73, reader 1973–87, prof of Hebrew and Old Testament studies 1987–94, emeritus prof 1994–; visiting prof of religion Dartmouth Coll USA 1991; memb Soc for Old Testament Study (pres 1994); *Books* Textbook of Hebrew and Moabite Inscriptions (1971), Language and Meaning (contrib, 1974), Textbook of Aramaic Inscriptions (1975), Canaanite Myths and Legends (1978), Genesis: Daily Study Bible (2 vols 1981 and 1982), Textbook of Phoenician Inscriptions (1982), Reader's Digest Family Guide to the Bible (ed, 1984), The Motherhood of God (contrib, 1984), Job: Daily Study Bible (1985), The Bible in Scottish Life and Literature (contrib, 1988), Ascribe to the Lord: In Memory of Peter C Craigie (contrib, 1988), Polytheistic Systems (contrib, 1989), Text as Pretext: Essays in Honour of Robert Davidson (contrib, 1992), Encyclopedia of Language and Linguistics (contrib, 1993), Understanding Poets and Prophets: Essays in Honour of G W Anderson (contrib, 1993), Ugarit and the Bible (contrib, 1994), Hebrew Syntax (1994); *Recreations* scottish literature, spy novels, golf; *Style—* Rev Prof John Gibson; ✉ 10 South Morton Street, Edinburgh EH15 2NB (☎ 0131 669 3635); Faculty of Divinity, University of Edinburgh, New College, Mound Place, Edinburgh EH1 2LX (☎ 0131 225 8400)

GIBSON, John King; s of Eric King Gibson (d 1982), and Ada Wills, *née* Danson (d 1982); *b* 23 July 1939; *Educ* Liverpool Inst HS for Boys, Univ of Leeds, Farnborough Coll of Technol; *m* 18 Dec 1965, Mari, da of Hovanes Postalian (d 1943); 1 s (Berdge King b 11 Jan 1968), 1 da (Miranda Jane b 22 March 1973); *Career* Nat Serv RAF 1959–61; entered Meteorological Office MOD 1961, asst experimental offr Civil Serv 1962; forecaster: Liverpool Airport 1966–70, Nicosia Airport Cyprus 1963–66; data processing meteorological office Bracknell 1970–76, Euro Centre for Medium-Range Weather Forecasts 1976–; project mangr ECMWF Re-analysis (ERA) Project 1993–; memb cmmn for basic systems' working gp on data mgmnt World Meteorological Orgn; FRMetS 1975, AFIMA 1982; *Recreations* musical appreciation, mountain walking; *Style—* John Gibson, Esq; ✉ 14 Hawkins Close, Bracknell, Berks RG12 2RF (☎ 01344 489254); European Centre for Medium-Range Weather Forecasts, Shinfield Park, Reading RG2 9AX (☎ 0118 949 9360, fax 0118 986 9360, telex 847908 ECMWF G)

GIBSON, Dr John Robin; s of Norman John Gibson (d 1983), and Marie Louise Elizabeth, *née* Edwards; *b* 16 Dec 1949; *Educ* Eastwood HS Glasgow, Univ of Glasgow (MB ChB, MRCP); *m* 25 April 1990, Sabina Silvia, da of Joachim Rosenthaler, of Basel, Switzerland; *Career* hosp MO Bulawayo Zimbabwe 1974–77, med registrar Glasgow 1977, hon conslt dermatologist London Hosp 1983–89 (hon dermatology registrar and sr registrar 1978–82), head Dermatology Section Wellcome Res Labs Beckenham 1978–89, vice pres of clinical res Bristol-Myers Squibb Co 1992–93 (dir 1989–90, exec dir 1990–92), sr vice pres pharmaceutical devpt Allergan Inc 1993–; clinical prof of dermatology State Univ of NY at Buffalo NY 1992–; author multiple book chapters and papers on: dermatology, therapeutics, pharmacology, allergy; Freeman City of London 1987, Liveryman Worshipful Soc of Apothecaries 1988 (Yeoman 1982); memb: BMA, BAD, ESDR, SPS; FRCPG 1987, FRSM; *Recreations* guitar playing, song writing, bridge, squash; *Style—* Dr John R Gibson; ✉ 2368 Glenneyre Street, Laguna Beach, California 92651, USA (☎ 714 376 9060); 9 Cabo Del Sol, Denia, Alicante, Spain; Pharmaceutical Development, Allergan Inc, 2525 Dupont Drive, PO Box 19534, Irvine, CA 92713–9534, USA

GIBSON, Dr Joseph; CBE (1980); s of George Gibson (ka 1918), and Mary Ann Scott, *née* Mordy (d 1980); *b* 10 May 1916; *Educ* Washington GS; King's Coll now Univ of Newcastle upon Tyne (MSc, PhD), Univ of Durham; *m* 22 Dec 1944, Lily McFarlane, da of late David McCutcheon Brown; 1 s (David McFarlane b 1950), 1 da (Carole Ann b 1954); *Career* res Northern Coke Res Lab 1938–47, head Chemistry Dept Sunderland Tech Coll 1948–55, lectr Univ of Durham 1948–55, chief scientist Northumberland and Yorkshire Divisions NCB 1956–64, dir Coal Research Establishment 1968–75, dir Coal Utilisation Research 1975–77; National Coal Bd: bd memb responsible for science 1977–81, dir several NCB subsids 1977–81, coal science advsr 1981–83; author of many articles on coal utilisation and conversion; pres Institute of Fuel 1975–76, pres BCURA 1977–81 and 1993– (chm 1972–77); meml lectures: Cadman 1980 and 1982, Prof Moore 1981; coal sci lectr and medal 1977, carbonization sci medal 1979; Hon DCL Univ of Newcastle 1981; Hon FIChemE 1977, FEng 1979; *Publications* jtly: Carbonisation of Coal (1971), Coal and Modern Coal Processing (1979), Coal Utilisation: Technology, Economics and Policy (1981); *Recreations* bridge, gardening; *Style—* Dr Joseph Gibson, CBE, FEng; ✉ 31 Charlton Close, Charlton Kings, Cheltenham, Glos GL53 8DH (☎ 01242 517832)

GIBSON, Lt-Col Kenneth Charles Robert; TD (1968, Bar 1974), DL (Glos 1996); s of Charles Robert Gibson (d 1974), and Jane Boyd Young, *née* Aitken (d 1978); *b* 16 Sept 1935; *Educ* Monkton Combe Sch Bath, Clare Coll Cambridge (MA, LLM); *m* 10 June 1964, Jill Seaton, da of Douglas Campbell Connor (d 1964); 3 s (Douglas b 1966, James b 1970, Mark b 1971), 1 da (Elizabeth b 1967); *Career* Nat Serv 5 Bn King's African Rifles Kenya 1954–56, Somerset LI (TA) 1956–71, CO 6 Bn LI (vol) 1971–74, Hon Col Avon ACF 1987–92; admitted slr 1962; ptnr: Wansbroughs 1985–90, Wansbroughs Willey Hargrave 1990–96; pres Bristol Law Soc 1984–85, memb Rule Ctee Supreme Ct 1993–96; reader Diocese of Bristol; missionary in Namibia with Africa Inland Mission International 1996–; DL Avon 1986–96; *Style—* Lt-Col Kenneth Gibson, TD, DL; ✉ Rosewell, Bitton, Bristol BS15 6LJ (☎ 0117 932 2122)

GIBSON, (Robert) Myles; OBE (1992), ERD (1973), TD (1980); s of Robert Gibson (d 1976), of Port Patrick and Oban, and Mary Elizabeth, *née* Harvey; *b* 6 May 1927; *Educ* Kilmarnock Acad, Univ of Glasgow, McGill Univ (MD, MSc); *m* 4 Aug 1962, Ena Edith

Christina, da of Dr Christian Balfour Fotheringham Millar (d 1965), of Newport, Gwent; 1 s (Alastair b 1967), 1 da (Stroma b 1965); *Career* RCAMC 1950–51, Lt-Col RAMC 1951–53, RAMC TA 1953–58, hon conslt neurosurgn to Army and BAOR 1960–; conslt neurosurgn Gen Infirmary Leeds 1959–, author of papers on surgery and neurosurgery; memb: BMA Cncl 1969–80, GMC, Cncl RCSEd (vice pres 1983–86); convenor Intercollegiate Bd (UK) of Neurosurgery, vice chm Med Protection Soc, chm Med Protection Europe; chief med advsr to Football League and FA, hon sec Mil Surgical Soc; Freeman City of London, Liveryman Worshipful Co of Apothecaries; fell Int Coll of Surgns; memb: RSM, Soc Br Neurological Surgns; FRCS, FRCSEd; CStJ 1970; *Books* Health Service Financing (jointly, 1972); *Recreations* golf, railways, railway travel; *Clubs* Athenaeum; *Style*— R Myles Gibson, Esq, OBE, ERD, TD; ✉ Department of Neurosurgery, General Infirmary, Leeds LS1 3EX (☎ 0113 2 32799); 152 Harley St, London W1 (☎ 0171 935 8868)

GIBSON, Baron (Life Peer UK 1975), of Penn's Rocks, Co of East Sussex; (Richard) Patrick Tallentyre Gibson; o s of Thornely Carbutt Gibson (d 1969), of 2 Kensington Gate, and late Elizabeth Anne Augusta, *née* Coit; *b* 5 Feb 1916; *Educ* Eton, Magdalen Coll Oxford (MA, hon fell 1977); *m* 14 July 1945, (Elisabeth) Dione, 3 da of Hon (Bernard) Clive Pearson (d 1965; 2 s of 1 Viscount Cowdray), and Hon Alicia Knatchbull-Hugessen, da of 1 Baron Brabourne; 4 s (Hon Hugh Marcus Thornely b 1946, Hon Clive Patrick b 1948, Hon William Knatchbull b 1951, Hon Piers Nathaniel b 1956); *Career* served WWII, Middx Yeo, Maj (POW 1941–43); sits as Ind Peer in House of Lords; Financial Times 1957–78 (chm 1975–77), dir Economist Newspaper Ltd 1957–78, chm S Pearson & Son 1978–83; chm: Arts Cncl of GB 1972–77, Nat Tst 1977–86; tstee Glyndebourne Festival Opera 1965–72 and 1977–87, memb Bd Royal Opera House 1977–87, treas Univ of Sussex 1983–87; Hon DLitt: Reading 1980, Keele 1992; Hon DUniv Sussex 1988; *Clubs* Brooks's, Garrick; *Style*— The Rt Hon Lord Gibson; ✉ 4 Swan Walk, London SW3 4JJ (☎ 0171 351 0344); Penn's Rocks, Groombridge, Tunbridge Wells TN3 9PA (☎ 01892 864 244)

GIBSON, Paul Alexander; s of Wing Cdr L P Gibson (d 1954), and Betty, *née* Peveler; *b* 11 Oct 1941; *Educ* Kingswood Sch Bath, King's Coll London, Canterbury Sch of Architecture, Regent Street Poly Sch of Architecture; *m* 29 Aug 1969, Julia Rosemary, da of Leslie Atkinson; *Career* architect; Farrell Grimshaw Partnership 1968–69, lectr N Dakota State Univ USA 1969–70, Foster Associates 1970–72, private practice Sidell Gibson Partnership 1973–; major projects incl: MEPC office buildings Frankfurt 1974, master plans Univ of Arack Iran and housing at Kermanshaw Iran 1976, 15 varied housing schemes English Courtyard Assoc 1976–91, office buildings and housing Frankfurt 1991, New Jewel House Tower of London 1993; appointed architect for Windsor Castle restoration 1994; winner major architectural competition for Grand Buildings Trafalgar Square 1987; RIBA 1969; *Recreations* painting, music; *Style*— Paul Gibson, Esq; ✉ Sidell Gibson Partnership, Fitzroy Yard, Fitzroy Rd, London NW1 8TP (☎ 0171 722 5009, fax 0171 722 0083)

GIBSON, Rear Adm Peter Cecil; CB (1968); 2 s of Alexander Horace Cecil Gibson (d 1968), and Phyllis Zéline, *née* Baume (d 1948); *b* 31 May 1913; *Educ* Ealing Priory; *m* 1938, Phyllis Anna Mary, da of Norman Haliburton Hume (d 1936); 2 s, 1 da; *Career* entered RN 1931; service mainly marine and aeronautical engrg, maintenance test flying, staff and Admty aviation appts; dir engr offr's appts 1961–63, dep controller aircraft (RN) Ministries Aviation and Technol 1966–69, ret RN 1969; business mgmnt conslt 1973–; *Recreations* bridge, fly-fishing; *Clubs* Army & Navy; *Style*— Rear Adm Peter Gibson, CB

GIBSON, Rt Hon Lord Justice Peter; Rt Hon Sir Peter Leslie Gibson; kt (1981), PC (1993); s of Harold Leslie Gibson (d 1972), and Martha Lucy, *née* Diercking (d 1971); *b* 10 June 1934; *Educ* Malvern, Worcester Coll Oxford (scholar, BA); *m* 4 Sept 1968, Katharine Mary Beatrice, da of Henry John Hadow; 2 s (Richard John b 1969, Nicholas Kenneth b 1972), 1 da (Annabel Martha Katharine b 1977); *Career* Nat Serv 2 Lt RA 1953–55; called to the Bar Inner Temple 1960, jr counsel to the Treasy (Chancery) 1972–81, bencher Lincoln's Inn 1975, judge of the High Court of Justice (Chancery Div) 1981–93, a Lord Justice of Appeal 1993–; judge of Employment Appeal Tbnl 1984–86, chm Law Cmmn 1990–92, treas Lincoln's Inn 1996; hon fell Worcester Coll Oxford; *Style*— The Rt Hon Lord Justice Peter Gibson; ✉ Royal Courts of Justice, Strand, London WC2A 2LL (☎ 0171 405 7641)

GIBSON, Prof Robert Edward; s of Edward Robert Ward (d 1941), of Felpham, W Sussex, and Ellen Constance Mack (d 1931), adopted s of John Gibson, and Mary, *née* Mack; *b* 12 May 1926; *Educ* Emanuel Sch, Battersea Poly, Imperial Coll London (BSc, PhD, DSc); *m* 10 Oct 1950, Elizabeth Jocelyn (d 1986), da of Donald Edward Bideleux; 2 s (Alastair Robert b 10 Oct 1952 d 1995, Jonathan Edward b 21 June 1963), 1 da (Caroline Lucy b 1 April 1957); *Career* Royal Aircraft Establishment Farnborough 1945–46, res student then asst Imperial Coll 1948–53, sr scientific offr Building Research Station 1953–56, lectr then reader in civil engrg analysis Imperial Coll 1956–65, King's Coll London 1965–83 (reader in civil engrg, prof of engrg sci), Cwlth visiting prof Univ of Sydney 1969–70, Rankine lectr British Geotechnical Soc 1974, sr princ and dir Golder Associates 1974–94, industl fell Wolfson Coll Oxford 1983–85, adjoint prof Univ of Colorado Boulder 1987–94, sr res fell Queen Mary and Westfield Coll 1988–; FEng 1984; *Recreations* travel, listening to music; *Clubs* Athenaeum; *Style*— Prof Robert Gibson, FEng; ✉ 23 South Drive, Ferring, West Sussex BN12 5QU (☎ 01903 700386, fax 01903 507122)

GIBSON, Rosemary (Rose); da of Donald Bruce Cameron (d 1987), of London, and Ruth Margaret, *née* Watson; *b* 16 Feb 1961; *Educ* Lady Margaret GS, Wadham Coll Oxford (BA, MA); *m* 31 July 1987, James Ernest Gibson, s of Joseph David Gibson, CBE (d 1992); 1 da (Leonora b 5 Jan 1993); *Career* news reporter and feature writer City of London Recorder 1982–84, account exec Communications Arc Ltd (subsid of General Advertising Ltd) 1984–85; Chambers Cox PR Ltd: sr account exec 1985–86, account dir 1986–89, dir 1989–93, md 1993–; awarded Daily Express Young Sportswriter of the Year 1978; MIPR, MInstD; *Recreations* theatre, cinema, music, drama, short story writing, cookery (finalist BBC Masterchef 1992), wine, literature, travel; *Style*— Ms Rose Gibson; ✉ Chambers Cox PR Ltd, 7/8 Rathbone Place, London W1P 1DE (☎ 0171 631 5414, fax 0171 580 7719)

GIBSON, Roy; s of Robert Gibson, OBE (d 1984), of Belfast, and Mary Gibson (d 1995); *b* 10 Sept 1933; *Educ* Royal Belfast Acad Inst, Queen's Univ Belfast (MB BCh, BAO); *m* 5 July 1962, Elizabeth Deirdre, da of William Jordan Addis (d 1981), of Belfast; 2 da (Lesley Deirdre b 1966, Jennifer Maxine b 1970); *Career* Royal Victoria Hosp Belfast: house surgn, registrar, conslt ENT surgn; clinical fellowship in otolaryngology Washington Univ St Louis Missouri USA 1965–66; memb: Central Ctee for Hosp Med Servs BMA 1980–85, Cncl BMA 1983–85; chm Royal Victoria Hosp Med Staff 1995, chm Med Advsy Ctee E Health and Social Servs Bd 1987–92, ex-officio memb E Health Bd NI 1986–90; FRCSEd 1962, FRCS 1964; *Recreations* watching rugby football and cricket, golf, gardening, reading; *Clubs* Instonians, RSM; *Style*— Roy Gibson, Esq; ✉ Consulting Rooms, 13 Ulsterville Avenue, Belfast BT9 7AS (☎ 01232 667741)

GIBSON, Ven Terence Allen (Terry); s of Fred William Allen Gibson, of Boston, Lincs, and Joan Hazel, *née* Bishop; *b* 23 Oct 1937; *Educ* Boston GS, Jesus Coll Cambridge (MA), Cuddesdon Coll Oxford; *Career* curate St Chad Kirkby Liverpool 1963–66, warden Centre 63 C of E Youth Centre and vicar for Youth Work 1966–75, rector of Kirkby Liverpool 1975–84, rural dean Walton Liverpool 1979–84; archdeacon of: Suffolk 1984–87, Ipswich 1987–; *Style*— The Ven The Archdeacon of Ipswich; ✉ 99 Valley Rd, Ipswich, Suffolk IP1 4NF (☎ 01473 250333, fax 01473 286877)

GIBSON, Thomas Herbert; s of Clement Herbert Gibson (d 1976), of England and Argentina, and Marjorie Julia, *née* Anderson (d 1982); *b* 12 April 1943; *Educ* Eton; *m* 1966, Anthea Fiona Catherine, da of late Lt-Col G A Palmer, RE; 3 s (Miles Cosmo Archdale b 1968, Sebastian Thomas Maximilian b 1972, Benjamin Hugh George b 1973); *Career* fndr chm Thomas Gibson Fine Art Ltd 1969–96, ret, fndr Thomas Gibson Fine Art Advsy Services 1996–; memb Soc of London Art Dealers (memb Exec Ctee 1987–89); *Recreations* tennis; *Style*— Thomas Gibson, Esq; ✉ Thomas Gibson Fine Art Advisory Services, 44 Old Bond St, London W1X 4HQ (☎ 0171 499 8572)

GIBSON, Sheriff William Erle; s of William Graham Gibson (d 1979), of Aberfeldy, and Robina Cruikshank, *née* Thomson (d 1949); *b* 30 Aug 1934; *Educ* Dollar Acad, Trinity Hall Cambridge (BA), Univ of Glasgow (LLB); *m* 29 Sept 1961, Anne Durie, da of late Lt Col Roy Mathieson, TD, DSO; 2 da (Fiona Jane b 3 June 1964, Clare Anne b 26 Jan 1966), 1 s (William Robert Graham b 10 Feb 1970); *Career* Nat Serv midshipman RN 1953–55; ptnr Buchanan & McIlwraith Slrs Glasgow 1961–89; sheriff S Strathclyde Dumfries & Galloway (at Hamilton) 1989–; sec Inc Glasgow Stirlingshire & Sons of the Rock Soc (charity) 1965–90, clerk Gen Cmmrs of Income Tax Glasgow Div 1966–89, clerk Gen Cncl Univ of Glasgow 1976–87; memb: Inc of Bakers Glasgow (deacon 1979–80), Inc of Wrights Glasgow; memb Law Soc of Scotland; *Recreations* hill walking, golf, fishing, piping and other music; *Clubs* Glasgow Golf; *Style*— Sheriff William Gibson; ✉ 7A Briarwell Road, Milngavie, Glasgow G62 6AW; Sheriff Court House, 4 Beckford Street, Hamilton ML3 6AA (☎ 01698 282957)

GIBSON, Hon William Knatchbull; 3 s of Baron Gibson, *qv*, and Elizabeth Dione, da of Hon Clive Pearson; *b* 26 Aug 1951; *Educ* Eton, Magdalen Coll Oxford (BA); *m* 1988, Lori Frances, o da of Herbert Mintz, of Miami, Florida, USA; 1 s (Matthew Charles b 6 Dec 1990), 1 da (Sarah Claire b 29 Aug 1992); *Career* newspaper mangr with Westminster Press (industl rels specialist 1976–82), Sloan fell London Grad Sch of Business Studies 1983, dir of admin Financial Times 1984–86, publisher of Financial Times magazines 1986–89, md Financial Times Business Information 1989–, chm and chief exec Westminster Press Ltd 1996–; *Recreations* opera, shooting, skiing; *Clubs* Garrick; *Style*— The Hon William Gibson; ✉ 46 Victoria Rd, London W8 5RQ; Financial Times, 1 Southwark Bridge, London SE1 9HL

GIBSON-CRAIG-CARMICHAEL, Sir David Peter William; 15 Bt (NS 1702), of Keirhill, Co Edinburgh, and 8 Bt (UK 1831), of Riccarton, Midlothian; s of Sir (Archibald Henry) William Gibson-Craig-Carmichael, 14 and 7 Bt (d 1969), and Rosemary Anita, *née* Crew (d 1979); *b* 21 July 1946; *Educ* Queen's Univ Kingston Canada (BSc); *m* 1973, Patricia, da of Marcos Skarnic, of Santiago, Chile; 1 s (Peter William b 1975), 1 da (Margaret Anne b 1977); *Heir* s, Peter William Gibson-Craig-Carmichael b 29 Dec 1975; *Style*— Sir David Gibson-Craig-Carmichael, Bt

GIBSON-WATT, Baron (Life Peer UK 1979), of The Wye, in the District of Radnor; (James) David Gibson-Watt; MC (1943 and 2 bars), PC (1974), DL (formerly Radnorshire 1968, now Powys); s of Maj James Miller Gibson-Watt, JP, DL (d 1929; gggs of James Watt the engineer and inventor of the steam engine), and Marjorie Adela, *née* Ricardo, MBE (gggda of David Ricardo, the political economist); *b* 11 Sept 1918; *Educ* Eton, Trinity Coll Cambridge (BA); *m* 10 Jan 1942, Diana, 2 da of Sir Charles Hambro, KBE, MC (d 1963); 3 s (Jamie b 1943 d 1946, Hon Julian David b 13 June 1946, Hon Robin (*qv*) b 25 March 1949), 2 da (Hon Claerwen (Hon Mrs Green) b 20 Oct 1952, Hon Sian Diana (Lady Biddulph) b 1 April 1962); *Career* served WWII Welsh Gds (North African and Italian campaigns); Parly candidate Brecon and Radnor 1950 and 1951, MP (C) Hereford 1956–74, lord cmmr of the Treasury 1959–61, min of state Welsh Office 1970–74; memb Historic Bldgs Cncl Wales 1975–79, a forestry cmmr 1976–86; chm: Cncl of Royal Welsh Agric Soc 1978–93, Cncl on Tribunals 1980–86; hon pres Timber Growers UK, vice pres Kennel Club; FRAgs; JP until 1988; *Clubs* Boodle's, Army and Navy; *Style*— The Rt Hon Lord Gibson-Watt, MC, PC, DL; ✉ Doldowlod, Llandrindod Wells, Powys LD1 6HF (☎ 01597 860208)

GIBSON-WATT, Hon Robin; 3 and yst s of Baron Gibson-Watt, MC, PC, JP, DL, *qv*; *b* 25 March 1949; *Educ* Eton; *m* 1971, Marcia Susan, da of Sir Roger Hugh Cary, 2 Bt, *qv*; 3 s (Anthony David b 1975, Edward Ricardo b 1978, Guy Charles b 1982), 1 da (Phoebe Charlotte b 1980); *Career* dep pres Powys Red Cross 1985–, pres Brecon and Radnor NSPCC 1992–95; Brecon and Radnor Cons Assoc: vice chm 1988–91, chm 1991–94, pres 1994–; memb Bd Devpt Bd for Rural Wales 1993–96; High Sheriff Powys 1981; memb Royal Welsh Agric Soc; *Style*— The Hon Robin Gibson-Watt; ✉ Gelligarn, Llanyre, Llandrindod Wells, Powys LD1 6EY (☎ 01597 822874, fax 01597 822875)

GIDADA, HE Dr Solomon; *b* 31 Jan 1935, Dimbo Dollo, Wollega, Western Ethiopia; *Educ* Haile Selassie I Secdy Sch Addis Ababa Ethiopia, York Central HS York NY USA, Washington & Jefferson Coll Univ of Rochester (BSc, MB), Syracuse Univ (DEd); *m*; 4 s, 2 da; *Career* Ethiopian Dip Serv; teacher Charlotte Jr HS Rochester NY 1967, teacher and vice princ Dimbo Dollo Ethiopia 1968–69 (sch sci teacher 1967), sci teacher Shale Jr HS Syracuse NY 1972–81, dir Bethel Evangelical Secdy Sch Dimbo Dollo 1972–81, dir Urban & Rural Devpt Ethiopian Evangelical Church Mekane Yesus Addis Ababa 1981–91; pres YMCA Dimbo Dollo 1973, co-ordinator Credit Union Dimbo Dollo 1974–76, chm Bethel Synod Admin 1984–91, chm Christian Relief and Devpt Assoc (CRDA) 1978–88, chm Jt Relief Partnership (consortium of Ethiopian Evangelical Church Mekane Yesus, Catholic Church, Ethiopian Orthodox Church, the Catholic Relief Servs and the Lutheran World Fedn); Ethiopian ambass to Ct of St James's 1992–; *Style*— HE Dr Solomon Gidada; ✉ Embassy of Ethiopia, 17 Princes Gate, London SW7 1PZ (☎ 0171 589 7212, fax 0171 584 7054)

GIDDINGS, Air Marshal Sir (Kenneth Charles) Michael; KCB (1975), OBE (1953), DFC (1945), AFC (1950, and bar 1955); s of Charles Giddings, and Grace, *née* Gregory; *b* 27 Aug 1920; *Educ* Ealing Co Sch, UCL; *m* 1946, Elizabeth, da of Joseph McConnell; 2 s, 2 da; *Career* conscripted RAF 1940, test pilot RAE 1947–50, Dep Chief Def Staff Op Requirements 1973–76; ind panel inspr DOE 1978–91, dir National Counties Building Society 1982–85; *Recreations* golf, gardening, music; *Style*— Air Marshal Sir Michael Giddings, KCB, OBE, DFC; ✉ 159 Long Lane, Tilehurst, Reading, Berks (☎ 0118 923012)

GIDDINGS, Robert; *Educ* Univ of Bristol (BA, MLitt, DipEd), Univ of Keele (PhD); *Career* sr English master Ryefields and St Nicholas Sch 1962–63; lectr: WEA South and West 1962–64, Extra Mural Dept Univ of Bristol 1963–65, in English and liberal studies Yeovil Tech Coll 1963–64, in English and communication studies City of Bath Coll of Further Educn 1964–82; researcher Educn Systems Ltd Bristol 1966–67, assoc tutor Sch of Educn Univ of Bath 1971–79, course tutor The Open Univ 1971–79, Fulbright Exchange prof St Louis Community Coll Florissant Valley 1975–76; author and journalist 1961– (contrib New Statesman, New Society, The Listener, Radio Times, Music and Musicians, The Guardian, Sunday Times, Radio Academy Journal, New Statesman - Society, Times Higher Education Supplement, Observer and various radio and television progs); researcher and writer: The Late Show, The Clive James Unit, The Late Review, various radio and television progs; radio and television scriptwriter and broadcaster 1966– (contrib Woman's Hour, Home for the Day, Does He Take Sugar?, Pebble Mill at One and The Late Show); radio columnist Tribune 1977–85, media columnist Music and Musicians 1980–84, professional attachment TVS Southampton 1987–88, contrib Classic CD 1982–; currently prof of communication and culture Sch of

Media Arts and Communication Bournemouth Univ (formerly Bournemouth Poly); *Books* incl: The Tradition of Smollett (1967), British Social and Political History (1967), You Should See Me in Pyjamas (autobiog, 1981), Mark Twain - A Sumptuous Variety (1987), The Changing World of Charles Dickens, JRR Tolkien - This Far Land, Who Was Really Who in Fiction (with Alan Bold), The War Poets 1914–1918 (1988), Screening the Novel, Literature and Imperialism (1990), Echoes of War (1991), The Author, the Book and the Reader (1991), Imperial Echoes (1995), Tobias Smollett 1721–1771 (1995), Charles Dickens 1812–1870 (1996); *Style*— Robert Giddings; ✉ School of Media Arts and Communication, Bournemouth University, Poole, Dorset BH12 5BB (☎ 01202 595240); c/o Sheila Watson, Authors Agents, 12 Egert St, London NW1 8LJ (☎ 0171 722 9514)

GIDDINS, Anthony David Chaffey (Pip); s of Dudley Dyster Chaffey Giddins (d 1979), of Mymms Hall, Herts, and Irene Dorothy, *née* Lock; *b* 19 July 1951; *Educ* Univ of Leicester (LLB); *m* 22 April 1978, Anne Patricia, da of Kenneth Raymond Coward, of Northbourne, Bournemouth; 1 s (David Robert Chaffey b 22 March 1980), 1 da (Fiona Victoria b 3 April 1979), 1 step s (Mark Andrew); *Career* admitted slr 1976; lectr law Coll of Law 1976–77, Bowmaker Ltd 1977–83, head legal servs British Credit Trust Ltd 1983–85, Warner Goodman & Streat and Trethowans 1985–88, ptnr Lester Aldridge 1988–, visiting lectr Bournemouth Univ 1988–; memb Examination Bd Fin and Leasing Assoc 1979–; *Style*— Pip Giddins, Esq; ✉ 28 Harrier Drive, Wimborne, Dorset BH21 1XE (☎ 01202 841723); Lester Aldridge, Russell House, Oxford Rd, Bournemouth, Dorset BH8 8EX (☎ 01202 786161, fax 01202 786170)

GIEDROYĆ, Michal Graham Dowmont (Miko); s of Michal Jan Henryk Giedroyć, of Oxford, and Rosemary Virginia Anna, *née* Cumpston; *b* 5 May 1959; *Educ* Ampleforth Coll York, New Coll Oxford (BA); *m* 1 Nov 1986, Dorothee Alexandra Ulrike, da of Dr Ernst Friedrich Jung, of Bonn; 2 s (Jan Tadeusz Friedrich William b 30 Oct 1994, Melchior Ernst Graham Mathias b 3 Jun 1996), 1 da (Anna Viva Magdalene b 25 Aug 1992); *Career* Investmt Div J Henry Schroder Wagg and Co Ltd 1980–83, vice pres Schroder Capital Management Inc 1984–85, dir Warburg Securities 1985–95, dir Deutsche Morgan Grenfell 1995–; *Recreations* jazz piano; *Style*— Miko Giedroyć, Esq; ✉ Deutsche Morgan Grenfell, 150 Leadenhall Street, London EC3V 4RJ (☎ 0171 588 4545, fax 0171 971 7465)

GIELGUD, Sir (Arthur) John; OM (1996), CH (1977), kt (1953); s of Frank Gielgud, stockbroker (d 1949), and Kate Terry Lewis (d 1958, niece of Dame Ellen Terry 1847–1928); *b* 14 April 1904; *Educ* Westminster, Lady Benson Sch of Drama, RADA; *Career* actor, stage director and producer; Special Award for services to theatre Lawrence Olivier Awards 1985, Shakespeare Globe Tst Award (first recipient) 1993; Hon LLD St Andrew's 1950, Hon DLitt Oxon 1953, Hon DLitt London 1977, Companion Légion d'Honneur 1960; fell BAFTA 1992; *Theatre* stage debut Old Vic 1921 as the herald in Henry V, suc Noel Coward as Nicky Lancaster in The Vortex 1925 and as Lewis Dodd in The Constant Nymph 1927, two Old Vic seasons 1929–30, Musical Chairs 1931, The Good Companions 1931, Richard II in Richard of Bordeaux 1932, Noah 1934, alternated Mercutio and Romeo with Laurence Olivier in Romeo and Juliet 1935 (also dir); appeared in Hamlet 1930, 1934, 1936, 1939, 1944, 1945 and 1946 (over 500 appearances in this role); Ernest Worthing in The Importance of Being Earnest 1930, 1939 and 1942; Prospero in The Tempest 1930, 1940, 1957 and 1974; King Lear 1931, 1950 and 1955; dir: The Heiress 1949, The Lady's Not For Burning 1949, The Cherry Orchard 1954, The Chalk Garden 1956, Hamlet (starring Richard Burton) USA 1964, Private Lives 1972, The Constant Wife 1973, The Gay Lord Quex 1975; played Oedipus in Seneca's Oedipus 1968, Headmaster in 40 Years On 1968, Home 1970, No Man's Land 1975, Julius Caesar 1977, Volpone 1977, Half-Life 1977, The Best of Friends 1988; *Television* incl: Brideshead Revisited 1981, Inside the Third Reich 1983, Neck 1983, The Scarlet and the Black 1983, Time After Time 1985, Marco Polo 1986, Oedipus the King 1986, The Canterville Ghost 1987, Quartermaine's Terms 1987, War & Remembrance 1988, Summer's Lease 1989, Under the Hammer 1993, Gulliver's Travels (Channel 4) 1996; *Films* incl: Richard III 1955, Chimes at Midnight 1966, Oh! What a Lovely War 1968, Murder on the Orient Express 1974, Providence 1977, The Elephant Man 1979, Arthur 1982 (Oscar for Best Supporting Actor), Wagner 1983, Plenty 1985, The Shooting Party 1985, Leave All Fair 1987, The Whistle Blower 1987, Arthur on the Rocks 1988, Getting Things Right 1988, Loser Takes All 1988, Prospero's Books 1991, First Knight 1995, Shine 1996; *Books* Early Stages (1938), Stage Directions (1963), Distinguished Company (1972), An Actor and His Time (autobiog 1979), Backward Glances (1989), Shakespeare - Hit or Miss (1991); *Recreations* music, painting; *Clubs* Garrick, Arts, Players (New York); *Style*— Sir John Gielgud, OM, CH; ✉ c/o ICM Ltd, Oxford House, 76 Oxford Street, London W1N 0AX (☎ 0171 636 6565, fax 0171 323 0101)

GIELGUD, Maina Julia Gordon; Hon AO (1991); da of Lewis Evelyn Gielgud (d 1953), and Elisabeth Sutton (author and actress under name of Zita Gordon); niece of Sir John Gielgud; *b* 14 Jan 1945; *Educ* BEPC France; *Career* ballerina with: Cuevas Co and Roland Petit Co to 1963, Grand Ballet Classique de France 1963–67; princ ballerina: Béjart Co 1967–71, Berlin 1971, London Festival Ballet 1972–76, Sadler's Wells Ballet 1976–78; freelance ballerina and guest artist 1978–82, rehearsal dir London City Ballet 1982; artistic dir: Australian Ballet 1983–96, Royal Danish Ballet March 1997–; creations and choreographies: Steps Notes and Squeaks (London) 1978, Petit Pas et Crac (Paris) 1979, Ghosties and Ghoulies (London City Ballet) 1982, The Sleeping Beauty (Australian Ballet) 1984, Giselle (Australian Ballet) 1986; *Style*— Miss Maina Gielgud; ✉ Stirling Court, 3 Marshall St, London W1

GIEVE, (Edward) John Watson; s of David Gieve, and Susan, *née* Best; *b* 20 Feb 1950; *Educ* Charterhouse, New Coll Oxford (BA, BPhil); *m* 25 March 1972, Katherine Elizabeth, Vereker, da of Charles Henry Vereker; 2 s (Daniel b 6 June 1980, Matthew b 31 Aug 1982); *Career* admin trainee Dept of Employment 1974–78, princ HM Treasy 1979–84; investmt controller Investors in Indust 1984–86; HM Treasy: asst sec Gen Expenditure Policy 1986–88, press sec 1988–89, princ private sec to the Chllr 1989–91, under sec Banking Gp 1991–94, dep dir Budget and Public Finances 1994–; *Recreations* golf, football; *Clubs* Arsenal; *Style*— John Gieve, Esq; ✉ HM Treasury, Parliament Street, London SW1P 3AG (☎ 0171 270 4499)

GIFFARD, Sir (Charles) Sydney Rycroft; KCMG (1984, CMG 1976); s of Walter Giffard, JP (d 1970), of Lockeridge, Wilts, and Minna, *née* Cotton (d 1966); *b* 30 Oct 1926; *m* 1, 1951 (m dis 1976), Wendy, *née* Vidal; 1 s (Berenger b 1959), 1 da (Theresa b 1960); m 2, 1976, Hazel Roberts, OBE; *Career* joined Foreign Serv 1951; HM ambass: Berne 1980–82, Tokyo 1984–86; hon fell Wadham Coll Oxford; *Books* Japan Among The Powers 1890–1990 (1994); *Style*— Sir Sydney Giffard, KCMG; ✉ Winkelbury House, Berwick St John, nr Shaftesbury, Dorset SP7 0EY

GIFFORD, Andrew Graham; s of Charles Henry Pearson Gifford, OBE (d 1993), of Edinburgh, and Margaret Laetitia Gifford, MBE, *née* Lyell (d 1995); *Educ* Bedales, Univ of Edinburgh; *m* Charlotte Montrésor, da of Michael White; 2 s (Henry (Harry) Montrésor, Charles Montrésor); *Career* PA to Rt Hon Sir David Steel, MP as Foreign Affrs Spokesman and Ldr of Lib Pty 1975–80 (memb Lib and SDP Ldrs' Campaign Staff 1979 and 1983 election campaigns), fndr ptnr and chief exec GJW Government Relations 1980–; directorships incl: Fleming Enterprise Investment Trust 1993–, London American Growth Trust 1995–, Fourth Estate (publishing co); chm Assoc of Professional Political Consultants 1994–; treas The Green Alliance; *Books* Handbook of World Development (1982); *Recreations* fishing, stalking, shooting, building; *Clubs* New, Beefsteak; *Style*— Andrew Gifford, Esq; ✉ 8 Hans Street, London SW1; GJW Government Relations, 2 Little Smith Street, London SW1

GIFFORD, 6 Baron (UK 1824); Anthony Maurice Gifford; QC (1982); s of 5 Baron Gifford (d 1961), and (Ellice) Margaret, *née* Allen (d 1990); *b* 1 May 1940; *Educ* Winchester, King's Coll Cambridge; *m* 1, 22 March 1965 (m dis 1988), Katherine Ann, da of Max Mundy, of 52 Hornton St, Kensington; 1 s, 1 da (Hon Polly Anna b 1969); m 2, 24 Sept 1988, Elean Roslyn, da of Bishop David Thomas, of Kingston, Jamaica; 1 da (Sheba Chanel b 1992); *Heir* s, Hon Thomas Adam Gifford b 1 Dec 1967; *Career* sits as Lab Peer in Lords; called to the Bar Middle Temple 1962; chm: Ctee for Freedom Mozambique, Angola and Guiné 1968–75, N Kensington Law Centre 1974–77, Legal Action Gp 1978–81, Mozambique Angola Ctee 1984; vice-chm British Defence and Aid Fund 1985; chm: Broadwater Farm Inquiry 1986, Liverpool 8 Inquiry 1989; attorney at law Jamaica 1990; sr ptnr Gifford Haughton & Thompson 1991–; *Books* Where's the Justice (1986); *Style*— The Lord Gifford, QC; ✉ 8 King's Bench Walk, Temple, London EC4Y 7DU (☎ 0171 797 8888); 21 Church Street, Kingston, Jamaica (☎ 809 922 6056, fax 809 967 0225)

GIFFORD, Joshua Thomas (Josh); MBE (1989); s of Thomas H Gifford (d 1968), and Dinah Florence, *née* Newman (d 1981); *b* 3 Aug 1941; *Educ* Huntingdon C of E Sch, Eaglehurst Coll Northampton; *m* 1969, Althea Meryl, da of George Roger Smith; 1 s (Nicholas b 1971), 1 da (Kristina b 1970); *Career* national hunt trainer; flat racing jockey 1951–58; first ride for Mr Beechner at Newmarket 1951, 56 winners Sam Armstrong's stable 1952–58, winner HM the Queen's Ten Bells 1956; nat hunt jockey 1958–70; 700 winners Capt Ryan Price's stable, champion jockey 1962, 1963, 1967 and 1968; nat hunt trainer 1970–; over 1175 winners incl: Grand Nat 1981 (Aldaniti), Hennessey Cognac Gold Cup, Whitbread Gold Cup, Tote Gold Trophy, SGB Chase Ascot, Black and White Whiskey, Queen Mother Champion Chase, Mackeson Gold Cup Handicap Chase; *Recreations* golf, shooting, cricket; *Clubs* Findon CC, Lords Taverners; *Style*— Josh Gifford, Esq, MBE; ✉ The Downs, Findon, Worthing, West Sussex BN14 0RR (☎ 01903 872226)

GIFFORD, Prof Paul Peerless-Dennis; s of David Arthur Gifford, of Norwich, and Vera Rosina, *née* Palmer; *Educ* King Edward VI Norwich, Univ of Cambridge (MA), Univ of Toulouse (Lès L, Dr 3e Cycle, Dès L); *m* 20 Sept 1969, (Irma) Cynthia Mary, da of Lt-Col AFS Warwick (d 1961); 1 s (Gregory b 27 May 1979), 2 da (Fiona b 20 Sept 1972, Joanne b 8 May 1975); *Career* Buchanan chair of French Univ of St Andrews 1987–; *Books* Valéry - Le Dialogue des Choses Divines (1989); *Recreations* sailing, skiing, golf, tennis; *Style*— Prof Paul Gifford; ✉ 51 Radernie Place, St Andrews, Fife KY16 8QR (☎ 01334 477243); Department of French, University of St Andrews, Buchanan Building, St Andrews, Fife KY16 9PH

GIFFORD, Zerbanoo; da of Bailey Irani, and Kitty Mazda; *b* 11 May 1950; *Educ* Roedean, Watford Coll of Technol, London Sch of Journalism, Open Univ (BA); *m* 14 Sept 1973, Richard David Gifford, s of David Arthur Gifford, of Norwich; 2 s (Mark Mazda b 28 Aug 1975, Alexander Justice (Wags) b 27 Feb 1979); *Career* Lib cncllr Harrow 1982–86; Parly candidate (Lib Alliance): Hertsmere 1983, Harrow East 1987; Parly candidate (Lib Dems) Hertsmere 1992; chm: Lib Pty Community Rels Panel 1985, Cmmn into Ethnic Involvement 1986; elected memb Lib Dem Federal Exec 1991–92, pres Hertsmere Lib Dems; memb Status of Women Cmmn 1987, community affairs advsr to leader of Lib Democrats; former ed Libas magazine, runner-up Special Interest Magazine Ed of the Year 1988, columnist Lib Democrat News; memb Advsy Cncl The Prince's Youth Business Tst, tstee Anti-Slavery Int, dir Charities Aid Fndn India; Freeman City of Lincoln Nebraska; Nehru Centenary Award from Non-Resident Indians' Assoc 1989, Asian City Club Annual Award 1990, nominee Women of Europe Award 1991; FRSA; *Books* The Golden Thread (1990), Dadabhai Naoroji (1992), Asian Presence in Europe (1995), Thomas Clarkson and the Campaign against Slavery (1996); *Recreations* collecting antique embroidery, meeting extraordinary people; *Style*— Mrs Zerbanoo Gifford; ✉ Herga House, London Road, Harrow on the Hill, Middlesex HA1 3JJ (☎ 0181 422 8556, fax 0181 423 3363)

GIGGALL, Rt Rev (George) Kenneth; OBE (1960); s of Arthur William Giggall (d 1959), and Matilda Hannah, *née* Granlese (d 1964); *b* 15 April 1914; *Educ* Manchester Central HS, Univ of Manchester (BA), St Chad's Coll Univ of Durham (Dip Theol); *Career* ordained deacon 1939, priest 1940; curate: St Alban's Cheetwood 1939–41, St Elisabeth's Reddish 1941–45; chaplain RNVR and RN: HMS Braganza 1945, 34 Amphibious Support Regt RM 1945–46, Sch of Combined Ops Fremington 1946–47, HMS Norfolk 1947–49, Ocean 1949– 50, Flotilla Cmd Med and HMS Phoenicia 1950–52, HMS Campania for Operation Hurricane 1952, BRNC Dartmouth 1952–53, HMS Centaur 1953–56, Ceylon 1956–58, Fisgard 1958–60, Royal Arthur and lectr RAF Chaplains' Sch 1960–63, HMS Eagle 1963–65, Drake 1965–69; QHC 1967–, dean of Gibraltar and officiating chaplain HMS Rooke and to Flag Offr Gibraltar 1969–73, Bishop St Helena 1973–79, consecrated St Saviours Church E London, Cape Province, RSA, chaplain San Remo with Bordighera 1979–81, Aux Bishop Diocese of Gibraltar (subsequently Europe) 1979–81, Asst Bishop Diocese of Blackburn 1982–; *Recreations* music; *Clubs* Commonwealth Soc, Exiles (Ascension Island); *Style*— The Rt Rev Kenneth Giggall, OBE; ✉ Fosbrooke House, Clifton Drive, Lytham St Annes FY8 5RQ (☎ 01253 735 683)

GIGNOUX, Peter Alan; s of Frederick Evelyn Gignoux, Jr (d 1968); *b* 17 June 1945; *Educ* St Albans Sch, The Gunnery Sch, Boston Univ, Columbia Univ; *m* 26 Jan 1984, Katherine Elizabeth Phillips; *Career* London fndr and mangr Int Energy Desk; md Smith Barney Ltd; MInstPet; *Recreations* shooting, travelling, yacht cruising; *Clubs* Buck's, Mark's, Hurlingham, St Anthony (New York); *Style*— Peter Gignoux, Esq; ✉ 53 Carlyle Court, Chelsea Harbour, London SW10 0UQ (☎ 0171 730 4132); Smith Barney Ltd, 10 Piccadilly, London W1V 9LA (☎ 0171 548 5555, fax 0171 548 5599)

GILBART, Andrew James; QC (1991); s of Albert Thomas Gilbart (d 1975), of Vinehall Sch, Robertsbridge, Sussex, and Carol, *née* Christie; *b* 13 Feb 1950; *Educ* Vinehall Sch, Westminster (Queen's Scholar), Trinity Hall Cambridge (MA); *m* 20 Jan 1979, Morag, da of Robert Thomas Williamson (d 1990), of Ayr, and Agnes Buchanan Williamson; 1 s (Thomas Christie b 1980), 1 da (Ruth Alexandra b 1982); *Career* called to the Bar Middle Temple 1972, in practice Northern Circuit 1973–, recorder 1996– (asst recorder 1992–96); memb Ctee Local Govt and Planning Bar Assoc 1988–92; *Recreations* history, theatre, walking, computing; *Clubs* Heaton Chapel Reform; *Style*— Andrew Gilbart, Esq, QC; ✉ 40 King Street, Manchester M2 6BA (☎ 0161 832 9082, fax 0161 835 2139)

GILBART-DENHAM, Lt-Col Seymour Vivian; s of Maj Vivian Vandeleur (d 1940), and Diana Mary, *née* Beaumont (d 1983); *b* 10 Oct 1939; *m* 1 April 1976, Patricia Caroline, da of Lt-Col and Mrs Granville Brooking, of E Sussex; 2 da (Sophie b 1977, Georgina b 1980); *Career* cmmnd Life Gds 1960 (Adjutant 1965–67), cmd Household Cavalry Regt 1986–87, Crown Equerry 1987; vice pres: Royal Windsor Horse Show, The Royal Parks Equitation Tst; Liveryman: Worshipful Co of Coachmakers & Coach Harness Makers, Worshipful Co of Loriners; *Recreations* carriage driving, shooting, skiing; *Clubs* RAC, White's; *Style*— Lt-Col Seymour Gilbart-Denham, CVO; ✉ The Royal Mews, Buckingham Palace, London SW1W 0QH (☎ 0171 930 4832, fax 0171 930 6129)

GILBERT, Brian Geoffrey; s of Donald William Gilbert (d 1968); *b* 18 July 1927; *Educ* Bishopshalt Sch Hillingdon, Middx; *m* 1978, Maxine, da of George Hadley (d 1971); 2 da; *Career* md and gp chief exec Low & Bonar plc 1973–84; chm: BMG Ltd, Randotte (No 204) Ltd, Richards plc, W M Gray & Co Ltd; dir: Abtrust Scotland Investment Co plc; CIMgt; *Recreations* golf, fishing; *Clubs* Royal and Ancient, Royal Northern and Univ;

Style— Brian Gilbert, Esq; ✉ Randotte (No 204) Ltd, Sutherland House, 108 Dundas Street, Edinburgh EH3 5DQ (☎ 0131 557 6003)

GILBERT, Christopher Gallard; s of Frank Lathe Gilbert, of Corbridge, Northumberland, and Ruth Gallard, *née* Ainsworth; *b* 7 Sept 1936; *Educ* Rydal Sch Colwyn Bay, St George's Harpenden, Univ of Keele (BA), Univ of Durham (MA); *m* 1, 1964 (m dis 1972), Clare Stamford, *née* Taylor; 2 da (Philippa Stamford b 17 July 1966, Miranda Gallard b 18 Nov 1968); m 2, Mary Catriona Murray Snaith, da of William Chalmers; 3 step c (Douglas, Julian, Polly); *Career* Temple Newsam House Leeds: asst keeper 1961–68, keeper 1968–74, princ keeper 1974–95, pt/t consIt 1995–; dir Leeds City Art Galleries 1983–95; curator Chippendale Soc 1974– (pres 1996–), chm Furniture History Soc 1991–, vice pres Regional Furniture Soc 1994–; ed: Furniture History 1975–83, Regional Furniture 1986–92; FMA 1970, FSA 1974; *Books* Life and Work of Thomas Chippendale (1978), Furniture at Temple Newsam House (1978), English Vernacular Furniture (1991), Dictionary of English Furniture Makers (1986), Pictorial Dictionary of Marked London Furniture (1996); *Recreations* bird watching, landscape, Shakespeare; *Style*— Christopher Gilbert, Esq, FSA; ✉ 8 North Park Grove, Leeds LS8 1JJ (☎ 0113 266 2165)

GILBERT, Dennis; s of Gordon S Gilbert (d 1973), and Beatrice Maskell-Hall (d 1968); *b* 7 Jan 1922; *Educ* Lewisham Sch, SW Essex Tech Coll, St Martin's Sch of Art; *m* 14 July 1949 (m dis 1976), Joan, da of Harold Musker, OBE, MC (d 1974); 3 s (Hugh b 1952, Michael b 1957, Joseph b 1963), 1 da (Mary b 1965); *Career* landscape and portrait painter; WWII Warrant Offr and Navigator RAF 1942–46; lectr (visiting): Hammersmith Coll of Art 1950–65, Wimbledon Coll of Art 1954–60, Kingston Coll of Art 1958–65; lectr Hammersmith Coll of Art 1965–75, sr lectr Chelsea Sch of Art 1975–84; memb: New English Art Club, Soc of Landscape Painters, Contemporary Portrait Soc (chm 1984–86), Nat Soc of Painters, Nine Elms Gp of Artists, Small Paintings Soc; *Exhibitions* incl: RA, Paris Salon, Royal Festival Hall, Royal Soc of Portrait Painters (annually 1959–81), Contemporary Portrait Soc, Royal Soc of Br Artists, Royal Inst of Oil Painters, New English Art Club (annually 1959–), Nat Soc of Painters (annually 1957–), Chelsea Art Soc, King Street Gallery, Medici Gallery, Browse and Darby Gallery, Chenil Gallery, Redfern Gallery, Wildenstein Gallery, W H Patterson Fine Art, Phoenix Gallery, Southwell Brown Gallery; *Clubs* Arts, Chelsea Arts; *Style*— Dennis Gilbert, Esq; ✉ Top Studio, 11 Edith Grove, London SW10 OJZ (☎ 0171 352 9476)

GILBERT, Prof Fiona Jane; da of Dr John Knight Davidson, OBE, of Glasgow, and Edith Elizabeth, *née* McKelvie; *b* 1 May 1956; *Educ* Hutchesons' Girls' GS, Univ of Glasgow (MB ChB), Univ of Aberdeen (DMRD); *m* 4 June 1982, Martin James Gilbert, *qv*, s of James Robert Gilbert, of Aberdeen; 1 s (Jamie b 1986), 2 da (Mhairi b 1989, Kirstin b 1992); *Career* conslt radiologist 1989–96, prof of radiology Univ of Aberdeen 1996–; dir NE Scotland Breast Screening Service; memb BMA 1978, FRCR 1986, FRCP 1991 (MRCP 1981), FRCPE 1994; *Recreations* sailing, skiing, tennis, theatre, classical music; *Style*— Prof Fiona Gilbert; ✉ 17 Rubislaw Den North, Aberdeen AB2 4AL; Department of Radiology, Aberdeen Royal Infirmary, Foresterhill, Aberdeen (☎ 01224 681818)

GILBERT, Francis Humphrey Shubrick; QC (1992); s of Cdr Walter Raleigh Gilbert, RN (d 1977), of Compton Castle, S Devon, and Joan Mary Boileau, *née* Willock; *b* 25 Jan 1946; *Educ* Stowe, Trinity Coll Dublin (MA); *m* 19 April 1975, Sarah Marian, da of Col Douglas Kaye, DSO, DL (d 1996), of Brinkley Hall, nr Newmarket, Suffolk; 1 s (Raleigh b 28 Oct 1982), 2 da (Emma b 11 Nov 1976, Rosella b 15 Feb 1979); *Career* called to the Bar Lincoln's Inn 1970, recorder on Western Circuit, head of chambers; memb Devon CC 1977–85; *Recreations* sailing, shooting; *Clubs* Royal Yacht Sqdn; *Style*— Francis Gilbert, Esq, QC; ✉ Walnut House, 63 St David's Hill, Exeter EX4 4DW (☎ 01392 279751, fax 01392 412080)

GILBERT, Maj-Gen Glyn Charles Anglim; CB (1974), MC (1944); s of C G G Gilbert, OBE, MC, and Marjory Helen Gilbert, MBE, of Bermuda; *b* 1920; *Educ* Eastbourne Coll, RMC Sandhurst; *m* 1943, Heather Mary, wid of Pilot Offr A E Jackson, DFM, and da of late F Green; 3 s, 1 da; *Career* served: NW Europe 1944–45, Palestine 1945–47, Cyprus 1951, Egypt 1951, Malaya 1955–56, Cyprus 1958–59, IDC 1966, Maj-Gen 1970, cmd 44 Para Bde Gp 1963–65, cmd Sch of Infantry 1967–70, GOC 3 Div 1970–72; cmd Jt Warfare Establishment 1972–74, ret 1974; dir: Riverside Holidays 1974–80, Fitness for Industry Ltd 1980–96; chief exec Airborne Forces Charities 1990–96; *Recreations* following the sun; *Clubs* Army & Navy; *Style*— Maj-Gen Glyn Gilbert, CB, MC; ✉ c/o Army and Navy Club, 36 Pall Mall, London SW1Y 5JN

GILBERT, James; s of Thomas C Gilbert (d 1959), of Edinburgh, and Mabel Gilbert (d 1945); *b* 15 May 1923; *Educ* Edinburgh Acad, Univ of Edinburgh, RADA; *m* 10 July 1951, Fiona, da of George Clyne (d 1958), Noss House, Wick, Caithness; 1 s (Colin b 3 April 1952), 2 da (Susan b 17 Nov 1953, Julia b 24 Nov 1962); *Career* Flt Lt RAF Pilot 519 Sqdn 1942–46; composer and lyricist: Grab me a Gondola (Lyric Theatre London) 1957, The Golden Touch (Piccadilly Theatre) 1960, Good Time Johnny (Birmingham Rep) 1972; BBC TV: prodr and dir 1957–73, head of comedy 1973–77, head Light Entertainment Gp 1977–82; Thames TV: head of comedy 1982–88, exec prodr 1988–91; BBC TV exec prodr 1993–95; BAFTA awards 1960, 1967 and 1973, Int Press prize Montreux 1963 and 1967, Golden Rose Montreux 1967, TV Critics award 1973, Int Emmy 1984; *Books* Grab me a Gondola (1958); *Recreations* golf, walking, music, theatre; *Clubs* RAF; *Style*— James Gilbert; ✉ 29 Sydney Rd, Richmond, Surrey TW9 1UB

GILBERT, John Arthur; *b* 11 Aug 1932; *Educ* King's Norton GS for Boys, Birmingham Coll of Technol (later Univ of Aston) (HNC, BSc); *m* 1, 19 Nov 1955, late Marion Audrey; 2 s (Simon Gerard b 11 April 1958, Andrew Boyd b 1 Feb 1960), 1 da (Rosamond Grace b 25 Feb 1964); m 2, 22 April 1983, Nicola Ann; *Career* trainee engr S Willis 1949, ptnr James-Carrington & Partners 1967–89 (assoc 1964–67); work incl: maj town redevelopment schemes, large retail stores, hosps, refurbishment of listed bldgs, developing on deep landfill sites; expert witness; awarded Inst of Civil Engrs George Stephenson medal for paper on maj Belfast project 1988; FICE 1961, FIStructE 1963, ACIArb 1979, MConsE 1979, FFB 1988; *Style*— John A Gilbert, Esq; ✉ White Lodge, Bevere, Worcs WR3 7RQ (☎ 01905 451285); Gilbert Consulting, The Stables, White Lodge, Bevere, Worcs WR3 7RQ (☎ 01905 755111, fax 01905 755112), and Birmingham (☎ 0121 321 1252)

GILBERT, Rt Hon Dr John William; PC (1978), MP (Lab) Dudley East (majority 9,200); *b* 5 April 1927; *Educ* Merchant Taylors', St John's Coll Oxford, New York Univ (PhD); *m* 1; 2 da; m 2, 1963, Jean Olive Ross Skinner; *Career* chartered accountant (Canada); Parly candidate (Lab): Ludlow 1966, Dudley 1968; MP (Lab): Dudley 1970–74, Dudley East 1974–; oppn front bench spokesman on Treasy affairs 1972–74, financial sec Treasury 1974–75, min for Transport DOE 1975–76, min of state MOD 1976–79; memb Select Ctees on: Expenditure 1970–74, Corporation Tax 1973, Defence 1979–87, Trade and Indust 1987–92; chm PLP Defence Gp 1981–83, vice chm Lab Fin and Indust Gp 1983–91; memb Ctee on Intelligence and Security; memb: RUSI, RIIA, IISS, Amnesty Int, GMBATU, WWF, Fabian Soc; tstee Cncl for Arms Control; Hon LLD Wake Forest (S Carolina) 1983; FRGS; *Clubs* Reform; *Style*— The Rt Hon Dr John Gilbert, MP; ✉ House of Commons, London SW1A 0AA

GILBERT, Jonathan Sinclair; s of Brian Hamlyn Gilbert (d 1978), and Joan, *née* Sinclair; *b* 29 Sept 1937; *Educ* Bilton Grange Sch, Rugby; *m* 10 Aug 1962, Lene, da of Palle Palsby (d 1988); 3 s (Andrew b 12 Nov 1964, Nicholas (twin) b 12 Nov 1964, Peter b 22 July 1967); *Career* Nat Serv, Lt King's Hussars 1955–57; bd dir Bland Payne Ltd 1968, dir Bland Payne Holdings Ltd 1978, chm Sedgwick Offshore Resources Ltd 1980, dir Sedgwick Group plc 1981–, dep chm Sedgwick Broking Services 1990–; chm: Sedgwick Energy Ltd 1992–, Sedgwick Payne Ltd Jan 1994–95 (dep chm and md 1992–94); *Recreations* golf; *Clubs* Burhill Golf, Royal St George's Golf, St George's Hill Golf, Lloyd's Golf, Lucifer Golfing Soc, MCC; *Style*— J S Gilbert, Esq; ✉ Sedgwick House, The Sedgwick Centre, London E1 8DX (☎ 0171 377 3153, fax 0171 377 3199, telex 882131)

GILBERT, Martin James; s of James Robert Gilbert, of Blairgowrie, Scotland, and Winifred, *née* Walker; *b* 13 July 1955; *Educ* Robert Gordon's Coll, Univ of Aberdeen (MA, LLB); *m* 4 June 1982, Prof Fiona Jane Gilbert, *qv*, da of Dr John K Davidson; 1 s (Jamie), 2 da (Mhairi, Kirstin); *Career* CA; Deloitte Haskins and Sells 1978–81, Brander and Cruickshank 1982–83, chief exec Aberdeen Trust plc 1983–; non-exec dir: Abtrust New Thai Investment Trust plc, Abtrust Preferred Income Trust plc, Abtrust Scotland Investment Co plc, Abtrust High Income Trust plc, Abtrust Latin America Investment Trust PLC, Abtrust Emerging Economies Investment Trust plc, Abtrust Emerging Asia Investment Trust plc, Radiotrust plc, Firstbus plc, Taverners Trust plc, Prior plc; MICAS; *Recreations* golf, hockey, skiing, sailing; *Clubs* Royal and Ancient (St Andrews), Royal Aberdeen Golf, Royal Selangor Golf, Gordonians HC, Royal Northern and Univ, Deeside Golf; *Style*— Martin Gilbert, Esq; ✉ 17 Rubislaw Den North, Aberdeen AB15 4AL; Aberdeen Trust plc, 10 Queen's Terrace, Aberdeen AB9 1QJ (☎ 01224 631999)

GILBERT, Sir Martin John; kt (1995), CBE (1990); s of Peter Gilbert (d 1976), of London, and Miriam, *née* Green; *b* 25 Oct 1936; *Educ* Highgate Sch, Magdalen Coll Oxford (BA); *m* 1, 1964 (m dis), Helen, da of Joseph Robinson, CBE; 1 da (Natalie b 1967); m 2, 1974, Susan, da of Michael Sacher; 2 s (David b 1978, Joshua b 1982); *Career* author; hon fell Merton Coll Oxford 1994– (fell 1962–94), official biographer of Sir Winston Churchill 1968–, visiting prof Univ Coll London 1995–96; FRSL; *Publications* author of 48 historical works and atlases incl: British History Atlas (1968), American History Atlas (1968), First World War Atlas (1970), Winston S Churchill Vols 3–8 (1971–88) and Churchill Document Vols (1973–), Sir Horace Rumbold, Portrait of a Diplomat (1973), Atlas of the Holocaust (1986), The Holocaust, The Jewish Tragedy (1986), Second World War (1989), Churchill: A Life (1991), Atlas of British Charities (1993), In Search of Churchill (1994), First World War (1994), The Day the War Ended (1995), Jerusalem in the Twentieth Century (1996), The Boys, Triumph over Adversity (1996); *Recreations* drawing maps; *Clubs* Athenaeum; *Style*— Sir Martin Gilbert, CBE, FRSL; ✉ Merton College, Oxford OX1 4JD

GILBERT, Michael Francis; CBE (1980), TD (1950); s of Bernard Samuel Gilbert (d 1927), and Berwyn Minna, *née* Cuthbert (d 1966); *b* 17 July 1912; *Educ* Blundell's, Univ of London (LLB); *m* 26 July 1947, Roberta Mary, da of late Col R M W Marsden; 2 s (Richard b 1956, Gerard b 1960), 5 da (Harriett b 1948, Victoria b 1950, Olivia b 1952, Kate b 1954, Laura b 1958); *Career* WWII HAC (Maj) served N Africa, Italy 1939–45 (despatches 1943); ptnr Trower, Still & Keeling 1952–83 (slr 1947), legal advsr to Ruler of Bahrain 1960; author of: 24 novels of detection and suspense, over 200 short stories, 4 stage plays, various critical articles; ed 2 anthologies; memb: Royal Literary Fund Ctee 1964, Cncl Soc of Authors 1975; pres Luddesdown Cricket Club 1965; *Recreations* walking; *Clubs* Garrick; *Style*— Michael Gilbert, Esq, CBE, TD; ✉ The Old Rectory, Luddesdown, Gravesend, Kent DA13 0XE

GILBERT, Richard Simon; s of Nigel John Gilbert, of Emsworth, Hants, and Mair, *née* James; *b* 1 Nov 1957; *Educ* Sevenoaks Sch Kent, Falmouth Sch of Art (BA), Wimbledon Sch of Art (BA), Chelsea Sch of Art (MA), Br Sch in Rome (Abbey Major scholar in painting), Sch of the Art Inst of Chicago (Harkness fell); *Career* self-employed fine artist; teacher Sch of Art and Design Wellington Coll Berks 1994; *Solo Exhibitions* Recent Work (Main Gallery Warwick Arts Trust London) 1986, Recent Work (Raab Gallery London) 1988, New Work (Raab Gallery London) 1992; *Group Exhibitions* incl: Wet Paint (Festival Gallery Bath) 1984, CAS Market (Smiths Gallery London) 1984–87 and 1990, John Moores Fourteenth Nat Exhibition (Walker Art Gallery Liverpool) 1985, Forty European Artists (Raab Gallery) 1986, Athena Arts awards (Barbican) 1987, Art for the City (Lloyd's Building London) 1987, Fellowship Exhibition (Sch of Art, Inst of Chicago) 1989, The Landscape and the Cityscape (Raab Gallery London) 1990, Rome scholars 1980–90 (Gulbenkian Gallery RCA London) 1990, The Discerning Eye (Mall Gallery London) 1990, Six Young British Artists (Oviedo, Madrid, Barcelona) 1991–92, Royal Over-Seas League Exhibition (Rosl Houe London) 1992, CAS Market (Smiths Galleries London) 1992 and 1993, The Blue Gallery 1994 and 1995; *Work in Collections* Contemporary Art Soc, Victoria Art Gallery Melbourne, Arthur Andersen plc, Barclays Bank plc, Business Design Centre, Leicester Educn Authy, Lloyds Bank of Spain and South America (Madrid), Pearl Life Assurance Co London, Rosehaugh Stanhope London, Clifford Chance London and NY, National Westminster Bank London, Caja de Ahorros de Segovia, Plymouth Art Gallery, Unilever plc and in private collections; Barclays Postgrad Painting award 1984; *Style*— Richard Gilbert, Esq; ✉ Acme Studios, 105 Carpenters Road, London E15 2DU (☎ 0181 519 5808)

GILBERT, Simon; *Career* drummer with Suede (joined 1991); 3 top twenty singles (Metal Mickey 1992, We are the Pigs 1994, The Wild Ones 1994), 2 top ten singles (Animal Nitrate 1993, Stay Together 1994, Trash 1996); albums: Suede (1993, UK no 1), Dog Man Star (1994), Coming Up (1996, UK no 1); Mercury Music Award 1993; *Style*— Simon Gilbert, Esq; ✉ c/o Interceptor Enterprises, 34–38 Provost Street, London N1 7NG (☎ 0171 490 8460, fax 0171 490 8372)

GILBERT, Stuart William; CB (1983); s of Rodney Stuart Gilbert (d 1978), and Ella Edith, *née* Esgate; *b* 2 Aug 1926; *Educ* Maidstone GS, Emmanuel Coll Cambridge (MA); *m* 1955, Marjorie Laws, da of Stanley Aloysius Vallance (d 1975); 1 s, 1 da; *Career* served WWII RAF, India, Burma; former civil servant; dep sec and dir Dept for Nat Savings 1981–86; chm Upkeep (formerly Bldg Conservation Tst) 1992– (tstee 1987–); FRSA; *Recreations* music, painting, woodwork; *Clubs* Oxford and Cambridge; *Style*— Stuart Gilbert, Esq, CB; ✉ 3 Westmoat Close, Beckenham, Kent BR3 5BX (☎ 0181 650 7213)

GILBERTSON, (Cecil) Edward Mark; s of Francis Mark Gilbertson, of Ham, Hungerford, Wilts, and Elizabeth Margaret, *née* Dawson; *b* 2 June 1949; *Educ* Eton; *m* 1, May 1975 (m dis 1980), Astrid Jane, da of late Lt-Col Tony Vaughan; m 2, 3 Sept 1986, Nicola Leslie Bellairs, yr da of Maj J A B Lloyd Philipps (d 1974), of Dale Castle, Dyfed; 1 da (Georgina Charlotte Bellairs b 29 Oct 1987), 1 s (Harry Edward Bellairs b 20 Feb 1990); *Career* dir: Brewin Dolphin Bell Lawrie Ltd, Pembroke Administration Ltd; memb Investment Ctee Rep Body The Church in Wales; MSI 1976; *Recreations* cricket, shooting, squash, tennis; *Clubs* MCC, Cardiff and County; *Style*— Edward Gilbertson, Esq; ✉ Cathedine Hill, Bwlch, Nr Brecon, Powys; Llangwarren Estate, Letterston, Dyfed SA62 5UL

GILBEY, Anthony James; s of Quintin Holland Gilbey (d 1979), of 19 Chelsea Lodge, Tite St, London SW3, and Rosemary Marguerite, *née* Hope-Vere (d 1990); *b* 2 April 1933; *Educ* Repton, Ecole des Roches, ChCh Oxford; *m* 1, 1958 (m dis 1971), Lenore, *née* Shatton; 2 s (Dennis b 1959, Paul b 1964), 1 da (Emma b 1961); m 2, 1981 (m dis 1984), Rena, *née* Ungley; m 3, 27 Sept 1984, Lady Penelope Ann Rous, da of Earl of Stradbroke (d 1983), of Henham, Wangford, Beccles, Suffolk; *Career* 2 Lt Grenadier Guards 1951; reporter Newcastle Chronicle and Newcastle Journal 1954–56, Paris correspondent Sunday Dispatch 1957–59, diarist Daily Telegraph 1959–60, Daily Sketch 1960–64 (NY correspondent 1962–64), dir Library of Imperial History 1970–75, chm Gilbey Collections

1975–; *Books* Champion Racehorses (ed, 1974), Champion Racehorses (ed, 1975); *Recreations* horseracing; *Clubs* Jockey Club Rooms, White's, MCC; *Style—* Anthony Gilbey, Esq; ✉ 13a St Loo Court, London SW3 5TJ (☎ 0171 351 1072); White Lion House, Wangford, Beccles, Suffolk NR34 8RL (☎ 0150 278 464); Gilbey Collections Ltd, White Lion Court, Wangford, Beccles, Suffolk (☎ and fax 01502 578416)

GILBEY, Hon Anthony William; s and h of 10 Baron Vaux of Harrowden, *qv*, by his 1 cous Maureen Gilbey; *b* 25 May 1940; *Educ* Ampleforth; *m* 4 July 1964, Beverley, o da of Charles Alexander Walton, of Cooden, Sussex; 2 s (Richard b 1965, Philip b 1967), 2 da (Victoria b 1969, Elizabeth b 1989); *Career* accountant, farmer; regnl cncllr Dumfries and Galloway; Liveryman Worshipful Co of Vintners; *Recreations* politics, fishing, shooting; *Style—* Hon Anthony Gilbey; ✉ Rusko, Gatehouse of Fleet, Kirkcudbrightshire

GILBEY, Sir (Walter) Gavin; 4 Bt (UK 1893), of Elsenham Hall, Essex; s of Sir (Walter) Derek Gilbey, 3 Bt (d 1991), and Elizabeth Mary, *née* Campbell; *b* 14 April 1949; *Educ* Eton; *m* 1, 1980 (m dis 1984), Mary, da of late William E E Pacetti, of Florida, USA; m 2, 1984, Anna, da of Edmund Prosser, of Cheshire; *Career* pres Gilbey's International (US based food and beverage import co); also works with abused children; *Recreations* golf, travel, anthropology; *Style—* Sir Gavin Gilbey, Bt; ✉ 8201 SW 115 Street, Miami, Fla 33156, USA

GILBEY, Hon Michael Christopher; 3 s of 10 Baron Vaux of Harrowden, and Maureen, *née* Gilbey (a first cous, da of Hugh Gilbey, yr bro of William Gilbey who m Baroness Vaux of Harrowden, m of 9 and 10 Barons); *b* 29 Dec 1949; *Educ* Ampleforth, St Andrews Univ (MA); *m* 1971, his third cousin once removed, Linda, da of Arthur Sebastian Gilbey (d 1964, ggs of Sir Walter Gilbey, 1 Bt); 3 s (Henry b 1973, Julian b 1975, William b 1979); *Career* chartered surveyor 1974–; dir: The Eton Wine Bar 1975–, Gilbey's Restaurant, M & W Gilbey Ltd (Wine Merchants) 1981–, The Gilbey Wine Club 1993–; ARICS; *Recreations* tennis, golf, English Wine grower; *Style—* Hon Michael Gilbey; ✉ Pheasant's Ridge, Hambleden, Henley-on-Thames, Oxon RG9 6SD (☎ 01491 573202); office (☎ 01494 411567, fax 01494 411560)

GILBEY, Walter Anthony; MHK (Glenfaba IOM 1982–); s of Sir Henry Walter Gilbey, 2 Bt, JP (d 1945), of Portman Square, London, and his 2 w Marion, *née* Roberts; hp to Sir (Walter) Gavin Gilbey, 4 Bt; *b* 26 Feb 1935, as Anthony Walter, names reversed by Deed Poll 1955; *Educ* Eton; *m* 2 April 1964, Jenifer Mary, eldest da of Capt James Timothy Noël Price, of Douglas, IOM, and his w, Hon Anne Younger, yr da of 2 Viscount Younger of Leckie; 1 s (Walter Anthony b 20 Jan 1966), 2 da (Caroline Anne b 2 Oct 1967, Sarah Elizabeth b 3 Nov 1969); *Career* merchant banker with Kleinwort Benson Ltd London 1954–62; fin dir Gilbeys Ltd and Int Distillers and Vintners Ltd 1962–72; chm: Mannin Trust Bank Ltd IOM 1972–82, Mannin International Ltd IOM 1982–88; dir and chm Vannin Int Securities Ltd IOM 1972–, dir IOM Steam Packet Co Ltd 1976–, chm Mannin Industries Ltd IOM 1972–, dir Gilbey Farms Ltd IOM 1974–, ptnr Gilbey Grianagh Horses IOM 1978–, chm Manx Telecom Ltd 1986–; chm Civil Service Cmmn and Whitley Cncl IOM 1985–90, memb Dept of Local Govt and the Environment IOM 1987–90, chm Planning Ctee Dept of Local Govt IOM 1987–90, memb Dept of Highways Ports and Properties IOM 1990–91, memb Dept of Indust IOM 1991–93, memb The Treasury IOM 1993–, chm London Harness Horse Parade 1985–, chm gp of almshouses; Sr Master IOM Bloodhounds, sec Manx Horse Cncl; memb: Euro Atlantic Gp, British Horse Fndn, Coaching Club, Br Driving Soc, Br Horse Soc, Shire Horse Soc, Masters of Drag Hounds Assoc; memb Berkshire CC 1966–74, Parly candidate (Cons) Ealing Southall 1971–74; Liveryman Worshipful Co of Vintners; *Recreations* horses, riding, driving; *Style—* Walter Gilbey, Esq, MHK; ✉ Ballacallin Mooar, Crosby, Marown, IOM (☎ 01624 851450, fax 01624 852852)

GILBODY, (Bryan) Martin; s of Thomas Gilbody (d 1985), of Norwich, and Iris Mary, *née* Bryan; *b* 5 Feb 1947; *Educ* Hawarden GS, Nottingham Coll of Educn; *m* 29 Dec 1971, Pamela Ann, da of Raphe Stuart Davies; 2 s (Oliver Bryan b 14 Dec 1976, Tristan Bryan 10 June 1980); *Career* hockey manager; player: South Nottingham Hockey Club 1969– (capt 1972–84), 162 appearances Nottinghamshire 1971–86, Midlands indoor squad 1976–84 (also capt, coach, mangr), Wales under 23 cap 1970, memb Wales sr squad 1977–78; mangr: Wales under 21 indoor 1981–89, Wales under 21 outdoor 1986–89, Wales sr indoor 1984–, Wales sr outdoor 1988–, Cannock HC Nat League Squad 1993– (nat champions 1996); asst teacher Alderman White Sch Nottingham 1970–74, head of modern languages Wilford Meadows Sch Nottingham 1974–87; gen mangr EMS International Ltd 1988–90; Signs UK Ltd (formerly EMS Signs Ltd): contract mangr 1987–88, gen mangr 1990–92, dir 1992–95, md 1995–; *Recreations* golf; *Style—* Martin Gilbody, Esq; ✉ Signs UK Ltd, Elson Street, Nottingham (☎ 0115 942 3050, fax 0115 942 3051)

GILCHRIST, Archibald (Archie); OBE (1996); s of James Gilchrist (d 1972); *b* 17 Dec 1929; *Educ* Loretto Sch, Pembroke Coll Cambridge (MA); *m* 1958, Elizabeth Jean, da of Robert Cumming Greenlees (d 1983); 2 s, 1 da; *Career* Capt Glasgow Yeomanry (TA); engr and shipbuilder, md Vosper Private Ltd Singapore 1980–86; non-exec dir: Caledonian MacBrayne Ltd, RMJM Ltd; vice chm Scottish Friendly Assurance Soc Ltd; vice chm Royal Scottish National Orchestra Society Ltd until 1994, chm Cncl St Leonard's Sch until 1995, bd memb Scottish Legal Aid Bd until 1996, memb Broadcasting Cncl for Scotland until 1995; *Recreations* golf, reading, music; *Clubs* Hon Co of Edinburgh Golfers, New (Edinburgh); *Style—* Archie Gilchrist, Esq, OBE; ✉ Inchmaholm, 35 Barnton Avenue, Edinburgh EH4 6JJ

GILCHRIST, Clive Mace; s of John Llewellyn Gilchrist (d 1984), and Ida, *née* Mace; *b* 27 Sept 1950; *Educ* LSE (BSc Econ); *m* 1979, Angela Rosemary, da of Roger Watson Hagger; 2 da (Philippa Jane (Pippa) b 1985, Julia Joy b 1987); *Career* stockbroker; J & A Scrimgeour & Co 1972–75, Joseph Sebag & Co 1975–78; dep dir of investmt Postel Investments Ltd 1978–87; dir: Argosy Asset Management plc 1987–91 (md Jan-May 1991), Aberdeen Trust plc 1991–; md BESTrustees plc 1992–; Nat Assoc of Pension Funds: vice pres 1992–94, chm Investment Ctee 1990–92, vice chm Cncl 1990–92 (memb 1988–); AIIMR 1979, MSI (Dip) 1992, FRSA 1993; *Recreations* gardening, music, travel; *Style—* Clive Gilchrist, Esq; ✉ Ashleigh Grange, off Chapel Lane, Westhumble, Dorking, Surrey; BESTrustees plc, The Cannon Centre, 78 Cannon Street, London EC4N 6HH (☎ 0171 623 3600, fax 0171 623 3900)

GILCHRIST, Graeme Elder; TD; s of Sir (James) Finlay Elder Gilchrist, OBE (d 1987), and (Dorothy) Joan, *née* Narizzano (d 1986); *b* 4 Dec 1934; *Educ* Sherborne, Queens' Coll Cambridge (MA); *m* 2 April 1981, Susie Elizabeth, da of Douglas William Fenwick (d 1992), and Billie (Eleanor), *née* Wade (1992); 1 s (Thomas William Elder b 1982); *Career* Lt RA 1953–55, Col HAC 1971–73, hon Col RA 1973–75; mangr Baring Bros 1963–71, md and dep chm Union Discount Company of London plc 1971–92, non-exec dir Sun Alliance Group plc 1991–94; govr Sherborne Sch 1989–; Cmmr Royal Hosp Chelsea 1992–; Freeman of Cities of London and Glasgow; hon fell City Univ; *Recreations* tennis, golf, music; *Clubs* HAC, Brooks's, MCC, Hurlingham; *Style—* Graeme Gilchrist, Esq, TD; ✉ 50 Holmbush Road, Putney, London SW15 3LE (☎ 0181 788 1667, fax 0181 788 1288)

GILCHRIST, (Sarah) Louise; da of Robert David Gilchrist, of W Compton, Somerset, and Constance May, *née* Hodgson; *b* 6 May 1961; *Educ* Corona Sch Lagos Nigeria, Godstowe Sch High Wycombe Bucks, Wells Cathedral Sch Somerset, Wells Blue Sch Somerset; *Career* copywriter J Walter Thompson 1981–82, PA/prodr Royds London Ltd 1982–86; head of TV: Harrison Agency (after merger with Royds) 1986–87, The Creative Business 1987–91; head of TV and bd dir Foote Cone and Belding (after merger with FCB) 1991–96; freelance prodr 1996–; Gold Award Int Public Tport Film Festival 1993, Silver Award Travel Advtg Awards 1993; *Recreations* cinema, swimming, galleries; *Style—* Miss Louise Gilchrist; ✉ 11 Worple Street, London SW14 8HE

GILCHRIST, Roderick Munn Renshaw; s of Ronald Renshaw Gilchrist (d 30 June 1971), and Vera, *née* Ashworth; *b* 6 Dec 1934; *Educ* Holt Sch Dumfriesshire, Mill Hill Sch; *m* 19 March 1959, Patricia Frances, da of late Robert Charles Durrant; 2 s (Adam Munn Renshaw b 1959, Luke Ronald Renshaw b 1965); *Career* admitted slr, cmmr for oaths; formerly princ Bennett and Gilchrist Slrs Guildford, currently princ Renshaw Gilchrist Slrs Fleetwood and Garstang; life govr Imperial Cancer Res Fund 1978–, tstee and clerk to the tstees W H King Alms Houses Garstang 1982–; memb: Clan Maclachlan Soc (life memb), The Law Soc, The Heraldry Soc of Scotland; FSA (Scot); *Recreations* hunting (beagle hounds), heraldry, celtic mythology; *Clubs* Old Millhillians; *Style—* Roderick Gilchrist, Esq; ✉ Sion Hill, Garstang PR3 1ZB (☎ 01995 602389); Renshaw Gilchrist Solicitors, 9 St Peters Place, Fleetwood FY7 6ED (☎ 01253 873569, fax 01253 777205)

GILDER, Eric George; s of David Richard Gilder (d 1971), of Westcliffe-on-Sea, and Minnie, *née* Walman (d 1974); *Educ* Henry Thornton Sch, RCM; *m* 23 Dec 1939, Jessica Lilian, da of Walter Clay (d 1946), of Hitchin, Herts; 2 da (Heather Melody b 1945, Paula June b 1949); *Career* served WWII RA 1939–45; composer; over 1000 broadcasts as author, composer, pianist, conductor, choir master and actor; composer of symphonic works, lyrics and musicals, princ of own sch of music 1959–87, author of critical essays in periodicals; memb: Royal Music Soc 1965, Composers' Guild 1966; *Books* Dictionary of Composers (1985, 1992 and 1993); *Recreations* gardening; *Style—* Eric Gilder, Esq; ✉ 21 Fieldend, Strawberry Hill, Twickenham TW1 4TF (☎ 0181 892 0742)

GILES, Prof Anthony Kent (Tony); OBE (1992); s of Harry Giles (d 1967), of Rochester, Kent, and Eva Gertrude, *née* Kent (d 1972); *b* 30 June 1928; *Educ* Sir Joseph Williamson's Mathematical Sch Rochester, Queen's Univ of Belfast (BScEcon); *m* 1, 2 Jan 1954 (m dis 1985), Helen Elizabeth Margaret, da of J Charles Eaton (d 1968), of Londonderry; 1 s (John b 1960), 3 da (Ann b 1954, Amanda b 1957, Alison b 1963); m 2, 6 Aug 1987, Heather Constance, da of Frank H J Pearce (d 1987), of Durban, SA; 1 step s (Sean Hewson b 1971), 1 step da (Linda Hewson b 1975); *Career* PO Personnel Selection RAF 1947–49; asst agric economist and lectr Univ of Bristol 1953–59; Univ of Reading: lectr 1960–68, sr lectr 1968–83, dir Farm Mgmnt Univ 1979–91, prof of farm mgmnt and provincial agric economist 1983–93 (prof emeritus 1993–), chm Sch of Applied Mgmnt Studies 1986–91, hon res fell Rural History Centre 1994–; UK country rep Int Soc of Agric Economists 1973–87, chm UK Farm Business Survey Ctee 1975–92, nat chm Centre Mgmnt in Agric 1987–89, pres Agric Econ Soc 1988; active in Samaritans 1972–82 (dir Reading Branch 1978–80); FIMgt 1989, FIAgrM 1992; *Books* professional: Agricultural Economics 1923–73 (1973), The Farmer as Manager (1980, 2 edn 1990), The Manager's Environment, Innovation and Conservation: Ernest Edward Cook and his Country Estates (jt ed, 1989), The Managers Environment (ed, 1990), Agricultural Economics at the University of Reading 1923–1993 (1993), Windows on Agricultural Economics and Farm Management (1993), See You at Oxford! A Celebration of Fifty Oxford Farming Conferences Over Sixty Years (1995), The Manager as Farmer - Wisdom from some I have known (1996); non-professional: One Hundred Years With the Clifton Rugby Football Club (princ author, 1972), About Twenty Five Years of Cricket (1983), The Publications of A K Giles, 1955–93 (1994), Never Mind the Frills - An Autobiographical Sketch (1995); *Recreations* watching sport (rugby and cricket), aviation, collecting books (especially early Penguins), allotment; *Clubs* Clifton Rugby Football, Penguin Collectors' Soc; *Style—* Prof Tony Giles, OBE; ✉ The Cottage, 63 Northumberland Ave, Reading, Berks RG2 7PS (☎ 0118 975 2763)

GILES, Brian John; s of Alfred Giles (d 1984) of Kent, and Constance, *née* Barndon (d 1996); *b* 22 Sept 1941; *Educ* Westlands Sittingbourne Kent; *m* 23 Feb 1963, Shirley Jennifer; 2 da (Sarah Louise b 24 June 1965, Philippa Clare b 30 April 1969); *Career* apprentice jockey Fairlawne Racing Stables 1958–62, ed Chaseform Raceform 1963–66; Daily Mail: equestrian corr 1967, racing ed as Robin Goodfellow (main tipster) 1987–; memb Sports Writers' Assoc; *Awards* Horse Trials Gp Award of the Year for Servs to Sport 1990; *Books* How to Win on the Flat, Twenty-Five Years in Showjumping - a Biography of David Broome, So You Think You Know About Horses, Behind The Stable Door, SR Direct Mail Book of Eventing (jtly with Alan Smith); *Recreations* golf, reading, classical music; *Style—* Brian Giles, Esq; ✉ Daily Mail, Northcliffe House, Derry St, Kensington, London W8 (☎ 0171 938 6203)

GILES, (John) David William; s of Herbert Giles (d 1965), of Shipley, Yorkshire, and Louise, *née* Proctor (d 1947); *b* 18 Oct 1926; *Educ* Bingley GS, The Northern Theatre Sch; *Career* television, stage and film director; worked at RADA under John Fernald, various regnl repertory cos, trained by BBC 1963; during early career directed Compact, The Newcomers, The Flying Swan; dir of prodns Lyric Theatre Hammersmith 1979; memb The Directors' Guild of GB; *Theatre* incl: Measure for Measure (Stratford Ontario) 1969, Twelfth Night (Windsor Festival) 1970, 'Tis Pity She's A Whore (Edinburgh Festival) 1972, Edward Bond's Lear (Yale Repertory Theatre) 1973, The Wood Demon (Edinburgh Festival) 1973, Gigi (West End) 1976, A Midsummer Night's Dream and The Tempest (Edinburgh Festival) 1978, Twelfth Night (Stratford Ontario) 1985, The Young Idea (Guildford) 1988, The Waltz of The Toreadors (Shaw Festival Theatre Niagara-on-the-Lake Canada) 1990, On Approval (Guildford) 1991; prodns for Lyric Hammersmith incl: You Never Can Tell 1979, The Potsdam Quartet 1980, Hobson's Choice 1981; *Television* incl: The Forsyte Saga (BBC) 1967, Vanity Fair (BBC) 1968, Resurrection (BBC) 1969, The First Churchills (BBC) 1970, Sense And Sensibility (BBC) 1971, Thursdays Child (Granada) 1971, Diary of an Encounter (BBC) 1971, Symphonic Variations (Granada) 1971, Facade (Granada) 1971, The Strauss Family (ATV) 1972, Hamlet (with Ian McKellan) 1972, Craven Arms (Granada) 1972, The Recruiting Officer (BBC) 1973, Twelfth Night (BBC) 1974, The Emigrants (BBC) 1975, When We Are Married (BBC) 1976, The Winslow Boy (BBC) 1976, Six Characters In Search of An Author (CBC) 1977, The Mayor of Casterbridge (BBC) 1977, The Wolf (CBC) 1978, Richard II (BBC) 1978, Henry IV Part I (BBC) 1979, Henry IV Part II (BBC) 1979, Henry V (BBC) 1979, On Approval (BBC) 1980, Fame is The Spur (BBC) 1981, The Barchester Chronicles (BBC, BAFTA nomination) 1982, Mansfield Park (BBC) 1983, King John (BBC) 1984, Drummonds (LWT) 1985, The Fools On The Hill (BBC) 1986, Hannay (BBC) 1986, The London Embassy (Thames) 1987, Forever Green (LWT) 1989, A Breath of French Air (YTV) 1990, Oh To Be In England (YTV) 1991, The Darling Buds of May (YTV) 1991, Mr Shaw's Missing Millions (The Drama House) 1992, Reith to the Nation (The Drama House) 1992; *Films* The Dance of Death (with Laurence Olivier and Geraldine McEwan) 1969, A Murder is Announced (BBC film) 1984; *Recreations* cooking; *Style—* David Giles, Esq

GILES, Frank Thomas Robertson; s of Col Frank Lucas Netlam Giles, DSO, OBE, of Barn Close, Finchampstead, Berks; *b* 31 July 1919; *Educ* Wellington, BNC Oxford; *m* 29 June 1946, Lady Katharine Pamela; 1 s (Sebastian b 1952), 2 da (Sarah b 1950, Belinda b 1958); *Career* Nat Serv WWII ADC to govr Bermuda, later WO Directorate of Mil Ops; FO 1945–46 (private sec to Ernest Bevin); The Times: joined 1946, asst corr Paris 1947, chief corr Rome 1950–53 and Paris 1953–60; Sunday Times: foreign ed 1961–77, dep ed 1967–81, ed 1981–83; dir Times Newspapers 1981–85; former memb Exec Ctee GB-USSR Assoc; govr: Sevenoaks Sch 1968–91, Wellington Coll 1968–89;

former chm Painshill Park Tst, memb Governing Body Br Inst in Florence, hon sec Grillions Club; author; *Books* A Prince of Journalists: the life and times of de Blowitz (1962), Sundry Times (autobiography, 1986), Forty Years On (ed, collection of essays to mark 40 anniversary Anglo-German Königswinter Conf, 1990), The Locust Years: the story of the Fourth French Republic (1991, Franco-British Soc Award), Corfu, the Garden Isle (ed, 1994); *Style*— Frank Giles, Esq; ✉ 42 Blomfield Road, London W9 2PF (☎ 0171 286 5706); Bunns Cottage, Lye Green, Crowborough, E Sussex TN6 1UY (☎ 01892 63701)

GILES, John Smart; s of Alexander Giles, of York, and Doreen, *née* Smart; *b* 30 March 1949; *Educ* Rutherford Coll Newcastle, Nunthorpe GS York; *m* 11 May 1971, Jacqueline, da of Gordon Leonard Clapham; 1 da (Claire Elizabeth b 1974); *Career* trainee/darkroom asst Westminster Press 1966–72, photographer Western Press/Yorkshire Evening Press 1972–88, staff photographer The Press Association (NE) 1988–; *Awards* Kodak, Fuji, Nikon, Canon Images of Life, UK Press Gazette, British Sports Cncl, Heineken Humour Awards, Whitbread Media Awards for sport, news and feature pictures; *Recreations* tennis, sport; *Clubs* Poppleton Tennis, Appleton Roebuck Tennis; *Style*— John Giles, Esq; ✉ The Press Association, 85 Fleet Street, London EC4P 4BE (☎ 0171 353 7440, fax 0171 353 1674, mobile 0860 167458)

GILES, Martin Peter; s of Peter James Wickham Giles (d 1977), and Jean Winifred, *née* Smith; *b* 13 Sept 1964; *Educ* Wymondham Coll, Lady Margaret Hall Oxford (MA PPE); *m* 1993, Isabelle Sylvie, da of Jacques Lescent; 1 s (Thomas b 31 Dec 1994); *Career* Midland Bank International 1983–85, J P Morgan 1985–86; The Economist Newspaper 1988–: banking corr 1988–89, Euro business corr 1989–93, fin ed 1994–; *Recreations* wine tasting, sport; *Style*— Martin Giles, Esq; ✉ The Economist Newspaper, 36 St James's Street, London SW1A 1HG (☎ 0171 830 7000, fax 0171 839 2968)

GILES, (James) Michael; *b* 9 Oct 1941; *Educ* Univ of Colorado (BA(Econ)), UCLA (MSc); *m* Diane Shubert; 1 da (Julie Elizabeth b 20 July 1966), 1 s (Mark Charles b 5 May 1969); *Career* with Citibank 1969–81; Merrill Lynch International Bank Ltd: exec dir banking 1981–83, md 1983–87, chm Merrill Lynch International Private Banking Group 1987–; *Style*— Michael Giles, Esq; ✉ Merrill Lynch International Bank Ltd, 33 Chester Street, London SW1X 7XD (☎ 0171 867 6788, fax 0171 867 6699)

GILES, Michael L; VRD (1987); *b* 1934, Woking, Surrey; *Educ* St Edward's Sch Oxford; *Career* designer; apprenticeship with Charles Hammond studying fabrics and antiques 1952; Nat Serv cmmnd RM 1953–54, RMR 1954–74, ret Maj; apprenticeship as interior designer Storey's of Kensington and Hamptons of Pall Mall 1955–58; md family practice (estab 1886) Godfrey Giles and Co 1964– (joined 1958); works incl: Hevingham Hall, Haberdashers' Hall, The Wren Church of St James Garlickhythe, The Holme Regent's Park, Chateau du Fey La Verenne Villicien France, Kensington Palace Gardens; Worshipful Co of Painter Stainers: Liveryman 1958, Renter Warden 1986, memb Ct of Assts 1987, Upper Warden 1990–91, Master 1992–93; FBID 1970 (pres 1985–86), FCSD 1988 (a vice pres 1992), ACIArb 1995; elected bro Artworkers' Guild 1988; watercolourist: studied under Laurence Toynbee 1949–51 and under Leslie Worth (past pres of Royal Water Colour Soc), fndr memb Nine Elms Gp of Artists 1987 (exhbns Oval 1987, Lambeth Palace 1988 and Painters' Hall 1989–93), fndr memb and sec The Painters' Co Freemans and Liverymans' Art Exhbn (exhbns at Painters' Hall 1989–92), one man exhbn Andorra 1992; memb Armed Forces Art Soc; *Clubs* Special Forces, East India; *Style*— Michael L Giles, Esq, VRD; ✉ Godfrey Giles & Co, No 3, 11 Chester Way, London SE11 4UT (☎ 0171 735 6025, fax 0171 793 1344)

GILES, (Derryck) Peter Fitzgibbon; s of Arthur Frederick Giles, CBE (d 1960), of 21 Princes Court, Knightsbridge, London, and Gladys Adelaide, *née* Hird; *b* 17 Nov 1928; *Educ* Sherborne, Univ of Bristol (LLB); *Career* called to the Bar Gray's Inn 1954; Stewarts and Lloyds Ltd 1955–62, Charity Cmmn 1962–69 and 1974–84 (asst cmmr 1967); legal advsr: Glaxo Holdings 1970–72, Soc of Authors 1973; govr BFWG Charitable Fndn (formerly Crosby Hall) 1992– (sec 1973, chm of Govrs 1992–95); memb: Heraldry Soc, Soc of Genealogists, Charity Law Assoc; FRSA; *Recreations* heraldry, genealogy, music, reading, pipe smoking; *Clubs* Savile; *Style*— Peter Giles, Esq; ✉ 22 Petworth Rd, Haslemere, Surrey GU27 2HR (☎ 01428 644425)

GILES, William George (Bill); OBE (1995); s of Albert William George Giles, of Brislington, Bristol, and Florence Ellen Christina, *née* James; *b* 18 Nov 1939; *Educ* Queen Elizabeth's Sch Crediton Devon, Bristol Coll of Sci and Technol; *m* 23 Dec 1961 (m dis 1992), Eileen Myrtle, da of John Henry Lake; 1 s (Philip John b 7 Aug 1969), 1 da (Helen Mary b 15 May 1971); m 2, 7 May 1992, Patricia Maureen Stafford, da of John Mabbott; *Career* Meteorological Office 1959–72, radio broadcaster London Weather Centre 1972–75, weather presenter BBC TV 1975–80, PR offr (sr sci offr) Met Office HQ Bracknell 1980–83, head Weather Centre (princ sci offr) BBC 1990– (offr in charge 1983–90); FRMetS 1985, FRSA 1995; *Awards* Scientific Prize Paris Festival of World Broadcast Meteorology 1994; *Books* Weather Observations (1980), The Story of Weather (1990); *Recreations* gardening, golf; *Style*— Bill Giles, Esq, OBE; ✉ BBC Weather Centre, Room 2050, BBC TV Centre, Wood Lane, London W12 7RJ (☎ 0181 576 7873, fax 0181 742 9432)

GILI, Jonathan Francesc; s of Joan Lluis Gili, and Elizabeth Helen, *née* Macpherson; *Educ* Dragon Sch Oxford, Bryanston, New Coll Oxford (MA); *m* 27 July 1968, Phillida Bovill, da of Alan Reynolds Stone, CBE (d 1979); 2 s (Oliver b 1972, Orlando b 1984), 1 da (Daisy b 1974); *Career* typographer and publisher Warren Editions 1967–, film ed Overlord 1974; BBC film dir: Public School - Westminster 1979, Year of the French 1982, She Married a Yank 1984, To the World's End 1985, The Great North Road 1988, Mixed Blessings 1988, All About Ambridge 1989, Chocolate! 1990, Fire in the Blood 1992, The Seven Deadly Sins 1993, Typhoid Mary 1994, Coming Home 1995, Pocahontas 1995, Gold Rush Memories 1996; *Clubs* Double Crown; *Style*— Jonathan Gili, Esq; ✉ BBC Television, 201 Wood Lane, London W12 7TS

GILKES, Dr Jeremy John Heming; s of Lt-Col Geoffrey Heming Gilkes, DSO, RA (d 1991), and Mary Stella, *née* Richardson; *b* 2 Dec 1939; *Educ* Charterhouse, St Bartholomew's Hosp Med Coll (MB BS), Univ of London (MD), FRCP; *m* 8 July 1978, Robyn Vanessa, da of Maj Nigel Bardsley (d 1962); 2 s (Alexander, Charles), 3 step da (Emma, Sara, Katrina); *Career* conslt dermatologist: Univ Coll Hosp 1976–95, Middx Hosp 1976–95, King Edward VII Hosp for Offrs, St Luke's Hosp for Anglican clergy, Eastman Dental Hosp 1976–95, London Foot Hosp 1976–95; memb: Br Assoc Dermatologists, RSM; *Clubs* The Hurlingham; *Style*— Dr Jeremy J H Gilkes; ✉ 115A Harley Street, London W1N 1DG (☎ 0171 935 6465, fax 0171 935 5014)

GILL, A A; s of Michael Gill, of London, and Yvonne, *née* Gilan; *b* 28 June 1954; *Educ* St Christopher's Sch Letchworth Herts, St Martin's Sch of Art London, Slade Sch of Fine Art London; *children* 1 da (Flora b 23 Dec 1991), 1 s (Hector b 30 April 1993); *Career* journalist, artist and cook; currently: TV and restaurant critic The Sunday Times, food writer Tatler; Columnist of the Year 1994, Food Writer of the Year (for work in Tatler) and Restaurant Writer of the Year (for work in The Sunday Times) Glenfiddich Awards 1996; *Books* Sap Rising (1996); *Clubs* Chelsea Arts; *Style*— A A Gill, Esq; ✉ The Sunday Times, 1 Pennington Street, London E1 9XW (☎ 0171 782 5000)

GILL, Sir Anthony Keith; kt (1991); s of Frederick William Gill (d 1955), of Colchester, Essex, and Ellen, *née* Davey; *b* 1 April 1930; *Educ* Colchester HS, Imperial Coll London (BSc); *m* 4 July 1953, Phyllis, da of Maurice Cook (d 1954), of Colchester; 1 s (Simon b 2 Oct 1964), 2 da (Joanna b 21 Feb 1958, Sally b 5 May 1960); *Career* engrg apprenticeship Davey Paxman 1945–51; REME (Nat Serv Offr) 1954–56; Lucas Industries plc: md Lucas Bryce Ltd 1965–72 (joined 1956), dir and gen mangr Lucas CAV Ltd 1974 (dir 1967–94), divnl md and dir Lucas Industries plc 1978, jt gp md 1980, gp md 1984, dep chm 1986, chm and chief exec 1987–94; chm Docklands Light Railway Ltd 1994–; non-exec dir: The Post Office 1989–91, National Power plc 1990–, Tarmac plc 1992–; chm Teaching Co Scheme Bd 1990–96; pro-chllr Cranfield Univ 1991–; memb Cncl (now Senate) Engrg Cncl 1988– (dep chm 1994–95); pres IProdE 1986–87; Inst of Mgmnt: hon vice pres 1993, chm Cncl 1996–; memb ACOST 1986–91; fell City of Birmingham Poly (now Univ of Central England) 1989; Hon DEng Univ of Birmingham 1990; Hon DSc: Cranfield Univ 1991, Univ of Southampton 1992, Univ of Warwick 1992; Hon DTech Univ of Coventry 1992, Hon Dr Sheffield Hallam Univ 1993; Hon FIEE, FIMechE, FCGI 1979, FEng 1983; *Recreations* boating, music; *Style*— Sir Anthony Gill, FEng; ✉ The Point House, Astra Court, Hythe Marina Village, Hythe, Hampshire SO45 6DZ (☎ 01703 840165)

GILL, Brett Richard Joseph; s of Richard Robert Gill (d 1959), of Hamble, and Dorothy, *née* Slade (now Mrs Turner); *b* 17 Oct 1942; *Educ* Blundell's; *m* 20 Nov 1965, Caroline Virginia, da of late James Herbert Bright; 1 s (William James b 15 Jan 1969), 1 da (Alice Kate b 25 April 1973); *Career* Woolley & Waldron Chartered Accountants Southampton: articled clerk 1961–65, seconded to Barton Mayhew London 1967, ptnr 1969–79; Ernst & Whinney: appointed staff ptnr following merger 1979–85, mktg ptnr 1985–88, office managing ptnr 1988–89; office managing ptnr Ernst & Young (following merger) 1989–; dir South C of C 1978–; FCA 1970 (ACA 1965), AMBIM 1968; *Recreations* rugby fives, sailing, archaeology, skiing, walking, bicycling; *Clubs* Royal Southern Yacht, Royal Southampton Yacht, Winchester Rugby Fives, Trojans Sports; *Style*— Brett Gill, Esq; ✉ Reapers, Duke St, Micheldever, nr Winchester, Hants (☎ 01962 774387); Ernst & Young, Wessex House, 19 Threefield Lane, Southampton SO14 3QB (☎ 01703 230230, fax 01703 390520, car 0836 774409)

GILL, Christopher J F; RD (1971), MP (C) Ludlow (majority 14,152); s of F A Gill, and D H Gill, *née* Southan; *b* 28 Oct 1936; *Educ* Shrewsbury; *m* 2 July 1960, Patricia, da of late E V Greenway; 1 s (Charles b 1961), 2 da (Helen b 1963, Sarah b 1967); *Career* Lt Cdr RNR 1952–79; butcher and farmer, chm F A Gill Ltd 1968–91; Wolverhampton BC: memb (C) 1965–72, chm Public Works Ctee 1967–69, chm Local Educn Authy 1969–70; MP (C) Ludlow 1987–, former vice chm Cons Euro Affairs Ctee, former vice chm Cons Agric Ctee; Liveryman Worshipful Co of Butchers, Freeman City of London; *Recreations* walking, sailing, skiing, golf, DIY; *Clubs* Carlton; *Style*— Christopher Gill, Esq, RD, MP; ✉ c/o House of Commons, Westminster, London SW1A 0AA

GILL, Rev Dr David Christopher; s of Alan Gill (d 1940), and Muriel, *née* Hodgson (d 1985); *b* 30 July 1938; *Educ* Bellevue GS Bradford, Univ of St Andrews (MB ChB), Salisbury Theol Coll, Univ of Nottingham (Dip Theol and Pastoral Studies); *Career* TA OTC 1956–61, RAMC 1961–66, 153 Highland Field Ambulance, Capt, RARO 1966–; house offr, sr house offr then registrar 1963–66: Perth Royal Infirmary, Bridge of Earn Hosp, King's Cross Hosp Dundee; medical supt and dist MO Mkomaindo Hosp Masasi Mtwara Region Tanzania 1966–72 (regnl leprosy offr 1967–72), clinical asst Herison Hosp and Yeovil Dist Hosp 1972–74, registrar then sr registrar psychiatry Knowle Hosp Fareham Hants 1974–78, conslt psychiatrist Mapperley Hosp Nottingham 1978–, clinical teacher Univ of Nottingham Med Sch 1978–95, currently med dir The Nottingham Clinic; ordained: deacon 1981, priest 1985, priest Russian Orthodox Church in GB 1995; priest in charge Orthodox Community of St Aidan and St Chad Nottingham; chm Collegiate Trainees Sub Ctee Royal Coll of Psychiatrists 1976–78, chm Senior Med Staff Ctee Mental Illness Unit 1980–85, memb Cncl Univ of St Andrews; DObstRCOG 1965, DTM&H (Liverpool) 1968, DPM 1975, MRCPsych 1976, FRCPsych 1986; *Recreations* sailing, theatre, opera; *Clubs* RAF Yacht, Royal Yachting Assoc, Army Sailing Assoc; *Style*— The Rev Dr David Gill; ✉ 1 Malvern Court, 29 Mapperley Road, Nottingham NG3 5SS (☎ 0115 962 2351); Knoydart, 2 Calligary, Ardvasar, Isle of Skye IV45 8RU; The Mandala Centre, Gregory Boulevard, Nottingham NG7 6LB (☎ 0115 960 6082); The Convent Hospital, 748 Mansfield Road, Nottingham NG5 3FZ (☎ 0115 920 9209)

GILL, Air Vice-Marshal Harry; CB (1979), OBE (1968); s of John William Gill, of Newark, Notts, and Lucy Gill; *b* 30 Oct 1922; *Educ* Barnby Rd Sch, Newark Tech Coll; *m* 1951, Diana Patricia, da of Colin Wood, of Glossop; 1 da; *Career* flying duties RAF 1941–49, Dir Gen of Supply RAF 1976–79; *Recreations* fishing, shooting, cycling; *Clubs* RAF; *Style*— Air Vice-Marshal Harry Gill, CB, OBE; ✉ Gretton Brook, S Collingham, Notts

GILL, Maj-Gen Ian Gordon; CB (1972), OBE (1959, MBE 1949), MC (1940, and Bar 1945); s of Brig Gordon Harry Gill, CMG, DSO (d 1962), and Doris Gill; *b* 9 Nov 1919; *Educ* Repton; *m* 1963, Elizabeth Vivian (Sally), MD, MRCP (d 1990), da of A F Rohr, of London; *Career* cmmnd 4/7 Royal Dragoon Gds 1938, served BEF France 1939–40, NW Europe 1944–45 (despatches), Palestine 1946–48, Tripolitania 1950–51, cmd 4/7 Royal Dragoon Gds 1957–59, Coll Cdr RMA Sandhurst 1961–62, Cdr 7 Armoured Bde 1964–66, dep mil sec (1) MOD 1966–68, head Br Def Liaison Staff Canberra 1968–70, Asst Chief Gen Staff Operational Requirements MOD 1970–72, ret 1972; Col 4/7 Royal Dragoon Gds 1973–78; Hon Liveryman Worshipful Co of Coachmakers and Coach Harness Makers; *Recreations* equitation, skiing, squash rackets, cricket; *Clubs* Cavalry & Guards', MCC; *Style*— Maj-Gen Ian Gill, CB, OBE, MC; ✉ Cheriton House, Thorney, Peterborough, PE6 0QD (☎ 01733 270246)

GILL, Jack; CB (1984); s of Jack Gill and Elizabeth Gill; *b* 20 Feb 1930; *Educ* Bolton Sch; *m* 1954, Alma Dorothy; 3 da; *Career* govt serv; under sec and princ fin offr Export Credits Guarantee Dept 1975–79, sec Monopolies and Mergers Cmmn 1979–81, dep sec and dir Industl Devpt Unit DOI 1981–83, chief exec Export Credits Guarantee Dept 1983–87; memb BOTB 1981–87; dir Govt Rels BICC plc 1987–91; advsr: Northern Engineering Industries plc 1987–89, British Aerospace plc 1987–89; memb Cncl CBI 1988–91 (chm Public Procurement Contact Gp 1990–91); *Recreations* music, chess problems, occasional Listener crossword setter; *Style*— Jack Gill, Esq, CB; ✉ 9 Ridley Rd, Warlingham, Surrey CR6 9LR (☎ 0188362 2688)

GILL, John Nichol; s of William Gill, MBE (d 1959), of Llandaff, Cardiff, and Jane Nichol, *née* Adamson; *b* 10 April 1930; *Educ* Boston GS, Chesterfield GS, St Edmund Hall Oxford (MA); *m* 20 Aug 1958, Ann Therese Frances, da of Charles Clifford Turner (d 1970), of Chesterfield; 1 s (Richard b 1963), 2 da (Susan (Mrs Micklethwaite) b 1960, Stephanie (Mrs Backhouse) b 1965); *Career* Nat Serv RCS 1948–49; admitted slr 1956; Stanton and Walker (Slrs) Chesterfield: articled clerk, asst slr 1956, ptnr 1959, sr ptnr 1978, ret 1995; chm Chesterfield Round Table 1967–68, pres Chesterfield and NE Derbyshire Law Soc 1980–81, pt/t chm Social Security Appeal Tbnls 1988–; memb: Law Soc 1956, Cmmn for Oaths 1962; *Recreations* golf, hill walking; *Clubs* Chesterfield Golf; *Style*— John N Gill, Esq; ✉ The White House, 38 Summerfield Road, Chesterfield, Derbyshire S40 2LJ (☎ 01246 232681)

GILL, (James) Kenneth; s of late Alfred Charles Gill and Isabel Gill; *b* 27 Sept 1920; *Educ* Highgate Sch; *m* 1948, Anne Bridgewater; 1 s; *Career* served RAC 24 Lancers and Intelligence Corps GSO II 1939–45, copywriter S T Garland Advertising Service 1938–39, chm Garland-Compton 1970–76; Saatchi & Saatchi Co plc: chm 1976–85, dir 1985–89, pres 1985–94; FIPA; *Clubs* RAC, MCC; *Style*— Kenneth Gill, Esq; ✉ c/o Cordiant plc, 83–89 Whitfield Street, London W1A 4XA (☎ 0171 436 4000)

GILL, Rt Rev Kenneth Edward; s of Fred Gill, of Ryton, Tyne and Wear, and Elsie, *née* Ezard (d 1984); *b* 22 May 1932; *Educ* Harrogate GS Hartley Victoria Coll Manchester;

m 20 April 1957, Edna, da of Harrison Hammond (d 1977); 1 s (Paul Robert b 1959), 2 da (Katharine Anne b 1961, Lynda Jane b 1964); *Career* Nat Serv RAF 1950–52; Karnataka South India: presbyter Hassan 1958–65, supt Vocational Training Centre Tumkur 1965–72, bishop of Central Diocese 1972–80; asst bishop of Newcastle 1980–; *Books* Meditations On The Holy Spirit (1979), Count Us Equal (1990); *Recreations* gardening; *Clubs* Rotary; *Style*— The Rt Rev Kenneth Gill; ✉ 83 Kenton Road, Gosforth, Newcastle upon Tyne NE3 4NL (☎ 0191 285 1502); Bishops House, 29 Moor Road South, Newcastle upon Tyne NE3 1PA (☎ 0191 285 2220)

GILL, Michael William Kennedy; s of Arthur K Gill (d 1991), and Peggy Gill (d 1966); *b* 20 June 1944; *Educ* Giggleswick Sch, Leeds Tech (Higher Dip); *m* 25 Feb 1969, Johanna Margrit, da of late Daniel Hilti; 1 s (Daniel b 8 May 1972); *Career* owner Pool Court (restaurant) Wharfedale 1966, ptnr Brasserie 44 Leeds 1991–, proprietor Pool Court at 42 1994–; dir of catering Harewood House, conslt Acad of Sports Health & Leisure Club; Restaurateur of the Year 1996, Pool Court at 42 awarded first Michelin Star in Leeds; memb Nat Ctee Restaurateurs Assoc GB; FHCIMA; *Books* Secret Recipes from Pool Court (1979); *Recreations* catering, travel, wine, fine dining; *Clubs* The Academy; *Style*— Michael Gill, Esq; ✉ Pool Court at 42, 42–44 The Calls, Leeds LS2 7EW (☎ 0113 244 4242, fax 0113 234 3332, mobile 0836 258800, e-mail 100621.617@COMPUSERVE.COM)

GILL, Peter; OBE (1980); s of George John Gill (d 1986, union rep Spillers Flower Mill Gen Strike 1926), and Margaret Mary, *née* Browne (d 1966); *b* 7 Sept 1939; *Educ* St Illtyd's Coll Cardiff; *Career* dramatic author and director; actor 1957–65; directed first prodn A Collier's Friday Night at the Royal Court 1965; plays directed since then incl: The Local Stigmatic 1966, Crimes of Passion 1967, The Daughter-in-Law 1967 (first prize Belgrade Int Theatre Festival 1968), The Widowing of Mrs Holroyd 1968, The Duchess of Malfi 1971, Twelfth Night 1974, As You Like It 1975, The Fool 1975, The Way of the World 1992, New England 1994, Uncle Vanya 1995, A Patriot for Me 1995; assoc artistic dir Royal Court Theatre 1970–72; dir Riverside Studios 1976–80: The Cherry Orchard (own version), The Changeling 1978, Measure for Measure 1979, Julius Caesar 1980; appointed assoc dir Nat Theatre 1980: A Month in the Country 1981, Don Juan 1981, Major Barbara 1982, Tales from Hollywood 1983, Venice Preserv'd 1984, Fool for Love 1984, The Garden of England 1985, The Murderers 1985, Mrs Klein 1988, Juno and The Paycock 1989; dir Nat Theatre Studio 1984–90; wrote and produced: The Sleepers Den 1966 and 1969, Over Garden's Out 1969, A Provincial Life (after Chekov) 1969, Small Change 1976 and 1983, As I Lay Dying (after Faulkner) 1985, In The Blue 1985, Mean Tears 1987, Certain Young Men 1992, Cardiff East 1996; *Style*— Peter Gill, Esq, OBE; ✉ c/o Casarotto Ramsay Ltd, National House, 4th Floor, 60–66 Wardour Street, Londo W1V 3HP (☎ 0171 287 4450, fax 0171 287 9128)

GILL, Robin Denys; CVO (1993); s of Thomas Henry Gill (d 1931), of Hastings, NZ, and Marjorie Mary, *née* Butler; *b* 7 Oct 1927; *Educ* Dulwich, BNC Oxford (MA); *m* 1, 5 Oct 1951, Mary Hope (d 1986), da of John Henry Alexander (d 1953), of Harrogate, Yorks; 3 s (Stephen b 23 July 1953, Richard b 9 Sept 1955, Jonathan b 25 March 1957 d 1992); m 2, 18 Feb 1991, Denise Spencer, *née* Waterhouse; *Career* sales mangr: Van den Berghs (Unilever Ltd) 1949–54, British International Paper Ltd 1954–59; fndr and md Border TV Ltd 1960–64, md Associated TV Corporation Ltd 1964–69; chm: ITN Ltd 1968–70, 1970 Trust Ltd 1970–93; dir: Reed Paper Group Ltd 1970–75, Hewlett Packard 1975–92; chm: Ansvar Insurance Co Ltd 1975–, Heidelberg Instr GmbH 1984–89, Systems Programming Holdings 1982–88, Baring Hambrecht Alpine Ltd 1986–, Baring Communications Equity Ltd 1993–; non-exec dir SD-Scicon plc 1988–91; chm Standard Industrial Trust 1970–81; memb: Ctee The Royal Family Film 1968–69, Nat Advsy Bd for Higher Educn, Visiting Ctee of RCA, Oxford Univ Appts Ctee, NW Regnl Cncl for Higher Educn, Bd IESTE (UK); memb Bd Claremont Fan Ct Sch; fndr and tstee The Royal Anniversary Tst 1990–; chm Orgn and Exec The Queen's 40th Anniversary Celebration 1992, chm Exec The Queen's Anniversary Prizes for Higher and Further Educn 1994–; pres The Brasenose Soc 1995–96; *Recreations* golf, sport, music, travel, art collecting, new projects; *Clubs* Vincent's (Oxford), St George's Hill Golf, Free Foresters CC; *Style*— Robin Gill, Esq, CVO; ✉ PO Box 61, East Horsley, Surrey KT24 6YG (☎ 01483 285290)

GILL, His Hon Stanley Sanderson; s of Sanderson Henry Briggs Gill, OBE (d 1966), of Snow Hill Grange, Wakefield, and Dorothy Margaret, *née* Bennett (d 1977); *b* 3 Dec 1923; *Educ* Queen Elizabeth GS Wakefield, Magdalene Coll Cambridge (MA); *m* 1954, Margaret Mary Patricia Grady, MB ChB, MRCPsych, da of James Grady (d 1976), of Coventry; 1 s, 2 da; *Career* RAF Bomber Command Europe 1942–46; called to the Bar Middle Temple 1950, in practice 1950–71; memb York Rent Assessment Ctee 1966–71, dep chm West Riding Quarter Sessions 1968–72; County Court judge 1971, circuit judge 1972–87, memb County Court Rule Ctee 1980–84; *Recreations* reading, walking, painting; *Style*— His Hon Stanley Gill; ✉ c/o Newcastle Crown Court, Quayside, Newcastle upon Tyne NE1 3LA

GILL, Air Vice-Marshal (Leonard) William George; DSO (1944); s of Leonard William Gill (d 1963), and Marguerite, *née* Dutton (d 1955); *b* 31 March 1918; *Educ* UC Sch London; *m* 1, 1943 (m dis), Joan Favill; 2 s (David b 1946, James b 1958), 2 da (Rosemary b 1945, Frances b 1947); m 2, 1982, Constance Mary Cull, da of late James Henry Button; *Career* RAF: Far East 1937–42 then UK, Cmd 68 Sqdn 1945 (despatches 1941), Cmd 85 and 87 Sqdn, DS RAF Staff Coll, Station Cdr Linton on Ouse 1957–60, dir Overseas Ops 1960–62, NDC of Canada 1962–63, dir of Orgn (Estabs) 1963–66; SASO RAF Germany 1966–68, DG Manning RAF MOD 1968–73, ret; planning advsr P&O Steam Navigation Co 1973–79; vice pres RAF Assoc 1973–89, chm Merton Associates (Consultants) Ltd 1985–94 (dir 1979–85), conslt Randle Cooke & Associates 1994–; chm River Thames Soc 1994–; awarded Order of King George of Bohemia 1991; FIPM, FIMgt; *Recreations* shooting, cricket, boats, amateur woodwork; *Clubs* Phyllis Court, RAF; *Style*— Air Vice-Marshal William Gill, DSO; ✉ Flat 15, 35 Cranley Gardens, Kensington, London SW7 3BD (☎ 0171 370 2716)

GILLAM, Patrick John; s of Cyril Bryant Gillam (d 1978), and Mary Josephine, *née* Davis; *b* 15 April 1933; *Educ* Clapham Coll, LSE (BA); *m* 23 Nov 1963, Diana, da of Dr Francis A Echlin (d 1988); 1 s (Luke b 1973), 1 da (Jane b 1970); *Career* 2 Lt RA 1954–56; FO 1956–57; md The BP Co plc 1981–91 (various appts 1957–81); chm: BP Shipping Ltd 1981–88, BP Minerals Int 1982–91, BP Coal Ltd 1986–88, BP Coal Inc 1988–91, BP America Inc 1989–91, BP Oil Int 1989–91, BP Nutrition 1989–91; dir: BP New Zealand Ltd 1981–89, BP Australia Holdings Ltd 1981–89, BP South Africa (Pty) Ltd 1981–89, BP Africa Ltd 1982–88, BP Exploration Co 1983–91, BP Canada Inc 1989–92; chm: Booker Tate Ltd 1991–93, Asda Group plc 1991–96, Standard Chartered plc 1993– (dep chm 1991–1993); non-exec dir Commercial Union plc 1991–; memb: Ct of Govrs LSE 1989–, The Cook Soc 1983, Appeal Ctee Queen Elizabeth's Fndn for the Disabled 1984–; chm ICC UK 1989–; Freeman City of London, Liveryman Worshipful Co of Shipwrights 1985; FRSA 1983, FInstD 1984; *Recreations* gardening, skiing, fine and decorative art; *Style*— Patrick Gillam, Esq; ✉ c/o Standard Chartered plc, 1 Aldermanbury Square, London EC2V 7SB (☎ 0171 280 7500, fax 0171 600 2546)

GILLAN, Cheryl; MP (C) Chesham and Amersham (majority 22,220); da of late Adam Mitchell Gillan, and Mona Gillan; *b* 21 April 1952; *Educ* Cheltenham Ladies' Coll, Coll of Law, Chartered Inst of Marketing; *m* 7 Dec 1985, John Coates Leeming, s of James Arthur Leeming; *Career* with International Management Group 1977–84, dir Br Film Year 1984–86, sr mktg conslt Ernst and Young 1986–91, mktg dir Kidsons Impey 1991; chm Bow Gp 1987–88, Euro Parly candidate (C) Greater Manchester Central 1989; MP (C) Chesham and Amersham 1992–; memb Select Ctee on: Science and Technol 1992–95, Procedures 1994–95; Parly under-sec of state Dept for Educn and Employment 1995–; memb: EDG, Euro Union of Women, Cons Highflyers' Gp; Liveryman Worshipful Co of Marketors; *Recreations* golf, music; *Style*— Cheryl Gillan, MP; ✉ House of Commons, London SW1A 0AA

GILLARD, David Owen; s of Robert Gillard (d 1983), of Croydon, Surrey, and Winifred, *née* Owens (d 1981); *b* 8 Feb 1947; *Educ* Tavistock Sch Croydon; *Career* arts writer and critic; scriptwriter and asst dir Assoc Br Pathé 1967–70, film and theatre critic Daily Sketch 1970–71, opera critic Daily Mail 1971– (ballet critic 1971–88), instituted Drama Preview Pages in The Listener 1982, fndr ed Friends (ENO magazine) 1983–92, radio corr Radio Times 1984–91; memb: NUJ 1963, Critics' Circle 1974, Broadcasting Press Guild 1995; *Books* Oh Brothers! (play, 1971), Beryl Grey: A Biography (1977); *Recreations* hill walking, collecting children's books; *Clubs* The Green Room; *Style*— David Gillard, Esq; ✉ 16 Grasmere Rd, Bromley, Kent BR1 4BA (☎ and fax 0181 464 6892)

GILLARD, Francis George (Frank); CBE (1961, OBE 1946); s of Francis Henry Gillard (d 1952), of Stockleigh Lodge, Exford, Somerset, and Emily Jane, *née* Burridge (d 1958); *b* 1 Dec 1908; *Educ* Wellington Sch Somerset, Univ of London (BSc), St Luke's Univ Coll Exeter; *Career* BBC: war corr N Africa, Italy, Normandy to Berlin 1940–45, head of progs Radio and TV Bristol 1945–55, controller S and W England 1956–62, dir then md Radio and dir Regions 1963–70, memb Bd of Mgmnt 1963–70; distinguished fell Corp for Public Broadcasting USA 1960–66, conslt to Public Broadcasting Interests USA 1966–; author of numerous articles for pubns incl The Listener; memb Cncl Educational Fndn Visual Aids 1968–87 (chm 1980–87), memb Fin Ctee Univ of Exeter 1968–86, chm Wellington Sch Somerset 1975–81 (govr 1960–91); Hon Citizen Creully Normandy 1995; Hon LLD Univ of Exeter 1987; FRSA 1972, fell Radio Acad 1995; *Recreations* country interests, walking, reading, music; *Clubs* Farmers'; *Style*— Frank Gillard, Esq, CBE; ✉ Trevor House, Poole, Wellington, Somerset TA21 9HN (☎ 01823 662890)

GILLARD, John Anthony; s of Sidney Mounsteven Gillard (d 1975), and Maisie Eleanor, *née* Stubbs (d 1983); *b* 14 Feb 1933; *Educ* Beckenham Sch of Art, RCA; *m* 26 Oct 1958, Rosalind Randall, da of William Francis Peele Bishop; 3 s (Paul Mounsteven b 4 July 1959, Claude William b 13 June 1964, Thomas John b 22 Dec 1965), 1 da (Sarah Randall b 20 April 1962); *Career* art dir The Whitefriars Press London 1958–61, creative consultancy 1961–76 (assignments for clients incl Access (new product devpt), BEA, Falcon International, Kaplan and Kasmin Galleries, London Symphony Orchestra, Rowntrees), concurrently visiting lectr Canterbury Coll of Art, Ealing Coll of Art, Medway Coll of Art, London Coll of Printing and Middx Poly 1958–61, co-fndr and mangr Creative Trg Unit J Walter Thompson Ltd 1968–74, princ lectr Berkshire Coll of Art & Design 1976–85, fndr princ Sch of Communication Arts London 1985–95, ret; recipient 4 D&AD Awards, Creative Circle's President's Award for servs to the communications indust 1986, Br Design & Art Direction Special Award for Servs to Educn 1995; ARCA; *Recreations* music, philosophy, reading, writing, travel; *Style*— John Gillard, Esq

GILLBERRY, Col George Kendall; s of George Kendall Gillberry (d 1965), of Liverpool, and Muriel, *née* Evans (d 1975); *b* 14 Aug 1936; *Educ* Liverpool Inst, RMA Sandhurst; *m* 1, 2 May 1959, Shirley (d 1994), da of Richard Sedgwick McDougall, CBE (d 1982), of Stevenage, Herts; 2 da (Susan Elizabeth (Mrs Taylor) b 1959, Margaret Anne (Dr Goodliff) b 1961); m 2, 30 Sept 1995, Margaret O'Brien, da of Frederick Briscoe Ramsbottom (d 1962); *Career* Army; 2 Lt 1956, Maj 1969, Lt-Col and Chief Planning Offr Central Ordnance Depot Bicester 1976, Cmdt and Chief Instr Petroleum Centre RAOC 1980, Col Directorate of Supply Mgmnt (Army) 1984, sr stores offr Central Ordnance Depot Bicester 1989; FInstPet 1976; *Recreations* travel, genealogy; *Style*— Col George K Gillberry; ✉ 20 Old Arncott Road, Ambrosden, Bicester, Oxon OX6 0LT (☎ 01869 246534)

GILLER, Norman; *b* 18 April 1940; *Educ* Raine's Fndn GS Stepney; *m* 8 April 1961, Eileen; 1 s (Michael), 1 da (Lisa); *Career* copy boy London Evening News 1955–56, reporter, sub ed and layout designer Boxing News 1959–61, sports ed and layout designer Stratford Express 1961–62, sports sub ed Evening Standard 1962, sports sub ed and layout designer Daily Herald 1962–64, football reporter Daily Express 1964–66 (chief football reporter 1966–74), TV sports columnist Evening News 1977–80, TV sports columnist Sunday Express 1991–, The Judge sports column The Sun 1995–; numerous freelance appts 1974–; deviser numerous newspaper games since 1974 and two board games (Namedropper! and Tiddlythinks!); script writer for This Is Your Life (scripts written for Dan Maskell, Richard Branson, Nigel Mansell, Jimmy Savile and many others); other TV credits incl: Stunt Challenge (ITV) 1984 and 1985, Stand and Deliver (Sky) 1995–96; writer and deviser: The Games of '48 (with Brian Moore, ITV), Eurovision Song Contest Preview 1992–93, Who's the Greatest (seven-part series, ITV); various video prodns; prodr and writer: Over the Moon (ITV), Frankly Bruno (Chrysalis), Football Trivial Pursuit (Telstar); PR for Joe Bugner and Frank Bruno; *Books* ghostwriter of numerous works with sporting personalities incl: Banks of England (with Gordon Banks), Watt's My Name (with Jim Watt), The Seventies Revisited (with Kevin Keegan), Olympic Heroes (with Brendan Foster), How to Box (with Henry Cooper), The Glory and the Grief (with George Graham), Top Ten Cricket Book (with Tom Graveney), Know What I Mean? and From Zero to Hero (with Frank Bruno); 16 books with Jimmy Greaves incl: This One's On Me, The Final (novel), The Boss (novel), The Sixties Revisited, It's A Funny Old Life, Saint and Greavsie's World Cup Special, Don't Shoot The Manager; among 40 other books: The Golden Milers, The Marathon Kings, The Olympics Handbook, This Sporting Laugh, Crown of Thorns, Mike Tyson, The Release of Power (with Reg Gutteridge), Six Carry On novels (1996); *Recreations* creating computer graphics, listening to opera, playing banana-fingered jazz piano, reading, following all major sports; *Style*— Norman Giller, Esq; ✉ Sunday Express, Ludgate House, 245 Blackfriars Road, London SE1 9UX

GILLESPIE, David Buchanan; s of William Hugh Gillespie (d 1986), of Littlehampton, Sussex, and Elizabeth, *née* Buchanan (d 1986); *b* 12 Dec 1938; *Educ* Dover Coll; *m* 1, 4 March 1967 (m dis 1976), Joanna Mary, da of Capt John Anthony Campbell Rupert (d 1993), of Montreux-Territet, Switzerland; 1 s (Benjamin b 6 March 1971), 1 da (Antonia b 20 Oct 1968); m 2, 20 June 1977, Elizabeth Mary, da of Maj James Malcolm Hay of Seaton (d 1987), of Edinglassie, Aberdeenshire; 1 s (Hamish b 10 Sept 1979); *Career* currently chief exec Kimpton Kitchens; FCA 1969 (ACA 1962); *Style*— David Gillespie, Esq; ✉ The Lodge, St Mary's Abbey, Woolmer Hill, Haslemere, Surrey GU27 1QA (☎ 01428 642621); Kimpton Kitchens, Fernhurst, Haslemere, Surrey GU27 3JL (☎ 01428 652043)

GILLESPIE, Prof Iain Erskine; s of John Gillespie (d 1974), of Glasgow, and Flora, *née* MacQuarie (d 1978); *b* 4 Sept 1931; *Educ* Hillhead HS, Univ of Glasgow (MB ChB, MD), Univ of Manchester (MSc); *m* 5 Sept 1957, (Mary) Muriel, *née* McIntyre; 1 s (Gordon McIntosh b 1963), 1 da (Rhona Kirstine b 1960); *Career* Nat Serv cmmnd Lt RAMC 1954, Regtl Med Offr then Capt until 1956; hon conslt Manchester Royal Infirmary 1970–92, dean Faculty of Med Univ of Manchester 1983–86 (prof of surgery 1970–92); memb Med Sub Ctee UGC 1975–86, former office bearer Br Soc of Gastroenterology; memb: Surgical Res Soc of GB and Ireland, Assoc of Surgns of GB and Ireland, Assoc of Profs of Surgery, Sub-Ctee Hong Kong Univs and Polys Grants Ctee 1985–89, editorial bds of several surgical and gastroenterological jls, North West RHA 1982–86, Central

Manchester Health Authy 1990–92; govr Stockport GS (formerly founding chm Parents Assoc), pres Manchester Branch Royal Scottish Dance Soc; FRCSE 1959, FRCS 1963, FRCSG 1970; *Books* Gastroenterology - An Integrated Course (ed with T J Thomson, 3 edn, 1983), Current Opinion in Gastroenterology - Stomach Duodenum (with T V Taylor, 1986, 1987, 1988), Guide to Surgical Principles and Practice (1992); *Recreations* golf, gardening, music; *Clubs* New Golf (St Andrews), Bramall Park Golf; *Style*— Prof Iain E Gillespie; ✉ 27 Athol Road, Bramhall, Cheshire SK7 1BR (☎ 0161 439 2811)

GILLETT, (John) Anthony Cecil Walkey; s of Eric Walkey Gillett, FRSL (d 1978), and Joan, *née* Edwards (d 1956); *b* 17 March 1927; *Educ* Malvern, Brasenose Coll Oxford (MA); *m* 18 Oct 1952, Jacqueline Eve, da of Philippe Leslie Caro Carrier, CBE (d 1975), of Lewes, Sussex; 2 s (Charles b 1954, John b 1958), 1 da (Amanda b 1961); *Career* served as Lt RM 1945–47; Colonial Serv dist offr Somaliland Protectorate 1950–58, called to the Bar Inner Temple 1955, magistrate Aden (sometime acting chief justice, puisne judge and chief magistrate) 1958–63, crown cnsl and asst attorney gen of Aden 1963–65, dep advocate gen Fedn of S Arabia 1965–68 (sometime acting attorney gen and advocate gen), temp legal asst Cncl on Tbnls (UK) 1968–70, legislative draftsman States of Guernsey 1970–83, stipendiary magistrate of Guernsey; played polo for Somaliland Protectorate and Aden; hon sec Oxford University Tennis Club (Royal Tennis); *Publications* State of Aden Law Reports (1959–60), The Juvenile Court of Guernsey; *Recreations* lawn tennis, reading; *Clubs* Royal Channel Islands Yacht, MCC, Vincents (Oxford); *Style*— Anthony Gillett, Esq; ✉ Bellieuse Farm, St Martin's, Guernsey, CI (☎ 01481 36986); The Magistrate's Chambers, Royal Court House, Guernsey, CI (☎ 01481 725277)

GILLETT, Christopher John; yr s of Sir Robin Danvers Penrose Gillett, 2 Bt, GBE, RD, *qv*; bro of Nicholas Gillett, *qv*; *b* 16 May 1958; *Educ* Durlston Court Sch, Pangbourne Coll, King's Coll Cambridge (choral scholar, MA), Royal Coll of Music (studied under Robert Tear and Edgar Evans), Nat Opera Studio; *m* 1984 (sep), Julia, yr da of late W H Holmes, of Tunbridge Wells; 1 da (Tessa Holmes b 1987), 1 s (Adam Holmes b 1989); *Career* operatic and concert tenor; has worked with various major opera companies incl: New Sadler's Wells (over 150 performances), Royal Opera, ENO, Glyndebourne Touring Opera, Kent Opera, Music Theatre Wales, Opera Northern Ireland; Liveryman Worshipful Co of Musicians; *Performances* operatic roles incl: Ferrando in Cosi fan Tutte (Glyndebourne Touring Opera), title role in Albert Herring (Glyndebourne Touring), Roderigo in Otello (Royal Opera House Covent Garden), Dov in The Knot Garden (Covent Garden), Pang in Turandot (Covent Garden), Hermes in King Priam (with Royal Opera Co in Athens), Nooni in The Making of the Representative for Planet Eight (with ENO at the London Colisseum and in Amsterdam), St Magnus in Peter Maxwell Davies' Martyrdom of St Magnus (Music Theatre Wales), Arbace in Idomeneo (English Bach Festival), Flute in A Midsummer Night's Dream (Aix-en-Provence Festival, Teatro Regio Turin, Ravenna Festival) and Lysander in the same for Netherlands Opera and New Israeli Opera, Vasek in The Bartered Bride (Opera Northern Ireland), Pysander in Ulisse (Vlaamse Opera, Netherlands Opera), Tikhon Kabanova in Katya Kabanova (Glyndebourne Touring Opera), Gigolo in Rosa (Netherlands Opera); recent concert performances incl: Stravinsky Cantata (with La Chapelle Royale under Philippe Herreweghe in Paris and Brussels), Haydn Creation (in Madrid), Handel Messiah (with The Sixteen Choir and Orch under Harry Christophers in the Netherlands), Nyman Songs, Sounds and Sweet Airs (with Michael Nyman Band in Japan), Bach St John Passion (Symphony Hall Birmingham and King's Coll Chapel Cambridge), Britten War Requiem (Teatro Colon Buenos Aires under Steuart Bedford); *Recordings* incl: Elgar The Kingdom (with London Philharmonic under Leonard Slatkin, RCA), The Beggar's Opera (Decca); *Style*— Christopher Gillett, Esq; ✉ c/o Harrison Parrott, 12 Penzance Place, London W11 4PA (☎ 0171 229 9166, fax 0171 221 5042)

GILLETT, Rev Canon David Keith; s of Norman Arthur Gillett (d 1996), of Rushden, Northants, and Kathleen, *née* Pitts; *b* 25 Jan 1945; *Educ* Wellingborough GS, Univ of Leeds (BA, MPhil); *m* 3 Sept 1988, (Susan) Valerie, da of Samuel Vernon Shannon (d 1981); *Career* curate St Luke's Watford 1968–71, northern sec Pathfinders and CYFA 1971–74, lectr St John's Coll Nottingham 1974–79, co-leader Christian Renewal Centre NI 1979–82, vicar St Hugh Lewsey Luton 1982–88, princ Trinity Coll Bristol 1988–, hon canon Bristol Cathedral 1991–; memb: Gen Synod C of E 1985–88 and 1990–, Gen Synod Bd of Mission 1990–96, C of E Inter-Faith Consultancy 1990–96, Gen Synod Advsy Bd of Ministry 1995–, Gen Synod Ctee for Minority Ethnic Anglican Concerns 1995–, Cncl Reference for Anglican Renewal Ministries; *Books* How Congregations Learn (1979), A Place in the Family (co-author, 1981), The Darkness where God is (1982), Whose Hand on the Tiller (co-author, 1984), Trust and Obey: Explorations in Evangelical Spirituality (1993), Treasure in the Field: The Archbishops' Companion for the Decade of Evangelism (jtly, 1993); *Recreations* gardening, photography, travel; *Style*— The Rev Canon David Gillett; ✉ 16 Ormerod Rd, Stoke Bishop, Bristol BS9 1BB (☎ 0117 968 2646); Trinity College, Stoke Hill, Bristol BS9 1JP (☎ 0117 968 2803, fax 0117 968 7470)

GILLETT, Nicholas Danvers Penrose; er s and h of Sir Robin Danvers Penrose Gillett, 2 Bt, GBE, RD; bro of Christopher Gillett, *qv*; *b* 24 Sept 1955; *Educ* Durlston Court Sch, Pangbourne Coll, Imperial Coll London (BSc); *m* 3 Jan 1987, Haylie, er da of Dennis Brooks, of Swansea, Glamorgan; *Career* British Aerospace: trials engr 1977–84, product assur mangr 1984–87, project mangr 1987–89, business devpt mangr 1989–91, EC Exec Trg Prog Japan 1991–92, project mangr 1993; Liveryman Worshipful Co of Coachmakers 1982; ARCS, FBIS; *Recreations* photography, sub-aqua, computing, reading, skiing, DIY; *Style*— Nicholas Gillett, Esq; ✉ 11 Tall Trees, St Ippolyts, Hitchin, Herts SG4 7SW (☎ 01462 451357)

GILLETT, Sir Robin Danvers Penrose; 2 Bt (UK 1959), of Bassishaw Ward, City of London, GBE (1976), RD (1965); s of Sir (Sydney) Harold Gillett, 1 Bt, MC, FCA (d 1976; Lord Mayor London 1958–59), and Audrey Isabel Penrose (d 1962), da of late Capt Edgar Penrose Mark-Wardlaw; *b* 9 Nov 1925; *Educ* Hill Crest Sch, Pangbourne NC; *m* 22 Sept 1950, Elizabeth Marion Grace, er da of late John Findlay, JP, of Busby House, Lanarks; 2 s (Nicholas, *qv*, Christopher, *qv*); *Heir* s, Nicholas Danvers Penrose Gillett b 24 Sept 1955; *Career* Canadian Pacific Steamships Ltd: cadet 1943–45, master mariner 1951–, staff cdr 1957–60; dir: Wigham Poland Home Ltd, Wigham Poland Management Services Ltd 1965–86; chm St Katharine Haven Ltd 1990–93, conslt Sedgwick Insurance Brokers 1987–89; underwriting memb Lloyd's 1965–, common councilman for Ward of Bassishaw 1965–69 (Alderman 1969–96), sheriff City of London 1973–74 (HM Lt 1975, Lord Mayor 1976–77); RLSS: UK pres 1979–82, dep Cwlth pres 1982–96; vice chm PLA 1979–84, er brother Trinity House 1978 (yr brother 1973–78), fell and fndr memb Nautical Inst, tstee Nat Maritime Museum 1982–92, pres Inst of Admin Mgmnt 1980–84; vice pres: City of London Red Cross, St John's Ambulance, City of London Outward Bound Assoc, KGFS 1993–; lay patron Missions to Seamen, churchwarden St Lawrence Jewry-next-Guildhall 1969–, tstee St Paul's Cathedral Tst; Hon Co of Master Mariners: memb 1962–, warden 1971–85, master 1979–80; Hon Cdr RNR, Hon DSc City of London Univ 1976 (chllr 1976–77); Offr Order of Leopard (Zaire) 1974, Cdr Order of Dannebrog 1974, Order of Johan Sedia Mahkota (Malaysia) 1974, Grand Cross Municipal OM (Lima) 1977, Gold medal Admin Mgmnt Soc (USA) 1983; FInstD; KStJ 1976; Gentleman Usher of the Purple Rod 1985–; FRCM 1991 (memb Cncl); *Recreations* sailing (yacht 'Lady Libby'); *Clubs* City Livery, Guildhall, City Livery Yacht (Adm), Royal Yacht Sqdn, Royal London Yacht (Cdre 1984–85), St Katharine Yacht (Adm), hon life memb Deauville Yacht; *Style*— Sir Robin Gillett, Bt, GBE, RD; ✉ 4 Fairholt St, London SW7 1EQ (☎ 0171 589 9860)

GILLFORD, Lord; Patrick James Meade; o s and h of 7 Earl of Clanwilliam, *qv*; *b* 28 Dec 1960; *Educ* Eton, RMA Sandhurst; *m* 1989 (m dis 1992), Serena Emily, da of Lt-Col Brian Lockhart; 1 da (Hon Tamara Louise Meade b 2 Dec 1990); *Career* Coldstream Gds 1979–83, Hanson plc 1983–90, Ian Greer Associates 1990–93, md Westminster Policy Partnership public affrs conslts 1993–; cncllr Royal Borough of Kensington and Chelsea 1990– (chm Traffic and Highways); *Recreations* golf, skydiving, sub-aqua; *Clubs* Turf, Mill Reef, Antigua, New Zealand Golf; *Style*— Lord Gillford; ✉ Westminster Policy Partnership Ltd, 49 Causton Street, London SW1P 4AT (☎ 0171 976 5555, fax 0171 976 5353)

GILLHAM, Anthony Kenneth (Tony); s of William Kenneth Gillham, of Essex, and Mary Joan, *née* Tuckwell; *b* 24 March 1951; *Educ* John Colet Sch Wendover Bucks, Thurstable Sch Tiptree Essex, Chelmsford Coll; *m* 1, 1976 (m dis), Linda Ann Quinlan; m 2, 1983 (m dis), Anna Aitken McElroy; 1 s (Anthony b 1987); 1 da (Layla b 23 Sept 1996); *Career* radio broadcaster: Radio Tees 1975–78, Radio Orwell 1978–80, Mercia Sound 1980–82, Chiltern Radio 1982–85, BBC Radio 2 1985, BBC Radio Beds 1985–, Brunel Classic Gold Radio 1988– (also head of music); currently presenter: Classic Gold Network, Gillham Gold (Sundays Classic Gold); *Style*— Tony Gillham, Esq; ✉ Brunel Classic Gold Radio, Canons Rd, Bristol BS99 7SN (☎ 0831 831966)

GILLHAM, Ian Robert; s of William Robert Gillham (d 1987), and Hilda Ivy Gillham (d 1966); *b* 18 Jan 1939; *Educ* Eltham Coll, Univ of Leeds (BA); *m* 1967, Pamela Mary, da of Arthur Robert Hill; 1 s (Andrew Robert b 7 Jan 1972), 1 da (Catherine Elizabeth b 22 April 1975); *Career* BBC: studio mangr 1961–66, scriptwriter 1966–73, organiser Italian progs 1973–75, asst head of central talks and features 1975–77, asst head of Eng World Serv 1977–84, head of prodns World Serv 1984–90, head of overseas admin 1990–94, chief advsr (Directorate) World Serv 1995–; chief exec Ascension Island Services, co sec Caribbean Relay Co; *Recreations* singing, reading, walking; *Style*— Ian Gillham, Esq; ✉ BBC World Service, Bush House, Strand, London WC2B 4PH (☎ 0181 257 2616, fax 0181 430 0374)

GILLHAM, Paul Maurice; s of Gerald Albert Gillham, and Doris, *née* Kinsey; *b* 26 Nov 1931; *Educ* RCM, GSM (LGSM), Christ's Coll Cambridge (BA, MA); *m* 3 Sept 1960, Jane Marion, da of Sir George Pickering (d 1982); 2 s (Adam b 27 Dec 1965, Dan b 13 April 1968), 1 da (Carola b 7 July 1963); *Career* chm: Keith Prowse Group 1970–80, St Giles Properties Ltd 1980–, Patent Developments International Ltd 1980–, Actonbarn Ltd 1983–92; dir Wren Underwriting Agencies Ltd 1993–; chm LPO Cncl 1983–87; *Recreations* playing cello and piano, walking; *Style*— Paul Gillham, Esq; ✉ Edmonds Farmhouse, Gomshall, Guildford, Surrey GU5 9LQ (☎ 0148641 2299); Patent Developments International Ltd, Southwick Business Centre, The Old Town Hall, Albion Street, Southwick, W Sussex BN42 4AX (☎ 01273 597411, fax 01273 595641)

GILLIAM, Terry Vance; s of James Hall Gilliam, and Beatrice, *née* Vance; *b* 22 Nov 1940; *Educ* Occidental Coll (BA); *m* 1973, Maggie Weston; 1 s (Harry Thunder), 2 da (Amy Rainbow, Holly Dubois); *Career* actor, director, writer, animator; assoc ed Help! magazine 1962–64, freelance illustrator 1964–65, advertising copywriter and art dir 1966–67; exec prodr Complete Waste of Time (Monty Python CD-Rom) 1995; contrib to Spellbound Hayward Gallery 1996; Hon DFA: Occidental Coll 1987, RCA 1989; *Television* resident cartoonist We Have Ways of Making You Laugh 1968, animator Do Not Adjust Your Set 1968–69, animator, actor and co-writer Monty Python's Flying Circus 1969–76 and 1979; animator: The Marty Feldman Comedy Machine 1971–72, The Do-It-Yourself Film Animation 1974; presenter The Last Machine (BBC series) 1995; *Films* co-writer, actor and animator: And Now For Something Completely Different 1971, Monty Python and The Holy Grail 1974 (also co-dir), Monty Python's Life of Brian 1978, Monty Python Live at The Hollywood Bowl 1982, Monty Python's The Meaning of Life 1983; animator and writer The Miracle of Flight 1974; co-writer/dir: Jabberwocky 1976, Time Bandits (also prodr) 1980, Brazil 1985, The Adventures of Baron Münchhausen 1988; dir: The Fisher King 1991, Twelve Monkeys 1995; *Albums* Monty Python's Flying Circus (jtly, 1970), Another Monty Python Record (jtly, 1971), Monty Python's Previous Record (jtly, 1972), The Monty Python Matching Tie and Handkerchief (jtly, 1973), Monty Python Live at Drury Lane (jtly, 1974), Monty Python and the Holy Grail (jtly, 1975), Monty Python Live at City Centre (jtly, 1976), The Monty Python Instant Record Collection (jtly, 1977), Monty Python's Life of Brian (jtly, 1979), Monty Python's Contractual Obligation Album (jtly, 1980), Monty Python Live at the Hollywood Bowl (jtly, 1981), Monty Python's The Meaning of Life (jtly, 1983), Monty Python The Final Rip Off (jtly, 1987), Monty Python Sings (jtly, 1989); *Books* The Cocktail People (1966), Monty Python's Big Red Book (jtly, 1977), Monty Python's Papperbok (jtly, 1977), Monty Python and The Holy Grail (jtly, 1977), Monty Python's Life of Brian (jtly, 1979), Animations of Mortality (1979), Time Bandits (jtly, 1981), Monty Python's The Meaning of Life (jtly, 1983), The Adventures of Baron Münchhausen (jtly, 1989), Monty Python's Just the Words (jtly, 1989); *Recreations* sitting extremely still for indeterminate amounts of time; *Style*— Terry Gilliam, Esq; ✉ c/o Poo Poo Pictures, Prominent Studios, 68A Delancey St, London NW1 7RY (☎ 0171 284 0242, fax 0181 341 5203); c/o CAA, 9830 Wilshire Boulevard, Beverly Hills, California 90212, 1825 USA (☎ 001 213 288 4545)

GILLIBRAND, Alec Lindow; OBE (1975); s of Harold Lindow Gillibrand (d 1953), of Accrington, Lancs, and May, *née* Ramsbottom (d 1983); *b* 30 March 1932; *Educ* Queen Mary's Royal GS Clitheroe; *m* 29 June 1957, Jennifer Bridget, da of Maj Jasper Cyril Holmes, MC (d 1976), of Tavistock, Devon; 1 s (Guy Nigel b 1962), 1 da (Susan Jane (Mrs Massie) b 1960); *Career* Nat Serv 1950–52; banker; served over 32 yrs overseas with British Bank of the Middle East and Hongkong and Shanghai Banking Corp in Bahrain, Doha, Aden, Jordan, Kuwait, Abu Dhabi, Beirut, Iran, Saudi Arabia, Hong Kong and India (ret as chief exec offr India); former dir British and South Asian Trade Assoc; memb: Exec Ctee British Cwlth Ex-Services League, Trade Advsy Ctee for S Asia; regnl dir Br Exec Service Overseas (BESO); memb Guild of Freemen of the City of London; ACIB 1975; *Recreations* walking, sport, reading, Arab affairs; *Clubs* Oriental, Bombay Gymkhana, Bombay Willingdon; *Style*— Alec Gillibrand, Esq, OBE; ✉ 181A Ashley Gardens, Emery Hill St, London SW1P 1PD (☎ 0171 834 5626)

GILLIBRAND, Sydney; CBE (1991); s of Sydney Gillibrand (d 1990), and Maud Gillibrand (d 1994); *b* 2 June 1934; *Educ* Preston GS, Harris Coll Preston, Coll of Aeronautics Cranfield (MSc); *m* 15 May 1960, Angela Ellen, da of Richard Williams (d 1982); 3 s (Paul b 1964, Simon b 1965, Jonathan b 1969); *Career* English Electric: apprentice 1950, chief stress engr 1966, works mangr Preston 1974; BAC (Preston) Ltd 1974–78 (gen mangr mfrg, special dir, dir mfrg Mil Aircraft Div); British Aerospace Aircraft Group: dep md Warton Div 1981, divnl md Kingston/Brough Div 1983, divnl md Weybridge Div 1984; British Aerospace plc: md Civil Aircraft Div 1986–88, gp dir 1987–95, chm BAe (Commercial Aircraft) Ltd 1988–92, chm BAe (Dynamics) Ltd 1990–92, chm Royal Ordance plc 1990–92, chm BAe (Consultancy) Ltd 1990–95, chm BAe (Liverpool Airport) Ltd 1990–95, chm BAe Inc 1988–90, gp vice chm 1992–95, ret from BAe 1995; non-exec dir AMEC plc 1995–; pres: AECMA 1992–95, Soc of Br Aerospace Cos 1990–91; FEng 1987, CIM 1992, Hon FRAeS 1994 (FRAeS 1975); *Recreations* golf; *Style*— Sydney Gillibrand, Esq, CBE, FEng; ✉ AMEC plc, Sandiway House, Northwich, Cheshire CW8 2YA (☎ 01606 883885, fax 01606 883996)

GILLIE, Dr Oliver John; s of John Calder Gillie, of Tynemouth, Northumberland, and Ann, *née* Philipson; *b* 31 Oct 1937; *Educ* Bootham Sch York, Univ of Edinburgh (BSc,

PhD), Stanford Univ; *m* 3 Dec 1969 (m dis 1988), Louise, da of Col Phillip Panton; 2 da (Lucinda Kathrine b 1970, Juliet Ann b 1972); *partner* Jan Thompson; 1 s (Calder Thompson b 1994); *Career* lectr in genetics Univ of Edinburgh 1961–65, Nat Inst for Med Res Mill Hill 1965–68, IPC Magazines 1968–70, Haymarket Publishing 1970–72, med corr The Sunday Times 1972–86; The Independent: med ed 1986–89, special corr 1989–94; freelance journalist 1994–; *Books* The Sunday Times Book of Body Maintenance (jtly, 1978), The Sunday Times Guide to the World's Best Food (jtly, 1981), The Sunday Times Self-Help Directory (jtly, 1982), The ABC Diet and Bodyplan (jtly, 1984), Regaining Potency (1995); *Recreations* sailing, wind-surfing; *Clubs* RSM; *Style*— Dr Oliver Gillie; ✉ 68 Whitehall Park, London N19 3TN (☎ 0171 561 9677)

GILLIES, (Maurice) Gordon; TD (1946 and bar 1952), QC (Scot 1958); s of James Brown Gillies (advocate in Aberdeen, ka 1916), and Rhoda Ledingham (d 1952); *b* 17 Oct 1916; *Educ* Aberdeen GS, Merchiston Castle, Univ of Edinburgh (MA, LLB); *m* 1954, Anne Bethea, da of Bryce McCall-Smith, OBE (d 1977), of Pencaitland, E Lothian; *Career* served RA 1939–46, Maj, France 1940, Europe 1944–46; advocate 1946, advocate depute 1953–58; sheriff of Lanarkshire at Lanark 1958–82, sheriff principal of South Strathclyde, Dumfries and Galloway 1982–88; *Recreations* golf, gardening; *Clubs* New (Edinburgh), Hon Co of Edinburgh Golfers; *Style*— Gordon Gillies, Esq, TD, QC; ✉ The Coach House, Broadgait, Gullane, East Lothian EH31 2DJ

GILLIES, Prof William; s of Iain Gillies (d 1989), of Oban, and Mary Kyle, *née* Cathie; *b* 15 Sept 1942; *Educ* Oban HS, Univ of Edinburgh (MA), Univ of Oxford (MA); *m* 24 June 1972, Valerie Roselyn Anna, da of Peter John Simmons, of Edinburgh; 1 s ((John) Lachlan b 1973), 2 da (Maeve b 1974, Mairi b 1982); *Career* Dublin Inst for Advanced Studies 1969–70, chair of Celtic Univ of Edinburgh 1979– (lectr 1970–79); dir: Scot Nat Dictionary Assoc Ltd 1982–, Comunn na Gaidhlig 1983–; FSA (Scot) 1975, FRSE 1990; *Books* Criticism and Prose Writings of Sorley Maclean (ed, 1985), Gaelic and Scotland (ed, 1989); *Style*— Prof William Gillies, FRSE; ✉ 67 Braid Avenue, Edinburgh EH10 6ED (☎ 0131 447 2876); University of Edinburgh, 19–20 George Square, Edinburgh EH8 9LD (☎ 0131 650 3621)

GILLIGAN, Timothy Joseph (Tim); OBE (1992), ERD (1989), DL (Hertfordshire); s of Timothy Gilligan (d 1928), of Rosscommon, Eire, and Mary, *née* Greevy (d 1924); *b* 18 April 1918; *Educ* Handsworth Tech Coll Birmingham; *m* 1944, Hazel (Bunty), da of William Ariel Farmer; 2 s (Simon, Peter), 2 da (Anita, Rosemary); *Career* Maj RASC WWII, served BEF France, ME and N Africa, Germany (despatches 1944 and 1945) 1939–46; exec offr (1 sec grade) FO (German Section) 1946–53; sales and mgmnt Dictaphone Co Ltd and WH Smith & Sons 1953–63; chm Pitney Bowes plc 1983–93 (joined 1963, chief exec 1967); chm The Tree Cncl 1983–85, fndr chm Conservation Fndn 1982–86, chm Herts Groundwork Tst 1984–89, chm Ridgehill Housing Assoc 1994–; memb Hertsmere BC 1983–91; CIMgt 1983, FRSA 1977, KSG 1990; *Recreations* the countryside and environment; *Style*— Tim Gilligan, Esq, OBE, ERD, DL; ✉ The White Cottage, Mimms Lane, Shenley, Radlett, Herts WD7 9AP (☎ 01923 857402, fax 01923 857307)

GILLILAND, Alan Howard; s of Wilfrid Howard Gilliland (d 1986), and Mary, *née* Miller; *b* 7 Jan 1949; *Educ* Bedford Sch, PCL, Architectural Assoc Sch; *m* 31 Oct 1975, Pauline, *née* Howkins; 5 s (Benjamin b 30 Jan 1976, Robert b 12 Dec 1980, Alexander b 4 Feb 1983, Oliver b 29 Jan 1985, Jack b 4 June 1988), 1 da (Emily b 24 Sept 1977); *Career* press photographer Evening Despatch Darlington 1979–86; editorial graphic artist: The Northern Echo 1986, London Daily News 1986–87; Daily and Sunday Telegraph: joined 1987, head Graphics Dept 1989–, graphics ed 1992–; winner: Graphic Artist of the Year Br Press awards 1988 and 1989 (commended 1990), Linotype award for text and graphics (The Daily Telegraph) Newspaper Indust awards 1990, Silver award for breaking news informational graphic Soc of Newspaper Design US 1989 (2 awards of excellence 1990, 1991 and 1994), jt winner Graphic Artist of the Year Br Press Awards 1991, highly commended Image of the Year Br Press Awards 1994; *Style*— Alan Gilliland, Esq; ✉ The Daily Telegraph, 1 Canada Square, Canary Wharf, London E14 5DT (☎ 0171 538 6432, fax 0171 538 7245)

GILLILAND, Elsie; da of James Lauder McCully (d 1985), of Belfast, and Mary Agnes, *née* Calvert (d 1991); *b* 6 Dec 1937; *Educ* Richmond Lodge, Queen's Univ Belfast (LLB); *m* 22 July 1961, His Hon Judge James Andrew David Gilliland, QC; 2 s (Jeremy b 1964, Jonathan b 1967); *Career* slr in private practice; pt/t chm VAT Tbnls; *Recreations* skiing, opera, painting; *Style*— Mrs Elsie Gilliland; ✉ The Shieling, Highfield, Prestbury, Cheshire (☎ 01625 828029); 30 Swedish Quays, London SE16 (☎ 0171 232 0144); Towns Needham & Co, John Dalton House, 121 Deansgate, Manchester M3 2AR

GILLINGHAM, Prof (Francis) John; CBE (1981, MBE 1945); s of Herbert John Gillingham (d 1958), of Elwell Lea, Upwey, Dorset and Lily Gillingham (d 1962); *b* 15 March 1916; *Educ* Hardye's Sch Dorset, Bart's Univ of London (MB BS); *m* 30 Aug 1945, Irene Judy, da of F W Jude (d 1947), of Norfolk; 4 s (Jeremy (d 1994), Timothy, Simon, Adam); *Career* house surgn Bart's 1940–41, surgn Mil Hosp (for head injuries) Oxford 1941–42, Maj RAMC (No 4 Mobile Neurosurgical Unit) 1942–45, conslt surgical neurologist Royal Infirmary & Western Gen Hosp Edinburgh 1950–80, conslt neurosurgn to the Army in Scotland 1963–81, prof of surgical neurology Univ of Edinburgh 1963–80 (now emeritus), hon conslt Bart's London 1980–, advsr MOD Saudi Arabia 1981–83, prof Univ of King Saud 1983–85 (now emeritus); co chm TV Educn and Communications Grampian TV/Univ of Edinburgh; pres RCS Edinburgh 1979–82 (currently memb Ct of Regents); hon pres World Fedn of Neurosurgical Socs; Colles lectr and medal Irish Coll of Surgns 1974, Medal City of Gdansk Poland 1978, Clark Fndn award 1979, Harveian oration Edinburgh 1980, 17 Elsberg lecture NY 1967, Adlington Syme oration Royal Aust Coll of Surgns 1981, Digby meml lecture and medal Univ of Hong Kong 1982, Obrador Fndn medal Madrid 1990; Hon MD (Thessaloniki); hon memb Royal Acad of Med (Valencia); Hon FRACS, Hon FCM (S Africa), Hon FRCSI; Hon FRCS: Australia, Glasgow; FRCS, FRSE 1970, FRSA 1991; *Publications* author of 85 papers on neurosurgical subjects and postgrad educn in learned magazines; ed 4 books; *Recreations* gardening, sailing, photography, travel; *Clubs* Bruntsfield Links Golfing Soc (Edinburgh), Club Nautico (Javea Spain); *Style*— Prof John Gillingham, CBE, FRSE; ✉ Easter Park House, Barnton Avenue, Edinburgh EH4 6JR (☎ 0131 336 3528); Las Colinas, Jesus Pobre 03749, Alicante, Spain (☎ and fax 00 34 65 75 70 62)

GILLINGHAM, Nicholas (Nick); MBE (1993); s of Frank Joseph Gillingham, of Walsall, and Hazel Eileen, *née* Burns; *b* 22 Jan 1967; *Educ* Blue Coat Comp Sch; *Career* swimmer; 200m breaststroke: Bronze medal Cwlth Games 1986, Silver medal Olympic Games 1988, Bronze medal Euro Championships 1989, Gold medal Euro Championships 1989, 1991 and 1993, Bronze medal Cwlth Games 1990 (also Bronze medal 100m), Euro Open champion 1990, Bronze medal World Championships 1991, Bronze medal Olympic Games 1992 (also finalist 100m), Euro champion 1993 (also Silver medal 100m and Bronze medal Relay), Gold medal Cwlth Games 1994, Silver medal 100m breaststroke Cwlth Games 1994, Bronze medal Olympic Games 200m breaststroke 1996; world record holder: 200m breaststroke short course 1990, 1991, 1992 and 1993, 200m breaststroke long course 1989 (also Euro and Cwlth record); Euro record holder 200m breaststroke short course, Cwlth champion 200m breaststroke 1994, current Cwlth record holder 100 and 200m breaststroke; memb England Amateur Swimming Assoc Ctee 1990–92 (memb Tech Ctee 1994); sports devpt offr (professional career); *Recreations* golf, theatre, music, new and old movies; *Style*— Nick Gillingham, Esq, MBE; ✉ 8 Old Langley Hall, Ox Leys Rd, Sutton Coldfield, W Midlands B75 7HP (☎ 0121 313 1230, mobile 0468 404345); Sports Development Officer, Birmingham Sports Centre, Balsall Heath Rd, Birmingham B12 9DL (☎ 0121 446 4659, fax 0121 440 2480)

GILLINGS, Ven Richard John; s of John Albert Gillings, MBE, of Scalby, N Yorks, and Constance Ford, *née* Weatherill (d 1991); *b* 17 Sept 1945; *Educ* Sale Co GS, St Chad's Coll Durham (BA, Dip in Biblical Studies), Lincoln Theol Coll; *m* 22 April 1972, Kathryn Mary, da of Frank George Hill, BEM; 1 da (Elizabeth Anne b 18 Feb 1974), 2 s (Stephen David b 28 Aug 1975, Scott Michael b 21 Nov 1988); *Career* curate St George's Altrincham 1970–75, rector St Thomas' Stockport 1977–83 (priest i/c 1975–77), priest i/c St Peter's Stockport 1978–83, rector of Birkenhead Priory 1983–93, rural dean of Birkenhead 1985–93, hon canon Chester Cathedral 1992–94, vicar St Michael and All Angels Bramhall 1993–, archdeacon of Macclesfield 1994–; memb Gen Synod 1980–; *Recreations* Rotarian, music, cinema, railways, theatre; *Style*— The Ven the Archdeacon of Macclesfield; ✉ The Vicarage, 5 Robins Lane, Bramhall, Stockport, Cheshire SK7 2PE (☎ 0161 439 2254)

GILLIONS, Paul; s of William Stanley Gillions (d 1972), and Marie Lilian, *née* Crawley; *b* 15 May 1950; *Educ* St Albans GS for Boys; *m* 5 June 1976, Grace Kathleen, da of David Adam Smith, and Kathleen Iris, *née* Towers; 2 da (Jennie b 1980, Laura b 1983); *Career* int PR conslt; Burson-Marsteller Ltd: main bd dir 1987–93, dir of issues mgmnt Burson-Marsteller Europe, memb Int Bd 1992–93; sr vice pres and dir public policy and issues mgmnt Fleishman-Hillard 1993–96, sr vice pres int public policy Fleishman-Hillard (Europe and USA) 1996–; memb IOD, MIPR; FRSA; *Recreations* reading, badminton; *Style*— Paul Gillions, Esq; ✉ 3 Whitehurst Ave, Hitchin, Herts (☎ 01462 621434); Fleishman-Hillard, 200 North Broadway, St Louis, Missouri, USA (☎ 001 314 982 1700)

GILLIS, Neil Duncan; s of Cyril Bertram Gillis, of Moreton Pinkney, Northamptonshire, and Jean, *née* Nunn; *b* 22 Jan 1965; *Educ* The Reading Blue Coat Sch, Oriel Coll Oxford (MA); *Career* mktg trainee Procter and Gamble 1985–86, brand mangr General Foods 1986–88, mktg controller RHM 1988–90, mktg dir Premier Brands 1990–; *Recreations* golf, badminton, cricket, gardening; *Style*— Neil Gillis, Esq; ✉ Premier Brands UK Ltd, Pasture Road, Moreton, Wirral L46 8SE (☎ 0151 678 8888)

GILLMAN, Tricia; da of Dr Theodore Gillman (d 1971), of Cambridge, and Selma, *née* Cohen (d 1993); *b* 9 Nov 1951; *Educ* Univ of Leeds (BA), Univ of Newcastle (MFA); *m* 1989, Alexander Ramsay, s of Frank Raymond Faber Ramsay (d 1977); 1 s (Thomas Jesmond b 3 Jan 1990); *Career* artist; teacher: 1977–83 (Newcastle Poly, Univ of Leeds, Ravensbourne Sch of Art, Lanchester Poly, Birmingham Poly, Edinburgh Sch of Art, Univ of Reading, Chelsea Sch of Art), St Martin's Sch of Art 1983–, RCA 1988–; *Solo Exhibitions* Parkinson Gallery Leeds 1978, Sunderland Arts Centre 1982, Arnofini Gallery Bristol 1985, Benjamin Rhodes Gallery London 1985, 1987 and 1993, Laing Gallery Newcastle (touring) 1989–90; *Gp Exhibitions* incl: Northern Art Assoc Exhibition (Shipley Art Gallery and tour) 1978, St Martin's Painters (Seven Dial Gallery) 1982, Summer Show II (Serpentine Gallery) 1982, John Moores Liverpool Exhibition XIV (Walker Art Gallery) 1985, Thirty London Artists (RA) 1985, Malaysian and British Exhibition Paintings and Prints (National Art Gallery, Kuala Lumpar, Singapore and Hong Kong) 1986, Summer Show (RA) 1987, London Group (RCA and tour) 1987, Homage to the Square (Flaxman Gallery) 1990, Works on Paper (Benjamin Rhodes Gallery) 1990, Forces of Nature (Manchester City Art Gallery and tour) 1990, Br Cncl and Royal Coll of Art touring exhibition of Eastern Europe 1990, Art '91 (London Contemporary Art Fair Olympia) 1991, Peter Stuyvesant Touring Exhibition (Zaragoza and Seville, Spain) 1991, The Discerning Eye (Mall Galleries) 1991, John Moores Exhibition (Liverpool) 1991, The New Patrons (Christie's London) 1992, 20th Century Women's Art (New Hall Cambridge) 1992, 3 Ways (RCA touring exhbn to Central Europe) 1992, London Group (Morley Coll London) 1992, Chicago Art Fair 1993; Tricia Gillman and Richard Gorman: Small Paintings (Benjamin Rhodes Gallery) 1989, Forces of Nature (Manchester City Art Gallery and tour) 1990; works in collections: Contemporary Arts Soc, Univ of Leeds, Television South West, The Stuyvesant Fndn, Stanhope Properties plc, Herbert Art Gallery Coventry, Unilever plc; private collections in: Britain, Belgium, Holland, Japan, Thailand, USA, Italy; *Style*— Ms Tricia Gillman; ✉ Benjamin Rhodes Gallery, 4 New Burlington Place, London W1X 1SB (☎ 0171 434 1768/9, fax 0171 287 8841)

GILLMER, Dr Michael David George; s of George Ernest Gillmer, of Pretoria, SA (d 1989), and (Adriana Margaretha) Janet, *née* Scholtz (d 1984); *b* 17 Jan 1945; *Educ* St Benedict's Sch Ealing, King's Coll Hosp (MA, MD); *m* 17 Aug 1968, Janet Yvonne, da of Leslie Francis Davis (d 1987); 1 s (David Michael b 1978), 1 da (Charlotte Jane b 1973); *Career* clinical reader in obstetrics and gynaecology Nuffield Dept Univ of Oxford 1979–84, conslt obstetrician and gynaecologist John Radcliffe Hosp Oxford 1984–; author of many publications on diabetes nutrition in pregnancy and contraception; hon memb Green Coll Oxford; memb Gynaecological Visiting Soc of GB and I, FRCOG 1984; *Books* 100 Cases For Students of Medicine (1979), Nutrition in Pregnancy (1982), 100 Case Histories in Obstetrics and Gynaecology (1991); *Recreations* ice skating, photography, music; *Style*— Dr Michael Gillmer; ✉ Felstead House, 23 Banbury Rd, Oxford OX2 6NX (☎ 01865 512776)

GILLMORE OF THAMESFIELD, Baron (Life Peer UK 1996), of Putney in the London Borough of Wandsworth; Sir David Howe Gillmore; GCMG (1994, KCMG 1990, CMG 1982); s of Air Vice-Marshal Alan David Gillmore, CB, CBE (d 1996), of Swallowfield, and Kathleen Victoria, *née* Morris (d 1993); *b* 16 Aug 1934; *Educ* Trent Coll, King's Coll Cambridge (MA); *m* 1964, Lucile, da of Jean Morin (d 1972), of Paris; 2 s (Hon Julian b 1967, Hon Paul b 1970); *Career* RAF 1953–55; Reuters 1958–60, Polypapier SA 1960–65, schoolmaster ILEA 1965–69; HM Dip Serv: FCO 1970–72, first sec Br Embassy Moscow 1972–75, cnsllr Br Delgn to MBFR Talks Vienna 1975–78, head of Def Dept FCO 1979–81, asst under sec of state FCO 1981–83, Br high cmmr to Malaysia 1983–86, dep under sec of state FCO 1986–90, visiting fell Harvard Univ 1990–91, perm under sec of state FCO and head of HM Dip Serv 1991–94, ret; currently: sr advsr Barclay de Zoete Wedd Ltd, non-exec dir The Prudential Corporation plc 1995–, non-exec dir Vickers plc, chm The Art and Antique Dealers' Assoc, govr Birkbeck Coll London, chm Cncl The Ditchley Fndn; *Recreations* books, music, exercise; *Clubs* Brooks's, RAC, Special Forces; *Style*— The Rt Hon Lord Gillmore of Thamesfield, GCMG; ✉ The House of Lords, London SW1A 0PW

GILLON, Dr John (Jack); s of William Millar Gillon, of Shotts, and Mary, *née* Wood; *b* 24 April 1949; *Educ* Wishaw HS, Univ of Edinburgh (MB ChB, MD); *m* 2 Sept 1972 (sep 1991), Sandria Joy, da of Alexander Headridge, of Byburn, Ecclesmachan; 1 s (Andrew b 1981), 1 da (Aimée b 1978); *Career* lectr dept of med and gastro-intestinal unit Western Gen Hosp Edinburgh 1977–84, conslt Blood Transfusion Serv 1985–; also chef and cookery writer; winner Observer/Mouton-Cadet Cookery Competition 1981; FRCP; *Books* Le Menu Gastronomique (1982), Chambers Scottish Food Book (1989); *Recreations* golf, wine and food; *Style*— Dr Jack Gillon; ✉ Edinburgh and SE Scotland Blood Transfusion Service, Royal Infirmary, Lauriston Place, Edinburgh EH3 9HB (☎ 0131 229 2585, telex 72163)

GILLOTT, Roland Charles Graeme; s of John Arthur Gillott (d 1982), of Northwood, Middx, and Ursula Mary, *née* Bailey (d 1983); *b* 22 Aug 1947; *Educ* Haileybury; *m* 25 Oct 1975, (Bridget) Rae, da of Lesley Bentley Jones (d 1959), of Northwood; 1 s (Adrian b 20 Oct 1979), 2 da (Shanta b 21 April 1978, Lissa b 1 Jan 1981); *Career* admitted slr 1972, ptnr Radcliffes Crossman Block 1979–; churchwarden St Michaels & All Angels

Amersham 1991–95; Liveryman: Worshipful Co of Merchant Taylors 1979, Worshipful Co of Info Technologists 1995; memb Law Soc; *Recreations* walking, photography; *Clubs* MCC, RAC, Travellers', City Livery; *Style*— Roland Gillott, Esq; ✉ Radcliffes Crossman Block, 5 Great College St, Westminster, London SW1P 3SJ (☎ 0171 222 7040, fax 0171 222 6208)

GILLUM, John Reginald; s of Sidney Julius Gillum (d 1953), of Reigate, Surrey, and Dorothea, *née* Smith (d 1952); *b* 25 Jan 1928; *Educ* Winchester, King's Coll Cambridge; *m* 17 June 1953, Mary Rosalind (Mary Rose), da of Alan Frederick Graham Ayling (d 1990); 3 s (Benedict John Nevile b 1954, Thomas Alan b 1955, Christopher Andrew b 1961); *Career* Lt The Buffs 1948, served Hong Kong and Sudan, ret 1951; joined Robert Benson Lonsdale & Co Ltd (subsequently Kleinwort Benson) 1956 (dir 1965), dir and head of corp fin Samuel Montagu & Co Ltd 1971, dir (corp fin) NM Rothschild & Sons Ltd 1981–88; dep chm Signet Group plc 1986–; dir: Blagden Industries plc 1985–93 (chm 1987–90), Kingsbury Group plc 1986–95, BR (Eastern) Bd 1987–92, GPG plc 1989–90 (chm), Ensign Trust plc 1990–92; memb Disciplinary Ctee Inst of Chartered Accountants 1978–96; Gen Cmmr for Taxes Hertford; memb Cncl Queen's Nursing Inst; *Recreations* golf; *Clubs* Brooks's; *Style*— John Gillum, Esq; ✉ Holwell Manor, Hatfield, Herts AL9 5RG (☎ 01707 261232)

GILMARTIN, John; *b* 5 Aug 1935; *Educ* Trinity Coll Dublin (BA, BCom); *Career* called to the Bar Lincoln's Inn 1972; *Style*— John Gilmartin, Esq; ✉ Cleves, nr Rodmell, Lewes, East Sussex BN7 3EZ (☎ 01273 477098); New Court, Temple, London EC4Y 9BE

GILMORE, Brian Terence; CB (1992); s of late John Henry Gilmore, of Sevenoaks, Kent, and Edith Alice, *née* Johnson; *b* 25 May 1937; *Educ* Wolverhampton GS, ChCh Oxford (MA); *m* 17 Feb 1962, Rosalind, da of Sir Robert Fraser (d 1986); *Career* ret civil servant; dep sec: Cabinet Office 1988–92, Dept of Social Security 1992–95; pt/t chm Prince's Youth Business Tst (E London); *Recreations* walking, music, Greece; *Clubs* Athenaeum; *Style*— Brian Gilmore, Esq, CB; ✉ c/o Athenaeum, Pall Mall, London SW1Y 5ER

GILMORE, David; s of David Gilmore, and Dora, *née* Baker; *b* 7 Dec 1945; *Educ* Alleyn's Sch; *m* 23 Sept 1978, Fiona, da of J P R Mollison; 3 s (Charles b 1982, George b 1985, Edward b 1989); *Career* artistic director; appts incl: Watermill Theatre, Nuffield Theatre Southampton; prodns incl: Nuts (Whitehall), Daisy Pulls it Off, Lend Me a Tenor (both Globe), The Resistible Rise of Arturo Ui, Beyond Reasonable Doubt (both Queen's), The Hired Man (Astoria), Cavalcade (Chichester), Song and Dance (Sydney, Melbourne and Adelaide), Glen Garry Glenross (Brussels), Fatal Attraction (Haymarket), Mandragola (RNT), Casablanca (Whitehall), A Swell Party (Vaudeville), Radio Times (Queen's), Grease (Dominion), As you Like it (Chicago), Chapter Two (Queen's), Alone Together (Hong Kong and Beijing), Là Haut (Theâtre des Celestins Lyon); memb: DGGB, TMA; *Recreations* golf, gardening; *Clubs* Garrick; *Style*— David Gilmore, Esq; ✉ 4 Wilton Crescent, Wimbledon, London SW19 3QZ

GILMORE, Fiona Catherine; da of Robin (Dick) Triefus (d 1983), and Jean Margaret, *née* Herring (da of Alfred Herring, VC); *b* 7 Nov 1956; *Educ* Queenswood Sch Hatfield Herts, Univ of Cambridge (scholar, MA); *m* 5 May 1979, Richard John Maurice, s of Richard Thomas Gilmore, of Maldon, Essex; 3 s (Daniel b 1986, Alexander b 1989, Edward b 1993); *Career* Ted Bates Advertising Agency London 1977–78, Benton & Bowles Advertising Agency London 1978–84, md Michael Peters & Ptnrs 1987–90 (devpt dir 1984, mktg dir 1985), md Lewis Moberly 1990–91, fndr ptnr and md Springpoint (brand and corp identity positioning and design consultancy) 1991–; speaker CBI conf 1986; memb: CBI Vision 2010 Gp 1986–87, NEDO Maker User Working Pty 1988, Milk Mktg Bd 1988, GCSE Modern Language Working Pty 1989; govr Centre for Info on Language Teaching and Res 1987, chm Design Effectiveness Awards Scheme 1988–89; non-exec dir RSPB 1994; advsr Lambeth Palace 1992–; memb: RSA, IOD; *Recreations* family, skiing, tennis, walking, music; *Style*— Mrs Fiona Gilmore; ✉ Springpoint, 31 Corsica Street, Highbury Fields, London N5 1JT (☎ 0171 704 2878, fax 0171 704 2874)

GILMORE, Dr Ian Thomas; s of Dr James M Gilmore, of Cullercoats, Tyne and Wear, and Jean, *née* Drummond; *b* 25 Sept 1946; *Educ* Royal GS Newcastle upon Tyne, King's Coll Cambridge (MA, MB BCh, MD), St Thomas' Hosp London (Beaney prize in surgery); *m* 18 Jan 1975, Hilary Elizabeth, *née* Douglas; 2 s (Alastair James b 20 March 1979, William Thomas b 15 May 1983), 1 da (Katherine Louise b 21 Jan 1981); *Career* house physician Southampton Gen Hosp 1971–72, house surgn St Thomas's Hosp 1972–73, house physician then SHO in neurology Whittington Hosp 1972–73, SHO Intensive Therapy Unit St Thomas's Hosp 1973, registrar in gen med Worthing Hosp 1973–74; St Thomas's Hosp: registrar in gen med and gastroenterology 1974–75, MRC research fell Gastrointestinal Lab and hon sr med registrar 1976–77; sr med registrar in gen med and gastroenterology Charing Cross Hosp 1978–79 and 1980, MRC travelling fell Univ of Calif San Diego 1979–80; Royal Liverpool and Broadgreen Hosps Liverpool: conslt physician and gastroenterologist 1980–, med dir 1995–; dir of R & D Royal Liverpool Univ Hosp 1993–95; Univ of Liverpool: hon lectr Dept of Med 1980–, chm Faculty of Med 1991–92; chm Standing Liaison Ctee Mersey RHA and Univ of Liverpool 1991–94; visiting prof: Univ of Calif San Diego 1989, Univ of S Carolina 1991; memb: Cncl Br Soc of Gastroenterology 1985–88, Specialist Advsy Ctee in Gastroenterology Jt Ctee for Higher Med Trg 1988– (sec 1989–95); regional advsr RCP 1992– (memb Cncl 1993–95); memb: American Assoc for the Study of Liver Disease, American Gastroenterology Assoc, Assoc of Physicians of GB and I, Br Assoc for the Study of the Liver, Br Soc of Gastroenterology, Euro Assoc for the Study of the Liver, Int Assoc for the Study of the Liver, Int Hepatobiliary Pancreatic Assoc; FRCP 1985; *Books* Gastrointestinal Emergencies (ed with R Shields); author of over 100 original articles, invited reviews and chapters; *Recreations* golf, travel; *Style*— Dr Ian Gilmore; ✉ Birchways, Oldfield Drive, Heswall, Wirral, Merseyside L60 6SS (☎ 0151 342 3264); Royal Liverpool University Hospital, Prescot Street, Liverpool L7 8XP (☎ 0151 706 3557)

GILMORE, Owen Jeremy Adrian (Jerry); s of Dr Owen Dermot Gilmore, of Inigo House, Highworth, Wilts, and Carmel, *née* Cantwell; *b* 27 Dec 1941; *Educ* Beaumont Coll, Bart's Med Sch (MB BS); *m* 1966 (m dis 1987), Hilary Ann Frances; 2 s (Hugh Inigo Jeremy b 1969, Quentin Roderick Zebedee b 1977), 6 da (Anna Benedicta Claire b 1967, Deborah Emma Frances b 1968, Katherine Laura Matilda b 1971, Natasha Olivia Polly b 1973); 3 subseq da (Georgia Alice Louise b 1990, Octavia Phoebe Hannah b 1993, Chiara Novena Jane b 1995); *Career* conslt surgn i/c breast clinic, groin and hernia clinic 108 Harley St, conslt gen surgn Bart's London 1976–91, conslt i/c Breast Unit Bart's 1981–91 prizes: Begley prize RCS 1966, Moynihan Prize and Medal Assoc Surgns GB 1975, Hamilton Bailey Prize Int Coll Surgeons 1975, Hunterian Prof RCS 1976; MRCS, LRCP (London) 1966, FRCS 1971, FRCSE 1971, MS (London) 1976, fell Inst of Sports Medicine 1995; *Books* Diagnosis and Treatment of Breast Disease, Diagnosis and Treatment of groin injuries in sportsmen (Gilmore's groin); *Recreations* children, skiing, rugby football, dining, travel; *Style*— Jerry Gilmore, Esq; ✉ 108 Harley Street, London W1N 2ET (☎ 0171 637 8820, fax 0171 436 2945)

GILMORE, Rosalind Edith Jean; CB (1995); da of Sir Robert Brown Fraser, OBE (d 1984), and Betty, *née* Harris (d 1984); *b* 23 March 1937; *Educ* King Alfred Sch London, Univ Coll London (BA), Newnham Coll Cambridge (BA, MA); *m* 17 Feb 1962, Brian Terence Gilmore, s of John Henry Gilmore; *Career* HM Treasy: appointed 1960, asst princ 1960–62, asst private sec to Chllr of Exchequer 1962–65, princ 1965, resigned to accompany husb to Washington; exec asst to Econ Dir International Bank for Reconstruction and Development 1966–67; HM Treasy: reinstated 1968, princ private sec to Paymaster Gen 1973, princ private sec to Chllr of Duchy of Lancaster 1974, asst sec 1975, head of Fin Inst Div 1977–80 (Banking Act 1979, Credits Unions Act 1979), press sec to Chllr of Exchequer 1980–82, head of Information 1980–82; gen mangr corp planning Dunlop Ltd 1982–83, dir of mktg National Girobank 1983–86, marketing conslt FI Group PLC (Software) 1986–89; memb Fin Servs Act Tbnl 1986–89, full-time chm and first cmmr Building Societies Cmmn 1991–94 (dep chm 1989–91), dir SIB 1993–, dir of regulation Lloyds of London 1995 (memb Bd 1996–); chm: Homeowners Friendly Soc Ltd 1996–, Arrow Broadcasting (CLT subsid) 1995–; dir: Mercantile Group plc, Mercantile Credit Co Ltd, London and Manchester Group plc 1986–89, BAT Industries plc 1996–; vice pres Building Soc Assoc 1995; fndr memb Forum UK 1990; memb Ct Cranfield Univ (formerly Cranfield Inst of Technol) 1992–; dir: Opera North 1993–, Moorfields Eye Hosp Tst 1994–; dir fell St George's House Windsor Castle 1986–89; hon memb City Womens Network 1993; fell UCL 1988, hon fell Newnham Coll Cambridge 1995 (assoc fell 1986); FRSA 1985, CIMgt 1992; *Recreations* music, reading, languages, Greece; *Style*— Mrs Rosalind Gilmore, CB; ✉ 3 Clarendon Mews, London W2 2NR

GILMOUR, Dr Alan Breck; CVO (1990), CBE (1984); s of Andrew Gilmour, CMG (d 1988), of Edinburgh, and Nelle, *née* Twigg (d 1984); *b* 30 Aug 1928; *Educ* Clayesmore Sch, King's Coll Hosp Univ of London (MB BS); *m* 8 June 1957, Elizabeth, da of late Henry Heath; 2 da; *Career* Nat Serv 1947–49; GP 1957–67, BMA Secretariat 1967–79, dir NSPCC 1979–89; formerly memb: Standing Med Advsy Ctee, Cncl BMA, Educn Ctee RCGP; former treas ASME, former chm Int Alliance on Child Abuse and Neglect; memb: Video Consultative Cncl Br Bd of Film Classification 1985–, Health Educn Authy 1989–95 (resigned); chm Michael Sieff Fndn 1990–96, former chm and tstee Kidscape, pres Parkinsons Disease Soc (Bridport Branch) 1992–, hon vice pres NSPCC 1990, patron Faithfull Fndn 1994– (tstee 1992–94), chm Dorset Forum on Domestic Violence 1996–; govr: Colfox Sch 1994– (chm 1995–), Clayesmore Sch 1995–; fell Dartington Centre for Social Policy 1994–; Liveryman Worshipful Soc of Apothecaries 1973; LMSSA 1956, FRCGP 1974; *Books* Innocent Victims - The Question of Child Abuse (1988); *Recreations* walking, gardening, music; *Clubs* RSM, IOD; *Style*— Dr Alan Gilmour, CVO, CBE; ✉ 106 Crock Lane, Bothenhampton, Bridport, Dorset DT6 4DH (☎ 01308 423116)

GILMOUR, Alexander Clement (Sandy); CVO (1990); s of Sir John Gilmour, 2 Bt (d 1977), and late Lady Mary Gilmour, da of 3 Duke of Abercorn; half bro of Lord Gilmour of Craigmillar, *qv*; *b* 23 Aug 1931; *Educ* Eton; *m* 1, 2 Dec 1954 (m dis 1983), Barbara Marie-Louise Constance, da of Hon Denis Gomer Berry, TD; 2 s, 1 da; m 2, 1983 (m dis 1990), Susan Janet, eld da of late Capt Voltelin James Howard Van der Byl, BSC, RN (ret), and formerly wife of (1) Alwyn Richard Dudley Smith and (2) 2 Baron Chetwode; *Career* stockbroker; dir and head Corp Fin Dept Carr Sebag and Co 1972–82; conslt with: Grieveson Grant 1982–83, Gilmour & Associates Ltd 1983–84, Equity Financial Trust 1984–86, Tide (UK) Ltd 1986; dir: London Wall Securities Ltd 1989–92, City and Provincial Securities 1991–93, Elmdale Investments Ltd 1991–; chm: Greys of Alnwick Ltd 1991–, Vulture Company 1 plc 1991–, Vulture Company 2 plc 1992–, Goldsborough Assured Properties plc 1992–, Sovereign Reversions plc 1992–; dir Tate Gallery Fndn 1986–88; govr LSE 1967–; *Recreations* fishing, gardening, tennis; *Clubs* White's, Hon Co of Edinburgh Golfers, MCC; *Style*— A C Gilmour, Esq, CVO; ✉ 1 Christopher Mews, Penzance St, London W11 4QZ (☎ 0171 602 7270)

GILMOUR, Col Sir Allan Macdonald; KCVO (1990), OBE (1961), MC (and bar 1942, 1943); s of Capt Allan Gilmour, of Rosehall, Sutherland (ka Salonica 1916), and Mary, *née* Macdonald, of Isle of Skye; *b* 23 Nov 1916; *Educ* Winchester; *m* 1941, Jean, da of Capt E G Wood (d 1980), of Gollanfield, Inverness-shire; 3 s, 1 da; *Career* WWII served Seaforth Highlanders ME, Sicily, Italy, NW Europe (despatches 1944), DSC (USA) 1944; Col Queen's Own Highlanders 1944–66: served Germany, ME, UK, instr Staff Coll Pakistan, CGS Ghana; memb Sutherland CC 1970–74, chm Sutherland District Cncl 1974–78, memb Highland Regional Cncl 1976–96; memb: Highland Health Bd 1974–86 (chm 1984–86), Highland River Purification Bd 1976–96 (chm 1994–96); pres Highland TAVRA 1989–91; HM Lord Lt of Sutherland 1972–91 (DL 1971); *Recreations* fishing; *Style*— Col Sir Allan Gilmour, KCVO, OBE, MC; ✉ Invernauld, Rosehall, Lairg, Sutherland (☎ 01549 441204)

GILMOUR, David Jon; s of Douglas Graham Gilmour, and (Edith) Sylvia, *née* Wilson; *b* 6 March 1946; *Educ* Perse Sch for Boys, Cambridge Coll of Arts & Technol; *m*; 6 c; *Career* musician and singer; with Pink Floyd 1968–; albums incl: Dark Side of the Moon (1973), The Wall (1979), The Division Bell (1994); solo albums 1978 and 1984; *Recreations* literature, films, aviation, sailing, scuba; *Style*— David Gilmour, Esq

GILMOUR, Hon David Robert; s and h to btcy of Lord Gilmour of Craigmillar (3 Bt), *qv*; *b* 14 Nov 1952; *Educ* Eton, Balliol Coll Oxford; *m* 1975, Sarah Anne, da of Michael Bradstock, of Whitefold, Clunas, Nairn; 1 s (Alexander b 1980), 3 da (Rachel b 1977, Katharine b 1984, Laura b 1985); *Career* writer; Alistair Horne fell St Anthony's Coll Oxford 1996–97; FRSL; *Books* Dispossessed: The Ordeal of The Palestinians 1917–80 (1980), Lebanon: The Fractured Country (1983), The Transformation of Spain: From Franco to the Constitutional Monarchy (1985), The Last Leopard: A Life of Giuseppe di Lampedusa (1988), The Hungry Generations (1991), Cities of Spain (1992), Curzon (1994, Duff Cooper Prize); *Style*— The Hon David Gilmour, FRSL; ✉ 27 Ann Street, Edinburgh EH4 1PL

GILMOUR, Ewen Hamilton; s of Lt Cdr Patrick Dalrymple Gilmour (d 1988), and Lorna Mary, *née* Dore; *b* 16 Aug 1953; *Educ* Rugby, Downing Coll Cambridge; *m* 3 June 1978, Nicola, da of Maarten Van Mesdag; 3 s (James b 27 Feb 1980, Rowallan b 3 April 1982, Fergus b 4 May 1985), 1 da (Iona b 19 Jan 1990); *Career* CA; Peat Marwick McLintock 1974–80, dir Charterhouse Bank Ltd 1987–93 (joined 1980), Lloyd's of London 1993–95, Murray Lawrence Holdings plc 1995–; FCA 1979; *Recreations* cricket, golf, tennis; *Clubs* Invalids, MCC; *Style*— Ewen Gilmour, Esq; ✉ 20 Arthur Rd, London SW19 7DZ (☎ 0181 947 6805); Murray Lawrence Holdings plc, 1 Whittington Avenue, London EC3V 1LE (☎ 0181 860 8600, fax 0171 860 8603)

GILMOUR, John; DL (Fife 1987); s and h of Col Sir John Edward Gilmour, 3 Bt, DSO, TD, JP, *qv*; *b* 15 July 1944; *Educ* Eton, Aberdeen Coll of Agric; *m* 6 May 1967, Valerie Jardine, yr da of late George Walker Russell and Mrs William Wilson, of Hilton House, Cupar; 2 s ((John) Nicholas b 1970, Patrick George William b 1980), 2 da (Corinna Valerie b 1972, (Victoria) Juliet b 1975); *Career* Capt Fife and Forfar Yeo/Scottish Horse (TA); farmer; memb Royal Co of Archers (Queen's Body Guard for Scotland); MFH 1972–; company dir; tstee The Moredun Fndn; *Recreations* fishing, racing, reading; *Clubs* New (Edinburgh); *Style*— John Gilmour, Esq, DL; ✉ Balcormo Mains, Leven, Fife KY8 5QF (☎ 01333 360229, fax 01333 360540)

GILMOUR, Col Sir John Edward; 3 Bt (UK 1897), of Lundin and Montrave, Parishes of Largo and Scoonie, Co Fife, DSO (1945), TD, JP (Fife 1957); s of Col Rt Hon Sir John Gilmour, 2 Bt, GCVO, DSO, sometime MP E Renfrewshire and Glasgow Pollok (d 1940), by his 1 w, Mary (d 1919), da of Edward Lambert, of Telham Court, Sussex; *b* 24 Oct 1912; *Educ* Eton, Trinity Hall Cambridge, Dundee Sch of Econs; *m* 24 May 1941, Ursula Mabyn, da of late Frank Oliver Wills, of Cote Lodge, Westbury-on-Trym; 2 s (John, *qv*, Andrew Frank b 1947); *Heir* s, John Gilmour b 15 July 1944; *Career* Cmd Fife and Forfar Yeo (TA) 1947–50, Bt-Col 1950; MP (C) E Fife 1961–79, chm Cons and Unionist Party Scot 1965–67; HM Lord-Lt Fife 1980–87 (vice Lord-Lt 1979–80, DL 1953); Lord High Cmmr to Gen Assembly of Church of Scot 1982 and 1983; Capt (ret) Royal Co of Archers

(Queen's Body Guard for Scot); *Recreations* hunting, gardening, shooting; *Clubs* Royal and Ancient (St Andrews); *Style*— Col Sir John Gilmour, Bt, DSO, TD, JP; ✉ Montrave, Leven, Fife KY8 5NZ (☎ 01333 426159)

GILMOUR, Nigel Benjamin Douglas; QC (1990); s of Benjamin Waterfall Gilmour (d 1967), and Barbara Mary, *née* Till; *b* 21 Nov 1947; *Educ* Tettenhall Coll, Univ of Liverpool (LLB); *m* 1972, Isobel Mary Harborow; 2 da (Katy b 28 Feb 1977, Alison b 1 Oct 1988); *Career* called to the Bar Inner Temple 1970, recorder 1990–, head of chambers; memb: Northern Arbitration Assoc, Hon Soc of Inner Temple; *Recreations* wine, gardening; *Style*— Nigel Gilmour, Esq, QC; ✉ Peel House, Ground Floor, 5/7 Harrington Street, Liverpool L2 9QA (☎ 0151 236 4321, fax 0151 236 3332)

GILMOUR, William; s of Gordon Scott Lauder Gilmour (d 1992), and Isabella, *née* Barrowman (d 1990); *b* 26 April 1951; *Educ* Dalziel HS Motherwell, Univ of Strathclyde (BA); *m* 11 Oct 1986, Katherine Margaret, da of Francis Trevor Gatefield; 1 da (Emily Isabella Gatefield b 26 Feb 1992); *Career* trainee accountant Coopers & Lybrand 1971, CA 1974, CA Price Waterhouse Lisbon 1977–79 (Los Angeles 1975–77), mangr Audit and Special Projects (Europe) Gulf & Western Corp 1979–80, fin dir Sleepeezee 1980–83, ptnr Price Waterhouse 1983–95, ptnr Consumer, Retail and Distribution Coopers & Lybrand 1995–; author of numerous articles on mgmnt control and IT in retailing; MICAS 1974, ACA 1989; *Recreations* motor sport, opera, travel; *Style*— William Gilmour, Esq; ✉ Coopers and Lybrand, 1 Embankment Place, London WC2N 6NN (☎ 0171 213 3192, fax 0171 213 2408)

GILMOUR OF CRAIGMILLAR, Baron (Life Peer UK 1992), of Craigmillar in the District of the City of Edinburgh; Sir Ian Hedworth John Little Gilmour; PC (1973); 3 Bt (UK 1926), of Liberton and Craigmillar, Co Midlothian; s of Sir John Little Gilmour, 2 Bt (d 1977), by his 1 w, Hon Victoria Laura, OBE, TD, *née* Cadogan (d 1991), da of Henry Arthur Cadogan, Viscount Chelsea and gda of 5 Earl Cadogan; *b* 8 July 1926; *Educ* Eton, Balliol Coll Oxford; *m* 10 July 1951, Lady Caroline Margaret Montagu Douglas Scott, da of 8 Duke of Buccleuch and Queensberry; 4 s (Hon David Robert b 1952, Hon Oliver John b 1953, Hon Christopher Simon b 1956, Hon Andrew James b 1964), 1 da (Hon Jane Victoria (Hon Mrs Peter Pleydell- Bouverie) b 1959); *Heir* s, David Robert Gilmour, *qv* b 14 Nov 1952; *Career* late Grenadier Gds; called to the Bar 1952; ed The Spectator 1954–59; MP (C): Norfolk Central 1962–74, Chesham and Amersham 1974–92; Parly under sec MOD 1970–71; min of state: for defence procurement MOD 1971–72, for defence 1972–74; sec of state for defence 1974, chm Cons Research Dept 1974–75, Lord Privy Seal and dep foreign sec 1979–81; Hon Degree Univ of Essex 1995; *Books* The Body Politic (1969), Inside Right - A Study of Conservatism (1977), Britain Can Work (1983), Riot, Risings and Revolution (1992), Dancing with Dogma (1992); *Style*— The Rt Hon Lord Gilmour of Craigmillar, PC; ✉ The Ferry House, Park Road, Old Isleworth, Middx TW7 6BD (☎ 0181 560 6769, fax 0181 560 0709)

GILROY, Angus Hugh; s of Donald Duff Gilroy (d 1963), and Margaret Campbell, *née* Forrester (d 1996); *b* 4 Sept 1936; *Educ* Harrow; *m* 30 Sept 1967, Elizabeth Hurst, da of late Richard Lumley Hurst; 1 s (Fergus Hugh b 29 March 1969), 1 da (Margaret Cecilia b 22 Dec 1970); *Career* Nat Serv 2 Lt The Black Watch RHR 1955–57; Binder Hamlyn & Co (now Binder Hamlyn): articled clerk 1958, ptnr 1972–95; dir: Colonial Mutual Life 1991–, Greenwich Lloyd's Underwriting 1996–; DTI inspr London United Investments plc 1990–93; memb: Royal Co of Archers (Queen's Body Guard for Scot) 1972, Worshipful Co of Bowyers 1991; FCA (ACA 1963); *Recreations* golf, shooting, fishing; *Clubs* MCC, West Sussex Golf, Buck's; *Style*— Angus Gilroy, Esq; ✉ Grainingfold, Five Oaks, Billingshurst, West Sussex RH14 9AT

GIMBLETT, (Frederick) Gareth Robert; CBE (1995, OBE 1989), DL (Berks 1988); s of Dan William Davies Gimblett (d 1980), of Tonyrefail, Mid Glam, and Annie, *née* Flook (d 1977); *b* 20 Dec 1931; *Educ* Tonyrefail GS, University Coll of Wales Aberystwyth (BSc, MSc), Univ of Manchester; *m* (Moreen) Margaret, da of Charles Cornford (d 1970); 3 s (Richard b 1959, Michael 1960, Jonathan 1965), 1 da (Briony b 1966); *Career* scientific offr RAE Farnborough Hants 1955–58, hon sr res fell Brunel Univ 1989–90 (lectr in physical chemistry 1958–82, sr res fell 1982–89), freelance sci ed 1989–; exec cncl memb ACC 1983–94; chm: Sub-Ctee Manpower 1985–87, Berks CC 1986–89 (memb 1977–95, ldr 1981–86 and 1991–92), LAMSAC 1988–89, Care Sector Consortium 1988–, Local Govt Trg Bd 1990–91; vice chm Local Govt Mgmnt Bd 1990–93, cncl memb Central Cncl for Educn and Trg in Social Work 1989– (vice chm 1990–), memb Ct Univ of Reading 1989–, memb Cmmn for Local Democracy 1993–95; Cdr Royal Order of Merit Norway 1988; FRSC 1989; *Books* Inorganic Polymer Chemistry (1962), Introduction to Kinetics of Chemical Chain Reactions (1970); *Recreations* hill walking, rugby football (spectator); *Style*— Gareth Gimblett, Esq, CBE, DL; ✉ 6 Park View Drive South, Charvil, Reading, Berks RG10 9QX

GIMENEZ, Raúl Alberto; s of Rodolfo Gimenez, of Argentina, and Aurora, *née* Rossi; *b* 14 Sept 1950; *Educ* Fondaccion del Teatro Colon Buenos Aires; *m* 1970, Mirta, *née* Ferrero; 1 s (Cesare b 2 June 1971), 1 da (Virginia b 17 Oct 1987); *Career* tenor; *Roles* incl: Ernesto in Don Pasquale (Teatro Colon Buenos Aires 1980, Turin 1988, Dallas Opera 1989, Royal Opera House Covent Garden 1990 and 1992, Paris and Rome 1994, Strasbourg Festival 1996), Elvino in La Sonnambula (Rome 1988, Paris 1989, Carnegie Hall NY 1991, Teatro Carlo Felice Genova 1995), Count Almaviva in The Barber of Seville (Vienna State Opera 1989, 1991, 1994 and 1996, Zurich 1989, Monte Carlo 1989, Covent Garden 1990 and 1993, Los Angeles 1991, Brussels 1992, Dallas 1993, Metropolitan Opera 1996, Hamburg State Opera 1996 and Teatro Comunale Florence 1996), Ferrando in Cosi fan Tutte (Verona 1989, Naples 1990, Colon 1992), Argirio in Tancredi (Geneva 1990, Rossini Festival Pesaro 1991, Schwetzingen Festival 1992, La Scala Milan 1993), Ramiro in La Cenerentola (Covent Garden) 1991/94, Teatro Communale Florence 1993, Monte Carlo 1995, Houston Grand Opera 1995), Viaggio a Rheims (Berlin Philarmonic/Abbado 1992), Capuleti ed i Monteechi (New York 1994), Lindaro in L'Italiana in Algeri (Venice 1992, Monte Carlo 1992, Berlin 1993 and 1995, Toulouse 1994, Vienna 1995 and 1996, Munich 1995 and 1996, Florence 1995), Nemorino in L'Elisir d'Amore (Opera Comique Paris) 1996; *Recordings* incl: L'Occasione fa il Ladro (Fonit Cetra) 1988, Rossini Arias (Nimbus) 1988, Argentinian Songs (Nimbus) 1988, Bellini and Donizetti Arias (with Scottish Chamber Orch under Michelangelo Veltri, Nimbus) 1989, Rossini Soirées Musicales (Nimbus) 1989, Mozart Arias (with Covent Garden Orch under Barry Wordsworth, Nimbus) 1991, Salieri's Les Danaides (EMI) 1991, Il Turco in Italia (Philips) 1992, Messa di Gloria (Philips) 1992, Il Barbiere di Seviglia (Teldec) 1993, Medea in Corinto (OperaRara) 1994, La Cenerentola (Teldec) 1995, Rossini's Petite Messe Solenelle (Philips) 1995, Rossini's Stabat Mater (DGG) 1996, La Cenerentola (video, Decca), Tancredi (video, BMG); *Style*— Raul Gimenez, Esq; ✉ c/o Patricia Greenan, 19B Belsize Park, London NW3 4DU (☎ 0171 794 5954, fax 0171 431 3503)

GIMPEL, Peter; s of René Gimpel (d 1945), and Florence, *née* Duveen (d 1978); *b* 26 Oct 1915; *Educ* Lycée Louis le Grand Paris, Le Rosay Switzerland; *Career* conscripted French Army 1936–40, joined Br Army 1940, cmmnd 60 Rifles KRRC 1941 (demob); fndr (with Charles Gimpel) Gimpel Fils Gallery London 1946, subsequently formed branches in Zurich and NY; Brazilian Govt Southern Cross for serv to the Arts 1946; *Recreations* sailing; *Clubs* Royal Corinthian Yacht (Cdre 1973–75), Royal Ocean Racing; *Style*— Peter Gimpel, Esq; ✉ Gimpel Fils, 30 Davies Street, London W1Y 1LG (☎ 0171 493 2488, fax 0171 629 5732)

GIMSON, (George) Stanley; QC (Scot 1961); s of George William Gimson (d 1949), of Glasgow, and Mary, *née* Hogg (d 1950); *b* 6 Sept 1915; *Educ* HS of Glasgow, Univ of Glasgow (BL); *Career* RA TA 1938, cmmnd 1941, Lt 1 HAA Regt Indian Artillery Singapore 1941–42, POW Changi (Singapore) and River Kwai (Thailand) 1942–45; called to the Scottish Bar (advocate) 1949; standing counsel Dept of Agric for Scotland and Forestry Cmmn 1956–61; Sheriff Princ: Aberdeen Kincardine and Banff 1972–74, Grampian Highland and Islands 1975–82; chm: Pensions Appeals Tbnls Scotland 1971–95, Med Appeals Tbnls Scotland 1985–91; dir Scottish National Orchestra Society Ltd 1962–80, chm RSPCC (Edinburgh) 1972–76; chm Bd of Mgmnt Edinburgh Central Hosps 1964–70 (memb 1960–70), vice chm Edinburgh Victoria Hosps 1970–74, tstee Nat Library of Scotland 1963–76; Hon LLD Univ of Aberdeen 1981; *Recreations* travel, forestry, sketching, history; *Clubs* Royal Northern and Univ (Aberdeen), Edinburgh Univ Staff; *Style*— Stanley Gimson, Esq, QC; ✉ 11 Royal Circus, Edinburgh EH3 6TL

GINGELL, Air Chief Marshal Sir John; GBE (1984, CBE 1973, MBE 1962), KCB (1978), KCVO (1992); eldest s of Ernest John Gingell; *b* 3 Feb 1925; *Educ* St Boniface's Coll Plymouth; *m* 1949, Prudence Mary, da of Brig Roy Frank Johnson; 2 s, 1 da; *Career* RAF 1943, Sub-Lieut RNVR Fleet Air Arm 1945–46, RAF 1951, Air Plans Staff HQ NEAF 1960–63, OC No 27 Sqdn (Vulcans) 1963–65, Defence Ops Staff MOD 1966–68, mil asst to chm Mil Ctee NATO Brussels 1968–70, AOA RAF Germany 1971–72, AOC No 23 Gp RAF 1973–75, asst chief of defence staff (Policy) MOD 1975–78, air memb for personnel 1978–80, AOC-in-C RAF support cmd 1980–81, Dep C-in-C Allied Forces Central Europe 1981–84; Gentleman Usher of the Black Rod and Serjeant at Arms House of Lords, sec Lord Great Chamberlain 1985–92; cmmr Cwlth War Graves Cmmn 1986–91; hon bencher Inner Temple 1990; *Clubs* RAF; *Style*— Air Chief Marshal Sir John Gingell, GBE, KCB, KCVO

GINGELL, Maj-Gen Laurie William Albert; CB (1980), OBE (1966, MBE 1959); s of Maj William George Gingell, MBE, MM (d 1960), and Elsie Grace Gingell (d 1989); *b* 29 Oct 1925; *Educ* Farnborough GS, Oriel Coll Oxford; *m* 2 June 1949, Nancy Margaret, da of Arthur Wadsworth (d 1966); 1 s (Richard William b 23 Aug 1961), 1 da (Sarah Louise b 15 June 1959); *Career* RTR: cmmnd 1945, cmd 1 RTR 1966–67, 7 Armd Bde 1970–71; MGA UKLF 1976–79; gen sec The Offrs Pensions Soc 1979–90, chm Victory Servs Club 1989–; Freeman City of London 1980; *Recreations* swimming, tennis; *Style*— Maj-Gen Laurie Gingell, CB, OBE

GINGER, Phyllis Ethel; da of Arthur James Ginger, of London, and Ethel, *née* Plimmer; *b* 19 Oct 1907; *Educ* Tiffin Girls' Sch Kingston upon Thames, Central Sch of Arts and Crafts (scholar); *m* 1940, Leslie Gordon James Durbin; 1 s (Paul Francis b 20 May 1944), 1 da (Eleanor Mary b 11 June 1949); *Career* artist; various commercial art and book illustration appts 1940s, lectr Bromley Sch of Art 1943–44; RWS 1953; *Collections* works in numerous private and public collections incl: V&A, Washington State Library, Dulwich Art Gallery, Worshipful Co of Goldsmiths; *Exhibitions* recent exhbns incl: Spring Exhbn RWS (featured artist) 1990, Nevill Gallery Canterbury 1990, Spanish Watercolour Soc touring exhbn of Spain with RWS membs 1992, various RWS exhbns Century Gallery Datchet Berks 1991–95; *Recreations* drawing, music, reading, theatre gp; *Style*— Miss Phyllis Ginger; ✉ 298 Kew Road, Kew, Richmond, Surrey TW9 3DU (☎ 0181 940 2221)

GINNINGS, Paul David; s of David John Ginnings, of Fordingbridge, Hants, and Betty Christina, *née* Ogle; *b* 22 July 1946; *Educ* Monkton Combe Sch; *m* Gillian, da of Leslie Saunders; 3 da (Alison b 8 Nov 1975, Hazel b 22 Sept 1978, Miriam b 10 Oct 1980); *Career* audit sr Norton Keen & Co 1969–72 (articled clerk 1964–69, qualified chartered accountant 1969), mangr Robson Rhodes 1972–74, mangr then ptnr Temple Gothard 1974–85, ptnr Touche Ross (now Deloitte & Touche) 1985–; FCA 1970; *Books* Financial Management of Housing Associations - A Practical Guide (1989), Tolley's Client and Advisor Guide on Housing Associations (1995); *Recreations* fly-fishing, church activities, skiing; *Style*— Paul Ginnings, Esq; ✉ 96 Clarence Rd, St Albans, Herts AL1 4NQ (☎ 01727 853468); Deloitte & Touche, Hill House, 1 Little New St, London EC4A 3TR (☎ 0171 936 3000, fax 0171 583 8517)

GINSBERG, Dr Lionel; s of Henry Ginsberg (d 1989), of London, and Rosalind, *née* Veltman; *b* 18 April 1955; *Educ* Haberdashers' Aske's Sch Elstree Herts, Middx Hosp Med Sch Univ of London (BSc, PhD, MB BS, Betuel prize, FRCP); *m* 8 June 1980, Dr Andrea Marguerite Cobon (d 1995), da of Herbert Frederick Cobon; 2 da (Amelia b 16 Feb 1984, Constance May b 1 June 1989), 2 s (Louis b 12 July 1985 d 26 Nov 1985, Tobias b 11 Jan 1988); *Career* MRC res student Dept of Biology as Applied to Med Middx Hosp Med Sch 1976–79, visiting specialist Nat Insts of Health Bethesda Maryland USA 1981, house physician The Middx Hosp 1982–83, house surgn N Middx Hosp 1983; SHO: in gen med (endocrinology and metabolism) Hammersmith Hosp 1983–84, in neurology The Nat Hosp Queen Square 1984; resident med offr in cardiology Nat Heart Hosp 1984–85, locum med registrar St Mary's Hosp Paddington 1985; registrar: in med (endocrinology) Hammersmith Hosp 1985, in neurology Royal Free Hosp 1985–87, in neurology The Nat Hosps 1987–88; visiting scientist Nat Insts of Health Bethesda Maryland 1988–89, clinical lectr in neurology Univ of Cambridge and hon sr registrar in neurology Addenbrooke's Hosp 1990–92, sr lectr in neurology Royal Free Hosp Sch of Med and Inst of Neurology Univ of London 1992–, conslt neurologist Royal Free Hosp, Nat Hosp for Neurology and Neurosurgery Queen Square and Queen Elizabeth II Hosp Welwyn Garden City 1992–; memb Assoc of Br Neurologists 1992; *Publications* author of numerous research articles in academic jls; *Recreations* pianoforte, walking, reading; *Style*— Dr Lionel Ginsberg; ✉ 26 High Street, Whittlesford, Cambridge CB2 4LT (☎ 01223 834702); Department of Clinical Neurosciences, Royal Free Hospital School of Medicine, Rowland Hill Street, London NW3 2PF (☎ 0171 830 2012, fax 0171 431 1577)

GINSBORG, Michael David; s of Samuel Ginsborg (d 1986), of Gerrards Cross, Bucks, and Rose, *née* Gabe; *b* 25 April 1943; *Educ* Westminster, King's Coll London, Central Sch of Art & Design (DipAD), Chelsea Sch of Art (Higher DipAD); *m* 1972, Rosamund (Robby) da of John Ducane Nelson; 2 da (Katharine (Teeny) b 3 Aug 1972, (Sonya) Charlotte b 2 Dec 1974); *Career* artist and educator; lectr and examiner numerous UK art schs 1969–, pt/t tutor Wimbledon Sch of Art until 1979, sessional lectr Univ of Reading, head of painting Ravensbourne Coll until 1984, head Sch of Fine Arts Birmingham Poly 1989–91 (course dir Masters Degree in Fine Arts 1984–89), head of fine art Wimbledon Sch of Art 1991–; *Solo Exhibitions* Lisson Gallery 1969, Serpentine Gallery 1973, City Museum Bolton 1976, Acme Gallery London 1980, Benjamin Rhodes Gallery 1986, 1989 and 1992; *Group Exhibitions* incl: British Painting (Royal Acad) 1977, Recent Acquisitions (Hayward) 1978, British Art Show 1979, British Abstract Art Part 1: Painting (Flowers East) 1994; *Work in Collections* Govt Art Collection, Br Cncl, Dept of the Environment, Arts Cncl of GB and in many other collections in UK, Europe and USA; cmmnd to paint St Charles' Hospital Centenary Murals 1981 and 1982, wall construction Glaxo Wellcome Medicines Research Centre Stevenage 1994; *Awards* incl: first prize Univ of London Painting Competition 1963, prizewinner Cleveland Drawing Biennale 1975, Visual Arts award Greater London Arts Assoc 1976, Arts Cncl Bursary 1977, Mark Rothko Meml award 1979; memb Register of Specialist Advsrs CNAA until 1992; *Style*— Michael Ginsborg, Esq; ✉ Jason and Rhodes Gallery, 4 New Burlington Place, London W1X 1SB (☎ 0171 434 1768/9, fax 0171 237 8841)

GIORDANO, Richard Vincent; Hon KBE (1989); s of late Vincent Giordano, and Cynthia Giordano; *b* 23 March 1934, March; *Educ* Harvard (BA), Columbia Univ Law

Sch (LLB); *m* 1956, Barbara Claire Beckett; 1 s, 2 da; *Career* lawyer Shearman & Sterling NYC until 1963; Airco Inc: joined as asst sec 1963, pres, chief operating off and bd dir 1971, chief exec 1978–79; BOC Group: dir following takeover of Airco 1978, gp md and chief exec 1979–91, chm 1985–91, non-exec dir 1991–96; non-exec dep chm Grand Metropolitan plc 1991– (dir 1984–), chm British Gas plc 1994–; also non-exec dir: National Power plc (formerly CEGB) 1982–92, Georgia Pacific Corp Atlanta GA 1984–, Reuters Holdings plc 1991–94, RTZ Corporation plc 1992– (non-exec dir CRA Ltd Dec 1995–), Lucas Lucas Industries plc 1993–94; *Recreations* ocean sailing, tennis; *Clubs* The Links, New York Yacht, Edgartown Yacht (Mass), Duquesne (Pittsburgh PA); *Style—* Richard Giordano, Esq, KBE; ✉ British Gas plc, The Adelphi, John Adam Street, London WC2N 6JT (☎ 0171 321 2880)

GIOVENE, Laurence (Duca di Girasole); s of Andrea Giovene, Duca Di Girasole (d 1995), of Palazzo Ciervo St Agata Del Goti, BV, Italy, and Adeline Constance, *née* Schuberth; *b* 21 Nov 1936; *Educ* Solihull Sch, St Catharine's Coll Cambridge (MA); *Career* barr; standing counsel to Italian Govt 1965–85, dep circuit judge 1978, recorder 1986; Parliamentary candidate (Cons) East-Ham North 1965, Fulham Borough cncllr 1962–64; pres Cambridge Union 1960; *Recreations* sailing, oil painting; *Clubs* Garrick, Bar Yacht; *Style—* Laurence Giovene, Esq; ✉ 2 Pump Court, Temple, London EC4 (☎ 0171 353 5597)

GIPPS, Dr Ruth Dorothy Louisa; MBE (1981); da of Gerard Cardew Bryan Gipps (d 1956), and Hélène Bettina, *née* Johner (d 1965); *b* 20 Feb 1921; *Educ* Bexhill Sch of Music, RCM (scholar, ARCM), Univ of Durham (external BMus and DMus); *m* 19 March 1942, Robert George Hugh Baker; 1 s (Lance Robert b 24 May 1947); *Career* professional solo pianist 1931–53, freelance oboist 1943, CBSO 1944–45, chorus master City of Birmingham Choir 1948–50, extramural lectr Univ of Oxford 1948–59, prof Trinity Coll London 1959–66, prof RCM 1967–77, princ lectr Kingston Polytechnic 1977–79; fndr and conductor: London Repertoire Orchestra (formerly One Rehearsal Orchestra) 1955–86, London Chanticleer Orch 1961–; conductor: Rondel Ensemble (ten wind) 1987–, Heathfield Choral Soc 1990–92, Chalvington Singers 1992–94, recording Music for the Rondel Ensemble 1993; organist: Holy Trinity High Hurstwood 1986–90, Ripe with Chalvington 1990–93; compositions incl: 5 symphonies, 5 concertos, choral works, chamber music; pres Hastings Festival 1956–87, chm Composers' Guild of GB 1967; FRSA 1950, Hon RAM 1966, FRCM 1972; *Recreations* country things, keeping animals, Tudor architecture; *Style—* Dr Ruth Gipps, MBE; ✉ Tickerage Castle, Pound Lane, Framfield, Uckfield, East Sussex TN22 5RT (☎ 01825 890348)

GIRAUD, André L Y; *b* 3 April 1925, Bordeaux; *Educ* Ecole Polytechnique Paris, Ecole Nationale Supérieure des Mines Paris, Ecole Nationale Supérieure du Pétrole Paris; *Career* trg in US petrochemical industry 1949–50, various research then mgmnt positions rising to exec vice pres Inst of Petroleum France 1951–64, head of Oil Directorate Miny of Industry France 1964–69, chief aide to Min of Educn 1969–70, chm Atomic Energy Commissariat 1970–78, sec of state for energy and industry under Valéry Giscard d'Estaing 1978–81, prof of geopolitics of energy and raw materials, industl policy and technol mgmnt Paris-Dauphine Univ and international conslt 1981–86, sec of state for defence under Jacques Chirac 1986–88, international conslt 1988–, pres Compagnie Générale d'Innovation et de Développement (COGIDEV) 1990–, chm Int Advsy Bd ELF Aquitaine 1994–; non-exec dir: GEC plc until 1995, Banque Arjil, Cristalleria Espanola, SOFRES; former dir: Regie Nationale des Usines Renault (dep chm), ELF, TOTAL, Electricité de France, Aérospatiale; chm French Scientific Cncl of Defence 1994, pres Ecole Polytechnique Paris 1974–78; memb US Nat Acad of Engrg; Henry de Wolfe-Smythe Award American Nuclear Soc, Foratom Award European Nuclear Soc, Hon Medal French Nuclear Soc; Cdr Légion d'Honneur; *Style—* A L Y Giraud, Esq; ✉ Compagnie Générale d'Innovation et de Développement (COGIDEV), 370 avenue Napoléon Bonaparte, 92500 Rueil-Malmaison, France (☎ 00 33 1 47 16 83 50, fax 00 33 1 47 16 83 60)

GIRDWOOD, Prof Ronald Haxton; CBE (1984); s of Thomas Girdwood (d 1933), of Polwarth Grove, Edinburgh, and Mary Elizabeth, *née* Haxton (d 1952); *b* 19 March 1917; *Educ* Daniel Stewart's Coll Edinburgh, Univ of Edinburgh (MB ChB, MD, PhD); *m* 1945, Mary Elizabeth, da of Reginald Ralph Williams (d 1965), of Calstock, Cornwall; 1 s (Richard), 1 da (Diana); *Career* RAMC Offr 1942–46, A/Lt-Col, served in India and Burma; Univ of Edinburgh: lectr in med 1946–51, sr lectr then reader 1951–62, prof of therapeutics and clinical pharmacology 1962–82, dean Faculty of Medicine 1975–79; conslt physician Royal Infirmary of Edinburgh 1951–82; Rockefeller research fell Univ of Michigan 1948–49; over 350 papers in med jls particularly relating to haematology, clinical pharmacology and med history; pres: RCPEd 1982–85 (vice pres 1980–82), Univ of Edinburgh Graduates' Assoc 1991–93; chm: Scot Nat Blood Transfusion Assoc 1980–95, Medico Pharmaceutical Forum 1985–87; memb Bd of Govrs St Columba Hospice 1985–; Oliver Meml Award for Services to Blood Transfusion 1991; Freedom of township of Sirajgunj Bangladesh 1984; Hon FRACP, Hon FACP, FRCPE, FRCPLond, FRCPI, FRCPath, FRSE 1978; *Books* Malabsorption (co-ed, 1969), Textbook of Medical Treatment (12 edn 1971, 15 edn 1987, Spanish ed 1992), Blood Disorders due to Drugs and other Agents (ed, 1973), Clinical Pharmacology (23 edn 1976, 25 edn 1984), Travels with a Stethoscope (1991); *Recreations* writing, photography, painting in oils; *Clubs* East India, Edinburgh Univ Staff; *Style—* Prof Ronald Girdwood, CBE, FRSE; ✉ 2 Hermitage Drive, Edinburgh EH10 6DD (☎ 0131 447 5137)

GIRLING, John Anthony (Tony); s of James William Girling, OBE, of Birchington, Kent, and Annie Doris, *née* Reeves; *b* 21 Aug 1943; *Educ* Tonbridge, Coll of Law Guildford; *m* 26 March 1965, Lynne, da of late Raymond Hubert Roland Davis; 1 da (Samantha Helen Dixon b 25 Nov 1968), 1 s (Richard Warwick b 19 March 1971); *Career* admitted slr 1966, ptnr Girlings 1966– (chm and managing ptnr 1985–96); pres Law Soc of England & Wales 1996–97 (memb Cncl 1980–96); High Court costs assessor 1982; pres: Kent Law Soc 1982, Isle of Thanet Law Soc 1987, Slrs' Benevolent Assoc; fndr memb Herne Bay Round Table (chm 1978), hon sec Herne Bay Rotary Club 1969–72; memb Law Soc 1966, NP 1968; *Recreations* skiing, golf, travel, reading; *Clubs* Canterbury Golf; *Style—* Tony Girling, Esq; ✉ Maypole House, Hoath, Canterbury, Kent CT3 4LN (☎ 01227 860332); Girlings, 158 High Street, Herne Bay, Kent CT6 5NP (☎ 01227 373874, fax 01227 365897)

GIROLAMI, Sir Paul; kt (1988); s of Peter Girolami (d 1956); *b* 25 Jan 1926; *Educ* LSE (BCom); *m* 1952, Christabel Mary Gwynne, *née* Lewis; 2 s, 1 da; *Career* Chantrey and Button CAs 1950–54, Coopers and Lybrand 1954–65; Glaxo Holdings: fin controller 1965, memb and fin dir 1968, chief exec 1980–85, dep chm 1985, chm 1985–94; pres Glaxo Finanziaria SpA Italy; dir: Nippon Glaxo Ltd Japan, Glaxo-Sankyo Ltd Japan, Credito Italiano International 1990–92, Forte plc 1992–96; memb: CBI Cncl 1986–93, Appeal Ctee of ICA 1987, Stock Exchange Listed Cos Advsy Ctee 1987–92; dir American C of C (UK) 1983, chm Senate of Bd for Chartered Accountants in Business 1989; Grande Ufficiale Ordine al Merito della Repubblica Italiana 1987, Cavaliere del Lavoro della Repubblica Italiana 1991; City and Guilds Insignia award in Technol 1988, Hon DSC Univ of Aston 1990, Accademico award Rome Acad of Med and Biological Sciences 1990, Hon DSc Trieste Univ 1991, Hon DSc Sunderland Poly 1991, Hon LLD Nat Univ of Singapore 1993; Order of the Rising Sun Gold Rays with Neck Ribbon (Japan) 1991; Freeman City of London 1980, Prime Warden Worshipful Co of Goldsmiths 1995 (memb Ct of Assts 1986), memb Worshipful Soc of Apothecaries 1993, Liveryman Worshipful Co of Chartered Accountants; hon fell LSE 1989; FCA; *Recreations* reading; *Style—* Sir Paul Girolami; ✉ Forte plc, 166 High Holborn, London WC1V 6TT

GIROUARD, Mark; s of Richard Désiré Girouard (d 1989; s of Col Sir Percy Girouard, KCMG, DSO, sometime govr N Nigeria and British E Africa Protectorates, and Mary, da of Hon Sir Richard Solomon, GCMG, KCB, KCVO), and his 1 w, Lady Blanche, *née* de la Poer Beresford, da of 6 Marquess of Waterford, KP; *b* 7 Oct 1931; *Educ* Ampleforth, ChCh Oxford (MA), Courtauld Inst of Art (PhD), Bartlett Sch UCL (BSc); *m* 1970, Dorothy N Dorf; 1 da; *Career* writer and architectural historian; Slade prof of fine art Univ of Oxford 1975–76; memb: Royal Fine Art Cmmn 1972–, Royal Cmmn on Hist Monuments 1976–81, Hist Bldgs Cncl 1978–84, Cncl Victorian Soc 1979– (fndr memb 1958); Hon DLitt Univ of Leicester 1982; FSA 1986, Hon FRIBA 1980; *Clubs* Beefsteak; *Style—* Mark Girouard, Esq, FSA; ✉ 35 Colville Rd, London W11 2BT

GIRVAN, Hon Mr Justice; Hon Sir (Frederick) Paul; kt (1995); s of Robert Frederick Girvan, of Holywood, Belfast, and Martha Patricia, *née* Barron (d 1989); *b* 20 Oct 1948; *Educ* Larne GS, Belfast Royal Acad, Clare Coll Cambridge (BA), Queen's Univ Belfast (barrister-at-law); *m* 20 July 1974, Karen Elizabeth, *née* Joyce; 1 da (Rebecca Jane b 19 March 1977), 2 s (Brian Richard b 12 Dec 1978, Peter Michael b 19 Jan 1980); *Career* called to the Bar NI 1971, called to the Inner Bar (QC) 1984, jr crown counsel (Chancery) 1981–84, judge of the High Court of Justice NI 1995–; memb: NI Cncl of Law Reporting 1985–, Standing Advsy Ctee on Human Rights 1985–87, NI Law Reform Advsy Ctee 1994–; *Recreations* reading, travel, badminton, cycling, walking, modern languages, cooking; *Style—* The Hon Mr Justice Girvan; ✉ The Royal Courts of Justice, Chichester Street, Belfast BT1 3JF (☎ 01232 32111)

GISBOROUGH, 3 Baron (UK 1917); Thomas Richard John Long Chaloner; JP (Langbaurgh East 1981); s of 2 Baron Gisborough, TD, JP (d 1951); *b* 1 July 1927; *Educ* Eton, RAC Cirencester; *m* 26 April 1960, Shane, er da of late Sidney Arthur Newton, of Hyde Park Gate, SW7 (2 s of Sir Louis Newton, 1 Bt); 2 s; *Heir* s, Hon Thomas Peregrine Long Chaloner; *Career* served 16th/5th Lancers, Northumberland Hussars TA; sits as Cons peer in House of Lords; former Lt-Col Green Howards (TA); farmer and landowner; cncllr of North Riding and then Cleveland 1964–77; Lord Lt Cleveland 1981–96; Lieut N Yorkshire 1996–; Hon Col Cleveland Cadet Force 1981–92; memb Devpt Cmmn 1985–89; pres Nat Ski Fedn 1985–90; KStJ; *Recreations* gliding, bridge, piano, tennis, field sports, skiing; *Clubs* White's; *Style—* The Rt Hon the Lord Gisborough, JP; ✉ 37 Bury Walk, London SW3 (☎ 0171 581 0260); Gisborough House, Guisborough, Cleveland (☎ 01287 632002)

GISH, Sheila; *Educ* Royal Sch for Daughters of the Offrs of the Army (Bath), RADA; *ptnr* Denis Lawson; 2 da (Louise, Kay); *Career* actress; *Theatre* incl: Twelfth Night (Prospect), Robert and Elizabeth (musical, Lyric), Confusions (Apollo, Clarence Derwent Award), Vieux Carre (Piccadilly), Stagestruck (Vaudeville), The Triumph of Death (Theatre Royal Birmingham) 1981, Rain from Heaven (Oxford Playhouse) 1982, Berenice (Lyric Hammersmith, Evening Standard Award nomination) 1982, Uncle Vanya (Haymarket) 1982, A Patriot for Me (Chichester Fest) 1983, A Street Car Named Desire (Greenwich, Mermaid, Evening Standard Award nomination) 1983–84, Rough Crossing (NT) 1984, Intermezzo (Greenwich) 1985, Biography (Greenwich) 1985, The Cocktail Party (Bath, West End) 1986, Ashes (Bush) 1986–87, When She Danced (Kings Head) 1988, The Debutante Ball (Hampstead) 1989, Sara (Cheek By Jowl) 1990, What the Butler Saw (Hampstead, Wyndhams) 1990–91, Electra (Riverside Studios & Bobigney) 1991–92, The Treatment (Royal Court) 1993, Les Parents Terribles (RNT, Evening Standard and Olivier Award nominations) 1994, Company (Donmar, Olivier Award for Best Supporting Actress in a Musical 1996) 1995, Company (Albery) 1996; *Television* incl: for LWT incl: Seven Faces of Woman, Affairs of the Heart, Helen - A Woman of Today (series), The Gentle Touch; for BBC Incl: That Uncertain Feeling 1985, Queenie - Born in the Gardens 1986, Anna Karenina, The House of Eliott 1991, Ghostbusters of East Finchley 1995, Jonathan Creek; other credits incl: The Sweeney (Euston Films), The Life Swappers (Thames), Small World (Granada) 1987, The Kept Man (TVS) 1989, Boon (Central) 1989, Stanley and the Women 1991, Jewels (NBC/De Luxe), Resnick (Central), Inspector Morse (Zenith Films) 1992, Brighton Belles (Carlton) 1993/94, The Perfect Match (Granada) 1995, Thin Blue Line (Tiger TV for ITV) 1995, Pie in the Sky (SelecTV); *Films* incl: Darling, The Reckoning, A Day in the Death of Joe Egg, Hitler - the Last Ten Days, Quartet, Highlander 1985, Separate Rooms 1989, Sea-Side (Tiger TV for ITV) 1995; *Style—* Ms Sheila Gish; ✉ c/o Conway van Gelder Robinson Ltd, 18–21 Jermyn Street, London SW1Y 6HP (☎ 0171 287 0077, fax 0171 287 1940)

GITTINGS, (Harold) John; s of Harold William Gittings (decd), of Surrey, and Doris Marjorie, *née* Whiting; *b* 3 Sept 1947; *Educ* Duke of Yorks Sch Dover; *m* 22 July 1988, Andrea Mary (d 1995), da of Arnold Fisher, of Surrey; 1 step s (Jonathan Charles English b 1969), 1 step da (Tracey Andrea English b 1965); *Career* Beecham Group 1971–73, Peat Marwick Mitchell Hong Kong 1973–74, N M Rothschild & Sons 1974–81, Continental Illinois Bank 1981–82, md Target Group plc 1982–85, sr md Touche Remnant & Co 1985–90, chm Greenfield Group Ltd 1992–96, chm Greenfield Film Development 1994–, dep chm Citigate Albert Frank Ltd 1996–; ACIS 1972; *Recreations* entertaining, travel, gardening, theatre, cinema; *Style—* John Gittings, Esq; ✉ Jacobs Ladder, Crockham Hill, Edenbridge, Kent TN8 6TD (☎ 01732 866267); Greenfield Group, 14 Floral Street, London WC2E 9DH (☎ 0171 379 1155, fax 0171 379 0851)

GITTUS, Dr John Henry; *b* 25 July 1930; *Educ* Univ of London (BSc, DSc), KTH Stockholm (DTech); *m* 23 May 1953, Rosemary Ann, da of John Geeves; 1 s (Michael John b 7 April 1954), 2 da (Sara Ann b 19 Aug 1956, Mary Ann b 8 Aug 1958); *Career* res worker Br Cast Iron Res Assoc 1951–56 (apprentice 1947–51), gp ldr Mond Nickel R & D Laboratories Birmingham 1956–60; UKAEA: res mangr Springfields 1960–80, head of water reactor fuel devpt 1980–81, head Atomic Energy Tech Branch Harwell 1981–83, dir of water reactor res Harwell 1981–83, dir of safety 1983–87, dir of communications 1987–89; dir gen Br Nuclear Industry Forum 1989–93 (currently conslt); fndr sr ptnr John Gittus & Associates (sci and public affrs consultancy) 1993–, sr ptnr NUSYS (nuclear conslts) Paris 1995–; working memb Lloyd's Nuclear Syndicate 1996–; conslt: Argonne Nat Laboratory Chicago 1968, Oak Ridge Nat Laboratory Tennessee 1969; visiting prof: Ecole Polytechnic Federale Lausanne Switzerland 1976, Univ of Nancy 1985; Regents prof UCLA 1990–; interpreter's certificate in French; FEng 1989, FIMechE, FIM, FIS, memb MENSA; *Books* Uranium (1963), Creep, Viscoelasticity and Creep-Fracture in Solids (1976), Irradiation Effects in Crystalline Solids (1980); *Recreations* old motor cars, swimming; *Clubs* IOD, RSM; *Style—* Dr John Gittus, FEng; ✉ British Nuclear Industry Forum, 22 Buckingham Gate, London SW1E 6LB (☎ 0171 828 0116, fax 0171 828 0110); NUSYS, 9 Rue Christophe Colomb, Paris 7508, France (☎ 00 33 1 40 69 76 00, fax 00 33 1 47 20 85 96)

GIVEN, Andrew Ferguson; s of Edward F Given, CMG, CVO, of Lymington, and Phillida Naomi, *née* Bullwinkle; *b* 14 Nov 1947; *Educ* Charterhouse, Lincoln Coll Oxford; *m* 18 Sept 1971, Morwenna, da of Frederic Neil Ritchie, of Italy; 2 da (Davina, Catriona); *Career* asst to md Union Corp UK Ltd 1969–73, exec dir James Finlay Corporation 1974–75; Northern Telecom Ltd (Canada): various positions 1977–82, asst treas 1982–83, treas and controller Bell-Northern Research 1984–87, vice pres fin Northern Telecom Europe 1987–88; gp fin controller Plessey Group plc 1988–89, gp fin dir Logica plc 1990–; *Recreations* sailing, photography, model building, running; *Style—* A F Given; ✉ Nahanni Gate, Dipley, Hartley Wintney, Hampshire RG27 8JP (☎ 01252 843265);

Logica plc, 75 Hampstead Road, London NW1 2NT (☎ 0171 637 9111, fax 0171 872 9947, telex 27200)

GIZIRIAN, Most Rev Archbishop Yeghishe; s of late Sarkis Gizirian, of Damascus, Syria, and Azniv, *née* Najarian; *b* 15 July 1925; *Educ* Damascus Syria, Seminary of the Armenian Catholicate of Cilicia Antelias Lebanon; *Career* ordained celibate priest 1947, assumed pastoral duties USA 1951–81 (served NY, Newark New Jersey, Worcester Mass, Detroit Michigan, Philadelphia Pa, Boston Mass and Toronto Canada), vicar gen Eastern Dio of America 1963–65, consecrated bishop (by His Holiness Vasken I, Catholicos and Supreme Patriarch of All Armenians) and appointed Primate of the Armenian Community in UK 1982, elevated to archbishop 1993; currently pres Cncl of Oriental Orthodox Churches in London; *Publications* numerous articles in Armenian and English periodicals on religious subjects; *Style—* The Most Rev Archibishop Yeghishe Gizirian; ✉ Armenian Vicarage, Iverna Gardens, Kensington, London W8 6TP (☎ 0171 937 0152); St Sarkis Armenian Church, Iverna Gardens, Kensington, London W8 6TP (☎ 0171 937 9049)

GLADMAN, Ronald John; s of Ronald Arthur Gladman (d 1940), of Deptford, and Johanna Patricia Fifield, *née* O'Connor; *b* 19 Feb 1941; *Educ* St Edmund's Coll Ware, Pembroke Coll Cambridge (MA, LLB); *m* 29 July 1972, Wendy Anne Urling, da of John Harold Stenning (d 1993), of Ringles Cross, Uckfield; 2 s (Anthony b 1974, Richard b 1977); *Career* admitted slr 1967, worked on Cmmn of Euro Communities 1971–74, asst sec and corporate slr Reuters Holdings plc 1976–96, conslt 1996–; memb Law Soc; *Recreations* reading, music, walking, skiing; *Style—* Ronald Gladman, Esq; ✉ 16 Taylor Avenue, Kew, Richmond, Surrey TW9 4ED (☎ 0181 255 7655, fax 0181 255 1443)

GLADSTONE, Charles Angus; s and h of Sir (Erskine) William Gladstone, 7 Bt, JP, *qv*; *b* 11 April 1964; *Educ* Eton, Worcester Coll Oxford; *m* 16 April 1988, Caroline M, o da of Sir Derek Morison David Thomas, KCMG, of Lower Sloane Street, London; 1 s (Jack William b 28 July 1989), 3 da (India Kate b 3 May 1991, Tara Rosamund b 12 Oct 1992, Xanthe Flora Mali b 23 June 1995); *Career* music mgmnt, estate mgmnt; *Recreations* theatre, film, music, food, television, shooting, fishing; *Style—* Charles Gladstone, Esq; ✉ Glen Dye Lodge, Strachan, nr Banchory, Kincardineshire (☎ 01561 340202, fax 01330 850348)

GLADSTONE, David Arthur Steuart; CMG (1988); s of Thomas Steuart Gladstone (d 1971), and Muriel Irene Heron, *née* Day; *b* 1 April 1935; *Educ* ChCh Oxford (MA); *m* 29 July 1961, (Mary Elizabeth) April, da of Wing Cdr Patrick O'Brien Brunner (d 1966), of Wotton House, nr Aylesbury, Bucks; 1 s (Patrick b 1969), 1 da (Perdita b 1965); *Career* Nat Serv 2 Lt 4 RHA 1954–56; articled to Annan Dexter & Co 1959–60; FO 1960–: Arabic language student MECAS Lebanon 1960–62, 3 sec political agency Bahrain 1962–63, FO 1963–65 and 1969–72, 2 later 1 sec HM Embassy Bonn 1965–69, 1 sec and head of chancery Cairo 1972–75, political advsr BMG Berlin 1976–79, head of Western Euro Dept FCO 1979–82, HM consul-gen Marseilles 1983–87, high cmmr Sri Lanka 1987–91, chargé d'Affaires Ukraine 1992; fndr memb and chm the Barnsbury Assoc 1964–65, chm Homes for Barnsbury 1970–72; *Recreations* domestic architecture, opera, German literature; *Style—* David Gladstone, Esq, CMG; ✉ 1 Mountfort Terrace, London N1 1JJ

GLADSTONE, Sir (Erskine) William; 7 Bt (UK 1846), of Fasque and Balfour, Kincardineshire; JP (Clwyd 1982); s of Sir Charles Andrew Gladstone, 6 Bt (d 1968), and Isla Margaret, *née* Crum (d 1987); ggs of Rt Hon William Ewart Gladstone, PM; *b* 29 Oct 1925; *Educ* Eton, ChCh Oxford (MA); *m* 10 Sept 1962, Rosamund Anne, yr da of Maj Robert Alexander Hambro (d 1943), of Milton Abbey, Dorset; 2 s (Charles Angus b 1964, Robert Nicolas b 1968), 1 da (Victoria Frances (Mrs Hugo Merison) b 1967); *Heir* s, Charles Angus Gladstone, *qv* b 11 April 1964; *Career* asst master Eton 1951–61, headmaster Lancing 1961–69, chief scout of the UK and Overseas Branches 1972–82 (ret 1982); chm: World Scout Ctee 1979–81, Representative Body of the Church in Wales 1977–92, Cncl Glenalmond Coll 1982–86; DL: Flintshire 1969, Clwyd 1974; HM Lord Lt of Clwyd 1985–; *Style—* Sir William Gladstone, Bt, JP; ✉ Hawarden Castle, Flintshire CH5 3PB (☎ 01244 520210)

GLADSTONE OF CAPENOCH, Robert Hamilton; er s of John Gladstone of Capenoch, TD (d 1977), and his 2 w, Diana Rosamond Maud Fleming, *née* Hamilton; gggs of Thomas Steuart Gladstone, JP, who acquired Capenoch 1850; *b* 17 July 1953; *Educ* Eton, Magdalene Coll Cambridge (MA); *m* 16 Jan 1982, Margaret Jane, da of Brig Berenger Colborne Bradford, DSO, MBE, MC, of Kincardine, Kincardine O'Neil, Aberdeenshire; 2 s (John b 3 March 1983, Harry (twin) b 3 March 1983), 1 da (Catharine b 13 April 1986); *Career* chartered surveyor; John Sale & Partners 1974–78, Smiths-Gore 1978–; memb: Scottish Landowners' Fedn Cncl 1984–87, Timber-Growers' UK South-West Scotland Ctee 1987–; vice pres Penpont Community Cncl 1986–; FRICS 1989 (ARICS 1977); *Clubs* Whistle, '71; *Style—* Robert Gladstone of Capenoch; ✉ Capenoch, Penpont, Dumfriesshire (☎ 01848 30261); Smiths-Gore, 28 Castle St, Dumfries (☎ 01387 63066)

GLADWIN, John Warren; *see:* Guildford, Bishop of

GLADWYN, 2 Baron (UK 1960); Miles Alvery Gladwyn Jebb; s of 1 Baron Gladwyn, GCMG, GCVO, CB (d 1996), and Cynthia, *née* Noble (d 1990); *b* 3 March 1930; *Educ* Eton, Magdalen Coll Oxford (MA); *Heir* none; *Career* author; 2 Lt Welsh Gds, Pilot Offr RAFVR; sr mgmnt with British Airways until 1983; *Books* The Thames Valley Heritage Walk (1980), A Guide to the South Downs Way (1984), Walkers (1986), A Guide to the Thames Path (1988), East Anglia, an Anthology (1990), The Colleges of Oxford (1992), Suffolk (1995), The Diaries of Cynthia Gladwyn (1995); *Recreations* long distance walking; *Clubs* Brooks's, Beefsteak; *Style—* The Rt Hon Lord Gladwyn; ✉ E1 Albany, Piccadilly, London W1V 9RH

GLAISTER, Lesley Gillian; da of Leonard Oliver Richard Glaister (d 1981), and Maureen Jillian, *née* Crowley; *b* 4 Oct 1956; *Educ* Deben HS Felixstowe Suffolk, Open Univ (BA), Univ of Sheffield (MA); *m* 1, 2 Oct 1976 (m dis 1984), Christopher French; 2 s (Joseph William French b 1978, Joshua James French 1981); 1 s by subsequent partner (Leo Stewart-Glaister b 1988); m 2, 14 April 1993, Dr Robert Murphy; *Career* adult educn tutor 1982–90, full time writer and teacher of creative writing 1990–; winner: Somerset Maugham Award 1991, Betty Trask Award 1991; memb Soc of Authors 1991; FRSL 1994; *Books* Honour Thy Father (1990), Trick-or-Treat (1991), Digging to Australia (1992), Limestone and Clay (1993), Partial Eclipse (1994), Private Parts of Women (1996); *Style—* Ms Lesley Glaister, FRSL; ✉ c/o Bill Hamilton, A M Heath & Co, 79 St Martin's Lane, London WC2N 4AA (☎ 0171 836 4271, fax 0171 497 2561)

GLAISYER, Ven Hugh; s of Canon Hugh Glaisyer (d 1981), of Bickley, and Edith Frances, *née* Campbell Thomson (d 1979); *b* 20 Jan 1930; *Educ* Tonbridge, Oriel Coll Oxford (MA); *m* 1962, Alison Marion Heap, JP, da of Hubert Leslie Heap; 1 s (Simon b 1967), 2 da (Judith b 1963, Hilary b 1965); *Career* Nat Serv Flying Offr RAF 1953–55; asst curate: St Augustine's Tonge Moor Bolton 1956–62, Sidcup 1962–64; vicar Christ Church Milton next Gravesend 1964–81, rural dean Gravesend 1974–81, vicar of Hove 1981–91 (rural dean 1982–91), hon canon Chichester Cathedral 1982–, archdeacon of Lewes and Hastings 1991–; *Recreations* Shetland sheepdogs, British shorthair cats; *Style—* The Ven the Archdeacon of Lewes and Hastings; ✉ 27 The Avenue, Lewes, E Sussex BN7 1QT (☎ 01273 479530, fax 01273 476529)

GLANUSK, 4 Baron (UK 1899); Sir David Russell Bailey; 5 Bt (UK 1852); s of Hon Herbert Crawshay Bailey (d 1936; 4 s of 1 Baron) and Kathleen Mary (d 1948), da of Sir Shirley Harris Salt, 3 Bt; suc 1 cous, 3 Baron, 1948; *b* 19 Nov 1917; *Educ* Eton; *m* 25 Jan 1941, Lorna Dorothy, da of late Capt Ernest Courtenay Harold Andrews, MBE, RA; 1 s, 1 da; *Heir* s, Hon Christopher Russell Bailey; *Career* Lt-Cdr RN 1935–51; MEL Ltd 1954–64, Elliott Automation Ltd 1964–66, md Wandel & Goltermann (UK) Ltd 1966–81, chm W & G Ltd 1981–87; Liveryman: Worshipful Co of Clockmakers, Worshipful Co of Scientific Instrument Makers; *Clubs* Army & Navy; *Style—* The Rt Hon Lord Glanusk; ✉ Po Anglada Camarasa 87–2B, 07470 Puerto Pollensa, Mallorca, Spain

GLANVILL-SMITH, John Seeley; s of Arthur Glanvill-Smith, MC (d 1965), of Madeira House, Littlestone, nr New Romney, Kent, and Margaret, *née* Harris (d 1930); *b* 26 June 1924; *Educ* Bishop's Stortford Coll; *m* 1, Alison Mary (d 1972), da of Charles Aldworth Gifford Campion (d 1963); 4 da (Virginia Mary b 1948, Mary b 1950, Angela Rosemary b 1955, Fiona Frances b 1958); m 2, 3 June 1978, Barbara Joan, *née* Young; *Career* WWII 1939–45, cmmnd Lt Royal Norfolk Regt 1943, wounded 1944; chm: Glanvill Enthoven & Co Ltd 1976–80 (dep chm 1973–76, dir 1954), Jardine Glanvill 1980–82; dep chm Jardine Matheson (Insurance Brokers) 1980–82; dir: Clarkson Puckle (Insurance Brokers) 1982–87, Harris & Dixon Ltd 1987–92; chm and md Glanvill Bullen Ltd 1992–95; memb Lloyd's 1956–; pres Buckingham Branch Br Limbless Ex-Servicemen's Assoc; Freeman City of London, memb Worshipful Co of Gardeners; *Recreations* golf, gardening, cricket; *Clubs* MCC, Surrey CCC, Landsdowne, Norwegian; *Style—* John Glanvill-Smith, Esq; ✉ Weycroft Manor, Weycroft, nr Axminster, Devon EX13 7LL

GLANVILLE, Brian Lester; s of James Arthur Glanville (d 1960), and Florence, *née* Manches (d 1984); *b* 24 Sept 1931; *Educ* Charterhouse; *m* 1959, Elizabeth Pamela de Boer, da of Fritz Manasse (d 1961); 2 s (Mark, Toby), 2 da (Elizabeth, Josephine); *Career* novelist, journalist, playwright; football corr and sports columnist: The Sunday Times 1958–92, The People 1992–96, The Times 1996–; lit advsr Bodley Head 1958–62; *Books* novels incl: Along The Arno, The Bankrupts, Diamond, The Olympian, A Roman Marriage, A Second Home, The Financiers, A Cry of Crickets, Kissing America; The Catacomb short story collections: A Bad Streak, The Director's Wife, The Thing He Loves, The King of Hackney Marshes, Love is Not Love; stage musical Underneath The Arches (co-author, 1982–83); play A Visit to the Villa (for stage and radio); *Recreations* playing football; *Clubs* Chelsea Casuals; *Style—* Brian Glanville, Esq; ✉ 160 Holland Park Avenue, London W11 4UH (☎ 0171 603 6908)

GLASBY, (Alfred) Ian; s of Frederick William Glasby (d 1942), of Doncaster, S Yorks, and Harriet Maria, *née* Claridge (d 1974); *b* 18 Sept 1931; *Educ* Doncaster GS, LSE (BSc); *m* 19 June 1970, Velia Herma Maureen, da of Harry Smith, of Bradford on Avon, Wiltshire; 1 da (Beth b 23 June 1973); *Career* Nat Serv Intelligence Corps BAOR 1950–52; Home Office 1953–68, FCO 1968–71, second and first commercial sec Br Embassy Washington DC 1971–76, dep high cmmr Kampala 1976, head Br Interests Section French Embassy Kampala 1976–77, first sec, head of chancery and HM consul Yaounde Cameroon 1977–81, non-resident charge d'affaires Gabon Equatorial Guineau and Central African Empire 1977–81, asst head Consular Dept FCO London 1981–84, dep consul gen Sydney Aust 1984–88, HM Ambassador Brazzaville People's Republic of Congo 1988–91; dir: Trust Company of Australia Ltd, Truco (Australia) Europe Ltd; currently int commercial affrs conslt; *Recreations* rugby, cricket, gardening; *Clubs* Australian Pioneers (Sydney), NSW Rugby (Aust), Royal Cwlth Soc; *Style—* Ian Glasby, Esq; ✉ High Pitch, Strande Lane, Cookham, Maidenhead, Berks SL6 9DW (☎ 016285 28054); 5 rue du Collet, 06530 Spéracèdes, Grasse, France (☎ 00 33 93 60 53 11)

GLASER, Dr Mark Gordon; s of Asher Alfred Glaser (d 1987), and Minnie, *née* Nasilewitz (d 1983); *b* 1 Dec 1944; *Educ* St Clement Dane's GS, Charing Cross Hosp Med Sch (MB BS, MRCS LRCP, DMRT); *Career* conslt in radiotherapy and oncology Charing Cross Hosp 1980–, hon conslt radiotherapist Hammersmith Hosp and Postgrad Med Sch 1980–, clinical teacher Univ of London 1981–, clinical dir Riverside Health Authy Cancer Servs 1990–, dir Depts of Radiotherapy Hammersmith and Charing Cross Hosp 1994–; visiting prof Yale Univ USA 1984; author of papers on cancer and radiation therapy; memb Univ of London Senate 1981–, Military Educn Ctee 1982–84, Central Res Fund Ctee 1982–84, Collegiate Cncl 1987–89, Academic Cncl 1989–; FFRRCSI 1977, FRCR 1978; *Recreations* walking, philosophy, comparative religion; *Clubs* Reform; *Style—* Dr Mark Glaser; ✉ Department of Radiotherapy and Oncology, Charing Cross Hospital, Fulham Palace Road, London W6 8RF (☎ 0181 846 1733)

GLASGOW, David George; s of Tom Glasgow, of Kingston-upon-Thames, Surrey, and Betty Madelaine, *née* Wells; *b* 18 Oct 1942; *Educ* King's Coll Sch Wimbledon, RNC Dartmouth; *m* 5 Oct 1985, Bridget Gay Elizabeth, da of Joseph Stanley (John) Watson, MBE, QC (d 1991), and Elizabeth Watson, of Mickleham, Surrey; *Career* Lt RN; qualified naval interpreter (Italian); served: HMS Arethusa 1965–67, rotary wing pilot 1967, HMS Albion 1967–70, HMS Cleopatra 1970–72, ret 1973; clerk Burge & Co Stockbrokers 1973–74, tech dir Schlesinger Tst Mangrs Ltd 1976–79 (joined 1974); Abbey Life Gp 1979–87: investmt mktg dir, md Abbey Unit Tsts Mangrs Ltd; dir Kleinwort Benson Investmt Mgmnt 1987–94, dep chm Kleinwort Benson Unit Tsts Ltd 1990–91; chief exec offr Creditanstalt-SCG Fund Management Warsaw 1994–96, currently pres and ceo Creditanstalt/BG 2 Korona Trust Fund Corp Warsaw; chm Unit Tst Customer Standards Ctee 1986–90, chm Unit Tst Assoc External Rels Ctee 1986–90, dir Insur Ombudsman Bureau 1989–91; hon sec Castaways Club 1983–94; memb Int Stock Exchange 1987; *Recreations* sailing, music, theatre, skiing; *Clubs* Royal Ocean Racing, Royal London Yacht; *Style—* David Glasgow, Esq; ✉ Inwardleigh Cottage, Rockbourne, Fordingbridge, Hants SP6 3ML (☎ 01725 518500, fax 01725 518700)

GLASGOW, Edwin John; QC (1987); s of Richard Edwin Glasgow, and Mary, *née* Markby; *b* 3 Aug 1945; *Educ* St Joseph's Coll Ipswich, UCL; *m* 1967, Janet, *née* Coleman; 1 s (Oliver Edwin James b 17 Jan 1971), 1 da (Louise Victoria Mary b 20 March 1972); *Career* Met Police 1961–64; called to the Bar Gray's Inn 1969; chm Fin Reporting Review Panel 1991–, bencher Gray's Inn 1994; tstee London Opera Players, chm Mary Glasgow Language Tst; *Recreations* music, family, France; *Clubs* RAC (steward); *Style—* Edwin Glasgow, Esq, QC; ✉ Copper Hall, Thames Ditton, Surrey KT7 0BX; Entrechaux, Vaulcluse, France; 39 Essex Street, London WC2R 3AT (☎ 0171 353 4741)

GLASGOW, 10 Earl of (S 1703); Patrick Robin Archibald Boyle; also Lord Boyle (S 1699), Lord Boyle of Kelburn (S 1703), Baron Fairlie (UK 1897); s of Rear Adm 9 Earl of Glasgow, CB, DSC (d 1984), and his 1 wife Dorothea, only da of Sir Archibald Lyle, 2 Bt, now Dorothea, Viscountess Kelburn; *b* 30 July 1939; *Educ* Eton, Sorbonne; *m* 29 Nov 1975, Isabel Mary, da of George Douglas James; 1 s (Hon David Boyle b 1978), 1 da (Lady Alice Dorothy b 1981); *Heir* s, Hon David Boyle (does not use courtesy title of Viscount of Kelburn); *Career* Sub-Lt RNR 1960; known professionally as Patrick Boyle; asst dir Woodfall Films 1961–64, freelance asst dir 1965–68, TV documentary producer/dir Yorkshire Television 1968–70; freelance TV documentary producer/dir working for BBC, Yorkshire Television, ATV, Central and Scottish Television 1971–81; formed Kelburn Country Centre (a leisure park created from part of the family estate) 1977, currently managing Kelburn Country Centre; chm: Largs & Dist Tourist Bd 1987–89, Largs Viking Festival 1981–85; *Recreations* theatre, cinema, skiing; *Style—* The Rt Hon the Earl of Glasgow; ✉ Kelburn, Fairlie, Ayrshire KA29 OBE (☎ 01475 568204); Kelburn Country Centre, Fairlie, Ayrshire KA29 OBE (☎ 01475 568685)

GLASGOW, Archbishop of (RC) 1974–; Most Rev Thomas Joseph Cardinal Winning; s of Thomas Winning (d 1959), and Agnes, *née* Canning (d 1954); *b* 3 June 1925; *Educ* Our Lady's HS Motherwell, Blairs Coll Aberdeen, St Peter's Coll Bearsden, Pontifical Scots Coll and Pontifical Gregorian Univ Rome (STL, DCL); *Career* ordained priest 1948; spiritual dir Pontifical Scots Coll Rome 1961–66, pres Scottish Catholic Tbnl 1970–71, aux bishop Glasgow 1971–74; pres Bishops Conf Scotland 1985; Hon DD Univ of Glasgow 1983, Hon DUniv Strathclyde 1992, Hon LLD Univ of Aberdeen 1996; hon fell Educnl Inst of Scotland 1986, Grand Prior of the Scottish Lieutenancy of the Equestrian Order of the Holy Sepulchre of Jerusalem 1989, cr a cardinal of the Holy Roman Church 1994; Hon FRSE 1996; *Recreations* golf, watching football; *Style*— His Eminence the Archbishop of Glasgow; ✉ 40 Newlands Rd, Glasgow G43 2JD; vicariate: Curial Office, 196 Clyde St, Glasgow G1 4JY (☎ 0141 226 5898, fax 0141 225 2600)

GLASGOW AND GALLOWAY, Bishop of 1991–; Rt Rev John Mitchell Taylor; *b* 23 May 1932; *Educ* Banff Acad, Univ of Aberdeen (MA), Edinburgh Theol Coll; *m* Edna Elizabeth; 1 da (Dr Alison Margaret Taylor b 20 Nov 1959), 1 s (Malcolm John b 21 Nov 1961); *Career* curate St Margaret's Aberdeen 1956–58; rector: Holy Cross Glasgow 1958–64, St Ninian's Glasgow 1964–73, St John's Dumfries 1973–91; *Recreations* fishing, sketching, hill walking, music; *Style*— The Rt Rev the Bishop of Glasgow and Galloway; ✉ Bishop's House, 25 Quadrant Road, Newlands, Glasgow G43 2QP (☎ and fax 0141 633 5877)

GLASS, Anthony Trevor; QC (1986); s of Percy Glass (d 1946); *b* 6 June 1940; *Educ* Royal Masonic Sch, Lincoln Coll Oxford (MA); *m* 30 April 1966, Deborah, da of late Dr William Wall, and late Katharine Wall, of Rocky Mount, North Carolina, USA; 1 s (James b 1969), 1 da (Emily b 1970); *Career* called to the Bar Inner Temple 1965, bencher 1995; recorder of the Crown Court 1985–; *Recreations* antique collecting, music; *Style*— Anthony Glass, Esq, QC; ✉ Queen Elizabeth Building, Temple, London EC4 (☎ 0171 583 5766, fax 0171 353 0339)

GLASS, David Peter; s of Max Glass, of Lisbon, Portugal, and Sigrid, *née* Dressler; *b* 9 Dec 1957, Zurich; *Educ* Boundstone Comp Sch, London Sch of Contemporary Dance, Ecole Etienne Decroux Paris, Alvin Ailey Sch New York, Jean Louis Barrault Carré Sch Paris; *m* 13 Aug 1993, Peta Lily; *Career* writer and dir 1982–; dancer and mime artist with Community Arts Theatre 1976–77, street theatre France, England and Italy 1977, began int solo career 1977; written and directed shows incl: Phoenix Dance Co, English Dance Theatre, Nottingham Playhouse, Crucible Theatre, Mime Theatre Project, Scottish Opera, Opera Circus, Scottish Chamber Orchestra, Hong Kong Symphony Orchestra; artistic dir David Glass Ensemble 1988–; David Glass Ensemble prodns incl: first adaptation of Popeye 1989, Gormenghast 1991, Les Enfants du Paradis 1993, The Mosquito Coast (Young Vic) 1995, Lucky (Young Vic) 1995, first musical adaptation of La Dolce Vita 1996; assoc dir feature film Beg!, movement conslt Mad and her Dad (Lyric) 1995; artistic dir Br Summer Sch of Mime, fndr and artistic dir of Southern Int Mime Festival; teacher Central Establishment of Physical Theatre; memb Panel Arts Cncl; *Style*— David Glass, Esq; ✉ David Glass Ensemble, 6 Aberdeen Studios, 22 Highbury Grove, London N5 2EA (☎ 0171 354 9200, fax 0171 354 0625)

GLASS, Martin; JP (1986); s of Harry Glass (d 1959), of Swansea, and Bella, *née* Cohen (d 1975); *b* 27 Sept 1935; *Educ* Swansea GS, UWIST (Dip Arch); *m* 12 May 1963, Norma Marcia, da of Hyman Corrick (d 1983), of Swansea; 2 da (Deborah b 1965, Judith b 1967); *Career* CA; princ of Martin Glass Chartered Architects 1960–96, conslt W Griffiths & Glass (architects and surveyors) 1996–; RIBA; *Clubs* Rotary (Swansea); *Style*— Martin Glass, Esq, JP; ✉ 6 Richmond Villas, Ffynone, Swansea, W Glamorgan SA1 6DQ (☎ 01792 472331); Martin Glass Chartered Architect, 101 Walter Rd, Swansea, W Glamorgan SA1 5QF (☎ 01792 464123/651532, fax 01792 470535, e-mail 100 534,3545)

GLASS, Norman Jeffrey; s of Philip Glass (d 1975), and Anne, *née* Stein; *b* 31 May 1946; *Educ* Stratford Coll Dublin, Trinity Coll Dublin (BA), Univ of Amsterdam (MSc); *m* 1974, Marieanne, *née* Verger; 1 da (Anne-Sophie b 21 Oct 1978), 1 s (Jerome b 11 Oct 1980); *Career* economist: Shell-Mex & BP Co Ltd 1969–70, Economic Models Ltd 1970–72; lectr Univ of Newcastle upon Tyne 1972–74, research scholar Int Inst for Applied Systems Analysis (IIASA) Austria 1974–75; economist: DHSS 1975–77, HM Treasy 1977–79, Exchequer and Audit Dept 1979–81; sr economist DHSS 1981–86, asst sec Dept of Health 1986–89, chief economist DSS 1989–92, chief economist DOE 1992–95, dep dir HM Treasy 1995–; *Recreations* windsurfing, choral singing, going for short walks; *Style*— Norman Glass, Esq; ✉ HM Treasury, Parliament Street, London SW1P 3AG (☎ 0171 270 4439, fax 0171 270 5807)

GLASSER, Cyril; s of late Phillip Glasser, and late Eva Glasser; *b* 31 Jan 1942; *Educ* Raine's Fndn GS, LSE (LLB, LLM); *Career* admitted slr 1967; Sheridans: ptnr and head of Litigation Dept 1977–, managing ptnr 1989–; Lord Chllr's Dept: special conslt Legal Aid Advsy Ctee 1974–77, memb Working Party to Review Legal Aid Legislation 1974–77; chm Legal Aid Fin Provisions Working Party Legal Aid Advsy Ctee 1975–77, memb Social Sci and Law Ctee SSRC 1979–83; visiting prof of law UCL 1987–; co-fndr and a dir Legal Action Gp 1972–74, memb Cncl of Mgmnt Inst of Judicial Admin Univ of Birmingham 1984–, tstee Legal Assistance Tst 1985–, memb Advsy Bd Centre of Advanced Litigation Nottingham Trent Univ 1991–, govr LSE 1996–; memb Editorial Bd: Modern Law Review 1992–, Int Jl of Evidence and Proof 1996–; memb Editorial Advsy Bd Litigator 1994–; FRSA 1995; *Style*— Cyril Glasser, Esq; ✉ 21 Holmes Rd, London NW5 3AA (☎ 0171 485 7821); Sheridans, 14 Red Lion Square, London WC1R 4QL (☎ 0171 404 0444, fax 0171 831 1982)

GLASSMAN, Rosslyn Angela; da of Sidney Glassman, of Hove, Sussex, and Millicant, *née* Goldstein; *b* 13 May 1947; *Educ* Wistons Sch Brighton Sussex; *Career* theatrical historian specialising in antique engravings relating to the performing arts; memb: Soc of Theatre Res, Soc of Dance Res, The Theatre Tst, American Soc of Theatre Research, Int Fedn of Theatre Research, Save the London Theatres; also advsr to museums and archives worldwide; exhibitions incl: 14 at Royal Festival Hall, 3 at Royal Opera House, 6 at Glyndebourne Festival Opera, Royal Nat Theatre Tenth Anniversary, Royal Shakespeare Meml Theatre Stratford on Avon, The Bear Garden Museum; Shakespeare Exhibition for Chichester Festival and at Henley Regatta; *Style*— Miss Rosslyn Glassman; ✉ 27 Chalcot Square, London NW1 (☎ 0171 586 4681); The Witch Ball, 2 Cecil Court, St Martins Lane WC2 (☎ 0171 836 2922, page 0171 884 3344/A007); The Witch Ball, 48 Meeting House Lane, Brighton, Sussex (☎ 01273 26618)

GLASSPOLE, Most Hon Sir Florizel Augustus; ON (1973), GCMG (1981), GCVO (1983), CD (1970); s of late Rev Theophilus A Glasspole, and Florence, *née* Baxter; *b* 25 Sept 1909; *Educ* Wolmer's Boys' Sch, Ruskin Coll Oxford; *m* 1934, Ina Josephine Kinlocke; 1 da; *Career* accountant 1932–44, dir City Printery Ltd 1944–50, gen sec Jamaica TUC 1939–52, memb House of Representatives Jamaica 1944–73, min of Educn 1957–62 and 1972–73, ldr of House 1955–62 and 1972–73, min of Labour 1955–57, govr-gen of Jamaica 1983–91; *Recreations* sports, gardening; *Style*— Most Hon Sir Florizel Glasspole,; ✉ c/o King's House, Kingston 10, Jamaica

GLASSPOOL, Frank Harry; s of Lesley William George Glasspool (d 1936), and Isobel, *née* Highfield (d 1992); *b* 14 May 1934; *Educ* Duke of York Royal Mil Sch; *m* 1, 1 April 1961 (m dis 1981), Olive, da of Charles Geddes (d 1982); 1 s (Stephen b 2 Nov 1964), 1 da (Wendy b 25 Jan 1963); m 2, 25 Feb 1984, Rosemary Esther, da of George Edward Saunders; 2 step s (Simon b 21 Dec 1963, Timothy b 7 Oct 1965), 1 step da (Juliette b 25 July 1971); *Career* sr engr Kellog Int 1961–68, sr ptnr Glasspool & Thaiss 1968–; pres Rotary Club Berkhamsted Bulbourne, pres Berkhamsted Lawn Tennis and Squash Rackets Club; CEng, FIStructE 1974, MConsE 1979; *Recreations* tennis, squash, photography, golf; *Clubs* British Tennis Umpires Assoc, Berkhamsted Lawn Tennis & Squash Rackets, Berkhamsted Bulbourne Rotary; *Style*— Frank Glasspool, Esq; ✉ Longcroft, Browns Lane, Hastoe, Tring, Hertfordshire HP23 6LX; Coughtrey House, 112–116 Broad St, Chesham, Bucks HP5 3ED (☎ 01494 771314, fax 01494 791455)

GLAUERT, Dr Audrey Marion; da of Hermann Glauert (d 1934), of Farnborough, Hants, and Muriel, *née* Barker (d 1949); *b* 21 Dec 1925; *Educ* Perse Sch for Girls Cambridge, Bedford Coll London (BSc, MSc), Clare Hall Cambridge (MA, ScD); *Career* asst lectr physics Royal Holloway Coll London 1947–50, Sir Halley Stewart fell and memb sci staff Strangeways Res Laboratory Cambridge 1950–89, fell Clare Hall Cambridge 1966–; ed: Practical Methods in Electron Microscopy 1972–, Jl of Microscopy 1986–89; chm: Br Jt Ctee for Electron Microscopy 1968–72, Fifth Euro Congress on Electron Microscopy 1972; pres Royal Microscopical Soc 1970–72; JP Cambridge 1975–88; hon memb: Société Française de Microscopie Electronique, Microscopy Soc of America (Distinguished Scientist in Biological Sciences award 1990), FRMS; *Books* Fixation, Dehydration and Embedding of Biological Specimens (1974); *Recreations* vol work prison reform tst, gardening, sailing; *Style*— Dr Audrey Glauert; ✉ 29 Cow Lane, Fulbourn, Cambridge CB1 5HB (☎ 01223 880463); 19 High St, Blakeney, Holt, Norfolk NR25 7NA; Clare Hall, University of Cambridge, Herschel Road, Cambridge CB3 9AL

GLAZE, Michael John Carlisle (James); CMG (1988); s of Derek Glaze (d 1970), and Shirley Winifred Gardner, formerly Glaze, *née* Ramsay; *b* 15 Jan 1935; *Educ* Repton, St Catharine's Coll Cambridge (MA), Worcester Coll Oxford; *m* 1965, Rosemary Duff; 2 da (Fiona, Deirdre); *Career* HM Overseas Civil Serv Lesotho 1959–70, dep perm sec Miny of Fin; Dip Serv: Abu Dhabi 1975–78, Rabat 1978–80, consul gen Bordeaux 1980–84; ambass: Republic of Cameroon 1984–87, Luanda 1987–89, Addis Ababa 1990–94 (concurrently (non-resident) to Eritrea 1993–94), ret; dep sec-gen Order of St John; *Style*— James Glaze, Esq, CMG; ✉ 32 Doods Park Road, Reigate, Surrey RH2 0QD

GLAZEBROOK, Benjamin Kirkland; s of Reginald Field Glazbrook (d 1986), and late Daisy Isobel, *née* Broad; *b* 27 Nov 1931; *Educ* Eton, Pembroke Coll Cambridge (BA); *m* Sara Ann, *née* Kentish; 2 s (Nicholas David Kirkland and James William); *Career* PA to chm Heinemann Publishers 1958–62 (joined 1955); Constable Publishers: bought controlling interest with Donald Hyde 1962, obtained sole controlling interest 1968, currently chm and md; memb Cncl Publishers Assoc 1989–91; *Recreations* reading, salmon fishing; *Clubs* Beefsteak, Garrick; *Style*— Benjamin Glazebrook, Esq; ✉ Constable Publishers, 3 The Lanchesters, 162 Fulham Palace Road, London W6 7ER (☎ 0181 741 3663, fax 0181 748 7562)

GLAZEBROOK, (Reginald) Mark; s of Reginald Field Glazebrook (d 1986), and late Daisy Isobel, *née* Broad; *b* 25 June 1936; *Educ* Eton, Pembroke Coll Cambridge (MA), Slade Sch of Fine Art; *m* 1, 1965 (m dis 1969), Elizabeth Lea, *née* Claridge; 1 da (Lucy b 22 April 1966); m 2, 27 Sept 1974, Wanda Barbara, da of Ignacy Piotr Osinski, of Warsaw, Poland; 1 da (Bianca b 25 March 1975); *Career* Nat Serv 2 Lt Welsh Gds 1953–55; exhbn organiser Arts Cncl 1962–65, art critic London Magazine 1967–68, dir Whitechapel Art Gallery 1969–71, head of Modern British Dept Colnaghi & Co Ltd 1972–75, gallery dir San José Univ USA 1976–78; dir: Editions Alecto 1979–81, Albemarle Gallery 1986–93; freelance writer and lectr 1996–; princ exhibition catalogues written and edited: Artists and Architecture of Bedford Park 1875–1900, John Armstrong (1957), David Hockney Paintings Prints Drawings 1960–70 (1970), Edward Wadsworth Paintings Drawings and Prints (1974), John Tunnard (1977), The Seven and Five Soc (1979), Unit One, Spirit of the 30's (1984); Mark Twain USA 1977; FRSA 1971; *Recreations* painting, cooking, tennis, swimming; *Clubs* Beefsteak, Chelsea Arts, Polish Hearth; *Style*— Mark Glazebrook, Esq; ✉ 18A Nevern Mansions, Warwick Road, London SW5 9TJ (☎ 0171 460 0728, fax 0171 460 3774)

GLAZEBROOK, Philip Kirkland; s of Francis Kirkland Glazebrook (d 1988), of Horsmonden, Kent, and Winifred, *née* Davison (d 1984); *b* 3 April 1937; *Educ* Eton, Trinity Coll Cambridge; *m* 5 Oct 1968, Clare Rosemary, da of Arthur Stewart Gemmell; 2 s (Augustin b 24 April 1973, Harry b 18 Dec 1980), 2 da (Olivia b 20 Jan 1976, Maisie b 3 April 1984); *Career* writer; *Fiction* Try Pleasure (1968), The Eye of the Beholder (1973), The Walled Garden (1977), Byzantine Honeymoon (1979), Captain Vinegar's Commission (1987), The Gate at the End of the World (1989); *Travel* Journey to Kars (1983), Journey to Khiva (1992); *Recreations* fishing; *Clubs* MCC, Travellers'; *Style*— Philip Glazebrook, Esq; ✉ Richard Scott Simon, 43 Doughty Street, London WC1N 2LF (☎ 0171 405 7379, fax 0171 831 2127)

GLAZER, Geoffrey; s of Benjamin Glazer (d 1979), of Croydon, and Dora, *née* Hornstein; *b* 11 Feb 1939; *Educ* Selhurst GS, St Mary's Hosp Med Sch (MB BS, MRCS, MRCP, MS); *m* Sandra Estelle, da of Bernard Lasky; 2 s (David Anthony b 1 July 1965, Simon Jonathon b 12 Oct 1968), 1 da (Debra Juliette b 7 April 1973); *Career* sr surgical registrar St Mary's Hosp London 1971–75, res fell Harvard Med Sch 1975, sr lectr in surgery St Mary's Hosp Med Sch 1976–77, conslt surgn St Mary's Hosp 1977–; Freeman: Worshipful Soc of Apothecaries 1990, City of London 1993; memb RSM 1977; FRCS, FACS; *Books* Acute Pancreatitis (1988); *Recreations* tennis, golf, dry fly fishing, travel, theatre, reading; *Clubs* MCC; *Style*— Geoffrey Glazer, Esq; ✉ 84A St John's Wood High Street, London NW8 7SH (☎ 0171 483 3020, fax 0171 483 3087)

GLAZIER, Barry Edward; s of Edward Thomas Glazier (d 1976), of San Antonio, Ibiza, Spain, and Gladys Mabel, *née* Faulkner; *b* 1 July 1941; *Educ* Hurstpierpoint, St Peter's Coll Oxford (MA); *m* 1, 5 Aug 1970 (m dis), Lesley (d 1990), da of John Richard Kirby (d 1986); 2 da (Anna b 1973, Rachael b 1976); m 2, 5 April 1984, Mrs Patricia McGregor, da of Cecil Mears (d 1977), of Wareham, Dorset; 1 da (Becky b 1985), 1 adopted step-da (Emma Sarah b 1981); *Career* admitted slr 1966; Clifford Turner 1966–70, ptnr Mooring Aldridge 1971–88 (sr ptnr 1984–88), managing ptnr Lester Aldridge 1994– (ptnr 1988–); pres: Bournemouth and Dist Law Soc 1991–92, Dorset Chamber of Commerce and Industry 1992–93; slr to and dir of Dorset Trg and Enterprise Cncl; former memb Dorset War Pensions Ctee; memb Law Soc 1966; *Recreations* concerts, piano, theatre, bird watching, gardening; *Style*— Barry Glazier, Esq; ✉ Quarter Jack House, 11 The Cornmarket, Wimborne Minster, Dorset BH21 1JL (☎ 01202 885128); Lester Aldridge, Russell House, Oxford Road, Bournemouth, Dorset BH8 8EX (☎ 01202 786161, fax 01202 786150)

GLEADELL, Colin Francis; s of Maj Gen Paul Gleadell, CB, CBE, DSO (d 1988), and Mary, *née* Montgomerie Lind (d 1994); *b* 17 Dec 1946; *Educ* Downside, Churchill Coll Cambridge (MA); *m* 1988, Sophie Barbara Estella, da of Ernle David Drummond Money; 1 da (Rose Montgomerie b 7 Sept 1993); *Career* res Paul Mellon Fndn for Br Art 1968–71, mangr Crane Arts London 1971–73, freelance art conslt and pt/t musical dir NEMS Records 1974–78, head Modern Art Dept Bonham's Auctioneers 1979–81, freelance art conslt 1982–85, features ed Galleries Magazine 1985–, salesroom corr Art Monthly 1986–; memb Advsy Ctee 20th Century Br Art Fair 1987–; conslt BBC TV: The Great Picture Chase 1990, Relative Values series 1991, Eric Hebborn, Portrait of a Master Forger 1991, Sister Wendy's Grand Tour 1993; memb Int Assoc of Art Critics 1987; *Publications* numerous exhibition catalogues and articles in specialist art magazines; *Style*— Colin Gleadell, Esq; ✉ c/o Barrington Publications, 54 Uxbridge Rd, London W12 8LP (☎ and fax 0181 740 7020)

GLEAVE, Prof (Michael) Barrie; s of John Thomas Gleave (d 1959), and Mildred, *née* Darbyshire (d 1992); *b* 22 July 1936; *Educ* Roundhay Sch Leeds, Univ of Hull (BA, MA, PhD), Univ of Reading (DipEd); *m* 21 Aug 1961, Jean, da of John Marsland (d 1965); 1 s (Jonathan b 1966), 1 da (Catherine b 1964); *Career* prof of geography Fourah Bay Coll Univ of Sierra Leone 1972–74; Univ of Salford: prof of geography 1982–95, chm of Dept 1983–94, research prof 1995–; treas African Studies Assoc of UK 1980–84; memb:

Inst of Br Geographers, Geographical Assoc; ASA UK; *Books* An Economic Geography of West Africa (jtly, 1971), Tropical African Development: Geographical Perspectives (ed, 1992); *Clubs* Lancs CCC; *Style*— Prof Barrie Gleave; ✉ Baldwin Croft, 36 Church Road, Leyland, Preston PR5 2AA (☎ 01772 422056); Department of Geography, University of Salford, Salford M5 4WT (☎ 0161 745 5000 ext 4780, fax 0161 745 5015, telex 668680 (SULIB))

GLEAVE, John Reginald Wallace; s of Rev Canon John Wallace Gleave (d 1979), of Cambridge, and Dorothy Littlefair, *née* Green (d 1978); *b* 6 April 1925; *Educ* Uppingham, Magdalen Coll Oxford (MA, BM BCh); *m* 6 Sept 1952, (Margaret) Anne, da of Michael Robert Newbolt (d 1956), of Chester; 3 s (Mark b 1957, Humphry b 1959, Arthur b 1964), 3 da (Frances b 1954, Charity b 1961, Emily b 1965); *Career* Nat Serv Maj RAMC OIC Army Neurosurgical Unit 1952–54; neurosurgeon; conslt neurosurgeon emeritus Addenbrooke's Hosp Cambs, conslt neurosurgn BUPA Hosp Cambs, lectr in neurosurgery Univ of Cambridge, praelector and emeritus fell St Edmund's Coll Cambridge, lectr and dir of med studies Magdalene Coll Cambridge; elected memb Magdalene Coll Cambridge 1995; memb: OUBC 1946–48 (won boat race 1946), Leander 1948–49 (won grand 1949); Freeman and Apothecary of City of London 1996; FRCS 1957, SBNS 1962, FRSM 1975; *Recreations* rowing, gardening, travel; *Clubs* Vincent's (Oxford), Hawks (Cambridge), Leander (Henley-on-Thames), Utd Oxford and Cambridge Univ; *Style*— John R W Gleave, Esq; ✉ Riversdale, Gt Shelford, Cambridge CB2 5LW (☎ 01223 843309); BUPA Hospital, Cambridge (☎ 01223 237474)

GLEDHILL, Anthony John; GC (1967); s of Harold Victor Gledhill (d 1990), of Portsmouth, Hants, and Marjorie Edith, *née* Prout; *b* 10 March 1938; *Educ* Doncaster Tech HS; *m* 3 Sept 1958, Marie Lilian, da of William Hughes, of Bromley, Kent; 1 s (Stewart b 1 Sept 1961), 1 da (Rachel b 13 Sept 1963); *Career* accounts clerk Offr's Mess RAF Bruggen Germany 1953–56; Met Police: cadet 1956–57, police constable 1957–75, detective sgt 1976–87; PO Investigation Dept 1987; divnl auditor NWS Bank plc 1993–; memb Royal Br Legion Kent; *Recreations* local football management, bowls, foreign travel; *Style*— Anthony Gledhill, Esq, GC; ✉ 98 Pickhurst Lane, Hayes, Bromley, Kent BR2 7JD (☎ 0181 462 4033); NWS Bank plc, NWS House, High Street, Purley, Croydon, Surrey CR8 2AF

GLEDHILL, Keith Ainsworth; MBE (1994), DL (Lancashire 1986); s of Norman Gledhill (d 1970), of Blackpool, and Louise, *née* Ainsworth (d 1988); *b* 28 Aug 1932; *Educ* Arnold Sch Blackpool; *m* 7 July 1956, Margaret Irene, da of Joseph Bramwell Burton (d 1970); 1 s (Ian C b 1958); *Career* jr offr MN 1950–54; Nat Serv RAF 1954–56; Norman Gledhill & Co Ltd 1956–65, Delta Metal Co Ltd 1965 (sr exec contract); fndr: Gledhill Water Storage Ltd 1972, Nu-Rad Ltd 1974, Thermal Sense (Energy Conservation Systems) Ltd 1979; chm Bd of Govrs Arnold Sch Ltd, vice chm Blackpool and Fylde Soc for the Blind, tstee Foxton Dispensary, govr Skelton Bounty Tst, chm Lancs St John Cncl, vice pres Lancs Cncl Vol Youth Servs; past chm Lancs Youth Clubs Assoc, past offr Rotary Int; High Sheriff of Lancs 1992; Freeman City of London, Liveryman Worshipful Co of Plumbers; OStJ 1995; FInstD 1968, MInstP 1970; *Recreations* golf; *Clubs* Royal Lytham and St Anne's Golf, Fylde RUFC; *Style*— Keith Gledhill, Esq, MBE, DL; ✉ Broken Hill, 35 South Park Drive, Blackpool, Lancashire FY3 9PZ (☎ 01253 764462); Gledhill Water Storage Ltd, Sycamore Estate, Squires Gate, Blackpool, Lancashire FY4 3RL (☎ 01253 401 494, fax 01253 407043)

GLEDHILL, Michael William; s of George Eric Louis Gledhill (d 1986), of Shelf, nr Halifax, W Yorks, and Sarah Jane, *née* Green (d 1979); *b* 28 Oct 1937; *Educ* Rishworth Sch Halifax; *m* 18 Oct 1962, Margaret, da of Cyril Ira Fletcher (d 1965), of Hanson Lane, Halifax, W Yorks; 3 s (Marc b Nov 1963, Andrew b May 1966, Jonathan b June 1969); *Career* slr; ptnr Finn, Gledhill & Co 1962–; Notary Public Halifax 1980; dir: G W Estates Ltd 1968–, Red Seal Ltd 1985–, Gold Seal (Conveyancing) Ltd 1985–; clerk: Waterhouse Charity Halifax 1965–, Tstees Abbotts Ladies Home Halifax 1967–; govr Wheelwright Charity (Rishworth Sch) 1991– (clerk 1985–91); *Recreations* golf, gardening, rugby; *Style*— Michael W Gledhill, Esq; ✉ Post Cottage, Warley Town, Warley, Halifax HX2 7RZ (☎ 01422 831890); Finn, Gledhill & Co, 1/4 Harrison Rd, Halifax HX1 2AG (☎ 01422 330000, fax 01422 342604)

GLEDHILL, Ruth; da of Rev Peter Gledhill, of Yr Hen Felin Pwllfanogl, LlanfairPG, Gwynedd, and Bridget Mary, *née* Rathbone; *b* 15 Dec 1959; *Educ* Thomas Alleyne's GS Uttoxeter, London Coll of Printing (HND), Birkbeck Coll London (Cert in Relgious Studies); *m* 1996, Andrew Daniels; *Career* indentured Birmingham Post & Mail 1982–84, gen news reporter Daily Mail 1984–87; The Times: home news reporter 1987–90, religion correspondent 1990–, columnist At Your Service (Times Weekend) 1996–, also ballroom dancing reporter for sports pages; regular radio and TV appearances on religious affrs; *Books* Birmingham is Not a Boring City (co-author, 1984), The Times Book of Best Sermons (ed and introduction, Cassell, 1995 and 1996), At A Service Near You (Hodder, 1996); *Recreations* ballroom dancing, music, reading and writing; *Clubs* Reform; *Style*— Ms Ruth Gledhill; ✉ The Times, 1 Pennington St, London E1 9XN (☎ 0171 782 5001, fax 0171 782 5988; home ☎ 01372 745092)

GLEESON, Dermot James; s of Patrick Joseph Gleeson, of Cheam, Surrey, and Margaret Mary, *née* Higgins; *b* 5 Sept 1949; *Educ* Downside, Fitzwilliam Coll Cambridge (MA); *m* 6 Sept 1980, Rosalind Mary Catherine, da of Dr Charles Edward Moorhead (d 1953), of Chipping Campden, Glos; 1 s (Patrick b 1984), 1 da (Catherine b 1981); *Career* Cons Res Dept 1974–77 (asst dir 1979), Euro Cmmn (cabinet of Sir Christopher Tugendhat) 1977–79, EEC rep of Midland Bank Brussels 1980–82, chief exec MJ Gleeson Group PLC 1988– (joined 1982, chm 1994–); dir The Housing Corporation 1990–95, dir Construction Industry Training Bd 1995–; *Clubs* Beefsteak, RAC; *Style*— Dermot Gleeson, Esq; ✉ Hook Farm, White Hart Lane, Wood Street Village, Surrey GU3 3EA (☎ 01483 236210); M J Gleeson Group plc, Haredon House, London Road, North Cheam, Sutton, Surrey SM3 9BS (☎ 0181 644 4321, fax 0181 644 6366, car 0836 777972, telex 927762)

GLEN, Sir Alexander Richard; KBE (1967, CBE 1964), DSC (1942, bar 1945); s of Richard Bartlett Glen, of Glasgow; *b* 18 April 1912; *Educ* Fettes, Balliol Coll Oxford; *m* 1, 1937 (m dis 1945), Nina, *née* Nixon; m 2, 1947, Baroness Zora Cartuyvels de Collaert, da of Ago Bukovac, of Dubrovnik; 1 s (Adrian d 1986); *Career* served RNVR 1939–59, Capt 1956; chm H Clarkson & Co 1958–73, dir BICC 1964–70, chm Br Tourist Authy 1969–77, dep chm Br Tport Hotels 1978–83; memb: Horserace Totalisator Bd 1976–84, Historic Bldgs Cncl 1976–80; chm V & A Museum Advsy Cncl 1978–83, vice pres Br Airline Pilots Assoc (pres 1980–94), vice pres Br Hospitality Assoc 1980–; former: explorer (Arctic), banker in New York, bd memb BEA and Nat Ports Cncl 1964–70; Gold medallist Royal Geographical Soc 1940, medallist Royal Soc of Edinburgh and Swedish Geographical and Anthropological Soc 1938, Polar medal 1935/36; Order of St Olav of Norway, Norwegian War Cross, Czech-Slovak War Cross; *Books* Under the Pole Star (1937), Footholds against a Whirlwind (1978); *Recreations* travel; *Clubs* City of London, Explorers (NYC); *Style*— Sir Alexander Glen, KBE, DSC; ✉ The Dower House, Stanton, Broadway, Worcs WR12 7NE

GLEN, Eric Stanger; s of William Kerr Glen (d 1952), and Annie Pullar Glen (d 1996); *b* 20 Oct 1934; *Educ* Univ of Glasgow (MB ChB); *m* 7 April 1965, Patricia Alexa Scott, da of Alexander Nicholson (d 1980), of Glasgow; 3 s (Jeremy b 26 Oct 1966, Stephen b 9 Sept 1968, Paul b 2 March 1971); *Career* ship surgn Royal Fleet Auxiliary 1962; conslt urological surgn, hon clinical sr lectr Univ of Glasgow; memb Examination Panel RCPS Glasgow, pt/t lectr Glasgow Caledonian Univ, fndr, past sec and hon memb Int Continence Soc, fndr and pres Urological Computing Soc, hon memb Italian Urodynamic Soc, chm Area Med Ctee Gtr Glasgow Health Bd 1992–94, med dir Gtr Glasgow Health Bd Continence Resource Centre, co-ordinator Scottish Task Force on Incontinence, past memb Audit Working Gp Br Assoc of Urological Surgns, pres Scottish Urological Soc 1993–95; memb BMA, FRSM, FRCSEd 1967, FRCS (Glasgow) 1967, ALCM; *Books* contrib: Advances in Diagnostic Urology (1981), Surgical Management (1984 and 1991), Female Stress Incontinence (1979); numerous papers on urodynamics, urology and computing; *Recreations* travel, computing applications, pottering about; *Style*— Eric Glen, Esq; ✉ 9 St John's Rd, Pollokshields, Glasgow G41 5RJ (☎ 0141 423 0759, fax 0141 423 1648); Walton Urological Teaching and Research Centre, Southern General Hospital, Glasgow G51 4TF (☎ 0141 201 1100, fax 0141 201 2987)

GLEN, James Robert; s of William Glen (d 1969), of Perthshire, and Irene Marjorie Stewart, *née* Sutherland; *b* 27 May 1930; *Educ* Merchiston Castle Sch Edinburgh; *m* 1956, Alison Helen Margaret, da of Robin Archibald Brown (d 1948); 3 s (Hamish b 1957, Graeme b 1959, Iain b 1961); *Career* 2 Lt RA 1955–56, served Hong Kong; CA; md The Scottish Investment Trust plc 1981–91 (non-exec dir 1991–), chm The Scottish Life Assurance Co 1987–93 (dir 1971–); *Recreations* golf, fishing; *Clubs* New (Edinburgh), Hon Co of Edinburgh Golfers; *Style*— James Glen, Esq; ✉ 18 Greenhill Park, Edinburgh EH10 4DW (☎ 0131 225 7781)

GLENAMARA, Baron (Life Peer UK 1977), of Glenridding in Co Cumbria; Edward Watson Short; CH (1976), PC (1964); s of Charles and Mary Short, of Warcop, Westmorland; *b* 17 Dec 1912; *Educ* Bede Coll Univ of Durham (LLB); *m* 1941, Jennie, da of Thomas Sewell, of Newcastle upon Tyne; 1 s (Hon Michael Christian b 1943), 1 da (Hon Jane Bronwen (Hon Mrs Fraser) b 1945); *Career* WWII Capt DLI; sits as Labour peer in House of Lords; MP (L) Newcastle upon Tyne Central 1951–76, oppn whip (N) 1955–62, dep chief oppn whip 1962–64, govt chief whip (and Parly sec Treasy) 1964–66, Postmaster Gen 1966–68, sec of state Educn and Sci 1968–70, Lord President of the Cncl and Ldr of the House of Commons 1974–76, dep ldr Lab Pty 1972–76, chllr Univ of Northumbria, pres Finchale Abbey Trg Coll for Disabled, chm Cable Wireless Ltd 1976–80; Hon DCL Durham, Hon DUniv Open Univ, Hon DLitt CNAA; *Books* The Story of the Durham Light Infantry (1944), The Infantry Instructor (1946), Education in a Changing World (1971), Birth to Five (1974), I Knew My Place (1983), Whip to Wilson (1989); *Style*— The Rt Hon Lord Glenamara, CH, PC; ✉ 21 Priory Gardens, Corbridge, Northumberland (☎ 0143 463 2880)

GLENARTHUR, 4 Baron (UK 1918); Sir Simon Mark Arthur; 4 Bt (UK 1903), DL (Aberdeenshire 1988); s of 3 Baron Glenarthur, OBE, DL (d 1976), by his 2 w, Margaret Risk, *née* Howie (d 1993); *b* 7 Oct 1944; *Educ* Eton; *m* 12 Nov 1969, Susan, yr da of Cdr Hubert Wyndham Barry, RN (d 1992), and Violet (d 1994), da of Col Sir Edward Ruggles-Brise, 1 Bt; 1 s, 1 da (Hon Emily Victoria b 1975); *Heir* s, Hon Edward Alexander Arthur b 9 April 1973; *Career* served 10th Royal Hussars (subsequently The Royal Hussars (PWO)): cmmnd 1963, Capt 1970, Maj 1973, ret; served Royal Hussars (PWO) TA 1975–80; Capt British Airways Helicopters Ltd 1976–82; dir Aberdeen & Texas Corporate Finance Ltd 1977–82, sr exec Hanson plc 1989–96 (conslt 1996–), dep chm Hanson Pacific Ltd 1994–; dir: The Lewis Group PLC 1993–94, Whirly Bird Services Ltd 1995–, Millenium Chemicals Inc 1996–; conslt: British Aerospace plc 1989–, Chevron UK Ltd 1994–, Imperial Tobacco Group plc 1996–; sits as Cons peer in House of Lords, Govt whip (lord in waiting) 1982–83; Parly under sec of state: DHSS 1983–85, Home Office 1985–86; min of state: Scotland 1986–87, FCO 1987–89; chm St Mary's Hosp Paddington NHS Tst 1991–; pres Nat Cncl for Civil Protection 1991–; chm: Br Helicopter Advsy Bd 1992–, Euro Helicopter Assoc 1996–; memb Cncl The Air League 1994–; memb (Brig) Queen's Body Guard for Scotland (Royal Co of Archers); Liveryman Guild of Air Pilots and Air Navigators; FRAeS, MCIT; *Recreations* field sports, flying, gardening, barometers, choral singing; *Clubs* Cavalry and Guards', White's, Pratt's; *Style*— The Rt Hon the Lord Glenarthur, DL; ✉ Northbrae Farmhouse, Crathes, Banchory, Kincardineshire AB31 6JQ (☎ 01330 844467, fax 01330 844465)

GLENCONNER, Baroness; Lady Anne (Veronica); *née* Coke; LVO (1991); eldest da of 5 Earl of Leicester, MVO (d 1976); *b* 16 July 1932; *m* 21 April 1956, 3 Baron Glenconner; 3 s, 2 da; *Career* train bearer to HM The Queen at the Coronation 1953 (maid of honour); an extra lady-in-waiting to HRH The Princess Margaret, Countess of Snowdon 1971–; pres: SOS 1979–83, Nat Assoc for Maternal and Child Welfare 1985; *Books* The Picnic Papers (with Susanna Johnstone, 1983); *Style*— The Rt Hon Lady Glenconner, LVO; ✉ East End Farm, Burnham Thorpe, King's Lynn, Norfolk PE31 8HW

GLENCONNER, 3 Baron (UK 1911); Sir Colin Christopher Paget Tennant; 4 Bt (UK 1885); s of 3 Baron Glenconner (d 1983), and his 1 w, Pamela, Baroness Glenconner, *qv*; *b* 1 Dec 1926; *Educ* Eton, New Coll Oxford; *m* 21 April 1956, Lady Anne Veronica Coke, LVO (*see* Glenconner, Baroness); 3 s (Hon Charles Edward Pevensey b 1957 d 1996, Hon Henry Lovell b 1960 d 1990, Hon Christopher Cary b 1967), twin da (Hon May and Hon Amy b 1970); *Heir* gs, Cody Charles Edward Tennant b 2 Feb 1994; *Career* Lt Irish Gds; governing dir Tennants Estate Ltd 1967–91, chm Mustique Co 1968–87; *Style*— The Rt Hon Lord Glenconner; ✉ Beau Estate, PO Box 250, Soufriere, St Lucia, West Indies

GLENCROSS, David; CBE (1994); s of John William Glencross, of Salford, Lancs (d 1962), and Elsie May, *née* Ward (d 1987); *b* 3 March 1936; *Educ* Salford GS, Trinity Coll Cambridge (BA); *m* 1965, Elizabeth Louise, da of Jack Turner Richardson (d 1977), of Birmingham; 1 da (Juliet b 1966); *Career* gen trainee various posts in radio and TV prodn BBC 1958–70, sr programme offr ITA 1970–76, head of programme servs 1976–77, dir of television IBA 1983–90 (dep dir 1977–83), chief exec Independent Television Cmmn 1991–96, ret; chm Br Screen Advsy Cncl 1996–; non-exec dir Independent Media Support Ltd; Hon MA Univ of Salford 1993; FRTS (vice pres); *Recreations* music, reading, walking, idling; *Style*— David Glencross, Esq, CBE; ✉ British Screen Advisory Council, 19 Cavendish Square, London W1M 9AB (☎ 0171 304 0040, fax 0171 306 0329)

GLENDEVON, 2 Baron (UK 1964), of Midhope, Co Linlithgow; Julian John Somerset Hope; er s of 1 Baron Glendevon, PC, ERD (d 1996), and Elizabeth Mary, o da of (William) Somerset Maugham, CH, FRSL; *b* 6 March 1950; *Educ* Eton, Christ Church Oxford; *Heir* bro, Hon Jonathan Charles Hope b 23 April 1952; *Career* operatic prodr; resident prodr Welsh National Opera 1973–75; assoc prodr Glyndebourne Festival 1974–81; prodns incl: San Francisco Opera, Wexford and Edinburgh Festivals; *Style*— The Rt Hon Lord Glendevon

GLENDINING, Rev Canon Alan; LVO (1979), QHC (1979); s of Vincent Glendining (d 1964), and Frida Alice, *née* Bery (d 1974); *b* 17 March 1924; *Educ* Radley, Westcott House Cambridge; *m* 8 May 1948, Margaret Locke, da of Lt-Col Claud McKinnon Hawes, DSO (d 1973); 1 s (David b 1950), 2 da (Sarah Jane b 1955 d 1981, Frances b 1962); *Career* Foreign Office 1942–45, newspaper publisher and ed 1945–58; deacon 1960, ordained priest Lincoln 1961, curate South Ormsby Gp of Parishes 1960; rector: Raveningham Gp of Parishes 1963, Sandringham Gp of Parishes 1970; domestic chaplain to HM the Queen 1970, rural dean Heacham and Rising 1972–76, hon canon Norwich Cathedral 1977, rector Lowestoft Gp of Parishes 1979, vicar Ranworth and Woodbastwick 1985, sr chaplain to Norfolk Holiday Indust 1985–90; sec Norfolk Water Safety Assoc 1987–91, chm West Norfolk Hospice Home Support 1990–92, hon curate St Margaret's King's Lynn 1990–; Queen's Jubilee Medal 1977; *Recreations* reading, writing; *Style*— The Rev Canon Alan Glendining, LVO, QHC; ✉ 7 Bellfosters, King's Staithe Lane, King's Lynn, Norfolk PE30 1LZ (☎ 01553 760113)

GLENDINNING, David Edward Hamilton; s of Dr David Glendinning, of Sleaford, Lincs, and late Kathleen Theresa, *née* Holmes; *b* 28 Dec 1946; *Educ* Carres GS Sleaford, UCH (BDS); *m* 1, 20 June 1971 (m dis 1974), Victoria Sorrell, da of Prof Raleigh Barcley Lucas, of Sevenoaks, Kent; m 2, 9 Oct 1976, Teresa Mary, da of Brendan James Bolger, of St Albans, Herts; 1 s (Andrew b 1986), 2 da (Laura b 1980, Sarah b 1982); *Career* house surgn UCH 1970, sr house offr in periodontology Royal Dental Hosp 1970–71, registrar Dental Dept St Bartholomew's Hosp 1972–74, sr registrar in oral surgery Manchester 1974–78, conslt oral surgn S Lincolnshire Pilgrim Hosp Boston and Grantham and Kesteven Gen Hosp 1978–; postgrad dental tutor to S Lincolnshire 1991–; various pubns in Br and US oral surgery press; fell BAOMS 1979, FDSRCS; *Recreations* golf, sailing, old cars, racing; *Clubs* Sleaford Golf, Fakenham Raceclub; *Style*— David Glendinning, Esq; ✉ Hill House, South Rauceby, Sleaford, Lincolnshire NG34 8QQ (☎ 01592 488625); Edinmore, Croc-An-Raer, North Bute, Isle of Bute PA20 0QT; Department of Oral Surgery, Pilgrim Hospital, Boston, Lincolnshire (☎ 01205 64801)

GLENDINNING, Hon Victoria (Hon Mrs de Vere White); *née* Seebohm; er da of Baron Seebohm, TD (Life Peer, d 1990), and Evangeline (d 1990), da of His Hon Sir Gerald Berkeley Hurst, QC; *b* 23 April 1937; *Educ* St Mary's Wantage, Millfield, Somerville Coll Oxford (BA, MA), Univ of Southampton (Dip Social Admin); *m* 1, 6 Sept 1958 (m dis 1981), Prof (Oliver) Nigel Valentine Glendinning; 4 s; m 2, 1982, Terence de Vere White (d 1994), s of Frederick S de Vere White; *Career* author and journalist; head Booker Prize panel 1992; Hon DLitt: Univ of Southampton 1994, Univ of Ulster 1995, Univ of Dublin 1995; FRSL; *Books* A Suppressed Cry, Elizabeth Bowen - Portrait of a Writer, Edith Sitwell - A Unicorn among Lions, Vita, Rebecca West, Hertfordshire, The Grown Ups, Trollope (Whitbread biography award 1992), Electricity (1995), Sons and Mothers (ed with Matthew Glendinning, 1996); *Recreations* gardening; *Style*— Victoria Glendinning; ✉ c/o David Higham Associates, 5–8 Lower John Street, London W1R 4HA (☎ 0171 437 7888)

GLENDYNE, 3 Baron (UK 1922); Sir Robert Nivison; 3 Bt (UK 1914); s of 2 Baron Glendyne (d 1967); *b* 27 Oct 1926; *Educ* Harrow; *m* 25 April 1953, Elizabeth, yr da of Sir (Stephen) Cecil Armitage, CBE, JP, DL, of Hawksworth Manor, Notts; 1 s, 2 da; *Heir* s, Hon John Nivison; *Career* WWII Lt Grenadier Gds; sr ptnr R Nivison & Co (stockbrokers) 1967–86, chm Glenfriars Unit Trust Managers Ltd 1971–93; *Clubs* City of London; *Style*— The Rt Hon the Lord Glendyne; ✉ Craigeassie By Forfar, Angus DD8 3SE

GLENNIE, Angus James Scott; QC (1991); s of Robert Nigel Forbes Glennie, of London and Sussex, and Barbara Scott, *née* Nicoll (d 1987); *b* 3 Dec 1950; *Educ* Sherborne, Trinity Hall Cambridge (exhibitioner, MA); *m* 3 Oct 1981, Patricia Jean, da of His Hon Andrew James Phelan, *qv*; 4 s (Alasdair Lewis Scott b 3 April 1983, Aishling Frances Robertson b 19 April 1985, Patrick James Nicoll b 27 July 1987, Pierce Nicholas Forbes b 11 Jan 1990); *Career* called to the Bar Lincoln's Inn 1974, called to the Scottish Bar 1992, practising advocate 1992–; farmer 1991–; assoc memb London Maritime Arbitrators' Assoc; *Recreations* sailing, real tennis, skiing; *Clubs* Queen's, Petworth House Tennis Court, Itchenor Sailing, Bar Yacht; *Style*— Angus Glennie, Esq, QC; ✉ 20 Essex Street, London WC2R 3AL (☎ 0171 583 9294, fax 0171 583 1341)

GLENNIE, Evelyn Elizabeth Ann; OBE (1993); da of Herbert Arthur Glennie, of Ellon, Aberdeenshire, and Isobel Mary, *née* Howie; *b* 19 July 1965; *Educ* Ellon Acad, Royal Acad of Music (GRSM, LRAM, James Blades prize for percussion and timpani, Hugh Fitch prize for percussion, Hilda Deane Anderson prize for orchestral playing, Queen's Commendation prize); *Career* musician (timpani and percussion); debut recital Wigmore Hall 1986, BBC Prom debut 1989; first ever solo percussion Last Night of the Proms 1994; concerts with numerous orchs worlwide incl: LSO, Philharmonia, London Sinfonietta, Northern Sinfonia, Eng Chamber, RTE (Dublin), Ulster Orch, BBC Scottish Symphony, Finnish Radio Symphony, Trondheim Symphony (Norway), Los Angeles Philharmonic, NY Philharmonic, Detroit Symphony, Nat Symphony (Washington), St Louis Symphony, Orchester der Deutschen Oper Berlin; concert tours of: Europe, Australia, USA, S America, Japan, Middle East, NZ, Far East, UK; composer: A Little Prayer, Giles, Light in Darkness; also orginal music for TV, radio and advertisements; numerous concerts and recitals as a soloist; guest appearances and presenter on TV and radio; recordings: Bartok Sonata for Two Pianos and Percussion (with Sir Georg Solti, Murray Perahia and David Corkhill 1987, Grammy award 1989), Rhythm Song (1989), Light in Darkness (1990), Last Night of the Proms 100th Season (1995), Dancin', Rebounds, Veni Veni Emmanuel, Wind in the Bamboo Grove, Drumming; several pieces composed for her by: John McLeod, Richard Rodney Bennett, Dominic Muldowney, James MacMillan, Geoffrey Burgon, Dave Heath, Thea Musgrave, Ney Rosauro, Askell Masson, John Psathas; awarded: Gold Medal Shell and LSO music scholarship 1984, Munster Trust scholarship 1986, Leonardo de Vinci Prize 1987, Charles Heidsick Instrumentalist of the Year Award 1991; voted by Jr Chamber as one of ten outstanding young people in the world 1989, Scotswoman of the Decade for the 1980's; Hon DMus: Univ of Aberdeen 1991, Univ of Portsmouth 1995, Univ of Bristol 1995, Univ of Loughborough 1995; Hon DLitt Univ of Warwick 1993, Hon LLD Univ of Dundee 1996; FRCM 1991, FRAM 1992; *Books* Good Vibrations (autobiography, 1990); *Recreations* reading, walking, music, antiques; *Style*— Dr Evelyn Glennie, OBE; ✉ PO Box 6, Sawtry, Huntingdon, Cambs PE17 5WE (☎ 01480 891772, fax 01480 891779)

GLENNY, (Alexander) Keith; s of Lt-Col Clifford Roy Glenny, TD, of 28 Crosby Rd, Westcliff On Sea, Essex, and Eileen Winifred, *née* Smith (d 1974); *b* 19 July 1946; *Educ* Charterhouse, Gonville and Caius Coll Cambridge (MA, LLM), King's Coll London (Dip of European Law); *m* 19 April 1975, Rachel Elizabeth, da of Rev A C Fryer, of Glebe House, Byfield, Northants; 2 s (Christopher b 5 Jan 1977, Matthew b 31 Oct 1986), 1 da (Anna b 24 May 1979); *Career* slr British Oxygen Co Ltd 1970–72; Hatten Asplin Glenny (Barking Essex): slr 1972–74, ptnr 1974–88, sr ptnr 1988–; clerk Barking and Ilford United Charities and Barking Gen Charities; Freeman Worshipful Co of Poulters 1978; memb Law Soc; *Clubs* Wig and Pen, City Livery; *Style*— Keith Glenny, Esq; ✉ Netherfield, Powdermill Lane, Leigh, Tonbridge, Kent TN11 8PY (☎ 01732 833 320); Hatten Asplin Glenny, 4 Town Quay Wharf, Abbey Rd, Barking IG11 7BZ (☎ 0181 591 4131, fax 0181 591 1912)

GLENTON, Anthony Arthur Edward; MBE (1983), TD (1974), DL (Northumberland, 1990); s of Lt-Col Eric Cecil Glenton (d 1978), of Gosforth, Newcastle, and Joan Lydia, *née* Taylor; *b* 21 March 1943; *Educ* Merchiston Castle Sch Edinburgh; *m* 8 April 1972, Caroline Ann, da of Maurice George Meade-King, of Clifton, Bristol; 1 s (Peter b 1977), 1 da (Sophie b 1974); *Career* joined TA 1961, Lt-Col 1984, cmd 101 (Northumbrian) Field Regt RA (V) 1984–86, Col 1986, dep cdr 15 Inf Bde 1986–89; ADC to HM the Queen 1987–89; TA Col advsr to GOC Eastern Dist 1990–94; sr ptnr Ryecroft Glenton & Co CAs Newcastle upon Tyne; chm: Newcastle Building Society 1993–, Port of Tyne Authy 1994–, SSAFA Northumberland Branch 1990–; Freeman City of London, Liveryman Worshipful Co of Chartered Accountants England and Wales; FCA 1971; *Recreations* shooting, skiing, contemporary art; *Clubs* Army & Navy; *Style*— Anthony Glenton, Esq, MBE, TD, DL; ✉ Whinbank, Rothbury, Northumberland (☎ 01669 620361); 27 Portland Terrace, Jesmond, Newcastle upon Tyne NE2 1QP (☎ 0191 281 1292)

GLENTORAN, 3 Baron (UK 1939); Sir (Thomas) Robin Valerian Dixon; 5 Bt (UK 1903), CBE (1992, MBE 1969), DL (1979); er s of 2 Baron Glentoran, KBE, PC (d 1995), and Lady Diana Mary Wellesley (d 1984), er da of 3 Earl Cowley; *b* 21 April 1935; *Educ* Eton; *m* 1, 12 Jan 1959 (m dis 1975), Rona Alice Gabrielle, da of Capt George Cecil Colville, CBE, RN, of Bishop's Waltham; 3 s (Hon Daniel George b 1959, Hon Andrew Wynne Valerian b 1961, Hon Patrick Anthony b 1963); m 2, 1979 (m dis 1988), Alwyn Gillian, da of Hubert A Mason, of Grove Lodge, Donaghadee, Co Down; m 3, 1990, Mrs Margaret Anne Murphy, *née* Rainey; *Heir* s, Hon Daniel George Dixon b 1959; *Career* 2 Lt Grenadier Gds 1954, Capt 1958, Maj 1966; non-exec chm Redland of N Ireland 1996– (md 1972–96); memb Millenium Cmmn; *Recreations* sailing (yacht 'Lazy Life'), squash, skiing; *Clubs* Kildare St and Univ (Dublin), Royal Cruising, Irish Cruising; *Style*— The Lord Glentoran, CBE, DL; ✉ Drumadarragh House, Ballyclare, Co Antrim, N Ireland; c/o Redland of N Ireland Ltd, 61 Largy Rd, Crumlin, Co Antrim, N Ireland BT29 4RR (☎ 01849 422791)

GLENTWORTH, Viscount; Edmund Christopher Pery; s and h of 6 Earl of Limerick, KBE; *b* 10 Feb 1963; *Educ* Eton, New Coll Oxford, Pushkin Inst Moscow, City Univ; *m* 21 July 1990, Emily K, o da of Michael Gavin Lynam Thomas, of Worcester; 2 s (Hon Felix Edmund b 16 Nov 1991, Hon Ivo Patrick Pery b 26 Oct 1993); *Career* called to the Bar Middle Temple 1987; HM Dip Serv: FCO 1987–88, Ecole Nationale d'Adminstration 1988–89, Quai d'Orsay 1990, second sec Dakar 1990–91, Amman 1991–92, resigned 1992; Clifford Chance slrs 1992–93, Freshfields slrs 1993–94, Milbank Tweed slrs Moscow 1994–96, Deutche Morgan Grenfell (Moscow) 1996–; *Recreations* windsurfing; *Style*— Viscount Glentworth; ✉ c/o Deutsche Morgan Grenfell (UK) Ltd (Moscow), 23 Great Winchester Street, London EC2P 2AX (☎ 007 503 230 6154)

GLENWRIGHT, (Harry) Donald; s of late Harry Glenwright, and Minnie Glenwright; *b* 25 June 1934; *Educ* Stockton-on-Tees Secdy Sch, Univ of Durham (BDS), Univ of Newcastle (MDS); *m* 29 Dec 1966, Gillian Minton, da of late Arthur Holland Thacker; 1 s (Robert b 1970), 1 da (Kate b 1973); *Career* house surgn Newcastle Dental Hosp 1957–58, Surgn Lt (D) RN 1958–61, registrar Eastman Dental Hosp 1961–63, lectr in dental surgery Univ of Birmingham 1963–66, lectr in periodontics Queen's Univ of Belfast 1966–69, Br Cncl scholar Univ of Oslo 1968, Cncl of Europe scholar Aarhus and Oslo Univs 1971, Br Cncl scholar Colombo Univ 1985; Univ of Birmingham: sr lectr in periodontology 1969–, acting head Dept of Restorative Dentistry 1989–91, chm Bd of Undergraduate Dental Educn 1989–92, chm Dental Curriculum Devpt Ctee 1992–96, asst dir (educn) 1994–96; external examiner: Univ of Dublin 1978, Univ of London 1979–81, Univ of Manchester 1979–86, Univ of Belfast 1980–83, Univ of Leeds 1985–87, RCS 1988–93; assessor Higher Educn Funding Cncl for Wales 1996–; pres: Br Soc of Periodontology 1980–81 (sr vice pres 1991–94), Section of Odontology Birmingham Med Inst 1981–82, Conslt in Restorative Dentistry Gp 1987–96 (memb Cncl, chm 1994–96); memb: Specialist Advsy Ctee in Restorative Dentistry 1987–92, Central Ctee for Hosp Dental Servs 1988, Dental Health and Sci Ctee 1988; FDSRCS; *Recreations* gardening, reading; *Style*— Donald Glenwright, Esq; ✉ White House, Rushbrook Lane, Tanworth-in-Arden, Warwickshire B94 5HP (☎ 01564 742578); The Dental School, St Chads Queensway, Birmingham B4 6NN (☎ 0121 236 8611)

GLICHER, Julian Harvey; s of Samuel Glicher (d 1982), and Dorothy Glicher (d 1983); *b* 15 June 1948; *Educ* Haberdashers' Aske's, Ashridge Sch of Mgmnt; *m* 18 Aug 1976, Adrienne, da of Phillip Rose, of Elstree; 2 s (Toby Oliver b 1978, Nicholas David b 1980); *Career* CA; sr exec Price Waterhouse Paris 1968–72, mangr Hambros Bank 1972–77, asst dir Lloyds Merchant Bank 1977–85, ptnr and nat dir corporate fin Clark Whitehill 1987–92 (dir 1985); dir: English Trust Company Ltd 1992–94, English Trust Group PLC 1992–94; fin dir LAMP Development Services Ltd 1994–; chm H C Holdings (Southampton) Ltd 1992–; FCA 1978, MSI 1993; *Recreations* badminton, cycling, sailing, family; *Style*— Julian H Glicher, Esq; ✉ Lawson-Price, Sir John Lyon House, 5 High Timber Street, London EC4V 3LN (☎ 0171 248 7464, fax 0171 248 1757)

GLICK, Ian Bernard; QC (1987); s of Dr Louis Glick (d 1989), and Phyllis Esty, *née* Barnett; *b* 18 July 1948; *Educ* Bradford GS, Balliol Coll Oxford (MA, BCL); *m* 14 Dec 1986, Roxane Olivia Sarah, da of Dr R Eban, and Mrs G Levin; 3 s (Louis Daniel b 22 March 1991, Joseph Adam b 30 May 1992, Saul David b 27 Dec 1994); *Career* called to the Bar Inner Temple 1970; jr counsel in common law to the Crown 1985–87, standing counsel in export credit cases to DTI 1985–87; *Style*— Ian Glick, Esq, QC; ✉ 1 Essex Court, Temple, London EC4Y 9AR (☎ 0171 583 2000, fax 0171 583 0118)

GLIDEWELL, Rt Hon Sir Iain Derek Laing; kt (1980), PC (1985); s of late Charles Norman Glidewell, and late Nora Glidewell; *b* 8 June 1924; *Educ* Bromsgrove Sch, Worcester Coll Oxford; *m* 1950, Hilary, da of late Clinton D Winant; 1 s, 2 da; *Career* called to the Bar 1949, QC 1969, recorder of the Crown Court 1976–80, appeal judge IOM 1979–80, judge of the High Court of Justice (Queen's Bench Div) 1980–85, memb Supreme Court Rule Ctee 1980–83, presiding judge NE Circuit 1982–85, Lord Justice of Appeal 1985–95; chm Panels for Examination Structure Plans: Worcs 1974, W Midlands 1975; chm Judicial Studies Bd 1989–92; conducted Heathrow Fourth Terminal Enquiry 1978; hon fell Worcester Coll Oxford 1986; *Style*— The Rt Hon Sir Iain Glidewell; ✉ 8 South Square, Gray's Inn, London WC1R 5EU

GLIN, 29 Knight of (The Black Knight, Irish hereditary knighthood dating c 1300–30, though first authenticated use dates from 1424); Desmond John Villiers FitzGerald; s of 28 Knight of Glin (Desmond Windham Otho FitzGerald, d 1949), descended from John Fitz-Thomas FitzGerald (d 1261), father of three bros, The White Knight, The Knight of Glin and The Knight of Kerry; *b* 13 July 1937; *Educ* Stowe, Univ of British Columbia, Harvard; *m* 1, 6 Oct 1966 (m dis 1970), Louise (Lulu) Vava Lucia Henriette, da of Alain, Marquis de la Falaise de la Coudraye, of Paris; m 2, 12 Aug 1970, Olda Anne, o da of Thomas Vincent Windham Willes, of Brompton Square, London; 3 da (Catherine b 1971, m 1995, Lord Durham, *qv*, Nesta b 1973, Honor b 1976); *Career* asst and dep keeper Furniture and Woodwork Dept Victoria and Albert Museum 1965–75, Irish agent Christie's 1975–; pres Irish Georgian Soc, chm and dir Irish Georgian Fndn, dir and past chm Irish Heritage Properties (formerly Historic Irish Tourist Houses Assoc), tstee Castletown Fndn, dir Irish Architectural Archive 1972–; author of books and numerous articles on Irish art and architecture; FSA; *Books* Ireland Observed (with Maurice Craig, 1975), Lost Demesnes (with Edward Malins, 1976), The Painters of Ireland (with Anne Crookshank, 1978), Vanishing Country Houses of Ireland (jtly, 1988), The Watercolours of Ireland (with Anne Crookshank, 1994); *Recreations* art history; *Clubs* White's, Beefsteak, Kildare St and Univ (Dublin); *Style*— The Knight of Glin, FSA; ✉ 52 Waterloo Rd, Dublin 4 (☎ 00 353 116 680 585, fax 00 353 116 680 271); Glin Castle, Co Limerick, Republic of Ireland (☎ 00 353 683 4173 and 34112, fax 00 353 683 4364)

GLOAK, Graeme Frank; CB (1980); s of Frank Gloak, MBE (d 1979), of Kent, and Lilian Phoebe (d 1991); *b* 9 Nov 1921; *Educ* Brentwood; *m* 1944, Mary Beatrice, da of Stanley James Thorne (d 1953), of Essex; 2 s (Nigel (decd), Malcolm b 1951), 1 da (Karen b 1960); *Career* RN 1941–46, Lt RNVR served Atlantic, North Sea, France; admitted slr 1947; slr for Customs and Excise 1978–82; vice chm Agric Wages Ctee for Essex and Herts 1987–90, chm Agric Dwellings Housing Advsy Ctee for Essex and Herts 1984–93; memb Barking and Havering: Family Practitioners' Ctee 1986–90, Family Health Service Authy 1990–96, Health Authy 1996–; *Publications* Customs and Excise Halsbury's Laws of England; *Recreations* badminton, walking, watching cricket; *Clubs* MCC, Essex CCC (Chelmsford); *Style*— Graeme Gloak, Esq, CB; ✉ Northwold, 123 Priests Lane, Shenfield, Essex CM15 8HJ (☎ 01277 212748)

GLOBE, Henry Brian; QC (1994); s of Theodore Montague Globe, of Liverpool, and Irene Rita, *née* Green; *b* 18 June 1949; *Educ* Liverpool Coll, Univ of Birmingham (LLB, hockey blue); *m* 11 June 1972, Estelle, da of Irene and Israel Levin; 2 da (Danielle Rebecca b 5 Feb 1976, Amanda Jane b 3 Sept 1978); *Career* called to the Bar Middle Temple 1972, jr Northern Circuit 1974; standing counsel to: Dept of Social Security 1985–94, HM Customs & Excise 1992–94; recorder 1991– (asst recorder 1988–90); govr King David Schs Liverpool 1979–, chm of govrs King David HS 1990–; *Recreations* tennis, bridge; *Style*— Henry Globe, Esq, QC; ✉ Exchange Chambers, Pearl Assurance House, Derby Square, Liverpool L2 9XX (☎ 0151 236 7747, fax 0151 236 3433)

GLOCK, Sir William Frederick; kt (1970), CBE (1964); s of William George Glock; *b* 3 May 1908; *Educ* Christ's Hosp, Gonville and Caius Coll Cambridge, studied with Artur Schnabel Berlin; *m* 1, 1944, Clemency, da of Swinburne Hale; m 2, 1952, Anne Genevieve, da of Charles Geoffroy-Dechaume; *Career* dir Summer Sch of Music: Bryanston 1948–52, Dartington Hall 1953–79; former music critic: The Observer, New Statesman; controller of music BBC 1959–72, former memb Bd Dirs Royal Opera House and Arts Cncl, dir Bath Festival 1975–84, chm London Orch Concerts Bd 1975–86; govr South Bank Bd 1986–90, hon memb Royal Philharmonic Soc; Albert Medal RSA 1971; Hon: DMus Univ of Nottingham 1968, DUniv York 1972, DLitt Univ of Bath 1984, DMus Univ of Plymouth 1993; *Publications* Notes in Advance, an Autobiography in Music (1991); *Style*— Sir William Glock, CBE; ✉ Vine House, Brightwell cum Sotwell, Wallingford, Oxon (☎ 01491 837144)

GLOIN, David Barclay; s of Barclay Arthur Gloin (d 1981), of Dulwich, and Dilys Margaret, *née* Williams; *b* 28 Feb 1946; *Educ* Alleyn's Sch Dulwich; *m* 25 July 1970, Elizabeth Mary, da of Leslie George Francis, MBE (d 1975), of Herne Hill, S London; 1 s (Peter b 1976), 1 da (Janet b 1980); *Career* slr; articled then ptnr Gaunt Foster and Hill 1964–70, legal asst then head of branch Post Office Slr's Office Conveyancing Dept 1970–82; BT: div slr Slr's Office Commercial Dept 1982–87, dir Property Law Dept 1987–89, dir Litigation and Advsy Dept 1989–90, dep slr and head of dept 1990–92; conslt Skillbase Ltd 1992–93, editorial team ldr statue law database Statutory Pubns Office Lord Chllr's Dept 1993–96, sec Advsy Ctee on Statute Law 1995–96, slr Building Societies Cmmn 1996–; memb: Law Soc, Int Bar Assoc; local preacher Methodist Church 1996–; Freeman City of London Slrs' Co 1989, Freeman City of London 1990; *Recreations* singing, reading, walking; *Style*— David B Gloin, Esq; ✉ Registry of Friendly Societies, 15 Great Marlborough Street, London W1V 2AX (☎ 0171 494 6633, fax 0171 437 1612)

GLOSSOP, (Charles Compton) Anthony; s of Col Alfred William Compton Glossop, OBE, TD (d 1980), of Chesterfield, Derbyshire, and Muriel Bradbury, *née* Robinson (d 1986); *b* 24 Nov 1941; *Educ* Eastbourne Coll, Queens' Coll Cambridge (MA); *m* 28 June 1969, Julia Margaret Anne, da of Capt William Forrester (d 1952), of Dalton-in-Furness, Cumbria; 2 da (Clare b 5 Jan 1971, Katharine b 21 Dec 1972); *Career* admitted slr 1967; asst sec Molins Ltd 1969–72, gp md St Modwen Properties plc (formerly Redman Heenan Int plc) 1982– (co sec 1972–82, dir 1976–); memb: Worcester Civic Soc, Law Soc 1967; *Recreations* walking, reading, gardening and bee-keeping; *Style*— Anthony Glossop, Esq; ✉ St Modwen Properties plc, Lyndon House, 58–62 Hagley Rd, Birmingham B16 8PE (☎ 0121 456 2800, fax 0121 456 1829, car 0860 206694)

GLOSSOP, Peter; s of Cyril Glossop, and Violet Elizabeth Glossop; *b* 6 July 1928; *Educ* High Storrs GS Sheffield; *m* 1, 1955 (m dis 1977), Joyce Elizabeth Blackham; m 2, 1977, Michèle Yvonne Amos; 2 da; *Career* baritone; princ baritone: Royal Opera House (Covent Garden) to 1967; guest artist: Royal Opera House (Covent Garden), La Scala (Milan), Met Opera (NY), Stasoper (Vienna), Colon Theatre (Buenos Aires), San Francisco, Chicago, San Diego, Paris Opera, San Carlo (Naples), Lyceo (Barcelona); *Films* Otello, Pagliacci; *Recordings* Otello, Billy Budd, Roberto Devereaux, Merrie England, Les Troyens, Dido and Aeneas; Hon DMus Univ Sheffield 1971; gold medal winner Opera Competition Sofia Bulgaria 1961; *Recreations* golf; *Style*— Peter Glossop, Esq

GLOSTER, Elizabeth (Mrs S E Brodie); QC (1989); da of Peter Gloster (d 1991), and Betty Mabel, *née* Read; *b* 5 June 1949; *Educ* Roedean Sch Brighton, Girton Coll Cambridge (BA); *m* 29 Oct 1973, Stanley Eric Brodie, QC, *qv*, s of Dr Abraham Brodie (d 1978); 1 da (Sophie Rebecca b 12 Sept 1978), 1 s (Samuel Rufus b 14 Jan 1981); *Career* called to the Bar 1971: Inner Temple, Bermuda, Gibraltar, IOM; memb Lincoln's Inn (ad eundem) 1974, memb Panel of Jr Counsel representing DTI in co matters 1982–89, recorder 1995– (asst recorder 1991–95), bencher Inner Temple 1992; assoc memb (as barr) Insolvency Lawyers' Assoc 1991–, pt/t memb Civil Aviation Authy 1992–93, judge of the Ct of Appeal of the Channel Islands (pt/t) 1994–; *Style*— Miss Elizabeth Gloster, QC; ✉ 1 Essex Court, Temple, London EC4Y 9BS (☎ 0171 583 2000, fax 0171 583 0118)

GLOUCESTER, Archdeacon of; *see:* Wagstaff, Ven Christopher John Harold

GLOUCESTER, Bishop of 1993–; Rt Rev David Edward Bentley; s of William Edward Bentley (d 1980), of Gorleston, and Florence Maud Marion, *née* Dalgleish (d 1978); *b* 7 Aug 1935; *Educ* Gt Yarmouth GS, Univ of Leeds (BA), Westcott House Cambridge; *m* 5 Sept 1962, Clarice May, da of Reginald Lahmers (d 1964), of KirkBride, Isle of Man; 2 s (Simon b 1964, Matthew b 1966), 2 da (Katharine (Mrs Martin Gorick) b 1963, Rachel (Mrs Michael Harrison) b 1964); *Career* Nat Serv 1956–58, 2 Lt 5 Regt RHA; curate: St Ambrose Bristol 1960–62, Holy Trinity with St Mary Guildford 1962–66; rector: All Saints, Headley 1966–73, Esher 1973–86; rural dean Emly 1977–82; hon canon Guildford Cathedral 1980–86, chm Diocesan Cncl of Social Responsibility 1980–86, Bishop of Lynn 1986–93; chm ACCM Candidates Cmmn 1987–91, chm ABM Recruitment and Selection Cmmn 1991–93; warden of All Hollows Convent Ditchingham 1990–93; *Recreations* music, theatre, sport, walking; *Clubs* MCC; *Style*— The Rt Rev the Lord Bishop of Gloucester; ✉ Bishopscourt, Pitt Street, Gloucester GL1 2BQ (☎ 01452 524598, fax 01452 310025)

GLOVER, Prof David Moore; *b* 28 March 1948; *Educ* Broadway Tech GS Barnsley, Fitzwilliam Coll Cambridge (BA), UCL (PhD); *Career* Damon Runyon postdoctoral res fell Stanford Univ 1972–75; Imperial Coll of Science and Technol: lectr in biochemistry 1975–81, sr lectr 1981–83, reader in molecular genetics 1983–86, prof of molecular genetics and dir Eukaryotic Molecular Genetics Gp Cancer Research Campaign 1986–89 (jt dir 1979–86), head Dept of Biochemistry 1988–89; Univ of Dundee: prof of biochemistry 1989–92, dir Cell Cycle Genetics Gp Cancer Research Campaign 1989–, prof of molecular genetics Dept of Anatomy and Physiology 1992–; ed Jl of Cell Science; memb Editorial Bd: Mechanisms of Development, Insect Molecular Biology; Cancer Research Campaign Career Devpt Award 1979–89; memb: Euro Molecular Biology Orgn 1978, Human Genome Orgn 1990; FRSE 1992; *Books* Frontiers in Molecular Biology (series ed); author of numerous scientific pubns; *Style*— Prof David M Glover, FRSE; ✉ Cancer Research Campaign Laboratories, Department of Anatomy & Physiology, Medical Science Institute, University of Dundee, Dundee DD1 4HN

GLOVER, Eric; s of William Arthur Glover (d 1965), of Liverpool, and Margaret, *née* Walker; *b* 28 June 1935; *Educ* Liverpool Inst HS, Oriel Coll Oxford (MA); *m* 1960, Adele Diane, da of Col Cecil Geoffrey Hilliard, of Harrogate; 3 s (Ian, Paul, Jason); *Career* sec gen Chartered Inst of Bankers 1982–94 (dir of studies 1968–82); chm Open and Distance Learning Quality Cncl 1993–, treas British Accreditation Cncl, sr conslt Fairplace Inst of Banking and Finance; hon fell Sheffield Hallam Univ; Hon MBA Univ of London; *Recreations* golf, squash, tennis; *Clubs* Overseas Bankers'; *Style*— Eric Glover, Esq; ✉ 12 Manor Park, Tunbridge Wells, Kent TN4 8XP (☎ 01892 531221);

GLOVER, Gen Sir James Malcolm; KCB (1981), MBE (1964); s of Maj-Gen Malcolm Glover, CB, OBE (d 1970), and Jean Ogilvie, *née* Will (d 1970); *b* 25 March 1929; *Educ* Wellington, RMA Sandhurst; *m* 1959, Janet Diones, da of Maj Hugo De Pree; 1 s (Jonathan), 1 da (Carolyn); *Career* cmmnd 1949, RHA 1950–54, instr RMA Sandhurst 1955–56, transferred to Rifle Bde 1956, Bde Maj 48 Gurkha Inf Bde 1960–62, memb Directing Staff Staff Coll 1966–68, CO 3 Bn Royal Green Jackets 1970–71, Col Gen Staff MOD 1972–73, Cdr 19 Airportable Bde 1974–75, Brig Gen Staff (Intelligence) MOD 1977–78, Cdr Land Forces NI 1979–80, Lt-Gen 1981, Dep Chief Def Staff (Intelligence) and memb Jt Intelligence Ctee 1981–83, Vice-Chief Gen Staff MOD and memb Army Bd of Def Cncl 1983–85, C-in-C UKLF 1985–87, Col Cmdt Royal Green Jackets 1983–88, ret 1987; non-exec dir British Petroleum plc 1987–, chm Royal Armouries International plc 1993–; memb Advsy Bd BTS Group 1996–; *Recreations* shooting, mountain walking, reading biographies; *Clubs* Boodle's; *Style*— Gen Sir James Glover, KCB, MBE; ✉ c/o Lloyds Bank Ltd, Cox's and King's Branch, 7 Pall Mall, London SW1

GLOVER, Dr Jane Alison; da of Robert Finlay Glover, TD, of Malvern, Worcs, and Jean, *née* Muir, MBE; *b* 13 May 1949; *Educ* Monmouth Sch for Girls, St Hugh's Coll Oxford (BA, MA, DPhil); *Career* freelance conductor; musical dir: Glyndebourne Touring Opera 1982–85, London Choral Soc 1983–; appeared with many orchs and opera cos incl: Glyndebourne Festival Opera 1982–, BBC Proms 1985–, Royal Opera House Covent Garden 1988–, Eng Nat Opera 1989–, Australian Opera 1996–, Glimmerglass Opera 1994–; artistic dir London Mozart Players 1984–91, princ conductor Huddersfield Choral Soc 1989–96; regular broadcaster on TV and radio, regular recordings; sr res fell St Hugh's Coll Oxford 1982 (hon fell 1991); govr BBC 1990–95; Hon DMus: Univ of Exeter 1986, Cncl for Nat Acad Awards 1991, Univ of London 1992, City Univ 1994; Hon DUniv Open Univ 1988; Hon DLitt: Loughborough Univ of Technol 1988, Univ of Bradford 1992; memb Worshipful Co of Haberdashers; RSA 1988, FRCM 1993; *Books* Cavalli (1978); *Recreations* Times crossword, theatre, walking, skiing; *Style*— Dr Jane Glover; ✉ c/o Lies Askonas Ltd, 6 Henrietta Street, London WC2E 8LA (☎ 0171 379 7700)

GLOVER, Julian Wyatt; s of (Claude) Gordon Glover (d 1975), of Arkesden, Essex, and Honor Ellen Morgan, *née* Wyatt; *b* 27 March 1935; *Educ* St Paul's, Alleyn's Sch Dulwich, RADA; *m* 1, 1957 (m dis 1966), Eileen Atkins, CBE *qv*; m 2, 28 Sept 1968, Isla Blair, *qv*; 1 s (Jamie Blair b 10 July 1969); *Career* actor; Nat Serv 2 Lt RASC 1954–56; started out as spear-carrier Shakespeare Memorial Theatre, Stratford-upon-Avon 1957; Liveryman Worshipful Co of Dyers 1956; *Theatre* incl: Aufidius in Coriolanus and Warwick in Henry VI (RSC) 1977, Habeas Corpus, Educating Rita, The Aspern Papers, Never The Sinner, title role in Henry IV Parts I and II RSC 1991–92 (winner Best Supporting Actor Olivier Award 1993), All My Sons 1992, Cyrano de Bergerac (Haymarket) 1992–93, An Inspector Calls (RNT, Aldwych) 1993–94; theatre seasons with: RSC (Cassius and Friar Lawrence 1995–96), Prospect, The Old Vic and Nat Theatre Companies; dir Hamlet (Norwich Playhouse) 1996; *Television* incl: An Age of Kings, Spytrap, Z-Cars, Dombey and Son, By The Sword Divided, Wish Me Luck, Spy Trap, Cover Her Face, Warburg, Man of Influence, Darling Buds of May, Money for Nothing, Degrees of Error, Taggart, The Chief 1995, The Infiltrator, Cadfael; *Films* incl: Tom Jones, For Your Eyes Only, The Fourth Protocol, I Was Happy Here, Cry Freedom, Treasure Island, Indiana Jones and the Last Crusade, King Ralph; *Books* Beowolf (1987 and 1995); *Style*— Julian Glover, Esq; ✉ c/o Conway van Gelder Robinson Ltd, 18–21 Jermyn Street, London SW1Y 6HP (☎ 0171 287 0077, fax 0171 287 1940)

GLOVER, Malcolm; *b* 3 Nov 1943; *Educ* Doncaster GS, Univ of Bristol (LLB); *m* 30 March 1973, Diane Marilyn; 1 s (Matthew b 1977), 2 da (Katie b 1975, Caroline b 1983); *Career* admitted slr 1968; Wilde Sapte 1970–: slr 1970–71, ptnr 1971–88, dep sr ptnr 1988–; memb Worshipful Co of Slrs; memb Law Soc; *Recreations* tennis, theatre; *Style*— Malcolm Glover, Esq; ✉ 31 Ossulton Way, Hampstead Garden Suburb, London N2 OJY; Wilde Sapte, Queensbridge House, 1 Fleet Place, London EC4M 7WS (☎ 0171 246 7000, fax 0171 246 7777, telex 887793 WILDES G)

GLOVER, (Herbert) Michael John; s of Herbert William Archibald Glover (d 1966), of Bideford, Devon and Ethel Alice, *née* Halbert; *b* 7 Sept 1943; *Educ* Belmont Coll Barnstaple, Bideford GS; *partner* Gillian Susan Pope; *Career* articled clerk H Barrett Son & Taylor Bideford and Barnstaple, qualified CA 1968, Cooper Bros & Co Bristol 1969–70; Turquand Young & Co: joined Exeter 1970, ptnr Torquay 1977–80, ptnr Bideford 1980–89; managing ptnr Ernst & Young N Devon Practice Bideford & Barnstaple 1989–90; ptnr Glover Pearce & Ross (following mgmnt buy-out) 1990–; FCA 1979 (ACA 1968); *Recreations* birdwatching, conservation and the countryside; *Style*— Michael Glover, Esq; ✉ Glover Pearce & Ross, 27 Bridgeland St, Bideford, Devon (☎ 01237 471881, fax 01237 470133)

GLOVER, Dr Richard Berry; s of Henry Graham Glover (d 1931), of Hove, Sussex, and Marjorie Florence, *née* Covell (d 1978); *b* 9 Dec 1928; *Educ* Charterhouse, Middx Hosp Univ of London (MB BS); *m* 24 April 1957, (Joan Elizabeth) Ann, da of C Stuart Chiesman (d 1969), of Bickley, Kent; 1 s (Mark Berry b 24 April 1959), 1 da (Sarah Jane (Mrs Tice) b 23 May 1962); *Career* Nat Serv Flt Lt Surgical Div Med Branch RAF 1954–58; house surgn and ENT house surgn Middx Hosp 1952–53, ptnr med practice Oxshott 1958–89; MO: Sandown Park Racecourse 1973, Epsom Racecourse 1978, Kempton Park Racecourse 1986, Lingfield Park 1989; MO Reed's Sch Cobham 1985–89; Liveryman Worshipful Co of Innholders 1961 (memb Ct 1989); MRCS, LRCP 1952; memb: BMA, Med Equestrian Assoc, Racecourse Med Offrs' Assoc; *Recreations* sailing, golf; *Clubs* RAC, Royal Lymington Yacht; *Style*— Dr Richard Glover; ✉ Scermer, Manor Way, Oxshott, Surrey KT22 0HU; 5 Totland Court, Victoria Rd, Milford-on-Sea, Hants SO41 ONR (☎ 01372 843088)

GLOVER, Richard Gordon Finlay; s of Robert Finlay Glover, of Malvern, Worcs, and Jean, *née* Muir; *b* 3 Aug 1952; *Educ* Tonbridge, Univ of Strasbourg, CCC Oxford (BA); *m* 4 Oct 1980, Teresa Anne, da of Richard Ingram Lindsell; 1 s (Thomas Finlay b 19 Jan 1984), 1 da (Alice Catherine b 31 July 1987); *Career* ICI 1974–80: variously asst works personnel offr Slough, gp personnel offr (Wall Coverings) and works personnel offr Newton Works Cheshire; Grand Metropolitan 1980–86: personnel mangr Watney's Brewery, employee relations offr Watney, personnel and admin dir Truman; nat ops dir Pizzaland Int (subsid of United Biscuits) until 1988 (joined as personnel dir 1986), sr search conslt Whithead Mann 1988–90, md BSM Group PLC 1990–; Liveryman The Worshipful Co of Haberdashers 1977; FRSA 1993; *Recreations* Welsh rugby, cinema, squash; *Style*— Richard Glover, Esq; ✉ British School of Motoring, 81/87 Hartfield Road, Wimbledon, London SW19 3TJ (☎ 0181 545 1420, fax 0181 545 0859, car 0850 655710)

GLOVER, Robert Edward; s of Ronald Glover, and Anne, *née* Richards; *b* 22 July 1936; *Educ* Bushey GS; *m* 1969 (m dis 1980); 1 da (Jessica Jane b 18 Oct 1972); *Career* photographer; trained as photogravure colour retoucher, fndr own commercial and social photography studio 1965; Portrait Photographer of the Year 1984 and 1991, Fox Talbot Award (first ever) 1996; chm Admissions and Qualifications Bd BIPP 1991–; FBIPP, FRSA; *Recreations* military history; *Clubs* MCC; *Style*— Robert Glover, Esq; ✉ Robert Glover Photography, Roundwood Farm, Near Kea, Truro, Cornwall TR3 6AS (☎ 01872 864587)

GLOVER, Stephen Charles Morton; s of Prebendary John Morton Glover (d 1979), and Helen Ruth, *née* Jones (d 1984); *b* 13 Jan 1952; *Educ* Shrewsbury, Mansfield Coll Oxford (MA); *m* 1982, Celia Elizabeth, da of Peter Montague; 2 s (Edmund b 1983, Alexander b 1987); *Career* leader and feature writer Daily Telegraph 1978–85 (parliamentary sketch writer 1979–81), foreign ed The Independent 1986–89, ed The

Independent on Sunday 1990–91, assoc ed (politics) The Evening Standard 1992–; dir Newspaper Publishing plc 1986–92; *Books* Paper Dreams (1993); *Clubs* Beefsteak; *Style—* Stephen Glover, Esq; ✉ c/o Aitken and Stone, 29 Fernshaw Rd, London SW10 0TG

GLOVER, Hon Sir Victor Joseph Patrick; *b* 5 Nov 1932; *Educ* Collège du Saint Esprit, Royal Coll Mauritius, Jesus Coll Oxford (BA); *m* M C Ginette Gauthier; 2 s; *Career* called to the Bar Middle Temple 1957, barr Mauritian Bar 1957–62, Attorney Gen Office 1962–76 (crown counsel, dist magistrate, sr crown counsel, princ crown counsel, Parly counsel), puisne judge Supreme Ct 1976–82, sr puisne judge 1982–88, chief justice 1988–94; sr legal conslt Price Waterhouse Mauritius; pt/t lectr Univ of Mauritius 1966–87, chm Cncl of Legal Educn 1985–88, hon prof of law Univ of Mauritius 1986, professeur invité Faculté de Droit Université d'Aix Marseille 1986; chm: Cmmn of Enquiry on Post-Primary and Secdy Educn, Cmmn of Enquiry on Educn 1982, Study Panel on Tertiary Educn 1985; chm Tertiary Educn Cmmn 1988–; pres Bd of Govrs Collège du Saint Esprit 1980–88, compiler and ed Abstract of Decisions of Supreme Ct of Mauritius 1966–; *Style—* The Hon Sir Victor Glover; ✉ 309 Chancery House, Port Louis, Mauritius

GLOVER, William James; QC (1969); s of Henry Percy Glover, KC (d 1938), and Martha, *née* Latham (d 1971); *b* 8 May 1924; *Educ* Harrow, Pembroke Coll Cambridge (BA); *m* 28 July 1956, Rosemary Dymond, da of Wilfrid Henry John Long (d 1971); 2 s (James William b 1957, Richard Michael b 1961); *Career* joined Army 1943, cmmnd RA 1944, served Royal West African Frontier Force (West African Artillery) W Africa and Burma 1944–47; called to the Bar Inner Temple 1950, second jr counsel to Inland Revenue 1963–69, recorder Crown Ct 1975–91, bencher 1977–; *Recreations* golf, photography; *Style—* William Glover, Esq, QC; ✉ 2 Mitre Court Buildings, Temple, London EC4Y 7BS (☎ 0171 583 1380, fax 0171 353 7772, car 0831 155216)

GLYN, Maj Sir Alan; kt (1990), ERD; s of John Paul Glyn (Lt Royal Horse Guards (Blues), Barr at Law Middle Temple, d 1938), and Margaret, *née* Johnston; *b* 26 Sept 1918; *Educ* Westminster, Gonville and Caius Coll Cambridge, St Bartholomew's Med Sch, St George's Hosp; *m* 4 Jan 1962, Lady Rosula Caroline, *née* Windsor-Clive, 3 da of 2 Earl of Plymouth, PC, and Lady Irene, *née* Charteris, da of 11 and 7 Earl of Wemyss and March; 2 da; *Career* WWII served UK 1939–42, Far East 1942–46, psc 1945, Bde Maj; re-employed as Capt (Hon Maj) RHG until 1967, attached French Foreign Legion 1960 (by special permission of French Govt); qualified doctor 1948, called to the Bar Middle Temple 1955; war corr in Vietnam; co-opted memb LCC Educn Ctee 1956–58, memb: No 1 LCC Divnl Health Ctee 1959–61, Chelsea Borough Cncl 1959–62, Inner London Med Ctee 1967–, GLC Valuation Panel 1967–91; MP (C): Wandsworth Clapham 1959–64, Windsor 1970–74, Windsor and Maidenhead 1974–92; former govr of Henry Thornton and Aristotle Schs; one of the Earl Marshal's Green Staff Offrs at Investiture of HRH The Prince of Wales at Caernarvon 1969; memb Governing Body of Br Postgrad Med Fedn Univ of London 1968–81, memb Bd of Govrs Nat Heart and Chest Hosps 1982–90; Freeman City of London 1961, Liveryman Worshipful Soc of Apothecaries 1961; awarded (with freedom fighters in Hungarian Revolution) Pro-Hungarian Medal of SMO of Malta 1956; *Publications* Witness to Vietnam (the Containment of Communism in SE Asia) (1968), Let's Think Again; *Clubs* Pratt's, Carlton, Special Services; *Style—* Maj Sir Alan Glyn, ERD; ✉ 17 Cadogan Place, London SW1X 9SA (☎ 0171 235 2957)

GLYN, Hon Andrew John; yr s of 6 Baron Wolverton, CBE (d 1988); bro and h of 7 Baron; *b* 30 June 1943; *Educ* Eton, New Coll Oxford (MA); *m* 1, 1965 (m dis 1986), Celia Laws; 1 s (Miles John b 1966), 1 da (Lucy Abigail b 1968); m 2, 1986, Wendy Carlin; 1 s (Jonathan b 1990), 1 da (Tessa b 1987); *Career* fell Corpus Christi Coll Oxford; *Style—* The Hon Andrew Glyn; ✉ c/o Corpus Christi College Oxford, University of Oxford, Oxford OX1 3DP (☎ 01865 276700)

GLYN, Sir Anthony Geoffrey Leo Simon; 2 Bt (UK 1927), of Berbice, British Guiana; s of Sir Edward Rae Davson, 1 Bt, KCMG (d 1937), and Margot Elinor, OBE (d 1966), da of Clayton Louis Glyn, and Elinor Sutherland (the novelist Elinor Glyn); assumed by deed poll 1957 the surname of Glyn in lieu of his patronymic and the additional forename of Anthony; *b* 13 March 1922; *Educ* Eton; *m* 2 Oct 1946, Susan Eleanor, da of Lt-Col Sir Rhys Rhys Williams, 1 Bt, DSO, QC; 1 da (Victoria Anne b 1951) (and 1 da decd); *Heir* bro, Christopher Michael Edward Davson b 26 May 1927; *Career* Capt Welsh Gds 1941–46; author; Book Society choice twice; Vermeil medal City of Paris 1985; *Books* major works: The Ram in the Thicket, Elinor Glyn: A Biography, I Can Take It All, The Seine, The Dragon Variation, The Blood of a Britishman, The Companion Guide to Paris (1985); *Recreations* skiing, music, chess; *Clubs* Pratt's; *Style—* Sir Anthony Glyn, Bt; ✉ Marina Baie des Anges, Ducal Apt U-03, 06270 Villeneuve-Loubet, Alpes Maritimes, France (☎ 00 33 93 73 67 52)

GLYN, Sir Richard Lindsay; 10 Bt (GB 1759), of Ewell, Surrey, and 6 Bt (GB 1800), of Gaunt's House; s of Sir Richard Hamilton Glyn, OBE, TD, 9 and 5 Bt (d 1980), and Lyndsay Mary Baker; *b* 3 Aug 1943; *Educ* Eton; *m* 1970 (m dis 1979), Carolyn Ann, da of Roy Frank Williams (d 1979), of Pasadena, Calif, USA; 1 s, 1 da (Eliza Jane Rose b 1975); *Heir* s, Richard Rufus Francis Glyn b 8 Jan 1971; *Career* 2 Lt Royal Hampshire Regt 1962–65; Studio Orange Ltd (photography and design) 1966–71, Gaunts Estate 1972, dir Gaunt's House 1989; farmer 1976–; underwriting memb Lloyd's 1976–; co-fndr High Lea Sch 1982; fndr Richard Glyn Foundation for Profound Learning 1995; *Style—* Sir Richard Glyn, Bt; ✉ Ashton Farmhouse, Stanbridge, Wimborne, Dorset (☎ 01258 840585, fax 01202 841959)

GLYN-JONES, Peter; s of Glyn Thomas Jones, of Abinger Hammer, Dorking, Surrey, and Annie, *née* Greenwood; *b* 27 April 1945; *Educ* Royal GS Guildford, Univ of Southampton (LLB), Guildford Law Sch; *m* 28 Sept 1968, Carolyn Mary, da of Joseph Frank Cox; 1 s (William Peter b 1 Dec 1972), 1 da (Annabel Roma (twin) b 2 Dec 1972); *Career* admitted slr 1969; Denton Hall: articled clerk 1967, ptnr 1973–94, opened and ran Docklands Office 1983–89; ptnr Osborne Clarke 1994–; chm Docklands Business Club 1990–92; memb: Law Soc 1969, Int Bar Assoc 1991, Br Cncl of Shopping Centres 1994, Int Cncl of Shopping Centres 1994, RPS (LRPS); *Recreations* photography, choral singing, marathon running, mountaineering, cycling, skiing, water-skiing; *Clubs* Royal Motor Yacht (Poole), Harewood Downs Golf, Pont Royal Golf and Country, Provence; *Style—* Peter Glyn-Jones, Esq; ✉ Osborne Clarke, Solicitors and Notaries, 6–9 Middle Street, London EC1A 7JA (☎ 0171 600 0155, fax 0171 726 2772, car 0850 383778, portable 0385 258044)

GLYNN, (Brian) David; s of William Arthur Glynn, CBE (d 1976), and Norah Haden, *née* Mottram; *b* 30 May 1940; *Educ* Epsom Coll, Guy's Hosp Dental School (BDS Univ of London, LDS RCS Eng, DGDP RCS Eng, represented hockey and shooting teams), Univ of Oregon Dental Sch (Newland Pedley scholar); *m* 16 May 1964, Judith Mary, da of George Charles English, CBE; 2 da (Amanda Jayne b 18 March 1968, Nicola Louise b 17 June 1970); *Career* dental surgeon; Dept of Conservation Dentistry Guy's Hosp: pt/t registrar 1967–74, pt/t jr lectr 1974–76, pt/t sr demonstrator 1976–79; in private practice 35 Devonshire Place W1 1979– (pt/t 1967–74); chm Compudent Ltd 1984–95; Federation Dentaire Internationale: conslt Scientific Programme Ctee 1989, conslt Cmmn of Dental Practice on Computer Aided Diagnostics 1990; lectr on use of computers in gen dental practice, author of numerous papers and courses on restorative dentistry, responsible for use of closed circuit TV in teaching at Guy's Hosp (prodr various films); memb: BDA, American Dental Soc of London (sec 1972–75, pres 1992–93); fell Int Coll of Dentists 1981 (gen sec Euro section 1984–92, vice pres 1992–93 and 1997, pres 1994–95); *Publications* Use of Closed Circuit TV (Medical and Biological Illustration, 1973); various papers to American Dental Soc of London; *Recreations* fly fishing, skiing, sailing, tennis, flying, twin & single engine aircraft; *Clubs* Fly Fishers; *Style—* David Glynn, Esq; ✉ Glynn Setchell and Allan, 35 Devonshire Place, London W1N 1PE (☎ 0171 935 3342/3, fax 0171 224 0558)

GLYNN, Prof Ian Michael; s of Hyman Glynn (d 1984), and Charlotte, *née* Fluxbaum (d 1990); *b* 3 June 1928; *Educ* City of London Sch, Trinity Coll Cambridge (MA, PhD, MD), Univ Coll Hosp; *m* 9 Dec 1958, Jenifer Muriel, da of Ellis Arthur Franklin, OBE (d 1964); 1 s (Simon b 1964), 2 da (Sarah b 1959, Judith b 1961); *Career* Nat Serv Flt Lt RAF Med Branch 1956–57; house physician Central Middx Hosp 1952–53; Univ of Cambridge: fell Trinity Coll 1955–, demonstrator in physiology 1958–63, lectr 1963–70, reader 1970–75, prof of membrane physiology 1975–86, vice master Trinity Coll 1980–86, prof of physiology 1986–95 (emeritus prof 1995–); visiting prof Yale Univ Sch of Med 1969; memb: MRC 1976–80, Cncl of Royal Soc 1979–81 and 1991–92, Agric and Food Res Cncl 1981–86; Hon MD Aarhus (Denmark) 1988; FRS 1970, FRCP 1987, hon foreign memb American Acad of Arts & Sciences 1984, hon memb American Physiological Soc 1990; *Books* The Sodium Pump (ed with C Ellory 1985), The Company of Biologists; *Style—* Prof Ian Glynn, FRS; ✉ Physiological Laboratory, Downing St, Cambridge CB2 3EG (☎ 01223 333 869, fax 01223 333 840, telex CAMSPL G)

GLYNNE, Alan; s of Daniel Glynne, and Lilian, *née* Swirsky; *b* 21 May 1941; *Educ* Univ of Edinburgh (BSc, MB ChB), RCP (MRCP); *m* 21 May 1969, Barbara, da of Philip Lee; 1 s (Paul Alexander b 1970), 1 da (Kathryn Antonia b 1971); *Career* registrar in cardiology Leeds Gen Infirmary 1967–69, registrar in endocrinology and gen med Univ Dept of Med Glasgow Royal Infirmary 1969–72, sr registrar in gen med Whithington Hosp and Royal Infirmary Manchester 1972–74, dir of clinical investigation and head of clinical pharmacology Lilly Research Centre UK 1974–82, hon conslt and lectr in med Guy's Hosp 1980–83, examiner RCP, currently conslt physician, pt/t conslt physician Cromwell Hosp; author of various contribs to sci jls; memb: Int Diabetes Fedn, Med and Scientific Section of Br Diabetic Assoc, The Thyroid Club, Chelsea Clinical Soc, Endocrine Section RSM; FFPM; *Recreations* golf, photography; *Clubs* Coombe Hill Golf; *Style—* Dr Alan Glynne; ✉ 97 Harley St, London W1N 1DF (☎ 0171 935 5896, fax 0171 935 6617)

GOAD, Sir (Edward) Colin Viner; KCMG (1974); s of late Maurice George Viner Goad, of Cirencester, Glos, and Caroline, *née* Masters; *b* 21 Dec 1914; *Educ* Cirencester GS, Gonville and Caius Coll Cambridge (BA); *m* 1939, Joan Olive Bradley (d 1980); 1 s; *Career* under sec Min of Tport 1963, sec gen Intergovernmental Maritime Consultative Orgn 1968–74 (dep sec gen 1963–68), ret 1974; dir International Registries Inc 1993–; *Style—* Sir Colin Goad, KCMG; ✉ The Paddock, Ampney Crucis, Cirencester, Glos (☎ 01285 851353)

GOAD, Brig Kevin John Watson; CBE (1997), ADC (1995); s of Maj Christopher Frederick Goad, of Portswood, Southampton, and Mary Merton, *née* Watson; *b* 8 May 1942; *Educ* Coatham Sch, Windsor Sch, RMA Sandhurst; *m* 31 July 1965, Anne Elizabeth, da of Maj Hugh Lewis Thomas; 2 da (Claire Emma b 5 Aug 1966, Annabelle Lavinia b 1 Oct 1968); *Career* cmmnd RAOC 1962, Lt 1963, Capt 1969, Staff Coll 1974, Maj 1975, Nat Def Coll Latimer 1980, Lt-Col 1980, tech weapons instr RMCS 1981–82, Col 1988, Brig 1991, Cdr Bicester Garrison/Base Ordnance Depot 1991–94, dir Base Depots 1994–95, chief exec Army Base Storage & Distribution Agency (ABSDA) 1995–; ADC to HM The Queen 1995–; served: UK, NI, Malaysia, Hong Kong, BAOR; MInstD 1994; FILog 1994; *Books* Brassey's Battlefield Weapons Systems and Technology Volume III (with D H J Halsey, 1982); *Recreations* water colours, military history, Arsenal FC, antiques; *Style—* Brig Kevin Goad, CBE, ADC; ✉ Chief Executive, ABSDA, Monxton Road, Andover, Hants SP11 8HT (☎ 01264 382424, fax 01264 383342)

GOAD, Timothy Francis; DL (Surrey 1995); s of Robert Francis Goad (d 1977), and Madeline, *née* Drew; *b* 14 Nov 1934; *Educ* Eton; *m* 1961, Sarah, da of Uvedale Lambert; 1 da (Cassandra (Mrs Erik Wetter Sanchez) b 1963), 2 s (Justin b 1965, Hallam b 1970); *Career* worked in family broking business 1955–70, farmer 1970–95; pres SE Region Winged Fellowship 1995–, chm Caterham Youth and Community Centre 1995–; High Sheriff Co of Surrey 1994–95; Liveryman Worshipful Co of Skinners, Freeman City of London 1956; Lord of the Manor of Blechingley 1995–; *Style—* Timothy Goad, Esq, DL; ✉ Prickloves Farmhouse, South Park, Bletchingley, Surrey RH1 4NE (☎ 01883 743660, fax 01883 744657)

GOBBO, Hon Sir James Augustine; AC (1993), kt (1982); s of Antonio Gobbo and Regina, *née* Tosetto; *b* 22 March 1931; *Educ* Xavier Coll, Melbourne Univ (BA), Rhodes Scholar 1952, Magdalen Coll Oxford (MA); *m* 1957, Shirley, da of S Lewis; 2 s, 3 da; *Career* barr 1956, ind lectr in evidence Melbourne Univ 1964–68, QC 1971, judge of the Supreme Ct of Victoria 1978–94, Lt-Govr of Victoria 1995–; chm: Aust Refugee Cncl 1977, Victoria's 150 Advsy Panel 1984–85, Aust Bicentenary Multicultural Task Force 1982, Mercy Private Hosp 1977–87, Supervisory Ctee Children's Protection Soc 1982–90, Italian Historical Soc 1980–93, Task Force for the Italian Aged 1983–, Caritas Christi Hospice 1986–, Order of Malta Hospice Home Care Serv 1986–92, Reference Gp into Public Library Funding 1987, Aust Cncl of Multicultural Affrs 1987–90, Aust Bicentennial Multicultural Fndn 1988–, Int Specialised Skills 1993–, Cncl of Aust Banking Indust Ombudsman 1994–; pres: Sovereign Mil Order of Malta (Aust) 1987– (vice pres 1984–87), CO-AS-IT Italian Assistance Assoc 1979–84 and 1986–93, Scout Assoc (Victorian Branch) 1987–; memb: Aust Population and Immigration Cncl 1975–83, Victoria Law Fndn 1972–84, Newman Coll Cncl 1970–85, RC Archdiocese Fin Advsy Cncl 1970–, Mercy Maternity Hosp Bd 1972–89, Sisters of Mercy Health Care Cncl 1977–90, Cncl of the Order of Aust 1982–92, Italo-Aust Educn Fndn 1974–, Exec Cncl of Judges 1986–89, Victorian Health Promotion Fndn 1988–, Palladio Fndn 1989–, Victorian Community Fndn 1992–; pt/t cmmr Law Reform Cmmn of Victoria 1985–88; tstee Opera Fund (Victoria) 1983–; chm Cncl of Electricity Indust Ombudsman 1995–, pres Order of Australia Assoc 1995–; hon fell Aust Inst of Valuers 1985; Commendatore all'Ordine di Merito of the Republic of Italy 1973; Knight of Magistral Grace Sovereign Mil Order of Malta; *Books* Cross on Evidence (ed Aust edn), numerous papers; *Style—* Hon Sir James Gobbo, AC; ✉ 6 Florence Ave, Kew, Victoria 3101, Australia (☎ 00 61 03 817 1669, business ☎ 00 61 03 349 4699)

GOBITS, Rolph; s of Ben Gobits (d 1957), and Ruth, *née* Reinheimer; *b* 19 Sept 1947; *Educ* Bournemouth & Poole Coll of Art (BA), RCA (scholar, MA, The Daily Telegraph Magazine Award); *m* 15 Dec 1978, Amanda, *née* Currey; 2 da (Tamara b 8 Sept 1974, Anoushka b 13 June 1981); *Career* photographer; clients incl: Mercedes Benz, BMW, Audi, Volkswagen, General Motors, IBM, Apple, British Airways, TWA, Hyatt Hotels, American Express, Forte Hotel Group, AT & T, Texaco, Spalding, Bosch, Morgan Grenfell Merchant Bank, Natwest, Orient Express, Gucci, IPC Publications; vice chm Assoc of Photographers; *Awards* Arts Council Bursary 1974; D & AD: Silver Award for most outstanding advertising colour photograph 1979, special mention for consumer campaign 1981, Silver Award (Netherlands club) for most outstanding advertising colour photograph 1984, Silver Award for most outstanding consumer campaign 1984, Silver Award (France club) for VW campaign 1992; Campaign Press Advertising: Silver Award for best use of colour 1983, Silver Award for best media advertisement 1983, Silver Award for best travel advertisement 1985, Silver and Bronze Awards for best business advertisement 1986; Advertising Festival Gold Award for best advertisement in Europe Cannes 1992, Assoc of Photographers Silver Award 1995; *Recreations* photography, reading, chess; *Style*— Rolph Gobits, Esq; ✉ Rolph Gobits Studio Limited, Bay Tree House, 73 West Hill Road, London SW18 1LE (☎ 0181 877 1800, fax 0171 877 1886)

GOBLE, James Blackley Hague; s of Leslie Herbert Goble, CMG (d 1969), of Ashford, Kent, and Lilian Miriam, *née* Cunningham (d 1963); *b* 21 July 1927; *Educ* Marlborough, Corpus Christi Coll Cambridge; *m* 1, 24 Nov 1951, Barbara Mary (d 1986), da of Sir Thomas Claude Harris Lea, Bt (d 1985), of Worcs; 2 s (Timothy b 1957, Jonathan b 1961); m 2, 4 June 1988, Yvonne Patricia Jane Coke-Wallis, da of Lt-Col Cecil Stone (d 1988); *Career* Coldstream Gds 1945, Gdsman O/Cadet Worcs Regt 1946–48, Capt; admin offr HM Overseas Civil Serv Gold Coast/Ghana 1950–61; J Walter Thompson London: joined 1962, dir 1971–86, sr int vice pres 1983–86; dir: Pillar Pubns 1987–91 (chm 1990–91), Winston Churchill Travelling Fellowships Fndn Inc USA 1988–; tstee Critical Care Trust 1989–96 (chm 1990–92), memb Br Standards Inst Advsy Panel on Publicity 1971–84, advsy cnsllr English Speaking Union 1976–83; MIPA 1971–86; *Recreations* ornithology, shooting, building; *Style*— James Goble, Esq; ✉ Court Farm, Upton Snodsbury, Worcs WR7 4NN (☎ 01905 381314, fax 01905 381319)

GODBER, (Robert) Christopher; s of Geoffrey Chapman Godber, CBE, DL, *qv*; *b* 3 Nov 1938; *Educ* Bedford Sch, Merton Coll Oxford; *m* 1962, Frances Merryn Candy, da of Capt Edward Howard Stanley Bretherton, MC (d 1960); 3 s, 1 da; *Career* Nat Serv King's Shropshire LI served Kenya and Mau Mau Emergency 1956–58; Travis & Arnold plc: branch mangr Cambridge 1967–69, branch mangr Rugby 1969–73, dir 1973–88; dir: King's Lynn Wood Preservation 1973–93, Sussex Timber Preservation 1975–93; chm E Anglian Timber Trade Assoc 1988–90; dir: Main Bd Travis Perkins plc 1988–94, Travis Perkins Trading Co Ltd 1988–93, Timber Trade Federation Ltd 1991–94, Anglo Norden Ltd 1995–96; memb: Inst Builders Merchants, Inst of Wood Sci; *Recreations* sailing (yacht 'Minnow'), shooting, bridge; *Clubs* Banbury Sailing, South Carnarvonshire Yacht, Leander, Royal Agric Soc of England; *Style*— Christopher Godber, Esq; ✉ Staverton Acres, Staverton, Daventry, Northamptonshire NN11 6JY (☎ 01327 871223)

GODBER, Geoffrey Chapman; CBE (1961), DL (W Sussex 1975); s of Isaac Godber (d 1957), of Willington Manor, Beds, and Bessie Maud, *née* Chapman; bro of Sir George Edward Godber, *qv*, and late Baron Godber, of Willington; *b* 22 Sept 1912; *Educ* Bedford Sch, Univ of London (LLB); *m* 1937, Norah Enid, da of Reginald John George Fletcher Finney (d 1945), of Derbyshire; 3 s (Christopher Godber *qv* b 1938, Jonathan b 1942, Peter b 1945); *Career* admitted slr 1936; clerk of CC and Lieutenancy Shropshire 1944–66 and West Sussex 1966–75; memb sundry govt ctees 1953–75 incl: Central Advsy Water Ctee 1961–70, SE Econ Planning Cncl 1969–75; chm Weald and Downland Museum 1975–82 (pres 1988–90), memb Br Waterways Bd 1975–81; dep chm: Chichester Harbour Conservancy 1975–78 (Hon Freeman of the Harbour 1988), Shoreham Port Authy 1976–82; *Recreations* sailing; *Clubs* Naval & Military, Sussex; *Style*— Geoffrey Godber, Esq, CBE, DL; ✉ Pricklows, Singleton, Chichester, W Sussex PO18 0HA (☎ 01243 811238)

GODBER, Sir George Edward; GCB (1971, KCB 1962, CB 1958); s of Isaac Godber (d 1957), of Willington Manor, Beds, and Bessie Maud, *née* Chapman; bro of Geoffrey Chapman Godber, *qv*, and late Baron Godber, of Willington; *b* 4 Aug 1908; *Educ* Bedford Sch, New Coll Oxford (BA, DM), London Hosp; *m* 1935, Norma Hathorne, da of W H T N Rainey; 2 s, 1 da (and 2 s, 2 da decd); *Career* dep chief med offr Miny of Health 1950–60, QHP 1953–56, chief med offr DHSS, DES and Home Office 1960–73; chm Health Educn Cncl 1976–78; DPH; FRCP, FFCM; *Style*— Sir George Godber, GCB; ✉ 21 Almoners' Avenue, Cambridge CB1 4NZ (☎ 01223 247491)

GODBER, Hon Richard Thomas; DL (Bucks 1993); s of Baron Godber of Willington, PC, DL (Life Peer; d 1980), and Miriam, *née* Sanders (d 1996); *b* 4 June 1938; *Educ* Bedford Sch; *m* 1962, Candida Mary, da of late Albert Edward Parrish; 1 s, 2 da; *Career* Lt Royal Lincs 1956–58 (served Malaya); farmer and horticulturist; vice pres Bucks Assoc Boys' Clubs (chm 1977–86); chm: CLA Game Fair Stowe 1981, Bucks CLA 1987–90; hon dir Royal Show 1987–92, vice pres Cncl RASE 1991– (memb 1970–91); *Recreations* shooting, gardening; *Clubs* Farmers', Bedford; *Style*— The Hon Richard Godber, DL; ✉ Hall Farm, Little Linford, nr Milton Keynes, Bucks MK19 7EA

GODBOLD, Brian Leslie; s of Leslie Robert Godbold (d 1970), of London, and Eileen Rosalie, *née* Hodgkinson; *b* 14 July 1943; *Educ* Elmbridge Sch Cranleigh Surrey, Walthamstow Sch of Art (NDD), RCA Fashion Sch; *Career* designer Jovi NY USA 1965–67, head designer Wallis Shops UK 1967–69; head of design: Cojana UK 1970–74, Baccarat/Wetherall UK (headed team that designed BA uniform 1976) 1974–76; divnl dir of design Marks & Spencer 1993– (design exec 1976–93); memb Cncl Royal Coll of Art; Hon Dr of Design Winchester Sch of Art 1994; pres RCA Soc; FRSA, FCSD; *Recreations* antique collecting, gardening, photography; *Clubs* Arts; *Style*— Brian Godbold, Esq; ✉ Marks and Spencer plc, Michael House, 67 Baker Street, London W1A 1DN (☎ 0171 268 8014, fax 0171 268 2625)

GODDARD, Her Hon Judge; Ann Felicity; QC (1982); da of Graham Elliott Goddard (d 1973), and Margaret Louise, *née* Clark (d 1995); *b* 22 Jan 1936; *Educ* Grey Coat Hosp Westminster, Univ of Birmingham (LLB), Newnham Coll Cambridge (LLM); *Career* called to the Bar 1960, recorder of the Crown Court 1979–93, circuit judge (SE Circuit) 1993–; bencher Gray's Inn 1990–; memb Criminal Justice Consultative Cncl 1992–93, pres Br Acad of Forensic Sciences 1995–96; *Recreations* travel; *Style*— Her Hon Judge Goddard, QC; ✉ Central Criminal Court, Old Bailey, London EC4M 7EH

GODDARD, Prof John Burgess; OBE (1986); s of Burgess Goddard, of Rickmansworth, Herts, and Maud Mary, *née* Bridge (d 1970); *b* 5 Aug 1943; *Educ* Latymer Upper Sch, UCL (BA), LSE (PhD); *m* 24 Sept 1966, Janet Patricia, da of Stanley James Peddle (d 1956), of Rickmansworth, Herts; 1 s (David Jonathan b 4 August 1976), 2 da (Jane Elizabeth b 1 Dec 1970, Jennifer Anne b 7 Nov 1974); *Career* lectr LSE 1968–75, Leverhulme fell Univ of Lund Sweden 1974; Univ of Newcastle Upon Tyne: Henry Daysh prof Regnl Devpt Studies 1975–, dir Centre of Urban and Regnl Devpt Studies 1977–, head Geography Dept 1980–87, memb Senate 1981–83 and 1992–, memb Cncl 1983–86, memb Res Ctee 1984–89, memb Planning and Resources Ctee 1988–93, dir Newcastle Initiative Ltd 1988–, dean Faculty of Law, Environment and Social Sciences 1994–; memb: N Econ Planning Cncl 1976–79, Exec Ctee Newcastle Common Purpose 1989–; govr and memb Employment and Fin Ctee Univ of Northumbria at Newcastle (formerly Newcastle Poly) 1989–; memb: Port of Tyne Authy 1990–93, Human Geography Ctee SSRC 1976–79, Editorial Bd Environment and Planning 1988–91; ed Regional Studies 1979–84; advsr: CBI Task Force on Urban Regeneration 1987–88, House of Commons Trade and Indust Select Ctee 1994–95; memb: Exec Ctee Regnl Studies Assoc 1979–84, Editorial Bd BBC Domesday Project 1985–86, Jt Ctee ESRC and Nat Sci Fndn of America on Large Scale Data Bases 1986–87; dir ESRC Prog on Info and Communication Technologies 1992–93; memb: Advsy Bd of the Natural Environment and Land Use Programme 1991–95, R & D Ctee Northern RHA 1993–94; chm The Assoc of Dirs of Res Centres in the Social Scis (DORCISS) 1990–; memb Econ Advsy Ctees: Newcastle City Cncl, Tyne and Wear C of C 1982–95; FRGS 1988 (Victoria medal 1992), MIBG 1966, memb Regnl Studies Assoc 1966, FRSA 1993; *Books* numerous books and pubns incl: Office Linkages and Location (1973), Office Location in Urban and Regional Development (1975), British Cities: An Analysis of Urban Change (with N A Spence, 1981), Economic Development Policies: an evaluation study of the Newcastle Metropolitan Region (with F Robinson and C Wren, 1987); *Recreations* rowing, walking; *Style*— Prof John Goddard, OBE; ✉ Centre for Urban and Regional Development Studies, University of Newcastle upon Tyne, Newcastle upon Tyne, NE1 7RU (☎ 0191 222 7955, fax 0191 232 9259)

GODDARD, Kay Louise; da of Lewis John Goddard (d 1991), of New Eltham, London, and Millient Eileen, *née* Jones; *b* 25 Jan 1954; *Educ* Hither Green Sch, Catford Co Sch for Girls, Wimbledon Coll (Pitmans cert); *Career* trainee The Job Newspaper 1970–72, trainee reporter, reporter then ed Woman's Page South London Advertiser 1972–75, fashion ed, features ed, dep ed then special projects ed IPC Magazines Youth Gp 1975–81, reporter/writer The Sun 1981–85, launch ed IPC Magazines 1985; Carlton Magazines: dep ed Woman's World 1986–88, dep ed Riva 1988; ed Me (GE Magazines) 1989–93 (dep ed 1988–89), women's ed The Sun 1993–95, assoc ed The Star newspaper 1995–; *Recreations* music, athletics, dancing, writing, reading; *Style*— Miss Kay Goddard; ✉ The Star, Express Newspapers, Blackfriars Road, London SE1 9LX (☎ 0171 922 7470)

GODDARD, (Harold) Keith; QC (1979); s of Harold Goddard (d 1979), of Stockport, Cheshire, and Edith Goddard (d 1982); *b* 9 July 1936; *Educ* Manchester GS, CCC Cambridge; *m* 1, 1963 (m dis), Susan Elizabeth, yr da of late Ronald Stansfield, of Wilmslow, Cheshire; 2 s; m 2, 1983, Maria Alicja, da of Czeslaw Lazuchiewicz (d 1981), of Lodz, Poland; *Career* called to the Bar 1959, recorder of the Crown Ct 1978–, head of chambers; memb Criminal Injuries Compensation Bd 1993–; *Recreations* golf; *Clubs* Wilmslow Golf; *Style*— Keith Goddard, Esq, QC; ✉ Deans Court Chambers, Cumberland House, Crown Square, Manchester M3 3HA (☎ 0161 834 4097)

GODDARD, Martyn Stanley; s of Thomas Raymond Goddard (d 1982), and Winifred Florence, *née* Eastman; *b* 9 Oct 1951; *Educ* Mandville Co Secdy Sch, Aylesbury Coll of Further Educn, Harrow Coll of Technol and Art (Dip Applied Photography); *m* Beverley Margret Ballard; 2 da (Lauren b 7 June 1985, Grace Natalie b 8 May 1990); *Career* photographer; asst to Gered Mankowitz and Denis Waugh 1975–76, freelance photographer IPC Young Magazine Group 1976–77; assignments 1977–91: Sunday Telegraph Magazine, Sunday Express Magazine, You Magazine, advtg projects (incl devpt of markets for car photography in Br and American magazines); ed and advtg work 1991–; exhibitions incl: Blondie in Camera (Mirandy Gallery) 1978, Montserrat Studio (Lincoln Centre NY) 1979, 10 x 6 Group (Battersea Arts Centre, Neal St Gallery) 1981, Polaroid Time Zero (tour of UK) 1981, Human Views 1977–81 (J S Gallery London) 1981, National Portraits (Nat Theatre) 1983, Faces of Our Time (Nat Theatre tour) 1985, The Car (V & A Museum) 1986; fell BIPP; *Recreations* historic rally car driving, black and white photographic diary; *Clubs* Alfa Romeo Club; *Style*— Martyn Goddard, Esq; ✉ Martyn Goddard Photography, 5 Jeffrey's Place, London NW1 9PP (☎ 0831 500477, fax 0171 485 0996)

GODDARD, Prof Peter; s of Herbert Charles Goddard (d 1971), and Rosina Sarah, *née* Waite (d 1991); *b* 3 Sept 1945; *Educ* Emanuel Sch London, Trinity Coll Cambridge (BA, MA, PhD); *m* 24 Aug 1968, Helen Barbara, da of Francis Fraser Ross (d 1991), of Alne, Yorks; 1 s (Michael b 1975), 1 da (Linda b 1973); *Career* res fell Trinity Coll Cambridge 1969–73, visiting scientist CERN Geneva Switzerland 1970–72 and 1978, lectr in applied mathematics Univ of Durham 1972–74; St John's Coll Cambridge: fell 1975–, lectr in mathematics 1975–91, tutor 1980–87, sr tutor 1983–87, master 1994–; Univ of Cambridge: univ asst lectr 1975–76, univ lectr 1976–89, reader in mathematical physics 1989–92, sr fell Isaac Newton Inst for Mathematical Sciences 1994– (dep dir 1991–94), prof of theoretical physics 1992–; visiting prof Univ of Virginia Charlottesville 1983; govr: Berkhamsted Sch and Berkhamsted Sch for Girls 1985–96, Emanuel Sch 1992–, Shrewsbury Sch 1994–; memb: Inst for Theoretical Physics Univ of Calif Santa Barbara 1986 and 1990, Inst for Advanced Study Princeton 1974 and 1988, London Mathematical Soc 1989; hon fell Trinity Coll Dublin 1995; FRS 1989, FInstP 1990; *Style*— Prof Peter Goddard, FRS; ✉ The Master's Lodge, St John's College, Cambridge CB2 1TP (☎ 01223 338635, fax 01223 338707, telex 81240); DAMTP, University of Cambridge, Silver Street, Cambridge CB3 9EW (☎ 01223 337883, e-mail p.goddard@joh.cam.ac.uk)

GODDEN, Rumer; OBE (1993); da of late Arthur Leigh Godden, of Lydd House, Aldington, Kent, and Katherine Norah Hingley; *b* 10 Dec 1907; *Educ* Moira House Eastbourne Sussex; *m* 1, 1934, Laurence Sinclair Foster; 2 da (Jane, Janaki); m 2, 1949, James Haynes-Dixon, OBE (d 1973); *Career* author; *Books* incl: Chinese Puzzle (1935), The Lady and The Unicorn (1937), Black Narcissus (1939), Breakfast with the Nikolides (1941), Fugue in Time (1944), The River (1946), A Candle for St Jude (1948), Kingfishers Catch Fire (1952), An Episode of Sparrows (1955), The Greengage Summer (1959), China Court (1961), The Battle of the Villa Fiorita (1963), In This House of Brede (1969), Prayers from the Ark (trans, 1962), Two Under the Indian Sun (autobiog, 1965), Swans and Turtles (1968), The Raphael Bible (1970), Shiva's Pigeons (with Jon Godden, 1979), Gulbadan (1980), The Dark Horse (1981), Thursday's Children (1984), Time To Dance: No Time to Weep (1987, autobiog Vol I), A House with Four Rooms (autobiog Vol II 1989), Indian Dust (short stories, 1989), Coromandel Sea Change (1991), Listen to the Nightingale (1993), Pippa Passes (1994), Premlata and the Festival of Light (1996), The Little Chair (1996), A Pocket Book of Spiritual Poems (1996), Cockcrow to Starlight (anthology, 1996); *Style*— Miss Rumer Godden, OBE; ✉ c/o Curtis Brown, Haymarket House, 28/29 Haymarket, London SW1Y 4SP

GODDIN, Richard William; s of William Frederick Goddin (d 1967), and Audrey Joan, *née* Stearn; *b* 17 May 1943; *Educ* Perse Sch, London Poly (DMS, Urwick medal 1969); *m* 15 June 1985, Margaret Ann, da of Reginald Barlow (d 1957); 2 s (James b 1987, Thomas b 1991); *Career* sr mangr Nat West Bank plc 1977–83, treas Lombard North Central plc 1983–86, dep treas Nat West plc 1986–87; County NatWest Ltd: exec dir 1987–88, head Global Funding Gp Treasury 1989–92, md Global Money Markets 1992–; ACIB; *Recreations* sailing, croquet, beekeeping, country life; *Style*— Richard Goddin, Esq; ✉ Belmington Close, Meldreth, Cambs SG8 6NT (☎ 01763 260061); National Westminster Bank plc, 135 Bishopsgate, London EC2M 3UR (☎ 0171 375 4888)

GODFREY, Andrew Paul; s of Bernard Russel Godfrey, of Dunblane, and Carol Emma Elise, *née* Leonhardt; *b* 12 Aug 1953; *Educ* Morrison's Acad Crieff Perthshire, Univ of Edinburgh (BSc Econ); *m* Irene, da of Robert Simpson, MBE; 2 s (Paul Douglas b 24 Oct 1982, Stuart Mark b 22 Feb 1985); *Career* Grant Thornton: corp fin ptnr, head of Growth & Devpt and memb Nat Corp Fin Panel; fin advsr and auditor various cos Scotland; ACA 1977; *Recreations* golf; *Clubs* Gleneagles Golf, Dunblane Golf; *Style*— Andrew Godfrey, Esq; ✉ 4 Newton Crescent, Dunblane, Perthshire FK15 0DZ (☎ 01786 823436); Grant Thornton, 112 West George Street, Glasgow G2 4QF (☎ 0141 332 7484, fax 0141 333 0581, mobile 0831 515571)

GODFREY, Bob; s of Roland Charles Godfrey (d 1967), of Middx, and Lucy Rachael, *née* Butler (d 1968); *b* 27 May 1921; *Educ* Cleveland Middle Sch, Leyton Art Sch; *m* 1947, Beryl Sonia, da of Percy Chapman; 4 da (Susan Ann b 1949 d 1994, Julia Melony b 1953 d 1970, Claire Beatrice b 1956, Tessa Jane b 1960); *Career* animated film maker; with Unilever Ltd 1937, Lintas advtg agency 1938–41; 10 Bn Royal Marines 1941–43, 47 Commando RM 1943–46, rejoined Lintas 1946–48, J Arthur Rank 1948–49, Film Producers' Guild 1949–54, Biographic Ltd 1955–65, Bob Godfrey Films Ltd 1965–; prof of animation Royal Coll of Art 1986–89, sr fell RCA 1989; hon pres Cardiff Int Film Festival 1992–; memb BAFTA; *Awards* Paom Fionnbarra Award Cork 1970, BAFTA awards 1970 and 1983, Academy Award (Oscar) 1975 (also nominated 1973, 1979 and 1994), Zagreb Critics' Award 1990, ASIFA Lifetime Achievement Award 1990, Zagreb Lifetime Achievement Award 1992, Cable ACE Award 1993; *Recreations* gardening;

Clubs Chelsea Arts; *Style*— Bob Godrey, Esq, MBE; ✉ Bob Godfrey Films Ltd, 199 Kings Cross Road, London WC1X 9DB (☎ 0171 278 5711, fax 0171 278 6809)

GODFREY, (William) Edwin Martindale; s of Ernest Martindale Godfrey (d 1974), of Chesterfield, Derbyshire, and Anna Lol Tedde, *née* Maas; *b* 20 Oct 1947; *Educ* Repton, Queens' Coll Cambridge (MA); *m* 10 Sept 1977, Helen Ann, da of Dr John Arthur Clement James (d 1996), of Northfield, Birmingham; 2 s (William b 1978, Thomas b 1980), 1 da (Alice b 1983); *Career* admitted slr 1971; asst slr Norton Rose Botterell and Roche 1971–72; Simmons and Simmons: asst slr 1972–76, ptnr 1977–, int managing ptnr 1995–96; Int Bar Assoc: vice chm Ctee on Anti Tst Law 1981–86, chm Sub-Ctee on Structure and Ethics of Business Law 1990–94 (vice chm 1988–90), memb Standing Ctee on Professional Ethics 1990–, memb Cncl Section on Business Law 1994–, memb Standing Ctees on Int Legal Practice and Multi-Disciplinary Practice 1995–; memb Advsy Bd Int and Comparative Law Center S Western Legal Fndn Dallas Texas 1991; hon legal advsr Hertford CAB until 1995; Freeman: City of London Solicitors' Co 1990, City of London 1991; memb: Law Soc 1971, UK Environmental Law Assoc 1989, City of London Law Soc 1990 (sec Commercial Law Sub-Ctee 1992–95, vice chm 1995–), British-Italian Law Assoc, British-Russian Law Assoc (sec 1993–95), Int Bar Assoc, Hertford Deanery Synod 1990–94; govr Abel Smith JMI Sch Hertford 1992–; FRSA 1994; *Books* Joint Ventures in Butterworths Encyclopaedia of Forms & Precedents (ed 5 edn, 1990), Der Schweizer Anwalt (contrib chapter Coping with Conflict, 1993), Law Without Frontiers (ed, 1995); *Style*— Edwin Godfrey, Esq; ✉ Simmons & Simmons, 21 Wilson Street, London EC2M 2TX (☎ 0171 628 2020, fax 0171 628 2070, telex 888562)

GODFREY, Frances Helen (Fran); da of John Leonard Thurlow Godfrey, of New Milton, Hampshire, and Joan, *née* Follebouckt; *b* 29 June 1953; *Educ* Convent of the Cross Bournemouth, PCL; *m* 1976 (m dis 1981), David Davies; *Career* trained as bi-lingual sec, sec/admin London and Bournemouth 1973–79; Two Counties Radio 1980–87: tech operator ILR Bournemouth 1980–82, commercial prodr 1982–84, presenter 1984–87; returned to admin and freelance work; announcer/newsreader BBC Radio 2 1990–; memb Equity 1984–; *Recreations* anything creative where I can see a result, old films (especially musicals); *Style*— Miss Fran Godfrey; ✉ BBC, Broadcasting House, London W1A 1AA (☎ 0171 765 4695)

GODFREY, Dr Gerald; s of Phillip Godfrey, of Stanmore, Middx, and Sophie, *née* Godfrey; *b* 22 Aug 1926; *Educ* Dunstable GS, Univ of Glasgow; *m* 9 April 1951, Florence, da of Leon Jaffé (d 1958), of Glasgow; 1 da (Leone b 1958); *Career* Southern Gen Hosp Glasgow (gen med, casualty surgery, psychiatry) 1951–52, civilian med offr RAF 1953–60, police med offr 1953–62, clinical asst med offr of Barking Hosp 1954–61, asst MOH Lewisham, Wandsworth and Croydon 1963–67; med referee for insur cos: Prudential, Colonial, Mutual, Crusader, Forester, Pearl, Royal London, NEM Assurance; GP: Dagenham and Streatham 1953–, Harley St 1966–; LRCP 1951, MRCS 1951, MRGP 1960, memb BMA; *Recreations* sail board, tennis, squash, sailing, shooting; *Clubs* Kensington Rifle and Pistol, Tir Club d'Antibes; *Style*— Dr Gerald Godfrey; ✉ Flat 2, 33–36 Chester Square, London SW1W 9HT (☎ 0171 730 6050); 68 Harley St, London W1N 1AE (☎ 0171 935 3980)

GODFREY, Howard Anthony; QC (1991); s of Emanuel Godfrey (d 1991), of London, and Amy, *née* Grossman; *b* 17 Aug 1946; *Educ* William Ellis Sch, LSE (LLB); *m* 3 Sept 1972, Barbara, da of John Ellinger, of London; 2 s (Timothy b 1975, James b 1980); *Career* called to the Bar Middle Temple 1970, practising SE Circuit 1972–, recorder Crown Ct 1992–; *Recreations* wine and food, humour; *Style*— Howard Godfrey, Esq, QC; ✉ The Red House, Swallowfield Rd, Arborfield Cross, Berks RG2 9JZ (☎ 0118 976 0657); 3 Hare Court, Temple, London EC4Y 7BJ (☎ 0171 353 7561, fax 0171 353 7741)

GODFREY, Louise Sarah (Mrs Stanley Bland); QC (1991); *b* 17 April 1950; *Educ* Tadcaster GS, St Hugh's Coll Oxford (MA), Cncl of Legal Educn; *m* 25 Aug 1977, Stanley Leslie Bland; 2 da (Rebecca Alice b 1979, Victoria Jane b 1982); *Career* called to the Bar Middle Temple 1972, recorder NE Circuit 1989–; chair Mgmnt Ctee Leeds Family Mediation Serv; *Recreations* walking, cooking; *Style*— Miss Louise S Godfrey, QC; ✉ 2 Park Court Chambers, 40 Park Cross St, Leeds, W Yorks LS1 2QH (☎ 0113 243 3277, fax 0113 242 1285)

GODFREY, Dr Malcolm Paul Weston; s of Harry Godfrey (d 1945), of London, and Rose Kaye; *b* 11 Aug 1926; *Educ* Hertford GS, Univ of London (MB BS); *m* 1955, Barbara, da of Louis Goldstein (d 1963), of London, and Brighton; 1 s (Richard), 1 da (Jennifer), 1 da decd (Claire); *Career* dean Royal Postgraduate Med Sch Univ of London 1974–83, second sec Med Res Cncl 1983–88; chm Public Health Laboratory Serv Bd 1989–; chm Cncl of Govrs UMDS Guy's and St Thomas' Hosps 1996–; memb Ct of Assts Worshipful Soc of Apothecaries (master 1989–90), Liveryman Worshipful Co of Goldsmiths; *Recreations* reading, theatre, walking; *Style*— Dr Malcolm Godfrey; ✉ 17 Clifton Hill, St John's Wood, London NW8 0QE (☎ 0171 624 6335, fax 0171 328 9474)

GODFREY, Prof Michael DeWitt; s of George H Godfrey, of Munich, and Augusta, *née* DeWitt (d 1983); *b* 30 May 1937; *Educ* Deerfield Acad, California Inst Technol (BSc), LSE (PhD); *m* 1 (m dis 1971); 1 s (Kent b 28 June 1958), 1 da (Christa b 19 Oct 1960); m 2, 2 Aug 1973, Ilse, da of Dr Wilhelm Pokorny, of 138 Hohenberg, Austria; *Career* asst prof and res assoc Econometric Res Prog Princeton Univ USA 1963–68, Bell Telephone Laboratories and AT&T Corp 1968–77, dir res Sperry Univac 1977–83, head res ICL 1983–87, Schlumberger prof of engrg software Imperial Coll 1987–92 (reader in statistics 1969–77), consulting prof of electrical engrg Stanford Univ 1993– (visiting prof 1990–93); *Books* An Incremental Cost Model of Message Toll Telephone Servs (with R L Breedlove, 1975), Machine-Independent Organic Software Tools (jtly, 2 edn, 1985); *Recreations* skiing; *Clubs* Athenaeum; *Style*— Prof Michael Godfrey; ✉ Stanford University, Electrical Engineering, ISL, Durand Building, Stanford, CA 94305, USA (☎ 415 723 3475, fax 415 723 8473)

GODFREY, Patrick Lindesay; s of Rev Canon Frederick Godfrey (d 1984), of Swithland, Leicestershire, and Lois Mary Gladys, *née* Turner (d 1973); *b* 15 Feb 1933; *Educ* Abbotsholme Sch Derbyshire, Central Sch of Speech and Drama; *m* 20 April 1960, Amanda Galafres Patterson Walker; 1 s (Richard Lindesay b 29 April 1961), 1 da (Kate b 12 Feb 1964); *Career* actor; Nat Serv 1951–53; *Theatre* repertory incl: Dundee, Coventry, Richmond, Hornchurch, RSC London and Stratford 1970–81; roles incl: Dr Dudakov in Summerfolk (by Gorky), Boyet in Love's Labours Lost, Ephraim Smooth in Wild Oats, Belarius in Cymbeline, Justice Shallow in Merry Wives of Windsor, Kulyghin in Three Sisters, Mr Kenwigs in Nicholas Nickleby (nine hour epic, later televised), Friar Lawrence in Romeo and Juliet, Polonius in Hamlet (RSC tour and repertory in Stratford) 1989, Paulet in Mary Stuart (RNT) 1996; *Films* incl: Heat and Dust, A Room with a View, Maurice, On The Black Hill, Clockwise, The Trial, The Remains of the Day; *Recreations* golf, restoring Islington house and shared house in Greece; *Clubs* Stage Golfing Soc; *Style*— Patrick Godfrey, Esq; ✉ c/o Markham & Froggatt Ltd, Julian House, 4 Windmill Street, London W1P 1HF (☎ 0171 636 4412, fax 0171 637 5233)

GODFREY, Paul; s of Peter Godfrey, of Exeter, and Valerie, *née* Drake; *b* 16 Sept 1960; *Career* playwright and director; dir Perth Repertory Theatre Scotland 1983–84, Eden Court Theatre Inverness 1985–87 (estab touring co); *Plays* Inventing A New Colour (NT Studio 1987, Royal Court 1988), A Bucket of Eels 1988, Once in a While the Odd Thing Happens (RNT) 1990, The Panic (Royal Opera) 1991, The Blue Ball (RNT) 1995, The Modern Husband (ATC) 1995, The Invisible Woman (The Gate) 1996, The Candidate 1996; *Awards* incl: Arts Cncl Trainee Directors bursary 1983, Arts Cncl Playwrights Award 1989, David Harlech Meml Bursary 1990, Stephen Arlen Award 1991, Arts Cncl Playwrights' Award 1992, Wingate Scholarship 1996; *Style*— Paul Godfrey; ✉ c/o Julia Kreitman, The Agency, 24 Pottery Lane, London W11 4LZ (☎ 0171 727 1346, fax 0171 727 9037)

GODFREY, Dr Richard Charles; s of Thomas Charles Godfrey (d 1965), of Watford, and Joan Eva, *née* Clayton; *b* 8 Sept 1940; *Educ* Watford GS, Peterhouse Cambridge (MA), UCL (MD); *m* 8 June 1968, Jane Catherine, da of Stanley Goodman, of Reigate; 3 s (Thomas b 1970, Robin b 1974, Matthew b 1975), 1 da (Sarah b 1971); *Career* clinical sub-dean Univ of Southampton 1984–89 (lectr in med 1972–76, conslt physician 1976–), Overseas Devpt Admin prof of med Moi Univ Kenya 1991–94, warden Farley Hosp Almshouses, memb Salisbury Diocesan Advsy Ctee; MD, FRCP, ARCO; *Recreations* music, organ building, squash; *Style*— Dr Richard Godfrey; ✉ The Wardenry, Farley, Salisbury SP5 1AH (☎ 01722 72231); Southampton General Hospital, Southampton SO16 6YD (☎ 01703 794838, fax 01703 701771)

GODFREY, Roger John; s of Rev Donald Vincent Godfrey (d 1964), and Dorothy Elizabeth, *née* Spivey (d 1993); *b* 22 July 1929; *Educ* Ashville Coll Harrogate, Univ of Nottingham (LLB); *m* 29 June 1955, Frances Christina, da of Frank Ironside; 2 da (Christina Jane (Mrs Brecknock) b 15 July 1956, Joanne Jill b 19 Feb 1964), 1 s (Duncan John Vincent b 16 Feb 1958); *Career* articled clerk 1947–52, admitted slr March 1953, Nat Serv RAF 1953–55, ptnr Cecil Godfrey & Son (later Tallents Godfrey & Co) 1955–93; Univ of Nottingham: pres Cncl 1983–93 (memb 1954–), chm Fin Ctee 1976–83, pro-chllr 1993–; pres Nottinghamshire Law Soc 1988–89, memb Law Soc 1955–93, Hon LLD Univ of Nottingham 1991; *Recreations* gardening, walking, reading and such sport as I can still manage; *Style*— Dr Roger Godfrey; ✉ Corse Cottage, Balmaclellan, Castle Douglas, Kirkcudbrightshire DG7 3QP (☎ 01644 420736); University of Nottingham, University Park, Nottingham NG7 2RD

GODFREY-ISAACS, Laura; *b* 22 July 1964; *Educ* Kingston Poly, Brighton Poly (BA), Slade Sch of Art London, RCA (PhD); *Career* artist; sr lectr: Winchester Sch of Art, Univ of Southampton, Kent Inst of Art and Design; visiting lectr at numerous art colls incl Tate Gallery, Whitechapel Gallery, Barbican and Camden Art Centre; artist in residence: Pratt Inst Brooklyn NYC 1988–89, Tate Gallery Liverpool 1990; public art projects with numerous galleries and museums; *Solo Exhibitions* Monima Gallery London 1987, Morgan's Gallery London 1987, Tate Gallery Liverpool 1990, Sue Williams Gallery London 1991 and 1993, John Milton Gallery London 1991, Physical Encounters (Gardner Arts Centre Univ of Sussex touring to Royal Festival Hall Galleries London) 1992, Robert Hossack Gallery London 1994, Condeso Lawler Gallery NYC 1994, John Jones Gallery London 1995; *Group Exhibitions* incl: Al Fresco Exhibition (RA) 1988, Whitechapel Open Studio Exhibition 1989, View of the New (Royal Over-Seas League London) 1991, John Moores Exhibition (Walker Art Gallery Liverpool) 1991, Roses are Red (Br Cncl touring exhbn of UK and Bulgarian artists to Polvdiv Bulgaria and London) 1991, invited artist Whitechapel Open 92, Festival International de la Peinture Cannes (Br Cncl rep artist with Saleem Arif, *qv*) 1992, Women's Art at New Hall Cambridge 1992, Somatic States (Middlesex Univ and Norwich Art Gallery) 1992, Riverside Open (Riverside Studios London) 1993, Skin (Antonio Barnola Gallery Barcelona) 1993, Wit and Excess (Sydney, Brisbane, Melbourne and Adelaide) 1994, It's a Pleasure (South Bank London) 1995, Stereo-Tip (Soros Centre for Contemporary Art Ljubljana Slovenia) 1995; *Collections* incl: Momart, New Hall, Arts Cncl of GB, Contemporary Arts Soc; *Awards* Jacob Mendelsohn scholarship 1986, McDonald fellowship from Pratt Inst NYC 1988, Boise fellowship from Slade Sch of Art London 1988, Fulbright fellowship for residency in NYC 1988, Momart fellowship for residency at Tate Gallery Liverpool 1990; *Style*— Ms Laura Godfrey-Isaacs; ✉ c/o 40 Crewdson Road, London SW9 0LJ

GODLEE, Dr (John) Nicholas; s of Philip Godlee (d 1952), of The White House, Didsbury, Manchester, and Barbara, *née* Lodge (d 1983); *b* 23 Jan 1928; *Educ* Marlborough, King's Coll Cambridge (MA, Jasper Ridley prize), UCH Med Sch (MB BChir); *m* 3 Nov 1951, (Dorothy) Barbara, da of Col J P Kellett, DSO, MC; 2 s (Rickman James Philip b 29 Dec 1953, Julian Raymond Lister b 15 April 1959), 2 da (Carolyn Jane b 25 Nov 1956, Fiona Nicolette b 4 Aug 1961); *Career* resident MO King Edward VII Hosp for Offrs 1956, registrar Radiotherapy Dept UCH 1957–59, registrar then sr registrar Royal Marsden Hosp 1959–63, post-doctoral fell Stanford Univ Med Center Calif 1961, conslt radiotherapist then conslt clinical oncologist UCH 1963–93 (dir Radiotherapy Dept 1979–93); hon conslt to: N London Hosps, Woolwich Hosps Gp, Gt Ormond St Hosp, Manor House Hosp, Royal Nat Orthopaedic Hosp, Cromwell Hosp, St Luke's Hosp for the Clergy; chm NE Thames RHA Ctee in Radiotherapy, memb Nat Bone Tumour Panel, sr clinical lectr UCL Faculty of Clinical Scis; memb: Br Inst of Radiology 1957, BMA 1990; FRCR 1960; *Recreations* music (piano, viola and composing), acting, collecting books, researching family history; *Style*— Dr Nicholas Godlee; ✉ 9 Meadowbank, Primrose Hill, London NW3 3AY (☎ 0171 586 5038); University College Hospital, Gower Street, London WC1E 6AU (☎ 0171 383 7911); Cromwell Hospital, Cromwell Road, London SW5 0TU

GODLEY, Hon Christopher John; s and h of 3 Baron Kilbracken, DSC, *qv*, of Killegar, Ireland; *b* 1 Jan 1945; *Educ* Rugby, Univ of Reading (BSc); *m* 10 May 1969, Gillian Christine, yr da of Lt-Cdr Stuart Wilson Birse, OBE, DSC, RN (d 1981), of Alverstoke, Hants; 1 s (James John b 1972), 1 da (Louisa Laheen b 1974); *Career* ICI: agriculturalist Agric Div 1968–78, gp buyer Central Purchasing Dept Head Office London 1978–82, int countertrade mangr ICI Agrochemicals Fernhurst Haslemere 1982–; *Style*— Hon Christopher Godley; ✉ Four Firs, Marley Lane, Haslemere, Surrey GU27 3PZ (☎ 01428 642814, office: 01428 655430, fax 01428 655097)

GODLEY, Georgina Jane (Mrs Conran); da of Michael Godley, and Heather, *née* Couper; *b* 11 April 1955; *Educ* Putney HS, Thames Valley GS, Wimbledon Art Sch, Brighton Poly (BA), Chelsea Sch of Art (MA); *m* 16 April 1988, Sebastian Conran, s of Sir Terence Conran; 2 s (Samuel Orby Conran b 12 May 1989, Maximillian Anthony Rupert Conran b 4 April 1995); *Career* picture restorer 1978–79, menswear designer Browns London and Paris 1979, ptnr designer Crolla London 1980–85, fndr and designer own label Georgina Godley (retail outlets from London to USA and Japan, and illustrations and articles in all maj fashion pubns); currently sr lectr St Martin's Sch of Art and Sch of Fashion and Textiles RCA; *Style*— Ms Georgina Godley; ✉ 7 Bedford Gardens, London W8 7ED (☎ and fax 0171 727 2217)

GODLEY, Kevin; *b* 7 Oct 1945; *Career* musician, composer, film director; former memb of 10CC (records incl I'm Not In Love and The Dean and I), left in 1976 with Lol Creme to form musical and directing partnership; music videos incl: Herbie Hancock's Rock It (Music Week award for Top Music Promo 1983, Billboard Best Music Video award and Best Art Direction 1983, MTV Music Video award - Best Concept Video, Best Special Effects, Best Art Direction, Best Editing, Most Experimental Video 1984), Duran Duran's Girls on Film (Grammy award for Best Video Short 1983), Frankie Goes to Hollywood's The Power of Love and Two Tribes (VPA Monitor award for Top Music Promo and Top Directors award 1984), The Police's Synchronicity, Wrapped around Your Finger and Every Breath You Take (MTV Best Cinematography award 1984); TV Commercials incl: Wrangler Jeans 1983 (Silver Lion Cannes award, Kodak Craft award), New York and Boston Yellow Pages 1987 (Clio award Best Utilities, The One Show Gold Pencil and Bronze Pencil, Golden Lion award), Reebok, Nissan, Audi, Ever Ready Batteries; working solo 1989–; commercials incl: Planters Peanuts, RCA Homes Theatres, Granada

TV Rentals; directed two hour music TV special One World One Voice 1990; *Style*— Kevin Godley, Esq; ✉ c/o Medialab Ltd, Chelsea Wharf, 15 Lots Rd, London SW10 0QH (☎ 0171 351 5814, fax 0171 351 7898)

GODLEY, Dr Margaret Joan; *b* 23 May 1953; *Educ* Univ of Liverpool (MB ChB), FRCOG; *Career* conslt in genitourinary med: Royal Berks Hosp Reading 1986–92, The Alexandra Hosp Redditch 1992–; hon sec: The Med Soc for the Study of Venereal Diseases 1989–92, The Assoc for Genitourinary Medicine 1992–; *Style*— Dr Margaret Godley; ✉ The Department of Genitourinary Medicine, The Alexandra Hospital, Redditch B98 7UB (☎ 01527 503030 ext 4118)

GODLEY, Lt Cdr Peter Brian; s of Brig Brian Richard Godley, CBE (d 1954), and Margaret Valiant, *née* Livingstone-Learmonth (d 1979); *b* 4 Oct 1933; *Educ* Cheltenham, RNC Dartmouth; *m* 7 Jan 1960, Jean, da of Col James Forbes Robertson, VC, DSO, MC; 1 s (John b 9 July 1962), 2 da (Sarah b 21 Dec 1960, Joanna b 25 Feb 1968); *Career* RN: submarines 1955–62, minesweepers 1963–65, RN Staff Coll 1966, First Lt HMS Minerva 1967–68, asst to Chief of Allied Staff Med 1969–70; RAF Coll Cranwell 1971–73; Charterhouse Group plc 1974–83 (md Charterhouse Pensions Ltd 1978–83); dir: Europa Investment Services Ltd 1987–88, Royal Br Legion 1988–; Liveryman Worshipful Co of Coachmakers and Coach Harness Makers 1976; *Recreations* off-shore sailing, walking; *Clubs* Army and Navy, Woodroffe's; *Style*— Lt Cdr P B Godley, RN; ✉ Down House, Westcott, Dorking, Surrey RH4 3JX (☎ 01306 881 555); Royal British Legion, 48 Pall Mall, London SW1Y 5JY (☎ 0171 973 7200)

GODLEY, Prof Hon Wynne Alexander Hugh; yr s of 2 Baron Kilbracken, CB, KC (d 1950), and his 1 wife Elizabeth Helen Monteith, *née* Hamilton; *b* 2 Sept 1926; *Educ* Rugby, New Coll Oxford (BA), Paris Conservatoire; *m* 3 Feb 1955, Kathleen Eleanora, da of Sir Jacob Epstein, KBE, and former w of the painter Lucian Freud; 1 da (Eve b 1967); *Career* economist; economist Metal Box Ltd 1954–56, various posts HM Treasy rising to dep dir Economic Section 1967–70; Univ of Cambridge: dir Dept of Applied Economics 1970–85 (actg dir 1985–87), fell King's Coll 1970–, prof of applied economics 1980–93; memb HM Treasy independent panel of economic forecasting advsrs 1992–; dir: Investing in Success Equities Ltd 1970–85, Royal Opera House (Covent Garden) 1976–86; visiting prof Alborg Univ Denmark 1987–88, distinguished scholar Jerome Levy Inst 1991–92 and 1993–95; former professional oboist, princ oboist BBC Welsh Orch 1952; *Style*— Prof Hon Wynne Godley; ✉ Jasmine House, Cavendish, Suffolk

GODMAN, Arthur; s of Arthur Andrew Godman (d 1958), of London, and Mary Adeline Newman (d 1946); *b* 10 Oct 1916; *Educ* UCL (BSc), Inst of Educn (DipEd); *m* 24 June 1950, Jean Barr, da of James Morton, OBE (d 1973), of Scotland; 2 s (Ian b 1951, Brian b 1953), 1 da (Diana b 1953); *Career* WWII Capt RA 1939: served France, India, Malaya (POW Far E 1946); Colonial Civil Serv Educn Dept Malaya, Hong Kong princ asst sec Miny of Educn Malaysia 1946–63; author 1963–; educn conslt Longman Group 1966–77; res fell Dept of SE Asian Studies Univ of Kent (hon fell Eliot Coll 1978); memb Canterbury Rotary Club 1980–; CChem, MRSC, FRAS; *Books* Dictionary of Scientific Usage (with E M F Payne, 1979), Illustrated Science Dictionary (1981), Illustrated Dictionary of Chemistry (1981), Cambridge Illustrated Thesaurus of Computer Science (1984), Health Science for the Tropics (1962), Chemistry: A New Certificate Approach (with S T Bajah, 1969), Human and Social Biology (1973), Energy Supply (1991); *Recreations* bridge, reading, Oriental languages; *Clubs* Royal Over-Seas League; *Style*— Arthur Godman, Esq; ✉ Sondes House, Patrixbourne, Canterbury, Kent CT4 5DD (☎ 01227 830322); Eliot College, University of Kent, Canterbury, Kent

GODMAN, Howard Anthony; s of Reginald Godman, of Hull, Yorks, and Brenda Godman (d 1975); *b* 11 March 1947; *Educ* Newton Hall GS Hull, Coll of Commerce Hull; *m* 1970, Gillian, da of Donald Macrae Sizen; 1 s (Alexander James b 15 Aug 1975), 1 da (Sarah Jane b 7 April 1978); *Career* mktg exec Norprint Ltd 1969–73, publicity mangr Glaxo 1973–78, dir of communications Schering Plough Inc Lucerne Switzerland 1978–85, account dir Shandwick PR 1985–86, account dir Edelman PR 1986–87, md Vox PR 1987–90, md Vox Prism Targis Ltd 1990–95, dep md Euro Prism 1990–95; MCIM 1975, MIPR 1985; *Clubs* RAC; *Style*— Howard Godman, Esq; ✉ The Hollies, Pilgrims Way, Westhumble, Surrey RH5 6AW (☎ 01306 883584)

GODMAN, Jo; da of Frank Alfred Leonard, of Dernford Hall, Swefling, Suffolk, and Amelia Emma, *née* Day; *b* 29 May 1944; *Educ* Camden Sch for Girls, Holborn Coll of Law, Languages and Commerce; *m* 11 March 1967, Keith William Godman, s of William Christopher Godman; *Career* girl friday Chapman Raper TV commercials prodn co 1965–67, prodn asst Geoffrey Forster Associates 1967–71, prodr for Tom Bussmann of Bussmann Llewelyn 1972–80 (prodn asst 1971–72), co-fndr Patterson Godman Ltd 1980–83, md RSA Films Ltd (Ridley Scott Associates) 1983–96; has produced numerous commercials winning awards at D&AD, British TV Awards, Cannes and Clio NY; *Recreations* cinema, gardening, ballet, cooking, swimming; *Clubs* Groucho, Women in Advertising; *Style*— Jo Godman

GODMAN, Dr Norman Anthony; MP (Lab) Greenock and Port Glasgow (majority 14,979); *b* 19 April 1937; *Educ* Westbourne St Boys' Sch Hull, Univ of Hull (BA), Heriot Watt Univ (PhD); *m* Patricia; *Career* former shipwright and teacher; joined Lab Pty 1962, Parly candidate (Lab) Aberdeen S 1979, MP (Lab) Greenock and Port Glasgow 1983–; *Style*— Dr Norman Godman, MP; ✉ House of Commons, London SW1A 0AA

GODSAL, Lady Elizabeth Cameron; *née* Stopford; DL (Berks 1994); 2 da of 8 Earl of Courtown, OBE, TD (d 1975), by his 1 w; *b* 10 April 1939; *m* 24 April 1962, Alan Anthony Colleton Godsal, o s of late Hugh Godsal, of Haines Hill, Twyford; 1 s (Hugh b 1965), 2 da (Lucy (Mrs Christopher Zeal) b 1964, Laura b 1968); *Career* chief pres St John Ambulance 1990–96 (cmmr Berks 1983–90), pres St John Fellowship 1996–; DJStJ; High Sheriff of Berks 1990–91, High Steward of Wokingham 1992–; *Style*— Lady Elizabeth Godsal, DL; ✉ Haines Hill, Twyford, Berks (☎ 0118 934 5678); 7 Herbert Crescent, London SW1 (☎ 0171 581 0937)

GODSAL, Philip Caulfeild; s of Maj Philip Hugh Godsal (d 1982), of Iscoyd Park, Whitchurch, Shropshire, and Pamela Ann Delisle, *née* Caulfeild; *b* 10 Oct 1945; *Educ* Eton; *m* 1, 29 Nov 1969 (m dis 1985), Lucinda Mary, da of Lt Cdr Percival Royston Dancy; 3 s (Philip Langley b 28 June 1971, Benjamin Rupert Wilmot b 17 June 1976, Thomas Henry b 3 Aug 1977), 1 da (Laura Sophie b 24 May 1973); *m* 2, 2 July 1986, Selina Baber, da of Thomas William Brooke-Smith (d 1991), of Canford Cliffs; 3 step da (Zoe Christina b 1974, Lucinda Selina b 1976, Christina Juliet b 1980); *Career* farmer, land agent and chartered surveyor; formerly ptnr Savills Norwich, ptnr John German Shrewsbury 1984–; chm Historic Houses Assoc for Wales 1989–91, chm N Wales Region Timber Growers UK 1989–91, memb Ctee Shropshire Branch CLA, sec Shropshire Rural Housing Assoc, pres Iscoyd and Fenns Bank CC; High Sheriff Clwyd 1993–94; FRICS; *Recreations* shooting, forestry, reading; *Clubs* MCC, Farmers', Salop, Lancashire CCC; *Style*— Philip Godsal, Esq; ✉ Iscoyd Park, Whitchurch, Shropshire SY13 3AT; John German, Chartered Surveyors, Black Birches, Hadnall, Shrewsbury SY4 3DH (☎ 01939 210440)

GODSIFF, Roger; MP (Lab) Birmingham Small Heath (majority 13,989); s of late George Godsiff, and Gladys Godsiff; *b* 28 June 1937; *Educ* Catford Comp Sch; *m* Julia Brenda; 1 s, 1 da; *Career* formerly political offr APEX then sr res offr GMB; Parly candidate Birmingham Yardley 1983, MP (Lab) Birmingham Small Heath 1992–; cncllr London Borough of Lewisham 1971–90 (Lab chief whip 1974–77, mayor 1977); *Recreations* sport, particularly football; *Clubs* Charlton Athletic Supporters', Rowley Labour; *Style*— Roger Godsiff, Esq, MP; ✉ House of Commons, London SW1A 0AA

GODWIN, Charles Richard; s of Maj John Percival Godwin (d 1961), and Nancy, *née* Lee (d 1992); *b* 23 Aug 1933; *Educ* Ardingly; *m* 19 Nov 1976, Gwendoline Janet, da of Geoffrey Thomas Le Butt (d 1991), of Leicester; *Career* Lt Essex Regt and Somaliland Scouts 1953–54; CA; sr ptnr Manchester Office Price Waterhouse 1975–89; dep chm Britannia Building Society 1994– (dir 1989–); chm Readicut International 1996– (dir 1989–), NWF Ltd 1989–; *Recreations* golf, skiing, wine, antiques; *Style*— Charles Godwin, Esq; ✉ c/o Britannia Building Society, PO Box 20, Britannia House, Cheadle Road, Leek, Staffs ST13 5RG (☎ 01538 399399)

GODWIN, Fay S; da of British diplomat and American artist; *b* 17 Feb 1931; *Educ* Univ of Copenhagen; *m* Tony Godwin; 2 s (Nicholas, Jeremy), 1 step da (Jennifer McEwan); *Career* photographer; fell Nat Museum of Photography Bradford 1986–87, hon fell RPS 1990, hon fell Royal Inst of Scottish Architects 1992; Arts Cncl award 1978, bursary Arnolfini Gallery Bristol 1985–86; first photographer featured South Bank Show (LWT); Ramblers' Assoc: pres 1987–90, life vice pres 1990–; Hon FRPS 1990, Hon FRIAS 1992; *Solo Exhibitions* Writers' Portraits/Young Music Makers (Swiss Cottage Library London) 1974, The Oldest Road (Anthony Stokes Gallery London and touring, purchased by V&A) 1975, The Drovers' Roads of Wales (Anthony Stokes Gallery and touring) 1977, The Oil Rush (Aberdeen Art Gallery and touring) 1977, The Calder Valley (Anthony Stokes Gall and touring, purchased by Mappin Gall Sheffield), Selected Landscapes and Portraits (Yuen Lui Gallery Seattle) 1979, Selected Landscapes (Aarhus Photographic Museum Denmark) 1980, East Neuk (Crawford Arts Centre Univ of St Andrews) 1980, Romney Marsh (Anthony Stokes Gallery and touring) 1981, The Saxon Shore Way (Photogallery Sussex and touring) 1983, The Whisky Roads of Scotland (Crawford Arts Centre and touring) 1983, Portraits of Writers (Midland Arts Centre Birmingham) 1983, Landscape Photographs (British Cncl int touring exhbn), Land (Serpentine Gallery and touring, inc Yale Center for British Art and Stanford Mus of Art Calif) 1985–88, Our Forbidden Land (RPS and touring) 1991–92; *Group Exhibitions* The Land - 20th c Landscape Photography (V & A) 1976, Sussex Photographers (Rye Art Gallery) 1978, Wales (Mostyn Art Gallery Llandudno) 1979, The Arts Cncl Collection 1942–78 (Hayward Gallery) 1980, Fairies (Brighton Arts Gallery and Museum) 1980, Presences of Nature (Carlisle Museum and touring) 1982, Nat Gall of Modern Art Edinburgh 1984 and others; *Public Collections* Aberdeen Art Gallery, Arts Cncl, Bibliothèque Nationale Paris, British Cncl, Creasey Collection of Contemporary Art Salisbury, Contemporary Arts Soc (first photographer in collection), DOE, Mappin Art Gallery Sheffield, Nat Gallery of Modern Art Edinburgh, Nat Portrait Gallery, Royal Library Copenhagen, V&A; *Books* The Oldest Road - An Exploration of the Ridgeway (with J R L Anderson, 1975), The Oil Rush (with Mervyn Jones, 1976), The Drovers' Roads of Wales (with Shirley Toulson, 1977), Islands (with John Fowles, 1978), Remains of Elmet - A Pennine Sequence (with Ted Hughes, 1979), Romney Marsh and the Royal Military Canal (with Richard Ingrams, 1980), Tess - The Story of a Guide Dog (with Peter Purves, 1981), The Whisky Roads of Scotland (with Derek Cooper, 1982), Bison at Chalk Farm (1982), The Saxon Shore Way from Gravesend to Rye (with Alan Sillitoe, 1983), The National Trust Book of Wessex (with Patricia Beer, 1985), Land (with essay by John Fowles, 1985), The Secret Forest of Dean (with intoduction by Edna Healey, 1986), Our forbidden land (1990, Green Book of the Yr Award from Books for a Change); *Recreations* walking, reading, photography, painting; *Style*— Mrs Fay Godwin; ✉ Fay Godwin/Network, 3–4 Kirby Street, London EC1N 8TS (☎ 0171 831 3633)

GODWIN, Lesley; da of Richard George Hewitt (d 1982), and Kathleen, *née* Ingall (d 1970); *b* 17 June 1945; *Educ* Sydenham HS for Girls; *Career* Glyn Mills and Co 1961–63, Ofrex Ltd 1963–70; Consumers' Association: advtg mangr 1980–88, direct mktg mangr 1988–91, mktg devpt mangr 1991–, head of mktg 1992–; Br Direct Mktg Assoc: memb 1988, memb Bd 1989, memb Membership and Mktg Ctee; *Recreations* cinema, theatre, swimming, tennis, badminton, reading, antiques, cats; *Style*— Ms Lesley Godwin; ✉ Consumers' Association, 2 Marylebone Rd, London NW1 4DX (☎ 0171 486 5544, fax 0171 383 5887)

GODWIN, Peter Raymond; CBE (1992); *b* 16 May 1942; *Educ* Harrow Co Boys' GS; *m* 3 June 1967, Wendy Dorothy; 1 s (Philip b 1972), 1 da (Helen b 1969); *Career* banker; md West Merchant Bank Ltd, chm WMB Export Fin Ltd, chm Compton Plough Limited 1996–; dir: Swindon Town Football Co Ltd 1995–, The Korea-Europe Fund Ltd 1996–; former dir: Merchant Banking Corp Seoul 1976–86, Lazard Bros & Co Ltd 1979–85, The Int Investmt Corp for Yugoslavia SA Luxembourg 1981 85, Fin Merchant Bank Ltd Lagos 1987–89; pres Anglo-Taiwan Trade Ctee 1986–92; chm Asia Pacific Advsy Gp (BOTB) 1992–; memb Br Overseas Trade Bd 1995–; organist St Andrew's Church Roxbourne Harrow; ACIB; *Style*— Peter R Godwin, Esq, CBE; ✉ 16 Newquay Crescent, Harrow, Middx HA2 9LJ (☎ 0181 422 1801); 33–36 Gracechurch St, London EC3V 0AX (☎ 0171 623 8711, fax 0171 626 1610)

GODWIN-AUSTEN, Dr Richard Bertram; s of R Annesley Godwin-Austen, CBE (d 1977), of The Manor House, Pirbright, Surrey, and Kathleen Beryl, *née* Odling (d 1995); *b* 4 Oct 1935; *Educ* Charterhouse, St Thomas's Hosp (MB BS); *m* 12 Aug 1961, Jennifer Jane (d 1996), da of Louis Sigismund Himely (d 1986), of Holne Brake, Bovey Tracey, Devon; 1 s (Jonathan Reade b 1962), 1 da (Alice Amelia b 1964); *Career* sr registrar Inst of Neurology Queen Sq London 1967–70, conslt neurologist Univ Hosp Nottingham 1970–; clinical teacher and chm of neurological sciences Nottingham, memb Cncl of Mgmnt Parkinson's Disease Soc, pres elect Assoc of British Neurologists; High Sheriff for County of Nottinghamshire 1994–95; MD 1968, FRCP (London) 1976; *Books* The Parkinson's Disease Handbook (1984), Medical Aspects of Fitness to Drive (contrib, 1985), The Neurology of the Elderly (1989); *Recreations* gardening, dessert wines; *Clubs* Garrick, RSM; *Style*— Dr Richard Godwin-Austen; ✉ Papplewick Hall, Nottinghamshire NG15 8FE; Department of Neurology, University Hospital, Queen's Medical Centre, Nottingham (☎ 0115 942 1421)

GOEHR, Prof Alexander; s of Walter and Laelia Goehr; *b* 10 Aug 1932; *Educ* Berkhamsted, Royal Manchester Coll of Music, Paris Conservatoire; *m* 1, 1954 (m dis 1971), Audrey Baker; 3 da; *m* 2, 1972, Anthea Staunton; 1 s; *m* 3, 1982, Amira Katz; *Career* composer; lectr Morley Coll 1955–57, music asst BBC 1960–67, Winston Churchill Tst fellowship 1968, composer-in-residence New England Conservatory Boston 1968–69, assoc prof of music Yale Univ 1969–70, West Riding prof of music Univ of Leeds 1971–76, prof of music and fell Trinity Hall Cambridge 1976–; artistic dir Leeds Festival 1975, visiting prof Peking Conservatoire of Music 1980, memb Bd of Dirs Royal Opera House 1982–, Reith lectr BBC 1987; hon pres SPNM 1983–, hon memb American Acad and Inst of Arts and Letters, Hon FRMCM, Hon FRAM 1975, Hon FRNCM 1980, Hon FRCM 1981; Hon DMus: Southampton 1973, Manchester 1989, Nottingham 1994; *Style*— Prof Alexander Goehr; ✉ Trinity Hall, Cambridge CB2 1TJ

GOFF, Martyn; OBE (1977); s of Jacob Goff (d 1971), and Janey Goff (d 1978); *b* 7 June 1923; *Educ* Clifton; *Career* author; dir Nat Book League 1970–86; fiction reviewer: The Daily Telegraph 1975–88, Evening Standard 1988–; chm Henry Sotheran 1988–; chm: Sch Bookshop Assoc, Soc of Bookmen; non-exec chm Book Tst (formerly Nat Book League) 1992–95 (chief exec 1986–88); Liveryman Worshipful Co of Stationers & Newspaper Makers; FRSA, fell Int Inst of Arts and Letters; *Books* novels: The Plaster Fabric, A Season with Mammon, A Sort of Peace, The Youngest Director, The Flint Inheritance, Indecent Assault, The Liberation of Rupert Bannister, Tar and Cement; music books: A Short Guide to Long Play, A Further Guide to Long Play, LP Collecting, Record Choice; others: Victorian Surrey, The Royal Pavilion, Why Conform? Prize

Writing; *Recreations* picture collecting, travel; *Clubs* Athenaeum, Savile, Groucho, Academy; *Style*— Martyn Goff, Esq, OBE; ✉ 95 Sisters Ave, London SW11 5SW (☎ 0171 228 8164)

GOFF OF CHIEVELEY, Baron (Life Peer UK 1986), of Chieveley, Co Berkshire; Sir Robert Lionel Archibald Goff; PC (1982), kt (1975); s of Lt-Col Lionel Trevor Goff, RA (d 1953), of Queen's House, Monk Sherborne, Basingstoke, Hants, and his wife, *née* Denroche-Smith; *b* 12 Nov 1926; *Educ* Eton, New Coll Oxford (MA, DCL); *m* 1953, Sarah, er da of Capt Gerald Roger Cousins, DSC, RN, of Child Okeford, Dorset; 1 s (Hon Robert Thomas Alexander b 1966) and 1 s decd, 2 da (Hon Katharine Isobel b 1959, Hon Juliet Mary Constance b 1961); *Career* served Scots Guards 1945–48; fell and tutor Lincoln Coll Oxford 1951–55; called to the Bar Inner Temple 1951, QC 1967, recorder of the Crown Court 1974–75, bencher 1975, judge of the High Court of Justice (Queen's Bench Div) 1975–82, judge i/c Commercial List and chm Commercial Ct Ctee 1979–81, Lord Justice of Appeal 1982–85, Lord of Appeal in Ordinary 1986–96, Senior Lord of Appeal in Ordinary 1996–; hon prof of legal ethics Univ of Birmingham 1980–81; Maccabaean lectr 1983, Lionel Cohen lectr (Jerusalem) 1987, Cassell lectr (Stockholm) 1993; hon fell: Lincoln Coll Oxford 1983, New Coll Oxford 1986; chm: Cncl Legal Educn 1976–82, Ct Univ of London 1986–91, Br Inst of Int and Comparative Law 1986–; pres: Chartered Inst of Arbitrators 1986–91, The Bentham Club 1986, The Holdsworth Club 1986–87; High Steward Univ of Oxford 1990–; Hon DLitt: City Univ, Univ of Reading; Hon LLD: Univ of Buckingham, Univ of London, Univ of Bristol; FBA 1987; *Books* The Law of Restitution (with Prof Gareth Jones, 1966); *Style*— The Rt Hon Lord Goff of Chieveley, PC, FBA; ✉ House of Lords, London SW1

GOFFEY, Chris Robert; s of Sqn Ldr Peter Scott Goffey, of Worcester, and Margaret Sydney, *née* Goffey (cousin); *b* 17 Oct 1945; *m* 1968 Linda Mary, *née* Nolan; 2 s (Nicholas Scott b 1970, Daniel Robert b 1973); *Career* reporter 1965–72: Ruislip Northwood Post, Bucks Advertiser, Evening Mail Slough; news ed The Autocar 1972–78, ed Motor Trader 1978–80; TV since 1980 incl: reporter and ed Wheels (Thames), presenter and co-prodr The Motor Show (C4), presenter and prodr Wheeltracks (C4), presenter Top Gear (BBC 2); memb: NUJ, Guild of Motoring Writers, British Actors' Equity; *Books* How to Pass the L Test, How to Buy a Good Used Car, How to Pass the Motorcycle L Test, Lucas Book of Roadside Repairs, Make the L Test Easy; *Recreations* classic cars, horse riding and breeding; *Clubs* MG Car, Citroen Owners', Traction Owners'; *Style*— Chris Goffey, Esq; ✉ Wheel Track TV Productions, Field House, Forest Hill, Oxford OX33 1EF (☎ 01865 873078, fax 01865 873593)

GOGUEN, Prof Joseph Amadee; s of Joseph Amadee Goguen (d 1988), and Helen Stratton Goguen (d 1985); *b* 28 June 1941; *Educ* Harvard (BA), Univ of California at Berkeley (MA, PhD); *m* 1, (m dis 1974), Nancy, da of Ernest Hammer (d 1985); 1 s (Healfdene b 25 Dec 1967), 1 da (Heather b 4 Jan 1963); m 2, 20 June 1981, Kathleen, da of Robert Morrow; 1 da (Alice b 29 Nov 1983); *Career* asst prof Ctee on Info Sci Univ of Chicago 1968–73, IBM postdoctoral fellowship T J Watson Res Centre 1971, prof Computer Sci Dept UCLA 1973–79, academic staff Naropa Inst Boulder Colorado 1974–78, sr visiting fell Univ of Edinburgh 1976, 1978 and 1983, memb Centre for Study of Language and Info Stanford Univ 1984–88, md Structural Semantics Palo Alto CA 1973–, sr sci staff SRI Int Menlo Park CA 1984–88 (Exceptional Achievement award 1984), prof of computing science Univ of Oxford 1988–96; author of over 125 publications, articles in professional jls; ACM, AMS, MAA, IEEE; *Books* Theory and Practice of Software Technology (ed, 1983); *Recreations* literature, music, philosophy; *Style*— Prof Joseph Goguen; ✉ Programming Research Group, Oxford University Computing Laboratory, Parks Road, Oxford OX1 3QD (☎ 01865 283504)

GOH, Dr Beng Tin; s of Pang Chuan Goh, of Malaysia; *b* 14 May 1953; *Educ* Univ of Singapore (MB BS), Univ of London (Dip Dermatology), Soc of Apothecaries (Dip in Venereology); *m* 17 Dec 1978, Dr Tiak Nyar Sim, da of Kuan Sui Sim, of Malaysia; 2 da (Po-Siann b 18 May 1983, Po-Laine b 20 Jan 1985); *Career* registrar in genitourinary med King's Coll Hosp London 1980–81, sr registrar in genitourinary med Royal London Hosp and Moorfields Eye Hosp London 1981–85, conslt genitourinary physician Royal London Hosp and Moorfields Eye Hosp London 1985–; chm N Thames (East) Regnl Advsy Ctee; examiner Soc of Apothecaries' Dip in Genitourinary Med; FRCP, FRCPI; *Recreations* travelling, photography; *Style*— Dr Beng Tin Goh; ✉ Ambrose King Centre, The Royal London Hospital, Whitechapel, London E1 1BB (☎ 0171 377 7310, fax 0171 377 7648); Moorfields Eye Hospital, City Rd, London EC1V 2PD

GOLD, Antony; s of Ellis Neville Gold, of Liverpool, and Sonya, *née* Greene; *b* 26 Aug 1958; *Educ* Birkenhead Sch, Univ of Manchester (LLB), Chester Law Coll; *m* 3 Oct 1983, Sally Jane, da of late Eddie Perkin; 1 da (Clara Wendy b 21 June 1989), 1 s (Alastair b 5 March 1992); *Career* asst slr Hammelburger Marks Manchester 1983–84 (articled clerk 1980–83); Eversheds: asst slr/assoc Alexander Tatham Manchester (now part of Eversheds) 1984–88, ptnr 1988–, UK head of litigation 1993–, head of litigation Eversheds Manchester 1995–; acted for investors in Barlow Clowes case 1988–89, for local authorities in BCCI case 1991–92 and numerous other cases involving financial collapse and professional negligence; memb: Law Soc 1983 (memb Legal Aid Area Ctee 1992–), Int Bar Assoc 1995; *Recreations* reading, mountaineering, chasing the dog, chasing the children; *Style*— Antony Gold, Esq; ✉ Eversheds, London Scottish House, 24 Mount Street, Manchester M2 3DB (☎ 0161 832 6666, fax 0161 832 5337, car 0468 883358)

GOLD, Sir Arthur Abraham; kt (1984), CBE (1974); s of late Mark Gold, and Leah Gold; *b* 10 Jan 1917; *m* 1942, Marion, da of late N Godfrey; 1 s (Jonathan); *Career* former international athlete (high jumper); chm Br Olympic Assoc 1988–92 (vice pres 1993–); leader Br Olympic Athletics Team Mexico 1968, Munich 1972, Montreal 1976; commandant: English Cwlth Games Team Brisbane 1982, Edinburgh 1986, Auckland 1990, Br Olympic Team Albertville 1992 and Barcelona 1992; Br Amateur Athletic Bd: hon sec 1965–77, life vice pres 1977; Euro Athletic Assoc: memb Cncl 1969–76, pres 1976–88, hon life pres 1988–; memb Sports Cncl 1980–88, chm Sports Cncl Drug Abuse Advsy Ctee 1981–92, chm Euro Sports Conf Drug Abuse Advsy Gp 1985–91, vice chm Cncl of Europe (Strasbourg) Ctee on Doping in Sport 1983–90; pres: Amateur Athletic Assoc 1984–, Counties Athletic Union 1983–, Universities Athletic Union 1984–, London Athletic Club 1962–63, Middx County AAA 1963; Liveryman Worshipful Co of Basketmakers; Hon DTech Loughborough Univ 1989, Hon LLD Univ of Sheffield 1991; Olympic Order (Silver) 1991; Hon FCP 1987; *Clubs* London Athletic, City Livery, MCC; *Style*— Sir Arthur Gold, CBE; ✉ 49 Friern Mount Drive, Whetstone, London N20 9DJ (☎ 0181 445 2848)

GOLD, David Laurence; s of Michael Gold (d 1980), and Betty, *née* Levitt; *b* 1 March 1951; *Educ* Westcliff HS, LSE (LLB); *m* 27 Aug 1978, Sharon; 2 s (Alexander b 23 Jan 1983, Edward b 5 Oct 1985), 1 da (Amanda b 30 March 1981); *Career* admitted slr 1975, ptnr Herbert Smith 1983–; Freeman City of London Slrs' Co; memb Law Soc; *Recreations* theatre, cinema, bridge, travel, family; *Style*— David Gold, Esq; ✉ Herbert Smith, Exchange House, Primrose St, London EC2A 2HS (☎ 0171 374 8000, fax 0171 496 0043, telex 886633)

GOLD, Henry Patrick; s of Patrick Hugh Gold (d 1976), of Holland Park, London, and Agnes Bisset, *née* Crowe (d 1991), ggn of Sir Walter Gilbey, 1 Bt; *b* 11 Aug 1936; *Educ* Eton; *m* 8 Oct 1966, Catherine Jane, da of Gp Capt A J Barwood, OBE; 1 s (Edward Henry b 15 June 1969), 1 da (Polly Augusta b 3 July 1972); *Career* CA; Nat Serv Lt Royal Berks Regt 1955–57; Turquand Youngs & Co CAs (later Turquands Barton Mayhew): articled 1957–62, mangr 1965–67, ptnr 1967–78; Royal Dutch Shell Group: head of accounting res 1978–81, dir of fin and admin Turkey 1981–84, regnl fin advsr Western Hemisphere & Africa and area co-ordinator certain S American countries 1984–88, dep gp controller 1988–91; ICAEW: tech dir 1991–94, memb Cncl 1980–81, chm Parly and Law Ctee 1980–81; chm London Soc of CAs 1979–80, chm of tstees Int Centre for Res in Accountancy Univ of Lancaster 1985–95; Accounting Standards Bd: memb Urgent Issues Task Force 1991–94, project conslt 1994–; memb Financial Instruments Task Force Financial Accounting Standards Bd (USA) 1989–94, tech advsr to UK Bd membs Int Accounting Standards Ctee 1991–94, dir and treas Colchester and NE Essex Bldg Preservation Tst 1995–, an advsr The Prince's Youth Business Tst 1995–; Freeman City of London 1981, memb Ct of Assts Worshipful Co of CAs 1995– (Liveryman 1981); FCA 1972 (ACA 1962), FRSA; *Books* British Accounting Standards - The First Ten Years (contrib, 1981); articles in nat and professional press; *Recreations* music (piano, cello and singing), skiing, walking, ornithology, fishing; *Clubs* Oriental, MCC, Ski Club of GB (memb Cncl 1993–96); *Style*— Henry P Gold, Esq; ✉ 1 The West Front, Abbey Precincts, Churchyard, Bury St Edmunds, Suffolk IP33 1RS

GOLD, Jack; *b* 28 June 1930; *Educ* Univ of London; *m* 1957, Denyse, *née* Macpherson; 2 s, 1 da; *Career* film director; ed Film Dept BBC 1955–60, dir TV/film documentaries and fiction 1960–; *Theatre* The Devil's Disciple (Aldwych) 1976, The Story of Yours (Hampstead) 1987, Danger! Memory (Hampstead) 1988, Three Hotels 1993; *Television* TV films incl: Death in the Morning (BAFTA Award) 1964, World of Coppard (BAFTA Award) 1968, Mad Jack (Grand Prix Monte Carlo, Monte Carlo Catholic Award) 1971, Stockers Copper (BAFTA Award) 1972, Catholics (Peaboday Award) 1974, The Naked Civil Servant (Italia Prize, Int Emmy and Critics Award) 1976, A Lot of Happiness (Int Emmy Award) 1981, Sakharov (Assoc of Cable Enterprises Award) 1984, Murrow (Assoc of Cable Enterprises Award) 1986, Escape from Sobibor (Golden Globe Award) 1987, She Stood Alone (Christopher Award) 1991, The Last Romantics 1992, The Return of the Native, Spring Awakening 1994, Heavy Weather 1995; Kavanagh QC 1996; Desmond Davies Award for servs to TV (BAFTA) 1976; *Films* incl: The Bofors Gun 1968, The Reckoning 1970, The National Health (Evening News Best Comedy Award) 1973, Aces High (Evening News Best Film Award) 1976, The Sailor's Return (jt winner Martin Luther King Meml Prize 1980, Karoly Vary Award, Monte Carlo Catholic and Critics Awards 1981), Little Lord Fauntelroy (Christopher Award) 1981, The Chain 1985, The Lucona Affair 1993; *Style*— Jack Gold, Esq; ✉ c/o The Artists' Index, BBC Television Centre, Wood Lane, London W12 7RJ; 24 Wood Vale, London N10 3DP

GOLD, Sir Joseph; kt (1980); *b* 12 July 1912; *Educ* Univ of London, Harvard Univ; *m* 1939, Ruth Schechter; 1 s, 2 da; *Career* IMF: joined 1946, gen counsel and dir Legal Dept 1960–79, sr conslt 1979–; author of numerous pubns on monetary matters; *Style*— Sir Joseph Gold; ✉ 7020 Braeburn Place, Bethseda, Maryland 20817, USA

GOLD, Nicholas Roger; s of Rev Guy Alastair Whitmore Gold, TD, of Gt Bealings, nr Woodbridge, Suffolk, and Elizabeth Weldon, *née* Maytham, JP; *b* 11 Dec 1951; *Educ* Felsted, Univ of Kent (BA), Coll of Law; *m* 23 April 1983, (Siena) Laura (Joy), da of Adam and Jane Arnold-Brown, of Salcombe, Devon; 1 s (James Mortimer Fearon b 8 Oct 1987), 2 da (Siena Jane b 9 Jan 1985, Elizabeth Harriet b 17 Oct 1991); *Career* CA Touche Ross & Co 1973–76, slr Freshfields 1977–86, dir Corp Fin Dept Baring Brothers International Ltd (formerly Baring Bros & Co Ltd) 1986–; FCA 1982 (ACA 1977); *Recreations* sailing, the arts, country pursuits, travel; *Clubs* Hurlingham; *Style*— Nicholas Gold, Esq; ✉ 14 Northumberland Place, London W2 5BS (☎ 0171 229 4773); North Sands Cottage, Salcombe, Devon; Baring Brothers International Ltd, 60 London Wall, London EC2M 5TQ (☎ 0171 767 1000, fax 0171 767 7222)

GOLDBERG, Prof Sir Abraham; kt (1983); s of Julius Goldberg (d 1953), and Rachel, *née* Varinofsky; *b* 7 Dec 1923; *Educ* George Heriot's Sch Edinburgh, Univ of Edinburgh (MB ChB, MD, Gold medal for thesis), Univ of Glasgow (DSc); *m* 1957, Clarice, da of late Jacob Cussin; 3 children; *Career* Maj RAMC ME; Univ of Glasgow: Regius prof of materia medica 1970–78, Regius prof of practice of med 1978–89, emeritus prof/sr hon res fell Dept of Modern History 1989–; chm Ctee on Safety of Med 1980–86, fndr pres Faculty of Pharmaceutical Med Royal Colls of Physicians of UK 1989–91; Lord Provost award for public service (Glasgow) 1988; FRCP (London, Edinburgh, Glasgow), FRSE 1971; *Books* co-author: Diseases of Porphyrin Metabolism (1962), Recent Advances in Haematology (1971), Disorders of Porphyrin Metabolism (1987), Pharmaceutical Medicine and the Law (co-ed, 1991); *Recreations* swimming, walking, writing; *Clubs* RSM (London); *Style*— Prof Sir Abraham Goldberg, FRSE; ✉ 16 Birnam Crescent, Bearsden, Glasgow G61 2AU

GOLDBERG, David Gerard; QC; s of Arthur Goldberg (d 1982), of Plymouth, and Sylvia, *née* Stone; *b* 12 Aug 1947; *Educ* Plymouth Coll, LSE (LLB, LLM); *m* 22 Dec 1981, Alison Ninette, da of Jack V Lunzer, of London; 1 s (Arthur b 1986), 1 da (Selina b 1984); *Career* called to the Bar Lincoln's Inn 1971, in practice at Revenue Bar; case note ed British Tax Review 1975–87, author of numerous articles on taxation and company law, chm of the tstees Surgical Workshop for Anatomical Prosection 1994–; Philip Hardman Meml Lecture 1995; *Books* An Introduction to Company Law (jtly, 1987), The Law of Partnership Taxation (jtly, 1987); *Recreations* reading, letter writing, thinking, working out; *Style*— David Goldberg, Esq, QC; ✉ Gray's Inn Chambers, Gray's Inn, London WC1R 5JA (☎ 0171 242 2642, fax 0171 831 9017)

GOLDBERG, Rabbi David J; s of Percy Selvin Goldberg (d 1981), and Frimette, *née* Yudt (d 1980); *b* 25 Feb 1939; *Educ* Manchester GS, Lincoln Coll Oxford (MA), Trinity Coll Dublin, Leo Baeck Coll London; *m* 1969, Carole-Ann, da of Sydney Marks; 1 s (Rupert Alexander Ian b 1 Feb 1974), 1 da (Emily Catherine Toby b 18 Jan 1977); *Career* rabbi Wembley and Dist Liberal Synagogue 1971–74, sr rabbi The Liberal Jewish Synagogue 1986– (assoc rabbi 1975–86); Robert Waley-Cohen travelling scholarship 1978; chm ULPS Rabbinic Conf 1983–85, vice chm Cncl of Reform and Liberal Rabbis 1984 and 1993–; *Books* The Jewish People (Viking 1987, Penguin 1989), To the Promised Land (Penguin 1996); *Recreations* fell walking, travel, tennis, watching cricket, listening to music, reading; *Style*— Rabbi David J Goldberg; ✉ The Liberal Jewish Synagogue, 28 St John's Wood Road, London NW8 7HA (☎ 0171 286 5181, fax 0171 266 3591)

GOLDBERG, Dr Jack; DL (Greater Manchester 1986); s of Morris Goldberg (d 1954), of Salford, Lancs, and Rachel, *née* Cornofsky (d 1978); *b* 16 May 1924; *Educ* Manchester GS, Magdalen Coll Oxford (MA, BCL); *m* 3 August 1952, Maria Luise, da of Dr Alfred Berthold Willy Wolff; 3 da (Ruth Anne b 4 August 1953, Patricia b 5 March 1957, Naomi Jane b 9 May 1964); *Career* articled to Betesh & Co slrs Manchester, admitted slr 1953, ptnr Betesh Singer & Goldberg 1953–58, Conn Goldberg & Co (fndr ptnr) 1958–72, sr ptnr Goldberg Blackburn (now Pannone & Ptnrs) 1972–87, ret 1987; pt/t chm Social Security Appeal Tbnls 1982–87; cnllr (Lab) City of Salford 1956–67; North West Arts: chm 1965–74, pres 1974–90; Cncl Salford Univ: memb 1967–87, dep chm 1987–92, chm 1992–; memb NW Econ Planning Cncl 1965–82; chm, vice chm or memb of numerous orgns in the Arts, voluntary serv, health serv and educn; memb Manchester Law Soc 1953–; Hon DLitt Univ of Salford 1981; *Recreations* music, walking, stamp collecting; *Style*— Dr Jack Goldberg; ✉ 1 Lullington Road, Salford, Lancashire M6 8GW (☎ 0161 736 1872)

GOLDBERG, Jonathan Jacob; QC (1989); s of Rabbi Dr Percy Selvin Goldberg (decd), and Frimette, *née* Yudt (decd); *b* 13 Nov 1947; *Educ* Manchester GS, Trinity Hall Cambridge (MA, LLB); *m* 7 Nov 1980 (m dis 1991), Alexis Jane, da of Sir George Martin, CBE, *qv*; 1 s (Saul Percy Laurence b 22 Sept 1985), 1 da (Natasha Jane Frimette b 22

Dec 1982); *Career* called to the Bar Middle Temple 1971, practising SE Circuit, recorder of the Crown Court 1993–, head of chambers; memb NY State Bar 1985; *Recreations* reading, films, music, wine; *Style*— Jonathan Goldberg, QC; ✉ 3 Temple Gardens, 2nd Floor, Temple, London EC4Y 9AU (☎ 0171 583 1155, fax 0171 353 5446)

GOLDENBERG, Philip; s of Nathan Goldenberg, OBE (d 1995), and Edith, *née* Dee; *b* 26 April 1946; *Educ* St Paul's, Pembroke Coll Oxford (MA); *m* 1, 16 Aug 1969 (m dis 1975), Dinah Mary Pye; m 2, 12 Oct 1985, Lynda Anne, *née* Benjamin; 3 s (Jonathan b 1986, Benjamin b 1990, Joshua b 1994), 1 da (Philippa b 1988); *Career* admitted slr 1972, asst slr Linklaters & Paines 1972–82, ptnr S J Berwin & Co 1983– (asst slr 1982–83); sec Oxford Univ Lib Club 1966, pres Watford Lib Assoc 1980–81, vice chm Home Counties Regnl Lib Pty 1976–78 and 1980–81; memb Lib Pty: Cncl 1975–88, Nat Exec Ctee 1977–87, Candidates Ctee 1976–85, Assembly Ctee 1985–87; Lib Democrats: memb Federal Conf Ctee 1988–92, Federal Policy Ctee 1990–92, pres Woking Lib Dems 1992–94; Parly candidate: (Lib) Eton and Slough 1974 (twice) and 1979, (Lib/SDP Alliance) Woking 1983 and 1987, (Lib Dem) Dorset and E Devon (Euro) 1994, Woking (Lib Dem) 1996; memb Woking Borough Cncl 1984–92 (chm Highways Ctee 1988–90); former memb Exec Ctee Wider Share Ownership Cncl, memb Cncl Electoral Reform Soc 1978–82; CBI: memb London Regnl Cncl 1989–95, memb Nat Cncl 1992–, memb Fin and Gen Purposes Ctee 1994–; legal advsr RSA's Tomorrow's Company Inquiry 1995; jt author original Constitution of the Lib Democrats 1988; jt ed New Outlook 1974–77, memb Editorial Advsy Bd Business Law Review 1994–; govr Slough Coll of Higher Educn 1980–86; memb Law Soc; FRSA 1992; *Books* Fair Welfare (1968), Sharing Profits (with Sir David Steel, 1986), Guide to Company Law (4 edn, 1996), The Business Guide to Directors' Responsibilities (1994); *Recreations* family, friends; *Clubs* National Liberal; *Style*— Philip Goldenberg, Esq; ✉ Toad Hall, White Rose Lane, Woking, Surrey GU22 7LB (☎ 01483 765377, fax 01483 764970); 222 Gray's Inn Rd, London WC1X 8HB (☎ 0171 533 2222, fax 0171 533 2000)

GOLDHILL, Flora Taylor; da of Thomas Kissock (d 1981), and Flora, *née* McKenzie; *b* 13 Feb 1953; *Educ* Morgan Acad Dundee, Univ of Edinburgh (MA); *m* 3 June 1978, Jonathan Paul Goldhill, s of Michael Goldhill; *Career* civil servant DHSS and Dept of Health 1976–90; chief exec Human Fertilisation and Embryology Authy 1991–96, Dept of Health 1996–; vice chair Canonbury Jr & Infants Schs; *Recreations* family and friends, walking, gardening, reading; *Style*— Mrs Flora Goldhill; ✉ Department of Health, Richmond House, 79 Whitehall, London SW1A 1NS (☎ 0171 210 4989, fax 0171 210 4995)

GOLDHILL, Jack Alfred; s of John Goldhill (d 1978), of London, and Sophie, *née* Hamburg (d 1973); *b* 18 Sept 1920; *Educ* Christ's Coll Finchley, Coll of Estate Mgmnt, Inst of Chartered Auctioneers; *m* 1, 1943, Aurelia (Rela) Freed (d 1966); 3 s (Michael b 1949, David b 1952, Simon b 1956); m 2, 1967, Grete Kohnstam; *Career* served WWII Royal Signals in France, Germany and Gold Coast 1939–46; commercial property advsr; fndr ptnr Leighton Goldhill Chartered Surveyors 1948–80 (conslt 1980–); fndr and admin Jack Goldhill Charitable Tst 1974–; exhibitor of paintings Royal Acad Summer Exhibition 1983, 1988, 1989 and 1991–96; estab: annual bursaries for Royal Academy Sch students without grants 1981–96, The Jack Goldhill Award for Sculpture 1987–; hon vice pres Jewish Care, involved (with Jewish Care) in the founding and building of the Rela Goldhill Lodge home and residential centre for young physically handicapped; fell Inst of Chartered Auctioneers 1951, FRICS 1970; *Recreations* painting, golf, keeping up with nineteen grandchildren; *Clubs* Arts, Coombe Hill Golf; *Style*— Jack Goldhill, Esq; ✉ 85 Kensington Heights, Campden Hill Road, London W8 7BD

GOLDIE, Ian William; *Educ* Trinity Coll Glenalmond, Jesus Coll Cambridge (BA, MA); *m* 14 Feb 1976, Susan Kay, *née* Moore; 2 s (Stuart Douglas b 7 May 1984, Daniel Scott b 22 Oct 1987) 1 da (Emily Louise b 29 Aug 1989); *Career* ptnr Slaughter and May 1983–; memb: Int Bar Assoc, Inst of Petroleum; *Recreations* golf, miscellaneous spectator sports; *Clubs* Royal St George's Golf, Woking Golf, Hong Kong, Royal Hong Kong Jockey; *Style*— Ian Goldie, Esq; ✉ Slaughter and May, 35 Basinghall St, London EC2V 5DV (☎ 0171 600 1200, fax 0171 726 0038/071 600 0289)

GOLDIE, Dr Lawrence; s of Bernard Goldie (d 1946), of Manchester, England, and Dora, *née* Sapper; *b* 8 Sept 1923; *Educ* Manchester Central GS, Univ of Manchester, Univ of Manchester Med Sch (MB ChB, MD); *m* 1, 12 July 1949, Lilian Fay (d 1991), da of Hyman Jaffa; 1 s (Boyd Stephen b 5 May 1967), 1 da (Helena Elspeth b 28 Sept 1954); m 2, Silvia Susana, da of Roberto and Sophia Oclander, of Buenos Aires, Argentina; 1 step s (Lorenzo), 1 step da (Natasha); *Career* serv WWII pilot RAF 1942–46; house offr in gen surgery: Park Hosp Manchester 1953, Withington Hosp Manchester 1954 (house offr in gen med 1954); sr house offr in gen psychiatry and at Geriatric Psychiatry Unit Bethlehem Royal Hosp 1955; registrar: Psychotherapy Unit (gp and individual) The Maudsley Hosp 1956, The Observation Ward (acute admissions) St Francis Hosp Dulwich London 1957, Neurosurgical Unit Guy's and Maudsley Hosps 1957, Paediatric Psychiatry Maudsley Hosp 1957; res asst in neurophysiology Dept of Clinical Neurophysiology Inst of Psychiatry 1957–61, lectr Inst of Child Health Postgrad Med Sch Hammersmith 1961–67, conslt psychiatrist Queen Mary's Hosp Carshalton Surrey 1961–74; conslt psychiatrist and conslt med psychotherapist: Inst of Laryngology and Otology Royal Nat ENT Hosp London 1966–89, The Royal Marsden Hosp 1971–89; sr lectr Inst of Obstetrics and Gynaecology The Hammersmith Hosp London 1974–89; course dir and symposium organiser Psychosexual Problems Course Inst of Obstetrics and Gynaecology 1988–95; currently: hon conslt Psychiatrist Tavistock and Portman NHS Tst, conslt med psychotherapist The Lister Hosp London, dir Caring for the Bereaved and the Dying Course Univ of Middx/Tavistock Inst of Human Relations, in private practice Harley Street; tstee Assoc of Psycho-Analysts in the NHS, memb Cncl Psychologie et Cancer Marseille France; hon memb Int Psycho-Oncology Soc; former memb: Cncl CRUSE (orgn for care of widows and widowers) 1977–91, Euro Working Gp for Psychomatic Cancer Res 1978–; med memb Steering Gp Kent Voluntary Serv Cncls' Project on Social Care of the Gravely Ill at Home 1980–81, visiting conslt on psychiatric problems St Joseph's Hospice 1982, former med advsr Cancer Link, memb Editorial Bd Medical Tribune Gp Br Jl of Sexual Med until 1989; considerable experience as teacher and lectr, author of numerous papers in learned jls; Freeman City of London 1987, Liveryman Worshipful Soc of Apothecaries 1987, memb Guild of Freemen of City of London 1988; grad memb Br Psychological Soc 1959, FRSM 1959, FRCPsych 1975, MAE 1993; *Recreations* theatre, music (jazz, classical, opera); *Clubs* RAC, The Aircrew Assoc; *Style*— Dr Lawrence Goldie; ✉ 111 Harley St, London W1N 1DG (☎ 0171 935 0977, fax 0171 935 0728)

GOLDIE-MORRISON, Keith Cooper; TD; s of Capt Wilfred Drury Goldie-Morrison (d 1933), and Elizabeth Gilmour Johnson, *née* McCall (d 1937); *b* 12 Nov 1920; *Educ* Wellingborough Sch, Airspeed Aeronautical Coll; *m* 12 Dec 1942, Synnöve, da of late Erling Monsen; 3 s (Duncan b 1955, Stewart b 1958, Angus b 1962), 2 da (Solveig b 1949, Karen b 1952); *Career* served Middx Yeomanry 1940–46 (despatches as Maj), Lt-Col TA 1947–59; sr ptnr: Carroll and Co 1968, Keith Bayley Rogers and Co 1968–78; elected to Cncl Stock Exchange 1984 (joined 1949), dir Securities Assoc (now Securities and Futures Authy) 1988–90; chm: Regal Hotel Group PLC 1992–96, Malaya Group PLC 1989–96; dir Rossmont plc; tstee: Douglas Haig Meml Home, Housing Assoc for Offrs' Families 1977–93; MSI; *Recreations* music, photography, painting; *Clubs* Special Forces, Hurlingham; *Style*— Keith Goldie-Morrison, Esq, TD; ✉ c/o Keith Bayley Rogers Co, 93–95 Borough High St, London SE1 1NL (☎ 0171 378 0657)

GOLDIN, (Jacob) Henry; *b* 21 Feb 1939; *Educ* Grey HS Port Elizabeth SA, Univ of Cape Town SA (MB ChB); *m* 8 Dec 1964, Elizabeth Ann; 1 s (Jonathan b 1965), 2 da (Diana b 1970, Rachel b 1974); *Career* conslt plastic surgn 1974–: Wordsley Hosp, E Birmingham Hosp, Good Hope Gen Hosp; conslt craniofacial surgn Children's Hosp and Queen Elizabeth Hosp Birmingham; memb: Br Assoc of Plastic Surgns, Br Assoc of Aesthetic Plastic Surgns, Euro Soc for Craniofacial Surgery, Int Soc of Craniomaxillofacial Surgery; memb: BMA, RSM; FRCSEd; *Books* Plastic Surgery - Pocket Consultant (1987); *Recreations* travel, pottery; *Style*— Henry Goldin, Esq; ✉ The Birmingham Nuffield Hospital, 22 Somerset Rd, Edgbaston, Birmingham B15 2QD (☎ 0121 643 9167, fax 0121 643 4206, mobile 0836 535686)

GOLDING, Dr Anthony Mark Barrington; s of Dr Mark Golding (d 1954), of 29 Dawson Place, London, and Marian Rosalie, *née* Benjamin (d 1965); *b* 21 Aug 1928; *Educ* Marlborough, Univ of Cambridge (MA, MB BChir), Middx Hosp Med Sch; *m* 29 Aug 1962, (Olwen) Valery, da of Reginald Francis Orlando Bridgeman, CMG, MVO (d 1968), of Pinner, Middx; 1 s (Richard b 1965), 3 da (Rosemary b 1963, Catherine b 1967, Charlotte b 1970); *Career* RAMC 1954–56; med offr DHSS 1968–72, princ asst sr med offr SE Met RHB 1972–74, dist community physician King's Health Dist (teaching) 1974–82, dist med offr Camberwell Health Authy 1982–86, sr conslt in community med 1986–88, hon conslt 1988–; hon sr lectr: King's Coll Hosp Med Sch, King's Coll Sch of Med & Dentistry 1977–; conslt in public health med Redbridge and Waltham Forest Health Authy 1989–96, ed Health and Hygiene 1988–; memb: Cncl RIPH & H 1987–, Cncl RSM 1990–92, 1993–94 and 1995–97, Cncl Section of Epidemiology and Public Health RSM 1987– (pres 1990–92, vice pres 1994–); tstee Ctee Against Drug Abuse; DO 1956, MFCM 1973, FFCM 1979, FRIPH & H 1983, MRCOphth 1989, FFPHM 1989; contrib to various pubns incl Public Health, The Lancet and British Medical Journal; *Recreations* walking the dog; *Style*— Dr Anthony Golding; ✉ 12 Clifton Hill, London NW8 0QG (☎ 0171 624 0504); Keepers, Byworth, nr Petworth, W Sussex

GOLDING, Dr (Harold) John; CBE (1992); s of Harold Samuel Golding (d 1990), and Dorothy Hamer (d 1991); *b* 10 Sept 1929; *Educ* Univ of Toronto (BA), Univ of London (MA, PhD); *Career* painter; lectr then reader in history of art Courtauld Inst Univ of London 1959–81, sr tutor Painting Sch RCA 1981–86; temp appts: Power lectr Aust 1974, Slade prof of fine art Univ of Cambridge 1978–79; FBA 1994; *One Man Exhibitions* Nishimura Gallery Tokyo 1982 and 1984, Coventry Gallery Sydney 1984, Juda Rowan Gallery London 1985, Mayor Rowan Gallery London 1988, Yale Centre for Br Art Conn 1989, Mayor Gallery London 1994; *Group Exhibitions* Museum of Modern Art Oxford 1971, British Painting '74 (Hayward Gallery) 1974, John Moores Exhibition (Liverpool) 1976 and 1978, British Painting 1952–77 (Royal Acad) 1977; *Works in Public Collections* incl: Tate Gallery, V & A, Museum of Modern Art NY, Nat Gallery of Aust, Fitzwilliam Museum Cambridge; *Exhibitions Selected and Organised* Léger and Purist Paris (Tate Gallery) 1970, Summer Show 2 (Serpentine Gallery) 1976, Picasso's Picassos (Hayward Gallery London) 1984, Braque Still Lifes and Interiors (Walker Gallery Liverpool and City Art Gallery Bristol) 1990, Picasso, Sculptor-Painter (Tate Gallery) 1994; *Publications* incl: Cubism 1907–1914 (1959, new edn 1988), Fauvism and the School Chatou (1980), Visions of the Modern (1994); *Style*— Dr John Golding, CBE, FBA; ✉ 24 Ashchurch Park Villas, London W12 9SP (☎ 0181 749 5221)

GOLDING, Llinos (Llin); MP (Lab) Newcastle-under-Lyme (majority 9,839); da of Rt Hon Ness Edwards (d 1968, MP for Caerphilly 1939–68), and Elina Victoria (d 1988); *b* 21 March 1933; *Educ* Caerphilly Girls' GS, Cardiff Royal Infirmary Sch of Radiography; *m* 1, June 1957 (m dis 1971), John Roland Lewis; 1 s (Steven), 2 da (Caroline (Mrs Hopwood), Janet); m 2, 8 Aug 1980, John Golding (MP for Newcastle-under-Lyme until 1986 and gen sec Union of Communication Workers 1986–88); *Career* sec Newcastle Dist Trades Cncl 1976–, memb N Staffs DHA 1983–; MP (Lab) Newcastle-under-Lyme 1986– (by-election), W Midlands whip 1987–92; oppn frontbench spokesperson on: Social Security 1992–93, Children and the Family 1993–95, Food Agriculture and Rural Affrs 1995–; vice chm: PLP Parly Affrs, All Pty Parly Gp on Children; jt chm All Pty Parly Gp on the Homeless; match sec Lords and Commons Fly Fishing Club, memb BBC Advsy Cncl 1989–92; memb: NUPE, Soc of Radiographers; *Style*— Mrs Llin Golding, MP; ✉ House of Commons, London SW1A 0AA

GOLDING, Brig Dame (Cecilie) Monica; DBE (1958), RRC (1950, ARRC 1940); o da of Ben Johnson, and Clara, *née* Beames; *b* 6 Aug 1902; *Educ* Croydon Secdy Sch; *m* 1961, as his 2 wife, Brig the Rev Harry Golding, CBE (d 1969); *Career* Royal Surrey County Hosp Guildford 1922–25, Louise Margaret Hosp Aldershot and Queen Victoria's Inst of Dist Nursing; joined Army Nursing Servs 1925: India 1929–34, France 1939–40, ME 1940–43 and 1948–48; Southern Cmd 1943–44 and 1950–52, WO 1945–46, Eastern Cmd 1955–56, matron-in-chief and dir of Army Nursing Serv 1956–60, ret 1960; Col Cmdt Queen Alexandra's Royal Army Nursing Corps 1961–66; OStJ; *Recreations* motoring, nature study; *Style*— Brig Dame Monica Golding, DBE, RRC

GOLDING, Dr Richard James Arthur; s of late Arthur Bertram Golding, and Bridget Elizabeth, *née* Mahoney; *b* 13 April 1952; *Educ* Queen Elizabeth's Sch for Boys Barnet, Wadham Coll Oxford (BA, MA, DPhil); *Career* stockbroker and investment banker 1976–; Simon and Coates 1976–81, ptnr Grieveson Grant and Co 1984–86 (joined 1981), dir Kleinwort Benson Ltd 1986–92, princ Fin Nomura International plc 1992–, Annington Holdings plc 1996–; *Clubs* Utd Oxford and Cambridge Univ; *Style*— Dr Richard Golding; ✉ Nomura International plc, Nomura House, 1 St Martin's-le-Grand, London EC1A 4NP (☎ 0171 521 2159, fax 0171 521 3565, telex 883119)

GOLDING, Terence Edward; OBE; s of Sydney Richard Golding, and Elsie Golding; *b* 7 April 1932; *Educ* Harrow Co GS; *m* 1955, Sheila Jean, *née* Francis; 1 s, 1 da; *Career* chief exec: Nat Exhibition Centre 1978–95, Int Convention Centre Birmingham 1990–95; dep chm Earls Court Olympia 1995–; dir: Br Exhibitions Promotions Cncl 1981–83, Birmingham Convention and Visitor Bureau 1981–93, Heart of England Tourist Bd 1984–91, Central England TEC 1990–92, Birmingham Marketing Partnership 1993–95; memb: Exhibition Liaison Ctee 1979–95, Nat Assoc of Exhibition Hall Owners 1988–, Exec Ctee Exhibition Indust Fedn 1988–; hon memb Cncl Birmingham Chamber of Commerce and Indust 1990–95; Midlander of the Year 1990; *Style*— Terence Golding, Esq, OBE; ✉ Pinn Cottage, Pinner Hill, Pinner, Middx (☎ 0181 866 2610, office 0171 370 8205)

GOLDINGAY, Rev Dr John Edgar; s of Edgar Charles Goldingay (d 1974), and Ada Irene, *née* Horton; *b* 20 June 1942; *Educ* King Edward's Sch Birmingham, Keble Coll Oxford (BA), Univ of Nottingham (PhD); *m* 28 Aug 1967, Ann Elizabeth, da of Arthur Wilson (d 1971); 2 s (Steven b 1968, Mark b 1971); *Career* ordained: deacon 1966, priest 1967; asst curate Christ Church Finchley 1966–69, princ St John's Coll Nottingham 1988– (lectr 1970–88); *Books* Approaches to Old Testament Interpretation (1981), Theological Diversity and the Authority of the Old Testament (1987), Daniel (1989), Models for Scripture (1994), Models for the Interpretation of Scripture (1995), After Eating the Apricot (1996); *Recreations* The Old Testament, Israel, France, rock music; *Clubs* Rock City (Nottingham); *Style*— The Rev Dr John Goldingay; ✉ 7 Peache Way, Bramcote, Nottingham NG9 3DX (☎ 0115 922 4046); St John's College, Bramcote, Nottingham NG9 3DS (☎ 0115 925 1114, fax 0115 943 6438)

GOLDMAN, Antony John (Tony); CB (1995); s of Sir Samuel Goldman, KCB, *qv*, of Wonersh, Surrey, and step s of Patricia Hodges (d 1990); *b* 28 Feb 1940; *Educ* Marlborough Coll, Peterhouse Cambridge (BA, Dip in Computing); *m* 1964, Anne Rosemary, *née* Lane; 3 s (Stephen b 1965, James b 1968, Timothy b 1975); *Career*

International Computers Ltd 1961–73; civil service: DOE 1973–76, private sec to Sec of State for Tport 1976–78, asst sec 1977, seconded to HM Treasy 1981–83, under sec 1984, DG Civil Aviation 1996–; *Recreations* music, sailing, poetry, wine; *Style*— Tony Goldman, Esq, CB; ✉ Department of Transport, Great Minster House, 76 Marsham Street, London SW1P 4DR (☎ 0171 271 4791, fax 0171 271 4962)

GOLDMAN, Ian John; s of Morris Lewis Goldman, of Liverpool, and Tina, *née* Kleinman (d 1992); *b* 28 Jan 1948; *Educ* Liverpool Coll, LSE (LLB); *m* 9 Sept 1970, Diane Elizabeth, JP, da of William Shipton (d 1984), of London; 3 da (Vikki b 1972, Katie b 1975, Charlotte b 1979); *Career* admitted slr 1971, princ Louis Godlove & Co 1971; dir: Commercial & Financial Investments Ltd 1972–, Goldman Investments Ltd 1972–90; sr ptnr Godlove Pearlman 1991–96, sr ptnr Godloves 1996–; memb: Leeds Family Practitioner Ctee 1985–90, Leeds East Health Authy 1988–90, Leeds Law Soc Ctee 1988–, Nat Exec Ctee Jewish Nat Fund of GB 1981–87 (chm Leeds Dist 1981–84); vice chm Leeds Family Health Services Authy 1990–96, chm Leeds Med Service Ctee 1985–96; hon slr Leeds Jewish Welfare Bd 1995–, hon treas Leeds Jewish Rep Cncl 1996–; memb Law Soc 1971–; FInstD 1990; *Style*— Ian Goldman, Esq; ✉ Russell House, 15 St Pauls St, Leeds, W Yorks LS1 2LZ (☎ 0113 243 3861, fax 0113 242 0714)

GOLDMAN, Prof John Michael; s of Dr Carl Heinz Goldman (d 1992), and Bertha Goldman; *b* 30 Nov 1938; *Educ* Westminster, Magdalen Coll Oxford (DM); *Career* prof of leukaemia biology and chm Dept of Haematology Royal Postgrad Med Sch, conslt physician and haematologist Hammersmith Hosp; med dir Anthony Nolan Res Centre, dir Leukaemia Res Fund Centre for Adult Leukaemia Hammersmith Hosp, ed Bone Marrow Transplantation; former pres: Int Soc for Experimental Hematology, Euro Bone Marrow Transplant Gp; sec World Marrow Donor Assoc; FRCP, FRCPath; *Books* Leukemia (1983); *Recreations* skiing, riding; *Style*— Prof John Goldman; ✉ Royal Postgraduate Medical School, Ducane Rd, London W12 0NN

GOLDMAN, Sir Samuel; KCB (1969, CB 1964); yst s of Philip Goldman (d 1958), and Sarah Goldman; *b* 10 March 1912; *Educ* Raine's Sch, LSE (BSc(Econs), Gladstone Memorial Prize, MSc(Econs)); *m* 1, 1933, Pearl Marre (d 1941); 1 s (Antony, *qv*, b 1940); m 2, 1943, Patricia Rosemary, *née* Hodges (d 1990); *Career* Bank of England 1940–47, Civil Serv 1947; Treasy: chief statistician 1948, asst sec 1952, under sec 1960–62, third sec 1962–68, second perm sec 1968–72; exec dir Orion Bank 1972–74 (md 1974–76); chm: Henry Ansbacher Ltd and Henry Ansbacher Holdings 1976–82, Covent Garden Mkt Authy 1976–81; hon fell LSE; *Books* Public Expenditure, Management and Control (1973); *Recreations* music, gardening; *Clubs* Reform; *Style*— Sir Samuel Goldman, KCB; ✉ 3 Little Tangley, Wonersh, Guildford, Surrey GU5 0PW (☎ 01483 568913)

GOLDREIN, Iain Saville; s of Neville Clive Goldrein, of Crosby, Liverpool, and Sonia Hannah Jane, *née* Sumner; *b* 10 Aug 1952; *Educ* Merchant Taylors', Pembroke Coll Cambridge; *m* 18 May 1980, Margaret Ruth, da of Josef De Haas, of Finchley, London; 1 s (Alastair Philip b 1 Oct 1982), 1 da (Alexandra Ann b 22 Feb 1985); *Career* called to the Bar Inner Temple 1975; in practice London and Northern Circuit, jt head Corn Exchange Chambers, asst recorder of the Crown Ct; visiting prof to the Sir Jack Jacob Chair in Litigation Nottingham Trent Univ, memb Exec Ctee Centre of Advanced Litigation Nottingham Law Sch; memb: Middle Temple, Br Insur Law Assoc, Union Internationale des Advocats; Companion Br Acad of Experts (BAE Register of Mediators); network counsel Environmental Law Fndn; ACIArb, FRSA; *Books* Personal Injury Litigation, Practice and Precedents (with Margaret de Haas, 1985), Ship Sale and Purchase, Law and Technique (1985, ed in chief 2 edn, 1993), Commercial Litigation, Pre-Emptive Remedies (with Dist Judge K H P Wilkinson, 1987 and 1991, with His Hon Judge Kershaw, QC, *qv*, 1996), Butterworths' Personal Injury Litigation Service (with Margaret de Haas), Pleadings: - Principles and Practice (with Sir Jack Jacob, 1990), Bullen and Leake and Jacob's Precedents of Pleadings (gen ed 13 edn with Sir Jack Jacob, 1990), Structured Settlements (ed in chief with Margaret de Haas, 1993), Medical Negligence (with Margaret de Haas, 1996); memb Advsy Bd: Environmental Law, The Litigator; *Recreations* law, new ideas, tennis, the family; *Clubs* Wig and Pen, Athenaeum (Liverpool); *Style*— Iain S Goldrein, Esq; ✉ 12 King's Bench Walk, Temple, London EC4Y 7EL (☎ 0171 583 0811, fax 0171 583 7228); 5th Floor, The Corn Exchange, Fenwick Street, Liverpool L2 7QS (☎ 0151 227 5009, fax 0151 236 1120, mobile 0831 703156); 4 Linden Avenue, Crosby, Liverpool L23 8UL (☎ 0151 924 2610); Flat 140, Clifford's Inn, Fetter Lane, London EC4

GOLDREIN, Neville Clive; CBE (1991); s of Saville Goldrein (d 1946), of Hull, and Nina, *née* Aronoff (d 1977); *Educ* Hymers Coll Hull, Pembroke Coll Cambridge (MA); *m* 30 Oct 1949, Sonia Hannah Jane, da of Myer Sumner (d 1966), of Newcastle upon Tyne, and Rebecca Sumner (d 1991); 1 s (Iain Saville b 1952), 1 da (Nadine (Mrs Simon Caplan) b 1954); *Career* served E Yorks Regt as Capt E Africa; admitted slr Supreme Ct, ret; former dep circuit judge memb: Crosby Borough Cncl 1957–71 (Mayor 1966–67, Dep Mayor 1967–68), Lancs CC 1965–74, NW Planning Cncl 1966–72, Cncl of Univ of Liverpool 1973–81, Merseyside CC 1973–86 (dep ldr Cons Gp 1975–77); ldr: Merseyside CC 1980–81 (vice-chm 1977–80), Cons Gp 1981–86; chm Crosby Constituency Cons Assoc 1986–89; dir Merseyside Economic Development Co Ltd 1980–87; memb Cncl Liverpool C of C and Indust (chm Rivers Ctee 1991–93, chm Environment and Energy Ctee 1993–, chm Police Liaison Ctee 1994–), memb Local and Regnl Affrs Ctee Br Assoc of Cs of C; govr Merchant Taylors' Schs 1965–74, vice pres Crosby Mencap; chm: South Sefton St John Ambulance 1965–87, NW Cons Social Affrs Forum 1986–93, Liverpool Royal Court Theatre Fndn; memb Bd of Deputies of British Jews; *Recreations* videography, current affairs, music, grandchildren; *Clubs* Athenaeum (Liverpool); *Style*— Neville C Goldrein, Esq, CBE; ✉ Torreno, St Andrew's Rd, Blundellsands, Merseyside L23 7UR (☎ and fax 0151 924 2065, e-mail goldrein@aol.com)

GOLDRING, John Bernard; QC (1987); s of Joseph Goldring (d 1980), and Marianne Goldring; *b* 9 Nov 1944; *Educ* Wyggeston GS Leicester, Univ of Exeter; *m* 2 Jan 1970, Wendy Margaret Lancaster, da of Ralph Lancaster Bennett (d 1980); 2 s (Jeremy b 1971, Rupert b 1974); *Career* called to the Bar Lincoln's Inn 1969 (bencher 1996), standing prosecuting counsel to Inland Revenue (Midland and Oxford Circuit) 1985–87, recorder Midland and Oxford Circuit 1987, dep sr judge Sovereign Base Areas Cyprus 1991, dep High Ct judge 1995; *Recreations* gardening, skiing; *Style*— John Goldring, Esq, QC; ✉ 9 Bedford Row, London WC1R 4AZ (☎ 0171 242 3555)

GOLDS, Anthony Arthur; CMG (1971), LVO (1961); s of Arthur Oswald Golds (d 1934), of Macclesfield, and Florence, *née* Massey (d 1943); *b* 31 Oct 1919; *Educ* The King's Sch Macclesfield, New Coll Oxford (MA); *m* 9 Oct 1944, Suzanne MacDonald, da of Dr John Miller Young, MC (d 1947), of Glasgow; 1 s (Richard b 1947), 1 da (Laura (Mrs Russell) b 1952); *Career* served RAC 1939–46; joined Cwlth Office 1948; first sec: Calcutta and Delhi 1951–53, Ankara 1957–59, Karachi 1959–61; cnsllr FCO 1962–65, Rome 1965–70, ambass Cameroon Gabon and Equatorial Guinea 1970–72, high cmmr Bangladesh 1972–74; sr civilian instr RCDS 1975–76, Br dir Int C of C 1977–83; *Recreations* golf, literature; *Clubs* Dulwich and Sydenham Hill Golf; *Style*— Anthony Golds, Esq, CMG, LVO; ✉ 4 Oakfield Gardens, London SE19 1HF (☎ 0181 670 7621)

GOLDSACK, His Hon Judge Alan Raymond; QC (1990); s of Raymond Frederick Goldsack, MBE (d 1985), of Hastings, and Mildred Agnes, *née* Jones; *b* 13 June 1947; *Educ* Hastings GS, Univ of Leicester (LLB); *m* 21 Aug 1971, Christine Marion, da of Frank Leslie Clarke, MBE; 3 s (Ian b 1974, Richard b 1977, Stephen b 1980), 1 da (Tessa b 1975); *Career* called to the Bar Gray's Inn 1970, recorder 1988–94, circuit judge (NE Circuit) 1994–; *Recreations* gardening, walking; *Style*— His Hon Judge Goldsack, QC; ✉ The Old Rectory, Braithwell, Rotherham (☎ 01709 812167)

GOLDSACK, John Redman; MBE (1971); s of Bernard Frank Goldsack (d 1975), and Dorothy Owen (d 1984); *b* 15 Aug 1932; *Educ* Sutton GS, Wye College Univ of London (BSc), Queens' Coll Cambridge (Dip Agric), Imperial Coll of Tropical Agriculture Trinidad (DTA); *m* 11 Aug 1962, Madeleine Amelia Rowena, da of Robert Stanley Kibbler (d 1968), and Grace Iris Kibbler (d 1988); 2 s (Mark b 1964, Robert b 1966), 1 da (Margaret b 1968); *Career* agric offr HMOCS Kenya 1956–63, head Land Devpt Div Miny of Agric Kenya 1963–70, asst agric advsr ODA London 1970–74; sr agric advsr: BDDSA Malawi 1974–78, MEDD Jordan 1979–81, EADD Kenya 1981–83, ODA London 1983–85; dep chief natural resources advsr and princ agric advsr ODA London 1986–88, minister and UK permanent rep to UNFAO Rome 1988–93, conslt in agric and rural devpt 1993–, natural resources advsr to CARE UK 1993–95, chm Programme Advsy Ctee ODA Natural Resources Systems Programme 1995–; *Recreations* golf, cricket, natural history; *Clubs* MCC, Farmers; *Style*— John R Goldsack, Esq, MBE; ✉ Bradford Peverell Farmhouse, Bradford Peverell, Dorchester, Dorset DT2 9SF (☎ and fax 01305 266543)

GOLDSACK, Prof Stephen James; s of Rev Eustace Redman Goldsack (d 1975), and Jean Stirling Smith (d 1958); *b* 6 Aug 1926; *Educ* Barnard Castle Sch, Univ of Durham (BSc), Univ of Manchester (PhD); *m* 27 May 1953, Ginette, *née* Steinert, da of Edouard Steinert (d 1976); 2 s (Patrick b 1957, Christopher b 1961, Luan Doan Minh (fostered)), 1 da (Anne b 1954); *Career* asst lectr Univ of Manchester 1949–53, res asst Univ of California Berkeley 1954, lectr Univ of Birmingham 1955–60; Imperial Coll of Sci Technol and Med London: reader in physics 1960–72, prof of computing sci 1972–92, prof emeritus 1992; FInstP, FBCS, FIEE, CEng, CPhys; *Books* Programming Embedded Computer Systems in Ada (with V A Downes, 1982), Ada for Specifications: Possibilities and Limitations (1985); *Style*— Prof Stephen Goldsack; ✉ 59 Rydens Ave, Walton on Thames, Surrey KT12 3JE (☎ 01932 220 418); Imperial Coll of Science, Technology and Medicine, Department of Computing, London SW7 2AZ (☎ 0171 589 5111, fax 0171 589 8024, e-mail sjg@doc.ic.ac.uk)

GOLDSCHEIDER, Gabriele Maria (Gaby); da of Ludwig Goldscheider (d 1973), of London, and Blanka, *née* Geiringer (d 1985); *b* 7 March 1929; *Educ* Convent of Our Lady of Sion Acton Burnell Salop, Blunt House Oxted, Ruskin Sch of Art Oxford Univ; *Career* writer and publisher, specialist bookseller of books by Sir Arthur Conan Doyle and books about Sherlock Holmes, fndr Sherlock Holmes Book Club of GB; articles in Antiquarian Book Monthly Review; memb Antiquarian Booksellers Assoc 1978–; *Books* Dolls (1977), Bibliography of Sir Arthur Conan Doyle (1977); *Recreations* book collecting, toy collecting, reading; *Style*— Miss Gaby Goldscheider; ✉ Deep Dene, Baring Rd, Cowes, IOW (☎ 01983 293598); 32 Hornton St, London W8 (☎ 0171 937 7311); The Charles Dickens Bookshop, 65 High St, Cowes, IOW (☎ 01983 280586)

GOLDSMITH, Alexander Kinglake (Alick); s of Maj-Gen Robert Frederick Goldsmith, CB, CBE (d 1995), of Winchester, and Brenda, *née* Bartlett (d 1983); *b* 16 Jan 1938; *Educ* Sherborne, Trinity Coll Oxford (minor scholar, MA); *m* 9 Jan 1971, Deirdre Maude Adelaide, da of Harold Stafford, of Wadhurst; 1 s (Crispin Kinglake b 1976), 1 da (Lucinda Jane b 1973); *Career* Nat Serv 2 Lt Queen's Own Nigeria Regt 1957–58; HM Dip Serv 1961–90: New Delhi 1963–66, FCO 1967–70, first sec (Info) Wellington 1971–74, asst head SE Asian Dept FCO 1975–77, head of chancery Br Embassy E Berlin 1978–80, asst head Perm Sec's Dept FCO 1980–82, head Cwlth Coordination Dept FCO 1982–83, dep sec Security Hong Kong Govt 1984–85, consul-gen Hamburg 1986–90; dir gen Export Group for the Constructional Industries 1991–; *Recreations* swimming, walking, family; *Clubs* RAC; *Style*— Alick Goldsmith, Esq; ✉ The Export Group for the Constructional Industries, Kingsbury House, 15–17 King St, St James's, London SW1Y 6QU (☎ 0171 930 5377)

GOLDSMITH, Lady Annabel; *née* Vane-Tempest-Stewart; da of 8 Marquess of Londonderry (d 1955), and Romaine, *née* Combe (d 1951); *b* 11 June 1934; *Educ* Southover Manor Lewes; *m* 1, 10 March 1954 (m dis 1975), Marcus Oswald Hornby Lecky Birley, s of Sir Oswald Hornby Lecky Birley, MC (d 1952); 2 s (Rupert b 1955, Robin b 1958), 1 da (Mrs Francis Pike b 1961); m 2, 1978, Sir James Michael Goldsmith, MEP *qv*; 2 s (Zacharias b 1975, Benjamin b 1980), 1 da (Jemima Marcelle (Mrs Imran Khan) b 1974); *Style*— Lady Annabel Goldsmith; ✉ Ormeley Lodge, Ham Common, Surrey TW10 5HB (☎ 0181 940 5677/8)

GOLDSMITH, Edward René David; s of Frank Benedict Hayum Goldsmith, OBE, TD (d 1967); MP (C) Stowmarket 1910–18), by his w Marcelle, *née* Mouiller (d 1985); er bro of Sir James Goldsmith, MEP, *qv*; *b* 8 Nov 1928; *Educ* Millfield, Magdalen Coll Oxford (MA); *m* 1, 1953, Gillian Marion Pretty; 1 s (Alexander), 2 da (Dido, Clio); m 2, 1981, Katherine Victoria, da of John Anthony James, CMG (d 1987), of Auckland, NZ; 2 s (Benedict, Zeno); *Career* author; publisher 1970–, ed The Ecologist 1970–89; vice pres Ecoropa, winner Honorary Right Livelihood Award Stockholm (known as the alternative Nobel Prize) 1991; Chevalier de la Legion d'Honneur 1991; *Books* Can Britain Survive? (ed, Tom Stacey 1971), A Blueprint for Survival (co-author 1972), The Stable Society (1977), The Social and Environmental Effects of Large Dams Vol I (with Nicholas Hildyard 1984) Vol II (co-ed, 1988) Vol III (co-ed, 1992), The Earth Report (with Nicholas Hildyard, 1988), The Great U Turn (1988), 5,000 Days to Save the Planet (with Nicholas Hildyard and others, 1990), The Way - An Ecological World-View (1992), The Case Against the Global Economy and for a turn towards the local (ed with Jerry Mander, 1996); *Clubs* Travellers' (Paris), Brooks's; *Style*— Edward Goldsmith, Esq; ✉ 9 Montague Road, Richmond, Surrey TW10 6QW

GOLDSMITH, Harvey Anthony; CBE (1996); s of Sydney Goldsmith, and Minnie Goldsmith; *b* 4 March 1946; *Educ* Christ's Coll, Brighton Coll of Technol; *m* 4 July 1971, Diana; 1 s (Jonathon b 28 July 1976); *Career* concert promoter and prodr; ptnr Big O Posters 1966–67, merged with John Smith Entertainments Ltd 1970, fndr Harvey Goldsmith Entertainments Ltd 1976, acquired Allied Entertainments Group 1985, formed Classical Productions (with Mark McCormack) 1986; staged first free open air concert Parliament Hill Fields 1968, fndr concerts Roundhouse Camden 1968, cr Crystal Palace Garden Party series 1969–72; promoter: Aida 1988, Carmen 1989, Pavarotti in the Park 1991, Tosca 1991, The 3 Tenors 1996; vice pres: Music Users Cncl, Prince's Tst, REACT; chm Concert Promoters Assoc; memb Bd: London First, London Tourist Bd, Prague Heritage Fund; tstee: Band Aid, Live Aid Foundation, Royal Opera House Tst; memb Communication Gp Red Cross; Int Promoter of the Year 1994–96; *Recreations* golf; *Clubs* RAC, Hartsbourne Golf, Vale de Lobo Golf; *Style*— Harvey Goldsmith, Esq, CBE; ✉ Allied Entertainments Group, Glass Works, 3–4 Ashland Place, London W1M 3JH (☎ 0171 224 1992, fax 0171 935 9595)

GOLDSMITH, Sir James Michael; MEP (France); s of Frank Benedict Hayum Goldsmith, OBE, TD (d 1967), and Marcelle, *née* Mouiller; yr bro of Edward Goldsmith, *qv*; *b* 26 Feb 1933; *Educ* Eton; *m* 1, 7 Jan 1954, Maria Isabel (d 15 May 1954), da of Don Antenor Patiño y Rodriguez (d 1982), sometime Bolivian ambass in London, and Maria Cristina, 3 Duchess of Durcal (*see* Vol I Burkes Royal Families of the World); 1 da (Isabel); m 2, Ginette Lery; 1 s, 1 da; m 3, 1978, as her 2 husband, Lady Annabel Goldsmith, *qv*; 2 s, 1 da; 2 step s, 1 step da; *Career* ret from active business; fndr and proprietor of numerous industrial, commercial and financial enterprises; MEP (France) 1994–; fndr Referendum Pty in UK; *Books* The Trap (1995), The Response (1995); *Clubs*

Brooks's, Travellers' (Paris); *Style*— Sir James Goldsmith, MEP; ✉ Ham Gate, Richmond, Surrey

GOLDSMITH, John Stuart; CB (1984); o s of R W Goldsmith, and S E Goldsmith; *b* 2 Nov 1924; *Educ* Whitgift Middle Sch, St Catharine's Coll Cambridge; *m* 1948, Brenda; 2 s, 1 da; *Career* Royal Signals 1943–47; WO 1948, joined MOD 1964, dir gen Def Accounts MOD 1980–84; *Style*— John Goldsmith, Esq, CB; ✉ 16 Church Lane, Rode, Somerset (☎ 01373 830681)

GOLDSMITH, Peter Henry; QC (1987); s of Sydney Elland Goldsmith, and Myra, *née* Nurick; *b* 5 Jan 1950; *Educ* Quarry Bank HS Liverpool, Gonville and Caius Coll Cambridge (MA), Univ Coll London (LLM); *m* Joy; 3 s (James b 1978, Jonathan b 1983, Benjamin b 1985), 1 da (Charlotte b 1981); *Career* called to the Bar Gray's Inn 1972, in practice SE Circuit, Master of the Bench (Gray's Inn) 1994–; jr counsel to the Crown in Common Law 1985–87, recorder of the Crown Ct 1991–; memb Gen Cncl of the Bar 1992– (vice chm 1994, chm 1995, chm Legal Servs Ctee 1991–93, chm Pro Bono Unit 1995–); memb: Fin Review Panel 1995–, Cncl Public Concern at Work 1995–; Int Bar Assoc: chm Standing Ctee on Globalisation of Law 1995–, chm Ctee 1 IBA Human Rights Inst 1995–; *Style*— Peter Goldsmith, Esq, QC; ✉ Fountain Court, Temple, London EC4Y 9DH (☎ 0171 583 3335, fax 0171 353 0329)

GOLDSMITH, Walter Kenneth; s of Lionel Goldsmith (d 1981), and Phoebe Goldsmith; *b* 19 Jan 1938; *Educ* Merchant Taylors'; *m* 1961, Rosemary Adele, da of Joseph Salter (d 1970); 2 s, 2 da; *Career* chartered accountant Mann Judd & Co 1964–66, mgmnt conslt McLintock Mann & Whinney Murray 1964–66; Black & Decker Ltd 1966–79: dir of investmt, fin and admin Europe 1967, gen mangr 1970, md 1974, chief exec and Euro dir 1975 (Black & Decker USA 1976–79), corporate vice pres and pres Pacific Int Operation; chm Korn Ferry International Ltd 1984–86 (chief exec 1984–85), gp planning and marketing dir Trusthouse Forte plc 1985–87; chm: Ansoll Estates Ltd 1990–, Flying Flowers Ltd 1990–, Ewart Parsons Ltd gp of companies 1992–, Nuffield Group 1994–; dep chm: Isys plc 1987–, British Food and Farming Ltd 1990–; dir: Bank Leumi (UK) plc 1984–, Chambers & Newman Ltd 1994–, CLS Services Ltd 1994–, Betterware Plc 1995– (chm 1990–95); memb Advsy Bd Kalchas Group; chm Governing Bd Marketing Quality Assurance 1990–; underwriting memb Lloyd's; memb: Eng Tourist Bd 1982–84, Br Tourist Authy 1984–86, Br Overseas Trade Gp for Israel 1984– (vice pres), Cncl Royal Agric Soc of Eng 1990–95; dir gen IOD 1979–84, chm Food From Britain 1987–90, Free Enterprise Award Aims for Indust 1984, fundraising chm St Luke's Hospice Grange Project 1995–; Liveryman Worshipful Co of CAs in England and Wales 1985; FCA; *Publications* The Winning Streak (with D Clutterbuck, 1984), The Winning Streak Workout Book (1985), The New Elite (with Berry Ritchie, 1987); *Recreations* music, boating, painting, property; *Style*— Walter Goldsmith, Esq; ✉ Ansoll Estates Ltd, 2nd Floor, Hillside House, 2–6 Friern Park, North Finchley, London N12 9BY

GOLDSPINK, Prof Geoffrey; s of James Albert Goldspink (d 1992), of 28 Dornoch Drive, James Reckitt Ave, Hull, Humberside, and Muriel, *née* Gee; *b* 2 April 1939; *Educ* Univ of Hull (BSc), Trinity Coll, Univ of Dublin (PhD, ScD), FRSC; *m* 31 Dec 1960, Barbara, da of Frederick Staniforth (d 1966); 3 s (Mark Richard b 6 Jan 1962, Paul Harvey b 28 April 1964, Andrew Jeffrey b 27 Jan 1966); *Career* prof and head of zoology Univ of Hull, visiting prof Univ of Nairobi, Agassiz visiting prof Harvard Univ, prof of anatomy and cell biology Tufts New England Med Centre Boston USA; Univ of London: fndr chair of veterinary molecular and cellular biol, dir of molecular and cellular biol RVC London, currently prof and head of anatomy and developmental biol Sch of Med The Royal Free Hosp; *Books* Growth and Differentiation of Cell in Vertebrate Tissues, Mechanics and Energetics of Animal Locomotion; *Recreations* restoration of houses of historical interest, music; *Style*— Prof Geoffrey Goldspink; ✉ Brambledene, East Common, Harpenden, Herts AL5 1DQ; Halsham House, Halsham, Humberside HU12 0DE; The Royal Free Hospital School of Medicine, University of London, Rowland Hill St, London NW3 2PS (☎ 0171 794 0500, fax 0171 794 1248)

GOLDSPINK, Robert Andrew; s of Canon R W Goldspink, of Lowestoft, Suffolk, and Kathleen Edith, *née* Betts; *b* 8 Aug 1949; *Educ* Eltham Coll, Fitzwilliam Coll Cambridge (Squire scholar, Rebecca Flower scholar, MA, LLM); *m* 1 Sept 1973, Dr Margo Diane Dunlop, da of Roy Graham Dunlop, MBE (d 1989), of Cambridge; 1 s (James Elliot b 1985), 1 da (Jesse Lorraine b 1991); *Career* articled clerk Wild Hewitson & Shaw Cambridge 1973–75, supervisor in constitutional legal studies Fitzwilliam and Christ's Colls Cambridge 1973–75, slr Freshfields 1975–80; Denton Hall: joined 1980, ptnr 1981–; lectr on legal subjects 1975–; memb: Marriot Ctee proposing revisions to English arbitration law, Advsy Cncl Centre for Advanced Litigation Nottingham Law Sch, Jt Working Pty Gen Cncl of the Bar and the Law Soc reviewing English civil courts and court procedures 1993; memb: Law Soc, City of London Law Soc, London Slrs' Litigation Assoc; *Recreations* gardening, music; *Style*— Robert Goldspink, Esq; ✉ Denton Hall, Five Chancery Lane, London EC4A 1BU (☎ 0171 242 1212, fax 0171 404 0087, telex 262738/263567 D H G)

GOLDSTAUB, Anthony; QC (1992); s of Henry Goldstaub (d 1977), and Hilda, *née* Bendix; *b* 25 May 1949; *Educ* Highgate Sch, Univ of Nottingham (LLB); *Career* called to the Bar Middle Temple 1972, criminal and common law civil litigation 1972–; *Style*— Anthony Goldstaub, Esq, QC; ✉ Ropewalk Chambers, 24 The Ropewalk, Nottingham NG1 5EF (☎ 0115 947 2581)

GOLDSTAUB, Thomas Charles; s of Werner Fritz Goldstaub, and Beate Charlotte, *née* Muller; *b* 2 Sept 1953; *Educ* Forest Sch; *m* 4 June 1985, Jane Hilary Elizabeth Procter, *qv*, da of Gordon Heslop Procter; 1 s (Rollo Alexander b 16 April 1989), 1 da (Tabitha Sophie b 11 Dec 1985); *Career* md Fred & Warner Ltd 1983–86 (sales and mktg dir 1979–82), special projects dir Garrard & Co 1987–88, mktg dir Mappin & Webb 1989–90, md Fintex of London 1993– (dep md 1991–93); Freeman City of London 1986, Liveryman Worshipful Co of Upholders 1986; *Books* What Do You Call A Kid (1985); *Recreations* sailing, skiing, classic cars; *Style*— Thomas Goldstaub, Esq; ✉ 34 The Chase, London SW4 0NH (☎ 0171 622 9634); Fintex of London, 19 Golden Square, London W1

GOLDSTEIN, Prof Harvey; s of Jack Goldsein (d 1991), and Millicent Goldstein (d 1945); *b* 30 Oct 1939; *Educ* Hendon GS, Univ of Manchester (BSc), UCL (Dip in Statistics); *m* 1970, Barbara, *née* Collinge; 1 s (Thomas Gregory b 1977); *Career* research asst Dept of Statistics UCL 1962–64, lectr in statistics Inst of Child Health Univ of London 1964–71, head of Statistics Section Nat Children's Bureau 1971–76; Inst of Educn Univ of London: prof of statistical methods 1977–, jt dir WHO collaborating centre on child growth and devpt 1989–, jt dir Int Centre for Research on Assessment 1992–, assoc dir Int Sch Effectiveness and Improvement Centre 1993–; visiting lectr in biostatistics Univ of Wisconsin June-Aug 1968; visiting prof: Ontario Inst for Studies in Educn Toronto Canada July-Aug 1983 and 1986 (adjunct prof 1987–90), UEA 1992–; memb Ed Bd Annals of Human Biology 1974–, assoc ed Jl of Educnl and Behavioural Statistics 1988–, exec ed Assessment in Educn 1993–; govr: St James' CE Primary Sch Haringey 1982–90, Tetherdown Primary Sch Haringey 1987–89; fndn govr William Ellis Sch London 1993–96; memb: Biometric Soc, Soc for the Study of Human Biology, American Statistical Assoc, Psychometric Soc, Soc for Social Med, Br Educnl Research Assoc, Nat Cncl on Measurement in Educn, Int Statistical Inst 1987–; CStat, FSS (memb Cncl 1973–77), FRSA 1991, FBA 1996; *Recreations* tennis, squash, walking, cycling, playing the flute; *Style*— Prof Harvey Goldstein, FBA; ✉ University of London, Institute of Education, 20 Bedford Way, London WC1H 0AL (e-mail h.goldstein@IOE.AC.UK)

GOLDSTEIN, Dr Michael; s of Jacob Goldstein (d 1945), of London, and Sarah, *née* Goldberg (now Mrs Hyman); *b* 1 May 1939; *Educ* Hackney Downs GS London, Northern Poly (BSc, PhD, DSc); *m* 5 May 1962, Janet Sandra, da of Henry Arthur Skevington (d 1979), of London; 1 s (Richard b 1968); *Career* successively lectr, sr lectr then princ lectr Poly of North London (formerly Northern Poly) 1963–73; Sheffield Poly: head Dept of Chemistry 1974–83, dean of the Faculty of Science 1979–83; vice chllr Coventry Univ (formerly Coventry Poly) 1987– (dep dir 1983–87); author of many scientific articles and several review chapters in books 1962–84; chm Chemistry Bd CNAA 1978–84, involved with local regnl and nat sections of Royal Soc of Chemistry (pres Educn Div 1993–95) and various local/regnl orgns and gps; dep chm: Polytechnics and Colleges Admissions System (PCAS), Universities and Colleges Admissions Service (UCAS) (following merger of PCAS and UCCA); memb Bd: Coventry and Warwickshire Trg and Enterprise Cncl (TEC), Universities and Colleges Employers Assoc (UCEA), Coventry and Warwickshire Partnerships Ltd, Coventry City Centre Mgmnt Co Ltd; CChem, MRSC 1967, FRSC 1973, Hon FCGI 1994; *Recreations* jogging, DIY, Coventry City FC; *Style*— Dr Michael Goldstein; ✉ Coventry University, Priory St, Coventry CV1 5FB (☎ 01203 838212, fax 01203 838638, telex 931210228 CP G)

GOLDSTEIN, Ronald Sidney; *b* 6 Jan 1937; *Career* fndr jt chm and md Superdrug (taken over by Kingfisher plc 1987) 1966–89, non-exec dir Kingfisher plc 1990–; dir 1990–: Burginhall 430 Limited, Memo Stationery Superstores Limited, Volume One Bookshops Limited, Volume One Holdings Limited; also currently dir: Solo Properties Limited, Tangier Wood Properties Limited, Heath Drive Properties Limited; *Style*— Ronald Goldstein, Esq; ✉ Kingfisher plc, 119 Marylebone Road, London NW1 5PX (☎ 0171 724 7749)

GOLDSTEIN-JACKSON, Kevin Grierson; JP (Poole 1990); s of Harold Grierson Jackson (d 1992), and Winifred Miriam Emily, *née* Fellows; *b* 2 Nov 1946; *Educ* Univ of Reading (BA), Univ of Southampton (MPhil); *m* 6 Sept 1975, Jenny Mei Leng, da of Ufong Ng, of Malaysia; 2 da (Sing Yu b 1981, Kimberley b 1984); *Career* Staff Rels Dept London Tport 1966, Scottish Widows Pension and Life Assurance Soc 1967, programme organiser Southern TV 1970–73, asst prodr HK-TVB Hong Kong 1973, freelance writer and TV prodr 1973–75, fndr and dir Thames Valley Radio 1974–77, head of film Dhofar Region TV Serv Sultanate of Oman 1975–76, asst to Head of Drama Anglia TV 1977–81; TSW - Television South West: fndr controller and dir of programmes 1981–85, jt md 1981–82, chief exec 1982–85; dir Independent TV Publications 1981–85, contrib Financial Times 1986–, dir of private cos; govr Lilliput First Sch Poole 1988–93; Freeman City of London 1996; FRSA 1978, FIMgt 1982, FInstD 1982, FFA 1988, FRGS 1989; *Books* incl: The Right Joke for the Right Occasion (1973), Experiments with Everyday Objects (1976), Dictionary of Essential Quotations (1983), Share Millions (1989), The Public Speaker's Joke Book (1991), The Astute Private Investor (1994); *Recreations* writing, TV, films, travel, music, walking; *Style*— Kevin Goldstein-Jackson, Esq, JP; ✉ c/o Alcazar, 18 Martello Rd, Branksome Park, Poole, Dorset BH13 7DH

GOLDSTONE, Dr Anthony Howard; *b* 13 Sept 1944; *Educ* Univ of Oxford (MA, BM BCh); *Career* house physician in med Chase Farm Hosp Enfield 1969, house surgn Edgware Gen Hosp 1969–70, resident clinical pathologist Guy's Hosp 1970, registrar in haematology Western Infirmary Edinburgh 1971–72 (SHO in med 1970–71), res fell in clinical immunology Cancer Research Campaign Edinburgh Royal Infirmary 1972–73, sr registrar in haematology Addenbrooke's Hosp and Dept of Haematological Med Univ of Cambridge 1973–76, postgraduate dean Sch of Med UCL 1984–87, currently conslt clinical haematologist, med dir and clinical dir Dept of Clinical Haematology and Bone Marrow Transplant Unit UCL Hosps; hon sr lectr Sch of Med Univ Coll and Middx Hosp; dir Clinical Directorate in Haematology Bloomsbury District 1991–; chm: Registry of Transplant in Lymphoma Euro Bone Marrow Transplant Gp 1984–92, Med Ctee UCH 1986–88, NE Thames Regnl Haematologists 1988–92, Working Gp Bloomsbury Haematologists 1988–92, FRCP(Edin) 1979, FRCP 1983 (MRCP 1971), FRCPath 1987 (MRCPath 1975); *Books* Leukaemia, Lymphoma and Allied Disorders (jtly, 1976), Examination Haematology 91977), Synopsis of Haematology (1983), Clinics in Haematology: Autologous Bone Marrow Transplantation (ed, 1986); author of numerous book chapters and papers in scientific jls; *Style*— Dr Anthony Goldstone; ✉ University College London Hospitals, Grafton Way, London WC1E 6AU (☎ 0171 387 6424, fax 0171 380 9911)

GOLDSTONE, Anthony Keith; s of Myer Charles Maurice Goldstone (d 1987), and Rose, *née* Kessley (d 1987); *b* 25 July 1944; *Educ* Manchester Grammar, Royal Manchester Coll of Music; *m* 26 July 1989, Caroline Anne Clemmow, pianist, da of David Menzies Clemmow; *Career* pianist; appears as soloist, in duo with wife Caroline Clemmow and as memb various chamber ensembles; fndr Musicians of the Royal Exchange 1978; has worked with all major Br symphony orchs, performed at numerous Br and international festivals and BBC Prom concerts (incl Last Night); FRMCM 1973; *Recordings* incl: three vols of Chopin Piano Solos (Oryx/Peerless), Schubert Piano Solos and Schumann Piano Solos (Oryx/Peerless), The Britten Connection (piano solos by Britten and others, Gamut Classics), Parry Piano Solos on Parry's Piano (Albany), Elgar Piano Solos on Elgar's Piano (Cobbe/NT), A Moyzes (solos and two pianos with Caroline Clemmow, Olympia), Holst and Lambert Piano Solos (Chandos), Holst Planets (two pianos with Caroline Clemmow, Albany), Russian Tableaux (solos and piano duets with Caroline Clemmow, Amphion), Paradise Gardens (solos and piano duets with Caroline Clemmow, Albany), George Lloyd Music for Two Pianos (with Caroline Clemmow, Albany), Virtuoso Variations (various piano duets with Caroline Clemmow, Symposium), Rimsky-Korsakov Scheherazade (piano duets with Caroline Clemmow, Amphion), Romantic Duet Sonatas (with Caroline Clemmow, Meridian), Duet Lollipops (with Caroline Clemmow, Meridian), Romantic Duet Waltzes (with Caroline Clemmow, Amphion), Romantic Duet Suites (with Caroline Clemmow, Amphion), Beethoven Fourth Concerto (with RPO under Norman Del Mar, BBC Radio Classics), Saint-Saëns' Carnival of Animals (with RPO under Owain Arwel Hughes, Enigma Classics), Berkeley and Debussy Duos (with James Galway on flute, RCA), Beethoven Piano Quartets (with Cummings String Trio, Meridian), Sibelius Piano Quintet (with Gabrieli String Quartet, Chandos), Alkan Concerto da Camera No 2 and Bombardo-Carillon (with Morhange Ensemble and Caroline Clemmow respectively, Symposium), Mendelssohn Complete Sonatas for Violin and Piano (with Yossi Zivoni, Meridian), Holst Quintet for Piano and Wind and Jacob Sextet for Piano and Wind (with Elysian Wind Quintet, Chandos); *Recreations* antique maps, birdwatching; *Style*— Anthony Goldstone, Esq; ✉ Walcot Old Hall, Alkborough, North Lincolnshire DN15 9JT (☎ 01724 720475, fax 01724 721599)

GOLDSTONE, (Leonard) Clement; QC (1993); s of Maurice Goldstone (d 1980), and Maree, *née* Lewis; *b* 20 April 1949; *Educ* Manchester GS, Churchill Coll Cambridge (BA); *m* 20 August 1972, Vanessa, da of Donald, and Muriel, Forster; 3 s (Simon Lewis b 27 Dec 1973, Jonathan Andrew b 11 Oct 1976, Maurice James b 24 May 1980); *Career* called to the Bar Middle Temple 1971, pupil to Ivor R Taylor (now His Hon Ivor R Taylor, QC), recorder 1992– (asst recorder 1988–92); *Recreations* golf, bridge, theatre, music; *Clubs* Dunham Forest Golf & Country (Altrincham); *Style*— L Clement Goldstone, Esq, QC; ✉ 28 St John Street, Manchester M3 4DJ (☎ 0161 834 8418, fax 0161 835 3929)

GOLDSTONE, David Joseph; s of Solomon Goldstone, and Rebecca, *née* Degotts; *b* 21 Feb 1929; *Educ* Dynevor Sch Swansea, LSE (LLB); *m* 21 March 1957, Cynthia, da of Walter George Easton; 1 s (Jonathan Lee b 3 Nov 1957), 2 da (Debra Ann b 24 Aug

1959, Karen Ella b 22 Oct 1964); *Career* legal practice 1955–66, chief exec Regalian Properties plc 1970–; memb: Football Assoc of Wales 1970–72, WNO 1984–89; memb Cncl Univ of London; memb Ct of Govrs: LSE 1985–, Atlantic Coll 1987–; fell LSE; *Recreations* family, reading, sport; *Clubs* Bath & Racquets, Riverside Racquet Centre; *Style*— David Goldstone, Esq; ✉ Regalian Properties plc, 44 Grosvenor Hill, London W1A 4NR (☎ 0171 493 9613, fax 0171 408 2096)

GOLDSWORTHY, Andy; s of Prof Fredrick Alan Goldsworthy, and Muriel, *née* Stanger; *b* 25 July 1956; *Educ* Wheatlands Secdy Modern Sch, Harrogate HS, Bradford Art Coll, Preston Poly; *m* Judith Elizabeth, da of Barry Gregson, and Audrey, *née* Jackson; 2 s (James b 8 Oct 1987, Thomas b 15 Dec 1994), 2 da (Holly b 4 April 1990, Anna b 5 Feb 1993); *Career* artist/sculptor; *Solo Exhibitions* Evidence (Coracle Press Gallery London) 1985, Rain, Sun, Snow, Mist, Calm (The Henry Moore Centre for the Study of Sculpture, Leeds City Art Gallery and Northern Centre for Contemporary Art Sunderland touring) 1985, Winter Harvest (Book exhibition with John Fowles, Scottish Arts Cncl) 1987, Fabian Carlsson Gallery London 1987, Gallery Takagi Nagoya Japan 1988, Yurakucho Asahi Gallery Tokyo and Osaka Japan 1988, Mountain and Coast Autumn into Winter Japan 1987 (Fabian Carlsson Gallery London) 1988, Touching North (Anne Berthoud Gallery London and Graeme Murray Gallery Edinburgh) 1989, Black in Black (Fabian Carlsson Gallery London) 1989, Snowballs in Summer (Old Museum of Tport Glasgow) 1989, Leaves (The Natural History Museum London) 1989, Garden Mountain (Centre D'Art Contenporain Castres France) 1990, Hand to Earth - Sculpture 1976–90 (retrospective exhibition touring Leeds City Art Gallery, Royal Botanic Garden Edinburgh, Stedelijke Musea Gouda Holland and Centre D'Art Contemporain Toulouse France) 1990–91, Drawings (Aline Vidal Gallery Paris) 1990–91, With Nature (Galerie Lelong NY and Chicago Arts Club) 1991, Sand Leaves (Chicago Arts Club) 1991, With Nature (Galerie Lelong NYC) 1991, Mid Winter Muster (Adelaide Festival Australia) 1992, Verden Und Vergehen (Museum Bellerine Zurich) 1992, California Project (Haines Gallery San Francisco) 1992, Stone Sky (Galerie St Anne Brussels) 1992, Ile de Lassiuiere France 1992, Flow of Earth (exhbn and film, Castlefield Gallery Manchester) 1992, Hard Earth (Turske Hue-Williams Gall London) 1992, Australia, NZ and Japan 1993, Mid-Winter Muster (Harwood House) 1993, Wood Land (Gallerie Lelong NY) 1993, Tochigi Museum of Fine Art Japan 1993, Setagaya Museum of Fine Arts Tokyo 1994, Aline Vidal Gallery Paris 1994, Hue-Williams Fine Art London 1994, Laumeier Sculpture Park St Louis 1994, Oriel Gallery Cardiff 1994, Haines Gallery San Francisco 1994, San Jose Museum of Art 1995, Galerij S65 Belgium 1995, Galerie Lelong NY 1995, Musée de Digne France 1995; *Group Exhibitions* incl: Place (Gimpel Fils Summer Show London) 1983, Sculpture in the Open Air (Yorkshire Sculpture Park) 1983, Salon D'Automne (Serpentine Gallery London) 1984, The Possibilities of Space - Fifty Years of British Sculptors' Drawings (Musee de Beaux Arts De Besancon, Kirlees Museums touring) 1987–88, Apperto 88 (Venice Biennale) 1988, Through the Looking Glass - Photographic Art in Britain 1945–1989 (Barbican Art Gallery London) 1989, Leaves (Atelier des Enfants, Centre Georges Pompidou Paris touring) 1990, Attitudes to Nature (Ile De Vassiviere France) 1991, Shared Earth (Br-Russian art, UK touring) 1991, Goldsworthy and Girke (Fruitmarket Gall Edinburgh) 1992, Galerie Lelong NY 1993, Impermanence (Alderich Museum of Modern Art) 1993, Parc de la Courneuve (Paris installation) 1993, Morecambe Bay Works (Lancaster, Scott Gallery and Storey Inst) 1993, Tikon (project, Denmark) 1993, Trees (Kunstierwerkstatt Lotheringstrasse Munich) 1993, Time Machine (British Museum London) 1994; *Films* Two Autumns (ACGB/Channel 4), Flow of Earth (Granada); *Publications* Rain sun snowhail mist calm (1985), Mountain and Coast Autumn into Winter (1987), Parkland (1988), Leaves (1989), Garden Mountain (1989), Touching North (1989), Andy Goldsworthy (1989), Sand Leaves (1991), Hand to Earth (1991), Ice and Snow Drawings (1992), Two Autumns (1993), Stone (1994), Black Stones, Red Pools (1995), Sheepfolds (1996), Wood (1996); *Style*— Andy Goldsworthy, Esq; ✉ c/o Michael Hue-Williams Fine Art Ltd, 21 Cork Street, London W1X 1HB (☎ 0171 434 1318, fax 0171 434 1321)

GOLDSWORTHY, Ian Francis; QC (1992); s of late Francis Charles Goldsworthy, and late Mary, *née* Williams; *b* 7 July 1943; *Educ* Clifton Coll, Univ Coll Oxford; *m* Lindsay Mary; 3 da (Francesca b 1969, Claudia b 1974, Flavia b 1979); *Career* called to the Bar Inner Temple 1968; *Recreations* master of Ratte Hounds, antiques, music; *Style*— Ian Goldsworthy, Esq, QC; ✉ 36 Essex Street, London WC2 (☎ 0171 413 0353)

GOLDTHORPE, Dr John Harry; s of Harry Goldthorpe (d 1989), of Great Houghton, Barnsley, and Lilian Eliza; *b* 27 May 1935; *Educ* Wath-upon-Dearne GS, UCL (BA), LSE, Univ of Cambridge (MA), Univ of Oxford (MA); *m* 1963, Rhiannon Esyllt, da of late Isaac Daniel Harry; 1 s (David Daniel Harry), 1 da (Siân Elinor); *Career* lectr Faculty of Econ and Politics Univ of Cambridge 1961–69 (fell King's Coll 1960–69), official fell Nuffield Coll Oxford 1969–; pres Int Sociological Assoc Ctee on Social Stratification 1982–85, fndr memb Soc for Comparative Research 1995; memb Academia Europaea 1988, Br Acad assessor ESRC 1988–92, chm Social Studies Section Br Acad 1992–94; FBA 1984, Hon Fil Dr Univ of Stockholm 1990; *Books* The Affluent Worker - Industrial Attitudes and Behaviour (with David Lockwood, 1968), The Affluent Worker - Political Attitudes and Behaviour (with David Lockwood, 1968), The Affluent Worker in the Class Structure (with David Lockwood, 1969), The Social Grading of Occupations - A New Approach and Scale (with Keith Hope, 1974), Social Mobility and Class Structure in Modern Britain (2 edn, 1987), The Constant Flux - A Study of Class Mobility in Industrial Societies (with Robert Erikson, 1992); *Recreations* lawn tennis, bird watching, computer chess; *Style*— Dr John Goldthorpe, FBA; ✉ 32 Leckford Rd, Oxford OX2 6HX (☎ 01865 556602); Nuffield College, Oxford OX1 1NF (☎ 01865 278559, fax 01865 278621)

GOMBRICH, Prof Sir Ernst Hans Josef; OM (1988), kt (1972), CBE (1966); s of Dr Karl B Gombrich (d 1950), and Prof Leonie Gombrich, *née* Hock; *b* 30 March 1909; *Educ* Theresianum, Univ of Vienna (PhD); *m* 1936, Ilse, da of Gustav Heller, of Neuötting, Bohemia; 1 s (Richard Francis b 1937); *Career* Slade prof of fine art: Univ of Oxford 1950–53, Univ of Cambridge 1961–63; dir of Warburg Inst and prof of history of the classical tradition Univ of London 1959–76 (emeritus prof 1976–); Ehrenkreuz für Wissenschaft und Kunst (Austria) 1975, Orden Pour le Mérite für Wissenschaften und Künste 1977, Ehrenzeichen für Wissenschaft und Kunst (Austria) 1984; Hon FRIBA 1971, FRSL 1969, FBA 1960, FSA 1961; *Books* incl; The Story of Art, Meditations on a Hobby Horse, Art and Illusion; *Style*— Prof Sir Ernst Gombrich, OM, CBE, FRSL, FBA, FSA; ✉ 19 Briardale Gardens, London NW3 7PN (☎ 0171 435 6639)

GOMBRICH, Prof Richard Francis; *b* 17 July 1937; *Educ* St Paul's (scholar), Magdalen Coll Oxford (Demy scholar, BA, MA, DPhil), Harvard Univ (AM); *Career* Univ of Oxford: lectr in Sanskrit and Pali 1965–76, governing body fell Wolfson Coll 1966–76, Boden prof of Sanskrit and professorial fell Balliol Coll 1976–; Benjamin Meaker visiting prof Univ of Bristol 1981–82, visiting prof Ecole des Hautes Etudes en Sciences Sociales 1982, Stewart visiting fell Princeton Univ 1986–87; memb: Advsy Cncl V & A 1978–83, Theological and Religious Studies Bd Cncl for Nat Academic Awards 1983–90, Cncl Soc for S Asian Studies 1986–92, Cncl Royal Asiatic Soc 1989–90, Academia Europaea 1990–, Pubns Ctee Royal Asiatic Soc 1991–92; pres Pali Text Soc 1994– (hon sec and treas 1981–94); Hon DLitt Kalyani Univ 1991; S C Chakraborty medal Asiatic Soc 1993, Sri Lanka Ranjana 1994; *Books* Precept and Practice: Traditional Buddhism in the Rural Highlands of Ceylon (1971), The World of Buddhism: Buddhist Monks and Nuns in Society and Culture (jt ed, 1984), Theravâda Buddhism: A Social History from Ancient Benares to Modern Colombo (1988), Buddhism Transformed: Religious Change in Sri Lanka (jtly, 1988), How Buddhism Began (1996); author of over 70 articles in learned jls; *Style*— Prof Richard Gombrich; ✉ Balliol College, Oxford OX1 3BJ

GOMER, Barry Edward; s of Philip Vincent Gomer (d 1984), of London, and Violet Eileen, *née* Long; *b* 4 Feb 1949; *Educ* Shooters Hill GS; *m* 3 Aug 1978, Marthe Lynne, da of Maj Jeffrey Max Allison; *Career* press photographer; Fin Control Dept London Borough of Greenwich 1965–67, press and commercial photographer Pace Photography Sidcup 1967–70 (apprentice on day-release 1965–67), proprietor own business Globe Photography 1970–73, freelance 1973–74, staff photographer Daily Express 1975–; assignments incl: Cannonball Run across USA in a Jaguar XJ40, refugee camps in Somalia, Brixton riots, taking tea with Charlie Cray on his release from Maidstone Prison, Madonna jogging in Hyde Park (published in A Day for Life), European Championships Sweden 1992, Olympic Games Barcelona 1992, Wimbledon Tennis 1992, 1994 and 1995, Cambodia Resurgence of Khmer Rouge 1995; hon dir Lakeland Ltd 1991–; memb Inst of Journalists; *Clubs* City Golf, Bradbourne Riding; *Style*— Barry Gomer, Esq; ✉ Daily Express, Ludgate House, 245 Blackfriars Rd, London SE1 9UX (☎ 0171 928 8000)

GOMEZ, Jill; *b* Br Guiana, of Br and Spanish parents; *Educ* RAM, Guildhall Sch of Music; *Career* opera and concert singer; FRAM; operatic debut with Glyndebourne Touring Opera 1968; *Opera roles* with Glyndebourne Festival Opera incl: Mélisande in Pelleas et Mélisande, title role in La Calisto, Ann Truelove in The Rake's Progress; roles with The Royal Opera, ENO and Scottish Opera incl: Pamina in The Magic Flute, Ilia in Idomeneo, Fiordiligi in Cosi fan Tutte, the Countess in The Marriage of Figaro, Elizabeth in Elegy for Young Lovers, Tytania in A Midsummer Night's Dream, Lauretta in Gianni Schicchi, Governess in The Turn of the Screw, cr role of Flora in Tippett The Knot Garden (Covent Garden) 1970, Governess in The Turn of the Screw (ENO) 1984; other roles incl: Countess in Thea Musgrave Voice of Ariadne (Aldeburgh) 1974, title role in Thaïs (Wexford) 1974, Jenifer in The Midsummer Marriage (WNO) 1976, cr title role in William Alwyn's Miss Julie for radio 1977, Tatiana in Eugene Onegin (Kent Opera) 1977, Donna Elvira in Don Giovanni (Ludwigsburg Festival) 1978, cr title role in BBC world première of Prokoviev Maddalena 1979, Fiordiligi in Cosi Fan Tutte (Bordeaux) 1979, 8th Book of Madrigals (première, Zurich Monteverdi Festival) 1979, Violetta in La Traviata (Kent Opera at Edinburgh Festival) 1979, Cinna in Lucio Silla (Zurich) 1981, Governess in The Turn of the Screw (Geneva) 1981, Cleopatra in Giulio Cesare (Frankfurt) 1981, Teresa in Benvenuto Cellini (Berlioz Festival, Lyon) 1982, Leïla in Les Pêcheurs de Perles (Scottish Opera) 1982–83, Helena in A Midsummer Night's Dream (Glyndebourne 1984, Opera London 1990), Donna Anna in Don Giovanni (Frankfurt Opera 1985, Kent Opera 1988), Amyntas in Il Re Pastore (Kent Opera) 1987, cr role of Duchess of Argyll in Powder her Face (Cheltenham Festival and Almeida Theatre) 1995; *Recitals* in: France, Austria, Belgium, Netherlands, Germany, Scandinavia, Switzerland, Italy, Spain, USA; festival appearances incl: Aix-en-Provence, Spoleto, Bergen, Versailles, Flanders, Netherlands, Prague, Edinburgh and BBC Proms; *Recordings* incl: Monteverdi Vespro della Beata Vergine 1610, Handel Acis and Galatea, Tippett The Knot Garden, three recital discs of French, Spanish and Mozart songs, Britten Quatre Chansons Françaises, Ravel Trois Poèmes de Mallarmé, Canteloube Chants d'Auvergne, Britten Les Illuminations, Villa Lobos Bachianas Brasileiras No 5, Samuel Barber Knoxville, Summer of 1915, Cabaret Classics with John Constable, South of the Border (...Down Mexico Way), Britten's Blues (incl songs by Cole Porter), cmmnd David Matthews work Cantiga - The Song of Inêz De Castro, Mahler Seven Early Songs, A Spanish Songbook (with John Constable); *Style*— Miss Jill Gomez; ✉ 16 Milton Park, London N6 5QA

GOMEZ, Dr Joan Rae; da of Maj Charles Harold McClelland, DSO (d 1951), and Florence Gertrude Victoria, *née* Baldwin; *b* 7 Oct 1921; *Educ* St Paul's Girls' Sch, King's Coll London (MB BS, DPM); *m* 1, 1943, Denis Charles Lendrum (ka 1944), s of Charles Lendrum; m 2 (m dis 1974), Dr George Gomez, s of Luis Gomez (d 1950); 4 da (Francesca b 1947, Lavinia b 1949, Vivienne b 1951, Anthea b 1953), 4 adopted s (Peter, Paul b 1952, George b 1955, Matthew b 1957), 2 adopted da (Coralie, Helena b 1964); *Career* jr pathologist W London Hosp 1946, sr house offr (psychiatry) St George's Hosp 1973–74, conslt psychiatrist Westminster Hosp 1982–87, hon consulting psychiatrist Chelsea and Westminster Hosp 1987–; currently also private conslt psychiatrist; memb Friends of The Wellcome Inst 1992–; memb: BMA 1970, Soc of Soc of Authors, London Writers' Circle; FRCPsych, FRSM 1980; *Books* Psychological & Psychiatric Problems in Men (1991), Homosexuality (1994), Living with Bulimia (1995), You and Your Grandchild (1996); *Recreations* walking, theatre, reading; *Style*— Dr Joan Gomez; ✉ Natterjack, Thursley Road, Churt, Farnham, Surrey GU10 2LG (☎ 01428 606354)

GOMMON, Peter Nicholas; s of David Edward Gommon (d 1987), and Jean, *née* Vipond; *b* 19 Dec 1945; *Educ* Northampton GS, Univ of Liverpool (BArch), City of Birmingham Poly (DipLA), Univ of Central England (MA); *m* 21 July 1973, Moira Joan, da of Leonard Thomas Maguire (d 1990), of Millhouses, Sheffield; 3 s (David b 28 Dec 1974, Joseph b 7 Aug 1976, d 2 Sept 1986, Edward b 19 Oct 1978); *Career* architect and landscape architect; Nelson & Parker 1968–69 and 1971–72, Johnson & Wright 1972–75, Merseyside Improved Houses 1975–79, ptnr Innes Wilkin Partnership 1979, pt/t studio instructor Univ of Liverpool 1980–85; ptnr: Innes Wilkin Ainsley Gommon 1981, Ainsley Gommon Wood 1989–; memb: St Saviour PCC Oxton, Wirral Scope epilepsy support gp; RIBA 1975, ALI 1982, FRSA 1992; *Recreations* art, theatre, music, agriculture, motor cycling, bass player with 'Low Flier'; *Clubs* RA Yacht; *Style*— Peter Gommon, Esq; ✉ 46 Shrewsbury Rd, Oxton, Birkenhead L43 2HZ (☎ 0151 653 7204); Ty Joseff, 6 Pen y Fron, Penmon, Ynys Môn, Gwynedd; Ainsley Gommon Wood - Architects and Landscape Architects, 1 Price St, Birkenhead Merseyside L41 6JN (☎ 0151 647 5511, fax 0151 666 2195); The Old Police Station, 15 Glynne Way, Hawarden, Clwyd CH5 3NS; Rex House, 354 Ballards Lane, North Finchley, London N12 0EG

GOMPERTZ, Jeremy; QC (1988); *b* 16 Oct 1937; *Educ* Univ of Cambridge (BA); *Career* called to the Bar Grays Inn 1962, head of chambers 5 Essex Ct, recorder of the Crown Ct 1987; chm Mental Health Review Tbnl Panel 1994–; *Recreations* horse racing and breeding, skiing, travel; *Style*— Jeremy Gompertz, Esq, QC; ✉ 5 Essex Court, Temple, London EC4Y 9AH (☎ 0171 410 2000, fax 0171 410 2010)

GONDRY, Michel; *b* 8 May 1963; *Career* music video dir London and Paris 1990– (clips for Bjork, Terence Trent D'Arby, Black Crows, Lenny Kravitz and Rolling Stones), commercials dir 1995– (spots for Levi's Drugstore, Adidas, Heineken, Smirnoff, Volvo and Polaroid); awards: Gold Lion Cannes 1995, 3 Silver Awards and winner Br Advertisement of the Yr D&AD 1995, Silver Award D&AD 1996, Grand Prix Clio Awards 1996, European MTV Best Director of 1996; memb D&AD; *Style*— Michel Gondry; ✉ Partizan Ltd, 7 Westbourne Grove Mews, London W11 2UR (☎ 0171 792 8483, fax 0171 792 8870)

GONET, Stella; *Educ* Royal Scottish Acad of Music; *Career* actress; *Theatre* various parts incl: Tonight We Celebrate (Dundee Rep), Bernadette in Slab Boy Trilogy (Traverse Theatre Edinburgh, transferred to the Royal Court) 1982, Platinum Sue in Trafford Tanzi (Mermaid) 1983, Lucy in The Holiday (Liverpool Playhouse) 1983, Points of Departure (trilogy, Traverse Theatre and tour Amsterdam) 1984, Phil in True Dare Kiss and Command or Promise (the National) 1985; RSC (Stratford and Barbican seasons) 1986–88 and 1994–: Irina in The Archbishop's Ceiling, Birdie in Heresies, Liz in Fashion, Bellamira in The Jew of Malta, Castitsa in Revenger's Tragedy, Irina in

Three Sisters, Angelique/Louise in Divine Gossip, Ophelia in Hamlet, Alice in The Voysey Inheritance, Frances Parnell in Racing Demon; most recently Titania and Hippolyta in A Midsummer Night's Dream 1994–95, Isabella in Measure for Measure 1995; *Television* Ellie in To Have and To Hold (5 episodes, LWT) 1985, Mairi in The Shutter Falls (BBC Scotland) 1986, Dr Claire Wainwright in Casualty (BBC) 1986, Down Where The Buffalo Goes (BBC Scotland) 1987, The Bill (Thames) 1988, Heading Home (BBC) 1990, Marigold in The Common Pursuit (BBC) 1990, Alex in The Advocates (3 part drama, STV) 1990, Beatrice in The House of Eliott (12 episodes, BBC) 1991, Trip Trap (BBC) 1995; *Radio* Kaleidoscope (BBC) 1989, Blood and Ice (BBC) 1990; *Film* Debbie in For Queen and Country 1987, Zena Ordzhonikidze in Stalin 1991; *Style—* Ms Stella Gonet; ✉ c/o Markham & Froggatt Ltd, Julian House, 4 Windmill Street, London W1P 1HF (☎ 0171 636 4412, fax 0171 637 5233)

GONSALKORALE, Dr Mahendra; s of Edwin Gonsalkorale, of Sri Lanka, and Anula, *née* Jayanetti; *b* 27 May 1944; *Educ* Royal Coll Colombo Sri Lanka, Univ of Ceylon (MB BS, MD), Univ of Manchester (MSc); *m* 10 Dec 1977, Wendy Mary, da of Geoffrey Lock, of Thingwall, Wirral; 2 s (Gehan Richard b 1982, Roshan Edward b 1983); *Career* registrar in neurology Addenbrooke's Hosp Cambridge, conslt neurologist Gen Hosp Kandy Sri Lanka, sr registrar in geriatric med Withington Hosp Manchester, conslt physician Salford Royal Hosps NHS Tst 1980–; memb: mgmnt bd Salford Royal Hosps NHS Tst (hon assoc lectr and med dir), Manchester Med Soc 1979, Br Geriatric Soc 1980, Int Continence Soc 1989; fndr memb Br Assoc of Continence Care; FRCP (MRCP 1975); *Recreations* squash, badminton, walking, computing; *Clubs* Galleon Leisure (Cheadle); *Style—* Dr Mahendra Gonsalkorale; ✉ Dept of Healthcare for the Elderly, Ladywell Hospital, Eccles New Rd, Salford M5 2AA (☎ 0161 789 7373 ext 4044, fax 0161 787 4031)

GOOCH, Brig Arthur Brian Sherlock Heywood; s of Col Brian Sherlock Gooch, DSO, TD, JP, DL (d 1968), of Tannington Hall, Woodbridge, Suffolk, and Monica Mary, *née* Heywood (d 1975); *b* 1 June 1937; *Educ* Eton; *m* 27 July 1963, Sarah Diana Rowena Gooch, JP, da of Lt-Col John Francis George Perceval (d 1980), of Templehouse, Co Sligo; 2 da (Rowena Elizabeth b 1965, Katherine Sarah (Mrs Edward J Hawkings) b 1967); *Career* cmmnd Life Gds 1956, Oman and Aden 1958–59, Adj 1960–63, instr RMA Sandhurst 1964–65, Malaysia and Hong Kong 1966–68, GS03 (Ops) HQ 4 Gds Armd Bde 1969–70, NI 1972, asst mil attaché Tehran 1973–75, CO Life Gds 1978–81, dir staff Army Staff Coll 1981–82, cmdt Jr Div Staff Coll 1982–86, cdr Royal Armd Corps Centre 1987–89, pres Regular Cmmns Bd 1989–92; ADC 1989–92; Hon Col Kent and Sharpshooters Yeomanry 1992–; regnl organiser Southern Regn Army Benevolent Fund 1992–, county organiser Wiltshire National Gardens Scheme 1993–; *Recreations* field sports, gardening, food and wine; *Style—* Brig Arthur Gooch

GOOCH, Charles Albert; s of Ernest Edward Gooch; *b* 15 Sept 1938; *Educ* Coleman St Ward Sch London; *m* 1974, June Margaret, *née* Reardon; 2 da (Charlotte b 1976, Jessica b 1978); *Career* former chm Shaw & Marvin plc, chm and md Buckland Securities Ltd Group of Cos; Liveryman Worshipful Co of Stationers & Newspaper Makers; *Style—* Charles Gooch, Esq; ✉ Buckland Securities Ltd, 28 Redchurch St, London E2 7DP (☎ 0171 739 3604, fax 0171 739 1962)

GOOCH, Graham Alan; OBE (1991); s of Alfred Gooch, and Rose Gooch; *b* 23 July 1953; *Educ* Cannhall Sch Leytonstone, Norlington Jr HS Leytonstone, Redbridge Tech Coll; *m* 23 Oct 1976, Brenda; 3 da (Hannah, Megan, Sally (twin)); *Career* professional cricketer; Essex CCC: debut 1973, awarded county cap 1975, capt 1986–87 and 1989–94, benefit 1985, county champions 1979, 1983, 1984, 1986, 1991 and 1992; Western Province SA winters 1982–84; England: debut 1975, over 110 test matches and one day ints, capt 1988–93, highest score 333 v India Lord's 1990 (third highest test score by Englishman, also scored 123 in second innings to create record test aggregate of 456, only player to score triple century and century in same first class match), ret from Test cricket 1995; England selector 1996–; tours: Aust 1978/79, Aust and India 1979/80, W Indies 1980/81, India and Sri Lanka 1981/82, Pakistan (incl World Cup) 1987/88, India and W Indies 1989/90, Aust 1990/91, NZ and Aust 1991/92 (incl World Cup), India and Sri Lanka 1992/93, Aust 1994/95; capt unofficial England team to SA 1981–82; *Books* Out of the Wilderness (autobiography, 1988), Test of Fire (1990); *Recreations* relaxing at home; *Style—* Graham Gooch, Esq, OBE; ✉ c/o TCCB, Lords Cricket Ground, London NW8 8QN

GOOCH, Sir (Richard) John Sherlock; 12 Bt (GB 1746), of Benacre Hall, Suffolk; JP (Suffolk 1970); s of Col Sir Robert Eric Sherlock Gooch, 11 Bt, KCVO, DSO, JP, DL (d 1978), and Katharine Clervaux (d 1974), da of Maj-Gen Sir Edward Walter Clervaux Chaytor, KCMG, KCVO, CB; *b* 22 March 1930; *Educ* Eton; *Heir* bro, Maj Timothy Robert Sherlock Gooch, MBE, *qv*; *Career* Capt Life Gds; *Style—* Sir John Gooch, Bt, JP; ✉ Benacre Hall, Beccles, Suffolk (☎ 01502 740333)

GOOCH, Nicholas John (Nicky); s of Ian Gooch, of Barnes, and Dawn Virginia, *née* Streeter; *b* 30 Jan 1973; *Educ* Shene Comp Sch; *Career* short track speed skater; achievements: European champion (1000m) 1991, Silver medal World Relay Championships 1992 (Bronze 1991), first Br Championships 1993, 1994 and 1996 (third 1990, 1991 and 1992, second 1995), first Euro Team Championships 1992 and 1993 (second 1995), European champion 1994 and 1996, Bronze medal (500m) Olympic Games 1994, Silver medal Euro Championships 1994 and 1995; Br record holder: 500m, 1000m, 1500m, 3000m; memb Nat Ice Skating Assoc; *Recreations* cycling, windsurfing, skiing; *Style—* Nicky Gooch, Esq; ✉ 107 Brookwood Avenue, Barnes, London SW13 0LU (☎ 0181 878 2606); Aldwych Speed Club, Spectrum Centre, Guildford, Surrey (☎ 01483 443340/1)

GOOCH, Maj Timothy Robert Sherlock; MBE (1970); s of Col Sir Robert Eric Sherlock Gooch, KCVO, DSO, JP, DL, 11 Bt (d 1978), of Benacre Hall, Suffolk, and Katharine Clervaux (d 1974), da of Maj-Gen Sir Edward Walter Clervaux Chaytor, KCMG, KCVO, CB; hp of bro, Sir (Richard) John Sherlock Gooch, 12 Bt, *qv*; *b* 7 Dec 1934; *Educ* Eton, RMA Sandhurst; *m* 17 Dec 1963, Susan Barbara Christie, da of Maj-Gen Kenneth Christie Cooper, CB, DSO, OBE (d 1981), of West End House, Donhead St Andrew, Wilts; 2 da (Lucinda b 1970, Victoria b 1974); *Career* Maj Life Gds; memb HM Body Gd of Hon Corps of Gentlemen at Arms 1986–; co dir; *Clubs* White's, Cavalry & Guards; *Style—* Maj Timothy Gooch, MBE; ✉ The Cedars, Covehithe, Wrentham, Beccles, Suffolk (☎ 01502 675266)

GOOCH, Sir Trevor Sherlock; 5 Bt (UK 1866), of Clewer Park, Berks; VRD; s of Charles Trevor Gooch (d 1963), and Hester Stratford, *née* Sherlock (d 1957); suc kinsman, Sir Robert Douglas Gooch, 4 Bt (d 1989); *b* 15 June 1915; *Educ* Charterhouse; *m* 1, 4 Dec 1956, Denys Anne (d 1976), o da of Harold Victor Venables (d 1993), of Edificio la Vileta Camino Vechinal la Vileta 215, Palma de Mallorca; 1 s (Miles Peter b 1963), 4 da (Beverly Jacqueline (Mrs Amy) b 1957, Vanda Madelaine b 1958, Yvonne Daryl Roote b 1961, Rowan Claire b 1971); m 2, 1978, Jean, da of late John Joseph Wright; *Heir* s, Miles Peter Gooch b 3 Feb 1963; *Career* Flt-Lt RAFVR; *Style—* Sir Trevor Gooch, Bt, VRD; ✉ Jardin de la Rocque, Mont de la Rocque, St Aubin, Jersey, CI

GOOD, Anthony Bruton Meyrick; *b* 18 April 1933; *Educ* Felsted; *m*; 2 da; *Career* mgmnt trainee Distillers Group 1950–52, editorial asst Temple Press Ltd 1952–55, PR offr Silver City Airways (PR/marketing Br Aviation Servs Ltd) 1955–60; fndr and chm: Good Relations Group plc 1961–89, Good Consultancy Ltd 1989–; chm: Cox & Kings Ltd 1975– (dir 1971–), Good Relations India Ltd 1988–, Cox & Kings (India) Ltd 1988– (dir 1980–), Foley Lodge Hotels plc 1989, Arcadian International plc 1995–; dir: IM Group Ltd 1977–, St James Court Hotel Ltd, Taj International Hotels Ltd, Millbank Public Relations Ltd 1994–, Matrix Public Affairs Consultants Ltd 1994–, T C Group plc 1996–; Liveryman: Worshipful Co of Coachmakers & Coach Harness Makers, Worshipful Co of Marketors; *Recreations* travel, reading, theatre; *Clubs* RAC; *Style—* Anthony Good, Esq; ✉ Clench House, Wootton Rivers, Marlborough, Wilts SN8 4NT; Good Consultancy Ltd, Clench Lodge, Wootton Rivers, Marlborough, Wilts SN8 4NT (☎ 01672 810126, fax 01672 810869)

GOOD, Ven Kenneth Roy; s of Isaac Edward Good (d 1972), of Fulmer, and Florence Helen Good (d 1974); *b* 28 Sept 1941; *Educ* Stamford Sch, KCL (BD, AKC), St Boniface Coll Warminster; *m* 18 May 1970, Joan Thérèse, da of late Cyril Bennett; 1 da (Suzanne Thérèse b 1 April 1971), 1 s (Andrew Roy b 12 Oct 1975); *Career* apprentice engr Newall Engineering 1957–60, asst curate St Peters Stockton on Tees 1967–70; port chaplain Missions to Seamen: Antwerp 1970–74, Kobe 1974–79; asst gen sec The Missions to Seamen 1979–85; vicar of Nunthorpe 1985–93, rural dean of Stokesley 1990–93, archdeacon of Richmond 1993–; hon canon: of Kobe 1985, of Ripon 1993; *Recreations* caravanning; *Style—* The Ven the Archdeacon of Richmond; ✉ 62 Palace Road, Ripon, N Yorks HG4 1HA (☎ 01765 604342, fax 01765 604342)

GOODACRE, (John) Michael Kendall; s of Kenneth Goodacre, TD, DL, of London, and Dorothy, *née* Kendall (d 1992); *b* 19 Aug 1941; *Educ* Shrewsbury, Keble Coll Oxford (MA); *m* 29 July 1967, Yvonne Scott, da of John Milsom (d 1985); 2 s (William Henry Kendall b 5 Mar 1971, Edward James Scott b 2 Feb 1972); *Career* admitted slr 1969; asst slr Messrs Coffin Mew & Clover 1969–71 (ptnr 1971); memb: Bd of Visitors HM Prison Kingston (chm 1987 and 1988), Promotion of Int Gastronomy Soc Portsmouth, Ctee Hants Inc Law Soc; memb Law Soc; *Recreations* eating, drinking, reading, skiing; *Style—* Michael Goodacre, Esq; ✉ Crofton Old Farm, Titchfield, Hants PO14 3ER (☎ 01329 843298); 43 High Street, Fareham, Hants PO16 7BQ (☎ 01329 825617, fax 01329 825619)

GOODALL, His Honour Anthony Charles; MC (1942), DL (Devon 1987); s of Charles Henry Goodall (d 1968), of Sutton Veny, Wilts, and Mary Helen, *née* Walker (d 1956); *b* 23 July 1916; *Educ* Eton, King's Coll Cambridge (BA, MA); *m* 8 April 1947, Anne Valerie, da of John Reginald Chichester (d 1968), of Tiverton, Devon; 1 s (Charles Roderick b 1948), 2 da (Clarissa Anne (Lady Clifford of Chudleigh) b 1950, Diana Mary Audrey b 1959); *Career* served WWII 1939–45, 1 Royal Dragoons in ME, Italy, France, Belgium, Holland (POW twice 1944), Capt; called to the Bar Inner Temple 1939, practised at the Bar 1946–67, judge County Ct 1968–72, circuit judge 1972–86; pres Plymouth Magistrates Assoc 1976–84, memb County Ct Rule Ctee 1978–83, jt vice pres Cncl of HM Circuit Judges 1985 (joint pres 1986), ret 1986; *Style—* His Honour Anthony Goodall, MC, DL; ✉ Hunt's Meadow, Moretonhampstead, Devon TQ13 8PA (☎ 01647 440239)

GOODALL, Caroline Mary Helen; da of Capt Peter Goodall, CBE, TD (d 1995), of Wetherby, W Yorks, and Sonja Jeanne, *née* Burt; sis of Charles Peter Goodall, *qv*; *b* 22 May 1955; *Educ* Queen Ethelburga's Sch, Newnham Coll Cambridge (MA); *m* 1 Oct 1983, (Vesey) John Hill, s of Maj Vesey Michael Hill (d 1972); *Career* asst slr Slaughter and May 1980–84 (articled clerk 1978–80), ptnr Herbert Smith 1987– (asst slr 1984–87); memb Worshipful Co of Slrs; memb Law Soc; *Recreations* tennis, theatre, sailing, fell walking; *Clubs* Roehampton, Brancaster Staithe Sailing Club; *Style—* Miss Caroline Goodall; ✉ Herbert Smith, Exchange House, Primrose St, London EC2A 2HS (☎ 0171 374 8000, fax 0171 496 0043, telex 886633)

GOODALL, Charles Peter; s of late Capt Peter Goodall, CBE, TD, of Wetherby, W Yorks, and Sonja Jeanne, *née* Burt; bro of Caroline Mary Helen Goodall, *qv*; *b* 14 July 1950; *Educ* Sherborne, St Catharine's Coll Cambridge (MA, LLM); *Career* asst slr Slaughter and May 1976–82 (articled clerk 1974–76), ptnr Simmons & Simmons 1984– (asst slr 1982–84); memb Law Soc; *Recreations* squash, golf, sailing; *Clubs* RAC, Hawk's; *Style—* Charles Goodall, Esq; ✉ Simmons & Simmons, 21 Wilson Street, London EC2M 2TX (☎ 0171 628 2020, fax 0171 628 2070)

GOODALL, Sir (Arthur) David Saunders; GCMG (1991, KCMG 1987, CMG 1979); o s of Arthur William Goodall (d 1968), of Whaley Bridge, Derbys, and Maisie Josephine, *née* Byers; *b* 9 Oct 1931; *Educ* Ampleforth, Trinity Coll Oxford (MA, hon fell 1992); *m* 1962, Morwenna, yst da of Percival George Beck Peecock (d 1972), of Goring, Sussex; 2 s, 1 da; *Career* 2 Lt 1 Bn KOYLI 1955–56 (Kenya, Aden, Cyprus); HM Dip Serv: head of W Euro Dept FCO 1975–79, min Bonn 1979–82, seconded to Cabinet Office, dep sec 1982–84, deputy under sec of state FCO 1984–87, Br High Cmmr to India 1987–91, ret; chm Leonard Cheshire Fndn 1995– (chm Int Ctee 1991–95); dir Govett India Fund 1993–, Br chm Anglo-Irish Encounter 1992–; pres Irish Genealogical Research Soc 1992– (fell 1986), tstee Rajiv Gandhi (UK) Fndn 1993–, vice chm Cncl Univ of Durham 1996– (memb 1992–), visiting prof Inst of Irish Studies Univ of Liverpool 1996–; Hon LLD Univ of Hull 1994; *Recreations* watercolour painting, social and family history; *Clubs* Garrick, United Oxford and Cambridge Univ; *Style—* Sir David Goodall, GCMG; ✉ Leonard Cheshire Foundation, 26–29 Maunsel Street, London SW1P 2QN (☎ 0171 828 1822, fax 0171 976 5704)

GOODALL, Elizabeth Ann; da of Maurice Edward Ogborn, and Olive Frances, *née* Deslandes; *b* 22 Dec 1949; *Educ* Ware GS, Univ of Leicester (BA), Portsmouth Poly (DMS); *m* 1983, Michael Ryan Goodall; 1 da (Laura b 1984); *Career* gallery asst Usher Gallery Lincoln 1972–74, sr keeper of art Southampton Art Gallery 1976–81 (keeper 1974–76); Southampton Museum and Art Gallery: asst curator 1981–88, princ arts offr 1988–90, dep head of cultural servs 1990–94, head of heritage, arts and entertainments 1994–96, environment policy mangr 1996–; fndr Southampton's Contemporary Collection 1975–; fifteen yrs of curatorship celebrated by donation of landscape/garden proposals to Southampton Art Gall by Ian Hamilton Finlay; estab Southampton NorthGuild (Arts Complex); MIMgt 1990, AMA 1976; *Books* Maxwell Armfield Catalogue (1978), Southampton City Art Gallery Collection (1980), One City a Patron Catalogue (1985); *Recreations* landscape photography; *Style—* Mrs Elizabeth Goodall; ✉ NorthGuild (Arts Complex), Commercial Road, Southampton SO9 4XF (☎ 01703 223855)

GOODALL, Francis Richard Cruice; s of William Cruice Goodall (d 1958), of Liverpool, and Joan Mary, *née* Berrill (d 1955); *b* 4 Oct 1929; *Educ* Ampleforth, Queens' Coll Cambridge (MA), Architectural Assoc (AADipl); *m* 21 Jan 1978, Vivienne, da of Thomas Vyvyan More (d 1956), of E London, South Africa; *Career* architect/arbitrator; Nat Serv 1948–49, cmmnd RE serv N Africa and Malta; ptnr Frederick MacManus & Partners 1963–94 (assoc 1958–63); memb Cncl: Soc of Construction Law 1988–94, Chartered Inst of Arbitrators 1990–93; Freeman City of London 1982, Liveryman Worshipful Co of Arbitrators 1982 (Master 1994); memb: Soc of Construction Law 1988 (treas 1991–94), Soc of Construction Arbitrators 1988 (sec 1992–95); FRIBA, FCIArb, FAE (MAE 1989); *Clubs* Garrick, Travellers'; *Style—* Francis Goodall, Esq; ✉ 37 Molyneux Street, Marylebone, London W1H 5HW (☎ 0171 724 6505, fax 0171 724 0608)

GOODALL, Dr Janet; da of Bernard Goodall (d 1978) of Notts, and Elizabeth Ellen, *née* Schofield (d 1948); *b* 20 July 1930; *Educ* Retford Co HS for Girls, Univ of Sheffield (MB ChB); *Career* med registrar Hosp for Sick Children Gt Ormond St 1963–66, secondment to Children's Hosp of Philadelphia 1964–65, sr med registrar Sheffield Children's Hosp 1966–69, conslt paediatrician: Mulago Hosp Kampala Uganda 1969–72, N Staffs Hosp Centre 1973–90; author of various pubns on paediatrics especially concerning the emotional needs of children and matters of med ethics; pres Christian Med Fellowship 1995–97 (chm 1985–87), hon memb Br Paediatric Assoc; FRCPE; *Books* Suffering in Childhood (1980), Help for the Family Who Have Lost a Cystic Fibrosis

Child (1988), Children and Grieving (1995); *Recreations* travel, photography, friendship; *Style*— Dr Janet Goodall; ✉ Melton, Burrington Drive, Trentham, Stoke-on-Trent, Staffs ST4 8SP

GOODAY, Prof Graham William; s of William Arnold Gooday (d 1947), of Colchester, and Edith May, *née* Beeton (d 1987); *b* 19 Feb 1942; *Educ* Hove GS for Boys, Univ of Bristol (BSc, PhD); *m* Margaret Ann, da of Stanley William Mealing; 1 s (Andrew James b 28 Aug 1969), 2 da (Rebecca Mary b 20 Feb 1971, Victoria Susan b 24 March 1973); *Career* res fell: Univ of Leeds 1967–69, Univ of Glasgow 1969–70, Univ of Oxford 1970–72; prof of microbiology Univ of Aberdeen 1984– (lectr 1972, sr lectr 1978, reader 1982); hon professorial fell Rowett Res Inst 1992, Williams Evans visiting fell Univ of Otago 1992; memb Soc for General Microbiology 1972, pres Br Mycological Soc 1993 (memb 1970, Centenary fell 1996); FRSE 1989, FIBiol 1995 (MIBiol 1980); *Books* Microbial Polysaccharides and Polysaccharases (1979), The Eukaryotic Microbial Cell (1980), Chitin in Nature and Technology (1986); *Style*— Prof Graham Gooday, FRSE; ✉ 126 Hamilton Place, Aberdeen AB2 4BB (☎ 01224 640293); Department of Molecular and Cell Biology, University of Aberdeen, Institute of Medical Sciences, Aberdeen AB25 2ZD (☎ 01224 273147, fax 01224 273144)

GOODBAND, Philip Haydon; s of Philip Aubrey Goodband, of Camberley, Surrey, and Edith Emma Haydon, *née* Cooper; *b* 26 May 1944; *Educ* Strodes Sch, Dijon France, Academie Du Champagne; *m* 18 Dec 1971, Lynne Wendy, da of Brig Lindsey Jerment Aspland, OBE, of Dorking, Surrey; 2 s (Charles Lindsey Haydon b 19 June 1976 d 24 Nov 1976, Henry Lindsey Charles b 24 Oct 1978), 1 da (Emily Victoria b 19 Sept 1973); *Career* Vintners scholarship; dir: Gilbey SA France 1972–73, Wine Devpt Bd 1980–92, purchasing and quality Stowells of Chelsea 1981–86 (buyer 1973–80); Grants of St James's: wine buying and quality logistics 1986–88, md Wine Div on Trade 1988–92, business devpt dir 1992–94; proprietor Goodband Wine Services and Consultancy 1994–; chm Inst of Masters of Wine 1984–85, tstee Wine and Spirit Trade Benevolent Soc 1986–89, lectr and broadcaster in London, Paris, Milan and San Francisco; chm Redbourn Tennis Club 1975–82, judge Newdigate Hort Soc; Freeman: City of London 1972, Worshipful Co of Haberdashers 1972 (Clothed 1975); FBBI 1968; Compagnon du Beaujolais 1978, membre de L'Ordre St Etienne France 1981, Cavaleiro da Confraria do Vinho do Porto Portugal 1987, Chevalier des Coteaux de Champagne 1989; Master of Wine; *Recreations* competition carriage driving, travel, tennis; *Clubs* Naval and Military; *Style*— Philip Goodband, Esq; ✉ Goodband Wine Services and Consultancy, Farnaby, Chichester Road, Dorking, Surrey RH4 1LR (☎ and fax 01306 740655)

GOODBODY, Michael Ivan Andrew; s of Llewellyn Marcus Goodbody (d 1989, see Burkes Irish Family Records), of Ardclough Lodge, Straffan, Co Kildare, Ireland, and Eileen Elizabeth, *née* Bourke; *b* 23 Jan 1942; *Educ* Kingstown Sch Dublin; *m* 9 March 1968, Susannah Elizabeth, da of Donald Guy Pearce (Capt Ayrshire Yeomanry RA, ka 1944); 1 s (Guy b 1972), 2 da (Sarah b 1970, Perry b 1976); *Career* Lt TA, 289 Parachute Battery RHA; stockbroker Smith Rice & Hill 1962–74, private client stockbroker Capel-Cure Myers 1974–88, dir Capel-Cure Myers Capital Management Ltd 1988–; MSI; *Books* The Goodbody Family of Ireland (1979); *Recreations* family history, genealogy; *Style*— Michael Goodbody, Esq; ✉ The Old Rectory, Wickham St Paul's, Halstead, Essex CO9 2PJ; Capel-Cure Myers Capital Management Ltd, The Registry, Royal Mint Court, London EC3N 4EY

GOODBURN, Andrew Robert; s of Robert Goodburn, of Camrose, Haverfordwest, and Peggy, *née* Barrett; *b* 5 Jan 1947; *Educ* Harrow HS, Monkton House Sch; *m* 28 June 1969, Elizabeth Ann, da of Joseph Henry Dunn; 3 s (Giles Andrew b 11 Nov 1972, Henry Robert b 18 April 1974, Benjamin Joseph b 24 June 1978), 1 da (Anne-Marie b 19 May 1980); *Career* Peat Marwick Mitchell & Co 1964–70 (articled clerk, audit sr); Bowthorpe Holdings plc 1970–81: gen mangr Hellermann Cassettes (fin controller), fin dir Hellermann Deutsch, commercial dir Bowthorpe EMP, mktg dir Hellermann Electric; ptnr Grant Thornton 1987–91 (joined as sr mgmnt consIt 1982), head of fin consultancy Price Waterhouse (Redhill Office) 1991–93, commercial dir Ricardo Hitec 1993–94, fin dir Ricardo Aerospace 1994, fin dir Ricardo Consulting 1995–; FCA (ACA 1969); *Recreations* tennis, travel, gardening; *Clubs* Richmond RFC, Haywards Heath RFC; *Style*— Andrew Goodburn, Esq; ✉ Deacons Hay, Beaconsfield Rd, Chelwood Gate, Sussex RH17 7LG (☎ 01825 740225); Ricardo Consulting Engineers Ltd, Bridge Works, Shoreham-by-Sea, West Sussex BN43 5FG (☎ 01273 455611, fax 01273 464124)

GOODCHILD, David Lionel Napier; CMG (1986); s of Hugh Napier Goodchild (d 1981), of Norwich, and Beryl Cynthia Maud, *née* Coller (d 1969); *b* 20 July 1935; *Educ* Eton, King's Coll Cambridge (BA, MA); *Career* HM Dip Serv 1958–73: third sec Tehran 1959–62, FO 1962–70 (second then first sec UK Delgn NATO 1964–66, dep political advsr Br Mil Govt Berlin 1970–72; dir Euro Cmmn Brussels 1979–86 (head of div 1973–79); *Style*— David Goodchild, Esq, CMG; ✉ Orchard House, Thorpe Morieux, Bury St Edmunds, Suffolk IP30 0NW (☎ 01284 828181)

GOODCHILD, Peter Robert Edward; s of Douglas Richard Geoffrey Goodchild, MBE (d 1989), of Angmering Village, W Sussex, and Lottie May, *née* Ager; *b* 18 Aug 1939; *Educ* Aldenham, St John's Coll Oxford (MA); *m* 1968, Penelope-Jane, da of Dr William Pointon-Dick (d 1956); 2 da (Abigail b 1971, Hannah b 1974); *Career* prodr Horizon BBC TV 1965–69 (winner Soc of Film and TV Arts Mullard Award for Science Broadcasting 1967, 1968 and 1969), ed Horizon BBC TV 1969–76 (winner BAFTA Award for Best Factual Series 1972 and 1974, winner Italia Prize for Factual Programmes 1973 and 1975), exec prodr drama prodns 1977–80 (including Marie Curie 1977 and Oppenheimer 1980 which both won BAFTA Awards for Best Series), prodr Bread or Blood 1980, head of Science and Features BBC TV 1980–84 (initiating programme QED), head of Plays BBC TV 1984–89 (initiating Screen Two, Sunday Premier (now Screen One) and Screenplay), exec prodr and prodr Film Dept BBC 1989–94; prodr: The March 1990 (winner One World TV Premier Network award), Adam Bede 1991, Trust Me 1992, Return to Blood River 1994, Black Easter 1994 (winner Gold Award Chicago Film Festival 1996); dir Stone City Films 1995–; CChem, FRSC; *Books* Shatterer of Worlds (the life of J Robert Oppenheimer, 1980); *Radio Plays incl* The Chicago Conspiracy Trial (1993, winner NY Radio Festival Gold Award 1995), Nuremburg (1996); *Recreations* tennis, music; *Clubs* Groucho's; *Style*— Peter Goodchild, Esq; ✉ Brockdale House, Cricketer's Lane, Warfield, Berks (☎ 01344 882492); Stone City Films, 23 Denmark Street, London WC2H 8NA

GOODCHILD, Tim; *Educ* Guildford Coll of Art, Wimbledon Coll of Art (Arts Cncl scholar); *Career* designer; *Theatre* over 50 West End prodns incl: Hadrian VII 1969, Richard II 1969, Cowardy Custard 1972, Gone with the Wind 1972, Show Boat, Hans Andersen, My Fair Lady 1979, Oklahoma (also Aust) 1980, Little Shop of Horrors 1983, Blondel 1983, Cafe Puccine 1986, Five Guys Named Moe (also Broadway and Aust) 1990, Pump Boys and Dinettes 1984, Wonderful Town, Bus Stop 1990, Henry IV 1990, Our Sing Song 1992, Chapter Two 1996; other prodns incl: Antony and Cleopatra (Egyptian Nat Theatre) 1978, The Taming of the Shrew (RSC) 1993/94, The Relapse (RSC) 1995, Zenobia (RSC) 1995, Cyrano de Bergerac (Stratford Ontario Festival Theatre), The Corsican Brothers (Abbey Theatre Co Dublin), Peter Pan (McLab Theatre Co Canada), R Love J, The Royal Baccarat Scandal (Chichester), Three Hours After Marriage 1996, The Merry Wives of Windsor (both RSC) 1996; *Opera* Sadler Wells Opera Co: The Mikado 1983, HMS Pinafore (also City Center NY) 1983, Gordolius 1984; other prodns incl: La Traviata (WNO), Mikado (Australian Opera Co), The Tales of Hoffman (Victoria State Opera Co), The Tales of Hoffman (Huston Grand Opera); *Ballet* numerous prodns incl: Swanlake (Moscow Classical Ballet) 1988; *Television* The Look of Love (BBC2), A Simple Man (BBC2), The Fool on The Hill (Aust); *Awards* Green Room Award Best Operatic Design (for The Tales of Hoffman, Aust); nominations incl: The Theatre LA Ovations Award for Best Set (for Five Guys Named Moe), Sammy Award Best TV Film (for The Fool on the Hill); *Style*— Tim Goodchild, Esq; ✉ c/o Simpson Fox Associates Ltd, 52 Shaftesbury Avenue, London W1V 7DE (☎ 0171 434 9167, fax 0171 494 2887)

GOODDEN, Benjamin Bernard Woulfe; o s of Cecil Phelips Goodden, JP, and Hylda Maud, da of Stephen Roland Woulfe, of Tiermaclane, Co Clare; *b* 16 July 1925; *Educ* Harrow, Trinity Coll Oxford (MA); *m* 1, 1952 (m dis 1966), Elizabeth Woodham-Smith; 1 s (James b 1958), 2 da (Caroline (Mrs Haworth) b 1953, Jane (Mrs Viney) b 1955); m 2, 1973, Rose Emma Margaret, 2 da of Lt Cdr Hon Douglas Vivian, DSC, RN, and formerly wife of J C Norman; 1 s (Timothy b 7 June 1980); *Career* served Royal Artillery 1943–47; called to the Bar 1951; ptnr James Capel & Co 1957–71, with M & G Group plc 1972– (dir M & G Securities Ltd 1974–94); memb Bach Choir (hon treas 1972–92); *Recreations* cricket (watching, discussing, reading about), music; *Clubs* MCC; *Style*— Benjamin Goodden, Esq; ✉ Ferryside, Riverside, Twickenham, Middlesex TW1 3DN (☎ 0181 892 1448)

GOODDEN, Robert Crane; yr s of John Henry Goodden (d 1974), of Compton House, and his 1 w, Valerie Mary, *née* Llewellyn-Evans (d 1959); bro of Rev John Maurice Phelips Goodden; *b* 2 April 1940; *Educ* Salisbury Cathedral Choir Sch, Dauntsey's Sch; *m* 1 June 1968, Rosemary Joan Frances, da of Lt-Col Arthur Edward Bagwell Purefoy (d 1986); 2 s (John b 5 April 1973, Michael b 23 June 1976), 1 da (Sally b 11 May 1971); *Career* trainee: L Hugh Newman, The Butterfly Farm Ltd Bexley Kent 1957, Harrods Knightsbridge 1959; fndr and md Worldwide Butterflies Ltd 1960; co-fndr, tstee and vice pres Br Butterfly Conservation Soc, owner Lullingstone Silk Farm, former advsr to Govt of Papua-New Guinea on butterfly farming, currently advsr to WWF Indonesia; fndr Conservation Worldwide (now Worldlife) 1993; memb: Mgmnt Ctee Almshouses of St John Sherborne, Sherborne Chamber Choir; FRES, FRHS; *Books* author of 10 books on lepidoptera and entomology incl: Butterflies (1971), The Wonderful World of Butterflies (1973), Field Guide to the Butterflies of Britain (1978), Beningfield's Butterflies (1978); *Recreations* gardening, music, photography, walking, natural history, botany, travel, computer programming, arts and crafts; *Style*— Robert Goodden, Esq; ✉ Compton House, nr Sherborne, Dorset DT9 4QN (☎ 01935 74608)

GOODE, Prof Anthony William; s of William Henry Goode, of Tynemouth, and Eileen Veronica, *née* Brannan; *b* 3 Aug 1944; *Educ* Corby Sch, Univ of Newcastle Med Sch (MB BS, MD); *m* 26 Sept 1987, Dr Patricia Josephine, da of late Michael Flynn, of Nutley Lane, Donnybrook, Dublin; *Career* surgical appts Newcastle upon Tyne teaching hosps and demonstrator anatomy Univ of Newcastle upon Tyne 1968–74, various appts Univ of London teaching hosps 1975–; currently: prof of endocrine and metabolic surgery Univ of London, hon conslt surgn Royal London Hosp and Bart's, hon prof Centre for Biological and Med Systems Imperial Coll London; res programmes related to: nutrition, metabolism, endocrinology in surgery, role of microgravity res in future med and surgical devpt; princ investigator NASA, hon sec and treas Br Assoc Endocrine Surgns (fndr memb 1980); Freeman City of London 1994; memb: RSM 1972, Int Soc Surgery 1985, New York Acad Scis 1987; FRCS 1972; *Books* contrib numerous surgical textbooks; ed-in-chief Medicine Sciences and the Law; *Recreations* music (especially opera), cricket, literature; *Clubs* Athenaeum, MCC, Cross Arrows CC; *Style*— Prof Anthony Goode; ✉ The Surgical Unit, The Royal London Hospital, Whitechapel, London E1 1BB (☎ 0171 377 7000); 2nd Floor, King George V Wing, St Bartholomew's Hospital, London EC1 (☎ 0171 601 7032)

GOODE, Graham Frederick; s of Frank Albert Goode (d 1975), and Ivy May, *née* Hodges (d 1989); *b* 16 March 1949; *Educ* Northampton Town & Country GS, Univ of Leicester (BA); *m* 24 July 1971, Gillian Margaret, *née* Waite; *Career* horse racing journalist and commentator; commentator Channel 4 Racing 1984–, journalist Daily Star until 1988, own syndicated racing column 1988–; public address racing commentator 1967–; proprietor Derwent News Agency, dir Nottingham Racecourse, chm Assoc of Racecourse Commentators; winner: Ciga Concours de la Press, Martell Grand National Press Tipping Competition 1992; *Recreations* golf, petanque, bridge; *Clubs* East India; *Style*— Graham Goode; ✉ 3 Digby Close, Tilton on the Hill, Leicester LE7 9LL (☎ 0116 259 7288, fax 0116 259 7488, mobile 0860 269436)

GOODE, Raymond Arthur; s of late Arthur Thomas Goode, of London, and Elsie Florence, *née* Hayes; *b* 24 April 1934; *Educ* Colindale Secdy Sch; *m* 1, 23 Aug 1956 (m dis 1976), Iris Margaret, da of Thomas Horn (d 1980); 2 da (Janette Ann b 15 July 1965, Karen Elizabeth b 4 Nov 1966); m 2, 28 Aug 1976, Yvonne, da of Philip Conway Cattrall; 2 da (Catherine b 27 Dec 1979, Helen b 23 April 1985); *Career* dir of photography; memb Br Soc of Cinematographers; Rank Orgn Ltd Pinewood Studios 1956–61, Granada TV Ltd 1961–89; series incl: Brideshead Revisited (BAFTA nominee) 1981, Jewel in The Crown (BAFTA nominee) 1984; *Recreations* golf; *Clubs* New North Manchester Golf; *Style*— Raymond Goode, Esq; ✉ 4 Johnson Grove, Archer Park, Middleton, Manchester M24 4BF (☎ and fax 0161 654 8262)

GOODE, Prof Royston Miles (Roy); CBE (1994, OBE 1972), QC (1990); s of Samuel Goode (d 1968), of Portsmouth, Hants, and Blooma, *née* Zeid (d 1984); *b* 6 April 1933; *Educ* Highgate, Univ of London (LLB, LLD); *m* 18 Oct 1964, Catherine Anne, da of Jean Marcel Rueff, and Marianne Rueff; 1 da (Naomi b 1965); *Career* Nat Serv RASC 1955–57; admitted slr 1955, ptnr Victor Mishcon & Co 1963–71 (conslt 1971–88); Queen Mary Coll: prof of law 1971–73, Crowther prof of credit and commercial law 1973–89, dean Faculty of Law and head dept 1976–86; fndr and dir Centre Commercial Law Studies 1979–89, Norton Rose prof of English law Univ of Oxford 1990–, fell St John's Coll Oxford 1990–, fell Queen Mary and Westfield Coll London 1991–, transferred to the Bar Inner Temple 1988 (hon bencher); chm Pension Law Review Ctee 1992–93; UK rep and memb governing Cncl UNIDROIT Rome 1989–; Freeman City of London; Hon DSc (Econ) London 1996; FBA 1988, FRSA 1990; *Books* Hire-Purchase Law & Practice (2 edn 1970), Commercial Law (1982, 2 edn 1995), Proprietary Rights & Insolvency in Sales Transactions (1985, 2 edn 1989), Legal Problems of Credit & Security (2 edn 1988), Principles of Corporate Insolvency Law; *Recreations* chess, walking, browsing in bookshops; *Clubs* Reform; *Style*— Prof Roy Goode, CBE, QC, FBA; ✉ 42 St John St, Oxford OX1 2LH (☎ 01865 515494); St John's College, Oxford OX1 3JP (☎ 01865 277399)

GOODENOUGH, Adrian John; *b* 16 May 1956; *Educ* John Ruskin GS Croydon, Oxford Poly (BA Business Studies); *Career* Tate & Lyle 1979–85, asst sec UniChem Ltd 1986–90, co sec UniChem plc 1990–; FICS; *Style*— A J Goodenough, Esq; ✉ UniChem plc, UniChem House, Chessington, Surrey KT9 1SN (☎ 0181 391 2323, fax 0181 391 7152)

GOODENOUGH, Alan; *b* 7 Dec 1943; *Career* unit gen mangr Excel Bowling 1964–66, gen mangr and regnl dir Bingo and Social Clubs Rank Organisation PLC 1966–71, main bd dir Pleasurama PLC 1972–88, md Casinos, Hotels and Holiday Businesses and main bd dir Mecca Leisure Group PLC 1988–90, fndr and chm Lyric Hotels 1990–, non-exec chm Time Line (bus and coach operator) 1990–, chief exec London Clubs International PLC 1993– (brought co to UK stock market 1994); MInstD 1990; *Style*— Alan Goodenough, Esq; ✉ London Clubs International plc, 30 Old Burlington Street, London W1X 2LN (☎ 0171 637 5464, fax 0171 631 3441, telex 27480LCLG)

GOODENOUGH, HE Anthony Michael; CMG (1990); s of Rear Adm Michael Grant Goodenough, DSO, CBE (d 1955), and Nancy Waterfield, *née* Slater; *b* 5 July 1941; *Educ* Wellington, New Coll Oxford (exhibitioner, BA, MA); *m* 22 July 1967, Veronica Mary, da of Lt-Col Peter Pender-Cudlip, LVO; 1 da (Eleanor Margaret b 1968), 2 s (Francis Nicholas b 1970, Robert Henry b 1979); *Career* VSO Sarawak 1963–64; HM Dip Serv: joined 1964, third sec FO 1964–67, second sec Br Embassy Athens 1967–71, private sec to Parly Under Sec FCO 1971–72, private sec to Min of State FCO 1972–74, first sec Br Embassy Paris 1974–77, first sec FCO 1977–80, cnsllr seconded to Cabinet Office 1980–82, head of Chancery Br Embassy Islamabad 1982–85, cnsllr FCO 1986–89, Br high commissioner Ghana and non-resident ambassador Togo 1989–92, asst under sec of state for Africa and the Cwlth FCO 1992–95, Br high cmmr Canada 1996–; *Style—* HE Mr Anthony Goodenough, CMG; ✉ c/o Foreign & Commonwealth Office (Ottawa), King Charles St, London SW1A 2AH

GOODENOUGH, Frederick Roger; DL (Oxfordshire 1989); 3 (but 2 surviving) s of Sir William Macnamara Goodenough, 1 Bt (d 1951), and Dorothea Louisa (d 1987), da of Ven the Hon Kenneth Gibbs, DD, 5 s of 1 Baron Aldenham; *b* 21 Dec 1927; *Educ* Eton, Magdalene Coll Cambridge (MA), Univ of Oxford (MA); *m* 15 May 1954, Marguerite June, o da of David Forbes Mackintosh, sometime headmaster of Loretto; 1 s (David b 1955), 2 da (Annabel b 1957, Victoria b 1961); *Career* RN 1946–48; joined Barclays Bank Ltd 1950; local dir: Birmingham 1958–60, Reading 1960–69, Oxford 1969–87; dir: Barclays Bank UK Ltd 1971–87, Barclays International Ltd 1977–87, Barclays plc 1985–89, Barclays Bank plc 1979–89; advsy dir Barclays Bank Thames Valley Region 1988–89, memb London Ctee Barclays Bank DCO 1966–71, Barclays Bank International Ltd 1971–80; sr ptnr Broadwell Manor Farm 1968–; curator Oxford Univ Chest 1974–93; pres Oxfordshire Rural Community Cncl 1993–; tstee: Nuffield Med Benefaction 1968– (chm 1987–), Nuffield Dominions Tst 1968– (chm 1987–), Oxford & Dist Hosps Improvement & Devpt Fund 1968– (chm 1982–88), Nuffield Orthopaedic Tst 1978– (chm 1981–), Oxford Preservation Tst 1980–89, Radcliffe Med Fndn 1987–; govr: Shiplake Coll 1963–74 (chm 1966–70), Wellington Coll 1968–74, London House for Overseas Graduates 1985–; patron Anglo-Ghanaian Society 1991–; fell Linnean Soc (memb Cncl 1968–75, treas 1970–75), hon fell Wolfson Coll Oxford 1995 (supernumerary fell 1989–95); High Sheriff of Oxfordshire 1987–88; FRSA, FCIB; *Recreations* shooting, fishing, photography, ornithology; *Clubs* Brooks's; *Style—* F R Goodenough, Esq, DL; ✉ Broadwell Manor, Lechlade, Glos GL7 3QS (☎ 01367 860326, fax 01367 860046)

GOODENOUGH, Sir William McLernon; 3 Bt (UK 1943), of Broadwell and Filkins, Co Oxford; s of Sir Richard Edmund Goodenough, 2 Bt (d 1996); *b* 5 Aug 1954; *Educ* Stanbridge Earls; *m* 12 June 1982, Louise Elizabeth, da of Capt Michael Ortmans, LVO, RN, of 48 Bishops Rd, Fulham; 1 s (Samuel William Hector b 11 June 1992), 2 da (Sophie Julia b 1986, Celia Isobel b 1989); *Heir* s, Samuel William Hector Goodenough b 11 June 1992; *Career* design conslt; currently jt md and gp sales dir Design Bridge; *Recreations* shooting, fishing, stalking; *Clubs* Boodle's, Royal Geographic Society; *Style—* Sir William Goodenough, Bt; ✉ Design Bridge, 18 Clerkenwell Close, London EC1R 0AA (☎ 0171 814 9922)

GOODEVE, (John) Anthony; s of Cdr Sir Charles Frederick Goodeve, OBE (d 1980), of London NW11, and Janet Irene, *née* Wallace (d 1993); *b* 4 Aug 1944; *Educ* Canford; *m* 2 Oct 1965, Susan Mary, da of Sydney John Tupper (d 1988), of Petts Wood, Kent; 1 da (Claire Michelle b 29 May 1982); *Career* RNR 1963–66; Shell Mex and BP Ltd 1964–68 (latterly with Shell UK Oil), md Dupré Vermiculite Ltd 1978–79, gp mktg exec Wood Hall Building Group Ltd 1979–80, chief exec and md Grosvenor Property & Finance Ltd 1980–, proprietor Mr Quickpix Photolabs 1985–91, regnl dir R J Temple plc 1991–; Freeman City of London 1969, Liveryman Worshipful Co of Salters 1969 (Renter Warden 1996); FInstD, MLIA (dip); *Recreations* work, photography, swimming; *Clubs* IOD; *Style* Anthony Goodeve, Esq; ✉ Highfields House, 4 Prospect Lane, West Common, Harpenden, Herts AL5 2PL

GOODFELLOW, John Graham; *b* 10 Jan 1947; *Educ* Allan Glen's Sch Glasgow; *Career* cashier rising to asst mangr programming Burnley Building Soc Glasgow 1964–82, asst gen mangr i/c IT National & Provincial Building Soc 1983–84; Skipton Building Society: asst gen mangr then gen mangr i/c IT and admin 1984–91, chief exec and dir 1991–; MIDPM, FRSA; *Style—* John Goodfellow, Esq; ✉ Skipton Building Society, The Bailey, Skipton, N Yorkshire BD23 1DN (☎ 01756 700500, fax 01756 700257)

GOODGER, Donald; s of Charles Thomas Goodger (d 1986), and Miriam, *née* Rowe (d 1979); *b* 1 Oct 1930; *Educ* Wyggeston GS Leicester, Leicester Coll of Tech (BSc(Eng)); *m* 29 Aug 1959, (Anne) Priscilla (d 1994), da of Percy Dalton (d 1968); 1 s (Anthony b 1963), 1 da (Katharine b 1960); *Career* engr; Scott Wilson Kirkpatrick 1957–64; Pick Everard: engr 1964–67, assoc 1967–82, ptnr 1982–92, conslt 1992–95; past chm: IStructE E Midlands Branch 1981–82, Concrete Soc E Midlands Region 1976–77; FIStructE 1972, FICE 1975; *Recreations* beagling, walking; *Clubs* Leicestershire; *Style—* Donald Goodger, Esq; ✉ 37 Grenfell Rd, Leicester LE2 2PA (☎ 0116 270 5150)

GOODHARDT, Prof Gerald Joseph; s of George Goodhardt (d 1978), of London, and Miriam, *née* Simmons (d 1978); *b* 5 April 1930; *Educ* Downing Coll Cambridge (MA, DipMathStat); *m* 27 Jan 1957, Valerie Yvonne, da of Walter Goldsmith (d 1968), of Hove; 1 s (Ian b 1961), 1 da (Catherine b 1958); *Career* res dir Young & Rubicam Ltd 1958–65, dir Aske Research Ltd 1965–75, reader in mktg Thames Poly 1975–81; City Univ Business Sch: Sir John E Cohen prof of consumer studies 1981–95 (emeritus prof 1995–), dean 1991–92; visiting prof Kingston Univ 1996–, research conslt S Bank Univ 1996–; chm Market Res Soc 1973–74, hon sec Royal Statistical Soc 1982–88, regnl cncllr for N Thames Gas Consumers Cncl 1986–95; FSS 1954, MMRS 1958, FCIM 1983; *Books* The Television Audience (1975 and 1987); *Recreations* grandchildren; *Style—* Prof Gerald Goodhardt; ✉ 68 Hamilton Terrace, London NW8 9UJ (☎ 0171 286 0677)

GOODHART, Hon Lady (Celia McClare); *née* Herbert; er da of 2 Baron Hemingford; *b* 25 July 1939; *Educ* St Michael's Sch Limpsfield, St Hilda's Coll Oxford (MA, hon fell); *m* 21 May 1966, Sir William Howard Goodhart, 2 s of Prof Arthur Lehman Goodhart, KBE (hon), QC, of Whitebarn, Boars Hill, Oxford; 2 da (Annabel Frances (Mrs Jim Dallas) b 1967, Laura Christabel b 1970), 1 s (Benjamin Herbert b 1972); *Career* Civil Serv (Miny of Agric and Treasy) 1960–66; history tutor 1966–81: Queen's Coll London, Westminster Tutors; selected as prospective Parly candidate (SDP) Kettering 1982, fought 1983 and 1987 Gen Elections for the SDP Liberal Alliance; memb: SDP Nat Ctee and Lib Dem Fed Exec, Data Protection Ctee 1976–78, Nat Gas Consumers Cncl (chm N Thames) 1978–81; pres: London Marriage Guidance Cncl 1990–95 (vice pres 1995–), Schoolmistresses and Governesses' Benevolent Instn; chm: Youth Clubs UK 1989–92 (vice pres 1992–), Exec Ctee Oxford Soc 1996–; principal Queen's Coll London 1991–; *Clubs* Reform, Cosmopolitan (NY); *Style—* The Hon Lady Goodhart; ✉ 11 Clarence Terrace, London NW1 4RD (☎ 0171 262 1319); Youlbury House, Boars Hill, Oxford OX1 5HH

GOODHART, Prof Charles Albert Eric; CBE (1997); s of Prof Arthur Lehman Goodhart, KBE (d 1978), sometime master Univ Coll Oxford, of NY, and Cecily Agnes Mackay, *née* Carter (d 1985); *b* 23 Oct 1936; *Educ* Eton, Trinity Coll Cambridge (BA, Adam Smith prize), Harvard Univ (PhD); *m* 2 July 1960, Margaret Ann (Miffy), da of Prof Sir Eric Smith, KBE (d 1990), of Plymouth; 1 s (William b 1965), 3 da (Lucy b 1963, Alice b 1968, Sophie b 1970); *Career* prize fell Trinity Coll Cambridge and asst lectr Univ of Cambridge 1963–65, economic advsr Dept of Econ Affrs 1965–66, lectr LSE 1966–68, advsr on domestic monetary policy then chief econ advsr Bank of Eng 1968–85; LSE: Norman Sosnow prof of banking and fin 1985–, convenor Economics Dept 1990–93; non-exec dir Gerrard & National Holdings plc; pres Confederation of European Economic Assocs 1994–95; FBA 1990; *Books* The New York Money Market and the Finance of Trade 1900–1913 (1969), The Business of Banking 1891–1914 (1972), Money Information and Uncertainty (1973, 2 edn 1989), Monetary Theory and Practice (1984), The Evolution of Central Banks (1988), The Central Bank and the Financial System (1995); *Recreations* sheep, walking; *Style—* Prof Charles Goodhart, CBE, FBA; ✉ 27 Abbotsbury Road, London W14 8EL (☎ 0171 603 5817); Halford Manor, South Tawton, Okehampton, Devon EX20 2LZ (☎ 01837 840354); London School of Economics, Houghton St, London WC2A 2AE (☎ 0171 955 7555, fax 0171 242 1006)

GOODHART, Rear Adm (Hilary Charles) Nicholas; CB (1973); s of Gavin Caird Goodhart (d 1974), of Newbury, Berks, and Evelyn Winifred Alphega, *née* Mahon (d 1989); ggf Jakob Emanuel Guthardt came to Eng in 1755 in Ct of George II; *b* 28 Sept 1919; *Educ* RNC Dartmouth, RN Engrg Coll Keyham; *m* 1975, Molly, da of Robert Copsey (d 1956), of Langstone, Farlington, Hants; 1 step s (Ian), 2 step da (Alyson, Fiona); *Career* Engrg Offr RN, served in Med 1941–43, Pilot 1944, Fighter Pilot Indian Ocean 1945, Test Pilot 1946, Naval Test Flying 1947–51, Br Naval Staff Washington 1952–55, Navy Staff Serv and MOD, Rear Adm 1970, ret 1973; dir: Brassey's Defence Publishers Ltd, Research Engineerings Ltd; competition glider pilot 1956–72, competed as memb Br team in 7 World Gliding Championships (world champion 1956, runner up 1958), competed in 9 Br Nat Championships (three times nat champion, three times runner up), competed in 2 US Nat Championships (winner 1955), first UK pilot to get Int Diamond Gliding Badge, Royal Aero Club Silver medal 1956, Fedn Aeronautique Int Tissandier Diploma 1972; invented mirror deck-landing system for aircraft carriers; designed and built 42m span man-powered aircraft, led team bldg the Sigma advanced glider; memb Worshipful Co of Grocers (Master 1981); FRAeS; Legion of Merit (US) 1958; *Recreations* computing; *Style—* Rear Adm Nicholas Goodhart, CB; ✉ Cable House, Lindridge Park, Teignmouth, Devon TQ14 9TF (☎ and fax 01626 779790)

GOODHART, Sir Philip Carter; kt (1981); eld s of late Prof Arthur Lehman Goodhart, KBE (hon), QC, FBA, and Cecily, *née* Carter; *b* 3 Nov 1925; *Educ* Hotchkiss Sch USA, Trinity Coll Cambridge; *m* 1950, Valerie Forbes, da of Clinton Winant, of NY; 3 s, 4 da; *Career* served KRRC and Para Regt 1943–47; editorial staff: Daily Telegraph 1950–54, Sunday Times 1955–57; contested (C) Consett Co Durham 1950, MP (C) Beckenham 1957–92; memb Cncl Consumers' Assoc 1959–68 and 1970–79, vice pres Consumers' Assoc 1983–; jt sec 1922 Ctee 1960–79; memb: Cons Advsy Ctee on Policy 1973–79, Exec Ctee Br Cncl 1974–79; chm Parly NI Ctee 1976–79, memb Advsy Cncl on Public Records 1976–79; Parly under-sec of state: NI Office 1979–81, MOD 1981; chm Sulgrave Manor Bd 1982–; chm Warship Preservation Tst 1987–; *Books* incl: Fifty Ships That Saved The World (1965), The 1922: The History of the 1922 Committee (1973), Full-Hearted Consent (1975); *Pamphlets* incl: Stand On Your Own Four Feet - a Study of Work Sharing and Job Splitting (1982); *Clubs* Beefsteak, Carlton, Garrick; *Style—* Sir Philip Goodhart; ✉ Whitebarn, Boars Hill, Oxford OX1 5HH (☎ 01865 735294); 25 Abbotsbury Road, London W14 8EJ (☎ 0171 602 8237, fax 0171 603 5118)

GOODHART, Sir Robert Anthony Gordon; 4 Bt (UK 1911), of Portland Place, St Marylebone, and Holtye, Sussex; s of Sir John Gordon Goodhart, 3 Bt, FRCGP (d 1979), and (Margaret Mary) Eileen, *née* Morgan; *b* 15 Dec 1948; *Educ* Rugby, Univ of London, Guy's Hosp Med Sch (MB BS); *m* 1972, Kathleen Ellen, eldest da of Rev Alexander Duncan MacRae (d 1979), of Inverness; 2 s (Martin Andrew b 1974, Iain Michael b 1980), 2 da (Kim Elaine b 1977, Rachel Alice b 1987); *Heir* s, Martin Andrew Goodhart b 9 Sept 1974; *Career* medical practitioner 1976–; MRCGP; *Recreations* cricket, sailing, music; *Style—* Sir Robert Goodhart, Bt; ✉ Orchard Hill, Netherbury, Bridport, Dorset DT6 5NB (☎ 01308 488248)

GOODHART, Sir William Howard; kt (1989), QC (1979); 2 s of Prof Arthur Lehman Goodhart, KBE (hon), QC (d 1978), and Cecily, *née* Carter; *b* 18 Jan 1933; *Educ* Eton, Trinity Coll Cambridge, Harvard Law Sch; *m* 21 May 1966, Hon Celia Herbert, da of 2 Baron Hemingford (d 1982); 1 s, 2 da; *Career* Nat Serv 1951–53; called to the Bar Lincoln's Inn 1957, bencher 1986, chm Exec Ctee Justice (Br Section Int Cmmn of Jurists) 1988–94 (vice chm 1978–88); memb: Cncl of Legal Educn 1986–92, Conveyancing Standing Ctee Law Cmmn 1987–89, Int Cmmn of Jurists 1993– (Exec Ctee 1995–); contested Kensington: SDP 1983, SDP/Alliance 1987, Lib Dem 1988, Lib Dem (Oxford West & Abingdon) 1992; chm: SDP Cncl Arrangements Ctee 1982–88, Lib Dem Conf Ctee 1988–91, Lib Dem Lawyers' Assoc 1988–91; memb Lib Dem Policy Ctee 1988–; tstee Campden Charities 1975–90, chm Cambridge Univ Ct of Discipline 1992–; *Style—* Sir William Goodhart, QC; ✉ 11 Clarence Terrace, London NW1 4RD; Youlbury House, Boars Hill, Oxford OX1 5HH

GOODHEW, Duncan Alexander; MBE; s of Donald Frederick Goodhew (d 1972), of Church House, Yapton, W Sussex, and Dolores Perle, *née* Venn; *b* 27 May 1957; *Educ* Millfield Sch, North Carolina State Univ USA; *m* 24 Dec 1984; *Career* swimmer; first int appearance Montreal Olympic Games 1976 (7th in 100m breast stroke final), capt Eng and GB Squad 1978–80; competitions: Commonwealth Games 1978 (3 Silver medals: 100m breast stroke, 200m breast stroke, 4 x 100 medley), World Championships 1978 (fourth 100m breast stroke, third 4 x 100 medley relay), Olympic Games Moscow 1980 (Gold medal 100m breast stroke, sixth 200m breast stroke, third 4 x 100 medley relay); memb 2 and 4 man bob sleigh team Euro Championships 1981; pres BT Swimathon; chm Ludorum Management Ltd (sports agent and conslt) 1996–; *Style—* Duncan Goodhew, Esq, MBE; ✉ c/o Ludorum Management Limited, 33 Tooley Street, London SE1 2QF (☎ 0171 403 8200)

GOODHEW, Prof Peter John; s of Philip Arthur Goodhew (d 1979), and Sheila Mary, *née* Maurau; *b* 3 July 1943; *Educ* Kings Coll Sch, Univ of Birmingham (BSc, PhD, DSc); *m* 27 July 1968, Gwendoline Diane, da of Frederick Fletcher; 1 s (Robert b 1972), 1 da (Laura b 1974); *Career* prof: Univ of Surrey 1986–89 (lectr 1968, reader 1982), Dept of Materials Sci and Engrg Univ of Liverpool 1990–; CEng 1978, FIM 1983, CPhys 1985, FInstP 1990; *Books* Specimen Preparation in Materials Science (1972), The Operation of The Transmission Electron Microscope (1984), Specimen Preparation for TEM of Materials (1984), Thin Foil Preparation for Electron Microscopy (1985), Electron Microscopy and Analysis (2 edn, 1988), Light Element Analysis in the TEM (1988); *Recreations* running, reading; *Style—* Prof Peter Goodhew; ✉ Department of Material Science and Engineering, University of Liverpool, PO Box 147, Liverpool L69 3BX (☎ 0151 794 4665)

GOODHEW, Sir Victor Henry; kt (1982); s of late Rudolph Goodhew, of Mannings Heath, Sussex, and late Rose, *née* Pullen; *b* 30 Nov 1919; *Educ* King's Coll Sch; *m* 1, 1940 (m dis 1951), Sylvia Johnson; 1 s, 1 da; m 2, 1951 (m dis 1972), Suzanne Gordon-Burge; m 3, 1972 (m dis 1981), Eva Rittinghausen; *Career* served WWII RAF, Sqdn Ldr; memb: Westminster City Cncl 1953–59, LCC 1958–61; contested (C) Paddington N 1955, MP (C) St Albans 1959–83; PPS to: Civil Lord Admty 1962–63, Jt Parly Sec for Tport 1963–64; asst Govt whip 1970, lord cmmr Treasy 1970–73; vice chm Cons Def Ctee 1965–70 and 1974–83; memb: Speaker's Panel of Chairmen 1975–83, Select Ctee House of Commons Servs 1978–83, House of Commons Cmmn 1979–83; jt sec 1922 Ctee 1979–83; *Style—* Sir Victor Goodhew; ✉ The Coach House, St Leonard's Dale, Winkfield Road, Windsor, Berkshire SL4 4AQ (☎ 01753 859073)

GOODIER, Roger Banks; s of Benjamin Bancroft Goodier (d 1967), and Ada Irene Goodier (d 1986); *b* 7 Sept 1944; *Educ* Moseley Hall GS, Univ of Sheffield (LLB); *m* 20

July 1974, Denise, da of Eric Forshaw; 2 s (Benjamin b 1975, Oliver b 1978); *Career* admitted slr 1970, sr ptnr Rowley Ashworth slrs; sec Assoc of Personal Injury Lawyers; *Recreations* soccer, rugby union, cricket; *Clubs* Wig & Pen, Twickenham CC; *Style*— Roger Goodier, Esq; ✉ 60 Hampton Road, Teddington, Middx (☎ 0181 977 0711); Rowley Ashworth, 247 The Broadway, Wimbledon, London SW19 1SE (☎ 0181 543 2277, fax 0181 543 0143, telex 8951693); Le Bourg, 14400 Le Manoir, France (00 33 31 92 62 88)

GOODING, Christopher Anderson; s of Frank L Gooding, of Brighton, and Maureen Gooding; *b* 27 May 1957; *Educ* St Lawrence Coll Ramsgate, Brünel Univ (LLBV); *m* Natasha Miriam, da of Jafr Khajeh, of Cyprus; *Career* admitted slr 1981; ptnr: Clyde & Co 1985–96 (joined 1981), LeBoeuf Lamb Greene & MacRae 1996–; memb Int Bar Assoc; *Recreations* motor racing, sailing; *Style*— Christopher Gooding, Esq; ✉ LeBouef Lamb Greene & MacRae, 6th Floor, No 1 Minster Court, Mincing Lane, London EC3R 7AA (☎ fax 0171 459 5000, fax 0171 459 5099)

GOODING, Mel; s of Frederick Gooding (d 1990), and Kathleen, *née* Cox; *b* 3 June 1941; *Educ* Northgate GS for Boys Ipswich, Univ of Sussex (BA, MA); *m* 1967, Esther Rhiannon Coslette, da of Ceri Richards; 2 s (Francis b 1974, Thomas b 1979); *Career* lectr in English, pedagogics and communication various London colls 1966– (notably Sidney Webb Coll of Education 1972–80 and City of London Poly 1980–94); contrib numerous articles to art press since 1980 incl: Arts Review, Artscribe, Flash Art, Art Monthly; contrib numerous introductions and essays to exhibition catalogues 1979–; curator of exhibitions incl: Ceri Richards (Tate Gallery) with Bryan Robertson 1981, Ceri Richards Graphics (Nat Gallery of Wales and tour) 1979–80, Poetry into Art (UEA and Nat Library of Wales) 1982, F E McWilliam (Tate Gallery) 1989, Michael Rothenstein Retrospective (Stoke-on-Trent City Art Gallery and tour); author and publisher (with Bruce McLean) of seven artists' books 1985–90; memb Int Assoc of Art Critics; *Publications* incl: Ceri Richards Graphics (1979), F E McWilliam (1989), Michael Rothenstein The Retrospective (1989), The Phenomenon of Presence Frank Auerbach (1989), The Experience of Painting (1989), Malevich A Box (with Julian Rothenstein, 1990), Bruce McLean (1990), John Hoyland (1990), William Alsop Architect (1992), Michael Rothenstein's Boxes (1992), Patrick Heron (1994), Mary Fedden (1995), Plecnik's National and University Library of Slovenia (1997); *Recreations* walking, birdwatching; *Style*— Mel Gooding, Esq; ✉ 62 Castelnau, Barnes, London SW13 (☎ 0181 748 4434)

GOODISON, Sir Alan Clowes; KCMG (1985, CMG 1975), CVO (1980); o s of Harold Clowes Goodison, and Winifred, *née* Ludlam; *b* 20 Nov 1926; *Educ* Colfe's GS Lewisham, Trinity Coll Cambridge (MA, DipTh); *m* 1956, (Anne) Rosemary (d 1994), o da of Edward Fitton, of Leeds; 1 s, 2 da; *Career* entered FO 1949; serv: Cairo, Tripoli, Khartoum, Lisbon, Amman, Bonn, Kuwait; head Southern European Dept FCO 1973–76, min Rome Embassy 1976–80, asst under sec of state FCO 1981–83, ambass to Irish Republic 1983–86; dir The Wates Fndn 1988–92, chm Charities Evaluation Servs 1993–; licensed lay reader Anglican Church 1959–; Grande Ufficiale dell'Ordine Al Merito (Italy); *Style*— Sir Alan Goodison, KCMG, CVO; ✉ 12 Gardnor Mansions, Church Row, London NW3 6UR

GOODISON, Sir Nicholas Proctor; kt (1982); yr s of Edmund Harold Goodison, of Longacre, Radlett, Herts, and Eileen Mary Carrington, *née* Proctor; *b* 16 May 1934; *Educ* Marlborough, King's Coll Cambridge (BA, MA, PhD); *m* 18 June 1960, Judith Nicola, o da of Capt Robert Eustace Abel Smith (ka 1940), Grenadier Gds (*see* Burke's Landed Gentry 1967); 1 s, 2 da; *Career* H E Goodison & Co (later Quilter Goodison & Co, now Quilter & Co Ltd): joined 1958, ptnr 1962, chm 1975–88; chm Stock Exchange 1976–88 (memb Cncl 1968–88), chm TSB Group plc 1989–95, dep chm Lloyds TSB Group plc (following merger) 1995–; dir: General Accident plc 1987–95, British Steel plc 1989– (dep chm 1993–), Burlington Magazine Ltd; pres: Int Fedn of Stock Exchanges 1985–86, British Bankers' Assoc 1991–96; dir ENO 1977– (vice chm 1980–), chm Courtauld Inst of Art 1982–; memb: Cncl Industl Soc, Nat Art Collections Fund 1976– (chm 1986–); tstee Nat Heritage Memorial Fund; pres Furniture History Soc, hon keeper of furniture Fitzwilliam Museum Cambridge; govr Marlborough Coll; Liveryman: Worshipful Co of Goldsmiths, Worshipful Co of Clockmakers; Hon DLitt City Univ 1985, Hon LLD Univ of Exeter 1989, Hon DSc Aston Univ 1994; hon fell Royal Academy, sr fell RCA 1991, Hon FRIBA 1992; CIMgt, FInstD 1989, FCIB 1989 (vice pres 1989–), FSA, FRSA; Chevalier Legion d'Honneur 1990; *Publications* English Barometers 1680–1860 (1968, 2 edn 1977), Ormolu - The Work of Matthew Boulton (1974), author of many papers and articles on the history of furniture, clocks and barometers; *Recreations* history of furniture and decorative arts, opera, walking, fishing; *Clubs* Arts, Athenaeum, Beefsteak; *Style*— Sir Nicholas Goodison; ✉ Lloyds TSB Group plc, 71 Lombard Street, London EC3P 3BS (☎ 0171 356 2074, fax 0171 356 2050)

GOODLAD, Rt Hon Alastair Robertson; PC (1992), MP (C) Eddisbury (majority 12,697); yst s of late Dr John Fordyce Robertson Goodlad, of Lincoln, and Isabel, *née* Sinclair; *b* 4 July 1943; *Educ* Marlborough, King's Coll Cambridge (MA, LLB); *m* 1968, Cecilia Barbara, 2 da of Col Richard Hurst (s of Sir Cecil Hurst, GCMG, KCB), by his w Lady Barbara, *née* Lindsay (6 da of 27 Earl of Crawford (and Earl Balcarres), KT, PC); 2 s; *Career* Parly candidate (C) Crewe 1970; MP (C): Northwich Feb 1974–83, Eddisbury 1983–; asst Govt whip 1981–82, a Lord Cmmr of the Treasy 1982–84, jt vice chm Cons Pty Trade Ctee 1979–81 (jt hon sec 1978–), hon sec All Party Heritage Gp 1979–81; memb Select Ctee Agriculture 1979–81, Parly under sec of state at Dept of Energy 1984–87; chm All Pty Gp for Refugees 1987–89; memb Select Ctee on Televising Proceedings of the House, comptroller Her Majesty's Household and sr govt whip 1989, treas of HM Household and dep chief whip 1990–92; min of state FCO 1992–95; Parly sec to the Treasy (Govt chief whip) 1995–; chm NW Area Cons Membs of Parly 1987–89, pres Water Companies Assoc 1989, memb House of Commons bridge team in matches against Lords 1982–85; *Clubs* Brooks's, Beefsteak, Pratt's; *Style*— The Rt Hon Alastair Goodlad, MP; ✉ c/o House of Commons, London SW1A 0AA

GOODLAND, Judith Mary; da of Rolf Thornton Ferro (d 1985), and Joan, *née* O'Hanlon; *b* 26 May 1938; *Educ* Howell's Sch Denbigh, Univ of Bristol (BA), Charlotte Mason Coll (CertEd); *m* 4 April 1961 (m dis 1983), Alan Thomas Goodland; 1 s (William Royse b 1966), 2 da (Helen Joanna b 1963, Deborah Clare b 1965); *Career* head of Modern Languages Dept Cartmel Priory Sch Cumbria 1968–72; headmistress: St George's Sch Ascot 1983–88, Wycombe Abbey Sch 1989–; vice chm Common Entrance Bd; expdn assessor Cumbria Panel DOE Award 1979–92, tstee SFIA; *Recreations* fell walking, golf, bridge; *Clubs* Lansdowne; *Style*— Mrs J M Goodland; ✉ Wycombe Abbey School, High Wycombe, Bucks HP11 1PE (☎ 01494 520381, fax 01494 473836)

GOODMAN, Andrew David; s of Bernard Goodman, and Heléne, *née* Greenspan (d 1984); *b* 4 June 1956; *Educ* Queen Elizabeth's Sch Barnet, Univ of Southampton (LLB); *m* 6 June 1982, Sandra Maureen, da of Charles Burney; 4 s (Adam Howard b 1986, Simon Nicholas b 1989, Sam Alexander b 1991, James Aidan Lewis b 1996); *Career* called to the Bar Inner Temple 1978; ACIArb 1989, accredited CEDR mediator 1992; *Books* The Court Guide (1980, 11 edn 1996), The Bar Diary (1982, 1983, 1984), Gilbert and Sullivan At Law (1983), The Royal Courts of Justice Guide (1985), Gilbert and Sullivan's London (1988); *Recreations* travel, music, Victorian theatre; *Clubs* Wig & Pen; *Style*— Andrew Goodman, Esq; ✉ 199 Strand, London WC2R 1DR (☎ 0171 379 9779, fax 0171 379 9481)

GOODMAN, Geoffrey George; s of Michael Goodman (d 1960), and Edythe, *née* Bowman (d 1976); *b* 2 July 1921; *Educ* LSE (BScEcon); *m* 1947, Margit, *née* Freudenbergova; 1 s (John Murray b 14 Feb 1949), 1 da (Karen Elizabeth Irene b 21 March 1951); *Career* RAF 1941–46; journalist, author and broadcaster; reporter: Manchester Guardian 1946–47, News Chronicle 1947–60; industl ed and columnist: Daily Herald 1960–64, The Sun 1964–69, Daily Mirror 1969–86 (asst ed 1976–86), ret; currently presenter and commentator various news and current affrs items for BBC and London News Radio, current affrs commentator various TV and radio progs; ed Br Journalism Review 1989–, assoc fell Nuffield Coll Oxford (fell 1974–76), memb and jt author of Minority report Royal Cmmn on the Press 1974–77, head Govt's Counter-Inflation Unit 1975–76; Hon MA Oxon; Descriptive Writer of the Year 1972, Gerald Barry Award for Journalism 1984–85; *Books* incl: The Awkward Warrior - life and times of Frank Cousins (1979), The Miners' Strike (1985); *Recreations* poetry, supporting Tottenham Hotspur FC; *Clubs* Savile; *Style*— Geoffrey Goodman, Esq; ✉ c/o The Savile Club, 69 Brook St, London W1

GOODMAN, Henry; twin s of late Hyman Goodman, and late Fay, *née* Tobias; *b* 23 April 1950; *Educ* CFS GS, RADA (J Barton Prize, Poel Prize, Shereck Award); *m*, Sue, *née* Parker; 1 s (Ilan b 31 Oct 1981), 1 da (Carla b 25 May 1986); *Career* teacher, director and actor; teacher and ldr various workshops incl: Guildhall Drama Sch, BADA, RNT, RNT Studio; artistic dir Peoples *Theatre* RNT: Roy Cohn in Angels in America, Mickey in After the Fall, Dr Baugh in Cat on a Hot Tin Roof, Steve/Les in Decadence, Beatrice and Benedick, Nathan Detroit in Guys and Dolls; RSC: Rocky Gravo in They Shoot Horses Don't They, Kitely in Every Man in his Humour, Lefer in Henry V, Prince de Condé in The Devils, Stalin/Azhog in Redstar, Dromio of Ephesus in Comedy of Errors (Best Newcomer Olivier Awards 1983), Voltore in Volpone, Harry in The Time of Life, Stravinsky in Astonish Me, Jacques in Jacques and His Masters, Arch of Canterbury and Norfolk in Henry VIII, Klyestakov in Government Inspector, Shylock in The Merchant of Venice, Tartuffe in Tartuffe, Lopakhin in Cherry Orchard, Groucho Marx in Groucho, Capt Hook in Peter Pan, Gellburg in Broken Glass; West End: Buddy Fidler in City of Angels, Hal in Kvetch; Tricycle Theatre: Agent in Lady Sings the Blues, Simon in A Free Country; other credits incl: Charles Guiteau in Assassins (Olivier Award for Best Actor in a Musical, Donmar Warehouse), Freud in Hysteria (Royal Court and Duke of Yorks, Olivier Best Actor Award nomination 1995); dir of various plays incl: The Promise (Arbazov), Metamorphosis, Agamemnon (Best Dir Award), Decadence, Bye Bye Blues, Neighbours, Epsom Wells, Berlin Kabarett; *Television* incl: Lovejoy, Rides, Spinoza, Maigret, The Gravy Train II, Zorro, El CID, Gentlemen and Players, London's Burning, This is David Lander, Bust, After the War, 99 to 1, Sherlock Holmes, The Chain, Pompei in Measure for Measure (BBC), David Siltz in Cold Lazarus (BBC/Channel 4), Xmas (TV film, Channel 4); *Radio* Gentlemen Prefer Blondes, The Prisoner in Prisoner of Papa Stour, André Gregory in Dinner with André, David Selzmik in Diaries of David Selzmik, Jackson in The Nuremberg Trials, title role in Beaumarchais, defence lawyer in No2 Goering, Woody Allen in Retribution, Cavoisier in Breath of Fresh Air, Teddy in Talking Towers; *Films* incl: Secret Weapon, Queen of Hearts, Son of the Pink Panther, Mary Reilly, The Saint, Private Parts, Broken Glass; *Style*— Henry Goodman, Esq; ✉ c/o Penny Wesson, Marmont Management Ltd, Langham House, 308 Regent Street, London W1R 5AL (☎ 0171 637 3183, fax 0171 323 4798)

GOODMAN, Prof John Francis Bradshaw; CBE (1995); s of Edwin Goodman (d 1979), and Amy Bradshaw, *née* Warrener (d 1989); *b* 2 Aug 1940; *Educ* Chesterfield Sch, LSE (BSc), Univ of Manchester (MSc), Univ of Nottingham (PhD); *m* 12 Aug 1967, Elizabeth Mary, da of Frederick William Towns (d 1993), of Romiley, Greater Manchester; 1 s (Richard b 1972), 1 da (Clare b 1970); *Career* personnel offr Ford Motor Co 1962–64, lectr in industl economics Univ of Nottingham 1964–69, industl rels advsr NBPI 1969–70, sr lectr in industl rels Univ of Manchester 1970–74; UMIST: Frank Thomas prof of industl rels 1975–, vice princ 1979–81, head Manchester Sch of Mgmnt 1977–79, 1986–88 and 1989–94; visiting prof of industl rels: Univ of WA 1981 and 1984, McMaster Univ 1985, Auckland Univ 1996; tstee Withington Girls Sch 1986– (govr 1980–92); pres: Manchester Industl Rels Soc 1984–, Br Univs Industl Rels Assoc 1983–86; dep chm Wood St Mission Manchester 1986–; memb: Cncl ESRC 1993–, Cncl ACAS 1988–, Panel of Arbitrators ACAS 1980–; CIPM 1986; *Books* Shop Stewards (1973), Rule-making and Industrial Peace (1977), Ideology and Shop-floor Industrial Relations (1980), Employee Participation (1981), Employment Relations in Industrial Society (1984), Unfair Dismissal Law and Employment Practice (1985); *Recreations* squash, fell walking; *Style*— Prof John Goodman, CBE; ✉ Manchester School of Management, UMIST, PO Box 88, Manchester M60 1QD (☎ 0161 200 3418, fax 0161 200 3623, telex 666094)

GOODMAN, Margaret Beatrice (Maggie); da of John Bertram Goodman (d 1985), and Cissie Phyllis, *née* Kay (d 1952); *b* 26 Nov 1941; *Educ* Plymouth HS for Girls, Coll of Commerce Univ of Birmingham; *m* 1988, Dr Anthony Harold Mercer Gaze, s of William Mercer Gaze; *Career* asst ed New Era Magazine 1960–62, Honey Magazine 1962–67 (sub ed, showbusiness ed, features ed, asst ed), asst ed rising to ed Petticoat magazine 1967–69, freelance feature writer 1969–71, dep ed Cosmopolitan 1971–79, fndr ed Company 1979–88, launch ed Hello! (with Maggie Koumi, *qv*) 1988–93, head Magazine Devpt Gp The National Magazine Company 1994–96, freelance conslt and writer 1996–; awards for Hello!: Consumer Magazine of the Year PPA and Media Week 1990, Magazine of the Year Br Press Circulation Awards 1991, Editors of the Year for gen interest magazine Br Soc of Magazine Editors 1991; memb Br Soc of Magazine Eds 1978–91 (chm 1982); *Books* Every Man Should Have One (jt author, 1971); *Recreations* sailing, socialising; *Clubs* The Groucho; *Style*— Ms Maggie Goodman; ✉ 12 Jeffrey's Place, London NW1 9PP (☎ 0171 267 3987)

GOODMAN, Prof Martin David; s of Cyril Joshua Goodman, and Ruth, *née* Sabel; *b* 1 Aug 1953; *Educ* Rugby, Trinity Coll Oxford (MA, DPhil); *m* 1976, Sarah Jane, da of John Lock; 2 s (Joshua b 1982, Alexander b 1984), 2 da (Daisy b 1987, Charlotte b 1992); *Career* Kaye jr research fell Oxford Centre for Postgrad Hebrew Studies 1976–77, lectr in ancient history Univ of Birmingham 1977–86; Univ of Oxford: fell Oxford Centre for Hebrew and Jewish Studies 1986–, sr research fell St Cross Coll 1986–91, lectr in Roman history Christ Church 1988–, Hebrew Centre lectr in ancient history 1990–91, univ reader in Jewish studies and professorial fell Wolfson Coll 1991–96, prof of Jewish Studies 1996–; fell Inst for Advanced Studies Hebrew Univ of Jerusalem 1993; pres Br Assoc for Jewish Studies 1995, acting pres Oxford Centre for Hebrew and Jewish Studies 1995–96; sec Euro Assoc for Jewish Studies 1994–; review ed Jl of Roman Studies 1993–, jt ed Jl of Jewish Studies 1995–; FBA 1996; *Books* State and Society in Roman Galilee, AD 132–212 (1983), On the Art of the Kabbalah (jt trans, 1983, 2 edn 1993), The History of the Jewish People in the Age of Jesus Christ (jt ed, 1986), The Ruling Class of Judaea: the origins of the Jewish revolt against Rome, AD 66–70 (1987, reprinted 1988, 1989, 1991, paperback 1993), The Essenes according to the Classical Sources (with Geza Vermes, 1989), Mission and Conversion: proselytizing in the religious history of the Roman Empire (1994); also author of over 35 articles and 100 reviews; *Style*— Prof Martin Goodman, FBA; ✉ The Oriental Institute, University of Oxford, Pusey Lane, Oxford OX1 2LE (☎ 01865 278208, fax 01865 278190)

GOODMAN, His Hon Judge Michael Bradley; s of Marcus Gordon Goodman (d 1971), of Manchester, and Eunice Irene May, *née* Bradley (d 1950), of London; *b* 3 May 1930; *Educ* Aldenham Sch, Sidney Sussex Coll Cambridge (MA); *m* 3 Jan 1967, Patricia Mary, *née* Gorringe; 2 da (Sarah Mary b 1 Dec 1967, Catherine Anne b 8 June 1971), 1 s (Paul Andrew Bradley decd); *Career* called to the Bar Middle Temple 1953, recorder 1973–83, circuit judge (SE Circuit) 1983–; chllr Dioceses of: Guildford 1968, Lincoln 1970, Rochester 1971; vicar gen Province of Canterbury 1977–83; chm: Ecclesiastical Judges Assoc, Legal Advsy Ctee of the Church of England; *Recreations* music, walking, tennis; *Clubs* Hurlingham; *Style*— His Hon Judge Goodman; ✉ Croydon Combined Courts Centre, Altyre Road, Croydon, Surrey (☎ 0181 681 2533)

GOODMAN, Richard Antony; s of Antony Marlow Goodman, of Tunbridge Wells, Kent, and Florence, *née* Sowry (d 1994); *b* 17 June 1952; *Educ* Dunstable GS, Selwyn Coll Cambridge (MA); *m* 14 April 1979, Julie, da of John Edwin Williams, of Chilham, Kent; 2 s (Thomas b 1982, William b 1986), 1 da (Charlotte b 1989); *Career* admitted slr 1976; ptnr Cameron Markby Hewitt 1981–; memb Law Soc; *Recreations* music, garden, photography; *Style*— Richard Goodman, Esq; ✉ Cameron Markby Hewitt, Sceptre Court, 40 Tower Hill, London EC3N 4BB (☎ 0171 702 2345, fax 0171 702 2303, telex 925779, e-mail rag@cmh.co.uk)

GOODMAN, Dr Ross Alfred; *b* 15 Dec 1937; *Educ* Endsleigh Sch Colchester, NE Essex Tech Coll Colchester, Sunderland Poly (BSc, PhD); *m* 26 May 1962, Nora Geraghty; 2 da (Oonagh b 13 March 1966, Zoë b 31 Dec 1967); *Career* student apprenticeship James & Stone Ltd Brightlingsea Essex 1953–58, asst experimental offr Ship Div Nat Physical Lab Teddington Middx 1958–64, asst chief ship surveyor Lloyd's Register of Shipping 1989– (joined 1964); Naval Architecture Res Ctee British Ship Res Assoc 1974–79, Design Philosophy Ctee Int Ship Structures Congress 1974–79, Wave Energy Steering Gp Dept of Energy 1985–88, dep ldr British Govt Inquiry into Hull Forms for Warships 1986–88; chm Cncl Royal Inst of Naval Architects 1989–91; Freeman City of London, Liveryman Worshipful Co of Shipwrights; FEng 1991, FRINA (vice pres, memb and chm Cncl 1989–91), FRSA 1994; *Recreations* tennis, reading, gardening; *Clubs* Byfleet Lawn Tennis; *Style*— Dr Ross A Goodman, FEng; ✉ 9 Oakfields, West Byfleet, Surrey KT14 6RZ (☎ 01932 349764); Lloyd's Register of Shipping, 71 Fenchurch Street, London EC3M 4BS (☎ 0171 709 9166, fax 0171 488 4796)

GOODRICH, David; s of William Boyle Goodrich (d 1984), of Sunderland, and Florence Bosenquet, *née* Douglas (d 1984); *b* 15 April 1941; *m* 5 June 1965, Margaret, da of Andrew Robertson Riley, of Sunderland; 1 s (John b 1981), 3 da (Helen b 1968, Kathryn b 1970, Alison b 1972); *Career* constructor RCNC MOD (Navy) 1970–80, md Br Ship Res Assoc 1980–85; British Maritime Technology Ltd: chief exec (formerly md) 1986–, dep chm 1995–; CEng, MBA, RCNC, FRINA; *Recreations* squash, walking; *Clubs* East India; *Style*— David Goodrich, Esq; ✉ British Maritime Technology Ltd, Orlando House, 1 Waldegrave Rd, Teddington, Middlesex TW11 8LZ (☎ 0181 943 5544, fax 0181 943 5347, telex 263118)

GOODRICH, Rt Rev Philip Harold Ernest; s of Rev Canon Harold Spencer Goodrich and Gertrude Alice Goodrich; *b* 2 Nov 1929; *Educ* Stamford Sch, St John's Coll Cambridge (MA); *m* 1960, Margaret, *née* Bennett; 4 da; *Career* curate Rugby Parish Church 1954–57, chaplain St John's Coll Cambridge 1957–61, rector South Ormsby Gp of Parishes 1961–68, vicar Bromley 1968–73, bishop suffragan of Tonbridge 1974–82, bishop of Worcester 1983–96; bishop protector Franciscan Order; chm Children's Soc; *Style*— The Rt Rev Philip Goodrich

GOODSON, Rear Adm (Frederick) Brian; CB (1996), OBE (1982); s of Frederick Orlando Goodson (d 1955), of Belfast, NI, and Edythe, *née* Hamer (d 1978); *b* 21 May 1938; *Educ* Campbell Coll Belfast, Britannia RNC Dartmouth Devon; *m* 25 Aug 1965, Susan Mary, (Sue), da of Reginald John Firmin (d 1981), of Dartmouth, Devon; 2 s (Simon b 1970, Hugo b 1973), 2 da (Pip b 1968, Becky b 1980); *Career* RN: coastal forces and cruisers and destroyers 1958–64, Aden 1964–65, Staff Britannia RNC Dartmouth 1970–72, exchange serv US Navy 1972–74, Cdr RN 1974, Supply Offr HMS Invincible 1980–81, Fleet Supply Offr 1981–82, Capt 1982, dir naval logistic planning 1985–87, chm Eurolog Naval Gp (NATO), Cdre and Cmdg Offr HMS Centurion (Naval Pay and Manning Centre) 1987–91, RCDS 1992, Asst Chief of Def Staff (Logistics) 1993–96, chm Western European Union Logistics Group 1993–; chm govrs St Francis Special Sch Fareham 1991; *Recreations* offshore sailing, squash, outdoor pursuits, family, reading; *Clubs* Lansdowne, Royal Naval Sailing Assoc; *Style*— Rear Adm Brian Goodson, CB, OBE

GOODSON, Sir Mark Weston Lassam; 3 Bt (UK 1922), of Waddeton Court, Parish of Stoke Gabriel, Co Devon; o s of Maj Alan Richard Lassam Goodson (d 1941, 2 s of 1 Bt), and Clarisse Muriel Weston, *née* Adamson; suc his uncle Sir Alfred Lassam Goodson, 2 Bt 1986; *b* 12 Dec 1925; *Educ* Radley, Jesus Coll Cambridge; *m* 4 May 1949, Barbara Mary Constantine, da of Surgn Capt Reginald Joseph McAuliffe Andrews, RN, of Crandel, Ferndown, Dorset; 1 s (Alan Reginald b 1960), 3 da (Phylida Mary (Mrs Timothy F Wright) b 1950, Hilary Frances b 1953, Christian Mary (Mrs Christopher Co[illegible]ns) b 1958); *Heir* s, Alan Reginald Goodson b 15 May 1960; *Style*— Sir Mark Goodson, Bt; ✉ Kilham, Mindrum, Northumberland TD12 4QS (☎ 01890 850217, fax 01890 850260)

GOODSON-WICKES, Dr Charles; MP (C) Wimbledon (majority 14,761); s of Ian Goodson Wickes, FRCP (d 1972), of Stock Harvard, Essex, and Monica Frances Goodson-Wickes; *b* 7 Nov 1945; *Educ* Charterhouse, St Bartholomew's Hosp, Inner Temple; *m* 17 April 1974, Judith Amanda, da of the late Cdr John Hopkinson, RN (d 1978), Sutton Grange, nr Stamford, Lincs; 2 s (Edward b 1976, Henry b 1978); *Career* house physician Addenbrooke's Hosp Cambridge 1972, Surgn Capt The Life Gds (served BAOR, NI, Cyprus) 1973–77, Silver Stick MO, Household Cavalry 1977, Capt RARO, re-enlisted as Lt-Col for Gulf Campaign 1991 (served Saudi Arabia, Iraq, Kuwait); called to the Bar 1972; specialist physician St Bartholomew's Hosp 1977–80, conslt physician BUPA 1977–86, occupational physician; med advsr: Barclays Bank, RTZ, Hogg Robinson, Standard Chartered, (UK) Norwegian Directorate of Health; previously med advsr: Br Alcan, McKinsey, Meat and Livestock Cmmn; MP (C) Wimbledon 1987–; PPS to Rt Hon Sir George Young, Bt, MP: as Min of State for Housing and Planning 1992–94, as Fin Sec to Treasy 1994–95, as Sec of State for Tport 1995–; former vice chm Def Ctee and Constitutional Affrs Ctee, memb Jt Ctee Consolidation of Bills, memb Select Ctee Armed Forces Bill 1990, chm Asbestos Licensing Regulations Appeals Tbnl, sec Arts and Heritage Ctee; BOC Industry and Parly Tst fell 1991; former memb: Med Advsy Ctee Indust Soc, Fitness Advsy Panel IOD; treas Dr Ian Goodson Wickes Fund for Handicapped Children 1979–88; chm BFSS 1994– (memb Public Affrs Ctee 1980–92); company dir Nestor-BNA plc and other int companies; govr Highbury Grove Sch 1977–85; *Books* The New Corruption (1984); *Recreations* hunting, shooting, real tennis, gardening, travel, history; *Clubs* Boodle's, Pratt's, MCC; *Style*— Dr Charles Goodson-Wickes, MP; ✉ Watergate House, Bulford, Wilts (☎ 01980 632344); 37 St James's Place, London SW1 (☎ 0171 629 0981); 8 Devonshire Place, London W1 (☎ 0171 935 5011)

GOODWAY, (John) Beverley; s of Cyril Clement Goodway (d 1991), of Birmingham, and Evelyn Debora Wilding, *née* Honor (d 1983); *b* 13 Aug 1943; *Educ* Seaford Coll, Regent St Poly Sch of Photography; *m* 1972, Karin Anne, da of Gordon Nisbett Hope-Mason; 2 da (Pollyanna b 29 June 1974, Saskia b 4 Nov 1977); *Career* photographer; news agency Cambridge 1965, The Daily Mail 1965–67, The Times 1967, The Sun 1967– (under IPC 1967–69, joined Murdoch launch 1969); Freeman City of London 1979; *Recreations* gardening, art exhibitions, Italy, opera and theatre, photography; *Style*— Beverley Goodway, Esq; ✉ c/o Picture Desk, The Sun, 1 Virginia St, London E1 9XP (☎ 0171 782 4110, fax 0171 242 1229)

GOODWAY, Nick Elston; s of Dr Keith Goodway, of Stone, Staffordshire, and late Cordelia Goodway; *b* 19 Aug 1959; *Educ* Newcastle-under-Lyme HS, Univ of Sheffield (BA); *m* 24 August 1991, Zoë Elizabeth Mary, *née* Biddick; 2 da (Francesca b 23 May 1992, Alexandra b 19 June 1995); *Career* journalist Investors Chronicle 1980–83, City news ed Evening Standard 1983–85; Observer Business: City journalist 1985–89, dep City ed 1989–93, City ed 1993–; *Recreations* opera, cricket, literature, cooking, France; *Style*— Nick Goodway, Esq; ✉ The Observer, 119 Farringdon Road, London EC1R 3ER (☎ 0171 713 4302, fax 0171 239 9508)

GOODWIN, David Pryce; eld s of Geoffrey Pryce Goodwin (d 1970), and Marjorie, *née* Perry (d 1975); *b* 10 May 1936; *Educ* Tonbridge, St Mary's Med Sch Univ of London (BSc, MB BS, MS); *m* 10 Oct 1970, Sarah Jane, da of Harold Morfee (d 1959), and Lorna, *née* Moon (d 1995); *Career* fell in surgery Tulane Univ New Orleans 1970–71, conslt surgn Royal Berks Hosp 1974–; author of various pubns in med jls; FRCS 1966, Hon FACS 1989; *Recreations* sailing, conjuring; *Clubs* Royal Southampton Yacht, Magic Circle (London); *Style*— David Goodwin, Esq; ✉ Royal Berkshire Hospital, Reading RG1 5AN (☎ 0118 987 7418)

GOODWIN, Frederick Anderson (Fred); s of Frederick Anderson Goodwin (d 1992), and Marylyn Marshall, *née* Mackintosh; *b* 17 Aug 1958; *Educ* Paisley GS, Univ of Glasgow (LLB); *m* 23 March 1990, Joyce Elizabeth, da of Norman McLean; 1 s (John Frederick Anderson b 2 Oct 1995); *Career* ptnr Touche Ross 1988–95, chief exec Clydesdale Bank PLC 1996– (dep chief exec 1995–96); MICAS 1983, FCIBS 1996; *Recreations* cars, shooting, golf; *Style*— Fred Goodwin, Esq; ✉ Clydesdale Bank PLC, 30 St Vincent Place, Glasgow G1 2HL (☎ 0141 248 7070, fax 0141 204 0828)

GOODWIN, Sir Matthew Dean; kt (1988), CBE (1980); s of Matthew Dean Goodwin (d 1965), of Bothwell, and Mary Gertrude, *née* Barrie (d 1965); *b* 12 Dec 1929; *Educ* Glasgow Acad; *m* 15 Sept 1955 (m dis 1993), Margaret Eileen, da of Harold Campbell Colvil (d 1959), of Bearsden; 2 da (Frances Margaret b 1957, Carol Elizabeth b 1959); m 2, 28 June 1995, Margaret Adamson; *Career* Nat Serv Flying Offr RAF; CA 1952; ptnr Davidson Down McGown 1959–68; chm: Hewden Stuart plc 1978–95 (fin dir 1968–78), Murray Enterprise plc 1984–, Scotcare Ltd 1988–; dir: Irvine Development Corporation 1980–90, Crestacare plc 1994– (chm 1995–), Rocep Holdings Ltd, Murray Ventures plc; dir East Park Children's Home, dep chm Scotish Cons Pty 1991–92 (treas 1984–90); *Recreations* shooting, farming, bridge; *Clubs* Western (Glasgow); *Style*— Sir Matthew Goodwin, CBE; ✉ 87 Kelvin Court, Anniesland, Glasgow G12 0AH (☎ 0141 339 7541); Hewden Stuart plc, 135 Buchanan St, Glasgow (☎ 0141 221 7331, fax 0141 248 5104)

GOODWIN, Neil; s of James Goodwin (d 1996), of Salford, and Dorothy Goodwin (d 1986); *b* 1 March 1951; *Educ* N Salford Co Secdy Sch, London Business Sch (MBA); *m* 1980 (m dis 1992), Sian Elizabeth Mary, *née* Holliday; 2 s (Matthew Thomas James b 17 Dec 1981, Owen David Neil b 29 March 1987); *Career* various NHS managerial positions Manchester, Liverpool and W Midlands 1969–81, St Albans 1981–84, gen mangr Central Middlesex Hosp 1985–88, gen mangr St Mary's Hosp Paddington 1988–92; chief exec: St Mary's Hosp NHS Trust 1992–94, Manchester Health Authy 1994–; hon fell Health Servs Mgmnt Unit Univ of Manchester; author of numerous articles on hosp mgmnt incl customer care, personal devpt for chief execs and public consultations; FRSA, MIMgt, FHSM 1991 (MHSM 1980); *Recreations* cycling, Coronation Street, theatre; *Clubs* Carlton, Richard III Soc, St James's (Manchester); *Style*— Neil Goodwin, Esq; ✉ Manchester Health Authority, Gateway House, Piccadilly South, Manchester M60 7LP (☎ 0161 237 2011, fax 0161 237 2264)

GOODWIN, (Trevor) Noël; s of Arthur Daniel Goodwin (d 1937), and Blanche, *née* Stephens (d 1956); more than three generations of master mariners and seafarers; *b* 25 Dec 1927; *Educ* France, Univ of London (BA); *m* 1, 1954 (m dis 1960), Gladys Marshall Clapham; m 2, 1963, Mrs Elizabeth Anne Myers, *née* Mason; 1 step s (Richard); *Career* freelance critic, writer, ed and broadcaster specializing in music and dance; asst music critic: News Chronicle 1952–54, Manchester Guardian 1954–55; music and dance critic Daily Express 1956–78, London dance critic Int Herald Tribune Paris 1978–83, exec ed Music and Musicians 1963–71, ed Royal Opera and Royal Ballet Yearbooks 1978, 1979 and 1980; frequent broadcaster on musical topics BBC Home and World Servs and Br Forces Broadcasting Serv (MOD) 1950–, interviewer and commentator on music and arts matters; prog annotator for: Royal Opera, Royal Ballet and other cos and major orchs; overseas news ed Opera 1985–91 (memb Editorial Bd 1991–); reg reviewer for: The Times, Dance and Dancers; memb Cncl Arts Cncl of GB 1979–81, chm Dance Advsy Panel (memb 1973–81), dep chm Music Advsy Panel (memb 1974–81); memb: Dance Advsy Panel Calouste Gulbenkian Fndn UK Branch 1972–76 (memb Fndn's Nat Enquiry into Dance Educn and Trg in Britain 1980), Drama and Dance Advsy Ctee Br Cncl 1973–89, HRH The Duke of Kent's UK Ctee for Euro Music Year 1985 (chm of its Sub-Ctee for Writers and Critics 1982–84); tstee and dir Int Dance Course for Professional Choreographers and Composers 1975–; pres The Critics' Circle 1977 (memb 1958–, jt tstee and memb Cncl 1977–); *Books* London Symphony: Portrait of an Orchestra (1954), A Ballet for Scotland (1979), A Knight at the Opera (1984), History of Theatre Music in Encyclopaedia Britannica (15 edn, 1976), Dance (Europe) in Britannica Books of the Year (1980–93), The New Grove Dictionary of Music and Musicians (area ed and contrib, 1981); contrib: Encyclopaedia of Opera (1976), The Dictionary of Composers (1977), Cambridge Encyclopaedia of Russia (1982, 2 edn 1994), The Concise Oxford Dictionary of Ballet (2 edn, 1982), Pipers Enzyklopädie des Musiktheaters (Munich, Vols 1–4 1987–91), A Portrait of the Royal Ballet (ed, 1988), The New Grove Dictionary of Opera (1992), The Metropolitan Opera Guide to Recorded Opera (New York, 1993), International Dictionary of Ballet (1993), New Shorter Oxford English Dictionary (specialist advsr, 1993); *Recreations* travel; *Style*— Noël Goodwin, Esq; ✉ 76 Skeena Hill, London SW18 5PN (☎ 0181 788 8794)

GOODWIN, Ronald Alfred (Ron); s of James Goodwin (d 1952), of Ruislip, Middx, and Bessie Violet, *née* Godsland (d 1966); *b* 17 Feb 1925; *Educ* Willesden Co Sch, Pinner Co Sch; *m* 1, 3 July 1947 (m dis 1986), Ellen Gertrude, da of William Drew, of Ruislip, Middx; 1 s (Christopher Russell b 16 Sept 1951); m 2, 22 Sept 1986, Heather Elizabeth Mary, da of Harold Wesley Dunsden, of Blewbury, Berks; *Career* composer and conductor; 61 film scores incl: Battle of Britain, 633 Squadron, Frenzy, Where Eagles Dare, Those Magnificent Men in their Flying Machines; other compositions incl: The New Zealand Suite, The Drake 400 Suite, The Armada 400 Suite, The Brimpton Suite, Suite No 1 for Brass Quintette; guest conductor with many orchestras incl: Royal Philharmonic Orchestra, The Bournemouth Symphony Orchestra, The Royal Scottish Nat Orchestra, The New Zealand Symphony Orchestra; vice pres: Br Acad of Songwriters Composers and Authors, The Stars' Orgn for Spastics; cncl memb The Composers' Guild of GB, bd memb Young Persons' Concert Fndn; pres Worthing Youth Orchestra, vice pres The Friends of the Hants Co Youth Orchestra, fell City of Leeds Coll of Music 1993 (pres Friends); Liveryman Worshipful Co of Musicians 1971; *Recreations* walking, swimming, amateur computer programming; *Style*— Ron Goodwin, Esq; ✉ Blacknest Cottage, Brimpton Common, Reading RG7 4RP (☎ 0118 981 5147, fax 0118 981 0770)

GOODWORTH, Simon Nicholas; s of Michael Thomas Goodworth, of Stratford-upon-Avon, Warwickshire, and Lorna Ruth, *née* Skerret; *b* 9 Aug 1955; *Educ* Solihull Sch W Midlands, Univ of Manchester (LLB); *m* 1991, Doris, da of Jun Yip Sew Hoy, of Outram, NZ; *Career* admitted slr 1980; Theodore Goddard: ptnr 1986–, res ptnr NY 1991, currently head Investment Tsts & Funds Gp and of MBO and Venture Capital

Gp; memb: Law Soc, City of London Young Slrs Soc; *Recreations* tennis, squash, theatre, music; *Style*— Simon N Goodworth, Esq; ✉ Theodore Goddard, 150 Aldersgate St, London EC1A 4EJ (☎ 0171 606 8855, fax 0171 606 4390)

GOODWYN, Charles Wyndham; *b* 11 March 1934; *Educ* Wellington Coll, Univ of London (LLB); *m* 18 Aug 1962, Judith Elisabeth Ann, da of Ernest Norman Riley; 2 da (Louisa Caroline (Mrs Wainwright) b 5 June 1963, Kate Judith b 18 Sept 1970), 2 s (Charles James Wyndham b 11 June 1965, Edward Christopher Wyndham b 10 July 1968); *Career* Wilks Head & Eve: joined 1956, ptnr 1960, sr ptnr 1990–95, conslt 1995–; Keeper of the Royal Philatelic Collection 1995–; Royal Philatelic Soc London: hon treas 1981–82, hon sec 1982, vice pres 1990–92, pres 1992–94, Society Medal 1994; divnl chm Gen Cmmrs of Income Tax 1956–, chm Land Inst, tstee Montgomery Sculpture Tst; FRICS (prizewinner 1958), IRRV, FCIArb, FLI; signatory Roll of Distinguished Philatelists, FRPSL; *Recreations* golf, tennis, cricket; *Clubs* Royal Philatelic, MCC; *Style*— Charles Goodwyn, Esq; ✉ Keeper of The Royal Philatelic Collection, Buckingham Palace, London SW1A 1AA

GOODYER, Prof Ian Michael; s of Mark Leonard Goodyer, and Belle, *née* Warwick; *b* 2 Nov 1949; *Educ* Kingsbury HS, Univ of London; *m* Jane Elizabeth, da of late Frank Goodliffe Akister; 1 s (Adam b 19 Nov 1981), 1 da (Sarah b 17 April 1983); *Career* clinical posts in med, surgery and paediatrics 1974–76, postgraduate trg in psychiatry Univ of Oxford 1976–79, res fell Brown Univ USA 1979–80, sr registrar Newcastle Health Authy 1980–83, conslt and sr lectr Univ of Manchester 1983–87, prof Univ of Cambridge 1992– (lectr 1987–92); fell Wolfson Coll Cambridge; vice pres Int Assoc of Child Psychiatry; FRCPsych; *Books* Life Experiences, Development and Child Psychiatry (1991), The Depressed Child Adolescent (1995); *Style*— Prof Ian Goodyer; ✉ Section of Developmental Psychiatry, Douglas House, 18b Trumpington Road, Cambridge CB2 2AH (☎ 01223 336098, fax 01223 324661)

GOOLD, George William; s and h of Sir George Leonard Goold, 7 Bt, and Joy Cecelia, *née* Cutler; *b* 25 March 1950; *m* 1973, Julie Anne, da of Leonard Powell Crack, of Whyalla; 2 s (George Leonard Powell b 1975, Jon b 1977); *Style*— George Goold, Esq; ✉ 2 Ambleside Ave, Mount Keira, NSW 2500, Australia

GOOLD, Baron (Life Peer UK 1987), of Waterfoot, in the District of Eastwood; Sir James Duncan Goold; kt (1983); s of John Goold (d 1934), and Janet Agnes, *née* Kirkland; *b* 28 May 1934; *Educ* Glasgow Acad, Inst of Chartered Accountants Scotland; *m* 1959, Sheena (d 1992), da of Alexander David Paton, OBE (d 1986), of Troon, Ayrshire; 2 s (Hon Michael Kirkland b 1966, Hon (James) David b 1968), 1 da (Hon (Anna) Jane (Hon Mrs McFadyen) b 1972); *Career* CA 1958; pres: Scottish Building Contractors' Assoc 1971, Scottish Building Employers' Fedn 1977; chm: CBI Scotland 1981–83, Mactaggart & Mickel Ltd; hon treas Scottish Cons Pty 1980–83 (chm 1983–89); dir: American Tst plc, Edinburgh Oil & Gas plc; former chm Royal Scot Nat Orchestra, former pres Glasgow Bn Boys' Bde; chm of Ct Univ of Strathclyde; Hon Col 71 (Scottish) Engineer Regt (V); Hon DUniv Strathclyde 1994; Lord Lt Renfrewshire 1994 (DL 1985); *Recreations* gardening, hill walking, golf; *Clubs* Carlton, RSAC, Royal Troon Golf; *Style*— The Rt Hon Lord Goold; ✉ Sandyknowe, Waterfoot, Clarkston, Glasgow G76 8RN (☎ 0141 644 2764); Mactaggart & Mickel Ltd, 126 West Regent St, Glasgow G2 (☎ 0141 332 0001, fax 0141 248 4921)

GOOLDEN, Michael Cyril Christopher; s of Douglas Cyril Aubrey Goolden, of Withyham, Hartfield, E Sussex, and The Hon Rosemary Goolden; *b* 7 Sept 1947; *Educ* Lancing, Oriel Coll Oxford (MA); *m* 17 Dec 1977, Siegrith, *née* Vickers; 3 da (Freya Polly Tamsin b 22 Oct 1980, Camilla Sophia Marique b 8 Sept 1984, Chloe Florence Basilia b 24 Feb 1988); *Career* Price Waterhouse: joined 1969, ptnr 1981–, sr tax ptnr Southampton 1981–90, ptnr i/c Corp Tax Gp London 1990–93, sr tax ptnr London 1993–; fndr Solent Business Fund 1984; MInstD, FCA 1972, ATII 1973; *Recreations* skiing, sailing, wine tasting, theatre, opera; *Clubs* MCC, Leander; *Style*— Michael Goolden, Esq; ✉ Foxes Bank Farm, Washwell Lane, Wadhurst, E Sussex TN5 6LN (☎ 01892 784494); Price Waterhouse, Southwark Towers, 32 London Bridge Street, London SE1 9SY (☎ 0171 939 2218, fax 0171 378 0647)

GOPAL-CHOWDHURY, Paul; *b* 1949; *Educ* Camberwell Sch of Art, Slade; *Career* artist; Boise Travelling Scholarship and French Govt Scholarship 1973–74; lectr: Chelsea Sch of Art 1973–74 (pt/t 1975–77), Fine Art Dept Univ of Leeds (pt/t) 1975–77, Byam Shaw Sch of Art (pt/t) 1975–77; Gregory fell Univ of Leeds 1975–77; artist-in-residence Gonville and Caius Coll Cambridge and Kettle's Yard Gallery Cambridge 1983–84; solo exhibitions: Art Gallery Newcastle Poly 1980, Arts Centre Folkestone 1980, Ian Birksted Gallery 1981 and 1984, Kettle's Yard Gallery Cambridge (and tour to Axiom Gallery Cheltenham and Oldham Art Gallery) 1984–85, Benjamin Rhodes Gallery 1986, 1988 and 1991, Quay Arts Centre IOW 1988; gp exhibitions incl: London Gp 1971, Royal Acad Summer Exhibition (1972, 1974, 1978, invited artist 1988), Royal Soc of Oil Painters 1973, John Moores Exhibition (Liverpool) 1974, Hayward Annual 1979 and 1981, Serpentine Summer Show 3 1979, Whitechapel Open (Whitechapel Gallery) 1980 and 1983, Imperial Tobacco Portrait awards (Nat Portrait Gallery) 1980, 1981 and 1985, A Taste of Br Art Today (Brussels) 1981, Ian Birksted Gallery (NY) 1981, Heads (Lamont Gallery London) 1992, Royal Acad Summer Exhibition (invited artist) 1992 and 1993, Beautiful Blooms (Lamont Gallery London) 1993; public collections: Bolton Art Gallery, Chase Manhattan Bank NY, Chelmsford and Essex Museum, Contemporary Art Soc, de Beers Ltd, Doncaster Museum and Art Gallery, Newcastle Poly; 2nd prize Imperial Tobacco Portrait Award (Nat Portrait Gallery) 1982; *Publications* articles incl: My Painting (Artscribe), Painting From Life (Hayward Annual 1979 Catalogue), Portrait of the Artist (Artist's and Illustrator's Magazine 1986), Reviving the Figurative Tradition (Landscape 1987); *Style*— Paul Gopal-Chowdhury, Esq

GORDIMER, Nadine; da of Isidore Gordimer (d 1961), of Springs, S Africa, and Nan, *née* Myers (d 1973); *b* 20 Nov 1923; *Educ* convent sch; *m* 1, 1949 (m dis 1952), Dr Gerald Gavronsky; 1 da (Oriane Taramasco b 1950); m 2, 29 Jan 1954, Reinhold Cassirer, s of Hugo Cassirer (d 1920), of Berlin; 1 s (Hugo b 1955); *Career* novelist and writer; eleven novels completed (incl My Son's Story, None to Accompany Me), nine short story collections (incl Something Out There), two non-fictional works (incl The Essential Gesture); vice pres Int PEN, hon memb American Acad of Arts and Sciences, hon memb American Acad and Inst of Arts and Letters, FRSL, patron and regnl rep Congress of S African writers; holder of fourteen honorary degrees incl: DLitt Harvard Univ 1986, DLitt Yale Univ 1986, DLitt Columbia Univ, DLitt Univ of Cambridge 1992, DLitt Univ of Oxford 1994; Commandeur de l'Ordre des Arts et des Lettres France 1986; winner Nobel Prize for Literature 1991; *Style*— Ms Nadine Gordimer, FRSL

GORDON, *see also:* Duff Gordon, Smith-Gordon

GORDON, Sir Alexander John (Alex); kt (1988), CBE (1974, OBE 1967); s of John Tullis Gordon (d 1959), of Swansea, and Euphemia Baxter Borrowman, *née* Simpson (d 1942); *b* 25 Feb 1917; *Educ* Swansea GS, Welsh Sch of Architecture; *Career* Maj RE 1940–46; architect in partnership with T Alwyn Lloyd 1948–60, sr ptnr Alex Gordon & Partners 1960–82, conslt The Alex Gordon Partnership 1982–88; memb: Welsh Arts Cncl 1959–73, Design Cncl 1973–77, Bd British Cncl 1980–87; Royal Fine Art Cmmr 1973–90; pres RIBA 1971–73; Hon LLD Univ of Wales 1972; FCSD 1975, ARICS 1987, hon fell ISE 1980, hon fell CIBSE 1975, hon memb BDA 1980, Soc of Mexican Architects 1972, and corresponding memb Danish Architects 1976, Hon FRAIC 1974, Hon FAIA 1974; *Recreations* reflecting on past skiing, visual arts; *Clubs* Arts, Cardiff and County; *Style*— Sir Alex Gordon, CBE; ✉ River Cottage, Llanblethian, nr Cowbridge, S Glam CF7 7JL (☎ 01446 773672)

GORDON, Anthony George; MBE (1979); s of Laurence Victor Gordon, MBE (d 1975), and Margaret Mary Gordon; *b* 21 April 1925; *Educ* The King's Sch Canterbury, Corpus Christi Coll Cambridge (BA); *m* 22 April 1966, (Mary) Sylvia (d 1995), da of William Edward Levers (d 1991), and Winifred Mary, *née* Tree (d 1975); 2 s (James b 25 Feb 1967, Jeremy b 8 Sept 1968); *Career* RAF pilot 1944–47; chm S American Freight Ctee 1958–, dir Int Meat Trade Assoc 1975–, chm Assoc of Br Meat Processors 1987–92, vice pres Assoc Européenne du Commerce en Gros des Viandes 1987–93, pres Euro Union of Abattoir Operators 1990–93; MInstM 1970; *Recreations* tennis, shooting, photography; *Style*— Anthony Gordon, Esq, MBE; ✉ 55 Fentiman Rd, London SW8 1LH (☎ 0171 735 9861); International Meat Trade Association, 217 Central Markets, London EC1A 9LH (☎ 0171 489 0005)

GORDON, Aubrey Abraham; s of Isaac Gordon (d 1962), of Sunderland, and Fanny, *née* Benjamin (d 1975); *b* 26 July 1925; *Educ* Bede Collegiate Boys' Sch Sunderland, Univ of Durham (LLB); *m* 28 June 1949, Reeva Rebecca, da of Myer Cohen (d 1941), of Sunderland; 1 s (David Myer b 1956), 2 da (Anne b 1950, Susan b 1950); *Career* admitted slr 1947; recorder of the Crown Ct 1978–; pres: Houghton le Spring Chamber of Trade 1955, Hetton le Hole Rotary Club 1967, Sunderland Law Soc 1976; chm: Houghton Round Table 1959, Sunderland Victims Support Scheme 1978–80, Sunderland Guild of Help 1984–92; pres: NE Joel Intract Memorial Home for Aged Jews 1990–93, Ethics Ctee Washington Hosp, Sunderland and S Tyneside Family Mediation Serv; *Recreations* communal activities, photography, walking; *Style*— Aubrey A Gordon, Esq; ✉ 1 Acer Court, Sunderland, Tyne & Wear SR2 7EJ (☎ 0191 565 8993)

GORDON, Catherine (Kate); JP (Inner Manchester 1969); da of William Alexander Keir (d 1963), of Ayr, Scotland, and Marion Watson, *née* Prentice (d 1987); *Educ* Ayr Acad, Open Univ (BA); *m* 20 Aug 1955, (Donald) Hugh McKay Gordon, s of James Bremner Gordon, of Huntly, Aberdeenshire; 1 s (Alistair Keir b 10 Sept 1956), 1 da (Marion Louise (Mrs Livingstone Jones) b 31 July 1959); *Career* Civil Serv and PA to chm of nationalised indust 1945–56; local and met dist cncllr 1969–95, chm Trafford Ethics Ctee 1984–96; memb: Trafford Health Authy 1976–89, Women's Nat Cmmn 1980–84, Trafford Cts Ctee 1972–88, Gtr Manchester Probation Ctee 1974–92, Cncl Nat Magistrates' Assoc 1985–92; chm Inner Manchester Magistrates 1985–89 (memb Exec 1976–92); YWCA: nat pres and chm Bd of Govrs 1980–84, govr 1970–95, del World Cncl YWCA Forces rep (BAOR and Cyprus) 1984–96; govr: St Vincent's Junior/Infants Sch 1984–, Altrincham Girls' GS 1994–; FRSA 1980; *Recreations* music, family, friends; *Clubs* YWCA; *Style*— Mrs Hugh Gordon, JP; ✉ 3 West Lynn, Devisdale Rd, Bowdon, Cheshire WA14 2AT (☎ and fax 0161 928 6038)

GORDON, Sir Charles Addison Somerville Snowden; KCB (1981, CB 1970); s of Charles Gordon Snowden Gordon, TD (d 1961); *b* 25 July 1918; *Educ* Winchester, Balliol Coll Oxford; *m* 1943, Janet Margaret (Jane) (d 1995), da of late Douglas Porteous Beattie, of Dewsbury, Yorks; 1 s (Oliver), 1 da (Maxine); *Career* served 1939–45 Fleet Air Arm (Lt (A) RNVR); House of Commons: asst clerk 1946, sr clerk 1947, fourth clerk at the Table 1962, princ clerk of the Table Office 1967, second clerk asst 1974, clerk asst 1976, clerk of the House of Commons 1979–83; *Books* ed 20th edition Erskine May's Parliamentary Practice (1983); *Style*— Sir Charles Gordon, KCB; ✉ 279 Lonsdale Rd, Barnes, London SW13 9QB (☎ 0181 748 6735)

GORDON, Christopher James; s of (Alexander) Esmé Gordon (d 1993), and Betsy Ballment, *née* McCurry (d 1990); *b* 3 Dec 1944; *Educ* Edinburgh Acad, Univ of St Andrews (MA), Br Sch of Archaeology Athens, Poly of Central London (Dip Arts Admin); *m* 27 June 1970, Susan Merriel, da of Bonham Bazeley; 1 da (Antonia b 4 Dec 1973), 3 s (Alexander b 4 Oct 1975, Rupert b 2 Sept 1978, Adam b 24 July 1981); *Career* trainee mangr Williamson Magor & Co (tea estates) Calcutta 1967–69, asst music offr Arts Cncl of GB 1969–72, theatre and mktg mangr Hampstead Theatre 1973, sr arts offr/festival admin London Borough of Camden 1973–77, co arts offr Hampshire CC 1977–85, exec dir Cncl of Regnl Arts Assocs 1985–91, chief exec Regnl Arts Bds Services Ltd 1991–; external examiner: MA Arts Admin Leicester Poly 1986–91, MA Euro Cultural Mgmnt Univ of Warwick 1993– (occasional lectr 1993–); lectr on cultural policy: Dijon, Barcelona, Turin, Salzburg; chair Festivals Panels Gr London Arts Assoc 1976–77, memb Nat Film & Video Forum BFI 1991–, memb Planning and Devpt Bd Arts Cncl of GB 1986–91 (memb Trg Ctee 1985–91), memb Fndr Steering Gp BP Arts Journalism Awards 1986–91; Southern Arts Assoc: chair General Arts, chair Festivals Panels, memb Exec Ctee, memb Gen Cncl; memb various Euro Arts Ctees, hon treas Euro Forum for the Arts & Heritage (EFAH) 1996–; memb: Univ of Southampton Arts Centre Ctee 1994–, Quality of Life Gp Hants Business Liaison Forum, Winchester Cathedral Fabric Ctee 1996–; tstee Portsmouth Theatre Royal 1985–, tstee and memb Exec Ctee Hants Sculpture Tst 1987–; FRSA; *Books* Cultural Policy in Italy (1995); *Recreations* travel, music, art, history; *Style*— Christopher Gordon, Esq; ✉ Laurel Cottage, Rectory Lane, Meonstoke, Hants SO32 3NF (☎ 01489 877772, fax 01489 877670); English Regional Arts Boards, 5 City Road, Winchester, Hants SO23 8SD (☎ 01962 851063, fax 01962 842033, e-mail info.erab@artsfb.org.uk)

GORDON, David Michael; s of Nathan Gordon (d 1990), of London, and Diana, *née* MacKoffsky; *b* 12 Dec 1940; *Educ* Davenant Foundation GS; *m* 9 June 1968, Patricia Anne, da of Alfred Melamed (d 1982); 1 s (Andrew b 27 Oct 1971), 1 da (Nicola b 2 July 1974); *Career* chief actuary Pearl Assurance Plc 1984–94 (asst actuary 1975–83, dep actuary 1983–84); dir: Pearl Assurance Plc 1987–94, Pearl Assurance (Unit Funds) Ltd 1987–94, Pearl Assurance (Unit Linked Pensions) Ltd 1987–94, Pearl Unit Trusts Ltd 1987–94, Pearl Group Plc 1988–94; non-exec dir Insur Ombudsman Bureaux 1988; memb various ctees Assoc of Br Insurers 1984–94; FIA 1968, FSS 1970; *Recreations* reading, gardening, swimming; *Clubs* 59, Denarius; *Style*— D M Gordon, Esq; (☎ 0181 953 9620)

GORDON, David Sorrell; s of Sholom Gordon (d 1965), and Tamara (Tania) Gordon (d 1994); *b* 11 Sept 1941; *Educ* Clifton, Balliol Coll Oxford (BA), LSE, Harvard Business Sch (AMP); *m* 1, 1963 (m dis 1969), Enid Albagli; m 2, 1974, Maggi McCormick; 2 s; *Career* articled clerk Thomson McLintock (now KPMG) 1965–68; The Economist: journalist 1968, financial ed 1972, dep business ed 1974–78, prodn and devpt dir The Economist Group 1978–81, gp chief exec The Economist Group 1981–93; chief exec Independent Television News Ltd (ITN) 1993–95; business advsr 1995–, sec Royal Academy of Arts 1996–; dir Target Group plc 1988–91, dir The Financial Times Group Ltd 1983–93, non-exec dir Profile Books 1996–; chm Contemporary Art Society 1992–, memb bd South Bank Centre 1986–, govr BFI 1983–91, memb Ct of Govrs LSE, tstee Tate Gallery 1993–; FCA; *Books* Newspaper Money (jtly with Fred Hirsch, 1975); *Recreations* movies, magic lanterns; *Clubs* Garrick, Harvard (NY); *Style*— David Gordon, Esq; ✉ Greenwood, 56 Duke's Avenue, Chiswick, London W4 2AF (☎ 0181 994 3126, e-mail 100607.2176@compuserve.com); Royal Academy of Arts, Burlington House, Piccadilly, London W1V 0DS (☎ 0171 439 7438)

GORDON, Donald; s of Nathan Gordon (d 1978), and Sylvia (Sheila), *née* Shevitz (d 1984); *b* 24 June 1930; *Educ* King Edward VII Sch Johannesburg, Univ of Witwatersrand; *m* 21 Jan 1958, Peggy, da of Max Cowan (d 1950); 2 s (Richard Michael b 1958, Graeme John b 1963), 1 da (Wendy Donna (Mrs Appelbaum)); *Career* CA, registered public accountant and auditor 1953; chm: Liberty Life Association of Africa Ltd (dir 1957), Liberty Holdings Ltd (dir 1968), Liberty Asset Management Ltd (dir 1969), Liberty

Investors Ltd (dir 1971), Liblife Strategic Investments Ltd (dir 1993), First International Trust Ltd (dir 1977), Guardian National Insurance Co Ltd (dir 1980), Guardbank Management Corporation Ltd (dir 1969), Liberty International Holdings plc (formerly TransAtlantic Holdings plc, UK dir 1981), Capital Shopping Centres PLC (UK dir 1994), Capital & Counties plc (UK dir 1982); dir: Guardian Royal Exchange plc 1971–94, Guardian Royal Exchange Assurance plc 1971–94, Premier Group Ltd 1983 (dep chm), South African Breweries Ltd 1982–, Standard Bank Investment Corp 1979– (dep chm), Beverage and Consumer Industrial Holdings Ltd 1989–, Sun Life Corporation plc 1992–95, Sun Life Assurance Society plc 1992–95; Doctorate of Econ Sci Univ of Witwatersrand 1991; *Recreations* tennis; *Clubs* Houghton Golf, Rand, Johannesburg Country, Plettenberg Bay Country; *Style*— Donald Gordon, Esq; ✉ Liberty Life Association of Africa Ltd, 4th Floor, Liberty Life Centre, 1 Ameshoff St, Braamfontein 2001, PO Box 10499, Johannesburg 2000, S Africa (☎ 00 27 11 408 2100, fax 00 27 11 403 3171); Liberty International Holdings plc, 40 Broadway, London SW1H 0BT (☎ 0171 222 5496, fax 0171 222 5554)

GORDON, (Robert) Douglas; s of late Robert Gordon, of Gourock, Scotland, and Helen, *née* McTaggart; *b* 31 July 1936; *Educ* Greenock Acad, Cardiff HS for Boys; *m* 1, 6 Aug 1960 (m dis 1990), Margaret, da of Jack Bruckshaw (d 1941); 1 s (Robert Christopher Cameron b 13 April 1961); m 2, 15 May 1990, Valerie Janet Brownlee, MVO, da of Dr Cecil Hugh Dickson, of Ilford, Essex (d 1989); *Career* Nat Serv RM 1955–57, 2 Lt Wiltshire Regt 1957; HM Dip Serv: joined FO 1954, Br Embassy Amman 1958, MECAS 1959–61, Political Office Abu Dhabi 1961–63, Br Embassy Vienna 1963–66, second sec (commercial) Kuwait 1966–69, second sec FCO 1969–73, second then first sec, head of Chancery and HM consul Doha 1973–76, asst to Dep Govr Gibraltar 1976–78, first sec FCO 1978, HM asst marshal of the Dip Corps 1982–84, first sec (commercial) Washington 1984–86, HM consul Cleveland 1986–88, HM ambass Aden 1989–90, consul gen Aden 1990, Br high cmmr Guyana and ambass Rep of Suriname 1990–93, HM ambass Repub of Yemen and ambass (non resident) Repub of Djibouti 1993–94, HM ambass Repub of Yemen 1993–95, ret; dip conslt Royal Garden Hotel London 1996–; Freeman City of London 1984; orders: Gorkha Dakshina Bahu (Nepal) 1980, King Abdul Aziz ibn Saud (Saudi Arabia) 1982, Officier de l'Ordre National du Mérite (France) 1984; *Recreations* golf, walking, photography; *Clubs* Royal Over-Seas League, Five Lakes Golf & Country, Tolleshunt Knights, Little Aden Golf; *Style*— Douglas Gordon, Esq; ✉ Melbrook, 73 North Road, Tollesbury, Essex CM9 8RQ

GORDON, Fiona Mary; da of Cdr David Leslie Gordon (d 1984), and Anne Josephine, *née* Haywood; *b* 2 June 1951; *Educ* Hurst Lodge Sunningdale Berks, Beechlawn Tutorial Coll Oxford; *Career* dir: Brook-Hart Advertising Ltd 1980–85, Hewland Consultants International Ltd 1980–85; md First Public Relations Ltd 1985–; MIPR, MIPA; *Clubs* Mortons, The Limelight; *Style*— Miss Fiona Gordon; ✉ First Public Relations Ltd, 2 Cinnamon Row, Plantation Wharf, York Place, London SW11 3TW (☎ 0171 978 5233, fax 0171 924 3134)

GORDON, George; s of Dr Adam Smith Gordon, RAMC (d 1951), of Ferniebank, Markinch, Fife, and Agnes Forbes, *née* Smith; *b* 4 Sept 1936; *Educ* Bell Baxter Sch Cupar Fife, Univ of Edinburgh (MB ChB); *m* 11 June 1966, Rosemary Gould, da of Rev Alexander Hutchison; 1 s (David b 4 Jan 1971), 1 da (Fiona b 27 March 1967); *Career* house surgn: Western Gen Hosp Edinburgh 1959–60, Royal Infirmary Edinburgh 1960; house physician Royal Hosp for Sick Children Edinburgh 1961, sr house offr Simpson Meml Maternity Pavilion 1962, registrar Eastern Gen Hosp Edinburgh 1962–66, sr registrar Western Gen Hosp Edinburgh 1966–69, conslt obstetrician and gynaecologist Dumfries 1969–, clinical dir for women and children Dumfries and Galloway Acute and Maternity NHS Tst 1994–; past pres Edinburgh Obstetrical Soc, chm Confidential Enquiry into Maternal Deaths Scot; fell BMA 1988; FRCSEd 1967, FRCOG 1977; *Recreations* Scots literature, gardening, golf, music; *Clubs* New (Edinburgh), Gynaecological Travellers'; *Style*— George Gordon, Esq; ✉ Dumfries & Galloway Royal Infirmary, Dumfries (☎ 01387 246246)

GORDON, George Park Douglas; s of George Park Gordon (d 1984), of Peterhead, and Chrissie Ann Gordon (d 1977); *b* 23 Oct 1937; *Educ* Peterhead Acad, Univ of Aberdeen (BSc Hons), Aberdeen Coll of Educn; *m* 16 July 1963, Karein Lawrence Mackenzie, da of Hector Mackenzie Fraser; 1 da (Anne Jacqueline b 3 Sept 1965), 1 s (David Neil b 11 Sept 1968); *Career* sci teacher Peterhead Acad 1961–64, princ sci teacher Dornoch Acad 1964–67, asst advsr in sci Glasgow 1967–69; HM Inspr of Schs: gen duties West Div 1969–73, Secdy Educn and Sch Building HQ 1973–77, nat specialist in sci 1977–82, dist inspr West Div 1982–86, chief inspr Basic and Special Educn 1986–88, 5–14 yr olds and Special Educnl Needs 1988–89, West Div and Special Educnl Needs 1989–92, chief inspr West Div 1992–95, ret 1996; memb: RSC 1961–82, Assoc for Sci Educn 1962–82; *Recreations* reading, gardening, theatre, walking, sport in general especially golf, football; *Clubs* Buchanan Castle Golf; *Style*— George Gordon, Esq; ✉ Suilven, 8 Ewing Walk, Fairways, Milngavie, Glasgow G62 6EG (☎ 0141 956 5131)

GORDON, Sheriff Gerald Henry; CBE (1995), QC (Scot 1972); er s of Simon Gordon (d 1982), of Glasgow, and Rebecca, *née* Bulbin (d 1956); *b* 17 June 1929; *Educ* Queen's Park Sr Secdy Sch Glasgow, Univ of Glasgow (MA, LLB, PhD), Univ of Edinburgh (LLD); *m* 1957, Marjorie (d 1996), yr da of Isaac Joseph, of Glasgow; 1 s (David), 2 da (Susan, Sarah); *Career* admitted Scots Bar 1953; Univ of Edinburgh: sr lectr 1965, head Dept of Criminal Law and Criminology 1965–72, personal prof of criminal law 1969–72, dean Faculty of Law 1970–73, prof of Scots Law 1972–76; Sheriff of: South Strathclyde, Dumfries and Galloway at Hamilton 1976–77, Glasgow and Strathkelvin 1978–; temp judge Court of Session and High Court of Justiciary 1992–; Hon LLD Univ of Glasgow; *Books* The Criminal Law of Scotland (1968, 2 edn 1978), Renton and Brown's Criminal Procedure (ed, 4 edn 1972, 5 edn 1983, 6 edn 1996); *Recreations* Jewish studies, swimming; *Style*— Sheriff Gerald H Gordon, CBE, QC; ✉ Glasgow Sheriff Ct (☎ 0141 429 8888)

GORDON, His Hon Judge; (Cosmo) Gerald Maitland; s of John Kenneth Maitland Gordon (d 1967), of Farnham, Surrey, and Erica Martia, *née* Clayton-East (d 1983), of London; *b* 26 March 1945; *Educ* Eton; *m* 4 July 1973, Vanessa Marie Juliet Maxine, *née* Reilly-Morrison; 2 s (James Cosmo Alexander b 11 Oct 1975, George William Robert b 6 June 1978); *Career* called to the Bar Middle Temple 1966, recorder of the Crown Court 1986–90 (asst recorder 1982–86), circuit judge (SE Circuit) 1990–; Cncl of Royal Borough of Kensington and Chelsea: memb 1971–90, chm Works and Town Planning Ctees, dep leader 1982–88, mayor 1989–90; *Style*— His Hon Judge Gordon; ✉ Central Criminal Court, Old Bailey, London EC4M 7EH (☎ 0171 248 3277)

GORDON, Giles Alexander Esmé; s of (Alexander) Esmé Gordon, RSA, FRIBA (d 1993), of Edinburgh, and Betsy, *née* McCurry (d 1990); *b* 23 May 1940; *Educ* Edinburgh Acad, Edinburgh Coll of Art; *m* 1, 1964, Margaret Anna Eastoe (d 1989); 2 s (one of whom d 1994), 1 da; m 2, 1990, Margaret Anne (Maggie), da of Frank McKernan (d 1985), and Bridget McKernan, of Glasgow; 2 da; *Career* trainee publisher Oliver & Boyd Edinburgh 1959–63, advtg mangr Secker & Warburg 1963–64, ed Hutchinson 1964–66, plays ed Penguin Books 1967–68, editorial dir Victor Gollancz 1967–72; lit agent and dir: Sheil Land Associates Ltd (formerly Anthony Sheil Associates) 1972–95, Curtis Brown Ltd 1995–; ed Bloomsbury Classics Short Story Vols 1995–, ed Clarion Tales 1995–; C Day Lewis fell in writing King's Coll London 1974–75, sec and chm Soc of Young Publishers; memb: Literature Panel Arts Cncl 1968–72, Ctee of Mgmnt Soc of Authors, Ctee Assoc of Authors' Agents, Ctee of Mgmnt Soc of Authors Scotland 1996–; lectr: Tufts Univ in London 1970–74, Hollins Coll in London 1983–86; theatre critic: Spectator, London Daily News, Drama (also ed); books columnist The Times 1993–95; memb Cncl Authors' Club 1992–; FRSL 1990 (memb Cncl 1992–94); *Books* Pictures from an Exhibition (1970), The Umbrella Man (1971), About a Marriage (1972), Girl with Red Hair (1974), Factions (ed with A Hamilton, 1974), Walter and the Balloon (for children, with Margaret Gordon, 1974), Beyond the Words (ed, 1975), Farewell, Fond Dreams (1975), Prevailing Spirits (ed, 1976), 100 Scenes from Married Life (1976), Members of the Jury (ed with Dulan Barber, 1976), You Always Remember the First Time (ed jtly, 1976), A Book of Contemporary Nightmares (ed, 1977), Enemies (1977), The Illusionist (1978), Modern Scottish Short Stories (ed with Fred Urquhart, 1978), Ambrose's Vision (1980), Shakespeare Stories (ed, 1982), English Short Stories 1940–80 (ed, 1982), Best Short Stories (ed annually with David Hughes, 1986–95), English Short Stories - 1900 to the present (ed, 1988), The Twentieth Century Short Story in English - a Bibliography (ed, 1989), Aren't We Due a Royalty Statement? (memoirs, 1993), Scotland from the Air (1996); *Recreations* walking, sleeping, the Arts, holidaying abroad; *Clubs* Garrick; *Style*— Giles Gordon, Esq, FRSL; ✉ 6 Ann Street, Edinburgh EH4 1PJ (☎ 0131 332 1993, fax 0131 315 2695)

GORDON, Hannah Campbell Grant; da of William Munro Gordon, of Edinburgh (d 1952), and Hannah, *née* Grant; *b* 9 April 1941; *Educ* St Denis Sch for Girls Edinburgh, Royal Coll of Music and Dramatic Art Glasgow (James Bridie Gold Medal); *m* 1970, Norman Warwick; 1 s (Ben b 19 July 1973); *Career* actress; Hon DLitt Univ of Glasgow 1993; FRSAMD; *Theatre* incl: various plays at Glasgow, Ipswich, Coventry and Windsor; West End: The Killing Game, The Jeweller's Shop, Can You Hear Me at the Back?, The Country Girl, Light Up the Sky, Shirley Valentine, Hidden Laughter, An Ideal Husband, The Aspern Papers; Othello (Chichester), Mary Stuart (Edinburgh Festival); *Television* incl: Johnson Over Jordan, David Copperfield, Great Expectations, Middlemarch, Abelard and Heloise, The Orkney Trilogy, The Exiles, Dear Octopus, My Wife Next Door, Telford's Change, Upstairs Downstairs, What Every Woman Knows, Good Behaviour, The Gay Lord Quex, The Day After the Fair, My Family and Other Animals, Joint Account; *Films* incl: Spring and Port Wine, The Elephant Man, Limited Edition; *Recreations* walking, gardening; *Clubs* St James, The Parrot; *Style*— Ms Hannah Gordon; ✉ c/o Conway van Gelder Robinson Ltd, 18–21 Jermyn Street, London SW1Y 6HP (☎ 0171 287 0077, fax 0171 287 1940)

GORDON, Ian; s of James Donald Gordon, of Montrose, Angus, and Winifred, *née* Thomson (d 1985); *b* 15 Aug 1957; *Educ* Biggar HS, Univ of Edinburgh (LLB); *m* 22 July 1988, (Mary) Angela Joan, da of Donald Macdonald, of Isle of Lewis; 1 s (James Alexander Donald b 22 April 1992), 1 da (Juliet Emily Katherine b 1 August 1994); *Career* McGrigor Donald (formerly Moncrieff Warren Paterson & Co Slrs Glasgow): apprentice 1979–81, slr 1981, ptnr 1983–; memb: Law Soc of Scotland 1981, Assoc of Pension Lawyers 1986 (memb Ctee and former chm Scottish Gp); NP 1981; *Recreations* getting out and about; *Style*— Ian Gordon, Esq; ✉ 25 Westbourne Gardens, Glasgow; Pacific House, 70 Wellington St, Glasgow G2 6SB (☎ 0141 248 6677, fax 0141 221 1390, telex 778744 MGDGLWG)

GORDON, Ian; OBE (1991), JP (Newcastle upon Tyne 1981); s of William Gordon (d 1984), and Elizabeth, *née* Brooks, of Carlisle; *b* 21 March 1939; *Educ* Carlisle GS; *m* 8 Sept 1962, Kathleen Verna, da of Ernest Francis Martin; 2 s (James Iain b 26 April 1968, Craig Martin b 23 Sept 1969), 1 da (Lindsay Kathryn b 6 Oct 1965); *Career* articled clerk N T O Reilly & Partners Carlisle 1956–61, qualified 1962; ptnr: Telfer & Co (formerly S W Telfer) 1963–70 (audit sr then mangr 1962–63), Winn & Co Newcastle (following merger) 1970–73, Tansley Witt & Co Newcastle 1973–80; sr ptnr Binder Hamlyn (following merger) 1980–96 (memb Nat Partnership Ctee 1980–89); North Tyneside MBC: cncllr (Cullercoats Ward) 1976–96, gp spokesman on finance 1976–80, ldr Cons Gp 1982–96 (dep ldr 1980–82); fndr memb North of Eng Assembly of Local Authorities 1985–90 and 1991–96 (ldr Cons Oppn Gp 1986–90 and 1991–96, Parly candidate (C) Newcastle North 1992, chm Tynemouth & Whitley Bay Cons Assoc Exec Ctee 1988–90 (pres 1985–88, dep chm 1995–); memb: N Area Exec Ctee (Cons) 1988–, Exec Ctee Nat Union 1989–90; vice chm Area Local Govt Ctee 1988–91 (memb 1982–, chm 1991–), memb Nat Local Govt Ctee, fndr and chm N Tyneside Political Ctee 1986–96; N Soc of Chartered Accountants: memb Exec Ctee 1971–80, chm Educ Training and Recruitment Sub Ctee, fndr memb & chm Fin Advice Scheme; memb: Juvenile Panel Newcastle upon Tyne Cmmn of the Peace, Magistrates' Courts Ctee 1991–, Lord Chllr's Advsy Ctee 1995–, Northumbria Police Authy 1995–96; fndr memb Northern Development Company, dir Cons Local Authy 1986–96; dir: Tyne and Wear Development Co Ltd 1985–90 and 1995–96, Signpost Europe Ltd 1989–94, Tyne & Wear Devpt Corp 1989–, North Tyneside City Challenge Partnership Ltd 1993–, Whitley Bay Playhouse Ltd 1996–; tstee Netherton Park Sch; fndr tstee: Cullercoats Educn Tst, Cedarwood Tst; govr: Preston Grange Primary Sch (chm of govrs), John Spence Community HS, N Tyneside Coll; former govr: Cullercoats Primary Sch, West Moor Middle Sch, Monkhouse Primary Sch; churchwarden St Hilda's Church Marden and Preston Grange 1984–88, lay vice chm Parish Church Cncl, memb Deanery Synod; FCA (ACA 1962); *Recreations* charity work, gardening, DIY; *Style*— Ian Gordon, Esq, OBE; ✉ 6 Beach Way, Beach Road, North Shields, Tyne & Wear NE30 3ED (☎ 0191 257 6879)

GORDON, James Stuart; CBE (1984); s of James Edward Gordon (d 1975), of Glasgow, and Elsie, *née* Riach (d 1984); *b* 17 May 1936; *Educ* St Aloysius' Coll, Univ of Glasgow (MA, winner Observer Mace and Best Individual Speaker 1957, pres of the Union 1958–59); *m* 1971, Margaret Anne, da of Andrew Kirkwood Stevenson (d 1968), of Glasgow; 2 s (Michael Stevenson b 1974, Christopher James b 1976), 1 da (Sarah Jane b 1972); *Career* political ed STV 1965–73; Radio Clyde: md 1973–96, chm Scottish Radio Holdings plc (parent co) 1996– (chief-exec 1991–96); chm Commercial Radio Companies Assoc; memb BP Scottish Advsy Bd, dir: Clydeport plc, Johnston Press plc, The AIM Trust plc; chm Scottish Exhibition Centre 1983–89; memb: Scottish Devpt Agency 1981–90, Ct Univ of Glasgow 1984–, Ctee of Inquiry into Teachers' Pay and Conditions 1986; DLitt Glasgow Caledonian Univ; *Recreations* walking, skiing, genealogy, golf; *Clubs* Caledonian, New (Edinburgh), Prestwick Golf, Buchanan Castle Golf; *Style*— James S Gordon, Esq, CBE; ✉ Deil's Craig, Strathblane, Glasgow G63 9ET (☎ 01360 770604); Scottish Radio Holdings plc, Clydebank Business Park, Clydebank, Glasgow G81 2RX (☎ 0141 306 2202, fax 0141 306 2322, telex 779537)

GORDON, John Edwin; s of Dennis Lionel Shute (d 1940); *b* 14 Dec 1939; *Educ* Tonbridge Sch, Queens' Coll Cambridge; *m* 1, 1968 (m dis 1994), Monica Anne, *née* Law; 1 s, 2 da; m 2, 1994, Fay Vere Harvey Hillier; *Career* dir: Robert Fleming & Co 1974–77, Laing & Cruickshank (stockbrokers) 1978–82, Jackson Exploration Inc 1982–85; head of corporate fin: Capel-Cure Myers 1985–89, Beeson Gregory 1989–96; dir: British Waterways Bd 1987–, Universal Ceramic Materials plc 1996–, Alizyme plc 1996–, Lavendor plc 1996–; FCA; *Recreations* fishing; *Clubs* Boodle's, Flyfisher's, Hawks', Leander; *Style*— John Gordon, Esq; ✉ Great Jenkins, Jenkins Lane, Bishop's Stortford, Herts CM22 7QL (☎ 01279 656686, fax 01279 655702)

GORDON, John Keith; s of Prof James Edward Gordon, and Theodora Mary Camilla, *née* Sinker; *b* 6 July 1940; *Educ* Marlborough, Trinity Coll Cambridge (MA), Yale Univ (Henry fell), LSE; *m* 14 Aug 1965, Elizabeth, da of Maj A J Shanks (d 1962); 2 s (Timothy Alan b 1971, Alexander Keith b 1973); *Career* Dip serv; entered FCO 1966, Budapest 1968–70, seconded to Civil Serv Coll 1970–72, FCO 1972–73, UK Mission Geneva

1973–74, head of Chancery and consul Yaoundé 1975–77 (concurrently Chargé d'Affaires Gabon and Central African Repub), FCO 1977–80, cultural attaché Moscow 1980–81, Office of UK Rep to EC Brussels 1982–83, UK Perm Del to UNESCO Paris 1983–85, head Nuclear Energy Dept FCO 1986–88, left FCO 1990; dep and policy dir Global Environment Res Centre 1990–94; independent conslt and analyst 1994–; prospective Parly candidate (Lib Dem) Daventry 1996; convenor St James's Alliance; conslt ed The Commonwealth Ministers Reference Book; memb: UNED-UK Exec Ctee, Friends of UNESCO Exec Ctee, Advsy Bd Int Security Info Serv; *Books* Institutions and Sustainable Development: Meeting the Challenge (with Caroline Fraser, 1991), 20/20 Vision: Britain, Germany and a New Environmental Agenda (with Tom Bigg, 1993), Canadian Round Tables (1994); author of other contributions to books, symposia and periodicals; *Recreations* theatre, jogging, sailing; *Clubs* RSA; *Style*— John Gordon, Esq; ✉ 68 Hornsey Lane, London N6 5LU

GORDON, John William; s of Norman Gordon (d 1981), and Margaret Elizabeth, *née* Reveley (d 1979); *b* 19 Nov 1925; *Educ* Wisbech GS; *m* 9 Jan 1954, Sylvia Ellen, da of Hubert Leslie Young; 1 s (Robert b 28 March 1965), 1 da (Sally b 30 Aug 1961); *Career* served RN 1943–46; journalist 1946–84 (Wisbech Advertiser, Bury Free Press, Western Evening Herald, Eastern Daily Press); author; memb Soc of Authors; *Books* The Giant under the Snow (1968), The House on the Brink (1970), The Ghost on the Hill (1976), The Waterfall Box (1978), The Spitfire Grave (1978), The Edge of the World (1983), Catch Your Death (1984), The Quelling Eye (1986), The Grasshopper (1986), Ride the Wind (1989), Secret Corridor (1990), Blood Brothers (1991), Ordinary Seaman (autobiog, 1992), The Burning Baby (1992), Gilray's Ghost (1995); *Recreations* reading, walking; *Style*— John Gordon, Esq; ✉ 99 George Borrow Rd, Norwich, Norfolk NR4 7HU (☎ 01603 452065); c/o A P Watt Ltd, 20 John St, London WC1N 2DR (☎ 0171 405 6774, fax 0171 831 2154)

GORDON, (George) Michael Winston; s of Winston Gordon, of Clonallon Rd, Warrenpoint, NI, and Marjorie Georgina Gordon; *b* 8 May 1937; *Educ* Queen's Univ Belfast (BSc, MSc), Univ of NSW (MEngSc); *m* 11 Aug 1966, Narelle Helen, da of Flt Lt Kenneth Charles Nicholl, of Sydney, NSW, Aust; 3 s (Matthew b 9 Sept 1967, Nicholas b 24 May 1969, Benjamin b 8 Feb 1976); *Career* graduate trainee Metropolitan Vickers 1958–60; design engr: Bristol Aircraft Co 1961–62, Amalgamated Wireless Australasia 1962–67; conslt: PA Management Consultants Aust, Singapore, Malaysia and NI 1967–76, Booz Allen and Hamilton Algeria 1976–77; dir: NI Devpt Agency 1977–80, American Monitor 1980–82, BIS London 1982–93 (chief operating offr); md LINK Training 1993–; dir: CRT plc 1994–, Murogen plc 1995–; MIEE (NY); *Style*— Michael Gordon, Esq; ✉ Kingfisher Cottage, Platt's Lane, Tattenhall, Cheshire CH3 9NT (☎ 01829 770087); Shell Cottage, 3 Collingwood Street, Manly, Australia; The LINK Organisation, Eastham Hall, 1 Eastham Village Road, Eastham, Wirral L62 0AF (☎ 0151 327 8080)

GORDON, Mildred; MP (Lab) Bow and Poplar (majority 8,404); da of late Judah Fellerman, and late Dora, *née* Cohen; *b* 24 Aug 1923; *Educ* Raines Fndn Sch, Pitmans Coll, Forest Teacher Trg Coll (Teaching Cert); *m* 1, 1948, Sam Gordon (decd); 1 s (David Ian); m 2, 1985, Nils Kaare Dahl; *Career* sec 1940–45, teacher LCC 1945–48, PA to Sec USA Plastering Industry Welfare Tst Fund 1948–52, teacher LCC (Barnet and Brent) 1952–85, MP (Lab) Bow and Poplar 1987–; memb Select Ctee on Educn 1991–; Gtr London Lab Pty: memb Exec 1983–86, jt chair Policy Ctee 1985–86; chair All Pty Parly Child Support Act Monitoring Gp, vice chair PLP Educn Ctee and Social Servs Ctee 1990–92; former advsr on older women GLC Women's Ctee; treas: Br Caribbean Gp, Br Estonian Gp, Older Women's Health Gp; memb: NUT, GMB, Co-operative Pty; *Recreations* reading, swimming, designing costume jewellery; *Style*— Ms Mildred Gordon, MP; ✉ House of Commons, London SW1A 0AA (☎ 0171 219 4125, fax 0171 219 2495)

GORDON, Prof Peter; s of Louis Gordon (d 1969), and Anne, *née* Schultz (d 1941); *b* 4 Nov 1927; *Educ* Univ of Birmingham (DipEd), LSE (BSc, MSc), Univ of London Inst of Educn (PhD); *m* 30 March 1958, Tessa Joan, da of Bernard Leton, of Aylmer Lodge, 3 Aylmer Drive, Stanmore, Middlesex; 1 s (David Nicholas b 12 April 1965), 1 da (Pauline Amanda b 24 June 1961); *Career* RAF in England and India 1945–48; teacher primary and secdy schs 1951–65, HM inspr of schs 1965–73; Univ of London Inst of Educn: lectr 1973–76, reader 1976–82, prof of history of educn 1982–93; FRHistS 1982, FSA 1991; *Books* The Victorian School Manager (1974), The Cabinet Journal of Dudley Ryder, Viscount Sandon (with Christopher Howard, 1974), Curriculum Change in the 19th and 20th Centuries (with Denis Lawton, 1978), Games and Simulations in Action (with Alec Davidson, 1978), Theory and Practice of Curriculum Studies (1978), Philosophers as Educational Reformers (with John White, 1979), Selection for Secondary Education (1980), The Study of Education: Inaugural Lectures (1980, 1988, 1995), The Red Earl: The Papers of the Fifth Earl Spencer of Althorp 1835–1910 (1981, 1986), The Study of the Curriculum (ed 1981), A Guide to English Educational Terms (with Denis Lawton, 1984), HMI (with Denis Lawton, 1987), A Dictionary of Educationists (with R Aldrich, 1989), History of Education: The Making of a Discipline (with R Szreter, 1989), Education and Policy in England in the Twentieth Century (ed 1991), Teaching the Humanities (ed 1991), The Wakes of Northamptonshire (1992), Dictionary of Education (with Denis Lawton, 1993), International Yearbook of History Education (jt ed, 1995), A Guide to Educational Research (ed, 1996); *Recreations* music, architecture; *Style*— Prof Peter Gordon, FSA; ✉ Birtsmorton, 58 Waxwell Lane, Pinner, Middx HA5 3EN (☎ 0181 868 7110); University of London Institute of Education, 20 Bedford Way, London WC1H 0AL (☎ 0171 580 1122)

GORDON, Peter David; s of Sydney Gordon (d 1984), and Sarah Gordon, *née* Paskin (d 1982); *b* 25 March 1939; *Educ* Hendon County GS, Univ of Sheffield (LDS RCS), DGDP(UK); *m* 28 Sept (m dis 1990), Ruth, *née* Summers; 2 s (Keith Michael b 20 Aug 1969, Jonathan Andrew b 6 Aug 1971); *Career* dental surgn 1964–; house surgn Charles Clifford Dental Hosp Sheffield 1964, clinical lectr Middlesex Hosp London 1985– (pt/t dental surgn to Nursing Staff 1969–85), private gen practitioner 1970–; hon clinical conslt to: 3M 1977–79, Bayer UK 1981–; dental advsr BDA 1991–; reg lectr in dental photography to postgrads; guest lectr: Asian Pacific Dental Congress Delhi 1987, Zoroastrian Dental Soc Bombay; lecture tour Bangkok, Kuala Lumpur, Singapore, Hong Kong 1988; memb: BDA, RSM; *Books* Dental Photography (with P Wander, 1987); *Recreations* theatre, music, bridge, swimming; *Clubs* RAC; *Style*— Peter Gordon, Esq; ✉ 12 Upper Wimpole Street, London W1M 7TD (☎ 0171 935 5454)

GORDON, Richard John Francis; QC (1994); s of John Bernard Basil Gordon, of London, and Winifred Josephine, *née* Keenan; *b* 26 Nov 1948; *Educ* St Benedicts Sch, Christ Church Oxford (MA), UCL (LLM); *m* 13 Sept 1975, Jane Belinda, da of Anthony George Lucey, of Welburn, Yorks; 2 s (Edmund John Anthony b 17 June 1982, Adam Richard Cosby b 25 Oct 1985); *Career* called to the Bar Middle Temple 1972; ed Crown Office Digest 1988–, broadcasts and articles on admin law in legal periodicals and other pubns; Freeman City of London; FRGS, ACIArb; *Books* The Law Relating to Mobile Homes and Caravans (second edn, 1985), Judicial Review Law and Procedure (1985); *Recreations* modern fiction, theatre, cricket; *Style*— Richard Gordon, Esq, QC; ✉ 39 Essex Street, London WC2R 3AT (☎ 0171 583 1111, fax 0171 353 3978)

GORDON, Sir Robert James; 10 Bt (NS 1706), of Afton and Earlston, Kirkcudbrightshire, probably next in remainder to the Viscountcy of Kenmure and Lordship of Lochinvar (dormant since 1872); s of Sir John Charles Gordon, 9 Bt (d 1982), and Marion, *née* Wright (d 1973); *b* 17 Aug 1932; *m* 1976, Helen Julia Weston, da of late John Weston Perry, of Cammeray, NSW; *Heir* none; *Style*— Sir Robert Gordon, Bt; ✉ Earlstoun, Guyra, NSW 2365, Australia

GORDON, Prof Robert Patterson; s of Robert Gordon (d 1976), and Eveline, *née* Shilliday; *b* 9 Nov 1945; *Educ* Methodist Coll Belfast, St Catharine's Coll Cambridge (Jarrett exhibitioner and scholar, John Stewart of Rannoch Hebrew scholar, sr scholar, Bender prize, Tyrwhitt's Hebrew scholar, Mason prize, MA, PhD); *m* 1970, Helen Ruth, *née* Lyttle; 2 s ((Christopher) Graham b 17 Nov 1975, Alasdair Robert b 3 Oct 1985), 1 da ((Nicola) Claire b 19 Sept 1977); *Career* lectr in Hebrew and Semitic languages Univ of Glasgow 1970–79 (asst lectr Hebrew and Old Testament 1969–70), regius prof of Hebrew Univ of Cambridge 1995– (lectr in Old Testament 1979–95); fell: St Edmund's Coll Cambridge 1985–89, St Catharine's Coll Cambridge 1995–; memb: Soc for Old Testament Study, Br Assoc of Jewish Studies; *Books* 1 and 2 Samuel (1984), 1 and 2 Samuel. A Commentary (1986), The Targum of the Minor Prophets (with K J Cathcart, 1989), Studies in the Targum to the Twelve Prophets (1994), Wisdom in Ancient Israel (jt ed, 1995), The Place is too Small for us (ed, 1995); *Recreations* jogging, local history (N Ireland); *Style*— Prof Robert Gordon; ✉ Faculty of Oriental Studies, University of Cambridge, Sidgwick Avenue, Cambridge, Cambs CB3 9DA (☎ 01223 335118, fax 01223 335110)

GORDON, Robert Smith Benzie; s of William Gladstone Gordon (d 1980), and Helen Watt, *née* Benzie; *b* 7 Nov 1950; *Educ* The Gordon Schs Huntly, Univ of Aberdeen (MA); *m* 2 July 1976, Joyce Ruth, da of Stephen Cordiner; 2 da (Rachel Joyce b 19 Oct 1978, Jennifer Claire b 18 March 1984), 2 s ((Robert Stephen) Niall b 20 March 1980, David William James b 20 May 1989); *Career* Scottish Office: admin trainee 1973, various trg appointments, princ Scottish Devpt Dept 1979–85, asst sec and private sec to Sec of State for Scotland 1985–87, asst sec Dept of Agric and Fisheries 1987–90, asst sec mgmnt and orgn and industrial relations 1990–91, dir of admin servs 1991–, under sec 1993–; Warden Incorporation of Goldsmiths City of Edinburgh; *Style*— Robert Gordon, Esq; ✉ The Scottish Office, Victoria Quay, Edinburgh EH6 6QQ (☎ 0131 244 7937, fax 0131 244 0380)

GORDON, Rt Rev (Archibald) Ronald McDonald; s of Sir Archibald McDonald Gordon, CMG (d 1974), and Dorothy Katharine (d 1959), da of Rev Charles Silvester Horne, MP, by his w Hon Katharine Maria, elder da of 1 Baron Cozens-Hardy; *b* 19 March 1927; *Educ* Rugby, Balliol Coll Oxford, Cuddesdon Theol Coll; *Career* deacon 1952, priest 1953, curate of Stepney 1952–55, chaplain Cuddesdon Coll 1955–59, vicar of St Peter Birmingham 1959–67, residentiary canon Birmingham Cathedral 1967–71, vicar of Univ Church of St Mary the Virgin with St Cross and St Peter in the East Oxford 1971–75, bishop of Portsmouth 1975–84, took seat in House of Lords 1981 (relinquished 1984), sr memb Archbishop of Canterbury's Staff 1984–91, bishop to HM Forces 1985–90, res canon and sub-dean Christ Church Oxford 1991–96; memb Church Assembly and Gen Synod and proctor in convocation 1965–71, chm ACCM 1976–83, select preacher Univ of Oxford 1985, 1993 and 1997; memb: Cncl St George's House Windsor Castle 1985–91, Court of Ecclesiastical Causes Reserved 1991–, Advsy Bd for Redundant Churches 1991–, Archbishops' Cmmn on Cathedrals 1992–94, Governing Body St Mary's Sch Wantage 1993–; *Style*— The Rt Rev Ronald Gordon; ✉ 16 East St Helen Street, Abingdon, Oxon OX14 5EA (☎ 01235 526956)

GORDON, Prof Siamon; s of Jonah Gordon (d 1955), of S Africa, and Liebe, *née* Solsky (d 1988); *b* 29 April 1938; *Educ* SACS Cape Town, Univ of Cape Town (MB, ChB), Rockefeller Univ (PhD); *m* April 1963, Lyndall Felicity, da of Harry Getz; 2 da (Anna b 9 Aug 1965, Olivia Jane b 26 Nov 1978); *Career* registrar Dept of Pathology UCT Med Sch 1963–64 (intern Dept of Med and Surgery 1962–63), res asst Wright-Fleming Inst of Microbiology St Mary's Hosp Med Sch 1964–65, asst prof and assoc physician Lab of Cellular Physiology and Immunology Rockefeller Univ 1971–76 (res assoc and asst physician Lab of Human Genetics 1965–66); Univ of Oxford: visiting scientist Dept of Biochemistry 1974–75, fell Exeter Coll 1976–, Newton-Abraham lectr in pathology 1976–91, reader in experimental pathology Sir William Dunn Sch of Pathology 1976–89, prof of cellular pathology 1989–91, Glaxo prof of cellular pathology 1991–; scholar Leukemia Soc of America Inc 1973–76 (special fell 1971), adjunct assoc prof Rockefeller Univ 1976–, Br Cncl visiting prof and lectr Hebrew Univ 1994; Friederich Sasse award in immunology 1990; memb: Lister Scientific Advsy Ctee 1987–92, Br Soc for Immunology, Br Soc for Cell Biology, American Soc for Cell Biology, Br Soc for Cancer Res, American Reticulo-endothelial Soc; memb Editorial Bd: Jl of Cell Science 1982–90, American Jl of Respiratory Cell and Molecular Biology 1989–91, Progress in Leukocyte Biology 1987–, Jl of Experimental Medicine 1993–; *Books* Macrophage Biology and Activation, Current Topics in Microbiology and Immunology (ed, 1992), Legacy of Cell Fusion (ed, 1994); author of articles in various scientific jls; *Recreations* reading, music, history; *Style*— Prof Siamon Gordon; ✉ Sir William Dunn School of Pathology, University of Oxford, South Parks Road, Oxford OX1 3RE (☎ 01865 275534, fax 01865 275501)

GORDON, Sir Sidney; kt (1972), CBE (1968, OBE 1965), JP (Hong Kong 1961); s of late P S Gordon, and Angusina Gordon; *b* 20 Aug 1917; *Educ* Hyndland Sch Glasgow, Univ of Glasgow; *m* 1950, Olive (d 1992), da of late T A Eldon; 2 da (Fiona, Carolyn); *Career* CA; sr ptnr Lowe Bingham & Matthews (chartered accountants) Hong Kong 1956–70, MLC Hong Kong 1962–66, MEC 1965–80, dir Sir Elly Kadoorie & Sons Ltd 1995– (chm 1970–94), chm China Light & Power Co 1992–; chm Univ and Poly Grants Ctee 1974–76, chm Standing Cmmn on Civil Service Salaries and Conditions of Service 1988–; hon steward Royal Hong Kong Jockey Club; Hon LLD Chinese Univ of Hong Kong 1970; *Recreations* golf, racing; *Clubs* Oriental, Hong Kong, Royal Hong Kong Jockey (hon steward), Royal Hong Kong Golf (former pres and hon life memb); *Style*— Sir Sidney Gordon, CBE, JP; ✉ 7 Headland Rd, Repulse Bay, Hong Kong (☎ 00 852 28122577)

GORDON, Tanya Joan (Mrs Tanya Sarne); da of Jean-Claude Gordon, of Bayswater, and Daphne Thomas, *née* Tucar (d 1976); *b* 15 Jan 1945; *Educ* Godolphin & Latymer Sch, Univ of Sussex (BA); *m* 1969 (m dis), Michael Sarne, *qv*, s of Alfred Schener; 1 s (William Gordon b 30 May 1972), 1 da (Claudia Aviva b 17 Jan 1970); *Career* model 1963–64, asst to Cultural Attaché Persian Embassy 1966–67, asst to Lit Agent Kramers 1967–68, freelance reader for Universal Film Studios 1967–68, supply teacher of history for GLC (mainly at St Martin's-in-the-Field) 1968–69, spent two years in Brazil helping husband make a film (Intimidade), working as a tour guide for Brazil Safaris and modelling 1973–75, sales dir Entrepas Ltd 1976–78, fndr Miz (fashion business) 1978–83, fndr Ghost 1984–; fndr memb Fashion Indust Action Gp, memb Br Fashion Cncl; *Recreations* cooking, tennis, acquiring property and the obvious; *Clubs* Groucho, Campden Hill Tennis; *Style*— Ms Tanya Gordon; ✉ Ghost Ltd, The Chapel, 263 Kensal Rd, London W10 5DB (☎ 0181 960 3121, fax 0181 960 8374)

GORDON, William John (Bill); s of Sidney Frank Gordon (d 1982), and Grace, *née* Louie; *b* 24 April 1939; *Educ* King Edward VI Sch Birmingham; *m* 17 Oct 1963, Patricia, da of Thomas Rollason; 2 s (Bruce b 1967, Lewis b 1971); *Career* Barclays Bank plc: joined 1955, asst gen mangr Barclaycard 1980–83, regnl gen mangr Central Region 1983–87, dir UK corporate servs 1987–90, gp personnel dir 1990–92, md UK banking servs 1992–, main bd dir Barclays plc and Barclays Bank plc 1995–; FCIB 1981 (ACIB 1959); *Recreations* bridge, golf, chess, music; *Style*— Bill Gordon, Esq; ✉ Barclays plc, 54 Lombard Street, London EC3P 3AH (☎ 0171 699 5000)

GORDON, Prof William Morrison; s of William Gordon (d 1967), of Inverurie, and Helen Morrison (d 1977); *b* 3 March 1933; *Educ* Inverurie Acad, Robert Gordon's Coll, Univ of Aberdeen (MA, LLB, PhD); *m* 1 June 1957, Isabella Evelyn Melitta, da of George Duguid Robertson (d 1976), of Glassford, Strathaven; 2 s (Malcolm b 1958, Mark b 1965), 2 da (Melitta b 1961, Elise b 1965); *Career* Nat Serv RN 1955–57; asst in jurisprudence Univ of Aberdeen 1957–60; Univ of Glasgow: lectr in civil law 1960–65, sr lectr in law 1965–69, Douglas prof of civil law 1969–, dean Faculty of Law 1974–76, senate assessor Univ Ct 1983–88; literary dir The Stair Soc 1984–; session clerk Jordanhill Parish Church 1989– (elder 1967–); memb Law Soc of Scotland 1956; FRSE 1995; *Books* Studies in Transfer of Property by Tradition (1970), Scottish Land Law (1989), Miscellany III (Stair Society, ed, 1992), European Legal History (jtly, 2 edn 1994); *Recreations* golf; *Style—* Prof William M Gordon, FRSE; ✉ School of Law, Stair Building, Glasgow University, Glasgow G12 8QQ (☎ 0141 339 8855 ext 5387, fax 0141 330 4900, e-mail W.Gordon@law.gla.ac.uk)

GORDON CUMMING, Alexander Penrose (Alastair); s and h of Sir William Gordon Gordon Cumming, 6 Bt, *qv*; *b* 15 April 1954; *m* 20 April 1991, Louisa, er da of Edward Geoffrey Clifton-Brown, of Glastonbury, Somerset; 1 s (William b 4 April 1993), 1 da (Sophie b 2 May 1995); *Style—* Alastair Gordon Cumming, Esq

GORDON CUMMING, Sir William Gordon; 6 Bt (UK 1804), of Altyre, Forres; s of Maj Sir Alexander Penrose Gordon Cumming, 5 Bt, MC (d 1939); *b* 19 June 1928; *Educ* Eton; *m* 1, 1953 (m dis 1972), Elisabeth, da of Maj-Gen Sir (William) Robert Norris Hinde, KBE, CB, DSO (d 1981); 1 s (Alexander Penrose b 1954), 3 da (Sarah (Mrs Dominic W Langlands Pearse) b 1955, Charlotte (Mrs Michael Edwards) b 1958, Henrietta (Mrs Donald Statham) b 1959); m 2, 1972 (m dis 1976), Lady Pauline Anne, sis of 13 Earl of Seafield, and former w of James Henry Harcourt Illingworth; m 3, 1989, Sheila Bates; *Heir* s, Alexander Penrose (Alastair) Gordon Cumming, *qv*; *Career* late Lt Royal Scots Greys; *Style—* Sir William Gordon Cumming, Bt

GORDON-DUFF-PENNINGTON, Patrick Thomas; OBE (1992), DL (Cumbria 1993); s of George Edward Gordon-Duff (d 1966), and Rosemary Estelle, *née* Craven; *b* 12 Jan 1930; *Educ* Eton, Trinity Coll Oxford (MA); *m* 1955, Phyllida Pennington, da of Sir William Pennington-Ramsden; 4 da; *Career* served Queen's Own Cameron Highlanders 1951–53; shepherd: Perthshire and Invernesshire 1953–55, Muncaster 1955–57; student land agent Sandringham 1957–59; farmer: Dumfriesshire 1959–82, Muncaster 1969–82; Scottish NFU: memb Cncl 1972–82, pres Dumfries and Galloway Area 1976–78, convenor Hill Farming 1976–82, vice-convenor Livestock Ctee 1976–80, hon pres 1981–83; county chm Cumbria NFU 1986, convenor Scottish Land Owners' Fedn 1988–91, md family estate Invernesshire 1990–; memb Lake District Special Planning Bd 1987–93, chm: Scottish Ctee Assoc of Electricity Producers 1991–, Park Mgmnt Ctee Lake District Special Planning Bd 1989–93, Red Deer Cmmn 1993–; vice pres Field Studies Cncl; *Style—* Patrick Gordon-Duff-Pennington, Esq, OBE, DL; ✉ Red Deer Commission, Knowsley, 82 Fairfield Road, Inverness IV3 5LH (☎ 01463 231751); Muncaster Castle, Ravenglass, Cumbria CA18 1RQ (☎ 01229 717203)

GORDON JONES, Air Marshal Sir Edward; KCB (1967, CB 1960), CBE (1956, OBE 1945), DSO (1941), DFC (1941); s of Lt-Col Dr Albert Jones, DSO, MC, of Dulverton House, Widnes; *b* 31 Aug 1914; *Educ* Wade Deacon Sch, Univ of Liverpool; *m* 1938, Margery Thurston Hatfield; 2 s; *Career* cmmnd RAF 1935, WWII (despatches), Air Vice-Marshal 1961, AOC RAF Germany 1961–63, AOC Malta and dep C-in-C (Air) Allied Forces Mediterranean 1965–66, Air Marshal 1966, AOC-in-C NEAF and admin Sovereign Base Areas 1966–69, Cdr Br Forces Near East 1967–69, ret; Greek DFC 1941, Cdr Order of Orange Nassau 1945; *Recreations* music, opera, photography, sport; *Clubs* RAF; *Style—* Air Marshal Sir Edward Gordon Jones, KCB, CBE, DSO, DFC; ✉ 20 Marlborough Court, Grange Road, Cambridge CB3 9BQ (☎ 01223 363029)

GORDON LENNOX, Maj-Gen Bernard Charles; CB (1986), MBE (1968); s of Lt-Gen Sir George Gordon Lennox (d 1988), and Nancy Brenda, *née* Darell (d 1993); *b* 19 Sept 1932; *Educ* Eton, Sandhurst; *m* 1958, Sally-Rose, da of John Weston Warner (d 1981); 3 s (Edward b 1961, Angus b 1964, Charles b 1970); *Career* cmd 1 Bn Grenadier Gds 1974–75, GSO 1 RAF Staff Coll 1976–77, Brig 1977, Cdr Task Force H, Dep Cdr and COS SE Dist UKLF 1981–83, Maj-Gen 1982, Br Cmdt and GOC Br Sector Berlin 1983–85, sr Army memb RCDS 1986–87, Lt-Col Grenadier Gds 1989–95; page of honour to HM The King 1946–49; dir Regions Motor Agents Assoc 1988–89; chm Guards' Polo Club 1993–; *Recreations* country sports, cricket, squash, music; *Clubs* Army and Navy, MCC; *Style—* Maj-Gen B C Gordon Lennox, CB, MBE; ✉ The Estate Office, Gordon Castle, Fochabers, Morayshire IV32 7PQ

GORDON LENNOX, Lord Nicholas Charles; KCMG (1986, CMG 1978), KCVO (1988, LVO 1957); yr son of 9 Duke of Richmond and (4 of) Gordon (d 1989), and Elizabeth Grace, *née* Hudson (d 1992); *b* 31 Jan 1931; *Educ* Eton, Worcester Coll Oxford; *m* 1958, Mary, o da of late Brig Hudleston Noel Hedworth Williamson, DSO, MC; 1 s, 3 da; *Career* late 2 Lt KRRC; entered HM Foreign Service 1954, ambass to Spain 1984–89; a govr of BBC 1990–; dir: Sotheby's, Foreign & Colonial Investment Trust; vice chm: MGM Assurance, Cañada Blanch Fndn (Spain); tstee Pallant House Gallery Tst Chichester; Hon Col 4 Royal Green Jackets (TA) 1990–95; Grand Cross Order of Isabel La Catolica (Spain); *Style—* The Lord Nicholas Gordon Lennox, KCMG, KCVO

GORDON OF LETTERFOURIE, George; s of Patrick Gordon Shee, 11 of Letterfourie (d 1938), and Louise Marie Caroline, *née* Van Dyck; descended from Sir James Gordon, 1 of Letterfourie, who cmd the Scots fleet 1513; officially recognised in the surname of Gordon of Letterfourie by the Lord Lyon 1949 (*see* Burke's Landed Gentry, 18 edn, vol III, 1972); *b* 14 Nov 1923; *Educ* Beaumont; *m* 23 April 1969, Joanna Mary, eldest da of Gerard Wilfrid Stanfield Bagshawe (d 1961), of Silwood Park Farm, Ascot, Berks; 3 s (Alexander b 1970, William b 1973, Oliver b 1975), 1 da (Emma b 1972); *Career* Irish Guards 1942–47, Lt 1943, Capt 1946, served Italy (Anzio) and NW Europe (wounded); *Style—* George Gordon of Letterfourie; ✉ Wester Pittendreich, Elgin, Morayshire IV30 3TF (☎ 01343 550464)

GORDON-SAKER, Andrew Stephen; s of Vincent Gordon-Saker, and Gwendoline Alice, *née* Remmers; *b* 4 Oct 1958; *Educ* Stonyhurst, UEA (LLB); *m* 28 Sept 1985, Liza Helen, *qv*, da of William James Marle; 1 s (Edward b 1991), 1 da (Francesca b 1989); *Career* called to the Bar Middle Temple 1981, in practice 1981–, dep taxing master of the Supreme Ct 1994–; memb Eastern Region Legal Aid Area Ctee 1995–; cncllr London Borough of Camden 1982–86; *Style—* Andrew Gordon-Saker, Esq; ✉ 4 King's Bench Walk, Temple, London EC4Y 7DL (☎ 0171 353 0478)

GORDON-SAKER, Liza Helen; da of William James Marle, of Chislehurst, Kent, and Doreen Maud, *née* Adams; *b* 30 Nov 1959; *Educ* Farrington's Sch Chislehurst, Univ of East Anglia (LLB); *m* 28 Sept 1985, Andrew Stephen Gordon-Saker, *qv*, s of Vincent Gordon-Saker, of Norwich; 1 s (Edward b 1991), 1 da (Francesca b 1989); *Career* called to the Bar Gray's Inn 1982; in practice 1983–; dir Bar Mutual Indemnity Fund Ltd 1988–; Freeman City of London 1984; *Recreations* golf; *Style—* Mrs Liza Gordon-Saker; ✉ Fenners Chambers, 3 Madingley Rd, Cambridge CB3 0EE (☎ 01223 68761)

GORDON-SAKER, Paul Declan; s of Vincent Gordon-Saker (d 1992), of Norwich, and Gwendoline Alice, *née* Remmers; *b* 6 Aug 1944; *Educ* Stonyhurst; *m* 4 Oct 1969, Victoria May, da of James Gordon Cresswell Wood; 1 s (Steven James b 20 Jan 1971), 1 da (Nicola Clare b 20 Feb 1972); *Career* head Litigation and Insolvency Dept Alsop Wilkinson 1988–96, head Corp Recovery and Insolvency Dibb Lupton Alsop 1996–; memb Law Soc 1970, memb Insolvency Lawyers Assoc 1990, MIPA 1991, MSPI 1992, memb American Bankruptcy Inst 1994; *Publications* Insolvency Procedure Notes (jtly with Michael Stubbs, 1987, revised edn 1991); *Recreations* theatre, opera, travel; *Clubs* Wig & Pen; *Style—* Paul Gordon-Saker, Esq; ✉ Dibb Lupton Alsop, 6 Dowgate Hill, London EC4R 2SS (☎ 0171 248 4141, fax 0171 623 8286)

GORDON SMITH, Prof Edward Colin (Ted); s of Gordon John Smith (d 1938), and Valentine Strange, *née* Waddington (d 1987); *b* 26 June 1938; *Educ* Oakham Sch, Epsom Coll, Exeter Coll Oxford (BA, BSc, BM BCh), Westminster Med Sch; *m* 1967, Moira Bernadette, da of Joseph Phelan; 2 s (Duncan Joseph b 1971, James Edward b 1973); *Career* house surgn then house physician Westminster Hosp 1963–64, SHO Nuffield Dept of Med Radcliffe Infirmary Oxford 1964–65, lectr in neurology Churchill Hosp Oxford 1965–67, registrar St James' Hosp Balham 1967, registrar in haematology RPMS 1968–70, MRC clinical training fell 1970–72, reader RPMS 1982–86 (sr lectr 1972–82), prof of haematology and hon conslt St George's Hosp Med Sch 1987–; res fell Metabolic Research Gp Oxford 1971; pres Euro Bone Marrow Transplant Gp 1980; ed Br Jl of Haematology 1983–86; memb: Br Soc of Haematology 1972– (pres 1994–95), Int Soc for Experimental Hematology 1984– (pres 1992), American Soc for Hematology 1987–, RSM 1980; FRCP 1978 (MRCP 1968), FRCPath 1987 (MRCPath 1985); *Recreations* golf, gardening, music; *Style—* Prof Ted Gordon Smith; ✉ Department of Cellular and Molecular Sciences, Division of Haematology, St George's Hospital Medical School, Tooting, London SW17 0RE (☎ 0181 725 3545, fax 0181 682 4217)

GORDON-SMITH, William Haydn; s of Cyril Smith, ISO (d 1993), and Joyce Muriel, *née* Davies; *b* 14 March 1944; *Educ* Richmond Hill Sch Sprotbrough, West End Co Sch Bentley, Doncaster Tech Coll; *Career* writer and local architectural historian; civil servant Ministry of Pensions & Nat Insurance 1962–89, proprietor The Lodge Gallery Cusworth Park Doncaster 1972–77, Clerk Parish Cncls of Norton and High Melton 1972–78, agent to Cusworth Estate and tstee Cusworth Church Lands 1971–; memb: Manorial Soc of GB, Doncaster Civic Trust; Lord of the Manors of Cusworth and Edlington in the former W Riding of Yorkshire, Arms granted by College of Arms London 1991; *Books* Cusworth Hall (1964), Sprotbrough Hall (1966), Askern Spa (1968), Sprotbrough Colliery (1968), Cusworth Hall and the Battie-Wrightson Family (1990), Cantley Hall (1992); series of fifty illustrated articles on the Country Houses of Doncaster (1964) for Doncaster Gazette and South Yorkshire Times; *Style—* W H Gordon-Smith, Esq; ✉ Church Cottage, Cusworth, Doncaster, South Yorkshire DN5 7TR (☎ 01302 782212, fax 01302 785343); Marine Court, St Leonards-on-Sea, E Sussex TN38 0BY

GORDON WALKER, Hon Alan Rudolf; er (twin) s of Baron Gordon-Walker, CH, PC (Life Peer, d 1980); *b* 1946; *Educ* Wellington Coll, ChCh Oxford (MA); *m* 1976, Louise Frances Amy, da of Gen Sir Charles Henry Pepys Harington, GCB, CBE, DSO, MC; 1 s (Thomas b 1978), 1 da (Emily b 1981); *Career* former md Pan MacMillan Ltd, currently md Cassells; *Clubs* MCC; *Style—* The Hon Alan Gordon Walker; ✉ Cassells, Wellington House, 125 The Strand, London WC2R 0BB (☎ 0171 420 5555)

GORE, Michael Balfour Gruberg; s of Dr Victor Gore (d 1985), of London, and Victoria, *née* Slavouski; *b* 25 Oct 1937; *Educ* Felsted, Peterhouse Cambridge (BA); *m* 11 April 1972, Mozella, da of Geoffrey Ransom; 2 s (Benjamin b 1974, Daniel b 1977), 1 da (Camilla (twin) b 1977); *Career* Kemp Chatteris & Co 1959–64, dir S G Warburg & Co Ltd 1969–95 (joined 1964); chm: S G Warburg & Co (Jersey) Ltd 1979–87, Rowe & Pitman Moneybroking Ltd 1986–91, S G Warburg Group Management Ltd 1986–93, S G Warburg Asia/Pacific Ltd 1993–95; vice chm S G Warburg Group plc (formerly Mercury International Group plc) 1991–95 (dir 1985–95, gp fin dir 1986–93); dep chm Potter Warburg Ltd Melbourne 1989–95; non-exec dir Zella Gallery 1991–, memb Cncl Friends of Peterhouse 1996–; FCA, FRSA; *Style—* Michael Gore, Esq; ✉ 19 Launceston Place, London W8 5RL (☎ 0171 938 1877, fax 0171 938 1183)

GORE, Michael Edward John; CVO (1994), CBE (1991); s of John Gore (d 1977), and Elsa Mary, *née* Dillon (d 1988); *b* 20 Sept 1935; *Educ* Xaverian Coll Brighton; *m* 19 May 1957, Monica, da of Caesar Shellish, MBE (d 1980); 3 da (Marina b 1958, Moira Jacqueline b 1960, Michelle Maria-Theresa b 1969); *Career* reporter Portsmouth Evening News 1952–55; Capt Army Gen List 1955–59; Dep Cmd Info Offr Air Miny Cyprus and Aden 1959–63; CRO (later FCO) 1963, served Jesselton 1963–66, FCO 1966–67, head of Chancery Seoul 1967–71, head of Chancery Montevideo 1971–74, dep high cmmr Banjul 1974–78, FCO 1978–81, consul gen Nairobi 1981–84, dep high cmmr Lilongwe 1984–87, HM ambass to Liberia 1988–90, FCO 1990–91, Br high cmmr Bahamas 1991–92, govr Cayman Is 1992–95, ret; wildlife photographer and author 1996–; memb Br Ornithologists' Union 1960–; tstee: The Tst for Oriental Ornithology; FRPS 1985; *Books* The Birds of Korea (with Pyong-Oh Won, 1971), Las Aves del Uruguay (with A R M Gepp, 1979), Birds of the Gambia (1981 and 1991), On Safari in Kenya: A Pictorial Guide to the National Parks and Reserves (1984); author of papers on birds and conservation; wildlife photographs published in books and magazines; *Recreations* ornithology, wildlife photography, fishing; *Clubs* Army and Navy; *Style—* Michael Gore, Esq, CVO, CBE; ✉ 5 St Mary's Close, Fetcham, Surrey

GORE, Sir Nigel Hugh St George; 14 Bt (I 1622), of Magherabegg, Co Donegal; yr s of St George Richard Gore (d 1952), who was gn of 9 Bt; suc his n, Sir Richard Ralph St George Gore, 13 Bt (d 1993); *b* 23 Dec 1922; *m* 3 Sept 1952, Beth Allison (d 1976), da of R W Hooper; 1 da (Seonaid Beth b 1955); *Heir* cousin, Dundas Corbet Gore b 1921; *Style—* Sir Nigel Gore, Bt; ✉ Hillhaven, Preston Road, M/S 852, Hodgsonvale, Qld 4350, Australia

GORE, Paul Annesley; CMG (1964), CVO (1961); s of Charles Henry Gore, OBE (d 1941), s of Sir Francis Gore, KCB, whose f (yr bro of 4 Earl of Arran) m Lady Augusta Ponsonby, 2 da of 4 Earl of Bessborough; hp of 9 Earl of Arran, *qv*; *b* 28 Feb 1921; *Educ* Winchester, Ch Ch Oxford (MA); *m* 1946, Gillian Mary, da of Tom Allen-Stevens (d 1941); 2 s (and 1 s decd); *Career* Capt 16/5 Lancers (N Africa, Italy) 1941–46; Colonial Admin Serv 1948–65, dep govr The Gambia 1962–65; JP: Oxford 1972–74, Suffolk 1976–84; *Recreations* sailing (yacht Malachite); *Clubs* Cruising Assoc; *Style—* Paul Gore, Esq, CMG, CVO; ✉ 1 Burkitt Rd, Woodbridge, Suffolk

GORE, (Francis) St John Corbet; CBE; s of Francis William Baldock Gore (gs of Rev William Gore, who was uncle of Sir St George Ralph Gore, 9 Bt, and gn of Lt-Gen Sir Ralph Gore, 6 Bt, who was cr Earl of Ross (1772), Viscount Bellisle (1768) and Baron Gore of Manor Gore (1764), all in the peerage of Ireland. His Lordship was C-in-C Ireland 1788 and d 1802, when his peerage honours became extinct); *b* 8 April 1921; *Educ* Wellington, Courtauld Inst of Art; *m* 1, 1951 (m dis 1976), Priscilla Margaret, da of Cecil Harmsworth King; 1 s (William b 1956), 1 da (Catharine (Mrs Richard Gayner)); m 2, 1981, Lady Mary Sophia Strachey; *Career* late Capt Royal Northumberland Fusiliers, served WWII; Nat Tst: advsr on pictures 1956–86, historic bldgs sec 1973–81; memb Exec Ctee Nat Art Collections Fund 1963–96; tstee: Wallace Collection 1975–89, Nat Gallery 1986–93; FSA 1979; *Recreations* sight-seeing; *Clubs* Brooks's, Beefsteak; *Style—* St John Gore, Esq, CBE, FSA; ✉ Grove Farm, Stoke-by-Nayland, Colchester, Suffolk CO6 4SL (☎ 01206 337234)

GORE-ANDREWS, Russell William; *b* 18 Jan 1928; *Career* chm until 1996: More O'Ferrall Sales (UK) Ltd, More O'Ferrall Development (UK) Ltd, More O'Ferrall plc, More O'Ferrall International Advertising Ltd, More O'Ferrall Publicité Int SA, SAGA SA, Adshel Ltd, More O'Ferrall SE Asia Ltd; dir Outdoor Advertising Assoc of GB Ltd; MInstD; *Style—* Russell Gore-Andrews, Esq

GORE-BOOTH, HE the Hon Sir David Alwyn; KCMG (1997, CMG 1990); er (twin) s of Baron Gore-Booth, GCMG, KCVO (Life Peer, d 1984), and Patricia Mary, o da of late Montague Ellerton, of Yokohama, Japan; hp to kinsman, Sir Josslyn Gore-Booth, 9 Bt, *qv*; *b* 15 May 1943; *Educ* Eton, ChCh Oxford (MA); *m* 1, 1964 (m dis 1970), Jillian Sarah, da of James Wyatt Valpy, of Somerset West, S Africa; 1 s (Paul Wyatt Julian b 1968); m 2, 7 Oct 1977, Mrs Mary Elisabeth Janet Gambetta, o da of Sir David Francis Muirhead, KCMG, CVO; 1 step s (Riccardo Gambetta b 1970); *Career* HM Dip Serv 1964–; third sec: FCO 1964, ME Centre for Arabic Studies 1964, Baghdad 1966; third then second sec Lusaka 1967; second sec: FCO 1969, Tripoli 1969; second later first sec FCO 1971, first sec UK permanent representation to European Communities Brussels 1974, asst head of Fin Relations Dept FCO 1978, cnsllr (Commercial) Jeddah 1980–83, cnsllr and head of chancery UK mission to UN NY 1983–86, head of policy planning staff FCO 1987–88, asst under sec (Middle East) 1989–92, ambass to Saudi Arabia 1993–96, high cmmr to Republic of India 1996–; *Recreations* tennis, current affairs, Island of Hydra (Greece); *Clubs* MCC, Travellers', Hurlingham; *Style*— HE the Hon Sir David Gore-Booth, KCMG; ✉ British High Commission, Chanakyapuri, New Delhi 1100–21, Republic of India (☎ 00 91 11 687 2161, fax 00 91 11 687 2882)

GORE-BOOTH, Sir Josslyn Henry Robert; 9 Bt (I 1760), of Artarman, Sligo; o s of Sir Angus Josslyn Gore-Booth, 8 Bt (d 1996), and Hon Rosemary Myra, *née* Vane, da of 10 Baron Barnard, CMG, OBE, MC, TD; *b* 5 Oct 1950; *Educ* Eton, Balliol Coll Oxford (BA), INSEAD (MBA); *m* 1980, Jane Mary, da of Hon Sir (James) Roualeyn (Hovell-Thurlow-) Cumming-Bruce, *qv*; 2 da (Mary Georgina b 1985, Caroline Sarah b 1987); *Heir* kinsman, HE the Hon Sir David Alwyn Gore-Booth, KCMG, *qv*; *Career* dir Kiln Cotesworth Corporate Capital Fund plc 1993–; *Recreations* shooting, fishing, cooking; *Clubs* Brooks's, Kildare Street and Univ (Dublin); *Style*— Sir Josslyn Gore-Booth, Bt; ✉ Selaby Hall, Gainford, Darlington, Co Durham DL2 3HF (☎ 01325 730206, fax 01325 730993); Lissadell House, Ballinfull, Co Sligo (☎ and fax 0035371 63150)

GORE BROWNE, Anthony Giles Spencer; s of (John) Giles Charles Gore Browne (d 1980), of Manton, Oakham, Leics, and Pamela Helen, *née* Newton; *b* 20 April 1944; *Educ* Rannoch Sch Perthshire; *m* 1, 14 March 1970, Penelope Anne Courtenay, da of Prebendary C E Leighton Thomson, of Chelsea, London; 1 s (Edward b 1973), 1 da (Alexandra b 1975); m 2, 6 Jan 1992, (Sarah) Gay, da of F G Salway, of W Felton, Shropshire; 1 s (George b 8 July 1993); *Career* stockbroker 1964–; Sheppards & Co 1964–65, Sheppards & Chase 1965–73, ptnr R C Greig & Co Glasgow (London Office) 1973–82, dir of dealing Greig Middleton & Co Ltd 1986– (ptnr 1982–86), dir Riverside Racquets plc 1988–93; Liveryman Worshipful Co of Fishmongers 1965, Freeman City of London 1965; MSI; *Clubs* City of London, Riverside Racquets; *Style*— Anthony Gore Browne, Esq; ✉ 8 Priory Gardens, Barnes, London SW13 0JU (☎ 0181 876 1531); Greig Middleton & Co Ltd, 66 Wilson St, London EC2A 2BL (☎ 0171 392 4000, fax 0171 392 4300, telex 887296)

GORE BROWNE, James Anthony; s of Sir Thomas Gore Browne (d 1988), and Lavinia, *née* Loyd (d 1995); *b* 26 March 1947; *Educ* Eton, Univ of Dundee (MA), Aston Univ (Dip Business Admin); *m* 16 April 1983, Jane Anne, da of Col Seton Dickson, of Symington, Ayrshire; 1 da (Marina b 19 Dec 1984); 2 s (Freddie b 21 Jan 1987, Harold b 20 April 1988); *Career* Cazenove & Co 1969–75, asst to Chm EMI Ltd 1976–79, Thames TV 1979–80, Lead Industries Group 1980–81; admitted slr 1986, fndr litigation practice Leicester 1991–; Parly candidate (SDP) Doncaster Central 1987, joined Lab Pty 1989 (resigned 1994), re-joined Cons Pty 1994; Liveryman Worshipful Co of Fishmongers; memb Law Soc; *Recreations* golf, studying portraiture; *Clubs* White's; *Style*— James Gore Browne, Esq; ✉ Vane House, Tugby, Leics LE7 9WD (☎ 0116 259 8382)

GORE-RANDALL, Philip Allan; s of Alec Albert Gore-Randall (d 1996), of Uxbridge, and Joyce Margaret, *née* Gore; *b* 16 Dec 1952; *Educ* Merchant Taylors', Univ Coll Oxford (MA); *m* 15 Dec 1984, Prof Alison Elizabeth While, *qv*, da of Harold Arthur Armstrong While, MBE, TD (d 1983); 2 s (William b 1986, Edward b 1987); *Career* Arthur Andersen: joined 1975, ptnr 1986–, head London Audit and Business Advsy 1994–, managing ptnr UK Audit and Business Advsy 1995–; MInstPet, FCA 1978; *Recreations* classical music, good food, travel, Cotswolds; *Clubs* Vincent's (Oxford); *Style*— Philip Gore-Randall, Esq; ✉ 21 Rylett Rd, London W12 9SS (☎ 0181 743 7054); Arthur Andersen, 1 Surrey St, London WC2R 2PS (☎ 0171 438 3601, fax 0171 438 2398, car 0860 380406, telex 8812711)

GORELL, 4 Baron (UK 1909); Timothy John Radcliffe Barnes; s of 3 Baron Gorell, CBE, MC, (d 1963), and (Maud) Elizabeth Furse (d 1954), eld da of Alexander Radcliffe, of Bag Park, S Devon; *b* 2 Aug 1927; *Educ* Groton Mass USA, Eton, New Coll Oxford; *m* 1954, Joan, da of John Collins, MC; 2 adopted da; *Heir* bro, Hon Ronald Barnes; *Career* late Lt Rifle Bde; called to the Bar 1951; sr exec Royal Dutch Shell Group 1959–84; various directorships until 1992, EEC Sub Ctee 1987; Upper Bailiff Worshipful Co of Weavers 1977–78; *Recreations* golf, sailing, gardening, skiing; *Clubs* Roehampton Golf; *Style*— The Rt Hon the Lord Gorell; ✉ 4 Roehampton Gate, London SW15 5JS (☎ 0181 876 5522)

GORHAM, Martin Edwin; s of Clifford Edwin Gorham (d 1983), and Florence Ada, *née* Wright; *b* 18 June 1947; *Educ* Buckhurst Hill Co HS, Queen Mary Coll London (BA); *Career* administrative trg NHS 1968–70; dep hosp sec: Scarborough Hosp 1970–72, Doncaster Royal Infirmary 1972–75; hosp administrator: Northern Gen Hosp Sheffield 1975–82, Lodge Moor Hosp Sheffield Jan-July 1983; head of corp planning Newcastle Health Authy 1983–86, unit gen mangr Norfolk and Norwich Hosps Acute Unit 1986–90, dep regnl gen mangr South West Thames Regional Health Authy 1990–92, chief exec London Ambulance Serv 1992–95, dir S Thames Regnl Office NHS Exec 1996–; memb Inst of Health Service Mangrs; *Recreations* walking, music, reading, gardening, travelling and the arts in general, sport (cricket); *Style*— Martin Gorham, Esq; ✉ South Thames Regional Office, NHS Executive, 40 Eastbourne Terrace, London W2 3QR (☎ 0171 725 2663, car 0860 627682)

GORICK, (Robert) Lionel; s of John Gorick, of Llandudno, N Wales; *b* 24 Feb 1927; *Educ* Blackburn Tech Coll; *m* 1968, Jean Audrey, da of Frank Harwood (d 1976), of Wilpshire, nr Blackburn; 3 c; *Career* chm and md: Liquid Plastics Ltd 1963– (mfr of plastics-based waterproof coatings and fire retardant finishes, Queen's Award for Export 1982), Flexcrete Ltd, Industrial Copolymers Ltd; *Recreations* reading, horticulture, modern music, wining and dining; *Clubs* Preston Rotary, Preston Golf; *Style*— Lionel Gorick, Esq; ✉ Liquid Plastics Ltd, PO Box 7, London Rd, Preston, Lancs PR1 4AJ (☎ 01772 259781); The Stone House, Whittingham Lane, Broughton, nr Preston, Lancs (☎ 01772 864872/864879)

GORING, George Ernest; OBE (1992); *b* 19 May 1938; *Educ* Cheltenham, Ecole Hoteliere Lausanne, Westminster Coll; *Career* md and proprietor The Goring Hotel and Manoir de Lezurec France; chm Master Innholders 1988, pres Reunion des Gastronomes 1988–90, chm London Div BHRCA 1989–92; govr Westminster Coll, Master Mid Surrey Farmers Draghounds 1994–; Hotelier of the Year 1990, membre d'honneur Clefs d'Or; Liveryman Worshipful Co of Distillers; fell Tourism Soc, Master Innholder, FHCIMA; *Recreations* horseracing, hunting, the sea; *Style*— George Goring, Esq, OBE; ✉ The Goring Hotel, Beeston Place, Grosvenor Gardens, London SW1W 0JW (☎ 0171 396 9000, fax 0171 834 4393)

GORING, Lesley Susan; da of Walter Edwin Goring (d 1983), and Peggy Lambert; *b* 23 March 1950; *Educ* Northfields Sch for Girls; *Career* fashion PR conslt; PA to Mangr Biba 1965–67, press offr Mr Freedom 1967–72, Lynne Franks PR 1972–75; fndr and proprietor: Goring Public Relations 1975–, Lesley Goring Fashion Show Production 1980–; *Recreations* music, social gatherings, pets; *Style*— Ms Lesley Goring; ✉ Lesley Goring PR+Show Production, Studio 17, 44 Earlham St, Covent Garden, London WC2 (☎ 0171 240 3022, fax 0171 379 0863)

GORING, Marius; CBE (1991); s of Dr Charles Goring; *b* 23 May 1912; *Educ* Perse Sch Cambridge, Univ of Frankfurt, Univ of Vienna, Univ of Munich, Univ of Paris; *m* 1, 1931 (m dis), Mary Steel; 1 da; m 2, 1941, Lucie Mannheim (d 1976); m 3, 1977, Prudence FitzGerald; *Career* served in Queen's Royal Regt 1940; joined FO, later Euro Serv BBC; actor (professional debut 1927), actor-manager 1939–; asst stage mangr Old Vic (also playing Macbeth and Romeo), joined Compagnie des Quinze touring France and Belgium (playing in French), co-fndr (with Michel Saint-Denis and George Devine) London Theatre Studio (later becoming Old Vic School), played in Satyr (West End) 1936, prodr A Doll's House (with Lucie Mannheim), first film Rembrandt, Bear (by Chekhov, TV debut) 1938, Hitler in Shadow of the Swastika (BBC), A Matter of Life and Death (film), The Scarlet Pimpernel (ITV), The Expert (BBC); recent credits: God in the Cycle of Mystery Plays (Canterbury Cathedral), Beyond Reasonable Doubt (Queen's Theatre), Loser Takes All (film), Toward's Zero (Churchill Theatre Bromley and nat tour); vice pres Equity 1975–82; Hon FRSL 1976; *Style*— Marius Goring, Esq, CBE, FRSL; ✉ c/o Film Rights Ltd, 483 Southbank House, Black Prince Road, Albert Embankment, London SE1 7SJ (☎ 0171 735 8171)

GORING, Sir William Burton Nigel; 13 Bt (E 1678, with precedency of 1627), of Highden, Sussex; s of Maj Frederick Yelverton Goring (d 1938, 6 s of 11 Bt), and Freda Margaret, *née* Ainsworth (d 1993); suc unc, Sir Forster Gurney Goring, 12 Bt, 1956; the Goring family is of great antiquity in Sussex and were MPs from fifteenth to the nineteenth century; *b* 21 June 1933; *Educ* Wellington; *m* 1, 1960 (m dis), Hon Caroline Thellusson, da of 8 Baron Rendlesham; m 2, 25 Oct 1993, Mrs Judith Rachel Walton Morison (d 1995), da of Rev Raymond John Walton Morris, OBE, of Shaftesbury, Dorset; *Heir* kinsman, Richard Harry Goring b 1949; *Career* Lt Royal Sussex Regt; memb London Stock Exchange 1963, ptnr Quilter Goodison Co 1976; Asst Worshipful Co of Woolmen; *Recreations* tennis, bridge; *Clubs* Hurlingham; *Style*— Sir William Goring, Bt; ✉ c/o Quilter Goodison Company, St Helens, 1 Undershaft, London EC3A 8BB

GORMAN, John Reginald; CVO (1961), CBE (1974, MBE 1959), MC (1944), DL; s of Maj J K Gorman, MC (d 1980); *b* 1 Feb 1923; *Educ* Rockport, Haileybury and ISC, Portora, Harvard Business Sch; *m* 1948, Norah Heather, *née* Caruth; 2 s, 2 da; *Career* Capt Irish Guards WWII; RUC 1945–60, personnel dir BOAC 1963–70 (chief of security 1960–63), vice chm and chief exec Northern Ireland Housing Exec 1979–85, chm Risk Management International NI; farmer; dir: Nationwide Building Society, NI Airports, NI IOD, Cooperation North; chm Forum for NI 1996–; High Sheriff Co Down 1987; FCIT, MIH; *Recreations* gardening, fishing, beekeeping; *Clubs* Cavalry and Guards', Ulster Reform; *Style*— John Gorman, Esq, CVO, CBE, MC, DL; ✉ The Forge, Jericho Road, Killyleagh, Co Down, NI (☎ 01396 821039, fax 01396 828766)

GORMAN, Michael; s of Thomas Gorman (d 1977); *Educ* Univ of Liverpool (BA, PGCE), Univ of London Inst of Educn (CertEd); *m* Rosemary, da of Eric Young McDonald; *Career* teacher Farnham Coll Surrey 1974–77, football coach Bahrain Nat Side 1977–80, various coaching tasks for Football Assoc 1980–82, advtg asst Ted Bates London 1982–86, various positions rising to media dir DMB&B 1986–91, head of client servs Portland Outdoor Advertising 1992–94, media dir Saatchi & Saatchi Advertising 1994–; author of articles for trade jls (reg contrib Media Week); *Recreations* football, cricket, golf, supporting Manchester Utd FC; *Style*— Michael Gorman, Esq; ✉ Saatchi & Saatchi Advertising Ltd, 80 Charlotte Street, London W1A 1AQ (☎ 0171 636 5060, fax 0171 287 5833, e-mail mgorman@bigfoot.com)

GORMAN, William Moore (Terence); s of Capt Richard Gorman (d 1927), of Lusaka, N Rhodesia, and Sarah Crawford, *née* Moore; *b* 17 June 1923; *Educ* Mount Temple Sch Dublin, Foyle Coll Derry, Trinity Coll Dublin (BA); *m* 29 Dec 1950, Dorinda Maud, da of Walter T Scott; *Career* RN 1943–46 (acting Petty Officer 1945); sr lectr in charge econometrics and social statistics Univ of Birmingham 1957 (asst lectr 1949, lectr 1951); prof of economics: Univ of Oxford 1962–67, LSE 1967–79; Nuffield Coll Oxford: fell 1962–67 and 1979–90, emeritus fell 1990–; visiting prof various univs; memb Human Sciences Sub Ctee SRC 1962–66, chm Econ Study Soc 1963–66, memb Econs Ctee SSRC 1972–76; Hon DSocSc Univ of Birmingham 1973, Hon DSc (Social Sci) Univ of Southampton 1974, Hon DEconSc Nat Univ of Ireland 1986; hon fell: Trinity Coll Dublin 1990, LSE 1994; fell Econometric Soc 1962 (Euro chm 1971–73, pres 1972); hon foreign memb: American Acad Arts and Scis 1986, American Econ Assoc 1987; memb Acadamea Europaeae 1990; FBA 1977; *Recreations* reading, talking; *Style*— Terence Gorman, FBA; ✉ 32 Victoria Rd, Oxford OX2 7QD (☎ 01865 56087); Moorfield, Fountainstown, Myrtleville, Co Cork, Republic of Ireland (☎ 00 353 21 831174)

GORMANSTON, 17 Viscount (I 1478, Premier Viscount of Ireland); Jenico Nicholas Dudley Preston; also Baron Gormanston (I 1365–70 and UK 1868, which latter sits as); s of 16 Viscount (ka 1940), and Pamela, *née* Hanly (whose mother was Lady Marjorie, *née* Feilding, da of 9 Earl of Denbigh); *b* 19 Nov 1939; *Educ* Downside; *m* 1974, Eva Landzianowska (d 1984); 2 s (Hon Jenico, Hon William b 3 May 1976); *Heir* s, Hon Jenico Francis Tara Preston b 30 April 1974; *Career* FRGS; *Clubs* Kildare St and University (Dublin); *Style*— The Rt Hon the Viscount Gormanston; ✉ 8 Dalmeny House, Thurloe Place, London SW7 2RY

GORMLEY, Antony Mark David; s of Arthur John Constantine Gormley (d 1977), of Hampstead, London, and Elspeth, *née* Braüninger; *b* 30 Aug 1950; *Educ* Ampleforth, Trinity Coll Cambridge (BA, MA), Goldsmiths' Coll Univ of London (BA), Slade Sch of Fine Art UCL (Higher Dip in Fine Art); *m* 14 June 1980, Emelyn Victoria (Vicken), da of Maj (Ian) David Parsons, of Baas Manor, Broxbourne, Herts; 2 s (Ivo b 16 March 1982, Guy b 17 June 1985), 1 da (Paloma b 20 July 1987); *Career* artist; winner Turner Prize 1994; *One Man Exhibitions* incl: Whitechapel Art Gallery 1981, Coracle Press 1983, Riverside Studios London, Chapter Cardiff 1984, Salvatore Ala Gallery NY 1985, 1986, 1987, 1989 and 1991, Stadtisches Gallerie Regensburg, Frankfurt Kunstverein 1985, Serpentine Gallery 1987, Burnett Miller LA 1988 and 1990, Louisiana Museum Denmark 1989, Scot Nat Gallery of Modern Art Edinburgh 1989, Art Gallery of NSW Sydney Aust 1989, Burnett Miller Gallery LA 1988, 1990 and 1992, Frith St Gallery London 1991, Isy and Christine Brachot Gallery Brussels 1991, Nordenhake Gallery Stockholm Sweden 1991, Shirakawa Gallery Kyoto Japan 1991, Field (Modern Art Museum Fort Worth 1991, Centro Cultural Arte Contemporaneo Mexico City 1992, Museum of Contemporary Art San Diego 1992, Corcoran Gallery of Art Washington 1993, Museum of Fine Arts Montreal 1993), Body and Soul: Learning to See (Contemporary Art Centre Tokyo) 1992, Learning to Think (Br Sch Rome) 1992, Galerie Thaddaeus Ropac Paris and Salzburg 1993, Galerie Nordenhake Stockholm 1993, European Field (Konsthall Malmö 1993, Centrum Sztuki Wspolczesnej Zagreb 1994, Ludwig Museum Budapest 1994, Prague Castle 1995, Bucharest 1995), Field for the British Isles (Tate Gallery Liverpool 1993, Irish Museum of Modern Art Dublin 1994, Oriel Mostyn Llandudno 1994, Scottish Museum of Modern Art Edinburgh 1994, Orchard Gallery Derry 1995, Ikon Gallery Birmingham 1995, Nat Gallery of Wales Cardiff 1995), Galeria Pedro Oliveira Oporto 1994, Kohji Ogura Gallery Nagoya 1995, Remise Vienna 1995, New Work (Obala Art Centar Bosnia) 1996, Inside the Inside (Galerie Xavier Hufkens Brussels Belgium) 1996, Arts 04 (St Remy de Provence France) 1996, Field for the British Isles (Hayward Gallery London) 1996, Still Moving (retrospective touring Japan) 1996–97; *Group Exhibitions* Objects and Sculpture (ICA) 1981, Br Sculpture of the 20th Century (Whitechapel Art Gallery) 1981, Venice Biennale 1982 and 1986, Biennale De

Sao Paulo 1983, Int Survey Museum of Modern Art NY 1984, The Br Show Aust 1985, Between Object and Image Madrid 1986, Documenta 8 Kassel 1987, ROSC Dublin 88, British Art Now: A Subjective View (6 museums in Japan) 1990–91, GB-USSR House of the Artist (Kiev and Moscow) 1990, Inheritance and Transformation (Irish Museum of Modern Art Dublin) 1991, Arte Amazonas (Museu de Arte Moderna Rio De Janeiro) 1992, Natural Order (Tate Gallery Liverpool) 1992, Images of Man (Isetan Museum of Art, Tokyo/Daimura Museum, Umeda-Osaka/Hiroshima City Museum of Contemporary Art) 1992, The Human Factor: Figurative Sculpture Reconsidered (Albuquerque Museum) 1993, Suite Substitute (Hotel du Rhone Geneva) 1993, The Fujisankei Biennale (Hakone Open-air Museum Japan) 1993, Klima Global: Arte Amazonas (Staatliche Kunsthalle Berlin, Technische Sammlungen Dresden, Ludwig Forum Aachen) 1993 and 1994, HA HA: Contemporary British Art in an 18th Century Garden (Killerton Park Devon) 1993, The Fujisankei Biennale (Hakone Open-Air Museum Japan) 1993, From Beyond the Pale: Part One (Irish Museum of Modern Art) 1994, Sculptors' Drawings from the Weltkunst Collection (Tate Gallery) 1994, Artists' Impressions (Kettles Yard Cambridge 1994, Castle Museum Nottingham 1995), ARS '95 (Helsinki Finland) 1995, Contemporary British Art in Print (Scottish Museum of Modern Art Edinburgh, Yale Center for British Art) 1995, Fredsskulptur 1995 (Jutland Denmark) 1995, Glaube, Hoffnung, Liebe und Tod (Kunsthalle Vienna) 1995, Un Siecle de Sculpture Anglaise (Jeu de Paume Paris) 1996; *Collections* incl: Arts Cncl of GB, Tate Gallery, CAS, Br Cncl, Southampton Art Gallery, Neue Museum Kassel, Stadt Kassel, Walker Arts Centre Minneapolis, Leeds City Art Gallery, Irish Museum of Modern Art Dublin, Louisiana Museum Denmark, Scottish National Museum of Modern Art, Moderna Museet Stockholm, Kunsthalle Mälmo Sweden, Modern Art Museum Fort Worth, Museum of Contemporary Art San Diego and Los Angeles, Iwaki Municipal Museum Fukushima Japan, The Hakone Open-air Museum Japan, Fundacio Gulbenkian Lisbon Portugal; *Catalogues* Salvatore Ala NY 1984 and 1985, Regensburg W Germany 1985, Contemporary Sculpture Centre Tokyo 1988, Louisiana 1989, Spoleto Festival Festival USA 1991, Field (Museum of Fine Arts Montreal) 1993, Antony Gormley (Konsthall Malmo/Tate Gallery Liverpool/Irish Museum of Modern Art Dublin) 1993, Antony Gormley (Phaidon Press London) 1995, Critical Mass (Stadt Raum Remise Vienna) 1995, Still Moving (Japan Assoc of Art Museums Tokyo) 1996; *Recreations* sailing, skiing, walking; *Style*— Antony Gormley, Esq; ✉ 13 South Villas, London NW1 9BS (☎ 0171 482 7383); 153 Bellenden Rd, London SE15 5NN (☎ 0171 639 1303, fax 0171 639 2674)

GORMLY, Allan Graham; CBE (1991); s of William Gormly, and Christina Swinton Flockhart, *née* Arnot; *b* 18 Dec 1937; *Educ* Paisley GS, Univ of Glasgow; *m* 30 June 1962, Vera Margaret, da of late Alexander Grant; 1 s (Alisdair William b 10 Sept 1965), 1 da (Lynn Margaret b 15 Nov 1963); *Career* chm John Brown Engineering Ltd 1983–92, gp md John Brown plc 1983–92, chm John Brown plc 1992–94, dir Trafalgar House Construction Holdings Ltd 1986–89; Trafalgar House plc (parent co of John Brown): head Engrg Div and main bd dir 1986–92, main bd dir and gp chief exec 1992–94, non-exec dir and jt dep chm 1994–96; non-exec chm Royal Insurance Holdings PLC 1994–96 (dir 1990–, dep chm 1992–94); non-exec dep chm Royal & Sun Alliance Insurance Group plc 1996–; non-exec dir: Brixton Estate plc 1994–, National Grid Co plc 1994–95, BPB Industries plc 1995–; chm Overseas Projects Bd 1988–91, dep chm Export Guarantees Advsy Cncl 1990–94; memb: Export Guarantees Advsy Cncl 1987–94, BOTB 1988–91, Top Salaries Review Body 1990–92; MICAS 1961; *Recreations* music, golf; *Style*— Allan Gormly, Esq, CBE; ✉ Royal Insurance Holdings PLC, 1 Cornhill, London EC3V 3QR (☎ 0171 283 4300, fax 0171 283 4841)

GORNA, Christina; da of John Gorna, of Oak Bank, Hill Top, Hale, Altrincham, Cheshire, and Muriel Theresa Gorna; *b* 19 Feb 1937; *Educ* Loreto Convent Llandudno, Univ of Manchester (LLB), Univ of Neuchâtel (Diploma in Swiss and Int Law), Univ of The Sorbonne Paris (Dip in French Civilisation), Br Cncl scholar, Harmsworth scholar of the Middle Temple; *m* 6 July 1963, Ian Davies (d 1996), s of Reginald Beresford Davies, of Timperly, Altrincham, Cheshire; 1 s (Caspar Dominick John b 11 May 1966), 1 da (Samantha Jane b 14 Jan 1964); *Career* barrister, writer, broadcaster and columnist; called to the Bar Middle Temple 1960; sr lectr Univ of Coventry 1973–79, in practice specialising in criminal, family, professional negligence, licensing and media law 1980–, head of Castle Chambers Exeter (estab 1990); numerous TV and radio appearances incl: Any Questions?, Woman's Hour, Kilroy, The Time The Place, Great Expectations, Behind the Headlines, Central Weekend, Advice Shop (BBC), Question Time (BBC) 1992 and 1994, The Verdict, Esther - You Are What You Wear 1996; presenter: Careering Ahead, Experts Exported, The Flying Brief (TV series) 1994–95, Check it Out (consumer series, West Country TV); regular contrib: GMTV, UK Living, Westcountry TV, Viva Radio, Talk Radio, London Talk Radio, Gemini Radio, Chanel 1, TLC, The Right Thing (Radio 5 Live); weekly legal column Chat, Carefree and Prospect Magazines, columnist The Universe; profile writer, gossip columnist, book, theatre and art reviewer, public speaker and debater; memb: Advsy Body Women in Prison, Prison Reform Tst; hon pres Network West; FRSA 1994; *Books* Company Law, Leading Cases on Company Law, Questions and Answers on Company Law; *Recreations* swimming, performing and visual arts, art collecting, visiting galleries, writing, painting, clothes (especially hats); *Clubs* Groucho, Western Circuit, Network, 300 Group, Charter 88, London Business Network, Association of Women Barristers, Thomas More Society, Fawcett Society, Association of Catholic Lawyers; *Style*— Miss Christina Gorna; ✉ 10a Kempsford Gardens, London SW5 9LH (☎ 0171 370 0434); The Old Warehouse, Denver Rd, Topsham, Exeter, Devon (☎ 01392 877736); 4 Paper Buildings, Temple, London EC4Y 7EX (☎ 0171 353 3366); Castle Chambers, 3 Queens Terrace, Exeter EX4 4HN (☎ 01392 420345); agent: Jacque Evans (☎ 0171 722 4700)

GORNALL, Alastair Charles; s of J I K Gornall, of Odiham, Hants, and E C Gornall, *née* Leighton; *b* 6 June 1956; *Educ* Stowe, RMA Sandhurst (RAF flying scholarship); *m* 1986, Sarah, *née* McCall; 3 c; *Career* Business Week International NY 1979–81; md: Scope Communications 1981–90, Consolidated Communications Management Ltd 1990–; bd dir PRCA; *Recreations* flying model helicopters; *Clubs* Cavalry and Guards', Annabel's; *Style*— Alastair Gornall, Esq; ✉ Consolidated Communications Management Ltd, 1–5 Poland Street, London W1V 3DG (☎ 0171 287 2087, fax 0171 734 0772)

GORNICK, Naomi; da of Abraham Harris (d 1989), and Rachel Harris (d 1992); *Educ* Montreal Canada, Willesden Sch of Art, PCL; *m* Bruce Gornick; 1 s (Simon), 1 da (Lisa); *Career* design mgmnt conslt; dir MA Design Strategy and Innovation Brunel Univ 1993–; advsr: Middlesex Univ, De Montfort Univ, industl clients incl Raychem, London Underground; ed Debrett's Interior Design Collection 1988 and 1989; Chartered Soc of Designers: memb Cncl 1992–, vice pres 1986–89, fndr chm Design Mgmnt Gp 1981–86; chm SIAD Design Mgmnt seminar series in 1983 and 1985 and the Design Mgmnt Conf for Indust Year 1986; course ldr RCA 1989–91; memb Steering Ctee on Design Mgmnt Courses CNAA, memb Bd of Tstees Worldesign Fndn USA 1993–, chm Design Selection Ctees Design Cncl, panel judge for Design Centre Awards 1989; FCSD, FRSA; *Clubs* Chelsea Arts; *Style*— Naomi Gornick

GORRINGE, Christopher John; s of Maurice Sydney William Gorringe (d 1981), of Newick, Nr Lewes, Sussex, and Hilda Joyce, *née* Walker; *b* 13 Dec 1945; *Educ* Bradfield, RAC Cirencester Glos; *m* 17 April 1976, Jennifer Mary, da of Roger Arthur Chamberlain (d 1979), of Ramsbury, Wilts; 2 da (Kim b 13 April 1978, Anna b 24 Feb 1981); *Career* asst land agent Iveagh Tstees Ltd (Guinness Family) 1968–73, chief exec The All Eng Lawn Tennis and Croquet Club Wimbledon 1983– (asst sec 1973–79, sec 1979–83); ARICS 1971; *Recreations* lawn tennis; *Clubs* The All England Lawn Tennis, The Queen's, Jesters, Int (GB), St George's Hill Lawn Tennis; *Style*— Christopher Gorringe, Esq; ✉ The All England Lawn Tennis Club, Church Road, Wimbledon, London SW19 5AE (☎ 0181 944 1066, fax 0181 947 3354, telex 265180 AELTC)

GORROD, Prof John William; s of Ernest Lionel Gorrod (d 1981), and Caroline Rebecca, *née* Richardson (d 1990); *b* 11 Oct 1931; *Educ* Univ of London (DSc, PhD), Chelsea Coll (Dip), Brunel Coll of Advanced Technol (HNC); *m* 3 April 1954, Doreen Mary, da of George Douglas Collins (d 1992); 2 s (Simon b 5 April 1962, Nicholas b 16 July 1966), 1 da (Julia b 8 June 1959); *Career* res fell Dept of Biochemistry Univ of Bari Italy 1964, res fell Royal Cmmn for the Exhibition of 1851 1965–67, lectr in biopharmacy Chelsea Coll Univ of London 1968–80 (reader 1980–84), prof of biopharmacy/head of Chelsea Dept of Pharmacy King's Coll London 1984–89, res prof Faculty of Life Sciences King's Coll London 1990– (head of Div of Health Scis 1988–90); Hon MRPharmS 1982; corresponding memb German Pharmaceutical Soc 1985; hon fell: Pan/Hellenic Pharmaceutical Soc 1987, Turkish Pharmaceutical Assoc 1988, Bohemslovaca Pharmaceutical Soc 1991; awarded Gold medal Comenius Univ Bratislava 1991; memb: Assoc for Res in Indoor Air 1989, Air Tport Users' Ctee CAA 1990–92, Assocs for Res in Substances of Enjoyment 1990, Cncl Indoor Air Int 1990–; fell King's Coll London 1996, Hon MRPharmS 1982; FRSC 1980, FRCPath 1984; *Books* Drug Metabolism in Man (1978), Drug Toxicity (1979), Testing for Toxicity (1981), Biological Oxidation of Nitrogen in Organic Molecules (1985), Biological Oxidation of Nitrogen (1978), Metabolism of Xenobiotics (1988), Development of Drugs and Modern Medicines (1986), Molecular Basis of Human Disease (1989), Molecular Basis of Neurological Disorders and Their Treatment (1991), Nicotine and Related Tobacco Alkaloids: absorption, distribution, metabolism and excretion (1993); *Recreations* reading biographies, running; *Clubs* Athenaeum, Hillingdon Athletic; *Style*— Prof John Gorrod; ✉ Kingsmead, 13 Park Lane, Hayes, Middx UB4 8AA (☎ an fax 0181 561 3851); The Rest Orchard, Polstead Heath, nr Colchester, Suffolk CO6 5BG; King's College London, Chelsea Department of Pharmacy, Manresa Rd, London, SW3 6LX (☎ 0171 333 4789, fax 0171 333 4881, e-mail udkjoo5@bay.cc.kcl.ac.uk)

GORST, John Marcus; s of Maj James Marcus Gorst (d 1995), of South Stack, Fornham All Saints, Bury St Edmunds, Suffolk, and Frances Gladys, *née* Espley; *b* 13 Jan 1944; *Educ* Culford Sch, Selwyn Coll Cambridge (MA); *m* June 1974 (m dis 1977), Marian, da of James Anthony Judge, of 2 Rockall Drive, Glasgow; *Career* md Drayson Property Holdings Ltd 1971–, chm Folkard and Hayward Commercial Ltd 1984–; Freeman Worshipful Co of Bakers; *Recreations* golf, shooting; *Style*— John Gorst, Esq; ✉ Folkard and Hayward Commercial Ltd, 25 Tedworth Square, London SW3 4DP

GORST, Sir John Michael; kt (1994), MP (C) Hendon North (majority 7,122); s of Derek Charles Gorst; *b* 28 June 1928; *Educ* Ardingly, Corpus Christi Coll Cambridge; *m* 1954, Noël Harington, da of Austin Walker, of E Kilbride; 5 s; *Career* advertising and PR mangr Pye Ltd 1953–63, PR conslt John Gorst and Assocs Ltd 1964–; fndr 1974: Telephone Users' Assoc, Local Radio Assoc; Parly candidate (C): Chester-le-Street 1964, Bodmin 1966; MP (C) Hendon North 1970–; memb Select Ctee: on Employment 1979–87, on Nat Heritage 1992–; vice chm All Pty War Crimes Ctee 1988–; chm: Cons Back Bench Media Ctee 1988–90, All Pty Br Mexican Gp; *Clubs* Garrick; *Style*— Sir John Gorst, MP; ✉ House of Commons, London SW1A 0AA

GORT, 9 Viscount (I 1816); Foley Robert Standish Prendergast Vereker; also Baron Kiltarton (I 1810); s of 8 Viscount Gort (d 1995), and Bettine, *née* Green; *b* 24 Oct 1951; *Educ* Harrow; *m* 1, 1979 (m dis 1987), Julie Denise, only da of D W Jones; m 2, 19 Oct 1991, Sharon Lyn, da of Arnold Quayle; 1 s (Hon Robert Foley Prendergast b 5 April 1993); *Heir* s, Hon Robert Foley Prendergast Vereker b 5 April 1993; *Career* gallery owner; *Style*— The Rt Hon the Viscount Gort

GORTY, Peter; s of Nathan Gorty, and Bella, *née* Lancet; *b* 3 Nov 1944; *Educ* Owens Sch Islington, LSE (LLB); *m* 20 Sept 1970, Mariana; 1 s (Andrew), 1 da (Helen); *Career* articled clerk Gilbert Samuel & Co 1967–69, asst slr Withers 1969–70, ptnr specialising in banking and energy law Nabarro Nathanson 1972– (asst slr 1970–72); *Recreations* all sports, reading, theatre, architecture; *Style*— Peter Gorty, Esq; ✉ Nabarro Nathanson, 50 Stratton St, London W1X 5NX (☎ 0171 493 9933, fax 0171 629 7900)

GOSCHEN, Edward Alexander; s and h of Sir Edward Christian Goschen, 3 Bt, DSO, and Cynthia, da of late Rt Hon Sir Alexander George Montagu Cadogan, OM, GCMG, KCB; *b* 13 March 1949; *Educ* Eton; *m* 1976, Louise Annette, da of Lt-Col Ronald Fulton Lucas Chance, MC, KRRC (d 1996), and Lady Ava, *née* Baird, da of 1 Viscount Stonehaven and Lady (Ethel) Sidney, *née* Keith-Falconer, who was Countess of Kintore in her own right; 1 da (Charlotte Leila, b 1982); *Style*— Edward Goschen, Esq; ✉ Pixton Stables, Dulverton, Taunton, Somerset TA22 9HW

GOSCHEN, Sir Edward Christian; 3 Bt (UK 1916), of Beacon Lodge, Highcliffe, Co Southampton, DSO (1944); s of Sir Edward Henry Goschen, 2 Bt (d 1933; s of Sir (William) Edward Goschen, 1 Bt, GCB, GCMG, GCVO, HM ambass in Berlin in 1914), and Countess Mary Danneskiold-Samsöe (d 1964), 7 da of 5 Count (Christian) Danneskiold-Samsöe; *b* 2 Sept 1913; *Educ* Eton, Trinity Coll Oxford; *m* 1946, Cynthia, da of Rt Hon Sir Alexander George Montagu Cadogan, OM, GCMG, KCB, PC, sometime perm under sec at the FO (7 s of 5 Earl Cadogan), by his w Lady Theodosia Acheson, da of 4 Earl of Gosford; 1 s (Edward Alexander b 1949), 1 da (Caroline Clare (Mrs Jonathan Mendham) b 1950); *Heir* s, (Edward) Alexander Goschen b 13 March 1949; *Career* memb Stock Exchange Cncl (dep chm 1968–71); Cwlth War Graves cmmr 1977–87; *Style*— Sir Edward Goschen, Bt, DSO; ✉ Lower Farm House, Hampstead Norreys, Newbury, Berks (☎ 01635 201270)

GOSCHEN, 4 Viscount (UK 1900); Giles John Harry Goschen; s of 3 Viscount Goschen, KBE (d 1977), and his 2 w Alvin, *née* England; *b* 16 Nov 1965; *m* 23 Feb 1991, Sarah, yr da of late A G Horsnail, of Clophill, Bedfordshire; *Heir* none; *Career* a Lord in Waiting to HM the Queen 1992–94; Parly under sec of state Dept of Tport 1994–; *Style*— The Rt Hon the Viscount Goschen; ✉ Hilton House, Crowthorne, Berks RG11 6AH

GOSDEN, John Harry Martin; s of John Montague Gosden (d 1967), of Sussex, and Peggie Gosden; *b* 30 March 1951; *Educ* Eastbourne Coll, Emmanuel Coll Cambridge (MA, Athletics blue); *m* 1982, Rachel Dene Serena Hood; 2 s (Sebastian b 1983, Thaddeus b 1995), 2 da (Serena b 1985, Theodora b 1990); *Career* racehorse trainer; asst trainer: Sir Noel Murless 1974–76, Dr Vincent O'Brien 1976–77; trainer: USA 1979–88, England 1989–; achievements as trainer USA: among top ten 1982–88, leading trainer Calif meets, 8 state champions, 2 Eclipse Award winners; Sussex Martlets schoolboy cricketer 1967–68, memb Blackheath Rugby Club 1969–70, memb Br under 23 rowing squad 1973; *Recreations* opera, skiing, environmental issues; *Style*— John Gosden, Esq; ✉ Stanley House Stables, Bury Rd, Newmarket, Suffolk CB8 7DF (☎ 01638 669944, fax 01638 669922)

GOSDEN, Prof Peter Henry John Heather; s of Alfred John Gosden (d 1980), of Fittleworth, and Elizabeth Ann Gosden (d 1962); *b* 3 Aug 1927; *Educ* Midhurst GS, Emmanuel Coll Cambridge (BA, MA), Birkbeck Coll London (PhD); *m* 2 Sept 1964, Dr (Margaret) Sheila Gosden, da of Charles Alfred Hewitt (d 1974), of Hull; *Career* Nat Serv RAF 1949–51; schoolmaster 1951–60, jt ed Journal of Educational Administration and History 1968–92, pro vice chllr Univ of Leeds 1985–87 (lectr 1960, sr lectr 1967, reader 1971, prof 1978); chm JMB Manchester 1988–92, academic sec Univ Cncl for Educn of Teachers 1991– (memb Exec 1978–91), chm Ripon Diocesan Bd of Educn 1992–, pres

History of Educn Soc 1993–; FRHistS 1969, FRSA 1989; *Books* incl: The Friendly Societies in England 1815–1875 (1961), The Evolution of a Profession (1972), Self-Help: Voluntary Associations in Nineteenth Century Britain (1973), Education in the Second World War: a study in policy and administration (1976), The Educational System since 1944 (1983), Education Committees (with George Cooke, 1986), The North of England Education Conference 1902–1992 (1992); *Recreations* music, gardening, walking; *Clubs* National Liberal; *Style*— Prof Peter Gosden; ✉ Orchard House, Creskeld Lane, Bramhope, nr Leeds LS16 9ES; Box Tree Cottage, Fittleworth, Pulborough, Sussex RH20 1JE; The University, Leeds LS2 9JT (☎ 0113 233 5061, fax 0113 233 4541)

GOSFORD, 7 Earl of (I 1806); Sir Charles David Nicholas Alexander John Sparrow Acheson; 13 Bt (NS 1628); also Baron Gosford (I 1776), Viscount Gosford (I 1785), Baron Worlingham (UK 1835, sits as), and Baron Acheson of Clancairny (UK 1847); s of 6 Earl of Gosford, OBE (d 1966), by his 1 w, Francesca, er da of Francesco Cagiati, of Rome; *b* 13 July 1942; *Educ* Harrow, Byam Shaw Sch of Drawing and Painting, Royal Academy Schs; *m* 1983, Lynnette Redmond; *Heir* unc, Hon Patrick Acheson; *Career* artist; one man shows: Barry Stern Exhibition Gallery, Sydney 1983 and 1986, Von Bertouch Galleries Newcastle NSW 1983 and 1986; *Style*— The Rt Hon the Earl of Gosford; ✉ c/o House of Lords, Westminster, London SW1 0PW

GOSKIRK, (William) Ian Macdonald; CBE (1986); s of William Arthur Goskirk (d 1984), of Scotby, Carlisle, and Flora Rennie, *née* MacDonald; *b* 2 March 1932; *Educ* Carlisle GS, Queen's Coll Oxford (MA); *m* 7 June 1969, Hope-Ann, da of John Knaizuk, of New York, USA; 1 da (Nadia Anna b 1970); *Career* REME 1950–52; Shell International Petroleum 1956–74, md Anschutz Petroleum Ltd 1974–76, British National Oil Corporation 1976–85, md BNOC (Trading) Ltd 1980–82 (chief exec 1982–85), dir Coopers & Lybrand Assocs 1986–90, ptnr Coopers & Lybrand 1990–92, ret; *Recreations* gardening; *Clubs* Athenaeum; *Style*— W I M Goskirk, Esq, CBE; ✉ c/o Athenaeum Club, 107 Pall Mall, London SW1Y 5ER

GOSLING, Christopher Spencer; DL (Essex 1995); *b* 22 Aug 1942; *Educ* Eton, Royal Agricultural Coll Cirencester; *m* 24 June 1967, Juliet Mary, *née* Stanton; 2 da (Venetia Rachel b 2 Oct 1969, Larissa Catherine b 9 Dec 1971), 1 s (Alexander Edward Spencer b 1 July 1975); *Career* farmer; family partnership (1,200 acres) 1964–, sole proprietor (500 acres) 1979–; assoc ptnr and conslt land agent and rural estate mgmnt Strutt & Parker Chelmsford 1964–; Country Landowners' Assoc: memb Cncl 1982–88, chm Essex Branch 1983–86, memb Agricultural & Land Use Sub-Ctee 1985–88; memb Cncl Essex Agricultural Soc (Essex Show) 1981– (chm 1991–95), chm Essex Branch Game Conservancy Cncl 1983–86, steward International Pavilion Royal Show 1987–92; memb: British Field Sports Soc, Essex Agric Assoc, Suffolk Agric Assoc, Royal Agric Soc of England; High Sheriff of Essex 1993–94; *Recreations* shooting, stalking, tennis, cricket, windsurfing, skiing, travel; *Clubs* Beefsteak, Farmers', Essex, Surveyors 1954; cricket clubs: Rickling Green, Gents of Essex, Eton Ramblers; *Style*— Christopher Gosling, Esq, DL; ✉ Byham Hall, Great Maplestead, Halstead, Essex CO9 3AR (☎ 01787 460134, fax 01787 461462)

GOSLING, Sir (Frederick) Donald; kt (1976); *b* 2 March 1929; *m* 1959 (m dis 1988), Elizabeth Shauna, *née* Ingram; 3 s; *Career* joined RN 1944, served Med HMS Leander; jt chm Nat Car Parks Ltd 1950–, chm Palmer & Harvey Ltd 1967–, dir Lovell Hldgs Ltd 1975–; memb Cncl of Mgmnt White Ensign Assoc 1970– (chm 1978–83, vice-pres 1983–93, pres 1993); chm Selective Employment Scheme 1976–; tstee: Fleet Air Arm Museum Yeovilton 1974–, RYA Seamanship Fndn, The Bernard Sunley Charitable Fndn; patron Submarine Meml Appeal 1978–; patron The Ark Royal Welfare Tst, chm Berkeley Square Ball Charitable Tst; Hon Capt RNR 1993; *Style*— Sir Donald Gosling; ✉ National Car Parks Ltd, PO Box 4NH, 21 Bryanston Street, Marble Arch, London W1A 4NH (☎ 0171 499 7050)

GOSLING, Justin Cyril Bertrand; s of Vincent Samuel Gosling (d 1945), of Brewood, Stafford, and Dorothy Mary Catherine, *née* Smith (d 1964); *b* 26 April 1930; *Educ* Ampleforth, Wadham Coll Oxford (BPhil), St John's Coll Oxford (MA); *m* 2 Sept 1958, (Angela) Margaret, da of Brig Sir Iltyd Clayton, KBE (d 1955), of Herefordshire; 2 s (Samuel b 18 May 1961, Thomas b 2 March 1970), 2 da (Rachel b 9 Aug 1962, Elizabeth b 9 April 1966); *Career* Univ of Oxford: Fereday fell St John's Coll 1955–58, lectr philosophy Wadham and Pembroke Coll 1958–60, fell in philosophy St Edmund Hall 1960–82, sr proctor 1977–78, princ St Edmund Hall 1982–96; Barclay Acheson prof Macalester Coll Minnesota 1964, visiting res fell ANU Canberra 1970; *Books* Pleasure and Desire (1969), Plato (1973), Plato, Philebus (ed 1975), The Greeks on Pleasure (with CCW Taylor, 1982); Weakness of the Will (1990); *Recreations* gardening, intaglio printing, recorder music; *Style*— Justin Gosling, Esq; ✉ Joymount, Northcourt Lane, Abingdon, Oxford OX14 1QA (☎ 01235 523310)

GOSLING, Paula Louise (Mrs John Hare); da of A Paul Osius (d 1986), and Sylvie, *née* Van Slembrouck (d 1986); *b* 12 Oct 1939; *Educ* Mackenzie HS, Wayne State Univ (BA); *m* 1, 1968 (m dis 1979), Christopher Gosling, s of Thomas Gosling; 2 da (Abigail Judith b 1970, Emily Elizabeth b 1972); m 2, 1981, John Anthony Hare, s of John Charles Hare; *Career* copywriter: Campbell-Ewald USA 1962–64, C Mitchell & Co London 1964–67, Pritchard-Wood London 1967–68, David Williams Ltd London 1968–70; copy conslt: C Mitchell & Co 1970–72, ATA Advertising Bristol 1977–79; crime writer 1979–; Arts Achievement Award Wayne State Univ 1994; Crime Writers' Assoc: memb Ctee 1984–90, chm 1988–89; memb: Soc of Authors, ALCS, Mensa; *Books* A Running Duck (1978, US title Fair Game, John Creasey Meml award for Best First Crime Novel 1978, made into film for Japanese TV and into film Cobra and film Fair Game 1995), The Zero Trap (1979), Mind's Eye (as Ainslie Skinner 1980, US title The Harrowing), Loser's Blues (1980, US title Solo Blues), The Woman in Red (1983), Monkey Puzzle (1985, Gold Dagger award for Best Crime Novel 1986), The Wychford Murders (1987), Hoodwink (1988), Backlash (1989), Death Penalties (1991), The Body in Blackwater Bay (1992), A Few Dying Words (1993), The Dead of Winter (1995); author of numerous serials and short stories incl Mr Felix (nominated for Best Short Story MWA 1987); *Recreations* needlework, kite-flying; *Style*— Ms Paula Gosling; ✉ c/o Greene and Heaton Ltd, 37 Goldhawk Road, London W12 8QQ (☎ 0181 749 0315, fax 0181 749 0318)

GOSLING, Prof William; s of Harold William Gosling (d 1980), of Cograve, Notts, and Aida Maisie, *née* Webb; *b* 25 Sept 1932; *Educ* Mundella Sch Nottingham, Imperial Coll London (BSc), Univ of Bath (DSc); *m* 5 July 1953, Patricia Mary, da of Charles Henry Best, of Rode, Somerset; 2 s (Richard b 1956 d 1958, Ceri b 1959), 1 da (Melanie b 1954); *Career* prof of electrical engrg Univ of Wales 1966, vice princ Univ Coll Swansea 1972, prof of electronic engrg Univ of Bath 1974; tech dir Plessey Co plc (formerly Plessey Electronic Systems Ltd) 1981–89, dir of electronic devpts Securicor Group 1990–, dir Venture Link Investors 1991–93; hon prof of communication engrg Southampton Univ 1981–89, visiting prof Univ of Bath 1990–; pres: Euro Convention of Electrical Engrs 1977–78, Inst of Electronic and Radio Engrs 1979–80; Freeman City of London 1980; Liveryman Worshipful Co of: Scientific Instrument Makers 1980, Engrs 1985; hon fell UMIST 1987; ARCS, FIEE 1968, FInstD 1982; *Books* Design of Engineering Systems (1962), Field Effect Electronics (1971), Radio Receivers (1986), Helmsmen and Heroes (1994); *Recreations* music, poetry; *Clubs* Athenaeum; *Style*— Prof William Gosling; ✉ White Hart Cottage, Rode, Bath (☎ 01373 830901, fax 01373 830172, mobile 0860 528859)

GOSPER, Brett; s of Richard Kevan Gosper, of Melbourne, Aust, and Gillian Mary, *née* Galwey (d 1981); *b* 21 June 1959; *Educ* Rutlish Sch, Scotch Coll Melbourne, Monash Univ Melbourne (BA Economics and Politics (Law Maj)); *m* 1989 (m dis), Laurence, *née* Albes; 1 s (Jonathan Kevan Thomas b 24 June 1990); *Career* advtg exec; account exec Ogilvy & Mather Melbourne 1981–82, gp account dir Ogilvy & Mather Paris 1982–89, dir rising to dep md BBDP Paris 1989–93, fndr md BBDP Frankfurt 1993–94, chief exec offr Euro RSCG Wnek Gosper London 1994–, memb Bd Euro RSCG Worldwide 1996–; *Recreations* rugby; *Clubs* Melbourne Rugby (Best Club Player Award 1978, 1979 and 1980, rep Victoria, Queensland and Aust), Melbourne Cricket, Racing Club de France (Best Club Player Award 1987, rep French Barbarians), Castel (Paris); *Style*— Brett Gosper, Esq; ✉ Euro RSCG Wnek Gosper, 11 Great Newport Street, London WC2H 7JA (☎ 0171 257 6002, fax 0171 465 0552)

GOSS, Prof Richard Oliver; s of Sqdn-Ldr Leonard Arthur Goss (d 1956), and Hilda Nellie, *née* Casson (d 1986); *b* 4 Oct 1929; *Educ* Christ's Coll Finchley, HMS Worcester, King's Coll Cambridge (BA, MA, PhD); *m* 1, 1958 (m dis 1983), Lesley Elizabeth, da of William Thomas Thurbon; 2 s (David Anthony b 1963, Stephen Peter b 1966), 1 da (Catherine Alice b 1960); m 2, 30 July 1994, Gillian Mary, *née* Page; *Career* MN: Cadet to Chief Offr 1947–56, Master Mariner 1956; statistics clerk then PA to gen mangr NZ Shipping Co Ltd (London) 1958–63, Civil Serv 1963–80 (successively econ conslt on shipping, shipbldg and ports, sr econ advsr on aviation, shipping and marine then under sec for advice on shipping, civil aviation, prices and consumer protection and wholesale prices), econ advsr Ctee of Inquiry into Shipping (Rochdale Ctee) 1967–70, prof of maritime economics Univ of Wales Coll of Cardiff 1980–95 (emeritus prof 1996); fndr memb Nautical Inst (cncl memb 1972–76), ed (later ed-in-chief) Maritime Policy and Mgmnt; Cristoforo Columbus Medal (Genoa) 1992; founding pres Int Assoc of Maritime Economists 1992; assoc RINA 1969 (vice pres 1995), FNI 1977; *Books* Studies in Maritime Economics (1968), Advances in Maritime Economics (1977); *Recreations* cruising; *Clubs* Wyre Mill (Pershore Worcs); *Style*— Prof Richard Goss; ✉ 1 Weir Gardens, Pershore WR10 1DX (☎ 01386 561140); Cardiff University of Wales, Department of Maritime Studies, Aberconway Building, Colum Drive, Cardiff CF1 3YP (☎ 01222 874000, fax 01222 874301)

GOSSAGE, Neal Trevor; *b* 11 Oct 1955; *Educ* Bemrose GS Derby, Univ of Lancaster (BA Accounting & Fin); *Career* gp fin controller Argos plc 1988–91; fin dir: Powerhouse Retail Ltd 1991–93, Specialist Computer Holdings Ltd 1993–96, Vaux Group plc 1996–; FCA (ACA 1979); *Style*— Neal Gossage, Esq; ✉ Vaux Group plc, The Brewery, Sunderland, Tyne & Wear SU1 3AN (☎ 0191 567 6277, fax 0191 514 2488, mobile 0468 812368)

GOSSCHALK, His Hon Judge; Joseph Bernard; s of Lionel Samuel Gosschalk (d 1955), of London, and Johanna, *née* Lion (d 1996); *b* 27 Aug 1936; *Educ* East Ham GS for Boys, Magdalen Coll Oxford (MA); *m* 1973, Ruth Sandra, da of Dr Harold Jarvis; 2 da (Juliette Stella b 30 April 1975, Louise Paula b 11 June 1977); *Career* admitted Hon Soc of Gray's Inn 1956 (Lord Justice Holker Jr Scholarship), called to the Bar Gray's Inn 1961, head of Chambers Francis Taylor Bldg Temple 1983–91, asst recorder 1983–87, recorder 1987–91, circuit judge (SE Circuit) 1991–; memb Hon Soc Inner Temple 1983; *Recreations* reading, tennis, foreign travel; *Style*— His Hon Judge Gosschalk; ✉ St Albans Crown Court, 4 Bricket Road, St Albans, Herts AL1 3LB (☎ 01727 834481, fax 01727 836263)

GOSSIP, Michael Arthur John; OBE (1991); JP; s of Rev Robin Arthur John Gossip (d 1962), of Edinburgh, and Elizabeth Ann, *née* Ness (d 1994); *b* 27 April 1933; *Educ* George Watson's Coll Edinburgh, Univ of Edinburgh (BL); *m* 10 Feb 1962, Margaret Helen, da of George McCall (d 1995), of Dumfries; 1 s (Robin b 1967), 2 da (Susan b 1963, Fiona b 1966); *Career* sr dep co clerk Dumfries CC 1960–71, co clerk Argyll CC 1972–75 (sr dep co clerk 1971–72), chief exec Argyll and Bute DC 1974–96, clerk to the Presbytery of S Argyll 1996–; memb Scot Records Advsy Ctee, pres Argyll Cncl of Vol Serv; Hon Sheriff at Dunoon; Bundesverdienstkreuz 1992; *Recreations* bowls, gardening; *Style*— Michael A J Gossip, Esq, OBE, JP; ✉ Tigh-Na-Coille, Ardrishaig, Argyll PA30 8EP (☎ 01546 603454)

GOSWELL, Sir Brian Lawrence; kt (1991); s of Albert George Goswell (d 1971), and Florence Emily, *née* Barnett (d 1980); *b* 26 Nov 1935; *Educ* St David's Sch High Wycombe, Univ of Durham; *m* 1961, Deirdre Gillian, da of Harold Stones, of Cadeby Hall, Cadeby, Leics; 2 s (Paul b 1964, Angus b 1967); *Career* dep sr ptnr Healey & Baker; chm: Healey & Baker France 1985–, Roux Restaurants Ltd 1989–, Avon City Ltd 1990–, Sunley Secure plc 1993–, Brent Walker Group plc 1994–, William Hill Group Ltd 1995–, Pubmaster Ltd 1996–; dir New Law Publishing Co plc; pres American C of C London 1994–; fell and past pres Incorporated Soc of Valuers and Auctioneers, past pres Br Cncl for Offices; Liveryman Worshipful Co of Gold & Silver Wyre Drawers; ACIArb, FRSA, FLI, FInstD, memb Urban Land Inst (USA); *Recreations* shooting, horse racing, cricket; *Clubs* Turf, Carlton (chm Political Ctee), City of London, City Livery, United & Cecil (hon sec), MCC, Cavalry & Guards, Royal Green Jackets London, Leander, Temple Golf; *Style*— Sir Brian Goswell; ✉ Healey & Baker, 27 Austin Friars, London EC2N 2AA (☎ 0171 514 2001, fax 0171 514 2399); Pipers, Camley Park Drive, Pinkneys Green, Berks SL6 6QF (☎ 01628 30768)

GOTCH, Prof Frances Margaret; da of Geoffrey Gore (d 1994), and Queenie, *née* Rawlings (d 1988); *b* 29 Jan 1943; *Educ* Univ of Oxford (MSc, DPhil), MRCPath; *m* 1 Feb 1964, Michael Gotch, s of Leonard Gotch; 3 da (Lisa Helen b 1966, Emma Sophie b 1969, Sharon Mandy (adopted 1973) b 1960); *Career* formerly research scientist Nuffield Dept of Med then univ lectr Inst of Molecular Med Oxford, currently prof and head Dept of Immunology Chelsea & Westminster Hosp London; author of over 100 pubns in peer reviewed jls since 1970; *Recreations* reading, painting, keep-fit; *Style*— Prof Frances Gotch; ✉ Department of Immunology, Chelsea & Westminster Hospital, 369 Fulham Road, London SW10 9NH (☎ 0181 746 8257, fax 0181 746 5997, e-mail f.gotch@cxwms.ac.uk)

GOTCH, Jeremy Millard Butler; s of Ralph Butler Gotch (d 1979), and Eileen Madge, *née* Millard (d 1956); *b* 6 June 1934; *Educ* Berkhamsted Sch, Jesus Coll Cambridge (MA); *m* 28 Dec 1957, Janet Phyllis, da of Eric Ralph Rich (d 1961); 1 s (Christopher b 1969), 2 da (Jennifer b 1960, Sarah b 1962); *Career* RASC 1952–54 (2 Lt 1952), Lt-Col ETSC (TA) 1989–; Shell International Petroleum Co 1957–59; Traffic Services Ltd: dir 1962, md 1968, chm 1978; md rail ops CAIB UK Ltd 1986–91, proprietor Gotch Consultancy tport conslts 1991–; first Br pres Union Internationale D'Associations de Propriétaires de Wagons Particuliers 1980–83 (memb 1969–91); tstee Jesus Coll Cambridge Soc; chm: Assoc of Private Railway Wagon Owners 1980–91, Friends of Dulwich Picture Gallery 1981–84, The Maitland Tst 1984–, Int Div Private Wagon Fedn 1991–93, Motorcycle Branch Save the Children Fund 1992–95, Lord Mayor's Appeal for St John Ambulance 1995–96; vice pres CIT 1990–93; chm Estates Govrs Alleyn's Coll of God's Gift 1994–96 (govr 1981–); govr: St Olave's and St Saviour's Schs, Dulwich Coll; sec Dulwich Sports Club 1964–73; Sheriff City of London 1993–94; Freeman City of London, Liveryman Worshipful Co of Carmen (memb Ct of Assts 1983–, Master 1996–97); Hon Dip London Coll of Advanced Tport Studies; underwriting memb Lloyd's 1974–; memb Royal Soc of St George; OStJ 1995; FCIT, FInstFF, FILog; *Recreations* music, squash, golf; *Clubs* MCC, City Livery, United Wards, Candlewick Ward, RAC, Dulwich Sports, Wig & Pen; *Style*— Jeremy Gotch, Esq; ✉ 21 Alleyn Road, Dulwich, London SE21 8AB (☎ and fax 0181 766 7999)

GOTHARD, Dr Richard Sherwin; s of late Henry Alexander Sherwin Gothard, and Amy Rubina, *née* Baxter; *b* 22 May 1923; *Educ* Cranbrook; *m* 1955, late Margaret Eileen

Milligan; 1 step s, 2 step da; *Career* joined RAF 1939, served 29 Sqdn, 174 Sqdn, 2 Tactical Airforce, 133 RAF/US Sqdn UK, RAFVR until 1963; ptnr Alexander Gothard and Ptnrs 1947, fndr md Adelphi Manufacturing Co; chm: Gothard House Publications Ltd, International Subscriptions Ltd; sr ptnr Hythe Books and Gothard Investment Co, dir Noyes Data Corp USA, chm and chief exec Gothard House Group of Cos Ltd; pres Fruit Culture Cncl 1982, past pres RNLI Henley-on-Thames; Freeman City of London, Freeman Liveryman and Archivist Worshipful Co of Fruiterers (Master 1982); former FInstD, former MInstM; memb: Assoc of Info Offrs in the Pharmaceutical Indust, Soc of Pharmaceutical Medicine, East Malling Res Assoc; *Books* Information Resources Guides Britain, Glossary of Terms Professionally and Commonly Used in Health, History of Worshipful Co of Fruiterers 1912–1975; *Recreations* sailing, engraving, gardening, writing; *Clubs* Royal Cinque Ports Yacht, MCC, RAF, City Livery, United Wards, Royal Soc of St George; *Style*— Dr Richard S Gothard; ✉ Sherwins, Park Place Farm, Remenham, Henley-on-Thames, Oxon; Gothard House, Henley-on-Thames, Oxon RG9 1AJ (☎ 01491 573602)

GOTO, John; *Educ* Berks Coll of Art, St Martin's Sch of Art (BA); *Career* artist; pt/t lectr: Camberwell Sch of Art 1979–81, Poly of Central London 1979–87, Oxford Brookes Univ 1979–, Ruskin Sch of Drawing & Fine Art Univ of Oxford 1987; visiting lectr to numerous art colls since 1979; Br Cncl scholar: Paris 1977, Prague 1978; artist fell Girton Coll Univ of Cambridge 1988–89, vice chm Visual Arts Panel S Arts Assoc 1989–90; *Solo Exhibitions* incl: Goto Photographs 1971–81 (The Photographer's Gallery) 1981, Goto Photographs 1975–83 (PPS Galerie Gundlac Hamburg) 1983, ULUV Gallery Prague (Br Cncl Exhibition) 1983, Moravian Gallery Bruno Czechoslovakia 1983 (touring Czechoslovakia and Spain 1983–85), Sites of Passage (Fischer Fine Art and Ashmolean Museum Oxford) 1986 and 1988, Terezin (Cambridge Darkroom, John Hansard Gallery Southampton, Cornerhouse Manchester and Raab Galerie Berlin) 1988–89, The Atomic Yard (Kettle's Yard Cambridge and Raab Gallery) 1993, The Scar (Banjamin Rhodes Gallery London, Manchester City Galleries and John Hansard Gallery Univ of Southampton) 1993, John Goto (touring Russia) 1994–95, The Framers' Collection (Portfolio Gallery Edinburgh) 1997; *Group Exhibitions* incl: Painting/Photography (Richard DeMarco Gallery) Edinburgh 1986, Next/Tomorrow (Kettle's Yard Cambridge) 1986, Fifteen Studios (Museum of Modern Art Oxford) 1986, Romantic Visions (Camden Arts Centre) 1988, Blasphemies Ecstasies & Cries (Serpentine Gallery) 1989, Photographic Art in Britain 1945–89 (Barbican), Metamorphosis (Raab Gallery Millbank) 1989, After Auschwitz: Responses to the Holocaust in Contemporary Art (Royal Festival Hall and UK tour) 1995–96; *Books* Shotover (1984), Terezin (1988), The Atomic Yard (1990), The Scar (1993); *Style*— John Goto, Esq; ✉ c/o Jason & Rhodes Gallery, 4 New Burlington Place, London W1X 1SB

GOTTELIER, (Catherine) Jane; da of Prof Charles Lewis Foster, of Chislehurst, Kent, and Margaret Louisa, *née* Woodward (d 1973); *b* 31 Aug 1951; *Educ* Stratford House Sch for Girls Bickley Kent, Croydon Coll of Art, St Martin's Sch of Art (BA), Central Sch of Art (Higher Dip in Textile Design); *m* 3 Dec 1982, Patrick George Campbell Gottelier, *qv*, s of Alfred John Dunhill Gottelier; 2 s (Thomas Charles Morehead b 13 Feb 1988, William John de Chermont b 13 April 1991); *Career* fashion designer specialising in knitwear, uses indigo dyed yarn and trompe d'oeil techniques; fndr dir (with husb) Artwork Apparel Ltd 1977–, estab diffusion label Artwork Blue 1990, expanded into menswear range Geo Trowark (retailed at flagship shop St Christopher's Place and at Thomas Neal Centre, Neal Street, Covent Garden) and lately childrenswear range Minor Artwork; stockists incl Harrods and Whistles of London and numerous others worldwide, show regularly London, NY and Paris; *Recreations* swimming, walking, interior design, antique hunting, reading, travel, cooking; *Style*— Mrs Jane Gottelier; ✉ Artwork Apparel Ltd, 103 Bermondsey Street, London SE1 3XB (☎ 0171 403 6332, fax 0171 403 0027)

GOTTELIER, Patrick George Campbell; s of Alfred John Dunhill Gottelier, of Penzance, Cornwall, and Freda Joan Gottelier; *b* 20 Nov 1951; *Educ* Birmingham Poly, Central Sch of Art (BA); *m* 3 Dec 1982, (Catherine) Jane Gottelier, *qv*, da of Prof Charles Lewis Foster; 2 s (Thomas Charles Morehead b 13 Feb 1988, William John de Chermont b 13 April 1991); *Career* fndr dir (with w) Artwork Apparel Ltd specialising in knitwear 1977–, estab diffusion label Artwork Blue 1990, expanded into menswear range Geo Trowark (retailed at flagship shop St Christophers Place) and lately childrenswear range Minor Artwork; stockists incl Harrods and Whistles of London and numerous others worldwide, show regularly London, NY and Paris; *Recreations* photography, sailing, walking, travel, cooking; *Clubs* Chelsea Arts; *Style*— Patrick Gottelier, Esq; ✉ Artwork Apparel Ltd, 103 Bermondsey Street, London SE1 3XB (☎ 0171 403 6332, fax 0171 403 0027)

GOUDIE, Prof Andrew Shaw; s of William Cooper Goudie, and Mary Isobel, *née* Pulman (d 1992); bro of (Thomas) James Cooper Goudie, QC, *qv*; *b* 21 Aug 1945; *Educ* Dean Close Sch Cheltenham, Trinity Hall Cambridge (BA, MA, PhD); *m* 21 March 1987, Heather Ann, da of John Viles, of Chelmsford; 2 da (Amy Louise b 7 June 1988, Alice May b 25 May 1991); *Career* Univ of Oxford: lectr in geography and fell Hertford Coll 1976–84, prof of geography and head of dept 1984–94, pres Oxford Univ Devpt Prog and pro-vice-chllr 1995–; FRGS 1970, MIBG 1970; *Books* The Human Impact, The Nature of the Environment, Environmental Change, Geomorphological Techniques, Duricrusts, The Warm Desert Environment, Land Shapes, Discovering Landscape in England and Wales, The Prehistory and Palaeogeography of the Great Indian Desert, Chemical Sediments in Geomorphology; *Recreations* old books, old records, gardening; *Clubs* Geographical; *Style*— Prof Andrew Goudie; ✉ University Offices, Wellington Square, Oxford OX1 2JD (☎ 01865 270000)

GOUDIE, (Thomas) James Cooper; QC (1984); s of William Cooper Goudie (d 1981), and Mary Isobel, *née* Pulman (d 1992); bro of Prof Andrew Shaw Goudie, *qv*; *b* 2 June 1942; *Educ* Dean Close Sch Cheltenham, LSE (LLB); *m* 30 Aug 1969, Mary Teresa, da of Martin Brick; 2 s (Martin b 5 July 1973, Alexander b 14 July 1977); *Career* slr 1966–70, called to the Bar Inner Temple 1970, SE Circuit 1970–, recorder 1985–, master of the Bench 1991–, dep High Ct judge (Queen's Bench Div) 1995–; memb Brent Cncl 1967–78 (latterly ldr), Party candidate (Lab) Brent North 1974; chm: Admin Law Bar Assoc, Law Reform Ctee, Bar Cncl, Soc of Labour Lawyers; FCIArb; *Style*— James Goudie, Esq, QC; ✉ 11 King's Bench Walk, Temple EC4Y 7EQ (☎ 0171 583 0610, fax 0171 583 9123/3690)

GOUGH, (Charles) Brandon; s of Charles Richard Gough (d 1957), and Mary Evaline, *née* Goff (d 1996); *b* 8 Oct 1937; *Educ* Douai Sch, Jesus Coll Cambridge (MA); *m* 24 June 1961, Sarah, da of Maurice Evans Smith (d 1987); 1 s (Richard b 1962) 2 da (Lucy (Mrs Peter Harris) b 1964, Katherine (Mrs Lee Medlock) b 1967); *Career* Nat Serv Army 1956–58; Coopers & Lybrand: joined 1964, ptnr 1968–94, chm 1983–94, chm Coopers & Lybrand Europe during 1989 and 1992–94, memb Exec Ctee Coopers & Lybrand International 1982–94 (chm 1985 and 1991–92); non-exec chm Yorkshire Water plc 1996–; non-exec dir: British Aerospace plc (govt dir) 1987–88, British Invisibles 1990–94, S G Warburg Group plc 1994–95 (dep chm 1995), De La Rue plc 1994–, National Power plc 1995–, George Wimpey PLC 1995–; chm Auditing Practices Ctee CCAB 1981–84 (memb 1976–84); memb: Accounting Standards Review (Dearing) Ctee 1987–88, Fin Reporting Cncl 1990–96, Cambridge Univ Careers Serv Syndicate 1983–86, Cncl for Indust and Higher Educn 1985–93; chm Higher Educn Funding Cncl for England 1993–; City Univ Business Sch: memb City Advsy Panel 1980–91 (chm 1986–91), chm Fin Ctee 1988–91, chm Cncl 1992–93 (memb 1986–93); chm Nat Trg Task Force working gp on The Role of Trg and Enterprise Cncls in local econ devpt 1991–92, chm Doctors' and Dentists' Pay Review Body 1993–; memb: Cncl of Lloyd's 1983–86 (Lloyd's Silver Medal 1986), Governing Cncl Business in the Community 1984–88, Mgmnt Cncl GB-Sasakawa Fndn 1985–96, Cncl Business in the Community 1988–94, CBI Task Force Vocational Educn and Trg 1989, UK Nat Ctee Japan-Euro Community Assoc 1989–94, Cncl Fndn for Educn Business Ptnrships 1989–91, CBI Educn and Trg Affrs Ctee 1990–94, Cncl City Univ 1991–93, Cncl of Mgmnt Royal Shakespeare Theatre Tst 1991–, President's Ctee of Business in the Community 1992–94, Cncl of The Prince of Wales Business Leaders Forum of Int Business in the Community 1992–94, Cncl London First 1993–94, Cncl Freshfields 1996–; tstee: Guildhall Sch Music and Drama Fndn 1989–95, Common Purpose 1989– (chm 1991–); Hon DSc City Univ 1994; Freeman: City of London 1983, Worshipful Co of CAs 1983; FCA 1974 (memb Cncl 1981–84); *Recreations* music, gardening; *Style*— Brandon Gough, Esq; ✉ Long Barn, Weald, Sevenoaks, Kent TN14 6NH (☎ 01732 463714)

GOUGH, Darren; *b* 18 Sept 1970; *m* 16 Oct 1993, Anna; 1 s (Liam James b 24 Nov 1994); *Career* professional cricketer; Yorkshire CCC: debut 1989, awarded county cap 1993, memb team to Barbados 1990, to S Africa 1991–92 and tour to Antigua 1994; England: first one day int (v New Zealand) 1994, test debut v S Africa 1994, memb team touring Aust 1994/95, memb team touring S Africa 1995–96, memb team World Cup India/Pakistan 1995–96, memb team touring Zimbabwe and New Zealand 1996–97; memb England YC tour to Aust 1989–90; *Style*— Darren Gough, Esq; ✉ c/o Yorkshire CCC, Headingley Cricket Ground, Leeds, W Yorks LS6 3BU (☎ 0113 2787394)

GOUGH, Prof Douglas Owen; s of Owen Albert John Gough, of Romford, Essex, and Doris May, *née* Camera; *b* 8 Feb 1941; *Educ* Hackney Downs GS, St John's Coll Cambridge (MA, PhD, Strathcona award); *m* 16 Jan 1965, Rosanne Penelope, da of Prof Charles Thurstan Shaw; 2 da (Karen Ione May b 30 July 1966, Heidi Natasha Susan b 25 Feb 1968); 2 s (Julian John Thurstan b 29 Sept 1974, Russell Edward William b 18 Aug 1976); *Career* res assoc Jt Inst for Laboratory Astrophysics and Dept of Physics and Astrophysics Univ of Colorado 1966–67, sr postdoctoral res assoc Goddard Inst for Space Studies 1967–69; Univ of Cambridge: memb graduate staff Inst of Theoretical Astronomy 1969–73, fell Churchill Coll 1972–, lectr in astronomy and applied mathematics 1973–85, reader in astrophysics 1985–93, prof of theoretical astrophysics 1993–; memb Bd of Dirs Møller Centre for Continuing Educn Churchill Coll Cambridge 1992–; SRC sr fell 1978–83, hon prof of astronomy Queen Mary and Westfield Coll 1986–, fell Jt Inst for Laboratory Astrophysics 1986–; Sir Joseph Larmor lectr Cambridge Philosophical Soc 1988, Wernher von Braun lectr Nat Aeronautics and Space Admin 1991, Morris Loeb lectr in physics Harvard Univ 1993, Bishop lectr Columbia Univ 1996, Halley lectr Univ of Oxford 1996; second prize Gravity Res Fndn 1973, James Arthur prize lectr Harvard Univ 1982, William Hopkins prize Cambridge Philosophical Soc 1984, George Ellery Hale prize American Astronomical Soc 1995; FRAS 1966; *Books* Problems of Solar and Stellar Oscillations (ed, 1983), Seismology of the Sun and the Distant Stars (ed, 1986), Challenges to Theories of the Structure of Moderate-Mass Stars (with J Toomre, 1991); author of 200 res papers in scientific jls and books; *Recreations* cooking, listening to music; *Style*— Prof Douglas Gough; ✉ 3 Oxford Road, Cambridge CB4 3PH (☎ 01223 360309); Institute of Astronomy, Madingley Road, Cambridge CB3 0HA (☎ 01223 337548, fax 01223 337523)

GOUGH, Janet; da of Clifford Gough (d 1983), of Craven Arms, Shropshire, and Sarah, *née* Allen; *b* 1 Aug 1940; *Educ* Ludlow HS, Newnham Coll Cambridge (state scholar); *Career* St Paul's Girls' Sch 1964–71, The Manchester GS 1972, Worcester HS for Girls 1973, St Paul's Girls' Sch 1973– (High Mistress 1993–); *Recreations* walking, architecture, opera; *Style*— Miss Janet Gough; ✉ St Paul's Girls' School, Brook Green, London W6 7BS (☎ 0171 603 2288)

GOUGH, John Osborne; MBE (1984); s of Reginald Osborne Gough (d 1972); *b* 26 March 1932; *Educ* Tonbridge, Univ of Bristol (BA); *m* 1, 1958 (m dis 1983), Patricia Annette, da of Kenneth Blandford Lalonde; 2 children; m 2, 1983, Susan Mary, da of Michael Hornby and Nicolette, gda of 1 Earl of Dudley (Susan m 1, 1951 (m dis), Marquess of Blandford, now 11 Duke of Marlborough; 1 s (Marquess of Blandford, *qv*), 1 da (Lady Henrietta Gelber); m 2, 1962, Alan Heber-Percy); *Career* chm: Kleeneze Holdings 1987–90, Quadron Services Ltd; non-exec dir: South Western Electricity plc, Baggeridge Brick plc; chm CBI (SW region) 1982–84, memb Cncl RSA 1988–94; dir of fundraising British Field Sports Soc; *Recreations* fishing; *Style*— John Gough, Esq, MBE; ✉ Church House, Little Coxwell, Faringdon, Oxon

GOUGH, Piers William; s of Peter Gough, of Lewes, E Sussex, and Daphne Mary Unwin, *née* Banks; gs of Leslie Banks, the actor; *b* 24 April 1946; *Educ* Uppingham, AA Sch (AADipl); *m* 8 June 1991, Rosemary Elaine Fosbrooke, da of Robert Bates; *Career* architect; ptnr Wilkinson Calvert and Gough 1968–72, in private practice 1972–75, ptnr CZWG 1975–; princ projects: Phillips West 2 London W2 1976, China Wharf London SE1 1988, CDT Building 1988 and Boarding Houses 1993–95 Bryanston Sch Dorset, Street-Porter House London EC1 1988, The Circle London SE1 1990, Cochrane Square Glasgow 1988–95, Crown Street Regeneration Project Gorbals Scotland 1991–, Westbourne Grove Public Lavatory 1993, ADT Building Uppingham Sch 1993–95, 1–10 Summers Street, London EC1 1994, Soho Lofts Wardour Street London 1995, Nat Portrait Gallery London 1995–; exhbns: Lutyens Exhbn (Hayward Gallery) 1982, Gilbert Exhbn (Royal Acad) 1985, CZWG 68–88 (RIBA Heinz Gallery) 1988; lecture tours: Australasia 1983, 1989 and 1992, Europe 1989, 1990 and 1991, N and S Americas 1986 and 1991; pres Cncl AA 1995– (memb 1970–71 and 1991–, vice pres 1993); memb: London Docklands Devpt Corp Design Gp 1989–, RIBA 1991– (awards regnl chm 1992–), English Heritage London Advsy Ctee 1995, Bd of Tstees Artangel and Chisenhale Gallery; FRSA; *Recreations* lunch; *Clubs* Groucho; *Style*— Piers Gough, Esq; ✉ CZWG Architects, 17 Bowling Green Lane, London EC1R 0BD (☎ 0171 253 2523, fax 0171 250 0594)

GOUGH, Richard; *b* 5 April 1962; *Career* professional footballer; over 150 appearances Dundee Utd 1980–86, 49 appearances Tottenham Hotspur 1986–87, transferred to Glasgow Rangers 1987–; Scotland: memb under 21 team, over 60 full caps; *Style*— Richard Gough, Esq; ✉ Glasgow Rangers FC, Ibrox Stadium, Edmiston Drive, Glasgow G51 2XD

GOUGH, 5 Viscount (UK 1849); Sir Shane Hugh Maryon Gough; 5 Bt (UK 1842); also Baron Gough of Chinkangfoo and of Maharajpore and the Sutlej (UK 1846); s of 4 Viscount Gough, MC, JP, DL (d 1951, ggs of Field Marshal 1 Viscount, KP, GCB, GCSI, PC, whose full title was Viscount Gough of Goojerat in the Punjaub and of the City of Limerick. His brilliant exploits in the two Sikh Wars resulted in the annexation of the Punjab to British India), by his w Margaretta Elizabeth (d 1977), da of Sir Spencer Maryon-Wilson, 11 Bt; *b* 26 Aug 1941; *Educ* Winchester; *Career* late Lt Irish Gds; stockbroker with Laurence Keen Ltd; local dir West End office Royal Insurance Group (UK) plc; chm: Mastiff Electronic System Ltd, Barwell plc and associate cos, Charlwood Leigh Ltd; memb Royal Co of Archers (Queen's Body Guard for Scotland); tstee: Gardners Tst for the Blind, Schizophrenia Research Tst; memb Exec Cncl RNIB; Sr Grand Warden United Grand Lodge of England 1984–86; FRGS; *Clubs* White's, Pratt's; *Style*— The Rt Hon the Viscount Gough; ✉ Keppoch Estate Office, Strathpeffer, Ross-shire IV14 9AD (☎ 01997 421224); 17 Stanhope Gardens, London SW7 5RQ; Laurence Keen Ltd, 49/51 Bow Lane, London EC4M 9LX (☎ 0171 489 9493)

GOULD, Bryan Charles; s of Charles Terence Gould, of Hamilton, NZ; *b* 11 Feb 1939; *Educ* Univ of Auckland, Balliol Coll Oxford; *m* 1967, Gillian Anne Harrigan; 1 s, 1 da; *Career* FO 1964–66, 2 sec Br Embassy Brussels 1966–68, fell Worcester Coll Oxford 1968–74, reporter TV Eye (Thames Television) 1979–83; MP (Lab): Southampton Test Oct 1974–79 (also contested Feb 1974), Dagenham 1983–94 (resigned May); PPS to Sec of State for: Trade 1975–76, Environment 1976–77; former memb Select Ctee on Euro Legislation, oppn front bench spokesman on trade and indust Nov 1985–86; memb Shadow Cabinet 1986–92; Lab Pty campaign co-ordinator 1986–87; shadow chief sec 1986–88; chief oppn spokesman on: trade and industry 1988–89, environment 1989–92, national heritage July-Sept 1992; candidate Lab Pty leadership and dep leadership elections 1992; vice-chllr Waikato Univ NZ 1994–; *Books* Goodbye to all That (1995); *Recreations* food, wine, walking, gardening; *Style—* Bryan Gould, Esq; ✉ Vice-Chancellor, Waikato University, Hamilton, New Zealand

GOULD, Edward John Humphrey; s of Roland Akehurst Gould, of London, and Winifred Ruth Lee, *née* Dixon; *b* 31 Oct 1943; *Educ* St Edward's Oxford, St Edmund Hall Oxford (MA, DipEd); *m* 4 April 1970, Jennifer Jane, da of Ian Hunter Lamb of Edinburgh; 2 da (Karen Penelope b 1971, Nicola Mary b 1973); *Career* Harrow Sch: joined 1967, asst master/head of Geography Dept 1974–79, housemaster 1979–83; headmaster Felsted Sch 1983–93, master Marlborough Coll 1993–; memb: Ind Schs Curriculum Ctee 1985–92 (chm 1990–92), Common Entrance Bd 1988–92, Ct of Univ of Essex 1985–93, Br Atlantic Educn Ctee 1987–89; chm ISIS East 1989–93; govr: St Andrew's Pangbourne, Cheam Sch Newbury, St Francis Sch Pewsey; former govr: Heathfield Sch Ascot, Orwell Park Sch Ipswich; JP Essex 1989–93; Oxford rugby blue 1963–66 and swimming half blue 1965, rep GB rowing 1967; FRGS, FRSA; *Recreations* music, sailing; *Clubs* East India, Devonshire Sports and Public Schools, Vincent's (Oxford); *Style—* Edward Gould, Esq; ✉ The Master's Lodge, Marlborough College, Marlborough, Wilts SN8 1PA (☎ 01672 892400)

GOULD, Prof Frank William; s of Frank Gould (d 1972), of London, and Bridget, *née* Tyler (1988); *b* 12 Aug 1937; *Educ* Glendale Co GS, UCL (BA), Univ of NSW (MA); *m* 1963, Lesley, da of Norman Hall; 2 da (Clio b 1968, Fiona b 1974), 1 s (Thomas b 1983); *Career* tutor in economics Univ of NSW 1964–66, economics journalist Beaverbrook Newspapers 1966–67, lectr in economics Kingston Poly 1967–73, princ lectr and dean of faculty Poly of Central London 1973–85, asst dir Leeds Poly 1985–88, pro-rector NE London Poly 1988–91, vice-chllr Univ of East London 1991–; dir London Docklands Business Sch 1994, chm and md UEL Training and Consultancy Company 1993, chm Bd of Dirs Open Learning Fndn Enterprises Ltd 1989–96, vice chm Open Learning Fndn 1991–96, memb London East TEC Bd 1993–96, memb Stratford Promoter Group 1995; contrib to books and scientific jls in economics, political science, social policy on govt and the economy and devpt of public expenditure; memb Int Inst of Public Finance 1981; *Recreations* horse riding, hill walking, jogging; *Clubs* Reform; *Style—* Prof Frank Gould; ✉ 8 Glenmore Road, London NW3 4DB (☎ 0171 722 1265); The University of East London, Romford Road, Stratford, London E15 4LZ (☎ 0181 849 3630, fax 0181 534 8151, car 0836 651676)

GOULD, Jonathan; s of Cedric Gould (d 1956), of London, and Joan Wilson, *née* Spiers (d 1983); *b* 1 April 1952; *Educ* Hurstpierpoint Coll, Univ of Bristol (LLB); *m* 4 May 1991, Elizabeth Ann Addison; *Career* Allen & Overy 1974–: articled 1974–76, asst slr 1976–81, ptnr 1982–, res ptnr Hong Kong 1988–96, ptnr London 1996–; memb City of London Slrs' Co; memb: Law Soc, Law Soc of Hong Kong; *Clubs* Hong Kong; *Style—* Jonathan Gould, Esq; ✉ Allen & Overy, One New Exchange, London EC4M 9QQ (☎ 0171 330 3000, fax 0171 330 9999)

GOULD, Jonathan Leon; s of Robert and Yvonne Gould, of Birmingham; *b* 5 June 1967; *Educ* Handsworth GS; *Career* reporter Supercall Sport 1988, sports ed Beacon Radio 1988–90, reporter BBC World Service, IRN, ITN, BFBS and BSkyB 1990–92, head of sport ITN Radio/IRN 1992–95, md Sportsmedia Broadcasting Ltd 1992–; presenter: Talk Radio, Live TV; memb Inst of Sports Sponsorship; *Recreations* travel, cinema, football; *Clubs* The Bushmen (BBC World Service), Sons of the Desert (Laurel and Hardy Appreciation Society); *Style—* Jonathan Gould, Esq; ✉ Sportsmedia Broadcasting Ltd, Suite 47, Canalot Production Studios, 222 Kensal Road, London W10 5BN (☎ 0181 962 9000, fax 0181 960 6999, mobile 0468 444422)

GOULD, Kenneth; CBE (1973), TD; s of Capt William Charles Gould (d 1929), and Ethel Edna, *née* Board; *b* 5 Feb 1919; *Educ* Manchester GS, Victoria Univ Manchester (LLB); *m* 1946, Kathleen Ann, da of Dr Thomas O'Connell (d 1975); 1 s, 1 da; *Career* Lt-Col RA (TA), served Pacific, Burma; slr 1947; advocate and slr Singapore and Malaya 1948; chm and md Borneo Berhad/Inchcape Berhad 1966–73, chm Singapore Int C of C 1971–73; govr London Sch of Oriental & African Studies 1975–93; dir: Inchcape plc 1971–81, Norwich Union Insurance Group 1976–89, Goal Petroleum plc 1985–93; *Recreations* shooting, golf, cricket; *Clubs* Oriental (tstee), MCC, Singapore Cricket, Royal Island Country (Singapore), Tanglin (Singapore); *Style—* Kenneth Gould, Esq, CBE, TD; ✉ Tithe Barn, Courts Mount Rd, Haslemere, Surrey GU27 2PP (☎ 01428 642879)

GOULD, Leonard Arthur; s of Arthur Leonard Gould (d 1981), of Walsall, Staffs, and Mary, *née* O'Neill (d 1975); *b* 3 Feb 1948; *Educ* St Patrick's RC Secdy Coatbridge; *m* 4 Aug 1969, Sandra, da of Neil Keegans; 1 s (Leonard Anthony b 19 April 1973), 2 da (Claire Louise b 14 June 1971, Jennifer Alexsandra b 23 July 1975); *Career* Scottish Daily Express: ed asst 1966, feature writer and sub ed 1967, news sub ed 1969–71, asst chief sub 1971–73, chief sub 1973–74; Daily Express: dep night ed Manchester 1974–81, asst night ed London 1981, dep sports ed Manchester 1982; exec ed Today 1986–88 (sports ed 1985), asst ed Daily Mail 1988–91 (dep sports ed 1988), ed The People 1996– (dep ed 1991–96); *Recreations* horse racing, reading, all sports, enjoying the talents of my family; *Clubs* Scribes West Int; *Style—* Leonard Gould, Esq; ✉ The People, Mirror Group Newspapers, One Canada Square, Canary Wharf, London E14 5AP (☎ 0171 510 3000)

GOULD, Michael Philip; s of John Gould (d 1989), of Clayhall, Ilford, Essex, and Amelia, *née* Cohen (d 1983); *b* 29 Jan 1947; *Educ* SW Essex Tech Coll; *m* 29 Aug 1971, Linda, da of Philip Keen, of Loughton, Essex; 2 da (Rosemary Julia b 1974, Jennifer Karen b 1977); *Career* CA; sr ptnr Haslers; dir: Brontree Ltd 1982, Tametree Properties Ltd 1982; FCA, ATII, MAE; *Recreations* amateur pianist, music generally, theatre, good food, skiing, travel, tennis; *Clubs* David Lloyd Tennis; *Style—* Michael P Gould, Esq; ✉ Laurels, Park Hill, Upper Park, Loughton, Essex IG10 4ES; Haslers, Johnston House, 8 Johnston Rd, Woodford Green, Essex IG8 0XA (☎ 0181 504 3344, fax 0181 506 1417)

GOULD, (Peter) Richard Douglas; s of John Charles Douglas Gould (d 1965), and Mollie Adela Ruth, *née* Blackstone; *b* 24 Sept 1943; *Educ* Sherborne, Univ of London (CertEd); *m* 20 Aug 1977, Alexandra Janet, da of Major A D Macpherson, RM (d 1991); 2 da (Zoë Alice Douglas b 19 Sept 1978, Annie Matilda Douglas b 23 Aug 1980); *Career* teacher: Bromsgrove Sch 1967–72, Summer Fields Oxford 1972–77; stipendiary steward: Jockey Club 1977–80, Royal Hong Kong Jockey Club 1980–83; headmaster Twyford Sch 1983–; played cricket for Hampshire 2nd XI and Dorset, played squash for Worcestershire; *Recreations* cricket, golf, horse racing (steward Newbury racecourse), reading; *Clubs* MCC; *Style—* Richard Gould, Esq; ✉ Springfields, Twyford School, Twyford, Winchester SO21 1NW (☎ 01962 712269)

GOULD, (John) Roger Beresford; s of John Cecil Beresford Gould (d 1978), and Dorothy, *née* Entwistle; *b* 1 Jan 1940; *Educ* Bolton Sch, Merton Coll Oxford (MA); *m* 21 Sept 1968, Catherine Celia, da of William Tetlow Faulkner; 1 s (Richard b 1973), 1 da (Diana b 1970); *Career* dep chm Seton Healthcare Group plc 1984– (co sec 1972–, fin dir 1974–80, dep md 1980–84); Inst of Mgmnt: chm Manchester Branch 1983–85, memb Nat Cncl 1984–90, chm NW Area 1985–87, vice chm Nat Cncl 1991–; memb Nat Cncl ICAEW 1995–; pres Manchester Soc of Chartered Accountants 1994–95, memb Bd of Govrs Manchester Met Univ 1995–; methodist local preacher; FCA 1966, CIMgt 1989 (MIMgt 1971); *Recreations* theatre, swimming, golf; *Clubs* United Oxford and Cambridge Univ; *Style—* Roger Gould, Esq; ✉ Seton Healthcare Group plc, Tubiton House, Oldham, Lancs OL1 3HS (☎ 0161 652 2222)

GOULD, Dr Terry Ronald; s of Sir Ronald Gould (d 1986), of Worthing, Sussex, and Nellie Denning, *née* Fish (d 1979); *b* 11 March 1934; *Educ* Culford Sch Bury St Edmunds, King's Coll London, St George's Hosp Med Sch (MB BS, DA, DObst, LRCP); *m* 18 June 1960, Shirley Anne, da of Robert Arthur Philip Bunce (d 1987), of Bournemouth; 2 s (Simon Mark b 1962, Nicholas James b 1965), 2 da (Caroline Emma b 1961, Sarah Kathryn b 1970); *Career* Nat Serv Lt Surgn RN 1960–63; consit anaesthetist: Royal Dental Hosp 1968–80, Atkinson Morley's Hosp 1968; St George's Hosp London: conslt anaesthetist 1968–95, chm Med Advsy Ctee 1976–79, hon archivist 1987–, hon conslt anaesthetist 1995–; hon conslt anaesthetist St Luke's Nursing Home for Clergy 1968–; Wandsworth Health Authy: chm Dist Med Exec Ctee 1980–83 (memb 1983–85), unit gen mangr Continuing Care Unit 1985–93; sec to Special Tstees St George's Hosp; memb: Cncl Trinity Hospice Clapham, Mgmnt Ctee Wandsworth Homes Assoc, History of Anaesthesia Soc, Assoc of Anaesthetists; memb BMA, DObstRCOG, MRCS, FRCA; *Books* Quality in Health Care - A Practical Guide (with H Merrett), A History of the Atkinson Morley's Hospital (with David Uttley), A Short History of St George's Hospital and the Origin of its Ward Names (with David Uttley); *Recreations* gardening, reading, art, history; *Clubs* Sloane; *Style—* Dr Terry Gould; ✉ St George's Hospital, Blackshaw Rd, Tooting, London SW17 0QT (☎ 0181 672 1255)

GOULDING, Sir (Ernest) Irvine; s of Dr Ernest Goulding (d 1938); *b* 1 May 1910; *Educ* Merchant Taylors', St Catharine's Coll Cambridge (MA); *m* 1935, Gladys Ethel (d 1981), da of Engr Rear Adm Marrack Sennett (d 1935); 1 s (Marrack Irvine, *qv*), 1 da; *Career* served as Instr Offr (Lt Cdr) RN 1931–36 and 1939–45; called to the Bar Inner Temple 1936, QC 1961, bencher Lincoln's Inn 1966 (treas 1983), judge of High Court (Chancery Div) 1971–85; hon fell St Catharine's Coll Cambridge 1971; *Clubs* Travellers'; *Style—* Sir Irvine Goulding; ✉ Penshurst, Wych Hill Way, Woking GU22 0AE (☎ 01483 761012)

GOULDING, Jeremy Wynne Ruthven; s of Denis Arthur Goulding (d 1979), of Nottingham, and Doreen Daphne, *née* Phizackerley; *b* 29 Aug 1950; *Educ* The Becket Sch Nottingham, Magdalen Coll Oxford (MA); *m* 24 Aug 1974, Isobel Mary, da of Arnold Samuel Fisher, of Worcester; 2 s (Richard b 1979, Paul b 1988), 2 da (Laura b 1983, Vanessa b 1988); *Career* asst master Abingdon Sch 1974–78, asst master Shrewsbury Sch 1978–89 (housemaster Oldham's Hall 1983–89), headmaster Prior Park Coll 1989–96, headmaster Haberdashers' Aske's Sch 1996–; memb: Oxford Soc, HMC; *Recreations* hillwalking, reading, cooking; *Style—* Jeremy Goulding, Esq; ✉ Headmaster's House, Haberdashers' Aske's School, Butterfly Lane, Elstree, Herts WD6 3AF (☎ 0181 207 4323)

GOULDING, Prof Kenneth Henry; *b* 26 Sept 1942; *Educ* Scarborough HS for Boys, Univ of London (external BSc, external MSc), Univ of Bradford (PhD); *m* 1962, Yvonne; 2 da (Paula Mary b 1966, Susanne b 1969); *Career* SERC research student Univ of Bradford 1964–67; pt/t lectr: Leeds Tech Coll 1964–65, Bradford Tech Coll 1965–67; Hatfield Poly: lectr 1965–68, sr lectr 1970–75, princ lectr 1975–81, dir of studies (biological scis) and head of dept 1979–85; Lancs Poly: head of dept 1985–87, actg dean of sci 1987–90, dean Faculty of Sci 1990–91; dep vice-chllr Univ of Middx 1992– (actg vice-chllr 1996); CNAA: memb and latterly vice chm Life Scis Ctee 1979–91, chm Environmental Sci Review Gp 1989–91, chm Biological Scis Review Gp 1991–92; Inst of Biol: vice chm NW Branch 1986–87 and 1989–92, chm NW Branch 1987–89, chm Working Gp on Continuing Professional Devpt 1993–; vice chm and memb Exec Ctee Ctee of Heads of Biology in Polytechnics 1986–88, fndr chm Deans of Sci Ctee 1989–92, Euro rep Euro Deans of Sci Ctee 1990–92; memb: Professional and Educn Ctee Biochemical Soc 1987–90, Educn Ctee Assoc for the Advancement of Br Biotechnology 1987–91, Sci Ctee Hong Kong Cncl for Accreditation 1989–92, Exec Ctee Save Br Sci 1989–92, Expert Ctee on Environmental Educn DES 1991–92 and 1996, HE Working Gp Assoc for Sci Educn 1993–95, Hendon Coll Corp 1994–, HEQC Steering Gp on External Examiners System 1994–95, SE England Consortium for Credit Accumulation and Transfer Working Gp 1994–96, Cncl Oak Hill Theol Coll 1995–, Working Gp on Continuing Professional Devpt 1995–, Southgate Coll Corp 1995–, HEQC Task Gp on Univ Awards 1996; memb: Soc for Gen Microbiology 1965, Br Phycological Soc 1969, Freshwater Biological Assoc 1971, Biochemical Soc 1982, Save Biological Scis 1988, Assoc for Sci Educn 1989; CBiol 1970, FIBiol 1986 (MIBiol 1970); *Books* Biotechnology - the Biological and Microbiological Principles (jtly, 1986, German translation), Horticultural Exploitation of Recent Biological Developments (contrib and ed, 1991), Principles and Techniques of Practical Biochemistry (ed with K Wilson, 4 edn 1995, various translations); author of various book chapters and numerous pubns in academic jls; memb: Editorial Advsy Bd Biological Reviews 1989–, Editorial Bd Jl of Health and Nursing Studies 1991–93; *Recreations* various sports; *Clubs* Hatfield Cricket; *Style—* Prof Kenneth Goulding; ✉ Trent Park Campus, University of Middlesex, Bramley Road, London N14 4YZ (direct ☎ 0181 362 5656, fax 0181 449 0798, e-mail KGoulding@mdx.ac.uk)

GOULDING, Sir (William) Lingard Walter; 4 Bt (UK 1904), of Millicent, Clane, Co Kildare, and Roebuck Hill, Dundrum, Co Dublin; er s of Sir (William) Basil Goulding, 3 Bt (d 1982), and Hon Valerie Hamilton Monckton, o da of 1 Viscount Monckton of Brenchley; Sir Lingard is tenth in descent from William Goulding, who arrived in Ireland as a member of Oliver Cromwell's army; *b* 11 July 1940; *Educ* Winchester, Trinity Coll Dublin; *Heir* yr bro, Timothy Adam Goulding, *qv*, b 15 May 1945; *Career* formerly with Conzinc Rio Tinto of Aust; former mangr Rionore; racing driver; headmaster Headfort Sch 1977– (asst master 1974–76); *Style—* Sir Lingard Goulding, Bt; ✉ Dargle Cottage, Enniskerry, Co Wicklow, Republic of Ireland

GOULDING, Marrack Irvine; CMG (1983); s of Sir (Ernest) Irvine Goulding, *qv*, and Gladys Ethel, *née* Sennett (d 1981); *b* 2 Sept 1936; *Educ* St Paul's, Magdalen Coll Oxford (BA); *m* 1961, Susan Rhoda, da of Air Marshal Sir John D'Albiac, KCVO, KBE, CB, DSO (d 1963); 2 s, 1 da; *Career* HM Dip Serv 1959–85, served Lebanon, Kuwait, London, Libya, Egypt, London (private sec to Min State FCO, seconded Cabinet Office CPRS), Portugal, UN (New York), ambass to Angola and (concurrently but non-resident) to São Tomé and Principé 1983–85; UN Secretariat NY 1986–97: under sec gen for peacekeeping 1986–93, under sec gen for political affairs 1993–97; warden St Antony's Coll Oxford 1997–; *Recreations* travel, bird-watching; *Clubs* Royal Over-Seas League; *Style—* Marrack Goulding, Esq, CMG

GOULDING, Robert Dennis (Bobbie); s of Robert Antony Goulding, and Lynn Veronica, *née* White; *b* 4 Feb 1972; *Educ* Fairfield HS; *m* 14 Aug 1992, Paula, da of Kenneth Rathbone; 1 s (Robert Carl (Bobbie) b 4 March 1993); *Career* professional Rugby League footballer; Wigan RLFC: signed 1988, debut March 1988, 40 appearances, Wembley appearances 1990 and 1991; Leeds RLFC: debut Sept 1991, 36 appearances (incl Regal Trophy final); Widnes RLFC: debut 1992, 6 appearances, Wembley appearance 1992; joined St Helens RLFC (for fee of £135,000) 1994–; for GB: 6 under

21 appearances, 6 full caps, memb touring team New Zealand (winning series 2–1) 1990 and Papua New Guinea (1–1) 1990, memb Ashes team 1994; winner: Daily Express Personality of the Year 1990, Wigan Young Player of the Year and Stones Bitter Young Player of the Year 1990, Leeds Player of the Year and Players' Player of the Year 1992, Widnes Supporters' Player of the Year 1992; *Recreations* golf, swimming, charitable activities; *Style*— Bobbie Goulding, Esq; ✉ St Helens RLFC, Knowsley Road, St Helens, Merseyside W10 4AD

GOULDING, Timothy Adam; s of Sir (William) Basil Goulding, 3 Bt (d 1982), and Hon Valerie Hamilton Monckton, o da of 1 Viscount Monckton of Brenchley; hp of bro, Sir (William) Lingard Goulding, 4 Bt, *qv*; *b* 15 May 1945; *Educ* Winchester; *m* 1971, Patricia Mohan, of Dublin; *Style*— Timothy Goulding, Esq; ✉ Dargle Cottage, Enniskerry, Co Wicklow

GOULSTONE, Very Rev (Thomas Richard) Kerry; s of Thomas Louis Goulstone (d 1989), of Llanelli, and Elizabeth Myfanwy Zenith, *née* Jones (d 1982); *b* 5 June 1936; *Educ* Llanelli Boys' GS, St David's UC Lampeter (BA, Tennis capt), St Michael's Coll Llandaff; *m* 27 April 1963, Lyneth Ann, da of James Eli Harris; 1 s (Simon James William b 24 Feb 1965), 1 da (Bridget Mary b 30 Nov 1969); *Career* ordained (St David's Dio): deacon 1959, priest 1960; curate: Llandbadarn Fawr 1959–61, St Peter's Carmarthen 1961–64; vicar: Whitchurch with Solva 1964–67, Gors-las 1967–76, Burry Port with Pwll 1976–84, St Peter's Carmarthen 1984–93; chaplain W Wales Gen Hosp 1984–93, canon St David's Cathedral Carmarthen 1986–93, rural dean of Carmarthen 1988–91, archdeacon of Carmarthen 1991–93, dean of St Asaph Cathedral 1993–; *Recreations* reading, collecting porcelain, sport; *Style*— The Very Rev Kerry Goulstone; ✉ The Deanery, St Asaph, Denbighshire, N Wales LL17 0RL (☎ 01745 583597)

GOURIET, Maj John Prendergast; s of Sqdn Ldr Alfred William Edward (Wings) Gouriet, RFC, RAF (d 1973), of Luxborough, Somerset, and Mary Douglas, *née* Prendergast (d 1977); *b* 1 June 1935; *Educ* Charterhouse, RMA Sandhurst, RMC Shrivenham and Staff Coll Camberley; *m* 4 April 1963, Sarah Julia Wheate, da of Maj Frank Henry Wheate Barnett (ka Dunkirk), of Glympton Park, Oxon; 3 s (James Edward Frank b 1966, Michael David b 1967, Rupert John b 1969); *Career* 15/19 Hussars, Sqdn Ldr and Ops Offr 1956–70, Co 2 i/c Somaliland Scouts 1959–60, Adj Trucial Oman Scouts 1961–63, Staff GSO 3 Intelligence, Dir of Ops Borneo 1965–66, DAA & QMG MOD (Ops and Plans) 1971–72; PA to Sir Walter Salomon Rea Brothers bankers 1973–75, dir Nat Assoc for Freedom 1975–78; md Naflita Ltd and Chine Consultants Ltd Lithuania (advsr Rep of Georgia, UK rep Georgian projects) 1994–, co-fndr Anglo Georgian Parly Gp; co dir and conslt incl: General Portfolio plc 1991–95, Park Air Travel Ltd, Stevens-Lefield Ltd (chm), Wild Life Conservation Project (USA); chm: Freedom in Action, Voters' Res Assoc; PR dir CHREST (Charity Film Making on Christian origins), govr Int Policy Forum (US); hon memb: Inst of Econ Affrs, Nat Right to Work Ctee (US), Colditz Soc; FRGS; awarded Polish Gold Cross 1976; *Books* incl Checkmate Mr President; *Recreations* all forms of sport, hunting, polo, racing, fishing, mountaineering, big game hunting, stalking; *Style*— Maj John Gouriet; ✉ Whites Meadow, Bichnoller, Nr Taunton, Somerset TA4 4EG (☎ and fax 01984 656256); London office (☎ 0171 371 9617, fax 0171 371 9521); Lithuania (☎ 00 3702 72 36 72, fax 00 3702 72 36 81)

GOURLAY, Gen Sir (Basil) Ian Spencer; KCB (1973), CVO (1990), OBE (1956, MBE 1948), MC (1944); s of Brig K I Gourlay, DSO, OBE, MC (d 1970), and Victoria May, *née* Oldrini (d 1986); *b* 13 Nov 1920; *Educ* Eastbourne Coll; *m* 1948, Natasha, da of late Col Dimitri Zinovieff, and late Princess Elisaveta Galitzine; 1 s (Michael b 1950), 1 da (Ann b 1954); *Career* cmmnd RM 1940, Capt 1949, Maj 1956, Lt-Col 1963, CO 42 Commando 1963, Col 1965, actg Brig 1966, Cdr 3 Commando Bde RM 1966, Maj-Gen 1968, Cdr Trg Gp RM 1968–71, Lt-Gen 1971, Gen 1973, Cmdt-Gen RM 1971–75, ret; vice pres Utd World Colleges 1990– (DG 1975–90); *Clubs* MCC, Army and Navy; *Style*— Gen Sir Ian Gourlay, KCB, CVO, OBE, MC

GOVETT, (Clement) John; LVO (1990); s of Clement Charles Govett (d 1963), and Daphne Mary, *née* Norman (d 1964); *b* 26 Dec 1943; *Educ* St Paul's, Pembroke Coll Oxford (MA); *m* 14 June 1975, Rosalind Mary, da of Geoffrey Fawn (d 1988); 3 da (Helen b 1977, Sarah b 1978, Joanna b 1981); *Career* Price Waterhouse 1966–69, dir J Henry Schroder Wagg & Co Ltd 1980–90 (joined 1969); Schroder Investment Management Ltd: dep chief exec 1987–94, chm 1995–; gp md asset mgmnt Schroders PLC 1996–; dir: New City & Commercial Investment Trust plc 1993–, Derby Trust plc 1995–; chm: Schroder Properties Ltd 1987–, Schroder Split Fund plc 1993–; *Recreations* bridge, tennis, gardening; *Clubs* Brooks's, Roehampton; *Style*— John Govett, Esq, LVO; ✉ 29 Marchmont Rd, Richmond, Surrey TW10 6HQ (☎ 0181 940 2876); Schroder Investment Management Ltd, 33 Gutter Lane, London EC2V 8AS (☎ 0171 382 6000)

GOVETT, William John Romaine (Bill); s of John Romaine Govett, and Angela Mostyn, *née* Pritchard; *b* 11 Aug 1937; *Educ* Sandroyd, Gordonstoun; *m* 1 (m dis 1970), Mary Hays; 2 s (Charles b 20 March 1965, Alexander b 3 May 1967), 1 da (Laura b 12 Aug 1968); m 2, 1970, Penelope Ann Irwin, *née* Connolly; 1 da (Romaine b 4 Jan 1973); *Career* Nat Serv cmmnd Royal Scots Greys; chm John Govett and Co Ltd 1974–86 (dep chm 1986–); directorships incl: Legal & General Group plc 1972–96, Govett Oriental Investment Trust 1972, Basinghall Securities Ltd 1975–, General Overseas Investments Ltd 1975–, Govett Equity Trust Ltd 1975–, Govett Strategic Investments Trust plc 1975–, Scottish Eastern Investment Trust plc 1977–, Corney & Barrow Ltd 1979–, Govett Atlantic Investment Trust plc 1979–, Energy & Resources International Ltd 1981–, Union Jack Oil Co Ltd 1981–, 3i Group plc 1984–, CIN Management Ltd 1985–, Berkeley Atlantic Income Ltd 1986–, Berkeley Govett & Co Ltd 1986–, Govett American Endeavour Fund Ltd 1988–, Ranger Oil (UK) Ltd 1988–, North British Canadian Investment Co 1991–; tstee Nat Arts Collection Fund 1985, tstee Tate Gallery 1988; *Recreations* modern art, fishing; *Style*— Bill Govett, Esq; ✉ Fosbury Manor, Marlborough, Wilts SN8 3JN

GOW, John Stobie; s of David Gow (d 1988), of Sauchie, Alloa, Scotland, and Ann Frazer, *née* Scott (d 1984); *b* 12 April 1933; *Educ* Alloa Acad, Univ of St Andrews (BSc, PhD); *m* 29 Dec 1955, Elizabeth, da of James Henderson (d 1963), of Alloa; 3 s (Iain b 1958, Alan b 1961, Andrew b 1964); *Career* prodn mangr Chem Co of Malyasia 1966–68; ICI: res mangr Agric Div 1968–72, gen mangr Catalysts Agric Div 1972–74, res dir Organics Div 1974–79, dep chm Organics Div 1979–84, md speciality chemicals 1984–86; non-exec dir W & J Foster Ltd 1984–93; sec gen Royal Soc of Chem 1986–93, memb Cncl Fedn Euro Chem Socs, assessor SERC 1987–93, sec CSTI; elder Utd Reformed Church; FRSE 1978, FRSC 1986, FRSA; *Style*— John Gow, Esq, FRSE; ✉ 19 Longcroft Ave, Harpenden, Herts AL5 2RD (☎ 01582 764889, fax 01582 461306)

GOW, Gen Sir (James) Michael; GCB (1983, KCB 1979), DL (Edinburgh 1994); s of J C Gow (d 1927); *b* 3 June 1924; *Educ* Winchester; *m* 1946, Jane Emily, da of Capt Mason H Scott, RN (ret); 1 s, 4 da; *Career* served WWII 2 Lt Scots Gds, Lt-Col cmdg 2 Bn Scots Gds 1964–67, Brig cmdg 4 Gds Bde 1967–70, Brig-Gen Staff (Intelligence & Security) HQ BAOR 1971–73, Col Cmdt Intelligence Corps 1973–86, GOC 4 Div 1973–75, dir Army Trg MOD 1975–78, GOC Scotland and Govr Edinburgh Castle 1979–80, C-in-C BAOR and Cdr NATO N Army Gp 1980–83, ADC Gen to HM The Queen 1981–84, Cmdt RCDS 1984–86, Brig Royal Co of Archers (Queen's Body Gd for Scotland); chm Queen Victoria Sch Dunblane 1979–80, cmmr Br Scouts Western Europe 1980–83; vice pres: Royal Patriotic Fund Corp 1984–88, The Scottish Nat Instn for the War Blinded 1995–; pres: Royal Br Legion Scot, Earl Haig Fund Scot 1986–96, Nat Assoc of Sheltered Employment 1993–; chm: Scottish Ex-Servs Charitable Organisations 1989–96, The Scots at War Tst 1994–; tstee Cairn Housing Assoc 1989–; Liveryman Worshipful Company of Painter-Stainers (Freeman 1980); FSA (Scot); *Books* Trooping the Colour: A History of the Sovereign's Birthday Parade (Souvenir Press, 1989), Jottings in a General's Notebook (Souvenir Press, 1989), General Reflections: A Military Man at Large (Souvenir Press, 1991); *Recreations* sailing, travel, music, reading; *Clubs* Pratt's, New (Edinburgh), Highland Society of London; *Style*— General Sir Michael Gow, GCB, DL; ✉ 18 Ann St, Edinburgh EH4 1PJ

GOW, Sheriff Neil; QC (Scot 1970); s of Donald Gow, of Glasgow; *b* 24 April 1932; *Educ* Merchiston Castle Sch, Univ of Edinburgh, Univ of Glasgow (MA, LLB); *m* 1959, Joanna, da of Cdr S D Sutherland, of Edinburgh; 1 s; *Career* Capt Intelligence Corps (BAOR); Carnegie scholar in History of Scots Law 1956, advocate 1957–76, Standing Cncl to Miny of Soc Security (Scot) 1964–70; Parly candidate (C): Kircaldy Burghs 1964 and 1966, Edinburgh East 1970; memb Regnl Cncl Scottish Cons Assoc, hon Sheriff of Lanarkshire 1971, Sheriff of South Strathclyde at Ayr 1976–; pres Auchinleck Boswell Soc; FSA (Scot); *Books* A History of Scottish Statutes (1959), An Outline of Estate Duty in Scotland (jt ed 1970); Crime and Prejudice (Channel 4, 1993), Tests of Evidence (Radio Scotland, 1995); numerous articles and broadcasts on legal topics and Scottish affairs; *Recreations* golf, books, antiquities; *Clubs* Prestwick Golf, Western (Glasgow); *Style*— Sheriff Neil Gow, QC; ✉ Sheriff Court House, Wellington Square, Ayr KA7 1DR (☎ 01292 268474)

GOWAN, David John; s of Prof Ivor Lyn Gowan, of Charlbury, and Gwendoline Alice, *née* Pearce; *b* 11 Feb 1949; *Educ* Nottingham HS, Ardwyn GS Aberystwyth, Balliol Coll Oxford (MA); *m* 10 Aug 1975, Marna Irene, da of Rhondda Williams; 2 s (Richard Vernon b 20 Sept 1978, Edward William b 29 April 1982); *Career* asst princ MOD 1970–73, Home Civil Serv 1973–75; HM Dip Serv: second sec FCO 1975–76, Russian language trg 1976–77, second then first sec Moscow 1977–80, first sec FCO 1981–85, head of chancery and HM consul Brasilia 1985–88, on secondment to Cabinet Office 1988–89, asst head Soviet Dept FCO 1989–90, on secondment as cnsllr Cabinet Office 1990–91, cnsllr (commercial and Know How Fund) Moscow 1992–95, cnsllr and dep head of mission Helsinki 1995–; *Recreations* reading, walking, travel, music, sailing; *Style*— David Gowan, Esq; ✉ c/o Foreign & Commonwealth Office (Helsinki), King Charles Street, London SW1A 2AH

GOWANS, Sir James Learmonth; kt (1981), CBE (1971); s of John Gowans, and Selma Josefina Ljung; *b* 7 May 1924; *Educ* Trinity Sch Croydon, King's Coll Hosp Med Sch, Lincoln Coll Oxford, Pasteur Inst Paris, Exeter Coll Oxford; *m* 1956, Moyra Leatham; 1 s, 2 da; *Career* hon dir MRC Cellular Immunology Unit 1963–77, sec Medical Research Cncl 1977–87, memb Advsy Bd for Res Cncls 1977–87, sec gen Human Frontier Sci Program Strasbourg 1989–93; Royal Soc Royal Medal, foreign associate US Nat Acad of Sciences, Gairdner Fndn Award Toronto, Paul Ehrlich Prize Frankfurt, Wolf Prize in Med Israel; hon fell: St Catherine's Coll Oxford, Exeter Coll Oxford 1983, Lincoln Coll Oxford 1984; Hon MD: Edinburgh, Southampton; Hon ScD Yale; Hon DSc: Chicago, Birmingham, Rochester NY, Hon LLD Glasgow; FRCP, FRS (research prof 1962–77, vice pres and memb Cncl 1973–75), FRSA, memb Academia Europaea; *Style*— Sir James Gowans, CBE, FRS; ✉ 75 Cumnor Hill, Oxford OX2 9HX

GOWAR, Martyn Christopher; s of T W Gowar (d 1987), of Ewell, Surrey, and M A Gowar, *née* Bower (d 1986); *b* 11 July 1946; *Educ* King's Coll Sch Wimbledon, Magdalen Coll Oxford (MA Jurisprudence); *m* 1971, Susan Mary, da of D B H Scotchmer; 3 s (Jonathan b 1973, Michael b 1975, Alexander b 1978); *Career* Lawrence Graham: articled clerk Lawrence Graham & Co 1967, ptnr 1973–, sr ptnr May 1997–; memb: Int Ctee Soc of Tsts & Estate Practitioners (STEP), Tax Ctee Assoc of Corp Tstees, Cncl Int Acad of Estate & Tst Law, Int Bar Assoc; taxation ed Law Soc Gazette 1979–94; frequent lectr on taxation and tst topics; clerk to the Govrs Wellington Coll, clerk to the Tstees Hamlyn Tst, memb Cncl St Paul's Cathedral Choir Sch, tstee Laura Ashley Fndn; memb Worshipful Co of Glaziers; memb Addington Soc; FInstT 1981 (AInstT 1976); *Publications* Butterworths Encyclopaedia of Forms & Precedents Vol 30 (ed Partnerships section), Simons Taxes (contrib); *Recreations* golf, cricket, gardening; *Clubs* MCC, Lord's Taverners, Hankley Common Golf, London Slrs' Golf Society; *Style*— Martyn Gowar, Esq; ✉ Lawrence Graham, 190 Strand, London WC2R 1JN (☎ 1071 379 0000, fax 0171 379 6854, e-mail martyn.gowar@lawgram.co.uk)

GOWDY, (David) Clive; s of Samuel David Gowdy (d 1977), and Eileen, *née* Porter (d 1996); *b* 27 Nov 1946; *Educ* Royal Belfast Academical Inst, Queen's Univ Belfast (BA, MSc); *m* 27 Oct 1973, Linda Doreen, da of Eric Anton Traub, of Belfast; 2 da (Claire b 1978, Alison b 1980); *Career* asst princ Miny of Fin 1970–73, dep princ Civil Serv Cmmn 1973–76, sec Rowland Cmmn 1978–79, princ NI Office 1976–81, exec dir Industl Devpt Bd for NI 1985–87, under sec Dept of Economic Devpt 1987–90 (asst sec 1981–85), Dept of Health and Social Servs 1990–93, Dept of Finance and Personnel 1994–; *Recreations* tennis, archery, music, reading; *Style*— Clive Gowdy, Esq; ✉ Department of Finance and Personnel, Rosepark House, Upper Newtownards Road, Belfast BT4 (☎ 01232 526514)

GOWENLOCK, Prof Brian Glover; CBE (1986); s of Harry Hadfield Gowenlock (d 1976), of Oldham, Lancs, and Hilda, *née* Glover (d 1977); *b* 9 Feb 1926; *Educ* Hulme GS Oldham, Univ of Manchester (BSc, MSc, PhD), Univ of Birmingham (DSc); *m* 24 July 1953, Margaret Lottie, da of Luther John Davies (d 1981), of Swansea; 1 s (Stephen David b 1958), 2 da (Cathren Elizabeth b 1959, Judith Margaret b 1964); *Career* lectr in chemistry Univ Coll of Swansea Univ of Wales 1951–55 (asst lectr 1948–51), sr lectr in chemistry Univ of Birmingham 1964–66 (lectr 1955–64); Heriot-Watt Univ Edinburgh: prof of chemistry 1966–90, dean Faculty of Sci 1969–72 and 1987–90, Leverhulme emeritus fell 1990–92; hon res fell Univ of Exeter 1992–; Erskine visiting fell Univ of Canterbury NZ 1976; memb Univ Grants Ctee 1976–85 (vice chm 1983–85); local preacher Methodist Church 1948–; FRSC 1966, FRSE 1969; *Books* Experimental Methods in Gas Reactions (with Sir Harry Melville, 1964), First Year at The University (with James C Blackie, 1964); *Recreations* genealogy; *Style*— Prof Brian Gowenlock, CBE, FRSE; ✉ 5 Roselands, Sidmouth, Devon EX10 8PB (☎ 01395 516864); Department of Chemistry, University of Exeter, Exeter EX4 4QD (☎ 01392 263263)

GOWER, David Ivon; OBE (1992); s of Richard Hallam Gower (d 1973), and Sylvia Mary, *née* Ford (d 1986); *b* 1 April 1957; *Educ* King's Sch Canterbury, Univ Coll London; *m* 18 Sept 1992, Thorunn Nash; 2 da (Alexandra Sylvia b 25 Sept 1993, Samantha Erna b 28 May 1996); *Career* former professional cricketer, now journalist and broadcaster; Leicestershire CCC 1975–89 (capt 1984–86 and 1988–89), Hampshire CCC 1990–93 (winners NatWest Trophy 1991 and Benson & Hedges Cup 1992); England: debut 1978, 117 test caps, capt 1984–86 and 1989 (total 32 tests as capt), 114 one day int appearances, highest score 215 v Aust Edgbaston 1985, second highest scoring English player in test matches with 8,231 runs incl 18 centuries (broke Geoff Boycott's previous record v Pakistan Old Trafford 1992), ret from first class cricket 1993; dir David Gower Promotions Ltd; cricket corr Sunday Express 1993–95; joined Test Match Special team BBC (for Ashes series in Australia) 1994, memb BBC TV Cricket Commentary Team; presenter: Gower's Cricket Monthly (BBC TV), David Gower's Cricket Weekly (BBC Radio 5); team capt They Think it's All Over (BBC TV) 1995; Hon MA: Univ of Southampton, Univ of Loughborough; *Books* David Gower: the Autobiography (with Martin Johnson, *qv*, 1992); *Recreations* tennis, golf, skiing, Cresta run; *Clubs* St Moritz Tobagganing, East India; *Style*— David Gower, Esq, OBE; ✉ c/o Park Associates, 6 George Street, Nottingham NG1 3BE (☎ 0115 948 3206)

GOWER, His Hon John Hugh; QC (1967); s of Henry John Gower, JP (d 1951), of Pembury, Kent, and Edith, *née* Brooks (d 1926); *b* 6 Nov 1925; *Educ* The Skinners' Co Sch Tunbridge Wells, Inns of Court Sch of Law; *m* 20 Feb 1960, Shirley Mameena, da of William Henry Darbourne (d 1977), of Carshalton Beeches, Surrey; 1 s (Peter b 30 Nov 1960), 1 da (Anne b 15 Feb 1962); *Career* RA Serv Corps 1945–48, Staff Sgt; called to the Bar Inner Temple 1948, bencher 1995–; dep chm Kent Quarter Sessions 1968–71, circuit judge (SE Circuit) 1971–96, resident judge and liaison judge East Sussex Crown Courts 1986–96, dep circuit judge 1996–; memb Lord Chancellor's Advsy Ctee on Legal Educn and Conduct 1991–96 (dep chm 1994–96); vice pres E Sussex Magistrates Assoc, chm Criminal Justice Liaison Ctee for Kent & Sussex 1992–96; pres: Kent Assoc of Parish Cncls 1962–71, pres Tunbridge Wells DC of Voluntary Serv 1974–88; vice pres Kent Cncl of Voluntary Serv 1971–86, chm Southdown and Eridge Hunt 1985–91; Freeman City of London (by purchase) 1960; *Recreations* fishing, riding, tapestry, gardening; *Style—* His Hon John Gower, QC; ✉ The Coppice, Lye Green, Crowborough, E Sussex TN6 1UY (☎ 01892 654395)

GOWER-SMITH, (Nicholas) Mark; s of Charles Samuel Smith (d 1983), of Tunbridge Wells, and Margaret Brenda, *née* Isaac; *b* 20 March 1955; *Educ* The Skinners' Sch Tunbridge Wells; *m* 25 July 1987, Christine Lorraine, da of Leslie Frank George Allan (d 1981); 2 s (Charles Edward b 1989, James Andrew b 1993); *Career* CA; sr ptnr Norman Cox & Ashby 1984–, proprietor Gower-Smith & Co 1984–; tstee The Gower Tst; organist and music co-ordinator St John's Church Tunbridge Wells 1992–96; Freeman City of London 1991, Liveryman Worshipful Co of Tobacco Pipe Makers and Tobacco Blenders 1991; FCA, FRSA; *Recreations* music, opera, heraldry, photography; *Clubs* Royal Cwlth Soc; *Style—* Mark Gower-Smith, Esq; ✉ Grosvenor Lodge, 72 Grosvenor Rd, Tunbridge Wells, Kent TN1 2AZ (☎ 01892 522551)

GOWERS, Andrew Richard David; s of Michael David Warren Gowers, of Haywards Heath, Sussex, and Florence Anne Dean, *née* Sykes; *b* 19 Oct 1957; *Educ* Trinity Sch Croydon, Gonville and Caius Coll Cambridge (MA); *m* 1982, Finola Mary, *née* Clarke; *Career* Reuters: grad trainee 1980, Brussels Bureau 1981–82, Zurich corr 1982–83; Financial Times: foreign staff 1983–84, agric corr 1984–85, commodities ed 1985–87, ME ed 1987–90, features ed 1990–92, foreign ed 1992–94, dep ed 1994–; jt winner Guardian/NUS Student Journalist of the Year award 1979; *Books* Behind the Myth: Yasser Arafat and the Palestinian Revolution (1990, reissued as Arafat: The Biography 1994); *Recreations* cinema, reading, opera, music of all kinds; *Style—* Andrew Gowers, Esq; ✉ Financial Times, 1 Southwark Bridge, London SE1 (☎ 0171 873 3000)

GOWERS, Gillian Carol; da of John Edward Gowers, and Irene, *née* Strong (d 1985); *b* 9 April 1964; *Educ* Hove GS, Chelsea Coll Eastbourne (BSc); *Career* badminton player; 105 England caps; Cwlth Games: team Gold medal (twice), ladies doubles Gold and Silver medals; Euro Championships: ladies doubles Gold medal, mixed doubles Silver medal; mixed doubles Bronze medal World Championships; GB Nat Championships: 6 times ladies doubles winner, 2 times mixed doubles winner; winner of 33 Grand Prix World titles; Silver medal World Team Championships (Uber Cup), finalist All England Ladies Doubles and Mixed Doubles, winner World Cup Mixed Doubles 1993; memb Br Olympic Team Barcelona 1992; *Style—* Ms Gillian Gowers

GOWING, Nik; s of Donald James Graham Gowing (d 1969), and Prof Margaret Mary Gowing, *née* Elliott; *b* 13 Jan 1951; *Educ* Latymer Upper Sch, Simon Langton GS Canterbury Kent, Univ of Bristol (BSc); *m* 10 July 1982, Judith Wastall, da of Dr Peter Venables, of Andover, Hants; 1 s (Simon Donald Peter b 9 Feb 1987), 1 da (Sarah Margaret b 21 Dec 1983); *Career* reporter Newcastle Chronicle 1973–74, presenter-reporter Granada TV 1974–78; ITN: joined 1978, Rome corr 1979, Eastern Europe corr 1980–83, foreign affrs corr 1983–87, dip corr 1987–89, dip ed and newscaster Channel 4 News 1989–96; co-presenter The World This Week 1990–92; presenter: BBC World TV 1996–, BBC News 1996–; conslt in media and conflict mgmnt, conslt Carnegie Cmmn on Prevention of Deadly Conflict 1996; memb Bd of Govrs Westminster Fndn for Democracy 1996–; fell Kennedy Sch of Govt Harvard Univ 1994; memb: IISS, RIIA, RTS; *Books* The Wire (1988), The Loop (1993); *Recreations* cycling, skiing, authorship; *Style—* Nik Gowing, Esq; ✉ BBC, Room 7520, BBC TV Centre, London W12 7RJ (☎ 0181 225 8137, fax 0181 287 4427, e-mail 100523.2530@compuserve.com)

GOWLAND, Robert George; s of George Fredrick Gowland (d 1978), of Enfield, Middlesex, and Meta, *née* Emck; *b* 27 Jan 1943; *Educ* Haileybury and ISC, Royal Agricultural Coll (CLAS); *m* Anne Sandra, da of Douglas Markes; 1 s (Benjamin Thomas George b 1976), 1 da (Nicola Louise b 1973); *Career* chartered surveyor; Strutt & Parker (Ipswich) 1961–62 and 1964–65, Weller Eggar & Co (Guildford) 1965–67, King & Co (London) 1968, WS Johnson & Co (Leighton Buzzard and Buckingham) 1969–70; ptnr: Wyatt & Son (Havant and Chichester) 1970–73, E J Brooks & Son (Oxford) 1973–79; Phillips International Auctioneers 1979–, pres Phillips New York 1980, md Phillips Chester and North West 1981–; main author Furniture and Works of Art Syllabus for RICS (chm Ctee 1984–87); auctioneer of historical golfing memorabilia 1982–; hon sec Soc of Fine Art Auctioneers 1976–80 and 1981–87 (chm 1987–), memb Br Hallmarking Cncl 1985–; Liveryman Worshipful Co of Clockmakers; FRICS 1974 (ARICS 1966); *Recreations* restoring historic golf clubs and furniture, golf, game fishing and shooting; *Clubs* Chester City, Artists' (Liverpool); *Style—* Robert Gowland, Esq; ✉ Phillips, 33 Botanic Road, Churchtown, Southport PR9 7NE (☎ 01704 507875, fax 01704 507877)

GOWLLAND, Robin Anthony Blantyre; s of Reginald Blantyre-Gowlland (d 1974), of London and Hawkley, Hants, and Pauline, *née* Broomfield (d 1981); *b* 6 Sept 1932; *Educ* RNC Dartmouth and Greenwich, IMEDE Lausanne (Dip), Harvard Business Sch (MBA); *m* 1994, Rosalie W Read, of Hackthorn, Lincs; *Career* mgmnt conslt and dir Egon Zehnder International 1969–92 (md UK 1969–81, chm 1981–92); dir Videotron Holdings Ltd 1985–93 (chm 1985–91), chm Robin Gowlland Consulting 1992–; md (Europe) Samanco International 1994–; dir FCCS 1989–; chm: GLS International 1992–, BGL Associates 1992–; sr res fell Cranfield Inst of Technol 1964–66; sr conslt and ptnr Harbridge House Inc 1966–69, vice chm London Fedn of Clubs for Young People 1976–96 (dir Int Fedn), memb Cncl Christian Assoc of Business Execs (chm 1976–80 and 1986), vice chm Inst of Business Ethics 1986–; chm Downside Settlement 1983– (hon sec 1966–73, vice chm 1973–83), vice chm Friends of Westminster Cathedral, dir InterAid, memb Cncl London Playing Fields Soc; govr St Michael's Sch Bermondsey; RN 1946–62, served UK, Med, Far East and Suez Campaign 1956 (ret as Lt); Hon Lt-Col Alabama State Militia (USA), Hon Citizen City of Mobile (USA); KSG, KCHS, GCLJ, CMLJ, FRSA, FIMgt, FInstD; *Recreations* cricket, squash, real tennis, sailing, travel, theatre, art; *Clubs* Brooks's, Royal Yacht Sqdn, MCC, Naval and Military, Royal Anglo-Belgian, Jesters; *Style—* Robin A B Gowlland, Esq; ✉ Tann House, Crondall, Hants GU10 5QU (☎ 01252 850700); 82 Kenyon Street, London SW6 6LB (☎ 0171 381 1725); Robin Gowlland Consulting, Abbott House, 1–2 Hanover Street, London W1R 9WB (☎ 0171 495 3683, fax 0171 495 2194)

GOWRIE, 2 Earl of (UK 1945); Alexander Patrick Greysteil Hore Ruthven; PC (1984); also Baron Ruthven of Gowrie (UK 1919), Baron Gowrie (UK 1935), and Viscount Ruthven of Canberra (UK 1945); in remainder to Lordship of Ruthven of Freeland (officialy recognised in the name of Ruthven by Warrant of Lord Lyon 1957); s of Maj Hon Patrick Hore Ruthven (s of 1 Earl of Gowrie, VC, GCMG, CB, DSO, PC, who was Govr Gen and C-in-C of Australia 1936–44 and 2 s of 9 Lord Ruthven of Freeland); suc gf 1955; *b* 26 Nov 1939; *Educ* Eton, Balliol Coll Oxford, Harvard; *m* 1, 1962 (m dis 1974), Xandra, yr da of Col Robert Bingley, CVO, DSO, OBE; 1 s; m 2, 1974, Countess Adelheid, yst da of Count Fritz-Dietlof von der Schulenburg; *Heir* s, Viscount Ruthven of Canberra, *qv*; *Career* former lectr and tutor: State Univ of New York, Harvard, UCL; Cons whip 1971–72, lord in waiting 1972–74, oppn spokesman Economic Affrs 1974–79; min of state: Dept of Employment 1979–81, NI Office 1981–83, Privy Cncl Office (and min for The Arts) 1983–84; chllr of the Duchy of Lancaster (and min for The Arts) 1984–85; chm: Sotheby's Int 1985–86, Sotheby's Europe 1987–93 (currently memb Bd), Really Useful Group 1985–90, Arts Cncl of England 1994–, Development Securities plc 1995–; provost Royal Coll of Art 1986–; non-exec: dir Ladbroke Group plc 1988–, Guinness Mahon plc 1986–; *Books* A Postcard from Don Giovanni (1971); jtly: The Genius of British Painting (1975), Derek Hill, An Appreciation (1985), The Conservative Opportunity (1976); *Style—* The Rt Hon the Earl of Gowrie, PC; ✉ Arts Council of England, 14 Great Peter Street, London SW1P 3NQ (☎ 0171 333 0100)

GOYDER, Daniel George; CBE (1996); s of George Armin Goyder, CBE, of Long Melford, Suffolk, and Rosemary Bernard Goyder; *b* 26 Aug 1938; *Educ* Rugby, Univ of Cambridge (MA, LLB), Harvard Law Sch (LLM); *m* 28 July 1962, Jean Mary, da of Kenneth Godfrey Arthur Dohoo (d 1944), of Malaysia; 2 s (Andrew b 1968, Richard b 1970), 2 da (Joanna b 1963, Elizabeth b 1965); *Career* admitted slr 1962, conslt Birketts Ipswich 1983– (ptnr 1968–83), pt/t lectr Dept of Law Univ of Essex 1981–91 (visiting prof 1991–), visiting prof in law King's Coll London 1991–; dep chm MMC 1991–97 (memb 1980–97), chm St Edmundsbury and Ipswich Diocesan Bd of Fin 1977–85; memb Law Soc; FRSA 1991; *Books* The Antitrust Laws of the USA (with Sir Alan Neale, 3 edn 1980), EEC Competition Law (1988, 2 edn 1992); *Recreations* sport, choral singing; *Clubs* Ipswich and Suffolk (Ipswich); *Style—* Daniel Goyder, Esq, CBE; ✉ Manor House, Old London Road, Capel St Mary, Ipswich, Suffolk (☎ 01473 310583); Birketts Solicitors, 24–26 Museum Street, Ipswich (☎ 01473 232300, fax 01473 230524)

GOYMER, Andrew Alfred; s of Richard Kirby Goymer (d 1986), of Keston, Kent, and Betty Eileen, *née* Thompson; *b* 28 July 1947; *Educ* Dulwich, Pembroke Coll Oxford (MA); *m* 30 Sept 1972, Diana Mary, da of Robert Harry Shipway, MBE, of Heathfield, E Sussex; 1 s (Patrick b 1977), 1 da (Eleanor b 1980); *Career* Gerald Moody entrance scholar 1968, Holker sr exhibitioner 1970, Arden Atkin and Mould prizeman 1971; called to the Bar Gray's Inn 1970, admitted to the Bar NSW Aust 1988; memb SE Circuit 1972–, asst recorder Crown Ct 1987–91, recorder 1991–; *Style—* Andrew Goymer, Esq; ✉ 6 Pump Court, 1st Floor, Temple, London EC4Y 7AR (☎ 0171 797 8400, fax 0171 797 8401)

GOZNEY, Richard Hugh Turton; CMG (1993); s of Thomas Leonard Gozney (d 1991), of Oxford, and Elizabeth Margaret Lilian, *née* Gardiner; *b* 21 July 1951; *Educ* Magdalen Coll Sch Oxford, St Edmund Hall Oxford (open scholar, BA); *m* 1982, Diana Edwina, da of David Brangwyn Harvey Baird; 2 s (James b 1987, Alexander b 1990); *Career* vol teacher Rusinga Secdy Sch Kenya 1970, student Univ of Oxford 1970–73; HM Dip Serv: joined FO 1973, third later second sec Jakarta 1974–78, second later first sec Buenos Aires 1978–81, first sec and head of Chancery Madrid 1984–88, asst private sec later private sec to Foreign Sec (Geoffrey Howe, John Major then Douglas Hurd) 1989–93, attachment to RIIA April-June 1993, high cmmr to Swaziland Aug 1993–96, head Security Policy Dept FCO 1996–; *Recreations* birdwatching, walking, windsurfing, learning to fish; *Style—* Richard Gozney, Esq, CMG; ✉ c/o Foreign & Commonwealth Office, King Charles Street, London SW1A 2AH

GRAAFF, David de Villiers; s and h of Sir de Villiers Graaff, 2 Bt, MBE, *qv*; *b* 3 May 1940; *Educ* Diocesan Coll S Africa, Stellenbosch Univ, Grenoble Univ, Magdalen Coll Oxford; *m* 1969, Sally, da of Robin Williams; 3 s (de Villiers b 16 July 1970, Robert b 1974, David John b 1977), 1 da (Leeza b 1973); *Career* farmer Hex River; dir: Graaff's Trust, Milnerton Estates, Deciduous Fruit Bd; MP Wynberg; dep min of Trade and Indust and Tourism 1991–; *Recreations* tennis; *Clubs* West Province Sports, West Province Cricket, City and Civil Service; *Style—* David Graaff, Esq, MP; ✉ PO Box 15192, Panorama 7506 (☎ 00 27 21 587030, fax 09 44 171 731 7768)

GRAAFF, Sir de Villiers; 2 Bt (UK 1911), of Cape Town, Cape of Good Hope Province of Union of South Africa; MBE (1947); s of Sir David Pieter de Villiers Graaff, 1 Bt (d 1931), sometime high cmmr for Union of S Africa in London, Cabinet minister and mayor of Cape Town; *b* 8 Dec 1913; *Educ* Diocesan Coll Cape Town, Univ of Cape Town (BA), Magdalen Coll Oxford (BCL, MA), Leyden Univ Holland; *m* 1939, Helena (Ena) le Roux, da of Frederick Carel Marthinus Voigt, of Claremont, Cape Province, S Africa; 2 s (David de Villiers b 1940, Johann Frederick de Villiers b 1946), 1 da (Genée de Villiers b 1948); *Heir* s, David de Villiers Graaff b 3 May 1940; *Career* war service in SA Forces 1941 (POW); advocate S African Supreme Ct 1938–, leader of the Oppn in SA 1957–77 (MP 1948–77); farmer of pedigree Friesian cattle; dir: Graaff's Trust, Milnerton Estates; Hon LLD Rhodes Univ, Hon DLit Univ of SA; Decoration for Meritorious Serv 1978; *Recreations* fishing, riding, cricket; *Clubs* Civil Service, Kelvin Grove, Western Province Cricket; *Style—* Sir de Villiers Graaff, Bt, MBE; ✉ PO Box 15192, Panorama 7506, S Africa

GRABHAM, Sir Anthony Herbert; kt (1987); *b* 19 July 1930; *Educ* St Cuthbert's GS Newcastle upon Tyne, Univ of Durham (MB BS); *m* 1960, Eileen Pamela; *Career* conslt Surgn Kettering Gen Hosp 1965–95; chm: BMA Services 1983–, Jl Ctee BMA, Jt Conslt Ctee 1984–90, BMA Cncl 1979–84; memb GMC; vice chm Private Patients' Plan; FRCS; *Clubs* Army and Navy; *Style—* Sir Anthony Grabham; ✉ Rothesay House, Headlands, Kettering, Northants NN15 6DG (☎ 01536 513299)

GRABINER, Anthony Stephen; QC (1981); s of Ralph Grabiner (d 1985), and Freda, *née* Cohen (d 1989); *b* 21 March 1945; *Educ* Central Fndn Boys' GS London, LSE, London Univ (LLB, LLM); *m* 18 Dec 1983, Jane Aviva, da of Dr Benjamin Portnoy, of Hale, Cheshire; 3 s (Joshua b 1986, Daniel b 1989, Samuel b 1994), 1 da (Laura Sarina b 1992); *Career* called to the Bar Lincoln's Inn 1968, bencher 1989, head of chambers 1995–; standing jr counsel to the DTI Export Credits Guarantee Dept 1976–81, jr counsel to the Crown 1978–81, recorder S Eastern Circuit 1990–; memb Ct of Govrs LSE 1990– (vice chm of Ct 1993–); *Books* Sutton & Shannon on Contracts (7 edn, 1970), Banking Documents in Encyclopedia of Forms and Precedents (1986); *Recreations* golf, theatre, swimming; *Clubs* Garrick, RAC, MCC; *Style—* Anthony Grabiner, QC; ✉ 1 Essex Court, Temple, London EC4Y 9AR (☎ 0171 583 2000)

GRABINER, Michael (Mike); s of Henry Grabiner, of London, and Renee, *née* Geller; *b* 21 Aug 1950; *Educ* St Albans Sch, King's Coll Cambridge (BA Econ, pres Students' Union 1972–73); *m* 30 May 1976, Jane Olivia, *née* Harris; 3 s (David b 15 Oct 1980, James b 30 Nov 1984, Benjamin b 7 Feb 1989), 1 da (Sophie b 5 Jan 1992); *Career* joined Post Office 1973, personal asst to MD Telecommunications 1979–80, London Business Sch (Sloan Programme) 1980; rejoined BT: controller of commercial fin Divnl HQ 1982–84, dep dir of mktg 1984–85, gen mangr Northern London Dist 1985–88, gen mangr City of London Dist 1988–90, dir quality and orgn 1990–92, dir global customer serv Business Communications Div 1992–94, dir BT Europe 1994; former memb Bd: BT Telecommunicaciones SA Spain, VIAG InterKom Germany, Telenordia Sweden, Albacom Italy; currently chief exec Energis Communications Ltd; cncllr London Borough of Brent 1978–82 (chm Devpt Ctee 1980–82), dir East London Partnership 1994–95, memb Public Policy Advsy Bd Queen Mary & Westfield Coll; Freeman City of London, memb Worshipful Co of Info Technologists; ACMA 1979; *Style—* Mike Grabiner, Esq; ✉ 35 Uphill Road, London NW7 4RA (☎ 0181 906 2930, fax 0181 959 5020); Energis Communications Ltd, 50 Victoria Embankment, London EC4Y 0DE (☎ 0171 206 5420, fax 0171 206 5050, mobile 0468 251188)

GRACE, Prof John; *b* 19 Sept 1945; *Educ* Bletchley GS, Univ of Sheffield (BSc, PhD); *m* Elizabeth, *née* Ashworth; 2 s (Stewart and Thomas), 1 da (Josephine); *Career* Univ of Edinburgh: lectr 1970–85, reader 1985–92, prof of environmental biology 1992–, convenor of ecological sci, currently convenor Faculty Post-Grad Studies Ctee; Br Ecological Soc: memb Cncl 1983–, co-ed Functional Ecology 1987–; Nat Environment Research Cncl (NERC): served on several ctees incl Terrestrial Life Scis Trg Ctee 1986–89, currently head UK consortium within Terrestrial Initiative in Global Environmental Research (TIGER); section ed Encylopedia of Ecology and Environmental Management; memb: Soc for Experimental Biology, Int Soc for Biometeorology; delivered Africanus Horton Meml lectr Freetown Sierra Leone 1988 (among others); awarded medal Univ of Helsinki 1994; FRSE 1994, FIBiol; *Books* Plant Response to Wind (1977), Plant Atmosphere Relationships (1983); also author of over 130 book chapters and papers in refereed jls; *Recreations* gardening, bridge, outdoor pursuits; *Style*— Prof John Grace, FRSE; ✉ Institute of Ecology and Resource Management, University of Edinburgh, Darwin Building, Mayfield Road, Edinburgh EH9 3JU (☎ 0131 650 5400, fax 0131 662 0478, e-mail jgrace@uk.ac.ed)

GRACE, John Oliver Bowman; QC (1994); s of Oliver Jelf Grace, MBE, TD, DL (d 1996), of Hollingbourne, Kent, and Marjorie Foster, *née* Bowman; *b* 13 June 1948; *Educ* Marlborough, Univ of Southampton (LLB); *m* 1973, Carol, da of Canon Jack Roundhill; 2 s (Edward Oliver b 2 Jan 1977, George William Jack b 11 June 1980), 1 da (Eleanor Rose b 26 Nov 1983); *Career* called to the Bar Middle Temple 1973; memb: Professional Negligence Bar Assoc, London Common Law and Commercial Bar Assoc; *Recreations* gardening, music, reading, cricket, France, bricklaying, modern art; *Clubs* 4 W's, Band of Brothers Cricket, Old Stagers; *Style*— John Grace, Esq, QC; ✉ 3 Serjeants' Inn, London EC4Y 1BQ (☎ 0171 353 5537)

GRACEY, Howard; s of Charles Douglas Gracey (d 1968), and Margaret Gertrude Gracey (d 1995); *b* 21 Feb 1935; *Educ* Birkenhead Sch; *m* 8 June 1960, Pamela Jean, da of William Thomas Bradshaw (d 1988); 1 s (Mark), 2 da (Kathryn, Rachel); *Career* Nat Serv 2 Lt RA 1959–61; Royal Insurance Co 1953–69, consulting actuary and ptnr R Watson & Sons 1970–95 (sr ptnr 1993–95); pres Pensions Mgmnt Inst 1983–85, chm Assoc of Consulting Actuaries 1991–93; memb: General Synod C of E 1970–85 (co-opted 1985–), C of E Pensions Bd 1970– (chm 1980–), Archbishops' Cmmn on the Orgn of the C of E 1994–95; church cmmr 1978–95, chm S American Missionary Soc 1994– (treas 1975–93), lay reader St Saviour's Guildford; FIA 1959, FIAA 1982, FPMI 1977, ASA 1978; *Recreations* fellwalking, photography; *Style*— Howard Gracey, Esq; ✉ Holmhurst Cottage, Back Lane, East Clandon, Guildford, Surrey GU4 7SD (☎ 01483 222798, fax 01483 211737)

GRACEY, John Halliday; CB (1984); s of Halliday Gracey, and Florence Jane, *née* Cudlipp; *b* 20 May 1925; *Educ* City of London Sch, Brasenose Coll Oxford (MA); *m* 1950, Margaret Procter; 3 s; *Career* served Army 1943–47; joined Inland Revenue 1950, HM Treasy 1970–73, cmmr Inland Revenue 1973–85, dir gen Bd of Inland Revenue 1981–85; hon treas Nat Assoc for Care and Resettlement of Offenders 1987–; *Recreations* walking, beekeeping; *Clubs* Reform; *Style*— John Gracey, Esq, CB; ✉ 3 Woodberry Down, Epping, Essex (☎ 01992 572167)

GRADE, Baron (Life Peer UK 1976), of Elstree, Co Herts; Sir Lew Grade; kt (1969); s of Isaac Winogradsky (d 1936), of Odessa, Russia, and Olga Winogradsky (d 1981); bro of Lord Delfont (d 1994); *b* 25 Dec 1906; *Educ* Rochelle St Sch London; *m* 1942, Kathleen Sheila, da of John Moody; 1 adopted s (Paul Nicholas b 1952); *Career* jt md Lew and Leslie Grade Ltd until 1955, chm and md ITC Entertainment 1958–82; chm and chief exec: ACC 1973–82, Embassy Communications International 1982–85, The Grade Company 1985–; dir Euro Disney SCA 1988–; chm: Bentray Investments 1979–82, Stoll Moss Theatres 1969–82, ACC Enterprises Inc 1973–82; pres ATV 1977–82, former govr Royal Shakespeare Theatre, vice pres Br Olympic Assoc; fell BAFTA 1979; Kt Cdr of St Silvester, OStJ; *Books* Still Dancing (autobiog, 1987); *Style*— The Rt Hon the Lord Grade; ✉ 34 Grosvenor Street, London W1X 9FG

GRADE, Michael Ian; s of late Leslie Grade and n of Lords Grade and Delfont; *b* 8 March 1943; *Educ* Stowe, St Dunstan's Coll; *m* 1, 1967 (m dis 1981), Penelope Jane, *née* Levinson; 1 s (Jonathan), 1 da (Alison); m 2, 1982 (m dis 1991), Hon Sarah Jane Lawson (*see* Hon Mrs Mayer), yst da of Lt-Col 5 Baron Burnham, JP (d 1993); *Career* sports columnist Daily Mirror 1964–66 (trainee journalist 1960), theatrical agent Grade Organisation 1966, jt md London Management and Representation 1969–73, dir of progs and bd memb LWT 1977–81 (dep controller of progs 1973), pres Embassy TV Los Angeles 1982–83, chm and chief operating offr The Grade Co (ind TV and motion picture prodn co) 1983–84, controller BBC 1 1984–86, dir of progs BBC TV 1986–87, chief exec Channel 4 1988–; non-exec chm: VCI plc 1994–, First Leisure plc 1995– (non-exec dir 1991–); memb Cncl LAMDA 1981–, pres RTS 1995–; *Recreations* entertainment; *Style*— Michael Grade, Esq; ✉ Channel Four Television Corporation, 124 Horseferry Road, London SW1P 2TX (☎ 0171 396 4444)

GRADIDGE, (John) Roderick Warlow; s of Brig John Henry Gradidge, OBE, and Lorraine Beatrice Warlow, *née* Warlow-Harry; *b* 3 Jan 1929; *Educ* Stowe, Arch Assoc Sch of Arch; *Career* architect specialising in repair, alteration and additions to major country houses (particularly work of Edwin Lutyens and contemporaries); other recent work incl: interior Bodelwyddan Castle Clwyd (Museum of the Year 1989), extension St Edmund's Coll Cambridge, new entrance Nat Portrait Gallery, recreation of Victorian interiors Northampton Guildhall; property corr: The Field 1984–87, Country Life 1988–93; memb: Ctee Victorian Soc, The Thirties Soc, Lutyens Tst; master Art Workers Guild 1987 (hon sec 1978–84); *Books* Dream Houses - The Edwardian Ideal (1980), Edwin Lutyens - Architect Laureate (1981), Surrey, A House and Cottage Handbook (1991); *Recreations* enjoyment of early twentieth century architecture and appreciation of its potential; *Clubs* Art Workers Guild; *Style*— Roderick Gradidge, Architect; ✉ Roderick Gradidge Architect, 21 Elliott Rd, London W4 1PF (☎ 0181 995 6490, fax 0181 995 6490)

GRAEF, Roger Arthur; s of Dr Irving Philip Graef (d 1978), of New York City, and Gretchen Waterman Graef (d 1984); *b* 18 April 1936; *Educ* Horace Mann Sch NY, Putney Sch Vermont, Harvard Univ (BA Hons); *m* 1, 26 Nov 1971 (m dis 1985), Karen Bergemann (d 1986); 1 s (Maximilian James b 26 July 1979), 1 da (Chloe Fay b 26 Nov 1972); m 2, 26 July 1986, Susan Mary, da of Sir Brooks Richards, KCMG, DSC, *qv*, of Dorset; *Career* writer, criminologist, producer, broadcaster and director; dir 26 plays and operas USA and two dramas for CBS TV; dir Period of Adjustment (Royal Court); co-designer London Transport Bus Map, pt/t lectr Assoc Sch of Architecture; memb Bd Govrs BFI 1975–79; memb Bd: London Transport Exec 1976–79, Channel 4 1980–85; memb Cncl: ICA 1971–83, BAFTA 1976–77, AIP 1987–90 (chm 1988–89), Howard League for Penal Reform; memb: Devpt Control Review (the Dobry Ctee) DOE 1975–77, Ctee for Control of Demolition DOE 1976; chm Study Gp for Public Involvement in Planning DOE 1975–77, fndr ICA Architectural Forum, expert memb Euro Analytical Coll of Crime Prevention 1993–, fell Mannheim Centre of Criminology LSE; memb Br Soc of Criminology, pres Signals Int Tst 1991–; tstee Koesoler Award Tst, memb Advsy Bd Oxford Probation Studies Unit, memb Advsy Bd Forensic Psychotherapy (post grad crse) UCL, memb Retail Action Gp Home Office; chm Theatre de Complicité 1991, chm Book Aid 1992–93; *Television* incl: The Space Between Words (BBC/KCET) 1972, A Law in the Making: Four Months Inside The Ministry (Granada) 1973, Inside The Brussels HQ (Granada) 1975, Is This the Way to Save a City? (BBC) 1976, Decision: Steel, Oil, Rates (ITV/Granada) 1976, Decision: British Communism (Royal TV Soc Award 1978), Pleasure (Her Majesty's, Amnesty/BBC) 1977, The Mermaids Frolics (Amnesty/ITV) 1977, The Secret Policeman's Ball (Amnesty Int) 1978, Italy: Chain Reaction (Granada) 1979, Police (series, BBC (BAFTA Award 1982)) 1980–82, Police: Operation Carter 1981–82, Nagging Doubt (Channel 4) 1984, Comic Relief 1985, Maybe Baby (BBC) 1985, Closing Ranks (Zenith/Central) 1987, The Secret Life of the Soviet Union (Channel 4) 1990, Turning the Screws (Channel 4) 1993, Look at the State We're In (BBC) 1995, In Search of Law and Order (Channel 4) 1995, Breaking the Cycle (ITV) 1996; series ed: Who Is? (BBC), Inside Europe (ITV), Signals (Channel 4); *Books* Talking Blues - The Police in Their Own Words (1989), Living Dangerously - Young Offenders in Their Own Words (1993); media columnist The Times 1992–94; numerous articles in: The Sunday Times, Times, Evening Standard, The Independent, The Observer, Daily Telegraph, Sunday Telegraph, Independent on Sunday, The Guardian, Police Review; *Recreations* tennis, music, photography; *Clubs* Beefsteak, Groucho; *Style*— Roger Graef, Esq; ✉ 72 Westbourne Park Villas, London W2 5EB (☎ 0171 286 0333 or 0171 727 7868)

GRAFFTEY-SMITH, John Jeremy (Jinx); s of Sir Laurence Barton Grafftey-Smith, KCMG, KBE (d 1989), and Mrs Vivien Isobel Tennant-Eyles, *née* Alderson (d 1995); bro of Roger Grafftey-Smith, *qv*; *b* 13 Oct 1934; *Educ* Winchester, Magdalen Coll Oxford (MA); *m* 23 Jan 1964, Lucy, da of Maj John Fletcher, MBE, of Sussex; 2 s (Alexander b 1967, Toby b 1970), 1 da (Camilla b 1968); *Career* 2 Lt Oxfordshire & Bucks LI 1953–55; banker; Samuel Montagu 1958–66, Wallace Bros 1966–76, res dir Allied Med Gp Saudi-Arabia 1977–81, London rep Nat Commercial Bank of Saudi-Arabia 1982–; memb Saudi Br Soc Ctee; *Recreations* golf, shooting, tennis, music, wine, bridge; *Clubs* Royal Automobile, City of London, Green Jackets, Ashridge Golf, Oxfordshire Golf, Mentmore Golf and Country, The Benedicts' Soc; *Style*— Jinx Grafftey-Smith, Esq; ✉ Burcott Hill House, Wing, Leighton Buzzard, Bedfordshire LU7 0JU; National Commercial Bank, 3rd Floor, 78 Cornhill, London EC3V 3QQ (☎ 0171 283 4233, fax 0171 929 4373)

GRAFFTEY-SMITH, Roger Tilney; s of Sir Laurence Barton Grafftey-Smith, KCMG, KBE (d 1989), and Mrs Vivien Isobel Tennant-Eyles, *née* Alderson (d 1995); elder bro of Jeremy Grafftey-Smith, *qv*; *b* 14 April 1931; *Educ* Winchester, Trinity Coll Oxford; *m* 28 March 1962, Jane Oriana Mary, da of Sir John Pollen, Bt; 2 s (Simon b 1968, Max b 1974), 1 da (Selina (m Charles Edward Hooton Faircloth) b 1971); *Career* 2 Lt Queen's Bays 1949–51; md Galban Lobo (England) Ltd 1962–72, vice chm N Wilts Dist Cncl 1980–82; managing ptnr Grafftey-Smith & Associates Financial Conslts 1982–, chm Unilab Corporation 1985; dir: Biolytic Systems Ltd 1990–92, Decora Industries Inc 1989–; *Recreations* shooting, fishing; *Style*— Roger T Grafftey-Smith, Esq; ✉ Monks Farm House, Sherborne, Cheltenham, Glos (☎ 01451 844604, fax 01451 844692); Grafftey-Smith & Associates, 133 Thomas More House, Barbican, London EC2Y 8BU (☎ 0171 638 1937, fax 0171 920 9262)

GRAFTON, Duchess of; (Ann) Fortune FitzRoy; GCVO (1980, DCVO 1970, CVO 1965); o da of late Capt (Evan Cadogan) Eric Smith, MC, LLD; *m* 12 Oct 1946, 11 Duke of Grafton, *qv*; 2 s, 3 da; *Career* SRCN Great Ormond St 1945, pres W Suffolk Mission to the Deaf, vice pres Suffolk Br Royal British Legion Women's Section; govr Felixstowe Coll, Riddlesworth Hall; JP: Co of London 1949, Co of Suffolk 1972; memb Bd of Govrs Hosp for Sick Children Great Ormond St 1952–66; patron: Great Ormond St Nurses League, West Suffolk Relate; vice pres Trinity Hospice (Clapham Common) 1951; lady of the bedchamber to HM The Queen 1953–66, mistress of the robes to HM The Queen 1967–; pres W Suffolk Decorative and Fine Art Soc; patron: Clarence River Historical Soc Grafton NSW Aust 1980, Guildhall String Ensemble 1988; pres Br Heart Fndn Bury St Edmunds Branch Suffolk 1992; *Style*— Her Grace the Duchess of Grafton, GCVO; ✉ Euston Hall, Thetford, Norfolk IP24 2QP (☎ 01842 753282)

GRAFTON, 11 Duke of (E 1675); Hugh Denis Charles FitzRoy; KG (1976), DL (Suffolk 1973); also Earl of Euston, Viscount Ipswich and Baron Sudbury (E 1672); patron of four livings; Hereditary Ranger of Whittlebury Forest; s of 10 Duke of Grafton (d 1970), and Lady Doreen Buxton, 2 da of 1 Earl Buxton; *b* 3 April 1919; *Educ* Eton, Magdalene Coll Cambridge; *m* 12 Oct 1946, Fortune (Duchess of Grafton, GCVO, *qv*); 2 s, 3 da; *Heir* s, Earl of Euston, *qv*; *Career* Grenadier Gds ADC to Viceroy of India 1943–46; memb: Historic Buildings Cncl for England 1953–84, Historic Buildings Advsy Ctee and Churches and Cathedrals Ctee English Heritage 1984–, Nat Tst Properties Ctee 1981–94, Royal Fine Art Cmmn 1971–94; chm: Cathedrals Advsy Cmmn 1981–91, Architectural Heritage Fund 1976–94; chm of tstees: Historic Churches Preservation Tst 1980–, Sir John Soane's Museum 1975–; vice chm of tstees Nat Portrait Gallery 1967–92; tstee: Tradescant Tst, Buildings at Risk Tst; pres: Soc for the Protection of Ancient Buildings 1989–, International Students House 1972–, Br Soc of Master Glass Painters, E Anglia Tourist Bd 1973–93, Suffolk Preservation Soc 1957–; patron: Historic Houses Assoc, Hereford Herd Book Soc; Hon DCL Univ of East Anglia 1990; *Clubs* Boodle's; *Style*— His Grace the Duke of Grafton, KG, DL; ✉ Euston Hall, Thetford, Norfolk IP24 2QW (☎ 01842 753282)

GRAFTON, Peter Witheridge; CBE (1972); s of James Hawkins Grafton and Ethel Marion, *née* Brannan; *b* 19 May 1916; *Educ* Westminster City Sch, Sutton Valence Sch, Coll of Estate Mgmnt; *m* 1, 1939, Joan (d 1969), da of late Rear Adm Hubert Bleackley, CBE, MVO; 3 da, 1 s (1 s and 1 da decd); m 2, 1971, Margaret Ruth, da of John Frederick Ward; 2 s; *Career* Nat Serv WWII Queen's Westminster Rifles, Dorsetshire Regt and RE, UK and Far E (Capt); chartered quantity surveyor; sr ptnr G D Walford & Partners 1978–82 (ptnr 1949); pres Royal Inst Chartered Surveyors 1978–79 (vice pres 1974–78, first chm Policy Review Ctee), memb and past chm Quantity Surveyors Cncl (first chm Building Cost Info Serv), memb Cncl Construction Industs Res and Info Assoc 1963–69, memb Res Advsy Cncl to Min of Housing and Construction 1967–71, memb Nat Cncl for Building and Civil Engrg Industs 1968–76, memb Nat Jt Consultative Ctee for Building Indust 1970–77 (chm 1974), memb Br Bd of Agrément 1973–88; tstee United Westminster Schs, govr Sutton Valence Sch 1971–96 (chm 1976–91), former chm Old Suttonians Assoc (pres 1996–); contested (Lib) Bromley 1950; fndr and chm Public Schs Old Boys' Golf Assoc 1962–94 (pres 1994–), co-donor Grafton Morrish Trophy, past capt Chartered Surveyors' Golfing Soc; Master Worshipful Co of Chartered Surveyors 1983–84; FRICS, FCIArB; *Recreations* golf, family; *Clubs* Reform, Rye Golf, Tandridge golf; *Style*— Peter Grafton, Esq, CBE; ✉ 57 Padbrook, Limpsfield, Oxted, Surrey RH8 0DZ (☎ 01883 716685)

GRAFTON GREEN, Patrick; s of George Grafton-Green (d 1990), of London, and Brigid Anna, *née* Maxwell (d 1991); *b* 30 March 1943; *Educ* Ampleforth, Wadham Coll Oxford (MA Jurisprudence); *m* 18 Sept 1982, Deborah Susan, da of Raymond Goodchild; 2 s (Nicholas Patrick James b 4 Nov 1983, Patrick William Peter b 18 April 1987), 2 da (Charlotte Brigid Kate b 3 Sept 1985, Lucy Anna Clare (twin) b 18 April 1987); *Career* Theodore Goddard: articled clerk 1966–68, staff slr 1969–73, ptnr 1973–, memb Mgmnt Ctee 1991–92, head Media & Communication Gp and Entertainment Gp 1992–; regular speaker at confs on taxation of entertainers and businesses operating in media sector; memb Law Soc 1969; *Recreations* music, cricket; *Clubs* MCC, Middlesex CCC; *Style*— Patrick Grafton Green, Esq; ✉ Theodore Goddard, 150 Aldersgate Street, London EC1A 4EJ (☎ 0171 606 8855, fax 0171 606 4390)

GRAHAM, Alan Philip; s of Aaron Goldstein (d 1981), of Edgware, Middx, and Helen, *née* Brown; *b* 4 Dec 1947; *Educ* Orange Hill Boys' GS; *m* Jennifer, da of Charles Phillips; 2 da (Caroline Louise b 14 Jan 1977, Lucie Vanessa b 11 April 1979); *Career* merchant banker; N M Rothschild & Sons Group: Credits Div 1967–68, money market dealer 1968–69, assigned to Manchester Branch 1969–71, Foreign Exchange and Bullion Dealing Room 1971–77, mangr 1974, md and chief exec NMR Metals Inc NY (memb Precious Metals Ctee NY Commodity Exchange) 1977–79, asst dir 1980, Int Banking Div London 1980–83, exec dir and head Banking Div N M Rothschild & Sons (CI) Limited Guernsey and dir Old Court Currency Fund Ltd 1984–88, exec dir N M Rothschild & Sons Limited 1988– (dir Treasy Div, head Treasy Admin, memb Northern Advsy Bd, chm Treasy Ctee, memb Credits Ctee), non-exec dir N M Rothschild & Sons (CI) Ltd, md N M Rothschild & Sons (Singapore) Ltd 1992–94; Freeman City of London 1977; memb Chartered Inst of Bankers 1967; *Recreations* soccer, music, theatre, tennis; *Clubs* Overseas Bankers'; *Style*— Alan Graham, Esq; ✉ N M Rothschild & Sons Ltd, New Court, St Swithin's Lane, London EC4P 4DU (☎ 0171 280 5000, fax 0171 929 1643)

GRAHAM, Sir Alexander Michael; GBE (1990), JP (City of London 1979); s of late Dr Walter Graham, and late Suzanne, *née* Simon; *b* 27 Sept 1938; *Educ* St Paul's; *m* 6 June 1964, Carolyn, da of Lt Col Alan Wolryche Stansfeld, MBE; 3 da; *Career* Nat Serv 1957–59, cmmnd Gordon Highlanders, TA 1959–67; Frizzell Group Ltd: joined 1957, md 1973–90, dep chm 1990–93; chm Firstcity Insurance Brokers Ltd 1993–; underwriting memb Lloyd's 1978–; chm: Employment Conditions Abroad Ltd 1993–, Folgate Insurance Company Ltd 1995– (dir 1975–), Euclidian plc; Mercers' Co: Liveryman 1971–, memb Ct of Assts 1980, Master 1983–84; memb Ct of Common Cncl City of London 1978–79, alderman Ward of Queenhithe 1979–, pres Queenhithe Ward Club 1979–, Sheriff City of London 1986–87, HM Lt City of London 1989–, Lord Mayor of London 1990–91; Hon Freeman Worshipful Co of Insurers 1992–, Hon Liveryman Worshipful Co of Chartered Secs and Admins 1992–; govr: Hall Sch Hampstead 1975–93, St Paul's Sch 1980–93, St Paul's Girls' Sch 1980–93, City of London Sch 1983–85, City of London Girls' Sch 1992–, Christ's Hosp Sch 1979–, King Edward's Sch Whitley 1979–; memb Cncl Gresham Coll 1983–93, chllr City Univ 1990–91; chm of Tstees: United Response 1993–, Morden Coll 1996– (tstee 1988–); tstee Temple Bar Tst 1992–, hon life memb Cancer Relief Macmillan Fund 1993–; memb Exec Ctee Army Benevolent Fund 1991–, chm Nat Employers Liaison Ctee for TA and Reserve Forces 1992–; chm Cncl Order of St John Herts; pres British Insurance Law Assoc 1994–; vice pres: Insurance Inst of London, N Herts Garden Hospice, Old Pauline Club; pres Civil Serv Motoring Assoc 1993–; Hon DCL City Univ 1990; FCII 1964, FBIIBA 1967, FInstD 1975, FCIS 1990, FRSA 1980, CIMgt 1991; KStJ 1990, Grand Cross Order of Merit (Chile) 1991, Order of Wissam Alouite (Morocco) 1987; *Recreations* wine, genealogy, music, reading, silver, bridge, sports (golf, swimming, tennis, shooting and getting daughters married); *Clubs* Garrick, City Livery, Highland Brigade, Royal Worlington Golf and Newmarket Golf, South Beds Golf; *Style*— Sir Alexander Graham, GBE, JP; ✉ Walden Abbotts, Whitwell, Hitchen, Herts SG4 8AJ (☎ and fax 01438 871223); Firstcity Insurance Brokers Ltd, 13–15 Folgate Street, London E1 6BX (☎ 0171 247 6495, fax 0171 410 4828)

GRAHAM, (John) Alistair; s of Robert Graham (d 1968), and Dorothy, *née* Horner (d 1995); *b* 6 Aug 1942; *Educ* Royal GS Newcastle upon Tyne; *m* 1967, Dorothy Jean, da of James Clark Wallace, of Morpeth, Northumberland; 1 s (Richard b 1974), 1 da (Polly b 1972); *Career* gen sec The Civil and Public Services Assoc 1982–86, dir The Industl Soc 1986–91, chief exec Calderdale and Kirklees Trg and Enterprise Cncl Ltd 1991–; *Recreations* music, theatre; *Style*— Alistair Graham, Esq; ✉ Calderdale and Kirklees Training and Enterprise Council Ltd, Parkview House, Woodvale Office Park, Woodvale Rd, Brighouse HD6 4AB (☎ 01484 400770, fax 01484 400672)

GRAHAM, Andrew Alexander Kenny; *see:* Newcastle, Bishop of

GRAHAM, Col Andrew John Noble; MBE (1993); s and h of Sir John Alexander Noble Graham, 4 Bt, GCMG, *qv*; *b* 21 Oct 1956; *Educ* Eton, Trinity Coll Cambridge; *m* 7 July 1984, Susan Mary Bridget, da of Rear Adm John Patrick Bruce O'Riordan, CBE, of Little Rectory, Whilton, Northants; 1 s (James Patrick Noble b 15 March 1990), 3 da (Katharine Rose b 1986, Louisa Christian b 1988, Isabella Alice b 1993); *Career* CO 1 Bn The Argyll and Sutherland Highlanders (Princess Louise's) 1995–96, Col HQ Land Cmd 1997–; *Recreations* outdoor sports, piping; *Clubs* MCC, New (Edinburgh), RGS; *Style*— A J N Graham, Esq; ✉ c/o Little Rectory, Whilton, Daventry, Northants NN11 5NN

GRAHAM, Andrew Winston Mawdsley; s of Winston Graham, OBE, of Abbotswood, Buxted, Sussex, and Jean Mary, *née* Williamson; *b* 20 June 1942; *Educ* St Edmund Hall Oxford (MA); *m* 1970, Peggotty, da of E L Fawssett; *Career* econ asst: Nat Econ Devpt Office 1964, Dept of Econ Affrs 1964–66; asst to the Econ Advsr To The Cabinet 1966–68, econ advsr to the PM 1968–69, fell and tutor in economics Balliol Coll Oxford 1969– (univ lectr 1970–), policy advsr to the PM 1974–76, estates bursar Balliol Coll Oxford 1978 (investmts bursar 1979–83, vice master 1988 and 1992–94), econ advsr to the Chief Oppn Spokesman on Economic Affairs 1988–92, econ advsr to the Ldr of the Lab Pty 1992–94; memb: The Wilson Ctee on the Functioning of Fin Instns 1977–80, Econs Ctee SSRC 1978–80; non-exec dir Br Tport Docks Bd 1979–82, memb ILO/JASPA Employment Advsy Mission to Ethiopia 1982, head Queen Elizabeth House Food Studies Gp advising the Govt of the Republic of Zambia 1984, conslt to BBC 1990–92; memb: Cncl Templeton Coll Oxford 1990–95, Econs Ctee Central European Univ 1991–, Media Advsy Ctee Inst for Public Policy; visiting scholar MIT and visiting fell Harvard 1994; *Publications* Government and Economies in the Postwar World (ed, 1990); *Recreations* windsurfing; *Style*— Andrew Graham, Esq; ✉ Balliol Coll, Oxford OX1 3BJ

GRAHAM, Charles Kenneth Colles; s of Malcolm Vaughan Graham, of Dublin, and Daphne Mary Nurmahal, *née* Dooley; *b* 24 April 1956; *Educ* Shrewsbury, Trinity Coll Cambridge; *m* 10 Aug 1991, Rosemary Jane, eld da of Walter Rich, of St Leonards, Exeter; *Career* admitted slr 1980, ptnr Cole and Cole 1986–, slr to Oxfordshire Health Authy 1986–; under sheriff Oxfordshire; memb Law Soc; *Recreations* golf, local church (former church warden); *Style*— Charles Graham, Esq; ✉ 29 Southdale Rd, Oxford OX2 7SE (☎ 01865 552039); Cole & Cole, 3 West Way, Botley, Oxford OX2 0SZ (☎ 01865 262600)

GRAHAM, Maj Sir Charles Spencer Richard; 6 Bt (GB 1783), of Netherby, Cumberland; s of Lt-Col Sir (Frederick) Fergus Graham, 5 Bt, KBE, TD (d 1978); *b* 16 July 1919; *Educ* Eton; *m* 1944, (Isabel) Susan Anne, o da of Maj Robert Lambton Surtees, OBE; 2 s (James Fergus Surtees b 1946, Malise Charles Richard b 1948), 1 da (Susanna Anne Mary b 1951); *Heir* s, James Fergus Surtees Graham b 29 July 1946; *Career* Maj Scots Gds, served 1940–50, NW Europe (despatches), Malaya; High Sheriff of Cumberland 1955–56, Lord-Lt Cumbria 1983–94 (DL Cumberland 1970); pres Country Landowners Assoc 1971–73, memb Nat Water Cncl 1973–83; Master Worshipful Co of Farmers 1982–83; KStJ; *Clubs* Brooks's, Pratt's; *Style*— Maj Sir Charles Graham, Bt; ✉ Crofthead, Longtown, Cumbria CA6 5PA (☎ 01228 791231)

GRAHAM, Colin; s of Fredrick Eaton Graham-Bonnalie (d 1975), of Edinburgh, and Alexandra Diana Vyvyan Findlay (d 1988); *b* 22 Sept 1931; *Educ* Stowe, RADA; *Career* artistic dir: English Opera Group 1966–75, Aldeburgh Festival 1968–90, English Music Theatre 1976–, Banff Opera Canada 1984–91, Opera Theatre of St Louis 1985–; asst dir of prodn Sadler's Wells Opera 1968–76, dir of prodn ENO 1979–84, vice pres Aldeburgh Festival 1990–; Orpheus Award for Prodn 1972, Winston Churchill Fellowship 1979, Opera America Award 1988, Arts and Educn Award 1992; Hon Dr of Arts: Webster Univ St Louis 1985, Univ of Missouri 1992; ordained min Christian Church 1987; memb: Br Actors' Equity, AGMA 1973; *Libretti* A Penny for a Song (1966), The Golden Vanity (1980), The Postman Always Rings Twice (1985), Joruri (1987); *Recreations* the Bible, movies, motor-cycles, weight-training; *Style*— Colin Graham, Esq; ✉ PO Box 191910, Saint Louis, Missouri 63119, USA (☎ 00 1 314 961 0171, fax 00 1 314 961 7463)

GRAHAM, (Stewart) David; QC (1977); s of Lewis Graham (d 1985), of Harrogate, and Gertrude, *née* Markman (d 1989); *b* 27 Feb 1934; *Educ* Leeds GS, St Edmund Hall Oxford (MA, BCL); *m* 20 Dec 1959, Corinne, da of Emile Carmona (d 1984), of London; 2 da (Jeanne (Mrs Zane), Angela (Mrs Marks)); *Career* called to the Bar Middle Temple 1957; Harmsworth Law scholar 1958, ret from Bar 1985, dir Coopers and Lybrand and Cork Gully 1985–92; chm: Law Parly and Gen Purpose Ctee of Bd of Deputies of Br Jews 1983–88, Editorial Bd of Insolvency Intelligence 1988–; memb: Cncl of Justice 1976–, Insolvency Rules Advsy Ctee 1984–86; ind memb Cncl Insurance Ombudsman Bureau 1993–; editor of various works on Insolvency Law, sr visiting fell Centre for Commercial Law Studies Queen Mary and Westfield Coll Univ of London; *Recreations* biography, travel, music, history of insolvency law; *Style*— David Graham, Esq, QC; ✉ 6 Grosvenor Lodge, Dennis Lane, Stanmore, Middx HA7 4JE (☎ 0181 954 8783)

GRAHAM, David; s of Philip Graham (d 1984), of London, and Annie, *née* Laport (d 1992); *b* 20 May 1926; *Educ* St Martin's Sch of Art, RCA; *Career* artist; teacher: Wimbledon Sch of Art 1951, Sir John Cass Sch of Art, City of London Poly 1963–90; RP; *Exhibitions* RA 1951–94, William Patterson Fine Art, Paintings of Israel (City of Coventry Art Gallery) 1987, Retrospective (Mall Galleries) 1990; *Collections* Museum of London, Barbican, Guildhall Art Gallery, Coca-Cola Ltd, Guinness plc, IBM, Belgrave House, Contemporary Art Soc, various private collections; *Recreations* painting; *Clubs* Chelsea Art; *Style*— David Graham, Esq, RP; ✉ 2 Curran Studios, Lucan Place, Chelsea, London SW3 (☎ 0181 699 3790)

GRAHAM, David Maurice; s of Jack Graham, of London, and Essie, *née* Fishberg; *b* 14 July 1947; *Educ* St Marylebone GS, Pembroke Coll Cambridge (MA); *m* 29 Aug 1982, Dr Jill Joanne Rowena Graham; 1 s (Michael James Nicholas b 5 Oct 1985), 1 da (Caroline Clare Jane b 17 Feb 1988); *Career* Blick Rothenberg & Noble CAs 1970–74 (qualified 1974), ptnr Price Waterhouse CAs 1981– (joined 1974); ACA 1974, memb Int Fiscal Assoc 1981; *Recreations* bridge (jr England int 1968), music, travel, watching live sport; *Style*— David M Graham, Esq; ✉ Price Waterhouse, Southwark Towers, 32 London Bridge Street, London SE1 9SY (☎ 0171 939 3000, fax 0171 939 2299)

GRAHAM, David Pottie; s of John Armstrong Graham (d 1965), and Isabella Robertson Graham (d 1988); *b* 25 Sept 1937; *Educ* Dalziel HS Motherwell, Coll of Commerce Newcastle upon Tyne; *m* 18 Jun 1960, Jean, da of Ralph Henry Boggon; 1 da (Tracey Lynne b 10 April 1964), 1 s (Fraser John b 15 March 1966); *Career* divnl fin mangr Northumbrian Water Authy 1974–77, md Sunderland and South Shields Water Company 1988–91 (sec accountant 1978–88); chm: City Hosp Sunderland NHS Tst 1993–, Age Concern Sunderland 1982–; FCIS 1963, FCMA 1967; *Recreations* golf, hill walking, music, reading; *Clubs* Sunderland, Landsdowne; *Style*— David Graham, Esq; ✉ City Hospitals Sunderland NHS Trust, Kayll Road, Sunderland, Tyne & Wear SR4 7TP (☎ 0191 565 6256, fax 0191 569 9642)

GRAHAM, Lord Donald Alasdair; s of 7 Duke of Montrose (d 1992), and his 2 w, Susan Mary Jocelyn, *née* Semple; *b* 28 Oct 1956; *Educ* St Andrew's Coll Grahamstown, Univ of St Andrews Scotland (BSc), INSEAD (MBA); *m* 1981, Bride Donalda Elspeth, yst da of Maj Allan John Cameron, of Allangrange, Munlochy, Ross-shire; 1 s (Alasdair John Cameron b 1986, d 1988), 3 da (Caitriana Mary Alice b 1984, Violet Elizabeth Helen b 1992, Jennie Alexandra Cameron b 1993); *Career* dir: Adam & Co plc (bankers), The Fruitmarket Gallery Edinburgh 1993–, The Children's Music Fndn in Scotland Ltd 1995–; MBCS 1988; *Recreations* shooting, piping, music; *Clubs* New (Edinburgh); *Style*— Lord Donald Graham; ✉ Nether Tillyrie, Milnathort, Kinross-shire, Scotland; Adam & Company plc, 22 Charlotte Square, Edinburgh EH2 4DF

GRAHAM, (Malcolm Gray) Douglas; s of Malcolm Graham (d 1993), of Farmcote Hall, Claverley, nr Wolverhampton, and Annie Jeanette Sankey, *née* Robinson (d 1976); *b* 18 Feb 1930; *Educ* Shrewsbury; *m* 18 April 1980, Sara Ann, da of William Patrick Whitelaw Anderson (d 1976), of Feckenham, Worcs; 2 step s (Colin William Edward Elwell b 12 Jan 1971, James Peter Elwell b 24 April 1973); *Career* chm: Claverley Co 1993, The Midland News Assoc Ltd 1984–, Express & Star Ltd, Shropshire Newspapers Ltd 1980–, Stars News Shops Ltd 1994–; pres: Young Newspapermen's Assoc 1969, W Midlands Newspaper Soc 1973–74; chm Evening Newspaper Advtg Bureau 1978–79; *Recreations* shooting; *Style*— Douglas Graham, Esq; ✉ Roughton Manor, Worfield, nr Bridgnorth, Shropshire WV15 5HE (☎ 0174 716209); Express and Star, Queen St, Wolverhampton, W Midlands (☎ 01902 313131)

GRAHAM, Prof Duncan Gilmour; CBE (1987); s of Robert Gilmour Graham, of Glasgow, and Lilias Turnbull, *née* Watson; *b* 20 Aug 1936; *Educ* Hutchesons' Sch Glasgow, Univ of Glasgow (MA), Jordanhill Coll of Educn (CertEd); *m* 1, 1962 (m dis 1990), Margaret Gray, da of Maj James Brown Cairns, RE (d 1984), of Eaglesham; 2 s (Roderick b 1966, Duncan b 1969), 1 da (Kirsty b 1967); m 2, 1991, Wendy Margaret, *née* Wallace; *Career* teacher of history Whitehill and Hutchesons' Schs Glasgow 1959–65, lectr Craigie Coll of Educn Ayr 1965–68, asst then sr dep dir of educn Renfrewshire 1968–74, sr dep dir of educn Strathclyde Regnl Cncl 1974–79, co educn offr Suffolk CC 1979–87, chief exec Humberside CC 1987–88, chm and chief exec Nat Curriculum Cncl 1988–91, sr ptnr Duncan Graham Conslts 1992–; visiting prof: Manchester Univ Sch of Educn 1992–, Univ of Exeter 1993–; advsr to Convention of Scottish Local Authys and Scottish Teachers' Salaries Ctee 1974–79, advsr Assoc of CC 1983–88, memb Burnham Ctee 1983–87, chm Assoc of Educn Offrs 1984, sec Soc of Co Educn Offrs 1985–87, Arts Cncl nominee on Lincoln and Humberside Arts 1987–91; memb: Yorks and Humberside Arts 1991–94, BBC North Advsy Panel, Cncl Industl Soc; FIMgt 1972, FRSA 1981; *Books* Those Having Torches (1985), In the Light of Torches (1986), The National Curriculum - A Lesson For Us All (1992), Sense, Nonsense and the National Curriculum (1993), Sunset on the Clyde (1993), The Education Racket (1996); *Recreations* amateur radio (GOVGJ), fly-fishing, the Arts; *Style*— Prof Duncan Graham, CBE; ✉ Gilmour Mews, Battlebarrow, Appleby, Cumbria CA16 6XT (☎ and fax 017683 52920)

GRAHAM, (Norman) Garrick; s of Cecil Davies Graham (d 1969), and Martha Berneice Isabel, *née* Glass, of Auckland, New Zealand; *b* 15 Dec 1932; *Educ* King's Coll Auckland NZ, Otago Univ Med Sch Dunedin NZ (MB ChB, univ cricket XI); *m* 15 Dec 1956, Joy Frances, *née* Bayly; 1 s (Michael Ian b 24 Oct 1958), 2 da (Kathryn Denise b 22 Nov 1960, Jacky Joy b 20 Dec 1965); *Career* house surgn Auckland Hosps NZ 1957–58, surgical registrar Auckland Public Hosp NZ 1959, anatomy demonstrator Otago Univ Med Sch 1960, rotating surgical registrar Auckland Hosps 1961–62, surgical registrar St Mary's Hosp Portsmouth Eng 1963–64, lectr and sr registrar Professorial Surgical Unit The Gen Infirmary Leeds 1964–67, conslt gen surgn Huddersfield Hosps 1967–93, pt/t unit gen mangr Huddersfield Royal Infirmary 1986–91, chm Huddersfield NHS Tst 1993–; memb: Huddersfield Med Soc (pres), BMA; FRACS 1962, FRCS (Eng) 1963; author of numerous papers in med jls relating to gastro-intestinal and biliary tract surgery and NHS mgmnt; *Recreations* golf, cricket, travel, reading; *Style*— Garrick Graham, Esq; ✉ 26 Thornhill Road, Marsh, Huddersfield, W Yorks HD3 3DD (☎ 01484 428349); Chairman, Huddersfield NHS Trust, Trust HQ, Huddersfield Royal Infirmary, Lindley, Huddersfield, W Yorks HD3 3EA (☎ 01484 482245)

GRAHAM, (William) Gordon; MC (1944 and Bar 1945); s of Thomas Graham (d 1944), and Marion Walker Hutcheson (d 1979); *b* 17 July 1920; *Educ* Hutchesons' GS Glasgow,

Univ of Glasgow (MA); *m* 1, 1943, Margaret (d 1946), da of Alexander Milne (d 1965); 1 da (Fiona); m 2, 1948, Friedel (d 1992), da of Emil Gramm (d 1966); 1 da (Sylvia); m 3, 1994, Betty, da of Charles Cottrell (d 1951); *Career* Nat Serv 1940–41, served Queen's Own Cameron Highlanders 1941–46, Capt 1944, Maj 1945, GSO II India Office 1946 serving in India and Burma; newspaper corr and publishers' rep in India 1946–56; vice pres McGraw-Hill Book Co NY 1961–74 (int sales mangr 1956–63); md McGraw-Hill UK, Europe, ME and Africa 1963–74; chief exec Butterworth Publishers 1975–88 (gp chm 1975–90), ed Logos 1990–; non-exec dir PWN Warsaw 1993–; chm: International Electronic Publishing Research Centre Ltd 1981–84, Publishers Databases Ltd 1982–84, R R Bowker NY 1985–90, Kraszna-Krausz Fndn 1990–95; dir: W & R Chambers Edinburgh 1974–83, International Publishing Corporation 1975–82, Reed Publishing Group 1982–90; pres Publishers' Assoc of GB 1985–87 (memb Cncl 1972–88), memb Bd Br Library 1980–86; Hon DUniv Stirling 1993; FRSA; *Recreations* reading, writing, skiing, gardening; *Style*— Gordon Graham, Esq, MC; ✉ 5 Beechwood Drive, Marlow, Bucks SL7 2DH (☎ 01628 483371)

GRAHAM, Lady; Halina; da of late Maj Wiktor Grubert, diplomat; *Educ* LSE (BA), Univ of Sussex (grad cert in educn), Courtauld Inst (MA); *m* 1986, Sir James Bellingham Graham, 11 Bt, *qv*; *Career* asst educn offr Walker Art Gall Liverpool 1968–70, sr asst curator The County Museum Buckingham 1970–71, curator Cecil Higgins Art Gallery and Museum Bedford 1971– (three awards for new wing and redisplay 1976, three awards for recreated Victorian Mansion 1978–84, Sandford Award 1989 and 1993), purchased Handley Read collection of Victorian and Edwardian decorative arts 1972, has subsequently made regular acquisitions of Euro fine and decorative arts; assessor BA (Architecture) Univ of Liverpool 1972; *Books* Cecil Higgins - Collector Extraordinary, Guide to the Cecil Higgins Art Gallery (with Sir James Graham, Bt); author of articles in Burlington Magazine, Apollo, Arts Review, Antique Collector and other jls; *Recreations* travel, theatre and opera; *Style*— The Lady Graham; ✉ Norton Conyers, nr Ripon, N Yorks HG4 5EH

GRAHAM, Col Ian Derek; TD, DL (E Yorks 1974); s of Maj Ernest Frederic Graham, MBE, MC (d 1985), of Rowan, The Park, Swanland, N Humberside, and Muriel, *née* Fell (d 1970); *b* 27 Feb 1928; *Educ* Sedbergh, Univ Coll Hull, Univ of London (LLB); *m* 1, 24 July 1954 (m dis 1984), Margaret Edwards; 3 da (Fiona Clare b 1955, Janet Elaine b 1958, Sally Anne b 1962); m 2, 1985, Betty, da of Thomas Vessey Whittaker (d 1954); *Career* cmmnd RA 1947, TA 1949–71, Lt-Col 440 LAD Regt RA (TA) 1967, Col Cmdt Humberside ACF 1971–79; admitted slr 1954; sr ptnr Graham & Rosen; memb Nat Cncl ACF Assoc, vice chm Yorks and Humberside TAVRA 1987–90; local chm Social Security Appeal Tbnl and Disability Appeal Tbnl 1970–; memb Law Soc; *Recreations* game shooting; *Style*— Col Ian Graham, TD, DL; ✉ Kelsey Cottage, Hariff Lane, Burstwick, E Yorks (☎ 01964 622429); Graham & Rosen, 8 Parliament St, Hull (☎ 01482 23123)

GRAHAM, Marquess of; James Alexander Norman Graham; s and h of 8 Duke of Montrose, *qv*; *b* 16 Aug 1973; *Educ* Belhaven Hill, Eton, Univ of Edinburgh (BSc); *Style*— Marquess of Graham; ✉ Auchmar, Drymen, Glasgow

GRAHAM, Sir James Bellingham; 11 Bt (E 1662), of Norton Conyers, Yorkshire; er s of Wing Cdr Sir Richard Bellingham Graham, 10 Bt, OBE, JP, DL (d 1982), and Beatrice Mary, OBE, *née* Hamilton-Spencer-Smith (d 1992); *b* 8 Oct 1940; *Educ* Eton, Christ Church Oxford; *m* 1986, Halina (*see* The Lady Graham), yr da of late Major Wiktor Grubert, diplomat; *Heir* bro, William Reginald Graham, *qv*; *Career* keeper of Fine and Decorative Arts Cecil Higgins Museum and Art Gallery Bedford; *Books* Cecil Higgins, Collector Extraordinary (jtly with wife, 1983), A Guide to the Cecil Higgins Museum and Art Gallery (jtly with wife, 1987), Guide to Norton Conyers (1988); *Recreations* history, travel; *Style*— Sir James Graham, Bt; ✉ Norton Conyers, nr Ripon, N Yorks HG4 5EH

GRAHAM, James Fergus Surtees; s and h of Maj Sir Charles Spencer Richard Graham, 6 Bt, *qv*; *b* 29 July 1946; *Educ* Milton Abbey; *m* 1975, Serena Jane, da of Maj Ronald Frank Kershaw; 1 s (Robert Charles Thomas b 19 July 1985), 2 da (Catherine Mary b 1978, Iona Susan Alice b 1980); *Style*— James Graham, Esq; ✉ The Tower, Kirkandrews-on-Esk, Longtown, Cumbria CA6 5NP (☎ 01228 791262)

GRAHAM, Jefferson (Jeff); *b* 24 Feb 1960; *Educ* Ardrossan Acad Ayrshire; *m* 3 May 1991, Inge Renée Van Zijll De-Jong; 1 s (Stanley b 29 Sept 1992); *Career* residential care offr Strathclyde Regnl Cncl 1978–84, freelance presenter BBC Radio Scotland Glasgow 1982–84, guest presenter Radio Forth Edinburgh 1983, presenter and head of music West Sound Radio Ayr 1984–85, presenter Moray Firth Radio Inverness 1985, prodr/presenter Capital Radio London 1985–87; Radio Luxembourg: joined as presenter (based Luxembourg) 1987, head of on-air promotion 1987, head of progs (based London) 1988–91, presenter and programming conslt Atlantic 252 Dublin (co-owned by Radio Luxembourg) 1989–90, prog controller Radio Luxembourg 1991–93, also dep gen mangr (based Luxembourg) 1991–93; Red Rose Radio plc: prog dir Red Rose Gold and Red Rose Rock FM 1993–94, main bd dir 1994; tstee Red Rose Community Tst 1993–94; exec prodr daytime progs and music manager BBC Radio 1 1995; gp programme dir Independent Radio Group 1996–; winner New York Festival International Programming Award 1993; memb: Radio Acad, Brit Award Voting Acad, Equity; tutor in radio Univ of Westminster; *Style*— Jeff Graham, Esq; ✉ Scot FM, 1 Albert Quay, Leith, Edinburgh EH6 7DN (☎ 0131 554 6677, fax 0131 554 2266)

GRAHAM, Sir John Alexander Noble; 4 Bt (UK 1906), of Larbert; GCMG (1986, KCMG 1979, CMG 1972); s of Sir (John) Reginald Noble Graham, 3 Bt, VC, OBE (d 1980), and Rachel, *née* Sprot (d 1984); *b* 15 July 1926; *Educ* Eton, Trinity Coll Cambridge; *m* 1, 1956, Marygold Ellinor Gabrielle (Meg) (d 1991), da of Lt-Col Clive Grantham Austin, JP, DL (d 1974), and Lady Lilian Lumley, sis of 11 Earl of Scarbrough, KG, GCSI, GCVO, TD, PC; 2 s (Andrew John Noble b 1956, George Reginald Clive b 1958), 1 da (Christian Rachel (Mrs Matthew Scott Dryden) b 1961); m 2, 27 June 1992, Jane, widow of Christopher Howells; *Heir* s, Col Andrew John Noble Graham, MBE, *qv* b 21 Oct 1956; *Career* joined FO 1950, served Amman, Kuwait, Bahrain, Belgrade, Benghazi, and as cnsllr and head of Chancery Washington; ambass Iraq 1974–77, FCO dep under sec 1977–79 and 1980–82, ambass Iran 1979–80, ambass and UK perm rep NATO Brussels 1982–86; dir Ditchley Fndn 1987–92, chm Countrywide Workshops Charitable Trust 1992–; *Recreations* outdoor activities; *Clubs* Army and Navy; *Style*— Sir John Graham, Bt, GCMG; ✉ Salisbury Place, Church Street, Shipton-under-Wychwood, Oxon OX7 6BP

GRAHAM, Maj-Gen John David Carew; CB (1978), CBE (1973, OBE 1967); s of Col John Alexander Graham (d 1957), of The White House, Nettlestone, IOW, and Constance Mary, *née* Carew-Hunt (d 1987); *b* 18 Jan 1923; *Educ* Fernden Sch Haslemere, Cheltenham; *m* 17 Nov 1956, Rosemary Elaine, da of James Basil Adamson (d 1945), of Georgetown, British Guiana; 1 s (John Christopher Malcolm b 1959), 1 da (Jacqueline Patricia Anne b 1957); *Career* cmmnd Argyll and Sutherland Highlanders 1942 (despatches), served 5 Bn The Parachute Regt 1946–49, Br Embassy Prague 1949–50, HQ Scottish Cmd 1956–58, mil asst to CINCENT Fontainebleau 1960–62, cmd 1 Bn The Parachute Regt 1964–66, instr Staff Coll Camberley 1967, Regtl Col The Parachute Regt 1968–69, Cdr Sultan's Armed Forces Oman 1970–72, Indian Nat Def Coll 1973, asst Chief of Staff HQ AFCENT 1974–76, GOC Wales 1976–78; admin Chevening Estate 1978–87; Hon Col Kent ACF 1981–88 (chm Kent ACF Ctee 1979–86), Hon Col 203 Welsh Gen Hosp, RAMC, TA 1983–89; chm St John Cncl for Kent 1978–86; memb: Cncl Royal Cwlth Soc (Barbados), Barbados Legion of Cwlth Ex-Servicemen and Women 1992–; CStJ; Freeman City of London 1992; Order of Oman; *Recreations* gardening, travel; *Style*— Major-General John Graham, CB, CBE; ✉ Fintry, 6 Sheraton Park, Christ Church, Barbados, West Indies (☎ 00 1 809 246 437 0618)

GRAHAM, John Malcolm; s of Malcolm Pullen Graham (d 1989), of Oxford, and Edna Stanhope, *née* Davis; *b* 9 Feb 1940; *Educ* Uppingham, Pembroke Coll Oxford (MA, BM BCh), Middx Hosp; *m* 15 Jan 1966, Sandy Judy, da of Wing Cdr Eduardo Walpole Whitaker, DFC (d 1985); 1 s (Alastair b 25 April 1966), 2 da (Harriet b 9 June 1976, Emily b 17 Jan 1978); *Career* conslt ENT surgn UCH, Middlesex and Royal London Homeopathic Hosp 1979–; ENT conslt Med Fndn for Victims of Torture 1991–, chm Med Ctee and memb Cncl St Luke's Hosp for the Clergy London 1992–; fndr pres Br Assoc for Paediatric Otorhinolaryngology 1991–93; author of various sci papers, contrib chapters on subjects incl: tinnitus in adults and children, cochlear implants, electric response audiometry; Freeman City of London 1988, Liveryman Worshipful Soc Apothecaries; memb: BMA, RSM; FRCS, FRCSE; miembro correspondiente Societad del ORL de Uruguay; *Recreations* music, construction; *Style*— John Graham, Esq; ✉ 16 Upper Wimpole Street, London W1M 7TB (☎ 0171 486 9583)

GRAHAM, Sir John Moodie; 2 Bt (UK 1964), of Dromore, Co Down; s of Sir Clarence Johnston Graham, 1 Bt (d 1966); *b* 3 April 1938; *Educ* Trinity Coll Glenalmond, Queen's Univ Belfast (BSc); *m* 1970 (m dis 1982), Valerie Rosemary, da of late Frank Gill, of Belfast; 3 da (Suzanne Margaret b 1971, Alyson Rosemary b 1974, Lucy Christina b 1978); *Heir* none; *Career* pres N Ireland Leukaemia Res Fund, dir John Graham (Dromore) Ltd, Electrical Supplies Ltd, Concrete (NI) Ltd, Ulster Quarries Ltd, G H Fieldhouse Plant (NI) Ltd; memb Lloyds 1978–; ret 1983; *Style*— Sir John Graham, Bt; ✉ Les Bordes d'Arinsal, Arinsal, Principat d'Andorra (☎ and fax 00 376 837863); Portofino, 77 South Birch Road 11D, Fort Lauderdale, Florida 33316 (☎ and fax 00 1 954 728 8720)

GRAHAM, John Strathie; s of Sir Norman Graham, CB, FRSE, *qv*, and Catherine Mary, *née* Strathie; *b* 27 May 1950; *Educ* Edinburgh Acad, CCC Oxford (BA); *m* 1979, Anne, da of James Stenhouse; 1 da (Kate b 1982), 2 s (Philip b 1985, Robert b 1986); *Career* SO: joined 1972, private sec to Min of State 1975–76, princ Scottish Economic Planning Dept 1976–82, asst sec 1982–83, private sec to Sec of State 1983–85, under sec (local govt gp) Devpt Dept (formerly Environment Dept) 1991–96, princ fin offr 1996–; *Recreations* exploring Scotland, music; *Style*— John Graham, Esq; ✉ Scottish Office, Finance Group, Victoria Quay, Edinburgh, Scotland EH6 6QQ

GRAHAM, Kenneth; CBE (1987, OBE 1971); s of Ernest Graham (d 1981), of Cleator, Cumbria, and Ivy, *née* Hutchinson (d 1987); *b* 18 July 1922; *Educ* Workington Tech Sch, Leyton Tech Coll, Univ of London (external); *m* 24 Nov 1945, Ann Winifred Muriel, *née* Taylor; *Career* engrg apprentice 1938–42, Radar Res Unit WO 1942–45, Air Training Sch, licensed engr Air Registration Bd, BOAC 1945–50, RN Scientific Serv Admiralty Res Estab 1950–61, pt/t tutor Univ of Southampton and WEA 1958–61; TUC: offr 1961, head Organisation and Industl Relations Dept 1966–77, asst gen sec 1977–85, dep gen sec 1985–87; memb: Cncl Inst for Employment Studies (formerly Inst of Manpower Studies) 1975–, Cncl Templeton Coll (Oxford Centre for Mgmnt Studies) 1984–95, Nat Cncl for Vocational Qualifications 1986–92, Bd The Open Coll 1987–, Bd Remploy Ltd 1987–92, Bd Universities' Staff Devpt Unit 1989–93, Professional Conduct Ctee Gen Cncl of the Bar 1990–95; a vice pres Airborne Forces Charities Appeal 1990–, hon friend Airborne Forces 1996–; Hon LLD CNAA 1986; FRSA 1987; *Books* Job Satisfaction - Challenge and Response in Modern Britain (contrib, 1976); *Recreations* military and aviation history, music, racing; *Style*— Kenneth Graham, Esq, CBE; ✉ 90 Springfield Drive, Ilford, Essex IG2 6QS (☎ 0181 554 0839)

GRAHAM, (John) Michael Denning; s of William Graham (d 1962), of Glasgow, and Inez Reid (d 1988); *b* 7 Sept 1944; *Educ* Royal Belfast Academical Inst, Queen's Univ Belfast (LLB); *m* 25 July 1970, Christina Jeanne, da of Ronald Ernest Sinclair, of Cladyhood, NI; 2 s (David William Denning b 1974, Richard Anthony Denning b 1976); *Career* sr ptnr Paterson Robertson & Graham Slrs (Glasgow, Kirkintilloch, Clydebank, Lennoxtown and Johnstone), non-exec dir John Smith & Son (Glasgow) Ltd 1988–, dir Select Assured Properties plc 1989–; sr tutor of professional responsibility and ethics Univ of Glasgow 1988–94; returning offr Community Cncl Elections 1982–, chm Rent Assessment Ctee Glasgow and West of Scotland 1983–, dir Glasgow Slrs' Property Centre 1993–; chm: Child Support Appeal Tbnl 1993–, Social Security Appeal Tbnl 1995–; non-exec dir W Glasgow Hosps Univ NHS Tst 1994–; govr Caledonian Univ Glasgow 1991–; deacon Incorporation of Fleshers of Glasgow 1993–94; memb Law Soc of Scotland 1970; *Recreations* tennis, skiing, golf, hang-gliding; *Clubs* Western (Glasgow); *Style*— Michael Graham, Esq; ✉ St Michaels, Garngaber Avenue, Lenzie, Glasgow G66 (☎ 0141 777 8224); Dunmhor, Lochgoilhead, Argyll; Paterson Robertson & Graham, 12 Royal Crescent, Glasgow G3 7SL (☎ 0141 353 0550, fax 0141 331 2231)

GRAHAM, Prof Neil Bonnette; s of George Henry Graham (d 1979), of Liverpool, and Constance, *née* Bonnette (d 1986); *b* 23 May 1933; *Educ* Alsop HS Liverpool, Univ of Liverpool (BSc, PhD); *m* 16 July 1955, Marjorie, da of William Edwin Royden (d 1937), of Liverpool; 1 s (Paul b 19 Sept 1957), 3 da (Kim b 7 Oct 1959, Michele b 14 May 1965, Lesley b 6 Aug 1967); *Career* res scientist Canadian Industries Ltd McMasterville PQ Canada 1956–67, gp head ICI Petrochemical and Polymer Laboratory Runcorn Cheshire 1967–73 (former assoc gp head), res prof of chemical technol Univ of Strathclyde 1983– (Young prof 1973–83), fndr and tech dir Polysystems Ltd Clydebank 1980–90; expert advsr on active med implants to Sec of State 1993–; memb Dept of Health Medicines Div Regulatory Advsy Ctee on Dental and Surgical Materials 1978–86; tstee: McKinnon McNeil Tst, James Clerk Maxwell Tst; govr Keil Sch; holder of more than 60 patents; ALCM, CChem, FRSC, FIM, FRSE; *Recreations* walking, sailing, music; *Style*— Prof Neil Graham, FRSE; ✉ 6 Kilmardinny Grove, Bearsden, Glasgow G61 3NY (☎ 0141 942 0484); 5 Clyde St, Millport, Cumbrae Island, Scotland; University of Strathclyde, Department of Pure & Applied Chemistry, Thomas Graham Building, 295 Cathedral St, Glasgow G1 1XL (☎ 0141 552 4400, fax 0141 552 5664, telex 77472 UNSLIB G, e-mail 100721,314@compuserv.com)

GRAHAM, Sir Norman William; kt (1971), CB (1961); s of late William McLeod Graham; *b* 11 Oct 1913; *Educ* Glasgow HS, Univ of Glasgow; *m* 1949, Catherine Mary, *née* Strathie; 2 s, (one of whom John Strathie, *qv*, b 27 May 1950), 1 da; *Career* PPS to Min of Aircraft Prodn 1944–45, asst sec Dept of Health for Scotland 1945, under sec Scottish Home and Health Dept 1956–63, sec Scottish Educn Dept 1964–73; FRSE 1972; *Clubs* New (Edinburgh); *Style*— Sir Norman Graham, CB, FRSE; ✉ Chesterhall Steading, Longniddry, East Lothian (☎ 01875 52130)

GRAHAM, Sir Peter; KCB (1993, CB 1982), QC (1990); o s of Alderman Douglas Graham, CBE (d 1981), of Huddersfield, Yorkshire, and Ena May, *née* Jackson (d 1982); f was Mayor of Huddersfield 1966–67, and Freeman of Borough 1973; *b* 7 Jan 1934; *Educ* St Bees Sch Cumberland (scholar), St John's Coll Cambridge (scholar, MA, LLM); *m* 1, Judith Mary, da of Charles Dunbar, CB; 2 s (Ian b 1960, Alistair b 1962); m 2 (sep 1993), Anne Silvia, da of Benjamin Arthur Garcia; *Career* called to the Bar Gray's Inn 1958, bencher 1992; Parly counsel 1972–86, second Parly counsel 1987–91, first Parly counsel 1991–94, conslt in legislative drafting 1994–; *Recreations* village organist, gardening, classic cars; *Clubs* The Sette of Odd Volumes; *Style*— Sir Peter Graham, KCB, QC; ✉ Le Petit Château, La Vallette, 87190 Magnac Laval, France

GRAHAM, Sir Peter Alfred; kt (1987), OBE (1969); s of Alfred Graham and Margaret, *née* Winder; *b* 25 May 1922; *Educ* St Joseph's Coll Beulah Hill; *m* 1953, Luned Mary, *née* Kenealy-Jones; 2 s, 2 da; *Career* chm: Standard Chartered Merchant Bank 1977–83, Standard Chartered Bank and Standard Chartered PLC 1987–88, Crown Agents 1983–90, Equatorial Bank 1989–93; dir: ECA 1989–94, Dolphin Management Services 1995–; pres Inst of Bankers 1981–83; chm Cncl City Univ Business Sch 1986–92; Hon DSc City Univ 1985; Freeman City of London 1982; FCIB, CIMgt, FRSA; *Recreations* golf, skiing, tennis; *Clubs* Royal Automobile, Naval, Hong Kong; *Style*— Sir Peter Graham, OBE; ✉ Heron Lea, Hobbs Lane, Beckley, nr Rye, Sussex TN31 6TT

GRAHAM, Peter Louis; s of David Barnett Graham, and Hannah, *née* Hyams; *b* 15 June 1946; *Educ* St Paul's, Magdalene Coll Cambridge (exhibitioner, scholar, BA, LLB, MA); *m* 25 June 1981, Susan Jane, da of Dr Benjamin Gottlieb; 1 s (Edward James b 21 June 1982); *Career* Norton Rose (formerly Norton Rose Botterell & Roche: articled clerk 1969–71, asst slr 1971–76, ptnr 1977–; on secondment to Cleary Gottlieb Steen & Hamilton Paris 1973–74; assoc memb Inst of Taxation 1971, memb Company Law Ctee Law Soc 1980–; Freeman City of London Slrs' Co 1977; memb: Law Soc 1971, Int Bar Assoc 1985; *Recreations* theatre, chess, classical music; *Style*— Peter Graham, Esq; ✉ Norton Rose, Kempson House, Camomile Street, London EC3A 7AN (☎ 0171 283 6000, fax 0171 283 6500)

GRAHAM, Lt-Gen Sir Peter Walter; KCB (1991), CBE (1981, OBE 1978, MBE 1972); s of Dr Walter Graham (d 1985), of Aberdeen and London, and Suzanne, *née* Simon (d 1976); *b* 14 March 1937; *Educ* Fyvie Sch Aberdeenshire, Hall Sch Hampstead, St Paul's Sch London, RMA Sandhurst; *m* 23 March 1963, Dr Alison Mary Morren, da of David Begg Morren, TD, of Huntly, Aberdeenshire; 3 s (James b 1964, Roderick b 1967, Douglas b 1970); *Career* cmmnd The Gordon Highlanders 1956; regtl appts 1957–62: Dover, BAOR, Scotland, Kenya; Staff Capt HQ Highland Bde Perth 1962; Adj 1 Gordons 1963–66: Kenya, Scotland, Borneo (despatches); Staff Capt HQ 1 Br Corps BAOR 1966–68, Staff Coll Aust 1968, Co Cdr 1 Gordons BAOR 1969, BM 39 Inf Bde Ulster 1970–72; 2 i/c 1 Gordons 1972–74: Scotland, Ulster, Singapore; MA to Adj-Gen MOD 1974–76; CO 1 Gordons 1976–78: Scotland, Ulster, Chester; COS HQ 3 Armd Div BAOR 1978–82, Cdr UDR (despatches) 1982–84, Nat Def Coll Canada 1984–85, Dep Mil Sec B MOD 1985–87, Col The Gordon Highlanders 1986–94, GOC Eastern Dist 1987–89, Cmdt RMA Sandhurst 1989–91, Col Cmdt Scottish Div 1991–93, GOC Scotland and Governor Edinburgh Castle 1991–93; chm The Gordon Highlanders Regtl Tst Fund 1986–; memb The Queen's Body Guard for Scotland (The Royal Co of Archers) 1985, Burgess of Guild City of Aberdeen 1994; *Books* Gordon Highlanders Pipe Music Collection (with Pipe Major B McRae, vol 1 1983, vol 2 1985); *Recreations* shooting, stalking, fishing, hill walking, reading, gardening under wife's supervision, pipe music; *Clubs* Caledonian; *Style*— Lt-Gen Sir Peter Graham, KCB, CBE; ✉ c/o HQ Scotland (Army), Edinburgh EH1 2YX

GRAHAM, Sir Ralph Stuart; 14 Bt (E 1629), of Esk, Cumberland; er s of Sir Ralph Wolfe Graham, 13 Bt (d 1988), and his 2 w, Geraldine, *née* Velour; *b* 5 Nov 1950; *Educ* Hofstra Univ; *m* 1, 1972, Roxanne (d 1978), da of Mrs Lovette Gurzan, of Elmont, Long Island, New York; 1 adopted s (Gabriel Lawrence b 1974); m 2, 1979, Deena Louise, da of William Robert Vandergrift, of 2903 Nemesis, Waukegan, Illinois; *Heir* bro, Robert Bruce Graham b 14 Nov 1953; *Career* self-employed (maintenance company); singer/songwriter (recorded three gospel albums, including Star of the Show, One by One); *Recreations* bible fellowships, performing music; *Style*— Sir Ralph Graham, Bt; ✉ 115 Bear Track, Nashville, Tennessee 37221, USA

GRAHAM, Col Richard Harold; MBE (1979); s of Harold Ernest Graham (d 1970), and Vera Irene Greta, *née* Wenman (d 1994); *b* 20 Jan 1941; *Educ* Gillingham Sch, Jesus Coll Cambridge (MA, MPhil), Staff Coll Camberley, Nat Defence Coll Latimer; *m* 28 Dec 1963, Ruby Primula Cécile, da of Walter Edwin Down, of Guernsey; 1 s (Justin Émile b 15 Oct 1969), 1 da (Sarah Louise b 10 Aug 1965); *Career* cmmnd Middlesex Regt 1964, served in Gibraltar, Libya, Br Guiana, NI, BAOR 1964–83, DAA and QMG 8 Inf Bde 1974–76 (despatches 1977), CO 3 Bn The Queen's Regt 1981–83, Cdr Battle Gp Trainer 1984–86, COS 1 Armed Div 1986–88, Cmdt Jr Div The Staff Coll 1989–92, Dep Col The Queen's Regt 1989–92, Dep Col The Princess of Wales's Royal Regt 1992–94; Croix d'Honneur avec Rosette de l'Ordre de la Maison d'Orange Netherlands 1983; *Recreations* long-distance walking, writing, golf, music; *Clubs* Royal Guernsey Golf; *Style*— Col Richard Graham, MBE; ✉ Veue du Guet, Rue de la Lande, Albecq, Catel, Guernsey GY5 7EH (☎ 01481 54784)

GRAHAM, (George Malcolm) Roger; OBE (1987); s of William George Blampied Graham (d 1943), and Enid, *née* Townsley (d 1970); *b* 10 May 1939; *Educ* Mill Hill Sch, Fitzwilliam Coll Cambridge; *m* Irene Helen Leyden, *née* Martin; 1 s, 2 da; *Career* various appts in heavy electrical and aircraft industs 1961–62, major account mangr IBM 1965–67 (joined 1962), md ASAP Consultants Ltd 1967–69; BIS Group Ltd: joined 1969, involved in mgmnt buy-in 1980 and sale to NYNEX Corp 1986, various positions rising to chm and chief exec until 1993; currently exec dir Close Brothers Corporate Finance Ltd; chm: Braid Systems Ltd, Mantix Systems Ltd; pres: UK Computing Servs Assoc 1981–82, European Computing Servs Assoc 1986–88, first chm World Computing Serv Indust Forum, fndr chm Computing Servs Indust Trg Cncl; Freeman City of London 1988; Liveryman: Worshipful Co of Information Technologists 1987, Worshipful Co of Glovers 1988; *Books* The Handbook of Computer Management (with R B Yearsley, 1973), Information 2000 - Insights into the Coming Decades in Information Technology (1989); *Recreations* landscape gardening, opera, private flying; *Clubs* United Oxford and Cambridge; *Style*— Roger Graham, Esq, OBE; ✉ Close Brothers Corporate Finance Ltd, 12 Appold Street, London EC2A 2AA (☎ 0171 426 4000, fax 0171 426 4385)

GRAHAM, Ronald Cairns; CBE (1992); s of Thomas Graham (d 1967), of Airdrie, Lanarkshire, and Helen Waugh, *née* Cairns (d 1989); *b* 8 Oct 1931; *Educ* Airdrie Acad, Univ of Glasgow (MB, ChB), Univ of Edinburgh (Dip Social Med); *m* 9 Oct 1959, Christine Fraser, da of James Cunningham Osborne (d 1982), of Airdrie; 2 s (Colin Thomas b 1961, Alistair James b 1971), 1 da (Rhona Osborne Ritchie b 1963); *Career* Nat Serv Capt RAMC 1957–59; dep med supt Royal Infirmary of Edinburgh 1962–65, asst sr med offr S Eastern Regnl Hosp Bd 1965–69, dep MO rising to sr MO Eastern Regnl Hosp Bd 1969–73, gen mangr Tayside Health Bd 1985–93 (chief med offr 1973–85); memb Ct Univ of Dundee 1995–; FFPHM 1973, FRCP (Edinburgh) 1983; *Recreations* golf, fishing; *Style*— Dr Ronald Graham, CBE; ✉ 34 Dalgleish Rd, Dundee DD4 7JT (☎ 01382 455426)

GRAHAM, (George) Ronald Gibson; CBE (1986); s of Dr James Gibson Graham (d 1987), and Elizabeth, *née* Waddell (d 1987); *b* 15 Oct 1939; *Educ* Glasgow Acad, Loretto, Oriel Coll Oxford (MA), Univ of Glasgow (LLB); *m* 23 July 1965, Mirren Elizabeth, da of (James) Forrest Carnegie, of Edinburgh; 3 s (Peter Carnegie Gibson b 4 Jan 1967, Alan Ronald b 18 Nov 1969, Douglas James Gibson b 28 May 1974); *Career* sr ptnr Maclay Murray & Spens Solicitors Glasgow Edinburgh and London 1996– (ptnr 1968–); dir Scottish Widows' Fund and Life Assurance Society 1984–; memb Ct Univ of Glasgow 1996– (clerk to Gen Cncl 1990–); govr Jordanhill Coll of Educn Glasgow until merger with Univ of Strathclyde 1993; coordinator of Dip in Legal Practice Univ of Glasgow 1979–83; Law Soc of Scotland: memb 1965, memb Cncl 1977–89, pres 1984–85; *Books* Stair Memorial Encyclopaedia of the Laws of Scotland (contrib); *Recreations* fishing, golfing, swimming; *Clubs* Western, Western Baths (Glasgow); *Style*— Ronald G Graham, Esq, CBE; ✉ Maclay Murray & Spens, 151 St Vincent St, Glasgow G2 5NJ (☎ 0141 248 5011, fax 0141 248 5819)

GRAHAM, Sandra Denise (Mrs John Bridger); da of James Graham, of Poole, Dorset, and Joyce N Elizabeth, *née* Botham; *b* 28 Sept 1957; *Educ* Fylde Lodge HS Stockport Cheshire, Manchester Poly (BA); *m* 13 Sept 1986, John Christopher Bridger, s of Lt Henry Chris Bridger, of Bournemouth, Dorset; 2 da (Sarah b 4 Nov 1990, Rachael b 13 April 1993), 1 s (David b 9 April 1996); *Career* admitted slr 1984; formerly ptnr Penningtons (Bournemouth), currently conslt Fynn & Partners (formerly Penningtons), specialist in liquor licensing and entertainment law and food law, memb Good Law Gp; nominated as one of ldrs in their field by chambers and ptnrs in directory 1995–96; chm Bournemouth & Dist Young Slrs' Gp 1991–92, treas Nat Young Slrs' Gp 1990–92 (Bournemouth & Dist rep 1985–92); memb: Bournemouth and Dist Law Soc (memb Gen Ctee 1990–93), Law Soc; *Recreations* squash, cake decorating (memb Br Sugarcraft Guild), sailing, music, travel; *Style*— Ms Sandra Graham; ✉ 70 Richmond Hill, Bournemouth, Dorset BH2 6JA (☎ 01202 551991, fax 01202 557742, car 0831 168951)

GRAHAM, Susan Alesta; da of Floyd Ben Graham, of Midland, Texas, and Betty Fort; *b* 23 July 1960; *Educ* Midland Lee HS, Texas Tech Univ, Manhattan Sch of Music; *Career* mezzo soprano; opera debut in Vanessa (St Louis) 1988; recordings: Beatrice et Benedict (Opera de Lyon) 1991, Damnation de Faust (Opera de Lyon) 1994, Falstaff (Berlin Philharmonic) 1994, La Damoiselle Elue (Boston Symphony Orch) 1995; winner Schwabacher Grand Prize Merola Finals 1987, awarded Richard Tucker Fndn Career Grant 1988, winner Metropolitan Opera Nat Cncl Award 1988; *Recreations* computers, roller-blading, reading, bicycling; *Style*— Ms Susan Graham; ✉ c/o Matthew Epstein, CAMI, 165 W 57th St, New York, NY 10019, USA (☎ 00 1 212 841 9550)

GRAHAM, Teresa Colomba; da of Albert Rea (d 1986), and Anna, *née* Mastroianni; *b* 8 March 1956; *Educ* La Sagesse Convent GS Newcastle upon Tyne, Univ of Newcastle upon Tyne (BA); *m* (m dis); *Career* Price Waterhouse CAs: Newcastle upon Tyne Office 1977–88 (qualified 1980), seconded to Govt's Enterprise and Deregulation Unit 1987, London Office 1988–90 (advsr to Govt on deregulation); currently managing ptnr Bromley Office and head of business servs London office Baker Tilly; chm London Soc of CAs 1994–95; memb: Educnl Policy Ctee RSA 1989–94, Govt's Deregulation Task Force 1994–; govr Bromley Coll 1993–94; Young Accountant of the Year 1988; FCA 1992 (ACA 1982), FRSA 1993; *Recreations* opera, driving, reading; *Style*— Mrs Teresa Graham; ✉ Baker Tilly, 2 Bloomsbury Street, London WC1B 3ST (☎ 0171 413 5100, fax 0171 413 5101)

GRAHAM, Thomas; MP (Lab) Renfrew West and Inverclyde (majority 1,744); *Career* MP (Lab) Renfrew W and Inverclyde 1987–; *Style*— Thomas Graham, Esq, MP; ✉ House of Commons, London SW1A 0AA (☎ 0171 219 3000)

GRAHAM, Timothy Richard (Tim); s of Herbert Maurice Graham (d 1987), and Florence Mary Warrington, *née* Winship (d 1984); *b* 23 Nov 1948; *m* 10 July 1976, Eileen Mary, da of George Tyner Fitzpatrick; 1 da (Lucy Mary b 24 Jan 1983), 1 s (Thomas Andrew b 15 Sept 1984); *Career* freelance photographer specialising in the Royal Family; Fox Photos 1965–70, staff photographer Daily Mail 1975–78; subjects incl: Royal Family, Heads of State, VIPs; sittings: HM The Queen and HRH Prince Philip, The Prince and Princess of Wales and Family, Princess Alice, Prince Edward, The Duke and Duchess of Gloucester and family, Prince and Princess Michael of Kent and family, Prince Albert of Monaco, Margaret Thatcher; exhibition Royal Photographs Royal Acad 1984; *Books* On the Royal Road (1984), The Prince and Princess of Wales - In Person (1985), The Prince and Princess of Wales - In Private, In Public (1986), Diana - HRH The Princess of Wales (1988), Charles and Diana - A Family Album (1991), The Royal Year (annually); *Recreations* photography, wine, food, travel, fast cars, countryside, preservation of the environment and our wildlife; *Style*— Tim Graham, Esq; ✉ Tim Graham Picture Library (☎ 0171 435 7693, fax 0171 431 4312)

GRAHAM, William Reginald; 2 s of Wing Cdr Sir Richard Bellingham Graham, 10 Bt, OBE, RAFVR (d 1982); bro and h of Sir James Bellingham Graham, 11 Bt, *qv*; *b* 7 July 1942; *Educ* privately; *Style*— William Graham, Esq; ✉ Badger Bank, Norton Conyers, Ripon, North Yorkshire

GRAHAM, Winston Mawdsley; OBE (1983); s of Albert Henry Graham, and Anne, *née* Mawdsley; *b* 30 June 1912; *m* 1939, Jean Mary, da of Cdr Samuel Arthur Williamson, RN; 1 s (Andrew), 1 da (Rosamund); *Career* published novelist since age of 23, books translated into 17 languages, six novels made into feature films incl Marnie (dir Alfred Hitchcock); TV films: The Sleeping Partner 1967, The Forgotten Story (six instalments) 1983, The Poldark novels (twenty-nine instalments) 1975–77, The Stranger from the Sea (a Poldark novel) 1996; other works incl: Angell, Pearl and Little God, The Walking Stick, The Grove of Eagles, The Spanish Armadas, Poldark's Cornwall, The Green Flash, The Tumbled House, The Twisted Sword, Stephanie, Tremor; FRSL; *Clubs* Savile, Beefsteak, Pratt's; *Style*— Winston Graham, Esq, OBE, FRSL; ✉ Abbotswood House, Buxted, Sussex TN22 4PB

GRAHAM-BOWMAN, Judyth Jacqueline; *see:* Thomas, Judyth Jacqueline

GRAHAM-BROWN, Dr Robin Alan Charles; s of Maj Lewis Hilary Graham-Brown, of Burton on the Wolds, Leics, and Elizabeth Constance, *née* Blaxland; *b* 14 Aug 1949; *Educ* Sevenoaks Sch, Royal Free Hosp Sch of Med (BSc, MB BS); *m* 13 Sept 1975, Dr Margaret Marie Rose Anne Graham-Brown, da of Dr Robert Graham, of Loughborough, Leics; 3 s (James Robert Philip b 1980, Matthew Paul Mark b 1982, John Joseph Dominic b 1986); *Career* conslt dermatologist 1982–; Leicester Royal Infirmary, Leicester Gen Hosp, Market Harborough Hosp, BUPA Hosp Leicester; hon sr lectr Univ of Leicester Sch of Med 1993–; local sec Br Assoc of Dermatologists 1987–88; FRCP 1990 (MRCP 1974); *Books* Skin Disorders in the Elderly (1988), Lecture Notes on Dermatology (1990); *Recreations* horseriding, cricket, opera; *Clubs* MCC, Dowling; *Style*— Dr Robin Graham-Brown; ✉ Killiecrankie, 46 Barrow Road, Burton on the Wolds, nr Loughborough, Leicestershire LE12 5TB (☎ 01509 880558); Department of Dermatology, Leicester Royal Infirmary, Leicester LE1 5WW (☎ 0116 254 1414)

GRAHAM-BRYCE, Dr Ian James; s of late Alexander Graham-Bryce, and Dame Isabel Graham-Bryce; *b* 20 March 1937; *Educ* William Hulmes' GS, Univ of Oxford (BA, MA, BSc, DPhil); *m* 1959, Anne Elisabeth; 1 s, 3 da; *Career* res asst Univ of Oxford 1958–61, lectr Dept of Biochemistry and Soil Science Univ Coll of N Wales 1961–64, sr scientific offr Rothamsted Experimental Station 1964–70, sr res offr ICI Plant Protection Div Jealott's Hill Res Station Bracknell 1970–72, special lectr in pesticide chemistry Imperial Coll of Sci and Technol Univ of London 1970–72, dep dir Rothamsted Experimental Station 1975–79 (head Dept of Insecticides and Fungicides 1972–79), visiting prof Imperial Coll of Sci and Technol Univ of London 1976–79, hon lectr Univ of Strathclyde 1977–80, dir East Malling Res Station 1979–85, conslt dir Cwlth Bureau of Horticulture and Plantation Crops 1979–85, hon conslt Zoecon Corp Calif 1980–86, head Environmental Affairs Div Shell Internationale Petroleum Maatschappij BV 1986–94, princ and vice-chllr Univ of Dundee 1994–; pres: Soc of Chemical Indust 1982–84, Assoc of Applied Biologists 1988–89, Br Crop Protection Cncl 1996–; chm: Agrochemical Planning Gp Int Orgn for Chem Scis in Devpt 1985–87, Working Gp on Environmental Auditing, Environmental Cmmn Int C of C 1988–92; vice chm: Global Warming Gp Int Petroleum Indust Environmental Conservation Assoc 1988–94, Environmental Res Working Gp Industl Res and Devpt Advsy Ctee to the Euro Communities 1988–91; memb: Br Nat Ctee for Chemistry 1982–84, Scientific Ctee Euro Chem Indust Ecology and Toxicology Centre 1988–94, Cncl UK Natural Environment

Res Cncl 1989–96 (chm Polar Scis and Technol Bd 1995–96), Tech Assoc Coal Indust Advsy Bd Global Warming Ctee 1989–94; govr: Long Ashton Res Station 1979–85, Imperial Coll of Sci Technol Univ of London 1985–; tstee Devpt and Endowment Fund Br Soc for Horticultural Res 1987–; Freeman City of London 1981, Liveryman Worshipful Co of Fruiterers 1981; FRCS 1981, FRSE 1996, FRSA 1996; *Books* Physical Principles of Pesticide Behaviour; *Recreations* music (especially opera), tennis, fly-fishing, windsurfing; *Clubs* Athenaeum, Caledonian; *Style*— Dr Ian Graham-Bryce, FRSE; ✉ Principal's Office, University of Dundee, Dundee DD1 4HN (☎ 01382 345555, fax 01382 229948)

GRAHAM BRYCE, Dame Isabel; *née* Lorrain-Smith; DBE (1968); da of late Prof J Lorrain-Smith, FRS; *b* 30 April 1902; *Educ* St Leonards Sch St Andrews, Univ of Edinburgh (MA); *m* 1934, Alexander Graham Bryce (d 1968); 2 s; *Career* investigator Industl Fatigue Res Bd 1926–27, HM inspector of factories 1928–34, organizer WRVS Manchester 1938–39, dir of orgn Ontario div Canadian WRVS 1941–42, tech advsr American WRVS 1942–43, res fell Fatigue Lab Harvard Univ 1943–44; Nat Cncl of Women: chm Manchester Branch 1947–50, vice chm Educn Ctee 1950–51, memb Oxford Branch 1987–; life vice pres Princess Christian Coll Manchester, JP and memb Juvenile Ct Panel Manchester City 1949–55, vice chm Assoc of HMC's 1953–55; memb: Nurses and Midwives Whitley Cncl 1954–60, Gen Nursing Cncl 1956–61, Public Health Inspectorate Educn Bd 1958–64, ITA 1960–65 (chm Gen Advsy Cncl 1964–65), Bd ATV Network Ltd 1968–72; chm: Oxford Regnl Hosp Bd 1963–72, Nat Staff Ctee and Nat Nursing Staff Ctee of NHS 1967–75; vice chm Visitors Grendon Prison 1962–67; memb: Bd of Govrs Eastman Dental Hosp 1957–63, Ancillary Dental Workers Ctee 1956–68, Experimental Scheme for Dental Auxiliaries 1958–69, Bd Br Tport Hotels 1962–78, Bd Oxford Poly 1969–70; pres Goring & Dist Day Centre for the Elderly, life memb Br Fedn of Univ Women, hon memb Oxford Br Zonta Int, memb Oxford Branch Edinburgh Univ Graduates' Assoc; vice pres League of Friends Radcliffe Infirmary Oxford, patron Oxford Branch Motor Neurone Disease Assoc; *Recreations* National Trust, music, needlework, various; *Style*— Dame Isabel Graham Bryce, DBE; ✉ 1 Quinton House, 98 Woodstock Rd, Oxford OX2 7NE (☎ 01865 513168)

GRAHAM-DIXON, Andrew Michael; s of Anthony Philip Graham-Dixon, QC, *qv*, and Margaret Suzanne, *née* Villar; *b* 26 Dec 1960; *Educ* Westminster, Christ Church Oxford (MA), Courtauld Inst (since 1981); *m* 8 June 1985, Sabine Marie, *née* Pascale Tilly; 1 s (Arthur b 1992), 2 da (Eleanor b 1986, Florence b 1989); *Career* art critic The Independent 1986–; BP Arts Journalist of the Year 1987 and 1988, Hawthornden Prize for Art Criticism 1991; memb Advsy Ctee Hayward Gallery 1991–; writer and presenter A History of British Art (6–part series, BBC 2) 1996; *Books* Howard Hodgkin (1992), A History of British Art (1996), Paper Museum (1996); *Recreations* snooker; *Style*— Andrew Graham-Dixon, Esq; ✉ 21 Croftdown Road, London NW5 1EL

GRAHAM-DIXON, Anthony Philip; QC (1973); s of Leslie Charles Graham-Dixon, QC (d 1986), and Dorothy, *née* Rivett (d 1979); *b* 5 Nov 1929; *Educ* Westminster, ChCh Oxford (MA); *m* 15 Dec 1956, Margaret Suzanne, da of Edgar Hurmon Villar (d 1953); 1 s (Andrew Graham-Dixon, *qv* b 1960), 1 da (Elizabeth b 1965); *Career* Mid Special Branch RN 1953–55, Lt Special Branch RNVR 1956; called to the Bar Inner Temple 1956, bencher 1982; memb Advsy Bd Competition Law in Western Europe and the USA 1976–87; chm London Concertino Ltd 1982–90; memb Cncl Charing Cross Hosp Med Sch 1976–83, dep chm Public Health Laboratory Serv 1988–96 (bd memb 1987–96), chm of tstees Soc for Promotion of New Music 1994– (tstee 1988–), govr Bedales Sch 1988–; Liveryman Worshipful Co of Goldsmiths; *Recreations* music, gardening, tennis, walking, trees; *Style*— Anthony Graham-Dixon, Esq, QC; ✉ 31 Hereford Square, London SW7 4NB (☎ 0171 370 1902, fax 0171 373 5912); Masketts Manor, Nutley, East Sussex TN22 3HD (☎ 01825 712719, fax 01825 712241)

GRAHAM-DIXON, Francis; s of Michael Stuart Graham-Dixon, of Asthall, Oxfordshire, and Anita, *née* Falkenstein; *b* 21 March 1955; *Educ* Stowe; *children* 2 s (Freddie Francis b 1981, Charles Isaac b 1984), 1 da (Celia Rosie b 1989); *Career* Sotheby's London 1973–78, Record Merchandisers 1978–79, Warner Brothers 1979–80, Heiman Music 1980–81, BBC 1982–87, opened Francis Graham-Dixon Gallery London 1987; govr Winchester Sch of Art 1989–93; *Recreations* art, music, cinema, cricket; *Clubs* MCC; *Style*— Francis Graham-Dixon, Esq; ✉ Francis Graham-Dixon Gallery, 17–18 Great Sutton St, London EC1V ODN (☎ 0171 250 1962, fax 0171 490 1069)

GRAHAM-HARRISON, Robert Montagu; s of Francis Laurence Theodore Graham-Harrison, CB, of London, and Carol Mary St John, *née* Stewart; *b* 16 Feb 1943; *Educ* Eton, Magdalen Coll Oxford (BA); *m* 30 April 1977, Kathleen Patricia, *née* Maher; 2 da (Emma b 24 July 1978, Laura b 15 Aug 1980); *Career* VSO India 1965, ODA (formerly Miny of Overseas Dept) 1967, World Bank Washington 1971–73, private sec Min of Overseas Devpt 1978, asst sec ODA 1979; head: Br Devpt Div Eastern Africa 1982, Eastern Asia Dept ODA 1986, UK alternate exec dir World Bank 1989–92, UK exec dir European Bank for Reconstruction and Development 1992–; *Style*— Robert Graham-Harrison, Esq; ✉ European Bank for Reconstruction and Development, 1 Exchange Square, London EC2 (☎ 0171 338 6475)

GRAHAM-JONES, Oliver; s of late Andrew Vaughan Jones, and Ethel Mabel, *née* Smith; *b* 17 Feb 1919; *Educ* King Edward's GS, RVC London Univ; *m* 1, 23 March 1958, Gillian Margaret (d 1990), da of Basil Dent (d 1948); 2 s (Piers Dominic b 1965, Peregrine Jasper b 1967); m 2, 15 June 1993, Josephine Bowen, da of U T de la Hay; *Career* cmmnd RAVC, served Italy 1943–44; vet surgn in private practice 1941–50, sr vet offr Zoological Soc of London 1960–66 (vet offr 1951–60), sr lectr RVC 1966–79 (asst lectr 1950–51); conslt vet offr: Nat Hosp for Nervous Diseases 1967–, London Hosp Med Sch 1967–, Royal Nat Orthopaedic Hosp; prof vet med and surgn to Sultan of Oman 1972–79; past pres: Br Small Animal Vet Assoc, Central Vet Soc; fndr pres BVZS, vet steward Nat Greyhound Racing Club; expert witness in many cases involving wild and domestic animals, licensed zoo inspector; awards: Livesey Medal RCVS, Victory Medal CVS, Sir Arthur Keith Medal RCS; hon fell: Fedn of Nat Zoological Gardens, CVS 1993; Hon Col Legion of Frontiersmen Mounted Sqdn; hon fell: CVS, BVZS, Fedn of Br Zoos; FRCVS; *Books* First Catch Your Tiger; author of numerous contributions to learned journals and magazines; *Recreations* horse driving, polo; *Clubs* RSM; *Style*— Oliver Graham-Jones, Esq; ✉ The Drey, 16 Park Lane, Selsey, Chicester, W Sussex PO20 0HD (☎ and fax 01243 606646)

GRAHAM-MOON, Sir Peter Wilfred Giles; 5 Bt (UK 1855), of Portman Square, Middx; s of Sir Wilfred Graham Moon, 4 Bt (d 1954), by his 2 w, Doris, *née* Jobson (d 1953); *b* 24 Oct 1942; *Educ* Lancing; *m* 1, 1967 (m dis 1992), Mrs Sarah Gillian Chater, da of Lt-Col Michael Smith, MC, of The Grange, Headley, Hants (gs of Sir Thomas Smith, 1 Bt, KCVO, Hon Serjeant-Surgeon to King Edward VII); 2 s (Rupert Francis Wilfred b 1968, Thomas Edward Bradshaw b 1972); m 2, 30 Oct 1993, Mrs Terry Lynn de Vries, da of W Coetzee, of Brackenfell, Cape Town, S Africa; *Heir* s, Rupert Graham-Moon; *Career* chm Trans Continental Corp Ltd, md Langbury Property Investments (Pty) Ltd SA; *Recreations* golf, shooting, horse racing; *Clubs* Royal Cork Yacht; *Style*— Sir Peter Graham-Moon, Bt; ✉ Holdfast House, Holdfast, nr Upton-on-Severn, Worcs WR8 0RA

GRAHAM-MOON, Rupert Francis Wilfred; s and h of Sir Peter Graham-Moon, 5 Bt, *qv*; *b* 29 April 1968; *Educ* Marlborough, Exeter Univ; *partner* Denise; 1 s (Arthur Sidney b 21 Oct 1992), 1 da (Tansy); *Style*— Rupert Graham-Moon, Esq

GRAHAM OF EDMONTON, Baron (Life Peer UK 1983), of Edmonton in Greater London; (Thomas) Edward Graham; s of Thomas Edward Graham, of Newcastle-upon-Tyne; *b* 26 March 1925; *Educ* WEA Co-Op Coll, Open Univ (BA); *m* 1950, Margaret Golding, da of Frederick and Alice Golding, of Dagenham; 2 s (Hon Martin Nicholas b 1957, Hon Ian Stuart b 1959); *Career* various posts Co-operative Movement 1939–; memb and leader Enfield Cncl 1961–68, national sec Co-Op Party 1967–74, MP (Lab and Co-Op) Enfield Edmonton Feb 1974–83, PPS to Min of State Prices and Consumer Protection 1974–76, lord cmmr Treasury 1976–79; oppn front bench spokesman on Environment 1980–83; oppn House of Lords spokesman on Sport, Defence, N Ireland 1983; oppn whips office, oppn chief whip 1990–; Hon MA 1989; pres Inst of Meat; Hon Freeman Worshipful Co of Butchers; FIMgt, FRSA; *Style*— The Rt Hon the Lord Graham of Edmonton; ✉ 2 Clerks Piece, Loughton, Essex IG10 1NR (☎ 0181 508 9801); House of Lords, London SW1 (☎ 0171 219 3234)

GRAHAM-SMITH, Prof Sir Francis; kt (1986); s of Claud Henry Smith, of April Cottage, Fairlight, Sussex (d 1963), and Cicely Winifred Kingston (d 1946); *b* 25 April 1923; *Educ* Epsom Coll, Rossall Sch, Downing Coll Cambridge (MA, PhD); *m* Dorothy Elizabeth, da of Reginald Palmer, of Ecclestone House, Mildenhall, Suffolk (d 1949); 3 s, 1 da; *Career* dir Royal Greenwich Observatory 1976–81, pres Royal Astronomical Soc 1975–77, prof of radio astronomy Univ of Manchester 1964–74 and 1981–90, dir Nuffield Radio Astronomy Laboratories 1981–88, Astronomer Royal 1983–90; vice pres and physical sec Royal Soc 1988–94, pro vice chllr Univ of Manchester 1988–90; hon fell Downing Coll Cambridge 1970; Royal Soc Royal Medal 1987, Inst of Physics Glazebrook Medal 1991; Hon DSc: Queen's Univ Belfast, Univ of Keele, Univ of Birmingham, Univ of Nottingham, Trinity Coll Dublin, Univ of Manchester; FRS; *Recreations* bee-keeping, gardening; *Style*— Prof Sir Francis Graham-Smith, FRS; ✉ Old School House, Henbury, Macclesfield, Cheshire SK11 9PH (☎ 01625 612657); Nuffield Radio Astronomy Laboratories, Jodrell Bank, Macclesfield, Cheshire (☎ 01477 571321)

GRAHAME-SMITH, Prof David Grahame; CBE (1993); s of George Edward Smith (d 1968), Leicester, and Constance Alexandra Smith (d 1974); *b* 10 May 1933; *Educ* Wyggeston GS for Boys Leicester, St Mary's Hosp Med Sch Univ of London (MB BS, MRCS, LRCP, MRCP, PhD), Univ of Oxford (MA); *m* 25 May 1957, Kathryn Frances, da of Dr Francis Robin Beetham (d 1985), of Leeds; 2 s (Harvey Neil b 1958, Henry Peter b 1964); *Career* Capt RAMC 1957–60; house physician Paddington Gen Hosp 1956, house surgn Battle Hosp Reading 1956–57, H A M Thompson scholar Royal Coll of Physicians 1961–62, hon med registrar Professorial Medical Unit St Mary's Hosp Paddington 1961–66 (registrar and sr registrar in medicine 1960–61), Saltwell res scholar Royal Coll of Physicians 1962–65, Wellcome Tst res fell 1965–66, MRC travelling fell Dept of Endocrinology Vanderbilt Univ Nashville Tennessee 1966–67, sr lectr and reader in clinical pharmacology and therapeutics St Mary's Hosp Med Sch Univ of London 1967–71, hon conslt physician St Mary's Hosp Paddington 1967–71, Rhodes prof of clinical pharmacology Univ of Oxford 1971–, hon dir MRC Unit of Clinical Pharmacology Radcliffe Infirmary Oxford 1971–93, hon conslt physician in gen internal medicine and clinical pharmacology Oxford AHA 1971–, fell Corpus Christi Coll Oxford 1971–, hon dir Oxford Univ/SmithKline Beecham Centre for Applied Neuropsychobiology 1989–; conslt clinical pharmacologist RAF 1985–95, visiting prof in clinical pharmacology Peking Union Med Coll Beijing China 1985–, conslt in pharmacology to the Army 1986–, William Potter lectr Thomas Jefferson Univ of Philadelphia 1988; examiner in therapeutics UK and abroad, principal examiner final BM BS Examinations Univ of Oxford 1990–94; memb Editorial Bd: Archives Internationale de Pharmacodynamic et de Therapie (Belgium), Pharmacopsychiatria (Berlin), Br Journal of Clinical Pharmacology (chm 1987–95), Pharmacology and Therapeutics, Psychological Medicine; memb: Br Nat Pharmacological Ctee 1974–79, Clinical Trials and Toxicity Sub Ctee of Ctee on Safety of Medicines 1974–86 (memb Main Ctee 1975–86), Clinical Medicine Faculty Bd 1976–80; vice chm Clinical Medicine Faculty Bd Univ of Oxford 1978–80; memb: Res Ctee Mental Health Res Fund 1978–80, Ctee Clinical Pharmacology Section Br Pharmacological Soc 1978–81, Scientific Ctee Migraine Tst 1980–86; tstee Sheik Rashid Diabetes Tst Oxford 1986; cnllr: Collegium Internationale Neuro-Psychopharmacologium 1988–, Clinical Section International Union of Pharmacology 1988–; pres Oxford Div BMA 1989–90; chm UK Advsy Ctee on Misuse of Drugs 1988–; Die Anna Monica Stiftung 2nd prize (jtly with A R Green) 1977, Paul-Martini prize in Clinical Pharmacology (jtly with J K Aronson) 1980, Lilly prize of the Clinical Section 1995; memb: Br Pharmacological Soc, Biochemical Soc 1964–95 (memb Neurochemical Gp Sub Ctee 1971–74), Med Res Soc 1961–95, Assoc of Physicians of GB and Ireland, Int Soc of Neurochemistry, Brain Res Assoc, Br Assoc of Psychopharmacology; assoc memb Royal Coll of Psychiatrists, foreign corr memb American Coll of Neuropsychiatry; FRCP; *Books* Carcinoid Syndrome (1972), Oxford Textbook of Clinical Pharmacology and Drug Therapy (with JK Aronson, 1984); *Recreations* piano, horse riding; *Style*— Prof David Grahame-Smith, CBE; ✉ University Department of Clinical Pharmacology, Radcliffe Infirmary, Woodstock Rd, Oxford OX2 6HE (☎ 01865 241091, fax 01865 791712)

GRAINGER, (Leonard) Cherry; s of George Grainger (d 1936), and Lucy, *née* Cherry (d 1974); *b* 12 March 1919; *Educ* Westminster Catering Coll (Dip), Ecole Des Hoteliers Zurich; *m* 17 June 1944, (Yvonne) Claudia Marshall, da of Victor Stanley Chambers, OBE (d 1954); 1 s (Cdr RN Robert Marshall b 1955), 2 da (Lynne b 1945, Jacki b 1947); *Career* RN: Fleet Air Arm 1940–42, Paymaster 1942–46; fndr and chm Graison (Caterers) Ltd 1946–; chm: London Ctee Catering Trades Benevolent Assoc, tstees Reunion Des Gastronomes (former pres); memb: Ctee Br Hotels & Restaurants Assoc, Mgmnt Ctee City & Guilds; govr Westminster Coll 1981–; Freeman City of London 1964, Liveryman Worshipful Co of Distillers 1964–, Master Worshipful Co of Cooks 1988–89; Chevalier Du Tastevin 1964; FCA, FHCIMA, FRSH; *Recreations* swimming, travel; *Clubs* City Livery, RAC; *Style*— Cherry Grainger, Esq; ✉ 102 Hayes Way, Beckenham, Kent BR3 2RS (☎ 0181 650 4727)

GRAINGER, Frederick George Edward (Stewart); s of Frederick Thomas Grainger (d 1978), of Ashcott, Somerset, and Alice Mary, *née* Syrett; *b* 23 June 1936; *Educ* Dr Mogan's Sch Bridgwater, RMA Sandhurst, Medway Coll of Technol (Dip Civil Engrg), Open Univ (BA), RMCS Shrivenham, RAF Staff Coll, Nat Def Coll; *m* 31 Oct 1959, Shirley Dorothy, da of Harold Pole (d 1965), of Bridgwater, Somerset; 2 s (Ian Anthony b 10 April 1968, Peter Edward b 8 Feb 1971), 1 da (Karen Shirley b 1 Aug 1965); *Career* Paratrooper 1959–62, army pilot 1965–68, jr exec Directorate of Army Air Corps 1970–72, offr i/c 60 Field Sqdn 1972–73, CO 72 Engr Regt (Vol) 1976–78, mil advsr to Chief Scientist of the Army 1979–80, sr mil advsr to Dir RAE Farnborough 1983, Chief Royal Engr 1 Armd Div 1983–86, Col Doctrine and Weapons RE 1986–89; Royal Ordnance plc: business mangr barrier systems 1989–90, dir Explosive Ordnance Disposal (EoD) Contract Kuwait 1991, project mangr 1992–94, EoD projects dir Mozambique 1994, engrg liaison mangr 1995–; chm Army Canoe Union 1975–83 (sec 1970–72); FIMgt 1980, AMRAeS 1983; *Recreations* canoeing, skiing; *Clubs* Civil Service, Royal Aeronautical Soc; *Style*— Stewart Grainger, Esq; ✉ 24 Studley Crescent, New Barn, Longfield, Kent DA3 7JL; Royal Ordnance plc, DRA Fort Halstead, Sevenoakes, Kent TN14 7BP (☎ 01959 514910)

GRAINGER, Margaret Ethel; CBE (1991, OBE 1979); da of Walter James Grainger (d 1980), and Mabel Ethel, *née* Peacock (d 1986); *b* 28 Oct 1922; *Educ* Ealing Co Sch for Girls; *Career* meteorologist WAAF 1942–46, section offr 1944–46, flying offr WRAF VR

1949–54; HM Civil Serv: sr princ Dept of Social Security 1978–80, asst sec, sec and controller of the exec office to the Occupational Pensions Bd 1980–82; emeritus fell pensions Mgmnt Inst, fndr chm The Occupational Pensions Advsy Serv 1982–91 (pres 1991–93), public speaker, TV and radio appearances, writer on occupational pensions; vice chm Civil Serv Sports Cncl, life vice pres of Dept of Social Security Recreational Assoc; memb: Nat Tst, RSPB, Eng Heritage; Freeman City of London 1993; *Recreations* golf, conservation; *Clubs* RAF; *Style*— Miss Margaret Grainger, CBE; ✉ 7 Chester Gardens, Argyle Road, Ealing, London W13 8EP (☎ 0181 997 6971)

GRAMMENOS, Prof Costas Theophilos; Hon OBE (1994); s of Cdr Theophilos C Grammenos, and Argyro, *née* Spanakos; *b* 23 Feb 1944; *Educ* State School in Athens, Pantion Univ (BA), Univ of Wales (MSc); *m* 20 Nov 1972, Anna, da of Prof Constantinos A Papadimitriou; 1 s (Theophilos b 6 April 1975); *Career* Nat Serv Greek Navy 1968–70; Nat Bank of Greece 1962–75 (shipping fin expert, head office 1973–74); City Univ Business Sch London: visiting prof 1982–86, fndr and head Dept of Shipping, Trade and Finance 1984–, prof of shipping, trade and finance 1986–; Archon of Ecumenical Patriarchate of Constantinople 1994; visiting prof World Maritime Univ Malmo 1990–; memb Bd of Dirs Alexander S Onassis Public Benefit Fndn 1995–; *Books* Bank Finance for Ship Purchase (1979), various studies in shipping investment and finance; *Recreations* music, theatre, walking; *Clubs* Travellers'; *Style*— Prof Costas Th Grammenos, OBE; ✉ City University Business School, Frobisher Crescent, Barbican Centre, London EC2Y 8HB (☎ 0171 477 8671, fax 0171 477 8895)

GRAMS, Gerry; *b* 29 July 1959; *Educ* Mackintosh Sch of Arch Glasgow Sch of Art (DipArch, W Sommerville Shanks legacy, Bram Stoker medal, ARIAS (Rowan Anderson Award); *Career* architectural apprentice: Murray and Manson Architects Glasgow 1980–81, McGurn Logan and Duncan Architects Glasgow 1982; architect McGurn Logan Duncan and Opfer Glasgow 1983–96 (assoc dir 1988–96), fndr ptnr Bonar & Grams Architects 1996–; past projects incl: Tron Theatre, Glassford Court; recent projects incl: private house for Robbie Coltrane, new Glasgow HQ for IBM; current projects incl: Bellgrove Cross/Graham Square housing for Molendinar Park HA, The Piping Centre Glasgow; pt/t design tutor (fndn course) Dept of Architecture Univ of Strathclyde 1989–; dir Workshop and Artists Studio Provision Scotland Ltd (WASPS); *Competitions* second prize Crown Street Masterplan 1990, first prize Darnley Masterplan 1991; *Exhibitions* Royal Scottish Acad Summer Exhibition 1984, For a Wee Country.... (RIAS Jubilee Travelling Exhibition) 1990; *Style*— Gerry Grams, Esq; ✉ Bonar & Grams Architects, 2nd Floor, 14 Elliot Place, The Clydeway Centre, Glasgow G3 8EP (☎ 0141 221 4090)

GRAN, Maurice Bernard; s of Mark Gran (d 1965), of London, and Deborah, *née* Cohen (d 1986); *b* 26 Oct 1949; *Educ* William Ellis GS London, UCL (BSc); *m* Carol, *née* James; 1 da (Jessica b 21 June 1985), 1 s (Thomas b 23 May 1988); *Career* mgmnt trainee Dept of Employment, various mgmnt appts Employment Agency 1974–80, television scriptwriter 1980–; creator and writer (with Laurence Marks, *qv*): Holding the Fort 1979–82, Roots, Shine on Harvey Moon 1982–85 and 1995–, Roll Over Beethoven, Relative Strangers, The New Statesman 1987–91, Birds of a Feather 1989–, Snakes and Ladders, So You Think You've Got Troubles, Get Back, Love Hurts 1991–93, Wall of Silence (film) 1993, Goodnight Sweetheart 1994–; fndr (with Laurence Marks and Allan McKeown, *qv*) Alomo Productions 1988 (now part of Pearson Television PLC); memb Cncl BAFTA 1994–95; *Awards* Silver Medal Int Film and TV Festival NY for Relative Strangers 1985, Int Emmy for The New Statesman 1988, BAFTA Best Comedy Award for The New Statesman 1990, Mitsubishi TV Sitcom of the Year for Birds of a Feather 1991, Mitsubishi TV Drama of the Year for Love Hurts 1991, BAFTA Writer's Award (jtly with Laurence Marks) 1992; *Books* Holding the Fort (with Laurence Marks, 1981), The New Statesman Scripts (with Laurence Marks, 1992), Dorien's Diary (with Laurence Marks, 1993); *Recreations* watching football, buying clothes, fell walking; *Clubs* Groucho, Arsenal FC; *Style*— Maurice Gran, Esq; ✉ Alomo Productions Ltd, 45 Foubert's Place, London W1V 2DN (☎ 0171 434 3060)

GRANARD, 10 Earl of (I 1684); Sir Peter Arthur Edward Hastings Forbes; 11 Bt (S 1628); also Viscount Granard and Baron Clanehugh (I 1675), and Baron Granard (UK 1806); er s of Hon John Forbes (d 1982), and Joan, *née* Smith; suc unc, 9 Earl of Granard, 1992; *b* 15 March 1957; *m* 1 Sept 1980, Nora Ann (Noreen), da of Robert Mitchell, of Portarlington, Co Leix; 2 s (Jonathan Peter Hastings, Viscount Forbes b 24 Dec 1981, Hon David Robert Hastings b 8 Feb 1984, Hon Edward Hastings b 13 June 1989), 1 da (Lady Lisa Ann b 2 July 1986); *Heir* s, Viscount Forbes b 24 Dec 1981; *Style*— The Rt Hon the Earl of Granard; ✉ Strathallan Cliff, Strathallan Road, Onchan, Isle of Man

GRANBY, Marquess of; David Charles Robert Manners; s and h of 10 Duke of Rutland, CBE, JP, DL, *qv*, by his 2 w, Frances; *b* 8 May 1959; *Educ* Wellesley House Broadstairs Kent, Stanbridge Earls; *m* 6 June 1992, Emma L, da of John Watkins, of Heartsease, Knighton, Powys; 2 da (Lady Violet Diana Louise b 18 Aug 1993, Lady Alice Louisa Lilly b 27 April 1995); *Career* dir: Belvoir Management Ltd; chm Historic Houses Assoc in E Midlands; parish cncllr Belvoir, Knipton and Harston; memb Leics Cttee CLA; memb civilian cttee ATC Sqdn Grantham Lincs (47F Sqdn); pres Grantham branch Air Crew Assoc; agent Elderkins (gunsmiths) Spalding Lincs, co-fndr Parklands Ltd (conservatory and garden furniture) Knipton; Freeman City of London, Liveryman Worshipful Co of Gunsmiths; *Recreations* shooting, fishing; *Clubs* Turf, Annabel's; *Style*— Marquess of Granby; ✉ Knipton Lodge, Knipton, nr Grantham, Lincs NG32 1RE

GRANBY, Nicholas Charles; s of Paul Granby (d 1982), of London, and Lydia Barbara, *née* Goulding; *Educ* Westminster Sch, London Sch of Film Technique (Dip); *m* 1, (m dis), Pauline Sylvia, da of Arthur Hapgood Rice (d 1975); 1 da (Sarah b 1967); m 2, Corinna Elvira, da of Dr Renato Asti (d 1991); *Career* film & TV dir, writer and prodr; films incl: Closed Circuit (prize winner Barcelona Film Festival); documentaries incl: The Queen in Arabia, To Win at all Costs - The Story of the America's Cup (prize-winner Houston Int Film Festival and UK Video Awards), The Queen in Jordan; stage musical Mesmer; dir Nicholas Granby Productions Ltd; *Clubs* BAFTA; *Style*— Nicholas C Granby, Esq; ✉ Via Bellinzona 21, 20155 Milan, Italy

GRANDY, Marshal of the RAF Sir John; GCB (1967, KCB 1964, CB 1956), GCVO (1988), KBE (1961), DSO (1945); s of Francis Grandy (d 1932), and Nell, *née* Lines (d 1948); *b* 8 Feb 1913; *Educ* Univ Coll Sch; *m* 1937, Cécile Elizabeth Florence, CStJ (d 1993), yr da of Sir Robert Rankin, first and last Bt (d 1960); 2 s (John b 1947, William b 1948); *Career* RAF 1931, Adj and Flying Instr London Univ Air Sqdn 1937–39, cmd 249 Sqdn Battle of Britain, Wing Cdr Flying RAF Coltishall 1941, cmd RAF Duxford 1942, cmd HQ 210 Gp, No 73 Operational Training Unit and Fighter Conversion Unit Abu Sueir 1943, cmd 341 Wing SE Asia 1944–45, Air Cdre 1956, AVM 1958, Cdr 2 ATAF and C-in-C RAF Germany 1961–63, Air Marshal 1962, AOC-in-C Bomber Cmd 1963–65, C-in-C Br Forces Far East and UK Mil Advsr SEATO 1965–67, Air Chief Marshal 1965, Chief of Air Staff 1967–71, Marshal of RAF 1971, govr and C-in-C Gibraltar 1973–78, constable and govr Windsor Castle 1978–88; dep chm Cncl RAF Benevolent Fund 1972–96, chm of tstees Imperial War Museum 1978–89, RAF tstee Burma Star Assoc 1990–96; tstee: St Clement Danes RAF Church, Shuttleworth Remembrance Trust (chm Aerodrome Ctee) 1978–88, Prince Philip Trust Fund Royal Borough of Windsor and Maidenhead 1982–92; past sr pres Offrs' Assoc; pres: Air League 1984–87, Disablement in City; vice pres: Offrs' Pension Soc, Nat Assoc of Boys' Clubs; life vice pres RNLI; dir Brixton Estate 1971–73 and 1978–83; patron Polish Air Force Assoc in GB; dir Brixton Estate 1971–73 and 1978–83; memb Ctee Royal Humane Soc 1972–95; Freeman City of London, Hon Liveryman Haberdashers' Co; KStJ; *Clubs* White's, Pratt's, Royal Yacht Sqdn, RAF; *Style*— Marshal of the RAF Sir John Grandy, GCB, GCVO, KBE, DSO; ✉ c/o White's, St James's St, London SW1

GRANGE, Anna Ruth; JP (1979); da of Edward Buckley Hetherington (d 1967), and Kathleen Clare, *née* Stuart (d 1962); *b* 27 April 1937; *Educ* Westonbirt Sch, Charlotte Mason Coll of Educn; *m* 4 July 1959, David John Hudson Grange, s of George Grange; 1 s (Jonathan Edward Charles b 23 June 1961), 2 da (Georgina Fiona Clare b 18 Aug 1963, Candida Jane Louise b 5 June 1965); *Career* teacher 1958–59, various jobs in farming and tourism 1969, dir Stuart & Sons 1987–95; High Sheriff for Co of Wiltshire 1994–95; *Recreations* gardening, needlework, tennis, sheep; *Style*— Mrs Anna Grange, JP

GRANGE, Hugh; s of James Grange (d 1968), of Inver Green House, Inver, Larne, Co Antrim, and Ruth, *née* Gourley (d 1996); *b* 26 Nov 1943; *Educ* Trinity Coll Dublin (MA, LLB); *m* 18 Sept 1971, Janet, da of Maj K C B Golding, TD, JP (d 1977), of Court Farm, Hedgerley, Bucks; *Career* called to the Bar NI 1970, practised NI 1970–73, called to the Bar Gray's Inn 1973, worked for HM Procurator Gen and Treasy Slr 1974–87, seconded to Attorney Gen's Chambers Law Offrs' Dept 1987–; memb compilation team Burke's Irish Family Records 1975; memb RSL; *Recreations* history, literature, genealogy, walking, pictures, travel; *Style*— Hugh Grange, Esq; ✉ c/o Attorney General's Chambers, 9 Buckingham Gate, London SW1E 6JP

GRANGE, Kenneth Henry; CBE (1984); s of Harry Alfred Grange, and Hilda Gladys, *née* Long; *b* 17 July 1929; *Educ* Willesden Coll of Art; *m* 21 Sept 1984, Apryl Jacqueline, da of Deric Swift; *Career* tech illustrator RE 1947–48; architectural asst Bronek Katz & Vaughan 1949–50; designer: Gordon Bowyer 1950–52, Jack Howe & Partners 1952–58; fndr Kenneth Grange Design London 1958–72, fndr ptnr Pentagram Design Ltd 1972–; conslt design dir Wilkinson Sword Ltd; winner: 10 Design Cncl awards, Duke of Edinburgh Prize for Elegant Design 1963, CSD Gold Medal (for lifetime's achievement in design) 1996; work represented in collections of: V & A, Design Museum London, State Museum Munich; one man shows: Kenneth Grange at the Boilerhouse V & A 1983, The Product Designs of Kenneth Grange of Pentagram XSITE Tokyo Japan 1989; juror BBC Design Awards 1996; Master Faculty of Royal Design for Indust 1985–87 (memb 1969); memb Cncl and memb Advsy Bd on Product Design Design Cncl (industl design advsr 1971), memb Cncl and Ct RSA; Hon Doctorate RCA 1985, Hon DUniv Heriot-Watt 1986; FCSD 1965 (pres 1987–89), RDI 1969; *Books* Living by Design (jtly 1977), The Compendium (jtly, 1993); *Recreations* skiing, building; *Clubs* RAC; *Style*— Kenneth Grange, CBE; ✉ Pentagram Design Ltd, 11 Needham Rd, London W11 2RP (☎ 0171 229 3477, fax 0171 727 9932)

GRANGER, Derek Harold; s of Thomas Edgar Granger (d 1959), and Bertha Winifred, *née* Ashcroft (d 1987); *b* 23 April 1921; *Educ* Eastbourne Coll; *Career* Ordinary Seaman then Lt RNVR 1939–46; reporter and feature writer Sussex Daily News and Brighton Evening Argus 1947–52, theatre and film critic Financial Times 1952–68 (fndr writer Arts Page), writer and prodr Granada TV 1958–67, prodr LWT 1967–69, literary conslt National Theatre 1969–71, prodr Granada TV 1971–81, exec prodr Goldcrest Films and Televison 1982–84, fndr dir Stagescreen Productions Ltd 1984–; prodr TV progs incl: Insanity or Illness, Surgeon, Sir Thomas Beecham, Coronation Street, World in Action, Seven Up, The Beatles in New York, Put Out The Lights, Pardon The Expression, The Inside Man, Wicked Women, Haunted; writer and presenter Cinema, prodr and script ed Country Matters (2 series 1972–73, Best Drama Series SFTA 1972, Best Drama Adaptation Critic's Circle 1972 and 1973), co-prodr with Laurence Olivier The Best Play of the Year (series 1976, Int Emmy for TV Fiction The Collection 1977); prodr and co-scriptwriter: Brideshead Revisited (1981, BAFTA Award 1982, IBA Prog of the Year 1982, Grand Award Int Film and TV Festival NY 1983, Golden Globe Award Best TV Mini Series 1983, Media Award Alliance for Gay Artists 1983), A Handful of Dust (film) 1989, Where Angels Fear To Tread (film) 1991; co-prodr West End: The Normal Heart 1986, Drood 1987, The Vortex 1988; memb: Drama Panel Arts Cncl of GB 1956–62, Cncl English Stage Co (Royal Court Theatre) 1979–90; co-chm West End Cares, chm Fundraising Ctee Crusaid; *Recreations* reading, looking at architecture and painting, swimming, cats; *Clubs* YMCA; *Style*— Derek Granger, Esq; ✉ 82 Palace Gardens Terrace, London W8 4RS (☎ 0171 229 3060)

GRANT, Alexander Marshall; CBE (1965); s of Alexander Gibb Grant, and Eleather May, *née* Marshall; *b* 22 Feb 1925; *Educ* Wellington Coll New Zealand; *Career* princ dancer Sadler's Wells Ballet (now Royal Ballet) 1946–76, dir Ballet for All 1971–76, artistic dir Nat Ballet of Canada 1976–83; princ dancer: London Festival Ballet 1985–90, English Nat Ballet 1991; judge at int ballet competitions: Moscow, Jackson Mississippi, Paris, Helsinki, Varna and Budapest; created many ballet roles particularly for Sir Frederick Ashton, guest artist with Royal Ballet, Joffrey Ballet and English Nat Ballet; *Recreations* gardening, cooking; *Style*— Alexander Grant, Esq, CBE

GRANT, Sir (Matthew) Alistair; kt (1992); s of John and Jessie Grant, of Louth; *b* 6 March 1937; *Educ* Woodhouse Grove Sch Yorkshire; *m* Judith Mary, *née* Dent (Lady Grant); 2 s, 1 da; *Career* Nat Serv 2 Lt Royal Signals 1955–57, served Cyprus and Aden; joined Unilever 1958; Safeway plc (formerly Argyll Group plc, parent co of Safeway, Lo-Cost and Presto stores): fndr and dir 1977–96, dep chm and chief exec 1986–88, chm and chief exec 1988–93, chm 1993–96; non-exec dir: Bank of Scotland plc, Scottish & Newcastle plc 1994–; chm Biotechnology and Biological Sciences Res Cncl (formerly Agric and Food Research Cncl); visiting prof Univ of Strathclyde; pres: Inst of Grocery Distribution 1991–94, Royal Agric Soc of England 1993–94; vice pres Chartered Inst of Mktg; tstee: Nat Museums of Scotland, Scottish Business Achievement Award Tst; regent Royal Coll of Surgns Edinburgh; Hon DBA Univ of Strathclyde 1992, Hon DSc Cranfield Inst of Technol 1993, Hon DUniv Edinburgh 1993, Hon DBA Napier Univ Edinburgh 1994; *Recreations* hunting, fishing, painting, reading, music; *Clubs* Caledonian; *Style*— Sir Alistair Grant; ✉ Bank of Scotland, PO Box 5, The Mound, Edinburgh EH1 1YZ (☎ 0131 442 7777, fax 0131 243 5546)

GRANT, Prof (Duncan) Alistair Antoine; s of Duncan George Grant (d 1968), of London, and Germaine Victoria, *née* Ramet Cousin (d 1970); *b* 3 June 1925; *Educ* Froebel Inst East Sheen, Whitehall Glasgow, Birmingham Sch of Art, RCA; *m* 1, Phyllis (d 1988), da of late William Fricker, of Guildford; 1 da (Emma b 12 Sept 1954); m 2, 23 April 1991, Joan Strickland; *Career* Aircrew RAF 1943–47; artist, painter and printmaker; art teacher 1951–53: St Martin's Sch of Art, Hammersmith Sch of Art, Sidcup Sch of Art, Colchester Sch of Art; RCA: tutor Printmaking Dept 1955–70, head Printing Dept 1970–84, prof of Printmaking 1984–90, prof emeritus 1990–; numerous exhibitions since 1951 including: Redfern Gallery London 1952–87, Nat Arts Cncl of Southern Rhodesia 1957, Tel Aviv Museum Israel 1959, Zwemmer Gallery London 1961 and 1962, AAA Gallery NY 1967, Portland Museum Oregon 1971, Cracow Print Biennale (prize) 1972, Calgary Graphics Canada 1973, Limited Editions London 1979, Mullhouse Print Biennale 1982 and 1986, Le Cadre Gallery Hong Kong 1985, Scottish Gallery London 1990, William Jackson Gallery 1991 and 1992, retrospective exhibition Le Touquet Museum France 1993 and 1994, Art First London 1995, Galerie Mischkind Lille France 1995, New Academy Gallery 1996; works in the collection of: V & A Museum, The Arts Cncl, The Tate Gallery, Dallas Museum USA, Museum of Modern Art NY USA, Vancouver Art Gallery Canada, Tel Aviv Museum Israel, Cairo Art Gallery Egypt, Nat Gallery of South Australia, Mobil Oil, BP International, Unilever, Br Museum, Hunterian Museum

Glasgow; memb: RBA, Royal Soc of Arts; *Clubs* Arts, Chelsea Arts; *Style*— Prof Alistair Grant

GRANT, Hon Anne Margaret; da of Maj Sir Arthur Lindsay Grant, 11 Bt (ka 1944), and Baroness Tweedsmuir of Belhelvie (Life Peeress d 1978); *b* 1937; *Educ* Lady Margaret Hall Oxford (MA); *m* 1965 (m dis 1983), Nicolas Mangriotis; 2 s (Paraskevas b 1971, Arthuros b 1974); *Career* econ conslt to OECD Paris and to Greek Govt 1962–70, dir mgmnt consultancy Athens 1975–85, mgmnt conslt (London) 1985–; dir: PLAN International (UK) 1989–, Green Cross 1995–; FIMgt, MCIM; *Style*— The Hon Anne Grant; ✉ 24 Amity Grove, London SW20 OLJ (☎ 0181 946 9887, fax 0181 944 1690)

GRANT, Sir (John) Anthony; kt (1982), MP (C) Cambridgeshire SW (majority 19,637); s of Arthur Ernest Grant; *b* 29 May 1925; *Educ* St Paul's, BNC Oxford; *m* 1953, Sonia Isobel, da of late George Henry Landen; 1 s, 1 da; *Career* served WWII Capt 3 Dragoon Gds; admitted slr 1952; MP (C): Harrow Central 1964–83, Cambridgeshire SW 1983–; oppn whip 1966–70, Parly sec BOT 1970; Parly under-sec: trade 1970–72, industl devpt 1972–74, DTI; chm Cons Back Bench Trade Ctee 1979–83, memb Foreign Affrs Select Ctee 1980–83, chm Econ Ctee Cncl of Europe 1980–84; memb Trade and Indust Select Ctee 1987–, pres Guild of Experienced Motorists 1987–; Freeman City of London (Master 1978–79), Liveryman Worshipful Co of Slrs; memb Law Soc; *Clubs* Carlton, Walton Heath Golf, Meridien Golf; *Style*— Sir Anthony Grant, MP; ✉ House of Commons, London SW1A 0AA

GRANT, Anthony Ernest; s of Ernest Grant (d 1986), of Sheffield, and Doris, *née* Hughes (d 1990); *b* 23 April 1940; *Educ* King Edward VII GS Sheffield, Keble Coll Oxford (MA); *m* 14 April 1962, Darel Avis, da of Frederick John Atkinson (d 1980), of Sheffield; 3 da (Henrietta (Mrs Michael Flood) b 1965, Sarah (Mrs Angus Ward) b 1966, Philippa b 1969); *Career* Coopers & Lybrand CAs 1961–96 (head of regnl ops 1994–96); chm: Tundra Ltd 1996–, Wilton Investments Ltd 1996–; non-exec dir: Leeds & Holbeck Building Soc 1996–, Rocom Ltd 1996–, Leeds Financial Services Initiative 1993– (chm 1993–94), Leeds C of C 1986– (pres 1996–), Leeds Metropolitan Univ 1989–91 (dep chm 1990–91); pres W Yorks CAs 1993–94; FCA (ACA 1965); *Recreations* riding, bridge; *Clubs* United Oxford and Cambridge, Leeds; *Style*— Anthony Grant, Esq; ✉ Wilton Investments Ltd, 3 The Embankment, Leeds LS1 4BP (☎ 0113 297 0800, fax 0113 297 0808)

GRANT, Bernard Alexander Montgomery (Bernie); MP (Lab) Tottenham (majority 11,968); s of Eric and Lily Grant; *b* 17 Feb 1944; *Educ* Stanislaus Coll Guyana, Tottenham Tech Coll; *m* (m dis); 3 s; *Career* analyst Demerara Bauxite Co Guyana 1961–63, clerk BR 1963–65, telephonist International Telephones 1969–78, area offr NUPE 1978–83, devpt worker Black Trade Unionists Solidarity Movement 1983–84, sr housing offr London Borough of Newham 1985–87, ldr London Borough of Haringey London 1985–87, MP (Lab) Tottenham 1987–; fndr memb and chair Parly Black Caucus 1987, memb Nat Exec Anti-Apartheid Movement 1988, fndr ed The Black Parliamentarian magazine 1989, chair Standing Conf on Racial Equality in Europe 1990–, elected chair Socialist Campaign Gp of Lab MPs 1990, chm Nat Ctee on Reparations for Africa 1993–, chair All Pty Gp on Race and Community 1995–; LLD (HC) Pace Univ NY 1993; *Style*— Bernie Grant, Esq, MP; ✉ House of Commons, London SW1A 0AA

GRANT, His Hon (Hubert) Brian; *b* 5 Aug 1917; *Educ* Trinity Coll Cambridge (MA); *m* 1946, Jeanette Mary; 1 s (Paul), 3 da (Susan, Elizabeth, Jane); *Career* served WWII No 10 Commando 1942–44; called to the Bar Gray's Inn 1945, circuit judge Sussex and Kent (formerly judge County Courts) 1965–82, memb Lord Chllr's Law Reform Ctee 1970–74; vice chm Nat Marriage Guidance Cncl 1970–72; fndr pres Parenthood 1979; hon librarian Br Deaf Assoc 1985–88; FRSA 1991; *Publications* Marriage, Separation and Divorce (1946), Family Law (1970), Conciliation and Divorce (1981), The Quiet Ear (1987), The Deaf Advance (1990), Not Guilty (1994); *Clubs* Penrith Golf; *Style*— His Hon Brian Grant; ✉ Eden Hill, Armathwaite, Carlisle CA4 9PQ

GRANT, David James; CBE (1980), JP (1988); s of Frederick Grant, MC, QC (d 1954), of London, and Grace Winifred, *née* McLaren (d 1966); *b* 18 Jan 1922; *Educ* Fettes, Oriel Coll Oxford (MA); *m* 10 Sept 1949, Jean Margaret, da of Gp Capt T E H Birley, OBE (d 1985); 2 s (James b 1951, Frederick b 1954), 1 da (Rosalind b 1958); *Career* joined RAF 1940, cmmnd navigator 1941; served: 218 Sqdn 1941–42, 215 Sqdn 1942–43, 271 Sqdn 1944, Navigation Offr 267 Sqdn 1945; demobbed Flt Lt 1945; md Darchem Ltd 1959–88, dep chm William Baird PLC 1981–92 (dir 1961–92); memb Cncl Univ of Durham 1978–92 (chm 1985–92), govr Univ of Teesside 1989; High Sheriff Co Durham 1985–86, Lord-Lt Co Durham 1988– (Vice Lord Lt 1987, DL 1980); Hon DCL: Univ of Durham 1988, Univ of Newcastle upon Tyne 1989; KStJ 1988; CIMgt (FIMgt 1978); *Clubs* Naval and Military; *Style*— David Grant, Esq, CBE, JP; ✉ Aden Cottage, Whitesmocks, Durham DH1 4HJ (☎ 0191 386 7161, fax 0191 386 0877)

GRANT, Dr Douglas; TD; s of Robert Grant (d 1959), and Ierne Grant (d 1963); *b* 6 Jan 1918; *Educ* George Watson's Coll, Univ of St Andrews; *m* 1948, Enid Whitsey, da of Raymond Whitsey Williams (d 1985); 3 s (William Neil b 1953, Richard Martin b 1955, Peter Michael b 1958); *Career* WWII Lt-Col RA (served W Africa and staff) 1939–46; Scottish Widows Fund 1936–39; dir: Oliver and Boyd Ltd 1947–67, Edinburgh C of C 1952–56, New Education Ltd 1962–66, Bracken House Publications Ltd 1963–67, Sprint Productions Ltd 1963–80, E & S Livingston Ltd 1963–67, Darien Press Ltd 1963–68, R & R Clark Ltd 1963–80, Port Seton Offset Printers Ltd 1965–75, T & A Constable Ltd 1965–75, Br Jl of Educnl Psychology 1970–91, Pindar (Scot) Ltd 1986–89, Macdonald Lindsay (Printers) Ltd 1988–89; chm: Scot Journal of Theology Ltd 1948–91, Robert Cunningham & Sons Ltd 1952–76, Hunter and Foulis Ltd 1963–75, Port Seton Offset Printers Ltd 1965–75, Multi Media (AU) Services Ltd 1967–75, Church of Scotland Publications Ctee 1971–76; Scottish Academic Press Ltd 1969–91, Scottish International Review Ltd 1970–75, The Handsel Press Ltd 1975–91, Scottish Academic Press (Jls) Ltd 1976–91, Clark Constable Printers Ltd 1978–89; conslt ed Scottish Academic Press 1991–; tstee: The Lodge Tst (Natural History) 1949–85, Darling (Ogilby) Investment Tst 1955–78, Kilwarlin Tst 1964–, Esdaile Tst 1975–, The Soc for the Benefit of Sons and Daughters of the Clergy of the Church of Scotland 1990–; memb Ctee: The Scot Cncl of Law Reporting 1950–93 (conslt 1993–), Police Dependents' Tst (Lothian and Borders Police) 1956–, NEDO 1968–75, New Coll Univ of Edinburgh Bd 1970–, Univ of Edinburgh Ct 1972–84, The Scot Arts Cncl 1975–79; pres: Edinburgh Master Printers' Assoc 1962–64, Edinburgh Bookseller Soc 1977–80, Edinburgh Amateur Angling Club 1978–80; hon fell Edinburgh Geological Soc 1992; Hon DLitt Univ of St Andrews 1986; MBOU 1944, FRSE 1949, FSA Scot 1949; *Clubs* New (Edinburgh), Hon Co of Edinburgh Golfers; *Style*— Dr Douglas Grant, TD, FRSE; ✉ Flat G, The Lodge, 2 East Road, North Berwick, East Lothian EH39 4HN (☎ 01620 894972)

GRANT, Francis Tollemache; s of late Capt Sir Francis Grant, 12 Bt; hp of bro, Sir Archibald Grant, 13 Bt; *b* 18 Dec 1955; *m* 4 Dec 1993, Virginia E, da of R Scott Russell, of East Hanney; 1 s (Alexander William b 28 Nov 1996), 1 da (Elizabeth Charlotte b 2 Nov 1994); *Books* Salmon Flyfishing, The Dynamics Approach (1993); *Recreations* salmon fly-fishing; *Style*— Francis Grant, Esq; ✉ Kingston Bagpuize House, Kingston Bagpuize, nr Abingdon, Oxon 0X13 5AX

GRANT, Hugh John Mungo; s of James Murray Grant, of Chiswick, and Fynvola Susan, *née* MacLean; *b* 9 Sept 1960; *Educ* Latymer, New Coll Oxford (scholarship, BA Hons Eng); *Career* actor; began career in theatre performing Jockeys of Norfolk (written with Chris Lang & Andy Taylor); *Films* incl: Privileged, Maurice, White Mischief, Rowing with the Wind, The Dawning, The Bengali Night, The Lair of the White Worm, Impromptu, The Big Man, Bitter Moon, Night Train to Venice, The Remains of the Day, Sirens, Four Weddings & A Funeral, An Awfully Big Adventure, Restoration, The Englishman Who Went Up A Hill But Came Down A Mountain, Nine Months, Sense & Sensibility; *Awards* incl: Best Actor Venice Film Festival 1987 (jtly with James Wilby), Golden Globe Award 1995 Best Actor in a Comedy (for Four Weddings & A Funeral), BAFTA Best Actor Award 1995; *Recreations* trapeze, singing; *Style*— Hugh Grant, Esq; ✉ c/o Simian Films, 3 Cromwell Place, London SW7 2JE (☎ 0171 589 6822, fax 0171 589 9405)

GRANT, Ian David; CBE (1988); s of Alan Howison Brewster Grant (d 1974), and Florence Ogilvie, *née* Swan; *b* 28 July 1943; *Educ* Strathallan Sch, East of Scotland Coll of Agric (dip); *m* 19 July 1968, Eileen May Louisa, da of Alexander Yule; 3 da (Catherine Louise b 10 Jan 1970, Jane Belle b 14 July 1971, Rosanne Elaine b 1 March 1974); *Career* pres (vice pres 1981–84) NFU Scotland 1984–90; dir: East of Scotland Farmers 1976–, Clydesdale Bank plc 1989–, NFU Mutual Insurance Soc 1990–, Scottish Hydro Electric plc 1992–; chm: Copa Cereals Gp Brussels 1982–86, Grains Gp Int Fedn of Agric Producers 1984–89, Scottish Tourist Bd 1990– (memb Bd 1988–); Crown Estate Cmmr 1996–; memb Bd BTA, memb Cncl CBI Scotland 1984–96; *Recreations* shooting, swimming, travel, reading, music; *Style*— Ian Grant, Esq, CBE; ✉ Scottish Tourist Board, 23 Ravelston Terrace, Edinburgh EH4 3EU (☎ 0131 332 2433, fax 0131 332 4441)

GRANT, Prof Ian Philip; s of Harold H Grant (d 1981), and Isabella Henrietta, *née* Ornstien (d 1980); *b* 15 Dec 1930; *Educ* St Albans' Sch Herts, Wadham Coll Oxford (Open scholar, MA, DPhil); *m* 1958, Beryl Cohen; 2 s (Paul Simon b 1960, David Michael b 1962); *Career* princ scientific offr UKAEA Aldermaston 1961–64 (sr scientific offr 1957–61), Atlas research fell (jt appt with SRC Atlas Computer Lab) Pembroke Coll Oxford 1964–69; Univ of Oxford: univ lectr in mathematics 1969–90, reader in mathematical physics 1990–92, prof of mathematical physics 1992–; Pembroke Coll Oxford: tutorial fell in mathematics 1969–, actg master 1984–85; visiting prof: McGill Univ 1976, Åbo Akademi Finland 1977, Inst de Fisica Univ Nacional Autónoma de México 1981; chm Oxford Synagogue and Jewish Centre; govr: Royal GS High Wycombe 1981–, St Paul's Sch London 1993–; memb London Mathematical Soc 1977; CMath 1992; FRAS 1966, FRS 1992; *Publications* author of papers in learned jls on relativistic quantum theory in atomic and molecular physics, and on radiative transfer theory in astrophysics and astrospheric science; *Recreations* walking, gardening, music, theatre going and travel; *Style*— Prof Ian Grant, FRS; ✉ Mathematical Institute, University of Oxford, 24/29 St Giles, Oxford OX1 3LB (☎ 01865 273551, fax 01865 273583, e-mail ipg@maths.ox.ac.uk)

GRANT, Dr James Shaw; CBE (1968, OBE 1956); s of William Grant (d 1932), of Stornoway, Isle of Lewis, and Johanna, *née* Morison (d 1952); *b* 22 May 1910; *Educ* Nicolson Inst Stornoway, Univ of Glasgow (MA); *m* 25 July 1951, Catherine Mary (d 1988), da of Norman Stewart (d 1945), of Back, Isle of Lewis; *Career* journalist and author; ed Stornoway Gazette 1932–63, chm Crofters Cmmn 1963–78, dir Grampian TV 1969–80; memb: Highlands and Islands Advsy Panel 1954–65, Highlands and Islands Devpt Bd 1970–82, Scottish Advsy Ctee Br Cncl 1972–94; chm Pitlochry Festival Theatre 1971–83, vice chm Eden Court Theatre 1987–96; Hon LLD Univ of Aberdeen 1979; FRSE 1982, FRAgS 1973; *Plays incl* Tarravore (1944), The Magic Rowan (1947), Legend is Born (1948), Comrade the King (1951); *Books* incl: Highland Villages (1977), Their Children will See (1979), The Hub of My Universe (1982), Surprise Island (1983), The Gaelic Vikings (1984), Stornoway and the Lews (1985), Discovering Lewis and Harris (1987), Enchanted Island (1989), A Shilling for Your Scowl (1992); *Recreations* walking, photography; *Clubs* Royal Over-Seas League; *Style*— Dr James Shaw Grant, CBE, FRSE; ✉ Ardgrianach, Inshes, Inverness (☎ 01463 231476)

GRANT, James Stevenson; s of James Grant (d 1981), of Muirkirk, and Margaret Baird, *née* Fisher (d 1989); *b* 27 Nov 1937; *Educ* Cumnock Acad, Univ of Strathclyde (BSc); *m* 26 April 1962, Christine Mary, da of John Sydney Hodges, OBE; 1 da (Tracey Belinda b 16 Dec 1966), 1 s (Andrew Stevenson b 18 Dec 1969); *Career* GEC Witton (subsequently CA Parsons Ltd, then Parsons Peebles Ltd): post graduate trg 1959–60, generator design engr 1960–62, sr generator design engr 1962–66, chief of central planning 1966–69, prodn controller 1969–70, chief of test inspection 1970–72; South of Scotland Electricity Bd (SSEB): Electrical Rotating Plant engr 1972–78, Electrical and Instrumentation engr 1978–81, seconded as tech servs mangr 1980–81, tech servs mangr 1981–88, engrg servs mangr 1988–89; chief engr designate Nuclear Div SSEB 1990 (devpt and engrg mangr designate 1989–90); dir of engrg Scottish Nuclear Ltd 1990–95, tech dir Scottish Nuclear Ltd 1995–; FIEE 1983 (MIEE 1967), FEng 1994; *Recreations* golf, bridge; *Clubs* Ex Round Table & Rotary; *Style*— James Grant, Esq, FEng; ✉ 24 Davieland Road, Whitecraigs, Glasgow G46 7LL (☎ 0141 638 0980); Scottish Nuclear Ltd, 3 Redwood Crescent, Peel Park, East Kilbride G74 5PR (☎ 013552 62408, fax 013552 62419, car 0831 503578)

GRANT, Jane Wentworth; *Educ* Univ of Bristol (BA), Inst of Educn Univ of London (PGCE), Univ of Essex (MA, MPhil), Univ of Lagos (Cert in Yoruba); *m*; 3 c; *Career* various English teaching posts in Dar-es-Salaam and England 1964–69, lectr Univ of Lagos 1971–73, educn offr/admin African Arts in Educn Project 1980–84, devpt offr Policy and Promotions Dept Nat Cncl for Voluntary Orgns 1984–89, dir Nat Alliance of Women's Orgns 1989–94, currently conslt and researcher on governance of women's orgns Univ of Kent; memb: Women's Advsy Gp RSA, Women in Arts Monitoring Ctee Arts Cncl, Advsy Cncl Global Fund for Women, Club of Rhodes, ACENVO, Women's Studies Network; tstee: Friends for Young Deaf People (FYD), Greengates Homes Greenwich, Women's Art Library; author of numerous articles on multi-cultural educn and women's issues; FRSA; *Style*— Ms Jane Grant; ✉ 13 Glenluce Road, Blackheath, London SE3 7SD (☎ 0181 858 8489, fax 0181 293 4808)

GRANT, Prof John; s of John Grant, of Bedlington, and Ivy Grant; *b* 8 Jan 1948; *Educ* Bedlington GS, Univ of Leeds (BSc, Brodetsky Prize), Univ of Newcastle (PhD); *m* Elizabeth, da of Robert Foster; 2 da (Julie b 22 Nov 1972, Lara b 11 July 1974), 1 s (David b 8 May 1981); *Career* senior sci offr RAE Farnborough 1972–79; Parsons Power Generation Systems (Rolls-Royce Industrial Power Group): princ design engr 1979, chief devpt engr 1991, dir Turbine-Generator Devpt 1994, tech dir 1996–; visiting prof in principles of engrg design Univ of Newcastle-upon-Tyne; chm Steam Plant Ctee Power Industs Div IMechE; author of numerous tech papers in jls and conf and seminar proceedings; winner Alan Marsh Meml Award Royal Aeronautical Soc 1976; FIMechE 1991, FEng 1996; *Recreations* football, golf, gardening, church; *Style*— Prof John Grant, FEng; ✉ Parsons Power Generation Systems Ltd, Heaton Works, Shields Road, Newcastle-upon-Tyne NE6 2YL (☎ 0191 275 2077, fax 0191 265 2532)

GRANT, John Albert Martin; s of Walter Grant, of Sandiway, Cheshire, and Irene, *née* Smyth; *b* 13 Oct 1945; *Educ* Campbell Coll Belfast, Queen's Univ Belfast (BSc Econ), Cranfield Sch of Mgmnt (MBA); *m* 1971, Corinne, da of John and Sally Porter; 2 da (Joanna b 27 March 1974, Nicola b 9 June 1976), 1 s (James b 23 April 1979); *Career* Ford of Europe: treas 1985–87, vice pres Business Strategy 1987–88; exec dir Corp Strategy Ford Motor Co (US) Jan-Dec 1989, exec dep chm Jaguar Ltd 1990–92; fin dir: Lucas Industries plc 1992–96, Lucas Varity plc 1996; non-exec dir National Grid Group plc 1995–; memb Advsy Bd City of Birmingham Symphony Orchestra, ptnr Northern

Ireland Partnership; FACT 1976; *Recreations* opera, music, theatre, motor sport, skiing; *Clubs* British Racing & Sports Car; *Style—* John Grant, Esq

GRANT, Prof John Paxton; s of John Dickson Grant (d 1968), and Jean Ramsay, *née* Paxton (d 1993); *b* 22 Feb 1944; *Educ* George Heriot's Sch, Univ of Edinburgh (LLB, Lord President prize), Univ of Pennsylvania (LLM); *m* 1983, Elaine Elizabeth, da of Eric Roy McGillvray Sutherland; *Career* lectr in public law: Univ of Aberdeen 1967–71, Univ of Dundee 1971–74; Faculty of Law Univ of Glasgow: sr lectr 1974–88, prof 1988–, dean 1985–89 and 1992–96; ed The Juridical Review 1988–; *Books* Independence and Devolution: The Legal Implications for Scotland (1976), The Impact of Marine Pollution (1980), The Encyclopaedic Dictionary of International Law (1986), Legal Education 2000 (1989), English-Estonian Law Glossary (1993), English for Lawyers (1994); *Recreations* walking, travelling; *Style—* Prof John Grant; ✉ 87 Warrender Park Road, Edinburgh EH9 1EW (☎ 0131 229 7705); Faculty of Law and Financial Studies, University of Glasgow, Glasgow G12 8QQ (☎ 0141 330 4181, fax 0141 330 5140)

GRANT, Dr John William; s of late John MacDonald Grant, and Isabella Grigor Clark, *née* Morrison; *b* 27 May 1953; *Educ* Dingwall Acad Ross & Cromarty, Univ of Aberdeen (MB ChB, MD); *m* 14 Nov 1980, Daniela, da of Hans Felix, of Bex, Switzerland; 2 da (Joanna b 1983, Marsali b 1986); *Career* registrar pathology Ninewells Hosp Dundee 1979–81, sr registrar in neuropathology and histopathology Southampton Gen Hosp 1981–86, Oberarzt Inst of Pathology Univ of Zürich Switzerland 1986–88; conslt histopathologist Addenbrooke's Hosp Cambridge 1988–, assoc lectr Univ of Cambridge 1989–, fell Emmanuel Coll Cambridge; MA Univ of Cambridge 1995; memb: BMA, Pathological Soc, Br Neuropathology Soc, Swiss Neuropathology Soc, ACP; FRCPath 1996 (MRCPath 1984); *Recreations* skiing, photography, squash; *Style—* Dr John W Grant; ✉ 4 The Stakings, Mill Lane, Sawston, Cambridge CB2 4TF (☎ 01223 835383); Histopathology Dept, Addenbrooke's Hosp, Hills Rd, Cambridge CB2 2QQ (☎ 01223 216744, fax 01223 216980)

GRANT, Keith Wallace; s of Randolph Grant (d 1977), and Sylvia, *née* Hawks (d 1983); *b* 30 June 1934; *Educ* Trinity Coll Glenalmond, Clare Coll Cambridge (MA); *m* 1968, Deanne, da of Dr Arnold Bergsma (d 1972), of S Africa; 1 s (Sam b 1975), 1 da (Katherine b 1977); *Career* account exec W S Crawford Ltd 1958–62, gen mangr Royal Opera Co Covent Garden and English Opera Gp 1962–73, sec RSA 1973–77, dir Design Cncl 1977–88, dean Faculty of Design Kingston Univ 1988–; *Recreations* music, reading, gardening; *Clubs* Garrick, Arts; *Style—* Keith Grant, Esq; ✉ Dean of Faculty of Design, Kingston University, Knights Park, Kingston upon Thames, Surrey KT1 2QJ; c/o Garrick Club, Garrick St, London WC2E 9AY

GRANT, Very Rev Malcolm Etheridge; s of Donald Etheridge Grant, and Nellie Florence May, *née* Tuffey; *b* 6 Aug 1944; *Educ* Dunfermline HS, Univ of Edinburgh (BSc, BD); *m* 1984, Katrina Russell, da of David Burn Skinner Dunnett; 1 s (Iain b 1989), 1 da (Alison b 1987); *Career* asst curate St Mary's Cathedral Glasgow 1969–72, team vicar of Earlesfield Grantham 1972–78, priest-in-charge St Ninian's Invergordon 1978–81, examining chaplain to Bishop of Moray Ross and Caithness 1979–81, provost and rector St Mary's (Scot Episcopal) Cathedral Glasgow 1981–91, provost and rector St Andrew's (Scot Episcopal) Cathedral Inverness 1991–, rector St Paul's Strathnairn and priest-in-charge St Mary's-in-the-Fields Culloden 1991–; memb Highland Cncl Educn Ctee 1979–81; *Style—* The Very Rev Malcolm Grant; ✉ 15 Ardross Street, Inverness IV3 5NS (☎ 01463 233535)

GRANT, Prof Malcolm John; s of Francis William Grant (d 1987), and Vera Jessica, *née* Cooke; *b* 29 Nov 1947; *Educ* Waitaki HS Oamaru NZ, Univ of Otago (LLB, LLM, LLD); *m* 13 July 1974, Christine Joan, da of Thomas John Endersbee, ISO (d 1986); 2 s (Nikolas b 1976, Thomas b 1980), 1 da (Joanna b 1978); *Career* sr lectr in law (former lectr) Univ of Southampton 1972–86, prof of law UCL 1988–91 (sr lectr 1986–88), prof of land economy Univ of Cambridge 1991–; fell Clare Coll Cambridge 1991–, cmmr for local govt for England 1992–; chm Local Govt Cmmn 1996– (dep chm 1995–96); ed Encyclopaedia of Planning Law and Practice 1982–, jt ed Encyclopaedia of Environmental Law 1993–; Hon MRTPI 1994, Hon ARICS 1995; *Books* Planning Law Handbook (1981), Urban Planning Law (1982, supplement 1989), Rate Capping and the Law (2nd edn, 1986), Permitted Development (1989, 2 edn 1996); *Recreations* travelling; *Style—* Prof Malcolm Grant; ✉ 10 Grange Road, Cambridge CB3 9DU (☎ 01223 562903); Department of Land Economy, 19 Silver St, Cambridge (☎ 01223 337134, fax 01223 337132)

GRANT, Dr Michael; CBE (1958, OBE 1946); s of late Col Maurice Harold Grant, and late Muriel, *née* Jörgensen; *b* 21 Nov 1914; *Educ* Harrow, Trinity Coll Cambridge (MA, LittD); *m* 1944, Anne Sophie Beskow, of Norrköping, Sweden; 2 s; *Career* fell Trinity Coll Cambridge 1938–49, acting Capt War Office 1939–40, first Br Cncl Rep Turkey 1940–45, prof of humanity Univ of Edinburgh 1948–59, first vice-chllr Univ of Khartoum 1956–58, pres and vice-chllr Queen's Univ Belfast 1959–66; medallist Royal Numismatic Soc 1962 (pres 1953–56), J H Gray lectr Cambridge 1955; chm: Cwlth Conf on Teaching of English as Second Language Makerere Uganda 1961, Nat Cncl for Supply of Teachers Overseas 1963–66; pres: Virgil Soc 1963–66, Classical Assoc 1977–78; Hon LittD Dublin 1961, Hon LLD Queen's Univ Belfast 1967; hon fell Royal Numismatic Soc 1984; memb American Numismatic Soc (Huntingdon medallist) 1965, Gold medal for Educn (Sudan) 1977, Premio del Mediterraneo, Premio Latina and Premio delle Muse (Italy); FSA; *Books* From Imperium to Auctoritas (1946), Aspects of the Principate of Tiberius (1950), Birth of Western Civilization (ed, 1964), Who's Who in Classical Mythology (with J Hazel, 1973), A Guide to the Ancient World - Dictionary of Ancient Place Names (1986), Civilization of the Ancient Mediterranean (with R Kitzinger, 1988), The Visible Past (1990), Short History of Classical Civilization (US title The Founders of the Western World, 1991), Greeks and Romans - A Social History (1992), Readings in the Classical Historians (ed, 1992), The Emperor Constantine (1993), Saint Peter (1994), My First Eighty Years (1994), The Sayings of the Bible (1994), Greek and Roman Historians: Information and Misinformation (1995), Art in the Roman Empire), The Severans (1996); *Clubs* Athenaeum; *Style—* Dr Michael Grant, CBE, FSA; ✉ Le Pitturacce, 351 Via della Chiesa, Gattaiola, Lucca 55030, Italy

GRANT, Newton Keene; OBE, JP (City of London 1974); s of Cyril Ernest Newton Oscar Grant (d 1947), of London, and Ethel, *née* Keene (d 1958); *b* 25 June 1931; *Educ* Eggars GS Alton Hants; *m* 30 Aug 1958, Mary Elizabeth, da of Joseph Henri Jules Romagny (d 1971), of Soissons, France; 3 da (Nicole Mary (Mrs Corbin) b 1962, Carolyn Gillian b 1966, Marie-Anne Hélène b 1969); *Career* Nat Serv RAPC; sr ptnr: Pridie Brewster CAs (ptnr 1960); pres Chartered Assoc of Certified Accountants 1983–84, chm Hearing Aid Cncl 1985–91; formerly JP Surrey; memb Worshipful Co of Horners 1971 (memb Ct of Assts, Master 1990–91); FCCA 1955, FCA 1960, FCIArb 1970; *Recreations* music, cookery, antique silver; *Clubs* Savage, City Livery; *Style—* Newton Grant, Esq, OBE, JP; ✉ Treworlas House, Ruanhighlanes, Truro, Cornwall TR2 5LN (☎ 01872 501759); 96 Thomas More House, Barbican EC2Y 8BU; Carolyn House, 29–31 Greville St, London EC1N 8RB (☎ 0171 831 8821, fax 0171 404 3069)

GRANT, Nicholas; s of Hugo Moore Grant (d 1987), of Herts, and Cara Phyllis, *née* McMullen-Pearson; *b* 24 March 1948; *Educ* Durham Sch, Univ of London (LLB), Univ of Warwick (MA); *m* 5 Nov 1977, Rosalind Louise, da of Winston Maynard Pipe; 1 s (Robert b 1979), 1 da (Rosemary b 1981); *Career* head of res and PR Confedn of Health Serv Employees 1972–82, dir of info Lab Pty 1983–85, public affrs advsr to Mirror Group Newspapers 1985–89; currently: md Mediatrack Ltd, chm Pearson Grant Associates, dir Kaleidoscope Television Ltd; memb: (Lab) Lambeth Borough Cncl 1978–84, West Lambeth Dist Health Authy 1982–84; Parly candidate (Lab) Reigate 1979; *Books* Economics of Prosperity (1980), Political Communication for British General Election (1983); *Recreations* walking, music, photography; *Clubs* Reform; *Style—* Nicholas Grant, Esq; ✉ Mediatrack Ltd, 9 Lincoln's Inn Fields, London WC2A 3BP (☎ 0171 430 0699, fax 0171 404 1493)

GRANT, Prof Nigel Duncan Cameron; s of Alasdair Cameron Grant (d 1957), of Inverness, and Anne Blythe Munro, *née* Blythe (d 1989); *b* 8 June 1932; *Educ* Inverness Royal Acad, Univ of Glasgow (MA, MED, PhD); *m* 15 July 1957, Valerie Keeling, da of Dr W S Evans (d 1952), of Glasgow; 1 s (David b 2 Feb 1966), 1 da (Alison b 25 Oct 1963); *Career* Nat Serv gunner RA 1955–57; teacher of English in Glasgow secdy schs 1957–60, lectr in educn Jordanhill Coll 1960–65, lectr then reader Univ of Edinburgh, prof of educn Univ of Glasgow 1978–95 (prof emeritus 1995); memb: Lab Pty, Br Comparative and Int Educn Soc (past chm and pres), Scottish Educnl Res Assoc (past chm), Advsy Cncl for the Arts in Scotland; past chm Scottish Univs Cncl for Studies in Educn; Joannes Amos Comenius Prize of Czech and Slovak Federal Republic 1992; memb: AUT, SERA, BCIES, CESE, Glasgow Educnl Colloquium (hon pres 1989–93), Urras Foghlam na Gàidhlig; FRSE 1992; *Books* Soviet Education (1964, 4 edn 1979), Society, Schools and Progress in Eastern Europe (1969), Education and Nation-building in the Third World (jtly, 1971), A Mythology of British Education (jtly, 1973), Scottish Universities: The Case for Devolution (jtly, 1975), Patterns of Education in the British Isles (jtly, 1977), The Crisis of Scottish Education (1982), Scottish Education: a Declaration of Principles (jtly, 1989); *Recreations* languages, poetry, music, theatre, ornithology, travel, history; *Clubs* Glasgow University College; *Style—* Prof Nigel Grant, FRSE; ✉ 4A Sydenham Rd, Glasgow, Scotland G12 9NS (☎ 0141 357 1549); Department of Education, The University, Glasgow G12 8QQ (☎ 0141 339 8855 ext 6030 5528)

GRANT, (Alastair) Norman; s of Alexander Grant (d 1985), of Carrbridge, Scotland, and May Grant, *née* Robertson; *b* 18 Nov 1943; *Educ* Royal Acad Inverness, Gray's Sch of Art Aberdeen, (Dips Silversmithing and Graphic Design); *m* 3 July 1965, Jess Sloss Innes, da of Dr William Paterson (d 1968), of Glenrothes, Fife; 1 s (Rob b 1973), 1 da (Romany b 1966); *Career* fndr and md Dust Jewellery Ltd 1966–88, co fndr and md Grant Walker Ltd (the first jewellery design conslt working internationally for UN, EC, UK and other govts and private companies), art coll business studies advsr; Freeman: City of London 1981, Worshipful Co of Goldsmiths 1981; *Recreations* travel, Scottish cottage; *Style—* Norman Grant, Esq; ✉ 55 Ridge Rd, London N8 9LJ (☎ 0181 341 6104); Grant Walker Ltd, 4–5 Broadbent Close, Highgate Village, London N6 5JP (☎ 0181 341 9119, fax 0181 348 0078)

GRANT, Patricia (Trista); da of N A D Grant, and M A R Grant, *née* Spence; *Educ* St Swithun's Sch Winchester, Univ of Reading (BA Politics); *Career* TMD/Carat Advertising 1986–89, McCann-Erickson Advertising 1992–94, media dir HK McCann 1992–94, exec media dir McCann-Erickson Advertising 1994–95, md Universial McCann 1996–; memb Media Policy Gp IPA 1996–; finalist Cosmopolitan Women of the Year 1995; *Recreations* skiing, paragliding, tennis; *Clubs* Carlton Tennis, Lambton Place Health; *Style—* Ms Trista Grant; ✉ Universal McCann, 36 Howland Street, London W1A 1AT (☎ 0171 436 7711, fax 0171 915 2165)

GRANT, Prof Peter Mitchell; s of George Mitchell Grant, of Leven, Fife, and Isobel Margaret, *née* Wilkinson (d 1973); *b* 20 June 1944; *Educ* Strathallan Sch, Heriot-Watt Univ (BSc), Univ of Edinburgh (PhD); *m* 12 Jan 1974, Marjory, da of Ness Renz (d 1991); 2 da (Lindsay Isobel b 1975, Jennifer Alison b 1977); *Career* devpt engr Plessey Company Ltd 1966–70; Univ of Edinburgh: res fell 1971–76, lectr 1976–82, reader 1982–87, prof of electronic signal processing 1987–; chm IEE Proceedings Editorial Panel, chm Editorial Panel IEE Electronics Jl; FIEE, FIEEE; *Books* Adaptive Filters (1985), Analogue and Digital Signal Processing and Coding (1989), Digital Communications (1996); *Style—* Prof Peter Grant; ✉ Department of Electrical Engineering, University of Edinburgh, King's Building, Mayfield Rd, Edinburgh EH9 3JL (☎ 0131 650 5569, fax 0131 650 6554, telex 727442 UNIVED G, e-mail pmg@ee.ed.ac.uk)

GRANT, Richard E; *b* 5 May 1957; *Educ* Waterford-Kamthlaba Mbabane Swaziland, Cape Town Univ SA (BA); *m* 1 Nov 1986, Joan Washington, *qv*; 1 da (Olivia b 4 Jan 1989); *Career* actor; *Theatre* co-fndr Troupe Theatre Co Cape Town 1980–82; credits incl: Man of Mode (Orange Tree) 1983, A Midsummer Night's Dream and Merry Wives of Windsor (Regents Park) 1984, Tramway Road (Lyric Hammersmith) 1984, The Importance of Being Earnest (Aldwych) 1993; *Television* Honest Decent and True (BBC) 1985, Here is the News (BBC) 1988, Suddenly Last Summer (BBC) 1992, Bed (BBC) 1994, Karaoke (BBC/Channel 4) 1995, A Royal Scandal 1996; *Films* incl: Withnail and I 1986, Warlock 1988, How to Get Ahead in Advertising 1988, Mountains of the Moon 1988, Killing Dad 1989, Henry and June 1989, LA Story 1990, Hudson Hawk 1990, The Player 1992, Age of Innocence 1992, Dracula 1993, Prêt a Porter 1994, Cool Light of Day 1994, title role in Jack & Sarah 1995, Portrait of a Lady 1995, Twelfth Night 1995, The Serpent's Kiss 1996, Food of Love 1996; *Books* With Nails (1996); *Recreations* scuba diving, building dolls houses, photography; *Style—* Richard E Grant, Esq; ✉ c/o ICM Ltd, Oxford House, 76 Oxford Street, London W1N 0AX (☎ 0171 636 6565, fax 0171 323 0101)

GRANT, Russell John d'Ammerall; s of Frank William Grant, and Joan Alice Peverall; *b* 5 Feb 1952; *Educ* Abbotsfield Hillingdon Middx; *Career* astrologer and television presenter; shows incl: Star Choice (ITV), The Zodiac Game (ITV), People Today (BBC), This Morning (Granada), Russell Grant's All Star Show (ITV), FX Cable (Fox TV USA); radio presenter Believe It or Not (BBC Radio 4); currently presenter/prodr: Get Away! (Granda Sky Broadcasting), Question of Taste (Granada Sky Broadcasting); original presenter BBC Breakfast Time, amateur sports corr BBC Radio 5 Live; columnist: Daily Mirror, Sunday Mirror Magazine, TV Quick; pres emeritus Br Astrological Psychic Soc, hon life memb Astrologers' Guild of GB, patron emeritis The County of Middlesex Tst; pres: Br Astrological Psychic Soc, Northern Lights Astrological Soc, Assoc of Br Counties; hon pres: Fedn of Middlesex Sports, The Middlesex Soc; fndr Friends of the County of Middlesex; Lord of the Manor of Ashford Middx; *Books* Your Sun Signs, Your Love Signs, Real Counties of Britain (1990, 2 edn 1996), Dreams Dictionary (1991), Astro-Tarot Pack (1992), Astrology Kit (1994), Illustrated Dream Dictionary (1995); *Recreations* collector of British maps and gazetteers, county of Middlesex memorabilia; *Style—* Russell Grant, Esq; ✉ PO Box 5757, Royal Lytham St Annes FY8 2TE; Jacque Evans Management, 11A St Johns Wood High Street, London NW8 7NG (☎ 0171 722 4700, fax 0171 722 4316)

GRANT, Susan Lavinia; da of Donald Blane Grant, of Dundee, Scotland, and Lavinia Ruth, *née* Ritchie; *b* 29 Jan 1948; *Educ* St Leonard's Sch St Andrews Scotland, Goldsmiths' Coll London; *m* 1, 1969 (m dis 1973), Charles Sharpe; *m* 2, 1975 (m dis 1983), Ian Woolgar; 1 s (Edward Rupert b 1980), 1 da (Lavinia Unity b 1977); *Career* res exec J Walter Thompson 1968–74, researcher BBC Publications then publicity exec BBC TV 1974–78, publicity mangr Hamlyns 1978–82, account mangr then account dir Good Relations 1982–86, fndr dir and memb Bd The Communication Group 1986–; MIPR; *Recreations* tennis, golf, waterskiing, Scotland, painting; *Clubs* Riverside Racquets, Panmure Golf; *Style—* Ms Susan Grant; ✉ The Communication Group, 19 Buckingham Gate, London SW1E 6LB (☎ 0171 630 1411)

GRANT, William; s of A S Grant (d 1967), and Dr F M Grant (d 1962); *b* 27 March 1938; *Educ* Wellington, Univ of Cambridge (MA); *m* 1 Sept 1961, Jane Margaret; 3 da (Louise b 6 Jan 1966, Polly b 5 July 1969, Belinda b 5 Jan 1972); *Career* Nat Serv RAF 1956–58; admitted slr 1965, ptnr Linklaters & Paines 1970–96; Freeman City of London, memb Ct of Assts Worshipful Co of Pewterers; memb Law Soc; *Recreations* skiing, walking, art; *Clubs* Roehampton; *Style—* William Grant, Esq; ✉ 11 Gwendolen Avenue, Putney, London SW15 6ET (☎ 0181 788 9669, fax 0181 780 1445)

GRANT-ADAMSON, Lesley Ann; da of late Edwin Bethuel Heycock, and Edna May, *née* Puddefoot; *b* 26 Nov 1942; *Educ* Trealaw Junior Sch Rhondda, Dame Alice Owen Sch Islington; *m* 14 Dec 1968, Andrew Duncan Grant-Adamson; *Career* author; journalist for several trade and technical magazines and local newspapers 1960–73, staff feature writer The Guardian 1973–80, freelance writer (The Times, The Observer, The Sunday Times, The Guardian) 1980–, writer in residence Nottingham Trent Univ and E Midland Arts 1994; writer and prodr of documentaries for Channel 4 and S4C, teaches and lectures on writing popular fiction; memb: Welsh Acad, Soc of Authors, PEN, Crime Writers' Assoc (memb Ctee 1987–90), Royal Soc of Literature; *Books* Patterns in the Dust (1985), The Face of Death (1985), Guilty Knowledge (1986), Wild Justice (1987), Threatening Eye (1988), Curse the Darkness (1990), Flynn (1991), A Life of Adventure (1992), The Dangerous Edge (1993), Dangerous Games (1994), A Season in Spain (with Andrew Grant-Adamson, 1995), Wish You Were Here (1995), Evil Acts (1996), Writing Crime and Suspense Fiction (1996), The Girl in the Case (1997); play: Blood Red; short stories in numerous anthologies and magazines, essays on crime and suspense fiction in various anthologies and magazines; *Recreations* art galleries, reading much too slowly, travelling; *Clubs* English Pen, Yr Academi Gymraeg; *Style—* Ms Lesley Grant-Adamson; ✉ 30 Bewdley Street, Islington, London N1 1HB (☎ 0171 607 4193); Stoddens Cottage, 32 High Street, Stogursey, Bridgwater, Somerset; c/o Clare Roberts, Rogers, Coleridge & White, 20 Powis Mews, London W11 1JN (☎ 0171 221 3717)

GRANT OF DALVEY, Sir Patrick Alexander Benedict; 14 Bt (NS 1688), of Dalvey; Chieftain of Clan Donnachaidh Grants; s of Sir Duncan Alexander Grant of Dalvey, 13 Bt (d 1961), of Polmaily, Glen Urquhart, Inverness-shire, and Joan Penelope, *née* Cope (d 1991); *b* 5 Feb 1953; *Educ* Fort Augustus Abbey Sch, Glasgow Univ (LLB); *m* 1981, Dr Carolyn Elizabeth, da of Dr John Highet, of Pollokshields, Glasgow; 2 s (Duncan Archibald Ludovic b 1982, Neil Patrick b 21 Oct 1983); *Heir* s, Duncan Archibald Ludovic Grant of Dalvey b 19 April 1982; *Career* deerstalker/gamekeeper 1969–71, inshore fisherman/skipper Scottish Highlands W Coast 1971–76; chm and md Grants of Dalvey Ltd 1987–; chm: The Clan Grant Soc, The Clan Grant Museum Tst; winner Queen's Award for Export 1992, Highland Business Award 1995; *Recreations* deerstalking, Scottish piping; *Clubs* New (Edinburgh); *Style—* Sir Patrick Grant of Dalvey, Bt; ✉ Tomintoul House, Flichity, Farr, Inverness-shire IV1 2XD; Grants of Dalvey Ltd, Alness, Ross-shire IV17 0XT

GRANT OF GARTENBEG, Rear Adm John; CB (1960), DSO (1942); s of Maj-Gen Sir Philip Grant, KCB, CMG (d 1943), and Lady Annette Mary Grant (d 1963), da of John Coventry, JP, descendant of 6 Earl of Coventry; *b* 13 Oct 1908; *Educ* St Anthony's Eastbourne, RNC Dartmouth, RNC Greenwich, JSSC, RCDS; *m* 1935, Ruth, da of Richard Slade (d 1915); 2 s (Duncan, Andrew), 2 da (Tessa, Grizel); *Career* RN: successively CO HM Ships Beverley (ex-USS Branch), Philante, Opportune, Fame, Crispin and Cleopatra (Atlantic, Med and Russia), MOD, Flag Offr Cmdg Reserve Fleet, ret 1961; Rank Organisation 1961–65, dir Conf of Electronics Industry 1965–71; CBIREE, FRSA until 1970; *Clubs* Hurlingham; *Style—* Rear Adm John Grant, CB, DSO; ✉ 9 Rivermead Court, Ranelagh Gardens, London SW6 3RT

GRANT OF GLENMORISTON, (14 Laird of) Ian Faulconer Heathcoat; JP (1982), DL; s of John Augustus Grant, DL (d 1978), and Gwendolen Evelyn Mary Knight; *b* 3 June 1939; *Educ* Sedbergh, Liverpool Coll of Commerce; *m* 1964, Sarah Bonita, da of Peter Mair D'Arcy Osborne (d 1974); 1 s (John b 1976), 3 da (Amabel b 1966, Miranda b 1968, Iona b 1970); *Career* md Glenmoriston Estates Ltd, chm Pacific Assets Trust plc; dir: The Royal Bank of Scotland Group plc, Banco Santander SA, Worldwide Value Fund Inc, Holland Pacific Fund NV, Dransfield Holdings Ltd; *Recreations* gardening; *Clubs* New (Edinburgh); *Style—* Ian Grant of Glenmoriston, JP, DL; ✉ Bhlaraidh House, Glenmoriston, Inverness; Duncow House, Kirkmahoe Dumfries DG1 1TA; Glenmoriston Estates Ltd, Glenmoriston, nr Inverness (☎ 01320 351202, fax 01320 351209)

GRANT OF GRANT, Hon Michael Patrick Francis; s of 5 Baron Strathspey (d 1992), and his 2 w, Olive, *née* Grant; *b* 22 April 1953; *Educ* Harrow, Oriel Coll Oxford (MA); *Career* chartered surveyor, mktg and franchise conslt; dir Blythe Management Ltd 1984–, dir Independent Valuation Surveyors; Liveryman Worshipful Co of Grocers; ARICS; *Recreations* sailing; *Style—* The Hon Michael Grant of Grant; ✉ 3 Ifield Road, London SW10 9AZ; Elms Cottage, Elms Ride, West Wittering, Sussex, PO20 8LP (☎ 01243 513246); PO Box 3945, Dubai, UAE (☎ 00 9714 823997, fax 00 9714 274633)

GRANT OF MONYMUSK, Sir Archibald; 13 Bt (NS 1705), of Cullen, Co Buchan; s of Capt Sir Francis Cullen Grant, 12 Bt (d 1966, himself tenth in descent from Archibald Grant, whose f d 1553 and whose er bro John was ancestor of the Barons Strathspey), by his w Jean, only da of Capt Humphrey Tollemache, RN (s of Hon Douglas Tollemache, 8 s of 1 Baron Tollemache); *b* 2 Sept 1954; *Educ* Trinity Coll Glenalmond, RAC Cirencester (Dip Farm Mgmnt); *m* 31 Dec 1982, Barbara Elizabeth, eldest da of Andrew Garden Duff Forbes, of Druminnor Castle, Rhynie, Aberdeenshire, and Mrs Alison Forbes; 2 da (Christian Mariot b 31 March 1986, Catriona Elizabeth b 14 April 1988); *Heir* bro, Francis Tollemache Grant b 18 Dec 1955; *Career* farmer; *Recreations* hill-walking, shooting, water-divining; *Clubs* Royal Northern; *Style—* Sir Archibald Grant of Monymusk, Bt; ✉ House of Monymusk, Monymusk, Inverurie AB51 7HL (☎ 01467 651220, office 01467 651333, fax 01467 651250)

GRANT OF ROTHIEMURCHUS, John Peter; DL (Inverness-shire 1986); s of Lt-Col John Grant of Rothiemurchus, MBE (d 1987), and Lady Katherine Grant of Rothiemurchus, *qv*; *b* 22 Oct 1946; *Educ* Gordonstoun; *m* 1971, Philippa, da of John Chance, of Widmer Lodge, nr Princes Risborough; 1 s, 2 da; *Career* dir and chm Scottish Trout Ltd 1989–95; memb: Bd NE River Purification Bd 1990–96, Tourism Trg Scotland 1993–95, Native Woodlands Advsy Panel to the Forestry Cmmn 1993–, Aviemore Partnership 1994–, Cairngorm Partnership 1995–; Nat Tst for Scotland: memb Cncl 1990–95, memb Countryside and Nature Conservation Ctee 1992–, memb Exec Ctee 1994–; vice pres Scottish Landowners' Fedn 1991–, chm Tourism and Environment Task Force 1995–, pres Royal Zoological Soc of Scotland 1996–; patron Highland Hospice; *Style—* John Grant of Rothiemurchus, DL; ✉ The Doune of Rothiemurchus, by Aviemore, Inverness-shire PH22 1QP

GRANT OF ROTHIEMURCHUS, Lady Katherine; *née* Greaves; 2 da of Countess of Dysart (d 1975, the 10 holder of the title) and Maj Owain Greaves, DL, RHG (d 1941); hp to sis, Countess of Dysart (11 holder of the title); *b* 1 June 1918; *m* 1941, Lt-Col John Peter Grant of Rothiemurchus, MBE (d 1987), s of late Col John P Grant of Rothiemurchus, CB, TD, JP, DL; 1 s (John Peter Grant of Rothiemurchus, *qv*), 1 da (Jane (Mrs A R F Buxton)); *Style—* The Lady Katherine Grant of Rothiemurchus; ✉ Rothiemurchus, Aviemore, Inverness-shire

GRANT-SUTTIE, James Edward; s and h of Sir (George) Philip Grant-Suttie, 8 Bt, *qv*; *b* 29 May 1965; *m* 10 Nov 1989 (m dis 1996), Emma Jane, yr da of Peter Craig, of Innerwick, E Lothian; 1 s (Gregor Craig b 29 Oct 1991); *Style—* James Grant-Suttie, Esq; ✉ Sheriff Hall Farm, North Berwick, E Lothian

GRANT-SUTTIE, Sir (George) Philip; 8 Bt (NS 1702); s of late Maj George Grant-Suttie, gs of 2 Bt; suc kinsman, Sir George Grant-Suttie, 7 Bt, 1947; *b* 20 Dec 1938; *Educ* Sussex Composite HS New Brunswick, McGill Univ; *m* 1962 (m dis 1969), Elspeth Mary, da of Maj-Gen Robert Elliott Urquhart, CB, DSO; 1 s; *Heir* s, James Grant-Suttie, *qv*; *Career* farmer, writer, pilot; *Recreations* fishing, forestry, flying (owner: Cessna 206); *Style—* Sir Philip Grant-Suttie, Bt; ✉ The Granary, Sheriff Hall, North Berwick, E Lothian EH39 5BP (☎ 01620 89 2569; office 3750)

GRANTCHESTER, 3 Baron (UK 1953); Christopher John Suenson-Taylor; s of 2 Baron Grantchester, CBE, QC (d 1995), and Betty, *née* Moores; *b* 8 April 1951; *Educ* Winchester, LSE (BSc); *m* 1973, Jacqueline, da of Dr Leo Jaffé; 2 s (Hon Jesse David b 1977, Hon Adam Joel b 1987), 2 da (Hon Holly Rachel b 1975, Hon Hannah Robyn b 1984); *Heir* s, Hon Jesse David Suenson-Taylor b 1977; *Career* dairy farmer and cattle breeder; former memb Cncl Holstein Soc Exec; memb Cncl: RASE, Cheshire Agric Soc; Supreme Dairy Female RASE 1990 and 1991; dir: The Littlewoods Organisation plc, Everton FC; *Recreations* soccer; *Style—* The Rt Hon the Lord Grantchester; ✉ Lower House Farm, Back Coole Lane, Audlem, Crewe, Cheshire (☎ 01270 811363)

GRANTHAM, Leslie Michael; s of Walter William Grantham, of Farnborough, Hampshire, and Adelaide Victoria Grantham; *b* 30 April 1947; *Educ* St Mary Cray Secdy Modern, Webber Douglas Acad of Dramatic Art; *m* 29 Dec 1981, Jane Mary, da of Alan David Hickinbotham; 2 s (Michael Leslie b 30 Sept 1986, Jake Edward b 3 Sept 1988); *Career* actor; winner Best Actor Pye TV Awards 1985–86; wine writer Sunday Mirror Magazine; *Theatre* Belgrade Theatre Coventry: Who's life is it anyway?, A Little Night Music, The Visitors, Lady Chatterley's, Brighton Rock; TK9 Bridge Lane Theatre London, Rick's Bar Churchill Theatre Bromley (and Whitehall Theatre London), Cold Sweat Queen's Theatre Hornchurch; *Film and TV* Jakes End (BBC), The Jewel in the Crown (Granada), Goodnight and Godbless (ATV), Hello I Thought You'd Gone (Central), Night of the Narrow Boats (Central), Dr Who (BBC), Morons from Outer Space, Knockback (BBC), Bulman (Granada), Eastenders (BBC), Nightwatch (BBC), Winners and Losers (Scottish), Paradise Club (2 series, BBC), Good Guys (LWT), Woof (Central), Runaway Bay (Yorkshire), Gummed Labels (Channel 4), Wild Oats (Carlton), The Detectives (BBC), Good Parent Guide (LWT), Cluedo (Granada), 99 to 1 (Carlton); *Recreations* wine, golf; *Style—* Leslie Grantham, Esq; ✉ c/o Michael Whitehall Ltd, 125 Gloucester Road, London SW7 4TE (☎ 0171 244 8466, fax 0171 244 9060)

GRANTLEY, 8 Baron (GB 1782); Richard William Brinsley Norton; s of 7 Baron Grantley, MC (d 1995), and Lady Deirdre Elisabeth Freda Hare, da of 5 Earl of Listowel; *b* 30 Jan 1956; *Educ* Ampleforth, New Coll Oxford (MA, pres Union); *Heir* bro, Hon Francis John Hilary Norton b 1960; *Career* merchant banker; Conservative Research Dept 1977–81, cllr Royal Borough of Kensington and Chelsea 1982–86, Conservative candidate for Wentworth in 1983 general election; dir Morgan Grenfell Int Ltd; Kt SMOM; *Recreations* Bridge; *Clubs* White's, Pratt's; *Style—* The Rt Hon the Lord Grantley; ✉ 8 Halsey St, London SW3

GRANVILLE, 6 Earl (UK 1833); Granville George Fergus Leveson Gower; also Viscount Granville, of Stone Park (UK 1815), and Baron Leveson, of Stone (UK 1833); s of 5 Earl Granville, MC (d 1996), and Doon Aileen, *née* Plunket; *b* 10 Sept 1959; *Educ* Eton; *Heir* bro, Hon Niall James Leveson-Gower b 1963; *Career* former page of honour to HM The Queen; *Style—* The Rt Hon the Earl Granville

GRANVILLE, Richard de la Bere; JP; s of Richard St Leger Granville (d 1972), of Frays, Weston, Herts, and Barbara Lempriere, *née* Wells (d 1983); *b* 20 June 1938; *Educ* Eton; *m* 1966, Christina Veronica, da of Philip Debell Tuckett (d 1967); 1 da (b 1968); *Career* Lt Coldstream Gds 1957–59; assoc memb Hoare Govett Ltd (stockbrokers) 1986 (joined Hoare & Co 1959), dep chm Neilson Cobbold Ltd 1988–92 chm Throgmorton Dual Trust PLC 1994, dir The New Throgmorton Trust PLC 1994; MSI (memb Stock Exchange 1964, memb Cncl 1981–84); *Recreations* country pursuits; *Clubs* Boodle's, Pratt's; *Style—* Richard Granville, Esq, JP; ✉ 5 Rutland Gardens, London SW1 1BS; 15/17 King Street, St James's, London SW1Y 6QU (☎ 0171 930 8786, fax 0171 839 3649)

GRANVILLE OF EYE, Baron (Life Peer UK 1967), of Eye, Co Suffolk; Edgar Louis Granville; s of Reginald Granville, of Brighton; *b* 12 Feb 1899; *Educ* High Wycombe, Melbourne Australia; *m* 1943, Elizabeth, da of late Rev William Cecil Hunter; 1 da (Hon Linda Elizabeth Mary b 1949); *Career* sits in Lords as an Independent Peer; served WWI and II; former md E L Granville & Co; MP (Lib) Suffolk Eye 1929–51; PPS to: Sir Herbert Samuel 1931, Sir John Simon (National Govt) 1931–36; *Recreations* skiing, writing autobiographies, poetry and novels, watching 3 day events; *Style—* The Rt Hon the Lord Granville of Eye; ✉ Charlton Lane, Cheltenham, Glos

GRATTAN, Dr Donald Henry; CBE (1989); s of Arthur Henry Grattan (d 1980), and Edith Caroline, *née* Saltmarsh (d 1980); family of Henry Grattan, Irish PM; *b* 7 Aug 1926; *Educ* Harrow County GS, King's Coll London (BSc), Open Univ (DUniv); *m* 1950, Valmai, da of Richard Edward Morgan (d 1978); 1 s (David), 1 da (Jennifer); *Career* jr res offr TRE Gt Malvern 1945–46; sch master Chiswick GS 1946–50, sr master Downer GS 1950–56; television prodr BBC 1956–61, ed further educn BBC 1961–63, head of continuing educn BBC TV 1963–71, controller educnl broadcasting BBC TV 1971–84; memb: Cncl Open Univ 1972–84, Cncl Educnl Technol 1972–84, Advsy Cncl for Adult and Continuing Educn 1979–83; chm: UDACE (Unit for Devpt of Adult Continuing Educn) 1984–91, Nat Cncl for Educnl Technol 1985–91; memb: Open Univ Visiting Ctee 1987–92, Open Coll Cncl 1987–89, RTS, Assoc for Sci Educn, Marlow Soc; FRSA 1988; *Publications* Science and the Builder, Mathematics Miscellany; *Recreations* foreign travel; *Style—* Dr Donald Grattan, CBE; ✉ Delabole, Gossmore Close, Marlow, Bucks SL7 1QG (☎ 01628 473571)

GRATTAN, Prof Kenneth Thomas Victor; s of William Grattan (d 1983), and Sarah Jane Grattan (d 1978); *b* 9 Dec 1953; *Educ* Watt's Endowed Sch Lurgan Co Armagh, Queen's Univ Belfast (BSc, Dunville Scholar, PhD), City Univ (DSc); *m* 28 Sept 1979, Lesley Sharon, da of Robert George Allen; *Career* postdoctoral research asst Dept of Physics Imperial Coll of Sci and Tech London 1978–83; City Univ London: lectr in measurement and instrumentation 1983–87, sr lectr 1987–88, reader 1988–91, prof of measurement and instrumentation 1991–, head Dept of Electrical, Electronic & Information Engrg 1991–; Liveryman Worshipful Co of Scientific Instrument Makers 1995; FInstP 1992 (memb 1984), FIEE 1993 (memb 1985), FInstMC 1995 (memb 1986, Callendar Medal 1992); *Books* Concise Encyclopedia of Measurement and Instrumentation (with L Finkelstein, 1994), Optical Fiber Sensor Technology (with B T Meggitt, 1995), Fiber Optic Fluorescence Thermometry (with Z Y Zhang, 1995); *Recreations* philately, travel, church affairs; *Style—* Prof Kenneth Grattan; ✉ Department of Electrical, Electronic & Information Engineering, City University, Northampton Square, London EC1V 0HB (☎ 0171 477 8120, fax 0171 477 8121)

GRATWICK, John; OBE (1978); s of Percival John Gratwick (d 1957), of Brands Hatch Place, Fawkham, Kent, and Kathleen Mary, *née* Lunnon (d 1970); *b* 23 April 1918; *Educ* Cranbrook, Imperial Coll London (BSc Eng); *m* 14 Feb 1944, Ellen Violet, da of W H Wright (d 1942), of Coventry, Warwicks; 2 s (John Michael b 1948, Christopher Andrew b 1950), 2 da (Susan Anne b 1953, Jennifer Jane b 1955); *Career* asst prodn mangr Armstrong Siddeley Motors Ltd 1941–45; Urwick Orr & Partners Ltd: joined 1945, dir 1959, md 1968, vice chm 1971–72; vice chm: Lake & Elliot Ltd 1971–85, George Bassett Holdings plc 1977–80; dir: R Kelvin Watson Ltd 1976–86, The Export Finance Co Ltd 1984–89, New Law Publishing Co plc 1993–; chm: Empire Stores Group plc 1973–90, Guild Sound & Vision Ltd 1976–85, Lovat Enterprise Fund Ltd 1980–88; chm Clothing

Indust Econ Devpt Ctee 1985–90 (memb 1967–90); ret 1990; dir Bd of Fin Guildford Diocese; memb: Senate of Univ of London 1967–95 (memb Ct 1987–95), MMC 1969–76, Bd of CAA 1972–75; FCGI, CEng, MIMechE, CIMgt; *Recreations* golf, sailing, photography, philately; *Clubs* City Livery, Wentworth; *Style*— John Gratwick, Esq, OBE

GRAVES, 9 Baron (I 1794); Evelyn Paget Graves; o s of Alweyn Montagu Graves (d 1956), and Kathleen Eleanor Cowle, *née* Priest (d 1974); suc his kinsman, 8 Baron Graves 1994; *b* 17 May 1926; *m* 13 March 1957, Marjorie Ann, OAM (1992), da of late Dr Sidney Ernest Holder, of Wallingford, Berks: 2 s (Hon Timothy Evelyn b 27 March 1960, Hon Simon Paget b 29 May 1963), 2 da (Hon Wendy Susan b 9 July 1958, Hon Philippa Ann b 14 Feb 1962); *Heir* s, Hon Timothy Evelyn Graves b 27 March 1960; *Style*— The Rt Hon the Lord Graves; ✉ Woodlands, 405 Mole Creek Road, Deloraine, Tasmania, Australia (☎ (03)6362 2009)

GRAVES, Francis Charles; OBE (1983), DL (West Midlands 1982); s of Capt Jack Graves (d 1942), of Whitby, Yorkshire, and Lily, *née* Porter (d 1980); *b* 9 June 1929; *Educ* Whitby GS, Birmingham Coll of Technol (now Aston Univ), Coll of Estate Mgmnt London; *m* 24 Nov 1951, Phyllis May, da of Abraham Arthur Woolhouse (d 1940), of Birmingham; 1 s (Richard John Charles b 22 March 1956), 1 da (Helen Margaret b 28 June 1953); *Career* Capt RE 1953–56; chartered quantity surveyor; articled pupil Maxwell Harrison & Ptnrs 1948–52, asst surveyor Wilfred Hiles & Son 1952–53, chm and ptnr Francis C Graves & Ptnrs 1956–; chm: Midlands Cable Communications Ltd 1988–94, Midlands Residential Corporation Ltd 1988–, The Ironbridge (Telford) Heritage Foundation Ltd 1991–; dir: Golf Fund PLC 1989–93, Midlands Electricity plc 1990–, Beeches Homes Ltd; West Midlands RICS 1960–: chm Junior Organisation Branch Ctee 1960–61, chm Quantity Surveyors Branch Ctee 1969–71, chm Branch Ctee 1973–74, nat pres Quantity Surveyors Div 1980–81; memb Cncl: Royal Soc of Health 1969–75, Birmingham Engrg and Bldg Centre 1969–83, Univ of Birmingham 1989–; project controller construction NEC Birmingham 1972–76 (project controller extensions 1978–90), memb W Midlands Economic Planning Cncl 1975–79; chm: Building Ind Gp W Midlands 1976–80, NEDO report Construction for Industrial Recovery 1977–78; dir Birmingham Hippodrome Theatre Tst 1979–; memb: Redditch Development Corp 1981–85, PSA Advsy Bd 1981–85; pres Birmingham Chamber of Indust and Commerce 1985–86 (memb 1977–, vice pres 1983–85), memb Home Office Prison Bldg Bd 1987–; chm South Birmingham Health Authy 1991–93; memb Bd Cmmn for the New Towns 1992–; High Sheriff Co of West Midlands 1988–89; Freeman City of London, Liveryman Worshipful Co of Paviors 1977; FRICS 1961, FRSH 1965, FCIOB 1980; *Recreations* sport generally, cricket (memb Ctee Warwicks CCC), golf, football (vice pres Aston Villa FC), gardening, travelling; *Style*— Francis Graves, Esq, OBE, DL; ✉ Aldersyde, Broad Lane, Tanworth in Arden, Solihull, W Midlands B94 5DY (☎ 01564 742324); 14 The Square, Broad Street, Edgbaston, Birmingham B15 1TW (☎ 0121 603 9000, fax 0121 643 9190, telex 338024)

GRAVES, Prof Norman John; s of George Alfred Graves (d 1977), of Worthing, Sussex, and Andrée Adèle Céline, *née* Carrel (d 1986); *b* 28 Jan 1925; *Educ* Highbury County Sch, LSE, Univ of London (BSc, MA, PhD); *m* 28 July 1950, Mireille Camille, da of Camille Joseph Dourguin, Croix de Guerre, of Saint Rémy de Provence (d 1991); 1 s (Francis Alan b 26 Feb 1954), 1 da (Hélène Monica (Mrs Scott) (twin) b 26 Feb 1954); *Career* school teacher 1950–60, lectr in educn Univ of Liverpool 1961–63, prof (formerly sr lectr, reader) Inst of Educn Univ of London 1963–, prof and pro dir Inst of Educn 1984–90; pres Geographical Assoc 1979, chm World Educn Fellowship 1985–90; FRGS (awarded Victoria Medal 1993); *Books* Geography in Secondary Education (1970), Geography in Education (1975–84), Curriculum Planning in Geography (1979), The Educational Crisis (1988), New UNESCO Source Book for Geography Teaching (ed, 1982), Initial Teacher Education: Politics and Progress (ed, 1990), Learner-Managed-Learning: Practice, Theory and Policy (ed, 1993); *Recreations* walking, gardening, decorating; *Style*— Prof Norman Graves; ✉ Institute of Education, University of London, 20 Bedford Way, London WC1H OAL (☎ 0171 580 1122, fax 0171 612 6126, e-mail gnjseen@ioe.ac.uk)

GRAVES, Rev Dr Peter Charles; s of Walter Graves, and Eileen, *née* Weir; *b* 23 March 1943; *Educ* Eltham Green Sch, Handsworth Theol Coll Birmingham, Union Theol Seminary Richmond Virginia USA (ThM, DMin), Garnet Coll Univ of London (CertEd); *m* 17 July 1976, Patricia Mary, *née* Campbell; 2 s (Matthew Peter b 31 Oct 1978, Luke Daniel b 3 Aug 1980), 1 da (Eleanor Ruth b 12 July 1982); *Career* Methodist min Enfield Circuit (Goffs Oak and St John) 1968–69, Methodist min Highgate Circuit (Holly Park) and chm Highgate Counselling Centre 1969–72, chaplain and assoc lectr Enfield Coll of Technol 1969–72, sr lectr and head of student welfare Middx Poly 1977–79 (chaplain and lectr 1972–77); min: Sutton Circuit (Epsom) 1979–89, N Shields and Whitley Bay Circuit (Cullercoats) 1989–95; supt min Methodist Central Hall Westminster 1995–; tutor: N Eastern Ordination Course 1990–94, Wesley Study Centre Durham 1991–95; ldr Methodist Parly Fellowship 1995–; Freeman City of London; *Recreations* travel, theatre, reading, family life; *Style*— The Rev Dr Peter Graves; ✉ Methodist Central Hall, Storey's Gate, Westminster, London SW1H 9NH (☎ 0171 222 8010, fax 0171 222 3392)

GRAVES, Richard Perceval; s of John Tiarks Ranke Graves (d 1980), of Amesbury, and Mary, *née* Wickens; *Educ* Charterhouse, St John's Coll Oxford (MA); *m* 1, 1970 (m dis 1988), Anne Katharine, da of Richard Lewis Fortescue; 2 s (David John Perceval b 21 Aug 1972, Philip MacCartney b 26 March 1974), 1 da (Lucia Mary b 17 Jan 1977); m 2, 1995, Elizabeth Richmond, da of Cdr Michael William Richmond Nicholas; *Career* writer; temp teaching posts: Arnold Lodge Prep Sch 1968, Harrow 1969; teacher: Holme Grange Prep Sch 1969–71, Ellesmere Coll 1971–73; memb: Whittington Parish Cncl, Oswestry Borough Cncl 1976–83, Shropshire Community Health Cncl 1987–91; memb Soc of Authors; *Books* Lawrence of Arabia and his World (1976), A E Housman - The Scholar-Poet (1980), The Brothers Powys (1983), Robert Graves - The Assault Heroic 1895–1926 (1986), Robert Graves - The Years with Laura 1926–1940 (1990), Richard Hughes (1994), Robert Graves and the White Goddess 1940–1985 (1995); *Recreations* reading, walking, watching films, talking to strangers in pubs; *Clubs* Salop; *Style*— Richard Graves, Esq; ✉ Brook House, Ballygarvan, Co Cork, Eire (☎ 00 353 21 888434, fax 00 353 21 888510); c/o Rachel Calder, Tessa Sayle Agency, 11 Jubilee Place, London SW3 3TE (☎ 0171 823 3883, fax 0171 823 3363)

GRAVES, Rodney Michael; s of Brian William Graves (d 1971), of Surrey, and Helen, *née* O'Brien (d 1986); *b* 13 Jan 1941; *Educ* Downside, Pembroke Coll Cambridge (MA, Boxing blue); *m* 1 (m dis 1984); 1 s (Julian Philip David b Sept 1966); m 2, July 1993, Elisabeth Kay Coleman, OBE; *Career* articled clerk Cooper Brothers 1963–69; ptnr Singleton Fabian Derbyshire & Co 1969–74, ptnr Binder Hamlyn (following merger) 1974–96 (sr specialist and corp fin ptnr, dir mgmnt consultancy); memb Exec Ctee CISCO; dir John Mansfield Group plc 1994–; dir and memb Cncl The Downside Settlement 1991–; Liveryman Worshipful Co of Tylers and Bricklayers; FCA; *Recreations* travel, bridge, horse-racing, dealing on the stockmarket, gardening, bonfires; *Clubs* Hawks; *Style*— Rodney Graves, Esq; ✉ Tudor Lodge, Leicester Road, Hale, Cheshire WA15 9PS

GRAVESTOCK, Peter Stanley; s of Herbert Stanley Gravestock (d 1993), of West Bromwich, W Midlands, and Phyllis Gwendoline, *née* Bye (d 1995); *b* 6 June 1946; *Educ* West Bromwich GS; *m* 9 Dec 1973, Cynthia Anne, da of Maj Philip John Radford (d 1993), of Walsall, W Midlands; 1 da (Elisabeth b 1977); *Career* sr lectr West Bromwich Coll of Commerce and Technol 1971–79 (lectr 1967–71), fndr ptnr Gravestock and Owen 1974–95, dir G & O Insurance Services Ltd 1995–; lectr in taxation; pres Assoc of Taxation Technicians; memb Cncl: Chartered Inst of Taxation, Assoc of Taxation Technicians; FCA 1967, FTII 1978, ATT 1990; *Books* Tolleys Guide to Self Assessment, Tolleys Taxwise (jtly, published annually); *Recreations* travelling, walking, reading; *Clubs* National Trust; *Style*— Peter Gravestock, Esq; ✉ 2 Grasmere Ave, Little Aston, nr Lichfield, Staffs (☎ 0121 353 5482); G & O Insurance Services Ltd, 75 New Road, Willenhall, W Midlands (☎ 01902 636111, fax 01902 606925, car 0831 552377)

GRAY, Alasdair James; s of Alex Gray (d 1973), and Mary, *née* Fleming (d 1952); *b* 28 Dec 1934; *Educ* Whitehill Secdy Sch, Glasgow Sch of Art (BA); *m* 1, 1960, Irge Sørensen; 1 s (Andrew); m 2, 1991, Morag McAlpine; *Career* pt/t art teacher and muralist 1958–62, theatrical scene painter Pavilion Vaudeville and Glasgow Citizens' Theatre 1963–64, painter and playwright 1964–76, artist recorder Peoples' Palace Glasgow (local history museum) 1977, writer in res Univ of Glasgow 1977–80, novelist and playwright 1981–; murals in: Scottish USSR Friendship Soc, Greenfedd Church of Scotland, Belleisle Street Synagogue Glasgow, Palacerigg Nature Reserve, Abbots House History Museum Dunfermline 1995; memb Soc of Authors; *Awards* for writing incl: Scottish Arts Cncl, Saltire Soc, Times, Guardian 1993, Whitbread 1993; *Books* Lanark - A Life in Four Books (1981), Unlikely Stories Mostly (1983), Janine (1984), The Fall of Kelvin Walker (1985), Lean Tales (with James Kelman and Agnes Owen, 1985), Saltire Self Portrait (1988), Old Negatives - 4 Verse Sequences (1989), Something Leather (1990), McGrotty and Ludmilla (1990), Why Scots Should Rule Scotland (1992), Poor Things (1992), Ten Tales Tall and True (1993), A History Maker (1994), Mavis Belfrage and Four Shorter Stories (1996); *Recreations* my work; *Style*— Alasdair Gray, Esq; ✉ c/o Toby Eadie Associates, 3 Floor, Orme Court, London W2 4RL

GRAY, Alison Vaudine; da of Ian Gray (md and chief exec Welsh Devpt Agency, d 1983), of Edinburgh, and Vaudine Angela, *née* Harrison-Ainsworth; *b* 8 Feb 1955; *Educ* Howell's Sch Llandaff, Bedford HS, Trevelyan Coll Durham (BA Law); *Career* articled clerk Edward Lewis Possart and Co Slrs Cardiff 1978–80, admitted slr 1980, commercial slr in private practice 1980–84, legal advsr/dep co sec Soc of West End Theatre (now Soc of London Theatre) and Theatrical Mgmnt Assoc 1984–87, ptnr in private practice specialising in entertainment/media law 1988–93, gen sec Writers' Guild of GB 1993–; memb: Law Soc, Slrs' Euro Gp; *Recreations* reading, film, theatre, opera, Francophile, swimming; *Clubs* Groucho; *Style*— Miss Alison Gray; ✉ The Writers' Guild of Great Britain, 430 Edgware Road, London W2 1EH (☎ 0171 723 8074, fax 0171 706 2413)

GRAY, Alistair William; s of John Lambert Gray (d 1980), of St Andrews, and Agnes Roberts, *née* Pow; *b* 6 Sept 1948; *Educ* The Madras Coll St Andrews Fife, Univ of Edinburgh (MA); *m* 7 April 1972, Sheila Elizabeth, da of Walter Harold Rose, of Preston, Lancs; 2 da (Kathryn Julia b 1976, Nicola Elizabeth b 1978); *Career* asst mill mangr Wiggins Teape Ltd 1970–72, divnl mangr Unilever Ltd 1972–78, exec dir John Wood Group plc 1978–81, dir strategic mgmnt consltg Arthur Young 1982–87, dir of strategy PA Consulting Group 1987–91 (assoc 1991–), fndr own co Genesis Consulting 1991–; non-exec dir Highland Distilleries plc 1992; chm: Scottish Sport - World Class Scottish Sports Cncl, Devpt Ctee Euro Hockey Fedn (memb Exec); memb GB Olympic Hockey Bd; visiting lectr Univ of Strathclyde, pres Scottish Hockey Union; Burgess of Aberdeen 1980; FInstM, ACMA, MInstD, MIMgt, FIMC, MRSH; *Books* The Managers Handbook (1986); *Recreations* hockey, golf, squash; *Clubs* Western Hockey, New Golf (St Andrews), Royal Northern and Univ; *Style*— Alistair Gray, Esq; ✉ Genesis Consulting, The Pottery, Saltoun Lane, 24 Ruthven Street, Glasgow G12 9BT (☎ 0141 337 3778)

GRAY, Master of; Hon Andrew Godfrey Diarmid Stuart Campbell-Gray; Master of Gray; s and h of 22 Lord Gray; *b* 3 Sept 1964; *Educ* Trinity Coll Glenalmond, Univ of Exeter (BA); *m* 11 Dec 1993, Hon Lucy Elton, yst da of 2 Baron Elton, TD; *Style*— The Master of Gray

GRAY, 22 Lord (S 1445); Angus Diarmid Ian Campbell-Gray; s of Maj the Hon Lindsay Stuart Campbell-Gray, Master of Gray, MC (d 1945), and Doreen, *née* Tubbs (d 1948); suc grandmother, Lady Gray, 21 holder of the title 1946; *b* 3 July 1931; *Educ* Eton; *m* 1, 1959, Patricia Margaret (d 1987), da of Capt Philip Alexander (d 1953, gs of 3 Earl of Caledon), of Lismore, Co Waterford, Ireland; 1 s, 3 da; m 2, 12 Aug 1994, Cecilia Wilfrida, *née* Dimsdale, widow of Paul Williams; *Heir* s, The Master of Gray; *Clubs* Carlton, MCC; *Style*— The Rt Hon the Lord Gray; ✉ Airds Bay House, Taynuilt, Argyll PA35 1JR

GRAY, Charles Antony St John; QC (1984); s of Charles Gray (d 1982), and Catherine, *née* Hughes (d 1986); *b* 6 July 1942; *Educ* Winchester, Trinity Coll Oxford (MA); *m* 1, 7 Sept 1967 (m dis 1990), Rosalind Macleod, da of Capt R F Whinney, DSO, RN, of Lymington, Hants; 1 s (Alexander Charles Macleod b 14 Dec 1974), 1 da (Anya Catherine Macleod b 2 Nov 1972); m 2, 4 May 1995, Susan, da of late Maj Michael Eveleigh, and formerly w of Hon Sir John Jacob Astor, MBE, ERD, DL; *Career* called to the Bar Lincoln's Inn 1966, in practice London, recorder 1990, bencher Lincoln's Inn 1991; *Recreations* tennis, skiing, walking; *Clubs* Brooks's; *Style*— Charles Gray, Esq, QC; ✉ 4 Priory Walk, London SW10 9SP (☎ 0171 373 9550); 5 Raymond Buildings, Gray's Inn, London WC1R 5BP (☎ 0171 242 2902, fax 0171 831 2686)

GRAY, Charles Donald Marshall; s of Capt Donald Gray, RE (d 1975), of Bournemouth, and Maude Elizabeth Gray; *b* 29 Aug 1928; *Career* actor; stage debut Regents Park Open Air Theatre; *Theatre* roles incl: Achilles in Troilus and Cressida, Bolingbroke in Richard II; West End plays incl: Expresso Bongo, Everything in the Garden, Poor Bitos, The Philanthropist; Broadway: Right Honourable Gentlemen, Kean, Poor Bitos; *Television* numerous credits incl: Hay Fever, The Moon and Sixpence, Ross, Richard II, Julius Caesar, An Englishman Abroad, Comedy of Errors, Sherlock Holmes, Bergerac, Small World, Blind Justice, Absolute Hell, Scarlett, Madson; *Films* incl: You Only Live Twice, The Man Outside, The Night of the Generals, Secret War of Harry Frigg, The Devil Rides Out, The Executioner, Cromwell, Diamonds are Forever, The Beast Must Die, The Rocky Horror Picture Show, The Seven Per Cent Solution, Seven Nights in Japan, The Silver Bears, The Legacy, The Mirror Crack'd, Shock Treatment, The Jigsaw Man; *Style*— Charles Gray, Esq; ✉ c/o London Management, 235–241 Regent St, London W1A 2JT (☎ 0171 493 1610)

GRAY, Charles Ireland; CBE (1994), JP; s of Timothy Gray (d 1971), and Janet McIntosh, *née* Brown (d 1968); *b* 25 Jan 1929; *Educ* Coatbridge HS; *m* 14 June 1952, Catherine Creighton, da of James Gray; 3 s (Donald b 22 March 1953, James b 30 Sept 1955, Charles b 17 Sept 1958), 2 da (Rosemary b 12 July 1960, Jacqueline b 2 Oct 1964); *Career* served BR 40 years, ret; rep Chryston Lanark CC until 1974, first Lab chm Lanark's Ninth Dist Cncl, regnl memb Chryston/Kelvin Valley 1974, first vice convener Strathclyde (former first chm Planning and Devpt Ctee), currently convener Euro Ctee N Lanark Cncl; memb Bd Clydeport Authy 1974–85, former memb Sec of State's Advsy Ctee for Travelling People, chm Scottish National Housing and Town Planning Cncl 1975–85, vice chm East Kilbride Devpt Corp 1974–86 (vice chm Planning Exchange 1976–86), chm Local Govt Int Bureau (UK) 1992–, vice chm Bureau of Cncl Euro Municipalities and Regions (CEMR), ldr and vice pres UK Delgn to Euro-Ctee of Regions 1994–; memb Bd: Scot Devpt Agency 1975–85, SECC 1986–92; COSLA: ldr Lab Gp 1988, pres 1992–94; memb: Single Market Ctee Scottish Econ Cncl 1989, Euro Consultative Cncl Local and Regnl Authys 1989; FRSA; *Recreations* politics, music and reading; *Style*— Charles Gray, Esq, CBE, JP; ✉ 9 Moray Place, Chryston, Glasgow G69 (☎ 0141 779 2962, fax 0141 779 3142); North Lanark Council, Civic Centre, Motherwell ML1 1TW (☎ 01698 302222, fax 01698 275125)

GRAY, Christopher Antony (Chris); s of William Gray, of Barnlea, Dunbar, Scotland, and Sheila Isabel, *née* Brown; *b* 11 July 1960; *Educ* Gordonstoun, Edinburgh Acad, Univ of Edinburgh (BDS); *m* Judith Marie, *née* Bunten; 2 s (Jamie b 28 Oct 1991, Nicholas b 2 Feb 1995); *Career* rugby union player; Edinburgh Academicals 1978–83; Nottingham 1985– (capt 1995–96): debut in Co Championship Final for Notts/Lincs/Derby v Middx; Anglo-Scots 1986–91 (capt 1987); Scotland: 5 B caps 1986–88, full debut v Wales 1989, 22 caps at lock forward, scored 3 tries, Grand Slam winners 1990, World Cup 1991 (fourth); also represented: Co-optimists, Penguins, Barbarians, Edinburgh Acads, Steele Bodgers XV; formerly assoc dental practice Derby, currently ptnr dental practice Nottingham; *Recreations* golf, reading, tennis; *Style—* Chris Gray, Esq; ✉ Wollaton Dental Care, 152 Bramcote Lane, Wollaton, Nottingham NG8 2QP (☎ 0115 928 3253, fax 0115 928 3253)

GRAY, David Francis; s of John Morris Gray (d 1975), and Alice Kathleen, *née* Winsor (d 1982); *b* 18 May 1936; *Educ* Rugby, Trinity Coll Oxford (MA); *m* 11 Sept 1970, Rosemary Alison Elizabeth, da of Horace William Parker (d 1987); 2 s (James b 1975, Oliver b 1981), 1 da (Fiona b 1977); *Career* admitted slr 1960; articled clerk Coward Chance 1957–60; slr: Coward Chance 1960–62, Bischoff & Co 1962–63; ptnr: Lovell White & King 1966–88 (slr 1963–65), Lovell White Durrant 1988–93; sec Fieldings Investment Management Limited 1993–; memb Securities Inst asst treas Int Bar Assoc 1988–94 (memb 1972–), tstee Int Bar Assoc Educnl Tst 1987–, hon auditor Law Soc 1988–90 (memb 1960–); City of London Slrs' Co: asst to the Ct 1974–, Master 1984–85, Almoner 1988–; vice pres, jt sec and chm ctee City of London Law Soc 1985–88; memb Mgmnt Ctee City Slrs' Educnl Tst, tstee Trinity Coll Oxford Soc (hon sec 1979–88); Liveryman: Worshipful Co of Slrs, Worshipful Co of Glaziers and Painters of Glass (asst to the Ct 1994–); *Recreations* skiing, golf, tennis, swimming; *Clubs* Ski of GB, Liphook Golf; *Style—* David Gray, Esq; ✉ Fieldings Investment Management Limited, Founders Hall, 6 Kinghorn Street, London EC1A 7HT (☎ 0171 606 7711, fax 0171 606 4313)

GRAY, David John; s of James Vincent Gray (d 1989), of Liverpool, and Jeanne Winifred Veronica, *née* Lamb; *b* 2 March 1959; *Educ* Liverpool Bluecoat Sch, Univ of Bristol (BA); *m* 18 April 1962, Hilary Jane Rosemary, *née* Fletcher; 1 da (Olivia Scarlet b 22 Aug 1994); *Career* display sales exec Centaur Communications 1984–85, account mangr Pilgrim Communications 1985–87, planning dir Design in Action until 1996 (joined 1987); *Recreations* mountaineering, cookery; *Style—* David Gray, Esq

GRAY, Dr Denis Everett; CBE (1983, MBE 1972), JP (Solihull 1962–); s of late Charles Norman Gray, and Kathleen Alexandra, *née* Roberts; *b* 25 June 1926; *Educ* Bablake Sch Coventry, Univ of Birmingham (BA), Univ of London, Univ of Manchester (PhD); *m* 1949, Barbara Joyce, da of Edgar Ewart Kesterton (d 1970); *Career* sr lectr Univ of Birmingham 1957–84, chm of Bench 1971–75; chm: Jt Negotiating Ctees for Justices' Clerks and Magistrates Courts Staff 1978–86, Central Cncl of Magistrates' Courts Ctees 1980–86; memb Magistrates' Courts Rule Ctee 1982–86; *Books* Spencer Perceval - The Evangelical Prime Minister (1963); *Recreations* travel, church architecture, reading; *Style—* Dr Denis Gray, CBE, JP; ✉ 11 Brueton Ave, Solihull, West Midlands (☎ 0121 705 2935)

GRAY, (John) Desmond; s of Abraham Gray (d 1985), of Rostrevor, Co Down, and Olivia, *née* Miller (d 1984); *b* 19 Aug 1937; *Educ* Portora Royal Sch, Queen's Univ (NI rowing crew Cwlth Games 1958), Open Univ (BA); *m* 1986, Angela (Jill) Gilmour; 1 step da (Nicola Joy b 1969), 1 step s (Lt John Ferguson, RN b 1971); *Career* games coach Methodist Coll Belfast 1959–60, head of mathematics and housemaster Brympton Sch Somerset 1960–76; Terrington Hall Sch: dep headmaster 1976–86, headmaster 1986–; memb: IAPS 1980–, NAHT 1988–; *Recreations* sailing, walking, travelling; *Clubs* Yorkshire RFU; *Style—* Desmond Gray, Esq; ✉ Terrington Hall Trust, Terrington, York YO6 4PR (☎ 01653 648227, fax 01653 648458)

GRAY, Rev Canon Dr Donald Clifford; TD (1970); s of Henry Hackett Gray (d 1959), of Manchester, and Constance Muriel, *née* Bullock; *b* 21 July 1930; *Educ* Newton Heath Tech HS Manchester, King's Coll London (AKC), Univ of Liverpool (MPhil), Univ of Manchester (PhD); *m* 1955, Joyce, da of Walter Mills Jackson (d 1979), of Oldham; 1 s (Timothy), 2 da (Clare, Alison); *Career* curate Leigh Parish Church 1956–60, chaplain TA & TAVR 1958–77, vicar St Peter Westleigh 1960–67, vicar of All Saints' Elton 1967–74, rector of Liverpool 1974–87, hon chaplain to HM The Queen 1974–77, proctor in convocation 1964–74 and 1980–87, rural dean of Liverpool 1975–81, canon Diocesan of Liverpool 1982–87, chaplain to HM The Queen 1982–, canon of Westminster, rector of St Margaret's Westminster Abbey and chaplain to the Speaker of the House of Commons 1987–; memb Liturgical Cmmn 1968–86; chm: Soc for Liturgical Study 1978–84, Jt Liturgical Gp 1989–96 (memb 1969–, sec 1980–89), Alcuin Club 1987–; pres Societas Liturgica 1987–89; memb Cathedrals' Fabric Cmmn for England 1991–96; FRHistS; ChStJ 1990 (OStJ 1982); *Books* Earth and Altar (1986), Chaplain to Mr Speaker (1991), Ronald Jasper, His Life, His Work and the ASB (1997); contrib: Worship and the Child (1975), Getting the Liturgy Right (1982), Liturgy Reshaped (1982), Nurturing Children in Communion (1985), The Renewal of Common Prayer (1993), Children at the Table (1995); ed: Holy Week Services (1983), The Word in Season (1988); *Recreations* watching cricket, reading modern poetry; *Clubs* Liverpool Artists', Liverpool Raquets; *Style—* The Rev Canon Dr Donald Gray, TD; ✉ 1 Little Cloister, Westminster Abbey, London SW1P 3PL (☎ 0171 222 4027, fax 0171 233 2072); 3 Barn Hill Mews, Stamford, Lincs PE9 2GN (☎ 01780 765024)

GRAY, Prof Douglas; s of Emmerson Walton Gray, and Daisy Gray; *b* 17 Feb 1930; *Educ* Wellington Coll NZ, Victoria Univ of Wellington (MA), Univ of Oxford (MA); *m* 3 Sept 1959, Judith Claire, da of Percy Campbell; 1 s (Nicholas b 1961); *Career* asst lectr Victoria Univ of Wellington 1953–54; Univ of Oxford: lectr in English Pembroke and Lincoln Colls 1956–61, fell in English Pembroke Coll 1961–80 (emeritus fell 1980–), univ lectr in English language 1976–80, JRR Tolkien prof of English literature and language 1980–, professorial fell Lady Margaret Hall 1980–; Hon LitD Victoria Univ of Wellington 1995; FBA 1989; *Books* Themes & Images in the Medieval English Religious Lyric (1972), A Selection of Religious Lyrics (1975), Robert Henryson (1979), The Oxford Book of Late Medieval Verse and Prose (1985); *Style—* Prof Douglas Gray, FBA; ✉ Lady Margaret Hall, Oxford OX2 6QA (☎ 01865 274300)

GRAY, Dulcie Winifred Catherine (Mrs Michael Denison); CBE (1983); da of Arnold Savage Bailey, CBE (d 1935), of Kuala Lumpur, and Kate Edith, *née* Clulow-Gray (d 1942); *b* 20 Nov 1920; *Educ* St Anthony's Wallingford Oxfordshire, Luckley Wokingham Berks, Leeson House Langton Matravers Dorset, St Mary's Kuala Lumpur; *m* 29 April 1939, (John) Michael Denison, CBE, *qv*, s of Gilbert Dixon Denison (d 1959); *Career* actress and author 1939–; memb exec Cncl and Fin Ctee Actors' Charitable Tst; FLS, FRSA; *Theatre* first part Sorel in Hay Fever at His Majesty's Aberdeen; more than 50 plays in West End incl: Brighton Rock, Candida, Where Angels Fear to Tread, Bedroom Farce, School for Scandal, Tartuffe; most recently An Ideal Husband (Theatre Royal Haymarket, Barrymore Theatre NY) 1996; *Television* incl: The Governess, The Letter, Beautiful for Ever, Three Up Two Down, Kate Harvey in Howards' Way (6 years, BBC); *Books* 24 published books incl: Baby Face, Murder in Mind, The Murder of Love, Butterflies on My Mind (winner Times Educnl Supplement Sr Info Award 1978), The Glanville Women, Looking Forward - Looking Back (autobiography); *Recreations* swimming, butterflies; *Clubs* The Lansdowne; *Style—* Miss Dulcie Gray, CBE; ✉ Shardeloes, Amersham, Bucks, HP7 0RL; c/o Barry Burnett Organisation Ltd, Suite 42–43, Grafton House, 2–3 Golden Square, London W1 (☎ 0171 437 7048/9, fax 0171 734 6118)

GRAY, Edward Earl; s of Edward Earl Gray (d 1969), of Shoreham-by-Sea, W Sussex, and Marie Cicelia Loftus, *née* Jones; *b* 24 Oct 1933; *Educ* Shoreham GS; *m* Brenda Mary, da of John Lewis; 2 s (Edward Earl b 24 June 1964, Simon Lewis b 27 April 1967); *Career* Nat Serv RA 1952–54; apprenticed Gloucester Hotel Weymouth 1954–57, asst mangr trainee Hotel Angleterre Nice 1958–59; asst mangr: Royal Albion Brighton 1960–61, Great Eastern Hotel 1961–64; mangr then md Coburg Hotel London 1964–89, hotel conslt Edward Gray & Associates 1989–; past chm: London branch HCIMA, SE region Best Western Hotels and London Hotel Mangrs' Club; fndr and past chm West London branch Hotel and Catering Trg Bd; Freeman City of London 1979; FHCIMA 1971, MI 1979, memb Reunion des Gastronomes 1980; *Recreations* practising Christian; *Clubs* MCC; *Style—* Edward Gray, Esq; ✉ Edward Gray & Associates, 50 Westbourne Gardens, London W2 5NS (☎ 0171 221 9514, fax 0171 792 3177)

GRAY, (Edna) Eileen Mary; OBE (1978); da of William Thomas Greenway (d 1957), of Reigate, Surrey, and Alice Evelyn Mary, *née* Jenkins (d 1983); *b* 25 April 1920; *Educ* St Saviour's and St Olave's GS for Girls London; *m* 24 Aug 1946, Walter Herbert Gray, s of Walter James Gray (d 1947), of London; 1 s (John Andrew b 25 Nov 1947); *Career* inspectorate fighting vehicles 1940–45; invited to ride abroad Br women's cycling team 1946, int del Paris 1957, organiser first int competition for women in UK 1957, campaigner for int recognition of women in cycling and team mangr inaugural women's world championship 1958, memb Exec Ctee Br Cycling Fedn 1958–87 (chm Fin Ctee, pres), elected to Fedn International Amateur de Cyclism 1977, vice pres BOA 1992– (vice chm 1988–92), chm Br Sports Forum 1991, memb Manchester Olympic Bid Ctee 1991, dep cmdt British Olympic Team 1992; int official Cwlth Games Edmonton and Brisbane, special Gold award Min of Educn Taiwan; tstee London Marathon Tst; chm London Youth Games; Royal Borough Kingston-upon-Thames: cncllr 1982–, pres Kingston Sports Cncl, Mayor 1990–91; awarded Olympic Order IOC 1993; Freeman City of London 1987, Grandmaster Hon Fraternity Ancient Freemasons (women) and tstee of it's charity; *Style—* Mrs Eileen Gray, OBE; ✉ 129 Grand Ave, Surbiton, Surrey KT5 9HY (☎ 0181 399 0068)

GRAY, George Bovill Rennie; OBE (1991), DL (E Lothian 1984); s of John Rennie Gray (d 1937), of Smeaton-Hepburn, E Lothian, and Margaret, *née* Bovill (d 1958); *b* 5 March 1920; *Educ* Clayesmore Iwerne Minster, E of Scotland Coll of Agric; *m* 30 Jan 1946, Anne Constance, da of John Robert Dale, of Auldhame, N Berwick; 4 s (John b Dec 1946, Kenneth b May 1948, Duncan b Sept 1949, Quentin b Feb 1954), 2 da (Ruth b June 1952, Joanna b Sept 1956); *Career* chm: G B R Gray Ltd (farmers) 1952–, Hanover (Scotland) Housing Association Ltd 1991–95; dir Moredun Scientific Ltd 1989–; convenor Cereals Ctee NFU Scot 1955–58; dir: Animal Diseases Res Assoc Moredun 1958–93, Scottish Soc for Res in Plant Breeding 1957–87; memb: Pig Indust Devpt Authy 1958–68, Agric and Vet Sub-ctee of UGC 1972–82, Scottish Advsy Bd Br Inst of Mgmnt 1978–90; elder Church of Scotland 1952–; tstee Scottish Soc for Crop Research; memb: Boy Scout Assoc E Lothian, Cncl Garleton Div Lothian Regnl Cncl 1974–82; FIMgt 1978; *Recreations* gardening, arboriculture; *Clubs* Caledonian; *Style—* George Gray, Esq, OBE, DL; ✉ Smeaton-Hepburn, East Linton, East Lothian EH40 3DT (☎ 01620 860275)

GRAY, Dr George Gowans; *b* 21 Jan 1938; *Educ* Linlithgow Acad, Univ of Edinburgh (BSc), Univ of Cambridge (PhD); *Career* engr: Pratt & Whitney Canada 1960–63, RCA Limited Canada 1963–69; researcher Univ of Cambridge 1969–71, md Serv Div RCA Limited Sunbury-on-Thames 1974–87 (mangr 1971–74), chm Serco Group plc 1987–; FIMechE; *Publications* contrib with K L Johnson: Journal of Sound and Vibration (1972), The Institution of Mechanical Engineers Proceedings (1975); *Clubs* Oxford and Cambridge; *Style—* Dr George Gray; ✉ Serco Group plc, Serco House, Hayes Road, Southall, Middx UB2 5NJ (☎ 0181 843 2411)

GRAY, Harold James; CMG (1956); s of John William Gray (d 1930), and Amelia Francis, *née* Miller (d 1961); *b* 17 Oct 1907; *Educ* Dover County Sch, Univ of London (BSc, MSc, LLB), Gray's Inn, Harvard (MPA); *m* 1928, Katherine, da of Sydney George Starling (d 1956); 1 da (Ann); *Career* civil servant 1927–61, examiner Patent Office 1935–39, asst sec Miny of Supply 1939, Cwlth Fund Fellowship 1949–50, under sec BOT 1954, UK sr trade cmmr; econ advsr to: UK High Cmmr Aust 1954–58, S Africa 1958–60; dir: Nat Union of Mfrs 1961–65, CBI 1965–72; chm Numas Management Service Ltd 1970–74 (dir 1961–70); ret; author of various booklets on small firms in UK 1965–72; CPhys, MInstP, FRSA; *Books* Electricity in Service of Man (1949), Economic Survey of Australia (1955), Dictionary of Physics (1956), New Dictionary of Physics (1975); *Recreations* horse riding, swimming, golf; *Style—* Harold Gray, Esq, CMG; ✉ Copper Beeches, 58 Tudor Avenue, Maidstone, Kent ME14 5HJ (☎ 01672 685978)

GRAY, Henry Withers; s of Henry Withers Gray (d 1958), and Jean Allen, *née* Cross (d 1994); *b* 25 March 1943; *Educ* Rutherglen Acad, Univ of Glasgow (MD); *m* 5 July 1967, Mary Elizabeth, da of Angus Henry Shaw, BEM (d 1996), of Arbeadie Rd, Banchory, Aberdeenshire; 1 s (Stuart Henry b 1968), 2 da ((Elizabeth) Anne b 1970, Karen Louise b 1981); *Career* conslt physician in med and nuclear med 1977–; FRCP 1978, FRCPG 1984; *Style—* Henry Gray, Esq; ✉ 4 Winton Park, E Kilbride, Glasgow G75 8QW (☎ 013552 29525); The Department of Nuclear Medicine, The Royal Infirmary, Alexandra Parade, Glasgow (☎ 0141 211 4761, fax 0141 211 4386)

GRAY, Dr James Allan; s of Maj (James) Douglas Allan Gray, TD (d 1993), of Edinburgh, and Agnes Dorothy, *née* Sloan (d 1985); *b* 24 March 1935; *Educ* St Paul's, Faculty of Med Univ of Edinburgh (MB ChB); *m* 17 Sept 1960, Jennifer Margaret Newton, da of Maj Eric Newton Hunter, MC, TD, DL (d 1983), of Badachro, Westerross; 1 s (Hugh Douglas Allan b 5 March 1962), 2 da (Emma Elizabeth Dorothea b 15 Sept 1966, Alison Lucy McLullich (Mrs Holden) b 11 Nov 1967); *Career* cmmnd Flying Offr RAF, unit MO RAF Finningley Yorks 1960–62, Flt Lt OC Med Div RAF Hosp Khormaksar Beach Aden 1962–63; house surgn and physician posts Edinburgh and Middlesbrough 1959–60, house physician sr house offr and res fell posts Edinburgh 1964–67, registrar Bristol Royal Infirmary 1967–68, sr registrar Dept of Infectious Diseases Royal Free Hosp London 1968–69, conslt in communicable diseases Regnl Infectious Diseases Unit City Hosp Edinburgh 1969–95, pt/t sr lectr Dept of Med Univ of Edinburgh 1969–92 (hon sr lectr 1992–95), asst dir of med studies Edinburgh Postgrad Bd for Med 1976–84, PMO Scottish Widows Fund Edinburgh 1990– (asst PMO 1979–1990); fndr and ed Res Medica 1957–58, asst ed Journal of Infection 1979–86, numerous pubns on infection, immunisation and antimicrobial chemotherapy; FRCPE 1974, fell Royal Med Soc, sr pres Royal Med Soc 1958–59, pres Br Soc for the Study of Infection 1989–91 (vice pres 1987–89); Freeman City of London, Liveryman Worshipful Soc of Apothecaries London (Yeoman 1958); *Books* Antibacterial Drugs (jtly, 1983), Colour Guides: Infectious Diseases (jtly, 1984, 2 edn 1992); *Recreations* hill walking, pottery collecting; *Style—* Dr James Gray; ✉ St Andrews Cottage, 15 Lauder Rd, Edinburgh EH9 2EN (☎ 0131 667 4124)

GRAY, James Laird; s of John Marshall Gray (d 1957), of Glasgow, and Jessie Cameron Smith (d 1968); *b* 11 Jan 1926; *Educ* Hyndland Secdy Sch Glasgow, Univ of Glasgow (BSc); *m* 1954, Mary, da of Thomas Magee; 2 s (Thomas Alexander b 1955, John James b 1964), 1 da (Susan b 1956); *Career* apprentice Yarrow and Co Glasgow, asst engr Steam Turbine Design Dept English Electric Co Ltd (now GEC) 1946–48, Br Electricity Authy (and successors) 1948–75 (latterly head Turbine-Generator Design Branch), chief engr Generation Design and Construction South of Scotland Electricity Bd 1989–90 (mangr of Generation Design and Tech Servs 1975–89), ret 1990; Thomas Hawksley Gold Medal, James Clayton Award of IMechE; FIMechE 1960, FEng 1985; *Recreations* sailing, gardening; *Clubs* Royal Northern and Clyde Yacht; *Style*— James L Gray, Esq, FEng; ✉ Woodburn, Garelochhead, Helensburgh G84 0EG (☎ 01436 810403)

GRAY, Maj-Gen (Reginald) John; CB (1973); s of Dr Cyril Gray (d 1951), and Frances Anne, *née* Higgins (d 1953), of Higginsbrook, Trim, Co Meath; *b* 26 Nov 1916; *Educ* Ascham House Gosforth, Rossall Sch, Durham Univ; *m* 1943, Esme, da of late Maj G R G Shipp; 1 s, 1 da; *Career* served 1939–45 in India, Burma, later in NW Europe, Egypt, Malta, BAOR; Gold Staff Offr 1953, dep dir-gen AMS 1969–72, QHS 1970–73, med dir UKLF 1972–73, CMO BRCS 1974–83, dir International Generics Ltd 1974–83, Col Cmdt RAMC 1977–81; chm: RAMC Assoc 1980–88, BMA Armed Forces Ctee 1981–85; memb BMA and BAEM; hon memb St AAA and Inst of Civil Defence; FRSM, FFCM (fndr fell), FFPHM; CStJ 1971 (OStJ 1957); *Recreations* growing old reasonably gracefully; *Style*— Maj-Gen John Gray, CB; ✉ 11 Hampton Close, Wimbledon, London SW20 0RY (☎ 0181 946 7429)

GRAY, Sir John Archibald Browne; kt (1973); s of Sir Archibald Montague Henry Gray, KCVO, CBE (d 1967); *b* 30 March 1918; *Educ* Cheltenham, Clare Coll Cambridge (MA, MB, ScD); *m* 1946, Vera Kathleen, da of Charles Anthony Mares, of Highgate; 1 s, 1 da; *Career* Surgn Lt RN Pacific Fleet; physiologist; prof of physiology UCL London 1959–66, sec MRC 1968–77, memb external scientific staff MRC Marine Biological Assoc Laboratories Plymouth 1977–83; hon fell Clare Coll 1976; Hon DSc Exeter 1985; FIBiol, FRCP, FRS; *Recreations* sailing (35 ft sloop 'White Seal II'); *Clubs* Royal Cruising, Royal Plymouth Corinthian Yacht; *Style*— Sir John Gray, FRS; ✉ Seaways, Kingsway, Kingsand, Torpoint, Cornwall (☎ 01752 822745)

GRAY, John Malcolm; CBE (1996); s of Samuel Alexander Gray (d 1958), and Ellen Christina, *née* Mackay-Sim (d 1990); *b* 28 July 1934; *Educ* Strathallan Sch; *m* 1, 1966 (m dis 1979), Nicole de Fournier, da of Ellis Melville Quinn, of Tasmania; 2 da (Siobhan Laetitia Mackay b 1967, Katrina Mackay b 1970); m 2, 1984, Ursula Wee Siong Koon, da of Dato Wee Khoon Hock, of Khota Bahru, Malaysia; 1 da (Alexandra Mackay b 1985); *Career* served RAF 1952–54; Hongkong and Shanghai Banking Corporation Ltd: joined 1954, accountant Hamburg 1970–73, mangr Frankfurt 1973–75, mangr foreign exchange Hong Kong 1975–79, chief accountant 1979–81, asst gen mangr finance 1981–85, gen mangr gp finance 1985–86, exec dir finance 1986–90, dep chm 1990–92, chm and chief exec 1993–May 1996; dir: HSBC Holdings plc until 1996, Hang Seng Bank Ltd, Swire Pacific Ltd, HSBC Investment Bank Asia Holdings Ltd; memb Hong Kong Exec Cncl, chm Hong Kong Port Devpt Bd, memb Hong Kong Provisional Airport Authy; *Recreations* golf, reading; *Clubs* Hong Kong, Royal Hong Kong Golf, Shek-O, Oriental (London); *Style*— John Gray, Esq, CBE; ✉ c/o The Hongkong and Shanghai Banking Corporation Ltd, Level 34, 1 Queen's Road, Central, Hong Kong (☎ 00 852 822 1134)

GRAY, Vice Adm Sir John Michael Dudgeon; KBE (1967, OBE 1950), CB (1964); s of Col Arthur Claypon Horner Gray, OBE (d 1963), of Nayland, Suffolk, and Dorothy, *née* Denham; *b* 13 June 1913; *Educ* RNC Dartmouth; *m* 1939, Margaret Helen (d 1994), da of Arthur Purvis, of Cairo; 1 s (Michael), 1 da (Caroline); *Career* joined RN 1926, served WWII: in HMS Hermes and Spartan, with US in Anzio, with 8 Army in Italy, with French Army in France (despatches); Cdr 1947, Capt 1952, cmd HMS Lynx 1955, cmd HMS Victorious 1960, Rear Adm 1962, dir gen Trg MOD (RN) 1962–65, Vice Adm 1965, C-in-C S Atlantic and S America 1965–67; *Clubs* Naval and Military; *Style*— Vice Adm Sir John Gray, KBE, CB; (☎ 0171 352 1757)

GRAY, Sir John Walton David; KBE (1995), CMG (1986); s of Myrddin Gray (d 1943), of Llanelli, and Elsie Irene, *née* Jones (d 1983); *b* 1 Oct 1936; *Educ* Queen Elizabeth GS Devon, Blundell's Sch Tiverton Devon, Christ's Coll Cambridge (BA, MA), ME Centre Oxford, American Univ Cairo; *m* 22 Sept 1957, Anthoula, da of Nicholas Yerasimou, of Nicosia, Cyprus; 1 s (Nicholas Myrddin Christopher b 1971), 2 da (Helen Irene (Mrs Carless) b 1961, Clare Marian (Mrs Rees) b 1963); *Career* 2 Lt RASC 1954–56; Foreign Serv: joined 1962, serv MECAS 1962–63, political offr Bahrain 1964–67, FO 1967–70, Geneva 1970, UK delgn to Conf on Security and Co-operation in Euro 1973–74, head of chancery Sofia 1974–77, cnsllr Jedda 1978–81, head of dept FCO 1982–85, ambass Beirut 1985–88, UK permanent rep OECD Paris 1988–92, ambass Belgium 1992–96, ret; assoc dir IRC Consulting Group Cardiff 1996–, advsr to the Chief Exec Hyder plc 1996–; vice chm Welsh Centre for Int Affrs; vice-pres: Cardiff Business Club, Crawshay's Welsh RFC; govr Cheltenham Coll; *Recreations* watching sport, reading history, Wales; *Clubs* Royal Inst for Int Affairs, Athenaeum, Royal Cwlth Soc, Anglo-Belgian (London), Cardiff and County (Cardiff), Cercle Royal Gaulois, Cercle des Nations (Brussels), Llanelli RFC; *Style*— Sir John Gray, KBE, CMG; ✉ 35 Royal Avenue, London SW3 4QE

GRAY, Rt Rev Joseph; s of late Terence Gray, and Mary, *née* Alwill; *b* 20 Oct 1919; *Educ* St Patrick's Cavan, Oscott Coll Sutton Coldfield, Maynooth Coll, Pontifical Univ Rome (DCL); *Career* ordained RC priest 1943, vicar gen of Birmingham 1960–69, aux Bishop of Liverpool 1969–80, bishop of Shrewsbury 1980–95 (emeritus bishop of Shrewsbury 1995–); *Recreations* music, reading, travel; *Style*— The Rt Rev Joseph Gray; ✉ 99 Eleanor Rd, Birkenhead L43 7QW (☎ 0151 653 3600, fax 0151 670 0338)

GRAY, Joseph Anthony (Tony); s of Abraham Gray (d 1985), of Rostrevor, Co Down, and (Frances) Olivia, *née* Miller (d 1984); *b* 23 April 1944; *Educ* Portora Royal Sch Enniskillen, Trinity Coll Dublin (MA); *m* 15 July 1972, Amanda Susan, da of Wing Cdr D W Edmonds, OBE, DFC, AFC; *Career* golf administrator; fin analysis mangr General Foods Banbury 1967–74, tournament dir and chief referee PGA Euro Tour 1974–90, md PGA Euro Seniors Tour 1990–94, conslt PGA Euro Tour; *Recreations* golf, rowing; *Clubs* Tadmarton Heath Golf, Sunningdale Golf, Leander (assoc); *Style*— Tony Gray, Esq; ✉ Killowen House, South Newington Rd, Bloxham, Banbury, Oxon OX15 4QF (☎ 01295 721179, fax 01295 720610); PGA European Tour, Wentworth Drive, Virginia Water, Surrey GU25 4LS (☎ 01344 842881, fax 01344 842929)

GRAY, Dr Kenneth Walter (Ken); CBE (1992); s of Robert Walter Gray (d 1994), of Bracklesham Bay, Sussex, and Ruby May, *née* Rofe (d 1978); *b* 20 March 1939; *Educ* Blue Coat Sch Liverpool, Univ of Wales (BSc, PhD), RCDS 1981; *m* 29 Dec 1962, Jill, da of William Hartley Henderson; 1 da (Carole Elizabeth b 1964), 2 s (Neil Kenneth b 1966, Ian Kenneth b 1968); *Career* Nat Research Cncl of Canada post-doctoral fell in magnetic resonance Univ of Br Columbia Vancouver 1963–65, researcher in semi-conductor devices and radiometry N American Rockwell Science Center California 1965–70; Royal Signals and Radar Estab (RSRE): research in devices and systems 1971, supt Solid State Physics and Devices Div 1976–79, head Physics Gp 1979–82, dep dir applied physics (CSO) RSRE/MOD 1982–84, dep dir info systems (under sec) 1984; EMI Group plc (formerly Thorn EMI plc): dir of research 1984–86, tech dir 1986–, exec chm Thorn Software 1987–89, tech dir Thorn Security and Electronics 1991–93, md Thorn Transaction 1993–; non-exec dir British Steel plc 1995–; visiting research fell Univ of Newcastle 1972–74, visiting research fell Univ of Leeds 1976–, visiting prof Univ of Nottingham 1986–; author of over 30 scientific and technical papers in learned jls; memb: Innovation Advsy Bd DTI 1988–93, SERC 1991–94, Technology Foresight Steering Gp 1992–; FInstP 1991, FIEE 1992, FEng 1996; *Style*— Dr Ken Gray, CBE, FEng; ✉ Broadgates, Manor Road, Penn, Bucks HP10 8JA (☎ 01494 814537); EMI Group plc, Dawley Road, Hayes, Middx UB3 1HH (☎ 0181 848 6666)

GRAY, Prof Kevin John; s of Bryce Holmes Gray, and Priscilla Margaret, *née* McCullough; *b* 23 July 1951; *Educ* Trinity Hall Cambridge (MA, PhD, LLD, Yorke prize), Univ of Oxford (DCL); *Career* Univ of Cambridge: fell Queens' Coll 1975–81, lectr in law 1978–90, fell Trinity Coll 1981–90, advocate 1986–88, prof of law 1993–, professorial fell Trinity Coll 1993–; res fell Australian Nat Univ 1990 (visiting fell 1979 and 1989), Drapers' prof of law Univ of London 1991–93, sr res fell St John's Coll Oxford 1993–94; called to the Bar Middle Temple 1993; memb Soc of Public Teachers of Law 1975, assoc memb Académie Internationale de Droit Comparé 1995; *Books* Reallocation of Property on Divorce (1977), Elements of Land Law (1987, 2 edn 1993); *Recreations* mountaineering and rock climbing; *Style*— Prof Kevin Gray; ✉ Trinity College, Cambridge CB2 1TQ (☎ 01223 338497/330074, fax 01223 338564)

GRAY, (Stephen) Marius; s of Basil Gray, CB, CBE (d 1989), of Long Wittenham, Oxford, and Nicolete Mary Gray, *née* Binyon; *b* 3 Aug 1934; *Educ* Westminster, New Coll Oxford (MA); *m* 2 Sept 1961, Clare Anthony, da of Sir Anthony Horace Milward, CBE (d 1981); 1 s (Theodore b 1964), 3 da (Emma b 1962, Bridget b 1967, Jacquetta b 1971); *Career* Nat Serv 2 Lt RCS 1953–55; CA 1962; sr ptnr Dixon Wilson 1981– (ptnr 1967–81); non-exec dir: Davies Turner Ltd 1970–, Abingworth Management Ltd 1973– (chm 1994–), Folkestone Ltd 1977–94, British Biotech plc 1982–, Associated Newspapers Holdings plc 1983–, Daily Mail and General Tst plc 1985–, East German Investment Trust plc 1993–; chm of special tstees The London Hosp 1974–, chm mgmnt ctee The King's Fund 1985–; govr The London Hosp Med Coll 1984–89; FCA; *Clubs* Savile; *Style*— Marius Gray, Esq; ✉ 47 Maze Hill, London SE10 8XQ; Dixon Wilson, Rotherwick House, PO Box 900, 3 Thomas More St, London E1 9YX (☎ 0171 628 432, fax 0171 702 9769)

GRAY, (H) Martin V; *Career* chief exec NatWest UK and main bd dir National Westminster Bank plc 1993–; *Style*— Martin Gray, Esq; ✉ National Westminster Bank plc, Drapers Gardens, 12 Throgmorton Avenue, London EC2N 2DL (☎ 0171 920 5555)

GRAY, Dr Michael Ian Hart (Mike); s of Harry Lesley Gray, of London, and Edith Louise, *née* Hart; *b* 12 July 1940; *Educ* Dartford GS, Univ of St Andrews (MB ChB), RAF Inst of Aviation Med (DAvMed); *m* 22 July 1964, Patricia Margaret (Trish), da of Capt William Thompson Stewart, of Dundee, Scot; 1 s (Jeremy Rupert Andrew Hart b 1968); *Career* cmmnd RAMC 1963, Regtl MO 4/7 Royal Dragoon Gds 1966–68, pathologist Queen Alexandra Mil Hosp London 1971–72 (trainee 1969), pathologist Tidworth Mil Hosp 1972–74, trainee in aviation med Army Air Corps Centre 1974–76, awarded Helicopter Wings 1975, specialist in aviation med Army Air Corps Centre 1976–77, advsr in aviation med (Lt-Col) to dir Army Air Corps 1977–79, conslt in aviation med (Flt Surgn) King Abdul Aziz Mil Hosp Tabuk Saudi Arabia 1979–83; chief med offr Gulf Air Bahrain 1986–88 (sr med offr 1983–86), aviation med specialist Military Aircraft Div British Aerospace 1989–96; memb: Br Acad of Forensic Scis 1971, Aerospace Med Assoc 1975; MFOM 1981, MRAeS 1984; *Recreations* reading, gardening, sailing, shooting; *Clubs* Cavalry and Guards, Royal Over-Seas League; *Style*— Dr Michael Gray; ✉ Nut Tree Cottage, Lower Chicksgrove, Tisbury, Wiltshire SP3 6NB (☎ 01722 714382)

GRAY, Lt-Gen Sir Michael Stuart; KCB (1986), OBE (1971); s of Lt Cdr Frank Gray, RNVR (ka 1940); *b* 3 May 1932; *Educ* Christ's Hosp Horsham, RMA Sandhurst; *m* 1958, Juliette Antonia; 3 children; *Career* cmmnd E Yorks Regt 1952, transferred Parachute Regt 1956, Army Staff College 1963, CO 1 Para 1969–71, instr Staff Coll 1971–73, RCDS 1976, Cdr 16 Parachute Bde 1977, Cdr 6 Field Force and COMUKMF 1977–79, Cdr Br Army Staff and Mil Attaché Washington DC (with additional responsibilities of Head Br Def Staff and Def Attaché 1980 and Mil Advsr to the Govr of Bermuda) 1979–81, GOC SW Dist 1981–83, COS HQ BAOR 1984–85, GOC SE Dist (cmd Joint Force HQ) 1985–88, ret 1988; Hon Col 10 Para (V) 1984–90, Col Cmdt The Parachute Regt 1990–93, Hon Col 250 (Hull) Field Ambulance (V) RAMC 1991–; chief exec Rainford Developments 1992–, non-exec chm June Cadman Homes 1985–, conslt Brittany Ferries 1988–, defence industs advsr Wardle Storeys plc and GQ Parachutes Ltd 1989–; Lt HM Tower of London 1985–; chm: Airborne Assault Normandy Tst 1978–, Mil and Aerospace (Aldershot) Tst 1989–, King George's Fund for Sailors E Yorks Ctee 1990–, June Cadman Charitable Tst 1994–; Normandy Veterans Assoc: national vice pres, pres Leeds and York branches, vice pres Goole branch; tstee: Airborne Forces Charities Tst, Airborne Forces Museum, Airborne Forces Security Fund, Br Support Ctee Meml Museum Caen Normandy; pres PRA York Branch, vice pres Army Parachute Assoc, patron Combined Ex Services Assoc Bridlington, memb Amicable Soc of Blues; Freeman City London; Officier de l'Ordre National de la Legion d'Honneur France 1994; FIMgt, FInstD, MICFM; *Recreations* military history, photography, gardening and house maintenance; *Style*— Lt-Gen Sir Michael Gray, KCB, OBE; ✉ c/o National Westminster Bank plc, 60 Market Place, Beverley, North Humberside

GRAY, Milner Connorton; CBE (1963); s of Archibald Campbell Gray (d 1952), of Eynsford, Kent, and Katherine May, *née* Hart; *b* 8 Oct 1899; *Educ* Privately, Colfe Sch Lewisham, Goldsmiths' Coll London; *m* 12 July 1934, Gnade Grace, da of William Osbourne-Pratt, of Northampton; *Career* 19 London Regt 1917, transferred RE Experimental Section Sch of Camouflage 1917–19, gunner HAC (TA) 1923–31, admitted Veteran Co 1931; fndr and sr ptnr Basset Gray (multi-discipline design practice) 1922–35, sr ptnr Industl Design Ptnrship (reorganisation of former practice) 1935–40, princ Sir John Cass Sch of Art 1937–40, head and princ design advsr Exhibitions Branch Miny of Info 1940–44, fndr ptnr Design Res Unit 1945–80, conslt 1980–; work incl: rendering of Royal Coat of Arms Crown and Royal Cipher for Coronation Souvenirs 1952–53, design conslt Royal Mint for coin inscriptions 1961–86, design of armorial bearings and common seal PO 1970, design of official emblem for Queen's Silver Jubilee for use on street decorations and souvenirs; fndr memb CSD 1930 (pres 1943–49 and 1966–67); memb Cncl: Design and Industs Assoc 1935–38, RSA 1959–65; memb: Miny Educn Advsy Ctee for Art Examinations 1947–52, Alliance Graphique Internationale 1950 (Br pres 1963–71), Royal Mint Advsy Ctee 1952–86, Fndn Ctee Int Cncl Soc Industl Design 1956, Miny Educn Advsy Cncl on Art Educn 1973–76; Design Centre award 1957, Queen's Silver Jubilee medal 1977; Freeman City of London 1981; Hon DA Manchester 1965, hon fell Soc Typographic Designers 1979, Hon Dr RCA 1979; RDI 1937, FInstPack 1947, AGI 1950; *Books* numerous publications, lectures and broadcasts on design; *Clubs* Arts; *Style*— Milner Gray, Esq, CBE; ✉ Felix Hall, Kelvedon, Essex CO5 9DG; 8 Holly Mount, Hampstead, London NW3 6SG (☎ 0171 435 4238)

GRAY, Paul Richard Charles; s of Rev Sidney Albert Gray (d 1981), of Thaxted, Essex, and Ina, *née* Maxey; *b* 2 Aug 1948; *Educ* Wyggeston Boys Sch, LSE (BSc); *m* 15 April 1972, Lynda Elsie, da of James Benjamin Braby, of Loughton, Essex; 2 s (Simon b 1978, Adam b 1980); *Career* HM Treasy 1969–77, corp planning exec Booker McConnell Ltd 1977–79; HM Treasy: princ Agric Div 1979–83, asst sec Gen Expenditure Div 1984–86, asst sec Indust and Employment Div 1987, econ affrs private sec to PM 1988–90, under sec Monetary Gp 1990–93, dir of personnel fin and support 1994–95, dir of budget and public finances (grade 2) 1995–; non-exec dir Laing Management Ltd 1993–94; *Recreations* family, walking, gardening; *Style*— Paul Gray, Esq; ✉ HM Treasury, Parliament Street, London SW1P 3AG

GRAY, Prof Peter; s of Ivor Hicks Gray (d 1954), and Rose Ethel, *née* Adcock (d 1935); *b* 25 Aug 1926; *Educ* Newport HS, Gonville and Caius Coll Cambridge (BA, PhD, ScD); *m* 1, 13 Dec 1952, Barbara Joan (d 1992), da of late John Basil Hume (d 1974); 2 s (Andrew b 1956, David b 1958), 2 da (Christine b 1954, Sally b 1960); m 2, 4 May 1996, Rachel Katharine Herzig, *née* Buxton; *Career* Univ of Cambridge: Ramsay fell 1949–51, res fell Gonville and Caius Coll 1949–53, demonstrator in chem engrg 1951–55; Univ of

Leeds: lectr in physical chemistry 1955–59, reader 1959–62, prof 1962–88, head Dept of Physical Chemistry 1965–88, hon visiting prof 1988–; master Gonville and Caius Coll Cambridge 1988–96 (life fell 1996–); visiting prof: Univ of BC 1958–59, Univ of Göttingen 1979 and 1986, Univ of Paris 1986, Univ of Calabria 1988; visitor Fire Res Orgn 1984–89; pres: Faraday Div RSC 1983–85, Cambridge Philosophical Soc 1992–94; Meldola Medal Royal Inst of Chemistry 1956, Marlow Medal Faraday Soc 1959, Lewis Gold Medal Combustion Inst 1978, RSC Award for Combustion 1986, Italgas Prize for Chemistry 1987, Chaire Bruylants 1994, Larmor lectr 1995; FRS 1977; *Publications* Chemical Oscillations and Instabilities (S K Scott, 1990); *Recreations* fell walking, music; *Style*— Prof Peter Gray, FRS; ✉ Gonville and Caius College, Cambridge CB2 1TA (☎ 01223 332400, fax 01223 332336); 13A The Causeway, Horsham, West Sussex RH12 1HE (☎ 01403 265239)

GRAY, Peter Francis; s of Rev George Francis Selby Gray; *b* 7 Jan 1937; *Educ* Marlborough, Trinity Coll Cambridge; *m* 1978, Fiona Bristol; 2 s (Augustus b 1979, Julius b 1981); *Career* Nat Serv Lt Royal Fus attached to 4 King's African Rifles Uganda 1956–58; Coopers & Lybrand 1967–69, Samuel Montagu & Co 1970–77, head of Investmt Div Crown Agents for Oversea Govts and Admins 1977–83, md Touche Remnant & Co 1983–87, dir TR Industrial & General Trust plc 1984–88; dep chm The Assoc of Investmt Tst Cos 1985–87; chm: Exmoor Dual Investment Trust 1988–, Abtrust Lloyd's Insurance Trust 1993–, Contra-Cyclical Investment Trust 1994–; dir: New Zealand Investment Trust 1988–, Second Consolidated Trust 1992–, Gartmore Shared Equity Trust 1993–, Foreign & Colonial Private Equity Trust 1994–, Liberty Newport World Portfolio SICAV 1995–; FCA; *Recreations* literature and music; *Clubs* Brooks's; *Style*— Peter Gray, Esq; ✉ 1 Bradbourne St, London SW6

GRAY, Philip Malcolm James; s of James Carter Gray (d 1932), and Lucy Venetia Emily, *née* Robson (d 1972); *b* 17 Jan 1927; *Educ* Eastbourne Coll, Royal Sch of Mines, Univ of London (BSc); *m* 18 Aug 1949, Joan, da of Alfred Thomas Houldsworth; *Career* scientific offr AERE Harwell 1947–51, res offr Cwlth Scientific and Res Orgn Melbourne Aust 1951–55, metallurgist and devpt mangr Imperial Smelting Corporation Avonmouth UK 1955–64 (tech mangr 1964–71), chief metallurgist Non-Ferrous Div Davy Corporation London 1971–78, metallurgical conslt and ptnr Philip M J Gray and J Gray London 1978–, md Zinc Metallurgy Ltd 1992–95, tech dir The Zinc Corporation Ltd 1996–; pres Inst of Mining and Metallurgy 1984–85 (Capper Pass award 1952 and 1955), Waverly Gold medal 1955; Freeman City of London 1984, Liveryman Worshipful Co of Engineers; ARSM, Hon FIMM 1992 (MIMM 1953, FIMM 1973), fell Aust Inst Mining and Metallurgy 1970 (memb 1952), FEng 1984; *Books* The Profitable Development of Sulphide Ore Resources (with P Loffler and G Bielstein, 1985), numerous contribs to learned pubns (1951–); *Recreations* bell ringing, opera, musical appreciation, looking at paintings, golf, cricket, travel; *Clubs* Lansdowne; *Style*— Philip Gray, Esq, FEng; ✉ 2 The Avenue, Backwell, Bristol BS19 3NB (☎ 01275 464192, fax 01275 464219)

GRAY, Prof Richard John; s of George Ernest Gray (d 1991), and Helen, *née* Cox; *b* 5 Jan 1944; *Educ* Tiffin Sch, St Catharine's Coll Cambridge (Open scholar, BA), Univ of Cambridge (PhD); *m* 1, 1965 (m dis), Joyce Mary, *née* Gray; 1 da (Catharine Emma b 6 April 1966), 1 s (Ben Thomas b 21 May 1972); m 2, 1990, Sheona Catherine, da of Ian Binnie; 1 da (Jessica Vivien b 7 April 1991), 1 s (Jack Ewan George b 12 March 1993); *Career* sr res scholar St Catharine's Coll Cambridge 1966–67, Harkness fell Univ of N Carolina and Univ of California 1967–69; Dept of Literature Univ of Essex: lectr 1969–76, sr lectr 1976–80, reader 1981–90, prof 1990–; Robert E McNair visiting prof Univ of S Carolina 1993; memb Int Cncl Centre for the Study of Southern Culture Univ of Mississippi 1979, assoc ed Jl of American Studies 1990, ed Jl of American Studies 1997; FBA 1993; *Books* American Verse of the Nineteenth Century (ed, 1973), American Poetry of the Twentieth Century (ed, 1976), The Literature of Memory: Modern Writers of the American South (1977), Robert Penn Warren: A Collection of Critical Essays (ed, 1980), American Fiction: New Readings (ed, 1983), Writing the South: Ideas of an American Region (1986, C Hugh Holman Award), American Poetry of the Twentieth Century (1990), The Complete Poems and Selected Essays of Edgar Allan Poe (ed, 1993), The Life of William Faulkner: A Critical Biography (1994), The Selected Poems of Edgar Allan Poe (ed, 1996); *Recreations* cinema, wine tasting, running, tennis, gardening; *Style*— Prof Richard Gray, FBA; ✉ Berri-Dene, Anglesea Road, Wivenhoe, Colchester, Essex CO7 9JS (☎ 01206 823118); Department of Literature, University of Essex, Wivenhoe Park, Colchester, Essex CO4 3SQ (☎ 01206 872590, fax 01206 873598, e-mail grayr@essex.ac.uk)

GRAY, Richard Paul; QC (1993); s of Dr J M Gray (d 1984), and Margaret Elizabeth, *née* Welsh (d 1986); *b* 1 Nov 1945; *Educ* Tonbridge Sch, Univ of St Andrews (LLB); *m* April 1976, Emma Serena, da of W R C Halpin; 1 s (Jocelyn b 9 Sept 1985); *Career* called to the Bar Inner Temple 1970; *Recreations* golf, tennis, gardens; *Style*— Richard Gray, Esq, QC; ✉ 39 Essex Street, London WC2R 3AT (☎ 0171 583 1111, fax 0171 353 3978)

GRAY, Ronald George; s of Henry Gray (d 1958), and Elizabeth Campbell Cowan, *née* Watson (d 1942); *b* 12 July 1929; *Educ* Royal HS Edinburgh, Univ of Edinburgh (MA); *m* 26 June 1954, Diana Ravenscroft, da of Francis Henry Houlston (d 1983); 3 da (Karen b 14 Oct 1955, Francesca b 14 Sept 1958, Fiona b 10 March 1960); *Career* trainee Unilever 1953; dir: Elida Gibbs Ltd 1967–72, Unilever Co-ordination 1973–80; chm: Elida Gibbs (Germany) 1981–84, Lever Bros Ltd 1984–91; chm: CTFA (Cosmetic Toiletry and Fragrance Assoc) 1970–72, SDIA (Soap and Detergent Industry Assoc) 1985–89; pres ISBA 1988–90, memb IBA Advertising Advsy Ctee 1985–90; govr Dulwich Estate, chm Alleyns Sch; FIGD 1985; *Style*— Ronald Gray, Esq; ✉ 4 Dulwich Village, London SE21 7AL (☎ 0181 693 1764)

GRAY, (Clemency Anne) Rose; da of Clement Nelson Swann (d 1939), of Bedford, and Elizabeth Anne, *née* Lawrence (d 1985); *b* 28 Jan 1939; *Educ* Manor House Sch Guildford, Guildford Sch of Art; *m* 1961 (m dis), Michael Selby Gray; 1 s (Ossian), 2 da (Hester (Mrs Justin Guest Albert), Lucy); *partner* David MacIlwaine; 1 s (Dante MacIlwaine-Gray); *Career* chef/restaurant owner; teacher of fine art London 1960–63, designer and manufacturer of paper lights and furniture 1963–68, importer of French stoves and cookers (concurrently introduced series of French creperie mobile units for pop concerts) 1969–72, dir Home Stoves Ltd (mfrg and exporting wood burning stoves) 1973–81, resided Lucca Italy 1981–85; chef: Italian restuarant within Nells nightclub NY 1985–86, River Cafe (with Ruth Rogers, *qv*) 1987–; Italian Restaurant of the Year (The Times) 1988, Best New Restaurant (Courvoisier Best of Best Awards) 1989, Eros Awards (Evening Standard) 1994 and 1995; *Books* Hot Chefs (BBC, contrib, 1992), The River Cafe Cook Book (with Ruth Rogers, 1995, Food Book of the Yr Glenfiddich Awards 1996), Great British Chefs 2 (contrib chapter, 1995); *Recreations* gardening, sailing; *Clubs* Groucho, Green Street, Pegg's; *Style*— Rose Gray; ✉ Flat E, No 7 Plympton Street, London NW8 8AB (☎ 0171 258 1780)

GRAY, Prof Sidney John; s of Sidney George Gray (d 1978), and Mary Angeline, *née* Birch (d 1974); *b* 3 Oct 1942; *Educ* Bedford Modern Sch, Univ of Sydney (BEc), Univ of Lancaster (PhD); *m* 23 July 1977, Hilary Fenella, da of William Leonard Jones (d 1995); 1 s (Peter b 1985), 1 da (Helen b 1981); *Career* exec: Peirce Leslie & Co Ltd UK and India 1961–67 (factory mangr 1966–67), Burns Philp & Co Ltd Aust 1967–68; tutor in accounting Univ of Sydney 1972, lectr Univ of Lancaster 1974–78 (res scholar 1973–74), prof of accounting and fin Univ of Glasgow 1978–92 (head of dept 1980–87), prof of int business Univ of Warwick 1992–; sec gen Euro Accounting Assoc 1982–83, memb UK Accounting Standards Ctee 1984–87, chm Br Accounting Assoc 1987, pres Int Assoc for Accounting Educn and Res 1992–; ACIS 1971, FCCA 1980, MIMgt 1973; *Books* Information Disclosure and the Multinational Corporation (1984), International Financial Reporting (1984), Mega-Merger Mayhem (1989), Handbook of International Business and Management (1990), International Accounting and Multinational Enterprises (1993); *Recreations* tennis, golf; *Clubs* East India; *Style*— Prof Sidney Gray; ✉ Warwick Business School, University of Warwick, Coventry CV4 7AL (☎ 01203 524580, fax 01203 524628)

GRAY, Simon James; s of James Gray, of Southport, and Maureen Constance Gail, *née* Cook; *b* 26 Jan 1970; *Educ* Birkdale HS Southport, King George V 6 Form Coll Southport, Birmingham Conservatoire (GBSM, MA); *Career* composer and prodr; composer in res Windsor HS Halesowen 1991–92, lectr in composition music technol and folk music Birmingham Conservatoire Univ of Central England 1993–, lectr in music technol Coventry Univ 1994–96; vice pres Student's Union 1992–93; works published by Mahayana Music; memb committee@usenet.org.uk (body managing UK Internet news hierarchy); memb Performing Right Soc; *Recreations* photography, motor scootering, IT, media, publishing, politics and current affairs, comparative religion and philosophy, ancient history; *Style*— Simon Gray, Esq; ✉ 7 Mossfield Road, Kings Heath, Birmingham B14 (☎ 07050 135175); Birmingham Conservatoire, Paradise Place, Birmingham B3 3HG (☎ 0121 331 5901, fax 0121 331 5906, mobile 0956 854959, e-mail simon@star-one.org.uk, web http://www.mahayana.demon.co.uk)

GRAY, Simon James Holliday; s of Dr James Davidson Gray, and Barbara Cecelia Mary, *née* Holliday; *b* 21 Oct 1936; *Educ* Westminster, Dalhousie Univ, Trinity Coll Cambridge (MA); *m* 1965, Beryl Mary, *née* Kevern; 1 s (Ben), 1 da (Lucy); *Career* res student and Harper-Wood travelling student 1960, sr instr in English Univ of Br Columbia 1963–64, lectr QMC London 1965–85; author and playwright; *Stage Plays* Wise Child (1968), Sleeping Dog (1968), Dutch Uncle (1969), The Idiot (1971), Spoiled (1971), Butley (1971), Otherwise Engaged (1975, voted Best Play 1976–77 by NY Drama Critics' Circle), Plaintiffs and Defendants (1975), Two Sundays (1975), Dog Days (1976), Molly (1977), The Rear Column (1978), Close of Play (1979), Stage Struck (1979), Quartermaine's Terms (1981), The Common Pursuit (1984), Plays One (1986), Melon (1987), Hidden Laughter (and dir London and Brighton, 1990), The Holy Terror (Melon Revised) (1990), Tartuffe - An Adaptation (1990), Old Flames (1990), Cell Mates (1995), Simply Disconnected (sequel to Otherwise Engaged, 1996); *Television Plays* After Pilkington (1987), Old Flames (1990), A Month in the Country (1990), They Never Slept (1991), Running Late (1992), Unnatural Pursuits (1993), Femme Fatale (1993); *Radio Plays* The Holy Terror (revised, 1989), The Rector's Daughter (adaption, 1992), Suffer The Little Children (1993), With A Nod and A Bow (1993); *Books* Colmain (1963), Simple People (1965), Little Portia (1967, as Hamish Reade), A Comeback for Stark (1968), An Unnatural Pursuit and Other Pieces (1985), How's That For Telling 'em Fat Lady? - A Short Life in the American Theatre (1988), Fat Chance (1995); *Recreations* watching cricket and soccer; *Clubs* Dramatist, Groucho; *Style*— Simon Gray, Esq; ✉ c/o Judy Daish Associates, 2 St Charles Place, London W10 6EG (☎ 0181 964 8811, fax 0181 964 8966)

GRAY, Simon Talbot; s of Dr John Talbot Carmichael Gray (d 1961), of Ealing, and Doris Irene, *née* Baker; *b* 1 June 1938; *Educ* Westminster; *m* 1963, Susan, da of Felix William Grain, of Ealing; 2 s (Nicholas b 1965, Julian b 1968); *Career* CA; sr ptnr Smith & Williamson; dir: S & W Securities, S & W Trust Corporation, Yattendon Investment Trust Ltd, Syndicate Administration Ltd; special tstee of St Bartholomew's and St Mark's Hospitals 1982– (chm 1992–); memb City & Hackney Health Authy 1983–90; memb Ct Worshipful Co of Glass Sellers (Master 1978); *Recreations* yachting (yacht 'Fast Anchor'); *Clubs* City of London, City Livery, Royal Lymington Yacht, Royal Thames Yacht, Royal Automobile; *Style*— Simon Gray, Esq; ✉ Brackens, Captains Row, Lymington, Hants SO41 9RP (☎ 01590 677101); Smith & Williamson, 1 Ridinghouse St, London W1A 3AS (☎ 0171 637 5377, fax 0171 631 0741)

GRAY, Sir William Hume; 3 Bt (UK 1917), of Tunstall Manor, Hart, Co Durham; s of late William Talbot Gray (d 1971), s of 2 Bt, and Rosemarie Hume, *née* Elliott-Smith; suc gf, Sir William Gray, 2 Bt, 1978; Sir William Cresswell Gray, 1 Bt, was chm William Gray & Co Ltd, a memb of Lloyd's Register Ctee and fndr of the S Durham Steel and Iron Co Ltd in 1889; *b* 26 July 1955; *Educ* Eton, Poly of Central London (DipArch); *m* 1984, Catherine, yst da of late John Naylor, of The Mill House, Bramley, Hants; 1 s (William John Cresswell b 1986), 2 da (Octavia b 1987, Clementine b 1990); *Heir* s, William John Cresswell Gray b 24 Aug 1986; *Career* architect William Gray Associates; dir Hartlepool Water plc; *Style*— Sir William Gray, Bt; ✉ Eggleston Hall, Eggleston, Barnard Castle, Co Durham

GRAY, Sir William Stevenson; kt (1974), JP (Glasgow 1965), DL (City of Glasgow 1976); s of William Gray; *b* 3 May 1928; *Educ* Univ of Glasgow (BL); *m* 1958, Mary Rodger; 1 s, 1 da; *Career* slr and NP Gray & Co; City of Glasgow: hon treas 1971–72, magistrate 1961–64, memb Corp 1958–75, chm Property Mgmnt Ctee 1964–67; former chm Irvine New Town Devpt Corp; chm: Gap (formerly World of Property Housing Scottish Housing Assoc) 1974–, Third Eye Centre 1975–85, Scottish Devpt Agency 1975–79, The Oil Club 1975–, Glasgow Ind Hosp 1982–89, The Barrel Selection 1986–, WPHT Scotland Ltd 1987–, Norcity Homes plc 1988–95, Clan Homes plc 1988–, Norhomes plc 1989–, Manchester Village Homes plc 1989–, Gap Housing Association (Ownership) Ltd 1989–, First Tax Homes to Fourth Tax Homes plc 1990–, Norcity II plc 1989–, Norcity III plc 1993–, Norcity IV plc 1993–, Paragon Protected Growth 1993–; vice pres Glasgow Citizens' Theatre 1975–; memb: Scottish Opera Bd 1971–72, Nat Tst Scotland 1971–72, Ct of Glasgow Univ 1972–75, Clyde Port Authy 1972–75, Advsy Cncl Energy Conservation 1974–85, Glasgow Advsy Ctee on JPs 1975–, Scottish Advsy Ctee on JPs 1975–96 (patron), Scottish Youth Theatre 1976–86, Scottish Pakistani Soc 1983–; vice pres: Charles Rennie Mackintosh Soc 1974–, Scottish Assoc for Care and Resettlement of Offenders 1975–82; Lord Provost City of Glasgow, Lord-Lt Co of the City of Glasgow 1972–75 (DL 1971–); Hon LLD: Univ of Strathclyde 1974, Univ of Glasgow 1980; FRSA 1991; *Style*— Sir William Gray, JP, DL; ✉ Gray & Co, 13 Royal Terrace, Glasgow G3 7NY (☎ 0141 332 8877, fax 0141 332 2809)

GRAY-CHEAPE, Hamish Leslie; JP (Warwickshire 1985), DL (Warwickshire 1990); s of Lt-Col Leslie George Gray-Cheape, MBE, JP, DL (d 1991), of Carse Gray, Forfar, Angus, and Dorothy Evelyn, *née* Thomas (d 1986); *b* 18 March 1942; *Educ* Eton; *m* 6 Oct 1965, Fiona Mariella, da of Brig Sir Harry Ripley Mackeson (d 1964, 1 Bn late Royal Scots Greys); 2 s (James b 1968, George b 1971); *Career* Capt Grenadier Gds 1961–71; High Sheriff of Warwickshire 1984; farmer 1972–; memb Queen's Body Guard for Scotland (The Royal Co of Archers) 1972; *Style*— Hamish Gray-Cheape, Esq, JP, DL; ✉ Great Alne, Warwickshire (☎ 01789 488420); Hill House, Walcote, Alcester, Warwickshire B49 6LZ

GRAY OF CONTIN, Baron (Life Peer UK 1983), of Contin in the District of Ross and Cromarty; Hamish James Hector Northey Gray; PC (1982); s of James Northey Gray, JP (d 1979), of Inverness, and M E Gray (d 1990); *b* 28 June 1927; *Educ* Inverness Royal Acad; *m* 1953, Judith Waite, da of Noel M Brydon, MBE, of Ayr; 2 s (Hon (James Northey) David b 1955, Hon Peter b 1959), 1 da (Hon Sally (Hon Mrs Brown) b 1957); *Career* served Queen's Own Cameron Highlanders (Lt) 1945–48; memb Inverness Cncl 1965–70; former dir: Drumry Testing Co Hillington, James Gray (Inverness) Ltd, and others; MP (C) Ross and Cromarty 1970–83; asst govt whip 1971–73,

Lord Cmmr of the Treasury 1973–74, oppn whip 1974–75, oppn spokesman on energy 1975–79; min of state: Dept of Energy 1979–83, Scottish Office 1983–86; public affrs, business and Parly conslt 1986–; Lord-Lieut of Inverness 1996– (DL 1989); *Recreations* golf, cricket, walking; *Clubs* Highland (Inverness); *Style*— The Rt Hon Lord Gray of Contin, PC; ✉ Achneim House, Flichity, Inverness-shire IV1 2XE (☎ 018083 211); House of Lords, London SW1A OPW

GRAYBURN, Jeremy Ward; s of Sqdn Ldr Robert William Grayburn (d 1982), of Silverdale, Lancs, and Moira Wendy, *née* Rice; *b* 24 Aug 1952; *Educ* Lancaster Royal GS; *m* 7 Feb 1976, Pamela Anne, da of Flt Lt Graham Ross; 2 da (Nichola, Caroline); *Career* Allied Dunbar Assurance plc: joined 1971, divnl dir 1984–85, exec dir 1985–, sr exec dir 1990, mktg ops dir 1991–, mktg dir 1992–; *Style*— Jeremy Grayburn, Esq; ✉ York Cottage, Long Lane, Shaw, Newbury, Berks RG14 2TA (☎ 01635 34437); Allied Dunbar Assurance plc, Allied Dunbar Centre, Swindon, Wiltshire (☎ 01793 514514, fax 01793 502021)

GRAYDON, Air Chief Marshal Sir Michael James; GCB (1993, KCB 1989), CBE (1984), ADC (1992); s of James Julian Graydon (d 1985), and Rita Mary, *née* Alkan; *b* 24 Oct 1938; *Educ* Wycliffe Coll; *m* 25 May 1963, (Margaret) Elizabeth, da of Arthur Ronald Clark (d 1972); *Career* RAF Coll Cranwell 1957–59, QFI No 1 Fts 1960–62, No 56 Sqdn Wattisham 1963–64, 226 OCU 1965–67, Flt-Cdr No 56 Akrotiri 1967–69, RAF Staff Coll Bracknell 1970, PSO to D/CINCENT HQAFCENT 1971–73, Ops Staff MOD 1973–75, NDC Latimer 1975–76, OC No 11 Sqdn Binbrook 1977–79, MA to CDS MOD 1979–81, OC RAF Leuchars 1981–83, OC RAF Stanley FI 1983, RCDS London 1984, SASO HQ 11 Gp Bentley Priory 1985–86, ACOS Policy SHAPE Belgium 1986–89, AOC-in-C RAF Support Cmd 1989–91, AOC-in-C Strike Cmd and C-in-C UK Air Forces 1991–92, Chief of Air Staff 1992–; vice chm Govrs Wycliffe Coll; Freeman City of London; FRAeS, FRSA; *Recreations* golf, photography; *Clubs* RAF, Royal and Ancient Golf (St Andrews); *Style*— Air Chief Marshal Sir Michael Graydon, GCB, CBE, ADC; ✉ Chief of Air Staff, Ministry of Defence, Main Building, London SW1A 2HB (☎ 0171 218 6314)

GRAYSON, Edward; *Educ* Taunton's Sch Southampton, Exeter Coll Oxford; *m* 27 May 1959, (Myra) Wendy Shockett; 1 s (Harry b 26 March 1966); *Career* RAF 1943–45; called to the Bar Middle Temple 1948; uninterrupted practice: Lincoln's Inn 1949–53, Temple and International 1953–; author and communicator; contrib: legal, sporting and nat jls, newspapers, BBC, ITV, various radio stations; contrib and conslt to Central Cncl of Physical Recreation and Sports Cncl; pres Br Assoc for Sport and Law, memb Br Assoc of Sport and Med; fell RSM; *Books* Corinthians and Cricketers (1955, re-issued as Corinthian-Casuals and Cricketers 1983), The Royal Baccarat Scandal (jtly, second edn 1988), The Way Forward: The Gleneagles Agreement (1982), Sponsorship of Sport, Arts and Leisure (jtly, 1984), Medicine, Sport and the Law (1990), Medico-Legal Hazards of Rugby Union (1991), Sport and the Law (3 edn, 1994); *Recreations* working and creative thinking about sports medicine and the law; *Clubs* MCC, Harlequins, Corinthian-Casuals, Sussex, Surrey CC, Littlehampton Town FC; *Style*— Edward Grayson, Esq; ✉ 9–12 Bell Yard, London WC2A 2LF (☎ 0171 400 1800, fax 0171 404 1405)

GRAYSON, Sir Jeremy Brian Vincent; 5 Bt (UK 1922), of Ravenspoint, Co Anglesey; s of Brian Harrington Grayson (d 1989), and his 1 w, Sofia, *née* Buchanan; suc uncle, Sir Rupert Stanley Harrington Grayson, 4 Bt 1991; *b* 30 Jan 1933; *Educ* Downside; *m* 1958, Sara Mary, da of late C F Upton, of Monte Carlo; 3 s (Simon Jeremy b 1959, Paul Francis b 1965, Mark Christopher b 1968), 4 da (Caroline Mary b 1961, Anna Katherine (Mrs Christopher Turner) b 1962, Mary b and d 1964, Lucy Kate b 1970); *Heir* s, Simon Jeremy Grayson b 12 July 1959; *Style*— Sir Jeremy Grayson, Bt; ✉ 54 Bucharest Road, London SW18 3AR

GRAZEBROOK, Adrian Michael; TD (1974); s of Brig (Tom) Neville Grazebrook, CBE, DSO (d 1967), of Sheepscombe House, Gloucestershire, and (Marion) Betty, *née* Asplin; *b* 25 March 1943; *Educ* Sherborne; *m* 22 Sept 1984, Susan Mary, da of (Frank) Geoffrey Outwin, of Barnwood, Gloucester; *Career* cmmnd TA 1962, Lt-Col 1984–90; admitted slr 1966; ptnr Wilmot & Co 1968–; vice pres Racehorse Owners' Assoc 1995–96; memb Law Soc 1966; *Recreations* racing, choral singing; *Clubs* Army and Navy, Turf; *Style*— Adrian Grazebrook, Esq, TD; ✉ The Shepherd's Cottage, Hilcot End, Ampney Crucis, Cirencester, Gloucestershire GL7 5SG (☎ 01285 851507); Wilmot & Co, 38 Castle St, Cirencester, Gloucestershire GL7 1QH (☎ 01285 650551, fax 01285 654007, car 0831 496608)

GRAZEBROOK, Donald McDonald Denis Durley; s of Kenrick Denis Durley Grazebrook (d 1957), and Evelyn, *née* Griffiths; *b* 17 Jan 1927; *Educ* privately, UCL (LLB); *m* 17 April 1953, Mabel, da of Charles Gawler (d 1970), of Stalbridge, Dorset and Anglesey; *Career* called to the Bar Lincoln's Inn 1952, entered Govt Legal Serv 1952; served: Miny of Nat Insur 1952–61, Miny of Lab (later Dept of Employment) 1961–78; UKAEA: dep legal advsr 1979–82, legal advsr 1982–88, conslt 1988–; hon life pres Conseil d' Administration Association International du Droit Nucléaire 1994 (memb 1983, 2 vice pres 1987, pres 1990, vice pres 1992); *Recreations* fox and stag hunting; *Clubs* East India, Pegasus; *Style*— Donald Grazebrook, Esq; ✉ Pine Ridge, Peaslake, Surrey; AEA Technology, Harwell Didcot, Oxon

GREATOREX, Raymond Edward (Ray); s of Percy Edward Greatorex (d 1985), and Lilian Alice Greatorex (d 1986); *b* 28 May 1940; *Educ* Westcliff HS, Lewes County GS; *m* Barbara Anne, da of Mark Booth; 1 da (Joanna b 16 Sept 1974); *Career* FCA; ptnr Kidsons Impey CAs, chm HLB International Ltd; Freeman City of London, memb Ct of Assts Worshipful Co of Farriers; *Recreations* horse racing, cricket, travelling, gardening, reading; *Clubs* East India; *Style*— Ray Greatorex; ✉ Beeches Brook, Wisborough Green, W Sussex RH14 OHP (☎ 01403 700 796); Kidsons Impey, Peel House, Barttelot Rd, Horsham, W Sussex RH12 1BW (☎ 01403 251666, fax 01403 251466)

GREAVES, James Peter (Jimmy); s of James Greaves (d 1989), and Mary Greaves; *b* 20 Feb 1940; *Educ* Kingswood Secdy Sch Hainault; *m* Irene, *née* Barden; 3 s (Jimmy b and d 1960, Daniel b 1962, Andrew b 1966), 2 da (Lynn b 1959, Mitzi b 1964); *Career* professional footballer 1957–71: debut Chelsea Aug 1957, AC Milan Italy, Tottenham Hotspur, West Ham Utd; non-league clubs: Chelmsford, Brentwood, Barnet, Woodford Town; 57 full England caps (44 goals) 1959–67; scored total of 491 goals in first class games (357 in Div 1) 1957–71; honours with Tottenham Hotspur: FA Cup winners' medal 1962 and 1967, Euro Cup Winners' medal 1963; TV presenter and football analyst 1980–, TV previewer TV-am then GMTV 1983–; jt presenter: Saint and Greavsie Show ITV 1985–92, Saint and Greavsie's World of Sport 1995; currently football journalist The Sun; three times winner TV Times Readers Popularity awards; *Books* 14 with Norman Giller incl: This One's On Me (autobiography, 1981), It's A Funny Old Life (autobiography, 1990); *Recreations* watching football, cricket and rugby, playing golf, gardening, trying to keep pace with seven grandchildren; *Clubs* Alcoholics Anonymous; *Style*— Jimmy Greaves, Esq

GREAVES, (Ronald) John; s of Ronald Greaves, and Rose Mary, *née* Nugent; *b* 7 Aug 1948; *Educ* Douay Martyrs Ickenham Middx, Central London Poly (LLB); *m* 1, 3 July 1970 (m dis 1980), Angela, da of Stanley Menze; m 2, Margaret Dorothy, da of Denis John O'Sullivan, of Lincolnshire; 1 da (Caroline Frances b 28 July 1984), 1 s (Patrick John b 30 Sept 1987); *Career* called to the Bar Middle Temple 1973; currently in practice SE Circuit; Parly candidate (Lab) St Albans 1979; memb: Justice Ctee of Compensation for Wrongful Imprisonment, Soc of Labour Lawyers; *Style*— John Greaves, Esq; ✉ Adams House, London Rd, Rickmansworth, Herts WD3 1JT (☎ 01923 776878); 9–12 Bell Yard, London WC2A 2LF (☎ 0171 400 1800, fax 0171 404 1405, DX LOE 390)

GREEN, Alan Michael; s of Frank Joseph Green (d 1966), and Hilda, *née* Bowden (d 1992); *b* 22 Dec 1932; *Educ* Colfes GS Lewisham, Beckenham Sch of Art (NDD), RCA (major travelling scholar, ARCA); *m* 30 Aug 1958, June, da of Oswald Barnes; 2 da (Paula b 5 July 1960, Julia b 26 July 1961); *Career* artist, pt/t and full time teacher in art colls until 1972; regular solo exhibitions in Europe America and Japan 1963–; paintings in perm museum collections worldwide incl: The Tate Gallery London, Solomon R Guggenheim Museum New York, Tokyo Metropolitan Art Museum; Grand Prix 4th Norwegian Int Print Biennale, Nat Museum of Art Osaka prize 11th Print Biennale Tokyo; *Style*— Alan Green, Esq; ✉ Annely Juda Fine Art, 23 Dering St, London W1R 9AA (☎ 0171 629 7578, fax 0171 491 2139)

GREEN, Alison Anne; da of Sam Green, CBE, of Bromley, Kent, and Lilly, *née* Pollak; *b* 18 March 1951; *Educ* Bromley HS, UCL (LLB, LLM), Univ of Louvain; *m* 20 April 1991, Thomas Francis Conlon; 1 da (Samantha Alice Green Conlon); *Career* called to the Bar Middle Temple 1974; lectr in law Univ of Surrey 1976–78; tutor in law: QMC London 1978–79, UCL 1979–81; chair Br Insur Law Assoc 1994– (vice chair 1992–94); memb: Ctee Bar Law Reform Ctee, Insurance Law Sub-ctee Law Soc; UK corr International Insurance Law Review; *Books* Insurance Contract Law (ed advsr 1988), Current Law (ed Euro Union section); *Recreations* music, tennis, ballet; *Clubs* Hurlingham; *Style*— Miss Alison Green; ✉ 4 Field Court, Gray's Inn, London WC1R 5EA (☎ 0171 440 6900, fax 0171 242 0197)

GREEN, Sir Allan David; KCB (1991), QC (1987); s of Lionel Green (d 1991), and Irene Evelyn, *née* Abrahams (later Mrs Axelrad, d 1975); *b* 1 March 1935; *Educ* Charterhouse, St Catharine's Coll Cambridge (MA); *m* 21 Feb 1967, Eva Brita Margareta (d 1993), da of Prof Artur Attman (d 1988), of Gothenburg, Sweden; 1 s (Robin b 1969), 1 da (Susanna b 1970); *Career* served RN 1953–55; called to the Bar Inner Temple 1959; sr prosecuting counsel to the Crown Central Criminal Ct 1979–85 (jr prosecuting counsel 1977–79), recorder of the Crown Ct 1979–87, bencher 1985, first sr prosecuting counsel to the Crown 1985–87, dir of Public Prosecutions and head Crown Prosecution Serv 1987–91; non-exec dir Windsmoor plc 1986–87; *Recreations* music, studying calligraphy; *Style*— Sir Allan Green, KCB, QC; ✉ No 1 Hare Court, Temple, London EC4Y 7BE

GREEN, HE Andrew Fleming; CMG (1991); s of Gp Capt Joseph Henry Green, CBE (d 1970), and Beatrice Mary, *née* Bowditch; *b* 6 Aug 1941; *Educ* Haileybury, Magdalene Coll Cambridge (BA, MA); *m* 21 Sept 1968, Catherine Jane, da of Lt Cdr Peter Norton Churchill, RN (d 1940); 1 s (Stephen b 1973), 1 da (Diana b 1970); *Career* short serv cmmn Royal Greenjackets 1962–65; joined Dip Serv 1965, MECAS Lebanon 1966–68, second sec Aden 1968–70, asst political agent Abu Dhabi 1970–72; first sec: FCO 1972–77, UK Delgn OECD Paris 1977–79, FCO 1979–82; political cnsllr Washington 1982–85, consul gen and head of chancery Riyadh 1985–88, cnsllr FCO 1988–91, HM ambass Syria 1991–94, asst under sec (Middle East) FCO 1994–96, HM ambass Saudi Arabia 1996–; *Recreations* tennis, sailing, bridge; *Style*— HE Mr Andrew Green, CMG; ✉ c/o Foreign & Commonwealth Office (Riyadh), King Charles Street, London SW1A 2AH

GREEN, Anthony Eric Sandall; s of Frederick Sandall Green (d 1961), of London, and late Marie-Madeleine (Mrs Joscelyne), *née* Dupont; *b* 30 Sept 1939; *Educ* Highgate Sch, Slade Sch of Fine Art UCL (Dip Fine Art); *m* 29 July 1961, Mary Louise, da of Gordon Roberts Cozens-Walker (d 1981); 2 da (Katharine Charlotte b 1965, Lucy Rebecca b 1970); *Career* artist; Harkness fellowship USA 1967–69, fell UCL 1991–; over 50 one-man shows worldwide; recent exhbns incl Piccadilly Gallery 1996; UK public collections: Tate, V & A, Arts Cncl of GB, Br Cncl, and others; foreign public collections: The Metropolitan Museum of Art NYC, various museums in Japan and Brazil, and others; RA 1977; *Books* A Green Part of the World (with Martin Bailey, 1984); *Recreations* family, travel; *Style*— Anthony Green, Esq, RA; ✉ Mole End, 40 High Street, Little Eversden, Cambridge CB3 7HE (☎ 01223 262292)

GREEN, Antony John Stephen; s of Edwin Stephen Green, of Lyndhurst, and Eileen, *née* Rigby; *b* 6 Jan 1935; *Educ* Merchant Taylors' Sch Crosby, Univ of Bristol; *m* 30 March 1962, Valerie Anne, da of late Herbert Stanley Exworth; 2 c (Sarah Caroline b 14 Sept 1964, Christopher Stephen Antony b 19 Jan 1966); *Career* Nat Serv RN 1958–59; mgmnt apprentice Trust Houses Ltd 1959–62, various admin and mgmnt posts Trust House Forte Ltd 1962–84, dir Evergreen Hotels Ltd (fndr 1984, proprietor Crown Hotel Lyndhurst); memb Mgmnt Ctee New Forest Tourism Assoc; Master Innholder 1987, Freeman City of London 1987; MIMgt 1968, FHCIMA 1972; *Recreations* sailing, cooking; *Clubs* Island Cruising (Salcombe); *Style*— Antony Green, Esq; ✉ Crown Hotel, High St, Lyndurst, Hants SO43 7NF (☎ 01703 282922, fax 01703 282751)

GREEN, (Michael James) Bay; s of Patrick Green, OBE, DFC, and Eileen Brenda, *née* Green; *b* 4 June 1943; *Educ* Harrow; *m* 26 Aug 1971, Ann Eila, da of James Kennedy Elliott, OBE; 1 s (Edward James Patrick b 27 Nov 1973), 1 da (Caroline Eila b 6 Oct 1975); *Career* articled clerk Peat Marwick Mitchell & Co 1960–65, mangr G W Green & Sons 1965–71; Kleinwort Benson Ltd: joined 1971, dir 1978, chm and md Kleinwort Benson Australia Ltd 1981–84; head of corporate finance and md Hill Samuel Bank Ltd 1988–91; Kleinwort Benson Group plc: dir 1991–, head of Financing and Advsy Div 1994–96, gp vice chm 1996–; FCA; *Recreations* opera, tennis, shooting, flying (PPL); *Style*— Bay Green, Esq; ✉ Kleinwort Benson Ltd, PO Box 560, 20 Fenchurch St, London EC3P 3DB (☎ 0171 623 8000, fax 0171 623 5535)

GREEN, Prof Brynmor Hugh (Bryn); OBE (1995); s of Albert Walter Green (d 1971), and Margaret Afona, *née* Griffiths (d 1971); *b* 14 Jan 1941; *Educ* Dartford GS, Univ of Nottingham (BSc, PhD); *m* 14 Aug 1965, Jean, da of (Thomas) Norman Armstrong (d 1981); 2 s (David Ellis, Simon Gareth); *Career* lectr Dept of Botany Univ of Manchester 1965–67; Nature Conservancy Cncl: dep and SE regnl offr 1967–74, chief sci team 1974; Wye Coll Univ of London: lectr and sr lectr 1974–87, Sir Cyril Kleinwort prof of countryside mgmnt 1987–96, emeritus prof 1996–; memb Eng Ctee Nature Conservancy Cncl 1983–90, countryside cmmr 1984–93, chm Landscape Conservation Working Gp Int Union for the Conservation of Nature 1992–, vice chm Kent Farming and Wildlife Advsy Group, chm White Cliffs Countryside Mgmnt Project; *Books* The Diversion of Land (with C Potter et al, 1991), The Changing Role of the Common Agricultural Policy (with J Marsh et al, 1991), Countryside Conservation (6 edn, 1996); contrib sci papers to numerous jnls and books; *Recreations* golf, watercolour sketching, ornithology; *Style*— Prof Bryn Green, OBE; ✉ Selsfield, Oxenturn Rd, Wye, Ashford, Kent TN25 5AZ (☎ 01233 812575); Department of Agriculture, Horticulture and Environment, Wye Coll, Univ of London, Wye, Ashford, Kent TN25 5AH (☎ 01233 812401, fax 01233 813320, telex 96118 ANZEEC G)

GREEN, Charles; s of Jacob Green, of Leicester, and Anna, *née* Ostersetzer; *b* 26 March 1950; *Educ* London Sch of Film Technique; *m* 28 May 1972, Toni, da of Leibish Engelberg, of Antwerp, Belgium; 1 s (Kenny b 23 Jan 1975), 2 da (Michelle b 4 June 1977, Davina b 6 Jan 1986); *Career* photographer; opened portrait studio Edgware 1978; Master Photographer of the Year Award 1985, Court of Honour Award of Excellence Professional Photographers Soc of NY USA 1986, 12 Kodak Gold Awards for tech excellence and creativity 1988–95, Gold Certificate for Achievement World Cncl of Professional Photographers 1989; exhibitions: The Forgotten People 1990, Epcot Centre Florida (portraits chosen by Professional Photographers of America) 1990–91, Leaders of GB Into the 21st Century 1995; awarded Masters and Craftsman Degree in Photography Professional Photographers of America 1991, official photographer for investitures at Buckingham Palace 1992–; FBIPP 1985 (assoc BIPP 1983), FMPA, FRPS,

FRSA; *Books* Shooting For Gold (1987); *Style*— Charles Green, Esq; ✉ 309 Hale Lane, Station Rd, Edgware, Middlesex HA8 7AX (☎ 0181 958 3183, fax 0181 958 1947)

GREEN, Charles Frederick; s of George Frederick Green (d 1987), and Ellen Maud Mary, *née* Brett (d 1987); *b* 20 Oct 1930; *Educ* Harrow Co Sch; *m* 1956, Elizabeth Pauline Anne, da of Egbert Joseph William Jackson, CB, MC (d 1975); 2 s (Nicholas b 1957, Martin b 1959), 1 da (Mary b 1963); *Career* sec National Provincial Bank 1967–70 (joined 1946); National Westminster Bank: head of planning 1970, md Centre File 1974–76, gen mangr Financial Control Div 1982, dir 1982–89, dep gp chief exec 1986–89; chm: Multinational Affrs Panel CBI/ICC 1982–87, Overseas Ctee CBI 1987–89; dir Business in the Community 1983–90 (vice chm 1983–89), memb Cncl Policy Studies Inst 1984– (treas 1984–93); Church of England: memb General Synod 1980–90, vice chm Bd for Social Responsibility 1983–91 (memb 1980–93), chm Industl and Econ Affrs Ctee 1986–93, chm Central Stewardship Ctee 1993–; vice chm Gloucester Diocesan Bd of Fin 1992–; chm: County of Glos Community Fndn 1991–, Mgmnt Ctee Glenfall House 1991– (chm of Tstees 1996–); tstee: Small Business Research Tst 1986–, Church Urban Fund 1987–89, Monteverdi Tst 1986–, Charities Aid Fndn 1989–; govr: Westonbirt Sch 1990–, Monkton Combe Sch 1990–96, Old Sodbury C of E Primary Sch 1992–; vice chm Cheltenham and Gloucester Coll of HE 1994– (memb Cncl 1993–); FCIB, FIMgt, FRSA, Hon FLCM; *Recreations* opera, concert music, drama; *Clubs* Athenaeum, National; *Style*— Charles Green, Esq; ✉ The Old House, Parks Farm, Old Sodbury, Bristol BS17 6PX (☎ 01454 311936)

GREEN, Christopher Edward Wastie (Chris); s of James Wastie Green, and Margarita, *née* Mensing; *b* 7 Sept 1943; *Educ* St Paul's, Oriel Coll Oxford (MA); *m* 1966, Mitzie, da of Dr Petzold; 1 s (James b 1971), 1 da (Carol b 1969); *Career* British Rail: mgmnt trainee 1965, area mangr Hull 1973, passenger ops mangr BRB 1978, regnl ops mangr Scotland 1980, dep gen mangr ScotRail 1983, gen mangr ScotRail 1984, md Network South East 1990–91 (dir 1986), md InterCity 1992–94, md ScotRail 1994–95; chief exec English Heritage March 1995–96 (cmmr July 1995–96), md (business consulting) Gibb Ltd (formerly Sir Alexander Gibb & Partners) 1996–; currently dir: Eurotunnel plc, Connex Rail Ltd; FCIT; *Recreations* canal boating, architecture, music, hill walking; *Style*— Chris Green, Esq; ✉ Gibb Ltd, Gibb House, London Road, Reading, Berks RG6 1BL (☎ 0118 963 5000)

GREEN, Prof Christopher John Charles; OBE (1995); s of Eric Frederick Green, and Muriel Mary, *née* Rice; *b* 3 Nov 1942; *Educ* Northgate GS for Boys Ipswich, Univ of Leeds (BA, PhD); *m* 3 Aug 1968, Sylvia Alice, da of Robert Buckenham; 2 s (Jonathan James b 13 Dec 1971, Richard Charles b 27 April 1975); *Career* lectr Enfield Coll of Technol 1971–73 (Hockerill Coll 1968–71), sr lectr Middx Poly 1973–76, head of dept Essex Coll of Higher Educn 1981–89 (Chelmer Coll of Higher Educn 1976–81), project dir Essex Centre Anglia Coll of Higher Educn 1989–91, prof of continuing and adult educn Anglia University (formerly Anglia Poly) 1991– (dir Regnl Office 1992–); sr music critic E Anglian Daily Times; dep chm Essex Radio plc; artistic dir Trianon Music Gp 1959–, chm Nat Assoc of Youth Orchestras 1975–78, artistic dir Ipswich Festival 1980–83, chm Chelmsford and Dist Mental Health Centre 1983–, chm Essex Radio Helping Hands Tst 1989–, chm Ipswich Arts Assoc 1989–; assoc fell Br Psychological Soc 1989, FRSA; *Recreations* reading, music, theatre; *Style*— Prof Christopher Green, OBE

GREEN, Colin Raymond; s of Dr Gerald Herman Green, of London, and Maisie, *née* Benkwich; *b* 16 April 1949; *Educ* Hampton GS, LSE (LLB), Coll of Law, Wujs Inst Arad Israel; *m* 1975, Hazel Ruth, *née* Lateman; 1 s (Samuel Nathan b 1983), 1 da (Hanna Judith b 1985); *Career* admitted slr 1973, asst slr Paisner & Co 1973–74 (articled clerk 1971–73), ptnr Clintons 1975–77 (asst slr 1974–75); British Telecommunications plc: legal asst The Post Office (before demerger of British Telecom) 1977–81, head of privatisation Legal Div British Telecom 1981–84, head of M&A Legal Div 1984–85, dir Commercial Dept 1985–89, slr and chief legal advsr 1989–94, sec and chief legal advsr 1994–; dir BT Property Ltd 1991–, tstee BT Pension Scheme 1994–, memb Exec Ctee BT 1996–; dir Centre for Dispute Resolution (CEDR) 1995–; memb (former chm) Kingston JIA Ctee; memb Law Soc 1973; *Recreations* football, reading, theatre, walking, music; *Style*— Colin Green, Esq; ✉ British Telecommunications plc, Room A979, BT Centre, 81 Newgate Street, London EC1A 7AJ (☎ 0171 356 5237, fax 0171 356 6135)

GREEN, Damian Howard; s of Howard Green, of Billericay, Essex, and Audrey Edith, *née* Lyons; *b* 17 Jan 1956; *Educ* Reading Sch, Balliol Coll Oxford (MA, pres Oxford Union); *m* 1988, Alicia Hester Collinson, *qv*, da of late Judge Jeffreys Collinson; 2 da (Felicity Charlotte Hester b 1990, Verity Mary Sophie b 1993); *Career* prodr/presenter Financial World Tonight BBC Radio 4 1978–82, economics scriptwriter ITN Channel 4 News 1982–84, news ed (Business News) The Times 1984–85, business ed Channel 4 News 1985–87, dep ed Business Daily Channel 4 1987–92, special advsr PM's Policy Unit 1992–94; currently public affrs conslt; Parly candidate (Cons) Brent E 1992, prospective Parly candidate (Cons) Ashford; *Publications* ITN Budget Factbook (1984, 1985 and 1986), A Better BBC (pamphlet for Centre for Policy Studies, 1991), The Cross Media Revolution (co-author, 1995), Communities in the Countryside (Social Market Fndn, 1996); *Recreations* cricket, football, opera, theatre; *Clubs* Carlton, MCC; *Style*— Damian Green, Esq; ✉ c/o Ashford Conservative Association, Hardy House, The Street, Bethersden, Ashford, Kent TN26 3AG (☎ 01233 820454)

GREEN, (Gregory) David; s of Thomas Dixon Green, of Thornton Rust, nr Leyburn, N Yorks, and Mabella Mary, *née* Walley; *b* 2 Dec 1948; *Educ* The Leys Sch Cambridge, Keswick Hall Coll of Educn Norwich, Trinity Hall Cambridge (BEd); *m* 10 Sept 1977, Corinne, da of Anthony Bernard Butler; 3 da (Hannah Mabella b 1978, Emily Corinne b 1980, Frances Ethel Rosalind b 1982); *Career* teacher of English West Pakistan (VSO) 1967–68, teacher of art/head of first year Northcliffe Comp Sch 1972–75, teacher of art/head of year Aston Comp Sch Rotherham 1975–76, dir Children's Relief Int/The Cambridge Project Save the Children 1976–79; Save the Children: staff devpt and trg offr 1979–82, dep dir of personnel 1983, dir of personnel 1983–88, dir of personnel and admin 1988–90; dir VSO 1990–; memb Advsy Panel Mgmnt Devpt Unit NVCO 1985–86; MIPM 1987; exhibition of paintings held 1978, dir Cinderella (by Peter Maxwell Davies, Queen Elizabeth Hall) 1990; memb Laurence Olivier Award Panel 1985; FRSA, FRGS; *Recreations* theatre, music, painting, woodworking, travel; *Style*— David Green; ✉ Director, Voluntary Service Overseas, 317 Putney Bridge Road, London SW15 2PN (☎ 0181 780 2266, fax 0181 780 1326)

GREEN, David Anthony; s of Thomas Green, of Northgate, Sussex, and Leonora Green; *b* 15 Aug 1943; *Educ* Collyers GS, LSE (BSc(Econ)); *m* 1972, Alice, *née* Zawilenski; 2 da (Nicole b 18 May 1984, Tanya b 12 May 1990); *Career* auditor Arthur Andersen & Co 1964–69, financial controller Spain Dan-Air 1970–72, international fin dir Morton International Inc 1972–77, fin dir International Harvester 1978–85, dir then chm Taylor Woodrow Services Ltd 1985–89, gp fin dir Taylor Woodrow plc 1988–; FCA; *Recreations* theatre, travel; *Style*— David Green, Esq; ✉ Taylor Woodrow plc, 4 Dunraven Street, London W1Y 3FG (☎ 0171 629 1201, fax 0171 409 1764)

GREEN, David John Mark; s of John Geoffrey Green, of Woodford Green, Essex, and Margaret Green; *b* 8 March 1954; *Educ* Christ's Hosp Horsham, St Catharine's Coll Cambridge (MA); *m* 7 June 1980, Katherine, da of James Sharkey, of Woodford Green; 1 s (Dominic James Millican), 2 da (Clemency Alice, Leonora Isabel); *Career* Def Intelligence Staff MOD 1975–78; called to the Bar Inner Temple 1979; *Style*— David Green, Esq; ✉ 5 King's Bench Walk, Temple, London EC4 (☎ 0171 797 7600, fax 0171 797 7648)

GREEN, David Michael; s of John Barrington Green, of Brisbane, Australia, and Nance, *née* O'Brian; *b* 28 Feb 1960; *Educ* St Pauls Brisbane Australia; *m* 4 Dec 1981 (m dis 1992), Lucinda Jane, *qv*, da of Maj-Gen G E Prior Palmer; 1 s (Freddie David b 9 April 1985), 1 da (Lissa Bella b 3 Feb 1989); *Career* horserider; Badminton Horse Trials: 6 place (Mairangi Bay) 1982, 11 place (Walkabout) 1984; winner int three-day event Punchestown Ireland (Botany Bay) 1982, 5 place American three-day event championships Chesterland (Walkabout) 1983; Euro Championships: Burghley (Walkabout) 1985, (Count de Bolebec) 1987; winner Hasselt Belgium (The Bushby Solider) 1987, winner Saumur France (Ayres Rock) 1988, 10 place World Championships The Hague (Chatsby) 1994, winner Saumur France (Chatsby) 1995, winner Fairhill USA (Chatsby) 1995; memb Aust team: World Championships Luhmulen Germany (Mairangi Bay) 1982, Seoul Olympics (Ayres Rock) 1988, World Equestrian Games 1990, Barcelona Olympics 1992 (Gold); rep individual for Aust: Open Euro Champs Pratoni Italy (Chatsby) 1995, Atlanta Olympics (Chatsby) 1996; placed in top fifteen world ranking system 1987–88; *Recreations* scuba diving, skiing, golf; *Style*— David Green, Esq; ✉ Scotland Lodge Farm, Winterbourne Stoke, Salisbury, Wilts SP3 4TF (☎ 01980 621199, fax 01980 621188)

GREEN, David William; *b* 5 March 1950; *Career* conslt anaesthetist and chair Dept of Anaesthetics King's Coll Hosp London; visiting prof of regional anaesthesia Univ of Western Ontario Nov 1987; hon sec SE Thames RCSC; memb: BMA, POWAR King's Coll Hosp, American Soc of Anesthesiologists, Euro Acad of Anaesthesiology; FRSM; *Books* A New Short Textbook of Anaesthetics (jtly, 1986), Anaesthesia and Perioperative Care (jtly, 1994); *Recreations* classical music; *Clubs* IOD; *Style*— David Green, Esq; ✉ 34 Ponsonby Terrace, London SW1P 4QA; Department of Anaesthetics, King's College Hospital, Denmark Hill, London SE5 9RS (☎ 0171 346 3154/3358)

GREEN, Prof Dennis Howard; s of Herbert Maurice Green (d 1953), and Agnes Edith, *née* Fleming; *b* 26 June 1922; *Educ* Latymer Upper Sch London, Trinity Coll Cambridge (BA), Univ of Basel (DPhil); *m* 17 Nov 1972, Margaret, *née* Parry; *Career* teaching fell Trinity Coll Cambridge 1952–66 (res fell 1949–52); lectr Univ of St Andrews 1949–50; Univ of Cambridge: lectr 1950–66, prof of modern languages 1966–79, Schröder prof of German 1979–89; professorial fell Trinity Coll Cambridge 1966–; various visiting professorships in USA, Germany, Aust and NZ; hon pres Int Courtly Lit Soc; memb Wolfram-von-Eschenbach-Gesellschaft; FBA 1992; *Books* The Carolingian Lord (1965), The Millstätter Exodus (1966), Approaches to Wolfram von Eschenbach (1978), Irony in the Medieval Romance (1979), The Art of Recognition in Wolfram's Parzival (1982), Medieval Listening and Reading (1994); *Recreations* walking and foreign travel; *Style*— Prof Dennis Green, FBA; ✉ 7 Archway Court, Barton Road, Cambridge CB3 9LW (☎ 01223 514386)

GREEN, Derek; *b* 27 Jan 1940; *Educ* Leigh GS, Hyde County GS, Salford Royal Coll of Advanced Technol (Dip in Quantity Surveying); *m*; 1 s, 1 da; *Career* articled pupil quantity surveyor J Gerrard & Sons Ltd Manchester 1956–61, quantity surveyor Building Design Partnership 1961–63, sr surveyor/estimator Neill Construction Ltd 1963–64, sr quantity surveyor Kuwait International Airport Project Sab Roma 1964–65, construction mangr NW Area Costain Construction Ltd 1967–70 (sr quantity surveyor 1965–67), dir of project devpt Europe, N Africa and ME Holiday Inns Inc USA 1971–75 (dir of project devpt UK 1970–71); AMEC plc: memb Gp Exec Bd, dir Fairclough Building Ltd 1975–88, dir Fairclough International Construction Ltd 1978–81, chief exec AMEC International Ltd 1981–85, chief exec AMEC Projects Ltd 1981–88, chm Worley Engineering Ltd 1983–88, chm Mapel Ltd 1983–88; chief exec Aggregates Gp Tilcon Holdings Ltd (pt of BTR plc) 1988–92; United Utilities plc (formerly North West Water Group plc): dir 1992–, md North West Water Ltd 1992–95, exec chm Utility Div (North West Water and Norweb) 1996–; non-exec dir Graham Group plc (nat builders merchants) 1994–; FRICS; *Style*— Derek Green, Esq; ✉ United Utilities plc, Dawson House, Great Sankey, Warrington, Cheshire WA5 3LW (☎ 01925 233502, fax 01925 233382)

GREEN, Emily (Mrs Knox); da of Leon Green, and Eleanor, *née* Samuels; *b* 1 March 1956; *Educ* Univ of Grenoble, Univ of Maryland; *m* 19 Jan 1984, Ian Knox, s of Eric Knox; *Career* The Independent 1988–: successively restaurant listings ed, fndr ed Eating Out page, restaurant critic Weekend Food and Drink pages; *Style*— Ms Emily Green; ✉ The Independent, 1 Canada Square, Canary Wharf, London EC14 5AP (☎ 0171 253 1222)

GREEN, Ernest; s of Luke Green (d 1944), and Daisy Sarah Lydia, *née* Smeeton; *b* 22 Dec 1929; *Educ* Westminster Tech Coll; *m* 1 Sept 1951, May, da of John Menzies Kennedy (d 1959), of Scot; 3 s (Graham Ernest b 1955, Russell Ian b 1959, Elliot Luke b 1973), 1 da (Susan Debra (Mrs Wright) b 1957); *Career* Nat Serv Sgt RE 1949, MONS OTC, cmmnd 1952; served: 3 TRRE, 9 TRRE, 114 Army Engr Regt, 101 Field Engr Regt, ret RE TA 1957; gained experience in various civil and structural consulting offices, fndr own practice Ernest Green Holdings (first consulting engr listed on London Stock Exchange) 1985; memb Assoc of Consulting Engrs; Freeman City of London 1960, Liveryman Worshipful Co of Basketmakers 1960, Freeman Guild of Air Pilots and Navigators 1974; FIStructE 1955, FICE 1957; *Recreations* motor yachting, flying; *Clubs* City Livery, Belfry; *Style*— Ernest Green, Esq; ✉ The White House, L'Eree, St Peters in the Wood, Guernsey, CI (☎ 01481 64385, fax 01481 65085)

GREEN, Dr Frank Alan; s of Frank Green (d 1943), and Winifred Hilda, *née* Payne (d 1991); *b* 29 Oct 1931; *Educ* Mercers Sch, Univ of London (BSc, PhD); *m* 30 March 1957, Pauline Eleanor, da of George Edward Tayler (d 1980); 1 s (Paul b 19 July 1963), 2 da (Gail b 17 April 1958, Sally b 18 Sept 1960); *Career* md AE Group subsid 1962–66, tech dir Consormex SA Mexico City 1966–68, mfrg dir Stewart Warner Corp 1968–72, dir of market devpt Calor Group 1972–74, md British Twin Disc Ltd (and dir Twin Disc International SA) 1974–80, industl advsr (under sec) DTI 1981–84; currently: md Charing Green Ltd, princ ptnr Charing Green Associates, PR conslt Europa Consultancy Ltd; advsr to Mexican Govt on mfrg 1966–68, dep chm Newcastle Technol Centre 1983; memb: Kent CBI Ctee and CBI SE Regnl Ctee 1974–80, Professional Bd Inst of Metals 1986–91 (chm Gen Educn Ctee 1986–88, chm Initial Formation Ctee 1988–91), Cncl Inst of Materials 1991–94; CEng, FIM, FIMgt; *Recreations* wine, photography, hill walking, military and local history; *Clubs* Old Mercers; *Style*— Dr Frank Green; ✉ Courtwood House, Burleigh Rd, Charing, Kent TN27 0JB; Europa Consultancy Ltd, Kings Hill, West Malling, Kent ME19 6DU (☎ 01233 713152)

GREEN, Geoffrey Colin; s of Stephen Frederick Green (d 1983), and Betty Esther, *née* Lewis (d 1983); *b* 3 Dec 1947; *Educ* Churchill Sch Rhodesia, Salisbury Poly Rhodesia; *m* 18 July 1970, Patricia, da of Thomas James Dent; 1 s (Andrew Stephen Landon b 12 Oct 1972), 1 da (Catherine Elizabeth b 8 March 1977); *Career* articled clerk: Myers Clarke Birkett 1965, Tansley Witt & Co until 1970; CA 1970; Coopers & Lybrand: Johannesburg office 1970–73, sr audit mangr Reading 1976–78 (audit mangr 1974–76), ptnr 1978, ptnr in charge 1989, managing ptnr 1994–96, nat market leader energy water tport 1996–; memb S Regnl Cncl CBI 1992; FCA 1979 (ACA 1970), MInstD 1985; *Recreations* golf, watching motor racing, photography; *Style*— Geoffrey Green, Esq; ✉ Coopers & Lybrand, 9 Greyfriars Road, Reading, Berkshire RG1 1JG (☎ 0118 959 7111, fax 0118 960 7700)

GREEN, Geoffrey David; s of Ronald Green (d 1977), of Enfield, and Ivy May, *née* Steggles (d 1988); *b* 17 March 1946; *Educ* George Spicer Central Sch Enfield; *m* 3 April 1969, Rosmarie, da of Dominik Raber, of Affoltern Am Albis, Switzerland; 2 da (Natasha b 1970, Vanessa b 1972); *Career* dir: Bisgood 1985–, County Securities 1986–, County NatWest 1986–90, County NatWest Wood MacKenzie 1988–90; MSI 1992 (memb Stock Exchange 1970); *Recreations* cycling, gardening, travel, reading; *Style*— Geoffrey Green, Esq; ✉ Hadleigh, 35 Carnaby Rd, Broxbourne, Hertfordshire EN10 7EG

GREEN, Geoffrey Edward; s of Edward Bowyer Green (d 1990), of Beaconsfield, and Clara Jane, *née* Allen (d 1972); *b* 27 March 1929; *Educ* High Wycombe Royal GS, Univ of London (LLB), Law Society's Coll of Law; *m* 2 Jan 1954, Joy Anne, da of William Robert Willcocks (d 1963), of Beaconsfield; 1 da (Nichola Joy (Mrs Blunt) b 1955); *Career* admitted slr 1951, NP 1969; asst to late Sir Cullum Welch, Bt, PA to late Sir Frank Medlicott, CBE, MP 1952–54, sole practice and ptnr in central London 1954–61, practice in Beaconsfield 1962–; pt/t specialist law lectr 1983–94; underwriting memb Lloyd's 1972–; Parly candidate (C) Manchester Openshaw Gen Election 1974; fndr memb (former memb Cncl) Central and S Middx Law Soc; memb: Soc of Cons Lawyers (memb Exec Ctee 1974–77), Law Soc, Soc of Notaries, City of London Law Soc, Berks, Bucks and Oxon Law Soc; Freeman City of London 1951, Liveryman Worshipful Co of Slrs 1974; *Recreations* reading, travel, gardening; *Clubs* Arts, Wig & Pen; *Style*— Geoffrey Green, Esq; ✉ Tumblers Chase, 8 Stratton Rd, Beaconsfield, Bucks HP9 1HS (☎ 01494 674406)

GREEN, Dr Geoffrey Frederic; s of George Hanson Green (d 1987), of Guiseley, West Yorks, and Elizabeth, *née* Kershaw; *b* 22 Aug 1947; *Educ* Bootham Sch York, Univ of Edinburgh (MA, PhD); *m* 25 Nov 1974, Ellen Clare, da of Edmund Favre Hughes (d 1987), of New Orleans; 1 s (Christopher George b 24 April 1985), 1 da (Emily Anais b 31 Oct 1983); *Career* T&T Clark academic publishers: publishing dir 1977–87, md 1987–, proprietor 1991–; *Clubs* New (Edinburgh), Edinburgh Croquet, Carlton Cricket, Edinburgh Univ Staff; *Style*— Dr Geoffrey Green; ✉ 35 Dick Place, Edinburgh, Scotland (☎ 0131 667 2028); T&T Clark, 59 George St, Edinburgh (☎ 0131 225 4703, fax 0131 220 4260)

GREEN, Geoffrey Stephen; s of John Geoffrey Green, of Essex, and Margaret Rowena, *née* Millican; *b* 3 Sept 1949; *Educ* Forest Sch, St Catharine's Coll Cambridge (MA); *m* 1 (m dis 1980), Fiona Mary Inglis; m 2, 30 Dec 1982, Sarah Charlton Chesshire, da of Wing Cdr Arthur Chesshire; 3 s (Alexander Thomas Charlton b 29 Dec 1983, Frederick Robert b 3 June 1986, Henry George Rollo b 30 July 1990); *Career* admitted slr 1975; ptnr Ashurst Morris Crisp 1979– (currently head of Company and Commercial Dept); *Recreations* tennis, cricket, golf; *Clubs* Hurlingham; *Style*— Geoffrey Green, Esq; ✉ Ashurst Morris Crisp, Broadwalk House, 5 Appold Street, London EC2A 2HA (☎ 0171 638 1111)

GREEN, Gerald John; s of Alfred Stanley Green (d 1988), of Northleach, Glos, and Mary Ellen, *née* Flynn (d 1981); *b* 14 Sept 1928; *Educ* Westwoods GS; *Career* ROC 1944–45, Palestine Police Force 1946–48 (wounded 1947), GOC Haifa Volunteer Force 1948 (wounded); building control offr Local Govt Serv 1950–90; memb: Nat Cncl of Faculty of Architects and Surveyors 1967–88, Building and Civil Engrg Cncl BSI 1971–90, Construction Indust Annual Assembly BSI 1990–; tstee Northleach Town 1972– (hon surveyor to tstees 1974–), chm Glos Branch Faculty of Architects and Surveyors 1972–73, High Bailiff of Northleach Town 1979–81, memb Nat Cncl of Architects and Surveyors Inst 1989–90 (chm Glos Branch 1989–); cncllr Cotswold DC 1991–95, memb Cncl Anglo Jordanian Soc 1995; Andrew Byrne Cup from Faculty of Architects and Surveyors 1985; Freeman City of London 1978, fndr memb and Liveryman Worshipful Co of Arbitrators 1981; FASI 1960, FSVA 1963, FBEng 1983, FCIArb 1972, MIBC 1973; *Books* FAS Short Form of Building Contract (LA version with J W Stephenson, 1964); *Recreations* foreign travel, flying, collecting autographed first edition books; *Clubs* Special Forces; *Style*— Gerald Green, Esq; ✉ 5 Grace Drive, Northleach, Glos GL54 3HQ (☎ 01451 860272)

GREEN, Dr John Edward; s of John Green (d 1957), and Ellen, *née* O'Dowd (d 1974); *b* 26 Aug 1937; *Educ* Birkenhead Inst GS, St John's Coll Cambridge (BA, MA, PhD); *m* 12 June 1959, Gillian Mary, da of Harold Barker Jackson (d 1988); 1 s (John b 1966), 1 da (Imogen b 1964); *Career* student apprentice Bristol Aircraft Ltd 1956, tech asst De Havilland Engine Co 1959–61, dir of project time and cost analysis MOD (PE) HQ 1981–84, dep head of defence staff and min-cnsllr of defence equipment Br Embassy Washington 1984–85, dep dir of aircraft Royal Aircraft Estab 1985–87 (aerodynamics 1964–81, head of various res divs 1971–78, head of Aerodynamics Dept 1978–81); Aircraft Research Association Ltd: chief exec 1988–95, chief scientist 1995–; Royal Aeronautical Soc: memb Cncl, hon treas 1992–, vice pres 1992–95, pres-elect 1995–96, pres 1996–97; UK rep on Int Cncl of Aeronautical Sciences (pres 1996–98), memb Court and Cncl Cranfield Univ; CEng 1972, FRAeS 1978, FEng 1994; *Recreations* mountain walking (Munroist 1994), music; *Style*— Dr John Green, FEng; ✉ 1 Leighton Street, Woburn, Milton Keynes, Buckinghamshire MK17 9PJ (☎ and fax 01525 290631)

GREEN, John Michael; CB (1976); s of George Morgan Green (d 1949), and Faith Mary, *née* Sage (d 1988); *b* 5 Dec 1924; *Educ* Merchant Taylors', Jesus Coll Oxford (MA); *m* 1951, Sylvia, da of Rowland Yorke Crabb (d 1972); 1 s (David), 1 da (Barbara); *Career* Royal Armoured Corps, Capt 1943–46; entered Civil Serv (Inland Revenue) 1948, HM Treasy 1956–57; memb: Bd of Inland Revenue 1971–85 (dep chm of Bd 1973–85), NW Surrey Health Authy 1989–95; *Recreations* gardening; *Clubs* Reform; *Style*— John Green, Esq, CB; ✉ 5 Bylands, Woking, Surrey GU22 7LA

GREEN, Dr John Timothy; s of Thomas Albert Green (d 1978), of Birmingham, and Joan, *née* Chamberlain; *b* 1 Jan 1944; *Educ* King Edward's Five Ways Sch Birmingham, Queens' Coll Cambridge (Foundation scholar, MA, PhD); *m* 1985, Susan Mary, da of David Harold Shattock; 1 s (Thomas William b 16 Nov 1988); *Career* Queens' Coll Cambridge: Bye fell 1970–72, dean 1972–77, tutor 1977–80, sr tutor 1977–80, fell and lectr in mathematics 1972–93, life fell 1993–; chief exec Royal Society of Medicine 1993–; recruitment advsr FCO 1992–; dir: South Leicestershire Garages 1985–95, Pennant Hotels 1987–95, RSM Press Ltd 1993–, RSM Support Services Ltd 1993–, RSM Foundation Inc NY 1993–; tstee: Harpur Tst 1984–87, Project Hope 1995–, London First Medicine 1995–; govr Hills Road Sixth Form Coll Cambridge 1993–; contrib to Journal of Fluid Mechanics and other scientific pubns; *Recreations* opera, music, fell-walking; *Style*— Dr John T Green; ✉ 40 Newton Road, Cambridge CB2 2AL (☎ 01223 353756); Royal Society of Medicine, 1 Wimpole Street, London W1M 8AE (☎ 0171 290 2900, fax 0171 290 2909)

GREEN, Jonathon Simon; s of Arthur Green (d 1989), of London, and Salome, *née* Morris; *b* 20 April 1948; *Educ* Bedford Sch, Brasenose Coll Oxford; *partner* Susan Ford; 2 s (Lucien b 29 Sept 1977, Gabriel b 10 May 1982); *Career* freelance journalist, broadcaster, editor and writer 1969–; *Books* Contemporary Dictionary of Quotations (1982, revsd edn 1989), Newspeak - A Dictionary of Jargon (1983), The Dictionary of Contemporary Slang (1984, revsd edn 1993), The Slang Thesaurus (1986), The Dictionary of Jargon (1987), Days in the Life - Voices from the English Underground 1961–71 (1988), The Encyclopedia of Censorship (1990), Them - Voices from the Immigrant Community in Contemporary Britain (1990), Neologisms - A Dictionary of Contemporary Coinages (1991), It - Sex Since the Sixties (1993), Slang Down the Ages (1994), Chasing the Sun: Dictionary Makers and the Dictionaries they Made (1996); *Style*— Jonathon Green, Esq; ✉ c/o Jacintha Alexander Assoc, 47 Emperor's Gate, London SW7 4HJ (☎ 0171 373 9258, fax 0171 373 4374)

GREEN, Sir Kenneth; kt (1988); s of James William Green, and Elsie May Green; *b* 7 March 1934; *Educ* Helsby GS, Univ of Wales Bangor (BA), Univ of London (MA); *m* 1961, Glenda, *née* Williams; 1 da (Lindsey); *Career* Nat Serv 2 Lt S Wales Borderers 1955–57; trainee mangr Dunlop Rubber Co Birmingham 1957–58, asst teacher Speke Secdy Modern Sch Liverpool 1958–60; lectr: Widnes Tech Coll 1961–62, Stockport Coll of Technol 1962–64, Bolton Coll of Educn (Tech) 1964–68; head of educn City of Birmingham Coll of Educn 1968–72, visiting lectr Univ of Warwick 1972–73, dean Faculty of Community Studies and Educn Manchester 1973–81, vice-chllr The Manchester Metropolitan Univ 1992– (dir Manchester Poly 1981–92); memb: Cncl for Nat Academic Awards 1985–93, Ct Univ of Salford 1985–92, Univs Funding Cncl 1989–93, Bd of Govrs Sheffield Hallam Univ (formerly Sheffield City Poly) 1989–92, Mgmnt Bd Polytechnics and Colleges Employers' Forum 1989–92, Higher Educn Funding Cncl for England Working Gp on the Review of the Academic Year (Flowers Ctee) 1992–93; chm: Governing Body Victoria Road County Primary Sch 1993– (memb 1990–), Rathbone Community Industry Limited 1995– (formerly chm The Rathbone Soc 1993–95), Runcorn Branch Age Concern 1992–; vice chm Bd Manchester Trg and Enterprise Cncl 1989–93, hon memb Manchester Literary and Philosophical Soc 1991, Hon Memb RNCM 1987; Hon LLD Univ of Manchester 1992; CIMgt 1996; *Recreations* rugby football; *Style*— Sir Kenneth Green; ✉ 40 Royden Ave, Runcorn, Cheshire WA7 4SP (☎ 019285 75201); The Manchester Metropolitan University, All Saints, Manchester M15 6BH (☎ 0161 247 1560, fax 0161 247 6358)

GREEN, Kenneth David; s of William Haskell Green, of California, USA, and Zelma Grace, *née* Galyean; *b* 11 April 1944; *Educ* El Camino HS, UCLA (BA, MBA); *m* 12 April 1969, Anne Elizabeth, da of late William Fred Fremdling; 1 s (Michael b 1972), 1 da (Melissa b 1975); *Career* sr vice pres Bank of America 1968–86, md Bank of America International Ltd 1980–86; dir: Barclays de Zoete Wedd Holdings Ltd 1986–, md Barclays de Zoete Wedd Ltd 1986–; dir Barclays de Zoete Wedd Government Securities Inc 1987–; *Recreations* tennis, travel, family; *Clubs* St George's Hill Lawn Tennis,; *Style*— Kenneth Green, Esq; ✉ Barclays de Zoete Wedd Ltd, 2 Swan Lane, London EC4R 3TS (☎ 0171 956 3118, fax 0171 956 4612)

GREEN, Rt Rev Dr Laurence Alexander (Laurie); *see:* Bradwell, Bishop of

GREEN, Prof Leslie Leonard; CBE (1989); s of Leonard Green (d 1975), and Victoria, *née* Hughes (d 1978); *Educ* Alderman Newton's Sch Leicester, King's Coll Cambridge (MA, PhD); *m* 26 April 1952, Helen Therese Green, da of Francis Joseph Morgan (d 1962); 1 s (Paul Nicholas b 25 April 1959), 1 da ((Elizabeth) Sarah b 1956); *Career* Univ of Liverpool: lectr 1948, reader 1962, prof (now emeritus) 1964, dean Faculty of Sci 1967–70, pro-vice-chllr 1978–81; dir SERC Daresbury Laboratory 1981–88; FInstP, CPhys; *Style*— Prof Leslie Green, CBE; ✉ Seafield Cottage, De Grouchy St, West Kirby, Merseyside L48 5DX (☎ 0151 625 5167)

GREEN, Lucinda Jane; MBE (1977); da of Maj-Gen George Erroll Prior-Palmer, CB, DSO (d 1977), by his 2 w, Lady Doreen; *b* 7 Nov 1953; *Educ* St Mary's Wantage, Idbury Manor Oxon; *m* 1981 (m dis 1992), David Michael Green, yr s of Barry Green, of Brisbane, Australia; 1 s (Frederick b 1985), 1 da (Lissa b 1989); *Career* three day eventer; winner Badminton Horse Trials Championships 1973, 1976, 1977, 1979, 1983 and 1984, Individual Euro Championships 1975 and 1977, memb Olympic Team Montreal 1976, Euro Championship winning team Burghley 1977, World Championship team Kentucky 1978, memb World Championship winning Br 3–Day Event Team Luhmühlen W Germany 1982 (also winner of individual championship), Silver medallist Euro Championship Frauenfeld 1983, memb Silver medal winning Olympic Team 1984, winning Euro Championship Team Burghley 1985; TV co-presenter of 6 part documentary Horses 1987, regular contrib to Daily Telegraph and commentator for BBC and Satellite TV, commented on all equestrian events at: Barcelona Olympics for Channel 7 Australia 1992, Atlanta Olympics 1996; *Books* Up, Up and Away (1978), Four Square (1980), Regal Realm (1983), Cross Country Riding (1986), The Young Rider (1993); *Clubs* Mount Kenya Safari; *Style*— Mrs Lucinda Green, MBE; ✉ The Tree House Appleshaw, Andover, Hants SP11 9BS (☎ 0126 477 1133)

GREEN, Dr Malcolm; s of James Bisdee Malcolm Green, of Colchester, Essex, and Frances Marjorie Lois, *née* Ruffel; *b* 25 Jan 1942; *Educ* Charterhouse, Trinity Coll Oxford (BA, BSc, BM BCh, MA, DM), St Thomas' Hosp Med Sch; *m* 24 April 1971, Julieta Caroline, da of William Preston (d 1978); 2 s (Andrew b 28 Feb 1974, Marcus b 20 June 1979), 3 da (Nicola b 6 March 1972, Alexandra b 26 Dec 1975 d 1978, Camilla b 7 Aug 1980); *Career* lectr in med St Thomas' Hosp 1970–74 (house physician 1968–69), Radcliffe travelling fell Univ of Oxford to Harvard Univ Med Sch 1971–73, conslt physician and conslt i/c Chest Dept Bart's 1975–87, conslt physician in chest med and sr lectr Royal Brompton Hosp 1975–, dean Nat Heart & Lung Inst Univ of London 1988–90, dir Br Postgrad Med Fedn 1991–; chm Cncl Br Lung Fndn 1985–, pres United Hosps SC 1992– (hon treas 1977–87); author of chapters, reviews and articles on gen med, respiratory med and physiology; Freeman City of London 1968, Liveryman Worshipful Soc of Apothecaries 1965; FRCP 1980 (MRCP 1970); *Recreations* sailing, skiing; *Clubs* Royal Thames Yacht, Itchenor Sailing, Imperial Poona Yacht; *Style*— Dr Malcolm Green; ✉ 38 Lansdowne Gdns, London SW8 2EF (☎ 0171 622 8286); Royal Brompton Hospital, London SW3 6HP (☎ 0171 376 4985, fax 0171 351 8939)

GREEN, Malcolm Leslie Hodder; s of Leslie Ernest Green (d 1946), and Ethel Sheila, *née* Hodder; *b* 16 April 1936; *Educ* Denstone Coll, Acton Tech Coll (BSc), Imperial Coll London (PhD, DIC); *m* 2 Jan 1965, Jennifer Clare, da of Philip Leo Bilham (d 1956); 3 c (Russell Philip Malcolm b 1969, Sophie Anne Jennifer b 1970, Matthew Charles Hereward b 1973); *Career* res assocs fell Imperial Coll 1959–60, asst lectr in inorganic chemistry Univ of Cambridge 1960–63 (fell Corpus Christi Coll 1961); Univ of Oxford: septcentenary fell of inorganic chemistry Balliol Coll 1963–88, departmental demonstrator 1963, univ lectr 1965–88, vice master Balliol Coll 1987, prof of inorganic chemistry and head of dept 1989–, fell St Catherine's Coll; visiting prof: Univ of W Ontario 1971, Ecole de Chimie and Institute des Substances Naturelles 1972; A P Sloan visiting prof Harvard Univ 1973, Pacific W Coast lectr in inorganic chemistry, Br Gas Royal Soc sr res fell 1979–86, Sherman Fairchild visiting scholar Caltech 1981, Karl Ziegler Gastprofessor Max Planck Inst Mulheim 1983, Hutchinson lectr Univ of Rochester 1983, Univ lectr in chem Univ of W Ontario 1984, Wuhan Univ PRC 1985, Debye lectr Cornell Univ 1985, Julius Stieglitz lectr Univ of Chicago 1986, Frontiers of Science lectr Texas A & M Univ 1987, Sir Edward Frankland prize lectr 1989, Glenn T Seaborg lectr in inorganic chemistry Univ of Calif Berkeley 1991, SE lectr in inorganic chemistry USA 1991, Walter Heiber Gastprofessor Univ of Munich 1991; conslt to: Medisense, BP, ICI; Corday-Morgan medal and prize 1974, RSC medal in Organometallic Chemistry 1986, JC Bailar medal Univ of Illinois 1983, American Chemical Soc annual award for Inorganic Chemistry 1984, Tilden prize 1982, Karl-Ziegler prize of Gesellschaft Deutscher Chemiker Germany 1992, Davy medal Royal Soc 1995, American Chemical Soc annual award for Orgonometallic Chemistry 1996; hon doctorate Universidade Tecnica de Lisboa - Instituto Superior Tecnico 1996; CChem, FRSC, FRS 1985; *Recreations* family; *Style*— Prof Malcolm Green, FRS; ✉ St Catherine's College, Oxford OX1 3UJ; Inorganic Chemistry Laboratory, South Parks Road, Oxford OX1 3QR (☎ 01865 272649, fax 01865 272690, e-mail malcolm.green@icl.ox.ac.uk)

GREEN, Dr Malcolm Robert; s of Frank Green (d 1970), and Margery Isabel Green; *b* 4 Jan 1943; *Educ* Wyggeston GS Leicester, Magdalen Coll Oxford (MA, DPhil); *m* 18 Dec 1971, Mary Margaret, da of Leonard Charles Pratley (d 1987); 1 s (Alasdair Calum b 1981), 2 da (Eleanor b 1975, Sally b 1978); *Career* lectr in Roman history Univ of Glasgow 1967–; memb: Corpn of Glasgow 1973–75, Strathclyde Regnl Cncl 1975–96; chm: Scottish Teachers and Lectrs Negotiating Ctee 1977–90, Nat Ctee for In-Serv Trg of Teachers 1977–86, Scottish Ctee for Staff Devpt in Educn 1987–91, Educn Ctee of Convention of Scottish Local Authys 1978–90, Educn Ctee City of Glasgow Cncl 1995–; Scottish cmmr MSC 1983–85, fin chm Scottish Examination Bd 1984–90; active in community based housing assoc movement 1975–; FScotvec; *Style*— Dr Malcolm Green; ✉ 46 Victoria Crescent Rd, Glasgow G12 9DE (☎ 0141 339 2007); City Chambers, George Square, Glasgow G2 1DU (☎ 0141 287 5586)

GREEN, Dame Mary Georgina; DBE (1968); da of Edwin Green, of Wellingborough; *b* 27 July 1913; *Educ* Wellingborough HS, Westfield Coll London; *Career* govr BBC 1968–73, chm Gen Optical Cncl 1979–85, former headmistress Kidbrooke Sch London; *Recreations* gardening; *Style*— Dame Mary Green, DBE; ✉ 45 Winn Rd, London SE12 9EX

GREEN, Prof Michael Alan; s of Thomas Clifford Green (d 1987), and Anne, *née* Greaves (d 1994); *b* 26 June 1938; *Educ* Batley GS, Univ of Leeds (MB ChB), DCH, DObstRCOG, DMJ; *m* 1962, Jennifer Barbara, *née* Mencher; 2 da (Tana b 20 March 1963, Maia b 8 Nov 1964); *Career* MO Royal Flying Doctor Serv Aust 1967–68, MO forensic pathology NSW 1968–69, sr lectr in forensic pathology Univ of Leeds 1974–90 (lectr 1970–74), prof of forensic pathology Univ of Sheffield 1990–; Royal Coll of Pathologists: chm Forensic Specialist Advsy Ctee 1992–, memb Cncl 1995–; pres Br Assoc of Forensic Med 1993–95; FRCPath; *Books* Clinical Toxicology (with C J Polson and M R Lee, 1984), Dealing with Death (with J B Green, 1990), Pathology of Trauma (contrib, 1993); also numerous papers on forensic pathology since 1972; *Recreations* music, model railways, walking, motorcycle restoration; *Style*— Prof Michael Green; ✉ 5 Grosvenor Park, Allerton Hill, Leeds LS7 3QD (☎ 0113 268 0825, fax 0113 268 0825); Department of Forensic Pathology, University of Sheffield, The Medico Legal Centre, Watery Street, Sheffield S3 7ES (☎ 0114 273 8721, fax 0114 279 8942, mobile 0831 480233)

GREEN, Rev Dr (Edward) Michael Bankes; s of Rev Edward Bankes Green (d 1985), and Beatrice Emily, *née* Smith (d 1980); *b* 20 Aug 1930; *Educ* Clifton, Exeter Coll Oxford (scholar, BA), Queens' Coll and Ridley Hall Cambridge (BA, BD, Fencing blue, Carus New Testament and Selwyn New Testament prizes), Univ of Toronto (DD) 1992, DD (Lambeth) 1996; *m* 12 Sept 1957, Rosemary Wake, da of Lt-Col Charles Felix Stoehr, OBE (d 1932); 2 s (Timothy b 1960, Jonathan b 1966), 2 da (Sarah b 1962, Jenny b 1964); *Career* Nat Serv Lt RA 1953–55; ordained deacon 1957, ordained priest 1958, curate Holy Trinity Eastbourne 1957–60; tutor in New Testament: London Coll of Divinity 1960–69, Univ of London 1960–69, Univ of Nottingham 1969–75; princ St John's Coll Nottingham 1969–75, rector St Aldate's Church Oxford 1975–86, prof of evangelism Regent Coll Vancouver Canada 1987–92, advsr in evangelism to Archbishops of Canterbury and York 1992–; pres Christian Union Oxford 1955–57, memb Studiorum Novi Testamenti Societas 1960–69, conslt Lambeth Conf 1968, memb Anglican Doctrinal Cmmn 1969–75; Hon DD Univ of Toronto 1992; *Books* Called to Serve (1964), Evangelism in the Early Church (1970), I Believe in the Holy Spirit (1975), You Must Be Joking (1976), The Truth of God Incarnate (ed 1977), I Believe in Satan's Downfall (1981), To Corinth With Love (1982), Evangelism through the Local Church (1990), Who Is This Jesus? (1990), On Your Knees, My God, Good News is for Sharing, Acts for Today, New Testament Spirituality, How Can I Lead a Friend to Christ (1995), Critical Choices (1995); *Recreations* fishing, walking, squash, gardening; *Style*— Rev Dr Michael Green; ✉ 7 The Green, Chilwell, Nottingham NG9 5BE (☎ 0115 943 1738, fax 0115 943 1737)

GREEN, Prof Michael Boris; s of Absalom Green, of London, and Genia, *née* Osherovitz; *b* 22 May 1946; *Educ* William Ellis Sch, Churchill Coll Cambridge (BA, PhD); *Career* res fell: Inst for Advanced Study Princeton NJ USA 1970–72, Cavendish Laboratory Cambridge 1972–77, Dept of Theoretical Physics Oxford 1977–79; Nuffield Science fell 1984–86, prof Physics Dept Queen Mary Coll London 1985–93 (lectr 1979–85), John Humphrey Plummer prof of theoretical physics Cambridge 1993–; sr fell SERC 1986–91 (advanced fell 1977–79), Distinguished Fairchild fell California Inst of Technol 1990; Maxwell medal and prize Inst of Physics 1987, Hopkins prize Cambridge Philosophical Soc 1987, DIRAC medal Int Centre of Theoretical Physics 1989; FInstP, FRS 1989; *Books* Superstring Theory Vols 1 and 2 (with J H Schwarz and E Witten, Cambridge University Press, 1987); *Style*— Prof Michael Green, FRS; ✉ Department of Applied Mathematics and Theoretical Physics, Silver Street, Cambridge CB3 9EW (☎ 01223 330884)

GREEN, Michael Philip; s of Cyril Green, and Irene, *née* Goodman; *b* 2 Dec 1947; *Educ* Haberdashers' Aske's; *m* 1, 12 Oct 1972 (m dis 1989), Hon Janet Frances, da of Baron Wolfson (Life Peer), *qv*; 2 da (Rebecca b 1974, Catherine b 1976); m 2, 15 June 1990, Theresa (Tessa), *née* Buckmaster; 2 s (Oliver b 12 Jan 1992, Theodore Samuel b 21 Nov 1994); *Career* chm Carlton Communications Plc 1993–; dir: Independent Television News Ltd 1993–, Reuters Holdings PLC 1992–, GMTV Ltd; govr Theale Green Sch, chm Tangent Charitable Tst; *Recreations* bridge, television; *Clubs* Portland; *Style*— Michael Green, Esq; ✉ Carlton Communications plc, 25 Knightsbridge, London SW1X 7RZ (☎ 0171 663 6363, fax 0171 663 6300)

GREEN, Prof Mino; s of Alexander Green (d 1969), and Elizabeth Rachel Gorodetsky (d 1991); *b* 10 March 1927; *Educ* Dulwich, Univ Coll Durham (BSc, PhD, DSc, rugby XV); *m* 1951, Diana Mary, da of Rev Arthur William Allen; 1 s (David Mino Allen b 12 Aug 1952), 1 da (Penelope Susan b 31 Dec 1955); *Career* gp ldr Lincoln Laboratory MIT 1951–55, post-doctoral fell Chemistry Dept Imperial Coll London 1955–56, div chief (res) Zenith Radio Corp Chicago USA 1956–60, assoc dir Electrochemistry Laboratory Univ of Pennsylvania 1960–62, dir Zenith Radio Res Corp (UK) Ltd 1962–72; Electrical Engrg Dept Imperial Coll London: res fell 1972–73, lectr 1973–76, reader in electrical materials 1976–83, prof of electrical device sci 1983–92 (emeritus prof 1992), sr res fell Imperial Coll London; visiting prof in physical chemistry Univ of Bradford 1967–72; FIEE 1986; *Publications*: Solid State Surface Science (ed, 3 volumes, 1969, 1970, 1972), over 100 papers in scientific jls; *Recreations* walking, tennis, art appreciation; *Clubs* Hurlingham; *Style*— Prof Mino Green; ✉ 55 Gerard Rd, London SW13 9QH (☎ 0181 748 8689); Imperial College of Science, Technology and Medicine, Department of Electrical Engineering, Exhibition Rd, London SW7 2BT (☎ 0171 594 6212, fax 0171 594 6211, telex 929484)

GREEN, Sir Owen Whitley; kt (1984); *b* 14 May 1925; *m* Doreen Margaret Spark; 1 s, 2 da; *Career* chm BTR plc 1984–93 (formerly md); former Businessman of the Year; FCA; *Style*— Sir Owen Green; ✉ Edgehill, Succombs Hill, Warlingham CR6 9JG

GREEN, Pauline; MEP (Lab) London N (majority 48,348); da of Bertram William Wiltshire (d 1975), of Bracknell, Berks, and Lucy, *née* Vella; *b* 8 Dec 1948; *Educ* John Kelly Secdy Modern Girls' Sch, Kilburn Poly, Open Univ (BA), LSE (MSc); *m* 6 March 1971, Paul Adam Green, s of Charles Henry Green, of Southampton; 1 s (Simon Timothy b 23 April 1974), 1 da (Ruth Charlotte b 20 Oct 1976); *Career* met police offr 1969–74, subsequently asst teacher Special Educn Unit London Borough of Barnet, pt/t lectr Barnet Coll of FE 1980–85, asst Parly offr Co-operative Union (responsible for Euro affairs) 1985–89; MEP (Lab) London North 1989–; ldr: Euro Parly Lab Pty 1993–94, Parly Gp Pty of Euro Socialists 1994–; vice pres Socialist International 1994–; Lab Pty spokesperson on public health and consumer protection 1989–93, pres All-Pty Gp on Consumer Affairs 1989–94, memb Bureau of Socialist Gp 1991–; memb: Co-operative Pty, Parly Gp USDAW, Amnesty Int, CND, SERA, SHA; *Recreations* music, reading; *Style*— Pauline Green, MEP; ✉ Broad House, 205 Fore Street, London N18 2TZ (☎ 0181 803 7635, fax 0181 803 7549)

GREEN, Brig Percy William Powlett; CBE (1960, OBE 1956), DSO (1946); s of Brig Gen Wilfrith Gerald Key Green, CB, CMG, DSO (d 1937), and Minnie Lilian, *née* Powlett (d 1962); *b* 10 Sept 1912; *Educ* Wellington, RMC; *m* 27 Nov 1943, Phyllis Margery FitzGerald (d 1995), da of late Lt-Col Arthur Henry May, OBE; 1 s (Guy b 24 July 1947), 1 da (Susan b 20 Nov 1944); *Career* cmmnd Northamptonshire Regt, served ops NW Frontier India 1936–37, BEF France 1939–40; Cdr: 2 Bn W Yorks Regt Burma and Java 1945–46 (despatches), 1 Bn Malay Regt 1946–47, 4 Bn KAR (ops in Kenya) 1954–56 (despatches); Col Gen Staff WO 1956–57, Brig COS E Africa Cmd 1957–60, dep dir Mil Intelligence WO 1961–63, COS NI Cmd 1963–65, ADC to HM The Queen and Dep Cdr Aldershot Dist 1965–67, Dep Col Royal Anglian Regt 1966–76, ret 1967; *Recreations* field sports; *Style*— Brig Percy Green, CBE, DSO; ✉ Grudds, South Warnborough, Hook, Hants RG29 1RW (☎ 01256 862472)

GREEN, Prof Peter Morris; s of Arthur Green, CBE (d 1976), and Olive Emily, *née* Slaughter (d 1985); *b* 22 Dec 1924; *Educ* Charterhouse, Trinity Coll Cambridge (open major scholar, sr fndn scholar, res scholar, BA, MA, PhD); *m* 1, 28 July 1951 (m dis 1975), Lalage Isobel, da of late Prof R J V Pulvertaft; 2 s (Timothy Michael b 1955, Nicholas Paul b 1958), 1 da (Sarah Francesca b 1960); m 2, 18 July 1975, Carin Margreta, da of late G N Christensen, of Saratoga, USA; *Career* WWII RAFVR 1943–47; dir of studies in classics Selwyn Coll Cambridge 1952–53, fiction critic London Daily Telegraph 1953–63, literary advsr The Bodley Head 1957–58, sr conslt ed Hodder & Stoughton 1960–63, TV critic The Listener 1961–63, film critic John o'London's 1961–63, emigrated to Greece as full-time writer 1963–71, lectr in Greek history and lit Coll Year in Athens Greece 1966–71 (memb Bd of Advsrs 1984–); Univ of Texas: visiting prof of classics 1971–72, prof of classics 1972–, James R Dougherty jr centennial prof of classics 1982– (memb numerous univ ctees and Classics Dept ctees 1974–); sr fell Nat Educn in the Humanities (NEH) 1983–84, visiting prof UCLA 1976, Mellon prof of humanities Tulane Univ 1986; numerous public lectures; memb Book Soc Selection Ctee 1959–62; former memb selection ctees for literary prizes: Heinemann Award, John Llewelyn Rhys Prize, WH Smith £1000 Award for Literature; memb: APA, AIA, Classical Assoc UK, Soc for Promotion of Hellenic Studies UK; FRSL 1956 (memb Cncl 1958); *Books* The Expanding Eye (1953), Achilles His Armour (1955), Cat in Gloves (under pseudonym Denis Delaney, 1956), The Sword of Pleasure (W Heinemann award for Lit 1957), Kenneth Grahame 1859–1932: A Study of his Life, Work and Times (1959), Essays in Antiquity (1960), Habeas Corpus and Other Stories (1962), Look at the Romans (1963), The Laughter of Aphrodite (1965, reprinted 1993), Juvenal: The Sixteen Satires (trans, 1967, 2 edn 1974), Armada from Athens: The Failure of the Sicilian Expedition 415–413 BC (1970), Alexander the Great: A Biography (1970), The Year of Salamis 480–479 BC (1971, reprinted as The Greco Persian Wars, 1996), The Shadow of the Parthenon (1972), Alexander of Macedon 356–323 BC: An Historical Biography (1974, reprinted 1991), Ovid: The Erotic Poems (trans, 1982), Beyond the Wild Wood: The World of Kenneth Grahame (1982), Medium and Message Reconsidered: The Changing Functions of Classical Translation (1986), Classical Bearings: Interpreting Ancient History and Culture (1989), Alexander to Actium: The Historical Evolution of the Hellenistic Age (1990), Hellenistic History and Culture (ed, 1993), Yannis Ritsos' The Fourth Dimension (trans, 1993), Ovid: The Poems of Exile (trans, 1994); *Recreations* squash, tennis, travel, avoiding urban life; *Clubs* Savile; *Style*— Prof Peter Green, FRSL; ✉ 1619 Sunny Vale, Austin, Texas 78741, USA (☎ 00 1 512 445 2305); Department of Classics, The University of Texas, Austin, Texas 78712, USA (☎ 00 1 512 471 8502/5742, fax 00 1 512 471 4111, e-mail pmgreen@.utexas.edu)

GREEN, Richard Chevallier; DL (Hereford and Worcester 1991); s of Lionel Green, MBE, JP, DL (d 1969), of The Whittern, Lyonshall, Kington, Herefordshire, and Phyllis Chalmers, *née* Jameson, (d 1977); *b* 22 May 1924; *Educ* Wellington, RAC Cirencester; *m* 1959, Julia, da of Roger de Wesselow (d 1960); 1 s (Jonathan b 1966, d 1993), 3 da (Nicola, Joanna (Mrs Ian Hilditch), Sara); *Career* Lt RNVR 1942–46, Escort Vessels N Atlantic and MTBs English Channel; RAC Cirencester 1947–48, farmer, dir The Whittern Farms Ltd; Liveryman Worshipful Co of Farmers; High Sheriff Hereford and Worcester 1981–82; *Recreations* fishing, travel, boating (yacht 'Rondone'); *Clubs* Royal Yacht Squadron, Farmers', Army & Navy; *Style*— Richard Green, Esq, DL; ✉ The Whittern, Lyonshall, Kington, Herefordshire (☎ 01544 340241/205, fax 01544 340253); Cancello Rosso, Giuncarico (GR), Italy (☎ 00 39 566 887224)

GREEN, Richard David; s of Bernard Green, and late Flora Amelia, *née* Wartski; *b* 25 May 1944; *Educ* Highgate Sch, Queen's Coll Oxford (BA); *m* Jan 1994, Hazel Ann *née* Spittle; *Career* PA to Chairman/Managing Director John Wyeth & Co Ltd 1966–67; Keyser Ullman Investment Management Ltd: investmt analyst 1967–68, gp economist and fund mangr 1970–72; Hill Samuel Investment Management Ltd: economist Research and Unit Trust Management 1973, instn fund mangr 1974–76, sr investmt mangr 1976–77 (dir 1979); former dir Hill Samuel Investment Management (global investmt) 1981, sr exec advsr/exec dir and chief investmt offr Daiwa International Capital Management (UK) Ltd 1988–; memb: Soc of Business Economists, London Oil Analysts Gp, Inst of Investmt Mgmnt and Res; *Recreations* travel, dog walking, charities, reading, water sports, art, theatre; *Style*— Richard Green, Esq; ✉ The Cottage, Whitestone Lane, London NW3 1EA (☎ 0171 435 3497); Daiwa International Capital Management (UK) Ltd, 14 St Paul's Churchyard, London EC4M 8BD (☎ 0171 246 8222, fax 0171 248 1575)

GREEN, Richard Desmond; s of Walter Herbert Green, FCA, of Winchester, and late Nina Margaret, *née* Hellyar; *b* 3 June 1947; *Educ* Allhallows, Rousdon Devon; *m* 16 Aug 1986, Margaret Ann, da of Frederick Richard Lisle (d 1985); *Career* CA 1970; dir: Int Thomson Publishing Servs Ltd 1988–, Thomson Books Ltd 1988–; *Recreations* golf, amateur operatics and dramatics; *Style*— Richard Green, Esq; ✉ ITPS Ltd, Cheriton House, North Way, Andover, Hants SP10 5BE (☎ 01264 342850, fax 01264 332446)

GREEN, Richard Paul; s of Hugh Claude Green (d 1990), of Effingham, Surrey, and Betty Rosina, *née* Blake (d 1983); *b* 17 April 1950; *Educ* King's Coll Sch Wimbledon, City of Westminster Coll London; *m* 29 Sept 1973, (Sheila) Marilyn, da of Lionel Francis Guillem, of Fetcham, Surrey; 3 da (Nicola b 1976, Elizabeth b 1976, Susannah b 1981); *Career* CA; ptnr Arthur Young 1979–87, dir Svenska International plc 1987–89, gp fin dir Abaco Investments Plc 1989–91, gp fin dir Dunhill Holdings Plc 1991–94; ind conslt and dir 1994–; chm Guildford Round Table 1988–89, vice pres French C of C in GB 1984–89; chm of govrs Royal Russell Sch Croydon 1996– (govr 1987–), Freeman City of London 1981, Liveryman Worshipful Co of Glovers 1981; FCA 1971; *Recreations* gardening, family, golf, motor sport, classic cars; *Clubs* RAC; *Style*— Richard Green, Esq; ✉ Tanglewood, Aldersey Rd, Guildford, Surrey GU1 2ES (☎ 01483 32216, fax 01483 32221)

GREEN, Robert; s of Peter Royston Green (d 1976), and Mary Tunstill Green, of Chapel-en-le-Frith, Derbyshire; *b* 5 Jan 1953; *Educ* Buxton Coll GS, Univ of Sheffield (LLB); *m* Philippa Jane; 2 s (Benjamin Peter b 31 Oct 1989, Samuel Robert b 14 Aug 1993); *Career* golfing journalist and writer; private sec and press offr to DPP Sir Thomas Hetherington 1980–82 (joined Dept of DPP 1977); asst ed Golf World magazine 1982–86 (freelance contrib 1976–82), golf corr London Daily News 1986–87, ed Golf World 1988–95 (ed designate 1987–88), sometime gp ed EMAP golf magazines in London (Golf World, Golf Weekly, Golf Industry News), golf contrib Sunday Times 1991–93, The

Independent on Sunday 1993; also contrib: The Times, Golf Digest (USA), Golf Magazine (France); British Sports Journalism Awards: commended Magazine Sports Writer 1989, winner Sports Pages Design 1990, highly commended Magazine Sports Writer 1991; *Publications* Golf - An Illustrated History of the Game (1987), Classic Golf Holes (1989), Illustrated Encyclopaedia of Golf (1994); scripted videos: Seve Ballesteros - The Short Game (1990); *Recreations* playing golf badly, reading almost everything avidly and drinking wine enthusiastically; *Clubs* Groucho, Crockfords, Highgate Golf; *Style*— Robert Green, Esq; ✉ 125 Hemingford Rd, London N1 1BZ

GREEN, (Aylmer) Roger; s of Aylmer Green (d 1983), and Irene Cameron, *née* Hunt; *b* 15 April 1949; *Educ* Wycliffe Coll; *m* 27 July 1974, (Aud) Reidunn Teodora, da of Einar Alfred Pedersen (d 1968), of Sarpsborg, Norway; 2 s (Eric b 1978, Christian b 1988), 1 da (Elizabeth b 1976); *Career* conslt plastic surgn Mersey Regnl Plastic Surgery and Burns Centre Liverpool 1987–, clinical lectr in plastic surgery Univ of Liverpool 1987–; memb: Br Assoc of Plastic Surgns, Br Assoc of Aesthetic Plastic Surgns; LRCPI, LRCSI 1974, FRCS 1981, FRSM 1983; *Recreations* walking, skiing, fishing; *Style*— Roger Green, Esq; ✉ Mersey Regional Plastic Surgery and Burn Centre, Whiston Hospital, Prescot, Liverpool L35 5DR (☎ 0151 426 1600 ext 262)

GREEN, Roger; s of Ernest Charles Arthur Green (d 1992), of Wimbledon, London and Truro, Cornwall, and Edna Florence, *née* Baker; *b* 6 Feb 1937; *Educ* KCS Wimbledon, RVC London (Surrey Co scholar and agricultural scholar, BVetMed); *m* 1, 7 May 1960, Susan, da of Terence Hingston; 1 s (Richard Douglas b 31 Dec 1960), 3 da (Caroline b 1 May 1962, Nicola b 7 April 1964 (decd), Juliet b 21 April 1966); m 2, 17 May 1977, Carolyn Frances Drake, da of Alfred Clifford Gordon Bell; 1 s (Philip b 21 Aug 1971); *Career* asst vet surgn in mixed practice: Holsworthy N Devon 1960–61, Falmouth Cornwall 1961–65; ptnr (now sole princ) Heath Veterinary Clinic 1965–; breeder of Blonde d'Aquitaine Cattle, Whiteface Woodland Sheep and Tamworth Pigs; sec Blonde d'Aquitaine Breeders Society of GB Ltd 1972–75, md Artificial Insemination Breeders Services Ltd 1988–91 (vet dir 1977–91); UK del to Fedn of Veterinarians of Europe (FVE) 1977–, chm Animal Welfare Working Pty FVE and del to Standing Ctee (TAP) Cncl of Europe for the Protection of Animals Kept for Farming Purposes 1985–; tstee Rare Breeds Survival Tst 1977–; MRCVS 1960 (memb Cncl 1990–); memb: BVA 1960, BSAVA 1965 (pres 1975), Soc for Practising Vet Surgns (treas 1977–80); *Recreations* playing rugby football (county standard and referee), singing (especially choral); *Clubs* Farmers'; *Style*— Roger Green, Esq; ✉ Hornsdene Cottage, Pookbourne Lane, Sayers Common, Hassocks, W Sussex BN6 9HD (☎ 01273 832023); Heath Veterinary Clinic, 7 Queens Road, Haywards Heath, W Sussex RH16 1EH (☎ 01444 413482, fax 01444 416183)

GREEN, Ronald Arthur; s of Arthur Henry Green (d 1970), and Anne Elizabeth Green (d 1983); *b* 12 June 1927; *Educ* Glos Coll of Art, Architectural Assoc Sch of Architecture London (AADipl); *m* 1953, Margaret Patricia, *née* Muller; 1 s (Matthew b 31 July 1959); *Career* architect; ptnr Casson Conder Partnership architects 1962–92; projects incl: undergrad accommodation in Oxford, commercial devpt in Winchester (Civic Tst commendation), five banks incl head office in Manchester (RIBA regnl award), conversion and interior design projects incl conservation and listed building restoration for the Crown Estate in London (Civic Tst award), office building for publisher Tonbridge (Civic Tst commendation), museum design and consultancy services Science Museum London, Royal Naval and Royal Marines Museums Portsmouth; design coordination for int exhbns in Turkey, Greece, Brazil, Hong Kong and USA; memb: RIBA examinations ctee (and examiner in architecture), CSD (and assessor in interior design); practising conslt; painter and gallery exhibitor; Freeman City of London; FRIBA, FCSD (past vice pres and cncl memb); *Books* The Architect's Guide to Running a Job (1962, 5th edn 1995), The Architect's Guide to Site Management; *Clubs* Arts; *Style*— Ronald Green, Esq; ✉ 12 Cranleigh, 137 Ladbroke Road, London W11 3PX (☎ 0171 229 1842)

GREEN, Simon Charles; s of Thomas Eric Green, of The Manor House, Great Longstone, nr Bakewell, Derbys, and Barbara Ann, *née* Morritt (d 1975); *b* 8 Sept 1961; *Educ* Worksop Coll, Aberystwyth Univ, Manchester Poly; *m* 28 April 1990, Helen Claire, da of Rodney Jameson; 1 da (Sophie Roseanna b 28 April 1991), 1 s (Sam Thomas b 13 Oct 1993); *Career* jr art dir Saatchi & Saatchi advtg 1982–86; art dir rising to gp head/bd dir: WCRS 1986–90, Still Price Lintas 1990–93; fndr ptnr Addition Marketing until Sept 1993, jt creative/bd dir Butterfield Day Devito Hockney Nov 1993–; awards: numerous from annual awards incl British TV, Campaign Press & Poster, Cannes Film Festival, NY Festival, Creative Circle, One Show, Clio, etc, 1983–; memb D&AD; *Recreations* photography, painting; *Clubs* Hogarth Health; *Style*— Simon Green, Esq; ✉ Butterfield Day Devito Hockney, 47 Marylebone Lane, London W1M 5FN (☎ 0171 224 3000, fax 0171 935 9865)

GREEN, Lt-Col Sir Simon Lycett; 5 Bt (UK 1886), of Wakefield, Yorkshire, and Ken Hill, Norfolk, TD, JP (Wakefield), DL (W Riding Yorks); s of Sir Edward Arthur Lycett Green, 3 Bt (d 1941); suc bro, Sir (Edward) Stephen Lycett Green, 4 Bt (d 1996); *b* 11 July 1912; *Educ* Eton, Magdalene Coll Cambridge (BA); *m* 1, 3 Jan 1935 (m dis 1971), Gladys, eldest da of late Arthur Ranicar, JP, of Springfield, Wigan; 1 da (Diana Rose Frances (Mrs Ronald E Wallace) b 1935); m 2, 1971, Mary, da of late George Ramsden, of Dale House, Wakefield; *Heir* kinsman, Edward Patrick Lycett Green b 1950; *Career* Lt-Col cmdg Yorks Dragoons Yeo 1947–51; chm Green's Economiser Group Ltd 1956–83, ret; *Recreations* shooting, racing; *Style*— Lt-Col Sir Simon Green, Bt; ✉ Cliff Bank, N Rigton, Leeds LS17 OBZ (☎ 01423 734582)

GREEN, Stephen Edgar Alexander; s of Rev Ernest Edgar Montague Green (d 1974), of Ryde, IOW, and Frances Ethel Isabella, *née* Coryton (d 1972); *b* 24 May 1943; *Educ* Monkton Combe Sch, Brasenose Coll Oxford (BA, MA), Univ of Liverpool (Dip Archive Admin); *Career* asst archivist Northants Record Office 1966–68, curator, librarian and archivist MCC 1968– (seconded to Melbourne CC 1991–92); hon archivist St Martin in the Fields, former hon sec The Brasenose Soc, pres IOW Assoc of Cricket Umpires; memb: Soc of Archivists, Museums Assoc; *Books* St James' Church, Ryde, Isle of Wight - A Short History (1975), Backward Glances (1976), Cricketing Bygones (1982), Oxford and Cambridge Cricket (contrib, 1989), My Lord's (contrib, 1990), Lord's: The Official Pictorial Souvenir (1992); *Recreations* travel, exploring churches and local history; *Clubs* MCC; *Style*— Stephen Green, Esq; ✉ Flat 15, Richmond House, 4 The Strand, Ryde, Isle of Wight PO33 1JD (☎ 01753 889897); Lord's Cricket Ground, London NW8 8QN (☎ 0171 289 1611, fax 0171 289 9100, telex 297 329 MCCG G)

GREEN, Stephen Peter; s of James Dean Green (d 1968); *b* 2 Jan 1937; *Educ* Kingswood Sch Bath, Univ of Manchester (LLB); *m* 1 (m dis 1979); 3 da (Clarissa Jane b 1965, Philippa Lucy b 1967, Victoria Alice b 1971); m 2, Aug 1979, Margaret Owen, da of Cdr John Irwin (d 1995); *Career* admitted slr 1963; ptnr Pannone & Partners Manchester; pres Manchester Consular Assoc 1988 (sec 1990); Netherland Consul for: Greater Manchester, E Lancs, E Cheshire; NW rep Netherlands-Br C-of-C; dep chm Manchester and Dist Housing Assoc (chm No 2 Assoc); memb: Law Soc, Licensing Exec Soc; *Recreations* opera, music, gardening; *Clubs* St James' (Manchester), Royal Over-Seas League; *Style*— Stephen Green, Esq; ✉ Cottage of Content, Off London Rd, Buxton, Derbyshire SK17 9NP; Pannone & Partners, 123 Deansgate, Manchester (☎ 0161 832 3000, fax 0161 832 2655)

GREEN, Trevor Bernard; s of Leslie Henry Roland Green, of Wendover, Bucks, and Audrey Ellen, *née* Douch; *b* 27 Aug 1944; *m* 10 Aug 1968, Mavis Elsie Edith, da of George Chesher; 3 s (Adrian Lee b 12 Sept 1970, Christopher Daniel b 20 July 1972, Stuart Edward Trevor b 17 Oct 1977); *Career* buyer Green Shield Trading Stamp Co 1968–74; Argos Distributors Ltd: buyer 1974–77, chief buyer 1977–78, merchandise mangr 1978–83, merchandise dir 1983–1990, md 1992–; exec dir Argos plc 1992– (business devpt dir 1990–92); *Style*— Trevor Green, Esq; ✉ Argos plc, 489–499 Avebury Boulevard, Saxon Gate West, Central Milton Keynes MK9 2NW (☎ 01908 600007, fax 01908 204037, car 0374 181441)

GREEN, Rev Vivian Hubert Howard; the man on whom John Le Carré partly modelled the character of George Smiley in Tinker, Tailor, Soldier, Spy, The Honourable Schoolboy and Smiley's People; s of Hubert James Green (d 1963); *b* 18 Nov 1915; *Educ* Bradfield Coll Berks, Trinity Hall Cambridge (MA, DD); *Career* deacon 1939, priest 1940; former chaplain and asst master Sherborne Sch; Lincoln Coll Oxford: chaplain 1951–69, fellow and history tutor 1951–83, sr tutor 1953–62 and 1974–77, sub-rector 1970–83, rector 1983–87, hon fellow 1987–; FRHistS; *Publications* Bishop Reginald Pecock (1945), The Hanoverians (1948), From St Augustine to William Temple (1948), Renaissance and Reformation (1952), The Later Plantagenets (1955), Oxford Common Room (1957), The Young Mr Wesley (1961), The Swiss Alps (1961), Martin Luther and the Reformation (1964), John Wesley (1964), Religion at Oxford and Cambridge (1964), The Universities (1969), Medieval Civilization in Western Europe (1971), A History of Oxford University (1974), The Commonwealth of Lincoln College 1427–1977 (1979), Love in a Cool Climate, Letters of Mark Pattison and Meta Bradley 1879–1884 (1985), Memoirs of an Oxford Don, Mark Pattison (edited with an introduction, 1988), A Question of Guilt: the murder of Nancy Eaton (with William Scoular 1989), The Madness of Kings (1993); contrib to Dictionary of English Church History, The Oxford Dictionary of the Christian Church, The Oxford History of the University, Encyclopaedia of Oxford (ed C Hibbert), The Quest for Le Carré (ed Alan Bold, 1988), A New History of Christianity (1996); *Style*— The Rev Vivian Green; ✉ Lincoln College, Oxford OX1 3DR (☎ 01865 279830); Calendars, 25 Sheep St, Burford, Oxon (☎ 01993 823214)

GREEN-ARMYTAGE, John McDonald (Jock); *b* 6 June 1945; *Educ* McGill Univ Montreal (BA), Columbia Univ NY (MBA); *m* 1977, Susan Rosemary, da of Lt-Col Hugh Shelley Le Messurier and Rosemary Alice Champney (maternal gda of 21 Baron Forbes and paternal ggda of Sir James Walker, 1 Bt, of Sand Hutton); 1 s (Matthew b 1978), 3 da (Anna b 1981, Camilla b 1983, Elizabeth b 1985); *Career* exec dir N M Rothschild & Sons Ltd 1977–82, md The Guthrie Corporation 1982–88 (conslt 1988–), former jt chm and chief exec Kelt Energy plc, chief exec then dep chm William Baird plc 1995– non-exec dir Amec plc 1990–95, N M Rothschild & Sons Ltd, MCIT plc (chm), International Biotechnology Trust plc (chm); *Style*— Jock Green-Armytage, Esq; ✉ William Baird Plc, 79 Mount Street, London W1Y 5HJ (☎ 0171 409 1785, fax 0171 499 6788)

GREEN-PRICE, Sir Robert John; 5 Bt (UK 1874), of Norton Manor, Radnorshire; s of Capt Sir John Green-Price, 4 Bt (d 1964); *b* 22 Oct 1940; *Educ* Shrewsbury; *Heir* uncle, (Powell) Norman Dansey Green-Price, JP; *Career* Capt (ret) RCT; ADC to Govr of Bermuda 1969–72; lectr in English: Teikyo Univ 1975–82, Chiba Univ of Commerce 1982–; pt/t lectr: Keio Univ 1977–, Waseda Univ 1986–; guest lectr NHK Radio 1978–83, asst prof of English Chiba Univ of Commerce Japan; *Recreations* relaxing at my villa in Northern Luzon, Philippines; *Style*— Sir Robert Green-Price, Bt

GREENALL, Dr the Hon Gilbert; CBE (1993); 2 s of 3 Baron Daresbury (d 1996); *b* 16 Aug 1954; *Educ* Eton, RMA Sandhurst, Univ of Bristol (MB ChB), INSEAD (MBA); *m* 1983, Sarah Elizabeth, er da of Ian C Mouat, of Stetchworth, Suffolk, and former w of Robert Greville Kaye Williamson; 3 s (Gilbert Edward b 1984, Frederick John b 1986, Alexander b 1988), 1 da (Amelia Frances b 1990); *Career* humanitarian relief co-ordinator: Thai/Cambodian border 1979, Karamoja Uganda 1980–81, Iran 1991, Iraq 1991; UK relief co-ordinator Northern Iraq for ODA 1991, Br Govt rep on EC/UN Mission to Baghdad and Iran/Iraq border 1991, Br Govt advsr on humanitarian affairs 1992, Br Govt humanitarian relief prog for Bosnia 1992, Somalia 1993 and Angola 1993, head EC Task Force for the former Yugoslavia 1992–93, Br Govt assessment of humanitarian progs in Azerbaijan, Armenia and Georgia 1994–, Br Govt adviser on volcanic emergency Montserrat 1995, ODA advsr to GOC Multinational Div SW IFOR Bosnia 1996; non-exec dir The Greenalls Group plc; *Recreations* flying, skiing; *Clubs* White's, St Moritz Tobogganing; *Style*— Dr The Hon Gilbert Greenall, CBE; ✉ Bromesberrow Place, Ledbury, Herefordshire HR8 1RZ

GREENALL, John C; s of Thomas Patrick Greenall (d 1957), of St Helens, Lancs, and Mary Ann, *née* Anderton (d 1977); *b* 28 June 1935; *Educ* W Park GS St Helens (head prefect), Univ of Liverpool (BCom, ed Guild Gazette), DipCAM; *m* 1963 (m dis 1977), Lillian Marie, *née* Sammon; 1 s (Stephen Leo b 3 July 1971, 1 da (Suzanne Claire b 2 Oct 1972); *Career* Nat Serv RN 1956–58; PRO: Pilkington Brothers Ltd 1959–65 (statistician 1958–59), UMIST 1965–68; Gp PRO WS Atkins & Partners 1968–69, dir of PR The Open Univ 1969–87, in sole PR practice 1987–; FIPR 1978 (MIPR 1964), registered ind conslt PRCA 1992; *Books* Public Relations Management in Colleges, Polytechnics and Universities (with Dr Clive Keen, 1987); *Recreations* amateur dramatics (acting and directing), running (including marathon races); *Style*— John Greenall, Esq; ✉ John Greenall Public Relations, 10 Holywell Place, Springfield, Milton Keynes, Bucks MK6 3LP (☎ 01908 667664)

GREENALL, John Desmond Thomas; s of Thomas Henry Greenall (d 1941), and Joan Clare Walker, *née* Ridgway; *b* 11 April 1939; *Educ* Winchester; *m* 30 Jan 1965, Margaret Anne, da of Sir Iain Maxwell Stewart; 1 s (Damian b 1968), 2 da (Melissa b 1967, Cleonie b 1974); *Career* stockbroker; with Greig Middleton and Co Ltd until 1994, Henderson Crosthwaite Ltd 1994–; *Recreations* shooting, fishing, golf; *Clubs* Prestwick Golf, The Hon Co of Edinburgh Golfers, Royal and Ancient, MCC, White's; *Style*— John Greenall, Esq; ✉ Henderson Crosthwaite Ltd, 32 St Mary at Hill, London EC3P 3AJ (☎ 0171 283 8577, fax 0171 623 1997)

GREENAWAY, Prof David; s of David Greenaway (d 1986), and Agnes MacKechnie, *née* Parker; *b* 20 March 1952; *Educ* Eastbank Acad Glasgow, Henry Mellish GS Nottingham; *m* (Susan) Elizabeth, da of William Hallam, of Strelley, Nottingham; 2 s (Stuart David b 1978, Daniel Christopher b 1980); *Career* lectr in econs Leicester Poly 1975–78; prof of econs: Univ of Buckingham 1986–87 (lectr sr lectr and reader 1979–86), Univ of Nottingham 1987– (pro-vice-chllr 1994–); visiting prof: Lehigh Univ Pennsylvania 1982 and 1987, Claremont Graduate Sch California 1989, 1990 and 1991; conslt: UNIDO 1983 and 1985, World Bank 1986 and 1988, Euro Cmmn 1991, GATT 1992, HM Treasy 1993, UNCTAD 1993; jt managing ed The World Economy, assoc ed The Economic Jl; non-exec dir Nottingham Health Authy; govr NIESR 1995–; memb: Royal Econ Soc 1978 (memb Cncl and Exec 1991–), Euro Econ Assoc, American Economic Assoc; *Books* An Introduction to International Economics (1979), International Trade Policy (1983), Current Issues in International Trade (1985), The Economics of Intra Industry Trade (1986), Macroeconomics - Theory and Policy in the UK (2 edn with G K Shaw, 1988), Pioneers of Modern Economics in Britain (1989), Current Issues in Macroeconomics (1989), Economic Analysis of Regional Trading Agreements (1989), Trade and Industrial Policy in Developing Countries (1993); *Recreations* tennis, football, wine, travel; *Style*— Prof David Greenaway; ✉ 238 Ruddington Lane, Wilford, Nottingham (☎ 0115 981 0773), Dept of Economics, University of Nottingham, University Park, Nottingham NG7 2RD (☎ 0115 948 4848)

GREENAWAY, Sir John Michael Burdick; 3 Bt (UK 1933), of Coombe, Co Surrey; s of Sir Derek Burdick Greenaway, 2 Bt, CBE, TD, JP, DL (d 1994), and Sheila Beatrice, *née* Lockett; *b* 9 Aug 1944; *Educ* Harrow; *m* 1982, Susan Margaret, da of Henry Birch, of Lion House, Tattenhall, Cheshire; 1 s (Thomas Edward Burdick b 3 April 1985), 1 da (Camilla Helen b 6 July 1983); *Heir* s, Thomas Edward Burdick Greenaway b 3 April 1985; *Career* Lt Life Gds 1965–70; dir Daniel Greenaway & Sons Ltd 1970–79; farmer 1980–; *Recreations* skiing, tennis, riding; *Style*— Sir John Greenaway, Bt; ✉ Lois Weedon House, Towcester, Northants NN12 8PJ (fax 01327 860533)

GREENBERG, Joanna Elishever Gabrielle; QC (1994); da of Ivan Marion Greenberg (d 1966), and Doris, *née* Sandground (d 1990); *Educ* Brondesbury & Kilburn HS for Girls, King's Coll London (LLB); *Career* called to the Bar Gray's Inn 1972, recorder 1995– (asst recorder 1992–95); *Style*— Ms Joanna Greenberg, QC; ✉ 3 Temple Gardens, Temple, London EC4Y 9AU (☎ 0171 583 1155, fax 0171 353 5446, LDE 0064)

GREENBERG, Louise; da of Carl Lorenz Basch (d 1995), of S Orange, New Jersey, USA, and Helen, *née* Feldstein; *b* 13 May 1944; *Educ* Barnard Coll Columbia Univ NY (AB); *m* 3 May 1984, Harold Salmond Greenberg, s of Rev Barry Greenberg (d 1965); 2 s (Jonathan Barry b 22 Aug 1976, Alexander Solomon b 22 Nov 1985), 2 da (Naomi Philippa b 22 June 1974, Judith Beila (twin) b 22 Nov 1985); *Career* prodr: WNBC and WABC NY USA, Radio Bristol 1970–72; BBC Radio: prodr Today and Kaleidoscope (original team), sr prodr Talks and Documentaries Dept, acting chief prodr sci progs 1981, chief prodr documentaries 1982, currently chief prodr arts, science and features; FRSA; *Recreations* music, theatre, books, galleries; *Style*— Mrs Louise Greenberg; ✉ Room 7059, BBC Broadcasting House, London W1A 1AA (☎ 0171 765 4826)

GREENBOROUGH, Sir John Hedley; KBE (1979, CBE 1975); s of William Greenborough (d 1953), and Elizabeth Marie, *née* Wilson; *b* 7 July 1922; *Educ* Wandsworth Sch London; *m* 1951, Gerta Ebel; 1 step s; *Career* served WWII pilot RAF later Fleet Air Arm; exec vice pres Shell Argentina 1960–66, area co-ordinator (Far East) Shell International Petroleum Co 1967–68, md (mktg) Shell-Mex & BP Ltd 1969–71, chief exec and md Shell-Mex & BP Ltd 1971–75, md Shell UK 1976–78, dep chm Shell UK 1976–80; chm: Newarthill 1980–93, Bowater Industries 1984–87; dir: Lloyds Bank 1980–93 (dep chm 1985–92), Hogg Group 1980–91, Laporte Industries (Holdings) 1983–86; pres: CBI 1978–80, Nat Cncl for Voluntary Orgns 1980–86, Strategic Planning Soc 1986–92; govr Ashridge Mgmnt Coll 1972– (chm 1977–91, pres 1991–); chm: Governing Cncl United Med and Dental Schs of Guy's and St Thomas' Hosps 1982–90 (hon fell 1995), Nursing and Professions Allied to Medicine Pay Review Body 1983–86, Civic Tst 1983–86; Liveryman Worshipful Co of Distillers 1975, Freeman City of London; Hon LLD Univ of Birmingham 1983; *Style*— Sir John Hedley Greenborough, KBE

GREENBURY, Sir Richard; kt (1992); s of Richard Oswald Greenbury (d 1974), and Dorothy, *née* Lewis (d 1980); *b* 31 July 1936; *Educ* Ealing County GS; *m* 1, 1959 (m dis), Sian, da of Dr T Eames Hughes, CBE; 2 s (Jonathan Harri b 1963, Adam Richard b 1966), 2 da (Alyson Jane b 1960, Rosalind b 1970); m 2, 1985 (m dis), Gabrielle Mary, *née* McManus; m 3, 1996, Sian, da of Dr T Eames Hughes, CBE; *Career* Marks and Spencer plc: joined as jr mgmnt trainee in stores 1953, trainee merchandiser Head Office 1962, alternate dir 1970, full dir 1972, jt md 1978–86, chief operating offr 1986–88, chief exec offr 1988–91, chm and chief exec 1991–; non-exec dir: British Gas Corporation/plc 1976–87, MB Group plc (formerly Metal Box) 1985–89, Lloyds Bank plc (now Lloyds TSB Group plc) 1992– April 1997, ICI plc 1992–93, Zeneca plc 1993–; chm Greenbury Ctee on executive pay 1995; memb UK Advsy Bd Br-American C of C 1989–, patron The Samaritans 1990–, chm CORDA Heart Charity 1991–, appeal pres Cottage Homes 1992–93, tstee Royal Academy 1992–; Silver Rose Award for Business Enterprise (for Marks and Spencer) Bank Hapoalim 1988; Hon DSc: Univ of Ulster 1993, UMIST; Hon DBA: Univ of Greenwich 1993, Univ of Nottingham 1994; hon fell London Business Sch; *Recreations* tennis (played for Middx Co for 12 years and for Int Tennis Club of GB), reading, music; *Clubs* All England Lawn Tennis, Int Lawn Tennis of GB; *Style*— Sir Richard Greenbury; ✉ Marks & Spencer plc, Michael House, 47–57 Baker Street, London W1A 1DN (☎ 0171 935 4422, fax 0171 487 2679)

GREENBURY, Toby Jonathan; s of Coleman Leonard Greenbury (d 1989), of Henley-on-Thames, Oxon, and Hannah Judith Pamela Greenbury; *b* 18 Sept 1951; *Educ* Clifton, UCL; *Career* asst slr Stephenson Harwood 1976–79 (articled clerk 1974–76), seconded assoc Lord Day & Lord 1976–77, ptnr D J Freeman 1980– (asst slr 1979–80); Freeman: City of London 1987, Worshipful Co of London Slrs 1985; memb: Law Soc, NY Bar; *Recreations* gardening, polo, music; *Clubs* RAC, Checkendon Park Polo (fndr chm); *Style*— Toby Greenbury, Esq; ✉ D J Freeman, 43 Fetter Lane, London EC4A 1NA (☎ 0171 583 4055, fax 0171 353 7377, telex 894579)

GREENE, Dr Alice Mary; da of Col Charles Westland Greene, Indian Med Servs, ret (d 1984), and Dr Elizabeth M Greene, *née* Rees; *b* 19 Sept 1952; *Educ* Wesley Coll Dublin, Trinity Coll Dublin (MB BCh, BAO, BA); *Career* jr house offr Sir Patrick Dun's Hosp Dublin 1977–78, St James' Hosp 1978–79, paediatrics in med and surgery Crumlin Children's Hosp Dublin 1980, registrar in med Royal London Homoeopathic Hosp 1982–83, GP S Kensington 1983, GP clinical asst NHS practice 1983–87, opened private practice Hampstead 1983–89, Letchworth Centre for Homoeopathic and Complementary Medicine 1985–91, private practice Harley St 1989–; lectr: Faculty of Homoeopathy Royal London Homoeopathic Hosp 1985–, Br Assoc for Autogenic Trg and Therapy, Homeopathic Physicians Teaching Gp Dept of External Studies Univ of Oxford 1991–; postgrad qualifications: DCH NUI, DORCPI 1980, Family Planning Certificate 1980, Dip in Counselling; MRCGP 1981, MFHOM 1982; memb: Br Assoc for Autogenic Trg and Therapy 1988 (vice chm 1993–), Br Holistic Med Assoc, Scientific and Med Network, Psychosynthesis and Educn Tst 1995–; *Style*— Dr Alice Greene; ✉ The Fourth Floor Flat, 86 Harley St, London W1N 1AE (☎ 0171 580 4188)

GREENE, Graham Carleton; CBE (1986); er s of late Sir Hugh Carleton Greene; *b* 10 June 1936; *Educ* Eton, Univ Coll Oxford (MA); *m* 1, 1957 (m dis), Hon Judith Margaret, da of late Baron Gordon-Walker, CH, PC (Life Peer); m 2, 1976, Sally Georgina Horton, da of Sidney Wilfred Eaton; 1 s; *Career* merchant banking Dublin, New York and London 1957–58; publishing: Secker & Warburg Ltd 1958–62, Jonathan Cape 1962–90 (dir 1962–90, md 1966–88); dir: Chatto, Virago, Bodley Head and Jonathan Cape 1969–88 (chm 1970–88), Random House UK Ltd 1988–90, Jackdaw Publications (chm 1964–88), Cape Goliard Press 1967–88, Guinness Mahon Holdings 1968–79, Australasian Publishing Co Pty 1969–88 (chm 1978–88), Sprint Productions 1971–80, Book Reps (NZ) 1971–88 (chm 1984–88), CVBC Services Ltd (chm 1972–88), Guinness Peat Group plc 1973–87, Grantham Book Storage Ltd (chm 1974–88), Triad Paperbacks Ltd 1975–88, Chatto, Virago, Bodley Head and Jonathan Cape Australia Pty Ltd (chm 1977–88), Greene King plc 1979–, Statesman & Nation Publishing Co Ltd 1980–85 (chm 1981–85), Statesman Publishing Co Ltd 1980–85 (chm 1981–85), New Society (chm 1984–86), Random House Inc 1987–88, Jupiter Int Green Investment Trust plc 1989–, Henry Sotheran Ltd 1990–, Ed Victor Ltd 1991–, Rosemary Sandberg Ltd 1991–, Libra KFT (Budapest) 1991–; pres Publishers Assoc 1977–79 (memb Cncl 1969–88); memb: Book Devpt Cncl 1970–79 (dep chm 1972–73), Int Ctee Int Publishers Assoc 1977–88 (Exec Ctee 1981–88), Groupe des Editeurs de Livres de la CEE (EEC) 1977–86 (pres 1984–86), Arts Cncl Working Party Sub Ctee on Public Lending Right 1970, Paymaster Gen's Working Party on Public Lending Right 1970–72, Bd British Cncl 1977–88; chm Nat Book League 1974–76 (dep chm 1971–74), memb Gen Ctee Royal Literary Fund 1975; chm Museums and Galleries Cmmn 1991–96; British Museum: tstee 1978–, chm of tstees 1996–; vice chm British Museum Devpt Tst 1993– (chm 1986–93), pres British Museum Fndn Inc 1989–90, chm British Museum Co Ltd 1988–, dir American Friends of British Museum 1990–; chm GB-China Centre 1986–; Chevalier de l'Ordre des Arts et des Lettres France 1985; *Style*— Graham Greene, Esq, CBE; ✉ 6 Bayley Street, Bedford Square, London WC1B 3HB (☎ 0171 304 4101, fax 0171 304 4102)

GREENE, Jenny; da of Capt James Wilson Greene (d 1945), of Cork, and Mary Emily, *née* Dickson (d 1971); *b* 9 Feb 1937; *Educ* Rochelle Sch Cork, Trinity Coll Dublin (BA), Univ of Montpellier France (Dip d'Etudes Francaises); *m* 1, 1 April 1971 (m dis 1987), John Gilbert, s of Capt James Gilbert (d 1987), of Johannesburg; m 2, 19 July 1994, Michael Arthur Guys Boys, s of Walter Guys Boys (d 1956), of London; *Career* researcher 1963–64, account exec Central News 1964–65, Pembertons Advertisers 1965–66, publicity exec Revlon 1966–71, beauty ed Woman's Own 1971–75, features writer and drama critic Manchester Evening News 1975–77, asst ed Woman's Own 1977–78, ed Homes and Gardens 1978–86, fndr ed A la Carte 1984–85, ed Country Life 1986–92; freelance writer 1993–; *Recreations* gardening, cookery; *Style*— Mrs J E Boys-Greene; ✉ En Chau, 71520 Trivy, France

GREENE, Prof the Hon Judith Margaret; *née* Gordon Walker; er da of Baron Gordon-Walker, CH, PC (Life Peer, d 1980); *b* 1936; *Educ* N London Collegiate Sch, Lady Margaret Hall Oxford (MA), Univ Coll London (BA, PhD); *m* 1, 1957 (m dis 1975), Graham Carleton Greene, CBE, *qv*, s of late Sir Hugh Carleton Greene, KCMG, OBE; m 2, 1981, Prof Norman William Dawson-Gowar, s of Harold James Dawson-Gowar; 1 step s, 1 step d; *Career* lectr in psychology Birkbeck Coll London Univ 1966–76, prof of psychology Open Univ 1976–; *Publications* (as Judith Greene) Psycholinguistics: Chomsky and Psychology (1972), Thinking and Language (1975), Learning to use Statistical Tests in Psychology (with M d'Oliveira 1982), Basic Cognitive Processes (with Carolyn Hicks, 1984), Language Understanding (1986, 2 edn 1995); *Style*— Prof the Hon Judith Greene; ✉ Open University, Walton Hall, Milton Keynes, Bucks MK7 6AA

GREENE, Lesley; *b* 25 March 1950; *Career* exhibitions organiser Scottish Arts Council 1973–79, visual arts offr Greater London Arts 1979–83, fndr dir Public Art Development Trust 1983–91; public art conslt: Castle Park Bristol 1991–93, Bristol Royal Hosp for Sick Children 1996–; fndr chairwoman Public Art Forum 1991, tstee Forest of Dean Sculpture; memb: Govt Art Collection Ctee 1989–92, Art Advsy Ctee Br Library 1990–91, Percent for Art Steering Ctee Arts Cncl 1990–93, Art for Architecture Res Team DOE 1985–89, Art for Architecture Awards Scheme Ctee DOE/RSA 1989–93; cncllr Stroud DC 1994–; FRSA 1992; *Recreations* gardening, walking, reading; *Style*— Lesley Greene; ✉ Old Police House, Cheltenham Road, Bisley, Glos GL6 7BJ (☎ and fax 01452 770018)

GREENE, Patricia Honor; da of Edward Greene, of Derby (d 1984), and Agnes, *née* Johnson (d 1992); *b* 26 Jan 1931; *Educ* Parkfield Cedars GS Derby, Central Sch of Speech and Drama; *m* 1, 1959 (m dis 1965), George Selway; m 2, 1972, Austen Richardson (d 1986); 1 s (Charles Austen b 1972); *Career* actress; early repertory work at Oxford Playhouse; has played character of Jill in The Archers since 1957; extensive tour of UK with Archers play 1991, Euro tours to Venice, Switzerland and Belgrade; featured in numerous radio and TV interviews; *Books* Book of the Archers (jtly, 1994); *Recreations* reading, gardening, cooking, theatre; *Clubs* Local Horticultural, BBC, Wine Club; *Style*— Ms Patricia Greene; ✉ The Archers, Pebble Mill, Birmingham (☎ 0121 414 8400, fax 0121 414 8873)

GREENE OF HARROW WEALD, Baron (Life Peer UK 1974), of Harrow, Greater London; Sidney Francis Greene; kt (1970), CBE (1966); s of Frank James Greene, of London; *b* 12 Feb 1910; *m* 1936, Masel Elizabeth Carter; 3 da; *Career* gen sec NUR 1957–74, chm TUC 1969–70; dir: Bank of England 1970–78, Trades Union Unit Tst 1970–, RTZ 1975–80; independent nat dir Times Newspaper Holdings 1980–82; JP London 1941–65; FCIT; *Style*— The Rt Hon Lord Greene of Harrow Weald, CBE; ✉ 26 Kynaston Wood, Boxtree Rd, Harrow Weald, Middx

GREENER, Anthony Armitage; s of William Martin Greener, and Diana Marianne, *née* Muir; *b* 26 May 1940; *m* Audrey, da of Patrick Ogilvie (d 1944); 1 s (Charles b 5 May 1981), 1 da (Claire b 20 Oct 1977); *Career* dir and gp md Dunhill Holdings plc 1974–87; Guinness plc: dir 1986–87, jt gp md 1987–91, chief exec 1992–, chm 1993–; chm United Distillers plc 1996– (md 1987–91); dir: Reed International plc 1990–, Reed Elsevier plc 1993–, Louis Vuitton Moët Hennessy SA (LVMH); vice pres Chartered Inst of Mktg 1993–; *Recreations* ocean racing, skiing; *Clubs* Royal Ocean Racing, Royal Yacht Sqdn; *Style*— Anthony Greener, Esq; ✉ Holly House, Church St, Chiswick, London W4 2PH; Guinness plc, 39 Portman Square, London W1H 0EE (☎ 0171 486 0288, fax 0171 935 9846)

GREENER, Michael John; s of late Gabriel William Greener, and late Morfydd, *née* Morgan; *b* 28 Nov 1931; *Educ* Douai Sch Woolhampton, Univ of Wales Cardiff (BA), Open Univ (BA); *m* 17 May 1964 (m dis 1973), Heather, da of James Balshaw; 1 s (Matthew Dominic b 17 Feb 1965); *Career* sr clerk Deloitte Plender Griffiths Cardiff 1956–58 (articled clerk 1949–56), asst to Sec Western Mail and Echo 1958–59, asst lectr then lectr Coll of Commerce Wednesbury Staffs 1959–62, dir then md Greener & Sons Ltd 1963–; author of numerous articles in professional jls 1958–; FCA 1967 (ACA 1957); *Books* Problems for Discussion in Mercantile Law (1968), Between the Lines of the Balance Sheet (1968, revised 1980), The Red Bus (children's fantasy) (1973), Penguin Dictionary of Commerce (1970, revised 1980), Penguin Business Dictionary (1987, revised 1994); *Recreations* freelance journalism, reading, bridge, walking; *Style*— Michael Greener, Esq; ✉ 33 Glan Hafren, The Knap, Barry, South Glamorgan CF62 6TA (☎ 01446 732867); 10 Broad St, Barry, S Glamorgan CF6 8AA (☎ 01446 735747)

GREENFIELD, Dr Christopher John; s of Leonard George Greenfield (d 1991), of Oldland Common, Nr Bristol, and Betty Joan, *née* Griffiths; *b* 28 Dec 1948; *Educ* Kingswood GS, Univ of Leeds (BA), Michigan State Univ (MA), Univ of Bristol (MEd, EdD 1996); *m* 23 June 1984, Gillian, da of George Orme (d 1984), of Newcastle upon Tyne; 1 s (George b 1987), 1 da (Laura b 1989); *Career* researcher Rowntree Tst 1971–73, asst to Richard Wainwright MP 1974–77, teacher in Huddersfield and Bahrain 1978–82, Quaker ME sec 1982–86, headmaster Sidcot Sch 1986–; memb Leeds CC 1973–76, Lib Parly candidate Leeds NE 1974 and Leeds W 1979; chm Quaker Headteachers' Conf 1991–94; fell CCC Cambridge 1995–; memb: W Yorks CC 1976–80, Winscombe Parish Cncl 1988–; tstee Rowntree Reform Tst 1983–; memb Soc of Headmasters of Ind Schs 1986; FCP 1991, FRSA 1992; *Publications* White Robed Queen (1994); *Recreations* local history, local affairs; *Clubs* National Liberal; *Style*— Dr Christopher Greenfield; ✉ Sidcot School, Winscombe, North Somerset BS25 1PD (☎ 01934 842340, fax 01934 843527)

GREENFIELD, Jonathan (Jon); s of John Frederick Greenfield, of Hatfield, and Mary Decimer, *née* Metivier; *b* 17 April 1959; *Educ* Hatfield GS, Univ of Manchester Sch of Architecture (BA, BArch); *m* 10 Aug 1991, Margaret Mary; 1 s (Patrick Peter b 22 Sept 1992), 1 da (Rosemary Anne b 31 May 1994); *Career* architect; office jr Sir Basil Spence Partnership 1978, trg with Trevor Dannatt & Partners 1980–81; project architect Chapman Taylor Partners (shopping devpts in Stockport and Coventry), assoc dir Pentagram Design Ltd (reconstruction of Shakespeare's Globe in Southwark, campaign designs for the Rose Theatre Tst); UNESCO travelling scholar Verona 1980, winner Mid Herts Rotary debating competition 1976; RIBA; *Recreations* drawing and painting; *Clubs* Friends of Shakespeare's Globe, Charter 88; *Style*— Jon Greenfield, Esq; ✉ 12 Wolsey Road, London N1 4QH (☎ 0171 249 7539); Pentagram Design Ltd, 11 Needham Rd, London W11 2RP (☎ 0171 229 3477, fax 0171 727 9932)

GREENGROSS, Sir (David) Alan; kt (1986), DL (1986); s of Morris Philip Greengross, OBE (d 1970), and Miriam Greengross (d 1969); *b* 15 April 1929; *Educ* Univ Coll Sch, Trinity Coll Cambridge (sr scholar, MA); *m* 26 May 1959, Sally (Lady Greengross, OBE, *qv*); 1 s (Peter b 1962), 3 da (Gail b 1960, Joanna b 1961, Claire b 1964); *Career* chm Memfagimal Group; dir: Indusmond Ltd, Blazy and Clement Ltd, BC Blazy and Clement Ltd, Port of London Authy 1979–84; dep traffic cmmr 1968–71; memb Holborn Borough Cncl 1957–64; memb Cncl London Borough of Camden 1965–84: chm planning and communications 1967–71, dep oppn ldr 1971–74, oppn ldr 1974–79; memb GLC 1977–86: chm Covent Garden Ctee, chm N London Area Planning Ctee, ldr Planning and Communications Policy Ctee 1979–81, dep ldr of oppn 1982–83, ldr of oppn 1983–86; visiting prof City of London Poly, chm Bloomsbury and Islington Health Authy 1990–93; govr: Univ Coll Sch, Univ Coll London 1990– (chm The Bartlett Faculty of the Built Environment 1993–); bd memb London Inward, chm London Regnl Passenger Ctee, fndr memb Inst for Metropolitan Studies; hon fell UCL; memb RSM; *Clubs* Hurlingham; *Style*— Sir Alan Greengross, DL; ✉ 9 Dawson Place, London W2 4TD; Batworthy on the Moor, Devon

GREENGROSS, Lady; Sally R; *née* Michaels; OBE (1993); *b* 29 June 1935; *Educ* Brighton & Hove HS, LSE (BA); *m* 26 May 1959, Sir Alan Greengross, *qv*; 1 s (Mark Peter b 6 Nov 1962), 3 da (Stephanie Gail b 24 April 1960, Joanna Louise b 31 Oct 1961, Claire Juliet b 10 Feb 1964); *Career* former linguist, exec in indust, lectr and researcher; dir gen Age Concern England 1987– (asst dir 1977–82, dep dir 1982–87), sec gen Eurolinkage 1981–, currently Euro vice pres Int Fedn on Ageing (sec gen 1982–87), pres Action on Elder Abuse 1994–, vice pres Research Inst for Care of the Elderly Bath 1987–, coordinator Prog for Elderly People within Second EEC Prog to Combat Poverty 1985–89, memb Standing Advsy Ctee on Transport for Disabled and Elderly People 1986–88, jt chm Bd Age Concern Inst of Gerontology King's Coll London 1987–, tstee Br Assoc of Domiciliary Care Offrs (BADCO) 1989–; ind memb: UN Network on Ageing 1983–, WHO Network on Ageing 1983–; advsr Centre for Vol Orgns, editorial advsr Home Care 1993–, conslt Jl of Educational Gerontology 1989–, patron Home Concern 1993–, vice pres EXTEND Exercis Trg 1996–; memb: Advsy Ctee Euro Movement, Govt Advsy Gp of Older Workers, Govt Advsy Gp on the Health of the Nation, Advsy Panel LSE Centre for Voluntary Organisations 1991–, Advsy Ctee for Carnegie Inquiry into the Third Age 1992–93, BT Forum Devpt Advsy Gp 1994–, Health Educn Authy Advsy Gp for Health Promotion and Older People 1996–; former memb: Inner London Juvenile Ct Panel, Mgmnt Bd Hanover Housing Gp; UK Woman of Europe 1990; Hon DLitt Univ of Ulster 1994, Hon DUniv Kingston and St George's 1996; FRSH 1989, FRSA 1989; *Books* Ageing, an Adventure in Living (ed, 1985), The Law and Vulnerable Elderly People (ed, 1986), Living, Loving and Ageing (1989), and others; *Recreations* countryside, music; *Clubs* Reform, Hurlingham; *Style*— Lady Greengross, OBE; ✉ Age Concern England, Astral House, 1268 London Road, London SW16 4ER (☎ 0181 679 8000, fax 0181 679 6069)

GREENHALGH, David Anthony; s of Rowland William Greenhalgh (d 1972), and Barbara Emily, *née* Edwards (d 1989); *b* 4 Dec 1943; *Educ* Sedbergh; *m* 24 May 1980, Jill Marian, da of John Donaldson, of Walton-on-Thames, Surrey; 1 s (Thomas William Michael Iain b 26 Nov 1991); *Career* articled clerk March Pearson & Skelton Manchester 1963–68; admitted slr 1968; Linklaters & Paines: joined 1969, tax ptnr 1974–93, head of Tax Dept 1989–93, corp ptnr 1994–; memb: Law Soc 1968, Revenue Law Sub Ctee City of London Law Soc 1974–91; Freeman City of London 1991; *Recreations* golf, gardening; *Clubs* West Sussex Golf, St George's Hill Golf; *Style*— David Greenhalgh, Esq; ✉ Linklaters & Paines, Barrington House, 59–67 Gresham St, London EC2V 7JA (☎ 0171 606 7080, fax 0171 606 5113, telex 884349)

GREENHALGH, Dr Peter Andrew Livsey; s of Herbert Livsey Greenhalgh (d 1973), of Heywood, Lancashire, and Elsie, *née* Wright; *b* 18 Oct 1945; *Educ* Bury GS, King's Coll Cambridge (Douton scholar, sr scholar, BA, Carrington-Koe student, MA, PhD); *m* 1968, Anna Mary Beatrice, da of Prof Kendal Dixon; 1 da (Clare Elizabeth Jane b 1978); *Career* res student and coll supervisor in classics and ancient history King's Coll Cambridge 1967–70, mgmnt trainee Reckitt & Colman PLC 1970–71, asst mangr corporate fin Hill Samuel & Co Ltd London 1972–76, sr lectr then assoc prof of classics Univ of Cape Town 1977–82, conslt in corp fin systems QB On-Line Systems England 1979–, asst gen mangr (corp fin) Hill Samuel Merchant Bank S Africa 1982–84, dir Hill Samuel Securities London 1985, dir and head corp fin Arbuthnot Latham Bank London 1985–88, corp fin conslt London 1988–89, chief exec AAF Investment Corporation PLC and md AAF Consultants Ltd 1989–90, pres Mobibau Inc (USA) 1990, md (corp fin) Chartered WestLB Ltd London 1990–91, corp fin conslt London 1992–; non-exec dir: National Bolts Ltd (S Africa) 1983–90, Auspharm International Ltd (Aust) 1986–88, AAF Investment Corporation PLC (UK) 1988–89; chm: Premier Construction Co Ltd (UK) 1989–90, Diamond Engineered Space Inc (USA) 1990, Lister Best Care Ltd 1990–95, Diagnostic and Daycare Property Management Co Ltd 1993–95, Greenwich Medical Media Ltd 1995–, Peter Greenhalgh & Co Ltd 1996–, White Swan Tst Hotel Ltd 1996–, Greenwich Medical Online Ltd 1996–; non-exec dir: Mobilbau Inc (USA) 1990, Preferred Medical Enterprises Inc (USA) 1990, Namibian Minerals Corporation Ltd (Canada) 1993–94, Lister BestCare Ltd 1990–96; *Books* Early Greek Warfare (1973), The Year of the Four Emperors (1975), Pompey: The Roman Alexander (1980), Pompey: The Republican Prince (1981), Deep into Mani: A Journey to the Southern Tip of Greece (1985, German edn 1987), A Miracle of Healing (1994); radio plays: The Tragedy of King Oedipus (1983), The Wrath of Achilles (1983, SA Academy Award 1985), Pompey the Great (1984), The Return of Odysseus (1985); *Recreations* reading, writing, walking, travel, theatre; *Clubs* Athenaeum; *Style*— Dr Peter Greenhalgh; ✉ Westwood House, Highcross Road, Westwood, Southfleet, Kent DA13 9PH (☎ 01474 832278, fax 01474 834495)

GREENHALGH, Robert (Bob); s of Robert Greenhalgh (d 1994), of Lancs, and Bertha Platt (d 1980); *b* 15 March 1942; *Educ* Lancaster Royal GS, Open University (BA); *m* 17 July 1965, Elizabeth, da of John Richard Higdon (d 1995), of Kemsing, Kent; *Career* princ RNIB Nat Rehabilitation Centre 1975–83, UK and int conslt for Low Vision Int 1982–, princ of trg South Regnl Assoc for the Blind 1983–92, sr ptnr Bob Greenhalgh and Partners (t/a Iridian) 1992–94, specialist in visual disability 1994–, Intersight Project mangr Guide Dogs for the Blind Assoc 1995–; hon chm: Mobility of the Blind Assoc 1973–76, Partially Sighted Soc 1980–88; chm Nat Light for Low Vision Ctee 1995– (memb 1977–, ed Handbook), memb Nat Light and Health Panel 1981–; Freeman City of Lancaster; memb Br Assoc of Social Workers 1970; *Recreations* music, good food, writing; *Style*— Bob Greenhalgh, Esq; ✉ 15 Belsize Park Mews, London NW3 5BL (☎ 0171 794 4861)

GREENHALGH, Prof Roger Malcolm; s of Maj John Greenhalgh (d 1977), of IOM, and Phyllis, *née* Poynton; *b* 6 Feb 1941; *Educ* Ilkeston Sch, Clare Coll Cambridge (MA, MD MChir), St Thomas' Hosp; *m* 30 July 1964, Karin Maria, da of Dr Karl Gross, and Lucia, *née* Hammer; 1 s (Stephen John b 4 Sept 1967), 1 da (Christina Elizabeth b 26 June 1970); *Career* house surgn St Thomas' Hosp London 1967, lectr in surgery Bart's 1972, sr lectr in surgery Charing Cross Hosp Med Sch London 1976 (hon conslt surgn 1976–), head Dept of Surgery Charing Cross Hosp Med Sch 1981 (prof of surgery London Univ 1982), head Dept of Surgery Univ of London at Charing Cross and Westminster Hosp Med Schs 1989–, dean Charing Cross and Westminster Med Sch 1993– (clinical dean 1991–93), chm Med Cncl Charing Cross and Westminster Hosps 1992–93, chm Directorate of Surgery Hammersmith Hosp Tst; hon conslt surgn: Chelsea and Westminster Hosp Tst, Chelsea Royal Hosp; cncl memb Assoc of Surgns of GB and Ireland 1987–90 and 1993–, Hunterian prof RCS of Eng 1980, vice pres Section of Surgery RSM 1986; Protem prof Brigham Hosp Harvard 1984, Boare-Powell prof Baylor Univ Dallas 1984, Hunter Sweaney prof Duke Univ North Carolina 1991, Marrick prof Brigham Hosp Harvard 1996; chm Editorial Bd European Journal of Vascular Surgery 1987–93, chm of tstees Euro Soc for Vascular Surgery 1987– (offr and memb Cncl 1987–93), sec gen and chm Exec Ctee Assoc of Int Vascular Surgns 1982; hon memb: Soc for Vascular Surgery, Euro Soc for Vascular Surgery, Brazilian Soc of Angiology, Polish Surgical Soc, Hellenic Surgical Soc, Hellenic Vascular Surgical Soc, Canadian Vascular Soc, Southern Africa Vascular Surgery Soc, Mediterranean League of Vascular Surgeons; Liveryman: Worshipful Co of Barbers, Worshipful Soc of Apothecaries; FRCS 1971; *Books* Progress in Stroke Research (1978), Smoking and Arterial Disease (1979), Hormones and Vascular Disease (1980), Femoro Distal Bypass (1981), Extra Anatomical Bypass and Secondary Arterial Reconstruction (1982), Progress in Stroke Research 2 (1983), Vascular Surgical Techniques (1984), Diagnostic Techniques and Investigative Procedures (1985), Vascular Surgery - Issues in Current Practice (1986), Indications in Vascular Surgery (1987), Limb Salvage and Amputation in Vascular Surgery (1988), Vascular Surgical Techniques - An Atlas (2 edn 1989, 3 edn 1994), The Cause and Management of Aneurysms (1990), The Maintenance of Arterial Reconstruction (1991), Emergency Vascular Surgery (1992), Surgery for Stroke (1993), Vascular Imaging for Surgeons (1995), The Trials and Tribulations of Vascular Surgery (1996), Clinical Surgery (ed, 1996); *Recreations* tennis; *Clubs* Athenaeum; *Style*— Prof Roger Greenhalgh; ✉ 271 Sheen Lane, London SW14 8RN (☎ 0181 878 1110); Department of Surgery, Charing Cross Hospital, London W6 8RF (☎ 0181 846 7316, fax 0181 846 7330)

GREENHILL, Dr Basil Jack; CB (1981), CMG (1967); s of Basil Greenhill (d 1979), of Nailsea, Somerset, and Edith, *née* Holmes (d 1964); *b* 26 Feb 1920; *Educ* Bristol GS, Univ of Bristol (BA, PhD); *m* 1, 1950, Gillian (d 1959); 1 s (Richard); m 2, 1961, (Elizabeth) Ann, da of Walter Ernest Giffard, JP (d 1970), of Lockeridge, Wiltshire; 1 s (James); *Career* Lt RN (Air Branch) 1941–45; HM Dip Serv cnsllr 1946–67; dir Nat Maritime Museum 1967–83; chm: Dulwich Picture Gallery 1980–88, SS Great Britain Project 1982–92 (life vice pres 1992–), The Royal Armouries 1983–88, Univ of Exeter Maritime History Project 1985–, Univ of Bristol Maritime History Research Centre 1993–, Govt Advsy Ctee on Historic Wreck Sites 1986–, The Royal Air Force Museum 1987–; series conslt Conway's History of the Ship 1991–; princ advsr BBC TV series: The Commanding Sea 1980–81, Trade Winds 1985–86; BBC Radio series The British Seafarer 1980–81; frequent radio and television appearances; fell Univ of Exeter; Order of White Rose Finland 1980; *Books* Boats and Boatmen of Pakistan (1971), Westcountrymen In Prince Edward's Isle (3 edn 1990, filmed and televised, American Assoc award), Archaeology of the Boat (1976), The Merchant Schooners (4 edn 1988), The Life and Death of the Sailing Ship (1980), Seafaring Under Sail (1982), The Grain Races (1986), The British Assault on Finland 1854–55 (with Ann Giffard, 1988), The Evolution of the Wooden Ship (1988), The Mary Fletcher (ed and preface, 1990), The Herzogin Cecilie (1991, Swedish edn 1992, German edn 1993), The Maritime History of Devon (jt ed, 1993), The Arby Boat (1993), Steam, Politics and Patronage (with Ann Giffard, 1994), The Bertha L Downs (with S F Manning, 1995), The Archaeology of Boats and Ships (1995), The Evolution of the Sailing Ship (ed, 1995); *Recreations* gardening, walking, sailing ('Nugget'), travel; *Clubs* Arts (hon memb), Royal Western Yacht, Nautical (Mariehamn Finland); *Style*— Dr Basil Greenhill, CB, CMG; ✉ West Boetheric Farm, St Dominic, Saltash, Cornwall PL12 6SZ

GREENHILL, 3 Baron (UK 1950), of Townhead in the City of Glasgow; Malcolm Greenhill; yr s of 1 Baron Greenhill, OBE, LLD (d 1967), and Ida, *née* Goodman (d 1985); suc bro, 2 Baron 1989; *b* 5 May 1924; *Educ* Kelvinside Acad Glasgow, Univ of Glasgow (BSc); *Heir* none; *Career* chartered patent agent; memb UK Scientific Mission to Washington USA 1950–51, Miny of Aircraft Prodn (merged with Miny of Supply after WWII) 1944–54, UKAEA 1954–73, MOD 1973–89; *Recreations* gardening; *Style*— The Rt Hon the Lord Greenhill; ✉ 28 Gorselands, Newbury, Berks RG14 6PX (☎ 01635 45651)

GREENHILL OF HARROW, Baron (Life Peer UK 1974), of Royal Borough of Kensington and Chelsea; Sir Denis Arthur Greenhill; GCMG (1972, KCMG 1967, CMG 1960), OBE (mil 1941); s of late James Greenhill, of Ashfields, Loughton, Essex; *b* 7 Nov 1913; *Educ* Bishop's Stortford Coll, Christ Church Oxford (MA); *m* 1941, Angela Doris, da of late William Leitch McCulloch, of Helensburgh; 2 s ((Hon) Nigel Denis St George b 1942, Hon Robin James b 1945, d 1986); *Career* apprentice London North Eastern Railway 1935–39; Col RE; served WWII: ME, N Africa, Italy, Asia; HM Diplomatic Serv 1946–73, perm under sec FCO and head Dip Serv 1969–73; govr BBC 1973–78; dir: BP 1973–78, BAT Industries 1974–82, British Leyland 1974–77, Leyland International 1977–82, Clerical Medical & General Life Assurance 1973–86, advsy cttee First Chicago Bank 1976–81, Hawker Siddeley Group 1974–84, S G Warburg & Co Ltd 1974–87 (advsr 1987–95), The Wellcome Foundation Ltd 1974–85; dep chm BUPA 1978–84; chm: Governing Body SOAS 1978–85, King's Coll Hosp Med Sch Cncl 1977–83; memb select ctees House of Lords 1974–; pres: Royal Soc for Asian Affrs 1976–84, Anglo-Finnish Soc 1981–84; tstee Rayne Fndn 1974–; govr Wellington Coll 1974–83; hon student ChCh Oxford 1973, fell King's Coll 1984; Grand Cross Order of Finnish Lion 1984; *Books* More by Accident (memoirs); *Clubs* Travellers'; *Style*— The Rt Hon the Lord Greenhill of Harrow, GCMG, OBE; ✉ 25 Hamilton House, Vicarage Gate, London W8 4HL (☎ 0171 937 8362)

GREENING, Christopher Seymour; s of John Seymour Greening (d 1971), and Natalie, *née* Robertson; *b* 26 Nov 1938; *Educ* Highgate Sch, RCM, Clare Coll Cambridge (MA); *m* Jane, da of Eric and Sylvia Alexander; 2 c (Julia Natalie b 1974, Robert Charles Alexander b 1979); *Career* Nat Serv Irish Gds 1957–60; advertising exec; graduate trainee J Walter Thompson 1963, copywriter McLaren Dunkley Friedlander 1964–70, vice chm Charles Barker City 1980 (creative dir 1970–80), md Christopher Greening Ltd 1980–83, creative dir Valin Pollen 1983–91, ptnr Lawton Greening 1992–; *Recreations* music, family life; *Clubs* 23; *Style*— Christopher Greening, Esq; ✉ The Want House, Barkway, nr Royston, Herts SG8 8EG

GREENING, Rear Adm Sir Paul Woollven; GCVO (1992, KCVO 1985); s of late Capt Charles W Greening, DSO, DSC, RN, and Molly, *née* Flowers; *b* 4 June 1928; *Educ* Mowden Sch Brighton, Nautical Coll Pangbourne; *m* 1951, Monica, da of late W E West; 1 s, 1 da; *Career* RN: entered 1946, Midshipman HMS Theseus 1947–48, Sub Lt then Lt HM Ships Zodiac, Neptune, Rifleman, Asheldham (CO) and Gamecock 1950–58, Lt Cdr HM Ships Messina (CO), Loch Killisport, Urchin and Collingwood 1958–63, Cdr 1963, CO HMS Lewiston and SO 2 Minesweeping Sqdn 1963–64, jssc 1964, Naval Plans MOD (Navy) 1965–67, CO HMS Jaguar 1967–68, Fleet Plans Offr FE Fleet 1969–70, Capt 1969, CO HMS Aurora 1970–71, Capt Naval Drafting 1971–74, Sr Offrs War Course 1974, Dir of Offrs Appts (Seamen) MOD (Navy) 1974–76, Capt BRNC Dartmouth 1976–78, Rear Adm 1978, Naval Sec 1978–80, Flag Offr Royal Yachts 1981–85, ret 1985; ADC to HM The Queen 1978, Extra Equerry to HM The Queen 1983–, Master of HM's Household 1986–92; memb Cncl Missions to Seamen 1993–; yr bro Trinity House 1984–; *Recreations* golf, gardening, following cricket; *Style*— Rear Adm Sir Paul Greening, GCVO; ✉ Kingsmead Cottage, Kingsmead, Wickham, Hants PO17 5AU

GREENLAND, Prof Dennis James; s of James John Greenland (d 1976), and Lily Florence Greenland, *née* Gardener (d 1980); *b* 13 June 1930; *Educ* Portsmouth GS, ChCh Oxford (MA, DPhil); *m* 27 Aug 1956, (Edith) Mary, da of Albert Henry Johnston (d 1974); 1 s (Rohan James b 1961), 2 da (Judith Mary b 1956, Jennifer Helen b 1962); *Career* lectr Univ of Ghana 1956–60, reader Univ of Adelaide 1960–69, prof Univ of Reading 1970–79, dep DG Int RICE Res Inst 1979–87, dir sci servs CAB Int 1987–92, ret; visiting prof Univ of Reading 1988–; chm Scientific Advsy Panel Cwlth Devpt Corp 1992–95; Hon DAgSci Univ of Ghent 1982; hon memb: American Soc of Agronomy 1993, Soil Sci Soc of America 1993; FIBiol 1974, FWA 1987, FRS 1994; *Books* The Soil Under Shifting Cultivation (with P H Nye, 1960), Soil Conservation and Management in the Humid Tropics (ed with R Lal, 1977), Chemistry of Soil Constituents (ed with M H B Hayes, 1978), Soil Physical Properties and Crop Production in the Tropics (ed with R Lal, 1979), Characterization of Soils in Relation to their Classification and Management for Crop Production: Some Examples from the Humid Tropics (ed, 1981), The Chemistry of Soil Processes (ed with M H B Hayes, 1981), Soil Resilience and Sustainable Land Use (ed with I Szabolcs, 1994); *Recreations* golf, walking; *Style*— Prof Dennis Greenland, FRS; ✉ Low Wood, The Street, South Stoke, Oxfordshire (☎ and fax 01491 873259)

GREENLY, Simon Stafford; s of Raymond Henry Greenly, of Corsham, and Brenda Margaret Agnes, *née* Stafford (d 1986); *b* 2 March 1945; *Educ* Uppingham, Univ of London (BSc); *Career* Beecham Group 1967–71; dir: Stafford Robert and Partners 1972–, Lloyd Instruments plc 1985–87; chm: Les Routiers 1983–90, Greenly's Management Consultants 1983–, ATA Selection plc 1986–88, Greenly's Holdings 1988–, GSL Systems 1991–93; tstee Windsor Leadership Tst 1995–; FRSA; *Recreations* fly fishing, racing, riding, gardening; *Clubs* Carlton, RAC; *Style*— Simon Greenly, Esq; ✉ The Great Barn, Wokingham Road, Hurst, Reading RG10 0RX; Greenly's, 39 Thames St, Windsor, Berks SL4 1PR (☎ 01753 831818, fax 01753 620118)

GREENOCK, Lord; Charles Alan Andrew Cathcart; s and h of 6 Earl Cathcart, CB, DSO, MC, *qv*; *b* 30 Nov 1952; *Educ* Eton; *m* 1981, Vivien Clare, o da of Francis Desmond McInnes Skinner, of North Farm, Snetterton, Norfolk; 1 s (Hon Alan George b 16 March 1986), 1 da (Hon Laura Rosemary b 11 June 1984); *Heir* s, Hon Alan George Cathcart; *Career* cmmnd Scots Gds 1972–75; CA Ernst and Whinney 1976–83, Hogg Robinson plc 1983, dir Gardner Mountain and Capel-Cure Agencies Ltd 1987–94, Murray Lawrence Holdings Ltd 1995–; memb Queen's Body Guard for Scotland (Royal Co of Archers); ACA; Liveryman Worshipful Co of Merchant Taylors; *Clubs* City of London, Household Division Yacht; *Style*— Lord Greenock; ✉ 18 Smith Terrace, London SW3; Gateley Hall, Dereham, Norfolk

GREENOUGH, Alan Edward; s of Edward Greenough (d 1987), and Nancy Dewar, *née* Houghton; *b* 14 July 1949; *Educ* Cowley GS St Helens, Univ of Bristol (LLB); *m* 16 Aug 1975, Sheila Mary, da of Francis Thomas Collins, of Rainhill, Merseyside; 2 da (Emma b 10 June 1978, Kate b 16 April 1980); *Career* slr; Alsop Wilkinson: ptnr 1979, sr ptnr Manchester office 1989, sr corp fin ptnr NW 1989; non-exec dir Parkman Group Ltd 1991–, non-exec chm Inter Selection Group Holdings Ltd 1991–93, chm and chief exec Prime People plc 1991–93; corp fin ptnr: Davies Arnold Cooper 1993–94, Pinsent Curtis 1994–; memb Law Soc; *Recreations* rugby league, travel, cinema, most sports; *Style*— Alan Greenough, Esq; ✉ The Mullions, 110 Moor Hall Drive, Sutton Coldfield, West Midlands B73 6LS (☎ 0121 308 0602); Pinsent Curtis Solicitors, 3 Colmore Circus, Birmingham B4 6BH (☎ 0121 200 1050, fax 0121 626 1040)

GREENSLADE, Roy; *b* 31 Dec 1946; *Educ* Dagenham County HS, Univ of Sussex (BA); *Career* journalist; with Barking Advertiser 1962–66; sub ed: Lancashire Evening Telegraph 1966–67, Daily Mail Manchester 1967–69; dep chief sub ed The Sun 1969–71 and 1971–73, sub ed Daily Mirror 1971, pt/t sub ed Sunday Mirror 1975–79, news reader BBC Radio Brighton 1975–76, Daily Express and Daily Star 1979–81 (leaving as features ed), asst features ed The Sun 1981–86, managing ed (News) Sunday Times 1986–90, ed Daily Mirror 1990–91, conslt ed News International 1991, freelance 1992–, columnist The Guardian and The Observer 1995–, presenter Talk TV (Granada/BSkyB) 1996–; dir Impact Books 1993–; presenter Mediumwave (BBC Radio 4); *Books* Goodbye to the Working Class (1975), Maxwell's Fall (1992); *Style*— Roy Greenslade, Esq; ✉ c/o Peters, Fraser and Dunlop, Chelsea Harbour, London SW10 0XF (☎ 0171 344 1000)

GREENSTED, Stephen; s of Leslie Bryan Greensted (d 1994), and Myra, *née* Shearsmith; *b* 6 March 1953; *Educ* Cranleigh Sch, RAF flying scholarship 1970, Keble Coll Oxford (open exhibitioner, MA); *m* 29 Sept 1976, Sally Frances, da of Prof Sir Stanley Hooker, tech dir Rolls Royce Aero Engines (d 1984); 2 da (Kate b 5 April 1992, Anna b 6 Feb 1994); *Career* advtg exec; account mangr: Hobson Bates 1974–77, Young and Rubicam 1977–79; account supr Leo Burnett 1979–84, client servs dir Gold Greenlees Trott 1984–90, gp account dir Lowe Howard-Spink 1990–94, md Woollams Moira Gaskin O'Malley 1994–95, dir Osprey Park Agency 1995–; *Recreations* half marathon running; *Style*— Stephen Greensted, Esq; ✉ Osprey Park Agency, Osprey House, 10 Little Portland Street, London W1N 6LX (☎ 0171 208 1000)

GREENSTOCK, Jeremy Quentin; CMG (1991); s of (John) Wilfrid Greenstock (d 1992), of Sheepscombe, Glos, and his 1 w, Ruth Margaret, *née* Logan (d 1973); *b* 27 July 1943; *Educ* Harrow, Worcester Coll Oxford (exhibitioner, BA, rackets blue, tennis blue); *m* 12 April 1969, Anne Derryn Ashford Hodges, da of William Anthony Ashford Hodges, of Fritton, Norfolk; 1 s (Nicholas b 1973), 2 da (Katherine b 1970, Alexandra b 1975); *Career* asst master Eton 1966–69; HM Dip Serv: joined 1969, MECAS 1970–72, second then first sec Dubai 1970–74, private sec to HM Ambass Washington 1974–78, planning staff, personnel ops, Near E and N African Depts FCO 1978–83, commercial cnsllr Jeddah and Riyadh 1983–86, head of Chancery Paris 1987–90, asst under sec of state Western and Southern Europe FCO 1990–93, min Washington 1994–95, dep under sec Middle East and Eastern Europe FCO 1995, political dir FCO 1996–; *Recreations* travel, photography, golf, skiing; *Style*— Jeremy Greenstock, Esq, CMG; ✉ Foreign and Commonwealth Office, Whitehall, London SW1A 2AH (☎ 0171 270 3000)

GREENTREE, Hedley Anthony; s of Bertram Albert Greentree (d 1963), of The Crossways, Portchester, and Dolly, *née* Snell (d 1956); *b* 17 April 1939; *Educ* St John's Coll Southsea, Portsmouth Poly (DipArch); *m* 1 (m dis), Sandra Caroline, da of late Frank Paige; 1 s (Richard Anthony b 19 March 1971); m 2, 10 Jan 1976, Jennifer Mary, da of Douglas Stuart Edwin Gudgin, of Magnolia Cottage, Friarydene, Prinstead, nr Emsworth, W Sussex; 3 s (Benjamin Hedley b 4 Feb 1977, Thomas Anthony b 7 Aug 1979, Joseph Michael b 27 Oct 1981); *Career* Nat Serv Lance Corpl X-Technician Army Signals Regt 1959–61; fndr Hedley Greentree Ptnrship Hampshire 1968, chm HGP Greentree Allchurch Evans Ltd (incorporating HGP Consultants, Greentree Associates Ltd and Marintech) 1987–; dir: Foodparks UK Ltd, Portsmouth Partnership; fndr and memb Exec Ctee Hampshire Devpt Assoc; formerly: vice pres Portsmouth Junior C of C, pres Hampshire branch RIBA, chm Bd of Govrs Portsmouth Coll of Art Design and Further Educn; Hon DLitt Portsmouth 1996; RIBA; *Recreations* windsurfing, tennis, swimming; *Style*— Hedley Greentree, Esq; ✉ Dormers, Crofton Ave, Lee-on-Solent, Hampshire (☎ 01329 315668); HGP Greentree Allchurch Evans Ltd, Furzehall Farm, Wickham Rd, Fareham, Hampshire PO16 7JG (☎ 01329 283225, fax 01329 237004, car 0378 737203)

GREENWAY, 4 Baron (UK 1927); Sir Ambrose Charles Drexel Greenway; 4 Bt (UK 1919); s of 3 Baron (d 1975); *b* 21 May 1941; *Educ* Winchester; *m* 1985, Mrs Rosalynne Peta Schenk, da of Lt-Col Peter Geoffrey Fradgley, of Upcott Manor, Rackenford, N Devon; *Heir* bro, Hon Mervyn Greenway, *qv*; *Career* marine photographer and writer, chm The Marine Soc 1994; Yr Bro of Trinity House 1987; *Recreations* sailing, swimming; *Clubs* House of Lords Yacht; *Style*— The Rt Hon Lord Greenway; ✉ c/o House of Lords, London SW1

GREENWAY, Harry; MP (C) Ealing North (majority 5,966); s of late John Kenneth Greenway, and Violet Adelaide, *née* Bell; *b* 4 Oct 1934; *Educ* Warwick Sch, Coll of St Mark and St John London, Caen Univ; *m* 1969, Carol Elizabeth Helena, da of Maj John Robert Thomas Hooper, Metropolitan Stipendiary Magistrate (d 1975); 1 s, 2 da; *Career* former schoolmaster, chm British Atlantic Educn Ctee 1970–84; dep headmaster: Sir William Collins Sch 1971–72, Sedgehill Sch 1972–79; MP (C) Ealing North 1979–, chm All Party Adult Educn Ctee 1979–, memb Parly Select Ctee on Educn Science and Arts 1979–92, vice chm Greater London Members 1981–87, vice chm and hon sec Cons Parly Educn Ctee 1981–86, vice chm Cons Pty Sports Ctee 1987; memb Parly Select Ctee: on Employment 1992–96, on Educn and Employment 1996–; memb Cncl: Br Horse Soc 1973– (Award of Merit 1980), Open Univ 1982; pres: Nat Equine Welfare Cncl 1989–, Assoc of Br Riding Schs 1993–; Freeman City of London, Liveryman Worshipful Co of Farriers; *Recreations* riding, hockey (fndr Lords & Commons Hockey Club, capt 1982–), tennis, music, cricket, skiing; *Clubs* Ski Club of GB, St Stephen's Constitutional; *Style*— Harry Greenway, Esq, MP; ✉ House of Commons, London SW1 (☎ 0171 219 4598)

GREENWAY, John Robert; MP (C) Ryedale (majority 18,439); s of Thomas William, of 34 Melchett Cres, Rudheath, Northwich, Cheshire, and Kathleen Gregory; *b* 15 Feb 1946; *Educ* Sir John Deane's GS Northwich; *m* 24 Aug 1974, Sylvia Ann, da of James Francis Gant, of 4 Mulgrave Rd, Whitby, N Yorks; 2 s (Stephen, Anthony), 1 da (Louise); *Career* Midland Bank 1964–65, Met Police 1965–69, insur rep 1969–72, insur broker 1972; MP (C) Ryedale 1987–, PPS to Baroness Trumpington as Min of State at Ministry of Agriculture, Fisheries and Food 1991–92; memb House of Commons Select Ctee on Home Affrs; chm: All Party Insur and Fin Servs Ctee, All-Party Racing and Bloodstock Ctee; vice chm: All-Party Football Ctee, Cons Backbench Agric Ctee, Cons Home Affrs Ctee; cncllr N Yorks CC 1985–87; pres York City FC; *Recreations* opera, football, wine, travel; *Style*— John Greenway, Esq, MP; ✉ 11 Oak Tree Close, Strensall, York YO3 5TE (☎ 01904 490535); 109 Town St, Old Malton, YO17 OHD (☎ 01653 692023); House of Commons, London SW1A 0AA (☎ 0171 219 3000)

GREENWAY, Hon Mervyn Stephen Kelvygne; s of 3 Baron Greenway; bro and hp of 4 Baron Greenway, *qv*; *b* 19 Aug 1942; *Educ* Winchester; unmarried; 1 da (Philippa Mary b 1980); *Career* stockbroker; Freeman City of London, Liveryman Worshipful Co of Vintners; FCA; *Recreations* racing, bridge, golf, cricket, tennis; *Clubs* Turf, MCC; *Style*— The Hon Mervyn Greenway; ✉ 605 Howard House, Dolphin Sq, London SW1 (☎ 0171 821 1893, fax 0171 976 6172)

GREENWELL, Sir Edward Bernard; 4 Bt (UK 1906), of Marden Park, Godstone, Co Surrey and Greenwell, Wolsingham, Co Durham; DL (1988); s of Capt Sir Peter McClintock Greenwell, 3 Bt, TD, DL (d 1978), and (Jean) Henrietta Rose (who m 2, Hugh Kenneth Haig, TD), da of Peter Haig Thomas and Lady Alexandra, *née* Agar, 2 da of 4 Earl of Normanton, DL; *b* 10 June 1948; *Educ* Eton, Nottingham Univ (BSc), Cranfield Inst of Technology (MBA); *m* 1974, Sarah Louise, da of Lt-Col Philip Maitland Gore-Anley (d 1968), of Sculthorpe House, Fakenham; 1 s (Alexander Bernard Peter b 1987), 3 da (Belinda Clayre b 1977, Lucy Rose b 1979, Daisy Julia b 1983); *Heir* s, Alexander Bernard Peter Greenwell b 11 May 1987; *Career* farmer; sometime chm Suffolk Coastal District Cncl; *Clubs* Turf; *Style*— Sir Edward Greenwell, Bt, DL; ✉ Gedgrave Hall, Woodbridge, Suffolk (☎ 01394 450440)

GREENWELL, (Arthur) Jeffrey; CBE (1991); s of George Greenwell (d 1982), of Durham, and Kate Mary, *née* Fleming; *b* 1 Aug 1931; *Educ* Durham Sch, Univ Coll Oxford (MA); *m* 15 Aug 1958, Margaret Rosemary, da of Sidney David Barnard (d 1949); 1 s (David 1964), 2 da (Jane b 1960, Kate b 1962); *Career* Nat Serv RHA 1950–51; articled to Town Clerk Newcastle upon Tyne 1955–58, admitted slr 1958, law tutor Gibson and Weldon 1958–59, asst slr Birmingham Corporation 1959–61, dep clerk of the Cncl Hants CC 1967–74 (asst clerk 1964–67, asst slr 1961–64), dep clerk of the peace 1967–73, dep clerk Hants River Authy 1967–73, chief exec Northants CC 1973–96, clerk of Lieutenancy Northants 1977–96; pres Northants Assoc of Local Cncls 1976–96, memb Peterborough Diocesan Synod, govr Nene Coll, chm Central Festival Opera; hon sec Assoc of Co Chief Execs 1980–84, Soc of Local Authy Chief Execs 1984–88; chm Home Office Gp on Juvenile Crime 1987, chm Assoc of Co Chief Executives 1993–94, pres Soc of Local Authy Chief Execs 1991; Freeman Cities of London and Durham, Liveryman Worshipful Co of Chartered Secretaries & Administrators; FCIS 1982 (pres 1989); *Recreations* bridge, travel, local history; *Clubs* Cheyne Walk (Northants); *Style*— Jeffrey Greenwell, Esq, CBE; ✉ 2 Hillside Way, Northampton NN3 3AW (☎ and fax 01604 401858)

GREENWOOD, Maj (Arthur) Alexander; s of Dr Augustus Charles Greenwood (d 1938), of Horncastle, Lincs; kinsman of 2 Viscount Greenwood, cous of Gen Sir Roland Guy, *qv*, Maj-Gen Richard Gerrard-Wright, *qv* and Brian Beves, *qv*; *b* 8 March 1920; *Educ* Oakham, Sidney Sussex Coll Cambridge (PhD); *m* 1, 1946 (m dis 1970), Betty Doreen, da of Brig Sidney Albert Westrop, CBE, DSO, MC (d 1979), of Brattleby, Lincs; 1 s (Nicholas Alexander Westrop b 1948), 1 da (Jane Alexandra b 1947); m 2, 1976, Shirley Knowles, da of Wing Cdr Alec Knowles-Fitton, MBE, CC (d 1988), of Appletreewick, N Yorks; *Career* regular army, The Royal Lincs Regt 1939–59, serv WWII Norway 1940, Iceland 1940–41, India and Burma 1942–45 (despatches), ADC to Field-Marshal Sir Claude Auchinleck, GCB 1943–44, GSO 2 (Int) GHQ Middle East Land Forces 1953–54, chief instr Sch of Mil Intelligence 1954–56; memb London Stock Exchange 1963–76; co dir 1977–; dir: Allied City Share Trust plc 1964–74, Lincolnshire Chickens Ltd 1965–87; vice pres Reform Party of Canada 1994–95 (riding dir 1992–95); Liveryman Worshipful Co of: Pattenmakers 1965, Chartered Secretaries 1978; memb: Authors Soc, Heraldry Soc, Soc of Genealogists; FCIS, FSCA, FRSA, FRGS, FREconS, FInstD; *Books* The Greenwood Tree in Three Continents (1988), Field-Marshal Auchinleck (1990), The Greenwood Family, formerly of Haddenham Bucks (1996); *Recreations* cricket, golf, shooting, genealogy; *Clubs* Carlton, Pilgrims, MCC; *Style*— Maj A A Greenwood; ✉ RR 1, Box 40, Madrona Drive, Nanoose Bay, BC, V0R 2R0 Canada (☎ 00 1 250 468 9770 and 00 1 250 468 7476, fax 00 1 250 468 7476)

GREENWOOD, Allen Harold Claude; CBE (1974), JP (Surrey 1962, Hampshire 1977); s of Lt-Col Thomas Claude Greenwood (d 1958); *b* 4 June 1917; *Educ* Cheltenham, Coll of Aeronautical Engrg London; *Career* Lt Cdr (A) RNVR, pilot Fleet Air Arm 1942–52; chm: Sepecat SA 1964–73, Panavia GmbH 1969–72, Rookcliff Props 1973–87, Europlane Ltd 1974–83, British Aircraft Corp 1975–77, Remploy Ltd 1976–79, British Aerospace Inc (USA) 1977–81; dep chm British Aerospace 1977–83; pres: Euro Assoc Aero Cos 1974–76, Br Soc Aero Cos 1970–72; vice pres Engrg Employers' Fedn 1982–83, gen cmmr of Income Tax 1970–74; pres Cncl Cheltenham Coll, chm Cncl St John's Sch Leatherhead 1980–84; memb: Cncl Cranfield Inst of Technol 1970–79, Cncl CBI 1970–77, Ctee Governing Body of Public Schs 1981–84; Freeman City of London, Liveryman Coachmakers' Co, memb Guild of Air Pilots; *Recreations* sailing, motoring, travel; *Clubs* White's, RAC, Royal Lymington Yacht; *Style*— Allen Greenwood, Esq, CBE, JP; ✉ 2 Rookcliff, Milford-on-Sea, Lymington, Hampshire SO41 0SD (☎ 01590 642893)

GREENWOOD, Brian John; s of Ronald Greenwood (d 1979), and Marianne Luise, *née* Weiss; *b* 15 April 1950; *Educ* Forest Sch, Univ of Southampton (LLB); *m* 1 July 1978, Julia Le Messurier, da of Alan Le Messurier Scott; 4 s (Jonathan Ronald b 9 April 1981, James Alan b 1 Oct 1985, Alexander Brian b 5 Oct 1989, Benjamin John (twin) b 5 Oct

1989), 1 da (Jacqueline Rachel b 10 April 1983); *Career* articled clerk City of Westminster 1973–76, admitted slr 1976, asst slr S Yorks CC 1976–78, asst co slr Kent CC 1980–82 (sr asst slr 1978–80), chief slr Beds CC 1982–85, ptnr and head Planning and Environmental Law Gp Norton Rose 1988– (joined 1985); visiting lectr on planning and environmental law Coll of Law 1988–; chm: Planning and Environmental Law Ctee of the Law Soc 1989–, Planning and Environmental Law Sub-Ctee City of London Law Soc 1990–95, Environmental Law Sub-Ctee Law Soc 1995–; exec memb Local Govt Gp Law Soc 1979–85; memb CBI Environmental Protection Panel; memb Int Bar Assoc; Liveryman Worshipful Co of Slrs 1989; FRSA; *Books* Basic Planning Law and Practice (1989), Butterworths Planning Law Service (1990), Butterworths Planning Law Handbook, Planning and Compensation Act 1991 (1991), Environmental Regulation and Economic Growth (contrib), Planning Law and Practice; *Recreations* family, violin, classical music, sport; *Style*— Brian Greenwood, Esq; ✉ Norton Rose, Kempson House, PO Box 570, Camomile Street, London EC3A 7AN

GREENWOOD, Prof Christopher John; s of Capt Murray Guy Greenwood, of Singapore, and Diana Maureen, *née* Barron; *b* 12 May 1955; *Educ* Wellingborough Sch, Magdalene Coll Cambridge (MA, LLB); *m* 5 Aug 1978, Susan Anthea, da of late Geoffrey James Longbotham; 2 da (Catherine b 1982, Sarah b 1985); *Career* called to the Bar Middle Temple 1978, practising barr Essex Ct Chambers; Univ of Cambridge: fell Magdalene Coll 1978–96, dir of studies in law 1982–96, tutor 1989–96, dean 1982–87, lectr Faculty of Law 1984–96 (asst lectr 1981–84); prof of int law London Sch of Economics 1996–; dir of studies in public int law Hague Academy of Int Law 1989; visiting prof: West Virginia Univ 1986, Mississippi Univ 1989, Marburg Univ 1991; jt ed Int Law Reports; *Recreations* politics, reading novels, walking; *Style*— Prof Christopher Greenwood; ✉ Department of Law, London School of Economics, Houghton Street, London WC2A 2AE (☎ 0171 955 7250, fax 0171 955 7366); Essex Court Chambers, 24 Lincoln's Inn Fields, London WC2A 3ED (☎ 0171 813 8000, fax 0171 813 8080)

GREENWOOD, 2 Viscount (UK 1937); Sir David Henry Hamar Greenwood; 2 Bt (UK 1915); also Baron Greenwood (UK 1929); s of 1 Viscount Greenwood, PC, KC (d 1948), and Dame Margery Spencer, DBE, da of Rev Walter Spencer (decd), of Fownhope Ct, Herefordshire; *b* 30 Oct 1914; *Educ* privately and Bowers Gifford; *Heir* bro, Hon Michael Greenwood; *Career* farmer; *Recreations* reading, walking, shooting; *Style*— The Viscount Greenwood; ✉ 63 Portsea Hall, Portsea Place, London W2 2BY

GREENWOOD, Debra (Debbie); da of Ronald Arthur Greenwood, of Liverpool, and Mary Rosalie, *née* Davenport; *Educ* Aigburth Vale HS, Liverpool Poly (BA); *m* 17 Oct 1992, Paul Coia, s of Ferdinando Coia; 1 da (Annalie b 2 July 1994); *Career* receptionist Red Rose Radio Preston 1982–83, advtg sales rep Merseymart (free newspaper) Liverpool 1983–84, presenter Granada TV 1984–85, co-host Breakfast Time (BBC 1) 1985–86, quizmaster First Class (teenage gen knowledge quiz) 1986–88, co-host Tricks of the Trade (BBC 2) 1987, reporter Tom O'Connor Roadshow (BBC 1) 1987; co-host: Streetwise (Channel 4) 1989–90, You Can Do It (BSB) 1990, Garden Party (BBC 1) 1988, 1990 and 1991; regular presenter: BBC Radio 2 1987–, Pick of the Week (ITV) 1992; reporter TV Weekly 1992–94, presenter Weekend Breakfast Show (LBC) 1995–96, co-host Spellbound (live games show Sky One) 1995–96, presenter Live at 3 (magazine show UK Living); guest appearances incl: Paul McKenna Show, Wogan, Through the Keyhole, Wheel of Fortune, Pyramid Game, Win Lose or Draw, Blankety Blank, Open Air, Give Us A Clue; memb Equity 1984–; *Recreations* sport, cinema, theatre, eating out; *Style*— Miss Debbie Greenwood; ✉ c/o Jane Hughes Management, The Coach House, PO Box 123, Knutsford, Cheshire WA16 9HX (☎ 01565 723000)

GREENWOOD, Dr Duncan Joseph; CBE (1992); s of Herbert James Greenwood (d 1982), and Alison Fairgrieve Greenwood (d 1967); *b* 16 Oct 1932; *Educ* Hutton GS, Univ of Liverpool (BSc), Univ of Aberdeen (PhD, DSc); *Career* res fell Univ of Aberdeen 1957–59; Nat Vegetable Res Station: scientific offr Chemistry Section 1959–62, sr scientific offr 1962–66, head of soil sci 1966–87; head of soil science and plant nutrition Horticultural Research Int 1987–92 (emeritus fell 1992–); Blackman lectr Univ of Oxford 1982, Distinguished Scholar Queen's Univ of Belfast 1982, Hannaford lectr Univ of Adelaide 1985, Shell lectr Univ of Kent at Canterbury 1988, Amos lectr Wye Coll London 1989; visiting prof in plant scis Univ of Leeds 1985 and 1993, hon prof of agric chemistry Univ of Birmingham 1986–93; Res medal Royal Agric Soc of England 1979, Sir Gilbert Morgan medal Soc of Chemical Indust 1962; published over 160 scientific papers; pres: Int Ctee of Plant Nutrition 1978–83, British Soc of Soil Sci 1991–93; fell Royal Chemical Soc 1977, FRS 1985, FIHort 1986; *Style*— Dr Duncan Greenwood, CBE, FRS; ✉ 23 Shelley Rd, Stratford-upon-Avon CV37 7JR (☎ 01789 204 735); Horticulture Research International, Wellesbourne, Warwick CV35 9EF (☎ 01789 470382)

GREENWOOD, Prof Geoffrey Wilson; s of Richard Albert Greenwood (d 1987), of Bradford, W Yorkshire, and Alice Greenwood (d 1983); *b* 3 Feb 1929; *Educ* Grange GS Bradford, Univ of Sheffield (BSc, PhD, DMet, Brunton medal); *m* 1954, Nancy, *née* Cole; 2 s (John Stephen, Alan Richard), 1 da (Catherine Joyce); *Career* scientific then sr scientific offr AEA Harwell 1953–60, section head CEGB Berkeley Nuclear Laboratories 1960–65, res mangr of sciences Electricity Cncl Res Centre Capenhurst 1965–66, prof of metallurgy Univ of Sheffield 1966–94 (pro vice chllr 1979–83, emeritus prof 1994–); LB Pfeil prize of Inst of Metals and Iron and Steel Inst 1972, Rosenhain medal 1975, Griffith medal 1995; FRS 1992, FIM 1966, FInstP 1966, FEng 1990; pres Sheffield Metallurgical and Engrg Assoc 1981–82; *Recreations* music, oboe and piano playing, travel, various outdoor activities; *Clubs* Rotary; *Style*— Prof Geoffrey Greenwood, FRS, FEng; ✉ University of Sheffield, Department of Engineering Materials, Mappin Street, Sheffield S1 3JD (☎ 0114 222 5517, fax 0114 275 4325, e-mail g.w.greenwood@sheffield.ac.uk)

GREENWOOD, Gillian Patricia; da of Maj Henry Stuart Cousens, of W Chiltington, Pulborough, Sussex, and Pauline, *née* Hale; *b* 16 Dec 1941; *Educ* Dover GS, Aldershot HS for Girls, Folkestone GS for Girls, Leicester Poly, Coll of Furniture London; *m* 1961 (m dis 1973), Martin John Corbitt Greenwood, s of Raymond Ronald Greenwood, and Joan, *née* Corbitt King; 2 s (Richard Gordon Corbitt b 19 Feb 1962, David Paul b 15 April 1964); *Career* teacher in FE Catmose Village Coll Rutland 1969–73, self-employed antique dealer and furniture restorer 1972–74, trainee then qualified constituency agent and sec to Cons Assocs 1974–82 in: Brecon and Radnor, Kidderminster, Montgomery, Fulham; self-employed political conslt and researcher 1982–84, nat fund raiser Nat Assoc for the Welfare of Children in Hosp 1984–85, dir Children's Country Holidays Fund 1985–89, nat dir Alexandra Rose Day 1989–; regular bdcaster on local and national TV and radio; former: sch govr, volunteer St Thomas's Hosp, memb Nat Soc of Cons Agents, memb Cons Pty Nat Educn Advsy Ctee, memb Church Cncl Wigmore Abbey; chair Teme Valley Youth Club Tst, fndr Building Bridges (youth opportunity); memb: Leominster Cons Assoc, Cncl W Midlands Area Cons, Inst of Charity Fundraising Offrs, Inst of Supervisory Management, British Women Pilots Assoc, Herefordshire Aero Club; FRSA; *Recreations* furniture restoration, swimming; *Style*— Mrs Gillian Greenwood; ✉ Alexandra Rose Day, 2a Ferry Rd, Barnes, London SW13 9RX (☎ 0181 748 4824, fax 0181 748 3188)

GREENWOOD, Jeffrey Michael; s of Arthur Greenwood (d 1981), of London, and Ada, *née* Gordon (d 1964); *b* 21 April 1935; *Educ* Raine's Foundation Sch, Downing Coll Cambridge (MA, LLM); *m* 1964, Naomi, da of Leo Grahame; 3 s (Matthew b 1967, Joel b 1970, Ethan b 1973), 1 da (Abigail b 1965); *Career* articled clerk Bartlett and Gluckstein 1959–60, admitted slr 1960; Nabarro Nathanson: ptnr 1963–95, head of Property Dept 1972–87, sr ptnr 1987–95, conslt 1995–; chm: Jewish Welfare Bd 1986–90, Jewish Care 1990, Central Cncl for Educn and Trg in Social Work 1993–; memb Cncl: Business in the Community, Hampstead Garden Suburb Trust (Law Soc appointee 1984–87); dir: Bank Leumi (UK) plc, Jewish Chronicle Ltd; dir and chm Wigmore Property Investment Trust plc; Freeman City of London, Liveryman of Worshipful Co of Glovers 1984; memb Law Soc 1960; *Recreations* running, swimming, skiing, literature, travel; *Clubs* RAC; *Style*— Jeffrey Greenwood, Esq; ✉ c/o Nabarro Nathanson, 50 Stratton St, London W1X 5FL (☎ 0171 518 3323, fax 0171 629 7900)

GREENWOOD, Jeremy John; s of Basil Procter Greenwood (d 1963), of Langham, nr Holt, Norfolk, and Stephanie Kathleen, *née* Davidson Houston, MBE (d 1988); *b* 30 March 1936; *Educ* Haileybury, Peterhouse Cambridge (BA); *m* 26 Oct 1963, Annabel Elizabeth Marie-Gabrielle, da of Noel Carlile (d 1945); 1 s (Simon Harry b 1966), 2 da (Elinor Rose b 1971, Gemma Charlotte b 1972); *Career* publisher; various positions with Cassell, Pergamon and Hutchinson Presses; dir Trade Div Cassell Ltd 1977–81; proprietor and md Quiller Press 1981–; govr Runton Hill Sch for Girls 1984–88; *Books* Sefton - Horse For Any Year (1983); *Recreations* horses, shooting, golf, tennis, theatre; *Clubs* Cavalry and Guards', Royal West Norfolk Golf, MCC; *Style*— Jeremy Greenwood, Esq; ✉ Sparrow Hall, Hindringham, nr Fakenham, Norfolk; Quiller Press Ltd, 46 Lillie Rd, London SW6 1TN (☎ 0171 499 6529, fax 0171 381 8941)

GREENWOOD, John Kenneth; s of Kenneth Greenwood, and Iris, *née* Humphries; *b* 24 Dec 1948; *Educ* Wellington Coll, Univ of Manchester; *m* 21 June 1986, Jennifer Joy, da of R Hagan; 1 s (Maximilian Peter b 1982), 1 da (Tzigane Timanfaya Grace b 1984); *Career* dir Intercon Advertising 1971–78, shareholder Gen Advertising Co London Ltd 1978–87, proprietor Greenwood Hinds Advertising Ltd 1987–91, proprietor Greenwood Advertising and Marketing Services Ltd 1991–95, md General Advertising Ltd 1995–; MInstM, MInstD, MIMgt, MCAM; *Recreations* writing, golf; *Clubs* Foxhills, St George's; *Style*— John Greenwood, Esq; ✉ Pendrick, 16 Castle Rd, Weybridge, Surrey KT13 9QN (☎ 01932 858 652); General Advertising Ltd, Locke King House, Balfour Road, Weybridge, Surrey KT13 8HD

GREENWOOD, Hon Michael George Hamar; yr son of 1 Viscount Greenwood (d 1948); hp of bro, 2 Viscount; *b* 5 May 1923; *Educ* Eton, ChCh Oxford, Webber-Douglas Sch of Singing and Dramatic Art; *Career* actor; formerly with RCS; *Theatre* West End appearance in Joan of Arc at the Stake (with Ingrid Bergman); *Television* incl: Emergency Ward 10, Falstaff, Great Expectations, Charlie Drake Show, Dixon of Dock Green, Rob Roy, Lloyd George Documentary, Nixon at Nine, Adam Adamant Lives, Broaden Your Mind, Honey Lane, Gnomes of Dulwich, Eric Sykes Show, Nancy Astor; *Films* incl: The Big Money, House in the Woods, The Bank Raiders, Poor Cow, The Insomniac; *Recreations* walking, dancing, reading, writing and rhythm; *Style*— The Hon Michael Greenwood; ✉ 63 Portsea Hall, Portsea Place, London W2 2BY (☎ 0171 402 2975)

GREENWOOD, Dr Monica Hazel; da of Joseph Spring, of London, and Rose Joan, *née* Barnett; *b* 31 March 1943; *Educ* Camden Sch for Girls, St Mary's Med Sch London (Clothworkers' scholar, MB BS); *Career* research worker Inst of Psychiatry London 1972–74, conslt psychiatrist Shenley and Central Middx Hosps 1976–79, conslt psychiatrist The Middx Hosp 1979–, hon sr lectr UCL Med Sch and psychiatric advsr to Counsel and Care for the Elderly 1979–; author of various pubns on serotonin in man and on care of elderly people; memb BMA; FRCPsych 1986 (MRCPsych 1972); *Recreations* beekeeping, scuba diving, sailing, skiing; *Style*— Dr Monica Greenwood; ✉ Roma, Hendon Wood Lane, London NW7 4HR (☎ 0181 959 1541); 144 Harley Street, London W1N 1AH (☎ 0171 935 0023)

GREENWOOD, Prof Norman Neill; s of Prof John Neill Greenwood (d 1981), of Melbourne, Aust, and Gladys, *née* Uhland (d 1976); *b* 19 Jan 1925; *Educ* Univ HS Melbourne, Univ of Melbourne (BSc, MSc, DSc), Univ of Cambridge (PhD, ScD); *m* 21 Dec 1951, Kirsten Marie, da of Johannes Rydland (d 1978), of Bergen, Norway; 3 da (Karen b 1952, Anne b 1954, Linda b 1958); *Career* res tutor and lectr Trinity Coll Univ of Melbourne 1946–48, sr lectr (formerly lectr) in inorganic chemistry Univ of Nottingham 1953–61; prof and head Dept of Inorganic Chemistry Univ of Newcastle upon Tyne 1961–71; Univ of Leeds: prof and head Dept of Inorganic and Structural Chemistry Univ of Leeds 1971–90, emeritus prof 1990–, dean Faculty of Sci 1986–88; visiting professorships: Aust, Canada, USA, Denmark, China, Japan; author of numerous books and some 450 res papers; chm Int Cmmn on Atomic Weights 1969–75; pres: Inorganic Chemistry Div Int Union of Pure and Applied Chem 1977–81, Dalton Div Royal Soc of Chemistry 1979–81, Chemistry Section Br Assoc of Advancement of Science 1990–91; chm UK Ctee of Heads of Univ Chemistry Depts 1985–87, memb Cncl Royal Instn of GB 1993–96; awards: Dux Gold Medal Auburn Central Sch Melbourne 1938, Masson Meml Medal Royal Aust Chemical Inst 1945, Tilden Lectureship and Medal Chemical Soc London 1966, Medal for Main-Group Element Chemistry Royal Soc of Chemistry 1974, A W von Hofmann Lectureship Gesellschaft Deutscher Chemiker 1983, Liversidge Lectureship and Medal Royal Soc of Chemistry 1984, Egon Wiberg lectureship Univ of Munich 1989, Ludwig Mond Lectureship and Medal Royal Soc of Chemistry 1991, Tertiary Education Medal Royal Soc of Chemistry 1993; Hon Citizen of Nancy (France) 1977; Hon Doctorate l'Univ de Nancy 1977; memb American Chem Soc 1958, foreign memb l'Académie des Sciences de l'Institut de France 1992, memb NY Acad of Scis 1994; FRSC 1960, FRS 1987, CChem; *Books incl*: Ionic Crystals, Lattice Defects and Nonstoichiometry (1968), Mössbauer Spectroscopy (with T C Gibb, 1971), Contemporary British Chemists (with W A Campbell, 1971), Boron (1973), Chemistry of the Elements (with A Earnshaw, 1984); *Recreations* travel, music; *Style*— Prof Norman N Greenwood, FRS; ✉ School of Chemistry, University of Leeds, Leeds LS2 9JT (☎ 0113 233 6406, fax 0113 233 6565, telex 556473 UNILDS G, e-mail n.n.greenwood@chem.leeds.ac.uk)

GREENWOOD, Paul Michael; s of Ernest Charles Greenwood, of Glasgow, and Marie Patricia, *née* Dunn; *b* 2 Aug 1943; *Educ* Alexandra GS Singapore, Wymondham Coll; *m* 1 adopted da (Melissa); *Career* actor since 1965; *Theatre* RSC 1980–; roles incl: Antipholus of Syracuse in A Comedy of Errors, Lysander in A Midsummer Night's Dream, Polixenes in The Winter's Tale, Cromwell in Henry VIII, Kent in King Lear, Scarecrow in the Wizard of Oz, Boyet in Love's Labour's Lost, Alonso in The Tempest, Lelio in The Venetian Twins, Bob Cratchit in A Christmas Carol 1994, Feste in Twelfth Night 1996; *Television* appearances incl title role in Rosie (BBC), Yelland in 'Spender' (BBC); *Style*— Paul Greenwood, Esq; ✉ c/o A & B Personal Management Ltd, 5th Floor, Plaza Suite, 114 Jermyn Street, London SW1Y 6HJ (☎ 0171 839 4433/4)

GREENWOOD, Philip John; s of John Edward James Greenwood, and Betty, *née* Roberts (d 1944); *b* 20 Nov 1943; *Educ* Dolgellau GS, Harrow Coll of Art (NDD), Hornsey Coll of Art (ATC); *m* 19 Oct 1974, Valery Jane (d 1985), da of Maj James Francis Ratcliff, of Banstead, Surrey; 4 s (Huw b 27 Aug 1976, Jonathan b 26 Jan 1978, Owen (twin) b 26 Jan 1978, Ashley b 12 Oct 1981); *Career* artist; lectr in printmaking Herts Coll of Educn 1970–71; maj one-man exhibitions: Bohun Gallery UK 1974, Gallery Deux Têtes Canada 1976, Portland Gallery UK 1978, Galerie Tendenz Germany 1982, J One Fine Arts Japan 1983, CCA Japan 1985 and 1990, CCA Retrospective London 1994; maj gp exhibitions: RA, RE 1964–, RGI 1973, Br Cncl Gallery Greece 1976, Br Printmakers Aust 1976, V&A 1977, Tate Gallery 1981, Br Embassy Belgium 1983; public collections: Tate Gallery, Arts Cncl, Br Cncl, Nat Museum of Wales; memb Cncl Royal Soc of Painters

Etchers 1983–94; memb RE 1982 (ARE 1979); *Recreations* fishing, shooting; *Clubs* Arts; *Style*— Philip Greenwood, Esq; ✉ Oakleigh, 30 Leigh Hill Rd, Cobham, Surrey KT11 2HX (☎ and fax 01932 862383)

GREENWOOD, Richard Kay (Dick); s of John Herbert Kay Greenwood (d 1975), of Stalybridge, Cheshire, and Hilda, *née* Wild (d 1978); *b* 3 May 1928; *Educ* Manchester GS, Trinity Hall Cambridge (MA, MD, MChir); *m* 20 Feb 1961, Sandrina Margaruite, da of Lt-Col David Bishop Campbell, OBE (d 1969), of Sevenoaks, Kent; 1 s (Alastair b 11 Jan 1963), 1 da (Laura b 4 May 1968); *Career* jr surgical appts London, Exeter and Glos 1953–65; former: demonstrator of anatomy Univ of Cambridge, dep dir of Surgical Unit St Thomas' Hosp London, surgical tutor St Thomas' Hosp Med Sch, clinical tutor and examiner Leics Univ Hosp Med Sch, conslt in gen and peripheral vascular surgery Leics DHA, sr surgn and chm Div of Surgery Leics, ret; Wellcome res fell Mayo Clinic USA; contrib numerous articles in jls on: the gastroesophageal junction, gall bladder, fissure in ano, pilonidal sinus and peripheral vascular disease; former: ombudsman of the Jt Conslts Ctee, sub-chm of the Central Med Manpower Ctee, med examiner Health Ctee GMC and UKCC (Nursing), assessor of Health Serv Bd and Overseas Med Graduates, memb Ct of the Univ of Warwick; Freeman: City of London 1974, Worshipful Co of Makers of Playing Cards 1974; memb: BMA (former memb Cncl), RSM, Assoc of Surgns of GB and Ireland, Vascular Surgical Soc of GB and Ireland; FRCS; *Recreations* mountaineering, rowing, bridge, croquet, politics; *Clubs* Leander Rowing; *Style*— Dick Greenwood, Esq; ✉ Herongate, 30 The Ridgeway, Rothley, Leicester LE7 7LE (☎ 0116 230 3466)

GREER, Dr Germaine; *b* 29 Jan 1939, Melbourne; *Educ* Star of the Sea Convent Gardenvale Victoria Aust, Univ of Melbourne (Diocesan and Sr Govt scholar, BA), Univ of Sydney (MA), Univ of Cambridge (Cwlth scholar, PhD); *Career* sr tutor in English Univ of Sydney 1963–64, asst lectr then lectr in English Univ of Warwick 1967–72, broadcaster, journalist, columnist and reviewer 1972–79, lectr throughout N America with American Program Bureau 1973–78, prof of modern letters Univ of Tulsa 1980–83 (visiting prof Graduate Faculty of Modern Letters 1979), dir Stump Cross Books 1988–, special lectr and unofficial fell Newnham Coll Cambridge 1989–; columnist The Guardian until 1995; fndr ed of Tulsa Studies in Women's Literature 1981, fndr dir Tulsa Centre for the Study of Woman's Literature; *Publications* The Female Eunuch (1969), The Obstacle Race: The Fortunes of Women Painters and their Work (1979), Sex and Destiny: The Politics of Human Fertility (1984), Shakespeare (1986), The Madwoman's Underclothes (selected journalism, 1986), Kissing the Rod: An Anthology of Seventeenth Century Women's Verse (ed with Susan Hastings, Jeslyn Medoff, Melinda Sansone, 1988), Daddy, We Hardly Knew You (1989, winner J T Ackerley Prize and Premio Internazionale Mondello), The Uncollected Verse of Aphra Behn (ed, 1989), The Change: Women, Ageing and the Menopause (1991), Slip-Shod Sibyls: Recognition, Rejection and The Woman Poet (1995); *Style*— Dr Germaine Greer; ✉ c/o Aitken Stone & Wylie, 29 Fernshaw Road, London SW10 0TG (☎ 0171 351 7561)

GREER, Prof Ian Andrew; s of Andrew Greer (d 1991), of Glasgow, and Rebecca, *née* Hamilton; *b* 16 April 1958; *Educ* Allan Glen's Sch Glasgow, Univ of Glasgow (MB ChB, MD, MRCOG, MRCP(UK), FRCPG, MFFP); *children* 2 s; *Career* Royal Infirmary Glasgow: jr house offr in surgery 1980–81, jr house offr in med 1981; SHO in obstetrics Glasgow Royal Maternity Hosp 1981–82, SHO in gynaecology Royal Infirmary 1982; Univ Dept of Med Royal Infirmary: res fell/ hon SHO 1982–83, registrar in general med, haemotosis and thrombosis 1983–85; SHO in obstetrics Glasgow Royal Maternity Hosp 1985–86, registrar in obstetrics and gynaecology Royal Maternity Hosp and Royal Infirmary 1986–87, lectr and hon sr registrar in obstetrics and gynaecology Univ of Edinburgh, Edinburgh Royal Infirmary and Simpson Meml Maternity Pavilion 1987–90 (lectr and hon registrar 1987), clinical res scientist and clinical conslt MRC Reproductive Biology Unit Edinburgh, hon sr lectr Dept of Obstetrics and Gynaecology Univ of Edinburgh and hon conslt obstetrician and gynaecologist Simpson Meml Maternity Pavilion 1990–91, Muirhead prof and head Dept of Obstetrics and Gynaecology Univ of Glasgow, hon conslt obstetrician Glasgow Royal Maternity Hosp and hon conslt gynaecologist Glasgow Royal Infirmary 1991–; asst ed Scottish Medical Jl, UK ed Euro Jl of Endocrinology; Gold Medal RCOG 1987, William Blair Bell meml lectr RCOG 1989, Bernhard Baron travelling scholar RCOG 1989, Watson Prize lectr RCPS 1990; memb: Soc for Gynaecologic Investigation, Gynaecological Travellers, Edinburgh Obstetric and Gynaecological Soc (memb Cncl 1990–92), Glasgow Obstetrical and Gynaecological Soc (memb Cncl 1993–), Assoc of Profs of Obstetrics and Gynaecology, Munro Kerr Soc for Reproductive Biology, Scottish Soc for Experimental Med, British Soc for Haemostasis and Thrombosis, Soc for the Study of Fertility, BMA; *Books* Haemostasis and Thrombosis in Obstetrics and Gynaecology (ed, 1992); author of numerous medical pubns; *Style*— Prof Ian Greer; ✉ University of Glasgow, Department of Obstetrics & Gynaecology, Glasgow Royal Infirmary, 10 Alexandra Parade, Glasgow G31 2ER (☎ 0141 211 4703, fax 0141 553 1367)

GREETHAM, John Francis; CBE (1994); s of late Francis and Marjorie Greetham; *b* 17 July 1939; *Educ* Nunthorpe GS York; *m* Jill Elizabeth; 2 s (Justin Spencer, James Picton), 1 step s (Alexander Sandy), 1 da (Abigail Lindsay); *Career* Nat Serv RE 1957–59; self employed dental equipment designer and mfr 1959–77, dairy farmer 1977–87, chm Whitewater Leisure Group 1993– (chief exec 1987–93); memb N Yorks CC 1978–86 (ind 1978–82, Cons 1982–86); memb Scarborough DHA 1980–84, vice chm Yorks RHA 1987–90 (memb 1984–90), memb York DHA 1990–91; chm: St James's Univ Teaching Hosp NHS Tst 1991–94, Northern and Yorks RHA 1994–96; fndr chm NHS Tst Fedn 1991–93, memb Cncl NAHAT 1992–94; memb NHS: Audit Ctee 1993, Private Sector Fin Gp 1994, Estates Bd 1994–, Policy Bd 1996–; memb Multi Media Gp DTI 1995–; govr Leeds Metropolitan Univ 1991–, memb Ct Univ of Leeds 1991–; FInstD 1994, CIMgt 1995; *Recreations* riding, swimming, shooting, golf; *Style*— John F Greetham, Esq, CBE; ✉ Whitewater Leisure Ltd, Regent House, Lysander Close, Clifton, York YO3 4XB (☎ 01904 610303, fax 01904 610885, car 0831 585322)

GREEY, Edward Ronald; s of Derek Edward Horace Greey (d 1979), and Irene Osborne, *née* Taylor; *b* 26 April 1939; *Educ* Malvern Coll; *m* 1 Oct 1966, Gillian Frances Rippon, da of John Sargeant Hughes, of Longthorpe, Peterborough; 3 da (Sally b 1969, Wendy b 1972, Philippa b 1976); *Career* cmmnd 16/5 Queen's Own Royal Lancers, TA Queen's Own Staffs Yeo; stockbroker and co dir; memb Birmingham Stock Exchange 1965 (chm 1975–76); dir: Albert E Sharp, Securities Inst, Assoc of Private Client Investment Mangrs and Stockbrokers; non-exec chm Robinson Bros Ryders Green Ltd; guardian Birmingham Assay Office, chm Stock Exchange Midland and Western Unit 1979–80 (dep chm 1977–78), memb Governing Cncl London Stock Exchange 1985–88, chm Regnl Ctee Int Stock Exchange, chm London Stock Exchange Midland and Western Region; govr Malvern Coll; *Recreations* golf, fishing, shooting; *Clubs* Blackwell Golf, Edgbaston Golf, Royal West Norfolk Golf, Royal & Ancient Golf; *Style*— Edward Greey, Esq; ✉ Peewit Cottage, Bittell Farm Rd, Barnt Green, Worcestershire B45 8BS (☎ 0121 445 1672); Albert E Sharp, Temple Court, 35 Bull Street, Birmingham B4 6ES (☎ 0121 200 2244, fax 0121 683 7300)

GREGG, Hubert Robert Harry; s of Robert Joseph (d 1955), of London, and Alice Maud, *née* Bessant (d 1956); *b* 19 July 1914; *Educ* St Dunstan's Coll, Webber-Douglas Acad; *m* 1980, Carmel Josephine, da of Laurence Maguire, of Dublin; 1 s (Robert b 1983), 1 da (Katherine b 1981); *Career* actor, composer, lyric writer, author, playwright and director; WWII Private Lincs Regt 1939, cmd 60 Rifles 1940, seconded to Intelligence, with Political Warfare Exec 1942 (duties included broadcasting in German); first London appearance Julien in Martine 1933, Shakespearean roles in Open Air Theatre Regent's Park and Old Vic 1934–36, first NY appearance as Kit Neilan in French Without Tears 1937 (London 1938–39); directed, lectured and adjudicated at: Webber-Douglas Sch, Central Sch of Speech Training, RADA; patron: Cinema Theatre Assoc 1973–, Nat Assoc of Drama with the Visually Handicapped 1995–; pres: Northern Boys' Club 1975–, Concert Artists Assoc 1979–80; Gold Badge of Merit Br Academy of Composers, Authors and Song Writers 1982; Freeman City of London 1981; *Theatre* London appearances incl: Pip in The Convict 1935, Frederick Hackett in Great Possessions 1937, Peter Scott-Fowler in After The Dance 1939, Polly in Men In Shadow 1942, Michael Carraway in Acacia Avenue 1944, Earl of Harpenden in While the Sun Shines 1945–46, Tom D'Arcy in Off the Record 1946–47, Gabriel Hathaway in Western Wind 1949, John Blessington-Briggs in Chrysanthemum (musical) 1958, Lionel Toop in Fools Paradise 1961; Chichester Festival Theatre: Alexander MacColgie Gibbs in The Cocktail Party, Antonio in The Tempest, Announcer in The Skin of Our Teeth 1968, Sir Lucius O'Trigger in The Rivals, Brittannus in Caesar and Cleopatra, Marcellin in Dear Antoine (also London) 1971; as dir London: The Hollow (Agatha Christie's first stage success) 1951, The Mousetrap (on yearly contract) 1953–60, Speaking of Murder 1958, The Unexpected Guest 1958, From The French 1959, Go Back for Murder 1960, Rule of Three 1962; first solo performance Leicester 1970, subsequently performances in Britain and America (subjects include Shakespeare, Shaw, Jerome K Jerome, the London Theatre and the 20s, 30s, and 40s), Words By Elgar Music By Shaw (Malvern Festival 1978, Edinburgh Festival 1979); *Television and Radio* incl: announcer BBC Empire Service 1934–35; weekly radio programmes with accent on nostalgia 1965–, chm BBC TV Brains Tst 1955, 40 week radio series on London theatres 1974–75, biography series I Call it Genius, I Call It Style 1980–82, ITV solo series 1982, 50 Years of Broadcasting (BBC celebration programme) 1984, Sounds and Sweet Airs (BBC celebration of 60 years at the microphone) 1993, Hubert Gregg and the Forties (BBC celebration prog) 1994, Hubert Gregg and the Twenties, The Thirties 1995, The Fifties 1996; *Films* incl: In Which We Serve, Flying Fortress, Acacia Avenue (The Facts of Love, USA), The Root of all Evil, Vote for Huggett, Once Upon a Dream, Robin Hood (Walt Disney), The Maggie (High and Dry, USA), Svengali, Doctor at Sea (also wrote music and lyrics), Simon and Laura, Speaking of Murder, The Third Visitor, Final Appointment, Room in the House, Stars in Your Eyes (also co-dir and wrote music and lyrics); *Plays and Screenplays* We Have Company (dir and appeared in, 1953), Cheque Mate (dir and appeared in), Villa Sleep Four (dir and appeared in, 1965), From the French (as Jean-Paul Marotte), Who's Been Sleeping...? (dir and appeared in), The Rumpus (dir and appeared in, 1967), Dear Somebody (in Germany as Geliebtes Traumbild, 1984), After the Ball (screenplay adapted from own television biography of Vesta Tilley), Stars in your Eyes (screenplay), Sherry (music and lyrics for musical play based on life of Richard Brinsley Sheridan, 1993); *Songs* writer of over 200 songs incl: I'm Going to Get Lit Up (melody used as a bdcast signal to Euro Resistance that Allied invasion was about to be launched), Maybe it's Because I'm a Londoner; *Books* April Gentleman (1951), A Day's Loving (1974), Agatha Christie and all that Mousetrap (1980), Thanks for the Memory (1983); *Recreations* reading, writing and delving into yesterday; *Clubs* Garrick; *Style*— Hubert Gregg, Esq; ✉ c/o BBC, Broadcasting House, London W1A 1AA

GREGOR, Zdenek Jiri; s of Prof Ota Gregor, and Miroslava Gregor; *b* 27 March 1948; *Educ* Prague 7 HS, Westminster Med Sch of London; *m* 1 s (Benjamin b 1973), 1 da (Camilla b 1977); *Career* house appts Westminster Hosp 1971–72, res surgical offr Moorfields Eye Hosp 1976–79, asst prof Univ of Southern California LA 1980–82, sr lectr ophthalmology Univ of London 1982–83, conslt ophthalmic surgn Moorfields Eye Hosp 1983–, numerous pubns and chapters on disorders and surgical treatment of the retina and the vitreous 1975–; memb: Oxford Ophthalmological Congress 1979, Euro Flouroscein Angiography Club 1977, Macular Soc of the US, Retina Soc of the US, Scientific Advsy Cncl, Opportunities for the Disabled; LRCP 1971, FRCS 1977, FRSM 1986 (and memb), fell Coll Ophthalmologists 1988; *Recreations* music, skiing; *Style*— Zdenek Gregor, Esq; ✉ 94 Harley Street, London W1N 1AF (☎ 0171 935 0777, fax 0171 935 6860); Moorfields Eye Hospital, City Rd, London EC1V 2PD (☎ 0171 253 3411, fax 0171 253 4696, telex 266129)

GREGORY, David John; s of (Newton) John Gregory, of London, and Doris May, *née* Bennett; *b* 3 Dec 1942; *Educ* Loxford Sch, NE London Poly; *m* 20 Jan 1968, (Solveig) Anita, da of Artur John and Siri Niklasson, of Lerdala, Sweden; 2 da (Anna b 1971, Lisa b 1973); *Career* ptnr Keevil & Gregory Architects 1973–; chm Awards Ctee ARCUK; RIBA 1972; *Style*— David Gregory, Esq; ✉ The Old Rectory, 5 Blisworth Road, Gayton, Northampton NN7 3EY; Keevil & Gregory Architects, 53 Derngate, Northampton NN1 1UE (☎ 01604 239300, fax 01604 232748)

GREGORY, David Noel; s of Charles Cope Gregory, and Caroline Ada Gregory; *b* 25 Dec 1944; *Educ* Hillcroft Sch London; *m* 19 Aug 1972, Angela Mary, da of Ernest James Day; 1 s (Daniel Mark b 24 Feb 1977), 1 da (Claire Louise b 9 Feb 1975); *Career* CA; articled clerk Evans Peirson & Co, gp fin controller James Walker Goldsmith & Silversmith plc; fin dir: Instore Enterprises Ltd (subsid Debenhams), Eurobrands Ltd (UK distribution co of Remy Martin & Co) 1987–90; gp fin dir: Freetraders Group Ltd 1991–95, Oxbridge Group Ltd 1995–; FCA (ACA 1969), ATII 1971, FCCA 1980, MBCS 1981, JDipMA 1981, DipM 1990, MCIM 1992; *Clubs* IOD, Twickenham on Thames Rotary; *Style*— David Gregory, Esq; ✉ Oxbridge Group Ltd, Oxbridge House, Guildford Street, Chertsey, Surrey KT16 9ND

GREGORY, Derek Edward; s of Edward Gregory (d 1970), of Ilkeston, and Hilda, *née* Stokeley (d 1989); *Educ* Ilkeston GS; *m* 1, 16 June 1962, Marjorie (d 1984), da of Lloyd Priest Newcastle (d 1976); 1 s (Philip Edward b 1965), 1 da (Tina Louise b 1968); *m* 2, 13 Dec 1986, Kate; *Career* fndr and sr ptnr Gregory Priestley & Stewart CA's Ilkeston Long Eaton 1970–; treas Stanton by Dale CC 1958–; FCA 1961; *Recreations* golf, horse racing, cricket, gardening; *Style*— Derek Gregory, Esq; ✉ Rosemary Cottage, Bowling Close, Stanton By Dale, Ilkeston, Derby (☎ 0115 932 2047); Gregory Priestley & Stewart, 16 Queen St, Ilkeston, Derbys (☎ 0115 932 6726)

GREGORY, John Frederick; s of Arthur Frederic Gregory (d 1955), of London, and Marjorie Phyllis, *née* Williams (d 1995); *b* 7 April 1935; *Educ* Ashburton HS; *m* 9 June 1956, Ethel Currie, da of Robert Burns, of Preston, Lancs; 1 s (David Russell b 14 Nov 1965), 2 da (Linda Ann b 21 May 1957, Alison Joy b 8 Dec 1960); *Career* RAF 1953–55; Capel-Cure Myers: joined 1950, ptnr 1979–85, dir 1985–89; dir Beeson Gregory Ltd 1989–, non-exec dir Cussins Property Gp plc 1983–; MSI (memb Stock Exchange 1972); *Recreations* music, painting, fell walking; *Clubs* London Capital; *Style*— John Gregory, Esq; ✉ 185 Ballards Way, Croydon, Surrey (☎ 0181 657 6706); Sefton, Saltcote Lane, Rye, East Sussex; Beeson Gregory Ltd, The Registry, Royal Mint Court, London EC3

GREGORY, John James Conrad; s of Hubert Conrad Gregory (d 1955), of Bristol, and Mary McLachlan, *née* Drysdale (d 1976); *b* 3 April 1932; *Educ* Chipping Sodbury GS, Merchant Venturers' Tech Coll Bristol (ONC), Gosta Green Coll of Technol (HNC); *m* 9 April 1955, Marion Elizabeth, da of Gilbert H Mart, of Bristol; 1 s (Nigel James b 1959), 1 da (Sarah Louise b 1961); *Career* apprentice and draughtsman Gardiner Sons & Co 1948–55, sr draughtsman Boulton & Paul 1955–58, section ldr Metal Constructions Ltd 1958–61, sr design engr Norris Conslts 1961–64, chief draughtsman Johnson Structures 1964–65, princ Gregory & Associates 1965–; cmmns include: catering estabs, food and chemical plants, multi-storey office blocks, schools and sports facilities; pres Chamber of Indust & Commerce Swindon 1986–87, memb Bd Great Western Enterprise 1988–91, rep Br Standards Ctee, chm SE Midlands Branch IOD 1989–92; CEng, FIStructE (memb Cncl London 1978–82, branch chm 1971–72, 1983–84 and 1995–96), MConsE, FFB 1970 (sec, branch chm 1994–95); *Recreations* propagation of plants, cooking & presentation of food; *Style*— John Gregory, Esq; ✉ Redcliffe House, 14 Thrapston Rd, Spaldwick, Huntingdon, Cambridgeshire PE18 0TA (☎ 01480 890632); Gregory & Associates, Harpur House, 62 Harpur St, Bedford MK40 2RA (☎ 01234 360377/8, fax 01234 211121)

GREGORY, John Raymond; s of Raymond Gregory (d 1988), of Congleton, Cheshire, and Ivy Charlotte, *née* Bourne (d 1993); *b* 18 April 1949; *Educ* St Ambrose Coll Hale Barns Cheshire, Univ of Hull; *m* 11 April 1981, Fiona Mary Kristin, da of Donald Walker, of Chorlton, Manchester; 2 s (Gordon b 1981, Lawrence b 1984), 2 da (Victoria b 1983, Elizabeth b and d 1987); *Career* called to the Bar Middle Temple 1972, in practice 1973–; chm Stretford Constituency Cons Assoc 1980–82; selected as prospective Cons Parly candidate (Stretford and Urmston) 1996; *Recreations* swimming, archaeology, writing, painting; *Clubs* Lancashire CCC; *Style*— John Gregory, Esq; ✉ 1 Deans Court, Crown Square, Manchester (☎ 0161 834 4097)

GREGORY, Kenneth John; s of Frederick Arthur Gregory (d 1969), of Belper, Derbyshire, and Marion, *née* Yates (d 1981); *b* 23 March 1938; *Educ* Herbert Strutt Sch Belper Derbyshire, UCL (BSc, PhD, DSc); *m* 25 Aug 1962, Margaret (Christine), da of Lawrence Wilmot (d 1974), of Belper, Derbyshire; 1 s (Jonathon b 1971), 2 da (Caroline b 1964, Sarah b 1966); *Career* reader in physical geography Univ of Exeter 1972–76 (lectr 1962–72), prof Univ of Southampton 1976–92 (dean of sci 1984–87, dep vice chllr 1988–92), warden Goldsmiths' Coll London 1992–; visiting lectr Univ of New England Armidale NSW Aust 1975, distinguished visiting prof Arizona State Univ 1987, visiting prof Univ Kebangsan Malaysia 1987; FRGS 1962 (Back award 1980, Founder's Medal 1993); *Books* Southwest England (with A H Shorter and W L D Ravenhill, 1969), Drainage Basin Form and Process (with D E Walling, 1973), River Channel Changes (ed, 1977), Geomorphological Processes (with E Derbyshire and J R Hails, 1979 and 1980), Horizons in Physical Geography (ed with M J Clark and A M Gurnell, 1988), The Nature of Physical Geography (1985), Temperate Palaeohydrology (ed with L Starkel and J B Thornes, 1989); *Recreations* gardening, travel; *Clubs* Geographical, Athenaeum; *Style*— Prof Kenneth Gregory; ✉ 17 Ulundi Road, Blackheath, London SE3 7UQ; Warden, Goldsmiths' College, University of London, New Cross, London SE14 6NW (☎ 0171 919 7900, fax 0171 919 7903)

GREGORY, Capt (Alexander) Michael; OBE (1987); s of Vice Adm Sir George David Archibald Gregory, KBE, CB, DSO (d 1975), of Greymount, Alyth, Perthshire, and Florence Eve Patricia, *née* Hill; *b* 15 Dec 1945; *Educ* Marlborough, BRNC Dartmouth; *m* 13 June 1970, Jean Charlotte, da of Lt Cdr Gerald Robin Muir, OBE (d 1991), of Braco Castle, By Dunblane, Perthshire; 4 da (Charlotte b 1971, Katherine b 1973, Helen b 1979, Sarah b 1982); *Career* HMS Albion and HMS Aisne 1965–66, HMS Narwhale 1966–67, HMS Otter 1967–68, HMS Warspite 1968–70, HMS Courageous 1970–73, HMS Odin (based in Australia) 1973–75, i/c HMS Finwhale 1976–78, HMS Repulse 1978–80, staff of US Third Fleet Hawaii 1980–82, i/c HMS Renown 1982–85, Cdr Tenth Submarine Sqdn and i/c HMS Resolution 1985–86, Jt Servs Def Coll 1987, MOD Directorate of Naval Warfare 1987–88, i/c HMS Cumberland 1988–90, capt Tenth Submarine Sqdn 1990–92, MOD Naval Staff 1992–93, naval attaché Washington 1994–; memb Royal Co of Archers (Queen's Bodyguard for Scotland); *Recreations* shooting, fishing, skiing, stalking, gardening; *Style*— Capt Michael Gregory, OBE, RN

GREGORY, Michael Anthony; OBE (1990); s of Lt-Col Wallace James Ignatius Gregory (d 1972), and Dorothy Isabel, *née* Malyon (d 1990); *b* 8 June 1925; *Educ* Douai Sch, UCL (LLB); *m* 11 Aug 1951, Patricia Ann, da of Frank Thomas Hodges (d 1978); 3 s (Martin, Damien, Tristan), 5 da (Anne, Philippa, Lucy, Bernadette, Jane); *Career* Nat Serv WWII, joined RAF 1943, cmmnd 1945, Navigator 1945, demobbed as Flying Offr 1947; called to the Bar Middle Temple 1952, in practice 1952–60, Legal Dept Country Landowners' Assoc 1960–90 (chief legal advsr 1977–90); freelance journalist; chm: Mgmnt Ctee Catholic Social Serv for Prisoners 1960–71 and 1974–85 (memb 1952–92), Fleet Branch Int Help for Children 1967–77; hon legal advsr Nat Anglers' Cncl 1968–91, fndr memb Agric Law Assoc 1975–, tstee Country Landowners' Assoc Charitable Tst 1980–; memb: BSI Ctee on Installation of Pipelines 1965–83, Cncl Salmon and Trout Assoc 1980–90, Cncl Anglers' Conservation Assoc 1980–, Ctee Fedn for Promotion of Hort for Disabled People 1981–95 (tstee 1987), Thames Water Authy Regnl Fisheries Advsy Ctee 1974–89, Inland Waterways Amenity Advsy Cncl 1982–92, Fisheries Advsy Ctee Nat Rivers Authy (Thames Region) 1989–96, Fisheries Advsy Ctee Environment Agency (Thames Region) 1996–; pres: Douai Soc 1984–86, Basingstoke Canal Angling Assoc 1991–; chm Fleet Utd Bowling Club 1991–95; Papal medal Pro Ecclesia Et Pontifice 1988; *Books* Organisational Possibilities in Farming (1968), Joint Enterprises in Farming (with C Townsend, 2 edn 1973), Angling and the Law (2 edn 1974), All for Fishing (with R Seymour, 1970), Essential Law for Landowners and Farmers (with Margaret Parrish, 2 edn 1987, with Angela Sydenham, 3 edn 1990), Conservation Law in the Countryside (1994); *Recreations* ball games, bowls, angling, playing saxophones, watching wildlife; *Style*— Michael Gregory, Esq, OBE; ✉ Beam Ends, Dipley Common, Hartley Wintney, Hook, Hampshire RG27 8JS (☎ 01252 842559, fax 01252 845698)

GREGORY, Dr Paul Duncan; s of Thomas Gregory, of Troon, and Elsie, *née* Millward; *b* 1 Dec 1954; *Educ* Marr Coll Troon, Univ of Edinburgh (BCom, PhD); *m* 21 July 1978, Catherine Margaret, da of James Campbell, of Troon; 1 s (James Alexander b 1985), 1 da (Jennifer Alison b 1987); *Career* oil analyst Wood Mackenzie & Co Ltd 1981–85, asst dir Hill Samuel 1986–87; dir County Natwest Securities 1989–92 (assoc dir 1988–89), md Wood Mackenzie Consultants Ltd 1994– (dir 1992–94), md NatWest Markets 1995–; memb Inst of Petroleum, memb Edinburgh & Leith Petroleum Club; *Books* Factors Influencing the Export Performance of the Scottish Manufacturing Sector of the Offshore Supplies Industry (1982), World Offshore Markets: Can Britain Compete? (1986); *Recreations* golf, badminton; *Clubs* Morton Hall Golf; *Style*— Dr Paul Gregory; ✉ 25 Greenhill Gardens, Edinburgh EH10 4BL (☎ 0131 447 6480); Wood Mackenzie Consultants Ltd, Kintore House, 74–77 Queen St, Edinburgh EH2 4NS (☎ 0131 225 8525, fax 0131 243 4435, telex 72555)

GREGORY, Peter Roland; s of Tom Gregory, and Ruby, *née* Reynolds; *Educ* Univ Coll Swansea (BA), Univ of Manchester (PhD); *m* 23 Sept 1978, Frances Margaret, *née* Hogan; *Career* Welsh Office: joined as admin trainee 1971, asst sec Health Dept 1982–90, under sec i/c Tport, Planning and Environment Gp 1990–94, dir Health Dept 1994–; *Recreations* music, theatre, walking; *Style*— P R Gregory, Esq; ✉ Health Department, Welsh Office, Cathays Park, Cardiff CF1 3NQ (☎ 01222 823446, fax 01222 825021)

GREGORY, Peter William; s of William Henry Gregory, of Walton on Thames, Surrey, and Florence Mabel, *née* Peters; *b* 3 Oct 1934; *Educ* Surbiton GS, City & Guilds Inst, Imperial Coll Univ of London (BSc); *m* 16 Jan 1960, Angela Margaret; 1 s (Timothy b 10 March 1963), 2 da (Sarah b 14 March 1965, Susan b 22 April 1966); *Career* short service cmmn RAF 1958–61, Flt Lt 5003 Sqdn Alb in UK; dir John Laing Construction Ltd 1984–96, chm Laing Management Ltd 1994–96 (md 1984–94), assoc dir John Laing plc 1995–96; Liveryman Worshipful Co of Plumbers; CEng 1964; *Recreations* game shooting, salmon fishing, gardening, golf; *Style*— Peter W Gregory, Esq; ✉ Target House, Hexham, Northumberland NE46 4LD (☎ 01434 604689)

GREGORY, Dr Philippa; da of Arthur Percy Gregory (d 1955), of Nairobi, and Elaine, *née* Wedd (d 1983); *b* 9 Jan 1954; *Educ* Duncan House Sch for Girls' Clifton, Colston's Girls' Sch Bristol, Univ of Sussex (BA), Univ of Edinburgh (PhD); *m* 1 (m dis); 1 da (Victoria Elaine b 31 Jan 1982); m 2, 1991, Paul Stephen Carter; 1 s (Adam Gregory b 20 Jan 1993); *Career* work on: newspaper in Portsmouth 1972–75, BBC Radio Solent and BBC Radio Scotland 1978–82; freelance BBC Radio producer 1978–82; guest reviewer Sunday Times 1989–; fell Univ of Kingston 1995–; *Books* Wideacre (1987), The Favoured Child (1989), Princess Florizella (1989), Meridon (1990), Florizella and the Wolves (1991), The Wise Woman (1992), Mrs Hartley and the Growth Centre (1992), Florizella and the Giant (1992), Fallen Skies (1993), The Little Pet Dragon (1994), A Respectable Trade (1995), Diggory and the Boa Conductor (1996), Perfectly Correct (1996), The Little House (USA, 1996); screenplay: Mrs Hartley and the Growth Centre (BBC 2, 1995); *Style*— Dr Philippa Gregory; ✉ Rogers Coleridge & White, 20 Powis Mews, London W11 1JN (☎ 0171 221 3717)

GREGORY, Richard John; s of John Gregory, and Joan, *née* Slingsby; *b* 18 Aug 1954; *Educ* Danum GS, Doncaster; *m* 14 Aug 1976, Elaine Margaret, da of (Herbert Charles) Ronald Matthews (d 1971); 2 da (Anna Marie b 11 Feb 1979, Antonia Faye b 11 Dec 1987); *Career* industl corr Morning Telegraph 1977–79, news ed Granada TV 1979–81; Yorkshire Television: news ed 1981–82, prodr 1982–84, ed Calendar 1984, head of news 1991–92, controller of regnl progs 1992–93, dir of regnl progs and bd memb 1993–, dir of broadcasting 1995–96, md Yorkshire Television (Broadcasting) 1996–; hon fell Univ of Sheffield, govr and dep chm Sheffield Hallam Univ; vice pres and dir Ponies Assoc (UK); *Recreations* show ponies; *Style*— Richard Gregory, Esq; ✉ Brooklands, Castleton Road, Hope, Derbyshire; Yorkshire Television, Kirkstall Road, Leeds LS3 1JS (☎ 0113 243 8283)

GREGORY, Prof Richard Langton; CBE (1989); s of C C L Gregory (d 1969), and Patricia, *née* Gibson (d 1988); *b* 24 July 1923; *Educ* King Alfred Sch Hampstead, Downing Coll Cambridge; *m* 1, 1953 (m dis 1966); 1 s (Mark Foss Langton), 1 da (Romilly Caroline Langton); m 2, 1976 (m dis); *Career* Univ of Cambridge: res MRC Applied Psychology Res Unit 1950–53, demonstrator then lectr Dept of Psychology 1953–67, fell Corpus Christi Coll 1962–67; prof of bionics Dept of Machine Intelligence and Perception Univ of Edinburgh 1967–70 (chm 1968–70), prof of neuropsychology and dir Brain and Perception Laboratory The Med Sch Univ of Bristol 1970–88, emeritus prof Dept of Psychology Univ of Bristol; visiting prof: UCLA 1963, MIT 1964, NY Univ 1966; Freeman Worshipful Co of Spectacle Makers; FRSE 1969, FRS 1992; *Books* Recovery from Early Blindness (with Jean Wallace, 1963), Eye and Brain (1966, 5 edn 1997), The Intelligent Eye (1970), Illusion in Nature and Art (jt ed, 1973), Concepts and Mechanisms of Perception (1974), Mind in Science (1981), Oxford Companion to the Mind (1987); *Clubs* Athenaeum; *Style*— Prof Richard Gregory, CBE, FRSE, FRS; ✉ 23 Royal York Crescent, Clifton, Bristol BS8 4JX (☎ 0117 973 9701); University of Bristol, Department of Psychology, 8 Woodland Road, Clifton, Bristol BS8 1TN (☎ 0117 928 8461, fax 0117 928 8588)

GREGORY, Robert Davies; s of James Gregory (d 1962), and Marjorie, *née* Ingram (d 1959); *b* 23 Jan 1939; *Educ* King's Sch Canterbury; *m* Janet, da of James McVey; 1 s (James b 1 July 1970), 1 da (Fiona b 27 March 1973); *Career* The Times 1960–66, Hedderwick Hunt Cox 1966–70, Lopex 1970–87, Temple Communications 1987–93, dir Lowe Bell Financial 1993–; memb: Cncl London Borough of Bromley 1964–70, Fundraising Ctee Royal London Soc for the Blind; *Recreations* gardening; *Clubs* Carlton, Reform; *Style*— Robert Gregory, Esq; ✉ The Granary, Dunsdale, Westerham, Kent TN16 1LJ (☎ 01959 63327); Lowe Bell Financial Ltd, 20–21 Red Lion Court, London EC4A 3HE (☎ 0171 353 9203, fax 0171 353 2937)

GREGORY, Susan; da of Dennis Geoffrey Pymont, of Sussex, and Eileen Vera Doris, *née* Stewart; *b* 29 April 1952; *Educ* Bognor Regis GS, Chichester Coll; *children* (Leo b 22 Nov 1978, Julian, Eliot and Ryan (triplets) b 21 July 1984); *Career* self-employed fashion retailer, restaurateur and hotelier, business conslt; *Recreations* sport, theatre, cinema, reading, music; *Style*— Ms Susan Gregory; ✉ 14 Clitheroe Road, London SW9 9DZ (☎ and fax 0171 771 3221, e-mail susan.gregory@msrl.com)

GREGORY-HOOD, Peter Charles Freeman; *b* 12 Dec 1943; *m* 1966, Camilla Bethell; 3 da (b 1968, 1970 and 1973); *Career* HM Dip Serv: third sec CRO 1965, Dakar 1967, third later second sec Tel Aviv 1969, second later first sec FCO 1972, first sec (Commercial) Paris 1976, first sec FCO 1981, first sec (Info) New Delhi 1986, consul-gen Casablanca 1990–June 1995, dep high cmmr Colombo Sri Lanka June 1995–; *Recreations* golf, tennis, skiing; *Clubs* White's, RAC; *Style*— Peter Gregory-Hood, Esq; ✉ c/o Foreign and Commonwealth Office (Colombo), King Charles Street, London SW1A 2AA

GREGSON, Edward; s of Edward Gregson (d 1976), and May Elizabeth, *née* Eaves (d 1985); *b* 23 July 1945; *Educ* Manchester Central GS, RAM (GRSM, LRAM, Battison Haynes Prize for composition, Edward Hecht Prize for composition, Frederick Corder Memorial Prize for composition), Univ of London (BMus); *m* 1967, Susan Carole; 2 s (Mark Edward b 1968, Justin Serge b 1970); *Career* lectr in music Rachel McMillan Coll 1970–76, sr lectr then reader rising to prof of music Goldsmiths Coll Univ of London 1976–96, princ RNCM 1996–; also composer; dir Performing Right Soc 1995–; memb: Composers' Guild of GB (vice chm 1976–78), Assoc of Professional Composers (chm 1989–91); hon prof of music Univ of Manchester 1996; Hon DMus Univ of Sunderland 1996; FRAM 1990, FRSA 1996; *Compositions* incl: Oboe Sonata 1965, Brass Quintet 1967, Music for Chamber Orchestra 1968, Horn Concerto 1971, Essay for Brass Band 1971, Tuba Concerto 1976, music for York Cycle of Mystery Plays 1976 and 1980, Connotations for Brass Band 1977, Metamorphoses 1979, Trombone Concerto 1979, Trumpet Concerto 1983, Piano Sonata 1983, Contrasts for Orchestra 1983, Festivo 1985, Missa Brevis Pacem 1988, Celebration 1991, Blazon 1992, The Sword and the Crown (based on music from RSC history play prodns 1988 and 1990) 1993, Clarinet Concerto 1994, Concerto for Piano and Wind 1995, The Kings Go Forth 1996; *Recreations* food, wine, watching sport; *Clubs* Royal Over-Seas League; *Style*— Prof Edward Gregson; ✉ Royal Northern College of Music, 124 Oxford Road, Manchester M13 9RD (☎ 0161 273 6283, fax 0161 273 8188, e-mail pat.woods@rncm.ac.uk)

GREGSON, Baron (Life Peer UK 1975), of Stockport in Greater Manchester; John Gregson; DL (Gtr Manchester 1979); s of John Gregson; *b* 29 Jan 1924; *Career* Fairey Engineering Ltd: joined Stockport Base Subsidiary 1939, memb Fairey R&D team 1946, appointed to Bd 1966, md 1978–94; non-exec dir: Br Steel plc 1976–94, Fairey Group plc 1989–94, Otto-Simon Carves Ltd until 1995, NRA 1992–95 (chm Audit Ctee 1992–95), currently Innovtech Corporate Ventures Ltd; dir OSC Process Engineering Ltd until 1995; past vice pres Assoc of Metropolitan Authorities, pres Defence Mfrs' Assoc 1984– (chm 1980–84); memb: House of Lords Select Ctees on Sci and Technol, EC Sub-Ctee on Energy Indust and Tport; pres Parly and Scientific Ctee 1986–90, pres Finance and Indust Gp of Lab Party; chm: BNFL Expert Panel, Advsy Cncl RMCS Shrivenham, Waste Mgmnt Indust Trg and Advsy Bd; memb Court UMIST 1976–; hon fell Manchester Poly 1983, Hon FIProdE 1982, Hon DUniv Open Univ, Hon DSc Aston Univ, Hon DTech Brunel Univ, Hon DSc Cranfield; AMCT, Hon CIMgt, Hon FEng 1986; *Recreations* mountaineering, skiing, sailing, gardening; *Style*— The Rt Hon the Lord Gregson, DL; ✉ 12 Rosemont Road, Richmond-upon-Thames, Surrey TW10 6QL

GREGSON, Sir Peter Lewis; GCB (1996, KCB 1988, CB 1983); s of Walter Henry Gregson (d 1961), and Lillian Margaret, *née* Lees; *b* 28 June 1936; *Educ* Nottingham HS, Balliol Coll Oxford (MA); *Career* Nat Serv 1959–61 (2 Lt RAEC, attached Sherwood Foresters); BOT 1961–66, private sec to PM 1968–72, sec Industl Devpt Advsy Bd 1972–74, sec NEB 1975–77, under sec Dept of Trade 1977–80, dep sec Dept of Trade

1980–81, dep sec Cabinet Office 1981–85, perm under sec of state Dept of Energy 1985–89, perm sec DTI 1989–96; *Recreations* gardening, listening to music; *Style*— Sir Peter Gregson, GCB; ✉ 36a Elwill Way, Beckenham, Kent BR3 6RZ

GREGSON, William Derek Hadfield; CBE (1970), DL (1984); s of W Gregson (d 1929); *b* 27 Jan 1920; *Educ* King William's Coll IOM, Alpine Coll Villars Switzerland, Faraday House Engrg Coll (DFH); *m* 1944, Rosalind Helen (d 1994), da of R M E Reeves; 3 s (Michael, Peter, David), 1 da (Fiona); *Career* served RAF, Sqdn Ldr NW Europe 1941–45; dir: Ferranti New York 1969–83, Ferranti Holdings Ltd 1983–85 (asst gen mangr Ferranti (Scotland) Ltd 1959–83), Anderson Strathclyde plc 1978–86, Brammer plc 1983–88, BT (Scotland) 1977–85, East of Scotland Industrial Investments plc 1980–; conslt ICI 1984–88; dep chm Br Airports Authy 1975–85; former pres: Electronic Engrg Assoc, Br Electrical and Allied Mfrs Assoc; memb: Electronics EDC 1965–75, Scot Economic Planning Cncl 1965–71, Cncl Soc of Br Aerospace Cos 1966–83 (chm Equipment Gp Ctee 1967), Bd Livingston New Town 1968–76, Scot Cncl CBI 1975–79, Machine Tool Expert Ctee 1969–70, Cncl BIM 1975–80, Jt BIM and NEDO Professional Mgmnt Advsy Ctee on Industl Strategy 1976–78; chm: BIM Advsy Bd Scotland 1970–75, Scot GPs Res Support Unit 1971–79, Mgmnt Assoc of SE Scotland 1980–81; dep chm Scot Cncl (Devpt and Indust) 1982–88; cmmr Northern Lighthouse Bd 1975–80, dir Scot Nat Orch 1977–85 (chm 1984–85); memb: Scottish Design Cncl 1974–78, Design Cncl 1980–85; CEng, FIEE, CIMgt, FIIM; *Recreations* reading, cabinet-making, automation in the home; *Clubs* RAF, New (Edinburgh); *Style*— William Gregson, Esq, CBE, DL; ✉ Murrayfield House, 66 Murrayfield Avenue, Edinburgh EH12 6AY

GREIG, Sir (Henry Louis) Carron; KCVO (1995, CVO 1972), CBE (1986), DL (Hampshire, 1992); s of Gp Capt Sir Louis Greig, KBE, CVO, DL, of Thatched House Lodge, Richmond Park, Surrey; *b* 21 Feb 1925; *Educ* Eton; *m* 1955, Monica, da of Hon John Stourton, TD; 3 s (one of whom George Carron (Geordie) Greig, *qv*), 1 da (twin); *Career* Capt Scots Gds NW Europe 1945; gentleman usher to HM The Queen 1962–95; chm: H Clarkson & Co 1973–85 (dir 1954–85, md 1962–85) Horace Clarkson plc 1976–93, Baltic Exchange 1983–85 (dir 1978–85); dir: James Purdey & Sons 1972–, Williams & Glyn's 1983–85, Royal Bank of Scotland 1985–95; vice chm Not Forgotten Assoc 1979–96, chm Schoolmistresses & Governesses Benevolent Instn 1992– (vice chm 1966–92); *Clubs* White's; *Style*— Sir Carron Greig, KCVO, CBE, DL; ✉ Brook House, Fleet, Hants GU13 8RF

GREIG, George Carron (Geordie); s of Sir Carron Greig, *qv*, and Monica, *née* Stourton; *b* 16 Dec 1960; *Educ* Eton, St Peter's Coll Oxford (MA); *m* 1995, Kathryn Elizabeth, *née* Terry; *Career* reporter: South East London and Kentish Mercury 1981–83, Daily Mail 1984–85, Today 1985–87; The Sunday Times: reporter 1987–89, arts corr 1989–91, New York corr 1991–95, literary ed 1995–; *Clubs* White's, Colony Rooms; *Style*— Geordie Greig, Esq; ✉ The Sunday Times, 1 Pennington Street, London E1 9XW (☎ 0171 782 5774, fax 0171 782 5798)

GREIG, John S; *b* 1931; *Educ* Marlborough; *m*; 1 s, 4 da; *Career* Nat Serv 2 Lt Royal Artillery 1949–50; Greig Fester Group Ltd insurance brokers: office boy rising to chm W T Greig Ltd 1948–74, chm Greig Fester Group Ltd (following merger) 1974–; dir Syndicate Underwriting Management Ltd 1993–; Lloyd's of London: memb Cncl 1986–87 and 1989–, sr dep chm until end 1992, memb Disciplinary Ctee, dir Lloyd's of London Press Ltd 1988–, tstee Lloyd's Tercentenary Fndn; vice pres Insurance Inst of London, chm Reinsurance Brokers' Assoc (now part of Br Insurance & Investmt Brokers' Assoc) 1973, memb Cncl CII, govr CII Coll of Insurance; Freeman City of London, memb Ct of Assts Worshipful Co of Insurers 1982– (fndr Liveryman 1979, past Master); ACII 1956; *Recreations* opera and ballet, tennis, golf; *Style*— J S Greig, Esq; ✉ Greig Fester Group Ltd, Devon House, 58–60 St Katharine's Way, London E1 9LB (☎ 0171 488 2828, fax 0171 265 1234)

GREIG OF ECCLES, James Dennis; CMG (1967); s of Dennis George Greig of Eccles (d 1971), of Eccles House, Kelso, Roxburghshire, and his 1 w, Florence Aileen, *née* Marjoribanks (d 1959); *b* 14 July 1926; *Educ* Winchester, Clare Coll Cambridge, LSE and SOAS London; *m* 1, 11 Dec 1952 (m dis 1960), Pamela Marguerite, da of late Thomas David Stock; 1 s (Charles Andrew George b 9 June 1955), 1 da (Hilary Nicola Duncan (Mrs Chater) b 12 May 1954); m 2, 12 Oct 1960 (m dis 1967), Mrs Elizabeth Ettenger Brown, da of late Horace Melville Starke, of Charlotte, N Carolina, USA; 1 s (Nigel Lewis b 19 April 1963); m 3, 2 April 1968, Paula Mary Sterling, da of Percival Cook (d 1969), of Gillingham, Kent; 1 adopted s (Justin Simon b 20 Aug 1962); *Career* Lt The Black Watch RHR and Nigeria Regt 1944–47, served Burma; Colonial Serv: dist offr N Nigeria 1949–54, sr asst sec Fedn of Nigeria 1955–59, fin sec Mauritius 1964–67 (dep fin sec 1960–64); gen mangr Medport Ltd 1967–68, head of Africa and Middle East Bureau Int Planned Parenthood Fedn 1968–76, dir Population Bureau Miny of Overseas Devpt 1976–80; racehorse owner: Man o' Magic 1985–92 (winner 4 hurdles and 11 steeplechases), San Lorenzo 1992–94 (winner 7 hurdles and 5 steeplechases); *Books* The Politics of Family Planning in the Third World (contrib, ed T Smith 1971); *Recreations* national hunt racing, shooting, gardening, bowls; *Clubs* Hurlingham, Annabel's; *Style*— James D Greig of Eccles, CMG; ✉ The Braw Bothy, Eccles, Kelso, Roxburghshire (☎ 01890 840544); 6 Beverley Close, Barnes, London SW13 0EH (☎ 0181 876 5354)

GRENFELL, 3 Baron (UK 1902); Julian Pascoe Francis St Leger Grenfell; s of 2 Baron Grenfell, CBE, TD (d 1976), and his 1 w, Elizabeth (gda of 1 Baron Shaughnessy); *b* 23 May 1935; *Educ* Eton, King's Coll Cambridge; *m* 1, 1961, Loretta Maria Olga Hildegarde, da of Alfredo Reali, of Florence; 1 da (Hon Isabella Sarah Frances (Hon Mrs Pianini Mazzucchetti) b 1966); m 2, 1970, Gabrielle, o da of Dr Ernst Raab, of Berlin; 2 da (Hon Katharina Elizabeth Anne b 1973, Hon Vanessa Julia Claire b 1976); m 3, 27 June 1987, Mrs Elizabeth Porter, da of Buford Scott, of Richmond, Virginia; m 4, 28 Oct 1993, Mrs Dagmar Langbehn Debreil; *Heir* first cous, Francis Grenfell; *Career* 2 Lt KRRC (60 Rifles), Capt Queen's Westminsters (TA) KRRC; World Bank: chief of info and public affrs Europe 1970, dep dir European office 1973, special rep to UNO 1974–81, special advsr 1983–87, sr advsr 1987–90, head of external affairs European Office 1990–95, sr advsr Euro Affairs 1995–; *Books* Margot (1984); *Recreations* writing; *Clubs* Royal Green Jackets; *Style*— The Rt Hon the Lord Grenfell; ✉ 18 rue de Bourgogne, 75007 Paris, France (☎ 00 331 47 05 97 21)

GRENFELL, His Hon Judge Simon Pascoe; s of Osborne Pascoe, of Saltburn, N Yorkshire (d 1971), and Margaret Grenfell, *née* Morris; *b* 10 July 1942; *Educ* Fettes, Emmanuel Coll Cambridge (MA); *m* 13 April 1974, Ruth de Jersey, da of John Peter de Jersey Harvard (d 1981), of Carlton-in-Cleveland, N Yorkshire; 1 s (Robin b 1981), 3 da (Rachel b 1975, Amelia b 1976, Philippa b 1978); *Career* called to the Bar Gray's Inn 1965; recorder Crown Ct 1985–92; circuit judge (NE Circuit) 1992–; chllr Dio of Ripon 1992–; chm of govrs Ripon GS 1996–; Liveryman Worshipful Co of Vintners; *Recreations* music, sailing, coarse gardening; *Style*— His Hon Judge Grenfell; ✉ St John's House, Sharow Lane, Sharow, Ripon, N Yorks HG4 5BN (☎ 01765 605771, e-mail grenfl@globalnet.co.uk)

GRENIER, David Arthur; s of Rev George A Grenier (d 1973), and Dorothy Anita, *née* Burn (d 1990); *b* 12 Aug 1931; *Educ* St John's Sch Leatherhead, Jesus Coll Cambridge (MA), Sorbonne; *m* 25 Aug 1959, Janet Elizabeth, da of Ralph Thompson (d 1989); 3 s (Lewis b 1962, Julian b 1968, Michael b 1969); *Career* Capel-Cure Myers Ltd: dep chm 1975–77, chm 1977–79; ptnr Scott Goff Hancock & Co 1980–82, sr ptnr Scott Goff Layton & Co 1982–86, dir Smith New Court plc 1986–88, chief exec Independent Investment Management Ltd 1989–; assoc memb Inst of Investment Mgmnt and Res 1968, FRSA 1992; *Recreations* opera, gardening; *Clubs* Oxford & Cambridge, Coningsby; *Style*— David Grenier, Esq; ✉ Independent Investment Management Ltd, 11 Old Jewry, London EC2R 8DU (☎ 0171 606 2101, fax 0171 606 0499)

GRENIER, John Allan; s of Rev George Arthur Grenier; *b* 2 April 1933; *Educ* St John's Sch Leatherhead Surrey; *m* 1980 (m dis 1995), Valerie Aggett, *qv*, da of James William Cocksey; 2 c; *Career* chm The HLT Group Ltd (Queen's Award for Export 1982); elected chm of British Mgmnt Trg Export Cncl 1985; FCA; *Recreations* off-shore cruising, water skiing; *Clubs* RAC, IOD; *Style*— John Grenier, Esq; ✉ The HLT Group Ltd, 200 Greyhound Road, London W14 9RY (☎ 0171 385 3377, telex 266386, fax 0171 381 3377); Plovers, Horsmonden, Kent

GRENIER, Rear Adm Peter Francis (Frank); CB; s of Dr Frank William Henry Grenier (d 1964), and Mabel, *née* Burgess (d 1985); *b* 27 Aug 1934; *Educ* Blundell's; *m* 15 Aug 1957, Jane Susan, da of Bert Bradshaw (d 1973), of Kent; 3 s (Timothy Francis b 1959 d 1960, Stephen Marcel b 1961, Matthew Peter b 1965), 1 da (Juliet (Mrs Love) b 1963); *Career* BRNC Dartmouth special entry scheme 1952, submarine serv HMS Dolphin 1956, first cmd submarine HMS Ambush Far East 1964, 2 i/c HMS Resolution (Polaris) 1968, cmmnd HMS Valiant (Nuclear Attack) 1972–74, Capt 1976, cmd destroyer HMS Liverpool 1981, Capt Fleet 1983–85, Rear Adm 1985, COS to C in C Naval Home Cmd, Flag Offr submarines 1987–89; chm RNFC 1982–85, chm Bd of Govrs Blundells Sch 1991–96 (govr 1985–96); advsr to House of Commons Defence Ctee; Liveryman Worshipful Co of Painters and Stainers, Hon Liveryman Worshipful Co of Glass Sellers; Craft Memb Guild of Glass Engravers; *Recreations* painting, sketching, glass engraving, golf; *Clubs* Army and Navy, West Wilts Golf; *Style*— Rear Adm Frank Grenier, CB; ✉ c/o Army and Navy Club, 36–39 Pall Mall, London SW1Y 5JN

GRENSIDE, Sir John Peter; kt (1983), CBE (1974); s of Harold Cutcliffe Grenside (d 1953), and Muriel Grenside (d 1970); *b* 23 Jan 1921; *Educ* Rugby; *m* 1946, Yvonne Thérèse, da of Ernest Albert Grau (d 1959); 1 s, 1 da; *Career* Capt RA, served UK, Europe, India; sr ptnr Peat Marwick Mitchell & Co 1977–86, (ptnr 1960–86), chm Peat Marwick Int 1980–83; non-exec dir: Allied-Lyons 1986–93, Nomura International Bank 1987–95; pres ICAEW 1975–76; Hon Memb of Ct Worshipful Co of Chartered Accountants (Master 1987–88); FCA; *Recreations* tennis, bridge; *Clubs* All England Lawn Tennis, MCC, Hurlingham, Pilgrims'; *Style*— Sir John Grenside, CBE; ✉ 51 Cadogan Lane, London SW1X 9DT (☎ 0171 235 3372, fax 0171 235 9225)

GRENVILLE, Prof John A S; s of Adolf Abraham Guhrauer (d 1960), of London, and late Charlotte, *née* Sandberg; *b* 11 Jan 1928; *Educ* Cambridge Tech Sch, Birkbeck Coll London, LSE (BA, PhD, Hutchinson medal); *m* 1, 1960, Betty Anne, *née* Rosenberg (d 1974); 3 s (Murray Charles b 1962, Edward Samson b 1964, George Daniel b 1966); m 2, 5 May 1975, Patricia, *née* Conway; 1 da (Annabelle Charlotte b 1979), 1 step da (Claire Georgina Carnie b 1972); *Career* gardener Peterhouse Cambridge 1945–47, lectr and reader Univ of Nottingham 1953–66, Cwlth Fund fell 1959–60, postdoctoral fell Yale Univ 1961–64, prof of int history Univ of Leeds 1966–69, prof of German history 1994–96, head of dept 1969–94, professorial fell Inst for German Studies Univ of Birmingham 1994–; visiting prof City Univ of NY and Hamburg Univ; fndr Br Univs History Film Consortium 1968; conslt: American Biographical Serv Oxford and Santa Barbara Calif 1960–90, Second German Television Service ZDF and BBC (documentary history film productions) 1984–; formerly: memb Cncl Royal Hist Soc, dir of films Hist Assoc; dir Leo Baeck Inst London 1987–, ed Leo Baeck Year Book 1992–; FRHistS 1960; *Books* Lord Salisbury and Foreign Policy (1964), Politics, Strategy and American Diplomacy (with G B Young, 1966), Major International Treaties 1914–1974 (1974), Europe Reshaped 1848–1878 (1976), World History of the Twentieth Century 1900–45 (1980), Major International Treaties Since 1945 (with B Wasserstein, 1987), Collins History of the World in the Twentieth Century (1994); *Film Documentaries* Munich Crisis (1968), End of Illusion (with Nicholas Pronay, 1970), World of the Thirties (with Dieter Franck, 1986), Another War, Another Peace 1940–60 (with Dieter Franck, 1991); *Recreations* meeting international colleagues, listening to music, ballet and opera; *Clubs* Athenaeum, Elizabethan (New Haven), New Lunar Soc; *Style*— Prof John Grenville; ✉ Institute for German Studies, University of Birmingham, PO Box 363, Birmingham, B15 2TT (☎ 0121 414 5736, fax 0121 414 3656)

GRESHAM, Prof (Geoffrey) Austin; TD; s of Thomas Michael Gresham (d 1939), of Wrexham, N Wales, and Harriet Ann, *née* Richards (d 1945); *b* 1 Nov 1924; *Educ* Grove Pk GS, Gonville and Caius Coll Cambridge (MA, DSc, MB BChir, MD), King's Coll Hosp London; *m* 1 July 1950, Gweneth Margery, da of Louis Charles Leigh (d 1983), of Cambridge; 3 s (Christopher b 1951, Andrew b 1955, Robert b 1957), 2 da (Diana b 1954, Susan b 1959); *Career* Lt and Capt RAMC 1950–52, Maj and Lt-Col RAMC (V) 1954–66; house physician King's Coll Hosp London 1949–50 (house surgn 1949); Univ of Cambridge: demonstrator in pathology 1953–58, fell and coll lectr (and sometime pres) Jesus Coll, sec Faculty Bd of Med 1956–61, lectr in pathology 1958–62 (sometime dep assessor to Regius prof of physics and supervisor of res Student Dept of Pathology); univ morbid anatomist and histologist Addenbrooke's Hosp Cambridge 1962– (jr asst pathologist 1953, conslt pathologist 1960), Home Office pathologist to Mid Anglia 1966– (prof of morbid anatomy and histology 1973); ed of Atherosclerosis, sci fell Zoological Soc London; FRCPath, FRCP(Ed) 1994; *Books* A Colour Atlas of General Pathology (1971, 2 edn 1992) A Colour Atlas of Forensic Pathology (1979), Post Mortem Procedures (1979), A Colour Atlas of Wounds and Wounding (1987); *Recreations* gardening, organ playing, wine, silver; *Style*— Prof Austin Gresham, TD; ✉ 18 Rutherford Rd, Cambridge (☎ 01223 841326); Addenbrooke's Hosp, Hills Rd, Cambridge (☎ 01223 217168, fax 01223 216980)

GRESTY, Deborah Susan; da of Alexander William Gresty, and Barbara Joan Nash, *née* Perry; *b* 3 April 1953; *Educ* Birkenhead HS, Merchant Taylors' Sch, Univ of Nottingham (BA), Oxford Centre of Mgmnt Studies; *m* Peter Warland, s of Charles Warland; *Career* magazine publisher; Thomson Publications: grad trainee 1974, advertisement sales exec Pins & Needles 1975, dep advertisement mangr Living 1977 (advertisement sales exec 1976); Slimming Magazine: advertisement mangr 1979, advertisement dir 1980, dir 1981, publisher 1982–84; publisher/dir Working Woman 1984–85; publisher: Brides and Setting Up Home 1985–90, House & Garden 1990–; bd dir Condé Nast 1993–; *Recreations* tennis, cricket, classical music, opera, theatre; *Style*— Ms Deborah Gresty; ✉ Conde Nast, Vogue House, Hanover Square, London W1R 0AD (☎ 0171 499 9080)

GRESTY, Hilary Marion Bell; da of Allan Bell Gresty (decd), and Joy Margaret, *née* Coltham; *b* 24 Feb 1954; *Educ* Oxford Girls' HS, Univ of Exeter (BA), UCL (MA), Courtauld Inst London (MPhil); *partner* Edward Macready Dickinson; 2 s (Edmund Gresty Dickinson b 12 June 1992, Arthur Gresty Dickinson b 16 Feb 1994); *Career* research asst Royal Library Windsor 1977, library res asst Tate Gallery London 1978–81, curator Kettle's Yard Univ of Cambridge 1983–89, freelance writer, curator and visual arts conslt 1989–; currently pt/t dir VAGA (Visual Arts & Galleries Assoc); *Exhibitions* incl: 1965–1972 - when attitudes became form (1984), Pounds Artists (1985), C R W Nevinson (1988); progs incl work with Susan Hiller, Nan Hoover, Ron Haselden, Mary Kelly, Richard Layzell and Charlie Hooker; *Catalogues* incl: Christopher Wood - his early years (Newlyn Art Gallery, 1989), Ron Haselden (Serpentine Gallery, 1990), Alison Wilding (Newlyn Art Gallery, 1993); *Books* British Sculpture 1960–90 (contrib), Postmodern Art: theory into practice (contrib 1995, Routledge); *Style*— Ms Hilary Gresty; ✉ The Old Village School, Witcham, Ely, Cambs CB6 2LQ (☎ 01353 776356)

GRETTON, 4 Baron (UK 1944) John Lysander Gretton; o s of 3 Baron Gretton (d 1989); *b* 17 April 1975; *Educ* Shrewsbury; *Style*— The Rt Hon Lord Gretton; ✉ Holygate Farm, Stapleford, Melton Mowbray, Leicestershire LE14 2XQ

GRETTON, Vice Adm Michael; *b* 1946; *Educ* Ampleforth, Britannia RNC Dartmouth, Trinity Coll Oxford (MA); *m* Stephanie, *née* O'Neill; 3 da, 1 s; *Career* with RN; sometime CO HMS Bossington and HMS Ambuscade, served Directorate of Naval Plans MOD 1980–82, staff offr ops to COMASWSTRIKFOR (Commander NATO Anti-Submarine Warfare Striking Force) 1982–84, dep dir Naval Recruiting MOD 1984–86, RCDS 1987, Cabinet Office Top Mgmnt Prog 1988, successively commanded HMS Invincible then NATO Standing Naval Force Atlantic (STANAVFORLANT) 1988–91, dir Naval Staff Duties MOD 1991–93, Rear Adm 1993, COMUKTG (Commander UK Task Group) and COMASWSTRIKFOR 1993–94, Vice Adm 1994, SACLANTREPEUR (representative of Supreme Allied Commander Atlantic in Europe) 1994–; a vice-pres the Nautical Inst; govr: St Edward's Sch Oxford, Farleigh House Sch Andover; *Style*— Vice Adm Michael Gretton; ✉ c/o Naval Secretary, Victory Building, HM Naval Base, Portsmouth, Hants PO1 3LR

GREW, James; CBE (1989), JP (1974), DL (Co Armagh 1981); s of James Grew; *b* 25 Oct 1929; *Educ* Downside; *m* 1955, Pauline Peta, da of Prof John Cunningham; 2 s (Jonathan James b 1958, Christopher Nicholas b 1969), 2 da (Michaela Maria b 1962, Philippa Peta b 1967); *Career* md Abbicoil Spring Ltd 1957–95; memb: NI Econ Cncl 1970–74, NI Community Relations Cmmn 1971–74, Craigavon Devpt Cmmn 1971–73, Crawford Ctee on Bdcasting Coverage 1973–74; chm Bannside Development Co Ltd 1990–95; dir: Management Development Services Ltd 1975–90, Portadown Integrated Primary School Ltd 1990–91, NIR Leasing Ltd 1990–91, Novatech Ltd 1990–95; pres IACOLE USA 1991–95 (dir 1975–90); memb: BBC Advsy Ctee NI 1976–80, BBC Gen Advsy Cncl London 1976–80; chm Post Office Users' Cncl NI 1976–81; memb: Post Office Users' Nat Cncl London 1976–81, Standing Advsy Cmmn on Human Rights 1980–82, IBA Advsy Ctee N Ireland 1983–85; first chm Probation Bd for NI 1982–88, dir (Govt appointment) NI Transport Holding Co Ltd 1983–86, dir NI Railways 1986–92, chm TSB Fndn Bd N Ireland 1986; first chm Ind Cmmn for Police Complaints NI 1988, dir Abbey National NI Advsy Bd 1989–92; dir/sec NI Cncl for Integrated Educn 1991–93; tstee: UDR Benevolent Fund 1990, Royal Irish Regt Museum Ballymena 1993; memb: TAVRA NI, Army Cadet Force Assoc; FInstD 1989; *Recreations* sailing; *Clubs* Chief Exec Club at Queens, Armagh, Royal Irish Yacht; *Style*— James Grew, Esq, CBE, JP, DL; ✉ Peacefield, Ballinacorr, Portadown, Co Armagh, N Ireland BT63 5RJ (☎ and fax 01762 332277)

GREY, Sir Anthony Dysart; 7 Bt (UK 1814), of Fallodon, Northumberland; s of Capt Edward Elton Grey (d 1962), and Nancy, *née* Meagher; suc gf, Sir Robin Edward Dysart Grey, 6 Bt (d 1974); *b* 19 Oct 1949; *Educ* Guildford GS Perth (Aust); *m* 1, 1970 (m dis), Donna, da of Donald Daniels, of London; m 2, 1993, Alison Turner; 2 da (Matilda Jessie b 4 Jan 1994, Lucinda Jane b 25 Jan 1996); *Heir* none; *Recreations* fishing, painting; *Style*— Sir Anthony Grey, Bt; ✉ c/o 38 King's Park Road, Perth, Western Australia 6005, Australia

GREY, Dame Beryl Elizabeth; DBE (1988, CBE 1973); da of Arthur Ernest Groom (d 1983), and Annie Elizabeth, *née* Marshall (d 1952); *b* 11 June 1927; *Educ* Dame Alice Owen Professional Madeleine Sharp, Sadler's Wells Ballet Sch; *m* 15 July 1950, Dr Sven Gustav Svenson, s of Ernest Svenson (d 1967), of Heleneborg, Vadstena, Sweden; 1 s (Ingvar b 1954); *Career* former ballerina; danced Swan Lake at 15, Giselle at 16, Sleeping Beauty at 19; prima ballerina Sadler's Wells later Royal Ballet 1941–57; int guest ballerina 1957–66; first Western guest artist: Bolshoi Ballet Moscow 1957, Peking Ballet 1964; dir gen Arts Educn Schs and Teacher Trg Coll 1966–68, artistic dir London Festival Ballet 1968–79; dir/prodr: Swan Lake (London Festival Ballet) 1972, Giselle (West Australian Ballet) 1984 and 1986, Sleeping Beauty (Royal Swedish Ballet) 1985; Imperial Soc of Teachers of Dancing: memb Cncl 1962–91, chm 1984–91, pres 1991–; pres: Dance Cncl of Wales 1982–, East Grinstead Operatic Soc 1986–, Keep Fit Soc 1992–93 (vice pres 1968–92); vice pres: Royal Acad of Dancing 1980– (memb Exec Ctee 1982–89), Br Fedn of Music Festivals 1985–, PRO (dogs nat charity) 1991–; chm Royal Ballet Benevolent Fund; vice chm: Dance Teachers Benevolent Fund 1986– (tstee 1981–), London Coll of Dance (govr 1966–93), Govrs Royal Ballet 1995– (govr 1993–); tstee: London City Ballet 1970–92, DISCS (Diagnostic Investigation of Spinal Conditions and Sciatica) 1993–; patron: Nature Cure Clinic 1986–, Dancers Resettlement Fund 1988–, Benesh Inst 1988–, Language of Dance Centre 1988–, Friends of Sadler's Wells 1991–, Eurlong Research Fndn (hip replacement) 1993–, Amber Tst 1995–, Theatre Design Tst (Central St Martin's Coll London) 1995–; govr Dame Alice Owens Girls' Sch 1960–77; memb Bd Birmingham Royal Ballet 1995–; Hon DMus Univ of Leicester 1970, Hon DLitt City of London Univ 1974, Hon DEd CNAA 1989, Hon DLitt Univ of Buckingham 1993, Hon DMus Univ of London 1996; Imperial Award Imperial Soc of Teachers of Dancing 1987, Queen Elizabeth II Coronation Award Royal Acad of Dancing 1996; FRSA, FISTD; *Books* Red Curtain Up, Through the Bamboo Curtain, Favourite Ballet Stories (ed); *Recreations* swimming, reading, playing piano, painting; *Clubs* Anglo-Belgian, Royal Thames Yacht; *Style*— Dame Beryl Grey, DBE; ✉ Fernhill, Forest Row, East Sussex RH18 5JE (☎ 01342 822539)

GREY, John Egerton; CB (1980); s of John Grey (d 1979), and Nancy Augusta, *née* Nickalls (d 1984); *b* 8 Feb 1929; *Educ* Blundell's, BNC Oxford (MA, BCL); *m* 1961, Patricia, da of Col Walter Francis Hanna, MC (d 1963), and Kathleen Ethel Madelaine, *née* Grey (d 1976); 2 adopted s; *Career* called to the Bar Inner Temple 1954, practised at Chancery Bar 1954–59; various posts as clerk Parliament Office 1959–74, clerk asst and clerk of public bills House of Lords 1974–88; advsr Colchester CAB 1989–; *Recreations* gardening, boating; *Clubs* Arts, West Mersea Yacht; *Style*— J E Grey, Esq, CB; ✉ 51 St Peter's Rd, West Mersea, Colchester, Essex CO5 8LL

GREY, Maj-Gen John St John; CB (1986); s of Maj Donald John Grey, RM (d 1942), and Doris Mary Grey, *née* Beavan; *b* 6 June 1934; *Educ* Christ's Hosp Sch, Royal Coll of Defence Studies, Army Staff Coll Camberley, US Marine Corps Cmd and Staff Coll, Nat Defence Coll; *m* 1958, Elisabeth Ann, da of late Frederick Charles Langley; 1 s (Angus Matthew St John b 1968), 1 da (Emelia St John b 1969); *Career* cmmnd 1952; Commando Serv: Malta, Egypt, Cyprus 1955–58; Support Co Cmd 43 Commando RM 1962–64, Cruiser HMS Lion 1964–65, Instr Army Sch of Infantry 1967–69, Rifle Co Cmd 41 Commando RM 1969–70, US Marine Corps 1970–71, Directorate Naval Plans MOD 1971–74, CO 45 Commando RM 1976–79, Mil Sec and Col Ops and Plans MOD 1979–84, Maj-Gen cmd Commando Forces 1984–87, Chief of Staff RM 1987–88, ret Oct 1988; memb HAC 1991, memb Cncl OPS 1991, pres SSAFA Devon 1992; Rep Col Cmdt RM 1995; Clerk Worshipful Co of Pewterers 1989–96; *Recreations* sailing; *Clubs* Army and Navy, RNSA, RMSC; *Style*— Maj-Gen John Grey, CB; ✉ c/o Lloyds Bank Ltd, Teignmouth, Devon TQ14 8SL

GREY, 6 Earl (UK 1806); Sir Richard Fleming George Charles Grey; 7 Bt (GB 1746); also Baron Grey of Howick (UK 1801) and Viscount Howick (UK 1806); s of Albert Grey (ggs of Adm Hon George Grey, himself 4 s of 2 Earl Grey, who was PM 1830–34); suc 2 cous twice removed 1963; *b* 5 March 1939; *Educ* Hounslow Coll, Hammersmith Coll of Bldg; *m* 1, 1966 (m dis 1974), Margaret Ann, da of Henry Bradford, of Ashburton; m 2, 1974, Stephanie Caroline, da of Donald Gaskell-Brown, of Newton Ferrers, Plymouth, and formerly w of Surgn-Cdr Neil Leicester Denham, RN; *Heir* bro, Philip Grey; *Career* chm: Academy Beverage Co Ltd, Ballantyne Ross Ltd, The London Cremation Co plc, Chartdisc Ltd; dir: Covent Garden Quality Ltd, The Countess Grey Collection Ltd; pres Cost and Exec Accountants Assoc 1978, pres The Cremation Soc of GB; memb Liberal Pty; *Style*— The Rt Hon the Earl Grey; ✉ c/o House of Lords, London SW1

GREY, Robin Douglas; QC (1979); s of Dr Francis Temple Grey (d 1941), and Eglantine, *née* Ellice; *b* 23 May 1931; *Educ* Eastbourne Coll, King's Coll London (LLB); *m* 1, 1968 (m dis 1972), Gillian, da of late Maj Esme Austin Reeves Porch; m 2, 1972 (m dis 1992), Berenice Anna, da of Dennis Wheatley (d 1985); 1 s (Julian Alexander b 2 May 1970), 1 da (Louise Katherine b 20 Aug 1973); m 3, 24 Sept 1993, Annick, da of late Henri Kerbiriou and Lady Winskill; *Career* Nat Serv Army 1950–51; called to the Bar Gray's Inn 1957; crown counsel in Aden 1959–63 (acting attorney gen, acting registrar gen, acting sr crown counsel); in practice SE Circuit 1963–, dep circuit judge 1977–79, recorder 1979–; head FCO Team of Legal Experts to Moscow 1993, FCO conslt to Govt of Russian Fedn 1994–; chm Police Disciplinary Appeals Tbnls 1989–, legal assessor GMC 1995–; memb: Soc of Forensic Med 1976, Crime and Juvenile Delinquency Study Gp Centre for Policy Studies 1980, Ctee of Criminal Bar Assoc 1991–94 (chm Int Sub-Ctee 1993); co-author Professional Conduct pamphlet for Inns of Court Sch of Law 1991, 1992 and 1993; *Recreations* tennis, golf, fishing; *Clubs* Hurlingham; *Style*— Robin Grey, Esq, QC; ✉ Queen Elizabeth Building, 3rd Floor, Temple, London EC4Y 9BS

GREY EGERTON, Sir (Philip) John Caledon; 15 Bt (E 1617), of Egerton and Oulton, Cheshire; s of Sir Philip Reginald Le Belward Grey Egerton, 14 Bt (d 1962); *b* 19 Oct 1920; *Educ* Eton; *m* 1, 1951, Margaret Voase (d 1971), eldest da of late Rowland Rank, of Aldwick, Place, Aldwick, W Sussex, and wid of Sqdn Ldr Robert Ullman, RAF; m 2, 1986, Frances Mary, da of late Col Robert Maximilian Rainey-Robinson, of Broadmayne, Dorchester, Dorset, and wid of Sqdn Ldr William Dudley Williams, DFC, RAF; *Heir* bro, Brian Balguy Le Belward Egerton b 5 Feb 1925; *Career* late Capt Welsh Gds; *Style*— Sir John Grey Egerton, Bt; ✉ Meadow House, West Stafford, Dorchester, Dorset DT2 8AQ

GREY OF CODNOR, 6 Baron (E 1397); Richard Henry Cornwall-Legh; DL (Cheshire 1995); o s of 5 Baron Grey of Codnor, CBE, AE, DL (in whose favour the barony (abeyant since 1497) was terminated in 1989; d 1996), and Dorothy Catherine Whitson, *née* Scott (d 1993); *b* 14 May 1936; *Educ* Stowe; *m* 1974, Joanna Storm, 7 and yst da of Sir Kenelm Henry Ernest Cayley, 10 Bt (d 1967); 3 s (Hon Richard Stephen Cayley b 1976, Hon Kenelm Michael b 1978, Hon George Henry b 1982), 1 da (Hon Caroline Philadelphia b 1983); *Heir* s, Hon Richard Stephen Cayley Cornwall-Legh b 1976; *Career* RN 1955–57 (Gen Serv Medal, Suez); landowner, farmer and dir of private cos; memb British Ski Team 1959–61 (Capt 1960–61); High Sheriff Cheshire 1993–94; *Clubs* Boodle's, MCC; *Style*— The Rt Hon the Lord Grey of Codnor, DL; ✉ High Legh House, Knutsford, Cheshire WA16 0QR

GREY OF NAUNTON, Baron (Life Peer UK 1968), of Naunton, Co Gloucester; Sir Ralph Francis Alnwick Grey; GCMG (1964, KCMG 1959, CMG 1955), GCVO (1973, KCVO 1956), OBE (1951); s of Francis Arthur Grey (d 1917), an accountant in NZ, and Mary Wilkie, *née* Spence (d 1952); *b* 15 April 1910; *Educ* Scots Coll, Wellington Coll NZ, Auckland Univ Coll (LLB), Pembroke Coll Cambridge; *m* 1 Nov 1944, Esmé Mae, DStJ (d 1996), da of Albert Victor Kerry Burcher, of Remuera, NZ, and widow of Pilot Offr Kenneth Kirkcaldie, RAFVR; 2 s (Hon Jolyon Kenneth Alnwick b 1946, Hon Jeremy Francis Alnwick b 1949), 1 da (Hon Amanda Mary Alnwick (Hon Mrs Clapham) b 1951); *Career* barr and slr NZ; Colonial Serv Nigeria 1937, devpt sec 1952, sec to Govr-Gen and Cncl of Mins Nigeria 1954, chief sec Fedn of Nigeria 1955, dep govr-gen 1957–59; govr and C-in-C: British Guiana 1959–64, Bahamas 1964–68, Turks and Caicos Islands 1965–68, N Ireland 1968–73; chm: Cwlth Devpt Corp 1979–80 (dep chm 1973–78), Central Cncl Royal Over-Seas League 1976–81 (pres 1981–93, grand pres 1993–); hon bencher Inn of Ct of Northern Ireland, hon bencher Gray's Inn 1991; Hon Freeman City of Belfast and Borough of Lisburn, Freeman City of London; pres: Chartered Inst of Secs NI 1970–, Britain-Nigeria Assoc 1983–89, Overseas Serv Pensioners' Assoc 1983–; chllr: New Univ of Ulster 1980–84, Univ of Ulster 1984–93; Hon: LLD Queen's Univ Belfast, DLitt New Univ of Ulster, LLD Nat Univ of Ireland, DSc Univ of Ulster; GCStJ 1976; Lord Prior of the Order of St John 1988–91 (Kt Cdr of Commandery of Ards 1968–76), Bailiff of Egle 1975–87 (chllr 1987–88); Gd Cross of Merit Pro Merito Melitensi; *Recreations* golf; *Clubs* Travellers'; *Style*— The Rt Hon the Lord Grey of Naunton, GCMG, GCVO, OBE; ✉ Overbrook, Naunton, Glos GL54 3AX (☎ 01451 850263)

GRIBBON, Angus John St George; s of Maj-Gen Nigel St George Gribbon, OBE, *qv*, and Rowan Mary, *née* MacLiesh; *b* 25 Dec 1951; *Educ* Rugby, New Coll Oxford (MA); *m* 15 May 1976, Mary-Anne, da of Hugh Wynwel Gamon, CBE, MC, of Black Charles Underriver, nr Sevenoaks, Kent; 1 s (Edward b 1981), 2 da (Mary-Clare b 1983, Caroline b 1985); *Career* Clifford-Turner Slrs 1974–79, slr Allied-Lyons plc 1979–89, sr legal advsr Securicor plc 1989–; *Recreations* sailing, skiing; *Clubs* Law Society; *Style*— Angus Gribbon, Esq; ✉ Pedlam Brook, West Peckham, Maidstone, Kent ME18 5JS (☎ 01732 851732); Securicor plc, Sutton Park House, 15 Carshalton Rd, Sutton, Surrey SM1 4LD (☎ 0181 770 7000, fax 0181 770 1145)

GRIBBON, (Edward) John; s of Henry Derwent Gribbon, of Belfast, and Dorothy, *née* Boyd (d 1972); *b* 10 July 1943; *Educ* Coleraine Academical Inst Co Londonderry, Univ of London (LLB); *m* 1968, Margaret Nanette, da of Edmund Flanagan, of Belfast; 2 da (Deborah b 1970, Claire b 1973), 1 s (Philip b 1980); *Career* articled clerk Atkinson & Boyd CAs Belfast 1960–66, HM princ inspr of taxes 1981–90 (inspr 1966–81); Inland Revenue: under sec and dir of Business Profits Div 1991–, dir of Compliance Div 1996–; FCA (Ireland) 1976 (ACA 1965); *Recreations* photography, family, local church; *Style*— John Gribbon, Esq; ✉ Inland Revenue, Business Profits Division, 22 Kingsway, London WC2B 6NR (☎ 0171 438 6774, fax 0171 438 6073)

GRIBBON, Maj-Gen Nigel St George; OBE (1960); s of late Brig W H Gribbon, CMG, CBE; *b* 6 Feb 1917; *Educ* Rugby, RMC Sandhurst; *m* 1943, Rowan Mary, *née* MacLiesh; 2 s (Antony b 5 Sept 1949, Angus, *qv* b 25 Dec 1951), 1 da (Annette b 14 Sept 1944); *Career* cmmnd King's Own Royal Regt 1937, Iraq 1941 (wounded), Western Desert 1942, Staff Coll Quetta 1943, GSO 2 45 Inf Div 1944, AATDC 1945–46, BM 1 Para Bde Palestine 1946, 1 King's Own Trieste 1947–48, GSO 2 (JIS) GHQ FARELF, Malaysia 1948–50, RAF Staff Coll 1952, DAQMG WO 1953–55, 1 King's Own Hong Kong 1956–57; cmd 5 King's Own 1958–60, AMS War Office 1960–62, cmd 161 Bde TA 1963–65, Canadian Nat Defence Coll 1965–66, staff of CDS MOD 1966, BGS (Intelligence) BAOR and ACOS NORTHAG 1967–69, ACOS (Intelligence) SHAPE 1970–72, ret; vice pres King's Own Royal Border Regt 1974–88; md Partnerplan Public Affairs Ltd 1973–75, chm Sallingbury Ltd 1975–77 (md 1977–84, chm 1985), dir Gatewood Engrs 1976–84, dep chm Sallingbury Casey Ltd (Saatchi & Saatchi Group) 1985–87, dir Chancellor Insurance Co Ltd 1986–92; memb: Exec Ctee British Atlantic Ctee 1977–89 (Cncl 1977–93), Euro-Atlantic Group 1977–86; pres and memb Cncl Canada-UK C of C 1981–; chm Falkland Islands Tst 1982–97, co-chm Joint Ctee with Canadian C of C 1984–91, memb Mgmnt Ctee Canada Meml Fndn 1988–, memb Shackleton Scholarship Fund 1995–; organiser Orford Festal Chamber Music Concerts 1991–; Freeman City of London, Liveryman Worshipful Co of Shipwrights 1982; *Recreations* sailing, grandchildren's Boatman, formerly skiing, swimming, sketching; *Clubs* Army & Navy (memb Gen and Fin Ctee 1989–92), Little Ship (Rear Cdre Trg 1976–79), Orford Sailing; *Style*— Maj-Gen Nigel Gribbon, OBE; ✉ 99 Pump St, Orford, Woodbridge, Suffolk IP12 2LZ (☎ 01394 450413)

GRICE, Prof Roger; s of Francis Grice (d 1965), and Phyllis Dale, *née* Fell (d 1994); *b* 27 July 1941; *Educ* Ormskirk GS, Cambridge Univ (MA), Harvard Univ (PhD); *m* 15 Aug 1964, Patricia Margaret, da of James Edmund Lee, of Bathavon, Somerset; 3 da (Cordelia Kendal b 29 Sept 1967, Emma Dale b 19 April 1969, Guinevere Lee b 7 Nov 1974); *Career* lectr in theoretical chemistry Univ of Bristol 1968–69, sr asst and asst dir of res Univ of Cambridge 1969–76, prof of physical chem Univ of Manchester 1976–; author papers in: molecular physics, Faraday discussions, transactions of Royal Soc of Chemistry, Jl of Physical Chemistry; Faraday Cncl memb Royal Soc of Chemistry 1984–87; govr: Manchester GS, Withington Girls' Sch; *Recreations* fell walking, theatre, classical music; *Style*— Prof Roger Grice; ✉ Oaklea, 186 Grove Lane, Cheadle Hulme, Cheshire SK8 7NH; Chemistry Department, University of Manchester, Manchester M13 9PL (☎ 0161 275 4667, fax 0161 275 4598)

GRIDLEY, 3 Baron (UK 1955); Richard David Arnold Gridley; only s of 2 Baron Gridley (d 1996), and (Edna) Leslie, *née* Wheen; *b* 22 Aug 1956; *Educ* Monkton Combe Sch, Portsmouth Poly, Univ of Brighton (BA Business Educn with Qualified Teacher Status); *m* 1, 1979 (m dis), Amanda J Mackenzie; m 2, 1983, Suzanne Elizabeth, *née* Ripper; 1 s (Hon Carl Richard b 5 Feb 1981), 1 da (Hon Danielle Lauren b 1983); *Career* formerly project mangr: Rush and Tompkins Gp plc, Ballast Nedam Construction UK; currently lectr in business and IT South Downs Coll of FE; *Style*— The Rt Hon Lord Gridley; ✉ 79 Purbrook Gardens, Purbrook, Hampshire PO7 5LE

GRIER, (Hugh) Christopher; s of The Very Rev A R M Grier (d 1939), of Perth, Scotland, and Edith Mary, *née* Howes (d 1961); *b* 4 Dec 1922; *Educ* Glenalmond Coll, King's Coll Cambridge (MA, MusB); *m* 30 Nov 1950, Mary Elisabeth, da of Brig J C Martin, CBE, DSO, MC; 1 s (Nicholas John Macgregor b 8 Feb 1956); *Career* served WWII The Black Watch 1942–45; music offr Br Cncl Scandinavia 1947–49; music critic: The Scotsman 1949–63, The Evening Standard 1971–93; London drama critic The Scotsman 1984–93; freelance contrib London newspapers, magazines and music jls 1963–, involved with BBC progs and purveyor of prog notes to various orchs and festivals; memb Prog Ctee Edinburgh Festival 1951–63, lectr Royal Scot Acad of Music and Drama 1954–63, later prof at RCM and RAM, vice pres Int Ski-Club of Journalists 1982–84; memb: Critics' Circle 1958, Inst of Journalists, Royal Soc of Musicians of GB; hon memb: RCM, RAM; *Recreations* walking, skiing, reading; *Style*— Christopher Grier, Esq; ✉ 10 St Cross Hospital, Saint Cross Road, Winchester SO23 9SD (☎ 01962 851427)

GRIERSON, Robert McMorrine; s of Robert Grierson (d 1987), and Gertrude, *née* Warwick; *b* 4 May 1943; *Educ* Yewlands Sch; *m* 12 Oct 1968, Pamela Christine, da of Richard Prewett (d 1985); 1 s (John Robert McMorrine b 1980), 1 da (Heather Louise b 1976); *Career* CA Robert M Grierson & Co; dir: Upperdale Ltd, Sheffield Wednesday Football Club plc; formerly: chm Chapeltown Round Table, pres Chapeltown 41 Club; holder of Duke of Edinburgh's Gold Award; FCA; *Recreations* golf, football; *Style*— Robert M Grierson, Esq; ✉ 2 Croft Close, Whirlow, Sheffield S11 9QP (☎ 0114 236 1774); Moor Oaks Lodge, 6 Moor Oaks Rd, Sheffield S10 1BX (☎ 0114 268 0357, fax 0114 266 6010)

GRIEVE, Alan Thomas; s of Lewis Miller Grieve (d 1963), of Stanmore, Middx, and Doris Lilian, *née* Amner (d 1975); *b* 22 Jan 1928; *Educ* Aldenham, Trinity Hall Cambridge (MA, LLM); *m* 1, 1957 (m dis 1971), Anne, da of Dr Lawrence Dulake, of Reigate, Surrey; 2 s (Charles b 1960, Ivan b 1962), 1 da (Amanda (Baroness Harlech) b 1958); m 2, 1971, Karen Louise, da of Michael de Sivrac Dunn, of Honiton, Devon; 1 s (Thomas de Sivrac b 1973), 1 da (Lara b 1974); *Career* Nat Serv 2 Lt 14/20 King's Hussars, Capt City of London Yeo TA; admitted slr 1953; sr ptnr Taylor Garrett; dir: Baggeridge Brick plc, Wilson Bowden plc, Reliance Resources Ltd, Stenham plc 1971–94, Medical Insurance Agency Ltd 1976–92 and other cos; chm The Jerwood Fndn and Racehorse Owners' Award; patron Brendoncare for the Elderly; tstee: Oakham Sch 1973–93, Br Racing Sch 1986–94; RCP: memb Fin and Gen Purposes Bd 1986–92, friend; memb Educnl Assets Bd 1988–90; memb Law Soc; *Books* Purchase Tax (1958); *Recreations* skiing, racing, shooting; *Clubs* Boodle's, Baur au Lac; *Style*— Alan Grieve, Esq; ✉ Stoke Lodge, Clee Downton, Ludlow, Shropshire SY8 3EG (☎ 01584 823212, fax 01584 823419); Jerwood Foundation, 22 Fitzroy Square, London W1P 5HJ (☎ 0171 388 6287, fax 0171 388 6289)

GRIEVE, William Percival (Percy); QC (1962); s of 2 Lt W Percy Grieve (ka Ypres 1915), of Kirkcudbrightshire and Argentina, and Dorothy Marie, *née* Hartley, who m 2, Dr William Cunningham, of Monkseaton, Northumberland; *b* 25 March 1915, (posthumously); *Educ* privately, Trinity Hall Cambridge; *m* 1949, Evelyn (d 1991), da of Cmdt Hubert Mijouain, of Paris, and Liliane, da of Sir George Roberts, 1 and last Bt (d 1950); 1 s (Dominic), 1 da (Orlane Kerr-Dineen, decd); *Career* late Maj Middx Regt; called to the Bar Middle Temple 1938, Hong Kong 1960; bencher Middle Temple 1969; recorder: Northampton 1965–71, Crown Ct 1971–87; MP (Cons) Warwicks Solihull 1964–83, UK Delgn Cncl of Europe (chm Legal Affrs Ctee 1979–83) and WEU 1969–83, hon assoc Parly Assembly Cncl of Europe 1989 and WEU 1990; Officier de l'Ordre d'Adolphe de Nassau, Chevalier de l'Ordre de la Couronne de Chêne, Croix de Guerre avec Palmes Luxembourg 1945–46, Bronze Star USA 1945, Chevalier de la Légion d'Honneur France 1974, Cdr de l'Ordre de Mérite Luxembourg 1976, Offr de l'Ordre de la Couronne Belgium 1980, Cdr de L'Ordre de La Couronne de Chene 1990; *Recreations* swimming, travel, theatre; *Clubs* Carlton, Hurlingham, Special Forces; *Style*— Percy Grieve, Esq, QC; ✉ 32 Gunterstone Road, London W14 (☎ 0171 603 0376)

GRIEVE, Hon Lord; William Robertson Grieve; VRD (1958); s of William Robertson Grieve (ka 1917), of Glasgow; *b* 21 Oct 1917; *Educ* Glasgow Acad, Sedbergh, Univ of Glasgow; *m* 1947, Lorna (d 1989), da of Rear Adm Edward Benn, CB; 1 s, 1 da; *Career* late Lt Cdr RNVR; advocate 1947, QC 1957, Sheriff Princ Renfrew and Argyll 1964–72, judge of appeal Jersey & Guernsey 1971–72; senator Coll of Justice Scot (Lord of Session) 1972–88; chm Bd of Govrs: Fettes Tst 1978–86, St Columba's Hospice 1983–; procurator Church of Scotland 1968–72; *Recreations* golf, painting; *Clubs* New (Edinburgh), Hon Co of Edinburgh Golfers, W Sussex Golf; *Style*— The Hon Lord Grieve, VRD; ✉ 20 Belgrave Crescent, Edinburgh EH4 3AJ (☎ 0131 332 7500)

GRIEVES, John Kerr; s of Thomas Grieves (d 1979), of Littlehampton, Sussex, and Annie, *née* Davis (d 1976); *b* 7 Nov 1935; *Educ* King's Sch Worcester, Univ of Oxford (MA), Harvard Business Sch; *m* 21 Oct 1961, Ann Gorell, da of Vincent Charles Harris (d 1982), of London; 1 s (Thomas b 11 Jan 1969), 1 da (Kate b 25 May 1964); *Career* Pinsent and Co 1958–63; Freshfields: joined 1963, managing ptnr 1979, sr ptnr 1990–96; non-exec dir: British Invisibles 1992–96, Enterprise Oil plc 1996–, Northern Electric plc 1996–; advsr Apex Partners 1996–; *Recreations* the arts, sport; *Clubs* Athenaeum, Roehampton; *Style*— John Grieves, Esq; ✉ 7 Putney Park Ave, London SW15 5QN (☎ 0181 876 1207)

GRIFFIN, Brian James; s of James Henry Griffin (d 1985), of Lye, nr Stourbirdge, W Midlands, and Edith Moore; *b* 13 April 1948; *Educ* Halesowen Tech Sch, Dudley Tech Coll, Manchester Poly Sch of Photography (ONC, Dip Photography, Dip Assoc of Manchester); *m* July 1980, Frances Mary, da of Morris Newman; 1 s (Danz James Sky b Aug 1983), 1 da (Layla Sky b Jan 1982); *Career* trainee draughtsman 1964–66, trainee estimator 1966–69, photography student 1969–72, photographer 1972–90, film dir 1990–; writer and dir of short film: Claustrofoamia 1994, The Curl 1996; Premi Al Llibre Fotografic award for Work (Primavera Fotografica '90 Barcelona); Freeman City of Arles (France); memb BAFTA; *Books* Brian Griffin Copyright (1978), Power (1980), Open (1985), Portraits (1987), Work (1988); *Recreations* speedway racing; *Clubs* Groucho; *Style*— Brian Griffin, Esq; ✉ Film Produktion Ltd, 34 Cleveland Street, London W1P 5FB (☎ 0171 637 4567, fax 0171 637 3456, car 0836 687166, e-mail expose@produktion.co.uk)

GRIFFIN, Prof George Edward; s of Herbert Griffin (d 1973), of Hull, and Enid Mary, *née* Borrill; *b* 27 Feb 1947; *Educ* Malet Lambert Sch Hull, King's Coll London (BSc), St George's Hosp Med Sch (MB BS), Univ of Hull (PhD); *m* 15 April 1972, Daphne Joan, da of Lionel Haylor, of Romford; 2 s (James Edward b 1978, Andrew John b 1980), 1 da (Joanna Mary b 1983); *Career* Harkness fell Harvard Univ Med Sch 1975–76; St George's Hosp Med Sch: house physician 1974–79, lectr 1979–83, div head of communicable diseases 1990–, chm of med 1994–; Wellcome Tst: sr lectr 1983–89, reader in med 1989–92, conslt physician 1983–, prof of infectious diseases and med 1992–; sec MRS 1988–; memb: Public Health Lab Serv Bd 1995–, MRC (UK) Physiological Med and Infection Bd 1995–; various pubns on pathogenesis of infection, immunological and metabolic responses to infection and vaccines; memb Br Soc of Gastroenterology; FRCP; *Recreations* mountain walking, gardening; *Style*— Prof George Griffin; ✉ Division of Infectious Diseases, St George's Hospital Medical School, Tooting, London SW17 0RE (☎ 0181 672 9944, fax 0181 672 4864, telex 945291 SAGEMS G)

GRIFFIN, Prof Jasper; s of Frederick William Griffin, and Constance Irene, *née* Cordwell; *b* 29 May 1937; *Educ* Christ's Hospital, Balliol Coll Oxford (BA, MA); *m* 10 Sept 1960, Miriam Tamara, da of Leo Dressler, of New York; 3 da (Julia b 1963, Miranda b 1966, Tamara b 1969); *Career* Jackson fell Univ of Harvard 1960–61; Balliol Coll Oxford: Dyson res fell 1961–63, tutorial fell 1963–90, reader 1990–92, prof of classical literature 1992–, public orator 1992–; T S Eliot lectr Univ of Kent 1984; FBA 1986; *Books* Homer on Life and Death (1980), Homer (1980), Snobs (1982), Latin Poets and Roman Life (1985), Virgil (1986), The Mirror of Myth (1986), Oxford History of the Classical World (co-ed, 1986), Homer - The Odyssey (1987), Commentary on Iliad Book 9 (1995); *Style*— Prof Jasper Griffin; ✉ 17 Staverton Road, Oxford; Balliol College Oxford (☎ 01865 2777782, fax 01865 270708)

GRIFFIN, Dr John Parry; s of late David Joseph Griffin (d 1992), of Cardiff, and Phyllis May Griffin (d 1989); *b* 21 May 1938; *Educ* Howardian HS Cardiff, London Hosp Med Coll (BSc, PhD, MB BS), FRCP, FRCPath, FFPM; *m* 31 March 1962, Margaret, da of Frank Cooper (d 1975); 1 s (Timothy David b 1967), 2 da (Jane Rachel b 1963, Ruth Catherine b 1965); *Career* head of clinical res Riker Laboratories 1967–71, professional head of Medicines Div Dept of Health 1971–84, hon conslt Lister Hosp 1976–, dir Assoc of Br Pharmaceutical Industry 1984–94, currently dir John Griffin Associates Ltd; author of over 200 pubns; *Books* Iatrogenic Diseases (3 edns), Manual of Adverse Drug Interactions (5 edns), Medicines Regulation Research & Risk (2 edns), International Medicines Regulations, The Textbook of Pharmaceutical Medicine (3 edns); *Style*— Dr John Griffin; ✉ John Griffin Associates Ltd, Quatermans, Digswell Lane, Digswell, Welwyn, Herts AL7 1SP (☎ 01438 716160, fax 01438 716029)

GRIFFIN, Maj Sir (Arthur) John Stewart; KCVO (1990, CVO 1974, MVO 1967); s of Col Arthur Wilfrid Michael Stewart Griffin, MC (d 1962), and Florence May, *née* Pearson (d 1987); *b* 20 Feb 1924; *Educ* Harrow; *m* 1 May 1962, Henrietta, da of Col Claud Andrew Montagu-Douglas-Scott, DSO (d 1971); 2 s (Andrew Michael Stewart b 1963, Phillip Anthony Stewart b 1965); *Career* Reg Army Offr The Queen's Bays (later Queen's Dragoon Gds) 1942–56, press sec to HM Queen Elizabeth the Queen Mother 1958–91 (equerry 1956–58, currently extra equerry); *Recreations* fishing, cricket; *Clubs* MCC; *Style*— Maj Sir John Griffin, KCVO; ✉ Barton's Cottage, Bushy Park, Teddington, Middlesex TW11 0EA (☎ 0181 977 6683)

GRIFFIN, Kevin Anthony; s of Patrick Anthony Griffin, of Harrow, Middx, and Patricia Barbera, *née* Squirrell; *b* 13 Oct 1964; *Educ* Watford Coll; *m* 2 Dec 1994, Sharon Theresa, da of Robert Gumley; 3 s (Oliver Robert b 29 March 1991, Patrick Dennis Richard b 14 Sept 1992, Thomas b 14 Sept 1994); *Career* photographer; asst to Jerry Oke, Paul Wakefield and Don McCullin 1986–89, freelance 1989–; memb Assoc of Photographers 1995; *Exhibitions* various American galleries, Hamiltons Gallery 1993; *Awards* D&AD (for best use of colour photography in advtg) 1989, Assoc of Photographers (for best colour cmmnd series) 1995; *Recreations* football, reading, cooking; *Style*— Kevin Griffin, Esq; ✉ 43 Sampson Avenue, Barnet, Herts EN5 2RN (☎ 0181 449 4621); c/o Hamiltons Gallery, 13 Carlos Place, Grosvenor Square, London W1Y 5AG (☎ 0171 499 9493)

GRIFFIN, Patrick Charles Lake; s of John Griffin, of Highclere, Newbury, Berks, and Helen Evelyn, da of Sir Henry Bashford, Hon Physician to King George VI, knighted for servs to med 1937; *b* 15 Sept 1948; *Educ* Leighton Park Sch, Birmingham Sch of Architecture, Aston Univ (BSc); *m* 8 Sept 1973, Linda Dorothy, da of Reginald Mitchell (d 1955), of Yapton, W Sussex; 1 s (Thomas b 1978), 1 da (Joanna b 1980); *Career* chartered architect; chm Architectural Partnerships plc, md Sutton Griffin Morgan (architects, planners, landscape architects, surveyors) 1973–; received Civic Tst Award 1977, Berkshire Environmental Awards 1981, 1983, 1984, 1985, 1986, 1987 and 1988; RIBA Housing Award 1987; vice chm Berks Soc of Architects 1988; ARIBA; *Recreations* cricket; *Style*— Patrick Griffin, Esq; ✉ Whitewood, The Mount, Highclere, Newbury, Berkshire (☎ 01635 253155); Sutton Griffin Morgan, Albion House, Oxford St, Newbury, Berks (☎ 01635 521100, fax 01635 44188)

GRIFFIN, Paul; s of Reginald Stuart Griffin, and Sylvia Mary, *née* Toyn; *b* 29 Dec 1955; *Educ* Humberston Fndn GS, Magdalen Coll Oxford (MA, BCL); *m* 16 April 1983, Janet Mary, da of Cecil Sidney Turner; 1 s (Alexander Jake b 25 Sept 1994), 1 da (Leonie Sabrina b 20 May 1991); *Career* called to the Bar Gray's Inn 1979, practising barr; memb Bar Cncl of England and Wales 1995–, lay memb Practice Regulation Review Ctee ICA 1995–; memb: Ctee London Common Law and Commercial Bar Assoc, COMBAR; *Recreations* restoring our French property, collecting furniture art books and wine, gardening, travel, skiing, music; *Style*— Paul Griffin, Esq; ✉ 77 Highbury Hill, London N5 1SX (☎ 0171 359 8559); 4 Essex Ct, Temple London EC4Y 9AJ (☎ 0171 797 7970, fax 0171 353 0998, telex 8812528 ADROIT G)

GRIFFIN, (William) Thomas Jackson; s of Frederick James Griffin (d 1947), of Newton Court, Monmouth, and Violet Madeline Griffin (d 1973); *b* 24 May 1928; *Educ* Eton, Trinity Coll Cambridge (MA); *m* 1968, Merrie Angela, *née* Leeds; 1 s (Nicholas b 1971), 1 da (Alexandra b 1969); *Career* Foreign & Colonial Investment Trust Co Ltd 1956–69, chm GT Management plc 1969–89, dir Pantheon International Ltd (formerly GT Venture Management Ltd) 1989–; other directorships: GT Japan Investment Trust plc 1972– (chm), Perpetual UK Smaller Companies Investment Trust plc (formerly Berry Starquest plc) 1987–, Pantheon International Participations plc (formerly GT Venture Investment Co plc) 1987–, CCLA Investment Management Ltd (formerly Church Charity and Local Authority Fund Managers Ltd) 1990–, The ECU Trust plc 1990– (chm), The Establishment Trust 1992–, Foreign & Colonial US Smaller Companies plc 1993– (chm), Scudder Latin America Investment Trust plc 1994– (chm); tstee Educn 2000; chm Bd of Tstees: COIF Charities Investment Fund, COIF Charities Fixed Interest Fund, COIF Charities Deposit Fund; chm Bd of Govrs Research into Ageing; FCA 1960; *Recreations* shooting, music; *Clubs* Boodle's, City of London; *Style*— Thomas Griffin, Esq; ✉ Pantheon International Ltd, 43–44 Albermarle Street, London W1X 3FE (☎ 0171 493 5685, fax 0171 629 0844)

GRIFFIN DOUGALL, Prof Beverly Elayne Smith; da of Solon Edgar Smith (d 1961), of Delhi, Louisiana, USA, and Nina Lee, *née* Gilliland; *b* 23 Jan 1930; *Educ* Baylor Univ Texas USA (BA, BSc), Univ of Virginia USA (PhD), Univ of Cambridge (Marshall scholar, PhD, ScD); *m* 1961 (m dis 1981), Dr Donald Ross Dougall; *partner* Dr Tomas

Lindahl, FRS; *Career* lectr in chemistry Mount Holyoke Coll 1958–61; Girton Coll Cambridge: research fell 1961–65, official fell/lectr in chemistry 1965–73; scientific staff MRC Lab of Molecular Biology 1968–73; ICRF London: scientific staff 1973–78, head Nucleic Acid Lab 1978–84; prof and dir Dept of Virology Royal Postgraduate Med Sch 1984–Sept 1996; memb Bd of Govrs Inst of Animal Virology Pirbright 1985–88; first Denis Burkitt fell 1995–96; Hon MD Univ of Göteborg Sweden; *Books* numerous book chapters, book reviews and original scientific papers/articles in academic jls; *Recreations* skiing, music, modern art, cats, gardening; *Style—* Prof Beverly Griffin Dougall; ✉ Department of Virology, Royal Postgraduate Medical School, Hammersmith Hospital, Du Cane Road, London W12 0NN (☎ 0181 740 3248, fax 0181 743 8331)

GRIFFITH, David Vaughan; s of Arthur Vaughan Griffith (d 1995), of Bethesda, and Josephine Mary, *née* East; *b* 14 April 1947; *Educ* Cardiff HS, Kaiser Wilhelms Gymnasium Hanover, Balliol Coll Oxford (MA); *m* 21 May 1977, Tina, da of Edwin Frost (d 1968), of Epsom; 1 s (Owen b 1981), 5 da (Mary b 1980, Lucy b 1983, Sarah b 1985, Anna b 1987, Tessa b 1989); *Career* banker; with S G Warburg & Co Ltd 1970–73, Edward Bates & Sons Ltd 1973–75, Orion Bank Ltd 1975–76, Saudi Int Bank 1976–86, exec dir Banque Paribas 1986–91, md Arbuthnot Latham & Co Ltd (formerly Aitken Hume Bank) 1992–95; dir: North Kensington City Challenge Company Ltd 1994–, Griffith & Partners Ltd (antiquarian booksellers) 1996–; *Recreations* hill walking, theatre, railways; *Clubs* Reform; *Style—* David Griffith, Esq; ✉ 17 Matlock Court, Kensington Park Road, London W11 3BS

GRIFFITH, Kenneth; brought up by grandparents Ernest and Emily Griffith; *b* 12 Oct 1921; *Educ* Tenby Cncl Sch, Tenby Green Hill GS; *m* three times (all dis); 3 s (David, Jono, Huw), 2 da (Eva, Polly); *Career* actor, writer and film maker; *Films* incl: A Touch of Churchill, A Touch of Hitler (life of Cecil Rhodes), Hang Out Your Brightest Colours (life of Michael Collins - this film was suppressed but released on BBC 2 after 21 years), The Man on the Rock (last six years of Napoleon's life), The Sun's Bright Child (life of Edmund Kean), The Public's Right to Know (investigation into suppression of Collins films), Curious Journey (investigation into cause of Irish Republicanism - also suppressed), Black as Hell, Thick as Grass (the S Wales Borderers in the Zulu War of 1879), The Most Valuable Englishman Ever (the life of Thomas Paine), Clive of India, The Light (life of David Ben Gurion), Life of Jawaharlal Nehru, Zola Budd, The Heart of Darkness (the life of Roger Casement), The Untouchable (a life of Dr Ambedkar, BBC) 1995, Who Was George Rex? (an heir to the British throne, Channel Four) 1996; *Books* Thank God We Kept the Flag Flying (1974), Curious Journey (1982), The Discovery of Nehru (1989), The Fool's Pardon (autobiography, 1994); *Recreations* travelling around the world; *Style—* Kenneth Griffith, Esq; ✉ 110 Englefield Road, Islington, London N1 3LQ (☎ 0171 226 9013)

GRIFFITH, (Edward) Michael Wynne; CBE (1987), DL (Clwyd); s of Maj Humphrey Wynne Griffith, MBE (d 1986), and Phyllis Lilian Griffith, JP, *née* Theobalds; *b* 29 Aug 1933; *Educ* Eton, RAC; *m* 31 Oct 1959, Jill Grange, da of Maj D P G Moseley (d 1986), of Dorfold Cottage, Cheshire; 3 s (Edward James Wynne b 1964 d 1994, Anthony David Wynne b 1966, Martyn b 1968 d 1969); *Career* memb ARC 1973–82, dir Regnl Advsy Bd Nat West Bank 1974–92; chm: Wales Ctee Nat Tst 1984–91, Clwyd Health Authy 1980–90, Medical and Dental Post Graduate Educn Welsh Cncl 1990–93, Countryside Cncl for Wales 1991–, Glan Clwyd Hospital Tst 1993–; memb: Cncl Nat Tst 1988–, Higher Educn Fund Cncl for Wales 1992–95, Br Library Bd 1992–95; High Sheriff Denbighshire 1969, Vice Lord-Lt Clwyd 1989; FLS, FRSA; *Clubs* Boodle's; *Style—* Michael Griffith, Esq, CBE; ✉ Greenfield, Trefnant, Denbigh, Clywd (☎ 01745 730633)

GRIFFITH, Owen Glyn; CBE (1980, OBE 1969), MVO (1954); s of William Glyn Griffith, MBE (d 1960), and Glwadys May, *née* Picton Davies (d 1981); *b* 19 Jan 1922; *Educ* Oundle, Trinity Hall Cambridge; *m* 1 Feb 1949, Rosemary Elizabeth Cecil, da of Dr John Cecil St George Earl (d 1973); 2 s (David b 1955, Michael b 1957); *Career* cmmnd Welsh Gds 1941–43, served Tunisia (wounded twice); Colonial Serv (later HMOCS) Uganda 1944–63: dist offr 1944–51, private sec to Govr 1952–54, dist cmmr 1954–61, perm sec Miny of Commerce and Indust 1961–63; HM Dip Serv 1963–82: princ CRO 1963, first sec and head of Chancery Khartoum Embassy 1965, first sec (commercial) Stockholm Embassy 1969, dep high cmmr Malawi 1973, inspectorate 1976, high cmmr Lesotho 1978; local rep Forces Help Soc and Lord Roberts Workshops; *Recreations* golf, fishing; *Clubs* Denham Golf; *Style—* Owen Griffith, Esq, CBE, MVO; ✉ The Sundial, Marsham Way, Gerrard's Cross, Buckinghamshire SL9 8AD; Blaengwilym, Rhydwilym, Clynderwen, Dyfed SA66 7QH (☎ 01753 882438)

GRIFFITH GRIFFIN, *see:* Griffin

GRIFFITH WILLIAMS, John; QC (1985); s of Griffith John Williams, of Beer, E Devon, and Alison Rundle, *née* Bennett; *b* 20 Dec 1944; *Educ* King's Sch Bruton, The Queen's Coll Oxford (BA); *m* 3 April 1971, Mair, only da of Rt Hon Sir Tasker Watkins, VC, GBE, DL, *qv*; 2 da (Joanna Kate b 5 June 1972, Sarah Jane b 18 May 1974); *Career* called to the Bar Gray's Inn 1968, bencher 1994, memb Wales & Chester Circuit (treas 1993–95, ldr 1996–), recorder 1984–, asst cmmr to Parly Boundary Cmmn for Wales 1994–; memb Bar Cncl 1990–92; Lt Royal Welch Fus (TA) (cmmnd 1964), Welsh Volunteers (TAVR) 1967–71; *Recreations* golf; *Clubs* Army & Navy, Cardiff & County, Royal Porthcawl Golf; *Style—* John Griffith Williams, Esq, QC; ✉ Goldsmith Building, Temple, London EC4Y 7BL (☎ 0171 353 7881, fax 0171 353 5319)

GRIFFITHS, *see also:* Norton-Griffiths

GRIFFITHS, Alan Paul; s of Emrys Mathias Griffiths, and Jane, *née* Griffiths; *b* 21 Sept 1953; *Educ* St David's Sch, Jesus Coll Oxford (BCL, MA); *Career* fell and tutor in Law Exeter Coll Oxford 1977–88, called to the Bar Gray's Inn 1981, practising barrister; chm: Museum of Modern Art Oxford 1990–, Oxfordshire Community Rels Cncl 1978–80; memb: Exec Commercial Bar Assoc 1992–95, Nat Ctee Child Poverty Action Gp 1987–91; memb Oxford City Cncl 1980–88 (ldr and chm Fin Ctee); *Style—* Alan Griffiths, Esq; ✉ 1 Essex Court, Temple, London EC4Y 9AR (☎ 0171 583 2000, fax 0171 583 0118, 0171 353 8958)

GRIFFITHS, Rt Rev (Michael) Ambrose, OSB; *see:* Hexham and Newcastle, Bishop of (RC)

GRIFFITHS, Air Vice-Marshal Arthur; CB (1972), AFC (1964); s of Edward Griffiths (d 1960), of Saltney, Chester, and Elizabeth Griffiths; *b* 22 Aug 1922; *Educ* Hawarden GS; *m* 1950, Nancy Maud, da of Herbert Sumpter, of Wansford; 1 da (Sally); *Career* CO: No 94 (Fighter) Sqdn, No 101 (Bomber) Sqdn, RAF Waddington; AOA then COS Far E Air Force 1969–71; head of Br Defence Staffs Aust 1972–75, DG Security and Comdt Gen RAF Regt 1975–77; dir Trident Safeguards Ltd 1985–; *Clubs* RAF; *Style—* Air Vice-Marshal Arthur Griffiths, CB, AFC; ✉ Water Lane House, Castor, Peterborough, Cambs (☎ 01733 380 742)

GRIFFITHS, Bill (baptised Brian Bransom); s of William Eric Bransom Griffiths (d 1984), of Kingsbury, Middx, and Eileen Alexandra Hambleton; *b* 20 Aug 1948; *Educ* Kingsbury Co GS, UCL (BA), King's Coll London (MA, PhD); *Career* self employed writer and small press publisher, runs Amra Imprint specialising in lit and local history, memb Cncl and mangr Printshop Poetry Soc 1974, sec and chm Assoc of Little Presses 1989–91; poetry pubns incl: War with Windsor (1974), Tract Against the Giants (1984), Rousseau and the Wicked (1996); translator of Old English poems incl: Guthlac B, The Phoenix; other work in this field incl: Alfred's Metres of Boethius (1991), An Introduction to the Anglo-Saxon Laws (1994); jt winner Nat Poetry Centre's Alice Hunt Bartlett award 1974, winner Tha Engliscan Gesithas' Caedmon prize for Old English poetry 1988, artist in residence Westfield Coll London 1984; *Recreations* piano, keep-fit; *Style—* Bill Griffiths, Esq; ✉ 21 Alfred St, Seaham, Co Durham SR7 7LH (☎ 0191 581 6738)

GRIFFITHS, His Hon Bruce Fletcher; QC (1970); s of Edward Griffiths (d 1944), of Aberdare, Glamorgan, and Nancy Olga, *née* Fuell; *b* 28 April 1924; *Educ* Whitchurch GS Cardiff, King's Coll London (LLB, Jelf medal); *m* 1952, Mary Kirkhouse, da of Judge George Kirkhouse Jenkins, QC (d 1967), of Bath, Avon; 2 s (David Edward b 1954, Richard Bruce b 1956), 1 da (Branwen Jane b 1962); *Career* RAF 1942–47; called to the Bar Gray's Inn 1952, chm Local Appeals Tbnl (Cardiff) Miny Social Security 1964–70, vice chm Mental Health Tbnl Wales 1968–72; asst recorder: Birkenhead 1965, Cardiff Swansea & Merthyr Tydfil 1966–71; dep chm Glamorgan QS 1971, cmmr of Assize Royal Courts of Justice London 1971, memb Parole Bd 1983–85, circuit judge 1972–86; memb Welsh Arts Cncl 1972–79 (chm Art Ctee 1975–79), pres Prov Court Church of Wales 1979–92 (memb Governing Body 1978–92); chm: Welsh Sculpture Tst 1981–92, Contemporary Art Soc for Wales 1986–92 (purchaser 1975–76, vice chm 1976–86, vice pres 1992–); chllr Dio of Monmouth 1977–92, organising tstee Welsh Portrait Sculpture Fund; Silver medal for Services to Art (Czechoslovak Republic) 1986; *Clubs* Naval and Military, Cardiff and County (Cardiff); *Style—* His Hon Bruce Griffiths, QC; ✉ 15 Heol Don, Whitchurch, Cardiff CF4 2AR (☎ 01222 625001); Carrer Alaro 15, 07108 Port de Soller, Spain (☎ 00 34 71 633800)

GRIFFITHS, His Hon Judge David John; s of John Griffiths (d 1936), and Anne Virgo, formerly Griffiths, *née* Jones (d 1967); *b* 18 Feb 1931; *Educ* St Dunstan's Coll; *m* 1, 1959, Joyce, da of Charles Gosling (d 1963); 3 s (John b 1961, Huw b 1963, Bryn b 1965), 1 da (Jane b 1960); m 2, 1972, Anita, da of William John Williams (d 1967); *Career* Royal Tank Regt, 5 Bn BAOR 1949–51, TA City of London Yeo 1951–56; slr Supreme Court 1957, own practice Bromley Kent 1961, acquired Harveys of Lewisham practice 1970, HM recorder 1980–84, circuit judge (SE Circuit) 1984–, resident judge Maidstone Crown Ct Kent 1995–; hon slr Bromley Marriage Guidance Cncl 1969, vice chm Legal Aid Area Ctee 1983–84 (memb 1976), appt Panel of Chm of Nat Insur Local Tbnls, chm Bromley Cncl of Voluntary Servs 1980–87; Freeman City of London 1982, Liveryman Worshipful Co of Scriveners; *Recreations* riding, music (male voice); *Style—* His Hon Judge David Griffiths; ✉ Crosswell, Fosten Green, Biddenden, Ashford, Kent TN27 8ER; The Law Courts, Barker Road, Maidstone ME16 8EQ

GRIFFITHS, His Hon Judge; David Laurence; s of Edward Laurence Griffiths (d 1959), and Mary Middleton, *née* Ewens, of Crewkerne, Somerset; *b* 3 Aug 1944; *Educ* Christ's Hosp Horsham, Jesus Coll Oxford (MA); *m* 13 March 1971, Sally, da of Canon Gerald Hollis, of Salisbury, Wilts; 4 da (Kate b 4 June 1973, Jane b 29 Jan 1975, Emily b 20 June 1977, Lucy b 5 June 1981); *Career* called to the Bar Lincoln's Inn 1967, asst recorder 1981–85, recorder 1985, currently circuit judge (Western Circuit); *Recreations* gardening, opera, hash running, sailing, amateur dramatics, cricket, walking, skiing, rugby football, cycling; *Style—* His Hon Judge Griffiths; ✉ The Law Courts, Winchester SO23 9EL

GRIFFITHS, Ven Dr David Nigel; RD; s of late William Cross Griffiths, LDS; *b* 29 Oct 1927; *Educ* Cranbrook Sch, Worcester Coll Oxford (MA), Lincoln Theol Coll, Univ of Reading (PhD); *m* 1953, Joan, *née* Fillingham; 2 s (Martin Simon b 1955, Oliver Mark b 1959), 1 da (Rachel Helen (Mrs Peter Holmes) b 1957); *Career* ordained 1958, chaplain RNR 1963–77; clerk in Holy Orders, vice chllr and librarian of Lincoln Cathedral 1967–73, rector of Windsor 1973–87; officiating chaplain to: Household Cavalry 1973–87, 1 Bn Irish Guards 1977–80; chaplain to HM The Queen 1977–, rural dean of Maidenhead 1977–82 and 1985–87, hon canon of ChCh Oxford 1983–87 (emeritus 1992), archdeacon of Berkshire 1987–92 (emeritus 1992); warden of St Anne's Bede Houses Lincoln 1993–; tstee Lincolnshire Old Churches Tst; FSA; *Recreations* serendipity; *Style—* The Ven Dr David Griffiths, RD, FSA; ✉ 2 Middleton's Field, Lincoln LN2 1QP (☎ 01522 525753)

GRIFFITHS, Derek; *b* 15 July 1946; *Educ* Acland Burghley Comp, London Coll of Music; *Career* actor, lyricist and composer; teacher of drama: ILEA, Greenwich Theatre Co 1970–73; memb Performing Rights Soc; *Theatre* incl: Sing a Rude Song (Garrick) 1971, Two Gentlemen of Verona (Phoenix) 1972, Black Mikado (Cambridge Theatre), Aladdin (Shaftesbury and Canada), Travelling Music Show (Her Majesty's), Fagin in Oliver (Theatre Royal Plymouth), The Rise and Fall of Little Voice (Bristol Old Vic) 1993, Feste in Twelfth Night (RSC) 1994, Pompey in Measure for Measure (RSC) 1994, Engineer in Miss Saigon (Drury Lane) 1996; dir nat tour Twelfth Night; prodns at Royal Exchange Theatre Manchester: version of Dick Whittington (writer & composer), The Three Musketeers (composer, co-writer and lyricist), Government Inspector, Bluebird of Unhappiness, The Nerd, Twelfth Night, The Odd Couple, Recruiting Officer 1992; *Television* incl: BBC TV children's progs, Two By Two (composer & lyricist), Animal Album, Heads and Tails (award winning nature series, composer), Opposites Attract (composer), Mythical Magical Creatures (composer), Porkpie (Channel 4); extensive work in radio; *Films* numerous roles incl most recently Fierce Creatures (Universal Co); *Recreations* scuba diving, flying vintage aircraft (Tiger Moths, Stampes SV4B's); *Style—* Derek Griffiths, Esq

GRIFFITHS, Sir Eldon Wylie; kt (1985); s of Thomas Herbert Wylie Griffiths, of Dorset, and Edith May, *née* Jones; *b* 25 May 1925; *Educ* Ashton GS, Emmanuel Coll Cambridge, Yale Univ; *m* 1, 1949 (m dis 1985), Sigrid Gante; 1 s (John Henry Morgan Griffiths, *qv*), 1 da (Pamela); m 2, 1985, Elizabeth Marie Beatrix, da of Adriaan den Engelse (d 1985); *Career* former journalist; MP (C) Bury St Edmunds 1964–92, Parly sec Min of Housing and Local Govt 1970, Parly under-sec of state DOE and Min for Sport 1970–74, conslt Nat Police Fedn 1975–90; Regents prof Univ of California Irvine 1989–91; pres World Affrs Cncl Orange Co California, fndr dir Centre for International Business Chapman Univ Orange Co California; columnist Orange Co Register; chm Bardwell (Western States) Inc USA; chm Korea-America Friendship Soc, vice chm Indo-Br Assoc, hon pres Special Olympics (UK); Hon Freeman City of London, Hon Citizen Orange County California; Medal of Honour Republic of China Taiwan 1989; *Recreations* swimming, tennis, exploring wilderness America; *Clubs* Carlton; *Style—* Sir Eldon Griffiths; ✉ The Wallow, Great Barton, Bury St Edmunds, Suffolk; 29091 Ridgeview, Laguna Niguel, California 92691, USA

GRIFFITHS, Garry; s of Arthur Griffiths (d 1976), and Marion, *née* Taylor; *b* 12 June 1941; *Educ* Wellingborough GS, Leicester Poly (NDD); *m* 25 July 1964, Anna Margaret, da of Albert Hannington, of Priors Rd, Whittlesey, Peterborough, Cambs; 2 da (Catherine Ann b 1965, Lucy Ann b 1971); *Career* designer Design Res Unit 1963–66, lectr Middx Poly 1966–67, ptnr YRM 1986–93 (joined 1967), md YRM Interiors 1986–93, ptnr Building Design Partnership 1994–95; memb Nat Tst; FCSD, FRSA; *Recreations* photography, travel; *Style—* Garry Griffiths, Esq; ✉ The Willows, 15 Willow Drive, High Barnet, Herts EN5 2LQ (☎ 0181 449 6872)

GRIFFITHS, (William) Griffin Thomas; s of Maldwyn Thomas Griffiths, of Gwenddwr, Builth Wells, Powys, and Catherine Irene, *née* Powell; *b* 10 Nov 1940; *Educ* Univ Coll of Wales Aberystwyth (LLB); *Career* slr; sr ptnr Jeffreys & Powell; pres Herefords Breconshire and Radnorshire Law Soc 1989; *Recreations* farming; *Style—* Griffin Griffiths, Esq; ✉ Wye Lodge, Erwood, Builth Wells, Powys LD2 3PQ (☎ 01982 560307); 4 Lion St, Brecon, Powys LD3 7AU (☎ 01874 622106, fax 01874 623702)

GRIFFITHS, Howard; s of Bernard Griffiths (d 1984), and Olive, *née* Stokes (d 1982); *b* 20 Sept 1938; *Educ* Gowerton GS, LSE (MSc); *m* 27 July 1963, Dorothy, *née* Todd; 1 s (Andrew b 1968), 1 da (Emma b 1972); *Career* MOD: res offr 1963–69, princ Army Dept 1970–72, princ Central Staffs 1972–76, asst sec head Civilian Faculty Nat Def Coll

1976–78, asst sec Procurement Exec 1978–80, dep and cnsllr def UK Delgn Mutual and Balanced Force Reduction Talks Vienna 1980–84, asst sec Office Mgmnt and Budget 1984–86, head Def Arms Control Unit 1986–88, asst under sec (policy) 1988–91, under-sec Procurement Exec 1992–93, under sec RAF Logistics Orgn 1993–94, cmd sec RAF Logistics Cmd 1994–; fell Centre for Int Affairs Harvard Univ 1991–92; *Style*— Howard Griffiths, Esq

GRIFFITHS, Baron (Life Peer UK 1985), of Govilon, Co Gwent; Sir (William) Hugh Griffiths; kt (1971), MC (1944), PC (1980); o s of Sir Hugh Ernest Griffiths, CBE (d 1961), and Doris Eirene, da of W H James; *b* 26 Sept 1923; *Educ* Charterhouse, St John's Coll Cambridge (MA); *m* 1949, Evelyn, da of Col A F Krefting; 1 s; 3 da; *Career* Capt Welsh Gds 1941–46; called to the Bar Inner Temple 1949, QC 1964–70; judge: High Ct of Justice (Queen's Bench Div) 1970–80, Nat Industl Relations Ct 1973–74; memb Advsy Cncl on Penal Reform 1967–70, chm Tbnl of Inquiry on Ronan Point 1968, vice chm Parole Bd 1976–77, memb Chllr's Law Reform Ctee 1976–85, chm Lord Chllr's Advsy Ctee on Legal Educn and Conduct 1991–93; pres Senate of Inns of Court and the Bar 1982–; a Lord Justice of Appeal 1980–85, a Lord of Appeal in Ordinary 1985–93; chm Security Cmmn 1985–92; hon memb Canadian Bar Assoc 1981; hon fell: American Inst of Judicial Admin 1985, American Coll of Trail Lawyers 1988; Hon LLD: Univ of Wales 1987, De Montfort Univ 1993; hon fell St John's Coll Cambridge 1985; *Clubs* Garrick, MCC (pres 1990), Sunningdale Golf, R & A Golf (capt 1993); *Style*— The Rt Hon Lord Griffiths, MC, PC; ✉ House of Lords, London SW1A 0PW

GRIFFITHS, Dr Hugh William; s of Peter Griffiths, of Downham, Essex, and Gwyneth Margaret, *née* Roberts; *b* 20 March 1957; *Educ* Brentwood Sch Essex, Univ of Newcastle upon Tyne (MB BS); *m* 2, 30 May 1992, Caroline, da of James Evans, of Welwyn; *Career* house offr Darlington Meml Hosp 1980–81, Newcastle Rotational Trg Scheme in psychiatry 1982–85, res registrar MRC 1985–86, sr registrar Northern Regnl Rotation 1986–88, conslt psychiatrist: St George's Hosp 1988–92, Royal Victoria Infirmary Newcastle 1992–94; med dir Northumberland Mental Health Tst 1994–; hon clinical lectr Univ of Newcastle upon Tyne; MRCPsych 1984; *Recreations* rugby union, skiing, motor sport, photography, flying, music; *Clubs* Newcastle Aero Club; *Style*— Dr Hugh Griffiths; ✉ St George's Hospital, Morpeth, Northumberland (☎ 01670 512121)

GRIFFITHS, John Albert; s of Richard Griffiths, of Egham, Surrey, and Katie Joan, *née* Smithers; *b* 2 Dec 1943; *Educ* Tiffin Boys' Sch Kingston upon Thames; *m* Peggy-Ann Marie, *née* Waite, da of late Robert Mandel, of Calgary, Alberta, Canada; 2 s (James Richard b 28 Feb 1980, Charles Robert b 25 July 1984); *Career* reporter then sub-ed Surrey Herald Group 1961–64, ed Blackheath Reporter 1965–66, PR offr Mannix Heavy Construction Group Calgary Alberta 1966–67, news ed The Albertan (Calgary morning newspaper) 1967–68, night ed and motoring corr Calgary Herald 1968–70; Financial Times: foreign staff 1974–76, night foreign news ed 1977, dep foreign news ed 1978–80; specialist writer on world motor industry and motor sport 1980–; memb World Land Speed Record Team (Richard Noble, Black Rock Desert Nevada 1983, 468–633 mph) and writer subsequent film (For Britain and the Hell of it), holder World Land Speed Record for a fire engine (Black Rock Nov 2 1982, 130–157 mph); *Recreations* motor racing (as driver); *Style*— John Griffiths, Esq; ✉ Financial Times, 1 Southwark Bridge, London SE1 9HL (☎ 0171 873 3000, fax 0171 873 3085)

GRIFFITHS, John Calvert; CMG (1983), QC (1972); s of Oswald Hardy Griffiths (d 1952), and Christina Flora Littlejohn; *b* 16 Jan 1931; *Educ* St Peter's Sch York, Emmanuel Coll Cambridge (BA, MA); *m* 17 May 1958, Elizabeth Jessamy Jean, eld da of Prof G P Crowden, OBE (d 1967); 3 da (Amanda b 1963, Anna b 1970, Alyson b 1973); *Career* Lt RE 1949–51; called to Bar Middle Temple 1959 (bencher 1983), Hong Kong Bar 1979, attorney gen of Hong Kong 1979–83, chm Hong Kong Law Reform Cmmn 1979–83, memb Court Hong Kong Univ 1980–84; memb Exec Ctee Prince Philip Cambridge Scholarships 1980–84, patron Matilda Hosp Charity for Handicapped Children 1981–83, treas Bar Cncl 1987; memb: Exec Ctee Gen Cncl of Bar 1967–71, senate Inns of Court & The Bar 1984–86 (Exec Ctee 1973–77), Cncl of Legal Educn 1983–, Nat Cncl of Social Service 1974–79, Gtr London CAB Exec Ctee 1978–79; Liveryman Worshipful Co of Glovers; *Recreations* fishing, first edns, gardening; *Clubs* Fly Fishers', Hurlingham, Hong Kong; *Style*— John Griffiths, CMG, QC; ✉ c/o Brick Court Chambers, 15/19 Devereux Court, London WC2R 3JJ

GRIFFITHS, John Charles; JP (Cardiff 1959); s of Sir Percival Griffiths, KBE (d 1992), and Kathleen, *née* Wilkes (d 1979); *b* 19 April 1934; *Educ* Uppingham, Peterhouse Cambridge (MA); *m* 1, 1956, Ann; 4 s (Timothy b 1957, Christopher b 1958, Gavin b 1961, Jonathan b 1964); m 2, 1983, Carole Jane; 1 da (Emily b 1983); *Career* Thomson Newspapers 1958–61, BBC 1961–64; exec dir Nat Extension Coll 1964–67, PR advsr Br Gas 1969–73; chm and md: MSG PR Ltd 1973–78, Rodhales Ltd 1978–, Contact PR Ltd 1981–85, Minerva Vision and Arts Channel 1983–; dep gen mangr Press Assoc 1968–69; contested (Lib): Ludlow 1964, Wanstead & Woodford 1966, Bedford (Feb & Oct) 1974; pres Lib Pty 1982–83; *Books* The Survivors (1964), Afghanistan (1967), Modern Iceland (1969), The Science of Winning Squash, Three Tomorrows, Afghanistan, Key to a Continent (1980), The Queen of Spades (1983), Flashpoint Afghanistan (1987), The Third Man: The Life and Times of William Murdoch 1754–1839 (1992), Nimbus: Technology Serving the Arts, Fathercare: a handbook for single fathers; *Recreations* reading, talking, walking, music; *Clubs* RAC; *Style*— John Griffiths, Esq, JP; ✉ The Grove, Coxbury Lane, Redbrook, Monmouth, Gwent NP5 4LX (☎ and fax 01594 837135)

GRIFFITHS, John Egbert; s of Claude Griffiths (d 1975), of Bridgnorth, Shropshire, and Edith May, *née* Bradley; *b* 6 May 1939; *Educ* Tettenhall Coll Staffordshire, King's Coll Durham (BArch); *m* 12 Aug 1964 (m dis 1988); 2 da (Heidi Michelle b 1966, Sally Ann b 1969); *Career* architect and arbitrator; ptnr Mason Richards Partnership 1972–; RIBA 1965, ACIArb 1976; *Books* The Evolution of a Small Town (1962); *Recreations* countryside pursuits, painting & sketching, watching rugby union football, canoeing, running miniature steam trains on Welsh estate, conservation of ancient woodland and site of special scientific interest relating to bats on estate; *Clubs* Old Tettenhallians; *Style*— John Griffiths, Esq; ✉ The Fron, Glascwm, Bwlch-y-Cibau, Llanfyllin, Montgomeryshire, Powys, Wales SY22 5LU (☎ 01938 500204); Mason Richards Partnership, Architects Planners Consulting Engineers Landscape Architects, Highfield Court, 23/24 Highfield Rd, Edgbaston, Birmingham B15 3DP (☎ 0121 456 1544, fax 0121 456 1523, mobile 0836 515567); Salisbury House, Tettenhall Road, Wolverhampton WV1 4SG (☎ 01902 771331, fax 01902 21914); Severn House, Fountain Court, New Leaze, Almondsbury, Bristol BS12 4LD (☎ 01454 201303, fax 01454 616382)

GRIFFITHS, John Francis Philpin; s of James Maldwyn Griffiths (d 1993), of Hayes, Bromley, Kent, and Joan, *née* Philpin; *b* 16 Sept 1948; *Educ* St Dunstan's Coll London, Clare Coll Cambridge (MA, DipArch); *m* 16 Sept 1972, Fiona Barbara, da of Lt Cdr Hugh Desmond Campbell Gibson, of Kilmelford, Argyll, Scotland; 1 s (Leo b 27 July 1980), 1 da (Anna b 16 Jan 1977); *Career* architect; Scarlett Burkett Griffiths (formerly Scarlett Burkett Associates): joined 1972, assoc 1975, ptnr 1978–94; chm: London Region Assoc of Conslt Architects 1988–90 (vice pres 1991–), AA Part III Examination Bd 1989–; Freeman City of London 1987, Liveryman Worshipful Co of Arbitrators 1987; RIBA 1974, FCIArb 1986, ACA 1985, memb AA 1987; *Recreations* reading, railway memorabilia, woodworking; *Style*— John Griffiths, Esq; ✉ Lyndhurst, 98 Hayes Rd, Bromley, Kent BR2 9AB (☎ 0181 460 6246, fax 0181 466 9079)

GRIFFITHS, John Henry Morgan; s of Sir Eldon Wylie Griffiths, *qv*, and Sigrid, *née* Gante; *b* 3 Dec 1953; *Educ* Rugby, Emmanuel Coll Cambridge (MA); *m* 10 June 1994, Hilary R, elder da of John W Yeend, of Cheltenham; *Career* Lloyds Bank International 1975–79 (seconded to Bank of London & SA 1975–77, int mgmnt London 1977–79), Samuel Montagu & Co Ltd 1979–90 (syndications mangr 1981–83, dir and W Coast rep (USA) S M Inc 1983–87, exec dir 1986–90), dep gen mangr Nomura Bank International plc 1990–91; chief exec: Lynton Delancey & Partners 1991–, Lynton Bardwell Ltd 1993–; *Recreations* cricket, tennis, squash, shooting; *Clubs* San Francisco Bay, RAC; *Style*— John Griffiths, Esq; ✉ 44 Carlisle Mansions, Carlisle Place, London SW1P 1WY (☎ 0171 630 0520); Lynton Cottage, Ixworth Thorpe, Bury St Edmunds, Suffolk IP31 1QR (☎ 01359 269589, fax 01359 268520)

GRIFFITHS, John Pankhurst; s of William Bramwell Griffiths (d 1978), of Broadstairs, and Ethel Doris, *née* Pankhurst (d 1993); *b* 27 Sept 1930; *Educ* Torquay GS, King George V Sch Southport, Sch of Architecture Univ of Manchester (DipArch); *m* 1 Aug 1959, Helen Elizabeth, da of Leonard Ivor William Tasker (d 1976), of Bristol; 2 s (Jonathan b 1962, Matthew b 1963), 1 da (Janet b 1964); *Career* res architect Maxwell Fry N Nigeria 1956–58, staff architect Granada TV 1959, fndr and first dir Manchester Bldg Centre 1959–65, head of tech info MPBW (later DOE) 1965–77, fndr Bldg Conservation Tst (now Upkeep at Hampton Court Palace) 1977 (dir 1979–93); clerk: Worshipful Co of Chartered Architects 1995–, Worshipful Co of Tylers and Bricklayers 1996– (Freeman 1981); RIBA 1956; *Recreations* writing, designing odd things, examining buildings, cooking on solid fuel Aga; *Style*— John Griffiths, Esq; ✉ 28 Palace Road, East Molesey, Surrey KT8 9DL (☎ and fax 0181 224 9328)

GRIFFITHS, Prof Keith; s of Richard Griffiths (d 1975), and Lilian Griffiths, *née* Ebbs (d 1995); *b* 1 April 1935; *Educ* Sir William Turner's Sch Coatham N Yorks, Univ of Edinburgh (BSc, PhD, DSc); *m* 6 Sept 1958, Veronica, da of Robert Henry Williams, of Penarth, S Wales; 2 s (David b 7 Nov 1960, Timothy b 3 June 1962); *Career* res assoc Dept of Histochemistry Univ of Minnesota Minneapolis USA 1960–61, lectr Dept of Steroid Biochemistry Univ of Glasgow 1961–66, dir of res Tenovus Inst for Cancer Res Univ of Wales Coll of Med 1966–, dir of res and prof of cancer res 1971–; memb Biochemical Soc 1958–; chm: Welsh Office Welsh Scientific Advsy Ctee 1975–84, Liaison Ctee Br Endocrine Socs 1987–90, Soc of Endocrinology 1987– (memb 1960–); *Recreations* gardening, cricket, motoring; *Style*— Prof Keith Griffiths; ✉ Tenovus Cancer Research Centre, University of Wales College of Medicine, Heath Park, Cardiff CF4 4XX (☎ 01222 742579, fax 01222 747618)

GRIFFITHS, Rev Dr Leslie John; s of Sydney John Griffiths (d 1987), and Olwen, *née* Thomas (d 1976); *b* 15 Feb 1942; *Educ* Univ of Wales (BA), Univ of Cambridge (MA), Univ of London (PhD); *m* 26 July 1969, Margaret, da of Alfred Rhodes (d 1989); 2 s (Timothy b 24 Sept 1972, Jonathan b 7 Jan 1974), 1 da (Ruth b 29 Oct 1975); *Career* lectr Univ of Wales 1964–67; methodist minister: Cambridge 1969–70, Haiti 1970–74 and 1977–80, Reading 1974–77, Loughton 1980–86, London 1986–91; supt: Finchley and Hendon Circuit 1991–96, Wesley's Chapel 1996–; pres Methodist Conf 1994; regular contribs to radio and TV bdcasting; chm: Methodist Church Carribbean and Latin American Ctee 1981–89, Churches Advsy Cncl for Local Bdcasting 1996–; govr Kingswood Sch Bath 1981–90; memb Bd: Addiction Recovery Fndn 1987–, Christian Aid 1990–, Birnbeck Housing Assoc 1993–96; KStJ 1989; *Recreations* rugby, snooker, reading, conversation; *Clubs* The Graduate Centre (Cambridge); *Style*— The Rev Dr Leslie Griffiths; ✉ 49 City Road, London EC1Y 1AU (☎ 0171 253 2262, fax 0171 608 3825)

GRIFFITHS, Mervyn Christopher; TD (1976), DL (E Sussex 1994); s of Rev Leonard Lewis Rees Griffiths, of Haslemere, Surrey, and Eileen Clarice, *née* Diffey; *b* 28 May 1936; *Educ* St George's Sch Windsor Castle, Uppingham, Corpus Christi Coll Cambridge (MA), Harvard Business Sch (PMD); *m* 27 April 1974, Barbara Marchant, da of late Dr (Heneage) Marchant Kelsey, of Ramparts, Rudgwick, West Sussex; 1 step s (Mark Selway b 7 Feb 1964); *Career* 2 Lt 4/7 Royal Dragoon Gds 1954–56, Capt Queen's Own Warwickshire & Worcestershire Yeo 1956–68; special constable Met Police 1973–76, asst mktg mangr W & T Avery Ltd 1959–65, PR exec McLeish Associates 1965–66; Eurocard International SA Belgium: mktg mangr 1966–67, exec vice pres NY 1967–71, md London 1971–76; dir and dep chief gen mangr: Alliance Building Society 1976–85, Alliance & Leicester Building Society (also sec) 1985–89; dir Legal & General Mortgage Services 1990–94; registrar The Med Soc of London 1991–; exec sec: The Harveian Soc of London 1991–, The Assurance Med Soc 1994–; vice chm SE TA & VRA; memb: Isfield PCC, Nat Centenary Appeal Ctee NSPCC 1984; govr St Bede's Sch Eastbourne; FCIM 1975; *Recreations* gardening, travel; *Style*— Mervyn Griffiths, Esq, TD, DL; ✉ The Old House, Isfield, nr Uckfield, E Sussex TN22 5XU (☎ 01825 750446); The Medical Society of London, 11 Chandos Street, London W1M 0EB (☎ 0171 580 1043)

GRIFFITHS, Michael John; s of late Sqdn Ldr J C Griffiths, RAF, of Huntly, Bishopsteignton, Devon, and Winifred Ann, *née* Smith (d 1952); *b* 15 Dec 1934; *Educ* Peter Symond's Sch Winchester, London Business Sch; *m* 1, 10 Aug 1957, Jennifer Elizabeth (Jenny) (d 1994), da of late Lt-Col E E H Stafford, TD, of nr Atherstone, Warwicks; 2 s (Jeremy Michael Christian b 10 July 1960, Andrew James Christian b 7 Oct 1961), 3 da (Sara Elizabeth (Mrs Hicklin) b 20 Nov 1958, Caroline Jane (Rosie) (Mrs Thornton) b 13 April 1964, Rebecca Lucy (Biba) b 5 June 1969); m 2, 8 Oct 1995, Penelope, da of David Beecher, of Headington, Oxford; *Career* RAF Coll Cranwell 1952–55, GD Pilot 1955–62; md: Halls Oxford Brewery 1967, Benskins Brewery 1970, Taylor Walker 1979, Ind Coope 1985; dep chief exec Ansells Brewery Co 1974; dir: Friary Meux 1966, Allied Breweries 1979, Allied Lyons 1988–92; non-exec dir: Centric Pub Company Ltd 1992–94, Capital Consultants 1992–, Wilson and Stafford 1993–; chm: Victoria Wine Co 1988, Embassy Hotels 1989, J Lyons Catering Ltd 1989; non-exec chm Capital Group PLC 1994; memb Cncl Design Museum, chm London Brewers Cncl; Freeman City of London 1982, memb Ct of Assts Worshipful Co of Brewers (past Master); *Recreations* skiing, sailing, shooting, fishing; *Clubs* RAF; *Style*— Michael Griffiths, Esq; ✉ Mead Farm, Church Lane, Yarnton, Oxford (☎ 01865 373284)

GRIFFITHS, Mike; *b* 18 March 1962; *Educ* Blaenclydach Secdy Sch; *m* 27 Aug 1983, Anne, da of Haydn Arthur Griffiths; 2 s (Joel Michael b 25 Oct 1985, Luce Rhys b 29 Aug 1989); *Career* rugby union prop forward; clubs: Ystrad Rhondda RFC, Bridgend RFC, Cardiff RFC, Wasps RFC; rep: Saltires, Crawshays, Barbarians, Wales B; Wales: debut v Western Samoa 1988, Five Nations debut v Scotland 1989, memb World Cup squad 1991 and 1995; memb Br Lions tour Aust 1989; employed Whitbread Beer Co Ltd; *Recreations* mountain cycling, weight training, running; *Style*— Mike Griffiths, Esq; ✉ c/o Wasps RFC, Rangers Stadium, South Africa Road, Shepherd's Bush, London W12 7PA

GRIFFITHS, Nigel; JP (1984), MP (Lab) Edinburgh South (majority 4,176); s of Lionel Griffiths, of Edinburgh, and Elizabeth, *née* Murray; *b* 20 May 1955; *Educ* Hawick HS, Univ of Edinburgh (MA), Moray House Coll of Educn; *m* 1979, Sally, da of Hugh McLaughlin, of Kilmarnock; *Career* joined Lab Party 1970, pres Edinburgh Univ Lab Club 1976–77; rights advsr Mental Handicap Pressure Gp 1979–87, City of Edinburgh District cnCllr; MP (Lab) Edinburgh S 1987–, oppn whip 1987–89, oppn spokesman on consumer affairs 1989– (on trade and consumer affrs 1992–); chm: Housing Ctee, Decentralisation Ctee; convenor Fin Ctee Scottish Constitutional Convention 1990; vice pres Inst of Trading Standards Admin (ITSA) 1994–; memb: Edinburgh Festival Ctee, Wester Hailes Sch Cncl 1980; *Books* Council Housing on the point of Collapse (1982), Welfare Rights Guide (1982–86), A Guide to DHSS Claims and Appeal (1983);

Recreations travel, hill walking, rock climbing, architecture, politics; *Style—* Mr Nigel Griffiths, JP, MP; ✉ House of Commons, London SW1A 0AA

GRIFFITHS, Prof Paul David; *b* 30 Jan 1953; *Educ* St Bartholomew's Hosp Med Coll London (BSc, MB BS, MD, DSc (Med) 1995), FRCPath 1995; *m* 1979, Brenda, *née* Attenborough; 3 s (Jonathon b 3 Aug 1984, Jamie b 24 May 1986, Ben b 25 Sept 1988); *Career* Fogarty int scholar Birmingham Alabama 1980–81, lectr Virology Dept St Bartholomew's Hosp 1980–82, prof Virology Dept Royal Free Hosp Sch of Med 1982– (currently head of dept); ed-in-chief Reviews in Med Virology, memb editorial bds of 8 other specialist jls, holder of numerous research grant awards, invited lectr at many int meetings, memb numerous ctees (local, nat and int); Ian Howat Prize in Med Microbiology 1975, Wheelwright's Prize for Paediatrics 1977, Lawrence Postgrad Research Scholarship 1979, Wellcome Award for Rapid Viral Diagnosis 1988, William Julius Mickle Fellowship 1991; memberships incl: Soc of Gen Microbiology 1982, RSM 1986, Med Research Club 1988, Euro Gp for Rapid Viral Diagnosis, Br Soc for Antimicrobial Chemotherapy, Int AIDS Soc, Int Soc for Antiviral Research; *Publications* author of over 100 original scientific papers and over 60 book chapters and invited reviews; *Recreations* family, music, bridge; *Style—* Prof Paul D Griffiths; ✉ Department of Virology, Royal Free Hospital School of Medicine, Rowland Hill Street, London NW3 2PF (☎ 0171 794 0500 ext 3210, fax 0171 830 2854)

GRIFFITHS, Peter Anthony; s of Albert Griffiths (d 1981), of Swansea, and Grace, *née* Cousins (d 1962); *b* 19 May 1945; *Educ* Swansea Tech Coll; *m* 29 Oct 1966, Margaret, da of Alan Harris; 2 s (Neil b 9 Oct 1969, Kevin b 17 Aug 1971); *Career* dist administrator Medway Health Authy 1976–81, actg area administrator Kent Health Authy 1981–82, dist gen mangr Lewisham and N Southwark Health Authy 1984–88 (dist administrator 1982–84), regnl gen mangr SE Thames RHA 1988–89, dep chief exec Dept of Health Richmond House London 1989–91, chief exec Guy's and Lewisham NHS Trust London 1991–93, on secondment to Dept of Health 1993, dir King's Fund Mgmnt Coll and dep chief exec King Edward's Hosp Fund for London 1994–; AHSM, AIMgt, memb RSA; *Recreations* golf, reading, gardening; *Style—* Peter Griffiths; ✉ King's Fund Management College, 11–13 Cavendish Square, London W1M 0AN (☎ 0171 307 2400)

GRIFFITHS, Peter Harry Steve; MP (C) Portsmouth North (majority 13,881); s of the late W L Griffiths, of West Bromwich; *b* 24 May 1928; *Educ* West Bromwich GS, City of Leeds Trg Coll, Univ of London, Univ of Birmingham; *m* 1968, Christine Jeannette, *née* Rubery; 1 s (John Paul), 1 da; *Career* former: headmaster, sr lectr, pres Young Cons; alderman Smethwick Borough Cncl 1964–66 (memb 1955–64), MP (C) Smethwick 1964–66, Parly candidate (C) Portsmouth North Feb 1974, MP (C) Portsmouth N 1979–; *Recreations* motoring, camping; *Clubs* Cons, Sloane; *Style—* Peter Griffiths, Esq, MP; ✉ House of Commons, London SW1A 0AA

GRIFFITHS, Peter John; s of Ronald Hugh Griffiths (d 1987), of Sutton, Surrey, and Emily Vera, *née* Cockshutt (d 1980); *b* 19 April 1944; *Educ* Battersea GS, Univ of Leicester (BA), McMaster Univ (MA); *m* 19 Aug 1968 (m dis 1993), Lesley Florence, da of Albert Palmer (d 1963), of Hull; 2 da (Helen b 1969, Clare 1972); *Career* Univ of London: asst to Princ 1968–70, asst sec Ctee of Enquiry into the Governance of Univ of London 1970–72, special duties offr Vice Chllr's Office 1972–78, dep head Legal and Gen Div Court Dept 1978–82, asst clerk of the Ct 1982–85, dep clerk 1985–87, clerk 1987–91, dir of resources and planning 1991–93; sec and chief admin Charing Cross and Westminster Med Sch 1993–; memb Assoc of Heads of UK Univ Administrations; *Recreations* choral singing; *Style—* Peter Griffiths, Esq; ✉ Upland House, Upland Rd, Sutton, Surrey SM2 5HW (☎ 0181 643 3599); Charing Cross and Westminster Medical School, Reynolds Building, St Dunstan's Road, London W6 8RP

GRIFFITHS, Peter John; s of late Rowland Griffiths, of Bradford, Yorks, and Jessie, *née* Wade; *b* 1 May 1937; *Educ* Rotherham Tech Coll, Barnsley Tech Coll (HNC); *m* 5 Aug 1961, Sheena Anne Margaret, da of late Thomas Bretherton; 2 da (Ailsa Jane b 22 July 1965, Claire Fiona b 9 Aug 1967); *Career* Nat Serv Capt RE 1958–60; Parkgate Iron and Steel Co Ltd: tech apprentice 1954–58, designer steel works 1960–66, project engr 1966–68; divnl project engr BSC 1968–69; Engineering Industry Training Board: advsr 1969–76, mangr Midlands 1976–86, dir trg ops 1986–91; dir and chief exec Engineering Construction Industry Training Board 1991–; Freeman City of London; CEng, MIPM, MIMechE; *Recreations* badminton, golf; *Style—* Peter Griffiths, Esq; ✉ Engineering Construction Industry Training Board, Blue Court, Church Lane, Kings Langley, Herts WD4 8JP (☎ 01923 270612, fax 01923 270969)

GRIFFITHS, Peter Kevin; s of Denis Griffiths, of Cardiff, and Elsie Joyce, *née* Linck; *b* 15 Oct 1956; *Educ* Llanishen HS Cardiff, Univ Coll Cardiff (BA); *Career* studio mangr BBC 1978; prodr Radio 4: Womans Hour 1981–82, Features Dept 1982–83, presentation 1983–85, Network Features Dept Manchester 1985; sr prodr sport and outside bdcasts Radio 4 and 2 1985–90, sr prodr Features and Arts for Radio 4 and Radio 5 1990–, prodn consit to S African campaign for adult educn and estab radio network to offer opportunities for educn 1994–95; memb Radio Acad; *Recreations* music, friends; *Style—* Peter Griffiths, Esq; ✉ British Broadcasting Corporation, Broadcasting House, Portland Place, London W1A 1AA (☎ 0171 765 5180, fax 0171 765 3340)

GRIFFITHS, Peter Robert; s of Robert Amos Griffiths (d 1988), of Long Ridges, Shotover, Oxford, and Grace Margaret, *née* Wilson; *b* 1 Aug 1953; *Educ* Repton, St Catharine's Coll Cambridge (MA); *m* 11 Dec 1981, (Julie) Marguerite, da of Hyltje Andrew Kamstra (d 1993), of Beverley, Humberside; 3 da (Victoria b 1983, Catharine b 1985, Sarah b 1988); *Career* Lt Inns of Court and City Yeomanry 1981; called to the Bar Inner Temple 1977, joined chambers of T P E Curry, QC 1978; Freeman City of London 1985, Liveryman Worshipful Co of Merchant Taylors 1985; *Books* Atkins Court Forms (companies winding up, 1989), The Encyclopaedia of Forms and Precedents (Companies) (1993); *Recreations* walking; *Clubs* Hurlingham; *Style—* Peter Griffiths, Esq; ✉ 4 Stone Buildings, Lincoln's Inn, London WC2A 3XT (☎ 0171 242 5524, fax 0171 831 7907)

GRIFFITHS, Prof (Allen) Phillips; s of John Phillips Griffiths (d 1941), of Cardiff, and Elsie Maud, *née* Jones (d 1975); *b* 11 June 1927; *Educ* Univ Coll Cardiff (BA), Univ Coll Oxford (BPhil); *m* 1, 6 June 1948, Margaret (d 1974), da of John Henry Joseph Lock (d 1974); 1 s (John Benedict Phillips b 1960), 1 da (Sarah Katharine Phillips b 1961); m 2, 21 April 1984 (m dis 1990), Vera Clare, da of Patrick Dunphy; *Career* Sgt Intelligence Corps 1945–48 (despatches); lectr: Univ of Wales 1954–56, Birkbeck Coll London 1956–65; pro vice chllr Univ of Warwick 1970–76 (prof of philosophy 1965–92, prof emeritus 1992); visiting prof: Swarthmore Coll Pa USA 1963, Univ of California 1967, Univ of Wisconsin 1965 and 1970, Carlton Coll Minnesota 1985; dir Royal Inst of Philosophy 1979–94; hon fell Univ Coll Cardiff 1984; Queen's Jubilee medal 1977; *Books* Knowledge and Belief (ed, 1967), Of Liberty (1983), Philosophy and Literature (1984), Philosophy and Practice (1985), Contemporary French Philosophy (1988), Philosophical Themes (1989), and numerous articles in philosophical journals; *Style—* Prof Phillips Griffiths; ✉ c/o Department of Philosophy, University of Warwick, Coventry CV4 7AL (☎ 01203 523421)

GRIFFITHS, (William) Robert; QC (1993); s of the late William John Griffiths, of Haverfordwest, Dyfed, and Marjorie Megan, *née* Green; *b* 24 Sept 1948; *Educ* Haverfordwest GS, St Edmund Hall Oxford (open scholar, BA, BCL, MA); *m* 10 March 1984, Angela May, da of Robert Victor Crawford, of Manchester; 1 s (Charles William Alexander b 13 March 1991), 2 da (Anna-Victoria Sophia b 7 Oct 1986, Helena Elizabeth Rose b 13 Sept 1989); *Career* called to the Bar Middle Temple 1974, jr counsel to the Crown (common law) 1989–93; memb: Hon Soc of the Middle Temple, Hon Soc of the Cymmrodorion; *Recreations* reading, collecting modern first editions, cricket, playing tennis; *Clubs* MCC (memb Estates sub-ctee 1996–), Lord's Taverners'; *Style—* Robert Griffiths, Esq, QC; ✉ 4–5 Gray's Inn Square, Gray's Inn, London WC1R 5AY (☎ 0171 404 5252, fax 0171 242 7803)

GRIFFITHS, Robin John; s of David Gromweigh Morgan Griffiths, and Elizabeth Hope, *née* Limbert; *b* 15 Dec 1942; *Educ* Bedford Sch, Univ of Nottingham (BA); *m* 6 Jan 1968 (m dis 1995), Esme Georgina (Gina), da of Willim Hunter (d 1967); 4 s (Mark David b 24 Sept 1971, Paul Robin b 6 Sept 1974, David James b 4 Aug 1977, Andrew William b 29 Nov 1979); *Career* Phillips & Drew 1964–68, ptnr Grieveson Grant 1968–84 (formerly Carr Sebag, previously W I Carr), sr exec James Capel 1986– (currently on secondment to New York office); dir Int Fedn of Tech Analysts (former chm); memb Nippon Tech Analysts Assoc; author and fndr The Amateur Chartist Newsletter; sailed the Atlantic with Robin Knox Johnston setting a Br record at the time; memb: Stock Exchange 1971, FIMBRA 1987; fell Soc of Technical Analysts (former chm); *Recreations* sailing, skiing; *Style—* Robin Griffiths, Esq; ✉ HSBC James Capel, Thames Exchange, 10 Queen Street Place, London EC4R 1BL

GRIFFITHS, Prof Roderic Keith; s of Thomas Hughes Griffiths, and Olwen Gladys Jackson Griffiths; *b* 12 April 1945; *Educ* Bristol GS, Univ of Birmingham (BSc, MB ChB, Russell Meml Prize), FFPHM, FRCP; *m* 1, Margaret Susan Ash; 2 da (Tami, Sara), 1 s (Denzil); m 2, Lois May Parker; *Career* former basic sci research Dept of Anatomy then lectr in public health Univ of Birmingham, memb then chm Central Birmingham Community Health Cncl 1975–81, chm Assoc of Community Health Cncls for England and Wales 1979–91 (vice chm 1977–79), dir of public health Central Birmingham 1982–90; Univ of Birmingham: prof of public health 1990–96, prof of public health practice 1996–; dir of public health W Midlands RHA 1993–; memb CMO's Enquiry into the Public Health Function (Acheson Ctee) 1986–88; published and lectured widely on public health in the NHS; vice chm Faculty of Public Health Med 1992–95; King's Fund Prize for Public Health Reports; memb Lunar Soc; *Recreations* making wheel-thrown pots, skiing, surfing, very occasionally sailing; *Style—* Prof Roderic Griffith; ✉ NHS Executive, West Midlands Regional Office, Barthlomew House, 142 Hagley Road, Birmingham B16 9PA (☎ 0121 224 4607, fax 0121 224 4680)

GRIFFITHS, Roger; s of William Thomas Griffiths (d 1979), of Barry, S Wales, and Annie Evelyn, *née* Hill; *b* 25 Dec 1931; *Educ* Lancing, King's Coll Cambridge (BA, MA), New Coll Oxford (BA, MA, DipEd); *m* 2 April 1966, Diana, da of Capt John Frederick Beaufoy Brown, OBE, DSC, RN (d 1979), of Burgess Hill, Sussex; 3 da (Elizabeth b 1966, Helen b 1968, Caroline b 1970); *Career* asst master Charterhouse 1956–64, headmaster Hurstpierpoint Coll 1964–86, sec HMC 1986–, dep sec SHA 1986–90; JP Mid Sussex Bench 1976–86, memb Mgmnt Ctee Pallant House Chichester 1987–92; govr: Mill Hill Sch 1987–92, Tormead Sch Guildford 1987–94, Prebendal Sch Chichester 1987–, Worth Sch 1990–; Freeman City of London 1970, memb Ct of Assts Worshipful Co of Wax Chandlers (Master 1990–91); *Recreations* music, theatre, bowls, gardening; *Clubs* East India, Devonshire Sport, Public Schools, Sussex; *Style—* Roger Griffiths, Esq; ✉ Hanbury Cottage, Cocking, Midhurst, W Sussex GU29 0HF (☎ 01730 813503); The Headmasters' Conference, 1 Russell House, Bepton Road, Midhurst, W Sussex GU29 9NB (☎ 01730 815635, fax 01730 815225)

GRIFFITHS, Dr Siân Meryl; da of John Daniel Griffiths, of London, and Rosemary, *née* Quick; *b* 20 March 1952; *Educ* N London Collegiate, Univ of Cambridge (MA), King's Coll Hosp Med Sch (MB BCh), Univ of London (MSc); *m* 1, 1978 (m dis 1986), Anthony Chu; 2 da (Jessica b 1979, Alexandra b 1980); m 2, 1987, Ian Wylie; 1 s (Sam b 1987); *Career* jr doctor 1977–80, trainee in public health med 1981–85, conslt in public health/dist med offr City of Hackney DHA 1985–87, conslt in public health Oxford RHA 1988–90, regnl dir of public health SW Thames RHA 1990–94, dir of public health and health policy Oxfordshire Health Authy 1994–; hon sr lectr: St George's Hosp Med Sch Univ of London 1990–94, Dept of Public Health and Primary Care Univ of Oxford 1995–; treas Faculty of Public Health Med 1995–; co-chair Assoc of Public Health 1995–; memb: BMA, RSM, Med Women's Fedn; FFPHM; *Recreations* family, film; *Style—* Dr Siân Griffiths; ✉ 39 Leckford Road, Oxford OX2 6HY; Oxfordshire Health, Richards Building, Old Road, Headington, Oxford OX3 7LG (☎ 01865 226626, fax 01865 2266894)

GRIFFITHS, Stephen Gareth (Steve); s of Dr Thomas Edwin Teasdale Griffiths (d 1984), and Kathleen Isobel Maxwell (d 1989); *b* 2 Feb 1949; *Educ* Ysgol Syr Thomas Jones Amlwch Ynys Môn, Churchill Coll Cambridge (BA); *m* 25 March 1978, Lala Isla, da of Alfredo Isla Garcia, of Madrid; 1 s (Pablo Siôn Isla Griffiths b 20 July 1979); *Career* poet, social policy specialist; work published in many magazines incl: Stand, Poetry Wales, Poetry Review, Literary Review, Radical Wales, Pivot (NY), Tribune, 2Plus2 (Geneva), New Welsh Review, La Traductière (Paris); poetry readings in Britain, France, Spain and USA, various BBC broadcasts; fndr memb Welsh Union of Writers 1983, memb Exec Academi Gymreig (Eng Language Section Welsh Acad) 1989–95; *Publications* The Green Horse (contrib, 1978), Anglesey Material (1980), Anglo-Welsh Poetry 1480–1980 (contrib, 1984), Civilised Airs (1984), Uncontrollable Fields (1990), Poetry Book Society Anthology (contrib, 1990), The Bright Field (contemporary poetry from Wales, contrib 1991), Selected Poems (1993); numerous pubns in social policy field on poverty and social security incl Supporting Community Care: the Contribution of Housing Benefit (Nat Inst for Social Work, 1995); *Recreations* finding space and silence, eating and drinking, music, film; *Style—* Steve Griffiths; ✉ 3 John Campbell Road, London N16 8JY (☎ and fax 0171 249 9890)

GRIFFITHS, Trevor; s of Ernest Griffiths (d 1961), of Manchester, and Ann Veronica, *née* Connor (d 1976); *b* 4 April 1935; *Educ* St Bede's Coll Manchester, Univ of Manchester (BA); *m* 1, 13 March 1960, Janice Stansfield (d 1977); 1 s (Joss b 1968), 2 da (Sian b 1965, Emma b 1967); m 2, 6 June 1992, Gillian Cliff; *Career* playwright; work incl: The Wages of Thin (first prodn Stables Theatre Manchester 1969), The Big House (1972, BBC Radio 4 1969), Occupations (1980, Stables Theatre Manchester 1970), Lay By (jtly 1971, Traverse Theatre Edinburgh), Apricots (1978, Basement Theatre London 1971), Thermidor (1978, Edinburgh Festival 1971), Sam, Sam (1972, Open Space 1972), The Party (1974, NT 1973), All Good Men and Absolute Beginners (1977, BBC TV 1974), Comedians (1976, Nottingham 1975), Through The Night and Such Impossibilities (1977, BBC TV 1975), Bill Brand (Thames TV 1976), The Cherry Orchard (new Eng version 1978, Nottingham Playhouse 1977), Deeds (jtly, Nottingham Playhouse 1978), Sons and Lovers (1982, BBC TV 1981), Country (1981, BBC TV 1981), Reds (jtly with Warren Beatty, 1981), Oi For England (1982, Central TV 1982), The Last Place on Earth (Central TV 1985), published as Judgement Over The Dead 1986, Real Dreams (1987, Williamstown Theatre Festival 1984), Fatherland (1987), Collected Plays for Television (1988), Piano (1990, NT 1990), The Gulf Between Us (West Yorkshire Playhouse Leeds, 1992), Thatcher's Children (Bristol Old Vic 1993), Hope in the Year Two (1994, BBC TV 1994), Who Shall Be Happy....? (stage version of Hope in the Year Two, Belfast Festival 1995); memb: The Reality Club (USA), Charter '88 (fndr memb), Theatre Writers' Union, Writers' Guild of America (West); *Recreations* chess, bridge, music, photography; *Style—* Trevor Griffiths; ✉ c/o Peters Fraser & Dunlop, 503/4, The Chambers, Chelsea Harbour, Lots Rd, London SW10 0XF (☎ 0171 376 7676, fax 0171 351 1756)

GRIFFITHS, Trevor Thomas; s of Charles Griffiths (d 1973), of Cardiff, and Lilian, *née* Ray; *b* 3 Oct 1943; *Educ* Univ of Wales Cardiff (BDS, LLM), Dip in Gen Dental Practice; *m* Meifis, *née* Howell; 1 s (Elis b 29 April 1980); *Career* resident HO and SHO Morriston then SHO Cardiff Dental Hosp 1968–70, asst lectr and hon registrar Univ of

Wales Dental Sch 1970–73, dental practitioner Cardigan 1974–95; memb and past chm: local and dist dental ctees, Welsh Dental Ctee; memb Welsh Cncl BDA, elected memb for Wales GDC, elected diplomat Faculty of Gen Dental Practitioners 1992; memb Cardigan Town Cncl; *Recreations* Cardigan Town Brass Band (tuba), Cantorian Teify (bass); *Style*— Trevor Griffiths, Esq; ✉ Old Rectory, Llangoedmor, Cardigan, Ceredigion SA43 2LH (☎ 01239 613699, fax 01239 613699)

GRIFFITHS, Winston James (Win); MP (Lab) Bridgend (majority 7,326); s of late Evan George Griffiths and late Rachel Elizabeth Griffiths; *b* 11 Feb 1943; *Educ* Brecon Boys' GS, Univ Coll Cardiff; *m* 22 Aug 1966, Elizabeth Ceri, *née* Gravell; 1 s, 1 da; *Career* teacher: Mzumbe Secdy Sch Tanzania (educn offr) 1966–68, George Dixon Boys' GS 1969–70, Barry Boys' Comprehensive Sch 1970–76; head History Dept Cowbridge Comprehensive Sch 1976–79; memb Vale of Glamorgan BC (chm Leisure Servs Ctee) 1973–76, memb St Andrew's Major Community Cncl 1974–79; MEP (Lab) South Wales 1979–89 (vice pres Euro Parliament 1984–87), MP (Lab) Bridgend 1987–; memb Select Ctee on Educn, Sci and Arts 1987–90, chm PLP Educn, Arts and Sci Ctee 1988–90; an oppn spokesman on: Environment 1990–92, Educn 1992–94 (Environment 1990–92), Wales 1994–; sec All Party: East African Gp, Tanzania Gp; memb Ct of Govrs Univ Coll Cardiff 1981–; *Recreations* reading, formerly running, cultivating pot plants; *Style*— Win Griffiths, Esq, MP; ✉ House of Commons, London SW1A 0AA (☎ 0171 219 4461)

GRIFFITHS OF FFORESTFACH, Baron (Life Peer UK 1991), of Fforestfach in the County of West Glamorgan; Brian Griffiths; s of Ivor Winston Griffiths and Phyllis Mary, *née* Morgan; *b* 27 Dec 1941; *Educ* Dynevor GS, LSE (BSc, MSc); *m* 18 Sept 1965, Rachel Jane, da of Howard Jones; 1 s (Hon James Brian b 1970), 2 da (Hon Aeronwen Jane b 1968, Hon Owenna Mary Ruth b 1973); *Career* lectr in economics LSE 1968–76 (asst lectr 1965–68), prof of banking and int fin City Univ 1977–85, dir Centre for Banking and Int Finance 1977–82, dean Business Sch City Univ 1982–85, visiting prof Rochester Univ USA 1972–73, prof of ethics Gresham Coll 1984–87, dir Bank of England 1984–86, head of Prime Minister's Policy Unit (Rt Hon Margaret Thatcher) 1985–90; int advsr and vice chm Goldman Sachs (Europe) 1991–; non-exec dir: Times Newspapers, THORN EMI plc until 1996, Herman Miller, Service Master, Telewest Communications plc, Tarmac Service Master; chm Sch Examinations and Assessment Cncl 1991–93; *Books* The Creation of Wealth (1984), Morality and the Market Place (1989); *Clubs* Garrick; *Style*— The Rt Hon Lord Griffiths of Fforestfach; ✉ c/o House of Lords, London SW1A OPW

GRIGG, Hon Anthony Ulick David Dundas; yr s of 1 Baron Altrincham, KCMG, KCVO, DSO, MC, PC (d 1955), and hp to Barony of bro, John Edward Poynder Grigg, *qv* (2 Baron, who disclaimed Peerage for life 1963); *b* 12 Jan 1934; *Educ* Eton, New Coll Oxford; *m* 1965, Eliane, da of the Marquis de Miramon; 2 s (Sebastian b 1965, Steven b 1969), 1 da (Casilda b 1967); *Style*— The Hon Anthony Grigg; ✉ 11 Horbury Mews, London W11 3NL (☎ and fax 0171 229 6005)

GRIGG, John Edward Poynder; s of 1 Baron Altrincham, PC, KCMG, KCVO, DSO, MC (d 1955), and Hon Joan Dickson-Poynder, da of 1 Baron Islington; disclaimed Barony for life 1963; *b* 15 April 1924; *Educ* Eton, New Coll Oxford; *m* 1958, Patricia, da of Harold Campbell, CBE, of Belfast; 2 adopted s (Alexander b 1966, Edward b 1969); *Heir* bro, Hon Anthony Grigg, *qv*; *Career* served WWII Lt Grenadier Gds; Parly candidate (C) Oldham W 1951 and 1955; journalist; ed Nat and English Review 1954–60, columnist The Guardian 1960–70, on staff The Times 1986–93; chm London Library 1985–91; FRSL; *Books* Two Anglican Essays, The Young Lloyd George, Lloyd George - The People's Champion (Whitbread award, 1943), 1943 - The Victory That Never Was, Nancy Astor - Portrait of a Pioneer, Lloyd George - From Peace to War (Wolfson award), The Thomson Years, Vol VI in The History of The Times (1993); *Style*— John Grigg; ✉ 32 Dartmouth Row, London SE10 (☎ and fax 0181 692 4973)

GRIGGS, Rt Rev Ian Macdonald; s of Donald Nicholson Griggs (d 1967), of Gt Easton, Essex, and Agnes Elizabeth, *née* Brown (d 1994); *b* 17 May 1928; *Educ* Brentwood Sch, Trinity Hall Cambridge (BA, MA), Westcott House Cambridge; *m* 29 Aug 1953, Patricia Margaret, da of Ernest Charles Medland Vernon-Browne (d 1974), of Lindfield, Sussex; 3 s (Alistair b 1954, Mark b and d 1957, Julian b 1964), 3 da (Clare b 1956, Helen b 1959, Hilary b 1962); *Career* served Essex Regt 1947–49; ordained: deacon 1954, priest 1955; asst curate St Cuthbert Portsmouth 1954–59, domestic chaplain to Bishop of Sheffield 1959–64, diocesan youth chaplain Sheffield 1959–64, vicar of St Cuthbert Firvale Sheffield 1964–71, vicar of Kidderminster 1971–83, hon canon Worcs 1977–84, archdeacon of Ludlow 1984–87, priest-in-charge St Michael's Tenbury 1984–87, bishop of Ludlow 1987–94; memb Gen Synod 1984–87; hon asst bishop Dio of Carlisle 1994–; govr: Bedstone Coll 1987–93, Atlantic Coll 1988–; chm: Churches Cncl for Health and Healing 1990–, Coll of Ascension Selly Oak 1992–94; *Recreations* mountaineering, hill-walking; *Style*— The Rt Rev Ian Griggs; ✉ Rookings, Patterdale, Penrith, Cumbria CA11 0NP (☎ 017684 82064)

GRIGGS, His Hon Judge; Jeremy David; s of Celadon Augustine Griggs, of Elm Tree Farm, East Brent, Highbridge, Somerset, and Ethel Mary (Maisie), *née* Anderson (d 1996); *b* 5 Feb 1945; *Educ* St Edward's Sch Oxford, Magdalene Coll Cambridge (MA); *m* 1, 1971 (m dis 1982), Wendy Anne Russell, *née* Culham; 2 s (Christopher b 1972, Tom b 1974), 1 da (Beth b 1976); m 2, 7 Sept 1985, Patricia Ann (the actress Patricia Maynard), da of Thomas Maynard (d 1991); 2 step da (Hannah Waterman b 1975, Julia Waterman b 1979); *Career* called to the Bar Inner Temple 1968, memb Western Circuit, recorder of the Crown Court 1990–95, circuit judge (Western Circuit) 1995–; Bar's rep CCBE 1990–94, vice chm Br Romanian Legal Assoc 1991–; chm London Choral Soc 1986–90; *Recreations* playing the piano, sailing in wayfarer dinghy, walking on Dartmoor; *Clubs* Royal Western Yacht; *Style*— His Hon Judge Griggs; ✉ Exeter Combined Court Centre, The Castle, Exeter EX4 3TH

GRIGGS, Patrick John Spear; s of John Garson Romeril Griggs (d 1987), of Jersey, CI, and Inez Frances, *née* Cole; *b* 9 Aug 1939; *Educ* Stowe, Tours Univ France, Law Soc Sch of Law London; *m* 4 April 1964, Marian Patricia, da of John Pryor Birch, of Mere, Wilts; 3 s (Simon Richard b 1967, Edward John b 1969, William Robert b 1972); *Career* slr 1963; Ince and Co: joined 1958, ptnr 1966, sr ptnr 1989–95, conslt 1995–; sec and hon treas Br Maritime Law Assoc 1995–, vice pres Comité Maritime Int 1996–; Stanford Rivers parish cncllr; Freeman City of London; *Books* Limitation of Liability for Maritime Claims (jtly, 1987, 2 edn 1991); *Recreations* tennis, skiing, walking, cycling, golf; *Clubs* City of London; *Style*— Patrick Griggs, Esq; ✉ British Maritime Law Association, Knollys Ho, 11 Byward Street, London EC3 (☎ 0171 972 6223)

GRIGGS, Roy; s of Norman Edward Griggs, CBE, of 5 Gledhow Gardens, London SW5, and Livia Lavinia, *née* Levi; *b* 26 April 1950; *Educ* Westminster, Univ of Bristol (LLB); *m* 4 Jan 1975, Anita Gwendolyn, da of Humphrey Osmond Nunes (d 1972); 4 da (Flavia b 1979, Eleanor b 1982, Cordelia b 1986, Marina b 1989); *Career* slr: Norton Rose Botterell and Roche 1975–84 (seconded to Hong Kong office 1981–83), Cameron Markby Hewitt 1984– (ptnr 1985); memb City of London Slrs' Co; memb Law Soc; *Recreations* bridge, sailing, opera, skiing; *Clubs* Itchenor Sailing; *Style*— Roy Griggs, Esq; ✉ 2 Brechin Place, London SW7 4QA; Cameron Markby Hewitt, Sceptre Court, 40 Tower Hill, London EC3 (☎ 0171 702 2345, fax 0171 702 2303)

GRIGGS, Susan Hunter; da of Paul Wylie Hunter (d 1970), and Isabel, *née* Strong (d 1993), step da of John Cushman Fistere (d 1986); *b* 26 Nov 1934; *Educ* Staples HS Westport Connecticut, Abbot Acad Andover Mass, Smith Coll Northampton Mass, Universita di Firenze Florence, Beirut Coll for Women (BA); *m* 1959 (m dis 1963), Northam Lee Griggs, Jr; *Career* jr asst Art Dept Fortune Magazine NYC 1957–59, American Heritage Publishers NYC 1963–65 (picture librarian later picture ed Carousel series of illustrated books for children), picture ed Weekend Telegraph (London Telegraph Magazine) 1965–68, fndr proprietor The Susan Griggs Agency London (representing freelance photographers in UK and abroad for cmmnd work and stock picture sales) 1968–94; chm Ctee on Photographic Copyright 1974–88 (lobbied successfully for changes in the 1988 Copyright Act), chm Br Photographers Liaison Ctee 1988–90; hon memb: Assoc of Photographers (first non-photographer memb), Br Assoc of Picture Libraries and Agencies (fndr memb); *Recreations* books, films, theatre, galleries, travel, beach walking, friends; *Style*— Ms Susan Griggs; ✉ 17 De Vere Gardens, London W8 5AN (☎ 0171 937 0848)

GRIGSON, Dr Caroline; da of Geoffrey Edward Harvey Grigson (d 1985), of Broad Town, Wiltshire, and Frances Franklin, *née* Galt (d 1937); *b* 7 March 1935; *Educ* Dartington Hall Sch, UCL (BSc), Inst of Archaeology London (PhD); *m* 18 Sept 1961, Colin Banks, *qv*, s of William James Banks (d 1985), of Faversham, Kent; 1 s (Joseph Caxton b 1967), 1 da (Frances Jenny Harriet b 1964, d 1978); *Career* archaeozoologist; RCS: asst curator Odontological Museum 1973–87, Osman Hill curator Odontological Museum 1987–, asst conservator of the museums 1991–, princ curator of the museums 1996–; author of numerous scientific papers incl many on animal remains from archaeological sites in Br and the Near E and some on the Piltdown scandal; fndr memb Cncl of the Int Cncl for Archaeozoology (ICAZ); memb Cncl: Br Inst in Amman, Br Sch of Archaeology Jerusalem, Wainwright Fund; co-organiser Fourth Int Conf in Archaeozoology Univ of London 1982; organiser Aims in Archaeozoology London Univ Inst of Archaeology 1985; former govr Kidbrooke Comprehensive Sch; hon fell Inst of Archaeology 1996; memb: Prehistoric Soc, Assoc for Environmental Archaeology (AEA), Museums Assoc; FSA 1982; *Books* co-ed: Ageing and Sexing Animal Bones from Archaeological Sites (1982), Animals and Archaeology (4 vols, 1983 and 1984); Colyer's Variations and Diseases of the Teeth of Animals (jtly, 1990); *Recreations* excavation, travelling, gardening; *Style*— Dr Caroline Grigson, FSA; ✉ The Museums, Royal College of Surgeons of England, 35–43 Lincoln's Inn Fields, London WC2A 3PN (☎ 0171 937 2188 ext 3020, fax 0171 831 9438)

GRIGSON, Hester Sophia Frances (Sophie); da of Geoffrey Edward Harvey Grigson (d 1985), of Broad Town, Swindon, Wilts, and Jane, *née* McIntire (d 1990); *b* 19 June 1959; *Educ* Oxford HS, UMIST (BSc); *m* 19 June 1992, William Black, s of Brian Black; 1 da, 1 s; *Career* freelance food writer and broadcaster; cookery correspondent: Evening Standard 1986–93, Sunday Express Magazine 1988–91, Independent 1993–94, Sunday Times Magazine 1994–96; contrib various magazines, newspapers and radio progs incl Curious Cooks (Radio 4) 1994; own TV shows: Grow Your Greens/Eat Your Greens (Ch4) 1993, Travels à la Carte (with William Black, Ch4) 1994, Sophie's Meat Course (Ch4) 1995; Food Writer of the Year (Restauranteur Assoc of GB) 1992, Caroline Walker Award (Media) 1994; memb Guild of Food Writers; *Books* Food for Friends, Sophie's Table, Sophie Grigson's Ingredients Book, The Students' Cook Book, Eat Your Greens, The Carved Angel Cook Book (with Joyce Molyneux), Travels à la Carte (with William Black), Sophie Grigson's Meat Course; *Style*— Ms Sophie Grigson; ✉ c/o David Higham Associates, 5–8 Lower John Street, Gold Square, London W1R 4HA

GRILLS, District Judge; Michael Geoffrey; *b* 23 Feb 1937; *Educ* Royal GS Lancaster, Merton Coll Oxford (MA); *m* 1969, Ann Margaret Irene; 2 da (Alison, Victoria); *Career* ptnr Crombies, slr York 1965–73, dist registrar York and Harrogate 1973–90; recorder Crown Ct on N Eastern Circuit 1982–, district judge 1990–; *Recreations* tennis, music, skiing; *Style*— District Judge Grills; ✉ Aldwark House, Aldwark, off Goodramgate, York (☎ 01904 629935)

GRIMA, George Peter; s of John Grima (d 1945), and Leopolda, *née* Farnese (d 1984); *b* 31 July 1929; *Educ* St Joseph's Coll Beulah Hill, Northern Poly London (DipArch); *m* 14 Dec 1978, Christina Mary, da of Col Leslie Wright, TD, DL, of Bakewell, Derbyshire; *Career* Nat Serv RE 1955–57; architect; worked for Raymond Erith on reconstruction of 10, 11 and 12 Downing St 1960; ptnr with bro Godfrey in Grima 1962–78; work incl: commercial centre Pomezia Rome 1970, ski resort Grimentz Val d'Anniviers Valais Switzerland 1972, jewellery shops for bro Andrew in London, Zurich, Sydney; private practice 1979–; projects incl: Warwick Town Cncl, Archdiocese of Birmingham, Restoration of Clifford Manor, Coventry City Cncl Stratford on Avon DC, new house for Ms J Smith-Ryland; Royal Acad exhibitor 1970; ARIBA; *Recreations* gardening, antiquarian books, skiing, tennis; *Style*— George Grima, Esq; ✉ 33 Watery Lane, Sherbourne, Warwick CV35 8AL (☎ 01926 624 794)

GRIMALDI, Dr Barry; s of Angelo Grimaldi (d 1988), and Dorothy, *née* Coppola; *b* 10 Sept 1947; *Educ* Emanuel Sch, St Bartholomew's Hosp Med Sch and Univ of London (MB BS); *m* (m dis); *Career* RMO The London Clinic 1972–73, registrar in cardiology St Bartholomew's Hosp 1973, in private Gen Practice 1973–; med advsr Sports Cncl Working Party 1988, MRCS 1971, LRCP 1971, MRCP 1973, memb RSM 1986; *Publications* author of papers on med diagnosis and screening, and dance medicine; *Recreations* Renaissance art, the oboe, riding, sky diving; *Clubs* Leander, Groucho's; *Style*— Dr Barry Grimaldi; ✉ 49 Harley House, Marylebone Rd, London NW1 5HG (☎ 0171 637 7989, fax 0171 935 0406)

GRIMBLE, Prof Michael John; s of Reginald William Parsons, of Truro, Cornwall, and Queenie Pearson; *b* 30 Oct 1943; *Educ* Rugby Coll of Engrg Technol (BSc), Imperial Coll London (PhD), Univ of Birmingham (MSc, DSc), Open Univ (BA); *m* 30 July 1966, Wendy, da of Noel Huntley (d 1975), of Grimsby; 1 s (Andrew Michael b 1977), 1 da (Claire Louise b 1975); *Career* sr engr GEC Electrical Projects 1971–75, reader in control engrg Sheffield City Poly 1975–81, prof of industl systems and dir Industrial Control Centre Univ of Strathclyde 1981–; tech dir Industl Systems and Control Ltd 1987–, dir DTI Industl Club on Advanced Control Technol; over 150 papers on control systems engrg and estimation theory; chm: Control Applications Conf Glasgow IEEE 1994, Working Gp on Adaptive Systems IFAC; FIEE 1981, FIMA 1982, FIEEE 1993, FInstMC 1990; *Books* Control Systems Design II, Inst Measurement and Control (with M A Johnson and D H Owens, 1986), Optimal Control and Stochastic Estimation Vols I and II (with M A Johnson, 1988), Robust Industrial Control: Optimal Design Approach for Polynomial Systems, Prentice Hall International Series on Systems and Control Engineering (ed), Prentice Hall International Series on Signal Processing (ed), Springer Verlag Series on Industrial Control (ed); *Recreations* reading, theatre, time with family, country walks; *Style*— Prof Michael Grimble; ✉ Industrial Control Centre, University of Strathclyde, Graham Hills Building, 50 George St, Glasgow G1 1QE (☎ 0141 552 4400, fax 0141 553 1232, telex 77472 UNSLIB G)

GRIME, Geoffrey John; s of Sqdn Ldr John Frederic Grime, DFC, of Blackpool, Lancs, and José Thompson, *née* Bennett; *b* 7 Feb 1947; *Educ* Sedbergh; *m* 19 June 1971, Margaret Joyce, da of Stanley Hamilton Russell, of St Helier, Jersey; 1 s (Charles b 1975), 1 da (Caroline b 1973); *Career* Coopers & Lybrand: joined 1969, ptnr 1972–, sr ptnr 1990–; chm Abacus Financial Services Ltd 1995–; hon treas: Br Heart Fndn Jersey until 1987, Jersey Arts Cncl until 1985, Jersey Church Schs Soc 1987–; Freeman: City of London 1975, Worshipful Co of Musicians 1977; FCA 1969; *Recreations* veteran and vintage cars; *Clubs* Brooks's, Victoria (Jersey), United (Jersey), Muthaiga (Nairobi); *Style*— Geoffrey Grime, Esq; ✉ Pine Farm, Rue Des Landes, St Mary, Jersey, Channel Islands JE3 3EE (☎ 01534 863840); La Motte Chambers, St Helier Jersey, Channel Islands JE1 1BJ (☎ 01534 602000, fax 01534 602002, telex 4192231)

GRIME, Mark Stephen Eastburn; QC (1987); s of Roland Thompson, and late Mary Diana, *née* Eastburn, of Morfa Nefyn; *b* 16 March 1948; *Educ* Wrekin Coll, Trinity Coll Oxford (Scholar, MA); *m* 29 July 1973, Christine, da of J H A Emck, of West Wittering, Sussex; 2 da (Eleanor b 1977, Isabel b 1981); *Career* called to the Bar Middle Temple 1970, Northern Circuit 1970–, recorder 1990–; chm: Disciplinary Appeal Tbnl UMIST 1980–, Northern Arbitration Assoc 1994– (memb Cncl 1990–); FCIArb 1996; *Recreations* antiquarian horology, sailing; *Style*— Stephen Grime, Esq, QC; ✉ Deans Court Chambers, Cumberland House, Crown Square, Manchester M3 3HA (☎ 0161 834 4097, 07000 444873, fax 0161 834 4805)

GRIMLEY EVANS, Prof John; s of Harry Walter Grimley Evans (d 1972), of Birmingham, and Violet Prenter, *née* Walker (d 1976); *b* 17 Sept 1936; *Educ* King Edward's Sch Birmingham, St John's Coll Cambridge (MA, MD), Balliol Coll Oxford (MA, DM); *m* 25 March 1966, Corinne Jane, da of Leslie Bernard Cavender (d 1947), of Edenbridge, Kent; 2 s (Edmund, Piers), 1 da (Freya); *Career* res fell Med Unit Wellington NZ 1966–69, lectr London Sch of Hygiene and Tropical Med 1969–71, conslt physician Newcastle Health Authy 1971–73, prof of med (geriatrics) Univ of Newcastle upon Tyne 1973–84, prof of geriatric med Oxford Univ 1985– (fell Green Coll 1985–), conslt physician Univ of Oxford; ed Age and Ageing 1988–95; chm: Geriatric Med Ctee Royal Coll of Physicians 1985–94, Health Servs Res Ctee MRC 1989–92, Health Servs and Public Health Res Bd MRC 1992–94; vice-pres RCP 1993–95 (censor 1991–92); memb: MRC 1992–95, GMC 1994–; FSS 1970, FRCP 1976, FFPHM 1980; *Books* Care of the Elderly (jtly, 1977), Advanced Geriatric Medicine (jtly, 1981–88), Improving the Health of Older People - A World View (jtly, 1990), Oxford Textbook of Geriatric Medicine (jtly, 1992); *Recreations* fly-fishing, photography; *Clubs* RSM; *Style*— Prof John Grimley Evans; ✉ Department of Clinical Geratology, Radcliffe Infirmary, Oxford

GRIMMETT, Prof Geoffrey Richard; s of Benjamin John Grimmett, of Birmingham, and Patricia Winifred, *née* Lewis; *b* 20 Dec 1950; *Educ* King Edward's Sch Birmingham, Univ of Oxford (MA, MSc, DPhil), Merton Coll Cambridge (postmaster); *m* 2 Sept 1986, Rosine, da of Pierre Bonay; 1 s (Hugo b 16 May 1989); *Career* IBM res fell Univ of Oxford and New Coll Oxford 1974–76, prof of mathematics Univ of Bristol 1989–92 (lectr 1976, reader 1985), prof of mathematical statistics Univ of Cambridge 1992–; visiting prof: Cornell Univ, Univ of Arizona, Univ of Rome, Univ of Utah; memb: GB fencing team 1973–77, Olympic foil team 1976; nat under 21 foil champion 1970; *Books* Probability and Random Processes (1982, 2 edn 1992), Probability, An Introduction (1986), Percolation (1989); *Recreations* mountaineering, music; *Clubs* Climbers', Alpine, Oxford Alpine; *Style*— Prof Geoffrey Grimmett; ✉ Statistical Laboratory, University of Cambridge, 16 Mill Lane, Cambridge CB2 1SB (☎ 01223 337958, fax 01223 337956)

GRIMOND, Hon John Jasper; er s of Baron Grimond, TD, PC (Life Peer; d 1993), by his w, Laura, *née* Bonham Carter (d 1994); *b* 1946; *Educ* Eton, Balliol Coll Oxford, Harvard Univ (Nieman fellow); *m* 1973, Kate, er da of Lt-Col Peter Fleming, OBE (d 1971), of Nettlebed, Henley-on-Thames; 3 da (Mary Jessie b 1976, Rose Clementine b 1979, Georgia Celia b 1983); *Career* The Economist: joined 1969, asst ed 1975–, Br ed 1976–79, American ed 1979–88, foreign ed 1989–; dir Fleming American Investment Trust 1991–; tstee Prison Reform Tst 1995–; Harkness fell 1974–75; *Books* The Economist Pocket Style Book (ed); *Style*— The Hon John Grimond; ✉ 49 Lansdowne Rd, London W11 2LG

GRIMSBY, Bishop of 1979–; Rt Rev David Tustin; s of John Trevelyan Tustin (d 1983), and Janet Reynolds, *née* Orton (d 1996); *b* 12 Jan 1935; *Educ* Solihull Sch, Magdalene Coll Cambridge (MA), Univ of Geneva; *m* 15 Aug 1964, Mary Elizabeth, da of Rev Prebendary John Moreton Glover (Prebendary of Hereford Cathedral, d 1979); 1 s (Nicholas b 1969), 1 da (Juliet b 1971); *Career* curate of Stafford 1960–63, asst gen sec C of E Cncl on Foreign Rels 1963–67; curate St Dunstan-in-the-West Fleet St 1963–67; vicar: Wednesbury St Paul 1967–71, Tettenhall Regis 1971–79; rural dean of Trysull 1976–79; pres Anglican-Lutheran Soc, co-chm Anglican-Lutheran Int Cmmn 1986–, chm General Synod Cncl for Christian Unity 1993–; *Recreations* travel, music, European languages; *Style*— The Rt Rev the Bishop of Grimsby; ✉ Bishop's House, Church Lane, Irby upon Humber, Grimsby DN37 7JR (☎ 01472 371715, fax 01472 371716)

GRIMSEY, Colin Robert; s of Arthur William Grimsey, of Worthing, and Joan Hartridge, *née* Summers; *b* 24 Dec 1943; *Educ* Dartford GS (RAF flying scholar), King's Coll of London (BSc); *m* 11 Dec 1976, Elizabeth, da of late Arthur Sermon, and Betty Sermon; 1 da (Helen Catherine b 28 Sept 1977), 1 s (Edward David b 18 May 1979); *Career* asst princ Miny of Tport 1968–72, princ DOE 1972–79; Dept of Tport: asst sec 1979–89, under sec 1989–96, seconded to London Tport 1989–91, dir of fin 1991–93, under sec Railways Directorate 1993–96; *Recreations* family, opera, choral singing; *Clubs* Goldsmith's Choral Union; *Style*— Colin Grimsey, Esq; ✉ 33 Charlton Avenue, Walton on Thames, Surrey KT12 5LE

GRIMSHAW, Maj-Gen (Ewing) Henry Wrigley; CB (1965), CBE (1957, OBE 1954), DSO (1945); s of Lt-Col Ewing Wrigley Grimshaw (d 1916), and Geraldine Grimshaw; *b* 30 June 1911; *Educ* Brighton Coll, RMC Sandhurst; *m* 1943, Hilda Florence Agnes (d 1993), da of Dr Allison (d 1942), of Coleraine, NI; 2 s (Ewing, Roland), 1 da (Hilary); *Career* joined Indian Army 1931, served war 1939–45, Western Desert, Burma (despatches twice), transferred to The Royal Inniskilling Fus 1947, active service with Inniskillings (cmd) Egypt, Malaya and Kenya, cmd 9 Inf Bde active service Suez 1956 and Cyprus 1958, Imperial Def Coll 1960, GOC 44 Div (TA) and home counties dist 1962–65, Col The Royal Inniskilling Fus 1966–68, Dep Col The Royal Irish Rangers 1968–73; *Style*— Maj-Gen Henry Grimshaw, CB, CBE, DSO

GRIMSHAW, Dr John Stuart; s of Neville Stuart Grimshaw (d 1978), and Sylvia May, *née* Taylor (d 1963); *b* 22 Sept 1934; *Educ* Repton, Jesus Coll Cambridge (MA), UCH Med Sch (MB BChir, DPM); *m* 12 July 1958, Anne, da of William James Vince (d 1986); 1 s (Robert b 13 March 1961), 1 da (Caroline b 14 Jan 1963); *Career* maj and sr specialist RAMC 1960–65; house physician and house surgn UCH 1959, house physician Whittington Hosp 1960, sr registrar Dept of Psychological Med St Thomas' Hosp and Knowle Hosp 1965–67, conslt psychiatrist Southampton Univ Hosps 1967–90, hon clinical tutor Univ of Southampton 1973–90, chm Southampton Univ Hosps Med Exec Ctee 1977–80, chm Wessex Regnl Psychiatric Sub Ctee 1978–81, conslt rep Dist Mgmnt Team 1978–82; approval exercise convenor RCPsych 1973–77, examiner MRCPsych 1977–81 and 1983–87; memb: Mental Health Act Cmmn 1983–89 (second opinion appointed doctor 1983–, memb Central Policy Ctee 1986–89), Mental Health Review Tbnl South and West 1990–, Editorial Bd Tbnl Members' Guide; memb Panel of Observers MRCPsych exam 1987–, external examiner Final MMed (psych) Nat Univ of Singapore 1993–95; Freeman City of London, Liveryman Worshipful Soc of Apothecaries; FRCPE 1977, FRCPsych 1977; *Recreations* history, gardening, long distance walking and fell walking, numismatics; *Clubs* Royal Society of Medicine; *Style*— Dr John Grimshaw; ✉ The Orchard, Curdridge Lane, Curdridge, Southampton, Hampshire SO32 2BH (☎ 01489 782525)

GRIMSHAW, Jonathan Michael; MBE (1990); s of George Brian Grimshaw (d 1989), of Whitley Bay, Tyne and Wear, and Pamela, *née* Chapman; *b* 2 April 1954; *Educ* Repton, The King's Sch Tynemouth, Clare Coll Cambridge (BA, MA); *Career* TV prodn mangr 1981–84, co-fndr and sec Body Positive 1984–85, training offr of Nat AIDS Counselling Unit 1986–87, dir The Landmark 1987–92, chief exec S London AIDS Action 1992–94 (ret 1994); memb: Working Party on Ethical Aspects of AIDS Vaccine Trials MRC 1988–91, Working Party on AIDS Inst of Med Ethics 1988–92, Directorate of Prison Health Care AIDS Advsy Ctee Home Office 1988–, Local Authorities Assoc's Offr Working Gp on AIDS 1988–95, Min of Health's AIDS Action Gp 1991–92, Steering Ctee Pan-London HIV/AIDS Providers' Consortium 1992– (dep chm 1992–93), UK Forum on HIV and Human Rights 1992–, EU Working Gp on Discrimination Against People with HIV and AIDS: Implications for Legal and Public Health Serv Delivery 1995–; tstee: Body Positive 1988–91, Nat AIDS Tst 1987–, NAM Charitable Tst 1988–95 (chm 1994–95), NAM Publications 1995– (chm 1995–), The Globe Centre 1993–96, Red Hot AIDS Charitable Tst 1993–; patron: London Lighthouse, Red Admiral Project, Bournemouth Body Positive; *Recreations* travel, music, reading; *Style*— Jonathan Grimshaw, Esq, MBE; ✉ Flat 2, 16 Chesham Road, Brighton BN2 1NB

GRIMSHAW, Nicholas Thomas; CBE (1993); s of Thomas Cecil Grimshaw (d 1942), and Hannah Joan, *née* Dearsley; *b* 9 Oct 1939; *Educ* Wellington, Edinburgh Coll of Art, Architectural Assoc Sch (AADipl); *m* 20 Oct 1972, Lavinia, da of John Russell, CBE, of New York; 2 da (Chloe b 1973, Isabel b 1977); *Career* chm Nicholas Grimshaw & Ptnrs Ltd architects and industl designers 1980–; major projects incl: Terminal 1 redevelopment Manchester Airport, Zurich Airport redevelopment, Channel Tunnel terminal for BR Waterloo, Br Pavilion for Expo '92 in Seville, Berlin Stock Exchange, BA Combined Operation Centre Heathrow, Camden Superstore for J Sainsbury, HQ for BMW Bracknell, HQ for Igus GmbH Cologne, factory for Herman Miller Bath, Oxford Ice Rink, Gillingham Business Park for Grosvenor Devpts, res centre for Rank Xerox, printing plant for Financial Times; major awards and commendations incl: RIBA Awards 1975, 1978, 1980, 1983, 1986, 1989, 1990, 1991, 1994 and 1995, Financial Times Award for Industl Architecture 1977, 1980 and 1995, Br Construction Industry Awards 1988, 1989, 1992 and 1993, Structural Steel Design Awards 1969, 1977, 1980, 1989, 1993, 1994 and 1995, Civic Tst Award 1978, 1982, 1989, 1990 and 1991, Architectural Design Award 1974, 1982 and 1983, Royal Fine Arts Cmmn Sunday Times 1989, 1993, 1994 and 1995, BBC Design Awards finalist 1990, Business and Indust Award Certificate of Merit 1977, Euro Award for Steel Structure 1981, Constructa Preis for Industrial Architecture in Europe, Quaternario Fndn Int Award 1993, Mies van de Rohe Pavilion Award for Architecture 1994; Hon DLitt, Hon FAIA; memb AA 1965 (memb Cncl 1992, vice pres 1994), RIBA 1967, FCSD 1969, RA 1994; *Books* Nicholas Grimshaw & Partners Ltd: Product and Process (jtly, 1988), Structure, Space and Skin: the work of Nicholas Grimshaw & Partners Ltd 1988–93 (1993), Architecture, Industry and Innovation: the work of Nicholas Grimshaw & Partners Ltd 1966–88 (jtly, 1995); *Recreations* sailing, tennis; *Style*— Nicholas Grimshaw, Esq, CBE, RA; ✉ Nicholas Grimshaw & Partners Ltd, 1 Conway St, Fitzroy Square, London W1P 6LR (☎ 0171 631 0869, fax 0171 636 4866)

GRIMSTON, Viscount; James Walter Grimston; s and h of 7 Earl of Verulam, *qv*; *b* 6 Jan 1978; *Style*— Viscount Grimston

GRIMSTON, Neil Alexander; TD (1982); s of Flt Lt Victor Gordon Manners Grimston (d 1966), and Adeline Jean Margaret, *née* Esson (d 1992); *b* 8 Sept 1947; *m* 19 July 1975, Berylanne, da of David McNaught (d 1992), of Thames Ditton, Surrey; 1 s (Alexander b 1979), 1 da (Henrietta b 1984); *Career* Private HAC 1970 (vet memb 1971–), cmmnd 2 Lt TA RCT 1971, Lt 1972, Capt 1976, cmd ind unit with BAOR 1977–82, Capt RARO 1983–; with Hill Samuel 1967–70, discount broker Smith St Aubyn 1970–73, discount broker Page and Gwyther Group 1973–77; Chemical Bank 1977–92: vice pres and mangr World Insurance Group (Asia) 1982–84, head City Instns Gp 1985–87, dir Chemical Bank Trustee Co 1986–88, vice pres and head of Fin Instns Gp 1987–92, memb UK Management Ctee 1991–92; ptnr The Financial Planning Group 1992–94, dir FPG Fiscal Ltd 1992–94, sr conslt Telos 1993–94, gp fin dir and memb Exec Mgmnt Ctee Telos Bioinformatik AG (Lucerne) 1994–95, dir Telos Consulting Inc (USA) 1994–95, chm Isisquest Ltd 1995–96, marketing conslt Eastgate Group 1996–; vice chm Twickenham Cons Assoc 1969–74, cncllr (Cons) London Borough of Richmond-upon-Thames 1971–74; memb approved list of Cons Party potential candidates for Westminster and Euro Parliaments 1989–93; chm Oxshott and Stoke Cons Assoc 1989–91; Freeman City of London 1971, Liveryman and memb Ct Worshipful Co of Scriveners; memb HAC 1970–; *Recreations* collecting prints, Oriental rugs, wine, photography; *Clubs* Singapore Cricket; *Style*— Neil A Grimston, Esq, TD; ✉ 14 Phelps House, Felsham Road, Putney, London SW15 1DF (☎ 0181 785 0815, fax 0181 780 2453); Eastgate Group, Eastgate House, 40 Dukes Place, London EC3A 7LP (☎ 0171 204 7918, fax 0171 397 4588)

GRIMSTON, Hon Robert John Sylvester (Robin); er s and h of 2 Baron Grimston of Westbury, *qv*, and Hon June Mary, *née* Ponsonby, da of 5 Baron de Mauley; *b* 30 April 1951; *Educ* Eton, Univ of Reading (BSc); *m* 1984, Emily Margaret, da of Maj John Evelyn Shirley, of Ormly Hall, Ramsey, IOM; 2 da (Charlotte Elgiva b 23 March 1991, Philippa Margaret b 7 Oct 1995); *Career* Capt Royal Hussars (PWO) 1970–81; CA: Binder Hamlyn, Citicorp Scrimgeour Vickers Ltd, Matrix Securities Ltd; *Style*— The Hon Robin Grimston; ✉ 51 Alderbrook Rd, London SW12 8AD (☎ 0181 673 4293)

GRIMSTON OF WESTBURY, 2 Baron (UK 1964); Sir Robert Walter Sigismund Grimston; 2 Bt (UK 1952); s of 1 Baron Grimston of Westbury (d 1979, er s of Canon Hon Robert Grimston, 3 s of 2 Earl of Verulam), and Sybil (d 1977), da of Sir Sigmund Neumann, 1 Bt (later anglicised to Newman); *b* 14 June 1925; *Educ* Eton; *m* 21 June 1949, Hon June Mary Ponsonby, er da of 5 Baron de Mauley; 2 s, 1 da; *Heir* s, Hon Robert Grimston; *Career* former Lt Scots Gds, WWII served NW Europe; formerly in oil and publishing, Hinton Hill & Coles Agencies Ltd (now Stewart Members' Agency Ltd) 1962–90; dir: Hinton Hill & Coles 1962–83, Stewart L Hughman Ltd 1983–86, River Clyde Holdings Ltd 1986–88; chm Gray's Inn (Underwriting Agency) Ltd 1970–87; Freeman City of London, Liveryman Worshipful Co of Gold and Silver Wyre Drawers; *Clubs* Boodle's, City of London; *Style*— The Rt Hon the Lord Grimston of Westbury; ✉ The Old Rectory, Westwell, Burford, Oxon OX18 4JT

GRIMSTONE, Gerald Edgar; s of Edgar Wilfred Grimstone (d 1986), and Dorothy Yvonne, *née* Martin; *b* 27 Aug 1949; *Educ* Whitgift Sch, Merton Coll Oxford (MA, MSc); *m* 23 June 1973 (m dis 1995), Hon Janet Elizabeth Gudrun Suenson-Taylor, da of 2 Baron Grantchester, CBE, QC (d 1995); 1 s (Toby Stephen Gunnar b 1975), 2 da (Jenny Elizabeth May b 1979, Anna Rose Yvonne b 1982); *Career* Civil Serv 1972–86 (latterly asst sec HM Treasy); J Henry Schroder & Co Ltd: dir 1986–, head Int Fin and Advisory Dept 1994–95, dep chm Schroder Asia Ltd, head of investment banking Asia-Pacific region (based in Hong Kong) 1995–; MSI; *Clubs* Athenaeum, China, Hong Kong Jockey; *Style*— Gerald Grimstone, Esq; ✉ c/o J Henry Schroder & Co Ltd, 120 Cheapside, London EC2V 6DS (☎ 0171 382 6000)

GRIMTHORPE, 4 Baron (UK 1886); Sir Christopher John Beckett; 8 Bt (UK 1813), OBE (1958), DL (N Yorks, formerly E Riding, 1969), patron of 1 living; s of 3 Baron, TD (d 1963), by his 1 w Mary, *née* Archdale (d 1962); through his gf's sis, Maud, Lord Grimthorpe is 2 cous of 22 Baron Hastings; *b* 16 Sept 1915; *Educ* Eton; *m* 1954, Lady Elizabeth, DCVO (1995, CVO 1983), *née* Lumley, da of 11 Earl of Scarbrough (*see* Grimthorpe, Baroness); 2 s, 1 da; *Heir* s, Hon Edward Beckett, *qv*; *Career* Brig (ret) 9 Queen's Royal Lancers, Lt-Col cmdg 1955–58, Col 9/12 Lancers 1973–77; Brig RAC HQ W Cmmd 1961–64, dep Cdr Malta & Libya 1964–67; ADC to HM The Queen 1964–68; dir: Standard Bdcasting Corp Canada (UK) Ltd 1972–83, Thirsk Racecourse Ltd 1972–, Yorkshire Post Newspapers 1973–85; *Clubs* Cavalry & Guards', Jockey; *Style*— The Rt Hon Lord Grimthorpe, OBE, DL; ✉ Westow Hall, York YO6 7NE (☎ 01653 618225)

GRIMTHORPE, Baroness; Lady Elizabeth; *née* Lumley; DCVO (1995, CVO 1983); da of the late 11 Earl of Scarbrough, KG, GCSI, GCIE, GCVO, PC, TD, and Katharine,

Fedn of Free Journalists 1972–; memb Catholic Union of GB 1972–; Polonia Restituta (Cdr's Cross) 1992, Pro Ecclesia et Pontifice 1993; *Recreations* riding, tennis, swimming, travel; *Clubs* Special Forces, POSK (London); *Style—* The Count Grocholski; ✉ 27 Baalbec Road, London N5 1QN; Château de Valduc, 1320 Hamme-Mille, Belgium

GROCOTT, Bruce Joseph; MP (Lab) The Wrekin (majority 6,648); s of Reginald Grocott; *b* 1 Nov 1940; *Educ* Univ of Leicester, Univ of Manchester; *m* 1965, Sally Barbara, *née* Ridgway; 2 s; *Career* lectr in politics 1965–74, television journalist and prodr Central Television 1979–87; MP (Lab): Lichfield and Tamworth 1974–79, The Wrekin 1987–; PPS to: Min for Local Govt Planning 1975–76, Min of Agric 1976–78; currently PPS to The Rt Hon Tony Blair, MP; *Clubs* Trench Labour; *Style—* Bruce Grocott, MP; ✉ House of Commons, London SW1A 0AA

GRODEN, Dr Bernard Melville; s of Louis Groden (d 1979), and Esther, *née* Goldberg (d 1978); *b* 1 Nov 1933; *Educ* Hutchesons Boys' GS, Univ of Glasgow (MB ChB, MD); *m* 8 April 1964, Patricia Ruth, da of Cecil Freeman, of Newton Mearns, Glasgow; 3 da (Laura Rochelle b 1965, Carolyn Anne b 1967, Wendy Lorraine b 1969); *Career* conslt physician and cardiologist: Ballchmyle Hosp 1971–82, Crosshouse Hosp 1982–96; hon clinical sub dean Univ of Glasgow 1988–96 (hon clinical lectr 1985, hon clinical sr lectr 1990); dir Sanmex International PLC; memb Br Cardiac Soc; chm: Mearns Community Cncl 1976–83, Eastwood Advanced Drivers' Assoc 1983–87, Broom Cons Assoc 1986–89; memb BMA, FRCPGlas 1972, FRCPEd 1974; *Recreations* sailing, golf, photography; *Style—* Dr Bernard Groden; ✉ 7 Broom Road East, Newton Mearns, Glasgow G77 5RQ (☎ 0141 639 4432)

GROGONO, James Lyon; s of Dr Eric Bernard Grogono, and Clare Anderton Gregono, JP, *née* Jolly; *b* 5 July 1937; *Educ* Oundle, London Hosp Med Coll London (MB BS); *m* 21 April 1972, Catherine Margaret, da of Dr Richard Bertram Morton, of 6 Hawk's Road, Hailsham, E Sussex; 1 s (Angus b 1974), 2 da (Emma b 1973, Dorothy b 1981); *Career* conslt surgn Wycombe Health Dist, surgical tutor RCS Eng; author; chm Windsurfing Ctee Royal Yachting Assoc, vice chm Multihull Ctee Iant Yacht Racing Union; FRCS, LRCP, DCH; *Books* Hydrofoil Sailing (1972), Icarus: The Boat that Flies (1987); *Recreations* sailing, windsurfing, sculling, skiing, skating, tennis, unicycling; *Clubs* Aldeburgh Yacht, Leander, Chiltern Med Soc; *Style—* James Grogono, Esq; ✉ The Garden House, Riverside, Marlow, Bucks (☎ 0162848 4261)

GRONOW, Dr Michael; s of Vivian Gronow (d 1970), and Mary Amelia, *née* Chappell; *b* 26 July 1937; *Educ* Cardiff HS, Univ Coll of S Wales (BSc), Trinity Coll Cambridge (PhD); *m* 1968 (m dis 1991); 1 s (Simon Richard b 19 March 1972), 1 da (Kathryn Louise b 26 Dec 1973); *Career* Univ of Cambridge: MRC res asst Dept of Radiotherapeutics 1963–65, demonstrator Dept of Chem 1962–65; res assoc Dept of Pharmacology Baylor Univ Houston Texas USA 1965–66, res assoc and demonstrator Dept of Biochem Univ of Oxford 1966–69, lectr Dept of Experimental Pathology and Cancer Res Univ of Leeds 1969–75, permanent sr res fell Cancer Res Unit Univ of York 1975–79; conslt PA Tech Centre Int 1979–80, head of biosciences PA Centre for Advanced Studies 1980–81, jt md and fndr Cambridge Life Science plc 1981–88, md CRL Ltd 1989–96, dir Excell Diagnostics Ltd and Kognos Ltd 1992; tstee and fndr Cambridge Cancer Research Fund 1989–; author of 50 pubns, ed The Genetic Engineer and Biotechnologist; memb: Biochemical Soc 1967, Br Assoc Cancer Res 1969; *Recreations* travel, music, photography, hockey, chess, wine; *Style—* Dr Michael Gronow; ✉ Thornton House, 131 Waterbeach Rd, Landbeach, Cambridge CB4 4EA; Cambridge Research Laboratories, 181A Huntingdon Rd, Cambridge CB3 0DJ (☎ and fax 01223 277744)

GROOM, Brian William Alfred; s of Fred Groom (d 1978), of Manchester, and Muriel Edith, *née* Linfoot; *b* 26 April 1955; *Educ* Manchester GS, Balliol Coll Oxford (BA); *m* 1980, Carola May, da of Peter Withington; 1 s (Jack Edward b 4 Oct 1984), 1 da (Elinor Rose b 6 Aug 1987); *Career* trainee reporter and sports ed Goole Times 1976–78; Financial Times: Syndication Dept 1978–79, sub ed int edn 1979–81, labour reporter and mgmnt feature writer 1981–85, UK news ed 1985–88; ed Scotland on Sunday 1994– (dep ed 1988–94); Pfizer award NCTJ 1978; *Recreations* cricket, reading, hillwalking, cinema; *Style—* Brian Groom, Esq; ✉ Scotland on Sunday, 20 North Bridge, Edinburgh EH1 1YT (☎ 0131 243 3475, fax 0131 220 2443)

GROOM, Jeremy Richard; s of Peter Farrant Groom, of Walton on Thames, and Anne, *née* Dainty; *b* 2 May 1948; *Educ* King's Sch Canterbury, Lincoln Coll Oxford; *m* 9 April 1983, Jennifer, da of Sir Norman Richard Rowley Brooke, CBE (d 1989), of Cardiff; 1 s (Pelham b 1989), 1 da (Camilla b 1984); *Career* ptnr Seymour Pierce and Co 1977–87 (joined 1972), dir Seymour Pierce Butterfield Ltd 1987–94, sr div dir Brewin Dolphin & Co 1994–; memb Stock Exchange 1975, MSI (Dip) 1992; *Recreations* music, theatre, real tennis, cricket; *Clubs* MCC; *Style—* Jeremy Groom, Esq; ✉ Bachelor's Mead, Horton, Devizes, Wiltshire SN10 3NB (☎ 01380 860344); Brewin Dolphin & Co, Cross Keys House, The Parade, Marlborough, Wiltshire SN8 1NE (☎ 01672 516666, fax 01672 515550)

GROOM, Maj-Gen John Patrick; CB (1984), CBE (1975, MBE 1963); s of Samuel Douglas Groom (d 1975), and Gertrude Groom, *née* Clinton (d 1996); *b* 9 March 1929; *Educ* King Charles Sch Kidderminster, Rugby, RMA Sandhurst, Staff Coll Camberley, RCDS; *m* 1951, Jane Mary, da of Thomas Miskelly (d 1937); 3 da (Susan, Maryanne, Josephine); *Career* served Br Army N Africa, Egypt, UK, Aden, BAOR, Malaya, Singapore, Cyprus 1946–83 (despatches 1965); Col Cmdt Corps RE 1983–91, rep Col Cmdt 1986; dir gen Guide Dogs for the Blind Assoc 1983–89, vice pres Int Fedn Guide Dog Schs 1989; memb Advsy Bd Talking Newspapers 1989; chm: Reach Fndn 1992–95, Cncl Solent Protection Soc 1992–; non-exec chm BKP Environmental Services Ltd 1991–; Freeman City of London; *Recreations* sailing ('Anahita'), ornithology, country pursuits; *Clubs* Royal Ocean Racing, Royal Lymington Yacht, Royal Yachting Assoc, British Keil Yacht, Keiler Yacht; *Style—* Maj-Gen John Groom, CB, CBE; ✉ Bridge End Cottage, Walhampton, Lymington, Hants SO41 5RD (☎ 01590 675710)

GROOM, Michael John; s of Thomas Rowland Groom (d 1984), of Wolverhampton, and Elizabeth Groom (d 1971); *b* 18 July 1942; *Educ* St Chad's GS Wolverhampton, Cotton Coll N Staffs; *m* 4 June 1966, Sheila Mary, da of Harold Cartwright, of Wolverhampton; 2 da (Nichola b 1971, Sally b 1975); *Career* CA; Michael Groom & Co 1971–76 and 1981–, Tansley Witt 1976–80, Binder Hamlyn 1980–81, dir various cos, lectr in mgmnt and legislation; memb ICAEW (cncl memb 1975–); Freeman Worshipful Co of CAs; FCA 1964; *Books* ed/author 1975–81: Chartac Administration Manual, Chartac Accounting Manual, Chartac Auditing Manual, Chartac Taxation Manual, Chartac Accounting and Auditing Model File, Financial Management in the Professional Office, Cash Control in the Smaller Business, Budgeting and Cash Management; *Recreations* theatre, travel, food and wine, photography, dog obedience training; *Clubs* Wolverhampton Lawn Tennis and Squash; *Style—* Michael Groom, Esq; ✉ 10 Clarendon Street, Wolverhampton WV3 9PP (☎ 01902 773644, fax 01902 710321)

GROOTENHUIS, Prof Peter; s of Johannes Christiaan Grootenhuis (d 1986), and Anna Christina van den Bergh (d 1992); *b* 31 July 1924; *Educ* Netherlands Lyceum The Hague, Imperial Coll London (BSc Eng, DIC, PhD, DScEng); *m* 7 Aug 1954, Sara Joan, da of Maj Charles Campbell Winchester, MC, RR, Royal Scots (ka 1940); 1 s (Hugh John b 30 April 1958), 1 da (Carol Felicity b 2 June 1955); *Career* apprentice rising to asst project engr Bristol Aero Engine Co 1944–46; Imperial Coll London: lectr in mech engrg 1946–59, reader in mech engrg 1959–72, prof 1972– (latterly emeritus prof), sr res fell 1989–, memb Bd of Studies of Civil and Mech Engrg 1959–89, memb Engrg Bd of Studies 1972–89, memb Governing Body Imperial Coll 1974–79; fndr Derriton Electronics Ltd 1960 (later tech dir Derriton Ltd), dir Derriton Environmental Systems Ltd 1981–84; ptnr Grootenhuis Allaway Associates (consltg engrs) 1969–92; conslt: Binnie and Partners 1962–64, Royal Armament R & D Estab 1963–64, Absorbit Ltd 1964–69, City of London Corp 1964–91, Arup Assocs 1965–67, MOD 1965–84, Esso Chemicals Ltd 1968 and 1971, Union Electrica Madrid 1976–81; memb: Special Advsy Bd in Ergonomics Univ of London 1966–89, BSI Ctees 1967–, Editorial Advsy Bd Journal of Environmental Engrg 1969–89 (chm 1974–89), jt IMechE/Dutch Working Pty on Educn 1979–81; external examiner: The Coll of Technol Dublin 1971–79, Univ of Lagos Nigeria 1972–75, Univ of Bristol 1979–81; FIMechE 1979 (MIMechE 1952); Soc of Environmental Engrs: fndr memb 1959, fell 1964, pres 1964–67; MIM 1956–76, memb Br Acoustical Soc (now Inst of Acoustics) 1965 (memb Provisional Cncl 1964–66), AFRAeS 1950–75; Fell City and Guilds of London Inst 1976; FEng 1982; chm: Imperial Coll Wine Ctee 1975–89, Knightsbridge Branch Cons Pty Assoc 1974–77; pres: Old Centralians 1988–89; *Pubns* author of over 70 pubns in learned jls; *Recreations* gardening, sailing; *Clubs* Athenaeum; *Style—* Prof Peter Grootenhuis, FEng; ✉ Imperial College of Science, Technology & Medicine, Department of Mechanical Engineering, Exhibition Rd, London SW7 2BX (☎ 0171 594 7018, fax 0171 823 8845)

GROSE, Vice Admiral Sir Alan; KBE (1989); s of George William Stanley Grose (d 1986), and Anne May, *née* Stanford (d 1954); *b* 24 Sept 1937; *Educ* Strodes Sch, Britannia RNC Dartmouth; *m* 2 Sept 1961, Gillian Ann, da of Cdre Richard Paul Dryden Dymond (d 1992), of Simonstown, Cape Province, SA; 2 s (Jeremy b 1964, Matthew b 1968), 1 da (Sarah b 1969); *Career* S Atlantic and Med 1957–67, qualified navigation specialist 1964, exchange serv with RAN 1964–66, Home and Med Fleets 1967–71, Cdr 1972, Capt 1977; CO: HMS Eskimo 1974–75, HMS Bristol 1980–82, HMS Illustrious 1984–86; Rear Adm 1986, Asst Chief of Def Staff (Operational Requirements) MOD 1986–88, Flag Offr Flotilla Three 1988–90, Vice Adm 1989, Flag Offr Plymouth and Naval Base Cdr Devonport 1990, Cdr Central Atlantic and Channel Area 1990–92, ret 1992; gp exec diamond security Anglo American Corporation of South Africa Ltd and De Beers Consolidated Mines Ltd 1993–; hon fell Liverpool John Moores Univ; past pres RN and RM Rowing Assoc; memb RUSI 1964, RCDS 1980; MInstD, FIMgt; *Recreations* tennis, rowing (spectator), genealogy; *Clubs* RNR, Kimberley; *Style—* Vice Adm Sir Alan Grose, KBE; ✉ c/o Barclays Bank, Princess Street, Plymouth, S Devon (☎ 01752 263333)

GROSS, Howard Anthony; s of Harold Victor Gross, of Southgate, and Pamela Alicia Tamara, *née* Rosen (d 1994); *b* 24 May 1948; *Educ* Minchenden Sch, City of London Coll; *m* 4 Nov 1973, Beverley Myra, da of Bennett Teff, of Mill Hill; 2 da (Zoë b 1975, Amanda b 1978); *Career* CA; ptnr Gross Klein & Co 1968–; fndr chm Hartley (now Paxus) Computer User Gp 1979–82; chm: North London CAs 1984–85, Heathfield Sch Parents' Assoc (GPDST) 1985–89; London Soc ICAEW: memb 1984, chm PR Ctee 1986–88, chm Advice and Servs Ctee 1988–89, chm memb Relations Ctee 1989–90, hon treas 1990–93; Freeman City of London 1990; FCA 1971, ATII 1972, FCCA 1980; *Recreations* jogging (completed London marathon 1989); *Style—* Howard Gross, Esq; ✉ Gross Klein & Company, 6 Breams Buildings, London EC4A 1HP (☎ 0171 242 2212, fax 0171 404 4412)

GROSS, Dr Jeremy Martin; s of Donald Gross, and Sylvia, *née* Nussbaum; *b* 11 Nov 1939; *Educ* Spring Grove GS, Univ of Leicester (BSc, PhD); *m* 1 (m dis 1974), Diane Rose, *née* Jackson; 1 da (Deborah Sara b 20 Sept 1969); m 2, 1976 (m dis 1989), Pamela Margaret, *née* Davey; m 3, 1990, Diana Christine, da of Clement Trill; *Career* sr lectr Sir John Cass Coll Univ of London 1965–69; mangr: GEC Computers 1969–71, ICL 1971–73; Triad Systems 1973–74; Data Logic 1974–90: chief conslt, tech dir, tech and mktg dir, divnl md; independent computer conslt 1990–; memb Industl Advsy Gp: Brunel Univ, UMIST; various articles and chapters on computing; memb: Br Computer Soc, Worshipful Co of Info Technologists; FRIC 1963, MBCS 1970, FInstD 1989; *Books* Principles of Physical Chemistry (1971); *Recreations* music, sport; *Clubs* Cricketers' London, IOD; *Style—* Dr Jeremy Gross; ✉ 9 High Beeches, Gerrards Cross, Bucks SL9 7HU (☎ 01753 890732)

GROSS, John Jacob; s of Abraham and Muriel Gross; *b* 12 March 1935; *Educ* City of London Sch, Wadham Coll Oxford; *m* 1965 (m dis), Miriam Gross, *qv*, da of Kurt May; 1 s (Thomas b 1966), 1 da (Susanna b 1967); *Career* former asst lectr London Univ, fellow King's Coll Cambridge 1962–65, literary ed New Statesman 1973, ed Times Literary Supplement 1974–81, tstee Nat Portrait Gallery 1977–84, dep chm George Weidenfeld & Nicolson Ltd 1982–83, staff writer NY Times 1983–89, theatre critic Sunday Telegraph 1990–; *Books* The Rise and Fall of the Man of Letters (1969, awarded Duff Cooper Meml Prize), Joyce (1971), The Oxford Book of Aphorisms (ed, 1983); *Style—* John Gross, Esq; ✉ Sunday Telegraph, 1 Canada Square, Canary Wharf, London E14 5DT

GROSS, Dr Manfred Ferry; s of Leon Gross (d 1965), of London, and Else, *née* Schönfeld (d 1949); *b* 22 Dec 1907; *Educ* Das Graue Kloster Berlin Germany; Univs of: Berlin, Heidelberg, Würzburg and Edinburgh (MD, LRCP, LRCS, LRFPS (Edinburgh)); *m* 17 Aug 1963, Sylvia Edna, da of Lieut Patrick Webb (ka 1917); *Career* WWII despatches (Burma) 1945; res worker and conslt physician; worked as Br ex-patriate in Germany: Hufeland Hosp Berlin 1933–34, Virchow Hosp Berlin 1934–35, Hosp Persische Strasse Berlin 1935–36, Kerckoff Res Inst Bad Nauheim 1936–38; New End Hosp London 1942; War Serv RAMC 1943–46: 112 Br Gen Hosp India, 23 Indian Casualty Clearing Station Burma, cmd offr Mil Hosp Kodaicanal Mysore S India; hon conslt cardiologist New End Hosp London 1948–51, res work (with Prof Paul Niehans, Vevey, Switzerland) into Xenogenic cell implants (Cell Therapy) 1952–, res work into therapeutic application of ozone in cardio-vascular and other diseases 1965–; memb BMA 1942, FRSM 1952; memb: Med Assoc for Organo-Biotherapy (Germany) 1964, Med Assoc for Ozone Therapy (Germany) 1970; *Recreations* music and drawing cartoons; *Style—* Dr Manfred Ferry Gross; ✉ 3 Loom Place, Radlett, Hertfordshire WD7 8AF (☎ 01923 856339)

GROSS, Dr Michael Lester Phillip; s of Harold Victor Gross, of Southgate, and Pamela Alicia Tamar, *née* Rosen; *b* 31 March 1952; *Educ* Minchenden Sch Southgate, Sidney Sussex Coll Cambridge (BA, MA, MB BChir, MD), The London Hosp Med Coll; *m* 30 July 1974, Jennifer Ruth, da of Lawrence Hoffman, of Edgware; 2 da (Louise b 1977, Jemma b 1981); *Career* sr resident The Nat Hosp 1983–85, sr registrar St Mary's Hosp and The Nat Hosp 1985–89, conslt neurologist Clementine Churchill Hosp, chm Div of Neurological Sci and conslt neurologist Regnl Neurological Centre Royal Surrey Co Hosp Guildford and East Surrey Hosps (memb Regnl Neurosciences Advsy Ctee), clinical dir The Royal and East Surrey Neurology Research Unit, dir of neurophysiology The Clementine Churchill Harrow; scientific papers and int presentations on treatment of Guillain-Barre syndrome, inflammatory polyneuropathy, experimental allergic neuritis, plasma exchange, rejection encephalopathy, migraine and headache syndromes and gen neurology topics; memb: Assoc of Br Neurologists, Euro Neurological Soc, BMA, Int Headache Soc, World Fedn of Neurology; FRCP 1995; *Books* The Therapeutic Modification of Inflammatory Polyneuropathy (1987); *Recreations* bridge, tennis, photography, theatre; *Style—* Dr Michael Gross; ✉ Green Waters, Green Lane, Stanmore, Middlesex HA7 3AF (☎ 0181 954 0987, fax 0181 954 7220); Clementine Churchill Hospital, Sudbury Hill, Harrow, Middx (☎ 0181 422 3464)

GROSS, Miriam Marianna; da of Kurt May, of Frankfurt, Germany, and Vera Hermine, *née* Freiberg; *b* 12 May 1939; *Educ* Dartington Hall Sch, St Anne's Coll Oxford (BA, MA, DipEd); *m* 1, 1965 (m dis), John Jacob Gross, *qv*, s of Abraham Gross; 1 s (Thomas b 1966), 1 da (Susanna b 1967); m 2, 1993, Sir Geoffrey Owen; *Career* The Observer:

née McEwen, DCVO; *b* 22 July 1925; *m* 1954, 4 Baron Grimthorpe, *qv*; 2 s, 1 da; *Career* appointed lady of the bedchamber to HM Queen Elizabeth The Queen Mother 1973; *Style*— The Rt Hon the Lady Grimthorpe, DCVO; ✉ Westow Hall, York (☎ 01653 618225)

GRIMWOOD, Nigel Manning; s of Maj Basil Joseph Grimwood (d 1989), of Westhampnett, Sussex, and Kitty Nora, *née* Andrews (d 1986); *b* 10 March 1929; *Educ* King's Sch Ely, King's Coll London (LLB); *m* 3 Nov 1973, Diana Monica, da of Arthur Cecil Williams (d 1990), of Surrey; 2 s (Toby Basil b 1974 d Madagascar 1995, Hugo b 1985), 1 da (Lucy b 1976); *Career* admitted slr 1952, ptnr Clifford-Turner 1958–71, dir of public cos 1971–86; chm Edward Barnsley Workshop Tst 1987–; memb Cncl Friends of Chichester Cathedral 1972–75, dir Chichester Festivities 1975–94, tstee Boxgrove Priory 1989–96; *Recreations* travelling; *Clubs* Travellers'; *Style*— Nigel Grimwood, Esq; ✉ Mayfield, Strettington, Chichester, W Sussex PO18 0LA (☎ 01243 773214)

GRINDLEY, David Allan; s of Allan Grindley, of Wigan, and Margaret, *née* Tomlinson; *b* 29 Oct 1972; *Educ* Park High Secdy Sch, Winstanley Sixth Form Coll, Metroplitan Univ of Manchester; *Career* athlete (400m); memb Wigan Harriers; achievements incl: Silver medal 4 x 400m World Jr Championships Bulgaria 1991, Gold medal 400m and 4 x 400m Euro Jr Championships Greece 1992, Bronze medal 4 x 400m and finalist 400m Olympic Games Barcelona 1992, Gold medals 400m and 4 x 400m relay Euro Cup 1993, Bronze medal 4 x 400m World Student Games Japan 1995; set nat 400m record (44.47) Barcelona 1992; currently accounting and fin student; *Recreations* music, socialising, astronomy; *Style*— David Grindley, Esq; ✉ c/o Vicente Modahl, 53 Harley Rd, Sale, Cheshire (☎ 0161 962 2732, fax 0161 976 4361)

GRINLING, Jasper Gibbons; CBE (1978); s of Lt-Col Anthony Gibbons Grinling, MBE, MC (d 1982), by his w Jean Dorothy Turing; *b* 29 Jan 1924; *Educ* Harrow, King's Coll Cambridge; *m* 1950, Gertrude Jane Moulsdale; 1 s, 2 da; *Career* served WWII 12 Lancers 1942–46, Capt; W & A Gilbey Ltd: joined 1947, dir 1952, md 1964; md IDV Ltd 1967; dir: N British Distillery Co 1968–86, corp affrs Grand Met Ltd 1981–85, trade relations Grand Met plc 1985–86; chm London Jazz Radio plc 1985–91; vineyard proprietor; memb Cncl Scotch Whisky Assoc 1968–86; pres: EEC Confédération des Industs Agricoles et Alimentaires 1976–80, The Apple and Pear Devpt Cncl 1986–89; Chev l'Ordre National du Mérite (France) 1983; CIMgt; *Books* The Annual Report (1987); *Recreations* gardening, jazz drumming, painting; *Style*— Jasper Grinling, Esq, CBE; ✉ 94D Kensington Church St, London W8 (☎ 0171 221 5377); The Old Vicarage, Helions Bumpstead, nr Haverhill, Suffolk CB9 7AS (☎ 01440 730316)

GRINSTEAD, Sir Stanley Gordon; kt (1986); s of Ephraim Grinstead; *b* 17 June 1924; *Educ* Strodes Sch Egham; *m* 1955, Joyce Preston; 2 da; *Career* served WWII RN; chm and gp chief exec Grand Metropolitan plc 1982–86 (dep chm 1980–82, md 1980–86, with Grand Metropolitan 1957–62 and 1964–86), dir Reed International plc 1981–90 (chm 1988–89), chm and dir Harmony Leisure Group 1989–92; treas Surrey CCC 1986–94, tstee Fleet Air Arm Museum 1982–; Hon Asst Worshipful Co of Brewers (Master 1983–84); FCA, CIMgt; *Recreations* gardening, cricket, racing, thoroughbred horse breeding; *Clubs* Army & Navy, MCC, Surrey County Cricket; *Style*— Sir Stanley Grinstead

GRINYER, Prof John Raymond; twin bro of Prof Peter Hugh Grinyer, *qv*; *b* 3 March 1935; *Educ* Central Park Sch East Ham London, LSE (MSc); *m* 31 May 1958, Shirley Florence, da of Harry Alfred Marshall (d 1989), of Dagenham, Essex; 1 s (Christopher b 1967), 2 da (Julie b 1961, Sally b 1963); *Career* Nat Serv RAMC 1953–55; posts with LEB and Halifax Building Soc 1950–56, trg as CA Martin Redhead and Co, Hope Agar and Co 1956–61, sr audit asst Kemp Chatteris and Co 1962–63, lectr Harlow Tech Coll Essex 1963–66; sr lectr: City of London Poly 1967–71, Cranfield Sch of Mgmnt Bedfordshire 1971–76; Univ of Dundee 1976–: prof of accountancy and business finance, head of Dept 1976–90, dean Faculty of Law 1984–85 and 1991–93; author of numerous articles in jls; chm: Assoc of Univ Teachers of Accounting 1980–81, Br Accounting Assoc 1990 (vice chm 1989), Polack Travelling Scholarship Fund Dundee; FCA, MICAS, FRSA; *Recreations* golf, dinghy sailing; *Clubs* Broughty Ferry Golf, Royal Tay Yacht; *Style*— Prof John Grinyer; ✉ Department of Accountancy & Business Finance, The University, Dundee DD1 4HN (☎ 01382 344192, fax 01382 24419, telex 76293, home ☎ 01382 775743)

GRINYER, Prof Peter Hugh; s of Sydney George Grinyer, of Harston, Cambs, and Grace Elizabeth, *née* Formals (d 1988); twin bro of Prof John Raymond Grinyer, *qv*; *b* 3 March 1935; *Educ* East Ham GS, Balliol Coll Oxford (BA, MA), LSE (PhD); *m* 6 Sept 1958, Sylvia Joyce, da of William James Boraston, of Dagenham, Essex; 2 s (Paul Andrew b 27 July 1961, Nigel James b 12 May 1964); *Career* sr mgmnt trainee Unilever Ltd 1957–59, personal asst to md (later mangr of prodn planning and stock control) E R Holloway Ltd 1959–61, asst lectr (later lectr and sr lectr) Hendon Coll of Technol 1961–64, lectr (later sr lectr and reader) Graduate Business Centre City Univ 1964–74, prof of business strategy City Univ Business Sch 1974–79; Univ of St Andrews: Esmee Fairbairn prof of economics 1979–93, vice princ 1985–87, actg princ 1986, actg chm Dept of Mgmnt 1987–90; visiting prof Stern Sch New York Univ 1992 and 1996, Erskine fell Univ of Canterbury NZ 1994; memb Business and Mgmnt Studies Sub Ctee UGC 1979–85; non-exec dir: John Brown plc 1984–86, Don & Low Holdings (formerly Don Bros Buist plc) 1985–91, Ellis & Goldstein Hldgs plc 1987–88; fndr memb Glenrothes Enterprise Tst 1983–86; chm: St Andrews Mgmnt Inst 1989–96, St Andrews Strategic Management Ltd 1989–, McIlroy Coates Ltd 1991–95; memb: Scottish Legal Aid Bd 1992–, Acad of Mgmnt, Br Acad of Mgmnt, MInstD; *Books* Corporate Models Today (with J Wooller, 2 edn 1978), From Private to Public (with G D Vaughan and S Birley, 1977), Turnaround (with J C Spender, 1979), Sharpbenders (with D G Mayes and P McKiernan, 1988), Organising Strategy (with Foo Check Teck, 1994); author of some 55 papers in jls; *Recreations* golf, mountain walking; *Clubs* Royal and Ancient Golf; *Style*— Prof Peter Grinyer; ✉ Aberbrothock, 60 Buchanan Gardens, St Andrews, Fife KY16 9LX (☎ 01334 472966); St Andrews Management Institute, Kinnesburn, Kennedy Gardens, St Andrews KY16 9DY (☎ 01334 462871, fax 01334 462872)

GRISBROOKE, William Jardine; s of Joseph Henry Grisbrooke (d 1975), of Friern Barnet, Middx, and Lilian Maud, *née* Betts (d 1979); *b* 2 Feb 1932; *Educ* The Woodhouse Sch Finchley, Sidney Sussex Coll Cambridge (MA, BD); *m* 12 April 1955, Maureen, da of Albert Newton Tasker (d 1972), of Southport, Lancs; *Career* historian and theologian; lectr in theol Univ of Birmingham 1972–83 (res fell Inst for the Study of Worship and Religious Architecture 1967–72); lectr in liturgy: The Queen's Coll Birmingham 1972–80, St Mary's Coll Oscott Birmingham 1980–83; visiting lectr Pontifical Univ of Salamanca Spain 1974–80, visiting prof St George's Coll Jerusalem 1986–; author of numerous articles in jls and reviews; FRHistS; *Publications* Anglican Liturgies of the Seventeenth and Eighteenth Centuries (1958), Spiritual Counsels of Father John of Kronstadt (1967, 1981), The Liturgical Portions of the Apostolic Constitutions (1990), Saint John of Kronstadt: Counsels on the Christian Priesthood (1994); contrib to symposia: Dying, Death and Disposal (1970), A Dictionary of Liturgy and Worship (1972), The Oxford Dictionary of the Christian Church (1974), The Study of Liturgy (1978, new edn 1992), A Dictionary of Christian Spirituality (1983), The Study of Spirituality (1986), A New Dictionary of Liturgy and Worship (1986), Dizionario Patristico e di Antichità Cristiane (1985), The Unsealed Fountain: Essays in the Christian Spiritual Tradition (1987); *Recreations* music, reading, winemaking, cooking, walking; *Style*— William Jardine Grisbrooke, Esq; ✉ Jokers, Bailey St, Castle Acre, King's Lynn, Norfolk PE32 2AG

GRISEWOOD, Daniel; s of Gabriel Thomas Grisewood (d 1976), and Olive, *née* Bruce (d 1993); *b* 25 Oct 1934; *Educ* The Abbey Sch Fort Augustus, Univ of St Andrews (BSc); *m* Jane; 4 da (Rachel, Sara, Naomi, Jessica), 1 s (Joseph); *Career* publisher; science ed Macmillan Publishers 1960–62, mathematics lectr Royal Univ of Malta 1962–65, md African Univ Press Lagos 1965–68, publisher Macdonald Educational London 1968–72, md Macdonald & Co Ltd 1973–74, chm and md Grisewood & Dempsey Ltd Kingfisher Books 1974–93, chm and chief exec Larousse plc 1993–95; *Style*— Daniel Grisewood, Esq; ✉ c/o Larousse PLC, 24–30 Great Titchfield Street, London W1P 7AD

GRIST, Ian; s of the late Basil William Grist, MBE, and the late Leila Helen Grist; *b* 5 Dec 1938; *Educ* Repton, Jesus Coll Oxford; *m* 1966, Wendy Anne Grist, JP, *née* White; 2 s; *Career* former plebiscite offr S Cameroons and stores mangr United Africa Co in Nigeria; info offr Wales Cons Central Office 1963–74, CRD 1970–74; MP (C): Cardiff N Feb 1974–83, Cardiff Central 1983–92; chm Cons W Africa Ctee 1977–87 and 1991–92, vice chm Cons Clubs Assoc 1978–82, PPS to Nicholas Edwards as sec of state for Wales 1979–81, Parly under sec of state for Wales 1987–90; chm S Glamorgan Health Authy 1992–96; *Recreations* reading poetry, listening to music; *Style*— Ian Grist, Esq; ✉ 29 Oakfield Street, Roath, Cardiff CF2 3RE

GRIST, Prof Norman Roy; s of Walter Reginald Grist (d 1970), of Rothbury, Northumberland, and Florence Goodwin, *née* Nadin (d 1983); *b* 9 March 1918; *Educ* Shawlands Acad Glasgow, Univ of Glasgow (BSc, MB ChB); *m* 27 Feb 1943, Mary Stewart, da of Alexander McAlister (d 1926), of Cupertino, California; *Career* Univ of Glasgow: lectr in virus diseases 1952–62, reader in viral epidemiology 1962–65, prof of infectious diseases 1965–83; regnl advsr in virology to Scot Western Regnl Hosp Bd 1960–74, head regnl virus laboratory Ruchill Hosp Glasgow 1958–83; memb Expert Advsy Panel on Virus Diseases WHO 1967–; pres: Br Soc for the Study of Infection 1982–83, Soc for the Study of Infectious Diseases 1971–72; chm Advsy Gp on Epidemiological and Other Aspects of Infection, SHS Planning Cncl 1975–83; memb: Jt Cmmn on Vaccination and Immunisation DHSS 1970–83, Dangerous Pathogens Advsy Gp 1978–80, Ctee Glasgow Branch Scot Ornithology Club 1984–86, Cncl Glasgow Natural History Soc 1988– (gen sec 1989–91, vice pres 1992–93 and 1996–, pres 1993); Bronze Medal Univ of Helsinki 1973, Orden Civ de Sanidad cat Encomienda Spain 1974; memb: Soc Gen Microbiology, Assoc Clinical Pathologists (hon memb 1989–), Br Soc for the Study of Infection, Pathological Soc of GB and Ireland; MRCPEd 1950, FRCPEd 1958, MRCPath 1959, FRCPath 1967, MRCP (Glasgow) 1980, FRCP (Glasgow) 1983; *Books* Diagnostic Methods in Clinical Virology (jtly, 3 edn 1979), Infections in Current Medical Practice (with Reid and Pinkerton, 1986), Diseases of Infection (jtly, 2 edn 1993); *Recreations* music, natural history; *Clubs* Royal Scottish Automobile; *Style*— Prof Norman Grist; ✉ 5A Hyndland Court, 6A Sydenham Road, Glasgow G12 9NR (☎ 0141 339 5242); Scottish Centre for Infection and Environmental Health, Ruchill Hospital, Glasgow G20 9NB (☎ 0141 946 7120, telex 776373, fax 0141 946 4359)

GRIST, Maj Gen Robin Digby; CB (1994), OBE (1979), DL; s of Lt-Col Digby Berkeley Angus Grist, OBE (d 1990), of Alresford, Hants, and Shirley Anstruther, *née* Bruton (d 1995); *b* 21 Oct 1940; *Educ* Radley, RMA Sandhurst; *m* 18 Dec 1971, (Margaret) Louise, da of James Littlejohn (d 1980), of Scotland; 1 s (Charles Edward Digby b 30 Nov 1974), 2 da (Katharine Louise b 12 Jan 1973, Harriet Jane b 21 Jan 1977); *Career* Gloucestershire Regt: cmmnd 1960, CO 1 Bn 1979–82, mil dir of studies RMCS 1982–84, Cdr 6 Air Mobile Bde 1985–86, RCDS 1987, mil attaché Washington DC 1988–89, dir Army Air Corps 1989–92, Col Gloucestershire Regt 1991–94, dir gen Adj Generals Corps 1992–94, Col Royal Gloucestershire, Berkshire and Wiltshire Regt 1994–; regnl co-ordinator SW TECs 1994–, exec dir Business Link Gloucestershire 1995–; chm: Museum of Army Flying Ltd 1989–92, Tstees of Regiments of Gloucestershire Museum, Middle Wallop International Air Show Ltd 1989–92; memb Guild of Air Pilots and Navigators 1990; *Recreations* gardening, fly-fishing, walking; *Clubs* Army and Navy; *Style*— Maj Gen Robin Grist, CB, OBE, DL; ✉ Regimental HQ, The Royal Gloucestershire, Berkshire and Wiltshire Regiment, Custom House, Gloucester GL1 4HE (☎ 01452 522682)

GROB, Prof Paul Richard; s of Oscar Gottlieb Grob, KSG (d 1975), and Kathleen Anne, *née* Hogan (d 1993); *b* 11 Feb 1936; *Educ* Guy's Hosp, Univ of London; *m* 1 July 1961, June, da of Herbert Fawcett (d 1957), of Zanzibar, Tanzania; 1 s (Stephen b 1963), 1 da (Catharine b 1962); *Career* visiting prof of gen practice and health care res Univ of Surrey 1980, chm Int Primary Care Network 1986, Lasdon visiting prof RSM Fndn 1987, pres Compton Heavy Horse Appreciation Soc; FRCGP, FRSM; *Recreations* sailing; *Style*— Prof Paul Grob; ✉ Abbots Garden, Eastbury Lane, Compton, Surrey GU3 1EE (☎ 01483 810410); Department of General Practice & Health Care Research, Guildford (☎ 01483 502003, fax 01483 573704)

GROBLER, Richard Victor; CBE (1996); s of Harry Steyn Grobler (d 1970), and Edith Alice Grobler (d 1982); *b* 27 May 1936; *Educ* Diocesan Coll (Bishops) Cape Town, Univ of Cape Town (BA); *m* 1961, Julienne Nora Delacour, da of late Rev Canon Laurie Sheath; 1 s (Andrew b 1970), 3 da (Caroline b 1963, Rosemary b 1966, Elizabeth b 1975); *Career* barr Gray's Inn; dep clerk Central Criminal Ct 1970–72, dep courts admin 1972–74; courts admin: Inner London Crown Ct 1974–77, Central Criminal Ct 1977–79; dep circuit admin SE Circuit 1979–84; dep sec of Cmmns Lord Chancellor's Dept 1984–96, ret; Liveryman Worshipful Co of Gold & Silver Wyre Drawers; *Recreations* gardening, swimming, golf; *Clubs* Temple Golf; *Style*— Richard Grobler, Esq, CBE; ✉ Southside, 105 Victoria Street, London SW1E 6QT (☎ 0171 210 2192)

GROCHOLSKI, Count Alexander Luan; er s of Count Kazimierz Adam Grocholski (d 1994), and his 1 w, Elzbieta Zofia, *née* Countess Baworowska (d 1987); hp to uncle Count Stanislas Bohdan Karol Grocholski, *qv*; *b* 30 Aug 1949; *Educ* French Lycée London, Study Centre for the History of the Fine and Decorative Arts London; *m* 1979, Bridget Caroline, da of Capt John Hamilton Fleming (d 1971); 1 da (Katherine Rose Mary b 1980); *Career* Phillips Son & Neale Ceramics Dept 1969–73, Sotheby's Valuation Dept 1973–78; Grocholski & Co Fine Art Valuers and Consultants 1978–; *Recreations* reading, walking; *Style*— Count Alexander Grocholski; ✉ 27 Baalbec Road, London N5 1QN (☎ 0171 226 8806)

GROCHOLSKI, Count Stanislas Bohdan Karol; head of the family; s of Zdzislaw Henryk, Count Grocholski (d 1968), of Pietniczany and Poniatow, Poland, and Maria, *née* Countess Soltan (of an ancient Lithuanian-Ruthenian family of which Alexander Soltan, Treasurer and Court Marshal of the Gd Duchy of Lithuania, was a royal envoy to the courts of Europe in 15 cent); descendant of ancient Polish nobility of the Syrokomla clan known since 1347, who fought under their family banner at Grunwald against the Teutonic Knights in 1410, under the walls of Vienna against the Turks in 1683 and, after moving to Podolia in the 17 cent produced, among others, Martin, Palatine of Braclaw and Mikolaj, Govr of Podolia; gf Count Stanislaw Grocholski and his bro Count Tadeusz m Wanda and Zofia Zamoyski, while their sister Maria m Prince Witold Czartoryski and as a widow entered the Carmelite Order; hereditary title of Count confirmed in Russia 1881; *b* 4 Nov 1912; *Educ* Bielany Coll, Univ of Warsaw (MA), Warsaw Acad of Political and Social Studies; *m* 1980, Elisabeth Victoria Adelaide, da of Albert Edouard Janssen (d 1966), Belgian Min of State, and wid of Count Thaddée Plater-Zyberk; *Heir* nephew, Count Alexander Luan Grocholski, *qv*; *Career* Reserve Offr Polish Forces; vice consul Marseilles 1938–40, consul Dublin 1945–46, gen sec Fedn of Poles in Britain 1946–51, vice pres Anglo-Polish Soc 1955–, foreign affairs ed The Polish Daily 1959–74; chm Veritas Foundation 1965–89; memb Euro Movement 1953–, memb Polish Cncl Euro Movement (Warsaw) 1992–; vice-chm: Euro Liaison Gp 1970–, Int joined as asst literary ed, dep literary ed 1964–81, woman's ed 1981–84; ed Book Choice Channel 4 1986–90, arts ed Daily and Sunday Telegraph 1986–91, literary ed Sunday Telegraph 1991–; *Books* The World of George Orwell (1971), The World of Raymond Chandler (1976); *Recreations* painting; *Style*— Ms Miriam Gross; ✉ Sunday Telegraph, 1 Canada Square, Canary Wharf, London E14 5DT (☎ 0171 538 5000, fax 0171 513 2504)

GROSS, Peter Henry; QC (1992); s of Samuel Lewis Gross, and Fanny Alice, *née* Cohen; *b* 13 Feb 1952; *Educ* Herzlia Sch Cape Town, Univ of Cape Town (BBusSc, MBusSc, Rhodes scholar), Oriel Coll Oxford (MA, BCL, Eldon scholar); *m* 1985, Ruth Mary, *née* Cullen; 2 s (George William b 6 April 1989, Edmund Walter b 6 Aug 1992); *Career* called to the Bar Gray's Inn 1977, admitted to the Bar New South Wales 1986, recorder 1995– (asst recorder 1991–95); vice-chm London Common Law and Commercial Bar Assoc 1993–; *Books* Legal Aid and Its Management (1976); *Recreations* jogging, cricket, sailing; *Clubs* United Oxford and Cambridge University; *Style*— Peter Gross, Esq, QC; ✉ 20 Essex Street, London WC2R 3AL (☎ 0171 583 9294, fax 0171 583 1341)

GROSS, Philip John; s of Juhan Karl Gross, and Mary Jessie Alison, *née* Holmes; *b* 27 Feb 1952; *Educ* Devonport HS Plymouth, Univ of Sussex (BA), Poly of North London (Dip in Librarianship); *m* 1976, Helen, da of Leon Gamsa; 1 s (Jonathan Gamsa b 20 March 1982), 1 da (Rosemary Gamsa b 20 Aug 1978); *Career* worked in publishing and libraries; writer and creative writing educator; lectr in Creative Studies Bath Coll of HE; first prize National Poetry Competition 1982; *Poetry* Familiars (1983), The Ice Factory (1984), Cat's Whisker (1987), The Air Mines of Mistila (with Sylvia Kantaris, 1988), Manifold Manor (1989), The Son of the Duke of Nowhere (1991), The All-Nite Café (1993), I D (1994), Scratch City (1995), A Cast of Stones (1996); *Novels* The Song of Gail and Fludd (1991), Plex (1994), The Wind Gate (1995), Transformer (1996); *Plays* Internal Affairs (shared 1 prize BBC W of Eng playwriting competition), Rising Star (1995); *Clubs* Soc of Friends; *Style*— Philip Gross; ✉ 87 Berkeley Road, Bishopston, Bristol BS7 8HQ (☎ 0117 942 7190)

GROSSART, Angus McFarlane McLeod; CBE (1989), DL; s of William John White Grossart, JP (d 1980), and Mary Hay, *née* Gardiner; *b* 6 April 1937; *Educ* Glasgow Acad, Univ of Glasgow (MA, LLB); *m* 1978, (Marion) Gay Kerr, *née* Dodd; 1 da (Flure b 6 Dec 1982); *Career* CA 1962; advocate Scottish Bar 1963–69, chm and md Noble Grossart Ltd (merchant bank) 1969–, chm Scottish Investment Trust plc 1974–; directorships incl: American Trust plc 1973–, Royal Bank of Scotland plc 1982–, Edinburgh Fund Managers plc 1983– (dep chm), Royal Bank of Scotland Group plc 1985– (vice chm 1996–), Alexander & Alexander Inc NY 1985–, Hewden Stuart plc 1988–, BP Scot Advsy Bd 1990–; chm of tstees Nat Galleries of Scot 1989–; Livingston award Capt of Indust 1990; Hon LLD Univ of Glasgow 1985; *Publications* Climate for Leadership (1982), The Financial Catalyst (1984); *Recreations* golf, restoration of sixteenth century castle, decorative and traditional arts; *Clubs* New (Edinburgh), Royal and Ancient (St Andrews), Hon Co of Edinburgh Golfers; *Style*— Angus Grossart, Esq, CBE, DL; ✉ Noble Grossart Ltd, 48 Queen St, Edinburgh EH2 3NR (☎ 0131 226 7011, fax 0131 226 6032)

GROSSART, Hamish McLeod; s of Kenneth William McFarlane Grossart, of Fintry, W Stirlingshire, and Mairi, *née* Paterson; *b* 7 April 1957; *Educ* Glasgow Acad, Univ of Stirling (BA); *m* 14 May 1981 (sep), Fiona Jean, da of Alastair William McDonald; 2 da (Mhoraig Louise b 14 March 1987, Cathleen Maire b 28 May 1989); *Career* dir Noble Grossart Ltd 1982–83 (joined 1979, responsible for corp fin), fndr dir First Northern Corporate Finance Ltd 1983–86; EFT Group plc: dir (following merger with First Northern) 1986–, md 1987–92, chm 1992–; chm: Quality Care Homes plc 1992–94 (dir 1994–95), Scottish Highland Hotels Group Ltd 1992– (dir 1991–), Eclipse Blinds plc 1994–, Hicking Pentecost plc 1994– (dir 1991–); dep chm: Cairn Energy plc 1996– (dir 1994–), Scottish Radio Holdings 1996– (dir 1985–91 and 1993–); dir British Thornton Holdings plc 1991–94; *Style*— Hamish Grossart, Esq; ✉ Cairn Energy plc, Cairn House, 61 Dublin Street, Edinburgh EH3 6NL (☎ 0131 557 2299, fax 0131 558 8062)

GROSSMAN, Prof Ashley Barry; s of Sidney Grossman (d 1966), of London, and Rose, *née* Green; *b* 20 Feb 1948; *Educ* Hasmonean GS, St Catharine's Coll Cambridge (open exhibitioner), UCH Med Sch London (Atkinson scholar, BA, BSc, MB BS, MD, Belasco medal, Univ Gold medal); *m* 1, 1971 (m dis 1982), Susan, da of Dr Dennis Friedman; 1 da (Emily Priscilla Sidonie b 7 July 1978); m 2, 1984, Deborah Foster, da of John Clark; 4 da (Sophie Eleanor b 28 April 1985, Annabel Clare b 9 Oct 1986, Camilla Rose b 14 Nov 1992, Cordelia Anne b 23 Nov 1996); *Career* hon conslt Dept of Endocrinology Bart's 1986–, prof Bart's Med Coll 1993– (lectr 1982–86, sr lectr 1986–90, reader 1990–93); ed Clinical Endocrinology, memb Editorial Bds Endocrinology, Neuroimmunomodulation and Functional Neurology, section ed Current Opinion in Endocrinology and Diabetes; elected memb Assoc of Physicians, memb Cncl Endocrine Section RSM; FRCP; *Books* Neuroendocrinology: a Clinical Text (with Mary Forsling, 1986), Bailliere's International Clinics in Endocrinology: The Neuroendocrinology of Stress (1987), Psychoneuroendocrinology (1991), Clinical Endocrinology (ed, 1993 and 1997); *Recreations* riding, skiing, walking, daughters; *Style*— Prof Ashley Grossman; ✉ 8 Ringwood Avenue, London N2 9NS (☎ 0181 444 8918); Department of Endocrinology, St Bartholomew's Hosp, London EC1A 7BE (☎ 0171 601 8343, fax 0171 601 8505, e-mail A.B.GROSSMAN@mds.qmw.ac.uk)

GROSSMAN, Loyd Daniel Gilman; s of David K Grossman (d 1982), of Marblehead, Massachusetts, and Helen Katherine, *née* Gilman (d 1985); *b* 16 Sept 1950; *Educ* Boston Univ (BA), LSE (MSc); *m* 15 June 1985, Deborah Jane, da of Sir David Puttnam, CBE, *qv*, of London; 2 da (Florence Grace b 1989, Constance Catherine b 1992); *Career* Harpers & Queen: design ed 1981–84, restaurant critic 1981–89 and 1991–93; contrib ed The Sunday Times 1984–86; TV presenter: Through The Keyhole (ITV until 1995, Sky One since 1996) 1987–, Behind the Headlines (BBC) 1989–92, Master Chef (BBC) 1990–, Junior Masterchef (BBC) 1994–; writer and deviser The Dog's Tale (BBC) 1993; writer and presenter: Off Your Trolley (BBC) 1995, The World on a Plate (BBC) 1996; frequent miscellaneous bdcast appearances on ITV and BBC; writer for various pubns on food, design and architecture; memb Ct of Govrs LSE, chm The Campaign for Museums, memb Museums and Galleries Cmmn, patron Nat Canine Def League, vice pres The Sick Children's Tst, patron The Scuba Tst; chm LSE Media Gp; FSA Scot, FRSA; *Books* The Social History of Rock Music (1975), Harpers & Queen Guide to London's 100 Best Restaurants (1987), The Dog's Tale (1993), Loyd Grossman's Italian Journey (1994), Curvoisier's Book of the Best (ed, 1994–), The World on a Plate (1996); *Recreations* fishing, looking at buildings, scuba diving, tennis, chess; *Clubs* Flyfishers', Hurlingham; *Style*— Loyd Grossman, Esq; ✉ c/o Peter Schnabl, 72 Vincent Square, London SW1P 2PA (☎ 0171 630 6955, fax 0171 233 5674)

GROSVELD, Prof Franklin (Frank); s of Ferdinand Grosveld, of The Netherlands, and Neeltje, *née* Veenendaal; *b* 18 Aug 1948; *Educ* Univ of Amsterdam (MSc), McGill Univ Montreal (PhD); *m* Ernie De Boer; 2 s (Rik, Joep); *Career* prof and head Lab of Gene Structure and Expression National Inst for Medical Research; Jeantet Prize for Med 1991; FRS 1991, memb Dutch Royal Soc 1994; *Style*— Prof Frank Grosveld, FRS; ✉ National Institute for Medical Research, The Ridgeway, Mill Hill, London NW7 1AA (☎ 0181 959 3666, fax 0181 906 4477); Erasmus University, Department of Cell Biology and Genetics, PO Box 1738, 3000 DR, Rotterdam, Netherlands (☎ 00 31 10 408 7593, fax 00 31 10 436 0225)

GROSVENOR, Hon Julian Francis Martin; s and h of 6 Baron Ebury, *qv*, by his 1 w; *b* 8 June 1959; *m* 15 April 1987 (m dis 1989), Danielle, 6 da of Theo Rossi, of Sydney, NSW, Australia; *Style*— The Hon Julian Grosvenor; ✉ 25/16 Leichharot Street, Glebe Point, Sydney, NSW 2037, Australia

GROSVENOR, Peter George; s of George William Grosvenor, CBE (d 1979), of Combe Down, Bath, and Mabel Mary, *née* Mortimer (d 1976); *b* 4 May 1933; *Educ* Monkton Combe Sch Bath, Worcester Coll Oxford (MA), Univ of Indiana USA; *m* 28 April 1962 (m dis 1982), Rita Mary, da of Charles Becker (d 1983), of Ealing, London; 3 s (Simon George b 5 Sept 1963, Paul William b 1 Jan 1965, Matthew Thomas b 25 March 1967); *Career* reporter: Daily Sketch 1954–55 and 1957–58, News Chronicle 1958–60; feature writer Reveille 1956–57, literary ed Daily Express 1962–96 (diarist William Hickey 1960–62); freelance 1996–; *Books* The British Genius (1973), We Are Amused - A History of Royal Cartoons (1978), Ian Woosnam's Golf Masterpieces (with Peter Grosvenor, 1988), Fred Trueman's Cricket Masterpieces (with Peter Grosvenor, 1990); *Recreations* watching cricket, playing golf; *Clubs* MCC, Royal Mid Surrey Golf, Garrick; *Style*— Peter Grosvenor, Esq; ✉ 46 King Henrys Rd, London NW3 3RP (☎ 0171 586 8474)

GROTE, Dr John David; OBE (1991); s of Royal Calverton Grote (d 1996), of Sompting, W Sussex, and Fay Dorothy, *née* Judson; *b* 5 Sept 1945; *Educ* Rydens Co Secdy Sch Walton-upon-Thames, Univ of Southampton (BSc, PhD); *m* 1, 1970 (m dis 1979), Pauline, *née* Bolton; 1 s (Matthew John b 1973), 1 da (Sarah Katherine b 1975); m 2, Barbara, da of Prof Henryk Smigielski (d 1993); 1 da (Joanna Caroline b 1981); *Career* temp lectr Maths Dept Univ of Southampton 1970–71, research fell Univ of Warwick 1971–74; Br Cncl 1974–: advsr Sci and Technol Dept 1974–75, sci offr Poland 1975–79, inspr of mgmnt servs 1979–82, dep dir Systems Dept 1982–83, sci offr Germany 1983–86, sci offr Japan 1987–91, dir Hungary 1991–96, dir Singapore 1996–; *Style*— Dr John Grote, OBE; ✉ The British Council, 30 Napier Road, Singapore 258509

GROTRIAN, Sir (Philip) Christian Brent; 3 Bt (UK 1934), of Leighton Buzzard, Co Bedford; s of Sqdn Ldr Robert Philip Brent Grotrian (d on active service 1945, s of 1 Bt), and his 1 w, Elizabeth Mary, o da of late Maj John Hardy-Wrigley; suc unc, Sir John Appelbe Grotrian, 2 Bt (d 1984); *b* 26 March 1935; *Educ* Eton, Trinity Coll Toronto; *m* 1, 1960, Anne Isabel, da of Robert Sieger Whyte, of Toronto; 1 s (Philip Timothy Adam Brent b 1962); m 2, 1979, Sarah Frances, da of Reginald Harry Gale, of Montreal; 1 s (John Hugh Brent b 1982), 1 da (Frances Elizabeth b 1980); *Heir* s, Philip Timothy Adam Brent Grotrian, *qv*; *Style*— Sir Christian Grotrian, Bt; ✉ RR3 Mansfield, Ontario LON 1MO, Canada; Calle Ample 2, Regencós, Gerona, Spain

GROTRIAN, (Philip) Timothy Adam Brent; s and h of Sir (Philip) Christian Brent Grotrian, 3 Bt, *qv*; *b* 9 April 1962; *Style*— Timothy Grotrian, Esq; ✉ 28 Bishop Street, Toronto, Ontario, Canada, M5R 1N2

GROUND, (Reginald) Patrick; QC (1981); s of Reginald Ground (d 1975), of Pinner, Middx, and Ivy Elizabeth Grace, *née* Irving (later Mrs Alan Manser, d 1992); *b* 9 Aug 1932; *Educ* Beckenham and Penge County GS, Lycée Gay Lussac Limoges, Selwyn Coll Cambridge (exhibitioner, MA), Magdalen Coll Oxford (MLitt); *m* 1964, Caroline, da of Col J F C Dugdale (d 1991), of London; 3 s (Andrew b 1967, Richard b 1970, Thomas b 1974), 1 da (Elizabeth b 1969); *Career* Sub Lt RNVR Med Fleet 1955–56; called to the Bar Inner Temple 1960 (Inner Temple studentship and Foster Boulton prize 1958), bencher 1987; cncllr Hammersmith Borough Cncl 1968–71, chm Ctees responsible for Health and Social Servs 1969–71; MP (C) Feltham and Heston 1983–92, PPS to the Slr Gen 1987–92; pres Oxford Univ Cons Assoc 1958, chm Fulham Soc 1975–95; *Recreations* lawn tennis, sailing, theatre, forestry, travel; *Clubs* Carlton, Brooks's; *Style*— Patrick Ground, Esq, QC; ✉ 13 Ranelagh Ave, London SW6 3PJ; 2–3 Gray's Inn Square, London WC1R 5JH

GROVE, Sir Charles Gerald; 5 Bt (UK 1874), of Ferne, Wilts; s of Walter Peel Grove (d 1944, 3 s of 2 Bt), and Elena Rebecca, *née* Crosthwaite; suc bro, Sir Walter Felipe Grove, 4 Bt, 1974; *b* 10 Dec 1929; *Heir* bro, Harold Thomas Grove b 6 Dec 1930; *Style*— Sir Charles Grove, Bt

GROVE, Sir Edmund Frank; KCVO (1982, CVO 1974, MVO 4 Class 1963, MVO 5 Class 1953); s of Edmond Grove and Sarah Caroline, *née* Hunt; *b* 20 July 1920; *m* 1945, Grete Elisabet, da of Martinus Skou, of Denmark; 2 da; *Career* WWII RASC served ME (C-in-C's commendation); memb Royal Household 1946–82, chief accountant Privy Purse 1963–82, Sergeant-at-Arms to HM The Queen 1975–82, ret 1982; tstee: W Norfolk Hospice, Sandringham Horticultural Tst; chev Order of Dannebrog (Denmark) 1974, offr Order of the Polar Star (Sweden) 1975, chev Légion d'Honneur (France) 1976; *Recreations* gardening; *Style*— Sir Edmund Grove, KCVO; ✉ Chapel Cottage, West Newton, Norfolk

GROVE, Rear Adm John Scott; CB (1984), OBE (1964); s of late William George Grove, and late Frances Margaret Scott Grove; *b* 7 July 1927; *Educ* Dundee HS, Univ of St Andrews (BSc(Eng)); *m* 1950, Betty Anne Robinson; 1 s (Peter), 1 da (Diana, decd); *Career* RN 1948–85; qualified in submarines 1953, nuclear trg 1958–59, Cdr 1963, Capt 1970, Rear Adm 1980, first Sr Engr Offr HMS Dreadnought (first RN nuclear submarine) 1960–64, Naval Asst to Controller of the Navy 1970–73, RCDS 1974, CSO(E) to Flag Office Submarines 1975–77, Capt Fisgard 1977–79, Chief Strategic Systems Exec 1980–85, Chief Naval Engr Offr 1983–85, ret 1985; defence conslt Babcock Energy Ltd 1986–91, non-exec dir Devonport Management Ltd 1987–91, nuclear and engrg conslt 1991–; memb Bd of Govrs BMT Quality Assessors Ltd 1990–94; chm Friends of the RN Museum and HMS Victory 1995–; Master Worshipful Co of Engrs 1994–95; FIEE 1981; *Recreations* walking, gardening; *Clubs* Army and Navy; *Style*— Rear Adm John Grove, CB, OBE; ✉ Maryfield, 6 South Close, Wade Court, Havant, Hants PO9 2TD (☎ 01705 475116)

GROVE, Josceline Philip; s of Brig Geoffrey Reginald Grove (d 1972), and Barbara Constance, *née* Woodburn (d 1993); *b* 8 Nov 1938; *Educ* Hurstpierpoint Coll, RMA Sandhurst; *m* 8 April 1970, Jennifer Clifton, da of Maj E A Calvert, of Rose Cottage Farmhouse, Faygate, Sussex; 1 s (decd), 2 da (Miranda Clifton b 1974, Venetia Mary b 1976); *Career* RMA Sandhurst 1957–58, cmmnd 1 Bn Cheshire Regt 1958, Lt 1960, TA QRR 1963–66, 4 Vol Bn RGJ Capt 1966–71; mgmnt trainee J & P Coats Patons & Baldwins 1963, C T Bowring & Co 1964–65, The Economist 1966, The Sunday Times 1967–70, J Walter Thompson 1970–73, dir Charles Barker 1978–83 (joined 1974), md Grandfield Rork Collins Financial 1983–91, dir Cardew & Co 1991–95; exec sec Wider Share Ownership Cncl 1976–78; memb: City Branch Ctee BIM 1978–83, City Sponsor's Gp - Tower Hamlets Ltd, Business in the Community 1986–87; sec Secretan Names Assoc (Lloyd's Action Gp) 1992–; memb Ct of Assts Worshipful Co of Bowyers; *Recreations* ocean racing, deer stalking, grand opera; *Clubs* Army & Navy, Brooks's, Northern Meeting (Inverness-shire); *Style*— Josceline Grove, Esq; ✉ 34 Stevenage Road, London SW6 6ET (☎ 0171 736 1533); Fasnakyle, Cannich, Inverness-shire (☎ 01456 415202)

GROVE, Peter Ernest; s of Ernest Grove (d 1974), and Elsie May, *née* Silver; *b* 18 Nov 1949; *Educ* Heathcote Sch Chingford; *m* 27 Jan 1973, Catherine Anne, da of Joseph Frederick Jolly, of Wanstead, London E11; 1 s (Alexander b 28 April 1979), 2 da (Elizabeth b 10 Jan 1981, Caroline b 18 Jan 1982); *Career* dep underwriter: Willis Faber Underwriting Mgmnt Ltd 1977, Lloyd's Syndicates 197/726 561 & 566 1984, Bankside Syndicates Ltd 1987, active underwriter Lloyd's Syndicates 197 & 561 1988, dir Bankside Underwriting Agencies Ltd 1988; dir Garwyn Ltd 1995; *Recreations* chess, reading; *Style*— Peter Grove, Esq; ✉ Bankside Underwriting Agencies Ltd, 5 Floor, Beaufort House, 15 St Botolph St, London EC3A 7PA (☎ 0171 621 1862, fax 0171 621 9917, tlx 8814440)

GROVE, Peter Hulbert; TD (1975 and bar 1982), JP (1993); s of James Hulbert Grove (d 1985), and Elfrida, *née* Golby (d 1976); *b* 24 July 1936; *Educ* Whitgift Sch; *m* 1, 3 Oct 1964 (m dis 1984), Mary Frances, da of Harry Ingledew Hopper (d 1972); 1 s (William b 1967), 2 da (Catherine b 1969, Victoria b 1971); m 2, 19 Oct 1984, Mary, da of Dr Harry Graham Dowler (d 1989); *Career* joined HAC 1956, Nat Serv 15/19 Hussars 2 Lt 1958–60, resigned cmmn and rejoined HAC 1960, HAC re-cmmnd Lt 1964, Capt 1967; transferred: Queen's Regt 1972, CVHQ RA 1977; Maj 1979, attached Staff of London Dist as SO2 (TA liaison), ret 1986; Knox Cropper: articled clerk 1952–58, rejoined after Nat Serv 1960, ptnr 1968, sr ptnr 1988–95, ret; memb: Fin and Gen Purposes Ctee Royal Masonic Benevolent Inst 1987–, various mgmnt ctees Royal Masonic Hosp 1976–86, Ctee Surrey branch Army Benevolent Fund 1991–; Special Constable 1974–85 (Long Service medal), Divnl Offr i/c HAC Detachment Met Special Constabulary 1984–85; Freeman City of London 1972, Liveryman Worshipful Co of Scriveners 1975 (memb Ct of Assts 1994–); Freemason 1964; FCA 1965 (ACA 1958); *Recreations* horology, military vehicle preservation and restoration, Co of Pikemen and Musketeers HAC, canals, narrow boats, amateur dramatics and choral singing; *Clubs* HAC, XIX; *Style—* Peter Grove, Esq, TD, JP; ✉ 121 Old Woking Rd, Woking GU22 8PF (☎ 01932 340620)

GROVE, Valerie; da of Doug Smith (d 1973); *b* 11 May 1946; *Educ* Kingsbury Co GS, Girton Coll Cambridge (exhibitioner, MA); *m* 1, 1968, David Brynmor Jenkins; m 2, 1975, Trevor Charles Grove, s of Ronald Grove (d 1980); 1 s (Oliver b 1983), 3 da (Lucy b 1976, Emma b 1979, Victoria b 1981); *Career* reporter Shields Gazette 1965–66, feature writer Evening Standard 1968–87 (literary ed 1979–81 and 1984–87); columnist: Sunday Times 1987–91, The Times 1992–; *Books* Where I Was Young - Memories of London Childhoods (1977), The Compleat Woman (1987), Dear Dodie (1996); *Recreations* tennis, family; *Style—* Mrs Valerie Grove; ✉ 14 Avenue Road, Highgate, London N6 5DW (☎ 0181 348 2621, fax 0181 348 5172)

GROVE-WHITE, Robin Bernard; s of Charles William Grove-White, of Amlwch, Gwynedd, and Mary, *née* Dobbs; (*see* Burke's Irish Family Records); *b* 17 Feb 1941; *Educ* Uppingham, Worcester Coll Oxford (BA); *m* 1, 1970 (m dis 1974), Virginia Harriet, da of Christopher Ironside, OBE; 1 s (William b 1973); m 2, 1979, Helen Elisabeth, da of Sir Francis Graham Smith, of Henbury, Cheshire; 2 s (Simon b 1982, Francis b 1986), 1 da Ruth (b 1980); *Career* freelance writer for TV, radio, press in US, Canada and UK 1963–71, asst sec Cncl for the Protection of Rural England 1972–80 (dir 1981–87), vice chm Cncl for National Parks; research fell Centre for Environmental Technol Imperial Coll London 1987–89, dir Centre for Study of Environmental Change Lancaster Univ 1991–, forestry cmmr 1990–; chm Greenpeace UK 1996–; contributor to various publications including The Times, Guardian, New Scientist, Nature; *Recreations* reading, walking, cricket; *Style—* Robin Grove-White, Esq; ✉ Conder Mill Cottage, Quernmore, Lancaster LA2 9EE (☎ 01524 382501); University of Lancaster, Bailrigg, Lancs (☎ 01524 65201)

GROVER, Derek James Langlands; s of Donald James Grover, of Hove, E Sussex, and Mary Barbara, *née* Langlands (d 1990); *b* 26 Jan 1949; *Educ* Hove Co GS for Boys 1960–68, Clare Coll Cambridge (Fndn scholar, MA, Grene prize); *m* 8 July 1972, Mary Katherine, da of David Yorweth Morgan, OBE, of Limpsfield, Surrey; 1 s (Jonathan Richard b 1978); *Career* civil servant: Dept of Employment 1971–79, Cabinet Office 1979–81, MSC 1981–88 (head of personnel and staff trg 1986–88); Dept of Employment: under sec grade 3 1989–, dir of youth trg 1989, dir of trg strategy and standards 1989–94, dep chief exec and sr dir of ops Employment Service 1994–; FRSA 1991, MIPD 1993; *Recreations* music, reading, walking; *Style—* Derek Grover, Esq; ✉ Employment Service, Steel City House, West Street, Sheffield, S Yorks S1 4ER

GROVES, Alan; s of Norman Cyril Groves (d 1985), and Clara Martha, *née* Hobbins (d 1986); *b* 19 April 1936; *Educ* William Morris Sch Essex; *m* Pauline Betty, da of Donald Frank Seeley; 1 s (Stephen Andrew John b 18 June 1964), 1 da (Marianne Nicola b 9 June 1966); *Career* with CEGB 1956–64, mgmnt accountant South Western Electricity Bd 1964–66, treas and head of financial planning Electricity Cncl 1966–74, financial dir North Eastern Electricity Bd 1974–90, fin dir Northern Electric plc 1990–95; non-exec dir Universal Building Society 1984– (vice chm 1994–); memb 100 Group of Fin Dirs 1991–95; FCCA 1960, JDipMA 1970, IPFA 1975; *Publications* Pricing, Investment Appraisal and Depreciation Policy (1970); *Recreations* golf, badminton, walking, theatre; *Style—* Alan Groves, Esq; ✉ 37 Avondale Road, Ponteland, Newcastle upon Tyne NE20 9NA (☎ and fax 01661 824764)

GROVES, Brian Arthur; s of Alfred Edward Groves (d 1990), and Winifred May, *née* Sheen (d 1996); *b* 3 July 1933; *Educ* Bishop Wordsworth Sch Salisbury; *m* 1 Aug 1955, Daphne Frances, da of Frederick Gale (d 1957); 2 da (Heather b 1956, Beverley, b 1957); *Career* journalist 1950–71, motoring ed Daily Mail 1968–71, advtg and PR dir Nissan UK Ltd 1985–88 (mktg dir 1975–85), chm David Ruskin Ltd 1988–92, md AFG Ltd 1992–94, dir Nissan UK Ltd 1994–; *Recreations* golf, flying; *Style—* Brian A Groves, Esq; ✉ Benbow, Doyle Road, St Peter Port, Guernsey (mobile 0850 857595)

GROVES, Michael Jonathan; s of Patrick Groves, and Camilla, *née* Manson; *Educ* Univ of Durham; *Career* property developer; md M J Groves (Property) Associates 1987–; tstee numerous charitable tsts; *Recreations* motor sport, horse racing, good food and wine; *Style—* Michael Groves, Esq; ✉ 218 Fortis Green Road, London N10 3DU

GROVES, Philip Denys Baker; DL (Co of Hertford 1989); s of Joseph Rupert Groves (d 1958), of Watford, Herts, and Eva Lilian, *née* Baker (d 1986); *b* 9 Jan 1928; *Educ* Watford GS, Poly Sch of Architecture; *m* 21 June 1952, Yvonne Joyce, da of George Chapman (d 1971), of Rickmansworth; 2 s (Mark b 29 April 1957, Michael b 23 Sept 1965), 1 da (Sarah b 27 May 1961); *Career* RAF 1946–48; served: UK, Palestine, Egypt; chm Architects Co-Partnership 1980–95 (joined 1955, ptnr 1965); architect for educn and health care projects: UK, ME, Far East, Caribbean; vice pres RIBA Cncl 1972–75 and 1978–80 (memb 1962–81), chm Bd of Educn RIBA 1974–75 and 1979–80 (memb 1962–80), chm ARCUK 1971–74 (memb Cncl 1962–80); chm: Univ of York Centre for Continuing Educn 1978–81, CPD in Construction GP 1986–96, Construction Indust Cncl 1993–96; memb Comité De Liaison Des Architects du Marché Commun 1972–80; external examiner at several schools of architecture in UK and overseas; govr W Herts Coll 1993–; chm Herts C of C 1985–88 (pres 1989), chm Herts Community Tst 1988–; dir: Herts TEC 1989– (chm 1992–), Business Link Herts 1993–, TEC Nat Cncl 1996–; ARIBA 1955, FRIBA 1968, FRSA 1989; *Books* Design for Health Care (jtly, 1981), Hospitals and Health Care Facilities (jtly, 1990); *Recreations* walking, reading, architecture; *Style—* Philip Groves, Esq, DL; ✉ The Dingle, Whisperwood, Loudwater, Rickmansworth, Hertfordshire WD3 4JU (☎ 01923 775921)

GROVES, His Hon Judge; Richard Bebb; TD (1966), RD (1979); s of George Thomas Groves (d 1965), and Margaret Anne Underhill, *née* Bebb; *b* 4 Oct 1933; *Educ* Bancroft's Sch Essex; *m* 1958, Eileen Patricia, da of Capt Graham Payne Farley (d 1942); 1 s (Christopher b 1963), 1 da (Caroline b 1961); *Career* Nat Serv 1952–54; TA 1954–70, Maj Intelligence Corps (TAVR) RNR 1970–83; Lt Cdr (SP) RNR PI Gp; Nijmegen Medal Royal Netherlands League of Physical Culture 1965 and 1966; admitted slr 1960; ptnr: H J Smith & Co, Richard Groves & Co 1962–85; dep circuit judge 1978–80, recorder Crown Ct 1980–85, circuit judge (SE Circuit) 1985–; *Recreations* watching sport, playing tennis, walking, reading; *Clubs* RAC, Chelmsford; *Style—* His Hon Judge Groves; ✉ Chelmsford County Court, London House, New London Road, Chelmsford, Essex CN2 0QR

GROVES, Richard Laurence; s of Wilfred Groves (d 1980), of Sheffield, and Ann Groves (d 1994); *b* 21 July 1944; *Educ* Rowlinson Secondary Sch Sheffield, Sheffield Poly (Dip Municipal Admin), Manchester Poly (Dip Mgmnt Studies), Univ of Manchester (MA), MHSM; *m* 1976, Christine, da of Gerard Grady; 1 s (Jonathan b 4 Jan 1979); *Career* clerical offr Sheffield City Cncl 1961–68, admin Tport and Town Clerks Depts Manchester City Cncl 1968–73, various managerial posts Manchester Regnl Hosp Bd N Western Regnl Health Authy 1973–75 (regnl servs planning offr 1975–86); N Manchester Healthcare NHS Tst (formerly N Manchester Health Authy): head of planning and admin 1986–88, unit gen mangr 1988–90, gen mangr and dep chief exec 1990–95, exec dir 1995–; *Recreations* football: Sheffield Wednesday under 18's, Bradway FC, and Norton Woodseats FC, referee's sec Sheffield & District League; tennis, walking; *Style—* Richard Groves, Esq; ✉ North Manchester General Hospital, Delaunays Road, Manchester M8 6RB (☎ 0161 720 2424, fax 0161 720 2888)

GROVES, Ronald Edward; CBE (1972); s of Joseph Rupert Groves (d 1958), of Watford, and Eva Lilian, *née* Baker (d 1986); *b* 2 March 1920; *Educ* Watford GS; *m* 16 Nov 1940, Beryl Doris Lydia, da of Frank William Collins (d 1940), of Watford; 2 s (Peter Warland b 1941, Richard Michael b 1958); 1 da (Mary Delia Margaret b 1945); *Career* Nat Serv RAF 1940–46, Flt Lt, seconded BOAC 1942, Capt 1943–46; pres Timber Trade Fedn 1969–71; chm: Meyer International plc 1982–87, International Timber plc 1976–87; pres: Nat Cncl of Bldg Material Prodrs 1987–90, Cncl of Euro Prodrs of Materials for Construction (CEPMC) 1992–93; chm: Nat Sawmilling Assoc 1966–67, W Herts Main Drainage Authy 1970–74; dir Nat Bldg Agency 1978–82, Business in the Community 1984–87; memb: EDC for Bldg 1982–86, Cncl of London C of C 1982–94, LCCI London Regnl Affrs Ctee 1980–95, London Regnl Cncl CBI 1983–87; cncllr: Three Rivers Dist Cncl 1974–96 (chm 1977–78), Rickmansworth UDC 1950–74 (chm 1957–58, 1964–65, 1971–72); chm: Watford Boys' GS 1980–, Watford Girls' GS 1980–; *Style—* Ronald Groves, Esq, CBE; ✉ 8 Pembroke Rd, Moor Park, Northwood, Middx HA6 2HR (☎ 01923 823187)

GRUBB, David Herbert Watkins; *b* 9 Feb 1941; *Educ* St George's Sch Harpenden Herts, Culham Coll Oxon (Cert Ed), Univ of Exeter (MEd); *Career* headteacher Gillotts Sch Henley on Thames 1980–86, gen appeal dir Barnardo's 1986–90, exec dir Feed the Children 1990– (name changed to Children's Aid Direct July 1996); memb ACENVO; ed Jl of Applied Studies in Educn 1980–86; *Books* The Gifted Child at School (ed, 1984), An Idea of Bosnia (ed, 1986); also author of 4 novels and 18 collections of poetry; *Style—* David Grubb, Esq; ✉ Children's Aid Direct, 82 Caversham Road, Reading, Berks RG1 8AE (☎ 0118 958 4000, fax 0118 958 8988)

GRUBER, Christiana; da of Max Gruber, and Gloria Gruber; *b* 19 April 1953; *Career* former actress, TV presenter and character model for broadcast commercials; publicist: American Coll Leysan Switzerland, Montreux Jazz Festival, Formula One racing; coordinator VIP facility visits and tours UN Geneva, prodn asst to film dir Jean Négulesco Spain, researcher to Harry Gilmore Time Magazine; publicist: Los Monteros Health and Sports Complex, Saatchi & Saatchi, Ellis & Barton (film prodrs), celebrity charity golf and tennis tournaments; promoted lifestyle magazine Metropolitan for Eppingfield, Redwood, contrib travel and arts pubns; ind gen PR conslt and practitioner: mktg and economic feasibility studies, lobbying, book launches, artistic ventures, design promotions, city firm of consits, corp strategy recommendation for engrg co Egypt; currently with Capital Radio plc (music and programming); sponsorship collaboration articles: on art, wine, gen interest; memb: IPR, NUJ, Chartered Soc of Designers, Soc of Arts Publicists, Women in Art and Antiques, Inst of Mktg Travel and Indust Gp; *Recreations* current affairs, food and wine, sports, visual and performing arts; *Style—* Miss Christiana Gruber; ✉ c/o Capital Radio, 29–30 Leicester Square, London WC2

GRUBMAN, Wallace Karl; s of Samuel Grubman (d 1988), of Philadelphia, Pa, USA, and Mildred, *née* Lippe (d 1985); *b* 12 Sept 1928; *Educ* Univ of Columbia NY (BS), Univ of New York (MS); *m* 29 July 1950, Ruth, da of Lewis Winer (d 1965); 3 s (James Wallace b 1954, d 1979, Steven Lee b 1956, Eric Peter b 1958); *Career* Nat Starch and Chemical Corp USA 1950–91: corp vice pres 1971–75, gp vice pres 1976–77, dir 1978–91, pres and chief operating offr 1978–83, chm and chief exec offr 1983–85; dir: United National Bank NJ USA 1978–86 (conslt to Bd 1986–), Unilever US 1981–86; dir and chemicals co-ordinator Unilever plc and Unilever NV 1986–91, dir Courtaulds PLC 1991–, dir Chairman's Club Corporate Renewal Associates Ltd 1993–, dir Videotron PLC 1996–; memb: Business Cncl UN, Engrg Cncl Univ of Columbia NY, Chem Engrg Dept Studies Ctee Imperial Coll Sci and Technol 1989; memb: American Inst Chem Engrs, SCI; FInstD, FIChemE; *Recreations* sports, music; *Clubs* Wentworth Golf, Mid Ocean Bermuda, Roxiticus Golf (New Jersey), SKY and Princeton NY; *Style—* Wallace Grubman, Esq; ✉ PO Box 977, Ascot, Berks SL5 0RD

GRUEBEL-LEE, David Mark; s of Harry Gruebel-Lee (d 1959), of Johannesburg, SA; *b* 20 March 1933; *Educ* Parktown HS S Africa, Univ of Witwatersrand (MB BCh); *m* 14 April 1957, Lydia Deborah, da of Leonard Yule (d 1941), of Johannesburg; 1 s (Leonard b 1958), 2 da (Caroline b 1961 d 1984, Elizabeth b 1969); *Career* jr appts in orthopaedic surgery: St Mary's Hosp 1960–63, The London Hosp 1963–65; sr registrar St Thomas' Hosp 1965–70, orthopaedic surgn to Albert Einstein Coll of Med Bronx NY 1967; hon conslt orthopaedic surgn Frimley Park Hosp Tst; FBOA, FRCS, FRCSE; *Books* Disorders Of The Lumbar Spine (1978), Disorders Of The Foot (1980), Disorders Of The Hip (1983); *Recreations* sailing, photography, computers; *Style—* David Gruebel-Lee, Esq; ✉ Woodburn, 2 Middle Bourne Lane, Farnham, Surrey GU10 3ND; Consulting Suite, Hampshire Clinic, Basing Road, Basingstoke, Hants

GRUENBERG, Erich; OBE (1994); *b* Vienna; *Educ* Jerusalem Conservatoire; *Career* violinist; concertmaster Stockholm Philharmonic Orch 1956–58; leader: LSO 1962–65, Royal Philharmonic Orch 1972–76, London Ensemble 1975–82; prof RAM, formerly prof RCM and Guildhall Sch of Music; played with orchs incl: all major Br orchs, Sydney Symphony, Melbourne Symphony, Hungarian State Symphony; toured in: USA, Canada, S America, Aust, Holland, Germany, Spain, Italy, Scandinavia, Switzerland, USSR, Hungary, Far East; winner Carl Flesch Int Violin Competition; cmmnd numerous new works and given first performances incl: David Morgan Violin Concerto (with the Royal Philharmonic Orch and Sir Charles Groves, Royal Festival Hall) 1975, John McCabe Violin Concerto No 2 (cmmnd, performed with the City of Birmingham Symphony Orch and Chris Seaman) 1979, John Mayer's Sangit (cmmnd, performed with Bournemouth Symphony Orch) 1980 and Ragamalika for Violin and Tambura (cmmnd, performed Cheltenham Festival) 1989, Robin Holloway's Romanza (Promenade Concert, with Simon Rattle) 1982; *Recordings* incl: Beethoven Violin Concerto (with the Philharmonia and Jascha Horenstein), Kreisler Pieces (also with the Philharmonia), Complete Beethoven Violin and Piano Sonatas (first recording by a Br artist), various works by Bach, Stravinsky, Messiaen, Durko, Parry, Reizenstein and Vaughan-Williams; *Style—* Erich Gruenberg, Esq, OBE; ✉ c/o Intermusica Artists' Management, 16 Duncan Terrace, London N1 8BZ (☎ 0171 278 5455, fax 0171 278 8434, telex 93121 02058 SL

GRUFFYDD, Prof (Robert) Geraint; s of Moses Griffith (d 1973), of Menai Bridge, Ynys Môn, and Ceridwen, *née* Ellis (d 1982); *b* 9 June 1928; *Educ* Ardwyn GS Aberystwyth, Gordonstoun, UCNW Bangor (BA), Jesus Coll Oxford (DPhil); *m* 1 Oct 1953, (Elizabeth) Eluned, da of John Roberts (d 1965), of Holyhead; 2 s (Rhun b 4 March 1961, Pyrs b 26 Nov 1963), 1 da (Siân b 14 Oct 1957); *Career* asst ed Univ of Wales Dictionary of the Welsh Language 1953–55, lectr in Welsh UCNW Bangor 1955–70, prof of Welsh language and literature Univ Coll of Wales Aberystwyth 1970–79, librarian Nat Library of Wales 1980–85, dir Centre for Advanced Welsh and Celtic Studies Univ of Wales 1985–93; chm: Welsh Books Cncl 1980–85, Welsh Language Section Yr Academi Gymreig (Welsh Acad) 1986–90 (hon fell 1995), Univ of Wales Bd of Celtic Studies 1991–93; pres: Cambrian Archaeological Assoc 1991–92, Int Congress of Celtic Studies 1995–; memb Hon Soc of Cymmrodorion (ed of Transactions 1989–93); hon fell: Jesus Coll Oxford 1992, UCNW Bangor 1993; FBA 1991; *Books* Cerddi '73 (ed, 1973), Meistri'r Canrifoedd (ed, 1973), Bardos (ed, 1982), Cerddi Saunders Lewis (ed, 1986), Dafydd ap Gwilym (1987), Y Gair ar Waith (ed, 1988), Llenyddiaeth y Cymry (1989), Cyfres Beirdd y Tywysogion (Poets of the Princes series, ed, 1991–96); *Recreations* meditating upon the uses of leisure; *Style*— Prof Geraint Gruffydd, FBA; ✉ Eirianfa, Caradog Rd, Aberystwyth, Ceredigion (☎ 01970 623396); Centre for Advanced Welsh & Celtic Studies, The National Library of Wales, Aberystwyth, Ceredigion (☎ 01970 626717)

GRUGEON, Sir John Drury; kt (1980), DL (Kent 1986); s of Drury Grugeon (d 1969), of Broadstairs, Kent; *b* 20 Sept 1928; *Educ* Epsom GS, RMA Sandhurst; *m* 1, 1955 (m dis 1986), Mary Patricia, da of Walter James Rickards (d 1957), of Canterbury; 1 s, 1 da; m 2, 28 July 1989, Lois, widow of Dr Roland Phillips; *Career* served The Buffs 1948–60, Capt, Regimental Adj (later Adj 5 Bn); served: Europe, ME, Far East; Kent CC: elected 1967, ldr 1973–81, vice chm 1987–89, chm 1989–91; chm Policy Ctee Assoc of CCs 1978–80, vice chm Assoc of CCs 1980–82; dir Liverpool Int Garden Festival 1982–83, chm Tunbridge Wells Health Authy 1984–92; chm Kent Police Authy 1992–; dep chm Medway (Chatham) Dock Co 1983–92; memb: Medway Ports Authy 1977–92, Consultative Cncl Local Govt Fin; exec mangr Save & Prosper Group Ltd (joined 1960); Liveryman Worshipful Co of Ironmongers; *Recreations* shooting, cricket; *Clubs* Carlton, MCC, Kent CCC; *Style*— Sir John Grugeon, DL; ✉ 3 Eastgate, Tenterden, Kent TN30 7AH

GRUNBERG, Michael; s of Solomon Aaron Grunberg, and Greta, *née* Fox; *b* 23 Sept 1956; *Educ* City of London Sch, LSE (BSc); *Career* chartered accountant; ptnr BDO Stoy Hayward 1985–94; md: BDO Stoy Hayward Consulting 1985–94, BDO Hospitality Consulting 1991–94, Plaza 107 Ltd; past chm Steering Ctee Comic Relief, tstee Tommy's Campaign; fndr memb Guild of Mgmnt Consultants; FCA, FIMC 1986; *Recreations* fitness, squash, skiing, scuba diving; *Style*— Michael Grunberg, Esq

GRUNDY, David James; s of James Grundy, of Nantwich, Cheshire, and Edna, *née* Littler; *b* 27 Feb 1939; *Educ* St George's Hosp Med Sch London (MB BS); *m* 15 April 1972, Mary Ethel, da of Edmund Digby Buxton, of Alresford, Hants; 2 da (Katharine b 1973, Joanna b 1976); *Career* sr MO and med supt Wusasa Hosp Nigeria 1973–79, conslt surgn Duke of Cornwall Spinal Treatment Centre Salisbury Dist Hosp Salisbury 1983–; FRCSEd 1969, FRCS 1970; *Books* ABC of Spinal Cord Injury (jtly, 2 edn 1993); *Recreations* tennis, classical music; *Style*— David Grundy, Esq; ✉ The Old Post Office, Besomers Drove, Lover, Redlynch, Salisbury SP5 2PN (☎ 01725 512905); The Duke of Cornwall Spinal Treatment Centre, Salisbury Dist Hospital, Salisbury SP2 8BJ (☎ 01722 336262, fax 01722 336550)

GRUNDY, David Stanley; s of Walter Grundy, and Anne, *née* Pomfret; *b* 10 April 1943; *Educ* De la Salle Coll Manchester, Jesus Coll Cambridge (MA), Jesus Coll Oxford (MPhil); *m* 1965, Elizabeth Jenny Schadla, da of Richard Schadla Hall; 1 s (Nicholas John b 29 Dec 1965); *Career* asst princ Miny of Power 1967–70, asst private sec to Min of Technol 1970–71, princ DTI 1971–76, econ advsr FCO 1976–78, DOE 1978–79, chief econ advsr to Vanuatu Govt 1979–81; Forestry Cmmn: chief economist 1982–90, cmmr Policy and Resources 1992– (Admin and Fin 1990–92); *Recreations* angling, bird watching, gardening, tennis; *Clubs* Dean Tennis (Edinburgh), Scottish Ornithological; *Style*— David Grundy, Esq; ✉ Forestry Commission, 231 Costorphine Road, Edinburgh EH12 7AT (☎ 0131 334 0303, fax 0131 316 4891)

GRUNDY, Ven Malcolm Leslie; s of Arthur James Grundy (d 1993), and Gertrude Alice, *née* Carter (d 1995); *Educ* Sandye Place Sch, Mander Coll Bedford, King's Coll London (AKC), Open Univ (BA); *m* 1972, Wendy Elizabeth, da of Stanley Gibson (d 1977); 1 s (Stephen James b 1973); *Career* architectural asst Bedford BC 1959–63, Community Serv Vols 1963–64, King's Coll London 1964–69, curate Doncaster Parish Church 1969–72, chaplain then sr chaplain Sheffield Industl Mission 1972–80, dir of educn and community Dio of London 1980–86, team rector of Huntingdon 1986–91, hon canon of Ely 1987–94, dir Avec 1991–94, archdeacon of Craven (Dio of Bradford) 1994–; co-fndr: Edward King Inst for Miny Devpt, MODEM; fndr ed Ministry Forum jl 1986–; *Books* Light in the City (1990), An Unholy Conspiracy (1992), Community Work (1995), The Parchmore Partnership (ed, 1995); *Recreations* classic cars, gardening; *Style*— The Ven Malcolm Grundy; ✉ The Vicarage, Gisburn, Clitheroe, Lancs BB7 4HR (☎ 01200 445214, fax 01200 445816)

GRUNDY, (James) Milton; s of Edward Kelvin Grundy (d 1958), of St Helens, Merseyside, and May Lilian, *née* Cobham (d 1980); *b* 13 June 1926; *Educ* Cowley Sch St Helens, Sedbergh, Gonville and Caius Coll Cambridge (MA); *Career* called to the Bar Inner Temple 1954, head of chambers; fndr and chm Gemini Tst for the Arts 1959–66, fndr memb and pres Int Tax Planning Assoc 1975–, fndr and chm Warwick Arts Tst 1978–, charter memb Peggy Guggenheim Collection 1980–89, chm Int Mgmnt Tst 1986–96, tstee Nat Museums and Galleries of Merseyside 1987–96; ed: OFC Report 1992–, Offshore Red 1996–; *Books* Tax and the Family Company (1956, 3 edn 1966), Tax Havens: Offshore Business Centres (1968, 6 edn 1993), Venice (1971, 4 edn 1985), The World of International Tax Planning (1984), Mediterranean Vernacular (with V I Atroshenko, 1991); *Recreations* conversation; *Style*— Milton Grundy, Esq; ✉ Gray's Inn Chambers, Gray's Inn, London EC1R 5JA

GRUNDY, Stuart; s of Clifford Grundy (d 1981), of Doncaster, S Yorks, and Freda, *née* Clark; *b* 8 Nov 1938; *Educ* Doncaster GS, RADA; *m* 31 Aug 1963, Ann Patricia Dorothy, da of Col Harry T Stanley, MBE; 2 s (Julian Henry John b 8 Oct 1964, Simon Dominic 21 June 1967); *Career* served RAF 1956–60, announcer Br Forces Broadcasting Serv (BFBS) 1960–64, presenter/prodr Radio Luxembourg 1965–67, exec prodr BBC Radio 1 1976–92 (prodr 1967–76), exec prodr The Unique Broadcasting Company Ltd 1992–; prodn credits incl: Nelson Mandela 70th Birthday Concert, Jean Michel Jarre's Destination Docklands, Freddie Mercury Tribute Concert, Sound City concert series 1992–, Radio Acad Festival 1994–; *Awards* incl: NY International Radio Festival Gold for Best Talk/Interview Prog 1989 (as presenter Three at 30 - Marvin Gaye), Sony Radio Award for Best Outside Bdcast 1989 (as prodr Nelson Mandela Birthday Concert), NY Int Radio Festival Silver for Best Talk/Interview Prog 1990 (as presenter In Dreams - A Tribute to Roy Orbison), Sony Radio Award for Best Popular Music Prog 1993 (as presenter Unsung Heroes); *Books* Guitar Greats (with John Tobler) 1982, The Record Producers (with John Tobler) 1982; *Recreations* travel, writing, large-scale gardening; *Style*— Stuart Grundy, Esq; ✉ The Unique Broadcasting Company, 50 Lisson Street, London NW1 5DF (☎ 0171 402 1011, fax 0171 402 3259)

GRUNWELL, Peter Higson; s of Charles Arthur Grunwell (d 1959), of Worsley, Lancashire, and Elsie, *née* Higson; *b* 18 Dec 1936; *Educ* Canon Slade GS; *m* 20 Aug 1960, Vivian Mary, da of Roland Daintith (d 1974), of Mawdesley, Lancashire; 2 da (Ann Kathryn (Katy) b 26 Jan 1963, Joanne Mary b 11 Aug 1965); *Career* Pilkington plc: HQ ops 1961–70, dir Pilkington Flatglass Europe 1970–80, gp chief accountant 1980–85, dir Pilkington plc 1985–, dir The Americas 1993–; chm: Pilkington Visioncare Companies 1991–, Libbey-Owens-Ford Co 1994– (chm gp's Worldwide Automotive Mgmnt Bds); dir: Pilkington Holdings Inc 1993–, Pilkington Aerospace Inc 1993–, Vidrieria Argentina SA 1990–, Santa Lucia Cristal SACIF 1990–, Santa Lucia Cristais Blindex Ltda 1990–, Pilkington Vidros Ltda 1990–; memb CBI, FCA; *Recreations* golf, tennis, gardening, sports; *Style*— Peter Grunwell, Esq; ✉ Woodfield, Croasdale Drive, Parbold, nr Wigan WN8 7HR (☎ 01257 462626); Pilkington plc, Prescot Rd, St Helens WA10 3TT (☎ 01744 28882, fax 01744 20038, telex 627441)

GRYLLS, Sir (William) Michael John; kt (1992), MP (C) Surrey NW (majority 28,394); s of Brig (William) Edward Harvey Grylls, OBE (d 1994), and Rachel Elizabeth, *née* Knapp (d 1976); *b* 21 Feb 1934; *Educ* St Ronan's Sch and RNC Dartmouth, Paris Univ, Madrid Univ; *m* 1965, Sarah, da of Neville Montague Ford; 1 s, 1 da (Lara (Mrs James Fawcett); *Career* served RM 1952–55; Parly candidate (C) Fulham 1964 and 1966; memb GLC 1967–70 (chm Further and Higher Educn Ctee 1968–70), memb Nat Youth Employment Cncl 1968–70, dep ldr ILEA 1969–70; MP (C): Chertsey 1970–74, Surrey NW 1974–; memb Select Ctee on Overseas Devpt 1970–78; chm: Small Business Bureau 1979–, Cons Trade and Industry Ctee 1981– (vice chm 1975–81); *Recreations* gardening, shooting, sailing, skiing; *Clubs* Royal Yacht Sqdn; *Style*— Sir Michael Grylls, MP; ✉ House of Commons, London SW1A 0AA (☎ 0171 219 4193)

GUARD, Howard Anthony; s of Herbert William Guard, of Seaford, Sussex, and Lilian Maud Guard (d 1995); *b* 27 Feb 1946; *Educ* Ardingly Coll, Univ of Leeds (BA); *m* 1972, Sheila Kathleen, da of Reginald Hyder; 4 s (Thomas Benjamin b 1973, Charles William b 1975, Edward Oliver b 1979, George Henry Hubert b 1982); *Career* asst dir in feature films 1968–73, prodr working in advtg indust 1973–77, fndr Howard Guard Productions (making advtg films and documentaries) 1977–; recipient of various indust awards; tstee Nat Hosp Fndn of Neurosurgery London; Freeman City of London 1995, Liveryman Worshipful Co of Barber-Surgns 1995; *Clubs* Groucho; *Style*— Howard Guard, Esq; ✉ Howard Guard Productions, 2 Bourlet Close, London W1P 7PJ (☎ 0171 631 0163, fax 0171 631 3765)

GUASCHI, Francis Eugene; s of Gino Guaschi (d 1986), of Holborn, London, and Catherine Bridget, *née* Smith (d 1982); *b* 5 April 1931; *Educ* St Marylebone GS; *m* 25 June 1960, Sylvia Rose, da of Douglas Jones Willesden (d 1959); 1 s (John b 27 Sept 1965), 1 da (Jane b 11 Aug 1967); *Career* Nat Serv 1955–57; asst gen mangr Mercantile and General Reinsurance Co Ltd 1980–85, ptnr Bacon and Woodrow Consulting Actuaries 1985–93, private actuarial conslt; FIA; *Recreations* playing the piano, mathematics, computers; *Clubs* Actuaries; *Style*— Francis Guaschi, Esq; ✉ 87 Andrewes House, Barbican, London EC2Y 8AY (☎ and fax 0171 628 2759)

GUAZZELLI, Rt Rev Victor; s of Cesare Guazzelli (d 1941), of London, and Maria Angela, *née* Frepoli (d 1984); *b* 19 March 1920; *Educ* St Bernard's Central Sch, English Coll Lisbon Portugal; *Career* ordained priest 1945; asst priest St Patrick's Soho Square 1945–48, prof of sacred scripture English Coll Lisbon 1953–58 (prof of church history 1948–53), chaplain Westminser Cathedral 1958–68 (sub-admin and canon of the chapter 1964), parish priest St Thomas of Canterbury Fulham 1968–70, aux bishop (RC) of Westminster and titular bishop of Lindisfarne 1970–; pres: Pax Christi in GB, Handicapped Children's Pilgrimage Tst; chm Ctee for Faith and Culture (Bishops' Conf Dept of Mission and Unity); episcopal promotor of the Apostleship of the Sea for England and Wales; *Recreations* walking, golf, music; *Style*— The Rt Rev Victor Guazzelli; ✉ The Lodge, Pope John House, Hale Street, London E14 0BT (☎ 0171 987 4209/4663)

GUBBINS, Prof David; s of Albert Edmund Gubbins (d 1964), and Joyce Lucy Gubbins (d 1994); *b* 31 May 1947; *Educ* King Edward VI GS Southampton (fndn scholar), Trinity Coll Cambridge (exhibitioner, BA), Univ of Cambridge (PhD); *m* 20 May 1972, Margaret Stella, da of James Francis McCloy; 1 s (Matthew Jonathan b 5 Aug 1975), 2 da (Katherine Joyce b 6 April 1977, Clare Margaret b 1 Sept 1981); *Career* visiting research fell Univ of Colorado 1972–73, instr in applied mathematics MIT 1973–74, postdoctoral research asst and pt/t adjunct asst prof UCLA 1974–76; Univ of Cambridge: postdoctoral research asst Dept of Geodesy and Geophysics 1976–77, sr assoc in research Dept of Geodesy and Geophysics 1977–81, fell Churchill Coll and lectr in mathematics for natural sci 1978–90, asst dir of research Dept of Earth Sci 1981–89; Univ of Leeds: prof of geophysics Dept of Earth Sci 1989–, head of Geophysics 1989–; memb: Royal Astronomical Soc 1972–, Soc of Exploration Geophysicists 1992–; fell American Geophysical Union (FAGU) 1985 (memb 1972), FInstP 1996, FRS 1996; *Books* Seismology & Plate Tectonics (1990); *Recreations* swimming, sailing; *Clubs* Wigton Bay Sailing; *Style*— Prof David Gubbins, FRS; ✉ Department of Earth Sciences, University of Leeds, Leeds LS2 9JT (☎ 0113 233 5255, fax 0113 233 5259)

GUBERT, Walter Alexander; *b* 15 June 1947; *Educ* Univ of Florence (LLD), INSEAD (MBA); *m* Caroline, *née* Espagno; 2 da (Amelie b 9 Feb 1979, Elsa b 6 June 1981); *Career* J P Morgan: asst vice pres Fin Analysis Paris 1973–77, vice pres Treasy Mgmnt Advsy London 1977–81, sr vice pres Capital Markets NY 1981–87, chief exec J P Morgan Securities Ltd London 1987–90, chm London Mgmnt Ctee 1990–92, md J P Morgan Advisory Europe London 1990–92, md and co-head activities in Europe, ME and Africa (i/c Corp Fin/M&A activities) 1992–95, head of Europe, ME and Africa 1995–, memb Bd of Dirs J P Morgan España SA Madrid, J P Morgan GmbH Frankfurt and J P Morgan Securities Ltd London; memb Fin Law Panel; *Recreations* golf, tennis, sailing; *Clubs* Wentworth, Overseas Bankers, RAC; *Style*— Walter Gubert, Esq; ✉ J P Morgan, 60 Victoria Embankment, London EC4Y 0JP (☎ 0171 600 2300)

GUDKA, Naresh Zaverchand; s of Zaverchand Gosar, of Nairobi, Kenya, and Jiviben Zaverchand (d 1945); *b* 13 Jan 1942; *Educ* Duke of Gloucester Sch Nairobi Kenya, Balham and Tooting Coll of Commerce London; *m* 1 April 1967, Catherine Elizabeth, da of Michael Charles Tynan (d 1951), of Limerick; 2 da (Rita Claire b 13 Feb 1968, Michelle Christine b 11 Feb 1971); *Career* articled clerk Leslie Furneaux & Co 1961–66, qualified CA 1966, Peat Marwick McLintock 1967–68, J & A Scrimgeour & Co 1968–74, Quilter Goodison & Co (now Paribas Capital Markets Group) 1974–82, Citicorp Scrimgeour Vickers & Co 1982–89, Paribas Capital Markets Group 1989–96, Albert E Sharp 1996–; FCA 1967, AIIMR 1975, MSIdip 1975; *Recreations* gardening, sports; *Clubs* Middlesex CCC; *Style*— Naresh Gudka, Esq; ✉ 2 Aston Ave, Kenton, Middx HA3 ODB (☎ 0181 907 3226); Albert E Sharp, Temple Court, 35 Bull Street, Birmingham B4 6ES (☎ 0121 200 2244, fax 0121 683 7297, telex 336550)

GUEGUINOU, HE Jean; *b* 17 Oct 1941; *Educ* l'Ecole Nationale d'Administration; *Career* French diplomat; Miny of Foreign Affairs: Press and Information Dept 1967–69, second sec French Embassy London 1969–71, head of mission of Miny of State/Miny of Def 1971–73, head of cabinet and cnsllr 1973–76, dir of cabinet of Sec of State reporting to PM 1976–77, asst dir for Southern Africa and Indian Ocean 1977–82, consul gen Jerusalem 1982–86, dir Press and Information Serv 1986–90, French ambass to Prague 1990–93 (ambass to Czechoslavakia 1990–92, ambass to Czech Republic 1993), French ambass to the Ct of St James's 1993–; memb Admin Cncl Agence France-Presse 1986–90; Chev de la Légion d'Honneur 1991, Officier de l'Ordre Nat du Mérite 1995 (Chev 1979–95), Cdr Order of St Gregory the Great, Hon GCVO 1996; *Style*— HE Mr Jean Gueguinou; ✉ French Embassy, 58 Knightsbridge, London SW1X 7JT (☎ 0171 201 1000)

GUERITZ, Rear-Adm Edward Findlay; CB (1971), OBE (1957), DSC (1942, and Bar 1944); s of late Elton L Gueritz; *b* 8 Sept 1919; *Educ* Cheltenham; *m* 1947, Pamela Amanda Bernhardina, *née* Jeans; 1 s, 1 da; *Career* served WWII RN, Home, Med and Eastern Waters; Capt of Fleet Far East Fleet 1965–66, dir Def Plans (Navy) 1967, dir Jt Warfare Staff MOD 1968, Adm Pres RN Coll Greenwich 1968–70, Cmdt Jt Warfare

Estab 1970–72, ret 1973; memb Bd of War Studies Univ of London 1969–85, chief hon steward Westminster Abbey 1975–85; pres: Soc for Nautical Res 1975–90 (hon vice pres 1990), J and K Class Destroyer Assoc 1987–; dir Royal United Servs Inst for Def Studies 1979–81 (dep dir and ed 1976–79, dir and ed-in-chief 1979–81); vice chm: Cncl for Christian Approaches to Def and Disarmament 1974–80, Victoria League 1985–88, Marine Soc 1987–93 (vice pres 1991), vice pres RN Commando Assoc 1993–; *Publications* (jt ed) Ten Years of Terrorism, Will the Wells Run Dry?, RUSI/Brassey's Defence Year Book (1978/79, 1980, 1981, 1982), Nuclear Attack/Civil Defence (1982); contributor: The Third World War (1978), The Second World War (1982), NATO's Maritime Strategy (1987); *Clubs* Army & Navy, Commonwealth Trust; *Style*— Rear Adm Edward Gueritz, CB, OBE, DSC; ✉ 56 The Close, Salisbury, Wilts (☎ 01722 333649)

GUERNSEY, Lord; Charles Heneage Finch-Knightley; s and h of 11 Earl of Aylesford, *qv*; *b* 27 March 1947; *Educ* Oundle, Trinity Coll Cambridge; *m* 1971, Penelope Anstice, da of Kenneth A G Crawley (d 1988), of London; 1 s (Hon Heneage James Daniel b 29 April 1985); 4 da (Hon Rachel Louise b 1974, Hon Kate Pamela (twin) b 1974, Hon Alexandra Rosemary b 1977, Hon Laura Charlotte b 1982); *Heir* s, Hon Heneage James Daniel; *Recreations* shooting, archery, real tennis; *Style*— Lord Guernsey; ✉ Packington Hall, Meriden, nr Coventry, Warwicks CV7 7HF (☎ 01676 522274)

GUERRA, Maximiliano Guido; s of Guido Adolfo Guerra, of Buenos Aires, Argentina, and Maria del Carmen Maldonado; *b* 5 May 1967; *Educ* Superior Inst of the Arts, Colon Theatre Buenos Aires Argentina; *m* 28 May 1988, Sandra Beatrice, da of Gian Carlo Scanferlato; *Career* ballet dancer; princ dancer La Plata's Ballet del Teatro Argentino until 1985, with Colón Theatre's Ballet Buenos Aires 1985–88, princ dancer Eng Nat Ballet (formerly London Festival Ballet) 1988–91, princ dancer with Deutsche Oper Berlin 1991, princ guest artist London City Ballet performing Swan Lake and Stevenson's Romeo and Juliet, guest artist Kirov Theatre 1992; given performances at numerous international galas incl: Chicago Ballet Benefit Gala, XI Int Ballet Festival of Havana, V Ballet Royal Gala Amsterdam, Montreal, 40th Anniversary of Eng Nat Ballet London, XVIII Cervantino Int Festival; *Roles* with Ballet Buenos Aires incl: S American premiere of Dvorak Serenade, Balanchine's Four Temperaments, La Sylphide (with Prima Ballerina Eva Evdokimova, at III Int Dance Festival Rio de Janeiro), Bournonville's La Sylphide (Colón Theatre); with English National Ballet incl: Siegfried in Makarova's Swan Lake, Nutcracker Prince and the Cavalier in Schaufuss' The Nutcracker, Franz in Hynd's Coppelia, Mercutio and Romeo in Ashton's Romeo and Juliet, Etudes and Le Corsaire Pas De Deux, Christopher Bruce's Land, the Golden Slave in Schéhérezade, Bournonville's La Sylphide (in Washington on US tour 1989) Romeo in Ashton's Romeo and Juliet (Metropolitan Opera House NY, US premiere), Carter's Swan Lake (Colón Theatre Buenos Aires 1989), Giselle, Swan Lake, Don Quixote, Vassilev's Romeo and Juliet (all on USSR tour 1989–90); other recent work incl: Vaganova's Diana and Acteon 1990, Piazolla-Lopez's Contrabajo para Hombre Solo and El Renidero 1990, Grigorovich's Spartacus with Novosibirsk Ballet Opera at St Petersburg's Renaissance 1991 (first non-Soviet dancer to perform this version of the ballet), Grigorovich's Spartacus (tour of Spain and S America 1991), Swan Lake (with London City Ballet 1991), Stevenson's Romeo and Juliet (London City Ballet 1991); *Awards* incl: Grand Prix and Silver medal 5th Int Ballet Competition Ciudad de Trujillo Peru 1985, Silver medal NY Int Ballet Competition 1987, Gold medal at XIII Varna Int Ballet Competition 1988; *Recreations* sports; *Style*— Maximiliano Guerra, Esq

GUERRA-MALDONADO, Maximiliano Guido; *see:* Guerra, Maximiliano Guido

GUEST ALBERT, Revel Sarah; da of Hon Oscar Guest (d 1958), of Hereford, and Susan Kathleen, *née* Paterson (d 1982); *b* 14 Sept 1931; *Educ* Bedgebury Pk Sch, LSE; *m* 26 Aug 1963, Robert Alan Albert, s of James Albert, of Boston, USA; 1 s (Justin Thomas b 19 Feb 1965), 1 da (Corisande Charlotte b 10 March 1967); *Career* private sec to ldr Lib Pty (Jo Grimond) 1949–51, contested Gen Election and LCC 1951 and 1952, asst ed Time & Tide magazine 1953–55, researcher and prodr Panorama (BBC) 1961–67, bureau chief Public TV Laboratory of US 1967 and 1968, formed Transatlantic Films 1968; prodr and dir 1968–; work incl: History's Turning Points I & II, Greek Fire, The Horse in Sport, The Monastery of Mount Sinai, A Year in the Life of Placido Domingo, Four American Composers, In Search of Paradise, Paris Lost, Feliks Topolski, Self Encounter - Man in a Fog, Bold as Brass, If It Moves Shoot It, Makin' It, Norman Mailer v Fun City USA; MRTS; *Books* Lady Charlotte - A Biography of the Nineteenth Century (1989), History's Turning Points (1995); *Recreations* horse training, gardening; *Clubs* Turf; *Style*— Mrs Revel Guest Albert; ✉ Cabalva House, Whitney-on-Wye, Hereford HR3 6EX (☎ 01497 831232, fax 01497 831677, car 0378 474858, e-mail 100306.3023@compuserve.com)

GUEST, Dr Ann Hutchinson; da of Robert Hare Hutchinson (d 1975), of West Redding, Conn, USA, and Delia Farley, *née* Dana (d 1989); *b* 3 Nov 1918; *m* 20 Jan 1962, Ivor Forbes Guest, *qv*, s of Cecil Marmaduke Guest (d 1954), of Bickley, Kent; *Career* dancer in a series of successful musicals NY USA 1942–50; dance notator: Ballet Jooss 1938–39, NY City Ballet 1948–61; Dance Notation Bureau New York: fndr 1940, dir 1941–61, hon pres 1961–; fndr memb Int Cncl Kinetography Laban (pres 1985), fndr and dir Language of Dance Centre 1967–; dance reconstructor: Cachucha (Royal Ballet, Ballet for All 1967, Vienna Staatsoper 1969), Pas de Six, La Vivandière (Joffrey Ballet 1977, Sadler's Wells Royal Ballet 1982, St Petersburg State Academic Ballet 1992, Zürich Ballet 1993), L'Après-midi d'un faune (San Carlo Ballet Naples, Grands Ballets Canadiens, Juilliard Dance Ensemble 1989, Zürich Ballet 1993); Hon LHD Marygrove Coll Detroit Univ 1977, Hon DHum Ohio State Univ 1987; *Books* Labanotation (1954, 1970), Your Move (1983), Dance Notation (1984), Choreo-Graphics (1989), Advanced Labanotation (1991), Nijinsky's Faune Restored (1991); *Recreations* photography; *Style*— Dr Ann Guest; ✉ 17 Holland Park, London W11 3TD (☎ 0171 229 3780)

GUEST, Prof Anthony Gordon; CBE (1989), QC (1987); s of Gordon Walter Leslie Guest (d 1982), and Alice Marjorie, *née* Hooper (d 1995), of Maidencombe, Devon; *b* 8 Feb 1930; *Educ* Colston's Sch Bristol, St John's Coll Oxford (MA); *Career* Lt RA (reg Army and TA) 1948–50; called to the Bar Gray's Inn 1956; memb Lord Chllr's Law Reform Ctee 1963–84, UK del to UN Cmmn on Int Trade Law 1968–88, bencher Gray's Inn 1978–; dean Univ Coll Oxford 1963–64 (fell and praelector 1955–65), prof of English law Univ of London 1966–, reader in common law Cncl of Legal Educn (Inns of Ct) 1967–80, fell King's Coll London 1982–; memb Bd of Govrs Rugby Sch 1968–88; FCIArb 1986, FBA 1993; *Books* Anson's Law of Contract (21–26 edns, 1959–84), The Law of Hire-Purchase (1966), Chitty on Contracts (gen ed, 23–27 edns 1968–94), Benjamin's Sale of Goods (gen ed 1–5 edns 1974–97), Encyclopaedia of Consumer Credit (jt ed, 1975), Chalmers and Guest on Bills of Exchange (ed 14 edn, 1991), Only Remember Me (anthology, 1993); *Clubs* Garrick; *Style*— Prof Anthony Guest, CBE, QC; ✉ 16 Trevor Place, London SW7 1LB (☎ 0171 584 9260)

GUEST, Dr George Howell; CBE (1987); s of Ernest Joseph Guest (d 1966), and Gwendolen, *née* Brown (d 1965); *b* 9 Feb 1924, Bangor, Wales; *Educ* Friars Sch Bangor, Chester Cathedral Choir Sch, Kings Sch Chester, Saint John's Coll Cambridge (MA, MusB); *m* 31 Oct 1959, Nancy Mary, da of William Peters Talbot; 1 s (David b 26 June 1963), 1 da (Elizabeth b 11 Oct 1965); *Career* RAF 1942–46, served France and India; organist and dir of music St John's Coll Cambridge 1951–91, lectr in Music Univ of Cambridge 1956–82 (asst lectr 1953–56), examiner to Associated Bd of RSM 1959–92, univ organist Cambridge 1973–91, dir Arts Theatre Cambridge 1977–92; concerts with St John's Coll Choir incl: USA, Canada, Japan, Aust, Brazil, Western Europe; concerts with Community of Jesus (USA) Choir in Russia, Hungary and Yugoslavia; given masterclasses in: Philippines, S Africa, Canada, USA; pres: Royal Coll of Organists 1978–80, Cathedral Organists Assoc 1980–82, Inc Assoc of Organists 1987–89; hon RAM, aelod Gorsedd y Beirdd Eisteddfod Genedlaethol Cymru; Hon DMus Lambeth 1977, Hon DMus Univ of Wales 1989, hon fell UC N Wales 1990; FRCO 1942, FRSCM, fell Royal Canadian Coll of Organists, fell Welsh Coll of Music and Drama 1992; *Recreations* Welsh language, Association Football; *Clubs* United Oxford & Cambridge Univ, Clwb Ifor Bach (Cardiff); *Style*— Dr George Guest, CBE; ✉ 9 Gurney Way, Cambridge (☎ 01223 354932); Saint John's College, Cambridge (☎ 01223 338683)

GUEST, Ivor Forbes; s of Cecil Marmaduke Guest (d 1954); *b* 14 April 1920; *Educ* Lancing, Trinity Coll Cambridge; *m* 20 Jan 1962, Dr Ann Hutchinson Guest, *qv*, da of Robert Hare Hutchinson; *Career* slr, dance historian; sec Radcliffe Tst 1966–96 (tstee 1997–), chm Royal Acad of Dancing 1969–93, vice pres Royal Acad of Dancing 1993–, chm Soc of Dance Research 1982–; FRAD; *Books* incl: Napoleon III in England, The Ballet of the Second Empire, The Romantic Ballet in Paris, The Romantic Ballet in England, Fanny Elssler, Jules Perrot, Gautier on Dance, The Dancer's Heritage, Dr John Radcliffe and his Trust, Ballet in Leicester Square, The Ballet of the Enlightenment; *Clubs* Garrick, MCC; *Style*— Ivor Guest, Esq; ✉ 17 Holland Park, London W11 3TD (☎ 0171 229 3780)

GUEST, Melville Richard John; s of Sqdn Ldr Ernest Melville Charles Guest, DSO, DFC, and Katherine Mary, *née* Hustler; *b* 18 Nov 1943; *Educ* Rugby, Magdalen Coll Oxford (MA); *m* 23 May 1970, (Beatriz Eugenia) Jenny, da of Horacio Alberto Lopez Colombres; 4 s (Edward, Benjamin, Alexander, William); *Career* entered FCO 1966, Tokyo 1967–72, private sec to Parly Under Sec FCO 1972–75, first sec commercial Paris 1975–79, FCO 1979–80; md Lucas France SA and dir Thomson-Lucas SA 1980–85, dir Channel Tunnel Group 1985–86; commercial cnsllr Br Embassy Tokyo 1986–89, cnsllr (political) and consul gen Stockholm 1990–93, head of S Pacific Dept FCO 1993–94, head of SE Asian Dept 1994–; *Recreations* tennis, golf, skiing; *Clubs* MCC, Hurlingham; *Style*— Melville Guest, Esq; ✉ Foreign & Commonwealth Office, King Charles Street, London SW1A 2AH

GUILD, Ivor Reginald; CBE (1985), WS; s of late Col Arthur Marjoribanks Guild, DSO, TD, DL, and Phyllis Eliza, *née* Cox; *b* 2 April 1924; *Educ* Cargilfield, Rugby, New Coll Oxford, Univ of Edinburgh; *Career* ptnr Shepherd and Wedderburn WS 1950–94, procurator fiscal of Lyon Court 1961–94, clerk to Abbey Court of Holyroodhouse 1970–79, baillie of Abbey Ct 1979–95; chm: Nat Museum of Antiquities Scotland 1981–86, Dunedin Income Growth Investment Trust plc, Dunedin Worldwide Investment Trust plc, The Edinburgh Investment Trust plc 1964–94, Fulcrum Investment Trust 1977–, Scottish Oriental Smaller Companies Trust PLC 1995–; ed Scottish Genealogist 1959–94, chllr Diocese of St Andrews; FRSE 1991; *Recreations* golf, genealogy; *Clubs* New (Edinburgh); *Style*— Ivor Guild, Esq, CBE, WS, FRSE; ✉ New Club, 86 Princes Street, Edinburgh EH2 2BB (home ☎ 0131 220 1085)

GUILD, Stuart Alexander; TD (1955), WS (1950); s of William John Guild, WS (d 1958), of Belmont Gardens, Edinburgh, and Mary Margaret Morton Stuart (d 1967); *b* 25 Jan 1924; *Educ* Edinburgh Acad, George Watson's Coll, Queen's Univ Belfast, Univ of Edinburgh (BL); *m* 21 Nov 1950, Fiona Catherine, da of Andrew Francis MacCulloch, OBE (d 1952); 1 s (David b 1952), 2 da (Cathleen b 1955, Lesley b 1960); *Career* RA, served UK 1942–44, Far E 1944–47, TA RA 1947–65; ptnr Guild & Guild WS 1950–89; Notary Public; county cadet cmdt Lothian Bn ACF 1966–69, vice chm Army Cadet Force Assoc (Scot) 1995– (hon treas 1976–91), cncl memb Army Cadet Force Assoc 1976–91, memb RA Cncl of Scot 1982–84 and 1985–93, memb Lowland TAVR Assoc 1966–; pres Lothians and Peeblesshire HG Rifle Clubs Assoc 1980–91 (hon vice pres 1991–), vice pres Lothians Smallbore Shooting Assoc 1985–92, chm Scot Smallbore Rifle Assoc 1986–88, memb Scot Target Shooting Cncl 1986–88; govr Melville Coll Tst 1976–91 (hon life govr), chm Sandilands Memorial Tst 1985–94; memb Worshipful Co of Merchants of the City of Edinburgh (asst Master's Ct 1972–75, memb Educn Bd 1972–81); *Recreations* golf, target shooting, photography, collecting; *Clubs* Watsonian, Murrayfield Golf, Edinburgh Academical; *Style*— Stuart Guild, Esq, TD, WS; ✉ 7 Lockharton Gardens, Edinburgh EH14 1AU

GUILDFORD, Bishop of 1994–; Rt Rev John Warren Gladwin; s of Thomas Valentine Gladwin (d 1991), and Muriel Joan, *née* Warren (d 1988); *b* 30 May 1942; *Educ* Hertford GS, Churchill Coll Cambridge (MA), St John's Coll Durham (DipTheol); *m* 5 Sept 1981, Lydia Elizabeth, da of William Adam (d 1966), and Ivy Adam (d 1962); *Career* asst curate St John the Baptist Church Kirkheaton 1967–71, tutor St John's Coll Durham 1971–77, dir Shaftesbury Project 1977–82, sec Bd for Social Responsibility Gen Synod C of E 1982–88, Provost of Sheffield 1988–94; pres St John's Coll Durham, memb Gen Synod of C of E; *Books* God's People in God's World (1978), Dropping the Bomb (ed, 1983), The Good of the People (1987); *Recreations* gardening, music, theatre, supporter of Tottenham Hotspur FC; *Style*— The Rt Rev John Gladwin; ✉ Willow Grange, Woking Road, Guildford, Surrey GU4 7QS

GUILFORD, 9 Earl of (GB 1752); Edward Francis North; DL (Kent 1976); also Baron Guilford (E 1683); patron of three livings; s of Major Lord North (k in accident 1940, himself er s of 8 Earl of Guilford), and Joan (d 1993), da of Sir Merrik Burrell, 7 Bt, CBE; suc gf, 8 Earl; *b* 22 Sept 1933; *Educ* Eton; *m* 1956, (Osyth) Vere Napier (d 1992), da of Cyril Leeston Smith; 1 s; *Heir* s, Lord North; *Style*— The Rt Hon the Earl of Guilford, DL; ✉ Waldershare Park, Dover, Kent (☎ 01304 820244)

GUILOFF, Dr Roberto Jaime; s of Angel Guiloff-Luder (d 1980), of Chile, and Blanca Eva, *née* Davis; *b* 4 March 1943; *Educ* Instituto Nacional Santiago Chile, Univ of Chile (honour scholar, BSc, LMed Surg, MD, LPhil), LMSSA, MRCP; *m* 3 Feb 1968, Dr Marcela Contreras, da of Dr Eduardo Contreras-Trabucco (d 1993), of Chile; 1 s (Claudio b 10 Nov 1968), 1 da (Carolina b 1 May 1972); *Career* trg in neurology Univ of Chile Hosp 1967–72, asst prof of neurology Univ of Chile 1972–74, Queen Elizabeth II scholar (Br Cncl) Nat Hosp for Nervous Diseases 1972–73; registrar in neurology: St Thomas' Hosp 1973–74, Nat Hosps 1974–76; sr registrar in neurology Nat Hosps for Nervous Diseases, Royal Free Hosp and King's Coll Hosp 1976–81; conslt neurologist: Westminster and St Stephen's Hosp 1981–89, Westminster and Charing Cross Hosps 1989–93, Charing Cross and Chelsea and Westminster Hosps 1993–; hon conslt neurologist Royal Brompton Hosp London 1993–, hon sr lectr in med (neurology) Charing Cross and Westminster Med Sch London 1987–; dir: Neuromuscular Unit Charing Cross Hosp 1993–, Motor Neuron Disease Care and Research Centre Charing Cross Hosp 1994–; sec for int affrs Section of Neurology RSM 1993–, memb Cncl Br Soc for Clinical Neurophysiology 1994–; memb: Soc for Clinical Neurophysiology 1979, Assoc of Br Neurologists 1981, RSM 1989, Med Soc of London 1989; FRCP 1987; *Books* Sense Perception in Idealism and The Neurological Theory (1968), Neurological Aspects of Human Retroviruses (contrib chapter, 1992), Motor Neuron Disease (contrib chapter, 1994); *Recreations* opera, classical music, tennis, gym; *Clubs* David Lloyd Tennis; *Style*— Dr Roberto Guiloff; ✉ Charing Cross Hospital, Fulham Palace Road, London W6 8RF (☎ 0181 746 8319, 0181 846 1196, fax 0181 746 8420)

GUILOR, Ralph John; s of John Kenneth Guilor, and Ingeborg Elizabeth, *née* Bambach; *b* 1 Jan 1955; *Educ* Dartford GS, Portsmouth Sch of Architecture (BArch, DipArch); *m* 1, 1979 (m dis 1990); 1 s (Edward Charles b 1985), 1 da (Rachel Elizabeth b 1983), m 2, 1995; *Career* architect Ralph Guilor Architects Ltd; RIBA; *Recreations* music, art, sport;

Style— Ralph Guilor, Esq; ✉ Ralph Guilor Architects Ltd, The Architecture Studio, 111 London Road, Cheltenham, Glos GL52 6HL (☎ 01242 251469)

GUINNESS, Sir Alec; CH (1994), kt (1959), CBE (1955); *b* 2 April 1914; *Educ* Pembroke Lodge Southbourne, Roborough Eastbourne; *m* 1938, Merula Sylvia, da of M H Salaman; 1 s; *Career* actor; RN Combined Ops WWII; Hon Doctor of Fine Arts Boston Coll, Hon DLitt Univ of Oxford 1977, Hon LittD Univ of Cambridge 1991; fell Nat Film Inst 1991; *Theatre* recent credits incl: The Old Country, A Walk in the Woods; *Television* recent credits incl: Tinker Tailor Soldier Spy, Monsignor Quixote, Tales from Hollywood, A Foreign Field; *Films* incl: Oliver Twist, Kind Hearts and Coronets, The Lavender Hill Mob, The Bridge on the River Kwai, Tunes of Glory, Lawrence of Arabia, Star Wars, Little Dorrit; *Awards* incl: Oscar for Best Actor of the Year (for The Bridge on the River Kwai) 1957, BAFTA Awards for Best Actor 1979 and 1982, Special Oscar for Contribution to Film 1979, Olivier Award for Services to the Theatre 1989, English Standard Special Award 1995; *Books* Blessings in Disguise (1985), My Name Escapes Me (1996); *Clubs* Garrick, Athenaeum; *Style*— Sir Alec Guinness, CH, CBE; ✉ c/o Ken McReddie Ltd, 91 Regent Street, London W1 7TB (☎ 0171 439 1456, fax 0171 734 6530)

GUINNESS, Hon Desmond Walter; s of 2 Baron Moyne (d 1992), and Hon Lady Mosley; *b* 8 Sept 1931; *Educ* Gordonstoun, Ch Ch Oxford; *m* 1, 1954 (m dis 1981), HSH Princess Marie-Gabrielle Sophie Joti Elisabeth Albertine Almeria (d 1989), da of HSH Prince Albrecht Eberhard Karl Gero-Maria von Urach, Count of Württemberg; 1 s Patrick Desmond Karl Alexander b 1956), 1 da (Marina b 1957); m 2, 1985, Penelope, da of Graham Cuthbertson; *Career* pres Irish Georgian Soc 1958–91; Hon LLD Trinity Coll Dublin; *Books* Georgian Dublin (1979), Irish Houses and Castles (jtly, 1971), Mr Jefferson, Architect (jtly, 1973), Palladio - a Western Progress (jtly, 1976), The White House (jtly, 1980), Newport Restored (jtly, 1981), Great Irish Houses and Castles (jtly, 1992), Dublin - A Grand Tour (jtly, 1994); *Style*— The Hon Desmond Guinness; ✉ Leixlip Castle, Co Kildare

GUINNESS, (Cecil) Edward; CVO (1986); er s of John Cecil Guinness (d 1970, gs of Richard Samuel Guinness, whose great uncle Arthur was the founder of the family brewing firm), of Clarehaven, Parbold, nr Wigan, Lancs; *b* 1924; *Educ* Stowe, Univ of Belfast, Sch of Brewing Birmingham; *m* 1951, Elizabeth Mary Fossett, da of George Alan Thompson (d 1971), of Albrighton Hall, nr Wolverhampton; 3 da; *Career* served WWII Offr Cadet RA (invalided out); former vice chm Guinness Brewing Worldwide; dir: Guinness plc 1971–89 (joined as jr brewer 1945), Wolverhampton and Dudley Breweries 1964–87; chm Harp Lager 1971–87; vice pres Brewers' Soc (chm 1985–86); chm: UK Tstees Duke of Edinburgh's Cwlth Study Cons 1971–86, Fulmer Parish Cncl 1973–91, Licensed Trade Charities Tst 1981–92, Governing Body Dame Alice Owen's Sch Potters Bar 1981–92, Wine and Spirit Trade's Benevolent Soc 1989–90; Queen Elizabeth Fndn for Disabled People: chm of the Devpt Tst 1993–96, govr and memb Exec Ctee of the Fndn 1996–; former pres and memb Exec Ctee Licensed Victuallers Nat Homes (vice pres 1991–92), memb Governing Body Lister Inst, selected as original memb Amersham Area Advsy Team Thames Valley Police Authy 1994; Hon Asst Worshipful Co of Brewers (Master 1977–78); life memb Industl Soc; *Books* The Guinness Book of Guinness (1988); *Recreations* gardening, shooting, travel, writing; *Style*— C Edward Guinness, Esq, CVO; ✉ Huyton Fold, Fulmer Village, Bucks SL3 6HD (☎ 01753 663179)

GUINNESS, Lt Cdr Sir Howard Christian Sheldon; kt (1981), VRD (1953); s of Edward Douglas Guinness, CBE (d 1983), by his 1 w, Martha Letière, *née* Sheldon; er bro of John Guinness, CB, *qv*; *b* 3 June 1932; *Educ* Eton; *m* 1958, Evadne, da of Capt Evan Gibbs, Coldstream Gds (n of 1 Baron Wraxall); 2 s (Christopher b 1963, Dominic b 1966), 1 da (Annabel b 1959); *Career* served RNR, Lt Cdr; joined S G Warburg & Co 1955, exec dir 1970–85; dir: Harris & Sheldon GP 1960–81, Quality Milk Producers 1988–, Riyad Bank Europe 1993–; dir and dep chm Youghal Carpets (Hldgs) 1972–80; chm N Hants Cons Assoc 1971–74; Wessex Cons Assoc: vice chm 1974, chm 1975–78, treas 1978–81; dairy farmer, memb cncl English Guernsey Cattle Assoc 1963–72; *Clubs* White's; *Style*— Lt Cdr Sir Howard Guinness, VRD; ✉ The Manor House, Glanvilles Wootton, Sherborne, Dorset DT9 5QF

GUINNESS, James Edward Alexander Rundell; CBE (1986); s of Sir Arthur Guinness, KCMG (d 1951), of Hawley Place, Hants; *b* 23 Sept 1924; *Educ* Eton, Univ of Oxford; *m* 1953, Pauline, da of Vivien Mander; 1 s (Hugo), 4 da (Miranda (Mrs Keith Payne), Sabrina, Anita (Hon Mrs Amschal Rothschild), Julia (Hon Mrs Michael Samuel)); *Career* Sub Lt RNVR; formerly: chm Guinness Mahon Holdings, dir Guinness Peat Group; formerly chm Public Works Loan Bd, ret; Liveryman Worshipful Co of Goldsmiths; *Recreations* fishing; *Clubs* Brooks's, Royal Yacht Sqdn; *Style*— James Guinness, Esq, CBE; ✉ Coldpiece Farm, Mattingley, Basingstoke, Hampshire (☎ 0173 326 292)

GUINNESS, John Ralph Sidney; CB (1985); s of Edward Douglas Guinness, CBE (d 1983), by his 1 w, Martha Letière, *née* Sheldon; yr bro of Sir Howard Guinness, *qv*; *b* 23 Dec 1935; *Educ* Rugby, Trinity Hall Cambridge; *m* 1967, Valerie, da of Roger North, JP; 1 s, 1 da (and 1 s decd); *Career* Overseas Devpt Inst 1961–62; FO: joined 1962, Economic Relations Dept 1962–63, third sec UK Mission to UN NY 1963–64, seconded to UN Secretariat as special asst to Dep Under Sec (later Under Sec Econ and Social Affrs) 1964–66, FCO 1967–69, first sec (econ) High Cmmn Ottawa 1969–72, seconded to Central Policy Review Staff (Cabinet Office) 1972–75 and 1977–79, alternate UK rep to Law of the Sea Conf 1975–77; transferred to Domestic Civil Serv 1980; Dept of Energy: under-sec 1980–83, dep sec 1983–91, permanent under-sec 1991–92; chm British Nuclear Fuels plc 1992–; non-exec dir: Guinness Mahon Holdings plc 1993–, Ocean Group plc 1993–, Mithras Investment Trust 1994–; tstee Prince's Youth Business Tst 1994–, chm Reviewing Ctee on the Export of Works of Art 1995–; *Recreations* iconography; *Clubs* Brooks's, Beefsteak; *Style*— John Guinness, Esq, CB; ✉ British Nuclear Fuels plc, 65 Buckingham Gate, London SW1E 6AP (☎ 0171 222 9717)

GUINNESS, Kenelm Edward Lee; s and h of Sir Kenelm Guinness, 4 Bt; *b* 30 Jan 1962; *Educ* Embry-Riddle Aeronautical U (BSc); *Career* commercial pilot; fndr chief exec offr Bay Seaplane Service Ltd; *Recreations* sailing, motorcycle road racing; *Style*— Kenelm Guinness, Esq; ✉ Rich Neck, Claiborne, Maryland 21624, USA (☎ 00 1 410 745 5079, fax 410 745 5595)

GUINNESS, Sir Kenelm Ernest Lee; 4 Bt (UK 1867), of Ashford, Co Galway; s of Kenelm Edward Lee Guinness, MBE, RNVR (d 1937), and Josephine (d 1989), da of Sir Thomas Strangman, sometime Advocate Gen in Bombay; suc unc, Sir Algernon Arthur St Lawrence Lee Guinness, 3 Bt, 1954; *b* 13 Dec 1928; *Educ* Eton, MIT (BSc); *m* 1961, Mrs Jane Nevin Dickson; 2 s (Kenelm Edward Lee b 1962, Sean St Lawrence Lee b 1966); *Heir* s, Kenelm Edward Lee Guinness b 30 Jan 1962; *Career* late 2 Lt RHG; engr Int Bank for Reconstruction and Devpt (World Bank) 1954–75; ind consltg engr 1975–90; memb American Soc of Civil Engrs; *Recreations* sailing; *Clubs* Cavalry & Guards', Household Division Yacht, Cruising Club of America; *Style*— Sir Kenelm Guinness, Bt; ✉ Rich Neck, Claiborne, Maryland 21624, USA (☎ 00 1 410 745 5079)

GUINNESS, Lucinda Jane (Lulu); da of Miles James Rivett-Carnac, *qv*, of Martyr Worthy Manor, nr Winchester, Hants, and April Sally, *née* Villar; *b* 29 May 1960; *Educ* Riddlesworth Hall Diss Norfolk, Downe House Newbury Berks, Queens Gate Sch London, Cape Town Univ; *m* 11 Nov 1986, Valentine Guy Bryan Guinness, s of Lord Moyne, *qv*; 1 da (Tara Victoria); *Career* handbag designer 1989–; launched career with Lulu Bag (signature briefcase design), subsequently moved into high fashion showing seasonally at The London Design Show and The Coterie NY; numerous stockists worldwide incl London, NY, Paris and Hong Kong; *Recreations* travel, reading, shopping; *Style*— Mrs Lulu Guinness; ✉ Lulu Ltd, 66 Ledbury Road, London W11 2AJ (☎ 0171 221 9686)

GUINNESS, Timothy Whitmore Newton (Tim); s of Capt Eustace Guinness, DSC, RN, and Angela Beryl, *née* Hoare (d 1990); *b* 20 June 1947; *Educ* Eton, Magdalene Coll Cambridge (BSc), MIT (MSc); *m* 6 June 1974, Beverley Anne, da of George Mills, of Rotherfield, East Sussex; 2 s (Edward, Harry), 2 da (Mary, Katherine); *Career* Baring Bros & Co Ltd 1970–77, Guinness Mahon & Co 1977–87 (investmt dir 1982–87), jt md Guinness Flight Global Asset Management Ltd 1987–; memb Ct of Assts Worshipful Co of Grocers; *Recreations* sailing; *Clubs* City Univ, MCC, RYS; *Style*— Tim Guinness, Esq; ✉ Lighterman's Court, 5 Gainsford Street, London SE1 2NE

GUINNESS ASCHAN, Marit Victoria; da of Henry Samuel Howard Guinness (d 1975), of Chelsea, London, and Alfhild Holter (d 1983); *b* London; *Educ* PNEU, art schs in Munich, Florence and Paris; *m* (m dis 1963), Carl William Aschan, s of Judge Nils Aschan (d 1966), of Stockholm, Sweden; 1 s (David), 1 da (Juliet); *Career* Nat Serv MOI 1940–45; enamellist, painter and jeweller; individual exhibitions incl: Beaux Arts Gallery London 1948, Van Diemen Lilienfeld Galleries NY 1949, 1955, 1957, 1959, 1962, 1966 and 1968, Inter Art Gallery Caracus 1973, Galleri J Kraus Paris 1977, Roy Miles Gallery London 1979, Saga Gallery London 1990, Benney London 1996, Galleri Galtung Oslo 1974, 1981, 1984, 1990, 1991, 1993, 1994 and 1996; cmmns and collections in England incl: V & A, Worshipful Co of Goldsmiths London, Focal Point on the Cross for the High Altar Exeter Cathedral, J R Abbey Collection, Hugo and Reine Pitman Collection, Paul Oppé Collection, Royal Norwegian Embassy Collection, Iliffe Collection, John Studzinski Collection; in Norway: HM the late King Olav V of Norway, HM The Queen of Norway, Kunstindustrimuseet Oslo, Hans Rasmus Astrup Collection; in USA: Brooklyn Museum NY, Yale Univ Art Gallery, Nelson Gallery and Atkins Museum Kansas, New Orleans Museum of Art, North Carolina Museum of Art Raleigh, Ian Woodner Family Collection New York, Beal Fndn Collection Boston Mass, Martin and Els Wyler Collection Switzerland, Madame Jacques Koerfer Collection Switzerland; work in numerous other private collections worldwide; memb Chelsea Arts Club 1967, pres Artist Enamellers 1969–90; *Books* incl: Modern Jewellery (1963), The Art of Jewellery (1968), Enamels (ed, 1983), Marit Guinness Aschan - Enamellist of Our Time (biog by Graham Hughes, 1995); *Recreations* travelling; *Clubs* Chelsea Arts; *Style*— Mrs Marit Guinness Aschan; ✉ 25 Chelsea Park Gardens, London SW3 6AF (☎ 0171 352 2562); Studios 3 and 4, Moravian Close, 381 King's Rd, London SW10 0LP (☎ 0171 352 3790)

GUISE, Christopher James (Jamie); s of Sir Anselm Guise, 6 Bt (d 1970), and Nina Margaret Sophie, *née* Grant (d 1991); hp of bro, Sir John Guise, 7 Bt, *qv*; *b* 10 July 1930; *Educ* Stowe; *m* 7 Nov 1969, Carole Hoskins, er da of Jack Hoskins Master (d 1979), and Ruth Master (d 1994); 1 s (Anselm Mark b 1971), 1 da (Ruth Victoria Margaret b 1972); *Career* dir: Winglaw Group Ltd, Just Ice (UK) Ltd, Pasta Galore Ltd; *Recreations* golf, shooting, fishing, gardening; *Clubs* Turf, Beefsteak, MCC; *Style*— Jamie Guise, Esq; ✉ Easton Town Farm, Sherston, Malmesbury, Wilts SN16 OPS (☎ and fax 01666 840310)

GUISE, Sir John Grant; 7 Bt (GB 1783), of Highnam Court, Glos; s of Sir Anselm William Edward Guise, 6 Bt, JP (d 1970), and Margaret (d 1991), da of Sir James Grant, 1 and last Bt; *b* 15 Dec 1927; *Educ* Winchester, RMA Sandhurst; *m* 14 October 1992, Sally H M, da of late Cdr H G C Stevens, RN; *Heir* bro, Christopher James Guise, *qv*; *Career* Capt 3 Hussars (ret 1959); Jockey Club official 1968–92; patron of one living; *Clubs* Turf; *Style*— Sir John Guise, Bt; ✉ Elmore Court, Gloucester GL2 6NT (☎ 01452 720293)

GULBENKIAN, Boghos Parsegh (Paul); s of Krikor Parsegh Gulbenkian (d 1968), of Beaulieu, Hants, and Vergine Gulbenkian (d 1965); *b* 23 March 1940; *Educ* KCS Wimbledon, LSE (LLB); *m* 1; 1 da (Vergine b 24 Nov 1968); m 2, 1 da (Sylvia b 27 July 1972); m 3, 15 Dec 1990, Jacqueline, da of late Bedros Chamlian; *Career* admitted slr 1965; Isadore Goldman: ptnr 1970–89, sr ptnr 1989–; Gulbenkian Harris Andonian 1989–; pt/t immigration adjudicator appointed by Lord Chllr 1989–; asst recorder appointed by Lord Chllr 1992–; chm Serv Mgmnt Ctee Camden CAB 1978–83, pres Holborn Law Soc 1984–85, memb Legal Aid Appeal Panel 1984–89; tstee: St Sarkis Charity Tst, various tsts for benefit of Armenian Community, Fndn for Int Health; memb Law Soc 1968 (hon auditor 1988–89); fndr memb: Slrs' Family Law Assoc, Immigration Law Practitioners' Assoc, Euro Immigration Lawyers' Gp; FRSA; *Recreations* music, tennis, squash, walking; *Style*— Paul Gulbenkian, Esq; ✉ 4 The Square, High Pine Close, Weybridge, Surrey KT13 9EA; Gulbenkian Harris Andonia, 181 Kensington High St, London W8 6SH (☎ 0171 937 1542, fax 0171 938 2059)

GULL, Sir Rupert William Cameron; 5 Bt (UK 1872), of Brook Street; s of Sir Michael Swinnerton Cameron Gull, 4 Bt (d 1989), and his 1 w, Yvonne, *née* Heslop; *b* 14 July 1954; *Educ* Diocesan Coll Cape Town, Univ of Cape Town; *m* 1980, Gillian Lee, da of Robert Howard Gordon MacFarlaine; 3 da (Victoria Yvonne b 3 Nov 1984, Katie Alexandra b 9 Dec 1986, Olivia b 2 Dec 1993); *Heir* great uncle, John Evelyn Gull, MC b 26 March 1914; *Career* dir Kintail Capital Investment (Pty) Ltd; *Clubs* Western Province Sports, Western Province Cricket, Royal Cape Golf; *Style*— Sir Rupert Gull, Bt; ✉ Harcourt Road, Claremont, Cape Town, South Africa

GULLACHSEN, Lorentz; s of Willoughby (Gus) Gullachsen, of Stratford upon Avon, and Doris, *née* Price; *b* 18 March 1951; *Educ* Birmingham Poly Sch of Photography (Dip); *m* 1982 (m dis 1991), remarried 1992 (m dis 1993), Maxine; 1 da (Laurie-Mo b 23 Nov 1983), 1 s (Jack Gustav b 19 April 1988); *Career* photographer (specialising in location advtg shooting worldwide); fndr Pictures Studio Birmingham 1974–88, working from London 1988–; numerous gp/association exhbns, has published extensively in all continents; Association of Photographers Awards incl Silver/Merits 1988–93 and Gold 1989, Gold Benson and Hedges Professional Awards 1990; memb: Assoc of Photographers 1977, RPS 1991; *Recreations* photography; *Clubs* Birmingham Press; *Style*— Lorentz Gullachsen, Esq; ✉ The Peter Bailey Company, 2 Devonshire Mews West, London W1 (☎ 0171 935 2626, fax 0171 925 7557)

GULLAN, Richard Wilson; s of Archibald Gordon Gullan, OBE, of Rickmansworth, Herts, and (Mary) Helena, *née* Todd; *b* 22 June 1953; *Educ* Merchant Taylors', Med Coll of St Bartholomew's Hosp (BSc, MB BS, MRCP); *m* 28 July 1979, Christine, da of Leslie Douglas Prime, of Wimbledon; 2 s (James Hector b 1985, Archie Charles b 1987), 2 da (Laura Jane b 1983, Helena Clare b 1988); *Career* surgical training rotator St Bartholomew's Hosp 1979–82 (house surgn Professorial Surgical Unit 1977–78); lectr in anatomy Univ of Manchester 1978–79, neurosurgical SHO Addenbrooke's Hosp Cambridge 1982–83, supervisor in anatomy Gonville and Caius Coll Cambridge 1982–83, neurosurgical registrar Edinburgh 1983–85; neurosurgical sr registrar: Guy's 1985–87, King's Coll Hosp 1985–87, Brook Regnl Unit 1987–88; conslt neurosurgeon SE Thames Regnl Neurosurgical Unit 1988–, hon conslt neurosurgeon Maudsley Hosp London 1988– (sr registrar 1985–87); memb Soc of Br Neurological Surgns, fndr memb Br Cervical Spine Soc; FRCS 1982, FRSM, fell London Med Soc; *Recreations* music (violinist), golf; *Clubs* Moor Park Golf Herts, Royal Cinque Ports Golf; *Style*— Richard Gullan, Esq; ✉ South East Thames Regional Neurosurgical Unit, Brook Hospital, Shooters Hill, London SE18 4LW (☎ 0181 856 5555, fax 0181 312 6258)

GULLIVER, Ronald; s of Ronald Charles Gulliver (d 1974), and Helen Christiana Duval; *b* 12 Aug 1940; *Educ* Kelvinside Acad, King Alfred's Sch, Univ of London (LLB);

m Daphne, da of Sir Henry Lushington, Bt (d 1988); 1 s (Christopher Ronald b 5 April 1974), 1 da (Patricia Jean b 19 Jan 1976); *Career* articled clerk rising to ptnr Fryer Sutton Morris & Co Chartered Accountants 1957–65, asst tech offr ICAEW 1965–67, ptnr P A Thomas & Co Chartered Accountants 1967–70, sr tax ptnr Nabarro Nathanson Solicitors 1974–94 (articled clerk 1970–74); chm: Orr & Boss Ltd Management Consultants 1988–90, Forminster plc 1988–95, G Stow plc 1991–; ICAEW awards: Plender prize, Sir Harold Howitt prize, Morgan prize, certificate of merit; FCA 1973 (ACA 1963), memb Law Soc 1974; memb: HAC 1963–, Light Cavalry Troop HAC 1991–; *Recreations* farming, riding, wildlife, music and theatre; *Clubs* IOD, Naval and Military, Phyllis Court; *Style*— Ronald Gulliver, Esq; ✉ c/o The Old Chapel, New Mill, Eversley, Hants RG27 0RA (☎ home 0118 973 3194, office 0118 973 0300, fax 01734 730022)

GUMLEY, Frances; *see:* Gumley-Mason, Frances

GUMLEY, Kenneth Louis; s of Lindsay Douglas Gumley, JP (d 1973); *b* 7 Oct 1932; *Educ* Fettes; *m* 1959, Anne Hogg, da of Lt-Col Robert Hogg Forbes, OBE (d 1978); 1 s (John Lindsay Robert b 1967), 1 da (Sally Catherine b 1961); *Career* chartered surveyor; md: The Joint Properties Ltd, Gogar Park Curling Club Ltd; *Recreations* curling, sailing (yachts 'Bandit of Lorne' and ' Cromarty 36'); *Clubs* Royal Forth Yacht, Royal Highland Yacht, Royal Caledonian Curling; *Style*— Kenneth L Gumley, Esq; ✉ Almondfield, 18 Whitehouse Rd, Edinburgh EH4 6NN (☎ 0131 336 4839)

GUMLEY-MASON, Frances Jane Miriah Katrina; da of Franc Stewart Gumley (d 1981), and Helen Teresa McNicholas (d 1987); *b* 28 Jan 1955; *Educ* St Augustine's and St Benedict's Ealing, Newnham Coll Cambridge (MA); *m* 2 July 1988, Andrew Samuel Mason; 1 s (John Michael Gumley Mason b 1989), 1 da (Helena Jane Gumley Mason b 1991); *Career* journalist, broadcaster, radio & television prodr and headmistress; Parly res 1974, braille transcriber 1975; Catholic Herald: editorial asst 1975–76, staff reporter and literary ed 1976–79, ed 1979–81; sr prodr religious broadcasting BBC 1981–88, series ed Channel 4 1988–89, acting exec prodr Religion BBC World Service 1989, guest prodr and scriptwriter BBC Radio 4 1989–95; headmistress St Augustine's Priory Ealing 1995–; Mistress of the Keys (Catholic Writers' Guild) 1982–87; *Books* with Brian Redhead: The Good Book, The Christian Centuries, The Pillars of Islam, Protestors for Paradise; *Recreations* playing with my children's toys; *Style*— Mrs F J Gumley-Mason; ✉ 2 Rathgar Avenue, Ealing, London W13 9PL

GUMMER, Rt Hon John Selwyn; PC (1985), MP (C) Suffolk Coastal (majority 19,285); s of Rev Canon Selwyn Gummer, and (Margaret) Sybille Vera, *née* Mason (d 1993); bro of Baron Chadlington, *qv*; *b* 26 Nov 1939; *Educ* King's Sch Rochester, Selwyn Coll Cambridge; *m* 1977, Penelope Jane, yr da of John P Gardner; 2 s, 2 da; *Career* md EP Group of Companies 1975–80; chm: Selwyn Sancroft International 1976–81, Siemssen Hunter Ltd 1980 (dir 1973); MP (C): Lewisham W 1970–74, Eye Suffolk 1979–83, Suffolk Coastal 1983–; vice chm Cons Pty 1972–74, PPS to Min of Agric 1972, govt whip 1981–83, under sec of state Employment June-Oct 1983, chm Cons Pty 1983–85; min of state: Employment 1983–84, Agric Fisheries and Food 1985–88; paymaster gen 1984–85, min for Local Govt 1988–July 1989, min Agric Fisheries and Food July 1989–93, sec of state for the Environment 1993–; memb Parly Ecclesiastical Ctee 1993; memb Gen Synod C of E 1978–92, guardian of the Shrine of Our Lady of Walsingham 1983–; *Books* To Church with Enthusiasm (1969), The Permissive Society (1971), The Christian Calendar (1973), Faith in Politics (1987), Christianity and Conservatism (1990); *Recreations* reading, gardening, Victorian buildings; *Style*— The Rt Hon John Gummer, MP; ✉ House of Commons, London SW1A 0AA (☎ 0171 219 3000)

GUMMER, Peter Selwyn; *see:* Chadlington, Baron

GUN-MUNRO, Sir Sydney Douglas; GCMG (1979), kt (1977), MBE (1957); s of Barclay Gun-Munro, and Marie Josephine Gun-Munro; *b* 29 Nov 1916; *Educ* Grenada Boys' Secdy Sch, King's Coll Hosp London; *m* 1943, Joan, *née* Benjamin; 2 s, 1 da; *Career* house surgn Horton EMS Hosp 1943, MO Lewisham Hosp 1943–46; dist MO Grenada 1946–49, surgn Gen Hosp St Vincent 1949–71, dist MO Bequia 1972–76, govr St Vincent 1977, govr gen St Vincent and Grenadines 1979–85; FRCS 1985; *Style*— Sir Sydney Gun-Munro, GCMG, MBE; ✉ Bequia, St Vincent and the Grenadines, West Indies (☎ 00 1 809 45 83261)

GUNN, Dr Alexander Derek Gower; OBE (1989); s of Col Alexander Joseph Gunn (d 1978), of West Bridgford, Nottingham, and Cassandra Valerie, *née* Hines (d 1978); *b* 27 Aug 1933; *Educ* William Hulme's GS Manchester, Univ of Sheffield; *m* 4 Jan 1956, Sheila Mary, da of Wilfred Gearey (d 1976), of Sale, Manchester; 1 s (Mark Alexander Gower b 25 Aug 1958), 1 da (Jessica Mary Cassandra b 21 April 1960); *Career* asst GP Darbishire House Health Centre Manchester 1961–64, asst MO Univ Health Serv Sheffield 1964–67, dir Univ Health Serv Reading 1971– (dep dir 1967–71); temp advsr WHO Geneva 1982–; formerly pres: Br Assoc of Health Servs in Higher Educn (UK), Euro Union Sch and Univ Health Servs, Assoc of Welfare Offrs in Higher Educn (UK), Reading Diabetic Assoc; med advsr Berks Red Cross Soc; former govr: Nat Bureau for Handicapped Students, Norlands Trg Coll for Nursery Nurses Hungerford Berks; med author, ed and advsr to publishers; MRCS, LRCP, DPH, DObstRCOG; *Books* Privileged Adolescent (1970), International Handbook of Medical Science (1974), Uprooting - Psycho-Social Problems of Overseas Students (1983), Oral Contraception - 30 Year History (1986); *Recreations* wining, dining, gardening, boating; *Style*— Dr Alexander D G Gunn, OBE; ✉ University Health Centre, 9 Northcourt Ave, Reading RG2 7HE (☎ 0118 987 4551/2)

GUNN, Andrew; RD (1980); s of Andrew Gunn (d 1985), and Mary Anne Jane Murray Gunn (d 1979); *b* 6 March 1936; *Educ* Univ of Edinburgh (MB ChB); *m* 1 Dec 1962, Deirdre Elizabeth Mary, da of Edmond Richard Weld, of Kirkden House, By Letham, Angus; 1 s (Adrian Richard b 1965), 3 da (Hilary Mary b 1964, Clare Elizabeth b 1966, Phillippa Jane b 1967); *Career* RNR 1965–85, Lt Cdr; conslt surgn Tayside Health Bd, hon sr lectr Univ of Dundee, dir Iatros Ltd; pres Br Assoc of Endocrine Surgns 1988–90; FRCSEd 1962 (memb Cncl 1990–); *Books* Exploration of the Parathyroid Glands (1988); *Style*— Mr Andrew Gunn, RD; ✉ Kirkden House, By Letham, Angus DD8 2QF (☎ 01307 818296); Iatros Ltd, Prospect 2, Dundee Technology Park, Dundee DD2 1TY (☎ 01382 562111)

GUNN, Bryan James; s of James William Donald Gunn, of Invergordon, Ross-shire, and Jessie, *née* Sinclair; *b* 22 Dec 1963; *Educ* Invergordon Acad; *m* 11 June 1989, Susan Ruth, da of John Winnard; 2 da (Françesca b 28 April 1990 (d 1992), Melissa b 22 Nov 1991); *Career* professional footballer (goalkeeper); 40 appearances Aberdeen 1980–86 (memb Euro Cup Winner's Cup winning squad 1983), over 400 appearances Norwich City 1986–; charity fundraiser for leukaemia research; Scotland caps: schoolboy, under 18, under 19, 10 under 21, 3 B, 6 full; *Recreations* golf, listening to music, watching TV; *Style*— Bryan Gunn, Esq; ✉ Norwich City FC, Carrow Rd, Norwich, Norfolk NR1 1JE (☎ 01603 760760)

GUNN, Catherine Rachel (Cathy); da of John Sinclair Gunn, of Callow, Derbys, and Rosemary Elizabeth, *née* Williams; *b* 28 May 1954; *Educ* St Swithun's Sch Winchester, Univ of Durham (BA), Univ of Edinburgh (Dip Business Admin); *m* 1994, Charles Guybon Hutson; 1 s (Rollo Guybon Hutson, b 8 Nov 1994), 1 da (Tallulah Rosemary Hutson b 4 June 1996); *Career* investmt analyst Touche Remnant & Co 1976–78; fin writer: Investors Chronicle 1978–80, The Times 1980–81, freelance 1981–83; fin writer and dep ed Financial Weekly 1983–86, City ed Today 1987–91 (dep City ed 1986–87), writer, broadcaster and freelance conslt 1991–, fin ed The People 1993–; *Publications* Fraud: The Growth Industry of the Eighties (Unwin Hyman, with Mihir Bose, 1989), Nightmare on Lime Street: Whatever happened to Lloyd's of London (Smith Gryphon, 1992 and 1993), High Street Robbery - How the Banks hold up their Customers (Smith Gryphon, 1993); *Recreations* reading, travel, scribbling, entertaining; *Clubs* London Press; *Style*— Cathy Gunn; ✉ The People, One Canada Square, Canary Wharf, London E14 5AP

GUNN, Prof John Charles; CBE (1994); s of Albert Charles Gunn, of Charlwood, Surrey, and Lily Hilda Gunn (d 1990); *b* 6 June 1937; *Educ* Brighton, Hove and Sussex GS, Reigate GS, Univ of Birmingham (MB ChB, MD), Univ of London (DPM); *m* 1, 9 Sept 1959 (m dis 1987), Celia Ann Frances (d 1989), da of Harry Richard Willis, of Charlwood, Surrey; 1 s (Richard Charles b 10 March 1962), 1 da (Frances Margaret b 28 Sept 1964); m 2, 11 Nov 1989, Pamela Jane, da of Rev P Geoffrey Taylor, of Liverpool; *Career* Pouse offr Queen Elizabeth Hosp Birmingham 1961–63, registrar Maudsley Hosp London 1963–67; Inst of Psychiatry: res worker and lectr 1967–71, sr lectr 1971–75, prof of forensic psychiatry 1978–; dir Special Hosps Res Unit 1975–78; memb Home Sec's Advsy Bd on Restricted Patients 1982–91, advsr House of Commons Social Servs Ctee 1985–86 (Ctee on Violence in Marriages 1975), memb DH/Home Office Review of Servs for Mentally Disordered Offenders (The Reed Ctee), memb Royal Cmmn on Criminal Justice 1991–93; FRCPsych 1980 (MRCPsych 1971); *Books* Violence in Human Society (1973), Epileptics in Prison (1977), Psychiatric Aspects of Imprisonment (1978), Forensic Psychiatry (1993); *Recreations* walking, photography, theatre, opera, cinema; *Clubs* Athenaeum, RSM; *Style*— Prof John Gunn, CBE; ✉ Institute of Psychiatry, De Crespigny Park, Camberwell, London SE5 8AF (☎ 0171 919 3123, answerphone 0171 701 7063, fax 0171 277 0283)

GUNN, Prof Sir John Currie; kt (1982), CBE (1976); s of Richard Gunn, and Jane Blair Currie; *b* 13 Sept 1916; *Educ* Glasgow Acad, Univ of Glasgow, St John's Coll Cambridge; *m* 1944, Betty Russum, OBE; 1 s; *Career* WWII researching for Admty; former applied mathematics lectr Univs of Manchester and London; Cargill prof of natural philosophy Univ of Glasgow 1949–82 (head of dept 1973–82, emeritus prof 1982–, dean of faculties 1989–91); former memb: Sci Res Cncl, UGC; Hon DSc: Heriot-Watt Univ 1981, Univ of Loughborough 1983; Hon DUniv Open Univ 1989; FRSE 1959, FIMA, FInstP; *Style*— Prof Sir John Gunn, CBE, FRSE; ✉ 32 Beaconsfield Rd, Glasgow G12 0NY (☎ 0141 357 2001)

GUNN, (Alan) Richard; CBE (1991); s of Alan Leslie Gunn (d 1960), of St Vincent and The Grenadines, and Violet Adeline, *née* Hazell; *b* 19 Jan 1936; *Educ* Boys' GS St Vincent WI, Southern Coll of Art Portsmouth Hants, Regent St Poly London; *m* 28 April 1962, Flora Beryl, da of Charles Fitz-william Richardson (d 1962), of St Vincent and the Grenadines; 1 s (Anthony b 1962), 2 da (Cheryl b 1964, Beverley b 1970); *Career* dir Hazells 1964–74, chm and chief offr Property Investments Ltd 1974–87; high cmmr for Eastern Caribbean States to Ct of St James's 1987–94; pres St Vincent Chamber of Indust and Commerce 1984–86, dir Caribbean Assoc of Indust and Commerce 1984–87; *Recreations* sailing; *Style*— Richard Gunn, Esq, CBE; ✉ Fairhall, PO Box 126, St Vincent and the Grenadines

GUNN, Sir Robert Norman; kt (1995), DL (Notts 1995); s of Donald MacFie Gunn (d 1930), and Margaret, *née* Pallister (d 1965); *b* 16 Dec 1925; *Educ* Royal HS Edinburgh, Worcester Coll Oxford (MA); *m* 1956, Joan, da of Frederick Parry (d 1972); 1 da (Jane Victoria b 1961); *Career* Lt RAC 1944–47; The Boots Co plc: dir 1976–90, md Industl Div 1980–83, chief exec 1983–87, chm 1985–90; dir: Foseco plc 1984–91, E Midlands Electricity plc 1989–95, Nottingham Building Society 1990–; memb Bd: of Mgmnt Assoc Br Pharmaceutical Indust 1981–84 (vice pres 1983–84), Nottingham Devpt Enterprise 1988–91; memb Cncl CBI 1985–90; chm: Further Educn Funding Cncl for England 1992–, Higher Educn Funding Cncl for England 1992–94; Hon LLD Univ of Nottingham 1993; CIMgt 1983, FInstD 1985–90, PCFC 1988–93, FRSA 1995; *Style*— Sir Robert Gunn, DL; ✉ Tor House, Pinfold Lane, Elston, Newark, Notts NG23 5PD

GUNN, Thomson William (Thom); s of Herbert Smith Gunn, and Ann Charlotte, *née* Thomson; *b* 29 Aug 1929; *Educ* Univ Coll Sch Hampstead, Trinity Coll Cambridge (BA); *Career* poet; lectr then assoc prof of English Univ of California at Berkeley 1958–66, visiting/freelance lectr 1966–76, sr lectr in English Univ of California at Berkeley 1990– (lectr 1976–90); *Books of Poetry* Fighting Terms (1954), The Sense of Movement (1957), My Sad Captains (1961), Positives (with Ander Gunn, 1966), Touch (1967), Moly (1971), Jack Straw's Castle (1976), Selected Poems (1979), The Passages of Joy (1982), The Man with Night Sweats (1992, winner Forward Prize 1992), Collected Poems (1993); *Essays* The Occasions of Poetry (1982), Shelf Life (1993); *Style*— Thom Gunn; ✉ 1216 Cole St, San Francisco, Calif 94117, USA

GUNN, (Anthony) William; s of William Arthur Gunn, OBE (d 1988), of Alton, Hants, and Diana Elizabeth, *née* Taylor (d 1972); *b* 21 May 1946; *Educ* Radley, Corpus Christi Coll Oxford (MA), Walter Sichel scholarship, WSET dip (Rouyer Guillet cup); *m* 6 June 1970, Amanda Marson, 3 da of Anthony Stedman Till; 2 da (Fiona Elizabeth b 10 July 1973, Rachel Georgina b 20 July 1977); *Career* Grants of St James's Ltd 1968–81: product gp mangr Fine Wines 1974–77, wine buyer (with special responsibility for Victoria Wine Co) 1977–81, buying dir Hatch Mansfield & Co; controller Wines and Spirits ASDA Stores Ltd 1981–83; Dent & Reuss Ltd (H P Bulmer plc) 1983–90: dir and gen mangr 1983–86, devpt dir 1986–90; md Pol Roger Ltd 1990–; Inst of Masters of Wine: dir 1979–84 and 1995–, chm MW Educn Ctee 1979–80; Wine & Spirit Assoc: chm French Wines Ctee 1980–81, memb Cncl 1984–89; chm Champagne Agents Assoc 1993; jury memb Gault-Millau 'Olympiades of Wines' 1977, judge various nat and int wine shows and speaker at wine confs throughout Europe, occasional panel memb Decanter and Wine Magazines, expert witness int litigation 1986 and 1993; Liveryman Worshipful Co of Fishmongers 1987, Freeman City of London 1988; MW 1974; Chevalier de l'Ordre du Mérite Agricole 1983, Offr de l'Ordre des Coteaux de Champagne; *Books* contrib: Wines of the World (1981), The Wine Drinker's Handbook (1982), Which? Wine Guide (1983–86); author of articles in Wine & Spirit Magazine, Decanter and other trade pubns; *Recreations* fly fishing, travel, classical music and opera; *Clubs* United Oxford and Cambridge Univ; *Style*— William Gunn, Esq; ✉ The Stone Barn, Woolhope, Hereford HR1 4QR (☎ 01432 860624); Pol Roger Ltd, Lanark House, New Street, Ledbury, Herefordshire HR8 2DX (☎ 01531 636111, fax 01531 636146)

GUNNELL, (William) John; MP (Lab) Leeds S and Morley (majority 7,372); s of William Henry Gunnell (d 1961), of Kettering, Northants, and Norah, *née* Haughton (d 1965); *b* 1 Oct 1933; *Educ* King Edward Sch Birmingham, Univ of Leeds (BSc); *m* 8 Oct 1955, Jean Louise, da of Frank Lacey (d 1957); 3 s (Colin David John b 1957, Jeremy Mark William b 1961, Nicolas Daniel b 1965), 1 da (Sarah Imogen b 1966); *Career* teacher Leeds Modern Sch 1959–62, head Sci Dept UN Int Sch NY 1962–70, lectr Centre for Studies in Sci Educn Univ of Leeds 1970–88, chm Yorkshire Enterprise Ltd 1982–90 and 1994–96 (vice chm 1991–94); hon pres: Yorks and Humberside Devpt Assoc (chm 1981–93), N of Eng Regnl Consortium (chm 1984–92); MP (Lab) Leeds S and Morley 1992–; memb Select Ctee on: Bdcasting 1992–, Public Serv 1995–; jt chair All Party Opera Gp 1995–, chair All Party Panel on Social Servs 1996–; memb: W Yorks Metropolitan CC 1977–86 (leader 1981–86), spokesman for Metropolitan Cos in their campaign against abolition 1983–85, Leeds City Cncl 1986–92 (chair Social Servs Ctee 1990–92, chair Crown Point Foods 1988–90); memb: Audit Cmmn 1983–90, Leeds Devpt Corp 1988–92, Leeds Eastern Health Authy 1990–91, Leeds Healthcare 1991–92; advsr Assembly of Regions of Europe 1986– (memb Bureau 1984–86); dir: Opera North 1982–, Leeds Theatre Tst (now West Yorkshire Playhouse) 1986–93; *Publications* author of texts with E W Jenkins incl Selected Experiments in Advanced Level Chemistry (1975), contrib of Enterprise Boards: An Inside View to Local Economic Policy (ed M Campbell, 1990); *Recreations* opera, music, watching cricket and soccer; *Clubs* East Hunslet Labour, Warwickshire CCC, Yorkshire CCC; *Style*— John Gunnell, Esq, MP; ✉ 6 Arthington View, Hunslet, Leeds LS10 2ND (☎ 0113 277 0592; Constituency Office: Morley Town Hall, Leeds LS27 9DY (☎ 0113 247 7138, fax 0113 247 7190); Yorkshire Enterprise, St Martins House, 210–212 Chapeltown Rd, Leeds LS7 4HZ (☎ 0113 237 4774, fax 0113 237 4922); House of Commons, London SW1A 0AA (☎ 0171 219 4549, fax 0171 219 2552)

GUNNELL, Sally Jane Janet; MBE (1993); da of Leslie Robert Gunnell, of Old Farm, Green Lane, Chigwell, Essex, and Doris Rosemary, *née* Mason; *b* 29 July 1966; *m* 19 Oct 1992, Jon Bigg, s of John Bigg; *Career* athlete; Gold medal 100m hurdles Cwlth Games Edinburgh 1986; 400m hurdles: fifth place Olympic Games Seoul 1988 (first Briton to compete in the Olympic Games in 100m hurdles, 400m hurdles and 4x400m relay), Silver medal Euro Cup 1989, Gold medal Euro Indoor Championships 1989, Bronze medal World Cup 1989, Gold medal Cwlth Games Auckland 1990, Silver medal World Championships Tokyo 1991, Gold medal Olympic Games Barcelona 1992 (also Bronze medal 4 x 400m relay), Gold medal Euro Cup 1993, Gold medal World Championships (and new world record) 1993 (also Bronze medal 4 x 400m relay), Gold medal World Cup 1994 (also Gold medal 4 x 400m relay), Gold medal Euro Championships 1994 (also Bronze medal 4 x 400m relay), Gold medal Cwlth Games 1994 (Gold medal 4 x 400m relay); co-commentator (with Jeremy Guscott, *qv*) Body Heat (ITV) 1994; runner-up BBC Sports Personality of the Year 1993 and 1994; *Style*— Ms Sally Gunnell, MBE

GUNNING, Sir Charles Theodore; 9 Bt (GB 1778), CD (1964); s of Sir Robert Charles Gunning, 8 Bt (d 1989), and Ann (Helen Nancy), *née* Hallett; *b* 19 June 1935; *Educ* Royal Roads Mil Coll BC, RN Engrg Coll, Tech Univ of Nova Scotia; *m* 1, 1969 (m dis 1982), Sarah, da of Col Patrick Arthur Easton, of Tonbridge; 1 da (Caroline Ann b 1971); m 2, 1989, Linda, da of Theodore Kachmar, of Montreal; *Heir* bro, John Robert Gunning b 1944; *Career* Lt Cdr RCN/Canadian Armed Forces 1952–80; engrg conslt; pres Ottawa Branch Royal Cwlth Soc 1975–78, 1980–81 and 1995–96, chm Nat Cncl RCS in Canada 1990–93 (vice chm 1980–90); Silver Jubilee medal 1977; memb: Professional Engrs of Ontario, Canadian Inst of Marine Engrs; PEng; *Recreations* squash, gardening, cross-country skiing, music; *Clubs* RMC of Canada, Ottawa Athletic, Royal Cwlth Soc; *Style*— Sir Charles Gunning, Bt, CD; ✉ 2940 McCarthy Rd, Ottawa, Ontario K1V 8K6, Canada (☎ 00 1 613 737 2179, fax 00 1 613 737 0794)

GUNNING, Christopher; s of Alexis Lambertus Gunning (d 1962), of Cheltenham and London, and Janet Alice, *née* Bennett (d 1993); *b* 5 Aug 1944; *Educ* Hendon Co GS, Guildhall Sch of Music and Drama (BMus); *m* 17 June 1974, Annie Christine, da of Flt Lt Clifford William Cornwall Farrow (d 1985), of Bristol; 4 da (Olivia b 1975, Pollyanna b 1977, Verity b 1981, Chloe b 1985); *Career* composer; TV and film scores incl: Rogue Male 1975, Charlie Muffin 1979, Day of the Triffids 1981, Wilfred and Eileen 1981, Flame to the Phoenix 1982, East Lynne 1982, Children's Opera Rainbow Planet 1983, Rebel Angel 1987, Porterhouse Blue 1987 (BAFTA award for the Best Original TV Music), Agatha Christie's Poirot (BAFTA award for Best Original TV Music) 1989, When the Whales Came (Royal Premiere 1989, nominated British Film Institute Anthony Asquith award for Best Film Score 1990), Yorkshire Glory 1990, Under Suspicion 1991 (Ivor Novello award for Best Film Score), The Big Battalions 1992 (BAFTA nomination for Best TV Music), Midnight Movie 1993, All or NoLOGIN M0A award for Best Original TV Music) 1994, Black Tuesday 1995, The Glass Virgin 1995, Karaoke 1995, Cold Lazarus 1996, Firelight 1996; composer dir PRS, fndr memb Assoc of Professional Composers; ARCM, AGSM; *Books* First Book of Flute Solos, Second Book of Flute Solos, Really Easy Flute Book, Really Easy Trumpet Book, Really Easy Horn Book (1987); *Recreations* sailing, walking, reading, horticulture, wine; *Style*— Christopher Gunning, Esq; ✉ 24 Ranelagh Road, Ealing, London W5 5RJ

GUNSTON, Sir John Wellesley; 3 Bt (UK 1938), of Wickwar, Co Gloucester; o s of Sir Richard Wellesley Gunston, 2 Bt (d 1991), and his 2 w, Joan Elizabeth Marie, *née* Forde; *b* 25 July 1962; *Educ* Harrow, RMA Sandhurst; *m* 1 Sept 1990 (separated 1995), Rosalind Gordon, yst da of Edward Gordon Eliott, of Bower's Mill House, nr Guildford, Surrey; 1 s (Richard St George b 3 July 1992); *Heir* s, Richard St George Gunston b 3 July 1992; *Career* cmmnd 1 Bn Irish Gds; chm The Rory Peck Tst and Award 1995; FRGS 1988; *Clubs* Special Forces, Cavalry and Guards; *Style*— Sir John Gunston, Bt; ✉ 127 Piccadilly, London W1

GUNSTONE, Prof Frank Denby; s of (Edwin) Leonard Gunstone (d 1981), and Adeline, *née* Benington (d 1969); *b* 27 Oct 1923; *Educ* Univ of Liverpool (BSc, PhD), Univ of St Andrews (DSc); *m* 20 March 1948, Eleanor Eineen, da of Sidney John Hill (d 1949); 2 s (Douglas b 1950, John b 1952), 1 da (Penny b 1958); *Career* lectr Univ of Glasgow 1946–54, hon res prof Univ of St Andrews 1989–96 (lectr 1954–59, sr lectr 1959–65, reader 1965–70, personal prof 1971–89), hon res fell Scottish Crops Res Inst 1996–; memb: American Oil Chemists Soc, RSE, Royal Soc of Chemistry 1945, Soc of Chemical Industry 1945; FRSE 1972; *Books* incl: A Text-Book of Organic Chemistry (with J Read, 1958), An Introduction to the Chemistry and Biochemistry of Fatty Acids and their Glycerides (1 edn 1958, 2 edn 1967), Programmes in Organic Chemistry vols 1–3, 5 and 6 (1966–74), Guidebook to Stereochemistry (1975), Lipids in Foods; Chemistry, Biochemistry and Technology (with F A Norris, 1983), The Lipid Handbook (ed with F B Padley and J L Harwood, 1986, 2 edn 1994), Critical Reports on Applied Chemistry Vol 15, Palm Oil (ed, 1987), A Lipid Glossary (with B G Herslöf, 1992), Fatty Acid and Lipid Chemistry (1996); *Recreations* gardening; *Clubs* University; *Style*— Prof Frank Gunstone, FRSE; ✉ Nether Rumgally, Cupar, Fife KY15 5SY (☎ 01334 653613), Scottish Crops Research Institute, Invergowrie, Dundee DD2 5DA (☎ 01382 562731, fax 01382 561442)

GUNTER, John Forsyth; s of Dr Herbert Charles Gunter (d 1959), and Charlotte Rose Scott, *née* Reid; *b* 31 Oct 1938; *Educ* Bryanston, Central Sch of Art and Design; *m* 19 Dec 1969, Micheline, da of late Col Maxwell S McKnight; 2 da (Jessica b 4 June 1972, Nicolette b 16 Oct 1978); *Career* theatre designer; head of Theatre Dept Central Sch of Art and Design 1974–82, head of design RNT 1988–90, assoc designer RNT 1990–; FRSA 1982; *Theatre* 28 prodns Royal Court Theatre 1965–66 incl: D H Lawrence Trilogy, Saved, The Contractor, The Philanthropist, West of Suez, Inadmissible Evidence; RSC: Juno and the Paycock, All's Well that Ends Well (Broadway 1983), Mephisto 1986, Love's Labour's Lost 1993 and 1995, Christmas Carol 1994, Twelfth Night 1994, Julius Caesar 1995, Troilus and Cressida; RNT: Guys and Dolls (SWET Award Best Designer), The Rivals, The Beggar's Opera, Wild Honey (SWET Award Best Designer), The Government Inspector, Bay at Nice, Wrecked Eggs, The Seagull, Long Days Journey Into Night 1991, The Devil's Disciple 1994, Absolute Hell 1995, Skylight (also West End and Broadway) 1995; West End: Comedians, Stevie, The Old Country, Rose, Made in Bangkok, High Society, Mrs Klein, Secret Rapture, Piaf (Piccadilly) 1993; *Opera* incl: The Greek Passion (WNO), Faust (ENO), Peter Grimes (Teatro Colon Buenos Aries), The Meistersinger (Cologne), Un Ballo in Maschera (Sydney Opera House), The Turn of the Screw (Munich), Macbeth (Leeds), Norma (Scottish Opera), Figaro (Glyndebourne) 1994, Don Quixote (ENO) 1994; for Sir Peter Hall Glyndebourne: Albert Herring, La Traviata 1987, Falstaff 1988; for Trevor Nunn Glyndebourne: Peter Grimes 1992, Porgy and Bess (Emmy Award 1994); also Attila (Opera North) 1990, Marriage of Figaro (Salzburg Festival Opera) 1991, Madame Butterfly (Los Angeles Opera) 1991, The Flying Dutchman (Royal Opera House) 1992, West Side Story (Victoria State Opera), Don Quixote (ENO, Victoria State Opera 1995) 1994; *Style*— John Gunter, Esq; ✉ c/o agent: Peter Murphy, Curtis Brown Group Ltd, 28–29 Haymarket, London SW1Y 4SP (☎ 0171 396 6600, fax 0171 396 0110)

GUPTA, Dr Nirmal Kumar; s of Kanti Bhushan Gupta (d 1964), of Agartala, India, and Kamala, *née* Sen Gupta (d 1948); *b* 13 June 1934; *Educ* Calcutta Univ (MB BS); *m* 28 Jan 1962, Namita, da of Nibaran Chandra Das Gupta (d 1982), of Assam, India; 2 da (Chandreyi b 1967, Sharmila b 1972); *Career* Christie Hosp and Holt Radium Inst Manchester: conslt in radiotherapy and oncology 1975–88, currently dep dir in radiotherapy and oncology; memb Sociedad Peruana de Radiologicá Lima 1982, pres The 1951 Club 1986–87; memb: Sub-Ctee on Head and Neck Cancer UK Coordinating Ctee on Cancer Res 1988–, Int Collaborative Gp on Fractionation American Coll of Radiology Philadelphia 1988–96, Cncl Faculty Bd of Radiotherapy and Oncology RCR 1988–89 (memb 1986–88), Int Cmmn on Radiation Protection 1993; memb Bd of Tstees Museum of Science and Industry in Manchester 1994–; DMRT, FRCR, FFR, FRSM; *Publications* contrib: The Radiotherapy of Malignant Disease (1985 and 1990), Clinical Radiology (1987), The British Journal of Radiology (1990), Annals, Royal Coll of Surgeons (1992); *Recreations* tasting good food and wine; *Style*— Dr Nirmal Gupta; ✉ The Christie Hospital NHS Trust, Withington, Manchester M20 9BX (☎ 0161 446 3000, fax 0161 446 3352)

GUPTARA, Prabhu; *Career* univ lectr India 1970–79, mgmnt conslt and trainer 1979–, fndr chm Prabhu Guptara Associates 1984–, dir ADVANCE Management Training Ltd 1988–, gp dir Organisational Learning & Transformation Union Bank of Switzerland 1995–; fndr ed Organisations and People 1994–; given lectures at: UNCTAD, Cncl of Europe, Univs of London and Oxford, Sorbonne, Warwick, Assoc Bank Inst (Frankfurt), Henley Mgmnt Coll, Int Inst for Mgmnt Devpt (Lausanne), Int Mmgnt Assoc of Japan, Singapore Inst of Mgmnt; visiting prof European Inst of Purchasing Mgmnt INSEAD France 1992–95; contrib to Gower Handbook of Management, Gower Handbook on Quality, International Encyclopedia of Business and Management and other reference books, as well as to numerous newspapers and magazines incl: Financial Times, Daily Telegraph, The Times, The Guardian, The Spectator, International Mangement, Training & Development (columnist); memb Cncl: Inst of Mgmnt, Int Fedn of Trg and Devpt Orgns, Assoc for Mgmnt Educn and Devpt; vice-chm Guildford Branch Inst of Trg and Devpt, judge MSC Nat Trg Awards 1988, judge Deo Gloria Award for Fiction 1990 (chm judges panel 1991 and 1992); govr Univ of Westminster (formerly Poly of Central London) 1989–92; MIMgt, MIBPR, MSPS, FRComS, FInstD, FIPD, FRSA; *Books* The Basic Arts of Marketing (3rd edn, 1990), Becoming a Managing Director (1997); *Clubs* Rotary, Arts Centre Group; *Style*— Prabhu S Guptara, Esq

GURDON, Brig Adam Brampton Douglas; CBE (1980, OBE 1973), DL (Suffolk 1993); elder s of Maj-Gen Edward Temple Leigh Gurdon, CB, CBE, MC (d 1959), of Suffolk, and Elizabeth Madeleine, *née* Wilson (d 1967); *b* 4 May 1931; *Educ* Rugby; *m* 30 Aug 1958, Gillian Margaret, da of Col Charles Newbigging Thomson (d 1987), of Dundee; 4 da (Miranda (Mrs Sandy Barclay) b 1960, Madeleine (Lady Lloyd Webber) b 1962, Melanie b 1966, Mary Louise (Mrs John Aitchison) b 1968); *Career* cmmnd Black Watch 1950, Korean War 1953–53, Mau Mau Kenya 1953–55, Adj Berlin 1956–57, Cyprus 1958, cmmnd Regtl Depot Perth 1960, KAR Tanganyka and Zanzibar 1961–62, Staff Coll 1963, DAA & QMG Gurkha Bde 1964–66, UN Cyprus 1967, MOD Mil Ops 1968–72, GSO1 Eastern Dist 1973–76, Mil Ops 1976–79 (while at MOD became involved in Lancaster House Settlement on Rhodesia, formulated Cwlth Monitoring Force, went to Rhodesia as COS to Maj-Gen Sir John Acland), RCDS 1981, Cabinet Office 1982–85, ADC to HM The Queen 1984–85, ret as Brig 1985; dir: St Edmundsbury Cathedral Appeal 1986–90, Chelmsford Cathedral Appeal 1990–92, Nat Youth Music Theatre 1992–, The Open Churches Tst 1994–; High Sheriff for County of Suffolk 1994–95; *Recreations* shooting, fishing, gardening; *Clubs* Army and Navy (vice chm 1986); *Style*— Brig Adam Gurdon, CBE, DL; ✉ Burgh House, Woodbridge, Suffolk IP13 6PU (☎ 01473 735273, fax 01473 738343); 22 Tower Street, London WC2 (☎ 0171 240 0880)

GURDON, Prof Sir John Bertrand; kt (1995); s of late W N Gurdon, DCM, of Suffolk, and late Elsie Marjorie, *née* Byass; *b* 2 Oct 1933; *Educ* Eton, ChCh Oxford (BA, DPhil, Beit meml fell); *m* 1964, Jean Elizabeth Margaret Curtis; 1 s, 1 da; *Career* Gosney res fell Calif Inst of Technol 1962; Univ of Oxford: department demonstrator Dept of Zoology 1963–64, res fell Christ Church 1962–72, lectr Dept of Zoology 1965–72; visiting res fell Carnegie Inst Baltimore 1965, head Cell Biology Div MRC Laboratory of Molecular Biology Cambridge 1979–83, Fullerian prof of physiology and comparative anatomy Royal Inst 1985–91, John Humphrey Plummer prof of cell biology and chm Wellcome/CRC Inst Cambridge 1991–, master Magdalene Coll Cambridge 1995–; fell: Churchill Coll Cambridge 1973–94, Eton Coll 1978–93; govr Wellcome Tst 1995–; hon foreign memb: American Acad of Arts and Sciences, US Nat Acad of Sciences, Belgian Acad of Letters and Fine Arts 1984; foreign memb American Philosophical Soc 1983, hon fell Christ Church Oxford; Hon DSc: Chicago 1978, Paris 1982, Oxford 1985; Albert Brachet Prize Belgian Royal Acad 1968, Scientific Medal Zoological Soc 1968, Feldberg Fndn Award 1975, Paul Ehrlich Award (Germany) 1977, Comfort Crookshank Award for Cancer Res 1983, William Bate Hardy Prize Cambridge Philosophical Soc 1984, Prix de Charles Leopold Mayer Acad des Scis France 1984, Ross Harrison Prize 1985, CIBA Medal Biochemical Soc 1985, Royal Medal Royal Soc 1985, Emperor Hirohito International Prize (Japan) 1987, Wolf Prize in Medicine (Israel) 1989; Liveryman Worshipful Co of Goldsmiths; FRS 1971; *Books* Control of Gene Expression in Animal Development (1974); author of articles in numerous scientific journals (especially on nuclear transplantation); *Recreations* tennis, skiing, horticulture, lepidoptera; *Clubs* Eagle Ski; *Style*— Prof Sir John Gurdon, FRS; ✉ Master's Lodge, Magdalene College, Cambridge CB3 0AG (☎ 01223 332154)

GURNEY, Maj Carol James Hay; DL (Suffolk 1995); s of Brig Cecil Hay Gurney, CBE, and Elnyth Meryl, *née* Segar-Owen (d 1993); *b* 24 Nov 1936; *Educ* Harrow; *m* 6 March 1964, Elizabeth Sara Ann, da of Brig Sir Frederick Coates, 2 Bt (d 1994), of Launchfield, Bryantspuddle, Dorchester, Dorset; 1 s (Christopher Hay b 22 April 1968), 1 da (Sara Catherine b 30 Aug 1965); *Career* served 60 Rifles and Royal Green Jackets 1955–69, seconded to Kenya Regt 1960–63, attended Indian Staff Coll 1967, memb HM Body Guard of Hon Corps of Gentlemen at Arms 1989; Barclays Bank 1969– (local dir Norwich), farmer; High Sheriff Suffolk 1993–94; *Recreations* field sports, gardening and forestry, travel; *Clubs* Army and Navy; *Style*— Maj Carol Gurney, DL; ✉ Higham Lodge, Higham, Stratford St Mary, Suffolk CO7 6ND

GURNEY, David Quintin; s of Richard Quintin Gurney (d 1980), and Elisabeth Margaret, *née* Boughey (d 1985); *b* 6 Feb 1941; *Educ* Harrow, Trinity Coll Cambridge, Grenoble Univ; *m* 1965, Jacqueline McLeod, *née* Rawle; 1 s, 2 da; *Career* banker; personal sector dir Barclays Bank Ltd Norwich 1988–96, ret; farmer; chm and dir Bawdeswell Farms Ltd, managing ptnr Breck Farms; chm Camphill Communities E Anglia Ltd; dir: Cecil Estate Farms Ltd, Fakenham Race Course Ltd, Norwich Diocesan Board of Finance Ltd; pres Norfolk Branch Br Red Cross Soc 1989–; *Recreations* field sports; *Clubs* Farmers', MCC, Norfolk; *Style*— David Gurney, Esq; ✉ Bawdeswell Hall, East Dereham, Norfolk (☎ 01362 688307); office (☎/fax 01362 688308)

GURNEY, Jane; *b* 25 June 1947; *Educ* Thomas Bennett Sch Crawley, Univ of Sussex (BA), St John's Coll York (postgrad CertEd); *m* (m dis), Richard Sandars; 1 da (Alison b 26 Sept 1971), 1 s (John b 16 June 1973); *Career* writer; over 350 short stories for

British and foreign magazines; memb Romantic Novelists' Assoc 1985–; *Books* Paris Fever (1986), The Green of the Spring (1991), Gone Tomorrow (1997); *Style*— Ms Jane Gurney; ✉ c/o Caroline Sheldon Literary Agency, 71 Hillgate Place, London W8 7SS

GURNEY, John; s of Sir Eustace Gurney, JP (d 1927); *b* 3 July 1905; *Educ* Eton, New Coll Oxford; *m* 1932, Ann, da of Capt Frederick Ogilvy, RN (3 s of Sir Reginald Ogilvy, 10 Bt, JP, DL, by his w Hon Olivia, da of 9 Lord Kinnaird, KT, PC); 4 da (Priscilla (Mrs Meath-Baker), Jean (Lady Mayhew), Elizabeth Olivia (Mrs Bristol), Christian (Mrs Forestier-Walker)), and 1 da decd (Elizabeth); *Career* served with Royal Norfolk Regt and W Africa Frontier Force 1939–43; chm and md Walsingham Estate Co 1928–, md Medici Soc 1935–94; JP Norfolk 1930–75; *Recreations* photography; *Style*— John Gurney, Esq; ✉ The Abbey, Walsingham, Norfolk NR22 6DQ

GURNEY, Prof Oliver Robert; s of Robert Gurney (d 1950), of Bayworth Corner, Boars Hill, Oxford, and Sarah Gamzu, *née* Garstang, MBE (d 1973); *b* 28 Jan 1911; *Educ* Eton, New Coll Oxford (MA, DPhil); *m* 23 Aug 1957, Diane Hope Grazebrook, da of Rene Esencourt; *Career* Capt RA 1939–45, Bimbashi Sudan Def Force 1940–44; Shillito reader in Assyriology Oxford 1946– (prof 1965–78), fell Magdalen Coll 1963, pres Br Inst of Archaeology at Ankara; Freeman City of Norwich; FBA 1959; *Books* The Hittites (latest edn 1990), Some Aspects of Hittite Religion (1977), The Middle Babylonian Legal and Economic Texts From Ur (1983); Literary and Miscellaneous Texts in the Ashmolean Museum (1989); *Recreations* golf; *Style*— Prof Oliver Gurney, FBA; ✉ Fir Tree House, Milton Lane, Steventon, Abingdon, Oxon OX13 6SA (☎ 01235 831212)

GURR, Prof Michael Ian; s of Henry Ormonde Gurr (d 1988), of Great Brickhill, Bletchley, Bucks, and Hilda Ruth Gurr (d 1978); *b* 10 April 1939; *Educ* Dunstable Sch, Univ of Birmingham (BSc, PhD); *m* 2 Aug 1963, (Elizabeth) Anne, da of Reginald Mayers, of Morden, Surrey; 2 s (Nicholas b 5 Jan 1965, Stephen b 9 March 1968), 1 da (Eleanor b 18 April 1969); *Career* sr scientist Unilever Res 1967–78, head nutrition Nat Inst Res in Dairying Shinfield Reading 1979–85, head laboratory AFRC Inst Food Res Shinfield Reading 1985–86, nutrition conslt Milk Mktg Bd Thames Ditton Surrey 1986–90, ptnr in nutrition consultancy business; visiting prof: Univ of Reading 1986–, Oxford Brookes Univ 1990–; memb: Ctee Med Aspects Food Policy 1985–90, Advsy Ctee Br Nutrition Fndn 1983–90; chm Editorial Bd: Br Jl Nutrition 1987–90, Nutrition Research Reviews 1990–; chm Sharnbrook Parish Cncl 1976; FIBiol 1980; memb: Biochemical Soc 1961, Nutrition Soc 1974, RSM 1987; *Books* Lipid Biochemistry: An Introduction (1971, 4 edn 1991), The Role of Fat in Food and Nutrition (1984, 2 edn 1992); *Recreations* sailing, walking, piano playing, reading; *Style*— Prof Michael Gurr; ✉ Vale View Cottage, Maypole, St Mary's, Isles of Scilly TR21 0NU (☎ 01720 422224); Maypole Scientific Services, Vale View Cottage, Maypole, St Mary's, Isles of Scilly TR21 0NU

GURTON, Michael John; s of Percy William Gurton, of Chelmsford, and Margaret Elsie, *née* Sargent; *b* 3 July 1950; *Educ* Chelmsford Tech HS, Chelmer Inst; *m* 10 Aug 1974, Gillian, da of Christopher Stone; 2 s (Timothy Michael b 21 March 1980, Christopher John 16 Aug 1982), 1 da (Jennifer Clare b 6 June 1989); *Career* apprentice Marconi Co Ltd 1966–71, Roff Marsh & Partners (architects) 1972–76, ptnr Purcell Miller Tritton & Partners 1989– (joined 1976); memb Wakes Colne Parish Cncl; memb: Inst of Engrs & Technicians 1971, Br Inst of Architectural Technicians 1977; FFB 1988; *Recreations* fishing, shooting; *Clubs* Chappel & Wakes Colne Cricket (vice pres); *Style*— Michael Gurton, Esq; ✉ Russets, Colchester Road, Wakes Colne, Colchester, Essex CO6 2AF (☎ 01206 240395); Purcell Miller Tritton & Partners, St Mary's Hall, Rawstorn Road, Colchester, Essex CO3 3JH (☎ 01206 549487, fax 01206 763408, car 0860 304498)

GURUSINGHE, Nihal Trevor; s of Hector Kingsley Gurusinghe, of Panadura, Sri Lanka, and Supriya, *née* Perera Vitachchi; *b* 30 Oct 1946; *Educ* Univ of Ceylon (MB BS); *m* 6 Aug 1973, Indrani Lucille, da of Martin Kumaraperu (d 1975); 2 s (Dilnath b 1976, Lakmal b 1980); *Career* sr registrar in neurosurgery: Atkinson Morley's Hosp Wimbledon, Nat Hosp for Nervous Diseases London, Gt Ormond St Hosp London; conslt neurosurgn Royal Preston Hosp 1985–; chm Whittingham CC Preston, govr Queen Elizabeth GS Blackburn; FRCSEd 1980; memb: BMA, Soc of Br Neurological Surgns; *Recreations* cricket; *Style*— Nihal Gurusinghe, Esq; ✉ Neurosurgery Department, Royal Preston Hospital, Sharoe Green Lane, Preston, Lancs PR2 4HT (☎ 01772 710574)

GUSCOTT, Jeremy Clayton; s of Henry Guscott, of Bath, and Susan Vivian, *née* Taylor; *b* 7 July 1965; *Educ* Ralph Allen Sr Sch Bath; *m* 14 July 1990, Jayne Irene Aland, da of Frederick Richard Simkiss; 2 da (Imogen Lily b 4 Aug 1992, Holly Jayne b 16 April 1995); *Career* rugby union centre threequarters; clubs: Bath RFC 1982– (won Pilkington Cup 1985, 1987, 1989/90, 1992, 1995 and 1996), Barbarians RFC; rep England B (2 caps) 1989; England: tour Romania 1989, debut v Romania 1989 (scored 3 tries), Five Nations debut v Ireland 1990, memb runners-up team World Cup 1991, memb Grand Slam winning team 1991, 1992 and 1995, 4th place World Cup S Africa 1995, 42 caps; British Lions tour Aust 1989 (3 test appearances) and tour NZ 1993 (3 test appearances); co-presenter (with Sally Gunnell, *qv*) Body Heat (ITV) 1994, 1995 and 1996, presenter Top Score (BBC 2), journalist Radio 5 Live; *Recreations* golf; *Style*— Jeremy Guscott, Esq; ✉ c/o MP Associates, 156 Sutherland Avenue, London W9 1HP (☎ 0171 286 1793)

GUTCH, Richard Evelyn; s of Sir John Gutch (d 1988), of Farnham, Surrey, and Diana Mary, *née* Worsley; *b* 17 Nov 1946; *Educ* Winchester, Gonville & Caius Coll Cambridge (BA), UCL (MPhil); *m* 15 May 1971, Rosemary Anne Capel, da of John Alexander Pike; 2 s (James Alexander b 1974, Adam William b 1978); *Career* jr planning asst Local Planning London Borough of Camden 1970–71, sr planning asst Devpt Control Sheffield Borough Cncl 1971–72, sr planning offr Land Use/Tport Rotherham Borough Cncl 1972–73, princ planning offr Public Participation South Yorks Met Cncl 1973–76, sr lectr Planning Unit PCL 1976–80, policy coordinator (then asst to chief exec) London Borough of Brent 1980–85; NCVO 1985–92: head of info, then asst dir (Local Vol Action), latterly asst dir Resource Devpt; chief exec Arthritis Care 1992–; chm Consortium on Opportunities for Volunteering Bd 1990–92, non-exec dir Hounslow and Spelthorne Community and Mental Health Tst 1992–94, chm then treasurer Long Term Med Conditions Alliance 1993–96, chm then vice chm ACENVO 1995–; MRTPI 1972–80; FRSA 1992; *Publications* incl: Getting in on the Act (NCVO, 1987), Partners or Agents? (NCVO, 1990), Contracting Lessons from the US (NCVO, 1992); *Recreations* the arts, walking, golf; *Style*— Richard Gutch, Esq; ✉ Chief Executive, Arthritis Care, 18 Stephenson Way, London NW1 2HD (☎ 0171 916 1500, fax 0171 916 1505)

GUTHRIE, Gen Sir Charles Ronald Llewelyn; GCB (1994, KCB 1990), LVO (1977), OBE (1980), ADC Gen (1993); s of Ronald Dalglish Guthrie (d 1982), of Chelsea, and Nina, *née* Llewelyn (d 1987); *b* 17 Nov 1938; *Educ* Harrow, RMA Sandhurst; *m* 11 Sept 1971, Catherine, da of Lt-Col Claude Worrall, MVO, OBE, Coldstream Gds (d 1973), of Avon Bassett, Warwicks; 2 s (David Charles b 21 Oct 1972, Andrew James b 3 Sept 1974); *Career* cmmnd Welsh Gds 1959, served BAOR and Aden, 22 SAS Regt 1965–69, psc 1972, mil asst to Chief of Gen Staff MOD 1973–74, Bde Maj Household Div 1976–77, CO 1 Bn Welsh Gds served Berlin and NI 1977–80, Col gen staff mil ops MOD 1980–82, cmd Br Forces New Hebrides 1980, 4 Armd Bde 1982–84, Chief of Staff 1 (Br) Corps 1984–86, GOC NE Dist cmd 2 Inf Div 1986–87, Asst Chief of the Gen Staff MOD 1987–89, Cmd 1 Br Corps 1990–91, C in C BAOR 1992–94, cmd Northern Army Gp 1992–93 (NORTHAG, now disbanded), Chief of the Gen Staff 1994–97, Chief of the Defence Staff April 1997–; Col Cmdt Intelligence Corps 1986–95; ADC Gen to HM The Queen 1993–; pres: Army Saddle Club 1991, Army LTA; Freeman City of London, Liveryman Worshipful Co of Painter-Stainers; *Recreations* tennis, skiing, travel; *Clubs* White's, Beefsteak, All England Lawn Tennis and Croquet; *Style*— General Sir Charles Guthrie, GCB, LVO, OBE, ADC Gen; ✉ c/o Lloyds Bank, 79 Brompton Rd, London SW8 1LH

GUTHRIE, James Dalglish; QC (1993); s of Ronald Dalglish Guthrie (d 1982), and Nina, *née* Llewelyn (d 1987); *b* 21 Feb 1950; *Educ* Harrow, Worcester Coll Oxford (BA); *m* 1981, Lucille Gay, da of Mr and Mrs Nigel Page-Roberts; 1 da (Charlotte Elizabeth b 31 July 1985), 1 s (Robert James b 17 June 1989); *Career* called to the Bar Inner Temple 1975, memb chambers 1 Crown Office Row 1975–; *Recreations* fishing, painting, travel; *Clubs* Turf; *Style*— James Guthrie, Esq, QC; ✉ 1 Crown Office Row, Temple, London EC4Y 7HH (☎ 0171 583 9292, fax 0171 353 9292)

GUTHRIE, Sir Malcolm Connop; 3 Bt (UK 1936), of Brent Eleigh Hall, Co Suffolk; s of Sir Giles Connop McEacharn Guthrie, 2 Bt, OBE, DSC (d 1979), and Rhona, *née* Stileman; *b* 16 Dec 1942; *Educ* Millfield; *m* 1967, Victoria, da of late Douglas Willcock; 1 s (Giles Malcolm Welcome b 1972), 1 da (Islay Mary Welcome b 1968); *Heir* s, Giles Malcolm Welcome Guthrie b 16 Oct 1972; *Career* memb Firearms Consultative Ctee 1991–94, Liveryman Worshipful Co of Gunmakers; *Recreations* competitive shooting, deer stalking, big game hunting; *Style*— Sir Malcolm Guthrie, Bt; ✉ Brent Eleigh, Belbroughton, Stourbridge, Worcestershire DY9 0DW

GUTHRIE, (Garth) Michael; s of Henry Morton (d 1957), of Bolton, and Ann, *née* Baxter (d 1993); *b* 30 April 1941; *Educ* Isis Sch, Bolton & Blackpool Catering Coll (FHCIMA); *m* 7 Sept 1963, Joyce; 1 s (Paul b 8 May 1965), 2 da (Lynn b 11 April 1967, Julia (Mrs Hook) b 20 Sept 1968); *Career* Mecca Leisure Group Ltd: joined as trainee mangr 1961, md catering 1969–73, md entertainment 1973–80, gp md 1980–81, chm and chief exec 1981–90; chm BrightReasons Group Ltd 1991–, chm Tomorrow's People Tst 1996; hon visiting fell Oxford Brookes Univ 1996–; *Recreations* skiing, reading, gardening, opera, theatre; *Style*— Michael Guthrie, Esq; ✉ BrightReasons Group plc, Bakers House, 25 Bakers Road, Uxbridge, Middx UB8 1RG (☎ 01895 811911, fax 01895 812049)

GUTHRIE, Robert Brown; s of Robert Brown Guthrie, of Harlow, Essex, and Doreen Oswald, *née* Dixon; *b* 8 April 1942; *Educ* Eton House Sch Thorpe Bay Essex; *m* 24 Jan 1970, Ulla Margareta, da of Anders Forsblom; 2 s (Robert Adrian Anders b 31 July 1976, Andrew Erik b 3 June 1980), 1 da (Anna Karina b 17 Aug 1974); *Career* Willis Faber & Dumas Ltd: joined 1958, property mangr Bristol Office 1964–68, specialist in insurance of multinational cos Head Office London, chm and md Willis Wrightson Construction Risks Ltd 1989–91, chm and md Willis Corroon London Ltd 1991–93 (jt md 1989–91), currently chief exec Willis Corroon Ltd, dir Willis Corroon International Holdings, dir Willis Corroon Japan; memb Lloyd's 1985–; *Recreations* tennis, badminton, swimming; *Clubs* Lloyd's Lawn Tennis (chm); *Style*— Robert Guthrie, Esq; ✉ Willis Corroon Ltd, Ten Trinity Square, London EC3P 3AX (☎ 0171 488 8458, fax 0171 975 2819, car 0836 723659)

GUTHRIE, Robert Isles Loftus (Robin); s of Dr William Keith Chambers Guthrie (d 1981), Master of Downing Coll Cambridge, and Adele Marion, *née* Ogilvy (d 1992); *b* 27 June 1937; *Educ* Clifton, Trinity Coll Cambridge (MA), Univ of Liverpool (CertEd), LSE (MSc); *m* 1963, Sarah Julia, da of J Weltman, OBE; 2 s (Andrew b 1965, Thomas b 1970), 1 da (Clare b 1969); *Career* 2 Lt Queen's Own Cameron Highlanders 1956–58; head Cambridge House South London 1962–69, schoolteacher Kennington Sch Brixton 1964–66, social devpt offr Peterborough Devpt Corpn 1969–75, asst dir social work serv DHSS 1975–79, dir Joseph Rowntree Meml Tst 1979–88, chief charity cmmr England and Wales 1988–92, dir of social and economic affairs Cncl of Europe 1992–; memb Arts Cncl of GB 1979–81 and 1987–88, chm Yorks Arts Assoc 1984–88; chm Cncl: Regnl Arts Assoc 1985–88, Univ of York 1980–94, Policy Studies Inst 1979–88; Hon LLD Univ of Bradford 1991; *Recreations* music, mountaineering, archaeology, travel; *Style*— Robin Guthrie, Esq; ✉ Braeside, Acomb, York YO2 4EZ

GUTTERIDGE, Reginald George (Reg); OBE (1995); s of Dick Islington (d 1946), and Linda, *née* Smith (d 1963); *b* 29 March 1924; *m* 26 Sept 1953, Constance, *née* Chamberlain; 2 da (Sammi, Sally-Ann); *Career* London Evening News: joined as jr then copy-boy, sportswriter (boxing) 1938; Nat Serv incl Royal Artillery 1942–44; rejoined London Evening News as journalist, subsequently commentator (boxing, greyhound racing, stunt jumping) ITV and also Sky TV; contrib: Sunday Express, Boxing News; life memb: Sportswriters' Assoc (chm 1969–70), NUJ; *Awards* Sports Presenter of the Year 1992, Excellence in Bdcast Journalism American Boxing Writers' Assoc; *Books* Great One's, Big Punchers, Norman Wisdom and Jimmy Greaves; *Clubs* Silver-Heart Variety, RAC; *Style*— Reg Gutteridge, Esq, OBE; ✉ ITV Network Centre, 200 Gray's Inn Road, London WC1X 8HF (☎ 0171 843 8113)

GUTTERIDGE, Tom Michael Gillan; s of Herbert Thomas Gutteridge (d 1972), of Tynemouth, and Ethelie, *née* Boucher; *b* 2 Feb 1952; *Educ* Royal GS Newcastle upon Tyne, Univ of York (BA); *m* 1981 (m dis 1993), Jillian, da of Capt C Carrington Barber; 1 s (Benjamin Leo Thomas), 2 da (Rebecca Holly, Anya); *Career* BBC: news trainee 1973–75, dir Nationwide, Tonight and Panorama 1975–79, prodr/dir Tonight in Town 1979, prodr Harty 1980, prodr/dir A Kick up the Eighties and The Hot Shoe Show 1981, exec prodr BBC TV Music & Arts 1982–85, dir coverage of Gen Election 1983; Mentorn Films: fndr chm and chief exec 1985–, chm and chief exec Mentorn Films Group 1991–, chm West One Television editing and facilities subsid 1991–, chm Javelin Production Partnership (corp prodn subsid); jt chm Space Productions 1994–, bdcasting conslt Camelot (National Lottery); Mentorn prodns incl: Gerry Anderson's Space Precinct, 01 for London, Challenge Anneka, Passport, Today's the Day, The Bullion Boys, Capital Woman, You Decide, Scratchy & Co; prodns as freelance dir incl: Fire & Ice (LWT) 1985, The Sleeping Beauty (Anglia) 1986; chm Producers' Alliance for Cinema and Television (PACT) 1993–94, memb Cncl Br Screen Advsy Cncl 1994–; memb BAFTA, FRTS 1996; *Awards* BAFTA award for The Hot Shoe Show 1984, Bronze Rose of Montreux for Fire & Ice 1985, Best Dir International Monitor Awards Los Angeles for Fire & Ice 1985, Best Prog International Monitor Awards for Sleeping Beauty 1986, Int Emmy nomination for I Drew Roger Rabbit 1987, Bronze Rose of Montreux, Best Prog Nat Viewers and Listeners' Assoc Awards for Challenge Anneka 1991, Silver Hugo award Chicago and NY Film Festival Bronze medal for Passport 1994, Silver medal for Best Children's Series NY Film and TV Festival for Early Bird 1994, Int Emmy for Best Drama for The Bullion Boys 1994; *Clubs* Chelsea Arts, Groucho; *Style*— Tom Gutteridge, Esq; ✉ Mentorn Films Ltd, Mentorn House, 140 Wardour Street, London W1V 4LJ (☎ 0171 287 4545, fax 0171 287 3728)

GUY, Diana; da of Charles Stanley Eade (d 1964), of Broadstairs, Kent, and Vera Dorothy, *née* Manwaring; *b* 27 March 1943; *Educ* Queen Anne's Sch Caversham, Lady Margaret Hall Oxford (MA); *m* 25 May 1968, (John) Robert Clare Guy, s of Wilfred Guy (d 1965), of Sydenham, London; 2 s (Jonathan b 1972, Matthew b 1975); *Career* admitted slr 1968, ptnr Theodore Goddard 1973–95, conslt 1995–; chm: Law Soc: Slrs' Euro Gp 1985, 1992 Working Pty 1988–92; memb City of London Slrs' Co 1985; memb Law Soc 1968; *Books* The EEC and Intellectual Property (with G I F Leigh, 1981); *Recreations* reading, opera, theatre; *Style*— Mrs Diana Guy; ✉ 29 Ennerdale Rd, Kew Gdns, Richmond, Surrey TW9 3PE (☎ 0181 948 3594); Theodore Goddard, 150 Aldersgate St, London EC1A 4EJ (☎ 0171 606 8855, fax 0171 606 4390, telex 884678)

GUY, Prof John Alexander; *b* 16 Jan 1949; *Educ* Univ of Cambridge (Greene Cup Clare Coll, MA, PhD, York Prize for published work in legal history); m; 2 c; *Career* research fell Selwyn Coll Cambridge 1970–73, asst keeper of public records Public Record Office London 1973–78, visiting lectr in Br history Univ of California at Berkeley 1977; Univ of Bristol: lectr in modern Br history 1978–82, awarded tenure 1981, reader in Br history 1982–90; John Hinkley visiting prof Johns Hopkins Univ 1990, Richard L Turner prof of humanities and prof of history Univ of Rochester 1990–92; Univ of St Andrews: prof of modern history 1992–, head Sch of History and Int Relations 1992–94, provost St Leonard's Coll 1994–, vice-princ 1996–; Marc Fitch research reader British Acad 1987–89; co-ed: Cambridge Studies in Early Modern British History, Royal Historical Soc British Bibliographies series for period 1500–1700; editorial conslt Massachusetts Studies in Early Modern Culture; memb: Royal Historical Soc, Br Nat Ctee Int Congress of Historical Scis, Editorial Bd Tudor Textbase and Lexicon Project Univ of Otago, Exec Ctee Folger Inst for Renaissance and 18th Century Studies Washington DC, Continuation Ctee Br Legal History Conf (co-convener Fifth Br Legal History Conf Univ of Bristol 1981); govr Caledonian Research Fndn; assessor: British Acad, Nat Endowment for the Humanities, Cambridge Univ Press, Oxford Univ Press and numerous other publishers and jls; FRHistS 1977; *Books* The Public Career of Sir Thomas More (1980), Tudor England (1988, paperback edn, 1990), The Reign of Elizabeth I: Court and Culture in the Last Decade (1995); also author of eight other books, 46 articles and numerous book reviews; *Style*— Prof John Guy; ✉ Principal's Office, University of St Andrews, St Andrews, Fife KY16 9AJ

GUY, Prof Keith William Arthur; s of Kenneth Leonard Guy (d 1977), of Portsmouth, and Margaret Olive Jesse, *née* Rose; *b* 14 Dec 1943; *Educ* Southern GS, Imperial Coll London (BSc, MSc, PhD, ACGI, DIC); *m* 1, 5 April 1968 (m dis 1989), Penelope Ann, da of Peter Desmond Greenyer; 3 da (Tabitha Kate b 11 Sept 1971, Victoria Rose b 31 May 1973, Hannah Roberta b 9 Sept 1976); m 2, 25 May 1991, Kathryn Elizabeth, da of Dr Norman Lawrence Franklin, CBE, FRS, FEng (d 1987); *Career* Air Products plc: joined 1970, mangr Staff Engrg 1974, mangr Engrg Design 1977, mangr Process and Proposals 1983, gp mangr Engrg 1985, tech dir 1987, mktg dir 1989, business devpt dir 1995–; pres Mitcham and Morden Cons Assoc 1996– (chm 1983–88 and 1993–95); memb CEI 1979–83; Inst of Chem Engrs: chm London and South East Branch 1985–87, chm Engrg Practices Ctee 1989–, chm Tech Bd 1996–; SERC (now EPSRC): appointments to Interdiciplinary Res Centre at Imperial Coll 1989–, chm Process Engrg Ctee 1993–94, chm Chem Engrg Sub-Gp 1991–93, memb Clean Technol Mgmnt Ctee 1992–94; IMI (Process) STAG memb 1995–; memb Steering Panel Process Systems Gp Univ of Edinburgh 1992–96; external examiner: in chem engrg Univ of Bradford 1992–, MSc int polution mgmnt UMIST; visiting prof Dept of Chem Engrg Univ of Bath 1994–; memb Res Assessment Panel (Chemical Engrg) and teaching assessment specialist assessor (Chemical Engrg) Higher Educn Funding Cncl for England 1995–, memb Chemicals Foresight Panel 1996–, chm Mgmnt Bd Inst of Applied Catalysis 1996–; FIChemE 1981, FEng 1988; *Books* numerous papers and co authorships on engrg; *Recreations* bridge, politics, golf, book collecting, church, music, travel, food; *Style*— Prof Keith Guy, FEng; ✉ Air Products plc, Hersham Place, Molesey Rd, Walton-on-Thames, Surrey KT12 4RZ (☎ 01932 249591, fax 01932 249565)

GUY, Richard Perran; s of Rev Wilfred Guy (d 1965), of Newlands Park, London, and Winifred Margaret Guy, *née* Hardisty (d 1988); *b* 10 May 1936; *Educ* Kingswood Sch Bath, Wadham Coll Oxford (MA); *m* 26 Sept 1981, Deborah Ann, da of Kenneth Owen, of Adlestrop, Glos; 1 s (Benjamin b 1983), 1 da (Georgina b 1986); *Career* Nat Serv 2 Lt CRMP 1955–57; ICI Ltd 1961–65, New Science Publications 1965–68; called to the Bar Inner Temple 1970; memb Hon Soc Inner Temple; *Recreations* tennis, theatre, skiing; *Clubs* RAC; *Style*— Richard Guy, Esq; ✉ 108 Barnsbury Rd, London N1 0ES (☎ 0171 278 7220); Queen Elizabeth Buildings, Temple, London EC4 (☎ 0171 353 7181, fax 0171 353 3929); Godolphin Chambers, 50 Castle Street, Truro, Cornwall (☎ 01872 76312, fax 01872 71922)

GUY, Gen Sir Roland Kelvin; GCB (1987, KCB 1980), CBE (1978, MBE 1955), DSO (1972); s of Lt-Col Norman Greenwood Guy; cous of Maj (Arthur) Alexander Greenwood, *qv*; *b* 25 June 1928; *Educ* Wellington, RMA Sandhurst; *m* 1957, Deirdre, da of Brig P Graves-Morris, DSO, MC; 2 da (Gillian, Nicola); *Career* cmmnd KRRC 1948, CO IRGJ 1969, Col GS HQ Near East Land Forces 1971, cmd 24 Airportable Bde 1972, RCDS 1975, princ staff offr to Chief of Def Staff 1976–78, Chief of Staff HQ BAOR 1978–80, Col Cmdt Small Arms Sch Corps 1981–87, mil sec MOD 1980–83, Col Cmdt 1 Bn Royal Green Jackets 1981–86; rep Col Cmdt Royal Green Jackets 1985–86, Adj Gen MOD 1984–86, ADC Gen to HM the Queen 1984–87, govr Royal Hosp Chelsea 1987–93; chm: Army Benevolent Fund 1987–93, Cncl of Mgmnt People's Dispensary for Sick Animals (PDSA) 1994–; vice pres Wellington Coll 1990–, govr Milton Abbey Sch 1987–; *Recreations* music, travel; *Clubs* Army & Navy; *Style*— Gen Sir Roland Guy, GCB, CBE, DSO

GUZ, Prof Abraham; s of Akiwa Guz (d 1970), of London, and Esther Guz (d 1986); *b* 12 Aug 1929; *Educ* Grocers' Sch, Charing Cross Hosp Med Sch, Univ of London (MB BS, MD, MRCP); *m* 5 Nov 1989, Nita Florenz, da of Aaron Hollander (d 1973), of London; 3 da (Deborah b 1959, Gabrielle b 1961, Stephanie b 1964); *Career* Nat Serv 1954–56: Lt (later Capt) RAMC Br Army Hosp Hostert HQ BAOR; jr hosp appts 1952–53, asst lectr in pharmacology Charing Cross Hosp Med Sch 1953–54, sr house offr Royal Posgrad Med Sch Hammersmith Hosp 1956–57; res fell: Harvard Med Sch 1957–59, Cardiovascular Res Inst Univ of California 1959–61; Charing Cross Hosp Med Sch 1961–82: lectr, sr lectr, reader, prof; prof of med and head Dept of Med Charing Cross and Westminster Med Sch 1982–94, prof emeritus and hon conslt Charing Cross Hosp 1994–; visitor Dept of Physiology Univ of Oxford; hon sec MRS 1965–70, censor RCP 1979–81; memb Ctee Physiological Soc 1992–; FRCP 1969; memb: Assoc of Physicians, RSM, MRS; *Recreations* family, violin in quartet, Jewish culture study; *Style*— Prof Abraham Guz; ✉ 3 Littleton Rd, Harrow, Middlesex HA1 3SY (☎ and fax 0181 422 2786); Room 1911N, Charing Cross Hospital, Fulham Palace Rd, London W6 8RF (☎ 0171 846 7337, fax 0171 846 7326, e-mail a.guz@cxwms)

GWENLAN, Gareth; s of Charles Aneurin Gwenlan (d 1939), and Mary, *née* Francis (d 1980); *m* 1, 1962 (m dis); 1 s (Simon); m 2, 1986 (m dis 1993), Sarah Elizabeth Fanghanel; *Career* producer and director; former head Comedy Dept BBC TV; over 200 programme credits incl: Woodhouse Playhouse 1977, The Fall and Rise of Reginald Perrin 1978–80, Butterflies 1979–81, To The Manor Born 1978–81, Solo 1980, Waiting for God 1990–, Only Fools and Horses, The Legacy of Reginald Perrin 1996; *Recreations* dressage, eventing; *Clubs* Garrick; *Style*— Gareth Gwenlan, Esq; ✉ Alderbourne Manor, Fulmer Lane, Gerrards Cross, Bucks; Putley Court, Putley, Nr Ledbury, Herefordshire

GWILLIAM, Kenneth Mason; s of John Gwilliam (d 1987), of Farnham, Surrey, and Marjorie, *née* Mason (d 1982); *b* 27 June 1937; *Educ* Latymer Upper Sch London, Magdalen Coll Oxford (BA); *m* 1, 1961 (m dis 1987), Jennifer Mary Bell; 2 s (David Richard b 30 Dec 1964, Michael James b 9 Jan 1967); m 2, 18 Dec 1987, Sandra, da of late John Robert; *Career* econ asst Fisons Ltd Felixtowe 1960–61, lectr in industl economics Univ of Nottingham 1961–65, lectr in economics Univ of E Anglia 1965–67, prof of transport economics Univ of Leeds 1967–89, prof of the economics of transport and logistics Erasmus Univ Rotterdam 1989–93, princ transport economist Infrastructure, Water and Transport Div World Bank 1993–; dir: National Bus Company 1978–83, Yorkshire Ride 1985–87; specialist advsr to House of Commons Tport Ctee; FCIT; *Books* Transport and Public Policy (1964), Economics of Transport Policy (1975); *Recreations* tennis, golf, walking; *Style*— Kenneth Gwilliam, Esq; ✉ Principal Transport Economist, The World Bank, Infrastructure, Water & Transport Division, 1818 H Street NW, Washington DC 20433, USA

GWILT, George David; s of Richard Lloyd Gwilt (d 1972); *b* 11 Nov 1927; *Educ* Sedbergh, St John's Coll Cambridge; *m* 1956, Ann Dalton, da of Arthur J Sylvester, of Connecticut, USA (d 1973); *Career* actuary; Standard Life Co 1949–88: asst official 1956, asst actuary 1957, statistician 1962, mechanisation mangr 1964, systems mangr 1969, dep pensions mangr 1972, pensions actuary 1973, asst gen mangr and pensions mangr 1977, asst gen mangr (fin) 1978, gen mangr and actuary 1979, md and actuary 1985, ret 1988; dir: Hammerson plc 1979–94, European Assets Trust 1979–, Scottish Mortgage and Trust plc 1983–, Hodgson Martin Ltd 1989–; tstee TSB S Scotland 1966–83, pres Faculty of Actuaries 1981–83, memb Monopolies and Mergers Cmmn 1983–87, convener Scottish Poetry Library 1988–; *Recreations* flute playing; *Clubs* RAF, New (Edinburgh); *Style*— George Gwilt, Esq; ✉ 39 Oxgangs Rd, Edinburgh EH10 7BE (☎ 0131 445 1266)

GWYN, Capt Charles Anthony Hugh; s of Brig Rhys Anthony Gwyn, OBE (d 1987), of Port of Menteith, Perthshire, and Dorothy Eileen, *née* Macmillan; *b* 10 May 1943; *Educ* Abbotsholm Sch, Mons OCS; *m* 24 April 1971, Charnisay Ann, da of Col Sir Delaval Cotter, DSO, 6 Bt, of Child Oakford, nr Blanford, Dorset; 1 s (Simon Anthony Delaval b 19 March 1979), 3 da (Victoria Ann b 28 Nov 1972, Rebecca Louise b 13 Feb 1974, Jessica Harriett b 20 May 1976); *Career* cmmnd 2 Lt Scots Gds 1963, served Malaysia, Germany, UK, ret Capt 1971; mangr Scottish and Newcastle Breweries Ltd 1971–74; dir: Christie & Co Ltd 1978–83 (mangr 1974–78), Christie Group plc 1983–88; chm and dir Town & Country Hotels Ltd 1988–; chm Interchange Hotels Ltd 1992–, dir Picture of Health Ltd 1989–; memb Queen's Body Guard for Scotland (Royal Co of Archers); Freeman Worshipful Co of Merchants of Edinburgh 1983; memb: ISVA 1976–88, BHRCA 1988; *Recreations* shooting, tennis, collecting trees; *Clubs* New (Edinburgh), Luffness New Golf; *Style*— Capt Charles Gwyn; ✉ The Walled Garden, Tyninghame, Dunbar (☎ 01620 860559), 69/74 Bruntsfield Place, Edinburgh EH10 4HH (☎ 0131 229 1393, fax 0131 229 5634, telex 727897, car 0860 230751)

GWYNEDD, Viscount; David Richard Owen Lloyd George; s and h of 3 Earl Lloyd George of Dwyfor, *qv*; *b* 22 Jan 1951; *Educ* Eton; *m* 29 June 1985, Pamela Alexandra, o da of late Alexander Kleyff; 2 s (Hon William Alexander, Hon Frederick Owen b 15 Aug 1987); *Heir* s, Hon William Alexander Lloyd George b 16 May 1986; *Career* insurance broker; *Style*— Viscount Gwynedd

GWYNN-JONES, Peter Llewellyn; LVO (1994); s of Maj Jack Llewellyn Gwynn-Jones, of Kalk Bay, Cape Town, SA (d 1981); stepson and ward of Lt-Col Gavin David Young (d 1978), of Spring House, Long Burton, Dorset; *b* 12 March 1940; *Educ* Wellington, Trinity Coll Cambridge (MA); *Career* Bluemantle Pursuivant of Arms 1973–83, Lancaster Herald of Arms 1982–95, House Comptroller College of Arms 1982–95, Garter Principal King of Arms 1995–; Genealogist Order of the Bath 1995–, Inspr of Regimental Colours 1995–, KStJ (Genealogist Order of St John) 1995, Hon Genealogist Order of St Michael and St George 1995, Inspr RAF Badges 1996; *Recreations* local architecture, tropical forests, wildlife conservation, fishing; *Clubs* Travellers; *Style*— Peter Gwynn-Jones, Esq, LVO, Garter Principal King of Arms; ✉ College of Arms, Queen Victoria St, London EC4 (☎ 0171 248 1188, fax 0171 248 6448); 79 Harcourt Terrace, London SW10 (☎ 0171 373 5859)

GWYNNE, Haydn; da of Guy Thomas Haydn Gwynne (d 1994), and Rosamond Noelle, *née* Dobson; *Career* actress; lecturer Facoltà di Economia E Commercio Rome University 1983–85; *Theatre* incl: debut Susan Dunedin in His Monkey Wife (Stephen Joseph Theatre, Scarborough) 1986, West End debut Billie Burke in Ziegfeld (London Palladium) 1988; other roles incl: Millamant in The Way of the World (Theatre Royal Northampton) 1990, title role in Hedda Gabler (Bolton Octagon) 1990, Lady Macbeth in Macbeth (Ludlow Festival) 1991, Oolie/Donna in City of Angels (Prince of Wales) 1993, The Memory of Water (Hampstead) 1996; Manchester Royal Exchange incl: The Bluebird of Unhappiness 1987, Mrs Gaylustre in The Cabinet Minister 1988, Sylvia in The Recruiting Officer 1992; RSC incl: Olivia in Twelfth Night (Stratford, Barbican) 1994–95, Helena in A Midsummer Night's Dream (Stratford) 1994–95, Solveig/Mother Aase in Peer Gynt (Swan, Stratford, Young Vic) 1994–95; *Television* incl: What Mad Pursuit (BBC) 1986, Lovejoy (BBC) 1986, Call Me Mister (BBC) 1986, The Great Writers - Thomas Mann (LWT/Channel Four) 1987, After the War (Granada) 1989, Robyn Penrose in Nice Work (BBC) 1989, B B Miller in Time Riders (Thames) 1991, Alex in Drop the Dead Donkey (Channel Four) 1991–93, Portia in The Merchant of Venice (Channel Four) 1995; *Films* incl: The Pleasure Principle 1990, Remember Me? 1996; *Awards* nominations incl: for City of Angels (Olivier Award for Best Actress in A Musical) 1993, for Drop the Dead Donkey (British Comedy Award and BAFTA); *Style*— Ms Haydn Gwynne; ✉ c/o Markham & Froggatt Ltd, Julian House, 4 Windmill Street, London W1P 1HF (☎ 0171 636 4412, fax 0171 637 5233)

GWYNNE, Richard; s of Dr Edward Ieuan Gwynne, of Ystrad-Rhondda, Mid Glamorgan, and Mary Therese, *née* Downey; *b* 9 March 1955; *Educ* Porth County GS, Trinity Coll Cambridge (MA); *m* 6 May 1995, Susan Mary, *née* Paton; *Career* admitted slr 1979, ptnr Stephenson Harwood 1986–, chm Mgmnt Ctee Fulham Legal Advice Centre 1987–91; memb Worshipful Co of Slrs; memb IBA; *Publications* International Execution Against Judgement Debtors (contrib, 1993); *Recreations* opera, theatre, golf; *Style*— Richard Gwynne, Esq; ✉ 46 Lytton Grove, Putney, London SW15 2HE (☎ 0181 788 7567); Stephenson Harwood, One St Paul's Churchyard, London EC4M 8SH (☎ 0171 329 4422, fax 0171 606 0822, telex 886789)

GYLLENHAMMAR, Pehr G; *b* 28 April 1935, Gothenburg, Sweden; *Educ* Lund Univ (LLB), Centre d'Etudes Industrielles Geneva; *Career* md and chief exec Skandia Insurance Co 1970–83, exec chm AB Volvo 1990–93 (chm and chief exec 1983–90), chm MC European Capital SA 1994–95, sr advsr Lazard Frères & Co LLC 1996–; non-exec dir: United Technologies Corp, Kissinger Associates Inc, Pearson plc 1983–, Reuters Holdings plc 1984–; fndr memb European Round Table of Industrialists; Hon MD Gothenburg Univ 1981, Hon DTech Brunel Univ 1987, Hon DEng Tech Univ of Nova Scotia 1988, Hon DSocSci Univ of Helsinki 1990, Hon LLD Univ of Vermont 1993; *Style*— Pehr G Gyllenhammar, Esq; ✉ Lazard Freres & Co LLC, 21 Moorfields, London EC2P 2HT (☎ 0171 448 2555, fax 0171 374 6614)

GYNGELL, Bruce; *b* 8 July 1929; *m* 1, 1957 (m dis), Ann Barr; 1 s, 2 da; m 2, 1986, Kathryn Rowan; 2 s; *Career* chief exec National Channel 9 Network Australia until 1969, md Seven Network 1969–72, dep chm and jt md ATV London 1972–75, fndr chm Aust Bdcasting Tbnl 1977–80, chief exec Special Broadcasting Service (Australia) 1980–83, chm TV-am (UK) 1990–93 (md 1984–93), chm Nine Network Australia 1993–95, group md Yorkshire-Tyne Tees Television Holdings plc 1995–, chm BRITE (British Independent TV Enterprise) 1995–; *Style*— Bruce Gyngell, Esq; ✉ YTT TV Holdings plc, The Television Centre, Leeds LS3 1JS (☎ 0113 243 8283, fax 0113 242 1069)

H

HAACKE, Norman Patrick von; s of Frederick and Margaret Haacke; *b* 15 March 1952; *Educ* St Joseph's Acad Blackheath, London Coll of Music (jr exhibitioner), St Catharine's Coll Cambridge (MA), Bart's Med Coll (MB BChir); *m* 17 Feb 1979, Jennifer Mary, da of Mathew Finbar Hunt (d 1986); 1 s (Samuel James Finbar b 22 Aug 1982), 1 da (Georgina Alexandra Morgan b 4 Nov 1984); *Career* house surgn Bart's 1976–77, house physician Royal Berkshire Hosp 1977, SHO Addenbrooke's 1977–78, sr registrar Royal Nat Throat, Nose and Ear Hosp 1983 (SHO 1980, registrar 1980–83), sr registrar Edinburgh Royal Infirmary 1983–87; currently: conslt ENT surgn Southampton Univ Hosps 1987–, sr lectr in otolaryngology Univ of Southampton, examiner in fellowship Royal Coll of Surgns in Ireland; Lionel Colledge meml fell RCSE 1985–86; memb: Br Assoc of Academic Otolaryngologists, Br Assoc of Otolaryngologists, Br Assoc for Paediatric Otorhinolaryngology, Br Soc of Audiology, Otolaryngology Research Soc, S Western Laryngological Soc, Scottish Otolaryngological Soc, BMA; FRCSI 1982, FRCS 1983, FRSM; *Publications* author of 3 chapters and over 40 papers on cochlear implantation, endoscopic sinus surgery and other aspects of ENT surgery; *Recreations* sculpture and painting, music, golf, tennis; *Style*— Norman Haacke, Esq; ✉ 2 Blackwater House, Emery Down, Lyndhurst, Hants SO43 7FJ (☎ 01703 282975); Chalybeate Hosp, Chalybeate Close, Tremona Close, Tremona Road, Southampton SO16 6UY (☎ 01703 764308, fax 01703 785621)

HAAN, Christopher; *Career* slr; formerly sr ptnr S J Berwin & Co, ptnr Coudert Brothers until 1994, ptnr Hammond Suddards 1995–; *Style*— Christopher Haan, Esq; ✉ Hammond Suddards, 119 London Wall, London EC2Y 5ET (☎ 0171 448 1000)

HAAN, Michael Robert Anthony; s of Joseph Patrick Haan (d 1989), and Mary Ailsa, *née* Richardson; *b* 24 Sept 1944; *Educ* Ledbury GS; *m* 26 May 1969, Margaret Mabel Haan, da of James Richard Dixon Delahay; 3 c (Rachel Elizabeth b 20 July 1971, Matthew Anthony b 12 June 1974, John Edward b 9 Aug 1978); *Career* chartered accountant Herbert Hill & Co 1969–71 (articled clerk 1964–69); Stoy Hayward: joined as supervisor following a merger 1971, ptnr 1974, currently memb Exec Ctee, head Professional Servs; FCA (ACA 1969); *Recreations* golf, cricket and watching most sports, philately; *Style*— Michael Haan, Esq; ✉ Stoy Hayward, 8 Baker St, London W1M 1DA (☎ 0171 486 5888, fax 0171 487 3686)

HABAKKUK, Sir John Hrothgar; kt (1976); s of Evan Guest Habakkuk; *b* 13 May 1915; *Educ* Barry Co Sch, St John's Coll Cambridge; *m* 1948, Mary Richards; 1 s, 3 da; *Career* lectr Faculty of Economics Cambridge Univ 1946–50, dir of studies in history and librarian Pembroke Coll Cambridge 1946–50 (fell 1938–50, hon fell 1973), Chichele prof of econ history Oxford and fell All Souls 1950–67, princ Jesus Coll Oxford 1967–84, pres Univ Coll Swansea 1975–84 (hon fell 1991), pro vice chllr Oxford Univ 1977–84 (vice chllr 1973–77); memb: Advsy Cncl Public Records 1958–70, SSRC 1967–71, Nat Libraries Ctee 1968–69, Admin Bd Int Assoc of Univs 1975–84, Royal Cmmn on Historical Manuscripts 1978–90; fell All Souls Coll Oxford 1988–; chm: Ctee of Vice Chllrs and Principals of Univs of UK 1976–77, Oxfordshire DHA 1981–84; former pres Royal Hist Soc; Hon DLitt: Wales 1971, Cambridge 1973, Pennsylvania 1975, Kent 1978, Ulster 1988; *Style*— Sir John Habakkuk; ✉ 28 Cunliffe Close, Oxford (☎ 01865 56583)

HABERMAN, Prof Steven; s of Louis Haberman, of Essex, and Rita Lily, *née* Kaminsky; *b* 26 June 1951; *Educ* Ilford Co HS, Trinity Coll Cambridge (MA), City Univ (PhD); *m* 11 April 1976, Mandy Nicola, da of Arnold and Sylvia Brecker, of Herts; 1 s (Benjamin Adam b 18 Aug 1978), 2 da (Nadia Lia (twin) b 18 Aug 1978, Emily Michal b 15 Feb 1980); *Career* Prudential Assurance Co 1972–74; City Univ: lectr Dept of Actuarial Sci 1974–79, sr lectr 1979–83, reader 1983–85, prof 1985–, dean Sch of Mathematics 1995–; memb Cncl Inst of Actuaries 1986–91, 1993–; FIA 1975, ASA 1976, FSS 1979, FRSA 1989, FIMA 1996; *Books* Pensions: The Problems of Today and Tomorrow (1987), Actuarial Mathematics (1993), History of Actuarial Science (1995); *Recreations* badminton, walking, reading, music; *Style*— Prof Steven Haberman; ✉ Dean School of Mathematics, City University, Northampton Square, London EC1V 0HB (☎ 0171 477 8471, fax 0171 477 8572)

HABGOOD, Anthony John; s of John Michael Habgood, MC, and Margaret Diana Middleton, *née* Dalby; *b* 8 Nov 1946; *Educ* Gonville and Caius Coll Cambridge (MA), Carnegie Mellon Univ Pittsburgh USA (MS); *m* 29 June 1973, Nancy, da of Ray Nelson Atkinson, of San Mateo, California, USA; 2 s (John Alan b 14 Nov 1979, George Michael (twin) b 14 Nov 1979), 1 da (Elizabeth Ann b 21 Sept 1975); *Career* memb Mgmnt Exec Ctee Boston Consulting Gp Inc 1979–86 (dir 1976–86), chief exec Tootal Group plc 1990–91 (dir 1986–91); Bunzl plc: chief exec 1991–, chm 1996–; dir: Geest plc 1988–93, Powergen plc 1993–, Schroder Ventures International Investment Trust plc 1996–; *Clubs* Royal Norfolk and Suffolk Yacht; *Style*— Anthony Habgood, Esq; ✉ Bunzl plc, 110 Park Street, London W1Y 3RB (☎ 0171 495 4950)

HABGOOD, Baron (Life Peer UK 1995), of Calverton, in the Co of Bucks; Rt Rev and Rt Hon John Stapylton Habgood; PC (1983); s of Arthur Henry Habgood, DSO, MB, BCh, and Vera (d 1968), da of Edward Chetwynd-Stapylton (d 1938), gggs of 4 Viscount Chetwynd; *b* 23 June 1927; *Educ* Eton, King's Coll Cambridge, Cuddesdon Theol Coll Oxford; *m* 7 June 1961, Rosalie Mary Anne, elder da of Edward Lansdown Boston, of Deeside, Neston, Chester; 2 s (Hon Francis John Stapylton b 1964, Hon Adrian George Chetwynd b 1971), 2 da (Hon Laura Caroline b 1963, Hon Ruth Barbara (Mrs Kenyon-Slade) b 1967); *Career* former demonstrator in pharmacology Cambridge; ordained deacon 1954, priest 1955; curate of St Mary Abbots with St George's London 1954–56, vice-princ Westcott House Cambridge 1956–62, rector St John's Jedburgh 1962–67, princ Queen's Coll Birmingham 1967–73, hon canon of Birmingham Cathedral 1971–73, bishop of Durham 1973–83, Archbishop of York 1983–95, ret; hon fell King's Coll Cambridge 1986; Hon DD Durham 1975, Camb 1984, Aberdeen 1988, Huron 1990, Hull 1991, Oxford 1996, Manchester 1996, York 1996; *Books* Religion and Science (1964), A Working Faith (1980), Church and Nation in a Secular Age (1983), Confessions of a Conservative Liberal (1988), Making Sense (1993); *Recreations* DIY, painting; *Clubs* Athenaeum; *Style*— The Rt Rev and Rt Hon the Lord Habgood, PC; ✉ 18 The Mount, Malton, N Yorkshire YO17 0ND

HABIBIE, HE Junus Effendy; *b* 11 June 1937; *Educ* US Naval Acad, Nat Defence Inst; *m*; 3 c; *Career* Indonesian diplomat; Indonesian Navy 1962–66, head Military Dept Acad of Navigation 1966–69, security asst Harbour Territory III 1969–70, harbour admin Tanjung Priok Harbour 1972–78 (dep admin 1970–71); Directorate Gen of Sea Communication: head regnl office for Region III 1978, acting sec 1978–80, sec 1980–84, DG of sea communication 1984–91; sr official attached to Min of Communications 1991–93, Indonesian ambass to the Ct of St James's and Ireland 1993–; Satya Lencana Satya Dharma (Medal of Honour for Distinguished Services), Satya Lencana Pembangunan (Medal of Honour for Devpt); *Style*— HE Mr Junus Habibie; ✉ Indonesian Embassy, 38 Grosvenor Square, London W1X 9AD (☎ 0171 499 7661)

HACKER, Alan Ray; OBE; s of Kenneth Ray Hacker, and Sybil Blanche, *née* Cogger; *b* 30 Sept 1938; *Educ* Dulwich, RAM; *m* 1 (m dis 1976), Anna Maria, *née* Skoks; 2 da (Katy, Sophie); m 2 (m dis), 1977, Karen Wynne, *née* Evans; 1 s (Alcuin); m 3, 23 Sept 1995, Margaret Shelley, *née* Lee; *Career* prof RAM, sr lectr Univ of York, conductor and teacher Royal Northern Coll; revived Mozart bassett clarinet in the 1960s, pioneer of authentic classical performances in England, many first modern performances of classical works in the 1970s (Haydn to Mendelssohn); operatic conductor 1986–; new prodns incl: Halström's Den Bergtagna (Sweden), Mozart's La Finta Giardiniera (England), Weir's The Vanishing Bridegroom (Scotland), Mozart's Cosi fan Tutte (Stuttgart), Monteverdi's Ulisse (Stuttgart), Handel's Julius Caesar (Halle), Bizet's Carmen (Canada), Rossini's La Cenerentola (Spain), King Arthur (Stuttgart); fndr: York Early Music Festival (dir), York Clarion Band; memb of various arts Cncl Ctees, host Br Cncl; FRAM; *Books* scores of: Mozart's Clarinet Concerto, Schumann's Fantasy Pieces (Soirėestücke); *Recreations* cooking; *Style*— Alan Hacker, Esq, OBE; ✉ Hindlea, Broughton, Malton, N Yorks YO17 0QJ (☎ and fax 01653 696163); Haydn Rawstron Int Management, 36 Station Road, London SE20 7BQ

HACKER, Richard Daniel; s of Samuel Hacker, of London, and Lilli Paula, *née* Eick; *b* 26 March 1954; *Educ* Haberdashers' Aske's, Downing Coll Cambridge (MA), Wiener Anspach scholar 1976, Université Libre De Bruxelles (Licencié Speciale En Droit Européen); *m* 25 March 1988, Sarah Anne, da of Richard Millar, of Bath; 1 da (Rebecca Leonora b 23 Jan 1993); *Career* called to the Bar Lincoln's Inn 1977; Hardwicke scholar 1977, Lincoln's Inn Student of the Year Prize 1977, Gray's Inn 1989; *Recreations* travel, gastronomy, opera; *Style*— Richard Hacker, Esq; ✉ 31 Carlton Hill, London NW8 0JX; 3–4 South Square, Gray's Inn, London WC1R 5HP (☎ 0171 696 9900, fax 0171 696 9911)

HACKETT, Dennis William Patrick; s of James Joseph Hackett (d 1961), of Sheffield, South Yorks, and Sarah Ellen, *née* Bedford (d 1982); *b* 5 Feb 1929; *Educ* De La Salle Coll Sheffield; *m* 1, 1953 (m dis 1970); 2 s (Sean James b 15 Sept 1956, Michael Simon b 30 May 1961), 1 da (Anne-Marie b 10 Jan 1955); m 2, 10 Aug 1974, Jacqueline Margaret Totterdell; 1 da (Clare Siobhan b 11 Sept 1976); *Career* RN 1947–49; art ed The Observer 1960–62; ed: The Queen 1963–65 (dep ed 1962–63), Nova 1965–69; editorial dir George Newnes (IPC) 1966–69, dir IPC Mirror Group Newspapers 1969–71, assoc ed Daily Express 1973–74, dir HK Communications 1974–82, editorial conslt Associated Newspapers 1982–86, TV critic The Times 1981–85; ed-in-chief: Today and Sunday Today 1986–87, The Observer Magazine 1987–88; ptnr Dennis Hackett Consultants 1982–86 and 1988–, dir Media Search & Selection 1988–, ed Management Today 1992–94; chm D&AD 1968–69; FRSA; *Books* The History of the Future: A History of the Bemrose Corporation 1826 (1976), The Big Idea: The Story of Ford in Europe (1978); *Recreations* reading, walking; *Clubs* RAC; *Style*— Dennis Hackett, Esq; ✉ 39 Denning Road, London NW3 1ST (☎ 0171 794 1015, fax 0171 435 9291)

HACKETT, Capt Edward Middleton; s of Maj Peter Middleton Hackett, of Broadstone, Dorset, and Margaret, *née* Thomas; *b* 28 Oct 1942; *Educ* Dauntsey's Sch, Britannia RNC; *m* 12 Dec 1981, Philippa Ann, da of Dr John Norcliffe Roberts, of London; 1 s (Jamie b 1987), 1 da (Flavia b 1984); *Career* RN: Dartmouth 1961, HMS Puncheston 1965, served Borneo and Singapore Indonesian confrontation (Lt 1966), specialised aviation flying Buccaneers 801 Sqdn HMS Hermes 1968, Air Warfare Instr 1972, 809 Sqdn HMS Ark Royal 1972, Staff Course RNC Greenwich 1974 (Lt Cdr 1974), Sr Pilot 809 Sqdn HMS Ark Royal 1975, instr Maritime Tactical Sch HMS Dryad 1977 (Cdr 1977), cmd HMS Rhyl 1978, Directorate Naval Air Warfare MoD 1980, Cdr Air HMS Illustrious 1982, Staff Aviation Offr Staff of Flag Offr Third Flotilla 1984 (Capt 1985), COS to Flag Offr Gibraltar 1985, cmd HMS Coventry 1988, Dep Dir Naval Warfare (Air) MOD 1990; Queen's Harbour Master and Captain of the Port Portsmouth 1992–94, ret; memb: Guild of Air Pilots and Air Navigators, Fleet Air Arm Offrs Assoc; FIMgt, MNI; *Recreations* sailing, fishing, shooting; *Clubs* Royal Yacht Squadron, RN Sailing Assoc, The Royal Navy of 1765 And 1785, The Naval; *Style*— Captain Edward Hackett, RN; ✉ The Coach House, Stoner Hill Road, Froxfield, Petersfield, Hants GU32 1DX (☎ 01730 260072, fax 01730 262021)

HACKETT, John Charles Thomas; s of Thomas John Hackett (d 1996), and Doris, *née* Whitefoot (d 1978); *b* 4 Feb 1939; *Educ* Glyn GS Epsom, Univ of London (LLB); *m* 27 Dec 1958, Patricia Margaret, da of Eric Ronald Clifford Tubb (d 1992), of Surrey; *Career* prodn planning mangr Rowntree Group 1960–64, prodn controller Johnson's Wax 1964, commercial sec Heating and Ventilating Contractors Assoc 1964–70, sec Confedn of Assocs of Specialist Engrg Contractors 1968–79, dir Br Constructional Steelwork Assoc 1980–84 (dep dir 1970–79); DG: Br Insur and Investmt Brokers Assoc 1984–91, Fedn of Civil Engrg Contractors 1992–; memb Cncl CBI 1980–88 and 1992–; MInstD 1979, FIMgt 1981, FRSA 1992; *Books* BCSA Members Contractual Handbook (1972, 1979); *Recreations* music, reading, walking, motoring; *Style*— John Hackett, Esq; ✉ 15 Downsway Close, Tadworth, Surrey KT20 5DR (☎ 01737 813024); The Federation of Civil Engineering Contractors, Cowdray House, 6 Portugal Street, London WC2A 2HA (☎ 0171 404 4020, fax 0171 242 0256)

HACKETT, Gen Sir John Winthrop; GCB (1967, KCB 1962, CB 1958), CBE (1953, MBE 1938), DSO (1942, Bar 1945), MC (1941), DL (Glos 1982); s of Hon Sir John Winthrop Hackett, KCMG, MLC (d 1916), of Perth, WA, and Deborah Vernon (d 1965, having m 2, 1918, Ald Sir Frank Beaumont Moulden, Lord Mayor of Adelaide (d 1932)), 2 da of Frederick Slade Drake-Brockman, of Guildford, WA; *b* 5 Nov 1910; *Educ* Geelong GS, New Coll Oxford (MA, BLitt); *m* 21 March 1942, Margaret, da of Joseph Frena (d 1953), of Graz, Austria, and widow of Friedrich Grossman; 1 da and 2 adopted step da; *Career* 2 Lt 8 Hussars 1931, served Palestine 1936 (despatches), seconded Transjordan Frontier Force 1937–39 (despatches), Syria (wounded), Western Desert (wounded), Italy 1943 (despatches), OC 4 Parachute Bde Arnhem 1944 (wounded), Temp Lt-Col 1942, Brig 1943, BGS (1) Austria 1946, OC Transjordan Frontier Force 1947, IDC 1951, Dep QMG BAOR 1952, OC 20 Armoured Bde 1954, Gen OC 7 Armd Div 1956, Maj-Gen

1957, Cmdt RMC of Sci 1958–61, Gen OC NI Cmd 1961–62, Dep Chief Imperial Gen Staff 1963–64, Dep Chief Gen Staff 1964–66, Gen 1966, C-in-C BAOR and Cdr Northern Army Gp in NATO 1966–68, ADC Gen to HM The Queen 1967–68, Col QRIH 1969–75, Hon Col Univ of Oxford OTC 1967–78, 10 Para Bn TA 1967–78, Col Cmdt REME 1961–66, ret; princ King's Coll London 1968–75; pres: UK Classical Assoc 1971, UK English Assoc 1974; visiting prof of classics King's Coll; vice pres Wildfowl & Wetlands Tst; Hon LLD: Univ of Western Australia, Queen's Univ Belfast, Univ of Exeter, Univ of Buckingham; Freeman City of London 1976; FRSL 1982; author; *Books* I Was A Stranger (1977), The Third World War (jtly, 1978), The Untold Story (1982), The Profession of Arms (1983), Warfare in the Ancient World (ed, 1989); *Recreations* music, wine, reading, travel, salmon and trout fishing; *Clubs* Cavalry and Guards, Carlton, United Oxford and Cambridge Univ, White's; *Style*— Gen Sir John Hackett, GCB, CBE, DSO, MC, DL; ✉ Coberley Mill, nr Cheltenham, Glos GL53 9NH (☎ 01242 870207)

HACKETT, Dr Peter; OBE, DL (Cornwall 1993); *b* 1 Nov 1933; *Educ* Univ of Nottingham (BSc, PhD); *m* 2 Jan 1958, Esmé Doreen, *née* Lloyd; 2 c (Nicholas Roger b 4 Oct 1964, Catherine Lesley b 16 April 1966); *Career* lectr Univ of Nottingham 1958–70, princ Camborne Sch of Mines Cornwall (Univ of Exeter) 1970–94 (advsr 1994–); visiting lectr: Univ of Minnesota 1979, Univ of California at Berkeley 1979; hon fell Instn of Mining & Metallurgy 1993 (memb 1964), FEng 1983; *Style*— Dr Peter Hackett, OBE, DL, FEng; ✉ University of Exeter at Camborne School of Mines, Redruth, Cornwall TR15 3SE (☎ 01209 714866, fax 01209 612329)

HACKING, 3 Baron (UK 1945); Sir Douglas David Hacking; 3 Bt (UK 1938); s of 2 Baron Hacking (d 1971); n of Hon Lady Waller; *b* 17 April 1938; *Educ* Aldro Sch, Charterhouse, Clare Coll Cambridge, (BA, MA); *m* 1, 31 July 1965 (m dis), (Rosemary) Anne (who m subsequently, 1982, Antony Askew, of Highgate), da of the late Frank Penrose Forrest, FRCSE, of Lytchett Matravers, Dorset; 2 s (Hon Douglas Francis b 8 Aug 1968, Hon Daniel Robert b 27 May 1972), 1 da (Hon Belinda Anne b 1966); m 2, 1982, Dr Tessa Margaret Hunt, MB, MRCP, FRCA, er da of Roland Hunt, CMG, of Whitchurch Hill, Reading, Berks; 3 s (Hon Alexander Roland Harry b 20 Jan 1984, Hon (Maxwell David) Leo b 8 July 1987, Hon Christian Eric George b 7 Dec 1989); *Heir* s, Hon Douglas Francis Hacking; *Career* Nat Serv RN 1956–58; Lt RNR (ret); sits as Cons peer in House of Lords (memb Select Ctee on Euro Community 1989–93 and 1995–); barr 1963–76, Harmsworth Major Entrance exhibitioner and Astbury scholar; attorney: New York State 1975, Simpson Thacher and Bartlett New York 1975–76; slr Supreme Court of Eng & Wales 1977; ptnr Richards Butler 1981–94, managing ptnr Sonneschein 1994–; Freeman: Worshipful Co of Merchant Taylors', City of London; FIArb 1979; *Clubs* MCC, Century (New York); *Style*— The Rt Hon the Lord Hacking; ✉ Sonnescheins, Royex House, Aldermanbury Square, London EC2V 7HR (☎ 0171 600 2222); 27 West Square, Kennington, London SE11 4SP (☎ 0171 735 4400)

HACKNEY, Arthur; s of John Thomas (d 1971), of Stoke on Trent, and Annie, *née* Morris (d 1979); *b* 13 March 1925; *Educ* Burslem Sch of Art, RCA; *m* 14 Aug 1954, Mary Cecilia, da of Ernest Baker (d 1946), of Coventry; 2 da (Rosalind b 27 July 1956, Clare b 17 May 1961); *Career* WWII RN, served Western Approaches 1943–46; artist; RCA travelling scholarship 1949, lectr then princ lectr and head of dept W Surrey Coll of Art and Design 1949–85; work in public collections incl: Bradford City Art Gallery, V & A, Ashmolean Gallery, Wellington Nat Gallery NZ, Nottingham Art Gallery, Keighley Art Gallery, Wakefield Art Gallery, Preston Art Gallery, Stoke on Trent Gallery; memb Fine Art Bd CNAA 1975–78; RWS, RE, ARCA; *Clubs* Chelsea Arts; *Style*— Arthur Hackney, Esq; ✉ Woodhatches, Spoil Lane, Tongham, Farnham, Surrey (☎ 01252 23919)

HACKNEY, Jeffrey; s of Reginald Thomas Hackney, of Stoke-on-Trent, and Mildred Anne, *née* Stanway; *b* 5 Jan 1941; *Educ* Newcastle HS Staffs, Wadham Coll Oxford (BA, BCL, Vinerian scholar), UCL (Churchill Jenkinson prize); *m* 27 Oct 1962, Dr Ann Christine, da of Frank Swindells; 1 s (Daniel b 3 Nov 1965), 1 da (Lucy b 2 April 1967); *Career* called to the Bar Middle Temple 1966 (Blackstone scholar, Colombos prize), pupillages with Martin Nourse (now Lord Justice Nourse) and Nicolas Browne-Wilkinson (now Lord Browne-Wilkinson); St Edmund Hall: fell and tutor in law 1964–76, librarian 1966–72, sr tutor 1972–76; Wadham Coll Oxford: fell and tutor in law 1976–, sec to Governing Body 1981–84, sr tutor 1986–88; University of Oxford: chm Law Faculty Bd 1977–79, Keeper of the Archives 1987–96, chm Libraries Bd 1988–91, Bodleian curator 1986–91, chm Gen Bd of the Faculties 1991–93, memb Hebdomadal Cncl 1991–95, chm Curators of the Sheldonian Theatre 1993–; *Books* Understanding Equity and Trusts (1987); *Recreations* music, theatre; *Style*— Jeffrey Hackney, Esq; ✉ 25 Barton Lane, Headington, Oxford OX3 9JW (☎ 01865 61458); Wadham College, Oxford OX1 3PN (☎ 01865 277918)

HACKNEY, Dr Roderick Peter (Rod); s of William Hackney, and Rose, *née* Morris; *b* 3 March 1942; *Educ* John Bright's GS Llandudno, Sch of Architecture Univ of Manchester (MA, BA, ARCH, PhD 1979); *m* Christine (Tina); 1 s (Roan b 27 April 1982); *Career* architect Expo 1967 monorail stations Montreal Canada 1965–66, housing architect Libyan Govt Tripoli 1967–68, asst to Arne Jacobson Copenhagen 1968–71, established practice of Rod Hackney Architect in Macclesfield 1972, established a number of offices throughout the UK 1975–87, set up Castward Ltd (building and devpt) 1983; RIBA: elected nat memb to the Cncl 1978, vice pres 1981–83, memb 3 man delgn to USSR under Anglo-Soviet Cultural Agreement 1984, chm The Times-RIBA Community Enterprise Scheme 1985–89, pres 1987–89, memb Cncl 1991–, vice pres international affrs 1992–; UIA: elected Cncl for Gp 1 1981, memb Editorial Bd Int Architect 1983 (Jl of Architect Theory and Criticism 1988), vice pres 1985, pres 1987–90, immediate past pres and cncl memb 1991–, Gold Medal jury memb 1993; advsr on regeneration and inner city problems in Sweden, Italy and USA 1990–, conslt BBC TV documentary series Europe by Design 1991, conslt World Architecture Review Agency Shenzen China 1992–, int advsr Centre for Int Architecture Studies Univ of Manchester Sch of Architecture 1992–; visiting prof UP6 Paris 1984, pres Young Architect World Forum Sofia 1985, pres Building Communities Int Community Architecture Conf 1986, special prof in architecture Univ of Nottingham 1987–91, lectr tour of India (sponsored by Br Cncl) 1991, advsr to Mayor of Trento Italy 1991, lectures in Sri Lanka (sponsored by Br Cncl) 1992, juror and advsr to DVA Int Competition Netherlands 1992, advsr to Mayor of City of Meridian USA (Livable Southern Communities Conf) 1992, lecture Int Biennale for Architecture BA/93 Buenos Aires Argentina 1993, lecture Univ of Shenzhen World Architecture Review Agency China 1993, lecture Inst of Architects Karachi Pakistan 1993, conslt speaker Livable City Conf Meridian Mississippi 1994 and 1996, advsr Centre for Human Settlements International India 1994, conslt Chapman Clarke Films (Forever England, Central TV) 1995, visiting prof Royal Danish Acad of Fine Arts Copenhagen 1995, lectr Br-American-Canadian Assocs tour USA 1995, Int Conf Writers & Intellectuals Pakistan 1995, lecture Hogeschool Mideen Brabant & IHS Netherlands 1996, lecture Acad of Architecture Rotterdam 1996, contrib Common Ground (Radio 4 debate); first prize: DOE Awards for Good Design in Housing 1975, St Ann's Hospice Architectural Competition 1976; Prix Int d'Architecture de l'Institut National du Logement 1979, commended RICS and The Times Conservation Awards 1980, highly commended DOE Awards 1980, commended The Civic Tst Awards 1980, hon mention Sir Robert Matthews Award 1981, commended Civic Tst Awards 1981, President's award Manchester Soc for Architects 1982, commended Otis Award 1982; commendation Business Enterprise award 1993, short listed Millennium Expo Competition Greenwich 1995, commended Natural Stone Award 1995, 96 citation World Habitat Awards 1995; Gold medal: Bulgarian Inst of Architects 1983, Young Architect of the Biennale Sofia 1983; award of commendation Civic Tst Awards 1984, Grand medal of the Federation de Colegios de Arquitectas de la Republica Mexicana 1986, PA award for Innovation in Building Design and Construction 1988; hon fell: American Inst of Architects 1988, Federacion de Colegias de Arquitectos de la Republica Mexicana 1988, Utd Architects of the Philippines 1988, Royal Architectural Inst of Canada 1990, Indian Inst of Architects 1990; chm of Tstees Inner City Tst 1986–, presented the case for Int Year of Shelter for the Homeless to all Pty Confs 1986, pres Snowdonia Nat Park Soc 1987–, patron Llandudno Museum and Art Gallery 1988–, pres North Wales Centre of the Nat Tst 1990–, hon memb Rural Buildings Preservation Tst 1994, memb Assoc of Planning Supervisors 1996; FCIArb 1977, MCIOB 1987, FFB 1987, PPRIBA (ARIBA 1969, PRIBA 1987); *Books* The Good, The Bad and The Ugly (1990), music play (based on own work) Good Golly Miss Molly (West End, 1991); *Recreations* photography, butterflies, travelling, walking, outdoor pursuits, looking at buildings, speaking at conferences; *Clubs* Cwlth; *Style*— Dr Rod Hackney, PPRIBA; ✉ St Peter's House, Windmill St, Macclesfield, Cheshire SK11 7HS (☎ 01625 431792, fax 01625 616929, e-mail mail@stpeter.demom.co.uk)

HADDACKS, Vice Adm Paul Kenneth; s of Kenneth Alexander Haddacks, and Edith Lillian, *née* Peardon (d 1979); *b* 27 Oct 1946; *Educ* Kingswood Sch Bath, Britannia RNC Dartmouth, RN Staff Coll, Staff Coll Camberley, RCDS; *m* 1970, Penny Anne, da of late Prof D Robertson; 1 s (David Paul b 1973); *Career* joined RN 1964; commanded HM Ships: Scimitar 1971–72, Cleopatra 1981–82, Naiad 1982–83, Intrepid 1986–88; Cdr 1979, instructor US Naval Acad 1979–80, Capt 1984, asst dir Naval Plans 1984–86, dep dir Naval Warfare 1988–89, commander RN Task Force Gulf 1990, Capt of the Fleet 1991–94, Rear Adm 1994, ACOS (Policy) to SACEUR 1994–97, Vice Adm 1997, UK Mil Rep at NATO HQ 1997–; *Recreations* family and travel; *Clubs* Naval and Military, Royal Naval Sailing Association; *Style*— Vice Adm Paul Haddacks; ✉ c/o Naval Secretary, Victory Building, HM Naval Base, Portsmouth, Hants PO1 3LR

HADDAD, (Patricia) Faith; da of Lawrence Atkin (d 1987), and Letitia, *née* Green; *b* 7 Nov 1943; *Educ* Cleethorpes Girls' GS, Univ of Sheffield (MB ChB, MD, Dip Obstetrics); *m* 21 Feb 1972, Joseph Haddad; 1 da (Samantha Faith b 19 July 1976); *Career* pre-registration house offr Nottingham City Hosp 1967–68, pre-registration house surgn Sheffield City Gen Jan-July 1968; sr house offr: in obstetrics and gynaecology Jessop Hosp Sheffield 1968–70, in surgery Scunthorpe Gen Hosp 1970–71; registrar in obstetrics and gynaecology Grimsby Gen Hosp 1971–72, sr med offr Hounslow and Surrey Public Health Dept 1972–75; registrar in obstetrics and gynaecology Hillingdon Hosp 1975–76, W Middx Hosp 1976–79 (acting sr registrar); assoc specialist W London Hosp and Charing Cross Hosp 1982–85 (lectr in obstetrics and gynaecology 1979–82), conslt gynaecologist Garden Hosp London 1985–; chair person Forum on Maternity and Newborn RSM; memb: Working Pty for Change in Antenatal Care NCT 1981, Advsy Ctee on Current Fertility Royal Coll of Gynaecologists 1984–86, Advsy Ctee for First Symposium on Preconception Care 1985, Advsy Ctee for Preconception Care Symposium City Univ 1987, recognized lectr to midwives; Lecture of the Year prize N of England Soc for Obstetrics and Gynaecology 1970; MRCOG 1972; memb: Inst of Psychosexual Med 1985, RSM, N of England Soc of Obstetrics and Gynaecology, Med Women's Fedn; fell Royal Coll of Gynaecologists; author of numerous articles in various learned jls; *Recreations* music, sport; *Style*— Mrs Faith Haddad; ✉ Tara, Trout Rise, Loudwater, Rickmansworth, Herts WD3 4JY (☎ 01923 772971); Hospital of St John and St Elizabeth, 60 Grove End Road, St John's Wood, London NW8 (☎ 0181 286 5126)

HADDAOUI, HE Khalil; *b* 21 April 1937; *Educ* Sch of Higher Business Studies Paris, Inst of Int Relations Paris; *m*; 3 c; *Career* Moroccan diplomat; Econ Section Miny for Foreign Affairs Rabat 1966–69, econ counsellor Embassy Rome 1969, 1st counsellor Embassy London 1969–70; minister-counsellor: Embassy Algiers 1970–71, Embassy Madrid 1971–74, Embassy London 1974–76; advsr to Minister for Foreign Affairs Rabat 1976–82, ambassador to Liberia and Sierra Leonne 1982–85, ambassador to UN 1985–86, dir Int Orgns Miny of Foreign Affairs Rabat 1986–90, dir of Euro and American affairs Miny for Foreign Affairs Rabat 1990–91, ambassador to Ct of St James's 1991–; *Style*— HE Mr Khalil Haddaoui; ✉ Embassy of Morocco, 49 Queen's Gate Gardens, London SW7 5NE (☎ 0171 581 5001)

HADDEN, Abel Robert; s of Alan Edwin Robert Hadden, of Andorra, and Carmen Clare, *née* Masters (d 1995); *b* 4 June 1953; *Educ* Westminster; *m* 1, 1977 (m dis 1984), Katherine, *née* Taylor; 1 s (Leo b 1983); m 2, Belinda, da of Dr Sir Reginald Frederick Brittain Bennett, VRD, *qv*; 1 da (Camilla b 1991); *Career* articled clerk Touche Ross 1972–75, Odhams & Gunn 1975–76, Charles Barker 1976–81, Abel Hadden Associates Ltd 1981–83, Good Relations Group/Lowe Bell Communications 1983–94, md Edelman London 1994–; IPR: memb 1976, memb Conslts' Gp 1979–84, memb Cncl 1981–84, fell 1993; DipCAM 1980, CAM examiner 1984–92 (chief examiner 1988–92), memb Mktg Soc 1984; non-exec dir Raleigh International 1990–; tstee Juvenile Diabetes FNdn 1995–; memb Charity Projects 1986, memb Bd of Visitors HMP Wandsworth 1995–; *Recreations* squash, tennis, fishing, skiing; *Clubs* Hurlingham, Naval & Military, Bembridge Sailing; *Style*— Abel Hadden, Esq; ✉ Edelman UK, Haymarket House, 28–29 Haymarket, London SW1Y 4SP (☎ 0171 344 1265, fax 0171 344 1295)

HADDEN, Prof David Robert; s of Robert Evans Hadden (d 1978), of Portadown, and Marianne Baird, *née* Johnston; *b* 24 May 1936; *Educ* Campbell Coll, Queen's Univ Belfast (MB BCh, BAO, MD); *m* 7 April 1967, Diana Sheelah Mary, da of William Herbert Martin (d 1987), of Belfast; 1 s (Robert b 1968), 2 da (Katharine b 1970, Emily b 1971); *Career* house physician and res fell Royal Victoria Hosp Belfast 1959–62, Fulbright travelling fellowship Johns Hopkins Hosp Baltimore USA 1962–64, MRC Infantile Malnutrition Res Unit Kampala Uganda 1965–66, Dept of Experimental Med Univ of Cambridge 1966–67, conslt physician Royal Victoria Hosp Belfast 1967–, prof of endocrinology Queen's Univ of Belfast 1990–; pres Ulster Med Soc 1996; memb: RSM, Assoc of Physicians of GB and I, Diabetes and Endocrinology Socs of GB and I, Europe and USA; FRCPEd 1969, FRCP 1987; *Publications* Diabetes and Frequancy - An International Approach to Diagnosis and Management (ed, 1996); articles and chapters on diabetes and endocrinology in med lit; *Recreations* restoration and care of old houses and gardens; *Style*— Prof David Hadden; ✉ 10 Mount Pleasant, Belfast BT9 5DS (☎ 01232 667110); Sir George E Clark Metabolic Unit, Royal Victoria Hospital, Belfast BT12 6BA (☎ 01232 894798, fax 01232 310111)

HADDINGTON, 13 Earl of (S 1619) John George Baillie-Hamilton; also Lord Binning (S 1613) and Lord Binning and Byres (S 1619); only s of 12 Earl of Haddington, KT,MC,TD (d 1986), and Sarah, *née* Cook (d 1995); *b* 21 Dec 1941; *Educ* Ampleforth, Trinity Coll Dublin, RAC Cirencester; *m* 1, 19 April 1975 (m dis 1981), Prudence Elizabeth, da of Andrew Rutherford Hayles, of Bowerchalke, Wilts; m 2, 8 Dec 1984, Susan Jane Antonia, da of John Heyworth, of Bradwell Grove, Burford, Oxon; 1 s (George Edmund Baldred, Lord Binning b 1985), 2 da (Lady Susan Moyra b 15 July 1988, Lady Isobel Joan b 16 June 1990); *Heir* s, George Edmund Baldred, Lord Binning b 27 Dec 1985; *Career* farmer, horse breeder; *Recreations* beekeeping, keeping finches, field sports, photography, racing, cerealogy; *Clubs* Turf, New, Puffins, Chelsea Arts; *Style*— The Rt Hon the Earl of Haddington; ✉ Mellerstain, Gordon, Berwicks TD3 6LG

HADDO, Earl of; Alexander George Gordon; s and h of 6 Marquess of Aberdeen and Temair, *qv*; *b* 31 March 1955; *Educ* Harrow, Poly of Central London (Dip of Bldg Econs); *m* 30 May 1981, Joanna Clodagh, da of late Maj Ian George Henry Houldsworth, of Dallas Lodge, Forres, Moray; 3 s (George Ian Alastair, Hon Sam Dudley b 25 Oct 1985, Hon Charles David b 8 June 1990), 1 da (Lady Anna Katharine b 2 Sept 1988); *Heir* s, George Ian Alastair, Viscount Formartine b 4 May 1983; *Career* London & Edinburgh Trust plc 1986–94, chm Kellie Estates Ltd 1995–; dir Mobile Cardiovascular Science PLC 1993–; landowner (10,000 acres); ARICS; *Recreations* sport, music, art; *Clubs* MCC, Huntercombe Golf, Royal Aberdeen Golf; *Style*— Earl of Haddo; ✉ House of Formartine, Methlick, Ellon, Aberdeenshire AB41 0EQ (☎ 01651 806897); Estate Office, Haddo House, Aberdeen (☎ 01651 851664)

HADDON, Martin Thomas; s of Brig Thomas Haddon (d 1993), and Clodagh, *née* Russell; *b* 8 Dec 1944; *Educ* Beaumont Coll Old Windsor, Worcester Coll Oxford (BA); *m* 1977, Helen, da of Hugh Parry (d 1980); 2 da (Susanna b 31 Dec 1978, Jessica b 19 July 1981), 1 s (Nicholas b 19 July 1981); *Career* MAFF: asst princ 1966–71, princ Land Tenure and Land Improvements Divs 1971–74, seconded to European Secretariat Cabinet Office 1974–76, Sugar Div 1976–77, on staff Mgmnt Review 1977–80, asst sec 1980–81, head of EC Div 1981–83, head of Fisheries 1983–88, head of Mgmnt Div and sec Departmental Mgmnt Bd 1988–90, Mgmnt Servs Gp 1990–91, under sec Animal Health and Vet Gp 1991–96, ret; *Recreations* reading, music, cooking, voluntary work; *Clubs* Soc of Recorder Players; *Style*— Martin Haddon, Esq

HADDON-CAVE, Charles Anthony; s of Sir Philip Haddon-Cave, KBE, CMG, *qv*, of Tackley, Oxford, and Elizabeth, *née* Simpson; *b* 20 March 1956; *Educ* The King's Sch Canterbury, Pembroke Coll Cambridge (MA); *m* 2 Aug 1980, Amanda Charlotte, da of Timothy James Law, of Godalming, Surrey; 2 da (Alexandra Charlotte b 11 Feb 1987, Florence Caroline b 8 Jan 1991); *Career* called to the Bar: Gray's Inn 1978, Hong Kong 1980; *Recreations* tennis, running, swimming; *Clubs* RAC; *Style*— Charles Haddon-Cave, Esq; ✉ Hunters Moon, Grayshott, Hampshire GU26 6EG (☎ 01428 605189); 4 Essex Court, Temple, London EC4Y 9AP (☎ 0171 797 7970, fax 0171 353 0998, telex 8812528)

HADDON-CAVE, Sir (Charles) Philip; KBE (1980), CMG (1973); s of Francis Macnamara Haddon-Cave; *b* 6 July 1925; *Educ* Univ of Tasmania, King's Coll Cambridge; *m* 1948, Elizabeth Alice May, da of Frederick Alfred Simpson; 2 s, 1 da; *Career* joined Colonial Admin Service 1952, chief secretary Hong Kong 1981–85 (financial sec Hong Kong 1971–81); dir Kleinwort Benson Group 1986–95, chm Fleming Overseas Investment Trust 1988– (dir 1986–95); *Books* Air Transport in Australia (with D M Hocking, 1951); *Clubs* Oriental, Hong Kong; *Style*— Sir Philip Haddon-Cave, KBE, CMG; ✉ The Old Farmhouse, Nethercote Rd, Tackley, Oxon OX5 3AW

HADDOW, Christopher; QC (Scot 1985); *b* 15 May 1947; *Career* admitted Faculty of Advocates 1971; *Style*— Christopher Haddow, QC; ✉ Advocates' Library, Parliament House, Edinburgh EH1 1RF (☎ 0131 226 5071)

HADEN, Harold John; s of Harold Stanley Haden (d 1979), and Eunice Escott, *née* Wood (d 1962); *b* 14 Feb 1941; *Educ* Wrekin Coll, Hackley Sch NY (ESU Exchange Scholar), Univ of Birmingham (LLB); *m* 4 April 1964, (Elizabeth) Jane, da of George Noel de St Croix, MBE; 1 s (Rupert b 1974), 2 da (Rachel b 1967, Philippa b 1970); *Career* pupillage practice 1964–65, barr 1966–69, loss adjuster 1970–72, M & G 1973, currently personnel legal and compliance dir M & G Group PLC (co sec until 1990); *Recreations* shooting, travel, theatre; *Style*— Harold Haden, Esq; ✉ M & G Limited, 7th Floor, 3 Minster Court, Great Tower Street, London EC3R 7XH (☎ 0171 626 4588, fax 0171 623 8615)

HADEN-GUEST, 5 Baron (UK 1950); Christopher Haden-Guest; s of 4 Baron Haden-Guest (d 1996), and his 2 w, Jean Pauline, *née* Hindes; *b* 5 Feb 1948; *m* 1984, Jamie Lee Curtis, the actress, da of Tony Curtis the actor, and Janet Leigh, the actress; 1 adopted s, 1 adopted da (Anne b 1986); *Heir* bro, Hon Nicholas Haden-Guest b 5 May 1951; *Career* actor, director, writer and humour conslt; writer of comedy for: National Lampoon (in print and for National Lampoon Radio Hour), Lily Tomlin (Emmy Award), Saturday Night Live; *Films* as as actor incl Nigel Tufnel in This is Spinal Tap 1984 (also scriptwriter); as dir incl: The Big Picture, Attack of the 50ft Woman, Waiting for Guffman; *Recreations* playing clarinet, mandolin, guitar, piano, electric bass, drums and harp; *Style*— The Rt Hon Lord Haden-Guest

HADEN-GUEST, Hon Nicholas; yst s of 4 Baron Haden-Guest (d 1996); hp to bro, 5 Baron; *b* 5 May 1951; *Educ* The New Sch for Social Research American Coll in Paris (BA), Stella Adler Inst, Herbert Berghof Studio; *m* 1, 11 May 1980 (m dis 1989), Jill Demby; 1 da (Julia b 23 Sept 1988); m 2, 26 Nov 1989, Mrs Pamela Ann Seamon Rack, da of Lt Joseph G Seamon, USN, of Akron, Ohio, USA; 1 da (Elizabeth b 30 May 1990), 1 step s (William Rack b 24 Sept 1983); *Career* actor; feature films: The Long Riders 1979, Trading Places 1982, Appointment with Death 1987, The Assassin 1988, National Lampoon's Christmas Vacation 1989, The Grand Tour 1989, Au Pair 1990, Dollman 1991, Hollywood Land 1991, Chrome Soldiers 1991, The Legend of O B Taggart 1994; TV shows: Fathers and Sons 1986, The Return of Sherlock Holmes 1987, Zorro 1989, Hunter 1989, Blossom 1991, Midnight Caller 1991; theatre: Vivien (Los Angeles) 1986; pop video Aerosmith's Janie's Got a Gun 1989 wrote song Oralee Cookies for film Trading Places; memb: Screen Actors' Guild, Actors' Equity Assoc, American Federated Television and Radio Artists, American Soc of Composers, Artists and Performers, BAFTA; *Style*— The Hon Nicholas Haden-Guest; ✉ P O Box 1069, Burbank, CA 91507, USA (☎ 001 818 766 5432, fax 001 818 760 2801)

HADEN-TAYLOR, Dr Anthony St John; s of Frank Pacey Haden-Taylor (d 1971), of Broughton House, Broughton Gifford, nr Melksham, Wilts, and Enid Christine, *née* Bushnell (now Mrs Bousfield); *b* 26 March 1948; *Educ* King's Sch, Sherborne, Pacific Western Univ of California (BSc, MSc, PhD); *m* 15 April 1989, Hon Susan Rosemary, *née* Greenall, da of 3 Baron Daresbury (d 1996), and sis of Peter, 4 Baron Daresbury, and former w of David St C O Bruton; 2 da (Pandora Eleanor Christine b 7 Nov 1989 d 1990, Annabella Margaret Christine b 28 July 1995); *Career* sr ptnr International Management Consultants SA 1970–82, chief exec Taylor Downs & Co 1987–91, sr ptnr The H T Partnership; chm: Re-Cycled Refuse Ltd, Re-Cycled Refuse (Holdings) Limited, RCR (Finland) OY, Richard Paxton Associates Ltd, Global Offshore Services Limited; Freeman City of London, Liveryman Worshipful Co of Basket Makers; *Recreations* polo, shooting, sailing, golf; *Clubs* Annabel's, Cotswold Edge Golf; *Style*— Dr Anthony Haden-Taylor; ✉ White Oaks, Park Estate, St Brelades, Jersey JE3 8EQ, Channel Islands (☎ 01534 43416); office (☎ 01534 498123, fax 01534 498124, mobile 0385 330428)

HADFIELD, Antony; s of Thomas Henry Hadfield, and Edna Hadfield; *b* 9 Sept 1936; *Educ* Sheffield, Brighton, Middx Poly (BA); *m* 1959, Dorothy Fay, da of Charles Edwin Osman (d 1976); 1 s (Warren b 1966); *Career* design engr Plessey 1958–62, design and project engr Metal Industries Group 1962–65, design engr CEGB 1965–67, sr engr and mangr Eastern Electricity 1967–77, area mangr Yorks Electricity 1977–79, dir of engrg Midlands Electricity 1979–85, dep chm and chief exec N Ireland Electricity 1985–91, chief exec Northern Electric plc 1994– (md 1991–94), dir Teesside Power Ltd, chm Sovereign Exploration Ltd; former chm Power Div IEE; CEng, CIMgt, FIEE, FRSA; *Recreations* mountaineering, sailing; *Clubs* Northern Counties, Royal North of Ireland Yacht; *Style*— Antony Hadfield, Esq; ✉ Northern Electric plc, Carliol House, Market St, Newcastle upon Tyne NE1 6NE (☎ 0191 210 2103)

HADFIELD, James Irvine Havelock; s of Prof Geoffrey Hadfield (d 1970), Henley-on-Thames, Oxon, and Sarah Victoria Eileen, *née* Irvine (d 1975); *b* 12 July 1930; *Educ* Radley, Brasenose Coll Oxford (BA), St Thomas' Hosp Med Sch (MA, BM BCh, MCh); *m* 5 Jan 1957, Ann Pickernell, da of Dr G C Milner (d 1974), of Rye, Sussex; 1 s (Geoffrey Irvine Havelock b 10 Jan 1964), 2 da (Esme Victoria b 12 Sept 1960, Helen Sarah (twin)); *Career* St Thomas' Hosp 1955–57: house surgn, casualty offr, lectr Dept of Anatomy; RAS St Thomas' Hosp Hysestile 1962, RSO Leicester Royal Infirmary 1962–64, surgical tutor Univ of Oxford 1964–66, first asst Nuffield Dept of Surgery 1964–66, conslt surgn and urologist Bedford Gen Hosp 1966, surgical and clinical tutor N Bedfordshire 1968–78; examiner: pathology MRCS and LRCP 1971–77, surgery Univ of Cambridge 1974–84; Univ of Cambridge: pt/t departmental demonstrator Dept of Anatomy, recognised teacher surgery 1974–; Arris and Gale lectr RCS 1975, conslt memb DMT 1979–84, chm Med Exec Ctee Bedford Gen Hosp 1979–84; memb: Ed Bd Health Trends 1972–77, Res and Devpt Ctee King Edwards Fund for London 1973–79; tstee Bedford Charity 1970–85, vice chm Estate Ctee Harpur Tst 1980–85 (govr 1970–85), pres Bedford Med Soc 1988; fell: Assoc Sports in Medicine, Assoc of Surgns Pakistan; FSZ (London), memb Anatomical Soc of GB, Ireland; boat club winner St Thomas' Hosp: sr fours, sr pairs, sr sculls, double sculls, United Hosps Regatta 1956 (15 races in 1 day); coach: Brasenose Coll 1951–80, St Thomas' Hosp Boat Club 1955–70, Oriel Coll Eight 1975–80; vice pres: Bedfords CC, Bedford RFC (qualified umpire ARA); memb Ctee Bedford Regatta; Freeman City of London, Liveryman Worshipful Co of Feltmakers 1975–; FRCS, FRCSE 1960, FRSM, fell Soc Clinical Anatomists, memb Assoc Urological Surgns; *Publications* articles in med jls on: Venous Thrombosis, Intravenous Feeding and Topics in Urology; *Recreations* shooting, fishing, watching rowing, sport in general, hates gardening; *Clubs* London Rowing, Leander, Henley-on-Thames, Vincent's (Oxford); *Style*— James Hadfield, Esq; ✉ Baker's Barn, Stagsden West End, Bedford MK43 8SZ (☎ 012302 4514); Porthiddy Cottage, St Davids, North Pembrokeshire SA62 6OW (☎ 013483 345)

HADFIELD, Hon Mrs (Maureen); elder da of Baron Segal (Life Peer; d 1985), and Molly, *née* Rolo (d 1989); *b* 15 Feb 1935; *Educ* St Anne's Coll Oxford (MA); *m* 6 Dec 1956, Jeremy Hadfield (d 1988), s of John Hadfield; 2 s; *Career* dir Economic Assocs 1969–76, economic advsr Price Cmmn 1976–78, ptnr/proprietor Hadfield Associates 1979–, mgmnt conslt Pannell Kerr Forster Associates 1985–88, advsr UNESCO 1989–; ptnr Business Dispute Resolution 1995–; chm Int Consulting Economics Assoc 1986–89; *Clubs* The Groucho; *Style*— The Hon Mrs Hadfield; ✉ 2 Park Town, Oxford OX2 6SH

HADFIELD, (John) Peter Brookes; OBE (1994), JP (1969), DL (Gtr Manchester 1986); s of John William Claude Hadfield (d 1965), of Devon, and Edith Annie, *née* Brookes; *b* 9 March 1926; *Educ* Brighton GS, Sandhurst; *m* 1949, Iris (d 1995), da of Frederick Arthur Brailsford (d 1947), of Chesterfield; 2 da (Vivienne b 1954, Sarah b 1957); *Career* Mil Serv 1943–47 Sandhurst, 2 Recce Regt, 25 Dragoons RAC Capt served Far East 14 Army India, Malaya, Singapore, Sumatra; joined Bass Ratcliffe & Gretton Ltd 1947, md Bass Mitchells and Butlers (Northern) Ltd 1966; dir: Mitchells and Butlers Ltd, Bass Marketing Ltd, Bass UK Ltd 1968; md Bass (South West) Ltd 1975; chm and md Bass North West Ltd 1976–86, vice chm Bass North Ltd 1986 (ret March 1986); chm 1976–86: Bass Mitchells and Butlers (North West) Ltd, Bents Brewery Co Ltd, Catterall and Swarbricks Brewery Ltd, Fred Anderton Ltd, Gartsides (Brookside Brewery) Ltd, Masseys Burnley Brewery Ltd, Park Hall Leisure; dir: Telecable (Stockport) Ltd 1988–92, Telecable (Macclesfield) Ltd 1988–92; chm NW Regnl Bd Br Inst of Mgmnt and Nat Cncl 1981–86; memb CBI: National Cncl, NW Regnl Cncl 1984; pres North Cheshire Branch Inst of Mgmnt 1985; chm: Gtr Manchester Residuary Body 1985–89, Trafford Park Devpt Corp 1987–90, Mainkind Ltd 1985–89, Gtr Manchester Property Tst 1985–89, South Manchester Univ Hosps NHS Tst 1994–; dir: Gtr Manchester Economic Devpt Cncl 1985–89, Central Station Properties Ltd 1985–89, Lloyds Bank plc (NW Region) 1985–89, Burtonwood Brewery plc 1985–, Petros Devpts Ltd 1986–91, Prestbury Golf Club, Savoy Hotel (Blackpool) plc 1977–90, Manchester Chamber of Commerce; memb: Ctee Pattison Research Inst Manchester 1990–91, Ct Univ of Manchester, Ct UMIST, Midland Hotel Crown Plaza Manchester 1985–89; chm S Manchester Health Authy 1990–94; tstee The Hammond Sch Chester, dir David Lewis Centre 1992; patron Henshaws Soc for the Blind; memb Inst of Brewing; CIMgt, FRSA; *Recreations* golf, shooting, gardening; *Clubs* St James's Manchester, Prestbury Golf, Athenaeum; *Style*— Peter Hadfield, Esq, OBE, JP, DL

HADFIELD, Sir Ronald; kt (1995), QPM (1989), DL (W Midlands 1994); s of George Hadfield (d 1975), of Oldham, Lancs, and Phyliss Marjorie Hadfield (d 1983); *b* 15 July 1939; *Educ* Chadderton GS; *m* 1 April 1961, Anne Phylissia, da of Ernest Frederick Worrall, of Royton Lancs; 1 s (Neil Stuart b 25 April 1964), 1 da (Elaine Louise b 29 Dec 1962); *Career* Oldham Borough Police 1958–69 (Sgt 1965–67, Inspr 1967–69), Lancs Constabulary 1969–74 (Chief Inspr 1973), Greater Manchester Police 1974–81 (Supt 1975, Chief Supt 1980), Acting Dep Chief Constable Derbyshire 1984–86 (Asst Chief Constable 1981–84), Chief Constable Notts 1987–90 (Dep Chief Constable 1986–87), Chief Constable W Midlands Police 1990–96; int vice pres Int Assoc of Chiefs of Police 1994–96; chm: Int Affairs Advsy Ctee ACPO, No 4 Regnl Crime Squad Mgmnt Ctee, ACPO No 3 Region, NCIS and RCS Steering Gps, PAA Cricket, PAA Clay Pigeon; memb: Int Steering Gp Revi, HO Central Conf of Chief Constables, PO & GP Ctee Central Conf, ACPO Chief Constables' Cncl, Chief Constables' Cytee Ryton, ACPO PO Sub-Ctee, Nat Ctee Police Athletic Assoc; conslt to: Edge & Ellison Slrs Birmingham, Sonic Communications (International) Birmingham; police advsr to Tbnl on Child Abuse N Wales; *Recreations* golf; *Clubs* Warwickshire Co Cricket (vice pres); *Style*— Sir Ronald Hadfield, QPM, DL

HADGRAFT, Prof Jonathan; s of John William Hadgraft (d 1984), and Doris, *née* Ayres; *b* 13 Dec 1950; *Educ* Queen Elizabeth's Sch Barnet, University Coll Oxford (MA, DPhil, DSc); *m* 3 May 1975, Pauline Joyce, da of Thomas Henry Bilton, of Penarth, S Glamorgan; 1 da (Eleanor Tamsin); *Career* lectr in pharmaceutical chemistry Univ of Strathclyde 1977–79, lectr in pharmacy Univ of Nottingham 1979–85, prof The Welsh Sch of Pharmacy 1985–; CChem, FRSC 1983; *Recreations* cycling; *Style*— Prof Jonathan Hadgraft; ✉ The Welsh School of Pharmacy, University of Wales, Cardiff CF1 3XF (☎ 01222 874180)

HADID, Zaha M; *b* 1950, Baghdad; *Educ* AA Sch of Architecture (AADipl); *Career* architect; memb Office for Metropolitan Architecture 1977, in sole practice 1979–; tutor AA 1977–87 (initially with Rem Koolhaas and Elia Zenghelis, latterly head of own studio), visiting design critic Harvard Graduate Sch of Design 1986 (Kenzo Tange chair 1994), visiting prof Columbia Univ 1987, holder of various master classes and lectr on architecture at venues worldwide; Special Award Royal Acad Summer Exhbn 1995; *Projects* incl: 59 Eaton Place London 1980 (Architectural Design Gold Medal 1982), furniture and interiors for W Bitar London 1985, design of several bldgs in Japan incl two projects in Tokyo 1988, a folly for Expo '90 Osaka and interior work for Moonsoon Restaurant Sapporo 1990, Vitra fire station Weil am Rhein 1988–93, IBA housing scheme in Berlin 1993, various large scale urban studies for harbour devpts in Hamburg, Bordeaux and Cologne since 1989; *Competitions* incl: The Peak Competition Hong Kong 1982, art and media centre project Düsseldorf 1989–94, Cardiff Bay Opera House project 1994–95, habitable bridge across The Thames 1996; *Exhibitions of Paintings and Drawings* incl: Guggenheim Museum NY 1978, AA (retrospective) 1983, GA Gallery Tokyo 1985, Museum of Modern Art NY (Deconstructive Architecture show) 1988, Graduate Sch of Design Harvard Univ 1994, The Waiting Room Grand Central Station NY 1995, Kunsthalle Vienna (Wish Machine exhibition) 1996; *Work in Perm Collections* incl: Museum of Modern Art NY, Deutsches Architecktur Museum Frankfurt, Getty Museum Los Angeles, FRAC collection France; *Style*— Ms Zaha Hadid; ✉ Studio 9, 10 Bowling Green Lane, London EC1R 0BD (☎ 0171 253 4147, fax 0171 251 8322)

HADINGHAM, Reginald Edward Hawke (Buzzer); CBE (1988, OBE 1971), MC and bar (1944), TD; 2 s of Edward Wallace Hadingham (d 1973), and Ethel Irene Penelope (d 1936), 5 da of Sir William Gwynne-Evans, 1 Bt; *b* 6 Dec 1915; *Educ* St Paul's; *m* 1940, Lois, da of Edward Pope, of Montreal, Canada; 2 da (Susan, Stephanie); *Career* 67 ATK TA RA, served UK, Iraq, N Africa, Italy, actg Lt-Col; Slazengers Ltd: joined 1933, Euro sales mangr 1936, export mangr 1949, sales dir 1952, joined bd 1952, md 1967, chm and md 1973, non-exec chm 1976–83; life pres SPARKS (the Sportsman's Charity), vice pres PHAB, sr memb and treas Sette of Odd Volumes (a dining club founded in 1878) 1957–; All Eng Lawn Tennis Club: elected Ctee 1976, chm 1984–89, vice pres 1990–; pres Int Lawn Tennis Club of GB 1990–; *Recreations* lawn tennis; *Clubs* All Eng Lawn Tennis, Queens LTC, Hurlingham, Lord's Taverners'; *Style—* Buzzer Hadingham, Esq, CBE, MC, TD; ✉ 15 Harrowdene Court, 6 Belvedere Drive, Wimbledon SW19 7BY

HADLEE, Roger Barrington; s of Barrington William Hadlee (d 1981), of Bishops Stortford, Herts, and Hilda Joan, *née* Newman; *b* 8 Jan 1935; *Educ* St Edward's Sch Oxford, Trinity Coll Oxford (MA); *m* 6 July 1960, (Alison) Jill, da of Harold Nettleton Broadley, of Folkestone, Kent; 3 da (Georgina b 1961, Caroline b 1964, Fiona b 1966); *Career* Subaltern 1 Royal Dragoons 1956–58; mktg exec: Pfizer Ltd 1958–63, Nabisco Foods 1963–65, Donald MacPherson Gp 1965–68, Br Printing Corp 1968–74 (dir Publishing Gp); fndr Royal Exchange Art Gallery 1974; *Recreations* tennis, sailing, cricket; *Clubs* MCC, Free Foresters; *Style—* Roger Hadlee, Esq; ✉ The Old Rectory, Fairstead, Nr Chelmsford, Essex CM3 2BW (☎ 01245233 246); Royal Exchange Art Gallery, 14 Royal Exchange, London EC3V 3LL (☎ 0171 283 4400)

HADLEY, David Allen; CB (1991); s of Sydney Hadley (d 1980), and Gwendoline Alice, *née* Rodwell (d 1987); *b* 18 Feb 1936; *Educ* Wyggeston GS Leicester, Merton Coll Oxford (MA); *m* 1965, Veronica Ann, da of Stanley Hopkins, of Sussex; 1 s (Christopher b 1970); *Career* Miny of Agric: 1959–75, 1979–89, dep sec (Agricultural Commodities, Trade and Food Prodn 1993–96; Treasy 1975–78, Cabinet Office 1989–93; ret 1996; *Recreations* music, gardening; *Style—* David Hadley, Esq, CB; ✉ Old Mousers, Racecourse Road, Dormansland, Lingfield, Surrey RH7 6PP (☎ and fax 01342 832259)

HADLEY, Graham Hunter; s of Albert Leonard Hadley (d 1973), and Lorna Elizabeth, *née* Hunter; *b* 12 April 1944; *Educ* Eltham Coll, Jesus Coll Cambridge (BA); *m* 1971, Lesley Mary Ann, da of Stanley Anthony Andrew Smith, of Kingston; 1 s (Andrew Hunter b 1978); *Career* Civil Service; asst princ: Miny of Aviation 1966, Miny of Technology 1968; princ: Miny of Aviation Supply 1971, Dept of Energy 1974; seconded to Civil Serv Cmmn 1976, asst sec Dept of Energy 1977, seconded to British Aerospace HQ Weybridge 1980, under sec Electricity Div Dept of Energy 1983, bd sec CEGB 1983–90; National Power plc (following privatisation of CEGB): exec dir 1990–95, md International Business Development 1993–95; independent conslt and sr advsr to Nat Econ Research Assocs (NERA) 1996–; *Recreations* cricket, golf, architecture, theatre; *Clubs* London Capital; *Style—* Graham Hadley, Esq; ✉ 11 Grange Park Place, Wimbledon, London SW20 0EE; NERA, 15 Stratford Place, London W1N 9AF

HADSLEY-CHAPLIN, (Edwin) Hadsley; s of Arthur Hadsley-Chaplin (d 1965), of Surrey, and Annie Violet Lewis (d 1983); *b* 27 Aug 1922; *Educ* Radnor House; *m* 1954, Margaret Mary, da of Robert Potter (d 1951); 2 s (Peter b 1957, Mark b 1961), 1 da (Anne b 1955); *Career* Capt RE 1941–46; chm: Rowe Evans Investment plc, Sungkai Holdings Ltd 1978, Bertam Holdings plc 1980, Beradin Holdings plc 1982, Lendu Holdings plc 1983, Padang Senang Holdings plc, The Singapore Para Rubber Estates plc; chm Tropical Growers' Assoc 1973–74 (memb); FCIS; *Recreations* watching cricket, travel, model railways, theatre; *Clubs* Oriental, Royal Solent Yacht; *Style—* Hadsley Hadsley-Chaplin, Esq; ✉ Norton House, Gatton Road, Reigate, Surrey RH2 0HB (☎ 01737 246217); Hulverstone Farm, Hulverstone, Newport, IOW PO30 4EH (☎ 01983 741161)

HAENDEL, Ida; CBE (1991); *b* 15 Dec 1928; *Educ* Warsaw Conservatoire (Gold Medal at age 7); *Career* violinist; began playing aged 3 1/2, studied with Carl Flesch and George Enescu in Paris, Br debut Brahm's Concerto Queen's Hall with Sir Henry Wood, gave concerts for Br and US troops and in factories WWII, has toured throughout Europe, N and S America, Scandinavia, Turkey, Israel, USSR and Far East; toured with orchs incl: London Philharmonic, BBC Symphony, English Chamber (foreign tours incl Hong Kong, China, Aust and Mexico); has played with numerous foreign orchs incl: Bayerishe Rundfunk, Berlin Philharmonic, Concertgebouw Orchestra, Israel Philharmonic, Boston Symphony, New York Philharmonic, Montreal Symphony; numerous recordings with EMI; memb Jury: Carl Flesch Competition London, Sibelius Competition Helsinki Finland, International Violin Competition Cologne; winner Sibelius medal Sibelius Soc of Finland (on 25 Anniversary of Sibelius' Death); *Books* Woman with Violin (autobiog, 1970); *Style—* Miss Ida Haendel, CBE; ✉ Harold Holt Limited, 31 Sinclair Road, London W14 ONS (☎ 0171 603 4600)

HAGAN, David Lloyd; s of William Hamill Hagan (d 1984), of Liverpool, and Miriam Dilys, *née* Lloyd; *b* 21 May 1946; *Educ* Merchant Taylors' Sch Crosby, Emmanuel Coll Cambridge; *m* 5 Dec 1981, Anita Janet Shepstone, da of Lennart Pettersson, of Karlstad, Sweden; 2 s (Charles b 1 Nov 1982, Felix b 14 Mar 1987), 1 da (Isabel b 4 Aug 1984); *Career* chm and chief exec Marlon House Holdings Ltd 1974–83, dir Medical and Professional Software Ltd 1984–, chm David Hagan Ltd 1986–, md Tullett & Tokyo Equities Ltd 1986–91, chm Trio Holdings PLC 1992–; FCA 1970, ATII 1970, MSI; *Recreations* offshore powerboat racing (Class II World Champion 1979), boatbuilding; *Clubs* Royal Thames Yacht, Royal Lymington Yacht, The South West Shingles Yacht (Vice Cdr); *Style—* David Hagan, Esq; ✉ 4 Deans Court, London EC4V 5AA (☎ 0171 489 8033, fax 0171 236 6018, car phone 0836 288 421)

HAGART-ALEXANDER, Claud; s and h of Sir Claud Hagart-Alexander, 3 Bt, *qv*; *b* 5 Nov 1963; *Educ* Trinity Coll Glenalmond, Univ of Glasgow (BSc); *m* 24 June 1994, Elaine Susan, only da of Vincent Park, of Winnipeg, Canada; *Career* electronics and electrical engr; *Style—* Claud Hagart-Alexander, Esq; ✉ c/o Coutts & Co, Adelaide Branch, 440 Strand, London WC2R 0QS

HAGART-ALEXANDER, Sir Claud; 3 Bt (UK 1886), of Ballochmyle, Co Ayr; JP (1985), DL (Ayrshire); s of late Wilfred Archibald Alexander, 2 s of 2 Bt; suc gf 1945; additional surname Hagart recognised by decree of Lord Lyon 1948; Maj-Gen Sir Claud Alexander, 1 Bt, served in the Crimea and was Cons MP for S Ayrshire 1874–85; *b* 6 Jan 1927; *Educ* Sherborne, CCC Cambridge (BA); *m* 16 April 1959, Hilda Etain, yr da of late Miles Malcolm Acheson, of Ganges, BC, Canada; 2 s (Claud b 1963, Boyd John b 1966), 2 da (Helenora Etain (Mrs Carl C Smith) b 1960, Anna Joanna Elizabeth (Mrs Michael C L Adam) b 1961); *Heir* s, Claud Hagart-Alexander, *qv*; *Career* Vice Lord-Lt Ayrshire and Arran 1983–97; memb Inst of Measurement and Control (MInstMC); *Clubs* New (Edinburgh); *Style—* Sir Claud Hagart-Alexander of Ballochmyle, Bt, JP, DL; ✉ Kingencleuch House, Mauchline, East Ayrshire KA5 5JL (☎ 01290 550217)

HAGDRUP, Alan; s of Sofus Vilhelm Hagdrup (d 1983), of Cheam; *b* 19 May 1932; *Educ* Epsom Coll, UCL; *m* 1958, Elizabeth, da of Lt-Col Harold Mason, OBE, TD (d 1960); 1 s, 2 da; *Career* ptnr Gouldens (slrs) 1962–69; dir: Hanson Transport Group 1969–, Hanson plc 1974–92; chm Cncl Epsom Coll; *Recreations* golf, skiing, bridge, music; *Clubs* Walton Heath Golf, Wisley Golf; *Style—* Alan Hagdrup, Esq; ✉ The Mill House, Dorking Road, Tadworth, Surrey (☎ 01737 814522)

HAGER, David Paul; s of Donald Charles Hager, of Bournemouth, and Betty Kathleen, *née* Hewitt; *b* 7 Jan 1951; *Educ* Bournemouth Sch, Univ of Oxford (MA); *m* 10 Sept 1951, Jeanette Carolyn, da of Alan Peter Hares, of Chilbolton, Hants; 1 s (Tristram b 1984); *Career* investmt advsr N M Rothschild and Sons Ltd 1972–74; Bacon & Woodrow: joined 1975, ptnr in Investmt Dept 1976–85, ptnr 1987–94, managing ptnr 1995–; dir County Investment Management 1985–87 (dir County Group Ltd 1986–87); Liveryman Worshipful Co of Actuaries; FIA 1975, FPMI 1982; *Books* An Introduction to Institutional Investment (with A J Frost, 1986), Debt Securities (with A J Frost, 1990), Pension Fund Investment (with C D Lever, 1989); *Recreations* flying light aircraft; *Clubs* Oxford and Cambridge, Guild of Air Pilots and Navigators; *Style—* David Hager, Esq; ✉ Bacon and Woodrow, St Olaf House, London Bridge, London SE1 2PE (☎ 0171 357 7171)

HAGERTY, William John Gell (Bill); s of William Hagerty, and Doris Julia, *née* Gell; *b* 23 April 1939; *Educ* Beal GS Ilford Essex; *m* 1, 1965 (m dis 1990), Lynda Ann, *née* Beresford; 1 s (William Daniel b 22 Jan 1970), 1 da (Faith Georgia b 5 March 1975); m 2, 1991, Elizabeth Ann Vercoe, *née* Latta; 1 s (Adam Benedict b 1 Dec 1993); *Career* Nat Serv RAF 1958–60; local newspapers 1955–58; local newspapers: Sunday Citizen, Daily Sketch, Daily Mirror 1960–67, various editorial positions The Mirror Group 1967–85, managing ed (features) Today 1986–87, ed Sunday Today 1987–88, conslt and advsr to the publisher Hola! Magazine (conslt Hello! Magazine) 1987–88; dep ed: Sunday Mirror 1988–90, Daily Mirror 1990–91; ed The People 1991–92, theatre critic Today 1993–95, film critic Today 1994–95; theatre critic News of the World 1996–, ed Voyager magazine 1996–; conslt ed Tribune 1993–; *Books* Flash Bang Wallop! (with Kent Gavin, 1978); *Recreations* watching cricket, jazz, lunch; *Style—* Bill Hagerty; ✉ Bull Cottage, 10/11 Strand on the Green, Chiswick, London W4 3PQ (☎ 0181 994 4966)

HAGGARD, Prof Mark Peregrine; s of Capt Stephen H A Haggard (d 1943), and Morna Christian, *née* Gillespie (d 1977); *b* 26 Dec 1942; *Educ* Dollar Acad, Univ of Edinburgh (MA), Univ of Cambridge (PhD); *m* 22 Sept 1962, Elizabeth Gilmore, da of Thomas Jackson Houston (d 1943), of Hong Kong; 2 s (Stephen b 1963, Patrick b 1965); *Career* teaching offr and fell CCC Cambridge 1967–71, prof Queen's Univ of Belfast 1971–76, dir MRC Inst Hearing Res, chief advsr Hearing Res Tst, memb Neurosciences Bd MRC 1989–93, dep chm Health Serv and Public Health Res Bd MRC 1990–93; FRSM 1977, FIOA 1978, fell Acoustical Soc America 1982; *Books* Hearing Science and Hearing Disorders (with M E Lutman, 1983), British Medical Bulletin: Hearing (with E F Evans, 1987), Screening Children's Hearing (with E A Hughes, 1991), Research in the Development of Services for Hearing-Impaired People (1993); *Recreations* extreme skiing, choral singing, Byzantine art; *Clubs* Ski Club of GB; *Style—* Prof Mark Haggard; ✉ MRC Institute of Hearing Research, University of Nottingham, University Park, Nottingham NG7 2RD (☎ 0115 922 3431, fax 0115 942 3710)

HAGGARD, Piers Inigo; s of Capt Stephen Haggard (d 1943), of London, and Morna Christian, *née* Gillespie (d 1977); *b* 18 March 1939; *Educ* Dollar Acad Scotland, Univ of Edinburgh (MA); *m* 1, 1960, Christiane, *née* Stokes; 1 s (Philip Charles Napier b 1962), 3 da (Sarah Clemence b 1960, Claire Imogen b 1961, Rachel Lindsay b 1961); m 2, Anna Maud, da of Grisha Sklovsky; 1 s (William Godfrey Abraham b 1975), 1 da ((Celia) Daisy Morna b 1978); *Career* theatre, television and film director; started as asst dir Royal Court Theatre 1960; resident dir: Dundee Repertory 1960–61, Glasgow Citizens 1961–62; asst The Nat Theatre 1963–65, dir Ticket of Leave Man 1981; trained with BBC TV 1965; fndr The Directors' Guild of GB and assoc organization The Directors' and Producers' Rights Soc; *Television* UK prodns incl: Pennies From Heaven (UK BAFTA Award 1979) 1978, Mrs Reinhart 1981, Knockback (US ACE Award 1985) 1984, Visitors 1987, Centrepoint 1990, Heartstones 1994–95, Eskimo Day 1995; USA prodns incl: Back Home (Emmy nomination, Gold Award NY Film and TV Festival) 1989, Four Eyes 1991–92, The Breakthrough 1993; *Films* incl: Wedding Night 1969, The Blood on Satan's Claw 1970, The Quatermass Conclusion (Triest Festival Award 1980) 1979, The Fiendish Plot of Dr Fu Manchu 1980, Venom 1982, A Summer Story 1988; The Double (screenplay)1996; *Recreations* swimming, landscape gardening, human nature; *Style—* Piers Haggard, Esq; ✉ Piers Haggard Productions Ltd, 26 Stockwell Park Crescent, London SW9 ODE (☎ 0171 733 4500, fax 0171 737 4619)

HAGGER, Jonathan Osborne; s of Cyril Francis Osborne Hagger (d 1957), of Loughton, Essex, and Norah Harrison, *née* Broadley (d 1981); *b* 3 Feb 1949; *Educ* Chigwell Sch; *m* 27 April 1974, (Carol) Anne, da of Alan David Luton, of Loughton, Essex; 2 s (William b 1981, James b 1984); *Career* CA; Edward Moore & Sons (CAs) 1968–72, BUPA 1972–75, Willis Faber 1976–85; fin dir: Bain Clarkson 1985–89, FKB Group Plc 1990, Grosvenor Estate Holdings 1991–; chm: King Charles Music Soc 1988–, Realty Insurances 1994–, English Sinfonia 1995–; ARCM 1968, FCA 1972, FCT 1993; *Recreations* music, tennis, organ-playing; *Style—* Jonathan Hagger, Esq; ✉ 104 Warwick Park, Tunbridge Wells, Kent TN2 5EN (☎ 01892 529161)

HAGGETT, Prof Peter; CBE (1993); s of Charles Frederick Haggett (d 1966), and Ethel Elizabeth Haines (d 1971); *b* 24 Jan 1933; *Educ* Dr Morgan's GS Somerset, St Catharine's Coll Cambridge (MA, PhD, ScD); *m* 28 July 1956, Brenda Mavis, da of Cyril Robert Woodley (d 1976); 2 s (Timothy b 1961, Andrew b 1965), 2 da (Sarah b 1960, Jacqueline b 1963); *Career* asst lectr UCL 1955–57, lectr Univ of Cambridge 1957–66, prof of urban and regnl geography Univ of Bristol 1966– (acting vice chllr 1984–85); memb: SW Econ Planning Cncl, UGC 1985–89, Nat Radiological Protection Bd 1985–; winner Prix Internationale Géographique 1991; Hon DSc York Canada 1983, Hon LLD Bristol 1985, Hon DSc Durham 1989; hon fell Fitzwilliam Coll Cambridge 1991; memb Euro Acad 1988, FBA 1992 (vice pres 1995–); *Books* Locational Analysis in Human Geography (1965), 15 further volumes on geographical research; *Clubs* United Oxford and Cambridge Univ; *Style—* Prof Peter Haggett, CBE, FBA; ✉ 5 Tunbridge Close, Chew Magna, NE Somerset (☎ 01275 332780); Department of Geography, University of Bristol, Bristol BS8 1SS (☎ 0117 930 3751)

HAGGETT, Stuart John; s of Wilfred Francis Haggett (d 1991), of West Kirby, Wirral, and Doreen Ada, *née* New; *b* 11 April 1947; *Educ* Dauntsey's Sch West Lavington, Downing Coll Cambridge (MA); *m* 2 Jan 1971, (Hilary) Joy, da of Maj Albert Hammond (d 1963), of Weymouth; 2 da (Laura Louise b 26 Feb 1978, Emily Frances b 23 Sept 1979); *Career* head of modern languages and housemaster Canford Sch Dorset 1973–83, second master King's Sch Rochester 1983–88, headmaster Birkenhead Sch 1988–; chm: Interact Club, Rotary Club of Birkenhead; memb: Medical Service Ctee, Wirral Family Health Services Authy, Secondary Heads Assoc 1983, Headmasters' Conference 1988; *Recreations* sport, reading and theatre, DIY, East India; *Style—* Stuart Haggett, Esq; ✉ Birkenhead School, 58 Beresford Rd, Oxton, Birkenhead, Merseyside L43 2JD (☎ 0151 652 4014, fax 0151 653 7412)

HAGMAN, Eric; s of Harald Hagman (d 1989), of Fairlie, Ayrshire, and Jessie Munro, *née* Henderson; *b* 9 July 1946; *Educ* Kelvinside Acad, Univ of Glasgow; *m* 1; 2 s (Christian b 1972, Robin b 1974), 1 da (Victoria b 1978); m 2, Valerie Hagman; 2 step s (George b 1971, John b 1973); *Career* CA; trained Thomson McLintock, qualified 1969; Arthur Andersen & Co: joined 1969, ptnr in Scot 1978, managing ptnr Glasgow 1979, regnl managing ptnr Scot 1983–; past chm: Audit Practice Ctee ICAS, Technical Liaison Ctee ICAS; memb Cncl of CBI Scotland, dir Scottish Financial Enterprise; bd memb Strathclyde 2000 Advsy Cncl, past bd memb Glasgow Sch of Art, memb Glasgow and West of Scotland Inst of Public Admin; pres Royal Glasgow Inst, treas Police Dependents Tst, tstee Scottish Nat Galleries, memb ICA; past chm RSAC; *Recreations* sailing, skiing, tennis, squash, art, travelling; *Clubs* RSAC, Clyde Corinthian Yacht; *Style—* Eric Hagman, Esq; ✉ Arthur Andersen & Co, 199 St Vincent St, Glasgow G2 5QD (☎ 0141 248 7941, fax 0141 248 6155)

HAGSTON, Prof Winston Edwin; s of Thomas Hagston, and Florence Maud, *née* Kirby; *b* 30 Nov 1941; *Educ* Beverley GS, Imperial Coll London (BSc), Univ of Hull (PhD), Univ of London (DSc); *m* 9 Nov 1963, (Sylvia) Heather, da of Harold Robinson (d 1982), of Melbourne, York; 2 s (Winston b 19 April 1964, Paul b 21 March 1967), 1 da (Michelle b 23 March 1966); *Career* postdoctoral res fell SRC 1966–68; Physics Dept Univ of Hull: lectr 1968–73, sr lectr 1973–80, reader in theoretical physics 1980, personal chair in theoretical physics 1986–; ARCS; *Recreations* fishing, shooting; *Style*— Prof Winston Hagston; ✉ The Wildfowlers, 7 Millbeck Close, Market Weighton, York YO4 3HT (☎ 01430 873158); Department of Applied Physics, The University, Cottingham Rd, Hull HU6 7BX (☎ 01482 46311 ext 5823)

HAGUE, Prof Sir Douglas Chalmers; kt (1981), CBE (1978); s of Laurence and Marion Hague; *b* 20 Oct 1926; *Educ* Moseley GS, King Edward VI HS Birmingham, Univ of Birmingham; *m* 1947 (m dis 1986), Brenda Elizabeth Fereday; 2 da; m 2, 1986, Janet Mary Leach; *Career* economist (mgmnt prof, conslt, co dir); chm Manchester Industl Relations Soc, dep chm Price Cmmn and pres NW Operational Res Gp, rapporteur to IEA 1953–78 (ed gen 1981–86), reader in political economy Univ of London 1957, Newton Chambers prof of economics Univ of Sheffield 1957–63, visiting prof of economics Duke Univ N Carolina USA 1960–61, head Business Studies Dept Univ of Sheffield 1962–63, prof of applied economics Univ of Manchester 1963–65, memb Cncl Manchester Business Sch 1964–81 (prof of managerial economics 1965–81, dep dir 1978–81); visiting prof: Manchester Business Sch 1981–, Imperial Coll London 1987–91; fell Templeton Coll Oxford 1981–84 (assoc fell 1984–); personal econ advsr to Rt Hon Margaret Thatcher 1967–79 (incl Gen Election 1979), advsr PM's Policy Unit 1979–83; chm: ESRC 1983–87, Oxford Strategy Network 1984–, Metapraxis Ltd 1984–90, Doctus Consulting Europe 1991–93, CRT plc 1992–93 (dir 1990–96), Professional Devpt Ctee IOD 1993–96; tstee Demos 1995–; *Recreations* Manchester Utd supporter, organist of classical music (granted permission to play at Blenheim Palace); *Clubs* Athenaeum; *Style*— Prof Sir Douglas Hague, CBE; ✉ Templeton College, Oxford OX1 5NY

HAGUE, His Hon Judge Nigel Thornton; QC (1981); s of Sir (Charles) Kenneth Felix Hague (d 1973), and Lady Marjorie Hague, *née* Thornton; *b* 29 May 1930; *Educ* Gayhurst Sch Gerrards Cross, Charterhouse, Pembroke Coll Cambridge (exhibitioner, MA, LLB); *m* 7 May 1960, Patricia Anne, da of John Mortimer Bowick; 4 s (James Mortimer b 16 Nov 1961, Philip Thornton b 14 Nov 1962, John Nigel Archibald b 12 May 1964, Richard Charles b 1 June 1965); *Career* called to the Bar Lincoln's Inn 1956; bencher 1988; practised Chancery Bar: London 1956–59, Cardiff 1959–64, London 1964–89; circuit judge (SE Circuit) 1989–; has sat as High Ct Judge (Chancery Div) and as judge of Employment Appeal Tbnl; memb Anglo-American Real Property Inst 1985; govr Gayhurst Sch; *Books* Leasehold Enfranchisement (1968, 2nd edn 1987); *Recreations* golf, opera, singing, bridge, cricket; *Clubs* Denham Golf; *Style*— His Hon Judge Hague, QC; ✉ Slough County Court, The Law Courts, Windsor Road, Slough SL1 2HE

HAGUE, Paul Nicholas; s of Bernard Hague, and Annie Nichols; *b* 3 Aug 1947; *Educ* Belle Vue Boys GS, Hatfield Coll, Univ of Durham (BA); *m* 1969, Alice Christine, da of Alf Tyreman; 1 s (Nicholas James b 1974), 1 da (Chrissie Anne b 1976); *Career* former chm Business & Market Research plc, currently dir Hague Jackson Ltd; *Books* The Industrial Market Research Handbook (1987), Do Your Own Market Research (1987), How To Do Market Research (1990), Handbook of Market Research Techniques (1991), Marketing Research in Practice (1992), Questionnaire Design (1993), Sampling and Statistics (1993), Interviewing (1993); *Recreations* athletics; *Style*— Paul Hague, Esq; ✉ Daleacre, Nab Lane, Dale Rd, Marple, Stockport, Cheshire (☎ 0161 427 7552)

HAGUE, Rt Hon William Jefferson; PC (1995), MP (C) Richmond Yorkshire (majority 23,504); s of Timothy Nigel Hague, of Wentworth, S Yorks, and Stella, *née* Jefferson; *b* 26 March 1961; *Educ* Wath upon Dearne Comp Sch, Magdalen Coll Oxford (BA, pres Oxford Union), INSEAD (MBA); *Career* temp special advsr to Chancellor of Exchequer 1983, mgmnt conslt McKinsey and Co 1983–88, MP (C) Richmond (Yorks) 1989–, PPS to Rt Hon Norman Lamont as Chancellor of the Exchequer 1990–93, under sec of state for social security 1993–94, min of state Dept of Social Security 1994–95, sec of state for Wales 1995–; *Style*— The Rt Hon William Hague, MP; ✉ House of Commons, London SW1A 0AA (☎ 01609 779093, fax 01609 778172)

HAGUENAUER, Hon Mrs (Elizabeth Cecilia Jane); *née* Fremantle; da of 4 Baron Cottesloe, GBE, TD, and his 2 w, Gloria Jean Irene Dunn; *b* 28 Aug 1962; *Educ* Heathfield; *m* 21 Dec 1991, Olivier Philippe Hagenauer, eldest s of Dr Pierre Haguenauer, of Neuilly-sur-Seine; 1 s (Raphael John b 27 July 1996), 1 da (Alice Flora Vivette b 11 Feb 1994); *Career* fashion ed: Vogue (UK) 1989–91, freelance 1991– (working for titles incl Vogue and The Sunday Times); *Style*— The Hon Mrs Haguenauer; ✉ 73 Rue des Vignes, 75016 Paris, France (☎ 4449 9282)

HAHN, Dr Carl H; *Career* exec chm Volkswagen AG until 1992 (currently non-exec dir), chm Saurer; also non-exec dir: British Petroleum plc 1990–, Benetton SA, Commerzbank AG, Gerling, Paccar, Perot Systems Corporation, Thyssen, TRW; *Style*— Dr Carl Hahn; ✉ c/o British Petroleum Co plc, 1 Finsbury Circus, London EC2M 7BA (☎ 0171 920 8000)

HAHN, Prof Frank Horace; s of Dr Arnold Hahn; *b* 26 April 1925; *Educ* Bournemouth GS, LSE (BSc(Econ), PhD), MA (Cantab); *m* 1946, Dorothy Salter; *Career* lectr in econs Univ of Birmingham 1948–58 (reader in mathematical econs 1958–60), lectr in econs Univ of Cambridge 1960–65 (fell Churchill Coll 1960–); prof of economics: LSE 1967–72, Univ of Cambridge 1972–92 (prof emeritus 1992), Univ of Siena Italy 1989–; visiting prof of econs: Mass Inst of Technol 1956–57, 1971–72 and 1982, Univ of California Berkeley 1959–60; fell Center for Advanced Study in Behavioural Sciences Stanford Calif 1966–67, Taussig res prof Harvard Univ 1974, Schumpeter prof Vienna 1984, memb Workshop in Mathematical Econs Stanford Univ, memb Cncl for Scientific Policy (later Advsy Bd of Res Cncls) 1972–75; managing ed Review of Economic Studies 1965–68, asst ed Journal of Economic Theory 1971–76; pres: Econometric Soc 1968–69, Royal Economic Soc 1986–89, Section F British Assoc for the Advancement of Science 1990; Palacky Gold medal Czechoslovak Acad of Sciences 1991; Hon DSocSci Birmingham 1981, Hon DUniv Strasbourg 1984, Hon DLitt UEA 1984, Hon DSc London 1985, Hon DUniv York 1991, Hon DLitt Leicester 1993, Hon DPhil Athens 1993; corresponding fell American Acad of Arts and Sciences 1971, hon memb American Economic Assoc 1986, foreign assoc US Nat Acad of Sciences 1988, hon fell LSE 1989, memb Academia Europaea 1989; FBA 1975; *Books* The Theory of Interest Rates (ed with F P R Brechling, 1965), General Competitive Analysis (with K J Arrow, 1971), Readings in the Theory of Growth (ed, 1971), The Share of Wages in the National Income (1972), Money and Inflation (1982), Equilibrium and Macroeconomics (1984), Money Growth and Stability (1985), The Economics of Missing Markets Information and Games (ed, 1989), Handbook of Monetary Economics (ed with Ben Friedman, 1990), The Market: Practice and Policy (ed, 1992), Ethics and Economics (ed with F Farina and S Vannucci, 1995), A Critical Essay on Modern Macroeconomic Theory (jtly with Robert Solow, 1995); *Style*— Prof Frank Hahn, FBA; ✉ 16 Adams Rd, Cambridge CB3 9AD; Churchill College, Cambridge CB3 0DS

HAIG, 2 Earl (UK 1919); George Alexander Eugene Douglas Haig; OBE (1965), DL (Roxburghshire, Ettrick and Lauderdale 1976); also Viscount Dawick, Baron Haig (both UK 1919) and thirtieth Laird of Bemersyde Chief of the Haig family; s of Field Marshal 1 Earl Haig, KT, GCB, OM, GCVO, KCIE (d 1928), by his w, Hon Dorothy, GCStJ (d 1939), 2 da of 3 Baron Vivian; *b* 15 March 1918; *Educ* Stowe, Ch Ch Oxford (MA), Camberwell Sch of Arts and Crafts; *m* 1, 19 July 1956 (m dis 1981), Adrienne Thérèse, da of Derrick Morley; 1 s, 2 da; m 2, 1981, Donna Gerolama Lopez y Royo di Taurisano; *Heir* s, Viscount Dawick; *Career* Capt Royal Scots Greys M East Force 1939–42, POW 1942–45, Maj on disbandment of Home Gd; sits as Conservative Peer in House of Lords, train bearer at Coronation of King George VI; painter; holds exhibitions at regular intervals; memb: Royal Fine Art Cmmn for Scotland 1958–61, Scottish Arts Cncl (chm Art Ctee 1969–76); tstee: Nat Galleries of Scotland 1963–73, Scottish Nat War Meml 1961– (chm Bd of Tstees 1983–); pres: Border Area RBLS 1955–61, Scottish Crafts Centre 1953–74; chm: Disablement Advisory Ctee SE Scotland 1960–73, Berwickshire Civic Society 1970–76; memb Bd of Dirs Richard DeMarco gallery 1986–87; chm Offr's Assoc (Scottish Branch) 1977–87; pres: OA Scottish Branch 1987–, Royal British Legion Scotland 1979–86 (nat chm 1963–66), The Earl Haig Fund Scotland 1979–86; vice-pres: Royal Blind Asylum, Scottish Nat Inst for War Blinded; DL Berwickshire 1953–76, Vice Lieut Berwicks 1967–70; memb Royal Co of Archers (Queen's Body Guard for Scotland), Liveryman Worshipful Co of Mercers; ARSA 1988, FRSA; KStJ; *Recreations* fishing, shooting; *Clubs* New (Edinburgh), Cavalry & Guards', Beefsteak; *Style*— The Rt Hon the Earl Haig, OBE, DL; ✉ Bemersyde, Melrose, Roxburghshire (☎ 01835 822762)

HAIGH, Dr Clement Percy; *b* 11 Jan 1920; *Educ* Univ of Leeds (BSc), King's Coll London (PhD); *m* 8 June 1945, (Ruby) Patricia, *née* Hobdey; 3 s ((Julian) Robin David b 5 July 1950, (Stephen) Patrick Hobdey b 19 Nov 1957, Jeremy Rupert Michael b 6 June 1961); *Career* with Radiochem Centre Thorium Ltd 1943–49, med physicist Barrow Hosp Bristol 1949–56; CEGB: joined 1956, dir Berkeley Nuclear Labs 1959–73, dep dir gen Design and Construction Div Gloucester 1973–78; dir of res BNOC 1978–81 (conslt 1981–87), dir S Western Industl Res 1981–86; distinguished lectr American Nuclear Soc San Francisco 1965, assessor Nuclear Safety Advsy Ctee 1972–76; memb: BBC W Advsy Cncl 1972–76, Mech Engrg and Machine Tools Requirements Bd 1972–76, UK chm Jt UK/USSR Working Gp on Problems of Electricity Supply 1974–78, Offshore Engrg Technol Bd 1978–81, Nat Maritime Inst 1981–82; chm Programme Steering Ctee UK Offshore Steels Res Project 1981–87; CPhys, FInstP 1953, FRSA 1985; *Recreations* music; *Clubs* Savile; *Style*— Dr C P Haigh; ✉ Painswick, Old Sneed Park, Bristol BS9 1RG (☎ 0117 968 2065); Duncombe, Wetherby Road, Harrogate, N Yorks HG2 7SH (☎ 01423 883266)

HAILES, Julia Persephone; da of Lt-Col John Martin Hunter Hailes, DSO (d 1995), of Chiselborough House, Stoke-sub-Hamdon, Somerset, and Marianne Carlyon, *née* Coates; *b* 23 Sept 1961; *Educ* St Mary's Sch Calne Wilts; *m* Edward de Courcy Bryant; 1 s (Connor Carlyon b 1 Jan 1995); *Career* Leo Burnett Advertising 1981–83; dir: SustainAbility Ltd 1990–95 (memb Cncl 1995–), Creative Consumer Co-operative Ltd (t/a Out of This World) 1994–; memb: UK Eco-Labelling Bd 1992–, Cncl Global 500 Forum 1992–96, Packaging Standards Cncl 1993–; elected to UN Global 500 Roll of Honour (for outstanding environmental achievements) 1989; FRSA; *Books* Green Pages, The Business of Saving The World (1988), The Green Consumer Guide (1988), The Green Consumer's Supermarket Shopping Guide (1989), The Young Green Consumer Guide (1990), The Green Business Guide (1991), Holidays that Don't Cost The Earth (1992); *Recreations* walking, travel, bridge; *Style*— Ms Julia Hailes; ✉ Tintinhull House, Tintinhull, Somerset BA22 8PZ (☎ 01935 823972, fax 01935 826176, e-mail 101363.1001@compuserve.com)

HAILEY, Arthur; AE; s of George Wellington Hailey, and Elsie Mary Wright; *b* 5 April 1920; *m* 1, 1944 (m dis 1950), Joan Fishwick; 3 s; m 2, 1951, Sheila Dunlop; 1 s, 2 da; *Career* author; Pilot RAF 1939–47, Flt Lt, emigrated to Canada 1947, cmmnd RCAF Reserve, Flt Lt 1951; various positions in indust and sales until becoming freelance writer 1956; books published in 39 languages, estimated 160 million copies in print; *Books* Flight into Danger (with John Castle, 1958), The Final Diagnosis (1959), Close-Up (collected plays, 1960), In High Places (1962), Hotel (1965, film 1966), Airport (1968, film 1970), Wheels (1971, film 1978), The Moneychangers (1975, film 1976), Overload (1979), Strong Medicine (1984, film 1986), The Evening News (1990), Detective (1997); *Other Films* Zero Hour (1956), Time Lock (1957), The Young Doctors (1961); TV series Arthur Hailey's Hotel (based on novel); *Clubs* Lyford Cay (Bahamas); *Style*— Arthur Hailey, Esq, AE; ✉ Lyford Cay, PO Box N7776, Nassau, Bahamas; c/o Nancy Stauffer Associates, 171 Newbury Street, Boston, MA 02116, USA

HAILSHAM, Viscountcy of (UK 1929) *see:* Hailsham of St Marylebone, Baron

HAILSHAM OF ST MARYLEBONE, Baron (Life Peer UK 1970); Quintin McGarel Hogg; KG (1988), CH (1974), PC (1956); s of 1 Viscount Hailsham (d 1950) by his 1 w Elizabeth, da of Judge Trimble Brown, of Nashville, Tennessee, and widow of Hon Archibald Marjoribanks (4 s of 1 Baron Tweedmouth); disclaimed both Viscountcy and Barony for life 1963; 1 cous of Sir John Hogg, TD, *qv*; *b* 9 Oct 1907; *Educ* Eton, ChCh Oxford; *m* 1, 1931 (m dis 1943), Natalie Antoinette (d 1987), da of Alan Sullivan, of Sheerland House, Pluckley, Kent; m 2, 1944, Mary Evelyn (d 1978), o da of Richard Martin, of Kensington; 2 s, 3 da (one of whom Mary Claire Hogg (Hon Mrs Justice Hogg, DBE, *qv*); m 3, 1986, Deirdre, er da of Mrs Margaret Briscoe and late Capt Peter Shannon; *Heir* (to Viscountcy and Barony of Hailsham, UK cr respectively 1928 & 1929, only) s, Rt Hon Douglas Hogg, QC, MP, *qv*; *Career* served WWII Rifle Bde; barrister 1932, jt under sec of state for Air 1945, QC 1953; MP (C) Oxford City 1938–58, St Marylebone 1963–70; first lord Admiralty 1956–57, min for educn 1957, Lord Pres of Cncl 1957–59 and 1960–64, Lord Privy Seal 1959–60, min for Science and Technology 1959–64, ldr House of Lords 1960–63 (dep ldr 1957–60), Lord Chllr 1970–74 and 1979–87 (3 in precedence in Cabinet); chm Cons Pty Orgn 1957–59; rector Univ of Glasgow 1959; ed Halsbury's Laws of England (4th edn) 1972–; fellow All Souls Coll Oxford 1951–38 and 1962–; Hon Freeman Worshipful Co of Merchant Taylors; Hon DCL Oxford, Hon LLD Cambridge; FRS 1973; *Style*— The Rt Hon the Lord Hailsham of St Marylebone, KG, CH, PC, FRS; ✉ Corner House, Heathview Gardens, London SW15 3SZ (☎ 0181 789 3954/788 2256)

HAILSTONE, Dr (John) Donovan; s of Capt Frank Hailstone (d 1944), and Maud Eunice, *née* Greenhough; *b* 26 Feb 1930; *Educ* Univ of Nottingham (BSc), Univ of London (DipEd, DPM, MB BS); *m* 1, 2 Sept 1951 (m dis 1978), Pamela Margaret, da of Michael John Gray (d 1971), of Andover, Hants; 1 s (Julien John b 1965); m 2, 14 April 1979, (Beatrice) Jane; *Career* St George's Hosp London 1961–62, med resident NY and Boston 1962–63, sr registrar St Mary's Hosp London 1964–69, conslt physician in psychological med the Royal Free Hosp London 1970–, hon sr lectr Royal Free Hosp Med Sch 1970–; chm Hampstead Dist Med Ctee and Dist Mgmnt Team 1983–85, memb Hosp Advsy Serv 1989–, Lord Chllr's Med Visitor 1989–, memb Mental Health Tribunal 1990–; MRCS, LRCS 1960, MRCPsych 1973, FRCPsych 1983; *Books* Psychiatric Illness in the Medical Profession and the Clergy (1969); *Recreations* sailing, private flying; *Clubs* Royal Ocean Racing Club (RORC); *Style*— Dr Donovan Hailstone; ✉ Edward House, Charter Nightingale Hospital, 7 Lisson Grove, London NW1 6SH (☎ 0171 723 1987/1918, fax 0171 435 3488)

HAIN, Peter Gerald; MP (Lab) Neath (majority 23,975); s of Walter Hain, and Adelaine Hain; *b* 16 Feb 1950; *Educ* QMC London (BScEcon), Univ of Sussex (MPhil); *m* 1975, Patricia Western; 2 s; *Career* head of res Union of Communication Workers 1987–91 (asst res offr 1976–87), MP (Lab) Neath 1991–; oppn whip 1995–96, oppn spokesman on employment 1996–; chm Stop the Seventy Tour campaign 1969–70, nat chm Young Libs 1971–73, press offr Anti-Nazi League 1977–80; Parly candidate (Lab) Putney 1983 and 1987; *Books* Don't Play with Apartheid (1971), Community Politics (1976), Mistaken

Identity (1976), Policing the Police (ed vol I, 1978, vol II 1980), Neighbourhood Participation (1980), Crisis and Future of the Left (1980), Political Trials in Britain (1984), Political Strikes (1986), A Putney Plot? (1987), The Peking Connection (1995), Ayes to the Left (1995), Sing the Beloved Country (1996); *Recreations* soccer, cricket, rugby, supporting Chelsea FC and Neath RFC, motor racing, rock and folk music; *Clubs* Neath Working Mens', Resolven Rugby, Resolven Royal British Legion Institute, Ynysygerwn CC; *Style—* Peter Hain, Esq, MP; ✉ House of Commons, London SW1A 0AA (☎ 0171 219 3925); 14 The Parade, Neath, W Glamorgan SA11 1RA (☎ 01639 630152)

HAINES, Prof Andrew Paul; s of Charles George Thomas Haines, of 75 Tentelow Lane, Southall, Middx, and Lilian Emily, *née* Buck; *b* 26 Feb 1947; *Educ* Latymer Upper Sch, KCH Med Sch London (MB BS, MD); *m* 12 Feb 1982 (m dis 1989), June Marie Power; *Career* house physician and surgn KCH 1969, sr house offr Nat Hosp for Nervous Diseases 1972, MO Br-Nepal Med Tst 1973, memb scientific staff MRC, Epidemiology and Med Care Unit Northwick Park Hosp 1974–86; pt/t sr lectr in gen practice: Middx Hosp Med Sch 1980–84, St Mary's Hosp Med Sch 1984–87; prof of primary health care UCL Med Sch 1987–; dir of R&D: NE Thames RHA (pt/t secondment) 1993–95, NHS Exec N Thames 1995–; author of papers on med subjects incl cardiovascular prevention, alcohol, care of the elderly and environmental issues; memb: Public Health Laboratory Serv Bd 1983–86, Cncl Inst of Physicians for the Prevention of Nuclear War 1982–85 (winners of Nobel Peace Prize 1985), Cncl Pugwash Orgn for Sci and World Affrs 1987–92 (winners of Nobel Peace Prize 1996), Working Pty on Prevention RCP 1989–91, WHO/UNEP/WMO Task Gp on Health Impacts of Climate Change 1993–, Intergovernmental Panel on Climate Change Working Gp 2 1993–, NHS Central R&D Ctee 1995–; MRC: memb Health Servs Research Ctee 1989–92, memb Cncl 1996–, chm Health Servs and Public Research Bd 1996–; hon dir Action In Int Med 1989–; vice pres MEDACT 1992–; FFPHM 1991 (MFPHM 1987), FRCGP 1991 (MRCGP 1976), FRCP (Lond) 1992 (MRCP 1971); *Recreations* foreign travel, environmental and security issues; *Style—* Prof Andrew Haines; ✉ 45 Lisburne Road, London NW3 2NS (☎ 0171 485 1905); Department of Primary Care and Population Sciences, University College London Medical School and Royal Free Hospital School of Medicine, Whittington Hospital, Highgate Hill, London N19 5NF (☎ 0171 288 3475, fax 0171 281 8004); Royal Free Hospital School of Medicine, Rowland Hill Street, London NW3 2PF (☎ 0171 830 2391, fax 0171 830 2339)

HAINES, Dr Charles Ian; s of Col George Harris Haines, MC, RAMC (d 1974), and (Laura) Ailsa, *née* MacPhail (d 1979); *b* 15 Sept 1934; *Educ* Marlborough, St Mary's Hosp Med Sch and Univ of London (MB BS); *m* 14 Sept 1963, Mollie Cynthia, da of James Reid Wheeler (d 1973); 1 s (Rupert b 1967), 3 da (Alexandra b 1965, Ruth b 1971, Lucy b 1974); *Career* Surgn Lt RN 1960–63; princ in gen practice 1963–66; consltpaediatrician: Bromsgrove and Kidderminster Gen Hosps, Alexandra Hosp Redditch 1974–94; emeritus conslt paediatrician Alexandra NHS Health Care Tst 1994–; sr clinical lectr Dept of Paediatrics Univ of Birmingham 1988–94; FRCP 1984; *Recreations* gardening, golf, fishing, opera; *Style—* Dr Charles Haines; ✉ 34 Greenhill, Blackwell, Bromsgrove, Worcs B60 1BJ (☎ 0121 445 1729)

HAINES, Christopher John Minton; s of Capt Geoffrey Francis Minton Haines (d 1941), and Daphne Joan Thal, MBE (d 1980); *b* 14 April 1939; *Educ* Stowe; *m* 1967, Mary Christine, da of Maj Robert Cobbold, late of Welsh Gds (d 1942); 2 s (Vivian b 1971, Robert b 1984), 2 da (Miranda b 1969, Philippa b 1975); *Career* Rifle Bde: joined as Nat Serv 1957, cmmnd 1959, served Cyprus, Malaya, Hong Kong, Canada, Germany, UK and Africa, ret Maj 1968 (formerly ADC, Adj, Co Cdr and Chief Instr Inf Weapons RM Commando Trg Centre); with E A de Pass & Co Ltd sugar brokers 1968–70, md Tower Hill Merchants 1970–74; James Budgett & Co Ltd sugar and produce merchants/process: gp md 1974–82, md 1982–85, chm 1985–89; chief exec The Jockey Club 1989–92; chm Sterling Publishing Group plc 1996–; dir: Yorkshire Food Group 1991–94, Devonshire Arms (Bolton Abbey) Ltd 1993–; formerly: memb Cncl W Indian Ctee, chm Export Houses Ctee London C of C, a chm UK Sugar Merchants' Assoc, memb Overseas Relief and Welfare Ctee Save the Children Fund; *Recreations* clarinet, gardening; *Clubs* Turf; *Style—* Christopher Haines, Esq; ✉ Cheshunts, Boxted, Colchester, Essex CO4 5SY; Sterling Publishing Group plc, 86–88 Edgware Road, London W2 2YW (☎ 0171 258 0066)

HAINES, Rev Dr Daniel Hugo; TD (1989); s of Dr Richard Wheeler Haines (d 1995), of London SE15, and Ellen Stephanie, *née* Swift (d 1989); *b* 16 May 1943; *Educ* Abbotsholme Sch Derbyshire, Guy's Hosp Dental Sch Univ of London (BDS, LDS), London Hosp Med Coll Univ of London, Staff Coll Camberley; *m* 20 July 1968, Dr Hilary Margaret Haines, da of Tudor Isaac, of Maesteg, Mid Glamorgan; 2 s (Tudor b 1972, Gwyn b 1977), 1 da (Catherine b 1974); *Career* Univ of London OTC 1962, Dental Offr 221 (Surrey) Field Ambulance RAMC (Capt) 1968, MO 217 (London) Gen Hosp RAMC (Maj) 1984; hon lectr in forensic dentistry London Hosp Med Coll 1968–75, med offr Govt of the Cayman Is 1975–77, chief med offr Usutu Forests Swaziland 1977–80, sr med offr Govt of the Falkland Is 1980–82, med and dental practitioner 1982–; ordained priest Southwark Cathedral 1984, hon curate St Catherine's Hatcham 1984–; Freeman City of London 1968, Liveryman Worshipful Soc of Apothecaries 1970; memb: BMA, BDA; tacsc, LRCP, MRCS, DRCOG; *Recreations* gardening, walking; *Style—* The Rev Dr Daniel Haines, TD; ✉ 56 Vesta Road, London SE4 2NH (☎ 0171 635 0305); The Surgery, 58 Vesta Road, London SE4 2NH (☎ 0171 639 0654)

HAINES, Joseph Thomas William (Joe); s of Joseph Haines, and Elizabeth Haines; *b* 29 Jan 1928; *m* 1955, Irene Lambert; *Career* political corr: The Bulletin (Glasgow) 1958–60 (Parly corr 1954–58), Scottish Daily Mail 1960–64, The Sun 1964–68; chief leader writer Daily Mirror 1978–90 (feature writer 1977–78), asst ed The Mirror 1985–90; dir: Scottish Daily Record and Sunday Mail Ltd, Mirror Group Newspapers 1986, MGN plc 1991–92 (gp political ed 1984–90); columnist: Today 1974–95, Daily Mirror until 1991; chief press sec to Harold Wilson as PM 1969–70 and 1974–76 and as Leader of Oppn 1970–74 (dep press sec 1969); former chm Tonbridge & Malling Lab Pty (resigned), former memb Tonbridge UDC and Royal Cmmn on Legal Servs; *Books* The Politics of Power (1977), Malice in Wonderland (ed, 1986), Maxwell (1986); *Style—* Joe Haines, Esq; ✉ 1 South Frith, London Rd, Southborough, Tunbridge Wells, Kent (☎ 01732 365919)

HAINES, Prof Michael; *b* 13 Aug 1939; *Career* various appts Nat Agric Advsy Serv MAFF 1963–71; UCW Aberystwyth: lectr 1971–81, prof of agricultural and food mktg 1981–91, prof of agricultural mktg and business 1991–, dir Welsh Inst of Rural Studies 1995–; dir: Welsh Food Promotions Ltd 1993–, Northern Milk Partnership 1994–; advsr Dyfed CC Econ Devpt Ctee 1983–90, memb Agric Advsy Panel to Sec of State for Wales 1981–90, memb Bd Seafish Indust Authy 1987–, memb Cncl Food From Britain 1994–; MInstM 1979–89, FCIM 1989, FSA 1989; *Books* An Introduction to Farming Systems (1982), Diversifying The Farm Business (1987); *Recreations* history, industrial archaeology; *Clubs* Farmers; *Style—* Prof Michael Haines, FSA; ✉ University of Wales, Aberystwyth, Dyfed SY23 3DD (☎ 01970 622242, fax 01970 622238, tlx 35181 ABYUCW G)

HAINES, Michael Geoffrey Minton; s of Geoffrey Francis Minton Haines (d 1941), and Daphne Joan, *née* Thal, BEM (d 1979); *b* 30 Dec 1935; *Educ* Stowe; *m* 21 Dec 1973, Elizabeth, da of Lt-Col John Matthew Blakiston Houston, of Beltrim Castle, Gortin, Co Tyrone (d 1983); 2 s (Francis b 1975, Richard b 1977), 1 da (Rosie b 1979); *Career* Nat Serv cmmnd 2 Lt Rifle Bde 1959, 4 (Vol) Bn Royal Green Jackets TAVR 1961–70 (ret Maj 1970); ptnr KPMG Peat Marwick 1969–93 (joined 1954); chm: Royal London NHS Tst 1993–94, Homerton Hosp NHS Tst 1995–; dir: Shires Investment Trust 1971–80, Nationwide Building Soc 1984–88, Cluff Resources plc 1993–95, Andrew Sykes Group plc 1994–, Tom Hoskins plc; dep dir Ind Devpt Unit 1975–76; chm Lambeth Building Society 1993–; treas: London & Quadrant Housing Tst 1970–95, E London Housing Assoc 1982–87, Sanctuary Housing Gp 1988–90; govr Peabody Tst 1996–; memb Overseas Projects Bd 1987–90; chm: London Sinfonietta 1990–, Oxford House 1990–; Freeman City of London 1982, memb Worshipful Co of Playing Card Makers 1983; MICAS 1959; *Recreations* music, theatre, literature, military history, golf, squash; *Clubs* Brooks's, City of London; *Style—* Michael Haines, Esq; ✉ 82A Mortimer Rd, London N1 4LH (☎ and fax 0171 254 2339)

HAINING, Thomas Nivison; CMG (1982); s of late William Haining, of Ayrshire (d 1977), and Agnes Nivison, *née* Williamson; *b* 15 March 1927; *Educ* Univ of Edinburgh, Göttingen Univ; *m* 1955, Dorothy Patricia, da of late Leslie Robson, and A Dorothy Robson, of Whitley Bay; 1 s (Nicholas); *Career* HM Dip Serv 1952–82, ambass and consul gen to Mongolian People's Republic 1979–82, ret; consltt on int and personnel questions 1982–87; hon res fell Dept of History and Economic History Univ of Aberdeen 1991– (hon res assoc 1988–89), pres Chinese Studies Gp; Freeman City of Rochester (NY State) 1972; FRAS; *Publication* Genghis Khan: His Life and Legacy (trans and ed, 1991); *Recreations* reading, historical travel studies, local historical studies, music, golf; *Clubs* RAC, Royal Northern and University (Aberdeen); *Style—* Thomas N Haining, Esq, CMG; ✉ Carseview, 7 The Banks, Brechin, Angus DD9 6JD (☎ 01356 622584)

HAINSWORTH, Prof Roger; s of Edward Trevor Hainsworth (d 1991), of Wakefield, and Constance Mary, *née* White; *b* 23 Dec 1938; *Educ* Queen Elizabeth GS Wakefield, Univ of Leeds (MB ChB, PhD, DSc), Cardiovascular Res Inst San Francisco USA; *m* 24 July 1965, Janet Ann, da of Frederick Fisher (d 1985), of Cheadle, Cheshire; 2 s (Christopher Roger b 1967, Jonathan Peter b 1968), 2 da (Caroline Ann b 1971, Lucy Jane b 1982); *Career* house offr Leeds 1963–64; Univ of Leeds: lectr in physiology 1964–69, lectr Dept of Cardiovascular Studies 1970–76, sr lectr 1976–87, reader 1987–90, prof 1990–; Br-American res fell San Francisco 1969–70, hon conslt in clinical physiology Leeds Western DHA and Leeds Eastern DHA 1979–; memb: Physiological Soc, Med Res Soc, Clinical Autonic Res Soc; *Books* Cardiac Receptors (with C Kidd and R J Linden, 1979), Acid Base Balance (1986), Cardiogenic Reflexes (with P N McWilliam and D A S G Mary, 1987), Cardiovascular Reflex Control in Health and Disease (with A L Mark); *Recreations* travel, photography, wine making; *Style—* Prof Roger Hainsworth; ✉ Academic Unit of Cardiovascular Studies, University of Leeds, Leeds LS2 9JT (☎ 0113 233 4820, fax 0113 233 4803, telex 556473)

HAIR, Prof Paul Edward Hedley; s of Thomas Edward Couchman Hair (d 1972), and Florence, *née* Hedley (d 1946); *b* 27 Jan 1926; *Educ* Berwick-upon-Tweed GS, St John's Coll Cambridge (MA), Nuffield and Balliol Colls Oxford (DPhil); *m* 5 Dec 1959, Margaret, da of Kenneth Alfred Edward Robinson (d 1961); 1 s (Christopher b 1963), 1 da (Ruth b 1966); *Career* res fell Univ of Ibadan Nigeria 1952–55, lectr Univ of Sierra Leone 1961–63, sr lectr in African hist Univ of Khartoum 1963–65; Univ of Liverpool: lectr, sr lectr then reader Dept of History 1965–79, Ramsay Muir prof of modern history 1979–90, emeritus prof and sr fell 1990–; pres Hakluyt Soc, chm Fontes Historiae Africanae Ctee Br Acad, chm Liverpool NHS Tsts Archive Ctee; FRHistS; *Books* The Early Study of Nigerian Languages (1967 and 1994), Before the Bawdy Court (1972), Liverpool, The African Slave Trade and Abolition (ed, 1976 and 1989), The Westward Enterprise (ed, 1978), East of Mina (1988), Coals on Rails (1988), To Defend Your Empire (1990), Barbot on Guinea (ed, 1992), English Seamen and Traders in Guinea 1553–1565 (ed, 1992), The European Outthrust and Encounter: the first phase c1400–c1700 (ed, 1994), The Founding of the Castelo de São Jorge da Mina (1994); *Recreations* reading, television; *Style—* Prof Paul Hair; ✉ 17 Abbey Rd, West Kirby, Merseyside L48 7EN (☎ and fax 0151 625 5745); Department of History, University of Liverpool, PO Box 147, Liverpool L69 3BX

HAITINK, Bernard; Hon KBE (1977); *b* 1929; *Career* conductor; chief conductor Concertgebouw Orchestra Amsterdam 1964–88, artistic dir and princ conductor London Philharmonic Orchestra 1967–79, musical dir Glyndebourne Opera 1978–88, musical dir Royal Opera House Covent Garden 1988– (debut 1977), pres London Philharmonic Orchestra 1990–, music dir European Union Youth Orch 1994–; princ guest conductor Boston Symphony 1995–; guest conductor: Berlin Philharmonic, Bayerische Rundfunk, Vienna Philharmonic, Concertgebouw, Salzburg Festival, Berlin Festival, re-opening of Glyndebourne Opera 1994, Tanglewood Festival; numerous recordings for EMI and Philips; awarded Bruckner Medal of Honour Bruckner Soc, hon gold medal Gustav Mahler Soc 1970, Erasmus prize Holland 1991, gold medal Royal Philharmonic Soc 1991, Olivier Award for Oustanding Achievement in Opera 1996; Hon DMus Univs of Oxford and Leeds; Order of Orange (Nassau), chev Ordre des Arts et des Lettres, offr Order of the Crown (Belgium); RAM, FRCM; *Style—* Bernard Haitink, Esq, KBE; ✉ Harold Holt Ltd, 31 Sinclair Road, London W14 0NS (☎ 0171 603 4600, fax 0171 603 0019)

HAJDUCKI, Andrew Michael; QC (Scot 1994); *b* 12 Nov 1952; *Educ* Dulwich Coll, Downing Coll Cambridge (MA); *m*; 3 s (1 decd), 1 da; *Career* called to the Bar Gray's Inn 1976, admitted Faculty of Advocates 1979, pt/t tutor Univ of Edinburgh 1979–81, reporter session cases 1980, temp sheriff 1987–; safeguarder: Lothian Children's Panel 1987–96, East, West & Midlothian & City of Edinburgh 1996–; candidate and agent (Lib) Scot 1978–85; FSA (Scot) 1990; *Publications* Scottish Civic Government Licensing Law (1994), also author of three books on railways of East Lothian and Berwickshire, author of various articles in legal, history and railway jls and magazines; *Recreations* reading, running, writing, travel by train, tram and landrover; *Style—* Andrew Hajducki, Esq, QC; ✉ c/o Advocates' Library, Parliament House, Edinburgh EH1 1RF

HALAKA, Ahmed Nageeb; s of Ali Mohamed Halaka (d 1983), of Mansura, Egypt, and Nafisa Osman Abou-El-Khier (d 1983); *b* 8 Feb 1949; *Educ* Lycée la Liberté Mansura, Mansura Faculty Med Cairo Univ (MB BCh), Univ of Leeds (PhD); *m* 31 March 1979, Catherine Anne, da of Alan Hibbert, of Woodley, Stockport; 3 da (Sarah b 24 Aug 1980, Sophie b 7 June 1982, Suzanne b 29 March 1986); *Career* sr house offr orthopaedics Swansea 1973 (sr house offr neurosurgery 1972–73), sr house offr gen surgery N Allerton 1974–75, registrar Cardiff and Swansea 1975–77, conslt neurosurgn Leeds 1982– (sr registrar in neurosurgery 1977–82), author of papers on meningitis, pituitary absess and intracranial tumours; memb: SBNS, NENA, Egyptian Soc Neurosurgeons; FRCSEd; *Style—* Ahmed Halaka, Esq; ✉ BUPA Hospital, Roundhay Hall, Jackson Ave, Leeds LS8 1NT (☎ 0113 269 3939, fax 0113 268 1340)

HALAM, Ann; *see:* Jones, Gwyneth Ann

HALBERT, His Hon Judge; Derek Rowland; s of Ronald Halbert, and Freda Mabel, *née* Impett; *b* 25 March 1948; *Educ* King's Sch Chester, Selwyn Coll Cambridge (MA), Open Univ (BA); *m* 28 Sept 1972, Heather Rose, da of late Samuel Walter Ashe; 2 da (Sarah Lucy b 21 Jan 1979, Elizabeth Amy b 17 May 1983); *Career* called to the Bar Inner Temple 1971, in practice Wales & Chester Circuit 1972–95, recorder of the Crown Court 1991–95, circuit judge (Wales & Chester Circuit) 1995–; *Clubs* Leander; *Style—* His Hon Judge Halbert; ✉ The Crown Court, The Castle, Chester CH1 2AN

HALDANE OF GLENEAGLES, (James) Martin; 28th of Gleneagles; er s of James Haldane (d 1990), of The Old Schoolhouse, Gleneagles, Auchterarder, and Joanna Margaret, *née* Thorburn; suc his kinsman, Alexander Chinnery Haldane, 27th of Gleneagles (d 1994); *b* 18 Sept 1941; *Educ* Winchester, Magdalen Coll Oxford; *m* 5 Oct

1968, Petronella Victoria, da of Sir Peter Scarlett, KCMG, KCVO; 1 s, 2 da; *Career* chartered accountant; ptnr: Arthur Young 1970–89, Chiene & Tait 1989–; chm: Craighead Investments plc 1982–90, Queen's Hall (Edinburgh) Ltd 1992–; dir: Northern and Scottish Bd Legal and General Assurance Soc 1984–87, Scottish Life Assurance Co 1990–, Investors Capital Trust plc 1995–, Wellington Members Agency Ltd 1995–96, Shires Income plc 1996–, Stace Barr Wellington Ltd 1996–; chm: Scottish Philharmonic Soc 1978–85, Scottish Chamber Orchestra 1981–85; memb: Cncl Edinburgh Festival Soc 1985–89, D'Oyly Carte Opera Tst 1985–92, Cncl Nat Tst for Scotland 1992–; treas Royal Co of Archers (Queen's Body Guard for Scotland); FRSA; *Recreations* music, golf; *Clubs* Brooks's, New (Edinburgh); *Style*— Martin Haldane of Gleneagles; ✉ Gleneagles, Auchterarder, Perthshire PH3 1PJ (☎ 01764 682388); 23 Northumberland Street, Edinburgh EH3 6LR (☎ 0131 556 2924)

HALDANE-STEVENSON, Rev (James) Patrick; TD (1948, Bar); 8th of Airthrey, Stirling; s of Graham Morton Stevenson (d 1939), Southbourne, and Jane Haldane (d 1941), da of James Thomson, of Airdrie; *b* 17 March 1910; *Educ* King Edward's Sch Birmingham, St Catherine's Coll Oxford (MA); *m* 1, 1938 (m dis 1967), Leila Mary, da of Arthur Flack; 2 s (Alan b 1940, Keith b 1941), 1 da (Janet b 1944); m 2, 1983, Mrs Joan Talbot Smith, o da of late Lt Cdr C W Wilson, of Par, Cornwall; *Career* served Br Reg Army 1946–55; Westminster Bank 1927–30; ordained Southwark 1935; rector: Hillington Norfolk (but on active serv 1939–46), Wongan Hills Australia 1956–59; vicar N Balwyn Melbourne; Aust corr Le Monde 1969–73, contrib to various books and jls incl New Statesman, The Spectator and Yr Enfys; pres Cambrian Soc of ACT 1985–88; assoc memb Inst RE; memb: Ctee Hunt Clubs Assoc of NSW, Thomas Hardy Soc; fell Australasian Canon Law, companion Inst of Engrs (Aust) 1992; FRSL 1994; Order of St Stanislas of Poland (Class II) and Prelate for Aust; *Books* In Our Tongues (1944), Religion and Leadership (1948), Crisanzio and Other Poems (1948), Beyond the Bridge (1973), The Backward Look (1976); *Recreations* foxhunting, English and Latin verse; *Clubs* Athenaeum, Quorn Hunt, Melbourne (Melbourne Australia), National Press (Canberra); *Style*— The Rev Patrick Haldane-Stevenson, TD, FRSL; ✉ 3 Argyle Square, Ainslie Avenue, Canberra 2601, Australia; c/o Coleg Mihangel Sant, Llandâf CF5 2YJ

HALE, Hon Mrs Justice; Hon Dame Brenda Marjorie; DBE (1994); da of Cecil Frederick Hale (d 1958), and Marjorie, *née* Godfrey (d 1981); *b* 31 Jan 1945; *Educ* Richmond (Yorks) HS for Girls, Girton Coll Cambridge (MA); *m* 1, 1968 (m dis 1992), Dr (Anthony) John Christopher Hoggett, QC, *qv*, s of Christopher Hoggett (d 1989), of Grimsby; 1 da (Julia b 1973); m 2, 1992, Dr Julian Thomas Farrand, Pensions Ombudsman, s of John Farrand; *Career* called to the Bar Gray's Inn 1969, QC 1989, asst recorder 1984–89, recorder of the Crown Court 1989–93, bencher Gray's Inn 1994, judge of the High Court of Justice (Family Div) 1994–; Univ of Manchester: asst lectr 1966, lectr 1968, sr lectr 1976, reader 1981, prof of law 1986–89; prof of English law King's Coll London 1989–90 (visiting prof 1990–); memb Cncl of Tribunals 1980–84, jt gen ed Journal of Social Welfare Law 1978–84, law cmmr 1984–93; managing tstee Nuffield Fndn 1987–, pres Nat Assoc Family Mediation and Conciliation Servs 1994– (chm 1989–93), memb Human Fertilisation and Embryology Authy 1990–93; Hon LLD: Sheffield 1989, London Guildhall Univ 1996; *Books* Mental Health Law (1976, 4 edn 1991), Parents and Children (1977, 4 edn 1993), The Family Law and Society - Cases and Materials (with D S Pearl 1983, 4 edn 1996), Women and the Law (with S Atkins 1984), From the Testtube to the Coffin - Choice and Regulation in Private Life (The Hamlyn Lectrs, 1996); many contribs to legal texts and periodicals; *Recreations* bridge, etc; *Style*— The Hon Mrs Justice Hale, DBE; ✉ Royal Courts of Justice, Strand, London WC2A 2LL

HALE, Charles Martin; s of Charles Sidney Hale (d 1981), and Carmen, *née* de Mora; *b* 19 Jan 1936; *Educ* St Bernard's Sch NY, Culver Mil Acad, Stanford Univ (BSc), Harvard Business Sch (MBA); *m* 11 Feb 1967, Kaaren Alexis; 2 da (Melissa b 18 May 1971, Amanda b 9 Nov 1976); *Career* USN: serv USS Union, Ensign i/c Boat Gp Div 1958, Lt 1960; gen ptnr Hirsch & Co London 1963–71, md and sr offr Europe AG Becker Inc 1971–83, gen ptnr Lehman Bros Kuhn Loeb Inc 1983–84, md and head of Int Div Donaldson Lufkin & Jenrette Securities Corp 1984–95, chm Donaldson Lufkin & Jenrette International Ltd 1996–; chm UK Assoc of NY Stock Exchange Membs 1989–91; memb: The Pilgrims, Harvard Business Sch Club of London, Stanford Univ Club of GB; *Recreations* tennis, travel and philately; *Clubs* Hurlingham, Vanderbilt, Annabel's, Harvard (New York), Harry's Bar; *Style*— Charles Hale, Esq; ✉ 33 Lyall Mews, London SW1X 8DJ (☎ 0171 245 9916); Donaldson, Lufkin & Jenrette International Ltd, Moorgate Hall, 155 Moorgate, London EC2M 6XB (☎ 0171 638 5822, fax 0171 628 1027)

HALE, John Hampton; s of Dr John Hale, and Elsie Ledbrooke Coles; *b* 8 July 1924; *Educ* Eton, Magdalene Coll Cambridge (MA), Harvard Business Sch; *m* 1, 1950; 1 s (Jonathan), 2 da (Susan, Anne); m 2, 1980, Nancy Ryrie Birks; *Career* dir: Alcan Aluminium Ltd 1970–85 (joined 1949, exec vice pres Fin 1970–83), Pearson plc 1983–93 (md 1983–86), Economist Newspaper Ltd 1984–95, Bank of Montreal 1985–95, SSMC Inc 1986–89; lay memb Cncl Int Stock Exchange (London) 1987–91, memb Ct of Assts Worshipful Co of Armourers and Brasiers 1985– (Master 1990), tstee Royal Armouries 1992–95; *Recreations* skiing, fishing, shooting; *Clubs* Royal Thames Yacht, Mount Royal, Toronto; *Style*— John Hale, Esq; ✉ 71 Eaton Terrace, London SW1W 8TN (☎ 0171 730 2929, fax 0171 823 4454)

HALE, Prof Sir John Rigby; kt (1984); *b* 17 Sept 1923; *Educ* Eastbourne Coll, Jesus Coll Oxford (DLitt); *m* 1, 1952, Rosalind Williams; 1 s, 2 da; m 2, 1965, Sheila Haynes MacIvor, the journalist; 1 s; *Career* prof of Italian history Univ Coll London 1970–89 (emeritus prof 1989–); chm of Tstees Nat Gallery 1974–80 (tstee 1973–80); tstee: V & A 1983–87, British Museum 1985–93; chm Govt Art Collection Advsy Cncl 1982–92, cmmr Museums and Galleries Cmmn 1983–92; hon fell Jesus Coll Oxford 1986; author; FSA, FRHistS, FRSA, FBA, FRSL; *Books* incl: Artists and Warfare in the Renaissance (1990), The Civilization of Europe in the Renaissance (1993); *Recreations* novels, museums; *Clubs* Beefsteak; *Style*— Prof Sir John Hale, FSA, FBA; ✉ 26 Montpelier Row, Twickenham, Middx TW1 2NQ (☎ 0181 892 9636, fax 0181 891 6778)

HALE, (Mathew) Joseph Hovey; OBE (1994), MC (1945), TD (1974); s of Mathew Robert Hale (d 1926), of Bognor Regis, and Grace Muriel, *née* Hovey (d 1962); *b* 14 Oct 1918; *Educ* St John's Coll Hurstpierpoint; *m* 28 Jan 1950, Gwenda, da of Sidney Herbert Roberts (d 1972), of Worthing, W Sussex; 2 da (Sheila b 1950, Sally b 1955); *Career* WWII 1939–46, cmmnd RA 1939, served N African and Italian Campaigns, Maj 1944; admitted slr 1947, in private practice; dir T R Beckett Ltd 1959–96; chm: Beckett Newspapers Ltd 1967–96, T R Beckett Ltd and subsid cos 1969–96, Today Interiors Ltd 1976–; dir Johnston Press PLC 1992–96; pt/t sec London Master Stevedores Assoc 1946–77, vice pres Worthing Area Guild for Voluntary Serv, chm Bd of Govrs Our Lady of Sion Sch Worthing 1984–; memb Law Soc 1947; *Recreations* golf, walking, gardening; *Clubs* Army and Navy; *Style*— Joseph Hale, Esq, OBE, MC, TD; ✉ Stortford, Little Drove, Steyning, W Sussex (☎ 01903 814852)

HALE, Julian Anthony Stuart; s of James Peter Rashleigh Hale (d 1981), and Gillian Mariette Stuart, *née* Mason; *b* 27 Nov 1940; *Educ* Winchester, Christ Church Oxford (MA); *m* 1, 1963 (m dis 1970), Jennifer Monahan; m 2, 1971, Mary Kathleen Benét (d 1984); m 3, 18 April 1987, Helen Elizabeth Grace, da of Julian Likierman, of London; 1 s (Felix b 1990), 2 da (Laura b 1972, Tamara b 1988); *Career* books ed G G Harrap 1963–65, Italian prog organiser BBC External Servs 1972–73 (prodr and scriptwriter 1968–72), ed European Gazette 1973, writer 1973–; prodr BBC Radio 3 and 4 incl: In The Air, Wilko's Weekly, File On 4, Third Ear, Radio Lives 1979–94 (also presenter European Journeys); independent radio prodr 1994–; prodr Icon Books audiotapes 1996–; *Books* incl: Ceausescu's Romania (1971), Radio Power (1975), Snap Judgement (1974), Vicious Circles (1978), Midwinter Madness (1979), Black Summer (1982); *Clubs* MCC; *Style*— Julian Hale, Esq; ✉ 11 Alexander Street, London W2 5NT (☎ 0171 229 0671, fax 0171 243 0001)

HALE, Michael; s of Bertram Hale (d 1986), of Dudley, W Midlands, and Nellie, *née* Cartwright (d 1977); *b* 20 June 1942; *Educ* Sir Gilbert Claughton GS; *m* 19 June 1965, Maureen Janet, da of John Thomas Shipley (d 1978), of Dudley; 1 s (Stephen Michael b 20 Nov 1971), 1 da (Helen Louise b 26 Oct 1975); *Career* dir: Central Manufacturing & Trading Group 1975–80, Caparo Industries plc 1980–83, Glynwed Distribution Ltd 1983–86; chief exec GEI International plc 1986–95; currently non-exec dir: GBE International plc, London Linen Supply Ltd, Englass Group Ltd; FCMA 1969, ACIS 1971; *Recreations* tennis, golf, walking; *Style*— Michael Hale, Esq; ✉ Lower House, 57A Norton Road, Stourbridge DY8 2TB (☎ 01384 373789)

HALE, Norman Morgan; CB (1992); s of Thomas Norman Hale (d 1961), of Worcs, and Ada Emily, *née* Morgan (d 1969); *b* 28 June 1933; *Educ* Prince Henry's GS, St John's Coll Oxford (MA); *m* 1965, Sybil Jean, da of Stephen Leonard Maton (d 1974), of Glos; 1 s (Roger b 1966), 1 da (Alison b 1968); *Career* Miny of Pensions and Nat Insur 1955, asst sec Assistance Bd 1966, Miny of Social Security 1966–70, Civil Serv Dept 1970–72, under sec (grade 3) Dept of Health 1977–93 (head Mental Health Div 1978–82, head Medicines Div 1982–87, head Health Promotion (Administrative) Div 1987–93); conslt: MOD 1994, Meds Control Agency 1994–, Nat Tst 1995–; *Recreations* gardening, historical geography; *Clubs* United Oxford & Cambridge Univ; *Style*— Norman Hale, Esq, CB; ✉ 64 Castle Avenue, Ewell, Epsom, Surrey KT17 2PH (☎ 0181 393 3507)

HALE, Robert; s of Roland Gilbert Hale, of Brierley Hill, and Ida Dorothy, *née* Atkins; *b* 29 Aug 1943; *Educ* Sir Gilbert Claughton GS Dudley; *m* 21 Sept 1968, Diane Elizabeth, da of William Henry Morris; 1 s (Simon Robert b 28 Nov 1972), 1 da (Rachel Elizabeth b 11 May 1970); *Career* Robson Rhodes: articled clerk 1962–67, qualified 1967, gen serv mangr 1970–73, ptnr Gen Servs 1974–88, ptnr Corp Fin Servs 1989–95; FCA (ACA 1967); *Recreations* golf, cricket, rugby, snooker; *Clubs* Forest of Arden Golf & Country; *Style*— Robert Hale, Esq; ✉ Battendown, Coton Rd, Nether Whitacre, Coleshill, Birmingham B46 2HH

HALES, Antony John (Tony); s of Sidney Alfred Hales (d 1985), and Margaret Joan, *née* Wood; *b* 25 May 1948; *Educ* Repton, Univ of Bristol (BSc); *m* Linda Christine, da of Hugh Churchlow; 4 c; *Career* Cadbury Schweppes: food salesman 1969–70, asst brand mangr milk products 1970–71, brand mangr biscuits 1971–74; foods mktg mangr Cadbury Typhoo 1974–79, mktg dir Joshua Tetley & Son Ltd 1979–83, md Halls Oxford and West Brewery Co 1983–85, md Ind Coope-Taylor Walker Ltd 1985–87, retail dir Allied Breweries Ltd 1987, md Ansells Ltd 1987–89; Allied Domecq plc (Allied-Lyons plc until 1994): dir 1989–, chief exec J Lyons & Co Ltd 1989–91, gp chief exec 1991–; non-exec dir: Hyder plc, Midland Bank 1994–; chm CBI Nat Manufacturing Cncl 1993–95; memb Ct of Assts Worshipful Co of Brewers (Liveryman 1986), Freeman City of London 1986; *Style*— Tony Hales, Esq; ✉ Allied Domecq plc, 24 Portland Place, London W1N 4BB (☎ 0171 323 9000, fax 0171 323 1742)

HALES, Lady Celestria Magdalen Mary; da of 5 Earl of Gainsborough; *b* 27 Jan 1954; *Educ* St Mary's Convent Ascot, St Hilda's Coll Oxford; *m* 1 March 1990, Timothy Manville Hales, o s of late S W M Hales, MC; 1 da (Catherine Rose Mary b 11 June 1990); *Career* social ed (as Lady Celestria Noel) Jennifer's Diary in Harpers & Queen 1992–; *Books* The Harpers & Queen Book of the Season (1994); *Style*— The Lady Celestria Hales; ✉ 8 Peel St, London W8

HALES, Christopher Atherstone; s of Lt-Col Herbert Marwicke Atherstone Hales (d 1956), of Turweston, Bucks, and Mary, *née* Bell (d 1970); *b* 26 Aug 1931; *Educ* Wellingborough, HMS Worcester; *m* 17 May 1956, Barbara Mary, da of Edwin Arthur Ryan (d 1963), of London N18; 2 s (Julian b 1963, Adrian b 1966), 4 da (Katherine b 1958, Caroline b 1959, Antonia b 1961, Marie Louise b 1964); *Career* MN, Midshipman to 2 Offr Blue Funnel Line 1949–58, Master Mariner 1957; called to the Bar Gray's Inn 1960, articled clerk Alsop Stevens and Co 1961–64, admitted slr 1964, asst slr Alsop Stevens and Co 1964; Holman Fenwick & Willan: asst slr 1965–67, ptnr 1968–92, conslt 1992–; dep dist judge of the High Ct and County Cts; Freeman City of London, Freeman City of London Solicitors' Co, Liveryman Hon Co of Master Mariners; memb Law Soc; *Recreations* concert and theatregoing, history, following cricket; *Style*— Christopher Hales, Esq; ✉ Farthing Green, Elmdon, Saffron Walden, Essex CB11 4LT; 69 Bessborough Place, London SW1V 3SE; Holman, Fenwick & Willan, Marlow House, Lloyds Ave, London EC3N 3AL (☎ 0171 488 2300, fax 0171 481 0316)

HALES, Christopher James; s of James Camille Hales (d 1968), and Genefer Enid, *née* Ratcliff; *b* 12 Nov 1952; *Educ* Westminster, Univ Hall London (external BA); *Career* called to the Bar Gray's Inn 1979, Treasy slr 1990–; *Recreations* composing songs, sport, art, karate, painting; *Style*— Christopher Hales, Esq; ✉ Treasury Solicitor, Queen Anne's Chambers, 28 Broadway, London SW1 (☎ 0171 210 3000)

HALES, Prof (Charles) Nicholas; *b* 25 April 1935; *Educ* King Edward VI GS Stafford, Trinity Coll Cambridge (scholar, BA, MB BChir, MA, PhD, MRCPath, MRCP, MD); *Career* house physician UCH 1960 (house surgn 1959), Stothert res fell Royal Soc 1963–64, lectr in biochemistry Univ of Cambridge 1964–70, fell Downing Coll Cambridge 1964–70 and 1977–, hon conslt in clinical biochemistry Addenbrooke's Hosp Cambridge 1968–70 (clinical asst 1961–68), prof in chem pathology Welsh Nat Sch of Med 1970–77, hon conslt in chem pathology Univ Hosp of Wales 1970–77, prof in clinical biochemistry Univ of Cambridge 1977–, hon conslt in clinical biochemistry Cambridge AHA 1977–; FRCP 1976, FRCPath 1980, FRS 1992; *Recreations* music, fishing; *Style*— Prof Nicholas Hales, FRS; ✉ Dept of Clinical Biochemistry, Addenbrooke's Hospital, Hills Road, Cambridge CB2 2QR (☎ 01223 336787)

HALEY, Prof (Keith) Brian; s of Arthur Leslie Haley (d 1972), and Gladys Mary, *née* Robson (d 1957); *b* 17 Nov 1933; *Educ* King Edward VI GS Birmingham, Univ of Birmingham (BSc, PhD); *m* 2 April 1960, Diana Elizabeth Haley, JP, da of Albert Bottrell Mason (d 1981); 1 s (Alan John b 1962); *Career* operational res scientist NCB 1957–59; Univ of Birmingham: lectr 1959, sr lectr 1963, prof of operational res 1968, head of Dept of Engrg Prodn 1980, head Sch of Manufacturing and Mechanical Engrg 1994–96, dir Centre for Applied Gerontology, dep dean Faculty of Engrg; pres: Operational Res Soc 1982–83, Int Fedn of Operational Res Socs 1992–94 (vice pres 1983–86); govr and tstee Bromsgrove Sch 1969–; FIMA 1968, FOR 1970, FIEE 1982; *Books* Mathematical Programming for Business & Industry (1964), Operational Research 75 (1975), Operational Research 78 (1978), Operational Research in Search (1980), Operational Research in Fishing (1981); *Recreations* squash, bridge; *Style*— Prof Brian Haley; ✉ 22 Eymore Close, Selly Oak, Birmingham B29 4LB (☎ 0121 475 3331); School of Manufacturing and Mechanical Engineering, The University of Birmingham, Edgbaston, Birmingham B15 2TT (☎ 0121 414 4542)

HALEY, Geoffrey Norman (Geoff); s of Norman Haley (d 1966), of Pudsey, Yorkshire, and Grace Ward, *née* Cooke (d 1983); *b* 12 Oct 1944; *Educ* Accrington GS, Univ of London (BL), Brunel Univ and Henley Mgmnt Coll (MBA), Inst of Mktg (Dip Mktg); *m* 22 Oct 1966, Doreen Haley, da of Leslie Veitch; 1 s (Paul b 5 Sept 1974), 1 da (Julie b 24 June 1977); *Career* admitted slr 1971, dep gp legal advsr Costain Gp 1974–78, dir Costain UK 1980–86 (legal advsr 1978–86), gen mangr Costain Ventures 1986–89, ptnr

Theodore Goddard 1989–93, ptnr S J Berwin & Co 1993–; legal advsr: Thames Barrier Consortium 1979–86, Channel Tunnel contractors Transmanche Link 1985; dir GKN Kwikform Ltd 1986–89, alternate dir Br Urban Devpt 1988–89; expert to European Cmmn; consult advsr: UNCTAD Geneva, UNIDO Vienna; memb: Law Soc, Strategic Planning Soc, Inst of Mktg, Soc of Construction Law, Br Urban Regeneration Assoc, Greenlands Assoc, Ascot Round Table, Panel Euro Centre for Infrastructure Studies Rotterdam; numerous articles in the field of construction law and private fin for transportation and infrastructure projects; MIStructE (memb Ctee on Design and Construction of Deep Basements), MInstPet; *Recreations* swimming, cycling, walking; *Clubs* RAC, Ronnie Scots; *Style—* Geoffrey Haley, Esq; ✉ Tanglewood, 39A Llanvair Drive, S Ascot, Berks SL5 9LW (☎ 01344 27311); S J Berwin & Co, 222 Grays Inn Road, London WC1V 8HB (☎ 0171 837 2222, fax 0171 833 2860)

HALFORD, William Timothy (Tim); s of John Halford, of Ripon, and Beatrice Margery Halford (d 1959); *b* 19 Feb 1947; *Educ* Leys Sch Cambridge; *m* 1969, Andrea Rosemary, da of John Henry Lee (d 1968); 3 da (Amy Katharine b 15 Dec 1971, Joanna Alice b 8 Aug 1973, Harriet Louise b 15 Nov 1975); *Career* PR consultancy 1966–75, vice pres of Euro public affairs Occidental Petroleum Corp 1975–84, dir group public affairs Grand Metropolitan plc 1984–92, dir group PR Trafalgar House plc 1992–94, dir group corporate affrs Standard Chartered PLC 1995–; dir College Hill Associates Ltd 1994–; chm Crechendo Ltd 1992–; FIPR, FIMgt; *Recreations* sailing, walking, theatre; *Clubs* HAC; *Style—* Tim Halford, Esq; ✉ Standard Chartered PLC, 1 Aldermanbury Square, London EC2V 7SB

HALIFAX, Archdeacon of; *see:* Inwood, Ven Richard Neil

HALIFAX, 3 Earl of (UK 1944); Sir Charles Edward Peter Neil Wood; 7 Bt (GB 1784); DL (Humberside 1983); also Viscount Halifax (UK 1866), Baron Irwin (UK 1925); s of 2 Earl of Halifax (d 1980); *b* 14 March 1944; *Educ* Eton, ChCh Oxford; *m* 1976, Camilla, da of Charles Frank Johnston Younger, DSO, TD (d 1995), of Gledswood, Melrose, Roxburghshire; 1 s, 1 da (Lady Joanna b 1980); *Heir* s, Lord Irwin, *qv*; *Career* dir Hambros Bank; JP; High Steward of York Minster 1988; KStJ; *Style—* The Rt Hon the Earl of Halifax, DL; ✉ Garrowby, York YO4 1QD

HALL, Adrian Charles; s of Alexander Stephenson Hall (d 1995), of Boarstall Tower, Boarstall, Aylesbury, Bucks, and Edith Mary Partington, *née* Smith (d 1975); *b* 8 June 1945; *Educ* Dragon Sch Oxford, Eton, Mansfield Coll Oxford (MA); *m* 17 Oct 1981, Magdalena Mary, da of Maj Edward Lewis Fiteni (ret RMA), of Morpeth Mansions, Morpeth Terrace, London SW1; 2 s (Richard b 27 June 1985, Edward (twin) b 27 June 1985), 1 da (Mary b 3 Dec 1982); *Career* asst slr Norton Rose (London) 1971–75, assoc barr/slr Borden & Elliot (Toronto) 1975–78, asst slr Allen & Overy 1978–82, sr legal mangr Standard Chartered Bank 1982–86, ptnr Turner Kenneth Brown Slrs 1986–94, asst slr McGrigor Donald Scottish Slrs 1994–96, conslt slr 1996–; memb: Law Soc of England and Wales 1971, International Bar Assoc, Canadian Bar Assoc; memb Worshipful Co of Slrs; *Recreations* historic motor racing and rallying, field game, wall game, cricket, classical music (oboe and cor anglais); *Clubs* MCC, Historic Sports Car, Classic Saloon Car, Eton Ramblers, Raffles, Alfa Romeo Owners'; *Style—* Adrian C Hall, Esq; ✉ 66 Mayford Road, London SW12 8SN (☎ 0181 675 0182)

HALL, Col Alan Edmund Matticot; TD (1975), DL (London 1985); s of Maj Edmund Hall (d 1983), of Helston, Cornwall, and Norah, *née* Carrick (d 1985); *b* 7 Oct 1935; *Educ* Emanuel Sch, Churchers Coll Petersfield, The Grammar Sch Enfield; *m* 8 Feb 1958, Diane Mary, da of Robert William Keyte (d 1969), of Cliftonville; 2 da (Amanda b 1959, Nicola b 1962), 1 s (James b 1968); *Career* Nat Serv 1955–57, Territorial Serv Royal Mil Police 1961–82; OC 44 Parachute Bde Provost Co 1965–67, OC 253 Provost Co 1969–76; appt Hon Col Royal Mil Police TA 1977–82; memb Ctee Greater London TAVRA: exec & fin, gen purpose & fin, HQ; vice chm Army Greater London TAVRA; Hon Col 36 Signal Regt 1990; md: Ind Coope London 1973–77, Ind Coope Ltd 1978–80, Ind Coope East Anglia Ltd 1981–84, J & W Nicholson & Co 1984, Löwenbräu (UK) Ltd 1993–94; dir of UK sales Löwenbräu Lager 1986–93; dir Infomatrix Ltd 1994–; estab Alan Hall Associates 1994; pres The Licensed Victuallers National Homes 1990, pres Soc of Past Chairmen 1991 and 1995, former pres The Percheron Horse Soc, regnl chm The Wishing Well Appeal, pres NE London SSAFA & FHS, pres Co of Gtr London NE Scout Assoc; ctee memb NE London Nat Employers Liaison Ctee; rep DL London Borough of Redbridge; Freeman City of London 1984, Liveryman Worshipful Co of Broderers; FIMgt 1979; *Recreations* shooting, wood working, curry cooking; *Clubs* Wig and Pen; *Style—* Col Alan Hall, TD, DL; ✉ Pippins, Tye Green, Good Easter, Essex (☎ and fax 01245 231280)

HALL, Alan Vivian; s of Walter Hall (d 1963), of Hull, and Vera, *née* Thompson (d 1978); *b* 5 April 1930; *Educ* Hull GS, Univ of Nottingham (BSc); *m* 26 June 1954, June Kathleen, da of William Redvers Beck (d 1977), of Hull; 2 s (Richard Guy b 1958, Jonathan Charles b 1961); *Career* RAF 1948–50; Shell-Mex and BP Ltd 1961–72, investmt mangr Shell International Petroleum Co Ltd 1973–90, memb Bd of Tstees Coll Retirement Equities Fund (USA) 1978–90, princ rep UK First Quadrant Corporation 1990–92, chm First Quadrant Ltd 1992–94; Freeman City of London 1979, memb Ct of Assts Worshipful Co of Actuaries (Master 1993–94); AIA 1958, FSS 1962, AIIMR 1961, FPMI 1978; *Recreations* travel, golf; *Clubs* MCC, City Livery, Burhill Golf; *Style—* Alan Hall, Esq; ✉ 50A Palace Road, East Molesey, Surrey KT8 9DW (☎ 0181 783 1134, fax 0181 783 0958)

HALL, Anthony Arthur; *b* 25 May 1939; *Educ* Sir George Monoux GS Walthamstow; *m* Valerie Christine; 1 s (Graham Anthony), 2 da (Alison Lindsay, Kathryn Lorna); *Career* with Barclays Bank Ltd 1955–70, Barclays Bank DCO (Dominion Colonial & Overseas, now Barclays International) 1965, N M Rothschild (CI) Ltd Guernsey 1971–72, Bank of London and Montreal Nassau Bahamas 1972–73, Italian International Bank (CI) Ltd Guernsey 1974–76; Rea Brothers: md Rea Brothers (Guernsey) Ltd 1976–95 (chm 1995–), also currently dir Rea Brothers Group plc London, dir Rea Brothers (Isle of Man) Ltd; memb Lloyd's; ACIB; *Recreations* flying (multi-engine instrument rating pilot), target pistol shooting, golf, chess, swimming; *Clubs* United (Guernsey); *Style—* Anthony Hall, Esq; ✉ Rea Brothers (Guernsey) Ltd, Commerce House, Les Banques, St Peter Port, Guernsey, Channel Islands (☎ 01481 726014, fax 01481 727645)

HALL, Anthony John; s of late Maj Percy Edwin John Hall, and late Mabel, *née* Webster; *b* 27 Feb 1938; *Educ* Harrogate GS, UCL (MB BS); *m* 19 Aug 1967, Avis Mary, da of Dennis John Harbour (d 1973); 2 s (Simon John Webster b 3 March 1969, Charles b 9 Sept 1970), 1 da (Julia b 26 April 1974); *Career* conslt orthopaedic surgn Chelsea and Westminster Hosp, hon conslt Royal Marsden and Queen Charlotte's Hosps 1973–, regnl advsr in orthopaedics to NW Thames RHA 1987–93; memb: Ct of Examiners RCS 1985–91, Editorial Bd International Orthopaedics 1987, Cncl Br Orthopaedic Assoc 1989–91, Int Soc of the Knee, Int Arthroscopy Assoc; sec gen Société Internationale de Chirurgie Orthopedique et de Traumatologie (SICOT); chm NW Thames Trg Ctee in Orthopaedics, examiner for Univ of London (MB BS and MSc (Orth)), examiner fo the intercollegiate FRCS (Orth); past pres W London Medico Chirurgical Soc; FRCS; *Books* Manual of Fracture Bracing (ed, 1985), Orthopaedic Surgical Approaches (ed with C L Colton, 1991); *Recreations* sailing; *Style—* Mr Anthony Hall; ✉ 4A Durward House, 31 Kensington Court, London W8 5BH (☎ 0171 937 6225); 126 Harley St, London W1N 1AH (☎ 0171 486 1096, fax 0171 224 2520, mobile 0836 520996)

HALL, Anthony Stewart (Tony); s of Albert Hall (d 1970), of Gillingham, Kent, and Dora Rose Ellen, *née* Rundle (d 1987); *b* 26 Oct 1945; *Educ* Gillingham GS, LSE (BSc); *m* 28 Dec 1968, Phoebe Katharine, da of John Leonard Souster; 1 s (Simon Anthony b 19 Dec 1973), 1 da (Katharine Phoebe b 17 May 1976); *Career* lectr in mgmnt and orgn studies Nat Inst for Social Work Trg 1971–73, lectr in social admin Univ of Bristol 1971–78, dir Assoc of Br Adoption and Fostering Agencies 1978–80, dir and sec Br Agencies for Adoption and Fostering 1980–86, dir Central Cncl for Education and Training in Social Work 1986–97; *Books* The Point of Entry: A Study of Client Reception in the Social Services (1974), Part-Time Social Work (with Phoebe Hall, 1980); *Recreations* photography, music, old films, genealogy, sport, stamps; *Style—* Tony Hall, Esq; ✉ 115 Babington Rd, Streatham, London SW16 6AN (☎ 0181 769 1504)

HALL, Anthony William (Tony); s of Donald William Hall, and Mary Joyce, *née* Wallwork; *b* 3 March 1951; *Educ* King Edward's Sch Birmingham, Birkenhead Sch, Keble Coll Oxford (MA); *m* 6 Aug 1977, Cynthia Lesley, da of Arthur Robin Davis; 1 s (William Arthur Henry b 5 June 1989), 1 da (Eleanor Alice Mary b 30 Jan 1986); *Career* BBC TV: news trainee 1973, sr prodr World at One 1978, output ed Newsnight 1980, sr prodr Six O'Clock News 1984, ed Nine O'Clock News 1985, ed News and Elections '87 1987, dir News and Current Affrs 1990– (ed 1987–90), md BBC Bd of Mgmnt 1993–; contrib various pubns; Liveryman Worshipful Co of Painter Stainers 1985, Freeman City of London 1988; FRTS (vice chm); *Books* King Coal - A History of The Miners (1981), Nuclear Politics (1984); *Recreations* opera, church architecture, walking; *Clubs* Reform; *Style—* Tony Hall, Esq; ✉ BBC TV Centre, Wood Lane, London W12 (☎ 0181 576 7312, fax 0181 743 7882)

HALL, Sir Arnold Alexander; kt (1954); s of Robert Alexander Hall (d 1960), of Wirral, Cheshire, and Ellen Elizabeth, *née* Parkinson; *b* 23 April 1915; *Educ* Alsop HS, Clare Coll Cambridge (MA); *m* 29 Nov 1946, (Moira Constance) Dione (decd), da of Rev J A Sykes, of Mugginton, Derby; 3 da (Caroline, Elizabeth, Veronica); m 2, 1986, Iola Mary Nealon; *Career* RAE Farnborough: princ sci offr 1938–45, dir 1951–55; Zararoff prof of aviation Imperial Coll London; Hawker Siddeley Group: dir 1955–86, vice chm 1963–67, md 1967–81, chm 1981–86, chm various subsidiary cos; md Bristol-Siddeley Engines 1959–63; dir: ICI, Lloyds Bank 1966–85, Phoenix Assurance 1969–86, Lloyds Bank UK Management 1979–84, Rolls-Royce 1983–88; memb: Air Registration Bd 1963–73, Electricity Supply Res Cncl 1963–72, Advsy Cncl on Technol 1964–67, Def Industs Cncl 1969–77, Industl Devpt Advsy Bd 1973–75; dep chm Engrg Industs Cncl 1975–78, chm Bd of Tstees Sci Museum 1984–86; pro chllr Univ of Warwick 1964–70, foreign assoc US Nat Acad of Engrg 1976–, chllr Loughborough Univ of Technol 1980–89; Von Baumhauer Medallist of Royal Netherlands Aero Club 1959; Gold Medal: Royal Aeronautical Soc 1962, Br Inst of Mgmnt 1982; Hambro Award for Businessman of the Year 1975, Albert Medal Royal Soc of Art 1983; Freeman City of London 1988, Hon Freeman Worshipful Co of Armourers and Brasiers; hon fell Clare Coll Cambridge 1966, hon fell American Institute of Aero Astronautics, hon memb American Soc of Mech Engrs 1981, Hon FIMechE, Hon ACGI, Hon FIEE, Hon FRAeS, FRS 1953, FEng 1976 (fndr fell); *Recreations* sailing; *Style—* Sir Arnold Hall, FRS, FEng; ✉ Wakehams, Boveney Road, Dorney, nr Windsor, Berks SL4 6QD (☎ 01753 864916)

HALL, Col Austin Patrick; TD (1970); s of Austin Percy Stuart Hall (d 1984), of Harrogate, Yorks, and Lily, *née* Melloy (d 1981); *b* 13 March 1932; *Educ* King James GS Knaresborough, Bradford Coll of Advanced Technol (DipEng); *m* 1957, Dorothy, da of George Alfred Whitfield (d 1961), of Harrogate; 1 s (Richard), 2 da (Sarah, Fiona); *Career* Col Engr and Tport Staff Corps RE (TA); chartered civil engr and builder, chief exec Bovis Civil Engineering 1974–81, dir Bovis Ltd 1977–81, gp md Turriff Corporation plc 1981–84, chm The Bath & Portland Group plc 1984–91; currently chm: E Roland Gurney and Partners Ltd, AHA Construction Services Ltd, Westec Ltd, St Mellion International, Jackson Vending (Holdings) Ltd, Equality Foundaiton Ltd; dir Investors In People (UK) Ltd; govr Dauntsey's Sch; Freeman City of London, Liveryman Worshipful Co of Arbitrators; Hon Col Legion of Frontiersmen of the Cwlth; Eur Ing, CEng, FICE, FCIOB, FCIArb, FRSA; *Recreations* golf, sailing, philately; *Clubs* Army & Navy, St Mellion Golf & Country, City Livery; *Style—* Col Austin Hall, TD; ✉ E Roland Gurney and Partners Ltd, 10 Dunstan Lane, St Mellion, Saltash, Cornwall PL12 6UE (☎ business 01579 351455, home 01579 351051)

HALL, Prof (John) Barrie; s of John Hall (d 1980), and Kathleen, *née* Glentworth (d 1989); *b* 7 Nov 1937; *Educ* Watford GS, St John's Coll Cambridge (MA, PhD); *m* 1, 1962 (m dis 1991), Jennifer Anne, da of Maurice George Biggs; 1 da (Penelope Anne b 7 April 1972); m 2, 1994, Annabel Louise Ritchie; *Career* Bedford Coll Univ of London: asst lectr in Latin 1962–65, lectr in Latin 1965–74, reader in Latin 1974–87; Hildred Carlile prof of Latin Univ of London 1987–94, Hildred Carlile research prof of Latin Univ of London 1994–; *Books* Claudian de Raptu Proserpinae (ed, 1969), Claudii Claudiani Carmina (ed, 1985), Prolegomena to Claudian (1986), John of Salisbury, Metalogicon (ed, 1991), Ovid, Tristia (ed, 1995); *Recreations* walking, opera, watching cricket; *Style—* Prof Barrie Hall; ✉ 2 Windmill Row, Kennington, London SE11 5DW (☎ 0171 735 3486); Department of Classics, Royal Holloway and Bedford New College, University of London, Egham Hill, Surrey TW20 0EX (☎ 01784 443209)

HALL, Sir Basil Brodribb; KCB (1976), MC (1944), TD; s of Alfred Brodribb Hall; *b* 2 Jan 1918; *Educ* Merchant Taylors', London Univ (LLB); *m* 1955, Jean Stafford, da of Edgar Frederick Gowland; 2 s, 1 da; *Career* 12 Lancers France 1940, Maj 27 Lancers UK 1940–44, Italy 1944–45, Inns of Ct TA; admitted slr 1942, entered Treasy Slrs Dept 1946, HM procurator-gen and treasy slr 1975–80, chm Civil Serv Appeal Bd 1981–84 (former dep chm); legal advsr Broadcasting Complaints Cmmn 1981–93, memb Euro Cmmn of Human Rights 1985–93; memb Cncl Nat Army Museum 1981–92, chm gen ctee Athenaeum 1983–86; *Recreations* military history; *Clubs* Athenaeum; *Style—* Sir Basil Hall, KCB, MC, TD; ✉ Woodlands, 16 Danes Way, Oxshott, Surrey KT22 OLX (☎ 01372 842 032)

HALL, Capt Christopher John Pepler; RD (1976, Bar 1986); s of Cdr Harry John Hall, DSO, DSC, RD (d 1994), of Salisbury, Wilts, and Kathleen Gwladys, *née* Pepler (d 1994); *b* 30 Dec 1940; *Educ* Marlborough, Univ of Edinburgh; *m* 8 July 1967, Patricia Valerie (d 1992), da of Capt William Neil Kennedy Mellon Crawford, VRD (d 1978); 5 s (Richard b 1969, Ian b 1970, David b 1972, Alistair b 1976, Stephen (twin) b 1976); *Career* RNR 1960–92; cmmnd 1961, Cdr 1978, Capt 1988, CO HMS Claverhouse Forth Division RNR 1984–89, Capt Mobilisation and Recruiting (Reserves) 1989–92, Hon ADC to HM The Queen 1991–92, Naval Vice Chm Lowland TAVRA 1992–; qualified CA 1966, Cooper Bros Mombasa 1967–68; ptnr: Davidson Smith Wighton and Crawford Edinburgh 1970–78, Turquands Barton Mayhew 1978–80, Ernst & Whinney 1980–82; md: Hall Management Services Ltd 1982–93, CJP Hall chartered accountant 1989–; Scot Episcopal Church: convenor Finance Ctee, diocesan sec and treas Diocese of Argyll and the Isles; *Recreations* sailing, travel, reading, theatre; *Clubs* Caledonian (Edinburgh), RNSA; *Style—* Christopher J P Hall, RD*; ✉ 31 Stirling Rd, Edinburgh EH5 3JA (☎ 0131 552 5991); 25 Dublin St, Edinburgh EH1 3PG (☎ 0131 557 2400, fax 0131 557 3285)

HALL, Christopher Myles; s of late Gilbert Hall, of Gt Cutts Farmhouse, East Hyde, Beds, and Muriel, *née* Filsell; *b* 21 July 1932; *Educ* Berkhamsted, New Coll Oxford (BA); *m* 24 March 1957 (m dis 1980), Jennifer Bevan, da of late Harold Keech, of Woodbury, Devon; 1 s (Gilbert), 1 da (Jessica); *Career* Nat Serv RA 1951–52; reporter and feature writer Daily Express, sub ed and ldr writer Daily Mirror, feature and ldr writer Daily Herald and Sun; special asst (info) to: Min of Overseas Devpt, Miny of Tport 1965–69; chief info offr Miny of Tport 1968, ed The Countryman 1981–; Ramblers' Assoc: sec

1969–74, memb Exec Ctee 1982–, chm 1987–90, pres 1990–93; dir Cncl for Protection of England 1974–80, ed South Eastern Rambler 1974–82; chm Save The Broad St Line Ctee 1963–65, hon sec Chiltern Soc 1965–68, memb Common Land Forum 1984–86; memb NUJ 1959–; *Recreations* country walking; *Style*— Christopher Hall; ✉ The Countryman, Sheep St, Burford OX18 4LH (☎ 01993 82258, fax 01993 822703)

HALL, Christopher Sandford; TD (1970), DL (East Sussex 1986); s of Brig Geoffrey Sandford Hall, TD, DL (d 1975), and Christine, *née* March (d 1993); *b* 9 March 1936; *Educ* Rugby, Trinity Coll Cambridge (MA); *m* 8 July 1967, Susanna Marion, da of Richard Harry Bott, of Benington Lordship, Stevenage, Herts; 3 s (David b 1968, Colin b 1970, Philip b 1973); *Career* Nat Serv 5 Royal Inniskilling Dragoon Gds 1954–56 (TAVR 1956–70); admitted slr 1963, ptnr Cripps Harries Hall Tunbridge Wells 1964– (currently conslt); dir South East Water Ltd; chm: A Burslem & Son Ltd, S of Eng Agric Soc 1984–90; chm Tstees Temple Grove Sch; memb CLA Ctee for Sussex, steward (chm Disciplinary Ctee) Jockey Club 1996–; memb Law Soc; memb Ct of Assts Worshipful Co of Broderers; *Recreations* hunting, racing, farming; *Clubs* Cavalry and Guards'; *Style*— Christopher Hall, Esq, TD, DL; ✉ Great Danegate, Eridge Green, Tunbridge Wells, Kent (☎ 01892 750385); 84 Calverley Rd, Tunbridge Wells, Kent (☎ 01892 515121)

HALL, Colin; s of Arthur Graham Henry Hall, of Enfield, Middlesex, and Winifred Martha, *née* Gray (d 1979); *b* 23 April 1945; *Educ* Stationers' Company's Sch, Univ of Bristol (LLB); *m* 29 Sept 1973, Philippa Margaret, da of Hac Collinson, of Sway, Hants; 4 s (Nicholas Justin b 1976, Oliver Rupert b 1978, Giles Edward b 1981, Rupert Charles (twin) b 1981); *Career* HM Dip Serv 1966–68, admitted slr 1971, ptnr Slaughter and May slrs 1978– (joined 1969); tstee The Tree Register of the British Isles 1992–; *Recreations* sailing, gardening, conservation; *Style*— Colin Hall, Esq; ✉ Slaughter and May, 35 Basinghall St, London EC2V 5DB (☎ 0171 600 1200, fax 0171 600 0289, telex 883486)

HALL, David; CBE (1983), QPM (1977); s of Arthur Thomas Hall (d 1974), of London, and Dorothy May, *née* Bryant (d 1965); *b* 29 Dec 1930; *Educ* Richmond and East Sheen GS for Boys; *m* 14 June 1952, Molly Patricia, da of Roland Knight (d 1981), of London; 2 s (Philip David b 17 Oct 1956, Nicholas Peter b 29 Nov 1958); *Career* joined Met Police 1950, supt 1965; staff offr to Col Eric St Johnstone (chief inspr of Constabulary), asst chief constable Staffordshire 1970 (later dep chief constable), chief constable Humberside 1976–92, ret; memb St John Cncl; Freeman City of London 1987; CIMgt 1987; *Recreations* music (playing the piano), gardening; *Clubs* Sloane; *Style*— David Hall, Esq, CBE, QPM

HALL, David Bernard; s and h of Sir John Bernard Hall, 3 Bt, and his w Delia Mary, da of Lt-Col James Archibald Innes, DSO; *b* 12 May 1961; *Educ* Eton, Univ of York; *Career* clerk Bank of America (Hamburg) 1980, Sales Dept United Biscuits 1985–87, proprietor Sunlite Blinds 1988–; *Recreations* rugby, tennis; *Clubs* Lansdowne; *Style*— David Hall, Esq; ✉ Rose Cottage, Holly Lane, Haughton, Stafford ST18 9JS

HALL, David Christopher; s of Sir Frederick Hall, 2 Bt (d 1949), and bro and h of Sir (Frederick) John Frank Hall, 3 Bt; *b* 30 Dec 1937; *m* 1, 24 Nov 1962 (m dis 1987), Irene, da of William Duncan, of Kincorth, Aberdeen; 1 s (John Christopher b 22 May 1965), 1 da (Olwen Evelyn b 1967); m 2, 31 Dec 1991, Annie Madelaine Renée Olivier, adopted da of late Bottemanne Raould, of Thieusies-Lez Soignies (Mons), Belgium; *Career* joiner/cabinet maker 1962–79, woodwork teacher 1980–, antique restorer 1982–; *Style*— David Hall, Esq

HALL, David (Davey); s of Ralph Hall (d 1975), and Marjorie, *née* Jarvis; *b* 27 June 1951; *Educ* St Aiden's Sch Gateshead; *m* 22 Aug 1970, Janet, da of John Hollows; 2 da (Gillian Amanda b 17 Feb 1971, Carolyn Tracy b 5 Feb 1973); *Career* time served mechanical engr C A Parsons (steam turbine manufacturers); Amalgamated Engineering & Electrical Union (AEEU): memb 1960–, memb Branch Ctee 1979–88, delegate District Ctee 1979–88, Swan Hunter Shipbuilders shop steward/safety rep 1979–88, shop steward 1979–88, convener 1980–88, pension tstee 1982–, national liaison offr Lab Pty 1984–87, district sec Tyneside & Sunderland 1988–96, pres (representing 750,000 members) 1996–; other positions currently held incl: memb IMF Finance Ctee and Br Section, memb Int Metalworkers' Fedn, exec memb Euro Metalworkers' Fedn, memb Nat Cncl for Vocational Qualifications, hon pres Tyneside One Fund For All, hon pres Int Needs for the Disabled Fellowship, signatory Nat Small Business Awards, exec memb Confedn of Shipbuilding and Engrg Unions (chm Nat Engrg Ctee), memb TUC Nat Exec, memb Nat TUC Gen Cncl Exec, memb Inst of Employment Rights, dir Engrg Trg Authy/Engrg Marine Trg Authy, former positions held incl: memb Northern Regnl TUC Exec, dir and pensions tstee Northumberland TEC, dir North East Innovation Centre, sec Tyne and Blyth Confedn of Shipbuilding and Engrg Unions, chm Wear Confedn of Shipbuilding and Engrg Unions, fndr memb Ctee Northern Pensions Resource Gp; *Recreations* DIY, tennis, socialising, gardening, driving, football, TV, ornithology; *Clubs* Forest Hall Social; *Style*— Davey Hall, Esq; ✉ Amalgamated Engineering and Electrical Union, Hayes Court, West Common Road, Bromley, Kent BR2 7AU

HALL, Prof David Michael Baldock; s of Ronald Hall, and Gwen, *née* Baldock; *b* 4 Aug 1945; *Educ* Reigate GS, St George's Med Sch (MB BS); *m* 24 Aug 1966, Susan Marianne, da of Gordon Howard Luck; 2 da (Emma b 1969, Vanessa b 1971); *Career* paediatrician Baragwanath Hosp Johannesburg 1973–76, sr registrar Charing Cross Hosp 1976–78, conslt St George's Hosp 1978–93, prof of community paediatrics Children's Hosp Sheffield 1993–; hon conslt: The Spastics Soc (now Scope) 1982–86, Tadworth Ct 1986–; med advsr Assoc for All Speech-Impaired Children 1981–86, academic vice pres Br Paediatric Assoc 1994–, fndr memb Children's Head Injury Tst; memb BPA, MRCP 1972, FRCP 1986; *Books* Health for all Children (1989, 3 edn 1996), Child Surveillance Handbook (1995), The Child with a Disability (1996); *Recreations* travel, reading, music, plumbing; *Style*— Prof David Hall; ✉ Storrs House Farm, Storrs Lane, Sheffield, South Yorkshire S6 6GY (☎ 0114 285 3177, fax 0114 285 4054); Children's Hospital, Sheffield S10 2TH (☎ 0114 271 7344)

HALL, David Nicholas; s of William Noel Hall (d 1981), of London, and Louisa Augusta, *née* Palma; *b* 19 Nov 1933; *Educ* London Choir Sch, Carlisle & Gregson (Jimmy's), RMA Sandhurst; *m* 28 Dec 1963, Harriet Mary Arden, da of William Lloyd McElwee, MC, TD (d 1978); 3 da (Susannah b 25 Feb 1965, Phillie b 13 April 1967, Christina b 17 Oct 1969); *Career* active serv Korean War 1953, cmmnd RE, served Cyprus, Congo (Zaire) and Ghana, instr RMA Sandhurst, Staff Coll, staff appt with Engr-in-Chief, Sqdn Cdr Scotland and Gibraltar, Kirkcudbright, CO RE Depot 1974–77, technical staff appt 1977–79, Record Office RE 1979–81, ret Lt-Col 1981; author of various pubns on land navigation and expeditions; dir Fndn for Science and Technol 1981–, liaison offr Learned Socs 1981–; chm: Palestine Exploration Fund 1990–95 (hon treas 1983–90), Expeditions & Research Ctee RGS 1984–91 (memb 1991–95, hon foreign sec 1973–83, vice pres 1984–87 and 1991–94, hon treas RGS 1996–); first pres The Desert Dining Club 1980–, chm Young Explorers' Tst Screening 1983–93; memb Cncl Br Sch of Archaeology in Jerusalem 1992–94; tstee: Frederick Soddy Tst 1985–, Young Explorers' Tst 1990–94; organiser and ldr: Br Expedition to Aïr Mountains (Southern Sahara) 1970, various camel journeys and scientific expeditions to arid regions; RMCS Heilbron Prize 1966, RGS Ness Award 1972; hon fell RGS 1992; FICS, FRGS; *Books* contrib: Expeditions (1977), Tales from the Map Room (1993); *Recreations* exploration, fishing, wine, music; *Clubs* Athenaeum; *Style*— David Hall, Esq; ✉ 3 Spencer Rd, London SW18 2SP (☎ 0171 228 8476); Foundation for Science and Technology, Buckingham Court, 78 Buckingham Gate, London SW1E 6PE

HALL, Col David Stevenson; CBE (1993), TD (1971); s of late Robert and Maude Hall; *b* 29 March 1938; *Educ* Scarborough Coll; *m* 1962, Marion Esmé, *née* Blundstone; 1 s, 1 da; *Career* Nat Serv RAOC 1956–58; RAOC (TA) 1958–93: ADC (TA) 1986–91, Col RAOC TA 1985–89, TA Col Logistics MOD/UK Land Forces 1989–93, Hon Col RAOC Specialist Units 1991–93; Combat Servs Support Gp Royal Logistics Corps Vols 1995–; md UDS Tailoring Ltd 1979–81, chm and md Collier Holdings plc 1982–85, chm Meadowcroft Management Ltd 1985–; non-exec dir: Sharp and Law plc 1989–90, Toye plc 1994–95; chm United Leeds Teaching Hosps NHS Tst 1995–; tstee RAOC Charitable Tst 1993–; Freeman City of London 1993; *Recreations* cricket, reading; *Clubs* Army and Navy, MCC; *Style*— Col David Hall, CBE, TD; ✉ Meadowcroft, Elmwood Lane, Barwick in Elmet, Leeds LS15 4JX (☎ 0113 281 3587); United Leeds Teaching Hospitals NHS Trust, Trust HQ, Leeds General Infirmary, Great George Street, Leeds LS1 3EX (☎ 0113 231 6446, fax 0113 231 6336)

HALL, Prof Denis R; *b* 1 Aug 1942, Cardiff; *Educ* Univ of Manchester (BSc), Med Coll St Bartholomew's Hosp London (MPhil), Case Western Reserve Univ Cleveland Ohio (PhD); *m*; 2 c; *Career* graduate asst/postdoctoral fell Dept of Electrical Engrg Case Western Reserve Univ Cleveland Ohio 1967–71, postdoctoral research fell (Nat Acad of Scis Award) NASA Goddard Space Flight Center Greenbelt Maryland 1971–72, sr research scientist Avco Everett Research Lab Boston Mass 1972–74 (summer visiting research scientist 1986 and 1988), princ scientific offr Royal Signals and Radar Estab MOD 1974–79, sr lectr/reader in applied laser physics Dept of Applied Physics Univ of Hull 1979–87, prof of optoelectronics Dept of Physics Heriot-Watt Univ Edinburgh 1987–; pt/t GS teacher in physics and physical educn 1965–67; conslt Systems Electronics Inc Cleveland Ohio 1969–74; MOD research contract monitor (industl and univ contracts) 1974–79, MOD del on Int Tech Cooperation Panel (lasers and IR systems) 1975–79, chief project scientist UK Satellite Laser Ranging Facility Royal Greenwich Observatory 1979–83; dir Laser Applications Ltd Hull 1980–86; memb: Satellite Laser Ranging Steering Ctee Astronomy, Space and Radio Bd SERC 1979–84, Quantum Electronics Bd Euro Physical Soc 1988–94, E13 Gp Ctee IEE 1993–; chm Quantum Electronics Gp Ctee Inst of Physics 1991–94 (memb 1977–81 and 1986–89); memb: Sigma Xi (elected) 1971, IEEE-LEOS 1991, Optical Soc of America; CEng, FInstP 1985 (MInstP 1974), FIEE 1986 (MIEE 1985), FRSE 1991; *Publications* author/jt author of numerous pubns in learned jls and of invited and contributed papers; *Style*— Prof Denis R Hall, FRSE; ✉ Department of Physics, Heriot-Watt University, Riccarton, Edinburgh EH14 4AS (☎ 0131 451 3081)

HALL, Derek Gordon; s of Gordon Ivor Hall (d 1986), of Dinas Powys, S Glam, and May Magaretta, *née* Horsey; *b* 17 April 1944; *Educ* Penarth Co Sch, UCL (BSc, PhD); *m* 1, 1967 (m dis 1971), Pauline Margaret Vivienne, *née* Coombe; 1 da (Samantha Kate b 1969); m 2, 6 Oct 1979, Susan Olga, da of Eric and Olga Victoria May Eaton, of Cheltenham, Glos; 2 s (Guy Sebastian b 1968, Daniel Gordon b 1973); *Career* with Arthur Andersen Mgmnt Consultants 1970–76; J P Morgan: joined 1976, vice pres 1978–87, md 1987–; *Style*— Derek Hall, Esq; ✉ Morgan Guaranty Trust Company, 60 Victoria Embankment, London EC4Y (direct ☎ 0171 325 8922)

HALL, Dinny; da of David Alexander Hall, of Shantock House, Bovingdon, Hertfordshire, and Susan Anne, *née* Martyr; *b* 28 April 1959; *Educ* Bourne Valley Comp Herts, Herts Sch of Art and Design St Albans, Central Sch of Art and Design (BA); *Career* jewellery designer; set up own business in Soho London 1983, launched first range of jewellery using gold and precious stones 1990, opened first shop Notting Hill 1992, second shop Chelsea 1995; clients incl Harvey Nichols, Browns, Harrods and many other prestigious stores worldwide; collections featured since 1985 in magazines incl: Vogue, Harpers & Queen, Elle, Sunday Times, Sunday Telegraph; Br Accessory Designer of the Year 1989; *Books* Creative Jewellery (1986); *Recreations* cooking, travelling, walking; *Clubs* Groucho's; *Style*— Ms Dinny Hall; ✉ Dinny Hall Ltd, 200 Westbourne Grove, London W11 2RH (☎ 0171 792 3913, fax 0171 792 8322)

HALL, Air Marshal Sir Donald Percy; KCB (1984, CB 1981), CBE (1975), AFC (1963); s of William Reckerby Hall, and Elsie Hall; *b* 11 Nov 1930; *Educ* Hull GS, RAF Coll; *m* 1953, Joyce, *née* Warburton; 2 da; *Career* AOC 38 Gp RAF 1980–83, dep CDS 1983–86, ret 1986; chm Marconi Def Systems 1987, dep chm GEC Marconi 1990–95; Warden Guild of Air Pilots and Air Navigators; FRAeS; *Style*— Air Marshal Sir Donald Hall, KCB, CBE, AFC

HALL, Sir Douglas Basil; 14 Bt (NS 1687), of Dunglass, Haddingtonshire; KCMG (1959, CMG 1958), JP (Devon 1964); s of Capt Lionel Erskine Hall (d 1948); suc bro Sir Neville Reynolds Hall, 13 Bt, 1978; *b* 1 Feb 1909; *Educ* Radley, Keble Coll Oxford (MA); *m* 25 April 1933, Rachel Marion (d 1990), da of late Maj Ernest Gartside-Tippinge, RA; 1 s (John Douglas Hoste b 1945) and 1 s decd, 2 da (Marion (Mrs John F Fuller-Sessions) b 1940, Ruth (Mrs Anthony B Cragg) b 1942); *Heir* s, John Douglas Hoste Hall, *qv*; *Career* entered HMOCS as a cadet N Rhodesia 1930, dist offr 1932–50, sr dist offr 1950–53, provincial cmmr 1953, admin sec 1955–56, sec for Native Affrs 1956, govr and C-in-C of Somaliland Protectorate 1959–60; memb Police Authy for Devon and Cornwall 1971–79; *Style*— Sir Douglas Hall, Bt, KCMG, JP; ✉ Barnford, Ringmore, nr Kingsbridge, Devon (☎ 01548 810401)

HALL, Sir Ernest; kt (1993), OBE (1986), DL (W Yorks 1991); s of Ernest Hall, and Mary Elizabeth Hall; *b* 19 March 1930; *Educ* Bolton Co GS, Royal Manchester Coll of Music (ARMCM, Royal Patron's Fund Prize for composition); *m* 1, 1951, June, *née* Annable (d 1994); 2 s (Jeremy b 1962, Tom b 1967), 2 da (Virginia b 1959, Vivian b 1961); m 2, 1975, Sarah, *née* Wellby; 1 s (Leopold b 1984); *Career* pianist and composer 1954–; textile manufacturer 1961–71; fndr Dean Clough enterprise educn and arts centre Halifax 1983; dep chm Eureka! Children's Museum 1989–, tstee Yorks Sculpture Park 1989–, pres Yorks Business in the Arts 1990–, chm Yorks and Humberside Arts 1991–, vice pres RSA 1995–; memb: President's Ctee Business in the Community 1990–, Arts Cncl of England 1990–, Design Cncl 1994–, Northern Ballet Theatre 1994–; Hon DUniv Univ of York 1986, Hon DLitt Univ of Bradford 1990, Hon DUniv Leeds Metropolitan Univ 1996, Hon LLD Univ of Leeds 1996; Hon Dr of Arts: CNAA 1991, Univ of Humberside 1995; hon fell: Huddersfield Univ 1989, Leeds Metropolitan Univ 1991, Univ of Central Lancashire 1996; Albert Medal (RSA) 1994; *Recreations* equestrianism, gardening, art collecting, theatre, languages; *Style*— Sir Ernest Hall, OBE, DL; ✉ Dean Clough, Halifax, W Yorkshire HX3 5AX (☎ 01422 250250, fax 01422 323250)

HALL, Rear Adm Geoffrey Penrose Dickinson; CB (1973), DSC (1943), DL (1982); s of Maj Arthur Kenrick Dickinson Hall (d 1945), of Legbourne Abbey, Louth, Lincs, and Phyllis Mary, *née* Penrose (d 1969); maternal gf Brig-Gen Cooper Penrose, CB, CMG, cmd RE Southern Cmd; maternal ggf Thomas Greene DD was sec of the Gen Synod of the Church of Ireland for 40 years; ggf Thomas Dickinson Hall was High Sheriff of Nottingham & Leicester, gf Frederick Dickinson Hall was rector of Manby and rural dean of Louthesk; *b* 19 July 1916; *Educ* Haileybury; *m* 1945, Mary Ogilvie, da of Dr Henry George Carlisle (d 1954), of Ardlair, Heswall, Cheshire; 2 s (Nicholas, Adrian), 1 da (Virginia); *Career* Naval Offr 1934–75, cmd six of HM ships 1945–67, Hydrographer of the Navy 1971–75, served in Atlantic, Iceland, W Africa, India, Burma & Far East 1939–45, hydrographic surveying in N and S Atlantic, Antarctic, Indian Ocean and NZ 1938–67, combined ops 1943–45, various appts within Admty and MOD 1954–75; *Recreations* walking, golf, croquet, dogs; *Clubs* Naval and Military, Royal Navy, Louth;

Style— Rear Adm Geoffrey Hall, CB, DSC, DL; ✉ Manby House, Manby, Louth, Lincs LN11 8UF (☎ 01507 327777)

HALL, Prof Geoffrey Ronald; CBE (1985); s of Thomas Harold Hall, JP (d 1974), of Douglas, IOM; *b* 18 May 1928; *Educ* Douglas HS, Univ of Manchester (BSc); *m* 1950, Elizabeth, da of Thomas Day Sheldon (d 1951), of Manchester; 3 c; *Career* Colombo plan expert India 1956–58; prof (formerly reader) of nuclear technol Imperial Coll 1958–70, dir and prof Brighton Poly 1970–90; higher educn conslt; pres: Br Nuclear Energy Soc 1970–71, Inst of Fuel 1976; memb: Engrg Cncl 1981–86, SERC 1982–86, Nat Cncl for Vocational Qualification 1986–89; hon fell Brighton Poly 1991, FEng 1976 (fndr fell); *Recreations* travel, golf; *Style—* Prof Geoffrey Hall, CBE, FEng; ✉ 23 Firsdown Rd, High Salvington, Worthing BN13 3BG

HALL, Prof George Martin; s of George Vincent Hall (d 1971), of Bridlington, Yorks, and Dora Hortensia, *née* Beauchamp; *b* 14 May 1944; *Educ* King Edward VI Sch Lichfield, UCL (MB BS, PhD); *m* 9 Jan 1964, Marion Edith, da of Frank Gordon Burgin, MBE, of Gt Missenden, Bucks; 1 da (Katherine Elizabeth b 1965); *Career* prof of clinical anaesthesia Royal Postgrad Med Sch Univ of London 1989–92 (sr lectr 1976–85, reader 1985–89), fndn prof of anaesthesia St George's Hosp Med Sch Univ of London 1992–; chm to British Journal of Anaesthesia; contrib research papers on anaesthesia; *Recreations* running, steam locomotives; *Clubs* Farmers'; *Style—* Prof George Hall; ✉ Department of Anaesthetics, St George's Hospital Medical School, London SW17 0RE (☎ 0181 725 2615)

HALL, Janice Elizabeth (Jan); OBE (1996); da of John Brian Hall, and Jean, *née* Chadwick; *b* 1 June 1957; *Educ* Rutland Girls' HS, St Anne's Coll Oxford (MA); *m* David Winston Costain; 1 s (Theo Costain b 15 Feb 1996); *Career* mktg mangr Paints Div ICI 1979–83, chm and chief exec Coley Porter Bell 1983–94, Euro chief exec The GGT Group plc 1994–; non-exec dir: Allied Maples Group Ltd 1988–91, BSM Group plc 1992–, First Choice Holidays plc 1994–, London First 1993–95; teaching assoc Ashridge Management Coll 1986–; chm: Design Business Assoc 1988–90, Ashridge Coll Assoc 1990–92, DTI BOTB Small Firms Ctee 1992–96; memb: DTI Small Firms Advsy Gp on the Single Market 1988–90, Southern Bd BR 1990–93, Forum UK 1990–, FO/DTI Br Overseas Trade Bd 1993–96, Dept of Employment TEC Assessors Ctee 1993–95, Advsy Bd Warwick Business Sch 1993–, Cmmn on Public Policy and Br Business 1995–; memb Cncl: CSD 1988–91, IOD 1991–; hon sec and treas Mktg Gp of GB 1991–, vice pres Strategic Planning Soc 1995–; FCSD 1989, FRSA 1990; *Recreations* travel, food, opera; *Style—* Ms Jan Hall, OBE; ✉ 64 Courtenay St, London SE11 5PQ (☎ 0171 582 3541); The GGT Group plc, 82 Dean Street, London W1V 5AB (☎ 0171 437 0434)

HALL, Jerry Faye; da of John P Hall (d 1977), and Marjore, *née* Sheffield; *b* 2 July 1956; *m* 21 Nov 1991, Michael Philip (Mick) Jagger, *qv*; 1 s (James b 28 Aug 1985), 2 da (Elizabeth b 2 March 1984, Georgia b 12 Jan 1991); *Career* actress and model 1973–; *Theatre* Bus Stop (New Jersey USA 1988, West End 1990); *Television* numerous appearances incl: Merv Griffin 1979, Good Day Show - Boston 1982, The Morning Show 1983 and 1985, Live at Five 1984 and 1985, Andy Warhol Television (host) 1985, Independent Network News 1985, ABC La Television 1985, CBS News Nightwatch 1985, CBS News - Jim Brady 1985, Cable News Network Showbiz 1985, PM Magazine 1985, Entertainment Tonight 1985, Good Morning America 1985, The Phil Donahue Show 1985, The David Letterman Show 1985, MTV Music News 1986, She's With Me (NBC pilot) 1986, Entertainment Tonight 1986, Saturday Night Live (host) 1986, Lifestyles of the Rich and Famous 1986, The Last Resort with Jonathan Ross 1987, The Dame Edna Experience 1987, Wogan 1988, Hysteria II 1989, Clive James on the 80's (co-presenter) 1989, 01 For London 1990, French and Saunders 1990, Bejewelled (TVS/Disney) 1990, The Detectives 1992, Cleudo (Granada) 1993, Noel's House Party 1994; *Radio* The Betty Grable Story (Radio 3) 1995; *Video* Let's Stick Together (Bryan Ferry) 1976, The Price of Love (Bryan Ferry) 1977; *Films* St Germain Des Pres Apres Le Guerre 1974, Willie and Phil 1978, Urban Cowboy 1979, Dream Cowboy 1980, Jack and the Beanstalk 1982, The Emperor and the Nightingale 1982, Running out of Luck 1984, Galileus Mouse 1987, Batman 1988, Princess Caraboo 1994, Savage Hearts 1994, Vampire in Brooklin 1994, Diana and Me 1996, RPM 1996; *Books* Tall Tales (1985); *Style—* Ms Jerry Hall; ✉ c/o ICM Ltd, Oxford House, 76 Oxford Street, London W1N 0AX (☎ 0171 636 6565, fax 0171 323 0101); c/o Models One, Omega House, 471–473 Kings Road, London SW10 0LU (☎ 0171 351 1195, 0171 351 6033, fax 0171 376 5821)

HALL, Joan Valerie; CBE (1990); da of Robert Hall (d 1979), and Winifred Emily, *née* Umbers (d 1991); *b* 31 Aug 1935; *Educ* Queen Margaret's Sch Escrick nr York, Ashridge House of Citizenship; *Career* Parly candidate (Cons) Barnsley 1964 and 1966, MP (Cons) Keighley 1970–74; PPS to Min of State MAFF 1972–74; memb Cncl: Univ Coll Buckingham 1977–83, Central Tport Users' Consultative Ctee 1981–86; chm Sudan Studies Soc of the UK 1989–92; *Style—* Miss Joan Hall, CBE; ✉ 7 Greenland, High Hoyland, Barnsley, South Yorks S75 4AZ (☎ 01226 380117)

HALL, John Anthony Sanderson; DFC (1944, Bar 1945), QC (1967); s of Rt Hon William Glenvil Hall, MP (d 1962), of Heath Mansions, Hampstead, and Rachel Ida, *née* Sanderson (d 1950); *b* 25 Dec 1921; *Educ* Leighton Park Sch, Trinity Hall Cambridge (MA); *m* 1, 27 Oct 1945 (m dis 1974), Nora Ella, da of Arthur Ulrich Crowe (d 1941); 1 s (Jonathan Mark Glenvil b 1950), 2 da (Sally Anne b 1946, Pamela Mary b 1952); m 2, 10 July 1976, Elizabeth Mary, da of E R T Wells (d 1993), and widow of late Alan Maynard; *Career* called to the Bar Inner Temple 1948, bencher Inner Temple 1975, dep chm Hants QS 1967–72, recorder Swindon 1971, recorder of the Crown Ct 1972–78; memb: Gen Cncl of the Bar 1964–68 and 1970–74, Senate Inns of Ct 1966–68 and 1970–74; chm UK Delgn Consultative Ctee of European Bars and Laws Socs 1978–79, memb Foreign Compensation Cmmn 1983–91; dir City Disputes Panel 1994–, chm Panel of Arbitrators SFA 1994–; govr St Catherine's Sch Guildford 1967–88; actg deemster Isle of Man 1991–; FCIArb 1982; *Recreations* fly fishing, book collecting; *Clubs* RAF; *Style—* John Hall, Esq, DFC, QC; ✉ Swallows, Blewbury, Oxon OX11 9PY (☎ and fax 01235 850511)

HALL, Sir John Bernard; 3 Bt (UK 1919), of Burton Park, Sussex; s of Lt-Col Sir Douglas Montgomery Bernard Hall, 2 Bt, DSO (d 1962), and his 2 w, Nancie Walton (who m 2, 1962, Col Peter J Bradford, DSO, MC, TD (d 1990)), o da of Col John Edward Mellor, CB, JP, DL; *b* 20 March 1932; *Educ* Eton, Trinity Coll Oxford (MA); *m* 19 Oct 1957, Delia Mary, da of Lt-Col James Archibald Innes, DSO (d 1949); 1 s (David Bernard b 1961), 2 da (Caroline Evelyn (Mrs Martin Dixon-Ward) b 1959, Julia Nancy b 1965); *Heir* s, David Bernard Hall b 12 May 1961; *Career* Lt Royal Fus RARO; joined J Henry Schröder & Co (later J Henry Schroder Wagg & Co Ltd) 1955 (dir 1967–73), dir Bank of America Int 1974–82, vice pres Bank of America NT & SA 1982–90, md European Brazilian Bank 1983–89; The Nikko Bank (UK) plc: md 1990–92, chm 1992–95, advsr to the Bd 1995–96; former chm: Anglo-Colombian Soc, Assoc of British Consortium Banks; Liveryman and memb Ct of Assts Worshipful Co of Clothworkers (Warden 1987–89), govr The Clothworkers' Fndn (chm Tst and Grants Ctee); memb: St Alban's Diocesan Synod and Diocesan Bd of Fin, Bishop's Stortford Deanery Synod, Albury PCC; FCIB 1976, FRGS 1988, FRSA 1989; *Recreations* travel, fishing; *Clubs* Boodle's, Lansdowne, Bankers'; *Style—* Sir John B Hall, Bt; ✉ Penrose House, Patmore Heath, Albury, Ware, Herts SG11 2LT (☎ 01279 771 255); Inver House, Lochinver, Lairg, Sutherland IV27 4LJ (☎ 01571 844349)

HALL, John Douglas Hoste; s and h of Sir Douglas Basil Hall, 14 Bt, KCMG, *qv*, of Barnford, Ringmore, Kingsbridge, Devon; *b* 7 Jan 1945; *Educ* Dover Coll, Gonville and Caius Coll Cambridge (BA), Univ of Southampton (Cert Ed); *m* 1972, Angela Margaret, da of George Keys, of 2 Barnsfield Lane, Buckfastleigh, S Devon; 2 s (Thomas James b 10 Dec 1975, Bernard Neville b 19 Feb 1979); *Career* poet; vice princ (academic) Dartington Coll of Art; *Books of Poetry* Between the Cities, Days, Malo-Lactic Ferment, Couch Grass, Repressed Intimations, Meaning Insomnia; *Style—* John Hall, Esq; ✉ Brook Mill, Buckfastleigh, S Devon TQ11 0HL (☎ 01364 642985)

HALL, Sir (Frederick) John Frank; 3 Bt (UK 1923), of Grafham, Co Surrey; s of Sir Frederick Henry Hall, 2 Bt (d 1949), and Olwen Irene, *née* Collis, who subsequently m Arthur Borland Porteous; *b* 14 Aug 1931; *Educ* Bryanston; *m* 1, 3 April 1956 (m dis 1960), Felicity Anne, da of late Edward Rivers-Fletcher, of Norwich; m 2, 3 June 1961 (m dis 1967), Patricia Ann, da of Douglas Atkinson (d 1973), of Carlisle; 2 da (Nicola Jane b 1962, Samantha Mary b 1965); re-m 9 Nov 1967, his 1 w, Felicity Anne; 2 da (Antonia Anne b 1970, Victoria Joy b 1973); *Heir* bro, David Christopher Hall b 30 Dec 1937; *Career* personnel mangr Universal Pattern & Precision Engineering Co Ltd 1955–59, personnel offr The Nestlé Co Ltd 1959–63, personnel mangr Johnson Wax Ltd 1963–65; The Nestlé Co Ltd: trg and mgmnt devpt mangr Nestlé UK Head Office 1965–67, gp personnel mangr Findus Ltd 1967–69; sr mangr McLintock Mann & Whinney Murray 1969–76, dir Thomson McLintock Associates 1976–87, fndr and head KPMG Career Consultancy Services 1983–93, ptnr KPMG Peat Marwick 1987–93; dir Roffey Park Inst 1978–90 (vice chm 1983–85, chm 1985–87); *Recreations* music, collecting antique gramophone records, magic (memb The Magic Circle); *Style—* Sir John Hall, Bt; ✉ Carradale, 29 Embercourt Rd, Thames Ditton, Surrey KT7 0LH (☎ 0181 398 2801)

HALL, John Michael; s of Ernest Smith Hall (d 1964), of Aston Cantlow, Warwickshire, and Joyce Kathleen, *née* Butler; *b* 30 Jan 1936; *Educ* Bloxham Sch; *m* 20 Oct 1962, Angela Phyllis, da of Ralph Dixon Coates, MBE, of Milford on Sea, Hampshire; 4 da (Katherine b and d 23 Jan 1964, Sophie b 6 Feb 1965, Lucy b 11 Nov 1967, Charlotte b 14 Nov 1969); *Career* Nat Serv 2 Lt RAPC 1959–61; CA; chm Baker Tilly 1995–96; non-exec dir Marley plc; govr St Martin's Sch Solihull; FCA 1959; *Recreations* vintage and classic cars; *Style—* John M Hall, Esq; ✉ Baker Tilly, Scottish Life House, 154 Great Charles St, Birmingham B3 3HN (☎ 0121 233 2323, fax 0121 236 9720, car 0860 952330)

HALL, John Peirs; s of Dr Robert Noel Hall, of Park Farm House, Upper Harlestone, Northampton, and Doreen Cecilia, *née* Russell; *b* 26 June 1940; *Educ* Dragon Sch Oxford, Stowe; *m* 1965, Sarah Gillian, da of Gerard Thorpe Page; 4 s (James b 6 April 1966, Charles b 6 May 1968, Freddie b 12 May 1977, Thomas b 1 April 1985); *Career* trainee Read Hurst & Brown Stockbrokers 1958–65; Wontner Dolphin & Francis (became Brewin Dolphin 1974 and then Brewin Holdings PLC 1994): joined 1965, md 1987–; Freeman City of London 1970, memb Ct of Assts Worshipful Co of Merchant Taylors; memb IMRO, MSI (memb Stock Exchange 1965); *Recreations* breeding British White cattle, sailing Dragons, golf; *Clubs* City of London, Royal Yacht Squadron, Royal Torbay Yacht, Island Sailing, Huntecombe Golf; *Style—* John Hall, Esq; ✉ Brewin Dolphin Holdings PLC, 5 Giltspur St, London EC1A 9BD (☎ 0171 248 4400, fax 0171 236 2034)

HALL, Maj Gen Jonathan Michael Francis Cooper; OBE (1987); s of (Charles) Richard Hall (d 1982), of Horsham, and Rosemary Elizabeth, *née* Beckwith (d 1979); *b* 10 Aug 1944; *Educ* Taunton Sch, RMA Sandhurst; *m* 5 Oct 1968, Sarah Linda, da of Laurence Whitmarsh Hudson, of Cheltenham; 2 da (Candida Sarah b 1971, Rachel Katharine b 1973); *Career* cmmnd 3 Carabiniers 1965, Staff Coll Camberley 1977, Cmd Offr Royal Scots Dragoon Guards 1984–86, Higher Cmd and Staff Course 1988, Cmd 12 Armoured Bde 1989–90, Royal Coll of Def Studies 1991, Dep Mil Sec (A) 1992–94, Dir RAC 1994–95, GOC Scotland and Govr Edinburgh Castle 1995–; Col Cmdt: Scottish Div 1995–, Royal Army Vet Corps 1995–; HM's Cmmr Queen Victoria Sch Dunblane 1995–; memb Cavalry and Guards' Gen Ctee 1981–; *Recreations* country pursuits, tennis, skiing, travel; *Clubs* Cavalry & Guards', New (Edinburgh), Royal Scottish Automobile, Caledonian; *Style—* Maj Gen Jonathan Hall, OBE; ✉ c/o Home Headquarters, The Royal Scots Dragoon Guards, The Castle, Edinburgh EH1 2YT

HALL, His Hon Judge Julian; s of Alexander Stephenson Hall (d 1995), of Bucks, and Edith Mary Partington, *née* Smith (d 1975); *b* 13 Jan 1939; *Educ* Eton, Ch Ch Oxford (MA), Trinity Coll Dublin (LLB); *m* 1, 1968 (m dis 1988), Margaret Rosalind; 1 s (Benjamin b 1971), 1 da (Rebecca b 1969); m 2, 11 March 1989, Ingrid; *Career* industl res chemist 1961–63; called to the Bar Gray's Inn 1966; practising Northern Circuit 1966–86, recorder Crown Court 1982–86, prosecuting counsel Inland Revenue Northern Circuit 1985–86, circuit judge (Midland and Oxford Circuit) 1986–; ARCM; *Recreations* making music; *Clubs* Buxton Musical Soc, Music Camp; *Style—* His Hon Judge Julian Hall; ✉ Crown and County Courts, 85–87 Ladys Lane, Northampton NN1 3HQ (☎ 01604 250131)

HALL, Prof Laurance David; s of Daniel William Hall, of Stevenage, and Elsie, *née* Beard; *b* 18 March 1938; *Educ* Leyton Co HS, Univ of Bristol (BSc, PhD); *m* 1 Aug 1962, (Winifred) Margaret, da of Henry Arthur Golding; 2 s (Dominic Courtney St John b 15 Dec 1971, Brecken Guy D'Arcy (twin) b 15 Dec 1971), 2 da (Gwendolen Judith Virginia b 21 May 1963, Juliet Katharine Olivia b 1 July 1964); *Career* post doctoral fell Univ of Ottawa 1962–63, prof of chemistry Univ of Br Columbia Vancouver Canada 1963–84, first holder Herchel Smith prof of medicinal chem Univ of Cambridge Clinical Sch 1984–; FCIC 1974, FRS (Canada) 1982, CChem, FRSC 1985; *Recreations* wine-making, skiing, scientific research; *Clubs* Emmanuel Coll Cambridge; *Style—* Prof Laurance Hall; ✉ Herchel Smith Laboratory for Medicinal Chemistry, University Forvie Site, Cambridge CB2 2PZ (☎ 01223 336 805, fax 01223 336748)

HALL, Mervyn Douglas; s of Matthew Douglas Hall (d 1965), of Windsor, and Maisie Eileen, *née* Allen; *b* 4 Jan 1949; *Educ* Windsor GS; *m* 14 April 1984, Valerie, *née* Nealson; 1 s (Nicholas James b 19 June 1974), 1 da (Suzannah Elizabeth b 27 July 1977); *Career* reporter: Windsor, Slough and Eton Express 1965–69, Shropshire Star 1969–70, Evening Post Luton 1970–73; sports ed LBC 1973–78; ITN: sports ed 1978–84, news ed 1984–89, ed Radio 1989–90, chief ed IRN 1990–93, sales dir 1993–95; commercial dir Reuters Television 1995–; memb: RTS, Radio Acad; *Recreations* golf, reading, food and wine, theatre; *Style—* Mervyn Hall, Esq; ✉ Reuters Television, 85 Fleet Street, London EC4P 4AJ

HALL, (Haddon) Michael; s of William Haddon Hall (d 1972), and Mildred, *née* Brown, of London; *b* 28 June 1945; *Educ* Aristotle Sch; *m* 1, 24 Jan 1970 (m dis 1976), Kathleen Mary, da of William Suggitt; m 2, 25 April 1981 (m dis 1986), Suzanne Marie, da of Ronald M Bell; m 3, 11 May 1989, Victoria Ann, da of Bryan John Vallas (d 1984); 1 s (Stephen b 6 Aug 1992); *Career* CA Barsham Nixon & Hamilton 1969–72 (joined as articled clerk 1961), qualified sr Stoy Hayward & Co 1972–74; Boty Cox Crawford & Ridley (merged Edward Moore & Sons 1975, which merged Rowland Nevill 1985 to become Moores Rowland): audit mangr 1974–79, ptnr 1979–, equity ptnr 1983–; non-exec dir Croydon Business Venture Ltd 1990–96; FCA (1979, ACA 1969); *Recreations* applied philosophy, shooting, reading science fiction, collecting collectables; *Clubs* Historical Breechloading Small-Arms Assoc (hon treas); *Style—* Michael Hall, Esq; ✉ Moores Rowland, 6 Bedford Park, Croydon, Surrey CR0 2AP (☎ 0181 686 9281, fax 0181 760 0411, car 0378 406598)

HALL, Prof Michael Anthony; s of Frederick Lancelot Hall (d 1982), and Eva, *née* Bridgewood-Jeffes (d 1992); *b* 7 July 1940; *Educ* Rutherford GS, Imperial Coll London (BSc, PhD, DSc); *m* 25 Aug 1964, Gillian, da of Frederick Barrone (d 1975); 1 da (Sara Jayne Barrone b 1 June 1969); *Career* Univ of California Riverside 1964–67, Scottish

Hort Res Inst 1967–68, dir and prof Inst of Biological Sciences Univ Coll of Wales Aberystwyth 1968–; memb Malaysian Rubber Research Devpt Bd; 150 pubns in professional jls; FIBiol, FRSA, ARCS; *Books* Plant Structure, Function and Adaptation (1976); *Recreations* skiing, music; *Style*— Prof Michael Hall; ✉ Glascoed, Piercefield Lane, Penparcau, Aberstwyth, Dyfed SY23 1RX (☎ 01970 612465); Institute of Biological Sciences, University College of Wales, Aberystwyth, Dyfed SY23 3DA (☎ 01970 622313, telex 83147 VIAOR G Attn UWA, fax 01970 622350)

HALL, Michael Robert; s of Robert Hall (d 1980), of Cheshire, and Hannah Hall; *b* 9 May 1942; *Educ* William Hulme's Manchester; *m* 1969 (m dis 1996), Irene Mavis, da of Percy Cuthbert Archer (d 1993), of Cheshire; 1 s (Robert Anthony b 1974), 1 da (Kathryn Elizabeth b 1971); *Career* currently dep vice-chllr Univ of Derby; currently dir: Selective Fin Servs Ltd 1987–, Spiralgem Ltd, Twinrare Ltd, Blackbrook House Ltd, and various other companies relating to Univ of Derby; md: Advanced Energy Systems Ltd 1993–, Advanced Energy Systems Marketing Ltd 1993–; chm: W Hawley & Son Ltd 1987–, Construction Cosmetics Ltd 1988–, Derbyshire College Estates Ltd 1992–, Derby Univ Estates Ltd 1993–; dir: South Derbyshire Chamber of Commerce Training and Enterprise Ltd, South Derbyshire Business Link Ltd, Derbyshire Ambulance Service Ltd; regional dir CBI; FCT, FCA, FCMA; *Recreations* squash, walking, sailing; *Clubs* Duffield Derbyshire, Stakis Regency International; *Style*— Michael R Hall, Esq; ✉ Ecclesbourne House, Windley, Derbyshire DE56 2LP; University of Derby, Kedleston Road, Derby DE22 1GB (☎ 01332 622222, fax 01332 622299)

HALL, Michael Robert (Mike); s of Antony David Hall, of Bridgend, and Julia, *née* Hayes; *b* 13 Oct 1965; *Educ* Brynteg Comp Sch, Univ Coll Cardiff (BSc), Wolfson Coll Cambridge (BA, Rugby blue); *Career* rugby union player (centre and wing); former teams: Maesteg RFC, Bridgend RFC, Welsh Students, Welsh Univs (capt), Cambridge Univ, Br Univs (capt), Cardiff RFC until 1995 (capt 1993–94); current club Cardiff RFC; Wales: under 20's rep, capt under 21's, full debut tour to NZ 1988, memb tour to Aust 1991, memb World Cup squad 1991, capt World Cup squad S Africa 1995, memb tour to Canada and S Seas 1994, 42 caps; also represented: Barbarians Hong Kong Sevens 1989, Br Lions tour Aust (1 test) 1989, World XV v SA (2 tests) 1989; chartered surveyor; ARICS; *Recreations* golf, gorge walking, Ringos, bungie jumping; *Style*— Mike Hall, Esq; ✉ Cardiff Rugby Football Club, Cardiff Arms Park, Westgate St, Cardiff

HALL, Michael Thomas (Mike); MP (Lab) Warrington South (majority 191); s of Thomas Hall, and Veronica Hall; *b* 20 Sept 1952; *Educ* St Damien's Secdy Modern Sch Ashton-under-Lyne, Ashton-under-Lyne Coll of FE, Stretford Tech Coll, Padgate Coll of HE (BEd), N Cheshire Coll, UCNW Bangor; *m* Lesley Hall; 1 s (Thomas Allen); *Career* scientific asst chemical indust 1969–73, teacher Bolton 1977–85, support teacher Halton Community Assessment Team 1985–92; ldr Warrington BC 1985–92 (cncllr 1979–93, chm Environmental Health Ctee 1981–84, chm Policy and Resources Ctee 1985–92), MP (Lab) Warrington S 1992–, memb Public Accounts Ctee 1992–; *Recreations* tennis, camping, walking, swimming, reading; *Style*— Mike Hall, Esq, MP; ✉ House of Commons, London SW1A 0AA

HALL, Nigel John; s of Herbert John Hall, of Chipping Sodbury, Avon, and Gwendoline Mary, *née* Olsen; *b* 30 Aug 1943; *Educ* Bristol GS, West of England Coll of Art (NDD), RCA (MArtRCA), Harkness fellowship to USA; *m* 1986, Manijeh Yadegar; *Career* artist; tutor RCA 1971–74, princ lectr Chelsea Sch of Art 1974–81; solo exhibitions incl: Galerie Givaudan Paris 1967, Robert Elkon Gallery NY 1974, 1977, 1979 and 1983, Annely Juda Gallery London 1978, 1981, 1985, 1987, 1991 and 1996, Galerie Maeght Paris 1981 and 1983, Staatliche Kunsthaus Baden-Baden 1982, Nishimura Gallery Tokyo 1980, 1984 and 1988, Hans Mayer Gallery Dusseldorf 1989, Garry Anderson Gallery Sydney 1987 and 1990, Galerie Ziegler Zurich 1995, Fondation Veranneman Belgium 1995; gp exhibitions incl: Documenta VI (Kassel) 1977, British Sculpture in the Twentieth Century (Whitechapel Gallery London) 1981, Aspects of British Art Today (Tokyo Metropolitan Museum) 1982, Carnegie International (Carnegie Inst Pittsburgh) 1982, Britannica: Thirty Years of Sculpture (Le Havre Museum of Fine Art) 1988; work cmmnd by: Aust Nat Gallery Canberra, IBM London, Airbus Industrie Toulouse, Olympic Park Seoul, Museum of Modern Art Hiroshima, British Petroleum London, Glaxo Research; represented in numerous public collections incl: Tate Gallery London, Musée Nat d'Art Moderne Paris, Nat Galerie Berlin, Tel Aviv Museum, Power Inst Sydney; memb: Panel CNAA 1975–76, Faculty of Prix de Rome 1979–83; *Style*— Nigel Hall, Esq; ✉ 11 Kensington Park Gardens, London W11 3HD (☎ 0171 727 3162); Annely Juda Fine Art, 23 Dering St, London W1R 9AA (☎ 0171 629 7578, fax 0171 491 2139)

HALL, Dr Peter; s of Arnost Hall (d 1971), of Bournemouth, and Margit, *née* Weiss (d 1979); *b* 30 Dec 1931; *Educ* Wyggeston Sch Leicester, Univ of Birmingham (MB ChB), Univ of Sheffield (PhD); *m* 12 Jan 1957, Gwynneth Anne, da of Harold Wallhouse (d 1989), of Warwick; 3 s (Nicholas b 1957, Jonathan b 1960, Timothy b 1963); *Career* Med Branch RAF 1956–59, RAFVR 1959–69, Wing Cdr 1969; fndn res fell Univ of Sheffield 1959–62, sr conslt psychiatrist Worcester 1963–91, Upjohn lectr Canadian Med Assoc 1979, advsr Med Res Cncl 1981–84, memb Worcester Health Authy 1983–89; appointed doctor Mental Health Cmmn 1984–85, advsr on mental health WHO 1985–89, regnl tutor in psychiatry W Midland Health Authy 1986–91, advsr on psychiatry Univ of Birmingham 1986–91, med dir Woodbourne Clinic Edgbaston 1991– (sr visiting consIt 1984–91); memb Hosp Advsy Serv 1987, med examiner Gen Nursing Cncl 1988–, chm Individual Membs World Psychiatric Assoc 1989–90; DPM (RCP) 1961, FAmGerSoc 1972, FRCPsych 1973 (memb Bd of Examiners), FICA 1977, FAASP 1980, MAE 1996; *Books* Assessment in Cerebrovascular Insufficiency (1971), Chemotherapy of Schizophrenia (1983), Perspectives in Psychiatry (1988), The Closure of Mental Hospitals (1990); *Recreations* inept gardening, package tourism, hopeless fishing; *Style*— Dr Peter Hall; ✉ Medical Director, Woodbourne Clinic, 21 Woodbourne Road, Edgbaston, Birmingham B17 8BY (☎ 0121 434 4343, fax 434 3270); Winfield Hospital, Gloucester; South Bank Hospital (BUPA), Worcester; BUPA Hospital, Parkway, Solihull

HALL, HE Sir Peter Edward; KBE (1993), CMG (1987); s of Bernard Hall (d 1993), of Kings Langley, Herts, and Katherine Monica, *née* Blackbourn (d 1972); *b* 26 July 1938; *Educ* Portsmouth GS, Pembroke Coll Cambridge; *m* 6 May 1972, Marnie, da of Herbert Brumby Kay (d 1971); 1 s (Barnaby b 1975), 1 da (Amanda Hall b 1973); *Career* Nat Serv RAF 1956–58, offr cadet Jt Servs Sch for Linguists, cmmnd RAFVR 1958; FO 1961–63, third then second sec Warsaw 1963–66, second sec New Delhi 1966–69, first sec FCO 1969–72, first sec Brussels EEC 1972–76, first sec FCO 1976–77, cnsllr for econ and political affrs Caracas 1977–78; cnsllr and head of Br Info Servs: New York 1978–81, Washington 1981–83; dir of research FCO 1983–86, under sec Cabinet Office 1986–88, sabbatical visiting scholar Stanford Univ 1988–89, HM ambass Yugoslavia 1989–92; advsr to: Lord Carrington 1992, Lord Owen 1992–93, Peace Conf on Yugoslavia; HM ambass Argentina 1993–; memb: ESRC Govt and Law Ctee 1983–86, Exec Ctee Br Int Studies Assoc 1983–86; *Recreations* reading, music; *Clubs* Royal Air Force; *Style*— HE Sir Peter Hall, KBE, CMG; ✉ c/o FCO (Buenos Aires), King Charles Street, London SW1

HALL, Prof Peter Geoffrey; s of Arthur Vickers Hall (d 1973), of Blackpool, and Bertha, *née* Keefe (d 1979); *b* 19 March 1932; *Educ* Blackpool GS, St Catharine's Coll Cambridge (MA, PhD); *m* 1, 7 Sept 1962 (m dis 1967), Carla Maria, da of Frank Wartenberg (d 1986); m 2, 13 Feb 1967, Magda, da of Antoni Mróz (d 1989), of Warsaw; *Career* asst lectr then lectr Birkbeck Coll Univ of London 1957–65, reader in geography LSE 1966–67, prof of geography Univ of Reading 1968–89 (emeritus prof 1989–), prof of city and regnl planning Univ of California 1980–92 (emeritus prof 1993–), dir Inst of Urban and Regnl Devpt 1989–92, prof of planning UCL 1992–; memb various govt bodies incl SE Regnl Econ & Planning Cncl 1960–79; special advsr to Sec of State for the Environment 1991–94; FBA 1983, FRGS; *Books* London 2000 (1963), The Containment of Urban England (1973), Europe 2000 (1977), Great Planning Disasters (1980), High-Tech America (1986), Western Sunrise (1987), Cities of Tomorrow (1988), London 2001 (1989), The Rise of the Gunbelt (1991), Technopoles of the World (1994); *Recreations* walking; *Clubs* Athenaeum, RGS; *Style*— Prof Peter Hall, FBA; ✉ The Barlett School of Planning, University College London, 22 Gordon Street, London WC1H 0QB (☎ 0171 380 7456, fax 0171 380 7502)

HALL, Sir Peter Reginald Frederick; kt (1977), CBE (1963); s of Reginald Edward Arthur Hall, and Grace, *née* Pamment; *b* 22 Nov 1930; *Educ* Perse Sch Cambridge, St Catharine's Coll Cambridge (MA); *m* 1, 1956 (m dis 1965), Leslie Caron, the actress; 1 s (Christopher), 1 da (Jennifer); m 2, 1965 (m dis 1981), Jacqueline Taylor; 1 s (Edward), 1 da (Lucy); m 3, 1982 (m dis 1990), Maria Ewing, the mezzo-soprano; 1 da (Rebecca b 1982); m 4, 1990, Nicola (Nicki) Frei; 1 da (Emma b June 1992); *Career* director and producer of plays, films and operas; dir: Oxford Playhouse 1954–55, Arts Theatre London 1955–57; fndr Int Playwrights' Theatre 1957, md RSC 1960–68 (created the RSC as a permanent ensemble, and opened the RSC's London home at the Aldwych Theatre), co-dir RSC 1968–73, dir Nat Theatre of GB 1973–88, artistic dir Glyndebourne Festival Opera 1984–90, formed own prodn co Peter Hall Co Ltd 1988, artistic dir Old Vic 1996–; assoc prof of drama Univ of Warwick 1966–; memb Arts Cncl of GB 1969–72, fndr memb Theatre Directors' Guild of GB 1983; Hon DLitt Univ of Reading 1973; Hon LittD: Univ of Liverpool 1974, Univ of Leicester 1977, Univ of Essex 1995; Hon DUniv York 1966, Hon DUniv Cornell USA; Chevalier de l'Ordre des Arts et des Lettres (France); *Theatre* has directed over 150 major prodns in London, Stratford-upon-Avon and New York, including 19 Shakespeare plays, and the premieres of plays by Samuel Beckett, Harold Pinter, Tennessee Williams, Edward Albee, Jean Anouilh, Peter Shaffer, John Mortimer, John Whiting, Alan Ayckbourn; first prodns incl: Waiting for Godot (Arts Theatre London) 1955, Gigi 1956, Love's Labours Lost 1956, Cat on a Hot Tin Roof 1958; RSC prodns incl: Twelfth Night 1958, 1960 and 1991, A Midsummer Night's Dream 1959 and 1963, Beckett 1961, The Collection 1962, The Wars of the Roses 1964 (televised for BBC 1965), The Homecoming 1965 and 1973, Macbeth 1967 and 1982, A Delicate Balance 1969, All's Well That Ends Well, The Gift of the Gorgon (also Wyndhams), Julius Caesar 1995; NT prodns incl: Bedroom Farce 1977, The Cherry Orchard 1978, Betrayal 1978 and 1980, The Importance of Being Earnest 1982, Yonadab 1985, Entertaining Strangers 1987, Antony and Cleopatra 1988, The Winter's Tale 1988, Cymbeline 1988, The Tempest 1988; Peter Hall Co prodns incl: Orpheus Descending (NY) 1988, The Merchant of Venice 1989, The Wild Duck (Phoenix) 1990, The Homecoming (Comedy Theatre) 1991, The Rose Tattoo (Playhouse) 1991, Tartuffe (Playhouse) 1991, Sienna Red 1992, An Ideal Husband (Globe) 1992, Four Baboons Adoring the Sun (NY) 1992, Lysistrata (Old Vic, Wyndhams) 1993, Separate Tables (Queens) 1993, Piaf (Piccadilly) 1993, An Absolute Turkey (Globe) 1993, On Approval (Playhouse) 1994, Hamlet (Gielgud Theatre) 1994, The Master Builder (Haymarket) 1995, Mind Millie for Me (Haymarket) 1996, The Oedipus Plays (Epidaurus and RNT) 1996, School for Wives 1996; *Operas* incl: The Magic Flute (Covent Garden) 1966, Eugene Onegin (Covent Garden) 1971, The Marriage of Figaro (Glyndebourne) 1973 and 1989, A Midsummer's Night Dream (Glyndebourne) 1981 and 1989, Macbeth (Metropolitan Opera NY) 1982, The Ring (Bayreuth) 1983, Figaro (Geneva) 1983, Carmen (Glyndebourne) 1985, Albert Herring (Glyndebourne) 1985 and 1986, (Covent Garden) 1989, Salome (LA 1986, Covent Garden 1988 and 1992, Chicago 1988), New Year (world premiere, Houston) 1989,The Magic Flute (LA) 1993; *Films and Television* Work is a Four Letter Word 1968, A Midsummer Night's Dream 1969, Three into One Won't Go 1969, Perfect Friday 1971, The Homecoming 1973, Akenfield 1974, She's Been Away 1989, Orpheus Ascending 1991, The Camomile Lawn (Channel 4) 1991, Jacob (TNT/LUX) 1993, Never Talk to Strangers (TriStar Pictures) 1994–95, The Final Passage (Channel 4) 1995; *Awards* Tony Award: 1967 for Pinter's Homecoming, 1981 for Shaffer's Amadeus; Hamburg Univ Shakespeare Prize 1967, Standard Special Award 1979, Standard Award for Best Director 1981 and 1987, Standard Award for outstanding achievement in Opera 1981, Sidney Edwards Award for NT prodn of The Oresteia 1982; *Publications* The Wars of the Roses (with John Barton, 1970), translation of Ibsen's John Gabriel Borkman (with Inga-Stina Ewbank, 1975), Peter Hall's Diaries (1983), adaptation of George Orwell's Animal Farm (1986), adaptation of Ibsen's The Wild Duck (with Inga-Stina Ewbank, 1990), Making an Exhibition of Myself (autobiography, 1993), translation of Feydeau's An Absolute Turkey (with Nicki Frei, 1993), translation of Ibsen's The Master Builder (with Inga-Stina Ewbank, 1995), translation of Feydeau's L'Occupe toi d'Amelie - Mind Millie for Me (with Nicki Frei, 1996); *Clubs* Garrick, RAC; *Style*— Sir Peter Hall, CBE; ✉ Peter Hall Company Ltd at The Old Vic, Waterloo Road, London SE1 8NB (☎ 0171 928 2651, fax 0171 261 9161)

HALL, Philip David (Phil); s of Norman Philip Hall, of Chadwell Heath, Essex, and Olive Jean Hall; *b* 8 Jan 1955; *Educ* Beal GS, NCTJ Course Harlow Coll; *Career* reporter: Dagenham Post 1974–77, Ilford Recorder 1977–80; sub ed: Newham Recorder 1980–84, Weekend Magazine 1984–85; The People: reporter 1985–86, chief reporter 1986–89, news ed 1989–92, news ed Sunday Express 1992–93; News of the World: asst ed (features) 1993–94, dep ed 1994–95, ed Sept 1995–; *Recreations* golf, cinema, theatre; *Style*— Phil Hall, Esq; ✉ News of the World, 1 Virginia Street, London E1 9XR (☎ 0171 782 4406, fax 0171 481 3384)

HALL, Raymond Walter; CBE (1993); s of Alfred Henry Hall, and Elsie Frieda, *née* Lake; *b* 24 Sept 1933; *Educ* Portsmouth & Grays Thurrock Tech Coll; *m* 29 Oct 1955, Diane, *née* Batten; 1 s, 3 da; *Career* early experience in electricity generation indust incl power stations, nuclear safety advsy work and tech and mgmnt servs support; station mangr: Trawsfynydd Nuclear Power Station 1975–77, Hinkley Point A & B Nuclear Power Stations 1978–82; CEGB: corp trg mangr 1983–85, corp dir of personnel 1986–88, divnl dir of generation 1988, chief exec Nat Power Nuclear Div 1989–90; exec dir Ops Nuclear Electric plc 1990–96, chief exec Magnox Electric plc 1996–; author of various papers in the field of nuclear power ops; a govr World Assoc of Nuclear Operators (WANO) and chm Paris Centre WANO; FEng 1993, FIEE, FIMechE, FINucE, FIMgt, FIPM, FRSA; *Recreations* music, gardening, walking; *Style*— Raymond Hall, Esq, CBE, FEng; ✉ Magnox Electric plc, Berkeley Centre, Berkeley, Gloucestershire GL13 9PB (☎ 01453 813372, fax 01453 813371)

HALL, Richard John Jeaffreson; s of Francis James Thomas Hall (d 1981), and Patricia Musgrave, *née* Parry; *b* 31 July 1945; *Educ* Westminster Sch, ChCh Oxford (MA); *m* 1, 25 July 1970, Wendy Jane, *née* Thomas; 1 da (Rebecca b 28 Feb 1973), 1 s (Crispian b 15 Jan 1975); m 2, 17 June 1995, Sally Frances Mary, da of Geoffrey Cass; *Career* articled Smallfield Fitzhugh Tillett 1968–71; Binder Hamlyn: joined 1971, ptnr 1978–, audit ptnr 1978– (seconded to Milan Div 1979–81), head Corp Services Div 1989–91, marketing ptnr 1992–94; memb Urgent Issues Task Force of Accounting Standards Board 1991–95; FCA (ACA 1971); *Recreations* tennis, squash, Italian opera; *Clubs* Hurlingham, Cumberland Lawn Tennis; *Style*— Richard Hall, Esq; ✉ Binder Hamlyn, 20 Old Bailey, London EC4M 7BH (☎ 0171 489 6150)

HALL, Robert; s of Lt-Col Henry Robert Hall, OBE, TD, DL, of La Landelle, Route Des Landes, St Ouen, Jersey, CI, and Margaret Lucy, *née* Stobart; *b* 14 Aug 1954; *Educ* Radley, Univ of Leeds (BA); *Career* reporter and presenter: Channel TV 1977–80,

Yorkshire TV 1980–88; S of England corr ITN 1991–; *Recreations* walking, tennis, swimming; *Style*— Robert Hall, Esq; ✉ Independent Television News, 200 Gray's Inn Rd, London WC1 8XZ (☎ 0171 833 3000)

HALL, Robin Alexander; s of Leslie Alexander Hall (d 1984), and Sheila Mary, *née* Martin; *b* 19 May 1948; *Educ* Highbury Co GS; *m* 25 March 1977, Hazel Ann, da of Ronald William George Maidman; 2 s (James Alexander b 1978, Richard William b 1983), 1 da (Emma Rebecca b 1980); *Career* CA; audit mangr Arthur Young & Co 1969–75, investmt exec Nat Enterprise Bd 1976–79, fin dir Insac Products Ltd 1980–81, md Cinven Ltd 1981–; non-exec dir: Citylink Group plc 1983–94, Sema Group plc 1985–, Gardner Marchant Services Group Ltd 1993–95; FCA 1972; *Style*— Robin Hall, Esq; ✉ Cinven Ltd, Pinners Hall, 105–108 Old Broad Street, London EC2N 1EH (☎ 0171 661 3333)

HALL, Ronald; s of John Hall (d 1960), and Amy Hall (d 1975); *b* 28 July 1934; *Educ* Dronfield GS, Pembroke Coll Cambridge (BA); *m* 1982, Christine; *Career* chief sub ed Topic Magazine 1962; Sunday Times: co-fndr Insight Team 1963, Insight ed 1964–66, asst ed 1966–68, managing ed of features 1969–77; ed Sunday Times Magazine 1978–81, jt dep ed Sunday Times 1981–82, ed Sunday Express Magazine 1982–86, associate ed London Daily News 1986–87, London ed Condé Nast Traveler New York 1987–, conslt ed Scotland on Sunday 1988–89; *Books* Scandal 63, A Study of The Profumo Affair (jtly), The Strange Voyage of Donald Crowhurst (with Nicholas Tomalin, 1970); *Recreations* chess, travel, building; *Style*— Ronald Hall, Esq

HALL, Simon Andrew Dalton; s of Peter Dalton Hall, CB, of Milton Keynes, Bucks, and Stella Iris, *née* Breen; *b* 6 Feb 1955; *Educ* Ampleforth, St Catharine's Coll Cambridge (MA), Coll of Law; *m* 26 Aug 1978, Teresa Ann, da of John Edmund Bartleet, of Great Tey, Colchester, Essex; 2 s (Eddie b 8 Dec 1980, Harry b 31 March 1983), 2 da (Rachael b 16 June 1979, Sophie b 18 March 1988); *Career* slr; articled clerk Freshfields 1977–79, seconded to Cravath Swaine & Moore 1983–84, Freshfields NY office 1984–85 (ptnr 1985–); memb: Law Soc, American Bar Assoc, City of London Slrs Co; *Books* Aircraft Financing (ed, 1993), Leasing Finance (jtly, 1991); *Style*— Simon Hall, Esq; ✉ Freshfields, 65 Fleet Street, London EC4Y 1HS (☎ 0171 936 4000, fax 0171 832 7001, telex 889292)

HALL, Stephen Hargreaves; TD (1969); s of Walter Brian Hall (d 1987), and Marjorie Marian (d 1995), *née* Hargreaves; *b* 30 April 1933; *Educ* Rugby, Christ's Coll Cambridge (MA); *m* 9 July 1960, Nuala, da of Edward James Walker Stanley (d 1985); 2 s (Niall James b 1961, Patrick Thomas b 1963), 1 da (Victoria Jane b 1972); *Career* Nat Serv 2 Lt KOYLI Korea 1951–53 (despatches), Maj TA 1953–70; ptnr Ernst & Young 1962–93, dir of fin Lloyds of London 1993–95, DG Br Venture Capital Assoc 1995–96; non-exec dir: Yorkshire Television Ltd 1973–, Yorkshire-Tyne Tees Television Holdings plc 1986–, Hiscox PLC 1995–; memb Cncl Univ of Hull 1972–84; High Sheriff of Humberside 1981–82; FCA; *Recreations* fishing; *Clubs* City of London, Army and Navy; *Style*— Stephen H Hall, Esq, TD; ✉ Malting Farm, Little Waldingfield, Sudbury, Suffolk (☎ 01787 248369, fax 01787 248378)

HALL, Prof the Rev Stuart George; s of George Edward Hall (d 1980), of London, and May Catherine, *née* Whale; *b* 7 June 1928; *Educ* Univ Coll Sch, New Coll Oxford (BA, MA, BD); *m* 9 April 1953, Brenda Mary, da of Walter McLaren Henderson, OBE (d 1975), of Glasgow; 2 s (Lindsay b 1954, Walter b 1965), 2 da (Nicola (Mrs Nicholson) b 1956, Edith b 1959); *Career* Nat Serv RA/RAEC 1947–48; ordained: deacon 1954, priest 1955; asst curate Newark-upon-Trent 1954–58, tutor The Queen's Coll Birmingham 1958–62, lectr in theology Univ of Nottingham 1962–73 (sr lectr 1973, reader 1978), prof of ecclesiastical history King's Coll London 1978–90, priest i/c Pittenweem and Elie (Fife) 1990–; hon prof Univ of St Andrews 1993–; ed Theologische Realenzyklopädie 1977–; memb: Studiorum Novi Testamenti Societas 1969–90, Ecclesiastical History Soc 1978–, Académie Internationale des Sciences Religieuses 1983–; *Books* Melito of Sardis and Fragments (1979), Doctrine and Practice in the Early Church (1991), Gregory of Nyssa, Homilies on Ecclesiastes (1993); *Recreations* gardening, choral music; *Clubs* Golf House (Elie); *Style*— Prof the Rev Stuart Hall; ✉ 15 High St, Elie, Leven, Fife KY9 1BY (☎ and fax 01333 330145)

HALL, Prof Stuart McPhail; s of Herman McPhail Hall (d 1980), of Kingston, Jamaica, and Jesse Merle, *née* Hopwood; *b* 3 Feb 1932; *Educ* Jamaica Coll, Merton Coll Oxford (Rhodes scholar, Jamaica scholar, BA, MA, DPhil); *m* 15 Dec 1964, Catharine Mary, da of Rev John Barrett; 1 s (Jesse b 1970), 1 da (Rebecca b 1968); *Career* lectr film and TV studies Chelsea Coll London 1961–64, dir Centre for Cultural Studies Univ of Birmingham 1968–79 (res fell 1964–68), prof of sociology The Open University 1979–; Hon DLitt: Univ of Massachusetts 1988, Kingston Univ 1993, City Univ 1993, Oxford Brookes Univ 1993, Univ of Sussex 1994, De Montfort Univ 1994, Univ of the South Bank 1995, Univ of Keele 1995, Univ of Leeds 1996; pres British Sociological Assoc 1995–97, chm Inst of Int Visual Arts; hon fell Portsmouth Poly 1989, Centenary fell Thames Poly 1990; *Style*— Prof Stuart Hall; ✉ 5 Mowbray Road, London NW6 7QX (☎ 0181 459 5372); Faculty of Social Science, The Open University, Walton Hall, Milton Keynes MK7 6AA (☎ 01908 654457)

HALL, Dr Vernon Frederick; CVO (1960); s of Cecil Septimus Hall, and Maud Mary, *née* Fuller; *b* 25 Aug 1904; *Educ* Haberdashers' Aske's, King's Coll London, King's Coll Hosp Med Sch; *m* 19 Jan 1935, Constance Marcia, da of Rev H T Cavell, rector of Woodford Green, London; 1 s (Desmond Lawrence b 1937), 2 da (Judith Margaret b 1939, Janet Elizabeth b 1943); *Career* WWII RAMC advsr in anaesthetics to SE Asia Cmd, late dir of anaesthetics Indian and Burma Cmd, Brig; fell King's Coll London, fndr memb Faculty of Anaesthetists RCS, pres Assoc of Anaesthetics of GB & Ireland; anaesthetist to HM The Queen for births of her four children, also HRH The Princess Margaret and HRH Duchess of Kent, conslt anaesthetist King's Coll Hosp 1930 (dean Med Sch 1937–66); vice pres The Exmoor Soc; Univ of London: memb Senate, chm Bd of Advanced Med Studies, hon fell Faculty of Anaesthetists 1975, pres Assoc of Anaesthetists 1962–65 (hon fell); MRCS, LRCP, FARCA (hon); *Books* History of King's College Hospital Dental School, Scrapbook of Snowdonia, The Story of King's; *Recreations* rugby, squash, tennis, riding; *Clubs* RAC; *Style*— Dr Vernon F Hall, CVO; ✉ 164A Kings Hall Road, Beckenham, Kent BR3 1LN (☎ 0181 776 7066)

HALL, His Hon Judge; Victor Edwin; s of Robert Arthur Victor James Hall (d 1978), of Selsey, Sussex, and Gladys, *née* Fukes (d 1986); *b* 2 March 1948; *Educ* Chichester HS for Boys, Univ of Hull (LLB); *m* 11 May 1974, Rosemarie Berdina, da of Walter Raymond Jenkinson, of Stoneygate, Eaton Hill, Baslow, Derby; 2 s (Timothy James b 24 July 1981, Matthew Peter b 16 Feb 1984); *Career* called to the Bar Inner Temple 1971; tenancy in chambers: Leicester 1972–89, London 1990–94; recorder of the Crown Ct 1988–94 (asst recorder 1983–88), asst boundary cmmr 1992–94, circuit judge (Midland & Oxford Circuit) 1994–; vice chm E Farndon Parish Cncl 1987– (chm 1985–87), deacon Harborough Evangelical Church 1989–; memb Inner Temple Soc; *Recreations* skiing, fell walking, cooking, music, computers, football; *Style*— His Hon Judge Hall

HALL, William; CBE (1991), DFC (1944); s of Archibald Hall (d 1956), and Helen Macfadyen (d 1977); *b* 25 July 1919; *Educ* Paisley GS, Coll of Estate Mgmnt; *m* 1945, Margaret Semple, da of Robert Gibson (d 1965); 1 s (David b 1954), 3 da (Elinor b 1947, Elaine b 1951, Maureen b 1959); *Career* pilot RAF Bomber Cmd, served in Europe, M East and Burma (despatches); memb Lands Tbnl: Scotland 1971–91, England & Wales 1979–91; sr ptnr R & W Hall (chartered surveyors) 1949–79; chm RICS Scotland 1972; Hon Sheriff Paisley; FRICS; *Recreations* golf; *Clubs* RAF; *Style*— William Hall, Esq, CBE, DFC; ✉ Windyridge, Brediland Road, Paisley PA2 9HF (☎ 01505 813614)

HALL, Willis; s of Walter Hall, and Gladys, *née* Gibbon; *Educ* Cockburn HS Leeds; *m* 2 Nov 1973, Valerie Shute; 4 s (Peter, Macer, Daniel, James); *Career* writer; *Books* The Incredible Kidnapping (1975), The Summer of the Dinosaur (1977), The Last Vampire (1982), The Inflatable Shop (1984), The Return of the Antelope (1985), Dragon Days (1985), The Antelope Company Ashore (1986), The Antelope Company At Large (1987), Dr Jekyll and Mr Hollins (1988), Spooky Rhymes (1989), The Vampire's Holiday (1992), The Vampire's Revenge (1993), The Vampire's Christmas (1994), The Vampire Vanishes (1995), Vampire Park (1996); *Plays incl* The Long and the Short and the Tall 1959, The Royal Astrologers, A Glimpse of the Sea 1960, Kidnapped at Christmas, Walk On Walk On 1975, Stag Night, Christmas Crackers 1976; with Keith Waterhouse: Billy Liar 1960, Celebration 1961, All Things Bright and Beautiful, England Our England 1962, Say Who You Are 1965, Saturday Sunday Monday (adapted from de Filippo) 1973, Filumena (adapted from de Filippo) 1977, Jane Eyre (adaptation, 1992), Mansfield Park (adaptation, 1993), The Three Musketeers (adaption, 1994), Mansfield Park (dramatisation Chichester Festival, 1996); *Musicals incl* The Card (with Keith Waterhouse) 1973, Treasure Island (with Denis King) 1985, The Wind in the Willows (with Denis King) 1986, The Water Babies (with John Cooper) 1987; *Clubs* Garrick, Savage, Lansdowne; *Style*— Willis Hall, Esq; ✉ c/o Alexandra Cann Representation, 200 Fulham Road, London SW10 9TW

HALL-SMITH, Martin Clive William; s of (Sydney) Patrick Hall-Smith, of 30 The Drive, Hove, Sussex, and Angela Wilma, *née* Hall (d 1996); *b* 21 July 1948; *Educ* Eton, Univ of Edinburgh (LLB), Selwyn Coll Cambridge (MA); *m* 1983, Victoria Mary, da of John Sherwood Stephenson (d 1992), of West Mews, Wylam, Northumberland; 1 s (Edward b 1989), 2 da (Rose b 1985, Katharine b 1987); *Career* called to the Bar 1972; pt/t chm Industrial Tbnls; Freeman City of London 1978, Liveryman Worshipful Co of Loriners; *Recreations* music, skiing, walking, family life; *Style*— M C W Hall-Smith, Esq; ✉ Goldsmith Building, Temple, London EC4 (☎ 0171 353 7881, fax 0171 353 5319)

HALLADAY, Eric; s of Rev Albert Raymond Halladay (d 1969), of Loversal, Yorks, and Helena Nicholson, *née* Renton; *b* 9 July 1930; *Educ* Durham Sch, St John's Coll Cambridge (BA, MA), Ripon Hall Oxford; *m* 1 Aug 1956, Margaret Leslie, da of Leslie Baister (d 1946), of Newcastle; 1 s (Richard b 1963), 2 da (Claire b 1962, Katharine b 1966); *Career* Nat Serv 2 Lt 5 Regt RHA 1948–50; Exeter Sch 1954–60 (sr history master 1956–60), sr lectr RMA Sandhurst 1960–64; Grey Coll Univ of Durham 1964–91: sr tutor 1964–80, vice master 1967–80, master 1980–89, rector 1989–91, rector St Aidan's Coll 1990–91, hon lectr in history; princ St Chad's Coll Durham 1991–94; sec Durham Branch Soldiers Sailors and Airmen's Families Assoc 1976–89, memb N Eastern TA Volunteer Res Assoc 1978, pres and chm Durham Regatta 1982–88, steward Henley Royal Regatta 1993; *Books* The Buildings of Modern Africa (with D D Rooney, 1966), The Emergent Continent (1972), Rowing in England - A Social History (1990); *Recreations* rowing, gardening; *Clubs* Leander (Henley-on-Thames); *Style*— Eric Halladay, Esq; ✉ The Coign, Corbridge, Northumberland (☎ 01434 632838)

HALLAM, Robert William; s of Joseph Paul Hallam (d 1991), and Leila Babette, *née* Powe; *b* 25 Jan 1961; *Educ* Clifton, Plymouth Coll of Art and Design (BTEC OND and HND in Photography); *m* 17 Sept 1994, Elisabeth Anne, da of Rev Dennis Henry Ronald Cornish; *Career* freelance photographer with The Independent and The Independent on Sunday 1989–; Sports Photographer of the Yr 1994; *Style*— Robert Hallam, Esq; ✉ c/o The Sports Desk, The Independent, 1 Canada Square, Canary Wharf, London E14 5DL (☎ 0171 293 2000)

HALLARD, Steven Leslie; s of Stanley Leslie Hallard, of Rugby, and Grace, *née* Williams; *b* 22 Feb 1965; *Educ* Dunsmore Sch for Boys, E Warks Coll; *m* 14 Jan 1989, Julie Karen, da of Stephen George Lingwood; 1 s (Samuel Luke b 2 Oct 1993); *Career* target archer; memb Dunlop Archery Club, 49 int appearances (debut 1981); honours incl: team Bronze medal Olympic Games Seoul 1988, Silver medal World Championships Switzerland 1989, Silver medal Euro Grand Prix Germany 1990, Bronze medal Danish Open 1991, Bronze medal Euro Grand Prix Denmark 1991, Bronze medal Euro Grand Prix Italy, team Bronze medal Olympic Games Barcelona 1992, Gold medal Euro Grand Prix Turkey 1993, Silver medal Euro Grand Prix Switzerland, 9 times Br Target champion, 9 times UK Masters champion; Br No 1 male archery 1981–; Br records: FITA single (1323) and double (2616), York single (1192) and double (2356) Br Championships, 16 distance awards; technician apprentice GEC Turbines 1981–85, design draughtsman GEC Alsthom 1985–95, section ldr TDO 1995–; *Recreations* cycling, jogging; *Style*— Steven Hallard, Esq; ✉ c/o Mr S Lingwood, High Quality Joinery Ltd, Lynchford Lane, Farnborough, Hants (☎ 01252 548702)

HALLATT, Rt Rev David Marrison; *see:* Shrewsbury, Bishop of

HALLCHURCH, The Hon the Chief Justice; David Thomas; TD; s of Walter William Hallchurch (d 1962), and Marjorie Pretoria Mary, *née* Cooper (d 1978); *b* 4 April 1929; *Educ* Bromsgrove, Trinity Coll Oxford (MA); *m* 1, 1954 (m dis 1972), Cherry, da of Basil Jagger (d 1980); 3 s (Nicholas b 1958, Nigel b 1960, Adrian b 1966); m 2, 1972, Susan Kathryn Mather Brennan, *née* Wilson; 2 step children (Myles b 1967, Kathryn b 1964); *Career* Maj Staffs Yeo (QORR) TA 1962; called to the Bar 1954, recorder of the Crown Ct 1980–; High Ct judge of Botswana 1986–88, pt/t immigration adjudicator 1990, asst cmmr to Parly Boundary Cmmn for Eng 1992, chief justice Caicos Islands WI 1996–; chm MHRT for West Midlands 1979–86; *Recreations* tennis, cartoon drawing; *Clubs* Vincent's (Oxford); *Style*— The Hon the Chief Justice Hallchurch, TD; ✉ Chief Justice Chambers, Grand Turk, Turks & Caicos Islands, West Indies

HALLETT, *see also:* Hughes Hallett

HALLETT, Heather Carol; QC (1989); da of Hugh Victor Dudley Hallett, QPM (d 1991), of Maidstone, Kent, and Doris Viola, *née* Churchill; *b* 16 Dec 1949; *Educ* Brockenhurst GS, St Hugh's Coll Oxford, (MA); *m* 20 April 1974, Nigel Vivian Marshall Wilkinson, QC, *qv*, s of John Marshall Wilkinson (d 1993), of Surrey; 2 s (James b 4 June 1980, Nicholas b 20 April 1982); *Career* called to the Bar Inner Temple 1972, bencher Inner Temple 1993; recorder Crown Court 1989, leader SE Circuit 1995; dir Public Affairs Bar Cncl 1993; *Recreations* theatre, music; *Style*— Ms Heather Hallett, QC; ✉ 6 Pump Court, Temple, London EC4 (☎ 0171 797 8400, fax 0171 797 8401)

HALLETT, Jeffrey Paul; s of Raymond George Hallett (d 1985), of Weymouth, Dorset, and Norma Joan, *née* Humphries; *b* 14 Dec 1946; *Educ* Hardye's Sch Dorchester, St Peter's Coll Oxford (MA, BM BCh), Univ Coll Hosp Med Sch; *m* 21 March 1970, Margaret Elizabeth, da of Dr Henry Renwick Vickers; 1 s (David b 1974), 2 da (Mary b 1976, Susan b 1983); *Career* sr orthopaedic registrar on trg rotation of UCH and Westminster Hosp 1978–83, conslt orthopaedic surgn Ipswich Hosp 1983–; author of various pubns in jls; Br Orthopaedic Assoc: chm BSI Ctee CH/22, rep BSI Ctee CH/18, CH/25 and CH/49, chm Central (Med) Manpower Ctee, chm E Anglian (Med) Taskforce on Jr Drs Hours; memb: Br Orthopaedic Assoc, BMA, RSM, Sesamoid Soc, UCH/Westminster Orthopaedic Club; FRCS; cncllr and vice chm Pettistree Parish Cncl, church warden Pettistree PCC; *Books* Traction and Orthopaedic Appliances (jtly, 1983), Use of the Tourniquet in Hand Surgery (1984); *Recreations* sailing, bell ringing, sheep farming, Suffolk Punch horses, domestic poultry; *Clubs* Aldeburgh Yacht, Oxford & Cambridge Sailing Soc, Ipswich & Suffolk; *Style*— Jeffrey Hallett, Esq; ✉ The Ipswich Hospital, Heath Road, Ipswich, Suffolk IP4 5PD (☎ 01473 712233); 89 Berners Street, Ipswich, Suffolk IP1 3LN (☎ 01473 251135)

HALLETT, Jeremy Norman; s of Maj Howard Samuel Hallett (d 1979), of Stourbridge, and Majorie Winnifred, *née* Harris (d 1981); *b* 3 May 1948; *Educ* Grange Secdy Modern Sch, Bluecoat Boys' Sch Stourbridge, Bromsgrove Coll of Educn, Inst of Health Servs Mgmnt (dip in public admin), Harvard Business Sch; *m* 1971, Pamela Anne Stephenson; 1 s (James Dominic), 1 da (Rebecca Louise); *Career* admin asst Warley BC 1970–71 (mgmnt grad trainee 1969–70), chief admin offr Walsall Co Borough 1971–74, unit admin Walsall Health Authy 1974–77; Kidderminster Health Authy: dep dist gen mangr 1978–82, dist admin 1982–83, dist gen mangr 1983–87; jt chief exec Gwent Health Cmmn 1993–96 (dist gen mangr 1988–92), chief exec Wiltshire Health Authy 1996–; memb Nat Tst; MHSM; *Recreations* family, fishing, tennis, music; *Clubs* Harvard Business; *Style—* Jeremy N Hallett, Esq; ✉ Holly Bank, Old Ross Road, Whitchurch, Ross-on-Wye HR9 6DD (☎ 01600 891030, fax 01600 891040); Wiltshire Health Authority, Southgate House, Pans Lane, Devizes SN10 5EQ (☎ 01380 728899, fax 01380 733760, mobile 0850 234760)

HALLETT, Michael John; s of Arthur Ronald Hallett (d 1979), of Weymouth, Dorset, and Dorothy Muriel, *née* Stone; *b* 29 April 1940; *Educ* Weymouth GS, Bournemouth Municipal Coll of Art (Dorset County Athletics Colours), Manchester Poly UMIST (MPhil), Birmingham Poly (Dip in History of Art and Design); *m* 1970, Carol Ann, da of Norman Maurice Flint; 1 s (William James b 11 July 1977), 1 da (Emily Jane b 22 May 1975); *Career* photographer Studio 5 1959–60; lectr in photography: Leicester Coll of Art and Design 1960–65, Bournemouth and Poole Coll of Art 1965–66; lectr then sr lectr in photographic studies Manchester Coll of Art and Design and Manchester Poly 1966–69 and 1970–75, visiting prof Sch of Photographic Arts and Scis Rochester Inst of Technol NY 1969–70; Univ of Central England in Birmingham (formerly Birmingham Poly): princ lectr Dept of Visual Communication 1975–82, head Sch of Photography 1975–78, dir BA (Hons) Graphic Design Course 1979, princ lectr Sch of Theoretical and Historical Studies in Art and Design Birmingham Inst of Art and Design 1982–; publishing ed Article Press 1990–; memb: Nat Cncl Inst of Incorporated Photographers 1966–69, Associateship Panel and Fellowship Panel of History of Photography and Critical Writing Category RPS 1990–; dep chm Sector 7 Admissions and Qualifications Bd BIPP 1989–; Kodak Colour scholar Eastman Kodak Co 1964, life memb Stockport Harriers & Athletic Club 1975; FRSA 1964, FRPS 1967, FBIPP 1969, MIMgt 1976, FCSD 1977; memb Euro Soc for the History of Photography 1981; *Books* Programmed Photography (with Jack Tait, 1967), Programmed Colour Photography (1970), Worcester Cathedral: A Grand View (1987), Arts Council Independent Photography Directory (with Barry Lane, 1989), Where to Study: Photography Film Video TV (1990), Rewriting Photographic History (1990), The Real Story of Picture Post (1994), A Hungarian in England (1997); reg contrib British Journal of Photography, contrib British Journal of Photography Annual 1970–94; *Style—* Michael Hallett, Esq; ✉ Holm Oak, 134 Henwick Rd, St John's, Worcester, WR2 5PB (☎ and fax 01905 425547); Birmingham Institute of Art and Design, University of Central England, Corporation Street, Gosta Green, Birmingham B4 7DX (☎ 0121 331 5881, fax 0121 331 5880)

HALLEY, Ian Alexander; s of Alexander Halley, of St Michael, Suffolk, and Betty, *née* Sheward; *b* 7 Jan 1957; *Educ* Dr Challoner's GS, Univ of Nottingham (BA); *m* 29 Oct 1983, Diana Mary, da of Henry Colbert; 1 da (Emily Diana b 10 April 1989), 1 s (Daniel Alexander b 5 July 1992); *Career* advtg exec; Allen Brady & Marsh 1979–86, J Walter Thompson 1986–88, Ogilvy & Mather 1988–95, dir Collett Dickenson Pearce & Partners 1995–; *Recreations* football, cars, Art Deco, cinema; *Style—* Ian Halley, Esq; ✉ Collett Dickenson Pearce & Partners, 33–34 Soho Square, London W1V 6DP (☎ 0171 292 4146, fax 0171 292 4012, mobile 0378 049094)

HALLGARTEN, His Hon Judge Anthony Bernard Richard; QC; s of Siegfried Salomon (Fritz) Hallgarten (d 1991), and Friedel Liselotte, *née* Liebmann (d 1986); *b* 16 June 1937; *Educ* Merchant Taylors', Downing Coll Cambridge (BA); *m* 16 Dec 1962, Katherine Anne, da of Kurt Borchard, and Ruth Borchard; 1 s (Joseph b 22 May 1970), 3 da (Ruth b 1 Feb 1965, Judy b 24 Oct 1966, Emily b 26 Oct 1972); *Career* called to the Bar, jr counsel 1962–78, leading counsel 1978–93, circuit judge (SE Circuit) 1993–; bencher Middle Temple; *Recreations* cricket, cycling, historical novels, visiting the Ariège; *Clubs* Garrick, MCC; *Style—* His Honour Judge Hallgarten, QC; ✉ Central London County Court, 13–14 Park Crescent, London W1N 3PD

HALLGARTEN, Dr Peter Alexander; s of Siegfried Salomon (Fritz) Hallgarten (d 1991), and Friedel Liselotte, *née* Liebmann (d 1986); *b* 29 Sept 1931; *Educ* Merchant Taylors', Univ of Zurich, Univ of London (PhD), Univ of Chicago; *m* 3 July 1960, Elaine, da of Sqdn Ldr Philip Braham, MBE; 2 s (Daniel Arthur b 1961, Simon Alfred b 1963), 1 da (Lisa Ann b 1966); *Career* chm Hallgarten Wines Ltd 1985–96 (joined 1958, md 1967); chm Wine and Spirit Assoc of GB and NI 1978–79; Master Worshipful Co of Distillers 1995–96 (Liveryman 1968); FRSC, CChem; Chevalier de l'Ordre Du Mérite Agricole France 1982, Chevalier de l'Ordre National National du Mérite France 1996; *Books* Liqueurs (1967 and 1973), Guide To The Wines Of The Rhone (1979, French and Danish edns), Spirits & Liqueurs (1979), Spirits and Liqueurs (special edn, 1983); *Recreations* golf, travel, music, theatre; *Style—* Dr Peter Hallgarten; ✉ 14 Antrim Grove, London NW3 4XR (☎ 0171 722 1077); Dallow Rd, Luton, Beds LU1 1UR (☎ 01582 22538, fax 01582 23240)

HALLIBURTON, Rev Canon (Robert) John; s of Robert Halliburton (d 1953), and Katherine Margery, *née* Robinson (d 1968); *b* 23 March 1935; *Educ* Tonbridge, Selwyn Coll Cambridge (MA), Keble Coll Oxford (DPhil); *m* 15 April 1968, Jennifer Ormsby, da of John Walter Turner (d 1978); 2 s (Rupert Sinclair b 1969 d 1969, Julian Alexander John b 1972), 3 da (Rachel Helen b 1970, Naomi Katherine b 1975, Charlotte Sophia Louise b 1979); *Career* Nat Serv RCS 1956–58; asst curate St Dunstan's and All Saints Stepney 1961–67, vice princ St Stephen's House Oxford 1970–75 (tutor 1967–70), princ Chichester Theol Coll 1975–82, canon Chichester 1976–82, p-in-c All Souls St Margaret's-on-Thames 1982–90, chllr and canon residentiary St Paul's Cathedral London 1990–; conslt Anglican Roman Catholic Int Cmmn 1971–82, memb Doctrine Cmmn of C of E 1977–86; *Books* The Authority of a Bishop (1987), Educating Rachel (1988); contrib to: The Eucharist Today (1975), The Study of Liturgy (1979), Believing in the Church (C of E Doctrine Commission, 1982), We Believe in God (C of E Doctrine Commission, 1987), The Sacrament of Penance (Church Union Theological Committee, SPCK, 1990), The Oil of Gladness (Church Union Theological Ctee, SPCK, 1993); *Recreations* music, gardening; *Clubs* Athenaeum; *Style—* The Rev Canon John Halliburton; ✉ 1 Amen Court, London EC4M 7BU (☎ 0171 248 1817)

HALLIDAY, Charlotte Mary Irvine; da of Edward Irvine Halliday (d 1984), of St John's Wood, London, and Dorothy Lucy, *née* Hatswell (d 1986); *b* 5 Sept 1935; *Educ* Froebel Sch, Wester Elchies Craigellachie, Francis Holland Sch London, Royal Acad (Silver Medal for drawing); *Career* artist; keeper of New English Art Club 1989–; topographical cmmns incl: Royal Hospital Chelsea 1959, Shell Centre 1957–59, head office Barclays Bank 1961–68, headquarters BP, Barbican 1964, head office Willis Faber Dumas Tower Hill and Ipswich 1978, Mowlem Nat West Tower 1980, head office Singer & Friedlander 1982, Dixons 1982–86, Royal Opera House 1984, RAC Pall Mall 1985–86, Royal Soc of Medicine 1987, United Newspapers 1989, Union Discount Co Cornhill 1990, Salisbury Cathedral 1991, Selfridges 1991, Lord's Pavilion 1994, Trinity Coll of Music 1994, The Great Hall Lincoln's Inn 1994, The Monument for Mercury Asset Management 1995; contrib to various gp exhbns and Summer Exhbns RA 1956–; memb NEAC 1961, RBA 1961–92, RWS 1976 (assoc 1971); *Awards* Lord Mayor's Art Awards 1962, 1963 and 1976, de Laszlo Medal RBA 1973, Spirit of London Awards 1978 and 1979; *Books* illustrations for Edwardian Architecture, A Biographical Dictionary (by A Stuart Gray, 1985), Fanlights - A Visual Architectural History (with A S Gray, 1990); *Recreations* amateur choral singing, walking in the Sussex Downs; *Style—* Miss Charlotte Halliday; ✉ 36a Abercorn Place, St John's Wood, London NW8 9XP (☎ 0171 289 1327)

HALLIDAY, David Ralph; s of Walter Henry Halliday (d 1976), and Isabel Kathleen, *née* Blagdon; *b* 28 Sept 1952; *Educ* Devonport HS, Selwyn Coll Cambridge (MA); *Career* pension fund actuary; ptnr Bacon and Woodrow 1987–93 (joined 1974); FIA 1979; *Recreations* reading, bridge, opera, swimming, drinking; *Style—* David Halliday, Esq

HALLIDAY, Rt Rev Robert Taylor; s of James Halliday (d 1967), and Agnes Logan, *née* Scott (d 1981); *b* 7 May 1932; *Educ* Glasgow HS, Univ of Glasgow (MA, BD, George Neilson prize in Scottish history), Trinity Coll Glasgow, Episcopal Theol Coll Edinburgh; *m* 1960, Dr Georgina Mabel Chadwin, da of James William Chadwin; 1 da (Fiona Marion b 1964); *Career* asst curate St Andrew's St Andrews 1957–60, sr curate St Margaret's Newlands Glasgow 1960–63, rector Holy Cross Davidson's Mains Edinburgh 1963–83, canon of St Mary's Cathedral Edinburgh 1973–83, rector St Andrew's St Andrews 1983–90, hon canon Trinity Cathedral Davenport Iowa 1990–; external lectr in New Testament studies Episcopal Theol Coll Edinburgh 1963–74, tutor in biblical studies Univ of St Andrews 1984–90, bishop of Brechin 1990–96, ret; memb Anglican-Reformed Int Cmmn 1981–84, convener Inter-Church Rels Ctee Scottish Episcopal Church 1982–88; *Recreations* walking, reading, gardening; *Style—* The Rt Rev Robert Halliday; ✉ 28 Forbes Road, Edinburgh EH10 4ED (☎ 0131 221 1490)

HALLIDAY, Vice Adm Sir Roy William; KBE (1980), DSC (1944); *b* 27 June 1923; *Educ* William Ellis Sch, Univ Coll Sch; *m* 1945, Dorothy Joan Meech; *Career* joined RN 1941, served WWII Fleet Air Arm (fighter pilot), test pilot Boscombe Down 1947–48, naval asst to Chief of Naval Info 1962–64, Cdr (Air) HMS Albion 1964–66, Capt 1966, Dep Dir Naval Air Warfare 1966–70, Capt D3 Far East Fleet and D6 Western Fleet 1971–73, Cdre (Intelligence) Def Intelligence Staff 1973–75, ADC to HM The Queen 1975, cmd Br Navy Staff Washington and naval attaché and UK nat liaison rep to SACLANT 1975–78, Dep CDS (Intelligence) 1978–81, dir gen Intelligence 1981–84; *Clubs* Royal Navy; *Style—* Vice Adm Sir Roy Halliday, KBE, DSC; ✉ Willow Cottage, Bank, nr Lyndhurst, Hants

HALLINAN, Sir (Adrian) Lincoln; kt (1971), DL (Glam 1969); s of Sir Charles Hallinan, CBE (d 1981), of Cardiff, and his 1 w, Theresa Doris, JP (d 1961), da of Frederick William Holman, of Knole Park, Almondsbury, nr Bristol; *b* 13 Nov 1922; *Educ* Downside; *m* 1955, Mary Alethea (*see* Parry Evans, Mary), da of Dr Evan Parry-Evans, JP; 2 s, 2 da; *Career* called to the Bar 1950, recorder 1972–82, stipendiary magistrate S Glam 1976–93; Lord Mayor Cardiff 1969–70; chm Commemorative Collectors Soc 1973–; fndr pres Cardiff 2000 Civic Soc, patron S Wales Victorian Soc; Chevalier Palmes Académiques 1965, Chevalier Legion d' Honneur 1973; *publications* British Commemoratives; *Recreations* music, the arts; *Style—* Sir Lincoln Hallinan, DL; ✉ Cotham Lodge, Newport, Pembrokeshire SA42 0TD

HALLINAN, Lady (Mary); *see:* Parry Evans, Mary Alethea

HALLING, Prof Peter James; s of John Halling, of Heswall, Merseyside, and Enid Joyce, *née* Rutherford; *b* 30 March 1951; *Educ* Calday GS, Univ of Cambridge (BA), Univ of Bristol (PhD); *Career* research asst Biochemical Engrg Section UCL 1975–78, scientist Unilever Research Lab 1978–83; Univ of Strathclyde: lectr 1983–89, sr lectr 1989–90, prof 1990–; MRSC; FRSE 1996; *Recreations* orienteering; *Style—* Prof Peter Halling, FRSE; ✉ 2/2, 34 Montague Street, Glasgow G4 9HX; Department of Bioscience & Biotechnology, University of Strathclyde, The Royal College Building, 204 George Street, Glasgow G1 1XW (☎ 0141 552 4400, fax 0141 553 1161, e-mail p.j.halling@strath.ac.uk)

HALLISSEY, Michael; s of John Francis Hallissey, MBE (d 1986), and Mary, *née* Kendall; *b* 6 March 1943; *Educ* Royal GS Lancaster, Magdalen Coll Oxford (MA); *Career* CA; Price Waterhouse: staff accountant 1964–68, asst mangr Melbourne 1969–70, mangr Milan 1970–71, sr mangr London 1971–74, audit ptnr London 1974–79, practice devpt ptnr UK 1979–81, strategic planning ptnr UK 1981–82, corp fin ptnr London 1982–85, head of corp fin servs UK 1985–87, head of strategic planning for world firm 1987–88, dir of strategy Price Waterhouse Europe 1988–; FCA 1968, FRSA; *Books* numerous articles on corporate strategy, strategic planning, mergers and acquisitions; *Recreations* politics, sailing, music, opera, good food; *Style—* Michael Hallissey, Esq; ✉ 66 Waterside Point, Albert Bridge, London SW11 4PD; Price Waterhouse, Southwark Towers, 32 London Bridge Street, London SE1 9SY (☎ 0171 939 3000, fax 0171 939 3805, telex 884657)

HALLIWELL, Brian; s of Norman Halliwell (d 1980), of Preston, Lancs, and Emma, *née* Kay (d 1981); *b* 17 Dec 1930; *Educ* Preston GS, Central London Poly Sch of Mgmnt (DMS); *m* 2 March 1957, Agnes, *née* Lee; *Career* RAOC 1949–51; HM Customs and Excise: joined 1947, princ 1969, asst sec 1973, dep accountant gen 1976, accountant and comptroller gen 1980–85; VAT conslt KPMG 1985–; pres Customs Annuity and Benevolent Fund Inc 1985–95 (dir 1981–95); FIMgt 1985; *Recreations* chess, reading, sport; *Style—* Brian Halliwell, Esq; ✉ Waverlee, Great Heads Road, Grange-over-Sands, Cumbria LA11 7EA (☎ 015395 34335, fax 015395 35799); KPMG, PO Box 486, 1 Puddle Dock, Blackfriars, London EC4V 3PD (☎ 0171 311 2467, fax 0171 311 2943)

HALLIWELL, Prof Neil; *b* 20 July 1948; *Educ* Univ of Liverpool (BSc Mathematics, PhD Engrg Sci); *m* 1987, Tessa Jane; 2 da (Katherine b 18 June 1990, Elisabeth b 21 Jan 1993), 1 s (Andrew b 31 July 1995); *Career* scientific offr Atomic Energy Authy 1972–74; Univ of Southampton: research fell Dept of Aeronautics 1974–77, lectr Inst of Sound & Vibration Research 1977–87 (sr lectr 1987–90); head Dept of Mechanical Engrg Univ of Loughborough 1992– (prof of optical engrg 1990); author of over 150 published research papers in field of laser technol for engrg application; FInstP 1990, FIMechE 1991, FEng 1996; *Awards* UK Prize for Metrology Nat Physical Laboratory 1992, Higher Doctorate (DSc) Univ of Southampton 1992; *Recreations* match angling; *Style—* Prof Neil Halliwell, FEng; ✉ Department of Mechanical Engineering, University of Loughborough, Leicestershire LE11 3TU (☎ 01509 223210, fax 01509 223934)

HALLS-DICKERSON, Peter George; s of Woolmer George Halls-Dickerson (d 1971), of Newquay, Cornwall, and Elsie, *née* Fiddick (d 1995); *b* 29 March 1937; *Educ* Newquay Boys' GS, Wadham Coll Oxford (MA), Univ of Leeds (PGCE); *m* 29 July 1961, Ruth, da of Charles Libby; 2 da (Deborah Jayne b 1964, Nicole Clare b 1966); *Career* head of English and French Snapethorpe Sch Wakefield 1960–63, head of English and head of house Fairfax HS Bradford 1963–65, dep head The Weald Sch W Sussex 1966–70, headmaster Townfield Sch Middx 1970–74, princ Collingwood Coll Surrey 1974–95, conslt PH-D Associates 1995–; Cons Pty: memb Nat Union Exec Ctee 1987–, chm Nat Advsy Ctee on Educn 1991–94, first chm Nat Educn Soc 1994–95; first vice pres CNES 1995–; memb St John Nat Schs' Ctee 1987–94, dir Surrey Crimestoppers 1993–95, pres Camberley Branch Br Heart Fndn 1994– (memb Br Heart Fndn Ctee on Emergency Aid 1989–94); memb: NAHT 1970–95, PCC St Lawrence and St Saviours Chobham; SBStJ 1991; FCollP 1984, FRSA 1994; *Recreations* motor caravaning, windsurfing, speedboating; *Clubs* RYA; *Style—* Peter Halls-Dickerson, Esq; ✉ Sparrow Cottage, Sparrow Row, Chobham, Surrey GU24 8TA (☎ 01276 857169, fax 01276 858065)

HALLSTRÖM, Dr Cosmo Oliver Sven; s of Björn Hallstrom (d 1969), and Lolo, *née* Bergenthal; *b* 21 Oct 1946; *Educ* Haberdashers' Aske's, Univ of Liverpool (MB ChB, MD), MRCP, FRCPsych; *m* 1 Sept 1984, Diana Wendy, da of Derek Buckland, of Esher, Surrey; 1 s (Oliver b 1989), 2 da (Sophie b 1987, Louisa b 1992); *Career* lectr Inst of Psychiatry 1977–79, res psychiatrist Rockland Res NY USA 1979–81, clinical asst prof of psychiatry Univ of NY 1980–82, conslt psychiatrist and sr lectr Charing Cross Hosp 1982–; pubns on tranquillizer addictions and the psychopharmacology of depression and anxiety; past memb Cncl Br Assoc for Psychopharmacology; fndr memb The Homeless Tst; *Recreations* countryside, family, friends, skiing, travel; *Style*— Dr Cosmo Hallström; ✉ Charter Clinic, 7 Radnor Walk, London SW3 4PB (☎ 0171 351 1272, fax 0171 622 5402)

HALLWORTH, David Malcolm; s of Frank Hallworth (d 1961), of Hale, Altrincham, Cheshire, and Irene Mildred, *née* Perry (d 1973); *b* 17 April 1930; *Educ* Shrewsbury, Univ of Oxford (MA, Golf half blues 1951 and 1953 and full blue 1952, Eton fives half blue); *m* 16 May 1959, Joan Stewart, da of Leslie Arnold (d 1968), of Timperley, Altrincham, Cheshire; 3 da (Alison b 1961, Claire b 1963, Sarah b 1965); *Career* slr 1957; ptnr: Hall Brydon and Co Slrs Manchester 1959–79, Foysters Slrs Manchester 1979–89; conslt Davies Wallis Foyster Slrs 1989–; former memb Cncl Manchester Law Soc 1966–78 (hon treas 1976–78); memb: Law Soc 1957–, Manchester Law Soc 1960–; became a Christian 1977, received into Roman Catholic Church 1979; *Recreations* physical exercise, singing; *Clubs* Royal St David's Golf (Harlech), Vincent's (Oxford), Oxford and Cambridge Golfing Soc; *Style*— David Hallworth, Esq; ✉ Redcroft, Belmont Rd, Hale, Altrincham, Cheshire (☎ 0161 928 2346); 34 Ty Canol, Harlech, Gwynedd, N Wales; Davies Wallis Foyster, Harvester House, 37 Peter St, Manchester M2 5GB (☎ 0161 228 3702, fax 0161 835 2407)

HALPERN, Sir Ralph Mark; kt (1986); *b* 24 Oct 1938; *Educ* St Christopher Sch Letchworth; *m* Joan Halpern, JP, *née* Donkin; 1 da; *Career* trainee with Selfridges; The Burton Group 1961–90: joined Peter Robinson 1961, developed Top Shop chain 1968, chief exec Burton Retail, chm Peter Robinson and Top Shop 1977, chm The Burton Group plc 1981–90 (md 1978, chief exec 1978–90); Confederation of British Industry: chm Mktg and Consumer Affairs Ctee 1984–, memb City-Industry Task Force 1986–, memb President's Ctee; chm British Fashion Cncl 1990–94; Liveryman Worshipful Co of Marketors; FInstD, CIMgt; *Clubs* Reform; *Style*— Sir Ralph Halpern; ✉ c/o The Reform Club, 104 Pall Mall, London SW1Y 5EW

HALSBURY, 3 Earl of (UK 1898); John Anthony Hardinge Giffard; also Baron Halsbury (UK 1885), and Viscount Tiverton (UK 1898); s of 2 Earl of Halsbury (d 1943; himself s of 1 Earl, lawyer, MP, solicitor-gen and lord chllr of three Conservative administrations), and Esmé Stewart Wallace (d 1973); *b* 4 June 1908; *Educ* Eton; *m* 1, 1 Oct 1930 (m dis 1936), Ismay Catherine, da of Lt-Col Lord Ninian Crichton-Stuart; 1 s; m 2, 12 Dec 1936, Elizabeth Adeline Faith (d 1983), da of Maj Harry Godley, DSO, and his w Elizabeth Mary (great niece of 3 Earl Annesley); 2 da; *Heir* s, Adam Edward Giffard (Viscount Tiverton, but does not use title); *Career* sits as Independent peer in House of Lords; md Nat Research Devpt Corp 1949–59; memb: DSIR Advsy Cncl 1950–55, SRC 1967–71; chm Science Museum Advsy Cncl 1951–65, first chllr Brunel Univ 1966, chm Meteorological Ctee 1970–82; memb: Standing Cmmn on Museums and Galleries 1960–76, MRC 1973–77, Ctee of Mangrs Royal Instn 1976–79; govr: LSE 1959–88, BBC 1960–62, UMIST 1966–; pres: Inst of Prodn Engrs 1960–62, Inst of Nuclear Engrs 1961; sr past pres IEE; Hon Liveryman Worshipful Co of Saddlers; Hon DTech Brunel 1966, Hon DUniv Essex 1968; Hon Fell Inst of Biology; Hon FRSC, FEng 1976 (fndr fell), FRS; *Recreations* music, philosophy, mathematics; *Clubs* Athenaeum, RAC (steward); *Style*— The Rt Hon the Earl of Halsbury, FEng, FRS; ✉ 4 Campden House, 29 Sheffield Terrace, London W8 7NE (☎ 0171 727 3125)

HALSEY, Prof Albert Henry; s of William Thomas Halsey, and Ada, *née* Draper (d 1976); *b* 13 April 1923; *Educ* Kettering GS, LSE (BSc, PhD); *m* 12 April 1944, (Gertrude) Margaret, da of Herbert Arthur Littler (d 1979), of Winsford, Cheshire; 3 s (Robert William b 13 July 1958, David b 16 Feb 1966, Mark b 22 Dec 1967), 2 da ((Catherine) Ruth b 10 April 1955, Lisa Jane b 13 Oct 1964); *Career* RAF: Cadet Pilot 1942–45, Sgt 1945, Flt Sgt 1946–47; lectr in sociology Univ of Liverpool 1952–54, sr lectr in sociology Univ of Birmingham 1954–62; Univ of Oxford: dir Dept of Social and Admin Studies 1962–78, professorial fell Nuffield Coll 1962–90, prof of social and admin studies 1978–90, emeritus fell Nuffield Coll; advsr to Sec of State for Educn 1964–66; Hon DSocSc Univ of Birmingham 1987, Hon DUniv Open Univ 1990; Hon DLitt: Glamorgan 1994, Warwick 1995, Leicester 1995; hon fell: Goldsmith's Coll 1992, LSE 1993; foreign memb American Acad of Arts and Sciences 1988, Senior FBA 1995; *Books* Social Class and Educational Opportunity (with J E Floud and F M Martin, 1956), Technical Change and Industrial Relations (with W H Scott et al), The Sociology of Education - A Trend Reports and Bibliography (with J E Floud, 1958), Education, Economy and Society (with J E Floud and C A Anderson, 1961), Ability and Educational Opportunity (1962), Power in Co-operatives (with G N Ostergaard, 1965), Social Survey of the Civil Service (with Ivor Crewe, 1966–68), The British Academics (with Martin Trow, 1971), Trends in British Society Since 1900 (ed, 1972), Educational Priority (ed, 1972), Traditions of Social Policy (ed, 1976), Power and Ideology in Education (with J Karabel, 1977), Heredity and Environment (1977), Change in British Society (1978, 1981, 1986 and 1995), Origins and Destinations (with A F Heath and J M Ridge, 1980), Faith in the City (1985), British Social Trends Since 1900 (1988), English Ethical Socialism: from Thomas More to R H Tawney (with N Dennis, 1988), The Decline of Donnish Dominion (1992 and 1995), No Discouragement: an autobiography of A H Halsey (1996); author of over 250 articles in various learned jls; *Recreations* gardening and walking; *Style*— Prof A H Halsey, FBA; ✉ 28 Upland Park Road, Oxford OX2 7RU (☎ 01865 58625); Nuffield College, Oxford OX1 1NF (☎ 01865 278521, fax 01865 278557)

HALSEY, Rev Sir John Walter Brooke; 4 Bt (UK 1920), of Gaddesden, Co Hertford; s of Sir Thomas Edgar Halsey, 3 Bt, DSO (d 1970); *b* 26 Dec 1933; *Educ* Eton, Magdalene Coll Cambridge (BA); *Heir* kinsman, Nicholas Guy Halsey, TD, b 1948; *Career* deacon 1961, priest 1962 Diocese of York, curate Stocksbridge 1961–65, little brother of the Common Life 1965–; *Style*— Brother John Halsey; ✉ The Hermitage, 23 Manse Road, Roslin, Midlothian EH25 9LF

HALSEY, Nicholas Guy; TD (1987); s of Lt-Col Guy Marsden Halsey, TD (d 1990), of The Golden Parsonage, Hemel Hempstead, and Juliet Mary Gough, *née* Arbuthnot; *b* 14 June 1948; *Educ* Eton, Royal Agric Coll Cirencester (MRAC); *m* 7 Aug 1976, Viola Georgina Juliet, da of Maj George Thorne, MC, ERD, DL, *qv*, of Reading; 1 s (Guy Francis Johnston b 4 Oct 1981); *Career* land agent Savills 1970–76, mangr Gaddesden Estate 1976–; chm: W Herts Cons Assoc 1985–88, CLA (Herts and Middx) 1986–89; memb: Regnl Advsy Ctee (Eng East) Forestry Cmmn 1990–94, Agric Land Tbnl (East) 1994; govr Berkhamsted Schs 1981–89; National Tst: chm Local Mgmnt Ctee Ashridge Estate 1981–, memb Regnl Ctee (Thames & Chilterns) 1986–92, memb Estates Panel 1992–; High Sheriff of Herts 1995–96; Duke of Cornwall's Award (Silver Medal) for Forestry and Conservation 1988; TA: served 5 (V) Royal Anglian Regt 1972–77, 4 (V) Royal Green Jackets 1977–90, Maj, Dep Hon Col (Herts) Royal Anglian Regt 1996; FRICS 1984; *Recreations* shooting, sketching, sailing, landscape history, architecture; *Clubs* Brooks's, Farmers'; *Style*— Nicholas Halsey, Esq; ✉ The Golden Parsonage, Gaddesden Row, Hemel Hempstead, Herts HP2 6HG (☎ 01582 840315); Halsey & Partners, Gaddesden Estate Office, The Home Farm, Great Gaddesden, Hemel Hempstead HP2 6EZ (☎ 01442 242421, fax 01442 231787)

HALSEY, Simon Patrick; s of Louis Arthur Owen Halsey, of Kingston-upon-Thames, and Evelyn Elisabeth, *née* Calder; *b* 8 March 1958; *Educ* chorister New Coll Oxford, Winchester (music scholar), King's Coll Cambridge (choral scholar), RCM (conducting scholar); *m* 14 June 1986, Lucy Jane, da of Norman Linsley Lunt; 1 s (Jack b 31 July 1989), 1 da (Harriet b 10 June 1992); *Career* conductor Scottish Opera-Go-Round 1980–81, dir of music Univ of Warwick 1981–88; chorus dir: CBSO 1983–, Acad of Ancient Music 1988–91, Flemish Opera Antwerp 1990–94; assoc dir Philharmonia Chorus 1986–, music dir City of Birmingham Touring Opera 1986–; artistic dir: Salisbury Festival 1988–93, BBC Nat Chorus of Wales 1995–; princ guest conductor Netherlands Radio Choir 1995–; has appeared as guest conductor with various major choirs and orchs incl: LSO, CBSO, English Chamber Orch, Scottish Concert Orch, London Symphony Chorus, French, Dutch, Danish and Belgian Radio Choirs, Australian Chamber Orch; has made over 40 recordings on EMI, Chandos, Oiseau-Lyre and Hyperion as chorus master and on Conifer as conductor; consultant ed Faber Music Ltd; *Recreations* architecture, food and wine, sport, English literature, travel; *Style*— Simon Halsey, Esq; ✉ Granby House, 279 High Street, Henley-in-Arden, Warwickshire B95 5BG (☎ 01564 794873); c/o John Bickley, Magenta Music International, 4 Highgate High Street, Highgate Village, London N6 5JL (☎ 0181 340 8321, fax 0181 340 7823)

HALSTEAD, Dr Michael Peter; s of Ronald Halstead, and Edna, *née* Calvert; *b* 10 March 1942; *Educ* Wolstanton Co GS Newcastle under Lyme, Gonville & Caius Coll Cambridge (state scholar, MA, PhD); *m* 1965, Christine, da of Sim Quinton; 2 s (David Edward Michael b 1968, John Simon b 1971); *Career* res fell Dept of Chemistry Univ Coll of Swansea 1967–69; Royal Dutch Shell Group: sr scientist Thornton Res Centre Shell Research Ltd Chester 1969–77, business devpt mangr Speciality Chemicals Div Shell International Chemical Co Ltd London 1977–81, planning mangr Western Regnl Orgn Shell International Petroleum Co Ltd London 1981–85; treas Univ of Cambridge 1985–93, chief exec and sec gen Univ of Cambridge Local Examinations Syndicate 1993–; tstee: Cambridge Cwlth Tst 1993–, Cambridge Overseas Tst 1993–; non-exec dir: CAD Centre Ltd 1987–94 (chm CAD Centre Pension Trustee Ltd 1992–), Cambridge Water Company 1993– (chm 1995–); author of papers in scientific jls on reaction kinetics; fell Gonville & Caius Coll 1985–; FCCA, CChem, FRSC (chm Investments Ctee 1989–, memb Fin Ctee); *Recreations* music, especially organ (ARCO), travel and walking in the Alps; *Style*— Dr Michael Halstead; ✉ 26 Newton Road, Cambridge CB2 2AL (☎ 01223 327861); University of Cambridge Local Examinations Syndicate, 1–3 Hills Road, Cambridge CB1 2EU (☎ 01223 553400)

HALSTEAD, Sir Ronald; kt (1985), CBE (1976); s of Richard Halstead, of Burton-in-Lonsdale, Lancs, and late Bessie, *née* Harrison; *b* 17 May 1927; *Educ* Lancaster Royal GS, Queens' Coll Cambridge; *m* 1968, Yvonne Cecile (d 1978), da of Emile de Monchaux (d 1970), of Australia; 2 s; *Career* chm Beecham Products 1967–84; Beecham Group plc: md Consumer Products 1973–84, chm and chief exec 1984–85; non-exec dir: British Steel plc 1979–94 (dep chm 1986–94), The Burmah Oil plc 1983–89, Davy Corporation plc 1986–91, Gestetner Holdings plc 1983–, American Cyanamid Co 1986–95, Laurentian Financial Group plc 1991–95; chm: Knitting Sector Gp NEDC 1978–90, Garment and Textile Sector Gp NEDC 1991–92, Nat Coll of Food Technol 1978–83, Bd for Food Studies Univ of Reading 1978–83, Industl Devpt Advsy Bd DTI 1985–93 (memb 1983–93), CAB Int 1995–; memb Cncl and Exec Ctee Food Mfrs Fedn Inc 1966–86 (pres 1974–76); memb Cncl: CBI 1970–86, Univ of Buckingham 1973–95, Univ of Reading 1978–, Trade Policy Res Centre 1985–89, Fndn for Science and Technology 1987–, European Policy Forum 1993–; vice chm The Advertising Assoc 1973–81, dir and hon treas Centre for Policy Studies 1984–93, memb Priorities Bd for R & D in Agric and Food for MAFF 1984–87, tstee Inst of Econ Affrs 1980–93, vice pres Chartered Inst of Mktg, pres Engineering Industries Assoc 1991–; govr: Ashridge Mgmnt Coll 1970– (vice chm 1977–), De Montfort Univ 1989–; memb: Newspaper Panel Monopolies and Mergers Cmmn 1980–92, Monopolies and Mergers Cmmn 1993–; memb Cncl and Exec Ctee Imperial Soc of Knights Bachelor 1986–; Hon DSc: Reading 1982, Lancaster 1987; hon fell Queens' Coll Cambridge 1985; FIMgt, FRSA, FRSC, FInstM (Hon 1982), FIGD, fell Mktg Soc, FCIM, Hon FIFST; *Recreations* squash racquets, skiing; *Clubs* Brooks's, Athenaeum, Carlton, Lansdowne, Royal Thames Yacht, Hurlingham; *Style*— Sir Ronald Halstead, CBE; ✉ 37 Edwardes Square, London W8 6HH (☎ 0171 603 9010, fax 0171 371 2595)

HALSTED, Nicolas (Nick); s of Erik Jacob Halsted (d 1976), and Winifred Lena Henrietta, *née* Lever; *b* 24 Oct 1942; *Educ* Westminster, Wadham Coll Oxford (MA); *m* 23 Sept 1972, Clare June, da of Sir Douglas Henley, KCB, of Banstead, Surrey; 2 s (Benjamin b 1977, Laurence b 1984), 1 da (Alexandra b 1981); *Career* admitted slr 1968; past pres Amateur Fencing Assoc; memb Law Soc; *Style*— Nick Halsted, Esq

HALTON, Nicholas Allen; s of Eric Creighton Halton (ka 1941), of Carlisle, and Diana Mabel, *née* Carr (now Mrs Wilkinson); *b* 26 Aug 1940; *Educ* Marlborough, Emmanuel Coll Cambridge; *m* 1; 1 da (Candida b 27 Feb 1974); m 3, 30 July 1992, Maureen, *née* Robinson; *Career* admitted slr 1966; Esso Group 1968–94: legal advsr and co sec Esso Petroleum Co Ltd 1979–82, sr cncl Esso Europe Inc 1982–86, gen cncl Esso Europe-Africa Servs Inc 1986–94; memb Putney Soc, hon treas Putney Cons Assoc 1985–90, p/t chm Indust Tribunals 1993–, exec tstee Petroleum and Mineral Law Educn Tst 1981–, chm Insolvency Practitioners Tribunal 1987–, vice chm and treas Section on Energy Law Int Bar Assoc 1990–94; memb Law Soc 1966; *Recreations* sport, walking, reading; *Clubs* Roehampton; *Style*— Nicholas Halton, Esq; ✉ 36 Granard Ave, Putney, London SW15 (☎ 0181 788 2985, fax 0181 785 9415)

HALUCH, Stefan James (Jim); s of Stefan L Haluch, and Elizabeth, *née* Wallace; *b* 9 March 1944; *Educ* St Mary's Acad Bathgate; *m* 25 May 1968, Joyce Vevers, da of late George S McClelland; 2 s (James b 1969, Eoin b 1974), 2 da (Helena b 1965, Shelagh b 1971); *Career* sales mangr (advertising) Scotsman Publications Ltd 1965–70, sr ptnr Athol Business Consultants 1970–75, md Athol Restaurants Ltd (Hoteliers) 1975–88, chm Highland Coach Tour Hotels Ltd 1987–88, UK trg mangr Sight & Sound Education Ltd 1988–91, business and mktg conslt 1988–, mktg and contracts mangr Edinburgh's Telford College 1991–; chm Isle of Arran Tourist Bd 1980–83, pres Isle of Arran Licensed Trade Assoc 1983–86; former councillor: Bathgate Town Cncl, W Lothian CC; FInstSMM, MIMgt, MIPD; *Recreations* music, travel; *Style*— Jim Haluch, Esq; ✉ 4 Bankton Grove, Livingston, West Lothian, Scotland EH54 9DW

HAMADAH, Dr Kamel; s of His Honour Judge Ahmad Hamadah (d 1972), of Cairo, and Khadouga, *née* El Gindi (d 1950); *b* 20 April 1929; *Educ* Khaediveyah Sch Cairo, Cairo Univ Med Sch (MB BCh), Ain Shams Univ Cairo (DPM & Neurology); *m* 27 March 1969, Brenda Olive, da of Capt Alfred Mullinger, DCM (d 1980), of London; *Career* conslt psychiatrist: SW Metropolitan Regnl Hosp Bd 1973–75, St Thomas' Health Dist 1975–92; clinical tutor Tooting Bec Hosp 1973–74, hon assoc clinical tutor 1975–77, med administrator 1973–77; emeritus conslt St Thomas' Hosp 1992–; chm: Tooting Bec & St Thomas' Health Dist Rehabilitation Ctee 1975–85, Psychiatrists Ctee St Thomas' Health Dist 1979–82 (Psychiatry Mgmnt Team 1978–79), Southern Div RCPsych 1980–84 (hon sec 1977–80); examiner of RCPsych 1980–85 (sr organiser of membership examination 1978–92), med advsr to Health Ctee GMC 1980– (med examiner 1980–), recognised teacher Univ of London 1982–92, memb Visiting Team Health Advsy Serv 1984, dep regnl advsr in psychiatry South East Thames RHA 1984–90, nat advsr Nat Counselling and Welfare Serv for Sick Doctors 1985–92, cmmr Mental Health Act Cmmn 1986–92 (appointed doctor 1983–92), memb Wise Men Procedure St Thomas' Hosp 1988–92; contrib: The Lancet, British Medical Journal, Biochem Journal, Biochem Society Transcripts, British Journal of Psychiatry; LMSSA 1967, MRCPsych 1972, FRCPsych 1977; *Recreations* shooting, walking; *Clubs* Reform; *Style*— Dr Kamel Hamadah; ✉ St Thomas' Hospital, London SE1 7EH (☎ 0171 928 9292)

HAMBLEDEN, 4 Viscount (UK 1891); William Herbert Smith; s of 3 Viscount (d 1948), and Lady Patricia Herbert, GCVO (d 1994), da of 15 Earl of Pembroke and (12 Earl of) Montgomery; *b* 2 April 1930; *Educ* Eton; *m* 1955 (m dis 1988), Donna Maria Carmela Attolico di Adelfia, da of Conte Bernardo Attolico, of Rome; 5 s; m 2, 1988, Mrs Lesley Watson; *Heir* s, Hon (William) Henry Bernard Smith, *qv*; *Style*— The Rt Hon the Viscount Hambleden; ✉ The Estate Office, Hambleden, Henley-on-Thames, Oxon RG9 6RJ

HAMBLEN, Prof David Lawrence; s of Reginald John Hamblen, of Woolwich, London, and Bessie, *née* Williams; *b* 31 Aug 1934; *Educ* Roan Sch Greenwich, The London Hosp Med Coll (MB BS); *m* 16 Nov 1968, Gillian Frances, da of Edgar Leonard Bradley, OBE, of Bearsden, Glasgow; 2 da (Sarah Catherine b 1970, Clare Alison b 1974), 1 s (Neil Andrew b 1975); *Career* Nat Serv RAMC 16 Para Bde, Maj TA 44 Para Bde, reg army res offr 1972–89; fell in orthopaedics Harvard Med Sch, clinical and res fell Mass Gen Hosp Boston USA 1966–67, lectr in orthopaedics Univ of Oxford 1967–68, sr lectr in orthopaedic surgery Univ of Edinburgh 1968–72, prof of orthopaedic surgery Univ of Glasgow; past pres Br Orthopaedic Assoc 1990–91, chm Cncl of Mgmnt Journal of Bone and Joint Surgery; non-exec dir West Glasgow Hosps Univ NHS Tst 1994–; FRCS, FRCS Edinburgh, FRCS Glasgow; *Books* Outline of Fractures (co-author, 10 edn 1992), Outline of Orthopaedics (co-author, 12 edn 1995); *Recreations* golf, music; *Clubs* RSM; *Style*— Prof David Hamblen; ✉ 3 Russell Drive, Bearsden, Glasgow G61 3BB (☎ 0141 942 1823); University Department of Orthopaedic Surgery, Western Infirmary, Glasgow G11 6NT (☎ 0141 211 2678/2264)

HAMBLETON, Prof Kenneth George; s of George William Hambleton (d 1972), of Chesterfield, Derbys, and Gertrude Ellen, *née* Brighouse (d 1981); *b* 15 Jan 1937; *Educ* Chesterfield GS, Queens' Coll Cambridge (MA); *m* 4 April 1959, Glenys Patricia, da of Horace Smith, of Hayling Island, Hants; 1 s (Neil b 1963), 1 da (Lindsey b 1965); *Career* res and devpt of semiconductor materials devices and applications Servs Electronics Res Lab Herts 1958–73, res and devpt on naval radars weapon systems and computers Admty Surface Weapons Estab 1973–81 (dep dir 1981–82), dir strategic electronics MOD 1982–85, asst chief sci advsr MOD (responsible for advising on sci content of all def projects and long term res progs) 1985–86; dir gen: Air Weapons and Electronic Systems 1986–90, Aircraft 3 1990–91; prof of def engrg UCL 1991–; Freeman City of London 1993, Liveryman Worshipful Co of Engrs 1993; FIEE 1982, FRAeS 1993, FEng 1994; *Recreations* bridge, chess, music, computing, golf; *Clubs* 2; *Style*— Prof Kenneth Hambleton, FEng; ✉ Defence Engineering Group, University College London, 66–72 Gower Street, London WC1E 6BT (☎ 0171 380 7614, fax 0171 380 7622)

HAMBLIN, Brian James; s of Philip James Arthur Hamblin, of Orpington, and Freda Mary Hamblin; *b* 17 Feb 1954; *Educ* Cray Valley Tech HS, Lanchester Poly (BA); *m* 1977, Jane Karen, da of W Alan Sutherland; 2 da (Elizabeth Jane b 7 April 1983, Victoria Claire b 6 Feb 1985), 1 s (Phillip James b 4 July 1987); *Career* articled clerk Warley & Warley 1975–76; Pannell Kerr Forster Leicester 1979–: asst mangr then sr audit mangr 1984–85, ptnr 1985–, managing ptnr and sr corp recovery ptnr 1986–; Hon BA Coventry Poly 1976; ACA 1979, memb Inst of Taxation 1981, MIPA 1990, MSPI 1990 (chm Midlands Region); *Recreations* playing the trumpet, badminton, golf, church steward; *Clubs* Leicester Rotary; *Style*— Brian Hamblin, Esq; ✉ Pannell Kerr Forster, Pannell House, 159 Charles Street, Leicester, Leics LE1 1LD (☎ 0116 285 6611, fax 0116 285 4651)

HAMBLIN, Prof Terence John (Terry); s of John Gordon Hamblin (d 1978), of Farnham, Surrey, and Gladys Marjorie, *née* Allies; *b* 12 March 1943; *Educ* Farnborough GS, Univ of Bristol (MB ChB), Univ of Southampton (DM); *m* 22 July 1967, Diane Vivienne, da of George William Lay, of Farnham, Surrey; 2 s (Richard b 1971, David b 1980), 2 da (Karen b 1968, Angela b 1977); *Career* house physician Southmead Hosp Bristol 1967, house surgn Bristol Royal Infirmary 1968, MRC registrar in med Univ of Bristol 1970–72, sr registrar in haematology Poole Gen Hosp 1972–74, conslt haematologist Bournemouth 1974–, prof of immunohaematology Univ of Southampton 1987– (sr lectr in immunology 1980–87), chm Tenovus Res Inst Southampton Gen Hosp; memb: Examining Panel RCPath 1986–, Working Pty Adult Leukaemia MRC 1989–; sr ed Transfusion Sci 1985–, ed Leukaemia Res 1986–; pres Euro Soc of Haemapheresis 1986; elder Lansdowne Baptist Church Bournemouth; FRCPath 1985 (MRCPath 1973), FRCP 1985 (MRCP 1971); *Books* Plasmapheresis and Plasma Exchange (1979), Immunological Investigation of Lymphoid Neoplasms (1983), Haematological Problems in the Elderly (1987), Immunotherapy of Disease (1990); *Recreations* reading theology, writing funny articles, preaching, pond gardening, listening to Mozart and Buddy Holly records; *Style*— Prof Terry Hamblin; ✉ 15 Queens Park, South Drive, Bournemouth BH8 9BQ (☎ 01202 391844); Department of Haematology, Royal Bournemouth Hospital, Castle Lane East, Bournemouth BH7 7DW (☎ 01202 704790, fax 01202 309975); Tenovus Research Institute, Southampton General Hospital, Shirley, Southampton SO9 4XY (☎ 01703 777222)

HAMBLING, Gerald James; s of Ernest James Hambling (d 1965), and Elsie Maud, *née* Sedman (d 1971); *b* 14 June 1926; *Educ* Whitgift Middle Sch Croydon, Selhurst GS Thornton Heath Surrey; *m* 23 May 1953, Margaret, da of George Speakman (d 1945); 1 s (Robert b 31 July 1957), 1 da (Belinda b 18 Oct 1954); *Career* film editor; memb: Br Guild of Film Eds 1966–, American Acad of Arts and Scis 1980–, American Cinema Eds Guild 1980–; Coldstream Gds 1944–47; asst ed J Arthur Rank Two Cities Films 1947–50; sound ed: Herbert Wilcox Films 1950–54, Alexander The Great 1954, Freud - The Passion 1962, The Servant 1964, Pretty Polly 1966, Night of the Iguana 1966, Wuthering Heights 1970; film ed: Dry Rot 1955, The Whole Truth 1956, The Story of Esther Costello 1957, Sally's Irish Rogue 1958, Left Right and Centre 1959, The Bulldog Breed 1960, She'll Have to Go 1961, The Early Bird 1963, A Stitch in Time 1965, The Intelligence Men 1967, That Riviera Touch 1968, The Magnificent Two 1969, Roger Cherrill Ltd documentaries and commercials 1971–74, Bugsy Malone 1975, Moses - The Lawgiver 1976, Midnight Express 1977 (Br Acad Award and American Acad nomination), Fame 1979 (Br and American Acad nominations, Br Guild of Film Eds Award, American Eds Guild nomination), Heartaches 1980, Shoot the Moon 1981, Pink Floyd - The Wall 1982, Another Country 1983 (Br Acad nomination), Birdy 1984 (Br Guild of Eds Award), Absolute Beginners 1985, Angel Heart 1986 (Br Guild of Eds nomination), Leonard VI 1987, Mississippi Burning 1988 (Br Acad Award), The Commitments 1991 (Br Acad Award, American Acad nomination), In The Name of the Father 1993 (American Acad nomination), The Road to Welville 1994, White Squall 1995, Evita 1996; *Recreations* horology, fishing, antiques, photography; *Style*— Gerald Hambling, Esq; ✉ Ramblers, Skirmett, Nr Henley-on-Thames, Oxon RG9 6TG (☎ 01491 638316, fax 01491 638316)

HAMBLING, Sir (Herbert) Hugh; 3 Bt (UK 1924), of Yoxford, Co Suffolk; s of Sir (Herbert) Guy Musgrave Hambling, 2 Bt (d 1966), and Olive Margaret Gordon, *née* Carter (d 1969); *b* 3 Aug 1919; *Educ* Eton; *m* 1, 23 Sept 1950, Anne Page (d 1990), da of Judge Hugo Edmund Oswald (d 1932), of Seattle, USA; 1 s; m 2, 21 June 1991, Helen Seymour, da of Donald Mackinnon, of Marida Yallock, Victoria, Australia, and widow of David Maitland Gavin, of Clabon Mews, London SW1; *Heir* s, (Herbert) Peter Hugh Hambling b 6 Sept 1953; *Career* RAF Training and Atlantic Ferry Cmd 1939–45; airline rep: British Airways 1956–74, Royal Brunei Airlines 1975–; mangr Sir Guy Hambling & Son 1956–; *Style*— Sir Hugh Hambling, Bt; ✉ Rookery Park, Yoxford, Suffolk IP17 3LQ; 1219 Evergreen Point Road, Medina, Washington 98039, USA

HAMBLING, Maggi; OBE (1995); da of Harry Leonard Hambling, of Wistaria House, Hadleigh, Suffolk, and Marjorie Rose, *née* Harris (d 1988); *b* 23 Oct 1945; *Educ* Hadleigh Hall Sch, Amberfield Sch, Ipswich Sch of Art, Camberwell Sch of Art (DipAD Painting), Slade Sch of Fine Art (Higher Dip in Fine Art), Boise travel award NY 1969; *Career* artist; first artist in residence Nat Gallery London 1980–81; Jerwood Painting Prize 1995; *Works in Public Collections* incl: Arts Cncl of GB, Birmingham City Art Gallery, Br Cncl, Br Museum, Christchurch Mansion Ipswich, Clare Coll Cambridge, Chelmsford and Essex Museum, Contemporary Art Soc, Eastern Arts Collection, Euro Parliament Collection, Fndn Du Musee De La Main Lausanne, GLC, Greene King Breweries, Gulbenkian Fndn, Haddo House Aberdeen, Harris Museum and Art Gallery Preston, HTV Bristol Imperial War Museum, Leics Educn Ctee, Minories Colchester, Morley Coll London, Nat Gallery, Nat Portrait Gallery, Petworth House, Rugby Museum, RAMC, Scottish Nat Gallery of Modern Art Edinburgh, Scottish Nat Portrait Gallery, Southampton Art Gallery, St Mary's Church Hadleigh Suffolk, St Mary's Coll Strawberry Hill London, St Mary's Hosp London, Tate Gallery, Unilever House London, Usher Gallery Lincoln, Whitworth Art Gallery Manchester, William Morris Sch London, Aust Nat Gallery Canberra, Hereford Cathedral, New Hall Cambridge, Yale Center for Br Art New Haven Conn, Templeton Coll Oxford, Univ of Warwick, Wakefield Art Gallery; *Exhibitions* solo: Sculpture in Bronze (Marlborough Fine Art) 1996; group: Hadleigh Gallery Suffolk 1967, Morley Gallery London 1973, Warehouse Gallery London 1977, Nat Gallery London 1981, Nat Portrait Gallery London and Tour 1983, Serpentine Gallery London 1987, Richard Demarco Gallery Edinburgh 1988, Maclaurin Art Gallery Ayr 1988, Arnolfini Gallery Bristol and Tour 1988, Bernard Jacobson Gallery London 1990, Yale Center for British Art New Haven Conn USA 1991, CCA Galleries London 1993, Northern Centre for Contemporary Art Sunderland 1993, Cornerhouse Manchester 1993, Angel Row Nottingham 1994, Christchurch Mansion Ipswich 1994, Harris Museum Preston 1994, Barbican Centre London 1994; *Clubs* Chelsea Arts, Green Street; *Style*— Miss Maggi Hambling, OBE; ✉ c/o Marlborough Fine Art, 6 Albermarle Street, London W1X 4BY

HAMBLING, (Herbert) Peter Hugh; s and h of Sir (Herbert) Hugh Hambling, 3 Bt, *qv*; *b* 6 Sept 1953; *Educ* Univ of Washington (BSc), von Karman Inst for Fluid Dynamics (Dip), Yale Sch of Orgn and Mgmnt (Master Public & Private Mgmnt); *m* 1, 1982 (m dis 1989), Jan Elizabeth, da of Stanton Frederick, Jr, of Seattle, Washington, USA; m 2, 1991, Lorayn Louise, da of Frank Joseph Koson (d 1971), of Ecorse, Michigan, USA; 2 s (Colin Hugh b 16 Dec 1991, Austin Peter b 26 Oct 1993); *Career* high technol mgmnt; Strategic Planning Associates 1982–84, 3M Co 1984–87, Orbital Sciences Corp 1987–91, Digital Control Inc Seattle Washington 1991– (pres, chief operating offr and fndr); *Recreations* flying, sailing, skiing; *Clubs* Seattle Tennis, Corinthian Yacht (Seattle), Wings Aloft Flying, Felthorpe Flying; *Style*— Peter Hambling, Esq; ✉ Rookery Park, Yoxford, Suffolk

HAMBRO, Baron (Life Peer UK 1994), of Dixton and Dumbleton in the County of Gloucester; Charles Eric Alexander Hambro; o s of Col Sir Charles Jocelyn Hambro, KBE, MC, DL (d 1963), of Dixton Manor, Glos, and his 1 w, Pamela Cobbold (d 1932); *b* 24 July 1930; *Educ* Eton; *m* 1, 4 July 1954 (m dis 1976), Rose Evelyn, er da of Lt-Col Sir Richard Charles Geers Cotterell, 5 Bt, CBE, TD (d 1978); 2 s (Hon Charles Edward b 20 Nov 1959, Hon Alexander Robert b 17 Jan 1962), 1 da (Hon Clare Evelyn (Hon Mrs Rabben) b 4 June 1957); m 2, 1976, Cherry Felicity, 2 da of Sir John Huggins, GCMG, MC (d 1971), and former w of Peter Twiss; *Career* Coldstream Gds 1949–51; Hambros Bank Ltd: joined 1952, md 1957, dep chm 1965, chm 1972–83; chm Hambros plc 1983–; non-exec dir: Taylor Woodrow plc 1962–, Guardian Royal Exchange Assurance plc 1968– (dep chm 1974–88, chm 1988–), Peninsular & Oriental Steam Navigation Co 1987–, San Paolo Bank Holdings SpA, General Oriental Investments Ltd; chm Royal Nat Pension Fund for Nurses 1968, tstee Br Museum 1984–94; Liveryman Worshipful Co of Fishmongers; *Clubs* MCC, White's, Carlton; *Style*— The Rt Hon the Lord Hambro; ✉ Dixton Manor, Gotherington, Cheltenham, Glos GL52 4RB

HAMBRO, James Daryl; s of Jocelyn Olaf Hambro, MC (d 1994), and his 1 w, Ann Silvia, *née* Muir (d 1972); *b* 22 March 1949; *Educ* Eton, Harvard Business Sch; *m* 3 c; *Career* exec dir Hambros Bank 1972–85, dir J O Hambro & Co 1986–, md J O Hambro Magan & Co 1988–94, md J O Hambro & Co 1994–, Australian Opportunities Investment Tst 1996–, Primary Health Properties plc 1996–; *Clubs* White's, Pratt's, Royal West Norfolk; *Style*— James Hambro, Esq; ✉ J O Hambro & Co, 10 Park Place, London SW1A 1LP (☎ 0171 222 2020, fax 0171 233 1503)

HAMBRO, Peter Charles Percival; elder s of Lt-Col Everard Bingham Hambro, MBE (d 1971, ggs of Baron Hambro, cr a Danish Baron 1851, and fndr of the Hambros as British bankers, by his 1 w), of Durrington House, Old Harlow, Essex; *b* 18 Jan 1945; *Educ* Eton, Université d'Aix-Marseille; *m* 1968, Karen Guinevere Gould, da of Capt George Brodrick, of Dunley Manor, Whitchurch, Hants; 3 s; *Career* md: Smith St Aubyn & Co Holdings until 1983, Richco Bullion Ltd 1982–83; dir Mocatta & Goldsmid Ltd 1985–90, md Peter Hambro Plc 1990–, dir City of Oxford Investment Tst, pres Mines d'Or de Salsigne SA 1992–, dir Bakyrchik Gold PLC 1993–95, chm Zoloto Mining Ltd 1995–; *Recreations* shooting, fishing, painting; *Clubs* Pratt's, White's; *Style*— Peter Hambro, Esq; ✉ Peter Hambro PLC, 7 Eccleston Street, London SW1W 9LX (☎ 0171 393 0102, fax 0171 393 0103)

HAMBRO, (Alexander) Richard; s of Jocelyn Olaf Hambro, MC (d 1994), by his 1 w, Ann Silvia, *née* Muir (d 1972); *b* 1 Oct 1946; *Educ* Eton; *m* 1, 1973 (m dis 1982), Hon Charlotte, da of Baron Soames, GCMG, GCVO, CH, CBE, PC; 1 da (Clementine b 1976, bridesmaid to Lady Diana Spencer at her marriage to HRH The Prince of Wales 1981); m 2, 12 July 1984 (m dis 1992), Juliet Mary Elizabeth Grana, da of Maj Thomas Harvey and Lady Mary Harvey; m 3, Mary Christine James, *née* Briggs; *Career* dir Hambros Bank 1979– (joined 1966), pres Hambro America Inc 1975–83, co-fndr J O Hambro & Co 1986; chm: J O Hambro Investment Management Co, I Hennig & Co diamond brokers; chm Cancer Relief Macmillan Fund; *Style*— Richard Hambro, Esq; ✉ 4 Egerton Place, London SW3

HAMBRO, Rupert Nicholas; eldest s of Jocelyn Olaf Hambro, MC (d 1994), and his 1 w, Ann Silvia, *née* Muir (d 1973); *b* 27 June 1943; *Educ* Eton, Aix-en-Provence; *m* 1970, Mary Robinson, da of late Francis Boyer; 1 s, 1 da; *Career* Hambros Bank Ltd: dir 1969–86, chm 1983–86; J O Hambro & Co Ltd: md 1986–94, chm 1994–; chm: J O Hambro Magan & Co Ltd 1988–93, J O Hambro Magan Irby Holdings Ltd 1988–, Mayflower Corporation plc 1989–, Fenchurch plc 1993–; dir: Hamleys PLC until 1996 (chm 1989–94), Anglo American Corp of SA Ltd 1981–, Racecourse Holdings Trust 1985–94, The Telegraph plc 1984–, Sedgwick Group plc 1987–92, Asset Trust plc 1987–90, Pioneer Concrete plc 1988–, CTR plc 1990–; chm Assoc of Int Bond Dealers 1979–82; chm of tstees: Garfield Weston Boys' Club Tst 1993–, The Silver Tst 1988–; chm Soc of Merchant Trading to the Continent; tstee Partners of the World; treas Nat Arts Collection Fund 1992–; Liveryman Worshipful Co of Goldsmiths; *Recreations* racing, shooting; *Clubs* White's, Pratt's, Jupiter Island; *Style*— Rupert Hambro, Esq; ✉ J O Hambro & Company Ltd, 30–32 Queen Anne's Gate, London SW1H 9AB (☎ 0171 233 1400, fax 0171 222 1993)

HAMBURGER, Michael Peter Leopold; OBE (1992); s of late Prof Richard Hamburger, and Mrs L Hamburger, *née* Hamburg; *b* 22 March 1924; *Educ* Westminster, ChCh Oxford (MA); *m* 1951, Anne Ellen, *née* File; 1 s, 2 da; *Career* Army Serv 1943–47; freelance writer 1947–52, asst lectr in German UCL 1952–55, lectr rising to reader in

German Univ of Reading 1955–64, Florence Purington lectr Mount Holyoke Coll Mass 1966–67, visiting prof State Univ of NY 1969, visiting fell Centre for Humanities Wesleyan Univ Conn 1970, Regent's lectr Univ of Calif San Diego 1973; visiting prof: Univ of S Carolina 1973, Boston Univ 1975–77; pt/t prof Univ of Essex 1978, Bollingen Fndn fell 1959–61 and 1965–66; translation prizes: Deutsche Akademie für Sprache und Dichtung Darmstadt 1964, Arts Cncl 1969, Arts prize Inter Nationes Bonn 1976, medal Inst of Linguists 1977, Schlegel - Tieck prize London 1978 and 1981, Wilhelm-Heinse prize Mainz 1978, Goethe medal 1986, Austrian State prize for literary translation 1988, Euro Cmmn Translation prize 1990, Hölderlin prize 1991, Petrarca prize 1992; Hon DLitt UEA, Hon Dr Phil Technische Universität Berlin 1995; corresponding memb: Deutsche Akademie für Sprache und Dichtung Darmstadt 1973; FRSL 1972–86; *Books* incl: Flowering Cactus (1950), Poems 1950–51 (1952), The Dual Site (1958), Weather and Season 1963, Feeding the Chickadees (1968), Penguin Modern Poets (with A Brownjohn and C Tomilinson, 1969), Travelling (1969), The Truth of Poetry (1969, trans into German, Italian and Spanish), Travelling I-V (1973), Ownerless Earth (1973) Travelling VI (1975), Real Estate (1977), Moralities (1977), Variations (1981), Collected Poems (1984), Trees (1988), Selected Poems (1988), Roots in the Air (1991); A Mug's Game (memoirs, 1973, new version as String of Beginnings, 1991, Collected Poems 1941–94 (1995); translator of various poems, plays and short prose incl work by: Bertold Brecht, Goethe, Beethoven, Hölderlin, Celan, Enzenberger, N Sachs, P Bichsel; *Recreations* gardening, walking; *Style*— Michael Hamburger, Esq, OBE

HAMBURGER, Sir Sidney Cyril; kt (1981), CBE (1966), JP (Salford 1957), DL (Greater Manchester 1981); s of Isidore Hamburger (d 1953); *b* 14 July 1914; *Educ* Salford GS; *m* 1940, Gertrude, da of Morris Sterling (d 1951); 3 s; *Career* cncllr and alderman Salford City Cncl 1946–71 (Mayor of Salford 1968–69); memb: North Western Electricity Consultative Cncl 1953–70 (chm Manchester Area Ctee 1963–68, dep chm Cncl 1968–70), Manchester Regnl Hosp Bd 1965–74 (chm Fin Ctee 1971–74), Supplementary Benefits Cmmn 1966–75; chm: NE Manchester Hosp Mgmnt Ctee 1970–74, NW Regnl Health Authy 1974–82, Hillel Ctee for Students 1975, NW ASH 1977–, Age Concern Salford 1984, Manchester Cncl for Soviet Jewry 1984–93, Gtr Manchester Citizens Advice Bureau 1985–90 (pres 1990–); life pres: Manchester Jewish Homes for the Aged 1965, Zionist Central Cncl 1976 (pres 1967–70 and 1974–75), JIA 1975; pres: Jewish Day Centre for the Elderly, Jewish Rep Cncl 1962–65, Trades Advsy Cncl 1984–94; vice pres: Mizrachi Fedn 1976, Labour Friends of Israel, Br Lung Fndn 1987; memb: Bd of Govrs Ben Gurion Univ 1979–84, Ct Univ of Manchester 1972–83, Advsy Bd Salvation Army 1983–; former memb BBC Advsy Cncl, govr King David Schs (vice pres 1993), pres Manchester Ctee Bar-Ilan Univ Jerusalem; hon fell Bar-Ilan Univ 1979; Hon MA Salford 1979, Hon LLD Univ of Manchester 1983; Papal Award Cross Pro Ecclesia et Pontifice 1983, Bnei Brith Award 1984; *Recreations* reading, public service, football; *Style*— Sir Sidney Hamburger, CBE, JP, DL; ✉ 26 New Hall Rd, Salford M7 0JU (☎ 0161 834 5452)

HAMELIN, Marc-André; *b* 1961; *Educ* Vincent d'Indy Sch of Music Montreal, Temple Univ Philadelphia (BA, MA); *m* Jody Karin Applebaum; *Career* pianist; worked with conductors incl: Charles Dutoit, Dennis Russell Davies, Güther Herbig, Emmanuel Krivine, Stanislaw Skrowaczewski, Hugh Wolff, David Zinman; orchs worked with incl: Royal Concertgebouw Amsterdam, Philadelphia Symphony Orch, Montreal Symphony Orch, BBC Scottish Symphony Orch (BBC Proms) 1994, Indianapolis Orch, Minneapolis Orch, Vancouver Symphony; recitals incl: Virtuoso Romantics Series Wigmore Hall 1994, Masterconcert Series Wigmore Hall 1996, Merkin Hall NY 1996, BBC World Service Celebrity Recitals Series Konzerthaus Vienna, BBC Lunchtime Series St John's Smith Square, Balldemossa Chopin Festival; broadcasts for CBC, Radio France, Swedish Radio; winner Int American Music Competition Carnegie Hall 1985; *Recordings* incl: Eckhardt-Gramatté (winner Preis Der Deutschen Schalplatten Kritik 1992), Alkan Concerto for solo piano (nominated Grammy Award 1994), Alkan and Henselt Piano Concertos (with BBC Scottish Symphony Orch and Martyn Brabbins, nominated Gramophone Award 1996), Live at Wigmore Hall (nominated Gramophone Award 1995), Ives Concord Sonata, Sorabji Sonata No 1 (winner Diapason D'or), An Alkan Solo Album (Canadian Juno Award 1996), complete Scriabin Sonatas, works by Godowsky, Bolcom, Wolpe; *Style*— Marc-Andre Hamelin; ✉ c/o Georgina Ivor Associates, 66 Alderbrook Road, London SW12 8AB (☎ 0181 673 7179, fax 0181 675 8058)

HAMER, (Michael Howard) Kenneth; s of Mark Hamer (d 1970), and Feodora Leonora, *née* Abrahams (d 1958); *b* 27 July 1945; *Educ* Cheltenham Coll, Sidney Sussex Coll Cambridge; *m* 20 Sept 1986, Victoria, da of Dr Thomas Walsh (d 1988); 1 da (Clara b 1989); *Career* admitted slr 1968, called to the Bar Inner Temple 1975, asst recorder Crown Ct 1991–; Westminster City cncllr 1974–78; *Recreations* cooking, opera, arts; *Clubs* Carlton; *Style*— Kenneth Hamer, Esq; ✉ 2 Harcourt Buildings, Temple, London EC4Y 9DB (☎ 0171 583 9020, fax 0171 583 2686); Iford Manor, Iford, nr Lewes, E Sussex BN7 3EU (☎ 01273 472832, fax 01273 478119)

HAMER-HODGES, David William; s of Dr Robert James Hamer-Hodges (d 1961), of Portsmouth, and Priscilla, *née* Fowler; *b* 17 Oct 1943; *Educ* Portsmouth GS, UCH (MB BS, MS); *m* 10 Oct 1969, Gillian Landale, da of Richard Cameron Kelman (d 1978), of Aberdeen; 3 s (Christopher James b 1970, Gareth William b 1973, Anthony Paul b 1975), 1 da (Clair Gillian b 1980); *Career* res fell surgery Harvard 1973, sr registrar surgery Aberdeen 1974, res surgical offr St Mark's Hosp London 1977, conslt surgn and hon sr lectr surgery Edinburgh 1979–; memb socs involving gastroenterology, endocrinology and transplantation; FRCS, FRCSEd; *Recreations* gardening; *Style*— David Hamer-Hodges, Esq; ✉ 38 India Street, Edinburgh EH3 6HB (☎ 0131 226 5720)

HAMILL, Sir Patrick; kt (1984), QPM (1979); s of late Hugh Hamill; *b* 29 April 1930; *Educ* St Patrick's HS Dumbarton, Open Univ (BA); *m* 1954, Nell Gillespie; 4 s, 1 da; *Career* Dunbartonshire Police 1950, asst chief constable City of Glasgow Police 1972, chief constable Strathclyde Police 1977–85 (joined 1975), RCDS 1976; memb Bd of Govrs: Scot Police Coll 1977–85, St Aloysius Coll Glasgow 1983–90; Assoc of Chief Police Offrs (Scotland): rep to Interpol 1977–81, pres 1982–83, hon sec 1983–85; chm: Bd of Mgmnt St Margaret's Hospice Clydebank 1986–, Bd of Govrs St Andrew's Coll of Educn Bearsden 1987–88; OStJ 1977; *Recreations* walking, reading history, golf; *Style*— Sir Patrick Hamill, QPM

HAMILTON, *see also:* Douglas-Hamilton, Stirling-Hamilton

HAMILTON, Duke of *see:* Hamilton and Brandon

HAMILTON, Abe; s of Roberta Austin (d 1993); *b* 4 Jan 1962; *Educ* High Peak Coll of FE Buxton Derbys, Bournemouth & Poole Coll of Art & Design, Middx Poly; *Career* former chef; fashion designer 1986–; cmmnd by Browns to design a capsule collection for new store 1993, first show Harvey Nichols 1993, winner British Design - The New Generation category (British Fashion Awards) 1993; *Style*— Abe Hamilton, Esq; ✉ 4th Floor, 22 Charlotte Road, London EC2 (☎ 0171 613 4710, fax 0171 739 7631)

HAMILTON, Adrian Walter; QC (1973); s of Walter George Morrell Hamilton (d 1957), and Sybil Emily, *née* Thomson (d 1972); *b* 11 March 1923; *Educ* Highgate, Balliol Coll Oxford (MA); *m* 1966, Jill Margaret Beverlie, da of Stanley Richard Brimblecombe, of Eastbourne; 2 da (Sarah b 1967, Philippa b 1970); *Career* Lt RNVR (Atlantic, Mediterranean, English Channel, FE); called to the Bar: Lincoln's Inn 1949 (bencher 1979), Middle Temple and Inner Temple; recorder of the Crown Court 1974–95, dep High Ct judge 1982; head of chambers; memb: Senate and Inns of Ct and the Bar 1976–82 (treas 1979–82), Cncl of Legal Educn 1977–87; inspr Peek Foods Ltd 1977–81; *Recreations* golf, sailing, family; *Clubs* Garrick, Roehampton, Piltdown Golf; *Style*— Adrian Hamilton, Esq, QC; ✉ 7 King's Bench Walk, Temple, London, EC4Y 7DS (☎ 0171 583 0404, fax 0171 583 0950)

HAMILTON, Alex John; *b* 5 Nov 1936; *Educ* Brazil and Argentina, The Queen's Coll Oxford (Neale scholar, BA); *m* Stephanie Nettell; 2 s; *Career* novelist, journalist and broadcaster; work incl: ed Books and Bookmen, columnist The Times and The Glasgow Herald, various BBC World Service programmes, travel ed The Guardian 1981–96 (formerly features writer); winner James Fitzgerald Travel Writer of the Year award 1985 and 1994/95; *Books* The Siberian Track, Tall Dark and Gruesome, As If She Were Mine, Wild Track, Town Parole, If You Don't Watch Out (USA), Beam of Malice, Fly On The Wall, The Dead Needle, The Christmas Pudding That Shook the World; ed: Triangles, Splinters, Factions, The Cold Embrace, Best Horror Stories; *Recreations* photography; *Style*— Alex Hamilton, Esq; ✉ 24 Weymouth St, London W1N 3FA (☎ 0171 580 3479)

HAMILTON, Prof (William) Allan; s of Vernon Hamilton (d 1980), and Jean Mair Murdoch Logan, *née* Hood (d 1988); *b* 4 April 1936; *Educ* Hutchesons' GS, Univ of Glasgow (BSc(Hons), PhD); *m* 1992, Evie, *née* Stewart; 2 step da (Marsali Ann Stewart b 1971, Victoria Elidh Stewart b 1974); *Career* Dept of Biochemistry Univ of Glasgow: ARC scholar 1958–60, MRC research asst 1960–61; US Public Health Serv research fell Dept of Biochemistry Univ of Illinios 1961–62, WHO research fell Dept of Phthisiology and Pneumology Univ of Brazil 1962–63, scientist Unilever Colworth House Bedford 1963–67, pt/t lectr Luton Coll of Technol 1964–65; Univ of Aberdeen: lectr Dept of Biochemistry 1967–70, sr lectr Dept of Biochemistry 1970–73, sr lectr Unit of Microbiology Dept of Biochemistry 1973–75, sr lectr and head Dept of Microbiology 1975–77, reader and head Dept of Microbiology 1977–80, prof of microbiology 1980–, head Dept of Genetics and Microbiology 1986–88, vice princ 1988–90; chm: Micran Ltd 1982–86, Nat Collections of Industrial and Marine Bacteria Ltd 1983–, Aberdeen University Research and Industrial Services Ltd 1989–91 (dir 1984–); Soc for Gen Microbiology: memb Cncl 1972–76 and 1985–89, memb Ctee of Cell Surfaces and Membranes Gp 1973–76, memb Editorial Bd 1981–86, treas 1992–99; memb: Cncl Scottish Assoc for Marine Scis 1987–93 (chm Fellowship and Bursary Ctee 1990–93), Aquatic Life Scis Ctee NERC 1990–93, Biochemical Soc (Ctee of Bioenergetic Orgelle Gp 1975–81), American Soc for Microbiology, Soc for Gen Microbiology (treas 1992–98); FRSE 1980 (convener Biological Sub-Ctee 1990–93, memb Cncl 1991–94), FIBiol 1983; *Publications* Bacterial Energetics (SGM symposium, with B A Haddock, 1977); *Recreations* sailing, fly fishing, wine tasting, skiing; *Style*— Prof Allan Hamilton, FRSE; ✉ Kinellar House East, Kinellar, Aberdeen AB2 0RY (☎ 01224 791054); Department of Molecular and Cell Biology, Marischal College, University of Aberdeen, Aberdeen AB9 1AS (☎ 01224 273143, fax 01224 273144)

HAMILTON, Andrew; s of Peter Hamilton, of Sussex, and Susie, *née* Blackwell; *b* 15 Jan 1950; *Educ* Univ Coll Sch, Coll of Estate Mgmnt Univ of Reading; *m* 23 July 1983, Fiona Ann, da of John Scott-Adie, of Perthshire; 2 s (Charles Scott-Adie b 1988, Malcolm Scott-Adie b 1991); *Career* dir: John D Wood SA 1975–77, Haslemere Estates plc 1985–86, Ranelagh Development Ltd 1986–95; chm Culverin Holdings Ltd 1986–; Poundbury Devpt Dir Duchy of Cornwall 1991–; FRICS 1986; *Recreations* opera, conservation, shooting; *Clubs* RAC; *Style*— Andrew Hamilton, Esq; ✉ c/o Culverin Holdings Ltd, 1 Tower Hill Terrace, London EC3 (☎ 0171 680 0084)

HAMILTON, Andrew Caradoc; s and h of Sir (Robert Charles) Richard Caradoc Hamilton, 9 Bt, *qv*; *b* 23 Sept 1953; *Educ* Charterhouse, St Peter's Coll Oxford (BA); *m* 26 Oct 1984, Anthea Jane, da of Frank Huntingford, of Hindhead, Surrey; 3 da (Alice b 4 Dec 1986, Harriet b 18 March 1989, Imogen Rosie b 6 Nov 1993); *Career* schoolmaster 1976–89; restored Wellesbourne Watermill to full working order 1988–90, now promoting mill's stoneground products and mill as tourist attraction; *Recreations* cricket, real tennis, art, music, family; *Clubs* MCC, Leamington Cricket, Leamington and Moreton Morrell Real Tennis; *Style*— Andrew Hamilton, Esq; ✉ c/o Wellesbourne Watermill, Mill Farm, Kineton Road, Wellesbourne, Warwickshire CV35 9HG (☎ 01789 470237)

HAMILTON, Lord (Claud) Anthony; DL (Co Fermanagh 1979); s of 4 Duke of Abercorn (d 1979), and Lady Mary Kathleen, GCVO, *née* Crichton (d 1990), sis of 5 Earl of Erne; *b* 8 July 1939; *Educ* Eton; *m* 17 April 1982, Catherine Janet, eldest da of Sir Dennis Faulkner, CBE, of Ringhaddy House, Killinchy, Co Down; 1 s (Alexander James b 1987), 1 da (Anna Kathleen b 1983); *Career* Lt Irish Gds; Capt RARO Ulster Def Regt 1979–; HS Co Fermanagh 1990; *Clubs* Kildare St and University; *Style*— The Lord Anthony Hamilton, DL; ✉ Killyreagh, Tamlaght, Enniskillen, Co Fermanagh, N Ireland (☎ 01365 87 221)

HAMILTON, Rt Hon Sir Archibald Gavin (Archie); kt (1994), PC (1991), MP (C) Epsom and Ewell (majority 20,021); yr s of 3 Baron Hamilton of Dalzell, GCVO, MC, JP (d 1990), and Rosemary Olive, *née* Coke (d 1993); *b* 30 Dec 1941; *Educ* Eton; *m* 14 Dec 1968, Anne, da of late Cdr Trevelyan Napier, DSC, RN; 3 da; *Career* cncllr London Borough of Kensington & Chelsea 1968–71, MP (C) Epsom and Ewell 1978–; PPS to: Sec of State Energy 1979–81, Sec of State Tport 1981–82; asst govt whip 1982–84, lord cmmr to the Treasy 1984–86, Parly under sec of state (Def Procurement) 1986–87, PPS to PM 1987–88, min of state (Armed Forces) Min of Defence 1988–93; currently memb: Exec 1922 Ctee, Select Ctee on Standards and Privileges; dir: Crown Ridge Industries, Saladin Holdings, Leafield Engineering, Woodgate Farms Dairy, First Phillipine Investment Trust, Siam Selective Growth Trust; memb Bd of Govrs Westminster Fndn for Democracy; *Style*— The Rt Hon Sir Archie Hamilton, MP; ✉ House of Commons, London SW1A 0AA

HAMILTON, Hon Lord; Arthur Campbell; s of James Whitehead Hamilton (d 1954), of Glasgow, and Isobel Walker, *née* McConnell; *b* 10 June 1942; *Educ* Glasgow HS, Univ of Glasgow, Worcester Coll Oxford (BA), Univ of Edinburgh (LLB); *m* 12 Sept 1970, Christine Ann, da of Thomas Carlyle Croll, of St Andrews, Fife; 1 da (Miranda b 1975); *Career* memb Faculty of Advocates 1968; standing jr counsel: Scot Devpt Dept 1975–78, Bd Inland Revenue (Scot) 1978–82; QC (Scot) 1982; Advocate Depute 1982–85, judge of the Courts of Appeal of Jersey and Guernsey 1988–95, pres Pensions Appeal Tbnls for Scot 1992–95, senator of the Coll of Justice 1995–; *Recreations* hill walking, fishing, music, history; *Style*— The Hon Lord Hamilton; ✉ 8 Heriot Row, Edinburgh EH3 6HU (☎ 0131 556 4663)

HAMILTON, Dr Barbara; da of Herbert H Hunter, OBE (d 1980), of Belfast, and Margretta, *née* Hemphill; *b* 19 Feb 1944; *Educ* Methodist Coll Belfast, Queen's Univ Belfast (MB BCh, BAO), Univ of Aberdeen (DipFP, Dip Psychotherapy); *m* 20 March 1971, David Stewart, s of David Hamilton (d 1981); 2 s (Michael b 1974, Colin b 1983), 3 da (Lisa b 1972, Barbara-Anne b 1973, Emma b 1977); *Career* hon lectr Univ of Aberdeen (former trainee psychiatrist and sr registrar), presently conslt psychiatrist; memb Exec RCPsych, gp supervision ldr Marriage Guidance Cncl Ayrshire; memb: BMA, AFT; MRCPsych; *Recreations* golf, music, dancing; *Clubs* Turnberry Golf; *Style*— Dr Barbara Hamilton; ✉ St Johns, Maybole, Ayrshire KA19 7LN (☎ 01655 82284); Isla Bank House, Keith, Banffshire AB5 3BS (☎ 01542 22322); Crosshouse Hospital, Kilmarnock (☎ 01563 21133)

HAMILTON, Bryan; *Career* former professional footballer and manager; clubs as player: Distillery (1st team), Linfield, Ipswich Town, Everton, Millwall, Swindon Town; player-manager Tranmere Rovers; clubs as manager: Wigan Athletic (chief exec), Leicester City; N Ireland: 50 full caps, appointed mangr National Team Feb 1994–;

Style— Bryan Hamilton, Esq; ✉ c/o The Irish Football Association, 20 Windsor Avenue, Belfast, N Ireland BT9 6AA (☎ 01232 669458)

HAMILTON, (Baron) Carl-Diedric Hugo Gustaf; s of Baron Fredrik Adolf Hugo Johan Hamilton (d 1968), and Karin Odelstierna; *b* 7 Aug 1948; *Educ* Sigtuna Skolan, Stockholm Sch of Business; *m* 1976, Astrid Gudrun Ebba Charlotte, da of Erik Carleson (d 1959), and Astrid Hagberg; 1 s (Carl-Johan b 1977), 2 da (Ebba b 1980, Louise b 1982); *Career* Capt Reserve Royal Swedish Lifeguards; dir Hambros Bank Ltd 1976–82; fndr and exec dir Enskilda Securities 1982–86; chm: Enskilda Fondkommission 1987–89, Enskilda Asset Management 1989–91, Enskilda Group 1991–93; Enskilda: vice chm 1989–91, chief exec 1991–93; memb Gp Exec Ctee Skandinaviska Enskilda Banken 1991–93, dep chief operating offr Enskilda Corporate (div of Skandinaviska Enskilda Banken) April-Dec 1993, chief exec Alfred Berg 1995–96; chm Global Equity Directorate ABN AMRO Bank NV 1996–; chm: C-D Hamilton AB fin and corp advsy servs 1994–, Multimedia Software Scandinavia AB; *Style—* Carl-Diedric Hamilton; ✉ Vårgårdsvägen 62A, S-133 36 Saltsjöbaden, Sweden (☎ 00 46 8 717 0500, fax 00 46 8 717 4877); business: ABN AMRO Bank NV, Global Equity Directorate, 4 Broadgate, London EC4M 7LE (☎ 0171 374 7777, fax 0171 374 4678)

HAMILTON, David; s of C J Pilditch (d 1967), and Joyce Mary Hamilton (d 1970); *b* 10 Sept 1938; *m* 1, 5 Nov 1962 (m dis 1977), Sheila Moore; 1 s (David b 1964), 1 da (Jane b 1963); m 2, 1993, Dreena Shrager; *Career* writer weekly column in nat football magazine whilst at school, script-writer ATV 1956 (scripted Portrait of a Star 1957); Nat Serv RAF, broadcaster Br Forces Broadcasting Serv Germany 1959; continuity announcer: Tyne-Tees TV 1961, ABC TV (Manchester) 1962; former freelance announcer several ITV stations; host of pop and sports shows, beauty contests and quizzes incl: Top of the Pops, Seaside Special, TV Times Gala Awards, Up for the Cup and All Clued Up ITV 1988–91; radio: first broadcast for BBC 1962, presented own daily show on Radio 1 and Radio 2 1973–86, subsequently presenter daily show for Capital Gold Radio London, currently presenter daily show for Melody FM Radio London; several appearances in films and maj pantomimes; hon pres Showbiz XI Football Team (memb for twenty years); memb Mgmnt Ctee Dogs Home Battersea; *Books* The Music Game (autobiography, 1986); *Recreations* tennis; *Style—* David Hamilton, Esq; ✉ M P C Artists, 15/16 Maple Mews, London NW6 5UZ (☎ 0171 624 1184)

HAMILTON, Dr David Stewart; s of David Hamilton (d 1981), of Belfast, and Anne, *née* Stewart; *b* 3 June 1944; *Educ* Belfast Royal Acad, Queen's Univ Belfast (MB BCh, BAO, DRCOG); *m* 20 March 1971, Barbara, da of Herbert Hunter, OBE (d 1980), of Belfast; 2 s (Michael b 1974, Colin b 1983), 3 da (Lisa b 1972, Barbara b 1973, Emma b 1977); *Career* princ GP Belfast 1972–77, trainee psychiatrist Aberdeen 1977–84, conslt psychiatrist and sr lectr Univ of Aberdeen 1984–87, conslt psychiatrist Ayrshire 1987–; sec Mental Handicap Section RCPsych Scotland, vice chm Div of Psychiatry Ayrshire; memb: BMA, AFT; assoc RCGP 1978, MRCPsych; *Recreations* golf, music, restoration of mansion houses; *Clubs* Turnberry, Ayrshire Symphony Orch; *Style—* Dr David Hamilton; ✉ St John's, Maybole, Ayrshire KA19 7LN (☎ 01655 82284); Isla Bank House, Seafield Ave, Keith AB5 3BS (☎ 01542 22322); Crosshouse Hospital, Kilmarnock (☎ 01563 21133)

HAMILTON, His Hon Judge Donald Rankin Douglas; s of Allister McNicoll Hamilton (d 1973), and Mary Glen, *née* Rankin; *b* 15 June 1946; *Educ* Rugby, Balliol Coll Oxford (BA); *m* 11 May 1974, (Margaret) Ruth, *née* Perrens; 1 da (Sarah Margaret b 2 June 1977), 1 s (Ian Allister b 1 Nov 1979); *Career* called to the Bar Gray's Inn 1969 (Atkin scholar), pupillage 1970–71, in practice 1971–94, recorder 1991–94, head of chambers 3 Fountain Ct 1993–94, circuit judge (Midland & Oxford Circuit) 1994–; dir City of Birmingham Symphony Orchestra Soc Ltd 1984– (memb Cncl of Mgmnt of the former CBSO Friendly Soc 1974–80); *Recreations* music; *Style—* His Hon Judge Hamilton; ✉ 3 Fountain Court, Steelhouse Lane, Birmingham B4 6DR (☎ 0121 236 5854, fax 0121 236 7008)

HAMILTON, Douglas Owens; s of Oswald Hamilton (d 1949), and Edith Florence Hamilton (d 1987); *b* 20 April 1931; *Educ* John Fisher Sch Purley Surrey, London Univ (LLB); *m* 15 Sept 1962, Judith Mary, da of Harold Arthur Benjamin Wood (d 1979); 3 s (Giles Alexander Douglas, Angus James Douglas, Benjamin Charles Douglas); *Career* sr ptnr Norton Rose Slrs 1982–94 (ptnr 1959, fin ptnr 1970–76, exec ptnr 1976–82); memb Court of Benefactors of Oxford Univ 1990–94, treas Br Polish Legal Assoc 1989–93; hon treas Br Maritime Charitable Fndn 1987–; memb: Law Soc 1955–94, Baltic Exchange 1970–94; vice chm Marine Soc 1994–, chm Thames Nautical Training Trust Ltd 1995–; *Recreations* tennis, golf, travelling; *Style—* Douglas Hamilton, Esq; ✉ Boarsney, Salehurst, nr Robertsbridge, E Sussex TN32 5SR (☎ and fax 01580 860131)

HAMILTON, (James) Dundas; CBE (1985); s of late Arthur Douglas Hamilton, and Jean Scott Hamilton; *b* 11 June 1919; *Educ* Rugby, Clare Coll Cambridge; *m* 1954, Linda Jean, da of late Sinclair Frank Ditcham; 2 da; *Career* Lt-Col RA Europe and Far East 1939–46; memb Stock Exchange 1948–94 (cncl memb 1972–78, dep chm 1973–76), sr ptnr Fielding Newson-Smith & Co 1977–85, dep chm Br Invisible Exports Cncl 1976–86; chm: TSB Commercial Holdings Ltd 1984–90, United Dominions Trust Ltd 1984–90, Wates City of London Properties plc 1984–94, LWT Pension Trustees Ltd 1992–95, WIB Publications Ltd 1991–; dir: TSB plc 1985–90, Camp Hopson Ltd 1991–, LWT (Holdings) plc 1981–91; memb: Exec Ctee City Communications Centre 1977–87, Advsy Bd Royal Coll Def Studies 1980–87; chm City and Industl Liaison Cncl 1991–95, govr Pasold Res Fund 1976–90; Parly candidate (C) East Ham North 1951; novelist and playwright; *Recreations* swimming, writing, golf, watching tennis; *Clubs* City of London, All England Lawn Tennis and Croquet, Royal and Ancient, Hurlingham, Worplesdon, Hankley Common Golf; *Style—* Dundas Hamilton, Esq, CBE; ✉ 45 Melbury Court, London W8 6NH (☎ 0171 602 3157)

HAMILTON, Eben William; QC (1981); s of Rev John Edmund Hamilton, MC (d 1981), of Edinburgh, and Hon Lilias Hamilton, *née* Maclay (d 1966); *b* 12 June 1937; *Educ* Winchester, Trinity Coll Cambridge (MA); *m* 1985, Themy Rusi, da of Brig Rusi Bilimoria (d 1963), of Bellagio, Warden Rd, Bombay, India; *Career* 4/7 Royal Dragoon Gds 1955–57, Fife and Forfar Yeo Scottish Horse TA 1957–68; called to the Bar Inner Temple 1962 (bencher 1985), head of chambers; admitted: Hong Kong Bar 1978, Singapore Bar 1982; DTI inspector Atlantic Computers plc 1990–93; FRSA 1989; *Clubs* Garrick; *Style—* Eben Hamilton, Esq, QC; ✉ Chesworth House, Horsham, W Sussex RH13 7AA; Priests Island, Co Longford, Ireland; 1 New Square, Lincoln's Inn, London WC2

HAMILTON, Sir Edward Sydney; 7 Bt (GB 1776), of Marlborough House, Hampshire, and 5 Bt (UK 1819), of Trebinshun House, Brecknockshire; s of Sir (Thomas) Sydney Perceval Hamilton, 6 and 4 Bt (d 1966); *b* 14 April 1925; *Educ* Canford; *Heir* none; *Career* RE 1943–47, 1 Royal Sussex Home Guard 1953–56; *Style—* Sir Edward Hamilton, Bt; ✉ The Cottage, East Lavant, nr Chichester, West Sussex PO18 0AL (☎ 01243 527414)

HAMILTON, Francis Rowan Oldfield de Courcy; s of James Percival de Courcy Hamilton, of Watlington, Oxon (d 1995), and Elizabeth Millicent, *née* Oldfield (d 1991); *b* 11 Feb 1940; *Educ* Winchester, Christ Church Oxford; *m* 22 July 1972, Catherine Rae, da of Lt Cdr William Alastair Robertson, CBE, DSC, RN, of Gifford, East Lothian; 1 s (Thomas b 1983), 2 da (Antonia b 1977, Olivia b 1979); *Career* The Economist Intelligence Unit 1965–72 (dir Mexico Office from 1967), dir Samuel Montagu & Co Ltd 1978–86; chief of div and sr advsr Int Finance Corp Washington DC 1986–; *Clubs* Travellers'; *Style—* Francis de C Hamilton, Esq; ✉ 30 Sussex Street, London SW1V 4RL (☎ 0171 821 7175)

HAMILTON, (Alexander) Gordon Kelso; s of Arthur Hamilton Kelso Hamilton (d 1996), of Weybridge, Surrey, and Elizabeth Evelyn, *née* Williams; *b* 27 Aug 1945; *Educ* Charterhouse, Pembroke Coll Cambridge (MA); *m* 12 July 1980, France Elisabeth Mary Colette, da of Pierre Laurent Millet, of Paris, France; 1 s (Edward b 1984), 1 da (Georgina b 1986); *Career* CA; ptnr Mann Judd 1975–79, following merger ptnr Touche Ross (now Deloitte & Touche) 1979–; tstee Pembroke Coll Cambridge (The Valence Mary (1997) Endowment Fund) 1985–90; Royal Nat Inst for Deaf People: memb Cncl of Mgmnt 1990–92, memb Fin Ctee 1990–96, tstee 1992–96, hon treas 1993–96; dir St George's Hill Golf Club Ltd; tstee Action on Addiction 1996–; FCA; *Recreations* golf; *Clubs* R & A, St George's Hill Golf; *Style—* Gordon Hamilton, Esq; ✉ 19 Elm Park Road, London SW3 (☎ 0171 352 2228)

HAMILTON, Hugo; *b* 28 Jan 1953; *Career* ex-journalist with Irish Press, work in music publishing business with Gael Linn; Rooney Prize 1992; *Books* Surrogate City (1990), The Last Shot (1991), The Love Test, Headbanger (1997); Dublin Where the Palm Trees Grow (collected short stories); *Style—* Hugo Hamilton, Esq; ✉ c/o Charles Walker, Peters Fraser & Dunlop Ltd, 503 The Chambers, Chelsea Harbour, Lots Road, London SW10 0XF (☎ 0171 344 1000, fax 0171 352 7356)

HAMILTON, Iain Ellis; s of James Hamilton (d 1951), of London, and Catherine, *née* Ellis (d 1979); *b* 6 June 1922; *Educ* Mill Hill Sch, Royal Acad of Music (LRAM, ARAM), Univ of London (BMus); *Career* engr Handley Page Aircraft Co 1939–46; lectr: Morley Coll 1952–60, Univ of London 1952–60; Mary Duke Biddle prof of music Duke Univ N Carolina USA 1962–78; composer; works incl: Symphony No 1 (1948), Concerto for Clarinet and Orchestra (1949–50), Symphony No 2 (1951), The Bermudas (for chorus and orchestra, 1957), Sinfonia for Two Orchestras (1958), The Royal Hunt of the Sun (opera in two acts, 1967–69), Alastor for Orchestra (1970), Anna Karenina (opera in three acts, 1979), St Mark Passion (1982), Piano Concerto No 2 (1988); Hon Doctorate of Music Univ of Glasgow 1970; FRAM; *Recreations* reading, walking; *Style—* Iain Hamilton, Esq; ✉ 85 Cornwall Gardens, London SW7 4XY (☎ 0171 589 4788)

HAMILTON, (Robert) Ian; s of Robert Tough Hamilton (d 1951), and Daisy, *née* Mackay; *b* 24 March 1938; *Educ* Queen Elizabeth GS Darlington, Keble Coll Oxford (BA); *m* 1, 1963 (m dis 1979), Gisela Dietzel; 1 s (Matthew William b 1967); m 2, 1981, Ahdaf Soueif; 2 s (Robert b 1984, Richard b 1989); *Career* Nat Serv RAF 1956–58; poet and author; ed: The Review 1962–72, The New Review 1974–79; *Books* incl: The Visit (poems, 1970), A Poetry Chronicle (1973), The Little Magazines (1976), Robert Lowell: A Biography (1983), In Search of J D Salinger (1988), Fifty Poems (1988), Writers in Hollywood 1915–51 (1990), Keepers of the Flame (1992), Walking Possession: Essays and Reviews 1968–93 (1994), Gazza Italia (1994), The Oxford Companion to Twentieth Century Poetry in English (1994); *Style—* Ian Hamilton, Esq; ✉ 54 Queens Road, London SW19 8LR (☎ 0181 946 0291)

HAMILTON, Ian Gordon; s of Forrest Hamilton (d 1943), of Glasgow, and Jane Isobel Cameron (d 1964); *b* 2 Dec 1925; *Educ* Market Harborough GS, Royal Tech Coll Glasgow (BSc); *m* 2 July 1952, Jean, da of Duncan MacMillan; 1 s (Gordon Macmillan b 6 Feb 1954); *Career* metallurgist Stewarts & Lloyds Ltd 1946–51, asst to Chief Metallurgist Babcock & Wilcox Ltd 1951–56, chief metallurgist and welding engr Motherwell Bridge & Engineering Co Ltd 1956–57, dir Problematics Ltd (engrg conslts) 1957–59, dep chief metallurgist Babcock & Wilcox Ltd 1959–67, chief metallurgist Babcock & Wilcox (Operations) Ltd 1967–77, gp chief metallurgist Babcock Energy 1977–87, sr engr assoc CAPCIS-UMIST 1988–90, sr conslt CAPCIS Ltd 1990–95, ret; pres Scottish Assoc for Metals 1978–79, awarded Brooker medal The Welding Inst; ARTC, FEng 1989, FIM, FWeldI; *Recreations* hill walking, literature, music; *Style—* Ian Hamilton, Esq, FEng; ✉ 2 Holm Road, Crossford, Carluke ML8 5RG (☎ 01555 860877)

HAMILTON, Ian Robertson; QC (Scotland 1980); s of John Harris Hamilton (d 1968), of Paisley, Renfrewshire, and Martha, *née* Robertson (d 1976); *Educ* John Neilson Sch Paisley, Allan Glens Sch Glasgow, Univ of Glasgow (BL), Univ of Edinburgh; *m* 1 and 2; 1 s, 2 da; m 3, 4 April 1974, Jeanette Patricia Mairi, da of Sqdn Ldr James Mitchell Watson Stewart, MBE (d 1966), of Dimbula, Ceylon; 1 s (Ian Stewart b 26 Oct 1975); *Career* RAFVR 1944–48; called to the Scottish Bar 1954, advocate depute 1964, state advocate Zambia 1966, hon sheriff Lanarkshire 1968, called to the Canadian Bar 1982, sheriff of Strathclyde and Kelvin 1985 (resigned to return to private practice); fndr Castlewynd Printers Ltd 1954, fndr chm Whichway Tst for Young Offenders 1988; chief pilot Scottish Parachute Club 1978–81, hon student pres Heriot-Watt Univ 1991–, rector Univ of Aberdeen 1994–; *Books* No Stone Unturned (1952), The Tinkers of the World (1958), A Touch of Treason (1990), The Taking of the Stone of Destiny (1991), A Touch More Treason (1994); *Recreations* motor biking; *Style—* Ian Hamilton, Esq, QC; ✉ Parliament House, Edinburgh (☎ 0131 226 2881, car 0860 820869)

HAMILTON, James; CBE (1979); s of late George Hamilton, of Baillieston, Lanarkshire; *b* 11 March 1918; *Educ* St Bridget's, St Mary's HS; *m* 1945, Agnes, da of Constantine McGhee; 1 s (and 1 s decd), 3 da; *Career* Reconnaissance Corps 1939–46; constructional engr; pres Constructional Engineering Union 1968–74, former co cncllr Lanarkshire; MP (Lab): Bothwell 1964–83, Motherwell North 1983–87; asst govt whip 1969–70, oppn whip 1970–74, lord cmmr of the Treasury 1974; vice chamberlain HM Household 1974–78, comptroller 1978–79; former chm PLP Trade Union Gp, memb Select Ctee on Selection; *Style—* James Hamilton Esq, CBE; ✉ 12 Rosegreen Crescent, Bellshill, Lanarkshire (☎ 01698 842071)

HAMILTON, Sir James Arnot; KCB (1978, CB 1972), MBE (1952); *b* 2 May 1923; *Educ* Lasswade Sch, Univ of Edinburgh (BSc); *m* 5 Sept 1947 (m dis 1977), Christine Mary, da of Robert McKean, of Glasgow; 3 s (Robin b 1949, Gordon b 1954, Angus b 1957); *Career* Marine Aircraft Estab 1943–52 (head of Flt Res 1948), Royal Aircraft Estab 1952 (head of Projects Div 1964), dir Anglo-French Combat Aircraft Miny of Aviation 1965, dir gen Concorde Miny of Technol 1966–70, dep sec DTI 1971–73, dep sec Cabinet Office 1973–76, perm sec Dept of Educn and Sci 1976–83; dir: Hawker Siddeley Group 1983–91, Smiths Industries 1984–93, Devonport Royal Dockyard 1987–; memb Advsy Bd Brown & Root (UK) Ltd; tstee Br Museum (Natural History) 1984–88; vice chm Cncl UCL 1985–, vice pres Cncl Univ of Reading 1985–96; Hon DUniv Heriot-Watt 1983, Hon LLD CNAA 1983; FRSE 1981, FEng 1981, Hon FIMechE 1982, FRAeS 1960; *Clubs* Athenaeum; *Style—* Sir James Hamilton, KCB, MBE, FRSE, FEng; ✉ Pentlands, 9 Cedar Rd, Farnborough, Hants (☎ 01252 543254)

HAMILTON, Marquess of; James Harold Charles Hamilton; s and h of 5 Duke of Abercorn; *b* 19 Aug 1969; *Educ* Harrow, Middlebury Coll Vermont USA; *Heir* bro, Lord Nicholas Hamilton; *Career* Page of Honour to HM The Queen 1982–84; *Style—* Marquess of Hamilton

HAMILTON, Jeremy Ian Macaulay (Jim); s of Zachary Macaulay Hamilton (d 1986), and Pamela Lucie, *née* Robson (d 1983); *b* 6 Jan 1944; *Educ* Canford Sch, Univ of Bristol (LLB); *m* 12 March 1977, Janet Lorna Joanna, da of David Morrice Man (d 1957), of Alresford, Hants; 2 s (James b 1977, Kit b 1979), 1 da (Nina b 1981); *Career* slr Beaumont & Son 1969–70, asst sec Tioxide plc 1970–73, ptnr Grieveson Grant and Co 1980–85 (joined 1973); dir Kleinwort Benson Ltd 1986–; memb Law Soc 1970; *Recreations* salmon and trout fishing, wine; *Style—* Jim Hamilton, Esq; ✉ Kleinwort Benson Ltd, 20 Fenchurch Street, EC3P 3DS (☎ 0171 623 8000)

HAMILTON, His Hon Judge John; s of Cdr John Ian Hamilton, Knight SMOM, RN, of Bognor Regis, Sussex, and Margaret Elaine, *née* Rowe (d 1959); *b* 27 Jan 1941; *Educ* Harrow, Hertford Coll Oxford (MA); *m* 19 Feb 1965, Patricia Ann, da of Cedric Walter Clive Henman, of Pulham Market, Norfolk; 2 s (Mark b 1967, Rupert b 1969), 1 da (Stephanie b 1972); *Career* called to the Bar Gray's Inn 1965, recorder of the Crown Court 1983, circuit judge (SE Circuit) 1987–; English under 18 golf int 1958, winner of Carris trophy 1958; Freeman City of London, Liveryman Worshipful Co of Merchant Taylors; Knight SMOM; *Recreations* golf, bridge, cycling, gardening; *Style—* His Hon Judge John Hamilton; ✉ Red Stack, Anstey, nr Buntingford, Herts SG9 0BN (☎ 01763 848536); Luton County Court, Cresta House, Alma Street, Luton, Bedfordshire

HAMILTON, (John Robert) Leslie; *b* 15 June 1952, Toronto, Canada; *Educ* Lurgan Coll NI, Queen's Univ Belfast (MB BCh, BAO), FRCS (Eng) 1981, FRCSEd 1988; *m* Joy; 1 s (Stuart b 28 July 1981), 3 da (Suzanne b 5 Sept 1983, Carolyn b 3 July 1986, Fiona b 14 June 1988); *Career* successively: jr house offr Royal Victoria Hosp Belfast, tutor Dept of Physiology Queen's Univ Belfast, sr house offr Belfast, surgical registrar NI, sr surgical registrar Yorks RHA Leeds 1985–91 (incl one year post at Hosp for Sick Children Great Ormond Street 1988–89), conslt cardiac surgn with special interest in congenital heart disease Freeman Hosp Newcastle upon Tyne 1991–; numerous invited lectures, presentations to learned socs and published articles; memb: BMA, Soc of Cardiothoracic Surgns of GB and I, Br Paediatric Cardiac Assoc; *Recreations* family activities, local church; sport - ex athletics and rugby, now occasional football (goalkeeper), golf, skiing and sailing (dinghy); *Style—* Leslie Hamilton, Esq; ✉ Freeman Hospital, High Heaton, Newcastle upon Tyne NE7 7DN (☎ 0191 284 3111 ext 26109, fax 0191 213 2167)

HAMILTON, Loudon Pearson; CB (1987); s of Vernon Hamilton (d 1980), of Glasgow, and Jean Mair (d 1987); *b* 12 Jan 1932; *Educ* Hutchesons' GS Glasgow, Univ of Glasgow (MA); *m* 15 Aug 1956, Anna Mackinnon (d 1993), da of Hugh Young (d 1955), of Glasgow; 2 s (Hugh Vernon b 1958, Gavin Patrick b 1964); *Career* Nat Serv 2 Lt RA 1954–55; Dept of Agric (Scottish Office) 1960, private sec to Parly Under Sec of State for Scotland 1963–64, first sec Agric Br Embassy Copenhagen 1966–70, asst sec Dept of Agric and Fisheries for Scotland 1973–79, princ estabs offr Scottish Office 1979–84, sec Scottish Office (Agric and Fisheries Dept) 1984–92; memb Agric and Food Res Cncl 1984–92; chm: Corstorphine Tst 1990–95, Scottish Agricultural & Rural Devpt Centre 1992–, Scottish Milk Mktg Bd 1994–, Scottish Food Quality Certification Ltd 1995–; *Recreations* hillwalking, bad bridge; *Style—* Loudon Hamilton, Esq, CB; ✉ 5 Belgrave Road, Edinburgh EH12 6NG (☎ and fax 0131 334 5398, fax 0131 334 7907)

HAMILTON, Sir Michael Aubrey; kt (1983); s of Rt Rev Eric Hamilton, KCVO, Dean of Windsor, by his w Jessie, da of Sir Walter Cassels; *b* 5 July 1918; *Educ* Radley, Univ Coll Oxford; *m* 16 May 1947, Lavinia, da of Sir Charles Ponsonby, 1 Bt, TD; 1 s, 3 da; *Career* served WWII 1 Bn Coldstream Gds; MP (C): Wellingborough 1959–64, Salisbury 1965–83; asst govt whip 1961–62, Lord Cmmr of the Treasy 1962–64; UK rep: UN Gen Assembly 1970, US Bicentennial Celebrations 1976; PPS to Francis Pym (Foreign Sec) 1982–83; former dir: Army & Navy Stores, Royal Exchange Assurance, Hops Marketing Board; *Style—* Sir Michael Hamilton; ✉ Lordington House, Chichester, W Sussex (☎ 01243 371717)

HAMILTON, Michael John; s of William E Hamilton (d 1985), of Guelph, Canada, and Jean, *née* Clark; *b* 24 Oct 1939; *Educ* Univ of Western Ontario (BA), Univ of Oxford (MA); *m* 20 Sept 1967, Irena, da of Albert Rudusans (d 1962); 1 s (Andrew), 3 da (Katharine, Anna, Nina); *Career* jt md Manufacturers Hanover Ltd 1969–73; exec dir: First Boston Corporation Europe Ltd 1973–78, Blyth Eastman Dillon Inc 1978–79; md Wallace Smith Trust Co Ltd 1980–91, fndr M J Hamilton & Co 1991–; dir: Midland Expressway Ltd 1992–, Autostrade International SA 1993–94, Autostrade UK Ltd 1993–; pres Autostrada International Equity Inc 1993–94; memb: Euro Advsy Bd Nippon Telephone and Telegraph Inc 1986–92, Bd of Mgmnt Dulles Greenway Virginia 1993–94; chm of tstees Kempton Great Engine Tst, tstee Guildhall Sch of Music and Drama Fndn; *Recreations* tennis, opera, cottage; *Clubs* City of London; *Style—* Michael Hamilton, Esq; ✉ M J Hamilton & Co, 18th Floor, St Alphage House, 2 Fore Street, London EC2Y 5DA (☎ 0171 374 8985, fax 0171 920 0015)

HAMILTON, (Mostyn) Neil; MP (C) Tatton (majority 15,860); s of Ronald Hamilton, of Southsea, Hants, and Norma, *née* Jones; *b* 9 March 1949; *Educ* Amman Valley GS, UCW Aberystwyth (BSc, MSc), CCC (LLB); *m* 4 June 1983, (Mary) Christine, da of Dr Edward Theodore Holman, of Manaccan, Cornwall; *Career* called to the Bar Middle Temple 1978; dir IOD 1982–83; Parly candidate (C): Abertillery 1974, Bradford N 1979; MP (C) Tatton 1983–, PPS to Min for Public Tport 1986–87, memb Treasy and Civil Serv Select Ctee 1987–90, sec Cons Pty Fin Ctee 1987–90, vice chm Cons Pty Trade and Industry Ctee 1987–90 and 1994, govt whip 1990–92, under sec of state DTI 1992–94 (resigned); vice patron Small Business Bureau 1983–; *Books* The Facts of State Industry, US/UK Double Taxation Treaty (1980); *Recreations* bibliomania, gardening, architecture and conservation, silence; *Style—* Neil Hamilton, Esq, MP; ✉ House of Commons, London SW1A 0AA (☎ 0171 219 3000)

HAMILTON, Prof Nigel; s of Sir Denis Hamilton (d 1988), and Olive, Lady Hamilton, *née* Wanless; *b* 16 Feb 1944; *Educ* Westminster Sch, Univ of Munich, Trinity Coll Cambridge (BA, MA); *m* 1, 1966, Hannelore Pfeifer (d 1973); 2 s (Alexander b 1967, Sebastian b 1970); m 2, 1976, Outi Palovesi; 2 s (Nicholas b 1977, Christian b 1980); *Career* slave Andre Deutsch Publishing House 1965–66; fndr: The Greenwich Bookshop 1966, The Biography Bookshop 1987; author, lectr and broadcaster 1969–; visiting prof Univ of Massachusetts Boston 1989–94, visiting prof of history Royal Holloway Coll Univ of London 1995–; dir British Inst of Biography 1996–; *Awards* Whitbread Prize for Best Biography 1981, Templer Award for Best Contrib to Mil History 1987, Blue Ribbon Award for Best Documentary (NY Film and Video Assoc) 1987; *Books* Royal Greenwich (with Olive Hamilton, 1969), The Brothers Mann, The Lives of Heinrich and Thomas Mann (1978), Monty: The Making of a General (1981), Monty: Master of the Battlefield (1983), Monty: The Field-Marshal (1986), Monty, The Man Behind the Legend (1987), JFK: Reckless Youth (1992), Monty: The Battles of Field-Marshal Bernard Montgomery (1994); currently working on a biography of Jawaharlal Nehru; *Television* writer and narrator of films incl: Monty, In Love and War (BBC TV, 1987), Frontiers, Finland and the Soviet Union (BBC TV, 1989); *Recreations* lake sailing; *Style—* Prof Nigel Hamilton; ✉ 12 Churton Place, London SW1V 2LN (☎ 0171 630 6402, fax 0171 630 6466)

HAMILTON, Nigel James; *b* 27 March 1941; *Educ* Loretto; *m* 1966, Valerie Joan Moorwood; 1 s (James Andrew b 1968), 1 da (Fiona Allison b 1972); *Career* Graham Proom & Smith Newcastle upon Tyne 1959–64, ptnr Ernst & Young 1975– (currently nat ptnr i/c insolvency, lead administrator Barings plc 1995); past pres Soc of Practitioners of Insolvency, chm Insolvency Practitioners' Ctee ICAEW (memb Cncl until 1996); ACA 1965, FCA; *Recreations* rugby football, golf, boats, opera, theatre; *Clubs* RAC, Salcombe Yacht; *Style—* Nigel J Hamilton, Esq; ✉ Ernst & Young, Becket House, Lambeth Palace Rd, London SE1 7EU (☎ 0171 928 2000)

HAMILTON, Nigel John Mawdesley; QC (1981); s of Archibald Dearman Hamilton, OBE, of 21 Briant's Piece, Hermitage, nr Newbury, Berks, and Joan Worsley, *née* Mawdesley; *b* 13 Jan 1938; *Educ* St Edward's Sch Oxford, Queens' Coll Cambridge (BA, MA); *m* 31 Aug 1963, Leone Morag Elizabeth, da of William Smith Gordon, CBE; 2 s (Andrew b 5 Oct 1966, William b 5 May 1970); *Career* Nat Serv 2 Lt RE; asst master: St Edward's Sch Oxford 1961–65, King's Sch Canterbury 1963–65; called to the Bar Inner Temple 1965, in practice Western Circuit, bencher Inner Temple 1989–; memb (C) Avon CC 1989–93; memb Bar Cncl 1989–93; *Recreations* fishing; *Clubs* Flyfishers'; *Style—* Nigel Hamilton, Esq, QC; ✉ St John's Chambers, Small St, Bristol BS1 1DW (☎ 0117 921 3456, fax 0117 929 4821)

HAMILTON, Peter Boris; *b* 17 Oct 1928; *Educ* Bedford Sch, Univ of St Andrews (BSc), Harvard Univ (MBA); *m* 1951, Gwendolen Mary, *née* Clark; 1 s (Michael), 1 da (Susan); *Career* chm and chief exec: Firth Cleveland Ltd 1977–79, GKN Engineering and Construction Services Ltd 1978–79; gp chief exec APV plc 1980–84, dir Fenner plc 1984–95, chief exec Carrier Holdings Ltd 1985–91; *Recreations* sailing (TSMY 'Moorea IV'); *Clubs* Royal Yacht Sqdn; *Style—* Peter B Hamilton, Esq; ✉ 31 Chantry View Rd, Guildford, Surrey GU1 3XW (☎ 01483 65318)

HAMILTON, Peter Brian; s of late Lt-Col Brian Hamilton, of Briar Lodge, Galmpton, S Devon, and Clara Maria, *née* Ertelthaler; *b* 7 Feb 1941; *Educ* Beaumont Coll Windsor, Plymouth Coll of Navigation (Diploma); *m* 1 (m dis); 1 s (James Drummond Alexander b 11 Sept 1977); m 2, 1979, Rosalind Mary, da of Bernard James Sanger (d 1990); 1 s (Edward Peter Willoughby b 14 Nov 1980), 1 step s (Charles Lindsay Jerrom b 11 May 1973), 1 step da (Amanda Suzanne Jerrom b 25 Aug 1970); *Career* PR exec; navigating cadet Shell Tankers Ltd 1957–60, reporter and feature writer Financial Times 1960–63, Planned Public Relations International (Young and Rubicam) 1963–75 (exec, account dir, md), dir public affairs Gulf Oil Corporation (Europe Africa and ME) 1975–80, dir Good Relations Group plc 1980–84; md: Hill & Knowlton Ltd London 1984–85, The Communication Group plc 1985–; winner of various awards for UK community affairs prog for Gulf Oil; author of various articles and essays on public relations; MIPR 1967, memb Int PR Assoc 1971; *Recreations* sailing, gardening, music, French railways; *Clubs* Royal Cornwall Yacht, Mylor Yacht; *Style—* Peter Hamilton, Esq; ✉ Moggs Farm, Wyke Champflower, nr Bruton Somerset BA10 0PW (☎ 01749 813829, fax 01749 813827); The Communication Group plc, 19 Buckingham Gate, London SW1E 6LB (☎ 0171 630 1411, fax 0171 931 8010)

HAMILTON, Maj Peter James Sidney; MBE (Mil 1953); s of Maj Frank Carr Hamilton (d 1946), late RGA, of Bishop's Stortford, Herts, and Alice Joan, *née* Trumper (d 1973); *b* 19 Nov 1917; *Educ* Bishop's Stortford Coll; *m* 1962, Patricia Douglas, da of Robert Hirst (d 1940), of Croydon; 2 s (Andrew, Hamish), 2 da (Rosamond, Penelope); *Career* banker 1936–39; served WWII with Prince of Wales's Own Regt of Yorkshire and on Gen Staff: N Africa, Palestine, Iraq, India, Burma, China, Austria, Malaya, Cyprus, attained rank of Maj; instr Mons Offr Cadet Sch 1951–54, Cyprus 1957–60, security advsr to PM of S Rhodesia 1961–62, dir Chubb Security Services Ltd 1972–78, md Zeus Security Consultants Ltd 1978–83, dep chm Zeus Security Ltd 1980–83, md Peter Hamilton (Security Consultants) Ltd 1983–89, jt md (with John Ingram) Hamilton Ingram Ltd 1989–90 (dep chm 1990–91); twice chm Euro Chapter American Soc for Industl Security (life memb 1993); has lectured widely in Europe, USA and Canada; hon fell Inst of Professional Investigators, hon memb Br Security Indust Assoc; assoc memb Nat Supervisory Cncl for Intruder Alarms; FRSA, FIPI, FInstD; *Books* Handbook of Security (founding ed), Espionage Terrorism and Subversion in an Industrial Society (1968 and 1980), Computer Security (1972), Business Security (1980), The Adminstration of Corporate Security (1987); several works translated into Japanese, Finnish and Italian; *Recreations* country life, fishing; *Clubs* Athenaeum, Army and Navy; *Style—* Maj Peter Hamilton, MBE; ✉ c/o The Army and Navy Club, 36 Pall Mall, London SW1Y 5JN

HAMILTON, Sir (Robert Charles) Richard Caradoc; 9 Bt (NS 1646), of Silvertonhill, Lanarkshire; s of Maj Sir Robert Caradoc Hamilton, 8 Bt (d 1959), and Irene (d 1969), 2 da of Sir Charles Mordaunt, 10 Bt; *b* 8 Sept 1911; *Educ* Charterhouse, St Peter's Coll Oxford; *m* 16 April 1952, Elizabeth Vidal, da of Sir William Pell Barton, KCIE, CSI, formerly of Lower Lodge, Ardingly, Sussex; 1 s (Andrew), 3 da (Susanna Eve b 1956, Sophia Louisa b 1964, Penelope Katherine b 1966); *Heir* s, Andrew Caradoc Hamilton, b 23 Sept 1953; *Career* Intelligence Corps 1940–45; taught French and drama at Ardingly Coll 1945–61; churchwarden Walton d'Eivile 1970–, memb Warwickshire Co Cncl Educn Ctee 1965–73; govr Westham House Adult Educn Coll, memb Warwickshire CLA; plays acted at Margate, Dundee and Farnham Reps, five Shakespeare plays directed at the Minack Theatre; landowner (4000 acres); *Publications* de Luze's A History of the Royal Game of Tennis (trans, 1979), Barcellon's Rules and Principles of Tennis (trans, 1987); *Recreations* real tennis, playwright; *Style—* Sir Richard Hamilton, Bt; ✉ The Old Rectory, Walton, Warwick CV35 9HX (☎ 01789 840460)

HAMILTON, His Hon Judge; Richard Graham; s of Henry Augustus Rupert Hamilton (d 1970), and Frances Mary Graham, *née* Abercrombie; *b* 26 Aug 1932; *Educ* Charterhouse, Univ Coll Oxford (MA); *m* 16 April 1960, Patricia Craghill, da of William Newton Ashburner (d 1954); 1 s (William Graham b 1963), 1 da (Susan Elizabeth b 1965); *Career* recorder of Crown Court 1974, circuit judge (Northern Circuit) 1976–, chllr Diocese of Liverpool 1979; *Books* Foul Bills and Dagger Money (1979), All Jangle and Riot (1986), A Good Wigging (1988); *Radio Plays* Van Gogh in England (1981), Voices from Babylon (1983), A Longing for Dynamite (1984), The Maybrick Trial (1988), The Veronica Mutiny (1990); *Recreations* reading, walking, films; *Clubs* Athenaeum (Liverpool); *Style—* His Hon Judge Hamilton; ✉ c/o Northern Circuit Office, 15 Quay Street, Manchester M60 9FD

HAMILTON, Stewart McKee; JP (Sheffield 1972); s of Ian Hamilton (d 1990), of Sheffield, and Marjorie, *née* McKee (d 1994); *b* 12 Jan 1937; *Educ* Oundle, King's Coll Cambridge (MA Mech Scis Tripos); *m* 21 July 1960, Susan Marie, da of late Ernest Lilleyman; 1 s (Bruce b 1 Nov 1962), 2 da (Madeleine b 1 Feb 1964, Tania b 29 June 1967); *Career* Nat Serv cmmnd Sub Lt RN, served Cyprus and Near East 1955–57; Rolls Royce Motors Ltd Crewe: devpt engr 1960–62, PA to Serv Dir 1962–63, tech serv mangr 1963–65; prodn mangr Tubewrights Ltd Liverpool 1965–66; T G Lilleyman & Son Ltd Sheffield: prodn dir 1966–76, md 1977–93, chm 1987–; chm Thornton Precision Forgings Ltd Sheffield 1995– (md 1994–95); chm: Cncl Sheffield Cutlery Research Assoc 1980–90, Central Sheffield Univ Hosps NHS Tst 1995– (non-exec dir 1991–95); tstee: Sheffield Church Burgesses Tst, J G Graves Charitable Tst, Cavendish Fellowship in Hip Surgery; special tstee for the former United Sheffield Hosps; Freeman: City of London, Worshipful Co of Cutlers in Hallamshire; High Sheriff of S Yorks 1990–91; CEng, FIMechE 1996 (MIMechE 1969), FRSA 1995, fell Inst of Forging Technol 1996; *Recreations* walking, dry stone-walling, classical music, opera, theatre; *Style—* Stewart Hamilton, Esq, JP; ✉ Swinglee Grange, Hollow Meadows, Sheffield S6 6GH (☎ 0114 230 1014, fax 0114 230 7783); Central Sheffield University Hospitals NHS Trust, Royal Hallamshire Hospital, Glossop Road, Sheffield S10 2JF (☎ 0114 271 3436, fax 0114 271 3519, mobile 0831 677056)

HAMILTON, Thomas Gottfried Louis; s of Louis Hamilton (d 1948), of London, and Johanna Agnes Lucia, *née* Jahn (d 1956); *b* 29 March 1930; *Educ* The King's Sch Canterbury, UCL (BA); *m* 23 March 1957, Georgina Vera, da of Hugh Millen Craig (d 1956), of Belfast; 1 s (Richard b 1964), 1 da (Julia b 1962); *Career* asst architect: Bertram Carter 1956–58, Campbell-Jones & Ptnrs 1958–60; ptnr Hammett & Norton 1960–64, fndr ptnr McDonald Hamilton & Montefiore 1964–86, dir MHM Partnership Ltd 1986–91, conslt MHM Architects Ltd 1992; RIBA; *Recreations* painting, theatre, music, literature, winter sports; *Clubs* Arts (ctee memb); *Style—* Thomas Hamilton, Esq; ✉ 55 Addison Avenue, London W11 4QU; Dorking Tye Cottage, Dorking Tye, Bures, Suffolk

CO8 5JY; Marlborough House, Tower Street, London WC2H 9LN (☎ 0171 240 3506, fax 0171 240 3498)

HAMILTON, Prof William Donald; *b* 1 Aug 1936; *Educ* Tonbridge Sch, St John's Coll Cambridge (state scholar, BA, PhD); *Career* Nat Serv RE 1955–57; lectr Dept of Zoology Imperial Coll London 1964–77, museum prof of evolutionary biology Museum of Zoology and Biological Sciences Univ of Michigan 1978–84, Royal Soc res prof Univ of Oxford 1984–, professorial fell New Coll Oxford 1984–; nine months in Brazil with Royal Soc and RGS Xavantina-Cachimbo expedition 1968–69, Leverhulme visiting prof Faculdade de Medicina de Ribeirão Preto Universidade de São Paulo Brazil 1975–76, visiting Agassiz prof Museum of Comparative Zoology Harvard Univ 1978; Scientific Medal Zoological Soc of London 1975, Newcomb Cleveland Prize American Assoc for the Advancement of Science (jtly with Robert Axelrod) 1982, Darwin Medal Royal Soc 1988, Scientific Medal Linnean Soc 1989, Frink Medal Zoological Soc of London 1991, lectr and prize Albert Wander Fndn and Univ of Bern 1992, Crafoord Prize and Medal Swedish Acad of Sciences (jtly with Seymour Benzer) 1993, Kyoto Prize for Basic Sciences Inamori Fndn 1993, Fyssen Prize Fyssen Fndn Paris 1996; first pres Human Behaviour and Evolution Soc 1988; foreign hon memb American Acad of Arts and Sciences 1978, memb Royal Soc of Sciences of Uppsala Sweden 1987; corresponding memb Brazilian Acad of Sciences 1994; Hon Doctorate Univ of Guelph 1994; FRS 1980; *Books* Narrow Roads of Gene Land (1995), author of numerous pubns and reviews on evolution theory in scientific jls; *Style*— Prof William Hamilton, FRS; ✉ Department of Zoology, South Parks Road, Oxford OX1 3PS

HAMILTON, William McDonald (Bill); s of Cdr James Hamilton, VRD, RNR (ret), of St Andrews, Fife, Scotland, and Emily, *née* McDonald; *b* 22 Sept 1943; *Educ* Dundee HS, Monkwearmouth Coll Sunderland; *m* 5 Feb 1972, Gertrude Veronica, da of Michael Lee (d 1963), of Aughrim, Co Wicklow; 1 s (David b 1980), 1 da (Claire b 1973); *Career* reporter/newsreader Tyne Tees TV 1966–70, sports prodr BBC radio 1970–71, reporter/presenter Border TV 1971–73, reporter/presenter BBC TV Scotland 1973–80, home affrs corr BBC TV News 1981–88, news and sports corr BBC TV News 1988–, presenter Now The Good News (BBC Radio 5 Live); vice pres Anglo-Albanian Assoc; memb Football Referees' Assoc; Paul Harris fell Rotary Int; Order of Mother Teresa (Albania); *Books* I Belong to Glasgow (1975), Albania - Who Cares? (1992); *Recreations* association football referee (class 1); *Style*— Bill Hamilton, Esq; ✉ 39 Waverley Road, St Albans, Hertfordshire, AL3 5PH (☎ 01727 869604); BBC Television Centre, Wood Lane, London W12 7RJ (☎ 0181 576 1314, fax 0181 749 7872)

HAMILTON AND BRANDON, 15 and 12 Duke of (S 1643, GB 1711); Angus Alan Douglas Douglas-Hamilton; also Earl of Arran (S 1503), Marquess of Douglas, Lord Abernethy and Jedburgh Forest (both S 1633), Marquess of Clydesdale, Earl of Arran and Cambridge, Lord Aven and Innerdale (all S 1643), Earl of Lanark, Lord Machansire and Polmont (both S 1661), Baron Dutton (GB 1711); Premier Duke in the Peerage of Scotland; Hereditary Keeper of Holyrood House; 18 Duke of Châtelherault (France 1549); s of 14 and 11 Duke of Hamilton and Brandon, KT, GCVO, AFC, PC (d 1973), and Dowager Duchess of Hamilton and Brandon; *b* 13 Sept 1938; *Educ* Eton, Balliol Coll Oxford (MA); *m* 1, 1972 (m dis 1987), Sarah Jane (d 1994), da of Sir Walter Scott, 4 Bt (d 1992); 2 s (Alexander b 1978, John b 1979), 2 da (Eleanor b 1973, Anne b 1976); m 2, 1988, Jillian, da of Noel Robertson, formerly w of (1) Martin Page and (2) Edward Hulton; *Heir* s, Alexander, Marquess of Douglas and Clydesdale, *qv*, b 1978; *Career* joined RAF 1956, Flt Lt 1963, flying instructor 1965, instrument rating examiner 1966, invalided 1967, sr commercial pilot's licence 1968, test pilot Scottish Aviation 1970–72; KStJ 1974 and Prior Order of St John in Scotland 1975–82; memb EC sub-ctee on Energy and Transport 1975–77; hon memb Royal Scottish Pipers Soc 1977, memb Piobaireachd Soc 1979, patron British Airways Pipe Band 1977–; memb cncl Cancer Research Campaign 1978; Hon Air Cdre No 2 (City of Edinburgh) Maritime HQ Unit RAuxAF 1982–; memb The Queen's Body Guard for Scotland (Royal Co of Archers) 1975–; CEng, MIMechE, FBIS; *Books* Maria R (1991); *Recreations* motorcycling, diving, piping; *Clubs* New (Edinburgh), RAF; *Style*— His Grace the Duke of Hamilton; ✉ Lennoxlove, Haddington, E Lothian EH41 4NZ (☎ 01620 823720); Archerfield, by Dirleton, E Lothian EH39 5HQ (☎ 01620 850298)

HAMILTON-BURKE, Ian Douglas; s of John Douglas Burke (ka 1944), and Jean Hamilton, *née* Drane; *b* 14 Oct 1943; *Educ* Liverpool Coll; *m* Joan, da of Harold Planche; 2 s (James Patrick Ian, Andrew Charles Raoul), 1 da (Victoria Roisin); *Career* Poulsoms CAs 1968–86; dir Minster Executive Ltd 1978–86; ptnr: Hodgson Impey CAs 1986–90, Pannell Kerr Forster CAs 1990–91, Hamilton-Burke Dufau CAs 1991–; dir Curtins Holdings plc 1990–; bd memb Liverpool Marie Curie Home, govr Liverpool Coll; Freeman City of London 1982, Liveryman Worshipful Co of Pipe Makers and Tobacco Blenders; FCA, FInstD; *Recreations* hockey, marathon running, fell walking; *Clubs* Liverpool Racquet, Rotary (Liverpool); *Style*— Ian Hamilton-Burke, Esq; ✉ Bellisle, Quarry St, Liverpool L25 6DY (☎ 0151 428 3199); Hamilton-Burke Dufau, Gladstone House, 2 Church Road, Liverpool L13 2BB (☎ 0151 733 0864, fax 0151 735 0370)

HAMILTON-DALRYMPLE, Sir Hew Fleetwood; 10 Bt (NS 1698), of North Berwick, Haddingtonshire; KCVO (1985, CVO 1974), JP (1987); s of Sir Hew Clifford Hamilton-Dalrymple, 9 Bt (d 1959), and Anne Dorothea Dyce Nicol, *née* Thorne (d 1979); *b* 9 April 1926; *Educ* Ampleforth; *m* 25 Sept 1954, Lady Anne-Louise Mary Keppel; 4 s (Hew Richard b 1955, John James b 1957, Robert George b 1959, William Benedict b 1965); *Heir* s, Hew Richard Hamilton-Dalrymple, *qv*, b 3 Sept 1955; *Career* Maj Grenadier Gds, ret 1962; The Queen's Body Guard for Scotland (Royal Co of Archers): Adjt 1964–85, pres Cncl 1988–96, Capt-Gen and Gold Stick for Scotland 1996–; dir: Scottish & Newcastle Breweries 1967–86 (vice chm 1983–86), Scottish American Investment Co 1967–93 (chm 1985–91); DL East Lothian 1964–87, Vice Lord-Lieut East Lothian 1973–87, Lord Lieut East Lothian 1987–; *Clubs* Cavalry and Guards'; *Style*— Major Sir Hew Hamilton-Dalrymple, Bt, KCVO, JP; ✉ Leuchie, North Berwick, East Lothian (☎ 01620 89 2903)

HAMILTON-DALRYMPLE, Hew Richard; s and h of Sir Hew Fleetwood Hamilton-Dalrymple, 10 Bt, KCVO, *qv*; *b* 3 Sept 1955; *Educ* Ampleforth, Corpus Christi Coll Oxford (MA), Clare Hall Cambridge (MPhil), Birkbeck Coll London (MSc); *m* 1987, Jane Elizabeth, yr da of Lt-Col John Morris, of Leighterton, Glos; 1 s (Hew John Lucian b 28 Aug 1990), 3 da (Hero Cecilia b 1989, Theophania Mary Anne b 1992, Lydia Diana Jane b 1996); *Career* Overseas Devpt Inst fellowship Swaziland 1982–84, Peat Marwick Management Consultants 1984–91, Scottish and Newcastle PLC 1992–; *Style*— Hew Dalrymple, Esq; ✉ Blackdykes, North Berwick, E Lothian

HAMILTON-GRIERSON, Philip John; OBE (1994); s of Philip Francis Hamilton Grierson (d 1963), of Edinburgh, and Margaret Bartholomew (d 1969); *b* 10 Oct 1932; *Educ* Rugby, CCC Oxford (MA); *m* 1963, Pleasaunce Jill, da of Peter Gordon Cardew, of Somerset; 2 da (Sophie b 1964, Katherine b 1966), 1 s (Philip b 1967); *Career* PO RAF (Asst Adjutant 207 AFS); sec to Lib Party 1962–65; dir Gallaher Ltd 1978–88, dep chm Highlands and Islands Devpt Bd 1988–91, dir Highlands and Islands Enterprise 1991–93; chm: Highland Hospice Ltd 1988–95, Northern Coll 1991–95, State Hospital Carstairs 1991–; dir: Cromarty Firth Port Authority 1989–, Investors in People Scotland 1992–, AI Welders Ltd 1992–, Moray Firth Service Company Ltd 1994–; *Recreations* tennis, music, sailing; *Clubs* Highland; *Style*— Philip Hamilton-Grierson, Esq, OBE; ✉ Pitlundie, North Kessock, By Inverness IV1 1XG (☎ 01463 731392, fax 01463 731729)

HAMILTON-JONES, Major General John; CBE (1976); s of Capt George Hamilton-Jones, MBE (d 1985), of London, and Lilian, *née* Bolton (d 1981); *b* 6 May 1926; *Educ* Cranbrook Sch, Univ of Edinburgh; *m* 15 Nov 1952, Penelope Ann Marion (d 1993), da of Robert Lawrie Derry (d 1980), of Norfolk; 3 da (Janet b 1956, Diana b 1958, Kaye b 1963); m 2, 29 Oct 1993, Frances Helen, da of Frank Edgar Griffiths; 1 da (Charlotte b 1968); *Career* commissioned 1945; served: India, Burma and Malaya 1945–50, USA 1957, ME 1963–64; Staff Coll 1959, DS 1966, cmd Artillery Regt 1967–70, MOD staff from Col to Brig 1971–79, ret as Major General 1981; vice pres of int mktg: Gen Defence Corpn 1981–89, Olin Ordnance 1989–90; conslt Cubic Defence Systems 1990–; Lefroy Gold medallist 1972; MIERE 1960, FRAeS 1980, FIMgt 1981, FInstD 1982; Cdr Assoc Franco Britannique 1980; *Recreations* rugby, rowing, flying, music; *Style*— Major General John Hamilton-Jones, CBE, (Ret); ✉ Lloyds Bank, Cox's and Kings Branch, 7 Pall Mall, PO Box 1190, London SW1Y 5NA

HAMILTON OF DALZELL, 4 Baron (UK 1886); James Leslie Hamilton; DL (Surrey 1993); s of 3 Baron Hamilton of Dalzell, GCVO, MC (d 1990), and Rosemary Olive, *née* Coke (d 1993); *b* 11 Feb 1938; *Educ* Eton; *m* 29 March 1967, (Ann Anastasia) Corinna Helena, DL (Surrey 1996), da of Sir Pierson John Dixon, GCMG, CB (d 1965), and sis of Piers Dixon; 4 s (Hon Gavin b 8 Oct 1968, Hon Robert b 29 July 1971, Hon John b (twin) 29 July 1971, Hon Benjamin b 5 Nov 1974); *Heir* s, Hon Gavin Hamilton b 8 Oct 1968; *Career* 2 Lt Coldstream Gds 1956–58; memb Stock Exchange 1967–80; dir Rowton Hotels plc 1978–82; memb Exec Ctee CLA 1991–96 (chm Surrey Branch 1989–91), chm Queen Elizabeth's Fndn for the Disabled 1993– (govr 1978–, chm of Appeals 1980–88, chm of Exec 1989–93), pres Ludlow Conservative Assoc 1996; Freeman City of London, Liveryman Worshipful Co of Drapers 1977; *Recreations* shooting, gardening; *Clubs* Boodle's, Pratt's; *Style*— The Rt Hon the Lord Hamilton of Dalzell, DL; ✉ Stockton House, Norton Shifnal, Shropshire (☎ 01952 730270); Betchworth House, Betchworth, Surrey RH3 7AE (☎ 01737 843324)

HAMILTON-RUSSELL, Col James Gustavus; MBE (1976); s of Maj Hon John Hamilton-Russell (ka 1943), and Lady Diana, *née* Legge (d 1970); *b* 11 Sept 1938; *Educ* Eton; *m* 30 Oct 1965, Alison Mary, da of Dr Sydney Haydn Heard, MBE, of Channel Islands; 2 s (Mark b 1969, Edward b 1969), 1 da (Julia b 1967); *Career* Col; cmmnd Royal Dragoons 1958; served Middle East, Far East, Europe 1958–78; mil asst to Dep Supreme Allied Cdr Europe Shape 1978–80; CO The Blues and Royals 1980–82; Cdr Household Cavalry and Silver Stick-in-Waiting 1983–86, Cdr Br Contingent UN Force in Cyprus 1986–88; asst mil attaché Br Embassy Washington 1988–91, COS HQ London Dist 1991–93; FIMgt; *Recreations* shooting, fishing, travel, golf, music; *Clubs* Pratt's; *Style*— Col James G Hamilton-Russell, MBE; ✉ The Brewhouse, Dudmaston, Bridgnorth, Shropshire (☎ 01746 780094)

HAMILTON-RUSSELL, Brig Hon Richard Gustavus; DSO (1943, and Bar 1944), LVO (4 Class 1977), DL (N Yorks 1973); 2 s of 9 Viscount Boyne, JP, DL; hp to great-nephew, 11 Viscount Boyne, *qv*; *b* 4 Feb 1909; *Educ* Eton, RMC Sandhurst; *m* 17 July 1939, Hon Pamela Cayzer (d 1987), da of 1 Baron Rotherwick; 2 s (Brian, Richard), 1 da (Veronica); *Career* WWII N Africa & Italy (despatches 1945); Brig late 17/21 Lancers (Col 1957–65); memb HM's Body Guard of Hon Corps of Gentlemen at Arms 1956–79 (standard bearer 1977); High Sheriff Yorks 1968; *Clubs* Cavalry and Guards'; *Style*— Brig the Hon Richard Hamilton Russell, DSO, LVO, DL; ✉ South Hill House, Cornbury Park, Charlbury, Oxfordshire OX7 3EU

HAMILTON-TURNER, William Allen; s of Dr Claude Frederic Hamilton-Turner (d 1988), of Castletown, IOM, and Mary Eileen, *née* Allen; *b* 16 July 1947; *Educ* Eton; *m* 4 Dec 1976, Dulcie Jill, *née* Procter; 1 s (Henry b 1978), 1 da (Lucy b 1980); *Career* Brown Shipley & Co Ltd 1966–74, Singer & Friedlander (IOM) Ltd 1974–80; Rea Bros (IOM) Ltd: md 1986–95, dep chm 1995–; pres Assoc of Manx Bankers 1995–; memb Viewer Consultative Cncl ITC 1990–93; Hon ADC to HE The Lieut Govr of the Isle of Man; Liveryman Worshipful Co of Skinners; ACIB 1972; *Recreations* golf; *Clubs* MCC, NMRA, Rotary International; *Style*— Bill Hamilton-Turner, Esq; ✉ Ballaquayle, Princes Rd, Douglas, IOM IM2 4HY (☎ 01624 624063); Rea Bros (IOM) Ltd, 29 Athol St, Douglas, IOM IM99 1RB (☎ 01624 643200, fax 01624 622039, telex 627752)

HAMILTON-WEDGWOOD, Kenneth Roy; s of Thomas Hamilton-Wedgwood (d 1978), of Rustington, W Sussex, and Elsie Maude, *née* Kershaw (d 1978); *b* 11 Dec 1931; *Educ* Warwick and Whitgift Schs; *m* 19 May 1973 (m dis 1979), Rita, da of George William Gransden, of Hyde Home Farm, East Hyde, Luton, Bedfordshire; *Career* conslt/tech author (electronics) Environmental Instrumentation Satellite Data Collection (Argos) Oceanography; Nat Serv RAF; SAC airborne wireless communciations, early experimental Decca navigator 1950–52; with Whessoe Ltd Darlington Co Durham, resident engr i/c instrumentation installation data measurement and transmission system for Esso West London Terminal (bulk fuel storage) 1960–67, with Ultra Electronics London 1968–69, Marine Electronics Ltd 1971–72, Partech Electronics Ltd 1982, fndr Camba Consultants; *Recreations* fully licensed radio amateur G3XKW, country walking, music, photography; *Style*— Kenneth Hamilton-Wedgwood, Esq; ✉ Rosedale, Redmoor, Bodmin, Cornwall PL30 5AR (☎ 01208 872608); Partech Electronics Ltd, Eleven Doors, Charlestown, St Austell, Cornwall PL25 3NN (☎ 01726 74856, telex 45362 G a/G PARTEK, fax 01726 68850)

HAMLIN, Prof Michael John; CBE (1994); *b* 11 May 1930; *Educ* Univ of Bristol (BSc), Imperial Coll London (DIC); *m* 1951, Augusta Louise, da of late Thomas, and Rose Louise, Tippins; 3 s (b 1952, b 1954, b 1957); *Career* water engrg conslt; asst under agreement Messrs Lemon & Blizard consulting engrs Southampton 1951–53, The Anglo American Corp of SA 1954–55, Messrs Stewart Sviridov and Oliver consulting civil engrs Johannesburg 1955, Dr E J Hamlin and Ptnrs consulting engrs Johannesburg 1955–57, ptnr Rowe and Hamlin consulting civil engrs Johannesburg 1957–59, lectr Dept of Civil Engrg Univ of the Witwatersrand SA 1959–60; Dept of Civil Engrg Univ of Birmingham: lectr 1961–66, sr lectr 1966–70, prof of water engrg 1971–87, head of dept 1980–87, pro-vice chllr 1985–86, vice-princ 1986–87, acting vice-chllr autumn term 1986; princ and vice-chllr Univ of Dundee 1987–94; independent conslt 1994–; chm: Bd of Govrs Scottish Centre for Children with Motor Impairments 1990–94, Ctee of Scottish HE Principals 1992–94; memb: Ctee of Vice-Chllrs and Principals 1987–94, Programme Bd Br Geological Survey 1988–93, Int Relations Ctee Royal Soc 1992–; UK nat corr Union of Geodesy and Geophysics nominated by The Royal Soc 1992–; author of numerous articles and pubns on public health engrg and water resources engrg; Hon LLD: St Andrews, Dundee 1996; Hon DEng Birmingham 1995; FIWEM (FIWES 1973), FICE 1981, FEng 1985, FRSE 1990, FRCPS(Glas) 1992, Hon FRCGP (London) 1993; *Style*— Prof Michael Hamlin, CBE, FRSE, FEng; ✉ The Coombs, nr Ludlow, Shropshire SY8 3AQ

HAMLIN, Patrick Lindop; s of Thomas Patrick Hamlin (d 1985), of Hong Kong, and Zehra Emena, *née* Mahmoud (d 1987); *b* 4 Aug 1947; *Educ* Birkenhead Sch, Inns of Ct Sch of Law; *m* 11 Sept 1976, Shelagh Joan, da of William Bernard Fitzpatrick (d 1985), of Wallasey; 1 s ((Edward) Ruari b 1985), 1 da (Georgina Louise b 1982); *Career* called to the Bar Gray's Inn (McCaskie scholar) 1970; private practice in common law and local authy, asst recorder 1990, recorder 1993; memb Lincoln's Inn Bar Rep Ctee, former memb Ctee London Common Law Bar Assoc, asst Parly Boundary Cmmn; memb Lincoln's Inn and Gray's Inn; *Recreations* skiing, reading, Eng furniture; *Style*— Patrick Hamlin, Esq; ✉ 22 Old Buildings, Lincoln's Inn, London WC2A 3UJ (☎ 0171 831 0222, fax 0171 831 2239)

HAMLYN, Michael John; s of Jack Trelawney Hamlyn (d 1990), and Agnes, *née* Ecob (d 1993); *b* 26 March 1936; *Educ* Kimbolton Sch Cambs, St Peter's Coll Oxford (BA); *m* 1 July 1961, Claire Honor Annabel, da of Silvester Bolam; 2 s (Nicholas b 5 Dec 1961, Alexander b 12 Aug 1964), 1 da (Victoria b 28 Feb 1963); *Career* reporter The Journal Newcastle upon Tyne 1959–61; The Sunday Times: reporter 1961–65, news ed 1965–68, asst ed (news) 1968–70; The Times: asst ed (night) 1970–73, exec ed (night) 1973–81, chief of bureau US Bureau News Ltd and Times Newspapers 1981–83, South Asia corr 1983–89, dep foreign ed 1989, chief night ed 1989–90, exec ed (news) 1990–92, Southern Africa corr 1992–95; *Clubs* Savile; *Style*— Michael Hamlyn, Esq; ✉ 45 Upper Orange Street, Oranjezicht, Capetown 8001, South Africa (☎ 00 27 21 461 9955, fax 00 27 21 462 2085)

HAMLYN, Paul Bertrand; CBE (1993); *b* 12 Feb 1926; *Educ* St Christopher's Sch Letchworth; *m*; 1 s, 1 da; *Career* dir Paul Hamlyn Ltd 1970– (fndr 1950), chm Hamlyn Publishing Group 1986– (co sold 1965, repurchased 1986); fndr and chm Octopus Publishing Group 1971–, co-fndr and co-chm Conran Octopus 1983–; other directorships incl: Reed Book Publishing Ltd 1971–, Reed International Books Ltd 1983–, Reed International plc 1987–, Reed Elsevier plc 1993–, Michelin House Development Ltd 1985–, Bibendum Restaurant Ltd 1986–, Brandchart Ltd 1987–, Chateau de Bagnols Ltd 1988–, Michelin House Investment Company Ltd 1989–, Book Club Associates (chm) 1993–; fndr The Paul Hamlyn Fndn 1972 (concentrating support on the arts, education and book publishing projects in the UK and continental Europe together with a number of projects in the Third World, mainly in the Indian sub-continent); chllr Thames Valley Univ 1993–; Hon DLitt: Univ of Keele 1988, Univ of Warwick 1991; RSA Albert Medal 1993; *Recreations* opera; *Style*— Paul Hamlyn, Esq, CBE; ✉ Sussex House, 12 Upper Mall, London W6 9TA (☎ 0181 741 2749, fax 0181 741 2263)

HAMMER, James Dominic George; CB (1983); s of E A G Hammer, and E L G Hammer; *b* 21 April 1929; *Educ* Dulwich, Corpus Christi Coll Cambridge; *m* 1955, Margaret Eileen Halse; 2 s, 1 da; *Career* conslt in occupational health and safety; dep dir gen Health & Safety Exec 1985–89, assoc memb King's Healthcare Tst 1991–, vice chm Southwark MENCAP 1975–, pres Int Assoc of Labour Inspection 1984–93, tech dir UK Skills 1990–; chm: Nat Accreditation Cncl for Certification Bodies 1992–95, Nat Examination Bd in Occupational Safety and Health 1992–95, UK Nat Organising Ctee for the Euro Year of Safety Hygiene and Health at Work 1992–93; chm Mgmnt Ctee: Athol House (Leonard Cheshire Fndn) 1995–, S London Servs for People with Learning Disabilities 1996–; FRSA; *Style*— James Hammer, Esq, CB; ✉ 10 Allison Grove, Dulwich, London SE21 7ER

HAMMERBECK, Brig Christopher John Anthony; CB (1991); s of Sqdn Ldr Olaf Rolf William Hammerbeck (d 1988), of Frinton on Sea, Essex, and Ivy Mary, *née* Musker; *b* 14 March 1943; *Educ* Mayfield Coll; *m* 23 March 1974 (m dis 1996), Alison Mary, da of Capt John Edward Felice, VRD, JP, RNR, of Southport, Lancs; 1 s (Christian b 7 July 1976), 2 da (Lucy b 5 Oct 1977, Leonora b 26 Oct 1984); *Career* articled to firm of slrs 1961–64; cmmnd 1965, Staff Coll 1975, DAA and QMG 12 Mech Bde 1976–78, DS Army Staff Coll 1982–84, CO 2 Royal Tank Regt 1984–87, ACOS G3 HQ 1 BR Corps 1987–88, RCDS 1989, cmd 4 Armd Bde Gulf War 1990–91, dep cdr Br Forces Hong Kong 1992–94, exec dir British C of C 1994–; MIMgt 1981; *Recreations* golf, sailing, cricket, skiing, bobsleigh; *Clubs* Army and Navy, Royal Over-Seas League, Hong Kong, Tripehounds; *Style*— Brig Christopher Hammerbeck, CB; ✉ British Chamber of Commerce, 1401 Tung Wai Commercial Building, 111 Gloucester Road, Hong Kong

HAMMERSLEY, Rear Adm Peter Gerald; CB (1982), OBE (1965); s of the late Capt Robert Stevens Hammersley, of Endon, Stoke-on-Trent, and Norah, *née* Kirkham; *b* 18 May 1928; *Educ* Denstone Coll, RN Engrg Coll, RN Coll Greenwich, Imperial Coll London (DIC); *m* 1959, (Audrey) Cynthia Henderson, da of late Pelham Bolton, of Wilmslow, Cheshire; 1 s (Robert), 1 da (Daphne); *Career* RN 1946–82, First Engr Offr First Br Nuclear Submarine HMS Dreadnought 1960–64, Capt RN Engrg Coll 1978–80, CSO (Engrg) to C-in-C Fleet 1980–82; chief exec Br Internal Combustion Engine Mfrs Assoc 1982–85, dir Br Marine Equipment Cncl 1985–92; fell Woodard Corp, chm Denstone Sch Cncl 1995–; Master Worshipful Co of Engrs 1988–89 (Freeman); *Recreations* walking, gardening; *Clubs* Army and Navy; *Style*— Rear Adm Peter Hammersley, CB, OBE; ✉ Wistaria Cottage, Linersh Wood, Bramley, nr Guildford, Surrey GU5 0EE (☎ 01483 898568)

HAMMERSLEY, Philip Tom; OBE (1989); s of Tom Andrew Hammersley (d 1959), of Buckhurst Hill, Essex, and Winifred Alice, *née* Moyns (d 1970); *b* 10 Feb 1931; *Educ* Bancroft's Sch Woodford Essex, Imperial Coll London (BSc); *m* 24 July 1954, Lesley Ann, da of Norman Stuart Millage; 2 s (Mark Andrew b 10 April 1957, Paul David b 22 May 1962), 1 da (Alison Clare b 18 May 1960); *Career* plant then design engr ICI Plastic Div 1954–65; Clarks Ltd Street Somerset: chief engr 1965–68, prodn servs mangr 1968–70, dir Children's Div 1971–79; pres Stride Rite Footwear Inc (Stride Rite Corp) Boston Mass 1979–81; British Shoe Corporation Ltd: factories dir 1981–85, dir responsible for mfrg, personnel and info systems 1985–87, md Freeman Hardy Willis and Trueform 1987–89, commercial dir 1989–90; non-exec chm BSS Group plc Leicester 1995– (non-exec dir 1991–); chm: Cncl Shoe and Allied Trades Research Assoc 1983–86, E Midlands Regnl Cncl CBI 1988–90; pres Br Footwear Mfrs Fedn 1986–87; vice chm Leics Health Authy 1990–92, chm Leicester Royal Infirmary 1992–; memb Cncl Univ of Leicester 1991–; Freeman City of London, memb Worshipful Co of Pattenmakers 1983; CEng, MIMechE 1961, FRSA 1993; *Clubs* MCC, East India; *Style*— Philip Hammersley, Esq, OBE; ✉ Leicester Royal Infirmary NHS Trust, Infirmary Close, Leicester LE1 5WW (☎ 0116 258 5078)

HAMMERTON, His Hon Rolf Eric; s of Eric Maurice Hammerton (d 1967), and Dorothea Alice, *née* Zander (d 1970); *b* 18 June 1926; *Educ* Brighton and Hove GS, Peterhouse Cambridge (MA, LLB); *m* 1953, Thelma Celèstine, da of Vernon Peters Appleyard (d 1955); 1 s (Alastair Rolf b 1960), 3 da (Veronica Lesley b 1954, Andrea Frances b 1956, Lorraine Hilary b 1958); *Career* Capt R Sussex Regt seconded RWAFF 1946–47; called to the Bar Inner Temple 1952, circuit judge (SE Circuit) 1972–94, designated judge children's cases Sussex area 1990–94, principle judge civil matters Sussex 1992–94; contrib to Butterworth Co Ct Precedents; chm Mgmnt Ctee Copper Cliff Hospice 1993; memb Ct of Assts Worshipful Co of Cooks; Philip Teichman Prizeman 1953; *Recreations* cooking; *Style*— His Hon Rolf Hammerton; ✉ The Old Rectory, Falmer, nr Brighton, Sussex BN1 9PG

HAMMETT, Sir Clifford James; kt (1969); s of late Frederick John Hammett; *b* 8 June 1917; *Educ* Woodbridge Sch; *m* 1946, Olive Beryl, da of Frank A Applebee; 4 s, 1 da; *Career* serv WWII 1 Punjab Regt (despatches), POW Siam Railway 1942–45; called to the Bar Middle Temple 1948; chief justice: Tonga 1956–68, Fiji 1967–72; acting govr-gen Fiji 1971; regnl legal advsr Br Devpt Div Barbados 1976–92, dir West Indian Legislative Judiciary Project Law Faculty of the WI Barbados 1982; *Style*— Sir Clifford Hammett

HAMMICK, Paul St Vincent; s and h of Sir Stephen George Hammick, 5 Bt, *qv*; *b* 1 Jan 1955; *Educ* Sherborne, RAC Cirencester; *m* 11 July 1984, Judith Mary, da of Ralph Ernest Reynolds, of Wareham, Dorset; *Recreations* fishing, shooting, wine; *Style*— Paul Hammick Esq

HAMMICK, Sir Stephen George; 5 Bt (UK 1834), of Cavendish Square, London; DL (Dorset 1989); s of Sir George Frederick Hammick, 4 Bt (d 1964), and Mary Adeliza, *née* Welch-Thornton (d 1988); *b* 27 Dec 1926; *Educ* Stowe, RAC Cirencester; *m* 16 April 1953, Gillian Elizabeth, yr da of Maj Pierre Elliot Inchbald, MC (d 1959); 2 s (Paul St Vincent b 1955, Jeremy Charles b 1956), 1 da (Wendy Jane (Mrs Bob Koster) b 1960); *Heir* s, Paul St Vincent Hammick b 1 Jan 1955; *Career* RN 1944–48, RAC Cirencester 1949–50, MFH Cattistock Hunt 1961 and 1962, CC Dorset 1958, farmer; High Sheriff Dorset 1981; vice chm Dorset CC (chm 1988), chm Dorset Police Force; chm Cattistock Hunt; *Recreations* hunting, fishing, music; *Style*— Sir Stephen Hammick, Bt, DL; ✉ Badgers, Wraxall, Dorchester, Dorset DT2 0HN (☎ 01935 83343)

HAMMON, Michael Antony; s of Arthur Stanley Hammon (d 1985), and Mary Augusta, *née* Salter (d 1993); *b* 5 March 1937; *Educ* Oundle; *m* 8 Oct 1966 (m dis 1993), Letitia Sara, da of Henry Leslie Johnson (d 1991); 2 s (Charles b 1969, George b 1973), 2 da (Sara b 1970, Elizabeth b 1972); *Career* slr and farmer; cncllr: Warwick RDC 1965–70, Warwickshire CC 1967–81 (chm Finance, Educn and Policy and Resources Ctees, ldr of Cncl 1976–81), Coventry City Cncl 1987–96; vice chm Warwick, Leamington and Kenilworth Cons Assoc 1970–73, lawyer memb W Midlands Rent Assessment Panel 1982–86; press and PR offr Warwickshire Law Soc 1984–89; dir: H H Goddard Ltd, Marath Developments Ltd; *Recreations* gardening, photography; *Clubs* Naval and Military; *Style*— Michael Hammon, Esq; ✉ Hammon & Co, 403 Walsgrave Road, Coventry CV2 4AH (☎ 01203 448585, fax 01203 441611)

HAMMOND, Anthony Hilgrove; CB (1992); s of Col Charles William Hilgrove Hammond (d 1985), and Jessie Eugenia, *née* Francis (d 1940); *b* 27 July 1940; *Educ* Malvern, Emmanuel Coll Cambridge (open scholar, BA, LLB); *m* 29 Sept 1988, Avril, *née* Collinson; *Career* admitted slr 1965, asst slr GLC (formerly London CC) 1965–68 (articled clerk 1962–65); Home Office: legal asst 1968–70, sr legal asst 1970–74, asst legal advsr 1974–80, princ asst legal advsr to Home Office and NI Office 1980–88, dep under sec of state and legal advsr 1988–92 (legal advsr NI Office 1988–92); slr DTI 1992–; Freeman City of London 1991, memb Worshipful Co of Glass Sellers 1990; *Recreations* bridge, music, birdwatching; *Clubs* Athenaeum; *Style*— Anthony Hammond, Esq, CB; ✉ Solicitor's Office, Department of Trade and Industry, 10–18 Victoria Street, London SW1H 0NN (☎ 0171 215 3039)

HAMMOND, Dr Brian Robert; s of Dennis Francis Hammond, of Rustington, W Sussex, and Iris Margaret Rose Hammond; *b* 28 May 1953; *Educ* Battersea GS, Anglo-Euro Coll of Chiropractic (DC, Canadian Award for Academic Distinction), Univ of Surrey (PhD); *m* 5 Nov 1975, Elizabeth-Jane, da of David Frederick Vincent Craig; 1 s (Daniel Michael b 29 June 1980), 1 da (Samantha Danielle b 26 July 1978); *Career* practising chiropractor; clinic dir Sutton Chiropractic Clinic 1975–, ed Euro Jl of Chirpractic 1976–80, govr Anglo-Euro Coll of Chiropractic 1976–80, memb Gen Cncl Euro Chiropractors' Union 1976–80, external lectr Anglo-Euro Coll of Chirpractic 1980–, external examiner CNAA 1989–92, memb Euro Cncl on Chiropractic Educn 1989–96; memb Br Chiropractic Assoc 1975– (treas 1987–89), Soc for Back Pain Res 1977–, Nat Back Pain Assoc 1977–; *Books* The Detection of Spondylolysis using Lumbar Sonography (1984); *Recreations* bridge, badminton; *Clubs* New Malden Bridge; *Style*— Dr Brian Hammond; ✉ Sutton Chiropractic Clinic, 137 Brighton Road, Sutton, Surrey SM2 5SW (☎ 0181 661 1613, fax 0181 770 9517)

HAMMOND, Col Catherine Elizabeth; CBE (1950); da of late Frank Ernest Rauleigh Eddolls; *b* 22 Dec 1909; *Educ* Lassington House Highworth, Chesterville Sch Cirencester; *m* 1, 1930, Albert Edward Haynes (decd); 1 s, 1 da; m 2, 1949, Aldwyn Hammond (d 1958), farmer and racehorse trainer; *Career* Col WRAC, dep dir HQ Eastern Cmd 1947–50, Hon Col 54 (E Anglian) Div/Dist WRAC (TA) 1964–68; chm WRAC Assoc Cncl 1966–70, life vice pres WRAC Assoc 1971–; chm Highworth Branch RNLI 1971–; pres: Highworth Royal Br Legion (Women's Section) 1977–86, Highworth Amateur Dramatic Soc 1982–86; town mayor Highworth 1979–81 and 1984–85; SSStJ 1986; *Recreations* racing, hockey; *Style*— Col Catherine Hammond, CBE; ✉ Red Down, Highworth, Wilts SN6 7SH (☎ 01793 762331)

HAMMOND, Donald William; *b* 5 March 1948; *Educ* King's Sch Macclesfield, Univ of Lancaster (BA), Manchester Business Sch (DBA); *m* 19 March 1982, Carole Isobel Hammond; *Career* T & N PLC 1969–73, Citibank NA 1974–76, Banco Hispano Americano Ltd 1976–86; dir: Edington plc 1986–90, Henry Cooke Group plc 1988–90, Waterwise Technology Ltd 1993–; chm Halton Gen Hosp Tst 1993–; chm Fin Ctee and dep ldr London Borough of Ealing 1983–86 (cncllr 1978–86), vice chm Gt Budworth Parish Cncl 1995–; FInstD, Assoc MBA; *Recreations* riding, shooting, venture capital; *Style*— Donald Hammond, Esq; ✉ The Butts, Smithy Lane, Great Budworth, Northwich, Cheshire CW9 6HL; Halton General Hospital NHS Trust, Runcorn, Cheshire WA7 2DA (☎ 01928 714567, fax 01928 753104)

HAMMOND, Eric Albert Barratt; OBE (1977); s of Arthur Edgar Hammond (d 1963), and Gertrude May, *née* Barratt (d 1983); *b* 17 July 1929; *Educ* Corner Brook Public Sch Newfoundland; *m* 26 Sept 1953, Brenda Mary, da of George Edgeler; 2 s (Ivan b 1958, Shaun b 1961); *Career* Nat Serv REME 1950–52; EETPU: electrician 1952–64, exec cncllr 1964–84, gen sec 1984–92; vice-pres Industl Participations Assoc 1986–; chm Electronic Components Sector Gp 1978–92; memb: Advsy Cncl on Energy Conservation 1974–77, Electronics EDC 1976–92, Industl Devpt Advsy Bd 1977–87, MMC 1978–84, Econ and Social Ctee of EU 1983–90, Engrg Cncl 1984–90, ACARD 1985–87, CBI Task Force on Wider Share Ownership 1989–90, Lord Chllr's Advsy Ctee on Legal Educn and Conduct 1991–, Employment Appeal Tbnl 1992–; chm 5 Northfleet Scout Gp 1979–84, chm Gravesend GS for Boys 1994–; cncllr: Gravesend Borough DC 1957–60, Northfleet UDC 1960–63; *Recreations* gardening, photography, watching rugby, reading; *Clubs* Gravesend Rugby; *Style*— Eric Hammond, Esq, OBE; ✉ 9 Dene Holm Road, Northfleet, Kent DA11 8LF

HAMMOND, Jane Dominica; da of Reginald Egbert Rolt Hammond (d 1967), and Nancy Mildred, *née* Hawtrey (d 1983); *b* 6 April 1934; *Educ* Queen Anne's Sch Caversham, Hampstead Secretarial Coll, CAM (Dip in PR); *m* 1970, Rudolph Samuel Brown, JP (d 1986); 1 da (Louisa Catherine b 5 March 1974); *Career* secretarial work Publicity Dept BBC and latterly Press Office Swissair 1953–61, asst ed Dairy Industries 1961–64; NALGO (now UNISON): reporter Public Service (newspaper) 1964–65, Health Service PRO 1965–68; PRO St Teresa's Hosp 1968–70; sr information offr: London Borough of Hammersmith 1971–73, Community Rels Cmmn 1973–77 and its successor body Cmmn for Racial Equality 1977–78; ed Hollis PR Weekly 1978–80; chm and md Trident Public Relations Ltd 1980–, proprietor Trident Training Services 1988–; PR conslt Enterprise UK 97 1996–; asst course dir annual Sr Int PR Courses 1991–, course dir twice-yearly London Management Training Centre Sr Secs' and Personal Assts' Courses 1992–; jt course dir annual int introductory and advanced PR courses 1994–; memb Cncl IPR 1995– (memb Professional Practices Ctee 1994–); lectr: Lansdowne Coll 1992–, The Queen's Business and Secretarial Coll 1994–; examiner CAM 1977–95, tutor PR Educn Tst (PRET) Distance Learning Prog 1991–, external moderator Birkbeck Coll 1995–; fndr memb Women's National Cancer Control Campaign; memb PR Educn Forum, memb NUJ, FIPR 1981 (MIPR 1968); *Recreations* reading, cooking, cycling, swimming, dog (as daughter Louisa in America); *Style*— Miss Jane Hammond; ✉ Trident Public Relations, Suite 5, 155 Fawe Park Road, London SW15 2EG (☎ 0181 874 3610)

HAMMOND, (John) Martin; s of Rev Canon Thomas Chatterton Hammond (d 1981), Rector of Beckenham, and Joan, *née* Cruse; *b* 15 Nov 1944; *Educ* Winchester, Balliol Coll Oxford; *m* 25 June 1974, Meredith Jane, da of Kenneth Wesley Shier, of Ontario, Canada; 1 s (Thomas b 1976), 1 step da (Chantal b 1970); *Career* asst master St Paul's 1966–71, teacher Anargyrios Sch Spetsai Greece 1972–73, asst master Harrow 1973–74, master in coll Eton 1980–84 (head of Classics Dept Eton 1974–80); headmaster: City of London Sch 1984–90, Tonbridge Sch 1990–; *Books* Homer - The Iliad, A New Prose Translation (1987); *Style*— Martin Hammond, Esq; ✉ Tonbridge School, Tonbridge, Kent TN9 1JP (☎ 01732 365555)

HAMMOND, Michael Harry Frank; CBE (1990), DL (Nottinghamshire 1990); s of Cecil Edward Hammond (d 1963), and Kate Hammond, *née* Lovell (d 1984); *b* 5 June 1933; *Educ* Leatherhead Co Secdy Sch, Univ of Nottingham (LLM Int Law); *m* 21 Aug 1965, Jenny, da of Dr George Macdonald Campbell (d 1981); 2 s (Ralph b 1968, Richard b 1971), 1 da (Sara b 1966); *Career* slr; dep town clerk: Newport Monmouthshire 1969–71, Nottingham 1971–73; chief exec and town clerk Nottingham City Cncl 1973–90 (prosecuting slr 1963–66); election supervisor Rhodesia Independence Elections 1980; chm Assoc of Local Authy Chief Execs 1984–85 (chm E Midlands Branch 1988–90), pres Notts Law Soc 1989–90; tstee: Hillsborough Disaster Appeal Fund 1989–95, Notts Branch Red Cross 1992– (dep pres 1994–95, pres 1995–), Nottingham Almshouse and Annuity Charity 1994–; chm E Midlands Chair in Stroke Medicine Appeal 1990–92, govr Nottingham High Sch 1990–; memb: National Forest Advsy Bd 1990–94, Midlands Regnl Ctee N Br Housing Assoc 1993–, Ctee Nottingham Rugby Club 1994–; Zimbabwe Independence medal 1980, Rhodesia medal 1980; *Recreations* walking, gardening, bowling; *Clubs* Nottingham and Notts United Services, Queen Anne Bowling Green, Nottingham Proprietary Bowling Green; *Style*— Michael Hammond, Esq, CBE, DL; ✉ 41 Burlington Rd, Sherwood, Nottingham (☎ 0115 960 2000)

HAMMOND, Prof Norman David Curle; s of William Hammond, and Kathleen Jessie, *née* Howes; *b* 10 July 1944; *Educ* Varndean GS, Peterhouse Cambridge (Trevelyan scholar, Dip in Classical Archaeology, MA, PhD, ScD); *m* 1972, Dr Jean Wilson, FSA, *qv*, da of Alan Wilson, and Beryl, *née* Wagstaff; 1 s, 1 da; *Career* Univ of Cambridge: res fell Centre of Latin American Studies 1967–71, Leverhulme res fell Centre of Latin American Studies 1972–75, res fell Fitzwilliam Coll 1973–75; sr lectr Univ of Bradford 1975–77, visiting prof of anthropology Univ of California Berkeley 1977; Rutgers Univ USA: visiting prof 1977–78, assoc prof 1978–84, prof of archaeology 1984–88; Bushnell lectr Univ of Cambridge 1997; visiting prof Jilin Univ Changchun China 1981, visiting Irvine chair of anthropology Calif Acad of Sciences 1984–85, Curl lectr RAI 1985, visiting prof Univ de Paris (Sorbonne) 1987, fell in pre-Columbian studies Dumbarton Oaks Washington USA 1988, assoc in Maya archaeology Peabody Museum Harvard Univ 1988–, prof of archaeology Boston Univ 1988–, visiting fell Worcester Coll Oxford 1989, academic tstee Archaeology Inst of America 1990–93, visiting fell Peterhouse Cambridge 1991 and 1996–97, visiting prof Rheinische-Wilhelms-Universität Bonn 1994, visiting fell McDonald Inst for Archaeological Research Univ of Cambridge 1997; archaeology corr The Times 1967–, memb Editorial Bds various archaeological jls in UK and USA, contrib to various scientific jls, ed Afghan Studies 1976–79, consltg ed Library of Congress (HLAS) 1977–89, archaelogy conslt Scientific American 1979–95, memb various advsy bds Belize 1987–; excavations and surveys: Libya/Tunisia 1964, Afghanistan 1966, Belize 1970– (Lubaantun 1970, Nohmul 1973–86, Cuello 1976–93, La Milpa 1992–), Ecuador 1972–84; FRAS 1972, FSA 1974 (memb Cncl 1996–), Hon Phi Beta Kappa 1989; *Publications* South Asian Archaeology (ed, 1973), Mesoamerican Archaeology New Approaches (ed, 1974), Lubaantun: a Classic Maya Realm (1975), Social Process in Maya Prehistory (ed, 1977), The Archaeology of Afghanistan (ed with F R Allchin, 1978), Maya Archaeology and Ethnohistory (ed with G R Willey, 1979), Ancient Maya Civilization (1982, 5 edn 1994), Archaeology Proceedings (gen ed, 8 vols), 44th International Congress of Americanists (1983–84), Nohmul: a Prehistoric Maya Community in Belize - Excavations 1973–1983 (1985), Cuello: an Early Maya Community in Belize (1991); *Recreations* fine wine, intelligent women, opera; *Clubs* Athenaeum, Tavern (Boston), Cosmos (Washington); *Style*— Prof Norman Hammond, FSA; ✉ Wholeway, Harlton, Cambridge CB3 7ET (☎ and fax 01223 262376); 83 Ivy St, Apt 32, Brookline, MA 02146–4073, USA (☎ 00 1 617 739 9077, fax 00 1 617 353 6800)

HAMMOND, His Hon Judge Simon Tristram; s of Philip Jones Hammond (d 1986), of Leicester, and Sylvia Dina, *née* Sillem (d 1988); *b* 5 Jan 1944; *Educ* Eastbourne Coll, Coll of Law; *m* 10 July 1976, Louise, da of Charles Duncan Weir, FRCS, MC; 2 da (Pollyann Lucy b 8 Feb 1980, Alicia Francesca b 18 Nov 1992), 1 s (Edward Charles b 2 Aug 1981); *Career* articled to Philip Jones Hammond 1962–67, admitted as slr 1967, ptnr Victor Lissack London 1970–76, ptnr Philip J Hammond & Sons Leicester 1977–93, recorder 1990–93 (asst recorder 1985–90), circuit judge (Midland & Oxford Circuit) 1993–; memb: Law Soc's Standing Ctee on Criminal Law 1982–91, Crown Ct Rules Ctee 1988–93, Enforcement Sub-Ctee Home Office Review of Magistrates' Ct Procedure 1989–90, Coll of Law Advsy Bd 1992; asst cmmr to Parly Boundary Cmmn for England 1992; church warden; *Recreations* riding, hunting, skiing, vegetable gardening, food and wine; *Style*— His Hon Judge Simon Hammond; ✉ Lord Chancellor's Department, Midland & Oxford Circuit Office, Priory Court, 33 Bull Street, Birmingham B4 6DW (☎ 0121 681 3200)

HAMMOND, Suzanna Mary; *Educ* Convent of St Clotilde Lechlade Glos, Portsmouth Coll of Further Educn (Dip Business Studies), Univ of Sussex/Regent St Poly (Business Communications and Journalism Degree); *m*; 3 s; *Career* account exec Good Relations Ltd 1969–72, assoc dir heading Consumer Products Div Lexington International 1975–82 (account dir 1972–75); Hill & Knowlton (UK) Ltd (following merger with Lexington International): dir Consumer Mktg Gp 1982–84, dep md 1985–87; md Ogilvy Adams & Rinehart 1987–93, chief exec Hammond Communications (part of Abbott Mead Vickers Group) 1993–; non-exec dir Bd of Govrs Royal Brompton Hosp; *Style*— Ms Suzanna Hammond; ✉ Hammond Communications, 31 Welbeck Street, London W1M 7PG (☎ 0171 935 5404)

HAMMOND, Valerie June; *née* Amas; da of Stanley F Amas (d 1972), and Eileen M Amas (d 1995); *b* 22 Oct 1942; *Educ* Pendergast GS, Open Univ (BA); *m* 1982, A Knighton Berry; *Career* dir Ashridge Mgmnt Res Group 1980–93, chief exec Roffey Park Management Inst 1993–, past pres European Women's Mgmnt Devpt Network; previously: project mangr Petroleum Indust Training Bd, Mobil Oil, Friden Ltd, Rank Screen Servs; memb Cncl European Women's Fndn; dir/govr: Downe House Sch, Kingshurst CTC; author; FIMgt, FRSA, MInstD, AMED, EFMD, EWMD; *Books* Employment Potential - Issues in the Development of Women (with Ashridge team, 1980), The Computer in Personnel Work (with Edgar Wille, 1981), Tomorrow's Office Today (with David, Birchall 1981), No Barriers Here? (1982), Practical approaches to Women's Management Development (1984), Current Research in Management (1985), Men and Women in Organisations (with Tom Boydell, 1985); book chapters and jl articles from research and conferences; *Style*— Ms Valerie Hammond; ✉ Roffey Park Management Inst, Forest Road, Horsham, W Sussex RH12 4TD (☎ 01293 851644, fax 01293 851565)

HAMMOND INNES, Ralph; CBE (1978); s of William Hammond Innes, and Dora Beatrice, *née* Crisford; *b* 15 July 1913; *Educ* Cranbrook Sch; *m* 1937, Dorothy Mary, da of William Cape Lang (d 1989); *Career* Maj RA WWII, served in ME; journalist Financial News 1934–40; author (as Hammond Innes); landowner; Hon DLitt Univ of Bristol 1985; *Books* (all made into films): The Lonely Skier (1947), The White South (1949), Campbells Kingdom (1952), The Mary Deare (1956), Levkas Man (1971), Golden Soak (1973); other books incl: The Last Voyage: Captain Cook's Lost Diary (1978), Solomons Seal (1980), The Black Tide (1982), High Stand (1985), Medusa (1988), Isvik (1991), Target Antarctica (1993), Delta Connection (1996); non-fiction incl: Harvest of Journeys (1960), Scandinavia (with the eds of Life, 1963), Sea and Islands (1967), The Conquistadors (1969), Hammond Innes Introduces Australia (1971), Hammond Innes' East Anglia (1986); *Plays* incl: Campbells Kingdom (screenplay, 1957), The Story of Captain James Cook (TV play, 1975); *Clubs* Soc of Authors, PEN, Royal Yacht Sqdn, Royal Ocean Racing, Royal Cruising, Garrick; *Style*— Ralph Hammond Innes, Esq, CBE; ✉ Ayres End, Kersey, Suffolk IP7 6EB (☎ 01473 823294)

HAMMOND-STROUD, Derek; OBE (1987); s of Herbert William Stroud (d 1951), of Stanmore, Middx, and Ethel Louise, *née* Elliott (d 1988); *b* 10 Jan 1926; *Educ* Salvatorian Coll Harrow, Trinity Coll of Music; *Career* RWAFF India and Burma 1944–47; concert and opera baritone; private study with Elena Gerhardt and Prof Gerhard Hüsch; Glyndebourne Festival Opera 1959–, ENO 1960–, Covent Garden Opera 1971–, Netherlands Opera 1976–87, Metropolitan Opera NY 1977–80, Teatro Colón Buenos Aires 1981, Munich State Opera 1983; festivals: Edinburgh, Aldburgh, Vienna, Munich, Cheltenham, English Bach; concerts and recitals in Spain, Iceland and Denmark; recordings: EMI, Decca, Chandos, RCA, Philipps, Célèbre, Symposium Records; prof of singing RAM 1974–90; awarded Sir Charles Santley Memorial Gift by Worshipful Co of Musicians 1988; Freeman City of London 1952; ISM 1971; Hon: RAM 1976, FTCL 1982; *Recreations* chess, study of philosophy; *Style*— Derek Hammond-Stroud, OBE; ✉ 18 Sutton Rd, Muswell Hill, London N10 1HE (☎ 0181 883 2120)

HAMMONDS, Peter James Scott; *b* 1 Feb 1954; *Educ* Douglas HS for Boys Isle of Man, Bedford Coll London (BA), LSE (MSc); *m* 27 Sept 1980, Hazel Frances; 2 da (Sophie Elizabeth b 27 June 1985, Henrietta Ellen b 21 Aug 1990); *Career* Sec and Slr's Office Central Electricity Generating Bd 1977–79; Lloyds Bank plc: joined Sec's Dept 1979, asst sec 1981–87, dep sec 1987–91, sec Lloyds Merchant Bank Ltd 1985–91, sec German Smaller Companies Investment Trust plc 1985–91; co sec National Westminster Bank plc 1991–; ICSA: memb Co Secs' Panel 1993–, elected memb Int Cncl 1995–, vice chm Admissions Ctee 1995–; memb Co Affrs Ctee IOD 1996; 3 times prizewinner for Gilbart Lectures on Banking; FRGS 1977, FCIS 1991 (ACIS 1980); *Recreations* heavy gardening; *Style*— Peter Hammonds, Esq; ✉ Company Secretary, National Westminster Bank plc, 41 Lothbury, London EC2P 2BP (☎ 0171 726 1044, fax 0171 726 1035)

HAMNETT, Prof Andrew; s of Albert Edward Hamnett (d 1990), and Dorothy Grace, *née* Stewart; *b* 12 Nov 1947; *Educ* William Hulme's GS Manchester, University Coll Oxford (Open Scholar, BSc), St John's Coll Oxford (Chemistry Senior Scholar, DPhil); *m* 1976, Suzanne Marie, da of Charles Parkin (d 1993); 3 da (Erica b 1979, Hilary b 1981, Gillian (twin) b 1981); *Career* jr research fell The Queen's Coll Oxford 1972–77, Killam research fell Univ of British Columbia 1974–76; Univ of Oxford: departmental research asst Inorganic Chemistry Lab 1977–80, lectr in inorganic chemistry 1980–89, successively fell by special election, fell then dean St Catherine's Coll 1980–89; Univ of Newcastle Upon Tyne: prof of physical chemistry 1989–, pro-vice-chllr 1993–; memb then chm Physical Chemistry Sub-Ctee SERC 1988–94, dep chm Chemistry Ctee EPSRC 1993–94; FRSC 1990; *Books* Techniques and Mechanisms in Electrochemistry (with P A Christensen, 1994); *Recreations* music (organist and pianist); *Style*— Prof Andrew Hamnett; ✉ Department of Chemistry, Bedson Building, University of Newcastle Upon Tyne, Newcastle Upon Tyne NE1 7RU (☎ 0191 222 6786, fax 0191 222 5472)

HAMOND, *see:* Harbord-Hamond

HAMPDEN, 6 Viscount (UK 1884); Anthony David Brand; DL (E Sussex 1986); s of 5 Viscount Hampden (d 1975), and Hon Imogen Rhys, da of 7 Baron Dynevor; *b* 7 May 1937; *Educ* Eton; *m* 1, 27 Sept 1969 (m dis 1988), Cara Fiona, da of Capt Claud Proby, Irish Gds (d 1987), 2 s of Sir Richard Proby, 1 Bt, MC, JP, DL; 2 s (Hon Francis, Hon Jonathan Claud David Humphrey b 25 Aug 1975), 1 da (Hon Saracha Mary b 7 March 1973); m 2, 21 Oct 1993, Mrs Sally Snow, of Rosenau Crescent, Battersea, yst da of Sir Charles Jocelyn Hambro, KBE, MC (d 1963); *Heir* s, Hon Francis Anthony Brand b 17 Sept 1970; *Career* Lazard Brothers Co 1956–69, Hoare Govett 1970–82, land agent Glynde Estates 1984–; chm Govrs Emanuel Sch 1985–; *Books* Henry and Eliza; *Clubs* White's; *Style*— The Rt Hon the Viscount Hampden, DL; ✉ Glynde Place, Glynde, nr Lewes, E Sussex BN8 6SX (☎ 01273 858337)

HAMPEL, Sir Ronald Claus (Ronnie); kt (1995); s of Karl Victor Hugo Hampel (d 1960), and Rutgard Emil Klothilde, *née* Hauck (d 1975); *b* 31 May 1932; *Educ* Canford Sch, CCC Cambridge (MA); *m* 11 May 1957, Jane Bristed, da of Cdr Wilfred Graham Hewson, RN, of Wellington, Somerset; 3 s (Andrew b 1960, Rupert b 1962, Peter b 1962), 1 da (Katharine b 1958); *Career* Nat Serv 2 Lt 3 RHA 1951–52; ICI plc: joined 1955, vice pres Americas 1973–77, gen mangr Commercial Gp 1977–80, chm Paints Div 1980–83, chm Agrochemicals 1983–85, bd dir 1985–, chief operating offr 1991–93, chief exec and dep chm 1993–95, chm 1995–; non-exec dir: Powell Duffryn plc 1984–89, Commercial Union 1987–95, British Aerospace plc 1989–, Alcoa (USA) 1995–; memb: Br N American Ctee 1986– (Exec Ctee 1989), Bd American C of C 1988–91, Int Assoc for the Promotion and Protection of Private Foreign Investments (APPI), Euro Roundtable 1995–, Listed Cos Advsy Ctee London Stock Exchange, Nomination Ctee New York Stock Exchange; chm Ctee on Corp Governance 1995–; CIMgt 1985; *Recreations* skiing, tennis, golf; *Clubs* All England Lawn Tennis, MCC, Royal and Ancient; *Style*— Sir Ronnie Hampel; ✉ ICI plc, ICI Group HQ, 9 Millbank, London SW1P 3JF (☎ 0171 834 4444, fax 0171 834 2042, telex 21324 ICI HQ G)

HAMPSHIRE, Prof Michael John; CBE (1987); *b* 13 Oct 1939; *Educ* Heckmondwike GS, Univ of Birmingham (BSc, PhD); *m* 1962, Mavis, *née* Oakes; 1 da (Julie Louise b 1972); *Career* Univ of Salford: lectr 1964–71, sr lectr 1971–78, prof of solid state electronics 1978–83, prof of electronic info technol 1983–, chm Dept of Electronic and Electrical Engrg 1981–89, asst md Salford University Business Services (SUBS) Ltd tech conslts 1989–95; dir: SUBS Ltd 1995–, Vertec Ltd 1991– (fndr chm 1981–91, co awarded N of Eng first prize in BTG Academic Enterprise Competition 1982), Cedeta Research Ltd 1991–92; conslt: Ferranti Semiconductors Ltd 1970–74, Volex Group plc 1977–, Thorn EMI 1980–88; fndr chm: Mgmnt Ctee Calderdale Industl Microelectronics Centre 1984–88, Mgmnt Ctee NW Microelectronics Awareness Prog 1986–89; chm: Mgmnt Ctee Microelectronics Awareness Scheme 1983–86, R & D Ctee Volex Group plc 1988–92; memb: SERC Nat Mgmnt Ctee for Teaching Company Scheme 1983–88, Mgmnt Ctee Software Servs Div SUBS Ltd 1986–89, AMTEC Jt Bd of Studies 1986–88; Techmart Technology Transfer Trophy 1984; author of numerous papers, theses and reports; Hon MIED 1981; FInstP 1971, FIEE 1984, CEng 1984, CPhys 1984; *Recreations* music, golf; *Style*— Prof Michael Hampshire, CBE; ✉ Salford University Business Services Ltd, Technology House, Lissadel Street, Salford, Manchester M6 6AP (☎ 0161 957 0012, fax 0161 745 8362)

HAMPSHIRE, Sir Stuart Newton; kt (1979); s of G N Hampshire; *b* 1 Oct 1914; *Educ* Repton, Balliol Coll Oxford; *m* 1, 1961, Renée Ayer (decd); m 2, 1984, Nancy Cartwright; *Career* served WWII; fell All Souls Coll Oxford 1936–40, lectr in philosophy UCL 1947–50, fell New Coll Oxford 1950–55, domestic bursar and res fell All Souls Coll Oxford 1955–60, Grote prof of philosophy of the mind and logic Univ of London 1960–63, prof of philosophy Princeton Univ 1963–70, warden Wadham Coll Oxford 1970–84, prof of philosophy Stanford Univ 1984–91; FBA; *Books* Spinoza (1951), Thought and Action (1959), Freedom of the Individual (1965), Modern Writers (1969), Freedom of Mind and Other Essays (1972), The Socialist Idea (ed, 1975), Two Theories of Morality (1977), Morality and Conflict (1983), Innocence and Experience (1989); *Style*— Sir Stuart Hampshire, FBA; ✉ 7 Beaumont Road, The Quarry, Headington, Oxford

HAMPSHIRE, Susan; OBE (1995); da of George Kenneth Hampshire (d 1964), and June Hampshire (d 1967); *b* 12 May 1942; *Educ* Hampshire Sch Knightsbridge; *m* 1, 1967 (m dis 1974), Pierre Julian Granier-Deferre; 1 s, 1 da (decd); m 2, 1981, Sir Eddie Kulukundis, *qv*; s of George Elias Kulukundis (d 1978); *Career* actress; Hon DLitt: Univ of London 1984, Univ of St Andrews 1986; Hon DEd Univ of Kingston 1994, Hon DArts Pine Manor Coll Boston USA 1994; *Theatre* incl: Express Bongo, Follow That Girl, Fairy Tales Of New York, The Ginger Man, Past Imperfect, The Sleeping Prince, She Stoops to Conquer, Peter Pan, A Doll's House, The Taming of The Shrew, Romeo and Jeanette, As You Like It, Miss Julie, The Circle, Arms and The Man, Man and Superman, Tribades, An Audience Called Edward, Crucifer of Blood, Night and Day, The Revolt, House Guest, Blithe Spirit, Married Love, A Little Night Music, The King and I, Noel and Gertie, Relative Values, Suzanna Andler, Black Chiffon; *Television* incl: What Katy Did, The Andromeda Breakthrough, The Forsyte Saga 1970, Vanity Fair 1971, The First Churchills 1973, The Pallisers 1975, Dick Turpin 1980, Barchester Chronicles 1982, Leaving (2 series), Going to Pot I, II and III, Don't Tell Father; *Film* incl: During One Night, The Three Lives of Thomasina, Night Must Fall, The Fighting Prince of Donegal, Paris in August, Monte Carlo or Bust, Violent Enemy, David Copperfield, A Time For Loving, Living Free, Baffled, Malpertius, Neither The Sea Nor The Sand, Roses and Green Peppers, Bang; *Awards* winner 3 Emmy Awards for Best Actress; *Books* Susan's Story, The Maternal Instinct, Lucy Jane at the Ballet, Lucy Jane on Television, Lucy Jane and the Dancing Competition, Lucy Jane and the Russian Ballet, Trouble Free Gardening, Every Letter Counts, Easy Gardening; *Recreations* gardening, writing, water-skiing; *Style*— Miss Susan Hampshire, OBE; ✉ c/o Chatto & Linnit, Prince of Wales Theatre, Coventry Street, London W1V 7FE (☎ 0171 930 6677, fax 0171 930 0091)

HAMPSON, Christopher; CBE (1994); s of Harold Ralph Hampson (d 1972), of Montreal, Canada, and Geraldine Mary, *née* Smith (d 1984); *b* 6 Sept 1931; *Educ* Ashbury Coll Ottawa Canada, McGill Univ Montreal Canada (BEng); *m* 18 Sept 1954, Joan Margaret Cassils, da of Lt-Col Arthur C Evans (d 1960), of Montreal; 2 s (Christopher Geoffrey b 1957, Harold Arthur b 1965), 3 da (Daphne Margaret (Mrs Kearns) b 1955, Sarah Anne (Mrs Clarridge) b 1958, Aimée Joan Geraldine (Mrs Pitman) b 1966); *Career* CIL Inc Canada: vice pres and dir 1973–78, sr vice pres and dir 1982–; md and chief exec offr ICI Australia Ltd 1984–87, exec dir ICI plc 1987–94; non-exec chm: Yorkshire Electricity Group PLC 1994–, RMC Group plc 1996– (non-exec dir 1994–); non-exec dir: Environment Agency 1995–, SNC-Lavalin Group Inc 1993–, TransAlta Corporation 1994–; CIMgt 1990; *Recreations* tennis, skiing; *Clubs* York (Toronto), Hurlingham; *Style*— Christopher Hampson, Esq, CBE; ✉ 77 Kensington Court, London W8 5DT (☎ 0171 376 1906)

HAMPSON, Dr Keith; MP (C) Leeds North West (majority 7,671); s of Bert Hampson (d 1967), of Shildon, Co Durham; *b* 14 Aug 1943; *Educ* King James I GS Bishop Auckland, Univ of Bristol, Harvard Univ (PhD); *m* 1975, Frances Pauline Einhorn (d 1975); m 2, 1979, Susan, da of John Cameron; *Career* former chm Bristol Univ Cons Assoc, PA to Rt Hon Edward Heath 1966, 1968 and 1970, history (American) lectr Univ of Edinburgh 1968–74; MP (C): Ripon 1974–1983 (contested same at by-election July 1973), Leeds NW 1983–; vice chm Cons Educn Ctee 1975–79, vice pres WEA 1979–, vice chm Youthaid 1979–83; vice pres Assoc of Business Execs 1979–; memb: Educn Advsy Ctee of UK Cwlth for UNESCO 1980–84, Gen Advsy Cncl IBA 1980–88; PPS to Rt Hon Tom King as Min for Local Govt and Environmental Services 1979–83, PPS to Rt Hon Michael Heseltine Sec of State for Defence 1983–84; sec Cons Parly Def Ctee 1984–88; memb: Trade and Indust Select Ctee 1988–, Public Accountants Cmmn 1992–; *Recreations* tennis, gardening, DIY; *Clubs* Carlton; *Style*— Dr Keith Hampson, MP; ✉ House of Commons, London SW1A 0AA

HAMPSON, Prof Norman; s of Frank Hampson (d 1967), and Elizabeth Jane, *née* Fazackerley (d 1946); *b* 8 April 1922; *Educ* Manchester GS, Univ Coll Oxford (MA), Univ of Paris (Docteur de l'Université), Univ of Edinburgh (DLitt); *m* 22 April 1948, Jacqueline Juliette Jeanne Marguerite, da of Charles Hector Gardin (d 1933); 2 da (Françoise b 1951, Michèle b 1955); *Career* RNVR 1941–45, Lt 1943; asst lectr then sr lectr Manchester Univ 1948–67; prof: Univ of Newcastle 1967–74, Univ of York 1974–89; FRHistS 1970, FBA 1980; *Books* La Marine de l'An II (1959), A Social History of the French Revolution (1963), The Enlightenment (1968), The First European Revolution (1969), The Life and Opinions of Maximilien Robespierre (1974), A Concise History of the French Revolution (1975), Danton (1978), Will and Circumstance (1983), Prelude to Terror (1987), Saint-Just (1990); *Recreations* gardening; *Style*— Prof Norman Hampson, FBA; ✉ 305 Hull Road, York, YO1 3LB (☎ 01904 412661)

HAMPSON, Stephen; s of Dr Frank Hampson (d 1990), of Reading, and Helen, *née* Ellis; *b* 27 Oct 1945; *Educ* Leys Sch Cambridge, Univ Coll Oxford (MA, BPhil); *m* Gunilla, da of Sture Brunk; 1 da (Annika b 1975), 1 s (Nicholas b 1977); *Career* civil servant; lectr Univ of Aberdeen 1969–71, economist NEDO 1971–75, Scottish Office 1975–78, first sec FCO (New Delhi) 1978–81, currently under sec Scottish Office (re-joined 1981); *Recreations* far away places; *Style*— Stephen Hampson, Esq; ✉ Glenelg, Park Road, Kilmalcolm, Renfrewshire PA13 4EE (☎ 01505 872615); The Scottish Office, Victoria Quay, Edinburgh EH6 6QQ (☎ 0131 244 0779, fax 0131 244 7705)

HAMPSTEAD, Archdeacon of; *see:* Wheatley, Ven Peter William

HAMPTON, Christopher James; s of Bernard Patrick Hampton, and Dorothy Patience, *née* Herrington; *b* 26 Jan 1946; *Educ* Lancing, New Coll Oxford (MA); *m* 1971, Laura Margaret de Holesch; 2 da; *Career* res dramatist Royal Court Theatre 1968–70, freelance writer 1970–; *Plays* When Did You Last See My Mother? 1966, Total Eclipse 1968, The Philanthropist 1970 (Evening Standard Best Comedy Award, Plays and Players London Theatre Critics Best Play), Savages 1973 (Plays and Players London Theatre Critics Best Play, Los Angeles Drama Critics' Circle Award for Distinguished Playwriting 1974), Treats 1976, After Mercer 1980, The Portage to San Cristobal of A H (from George Steiner) 1982, Tales from Hollywood 1982 (Standard Best Comedy Award 1983), Les Liaisons Dangereuses (from Laclos) 1985 (Plays and Players London Theatre Critics Best Play, Standard Best Play Award 1986, NY Drama Critics' Circle Best Foreign Play Award 1987, Laurence Olivier Award 1986), White Chameleon 1991–92, Sunset Boulevard (adaption, 1993); *Television* Able's Will BBC 1977, The History Man (from Malcolm Bradbury) BBC 1981, The Price of Tea 1984, Hotel du Lac (From Anita Brookner) BBC 1986 (BAFTA Best TV Film Award 1987), The Ginger Tree (from Oswald Wynd) BBC 1989; *Films* A Dolls House 1973, Tales From the Vienna Woods 1979 (Screen International Award 1980), The Honorary Consul 1983, The Good Father 1986 (Prix Italia 1988), Wolf at the Door 1986, Dangerous Liaisons 1988 (Writers Guild of America Award, BAFTA Award Academy Award), Carrington (also dir) 1995 (Special Jury Award Cannes Film Festival 1995), Total Eclipse 1995, Mary Reilly 1996; *Translations* Marya (pby Isoac Babel) 1967, Uncle Vanya (by Chekhov) 1970, Hedda Gabler (by Ibsen) 1970, A Doll's House (by Ibsen) 1971, Don Juan (by Molière) 1972, Tales from the Vienna Woods (by Horváth) 1977, Don Juan Come Back from the War (by Horváth) 1978, Ghosts (by Ibsen) 1978, The Wild Duck (by Ibsen) 1979, The Prague Trial (by Chéreau and Mnouchkine) 1980, Tartuffe (by Molière) 1983, Faith, Hope and Charity (by Horváth 1989; *Recreations* travel, cinema; *Clubs* Dramatists'; *Style*— Christopher Hampton, Esq, FRSL; ✉ 2 Kensington Park Gardens, London W11

HAMPTON, Prof John Reynolds; s of Eric Albert Hampton (d 1979), of Gorleston, Norfolk, and Norah Kathleen, *née* Johnson (d 1981); *b* 8 Nov 1937; *Educ* Gresham's, Magdalen Coll Oxford (BA, DM, DPhil, MA, BM BCh, MRCP), Radcliffe Infirmary Oxford; *m* 25 July 1964, Pamela Jean, da of Edmund Joseph Wilkins (d 1980), of Tunbridge Wells; 2 s (Christopher, Philip), 1 da (Joanna); *Career* house physician and surgn and sr house offr Radcliffe Infirmary 1963–64, jr lectr and lectr in med Univ of Oxford 1965–68, instr in med and jr assoc in med Harvard Univ and Peter Bent Brigham Hosp Boston Mass USA 1968–69; Univ of Nottingham 1969–: lectr, sr lectr in med and hon conslt physician to Nottingham Hosps 1970–74, reader in med and conslt physician Queen's Med Centre 1974–79, prof of cardiology 1980–; sec Atherosclerosis Discussion GP 1978–81; memb: Br Cardiac Soc, Assoc of Physicians; FRCP 1975; *Books include* All About Heart Attacks: A guide for patients with heart disease and high blood pressure (1980), Integrated Clinical Science - cardiovascular disease (1983), The ECG in practice (1986), The ECG Made Easy (4 edn, 1992); *Recreations* sailing; *Style*— Prof John Hampton; ✉ Cardiovascular Medicine, D Floor, S Block, Queen's Medical Centre, Nottingham NG7 2UH (☎ 0115 970 9346, fax 0115 970 9384)

HAMPTON, Joshua Gerard Reynolds (Josh); s of Donald Lindsay Hampton (d 1994), of Sydney, Australia, and Judith Anne Cooling; *b* 21 Sept 1961; *Educ* Unley HS Adelaide S Australia, Regency Park Sch of Catering S Australia (cert of commercial cookery); *partner* Carole Anne Robertson; *Career* apprentice chef Caledonian Inn Robe S Australia 1978–81, chef saucier Feathers Hotel Adelaide 1981–84; sous chef: Colonial Restaurant Adelaide 1984–86, Noahs Northside Sydney 1986–87, Hakoah Club Sydney 1987; chef Troy's Catering Sydney 1987–89; sr sous chef: Braganza Restaurant Soho 1989–90, 192 Restaurant Notting Hill 1990–91; head chef The Canal Brasserie 1991–92 (nominated Time Out Modern British Restaurant of the Year 1992), personal and executive chef to Sir Andrew Lloyd Webber London/Newbury/Nice July-Oct 1992; head chef: 192 Restaurant 1992–94, Kartouche Restaurant 1994–95, The Ebury Wine Bar 1995–; Merit award winner (with Maddalena Bonino) Rothschild Menu Competition 1991; *Recreations* entertaining, travelling, the arts, current affairs; *Style*— Josh Hampton, Esq; ✉ The Ebury Wine Bar, 139 Ebury Street, London SW1 (☎ 0171 730 8206)

HAMPTON, 6 Baron (UK 1874); Sir Richard Humphrey Russell Pakington; 6 Bt (UK 1846); s of 5 Baron Hampton, OBE, FRIBA (d 1974), and Grace, da of Rt Hon Sir Albert Spicer, 1 Bt; *b* 25 May 1925; *Educ* Eton, Balliol Coll Oxford; *m* 25 Oct 1958, Jane Elizabeth Farquharson, da of late Thomas Arnott, OBE, TD; 1 s, 2 da; *Heir* s, Hon John Pakington, *qv*; *Career* Sub Lt (observer) Fleet Air Arm, RNVR WWII; in advertising until 1958, CPRE Worcs 1958–71, with Tansley Witt and Co 1971–73; sits as Liberal Democrat in House of Lords, Lib spokesman on NI 1977–87, pres South Worcestershire Lib Assoc 1978–88; *Books* The Pakingtons of Westwood (1975); *Style*— The Rt Hon Lord Hampton

HAMPTON, Robert Paul; s of Michael James Toop, of Barnet, Herts, and Jennifer Marie, *née* Slade; *b* 14 Feb 1962; *Educ* The Nicholas Legat Sch of Russian Ballet; *m* 1982 (m dis 1991); 1 s (Ross Michael b 17 June 1986); *Career* ballet dancer; first princ role James in Bournonville's La Sylphide 1983 (performed Spoleto Festival Charlston USA 1986); only Euro dancer Japan Ballet Festival 1988; patron Russian Ballet Soc Edinburgh 1991–; *Performances* performed Peter Darrell's prodns of: Othello 1984, Cinderella (as Prince) 1984, Don José 1985, Cheri 1985, The Nutcracker (as Prince) 1985, Seigfried 1986, Albrecht 1987, Tales of Hoffman 1987; others incl: Cranko's Romeo 1988, Balanchine's Concerto Barocco, Who Cares and Scotch Symphony, Jiri Kylian's Forgotten Land; *Style*— Robert Hampton, Esq; ✉ The Scottish Ballet Co, 261 West Princes St, Glasgow G4 9EE (☎ 0141 331 2931)

HAMPTON, Surgn Rear Adm Trevor Richard Walker; CB (1988); s of Percy Ewart Erasmus Hampton (d 1952), of King's Lynn, Norfolk, and Violet Agnes, *née* Neave (d 1987); *b* 6 June 1930; *Educ* King Edward VII GS King's Lynn, Univ of Edinburgh Sch of Med (MB ChB, MRCPE); *m* 1, 11 Aug 1952 (m dis 1976), (Celia) Rosemary, da of Stanley Day (d 1957), of Winchmore Hill; 3 da (Fiona, b 1956, Nicola b 1959, Judy b 1963); m 2, 12 Aug 1976, Jennifer Lily, da of Leonard R Bootle (d 1986), of Fillongley, Warwickshire; *Career* Surgn Lt RN 1955; serv: HMS Ganges, Harrier and Victorious; conslt physician RN Hosps: Plymouth, Haslar and Gibraltar; Surgn Cdr 1967, Surgn Capt 1977; med offr i/c RN Hosps: Gibraltar 1980–82, Plymouth 1982–84; Surgn Rear Adm 1984, Support Med Servs 1984–87, Operational Med Servs 1987–89; author of pubns on Waterhouse-Friderichsen Syndrome, inhalation injury, drowning and med screening; FRCPE 1975; *Recreations* professional and amateur theatre, music, writing; *Style*— Surgn Rear Adm Trevor Hampton, CB; ✉ Coombe House, Latchley, nr Gunnislake, Cornwall PL18 9AX (☎ 01822 832419)

HAMWEE, Baroness (Life Peer UK 1991), of Richmond-upon-Thames in the London Borough of Richmond-upon-Thames; Sally Rachel Hamwee; da of late Alec Hamwee, and Dorothy, *née* Saunders; *b* 12 Jan 1947; *Educ* Manchester HS for Girls, Univ of Cambridge (MA); *Career* slr; ptnr Clintons Slrs; cncllr London Borough of Richmond-upon-Thames 1978– (chm Planning Ctee 1983–87); chm London Planning Advsy Ctee 1986–94; pres ALDC (Liberal Democrat Councillors' Assoc) 1995–96; pres Town and Country Planning Association; memb Cncl of Mgmnt: Family Policy Studies Centre, Refuge; legal advsr The Simon Community; chm Xfm Ltd; memb Advsy Cncl London First; Liberal Democrat spokesperson in House of Lords on environment, local govt, housing and planning; former memb: Cncl Parents for Children, Bd London First, Joseph Rowntree Fndn Inquiry, Planning For Housing; *Style*— The Rt Hon Lady Hamwee; ✉ 101a Mortlake High Street, London SW14 8HQ

HAMYLTON-JONES, Keith; CMG (1979); s of G Jones, of Fairholm, Sussex; *b* 12 Oct 1924; *Educ* St Paul's, Balliol Coll Oxford; *m* 1953, Eira, da of B Morgan; 1 da; *Career* serv WWII Capt HM Welsh Gds (Italy, Germany and S France); HM Foreign Serv 1949–79: Warsaw, Lisbon, Manila, Montevideo, Rangoon; HM consul-gen to Katanga 1970–72; ambass: Costa Rica 1974–79, Honduras 1975–78, Nicaragua 1976–79; chm (for Devon and Cornwall) Operation Raleigh 1983–85 (led int expdn to Costa Rica 1985); nat chm: Anglo-Costa Rican Soc 1983–88; Anglo-Central American Soc 1988–91; *Recreations* reading, writing (pen-name Peter Myllent); *Clubs* Chelsea Arts; *Style*— Keith Hamylton-Jones, Esq, CMG; ✉ Morval House, Morval, nr East Looe, Cornwall (☎ 01503 262342)

HANBURY, Benjamin; *b* 25 March 1946; *m* 31 May 1969, Moira Elizabeth, da of Sir Arthur Pilkington; 2 da (Emma Jane b 15 Dec 1970, Amanda Aline b 9 March 1973); *Career* racehorse trainer; rode over 50 winners; formerly with: Ryan Price, D L Moore, B van Cutsem; trainer's licence 1974–; horses trained incl: Kala Dancer, Batshoof, Midway Lady, Matiya; major races won: Gold Seal Oaks, General Accident 1,000 Guineas, William Hill Dewhurst Stakes, Prix Marcel Boussac, May Hill Stakes, Tattersalls Rogers Gold Cup, Prince of Wales's Stakes, Irish 1,000 Guineas; *Recreations* golf, shooting, tennis; *Style*— Benjamin Hanbury, Esq; ✉ Green Man House, Cowlinge, Newmarket, Suffolk (☎ 01440 820396); Diomed Stables, Hamilton Rd, Newmarket, Suffolk CB8 0PD (☎ 01638 663193 or 664799, fax 01638 667209)

HANBURY-TENISON, Sir Richard; KCVO (1995), JP (Gwent 1979); s of Maj G E F Tenison (d 1954), sometime Jt MFH Essex and Suffolk, of Lough Bawn, Co Monaghan, Ireland, by his w Ruth (only c of John Capel Hanbury, JP, DL, who was n of 1 Baron Sudeley); *b* 3 Jan 1925; *Educ* Eton, Magdalen Coll Oxford; *m* 12 May 1955, Euphan Mary Hanbury Tenison, JP, er da of Maj Arthur Wardlaw Ramsay and Hon Mary, *née* Fraser, only da of 18 Lord Saltoun; 3 s (John b 1957, William b 1962, Capel b 1965), 2 da (Sarah b 1956, Laura b 1966); *Career* WWII Irish Gds NW Europe (wounded), Capt 1946; Foreign Serv 1949–75; first sec: Vienna, Phnom Penh, Bucharest; cnsllr: Bonn, Brussels;

head Aviation and Telecommunication Dept FCO 1970–71, ret 1975; dir Gwent TEC 1991–; Timber Growers' award for forestry and woodland management 1990; pres: Monmouthshire (later Gwent) Rural Community Cncl 1959–67, Gwent Community Servs Cncl 1975– (chm 1967–74), St John Cncl for Gwent 1979–; chm: Art Ctee Nat Museum of Wales 1986–91 (memb 1976–), S Wales Regnl Bd Lloyds Bank 1987–91; DL: Monmouthshire 1973, Gwent 1974; High Sheriff Gwent 1977, Lord Lt Gwent 1979–; Hon Col 3 Bn Royal Regt of Wales 1982–90, pres TA and VR Assoc for Wales 1985–90, South Wales Regn TAVRA 1990–, CStJ 1980, KStJ 1990, FRSA 1995; *Recreations* shooting, fishing, conservation; *Clubs* Boodles, Kildare St Univ (Dublin); *Style*— Sir Richard Hanbury-Tenison, KCVO, JP; ✉ Clytha Park, Abergavenny, Gwent (☎ 01873 840300); Lough Bawn, Co Monaghan, Ireland

HANBURY-TENISON, (Airling) Robin; OBE (1981); s of Maj Gerald Evan Farquhar Tenison (d 1954), of Co Monaghan, Ireland, and Ruth Julia Marguerite, *née* Hanbury; *b* 7 May 1936; *Educ* Eton, Magdalen Coll Oxford (MA); *m* 1, 14 Jan 1959, Marika (d 1982), da of Lt-Col John Montgomerie Hopkinson (d 1989), of Garwyns Farm, Sussex; 1 s (Rupert b 1970), 1 da (Lucy b 1960); m 2, 1983, Louella Gage, da of Lt-Col George Torquil Gage Williams, of Menkee, Cornwall; 1 s (Merlin b 1985); *Career* farmer, author, explorer, environmental and human rights campaigner; pres Survival Int 1984– (chm 1969–84), memb SW Regnl Panel MAFF 1993–96, chief exec British Field Sports Soc 1995–; Dr (hc) Univ of Mons-Hainant 1992; *Books* The Rough and The Smooth (1969), A Question of Survival (1973), A Pattern of Peoples (1975), Mulu - The Rain Forest (1980), The Yanomami (1982), Worlds Apart (1984), White Horses Over France (1985), A Ride along the Great Wall (1987), Fragile Eden (1989), Spanish Pilgrimage (1990), The Oxford Book of Exploration (1993), Jake's Escape (1996); *Recreations* travelling, conservation; *Clubs* Kildare Street and Univ (Dublin), Groucho, Geographical; *Style*— Robin Hanbury-Tenison, Esq, OBE; ✉ Cabilla Manor, Cardinham, Bodmin, Cornwall PL30 4DW (☎ 01208 821224, fax 01208 821267)

HANBURY-TRACY, (Desmond) Andrew John; er s of Maj Claud Edward Frederick Hanbury-Tracy-Domvile, TD (d 1987), and his 1 w Veronica May (d 1985), da of Cyril Grant Cunard; hp of kinsman 7 Baron Sudeley, *qv*; *b* 30 Nov 1928; *Educ* Sherborne, RAC Cirencester; *m* 1, 22 June 1957 (m dis 1966), Jennifer Lynn, o da of Dr Richard Christie Hodges; 1 s (Nicholas Edward John b 13 Jan 1959); m 2, 4 April 1967 (m dis), Lilian, da of late Nathaniel Laurie; 1 s (Timothy Christopher Claud b 25 March 1968); m 3, 28 July 1988, Mrs Margaret Cecilia White, da of late Alfred Henry Marmaduke Purse, MBE; *Style*— Andrew Hanbury-Tracy, Esq; ✉ 7 Gainsborough Drive, Sherborne, Dorset DT9 6DS

HANCOCK, Prof Barry William; s of George Llewellyn Hancock, of London, and Sarah Hancock (d 1973); *b* 25 Jan 1946; *Educ* E Barnet GS, Univ of Sheffield Med Sch (MB ChB, MD), Univ of London (DCH); *m* 5 July 1969, (Christine Diana) Helen, da of Alexander Moffatt Spray (d 1972); 1 s (David b 1974), 1 da (Caroline b 1971); *Career* medical registrar Professorial Therapeutics Unit Royal Infirmary Sheffield 1973–74, lectr in med and sr registrar Professorial Medical Unit Royal Hosp Sheffield 1974–78, hon conslt physician and oncologist Royal Hallamshire and Weston Park Hosps Sheffield 1978–88; Univ of Sheffield: sr lectr in med 1978–86, reader in med 1986–88, prof of clinical oncology 1988–, dir Supraregional Gestational Trophoblastic Tumour Serv; trial co-ordinator Br Nat Lymphoma Investigation, chm UK Co-ordinating Ctee on Cancer Research Melanoma Sub-Ctee; formerly: hon dir Trent Palliative Care Centre, divnl surgn N Derbys St John Ambulance Bde; MRCP 1973, FRCP (London) 1985, FRCR 1994, FRCP (Edinburgh) 1995; *Books* Assessment of Tumour Response (ed, 1982), Immunological Aspects of Cancer (jt ed, 1985), Lymphoreticular Disease (jt ed, 1985), Lecture Notes in Clinical Oncology (jtly, 1986), Cancer Care in the Community (ed, 1996), Cancer Care in the Hospital (ed, 1996); *Recreations* railways, photography, philately, tennis; *Style*— Prof Barry Hancock; ✉ Treetops, 253 Dobcroft Rd, Ecclesall, Sheffield S11 9LG (☎ 0114 235 1433); YCRC Dept of Clinical Oncology, Weston Park Hospital, Whitham Rd, Sheffield S10 2SJ (☎ 0114 267 0222, fax 0114 267 8140)

HANCOCK, Christine; *Educ* LSE; *Career* formerly: chief nursing offr Bloomsbury Health Authy, gen mangr Waltham Forest Health Authy; gen sec Royal Coll of Nursing 1989–; *Style*— Miss Christine Hancock; ✉ Royal College of Nursing, 20 Cavendish Square, London W1M 0AB (tel 0171 409 3333)

HANCOCK, Cyril James; s of Herbert James Hancock (d 1958), and Lilian, *née* Smith; *b* 9 Nov 1931; *Educ* Univ of Durham (BSc); *m* 9 July 1955, (Jean) Helen Spence, da of Samuel Steel (d 1967); 2 da (Karen b 1961, Ann b 1963); *Career* princ conslt and divnl dir PE Consulting Group 1961–78, dir Binder Hamlyn Fry 1979–81, princ Cyril Hancock Assocs 1981–; non-exec dir: William Tatham Ltd 1981–, Wrights and Dobson Bros 1981–84, Shackleton Engrg 1984–86; CEng, FIMechE, FIEE, FIMfgE, FIMC; *Recreations* walking, veteran bicycles and cycling, vintage cars; *Clubs* Vintage Sports Car; *Style*— Cyril Hancock, Esq; ✉ Fairacre, Bellingdon, Chesham, Bucks HP5 2XU (☎ 01494 758243)

HANCOCK, Sir David John Stowell; KCB (1985); s of Alfred George Hancock (d 1955), of Beckenham, Kent, and Florence, *née* Barrow (d 1988); *b* 27 March 1934; *Educ* Whitgift Sch, Balliol Coll Oxford (BA, MA); *m* 23 Dec 1966, Sheila Gillian (Gill), da of late Dr Even Finlay, of Walgrave, Northamptonshire; 1 s (John Farquharson b 1969), 1 da (Cordelia Jane b 1973); *Career* Nat Serv 2 Lt RTR 1953–54; BOT 1957–59; HM Treasy: joined 1959, under sec 1975–80, dep sec 1980–82; head Euro Secretariat Cabinet Office 1982–83, perm sec Dept of Educn and Science 1983–89, exec dir Hambros Bank Ltd 1989–, dir Hambros plc 1989–, chm Dyvell Holdings Ltd 1990–94, dir AXA Equity and Law 1992–95; chm: UK Selection and Advsy Ctee Harkness Fellowships 1988–92 (memb 1984–92), Fndn for Young Musicians 1990–, St Katharine and Shadwell Tst 1990–; tstee St Catharine's Fndn Cumberland Lodge 1989–; Freeman City of London 1989; Hon LLD Poly of E London (CNAA) 1990; FRSA 1986, CIMgt 1987; *Recreations* theatre, music, opera, reading, gardening, walking; *Clubs* Athenaeum; *Style*— Sir David Hancock, KCB; ✉ Hambros Bank Limited, 41 Tower Hill, London EC3N 4HA (☎ 0171 480 5000, fax 0171 702 9262)

HANCOCK, David Martin; s of Henry Charles Hancock (d 1973), and Constance Catherine, *née* Martin (d 1990); *b* 1 May 1936; *Educ* Sutton County GS; *m* 30 March 1963, June Noreen, da of William Thomas (d 1990); 1 s (Thomas b 1971), 1 da (Emma b 1969); *Career* fin dir and gp commercial dir McCann Erickson Advertising Ltd 1965–82, gp vice chm and chief fin offr Grey Communications Group Ltd 1984–94, dir Cronulla Creative and Management Services Ltd; FCCA 1961, FInstD 1977, FIPA 1990; *Recreations* music, reading, sport; *Clubs* Royal Automobile; *Style*— David Hancock, Esq

HANCOCK, Marion; da of Thomas Douglas Archibald Hancock (d 1994), and Doris, *née* Hornsby (d 1978); *b* 23 March 1954; *Educ* Gosforth GS Newcastle upon Tyne, Univ of Warwick (BA); *m* David Kirkpatrick; *Career* ed; PA to Dir Foyles Booksellers 1975–76; The British Council 1976–87: admin asst then project mangr design, prodn and publishing then dep ed press and info; ed Design Magazine The Design Council 1987–92, freelance editor and writer 1992–96, corp pubns mangr Health Educn Authy 1996–; memb Women in Marketing and Design, FRSA; *Books* How to Buy Design (1992); *Recreations* making lists; *Clubs* Chelsea Arts; *Style*— Ms Marion Hancock; (☎ 0181 340 8612, fax 0181 292 4208)

HANCOCK, Michael Anthony; s of Anthony Ilbert Hancock (d 1954), of Bickley, Kent, and Eileen Mary, *née* King (d 1994); *b* 11 Sept 1943; *Educ* Tonbridge; *m* 11 July 1967 (m dis 1975), Diana Margaret, da of Albert Edward Peter; 1 s (Froude), 2 da (Claire, Emma); *Career* Bank of England 1961–63, ptnr WN Middleton & Co and Stock Exchange memb 1969–75, chm and chief exec Chart Estates Ltd 1985–; *Recreations* vintage cars, fine wines, antique furniture; *Clubs* Wig and Pen, Kent Woolgrowers; *Style*— Michael Hancock, Esq

HANCOCK, Michael Thomas (Mike); CBE (1992); *b* 9 April 1946; *m* 1967, Jacqueline, da of Sidney and Gwen Elliott; 1 s, 1 da; *Career* memb Bd of Dirs Drug Rehabilitation Unit Alpha Drug Clinic Droxford 1971–; memb Portsmouth City Cncl 1971– (Fratton Ward 1973–, ldr Lib Dem Gp 1989–); Hampshire CC: memb 1973–, ldr of the oppn 1977–81 and 1989–, ldr Lib Dem Gp 1989–, ldr Hampshire CC 1993–; joined SDP 1981 (memb Nat Ctee 1984), Parly candidate (SDP) Portsmouth South 1983 (SDP/Alliance 1987), MP (SDP) Portsmouth South 1984–87; dir Daytime Club BBC 1987–90, chm Southern Branch NSPCC 1989–, dist offr for Hampshire, IOW and Channel Islands Royal Soc for Mentally Handicapped Children and Adults 1989–; memb: Br Delgn to UN 1983–84, Bureau of the Assembly of Euro Regions 1993–, Congress of Local and Regional Authorities of Europe (a body of the Cncl of Europe) 1994–; vice pres Atlantic Arc Cmmn of the Conf of Peripheral Maritime Regions 1994; tstee: Royal Marines Museum Portsmouth, Mary Rose; chm Portsmouth Contract Servs, dir the Beneficial Fndn Portsmouth; contrib to various jls; hon award for contrib to Anglo-German rels Homborn W Germany 1981; *Recreations* people, living life to the full; *Style*— Mike Hancock, Esq, CBE; ✉ Hampshire County Council, The Castle, Winchester, Hants SO23 8UJ (☎ 01962 847943, fax 01962 842368); office: Somerstown Health Centre, Blackfriars Close, Southsea, Hants PO5 4NJ (☎ 01705 830530); political office: (☎ 01705 834172); home: (☎ 01329 287340)

HANCOCK, Prof Peter; s of Ralph Hancock (d 1967), of Brooklands, Cheshire, and Annie, *née* MacAlister (d 1987); *b* 6 June 1933; *Educ* Manchester GS, UMIST (BSc), Univ of Cambridge (PhD); *m* 5 Jan 1957, Barbara, da of Ernest Hill; 1 da (Catharine Clare b 20 July 1961), 1 s (Michael John b 6 July 1963); *Career* res scientist International Nickel Co 1958–61, lectr then sr lectr Dept of Mechanical Engrg Univ of Glasgow 1961–70; Cranfield Univ (formerly Cranfield Inst of Science and Technol): prof of engrg metallurgy 1970–, dir and fndr Industrial Science Centre (ISC) 1979, head Materials Dept ISC 1981, dean Faculty of Science and Technol 1982–85, head Sch of Industl Science 1982–90, pro vice chllr 1989–92, head Sch of Industl and Manufacturing Science (following merger with Coll of Manufacturing) 1990–, chief exec CIM Inst 1992–; memb Cncl: Aeronautical Res Cncl 1977–80, Defence Scientific Advsy Cncl 1981–91; author of 110 res papers; memb: CIRP, Inst of Corrosion Science; FIM, FEng 1992; *Recreations* golf, walking, reading; *Clubs* Athenaeum, Bedfordshire Golf (pres, former capt); *Style*— Prof Peter Hancock, FEng; ✉ School of Industrial & Manufacturing Science, Cranfield University, Cranfield, Beds MK43 0AL (☎ 01234 754036, fax 01234 751346)

HANCOCK, Roger Markham; s of Howard Spencer Hancock, of Oxford, and Helen Marjorie, *née* Skelcher; *b* 4 Nov 1942; *Educ* Southfield Sch Oxford; *m* 14 Aug 1968, Marian Sheila, da of Arthur Herbert Holloway, of S Tawton; 1 s (Mark Peter Skelcher b 25 Jan 1978), 1 da (Kirsty Sheila Bevis b 14 Aug 1975); *Career* articled clerk Wenn Townsend CAs Oxford 1959–65, mgmnt accountant British Motor Corporation 1965, mangr Morris & Harper CAs 1966; Whitley Stimpson & Partners: ptnr 1967–, managing ptnr 1987–95, sr ptnr 1995–; ptnr Moores Rowland Banbury 1979–, memb Cncl Moores Rowland International 1985–; dir Nortec Training Agency Ltd 1986–; tstee Reed Coll of Accountancy 1988–; pres Banbury and District Chamber of Commerce 1989–90; FCA 1967 (ACA 1965); *Recreations* theatre, music, rugby football; *Style*— Roger Hancock, Esq; ✉ Whitley Stimpson & Partners, Penrose House, Oxford Rd, Banbury, Oxon OX16 7AB (☎ 01295 270200, fax 01295 271784)

HANCOCK, Ronald Philip; s of Philip Henry Hancock (d 1953), and Ann, *née* Lioni (d 1980); *b* 9 Aug 1921; *Educ* Epsom Coll; *m* 1, 1958, Stella Florence (d 1988), da of Arthur Howard Mathias, CBE (d 1970); 2 s (William, Richard), 1 da (Anne-Marie); m 2, Pauline Mary, da of William Leighton Jones (d 1980), wid of John Stenhouse Manuel (d 1982); 1 step da (Susan); *Career* Lt RNVR, served Atlantic and Pacific Oceans and with Coastal Forces in English Channel; int insur conslt (memb Lloyd's), farmer and forester; dep chm Bland Welch and Co Ltd 1955–70 (dir 1946–70); chm: Euro Risk Management Ltd 1972–77, A R M International Ltd 1972–84, Leumi Insurance Services (UK) Ltd 1983–87 (dir until 1990); dir: De Falbe Halsey and Co (Holdings) Ltd 1972–74, International Risk Management Ltd 1972–77, American Risk Management Inc (USA) 1972–77, Medical Insurance Agency Ltd 1974–93 (memb Cncl 1977–); forestry cmmr 1988–91; memb Cncl: Royal Med Fndn of Epsom Coll 1969–, Br Horse Soc 1980–87 (chm Horse Driving Trials Ctee 1983–87), Riding for the Disabled Assoc 1989–94; tstee and dir PHAB (Physically Handicapped and Ablebodied) 1979– (chm Surrey 1973–79); memb: Br Equestrian Fedn 1983–87, Int Paralympic Equestrian Ctee 1994–; Freeman City of London, Liveryman Worshipful Co of Carmen; *Recreations* ocean racing and cruising, horse driving trials; *Clubs* Royal Thames Yacht, Lloyd's Yacht; *Style*— Ronald Hancock, Esq; ✉ Hillside Farm, Shere Rd, West Horsley, Surrey KT24 6ER (☎ 01483 282098, fax 01483 284132)

HANCOCK, Stephen Clarence; s of Norman Harry Hancock, of Brymore, West Parade, Llandudno, Wales, and Jean Elaine, *née* Barlow; *b* 1 Nov 1955; *Educ* King Edward VI Lichfield Staffs, City of Stoke-on-Trent Sixth Form Coll, Univ of Sheffield (LLB); *Career* admitted slr 1980; ptnr Herbert Smith Slrs 1986– (articled clerk 1978–80, asst slr 1980–86); memb Worshipful Co of Slrs; *Style*— Stephen Hancock, Esq; ✉ Herbert Smith, Exchange House, Primrose St, London EC2A 2HS (☎ 0171 374 8000, fax 0171 496 0043)

HANCOX, Tony; s of Christopher Hancox (d 1957), of Nottingham, and Gwendoline, *née* Chapman (d 1975); *b* 1927; *Educ* Univ of Oxford (BA, MA); *m* 1949, Doreen, da of Thomas Bertie Anthony (d 1972), of London; 1 s (George b 1959), 1 da (Alcina b 1958); *Career* retail mangr (latterly in personnel mgmnt and trg) 1952–87, chm Hancox Managment Services 1987–; memb: Employers' Sides Retail Wages Cncls 1965–80, Cncl Assoc of Retail Distributors 1970–72; dep chm City of Westminster Local Employment Ctee 1969–72; memb: Univ of London Careers Advsy Bd 1970–80, Cncl Coll for the Distributive Trades 1981; assoc Templeton Coll Oxford 1983–85; memb: Mgmnt Bd Univ of Stirling distance learning MBA Degree 1986–, Ct of Govrs The London Inst 1986–89, Shadow Bd City Univ Business Sch mgmnt MBA Degree 1986–87, Faculty Euro Sch of Mgmnt Oxford 1987–91, Steering Gp Retail Mktg Degree Manchester Metropolitan Univ 1987, Devpt Gp Nat Cncl for Vocational Qualifications 1987; nat co-ordinator Nat Retail Trg Cncl 1987–89, chm Enterprise Steering Gp Oxford Brookes Univ 1991–97, nat verifier and advsr Pitman Examinations Inst 1991–94, memb Planning Gp Chairmen of Enterprise in HE Ctees Network 1993–95, co-fndr Employers for Higher Educn 1995; capt Thames Rowing Club 1958, memb of Eng Eight VIth Commonwealth Games (Bronze medallist) 1958; memb Soc of Authors 1995; FITD 1987, FIPD 1994 (FIPM 1975); *Recreations* music, reading, writing, rowing; *Clubs* Athenaeum, Leander; *Style*— Tony Hancox, Esq; ✉ c/o Athenaeum Club, Pall Mall, London SW1Y 5ER

HAND, John Lester; QC (1988); s of John James Hand (d 1965), and Violet, *née* Middleton; *b* 16 June 1947; *Educ* Huddersfield New Coll, Univ of Nottingham; *m* 1, 17 Dec 1971 (m dis 1989), Helen Andrea, *née* McWatt; m 2, 6 April 1990, Lynda (Ray) Ferrigno Hand, da of Gisbert Mills (d 1985); 1 da (Theodora Isobel b 1991); *Career* called to the Bar Gray's Inn 1972 (bencher 1996), practising barrister 1972–, recorder of the Crown Court 1991–, head of chambers; legal assessor: GMC 1991–, Gen Dental Cncl 1991–; *Recreations* travel, sailing; *Style*— John Hand, Esq, QC; ✉ 9 St John Street,

Manchester M3 4DN (☎ 0161 955 9000, fax 0161 955 9001, MDX 14326); Old Square Chambers, 1 Verulam Buildings, Gray's Inn, London WC1R 5LQ (☎ 0171 831 0801, fax 0171 405 1387)

HAND, Nicholas; s of Kenneth Robert Hand, of Bristol, and Josephine Mary, *née* Griffiths; *b* 4 Jan 1957; *Educ* Filton HS Bristol, King Edward XI GS Stafford, Stafford Coll of Further Educn, Bristol Poly (Post Graduate Dip in Graphic Design); *m* 10 April 1982, Katharine Elizabeth, da of Harry Graydon; 2 da (Eleanor Clare b 27 May 1984, Jessica Louise b 28 Nov 1986), 1 s (Laurence Daniel b 9 Nov 1990); *Career* designer; Creative Advertising 1978–80, ESL Bristol (design for audio visual presentations) 1980–82, sr designer Playne Design (graphic design for book packaging and gen print) 1982–85, freelance graphic design 1985–88, ptnrship with Len Upton forming Legend Design Consultants 1988–; lectured: Polytechnic of the South West, Bristol Poly, Gwent Coll of Higher Educn, Brunel Tech Coll; CSD: diploma memb 1977, chartered memb 1982, chm SW Region 1987–90, hon sec 1990–92; chm of govrs St Andrew's Sch 1994–96; *Recreations* walking in the countryside, gardening, reading; *Style—* Nicholas Hand, Esq; ✉ Legend Design Consultants, 33 Eastfield Rd, Westbury-on-Trym, Bristol BS9 4AE (☎ 0117 962 1333, fax 0117 962 1117)

HANDCOCK, John Eric; LVO (1991), DL (Royal Co of Berks 1986); s of Eric George Handcock (d 1979), and Gladys Ada Florence, *née* Prior, of Bolton Ave, Windsor; *b* 7 Oct 1930; *Educ* Aldenham, King's Coll London (LLB); *m* 1956, Joan Margaret, da of Wilfred Joseph Bigg, CMG (d 1983), of Swanage, Dorset; 2 s (David, Jonathan), 2 da (Sandra, Nicola); *Career* admitted slr 1954; sr ptnr Lovegrove and Durant of Windsor and Ascot (now Lovegrove & Eliot of Windsor, Ascot and Egham) 1966–96, conslt 1996–; pres Berks, Bucks and Oxon Incorporated Law Soc 1979–80, dir Solicitors' Benevolent Assoc 1981–88, pt/t chm Social Security Appeals Tbnls 1992–; Nat Assoc of Round Tables of GB and NI: chm Thames Valley Area 1964–65, memb Nat Cncl 1966–68, nat exec convenor Rules and Special Purposes 1968–70; chm Berks Bucks and Oxon Prof Cncl 1981–82; govr: Upton House Sch Windsor 1965–, St George's Choir Sch Windsor Castle 1975–96; capt lay stewards St George's Chapel Windsor Castle 1992– (dep capt 1977–92), tstee Prince Philip Tst for Windsor and Maidenhead 1978–; pres Windsor and Eton Operatic Soc 1961–, hon slr River Thames Soc 1962– (life memb 1986); Paul Harris fell Rotary International 1994; Citoyen d'Honneur de la Ville Royale de Dreux 1976; Freeman City of London 1984; *Recreations* history, travel, wine, books; *Clubs* Law Society; *Style—* John E Handcock, Esq, LVO, DL; ✉ c/o Lovegrove & Eliot, 4 Park St, Windsor, Berks SL4 1JF (☎ 01753 851133, fax 01753 850812, telex 849275 LOVDUR G)

HANDFORD, Rt Rev (George) Clive; s of Cyril Percy Dawson Handford (d 1974), of Gedling, Notts, and Alice Ethel, *née* Bullers; *b* 17 April 1937; *Educ* Henry Mellish Sch Nottingham, Hatfield Coll Durham (BA), Queen's Coll Birmingham, Univ of Birmingham (dip in theol); *m* 3 Sept 1962, (Anne Elizabeth) Jane, da of Rev Cecil Atherley Atherley; 1 da (Catherine Elizabeth b 26 Jan 1977); *Career* curate Mansfield PC 1963–66; chaplain: at Baghdad 1967, at Beirut 1967–73; res fell St Augustine's Coll Canterbury 1973, dean of St George Cathedral Jerusalem 1974–78, archdeacon in The Gulf and chaplain at Abu Dhabi and Qatar 1978–83, vicar of Kneesall with Laxton and Wellow 1983–84, rural dean of Tuxford and Norwell 1983–84, Bishop of Southwell's ecumenical offr 1983–84, archdeacon of Nottingham 1984–90, bishop of Warwick 1990–96, hon canon of Coventry 1990–96, bishop of Cyprus and The Gulf 1996–; *Recreations* bird watching, walking; *Style—* The Rt Rev the Bishop of Cyprus and The Gulf; ✉ 2 Grigori Afxentiou Street, PO Box 2075, Nicosia 1517, Cyprus

HANDFORD, Peter Thomas; MBE (1945); s of Rev Hedley William Mountenay Handford (d 1928), Vicar of Four Elms, Edenbridge, Kent, and Helen Beatrice, *née* Crosse (d 1964); *b* 21 March 1919; *Educ* Christ's Hosp; *m* 12 May 1974, Helen Margaret; 2 da (Lyn Patricia (Mrs Hedges), Pamela Anne (Mrs Kucel)), both by previous m; *Career* sound recordist; memb: Acad of Motion Picture Arts and Sciences 1986, Cinema Audio Soc (USA) 1991, Assoc of Motion Picture Sound 1993; WWII (Capt RA) serv incl 50 BEF and D Day landings 1939–46; London Film Prodns 1936–39; after war worked with various film companies before becoming freelance; responsible for sound recording on more than 60 films incl: Room at the Top, Billy Liar, Out of Africa (Academy (Oscar) and BAFTA Awards for sound track 1986), Murder on the Orient Express, Hope and Glory (BAFTA nomination for sound track 1987), Gorillas in the Mist (Academy nomination for sound track 1988), Dangerous Liaisons, White Hunter Black Heart, Havana; prodr Sounds of the Steam Age on records and CDs (awarded Grand Prix du Disque Paris 1964); *Books* The Sound of Railways (1980); *Recreations* gardening, sound recording, railway enthusiasm and travel, country pursuits; *Clubs* Academy of Motion Picture, Arts and Scis, Sloane; *Style—* Peter T Handford, Esq, MBE; ✉ c/o Casarotto Ramsay Ltd, National House, 4th Floor, 60–66 Wardour Street, London W1V 3HP (☎ 0171 287 4450, fax 0171 287 9128)

HANDFORTH, David Arthur; s of late Stanley Wilkinson Handforth, and Kathleen Alice, *née* Metcalfe; *b* 16 Nov 1936; *Educ* W Leeds HS, Clare Coll Cambridge (exhibitioner, MA), Univ of Cambridge (CertEd), Univ of Edinburgh (Dip in Applied Linguistics, MSc); *m* 1968 (m dis 1984), Christa Brigitta, *née* Hochreiter; 2 da (Caroline Elizabeth b 24 Aug 1970, Deborah Clare b 6 March 1974), 1 s (Nicholas Richard Dominic b 8 June 1975); *Career* asst master: St Alban's Sch 1959–61, Dulwich Coll 1961–65; pt/t lectr St Alban's Coll of FE 1960–65, conslt in English studies Royal Norwegian Miny of Educn 1965–69; British Council: joined 1969, seconded to Advanced Teachers' Coll Nigeria 1970–72, English language/educn offr Nepal 1972–76, Educn Liaison Unit 1977–80, regnl dir Hamburg 1980–84, regnl dir Oxford 1984–88, rep Tunisia 1988–93, dir Austria 1993–; *Recreations* travelling, theatre, music, reading, golf; *Clubs* United Oxford and Cambridge; *Style—* David Handforth, Esq; ✉ The British Council, Schenkenstrasse 4, 1010 Vienna, Austria

HANDLER, Thomas Joseph; s of Nicholas Handler (d 1958), of Budapest, Hungary, and Lily, *née* Singer (d 1986); *b* 25 May 1938; *Educ* Fort Street Boys' HS Sydney Australia, Univ of Sydney (Cwlth scholarship, BA, LLB); *m* 25 May 1970, Adrienne, da of Alajos Marxreiter, of Budapest; 2 da (Rebecca Louise b 21 Dec 1974, Sophie Melinda b 15 Aug 1976); *Career* slr; WC Taylor & Scott (Sydney) 1962–65 (articled clerk 1958–61), Simmons & Simmons (London) 1965–67; Baker & McKenzie (London): joined 1967, ptnr 1973–, admin ptnr 1975–76, 1978–79 and 1982–83; mediator accredited by Centre for Dispute Resolution; chm Environmental Resolve Ctee and memb Bd of Dirs The Environment Cncl, sr assoc Fndn for Int Environmental Law and Devpt, memb Exec Ctee Environmental Law Fndn; legal conslt ELFline; memb: Law Soc 1966, UK Environmental Law Assoc, Br-Hungarian Soc; *Recreations* reading, music, theatre, tennis, cross-country skiing, hiking, gardening; *Style—* Thomas Handler; ✉ Baker & McKenzie, 100 New Bridge Street, London EC4V 6JA (☎ 0171 919 1000, fax 0171 919 1999)

HANDLEY, *see:* Davenport-Handley

HANDLEY, Dr Anthony James; s of Wing Cdr Austyn James Handley, RAF (d 1985), of W Mersea, Essex, and Beryl Janet, *née* Ashling (d 1982); *b* 22 June 1942; *Educ* Kimbolton Sch, King's Coll London, Westminster Hosp Med Sch (MB BS, MD, DipIMC RCS(Ed), FRCP); *m* 3 Dec 1966, Jennifer Ann, da of Noël Lindsay Ross Kane (d 1986), of Colchester, Essex; 1 s (Simon b 1973), 1 da (Juliette b 1971); *Career* Maj RAMC (TA) 1970–94; conslt physician (cardiology) and clinical dir Essex Rivers Healthcare NHS Tst (formerly NE Essex Health Authy) 1974–, hon clinical tutor Charing Cross and Westminster Med Sch 1976–, clinical tutor Colchester Postgrad Med Centre 1980–85; med advsr Essex Ambulance Serv; pres and chief med advsr RLSS (UK); chm Basic Life Support Gp Euro Resuscitation Cncl 1993–; OStJ 1992; memb Br Cardiac Soc 1984, chm Resuscitation Cncl (UK) 1997– (hon ssec 1986–97); FRCP 1985, FRSM 1985; *Books* Thoracic Medicine (contrib, 1981), Life Support (ed, 1992), Advanced Life Support (ed, 1994), ABC of Resuscitation (ed, 1995); *Recreations* swimming, squash, music (euphonium player); *Style—* Dr Anthony J Handley; ✉ 40 Queens Road, Colchester, Essex CO3 3PB (☎ 01206 560910); 55 Turner Road, Colchester, Essex CO4 5JY (☎ 01206 752444)

HANDLEY, Prof Eric Walter; CBE (1983); s of Alfred Walter Handley (d 1974), and Ada Doris, *née* Cox (d 1944); *b* 12 Nov 1926; *Educ* King Edward's Sch Birmingham, Trinity Coll Cambridge (BA, MA); *m* 31 July 1952, Carol Margaret Handley, da of Claude Hilary Taylor (d 1966); *Career* UCL: lectr in Greek and Latin 1946–61, reader 1961–67, prof 1967–68, prof of Greek and head of dept 1968–84; dir Inst of Classical Studies Univ of London 1967–84, regius prof of Greek Univ of Cambridge 1984–94, fell Trinity Coll 1984–, hon fell UCL 1989, hon res fell Inst of Classical Studies 1995, prof of ancient lit Royal Acad of Arts 1990–, visiting lectr in classics Harvard 1966, visiting memb Inst for Advanced Study Princeton 1971, visiting prof Stanford 1977 and Melbourne 1978, sr res fell Princeton 1981; chm Cncl Univ Classical Depts 1975–78 (sec 1969–70); foreign memb Societas Scientiarum Fennica 1984, memb Academia Europaea 1988, hon memb Hungarian Acad of Sciences 1993, corr memb acad Athens 1995–, memb Norwegian Acad of Sci and Letters 1996, vice pres Union Académique Internationale 1994–; pres: Classical Assoc 1984–85, Hellenic Soc 1993–96; Dr hc Athens 1995; FBA 1969 (foreign sec 1979–88), FRSA 1971, Hon RA 1990; *Books* The Telephus of Euripides (with John Rea, 1957), The Dyskolos of Menander (1965 and 1992), Relire Ménandre (with André Hurst, 1990), Aristophane (with Jan-Maarten Bremer, 1993), Images of the Greek Theatre (with Richard Green, 1995); *Recreations* walking, travel; *Clubs* Utd Oxford and Cambridge Univ; *Style—* Prof Eric Handley, CBE, FBA; ✉ Trinity College, Cambridge CB2 1TQ (☎ 01223 338413, fax 01223 338564)

HANDS, Donald Christopher; s of Vincent Edwin Hands (d 1989), and Marjorie Elsie, *née* Witton; *b* 23 May 1944; *Educ* Colchester Royal GS, Southend Sch of Arch (DipArch), Architectural Assoc Sch of Arch; *m* 1, 1963, Keren Margaret, *née* Steady; 1 s (Simon Christopher b 30 Nov 1964), 1 da (Kirsty Sarah b 1 June 1969); m 2, 1991, Catherine Barbara, *née* Hutton; 1 da (Amy Lotus b 3 Feb 1996); *Career* architect; Gollins Melvin Ward 1969–70: memb BOAC Terminal J F Kennedy Airport project team and Royal Opera House design team; dir Rolfe Judd 1980– (joined 1971): responsible for restoration and refurbishment of notable historic bldgs incl RICS Parliament Square, St Olaf House Tooley St, 49 St James St, Spencer House, St James's Place; recipient Europa Nostra Award 1994 and Civic Tst Award 1996 (for restoration of Spencer House); RIBA 1970; *Recreations* historic sports car racing, coastal sailing, hill walking, cycling; *Clubs* Historic Sports Car (vice chm 1995–), Bentley Drivers'; *Style—* Donald Hands, Esq; ✉ Rolfe Judd, Old Church Court, Claylands Road, The Oval, London SW8 1NZ (☎ 0171 582 7070, fax 0171 735 5141, mobile 0850 644447, e-mail donh@ROLFE-JUDD.CO.UK)

HANDS, Jeremy Gyles Hargrave; s of Hargrave Patrick Hands, of Thatch End, Flempton, Bury St Edmunds, Suffolk, and Daphne Mary, *née* Bolton; *b* 4 April 1951, Torquay; *Educ* St Marylebone GS; *m* 1, 1977 (m dis 1991), Julia Rae, da of Stanley Edward Bennett, of Knaresborough, N Yorks; 1 s (Tom b 20 Aug 1978), 1 da (Lucy b 4 Sept 1980); m 2, 29 May 1992, Margaret Jane Gill, da of Jack Thomas, of Brecon; *Career* reporter: Hendon and Finchley Times 1970–74, Herald Express Torquay 1974; researcher Westward TV Plymouth 1974–77; reporter: Border TV Carlisle 1977 78, ITN 1978–89 (incl coverage of Falklands campaign, Gulf War, Lebanon, NI); presenter Anglia TV Norwich 1989–90 (ed News Programmes 1990–93), fndr and md Jeremy Hands Associates (Norwich and Aberdeen) 1993–; govr Norfolk Coll 1996–, churchwarden St Margaret's Hardley; *Books* with Robert McGowan: Don't Cry for Me, Sergeant Major (1983), Try Not to Laugh, Sergeant Major (1984); *Recreations* golf, writing, maritime history; *Clubs* Norwich City FC, RAFA Brecon; *Style—* Jeremy Hands, Esq; ✉ 16 The Street, Hardley, Norwich, Norfolk (☎ 01508 528259, fax 01508 520700)

HANDS, Terry; *b* 9 Jan 1941; *Educ* Univ of Birmingham (BA), RADA; *m* 1, 1964 (m dis 1967), Josephine Barstow (now Dame Josephine Barstow, *qv*); m 2, 1974, (m dis 1980), Ludmila Mikael; 1 da (Marina); m 3, 1988, Julia Lintott; 2 s (Sebastian, Rupert); *Career* theatre and opera director; fndr dir Liverpool Everyman Theatre 1964–66; RSC: artistic dir Theatreground (touring schs and community centres) 1966–68, assoc dir 1967, jt artistic dir 1978, chief exec 1986–91, dir emeritus 1991–; Hon DLitt; hon fell Shakespeare Inst; Chevalier des Arts et des Lettres; *Theatre* dir many prodns for RSC incl: The Merry Wives of Windsor 1968 (revived 1975/76), Pericles 1969, Henry V, Henry IV Parts I and 2 (all transfered to Aldwych (centenary season Stratford)) 1975, Henry VI (all 3 parts, Stratford (1st time in entirety since Shakespeare's day, SWET Award for Dir of the Year)) 1977, As You Like It, Richard II and Richard III (the latter two completing the entire Shakespeare history cycle, begun 1975, with Alan Howard in leading roles, Stratford) 1982, Much Ado About Nothing (Stratford) 1982, Poppy (Musical of the Year), Cyrano de Bergerac (SWET Award for Best Dir, Barbican) 1983, Red Noses 1985, Singer 1989, The Seagull 1990, Tamburlaine (Evening Standard Award for Best Dir, transferred to Barbican) 1992–93, The Importance of Being Earnest (Birmingham Rep and Old Vic) 1995; other credits incl: Richard III (Comedie Francaise) 1972 (Meilleur Spectacle de L'Année), Twelfth Night 1976 (Meilleur Spectacle de L'Année), Othello (Paris Opera, televised France 1978), Parsifal (Royal Opera House) 1979, Arden of Faversham (Schauspielhaus Zürich) 1992, Buffalo Bill Show (Recklinghausen) 1992, Simon Boccanegra (Bremen) 1992, Sag Mir Wo Die Blumen Sind (Berlin) 1993, Hamlet (Paris) 1994, Hadrian VII and The Visit (Chichester Festival Theatre) 1995, Merry Wives of Windsor (RNT 1995, NT Oslo 1995), The Pretenders (NT Oslo) 1996; consIt dir: Comedie Française 1975–80, Troilus and Cressida (Burgtheater Vienna) 1977, As You Like It (Burgtheater Vienna) 1979; *Style—* Terry Hands, Esq; ✉ Royal Shakespeare Company, Barbican Centre, Barbican, London EC2 (☎ 0171 628 3351)

HANDY, Charles Brian; s of Ven Brian Leslie Handy, Archdeacon of Kildare, and Joan Kathleen Herbert, *née* Scott; *b* 25 July 1932; *Educ* Bromsgrove Sch, Oriel Coll Oxford (BA, MA), MIT (SM); *m* 5 Oct 1962, Elizabeth Ann, da of Lt-Col Rowland Fenwick Ellis Hill (d 1978); 1 da (Kate b 1966), 1 s (Scott b 1968); *Career* mktg exec Shell International Petroleum Co Ltd 1956–65, economist Charter Consolidated Co Ltd 1965–66, int faculty fell MIT 1966–67, London Business Sch 1967– (prof 1978–94), warden St George's House Windsor Castle 1977–81, writer and broadcaster 1981–; chm RSA 1986–88, memb CNAA 1988–91; Hon DLitt Bristol Poly 1988, Hon DUniv Open Univ 1989, Hon DLitt Univ of E Anglia; *Books* Understanding Organizations (1983), Future of Work (1984), Gods of Management (1985), Understanding Schools (1986), Understanding Voluntary Organizations (1988), The Age of Unreason (1989), Inside Organisations (1990), The Empty Raincoat (1994), Waiting for the Mountain to Move (1995), Beyond Certainty (1995); *Recreations* theatre, cooking, travel; *Style—* Charles Handy, Esq; ✉ 73 Putney Hill, London SW15 3NT (☎ 0181 788 1610, fax 0181 789 3821); Old Hall Cottages, Bressingham, Diss, Norfolk (☎ 01379 687546); Le Bagnaie, 53011 Castellina in Chianti, Siena, Italy (☎ 39 577 743247)

HANDY, Prof Nicholas Charles; of Kenneth George Edwards Handy (d 1995), of Swindon, Wilts, and Ada Mary, *née* Rumming; *b* 17 June 1941; *Educ* Clayesmore Sch, St Catharine's Coll Cambridge (MA, PhD, ScD); *m* 19 Aug 1967, Elizabeth Carole, da of

Alfred Rennick Gates (d 1960); 2 s (Charles Paul b 1971, Julian John b 1973); *Career* Harkness fell Johns Hopkins Univ USA 1968–69; Univ of Cambridge: demonstrator 1972–77, lectr 1977–89, reader 1989–91, prof of quantum chemistry 1991–, pres St Catharine's Coll 1994–97 (fell 1965); memb Int Acad of Quantum Molecular Sci 1988, FRS 1990; *Recreations* travel, gardening; *Style—* Prof Nicholas Handy, FRS; ✉ University Chemical Laboratory, Lensfield Road, Cambridge CB2 1EW (☎ 01223 336373, fax 01223 336362)

HANDYSIDE, Robert Graham; s of George Robinson Handyside (d 1966), of Glasgow, and Marion Handyside, *née* Graham; *b* 1 Aug 1938; *Educ* Bassaleg GS; *m* 25 Feb 1963, (m dis 1993), Rhona Nancy; 1 s (Richard b 1968), 1 da (Julie b 1966); *Career* CA; chm: Argosy Finance & Co Ltd 1970, Argosy Finance and Guarantees Ltd 1970, Glenwood Securities Ltd 1975; *Recreations* golf; *Clubs* RAC, Cardiff and County; *Style—* Robert Handyside, Esq; ✉ The Mews, 4 Cathedral Rd, Cardiff CF1 9RF (☎ 01222 372331, fax 01222 222624)

HANGARTNER, Dr (John) Robert Wilfred; s of John Hangartner, and Ita Patricia, *née* Brett; *b* 5 Feb 1955; *Educ* Merchant Taylors', Guy's Hosp Med Sch Univ of London (BSc, MB BS, MRCS, LRCP), Open Univ (MBA); *m* 1980, Jillian Mary, da of Martin Frederick Ansell; 1 da (Caroline Emma b 27 Feb 1987), 1 s (Christopher Robert b 12 May 1991); *Career* house offr general medicine Lewisham Hosp 1979–80, sr house offr Guy's Hosp 1980–81 (house offr general surgery 1980); St George's Hosp: sr house offr 1981–82, registrar (pathology) 1982–83, clinical lectr in histopathology Med Sch 1983–88; Dept of Health: sr med offr 1988–91, sr princ med offr and divnl head 1993– (temp princ med offr 1991–93); hon sr registrar SW Thames RHA 1983–88; chm Hospital Jr Staff Ctee BMA 1984–85; former memb: Cncl BMA, Bd of Educn and Science BMA; MRCPath 1988, FRSA 1994; *Recreations* photography and singing; *Style—* Dr Robert Hangartner; ✉ Department of Health, Health Care Directorate, Medical Education, Training and Staffing Division, 2W59 Quarry House, Quarry Hill, Leeds LS2 7UE (☎ 0113 254 5000)

HANHAM, Prof Harold John (Harry); s of John Newman Hanham (d 1960), and Ellie, *née* Malone (d 1977); *b* 16 June 1928; *Educ* Mount Albert GS, Auckland Univ Coll, Univ of NZ (BA, MA), Selwyn Coll Cambridge (PhD); *m* 27 Jan 1973, Ruth Soulé, da of late Prof Daniel I Arnon, of Univ of California; *Career* asst lectr (latterly sr lectr) Univ of Manchester 1954–63, prof of politics Univ of Edinburgh 1963–68, prof of history Harvard Univ (also fell of Lowell House) 1968–73, prof of history and political sci and dean Sch of Humanities Social Sci MIT 1973–85, hon prof of history and vice-chllr Univ of Lancaster 1985–95; memb Econ and Social Res Cncl 1986–91, memb Cncl for Mgmnt Educn and Devpt 1988–; Guggenheim fell 1972–73; Hon AM Harvard Univ 1968; FRHistS, FAAAS; *Books* Elections and Party Management (1959), The Nineteenth Century Constitution (1969), Scottish Nationalism (1969), Bibliography of British History 1851–1914 (1976 awarded John H Jenkins Prize); *Clubs* Utd Oxford and Cambridge Univ, St Botolph (Boston); *Style—* Prof H J Hanham; ✉ c/o University House, University of Lancaster, Lancaster LA1 4YW

HANHAM, Sir Michael William; 12 Bt (E 1667), of Wimborne, Dorsetshire, DFC (1944); o s of Patrick John Hanham (d 1965, yst s of Col Phelips Brooke Hanham, bro of 9 Bt), and his 1 w, Dulcie, *née* Daffarn, formerly Hartley (d 1979); suc his kinsman, Sir Henry Phelips Hanham, 11 Bt, 1973; *b* 31 Oct 1922; *Educ* Winchester; *m* 27 Feb 1954, Margaret Jane, o da of Wing-Cdr Harold Thomas, RAF; 1 s (William John Edward b 1957), 1 da (Victoria Jane (Mrs David L Gross) b 1955); *Heir* s, William John Edward Hanham b 4 Sept 1957; *Career* Flying Offr RAF Pathfinder Force 1944–45, actg Flt Lt India 1946; BOAC 1947–61; own garden furniture workshop 1963–74; running family estate at Wimborne 1974–; *Style—* Sir Michael Hanham, Bt, DFC; ✉ Deans Court, Wimborne, Dorset

HANHAM, William John Edward; s and h of Sir Michael William Hanham, 12 Bt, DFC, *qv*; *b* 4 Sept 1957; *Educ* Winchester, Courtauld Inst of Art (BA); *m* 1, 1982 (m dis 1986), Elizabeth Ann, yr da of Paul Keyworth, of Farnham, Surrey; m 2, 15 June 1996, Jennifer T, da of Harold Henry Sebag-Montefiore, of Kensington; *Career* print dealer 1980–82, public relations offr Christie's 1983–91, art public relations conslt 1991–93, fine art agent 1993–; *Recreations* painting, photography, chess; *Style—* William Hanham, Esq; ✉ G2 Albany, Piccadilly, London W1V 9RL

HANKES-DRIELSMA, Claude Dunbar; *b* 8 March 1949; *Career* strategic advsr; Manufacturers Hanover 1968–72, Robert Fleming & Co Ltd 1972–77 (dir 1974–77), dep chm Leutwiler and Partners Ltd 1992–96; chm: Mgmnt Ctee Price Waterhouse and Partners 1983–89, Action Resource Centre 1986–91; bd memb Hotel Chesa Grischuna Klosters 1991–; memb Cncl of Govrs Business in the Community 1986–91 (memb Pres Ctee 1988–90), memb Deanery Synod 1984–93; assisted Dr Fritz Leutwiler in his role as independent mediator between the South African Govt and foreign banks 1985, initiated attempt to secure Thyssen Collection for Britain 1988; Nobel Report 1991; hon fell Corpus Christi Coll Oxford; *Publications* The Dangers of the Banking System: Funding Country Deficits (1975); *Recreations* gardening, walking, skiing, reading, ancient art; *Style—* Claude Hankes-Drielsma, Esq; ✉ Stanford Place, Faringdon, Oxon SN7 8EX (☎ 01367 240547, fax 01367 242853)

HANKEY, Dr the Hon Alexander Maurice Alers; s of 2 Baron Hankey, KCMG, KCVO (d 1996); hp of bro 3 Baron Hankey; *b* 18 Aug 1947; *Educ* Rugby, Trinity Coll Cambridge, MIT (PhD), MERU (MSCI); *m* 1970 (m dis 1990), Deborah, da of Myron Benson, of Mass, USA; *Career* Greenlaw fell MIT 1969–71, Lindemann fellowship 1972–73 (held at Stanford Linear Accelerator Center), teacher of transcendental meditation 1973; Maharishi Int Univ USA: asst prof of physics 1973–74, associate prof 1974–75, prof 1975–78; prof of physics Maharishi Euro Res Univ of Switzerland and UK 1975–82, govr Age of Enlightenment 1977–, co dir Academy for the Science of Creative Intelligence Mass 1978, dean Faculty Maharishi Int Academy UK 1985–86, registrar Maharishi Univ of Natural Law North of England Campus 1986–92, memb Exec Cncl Natural Law Party of GB 1992–, sec Natural Law Pty of Sussex 1994–, memb E Grinstead TM Centre 1993–; Leverhulme Foundation Res award 1986; *Recreations* skiing, tennis, hiking; *Clubs* Royal Tennis; *Style—* Dr the Hon Alexander Hankey; ✉ Hethe House, Cowden, Kent TN8 7DZ (☎ 01342 850086)

HANKEY, 3 Baron (UK 1939); Donald Robin Alers Hankey; s of 2 Baron Hankey, KCMG, KCVO (d 1996), and his 1 w, Frances Bevyl, *née* Stuart-Menteth (d 1957); *b* 12 June 1938; *Educ* Rugby, UCL (Dip Arch); *m* 1, 1963 (m dis 1974), Margaretha, yr da of Cand Jur H Thorndahl, of Copenhagen, Denmark; m 2, 1974 (m dis 1994), Eileen Désirée, da of Maj-Gen Stuart Hedley Molesworth Battye, CB, of Fensacre House, Ascot, Berks; 2 da (Hon Fiona Bevyl b 1975, Hon Beatrice Eileen b 1978); m 3, 9 July 1994, June, da of late Dr Leonard Taboroff, and of Mrs Elsie Taboroff, of Palo Alto, California; *Heir* bro, Hon Alexander Maurice Alers Hankey, *qv*; *Career* chm Intercol International 1970–72, fndr and chm Gilmore Hankey Kirke 1973–92, fndr GMI Ltd 1990 (involved in architecture, conservation, planning engrg, economics and mgmnt); conslt to: Royal Household, PSA, Parliamentary Works Office, Home Office, English Heritage, Overseas Devpt Administration, World Bank, UNCHS, Govt of Jamaica; memb: SPAB, EASA, ASCHB, APT, Cercles d'Etudes Architecturales; RIBA, FRSA, FRAI; *Recreations* tennis, painting, music; *Style—* The Rt Hon the Lord Hankey; ✉ 34 Sunray Avenue, London SE24 9PX

HANKEY, Hon Henry Arthur Alers; CMG (1959), CVO (1960); yst s of 1 Baron Hankey, GCB, GCMG, GCVO, PC (d 1963); *b* 1 Sept 1914; *Educ* Rugby, New Coll Oxford; *m* 1 Jan 1941, Vronwy, o da of late Rev Thomas Frederic Fisher, Rector of Stilton, Peterborough; 3 s (Christopher, Maurice, Peter), 1 da (Veronica); *Career* ambass to Panama 1966–69, under sec FCO 1969–74; dir: Lloyds Bank International 1975–80, Antofagasta (Chile) & Bolivia Railway Co 1975–82; sec Br N American Ctee 1981–85; *Clubs* Ski Club of GB, Utd Oxford and Cambridge Univ; *Style—* The Hon Henry Hankey, CMG, CVO; ✉ Hosey Croft, Hosey Hill, Westerham, Kent TN16 1TA

HANKINS, (Frederick) Geoffrey; s of Frederick Aubrey Hankins (d 1966), of Eltham, and Elizabeth, *née* Stockton (d 1957); *b* 9 Dec 1926; *Educ* St Dunstan's Coll; *m* 1951, Iris Esther, da of George Robert Perkins (d 1977), of Wotton-under-Edge; 2 da (Susan, Jane); *Career* cmmnd Army BAOR 1946–48; mgmnt trainee later mfrg mgmnt J Sainsbury 1949–55, gen mangr Allied Suppliers 1955–62, prodn dir Brains Food Products 1962–69, Kraft Foods 1966–69; W L Miller and Sons Poole: gen mangr 1970–72, md 1972–82, chm 1975–85; Fitch Lovell plc: dir 1975–90, chief exec 1982–89, chm 1983–90; non-exec dir Booker plc (following merger with Fitch Lovell) 1990–; Liveryman Worshipful Co of Poulters; *Recreations* genealogy, antiques, practical pursuits; *Style—* Geoffrey Hankins, Esq; ✉ 51 Elms Ave, Parkstone, Poole, Dorset BH14 8EE; Booker plc, Portland House, Stag Place, London SW1E 5AY (☎ 0171 411 5500, fax 0171 411 5555)

HANKINS, Prof Harold Charles Arthur; CBE (1996); s of Harold Arthur Hankins (d 1982), of Crewe, Cheshire, and Hilda Hankins (d 1959); *b* 18 Oct 1930; *Educ* Crewe GS, Univ of Manchester (BSc, PhD); *m* 23 July 1955, Kathleen, da of Alec Higginbottom (d 1983), of Glossop, Derbyshire; 3 s (Anthony b 22 Dec 1957, Matthew b 9 July 1961, Nicholas b 21 Dec 1962); *Career* asst chief engr Metropolitan Vickers Electrical Co Ltd 1955–68; UMIST: lectr in electrical engrg 1968–71, sr lectr in electrical engrg 1971–74, prof of communication engrg and dir of Med Engrg Unit 1974–84, vice princ 1979–81, dep princ 1981–82, acting princ 1982–84, princ and vice chllr 1984–95; non-exec dir: Thorn EMI Lighting Ltd 1979–85, Bodycote International PLC 1993–; dir Inward 1993–95; chm NW Centre Ctee Inst of Electrical Engrs 1977–78 (memb 1969–77); memb: Bd of Govrs Manchester Poly 1989–, Manchester Lit & Phil Soc 1983–, Engrg Cncl 1993–95; pres Cheadle Hulme Sch 1996–; Mitchell Meml medal 1990; hon fell Manchester Poly 1984; Hon DSc Univ of Manchester 1995, Hon DUniv Open University 1996, Hon DEng UMIST 1996; FIEE 1975, FEng 1993; *Recreations* hill walking, music, choral work; *Clubs* Athenaeum; *Style—* Prof Harold Hankins, CBE, FEng; ✉ Rosebank, Kidd Rd, Glossop, Derbyshire SK13 9PN (☎ 01457 43895)

HANKINSON, Alan; s of Robert Hankinson (d 1970), of Lancs, and Beatrice, *née* Nelson (d 1966); *b* 25 May 1926; *Educ* Bolton Sch, Univ of Oxford (MA); *m* 1952 (m dis 1984), Roberta Lorna, da of James Gibson (d 1977), of Bolton; 1 s (Robert James b 1958); *Career* author; news ed Nigerian Broadcasting Corp 1953–58, journalist ITN London 1958–75; *Books* The First Tigers (1972), The Mountain Men (1977), Man of Wars (1985), A Century on the Crags (1988), First Bull Run (1991), Coleridge Walks the Fells (1991), Geoffrey Wintrop Young (biography, 1995); *Recreations* rock climbing, reading, fell walking; *Style—* Alan Hankinson, Esq; ✉ 30 Skiddaw St, Keswick, Cumbria CA12 4BY (☎ 017687 73746)

HANLEY, Brian Michael; s of Eric Thomas Hanley, and Constance Mary, *née* Garnett; *b* 3 April 1943; *Educ* John Fisher GS; *m* 19 Oct 1973, Rosalyn Alice, da of James Hancock (d 1971); 1 s (Christopher b 5 March 1981), 2 da (Michelle b 7 August 1974, Susan b 14 March 1978); *Career* various sr sales and mktg mgmnt appointments Honeywell Information Systems Ltd 1969–82; Perkin Elmer: nat sales mangr 1982–83, chm and md 1984–87, gp md Europe 1989 (concurrent with responsibility for ME, S America and Africa); md UK & International Motorola Computer Systems 1990–, chief exec The Parc Group (a wholly owned subsid of Kleinwort Benson Merchant Bank) 1991–; *Recreations* water sports, tennis; *Style—* Brian Hanley, Esq; ✉ Parc International Limited, Edinburgh House, Windsor Rd, Slough, Berks SL1 2DU

HANLEY, Ellery; MBE (1990); step s of Vincent Wendell Adams, of Leeds, s of Orene Muriel Hanley; *b* 27 March 1961; *Career* rugby league player/coach; Bradford 1978–85, Wigan (capt) 1985–91, Leeds 1991; capt: Yorkshire, GB 1987–93 (over 30 test caps); GB coach 1994–95; winner Golden Boot (Player of the World) 1989, voted Man of Steel (Rugby League Personality of the Year) 1985, 1987 and 1989; *Recreations* chess, squash, badminton, reading; *Style—* Ellery Hanley, Esq, MBE

HANLEY, Jenny Jane; da of Jimmy Hanley (d 1970), and Dinah Sheridan, *qv*; sis of Rt Hon Jeremy Hanley, MP, *qv*; *b* 15 Aug 1947; *Educ* Sherrard's Wood Sch Welwyn Garden City, St Margaret's Sch Folkestone, Sibton Park Sch Sellinge Kent, Crofton Grange Sch Buntingford Herts, Villa Brillamont Lausanne Switzerland (TEFL Cert); *m* 12 Jan 1980 (sep), Trevor James (Herby) Clark; 2 s (Tobias James Barnes b 4 Jan 1984, Daniel Francis Hanley b 31 Jan 1987); *Career* actress; debut as model aged 3, trained as nanny, then photographic model; wrote weekly page for Daily Mirror for two yrs, book reviewer for numerous pubns; pres Reading Male Voice Choir; Ambass Hosptial Radio; *Television* as presenter incl: We Have Ways of Making You Laugh, Fashion Today, Saturday Night at the Mill, Help, Magpie (for 6 years), Collector's Corner, daily chat show on BSkyB (for 2 years); other credits incl: Man About the House, And Mother Makes Five, Zodiac, The Hanged Man, Emmerdale Farm, Softly Softly (for 6 years), Warship, The Two Ronnies, Morecambe & Wise Christmas Special, numerous game shows; author of children's TV show ...and Maisy Too (with Quentin Blake, 3 series); *Films* incl: On Her Majesty's Secret Service (debut), Tam Lin (with Ava Gardner and Ian McShane), Scars of Dracula (with Christopher Lee), The Private Lives of Sherlock Holmes, Soft Beds Hard Battles (with Peter Sellers); *Recreations* cooking, deep-sea and freshwater fishing, driving, reading, swimming; *Style—* Ms Jenny Hanley; ✉ c/o Mahoney Gretton Associates, Concord House, 18 Margaret Street, Brighton BN2 1TS (☎ 01273 685970, fax 01273 685971); c/o LWA, 52 Wardour Street, London W1V 3HL (☎ 0171 434 3944, fax 0171 287 5194)

HANLEY, Rt Hon Jeremy James; PC (1994), MP (C) Richmond and Barnes (majority 3,869); s of Jimmy Hanley (d 1970), and Dinah Sheridan; *b* 17 Nov 1945; *Educ* Rugby; *m* 1, 1968 (m dis), Helene; 1 s (Jason b 1970); m 2, 1973, Verna, Viscountess Villiers, da of Kenneth Stott (d 1992), of Jersey; 1 s (Joel b 1974), 1 step-da (Sophia b 1971); *Career* CA; Parly candidate (C) Lambeth Central (by-election) 1978 and 1979, MP (C) Richmond and Barnes 1983–; vice chm Cons Trade and Indust Ctee, memb House of Commons Select Ctee on Home Affrs; memb: House of Commons Select Sub Ctee on Race Relations and Immigration, Br-Irish Inter Parly Body; sec All Party Gp for Europe; PPS to: Min of State at Privy Cncl Office, Min for Civil Serv and the Arts (Rt Hon Richard Luce, MP) 1987–90, Sec of State for the Environment (Rt Hon Christopher Patten, MP) 1990; Parly under-sec of state NI Office 1990–93, min for Health, Social Servs and Agriculture 1990–92, min for Political Devpt, Educn and Community Relations 1992–93, min of state for Armed Forces MOD 1993–94, chm Cons Pty 1994–95, Cabinet min without portfolio 1994–95, min of state FCO 1995–; Parly advsr Inst of CAs in England and Wales 1986–90; Freeman City of London, Liveryman Worshipful Co of CAs; FCA; *Recreations* cookery, cricket, golf, chess, languages, the arts; *Clubs* Lord's Taverners, Garrick, Pilgrims; *Style—* The Rt Hon Jeremy Hanley, MP; ✉ House of Commons, London SW1A 0AA (☎ 0171 219 4099)

HANLEY, Sir Michael Bowen; KCB (1974); s of late Prof J A Hanley; *b* 24 Feb 1918; *Educ* Sedbergh, Queen's Coll Oxford; *m* 1957, Hon Lorna Margaret Dorothy; *Career* served WWII; attached to MOD; *Style—* Sir Michael Hanley, KCB; ✉ Ministry of Defence, Whitehall, London SW1

HANLEY, Shirley Ann; da of Gerard Farnworth, and Renee Winifred, *née* Royds; *b* 2 Oct 1956; *Educ* Notre Dame GS Blackburn Lancs, Univ of Leicester (BSc); *m* 25 June 1983, Dermot Joseph Hanley, s of Dr Donal Aloysius Hanley, and Honora Eileen, *née* O'Mahony; 3 s (Christopher Jon b 17 May 1987, William Gerard b 5 March 1990, Simon James b 22 Jan 1992); *Career* graduate trainee rising to PR account exec Octagon Marketing Consultants Ltd 1979–82, sr PR exec Byron Advertising Ltd 1982–84; The Quentin Bell Organisation plc: campaign mangr 1984–86, campaign dir 1986–87, associate dir 1987–89, bd dir 1989–, dep md 1991–; MIPR 1988; *Recreations* tennis, entertaining, family life, ballet; *Style—* Mrs Shirley Hanley; ✉ Bramley House, Church Road, Sunningdale, Ascot, Berkshire SL5 0NJ; The Quentin Bell Organisation plc, 22 Endell Street, Covent Garden, London WC2H 9AD (☎ 0171 379 0304, fax 0171 379 4732)

HANMER, (Wyndham Richard) Guy; s and h of Sir John Wyndham Edward Hanmer, 8 Bt, *qv*; *b* 27 Nov 1955; *Educ* Wellington; *m* 9 Aug 1986, Elizabeth A, yr da of Neil Taylor, of Frampton-on- Severn, Glos; 2 s (Thomas Wyndham William b 10 May 1989, George Hugh Richard b 13 July 1992), 1 da (Alicia Marina b 24 May 1994); *Career* Blues and Royals, ret 1981; now farming; *Style—* Guy Hanmer, Esq; ✉ The Stables, Bettisfield Park, Whitchurch, Shropshire SY13 2JZ

HANMER, Sir John Wyndham Edward; 8 Bt (GB 1774), of Hanmer, Flintshire, JP (Clwyd 1971), DL (1978); s of Lt-Col Sir (Griffin Wyndham) Edward Hanmer, 7 Bt (d 1977), by his 1 w, Aileen; *b* 27 Sept 1928; *Educ* Eton; *m* 1954, Audrey Melissa, eldest da of Maj Arthur Christopher John Congreve (d 1992), of the same family (which held land in Staffs from *temp* Edward II) as William Congreve, the Restoration playwright; 2 s ((Wyndham Richard) Guy b 1955, Edward Hugh b 1957); *Heir* s, (Wyndham Richard) Guy Hanmer, *qv*, b 27 Nov 1955; *Career* Capt late The Royal Dragoons; landowner and farmer; dir Chester Race Co 1978, Ludlow Race Club Ltd 1980; High Sheriff Clwyd 1977; *Recreations* shooting, racing; *Clubs* Army and Navy; *Style—* Sir John Hanmer, Bt, JP, DL; ✉ The Mere House, Hanmer, Whitchurch, Shropshire (☎ 01948 830383)

HANN, Judith; da of Ralph Hann, of Derby, and Connie, *née* Buxton; *b* 8 Sept 1942; *Educ* Univ of Durham (BSc); *m* 17 Oct 1964, John Exelby; 2 s (Jake b 7 Jan 1970, Daniel b 6 Dec 1971); *Career* journalist trg Northern Echo and Westminster Press, won Glaxo award for science writers in 1960s and 70s, reporter BBC Science and Features (former presenter Tomorrow's World, latterly presenter Watchdog Healthcheck); memb: IVF Ethics Ctee, Small Business Foresight Project, Bd Countryside Movement; patron of various scientific socs; *Books* But What About the Children, The Perfect Baby, Family Scientist, Total Health Plan, The Food of Love, How Science Works (1991); *Recreations* walking, herb gardening, cookery; *Style—* Ms Judith Hann; ✉ Baxters Farm, Fyfield, Nr Lechlade, Glos GL7 3NS (☎ 01367 850236)

HANNA, Robert James; CBE 1988 (OBE 1975), JP (Londonderry 1962); s of James Hanna (d 1973), of Draperstown, and Isabella Margaret, *née* Smyth (d 1978); *b* 9 May 1935; *Educ* Rainey Endowed Magherafelt Co Londonderry; *m* 1 Aug 1962, (Annie) Elizabeth (Betty), da of late James Faulkner, of Cookstown, Co Tyrone; 3 s (James Faulkner b 14 June 1963, (Robert) Gordon b 18 Oct 1964, (Wilfred) Sydney b 9 April 1967), 1 da (Muriel Elizabeth Margaret b 9 Dec 1969); *Career* farmer and landowner; memb: Londonderry CC 1965–73, Ulster Countryside Ctee 1965–89 (vice chm 1968–75, chm 1975–89); pres Ulster Farmers' Union 1972–73; memb: NI Economic Cncl 1972–77, NI Agricultural Tst 1973–81; cmmr Planning Appeals Cmmn 1973–86; memb: PO Users' Cncl NI 1978–81, BBC NI Agricultural Advsy Ctee 1978–84, Gen Consumer Cncl NI 1985–91 (dep chm 1991–92), Bd NI Electricity 1991–92; chm NI Northern Health and Social Servs Bd 1989–, dep chm Cncl for Nature Conservation and the Countryside 1989–, memb Cncl Nat Assoc of Health Authys and Tsts 1990–, pro-chllr Univ of Ulster 1994–; fndr memb Ulster Tst for Nature Conservation (now the Ulster Wildlife Tst), fndr and past chm Farming and Wildlife Advsy Gp NI; FRSA 1990; *Recreations* the Great Outdoors, local history, 19th and 20th century porcelain; *Clubs* Farmers'; *Style—* Robert J Hanna, Esq, CBE, JP; ✉ Northern Health and Social Services Board, County Hall, 182 Galgorm Road, Ballymena, Co Antrim BT42 1QB (☎ 01266 662318, fax 01266 43094)

HANNA, Vincent Leo; s of the Hon Francis Hanna (d 1987), of Dublin, and Ida Mary, *née* Conboy; *b* 9 Aug 1939; *Educ* Queen's Univ Belfast, Trinity Coll Dublin, Harvard Univ; *m* 1975, Hon Susan Joan, da of Lord Fitt of Bellshill; 2 da (Emily Elizabeth b 1975, Sinead Eileen b 1980); *Career* admitted slr of the Supreme Ct 1964, slr in family practice 1963–70, industl relations corr Sunday Times 1970–73, political journalist BBC TV 1973–87 (reporter numerous current affrs progs incl Panorama, Newsnight, election specials), formed independent TV prodn co 1987; presenter: A Week in Politics (Channel 4) 1990–, Hypotheticals (BBC2) 1992–, After Hours (BBC Radio 5 Live) 1994–, Medium Wave (BBC Radio 4) 1996–, numerous documentaries; non-exec dir London Borough of Tower Hamlets 1993–94, vice chm Family Holidays Assoc 1993–; independent conslt to: City of Leeds, City of Birmingham; *Recreations* France, music, food, family; *Style—* Vincent Hanna, Esq; ✉ 15 College Heights, St John Street, London EC1V 4PH (☎ 07000 842662)

HANNAFORD, Barry William; s of Albert Edward Hannaford (d 1984), and Ethel, *née* Cesana; *b* 25 June 1953; *m* Rowena; *Career* trainee lighting engr Thorn Lighting Ltd 1970–75, lighting engr Concord Lighting Ltd 1975–76, tech offr London Borough of Greenwich 1976–77, lighting engr and dep mangr Concord Lighting Ltd 1977–80, project sales mangr Erco Lighting Ltd 1980–85, dir Lighting Design Partnership 1987– (assoc 1985–86); major projects incl: James Bond film set Pinewood Studios, Newport and Sequoia Lodge Disney Hotels Paris, Mercury House London, UNESCO Nat Museum Libya, Pirelli Gardens V & A, Adelphi Building London (exterior), Opus Sacrum (exhibition) Warsaw, refurbishment Billingsgate Market; UK rep Int Assoc of Lighting Designers; *Publications* Lighting Design (jtly, Design Cncl); *Style—* Barry Hannaford, Esq; ✉ Lighting Design Partnership, 63 Gee Street, London EC1V 3RS (☎ 0171 250 3200, fax 0171 250 0824)

HANNAH, David Stuart; s of Daniel Hannah, of Appleton, Warrington, and Phyllis, *née* Mottershead; *b* 1 Jan 1953; *Educ* Royal GS Lancaster, Univ of Liverpool (LLB); *m* 26 March 1977, Joanne Alison, da of James Crichton, of Minchinhampton, Glos; 3 s (Daniel b 1981, Christopher b 1983, Michael b 1987), 1 da (Louise b 1979); *Career* admitted slr 1977; tutor in law of equity and trusts Univ of Liverpool 1974–78; memb Legal Aid Area Ctee Chester 1981–, chm Educn Ctee Slrs Family Law Soc 1996–; memb Nat Ctee SFLA 1996, fndr Ctee memb Br Assoc of Lawyer Mediators 1995; *Recreations* swimming, photography, restoring classic cars; *Style—* David S Hannah, Esq; ✉ 1 Marlfield Rd, Grappenhall, Warrington WA4 2JT (☎ 01925 264974); 1 Victoria Rd, Stockton Heath, Warrington (☎ 01925 261354)

HANNAH, Eur Ing Gordon Marshall; s of Dr Daniel Marshall Hannah (d 1971, former Wing Cdr), of Eccles, Manchester, and Kathleen Mary Hannah, JP, *née* Schaap; *b* 30 April 1940; *Educ* Ellesmere Coll Shropshire, Trinity Coll Cambridge (MA); *m* 14 March 1964, Carolyn Joyce, da of William Dancer (d 1989), of Axminster, Devon; 2 da (Juliette b 29 June 1966, Vanessa b 8 Oct 1968); *Career* chief engr The Dredging & Construction Co Contractors 1972–76; ptnr: Brown Crozier & Wyatt Consultant Engineers 1976–79, Hannah Reed & Assocs 1979–; memb Cncl Inst of Civil Engrs 1982–85 and 1991–92, past pres Rotary Club of Cambridge Rutherford; past chm: Cambridge Round Table, E Anglian Assoc of Inst of Civil Engrs; FICE 1981, MConsE 1982, FIHT 1983, FRSA 1986; *Recreations* golf, gliding, gardening, modelmaking; *Clubs* Gog Magog Golf, Cambridge Univ Gliding; *Style—* Eur Ing Gordon Hannah; ✉ 8 Linton Road, Great Abington, Cambridge CB1 6AA (☎ 01223 890654); Hannah Reed & Associates, Telford House, Fulbourn, Cambridge CB1 5HB (☎ 01223 882000, fax 01223 881888, car 0831 511665)

HANNAH, Prof Leslie; s of Arthur Hannah (d 1969), and Marie, *née* Lancashire; *b* 15 June 1947; *Educ* Manchester GS, St John's and Nuffield Colls Oxford (BA, MA, DPhil); *m* 29 Dec 1984, Nuala Barbara Zahedieh, da of Thomas Hockton, of Hove, Sussex; 1 s (Thomas b 1988), 2 step da (Sophie b 1977, Miranda b 1981); *Career* res fell St John's Coll Oxford 1969–73, lectr in econs Univ of Essex 1973–75, lectr Univ of Cambridge 1975–78 (fell Emmanuel Coll Cambridge, fin tutor 1977–78); LSE: dir Business Hist Unit 1978–88, prof 1982–, pro-dir 1995–, actg dir 1996–97; res fell Centre for Econ Policy Res London 1984–92, visiting prof Harvard Business Sch 1984–85, assoc fellow Centre for Business Strategy London Business School 1988–89, invited lectr at univs in USA Europe and Japan; dir various cos (dir NRG Victory Holdings 1987–93), dir London Economics 1992– (fndr memb, subsequently specialist res conslt); referee/tstee for various res funding agencies, charities and jls; memb Social Sci Res Cncl (UK) 1982–84, chm Editorial Advsy Bd Dictionary of Business Biography 1979–85; MInstD; *Books* The Rise of the Corporate Economy (1976, 2 edn 1983, Japanese edn 1987), Management Strategy and Business Development (ed, 1976), Concentration in Modern Industry: Theory, Measurement and the UK Experience (jtly, 1977), Electricity Before Nationalisation (1977), Engineers, Managers and Politicians (1982), Entrepreneurs and the Social Sciences (1984), Inventing Retirement: The Development of Occupational Pensions in Britain (1986), Electricity Privatisation and the Area Boards: the Case for 12 (jtly, 1987), Pension Asset Management: An International Perspective (ed, 1988); *Recreations* reading, walking, talking; *Style—* Prof Leslie Hannah; ✉ LSE, Houghton St, London WC2A 2AE (☎ 0171 955 7013, fax 0171 404 5510, telex 24655)

HANNAH, His Hon William; s of William Bond Hannah (d 1952), and Elizabeth Alexandra, *née* Farrow (d 1982); *b* 31 March 1929; *Educ* Everton Sch Nottingham; *m* 1 July 1950, (Alma) June, da of James Marshall (d 1969); 1 s (William Robert b 1960), 1 da (Kay b 1953); *Career* RAF 1946–52; police serv (UK) 1952–77; called to the Bar 1970, in practice Newcastle (chambers of David Robson, QC) 1977–88, recorder of the Crown Court 1987–88, circuit judge (NE Circuit) 1988–95, ret; *Recreations* golf, swimming, walking, theatre; *Clubs* South Shields Golf; *Style—* His Hon William Hannah; ✉ c/o The Courts Administrative Office, Westgate House, Newcastle NE1 1RR

HANNAM, Sir John Gordon; kt (1992), MP (C) Exeter (majority 3,045); s of Thomas William Hannam (d 1955), and Selina, *née* Young (d 1986); *b* 2 Aug 1929; *Educ* Yeovil GS; *m* 1, 19 June 1956 (m dis 1981), Wendy, da of late Thomas Lamont Macartney, of Beckenham; 2 da (Amanda b 1961, Katie b 1976); m 2, 1983, Mrs Vanessa Wauchope, da of Wing Cdr Henry Albert Anson, RAF (d 1955; gs of 2 Earl of Lichfield), and former w of John Wauchope; 1 step s, 3 step da; *Career* cmmnd 4 Royal Tank Regt 1947–48, 4 Bn Somerset LI (TA) 1949–51; md: Hotels & Restaurants Co 1952–61, Motels & Restaurants Co 1961–70; pres British Motels Fedn 1974–80 (chm 1967–74), memb Cncl Br Travel Assoc 1968–69; MP (C) Exeter 1970–, PPS to Min for Indust 1972–73, chief sec Treasy 1973–74; sec 1922 Ctee 1987–; chm: W Country Cons Backbench Ctee 1979–81, Cons Energy Ctee 1979–92, All-Pty Disablement Gp 1992– (sec 1975–92); capt: Lords and Commons Tennis Club 1975–, Lords and Commons Ski Club 1975–82; memb: Govt Advsy Ctee on Transport for Disabled, Cncl Action Res, Glyndebourne Festival Soc, Bd Nat Theatre 1979–92; vice pres Disabled Drivers' Assoc; Hon MA Open Univ 1986; *Recreations* tennis (ex Somerset Singles Champion), skiing, sailing, music, singing, reading; *Clubs* All England Lawn Tennis, Royal Yacht Sqdn; *Style—* Sir John Hannam, MP; ✉ House of Commons, London SW1A 0AA

HANNAY, Anthony Hewitt Scott; s of Thomas Scott Hannay (d 1975), of Chorlton-by-Backford, Chester, and Doreen, *née* Paul; *b* 2 May 1944; *Educ* Rugby, Univ of Liverpool (LLB); *m* 10 Oct 1970, Rosemary Susan, da of Maj Geoffrey Thomas St John Sanders, TD (d 1986), of Cirencester, Glos; 1 s (Andrew b 1975), 1 da (Diana b 1973); *Career* admitted slr 1968; ptnr: Laces & Co 1970–88, Lace Mawer 1988–93 (conslt 1993–96), Anthony Hanny (slr and notary) 1996–; dir Liverpool Cncl of Social Service Inc 1994–; memb: Mersey RHA 1988–90, RNLI Mgmnt Ctee 1986– (chm Port of Liverpool and Dist Branch 1989–); memb Law Soc; *Recreations* sailing, skiing, windsurfing; *Clubs* Liverpool Artists; *Style—* Anthony Hannay, Esq; ✉ The Stray, School Lane, Hinderton, Neston, South Wirral L64 7TX (☎ 0151 336 8455, fax 0151 353 1755)

HANNAY, David Hugh Alexander; GCMG (1995, KCMG 1986, CMG 1981); s of J G Hannay (d 1972), of Aston Tirrold, nr Didcot, Oxon, and E M Hannay (d 1986), *née* Lazarus; *b* 28 Sept 1935; *Educ* Winchester, New Coll Oxford; *m* 1961, Gillian Rosemary, da of H Rex (d 1962), of Exmouth, Devon; 4 s (Richard, Philip, Jonathan, Alexander); *Career* 2 Lt 8 King's Royal Irish Hussars 1954–56; HM Dip Serv: joined 1959, Tehran 1960–61, oriental sec Kabul 1961–63, Eastern Dept FO 1963–65, second then first sec UK Delgn to the EC 1965–70, first sec UK Negotiating Team with the Euro Community 1970–72, chef de cabinet to Sir Christopher Soames (vice pres of Cmmn of Euro Community) Brussels 1973–77, head Energy Sci and Space Dept FCO 1977–79, head ME Dept FCO 1979, asst under sec of state (Euro Community) FCO 1979–84, min Washington 1984–85, ambass and UK perm rep to Euro Community 1985–90, ambass and UK permanent rep to UN and rep on Security Cncl 1990–95, ret; Br Govt's special rep for Cyprus 1996–; *Recreations* photography, travel, gardening; *Clubs* Travellers'; *Style—* Sir David Hannay, GCMG; ✉ 3 The Orchard, London W4 1JZ (☎ 0181 994 7004)

HANNAY OF KIRKDALE AND THAT ILK, Ramsay William Rainsford; s of Col Frederick Rainsford-Hannay, CMG, DSO, JP (d 1959), of Cardoness, Gatehouse-of-Fleet, Kirkcudbrightshire, and Dorothea Letitia May, *née* Maxwell (d 1981); *b* 15 June 1911; *Educ* Winchester, Trinity Coll Cambridge; *m* 19 Sept 1936, Margaret, 2 da of Sir William Wiseman, 10 Bt (d 1962), of Content, Montego Bay, Jamaica; 1 s (David Wiseman Ramsay b 3 Jan 1939), 1 da (Jessica Margaret b 2 Sept 1937); *Career* served WWII, cmmnd Highland Light Inf, serv with SOE in US and Europe, attached to Kings Liverpool Regt, demob as Maj; called to the Bar 1934, legal asst Bd of Trade 1937–59, asst slr Bd of Trade 1959–64 (ret to look after family estates in Galloway); appointed Hon Sheriff substitute Stewartry of Kirkcudbright; appointed Chief of Clan Hannay 1980 as Hannay of Kirkdale and of that Ilk and relinquished the surname of Rainsford; pres Galloway Scouts; *Recreations* shooting, fishing, sailing; *Clubs* New (Edinburgh), Royal Ocean Racing; *Style—* Hannay of Kirkdale and of that Ilk; ✉ Cardoness Cottage, Gatehouse-of-Fleet, Kirkcudbrightshire DG7 2EP (☎ 01557 840 286); Estate Office, Cardoness, Gatehouse-of-Fleet, Kirkcudbrightshire DG7 2EP (☎ 01557 840 288)

HANNON, Rt Rev Brian Desmond Anthony; *see:* Clogher, Bishop of

HANNON, Timothy Joseph (Tim); s of Timothy Patrick Hannon, of Cork, Eire, and Teresa Rose, *née* McNamara (decd); *b* 29 Oct 1952; *Educ* Sir James Altham Watford; *m* 30 June 1984, Patricia Lucy Evelyn, da of John Cameron Norman; 2 da (Alice Teresa Lucy b 4 Nov 1986, Catriona Rose b 14 March 1990); *Career* former appts incl print buyer, photographic/retouching sales mangr, account mangr then prodn/traffic controller at advertising agencies Rex Stewart & Associates, Garland Compton, Saatchi & Saatchi, Young & Rubicam and Doyle Dane Bernbach, currently creative servs dir BMP DDB Worldwide; presentations to: French Bd of Trade (Printing in the UK) Feb 1995, Euro Rotagravure Assoc's 40th Anniversary (Print in Advertising) May 1996; chm Creative Servs Ctee IPA; FIPA 1996 (MIPA 1990); *Recreations* rugby (watching), jogging;

Clubs Tabard RFC; *Style*— Tim Hannon, Esq; ✉ 74 Eaton Drive, Kingston-upon-Thames, Surrey KT2 7QX (☎ 0181 549 3740); BMP DDB, 12 Bishop's Bridge Road, London W2 6AA (☎ 0171 258 4605, fax 0171 262 2615)

HANRAHAN, Brian; s of Thomas Hanrahan, and Kathleen, *née* McInerney; *b* 22 March 1949; *Educ* St Ignatius Coll, Univ of Essex (BA); *m* 4 Jan 1986, Honor Catherine, *née* Wilson; 1 da (Catherine); *Career* BBC: Far East corr 1983–85, Moscow corr 1986–89, diplomatic corr 1989–; *Style*— Brian Hanrahan, Esq; ✉ c/o BBC TV Centre, Wood Lane, London W12 7RJ (☎ 0181 743 8000)

HANRATTY, Dr James Francis; OBE (1989); s of Dr James Joseph Hanratty (d 1968), of Huddersfield, and Elsie May, *née* Lycett (d 1987); *b* 27 July 1919; *Educ* Stonyhurst, Univ of Leeds (MB ChB, MRCGP); *m* 26 May 1945, (Mary) Irene Evangeline, da of Andrew Belton (d 1977); 4 s (James b 1946, John b 1949, Patrick b 1952, Peter b 1957), 1 da (Mary b 1947); *Career* Surgn Lt RNVR 1943–46 (despatches 1944); serv HMS Cam: Atlantic, Med, Normandy invasion; GP N Derbys 1946–78, med dir St Joseph's Hospice Hackney 1978–88; lectr on terminal illness: RAMC, USA 1981, Sorbonne 1983, Hong Kong 1984, Brussels 1987, Hague 1987; former pres Derbys Branch BMA, memb Industl Injuries Med Bd Chesterfield 1949–78, master Guild of Catholic Doctors Nottingham 1975–78, govr Stonyhurst Coll 1975–81, pres Stonyhurst Assoc 1989; Knight of the Order of St Gregory the Great (Papal) 1988, Knight Cdr of the Order of the Holy Sepulchre of Jerusalem English Lieutenancy 1987; *Books* Control of Distressing Symptoms in the Dying Patient (1982), Palliative Care in Terminal Illness (ed, 1994); *Recreations* watching cricket, classical music; *Clubs* Naval, Hurlingham, Athenaeum; *Style*— Dr James Hanratty, OBE; ✉ 44 Westminster Gardens, Marsham St, London SW1P 4JG (☎ 0171 834 4660)

HANRATTY, Judith Christine; da of John Edward Hanratty (d 1981), of Wellington, NZ, and Joyce, *née* Proudfoot, of Waikanae, NZ; *b* 16 Aug 1943; *Educ* Chilton St James Sch, St Hilda's Collegiate Sch NZ, Victoria Univ of Wellington NZ (LLB, LLM); *Career* barrister: High Ct of NZ 1966, Supreme Ct of Victoria Australia 1980, Inner Temple 1987; currently co sec BP plc; dir: London Electricity plc 1995–, The Tanker Insurance Co Ltd, BP Pension Trustees Ltd, Ropemaker Properties Ltd, Jupiter Insurance Ltd; tstee: Lucy Cavendish Coll Cambridge, Waitangi Fndn; memb Insurance Brokers' Registration Cncl; FRSA 1994; *Recreations* golf, horticulture; *Clubs* Royal Mid-Surrey Golf, Roehampton, Wellington; *Style*— Miss Judith Hanratty; ✉ The British Petroleum Company plc, 1 Finsbury Circus, London EC2M 7BA (☎ 0171 496 4244, fax 0171 496 4678)

HANSCOMB, Christine; da of Ronald and Margaret Hanscomb, of Dorset; *b* 7 Jan 1946; *Educ* Ravensbourne Sch of Art Sunderland, Maidstone Sch of Art (BA Graphics); *m* David Versey, artist; 2 da (Crystal-Lily b 5 Nov 1976, Tara-Jade b 25 July 1984); *Career* Art Dept Vogue Magazine 1969–71, art dir Brides magazine 1971–76, art ed Vogue Magazine 1977, art dir Vogue Beauty Book 1978–81, freelance photographer 1979–; cmmnd by all maj advtg agencies in London, Paris and Milan 1981–, and by pubns incl Vogue (London, Paris and NY), Country Living, Interiors, House and Garden, The Observer and Sunday Times; commercials dir with The Producers prodn co; *Books* English Country Style (1987); photographic illustrations for numerous cookery books incl: Madhur Jaffrey's A Taste of India, Antonio Carluccio's A Taste of Italy, Sir Terence and Lady Conran's The Cook Book, Sainsbury's The Book of Food, Nathalie Hambro's Visual Delights; *Recreations* films, music, art, deepsea scuba diving, the countryside; *Style*— Ms Christine Hanscomb; ✉ 11 Perseverance Works, 38 Kingsland Road, London E2 8DD (☎ 0171 739 0132, fax 0171 729 7066)

HANSEN, Alan David; s of John McDonald Hansen, of Clackmananshire, Scotland, and Anne Peddie, *née* Gillon; *b* 13 June 1955; *Educ* Lornshill Acad; *m* 21 June 1980, Janette, da of James Harold Rhymes; 1 s (Adam John b 29 June 1981), 1 da (Lucy Grace b 23 Aug 1984); *Career* former professional footballer; signed for Partick Thistle 1973; Liverpool FC 1977–91: 621 appearances, 8 League Championship medals, 3 European Cup winner's medals (1 loser's), 2 FA Cup winner's medals (1 loser's); currently commentator BBC TV (Sportsnight and Match of the Day); *Recreations* golf, tennis; *Clubs* Hillside Golf, Southport and Birkdale Cricket; *Style*— Alan Hansen, Esq; ✉ c/o BBC TV Sports and Events Group, Kensington House, Richmond Way, London W14 0AX

HANSEN, Brent Vivian; s of Vivian Ernest Hansen (d 1988), of Christchurch, NZ, and Noeline, *née* Eathorne; *b* 14 Sept 1955; *Educ* St Andrew's Coll Christchurch NZ, Otago Univ Dunedin NZ (BA), Canterbury Univ Christchurch (MA), Christchurch Teachers' Coll (teaching cert); *m* 30 Aug 1986, Phillipa Jennie Dann, of NZ; 1 da (Marley Harriet b 22 April 1991), 1 s (Cassidy Jake b 8 Jan 1995); *Career* TV New Zealand: floor mangr, unit mangr, prodr and dir Radio With Pictures 1982–86; MTV: news prodr 1987, dir of news 1987–88, head of prodn 1988–89, dir of programming and prodn 1989–94, pres and creative dir MTV Networks Europe 1994–; memb Country Music Assoc Nashville; *Recreations* rugby, collecting music; *Style*— Brent Hansen, Esq; ✉ MTV Europe, Hawley Crescent, London NW1 8TT (☎ 0171 284 7777, fax 0171 284 7788)

HANSFORD, Jean-Paul; s of David John Hansford, of Bembridge, IOW, and Anne-Marie, *née* Hewison; *Educ* St John's Coll Southsea, London Coll of Printing (post grad dip in radio journalism); *Career* prog asst BBC Radio York 1985–86, prodr and presenter Ocean Sound Fareham Hants 1986–89, fndr and md (programming) Isle of Wight Radio 1989, programme controller 2CR Bournemouth 1992–94, prog controller Fox FM Oxford 1994, currently presenter BBC Radio Solent; BP Journalist of the Year 1986; *Recreations* reading, swimming, travel; *Style*— Jean-Paul Hansford, Esq; ✉ BBC Radio Solent, Broadcasting House, 10 Havelock Road, Southampton SO14 7PW (☎ 01703 631311)

HANSON, Sir Anthony (Leslie Oswald) Dominic Sean; 4 Bt (UK 1887), of Bryanston Square, Co Middlesex; s of Sir Gerald Stanhope Hanson, 2 Bt (d 1946), and his 3 w Flora Libre, *née* Blennerhassett (d 1956); suc half-bro Sir Richard Leslie Reginald Hanson, 3 Bt, 1951; *b* 27 Nov 1934; *Educ* Hawtrey's, Gordonstoun, Univ of Exeter (BEd); *m* 1964, Denise Jane, da of Richard S Rolph, BEM, of Stoke-sub-Hamdon, Somerset; 1 da (Charlotte Penelope Frances b 1971); *Heir* none; *Career* served RN; farming to 1967; teacher to 1983; serious motorcycle accident 1980; *Recreations* riding, avoiding rows with wife, reading, working for Amnesty Int and Greenpeace, talking; *Style*— Sir Anthony Hanson, Bt; ✉ Woodland Cottage, Woodland, Ashburton, Devon (☎ 01364 52711)

HANSON, Brian John Taylor; CBE (1996); s of Benjamin John Hanson (d 1978), of Norwood Green, Middx, and Gwendoline Ada, *née* Taylor; *b* 23 Jan 1939; *Educ* Hounslow Coll, Law Soc Coll of Law, Univ of Wales (LLM); *m* 10 June 1972, Deborah Mary Hazel, da of Lt-Col Richard Stewart Palliser Dawson, OBE (d 1994), of Shrubbery Cottage, Stowting, Kent; 2 s (James b 1973, Crispin b 1982), 3 da (Sarah b 1975, Rebecca b 1979, Alice b 1986); *Career* slr and ecclesiastical notary; slr in private practice 1963–65, slr Church Cmmrs for Eng 1965–70; Gen Synod of C of E: asst legal adviser 1970–74, legal advsr 1974– registrar 1980–; legal advsr House of Bishops 1974–; registrar to the Convocation of Canterbury 1982–; memb Legal Advsy Cmmn of the Gen Synod 1980– (sec 1970–86), guardian Shrine of Our Lady of Walsingham 1984–; memb Cncl: St Luke's Hosp for the Clergy 1985–, The Ecclesiastical Law Soc 1987–; fell Woodard Corp 1987–; govr: St Michael's Sch Burton Park 1987–94, Pusey House Oxford 1993–, Quainton Hall Sch 1994–; Bishop's nominee on Chichester Diocesan Synod 1987–; memb: Law Soc 1963, Canon Law Soc of GB 1980, Ecclesiastical Law Assoc 1980–; Freeman City of London, Liveryman Worshipful Co of Glaziers and Painters of Glass; *Books* The Opinions of the Legal Advisory Commission (ed 6 edn, 1985), The Canons of the Church of England (ed 2 edn 1975, 4 edn 1986), Norwood Parish Church - A Short History (1970), Garth Moore's Introduction to English Canon Law (jtly 3 edn, 1992), Atkin's Court Forms (ed Ecclesiastical vol, 1992, 1996); *Recreations* the family, gardening, genealogy; *Clubs* Royal Cwlth Soc; *Style*— Brian Hanson, Esq, CBE; ✉ Daltons Farm, Bolney, W Sussex RH17 5PG (☎ 01444 881890); Church House, Deans Yard, London SW1 (☎ 0171 222 9011, fax 0171 233 2660)

HANSON, Christopher John; s of Laurence William Hanson (d 1966), of Oxford, and Carola Mary, *née* Hawes (d 1985); *b* 20 April 1940; *Educ* The King's Sch Canterbury, Univ of Oxford (MA); *m* 26 May 1975, Jayne Gwenllian, da of Evan Morgan Lewis; 1 s (David William b 1976), 1 da (Elizabeth Jane b 1979); *Career* slr; ptnr Lovell White Durrant; memb Insolvency Law Sub-Ctee Law Soc, chm Insolvency Law Sub-Ctee City of London Law Soc; *Style*— Christopher Hanson, Esq; ✉ The Shaw, Brasted Chart, nr Westerham, Kent (☎ 01959 563763); Lovell White Durrant, 65 Holborn Viaduct, London EC1A 2DY (☎ 0171 236 0066, fax 0171 248 4212, telex 887122 LWD G)

HANSON, David; MP (Lab) Delyn (majority 2,039); s of Brian Hanson, and Glenda Hanson; *b* 5 July 1957; *Educ* Verdin Comp Sch Winsford, Univ of Hull (BA, CertEd); *m* 6 Sept 1986, Margaret, *née* Mitchell; 1 s, 2 da; *Career* vice pres Hull Univ Students' Union 1978–79, trainee Co-operative Union 1980–81, mangr Plymouth Co-operative 1981–82, various appts The Spastics Soc (now Scope) 1982–89, dir Re-Solv (Soc for Prevention of Solvent Abuse) 1989–92, MP (Lab) Delyn 1992– (also contested 1987), sec PLP Heritage Ctee 1995–, memb Leadership Campaign Team 1995–, memb Public Serv Select Ctee; Parly candidate (Lab) Eddisbury 1983, Euro Parly candidate Cheshire W 1984; cncllr: Vale Royal BC 1983–91 (chm Econ Devpt Ctee and ldr Lab Gp 1989–90), Northwich Town Cncl 1987–91; *Recreations* football, cinema, cooking; *Style*— David Hanson, Esq, MP; ✉ 64 Chester Street, Flint, Flintshire (☎ 01352 763159); House of Commons, London SW1A 0AA (0171 219 5064)

HANSON, Derek; *b* 17 June 1933; *Educ* Univ of Nottingham (BSc), Queen's Coll Cambridge (BA); *Career* various appts ICI plc 1957–71; John Brown plc: tech mangr 1971–78, md John Brown E & C Ltd 1979–90 (mktg dir 1978–79), dir 1989–; pres Chemetics International Co Ltd 1990–; FIChemE 1971, FEng 1986; *Recreations* sailing, cricket; *Clubs* MCC, Royal Naval; *Style*— Derek Hanson, Esq, FEng; ✉ John Brown plc, 4500 Parkway, Solent Business Park, Whiteley, Hants PO15 7AY (☎ 01489 614379, fax 01489 614504)

HANSON, Derrick George; s of late John Henry Hanson; *b* 9 Feb 1927; *Educ* Waterloo GS, Univ of London, Univ of Liverpool; *m* 1 1951, Daphne Elizabeth (decd); 1 s, 2 da; m 2, 1974, Hazel Mary (decd); m 3, 1986, Patricia; *Career* dir and gen mangr Martins Bank Trust Co 1968, Barclays Bank Trust Co 1969–76, chm Barclays Unicorn 1972–76, sr advsr (UK) Manufacturers Hanover Trust Co 1977–79, chm City of London and Euro Property Co Ltd 1980–86, dir Phillips Fine Art Auctioneers 1977–82; chm: Key Fund Managers Ltd 1984–87, Birmingham Midshires Building Society 1988–90 (dir 1982–90), Moneyguide Ltd 1978–, Br Leather Co Ltd 1993–94 (dir 1983–94); dir: Toye and Co plc 1981–92, Albany Investment Trust plc 1980–, James Beattie plc 1985–; memb Cncl Univ of Liverpool 1981–84, chm Southport and Formby DHA 1986–89; memb Nat Tst NW Regnl Cncl 1990–96, pres Assoc of Banking Teachers 1979–88, chm Christian Arts Tst 1980–86; hon fell City Univ Business Sch 1977–86, Hon FCIB 1987; *Books* Service Banking - The Arrival of the All-Purpose Bank (1982, Chartered Inst of Bankers sr prize for outstanding contribution to banking literature), Moneyguide - the Handbook of Personal Finance (1980), Dictionary of Banking and Finance (1985); *Recreations* golf, gardening, hill walking; *Clubs* RAC, Formby Golf; *Style*— Derrick Hanson, Esq; ✉ Bridgend, Deepdale Bridge, Patterdale, Cumbria CA11 0NS; Grasshopper House, Freshfield Road, Formby, Merseyside L37 7BJ

HANSON, Geoffrey; s of John Hanson (d 1967), of Witney, Oxfordshire, and Grace Emily, *née* Elphick (d 1977); *b* 9 Dec 1939; *Educ* Eastbourne GS, Itchen GS Southampton, Trinity Coll of Music London (GTCL, LTCL, ATCL); *m* 5 Aug 1961 (m dis 1994), (Alice) Janet, MBE, da of Frank Wyatt (d 1948), of Sussex; *Career* conductor and composer; conductor London Ripieno Soc 1962–, prof Trinity Coll of Music 1964–, conductor Square Singers of St James 1977–89; Telemann St Matthew Passion Camden Festival 1968; hon fell Trinity Coll of Music London 1972; memb City of Westminster Arts Cncl; memb: Performing Rights Soc 1981, Incorporated Soc of Musicians 1983, Composers' Guild of GB 1983; *Compositions* incl: 3 Pieces for Organ 1970, A Trilogy of Psalms for chorus and orchestra 1973, Brecon Ser 1974, concerto for piano and orchestra 1977, concerto for oboe and strings 1978, Sinfonia Amoris for soloists chorus and orchestra 1981, War! Cry War! for soloists chorus and orchestra 1986, concerto for violin and orchestra 1986, concerto for clarinet and strings 1987, concerto for viola and orchestra 1990, The Virgin Crown (opera) 1991, Te Deum (for Hanover Choir) 1993, Carols for Tring 1994; *Recreations* swimming, walking; *Style*— Geoffrey Hanson, Esq; ✉ 89 Fordington Rd, Highgate, London N6 4TH (☎ 0181 444 9214)

HANSON, James Donald (Don); s of Leslie Hanson (d 1977), of W Yorks, and Mary, *née* Haigh (d 1982); *b* 4 Jan 1935; *Educ* Heath GS Halifax W Yorks; *m* 1, 29 Aug 1959 (m dis 1977), (Patricia) Margaret, da of Frank Talent (d 1982), of Cheshire; 2 s (Steven b 1962, Scott b 1966); m 2, 8 July 1978, Anne Barbara Asquith; *Career* managing ptnr of strategical affrs and communications Arthur Andersen 1989– (joined 1958, estab NW practice 1966, manging ptnr 1968–82, sr ptnr of UK firm 1982–89); memb: Int Operating Ctee 1982–88, Int Bd of Ptnrs 1985–88; pres Manchester Soc of Chartered Accountants 1979 (memb 1967–81); memb: Cncl CBI 1982–, Cncl and Ct Univ of Manchester 1982–; FCA 1957 (ACA 1956); *Recreations* reading, tennis; *Clubs* Mark's, Groucho, Annabel's; *Style*— Don Hanson, Esq; ✉ Arthur Andersen & Co, 1345 Avenue of the Americas, New York, NY 10105, USA

HANSON, Baron (Life Peer UK 1983), of Edgerton, Co of W Yorks; Sir James Edward Hanson; kt (1976); s of Robert Hanson, CBE (d 1973), and late Louisa Ann (Cis), *née* Rodgers; *b* 20 Jan 1922; *m* 1959, Geraldine, *née* Kaelin; 2 s, 1 step da; *Career* served WWII 1939–46; chm: Hanson PLC 1965–, Hanson Transport Group Ltd 1965–96; memb Ct of Patrons Royal Coll of Surgeons of England, tstee Hanson Fellowship of Surgery Univ of Oxford, fell Cancer Research Campaign; life memb Royal Dublin Soc 1948; Freeman City of London 1964, Hon Liveryman Worshipful Co of Saddlers; Hon LLD Leeds 1984, Hon DBA Huddersfield 1991; hon fell St Peter's Coll Oxford 1996; FRSA, CIMgt; *Clubs* Brooks's, Huddersfield Borough, The Brook (New York), Toronto; *Style*— The Rt Hon the Lord Hanson; ✉ Hanson PLC, 1 Grosvenor Place, London SW1X 7JH (☎ 0171 245 1245)

HANSON, Sir John Gilbert; KCMG (1995), CBE (1979); s of Gilbert Fretwell Hanson (d 1981), and Gladys Margaret, *née* Kay (d 1991); *b* 16 Nov 1938; *Educ* Manchester GS, Wadham Coll Oxford (MA); *m* 1962, Margaret, da of Edward Thomas Clark, MBE, of Oxfordshire; 3 s (Mark b 1966, Paul b 1967, James b 1971); *Career* WO 1961–63; Br Cncl: Madras India 1963–66, MECAS Lebanon 1966–68, Bahrain 1968–72, London 1972–75, Tehran Iran 1975–79, London 1979–82, RCDS 1983; min (cultural affrs) Br High Cmmn New Delhi 1984–88, dep dir gen Br Cncl 1988–92, dir gen Br Cncl 1992–; memb Governing Cncl SOAS; patron GAP; Hon DLitt Oxford Brookes Univ 1995, Hon Doc Univ of Lincolnshire & Humberside 1996; FRSA, CIMgt; *Recreations* books, music, sailing, sport, travel; *Clubs* Athenaeum, MCC, Gymkhana (Madras); *Style*— Sir John Hanson, KCMG, CBE; ✉ c/o The British Council, 10 Spring Gardens, London SW1A 2BN (☎ 0171 930 8466)

HANSON, Prof Owen Jerrold; s of Lawrence Hanson-Smith (d 1972), of Cheltenham, and Edith Annette Audrey, *née* Waller (d 1995); *b* 2 Jan 1934; *Educ* Wallington Co HS, Univ of Cambridge (BA, MA), Univ of London (MSc), City Univ (PhD); *m* 14 July 1965, Barbara Maria Teresa, da of Maj Albin Srodzinski; 2 da (Annette b 31 Aug 1967, Ilona b 9 March 1971); *Career* jr technician RAF 1952–54; works metallurgist Wilkinson Sword Co Ltd 1957–60, mangr of works laboratory Gillette Industs UK Ltd 1962–64, systems analyst IBM UK Ltd 1964–70; City Univ: sr lectr 1970–89, chair in business computing 1989–, dir Centre for Business Systems Analysis 1983–88, head Dept of Business Systems Analysis 1988–94, dir Centre for Business Systems Applications 1994–; *Books* Basic File Design (1978), Design of Computer Data Files (1982, 2 edn 1988), Essentials of Computer Data Files (1985); *Recreations* cross country running, tennis, squash; *Clubs* South London Harriers, Purley Cricket; *Style*— Prof Owen Hanson; ✉ Centre for Business Systems Applications, City University, Northampton Square, London EC1V 0HB (☎ 0171 477 8403, fax 0171 477 8395)

HANSON, Prof Philip; s of Eric Hugh Cecil Hanson (d 1942), of London, and Doris May, *née* Ward (d 1980); *b* 16 Dec 1936; *Educ* Highgate Sch, Jesus Coll Cambridge (MA), Univ of Birmingham (PhD); *m* 22 Oct 1960, Evelyn, da of Sidney James Rogers (d 1968), of London; 2 s (Paul Edward b 1963, Nicholas James b 1972); *Career* Nat Serv Middx Regt and Intelligence Corps, Sgt mil interpreter (Russian); lectr in econs Univ of Exeter 1961–67, visiting prof of econs Univ of Michigan 1967–68; Univ of Birmingham 1968–: lectr, sr lectr, reader, currently prof of the political economy of Russia and Eastern Europe, dep dir Centre for Russian & East Euro Studies; first sec HM Embassy Moscow, sr res offr FCO 1971–72; visiting prof Univ of Michigan 1977, sr Mellon fell Harvard Univ 1986–87, economist UN Economic Cmmn for Europe Geneva 1991–92; conslt: Planecon Inc, Oxford Analytica, Radio Liberty; memb Ctee Birmingham Jazz 1978–83, memb E Europe Exec Birmingham C of C and Indust 1980–89, memb Cncl Univ of London Sch of Slavonic and East Euro Studies 1990–; MRIIA; *Books* Trade and Technology in Soviet-Western Relations (1981), The Comparative Economics of Research, Development & Innovation (with K Pavitt, 1987), Western Economic Statecraft in East-West Relations (1988), From Stagnation to Catastroika (1992); *Recreations* jazz, cricket; *Style*— Prof Philip Hanson; ✉ c/o CREES, University of Birmingham, Birmingham B15 2TT (☎ 0121 414 6353, fax 0121 414 3423, e-mail p.hanson@bham.ac.uk)

HANSON, Richard William Durrant; TD (1969); s of William Gordon Hanson, OBE (d 1990), and Dulce Durrant Hanson (d 1996); *b* 11 Aug 1935; *Educ* Eton; *m* 23 June 1961, Elizabeth Deirdre Dewar, da of late Dr A D Frazer; 1 s (James b 1969), 2 da (Arabella (Mrs Hugh Derrick) b 1962, Georgina (Mrs Magnus Laird) b 1963); *Career* 2 Lt 17/21 Lancers 1954–56, Maj Sherwood Rangers Yeo and Royal Yeo 1956–69; Hardys & Hansons plc (Kimberley Brewery Nottingham): dir 1962–, md 1973–, chm and md 1989–; High Sheriff Nottinghamshire 1980–81; Liveryman Worshipful Co of Brewers; *Recreations* shooting, tennis; *Clubs* MCC; *Style*— Richard Hanson, Esq, TD; ✉ Budby Castle, Newark, Notts NG22 9EU (☎ 01623 822293); Hardys & Hansons plc, Kimberley Brewery, Nottingham NG16 2NS (☎ 0115 938 3611, fax 0115 945 9055)

HANSON, Hon Robert William; s of Baron Hanson (Life Peer, *qv*); *b* 3 Oct 1960; *Educ* Eton, St Peter's Coll Oxford; *Career* NM Rothschild & Sons Ltd 1983–90, asst dir NM Rothschild Sons Ltd 1990; dir: Hanson PLC 1992– (assoc dir 1990–92), Hanson Transport Group 1991–; Liveryman Worshipful Co of Saddlers; *Recreations* hunting, polo, helicopter flying, golf; *Clubs* White's, Brooks's, The Berkshire, Cirencester Polo, The Brook (NY); *Style*— The Hon Robert Hanson; ✉ Hanson plc, 1 Grosvenor Place, London SW1X 7JH (☎ 0171 245 1245, fax 0171 235 3455)

HANSON, Sir (Charles) Rupert Patrick; 4 Bt (UK 1918), of Fowey, Cornwall; s of Sir (Charles) John Hanson, 3 Bt (d 1996), and his 1 w, Patricia Helen, *née* Brind; *b* 25 June 1945; *Educ* Eton, Central London Poly; *m* 1977, Wanda, da of Don Arturo Larrain, of Santiago, Chile; 1 s (Alexis b 1978); *Heir* s, Alexis Charles Hanson b 25 March 1978; *Career* tech, legal and commercial translator 1977–84, teacher of English as foreign language 1981–83; vol charity worker 1984–85; Inland Revenue: joined 1986, various positions in different offices, HM Inspr of Taxes Brighton 4 1993–; *Recreations* classical music, writing poetry, tennis, walking; *Style*— Sir Rupert Hanson, Bt; ✉ 125 Ditchling Rd, Brighton, E Sussex BN1 4SE (☎ 01273 697882)

HANWORTH, 3 Viscount (UK 1936); Sir (David) Stephen Geoffrey Pollock; 3 Bt (UK 1922); also Baron Hanworth (UK 1926); s of 2 Viscount Hanworth (d 1996), and (Isolda) Rosamond, *née* Parker; *b* 16 Feb 1946; *Educ* Wellington Coll, Guildford Tech Coll, Univ of Sussex; *m* 1968, Elizabeth, da of Lawrence Vambe, of Harare, Zimbabwe; 2 da (Hon Cecile Abigail Shona b 1971, Hon Charlotte Anne Catherine b 1973); *Heir* bro, Hon Richard Charles Standish Pollock b 1951; *Career* lectr QMC Univ of London; *Style*— The Rt Hon the Viscount Hanworth

HARAN, Maeve; da of Dr Thomas Haran (d 1984), of Worthing, and Dr Mary Christina Haran, *née* Walsh (d 1982); *b* 12 April 1950; *Educ* Mayfield Sch, St Anne's Coll Oxford (BA); *children* 2 da (Georgia b 24 Sept 1986, Holly b 20 Nov 1988), 1 s (James b 20 Nov 1993); *Career* publicity asst Secker & Warburg Publishers, freelance magazine journalist; TV researcher, prodr then editor; ed: Six O'Clock Show (LWT), The Good Life Guide (LWT), Friday Now (LWT); *Books* Having It All (1992, shortlist Romantic Novel of the Year), Scenes from the Sex War (1993), It Takes Two (1994); *Recreations* family life!; *Style*— Ms Maeve Haran; ✉ Blake Friedmann Inc, 37–41 Gower Street, London WC1E 6HH (☎ 0171 631 4331, fax 0171 322 1274)

HARARI, Sammy; s of René David Harari, and Sandrine, *née* Olifson; *b* 4 April 1950; *Educ* Univ of Reading, Univ of Montpellier (BA); *Career* with Dunlop Ltd 1972–74, account dir Darcy Masius Benton & Bowles advtg 1974–83, dir Yellowhammer 1983–86 (handled UK Govt's first anti-heroin campaign), chief exec TBWA 1986–89 (responsible for UK Govt's anti-AIDS campaign), fndr md Harari Page 1990–; MInstM, MIPA; *Style*— Sammy Harari, Esq; ✉ Harari Page, 42–46 Weymouth Street, London W1N 3LQ (☎ 0171 224 1980, fax 0171 224 1981)

HARBERT, Walter Bertram; s of Bertie Francis Harbert (d 1979), of Mitcham, Surrey, and Maud Lily May, *née* Marchant (d 1967); *b* 12 Feb 1931; *Educ* Mitcham GS, Univ of Hull (Dip Social Studies), Univ of Manchester (Cert Psychiatric Social Work); *m* 26 May 1962, Susan Pamela, da of Harold Hill (d 1976), of Birmingham; 2 s (Stephen b 1963, Richard b 1964), 3 da (Josephine b 1965, Gillian b 1968, Alison b 1970); *Career* Nat Serv radar operator RAF 1949–51; gen sec Liverpool Personal Serv Soc 1965–70; dir of social serv: London Borough of Hackney 1970–73, Avon CC 1973–90; Help the Aged: exec dir of UK ops 1990–93, dir of planning and devpt 1993–96; currently dir Age Care Consultancy; Home Office: memb Advsy Ctee on Probation and After Care 1968–72, memb Working Pty on Community Serv Orders; DHSS: memb Finer Ctee on One Parent Families, Tutt Working Pty on Observation and Assessment of Children, Nodder Ctee on Mgmnt of Mental Illness Hosps; UN advsr on care of elderly people in Yugoslavia, WHO advsr on care for elderly people in Bulgaria, advsr on new technol for elderly and disabled people Euro Union; memb: Assoc of Psychiatric Social Workers 1960, Assoc of Dirs of Social Servs 1970 (pres 1978–79); FRSA; *Books* Welfare Benefits Handbook (1968), Community-Based Care - The Avon Experience (1983), The Home Help Service (1983), The Welfare Industry (1988), Letters To My Staff (1989), A Lonely Death (1994), Child of the War (1995); *Recreations* writing, lecturing, walking, foreign travel; *Style*— Walter Harbert, Esq, OBE; ✉ 8 Button Street, Frome, Somerset BA11 3DR (☎ 01373 453837)

HARBERTON, 10 Viscount (I 1791); Thomas de Vautort Pomeroy; also Baron Harberton (I 1783); s of 8 Viscount Harberton, OBE (d 1956); suc bro, 9 Viscount, 1980; *b* 19 Oct 1910; *Educ* Eton; *m* 1, 1939 (m dis 1946), Nancy Ellen, o da of late C A Penoyer, of San Francisco; m 2, 1950, Pauline Stafford (d 1971), da of late Wilfred Sydney Baker, of Plymouth; m 3, 1978, Vilma (Wilhelmine), widow of Sir Alfred Butt, 1 Bt, and da of Heinrich Wahl; *Heir* bro, Hon Robert Pomeroy; *Career* Lt-Col: Welsh Gds 1931–41, RAOC 1941–; *Clubs* Cavalry and Guards'; *Style*— The Rt Hon the Viscount Harberton

HARBISON, Air Vice-Marshal William; CB (1977), CBE (1965), AFC (1956); s of William Harbison, of Garvagh, NI; *b* 11 April 1922; *Educ* Ballymena Acad; *m* 1950, Helen, da of William Blaine Geneva, of Bloomington, Illinois; 2 s; *Career* Cdr RAF Staff and air attaché Washington 1972–75, AOC HQ 11 Gp RAF 1975–77; vice pres Br Aerospace Washington DC 1979–92; *Recreations* motoring; *Clubs* RAF; *Style*— Air Vice-Marshal William Harbison, CB CBE, AFC; ✉ 3292 Annandale Road, Falls Church, VA 22042, USA

HARBOR, John Liming; s of Jack Liming Harbor, of Swanage, and Isabel Katherine, *née* Lauder; *b* 11 March 1947; *Educ* Hurstpierpoint Coll; *m* 4 July 1970, Christine Elizabeth, da of John Walter De Foix Rawle; 1 da (Lucy Elizabeth b 12 May 1973), 1 s (Andrew Liming b 7 May 1979); *Career* audit supervisor London and Madrid Barton Mayhew (later merged with Ernst & Young) 1970–75, conslt to shipowners UK and Netherlands 1975–80, ptnr Bagshaws 1982–91 (joined 1980), sr insurance ptnr Moore Stephens (following merger with Bagshaws 1991); FCA (ACA 1970); *Recreations* golf, walking, cooking; *Style*— John Harbor, Esq; ✉ Moore Stephens, St Paul's House, Warwick Lane, London EC4P 4BN (☎ 0171 334 9191, fax 0171 246 6059)

HARBORD, Richard Lewis; s of Lewis Walter Harbord, of Norwich, and Dorothy Florence, *née* Mobbs; *b* 30 April 1946; *Educ* Minchenden GS, Anglian Regnl Mgmnt Centre (MPhil), Henley Coll of Mgmnt (PhD); *m* 2 May 1970, Jenny Ann, da of Herbert John Berry (d 1988), of London; 3 s (Mark b 26 Aug 1971, Adam b 5 Oct 1975, Guy b 19 July 1984); *Career* chief exec London Borough of Richmond Upon Thames 1988– (fin dir 1981–88); memb: Cncl Ratings and Valuation Assoc 1987– (pres 1994–95), Ct Univ of Surrey; chm Windlesham Community House Project, hon treas Windlesham PCC; memb IPFA 1967, memb IDPM 1968, FCCA 1981, FRVA 1982, FRSA 1990; *Recreations* family; *Style*— Richard Harbord, Esq; ✉ Gooserye, Cooper Rd, Windlesham, Surrey GU20 6EA; London Borough of Richmond upon Thames, York House, Twickenham, Middx TW1 (☎ 0181 891 1411, fax 0181 891 7703)

HARBORD-HAMOND, Hon Charles Anthony Assheton; s and h of 11 Baron Suffield, MC; *b* 3 Dec 1953; *Educ* Eton; *m* 10 Sept 1983 (m dis), Lucy Lennox Scrope, yr da of Cdr A S Hutchinson, of Langford Grange, Lechlade, Glos; *Career* Capt Coldstream Gds 1972–79; temp equerry to HM The Queen 1977–79; md Christie Brockbank Shipton Ltd; OStJ; ACII; *Clubs* Pratt's, City of London; *Style*— The Hon Charles Harbord-Hamond; ✉ Park House, Gunton Park, Norfolk NR11 7HL

HARBORD-HAMOND, Hon John Edward Richard; 2 s of 11 Baron Suffield, MC, and Elizabeth Eve, *née* Edgedale; *b* 10 July 1956; *Educ* Eton, Coll of Law; *m* 1983, Katharine Margaret Lucy Seymour, only da of Maj Raymond and Hon Mrs Seymour, of Bucklebury, Berks; 3 s (Sam Charles Anthony b 4 Feb 1989, George Edward Seymour b 3 April 1991, William Henry Morden b 19 March 1996), 1 da (Alice Mary Elizabeth b 4 Oct 1986); *Career* memb Inner Temple; ptnr Cazenove & Co; MSI; *Style*— The Hon John Harbord-Hamond; ✉ 72 Brodrick Road, London SW17 7DY

HARBORNE, Prof Jeffrey Barry; s of Frank Percy Harborne (d 1969), of Bristol, and Phyllis Maud, *née* Sherriff (d 1987); *b* 1 Sept 1928; *Educ* Wycliffe Coll Stonehouse Glos, Univ of Bristol (BSc, PhD, DSc); *m* 15 June 1953, Jean Charlotte, da of Dr John Buchanan (d 1935), of Bristol; 2 s (Alan Jeffrey b 1954, Derek Jeremy b 1958); *Career* biochemist John Innes Inst 1955–65, res fell Univ of Liverpool 1965–68; Univ of Reading: reader 1968–76, prof in botany 1976–93, prof emeritus 1993–) visiting prof Univ of Texas 1976, plenary lectr IUPAC Nat Prods Symposium 1976, visiting prof Univ of California 1977; ed-in-chief Phytochemistry Jl 1972–; Gold Medal in Botany Linnean Soc London 1985, Silver Medal Phytochemical Soc of Euro 1986, Silver Medal Int Soc of Chemical Ecology 1993, Pergamon Phytochemistry Prize 1993; churchwarden Christ Church Reading 1972–85; memb: Royal Soc of Chemistry 1956, Biochemical Soc 1957; FLS 1986, FRS 1995; *Books* Biochemistry of Phenolic Compounds (1964), Comparative Biochemistry of the Flavonoids (1967), Phytochemical Phylogeny (1970), Phytochemical Ecology (1972), Phytochemical Aspects of Plant and Animal Coevolution (1978), Phytochemical Methods (2 edn, 1984), Plant Chemosystematics (1984), Introduction to Ecological Biochemistry (4 edn, 1993), The Flavonoids: Advances in Research Since 1986 (1994), Phytochemical Dictionary (1992), Dictionary of Plant Toxins (1994); *Recreations* rambling, classical music; *Style*— Prof Jeffrey Harborne; ✉ University of Reading, Plant Science Laboratories, Reading, Berks RG6 2AS (☎ 0118 931 8162, fax 0118 975 3676, telex 847813 RULIB G)

HARBORNE, HE Peter Gale; s of late Leslie Herbert Harborne, and late Marie Mildred Edith, *née* Suckling; *b* 29 June 1945; *Educ* King Edward's Sch Birmingham, Univ of Birmingham (BCom); *m* 24 July 1976, Tessa Elizabeth Harborne, da of Dennis Frederick Joseph Henri, of Solihull, West Midlands; 2 s (James b 1980, Alexander b 1981); *Career* Home Civil Service 1966–72, HM Dip Serv 1972, first sec Ottawa 1974–75, first sec (commercial) Mexico City 1975–78, Lloyds Bank Int 1979–81, FCO 1981–83, first sec and head of Chancery Helsinki 1983–87, counsellor and dep head of Mission Budapest 1988–91, FCO 1991–95, ambass Slovak Republic 1995–; *Recreations* cricket, tennis, cross country skiing; *Clubs* MCC; *Style*— HE Mr Peter Harborne; ✉ c/o Foreign and Commonwealth Office (Bratislava), King Charles Street, London SW1A 2AH; British Embassy, Panska 16, 814 99 Bratislava, Slovak Republic (☎ 00 42 531 9632/9633)

HARBOTTLE, Rev Anthony Hall Harrison; LVO (1984, MVO 1979); s of Alfred Charles Harbottle (d 1938), of Topsham, Devon, and Ellen Muriel, *née* Harrison (d 1955); *b* 3 Sept 1925; *Educ* Sherborne, Christ's Coll Cambridge (MA), Wycliffe Hall Oxford; *m* 1955, Gillian Mary, da of Hugh Goodenough (d 1975); 3 s (Charles, Jonathan, David), 1 da (Jane); *Career* serv WWII RM (Corpl) Holland, NW Germany; deacon 1952, priest 1953; asst curacies: Boxley 1952–54, St Peter-in-Thanet 1954–60; rector of Sandhurst with Newenden 1960–68, chaplain Royal Chapel Windsor Great Park 1968–81, priest-in-charge East Dean with Friston and Jevington 1995–96 (rector 1981–95); chaplain to: HM The Queen 1968–95, Co of Sussex, Royal Br Legion 1982–; memb: Br Entomological and Natural History Soc 1948–, Green Alliance 1984–; fndr memb Kent Tst for Nature Conservation 1954–; FRES; *Recreations* butterflies and moths, nature conservancy, entomology, ornithology, philately, coins, treasury and bank notes, painting, cooking, lobstering; *Style*— The Rev Anthony Harbottle, LVO; ✉ 44 Summerdown Road, Eastbourne, East Sussex BN20 8DG (☎ 01323 730881)

HARBOTTLE, (George) Laurence; s of George Harbottle, MC, of Newcastle upon Tyne, and Winifred Ellen, *née* Benson (d 1982); *b* 11 April 1924; *Educ* The Leys Sch Cambridge, Emmanuel Coll Cambridge (MA); *Career* cmmnd RA 1942, Capt and Adj 9 Field Regt RA 1945–47; conslt Harbottle and Lewis Slrs 1994– (sr ptnr 1955–94); chm: Theatre Centre Ltd 1959–88, Prospect Productions Ltd 1966–67, Royal Exchange Theatre Co Ltd 1968–83, Cambridge Theatre Co Ltd 1969–92 (pres 1992–); dir: The Watermill 1970–75, The Bush (Alternative) 1975–77; memb The Arts Cncl 1976–78 (memb Drama Panel 1974–78, chm Housing the Arts 1977–78, chm Trg Ctee 1977–78); pres Theatrical Management Assoc 1979–85 (hon vice pres 1992); chm: Central Sch of Speech and Drama 1982– (vice chm 1977–82), ICA 1986–90 (dep chm 1977–86), Theatres

Tst 1992– (memb 1980–); vice pres: Music Users Cncl 1985–, Theatres Advsy Cncl 1986–88, Theatres Nat Ctee 1986–91; govr City Literary Inst 1990–94; memb: The Law Soc; *Recreations* works of art, gardening; *Clubs* The Savile; *Style*— G Laurence Harbottle, Esq; ✉ Hanover House, Hanover Square, London W1R 0BE (☎ 0171 667 5000, fax 0171 667 5100)

HARBOTTLE, Brig Michael Neale; OBE; s of Capt Thomas Cecil Benfield Harbottle, RN (d 1968), and Kathleen Millicent, *née* Kent (d 1937); *b* 7 Feb 1917; *Educ* Marlborough, RMA Sandhurst, Staff Coll Pretoria SA (psc), Open Int Univ for Complementary Meds (PhD 1993); *m* 1, 1 Aug 1940 (m dis 1972), Alison Jean, *née* Humfress; 1 s (Simon Neale b 2 April 1942), 1 da (Carolyn Daphne b 6 Nov 1946); m 2, 5 Aug 1972, Eirwen Helen, da of Hugh Llewlyn Jones (d 1962); *Career* cmmnd The Oxfordshire and Buckinghamshire Light Inf 1937, WWII serv UK and Italy (despatches), GSO2 instr UK Army Staff Coll 1945, GSO2 staff duties WO 1950–52, GSO1 43 Inf Div TA/SW Dist 1957–59, CO 1 Green Jackets Regt 1959–62, Security Cdr and Cdr Aden Garrison 1962–64, Cdr 129 Inf Bde TA 1964–66, COS UN Peacekeeping Force Cyprus 1966–68, ret 1968; chief security offr Sierra Leone Selection Tst 1969–70, vice pres Int Peace Acad 1970–73, visiting sr lectr Sch of Peace Studies Univ of Bradford 1974–79; visiting prof: Univ of Cape Town SA 1976, Waterloo Univ 1979, Carleton Univ Canada 1979; head of dept Vietnamese Section Br Cncl for Aid to Refugees 1979–80, gen sec World Disarmament Campaign (UK) 1980–82, fndr and dir Centre for Int Peacebuilding 1983–, co-ordinator Worldwide Consultative Assoc of Retired Generals and Admirals 1993–, fndr memb The Global Action Plan (UK); memb Int Cncl Inst of Conflict Analysis and Resolution George Mason Univ USA; memb: Generals for Peace and Disarmament 1980–93, RIAA; FRSA 1994; *Books* The Impartial Soldier (1970), Blue Berets (1971), The Thin Blue Line (jtly, 1974), The Knaves of Diamonds (1976), The Peacekeepers' Handbook (1978), Reflections on Security in the Nuclear Age (jtly, 1988), What is Proper Soldiering? (1991); *Recreations* cricket, tennis, hockey, golf; *Clubs* MCC; *Style*— Brig Michael Harbottle, OBE; ✉ 9 West St, Chipping Norton, Oxon (☎ 01608 642335); Centre for Int Peacebuilding (fax 01608 644732)

HARBOTTLE, (Philip) Richard Milnes; s of Thomas Milnes Harbottle, CBE, MC (d 1961), of Ponteland, Northumberland, and Marion, *née* Learmount; *b* 19 March 1934; *Educ* The Leys Sch Cambridge, Trinity Hall Cambridge (MA); *m* 13 Aug 1960, (Jean Margaret) Elizabeth, da of John Talbot Hall (d 1958), of Sutton Coldfield; 3 da (Charlotte (Mrs Welch), Philippa (Mrs Sampson), Rebecca); *Career* ptnr Deloitte Haskins & Sells (and predecessor firms) 1962–89, non-exec chm Northumberland Health Authy 1986–92, chm Cheviot & Wansbeck NHS Tst 1994 (resigned); non-exec dir: Northern Rock Building Society 1988–, Yuill Group Ltd 1989–, Minster Sound Radio plc 1992–, Black Sheep Brewery plc 1993–; chm: Tyne & Wear Building Preservation Tst, Tyne & Wear Fndn 1993–; treas Soc of Antiquaries of Newcastle upon Tyne; FCA (ACA 1960); *Recreations* gardening, history, walking; *Clubs* Northern Counties; *Style*— Richard Harbottle, Esq; ✉ Caponscleugh House, Allerwash, Hexham, Northumberland NE47 5AB (☎ and fax 01434 674271)

HARCOURT, Prof Geoffrey Colin; AO (1994); s of Kenneth Kopel Harcourt (d 1988), of Gen Iris, Melbourne, Aust, and Marjorie Rahel, *née* Gans (d 1981); *b* 27 June 1931; *Educ* Wesley Coll Melbourne, Queen's Coll Univ of Melbourne (BCom, MCom), King's Coll Cambridge (PhD, LittD); *m* 30 July 1955, Joan Margaret, da of Edgar James Bartrop, OBE (d 1989), of Ballarat W, Victoria, Aust; 2 s (Robert Geoffrey b 1961, Timothy William b 1965), 2 da (Wendy Jane b 1959, Rebecca Mary b 1968); *Career* Univ of Adelaide: lectr in economics 1958–62, sr lectr 1963–65, reader 1965–67, prof (personal chair) 1967–85 (prof emeritus 1988); Univ of Cambridge: lectr in economics and politics 1964–66, fell Trinity Hall 1964–66, fell Jesus Coll 1982–, lectr in economics and politics 1982–90, pres Jesus Coll 1988–89 and 1990–92, reader in the history of economic theory (ad hominem) 1990–; memb Aust Labor Pty 1954–; Howard League for Penal Reform S Aust branch: sec 1959–63, vice pres 1967–74, pres 1974–80; chm Campaign for Peace in Vietnam S Aust 1970–72 (1968), fell Acad of the Social Sciences in Aust 1971, memb Cncl Royal Economic Soc 1990–95; *Books* incl: Economic Activity (jtly, 1967), Capital and Growth, Selected Readings (ed with N F Laing, 1971), Some Cambridge Controversies in the Theory of Capital (1972), Theoretical Controversy and Social Significance - An Evaluation of the Cambridge Controversies (1975), The Microeconomic Foundations of Macroeconomics (ed, 1977), The Social Science Imperialists. Selected Essays (1982), Keynes and his Contemporaries (ed, 1985), Readings in the Concept and Measurement of Income (jt ed 1969, 2 edn 1986), Controversies in Political Economy. Selected Essays (1986), International Monetary Problems and Supply-side Economics. Essays in Honour of Lorie Tarshis (jt ed, 1986), On Political Economists and Modern Political Economy. Selected Essays (1992), Post-Keynesian Essays in Biography: Portraits of Twentieth Century Political Economists (1993), The Dynamics of the Wealth of Nations. Growth, Distribution and Structural Change. Essays in Honour of Luigi Pasinetti (jt ed, 1993), Markets, Madness and a Middle Way (the second Donald Horne address, 1992), Income and Employment in Theory and Practice (jt ed, 1994), Capitalism, Socialism and Post-Keynesianism. Selected Essays (1995); *Recreations* cricket, running, reading, politics; *Clubs* Melbourne Cricket, S Aust Cricket; *Style*— Prof Geoffrey Harcourt, AO; ✉ 43 New Square, Cambridge CB1 1EZ (☎ 01223 360833); Austin Robinson Building, Faculty of Economics and Politics, University of Cambridge, Sidgwick Ave, Cambridge CB3 9DD (☎ 01223 335231); Jesus College, Cambridge CB5 8BL (☎ 01223 339436)

HARCOURT, Palma; *see:* Trotman, Palma Noreen Sarah

HARCOURT, Roger; s of Arthur James Harcourt, of Meldreth, Cambs, and Joan, *née* Luckett (d 1989); *b* 26 July 1939; *Educ* Perse Sch, Magdalene Coll Cambridge (MA), Univ of Reading (PGCE); *m* 1966, Joan, da of Edward Gates; 2 da (Jessica Constance b 30 Aug 1967, Olivia Joyce b 5 Dec 1972), 2 s (Edmund Colin b 20 Dec 1968, Benedick Douglas 30 Dec 1969 (adopted)); *Career* asst master Glyn GS Epsom 1963–67, head of English Gateway Sch Leicester 1967–72, dep headmaster Raynes Park High Merton 1972–74, headmaster Ward Freeman Sch Buntingford 1975– (Independent Parents' Choice Sch 1992, featured Sunday Mirror Best Schs 1993); has organised numerous sch Shakespeare prodns 1977–; churchwarden Strethall Church 1986–; *Books* Sharing Literature (Longmans, 1975); *Recreations* memb Liberal Democrat Party; *Style*— Roger Harcourt, Esq; ✉ Manor Cottage, Strethall, nr Saffron Walden, Essex (☎ 01799 525596); The Ward Freman School, Bowling Green Lane, Buntingford, Herts (☎ 01763 71818)

HARCOURT-SMITH, Air Chief Marshal Sir David; GBE (1989), KCB (1984), DFC (1957); *b* 14 Oct 1931; *Educ* Felsted, RAF Coll; *m* 1957, (Dorothy) Mary, *née* Entwistle; 2 s, 1 da; *Career* cmmnd RAF 1952, served with 11, 8 and 54 Squadrons, Staff Coll 1962, OC 54 Sqdn 1963–65, Cmdt RAF Coll Cranwell 1978–80, Asst CAS (Operational Requirements) 1980–84, Air Marshal 1984, Air Officer Commanding-in-Chief RAF Support Cmmd 1984, Controller Aircraft (MOD PE) and memb Air Force Bd 1986, Air Chief Marshal 1987–89 (ret); chm Chelworth Defence Ltd, dir DESC; *Recreations* music, golf; *Style*— Sir David Harcourt-Smith, GBE, KCB, DFC

HARDCASTLE, Prof Jack Donald; s of Albert Fenton Hardcastle, and Bertha, *née* Ellison; *b* 3 April 1933; *Educ* St Batholomew's GS Newbury, Emmanuel Coll Cambridge (BA, MB BChir, MA, MChir); *m* 18 Dec 1965, Rosemary, da of Col Cecil Hay-Shunker; 1 s (Philip b 3 May 1968), 1 da (Rachel b 19 June 1971); *Career* London Hosp: lectr and registrar 1963–65, sr registrar 1965–68; St Mark's Hosp: sr registrar 1968, sr lectr 1968–70; prof and head of Dept of Surgery Queen's Med Centre Univ of Nottingham 1970–; Sir Arthur Sims travelling prof 1985, Mayne visiting prof Univ of Queensland Aust 1987, Sir Alan Park visiting prof St Marks Hosp London 1991; Royal Coll of Surgeons of England: vice-pres 1995–, dir Raven Dept of Educn; MRCP 1961, FRCS 1962, FRCP 1984; *Books* Isolated Organ Perfusion (jtly, 1973); *Clubs* RSM; *Style*— Prof Jack Hardcastle; ✉ Department of Surgery, University Hospital, Queen's Medical Centre, Nottingham NG7 2UH (☎ 0115 970 9245, fax 0115 970 9428)

HARDCASTLE, Leslie Jesse; OBE (1978); s of Francis Ernest Hardcastle, and Dorothy Alma, *née* Schofield; *b* 8 Dec 1926; *Educ* St Joseph's Coll Croydon; *m* 14 Sept 1968, (Vivienne Mansel) Wendy, da of Maj Trevor Richards (d 1968), of Sussex; 2 s (Adam Alexander b 23 June 1972, Paul James b 3 Jan 1975); *Career* RN sick berth Br Pacific Fleet 1944–47; prodn Br Lion Film Studio 1943, admin Br Film Inst 1947, mangr Festival of Br Telekinema 1951, admin London Film Festival 1958–86, controller Nat Film Theatre 1968–91 (mangr 1952), creator Museum of Moving Image (MOMI) 1988, controller Br Film Inst South Bank (Nat Film Theatre and MOMI) 1989–91 (ret), museum and exhbn conslt MOMI 1992–; pres Soho Soc, chm Housing Mgmnt Soho Housing Assoc; Fell Br Film Inst 1991; *Recreations* theatre, music, community work; *Style*— Leslie Hardcastle, Esq, OBE; ✉ 37C Great Pulteney St, London W1R 3DE (☎ 0171 437 5149); Woodlands Cottage, Nursery Lane, Fairwarp, Sussex (☎ 01825 712887); NFT & MOMI, South Bank Arts Complex, London SE1 8XT (☎ 0171 928 3535)

HARDEN, Richard John; s of Christopher John Harden, and Elizabeth Anne, *née* Cottle; *b* 16 Aug 1965; *Educ* King's Coll Taunton Somerset; *m* 25 Sept 1992, Nicola Rae; *Career* right-hand batsman and left-arm bowler; Somerset CCC: debut 1985, county cap 1989, best bowling 2 for 7 Central Dists v Canterbury 1987–88, vice capt 1992–, best batting 187 v Nottinghamshire 1992; off-season business forms salesman for Pennine Dataforms; *Recreations* most sports particularly golf and squash; *Style*— Richard Harden, Esq; ✉ c/o Somerset County Cricket Club, The County Ground, St James Street, Taunton TA1 1JT

HARDEN, Prof Ronald McGlashan; s of Alexander Harden (d 1959), and Janet Roy, *née* McGlashan; *b* 24 Dec 1936; *Educ* Uddington GS, Univ of Glasgow (MB ChB, MD); *m* 4 Jan 1961, Sheila, da of James Harris (d 1956); 3 da (Susan b 28 Sept 1964, Valerie b 31 July 1966, Jennifer b 3 July 1968); *Career* res and clinical posts Western Infirmary Glasgow 1960–70, sr lectr in med Univ of Glasgow 1970–72, postgrad dean of med Univ of Dundee 1985– (dir centre for med educn and hon conslt physician 1972), ed Medical Teacher and int authy on med educn with over 200 papers in scientific jls; sec/treas Assoc for Med Educn Europe, memb Exec Assoc for Study of Med Educn; FRCPGlas 1975, FRCPS Canada 1988, FRCSEd 1994; *Recreations* gardening; *Clubs* Royal Society of Medicine; *Style*— Prof Ronald Harden; ✉ Director, Centre for Medical Education, Level 8, Ninewells Hospital and Medical School, Dundee (☎ 01382 660111, fax 01382 645748)

HARDER, Ian Gray; s of Robert William Harder (d 1940), and Gladys Dorothy, *née* Mawby (d 1980); *b* 3 June 1931; *Educ* E Barnet GS, Univ of Southampton, Univ of London (BSc); *Career* Corpl RAF 1953–55; head Econ and Fin Dept EIU 1955–65, md New Ventures (Investments) Ltd 1965–68, chm and md Maxwell Stamp PLC 1968–; *Recreations* music, theatre, walking; *Style*— Ian G Harder, Esq; ✉ 5 Blake Rd, New Southgate, London N11 2AD (☎ 0181 368 6417); Maxwell Stamp PLC, 2 Hat and Mitre Court, St John St, London EC1M 4EL (☎ 0171 251 0147, fax 0171 251 0140)

HARDIE, Andrew Rutherford; QC (Scot 1985); s of Andrew Rutherford Hardie, of Ashley Terrace, Alloa, and Elizabeth Currie, *née* Lowe; *b* 8 Jan 1946; *Educ* St Modan's HS Stirling, Univ of Edinburgh (MA, LLB); *m* 16 July 1971, Catherine Storrar, da of David Currie Elgin, of Crescent Wood Rd, London; 2 s (Ewan b 1975, Niall b 1981), 1 da (Ruth b 1977); *Career* admitted slr 1971, admitted memb Faculty of Advocates 1973; advocate depute 1979–83, standing jr counsel City of Edinburgh DC 1983–85 (sr counsel 1987–96), dean Faculty of Advocates 1994– (treasurer 1989–94), convener Children in Scotland 1994–96, hon pres The Muir Soc 1994–; *Clubs* Caledonian (Edinburgh), Murrayfield Golf; *Style*— Andrew R Hardie, Esq, QC; ✉ Dean of the Faculty of Advocates, 4 Oswald Road, Edinburgh EH9 2HF (☎ 0131 667 7542); Advocates Library, Parliament House, Edinburgh EH1 1RF (☎ 0131 260 5658)

HARDIE, Sir Charles Edgar Mathewes; kt (1970), CBE (1963, OBE 1943); s of Dr Charles Frederick Hardie (d 1964), of Barnet, Herts, and Mrs R F Hardie, *née* Moore; *b* 10 March 1910; *Educ* Aldenham; *m* 1, 1937, Dorothy Jean (d 1965), da of Montague Hobson; 1 s (Jeremy, *qv*), 3 da; m 2, 1966 (m dis 1975) Angela, wid of Raymond Paul Richli, and da of George Street; m 3, 1975, Rosemary Margaret Harwood; *Career* WWII Col; sr ptnr Dixon Wilson and Co 1975–81 (joined 1934); chm: White Fish Authy 1967–73, BOAC 1969–70 (dep chm 1964–69), British Printing Corporation 1969–76 (dir 1965–82), Fitch Lovell Ltd 1970–77; dir: Forte 1970–96 (dep chm 1983–93), Royal Bank of Canada 1969–81, Hill Samuel Group 1970–77; dir fifty other cos 1946–; Liveryman Worshipful Co of Fishmongers; FCA; Legion of Merit (USA); *Recreations* bridge; *Clubs* Phyllis Court; *Style*— Sir Charles Hardie, CBE; ✉ The Old School House, Sturminster Newton, Dorset DT10 1DG (☎ 01258 473983); 25 New St, Henley on Thames, Oxon RG92 2BP (☎ 01491 577944)

HARDIE, David; WS (1982); s of John Hardie, of Gourock, Renfrewshire, Scot, and Amy Alfreda, *née* Masey; *b* 17 Sept 1954; *Educ* Glasgow Acad, Greenock HS, Univ of Dundee (LLB); *m* 27 Feb 1981, Fiona Mairi, da of late Dr Alexander Donaldson Willox, MBE, of W Lothian, Scot; 3 s (Iain b 1981, Stewart b 1984, Alasdair b 1989); *Career* NP 1979, ptnr Dundas & Wilson CS 1983; memb: Law Soc of Scot, Int Bar Assoc; *Recreations* sailing, golf, swimming, cycling, motor cycling; *Style*— David Hardie, Esq, WS; ✉ Dundas & Wilson, Saltire Court, 20 Castle Terrace, Edinburgh EH1 2EN (☎ 0131 228 8000, fax 0131 228 8888)

HARDIE, Brig Donald Graeme; TD, JP; s of Graeme Hardie, BEM, of Helensburgh, and Sheila Ramsay McLennan (d 1965); *b* 23 Jan 1936; *Educ* Larchfield, Blairmore, Merchiston Castle; *m* 10 Feb 1961 (sep 1995), Rosalind Allan Ker; 2 s (Fergus Allan Graeme b 15 Sept 1962, Adam Ker b 2 June 1964); *Career* mgmnt trainee UTR 1956–59, F W Allan & Ker Shipbrokers 1960–61; dir: J & G Hardie & Co Ltd 1961–81, Gilbert Plastics 1973–76, Hardie Polymers Ltd 1981–, Ronash Ltd 1987–; Nat Serv cmmnd 41 Field Regt RA 1954–56; TA service: 277 (A & S H) Field Regt RA 1954–66, CO G & SUOTC 1966–73, Col Lowlands 1973–76, Col DES 1976–80, Col Scot 1980–84, ACF Brig Scot 1985–87; Hon Col: 105 AD Regt RA (V), Glasgow & Lanarkshire ACF; chm RA Cncl for Scot, vice pres ACFA Scot; pres: SSAFA Dunbartonshire, Scouts Dumbarton area; chieftain Baloch Games; Lord Lt Dunbartonshire 1990–; memb Grand Antiquity Soc; FPRI, FIM; *Recreations* shooting, fishing, skiing, sailing; *Clubs* Royal Northern & Clyde Yacht; *Style*— Brig Donald Hardie, TD, JP; ✉ Dun Ruadh Farm, Gartocharn, Dunbartonshire (☎ 01389 830399); Hardie Polymers Ltd, Gartocharn, Dunbartonshire (☎ 01389 830241, fax 01389 830410)

HARDIE, Maj (John) Donald Morrison; OBE (1987), DL; s of Capt John David Hardie (d 1949), of Dallas, Morayshire, late Scottish Horse and Skinner's Horse, and Gertrude Louise, *née* Morrison; *b* 27 Sept 1928; *Educ* Beckenham GS, Univ of St Andrews (MA), Indiana Univ USA (MSc); *m* 9 Aug 1952, Sally Patricia, da of Thomas Whipple Connally (d 1928), of Atlanta, Georgia, USA; 2 s (David b 1954, Robin b 1957), 1 da (Katharine b 1960); *Career* Lt 1 Bn Queen's Own Cameron Highlanders 1952–56, Maj TA Bn 1956–67; dir Wood and Hardie Ltd 1961–82; currently dir: Bute Fabrics Ltd, McCann Erickson (Scotland) Ltd, Corporate Risk plc; dir Scottish Div IOD 1980–, dep chm Pantrons' Cncl Museum of Scotland; organised Yes campaign in Scotland for EEC referendum 1975; session clerk Humbie Kirk 1960–; Scottish XI (hockey) 1950–53; FRSA 1994; *Recreations* golf, shooting; *Clubs* Hon Co of Edinburgh Golfers, Royal and Ancient Golf (St Andrews), New (Edinburgh), Piedmont Driving (Atlanta), Peachtree Golf (Atlanta); *Style*— Maj Donald Hardie, OBE, DL; ✉ Chesterhill House, Humbie, E Lothian EH36 5PL (☎ 01875 833648); Institute of Directors, 13 Great Stuart Street, Edinburgh EH3 7TP (☎ 0131 225 8101)

HARDIE, Sir Douglas Fleming; kt (1990), CBE (1979), JP (1970); s of late James Dunbar Hardie, JP, of Dundee, and Frances Mary, *née* Fleming; *b* 26 May 1923; *Educ* Trinity Coll Glenalmond; *m* 5 Sept 1945, Dorothy Alice, da of Frederick William Warner (d 1971), of Newcastle upon Tyne; 2 s (Michael b 1948, Christopher b 1954), 1 da (Hilary b 1947); *Career* Trooper 58 Trg Regt RAC 1941, cmmnd RMA Sandhurst 1942, 1 Fife and Forfar Yeo Flamethrowing Tank Regt NW Europe 1942–46 (despatches), Maj; chm Edward Parker and Co Ltd 1960–, dep chm Scottish Development Agency 1978–91; dir: H & A Scott (Holdings) Ltd 1964–84 (chm 1984–85), Dayco Rubber (UK) Ltd 1956–86, Clydesdale Bank plc 1981–92, The Alliance Trust plc 1982–93, The Second Alliance Trust plc 1982–93, Alliance Trust (Finance) Ltd 1982–93, SECDEE Leasing 1982–93, Alliance Trust (Nominees) Ltd 1982–93, A G Scott Textiles Ltd 1985–88, Drug Development (Scotland) Ltd 1994; chm Grampian TV plc 1989–93 (dir 1984–93); deacon convener Nine Incorporated Trades of Dundee 1951–54, pres Dundee Rotary Club 1967–68; memb: CBI Grand Cncl London 1976–85, Scot Econ Cncl 1977–91, Cncl Winston Churchill Meml Tst 1985–; vice pres Fife and Forfar Yeomanry Regtl Assoc, elder Dundee Parish Church (St Mary's), dir Prince's Scottish Youth Business Tst 1988, chm Music in Scotland Tst; Hon LLD Univ of Dundee 1992; FRSA 1988, CIMgt 1989; *Recreations* golf, fishing; *Clubs* Caledonian, Royal and Ancient Golf, Blairgowrie Golf, Panmure Golf; *Style*— Sir Douglas Hardie, CBE, JP; ✉ Norwood, 6 Norwood Terrace, West Park, Dundee DD2 1PB (☎ 01382 669107)

HARDIE, (Reginald) George; *b* 6 Dec 1938; *Educ* Stockport GS; *m* 1968, Christine; 2 s, 1 da; *Career* fin controller Richard Johnson & Nephew 1969–72, jt gp md Firth Rixson plc 1989–94 (fin dir 1972), chm and chief exec Harbury Group Ltd 1994–; FCA, FCT; *Recreations* golf, DIY, music, reading; *Style*— George Hardie, Esq; ✉ Harbury Group Ltd, Oliver House, Priestly, Worsley, Manchester M28 2LY (☎ 0161 794 9911, fax 0161 794 8111)

HARDIE, Gwen Waterston; da of James Waterston Hardie, and Anne, *née* Livingston; *b* 7 Jan 1962; *Educ* Inverurie Acad, Edinburgh Coll of Art (BA); *Career* artist; lectr and visiting artist to various art colls incl: Glasgow, Edinburgh, Sheffield Poly, St Martin's and Royal Coll of Art; pt/t lectr Oxford Brookes Univ; *Solo Exhibitions* Paton Gallery London 1986 and 1988, Fruitmarket Gallery Edinburgh (travelling Br show) 1987, Kettle's Yard Cambridge 1988, Scottish Nat Gallery of Modern Art Edinburgh 1990, Fischer Fine Art London 1990, Annely Juda Fine Art London 1994, Talbot Rice Gallery Univ of Edinburgh 1994, Jason and Rhodes Gallery London 1996; *Group Exhibitions* Contemporary Art for Museums - Contemporary Art Soc purchases 1982–84 (Sutton Place Guildford Surrey) 1985, Twelve British Artists (Künstlerhaus Vienna) 1986, The Human Touch (Fischer Fine Art London) 1986, Identity - Desire (Scottish Arts Cncl touring) 1986, The Self-Portrait - A Modern View (Artsite Bath) 1987, The Vigorous Imagination (Scottish Nat Gallery of Modern Art Edinburgh) 1987, The New British Painting (American touring) 1988–90, Scottish Art in the 20th Century (The Royal W of England Acad Bristol) 1991, Cabinet Paintings (Gillian Jason Gallery) 1991, Critics Choice (Bruton St Gallery) 1992, Artistic Associations (Gillian Jason Gallery) 1992, The Body Abstract - Somatic States (Quicksilver Gallery Univ of Middx) 1992, Festival Fourteen (Dunfermline Dist & City Museum) 1992, Foreground and Distances (Serpenti Galleria Rome and touring Europe) 1992–94, New Artists and Cabinet Art (both at Jason and Rhodes Gallery, London) 1995; *Work in Collections* Br Cncl London, Contemporary Art Soc London, Leicester CC, Scottish Nat Gallery of Modern Art Edinburgh, City Art Collection Edinburgh, Met Museum NYC, Gulbenkian Collection Lisbon, Scottish Arts Cncl Edinburgh, Unilever plc, Stanhope Properties plc, Sundridge Mgmnt Centre London, Glaxo Ltd; *Awards* Richard Ford Award Royal Acad 1983, Daad Annual Art Scholarship W Berlin 1984 and 1985, King Edward VII Br-German Fndn Award 1987; *Recreations* travel; *Clubs* Chelsea Arts; *Style*— Ms Gwen Hardie; ✉ Jason and Rhodes Gallery, 4 New Burlington Place, London W1X 1FB (☎ 0171 434 1768)

HARDIE, (Charles) Jeremy Mawdesley; CBE (1983); s of Sir Charles Hardie, CBE, *qv*; *b* 9 June 1938; *Educ* New Coll Oxford, Nuffield Coll Oxford; *m* 1, 1962 (m dis 1976), Susan Chamberlain; 2 s, 2 da; m 2, 1978, Xandra, Countess of Gowrie (m dis 1994); 1 da; m 3, 1994, Kirsteen Tait; *Career* Monopolies and Mergers Cmmn 1976–82 (dep chm 1980–82); National Provident Institution: dir 1972–90, dep chm 1977–80, chm 1980–90; W H Smith Group plc: non-exec dir 1988–, dep chm 1992–84, chm 1994–; dep chm Alexanders Discount Co (dir 1978–87), chm Alexander Syndicate Management Ltd 1982–95; also dir: Unilever Pensions Investment Management Ltd 1980–86, John Swire and Sons 1982–; ptnr Dixon Wilson and Co 1975–82, chm D P Mann Underwriting Agency 1983–; Parly candidate (SDP) Norwich South 1983 and 1987; memb Arts Cncl of GB 1984–86; tstee Esmee Fairbirn Charitable Tst 1972–; FCA; *Style*— Jeremy Hardie, Esq, CBE; ✉ The Old Rectory, Metton, nr Cromer, Norfolk (☎ 01263 76765); W H Smith Group plc, Audrey House, Ely Place, London EC1N 6SN (☎ 0171 404 4242, fax 0171 269 2631)

HARDIE, Michael John; OBE (1989); s of John Thomas Hardie (d 1966), and Ann, *née* Smethurst; *b* 14 July 1938; *Educ* St Ambrose Coll Hale Barns Cheshire, De le Salle Coll Salford; *m* 1 (m dis); 1 da (Shân Louise b 9 Jan 1969), 2 s (Simon James Nicholson b 20 July 1970, Richard Michael Houston b 12 Oct 1978); m 2, 1 Aug 1990, Jean, da of Thomas Hunter (d 1979), and Jessie Hunter; 1 step s (Jeremy Kenneth Fish b 13 July 1970), 1 step da (Nicola Jean Crane b 18 March 1972); *Career* Nat Serv Intelligence Corps 1957–59; joined FO 1956, Bahrain 1959–62, Personnel Dept FO 1962–64, pro-consul Elisabethville 1964–66, temp duty Bathurst 1966, vice consul and third sec Sofia 1966–68, third sec (commercial) Vienna 1968–69, vice consul (commercial) Munich 1969–73, Personnel Ops Dept FCO 1973–76, info and press offr Cape Town 1976–79, first sec (info and press) Berlin 1979–81, first sec (economic and commercial) Valletta 1981–83, Personnel Ops and Security Depts FCO 1983–86, first sec then cnsllr (mgmnt) Lagos 1986–89, cnsllr (mgmnt) New Delhi 1990–93, high cmmr The Gambia (Banjul) 1994–95; *Recreations* golf, ball sports, music and reading; *Style*— Michael Hardie, Esq, OBE; ✉ 17 Dunham Lawn, Bradgate Road, Altrincham, Cheshire WA14 4QJ

HARDIE, Michael Scott; s of Col Alan Scott Hardie, OBE, DL (d 1968), of Purves Hall, nr Greenlaw, Berwickshire, and Joan Lilian, *née* Powell (d 1968); *b* 31 Dec 1926; *Educ* Glenalmond Coll Perthshire; *m* 14 Feb 1953, Valerie Edith, da of Richard Everard Hambro (d 1967); 4 s (Nicholas A S b 19 Jan 1955, Christopher R S b 28 Feb 1957, Charles M S b 14 Nov 1961, Jonathan D S b 12 Feb 1965); *Career* RAF Hong Kong 1946–48, HAC 1953–58; qualified CA Scot 1951; Brown Fleming & Murray 1952–53, Mercantile Investment Tst 1955–57, Debenture Corporation Investment Tst 1953–55 and 1957–59, dep investmt mangr ICI Pension Fund 1959–71, investmt dir Friends Provident 1971–86; non-exec dir: Shires Income plc 1987–, Shires Smaller Companies plc 1992– (chm 1992–95), Glasgow Investment Managers Ltd; govr Glenalmond Coll; memb Honourable Artillery Co 1953; *Recreations* golf, travelling, shooting, skiing; *Clubs* Muirfield Golf, Royal Wimbledon Golf; *Style*— Michael Hardie, Esq; ✉ Wyndham Barns, Corton Denham, Sherborne, Dorset DT9 4LS (☎ 01963 220631, fax 01963 220738); Blue House, Trevose Estate, Constantine Bay, nr Padstow, Cornwall (☎ 01481 520331); c/o Shires Income plc, 29 St Vincent Place, Glasgow G1 2DR (☎ 0141 226 4585, fax 0141 226 3632)

HARDIE, Sean; s of Ven A G Hardie, and Shelagh, *née* Jacob; *b* 4 March 1947; *Educ* Trinity Coll Glenalmond, Trinity Coll Cambridge (MA); *m* 1, 1973 (m dis 1979), Janet, *née* Hall; 1 s (William); m 2, Kerry Jolley; *Career* prodr and dir current affairs BBC TV 1969–79 (incl 24 Hours, Panorama, Midweek), prodr light entertainment BBC TV 1979–81 (incl Not the Nine O'Clock News, later Spitting Image), contract writer and dir Video Arts Ltd; recent prodns incl: The Signal Box (RTE) 1995, Rory Bremner - Who Else? (Channel 4) 1996; TV awards incl: BAFTA, Silver Rose Montreux, US Emmy; chair: Kilkenny Art Gallery Soc, Duiske Concerts; *Books* Not!, Not the Royal Wedding (1981), Not 1982 (1982), The Last Supper (1990), Right Connections (1991), Till The Fat Lady Sings (1993), Falling Off a Log (1994); *Recreations* gardening, rock music, reading; *Clubs* Ballytighlea Social; *Style*— Sean Hardie, Esq; ✉ Milltown, Skeoghvosteen, Co Kilkenny, Eire (☎ 00 353 503 73194, fax 00 353 503 73622); c/o Alexandra Cann Associates, 200 Fulham Road, London SW10 9PN (☎ 0171 352 6266, fax 0171 352 2294)

HARDING, Charles Alvar; s of Charles Copeley Harding (d 1942), of 14 Holland Park, London, and Louise Victoria Alvar Woods, *née* Beckman (d 1966); *Educ* Westminster, Gonville and Caius Coll Cambridge; *Career* Capt Royal Fus, ADC to Govr of Madras 1942–46; dir Trafford Gallery 1948–75; *Recreations* skiing, tennis, architecture, theatre; *Clubs* Travellers, Buck's; *Style*— Charles Harding, Esq; ✉ 47 Cadogan Square, London SW1X 0HX (☎ 0171 235 7400)

HARDING, Cherry Jacinta; da of James Albert Harding, of Homer, Much Wenlock, Shropshire, and Pauline Mary, *née* Temlett; *b* 2 June 1956; *Educ* The Canon Slade GS Bolton Lancs, King's Coll London (LLB); *m* 8 July 1989, Michael Almond; 2 s (Vyvyan Kendrick b 31 March 1991, Benedict Ivo b 2 Aug 1995), 1 da (Genevieve Mary b 19 Jan 1994); *Career* called to the Bar Gray's Inn 1978, in practice (mainly in family area) 1980–; *Style*— Miss Cherry Harding; ✉ 5th Floor, Gray's Inn Chambers, Gray's Inn, London WC1 (☎ 0171 404 1111)

HARDING, Sir Christopher George Francis; kt (1991); s of Frank Harding (d 1986), of Amersham, Bucks, and Phyllis Rachel Pledger Wise; *b* 17 Oct 1939; *Educ* Merchant Taylors', Corpus Christi Coll Oxford (MA); *m* 1, 1963 (m dis 1977), Susan Lilian Berry (d 1989); 1 s (Rupert b 1965), 1 da (Louise b 1966); m 2, 1978 (m dis 1988); m 3, 21 Nov 1994, P Anne, da of Dr John Skelley; *Career* head office ICI Ltd London 1961–65, Agric Div ICI Billingham 1966–69; Hanson: with Hanson Trust Ltd 1969–74, md Hanson Transport Group 1974–91 (vice chm 1991–), non-exec dir Hanson plc 1979–; non-exec chm: British Nuclear Fuels Ltd 1986–92 (dir 1984–92), BET plc 1992–96, Newarthill plc 1993– (dir 1992–), Legal & General Group plc 1994– (dir 1993–); also non-exec dir: Proshare (UK) Ltd 1992–93, English China Clays plc 1992–94, Slough Estates plc 1992–94, GEC plc 1992–, Post Office 1993–; dir Foyer Federation for Youth 1992–; memb Cncl: CBI 1986, Business in the Community 1989, Prince's Youth Business Tst 1988 (chm 1994); memb: Br Energy Assoc 1986 (chm 1989–92), NACETT 1993; hon fell Univ of Huddersfield 1990; Freeman: City of London 1965, Worshipful Co of Merchant Taylors 1965 (Liveryman 1986); FRSA 1987, CIMgt 1988, Hon FCGI 1990, Hon FINucE 1992, Hon FIChemE 1992; *Recreations* theatre, music, travel, tennis, pocillovy; *Clubs* Brooks's; *Style*— Sir Christopher Harding; ✉ Hanson plc, 1 Grosvenor Place, London SW1X 7JH (☎ 0171 245 1245)

HARDING, Frank Alexander; s of Eric Harding (d 1980), and Elsie, *née* Alexander; *b* 20 Sept 1937; *Educ* Malvern, Ecole de Commerce de Neuchatel; *m* 30 Aug 1960, Belinda Ruth; 2 s (David b 1961, Thomas b 1968), 2 da (Kate b 1963, Amanda b 1967); *Career* CA 1961, ptnr KPMG (formerly KPMG Peat Marwick) 1967–96 (joined 1955); memb Cncl: ICAS 1980–85, ICAEW 1990–93; Int Fedn of Accountants: memb Cncl (UK rep) 1987–, dep pres 1995–; memb Exec Ctee Union of Euro Accountants 1983–86, memb Int Accounting Standards Advsy Cncl 1995–; *Recreations* golf, tennis, opera, bridge; *Style*— Frank Harding, Esq; ✉ KPMG, 1 Puddle Dock, London EC4V 3PD (☎ 0171 311 2255, fax 0171 311 2946, telex 8811541)

HARDING, Dr Geoffrey Wright; s of Jack Harding (d 1989), of Gravesend, Kent, and Ethel Florence, *née* Wilkinson; *Educ* King's Coll London (LLB, AKC), Northwestern Univ Sch of Law Chicago (LLM), QMC London (PhD); *m* 7 Oct 1972, Margaret June, da of Eric Oscar Danger; 1 s (Peter James John b 1980), 1 da (Kate Joanna b 1978); *Career* Nat Serv RAF 1951–53; called to the Bar Gray's Inn 1957; asst sec FCEC 1958–60, legal advsr Br Insur (Atomic Energy) Ctee 1960–63, exchange lawyer under Harvard Law Sch Prog Isham Lincoln and Beale Attorneys Chicago 1963–64, asst slr Joynson Hicks 1965–67, ptnr Wilde Sapte London and Brussels (specialising in banking, consumer credit, competition, IT and Euro Union law) 1967–94, conslt with Wilde Sapte and ind legal conslt 1994–; visiting prof in commercial law Univ of Greenwich 1995–; memb Law Soc Banking Law and Consumer Credit Sub-Ctees; business advsr The Prince's Youth Business Tst, vice chm and cncllr Greater London Region Nat Autistic Soc; memb: Kent Autistic Tst, Int Editorial Bd Utilities Policy (Butterworth-Heinemann);Gen Electric Fndn fell Northwestern Univ Sch of Law Chicago; Freeman City of London 1986, memb Guild of Freemen of City of London; memb Law Soc; *Books* Banking Act 1987 - Current Law Annotated (1987), Encyclopaedia of Competition Law (Euro contrib ed, 1987), Consumer Credit and Consumer Hire Law (1995); *Recreations* family, mountain biking, scuba diving, trying to understand autism, avoiding domestic DIY; *Style*— Dr Geoffrey Harding; ✉ Wilde Sapte, 1 Fleet Place, London EC4M 7WS (☎ 0171 246 7000, fax 0171 246 7777)

HARDING, Prof Graham Frederick Anthony; s of Frederick William Harding (d 1991), of Shenstone, and Elizabeth Louise Harding; *b* 19 March 1937; *Educ* Torquay GS, UCL (BSc), Univ of Birmingham (PhD), Univ of Aston (DSc); *m* 1, 4 March 1961 (m dis 1990), Margaret; 2 da (Catherine Louise b 25 Oct 1965, Laura Jane b 14 Aug 1969); m 2, 20 Sept 1991, Pamela Frances, da of Peter Frederick Evans, of Solihull; 1 s (Anthony Gray b 20 May 1993); *Career* hon conslt electroencephalographer Wolverhampton Area Health Authy 1974–, hon conslt neuropsychologist Birmingham Area Health Authy 1974–, hon conslt clinical neurophysiologist Royal Wolverhampton Hosps Tst 1995–, hon sr research fell Med Sch Univ of Birmingham; Univ of Aston: reader in neuropsychology 1973–78, head of neuropsychology unit 1969–78, prof of clinical neurophysiology 1978–, head of Clinical Neurophysiology Unit 1979–, head of Vision Sciences 1981–89; pres Ctee on Clinical Neurophysiology W Midlands RHA 1996– (memb 1975–); memb: Br Soc for Clinical Neurophysiology (formerly Electroencephalographic Soc) 1963– (memb Cncl 1971–75), Midland Opthalmological Soc 1985–, Int League Against Epilepsy 1983–, Int Soc for Clinical Electrophysiology of Vision 1973–, Nat Conf of Univ Profs 1989–, Birmingham Medico-Legal Soc 1992–; tstee Birmingham Eye Fndn 1989–, patron Birmingham Royal Inst for the Blind Appeal 1990–; FBPsS, CPsychol; *Books* Photosensitive Epilepsy (1975 and 1994); over 190 chapters and papers on electroencephalography, visual evoked responses, Alzheimer's disease, psychiatry, prematurity, ophthalmology and neuromagnetism; *Recreations* railways, model railways; *Style*— Prof Graham Harding; ✉ Electro Diagnostic Centre, Greenfields, Upton Snodsbury, Worcs WR7 4NR (☎ 01905 381335, fax 01905 381335)

HARDING, James Owen Glyn (Jim); s of Walter James Harding (d 1988), and Elizabeth May, *née* Davies; *b* 18 Oct 1942; *Educ* Harrow HS, Pinner GS, Univ of Sussex (BA English), Univ of Exeter (postgrad qualification in social work); *m* 11 Sept 1965, Sally, da of late Dr William Goldie; 1 s (Jamie b 14 Oct 1967), 2 da (Megan b 11 March 1970, Alice b 2 March 1974); *Career* trainee child care offr Bucks CC 1965–66, child care offr rising to sr child care offr Kensington & Chelsea Children's Dept 1968–71, area offr then asst dir (social work) Kensington & Chelsea Social Servs Dept 1971–85; NSPCC: dir of children's servs and dep chief exec 1986–95, dir and chief exec 1995–; memb Cmmn of Inquiry into circumstances surrounding death of Kimberley Carlile 1987; memb Exec Ctee ACENVO, Howard League cmmr (inquiry into violence in penal instns), tstee NCVCCO, memb Human Resources Gp City and Inner London North TEC, memb Professional Advsy Ctee Childline; *Publications* A Child in Mind: Protection of Children in a Responsible Society (jtly, 1987); *Recreations* writing, reading, walking and sport; *Style—* Jim Harding, Esq; ✉ NSPCC, National Centre, 42 Curtain Road, London EC2A 3NH (☎ 0171 825 2585, fax 0171 825 2587)

HARDING, Prof John Edmond; s of William Gordon Harding (d 1987), and Alice Eleanor Harding (d 1985); *b* 22 Nov 1948; *Educ* St Joseph's Coll Beulah Hill, Imperial Coll London (BSc(Eng), MSc, DIC, PhD); *m* 7 Jan 1978, Patricia Anne, da of late Henry Wigfull; 2 da (Emma Philippa b 18 Aug 1980, Laura Anne b 20 July 1982); *Career* lectr in structural engrg Imperial Coll London 1978–85 (research asst/research fell 1971–78); Univ of Surrey: prof of structural engrg 1985–, pro-vice-chllr 1991–; memb: US Structural Stability Research Cncl 1988–, Jt Bd of Moderators Instns of Civil and Structural Engrs, Bd of Govrs St Mary's Univ Coll Strawberry Hill; ed Int Jl of Constructional Steel Research 1980–, hon ed Structures and Buildings proceedings Instn of Civil Engrs until 1996; awarded Trevithick Premium Instn of Civil Engrs 1977; CEng, FIStructE 1986 (MIStructE 1980), FICE 1993 (MICE 1989); *Books* Bridge Management - Inspection, Maintenance, Assessment and Repair (ed 3 vols, 1990, 1993 and 1996), Traversely Stiffened Girder Webs Subject to Combined Loading (1991), Constructional Steel Design - an International Guide (ed, 1992), World Developments in Constructional Steel Design (ed, 1993); also author of numerous conference papers, and contribs to learned jls; *Style—* Prof John Harding; ✉ University of Surrey, Civil Engineering Department, Guildford, Surrey GU2 5XH (☎ 01483 259119, fax 01483 450984, e-mail j.harding@Surrey.ac.uk)

HARDING, John Richard Vincent; s of William Henry Harding (d 1981), and Winifred Elsie, *née* Brett; *b* 1 Sept 1939; *Educ* Enfield GS, Clare Coll Cambridge (MA); *m* 30 March 1965 (m dis 1983), Janet Ann, da of Albert Norman Roué, of Kempston, Bedford; 2 da (Clare b 1966, Susan b 1968); *Career* graduate trainee rising to asst mangr Martins Bank Ltd 1962–70, vice pres and asst gen mangr Republic Nat Bank of Dallas London 1970–76, mangr rising to dep gen mangr European Arab Bank Ltd 1977–85, gen mangr AK Int Bank (now Sabanci Bank) 1985–92, dir and gen mangr National Bank of Egypt International Ltd 1992–; FCIB 1990 (ACIB 1966); *Recreations* swimming, music, theatre, gardening, photography; *Style—* John Harding, Esq; ✉ National Bank of Egypt International Ltd, 16 Finsbury Circus, London EC2M 7DJ (☎ 0171 374 6446)

HARDING, Dr (Leslie) Keith; s of Leslie Charles Harding (d 1964), of West Bromwich, and Priscilla Olive, *née* Mason (d 1984); *b* 3 Feb 1939; *Educ* Handsworth GS, Univ of Birmingham Med Sch (BSc, MB ChB, FRCP, FRCR); *m* 18 Aug 1962, Carol Margaret, da of Dr Colin Starkie, of Kidderminster; 1 s (Nicholas b 1969), 1 da (Victoria b 1972); *Career* lectr in med Queen Elizabeth Hosp Birmingham, conslt in nuclear med Dudley Rd Hosp Birmingham 1982– (conslt physician in gen and nuclear med 1972–82), clinical sr lectr in med Univ of Birmingham 1982–, med dir/conslt in nuclear med City Hosp NHS Tst Birmingham 1994–; author of chapters on gastric emptying and bile reflux; papers on: gastro intestinal motility, the lung, radiation safety in nuclear med depts; memb Advsy Cncl Euro Assoc of Nuclear Med; chm: Nuclear Med Ctee RCP, Regnl Med Advsy Ctee; former chm: Med Exec Ctee W Birmingham Health Authy (also dep dist gen mangr), Admin of Radioactive Substances Advsy Ctee, Euro Task Gp exploring risks; past treas and pres Br Nuclear Med Soc; dep bailiff and fndn govr King Edward VI Schs Birmingham, chm of govrs Five Ways Sch; *Recreations* maintaining a country cottage, gardening; *Clubs* RSM, Woolhope; *Style—* Dr Keith Harding; ✉ Huntroyd, 27 Manor Rd North, Edgbaston, Birmingham B16 9JS (☎ 0121 454 2497); Birmingham Regional Radioisotope Centre, City Hospital NHS Trust, Dudley Road Hospital, Birmingham B18 7QH (☎ 0121 507 4430, fax 0121 507 5223, e-mail l.k.harding@bham.ac.uk)

HARDING, Kerry Richard Kerwan; s of (Albert Edgar) Kerry Harding (d 1994), and Daphne Wynne, *née* Mytton (d 1988); *b* 18 Jan 1936; *Educ* Prior Park Coll, RMA Sandhurst; *m* 1 Aug 1970, Mary Ann, da of Alexander Badenoch (d 1965), and Midi, *née* Berger (d 1994); 4 s (Jonathan b 28 May 1971, Alexander b 20 March 1973, Richard b 9 Feb 1978, Christopher b 8 Aug 1981), 1 da (Katie b 28 Feb 1979); *Career* King's Own Yorkshire Light Infantry: Platoon Cdr Cyprus and BAOR 1956–58, Trg Offr Trg Depot 1958–60, Platoon Cdr and Co 2 i/c Malaya then intelligence offr Borneo 1961–63, instr Small Arms Wing Sch of Infantry 1963–65, 2 i/c then Co Cdr Berlin 1965–67; Adjutant 5 Bn Light Infantry (TA) 1968–70, staff offr grade III 2 Div (latterly 1 (BR) Corps) BAOR 1970–72, Co Cdr Light Infantry Trg Depot 1973–75, trg Maj 6 Bn Light Infantry 1975–77, instr/staff offr grade II Tactics Wing Royal Sch of Military Engrg 1977–78; exec sec Glass and Glazing Fedn 1978–81, sec gen Chartered Inst of Arbitrators 1986– (dep sec 1981–86); memb Cncl Goring on Thames PC 1991–95; memb Soc of Association Execs 1978–87; MIPD 1978, FCIArb 1986, FRSA 1993, MInstD 1995; *Recreations* family, art, golf; *Clubs* Cavendish; *Style—* Kerry Harding, Esq; ✉ Chartered Institute of Arbitrators, 24 Angel Gate, City Road, London EC1V 2RS (☎ 0171 837 4483, fax 0171 837 4185, e-mail 71411.2735@COMPUSERVE.COM)

HARDING, Michael John; s of Maurice John Harding (d 1949), of Colombo, Ceylon, and Dorchester, Dorset, and Wanetse Harding (d 1974); *b* 24 Aug 1933; *Educ* Canford, Gonville and Caius Coll Cambridge (BA, MA); *m* 6 June 1964, Inga Elisabeth, *née* Eriksson; 1 s (Michael James b 11 Aug 1969); *Career* Nat Serv 2 Lt RA 1952–54; articled clerk Whinney Smith & Whinney 1958–62, seconded to Special Cmmn on Govt Ops Republic of Liberia 1962–63; Whinney Murray Ernst & Ernst: mangr Zurich 1964–67, ptnr Paris 1967–68, ptnr Frankfurt 1969–73, managing ptnr Germany 1974–85, pres Accountants' Gp in Germany 1974–85; ptnr Ernst & Young London 1985–94; tstee Knowles Tst 1994–96; memb Sch Teachers Review Body 1993–; FCA 1968 (ACA 1962), memb Institut der Wirtschaftspruefer 1968–85; *Recreations* golf, tennis, reading political and military biographies; *Clubs* RAC, Hankley Common Golf; *Style—* Michael Harding, Esq; ✉ Wellwaters, Dogmersfield, Hook, Hants RG27 8SS (☎ 01252 616717)

HARDING, Paul Anthony; s of Norman John Harding, and Yvonne Mary, *née* Rees; *b* 6 Oct 1955; *Educ* Hardye's GS Dorchester Dorset; *m* 18 Aug 1979, Deborah Anne, da of Roy William George Harvey, of Farnham, Surrey; 1 s (Benjamin James); 1 da (Alison Jane); *Career* slr: NCB 1979–82, Forsyte Kerman 1982–84, Titmuss Sainer Webb 1984–86 (ptnr 1986–); memb Law Soc; *Style—* Paul A Harding, Esq; ✉ Titmuss Sainer Dechert, 2 Serjeants' Inn, London EC4Y 1LT (☎ 0171 583 5353, fax 0171 353 3683)

HARDING, Peter Leslie; s of Leslie O'Brien Harding (d 1977), and Muriel Ellen, *née* Money (d 1966); *b* 22 Sept 1926; *Educ* Rugby, King's Coll Cambridge; *m* 6 Nov 1954, Nina Doris, da of Charles Downing Barnard (d 1965); 1 s (David b 30 July 1959), 1 da (Caroline b 23 March 1956); *Career* Union Castle Line 1947–53, dir Alexander Howden & Co Ltd 1960–67 (joined 1953); Baltic Exchange Ltd: dir 1969–73 and 1975–83, chm 1981–83; chm: JE Hyde & Co Ltd 1986– (ptnr 1968–86), Polak Gallery Ltd 1986– (ptnr 1977–86); Freeman City of London 1982, Liveryman Worshipful Co of Shipwrights 1984; FICS; *Recreations* gardening, fly-fishing; *Style—* Peter Harding, Esq; ✉ Martlets, Greenways, Walton-on-The-Hill, Tadworth, Surrey (☎ 01737 813766); J E Hyde & Co Ltd, 18 Mansell Street, London E1 8AA (☎ 0171 459 2000, fax 0171 459 2299, telex 885991)

HARDING, Marshal of the Royal Air Force Sir Peter Robin; GCB (1988, KCB 1983, CB 1980); s of Peter Harding, and Elizabeth, *née* Clear; *b* 2 Dec 1933; *Educ* Chingford HS; *m* 1955, Sheila Rosemary, da of Albert May; 3 s (Simon, Timothy, Stephen), 1 da (Katherine); *Career* joined RAF 1952, pilot 12 Sqdn 1954–57, QFI and Flt Cdr, RAF Coll Cranwell 1957–60, pilot 1 Sqdn RAAF 1960–62, Staff Coll 1963, Air Secretary's Dept MOD 1964–66, OC 18 Sqdn Gutersloh and Acklington 1966–69, Jt Serv Staff Coll Latimer 1969–70, Def Policy Staff MOD 1970–71, Dir Air Staff Briefing MOD 1971–74, stn cdr RAF Bruggen 1974–76, Dir of Def Policy MOD 1976–78, Asst Chief of Staff (plans and policy) SHAPE 1978–80, AOC 11 Gp 1981–82, Vice Chief of Air Staff 1982–84, Vice Chief of Def Staff 1985, Air Offr C-in-C Strike Cmd and C-in-C UK Air Forces 1985–88, Chief of Air Staff 1988–92, Chief of Defence Staff 1992–94; ADC to HM The Queen 1975–77, Air ADC to HM The Queen 1988–92; dep chm GEC-Marconi 1995; memb Advsy Bd GVT Investment Management Corporation (US); vice pres Guild of Aviation Artists, memb Cncl Winston Churchill Meml Tst 1990, memb Pilgrims Soc, memb Partnership Korea Forum; Legion of Merit (USA), Order of Blue Max (Chile); Freeman City of London, Liveryman Guild of Air Pilots and Air Navigators 1989; Hon DSc Cranfield 1990; FRAeS (Hon CRAeS), CIMgt 1984, FRSA 1988; *Recreations* pianoforte, bridge, birdwatching and shooting (normally separately); *Clubs* Beefsteak; *Style—* Sir Peter Harding, GCB

HARDING, Philip (Phil); s of Douglas Harding, and Leonora, *née* Browne; *b* 28 April 1947; *Educ* Univ of York (BA); *m* 1979, Margo, da of Morris Blythman; 1 da (Laura b 1980); *Career* dep ed Nationwide 1980–81, dep ed Panorama 1981–83 (sr prodr 1978–80), ed London Plus 1984–86, asst head current affrs BBC TV 1986–87 (prodr 1972–78), ed Today BBC Radio Four 1987–93, project dir Radio News Network 1993, ed Five Live News Progs 1993, BBC chief political advsr 1995–96, controller Editorial Policy 1996–; Broadcast Press Guild 1992; *Awards* Emmy Award for Best Documentary Who Killed Georgi Markov? (Panorama) 1980; Sony awards: Best Current Affrs Prog 1989, Best Response to a News Event 1989, Best Daily News Prog 1990, Best Response To A News Event 1990, Best Breakfast Prog 1992; *Recreations* thinking, walking, watching football and supporting QPR; *Style—* Phil Harding, Esq; ✉ BBC, Broadcasting House, London W1A 1AA (☎ 0171 580 4468)

HARDING, Air Vice-Marshal Ross Philip; CBE (1968); s of late Philip James Harding, of Salisbury, and late Ellen Alice, *née* Mann; *b* 22 Jan 1921; *Educ* Bishop Wordsworth's Sch Salisbury, St Edmund Hall Oxford (MA); *m* 29 March 1948, (Laurie) Joy, da of late Edward James Gardner, of Salisbury; 3 s (Russell b 1950, Murray b 1957, Stuart b 1963); *Career* WWII serv No 41 Sqdn Fighter Cmd and 2 TAF 1943–45 (despatches), RAF Staff Coll Andover 1951, ACAS (Ops) Air Miny 1952–54, CO No 96 Sqdn Germany 1955–58, dir staff RAF Staff Coll Andover 1958–60, CO Oxford Univ Air Sqdn 1960–62, dep chief Br Mil Mission Berlin 1963–65, CO RAF Valley 1965–68, sr dir staff (Air) Jt Servs Staff Coll 1968–69, def and air attaché Moscow 1970–72, dir Personal Servs I MOD (Air) 1973, sr RAF memb RCDS 1974–76, ret 1976; head Airwork Ltd Oman 1976–78, def advsr House of Commons Select Ctee on Def 1979–83; chm: Selection Bds Civil Serv and MOD 1979–95, Govrs Bishop Wordsworth's Sch 1983–92; pres Nat Ex-POW Assoc 1990–; *Recreations* bridge, skiing; *Clubs* RAF; *Style—* Air Vice-Marshal Ross Harding, CBE; ✉ 8 Hadrian's Close, Lower Bemerton, Salisbury, Wilts (☎ 01722 336075)

HARDING, Sir Roy Pollard; kt (1985), CBE (1978); s of William Foster Norman Harding, BEM (d 1966), of Cornwall, and Phebe Emma, *née* Pollard (d 1978); *b* 3 Jan 1924; *Educ* Liskeard GS, King's Coll London (BSc, DPA, AKC); *m* 1948, Audrey Beryl, da of Arthur Wimble Larkin (d 1973); 2 s (Alan, Paul), 1 da (Hilary); *Career* educationalist, ballistics res, sch and coll teacher until 1950; educn admin 1951–84: Wilts, Herts, Leics, Bucks (chief educn offr Bucks 1966–84); memb: Printing and Publishing Indust Trg Bd 1970–72, BBC Further Educn Advsy Ctee 1970–75, Burnham Ctee 1972–77, DES Local Authy Educnl Expenditure Gp 1976–84, Sec of State's Visiting Ctee Cranfield Inst of Technol 1976–81, Cncls and Educnl Press Eds Advsy Panel 1977–87, Teaching of Mathematics in Schools (Cockcroft) Ctee 1978–81, Educnl Mgmnt Info Exchange 1981–89, Bd Nat Advsy Body for Higher Educn 1982–84, Open Univ Cncl 1985–96 (chm Bd for Professional Devpt of Teachers 1983–87), Higginson Ctee (A Level) 1987–88, CBI Educn Fndn Cncl 1990–93, AEC Tst 1990–; advsr: CC Assoc 1972–74, Assoc of Co Cncls and Cncl of LEAs 1974–84; pres: Soc of Educn Offrs 1977–78 (exec 1974–79, chm Int Ctee 1978–83, gen sec 1984–89), Br Educnl Equipment Assoc 1980–83, Br Assoc Educn Section 1986–87, Nat Inst of Adult Continuing Educn 1988–94, Inst of Mathematics and Applications 1990–92 (memb Cncl 1983–); chm: Co Educn Offrs Soc 1978–79 (sec 1973–76), Educn Policy Interchange Ctee 1979–88, Governing Body The Staff Coll 1986–95, EMIS Ltd 1988–91, Royal Soc Trg and Support of Teachers Ctee 1991–94, Further Educn Funding Cncl Tariff Advsy Ctee 1993–; vice chm: Secdy Examinations Ctee 1983–86, Educn Ctee Royal Soc 1994–; Hon DUniv Open 1985, Hon LLD Univ of Leicester 1995; FIMA, CMath, FZS, FRSA; *Clubs* Royal Over-Seas League; *Style—* Sir Roy Harding, CBE; ✉ 27 King Edward Ave, Aylesbury, Bucks HP21 7JE (☎ 01296 23006)

HARDING, Timothy John Randolph; *Career* The Peninsular & Oriental Steam Navigation Co plc: main bd dir, md P & O Properties International Ltd, chm P & O Developments Ltd, chm P & O Properties Ltd, chm Laing Property Corporation Canada, chm P & O Shopping Centres Ltd; *Style—* T J R Harding, Esq; ✉ P & O Properties Ltd, 78 Pall Mall, London SW1Y 5EH (☎ 0171 930 4343)

HARDING, Sir (George) William; KCMG (1983, CMG 1977), CVO (1972); s of Lt-Col George Richardson Harding, DSO, MBE (d 1976), and Grace Henley, *née* Darby (d 1991); *b* 18 Jan 1927; *Educ* Aldenham, St John's Coll Cambridge; *m* 1955, Sheila Margaret Ormond, da of Maj John Ormond Riddel (d 1945), of Edinburgh; 4 s (Rupert, Simon, Martin, James); *Career* Lt Royal Marines 1945–48; entered Dip Serv 1950, served Singapore, Burma, Paris, Santo Domingo, Mexico City, Paris again, ambass Peru 1977–79, asst under sec of state FCO 1979–81, ambass Brazil 1981–84, dep under sec of state for Asia and the Americas FCO 1984–86; int advsr to bd and non-exec dir of Lloyds Bank plc 1988–93, dir Lloyds Merchant Bank Holdings Ltd 1988–93; chm: First Spanish Investment Trust plc 1987–, Thai-Euro Fund Ltd 1988–, Margaret Mee Amazon Trust 1988–94, Br-Thai Business Gp 1995–; visiting fell Harvard Univ Center for Int Affrs 1986; memb: Trilateral Cmmn 1987–94, Cncl of Royal Inst of Int Affrs 1988–94, Cncl of Royal Geographical Soc 1988–91 (vice pres 1991–93); *Clubs* Beefsteak, Sloane, Leander; *Style—* Sir William Harding, KCMG, CVO; ✉ La Dreyrie, 24510 Pezuls, France

HARDING-JONES, David; s of Rev William Harding Jones (d 1981), of Seaford, Sussex, and Gertrude Alice, *née* Roberts; *b* 3 Aug 1936; *Educ* Bancrofts Sch, Charing Cross Hosp Med Sch (MB BS); *m* 2 April 1960, (Josephine) June Mary, da of Henry Thomas Hitchens, of Exeter; 3 s (Andrew David b 1964, Ian Richard b 1965, Neil Robert b 1967), 2 da (Alison Margaret b 1969, Fiona Marie b 1971); *Career* orthopaedic registrar Oswestry and Hereford 1968–69 (Westminster Hosp 1964–67), orthopaedic sr registrar Cardiff 1969–70, conslt orthopaedic surgn W Wales Gen Hosp Carmarthen 1971–; regnl advsr in orthopaedics S Wales RCS England 1986–93, chm Orthopaedic Advsy Ctee Wales 1986–90; pres Rotary Club Saundersfoot 1980–81, past master Caerfyrddin Lodge 4928, previous convener S W Wales Orthopaedic Club 1972–88; memb: BMA, Hosp Conslts and Specialists Assoc; FRCS; *Recreations* travel; *Style—* David Harding-Jones, Esq; ✉ Department of Orthopaedics, W Wales General Hospital, Glangwili, Carmarthen SA31 2AF (☎ 01267 227531)

HARDING OF PETHERTON, 2 Baron (UK 1958); John Charles Harding; o s of Field Marshal 1 Baron Harding of Petherton, GCB, CBE, DSO, MC (d 1989), and Mary, *née* Rooke (d 1983); *b* 12 Feb 1928; *Educ* Marlborough, Worcester Coll Oxford; *m* 20 June 1966, Harriet, da of Maj-Gen James Hare, CB, DSO (d 1970); 2 s (Hon William Allan John, Hon David Richard John b 1978), 1 da (Hon Diana Mary b 1967); *Heir* s, Hon William Allan John Harding b 5 July 1969; *Career* Maj 11 Hussars, ret 1968; farmer, ret 1991; *Style—* The Rt Hon the Lord Harding of Petherton; ✉ Barrymore Farm House, Pict's Hill, Langport, Somerset TA10 9EZ (☎ 01458 250416)

HARDINGE, 6 Viscount (UK 1846); Sir Charles Henry Nicholas Hardinge; 8 Bt (UK 1801), of Lurran, Fermanagh; s of 5 Viscount Hardinge (d 1984), and his 1 w (m dis 1982), Zoe Ann (Mrs C M H Murray), da of Hartland de Montarville Molson, OBE, of Montreal, Senator of Canada; suc his kinsman, Sir Robert Arnold Hardinge, 7 Bt, in his baronetcy 1986; *b* 25 Aug 1956; *Educ* Upper Canada Coll, Trinity Coll Sch, McGill Univ Montreal; *m* 1985, Mrs Julie Therese Sillett, eld da of Keith Sillett, of Sydney, Aust; 2 da (Hon Emilie Charlotte b 1986, Hon Olivia Margaux b 1989), and 1 step s (Matthew b 1982); *Heir* bro, Hon Andrew Hartland Hardinge; *Career* sits as ind in House of Lords; sr mangr private banking The Royal Bank of Canada; *Clubs* Turf, Canada (hon sec); *Style—* The Rt Hon the Viscount Hardinge; ✉ 12 Streathbourne Road, London SW17

HARDINGE OF PENSHURST, 3 Baron (UK 1910); George Edward Charles Hardinge; s of 2 Baron, GCB, GCVO, MC, PC (d 1960), and Helen, Baroness Hardinge of Penshurst (d 1979); *b* 31 Oct 1921; *Educ* Eton, RNC Dartmouth; *m* 1, 22 July 1944 (m dis 1962), Janet (d 1970), da of Lt-Col Francis Balfour, CIE, CVO, CBE, MC (n of 1 and 2 Earls of Balfour); 3 s; m 2, 1966, Mrs Margaret Trezise, da of William Jerrum; 1 s, 1 adopted step s; *Heir* s, Hon Julian Hardinge; *Career* Lt Cdr RN, ret (served 1942 HMS Naiad, HMS Medway); page of honour to HM 1933–38, train bearer at Coronation of George VI; professional publisher with Collins, Longman and Macmillan for 30 years; ed to Agatha Christie, Ngaio Marsh, Nicholas Blake, Julian Symons, Ellis Peters and others, 'discoverer' of Nina Bawden, Colin Dexter, Peter Lovesey, E V Thompson, Mary Wesley, Iain Banks and others; fndr memb Booker Prize for Fiction; *Books* An Incompleat Angler (1976); *Recreations* reading, bridge, fishing; *Clubs* Brooks's; *Style—* The Rt Hon Lord Hardinge of Penshurst; ✉ Bracken Hill, 10 Penland Road, Bexhill-on-Sea, E Sussex TN40 2JG (☎ 01424 211866)

HARDINGHAM, Michael; s of Edmund Arthur Hardingham, and Winifred, *née* Leeding; *b* 16 Oct 1939; *Educ* West House and Solihull Sch, St Mary's Hosp Univ of London (MB BS, LRCP); *m* 25 Sept 1982, Ellen, da of William McCafferty, of Pennsylvania, USA; 1 s (Henry b 1984), 1 da (Isabel b 1986); *Career* postgrad med trg London, Edinburgh and Sweden, trg in otorhinolaryngology St Mary's Royal Marsden Hosp, conslt ENT surgn Cheltenham Gen Hosp and Gloucestershire Royal Hosp 1974– (special interest head and neck oncology); memb Cncl Sections of Laryngology and Otology RSM; hon sec Br Assoc of Head and Neck Oncologists, Gloucestershire Hosp rep to BMA Annual Rep Body Meeting, foreign corresponding memb American Soc of Head and Neck Surgns; fell and examiner for: DLO of RCS (Eng) and FRCSEd, Nursing Assoc of Midland Inst of Otology (formerly hon sec), BMA Gloucestershire Branch (formerly sec); contrib pubns to otolaryngolical clinics N America; FRCSEd, FRCS 1973; *Recreations* theatre, opera, skiing; *Style—* Michael Hardingham, Esq; ✉ Winfield Hospital, Tewkesbury Road, Gloucester GL2 9EE (☎ 01452 380358, fax 01452 331200)

HARDMAN, Blaise Noel Anthony; s of Air Chief Marshal Sir Donald Hardman, GBE, KCB, DFC (d 1982), and Dorothy, *née* Ashcroft Thompson; *b* 24 Dec 1939; *Educ* Eton; *m* 1967, Caroline Marion, da of Sir Donald Cameron of Lochiel, KT, CVO, of Inverness-shire; 1 s (Thomas b 1977), 4 da (Jane b 1969, Annabel b 1971, Elizabeth b 1974, Rosanna b 1979); *Career* 2 Lt HM Forces 1959, served 13/18 Royal Hussars 1959–61, Malaya 1961, BAOR; Morgan Grenfell and Co Ltd 1962–88, (dir 1971, chm 1987); dir: P & O Steam Navigation Co 1980–83, Matthew Clark plc 1982–91, Murray International Trust plc 1988, Murray Income Trust plc 1988, Murray Smaller Markets Trust plc 1988, Tokai Bank Europe Ltd 1989, Whiteaway Laidlaw Bank Ltd 1989, Murray Ventures plc 1989, Murray Johnstone Holdings Ltd 1990, The Birmingham Midshires Building Society 1991, Murray Split Capital Trust 1991, The Murray European Trust Plc 1992–, Fleming Japanese Investment Trust plc 1996, Elizabeth FitzRoy Homes 1993–; *Recreations* gardening; *Clubs* Boodle's; *Style—* Blaise Hardman, Esq; ✉ Farley House, Farley Chamberlayne, nr Romsey, Hants

HARDMAN, Sir Henry; KCB (1962, CB 1956); s of Harry Hardman (d 1957); *b* 15 Dec 1905; *Educ* Manchester Central HS, Univ of Manchester; *m* 1937, (Helen) Diana (d 1996), da of late Robert Carr Bosanquet; 1 s (Paul), 2 da (Anna, Charlotte); *Career* economics tutor Univ of Leeds 1934–45; Miny of Food 1940–: dep head Br Food Mission to N America 1946–48, under-sec 1948–53; min UK delegn to NATO Paris 1953–54, dep sec MAFF 1955–60; dep sec Miny of Aviation 1960 (perm sec 1961–63), perm under-sec of state MOD 1963–66; memb MMC 1967–70 (dep chm 1967–68), chm Covent Garden Market Authy 1967–75, govr and tstee Reserve Bank of Rhodesia 1967–79, chm Home-Grown Cereals Authy 1968–77; *Style—* Sir Henry Hardman, KCB; ✉ 9 Sussex Square, Brighton, East Sussex BN2 1FJ (☎ 01273 688904)

HARDMAN, John Nimrod; s of Harry John Hardman (d 1974), of Liverpool, and Florence Sybil Anne, *née* Dolby (d 1988); *b* 8 Oct 1939; *Educ* Quarry Bank HS, Univ of Liverpool (BCom); *m* 19 Feb 1966, Joan, da of Joseph McHugh; 1 s (Michael John b 18 Nov 1969), 1 da (Jacqueline Martha b 21 Aug 1973); *Career* audit mangr Duncan Watson & Short CAs Liverpool 1962–66, fin dir Thorn Colour Tubes Ltd 1967–74, dir Europe Africa and Far E RCA Corp NY 1974–77, dir of corp fin RCA Corp NY 1977–79, fin dir Oriel Foods UK 1979–81, md Asda Stores Ltd 1984–89 (fin dir 1981–84), chm and chief exec Asda Group plc 1989–91; dir: Yorkshire Electricity plc 1989–, Maples Stores plc; chm Dewhurst Butcher Ltd; dep chm Leeds Devpt Corp; FCA 1976 (ACA 1966), CIMgt 1988, FRSA 1988; *Recreations* field sports, golf; *Clubs* Royal Liverpool Golf, Pannal Golf, Liverpool Artists; *Style—* John Hardman, Esq; ✉ c/o Yorkshire Electricity plc, Wetherby Road, Scarcroft, Leeds, LS14 3HS (☎ 0113 289 2123)

HARDMAN, Victoria; da of Donald Hardman, of Lincolnshire, and Joan Frances, *née* Dolphin; *b* 5 Jan 1953; *Educ* Erdington GS Birmingham, Bournemouth Poly (BA); *m* 1989, Michael Fairey CB; *Career* trg in NHS 1978–81, asst admin Guy's Hosp 1981–83, health serv planner NE Thames RHA 1983–86, gen mangr The Royal London Hosp 1986–91; chief exec: Hampstead Health Authy 1991–92, Bloomsbury and Islington Health Authy 1992–93, Camden and Islington Health Authy 1993–96; memb Inst of Health Servs Mgmnt 1979; *Recreations* opera, ballet, gardening; *Style—* Miss Victoria Hardman

HARDSTAFF, Joseph (Joe); MBE (1968); s of Joseph Hardstaff (d 1990), of Nottingham, and Cissy, *née* Rose (d 1981); *b* 28 Feb 1935; *Educ* Brunts Sch Mansfield; *m* 21 Dec 1963, Olive Mary, da of Thomas Nancekievill, of Torrington, Devon; 1 s (Joseph b 21 Dec 1967), 1 da (Lisa Jane b 20 Nov 1965); *Career* gen duties offr pilot RAF 1953–88 (ret as Air Cdre); sec Middlesex CCC 1989–; cricket player: RAF 1953–73 (capt 1964 and 1967–69), Combined Servs 1964; FIMgt; *Recreations* golf, walking, reading; *Style—* Joe Hardstaff, Esq, MBE; ✉ 5 Dial Close, Seend, Melksham, Wiltshire SN12 6NP (☎ 01380 828458); Middlesex CCC, Lord's Ground, London NW8 8QN (☎ 0171 289 1300)

HARDSTAFF, Veronica; MEP (Lab) Lincolnshire and Humberside South (majority 13,745); *Educ* Univ of Manchester, Univ of Cologne; *Career* MEP (Lab) Lincolnshire and Humberside S 1994–; memb: Agric and Rural Devpt Ctee, Environment Ctee; vice-pres Jt Parly Ctee with Poland; *Style—* Ms Veronica Hardstaff, MEP; ✉ 397 High Street, Lincoln, LN5 7SS; c/o European Parliament, 93–113 Rue Belliard, 1040, Brussels, Belgium

HARDWICK, Mary Atkinson (Mollie); *née* Greenhalgh; da of Joseph Greenhalgh (d 1940), of Cheadle Hulme, Cheshire, and Anne Frances, *née* Atkinson (d 1959); *Educ* Manchester HS for Girls; *m* 1961, Michael Hardwick (d 1991), s of George Drinkrow Hardwick, of Leeds, W Yorks; 1 s (Julian); *Career* announcer BBC North Region 1940–45, BBC (Radio) Drama Dept 1945–62; freelance author 1962–; memb Soc of Authors; *Books* Stories from Dickens (1968), Emma, Lady Hamilton (1969), Mrs Dizzy (1972), Upstairs Downstairs: Sarah's Story (1973), The Years of Change (1974), The War to end Wars (1975), Mrs Bridges' Story (1975), The World of Upstairs Downstairs (1976), Alice in Wonderland (play, 1975), Beauty's Daughter (1976, Elizabeth Goudge Award for best historical romantic novel of year), The Duchess of Duke Street: The Way Up (1976), The Golden Years (1976), The World Keeps Turning (1977), Charlie is My Darling (1977), The Atkinson Heritage (1978), Thomas and Sarah (1978), Thomas and Sarah: Two for a Spin (1979), Lovers Meeting (1979), Sisters in Love (1979), Dove's Nest (1980), Willowwood (1980), Juliet Bravo 1 (1980), Juliet Bravo 2 (1980), Monday's Child (1981), Calling Juliet Bravo: New Arrivals (1981), I Remember Love (1982), The Shakespeare Girl (1983), By the Sword Divided (1983), The Merrymaid (1984), Girl with a Crystal Dove (1985), Malice Domestic (1986), Parson's Pleasure (1987), Uneaseful Death (1988), Blood Royal (1988), The Bandersnatch (1989), Perish in July (1989), The Dreaming Damozel (1990), Come Away Death (1997); with Michael Hardwick: The Jolly Toper (1961), The Sherlock Holmes Companion (1962), Sherlock Holmes Investigates (1963), The Man Who Was Sherlock Holmes (1964), Four Sherlock Holmes Plays (1964), The Charles Dickens Companion (1965), The World's Greatest Sea Mysteries (1967), Writers' Houses: a literary journey in England (1968), Alfred Deller: A Singularity of Voice (1968), Charles Dickens As They Saw Him (1969), The Game's Afoot (Sherlock Holmes Plays, 1969); *Recreations* theatre, reading detective novels; *Style—* Mollie Hardwick; ✉ c/o The Society of Authors, 84 Drayton Gardens, London SW10 9SB

HARDWICK, Dr Peter Bernard; QHP (1992); s of Arthur William Hardwick (d 1976), of Silverdale, Rayleigh, Essex, and Nellie, *née* Love (d 1960); *b* 21 Sept 1933; *Educ* Southend-on-Sea HS for Boys, The Royal Free Hosp Sch of Med (MB BS); *m* 1961 (m dis 1988), Nancy, *née* Peters; 2 s (Nigel Peter Arthur b 1967, Matthew James Gerald b 1969), 2 da (Deborah Claire b 1962, Julia Dawn b 1964, d 1989); *Career* The Royal Free Hosp London: conslt anaesthetist, conslt i/c clinic for pain relief 1969–92; memb Ct of Common Cncl Corp of City of London, Hon MO London and Schools ABA, dep dist surgn St John Ambulance Bde London (Prince of Wales) Dist; Liveryman: Worshipful Co of Barbers, Worshipful Soc of Apothecaries; OStJ; FRCA; *Recreations* private flying, horse riding, cricket and rugby; *Clubs* MCC; *Style—* Dr Peter Hardwick, QHP; ✉ 72 Harley Street, London W1N 1AE (☎ 0171 436 3764)

HARDWICKE, 10 Earl of (GB 1754); Joseph Philip Sebastian Yorke; also Baron Hardwicke (GB 1733) and Viscount Royston (GB 1754); s of Viscount Royston (d 1973, s and h of 9 Earl, who d 1974); *b* 3 Feb 1971; *Heir* kinsman, David John Napier Edward Yorke b 1919; *Career* dir World Cancer Fund; hon pres: The Wednesday Club, The Twenty-toe Shuffle Club; *Recreations* films, music, the Caribbean Islands, wine, shooting, football, cricket, water skiing, underwater ballet, ten pin bowling; *Style—* The Rt Hon Earl of Hardwicke; ✉ 48 Tite Street, London SW3 4JA

HARDY, Prof Barbara Gladys; da of Maurice Nathan (d 1962), and Gladys Emily Ann, *née* Abraham (d 1992); *b* 27 June 1924; *Educ* Swansea HS for Girls, UCL (BA, MA); *m* 14 March 1946, Ernest Dawson Hardy (d 1977); 2 da (Julia b 1955, Kate b 1957); *Career* lectr English Dept Birkbeck Coll London, subsequently prof of English Royal Holloway Coll Univ of London 1965–70, prof of English lit Birkbeck Coll London 1970–89; emeritus prof Univ of London, hon prof of English Univ Coll Swansea, hon fell Birkbeck Coll and Royal Holloway Univ of London; pres Dickens Soc 1987–88; vice pres: George Eliot Fellowship, Hardy Soc; memb Labour Pty; fell Welsh Acad; hon memb MLA; Hon DUniv Open Univ 1981; *Books* The Novels of George Eliot (1959), The Appropriate Form (1964), The Moral Art of Dickens (1970), The Exposure of Luxury: Radical Themes in Thackeray (1972), Tellers and Listeners: The Narrative Imagination (1975), A Reading of Jane Austen (1975), The Advantage of Lyric (1977), Particularities: Readings in George Eliot (1982), Charles Dickens - The Writer and His Work (1983), Forms of Feeling in Victorian Fiction (1985), Narrators and Novelists: Collected Essays (1987), Swansea Girl (1994), Henry James: The Later Writing (1996), London Lovers (1996), Shakespeare's Storytellers (1997); *Recreations* walking, theatre, galleries; *Style—* Prof Barbara Hardy; ✉ Birkbeck College, Malet Street, London WC1E 7HX

HARDY, Brian; s of Arthur Hardy (d 1986), and Muriel, *née* Michaelson (d 1975); *b* 31 Jan 1942; *Educ* LSE (BSc Econ), Stanford Graduate Sch of Business (MBA 1972); *m* 1970, Eirene, da of Evstratios Verganelakis; 1 s (Nicholas Alexander Stratis b 1985); *Career* Arthur Andersen: articled clerk London 1963–66, audit sr London 1966–67, sr then mangr Athens 1967–70, mangr then sr mangr 1972–76, seconded to BNOC as special asst to md in establishing fin dept 1976–77; head of gp audit then gp controller BICC plc 1977–82, gp financial controller Unigate plc 1982–84, fin dir Burmah Castrol plc 1990– (fin dir Castrol Ltd subsid 1984–90), non-exec dir Storehouse plc 1994–; FCA (ACA 1966); *Recreations* tennis, theatre, golf; *Clubs* RAC, Studley Wood Golf; *Style—* Brian Hardy, Esq; ✉ Director Finance, Burmah Castrol plc, Burmah Castrol House, Pipers Way, Swindon, Wilts SN3 1RE (☎ 01793 452210, fax 01793 453226)

HARDY, Rev Canon Brian Albert; s of Albert Charles Hardy (d 1969), of Skegness, Lincs, and Edith Maude Sarah, *née* Mabe (d 1989); *b* 3 July 1931; *Educ* Leicester City Boys' Sch, St John's Coll Oxford (MA, DipTheol); *Career* curate of Rugeley Staffs 1957–62, chaplain Downing Coll Cambridge 1962–66, Livingston Ecumenical Team Miny 1966–74, churches' planning offr Telford and prebendary Hereford Cathedral 1974–78, chaplain Coates Hall Theol Coll Edinburgh 1978–82, rector St Columba by the Castle Episcopal Church Edinburgh 1982–91, dean of the Dio of Edinburgh 1986–91, hon canon St Mary's Cathedral Edinburgh 1991–, rector All Saints' St Andrews 1991–; *Recreations* music, cycling; *Style—* The Rev Canon Brian Hardy; ✉ All Saints Rectory, North Street, St Andrews KY16 9AQ (☎ 01334 73193)

HARDY, David Gordon; s of Gordon Patrick Hardy, of 33a High St Auchtermuchty, Fife, and Margaret Maud, *née* Cunningham; *b* 5 July 1940; *Educ* Daniel Stewart's Coll Edinburgh, Univ of Edinburgh (BSc, MB ChB), Univ of Cambridge (MA); *m* 8 Aug 1967, Maria Rosa (Rosemary), da of Johann Breu (d 1965), of Appenzell, Switzerland; 1 s (James Patrick b 5 Oct 1971), 1 da (Ruth Maria b 10 Oct 1969); *Career* Fulbright Hayes scholar Univ of Florida 1977–78, sr lectr in neurosurgery London Hosp Med Coll 1979–80, conslt neurosurgn Addenbrooke's Hosp Cambridge 1980–, med dir Addenbrooke's Hosp NHS Tst, supervisor in anatomy Gonville and Caius Coll Cambridge (assoc lectr faculty of clinical med); visiting conslt Norfolk and Norwich Hosp; contrib various chapters and papers on various neurosurgical and anatomical subjects; memb Section of Neurology RSM, hon treas Soc of Br Neurosurgeons; FRCSEd 1970, FRCS 1971, FRSM; *Recreations* gardening, walking; *Style—* David Hardy, Esq; ✉ Department of Neurosurgery, Addenbrooke's Hospital, Hills Rd, Cambridge CB2 2QQ (☎ 01223 216302)

HARDY, David Malcolm; s of Roy Hardy, of Leigh-on-Sea, Essex, and Mary, *née* Ebsworth; *b* 16 July 1955; *Educ* Westcliff HS; *m* 1, 1981 (m dis); 1 s (Matthew James Cranmer b 1985), 1 da (Joanna Louise b 1989); m 2, 1995, Marion, da of Cecil and Dorothy Brazier; *Career* Barclays Bank plc 1973–81, Barclays Merchant Bank 1981–85; London Clearing House Ltd (formerly International Commodities Clearing House Ltd): on secondment from Barclays Bank 1985–87, md 1987–95, chief exec 1995–; also dir: London Commodity Exchange (1986) Ltd 1991–, International Petroleum Exchange of London Ltd 1993–, Futures and Options Association 1993–; memb Co of World Traders 1993; Freeman City of London 1995; ACIB 1976, FCT 1992; *Recreations* golf, photography; *Style—* David Hardy, Esq; ✉ The London Clearing House Ltd, Aldgate House, 33 Aldgate High Street, London EC3N 1EA (☎ 0171 426 7040, fax 0171 667 7354)

HARDY, Sir David William; kt (1992); s of Brig John Herbert Hardy, CBE, MC (d 1969), of Lancaster, and (Amy) Doris, *née* Bacon (d 1982); *b* 14 July 1930; *Educ* Wellington Coll, Harvard Business Sch (AMP); *m* 11 Sept 1957, Rosemary Stratford, da of Sir Godfrey Ferdinando Stratford Collins, KCIE, CSI, OBE (d 1952); 1 s (Alexander David b 11 May 1968), 1 da (Sarah Elizabeth b 28 May 1964); *Career* 2 Lt 2 Royal Horse Artillery Germany 1953–54; with Funch Edye Co Inc 1954–64 (dir 1960–64), vice pres fin and admin Imperial Tobacco 1964–70, HM Govt co-ordinator of industl affrs 1970–72, fin dir Tate and Lyle plc 1972–77; dir: Ocean Transport and Trading plc 1977–83, Waterford Wedgwood Group plc 1984–90, Paragon Group Ltd 1984–88, Tootal Group plc 1990–91; non-exec dir: Sturge Holdings plc 1985–95, Aberfoyle Holdings plc 1986–91, Ciba-Geigy PLC 1991–96, Hanson PLC 1991–, J Devenish plc 1991–93, James Fisher & Sons plc 1993–, Imperial Tobacco Group plc 1996–; chm: Ocean Inchcape Ltd 1980–83, Globe Investment Trust plc 1983–90 (dir 1976), London Park Hotels 1983–87, Docklands Light Railway 1984–87, Swan Hunter Ltd 1986–88, MGM Assurance 1986– (dir 1985), Leisuretime International 1988–89, Buckingham International 1989–95, London Docklands Devpt Corp 1988–92, Europa Minerals PLC 1991–, Bankers Trust Investment Management Ltd 1992–94, Burmine Ltd (Melbourne Australia) 1992–96, Y J Lovell Holdings PLC 1994–; dep chm: London Regnl Tport 1984–87, The Agricultural Mortgage Corp 1986–93 (dir 1973); advsy dir HSBC Samuel Montagu 1995; dir Sons of Gwalia Ltd 1996–; chm: 100 Gp of Fin Dirs 1986–88, DTI Engrg Markets Advsy Ctee 1988–90, Tport Research Fndn 1996–; memb: NEDC for Agriculture 1970–72, ECGD Advsy Cncl 1973–78, CBI Econs and Fiscal Ctee 1982–89, NACF Devpt Ctee 1990–, Fin Ctee London Fedn of Boys Clubs 1990–, Indust Development Advsy Bd DTI 1991–96; co-opted Cncl Inst CAs 1974–78; fndr dir: St Katherine & Shadwell Tst 1991, Royal Albert Dock Tst; Nat Maritime Museum: tstee 1993–, dep chm 1994–95, chm 1995–; co-opted govr Chelsea Open Air Sch 1992– (dep chm 1993); pres: Poplar, Blackwall and Dist Rowing Club 1991, Pitlochry Angling Club 1994–; Freeman City of London; Liveryman: Worshipful Co of CA's, Worshipful Co of Shipwrights; FCA, FCIT, CIMgt (chm Econs and Social Affrs Ctee 1974–78, memb Cncl 1974–79); *Recreations* flyfishing, shooting; *Clubs* Brooks's, MCC, HAC, Flyfishers; *Style—* Sir David Hardy; ✉ National Maritime Museum, Greenwich, London SE10 9NF

HARDY, Graham John; s of William A Hardy (d 1976), and Lettie, *née* Lovell (d 1984); *b* 5 March 1938; *Educ* Llandaff Cathedral Sch, Cathays HS, Welsh Sch of Architecture Univ of Wales (BArch), Univ of Bristol (DipArchCons); *m* 7 Sept 1963, Sara Maureen, da of David Metcalfe Morgan, of Archer Road, Penarth; 1 s (Keiron b 1972), 2 da (Bridget b 1966, Elise b 1968); *Career* chartered architect and ecclesiastical surveyor; Prince of Wales Awards 1984: St John Evangelist Church Grounds Cardiff, Eglwysilian Church Mid Glam; Catnic UK Restoration Award 1981, first prize Prince of Wales' Ctee (competition for Inner Areas) 1980, Civic Tst commendation Victoria Place Newport 1980, Lord Mayor's Civic Award Cardiff 1990, Porthcawl Civic Soc Award 1992; architect and surveyor to the Fabric: Margam Abbey, Old Priory Caldey Abbey, St Illtyds Church Llantwit Major, St Germans Church Cardiff; architect to the Cathedral Parish of Llandaff; former pres Rotary Club of Cardiff East, dist govr Wales Rotary 1150 1997–98; RIBA; *Clubs* Rotary; *Style—* Graham J Hardy, Esq; ✉ Timbers, 6 Cefn Coed Rd, Cyncoed, Cardiff CF2 6AQ (☎ and fax 01222 752960); Graham J Hardy and Associates, 6 Cefn Coed Rd, Cardiff CF2 6AQ

HARDY, Herbert Charles (Bert); s of Charles Hardy; *b* 13 Dec 1928; *Educ* Sandhurst; *m* 1960 (m dis 1992), Irene Burrows; 1 da; *Career* dir News Group Newspapers Ltd 1969–78, md and chief exec News International Ltd 1976–78 (dir 1972–78), md Evening Standard Co Ltd 1980–89, md Associated Newspapers Ltd and chm Evening Standard Co Ltd 1989–94; chief exec: The European 1995–, The Scotsman Publications Ltd 1995–; non-exec dir Channel Four Television Corporation; *Style—* Bert Hardy, Esq; ✉ The European, 200 Gray's Inn Road, London WC1X 8NE (☎ 0171 418 7777, fax 0171 713 1840)

HARDY, Howard; *b* 26 Oct 1936; *Educ* Henry Mellish GS Nottingham, St Edmund Hall Oxford (MA, Athletics Blue); *m* 1958, Audrey; 1 s (Steven Robert b 25 Aug 1965), 1 da (Karen (Mrs Snell) b 1960); *Career* admitted slr 1964, in house slr Boots and others 1964–67; Burton & Dyson: joined as ptnr 1969, sr ptnr 1980–94, conslt 1994–; memb Cncl (for Lincs) Law Soc 1990–; non-exec dir: Darby Group plc, Lomtex Industries Ltd, Law Society Services Ltd; tstee Whittons Charity, dir local community CCTV scheme; *Recreations* golf; *Clubs* United Oxford and Cambridge University; *Style—* Howard Hardy, Esq; ✉ Burton & Dyson, 5 Curtis Walk, Gainsborough, Lincolnshire DN21 2BX (☎ 01427 810183, fax 01427 617912)

HARDY, Maj Gen John Campbell; CB (1985), LVO (1978); s of Gen Sir Campbell Hardy, KCB, CBE, DSO (d 1984); *b* 13 Oct 1933; *Educ* Sherborne; *m* 1961, Jennifer Mary Kempton; 1 s, 1 da; *Career* joined RM 1952, 45 Commando 1954, HMS Superb 1956, instr NCOs' Sch at Plymouth 1957, 42 Commando 1959, 43 Commando 1962, Adj Jt Serv Amphibious Warfare Centre 1964, Co Cdr 45 Commando 1965, student RAF Staff Coll Bracknell 1966, instr RNC Greenwich 1967, extra equerry to HRH Prince Philip 1968–69, SO in Dept of Cmdt Gen RM 1969, Rifle Co Cdr 41 Commando 1971, student NDC Latimer 1972, staff of CDS 1973, SO HQ Commando Forces 1975, CO RM Poole 1977, Col 1978, COS and asst def attaché Br Def Staff Washington 1979, ADC to HM The Queen 1981–82, Maj Gen 1982, COS to Cmdt Gen RM 1982–84, dep COS HQ AFNORTH 1984–87; dir Br Digestive Fndn 1987–92, admin Sion Coll 1993–; *Recreations* walking, shooting; *Clubs* Army and Navy; *Style—* Maj Gen John Hardy, CB, LVO; ✉ c/o National Westminster Bank, 31 High Street, Deal, Kent CT14 6EW

HARDY, Peter; MP (Lab) Wentworth (majority 22,449); s of Lawrence Hardy, of Wath-upon-Dearne; *b* 17 July 1931; *Educ* Wath-upon-Dearne GS, Westminster Coll, Univ of Sheffield; *m* 1954, Margaret Anne, *née* Brookes; 2 s; *Career* MP (Lab): Rother Valley 1970–83, Wentworth 1983–; PPS to: Sec of State for Environment 1974–76, Foreign Sec 1976–79; former ldr of Lab delgn to Cncl of Europe (currently memb), Western Euro Union and CSCE Assemblies 1983–, chm Cncl of Europe Environment Ctee 1986–90, vice chm Socialist Gp Cncl of Europe (leader Lab delgn 1983–95); chm Energy Ctee PLP 1974–92, hon sec All-Pty Gp for Energy Studies 1992–, vice chm All-Pty Conservation Ctee; attachment RAF 1992–93; former Local Authy chm; memb Central Exec Cncl NSPCC 1986–94, hon memb Kennel Club; former memb: Cncl RSPB, Worldwide Fund for Nature (UK); patron Yorkshire Wildlife Tst; sponsored by NACODS 1983–; *Books* A Lifetime of Badgers (1975); *Style—* Peter Hardy, MP; ✉ 53 Sandygate, Wath-upon-Dearne, Rotherham, S Yorkshire (☎ 01709 874590)

HARDY, Peter B; *Career* former md (investment banking) S G Warburg Group; non-exec dir: Kingfisher plc 1992–, Land Securities plc, Foreign & Colonial PEP Investment Tst, Howard De Walden Estates Ltd 1995–; dir Barnardo's; *Style—* Peter B Hardy, Esq; ✉ Kingfisher plc, North West House, 119 Marylebone Road, London NW1 5PX (☎ 0171 724 7749)

HARDY, Richard Charles Chandos; s and h of Lt-Col Sir Rupert John Hardy, 4 Bt, *qv*; *b* 6 Feb 1945; *Educ* Eton; *m* 1972, Venetia Wingfield, da of Simon Wingfield Digby, TD, DL, MP, of Haydon Gate, Sherborne; 4 da (Arabella Venetia Jane b 1976, Jacquetta Anne b 1977, Georgina Charlotte b 1982, Henrietta Alicia Diana b 1986); *Career* insurance broker; *Recreations* hunting, point-to-pointing, racing; *Clubs* Turf; *Style—* Richard Hardy, Esq; ✉ Springfield House, Gillingham, Dorset

HARDY, (Timothy Sydney) Robert; CBE (1981); s of late Maj Henry Harrison Hardy, CBE, and Edith Jocelyn, *née* Dugdale; *b* 29 Oct 1925; *Educ* Rugby, Magdalen Coll Oxford (BA); *m* 1, 1952 (m dis), Elizabeth, da of late Sir Lionel Fox, and Lady Fox; 1 s; m 2, 1961 (m dis 1986), Sally, da of Sir Neville Pearson, 2 Bt, and Dame Gladys Cooper, DBE; 2 da; *Career* actor; tstee: Mary Rose Tst 1991– (conslt 1979–), WWF 1983–89; memb: Bd of Tstees Royal Armouries 1984–95, Battlefields Panel English Heritage 1993–; chm Berks Bucks and Oxon Naturalists Tst Appeal 1985–90; Hon DLitt Reading 1990; Master Ct Worshipful Co Bowyers 1988–90; FSA 1996; *Theatre* early work incl: Shakespeare (Memorial Theatre) 1949–51, West End 1951–53, Old Vic Theatre 1953–54, USA 1954, 1956–58 and 1963–64 (incl Hamlet and Henry V), Shakespeare (Memorial Theatre Centenary season) 1959; later work incl: Rosmersholm (Comedy Theatre) 1960, The Rehearsal (Globe Theatre) 1961, A Severed Head (Criterion Theatre) 1963, The Constant Couple (New Theatre) 1967, I've Seen You Cut Lemons (Fortune Theatre) 1969, Habeas Corpus (Lyric Theatre) 1974, Dear Liar (Mermaid Theatre) 1982, Winnie (Victoria Palace Theatre) 1988, Body and Soul (Albery) 1992; *Television* incl: David Copperfield 1956, Age of Kings 1960, Trouble-Shooters 1966–67, Elizabeth R 1970, Manhunt 1970, Edward VII 1973, All Creatures Great and Small 1978–90, Winston Churchill - The Wilderness Years 1981, Paying Guests 1986, Make and Break 1986, Churchill in The USA 1986, Hot Metal 1987–88, Northanger Abbey 1987, Sherlock Holmes 1991, Twilight of the Gods 1992, Middlemarch 1993, Gulliver's Travels 1995; author of TV documentaries: The Picardy Affair 1962, The Longbow 1972, Horses in our Blood 1977, Gordon of Khartoum 1982; *Films* incl: Torpedo Run 1956, The Spy Who Came in from the Cold, Ten Rillington Place, Young Winston, How I Won The War, Le Silencieux, La Gifle, The Far Pavilions 1983, The Shooting Party 1984, Jenny's War 1985, Paris by Night 1988, War and Remembrance 1988, A Feast at Midnight 1995, Sense and Sensibility (Columbia) 1995; *Books* Longbow (1976, 1986 and 1992); *Recreations* archery, horsemanship, bowyery; *Clubs* Buck's, Royal Toxophilite, Br Longbow; *Style—* Robert Hardy, Esq, CBE, FSA; ✉ c/o Chatto & Linnit, Prince of Wales Theatre, Coventry Street, London W1V 7FE (☎ 0171 930 6677, fax 0171 930 0091)

HARDY, Robert Hugh; JP (Berks 1984); s of Rev Charles Sidney Hardy (d 1965), of Curfew House, Sandwich, Kent, and Eva Meriel Violet, *née* Hodson (d 1993); *b* 15 Aug 1932; *Educ* Winchester, Merton Coll Oxford (BA, MA); *m* 18 July 1970, Penelope Jean Maxwell, da of Robert Sherston (d 1982), of Ringwell House, Ditcheat, Somerset; 1 s (James b 1975), 1 da (Caroline b 1972); *Career* house master Eton Coll 1969–84 (asst master 1956–87), headmaster Milton Abbey Sch 1987–95; govr N Foreland Lodge 1984; *Recreations* walking, fishing, cricket, antique glass; *Style—* Robert Hardy, Esq, JP; ✉ Hillcroft Cottage, Bicknoller, Taunton, Somerset TA4 4EF (☎ 01984 656738)

HARDY, His Hon Robert James; s of James Frederick Hardy and Annie, *née* Higinbotham; *b* 12 July 1924; *Educ* Mostyn House, Wrekin, Univ Coll London (LLB); *m* 1951, Maureen Scott; 1 s, 1 da; *Career* called to the Bar 1950, circuit judge 1979–94; *Style—* His Hon R J Hardy; ✉ Smithy House, Sandle Bridge, Little Warford, Cheshire SK9 7TY (☎ 01565 872535); Betlem, Mallorca

HARDY, Rosemary Helyn; da of Eric Hardy, of Burton-on-Trent, and Ella, *née* Sutton; *b* 19 May 1949; *Educ* Burton Girls' HS, Royal College of Music, Liszt Music Academy Budapest; *m* 8 Sept 1984, Hugo M Ramsten; 1 da (Hannah Maria b 9 March 1988); *Career* soprano; sometime memb Deller Consort; worked with Roger Norrington, John Eliot Gardiner, David Munro, Jonathan Miller, Peter Eötvös, Ronald Zollman and Kent Nagano; festival appearances incl: Venice Biennale, Holland Festival, Frankfurter Festspiele, Aldeburgh Festival, Glyndebourne (Max in Oliver Knussen's Where the Wild Things Are), Wien Modern, Helsinki Festival, Salzburg Festival 1992, Warsaw Autumn Festival (awarded Critics' Prize for concert with Schoenberg Ensemble under Reinbert de Leeuw 1993); concerts with LSO, LPO, BBC Symphony Orch, Hallé Orch, The Hague Philharmonic, Rheinlandpfalz, Swedish, Danish and Dutch Radio Symphony Orchs, Stockholm Philharmonic Orch; other performances incl: Messiaen Harawi Berwald Hall Stockholm, György Kurtag The Sayings of Peter Bornemisza, Benjamin Britten Owen Wingrave 1993, Berio Circles (with Ensemble Intercontemporain Paris) 1993, Kandinsky exhibition Murnau, Schoenberg Erwartung (with Stockholm Philharmonic Orch) 1994, works by Stravinsky, Webern, Delage and Szymanowsky, Hindemith Das Nusch Nuschi (with BBC Symphony Orch under Andrew Davis); recorded Kurt Weill songs and instrumental pieces Berlin in Licht; winner Artisjus Prize Hungary 1983; *Style—* Ms Rosemary Hardy; ✉ c/o Magenta Music International Limited, 4 Highgate Street, Highgate Village, London N6 5JL (☎ 0181 340 8321, fax 0181 340 7823)

HARDY, Lt-Col Sir Rupert John; 4 Bt (UK 1876), of Dunstall Hall, Co Stafford; s of Sir Bertram Hardy, 3 Bt (d 1953), and Violet (d 1972), da of Hon Sir Edward Chandos Leigh, KCB, KC, JP (2 s of 1 Baron Leigh); *b* 24 Oct 1902; *Educ* Eton, Trinity Hall Cambridge (BA 1925); *m* 2 June 1930, Hon Diana Joan, *née* Allsopp; 1 s (Richard Charles Chandos *qv*), 1 da (Rosemary Diana (Mrs Black) b 1931); *Heir* s, Richard Charles Chandos Hardy b 6 Feb 1945; *Career* Lt-Col Life Gds, served WWII 8 Army in W Desert, Palestine, Syria, France; ret from Army 1948; rejoined as RARO 1952, Lt-Col Cmdg Household Cavalry 1952–56; *Recreations* hunting, shooting; *Clubs* Turf; *Style—* Lt-Col Sir Rupert Hardy, Bt; ✉ Gulliver's Lodge, Guilsborough, Northampton (☎ 01604 375)

HARDY, Timothy (Tim); s of Robert Norman Hardy (d 1992), of Seer Green, Beaconsfield, Buckinghamshire, and Patricia Margaret May, *née* Keen (d 1985); *b* 17 Feb 1956; *Educ* Royal GS High Wycombe, Balliol Coll Oxford (MA); *Career* admitted slr 1982; slr Barlow Lyde & Gilbert 1982–87 (ptnr 1987–); chm Br Insurance Law Assoc 1996–; memb: Law Soc, London Slrs Litigation Assoc; *Recreations* literature, theatre, sports; *Clubs* Dulwich Hockey, Nepotists Cricket; *Style—* Tim Hardy, Esq; ✉ Barlow Lyde & Gilbert, Beaufort House, 15 St Botolph St, London EC3A 7NJ (☎ 0171 247 2277, fax 0171 782 8509, telex 913281)

HARDY-ROBERTS, Brig Sir Geoffrey Paul; KCVO (1972), CB (1945), CBE (1944, OBE 1941), JP (W Sussex 1960), DL (W Sussex 1964); s of late Alfred Roberts; *b* 16 May 1907; *Educ* Eton, RMC Sandhurst; *m* 1945, Eldred (d 1987), wid of Col John Ronald Macdonell, DSO (d 1944); *Career* regular cmmn 9 Lancers 1926–37, served WWII, ME, Sicily, Italy, NW Europe, Brig 1943; contested (C) Wimbledon 1945; sec superintendent Middx Hosp 1946–67; master of HM's Household 1967–73, extra equerry to HM The Queen 1967–, memb W Sussex AHA 1974–81, dep chm King Edward VII Hosp Midhurst 1967–81; High Sheriff Sussex 1965; Offr Legion of Merit (USA) 1945; *Style—* Brig Sir Geoffrey Hardy-Roberts, KCVO, CB, CBE, JP, DL; ✉ Pendean Convalescent Home, West Lavington, Midhurst, West Sussex GU29 0ES (☎ 01730 815739)

HARE, Christopher Peter; s of Reginald Charles Hare (d 1980), and Mary Euphemia, *née* Lefroy (d 1988); *b* 6 Nov 1947; *Educ* Dover Coll; *m* (Dorothy) Jane, da of Richard Gough Dowell (d 1996), of Middleton-on-Sea, Sussex; 2 s (Nicholas Anthony b 28 May 1977, Julian Charles b 17 Nov 1981), 1 da (Rebecca Anne b 14 Feb 1975); *Career* John Dickenson & Co 1966–68, Lyon Trail Attenborough (formerly Lyon Lohr & Sly) 1968–85; dir: Lyon Lohr Group Services 1979 (gp admin 1979–85), Lyon Lohr Int 1980, Minories Underwriting Agencies (formerly Fenchurch Underwriting Agencies) 1986 (joined 1985); memb Lloyd's 1977–, chm City Forum 1983 (memb 1978, memb Ctee 1980–83); govr Dover Coll 1982– (memb Cncl and Fin Ctee 1982–, vice chm 1991–94, chm 1994–), chm Ctee Old Dovorian Club 1984–90 (memb 1975–96); Freeman City of London, memb Ct Worshipful Co of Merchant Taylors 1978; *Recreations* cricket, tennis, squash, golf; *Clubs* MCC, RAC, Roehampton; *Style*— Chistopher Hare, Esq; ✉ 40 Doneraile Street, London SW6 6EP (☎ 0171 736 4218); Minories Underwriting Agencies Ltd, 18 Mansell Street, London E1 8AA (☎ 0171 264 7000, fax 0171 488 2789)

HARE, David; s of Clifford Theodore Rippon, and Agnes Cockburn Hare; *b* 5 June 1947; *Educ* Lancing, Jesus Coll Cambridge (MA); *m* 1970 (m dis 1980), Margaret Matheson; 2 s, 1 da; m 2, Nicole Farhi; *Career* playwright and director; fndr Portable Theatre 1968, literary mangr and resident dramatist Royal Court Theatre 1969–71, resident dramatist Nottingham Playhouse 1973, fndr Joint Stock Theatre Gp 1975, fndr Greenpoint Films 1982, assoc dir Royal Nat Theatre 1985–; US/UK Bicentennial fell 1976; FRSL 1985; *Plays* writer: Slag (Royal Court 1971, Evening Standard Drama Award 1970), The Great Exhibition (1972), Knuckle (Comedy Theatre 1974, John Llewellyn Rhys Award 1974, televised 1989), Fanshen (1975), The Secret Rapture (NT 1988, Best Play of the Yr Drama Award, Best Play London Critics Poll), Racing Demon (NT 1990, NYC 1995, Best Play of the Yr Olivier Award, Best Play of the Yr Plays and Players Award, Time Out Award, Best Play of the Year Critics' Circle), Murmuring Judges (RNT 1991 and 1993), Rules of the Game (adapted, 1992), The Absence of War (RNT, 1993) The Life of Galileo (adapted, 1994), Skylight (RNT 1995, NYC 1996 (Olivier Award for Best Play 1996)), Mother Courage (RNT, adapted, 1995), Amy's View (RNT 1997), Ivanov (adapted, 1997); writer and dir: Brassneck (with Howard Brenton, Nottingham Playhouse 1973), Teeth 'n' Smiles (Royal Ct 1975, Wyndhams 1976), Plenty (NT 1978, NYC 1983, NY Critics Circle Award), A Map of the World (NT 1983, NYC 1985), Pravda (with Howard Brenton, NT 1985, Evening Standard Award, Plays and Players Award, City Limits Award), The Bay at Nice (NT 1986); *Opera* The Knife (libretto with Nick Bicat and Tim Rose Price, NY 1987); *TV* Man Above Men (1973), Licking Hitler (also dir 1978, BAFTA Award), Dreams of Leaving (also dir 1980), Saigon - Year of the Cat (1983), Heading Home (1991); *Films* writer and dir: Wetherby (1985, Golden Bear Award Berlin), Paris By Night (1988), Strapless (1989); writer only: Plenty 1985, Damage (adapted from Josephine Hart novel, 1992), The Secret Rapture (1994); as dir only The Designated Mourner (1996); *Style*— David Hare, Esq, FRSL; ✉ c/o Casarotto Ramsay Ltd, National House, 4th Floor, 60–66 Wardour Street, London W1V 3HP (☎ 0171 287 4450, fax 0171 287 9128)

HARE, John Neville; s of late Capt Lancelot Geldart Hare, MC (d 1957), and Esther Maria, *née* Whales (d 1969); *b* 11 Dec 1934; *Educ* St Edward's Oxford; *m* 17 Sept 1966, Pippa, da of Harding McGregor Dunnett, of Eliot Vale, Blackheath, London; 3 da (Charlotte b 1968, Henrietta b 1970, Emily b 1974); *Career* Lt Oxford and Bucks LI, Royal W Africa Frontier Force 1954–55; sr dist offr Colonial Serv Northern Nigeria 1957–64; dir Macmillan Education Publishers 1966–74, author and conslt Hodder and Stoughton Publishers 1980–89; UN Environment Prog 1989–; memb: Jt Russian-Mongolian Scientific Expdn to the Gobi Desert 1993, Xinjiang Protection Bureau Expdn to the Gobi and Taklamakan Desert to survey the wild camel population 1995 and to Lop Nur 1996; fndr Wild Camel Protection Fndn; author of 38 books incl 24 novels/readers; FRGS; *Recreations* hunting, travel, writing; *Clubs* Muthaiga; *Style*— John Hare, Esq; ✉ School Farm, Benenden, Kent (☎ 01580 240755)

HARE, Sir Philip Leigh; 6 Bt (UK 1818), of Stow Hall, Norfolk; s of Edward Philip Leigh Hare (d 1954), and his 3 w, Lady Kathleen Florence Mary, *née* Stanhope (d 1971), da of 9 Earl of Harrington, and widow of Edward Morant, JP, of Brockenhurst Park, Hants; suc cous, Sir Thomas Hare, 5 Bt (d 1993); *b* 13 Oct 1922; *m* 4 Nov 1950, Anne Lisle, 2 da of Maj Geoffrey Nicholson, CBE, MC; 1 s (Nicholas Patrick b 1955), 1 da (Louisa Kathleen (Mrs Benson Whittle) b (twin) 1955); *Heir* s, Nicholas Patrick Hare b 27 Aug 1955; *Style*— Sir Philip Hare, Bt; ✉ The Nettings, Hook Norton, Banbury, Oxon OX15 5NP

HARE, Rosina Selina Alice; QC (1976); *m* 1971, Patrick Back, QC, *qv*; *Career* called to the Bar Middle Temple 1956, recorder 1973–; legal memb Mental Health Review Tbnls 1983; bencher Middle Temple 1986; *Recreations* fishing, golf; *Clubs* Hurlingham; *Style*— Miss Rosina Hare, QC; ✉ 3 Temple Gardens, Temple, London EC4Y 9AU (☎ 0171 353 3102, fax 0171 353 0960)

HARE DUKE, Rt Rev Michael Geoffrey; s of Arthur Robert Aubrey Hare Duke (d 1972), of United Service Club, Calcutta, India, and Dorothy Lee, *née* Holmes (d 1967); *b* 28 Nov 1925; *Educ* Bradfield, Trinity Coll Oxford (MA), Westcott House Cambridge; *m* 6 July 1949, Grace Lydia Frances McKean, da of Rev Walter Edward Fagan Dodd (d 1971); 1 s (Barnabas Martin b 1954), 3 da (Phillida Frances b 1950, Teresa Mary b 1956, Hilary Margaret b 1958); *Career* Sub Lt RNVR 1944–46; ordained: deacon 1952, priest 1953; curate St John's Wood Church 1952–56, vicar St Mark's Bury 1956–62, pastoral dir Clinical Theol Assoc 1962–64 (pastoral conslt 1964–69), vicar St Paul's Daybrook 1964–69, OCF E Midlands Dist HQ 1968–69, bishop of St Andrews, Dunkeld and Dunblane 1969–94; chm: Scottish Pastoral Assoc 1970–74, Scottish Assoc for Mental Health 1978–85, Age Concern Scotland 1994–; pres Br Region Christian Peace Conf 1982–94, vice pres Scottish Inst of Human Relations 1974–76; Hon DD Univ of St Andrews; *Books* The Caring Church (jtly, 1963), First Aid in Counselling (jtly, 1968), Understanding the Adolescent (1969), The Break of Glory (1970), Freud (1972), Good News (1976), Stories, Signs and Sacraments in the Emerging Church (1982), Praying for Peace - reflections on the Gulf crisis (1991), Hearing the Stranger (1994); contrib to: Expository Times, Blackfriars, New Christian, Church Quarterly Review, Church Times, Scotsman, Contact; *Recreations* broadcasting, journalism, walking; *Style*— The Rt Rev M G Hare Duke, DD; ✉ 2 Balhousie Avenue, Perth PH1 5HN (☎ and fax 01738 622642)

HAREWOOD, 7 Earl of (UK 1812); George Henry Hubert Lascelles; KBE (1986); also Baron Harewood (GB 1796) and Viscount Lascelles (UK 1812); s of 6 Earl of Harewood, KG, GCVO, DSO, TD (d 1947), and HRH Princess Mary (The Princess Royal), CI, GCVO, GBE, RRC, TD, CD (d 1965), only da of HM King George V, *see* Debrett's Peerage, Royal Family section; *b* 7 Feb 1923; *Educ* Eton, King's Coll Cambridge; *m* 1, 29 Sept 1949 (m dis 1967; she m 2, 1973, as his 2 w, Rt Hon Jeremy Thorpe), Maria Donata Nanetta Paulina Gustava Erwina Wilhelmina (Marion), o da of late Erwin Stein; 3 s (Viscount Lascelles b 1950, Hon James b 1953, Hon Jeremy b 1955); m 2, 31 July 1967, Patricia Elizabeth, o da of Charles Tuckwell, of Sydney, and former w of (Louis) Athol Shmith (d 1990); 1 s (Hon Mark b 1964); *Heir* s, Viscount Lascelles, *qv*; *Career* Capt late Grenadier Guards, serv WWII (wounded, POW); ADC to Earl of Athlone Canada 1945–46; ed Opera magazine 1950–53, asst to David Webster at The Royal Opera Covent Garden 1953–60; artistic dir: Leeds Festival 1956–74, Edinburgh Festival 1961–65, Adelaide Festival 1988; md ENO 1972–85 (chm 1986–95), govr BBC 1985–87; pres: Br Bd of Film Classification 1985–96, Leeds United FC 1962–, Football Assoc 1963–72; chllr Univ of York 1963–67; Hon LLD: Univ of Leeds 1959, Univ of Aberdeen 1966; Hon DMus Univ of Hull 1962, Hon DLitt Univ of Bradford 1983, Hon DUniv York 1983; Hon RAM 1983, hon fell King's Coll Cambridge 1984, hon memb Royal Northern Coll of Music 1984; Liveryman Worshipful Co of Musicians; Austrian Great Silver Medal of Honour 1959, Lebanese Order of the Cedar 1970, Janácek Medal 1978; *Books* Kobbé's Complete Opera Book (ed), The Tongs and the Bones (memoirs 1981), The Illustrated Kobbé; *Recreations* looking at pictures, shooting, watching cricket, football, films; *Style*— The Rt Hon the Earl of Harewood, KBE; ✉ Harewood House, Leeds LS17 9LG

HARFORD, Mark John; s and h of Sir Timothy Harford, 3 Bt; *b* 6 Aug 1964; *Style*— Mark Harford, Esq

HARFORD, Piers Scandrett; s of Sir George Arthur Harford, 2 Bt, OBE (d 1967), and Anstice Marion, *née* Tritton (d 1993); *b* 9 Sept 1937; *Educ* Eton, Worcester Coll Oxford (BA); *m* 1, Hyacinthe Cecilia, da of Nigel Walter Hoare; 1 s (Henry Scandrett b 17 July 1963), 1 da (Charlotte Anstice b 12 May 1965); m 2, Patricia Jane, da of Air Cdr Patrick Burnett; 1 s (William Patrick b 18 March 1976); *Career* stockbroker; ptnr B S Stock Son & Co Bristol 1965 (joined 1961), Albert E Sharp 1990–91, Singer & Friedlander 1991–95, Rowan Dartington & Co 1995–; MSI 1965; *Recreations* various; *Style*— Piers Harford, Esq; ✉ Church Farm, Great Somerford, nr Chippenham, Wilts (☎ 01249 720135, fax 01249 720059)

HARFORD, Sir (John) Timothy; 3 Bt (UK 1934), of Falcondale, Co Cardigan; s of Lt-Col Sir George Arthur Harford, 2 Bt, OBE (d 1967), and Anstice Marion, *née* Tritton (d 1993); *b* 6 July 1932; *Educ* Harrow, Worcester Coll Oxford, Harvard Business Sch; *m* 12 May 1962, Carolyn Jane, o da of Brig Guy John de Wette Mullens, OBE (d 1981), of North House, Weyhill, Andover; 2 s (Mark John b 1964, Simon Guy b 1966), 1 da (Clare Elisabeth (Mrs Nicholas Clatworthy) b 1963); *Heir* s, Mark John Harford b 6 Aug 1964; *Career* dir Singer & Friedlander Ltd 1970–88; chm Wesleyan Assurance Society 1993–; dep chm: Wolseley Group plc 1983–, Wagon Industrial Holdings plc 1991–, Kwiksave Group plc 1994–, Sandaire Investments plc 1995–; Liveryman Worshipful Co of Grocers; *Clubs* Boodle's; *Style*— Sir Timothy Harford, Bt; ✉ South House, South Littleton, Evesham, Worcs (☎ 01386 832827)

HARGRAVE, David Grant; s of (Frank) Edward Hargrave, of Cyncoed, Cardiff, and Margaret Constance Mabel, *née* Grant; *b* 11 April 1951; *Educ* Howardian HS Cardiff, Univ of Birmingham (BCom, MSc); *m* 13 Dec 1969, Celia, da of Harry Hawksworth (d 1963); 1 s (Neil David b 30 July 1974), 1 da (Emma Louise b 17 June 1970); *Career* actuary Duncan C Fraser & Co (later William M Mercer Fraser Ltd) 1973–79; Bacon & Woodrow (formerly TG Arthur Hargrave): ptnr 1979–95, head of employee benefits 1994–95; fndr David Hargrave Ltd 1995–; non-exec dir: Homeowner's Friendly Soc Ltd 1982–, NHP plc 1996–; sec and treas Birmingham Actuarial Soc 1979–81; Nat Assoc Pension Funds Ltd (W Midlands): treas 1982–85, sec 1985–87, chm 1987–89; FIA 1977; *Recreations* long distance running, swimming, windsurfing, rugby; *Style*— David Hargrave, Esq; ✉ David Hargrave Ltd, Trench Hill, Painswick, Stroud, Gloucester GL6 6TZ

HARGRAVE, Dr Philip John; s of Edward James Anthony Hargrave (d 1963), and Doris Elsie, *née* Jackson (d 1995); *b* 21 June 1950; *Educ* Hinchley Wood Sch Surrey, Univ of Bristol (BSc Physics (1st class)), Cavendish Laboratory Univ of Cambridge (PhD); *m* 5 Oct 1985, Maureen Joyce, da of Alfred James Brook; 1 s (David John b 13 Dec 1990); *Career* Sci Research Cncl research fell Cavendish Lab Cambridge 1975–77; Standard Telecommunications Laboratories (STL, part of STC UK R & D Lab for ITT): joined 1977, successively research engr, sr research engr, princ research engr and sr princ research engr 1977–84, departmental mangr Adaptive Antenna Systems 1984–86, successively chief research engr, mangr tech strategy and asst dir 1986–92; Advanced Technology Centre (following acquisition of STC by Northern Telecom): dir Govt and External Progs then dir Radio and High Integrity Communications 1992–94, dir Next Generation Architecture 1994–95, dir Next Generation Products Advanced Technology Centre (part of Nortel Technology from Jan 1996) 1995–; IEE: memb Professional Gp Ctee E15 (Radar, Sonar and Navigation) 1986–92 (chm 1990–92), memb Electronics Divnl Bd 1992–96, memb Schs Educn and Liaison Ctee 1993–96; sec Friends of St James the Great Thorley; fell Royal Astronomical Soc 1976, CEng 1983, CPhys 1987, FIEE 1995 (MIEE 1983), FEng 1996; *Publications include* Observations of Cygnus A with the 5-km Radio Telescope (with M Ryle, 1974), Design and Performance Evaluation of a Five Channel Navstar Receiver (jtly, 1982), Application of a Systolic Array to Adaptive Beamforming (jtly, 1984), A Novel Algorithm and Architecture for Adaptive Digital Beamforming (jtly, 1986), Adaptive Antennas for Modern Electronic Systems (1989), Systolic Beamforming - from Theory to Practice (1991); *Recreations* genealogy; *Style*— Dr Philip Hargrave, FEng; ✉ 60 The Paddock, Bishop's Stortford, Herts CM23 4JW (☎ 01279 657273); Nortel Technology, London Road, Harlow, Essex CM17 9NA (☎ 01279 402274, fax 01279 403206, e-mail P.J.Hargrave@nortel.co.uk)

HARGREAVE, Jeremy David Hamilton; s of Colin Oliver Hargreave, of Lytham, Lancs, and Averina Rachel Grace, *née* Hamilton (d 1987); *b* 26 Aug 1955; *Educ* Eton; *m* (m dis), Carolyn Margaret, da of Peter Geoffrey Airey; 1 s (James Oliver b 10 Sept 1985), 1 da (Lucy Victoria b 2 March 1987); *Career* Hargreave (Marsden W) Hale & Co Blackpool: joined 1976, actg sr ptnr 1992, sr ptnr 1993–; MSI(Dip) (memb Stock Exchange 1980); chm Blackpool Progress Business Club, govr Blackpool Sixth Form Coll; *Recreations* walking, tennis, horse riding, reading; *Style*— Jeremy Hargreave, Esq; ✉ Hargreave (Marsden W) Hale & Co, 8–10 Springfield Road, Blackpool FY1 1QN (☎ 01253 21575)

HARGREAVE, Dr Timothy Bruce; s of Lt Cdr John Michael Hargreave, VRD, and Margaret Isobel Hargreave; *b* 23 March 1944; *Educ* Harrow, Univ of London (MB BS, MS); *m* 27 March 1971, Molly; 2 da (Alison Lucinda b 1972, Sophie Louise b 1976); *Career* pt/t sr lectr Univ of Edinburgh, conslt urological surgn Western General Hosps NHS Tst; memb Scientific and Ethical Review Gp Human Reproduction Prog WHO, former chm Steering Ctee WHO Infertility Task Force, former chm Br Andrology Soc, memb Cncl Br Assoc of Urological Surgns, chm Audit Ctee Br Assoc of Urological Surgns, former sec Scot Urological Soc; FRCS, FRCSE, FEB (Urol); *Books* Practical Urological Endoscopy (1988), Management of Male Infertility (1990), Male Infertility (2 edn, 1994); *Recreations* skiing; *Style*— Dr Timothy Hargreave; ✉ Dept of Surgery, Western General Hospital, Edinburgh (☎ 0131 537 1580)

HARGREAVES, Andrew Raikes; MP (C) Birmingham Hall Green (majority 3,665); s of Col David William Hargreaves, and Judith Anne, *née* Currie; *b* 15 May 1955; *Educ* Eton, St Edmund Hall Oxford (MA); *m* 1978, Fiona Susan, da of Guy William Dottridge; 2 s (William b 1985, Thomas b 1986); *Career* auctioneer and valuer Christies 1977–81, exec Hill Samuel 1981–85; asst dir: Sawwa International 1983–85, Schroders 1985–87; MP (C) Birmingham Hall Green 1987–; *Recreations* fishing, gardening, walking; *Clubs* Boodle's; *Style*— Andrew Hargreaves, Esq, MP; ✉ House of Commons, London SW1A 0AA

HARGREAVES, David; s of Herbert Hargreaves (d 1959); *b* 3 June 1930; *Educ* Pocklington Sch; *m* 1978, Jill, da of Joseph Fuller (d 1977); 4 c; *Career* Lt E Yorks Regt Malaya; chm: Hirst and Mallinson until 1980, Hestair plc and subsidiaries until 1990; ptnr Acquest International; chm: Hozelock plc, Heathfield Hargreaves Ltd, Equity Leisure Group Ltd, Primetime Recruitment Ltd, Potter & Moore Ltd, Automotive Products Group Ltd 1995–, Flying Colours Leisure Group Ltd 1996–; dir The Rugby

Group plc; FCA; *Recreations* sailing, golf, gardening; *Clubs* Wisley Golf; *Style—* David Hargreaves, Esq

HARGREAVES, David; s of Harry Gregson Hargreaves (d 1975), and Cissie, *née* Hyde (d 1979); *b* 2 Feb 1940; *Educ* Glossop GS, City of Leeds Tech Coll, Central Sch of Speech and Drama; *m* 24 Oct 1966, Chloe Elizabeth, da of Edward Ashcroft; 1 s (Joseph b 13 March 1968), 1 da (b 12 April 1971); *Career* actor; *Theatre* RSC: Richard II, Richard III, Henry IV Part 1, Julius Caesar, The Lower Middle-Class Wedding Party; West End: The Wars of the Roses, Love for Love, Othello, Not Now Darling, Twelfth Night; NT: Othello, Mother Courage, Love for Love, Much Ado About Nothing, Juno and the Paycock, The Storm, A Flea in her Ear, Rosencrantz and Guildenstern; Moving Theatre: Casment, The Fire Raisers, Antony and Cleopatra; Repertory: St Joan, The Roaring Girl, The Recruiting Officer, It's a Madhouse, Wednesday, Devour the Snow, Happy Jack, Passion in Six Days, A View from the Bridge, The Father, Is this the Day, Raising Hell, A Passionate Woman, Antony & Cleopatra; dir of: Then and Now, Chekhov's Women, Save the Rose; *Television* BBC: The Last Man Out, Z-Cars, Softly Softly, Elizabeth R, The Brothers, The Visitors, A Life is Forever, Stronger than the Sun, Minor Complications, Juliet Bravo, When the Boat Comes In, Truckers, Casualty, All Creatures Great and Small, Harry, Midding Persons; Granada: Crown Court, Home and Away, Coronation Street, Strangers, Making Out, Thatcher the Final Days, Justice for Gemma, Some Kind of Life; Thames: Callan, The Sweeney, Minder, The Bill; Central: Crossroads, Shine On Harvey Moon, Saracen; LWT: The Professionals, Poirot, Expert Witness; YTV: Heartbeat, Home to Roost, The Cost of Loving, 1914 All Out; also Ruth Rendall Mysteries (Meridian), A Strike Out of Time (Channel 4); presenter: Science Workshop, Further Education, Playschool, Jackanory, Pie in the Sky; *Radio* Mrs Dale's Diary Poems by Post, Gregory Dawson - Bright Day, The Last Frontier, Sleeping Dogs Lie; *Films* incl: Othello, Agatha, She's Been Away; *Style—* David Hargreaves, Esq; ✉ c/o Richard Stone Partnership, 25 Whitehall, London SW1A 2BS (☎ 0171 839 6421, fax 0171 839 5002)

HARGREAVES, Prof David Harold; s of Clifford Hargreaves (d 1977), and Marion, *née* Bradley (d 1961); *b* 31 Aug 1939; *Educ* Bolton Sch, Christ's Coll Cambridge (MA, PhD), Univ of Oxford (MA, DPhil); *Career* reader Dept of Educn Univ of Manchester 1964–79 (formerly lectr and sr lectr), reader in educn Univ of Oxford 1979–84 (fell Jesus Coll), chief inspr ILEA 1984–88, prof of educn Univ of Cambridge 1988– (fell Wolfson Coll); memb Research Ctee Teacher Trg Agency 1995–; chm Regnl Arts Bd for the E of England 1991–94, memb ESRC 1991–95; chm Res Centres Bd 1992–94; FRSA 1984; *Books* Social Relations in a Secondary School (1967), Interpersonal Relations and Education (1972), Deviance in Classrooms (1975), The Challenge for the Comprehensive School (1982), The Empowered School (1991), The Mosaic of Learning (1994); *Recreations* the arts; *Style—* Prof David Hargreaves; ✉ Department of Education, University of Cambridge, 17 Trumpington St, Cambridge CB2 1QA (☎ 01223 332888)

HARGREAVES, Ian Richard; s of Ronald Hargreaves (d 1988), and Edna, *née* Cheetham; *b* 18 June 1951; *Educ* Burnley GS, Altrincham GS, Queens' Coll Cambridge; *m* 1, 20 May 1972 (m dis 1991), Elizabeth Anne, da of Charles Crago, of Cornwall; 1 s (Ben b 20 Oct 1975), 1 da (Kelda b 23 June 1977); m 2, 13 Feb 1993, Adele Blakebrough; *Career* Bradford & District Newspapers 1973–76, Financial Times 1976–87, dir BBC News and Current Affrs 1987–90, dep ed Financial Times 1990–94, ed The Independent 1994–95, ed New Statesman 1996–; *Recreations* tennis, football; *Style—* Ian Hargreaves, Esq; ✉ New Statesman, Foundation House, Perseverance Works, 38 Kingsland Road, London E2 8DQ (☎ 0171 739 3211, fax 0171 739 9307)

HARGREAVES, Prof John Desmond; s of Arthur Swire Hargreaves (d 1950), of Colne, Lancs, and Margaret Hilda, *née* Duckworth (d 1968); *b* 25 Jan 1924; *Educ* Ermysted's GS Skipton, Bootham, Univ of Manchester (BA, MA); *m* 30 Sept 1950, Sheila Elizabeth, da of George Samuel Wilks (d 1960), of Stockton, Warwickshire; 2 s (Alastair b 1952, Nicholas b and d 1957), 2 da (Sara b 1953, Catherine b 1959); *Career* 2 Lt The Loyal Regt 1944, served Germany 1945, Malaya 1945–46, T/Capt 1946; asst lectr and lectr in history Univ of Manchester 1948–52, sr lectr Fourah Bay Coll Sierra Leone 1952–54, Burnett-Fletcher prof of history Univ of Aberdeen 1962–85 (lectr 1954–62); visiting prof: Union Coll Schenectady NY 1960–61, Univ of Ibadan 1970–71; Hon DLitt Univ of Sierra Leone 1985; FRHistS 1963; *Books* Prelude to the Partition of West Africa (1963), West Africa Partitioned (two vols, 1974 and 1985), The End of Colonial Rule in West Africa (1979), Aberdeenshire to Africa (1981), Decolonisation in Africa (1988, 2 edn 1996), Academe and Empire (1994); *Recreations* hill walking, theatre; *Style—* Prof John Hargreaves; ✉ Balcluain, 22 Raemoir Rd, Banchory, Kincardine AB31 5UJ

HARGREAVES, John Geoffrey (Jack); CBE (1992); s of Gp Capt Geoffrey William Hargreaves (d 1976), of Chalfont St Peter, Bucks, and Eileen Mary, *née* Page (d 1984); *b* 17 March 1937; *Educ* Canford, RAF Coll Cranwell; *m* 30 Sept 1961, Patricia Anne, da of Maj R C Stowe, RE; 1 s (David Geoffrey b 8 June 1963), 1 da (Sally Gail b 2 March 1967); *Career* with RAF (Supply/Logistics Branch) 1956–93: Sqdn Ldr 1969, Wing Cdr 1976 (station cdr RAF Hendon 1981–83), Gp Capt 1983, Air Cdre 1989 (dir Logistics & Ops RAF 1989–92), ret 1993; sec gen Royal Air Forces Assoc 1993–; FCIT 1991, FIMgt 1992; *Recreations* travel, bridge, garden; *Clubs* RAF; *Style—* Jack Hargreaves, Esq, CBE; ✉ Secretary General, Royal Air Forces Association, 43 Grove Park Road, Chiswick, London W4 3RX (☎ 0181 994 8504, fax 0181 994 4862)

HARGREAVES, Dr (George) Kenneth; s of Albert Hargreaves (d 1969), of St Annes on Sea, Lancs, and Ada, *née* Lord (d 1989); *b* 24 Oct 1928; *Educ* King Edward VII Sch Lytham, Univ of Edinburgh (MB ChB); *m* 24 March 1956, Hazel, da of James Nutter (d 1982), of Clitheroe, Lancs; 2 s (Timothy b 17 Feb 1957, John b 23 Sept 1961), 2 da (Gillian b 27 Feb 1959, Catherine b 10 Sept 1964); *Career* Nat Serv RAMC 1952–54, Capt 1953, OC MRS Hook of Holland 1954; formerly conslt dermatologist: NW RHA 1962–93, Mersey RHA 1974–93, Trent RHA 1989–93, East Cheshire NHS Tst; currently hon conslt dermatologist Salford Royal Hosps NHS Tst; lectr Northern Coll of Chiropody 1962–86, hon lectr Univ of Manchester 1983; pres N of Eng Dermatological Soc 1981 (sec 1963–79), memb Medical Appeals Tbnl; FRCPE 1971; *Recreations* gardening, walking, music; *Style—* Dr Kenneth Hargreaves; ✉ 23 St John St, Manchester M3 4DT (☎ 0161 834 4205, fax 0161 834 4205)

HARGROVES, Brig Sir (Robert) Louis; kt (1987), CBE (1965), DL (Staffs 1974); s of William Robert Hargroves (d 1946), and Mabel Mary Pollock, *née* Lalonde (d 1949); *b* 10 Dec 1917; *Educ* St John's Coll Southsea; *m* 1940, Eileen Elizabeth, da of Lt-Col W M Anderson, CIE (d 1947); 4 da; *Career* cmmnd S Staffs Regt 1938, served WWII India, Sicily and Italy, Brig 1964, ret 1972, Col The Staffordshire Regt (The Prince of Wales's) 1971–77; *Recreations* gardening; *Style—* Brig Sir Louis Hargroves, CBE, DL; ✉ Hyde Cottage, Temple Guiting, Cheltenham, Glos GL54 5RT (☎ 01451 850242, fax 01451 850363)

HARINGTON, Gen Sir Charles Henry Pepys; GCB (1969, KCB 1964, CB 1961), CBE (1957, OBE 1953), DSO (1944), MC (1940); s of Col Hastings Harington (ka 1916), and Dorothy, da of Hon Walter Courtenay Pepys (d 1914), 5 s of 1 Earl of Cottenham (Lord High Chllr of England 1836–41 and 1846–50); *b* 5 May 1910; *Educ* Malvern, Sandhurst; *m* 1942, Victoire Williams-Freeman; 1 s (Guy b 1946), 2 da (Louise (Hon Mrs Alan Gordon Walker) b 1949, Clare (Mrs Julian Calder) b 1956); *Career* cmmnd Cheshire Regt 1930, served WWII NW Europe Co and Bn Cdr, CO 1 Para 1949, Cdr 49 Bde Kenya 1955, Cmdt Sch of Infantry 1958, GOC 3 Div 1959, Cmdt Army Staff Coll 1961, C-in-C Middle East Cmd 1963, DCGS 1966, Chief of Personnel and Logistics to the 3 Services 1968–71, ADC (Gen) to HM The Queen 1969–71; vice pres Star and Garter Home; pres Hurlingham Club; *Style—* Gen Sir Charles Harington, GCB, CBE, DSO, MC; ✉ c/o The Hurlingham Club, Ranelagh Gardens, London SW6

HARINGTON, David Richard; s of His Honour John Charles Dundas Harington, QC (d 1980), and Lavender Cecilia, *née* Denny (d 1982); hp of bro, Sir Nicholas John Harington, 14 Bt *qv*; *b* 25 June 1944; *Educ* Westminster, ChCh Oxford; *m* 1983, Deborah Jane, eldest da of Maurice William Catesby, MC, of Long Compton, Warks; 2 s (John Catesby b 7 Jan 1984, Christopher b 1986); *Style—* David Harington, Esq; ✉ 7 Vale Grove, London W3 7QP (☎ 0181 740 8382)

HARINGTON, Guy Charles; s of Gen Sir Charles Harington, GCB, CBE, DSO, MC, of London, and Victoire Marion, *née* Williams-Freeman; *b* 12 Dec 1946; *Educ* Malvern, Univ Coll Oxford (MA), Loughborough Univ of Technol (MSc); *m* 8 Sept 1984, Kay Elizabeth, *née* Humphreys; 1 s (Charles Hasting b 1986), 1 da (Zara Elizabeth b 1988); *Career* BP 1969–71, dir J Henry Schroder & Co Ltd 1985– (joined 1971); *Clubs* Hurlingham; *Style—* Guy Harington, Esq; ✉ J Henry Schroder & Co Ltd, 120 Cheapside, London EC2V 6DS (☎ 0171 382 6000)

HARINGTON, Sir Nicholas John; 14 Bt (E 1611), of Ridlington, Rutland; s of His Hon late John Charles Dundas Harington, QC (s of Sir Richard Harington, 12 Bt); suc uncle, Sir Richard Dundas Harington, 13 Bt, 1981; *b* 14 May 1942; *Educ* Eton, ChCh Oxford (MA); *Heir* bro, David Richard Harington, *qv*; *Career* called to the Bar 1969; joined Civil Serv 1972; *Style—* Sir Nicholas Harington, Bt; ✉ The Ring o'Bells, Whitbourne, Worcester WR6 5RT

HARKER FARRAND, Prof Margaret Florence; da of Dr Thomas Henry Harker (d 1947), of Southport, Lancs, and Ethel Dean, *née* Dyson (d 1975); *b* 17 Jan 1920; *Educ* Howell's Sch Denbigh (Drapers' Co), Southport Sch of Art, The Polytechnic Regent St London; *m* 20 Dec 1972, Richard George Farrand, s of Frederick George Farrand; *Career* photographer, lectr, historian, author; architectural photographer 1941–59; Univ of Westminster (formerly The Poly of Central London): lectr Sch of Photography 1943–59, head Sch of Photography 1959–74, prof of photography 1972–80, dean Sch of Communications 1974–75, pro rector (asst dir) 1975–80, emeritus prof of photography 1987–; RPS: memb Cncl 1951–76, pres 1958–60, chm Photographic Collection and hon curator of Photographs 1970–79 and 1982–86; memb Cncl: BIPP 1957–72 (pres 1964–65), RSA 1962–67; CNAA: memb Cncl and Ctee for Art & Design 1977–83, chm Photography Bd 1978–83 (memb 1971–83); pres Euro Soc for The History of Photography 1985–, memb Advsy Ctee Nat Museum of Photography Film and Television Bradford 1983–, chm Tstees Photographers' Gallery 1987–94, govr London Coll of Printing 1977–81 and 1982–85; Hon Dr of Arts CNAA 1987; hon fell Br Kinematograph Sound and TV Soc 1969; corresponding memb Deutsche Gesellschaft fur Photographie 1960; Hon FRPS 1960 (FRPS 1942), Hon FBIPP 1972 (FBIPP 1942); *Books* Henry Peach Robinson, Master of Photographic Art 1830–1901 (1988), The Linked Ring, the Secession in Photography 1892–1910 (1979), Victorian and Edwardian Photographs (1975), Julia Margaret Cameron (The Great Photographers series, 1983), W H Fox Talbot (I Grandi Fotografi series, 1983), E Chambré Hardman: Portrait of an Era (1994); *Recreations* gardening, swimming, choral singing; *Style—* Prof Margaret Harker Farrand; ✉ Egdean House, Egdean, nr Pulborough, Sussex RH20 1JU (☎ and fax 01798 865360); University of Westminster, 309–311 Regent St, London W1R 8AL

HARKINS, His Hon Judge Gerard Francis Robert; s of Francis Murphy Harkins (d 1977), and Katherine, *née* Hunt; *b* 13 July 1936; *Educ* Mount St Mary's Coll Spinkhill, King's Coll Univ of Durham (LDS); *Career* dental surgn in gen practice Yorks 1961–70; called to the Bar Middle Temple 1969, in practice NE Circuit 1970–86, asst recorder 1982, circuit judge (NE Circuit) 1986–; govr Mount St Mary's Coll 1990–94, pres The Mount Assoc 1991–92, memb Northumbria Probation Ctee 1993–; *Clubs* Lansdowne; *Style—* His Hon Judge Harkins; ✉ c/o The Law Courts, The Quayside, Newcastle upon Tyne (☎ 0191 201 2000, fax 0191 201 2001)

HARKNESS, Prof David William; OBE (1995); s of William Frederick Samuel Harkness, and Rita Alice, *née* Barrett; *b* 30 Oct 1937; *Educ* Campbell Coll Belfast, Corpus Christi Coll Cambridge (BA, MA), Trinity Coll Dublin (PhD); *m* 29 Aug 1964, Hilary Katherine Margaret, da of William Walker Land (d 1987), of Wilmslow; 1 s (Patrick b 1972), 2 da (Emma b 1967, Lucy b 1969); *Career* RE 1956–58 (2 Lt 1957–58); sr lectr (former asst lectr and lectr) Univ of Kent 1965–75, prof Queen's Univ Belfast 1975–96; memb: Irish Ctee of Historical Sciences 1976–96 (chm 1980–86), Bd of Tstees Ulster Folk and Tport Museum 1978–95 (chm 1985–95), BBC Gen Advsy Cncl 1979–84; jt ed Irish Historical Studies Jl 1978–88; FRHistS; *Books* The Restless Dominion (1969), The Post-War World (1974), The Town in Ireland (ed with M O'Dowd, 1981), Northern Ireland since 1920 (1983), Ireland in the Twentieth Century: divided island (1995); *Recreations* squash, running, tennis, travel; *Style—* Prof David Harkness, OBE; ✉ c/o Department of Modern History, Queen's University, Belfast BT7 1NN (☎ 01232 245133, fax 01232 314611)

HARKNESS, Very Rev James; CB (1993), OBE (1978); s of James Harkness, of Dumfries, and Jane McMorn, *née* Thomson; *b* 20 Oct 1935; *Educ* Dumfries Acad, Univ of Edinburgh (MA); *m* 1960, Elizabeth Anne, da of George Tolmie (d 1959); 1 s (Paul b 1965), 1 da (Jane b 1962); *Career* joined RAChD 1961; DACG: NI 1974–75, 4 Div 1974–78; staff chaplain HQ BAOR 1978–80, asst chaplain gen Scotland 1980–81; sr chaplain: 1 (Br) Corps 1981–82, BAOR 1982–84; dep chaplain gen 1985–86, chaplain gen 1987–95; Moderator of the Gen Assembly of the Church of Scotland 1995–96; Dean of the Chapel Royal in Scotland 1996–; extra chaplain to HM The Queen 1995–, chaplain in ordinary to HM The Queen 1996–; memb: Scotland Against Drugs Advsy Cncl 1996–, Scottish Advsy Ctee Imperial Cancer Research Fund 1995–, Exec Ctee Anglo Israel Assoc 1995–; patron: Napier Univ Craighouse Appeal 1995–, St Mary's Music Sch Appeal 1995–; nat chaplain: Br Limbless Ex-Servicemen's Assoc 1995–, Royal Br Legion Scotland 1995–; gen tstee Church of Scotland 1996–, pres Army Cadet Force Assoc Scotland 1996–; QHC 1982–95; OStJ 1988; FRSA 1992; *Recreations* walking, reading, watching sport; *Clubs* New (Edinburgh, hon memb); *Style—* The Very Rev James Harkness, CB, OBE; ✉ 13 Saxe Coburg Place, Edinburgh EH3 5BR (☎ 0131 343 1297)

HARLAND, (William) Bryce; QSO (1992); s of Edward Dugard Harland (d 1939), and Annie Mcdonald, *née* Gordon (d 1965); *b* 11 Dec 1931; *Educ* Victoria Univ of Wellington NZ (MA), Fletcher Sch of Law & Diplomacy Medford USA (AM); *m* 1, 15 June 1957 (m dis 1977), Rosemary Anne, *née* Gordon; 3 s (James b 1958, Andrew b 1960, d 1978, David b 1962); m 2, 29 June 1979, (Margaret) Anne, da of Andrew Blackburn, of Auckland NZ; 1 s (Thomas b 1981); *Career* joined NZ Foreign Serv 1953, third sec Singapore and Bangkok 1956–59, second sec NZ Mission to UN NY 1959–62, Dept External Affrs Wellington 1962–65, cnsllr NZ Embassy Washington 1965–69, Miny of Foreign Affrs Wellington NZ 1969–73, NZ ambass to China Peking 1973–75, asst sec Foreign Affrs NZ 1976–82, ambass and permanent rep to UN NY 1982–85, NZ high cmmr London 1985–91; chm Econ and Fin Ctee UN General Assembly 1984, visiting fell All Souls Coll Oxford Sept-Dec 1991; hon Liveryman Worshipful Co of Butchers 1986, Girdlers 1991, Freeman City of London 1987–; KStJ 1985; *Books* On Our Own - New Zealand in the Emerging Tripolar World (1992), East Asia - What Next? (1992), Collision Course: America and East Asia, in the Past and the Future (1996); *Recreations* history, music, walking; *Clubs* Royal Over-Seas League; *Style—* Bryce Harland, QSO; ✉ 9 Thordon Court, Harriet Street, Wellington, New Zealand

HARLAND, Air Marshal Sir Reginald Edward Wynyard; KBE (1974), CB (1972), AE; s of Charles Cecil Harland (d 1945); *b* 30 May 1920; *Educ* Stowe, Trinity Coll Cambridge (MA); *m* 1942, Doreen, da of William Hugh Cowie Romanis (d 1972); 2 s, 2 da (and 1 s decd); *Career* joined RAF 1939, served W Med 1942–45, Air Cdre 1965, Harrier project dir Miny Technol 1967–69, idc 1969, AOC 24 Gp 1970–72, Air Vice-Marshal 1970, AO i/c E Air Support Cmd 1972, Air Marshal 1973, AOC-in-C RAF Support Cmd 1973–77; tech dir W S Atkins and Partners Epsom 1977–82, engrg and mgmnt conslt 1982–; chm Suffolk Professional Engineers 1991–; Parly candidate (Alliance) Bury St Edmunds 1983 and 1987; chm: Suffolk Preservation Soc 1988–91, Bury St Edmunds Soc 1993–94; govr ESU 1993–; CEng, CIMgt, FIMechE, FIEE, FRAeS, FRSA, FAPM, FSEE (Soc of Environmental Engrs, pres 1974–77); *Recreations* better management, better government; *Clubs* RAF; *Style*— Air Marshal Sir Reginald E W Harland, KBE, CB, AE; ✉ 49 Crown St, Bury St Edmunds, Suffolk IP33 1QX (☎ 01284 763078)

HARLE, John Crofton; s of Jack Harle, and Joyce, *née* Crofton; *b* 20 Sept 1956; *Educ* Newcastle Royal GS, Royal Coll of Music (Fndn scholar, ARCM); *m* 1985, Julia Jane Eisner; 2 s; *Career* saxophonist, composer, conductor; ldr Myrha Saxophone Quartet 1977–82, formed duo with pianist John Lenehan 1979, saxophone soloist 1980–; appeared at numerous int venues incl: Carnegie Hall, South Bank Centre, BBC Proms, Germany, Switzerland, Far East; soloist Last Night of the Proms 1995 (world premiere of Sir Harrison Birtwistle's saxophone concerto Panic written for him); played with: LSO, English Chamber Orch, Basel Chamber Orch, London Sinfonietta, Northern Sinfonia, BBC orchs; princ saxophone London Sinfonietta 1987–, prof of saxophone Guildhall Sch of Music and Drama 1988–; composer of music for feature films (Butterfly Kiss, Breed of Horses), TV (Love Lies Bleeding, Family, Baby It's You) and advertising (Nissan, Harveys, Sony); regular broadcaster on BBC Radio, featured in One Man and his Sax BBC 2 TV 1988; EMI Classics artist 1990–; Decca recording artist 1991–; Dannreuther Concerto Prize Royal Coll of Music 1980, GLAA Young Musician 1979 and 1980; FGSM 1990; *Books* John Harle's Saxophone Album (1986); *Recreations* family life, cooking, tidying up kids' bedrooms; *Style*— John Harle, Esq; ✉ c/o Clarion/Seven Muses, 47 Whitehall Park, London N19 3TW (☎ 0171 272 4413, fax 0171 281 9687)

HARLECH, 6 Baron (UK 1876); Francis David Ormsby Gore; s of 5 Baron Harlech, PC, KCMG (d 1985), and his 1 w Sylvia (d 1967), da of late Hugh Lloyd Thomas, CMG, CVO; *b* 13 March 1954; *m* 1986, Amanda Jane, da of Alan Thomas Grieve, *qv*, of Stoke St Milborough, nr Ludlow, Shropshire; 1 s (Hon Jasset David Cody), 1 da (Hon Tallulah Sylvia Maria b 16 May 1988); *Heir* s, Hon Jasset David Cody Ormsby Gore b 1 July 1986; *Style*— The Rt Hon the Lord Harlech; ✉ The Mount, Race Course Rd, Oswestry, Shropshire SY10 7PH

HARLECH, Pamela, Lady; Pamela; *née* Colin; o da of Ralph Frederick Colin (d 1985), of NY; *b* 18 Dec 1934; *Educ* Smith Coll, Finch Coll; *m* 11 Dec 1969, as his 2 wife, 5 Baron Harlech, KCMG, PC (d 1985); 1 da (Hon Pandora b 19 April 1972); *Career* journalist/producer; London ed for American Vogue 1965–69, contributing ed to British Vogue 1970–84; tstee V & A 1986–94; memb: South Bank Bd 1986–94, Arts Cncl 1986–90, Cncl of Assoc for Business Sponsorship of the Arts, British-American Arts Assoc 1989–92; chm: Women's Playhouse Tst 1982–94, English Nat Ballet 1990–; *Books* Feast Without Fuss, Pamela Harlech's Complete Book of Cooking, Entertaining and Household Management, Vogue Book of Menus; *Style*— The Rt Hon Pamela, Lady Harlech

HARLEN, Prof Wynne; OBE (1991); da of Arthur Mitchell, and Edith, *née* Radcliffe; *b* 12 Jan 1937; *Educ* Pate's GS for Girls Cheltenham, Univ of Oxford (MA), Univ of Bristol (MA, PhD); *m* 14 Aug 1958, Frank Harlen (d 1987); 1 s (Oliver b 1 Jan 1965), 1 da (Juliet b 9 July 1967); *Career* teacher Cheltenham 1958–60; lectr: St Mary's Coll Cheltenham 1960–64, Glos Coll of Art 1965–66; res fell: Univ of Bristol 1966–73, Univ of Reading 1973–77; sr res fell Univ of London 1977–84, Sidney Jones prof of sci educn Univ of Liverpool 1985–90, dir Scottish Cncl for Res in Educn 1990–; pres BERA 1993–94; memb: Sec of State's Working Gp For Devpt of the Nat Sci Curriculum, Teaching Educn Ctee CNAA, ASE, SERA, EARLI, ASPE, BERA, EERA; *Books* incl: Science 5 to 13: A Formative Evaluation (1975), Guides to Assessment in Education: Science (1983), Teaching and Learning Primary Science (1985, revd edn 1993), Developing Primary Science (with S Jelly, 1989), Environmental Science in the Primary Curriculum (with Elstgeest, 1990), The Teaching of Science (1992, revised edn 1996), UNESCO Sourcebook for Science in the Primary School (1992), Enhancing Quality in Assessment (1994); *Recreations* listening to music, walking; *Style*— Prof Wynne Harlen, OBE; ✉ Scottish Council for Research in Education, 15 St John Street, Edinburgh EH8 8JR (☎ 0131 557 2944, fax 0131 556 9454, e-mail wynne.harlen@ed.ac.uk)

HARLEY, Lt-Gen Sir Alexander George Hamilton; KBE (1996, OBE 1981), CB (1991); s of Lt-Col William Hamilton Coughtrie Harley, 1 Punjab Regt and later Royal Indian Engineers, of Warnham, Sussex, and Eleanor Blanche, *née* Jarvis; *b* 3 May 1941, India; *Educ* Caterham Sch, RMA Sandhurst; *m* 12 Aug 1967, Christina Valentine, da of Edmund Noel Butler-Cole, of Cross-in-Hand, Sussex, and Kathleen Mary, *née* Thompson; 2 s (Oliver b 1973, Angus b 1974); *Career* cmmnd RA 1962; 1963–73: served 7 Para Regt RHA, instr Jr Ldrs, Staff Capt Miny of Def, Adj; Canadian Staff Coll, Mil Asst Miny of Def 1974–75, Battery Cdr 1975–78 (despatches 1978), Directing Staff Staff Coll 1978–79, CO 19 Field Regt RA 1979–82, Col Def Staff Miny of Def 1983–85, Cdr 33 Armd Bde 1985–88, Asst Chief of Staff Ops N Army Gp 1988–90, Asst Chief of Def Staff (Overseas) Miny of Def 1990–93, Cdr Br Forces Cyprus and Admin of the Sovereign Base Areas 1993–95, Dep Chief of Staff (Commitments) MOD 1995–; Regtl Col 19 Field Regt RA, pres Combined Servs Hockey, patron NORDICS Hockey; FIMgt 1982; *Recreations* country pursuits, clocks, hockey; *Clubs* Royal Cwlth Soc; *Style*— Lt-Gen Sir Alexander Harley, KBE, CB; ✉ Ministry of Defence (DCDS(C)), Whitehall, London SW1A 2HB

HARLEY, Basil Hubert; s of Mervyn Ruthven Harley, JP (d 1973), of Stud Farm, Lamb Corner, Dedham, Essex, and Marion, *née* Parkinson (d 1973); *b* 17 July 1930; *Educ* Harrow, St John's Coll Oxford (MA); *m* 10 Oct 1959, Annette, da of Edgar Wolstan Bertram Handsley Milne-Redhead, ISO, MBE, TD; 3 da (Jane Elizabeth b 12 Oct 1960, Emma Katherine b 7 June 1962, Harriet Susanna b 15 May 1965); *Career* Nat Serv RA 1949–50, cmmnd 2 Lt 1949, 17 Trg Regt Oswestry 1949–50, Capt TA Queen's Own Oxfords Hussars & Royal Bucks Yeo 1950–60; md Curwen Press Ltd 1964–82; dir: Curwen Prints Ltd 1970–92, Wedge Entomological Res Fndn US at Nat Museum Natural History Washington DC 1974–; chm and md Harley Books Natural History Publishers (BH & A Harley Ltd) 1983–; chm Wynken de Worde Soc 1975, memb Exec Ctee Nat Book League 1974–78; Liveryman Worshipful Co of Stationers & Newspaper Makers 1973–; fell Linnean Soc 1955, fell Royal Entomological Soc 1981; *Books* The Curwen Press A Short History (1970), Martin Lister's English Spiders, 1678 (co-trans from Latin and co-ed, 1992); *Recreations* natural history, reading; *Clubs* Utd Oxford and Cambridge Univ, Double Crown (pres 1996); *Style*— Basil Harley, Esq; ✉ Martins, Great Horkesley, Colchester, Essex CO6 4AH (☎ 01206 271 216, fax 01206 271 182)

HARLEY, Christopher Charles; s of Maj John Ralph Henry Harley, JP, DL (d 1960), of Brampton Bryan, and Rachel Mary, *née* Gwyer (d 1967); *b* 31 Dec 1926; *Educ* Eton, Magdalene Coll Cambridge; *m* 2 April 1959, Susan Elizabeth, da of Sir Roderick Barclay, GCVO, KCMG, of Latimer, Bucks; 4 s (Edward b 1960, John b 1961, Adrian b 1965, Philip b 1969); *Career* mech engr until 1956; landowner Brampton Bryan 1956–; past pres Herefordshire branch CLA; JP 1960, DL 1987, High Sheriff of Hereford and Worcs 1987–88; memb Nat Tst Severn Regnl Ctee 1968–93; CEng; *Recreations* shooting, forestry; *Style*— Christopher Harley, Esq; ✉ Brampton Bryan Hall, Bucknell, Shropshire SY7 0DJ (☎ 01547 530241)

HARLEY, Ian; *Educ* Falkirk HS, Univ of Edinburgh (BA, MA); *m*; 3 s; *Career* articled clerk Touche Ross & Co 1972, later in Corp Planning Dept Morgan Crucible Ltd; Abbey National plc: joined Abbey National Building Society as financial analyst 1977, SE regnl mangr Retail Ops Div 1984–86, commercial mangr for business devpt 1986, gp financial controller 1986–88, asst gen mangr fin 1988–91, fin dir retail ops 1991–92, ops dir 1992, gp treas 1992–93, gp fin dir and memb main bd 1993–; MICAS, FCA; *Style*— Ian Harley, Esq; ✉ Abbey National plc, Abbey House, Baker Street, London NW1 6XL (☎ 0171 612 4000, fax 0171 486 2764)

HARLEY, Prof Ian Allan; s of Gordon Nicoll Harley (d 1986), of Maryborough, Queensland, and Bessie Winifred, *née* Shapcott (d 1975); *b* 4 April 1932; *Educ* Maryborough State HS, Univ of Queensland (BSurv), Univ of London (PhD); *m* 11 Jan 1957 (m dis 1996), (Margaret) Wendy, da of Oswald Hoskin, (d 1941), of Brisbane, Queensland; 3 s (David b 1960, William b 1962, Robert b 1964), 1 da (Anne b 1966); *Career* surveyor Queensland Surveyor-Gen's Dept 1953–59, surveyor Mount Isa Mines Ltd 1959, head Dept of Surveying Univ of Queensland 1973–82 (staff memb 1963–82), res fell Alexander Von Humbolt Fndn Univ of Stuttgart 1969, dean Faculty of Engrg UCL 1985–88 (prof and head Dept of Photogrammetry and Surveying 1982–), vice dean Faculty of Engrg Univ of London 1991–94; pres British Aust Studies Assoc 1990–92; FISAust, FRICS, FRSA, FRGS; *Recreations* music (all kinds), reading, walking, swimming; *Style*— Prof Ian Harley; ✉ 37 Ridgmount Gardens, London WC1E 7AT (☎ 0171 580 3444); Department of Photogrammetry and Surveying, University College London, Gower St, London WC1E 6BT (☎ 0171 380 7225, fax 0171 380 0453, e-mail iah@ps.ucl.ac.uk)

HARLEY, Paul Stuart; s of Brian Erskine Harley (d 1972), of Melbourne, Australia, and Elizabeth Ann Charlton, *née* Allan; *b* 20 June 1939; *Educ* St Lawrence Coll Kent, Univ Coll of N Staffs Keele (IEE PtIII); *m* 15 April 1963, Sally Ann, da of Eugene Prosser, of Wilts; 2 s (Nicholas b 1965, Adam b 1970), 1 da (Cherie-Ann b 1973); *Career* electrical engr, inventor of Welliwarma; md: Wiltsavon Leisure Ltd 1984–86, Hammond Showjumps Ltd 1992–93; ptnr Draychem-Glostec, tech and mktg conslt to various cos; *Recreations* choral singing, riding; *Style*— Paul S Harley, Esq; ✉ April Cottage, The Street, Cherhill, Calne, Wilts SN11 8XR

HARLEY, Sophie Elizabeth; da of Dr Clifford Elliot Harley, and Anne Maureen, *née* Phillips; *b* 14 Jan 1965; *Educ* Bryanston, W Surrey Coll of Art & Design (BA), RCA (MA); *Career* jewellery designer 1990–, fndr memb The New RenaisCAnce (multi media co specialising in fashion and accessory design, display, styling and video prodn) 1991–; gp and solo exhbns incl: Taxidermy, Love and Letters (Southbank Crafts Gallery) 1990, Six of the Best (Barbican Centre) 1990, The Art Machine (McLellan Gallery Glasgow) 1990, Triennale Europeenne du Bijou (Musee du Luxembourg Paris) 1990, From the Heart (Fouts & Fowler Gallery) 1991, The Evening Standard Art Machine (Barbican) 1991, Celebration of Gold (Mappin & Webb London) 1991, De Beers Diamond Showcase (David Thomas London) 1991, Four Play - The World of New RenaisCAnce (Royal Festival Hall and Parco Gallery Tokyo) 1992, Decorative Arts Today (Bonhams Knightsbridge) 1992, Court Couture 1992 (Kensington Palace) 1992, The World of New RenaisCAnce (Tokyo) 1992, Dazzle (NT) 1992, Decorative Arts Today (Bonhams Knightsbridge) 1993, Crafts in Performance (Crafts Cncl touring exhbn) 1993; New Generation catwalk show as part of London Fashion Week (with The New RenaisCAnce) 1994; Greater London Arts Award 1992; lectr various colls of art nationwide incl RCA (actg conslt on course structure); *Style*— Ms Sophie Harley; ✉ Studio W2, Cockpit Studios, Cockpit Yard, London WC1N 2NP (☎ 0171 430 2070, fax 0171 916 2455)

HARMAN, Claire Patricia; da of John Edward Harman, of the Isle of Skye, and Patricia Josephine, *née* Mullins; *b* 21 Sept 1957; *Educ* Farnborough Hill Convent, Univ of Manchester (BA, Samuel James Wheeler Prize); *m* 1979, Michael Norton Schmidt, s of Carl Bernhardt Schmidt; 2 s (Charles b 21 March 1980, Benedict b 19 Oct 1985), 1 da (Isabel b 12 July 1982); *Career* with Carcanet Press Manchester 1979–81, co-ordinating ed PN Review Manchester 1981–84; awarded John Llewelyn Rhys Prize 1990; memb Soc of Authors 1990; *Books* Sylvia Townsend Warner - Collected Poems (ed, 1982, Carcanet), Sylvia Townsend Warner - A Biography (1989, Chatto & Windus), Robert Louis Stevenson - Essays and Poems (ed, 1992, Everyman), Robert Louis Stevenson - Selected Stories (ed, 1992, Everyman), Sylvia Townsend Warner - Diaries (ed, 1994, Chatto & Windus); *Style*— Ms Claire Harman; ✉ c/o Rachel Calder, Tessa Sayle Agency, 11 Jubilee Place, London SW3 3TE (☎ 0171 823 3883)

HARMAN, Harriet; MP (Lab) Peckham (majority 12,005); da of Dr John Bishop Harman (d 1994), and Anna Charlotte Malcolm Spicer; niece of Countess of Longford; *b* 20 July 1950; *Educ* St Paul's Girls' Sch, Univ of York; *m* Jack Dromey (sec of SE Area TUC, nat sec TGWU); 2 s, 1 da; *Career* lawyer, memb Liberty (formerly Nat Cncl for Civil Liberties); MP (Lab) Peckham 1982–; oppn front bench spokesperson: on health and social servs 1984–89, on health 1989–92; shadow chief sec to the Treasy 1992–94; chief oppn spokesperson on: employment 1994–95, health 1995–96, social security 1996–; elected to Lab NEC 1993–; *Books* The Century Gap (1993); *Style*— Ms Harriet Harman, MP; ✉ House of Commons, London SW1A 0AA

HARMAN, Hon Mr Justice; Hon Sir Jeremiah LeRoy Harman; kt (1982); s of Rt Hon Sir Charles Eustace Harman (d 1970), and Helen Sarah LeRoy Lewis (d 1992); *b* 13 April 1930; *Educ* Eton; *m* 1960 (m dis 1986), Erica, da of Hon Sir Maurice Bridgeman, KBE (d 1980, 3 s of 1 Viscount Bridgeman); 2 s (Charles Richard LeRoy b 1963, Toby John b 1967), 1 da (Sarah Jane (Mrs Hugh Lewis Evans) b 1962); m 1987, Katharine, da of late Rt Hon Sir Eric Sachs; *Career* served Coldstream Gds and Para Regt 1948–51; called to the Bar Lincoln's Inn 1954, QC 1968, bencher Lincoln's Inn 1977, barr Hong Kong 1978, Singapore Bar 1980, judge of the High Court of Justice (Chancery Div) 1982–, Keeper of the Black Book Lincoln's Inn 1997–; *Recreations* fishing, bird watching, reading; *Style*— The Hon Mr Justice Harman; ✉ The Royal Courts of Justice, The Strand, London WC2A 2LL

HARMAN, Robert Donald; QC (1974); s of late Herbert Donald Harman, MC; *b* 26 Sept 1928; *Educ* St Paul's, Magdalen Coll Oxford; *m* 1, 1960, Sarah Elizabeth (d 1965), da of late G C Cleverly; 2 s; m 2, 1968, Rosamond Geraldine, JP, da of late Cdr G T A Scott, RN; 2 da; *Career* called to the Bar Gray's Inn 1954 (bencher 1984), in practice SE Circuit, head of chambers; treasy counsel Central Criminal Ct 1967–74, recorder Crown Ct 1972–, judge Cts of Appeal Jersey and Guernsey 1986–; Liveryman Worshipful Co of Goldsmiths; *Clubs* Garrick, Beefsteak, Pratt's; *Style*— Robert Harman, Esq, QC; ✉ The Clock House, Sparsholt, Winchester, Hants SO21 2LX (☎ 01962 776461); 2 Harcourt Buildings, Temple, London EC4 (☎ 0171 353 2112)

HARMAN, Robert Lawrence; s of Roderick Frank Harman (Gp Capt RAF, d 1994), and Katharine Lawrence, *née* Leopold; *b* 30 July 1947; *Educ* Wellington, St Catharine's Coll Cambridge (MA); *m* 1972, Wendy; 1 s (Daniel b 1976), 1 da (Antonia b 1980); *Career* currently ptnr & head Property Department Travers Smith Braithwaite (joined 1970); memb Law Soc; *Clubs* City of London, Royal Society of Arts; *Style*— Robert Harman, Esq; ✉ Travers Smith Braithwaite, 10 Snow Hill, London EC1A 2AL (☎ 0171 248 9133, fax 0171 236 3728)

HARMAR-NICHOLLS, Baron (Life Peer 1974), of Peterborough, Cambs; Sir Harmar Harmar-Nicholls; 1 Bt (1960), JP; s of Charles Nicholls; *b* 1 Nov 1912; *Educ* Queen Mary's GS Walsall, Middle Temple; *m* 1940, Dorothy Elsie, eldest da of James Edwards, of Tipton, Staffs; 2 da (Hon Judith Ann (Hon Mrs Aspden) b 1941, Hon Susan Frances (Hon Mrs Eden) b 1943); *Career* takes Cons Whip in House of Lords; MP (C) Peterborough 1950–74; PPS to Asst Postmaster-Gen 1951–55; Parly sec: MAFF 1955–57, Miny of Works 1957–60; MEP (EDG) Gtr Manchester South 1979–84; chm: Nicholls and Hennessy (Hotels) Ltd, Malvern Festival Theatre Trust Ltd; dir: J and H Nicholls and Co, Radio Luxemburg (London) Ltd; Lloyd's underwriter; *Style*— The Rt Hon the Lord Harmar-Nicholls, JP; ✉ Abbeylands, Weston, Stafford (☎ 01889 270 252)

HARMAR-NICHOLLS, Hon Susan Frances; *see:* Nicholls, Susan

HARMER, Dr Clive Lucas; s of Cecil Norman Harmer (d 1986), and Elizabeth Mary, *née* Lucas (d 1989); *b* 18 Aug 1940; *Educ* Westminster Hosp Med Sch (MB BS, FRCP); *m* 9 Nov 1993, Pauline Ann Cattell; 2 da from prev m (Kasha b 1968, Victoria b 1971); *Career* instr Dept of Radiation Oncology Stanford Univ California 1970; conslt in radiotherapy and oncology: St Luke's Hosp Guildford 1970–73, St George's Hosp London 1973–; currently head Radiotherapy Servs and Thyroid Unit Royal Marsden Hosp London; chm of examiners for dip of oncology Univ of London; memb: RSM, Br Inst of Radiology; FRCR 1968; *Recreations* wildlife photography; *Clubs* Wig & Pen, Stocks; *Style*— Dr Clive Harmer; ✉ St George's Hospital, Blackshaw Rd, London SW17 0QT; Royal Marsden Hospital, Fulham Rd, London SW3 6JJ

HARMSWORTH, Hildebrand Esmond Miles; s and h of Sir Hildebrand Harold Harmsworth, 3 Bt, *qv*; *b* 1 Sept 1964; *Educ* Dean Close Sch Cheltenham, Crewe and Alsager Coll; *m* 23 Dec 1988, Ruth Denise, da of Dennis Miles, of Cheltenham; 1 s (Hildebrand Darcy Laurence b 16 July 1994), 2 da (Alice Katherine Elspeth b 23 March 1990, Grace Hester Elaine b 28 Dec 1991); *Recreations* hockey, golf; *Style*— Hildebrand Harmsworth, Esq; ✉ 14 Miles Road, Epsom, Surrey KT19 9AO

HARMSWORTH, Sir Hildebrand Harold; 3 Bt (UK 1922), of Freshwater Grove, Parish of Shipley, Co Sussex; s of Sir Hildebrand Alfred Beresford Harmsworth, 2 Bt (d 1977), and Elen, *née* Billenstein; *b* 5 June 1931; *Educ* Harrow, Trinity Coll Dublin; *m* 1960, Gillian Andrea, o da of William John Lewis, of Tetbury, Gloucs; 1 s (Hildebrand Esmond Miles b 1964), 2 da (Claire Elen Mary b 1961, Kirsten Elizabeth Ashley b 1963); *Heir* s, Hildebrand Esmond Miles Harmsworth, *qv*; *Style*— Sir Hildebrand Harmsworth, Bt; ✉ Ewlyn Villa, 42 Leckhampton Rd, Cheltenham, Gloucs

HARMSWORTH, Hon (Harold) Jonathan Esmond Vere; s and h of 3 Viscount Rothermere, *qv*, and his 1 wife, Patricia Evelyn Beverley, *née* Matthews (d 1992); *b* 3 Dec 1967; *m* 15 July 1993, Claudia C, da of T J and Patricia Clemence, of Wilton Crescent, London SW1; 1 s (Vere Richard Jonathan Harold b 20 Oct 1994); *Style*— The Hon Jonathan Harmsworth

HARMSWORTH, Madeleine Thérèse Margaret; da of Hon Eric Beauchamp Northcliffe Harmsworth (d 1988), and Hélène Marie, *née* Dehove (d 1962); *b* 10 July 1941; *Educ* Pole's Convent Ware Herts, Somerville Coll Oxford (MA); *Career* journalist; Sunday Mirror: gen reporter 1962, film critic 1965–93, theatre critic 1979–88, letters page ed 1985–93, travel corr 1991–93; freelance journalist (previously under pseudonym Hannah Carter) for nat newspapers and jls; memb BBC's Central Music Advsy Ctee 1973–80, govr Dr Johnson's House Tst 1982–; memb The Critics' Circle 1971–; *Recreations* cycling, trekking, swimming; *Style*— Ms Madeleine Harmsworth; ✉ 15 Sudeley St, London N1 8HP (☎ 0171 278 6022)

HARMSWORTH, 3 Baron (UK 1939); Thomas Harold Raymond Harmsworth; o s of Hon Eric Beauchamp Northcliffe Harmsworth (d 1988), and Hélène Marie, *née* Dehove (d 1962); suc uncle 2 Baron Harmsworth 1990; *b* 20 July 1939; *Educ* Eton, Christ Church Oxford; *m* 26 June 1971, Patricia Palmer, da of Michael Palmer Horsley, of Waltham House, Brough, N Humberside; 2 s (Hon Dominic Michael Eric b 18 Sept 1973, Hon Timothy Thomas John b 6 April 1979), 3 da (Hon Philomena Hélène Olivia b 10 Feb 1975, Hon Abigail Patricia Thérèse b 14 June 1977, Hon Pollyanna Mary Clare b 8 Sept 1981); *Heir* s, Hon Dominic Harmsworth; *Career* Nat Serv 2 Lt Royal Horse Gds 1957–59; in the City 1962–74, Civil Serv 1974–88, publisher 1988–; chm Dr Johnson's House Gough Square London; *Style*— The Lord Harmsworth; ✉ The Old Rectory, Stoke Abbott, Beaminster, Dorset DT8 3JT

HARNDEN, Prof David Gilbert; s of William Alfred Harnden (d 1934), of London, and Anne McKenzie, *née* Wilson (d 1983); *b* 22 June 1932; *Educ* George Heriot's Sch Edinburgh, Univ of Edinburgh (BSc, PhD); *m* 9 July 1955, Thora Margaret, da of Alexander Ralph Seatter (d 1945), of Burray, Orkney; 3 s (Ralph b 1957, Mark b 1960, Richard b 1965); *Career* lectr Univ of Edinburgh 1956–57, sci memb MRC Harwell and Edinburgh 1957–69, res fell Univ of Wisconsin USA 1963–64, prof of cancer studies Univ of Birmingham 1969–83, dir Paterson Inst for Cancer Res Manchester 1983–, prof of experimental oncology Univ of Manchester 1983–; chm Br Assoc Cancer Res 1984–87, pres Assoc Clinical Cytogeneticists 1985–88, chm Editorial Bd Br Journal of Cancer; many papers on cytogenetics and cancer published in learned jls and books; FIBiol 1970, FRCPath 1983, FRSE 1983, Hon MRCP 1987; *Recreations* sketching, a little gardening; *Style*— Prof David Harnden, FRSE; ✉ Tanglewood, Ladybrook Road, Bramhall, Stockport, Cheshire SK7 3NE (☎ 0161 485 3214); Paterson Institute for Cancer Research, Christie Hospital (NHS) Trust, Wilmslow Road, Manchester M20 9BX (☎ 0161 446 3101, fax 0161 446 3109, telex 934999 TXLINKG)

HARNEY, Desmond Edward St Aubyn; OBE (1968); s of Edward Augustine St Aubyn Harney, KC, MP (d 1929), of London, and Kathleen, *née* Anderson (d 1973); *b* 14 Feb 1929; *Educ* Corby Sch Sunderland, Univ of Durham (BSc), Univ of Cambridge, SOAS London; *m* 10 July 1954, Judith Geraldine, da of Daniel McCarthy Downing (d 1940), of Dublin; 1 s (Richard Tindle b 16 Oct 1958), 2 da (Geraldine Anne b 3 July 1955, Bridget Clare b 14 Sept 1957); *Career* Nat Serv RAF 1947–49; ICI 1954–56, cnsllr HM Dip Serv Iran and Kenya 1956–74, dir Morgan Grenfell & Co Ltd 1974–87; non-exec dir: London Brick plc 1981–85, Equatorial Bank plc 1986–93; chm Irano-British C of C 1976–79, pres Br Inst of Persian Studies 1995–; cnsllr Royal Borough of Kensington and Chelsea 1986– (mayor 1993–94); *Recreations* photography, astronomy, skiing; *Clubs* Garrick; *Style*— Mr Desmond Harney, OBE; ✉ 16 Stafford Terrace, London W8 7BH (☎ 0171 938 3291, fax 0171 937 0423); Broadwater, Sherborne, Cheltenham, Glos GL54 3DR (☎ 01451 844271)

HARNIMAN, John Phillip; OBE (1984); s of William Thomas Harniman (d 1941), and Maud Kate Florence, *née* Dyrenfurth (d 1980); *b* 7 May 1939; *Educ* Leyton CHS, Culham Coll (Dip Ed), Univ of London (BA), Université de Paris; *m* 26 August 1961, Avryl, da of Harold Hartley (d 1953); 1 s (Denzil b 20 Nov 1971), 1 da (Claire-Elise b 24 Dec 1968); *Career* teacher William Morris Sch Walthamstow 1960–62, lectr Ecole Normale Supérieure de St Cloud 1962–67; British Council: Algeria 1967–70, asst dir personnel 1970–76, dir Singapore 1976–81, cultural attaché Romania 1981–84, cultural cnsllr and dir Belgium and Luxembourg 1984–87, dir of trg Br Cncl London 1988–92, cultural cnsllr and dir Canada 1992–96; *Recreations* music, reading, letter writing, cats; *Style*— John Harniman, Esq, OBE; ✉ Shilling Orchard, Shilling Street, Lavenham, Sudbury, Suffolk CO10 9RH

HARPER, Alan Henry; s of Frank Dennis Harper (d 1969), of Essex, and Patricia May Harper; *b* 27 Jan 1943; *Educ* Southend GS; *m* 9 Oct 1965, Nicol Susan, da of Owen Jaques Reid; 3 da (Selina Anne b 24 Feb 1968, Anita Carol b 29 May 1970, Carol Ann b 6 May 1979); *Career* commodities broker; Louis Dreyfus & Co: post boy and contract clerk London Grain Market 1958–59, trainee trader London Oilseeds Market 1960–63, trader Jute Market Calcutta 1964–65; Andre & Co: trader Animal Feed Markets India 1964–66, trader London Rice and Grain Markets 1966–74; proprietor and md Coley & Harper Ltd futures brokers London 1974–89, md Jackson Son & Co rice brokers London 1989–; chm Baltic Exchange Ltd 1994–96 (dir 1982–87 and 1989–96); Freeman City of London, Liveryman Worshipful Co of Shipwrights; *Recreations* sailing, swimming, tennis, skiing; *Style*— Alan Harper, Esq; ✉ Ancas Commodities Ltd, Hillersdon, Hervines Road, Amersham, Bucks HP6 5HS (☎ 01494 434560, fax 01494 434577)

HARPER, Prof Anthony John; s of Maurice Colston Harper (d 1984), and Evelyn, *née* Thomas; *b* 26 May 1938; *Educ* Univ of Bristol (BA, MA), Univ of Edinburgh (PhD); *m* 4 April 1964, Sandra, da of Harold Green; 1 s (Stephen b 20 March 1971), 2 da (Veronica b 7 Oct 1965, Anne b 12 Nov 1967); *Career* lectr Univ of Edinburgh 1964–79 (asst lectr 1962–64), prof of German studies Univ of Strathclyde 1979– (head of German studies 1979–95); *Books* German Today (with E McInnes, 1967), David Schirmer - A Poet of the German Baroque (1977), Time and Change - Essays on German and European Literature (1982), Schriften zur Lyrik Leipzigs 1620–70 (1985), The Song Books of Gottfried Finckelthaus (1988), Studien zum weltlichen deutschen Kunstlied (with Gudrun Burch, 1992), The European Emblem - Tradition and Variety (with Alison Adams, 1992), Christian Brehme - edition of Lustige Gedichte (1994); *Style*— Prof Anthony J Harper; ✉ 101 Stirling Drive, Bishopbriggs, Glasgow G64 3PG (☎ 0141 772 2905); University of Strathclyde, Department of Modern Languages, 26 Richmond Street, Glasgow G1 1XH (☎ 0141 552 4400)

HARPER, Douglas Ross; s of Louis R Harper (d 1973), of Aberdeen, and Margaret Hall, *née* Cartwright; *b* 16 Feb 1940; *Educ* Aberdeen GS; *m* 19 July 1968, Dorothy Constance, da of Norman F Wisely (d 1991), of Methlick, Aberdeenshire; 1 s (Ross b 1973), 3 da (Caroline b 1969, Lorraine b 1971, Helen b 1977); *Career* jr surgical post Aberdeen Royal Infirmary 1967–73, sr surgical registrar Edinburgh Royal Infirmary 1973–76, conslt gen surgn Falkirk and Dist Royal Infirmary 1976–, med dir Falkirk and Dist Royal Infirmary Tst 1994–, clinical sr lectr Dept of Clinical Surgery Univ of Edinburgh 1976–; memb: Cncl of Mgmnt Strathcarron Hospice, Assoc of Surgns, Vascular Surgical Soc; FRCSE 1971, FRCS 1972, FRCS Glasgow 1985; *Recreations* hillwalking; *Style*— Mr Douglas Harper; ✉ Glenallan, 16 Upper Glen Rd, Bridge of Allan, Stirlingshire FK9 4PX (☎ 01786 832242); Falkirk & District Royal Infirmary, Major's Loan, Falkirk, Stirlingshire (☎ 01324 616059)

HARPER, Gerald George Frederick; s of Ernest George Harper, and Mary Elizabeth, *née* Thomas; *b* 15 Feb 1929; *Educ* Haileybury; *m* 1, 1958 (m dis), Jane Downs; 1 s (James), 1 da (Sarah b 1959); m 2, (m dis 1983), Carla, *née* Rabaiotti; *Career* actor; Nat Serv 2 Lt Army 1947–49; broadcaster Capital Radio for ten years, former presenter Saturday Selection BBC Radio 2; *Theatre* London stage debut How He Lied to Her Husband (Arts Theatre) 1951, Liverpool Repertory 1952, No News From Father (Cambridge Theatre London) 1955, Free as Air (Savoy) 1957, Broadway debut with Old Vic Co (tour) 1960, Boeing Boeing (Broadway) 1965; other theatre incl: House Guest (Savoy), Baggage (Vaudeville), Suddenly at Home (Fortune), Royal Baccarat Scandal (Sadler's Wells Royal), The Little Hut (Duke of York's), Murder By Misadventure (Vaudeville), one man show The King's Trumpeter (tour); *Television* series Adam Adamant, Hadleigh (most popular actor on TV award twice); *Films* incl: The Admirable Crichton, The Dambusters, The Young Ones, League of Gentlemen, The Lady Vanishes; *Style*— Gerald Harper, Esq; ✉ London Management, 2–4 Noel Street, London W1 (☎ 0171 287 9000)

HARPER, Heather (Mrs Eduardo Benarroch); CBE; da of Hugh Harper, of Belfast, and Mary Eliza, *née* Robb; *b* 8 May 1930; *Educ* Ashleigh House Sch Belfast, Trinity Coll of Music (FTCL); *m* 19 May 1973, Eduardo J Benarroch, s of Hector A Benarroch, of Buenos Aires; *Career* soprano; leading int opera and concert singer 1954–91, has sung at all major opera houses and with all major symphony orchs in the world; recent seasons incl: Japan, Hong Kong, Australia, New York, Geneva, Rome, Milan, Madrid, Vienna, Paris, Amsterdam, Los Angeles; soprano soloist: first BBC Symphony Orch Far East tour 1982, first BBC Philharmonic Orch South American tour 1989; regular soloist: Covent Garden, New York Met, Teatro Colon Buenos Aires; notable performances incl: Elsa in Lohengrin (Bayreuth debut, conducted by Kempe), Countess in The Marriage of Figaro, Deutsche Opera Berlin (conducted by Barenboim), Arabella and Chrysothemis, Die Marschallin and Die Kaiserin by Richard Strauss, farewell concert with LSO Barbican Hall 1991, came out of retirement to sing 2 concerts at The Henry Wood Promenade Concerts 100th Anniversary 1994; world premieres incl: Britten's War Requiem Coventry Cathedral 1962, Mrs Coyle in Britten's Owen Wingrave 1971, Tippett's Third Symphony 1972, Nadia in Tippett's The Icebreak Covent Garden 1975, Britten's Praise We Great Men 1985; recorded over 90 major works with all main recording cos in Britain and abroad; prof of singing and conslt RCM 1985–93, hon dir of singing studies Britten-Pears Sch Snape, visiting lectr RSAMD 1988, vice pres N Ireland Youth Symphony Orch; Hon DMus Queen's Univ Belfast 1964, DLitt Univ of Ulster 1991; Hon RAM 1972, Hon FTCL, Hon FRCM 1988, RSA 1989, Hon GSM 1995; *Awards* incl: Edison Award for Britten's Les Illuminations, Grammy nomination for Berg's Seven Early Songs, Grammy Award Best Solo Recording for Ravel's Scheherazade 1984, Grammy Award 1991 and Grand Prix du Disque for Peter Grimes,; *Recreations* reading, biographies, gardening; *Style*— Miss Heather Harper, CBE

HARPER, James Norman; s of His Hon Judge Norman Harper (d 1967), and Iris Irene, *née* Rawson (d 1989); *b* 30 Dec 1932; *Educ* Marlborough, Magdalen Coll Oxford (BA); *m* 1956, Blanka Miroslava Eva, da of Miroslav Sigmund, of Henley on Thames; 1 s, 1 da; *Career* Lt RA (Nat Serv and TA for 3 years); called to the Bar Gray's Inn 1957, recorder 1980, in practice NE Circuit, attorney gen North Eastern Circuit 1992–95; pres Northumberland Co Hockey Assoc 1982–; *Recreations* cricket, hockey; *Clubs* MCC; *Style*— James Harper, Esq; ✉ 59 Kenton Rd, Gosforth, Newcastle upon Tyne NE3 4NJ (☎ 0191 285 7611)

HARPER, Prof John Lander; CBE (1989); s of John Hindley Harper, and Harriet Mary, *née* Archer; *b* 27 May 1925; *Educ* Lawrence Sheriff Sch Rugby, Magdalen Coll Oxford (MA, DPhil); *m* 8 Jan 1954, Borgny, da of Toralf Lero; 1 s (Jonathan b 24 Sept 1960), 2 da (Belinda b 19 Jan 1955, Claire b 20 Jan 1957); *Career* univ demonstrator Dept of Agric Univ of Oxford 1948–60, prof of botany Univ of N Wales 1967–82 (prof of agric botany 1960–67), emeritus prof Univ of Wales 1982–; memb: NERC 1971–78 and 1987–90, AFRC 1980–90, JNCC 1990–94; ed Proceedings of the Royal Soc 1993–; tstee Natural History Museum 1990–; foreign assoc Nat Acad of Sci USA, foreign memb American Acad of Arts and Scis; Hon DSc Univ of Sussex 1984, Doctor (hc) Autonomous Univ of Mexico 1996; FRS 1978 (memb Cncl 1987–89, Darwin medal 1990); *Books* Population Biology of Plants (1977), Ecology: Individuals, Populations and Communities (with M Begon and C Townsend, 1986, 3 edn 1996); *Recreations* gardening; *Clubs* Farmers'; *Style*— Prof John Harper, CBE, FRS; ✉ Cae Groes, Glan-y-Coed Park, Dwygyfylchi, Penmaenmawr, Conwy LL34 6TL (☎ 01492 622362, fax 01492 623997)

HARPER, Prof John Martin; s of Geoffrey Martin Harper, of Wednesbury, W Midlands, and Kathleen, *née* Birks; *b* 11 July 1947; *Educ* King's Coll Sch Cambridge, Clifton (music scholar), Selwyn Coll Cambridge (organ scholar, MA), Univ of Birmingham (PhD); *m* 1, 1 July 1970 (m dis), Cynthia Margaret, da of George Dean, of Combe Down, Bath; 3 s (Edward John b 1976, William George b 1978, Joseph Martin b 1985); m 2, 21 Dec 1991, Sally Elizabeth, da of late John Stephen Roper; *Career* music tutor Ingestre Hall Stafford 1970–71, lectr in music Univ of Birmingham 1974–75 and

1976–81, asst dir of music King Edward's Sch Birmingham 1975–76, fell and tutor in music Magdalen Coll Oxford (also organist and informator choristarum) 1981–90, prof of music Univ of Wales Bangor 1991–; dir Edington Music Festival 1971–78, dir of music St Chad's Cathedral Birmingham 1972–78, musical advsr Panel of Monastic Musicians 1976–; memb: Cncl Plainsong and Medieval Music Soc 1994–, Guild of Church Musicians 1995–, Royal Musical Assoc, Royal Coll of Organists, Br Inst of Organ Studies; FRCO (CHM); Benemerenti Papal award 1978; *Books* Orlando Gibbons: Consort Music (Musica Britannica 48, 1982), The Forms and Orders of Western Liturgy (1991); *Recordings* The English Carol (1984), The English Anthem (5 vols, 1990), The Victorian Carol (1990), Hymns for Prayer and Praise (ed, 1996); *Recreations* walking, ecclesiastical architecture; *Style—* Prof John Harper; ✉ Department of Music, University of Wales, Bangor, Gwynedd LL57 2DG (☎ 01248 382181)

HARPER, Joseph Charles; QC (1992); s of Frederick Charles Harper (d 1967), and Kitty, *née* Judah (d 1983); *b* 21 March 1939; *Educ* Charterhouse, LSE (BA, LLB, LLM); *m* 1984 (m dis 1993), Sylvia Helen, *née* Turner; 2 da (Helen Jane b 5 May 1987, Anna Clare b 1 April 1989); *Career* formerly lectr and head Dept of Law Kingston Poly; barrister; memb Gray's Inn; Freeman Worshipful Co of Musicians; ARCM; *Books* Hill & Redman - Law of Landlord and Tenant (ed), Halsburg's Laws: Compulsory Practice vol 8 (ed, 4 edn); *Recreations* playing the French Horn, bibliomania; *Clubs* Garrick; *Style—* Joseph Harper, Esq, QC; ✉ 4 Breams Buildings, London EC4A 1AQ (☎ 0171 353 5835, fax 0171 430 1677)

HARPER, Martin John; OBE (1992); s of Frank Harper, of Welford-on-Avon; *b* 26 March 1925; *Educ* King Edward's GS Birmingham, LSE; *m* 1949, Stella, da of Francis Beavis, of Birkdale, Southport; 1 s, 2 da; *Career* merchant banker and conslt; dir: Keyser Ullmann 1971, Charterhouse Japhet 1980 (md 1984–86); chm: Charterhouse Japhet Credit 1983–86, Johnson Matthey Bankers 1984, Minories Finance 1986–; dir: London Interstate Bank 1980, RoyScot Finance Group 1986–90, RoyScot Trust 1990–94, Agricultural Mortgage Corp 1991–94; memb Appeal Ctee ICAEW; memb Ct of Assts Worshipful Co of Feltmakers; FCIB; *Recreations* reading, music, walking; *Clubs* Bankers'; *Style—* Martin Harper, Esq, OBE; ✉ Minories Finance, 123 Minories, London EC3N 1NT (☎ 0171 488 2671, fax 0171 481 3365); Martin Harper & Co, 46a Priestlands Park Rd, Sidcup, Kent DA15 7HJ (☎ and fax 0181 300 1264)

HARPER, Prof (Alexander) Murray; s of Rev Dr Thomas Harper (d 1959), of Eastwood, Glasgow, and Margaret Simpson, *née* Ross (d 1989); *b* 31 May 1933; *Educ* Hutchesons' GS, Univ of Glasgow (MB ChB, MD); *m* 1958, Charlotte Maria Fossleitner; 2 s (Peter Thomas b 25 Aug 1961, Murray Antony 27 Sept 1965), 1 da (Alison Margaret b 25 Feb 1964); *Career* Univ of Glasgow: dir Wellcome Surgical Inst 1963–96, Wellcome sr research fell in clinical sci and hon lectr in surgery 1963–68, sr lectr 1968–69, reader 1969–81, prof in surgical research 1981–96, dir Hugh Fraser Neuroscience Laboratories 1987–96, emeritus prof and sr research fell 1996–; hon conslt in clinical physiology Gtr Glasgow Health Bd 1970–96; visiting prof various med schs USA and Europe; David Patey Prize Surgical Research Soc 1966, Harold G Wolff Award American Assoc for the Study of Headache, Gold Medal Br Migraine Assoc 1976; memb: numerous prof bodies, Fachbeirat (int advsy ctee) Max-Planck Institut für Neurologische Forschung Cologne 1990–96; fell American Heart Assoc (Stroke Cncl) 1980; *Books* Journal of Cerebral Blood Flow and Metabolism (fndr ed-in-chief, 1981–88), Cerebrovascular and Brain Metabolism Reviews (fndr ed, 1989–), also author of over 200 books, book chapters and scientific papers; *Recreations* salmon fishing; *Clubs* College (Glasgow); *Style—* Prof Murray Harper; ✉ 2 Pollock Road, Bearsden, Glasgow G61 2NJ (☎ 0141 942 2510); University of Glasgow, Wellcome Surgical Institute, Glasgow G61 1QH (☎ 0141 339 8855 ext 5826, fax 0141 943 0215)

HARPER, Dr Peter George; s of Frederick Charles Harper (d 1965), of Bath, and Catherine Tryphosa, *née* McHattie; *b* 30 Aug 1945; *Educ* UCH and UCL (MB BS, LRCP, MRCP, MRCS); *m* 21 June 1971, Saga Margaret Elizabeth (d 1996), da of Peter Guise Tyndale; 3 s (Benjamin b 1974, Sebastian b 1976, Maximillian b 1988), 1 da (Harriet b 1980); *Career* house offr then sr house offr UCH and Addenbrooke's Hosp Cambridge 1969–71, sr house offr and med registrar St Mary's Hosp 1972–76, sr med registrar UCH 1976–82, conslt physician and med oncologist Guy's Hosp 1982–; MRC: memb Lung Cancer Ctee, memb Gynaecological Malignancies Ctee, memb Genito-Urinary Malignancies Ctee; memb: UK Central Coordinating Cancer Ctee, Br Prostate Gp, Hampstead Med Soc; FRCP 1987; *Books* numerous papers on aspects of cancer treatment; contrib chapters: The Treatment of Urological Tumours (1985), A Textbook of Unusual Tumours (1988); *Recreations* music (especially opera), walking, fly-fishing, shooting; *Style—* Dr Peter Harper; ✉ 97 Harley St, London W1N 1DF (☎ 0171 935 6698, fax 0171 224 6504)

HARPER, Peter J; *m*; 4 c; *Career* qualified CA 1958, Nat Serv Army 1958–60; Hanson plc 1970–80 (joined as dep financial controller 1970, successively chief exec Construction Equipment Div, chm Building Materials Div then chief exec UK industrial activities until 1980), main bd dir John Laing plc 1980–83, rejoined Hanson plc 1983, chm subsid UDS Group plc (now Allders) 1983–89, chm Imperial Tobacco Ltd 1986–87, chm Hanson Industrial Services Ltd 1987–94, exec dir Hanson plc 1990–94, currently dir of Parly affrs Hanson plc; chm Eversholt Leasing Ltd 1996–; currently non-exec dir: Lonhro plc, Victrex plc, John Laing PLC; non-exec dir London Clubs International plc 1992–95; vice pres Br Sports Tst, memb Exec Ctee Inst of Business Ethics, tstee Maurice Laing Fndn; FCA, FRSA; *Style—* Peter Harper, Esq; ✉ Hanson plc, 1 Grosvenor Place, London SW1X 7JH (☎ 0171 245 1245, fax 0171 823 1018)

HARPER, Rev Roger; s of Albert William Harper (d 1979), of Peel, IOM, and Joyce, *née* Griffiths (d 1990); *b* 10 Jan 1943; *Educ* Merchant Taylors' Crosby, UMIST (BSc); *m* 26 July 1966, Joan, da of John Worthington, of Freckleton, Lancs; 2 da (Charlotte b 1967, Camilla b 1969); *Career* CA; ordained priest 1988 in diocese of Sodor and Man, chm Diocesan Bd of Fin 1984–; dir: Roach Bridge Holdings plc, Manx Industrial Trust 1973–; FCA; *Recreations* jt master huntsman IOM bloodhounds drag hunt; *Style—* Rev Roger Harper; ✉ Ballahowin House, St Marks, Ballasalla, Isle of Man IM9 3AS (☎ 01624 851251); 18 St George's St, Douglas, Isle of Man IM1 1PL (☎ 01624 624945, fax 01624 624945)

HARPER, Prof (John) Ross; CBE (1986); s of Rev Thomas Harper (d 1960), and Margaret Simpson, *née* Ross; *b* 20 March 1935; *Educ* Hutchesons' Boys' GS, Univ of Glasgow (MA, LLB); *m* 26 Sept 1963, Ursula Helga Renate, da of Hans Gathmann (d 1966), of Zimerstrasse, Darmstadt; 2 s (Robin b 1964, Michael b 1969), 1 da (Susan b 1966); *Career* slr Scotland; sr ptnr Ross Harper & Murphy and Harper Macleod; pt/t prof of law Univ of Strathclyde; former pres: Law Soc of Scotland, Scottish Cons and Unionist Assoc, Glasgow Bar Assoc; former chm Tory Reform Gp Scotland; pres Int Bar Assoc 1994– (former chm Gen Practice Section); dep chm: Mining (Scotland) Ltd, Scottish Coal Company Limited; Parly candidate (Cons) Hamilton and W Renfrewshire 1970's; *Books* Practitioners' Guide to Criminal Procedure, A Guide to the Courts, The Glasgow Rape Case, Fingertip Guide to Criminal Law, Rates Reform, Devolution, New Unionism, My Client My Lord; *Recreations* angling, bridge; *Clubs* Western; *Style—* Prof Ross Harper, CBE; ✉ 23 Clabon Mews, Cadogan Square, London SW1X 0EG; Ca 'd'oro, 45 Gordon St, Glasgow G1 3PE (☎ 0141 221 8888, fax 0141 226 4198)

HARPER GOW, (Maxwell) Eric; s of Sir (Leonard) Maxwell Harper Gow, MBE (d 1996), and Lillan Margaret, *née* Kiaer; *b* 1 Aug 1945; *Educ* Rugby, Université de Grenoble France; *m* 1 July 1972, Celia Marjorie, da of James William Macleod (d 1978); 1 s (Robert b 1978), 2 da (Marianne b 1973, Amalie b 1975); *Career* CA; Graham Smart & Annan Edinburgh 1964–69, Cooper Brothers & Co London 1970–73, fin controller sound and vision div Hayes Middx EMI Ltd 1973–78, fin dir Edinburgh and Reading Nuclear Enterprises Ltd 1978–81, co sec A H McIntosh & Co Ltd Kirkcaldy 1981–82, assoc dir corporate fin servs Coopers & Lybrand Edinburgh 1982–95, dir of fin Common Servs Agency NHS Scot 1995–; memb Inst CA Scotland 1969; *Recreations* sailing, skiing, silviculture; *Clubs* New Edinburgh; *Style—* Eric Harper Gow, Esq; ✉ Common Services Agency, National Health Service in Scotland, Trinity Park House, South Trinity Road, Edinburgh EH5 3SE

HARPHAM, Sir William; KBE (1966, OBE 1948), CMG (1953); s of William Harpham, of Grimsby (d 1932); *b* 3 Dec 1906; *Educ* Wintringham Secdy Sch Grimsby, Christ's Coll Cambridge; *m* 1943, Isabelle, da of Maurice Droz; 1 s, 1 da; *Career* HM Foreign Serv: min UK delgn to OEEC 1953–56, min Tokyo 1956–59, min (econ) Paris 1959–63, ambass to Bulgaria 1964–66, ret 1967; dir GB East Europe Centre 1967–80; *Clubs* RAC; *Style—* Sir William Harpham, KBE, CMG; ✉ 9 King's Keep, Putney Hill, London SW15 6RA (☎ 0181 788 1383)

HARPUR, Oonagh Mary; da of Dr William Ware Harpur, of Drigg, Cumbria, and Patricia Elizabeth, *née* Coote; *b* 26 Sept 1953; *Educ* Univ of Keele (BA); *m* 1974 (m dis 1991), Peter Edward Clamp, s of Owen Gregory Edward Clamp, of Caversham, Reading, Berks; 1 da (Jennifer Sarah b 23 Nov 1978); *Career* held various posts, especially advising bd membs and ctees NCB 1976–85, ldr Professional Practices Consulting Gp Spicer & Oppenheim 1985–87, assoc Strategic Planning Assoc Washington DC 1987–88, princ exec Berwin Leighton 1988–94; co-fndr: Global Change Fndn 1994–, Architects for Change 1994–; ptnr The Love and Integrity Partnership 1995–; non-exec dir Hillingdon Health Authy 1992–96; memb: Forum, Scientific and Med Network; FRSA; *Recreations* opera, clarinet playing, singing; *Style—* Ms Oonagh Harpur; ✉ Global Change Foundation, The Velma Boathouse, Broom Close, Teddington, Middx TW11 9RL (☎ 0181 977 1946, fax 0181 940 0401)

HARRAP, Simon Richard; s of M W Harrap, of Marsh House, Bentley, and Cynthia Mary, *née* Darell; *b* 25 March 1941; *Educ* Harrow; *m* 24 May 1969, Diana, da of Ian Akers Douglas (d 1952); 1 s (Nicholas Guy 15 April 1975), 2 da (Louise Jane b 17 Oct 1971, Lara Sophie b 5 Jan 1979); *Career* Stewart Smith & Co 1960–71; dir: Stewart Wrightson N America Ltd 1971–88, Stewart Wrightson plc 1984–87, Willis Faber plc 1987–88, HSBC Gibbs 1988–; *Style—* Simon Harrap, Esq; ✉ HSBC Gibbs Ltd, 27–33 Artillery Lane, London E1 7LP (☎ 0171 247 5433)

HARREL, David T D; *b* 23 June 1948; *m* Julia Mary; 1 da (Rebecca b 1977), 2 s (Tom b 1979, Charlie b 1983); *Career* admitted slr 1974, asst slr then ptnr Messrs William Charles Crocker 1974–79, ptnr Messrs Burton & Ramsden 1979–82, currently sr ptnr and head Commercial Litigation Dept S J Berwin & Co (co-fndr and ptnr 1982); chm Devpt Fund Royal Coll of Music, memb Fin and Appeals Ctee London Fedn of Clubs for Young People; tstee: Clore Fndn, Vivien Duffield Fndn; *Recreations* shooting, fishing, golf, tennis, gardening, music, theatre; *Style—* David Harrel, Esq; ✉ S J Berwin & Co, 222 Grays Inn Road, London WC1X 8HB (☎ 0171 533 2222)

HARRHY, Eiddwen Mair; *b* 14 April 1949; *Educ* St Winifred's Convent Swansea, Royal Manchester Coll of Music; *m* 23 Jan 1988, Gregory Strange; 1 da; *Career* soprano; debut: Royal Opera House Covent Gdn 1974, English Nat Opera 1975; performances incl: Glyndebourne Festival, Scottish Opera, Welsh National Opera, Opera North, Teatro Colon Buenos Aires, Philharmonie St Petersburg, La Scala Milan, Amsterdam Concertgebouw, Sydney Opera House, Hong Kong, NZ, LA, BBC Promenade concerts; recordings: EMI, Harmonia Mundi, Erato, Deutsche Grammophon, Virgin Classics; awards: Imperial League of Opera Prize Gold Medal, Miriam Licette Prize; fndr convenor The Trust for Young Musicians, dir Crisis Messiah; *Recreations* chamber music concerts, watching rugby in Wales; *Clubs* Friends of the Musicians' Benevolent Fund; *Style—* Miss Eiddwen Harrhy; ✉ c/o Ron Gonsalves Personal Artists & Concert Management, 7 Old Town, Clapham, London SW4 0JT (☎ 0171 622 2244, fax 0171 622 2288)

HARRIES, Andy; *Career* television prodr, dir and exec prodr; scriptwriter/researcher/presenter Granada Television Manchester and London 1976–81, freelance prodr and dir 1982–92, controller of entertainment and comedy Granada Television 1994– (head of comedy 1992–94); *Programmes* dir and prodr/co-prodr: Africa - History of a Continent (2 progs in series, Channel 4) 1983, Resisting Apartheid and The Scramble for Cable (20/20 Vision strand, Channel 4) 1983–84, South Bank Show features on Malcolm McLaren, Truman Capote, The Penguin Cafe Orchestra and Lenny Henry (LWT) 1984–87, South of Watford: Sloanes on the Slopes (LWT) 1986, Animation (LWT, Silver Bear for Best Documentary Chicago Film Festival) 1986, A Short Sharp Shock (LWT) 1987, Our God the Condor (The World About Us strand, BBC2, winner Special Prog Category Barbara Myeroff Film Festival) 1987, Martin Chambi: Heirs of the Incas (Arena strand, BBC2, Gold Award Houston Film Festival, Silver Apple Nat Educn Film Festival San Francisco) 1987, The Incredibly Strange Film Show, Son of the Incredibly Strange Film Show and For One Week Only (series prodr and dir, Channel X for Channel 4/Discovery Channel) 1988, 1989 and 1990, Lenny Live and Unleashed (Lenny Henry live act, cinema and video release) 1989, Mario Vargas Llosa: The Novelist Who Would Be President (Omnibus strand, BUP for BBC1) 1990, Viva Elvis (Channel X for Channel 4) 1991; prodr for Granada: Rik Mayall Presents 1993, An Evening with Gary Lineker (special commendation Prix Italia) 1994; exec prodr for Granada: September Song (3 series) 1993–95, Watching 1993, Surgical Spirit 1993–, Up the Garden Path 1993, Rik Mayall Presents (series II) 1994, You've Been Framed 1994–, Stars In Their Eyes 1994–, The Perfect Match (comedy drama film) 1995, Jack Dee's Saturday Night 1995; exec prodr for other broadcasters: The Ghosts of Oxford Street (Christmas musical special, Channel 4) 1991, The World of Lee Evans (Channel 4) 1994, The Mrs Merton Show (BBC) 1994–; *Style—* Andy Harries, Esq; ✉ Granada Television Ltd, The London Television Centre, Upper Ground, London SE1 9LT (☎ 0171 620 1620)

HARRIES, Kathryn Gwynne; da of Stanley George Harries, of Pembroke, and Gwynneth Rosemary, *née* Hubbard; *b* 15 Feb 1951; *Educ* Surbiton HS, Royal Acad of Music (jr exhibitioner, then at Sr Acad), Univ of London (BMus); *m* 30 July 1977, Chirstopher Charles Lane, s of Charles Victor Lane; 1 da (Victoria Jessica Gwynne b 27 Dec 1979), 1 s (William Stanley Gwynne b 21 Sept 1981); *Career* opera singer; lectr Kingston Poly 1969–82, prof Jr Dept RAM 1976–82, presenter BBC Schools TV series Music Time 1977–83, also various concerts, oratorios and recitals 1969–83; Wigmore Hall debut 1972, Royal Festival Hall debut 1977, operatic debut as a Flower Maiden in Parsifal (with WNO under Reginald Goodall) 1983; Olivier Award nomination for Sieglinde and Gutrune in WNO's full Ring Cycle 1986; FRAM 1991 (ARAM 1988); *Performances* other operatic roles incl: Leonora in Fidelio (with WNO in Liverpool 1983, Scottish Opera 1984, Teatro Colon Buenos Aires under Franz Paul Decker 1988, ENO 1996), Sylvie in La Colombe (Buxton Festival under Anthony Hose) 1983, Irene in Rienzi (ENO debut directed by Nicholas Hytner) 1983, Sieglinde in Die Walküre (WNO under Reginald Goodall 1984, Nice Opera and Théâtre Champs Elysée 1988), Eva in Die Meistersinger (ENO) 1984, Female Chorus in The Rape of Lucretia (ENO) 1984, Adalgisa in Norma (WNO) 1985, title role in Hedda Gabler (Scottish Opera under Edward Harper) 1985, Gutrune in Götterdämmerung (WNO 1985, Met Opera NY under James Levine 1988 and 1989), Kundry in Parsifal (Met Opera debut under James Levine 1986, Netherlands Opera under Hartmut Hänchen 1990), Donna Elvira in Don Giovanni (Opera

North under David Lloyd Jones 1986, Stuttgart debut 1992), Sieglinde and Gutrune in WNO's full Ring Cycle (Covent Garden) 1986, Senta in Der Fliegende Holländer (Scottish Opera under Sir Alexander Gibson, Paris Opera debut Palais Garnier) 1987, Donna Anna in The Stone Guest (ENO) 1987, Didon in Les Troyens (Berlioz Festival under Serge Baudo, first complete prodn ever in France) 1987, title role in The Merry Widow (Opera North) 1988, Protaganista in Un Re in Ascolto (Covent Garden debut under Luciano Berio 1989, Opèra Bastille debut 1991), The Composer in Ariadne auf Naxos (WNO under Sir Charles Mackerras) 1989, title role in Katya Kabanova (ENO under Albert Rosen) 1989, Arianne in Arianne et Barbe Bleu (Netherlands Opera debut) 1989, Jocasta in Oedipus Rex (Los Angeles debut under Eza Pekka-Salonen) 1989, Judith in Bluebeard's Castle (Scottish Opera directed by Stefan Lazarides) 1990, Didon in Les Troyens (Scottish Opera and Covent Garden under John Hauceri 1990, La Monnaie Brussels debut 1992), title role in Cléopatre (Massenet Festival debut under Patrick Fournillier) 1990, Giulietta in The Tales of Hoffmann (Théâtre du Chatalet debut) 1991, Die Frau in 'Intolleranza 1960' (Stuttgart) 1992, title role in Carmen (Orange Festival debut under Michel Plasson) 1992, Principess di Bouillon in Adriana Lecouvreur (St Etienne) 1992, Geschwitz in Berg's Lulu (BBC Proms) 1996; incl: Flower Maiden and Voice from Above in Wagner's Parsifal (under Reginald Goodall), title role in Massanet's Cléopatre (under Patrick Fournillier), The Mother in Janacek's Osud (under Sir Charles Mackerras), Fevronia in Rimsky-Korsakov's The Invisible City of Kitezh (under Edward Downes); *Recreations* riding and competing on own horses, reading, DIY, supporting her children; *Clubs* Abinger Forest Riding; *Style—* Ms Kathryn Harries; ✉ c/o Ingpen & Williams Ltd, 14 Kensington Court, London W8 5DN (☎ 0171 937 5158, fax 0171 938 4175)

HARRIES, Rt Rev Richard Douglas; *see:* Oxford, Bishop of

HARRIMAN, Andrew Tuoyo (Andy); s of Chief H Harriman, of Windrush, Clare Hill, Esher, Surrey, and Irene, *née* Ogedegbe; *b* 13 July 1964; *Educ* Radley, Magdalene Coll Cambridge (exhibitioner, Rugby blue, Athletics blue); *Career* rugby player; Harlequins RFC: debut 1986, winner Middlesex seven (three times), winner John Player Cup 1988; divnl rugby debut for London Oct 1988, int debut England v Australia Nov 1988 (injured thereafter), represented Barbarians RFC 1989, capt winning England team World Cup sevens (Edinburgh) 1993 (highest try-scorer, voted player of the tournament); qualified chartered surveyor 1989–90, self-employed 1990–; GB U16 tennis doubles champion 1980; *Style—* Andy Harriman, Esq; ✉ Harlequins RFC, Stoop Memorial Ground, Craneford Way, Twickenham, Middlesex

HARRIMAN, Honorable Pamela Beryl; da of 11 Baron Digby, KG, DSO, MC, TD (d 1964); *b* 1920; *Educ* Downham Sch, Sorbonne; *m* 1, 1939 (m dis 1946), Maj the Hon Randolph Frederick Edward Spencer-Churchill, MBE (d 1968, eld s of Rt Hon Sir Winston Churchill KG, PC, OM, CH, TD, DL, and Baroness Spencer-Churchill (Life Peeress); 1 s (Winston Churchill, MP, *qv* b 1940); m 2, 1960, Leland Hayward (d 1971); m 3, 1971, (William) Averell Harriman (d 1986), sometime Govr of New York; *Career* Democratic Party: chm Democrats for the 1980s 1980–90, chm Democratic Senatorial Campaign Ctee's Annual Dinner 1988 and 1989, at-large memb Democratic Nat Ctee 1988–93, chm Quarterly Policy Issues Forum Democratic Govrs' Assoc 1990–92 a nat co-chair of Clinton/Gore presidential campaign 1992; US ambass to France 1993–, memb US Cncl on Foreign Relations; formerly: hon memb Exec Ctee Brookings Instn, vice chm Atlantic Cncl, tstee Rockefeller Univ, vice pres English-Speaking Union of the US, tstee Winston Churchill Fndn of the US; former memb: Tstees' Cncl Nat Gallery of Art, Bd of Friends of Kennan Inst for Advanced Russian Studies, Advsy Cncl W Averell Harriman Inst Columbia Univ, Bd of Dirs Franklin and Eleanor Roosevelt Inst; Hon LLD Columbia Univ; *Style—* The Honorable Pamela Harriman; ✉ United States Embassy, 2 avenue Gabriel, 75382 Paris, France; Willow Oaks, Middleburg, Virginia 22117, USA

HARRIMAN, (Joseph) William Fletcher; TD (1989); s of Flt-Lt Joseph Fletcher Harriman, MBE (d 1974), and Kathleen Harriman, *née* Robinson; *b* 27 April 1956; *Educ* Oakham Sch Rutland, Trent Poly Nottingham (BSc); *m* 25 June 1991, Janet, da of Albert Benson, of Nottingham; 1 da (Annabel b 30 May 1996); *Career* S Notts Hussars Yeomanry RHA TA 1974–, troop commander 1986–88, seconded Royal Yeomanry as artillery advsr 1989–91, Army reserve 1992–; head of Catalogue Dept and princ valuer Weller and Dufty Auctioneers 1984–90 (conslt 1987–), ind conslt valuer and identifier of firearms 1987–, expert witness in court cases for firearms and ballistics 1987–; head of firearms Br Assoc for Shooting and Conservation 1991–, conslt to BBC on arms and militaria; memb: Panel of Experts Antiques Roadshow, Home Office Working Gp reviewing Firearms Rules 1993–, Home Office Working Gp on Firearms Licensing by Category 1995; columnist Shooting Gazette magazine, contrib Shooting Times magazine, firearms conslt Gun Trade News magazine 1995; treas Br Shooting Sports Cncl 1993–, memb Cncl Historical Breechloading Smallarms Assoc 1995; assoc ISVA 1982–92 (memb Fine Arts & Chattels Ctee 1991–92); *Books* Experts on Antiques (contrib, 1987), Tiaras, Tallboys and Teddy Bears (contrib, 1990); *Recreations* shooting, riding, toxophily, wine, music; *Style—* William Harriman, Esq, TD; ✉ Pistyll Bank, Springfield Lane, Marford, Wrexham LL12 8TF; British Association for Shooting and Conservation, Marford Mill, Rossett, Wrexham LL12 OHL (☎ 01244 573010, fax 01244 573001)

HARRINGTON, Dr Christine Ida (Mrs Maddocks); da of Edward Thomas Harrington, of Braintree, Essex, and Ida Oxborough, *née* Richardson (d 1981); *b* 21 Sept 1947; *Educ* Braintree County HS, Univ of Sheffield (MB ChB, MD); *m* 8 March 1982, John Leyshon Maddocks, s of Thomas Maddocks, of Mumbles, S Wales; 2 s (Geraint b 1983, Owen b 1986); *Career* conslt dermatologist 1980–; studies on bullous diseases, written works and nat and int lectures on diseases of the vulva; memb: Br Assoc of Dermatologists, N England Dermatological Soc, Euro Acad of Dermatology and Venereology; fndr chm Br Soc for the Study of Vulval Disease; MRCP 1974, FRCP 1989; *Recreations* music, walking, gardening; *Style—* Dr Christine Harrington; ✉ Dermatology Department, Royal Hallamshire Hospital, Glossop Rd, Sheffield S10 (☎ 0114 271 1900)

HARRINGTON, Prof (John) Malcolm; CBE (1992); s of John Roy Harrington, of Newport, Gwent, and Veda Naomi, *née* Harris; *b* 6 April 1942; *Educ* Newport HS, King's Coll, Westminster Med Sch London (BSc, MB BS, MSc, MD); *m* 20 May 1967, Madeline Mary, da of Brinley Hunter Davies (d 1971); 1 da (Kate b 27 Sept 1975); *Career* various hosp appts 1966–69, visiting scientist US Public Health Serv 1975–77, sr lectr in occupational med London Sch of Hygiene and Tropical Med 1977–80 (lectr 1969–75), fndn prof of occupational health Univ of Birmingham 1981–; chm Industrial Injuries Advsy Cncl 1984–96, specialist advsr House of Lords select ctees; memb: Nat Radiological Protection Bd, Soc of Occupational Med, Soc of Epidemiological Res, Int Epidemiology Assoc, Br Occupational Hygiene Soc; MFPHM, FRCP (MRCP, LRCP), MRCS, FFOM (MFOM), FFOM(I), FACE USA; *Books* Recent Advances in Occupational Health (ed vol 2, 1984, ed vol 3, 1987), Occupational Health (with F S Gill, 1983, 4 edn 1997), Occupational Hygiene (with K Gardiner, 2 edn 1995); over 160 scientific papers published; *Recreations* music, theatre, gardening, cricket; *Style—* Prof Malcolm Harrington, CBE; ✉ Institute of Occupational Health, The University of Birmingham, Edgbaston, Birmingham B15 2TT (☎ 0121 414 6022, fax 0121 471 5208, telex 333762)

HARRINGTON, Mark Anthony; s of Terrence John Harrington, of Cardiff, and Joan Margaret, *née* Gore; *b* 3 Oct 1959; *m* Andrea Lee, da of Roger Hancock; 1 s (Tayo Jon), 2 da (Libby Jayne (twin), Chloe Louise); *Career* trainee chef rising to chef de partie Angel Hotel Cardiff 1976–79, chef de partie Garden House Hotel Cambridge Feb-Oct 1979, sous chef Angel Hotel Cardiff 1979–81, chef de partie Newstead Guest House Bermuda 1981–82, chef de partie Newstead Guest House Bermuda 1981–82, chef de partie Holiday Inn Toronto Canada March-Sept 1982, chef de cuisine Deri Restaurant Cardiff 1982–83, sous chef Hendon Hall Hotel London 1983–84, sous chef Ston Easton Park Hotel nr Bath 1984–85, head chef Hendon Hall Hotel 1985–86, chef de cuisine Ston Easton Park Hotel 1986–; supporter various charities incl CLIC (Cancer and Luekaemia in Children); *Awards* Hotel of the Year 1983, Egon Ronay Gold Plate, Egon Ronay 88%, AA 3 stars Rosette, Good Food Guide 3* out of 5, Ackerman's Guide White Cloves; *Recreations* golf, squash, tennis; *Style—* Mark Harrington, Esq; ✉ Ston Easton Park Hotel, Ston Easton, Somerset BA3 4DF (☎ 01761 241631, fax 01761 241377)

HARRINGTON, 11 Earl of (GB 1742); William Henry Leicester Stanhope; also Viscount Stanhope of Mahon, Baron Stanhope of Elvaston (both GB 1717), Baron Harrington (GB 1730), and Viscount Petersham (GB 1742); s of 10 Earl of Harrington, MC (d 1929, ggn of 4 Earl, inventor of the blend of snuff known as Petersham mixture, snuff being colour he used for his livery and equipage); suc kinsman, 7 and last Earl Stanhope, in the Viscountcy of Stanhope of Mahon and the Barony of Stanhope of Elvaston 1967; *b* 24 Aug 1922; *Educ* Eton; *m* 1, 1942 (m dis 1946), Eileen, da of Sir John Foley Grey, 8 Bt; 1 s (Viscount Petersham b 1945), 2 da (Lady Jane Cameron b 1942 d 1974, Lady Avena Maxwell b 1944); m 2, 1947 (m dis 1962), Anne, da of Maj Richard Chute, of Co Limerick; 1 s (Hon Steven b 1951), 2 da (Lady Trina b 1947, Lady Sarah Barry b 1951); m 3, 1964, Priscilla, da of Hon Archibald Cubitt (5 s of 2 Baron Ashcombe); 1 s (Hon John b 1965), 1 da (Lady Isabella Rachel (Countess Cawdor) b 1966); *Heir* s, Viscount Petersham, *qv*; *Career* Capt RAC serv WWII; landowner; adopted Irish citizenship 1965; *Clubs* Kildare Street (Dublin); *Style—* The Rt Hon the Earl of Harrington; ✉ The Glen, Ballingarry, Co Limerick, Ireland (☎ 0161 399162, fax 0161 399122)

HARRIOTT, Ainsley; s of Chester Leroy Harriott, of Manchester, and Peppy Petrona, *née* Strudwick (d 1993); *b* 28 Feb 1957; *Educ* Wandsworth Boys Sch, Westminster Catering Coll; *m* 4 Jan 1992, Clare Judy, da of Derek Fellows; 1 s (James Reuben b 24 June 1990), 1 da (Madeleine Joan Adaisma b 18 July 1993); *Career* trainee chef rising to commis chef Verreys Restaurant London 1975–78, demi chef de partie rising to chef tournant Strand Palace Hotel 1978–80, jr sous chef rising to sr sous chef Westbury Hotel 1980–85, chef de partie George V Paris, freelance chef and owner catering co 1985–95, presenter In the Kitchen with Ainsley Harriott 1996–; head chef Long Room Lords Cricket Ground 1985–95, head chef various ODC Cos; winner various team medals Westbury Hotel; charity work for: Help the Aged, Childline, Cancer Research, various hosp charities, Comic Relief, Barnardo's; *Books* In the Kitchen with Ainsley Harriott (1996); *Clubs* David Lloyd Tennis; *Style—* Ainsley Harriott, Esq; ✉ c/o Jeremy Hicks Associates, 53 Keyes House, Dolphin Square, London SW1V 3NA (☎ 0171 233 9569, fax 0171 630 8412)

HARRIS, Prof Adrian Llewellyn; s of Luke Harris, and Julia, *née* Wade; *b* 10 Aug 1950; *Educ* Liverpool Collegiate Sch, Univ of Liverpool (BSc, MB), Univ of Oxford (DPhil); *m* 7 July 1975, Margaret Susan, da of Rev Ronald Denman; *Career* clinical scientist Clinical Pharmacology Unit MRC Oxford 1975–78, lectr in med oncology Royal Marsden Hosp London 1978–80, visiting fell ICRF London 1981, prof of clinical oncology Univ of Newcastle 1981–88, ICRF prof of clinical oncology and dir of Molecular Laboratory Univ of Oxford 1988– (fell St Hugh's Coll); non-exec dir Xenova Group 1996–; FRCP; *Recreations* swimming, walking, films and theatre; *Style—* Prof Adrian Harris; ✉ Clinical Oncology Unit, Churchill Hospital, Headington, Oxford OX3 7LJ

HARRIS, Prof Sir Alan James; kt (1980), CBE (1968); s of Walter Harris; *b* 8 July 1916; *Educ* Owen's Sch Islington, Northampton Poly, Univ of London (BSc); *m* 1948, Marie Thérèse, da of Prof Paul Delcourt (d 1976), of Paris; 2 s; *Career* WWII RE served NW Europe (despatches), Maj 1945; local govt engr 1933–40, sr ptnr (later conslt) Harris & Sutherland 1955–; memb Engrg Cncl 1982–85, emeritus prof of concrete structures Imperial Coll London 1981 (prof 1973–81), tstee Imperial War Museum 1983–89, pres Hydraulics Res Ltd 1989– (chm 1981–89); Hon DSc; FEng 1979, FIStructE (pres 1978, Gold medal 1984), FICE, FCGI 1995; Croix de Guerre France 1945, Ordre du Mérite France 1978; *Style—* Prof Sir Alan Harris, CBE, FEng; ✉ 128 Ashley Gardens, Thirleby Rd, London SW1P 1HL (☎ 0171 834 6924)

HARRIS, Ann Gertrude; MBE (1984); da of Reginald Thompson Harris (d 1956), of North Crawley, Newport Pagnell, Bucks, and Beatrice Amy, *née* Inglis (d 1961); *b* 27 July 1923; *Career* war work with Echo Radio Firm Aylesbury and Glasgow; camphill Rudolf Steiner Schs nr Aberdeen 1946–: trained under fndr Dr Karl Konig, involved with people with special needs and children with handicaps, fndr memb first communities in England The Sheiling Schs (Ringwood and Thornbury nr Bristol), moved from Harley St office to Hertfordshire 1963 (responsible for arrangements for interviews, adults with mental handicaps and people who have undergone mental illness, addresses various gps of people to bring about a better awareness of people with handicaps); memb: N ionwide Counselling Serv, Nat Assoc for the Rehabilitation of Offenders, Nat Schizophrenic Fellowship, Assoc of Residential Communities, Assoc of Therapeutic Communities, Ctee Housing Assoc for Single People Islington; memb Bd of Dirs of several cos; former memb Disablement Advsy Ctee for Watford area, memb Cncl Anthroposophical Soc of Great Britain; *Recreations* travel, including taking parties of handicapped people abroad, keen interest in social problems and questions, but not biased politically; *Style—* Miss Ann Harris, MBE; ✉ The Camphill Village Trust, Delrow House, Aldenham, Watford, Herts WD2 8DJ (☎ 01923 856006)

HARRIS, Anthony David; CMG (1995), LVO (1979); s of Reginald William Harris (d 1983), and Kathleen Mary, *née* Daw; *b* 13 Oct 1941; *Educ* Plymouth Coll, Exeter Coll Oxford; *m* 1, 1970 (m dis 1988), Patricia Ann, *née* Over; 1 s (Stuart Alexander Hugh b 1978); m 2, 6 March 1988, (Ann) Sophie, da of Prof Erik Kisling (d 1995), of Denmark; 2 s (Andreas William b 1988, Alexander Matthias b 1990), 1 da (Amelia Katrine b 1993); *Career* Dip Serv; joined 1964, Arabic Sch Lebanon 1965–67, third then second sec Jedda 1967–69, info offr Khartoum 1969–72, first sec and head of Chancery and HM Consul Abu Dhabi 1975–79, first sec UK perm mission to UN Geneva 1979–82, cnsllr Home Inspectorate FCO 1982–83, regnl mktg dir Gulf States and Pakistan MOD 1983–86, cnsllr and dep head of mission Cairo 1986–90, cnsllr FCO 1990–94, ambass UAE (Abu Dhabi) 1994–; *Recreations* shooting (HM Queen's prize Bisley 1964), skiing, climbing, diving, travel, Roman history; *Clubs* Reform, North London Rifle (Bisley), British Cwlth Rifle (Bisley); *Style—* Mr Anthony Harris, CMG, LVO; ✉ c/o Foreign and Commonwealth Office (Abu Dhabi), King Charles St, London SW1A 2AH; British Embassy, PO Box 248, Abu Dhabi, United Arab Emirates (☎ 00 971 232 6600, fax 00 971 2 318138)

HARRIS, Anthony John David; s of Dr Edwin Gabriel Harris (d 1930), of London, and Adela Rachel, *née* Jacobs; *b* 9 Dec 1929; *Educ* Bryanston, Jesus Coll Cambridge (scholar, BA); *Career* journalist; asst London corr Nihon Keizai Shimbun Tokyo 1953–54, trainee rising to ed's PA Oxford Mail 1954–59, Financial Times 1959–68 (dep features ed, ed gossip column, industl reporter, feature writer, ed mgmnt page), economics ed The Guardian 1968–73; Financial Times: econ commenter 1973–77, chief domestic leader writer and asst ed 1977–87, Washington columnist 1987–90, home columnist and assoc ed 1990–92; freelance and columnist The Times 1992–; jt winner H Wincott prize for fin journalism 1974; *Recreations* sailing, bridge, walking; *Clubs* Reform; *Style—* Anthony Harris, Esq

HARRIS, Prof Anthony Leonard; s of Thomas Haydn Harris (d 1967), of Cardiff, and Dora, *née* Wilkinson (d 1989); *b* 11 May 1935; *Educ* Cardiff HS, Univ Coll of Wales Aberystwyth (BSc, PhD); *m* 29 Aug 1959, (Muriel) Noreen, da of Arthur Jones, of Rhondda; 1 da (Elisabeth Siân b 31 May 1964), 1 s (David Huw Mendus b 20 April 1967); *Career* geologist then princ geologist Geological Survey Edinburgh 1959–71; Univ of Liverpool 1971–: lectr, sr lectr, reader, personal chair 1987, prof of geology, head Dept of Earth Scis 1987–94, dean Faculty of Science 1994–: pres: Geological Soc of London 1990–92 (hon sec 1979–82), Geological Soc of Liverpool 1989–91; C T Clough Fund and Memorial Medal Geological Soc of Edinburgh, Murchison Fund and Major John Coke Medal Geological Soc of London; FGS 1966, CGeol 1991, FRSE 1988; *Books* The Caledonides of the British Isles (reviewed, ed and contrib, 1979), The Caledonian-Appalachian Orogen (ed and contrib, 1986); *Recreations* ornithology, hillwalking, gardening; *Style—* Prof Anthony Harris, FRSE; ✉ Department of Earth Sciences, University of Liverpool, PO Box 147, Liverpool L69 3BX (☎ 0151 794 5145(0), fax 0151 794 5170)

HARRIS, Rt Rev Augustine; s of Augustine Harris (d 1948), and Louisa Beatrice, *née* Rycroft (d 1951); *b* 27 Oct 1917; *Educ* Upholland Coll Lancs; *Career* ordained 1942, curate 1942–52, Prison Serv chaplain 1952–65, auxiliary bishop Liverpool 1966–78, bishop of Middlesbrough 1978–93; *Style—* The Rt Rev Augustine Harris; ✉ 17 Old Town Lane, Freshfield, Formby, Merseyside L37 3HJ

HARRIS, Ven (Reginald) Brian; s of Reginald George Harris (d 1985), of Kent, and Ruby C Harris; *b* 14 Aug 1934; *Educ* Eltham Coll, Christ's Coll Cambridge (MA), Ridley Hall Cambridge; *m* 1959, Anne Patricia, da of George Frederick Hughes (d 1986); 1 s (Nigel b 1962), 1 da (Celia b 1963); *Career* curate: Wednesbury 1959–61, Uttoxeter 1961–64; vicar of St Peter's Bury 1964–70, vicar and rural dean of Walmsley 1970–80, archdeacon of Manchester 1980–, canon residentiary of Manchester Cathedral 1980–, sub dean 1986–; dir Ecclesiastical Insurance Office; *Recreations* long distance walking, painting; *Style—* The Ven the Archdeacon of Manchester; ✉ 4 Victoria Ave, Eccles, Manchester M30 9HX (☎ and fax 0161 707 6444)

HARRIS, Brian Nicholas; s of Claude Harris (d 1976), and Dorothy, *née* Harris (d 1982); *b* 12 Dec 1931; *Educ* Coll of Estate Mgmnt Univ of London; *m* 18 March 1961, Rosalyn Marion, da of Geoffrey Alfred Caines (d 1982); 2 da (Suzanne (Mrs Richard Thompson) b 1961, Jennifer b 1965); *Career* chartered surveyor; Richard Ellis: ptnr 1961–96, chm 1984–93, conslt 1996–; vice chm: RICS Bldg Surveying Div 1976–77, RICS Continental Gp 1977–78; chm City Branch RICS 1984–85; London C of C: memb Cncl 1985–, memb Bd 1989–96, dep pres 1990–92, pres 1992–94; memb Cncl Aust Br C of C (UK) 1988–, memb Aust and NZ Trade Advsy Ctee 1991– (chm 1996–), first chm London Heathrow Support Gp 1993–, chm Southern Region Assoc of Br C of Cs 1993–96 (memb Bd 1994–), memb Bd Br C of C 1994– (dep pres 1996–), memb Ct of Common Cncl Corp of London 1996–; govr and dep chm Woldingham Sch 1986–93; Liveryman and memb Ct of Assts Worshipful Co of Glaziers and Painters of Glass 1975; FRSA; *Recreations* flyfishing, gardening, golf; *Clubs* Carlton, Flyfishers', City of London; *Style—* Brian Harris, Esq; ✉ Grants Paddock, Grants Lane, Limpsfield, Surrey RH8 0RQ (☎ 01883 723215); Richard Ellis, 55 Old Broad St, London EC2M 1LP (☎ 0171 256 6411, fax 0171 256 8328)

HARRIS, Brian Thomas; OBE (1983), QC (1982); s of late Thomas John Harris, and late Eleanor May, *née* Roffey; *b* 14 Aug 1932; *Educ* Henry Thornton GS, King's Coll London (LLB); *m* 6 April 1957, Janet Rosina, da of Herbert W Hodgson; 1 s (Neil Andrew), 1 da (Jane Eleanor); *Career* called to the Bar Gray's Inn 1960, London Magistrates' Ct 1963, clerk to the Justices Poole 1967–85; ICEAW: dir Professional Conduct Dept 1985–93, sec Exec Ctee Jt Disciplinary Scheme 1986–95; a chm Disciplinary Tribunals SFA and PIA; *Books* Clarke Hall and Morrison on Children (contrib ed 9 edn 1977, co-ed 1985), Criminal Jurisdiction of Magistrates (1986), The Rehabilitation of Offenders (1989) Halsburys Laws (contrib ed, Magistrates, 4 edn 1979), Disciplinary and Regulatory Proceedings (1995), The Tribunal Member (1995); *Style—* Brian Harris, Esq, OBE, QC; ✉ Church Barn, High Street, Yardley, Hastings, Northants NN7 1ER (☎ 01604 696387, fax 01604 696071); 4/5 Gray's Inn Square, London WC1

HARRIS, Cecil Rhodes; s of Frederick William Harris (d 1954); *b* 4 May 1923; *Educ* Kingston GS; *m* 1946, Gwenyth, da of Hugh Llewelyn Evans (d 1966); 1 s, 2 da; *Career* Commercial Union Assur Co: asst gen mangr 1969–73, dep gen mangr and asst sec 1973–74, co sec 1974–78, dir 1975, exec dir 1976–, dep chief gen mangr 1980–82, chief exec 1982–85; dep chm Trade Indemnity plc 1986–93; FCIS, FSCA; *Recreations* bible study; *Style—* Cecil Harris, Esq; ✉ Ashley, 35a Plough Lane, Purley, Surrey CR8 3QJ (☎ 0181 668 2820)

HARRIS, His Hon Judge (Geoffrey) Charles Wesson; QC (1989); s of Geoffrey Hardy-Harris (d 1994), and Joan, *née* Wesson (d 1979); *b* 17 Jan 1945; *Educ* Repton, Univ of Birmingham (LLB); *m* 25 July 1970, Carol Ann, da of J D Alston, CBE, of South Lopham Hall, Norfolk; 2 s (Roger, Hugh), 1 da (Kate); *Career* called to the Bar Inner Temple 1967, in practice (Common law) London and Midlands 1968–93, recorder 1990–93, circuit judge (Midland & Oxford Circuit) 1993–; memb Parole Bd 1995–; Parly candidate (C) Penistone 1974; govr St Clement Danes C of E Primary Sch 1976–79; *Books* contrib current edn Halsbury's Laws of England; author of various magazine articles; *Recreations* history, stalking, skiing, architecture, travel, fireworks; *Style—* His Hon Judge Charles Harris, QC; ✉ Westcot Barton Manor, Oxfordshire (☎ 01869 340624); 1 Harcourt Buildings, Temple, London EC4Y 9DA (☎ 0171 353 0375)

HARRIS, Prof Christopher John; s of George Henry Harris, BEM, and Hilda Winifred, *née* Ward; *b* 23 Dec 1945; *Educ* Portsmouth GS, Univ of Leicester (BSc), Univ of Oxford (MA), Univ of Southampton (PhD); *m* 10 Sept 1965, (Ruth) Joy, da of Robert Garrod (d 1986); 1 s (Philip Jonathan b 1971), 2 da (Caroline Louise b 1968, Kathryn Ruth b 1978); *Career* lectr in electronics Univ of Hull 1969–72, lectr in control engrg and maths UMIST 1972–75, lectr and fell in engrg sci Univ of Oxford and St Edmund Hall 1976–80, prof and dep chief scientist MOD 1980–84, prof and chm of sch Cranfield Inst of Technol 1984–87, Lucas prof of aerospace systems Univ of Southampton 1987–; author of several hundred scientific papers; CEng 1972, FIMA 1975, FIEE 1976, FEng 1996; *Books* Mathematical Modelling of Turbulent Diffusion in the Environment (1979), Stability of Linear Systems (1980), Self Tuning and Adaptive Control (1981), The Stability of Input/Output Dynamic Systems (1983), Advances in Command, Control and Communication Systems (1987), Application of Artificial Intelligence to Command and Control Systems (1988), Intelligent Control: aspects of fuzzy logic and neural nets (1993), Neurofuzzy Adaptive Modelling and Control (1994), Advances in Intelligent Control (1994), Advances and Adaptive Control (1995); *Recreations* gardening, golf; *Style—* Prof Christopher Harris, FEng; ✉ Dept of Electronics & Computer Sciences, University of Southampton, Highfield, Southampton, Hants (☎ 01703 592353, fax 01703 594498, telex 47661 SOTONU G, e-mail cjh@ecs.soton.ac.uk)

HARRIS, Prof Christopher John; s of Colin Christopher Harris, and Barbara Kay, *née* Hall; *b* 22 Sept 1960; *Educ* Oundle Sch, CCC Oxford (BA), Nuffield Coll Oxford (MPhil, DPhil); *m* 1993, Qun Li; *Career* Univ of Oxford: prize research fell in economics Nuffield Coll 1983–84, lectr in economics 1984–94, fell of Nuffield Coll 1984–94; prof of mathematical economics Univ of Cambridge 1995–, fell King's Coll Cambridge 1995–; visiting prof MIT 1990–91; *Publications* author of articles in academic journals; *Style—* Prof C J Harris; ✉ Faculty of Economics and Politics, University of Cambridge, Austin Robinson Building, Sidgwick Avenue, Cambridge, Cambridgeshire CB3 9DD (☎ 01223 335706, fax 01223 335475)

HARRIS, Christopher John Ashford; s and h of Sir Jack Wolfred Ashford Harris, 2 Bt, *qv*; *b* 26 Aug 1934; *m* 1957, Anna, da of F de Malmanche, of Auckland, NZ; 1 s (Andrew Frederick Ashford b 1958), 2 da (Charlotte Anna b 1960, Phoebe Jane Ashford b 1963); *Career* chief exec offr Bing Harris & Co, chief exec offr and exec chm North Pacific Securities Ltd, dep chm Renouf Properties Ltd, dir Exide Batteries Ltd, chm Southern Cross TV Ltd; *Clubs* Wellington, Royal Port Nicholson Yacht; *Style—* Christopher Harris, Esq; ✉ 21 Anne St, Wadestown, NZ 644 Wellington, New Zealand (☎ 472 232 12, fax 473 47 99)

HARRIS, Colin Charles; s of Charles Elwood Harris, of Bromley, Kent, and Ivy Kate, *née* Hutchinson (d 1981); *b* 25 Aug 1944; *Educ* St Dunstan's Coll, Univ of Exeter (BA), London Business Sch (MSc); *m* 17 April 1971, Susan Caroline, da of Frederick George Alchin; 3 s (David Alchin b 15 Nov 1974, Richard Colin b 11 May 1976, Jonathan Mark b 20 July 1978); *Career* branch banking and HO Econ Unit Lloyds Bank 1966–70; Legal & General: corp planning div 1970–72, asst controller admin of gp pension schemes 1972–73, controller pensions and support serv for mktg and sales 1973–74, asst gen mangr (ops) Legal and General (South Africa) 1974–77, life admin mangr UK 1977–80, head of personnel 1980–86, dir Life 1986–89, md (fin servs) Independent Intermediaries, Mortgage Co and L & G's Estate Agency 1989, currently md personnel servs; chm Bd of Surrey TEC 1992–, dep chm Exec Ctee Cncl of Mortage Lenders 1989–91; govr George Abbot Sch Guildford 1990–94; *Recreations* dinghy sailing; *Style—* Colin Harris, Esq

HARRIS, David Albert; s of Albert Edward Harris (d 1988), of Woodford Halse, Northants, and Edith Lilian, *née* Butler (d 1988); *b* 11 June 1938; *Educ* Magdalen Coll Sch Brackley Northants, UCL (ed Sennet London Univ student newspaper), DipCAM (PR); *m* 1965, Marjorie Ann, da of Arthur Ney, and Lotte, *née* Friedlaender (d 1996); 1 da, 1 s; *Career* editorial asst Furniture Record 1958–59, PRO Nat Union of Students 1960–62, freelance educational journalist 1962–64, on staff The Teacher (Nat Union of Teachers) 1964–66 (latterly dep ed), dep ed Focus (Consumer Cncl) 1966–67, account exec Max Redlich Ltd (PR conslts) 1967–69, info offr Consumer Cncl 1969–71, dir Braban Public Relations Ltd 1971–75, md Partnerplan Public Affairs Ltd 1975–77; dir of public affrs: The Advtg Assoc 1977–88, Market Research Soc 1988–89; dir The Hansard Soc for Parliamentary Govt 1989–; Lib/Lib Democrat Pty: agent for Finchley gen elections 1970 and Feb 1974, former chm Hendon South and memb Lib Nat Publicity Ctee; sometime memb Cncl Inst of PR (chm Govt Affrs Gp 1988–89); FIPR 1986 (MIPR 1972), FRSA 1994; *Recreations* watching cricket, family history, collecting political commemoratives; *Style—* David Harris, Esq; ✉ The Hansard Society for Parliamentary Government, St Philip's Building North, Sheffield Street, London WC2A 2EX (☎ 0171 955 7478, fax 0171 955 7492)

HARRIS, David Anthony; MP (C) St Ives (majority 1,645); s of Edgar Courtenay Harris (d 1980), and Betty Doreen Harris (d 1977); *b* 1 Nov 1937; *Educ* Mount Radford Sch Exeter; *m* 1962, Diana Joan, *née* Hansford (d 1996); 1 s (Justin b 1964), 1 da (Rebecca b 1967); *Career* journalist; formerly with W Country newspapers, political corr Daily Telegraph 1976–79 (joined 1961); MEP (EDG) Cornwall and Plymouth 1979–84, MP (C) St Ives 1983–; *Clubs* Farmers'; *Style—* David Harris Esq, MP; ✉ Alexandra House, Alexandra Road, Penzance, Cornwall (☎ 01736 63664); House of Commons, London SW1A 0AA (☎ 0171 219 3000)

HARRIS, David Anthony; s of Dr Samuel Harris (d 1996), and Joan, *née* Pegler; *b* 31 March 1954; *Educ* King Edward's Sch Birmingham, Univ of London (LLB); *m* 7 Nov 1987, Penelope Anne, da of Alfred Dalton, CB; 1 s (Edward Robert b 15 Dec 1991), 1 da (Sophie Olivia b 30 Sept 1988); *Career* admitted slr 1979; Field Fisher & Martineau 1977–82, ptnr Lovell White Durrant (formerly Lovell White & King) 1986– (joined 1982); Freeman Worshipful Co of Slrs; memb Section on Business Law Int Bar Assoc; MSI, memb Law Soc; *Recreations* riding, tennis, skiing; *Style—* David Harris, Esq; ✉ Lovell White Durrant, 65 Holborn Viaduct, London EC1A 2DY (☎ 0171 236 0066)

HARRIS, Prof David John; s of Sidney John William Harris, and Alice May, *née* Full (d 1955); *b* 3 July 1938; *Educ* Sutton HS Plymouth, King's Coll London (LLB), LSE (LLM, PhD); *m* 15 Aug 1964, Sandra, da of Denzil Nelson, of Arcadia, California; 2 s (Mark b 20 Sept 1967, Paul b 27 March 1972); *Career* asst lectr in law Queen's Univ Belfast 1962–63; Univ of Nottingham asst lectr in law 1963–65, lectr 1965–73, sr lectr 1973–81, prof of public int law 1981–, head Law Dept 1986–89; memb Ctee of Ind Experts Euro Social Charter 1990–; *Books* International Law - Cases and Materials (1973, 4th edn 1991), Civil Liberties - Cases and Materials (1979, 3rd edn 1991), The European Social Charter (1984); *Recreations* walking, travel; *Style—* Prof David Harris; ✉ c/o Department of Law, University of Nottingham, Nottingham (☎ 0115 951 5700)

HARRIS, Col David Keith; OBE (1987, MBE 1983), TD (1978), DL (Lincolnshire 1993–); s of Edwin Harris (d 1974), of Epworth, Doncaster, and Mona Doreen, *née* Sleight; *b* 27 Jan 1945; *Educ* Worksop Coll, King's Coll London (LLB); *m* 25 Jan 1975, Veronica Mary, da of Arthur Vernon Harrison (d 1983), of Manor Farm, Finningley, Doncaster; *Career* Univ of London OTC 1963–67, cmmnd Royal Lincolnshire Regt TA 1967; served: 5 Royal Anglian 1967–78, 7 Royal Anglian 1978–80, SO2 G3 7 Field Force 1980–82, SO2 G3 49 Inf Bde 1982; cmd 7 R Anglian 1984–87, dep cdr 49 Inf Bde 1987–90, TA Col RMAS 1991–94, Dep Col The Royal Anglian Regt TA 1992–; admitted slr 1969, sr ptnr Richmonds 1987– (co dir); Parly candidate (Cons) Bassetlaw: Oct 1974, May 1979; memb Law Soc 1967; ADC 1990–93; *Recreations* rugby union, shooting, gardening, good food and wine; *Style—* Col David Harris, OBE, TD, DL; ✉ Green Hill House, Haxey, Doncaster, S Yorks DN9 2JU (☎ 01427 752794); Richmonds, Richmonds House, White Rose Way, Doncaster, S Yorks DN4 5JH (☎ 01302 762900, fax 01302 762801, Gainsborough ☎ 01427 613831)

HARRIS, David Laurence; *b* 19 June 1944; *Educ* Liverpool GS, Coll of Law; *m* 1973, Maureen Ann, *née* Cocklin; 2 s, 1 da; *Career* admitted slr; Govt serv exec various appts 1963–73, ptnr Tax Law Dept Nabarro Nathanson 1973–82; dir N M Rothschild & Sons Ltd 1987–; chief exec Rothschild Trust Corporation Ltd 1982–, non-exec dir Rothschild Asset Management Ltd 1984–, pres Rothschild Trust (Canada) Inc 1989–, dir Rothschild Trust Switzerland AG 1992–; chm: Rothschild Trust Guernsey Ltd 1995– (dir 1992–), Rothschild Trust (Bermuda) Ltd 1996– (dir 1991–); memb Law Soc, FInstT; *Recreations* golf, opera, sport, gardening; *Clubs* IOD; *Style—* David Harris, Esq; ✉ Director, N M Rothschild & Sons Limited, PO Box 185, New Court, St Swithin's Lane, London EC4P 4DU (☎ 0171 280 5000, fax 0171 280 5948)

HARRIS, David Leslie; s of Leslie Godfrey Harris (d 1959), and Frances Olive, *née* Jones (d 1974); *b* 24 April 1938; *Educ* Watford GS, Westminster Hosp Med Sch (MB BS, MS); *m* 22 Jan 1966, Patricia Ann (Trish), da of William Charles David Hooper (d 1978); 1 s (Stephen b 1967, d 1986), 3 da (Vanessa b 1967, Joanna b 1968, Sally b 1976); *Career* conslt plastic surgn and head of Dept Derriford Hosp Plymouth 1972–, civilian conslt in plastic surgery RN Hosp Stonehouse Plymouth 1978–86, chm Div of Surgery Plymouth Health Authy 1981–84, hon visiting conslt in plastic surgery to Gibraltar Health Authy St Bernard's Hosp Gibraltar 1985–91, civilian conslt RN 1986–; numerous pubns on psychological aspects of cosmetic plastic surgery and treatment of hypospadias; memb: Ct of Examiners Intercollegiate Bd for Plastic Surgery 1993–, Br Assoc of Plastic Surgns, Int Soc of Aesthetic Plastic Surgns, Br Assoc of Aesthetic Plastic Surgns (pres 1989–90), Faculty Educnl Fndn; MRCS 1961, FRCS 1966;

Recreations garden, music, dining out, sailing; *Clubs* Plymouth Legal and Medical Dining, Royal Western Yacht; *Style—* David Harris, Esq; ✉ West Park House, Tamerton Foliot, Plymouth PL5 4NG (☎ 01752 773411); Nuffield Hospital, Derriford Rd, Plymouth PL6 8BG (☎ 01752 707345)

HARRIS, David Michael; QC (1989); s of Maurice Harris, of Liverpool, and Doris, *née* Ellis; *b* 7 Feb 1943; *Educ* Liverpool Inst HS for Boys, Univ of Oxford (BA, MA), Univ of Cambridge (PhD); *m* 16 Aug 1970, Emma Lucia, da of Dr Italo Calma, of Liverpool; 2 s (Julian b 3 July 1974, Jeremy b 9 May 1977), 1 da (Anna b 10 May 1980); *Career* asst lectr in law Univ of Manchester 1967–69, called to the Bar 1969, recorder 1988– (asst recorder 1984–88), head of chambers; *Books* Winfield & Jolowicz on Tort (co-ed, 1971), Supplement to Bingham's The Modern Cases on Negligence (co-ed, 1985); *Recreations* arts, travel, sport; *Style—* David M Harris, Esq, QC; ✉ Peel House, 3rd Floor, Harrington St, Liverpool L2 9XN (☎ 0151 236 0718, fax 0151 255 1085); 3 Paper Buildings, Temple, London EC4Y 7EU (☎ 0171 583 8055, fax 0171 353 6271)

HARRIS, Prof David Russell; s of Dr Herbert Melville Harris (d 1976), of Oxford, and Norah Mary, *née* Evans (d 1985); *b* 14 Dec 1930; *Educ* St Christopher Sch Letchworth Herts, Univ of Oxford (MA, BLitt), Univ of California Berkeley (PhD); *m* 5 July 1957, Helen Margaret, da of Dr Gilbert Ingram Wilson (d 1980), of Stafford; 4 da (Sarah b 1959, Joanna b 1962, Lucy b 1964, Zoë b 1969); *Career* Nat Serv RAF 1949–50; teaching asst and instr Univ of California 1956–58, lectr Queen Mary Coll London 1958–64; UCL: lectr and reader 1964–79, prof of human environment Inst of Archaeology 1979– (dir 1989–96); memb: Museum of London Archaeology Ctee 1984–93, English Heritage Sci and Conservation Panel 1985–, Dover Archaeological Advsy Bd 1989–; chm Science-Based Archaeology Ctee SERC 1989–92; pres: Prehistoric Soc 1990–94, Soc for Economic Botany UK Chapter 1995–97; FSA 1982; *Books* Plants, Animals and Man in the Outer Leeward Islands (1965), Africa in Transition (with B W Hodder, 1967), Human Ecology in Savanna Environments (1980), Foraging and Farming (with G C Hillman, 1989), Modelling Ecological Change (with K D Thomas, 1991), The Archaeology of V Gordon Childe (1994), The Origins and Spread of Agriculture and Pastoralism in Eurasia (1996); *Recreations* mountain walking, archaeo-ecological overseas travel; *Clubs* Athenaeum; *Style—* Prof David Harris, FSA; ✉ Institute of Archaeology, University College London, 31–34 Gordon Square, London WC1H 0PY (☎ 0171 380 7484, fax 0171 383 2572)

HARRIS, Prof Frank; CBE (1996); s of David Aaron Harris (d 1948), and Miriam, *née* Silber (d 1977); *b* 6 Oct 1934; *Educ* Univ of Capetown (MB ChB, MMed (paediatrics), MD); *m* 13 Mar 1963, Brenda Henriette, da of Samuel van Embden (d 1982); 2 s (David b 1964, Evan b 1965); *Career* Univ of Liverpool: prof of child health 1974–89, pro vice chllr 1981–84, dean Faculty of Med 1986–89; dean Sch of Med and prof of paediatrics Univ of Leicester 1990–; memb: Liverpool Health Authy 1977–83, CRM 1981–90, Mersey RHA 1983–89, CSM 1990–92, Trent RHA 1990, GMC 1989– (memb Review Bd Overseas Qualified Practitioners 1991–, Educn Ctee 1993–, PPC 1993–), Leicestershire Health Authy 1990– (vice-chm 1993–, chm Audit Ctee 1993–), JPAC Ctee 1990–94, Advsy Gp on Med Educn and Trg (AGMETS) 1995–; exec sec Cncl of Deans of UK Med Schs and Faculties 1990–96; memb: EC Advsy Cmmn on Med Trg 1994–, vice pres Assoc of Medical Schs in Europe 1992–; MCPCH 1996, FRCPE 1975, FRCP 1982; *Books* Paediatric Fluid Therapy (1973); *Recreations* golf, bridge; *Style—* Prof Frank Harris, CBE; ✉ Dean Faculty of Medicine, University of Leicester, PO Box 138, Maurice Shock Medical Sciences Building, University Road, Leicester LE1 9HN (☎ 0116 252 2962, fax 0116 252 5001)

HARRIS, Geoffrey Ronald; s of Clarence Edgar Harris (d 1966); *b* 10 Sept 1926; *Educ* Whitgift; *m* 1953, Joan Lyn, da of George Jarvis; 2 s (Nigel David, Mark Stephen), 1 da (Sally Elizabeth); *Career* WWII Lt served Germany and India; insur broker; dir: Stewart Wrightson (Marine) 1965–88, Codresa (Spain) 1973–88, Stewart Wrightson Chile Ltd 1978–88, Stewart Wrightson Cusur (Argentina) 1978–88, Golding Stewart Wrightson 1985–88, insur conslt Alexander Howden Reinsurance Brokers Ltd 1989–; *Recreations* sport, travel; *Style—* Geoffrey Harris, Esq; ✉ Rookwood, Lower Park Rd, Chipstead, Surrey (☎ 01737 553768); Alexander Howden Reinsurance Brokers Ltd, 8 Devonshire Square, London EC2M 4PL (☎ 0171 623 5500, telex 882171)

HARRIS, Graham Derek; s of Philip Henry Harris, of 16 Hardwick Rd, Folkestone, Kent, and May Dorothy, *née* Perovich; *b* 28 Sept 1956; *Educ* King's Sch Canterbury Kent, Oriel Coll Oxford (MA); *m* 14 Feb 1987, Katarine Maria, da of Boris Stanislaus Brandl (d 1955), of Garstang, Lancs; 1 da (Philippa Josephine Brandl b 28 Sept 1989); *Career* slr; articled clerk Norton Rose Botterell & Roche 1979–83, admitted 1981, ptnr Richards Butler 1988– (joined 1983); SSC; *Style—* Graham Harris, Esq; ✉ Richards Butler, Beaufort House, 15 St Botolph St, London EC3A 7QQ (☎ 0171 247 6555, fax 0171 247 5091, telex 949494 RBLAW G)

HARRIS, Harry; s of Jack Harris, and Sara, *née* Cohen; *b* 30 May 1952; *Educ* Davenant Fndn GS (soccer capt), Harlow Coll; *m* (m dis); 1 s (Simon Paul b 16 Nov 1975), 1 da (Jordanna b 17 Aug 1980); *Career* journalist; Express & Independent 1971–72, North London Weekly Herald 1972–79, Newcastle Journal 1979–80, London Evening News 1980–81, Daily Mail 1981–85, Daily Mirror 1985– (currently gp chief soccer writer); memb: Football Writers' Assoc, Sports Writers' Assoc; Great Britain's Sports Journalist of the Year 1993, Sports Cncl's Sports Reporter of the Year (jtly) 1993, highly commended Race in the Media Awards 1993, short-listed Br Sports Reporter of the Yr 1994, runner-up GB's Sports Journalist of the Yr 1996; *Books* ghost writer of books incl: Spurred to Success (with Glenn Hoddle), The Inside Story (with Terry Venables), Rock Bottom (with Paul Merson), Against All the Odds (with Gary Mabbutts), Macca Can (with Steve McMahon), Revelations of a Football Manager (with Terry Neill); also Bill Nicholson's autobiography (co-author), Jurgen Klinsman's Diary of a Season, Portrait of a Genius (Ruud Gullit's biography); *Style—* Harry Harris, Esq; ✉ Group Chief Soccer Writer, Daily Mirror, Mirror Group Newspapers, 1 Canada Square, London E14 5AP (☎ 0171 510 3000)

HARRIS, Prof Sir Henry; kt (1993); s of late Sam Harris, and late Ann Harris; *b* 28 Jan 1925; *Educ* Sydney Boys' HS, Univ of Sydney (Garton scholar BA (modern languages), MB BS, Freehill prize for Italian), Univ of Oxford (MA, DPhil, DM); *m* 1950, Alexandra Fanny Brodsky; 1 s, 2 da; *Career* resident med offr Royal Prince Albert Hospital Sydney Aust 1950, res offr Dept of Physiology Univ of Melbourne 1951, dir of res Br Empire Cancer Campaign at Sir William Dunn Sch of Pathology Oxford 1954–59, visiting scientist NIH USA 1959–60, head Dept of Cell Biology John Innes Inst 1960–63; Univ of Oxford: prof of pathology 1963–79, head of dept Sir William Dunn Sch of Pathology 1963–94, Regius prof of med 1979–92; visiting prof Vanderbilt Univ 1968, Walker-Ames prof Univ of Washington 1968, foreign prof Collège de France 1974; memb: Scientific Advsy Ctee CRC 1961–85, ARC 1968–78 (chm Animals Res Bd 1976–78), Cncl Royal Soc 1971–72, Cncl Euro Molecular Biology Orgn 1974–76; govr Euro Cell Biology Orgn 1973–75; lectr at numerous public lectures; corresponding memb: Aust Acad of Sci, American Assoc for Cancer Res, Waterford Striped Bass Derby Assoc (foreign correspondent); hon memb: American Assoc of Pathologists, German Soc for Cell Biology; foreign memb Max Planck Soc, foreign hon memb American Acad of Arts and Sciences, hon fell Cambridge Philosophical Soc; Hon DSc Univ of Edinburgh 1976; Hon MD: Univ of Geneva 1982, Univ of Sydney 1983; Hon FRCPath Aust, FRCP, FRCPath, FRS; *Publications* Nucleus and Cytoplasm (1968, 2 edn 1970, 3 edn 1974), Cell Fusion (1970), La Fusion Cellulaire (1974), The Balance of Improbabilities (1987), The Cells of the Body (1995); papers on cellular physiology and biochemistry; *Style—* Prof Sir Henry Harris, FRS; ✉ Sir William Dunn School of Pathology, South Parks Road, Oxford OX1 3RE (☎ 01865 275577)

HARRIS, Hugh Christopher Emlyn; s of T E Harris, CB, CBE (d 1955), and M A Harris (d 1980); *b* 25 March 1936; *Educ* The Leys Sch, Trinity Coll Cambridge (MA); *m* 7 Sept 1968, Pamela Susan, da of R A Woollard (d 1980); 1 s (William b 1972), 1 da (Kate b 1970); *Career* Nat Serv Lt RA 1954–56; dir: BE Services Ltd 1979–94, Houblon Nominees 1988–94, The Securities Management Trust Ltd 1988–95; Bank of England 1959–94: chief of corp servs 1984–88, assoc dir 1988–94; dir of ops London First 1995– (former gen mangr London First Centre 1995); dep chm Cmmn for Racial Equality 1996– (cmmr 1995–); special advsr CILNTEC 1994–; churchwarden St Margaret Lothbury 1988–94, hon treas Royal Br Legion Kemsing Branch, chm Solefield School Educational Trust Ltd, memb Advsy Cncl Windsor Fellowship; companion Business in the Community; Liveryman Worshipful Co of Turners; ACIB, FIPD, FRSA; *Recreations* rugby, tennis; *Style—* Hugh Harris, Esq; ✉ London First, Caxton House, 6 Tothill Street, London SW1H 9NA (☎ 0171 222 1445, fax 0171 222 1448)

HARRIS, Iain Grant Nicolson; *b* 17 March 1946; *Educ* George Heriot's Sch Edinburgh, Univ of Aberdeen (MA); *m* 8 Aug 1969, Jane Petrie, *née* Robertson; 1 s (Grant b 1975), 1 da (Rochelle b 1980); *Career* sales promotion mangr RMC Group 1968–73; dir: Parker PR Associates Ltd 1973–80, Shandwick Consultants Ltd 1980–82, Good Relations City Ltd 1982–85; chm: Lombard Communications Ltd 1985–90, Wolfe Lombard Ltd 1985–90, Lombard Group plc 1988–90, Lombard Consultants Ltd 1989–90, Lombard PR Ltd 1989–90, First Pacific Ltd 1990–, Valley Communications plc 1992–; dep chm Grandfield Rork Collins Ltd 1991–92; pres Lombard Communications Inc (USA) 1987–91; pres: Windsor Soc for Mentally Handicapped Children and Adults 1978–95, Windsor Talking Newspaper 1978–95; tstee New Windsor Community Assoc 1978–95, vice pres Royal Windsor Rose and Horticultural Soc, Mayor Royal Borough of Windsor and Maidenhead 1976–78 (borough cncllr 1970–79); Freeman City of London 1982; *Recreations* gardening supervision, travel; *Style—* Iain Harris, Esq; ✉ Redholme House, 20 Colinton Road, Edinburgh EH10 5EQ (☎ 0131 447 5111, fax 0131 447 6111)

HARRIS, Sir Ian Cecil; KBE (1967, CBE 1958), CB (1962), DSO (1945); s of late J W A Harris; *b* 7 July 1910; *Educ* Portora Royal Sch Enniskillen, RMC Sandhurst; *m* 1945, Anne-Marie Desmotreux; 2 s (1 decd); *Career* 2 Lt Royal Ulster Rifles 1930, NW Frontier of India (despatches) 1939, served WWII NW Europe, cmd 2 Bn Royal Ulster Rifles 1943–45, GSO 1 25 Ind Div and 7 Div Burma and Malaya 1945–46 (despatches), India and Pakistan 1946–47, AQMG Scot cmd 1949–51, cmd 6 Bn Royal Ulster Rifles (TA) 1951–52, chief of staff N Ireland 1952–54, cmd 1 Fed Inf Bde Malaya 1954–57 (despatches), dep dir of staff duties (A) WO 1957–60, GOC Singapore Base Dist 1960–62, chief of staff contingency planning SHAPE 1963–66, Lt-Gen 1966, GOC N Ireland 1966–69, ret; Hon Col: Royal Ulster Rifles 1962–68, Royal Irish Rangers 1968–72; chm: Irish Bloodstock Breeders Assoc 1977–79 (pres 1984–88), Br Support Ctee Memorial Museum of Caen 1988; Hon Citizen City of Caen Normandy 1984; *Clubs* Army & Navy; *Style—* Sir Ian Harris, KBE, CB, DSO; ✉ 24 Belgrave Square, Monkstown, Co Dublin, Ireland (☎ 00 353 1 280 7312)

HARRIS, Sir Jack Wolfred Ashford; 2 Bt (UK 1932), of Bethnal Green, Co London; s of Rt Hon Sir Percy Alfred Harris, 1 Bt, DL (d 1952); *b* 23 July 1906; *Educ* Shrewsbury, Trinity Hall Cambridge (BA); *m* 1933, Patricia, da of Arthur P Penman, of Wahroonga, nr Sydney, NSW; 2 s (Christopher John Ashford b 1934, Paul Percy Ashford b 1945), 1 da (Margaret b 1939); *Heir* s, Christopher John Ashford Harris b 26 Aug 1934; *Career* chm Bing Harris & Co NZ 1935–; past pres Wellington C of C; *Recreations* reading, gardening, swimming, writing; *Clubs* Wellington; *Style—* Sir Jack Harris, Bt; ✉ Flat 12, Quarterdeck, Carabella St, Kirribilli, NSW, Aust; Te Rama, Waikanae, New Zealand (☎ 00 64 4 293 5001)

HARRIS, Dr James Richard; s of James Derek Harris, and Valerie Olive Harris, of London; *b* 8 Aug 1960; *Educ* London Hosp Med Coll (MB BS, MRCGP), Inst of Aviation Med (CertAvMed); *m* 10 July 1983, Jill Elizabeth, da of Peter Charles Richards; 2 s (Edward James b 19 Dec 1986, William Peter b 10 Feb 1989), 1 da (Emily Rose Harris b 19 March 1993); *Career* formerly: various hosp posts Chelmsford and Essex Hosp, St George's Hosp London, St Peter's Hosp Chertsey and Llandough Hosp Penarth, gen practice trainee Dinas Powis S Glamorgan; currently: princ in gen practice Woodlands Surgery Crawley, publisher Network Medical Services Ltd Crawley; chm Nat Young Principals 1990–, memb Cncl RCGP 1991–, divnl pres BMA 1993–; *Recreations* golf, travel; *Style—* Dr James Harris; ✉ Plovers, Brantridge Forest, nr Balcombe, W Sussex RH17 6JY (☎ 01444 400440, fax 01444 401360); Network Medical Services Ltd, Ocean House, Hazelwick Avenue, Crawley, W Sussex RH10 1NP (☎ 01293 534411, fax 01293 612266)

HARRIS, Very Rev John; s of Richard Harris (d 1988), of Newport, Gwent, and Ivy Millicent, *née* Price (d 1961); *b* 12 March 1932; *Educ* Pontywain GS, St David's UC Lampeter (Phillips scholar, BA), Sarum Theol Coll; *m* 29 Dec 1956, Beryl June, da of late Ivor Edward Roberts; 2 s (Martin John b 22 Oct 1960, Timothy Edward b 27 Jan 1967), 1 da (Catherine b 2 Oct 1959); *Career* ordained: deacon 1957, priest 1958; curate: of Pontnewynydd 1957–60, of Bassaleg 1960–63; vicar: of Penmaen 1963–69, of St Paul Newport 1969–84; chaplain to Royal Gwent Hosp 1974–84, canon of Monmouth 1983, vicar of Maindee Newport 1984–93, dean of Brecon 1993–; *Recreations* archaeology, walking, serious music, ballet; *Style—* The Very Rev John Harris, Dean of Brecon; ✉ The Deanery, Cathedral Close, Brecon, Powys LD3 9DP (☎ 01874 623344)

HARRIS, Prof John Buchanan; s of John Benjamin Sargent Harris (d 1971), of Adelaide, Aust, and Mary Isobel, *née* Pratt; *b* 18 Jan 1940; *Educ* Tiffin Sch Kingston upon Thames, Univ of London (BPharm), Univ of Bradford (PhD); *m* 6 Sept 1965, Christine Margaret, da of Clifford Morton Holt (d 1983), of Bradford, W Yorks; 2 s (Joel b and d 1972, Jolyon Leo b 1974), 1 da (Danica Mathilde b 1981); *Career* res asst Univ of Bradford 1963–67; Univ of Newcastle: sr res asst 1967–72, princ res assoc 1972–74, sr lectr 1974–80, prof 1980–; res fell Univ of Lund Sweden 1970–71, UCLA America 1977–78, Monash Univ Melbourne Aust 1980; FIBiol, MRPharmS; *Books* Muscular Dystrophy and other Inherited Diseases of Muscle in Animals (1979), Natural Toxins (1986), Muscle Metabolism (with D M Turnbull, 1990); *Recreations* reading, philately, walking; *Style—* Prof John Harris; ✉ Head of School of Neurosciences, University of Newcastle School of Neurosciences, Muscular Dystrophy Group Laboratories, Regional Neurosciences Centre, Newcastle General Hospital, Newcastle upon Tyne NE4 6BE (☎ 0191 2738811 ext 22632, fax 0191 226 0775)

HARRIS, John Charles; DL (S Yorks 1986); s of Sir Charles Joseph William Harris, KBE (d 1986), and Emily Kyle, *née* Thompson (d 1992); *b* 25 April 1936; *Educ* Dulwich, Clare Coll Cambridge (MA, LLM); *m* 1 April 1961, Alison Beryl, da of Dr Kenneth Reginald Sturley; 1 s (Edward John Charles b 16 June 1968), 1 da (Susan Alison b 15 Sept 1966); *Career* Nat Serv 2 Lt Intelligence Corps 1954–56; with UKAEA (seconded to OECD) 1959–63, Poole Borough Cncl 1963–67, admitted slr 1966, dep town clerk Bournemouth CB 1971–73 (offr 1967–73); S Yorks CC 1973–86: co sec 1973–83, chief exec and co clerk 1983–86, non-exec dir S Yorks Passenger Tport Exec, clerk to Lord-Lieut S Yorks 1983–86; legal, mgmnt and recruitment conslt (incl for PA Conslt Group and Daniels Bates Partnership) 1986–, exec dir Solace International Ltd 1992–; freelance corr on public affrs; non-exec dir Pontefract Health Authy 1990–93; memb: Rampton Special Hosp Ctee 1989–96, Arts Cncl Touring Advsy Bd 1988–92, Bd

Northern Counties Housing Assoc 1990– (chair 1994–), Ctee Ackworth Gp Riding for the Disabled Assoc 1976–; fndr memb and sec Barnsley-Rockley Rotary Club 1976–79, vice chm and sec Friends of Opera North 1978–87; Opera North plc: memb Cncl 1979–88, memb Devpt Ctee 1987–94; nat chm Soc of Co Secs 1983, Hon PRO S Yorks and Humberside Region RDA 1983–92; memb: Cncl Soc of Local Authys Chief Exec 1984–86, RDA Nat Pubns Ctee 1988–90, W Yorks Police Authy (independent) 1994–; tstee Housing Assocs Charitable Tst 1995–96; Freeman City of London 1957; memb: Charter 88, Euro Movement; FRSA 1984; *Recreations* foreign travel, opera, competitive trail riding; *Clubs* Leeds; *Style*— John Harris, Esq, DL; ✉ Long Lane Close, High Ackworth, Pontefract, Yorkshire WF7 7EY (office ☎ 01977 707402, fax 01977 707409, home ☎ 01977 795450, fax 01977 795470)

HARRIS, John Clement; s of Norman Rees, and Leah Eastwood, *née* Clement; *b* 9 July 1936; *Educ* Seaford Coll, Petworth; *m* 19 Sept 1962, Shirley, *née* Anderson; 1 s (Jonathan b 17 May 1964); *Career* Nat Serv RAF 1955–57; own business: nursing homes 1957–62, furnishing and interior design 1962–84, commercial property devpt/mgmnt 1978–; Fedn of Small Businesses: fndr memb 1975, branch and vice chm, region and vice chm, nat cncllr and exec memb Bd of Dirs, policy chm, hon nat chm 1992–; chm Southern Water Consumer Consultative Ctee, memb OFWAT Southern Customer Servs Ctee; *Recreations* building, walking, travelling (particularily USA); *Style*— John Harris, Esq; ✉ Walnut Trees, Houghton, Arundel, W Sussex BN18 9LN (☎ 01798 831375); Federation of Small Businesses, Parliamentary Office, 2 Catherine Place, Westminster, London SW1E 6HF (☎ 0171 233 7900, fax 0171 233 7899)

HARRIS, Prof John Edwin (Jack); MBE (1981); s of John Frederick Harris (d 1978), and Emily Margaret, *née* Prosser (d 1980); *b* 2 June 1932; *Educ* Larkfield GS Chepstow, Univ of Birmingham (BSc, PhD, DSc); *m* 9 June 1956, Ann, da of Peter James Foote (d 1976); 2 s (Peter b 28 March 1957, Ian b 17 May 1962), 2 da (Wendy b 3 Feb 1962, Perlita b 6 April 1966); *Career* res worker AEI John Thompson 1956–59; Berkeley Nuclear Laboratories CEGB: res offr 1959–64, section head 1964–88, univ liaison offr 1988; visiting prof of nuclear engrg Univ of Manchester 1989–, visiting prof of corrosion UMIST 1992–, visiting prof of manufacturing and materials Univ of Plymouth 1992–; memb: Bd Br Nuclear Energy Soc, Cncl British Pugwash 1996–; ed Interdisciplinary Sci Review 1996–; memb Bd of Visitors Leyhill Open Prison 1967–93; FIM 1974, FEng 1987, FRS 1988, FInstP 1992; *Books* Physical Metallurgy of Reactor Fuel Elements (ed), Vacancies (ed 1976); *Recreations* writing popular articles on sci; *Clubs* Cam Bowling (non playing memb); *Style*— Prof Jack Harris, MBE, FRS, FEng; ✉ Church Farm House, 28 Hopton Rd, Upper Cam, Dursley, Glos GL11 5PB (☎ 01453 543165)

HARRIS, John Eric; MBE (1996); s of Jack Harris (d 1982), of Ilford, Essex, and Freda, *née* Jacobs (d 1979); *b* 29 April 1932; *Educ* Slough GS, Plaistow GS; *m* 1, 15 June 1958, Helene Hinda (d 1985), da of Aaron Coren (d 1960), of London; 1 s (Daniel Bruce b 1960), 1 da (Allyson b 1961); m 2, 10 Dec 1989, Jacqueline Maureen, da of Alfred Freeman (d 1989), of London, and wid of Philip Leigh; *Career* chm: Alba plc 1987–, Harvard International 1980–87, Bush Radio plc, Goodmans Industries Ltd, Satellite Technology Systems Ltd; md Harris Overseas Ltd 1963–82; dir: Alba France SA, Hinari Deutschland GmbH, Dirt Devil Ltd; chm and tstee Helene Harris Meml Tst promoting res into ovarian cancer; hon memb British Gynaecological Cancer Soc; *Recreations* reading, theatre, opera; *Clubs* Reform; *Style*— John Harris, Esq, MBE; ✉ 11 Blenheim Road, London NW8 OLU (☎ 0171 625 7600); Alba plc, Harvard House, 14–16 Thames Rd, Barking, Essex IG11 OHX (☎ 0181 594 5533, fax 0181 594 9845, car 0468 244309)

HARRIS, John Frederick; s of John Harris (d 1942), and Lily, *née* Heard (d 1985); *b* 9 Dec 1938; *Educ* Central GS Birmingham, Aston Tech Coll Birmingham, Aston Univ; *m* 27 Aug 1960, Diana Joyce, da of Stanley John Brown, of Nottingham; 1 s (Alastair Charles b 1961), 2 da (Mary Julia b 1963, Susan Elizabeth b 1977); *Career* dep chm NORWEB 1979–82, dir Saudi Arabia BEI Ltd 1978–84, dir BEI Ltd 1982–87, chm EMEB 1982–90, chm East Midlands Electricity plc 1990–94; dir Nottingham Devpt Enterprise, govr Nottingham Trent Univ, pres Nottinghamshire VSO; memb Cncl IEE; CEng 1967, FIEE 1982, CIMgt 1984; *Recreations* golf, opera, gardening; *Clubs* Reform; *Style*— John Harris, Esq

HARRIS, His Hon John Percival; DSC (1945), QC (1974); s of Thomas Percival Harris (d 1981), of Ebbor Hall, Somerset; *b* 16 Feb 1925; *Educ* Wells Cathedral Sch, Pembroke Coll Cambridge (BA); *m* 1959, Janet Valerie, da of Archibald William Douglas, of Jersey, CI; 1 s, 2 da; *Career* Sub Lt RNVR 1943–46, serv: Western Approaches, Far East, China, Japan; called to the Bar Middle Temple 1949, master of the bench 1970, recorder of the Crown Court 1972–80, circuit judge (SE Circuit) 1980–95, dep sr judge of the Ct of the Sovereign Base Area Cyprus; *Recreations* golf, reading, Victorian paintings; *Clubs* Woking Golf, Rye Golf, The Royal St George's Golf; *Style*— His Hon J P Harris, DSC, QC; ✉ Tudor Court, Fairmile Park Rd, Cobham, Surrey KT11 2PP (☎ 01932 864756)

HARRIS, John Robert; TEM (1945); s of Maj Alfred Harris, CBE, DSO, and Rosa Alfreda, *née* Alderson; *b* 5 June 1919; *Educ* Harrow, Architectural Assoc Sch of Architecture (AADipl); *m* 10 June 1950, Gillian, da of Col C W D Rowe, CB, MBE, TD, JP, DL (d 1954), of Peterborough; 1 s (Mark b 27 Sept 1952), 1 da (Georgina b 7 Aug 1956); *Career* active serv and TA 1939–45, Lt RE Hong Kong 1940–41 (POW of Japanese 1941–45); memb: Br Army Aid Gp China 1943–45, Hong Kong Resistance 1942–45; architect; fndr and sr ptnr J R Harris Partnership 1949– (fndr and sr ptnr assoc firms in Brunei, Dubai, France, Hong Kong, Oman, Qatar, Spain); projects won in int competition: State Hosp Qatar 1953, New Dubai Hosp 1976, Corniche Dev and traffic intersection Dubai 1978, HQ for Min of Social Affrs and Lab Oman 1979, Tuen Mun Hosp Hong Kong 1981; int assessment Rulers office dev Dubai 1985, architect and planner Zhuhai New Town Econ Zone Peoples Republic of China 1984, Q-Tel 1991; major UK works incl: Stoke Mandeville Hosp 1983, Wellesley House and St Peter's Court Sch redevpt 1975, Dorchester Hotel renovation 1985–90, North Quay Docklands 600 room hotel, Gloucester Park devpt (apartments, offices and retail) incl refurbishment on assoc underground station 1986–92, Natural History Museum refurbishment, Sheraton Grand Hotel Edinburgh redevpt, Strangeways Prison rebuild, various projects Royal Parks London; major overseas works incl: Int Trade Centre (40 storey) Dubai 1982, Br Embassy chancery offices and ambassador's residence Abu Dhabi 1982, Univ Teaching Hosp Maiduguri Nigeria 1982, dept stores 1973–93 (Antwerp, Brussels, Lille, Paris, Strasbourg, Hong Kong), Dubai Headquarters building British Bank of the Middle East 1993; pres Surveyors' Club 1968; FRIBA 1949, HKIA 1982, FRSA 1982; Membre de l'Ordre des Architectes Francais 1978; *Books* John R Harris Architects (jtly, 1984); *Recreations* architecture, sketching, sailing (Dream Lady); *Clubs* Royal Thames Yacht; *Style*— John R Harris, Esq; ✉ 24 Devonshire Place, London W1N 2BX (☎ 0171 935 9353, fax 0171 935 5709)

HARRIS, Joseph Hugh; JP (Penrith 1971), DL (1984); s of John Frederick Harris (d 1990); *b* 3 June 1932; *Educ* Harrow, RAC Cirencester (DipAg); *m* 1957, Anne, da of Brig L H McRobert (d 1981); 3 s; *Career* Lt 11 Hussars PAO; chm Cumbrian Newspapers Ltd 1987– (formerly dir); farmer, landowner; memb Miny of Agric Northern Regnl Panel 1977–83; RASE: sr steward 1957–77, hon dir Royal Show 1978–82, vice pres 1980–92, dep pres 1986–87, tstee 1992–; High Sheriff Cumbria 1976–77; chm: govrs Aysgarth Sch 1975–85, Grasmere Sports 1977–, Penrith and Alston Magistrates Bench 1991–96; memb Cumbria Rural Devpt Cmmn 1990–; Liveryman Worshipful Co of Farmers; Vice Lord Lt of Cumbria 1994–; *Recreations* shooting and field sports; *Style*— Joseph Harris, Esq, JP, DL; ✉ Brackenburgh, Calthwaite, Penrith, Cumbria CA11 9PW (☎ 01768 885253, fax 01768 885020)

HARRIS, Keith Reginald; s of Reginald Harris, and Doris Lillian, *née* Smith; *b* 11 April 1953; *Educ* Buckhurst Hill Co HS, Mgmnt Sch Univ of Bradford (Elijah Hepworth Prize, BSc), Univ of Surrey (PhD); *m* 12 Aug 1985, (Christine) Judith, da of David Morgan; 1 da (Francesca Alice b 30 May 1987), 1 s (Thomas Edward b 2 Sept 1993); *Career* assoc dir Orion Bank Ltd 1980 (credit analyst 1977–80); Morgan Grenfell & Co Ltd: asst director 1980–84, dir 1984–85, pres Morgan Grenfell Inc New York 1985–87; dir Drexel Burnham Lambert Holdings (UK) 1989–90 (md Drexel Burnham Lambert Inc 1987–89), md Apax Partners & Co Corporate Finance Ltd (formerly MMG Patricof & Co) 1990–94, chief exec Samuel Montagu & Co Ltd and dir HSBC Investment Bank Ltd 1994–96, chief exec Investment Banking HSBC Investment Bank plc 1996–; *Recreations* watching Manchester United, playing tennis, crossword puzzles, music, reading; *Style*— Keith Harris, Esq; ✉ HSBC Investment Bank plc, Vintners Place, 68 Upper Thames Street, London EC4V 3BJ (☎ 0171 336 4545, fax 0171 336 9990)

HARRIS, Lyndon Goodwin; s of late Sydney Ernest Harris, of Halesowen, and late Mary Elsie, *née* Tilley; *b* 25 July 1928; *Educ* Halesowen GS, Birmingham Coll of Art, Slade Sch of Fine Art (Dip Fine Art), Univ of London Inst of Educn (ATD), Courtauld Inst; *Career* artist; works exhibited at: Paris Salon (Gold medal in painting, hon mention in etching), RA, RSA, RI, RSW, RWA, RBA, RGI, NEAC; works in permanent collections incl: Govt Art Collection, UCL, Birmingham and Midland Inst; works reproduced in: Young Artists of Promise (Studio), The Artist (Masters of Water Colour and their Techniques), Royal Inst of Painters in Water Colours History and Membership List 1831–1981, Birmingham Post; scholarships: Leverhulme, Pilkington, Slade; Slade Anatomy Prizeman; memb: RI 1958, RSW 1952, RWA 1947; *Recreations* music (organ and pianoforte), cycling; *Style*— Lyndon Harris, Esq

HARRIS, Prof Malcolm; *b* 8 Nov 1934; *Educ* Univ of Leeds Dental Sch (BchD), London Hosp Med Sch (MB BS), Univ of London (MD); *m* 10 Jan 1965; 2 da, 1 s; *Career* prof Dept of Oral Surgery and Oral Medicine Eastman Dental Hospital and Univ Coll Hosp; FDSRCS (Eng), FFD RCS; *Books* Oral Surgery (with G R Seward and D M McGowan, 1988), Basic Manual of Orthognathic Surgery (with I Reynolds, 1990); *Recreations* work, painting, cooking and eating; *Clubs* Royal Society of Medicine; *Style*— Prof Malcolm Harris; ✉ 95 Wood Vale, London N10 3DL (☎ and fax 0181 883 1379); Eastman Dental Hospital, Gray's Inn Rd, London WC1 8LD (☎ 0171 935 1056, fax 0171 915 1259)

HARRIS, Mark; s of Solomon Harris (d 1982), of London, and Eva, *née* Lazarus (d 1990); *b* 23 Feb 1943; *Educ* Central Fndn Boys' GS, LSE (LLB), The Law Soc Coll of Law; *m* 8 Oct 1972, Sharon Frances, da of Alex Colin (d 1981), of Essex; 1 da (Emma Tanya b 1975); *Career* admitted slr 1967; Dept of Employment: legal asst 1968, sr legal asst 1973–78, asst slr 1978–87, legal advsr 1987–88; asst treasy slr Dept for Educn 1988–94, ret; memb Law Soc; *Recreations* travel, short-story writing (several published), painting, walking, London Jewish male choir (first tenor); *Clubs* Seaweed (vice pres); *Style*— Mark Harris, Esq; ✉ 17 Marlands Road, Clayhall, Ilford, Essex 1G5 OJL (☎ 0181 550 9894)

HARRIS, Prof Martin Best; CBE (1992); s of William Best Harris (d 1987), of Plymouth, and Betty Evelyn, *née* Martin; *b* 28 June 1944; *Educ* Devonport HS for Boys Plymouth, Queens' Coll Cambridge (MA), Univ of London (PhD); *m* 10 Sept 1966, Barbara Mary, da of Joseph Daniels (d 1971); 2 s (Robert b 1 July 1968, Paul b 13 June 1970); *Career* lectr in French linguistics Univ of Leicester 1967–72; Univ of Salford: sr lectr in French linguistics 1972–76, prof of Romance linguistics 1976–87, dean social science and arts 1978–81, pro vice chllr 1981–87; vice chllr: Univ of Essex 1987–92, Univ of Manchester 1992–; author of numerous books and articles on the Romance languages; memb UGC 1984–87 (chm NI sub ctee 1985–89); chm: UFC NI Ctee 1989–91, Nat Curriculum Working Party on Modern Languages 1989–90, Govrs Centre for Information on Language Teaching 1990–, Africa Ctee CICHE 1991–93, HEFCE Review of Postgraduate Educn 1995–96 (memb Libraries Review Ctee 1992–93), Clinical Standards Advsy Gp 1996–; vice chm CVCP 1995–97; dir USS (Universities Superannuation Scheme) Ltd 1991–; govr: Parrs Wood HS 1982–87, Anglia Poly 1989–92, SOAS 1990–93, Colchester Sixth Form Coll 1987–92, European Univ Inst 1992–; memb: Cncl Philological Soc 1985–92, Academia Europaea 1991–; hon fell: Queens' Coll Cambridge 1992, Bolton Inst 1996; Hon LLD Queen's Univ Belfast 1992, Hon DUniv Essex 1993, Hon DLitt Univ of Salford 1995; *Books* Evolution of French Syntax (1978), The Romance Verb (with N Vincent, 1983), The Romance Languages (with N Vincent, 1988, 2 edn 1990); *Recreations* walking, gardening, wine; *Style*— Prof Martin Harris, CBE; ✉ University of Manchester, Oxford Road, Manchester M13 9PL (☎ 0161 275 7399, fax 0161 272 6313)

HARRIS, Martin Richard; s of Col T B Harris, DSO (d 1965), of Bexhill-on-Sea, Sussex, and Phyllis Margaret, *née* Goode (d 1972); family members of Drapers' Co since 1760; *b* 30 Aug 1922; *Educ* Wellington Coll, Trinity Hall Cambridge; *m* 1952, Diana Moira, da of R W Gandar Dower (d 1967), of London SW1; 4 s (Andrew, Colin, Thomas, Peter); *Career* WWII Capt RE serv Middle East and Italy 1941–46; Price Waterhouse & Co 1946–74 (ptnr 1956–74), dir gen of the City Panel on Take-overs and Mergers 1974–77; dir: Reckitt and Colman 1977–82 (dep chm 1979–82), NatWest Bank 1977–93, NatWest Investment Bank 1977–92, Inmos International 1980–84, Equity and Law Life Assurance Society 1981–87 (dep chm 1983–87), De La Rue plc 1981–93, Westland 1981–85, TR Industrial and General Trust 1983–88, NatWest Smaller Companies Investment Trust 1991–; chm The Nineteen Twenty-Eight Investment Trust 1984–86; govr QMW London 1979–95 (chm 1989–95), memb Cncl RCM 1985–95; memb Ct: The Worshipful Co of Drapers 1978– (Master 1987–88), Co of CAs 1972– (Master 1983–84); FCA, FRCM, US Silver Star 1945; *Recreations* music, antique furniture and china, philately, keeping busy; *Clubs* Carlton, MCC, Pilgrims; *Style*— Martin Harris, Esq; ✉ 101 Church Road, Wimbledon, London SW19 5AL (☎ 0181 946 0951)

HARRIS, Matthew Edwin Charles; s of Lewis Martin Harris, of Hove, E Sussex, and Gaye, *née* Lloyd; *b* 31 May 1965; *Educ* Charterhouse, Brighton & Hove Tech Coll, Ecole le Nôtre Paris; *m* 4 May 1996, Donna Lynette, da of Donald Davies; *Career* chef Geneva 1984–85, Patisserie Sch Paris 1985–86, chef Hilaire Restaurant London 1986–87, exec head chef Bibendum Restaurant London 1995– (sous chef 1987–95); *Recreations* travel, eating out, cinema, swimming; *Style*— Matthew Harris, Esq; ✉ Bibendum, Michelin House, 81 Fulham Road, London SW3 6RD (☎ 0171 589 1481, fax 0171 823 7925)

HARRIS, Max; s of Harry Harris (d 1970), of London, and Tilly, *née* Stock (d 1975); *b* 15 Sept 1918; *m* 12 Aug 1953, Nanette Patricia May, da of Albert Rees (d 1946), of London WC1; 1 s (Paul Avrom), 1 da (Sarah Ann); *Career* Sgt RA 1942, Capt RASC 1943; pianist, composer, arranger; TV themes incl: Sherlock Holmes, Gurney Slade, Poldark, Porridge, Open All Hours, Black Eyes, Singing Detective; radio musical dir: Round The Horn 1969, Frankie Howerd 1976, Arthur Askey 1985; radio themes: The Spy Who Came In From The Cold, Tinker Tailor Soldier Spy, Smiley's People, A Perfect Spy, The Russia House; film themes: Carry On Sergeant, Baby Love, On The Buses, Christmas Wife; Novello award winner 1960–64, arranger on records by Stephan Grappelli and Yehudi Menuhin; memb Ctee Br Heart Fndn; Freeman City of London 1994; MCPS 1954, PRS 1961; *Recreations* golf, pictorial art; *Clubs* Betchworth Park Golf; *Style*— Max Harris, Esq

HARRIS, Michael Abraham Philip; s of Louis Harris (d 1974), of Southsea, Hants, and Rebecca, *née* Peter; *b* 14 March 1937; *Educ* Portsmouth GS, Queen's Coll Oxford (MA); *m* 11 Aug 1963, Sylvia Freda, da of Joshua Berman (d 1969), of Southsea, Hants; 2 s (David, Jonathan), 1 da (Claire); *Career* admitted slr 1965; memb Hants Inc Law Soc

1965–, tstee and hon slr Portsmouth and Southsea Hebrew Soc; memb Law Soc 1965–; *Recreations* all sport (especially cricket and soccer), bridge, classical music; *Clubs* Old Portmuthian; *Style*— Michael A P Harris, Esq; ✉ Harris Pascoe, 106 Victoria Road North, Portsmouth, Hants PO5 1QG (☎ 01705 828611, fax 01705 736978)

HARRIS, Michael Douglas Gerard; s of Gerard T Harris (d 1966), and Daphne Mary, *née* King; *b* 26 Nov 1940; *Educ* Millfield, École Hotelier Lausanne, Académie de Champagne; *m* Patsy Fiona Frazer Blair; *Career* hotelier; varied work experience England, France, Germany and Switzerland, attended short business course Georgetown Washington, subsequently asst mangr Bar Roc Montego Bay then food and beverage mangr Sunset Lodge Jamaica, proprietor The Bell Inn Aston Clinton 1966–; *Style*— Michael Harris, Esq; ✉ The Bell Inn, Aston Clinton, Bucks HP22 5HP (☎ 01296 630252, fax 01296 631250)

HARRIS, His Hon Judge Michael Frank; s of Joseph Frank Harris (d 1982), of Bridgend, Glamorgan, and Edna, *née* Walters; *b* 11 Jan 1942; *Educ* St Bartholomew's GS Newbury, Merton Coll Oxford (BA); *m* 23 Aug 1969, Veronica, da of Ronald Edward Brend; 1 da (Bronwen Sarah b 13 Sept 1970), 1 s (Owen Joseph b 4 Oct 1972); *Career* called to the Bar Middle Temple 1965, recorder 1990–92, circuit judge (SE Circuit) 1992–; *Recreations* piano playing, amateur dramatics, walking, music, theatre, travel, reading; *Style*— His Hon Judge Michael Harris; ✉ Southwark Crown Court, 1 English Grounds, off Battlebridge Lane, London SE1 2HU

HARRIS, Rear Adm Michael George Temple; s of Cdr Antony John Temple Harris, OBE, RN, of Wickham, Hants, and Doris, *née* Drake; *b* 5 July 1941; *Educ* Pangbourne, RNC Dartmouth; *m* 17 Oct 1970, (Caroline) Katrina, da of Gp Capt Patrick George Chichester, OBE, RAF (d 1983), of Hayne Manor, Stowford, Devon; 3 da (Tamsin b 1971, Rebecca b 1973, Emily b 1979); *Career* Sub Lt RN 1961, Lt 1963, Cdr 1975, Capt 1980, Rear Adm 1989; served: home, Med, submarines, Canada, Hawaii, long TAS course, cmd submarines Osiris and Sovereign, North Pole 1976, staff of flag offr submarines 1977–79, Capt HMS Cardiff 1980–82, Falklands Campaign, Capt 3 Submarine Sqdn 1982–85, central staff MOD 1985–87, Capt HMS Ark Royal 1987–89, asst chief of Def Staff (NATO UK) 1989–92; yr bro of Trinity House 1989; Liveryman Worshipful Co of Shipwrights 1991, Clerk to Worshipful Co of Clothworkers 1992–; FRGS 1978, FNI 1988; *Recreations* riding, fishing, reading, bellringing; *Clubs* Naval and Military; *Style*— Rear Adm Michael Harris; ✉ c/o Naval Secretary, Victory Building, HM Naval Base, Portsmouth, Hampshire PO1 3LS

HARRIS, Cdre Nicholas Richard; s of Sidney George Harris, and Jean Elliott (d 1986); *b* 24 Sept 1941; *Educ* South Africa KHS and Nautical Coll General Botha; *m* 31 Dec 1966, Philippa Joan Harris, da of Col Donald Friswell Easten, MC, of Wormingford, Essex; 2 s (Rupert b 20 Oct 1967, Giles b 16 July 1973), 2 da (Jessica b 24 April 1971, Emily b 9 July 1983); *Career* BNRC Dartmouth 1963, qualified fixed wing pilot 1964–65; HMS Eagle 899 Sqdn 1965–66, 766 Sqdn RNAS Yeovilton 1967–68, air warfare instr 764 Sqdn RNAS Lossiemouth 1969–70, USN VF121 and Topgun NAS Mirimar California 1971–72, HMS Devonshire 1973, RN Staff Coll Greenwich 1974, Directorate of Naval Air Warfare MOD (Sea Harrier) 1975–76, CO 892 Sqdn (Phantoms) 1977, Air Warfare Course RAF Cranwell 1978, RN presentation team 1979, Directorate of Naval Manpower Planning MOD 1980–81, HMS Bristol (Falklands Campaign) 1982–83, Royal Coll of Defence Studies 1984–85, Dep Sec Chief of Staff Ctee MOD 1986, Naval Attache Rome 1987–89, Dir Mgmnt Strategy (Naval Personnel) MOD 1990–91, Asst Dir (DNSD) Staff of First Sea Lord MOD 1992–93, Dir Defence Medical Services Restructuring MOD 1994–96, ret; chm Farringdon Harris Group 1996–; MInstD, MRUSI; *Recreations* most country pursuits, watching cricket and rugby, reading; *Clubs* Royal Over-Seas League, Royal Navy Club of 1765 and 1785, Royal Navy Sailing Assoc, Royal Acad of Arts (friend); *Style*— Nicholas Harris, Esq; ✉ c/o Coutts & Co, 440 Strand, London WC2R 0QS (☎ 0171 753 1000)

HARRIS, Nigel Henry; *b* 11 July 1924; *Educ* Perse, Trinity Coll Cambridge and Middx Hosp (MA, MB BChir, FRCS); *m* Aug 1949, Elizabeth; *Career* Nat Serv RAF 1949–52; house surgn: Orthopaedic Dept Middx Hosp 1947, N Middx Hosp 1952–53; in charge of Casualty and registrar to Orthopaedic Dept King Edward Meml Hosp Ealing 1953–55, surgical registrar Mile End Hosp 1955–56, surgical registrar Fulham Hosp 1958–59 (orthopaedic registrar 1956–58), sr registrar Royal Nat Orthopaedic Hosp 1960 (registrar 1959–60), Euro travelling scholar 1962, conslt orthopaedic surgn to Thames Gp of Hosps 1963, conslt orthopaedic surgn to St Mary's Hosp London and the London Foot Hosp 1964–90, asst hon orthopaedic surgn to the Hosp for Sick Children Gt Ormond St 1964–87, Geigy scholar 1967, hon conslt orthopaedic surgn St Mary's Hosp (after ret from NHS 1990); currently private conslt in Orthopaedic Practice and in Medico-Legal Practice; orthopaedic surgn to: Football Assoc, Arsenal Football Club; med examiner: for Football League Underwriters, to General and Medical Legal Services; tstee Metropolitan Police Convalescent and Rehabilitation Tst; memb: Br Orthopaedic Res Soc, Hosp Conslts and Specialists Assoc, Medico-Legal Soc; MIArb, fell Br Orthopaedic Assoc, FRSM, FAE; *Books* Postgraduate Textbook of Clinical Orthopaedics (ed, 1984, 2 edn 1995), Medical Negligence (jt ed, 1990, 2 edn 1994); *Recreations* horse racing (owner), cricket; *Clubs* Utd Oxford and Cambridge Univ, Athenaeum; *Style*— Nigel Harris, Esq; ✉ 14 Ashworth Rd, London W9 (☎ 0171 286 4725); 72 Harley St, London W1 (fax 0171 636 4015)

HARRIS, Patricia Ann; *b* 29 May 1939; *Educ* St Julian's HS Newport Monmouthshire, Trinity Coll Carmarthen (hon fell 1995); *m* 3 August 1963, The Rev James Nigel Kingsley Harris; 1 s (James Michael b 11 Oct 1967), 1 da (Sarah Ann b 25 June 1965); *Career* memb Diocesan: Houses Bd 1975–92, Synod 1980–, Pastoral Ctee 1984–89, Educn Ctee 1986–89; diocesan pres Mothers' Union 1980–85, memb Gen Synod (House of Laity) 1985–, central pres Mothers' Union 1989–94, memb Cncl of Churches for Britain and Ireland 1990–, exec memb Gen Synod Bd of Mission 1991– (vice chm 1996); Paul Harris fell 1995; awarded Cross of St Augustine by Archbishop of Canterbury 1995; *Recreations* watching Gloucester play rugby, swimming, embroidery; *Style*— Mrs Patricia Harris; ✉ The Vicarage, Elm Rd, Stonehouse, Gloucester GL10 2NP (☎ 014538 22332); The Mary Sumner House, 24 Tufton St, London SW1P 3RB (☎ 0171 222 5533, fax 0171 222 6143)

HARRIS, Paul Haydn Beverley; s of late Michael James Harris, and Vivien Diana, *née* Hoyland; *b* 4 Sept 1945; *Educ* Emanuel Sch, Univ of Kent at Canterbury (BA); *m* 27 Oct 1979, Amanda Helen, da of late Arthur Robert Charles Stiby, TD, JP; 2 s (Kit b 1988, James b 1991); *Career* broadcaster and writer; radio and TV newsreader and presenter 1973–86, BBC staff 1970–80, freelance 1980–, currently specialising in prodn of commercial educnl and med videos and films; widely involved in charity fund raising in S of England; *Recreations* cricket, carriage driving, writing, fine art, ceramics; *Clubs* MCC, Hants CCC; *Style*— Paul Harris, Esq; ✉ Mile Tree House, Crawley, Winchester, Hampshire SO21 2QF (☎ 01962 885916)

HARRIS, Paul Ian; s of Alexander Munsie (d 1988), and Sylvia, *née* Goodman (d 1989); *b* 13 Dec 1943; *Educ* Chatham House GS Ramsgate, Birmingham Univ (LLM); *m* 21 June 1967, Margaret Eve, *née* Roer; 1 s (Keith Daniel b 1971), 1 da (Ruth Caroline b 1974); *Career* admitted slr 1969, ptnr Linklaters & Paines; tstee World Student Drama Tst; memb: Law Soc, Slrs Benevolent Assoc; immediate past chm Ctee I Section of Business Law Int Bar Assoc; *Books* Day & Harris Unit Trusts (1974), Linklaters & Paines Unit Trusts The Law and Practice (1989); *Recreations* bridge, golf, cricket, watching football, theatre, cinema, sitting on committees; *Style*— Paul Harris, Esq; ✉ Linklaters & Paines, 59/67 Gresham St, London EC2V 7JA (☎ 0171 606 7080, fax 0171 606 5113, telex 884349)

HARRIS, Gp Capt Peter Langridge; CBE (1988), AE (1961, and clasp 1971), DL (Gtr London 1986); s of Arthur Langridge Harris (d 1975), of Eastbourne, and Doris Mabel, *née* Offen (d 1978); *b* 6 Sept 1929; *Educ* St Edward's Sch Oxford, Univ of Birmingham (BSc); *m* 29 Dec 1955, (Yvonne) Patricia, da of Arthur James Stone, DSM (d 1986), of Southsea; 2 da (Sally b 1960, Philippa b 1962); *Career* RAFVR 1947–60, RAuxAF 1960–88 (Gp Capt 1983, Inspr 1983–88), ADC to HM The Queen 1984–88, vice chm (air) TA & VR Assoc for Gtr London 1988–94; chartered engr; Elliott Bros (London) Ltd 1952–55, Decca Navigator Co Ltd 1955–59, Elliott-Automation/GEC plc 1959–89, ret 1989; chm Hatfield District IEE 1979–80, bd memb Milton Keynes Business Venture 1983–89, memb Bd of Mgmnt Princess Marina House Rustington 1990–; Freeman Guild of Air Pilots and Air Navigators 1987; Chevalier Sovereign Military Order of Temple of Jerusalem 1994; FIEE 1976; *Recreations* travel, gardening; *Clubs* RAF, Royal Naval and Royal Albert Yacht (Portsmouth); *Style*— Gp Capt Peter L Harris, CBE, AE, DL; ✉ 10 Dolphin Court, St Helen's Parade, Southsea, Hants PO4 0QL (☎ 01705 817602); 29 Davenham Ave, Northwood, Middx HA6 3HW

HARRIS, Peter Michael; s of Benjamin Warren Harris (d 1980), and Ethel Eveline, *née* Mabbutt (d 1982); *b* 13 April 1937; *m* 20 April 1963, Bridget; 1 s, 2 da; *Career* RN: Cadet BRNC Dartmouth 1953, ret as Lt Cdr 1972; called to the Bar Gray's Inn 1971, in private practice 1972–74; Lord Chancellor's Dept: legal asst 1974, under sec 1986, circuit admin Northern Circuit 1986–93, official slr to the Supreme Ct 1993–; asst ed County Court Practice 1985–; *Books* Harris and Scanlan: Children Act 1989 - A Procedural Handbook (1994); *Style*— Peter Harris, Esq; ✉ Office of the Official Solicitor, 81 Chancery Lane, London WC2A 1DD (☎ 0171 911 7116)

HARRIS, Philip Ian; s of Raymond Harris, of Hucknall, Nottinghamshire, and Cynthia, *née* Bunt; *b* 3 June 1965; *Educ* Friesland Comp Sch Sandiacre Notts, Mansfield Coll of Art & Design (DATEC dipl), Bradford Coll of Art & Design (BA); *Career* artist; *Solo Exhibitons* Tricycle Gallery London 1990, Merz Contemporary Art London 1990 and 1992, Paintings Drawings and Etchings Woodlands Art Gallery London 1991, Ghent Inernational Art Fair Belgium 1991; *Gp Exhibitions* Works on Paper (Central Space Gallery London) 1988, The Spectator Art Award (Spink & Son London) Portobello Open (Taberncale London) 1989, BP Portrait Award Exhbn (Nat Portrait Gallery London) 1990 and 1993; *Awards* BP Portrait Award 3rd Prize 1990, BP Portrait Award 1st Prize 1993; *Style*— Philip Harris, Esq

HARRIS, Philip James; s of Philip John Harris, of Avenue Decelles, Montreal, Canada, and Violet Edna May, *née* Fretwell; *b* 4 Oct 1936; *Educ* Northampton Sch of Art, Watford Coll of Technol; *m* 1, 20 April 1959 (m dis 1977), Audrey Mary, da of Richard Stanley Flawn (d 1968), of The Old Manor, Irthlingborough, Northants; 1 s (Philip Julian b 1964), 1 da (Susan Mary (Mrs Goodwin) b 1967); *m* 2, 21 March 1980, Esther Elizabeth, da of James Buchanan (d 1982), of Blunham, Beds; *Career* Northants Regt 1955, Parachute Regt 1955–58; active serv: Cyprus, Eoka Campaign, Suez (despatches); chief exec Reporter Newspapers Kent 1977–79, dir and gen mangr Middx Co Press 1979–83; md: B Lansdown & Sons Trowbridge 1983–87, Wessex Group of Newspapers Bath 1987–93; non-exec dir Southern and Western Press Ltd 1990–93; mangr NHS 1994–; past pres SW Fedn of Newspaper Owners, former vice pres Newsvendors Benevolent Inst, former memb CGLI Adjudication Ctee; HM Gen Cmmr of Taxes; tstee W Wiltshire Assoc for Mental Health; MIIM 1979, memb Inst of Printing 1981, memb IOD 1985; FIMgt 1983; *Recreations* horse racing, polo, rowing; *Clubs* Leander, Bath and County, Guards' Polo, Cirencester Park Polo; *Style*— Philip Harris, Esq; ✉ Wolery Twoo, 18 Palairet Close, Bradford-on-Avon, Wiltshire (☎ 01225 864223)

HARRIS, Phillip; s of Simon Harris (d 1970), of Edinburgh, and Leah Sarah, *née* Horovits (d 1984); *b* 28 March 1922; *Educ* Royal HS Edinburgh, Univ of Edinburgh; *m* 7 Nov 1949, Sheelagh Shena, da of Harry Joshua Coutts (d 1977), of Glasgow; 1 s (Harvey b 14 May 1953), 1 da (Frances b 27 Oct 1950); *Career* Capt RAMC 1945–48; Univ of Edinburgh: sr conslt neurosurgeon Dept of Clinical Neurosciences, sr lectr Dept of Surgical Neurology, lectr Dept of Linguistics; visiting prof in Univs worldwide; pres Br Cervical Spine Assoc, sr del Br Neurosurgeons to the World Fedn of Neurological Surgery, pres Scottish Sports Assoc for the Disabled, dir and tstee Scottish Tst for the Physically Disabled, hon memb Scottish Paraplegic Assoc, cncl memb Thistle Fndn Scotland, memb Med Appeals Tbnl Scotland; ed Paraplegia (the int jl on the spine); LRCP Edinburgh, LRCS Edinburgh, LRFP Glasgow, LRCS Glasgow, FRCS Edinburgh, FRCP Edinburgh, FRCS Glasgow, FRSE 1967; hon memb: American Assoc of Neurological Surgeons, The Hong Kong Surgical Soc, Middle East Neurosurgical Soc; *Books* Head Injuries (ed 1971), Epilepsy (ed 1974), Spine (ed 1987); *Recreations* art, music, travel, golf; *Clubs* New (Edinburgh), Royal Scottish Automobile (Glasgow), Bruntsfield Links Golfing Soc (Edinburgh); *Style*— Phillip Harris, Esq, FRSE; ✉ 4/5 Fettes Rise, Edinburgh EH4 1QH (☎ 0131 552 8900); Paraplegia Journal, Royal College of Surgeons, Nicolson Street, Edinburgh EH8 9DW (☎ 0131 668 2557)

HARRIS, Raymond Govette; s of Walter Henry Harris (d 1957), of Cambridge, and Ruth Olive, *née* Drake (d 1987); *b* 3 June 1928; *Educ* Perse Sch Cambridge, Architectural Assoc Sch of Architecture (AA Dip); *m* 16 Feb 1957, Rosemary, da of Rev Frederick Walter Palmer (d 1979), of Easebourne, W Sussex; 1 s (Thomas Edward Henry b 1964), 3 da (Katherine b 1958, Eleanor Rosemary b 1959, Hilary Juliet b 1962); *Career* architect; sr ptnr T P Bennett & Son 1982–85 (ptnr 1967–82), sr ptnr T P Bennett Partnership 1985–90 (conslt 1991–); architect to: The Middx Hosp, Rackhams Birmingham, Bentalls Kingston; works incl: Br Linen Bank Glasgow, Int Students House Park Crescent, Financial Times Bldg, Norwich Union HQ Norwich; chm Petworth Festival; FRIBA 1968 (ARIBA 1951), FRSA 1973; *Recreations* watercolour drawing, cabinet making, music; *Clubs* Garrick; *Style*— Raymond Harris, Esq; ✉ Somerset Lodge, North St, Petworth, W Sussex (☎ 01798 343842); T P Bennett Partnership, 262 High Holborn, London WC1V 7DU (☎ 0171 405 9277, fax 0171 405 3568, telex 21671)

HARRIS, Prof (Ivor) Rex; s of John Fredrick Harris (d 1977), and Margaret Emily Harris (d 1980); *b* 27 July 1939; *Educ* Larkfield GS Chepstow, Univ of Birmingham (BSc, PhD, DSc); *m* Vera Winifred, da of Leslie Boylin; 2 s (Christopher John Edward b 9 June 1966, David James Andrew b 22 Aug 1968), 1 da (Margaret Jane b 13 July 1972); *Career* University of Birmingham: ICI research fell 1964–66, lectr Dept of Physical Metallurgy 1966–74, sr lectr of metallurgy and materials 1974–87, prof of materials science 1988–, head of sch 1996– (actg head 1989–90); lectr NATO Summer Sch Italy 1990, visiting lectr various univs worldwide; memb: Editorial Advsy Bd Jl of Alloys and Compounds, Int Steering Ctee Metal Hydride Conf Series; gp co-ordinator Concerted Euro Action on Magnets (CEAM), mission ldr Overseas Tech Experts Mission (OSTEM) USA 1987; chm: UK Magnetics Club 1988–90, Euro Material Research Soc (Strasbourg) 1988, Magnetism and Magnetic Materials Initiative SERC 1992–94, 13th Int Workshop on Rare Earth Magnets and their Application 1994, 8th Int Symposium on Magnetic Anisotropy and Coercivity in Rare-earth Metal Alloys 1994; memb Metals and Magnetic Materials Ctee SERC 1991–94; pres Birmingham Metallurgical Assoc 1992; FIM 1992, MIEEE 1992, FEng 1994; *Books* Hydrogen in Metals (ed with J P G Farr, 1976), Rare Earth Permanent Magnets (ed, 1989), Concerted European Action on Magnets (co-ed, 1989), Magnet Processing: Rare-earth Iron Permanent Magnets (contrib, 1996); also author of over 340 scientific papers; *Style*— Prof Rex Harris, FEng; ✉ School of

Metallurgy & Materials, The University of Birmingham, Edgbaston, Birmingham B15 2TT (☎ 0121 414 5165, fax 0121 471 2207, e-mail IRHarris@bham.ac.uk)

HARRIS, Richard Leslie; s of William Leslie Freer Harris (d 1956), of Romsley, Worcs, and Lucy Penelope Harris (d 1976); *b* 31 March 1927; *Educ* Shrewsbury; *m* 1955, Jane, da of Herbert Charles Oxenham, of Rhuallt, St Asaph; 2 s; *Career* stockbroker and CA; formerly: ptnr Harris Allday Lea and Brooks, chm Royal Brierley Crystal Ltd; chm Newater Investments Ltd; dir: Tewksbury Marina Ltd, Thomas Jones Estates Ltd; memb Stock Exchange 1961 (memb Cncl); chm: Midlands and Western Stock Exchange 1969, Feoffees Old Swinford Hosp Sch; Freeman City of London; High Sheriff Co of West Midlands 1987; *Clubs* Birmingham; *Style—* Richard Harris, Esq; ✉ 23 Farlands Rd, Old Swinford, Stourbridge, W Midlands DY8 2DD (☎ 01384 395760); c/o Harris Allday Lea and Brooks, Stock Exchange Buildings, 33 Great Charles St, Queensway, Birmingham B3 3JN (☎ 0121 233 1222)

HARRIS, Richard Travis; 2 s of Douglas Harris (d 1964), and Emmeline, *née* Travis; *b* 15 April 1919; *Educ* Charterhouse, RMA Woolwich; *m* 1, 1941 (m dis 1953), June Constance, *née* Rundle; 2 da; m 2, 1953, Margaret Sophia Nye, *née* Aron; 1 s, 1 da; *Career* RCS 1939, France 1940, Western Desert 1941–43, Italy 1943, Staff Coll 1944, instr Sch of Inf 1944–45, BAOR 1945–46, Sudan Def Force 1947–50, ret Lt-Col 1950; md Rediffusion (Nigeria) Ltd 1951–54, dep gen mangr Assoc Rediffusion Ltd 1954–57, md Coates & Co (Plymouth) Ltd 1957–63, md Dollond & Aitchison Group Ltd 1964–70; dir: Dollond & Aitchison Group Ltd 1964–86 (chm and md 1970–78), Gallaher Ltd 1970–87 (dep chm 1978–84), Burton Group plc 1984–92; chm IOD 1982–85 (vice pres 1985–89), Wider Share Ownership Cncl 1988–91; govr Royal Shakespeare Theatre 1980–94, memb Cncl Univ of Birmingham 1978–93 (life memb of Court 1981); Liveryman Worshipful Co of Spectacle Makers, Hon Asst Worshipful Co of Coachmakers & Coach Harness Makers (Master 1963–64); *Recreations* flyfishing, theatre; *Style—* Richard Harris, Esq; ✉ 21 Lucy's Mill, Mill Lane, Stratford-upon-Avon, Warwicks CV37 6DE (☎ 01789 266016)

HARRIS, Robert Brinley Joseph (Bob); s of William Brinley Harris, of Hunstanton, Norfolk, and Doria Katherine, *née* Dow; *b* 11 April 1946; *Educ* Northampton Trinity GS; *m* 1; 2 s (Benjamin Brinley Howard b 17 Sept 1982, James David b 19 Nov 1986), 2 da (Mirelle b 23 Nov 1970, Emily b 2 Feb 1973); m 2, 24 April 1991, Trudie Myerscough-Harris, da of Simon Myerscough-Walker; 2 s (Miles Simon b 2 June 1992, Dylan Joseph b 2 Sept 1994); *Career* broadcaster; fndr Time Out magazine 1968, commenced broadcasting BBC Radio 1 1970, presenter Old Grey Whistle Test (weekly rock show) BBC 2 1972–79, Radio Luxembourg 1975, Radio 210 1977, Radio Oxford 1981, LBC London 1985, rejoined BBC Radio 1 1989, launched overnight serv midnight to 4am 1991–93, broadcasting on BBC GLR 1994–; interviewed: John Lennon 1975, Jimmy Carter 1976, John Major, Neil Kinnock; appeared in film Made 1971, produced 3 LP records for EMI and Atlantic 1973–74, released Best of The Test LP compilation 1991; *Books* Rock and Pop Mastermind (Orbis, 1985), Bob Harris Rock Dates (Virgin, 1992); *Recreations* music, cricket, rugby; *Style—* Bob Harris, Esq; ✉ c/o BBC Radio GLR, 35c Marylebone High Street, London W1A 4LG (☎ 0171 224 2424, fax 0171 487 2908)

HARRIS, Robert Dennis; s of Dennis Harris, and Audrey, *née* Hardy; *b* 7 March 1957; *Educ* King Edward VII Sch Melton Mowbray, Selwyn Coll Cambridge (BA, chm Cambridge Fabian Soc, pres Cambridge Union Soc); *m* 1988, Gillian, da of Sir Derek Hornby, *qv*; 1 s (Charlie Robert Nicholas b 17 April 1992), 2 da (Holly Miranda b 21 July 1990, Matilda Felicity b 5 Oct 1996); *Career* res and film dir Current Affairs Dept BBC TV (progs incl Tonight, Nationwide and Panorama) 1978–81; reporter: Newsnight 1981–85, Panorama 1985–87; political ed Observer 1987–89, political reporter This Week (Thames TV) 1988–89, political columnist Sunday Times 1989–92 and 1996–; commended Columnist of the Year Br Press Awards 1992; *Books* A Higher Form of Killing - The History of Gas and Germ Warfare (with Jeremy Paxman, 1982), Gotcha! - The Media, The Government and The Falklands Crisis (1983), The Making of Neil Kinnock (1984), Selling Hitler - The Story of the Hitler Diaries (1986, televised 1991), Good and Faithful Servant - The Unauthorised Biography of Bernard Ingham (1990), Fatherland (novel, 1992 (filmed 1994)), Enigma (novel, 1995); *Style—* Robert Harris, Esq; ✉ The Old Vicarage, Kintbury, Berks RG17 9TR

HARRIS, Robert Frederick (Bob); s of Frederick Cecil Harris (d 1972), of Ipswich, Suffolk, and Ellen Rose Mary, *née* Damant; *b* 8 Sept 1943; *Educ* Northgate GS Ipswich, Kingston Coll of Art (BA); *m* 26 July 1969, Jayne Susan, da of Frederick Gibson; 1 da (Eleanor Volante Harris b 2 April 1977); *Career* art dir (advtg agencies): Collett Dickenson Pearce 1968–73, Sharps Advertising 1974–76, Geers Gross 1976–77, Marsteller 1977–78, Davidson Pearce (now BMP DDB) 1978–85; freelance photographer 1985– (various clients incl Tesco, Sainsbury, King & Barnes Brewery and Northern Rock Building Society); Pilots and their Favourite Aircraft (solus exhbn) Biggin Hill Aerodrome; Freeman City of London 1987, Liveryman Worshipful Co of Loriners 1987; memb: D&AD, Assoc of Photographers (chm 1991, 1992 and 1993, chm Awards Ctee 1992, 1993 and 1994); *Recreations* gardening, aviation; *Clubs* Aldersgate Ward, Tiger; *Style—* Bob Harris, Esq; ✉ 26 Albany Park Road, Kingston upon Thames, Surrey KT2 5SW (☎ 0181 546 4018)

HARRIS, Prof Robert James; s of Charles William Harris (d 1996), of Sanderstead, Surrey, and Lucy Dorothea Emily, *née* Weller; *b* 10 March 1947; *Educ* The GS Enfield, Univ of Leeds (BA), McMaster Univ (MA), Univ of Manchester (DipAS), Univ of Birmingham (DSW); *m* 23 Feb 1974, Janet Nuttall, da of James Nuttall Horne (d 1987), of Ewell, Surrey; 1 s (George b 1982), 2 da (Ruth b 1978, Amelia b 1979); *Career* probation offr Middx 1973–75; lectr: in social work and criminology Brunel Univ 1975–77, in social work and criminal justice Univ of Leicester 1977–87; Univ of Hull: prof of social work 1987–, pro-vice-chllr 1993–; chm Assoc of Univ Profs in Social Work until 1994; memb Home Office Probation Trg Advsy Gp, chm Humberside Child Protection Ctee until 1991; *Books* Educating Social Workers (1985), Practising Social Work (1987), Welfare, Power and Juvenile Justice (1987), The Law Report (1988), Crime, Criminal Justice and the Probation Service (1992), Secure Accommodation in Child Care (1993), Probation Round the World (1995); *Recreations* antiquarian book collecting, travelling, talking, working; *Style—* Prof Robert Harris; ✉ Yew Tree House, Station Walk, Cottingham, East Yorkshire HU16 4QU (☎ 01482 849961); The University of Hull, Department of Social Policy, Hull HU6 7RX (☎ 01482 465784, fax 01482 466306)

HARRIS, Robert William (Bob); s of Frank Harris (d 1992), of Birmingham, and Joan, *née* Lee (d 1995); *b* 9 Nov 1944; *Educ* George Dixon GS Edgbaston Birmingham; *m* 1, Carol Lillian; 1 da (Zoë b 1971); m 2, Carol Ann; 2 s (Dominic b 1976, Adam b 1985); *Career* sports writer and sports ed: Birmingham Planet 1963–66, Thomson Regional Newspapers 1966–86; sports writer and chief football writer Today 1986–89, exec sports ed Sunday Mirror 1993–95 (sports ed 1989–93), ed Sport First 1996–; major events covered incl: 7 Olympic Games 1972–96, 6 football World Cups, 5 Cwlth Games, various world title fights, cricket World Cup; *Books* No Half Measures (with Graeme Souness, 1985), Touch and Go (with Steve Coppell, 1985), More Than Somewhat (with Bruce Grobbelaar, 1986), World Cup Diary (with Bobby Robson, 1986), Bring on the Clown (with Bruce Grobbelaar, 1988), Against the Odds (with Bobby Robson, 1990); *Style—* Bob Harris, Esq; ✉ 25 Broadheath Drive, Chislehurst, Kent BR7 6EU (☎ 0181 289 3000, fax 0181 467 0735); Sport First, 20–26 Brunswick Place, London N1 6DZ (☎ 0171 216 8600, fax 0171 490 1486)

HARRIS, Prof Robin Kingsley; s of Alfred William Harris (d 1964), of Hornchurch, Essex, and Nellie, *née* Missen (d 1987); *b* 23 Dec 1936; *Educ* Royal Liberty GS Romford, Magdalene Coll Cambridge (BA, MA, PhD, ScD); *m* 6 Aug 1960, Maureen Elizabeth, da of James Samuel Reardon (d 1968), of Langley, Berks; 1 s (Nigel b 1962); *Career* fell in independent res Mellon Inst Pittsburgh 1962–64; prof of chemistry: Univ of East Anglia 1980–84 (lectr 1964–70, sr lectr 1970–73, reader 1973–80), Univ of Durham 1984–; chm Ctee Sci and Engrg Res Cncl, sec gen Int Soc of Magnetic Resonance 1986–92; FRSC; *Books* Nuclear Magnetic Resonance Spectroscopy: A Physicochemical View (1983), Encyclopedia of Nuclear Magnetic Resonance (8 vols, jt ed-in-chief with D M Grant, 1996); *Recreations* gardening; *Style—* Prof Robin Harris; ✉ Department of Chemistry, University of Durham, South Road, Durham DH1 3LE (☎ 0191 374 3121, fax 0191 386 1127)

HARRIS, Prof Rodney; CBE (1996); s of Ben Harris (d 1966), and Toiby, *née* Davies (d 1958); *b* 27 May 1932; *Educ* Quarry Bank Sch, Univ of Liverpool (MD); *m* 1, Ruth, *née* Levy (d 1975); m 2, Hilary Jean, da of Eric Melsher, of Bowdon; 1 s (Richard Ben), 2 da (Alexandra Jane, Anne Tessa); *Career* prof of med genetics Manchester 1980–, advsr to Chief Med Offr at Dept of Health 1982–89; chm: Specialty Advsy Ctee JCHMT 1982–89, RCP Ctee on Clinical Genetics 1984–93, NWRHA Res Advsy Ctee 1994–, Nat Confidential Enquiry into Genetics Counselling, EC Concerted Action on Medical Genetics; dir of R&D Central Manchester Health Care Tst; memb Preston Health Authy 1986–90; FRCP 1964; *Style—* Prof Rodney Harris, CBE; ✉ Medical Genetics Department, 6th Floor, St Mary's Hospital, Manchester M13 0JH (☎ 0161 276 6262, fax 0161 248 8308, e-mail Rodney.Harris@man.ac.uk)

HARRIS, Dr Roger James; s of Sidney George Harris (ka 1940), of Northampton, and Alfreda Mabel, *née* Sibley; *b* 29 Nov 1937; *Educ* Northampton GS, Univ of Bristol Med Sch (MB ChB, MD); *m* 20 April 1963, Mary Jennifer Evans; 1 s (Simon John b 1967), 3 da (Sarah Jane b 1964, Katherine (Kate) Martha b 1980, Emmeline (Mimi) Louisa May b 1982); *Career* currently conslt The Royal Hosps Tst Royal London Hosp, sr lectr in child health London Hosp Med Coll 1975–; author of articles on paediatrics; examiner in paediatrics for RCP, rep for The Royal Hosps Tst Royal London Hosp on Regnl Advsy Paediatric Ctee; memb: Area Child Protection Ctee, London Hosp Res Advsy Ctee; FRCP 1986; *Recreations* theatre, opera, playing cricket; *Style—* Dr Roger Harris; ✉ The Children's Department, The Royal London Hospital, Whitechapel, London E1 1BB (☎ 0171 377 7428, fax 0171 377 7759, e-mail R.J.Harris@mds.qmw.ac.uk)

HARRIS, Rosemary; da of Stafford Berkeley Harris (d 1952), and Enid Maud, *née* Campion (d 1942); *Educ* St Helen's Sch Abingdon, All Hallows' Sch Ditchingham, RADA; *m* 1, 1960 (m dis 1967), Ellis Rabb; m 2, 1967, John Marsden Ehle; 1 da (Jennifer Anne b 1969); *Career* actress; hon doctorate Smith College 1968; *Theatre* incl: Climate of Eden (Broadway, Theatre World Award) 1952, The Seven Year Itch (London) 1953–54, Hamlet and Uncle Vanya (NT) 1964–65, The Lion in Winter (Broadway, Tony Award) 1966, Plaza Suite (London, Evening Standard Award) 1969, The Merchant of Venice (Broadway) 1973, A Streetcar Named Desire (Broadway) 1973, All my Sons (London) 1980, Heartbreak House (London and Broadway) 1983, A Pack of Lies (Broadway) 1984, Hayfever (Broadway) 1985, Best of Friends (London) 1989, Steel Magnolias (London) 1990, Lost in Yonkers (Broadway) 1991, Arsenic and Old Lace (Chichester) 1991, Preserving Mr Panmure (Chichester) 1991, Lost in Yonkers (London) 1992, In the Summer House (Lyric Hammersmith) 1993, An Inspector Calls (Broadway) 1994, Women of Troy (RNT) 1995; *Television* incl: Twelfth Night, A Tale of Two Cities, Dial M For Murder, Wuthering Heights, Notorious Woman (Emmy Award), The Holocaust (Golden Globe Award), To The Lighthouse, The Camomile Lawn, Summers Day Dream 1993; *Films* incl: The Shiralee, Beau Brummel, The Boys From Brazil, The Ploughman's Lunch, Crossing Delancey,The Bridge, Tom and Viv (Academy Award nomination) 1993; *Style—* Ms Rosemary Harris; ✉ c/o ICM Ltd, Oxford House, 76 Oxford Street, London W1N 0AX (☎ 0171 636 6565, fax 0171 323 0101)

HARRIS, Rosemary Jeanne; da of Marshal of the RAF Sir Arthur Harris, 1 Bt, GCB, OBE, AFC (d 1984), and Barbara Daisy Kyrle (d 1986), da of Lt-Col E W K Money, KSLI; g and g-uncs were the famous ten Fighting Battyes chronicled by Younghusband's Story of the Guides and by Evelyn Battye in her book The Fighting Ten; *b* 20 Feb 1923; *Educ* privately, Thorneloe Sch Weymouth, Chelsea Sch of Art, Dept of Technol Courtauld Inst; *Career* author of fiction, thrillers and children's books; picture restorer 1949, reviewer of children's books for The Times 1970–73; memb Soc of Authors 1956 (memb Ctee Children's Writers and Illustrators Gp 1986–90); *Plays* Peronik (1976), The Unknown Enchantment (1981); *Books* The Summer-House (1956), Voyage to Cythera (1958), Venus with Sparrows (1961), All My Enemies (1967), The Nice Girl's Story (1968), A Wicked Pack of Cards (1969), The Double Snare (1975), Three Candles for the Dark (1976); *Children's* Moon in the Cloud (winner Carnegie medal 1968), The Shadow on the Sun (1970), The Seal-Singing (1971), The Child in the Bamboo Grove (1971), The Bright and Morning Star (1972), The King's White Elephant (1973), The Lotus and the Grail (1974), The Flying Ship (1974), The Little Dog of Fo (1976), I Want to be a Fish (1977), A Quest for Orion (1978), Beauty and the Beast (1979), Greenfinger House (1979), Tower of the Stars (1980), The Enchanted Horse (1981), Janni's Stork (1982), Zed (1982), Heidi (adapted 1983), Summers of the Wild Rose (1987), Love and the Merry-go-Round (ed poetry anthology, 1988), Colm of the Islands (1989), Ticket to Freedom (1991), The Wildcat Strike (1995), The Haunting of Joey M'baso (1996); *Recreations* music, reading, gardening; *Style—* Miss Rosemary Harris; ✉ c/o A P Watt Ltd, Literary Agents, 20 John St, London WC1N 2DL

HARRIS, Rosina Mary; da of Alfred Harris, DSO, CBE (d 1976), and Rosa Alfreda, *née* Alderson (d 1987); *b* 30 May 1921; *Educ* St Swithin's Sch, St Hilda's Coll Oxford (MA, BCL); *Career* served with American Ambulance of GB 1940–45; called to the Bar Lincoln's Inn; solicitor; sr ptnr Joynson-Hicks 1977–86 (ptnr 1954–89), conslt Taylor Joynson Garrett 1989–96; dep chm Blundell-Permoglaze Holdings plc 1981–86, non-exec dir London Brick plc 1983–84; Queen's Jubilee medal 1977; *Recreations* gardening, opera, theatre; *Style—* Miss Rosina Harris; ✉ 23 Devonshire Place, London W1N 1PD (☎ 0171 935 6041)

HARRIS, Prof Roy; s of Harry Harris (d 1978), and Emmie Jessie, *née* Oaten (d 1978); *b* 24 Feb 1931; *Educ* Queen Elizabeth Hosp Bristol, St Edmund Hall Oxford (BA, MA, DPhil), Sch of Oriental & African Studies London (PhD); *m* 14 July 1955, Rita Doreen, *née* Shulman; 1 da (Laura Doe b 1959); *Career* lectr Univ of Leicester 1957–60; Univ of Oxford: lectr 1960–76, fell and tutor in romance philology Keble Coll Oxford 1967–76, prof of romance languages 1976–77, prof of gen linguistics 1978–88, emeritus prof 1988; prof of English language Univ of Hong Kong 1988–91, dir d'Etudes Associé Ecole Pratique des Hautes Etudes Paris 1991–92, fell of the univ profs and prof of modern foreign languages and lit Boston Univ 1993–95; hon fell St Edmund Hall Oxford 1987–; FRSA 1986–; *Books* Synonymy and Linguistic Analysis (1973), The Language-Makers (1980), The Language Myth (1981), F De Saussure, Course in General Linguistics (trans 1983), The Origin of Writing (1986), Reading Saussure (1987), The Language Machine (1987), Language, Saussure and Wittgenstein (1988), La Sémiologie de l'Ecriture (1994), Signs of Writing (1995), The Language Connection (1996); *Recreations* cricket, modern art and design; *Style—* Prof Roy Harris; ✉ 2 Paddox Close, Oxford OX2 7LR (☎ 01865 554256, fax 01865 513723)

HARRIS, Sandra; da of C Harris (d 1991), of Perth, Australia, and Rae, *née* McPherson; *b* 18 Jan 1946; *Educ* Methodist Ladies' Coll Perth Australia; *m* 1972, Jafar Ramini, of

Palestine and London; 2 s (Nidal Jafar b 1973, Tarek Jafar b 1975), 1 da (Kareema b 1982); *Career* reporter/interviewer World At One (BBC Radio 4) 1967–69; Thames TV 1969–81; reporter/interviewer Today Programme, Thames at 6 and Thames News, writer/researcher Take Two, prodr/presenter People in the News and Sandra; freelance bdcaster and writer work with Sunday Times, Channel 4 and others; Headway Publications: ed Global Business 1986–88, ed Dream Journeys, Above the Clouds (British Airways) and contrib ed Highlife Magazine (British Airways) 1988–89, ed In Britain Magazine 1989–92; Premier Magazines: ed Business Life 1992–, ed Dream Journeys (Japanese language magazine) 1992–, ed People page High Life Magazine; winner Silver award for travel writing England for Excellence Awards 1990; *Books* The Nice Girl's Handbook (1981), The Double Bed Book (1983); *Recreations* playing tennis badly, dead-heading roses, behaving foolishly with my children; *Style—* Ms Sandra Harris; ✉ Premier Magazines, Haymarket House, 1 Oxendon Street, London SW1Y 4EE (☎ 0171 925 2544, fax 0171 839 4508)

HARRIS, Prof Sandra Jean; *b* 16 Dec 1939; *Educ* State Univ of Iowa (BA, CertEd, Phi Beta Kappa), Univ of Michigan (MA, Woodrow Wilson fell, Horace Rackham fell), Queen's Univ Belfast (exchange scholar 1962–63), Univ of Nottingham (PhD); *Career* lectr then sr lectr Nottingham Coll of Educn 1966–75; Nottingham Trent Univ: sr lectr 1974–84, princ lectr 1984–85, head Dept of English and Media Studies 1985–, dean Faculty of Humanities 1989–96, dean of graduate studies 1996–; Standing Conf on English in Polys and Colls of HE: regnl rep 1985–86, vice-chair 1986–87, chair 1987–89, treas 1989–92; memb Exec Ctee Cncl of Univ Deans of Arts and Humanities 1992–96; fndr memb European Study for the Study of English; memb: Through the Glass Ceiling, Bd of Govrs Nottingham HS for Girls, Editorial Bd Over Here jl 1989–; FRSA 1993; *Books* Language Projects: an Introduction to Language Study (with Ken Morgan, 1979), Managing Language: the Discourse of Corporate Meetings (1996); contrib articles and chapters to numerous jls and pubns; *Style—* Prof Sandra Harris; ✉ Department of English and Media Studies, Faculty of Humanities, Nottingham Trent University, Nottingham NG11 8NS (☎ 0115 941 8418 ext 3286)

HARRIS, Simeon George (Sim); s of George Herbert Harris, of Birmingham, and Kathleen Mary, *née* Bull (d 1978); *b* 26 July 1946; *Educ* Kings Norton GS Birmingham; *m* Oct 1969, Helen Patricia, da of Howard George Barlow; 2 da (Eleanor Jane b 15 July 1973, Victoria Anne b 16 June 1977); *Career* BBC: joined 1965, trained as camera and sound technician in studio, outside bdcasts and film, asst sound recordist 1967–69, news sound recordist and cameraman 1969–82, memb project team introducing electronic news gathering (ENG) to BBC 1979, held hostage for six days in London Iranian Embassy Siege until rescued by SAS 1980; ops mangr TV-am 1982–83 (from start of franchise); Central Independent Television Birmingham: head of film and ENG 1983–86, head of operational resources 1986–88, controller of resources 1988–90, controller of operations 1990–92; controller of operations and engrg Westcountry Television Plymouth 1992–94; md Racecourse Technical Services 1994–; memb RTS 1983, FBKSTS 1990; *Books* Hostage (with Chris Cramer, 1981); *Recreations* golf, sailing; *Style—* Sim Harris, Esq; ✉ Racecourse Technical Services, 88 Bushey Road, Raynes Park, London SW20 0JH (☎ 0181 947 3333, fax 0181 879 7354)

HARRIS, Stewart Edwin; s of William James Harris (d 1967), of Tatsfield, Surrey, and Grace Mary, *née* Stewart (d 1973); *b* 27 March 1922; *Educ* Oxted Co GS Surrey; *m* 26 July 1942, Eileen Laura Mary, da of David Thomas Francis, of Llandyfaelog; 1 s (Stephen Andrew Francis b 5 June 1949), 2 da (Catherine Sandra b 4 Dec 1943, Rosalind Ann b 26 Nov 1945); *Career* flying duties RAF 1940–45 (cmmnd 1942, shot down 1943, evaded capture in Belgium and then POW Stalag Luft III Germany; malnutrition caused later blindness), Staff Offr Directorate of Orgn Air Ministry 1945–47; worked in mktg and budgetary planning depts of Shell, Texaco and Total 1947–60 in SA, UK and France; Chrysler Corp UK: PA to MD 1960–61, head of Economic Studies Dept 1961–62, purchasing & material control mangr Kew Plant 1962–63, UK truck & car sales mangr 1963–64; dir and gen mangr VIP Petroleum Ltd (later Elf UK Ltd) 1964–67, fndr and md Trident Petroleum Ltd (London) 1967–73, gen conslt to petroleum indust 1974–, chief exec Avia (UK) Ltd 1978–1981, md Pace Petroleum Ltd 1982–84, chief exec Flare (1980) Ltd 1986–87, md Proteus Petroleum Ltd (and chm of subsids) 1987–90; contrib articles on UK oil indust to various magazines 1966–75; chm Medium & Small Cos Mgmnt Trg Ctee Petroleum Indust Trg Bd 1967–73, FInstPet (memb Cncl 1981–87, chm London Branch 1978–80), FInstD; memb: Royal Inst of Navigation, St Dunstan's Orgn for the War-Blinded, Nat Appeal Ctee Talking Newspapers & Magazines for the Blind 1991–92; *Recreations* walking, gardening, Trollope and Thackeray, Gibraltar; *Clubs* RAF; *Style—* Stewart Harris, Esq; ✉ Woodhall House, Andover Down, Hampshire SP11 6LJ (☎ and fax 01264 350413)

HARRIS, HE Thomas George; CMG (1995); s of Kenneth James Harris (d 1995), of Ferndown, Dorset, and Dorothy, *née* Barrett; *b* 6 Feb 1945; *Educ* Mercers' Sch, Haberdashers' Aske's, Gonville and Caius Coll Cambridge; *m* 21 Oct 1967, Mei-Ling, da of Kono Hwang (d 1976), of Kobe, Japan; 3 s (Ian Kenneth b 1969, Paul David b 1970, Simon Christopher b 1984); *Career* asst princ Bd of Trade 1966–68, third sec Br Embassy Tokyo 1969–71, asst private sec to Min for Aerospace 1971–72, princ Dept of Trade and Indust 1972–76, Cabinet Office 1976–78, princ private sec to Sec of State for Trade and Indust 1978–79, asst sec Civil Aviation Policy DTI 1979–83, commercial cncllr Br Embassy Washington 1983–88, head of chancery Br High Cmmn Lagos 1988–90, Br dep high cmmr Nigeria 1990–91, head African Dept (Equatorial) FCO 1991–94, ambass Korea 1994–; *Recreations* reading; *Style—* HE Mr Thomas Harris, CMG; ✉ c/o Foreign & Commonwealth Office (Seoul), King Charles Street, London SW1A 2AH

HARRIS, Timothy Richard; s of Kenneth Morgan Harris, of Cardiff, and Margaret, *née* McLean; *b* 16 April 1945; *Educ* Cathays HS for Boys Cardiff; *m* 8 May 1971, (Marion) Julia, da of late Thomas Barlow; 2 da (Emma b 2 Dec 1975, Ellen Rachel b 19 June 1980); *Career* articled clerk Deloitte Plender Griffiths & Co Cardiff 1962; ptnr: Deloitte Haskins & Sells 1983–89, Coopers & Lybrand Deloitte (now Coopers & Lybrand) 1990– (following merger); vice pres London Welsh RFC; FCA 1969, FIPA 1980, MICM 1988, MSPI 1990; *Recreations* rugby union; *Style—* Timothy R Harris, Esq; ✉ Coopers & Lybrand, Plumtree Court, London EC4A 4HT

HARRIS, (Jonathan) Toby; s of Prof Harry Harris, FRS (d 1994), of Pennsylvania, USA, and Muriel, *née* Hargest; *b* 11 Oct 1953; *Educ* Haberdashers' Aske's, Trinity Coll Cambridge (BA); *m* 7 April 1979, Ann Sarah, da of Stephen Austen Herbert (d 1988); 2 s (James Phillip b 1981, Matthew Anthony b 1984); *Career* Econ Div Bank of England 1975–79, dep dir Electricity Consumers' Cncl 1983–86 (joined 1979), dir Assoc of Community Health Cncls for Eng and Wales 1987–; Haringey BC: cncllr (Lab) 1978–, chm Social Servs Ctee 1982–87, ldr 1987–; chm: Assoc of London Authys 1993–95 (chm Social Servs Ctee 1984–88, dep chm 1990–93), chm Assoc of London Govt 1995–; dep chm AMA 1991– (chm Social Servs Ctee 1986–93); chm LBTC - Trg for Care 1986–94, memb Ctee of the Regions of the Euro Union 1994–; chm Local Govt Anti-Poverty Unit 1994–, jt chm London Pride Partnership 1995–; chm Univ of Cambridge Lab Club 1973, pres Cambridge Union Soc 1974, nat chm Young Fabian Gp 1976–77, chm Hornsey Lab Pty 1978, 1979 and 1980, dep chm Nat Fuel Poverty Forum 1981–86, pres Haringey Foster Care Assoc 1982–87; memb: London Drug Policy Forum 1990–, Nat Nursery Examination Bd 1992–94, Home Office Advsy Cncl on Race Relations 1993–, Exec Cncl RNIB 1993–94, Lab Pty Nat Policy Forum 1992–, Ct Middx Univ 1995–, Jt London Advsy Panel (Cabinet sub-ctee for London 1996–); coopted memb: Lab Pty Local Govt Policy Ctee 1993–, Exec Ctee Royal Assoc for Disability and Rehabilitation 1990–93; memb Bd London First 1993–; tstee: Evening Standard Blitz Meml Appeal 1995–, Help for Health Tst 1995–, The Learning Agency 1996–; govr: St Mary's Jr and Infants Schs 1978–96, Sch of St David and St Katharine 1978–, Nat Inst for Social Work 1986–94; FRSA 1993; *Books* Why Vote Labour? (with Nick Butler and Neil Kinnock, 1979), The Economics of Prosperity (contrib, 1980), Energy and Social Policy (ed with Jonathan Bradshaw, 1983), Rationing in Action (contrib, 1993), Whistleblowing in the Health Service: Accountability, Law and Professional Practice (contrib, 1994); *Style—* Toby Harris, Esq; ✉ Association of Community Health Councils for England and Wales, 30 Drayton Park, London N5 1PB (☎ 0171 609 8405)

HARRIS, Valentina; da of Contessa Fiammetta Bianca Maria Sforza; *Educ* St George's English Sch Rome, Scuola di Alta Cucina Cordon Bleu Sch Rome (dips in teaching and cooking); *partner* Bruce J Williams; 2 s from previous m (Ben b 17 Sept 1982, Jamie b 19 Nov 1985); *Career* authority on Italian food and food culture; reg appearances on TV and radio, own TV series Italian Regional Cookery (BBC 2) 1990 (nominated Best Cookery Series Glenfiddich Awards), contrib numerous nat newspapers and magazines, lectr/numerous live cooking demonstrations across Europe and Australasia; mangr Edible Creativity (prodn of food and beverage mktg events), ptnr Tasting Italy specialist travel co; memb: Guild of Food Writers 1992, Int Assoc of Culinary Professionals 1993; *Books* Perfect Pasta (1984, 2 edn 1991), Pasta (1984, 2 edn 1985), Regional Italian Cookery (1986, one of series ed by Jill Norman, Glenfiddich Award 1987, 2 edn 1991), Edible Italy: A Travelling Gourmet's Guide (1988), Southern Italian Cooker (1988, 2 edn 1990), Recipes from an Italian Farmhouse (1989, nominated Best Euro Food Book James Beard Awards 1991), Valentina's Regional Italian Cookery (1990), Valentina's Italian Family Feast (1990), The Cooking of Tuscany (1992), Valentina's Complete Italian Cookery Course (1992), Instant Italian (1992), Southern Italian Cooking (1993); *Style—* Ms Valentina Harris; ✉ c/o Pavilion Books Ltd, 26 Upper Ground, London SE1 9PD (☎ 0171 620 1666, fax 0171 620 1314)

HARRIS, William Barclay; QC (1961); s of William Cecil Harris (d 1942), and Rhoda Mary, *née* Barclay (d 1961); landed gentry family formerly of Westcotes; *b* 25 Nov 1911; *Educ* Harrow, Trinity Coll Cambridge (MA); *m* 1937, Elizabeth Hermione, da of Capt Sir Clive Milnes-Coates, 2 Bt, OBE, JP, and Lady Celia Milnes-Coates, JP, *née* Crewe-Milnes, da of 1 and last Marquess of Crewe, KG; 1 s (Jonathan), 2 da (Jessica, Hermione); *Career* served WWII 1940–45 Coldstream Gds N Africa, Italy and Germany (despatches), demobbed as Maj; called to the Bar Inner Temple 1937, master of the Bench 1991; chm Rowton Hotels 1965–83; church cmmr 1966–82, chm Redundant Churches Ctee 1972–82, pres Georgian Gp 1990– (memb Exec Ctee 1967–90, chm 1985–90); Liveryman Worshipful Co of Merchant Taylors; *Recreations* shooting; *Clubs* Brooks's, Athenaeum, MCC; *Style—* William Harris, Esq, QC; ✉ Moatlands, East Grinstead, W Sussex RH19 4LL (☎ 01342 810228); 29 Barkston Gardens, London SW5 0ER (☎ 0171 373 8793)

HARRIS, Sir William Gordon; KBE (1969), CB (1963); s of Capt James Whyte Harris, RNR (d 1952); *b* 10 June 1912; *Educ* Liverpool Coll, Sidney Sussex Coll Cambridge (MA); *m* 1, 1938, Margaret Emily (d 1991), da of John Steel Harvie (d 1951); 3 s (Kennedy, John, Gordon), 1 da (Joy); m 2, 1992, Constance Rachel Mary Bishop, *née* Goucher; *Career* civil engr; joined Admty 1937, civil engr in chief Admty 1959, dir gen Navy Works Admty 1960–63; dir gen: Works MPBW 1963–65, Highways Miny of Tport (later Environment) 1965–73; ptnr Peter Fraenkel & Ptnrs 1973–78; chief Br del: Perm Int Assoc of Navigation Congresses 1969–85 (vice pres 1976–79), Perm Int Assoc of Road Congresses 1970–73; Hon Seabee (US Navy) 1961, Decoration for Distinguished Civilian Serv (US Army) 1985; pres: ICE 1974–75, Smeatonian Soc of Civil Engrs 1983–84; chm: Construction Indust Manpower Bd 1976–80, B & CE Holiday Mgmnt Co 1978–87, Dover Harbour Bd 1980–83; chm Br Sch of Osteopathy 1990–92; Hon DSc City Univ 1977; FEng 1977, FICE; *Recreations* gardening, walking, music, 15 grandchildren; *Style—* Sir William Harris, KBE, CB, FEng; ✉ 10 Church Lane, East Carlton, Market Harborough, Leics LE16 8YA (☎ 01536 771307)

HARRIS OF GREENWICH, Baron (Life Peer UK 1974); John Henry Harris; s of Alfred Harris; *b* 5 April 1930; *Educ* Pinner GS; *m* 1, 1952 (m dis 1982), Patricia, da of George Alstrom; 1 s (Hon Francis b 1961), 1 da (Hon Deborah b 1958); m 2, 1983, Angela, da of Joseph Arthur Smith; *Career* sits as Lib Democrat Peer in House of Lords; Lib Democrat Chief Whip 1994–; PA to Ldr of Oppn (Rt Hon Hugh Gaitskell) 1959–62, dir of publicity Lab Pty 1962–64; special asst to: Foreign Sec 1964–66, Home Sec 1966–67, Chllr of the Exchequer 1967–70, Min of State Home Office 1974–79; pres Nat Assoc of Sr Probation Offrs 1980–91; chm Parole Bd England and Wales 1979–82, memb House of Lords Select Ctee on Murder and Life Imprisonment 1988–89; memb House of Lords Select Ctee on the Public Service 1996–97; tstee Police Fndn (chm Exec Ctee); political corr The Economist 1970–74; *Clubs* Reform, MCC; *Style—* The Rt Hon the Lord Harris of Greenwich; ✉ House of Lords, London SW1A 0PW

HARRIS OF HIGH CROSS, Baron (Life Peer UK 1979); Ralph Harris; s of William Henry Harris (d 1954); *b* 10 Dec 1924; *Educ* Tottenham GS, Queens' Coll Cambridge (Foundation scholar); *m* 1949, Jose Pauline, da of Roger Fredrick Jeffery (d 1975); 1 da (and 2 s decd); *Career* sits as Independent Peer in Lords; contested (Lib Unionist): Kirkcaldy 1951, Edinburgh 1955; leader writer Glasgow Herald 1956, lectr in political economy Univ of St Andrews 1949–56, gen dir Inst of Econ Affrs 1957–87 (chm 1987–89, life pres 1990–), ind dir Times Newspapers 1988–; tstee: Ross McWhirter Fndn, Wincott Fndn, Centre for Res into Communist Econs, Atlas Fndn (UK); chm: FOREST 1989–, International Centre for Research into Economic Transformation (Moscow) 1990–; Hon DSc Univ of Buckingham 1984; *Books* Politics Without Prejudice, End of Government, Challenge of a Radical Reactionary, No Minister!; *Clubs* Political Economy, Mont Pelerin Soc; *Style—* The Rt Hon the Lord Harris of High Cross; ✉ 5 Cattley Close, Wood Street, Barnet, Herts EN5 4SN (☎ 0181 449 6212)

HARRIS OF PECKHAM, Baron (Life Peer UK 1995), of Peckham in the London Borough of Southwark; Sir Philip Charles Harris; kt (1985); s of Charles William Harris, MC, of Peckham, and Ruth Ellen, *née* Ward; *b* 15 Sept 1942; *Educ* Streatham GS; *m* 1960, Pauline Norma, da of Bertie William Chumley (d 1968); 3 s (Hon Charles William b 1963, Hon Peter Alexander b 1963, Hon Martin James b 1969), 1 da (Hon Susan Louise (Hon Mrs Sadler) b 1961); *Career* chm: Harris Queensway plc 1964–88 (chief exec 1987), Harris Ventures Ltd 1988–, Carpetright of London 1988–, CW Harris Properties 1988–, Furniture City 1988–; dir Harveys Holdings plc 1986–; non-exec dir: Great Universal Stores plc 1986–, Fisons plc 1986–, Molyneux Estates plc 1990–; memb: Br Showjumping Assoc, Ct of Patrons RGOG 1984–; chm Guy's and Lewisham NHS Tst 1991–93; Hambro Businessman of the Year 1983, hon fell Oriel Coll Oxford 1989; *Recreations* showjumping, cricket; *Style—* The Rt Hon Lord Harris of Peckham; ✉ Harris Ventures Ltd, 187/198 Sevenoaks Way, Orpington, Kent BR5 3AQ (☎ 01689 875135)

HARRISON, Prof Alan; TD (1983, bar 1989 and 1995); s of Lt-Col John Thomas West Harrison, TD, of West Kirby, Wirral, Merseyside, and Mona Evelyn, *née* Gee; *b* 24 July 1944; *Educ* Rydal Sch Colwyn Bay, Welsh Nat Sch of Med Dental Sch (BDS, PhD); *m* 1, (m dis 1980), Pauline Lilian, *née* Rendell; 1 s (Mark Richard b 26 Aug 1973), 1 da (Jane Lorrie b 11 March 1970); m 2, 1 Oct 1982, Margaret Ann, da of Alan William Frost (d 1973), of Leicester; 2 da (Kathryn Ruth b 24 Feb 1984, Sally Deborah b 24 April 1985);

Career OC 390 Field Dental Team 1971–73, CO 308 Evacuation Hosp RAMC (V) 1989–94 (2 i/c 1988–89, training offr 1984–88), CO 306 Field Hosp RAMC (V) 1994–95; lectr Dept of Restorative Dentistry Dental Sch Cardiff 1970–78, visiting asst prof Univ of S Carolina USA 1974–75, sr lectr and hon conslt Sch of Dentistry Univ of Leeds; Univ of Bristol: prof of dental care of the elderly and head Dept of Prosthodontics and Periodontology 1987–94, head Dental Sch 1990–, head Dept of Oral and Dental Science 1994–; memb General Dental Cncl 1994–; Hon Col Cmdt RADC 1996, QHDS 1996; fell Acad of Dental Materials 1992; FDSRCS; *Books* Overdentures in General Dental Practice (1988); *Recreations* tennis, walking, DIY schemes; *Style*— Prof Alan Harrison, TD; ✉ Department of Oral and Dental Science, Dental School, Lower Maudlin Street, Bristol BS1 2LY (☎ 0117 922 6056, fax 0117 925 3724)

HARRISON, Alan James; s of Maj James Harrison (d 1972); *b* 8 Jan 1942; *m* Oct 1978, Dioné Anne, da of Rev William Austin; 1 s (Martin Richard b 1969), 2 da (Yvonne Jane b 1966, Victoria Dioné b 1981); *Career* London branch mangr Bank Sanaye Iran 1978–82; Multibanco Comermex: gen mangr Singapore branch 1982–84, gen mangr London branch 1984, gen mangr NY and London branch 1993, currently with Banco Inverlat USA; Freeman City of London; assoc memb Chartered Inst of Bankers; *Clubs* Overseas Bankers', Guards' Polo; *Style*— Alan Harrison, Esq

HARRISON, Prof Bernard Joseph; s of William Bernard Harrison (d 1964), of Bristol, and Camilla Victoria, *née* Davis; *b* 29 May 1933; *Educ* Dursley GS, Cheltenham GS, Univ of Birmingham (BA, MA), Univ of Michigan Ann Arbor (PhD); *m* July 1956, Dorothy Muriel, da of George Harold White (d 1967), of Nottingham; 1 s (David Thomas b 24 Dec 1964), 2 da (Eva Tempe Jane b 1957, Katherine Lisa b 1960); *Career* lectr in philosophy Univ of Toronto 1960–62, asst lectr in philosophy Univ of Birmingham 1962–63, prof of philosophy Univ of Sussex 1985–92 (lectr 1963, reader 1972), E E Erickson prof of philosophy Univ of Utah 1991–; memb: Aristotelian Soc, American Philosophical Assoc; *Books* Meaning and Structure (1972), Form and Content (1973), Fielding's Tom Jones: The Novelist as Moral Philosopher (1975), An Introduction to the Philosophy of Language (1979), Inconvenient Fictions: Literature and the Limits of Theory (1991); *Style*— Prof Bernard Harrison; ✉ Department of Philosophy, University of Utah, Salt Lake City, Utah 84112, USA (Sept-Dec annually)

HARRISON, Dr Brian David Walter; s of Joseph Harrison (d 1955), and Constance Jennings, *née* Horsfall (d 1994), of Lytham St Annes; *b* 24 April 1943; *Educ* Shrewsbury, St John's Coll Cambridge (MA, MB BChir), Guy's Hosp (LRCP, MRCS); *m* 13 July 1968, Jennifer Anne, da of Dr John Fisher Stokes, of Stoke Row, Oxfordshire; 1 s (Ben b 1970), 1 da (Nicola b 1974); *Career* house physician Guy's Hosp 1967–68, house surgn Bolingbroke Hosp London 1968–69, sr house offr New Cross Hosp London 1969, jr registrar cardiology and gen med Guy's Hosp 1969–70, hon clinical lectr in physiology Brompton Hosp 1971–72 (house physician 1970–71), registrar to Med Professorial Unit Westminster Hosp 1971–72, clinical lectr in physiology Brompton Hosp 1973, sr med registrar Ahmadu Bello Univ Hosp Zaria Nigeria 1973–74, lectr and sr registrar in thoracic and gen med Middlesex Hosp 1974–77; conslt physician: Norfolk and Norwich Hosp 1978–, West Norwich Hosp 1978–; memb Cncl ASH 1983– (fndr and first chm Norfolk ASH 1979); British Thoracic Soc: memb Res Ctee 1980–86, clinical coordinator Nat Pneumonia Study 1981–87, memb Educn Ctee 1986–89 and 1994–, chm Pneumonia Standing Sub Ctee 1987–89, chm Standards of Care Ctee 1989–93, memb Cncl and Exec 1989–93, coordinator confs to produce guidelines on the mgmnt of asthma in Britain 1990, 1992 and 1995; pres East Anglian Thoracic Soc 1982–84; MRCP 1970, FRCP 1987; FCCP 1990; author of numerous med pubns on pneumonia, smoking, asthma, pulmonary function, respiratory failure, secondary polycythemia, chronic airflow obstruction, lung biopsy, sarcoidosis; *Recreations* gardening, sailing, theatre, travel; *Clubs* Stranger's (Norwich); *Style*— Dr Brian Harrison; ✉ The White House, Church Avenue East, Norwich NR2 2AF (☎ 01603 456508); Norfolk and Norwich Hospital, Brunswick Road, Norwich NR1 3SR (☎ 01603 289642, fax 01603 289640)

HARRISON, Prof Bryan Desmond; CBE (1990); s of John William Harrison (d 1963), and Norah, *née* Webster; *b* 16 June 1931; *Educ* Whitgift Sch Croydon, Univ of Reading (Wantage scholar, BSc), Rothamsted Experimental Station Harpenden, Univ of London (PhD); *m* 13 Jan 1968, Elizabeth Ann, da of Vivian Francis Latham-Warde (d 1981); 2 s (Peter William b 1969, Robert Anthony b 1972), 1 da (Claire Janet b 1977); *Career* res scientist: Virology Section Scot Horticultural Res Inst Dundee 1954–57, Plant Pathology Dept Rothamsted Experimental Station Harpenden 1957–66; Scot Crop Res Inst Dundee (formerly Horticultural Res Inst): res scientist and head Virology Dept 1966–91, sr pso 1969, dep chief scientific offr 1981; hon prof Univ of St Andrews 1986–, prof of plant virology Univ of Dundee 1991–96 (hon visiting prof 1988–91); Hon Doctorate in Agriculture and Forestry Univ of Helsinki 1990; hon memb: Assoc of Applied Biologists 1989, Soc for Gen Microbiology 1990, Phytopathological Soc of Japan 1992; FRSE 1979, FRS 1987; *Recreations* gardening; *Style*— Prof Bryan Harrison, CBE, FRS, FRSE; ✉ Scottish Crop Research Institute, Invergowrie, Dundee DD2 5DA (☎ 01382 562731, fax 01382 562426)

HARRISON, Cameron; s of Elias Harrison, and Herries, *née* Smith (d 1990); *b* 27 Aug 1945; *Educ* Cumnock Acad, Univ of Strathclyde (BSc), Univ of Stirling (MEd); *m* 1968, Pearl, da of Richard Leimon; 1 s (Keith b 1970), 1 da (Fiona b 1972); *Career* teacher Greenock Acad 1968–71, head of dept Graeme HS 1971–79, depute rector Kirkudbright Acad 1979–82, rector The Gordon Schs 1982–91, chief exec The Scottish Consultative Council on the Curriculum 1991–; sec-gen Consortium of Institutions for Development and Research in Education in Europe (CIDREE) 1993–; *Books* Managing Change (1988); *Recreations* singing, talking, listening, teaching, learning; *Style*— Cameron Harrison, Esq; ✉ Scottish Consultative Council on the Curriculum, Gardyne Road, Broughty Ferry, Dundee DD5 1NY (☎ 01382 455055, fax 01382 455046, car 0831 518291)

HARRISON, Christopher Peter Motte; s of Peter Motte Harrison (d 1943), and Joyce Marie, *née* Holtom; *b* 27 Sept 1943; *Educ* Michaelhouse Sch S Africa, Prince of Wales Sch Kenya, Univ of Aberdeen (MA), Makerere Univ (DipEd), Loughborough Univ (MLS); *m* 1986, Sarah Elizabeth, da of Bertram Pink; 1 s (Richard Mark Gervase b 1971), 2 da (Nicola Jane b 1977, Antonia Emily Rosalind b 1988); *Career* teacher of English Nairobi 1969–72, lectr Staff Trg Coll Office of the President Blantyre Malawi 1972–75; British Council: asst English language offr Yugoslavia 1975–79, head English Teaching Information Centre 1980–83, libraries and books offr Egypt 1983–87, information servs offr Turkey 1987–91, dir Enugu Nigeria 1991–94, cultural attaché Rangoon 1994–; memb Library Assoc; fell Inst of Mgmnt and Technol Enugu 1992; *Recreations* computing, music, travel; *Style*— Christopher Harrison, Esq; ✉ c/o FCO (Rangoon), King Charles Street, London SW1A 2AH

HARRISON, Claude William; s of Harold Harrison (d 1976), and Florence Mildred, *née* Ireton (d 1986); *b* 31 March 1922; *Educ* Hutton GS, Harris Art Sch Preston, Liverpool City Sch of Art, RCA (ARCA); *m* 1 March 1947, Audrey, da of Arthur John Johnson (d 1964); 1 s (Tobias b 1950); *Career* WWII RAF 1942–47; serv: India, Burma, China; painter of: conversation pieces, portraits, figure compositions; exhibitions: RA, London, Florida, NY, Chicago; RSPP 1961, Hon RP; *Books* The Portrait Painters Handbook (1968), Book of Tobit (1970); *Recreations* walking and reading; *Style*— Claude Harrison, Esq; ✉ Barrow Wife, Cartmel Fell, Grange over Sands, Cumbria LA11 6NZ (☎ 01539 531323)

HARRISON, Sir (Robert) Colin; 4 Bt (UK 1922), of Eaglescliffe, Co Durham; s of late Sir John Fowler Harrison, 2 Bt, and late Kathleen, *née* Livingston; suc bro, Sir (John) Wyndham Harrison, 3 Bt, 1955; *b* 25 May 1938; *Educ* Radley, St John's Coll Cambridge; *m* 1963, Maureen Marie, da of late E Leonard Chiverton, of Langley House, Lanchester, Co Durham; 1 s (John Wyndham Fowler b 1972), 2 da (Rachel Deborah (Mrs Waddell) b 1966, Claire Grace b 1974); *Heir* s, John Wyndham Fowler Harrison b 14 Dec 1972; *Career* Nat Serv cmmnd 5 Royal Northumberland Fusiliers 1957–59; chm John Harrison (Stockton) Ltd, vice chm Darlington Building Society; general cmmr of income tax; chm Young Master Printers Nat Ctee 1972–73; *Style*— Sir Colin Harrison, Bt; ✉ Stearsby Hall, Stearsby, York YO6 4SA (☎ 01347 888226)

HARRISON, Sir David; kt (1997), CBE (1990); s of Harold David Harrison (d 1987), of Exeter, Devon, and Lavinia, *née* Wilson (d 1993); *b* 3 May 1930; *Educ* Bede Sch Sunderland, Clacton Co HS, Selwyn Coll Cambridge (MA, PhD, ScD); *m* 11 Aug 1962, Sheila Rachel, da of Denis Richardson Debes, of Little Budworth, Cheshire; 2 s (Michael b 1963, Tony b 1966, d 1986), 1 da (Sarah b 1965); *Career* Nat Serv 2 Lt REME 1949; Univ of Cambridge: lectr 1956–79, master Selwyn Coll 1994– (sr tutor 1967–79, fell 1957–), chm Bd of Tstees Homerton Coll 1979–; visiting prof: Delaware Univ USA 1967, Sydney Univ Aust 1976; vice chllr: Univ of Keele 1979–84, Univ of Exeter 1984–94; chm: UCCA 1984–91, Ctee of Vice Chllrs and Princs 1991–93; pres Inst of Chem Engrs 1991–92, former memb Engrg Cncl; FEng 1987, FRSC, FRIC 1961, FIChemE 1968, FRSA 1985, CIMgt 1990; *Books* Fluidised Particles (with J F Davidson, 1963), Fluidization (with J F Davidson and R Clift, 2 edn 1985); *Recreations* music, tennis, hill walking, good food; *Clubs* Athenaeum, United Oxford and Cambridge, Foundation House (Stoke-on-Trent); *Style*— Sir David Harrison, CBE, FEng; ✉ 7 Gough Way, Cambridge; The Master's Lodge, Selwyn College, Cambridge (☎ 01223 335889, fax 01223 335888)

HARRISON, David Ernest; s of Ernest Harrison (d 1984), and Margaret Louise, *née* Robson (d 1976); *b* 14 July 1936; *Educ* Exeter Sch, St Catherine's Coll Oxford (MA), Stanford Univ Calif USA (MA); *m* 25 March 1961, Pamela Lilian, da of Stanley Brobyn; 1 s (Richard Stanley Ernest b 30 May 1964 d 1981), 2 da (Catherine Louise (Mrs Raba) b 21 Sept 1965, Rowan Jane b 11 April 1970); *Career* dep sales controller ATV 1959–68, sales dir Tyne Tees Television 1968–71, md British Posters 1971–73, md Media Div Lion International 1973, mktg dir Credcrest Ltd 1973–74, mktg dir E Gomme Ltd 1973–82, chm Posterscope Group 1982–; govr RSC 1979– (memb Cncl, chm Mktg Advsy Ctee); *Recreations* amateur dramatics, cricket; *Clubs* Somerset CCC (vice pres), Solus; *Style*— David Harrison, Esq; ✉ Posterscope Group, 55 North Wharf Rd, London W2 1LA (☎ 0171 724 7244, fax 0171 724 7620)

HARRISON, Sir Donald Frederic Norris; kt (1990); s of Frederick William Rees Harrison, OBE (d 1991), and Florence (d 1987); *b* 9 March 1925; *Educ* Newport HS Gwent, Guy's (MS, MD, PhD, Pembrey prize, 14 Gold medals); *m* 29 Jan 1948, Audrey Dixon, da of Percival Clubb (d 1970); 2 da (Susan Patricia Denny b July 1949, Zoë Clare b March 1965); *Career* Nat Serv ENT specialist RAF 1950–52; 1963–90: prof of laryngology and otology Univ of London, sr surgn Royal Nat ENT Hosp, emeritus ENT surgn Moorfields Eye Hosp London, dean Inst of Laryngology and Otology; emeritus prof of laryngology and otology Univ of London 1990; past pres Royal Soc of Med 1996 (Hon FRSM 1991); Master 8th Br Academic Conf in ENT 1991; memb Cncl Roedean Girls Sch 1982–89; Liveryman Worshipful Soc of Apothecaries; FRCS 1955, FCOpth 1993, FRCR 1995; FRCS(Aust) 1977, FRCSE 1981, FRCSI 1991, fell S African Coll of Med 1988, fell American Coll of Surgns 1990, fell or memb of 40 nat and int learned socs; *Publications* 46 book chapters, Scientific Basis of Otolaryngology (1976), Dilemmas in Otorhinolaryngology (1988), Neoplasms of the Upper Jaw (1993), Anatomy and Physiology of the Mammalian Larynx (1995); *Recreations* heraldry, model making, comparative anatomy; *Style*— Sir Donald Harrison; ✉ Springfield, 6 Fishers Farm, Horley, Surrey RH6 9DU (☎ 01293 784307)

HARRISON, Edward Peter Graham (Ted); s of Rev Peter Graham Harrison, of Bishops Lydeard, Somerset, and (Eleanor) Joan, *née* Rowland; *b* 14 April 1948; *Educ* Grenville Coll Bideford Devon, Univ of Kent at Canterbury (BA); *m* 1968, Helen Grace, da of Ronald Percy Waters (d 1986); 1 s (David Edward Graham b 1969), 1 da (Caroline Helen b 1971); *Career* writer, broadcaster and cartoonist; trainee journalist Kent Messenger and Evening Post 1968–72; reporter: Morgan-Grampian Magazines 1972, Southern TV 1970–73, You and Yours (BBC Radio 4) 1972–80, Sunday (Radio 4) 1972– (presenter 1986–88), BBC Scotland News and Current Affrs 1980–85 (also presenter), World Tonight (Radio 4) 1981–83, World at One and PM (Radio 4) 1983–87; presenter: numerous radio documentaries in Profile and Soundings series (Radio 4), Opinions (Radio 4) 1986–87, The Human Factor (ITV) 1986–, Does he take Sugar? (Radio 4) 1991–95; religious affrs corr BBC 1988–89, currently freelance reporter/presenter BBC Radio 4; ind radio and television prodr; dir Pilgrim Productions Canterbury; Parly candidate (Lib) Bexley 1970 and Maidstone Feb 1974; exhibition of caricatures London 1977, exhibition of watercolours Oxford and Canterbury 1981; *Books* Modern Elizabethans (1977), McIndoe's Army (with Peter Williams, 1979), Marks of the Cross (1981), Commissioner Catherine (1983), Much Beloved Daughter (1985), The Durham Phenomenon (1986), Living with Kidney Failure (1990), Kriss Akabusi - On Track (1991), Elvis People (1992), Members Only (1994), Stigmata (1994), Letters to a Friend I Never Knew (1995), Defender of the Faith (1996), Tanni (1996); *Recreations* watercolour painting; *Style*— Ted Harrison, Esq; ✉ 28 The Quay, Conyer, Sittingbourne, Kent ME9 9HR (☎ 01795 521752)

HARRISON, Sir Ernest Thomas; kt (1981), OBE (1972); s of late Ernest Horace Harrison, and Gertrude Rebecca, *née* Gibbons (d 1995); *b* 11 May 1926; *Educ* Trinity GS London; *m* 1960, Phyllis Brenda (Janie), *née* Knight; 3 s, 2 da; *Career* CA; Harker Holloway & Co, Voluntary Nat Savings Movement 1964–76; Racal Electronics plc: joined 1951, dir 1958, dep md 1961, chief exec 1966–92, chm 1966–; chm Racal Telecom plc 1988–91, chm Vodafone plc 1991– (following demerger from Racal), chm Chubb Security plc 1992– (also following demerger from Racal); dir Camelot Group plc 1993–; chm Ronald Raven Chair in Clinical Oncology Tst 1991–; Capt of Industry (Livingston Industl and Commercial Assoc Edinburgh) 1980, Hambro Businessman of the Year 1981, Aims of Industry Nat Free Enterprise award 1982, Br Enterprise award for Racal 1982, received The 1990 Founding Society's Centenary award by Inst of Chartered Accountants, first recipient of Mountbatten medal by National Electronics Cncl 1992; former memb Cncl Electronics Engrg Assoc and Nat Electronics Cncl; memb The Jockey Club; memb Worshipful Co of Scriveners; Hon DSc Cranfield Inst of Technol, Hon DUniv Surrey, Hon DSc City Univ, Hon DUniv Edinburgh, Hon FCGI; fell Royal Free Hosp Sch of Med Univ of London; memb RSA, FCA, CompIERE, CompIEE, Companion Inst of Mgmnt; *Recreations* horse racing (owner and breeder), gardening, wild life, all sports (particularly soccer); *Clubs* Jockey; *Style*— Sir Ernest Harrison, OBE; ✉ Racal Electronics plc, Western Rd, Bracknell, Berks

HARRISON, Sir Francis Alexander Lyle (Frank); kt (1974), MBE (1943), QC (NI), DL (Co Down 1973); s of Rev Alexander Lyle Harrison; *b* 19 March 1910; *Educ* Campbell Coll Belfast, Trinity Coll Dublin; *m* 1940, Norah Patricia Rea; 2 da; *Career* called to the Bar NI 1937, bencher Inn of Ct NI 1961, pres Lands Tbnl NI 1964–82; fndr memb NI Assoc of Mental Health 1959, chm Glendhu Children's Hostel 1969–81; cmmr: Local Govt Boundaries NI 1971–72 and 1983–84, Dist Electoral Areas 1984; *Style*— Sir Frank Harrison, MBE, QC, DL; ✉ Ballydorn Hill, Killinchy, Newtownards, Co Down, NI (☎ 01238 541 250)

HARRISON, Frank Ronald; s of Ronald Charles Gulley Harrison, of Helensburgh, Dumbartonshire, and Eva Louise Johanne, *née* Hornäffer; *b* 11 July 1962; *Educ* Eton,

Oxford Poly (BA); *m* Caroline Elizabeth, da of Malcolm B C Ward; 1 da (Emma Louise Elizabeth b 19 Feb 1990), 1 s (William Frank Ion b 20 April 1992); *Career* media research dir/bd dir Saatchi & Saatchi Advertising 1987–91, worldwide media info systems dir Zenith Media 1994– (media research dir 1992–94); speaker at numerous indust confs, author of various papers published on media; memb IPA/ISBA/AFVPA Working Pty on Equity Repeat Fee Agreement 1992 and 1996; memb MRS 1985 (DipMRS), FIPA 1996 (MIPA 1989); *Books* UK Media Yearbook (annually 1987–), UK Television Forecasts (annually 1988–), Interactive Media (1995), Television in Asia Pacific to 2000 (1995), Television in Europe to 2005 (1996); *Recreations* astronomy, multimedia, internet; *Style*— Frank Harrison, Esq; ✉ Chetwode, Burchetts Green Lane, Littlewick Green, Berks SL6 3QW (☎ 01628 829068); Zenith Media, 63–65 North Wharf Road, London W2 1LA (☎ 0171 753 6470, fax 0171 402 5703, e-mail frank_harrison@zenithmedia.co.uk)

HARRISON, (James) Graham; s of Col Alfred Marshal Langton Harrison, CBE, MC (d 1986), of West Malvern, Worcs, and Violet, *née* Robinson (d 1988); *b* 3 July 1930; *Educ* The Elms Colwall Worcs, Bishop Cotton Sch Simla India, Geelong GS Victoria Aust, Uppingham; *m* 26 July 1958, June Eveline, da of Robert Eustace Taylor (d 1958), of Woodford Wells, Essex; 2 s (Robert b 1962, Nicholas b 1973), 1 da (Sarah (Mrs Moloney) b 1959); *Career* Nat Serv 2 Lt RHA 1954–56; TA: L/Bdr HAC 1956–59, Capt S Nottingham Hussars 1959–64; CA; articled Wright & Westhead 1948–54, qualified 1954, Price Waterhouse 1956–59, Chamberlain & Merchant 1959–64; sole practitioner: Sacker & Harrison Bournemouth 1964–70, Bicker & Co 1970–84, Thornton Baker 1985; fndr Harrison & Co 1986–96, conslt 1996–; dir Portman Bldg Soc 1989–91; chm: Wessex Branch Inst of Taxation 1978–80, Courses Ctee S Soc of CAs 1979–82; treas St Saviour's PCC 1984–90 (sec 1974–79, churchwarden 1979–84); FCA 1954, ATII 1963; *Books* Handbook on Taxation of Land (1982), Taxation of Income Arising From Furnished Lettings (1985); *Recreations* sport, music, bridge; *Clubs* David Lloyd Club; *Style*— Graham Harrison, Esq; ✉ 45 Littledown Ave, Queens Park, Bournemouth, BH7 7AX (☎ 01202 393540); Fairview House, Hinton Rd, Bournemouth, BH1 2EE (☎ 01202 294162, fax 01202 295546)

HARRISON, Maj-Gen Ian Stewart; CB; s of Capt Leslie George Harrison (d 1930), and Evelyn Simpson, *née* Christie (d 1980); *b* 25 May 1919; *Educ* St Albans Sch; *m* 5 Dec 1942, Winfred (Wynne) Raikes, da of George Vose Stavert, of Endmoor, Kendal, Westmorland; 1 s (David Raikes Stewart b 11 June 1949), 1 da (Jenifer Anne b 15 April 1947); *Career* cmmnd RM 1937; serv at sea: Norway, ME, Sicily, BAOR 1939–45; student Staff Coll Camberley 1948, HQ 3 Commando Bde 1949–51 (despatches), dir Staff Coll Camberley 1953–55, Cmdt Signal Sch RM 1959–61, on staff of Cmdt Gen RM 1962–63, chief instr Jt Warfare Estab 1963–65, CO RM Barracks Eastney 1966–67, Br Def Staff Washington DC 1967–68, COS RM 1968–70; ADC to HM The Queen 1966–67; fndr tstee British Sch of Brussels 1969–, dir gen British Food Export Cncl 1970–78, dir Br Conslts Bureau 1978–88, chm Chichester Festivities 1979–89, Capt of Deal Castle 1980–; FIMgt; *Recreations* golf, real tennis, sailing; *Clubs* Royal Yacht Squadron, Army and Navy, Royal St George's Golf; *Style*— Maj-Gen Ian Harrison, CB; ✉ Manor Cottage, Runcton, Chichester, W Sussex PO20 6PU (☎ 01243 785 480)

HARRISON, Prof James Sumner; *b* 19 Jan 1929; *Educ* Univ of London (BSc), Loughborough Univ (DLC); *m* 1959, Sally, *née* Bennett; 2 da (Sarah b 1960, Polly b 1962), 1 s (Thomas b 1964); *Career* dir Coal Research Establishment until 1992; chm Nat Soc for Clean Air 1992, pres Inst of Energy 1993; FRIC 1952, FInstE 1957, FIChemE 1990, FEng 1994; *Recreations* music, French, hill walking; *Clubs* Athenaeum; *Style*— Prof James Harrison, FEng; ✉ Hetton Lawn, Cudnall Street, Cheltenham, Glos GL53 8HU (☎ 01242 238705, fax 01242 573498)

HARRISON, John; s of John Henry Jordan (d 1995), of Grantham, Lincs, and Margaret, *née* Harrison; *b* 20 Feb 1944; *Educ* Silverdale Secdy Modern Sch, Sheffield Tech Coll; *m* 13 July 1968, Vivien Ann Eveline, da of Frederick Charles Hardisty (d 1988), of Brighton; 1 s (Mark b 31 July 1976); *Career* asst electrician to chief engr Harold Fielding 1961–63, lighting designer Theatre Projects Ltd 1964–68, prodn mangr and tech dir ENO 1968–74, theatre conslt John Wyckham Associates 1975–76; tech dir: WNO 1976–88, Vancouver Opera Canada 1984–88, Royal Opera House Covent Garden 1989–; md Cardiff Theatrical Services Ltd 1984–88; memb: Soc of Br Theatre Designers 1964, Soc of Br Lighting Designers 1964, Assoc of Br Theatre Technicians 1968; *Recreations* travel, gardening; *Style*— John Harrison, Esq; ✉ 6 Summerswood Close, Kenley Lane, Kenley, Surrey CR8 5EY; Royal Opera House, Covent Garden, London WC2E 9DD (☎ 0171 240 1200, fax 0171 836 1762, telex 27988 COVGAR G)

HARRISON, John; s of Kenneth Ridley Harrison (d 1960), of Stockton on Tees, and Margaret, *née* Calvert; *b* 12 Nov 1944; *Educ* Grangefield GS, Univ of Sheffield (BA); *m* 4 June 1969, Patricia Alice Bridget, da of Dr Harry Raymond Alban (d 1974), of London; 1 s (Joseph b 1979), 2 da (Rachel b 1971, Philippa b 1973); *Career* articled clerk Coopers & Lybrand 1966–70, Tillotson corp planner 1970–72; Deloitte & Touche Consulting Group: mgmnt conslt 1972–92, ptnr 1981–, ptnr in charge Corp Special Servs 1992–94, ptnr in charge Financial Institutions Consulting; FCA 1969, FIMC 1973, FRSA 1991; *Recreations* fly fishing, skiing, sailing, shooting; *Style*— John Harrison, Esq; ✉ Goodwin Manor, Swaffham Prior, Cambridge CB5 0LG (☎ 01638 742850); Deloitte & Touche Consulting Group, Stonecutter Court, Stonecutter Street, London EC4A 4TR (☎ 0171 936 3000, fax 0171 480 6958)

HARRISON, Surgn Vice Adm Sir John Albert Bews; KBE (1981); s of Albert William Harrison (d 1959), of Dover, Kent, and Lilian Eda, *née* Bews (d 1973); *b* 20 May 1921; *Educ* St Bartholomew's Hosp; *m* 1943, Jane Harris (d 1988); 2 s; *Career* RN Med Serv 1947–83, after serv with RM and at sea, served in RN Hosps Plymouth, Hong Kong, Chatham, Malta and Haslar; conslt radiologist and advsr in radiology to Med DG Navy 1967–76, Dep Med DG and Dir Med Personnel and Logistics 1975–77, Dean Naval Med and Surgn Rear Adm in charge Inst of Naval Med 1977–80, QHP 1976–83, Med DG Navy and Surgn Vice Adm 1980–83; former memb MRC Decompression Sickness Panel, former memb Cncl for Med Postgrad Educn of Eng and Wales; pres Radiology Section RSM 1984–85; fell Med Soc London (pres 1985–86), FRCP, FRCR, DMRD; CStJ 1983 (OStJ 1975); *Recreations* fishing, cricket, photography; *Clubs* RSM, MCC; *Style*— Sir John Harrison, KBE; ✉ Alexandra Cottage, Swanmore, Hants SO32 2PB

HARRISON, HE John Clive; LVO (1971); s of Sir Geoffrey Wedgwood Harrison, GCMG, KCVO (d 1990), and Amy Katherine, *née* Clive; *b* 12 July 1937; *Educ* Winchester, Jesus Coll Oxford (BA); *m* 1967, Jennifer Heather, da of Cdr John Courtney Evered Burston, OBE, RN (d 1970); 1 s (James b 1968), 2 da (Carolyn b 1970, Sarah b 1972); *Career* HM Dip Serv; cnsllr and head of Chancery Lagos 1981–84, head of Consular Dept FCO 1985–89, dep high cmmr Islamabad 1989–93, high cmmr Mauritius (Port Louis) 1993–; *Recreations* gardening, golf, tennis; *Clubs* Royal Overseas League, Mannings Heath Golf; *Style*— HE Mr John C Harrison, LVO; ✉ c/o Foreign and Commonwealth Office, (Port Louis), King Charles Street, London SW1A 2AH

HARRISON, Eur Ing Dr John David; s of Alick Robin Walsham Harrison (d 1969) of Merton Coll Oxford, and Margaret Edith, *née* Ross (d 1989); *b* 23 Nov 1933; *Educ* Marlborough, Peterhouse Cambridge (scholar, MA, PhD); *m* 1957, Margaret Primrose, da of Rev Wilfred J C Armstrong; 2 s (Andrew David b 1959, Peter Alick b 1961), 1 da (Susan Margaret b 1964); *Career* design and site engr Freeman Fox and Ptnrs 1957–61; TWI (formerly Br Welding Res Assoc) 1962–: res engr 1962–69, head of fracture res 1969–77, head Engrg Res Dept 1977–84, mangr Engrg and Materials Gp 1984–92, assoc dir (consultancy servs) 1992–; chm: Cmmn XIII Int Inst of Welding 1974–89, Ctee WEE/37 BSI 1985–, UK Ctee on Structural Integrity 1990–94; co-chm Crack Tip Opening Displacement (fracture toughness) Testing Sub-Ctee American Soc for Testing Materials 1978–81; memb: Pressure Vessel Study Gp Nuclear Installations Inspectorate 1974–79, Fast Reactor Study Gp Advsy Ctee Safety in Nuclear Installations 1977–80, Structural Integrity Advsy Gp (Prototype Fast-Breeder Reactor) UKAEA 1990–94, Engrg Advsy Bd Univ of Aberdeen 1995; sec Royal Soc Working Party on sub-critical crack growth 1981–86; author of over 80 papers on fracture res etc; MICE 1962, FWeldI 1969, FIMechE 1989, MAE 1994, FEng 1995; *Awards* Sir William J Larke Medal Welding Inst 1980; *Recreations* golf, hill walking, gardening; *Style*— Eur Ing Dr John Harrison, FEng; ✉ TWI, Abington Hall, Abington, Cambridge CB1 6AL (☎ 01223 891162, fax 01223 892588)

HARRISON, Jonathan; s of Michael George Harrison, of York, and Pauline, *née* Mytum; *b* 2 March 1966; *Educ* Manor Secdy Sch York, York Coll of Arts & Technol (City & Guilds); *m* 20 July 1991; Janine Helen, da of David Alan Farnsworth; 1 da (Chloe Anna b 11 Oct 1996); *Career* chef; apprentice rising to chef de partie Judges Lodgings Hotel Lendal York 1982–86, first commis rising to demi chef de partie Longueville Manor Hotel Jersey 1986–87, chef de partie rising to jr sous chef Bilbrough Manor Country House Hotel York 1987–90, Le Louise XV Hotel de Paris Monte Carlo 1993, sr sous chef rising to chef de cuisine Swallow Hotel Birmingham 1990–; memb: Ctee Midlands Assoc of Chefs, Academie Culinaire de France; charity work for Macmillan Appeal; *Awards* Gold and Silver Medals Salon Culinaires 1990–96, Caterer & Hotelkeeper Catey Hotel of the Year Award 1992, English Tourist Bd Award for Hotel of the Year 1993, Johansens Annual Award for City Hotel of the Year 1993, winner Hotel & Caterers Acorn Award 1993, winner Roux Brothers Scholarship 1993, Br finalist Pierre Taittinger Culinaire Prize 1994; *Recreations* cycling, wine (memb Sunday Times Wine Club), food; *Style*— Jonathan Harrison, Esq; ✉ Swallow Hotel, 12 Hagley Road, Five Ways, Birmingham B16 8SJ

HARRISON, Karl; s of Michael Norman Harrison, and Janet, *née* Gough; *b* 20 Feb 1964; *Educ* Morley HS, Kitson Coll of Technol; *partner* Suzanne Black; 2 s (Samuel b 15 Sept 1992, James b 15 June 1996); *Career* rugby league player; clubs: Bramley RLFC 1982–85 (81 appearances), Featherstone Rovers RLFC 1985–89 (106 appearances), Hull FC 1989–91 (56 appearances), Halifax RLFC 1991– (109 appearances); GB: v Australia (8 caps), v New Zealand (5 caps), v France (1 cap), v Papua New Guinea (1 cap); England: debut v France 1995, 6 caps, runners up Rugby League Centenary World Cup 1995; memb Br Lions tour to Australia 1992 and France 1996; *Recreations* golf (memb West Bowling Golf Club); *Style*— Karl Harrison; ✉ Halifax RLFC, The Pavilion, Thrum Hall, Gibbet Street, Halifax HX1 4TL

HARRISON, Kenneth Arthur; TD (1965); s of Arthur Reginald Harrison (d 1969), and Agnes, *née* Hutcheson (d 1963); *b* 4 July 1930; *Educ* Denstone Coll Staffs, Univ of Manchester; *m* 12 Sept 1953, Christine Mary, da of Joseph Herrod; 2 s (Roger b 1955, Peter b 1960); *Career* Harrison Industries plc: sr engr 1951–61, building design conslt 1961–65, md (engrg) 1965–70, chm 1971–92; chm subsid co Bostwick Doors (UK) Ltd (Queen's award for Export 1980); chm and md Ensor Holdings PLC 1992–; *Recreations* tennis, parachuting, business, golf, garden design; *Clubs* St James's (Manchester), Carlton; *Style*— Kenneth Harrison, Esq, TD; ✉ White Cottage, Oldfield Road, Altrincham, Cheshire; Shippon, Moelfre, Anglesey; Chesaux-Dessous, St Cergues, Switzerland; Ensor Holdings PLC, Manchester M23 9NX (fax 0161 945 5851)

HARRISON, Kenneth Cecil; OBE (1980, MBE (Mil) 1946); s of Thomas Harrison (d 1967), of Hyde, Cheshire, and Annie, *née* Wood (d 1976); *b* 29 April 1915; *Educ* Hyde GS Cheshire, Coll of Technol Manchester, RMA Sandhurst; *m* 26 Aug 1941, Doris, da of Frank Taylor (d 1927), of Hyde, Cheshire; 2 s (David John b 25 Aug 1944, Timothy Michael b 28 Aug 1948); *Career* WWII served: S Lancs Regt 1940–42, offr cadet RMA 1942, 2 Lt W Yorks Regt 1942, Lt E Yorks Regt 50 Div Western Desert 1942, platoon cdr Sicily Landing 1943, Capt 1943, Maj 1944, company cdr D-Day landing (wounded) 1944, Normandy and Arnhem 1944, Italy and Austria 1945; demobbed Maj 1946; borough librarian: Hyde and Glossop 1939, Hove 1947, Eastbourne 1950, Hendon 1958; city librarian Westminster 1961–80, chief exec Cwlth Library Assoc 1980–83, conslt librarian Ranfurly Library Serv 1983–90; vice pres City of Westminster Arts Cncl 1980– (hon sec 1965–80); govr Westminster Coll 1962–80, pres Paddington Soc 1982–90; memb Rotary Club: Hyde 1939–47, Hove 1947–50, Eastbourne 1950–58 (pres 1957–58), Hendon 1958–61; memb: Past Rotarians Club of Eastbourne and Dist 1986– (hon sec 1992–), Assoc of Past Rotarians (hon sec 1996–), Eastbourne Local History Soc 1987–, Cwlth Library Assoc (pres 1972–75); fell Library Assoc 1938– (pres 1973); Knight First Class Order of the Lion of Finland 1976; *Books* Public Libraries Today (1963), Facts at your Fingertips (2 edn, 1966), British Public Library Buildings (1966), Libraries in Britain (1968), Libraries in Scandinavia (2 edn, 1969), The Library and the Community (3 edn, 1977), Prospects for British Librarianship (ed, 1977), First Steps in Librarianship (5 edn, 1980), Public Library Policy (ed, 1981), Public Relations for Librarians (2 edn, 1982), Public Library Buildings 1975–83 (ed, 1987), International Librarianship (1989), Library Buildings 1984–89 (ed, 1990); *Recreations* reading, writing, travel, wine-bibbing, crosswords, cricket; *Clubs* MCC, Cwlth Tst, Sussex CCC; *Style*— K C Harrison, Esq, OBE; ✉ 5 Tavistock, Devonshire Place, Eastbourne, East Sussex BN21 4AG (☎ 01323 726747)

HARRISON, Lyndon Henry Arthur; MEP (Lab) Cheshire W and Wirral (majority 47,176); s of Charles William Harrison, and late Edith Harrison, *née* Johnson; *b* 28 Sept 1947; *Educ* Oxford Sch, Univ of Warwick (BA), Univ of Sussex (MA), Univ of Keele (MA); *m* 1980, Hilary Anne, *née* Plank; 1 s (Adam b 1982), 1 da (Sara b 1985); *Career* mangr Students' Union NE Wales Inst of HE Wrexham; MEP (Lab): Cheshire W 1989–94, Cheshire W and Wirral 1994–; Euro Parl: memb Transport and Tourism Ctee, memb Economic and Monetary Ctee, socialist spokesperson Monetary Sub-Ctee, sec European Parly Lab Pty (EPLP) 1991–94; cncllr Cheshire CC 1981–90 (formerly chm Libraries and Countryside and Tourism Ctees), vice pres Assoc of CCs; *Recreations* chess, music, sport; *Style*— Lyndon Harrison, Esq, MEP; ✉ Watergate Building, Crane Wharf, Chester CH1 4JW (☎ 01244 320623 and 01244 343826, fax 01244 350355)

HARRISON, Prof Martin; s of Wilfrid Harrison (d 1968), of Darlington, Co Durham, and Isobel, *née* Armstrong (d 1991); *b* 19 April 1930; *Educ* Queen Elizabeth GS Darlington, Univ of Manchester (BA), Univ of Oxford (PhD), Univ of Paris (DRESSP); *m* 23 April 1957, Wendy Handford, da of Robert Wood Hindle (d 1974), of Madeley, Staffs; 2 s (Andrew b 1959, David b 1962), 1 da (Catherine b 1966); *Career* RAF 1952–54: PO 1953, flying offr 1954, Flt Lt 1954; res fell Nuffield Coll Oxford 1957–62, lectr then sr lectr Univ of Manchester 1963–66; Univ of Keele: prof and head Dept of Politics 1966–93, chm Bd of Social Scis 1976–79 and 1988–91, dep vice chllr 1979–82, pro vice chllr 1985–88 and 1991–94; chm Local Radio Advsy Ctee BBC Radio Stoke-on-Trent 1982–85; memb: BBC Gen Advsy Ctee 1983–85, BBC Midlands Advsy Co 1983–86; chm: Beth Johnson Housing Gp 1983–96, Editorial Bd Sociological Review; county controller Staffs Radio Amateur Emergency Network; *Books* Trade Unions and the Labour Party (1960), De Gaulle's Republic (1960), Politics and Society in De Gaulle's Republic (1972), French Politics (1969), TV News - Whose Bias? (1985); *Recreations* amateur radio (G3USF), walking; *Style*— Prof Martin Harrison; ✉ 1 Church Fields, Keele, Newcastle-Under-Lyme, Staffs ST5 5HP (☎ 01782 627396); Department of Politics, Keele University, Keele, Staffs ST5 5BG (☎ 01782 583354, fax 01782 583452)

HARRISON, (Robert) Michael; QC (1987); s of Robert William Harrison (d 1981), and Bertha, *née* Harrison; *b* 3 Nov 1945; *Educ* Heckmondwike GS, Univ of Hull (LLB); *m* 20 April 1974, Jennifer, da of Edward Armstrong, of Aston, Sheffield; 1 s (Christopher Edward b 24 June 1977); *Career* called to the Bar 1969, recorder of the Crown Ct 1985–; *Style*— Michael Harrison, Esq, QC; ✉ Park Court Chambers, 40 Park Cross St, Leeds LS1 2QH (☎ 0113 243 3277, fax 0113 242 1285)

HARRISON, Dr Michael; JP (Birmingham 1980); s of Frank Harrison (d 1973), of Leamington Spa, and Ruby Wilhelmina, *née* Proctor (d 1981); *b* 1 March 1939; *Educ* Leamington Coll, St Mary's Hosp Med Sch London (MB BS, LRCP, MRCS), Univ of Bristol (DPH), Open Univ (BA); *m* 23 April 1962, Ann, da of Eric Bertram Haiser (d 1963), of Leamington Spa; 2 da (Mary Jane b 1965, Susan Elizabeth b 1967); *Career* hosp med appts 1964–66, Public Health Dept City of Birmingham 1966–70, princ asst SMO Birmingham RHB 1971–74, specialist in community med West Midlands RHA 1974–76; Sandwell Health Authy: area med offr 1976–83, dist med offr 1983–88, gen mangr 1985–88; asst md and regnl dir of public health West Midlands RHA 1988–93, public health conslt 1993–96, med dir and chm Midlands Health Consultancy Network Ltd 1996–; sr clinical lectr Univ of Birmingham 1988–, visiting fell Business Sch Aston Univ 1988–, conslt advsr WHO 1989–; pres Lichfield Sci and Engrg Soc 1991; FRSH 1978, FRSM 1989, FIMgt 1984, LHSM 1985, FFPHM 1980; SBStJ 1977; *Recreations* sailing, photography, industrial archaeology; *Clubs* Reform, RSM; *Style*— Dr Michael Harrison, JP; ✉ 6 Moor Green Lane, Moseley, Birmingham B13 8ND (☎ 0121 449 1739, fax 0121 449 9731)

HARRISON, Michael Anthony; s of William Harrison (d 1981), and Gweneth Harrison; *b* 30 April 1947; *Educ* Royal GS Newcastle upon Tyne, Aylesbury GS, Oxford Coll of Technol, Univ of Nottingham (BA); *m* 25 Aug 1973, Marie-Claude, da of Léon Victor Bouquet; 3 s (Stéphane Daniel b 5 July 1974, Frank William b 8 July 1978, John-Gabriel b 21 Jan 1986), 1 da (Laura Rachel b 20 Nov 1975); *Career* technician Tate Gallery London 1970–71; Arts Cncl of GB: regnl arts offr 1971–73, exhbn organiser 1973–77, asst dir for regnl exhbns (with S Bank Centre) 1977–90; head of fine art Winchester Sch of Art 1990–92, dir Kettle's Yard Univ of Cambridge 1992–; *Recreations* art, architecture, reading, walking; *Style*— Michael Harrison, Esq; ✉ 49 City Road, Cambridge CB1 1DP; Kettle's Yard, Castle Street, Cambridge CB3 0AQ (☎ 01223 352124, fax 01223 324377)

HARRISON, The Hon Mr Justice; Hon Sir Michael Guy Vicat; kt (1993); s of Hugh Francis Guy Harrison, and Elizabeth Alban, *née* Jones; *b* 28 Sept 1939; *Educ* Charterhouse, Trinity Hall Cambridge; *m* 1966, Judith, da of late Fernley Edward Gist; 1 da (Sarah Louise b 11 March 1970), 1 s (William Vicat b 22 July 1972); *Career* called to the Gray's Bar 1965, QC 1983, recorder of the Crown Court 1989–93, judge of the High Court of Justice (Queen's Bench Div) 1993–; bencher Gray's Inn 1993; dep chm Boundary Cmmn for England 1996–; *Recreations* tennis, sailing, fishing, walking; *Style*— The Hon Mr Justice Harrison; ✉ Royal Courts of Justice, Strand, London WC2A 2LL

HARRISON, Sir Michael James Harwood; 2 Bt (UK 1961), of Bugbrooke, Co Northampton, JP (1993); s of Col Sir (James) Harwood Harrison, 1 Bt, TD (d 1980), MP (C) Eye 1951–79, of Little Manor, Hasketon, Woodbridge, Suffolk, and Peggy Alberta Mary, *née* Stenhouse (d 1993); *b* 28 March 1936; *Educ* Rugby; *m* 1967, (Rosamund) Louise, da of Edward Buxton Clive (d 1975), of Swanmore Lodge, Swanmore, Hants; 2 s (Edwin Michael Harwood b 1981, Tristan John b 1986), 2 da ((Auriol) Davina b 1968, Priscilla Caroline b 1971); *Heir* s, Edwin Michael Harwood Harrison b 29 May 1981; *Career* Nat Serv 17/21 Lancers 1955–56; insur broker Lloyd's 1958–92; dir of various private cos 1980–; memb Cncl Sail Training Assoc 1968–; Assoc of Combined Youth Clubs: vice pres 1983–, chm Management Ctee 1987–95; Freeman City of London 1964–, Master Mercers' Co 1986 (Liveryman 1967); *Recreations* sailing (yacht 'Falcon'), skiing, riding (horse and bicycle), Daily Telegraph crossword; *Clubs* Boodle's, MCC, Royal Harwich Yacht, Aldeburgh Yacht; *Style*— Sir Michael Harrison, Bt, JP; ✉ 35 Paulton's Square, London SW3 (☎ 0171 352 1760)

HARRISON, (Walter) Paul; s of Walter Harrison, of Morecambe, and Margaret Hildred, *née* Buttery; *b* 19 March 1955; *Educ* Skerton Co Boys' Sch Lancaster, Preston Poly (OND, HNC), Leicester Poly (BA, DipArch); *Career* architect; Cassidy & Ashton Partnership Preston 1973–75, W E Moore & Sons Leicester 1978–79, ptnr Robert Davies John West & Assocs Crawley 1987–90, dir RDJW Architects Ltd 1990–, fndr and jt md Pentagon Professional Services 1991–; RIBA, ARCUK; *Recreations* squash, badminton, cars, horse riding; *Style*— Paul Harrison, Esq; ✉ Denholme, Crawley Rd, Horsham, West Sussex (☎ 01403 262224); RDJW Architects Ltd, Quoin House, 11 East Park, Crawley RH10 6AN (☎ 01293 404300, fax 01293 404299); Pentagon Professional Services, Quoin House, 11 East Park, Crawley RH10 6AN (☎ 01293 548102)

HARRISON, Philip Vernon; s of Ronald Geoffrey Harrison, of Kent, and Beryl May, *née* Crisp; *b* 19 Nov 1952; *Educ* The Hill Sch Nuwara Eliya Sri Lanka, Worksop Coll Notts; *m* 4 Sept 1976, Jessica Jane, da of Peter Derrick Whiteley; 1 da (Alice Maria Casuarina b 25 Dec 1985); *Career* tea buying asst Lyons Groceries Ltd 1971–73; Lyons Tetley Ltd: asst brand mangr 1973–74, product mangr 1974, new product devpt mangr 1974–79, int mktg mangr 1979–83; commercial dir Spearhead Ltd 1983–86, mktg mangr Dixons Colour Laboratories Ltd 1986–88; mktg dir: Supasnaps Ltd 1989–90 (mktg mangr 1988–89), Dixons Finance plc and Dixons Financial Services Ltd 1990–92; brand mktg dir Dixons Stores Group 1992–94, mktg dir Allied Carpets Group 1994–; memb Mktg Soc 1990; *Recreations* cookery (City & Guilds 1991), sailing; *Style*— Philip Vernon Harrison, Esq

HARRISON, Philippa Mary; da of Charles Kershaw Whitfield (d 1972), and Alexina Margaret, *née* Dykes; *b* 25 Nov 1942; *Educ* Walthamstow Hall, Univ of Bristol (BA), Courtauld Inst; *m* July 1967 (m dis), James Fraser Harrison; *Career* jt ed in chief Penguin Books 1979–80, ed dir Michael Joseph 1980–85, md and publisher Macmillan London 1986–88, md V and A Enterprises 1990–91, chief exec and publisher Little Brown & Co (UK) 1996– (md 1992–96); dir Book Tokens Ltd 1996–; memb: Bd of Book Marketing Cncl 1983–88, Literature Panel Arts Cncl 1988–92, Cncl Publishers Assoc 1995–; tstee Eric & Salome Estovick Fndn 1996–; CIMgt 1987, FRSA 1992; *Books* Publishing: The Future (contrib, 1988); *Recreations* walking, theatre, reading, the arts; *Clubs* Groucho; *Style*— Mrs Philippa Harrison; ✉ 105 Lofting Rd, London N1 (☎ 0171 609 5516)

HARRISON, Prof Sir Richard John; kt (1984); er s of late Geoffrey Arthur Harrison, MD, and Theodora Beatrice Mary, *née* West; *b* 8 Oct 1920; *Educ* Oundle, Gonville and Caius Coll Cambridge (MA, MD), Univ of Glasgow (DSc), St Bart's; *m* 1, 1943 (m dis), Joanna Gillies; 2 s, 1 da; *m* 2, 1967, Barbara (d 1988), da of late James Fuller, of Neston, Cheshire; m 3, 3 March 1990, Gianetta, widow of Cdr John Drake, RN (ret); *Career* prof of anatomy Cambridge Univ 1968–82 (later emeritus), fell Downing Coll Cambridge 1968–82 (hon fell 1982); chm Farm Animal Welfare Cncl 1979–88, memb Bd of Tstees Br Museum (Natural History) 1984–89; pres Int Fedn of Assocs of Anatomists 1985–87; FRS 1973; *Books* Handbook of Marine Mammals (vols I-V, 1981–94), Research on Dolphins (1986), Whales, Dolphins and Porpoises (1988); *Recreations* gardening; *Style*— Prof Sir Richard Harrison, FRS; ✉ Milestone House, 58a High Street, Barkway, Royston, Herts SG8 8EE (☎ 01763 848974)

HARRISON, Prof Robert Graham; s of Robert Graham Harrison, of Essex, and Constance May, *née* Scott; *b* 26 Feb 1944; *Educ* Wanstead Co HS, Univ of London (BSc, PhD); *m* Rowena Indrania; 1 s (Samuel Scott b 1972), 1 da (Sophia Victoria b 1982); *Career* research fell Univ of London/Culham Lab UKAEA 1970–72, lectr Dept of Physics Univ of Bath 1972–76; Dept of Physics Heriot-Watt Univ: lectr then sr lectr 1976–83, reader 1983–87, prof 1987–; dir of several confs and advanced workshops; FRSE 1987, FInstP; *Publications* author of over 200 pubns in int scientific jls and ed of 4 books; *Style*— Prof Robert Harrison, FRSE; ✉ Department of Physics, Heriot-Watt University, Riccarton, Edinburgh EH14 4AS (☎ 0131 449 5111, fax 0131 451 3136)

HARRISON, (Desmond) Roger Wingate; s of Maj-Gen Desmond Harrison, CB, DSO, and Kathleen, *née* Hazley; *b* 9 April 1933; *Educ* Rugby, Worcester Coll Oxford (MA), Harvard Business Sch; *m* 1965, Victoria Harrison, MVO, da of late Rear Adm John Lee-Barber; 1 s (decd), 4 da (1 decd); *Career* 5 Royal Inniskilling Dragoon Guards 1955–57; The Times 1957–67 (freelance writer 1955–57); The Observer: joined 1967, dir 1970–, jt md 1977–84, chief exec 1984–87; dir: LWT Holdings plc (non-exec) 1976–94, Sableknight 1981–, Trinity Holdings International plc (non-exec) 1991–; dep chm Capital Radio plc 1991– (dir 1975–), non-exec dir Sterling Publishing Group PLC 1993– (chm 1993–96); exec dir The Oak Fndn (UK) Ltd 1987–89; cncl memb Newspaper Publishers' Assoc 1967–87; chm: Toynbee Hall 1989–, Asylum Aid 1990–, Royal Acad of Dancing 1992–; govr Sadler's Wells Theatre 1984–95; *Recreations* theatre, country pursuits, tennis; *Clubs* Beefsteak, Flyfishers', Queen's; *Style*— Roger Harrison, Esq; ✉ 35 Argyll Rd, London W8 7DA

HARRISON, Ronald Charles Gully; s of Ion Robinson Harrison (d 1952), of Helensburgh, Dunbartonshire, and Marie Louise, *née* Canonico (d 1977); *b* 11 June 1933; *Educ* Charterhouse, King's Coll Cambridge (MA); *m* 27 Dec 1957, Eva Luise Johanne, da of Adolf Johannes Friedrich Hornäffer; 3 s (Neal Francis Ion b 9 Dec 1960, Frank Ronald b 11 July 1962, Ivor John Anthony b 11 April 1965), 1 da (Corinna Eva Louise b 22 Sept 1966); *Career* Nat Serv 2 Lt Royal Scots Greys 1951–53; lectr in English Br Cncl Rio de Janeiro 1957–59; HM Dip Serv: entered 1960, Ibadan 1961–64, Malta 1964–67, Karachi 1967–70, FCO 1970–72, São Paulo 1972–74, Br Trade Devpt Office NY 1975–77, consul (commercial) Dallas 1977–79, FCO 1979–82, dep consul-gen Milan 1982–87, consul-gen São Paulo 1987–90, consul-gen Naples 1990–93; hon res fell Dept of Italian Univ of Glasgow 1994–; *Recreations* travelling, reading, theatre, skiing; *Style*— Ronald Harrison, Esq; ✉ Croft House, 41 George Street, Helensburgh G84 7EX (☎ 01436 678250, fax 01436 679455)

HARRISON, Sir Terence; kt (1995), DL (Tyne and Wear 1989); s of Roland Harrison (d 1985), and Doris, *née* Wardle; *b* 7 April 1933; *Educ* Univ of Durham (BSc); *m* 9 July 1956, June, da of Mathew Forster; 2 s (Peter Forster b 18 May 1959, Mark Terence b 20 June 1962); *Career* Clarke Chapman Ltd: dir 1976, md 1977, merged with Reyrolle Parsons Ltd to become Northern Engineering Industries 1977; Northern Engineering Industries plc: dir 1977, md UK ops 1980–83, chief exec 1983–86, chm 1986–89, merged with Rolls-Royce plc 1989; Rolls-Royce plc: dir 1989–April 1996, md Ind Power Gp 1991–92, chief exec 1992–96; chm Alfred McAlpine plc 1996– (non-exec dir 1996–); non-exec dir: local bd Barclays Bank plc 1986–, Northumbrian Water Group plc 1989–91, T & N plc 1995–; author of various tech and business papers on the mechanical engrg marine and mining industs; pres: BEAMA 1989–90, NE Coast Inst of Engrs and Shipbuilders 1988–90; fndr chm Northern Engrg Centre; Freeman City of London, memb Worshipful Co of Engineers; Hon DEng 1991, Hon DTech 1995, Hon DSc 1996; FIMarE 1973, FIMechE 1984, FEng 1988; *Recreations* fell walking, gardening, golf; *Style*— Sir Terence Harrison, DL, FEng; ✉ 2 The Garden Houses, Whalton, Morpeth, Northumberland NE61 3HB (☎ 01670 775400); Alfred McAlpine plc, 8 Suffolk Street, London SW1Y 4HG (☎ 0171 930 6255, fax 0171 839 6902)

HARRISON, Timothy David Blair (Tim); s of Blair Wilfred Wortley Harrison, of The Coach House, Banwell, Avon, and Sheelagh Margurite Hildergarde, *née* Woolford (d 1972); *b* 13 Dec 1944; *Educ* Blundell's; *m* 2 Nov 1991, Beverley, da of George William Brindle, of Bahrain; 2 s (Blair Edward Charles b 1976, Thomas George b 1992); *Career* UBM/MAC Group Bristol 1963–73, GKN Mills Building Services Ltd 1973–76, Norplant/Witpalm International Ltd 1976–79, Mallison-Denny Group 1979–86 (sales and mktg dir Formwood Ltd, md Bushboard Ltd), md GA Harvey Office Furniture Ltd 1986–88, Trafalgar House Building & Civil Engineering Holdings Ltd 1988–89 (dir, sector md), gp chief exec The Company of Designers plc 1989–92 (directorships and chm of 22 companies COD gp); currently: dir CAMAS UK Ltd (formerly part of English China Clays), md CAMAS Building Materials Ltd, pres Prefabricados de Hormigon Lurgain SA Spain, dir SMMO France; Freeman City of London, memb Worshipful Co of Builders Merchants; *Recreations* rugby (watching now), rally driving; *Style*— Tim Harrison, Esq; ✉ CAMAS Building Materials Ltd, Hulland Ward, Ashbourne, Derbys DE6 3ET (☎ 01335 370085, fax 01335 372222); Churchside House, Kirk Ireton, Ashbourne, Derbys DE6 3LD (☎ 01335 370948)

HARRISON, Tony; s of Harry Ashton Harrison (d 1980), and Florence Horner, *née* Wilkinson (d 1976); *b* 30 April 1937; *Educ* Leeds GS, Univ of Leeds (BA); *Career* poet and dramatist; FRSL; *Television* The Oresteia (Channel 4 1982), The Big H (BBC 1984), The Mysteries (Channel 4 1985), Yan Tan Tethera (Channel 4 1986), Loving Memory (BBC 1986), V (Channel 4 1987, Royal Television Soc Award), The Blasphemers' Banquet, The Gaze of the Gorgon (1992), Black Daisies for the Bride (1993, Prix Italia 1994), A Maybe Day in Kazakhstan (1994), The Shadow of Hiroshima (Channel 4, 1995); *Books and Plays* Earthworks (1964), Aikin Mata (1965), Newcastle is Peru (1969), The Loiners (1970), The Misanthrope (1973), Phaedra Britannica (1975), The Passion (1977), Bow Down (1977), from The School of Eloquence (1978), Continuous (1981), A Kumquat for John Keats (1981), US Martial (1981), The Oresteia (1981), Selected Poems (1984), The Mysteries (1985), V (1985), Dramatic Verse 1973–85 (1985), The Fire-Gap (1985), Theatre Works 1973–85 (1986), Selected Poems (augmented edn 1987), The Trackers of Oxyrhynchus (performed ancient stadium of Delphi 1988, NT 1990), A Cold Coming - Gulf War Poems (1991), The Common Chorus (1992), The Gaze of the Gorgon and other poems (Whitbread poetry award, 1992), Square Rounds (1992), Poetry or Bust (1993), The Kaisers of Carnuntum (1995), Permanently Bard (1995), The Labourers of Herakles (1995), The Shadow of Hiroshima and other film/poems (1995), The Prince's Play (1996); *Style*— Tony Harrison

HARRISON, William Robert (Bill); s of William Eric Harrison, and Catherine Frances, *née* Dyson; *b* 5 Oct 1948; *Educ* George Dixon GS Birmingham, LSE (BSc, MSc); *m* 18 July 1970, Jacqueline Ann, da of Marwood Eric Brown, of Birmingham; 1 s (Nicholas David b 1977), 1 da (Charlotte Ann b 1976); *Career* formerly: dir J Henry Schroder Wagg & Co Ltd, vice chm Lehman Brothers; chief exec of investment banking Robert Fleming & Co Ltd 1993–96, chief exec Barclays de Zoete Wedd Investment Banking Ltd 1996–; *Recreations* soccer, cricket, music, gardening; *Style*— Bill Harrison; ✉ Barclays de Zoete Wedd Ltd, Ebbgate House, 2 Swan Lane, London EC4R 3TS (☎ 0171 623 2323, fax 0171 623 6075)

HARRISON-CRIPPS, William Lawrence; s of William Harrison Harrison-Cripps, of Donnington, Berks, and Anne Elizabeth, *née* Graham Smith (d 1959); *b* 25 Jan 1950; *Educ* Marlborough; *m* 4 Nov 1977, Elizabeth Joy, da of Kenneth Henry Cornwell; 2 s (William Henry b 17 Aug 1979, Thomas Peter Seddon b 24 Oct 1987), 1 da (Alexandra Elizabeth b 9 April 1981); *Career* Price Waterhouse: articled clerk 1968–72, mangr 1976, ptnr 1982–, chm M/A Tax Servs (Europe) 1989, memb European Tax Bd and European Corp Fin Exec 1990, ptnr i/c Int Corp Tax Services Gp 1991, UK Tax Service Exec 1992, chm UK Tax Servs 1993, World Tax Service Exec 1993; memb Addington Soc 1992; FCA 1973, ATII 1975; *Books* Mergers and Acquisitions - The Complete Guide To

Principles and Practice (contrib, 1986); *Recreations* flying light aircraft, sailing, shooting, photography; *Clubs* Mayfair Gun, Papercourt Sailing, Shere Tennis; *Style—* William Harrison-Cripps, Esq; ✉ Price Waterhouse, Southwark Towers, 32 London Bridge Street, London SE1 9SY (☎ 0171 939 3907, fax 0171 357 8950)

HARRISON-HALL, His Hon Judge Michael Kilgour; DL (Warwicks 1985); s of Arthur Harrison-Hall (d 1953), and Isabella Harrison-Hall (d 1978); *b* 20 Dec 1925; *Educ* Dragon Sch Oxford, Rugby, Trinity Coll Oxford (MA); *m* 5 May 1951, (Jessie) Margaret, da of Rev Arthur William Brown (d 1961); 2 s (Giles Arthur b 1953, Oscar John Andrew b 1958), 2 da (Katharine Margaret (Mrs Cadbury) b 1955, Jessica Lucy Kilgour b 1965); *Career* called to the Bar Inner Temple 1949, dep chm Warwickshire QS 1968–71, recorder Crown Ct 1972, circuit judge (Midland and Oxford Circuit) 1972–; memb Cncl Univ of Warwick; *Clubs* United Oxford & Cambridge Univ, Leander; *Style—* His Hon Judge Harrison-Hall, DL; ✉ Ivy House, Church St, Barford, Warwick CV35 8EN (☎ 01926 624272)

HARRISSON, Tim; *b* 1952; *Educ* Hammersmith Coll of Art, Norwich Coll of Art (BA), Byam Shaw Sch of Fine Art, Sir John Cass Sch of Art; *Career* sculptor; *One/Two Person Exhibitions* Salisbury Art Centre 1984, The Showroom Gallery London 1986, Exhibition of Prints and Drawings (Halesworth Gallery Suffolk) 1987, South Hill Park Art Centre Bracknell 1988, The Flaxman Gallery Stoke on Trent 1988, Purdy-Hicks Gallery London 1988, Artsite Gallery Bath 1989, Recent Sculpture (New Art Centre London) 1991, Four Stone Sculptures (New Art Centre London) 1993; *Group Exhibitions* incl: Salisbury Library 1981, RIBA Sculpture Ct Winter Exhbn 1984, Still Life a New Life (Harris Museum Preston) 1985, Art for the Garden (Hannah Peschar Gallery Surrey) 1986–87, Coastlines (The Towner Museum Eastbourne) 1987, a winner in int art competition organised by Metro Art NYC 1987, Sculpture Open (The Minories Colchester) 1989, The Salisbury Festival 1991, The Economist Bldg Plaza London 1991, London Contemporary Art Fair 1991, Art 23 '92 Basel Switzerland 1992, Art on the Waterfront (Southampton Civic Centre) 1992; *Commissions* incl: Roche Ct Sculpture Garden 1989, The Millfield Cmmn (Millfield Sch with Artsite Gallery Bath) 1989, James Kirkham in Sussex 1989, Ivor Braka in Norfolk 1990, Russell Cotes Museum Bournemouth 1995, new terminal building Southampton Airport for BAA 1995, The Liverpool Victoria Friendly Soc Building Southampton 1996; *Style—* Tim Harrisson, Esq; ✉ c/o The New Art Centre, Roche Court, East Winterslow, Nr Salisbury, Wilts SP5 1BG

HARROD, Henry Mark; s of Sir (Henry) Roy Forbes Harrod (d 1978), and Wilhelmine Margaret Eve, *née* Cresswell; *b* 6 Jan 1939; *Educ* Eton, Christ Church Oxford (MA); *m* 1, 1965 (m dis 1973); 2 s ((Henry) Barnaby b 1965, Huckleberry Nathaniel b 1967); m 2, 1977, Tanya Olivia Ledger, PhD, da of Dr Peter Ledger, MD; 1 s (Hugo Roy Francis b 1979), 1 da (Horatia Mary b 1983); *Career* called to the Bar Lincoln's Inn 1963, pupil of Conrad Dehn 2 Crown Office Row Temple 1963; memb chambers of David Fenwick 46 Grainger St Newcastle upon Tyne 1964–68, chambers of Quintin Hogg 4 Paper Bldgs Temple 1968, chambers of John Brightman and others 2 New Sq Lincoln's Inn (chambers moved to 5 Stone Bldgs 1993): joined 1969, head of chambers 1990–; recorder 1993– (asst recorder 1989–93), conveyancing counsel of the Court 1991–; bencher of Lincoln's Inn 1991; *Clubs* Garrick; *Style—* Henry Harrod, Esq; ✉ 5 Stone Buildings, Lincoln's Inn, London WC2A 3XT (☎ 0171 242 6201)

HARROD, Lady (Wilhelmine Margaret Eve); *née* Cresswell; OBE (1992); da of Capt Francis Joseph (Joe) Cresswell (ka 1914), and Barbara, *née* ffolkes, wid of Gen Sir Peter Strickland, KCB; *b* 1 Dec 1911; *Educ* Langford Grove Maldon Essex; *m* 8 Jan 1938, Sir Roy Forbes Harrod (d 1978), s of Henry Harrod; 2 s (Henry b 1939, Dominick b 1940); *Career* involved in conservation of countryside and bldgs; memb: Georgian Gp, Oxford Preservation Tst, CPRE, Regnl Ctee Nat Tst, Historic Churches Preservation Tst, Norfolk Churches Tst (fndr and pres), various diocesan ctees; Hon DCL UEA 1989, Esher Award Soc for the Protection of Ancient Buildings 1992; *Books* Shell Guide to Norfolk (jtly 1957), The Norfolk Guide (1988); *Recreations* gardening; *Clubs* The Norfolk (Norwich); *Style—* Lady Harrod, OBE; ✉ The Old Rectory, Holt, Norfolk NR25 6RY (☎ 01263 712 204)

HARROLD, Timothy John (Tim); s of Col W G Harrold (d 1969), and Christine Russell, *née* Kilburn Scott (d 1994); *b* 12 May 1938; *Educ* Bryanston, Lausanne Univ Switzerland, Pembroke Coll Cambridge (MA); *m* 9 Sept 1967, Gillian Doris, da of Leslie Albert Cruttenden; 3 s (Simon Timothy b 14 March 1970, Michael Stephen b 24 March 1971, James Andrew b 15 Sept 1976), 1 da (Katherine b 2 Sept 1973); *Career* with ICI 1960–69, mktg dir Polydor Ltd London 1970–74, exec vice pres Phonodisc Inc NY 1974–75; pres: Polygram Inc Montreal 1975–81, Polydor International Hamburg 1981–83; exec vice pres Polygram International London 1983– (chm Polygram Classics, Decca International); *Recreations* skiing; *Style—* Tim Harrold, Esq; ✉ Farthings, Longdown Road, Guildford, Surrey (☎ 01483 564876); Polygram International, 8 St James's Square, London SW1Y 4JU (☎ 0171 747 4000, fax 0171 747 4499)

HARROP, Sir Peter John; KCB (1984, CB 1980); s of Gilbert Harrop (d 1971), and Frances May, *née* Dewhirst; *b* 18 March 1926; *Educ* King Edward VII Sch Lytham, Peterhouse Cambridge (MA); *m* 1975, Margaret Joan, da of E U E Elliott-Binns; 2 s (Andrew b 1976, Nicholas b 1978); *Career* Sub Lt RNVR 1945–48; asst princ: Miny of Town and Country Planning 1949, Miny of Housing and Local Govt 1951, DOE 1970; regnl dir and chm Yorks and Humberside Econ Planning Bd 1971–73, HM Treasy 1973–76, Cabinet Office 1979–80, second perm sec DOE 1981–86; chm UK Ctee Euro Year of the Environment 1987–88, chm Nat Bus Co 1988–91; non-exec dir: Thames Water plc 1986–95, National Home Loans plc 1987–91, Municipal Mutual Insurance Ltd 1988–; tstee Br Museum 1987–, chm Richmond upon Thames Churches Housing Tst 1990–96, chm Richmond upon Thames Coll 1993–96; *Recreations* golf, sailing; *Clubs* United Oxford and Cambridge, Roehampton, Island Cruising (Salcombe); *Style—* Sir Peter Harrop, KCB; ✉ 19 Berwyn Rd, Richmond, Surrey TW10 5BP

HARROP, Prof Stuart Reginald; s of Reginald Harrop, of E Yorkshire, and Valerie Mary, *née* Hotham; *b* 11 Jan 1956; *Educ* Beverley GS, Univ of Leeds (LLB); *m* 30 April 1983, Tracy Ann, da of Dennis Roy Green; 3 s (Lee Stuart b 11 May 1986, Joel William b 3 Feb 1990, Christian Sean b 7 Aug 1993); *Career* admitted slr 1980; slr Costain Group plc 1982–84, co slr Albright & Wilson Ltd 1984–86, ICI plc 1986–88; dir legal servs: Stock Exchange 1988–91, RSPCA 1991–96; prof of wildlife mgmnt law Univ of Kent at Canterbury 1996–; tstee Herpetological Tst 1995–; memb Law Soc; *Recreations* freelance photography (natural history and business lifestyle); *Style—* Prof Stuart Harrop; ✉ University of Kent at Canterbury, Canterbury, Kent CT2 7NS (☎ 01222 764000)

HARROWBY, 7 Earl of (UK 1809); Dudley Danvers Granville Coutts Ryder; TD (1953); also Baron Harrowby (GB 1776) and Viscount Sandon (UK 1809); er s of 6 Earl of Harrowby (d 1987), and Lady Helena Blanche, *née* Coventry (d 1974), sis of 10 Earl of Coventry; *b* 20 Dec 1922; *Educ* Eton; *m* 14 June 1949, Jeannette Rosalthé, yr da of Capt Peter Johnston-Saint (d 1974); 1 s, 1 da (Lady Rosalthé Rundall); *Heir* s, Viscount Sandon, *qv*; *Career* served WWII in NW Europe (wounded) and Far East with 59 Inf Div, 5 Para Bde, political offr India and Java 1941–45, 56 Armoured Div TA; Lt-Col RA cmdg 254 (City of London) Field Regt RA (TA) 1962–64; dir: Dinorwic Slate Quarries Co Ltd 1951–69, National Provincial Bank 1961–69, UKPI 1955–86 (dep chm 1956–64), Olympia Group 1968–73 (chm 1971–73), Powell Duffryn Group 1976–86 (chm 1981–86), Sheepbridge Engineering Ltd 1977–79; dep chm: Coutts & Co 1970–89 (md 1949), National Westminster Bank plc 1971–87 (dir 1968–87) chm: International Westminster Bank plc 1977–87, Orion Bank 1979–81, Bentley Engineering Co Ltd 1983–86, National Westminster Investment Bank 1986–87, The Private Bank & Trust Co Ltd 1989–92, Dowty Group plc 1986–91, Private Financial Holdings 1992–95; dir Saudi International Bank 1980–82 and 1985–87; chm Nat Biological Standards Bd 1973–88; memb: Trilateral Cmmn 1980–95, Ctee of Mgmnt Inst of Psychiatry 1953–73 (chm 1965–73); Bd of Govrs: Bethlem Royal and Maudsley (Postgraduate Teaching) Hosps 1955–73 (chm 1965–73), Univ of Keele 1956–68, Lord Chancellor's Advsy Investmt Ctee for Ct of Protection 1965–77, Advsy Investmt Ctee for Public Tstee 1974–77, Psychiatry Research Tst (tstee) 1982–, Institut Internationale d'Etudes Bancaires 1977–87, Kensington Borough Cncl 1950–65 (chm GP Ctee 1957–59), Kensington and Chelsea Borough Cncl 1965–71 (chm Finance Ctee 1968–71); govr Atlantic Inst of Int Affairs 1983–88; hon treas: Staffs Soc 1947–51, Exec Ctee London Area Conservative Assoc 1949–50, Family Welfare Assoc 1951–65, S Kensington Conservative Assoc 1953–56, Central Cncl for Care of Cripples 1953–60; mangr Fulham and Kensington Hosp Gp 1953–56, gen cmmr for Income Tax 1954–71; Freeman of City of London 1947, Liveryman Worshipful Co of Goldsmiths 1959; CBIM, MRIIA, hon fell Royal Coll of Psychiatrists 1983; *Style—* The Rt Hon the Earl of Harrowby, TD; ✉ 5 Tregunter Rd, London SW10 9LS (☎ 0171 373 9276, office 0171 370 0320); Sandon Hall, Stafford ST18 0BZ (☎ 01889 508338); Burnt Norton, Chipping Campden, Glos GL55 6PR (☎ 01386 840358)

HARSTON, Julian John Robert Clive; s of Lt-Col Clive Harston, ERD (d 1993), of Surrey, and Kathleen Mary, *née* Grace; *b* 20 Oct 1942; *Educ* The King's Sch Canterbury, Univ of London (BSc); *m* 1966, Karen Howard Oake, da of Col T E Longfield (ka 1941); 1 s (Alexander b 1978); *Career* mangr Br Tourist Authy Copenhagen and Vancouver 1965–71; FCO: joined 1971, first sec/consul Hanoi 1973–74, first sec Blantyre 1975–79, first sec Lisbon 1982–84, cnsllr Harare 1984–88, cnsllr UN Geneva 1991–95; political advsr to Special Rep of Sec-Gen for former Yugoslavia 1995, dir UN Liaison Office Belgrade 1996–; *Recreations* travel, photography, Switzerland; *Clubs* East India, RAC, Gremio Literario (Lisbon), Harare; *Style—* Julian Harston, Esq; ✉ c/o 33 Rosemont Road, Richmond, Surrey TW10 6QN

HART, Alan; s of Reginald Thomas Hart (d 1980), of Haddenham, Bucks, and Lilian Clara, *née* Hanson (d 1992); *b* 17 April 1935; *Educ* Univ Coll Sch Hampstead; *m* 16 Dec 1961, Celia Mary, *née* Vine, da of Raglan Keough; 2 s (David Alan b 31 Oct 1962, Andrew Dominic b 6 May 1965), 1 da (Gabrielle Louise b 13 Nov 1975); *Career* reporter: Willesden Chronicle and Kilburn Times 1952–58, Newcastle Evening Chronicle 1958, London Evening News 1958–59; editorial asst BBC Sportsview 1959–61, TV sports prodr BBC Manchester 1962–64, ed BBC Sportsview 1965–68 (asst ed 1964–65), ed Grandstand 1968–77, head of sport BBC TV 1977–81, controller BBC 1 1981–84, special asst to Dir Gen BBC 1985, controller Int Rels BBC 1986–91, bdcasting conslt 1991–, advsr to Euro Bdcasting Union on East European bdcasting 1991–93, exec dir Eurosport Consortium 1993–, dir Global Amg 1995–; memb Bd Eurosport (former chm) 1991–; vice pres Watford FC 1996–; FRTS; *Recreations* sport, walking, music; *Style—* Alan Hart, Esq; ✉ Cutwellwalls, Avonwick, Near South Brent, South Devon TQ10 9HA (☎ 01364 72552)

HART, Prof (Charles) Anthony; s of Edmund Hart, of Harrogate, N Yorks, and Alice Edna, *née* Griffin; *b* 25 Feb 1948; *Educ* St Michael's Coll Leeds, Royal Free Hosp Sch of Med Univ of London (MB BS, BSc, PhD); *m* 26 June 1971, Jennifer Ann, da of Keith Bonnett (d 1977); 3 da (Caroline Joanne b 23 March 1975, Rachel Louise b 6 Jan 1977, Laura Jane b 5 Feb 1980); *Career* res student and hon lectr Royal Free Hosp Sch of Med 1973–76, prof and hon conslt Dept of Med Microbiology and Genito-urinary Med Univ of Liverpool 1986– (lectr 1978–82, sr lectr and hon conslt 1982–86), visiting prof Univ of Santo Tomas Manila Philippines 1987–; FRCPath 1994 (MRCPath 1983), fell Royal Soc of Tropical Med, MCPCH 1996; *Books* A Colour Atlas of Paediatric Infectious Diseases (with R Broadhead, 1991), A Color Atlas of Medical Microbiology (with P Shears, 1996); *Style—* Prof Anthony Hart; ✉ 104 Thurstaston Rd, Thurstaston, Wirral L61 0HG (☎ 0151 648 1491); Dept of Medical Microbiology and Genito-Urinary Medicine, University of Liverpool, PO Box 147, Liverpool L69 3BX (☎ 0151 706 4381, fax 0151 706 5805, e-mail cahmnn@liv.ac.uk)

HART, (Thomas) Anthony Alfred; s of Rev Arthur Reginald Hart, and Florence Ivy Hart; *b* 4 March 1940; *Educ* City of Bath Sch, New Coll Oxford (BA, MA); *m* 1971, Daintre Margaret Withiel, *née* Thomas; 1 s, 1 da; *Career* served with VSO (Mzuzu Secdy Sch Nyasaland) 1959–60; asst princ rising to princ Miny of Tport 1964–69, seconded to Govt of Malawi as tport advsr 1969–70, princ DOE and Civil Serv Dept 1970–73, head Voluntary Servs Unit Home Office 1973–75, asst sec Civil Serv Dept and HM Treasy 1975–84; headmaster Cranleigh Sch 1984–; *Clubs* Travellers'; *Style—* Anthony Hart, Esq; ✉ The Headmaster's House, Cranleigh School, Cranleigh, Surrey GU6 8QQ

HART, Charles; s of George Hart, of Henley-on-Thames, and Juliet, *née* Byam Shaw; *b* 3 June 1961; *Educ* Desborough Comp Sch Maidenhead, Robinson Coll Cambridge (BA), Guildhall Sch of Music and Drama; *Career* composer and lyricist; composer: Show Piece (overture for small orch BBC Radio 2) 1984, Oman - Tracts of Time (film score, Shell Int Petroleum) 1993; lyrics: The Phantom of the Opera (musical) 1986, Doretta's Dream (aria) 1987, Aspects of Love (musical) 1988–89, Vampyr (opera, BBC TV) 1992; music and lyrics: Watching (title song, Granada TV) 1987, Love Songs (song cycle, BBC Radio 2) 1988–89, Split Ends (title song, Granada TV) 1989; winner for Phantom of the Opera: Olivier Award 1987, Standard Award 1987, Ivor Novello Award 1987, Tony Award 1987; winner Prix Italia 1993 for the Vampyr; *Clubs* Groucho, Soc of Distinguished Songwriters, West London Aero; *Style—* Charles Hart

HART, David Michael; OBE (1988); *b* 27 Aug 1940; *Educ* Hurstpierpoint Coll; *Career* slr in private practice 1963–78, gen sec and slr Nat Assoc of Head Teachers 1978–; memb Educn/Business Partnership Team Business in the Community; memb Law Soc 1963 (Herbert Rose prize 1962); Liveryman Worshipful Co of Lorimers; *Recreations* riding, tennis, cycling and walking; *Clubs* Wig & Pen; *Style—* David Hart, Esq, OBE; ✉ Whimby Cottage, Haltcliffe, Hesket Newmarket, Nr Wigton, Cumbria CA7 8JT; National Association of Head Teachers, 1 Heath Square, Boltro Road, Haywards Heath, W Sussex RH16 1BL (☎ 01444 416708, fax 01444 450257)

HART, Dr (Francis) Dudley; s of Rev Canon Charles Dudley Hart (d 1952), of Southwell Cathedral, and Kate Evelyn, *née* Bowden (d 1961); *b* 4 Oct 1909; *Educ* Grosvenor Sch Nottingham, Univ of Edinburgh (MB ChB, MD); *m* 18 Dec 1944, Mary Josephine (Maureen), da of Luke Tully (d 1956), of Carrigaline, Co Cork, Ireland; 1 s (Paul b 1950), 2 da (Elizabeth b 1946, Clare b 1948); *Career* house surgn: Royal Hosp for Sick Children Edinburgh 1933, Paddington Green Children's Hosp 1934; med registrar Royal Northern Hosp 1935–37 (house physician 1935), house physician Brompton Hosp 1937, med registrar Westminster Hosp 1939–42, Maj (med specialist) and Lt-Col i/c Med Div RAMC 1942–46, consulting physician and physician i/c rheumatism clinic Westminster Hosp 1946–74, civilian conslt physician Army 1972–74; currently hon conslt physician Chelsea Westminster Hosp and Hosp of St John and St Elizabeth St John's Wood London; former vice chm Ctee Review of Medicines, former pres Heberden Soc (rheumatism res and educn), former chm Ctee Tst Educn and Res Therapeutics, vice chm and memb Exec Ctee Arthritis and Rheumatism Cncl; Freeman City of London 1956, Liveryman Worshipful Soc of Apothecaries 1956; hon memb French, Italian, American and Australian Rheumatology Socs, FRCP 1949 (MRCP 1937), Hon FRSM; *Books* French's Index of Differential Diagnosis (ed 10–12 edns 1973–85), Drug Treatment of Rheumatic Diseases (3 edns, 1978–87), Overcoming Arthritis (1981), Colour Atlas of Rheumatology (1987), Clinical Rheumatology Illustrated (1987), Clinical

Problems in Rheumatology (1993); *Recreations* walking, snorkelling; *Style—* Dr Dudley Hart; ✉ 19 Ranulf Rd, London NW2 2BT (☎ 0171 794 2525); 24 Harmont House, 20 Harley St, London W1N 1AN (☎ 0171 935 4252)

HART, Garry Richard Rushby; s of Dennis George Hart (d 1984), and Evelyn Mary, *née* Rushby; *b* 29 June 1940; *Educ* Northgate GS Ipswich, UCL (LLB); *m* 1, 24 March 1966 (m dis 1986), Paula Lesley, da of Leslie Shepherd; 2 s (Alexander, Jonathan), 1 da (Kaley); m 2, 1986, Valerie Elen Mary, da of Cledwyn Wilson Davies; 2 da (Sarah, Stephanie (twins)); *Career* slr; ptnr Herbert Smith 1970– (head Property Dept 1988–); Freeman City of London, Liveryman Worshipful Co of Slrs; tstee Architecture Fndn; memb Law Soc 1966; *Books* Blundell and Dobrys Planning Applications Appeals and Proceedings (jtly, 5 edn); *Recreations* farming, travel; *Clubs* Reform; *Style—* Garry Hart, Esq; ✉ 36 Alwyne Road, London N1 2HW; Herbert Smith, Exchange House, Primrose Street, London EC2A 2HS (☎ 0171 374 8000, fax 0171 496 0043, telex 886633)

HART, Dr George; eld s of George Hart, of Golborne, Lancs, and Mary, *née* Britton; *b* 7 June 1951; *Educ* Boteler GS, Churchill Coll Cambridge (BA, MA), Trinity Coll Oxford and Oxford Univ Clinical Sch (BA, MA, BM BCh), St Peter's Coll Oxford (DM); *m* 19 Jan 1980, Dr Judy Hart, da of Alfred Alan Reynolds (d 1988), of Bognor Regis, West Sussex; 2 s (Samuel b 1985, Joseph b 1986), 1 da (Alice b 1982); *Career* jr hosp posts 1975–77; registrar: cardiology Papworth Hosp 1977–78, med Addenbrooke's Hosp 1978–79; lectr in physiology Balliol Coll Oxford 1979–80, MRC res trg fell Univ Laboratory of Physiology Oxford 1979–82, Sidney Perry jr res fell St Peter's Coll Oxford 1979–82, sr registrar in cardiology Yorkshire Regnl Health Authy 1982–86, BHF clinical reader in cardiovascular med Univ of Oxford 1986–, hon conslt physician and cardiologist John Radcliffe Hosp Oxford 1986–, supernumerary fell Lady Margaret Hall Oxford 1986–; chm Br Soc for Cardiovascular Res 1990–93; memb: Br Cardiac Soc, The Physiological Soc; FRCP 1990 (MRCP 1977); *Recreations* photography, walking; *Style—* Dr George Hart; ✉ 82 Southmoor Rd, Oxford OX2 6RB; Cardiac Department, John Radcliffe Hospital, Headington, Oxford OX3 9DU (☎ 01865 220257, fax 01865 68844)

HART, Gerry; s of Tom Hart (d 1993), and Sylvia, *née* Robinson; *Educ* Dartford GS; *m* 31 March 1973, Pamela Elizabeth; 1 da (Jane b 6 Dec 1976), 2 s (Robert Edwin b 6 Oct 1979, Jonathan William b 30 Dec 1990); *Career* tax trainee Nat West Bank 1963–66, tax mangr Temple Gothard 1970–73, gp tax asst Guthrie Corporation 1973–74, own tax practice 1980–, md The Tax Team Ltd 1994–; fndr UK Tax Congress (held 1981–87); popular lectr in tax; memb Editorial Bd The Tax Jl; Chartered Inst of Taxation: assoc 1968, fell 1970, nat pres 1995–96, fndr chm Sussex branch; *Books* Dictionary of Taxation (Butterworths, 1983), Tougy's Tax Planning For Family Companies (1995); *Recreations* jazz, horse riding, watching most sports, travel; *Clubs* Mortons; *Style—* Gerry Hart, Esq; ✉ The Tax Team Limited, 2 The Courtyard, London Road, Horsham, West Sussex RH12 1AT (☎ 01403 274400, fax 01403 218758)

HART, Guy William Pulbrook; OBE (1985); s of Ernest Guy Hart (d 1966), of Guildford, and Muriel Lily, *née* Walkington (d 1965); *b* 24 Dec 1931; *Educ* Cranleigh Sch Surrey; *m* 14 Aug 1954, (Elizabeth) Marjorie, da of Charles Bennett (d 1963), of Caerleon; 1 s (Guy), 2 da (Victoria (Mrs Eley), Alexandra (Mrs Miller)); *Career* Army Offr Intelligence Corps 1951–61; Br Cellophane Ltd London 1961–62; civil service career; Cwlth Relations Office London 1962–63, consular offr Br High Cmmn Kuala Lumpur 1963–67, News Dept FCO 1971–73, second later first sec Br Mil Govt Berlin 1974–78, first sec commercial Br High Cmmn Port of Spain 1979–82, first sec commercial Br Embassy Budapest 1982–85 (second sec information 1968–71), asst head Information Dept FCO London 1986, ambass Ulan Bator Mongolia 1987–89, Br High Cmmr Victoria Seychelles 1989–91; head Br Delgn European Community Monitor Mission in the former Yugoslavia 1993–94, memb UN Observer Mission at the South African elections 1994, memb CSCE Observer Mission in the former Yugoslav Republic of Macedonia 1994; *Books* White Month's Return - Mongolia Comes of Age (1993); *Recreations* Alpine sports, painting, gardening; *Style—* Guy Hart, Esq, OBE; ✉ 1 Marsh Mill, Wargrave Road, Henley-on-Thames RG9 3JD

HART, K Mortimer; s of Frank Mortimer (d 1969), of Bristol, and Minnie Anna, *née* Houlson (d 1968), of Abergavenny; *b* 24 March 1914; *Educ* Redland Hill House Sch Bristol; *m* 7 Dec 1946, Shirley, da of Percy Burkinshaw, of Wakefield and Sheffield; 1 da (Catherine Jane Mortimer b 23 June 1966); *Career* WWII RAFVR 1940–46, seconded Indian Air Force 1942–45; chartered surveyor and town planner; sr planning inspr: Miny of Housing and Local Govt, Welsh Office; surveyor and town planning conslt; chm Conwy Valley Civic Soc 1976–82; ARICS 1935, MRTPI 1945; *Books* Conwy Valley and the Lands of History (1988); *Recreations* formerly swimming, photography; *Clubs* Royal Cwlth Soc; *Style—* K Mortimer Hart, Esq; ✉ Pen Rhiw, Ro Wen, Conwy County Borough, Wales LL32 8TR (☎ 01492 650343)

HART, Matthew Jason; s of Colin Dennis Hart, and Susan Jean, *née* Ranson; *b* 13 July 1972; *Educ* Arts Educnl Sch London, Royal Ballet Upper Sch; *Career* dancer/choreographer; Royal Ballet: artist 1991–93, first artist 1993–95, soloist 1995–96; Rambert Dance Co 1996–; judge and patron BT Dance Award 1996–; memb Elephant Conservation Kenya 1994, memb Crusaid (HIV and AIDS awareness); *Roles* incl: The Trepak in The Nutcracker, head Fakir in La Bayerdare, Bratfisch in Mayerling, Jester in Cinderella, Squirrel Nutkin in Tales of Beatrix Potter, Solo Boy in Dances Concertantes, Beggar Cheif in Manon, Neopolitan Dance, lead Czardas, lead waltz in Swan Lake, 3 movement Symphony in C, Rhapsody, Stravinsky Violin Concerto, Les Noces, Petrouchka, cr role Steptext in Forsythe's Firstext, Bryaxis in Daphnis and Chloë; *Choreography* The Dream of the Cherry Blossom (Birds Gala Royal Opera House) 1991, Simple Symphony (Royal Ballet Sch) 1992, Forbidden Fruit (Royal Ballet) 1992, Solo (Royal Ballet) 1992, Street (Birmingham Royal Ballet) 1993, Fanfare (Royal Ballet) 1993, Caught Dance (Royal Ballet) 1994, Tusk (Royal Ballet) 1994, Peter and the Wolf (Royal Ballet Sch) 1995, Cinderella (London City Ballet) 1995, Sleepers (Royal Acad of Dancing 70 Anniversary) 1995, Dances with Death (Royal Ballet) 1996, Blitz (Eng Nat Ballet) 1996; *Awards* Cosmopolitan/C & A Dance Award 1988, winner Ursula Moreton Choreographic Competition 1991, winner Frederick Ashton Choreographic Award 1994; *Recreations* singing, painting, designing, swimming, eating out, cinema, theatre; *Style—* Matthew Hart, Esq; ✉ Rambert Dance Company, 94 Chiswick High Road, London W4 1SM (☎ 0181 995 4246)

HART, Prof Michael; CBE (1993); s of Reuben Harold Victor Hart, of Melbourne, and Phyllis Mary, *née* White; *b* 4 Nov 1938; *Educ* Cotham GS Bristol, Univ of Bristol (BSc, PhD, DSc); *m* 16 April 1963, Susan Margaret, *née* Powell; 3 da (Linda b 29 Sept 1964, Janet b 20 June 1966, Rachel b 1 Jan 1969); *Career* res assoc Cornell Univ NY USA 1963–65; Univ of Bristol: res assoc 1965–67, lectr in physics 1967–72, reader 1972–76; sr res assoc Nat Res Cncl USA 1969–70, special advsr CPRS Cabinet Office 1975–77, Wheatstone prof and head of physics King's Coll London 1976–84, prof of physics Univ of Manchester 1984–93, sci prog coordinator SERC Daresbury Laboratory 1985–87, hon prof of applied physics De Montfort Univ 1993–, hon prof in engrg Univ of Warwick 1993–; chm Nat Synchotron Light Source Brookhaven Nat Laboratory USA 1995–; winner CV Boys Prize of Inst of Physics and Warren Award of American Crystallographic Assoc; CPhys, FRS, FInstP; *Clubs* Athenaeum; *Style—* Prof Michael Hart, CBE, FRS; ✉ National Synchotron Light Source, Building 725B, Brookhaven National Laboratory, PO Box 5000, Upton, New York 11973, USA (☎ 00 1 516 282 4966, fax 282 5842)

HART, Michael Christopher Campbell; QC (1987); s of Raymond David Campbell Hart, and Penelope Mary, *née* Ellis; *b* 7 May 1948; *Educ* Winchester, Magdalen Coll Oxford (MA, BCL); *m* 12 Aug 1972, Melanie Jane, da of Richard Hugh Sandiford; 2 da (Jessie b 3 Oct 1973, Zoe b 13 Dec 1974); *Career* called to the Bar Gray's Inn 1970; fell All Soul's Coll Oxford 1970; *Style—* Michael Hart, Esq, QC; ✉ 5 Stone Buildings, Lincoln's Inn, London WC2A 3XT (☎ 0171 242 6201, fax 0171 831 8102)

HART, Michael John; s of Ernest Stanley Granville Hart (d 1982), of Theydon Bois, Essex, and Wilhelmine Patricia, *née* McClurg (d 1972); *b* 26 Dec 1932; *Educ* LSE (BSc); *m* 30 May 1964, (Ann) Sheila, da of William Severy Conrad Decker (d 1965), of Loughton, Essex; 1 s (Samuel b 19 Jan 1977), 1 da (Susan b 23 May 1975); *Career* Nat Serv RAF 1950–52; mangr Foreign and Colonial Investment Trust 1969–, chm Foreign and Colonial Management Ltd 1992– (dep chm 1986–92); chm Assoc of Investmt Tst Cos 1989–91; ACIS 1956; *Recreations* tennis, cricket, gardening, reading biographies; *Style—* Michael Hart, Esq; ✉ Springs, Water End, Ashdon, Essex (☎ 01799 84259); Foreign and Colonial Management Ltd, Exchange House, Primrose Street, London EC2A 2NY (☎ 0171 628 8000)

HART, Norman A; *Educ* Univ of Bradford (MSc Mgmnt and Business Admin (by research)); *Career* gp chief exec Roles and Parker Ltd (industl advtg agency) 1957–62, mktg servs mangr Unilever Ltd 1962–67, divnl gen mangr Morgan Grampian Ltd (publishers) 1967–68, chief mktg exec Industrial Advisors to the Blind (Govt mgmnt consultancy) 1968–72, the dir The CAM Educn Fndn 1972–84; md: Interact Communications Ltd (business-to-business advtg agency) 1984–86, Interact International Ltd (trg orgn) 1986–92, Norman Hart Associates (mktg consultancy) 1992–; speaker on mktg, advtg and PR and educn in Europe, USA, S America, the Far East and Africa; visiting fell: Univ of Bradford 1974–, Leeds Metropolitan Univ 1994–; course dir The Coll of Mktg 1984–, MBA course dir Hull Business Sch 1992–; chm Int PR Educn Fndn; FIPR, FCIM; *Books* incl: The Marketing Dictionary (1992, 5 edn 1996), Industrial Marketing Communications (5 edn, 1993), Effective Industrial Marketing (1994), How to get on in Marketing (3 edn, 1994), Strategic Public Relations (1995), The Practice of Advertising (4 edn, 1995); *Recreations* reading, writing, music, theatre, church, travel, swimming; *Style—* Norman Hart, Esq; ✉ Norman Hart Associates, 72 St James Road, Tunbridge Wells, Kent TN1 2HN (☎ and fax 01892 533066)

HART, Norman Antony (Tony); s of Norman Chandler Hart (d 1970), of Maidstone, and Evelyn Emma, *née* Dyke (d 1981); *b* 15 Oct 1925; *Educ* Clayesmore, Indian Military Acad, Maidstone Coll of Art; *m* 2 Sept 1954, Jean, da of Reginald Frederick Skingle; 1 da (Carolyn b 1957); *Career* Indian Army 1st Gurkha Rifles 1943–47; TV presenter and artist; former presenter Vision On, Take Hart, Hartbeat and The Artbox Bunch; *Awards* Society of Film and TV Arts (for Vision On) 1974, Int Children's TV Festival (for Vision On) 1972, BBC's Multi-Coloured Swap Shop Award (for Children's TV Star) 1979 and 1980, Br Acad Awards (nominated Best Children's TV Prog) 1979; *Films* prod by Video Arts: How to Lie with Statistics, The Average Chap, Man Hunt, Who Sold You This, Then?, It's All Right, It's Only a Customer, Meetings of Minds, The Balance Sheet Barrier, The Control of Working Capital, In Two Minds, When I'm Calling You, Will You Answer True?; memb 1st Gurkha Assoc 1947; *Books* Making Mosaics, Fun with Drawing, Fun with Art, Fun with Design, Fun with Picture Projects, Fun with Historical Projects, The Young Letterer, The Corporate Computer (by Norman Saunders, illustrations), Make It With Hart, Take Hart, The Art Factory (1980), Paint and Draw (1984), Art and Craft (1984), Lettercraft (1986), Small Hands Big Ideas (1988), Draw it Yourself (1989), The Tale of Billy Bouncer (1990); *Recreations* wine, building stone walls; *Style—* Tony Hart, Esq; ✉ c/o ROC Renals, 10 Heatherway, Crowthorne, Berks RG11 6HG

HART, Prof Oliver Simon D'Arcy; s of Philip Montagu D'Arcy Hart, and Ruth Hart; *b* 9 Oct 1948; *Educ* Univ Coll Sch, King's Coll Cambridge (BA), Univ of Warwick (MA), Princeton Univ (PhD); *m* 1974, Rita Goldberg; 2 s; *Career* lectr in economics Univ of Essex 1974–75, asst lectr then lectr in economics Univ of Cambridge 1975–81, fell Churchill Coll Cambridge 1975–81; prof of economics: LSE 1981–85, MIT 1985–93, Harvard Univ 1993–; visiting Scholar Harvard Law Sch 1987–88, Marvin Bower fell Harvard Business Sch 1988–89; memb: Coordinating Ctee Social Sci Res Cncl Econ Theory Study Gp UK 1975–79, Prog Ctee Fourth World Congress of the Econometric Soc 1980, Editorial Advsy Bd Review of Econ Studies 1975–88, Editorial Advsy Bd Cambridge Surveys of Economic Literature Cup 1984–, Cncl Econometric Soc 1983–89 (memb Exec Ctee at large 1984–87), Nat Sci Fndn Economics Panel 1987–, Advsy Cncl Princeton Univ Economics Dept 1989–; assoc ed: Jl of Economic Theory 1976–79, Econometrica 1984–87, Games and Economic Behaviour 1988–, Jl of Accounting Auditing and Finance 1989–; ed Review of Economic Studies 1979–83 (asst ed 1978–79), prog dir Centre for Econ Policy Res London 1983–84, res assoc Nat Bureau of Econ Res 1990–; Dr (hc): Free Univ of Brussels 1992, Univ of Basel 1994; fell: Econometric Soc 1979, American Acad of Arts and Scis 1988; *Books* Firms, Contracts, and Financial Structure (1995); also author of numerous articles and chapters in various books; *Recreations* playing and watching tennis; *Style—* Prof Oliver Hart; ✉ Littauer 220, Department of Economics, Harvard University, Cambridge, Mass 02138, USA

HART, Peter Dorney; s of Sydney Charles Hart (d 1974), of Fulham and Croydon, and Florence Jane, *née* Dorney; *b* 24 June 1925; *Educ* Dulwich, Regent St Poly; *m* 18 March 1958, Paulette Olga, da of Julian Pearmain (d 1971), of Hayes, Kent; *Career* RE 1943–48, Capt attached to Indian Army 1945–48, RARO 1949–75; Walfords Chartered Quantity Surveyors: joined 1950, ptnr 1967, jt sr ptnr 1982, sr ptnr 1987–89, conslt 1989–91; sr ptnr PD Hart & Partners 1989–95; dir: Surveyors Pubns 1984–90, CEM Courses Ltd 1990–, Inst and Coll Confs 1992–93; memb: Nat Jt Consultative Ctee for Bldg 1978–86, Bd Coll of Estate Mgmnt Reading 1985– (hon treas 1989–); pres Quantity Surveyor's Div RICS 1989–90 (vice chm 1987–89), memb General Cncl RICS 1988–91; tstee: Douglas Haig Meml Homes 1978– (chm 1992–), Housing Assoc for Offrs Families 1988–93; hon sec Surrey & N Sussex Beagles 1979–; pres The Surveyors' Club 1988; Freeman City of London 1977; Liveryman: Worshipful Co of Chartered Surveyors 1977, Worshipful Co of Carpenters 1984; FRICS 1965 (ARICS 1953); *Recreations* beagling, archaeology, local history; *Clubs* Athenaeum; *Style—* Peter Hart, Esq; ✉ The Coach House, 50 Lovelace Rd, Surbiton, Surrey KT6 6ND (☎ 0181 399 8423)

HART, Prof Robert A; s of James Hart (d 1980), and Kathleen Mary Hart; *b* 7 Jan 1946; *Educ* Univ of Liverpool (MA); m; 3 c; *Career* lectr in economics and statistics Univ of Aberdeen 1971–73 (lectr in economics 1969–71), lectr in economics Univ of Leeds 1974–75, sr lectr Univ of Strathclyde 1976–79, visiting assoc prof McMaster Univ 1979–80, sr res fell IIM Science Centre 1980–86; Univ of Stirling: prof of economics 1986–, head of dept 1986–91, head Sch of Mgmnt 1991–94; visiting res fell W E Upjohn Inst for Employment Research 1990; *Books* The Economics of Non-Wage Labour Costs (1984), Working Time and Employment (1987), Employment, Unemployment and Labour Utilization (1988), Human Capital, Employment and Bargaining (with T Moutos, 1995); author of numerous chapters in books and articles in jls; *Recreations* reading, walking, beer drinking; *Style—* Prof Robert Hart; ✉ Department of Economics, University of Stirling, Stirling FK9 4LA (☎ 01786 467471, fax 01786 67469)

HART, HE Roger Dudley; s of Alfred John Hart (d 1975), and Emma Jane, *née* Turner (d 1984); *b* 29 Dec 1943; *Educ* St Olave's GS London, Univ of Birmingham (BA); *m* 3 May 1968, Maria De Los Angeles De Santiago Jimenez (Angela), da of Lt-Col Arsenio De Santiago (d 1993), of Madrid, Spain; 2 s (Stephen Andrew b 1969, Christopher

Alexander b 1970); *Career* HM Dip Serv: third sec FO London 1965, third later second sec Br Mil Govt W Berlin 1967–70, second sec Political Residency Bahrain 1970–72, second later first sec FCO London 1972–75, first sec (Aid) Br High Commission Nairobi 1975–78, first sec (commercial) Br Embassy Lisbon 1978–83, asst head Def Dept FCO London 1983–85, memb Royal Coll of Defence Studies 1985, int advsr Br Nat Space Centre London 1986, HM consul-gen Rio de Janeiro 1986–90, cnsllr, consul gen and dep head of mission Br Embassy Mexico City Mexico 1990–93, head Nationality, Treaty and Claims Dept FCO London 1993–95, ambass Angola 1995– (concurrently non-resident ambass to Sao Tome); citizen of Rio de Janeiro 1989–; awarded Pedro Ernesto Medal Brazil 1990; *Recreations* travel, reading, music; *Clubs* Royal Over-Seas League; *Style*— HE Mr Roger Hart; ✉ c/o Foreign and Commonwealth Office (Luanda), King Charles Street, London SW1A 2AH

HART, Timothy Frederick (Tim); s of Louis Albert Hart (d 1977), of Dynes Hall, Halstead, Essex, and Theresa Elsie Hart (d 1994); *b* 7 Dec 1947; *Educ* Westminster, Jesus Coll Cambridge (MA); *m* Stefa Belitis, da of Vladimir Daskaloff; 3 s (Samuel b Sept 1974, Edward b Aug 1976, James b March 1982); *Career* Henry Ansbacher and Co 1969–73, Lehman Brothers Inc 1974–79; purchased Hambleton Hall 1979 (opened as Country House Hotel 1980); fndr chm and chief exec Hart Hambleton plc 1986, purchased and redeveloped Ram Jam Inn 1986; chm: Br Section of Relais ex Chateaux 1987–90, Smollensky's Balloon Ltd 1994–; govr Oakham Sch 1990–; *Recreations* hunting, shooting, fishing, gastronomy, oenology, literature, gardening, watercolour painting, deer stalking, tree climbing; *Style*— Tim Hart, Esq; ✉ Hart Hambleton plc, Hambleton Hall, Hambleton, Oakham, Rutland LE15 8TH (☎ 01572 756991, fax 01572 724721)

HART, Timothy Guy Collins; s of Dr Robert John Collins Hart (Lt-Col RAMC), of Budleigh Salterton, Devon, and Mary Winifred, *née* Sawday; *b* 31 Aug 1953; *Educ* The King's Sch Canterbury, Oxford Poly; *m* 2 Aug 1980, Judith Charlotte, da of Brig Bernard Cyril Elgood, MBE, of Pauntley, Glos; 2 s (Thomas b 1982, Nicholas b 1985), 1 da (Jennifer b 1988); *Career* Arthur Young 1974–83, Prudential Assurance 1983–85, ptnr Phildrew Ventures 1985–; ACA 1980; *Recreations* tennis, golf, skiing; *Style*— Timothy Hart, Esq; ✉ Phildrew Ventures, Triton Ct, 14 Finsbury Sq, London EC2A 1PD (☎ 0171 628 6366, fax 0171 638 2817)

HART-DAVIS, (Peter) Duff; s of Sir Rupert Hart-Davis, *qv*, of Marske-in-Swaledale, Yorks, and Comfort Borden, *née* Turner (d 1970); *b* 3 June 1936; *Educ* Eton, Univ of Oxford (BA); *m* 1961, Phyllida, da of Col John Barstow; 1 s (Guy b 1965), 1 da (Alice b 1963); *Career* journalist and author, graduate trainee Western Mail Cardiff 1960; Sunday Telegraph: asst to Literary Ed 1961–63, ed Close-Up (news background) team 1968–70, literary ed 1976–77, asst ed 1977–78, editorial advsr 1980–85; contrib Country Matters column The Independent 1986–; *Novels* The Megacull (1968), The Gold of St Matthew (1970), Spider in the Morning (1972), The Heights of Rimring (1980), Level Five (1982), Fire Falcon (1983), The Man-Eater of Jassapur (1985), Horses of War (1991); *Non-fiction* Peter Fleming (1974), Ascension (1976), Monarchs of the Glen (1978), Hitler's Games (1986), The Letters and Journals of Sir Alan Lascelles (ed 2 vols, 1986 and 1988), Armada (1988), Country Matters (1989), The House the Berrys Built (1990), Wildings: the Secret Garden of Eileen Soper (1991), Further Country Matters (1992); *Recreations* opera, gardening, deer stalking, splitting wood; *Clubs* Garrick; *Style*— Duff Hart-Davis, Esq

HART-DAVIS, Sir Rupert Charles; kt (1967); s of Richard Vaughan Hart-Davis and Sybil Cooper (sister of Rt Hon Sir Alfred Duff Cooper, GCMG, DSO, 1 Viscount Norwich, da of Sir Alfred Cooper, FRCS, and Lady Agnes, *née* Duff, 4 of da 5 Earl of Fife and sister of 1 Duke of Fife); *b* 28 Aug 1907; *Educ* Eton, Balliol Coll Oxford; *m* 1, 1929 (m dis), Dame Peggy Ashcroft; m 2, 1933 (m dis), Catherine Comfort Borden-Turner; 1 da (Lady Silsoe b 1935 *see* Rt Hon the Lord Silsoe, QC), 2 s ((Peter) Duff, *qv*, b 1936, Adam b 1943); m 3, 1964, Winifred Ruth (d 1967), da of C H Ware and wid of Oliver Simon; m 4, 1968, June, *née* Clifford, wid of David Williams; *Career* ed, author, publisher; dir Rupert Hart-Davis Ltd (and fndr) 1946–68 (former dir Jonathan Cape Ltd), vice pres Ctee of London Library 1971– (former chm); ed letters of: Oscar Wilde, Max Beerbohm, the Lyttelton Hart-Davis Letters, and Siegfried Sassoon Diaries (3 vols); *Books* Hugh Walpole - A Biography (1952), The Arms of Time - A Memoir (1979), A Beggar in Purple - a Commonplace Book (1989), The Power of Chance - A Table of Memory (1991); *Style*— Sir Rupert Hart-Davis; ✉ The Old Rectory, Marske-in-Swaledale, Richmond, N Yorks

HART-DYKE, Capt David; CBE (1990), LVO (1980); s of Cdr the Rev Eric Hart Dyke (d 1971), of Lavenham, Suffolk, and Mary, *née* Alexander; *b* 3 Oct 1938; *Educ* St Lawrence Coll; *m* 8 July 1967, Diana Margaret, da of Sir William Luce, GBE, KCMG (d 1977), of Fovant, Wilts; 2 da (Miranda b 1972, Alice b 1975); *Career* BRNC Dartmouth 1958, served Far E and ME, Exec Offr HMS Hampshire 1974–76, on staff of RN Staff Coll 1976–78, Cdr Royal Yacht Britannia 1978–80, Capt HMS Coventry 1981–82 (served Falklands conflict 1982), ACOS to C-in-C Fleet 1982–84, Asst Naval Attaché and COS Washington DC USA 1985–87, Dir of Naval Recruiting 1987–89, ADC 1988–90, ret 1990; Clerk to Worshipful Co of Skinners 1990–; *Recreations* painting, gardening, military history; *Clubs* Naval and Military; *Style*— Capt David Hart-Dyke, CBE, LVO, RN; ✉ Hambledon House, Hambledon, Hants PO7 4RU (☎ 01705 632380)

HART DYKE, Sir David William; 10 Bt (E 1677), of Horeham, Sussex; s of Sir Derek William Hart Dyke, 9 Bt (d 1987), and his 1 w, Dorothy, *née* Moses; 2 Bt m Anne, da and heir of Percival Hart of Lullingstone Castle, 5 Bt unsuccessfully claimed the Barony of Brayes of which he was a co heir through the Harts 1836; *b* 5 Jan 1955; *Educ* Ryerson Polytechnical Inst; *Heir* unc, (Oliver) Guy Hart Dyke b 9 Feb 1928; *Style*— Sir David Hart Dyke, Bt; ✉ 28 King St West, Apt B14, Stoney Creek, Ontario, Canada

HART-LEVERTON, Colin Allen; QC (1979); s of Morris Hart-Leverton, of London; *b* 10 May 1936; *Educ* Stowe; *m*; 1 s (David b 1 July 1967); m 1990, Kathi, *née* Davidson; *Career* called to the Bar Middle Temple 1957, dep circuit judge 1975, attorney-at-law Turks and Caicos Islands 1976, recorder of the Crown Ct 1979; occasional radio and TV broadcasts in UK and USA; memb Taxation Inst 1957; *Recreations* table tennis, jazz; *Style*— Colin Hart-Leverton, Esq, QC; ✉ 1 Dr Johnson's Buildings, London EC4Y 7AX (☎ 0171 353 9328)

HARTE, Dr Michael John; s of late Harold Edward Harte, of Sussex, and Marjorie Irene, *née* Scaife; *b* 15 Aug 1936; *Educ* Charterhouse, Trinity Coll Cambridge (BA), UCL (Dip Biochem Engrg, PhD); *m* 1, 1962 (m dis); m 2, 1975, Mrs Mary Claire Preston, da of D J Hogan (d 1972); 4 step da (Caroline b 1962, Emma b 1964, Abigail b 1966, Lucy (twin) b 1966); *Career* chm NATO Budget Ctees 1981–83; asst under sec: Dockyard Planning Team MOD 1985, Air Personnel MOD 1987, Resources MOD 1990–93; dir gen IT Systems MOD 1994–95, currently managing conslt Greenman Enterprise; *Recreations* wine, walking, weeding; *Clubs* Royal Soc of Arts; *Style*— Dr Michael Harte; ✉ Greenman Farm, Wadhurst, Sussex TN5 6LE (☎ 01892 783292)

HARTGILL, John Clavering; s of Maj-Gen William C Hartgill, CB, MC, OBE, KHS (d 1969), and Katherine Robertson, *née* Lowe, MM (d 1970); *b* 26 July 1925; *Educ* Wanganui Collegiate NZ, Univ of Otago NZ, The Royal London Hosp; *m* 1 July 1961, Unni, da of Otto Aass (d 1971), of Drammen, Norway; 2 s (Paul b 9 April 1963, Tom b 26 Sept 1966), 1 da (Katrina b 24 March 1968); *Career* sr registrar Dept of Obstetrics The Royal London Hosp 1958–61, asst Lege Ulleval Hosp Oslo Norway 1962–66, conslt obstetric and gynaecological surgn The Royal London Hosp 1966–90; sr lectr London Hosp Med Coll 1966–; examiner 1966–: Univ of Cambridge, RCOG, Univ of London; jt ed Int Journal of Lymphology 1967–72; memb: Gynaecological Visiting Soc of GB & I, Sydenham Med Club, The Blizard Club (London Hosp Med Sch); Liveryman Worshipful Soc of Apothecaries 1973, Freeman City of London; FRCSEd, FRCOG, MRCS, LRCP, FRSM 1958; awarded Norske Medicinske Seiskap Medal 1964; *Books* Ten Teachers Obstetrics (jtly 12, 13, 14 edns 1976–85), Diseases of Women (jtly 12 edn 1976), Ten Teachers Gynaecology (jtly 13 and 14 edns 1980–85); *Style*— John Hartgill, Esq; ✉ Bridge House Farm, Felsted, Great Dunmow, Essex CM6 3JF (☎ 01371 820349)

HARTILL, Rosemary Jane; da of Clement Augustus Hartill, of Shropshire, and Florence Margarita, *née* Ford (d 1989); *b* 11 Aug 1949; *Educ* Wellington Girls' HS Shropshire, Univ of Bristol (BA); *Career* editor Tom Stacey Ltd 1970–73, jr editor David & Charles 1973–75, sr non-fiction editor Hamish Hamilton Children's Books 1975–76, freelance dance and book reviewer Times Education Supplement 1976–79, BBC religious affrs corr 1982–88 (reporter 1979–82), reporter Human Factor (ITV) 1988–92; presenter of progs incl: Women's Hour (BBC Radio 4, NE editions) 1989–91, Meridian Books (BBC World Service); freelance bdcaster and writer; Sony Award nominations for: Best Radio Reporter of the Year 1988, Best Arts Feature 1990; Sandford St Martin Tst prizes 1992 and 1994 (incl personal award for outstanding contrib to religious bdcasting 1994), various other awards and nominations; Hon DLitt Hull 1995; *Books* Wild Animals, Emily Brontë - Poems (ed), In Perspective, Writers Revealed, Were You There?, Florence Nightingale: Letters and Reflections (ed); *Recreations* wildlife, walking, being in Northumberland; *Style*— Ms Rosemary Hartill; ✉ Old Post Office, 24 Eglingham Village, Alnwick, Northumberland NE66 2TX

HARTILL, (Edward) Theodore; s of Clement Augustus Hartill, of Shropshire, and Florence Margarita, *née* Ford (d 1989); *b* 23 Jan 1943; *Educ* Priory Sch for Boys Shrewsbury, Coll of Estate Mgmnt, Univ of London (BSc); *m* 1, 2 s (Jeremy b 1969, Richard b 1972); m 2, 1975, Gillian Ruth, da of Harold Todd (d 1963); 2 s (Andrew b 1977, Giles b 1981); *Career* joined Messrs Burd and Evans Land Agents Shrewsbury 1963; Estates Dept Legal and Gen Assurance Society 1964–73, Property Investmt Dept Guardian Royal Exchange Assurance Group 1973–85, The City Surveyor Corp of London 1985–; visiting lectr in law of town planning and compulsory purchase Hammersmith and West London Coll of Advanced Business Studies 1968–78; RICS: memb Gen Practice Divnl Cncl 1989–, memb Gen Cncl 1990–, pres Gen Practice Div 1992–93, memb Quantity Surveyors' Divnl Cncl 1993–, memb Mgmnt Bd 1994–95; chm: gp developing National and Scottish Vocational Qualification in Property Services, Local Govt Policy Panel 1996–; memb: Assoc of Chief Estates Surveyors na Property Managers in Local Govt 1988– (sr vice-pres 1995–96), Br Schs Exploring Soc, Property Co-ordination and Presentation Gp London First Centre; hon assoc Czech Chamber of Appraisers; hon memb Investment Property Forum, memb Ct of Assts Worshipful Company of Chartered Surveyors 1991 (Liveryman 1985); FRICS, FRSA; *Recreations* travel, hill walking, films; *Style*— E T Hartill Esq; ✉ 215 Sheen Lane, East Sheen, London SW14 8LE (☎ 0181 878 4494); The City Surveyor, City Surveyor's Department, Corporation of London, PO Box 270, Guildhall, London EC2P 2EJ (☎ 0171 332 1500, fax 0171 332 1536, telex 265608 LONDON G)

HARTINGTON, Marquess of; Peregrine Andrew Morny Cavendish; CBE (1997); s and h of 11 Duke of Devonshire, KG, MC, PC, and Hon Deborah (Debo) Freeman-Mitford (sis of Nancy, Jessica and Unity Mitford, *see* Treuhaft, Hon Mrs, and Hon Lady Mosley), da of 2 Baron Redesdale; *b* 27 April 1944; *Educ* Eton, Exeter Coll Oxford; *m* 28 June 1967, Amanda Carmen, da of late Cdr Edward Gavin Heywood-Lonsdale, RN; 1 s, 2 da (Lady Celina Imogen (m Alexander Carter 1995) b 1971, Lady Jasmine Nancy b 1973); *Heir* Earl of Burlington b 1969; *Career* owner Side Hill Stud; sr steward The Jockey Club 1989–94; chm British Horseracing Board, dep chm Sotheby's Holdings Inc; chm Diocese of Bradford Church Buildings Appeal; pres: Chesterfield and N Derbyshire NSPCC, Chesterfield and Dist Soc for the Deaf, Eastbourne Branch RNLI, S of England Agricultural Soc 1996; tstee Ascot Authy, tstee Yorkshire Dales Nat Park Millenium Tst, memb York Race Ctee; Liveryman Worshipful Co of Fishmongers; *Style*— Marquess of Hartington, CBE; ✉ Beamsley Hall, Skipton, N Yorks BD23 6HD (☎ 01756 710419/710424)

HARTLAND, Michael; *see:* James, Michael Leonard

HARTLAND-SWANN, Julian Dana Nimmo; CMG (1992); s of Prof John Hartland-Swann (d 1961), and Kenlis, *née* Taylour (d 1957); *b* 18 Feb 1936; *Educ* Stowe, Lincoln Coll Oxford (BA); *m* 22 Oct 1960, Ann Deirdre, da of Lt Cdr Robert Green, MBE, DSC (d 1991), of St Helier, Shotley Gate, nr Ipswich; 1 s (Piers b 1961), 1 da (Justina b 1963); *Career* Nat Serv RA 1955–57; Dip Serv 1960–95; 3 sec later 2 sec Bangkok Embassy 1961–65, 1 sec FO 1965–68, head of External Dept Br Mil Govt Berlin 1968–71, 1 sec and head of chancery Vienna 1971–74, FCO 1975–77, cnsllr 1977, ambass to Mongolian People's Republic 1977–79, cnsllr and dep head of mission Brussels 1979–83, head of SE Asian Dept FCO 1983–85, consul gen Frankfurt 1986–90, ambass to Union of Myanmar (Burma) 1990–95; exec dir European Business Information Centre Thailand 1995–; *Recreations* French food, sailing, restoring ruins; *Style*— Julian Hartland-Swann, Esq, CMG; ✉ European Business Information Centre, Vanissa Building, Soi Chidlom, Ploenchit, Bangkok, Thailand

HARTLEY, Air Marshal Sir Christopher Harold; KCB (1963, CB 1961), CBE (1957, OBE 1949), DFC (1945), AFC (1944); s of Brig-Gen Harold Hartley, GCVO, CH, CBE, MC, FRS (d 1972); *b* 31 Jan 1913; *Educ* Eton, Balliol Coll Oxford, King's Coll Cambridge; *m* 1, 1937 (m dis 1943), Anne Sitwell; m 2, 1944, Margaret Watson (d 1989); 2 s; *Career* zoologist Univ of Oxford Expeditions: Sarawak 1932, Spitsbergen 1933, Greenland 1936; asst master Eton 1937–39; joined RAFVR 1938, served WWII, Gp Capt 1952, Air Cdre 1958, AOC 12 Gp Fighter Cmd 1959, Air Vice-Marshal 1960, asst chief Air Staff (Operational Requirements) Air Miny 1961–63, Air Marshal 1963, dep chief of Air Staff 1963–66, controller of Aircraft Miny of Aviation 1966, ret 1970; dir Westland Aircraft Ltd 1971–83, dep chm British Hovercraft Corp 1979–83 (chm 1974–79); *Recreations* fishing; *Clubs* Travellers'; *Style*— Sir Christopher Hartley; ✉ c/o Barclays Bank, Bank Plain, Norwich, Norfolk

HARTLEY, Dr David Fielding; s of Robert Maude Hartley (d 1980), of Hebden Bridge, Yorks, and Sheila Ellen, *née* Crabtree (d 1977); *b* 14 Sept 1937; *Educ* Rydal Sch, Clare Coll Cambridge (MA, PhD); *m* 23 April 1960, Joanna Mary, da of John Stanley Bolton (d 1988), of Halifax; 1 s (Timothy b 1965), 2 da (Caroline (Mrs Eatough) b 1963, Rosalind (Mrs Fell) b 1968); *Career* Univ of Cambridge: sr asst in res 1964–65, asst dir of res 1966–67, lectr Mathematical Laboratory 1967–70, jr res fell Churchill Coll 1964–67, dir computing serv 1970–94, fell Darwin Coll 1969–86, fell Clare Coll 1987–; chief exec UK Educn and Research Networking Assoc 1994–; dir: Lynxvale Ltd 1982–94, CAD Centre Ltd 1983–94; chm and dir NAG Ltd; memb: Computer Bd for Univs and Res Cncls 1979–83, PM's Info Technol Advsy Panel 1981–86, BBC Sci Consultative Gp 1984–87, vice pres Br Computer Soc 1984–90; Freeman: City of London 1988, Co of Info Technologists 1988; FBCS 1967, CEng 1990; Medal of Merits Nicholas Copernicus Univ Poland 1984; *Style*— Dr David Hartley; ✉ 26 Girton Rd, Cambridge (☎ 01223 571717); UKERNA, Atlas Centre, Chilton, Didcot OX11 0QS (☎ 01235 822312)

HARTLEY, Sir Frank; kt (1977), CBE (1970); s of Robinson King Hartley (d 1916), and Mary, *née* Holt (d 1959); *b* 5 Jan 1911; *Educ* Nelson Municipal Secondary Sch, Sch of Pharmacy Univ of London, UCL, Birkbeck Coll London (PhD); *m* 1937, Lydia May England (d 1996); 2 s (incl Prof Frank Hartley, *qv*); *Career* dean Sch of Pharmacy Univ of London 1962–76, vice chllr Univ of London 1976–78; pres Royal Inst of Chemistry 1965–67; chm Br Pharmacopoeia Cmmn 1970–80, vice chm Medicines Cmmn 1974–83;

chm: Cmmrs Lambeth Southwark and Lewisham Health Area 1979–80, Consortium of Charing Cross and Westminster Med Schs 1981–84, Br Cncl for Prevention of Blindness 1988–95; memb Consultative Bd of Regents Univ of Qatar 1978–; fell: Birkbeck Coll London 1970, UCL 1972, Sch of Pharmacy London 1977; hon fell Imperial Coll London 1990, Hon FRCP (London) 1979, Hon FRCS (London) 1980, Hon FRSC 1981, life memb Soc Chem Indust 1994; Hon DSc Warwick 1978, Hon LLD Strathclyde 1980, Hon LLD London 1987; Charter Gold Medal Royal Pharmaceutical Soc of GB 1974; FRPharmS; Liveryman Worshipful Soc of Apothecaries 1958, Freeman City of London 1959; *Recreations* reading, watching sport; *Style*— Sir Frank Hartley, CBE; ✉ Flat 16, Town Thorns, Easenhall, Rugby CV23 0JE (☎ 01788 833483)

HARTLEY, Prof Frank Robinson; s of Sir Frank Hartley, CBE, *qv*, and Lydia May, *née* England (d 1996); *b* 29 Jan 1942; *Educ* King's Coll Sch Wimbledon, Magdalen Coll Oxford (MA, DPhil, DSc); *m* 12 Dec 1964, Valerie, da of George Peel (d 1984), of Silksworth, Co Durham, and Watchfield, Oxon; 3 da (Susan b 1967, Judith b 1971, Elizabeth b 1974); *Career* res fell Div of Protein Chem CSIRO (Aust) 1966–69, ICI res fell and tutor in chem UCL 1969–70, lectr in chem Univ of Southampton 1970–75, princ and dean RMCS 1982–89 (prof of chem 1975–82), vice chllr Cranfield Univ 1989–; chm CIM Technology Ltd 1990–, md CIT Holdings Ltd 1990–; dir: Cranfield Ventures Ltd 1990–, Cranfield Services Ltd 1994–, Shuttleworth Tst 1994–, Beds Trg and Enterprise Cncl 1994–96; non-exec dir: T & N plc 1989–, Eastern Regnl Bd National Westminster Bank plc 1990–92, Kalon plc 1994–, Kenwood Appliances plc 1995–; special advsr to PM on Defence Systems 1988–90; memb: Parly Scientific Ctee 1987– (Cncl 1992–, vice pres 1996–), Oxon Soc of Rugby Football Referees; chm Lorch Fndn 1995–; RFU touch judge; FRSC 1977, FRSA 1988, CIMgt 1991, FRAeS 1996; *Books* Chemistry of Platinum and Palladium (1973), Elements of Organometallic Chemistry (1974), Solution Equilibria (1980), Supported Metal Complexes (1985), Chemistry of the Metal-Carbon Bond (vol 1 1983, vol 2 1984, vol 3 1985, vol 4 1987, vol 5 1989), Chemistry of Organphosphorus Compounds (vol 1 1990, vol II 1992, vol III 1994), Chemistry of the Platinum Group Metals (1991); *Recreations* rugby, swimming, cliff walking, reading, gardening; *Clubs* Shrivenham, IOD; *Style*— Prof Frank Hartley; ✉ Cranfield University, Cranfield, Bedford MK43 0AL (☎ 01234 754013, fax 01234 752583)

HARTLEY, Rev Godfrey; s of Isaac Hartley, and Hannah, *née* Lowther; *b* 26 Aug 1937; *Educ* Clare Hall Sch, Univs of Manchester, Nottingham and Oxford, Cuddesdon Theological Coll Oxford; *m* 17 Aug 1963, Maureen Ruth, da of Norman Harding Goldsworth, of Nottingham; 2 s (António b 1965, Richard b 1974); *Career* Nat Serv RAF 1956–58; ordained: deacon 1964, priest 1965; curate St Giles Balderton Diocese of Southwell 1964–67, port chaplain Missions to Seamen, rector St George Beira Mozambique 1968–73, sr chaplain and sec for Scotland Missions to Seamen 1974–89, priest i/c St Gabriel's Govan 1974–89, chaplain Missions to Seamen in Cornwall 1989; chaplain RNR 1973–92 (ret list 1992–), Chaplain of the Fleets representative Ships Bldg Clyde 1974–89; memb: SSC, Int Christian Maritime Assoc, Euro Palm Soc, Botanical Soc of SA; Freeman City of Glasgow 1979, memb Incorporation of Coopers of Glasgow 1979; hon roughneck Beaumons Texas 1978; *Recreations* skiing, photography, painting, reading, horticulture, country life; *Clubs* Army and Navy, Ski Club of GB, Glasgow Press, Skål of Scotland; *Style*— The Rev Godfrey Hartley; ✉ Sandoes Gate, Feock, Truro, Cornwall TR3 6QN (☎ 01872 865863)

HARTLEY, Prof Keith; s of W Hartley, of Leeds, and Ivy, *née* Stead; *b* 14 July 1940; *Educ* Univ of Hull (BA, PhD); *m* 12 April 1966, Winifred; 1 s (Adam b 27 Feb 1969), 2 da (Lucy b 18 Oct 1970, Cecilia b 20 July 1975); *Career* Univ of York: dir Inst for Research in Social Scis 1982–94, prof of economics 1987–, fndr dir Centre for Defence Economics 1990–; visiting prof: Univ of Illinois, Univ of Malaysia, Univ of NSW; *Books* Economics of Defense (1995); *Recreations* angling, football, walking, reading; *Style*— Prof Keith Hartley; ✉ Centre for Defence Economics, University of York, York YO1 5DD (☎ 01904 433680, telex 01904 432300)

HARTLEY, Keith; s of Albert Hartley, MBE (d 1991), and Joan Winifred, *née* Dixson (d 1973); *b* 11 Oct 1956; *Educ* Chislehurst & Sidcup GS for Boys, KCL (LLB), Coll of Law; *m* 1986, Barbara Elizabeth Rundle-Smith, da of Capt Arthur Edmund Smith; 1 s (Dominic Edward b 23 Nov 1993); *Career* admitted slr 1982; Masons: articled clerk 1980–82, slr London 1982–84, Hong Kong office 1984–95 (ptnr 1986–); memb: Law Soc Hong Kong 1984, Inst of Arbitrators 1987, Asia Pacific Lawyers Assoc 1990; *Recreations* history, computing, family; *Style*— Keith Hartley, Esq; ✉ Masons, Minerva House, 29 East Parade, Leeds LS1 5TN (☎ 0113 233 8905, fax 0113 245 4285, mobile 0836 312314, email keithhartley@masons.com)

HARTMANN, Dr Reinhard Rudolf Karl; s of Walther Eduard Hartmann, of Vienna, Austria, and Gerta Emilia Stanislawa, *née* Müllner; *b* 8 April 1938; *Educ* Vienna GS, Vienna Sch of Economics (BSc and Doctorate), Univ of Vienna (Dip Translation), Southern Illinois Univ (MA); *m* 22 June 1965, Lynn, da of Kingston Vernon Warren, of Droylsden, Manchester; 1 s (Stefan b 1967), 1 da (Nasim b 1965); *Career* lectr in modern languages UMIST 1964–68, lectr in applied linguistics Univ of Nottingham 1968–74; Univ of Exeter: sr lectr in applied linguistics 1974–91, dir Language Centre 1974–92, dir Dictionary Res Centre 1984–, reader 1991–, head Dept of Applied Linguistics 1992–96; former fndr, sec and pres EURALEX; memb: BAAL 1967, LAGB 1970, SLE 1972, ALLC 1975, EURALEX 1983 (hon life memb 1994), DSNA 1984; *Books* Dictionary of Language and Linguistics (jtly, 1972), Contrastive Textology (1980); ed: Lexicography Principles and Practice (1983), LEXeter '83 Proceedings (1984), The History of Lexicography (1986), Lexicography in Africa (1990), The English Language in Europe (1996), Solving Language Problems (1996); *Recreations* listening to music, table tennis; *Style*— Dr Reinhard Hartmann; ✉ School of English and American Studies, University of Exeter, Queen's Building, Exeter, Devon EX4 4QH (☎ 01392 264303, fax 01392 264361, telex 42894 EXUNIVG, e-mail r.r.k.hartmann@exeter.ac.uk)

HARTNACK, Paul Richard Samuel; s of Carl Samuel Hartnack (d 1989), and Maud Godden Hartnack (d 1993); *b* 17 Nov 1942; *Educ* Hastings GS; *m* 1966, Marion, da of Peter Anthony Quirk; 2 s (Christopher Stephen b 1970, Michael David b 1971); *Career* clerical offr Bd of Trade 1961–62, Office of the Registrar of Restrictive Trading Agreements 1962–64, Commercial Relations and Exports Div Bd of Trade 1964–67, asst sec Ctee of Inquiry into Civil Air Tport 1967–69, Br Embassy Paris 1969–72, Export Servs Div DTI 1972–78, asst sec National Enterprise Bd 1978–80, sec British Technology Group 1980–85, fin and resource mangr DTI 1985–89, comptroller general and chief exec The Patent Office 1989–; *Recreations* gardening, watching rugby; *Style*— Paul Hartnack, Esq; ✉ The Patent Office, Concept House, Cardiff Road, Newport NP9 1RH (☎ 01633 814500, fax 01633 814504)

HARTNALL, Michael James; s of late James Inglis Hartnall, of Headley Down, Hants, and late Phylis Hartnall; *b* 10 July 1942; *Educ* Ryde Sch; *m* July 1968, Pamela Hartnall; 3 da; *Career* qualified CA 1965, Osborne Ward & Co, IMI then Goblin (BVC) 1965–70; Swift & Co/Esmark: fin dir 1970–79, md 1979–84; md Mayhew Foods plc 1987 (joined 1984), fin dir Rexam PLC (formerly Bowater plc) 1987–, non-exec dir Harrisons & Crosfield plc 1993–; Liveryman Worshipful Co of Butchers; FCA; *Recreations* opera, music, theatre, walking, snooker; *Clubs* Anglo Belgian; *Style*— Michael Hartnall, Esq; ✉ REXAM PLC, 114 Knightsbridge, London SW1X 7NN (☎ 0171 584 7070, fax 0171 581 1149)

HARTNELL, Dr George Gordon; s of Francis George Hartnell, of Holywell Lake, Somerset, and Margaret, *née* Gordon; *b* 19 July 1952; *Educ* Abingdon Sch, Univ of Bristol (BSc, MB ChB); *Career* registrar in cardiology Harefield Hosp 1979–81, registrar and sr registrar Royal Postgrad Med Sch Hammersmith Hosp London 1983–87, currently dir of cardiovascular and interventional radiology Beth Israel Deaconess Medical Center Boston and assoc prof Harvard Med Sch; memb Radiological Soc of North America, fell American Coll of Cardiology; MRCP 1982, FRCR 1985; *Recreations* sailing, skiing; *Style*— Dr George Hartnell; ✉ Department of Radiology, Beth Israel Deaconess Medical Center, Boston, Mass 02215, USA (☎ 00 1 617 754 2523, fax 00 1 617 754 2525)

HARTNETT, Frank Ernest Lawrence; OBE (1988); s of John Richard Hartnett (d 1966), of Odiham, Hampshire, and Eva Marjorie, *née* Maybanks (d 1970); *b* 3 Sept 1940; *Educ* Lord Wandsworth Coll, Univ of London (BSc), Univ of Southampton (CertEd), Univ of Sussex (DipEdTech); *m* 27 Dec 1961, Catherine Mary (d 1994), da of Thomas Adams; 1 s (Richard Lawrence b 25 Feb 1964), 1 da (Katherine Louise b 9 Nov 1966); *Career* head of economics Cheshunt GS 1962, cmmnd RAF 1965, post grad dip Sussex 1971, lead role in achieving organisational change in RAF trg 1972–75, involvement with fast jet ops RAF Germany 1975–78, introduction of Tornado into RAF serv 1979–81, chm Offr and Aircrew Selection Panel 1982; cmdg offr: Training Wing RAF Hereford 1982–85, Admin Wing RAF Cosford 1985–87; gen mangr: Maternity and Child Health Services Grampian 1987–89 (winner Sunday Times Hosp of the Year and UK's Best Teaching Hosp 1989), Mental Health Services Grampian 1990–91, Grampian Health Bd 1991– (currently bd gen mangr); *Recreations* hillwalking, badminton, golf, shooting; *Clubs* RAF, Royal Northern and Univ; *Style*— Frank Hartnett, Esq, OBE; ✉ Grampian Health Board, Summerfield House, 2 Eday Road, Aberdeen (☎ 01224 663456 ext 75224)

HARTOP, Barry; s of Philip William Hartop (d 1954), of Lowestoft, and Constance Winifred Hartop; *b* 15 Aug 1942; *Educ* Lowestoft GS, Univ of Durham (BSc); *m* 30 July 1966, Sandra, da of Alan Walter Swan (d 1976), of Lowestoft; *Career* mgmnt trainee Unilever, prodn mangr Lever Bros Ltd 1965–72, information and cost reduction mangr Unilever plc 1972–80, md Euro Business Centre Unilever plc 1980–83, chm/md Lever Industrial Ltd 1983–89, md Gestetner plc 1989–92; chief exec: Welsh Development Agency 1994–, Millennium Central 1996–; chm Hammicks Bookshops Ltd 1994–; govr Royal GS Guildford 1991–; *Recreations* keeping fit, tennis, squash, gardening; *Style*— Barry Hartop, Esq; ✉ Welsh Development Agency, Principality House, The Friary, Cardiff CF1 4AA (☎ 01222 828669); Millennium Central, 120 Old Broad Street, London EC2N 1AR

HARTSHORNE, Dennis; *b* 1946; *Educ* Heanor GS Derbyshire, Univ of Lancaster (BA), Univ of Southampton (PGCE), Univ of Leicester (MA); *m* Janet; 2 s (Edward, James); *Career* dir: Birmingham Technol Ltd, Aston Sci Park, W Midlands Enterprise Bd, Birmingham Innovation and Devpt Centre; ed Br Atlantic Publications; Parly candidate (C) Stoke-on-Trent South 1987; memb Birmingham City Cncl: Fin and Mgmnt Ctee, Business and Investmt Ctee, Educn Ctee, Tourism and Promotions Ctee, Jt Consultative Ctee, Employment Ctee (chm 1982–84), Personnel Ctee, Gen Purposes and Licensing Ctee, Aid-To-Indust Ctee; memb Cncl Br Atlantic Ctee; chm: SW Birmingham CPC 1973–83, Bournville Cons Assoc 1981–82 (pres 1983–88); memb Exec Ctee Birmingham Cons Gp (responsible for local policy and election planning), chm Govrs Cadbury Coll 1983–93; voluntary PR work for NATO, vice chm Atlantic Cncl 1993–; NATO fell 1980, MIMgt; *Recreations* historical research; *Style*— Dennis Hartshorne, Esq; ✉ Chenda, 59 Bittell Rd, Barnt Green, Worcs (☎ 0121 445 1645)

HARTSHORNE, (Bertram) Kerrich; s of Bertram Charles Hartshorne (d 1949), of Alexandria, Egypt, and Beatrice Mabel, *née* Spencer (d 1974); *b* 24 Nov 1923; *Educ* Charterhouse, Clare Coll Cambridge (MA), Birmingham Univ (MSc); *m* 27 Sept 1952, Jean Irving, da of Oswald Irving Bell (d 1946), of Dumfries; 3 s (David b 1954, Christopher b 1955, James b 1965), 1 da (Pamela b 1958); *Career* WWII RE 1942–47; cmmnd 1943, active serv with Royal Bombay Sappers and Miners in India, Burma and Indo-China (despatches 1946); commanded: Field Sqdn 1945, Depot Bn 1946–47; Sir William Halcrow & Partners civil engrs: joined 1949, assoc 1969–73, ptnr 1973–84; dir Halcrow Fox & Associates 1977–83; chm: Halcrow Surveys 1982–84, Sir William Halcrow & Partners Scotland 1983–84; sr ptnr The Hartshorne Partnership 1985–; involved with many major projects incl: Volta River Project Ghana 1950–60, Pangani River Basin and Nym Dam Tanzania 1961–68, Orange Fish Tunnel 1963–64, military and civil devpt projects Sultanate of Oman 1973–79; FICE 1968, FInstHE 1970, memb ACE 1973; *Books* Transport Survey of the Territories of Papua and New Guinea (1971); *Recreations* sailing, landscape gardening, travelling; *Style*— Kerrich Hartshorne, Esq; ✉ Mill House, Irongray, Dumfries DG2 9SQ (☎ 01387 730417); The Hartshorne Partnership, Oakwood Farm, Irongray, Dumfries DG2 9SQ (☎ 01387 730493)

HARTWELL, Sir (Francis) Anthony Charles Peter; 6 Bt (UK 1805), of Dale Hall, Essex; s of Sir Brodrick William Charles Elwin Hartwell, 5 Bt (d 1993), and his 1 w, Molly Josephine, *née* Mullins; *b* 1 June 1940; *Educ* Thames Nautical Trg Coll, HMS Worcester, Cadet RNR, Univ of Southampton Sch of Navigation (Master Mariner); *m* 1968 (m dis 1989), Barbara Phyllis Rae, da of Henry Rae Green (d 1985), of Sydney, Aust; 1 s (Timothy Peter Michael Charles b 1970); *Heir* s, Timothy Peter Michael Charles Hartwell b 1970; *Career* P&O/Inchcape Gp 1958–69 and 1972–75: Chief Offr/Cadet Trg Offr, Mate/Master, OCL (London) 1969–71, Cargo Supt 1975–, Overseas Managerial Services for marine and port ops contracts; marine conslt and surveyor; memb Fedn of Aust Underwater Instructors (FAUI), MCIT, MRIN, MNI; *Recreations* scuba diving, ocean sailing, photography; *Clubs* Master Mariners (Southampton), Old Worcester's Assoc; *Style*— Sir Anthony Hartwell, Bt; ✉ Trevean, Highlands Road, Barton-on-Sea, Hampshire

HARTWELL, Eric; CBE (1983); s of Alfred Hartwell (d 1932), of Holmleigh, West Parade, Worthing, Sussex, and Edyth Maud, *née* Brunning (d 1980); *b* 10 Aug 1915; *Educ* Mall Sch Twickenham, Worthing HS; *m* 1, 1937 (m dis 1951), Gladys Rose, *née* Bennett; 1 s (Anthony Charles b Jan 1939), 1 da (Susan b Jan 1946); *m* 2, 14 June 1952, Dorothy Maud, da of late Harold Mowbray, MM, of Edgware, Middx; 1 s (Keith Alan b Sept 1958), 1 da (Janine Erica b June 1956); *Career* served WWII with RE 1940–46 (QMSI); Trusthouse Forte plc (now Forte plc): vice chm 1972–93, chief exec 1978–83; chm Br Hotels Restaurants and Caterers' Assoc 1981–84, memb Cncl CBI 1972–87 (memb Fin and Gen Purposes Ctee and chm Fin Sub-Ctee 1980–87), fndr memb LV Catering Educnl Tst, vice chm Thames Heritage Tst 1983–87; memb Inner Magic Circle; Freeman City of London, Liveryman Worshipful Co of Upholders; life fell Br Hospitality Assoc 1992, CIMgt, FHCIMA, FRSA, MIMC; *Recreations* yachting, painting, photography, golf, magic; *Clubs* Thames Motor Yacht, South Herts Golf, Terenure Country, Inner Magic Circle; *Style*— Eric Hartwell, Esq, CBE; ✉ Tall Trees, 129 Totteridge Lane, London N20 8NS (☎ 0181 445 2321)

HARTWELL, Baron (Life Peer UK 1968), of Peterborough Court in the City of London; Sir (William) Michael Berry; 3 Bt (UK 1921), MBE (1945), TD; 2 s of 1 Viscount Camrose (d 1954), and Mary Agnes (d 1962), eldest da of Thomas Corns, of Bolton Street, London W1; suc bro, 2 Viscount Camrose, TD Feb 1995, but disclaimed that title for life March 1995; *b* 18 May 1911; *Educ* Eton, ChCh Oxford (MA); *m* 1936, Lady Pamela Margaret Elizabeth, *née* Smith (d 1982), yr da of 1 Earl of Birkenhead; 2 s (Hon Adrian Michael b 1937, Hon Nicholas William b 1942), 2 da (Hon Harriet Mary Margaret (Hon Mrs Cullen) b 1944, Hon Eleanor Agnes b 1950); *Heir* s, Hon Adrian Michael Berry, *qv* b 1937; *Career* ed Sunday Mail (Glasgow) 1934–35, managing ed Financial Times 1937–39; served WWII, Lt-Col RA (TA), despatches twice; chm Amalgamated Press Ltd 1954–59; chm and ed-in-chief: Daily Telegraph 1954–87,

Sunday Telegraph 1961–87; dir Daily Telegraph plc; tstee Reuters 1963–89; *Books* Party Choice (1948), William Camrose, Giant of Fleet Street (1992); *Clubs* White's, Royal Yacht Sqdn, Beefsteak; *Style*— The Lord Hartwell, MBE, TD; ✉ Oving House, Oving, Aylesbury, Bucks (☎ 01296 641307); 18 Cowley Street, London SW1 (☎ 0171 222 4673); office: 36 Broadway, London SW1 (☎ 0171 222 3833)

HARTY, Bernard Peter; s of William Harty (d 1975), and Eileen Nora, *née* Canavan; *b* 1 May 1943; *Educ* St Richard's Coll Droitwich, Ullathorne GS Coventry; *m* 12 Aug 1965, Glenys Elaine, da of Ernest Simpson (d 1969); 1 da (Sarah Jane b 1970); *Career* accountant Coventry City Cncl 1961–69; forward budget planning offr Derbys CC 1969–72, chief accountant Bradford City Cncl 1972–73, chief fin offr Bradford Met Dist Cncl 1972–73, co treas Oxon County Cncl 1976–83, Chamberlain and Banker Corp of London 1983–95, md Barbican Centre 1995, Town Clerk and Chamberlain Corp of London 1996–; non-exec dir CLF Municipal Bank plc; former chm: Fndn for IT in Local Govt, Superannuation Investment Panel and Treasy Mgmnt Panel Chartered Inst of Public Fin Accountants; Liveryman Worshipful Co of Tallow Chandlers, Hon Liveryman Worshipful Co of Info Technologists; IPFA 1966, MBCS 1983; *Recreations* National Trust, music, cricket; *Style*— Bernard Harty, Esq; ✉ Town Clerk and Chamberlain of London, Guildhall, London EC2P 2EJ (☎ 0171 332 1300, fax 0171 332 1991)

HARVARD TAYLOR, Nicholas; s of Paul Harvard Taylor (d 1980), and Esmée Mary, *née* Biggs (d 1980); *b* 4 Dec 1952; *Educ* Haileybury and Imperial Serv Coll, BA; *m* Tessa Ann Harvard Taylor, JP, *née* Moirs; 2 c (Jack Alfred and Katie Esmée (twins) b 3 Oct 1989); *Career* chm and chief exec offr Harvard Marketing Services 1981– (fndr 1979); chm: Harvard Public Relations Ltd 1982–, Harvard Marketing Services GmbH 1993–, Protech Communications Ltd; memb Parly Info and Technol Ctee; chm of govrs Harmondsworth Sch, memb British Red Cross Soc; Freeman City of London, Liveryman Worshipful Co of Merchant Taylors; MCIM, FRSA; *Recreations* classic cars, avoiding the ignorance of the Arts, tennis, keeping a lawn, favourite outdoor sport is the same as favourite indoor sport but with my coat on; *Clubs* East India, Foxhills County; *Style*— Nicholas Harvard Taylor, Esq; ✉ Kenwolde Manor, Callow Hill, Virginia Water, Surrey UB7 0AW; Harvard Public Relations, Harvard House, Summerhouse Lane, Harmondsworth, West Drayton, Middx UB7 0AW (☎ 0181 759 0005, fax 0181 897 3242, e-mail nick@harvard.co.uk)

HARVEY, Andrew; s of Patrick Harvey, and Margaret Harvey; *b* 26 July 1943; *Educ* Norwich Sch; *m* 1970, Valerie-Ann Collins; 2 da (Jessica, Fleur); *Career* journalist; Eastern Daily Press Norwich 1962–68; picture ed: Evening Standard 1970–77, Daily Express 1977–81 (showbusiness ed 1981–84), The Times 1986–89; ed The Times Saturday Review 1989–93, ed The European Magazine 1995–; *Books* Give My Regards to Broad Street (with Paul McCartney, 1984); *Style*— Andrew Harvey, Esq; ✉ 84 Selwyn Avenue, Richmond, Surrey TW9 2HD (☎ 0181 940 9989, fax 0181 948 8951)

HARVEY, Anthony Peter; s of Frederick William Henry Harvey, of Kettering, Northants, and Fanny Evelyn, *née* Dixon (d 1978); *b* 21 March 1940; *Educ* Hertford GS; *m* 16 Jan 1963, Margaret, da of Walter Henry Hayward, of Hastings, Sussex; 3 s (Terence b 7 Jan 1966, Iain b 7 June 1967, Kevin b 18 March 1972), 1 da (Joanne b 24 Sept 1970); *Career* British Museum (Natural History) now The Natural History Museum: head Dept of Library Servs 1981–88, coordinator of planning and devpt 1985–88, head Dept of Marketing and Devpt 1988–91, dir The Natural History Museum Devpt Tst 1990–91 (sec 1988–91); non-exec dir The Britain-Australia Bicentennial Tst 1986; chm The Broad Oak Consultancy 1992–, dir Bo'ness Devpt Tst 1994–96, treas Soc for History of Natural History; author of numerous papers in professional jls; Freeman City of London 1985, Liveryman Worshipful Co of Marketors 1990–; MInstInfSci, FRHS; *Books* Directory of Scientific Directories (1969, 2 edn 1972, 4 edn 1986), Guide to World Science (1974), Geoscience Information: an international state-of-the-art review (ed 1979), Walford's Guide to Reference Material (ed 1980), Natural History Manuscript Resources in the British Isles (jt ed 1980), European Sources of Scientific and Technical Information (jt ed 1981, 1983, 1984), The Petrology of Archaeological Artifacts (jt ed 1984); *Recreations* books, music, countryside, gardens and gardening, economic and social history of transport; *Style*— Anthony Harvey, Esq; ✉ Ragstones, Broad Oak, Heathfield, E Sussex TN21 8UD (☎ and fax 01435 862012)

HARVEY, Barbara Fitzgerald; da of Richard Henry Harvey (d 1960), of Teignmouth, and Anne Fitzgerald, *née* Julian (d 1974); *b* 21 Jan 1928; *Educ* Teignmouth GS, Bishop Blackall Sch Exeter, Somerville Coll Oxford (BLitt, MA); *Career* asst lectr Dept of Scottish History Univ of Edinburgh 1951–52, lectr Dept of History Queen Mary Coll London 1952–55; Somerville Coll Oxford: tutor in medieval history 1955–93, fell 1956–93 (emeritus fell 1993), vice princ 1976–79 and 1981–83, reader (ad hominem) Oxford Univ 1990–93; memb Royal Cmmn on Historical Manuscripts 1991–; Wolfson Fndn History Prize 1993; FRHistS 1960 (vice pres 1986–90), FBA 1982; *Books* Westminster Abbey and its Estates in the Middle Ages (1977), The Westminster Chronicle 1381–1394 (ed with L C Hector, 1982), Living and Dying in England 1100–1540: The Monastic Experience (1993); *Clubs* University Women's; *Style*— Miss Barbara Harvey; ✉ 66 Cranham Street, Oxford OX2 6DD (☎ 01865 554766); Somerville College, Oxford OX2 6HD (☎ 01865 270600)

HARVEY, Brian; *Career* singer; fndr memb East 17 with Anthony Mortimer, *qv*, John Hendy, *qv*, Terry Coldwell, *qv*; 14 top twenty singles; singles incl: House Of Love 1992, Gold, Slow It Down, Deep 1993, West End Girls 1993, It's Alright 1993, Around the World 1994, Steam 1994, Stay Another Day (UK no 1) 1994, Let It Rain 1995, Hold My Body Tight 1995, Thunder 1995, Do U Still 1996, Someone to Love 1996, Hey Child 1997; albums: Walthamstow (1993, UK no 1, platinum disc), Steam (UK no 4, 1994), Up All Night (UK no 7, 1995); *Style*— Brian Harvey, Esq; ✉ c/o London Records 90 Ltd, PO Box 1422, Chancellor's House, Chancellor's Road, London W6 9RS (☎ 0181 910 5111, fax 0181 741 2600)

HARVEY, Prof Brian Wilberforce; s of Gerald Harvey, and Noelle, *née* Dean; *b* 17 March 1936; *Educ* Clifton, St John's Coll Cambridge (choral scholar, MA, LLM); *Career* admitted slr 1961, lectr Univ of Birmingham 1962–63, sr lectr Nigerian Law Sch 1965–67, lectr, sr lectr then prof of law Queen's Univ of Belfast 1967–73; Univ of Birmingham: prof of property law 1973–, pro vice chllr 1986–92, dir of Legal Office 1990–; chm: Medical and Disability Appeal Tbnls and Social Security Appeals Tbnls Birmingham 1982–, Consumer Credit Appeals 1990–; memb Br Hallmarking Cncl 1989–91, tstee Ouseley Tst 1988–; *Books* Settlements of Land (1973), Law of Consumer Protection and Fair Trading (1978, 5 edn jtly, 1996), Law of Auctions (2 edn jtly, 1995), Law of Producing and Marketing Goods and Services (jtly, 1990), Violin Fraud - Deception, Forgery, Theft and the Law (1992), The Violin Family and its Makers in the British Isles (1995); *Recreations* theological speculation, studying violins, music; *Style*— Prof Brian Harvey; ✉ c/o Faculty of Law, The University, Birmingham B15 2TT (☎ 0121 414 6282)

HARVEY, Caroline; *see:* Trollope, Joanna

HARVEY, Prof (Sir) Charles Richard Musgrave; 3 Bt (UK 1933), of Threadneedle St, City of London; does not use title; s of Sir Richard Musgrave Harvey, 2 Bt (d 1978), and Frances, *née* Lawford (d 1986); *b* 7 April 1937; *Educ* Marlborough, Pembroke Coll Cambridge; *m* 1967, Celia Vivien, da of George Henry Hodson; 1 s, 1 da (Tamara b 1977); *Heir* s, Paul Richard Harvey b 2 June 1971; *Career* professorial fell Inst of Devpt Studies Univ of Sussex; *Style*— Prof Charles Harvey; ✉ IDS, University of Sussex, Brighton BN1 9RE (☎ 01273 606261, fax 01273 621202)

HARVEY, Colin Ivan; *Career* J Sainsbury plc: joined as tradesman 1958, area dir 1983–89, main bd dir 1989–, chm and md Savacentre 1995–; *Style*— Colin Harvey, Esq; ✉ Savacentre, 45–47 Peach Street, Wokingham, Berkshire RG11 1XJ (☎ 0118 977 8000)

HARVEY, Prof David Robert; s of Cyril Francis Harvey (d 1971), of Orpington, Kent, and Margarita, *née* Cardew-Smith (d 1986); *b* 7 Dec 1936; *Educ* Dulwich, Guy's Hosp Med Sch (MB BS); *Career* held jr appointments in paediatrics: Guy's Hosp, Gt Ormond St, Hammersmith Hosp; conslt paediatrician: Queen Charlotte's Maternity Hosp 1970–, St Charles' Hosp 1971–92, St Mary's Hosp 1987–92; prof of paediatrics and neonatal med Royal Postgrad Med Sch Hammersmith Hosp 1993–; hon sec: Neonatal Soc 1974–79, British Paediatric Assoc 1979–84, British Assoc for Perinatal Paediatrics 1983–86; dir: Terence Higgins Tst 1983–88, Radio Lollipop; Freeman of City of London, Liveryman Worshipful Soc of Apothecaries; MRCP 1963, FRCP 1976; *Books* articles on general and neonatal paediatrics and child health, A New Life (1979), New Parents (1988); *Recreations* opera, learning Chinese, using word processor; *Style*— Prof David Harvey; ✉ 2 Lord Napier Place, Upper Mall, London W6 9UB (☎ 0181 748 7900); Queen Charlotte's and Chelsea Hospital, Goldhawk Road, London W6 OXG (☎ 0181 740 3918)

HARVEY, Prof David Roberton; s of Capt John Harvey (d 1983), of New Milton, Hants, and Ann, *née* Dodgson; *b* 24 Oct 1947; *Educ* Berkhamsted Sch, Univ of Newcastle (BSc), Univ of Manchester (MA, PhD); *m* 1 (m dis 1984), Cathryn, *née* Whitehead; 2 s (Daniel b 1975, James b 1977); m 2, 9 April 1985, Joan, da of John Hayward, of Ripon, Yorks; 1 s (John b 1985); *Career* asst lectr Univ of Manchester 1972–73, sr agric economist Agriculture Canada (Ottawa) 1977–79 (agric economist 1973–76); prof: Univ of Reading 1984–86, Univ of Newcastle 1986– (lectr 1979–83, currently head Dept of Agric Economics and Food Mktg); memb Nat Ctee SDP 1983–87; *Books* Costs of The Common Agricultural Policy (1982), The CAP and the World Economy (ed, 1992); *Style*— Prof David Harvey; ✉ Head of Department, Department of Agricultural Economics and Food Marketing, The University, Newcastle upon Tyne NE1 7RU (☎ 0191 222 6872, fax 0191 222 6720, e-mail david.harvey@ncl.ac.uk)

HARVEY, Prof David William; s of Frederick Hercules Harvey, MBE (d 1963), and Doris Maude, *née* Morton (d 1977); *b* 31 Oct 1935; *Educ* Gillingham GS, St John's Coll Cambridge (MA, PhD); *Career* lectr Univ of Bristol 1961–69, prof of geography Johns Hopkins Univ Baltimore 1969–89, Halford Mackinder prof of geography Univ of Oxford 1987–93, sr res fell St Peter's Coll Oxford 1993– (fell 1987–93), prof of geography and environmental engrg GWC Whiting Sch of Engrg Johns Hopkins Univ 1993–; fell Inst of Br Geographers, memb Assoc of American Geographers; Anders Retzius Gold medal Swedish Anthropology and Geography Soc 1989, Gill Meml Royal Geographical Soc 1972, Patron's Medal Royal Georgraphical Soc 1995, Vautrin Lud Int Prize in Geography 1995; *Books* Explanation in Geography (1969), Social Justice and the City (1973), The Limits to Capital (1982), The Urbanisation of Capital (1985), Consciousness & The Urban Experience (1985), The Urban Experience (1989), The Condition of Postmodernity (1989); *Style*— Prof David Harvey; ✉ Department of Geography and Environmental Engineering, Johns Hopkins University, Baltimore, Md 21218, USA (☎ 00 1 410 516 5127, fax 00 1 410 516 8996)

HARVEY, Ian Alexander; s of Dr Alexander Harvey (d 1987), and Mona, *née* Anderson; *b* 2 Feb 1945; *Educ* Cardiff HS, Univ of Cambridge (MA), Harvard Business Sch (MBA); *m* 21 Nov 1976, Dr DeAnne Julius, da of Prof Marvin Julius, of Ames, Iowa, USA; 1 da (Megan b 1979), 1 s (Ross b 1980); *Career* apprentice mech engr Vickers Ltd 1963–69, project engr Laporte Industries 1969–73, sr loan offr World Bank 1975–82, ptnr Logan Associates Inc 1984–85, chief exec BTG plc (formerly British Technology Group plc) 1985–; memb: Cabinet Office Advsy Cncl on Sci and Technol 1989–93, Res and Mfrg Ctee CBI 1986–92, Sci and Industl Ctee BAAS, Advsy Bd Science Policy Res Unit Univ of Sussex 1988–; fell Univ of Nottingham 1994; CIMgt 1987; *Recreations* piano, skiing, sailing, windsurfing; *Style*— Ian Harvey; ✉ BTG plc, 101 Newington Causeway, London SE1 6BU (☎ 0171 458 3193, fax 0171 403 7586, telex 894397, e-mail harveyi@BTGplc.com)

HARVEY, Jake; *b* 3 June 1948; *Educ* Edinburgh Coll of Art (DA); *Career* sculptor; memb: Scottish Soc of Artists 1975, Fedn of Scottish Sculptors 1983; tstee Scottish Scupture Tst 1984–87; RSA 1989 (ARSA 1977); *Solo Exhibitions* incl: NORTH (Pier Arts Centre, Stromness Artspace and Peacock Printmakers Aberdeen) 1993, Scottish Gallery Edinburgh 1993, Retrospective (Talbot Rice Gallery Univ of Edinburgh) 1993, Recent Works (Christopher Boyd Gallery Galashiels) 1994; *Group Exhibitions* incl: RSA Award Winners (Artspace Aberdeen) 1980, Built in Scotland (Third Eye Centre, City Arts Centre Edinburgh and Camden Arts Centre London) 1983, Putting Sculpture on the Map (Talbot Rice Art Centre) 1984, Dublin/Ediburgh (Edinburgh Coll of Art) 1985, Works on Paper (RSA Edinburgh) 1990, Scottish Art in the 20th Century (Royal W of England Acad Bristol) 1990, Scottish Scupture Open (Kildrummy Castle Aberdeen) 1991, Virtue and Vision Festival Exhbn (Nat Gallery of Scotland) 1991, William Gillies Bursary Exhbn (RSA) 1992, A Collection of Self-Portraits (Pier Art Centre Stromness) 1994, The Art of the Garden (Greywalls, Scottish Gallery) 1994, Scandex (Aberdeen Art Gallery and Norway, Sweden and Finland) 1995, Jake Harvey Sculpture (Alkwood Tower Selkirk) 1995, A Battle for Hearts and Minds (Robson Gallery Selkirk) 1995; *Major Commissions* incl: Hugh McDiarmid Memorial Langholmn 1985, Charles Mackintosh Scupture Glasgow 1985, Compaq Computers Glasgow 1988, Poacher's Tree (Maclay Murray & Spens Edinburgh) 1991, Tools for the Shaman (Hunterian Museum Glasgow) 1996; *Public Collections* Scottish Arts Cncl, Edinburgh Museums and Galleries, Univ of Edinburgh, Contemporary Art Soc, Borders Educn Authy, Kelvingrove Museum Glasgow, Aberdeen Art Gallery, Motherwell Dist Cncl; *Awards* incl: Helen Rose Bequest 1971, Latimer award RSA 1975, Benno Schotz Sculpture prize RSA 1976, William Gillies bursary 1989; *Style*— Jake Harvey, Esq, RSA; ✉ c/o The Royal Scottish Academy, The Mound, Edinburgh EH1

HARVEY, Jean; da of Lt W J Harvey, DSM (d 1983), of Harrow, Middx, and Amy, *née* Benfield (d 1979); *b* 19 Sept 1936; *Career* Sunday Times 1963–69, fndr Jean Harvey Group 1969 (publishing, PR, fundraising, entertainment), publicity dir Methodist Homes for the Aged; MIPR 1988, MICFM 1990, MCIM 1994; *Books* Jean Harvey's Bedside Book (1986); *Videos* Charity Fundraising (1989 and 1990), Life in the Nineties (1994), A Mind to Care (1995); *Recreations* photography, antiquarian book collecting; *Clubs* Groucho, University Women of America; *Style*— Ms Jean Harvey; ✉ Primrose Cottage, Hunters Hill, Alkmonton, Derbyshire DE6 3DL (☎ 01335 330094, fax 01332 296925)

HARVEY, Prof Jonathan Dean; s of Gerald Harvey, and Noelle Heron, *née* Dean (d 1969); *b* 3 May 1939; *Educ* St Michael's Coll Tenbury, Repton, St John's Coll Cambridge (MA, DMus), Univ of Glasgow (PhD); *m* 24 Sept 1960, Rosaleen Marie, da of Daniel Barry (d 1949); 1 da (Anna Maria b 13 Jan 1964), 1 s (Dominic b 3 May 1967); *Career* composer; lectr Univ of Southampton 1964–77, Harkness fell Princeton Univ 1969–70; prof of music: Univ of Sussex 1980– (reader 1977–80), Univ of Stanford 1995–; works performed at many festivals and int centres; compositions: Persephone Dream (for orchestra, 1972), Inner Light (trilogy for performers and tape, 1973–77), Smiling Immortal (for chamber orchestra, 1977), String Quartet (1977), Veils and Melodies (for tapes, 1978), Magnificat and Nunc Dimitis (for choir and organ, 1978), Album (for wind quintet, 1978), Hymn (for choir and orchestra, 1979), Be(com)ing (for clarinet and piano, 1979), Concelebration (instrumental, 1979 and 1981), Mortuos Plango Vivos Voco (for tape, 1980), Passion and Resurrection (church opera, 1981), Resurrection (for double chorus and organ, 1981), Whom ye Adore (for orchestra, 1981), Bhakti (for 15 instruments and tape, 1982), Easter Orisons (for chamber orchestra, 1983), The Path of Devotion (for choir and orchestra, 1983), Nachtlied (for soprano piano and tape, 1984), Gong-Ring (for ensemble with electronics 1984), Song Offerings (for soprano and players, 1985), Madonna of Winter and Spring (for orchestra, synthesizers and electronics, 1986), Lightness and Weight (for tuba and orchestra, 1986), Forms of Emptiness (for choir, 1986), Tendril (for ensemble, 1987), Timepieces (for orchestra, 1987), From Silence (for soprano, six instruments and tape, 1988), Valley of Aosta (for 13 players 1988), String Quartet No 2 (1989), Ritual Melodies (for tape, 1990), Cello Concerto (for cello and orchestra, 1990), Serenade in Homage to Mozart (for wind ensemble, 1991), Fantasia (for organ, 1991), Inquest of Love (opera, 1992), Lotuses (for flute quartet, 1992), Scena (for violin and ensemble, 1992), One Evening (for voices, instruments and electronics, 1993), Advaya (for cello, keyboard and electronics, 1994), String Quartet No 3 (1995), Percussion Concerto (1996); memb Music Advsy Panel: Br Cncl 1992–95, Arts Cncl 1995–; memb Academia Europaea 1989; Hon DMus: Univ of Southampton 1990, Univ of Bristol 1994; Britten Award for Composition 1993; FRCM 1994; *Books* The Music of Stockhausen (1975); *Recreations* tennis, meditation; *Style*— Prof Jonathan Harvey; ✉ c/o Faber Music, 3 Queen Square, London WC1N 3AU

HARVEY, Jonathan Paul; s of Brian Harvey, of Liverpool, and Maureen, *née* Pratt; *b* 13 June 1968; *Educ* Blue Coat Sch Liverpool, Univ of Hull (BSc); *Partner* Richard Foord; *Career* writer; special needs teacher Abbey Wood Comp London 1990–93, writer in res Bush Theatre 1993–94; patron: London Lighthouse, The Food Chain, It's Queer Up North; *Awards* National Girobank/Liverpool Playhouse Young Writer of the Year 1987, Royal Court/Rank Xerox Young Writers Award 1988, George Devine Award for Babies 1993, Thames TV Bursary Award 1993, John Whiting Award for Beautiful Thing 1994, Evening Standard Most Promising Playwright for Babies 1994, London Lesbian & Gay Film Festival Best Film for Beautiful Thing 1996, Norway Film Festival Audience Award for Beautiful Thing 1996, Mike Rhodes Award for furthering the understanding of lesbian and gay life 1996; *Plays* The Cherry Blossom Tree (1987), Mohair (1988), Tripping and Falling (1989), Catch (1990), Lady Snogs The Blues (1991), Wildfire (1992), Babies (1993), Beautiful Thing (1993, released as film 1996), Boom Bang A Bang (1995), Rupert Street Lonely Hearts Club (1995); *Television* Going Underground (1993); *Recreations* clubbing, East Enders, reading; *Clubs* Trade, The Fridge, Heaven; *Style*— Jonathan Harvey, Esq; ✉ c/o Alan Radcliffe, William Morris Agency (UK) Ltd, 31–32 Soho Square, London W1V 6HH (☎ 0171 434 2191, fax 0171 437 0238)

HARVEY, Michael Anthony; s of Edgar Charles Harvey (d 1975), of Dorking, Surrey, and Evelyn May, *née* Klein (d 1976); *b* 22 Aug 1921; *Educ* Bryanston, Selly Oak Coll Woodbrooke Birmingham, Wimbledon Sch of Art (Intermediate Exam in Art and Crafts, Nat Dip in Design); *m* 30 Oct 1965 (m dis 1973), (Anne) Jennifer; 1 s (Anthony b 1966); *Career* Friends' Ambulance Unit 1940–42, Fishing Fleet 1942–43, MN 1943–55, awarded Africa Star 1945; artist; teacher: Royal Alexandra and Albert Schs Reigate 1957–59, Ewell Castle Sch Surrey 1959–64, Tollington Park Sch N1 1965–69, Court Lodge Sch Horley 1970–76; exhibited paintings: Qantas Gallery W1 1964, Royal Acad 1965, Fine Arts Gallery W1 1967, John Whibley Gallery W1 1969–70, Rutland Gallery W1 1970–71, Royal Inst of Oil Painters, Royal Soc of Br Artists, Royal Inst of Oil Painters Aust 1977, Silver Longboat Exhibition Portsmouth and Oslo 1988 and 1990, Eschweiler Germany 1984 and 1991, Chichester Centre of Arts 1993, Dortmund Germany 1996; Linton Prize for Painting 1972; art critic Surrey Mirror Group of Newspapers 1973–80, art corr Croydon Advertiser Group 1975–78; life memb Int Assoc of Art 1970, hon memb Bognor Art Soc; memb: Chichester Art Soc, Reigate Soc of Artists, Soc of Graphic Fine Art; FRSA; *Recreations* sailing; *Clubs* Royal Soc of Arts; *Style*— Michael A Harvey, Esq; ✉ 15 Waterloo Square, Bognor Regis, W Sussex (☎ 01243 863732)

HARVEY, Michael Llewellyn Tucker; QC (1982); s of Rev Victor Llewellyn Tucker Harvey, of Suffolk, and Pauline, *née* Wybrow; *b* 22 May 1943; *Educ* St John's Sch Leatherhead, Christ's Coll Cambridge (BA, LLB, MA); *m* 2 Sept 1972, Denise Madeleine, da of Leonard Walter Neary, of London; 1 s (Julian b 19 June 1976), 1 da (Alexandra b 30 June 1973); *Career* called to the Bar Gray's Inn 1966, recorder 1986, bencher 1991; memb Review Bd Cncl of Legal Educn 1993–94, additional memb Bar Cncl 1994–; *Books* Damages (jtly, in Halsbury's Laws of England 4 edn, 1975); *Recreations* shooting, golf; *Clubs* Athenaeum, Hawks (Cambridge); *Style*— Michael Harvey, Esq, QC; ✉ 2 Crown Office Row, Temple, London EC4Y 7HJ (☎ 0171 797 8100, fax 0171 797 8101)

HARVEY, Nicholas (Nick); MP (Lib Dem) North Devon (majority 794); s of Frederick Harvey, and Christine Harvey; *b* 3 Aug 1961; *Educ* Queen's Coll Taunton, Middx Poly; *Career* pres Middx Poly Students' Union 1981–82, nat vice chm Union of Liberal Students 1981–82, communications and marketing exec Profile PR Ltd 1984–86, Dewe Rogerson Ltd 1986–91, communications conslt 1991–92; Parly candidate (Alliance) Enfield Southgate 1987, MP (Lib Dem) N Devon 1992–; Lib Dem spokesman: on tport 1992–94, on trade and indust 1994–; chair of campaigns and communications 1994–; *Recreations* travel, football, walking, music; *Clubs* National Liberal; *Style*— Nick Harvey, Esq, MP; ✉ House of Commons, London SW1A 0AA

HARVEY, Prof Paul Dean Adshead; s of John Dean Monroe Harvey (d 1978), and Gwendolen Mabel Darlington, *née* Adshead; *b* 7 May 1930; *Educ* Bishop Feild Coll St John's Newfoundland, Warwick Sch, St John's Coll Oxford (MA, DPhil); *m* 6 July 1968, Yvonne, da of Howard Leonard Crossman (d 1965); *Career* asst archivist Warwick Co Record Off 1954–56, asst keeper Dept of Manuscripts Br Museum 1957–66, sr lectr Dept of History Univ of Southampton 1970–78 (lectr 1966–70), prof of medieval history Univ of Durham 1978–85 (emeritus prof 1985); gen ed: Southampton Records Series 1966–78, Portsmouth Record Series 1969–; vice pres Surtees Soc 1978, memb Advsy Cncl on Public Records 1984–89, chm Br Records Assoc 1995–; hon fell Portsmouth Poly 1987; FRHistS 1961, FSA 1963; *Books* The Printed Maps of Warwickshire 1576–1900 (with H Thorpe 1959), A Medieval Oxfordshire Village: Cuxham 1240–1400 (1965), Manorial Records of Cuxham Oxfordshire 1200–1359 (ed, 1976), The History of Topographical Maps (1980), The Peasant Land Market in England (ed, 1984), Manorial Records (1984), Local Maps and Plans from Medieval England (ed with R A Skelton, 1986), Medieval Maps (1991), Maps in Tudor England (1993), Guide to British Medieval Seals (with A McGuinness, 1996); contrib to: Victoria History of Oxfordshire Vol 10 (1972), History of Cartography Vol 1 (1987), Agrarian History of England and Wales Vol 3 (1991), Agricultural History Review, Economic History Review, English Historical Review, Past and Present; *Recreations* Br topography; *Clubs* Athenaeum; *Style*— Prof P D A Harvey, FSA; ✉ Lyndhurst, Farnley Hey Road, Durham DH1 4EA (☎ 0191 386 9396)

HARVEY, Prof Paul H; s of Edward Walter Harvey, of Kidderminster, Worcs, and Eileen Joan, *née* Pagett; *b* 19 Jan 1947; *Educ* Queen Elizabeth GS Hartebury Worcs, Univ of York (BA, DPhil), Univ of Oxford (MA, DSc); *m* 12 April 1969, Anna Margaret, da of John Lawrence Kirkby; 2 s (Joseph Edward b 2 April 1980, Benjamin Mark b 18 March 1982); *Career* lectr in biology Univ of Wales Swansea 1971–73, reader in biology Univ of Sussex 1984–85 (lectr 1973–84); Univ of Oxford: lectr in zoology 1985–89, fell and tutor in biology Merton Coll 1985–96, reader in biology 1989–96, professorial fell Jesus Coll 1996–, estab prof in zoology 1996–; visiting lectr Harvard Univ 1978–79; visiting prof: Harvard Univ 1980, Univ of Washington Seattle 1982, Princeton Univ 1984–85, Imperial Coll London 1995–; Scientific medal Zoological Soc 1986; FRS 1992; *Books* The Comparative Method in Evolutionary Biology (with M D Pagel, 1991); *Style*— Prof Paul H Harvey, FRS; ✉ Hall Place, Sparsholt, Oxon OX12 9PL (☎ 01235 751491); University of Oxford, Department of Zoology, South Parks Road, Oxford OX1 3PS (☎ 01865 271260, fax 01865 271249)

HARVEY, Peter; CB (1980); s of George Leonard Hunton Harvey (d 1948), and Helen Mary, *née* Williams (d 1973); *b* 23 April 1922; *Educ* King Edward VI HS Birmingham, St John's Coll Oxford (MA, BCL); *m* 1950, Mary Vivienne, da of John Osborne Goss (d 1971); 1 s (Roderick), 1 da (Vivienne); *Career* RAF 1942–45; called to the Bar Lincoln's Inn 1948, legal asst Home Office 1948, princ asst legal advsr Home Office 1971–77, legal advsr Dept of Educn and Sci 1977–83, conslt Legal Advsr's Branch Home Office 1983–86, asst counsel to the Speaker House of Commons 1986–94, conslt Slr's Office Dept of Trade and Indust 1994–96; memb Legal Affrs Ctee Inst for Citizenship Studies 1992–95; *Publications*contrib to 3 and 4 edns of Halsbury's Laws of England; *Recreations* walking, history, genealogy; *Style*— Peter Harvey, Esq, CB; ✉ Mannamead, Old Ave, Weybridge, Surrey KT13 0PS (☎ 01932 845133)

HARVEY, Peter Derek Charles; s of Norman Charles Harvey (d 1991), and Sheila June, *née* Curtis, of Stanmore, Middx; *b* 21 Dec 1958; *Educ* Haberdashers' Aske's Sch Elstree, Magdalen Coll Oxford, Guildhall Sch of Music and Drama (BP opera scholarship, Schubert Lieder prize); *m* 25 May 1985, Jean Patricia, da of John Hamilton Paterson; 2 s (William b 9 Oct 1987, Patrick b 2 May 1989); *Career* baritone; regularly appears as soloist with ensembles and choirs incl: Monteverdi Choir, London Baroque, Gabrieli Consort, Purcell Quartet, The Sixteen, The Hanover Band, Orch of the Age of Enlightenment, Yorkshire Bach Choir, La Chapelle Royale (Paris), Le Concert Spirituel (Paris), Il Seminario Musicale (Paris), Thomanerchor (Leipzig), L'ensemble Vocal de Lausanne, Collegium Vocale (Ghent), Gulbenkian Choir and Orch (Lisbon), various symphony orchs and cathedral choirs; numerous appearances in UK and Europe, also Japan, Israel and N America; *Recordings* over thirty incl: Bach St John Passion and Cantata No 21, C P E Bach Die Auferstehung, various Purcell works incl Dido and Aeneas and Hail Bright Cecilia, Fauré Requiem, Slook in Rossini opera La Cambiale di matrimonio, Charles Wood St Mark Passion, Janacek Mass, Puccini sacred duet Vexilla Regis, Henri Pousseur Traverser la forêt, numerous works by Charpentier, Lully, Du Mont, Campra, Gilles, Rameau and Blanchard; other baroque music recordings incl: Zelenka Lamentations, Teixeira Te Deum, Boismortier Motets, 17th Century Venetian ceremonial music, Galuppi Confitebor tibi Domine; *Recreations* not being on tour, attempting foreign languages when on tour, making and fixing things; *Style*— Peter Harvey, Esq; ✉ c/o Magenta Music International, 4 Highgate High Street, Highgate Village, London N6 5JL (☎ 0181 340 8321, fax 0181 340 7823)

HARVEY, Dr Peter Kenneth Philip; s of Philip and Leah Harvey, of London; *b* 22 Jan 1942; *Educ* Emanuel Sch Wandsworth, Gonville and Caius Coll Cambridge (MA, MB BChir, FRCP); *m* 5 June 1971, Lesley MacGregor, da of late George Henderson; 2 s (Alan b 24 May 1978, Johnny b 26 July 1980), 1 da (Zehra b 4 March 1984); *Career* successively: pre-registration posts Middx Hosp Mortimer St and Queen Elizabeth II Hosp Welwyn Garden City, post-registration house posts Middx, Brompton and Nat Heart Hosps, further studies Imperial Coll London, neurological trg Middx Hosp and Nat Hosp for Nervous Diseases Queen Square; currently conslt neurologist: Royal Free Hampstead NHS Tst (med dir 1991–93, chm Med Advsy Ctee 1991–94), Chase Farm Hosp NHS Tst Enfield; author of articles on neurological topics incl epilepsy in various learned jls; memb: BMA, RSM (memb Section Cncl 1980–90, hon sec for overseas affrs 1985–90); *Clubs* Savile; *Style*— Dr Peter Harvey; ✉ 134 Harley Street, London W1N 1AH (☎ 0171 486 8005, fax 0171 224 3905); Royal Free Hospital NHS Trust, Pond Street, London NW3 2QG (☎ 0171 794 0500)

HARVEY, Thomas Christopher (Tom); s of Wing Cdr Derek Leslie Harvey, RAF (ret), of Ringwood, Hants, and Peggy Eileen, *née* Aldis; *b* 7 Dec 1953; *Educ* Hurstpierpoint Coll Hassocks Sussex, Brasenose Coll Oxford (MA); *m* 9 Sept 1978, Amanda Julie, da of Capt J H H Mills, MBE; 1 da (Katie b 26 Sept 1981), 1 s (David b 18 Jan 1984); *Career* Barclays Bank Ltd 1976–78, Burroughs Machines Ltd 1978–79, Guinness Overseas Ltd 1979–82, account dir McCormick International 1982–84, bd dir D'Arcy Masius Benton and Bowles 1984–91, business devpt dir Butterfield Day Devito Hockney 1992–95, client servs dir WCT Live Communication (formerly World Conference Travel event mgmnt co) 1995–; MIPA; *Recreations* squash, classic cars; *Clubs* RAC; *Style*— Tom Harvey, Esq; ✉ World Conference Travel, 4 Buckingham Gate, London SW1E 6JP (☎ 0171 393 4950)

HARVEY, Maj Thomas Cockayne; CVO (1951), DSO (1944), ERD; s of Col John Harvey, DSO, whose mother, Rosa, was 6 da of Adm Hon Keith Stewart, CB (2 s of 8 Earl of Galloway), by Mary Fitzroy (paternally ggda of 3 Duke of Grafton and maternally gda of 4 Duke of Richmond); *b* 22 Aug 1918; *Educ* Radley, Balliol Coll Oxford; *m* 1940, Lady Mary Katherine Coke (d 1993), da of 4 Earl of Leicester (d 1949); 1 s (David Vincent b 1941), 2 da (Caroline Susan (Mrs Raison) b 1943, Juliet Mary Elizabeth (Mrs Juliet Hambro) b 1947); *Career* joined Scots Gds 1938, serv Norway 1940, Italy 1944; private sec to HM The Queen 1946–51; extra gentleman usher: to HM King George VI 1951–52, to HM The Queen 1952–; regnl dir Lloyds Bank 1980–85; capt The Royal and Ancient Golf Club of St Andrews 1976–77; *Recreations* golf, shooting; *Clubs* White's, Beefsteak; *Style*— Maj Thomas Harvey, CVO, DSO, ERD; ✉ Warham House, Warham, Wells-next-the-Sea, Norfolk (☎ 01328 710 457)

HARVEY, William Graeme; s of Jack William Harvey, and Grace, *née* Wilson; *b* 15 Jan 1947; *Educ* Simon Langton GS, Univ Coll Oxford (MA); *m* 1970 (m dis 1989), Pamela Joy, *née* Garnham; 1 s (Thomas Edward b 1971), 2 da (Amy Louise b 1974, Charlotte Luscia b 1977); *partner* Pauline Maria Hayes; *Career* British Council: asst rep Dar Es Salaam 1970–74, asst rep Jakarta 1974–76, asst Personnel Dept 1976–80, asst rep Madras 1980–83, dep dir Educnl Contracts Dept 1983–86, rep Bangladesh 1986–90, gen mangr Tech Cooperation Trg 1990–93, regnl dir Eastern Africa and dir Kenya 1993–; memb Br Ornithologists' Union 1973; *Books* Birds in Bangladesh (1990); *Recreations* bird watching, conservation, poetry, pop music and Coronation Street; *Clubs* Madras (India), Aberdares (Kenya); *Style*— William Harvey, Esq; ✉ The British Council, ICEA Building, Kenyatta Avenue, PO Box 40751, Nairobi, Kenya

HARVEY-JAMIESON, Rodger Ridout; TD (1982); s of Lt Col Harvey Morro Harvey-Jamieson, OBE, TD, of Edinburgh, and Maude Frances Wilmot, *née* Ridout; *b* 30 June 1947; *Educ* Edinburgh Acad, Univ of Edinburgh (LLB, MBA); *m* 9 Oct 1971, Alison Mary, da of Edward Whitworth, OBE (d 1968); 1 s (Edmund b 1975), 1 da (Susannah b 1973); *Career* 2 Lt RA TA 1970, Maj RARO 1989; slr; ptnr Messrs Murray Beith Murray WS 1973–; dir The Fruit Market Gallery; tstee The Seagull Tst (free canal cruising for disabled people), cdre Loch Earn Sailing Club; memb Queen's Body Guard for Scotland (Royal Co of Archers) 1978; FRSA; *Books* Dean Terrace - An Historical Sketch (1975); *Recreations* sailing, scuba diving, archery; *Clubs* New (Edinburgh); *Style*— Rodger Harvey-Jamieson, Esq, TD, WS; ✉ 19 Dean Terrace, Edinburgh EH4 1NL (☎ 0131 332 2933); Messrs Murray Beith Murray, 39 Castle St, Edinburgh EH2 3BH (☎ 0131 225 1200, fax 0131 225 9212)

HARVEY-JONES, Sir John Henry; kt (1985), MBE (1952); s of Mervyn Harvey-Jones, OBE, and Eileen Harvey-Jones; *b* 16 April 1924; *Educ* Tormore Sch Deal, RNC Dartmouth; *m* 1947, Mary Evelyn Atcheson, da of E F Bignell, and Mrs E Atcheson; 1 da; *Career* served RN 1937–56, submarines and naval intelligence, qualifying as German and Russian interpreter, resigned with rank of Lt Cdr; ICI: joined as work study offr 1956, dir 1973–87, dep chm 1978–82, chm 1982–87 (dep chm Heavy Organic Chemicals Div 1968, chm ICI Petrochemicals Div 1970–73); Hon LLD: Manchester 1985, Liverpool

1986, London 1987, Cambridge 1987; Hon DUniv Surrey 1985; Hon DSc: Bradford 1986, Leicester 1986, Keele 1989, Exeter 1989; Hon DCL Newcastle 1988, Hon DBA (Int Mgmnt Centres) 1990, Hon DTech Loughborough 1991, hon degree Open Univ 1996; hon fell Poly of Wales; Sr Ind Fellowship Leicester Poly 1990, hon memb City & Guilds of London Inst 1988, fell Smallpiece Tst 1988; hon fell: Royal Soc of Chemistry 1985, The Inst of Chemical Engrs 1985; memb Soc of Chemical Indust 1978; Cdr's Cross Order of Merit FRG; *Awards* BIM Gold Medal 1985, Soc of Chemical Indust Centenary Medal 1986, Jo Hambro Br Businessman of the Year 1986, Int Assoc of Business Communicators Award of Excellence in Communication 1987, Radar Man of the Year 1987, Pipesmoker of the Year 1991, City & Guilds Insignia Award in Technol (hc); *Current Appointments* chm Parallax Enterprises Ltd 1987–; vice pres Hearing and Speech Tst 1985–, vice pres Heaton Woods Tst 1986–, memb Royal Soc of Arts 1979– (vice pres 1988–92), memb Advsy Cncl Prince's Youth Business Tst 1986–; hon conslt: Royal Utd Servs Inst for Defence Studies 1987–, Steer Orgn; vice patron Br Polio Fellowship 1988–, hon pres Univ of Bradford MBA Alumni Assoc 1989–, vice pres Industl Participation Assoc 1983–, hon pres Friends of Brecon Jazz 1989–, patron Nat Canine Defence League 1990–, vice pres Tyne & Wear Fndn; *Previous Appointments* memb Tees and Hartlepool Port Authy 1970–73, chm Phillips-Imperial Petroleum 1973–75, dir ICI Americas Inc 1975–76, dir Fiber Industries Inc 1975–78, dir Grand Metroploitan 1983–94; chm: Didactacus Video Productions Ltd 1989–95, The Economist 1989–94, ProShare UK Ltd 1992–94; dep chm GPA Ltd 1989–93 (dir 1987–93); chm: Cncl Wildfowl Tst 1987–95 (now memb Cncl and vice pres), Book Tst Appeal Fund 1987–93; vice pres Conseil European des Fédérations de L'Industrie Chimique (CEFIC) 1982–84, memb President's Ctee CBI 1982–87 (pres 1984–86), vice chm Policy Studies Inst 1980–85, hon vice pres Inst of Mktg 1982–89, memb Bd Welsth Devpt Int 1989–93; non-exec dir: Reed International Plc 1975–84, Carrington Viyella Ltd 1974–79 (dir 1981–82); memb NEDO Ctee for the Chemical Indust 1980–82, memb Cncl Chemical Industries' Association Ltd 1980–82, memb NE Devpt Bd 1971–73, memb Ct Br Shippers' Cncl 1982–87, memb Cncl Br Malaysian Soc 1983–87, memb Fndn Bd Int Mgmnt Inst Geneva 1984–87, memb Cncl Youth Enterprise Scheme 1984–86, tstee the Conf Bd 1984–86, memb Int Cncl Euro Inst of Business Admin 1984–87, tstee Sci Museum 1983–87, vice chm Great Ormond Street Redevelopment Appeal, patron Halton Chemical Indust Museum Appeal 1986; non-exec dir: Nimbus Records April-July 1987, Burns Anderson 1987–91 (chm 1987–90), Police Fndn 1983–91 (chm of tstees 1984–88); vice pres Newnham Coll Appeal 1987, memb Ct of Govrs Kidney Res Unit for Wales Fndn 1989–90, govr ESU 1987–91, chm Cncl St James's and The Abbey Sch Malvern 1987–93; patron: Cambridge Univ Young Entrepreneurs Soc 1987–91, Manpower Servs Cmmn Nat Trg Awards 1987; chllr Bradford Univ 1986–91; non-exec chm: Business Int Bd Ctee 1988–91, Trendroute Ltd 1988–91, Wider Share Ownership Cncl 1988–92; vice chm BIM 1980–85; *Television Series* Troubleshooter 1990 and 1992, Troubleshooter Specials - Eastern Europe 1991, Troubleshooter Returns 1995; *Publications* Making it Happen, Reflections on Leadership (1987), Troubleshooter (1990), Getting it Together (1991), Troubleshooter 2 (1992), Managing to Survive, A Guide to Management Through the '90s (1993), All Together Now (1994), Troubleshooter Returns (1995); *Recreations* swimming, the countryside, cooking, contemporary literature; *Clubs* Athenaeum, Groucho's; *Style*— Sir John Harvey-Jones, MBE; ✉ c/o PO Box 18, Ross-on-Wye, Herefordshire HR9 7PH (☎ 01989 567171, fax 01989 567173)

HARVEY-KELLY, (Hugh) Denis; s of Lt-Col Charles Hamilton Grant Harvey-Kelly, DSO (d 1982), of Clonhugh, Mullingar, and Sybil Mary, *née* Nuttall (d 1980); paternal (Kelly) lineage listed in Burke's Irish Family Records; *b* 5 March 1932; *Educ* Wellington, RMA Sandhurst; *m* 20 June 1964, Jennifer Rosemary, da of John Elton-Phillips (d 1943); 1 da (Sarah b 1971); *Career* Capt 8KRI Hussars Germany and Aden 1949–57; Vickers da Costa Stockbrokers London 1958–84, Dudgeon & Sons Stockbrokers Dublin; dir: Investment Bank of Ireland 1968–85, Marlborough Productions plc 1985–87; chm: Ovidstown Bloodstock 1984–93, Dolormore plc 1985–87, BCP Group; master of foxhounds Westmeath Hunt 1979–83; *Recreations* hunting, shooting, fishing, painting; *Clubs* Kildare St and University; *Style*— Denis Harvey-Kelly, Esq; ✉ Corby House, Long Street, Sherborne, Dorset DT9 3DD (☎ 01935 817571, fax 01935 817572); 3 Sloane Square House, London SW1W 8NS (☎ 0171 730 6090, fax 0171 730 1025)

HARVEY OF TASBURGH, 2 Baron (UK 1954); Sir Peter Charles Oliver Harvey; 5 Bt (UK 1868); s of 1 Baron, GCMG, GCVO, CB, (HM Ambass to France 1948–54, d 1968), and Maud, da of Arthur Williams-Wynn (gn of Sir Watkin Williams-Wynn, 4 Bt); *b* 28 Jan 1921; *Educ* Eton, Trinity Coll Cambridge; *m* 1957, Penelope (d 1995), yr da of Lt-Col Sir William Makins, 3 Bt; 2 da (Hon Juliet (Hon Mrs Lee) b 1958, Hon Miranda b 1960); *Heir* nephew, Charles John Giuseppe Harvey b 1951; *Career* served WWII RA N Africa and Italy; investmt conslt Brown Shipley and Co 1978–81; formerly with: Bank of England, Binder Hamlyn & Co, Lloyds Bank International Ltd, English Transcontinental Ltd; FCA, AIIMR; *Clubs* Brooks's; *Style*— The Rt Hon the Lord Harvey of Tasburgh; ✉ Crownick Woods, Restronguet, Mylor, Falmouth, Cornwall TR11 5ST

HARVEY WOOD, (Elizabeth) Harriet; OBE (1993); da of Henry Harvey Wood, OBE, FRSE (d 1977), and Lily, *née* Terry; *b* 1 Oct 1934; *Educ* Cranley Sch for Girls, Univ of Edinburgh (MA, PhD); *Career* mangr Philomusica of London Orchestra 1959–66, sec Faculty of Music KCL 1966–68, head Literature Dept British Cncl 1980–94 (joined Br Cncl 1973); dir The Harvill Press; memb: Wingate Scholarship Ctee 1992–, Panel of Judges Booker Prize for Fiction 1992, Bibliographical Soc 1970–94, English PEN 1985– (memb Exec Ctee 1994–); *Books* James Watson's Choice Collection of Comic and Serious Scots Poems Vol I (1977), Vol II (1991), The Percy Letters: The Correspondence of Thomas Percy and John Pinkerton (1985); *Recreations* reading, music, gardening; *Clubs* United Oxford and Cambridge University; *Style*— Miss Harriet Harvey Wood, OBE; ✉ 158 Coleherne Court, Old Brompton Road, London SW5 0DX (☎ and fax 0171 373 2113)

HARVIE-WATT, Sir James; 2 Bt (UK 1945), of Bathgate, Co Linlithgow; er s of Sir George Steven Harvie-Watt, 1 Bt, TD, QC (d 1989), and Jane, *née* Taylor; *b* 25 Aug 1940; *Educ* Eton, ChCh Oxford (MA); *m* 28 May 1966, Roseline Gladys Virginia, da of Baron Louis de Chollet (d 1972), of Fribourg, Switzerland; 1 s (Mark Louis b 19 Aug 1969), 1 da (Isabelle Frances (m 1995, Nobile Carlo dei Marchesi Clavarino) b 19 March 1967); *Heir* s, Mark Louis Harvie-Watt b 19 Aug 1969; *Career* Lt London Scottish (TA) 1959–67; with Coopers and Lybrand 1962–70, exec Br Electric Traction Co Ltd and dir of subsid cos 1970–78, md Wembley Stadium Ltd 1973–78; memb: Exec Ctee London Tourist Bd 1977–80, Sports Cncl 1980–88 (vice chm 1985–88); chm Crystal Palace Nat Sports Centre 1984–88, dir Lake & Elliot Industries Ltd 1988–93; chm: Cannons Sports & Leisure Ltd 1990–93, A H Ball Group plc 1995–; dir Penna Holdings plc 1995–; memb of Mgmnt Ctee: The Nat Coaching Fndn 1984–88, The Nat Water Sports Centre Holme Pierrepont 1985–88; memb: Sports Cncl Enquiries into Financing of Athletics in UK 1983, Karate 1986, Cncl NPFA 1985–90; OStJ 1964 (memb London Cncl of the Order 1975–84); FCA 1975 (ACA 1965), FRSA 1978; *Recreations* tennis, golf, shooting, photography, philately; *Clubs* White's, Pratt's, Sunningdale, Queen's (vice chm 1987–90, chm 1990–93, dir 1987–), Swinley Forest; *Style*— Sir James Harvie-Watt, Bt; ✉ 15 Somerset Sq, London W14 8EE (☎ 0171 602 6944)

HARWOOD, Giles Francis; yr s of Basil Antony Harwood, QC (Senior Master Supreme Ct Queen's Bench Div and Queen's Remembrancer, d 1990), and Enid Arundel, *née* Grove (d 1990); *b* 31 Jan 1934; *Educ* Douai Sch, ChCh Oxford (MA); *m* 1, 5 Jan 1963 (m dis 1979), Ursula Mary, da of Norman Humphrey, OBE (d 1965), of Exeter; 3 s (Francis, Dominic, Nicholas), 2 da (Monica, Bridget); m 2, 31 March 1983, Diana Mary, da of Maj Gerald Cuthbert Galahad Roe (d 1957), of Birkdale; *Career* Nat Serv 2 Lt RA 1956–58, Asst Adj/BHQ Troop Cdr Sch of Anti-Aircraft Artillery and Guided Weapons Manorbier; (TA) HAC G Battery 1959–66, Veteran Co 1966–88; called to the Bar Inner Temple 1956; practised London and Western Circuit 1959–70, sr state counsel Kenya 1970–72, first Parly counsel Kenya 1972–75, legal advsr St Vincent and The Grenadines 1976–78, chief Parly draftsman Malawi 1978–83, chief justice Tonga 1983–85, pt/t chm Social Security Appeal Tbnls 1986–93, law revision cmmr Grenada 1988–93, judge of the Supreme Ct Gibraltar 1993–96; chm Registered Homes Tbnl 1987–93 and 1996–; JP N Avon 1989–93; *Books* Odgers' Principles of Pleading and Practice (17–20 edns, 1960–71); *Recreations* music, travel; *Clubs* Nairobi; *Style*— Giles Harwood, Esq; ✉ Fernhill House, Almondsbury, South Gloucestershire BS12 4LX

HARWOOD, Gillian Margaret; da of Herbert Norton Harwood, of Kyrenia, Cyprus, and Margaret, *née* Gadsby; *b* 29 Nov 1942; *Educ* Farrington Girls' Sch, Institut Britannique Paris; 2 da (Hester Allen b 4 April 1974, Flossie Allen b 28 Nov 1975); *Career* Mather & Crowther Ltd 1962–64, WGBH TV Boston USA 1964–66, CBC News London 1966–68; BBC drama and gardening business 1968–78, specialist in urban regeneration and the conversion of redundant industrial buildings into managed workspace for small and growing firms 1978–; md: Omnibus Workspace Ltd, Forum Workspace Chichester, The Old Needlemakers Lewes, Tideway Yard Mortlake, United House Islington; opened The Depot Winebar Mortlake 1986, opened Shillibeer's Brasserie Islington 1993; dir: City and Inner London North TEC, Business Link; winner: Options/TSB Tst Co Women Mean Business Award 1988, The Times/RICS Conservation Award, Business in the Community Environment Award 1990; FRSA; *Recreations* gardening, breeding Staffordshire Bull Terriers and Southdown sheep; *Style*— Miss Gillian M Harwood; ✉ 35 Gorst Road, London, SW11; Podmore's Farm, Tillington, Petworth, W Sussex; North Road, London N7 9DP (☎ 0171 700 4114, fax 0171 700 3921)

HARWOOD, Prof John Leander; s of Capt Leslie James Harwood, of Tunbridge Wells, and Lt Beatrice, *née* Hutchinson; *b* 5 Feb 1946; *Educ* King Edward's GS Aston, Univ of Birmingham (BSc, PhD, DSc); *m* 1, 27 Aug 1967, Gail (d 1991), da of Harry Burgess (d 1968); 1 s (Nicholas James b 27 Feb 1969); m 2, 14 April 1993, Bernice Adele (d 1994), da of Brian Alfred Andrews (d 1971); *Career* post doctoral res Univ of California Davis 1969–71 and Univ of Leeds 1971–73, personal chair Univ Coll Cardiff 1984– (lectr 1973–80, reader 1980–84), author of over 320 scientific pubns; guide book writer for S Wales Mountaineering Club and The Climbers Club; memb: Biochemical Soc, Phytochemical Soc, Soc of Experimental Biology; *Books* South East Wales - A Rock Climber's Guide (ed, 1977), Lipids of Plants and Microbes (1984), The Lipid Handbook (jt ed, 1986, 2nd edn 1994), Plant Membranes (jt ed, 1988), Methods in Plant Biochemistry (Vol 4, jt ed, 1990), Plant Lipid Biochemistry, Structure and Utilization (jt ed, 1990), Lipid Biochemistry (jt author, 1991); *Style*— Prof John Harwood; ✉ School of Molecular and Medical Biosciences, University of Wales, College of Cardiff, PO Box 911, Cardiff CF1 3US (☎ 01222 874108)

HARWOOD, John Warwick; s of Denis George Harwood, of West Camel, Somerset, and Winifred, *née* Hoatson; *b* 10 Dec 1946; *Educ* Catford Sch, Univ of Kent (BA), Univ of London (MA); *m* 1967; 1 s, 1 da; *Career* admin offr GLC 1968–73, private sec to Sir Ashley Bramall as Ldr ILEA 1973–77, asst chief exec London Borough of Hammersmith and Fulham 1979–82 (head Chief Exec's Office 1977–79); chief exec Lewisham Borough Cncl 1982–88, chief exec Oxfordshire CC 1989–; clerk of the lieutenancy for Oxfordshire 1989–; dir: N Oxfordshire Business Venture Ltd, Heart of Eng Trg and Enterprise Cncl, Thames Business Advice Centre, Oxfordshire Ethnic Minorities Enterprise Developments Ltd; memb: Exec Ctee Town and Country Planning Assoc 1981–89, Nat Cmmn on Future of Voluntary Sector 1995–96, Business Links Accreditation Bd 1996–; clerk S London Consortium 1983–89, memb SOLACE; Hon MA Univ of Kent 1995; *Recreations* walking, cooking, gardening; *Style*— John Harwood, Esq; ✉ County Hall, Oxford OX1 1ND (☎ 01865 815330, fax 01865 726155)

HARWOOD, Lee; s of Wilfrid Travers Lee-Harwood (d 1969), of Chertsey, Surrey, and Grace, *née* Ladkin; *b* 6 June 1939; *Educ* St George's Coll Weybridge Surrey, QMC London (BA); *m* 1 (m dis), Jenny Goodgame; 1 s (Blake b 1962); m 2 (m dis), Judith Walker; 1 s (Rafe b 1977), 1 da (Rowan b 1979); *Career* poet; collections published incl: The Man with Blue Eyes (1966), The White Room (1968), Landscapes (1969), The Sinking Colony (1971), HMS Little Fox (1976), Boston-Brighton (1977), All the Wrong Notes (1981), Monster Masks (1985), Dream Quilt (1985), Rope Boy to the Rescue (1988), Crossing the Frozen River - Selected Poems (1988), In the Mists: Mountain Poems (1993); translations: Tristan Tzara Selected Poems (1975), Tristan Tzara - Chanson Dada: Selected Poems (1987); chm: Nat Poetry Secretariat 1974–76, Poetry Soc London 1976–77; *Awards* Poetry Fndn NY annual award 1966, Alice Hunt Bartlett prize Poetry Soc London 1976; *Recreations* mountaineering and hill walking, the countryside; *Style*— Lee Harwood, Esq

HARWOOD, Richard Cecil; s of Cecil Albert Harwood, of Ashtead, Surrey, and Gladys Merrells, *née* Davis (d 1979); *b* 21 Sept 1943; *Educ* Sutton HS for Boys, Tiffin Boys' Sch Kingston-on-Thames, The City Univ London (BSc, Sir Walter Puckey Prize), The City Univ Business Sch (SSRC scholar, MSc); *m* 1, 26 Aug 1967, da of Egund Alexander Møller; 1 s (Alexander Richard b 27 June 1977), 2 da (Cordelia Anne b 16 April 1970, Amanda Kirsten b 28 Sept 1972); m 2, 5 Sept 1995, Caroline Sarah Thomson, da of Michael John Cleeve Brocklehurst; *Career* Smiths Industries: student apprentice 1962–67, asst works mangr 1967–68, Divnl Corp Planning 1968–69; res ptnr Scott Goff Hancock (investmt analyst 1969–73), dir Smith New Court Agency 1986, res dir Morgan Grenfell Securities 1986–89, dir UK Research Schroder Securities 1989–91, res dir Collins Stewart & Co 1991–; no 1 office equipment sector analyst Extel and Institutional Investor surveys 1973–88; memb Cncl Soc of Investmt Analysts 1981–89 (chm Educn Ctee 1984–87); memb: Stock Exchange 1971, Lloyd's 1987; MIProdE, CEng, FSIA; *Books* Institutional Investment Research; *Recreations* classic cars, family, travel; *Style*— Richard Harwood, Esq; ✉ Collins Stewart & Co, 21 New Street, Bishopsgate, London EC2M 4HR (☎ 0171 283 1133, fax 0171 283 8031)

HARWOOD, Richard Francis Wilson; s of Gerald Wilson Harwood, of Sutton Coldfield, and Ellen Margaret, *née* Small; *b* 7 Sept 1944; *Educ* Wycliffe; *m* 8 Sept 1967, Kathleen Janet, da of Edward Charles Shelley; 1 s (Charles Richard Louis b 23 Oct 1973); *Career* articled to C Herbert Smith & Russell 1961–66; subsequent positions with: Thos Bourne & Co 1967, Kenneth Hayes & Co 1967–68, Deloitte & Co 1968–81; ptnr Hart Harwood 1981–; pres Birmingham and W Midlands CAs 1991–92; Birmingham and W Midlands rep Nat Cncl ICAEW 1992–; chm ICAEW Trg Standards Ctee 1995– (dep chm 1993–95), dep chm Educn & Trg Directorate 1995–; dep chm of govrs Bishop Vesey's GS Sutton Coldfield, dep churchwarden St Mary, St Giles and All Saints Canwell 1993–, hon treas Quinney Hall (registered charity) 1995–; memb: Royal Agricultural Soc of England, Nat Trust; FCA; *Recreations* gardening, music, cricket umpiring; *Clubs* Walsall, Warwickshire CCC; *Style*— Richard F W Harwood, Esq; ✉ Canwell Edge Cottage, 6 Duttons Lane, Four Oaks, Sutton Coldfield, West Midlands B75 5RH (☎ 0121 308 1715); Hart Harwood, Ryknild House, Burnett Road, Streetly, Sutton Coldfield, West Midlands B74 3EL (☎ 0121 352 0901, fax 0121 353 8601)

HARWOOD, Ronald; s of Isaac Horwitz (d 1950), and Isobel, *née* Pepper (d 1985); *b* 9 Nov 1934; *Educ* Sea Point Boys' HS Capetown, RADA; *m* 1959, Natasha, da of William Charles Riehle, MBE (d 1979); 1 s (Antony), 2 da (Deborah, Alexandra); *Career* actor 1953–60; writer 1960–; artistic dir Cheltenham Festival of Lit 1975; chm Writers' Guild of GB 1969; memb Lit Panel Arts Cncl of GB 1973–78; visitor in theatre Balliol Coll Oxford 1986; pres PEN (Int) 1993 (PEN (Eng) 1989–93); Chevalier de l'Ordre des Arts et des Lettres, DFRSL; *Presenter* Kaleidoscope (BBC) 1973, Read All About It (BBC) 1978–79, All The World's A Stage for (also writer, BBC); *TV Plays* incl: The Barber of Stamford Hill (1960), Private Potter (1961), The Guests (1972), Breakthrough at Reykjavik (1987), Countdown to War (1989); *Screenplays* incl: A High Wind in Jamaica (1965), One Day in the Life of Ivan Denisovich (1971), Evita Peron (1981), The Dresser (1983), Mandela (1987), The Browning Version (1994), Cry The Beloved Country (1995); *Books* All the Same Shadows (1961), The Guilt Merchants (1963), The Girl in Melanie Klein (1969), Articles of Faith (1973), The Genoa Ferry (1976), César and Augusta (1978), Home (Jewish Quarterly Prize for Fiction, 1993); short stories: One Interior Day (adventures in the film trade 1978), New Stories 3 (ed, 1978); biography: Sir Donald Wolfit, CBE - his life and work in the unfashionable theatre (1971); essays: A Night at the Theatre (ed, 1983), The Ages of Gielgud (1984), Dear Alec (ed, 1989); others: All The World's A Stage (1984), The Faber Book of Theatre (ed, 1993); *Plays* Country Matters (1969), The Ordeal of Gilbert Pinfold (from Evelyn Waugh, 1977), A Family (1978), The Dresser (New Standard Drama Award, Drama Critics' Award, 1986), After the Lions (1982), Tramway Road (1984), The Deliberate Death of a Polish Priest (1985), Interpreters (1985), J J Farr (1987), Ivanov (from Chekov 1989), Another Time (1989), Reflected Glory (1992), Poison Pen (1993), Taking Sides (1995), The Handyman (1996); *Musical Libretto* The Good Companions (1974); *Recreations* tennis, watching cricket; *Clubs* Garrick, MCC; *Style—* Ronald Harwood, Esq, FRSL; ✉ c/o Judy Daish Associates, 2 St Charles Place, London W10 6EG (☎ 0181 964 8811, fax 0181 964 8966)

HARWOOD-SMART, Philip Mervyn Harwood; s of Harold Leslie Harwood Smart (d 1976), of High Point, Cuckfield, Sussex, and Moira Veronica, *née* Scanlon (d 1986); *b* 1 Oct 1944; *Educ* Eastbourne Coll, Univ of Lancaster (BA); *m* Juliet Marion Frances, da of Keith Mackay Campbell (d 1990), of West Bagborough, Somerset; 2 da (Venetia Louise b 14 June 1977, Davina Brietzcke b 17 Feb 1980); *Career* 4/5 Bn KORR Lancaster (TA) 1964–67, cmmnd 1965, memb HAC 1986–; admitted slr 1971, assoc ptnr Herbert Smith & Co 1973–75, asst slr Farrer & Co 1977–80; ptnr Ashurst Morris Crisp 1984–92, currently conslt Blake Lapthorn (joined as ptnr 1992); chm of the tstees Conder Pension Fund 1992; chm Owslebury and Morestead Cons Assoc 1990–93, hon sec Old Eastbournian Assoc 1970; sidesman of Winchester Cathedral; memb: Sussex Archaeological Soc, Cncl of Friends of Winchester Cathedral 1988–93, Owslebury PCC 1988–92, Sussex Record Soc, Royal Archaeological Inst, Alresford Agricultural Soc; Freeman: City of London 1973, Worshipful Co of Slrs 1973; *Books* The History of Jevington (1962, second edn, 1972), A Practical Legal Guide to Occupational Pension Schemes (with Caroline Williams, 1993); *Recreations* people, wine, heraldry, genealogy; *Clubs* Carlton, Hampshire, Bishopsgate Ward, Coleman Street Ward, Inns of Ct, City Yeo Luncheon, Henley Royal Regatta; *Style—* Philip Harwood-Smart, Esq; ✉ Thimble Hall, Owslebury, Winchester, Hants; Blake Lapthorn, New Court, 1 Barnes Wallis Road, Fareham, Hants PO15 5UA (☎ 01489 579990, fax 01489 529126, telex 86283)

HARYOTT, Richard Baskcomb; s of Reginald Arthur Haryott, OBE (d 1993), and Noreen Miller, *née* Baskcomb; *b* 28 March 1941; *Educ* Leys Sch Cambridge, Univ of Leeds (BSc, Dorman Long Prize); *m* 1966, Virginia Mary, da of late Charles Taylor; 1 da (Josephine (Hon Mrs de Grey) b 1968), 2 s (James b 1971, Charles 1977); *Career* Ove Arup & Partners: engr 1962–, md Arup Iran 1976–79, dir 1979–, dir Ove Arup Partnership (holding co) 1984–; major projects incl: Nat Exhibition Centre 1975, Sainsbury Wing Nat Gallery 1991, UK Pavilion Seville 1992, Glaxo Wellcome Medicines Research Labs 1995; chm Steel Construction Inst, memb Jt Bd of Moderators and Degree Accreditation Bd for Chartered Engrs; govr Leys Sch and St Faith's Sch Cambridge; FICE 1986, FIStructE 1993, FEng 1995; *Publications* Integrating the Professions at the NEC Building (1976), The National Exhibition Centre (Birmingham Int Arena), Proceedings of Institution of Civil Engineers (jtly, 1983), Solar-Powered Pavilion (RIBA Jl, 1992); *Recreations* golf, tennis, wine; *Style—* Richard Haryott, Esq, FEng; ✉ Wellpond Cottage, Brickendon, Hertford SG13 8NU (☎ and fax 01992 511575); Ove Arup Partnership, 13 Fitzroy St, London W1P 6BQ (☎ 0171 465 3139, fax 0171 465 3675, e-mail richard.haryott@arup.com)

HASAN, HE Wajid Shamsul; s of late Syed Shamsul Hasan, of Delhi, India, and Amir Begum; *b* 5 Jan 1941; *Educ* LLB, MA (Int Rels); *m* Zarine; 1 s (Zulfikaur Wajid b 2 March 1977); *Career* Pakistan diplomat and journalist; freelance journalist 1960–62, recipient Cwlth Press Union scholarship for journalistic trg in UK 1968, ed The News (English language daily) Karachi 1969–89 (joined as reporter 1962), fndr ed Mag (English weekly) 1981; chm Nat Press Tst 1989–90, press advsr to Benazir Bhutto as Ldr of the Oppn 1990–93; Pakistan high cmmr to the Ct of St James's 1994–; memb: Karachi Union of Journalists, Karachi Press Club, Royal Soc for Asian Affairs; *Recreations* book reading, cricket, travelling; *Clubs* Royal Over-Seas League; *Style—* HE Mr Wajid Shamsul Hasan; ✉ Pakistan High Commission, 35 Lowndes Square, London SW1X 9JN (☎ 0171 235 2044, fax 0171 235 7867, mobile 0973 750735)

HASELER, Prof Stephen Michael Alan; s of Maj Cyril Percival Haseler (d 1973); *b* 9 Jan 1942; *Educ* Westcliff HS for Boys, LSE (BSc, PhD); *m* 24 Feb 1968, Roberta Berenice Haseler; *Career* prof of govt: London Guildhall Univ (formerly City of London Poly) 1968–, Univ of Maryland 1982–; visiting prof: Georgetown Univ Washington DC 1978, John Hopkins Univ 1984; chm Gen Purposes Ctee GLC 1973–75 (memb 1973–77), fndr memb SDP 1981, chm Radical Soc 1987– (fndr memb); Parly candidate (Lab): Saffron Walden 1966, Maldon 1970; hon prof Univ of Maryland 1986–; *Books* The Gaitskellites (1969), The Tragedy of Labour (1976), Eurocommunism (1978), Thatcher & The New Liberals (1989); *Clubs* IOD; *Style—* Prof Stephen Haseler; ✉ 2 Thackeray House, Ansdell Street, Kensington, London W8 (☎ 0171 937 3976)

HASELHURST, Sir Alan Gordon Barraclough; kt (1995), MP (C) Saffron Walden (majority 17,424); s of late John Haselhurst, and late Alyse, *née* Barraclough; *b* 23 June 1937; *Educ* Cheltenham, Oriel Coll Oxford; *m* 1977, Angela, da of John Bailey; 2 s, 1 da; *Career* MP (C): Middleton and Prestwich 1970–74, Saffron Walden 1977–; PPS to Sec of State for Educn 1979–81; chm of Trustees Community Projects Fndn 1986–; hon sec All Pty Parly Cricket Gp 1993–; *Recreations* music, gardening, watching cricket; *Style—* Sir Alan Haselhurst, MP; ✉ House of Commons, London SW1A 0AA

HASELTINE, Barry Albert; s of Albert Edward Haseltine (d 1974), of Horsham, Sussex, and Lillian Sarah Louise, *née* Payne (d 1996); *b* 17 June 1933; *Educ* Collyers Sch Horsham, Imperial Coll London (BSc, DIC); *m* 7 July 1956, Sylvia Ethel, da of Arthur George Jones (d 1975), of Gloucester; 1 s (Richard Barry b 16 Feb 1963), 1 da (Susan Jane b 8 March 1966); *Career* Flying Offr RAF 1955–57; ptnr Jenkins and Potter Consulting Engrs 1967–94, conslt 1994–; chm: Euro Cmmn's Code of Practice Ctee for Masonry, several Br Standards Instn Ctees, Int Standards Orgn Ctee; FEng 1985, FICE, FIStructE, MConsE, FCGI; *Books* Bricks and Brickwork (1974), Handbook to BS5628: Part 1 (1980), Part II (1991); *Recreations* gardening, golf, skiing; *Clubs* RAF, Copthorne Golf (Sussex); *Style—* Barry Haseltine, Esq, FEng; ✉ Jenkins and Potter, 12–15 Great Turnstile, London WC1V 7HN (☎ 0171 242 8711, fax 0171 404 0742)

HASHEMI, Kambiz; s of Hussain Hashemi, of Tehran, Iran, and Aghdas, *née* Tehrani; *b* 13 Aug 1948; *Educ* Greenmore Coll Birmingham, Univ of Birmingham (MB ChB, MD); *m* 11 Sept 1974, Elahe, da of Dr Abbas Hashemi-Nejad, of Tehran, Iran; 1 s (Nima b 14 Nov 1978), 1 da (Neda b 14 May 1989); *Career* surgical registrar United Birmingham Hosp 1974–82, sr registrar in accident and emergency med Dudley Rd and East Birmingham Hosp 1982–85, dir of accident and emergency serv Mayday Univ Hosp 1985–, conslt in hand surgery Mayday Univ Hosp Croydon 1985–; author of numerous scientific pubns in med jls; univ clinical tutor Mayday Univ Hosp; regnl tutor in A/E med SW Thames RHA, SW Thames speciality rep to RCS, pres A/E section RSM, chm Medical Cmmn for Accident Prevention; memb: Manpower Advsy Ctee, Dist Child Accident Prevention Gp, Academic Ctee BAEM, BMA, BAEM, Emergency Med Res Soc, Iran Soc; FRCS, FRSM; *Books* Hazards of Forklift Truck (1989); *Recreations* squash, tennis, photography, theatre and opera; *Style—* Kambiz Hashemi, Esq; ✉ 16 Rose Walk, Purley, Surrey CR8 3LG (☎ 0181 668 8127); Accident and Emergency Unit, Mayday University Hospital, Mayday Rd, Thornton Heath, Surrey CR7 7YE (☎ 0181 401 3000, fax 0181 401 3092)

HASHMI, Dr Farrukh Siyar; OBE (1974); s of Dr Ziaullah Qureshi (d 1983), and Majida, *née* Mufti (d 1987); *b* 12 Sept 1927; *Educ* Punjab Univ (MB BS), King Edward Med Coll Lahore Pakistan (Dip Psychological Med); *m* 11 Feb 1972, Shahnaz Hashmi, JP, da of Khalifa M Nasimullah, of Karachi, Pakistan; 1 s (Zia b 2 Sept 1977), 2 da (Mahnaz b 1 Jan 1973, Noreen b 16 Sept 1974); *Career* asst med offr for health Berwickshire 1957, scholar Volkart Fndn Switzerland 1958–60, registrar Uffculme Clinic and All Saints Hosp 1960–63, res fell Dept of Psychiatry Univ of Birmingham 1969– (sr registrar 1966–69), conslt psychiatrist W Birmingham Health Authy 1969–92, psychotherapist HM Prison Stafford 1973–, conslt in trans-cultural psychiatry The Woodbourne Clinic Birmingham 1992–, currently conslt psychiatrist Eating Disorders Unit S Warwick Mental Health Servs; memb: Health and Welfare Advsy Panel Nat Ctee on Cwlth Immigrants 1966–81, Home Sec's Advsy Ctee On Race 1976–81; cmmr Cmmn for Racial Equality 1980–86, memb Working Pty on Community and Race Rels Trg Home Office Police Trg Cncl 1982–83, GMC memb Tbnl on Misuse of Drugs 1983–92, advsy conslt C of E Bd for Social Responsibility 1984–86; memb: Race Rels Bd W Midlands Conciliation Ctee 1968–81, Regnl Advsy Ctee BBC 1970–77; fndr and chm Iqbal Acad Coventry Cathedral 1972–86; memb: Warley Area Social Servs Sub Ctee 1973–81, Mental Health Servs Ctee RHA 1976–92; chm Psychiatric Div W Birmingham Health Dist 1977–83 and 1989, memb Central DHA Birmingham 1982–90; individual memb World Psychiatric Assoc, fndr pres and patron Overseas Doctors' Assoc UK, memb World Fedn for Mental Health; FRCPsych 1971, FRSM 1996; *Books* Pakistani Family in Britain (1965), Psychology of Racial Prejudice (1966), Mores Migration and Mental Illness (1966), Community Psychiatric Problems Among Birmingham Immigrants (1968), In a Strange Land (1970), Measuring Psychological Disturbance in Asian Immigrants to Britain (1977); *Recreations* writing, reading music; *Clubs* Oriental, Rotary Int, Edgbaston Priory (Birmingham); *Style—* Dr Farrukh Hashmi, OBE; ✉ Shahnaz, 5 Woodbourne Rd, Edgbaston, Birmingham B15 3QJ (☎ 0121 455 0011); The Woodbourne Clinic, Edgbaston, Birmingham B17 8BY (☎ 0121 434 4343)

HASKARD, Sir Cosmo Dugal Patrick Thomas; KCMG (1965, CMG 1960), MBE (1945); s of Brig-Gen John McDougall Haskard, CMG, DSO (d 1967), and Alicia Isabella, *née* Hutchins (d 1960); *b* 25 Nov 1916; *Educ* Cheltenham, RMC Sandhurst, Pembroke Coll Cambridge (MA); *m* 3 Aug 1957, Phillada, da of Sir Robert Christopher Stafford Stanley, KBE, CMG (d 1981), and Lady Stanley, *née* Ursula Cracknell (d 1981); 1 s (Julian Dominic Stanley b 1962); *Career* 2 Lt TA 1938; emergency cmmn RIrF, seconded KAR; served 2 Bn: E Africa, Ceylon, Burma; Maj 1944; Colonial Serv Tanganyika 1940 (released for War Serv), transferred Nyasaland 1946, dist cmmr 1948, memb Nyasaland Mozambique Boundary Cmmn 1951–52, provincial cmmr 1955, acting sec for African Affairs 1957–58; sec successively for: Labour and Social Devpt, Local Govt, Natural Resources 1961–64; Govr and C-in-C Falklands Is and High Cmmr for British Antarctic Territory 1964–70; tstee Beit Trust 1976–; *Style—* Sir Cosmo Haskard, KCMG, MBE; ✉ Tragariff, Bantry, Co Cork, Ireland

HASKELL, Prof Francis; *b* 1928; *Educ* Eton, King's Coll Cambridge; *m* 1965, Larissa Salmina; *Career* fell King's Coll Cambridge 1954–57, librarian Fine Arts Faculty Univ of Cambridge 1962–67, prof of history of art Univ of Oxford and fell Trinity Coll 1967–95 (now emeritus); tstee Wallace Collection 1976–; Serena Medal for Italian Studies British Acad 1985, Officer de L'Ordre des Arts et des Lettres 1990; hon fell King's Coll Cambridge 1986, foreign hon memb American Acad of Arts and Sciences 1979, foreign memb American Philosophical Soc 1994, hon degree Free Univ of Berlin 1993; corresponding memb: Academia Pontaniana Naples 1982, Ateneo Veneto 1986; hon memb Academia Clementina of Bologna 1990; FBA 1971; *Books* Patrons and Painters (1963), Rediscoveries in Art (1976), L' Arte e il Liguaggio Della Politica (1978), Taste and the Antique (with Nicholas Penny, 1981), Past and Present in Art and Taste (1987), The Painful Birth of the Art Book (1987), History and its Images: Art and the Interpretation of the Past (1993); *Style—* Prof Francis Haskell, FBA; ✉ Trinity College, Oxford OX1 3BH

HASKELL, HE (Donald) Keith; CMG (1991), CVO (1979); s of Lt Donald Eric Haskell, RN, of Southsea, Hants, and Beatrice Mary, *née* Blair (d 1985); *b* 9 May 1939; *Educ* Portsmouth GS, St Catharine's Coll Cambridge (BA, MA); *m* 7 Feb 1966, Maria Luisa Soeiro, da of Dr Augusto Tito de Morais (d 1981); 3 s (Donald Mark b and d 1972, Jonathan b 1974, Paul b 1976), 3 da (Lysa b 1970, Anne-Marie b 1979, one other unnamed b and d 1969); *Career* HM Dip Serv 1961–: language student MECAS Shemlan Lebanon 1961–62 and 1968–69, third sec Br Embassy Baghdad Iraq 1962–66, second sec FO London 1966–68, first sec and consul Br Embassy Benghazi Libya 1969–70, first sec Br Embassy Tripoli Libya 1970–72, first sec FCO London 1972–75, chargé d'affaires and consul gen Br Embassy Santiago Chile 1975–78, cnsllr and consul gen Br Embassy Dubai UAE 1978–81, head Nuclear Energy Dept FCO London 1981–83, head ME Dept FCO London 1983–84, cnsllr Br Embassy Bonn W Germany 1985–88, seconded to indust 1988–89, ambass to Peru 1990–95, ambass to Brazil 1995–; target rifle shooting half blue 1960–61, shot for Hampshire Eng and GB on various occasions; *Recreations* target shooting, squash, tennis, skiing, wine and food; *Clubs* Hawks (Cambridge); *Style—* HE Mr Keith Haskell, CMG, CVO; ✉ c/o Foreign and Commonwealth Office (Brasilia), King Charles Street, London SW1A 2AH

HASKELL, Mark John; s of John Harold Haskell, of Poole, Dorset, and Mary June, *née* Coombs; *b* 12 Nov 1959; *Educ* Poole GS, Univ of Warwick (BSc); *m* 1990, Jane Elizabeth, *née* Derry; *Career* chartered accountant KPMG 1981–92, fin dir Westcountry Television Ltd 1992–; ACA 1984; FRSA; *Recreations* golf, tennis; *Clubs* Teignmouth Golf, Broadstone Golf (Dorset); *Style—* Mark Haskell, Esq; ✉ Westcountry Television Ltd, Western Wood Way, Langage Science Park, Plymouth, Devon PL7 5BG (☎ 01752 333333, fax 01752 333444)

HASKELL, Richard; s of Jack Herbert Haskell (d 1982), and Marjorie Rose, *née* Damerum; *b* 19 June 1936; *Educ* King Edward VI Royal GS Guildford, KCH (MB BS, BDS, MRCP, FDSRCS, FRCP (Lond)); *m* 16 April 1959, Marion, da of John Lucas Gregory (d 1973); 1 da (Greer Myra b 2 June 1964); *Career* conslt oral and maxillofacial surgn Guy's Hosp and Greenwich Health Dist 1974–96, hon civilian conslt to Queen Elizabeth Mil Hosp Woolwich 1981–95; chm of FDS examiners RCS 1988–89; memb: Dental Advsy Bd Med Protection Soc, Bd of Faculty of Dental Surgery RCS 1990–, Cncl Br Assoc of

Oral and Maxillofacial Surgns (hon treas 1992–95); *Books* Atlas Of Orofacial Diseases (jtly 1971), Clinical Oral Medicine (2 edn jtly, 1977); *Style*— Richard Haskell, Esq; ✉ 19 Pembridge Square, London W2 4EJ (☎ 0171 229 3552)

HASKINS, Samuel Joseph (Sam); s of Benjamin George Haskins (d 1970), and Anna Elizabeth Haskins (d 1983); *b* 11 Nov 1926; *Educ* Helpmekaar HS SA, Witwatersrand Tech Coll SA, London Coll of Printing; *m* 1952, Alida Elzabe, da of Stephanus Johannes van Heerden; 2 s (Ludwig b 1955, Konrad b 1963); *Career* photographer; estab: freelance advertising studio Johannesburg SA 1952, Haskins Studio and Haskins Press London 1968; *Solo Exhibitions* incl: Haskins Photographs (Johannesburg) 1953, Sam Haskins (Pentax Gallery Tokyo) 1970, Haskins Posters (The Photographers Gallery) 1972, FNAC Gallery Paris 1973, The Camera Gallery Amsterdam 1974, Scandiniavian Landscape (Isetan Gallery Tokyo) 1973, Photo Graphics (Nat Theatre London) 1980, Sam Haskins a Bologna (Bologna) 1984, The Best of Sam Haskins (Pentax Forum Gallery Tokyo) 1986, The Image Factor (Pentax Forum Gallery Tokyo) 1990, Remember Barcelona (Pentax Forum Gallery Tokyo, Osaka Pentax Gallery then Interkamera Prague) 1992, Hearts (Pentax Forum Tokyo, Pentax Gallery Osaka) 1993, Sam Haskins - Monochrome (Pentax Forum Gallery Tokyo, Pentax Gallery Osaka) 1996; *Books* incl: Five Girls (1962), Cowboy Kate and Other Stories (1964, Prix Nadar), November Girl (1966), African Image (1967, Silver medal Int Art Book Competition 1969), Haskins Posters (1972, Gold medal NY Art Directors' Club 1974), Photographics (1980, Kodak Book of the Year award 1980), Sam Haskins a Bologna (1984), Barcelona '92 (1991); *Recreations* vintage car rallying, sculpting, joinery, painting, craft and antique collecting, horticulture; *Style*— Sam Haskins, Esq; ✉ (e-mail sam@haskins.com)

HASLAM, Dr David Antony; *b* 4 July 1949; *Educ* Monkton Combe Sch Somerset, Univ of Birmingham Med Sch (MB ChB, DObstRCOG, FPA Cert, MRCGP); *Career* house physician Warneford Hosp Leamington Spa 1972–73, house surgn N Staffs Royal Infirmary 1973; SHO: (obstetrics) Birmingham Maternity Hosp 1973–74, (paediatrics) Birmingham Children's Hosp 1974, (psychiatry) Midland Nerve Hosp 1974–75, (gen med) Birmingham Gen Hosp 1975; trainee GP 1975–76, GP in partnership Ramsey Health Centre Huntingdon Cambs 1976–; RCGP: memb Cncl 1987–, chm Examination Bd 1993–; patron Crysis (Parents' Self Help Gp); FRCGP 1989; *Books* Sleepless Children (1984), Eat it Up (1986), Travelling with Children (1987), ParentStress (1989), The Expectant Father (1990), Bulimia - A Guide for Sufferers and Their Families (1994); author of numerous articles and reg contrib various academic and non-academic jls, numerous appearances on local and nat radio and on TV; *Style*— Dr David Haslam; ✉ The Health Centre, Ramsey, Huntingdon, Cambs PE17 1AQ (☎ 01487 812611, fax 01487 813033)

HASLAM, Rear Adm Sir David William; KBE (1984, OBE 1964), CB (1979); s of Gerald Haigh Haslam (d 1962), and Gladys, *née* Finley (d 1973); *b* 26 June 1923; *Educ* Bromsgrove; *Career* RN 1941–85, Cdr 1957, Capt 1965, Rear Adm 1975, Hydrographer of the Navy 1975–85; actg conservator River Mersey 1985–87, pres Directing Ctee Int Hydrographic Bureau Monaco 1987–92; pres: Eng Schs Basketball Assoc 1973–96, Derbyshire CCC 1991–92; chm Bd of Govrs Bromsgrove Sch 1991–96; Freeman City of London 1983, Liveryman Worshipful Co of Chartered Surveyors 1983; FRIN 1974, FRGS 1975, FRICS 1975; *Style*— Rear Adm Sir David Haslam, KBE, CB; ✉ 146 Worcester Road, Bromsgrove, Worcestershire B61 7AS (☎ 01527 574068)

HASLAM, Jonathan; s of Arthur and Irene Florence; *b* 2 Oct 1952; *Educ* Cowbridge GS Glamorgan, Plymouth Poly, Croydon Coll of Art and Technology; *m* 1982, Dawn Rachel; 2 s (James Samuel Charles b 25 July 1991, George Michael Anthony 27 July 1994); *Career* with National Westminster Bank 1975–79; information offr: COI 1979–82, DTI 1982–84; sr information offr Home Office 1984–86, dep head of information and dep press sec to Sec of State Dept of Employment 1988–89 (princ information offr 1986–88), dep dir of information, dep press sec to Sec of State and head of news Home Office 1989–91, dep press sec to PM 1991–95, head of information and press sec to Minister for Agric, Fisheries and Food 1995, chief press sec to PM 10 Downing Street 1996–; *Recreations* golf, music, cinema, reading; *Style*— Jonathan Haslam, Esq; ✉ 10 Downing Street, London SW1A 2AA (☎ 0171 930 4433)

HASLAM, Dr Michael Trevor; s of Gerald Haslam (d 1946), of Leeds, England, and Edna Beatrice, *née* Oldfield; *b* 7 Feb 1934; *Educ* Sedbergh, St John's Coll Cambridge (MA, MD), Bart's (MB BChir, DPM, DMJ); *m* 2 May 1959, Shirley Dunstan, da of Alfred Walter Jefferies (d 1985); 1 s (Michael b 1965), 2 da (Fiona b 1962, Melanie b 1966); *Career* RAMC 1960–62, Lt, Capt, Actg Maj; registrar in psychiatry York 1962–64, sr registrar Newcastle upon Tyne 1964–67; conslt in psychological med: Doncaster 1967–70, York 1970–89; assoc clinical prof St George's Univ Grenada 1987–90; med dir: The Harrogate Clinic 1989–91, SW Durham Mental Health Tst 1993–; chm Soc of Clinical Psychiatrists; formerly: chm Clinical Tutors Ctee Royal Coll of Psychiatrists, hon sec and chm Leeds Regnl Psychiatrists Assoc; Liveryman Worshipful Soc of Apothecaries 1971, Freeman City of London 1971, Warden for the North Freemen of England and Wales; FRCPS (Glasgow) 1979, FRCPsych 1980; *Books* Psychiatric Illness in Adolescence (1975), Sexual Disorders (1978), Psychosexual Disorders (1979), Psychiatry Made Simple (1987); *Recreations* fives, squash, croquet, music; *Clubs* Soc of Authors; *Style*— Dr Michael Haslam; ✉ Chapel Garth, Crayke, York YO6 4TE; Medical Director, SW Durham Mental Health Trust, Winterton Hospital, Sedgefield, Co Durham (☎ 01740 620521)

HASLAM, Baron (Life Peer UK 1990), of Bolton in the County of Greater Manchester; Sir Robert Haslam; kt (1985); s of Percy Haslam (d 1971); *b* 4 Feb 1923; *Educ* Bolton Sch, Univ of Birmingham (BSc); *m* 1, 1947, Joyce (d 1995), da of Frederick Quin (d 1937); 2 s (Hon Roger b 1948, Hon Nigel b 1952); m 2, 20 July 1996, Elizabeth, widow of Hon Michael David Sieff, CBE, and da of late William Norman Pitt, of Hampton, Middx; *Career* dep chm ICI plc 1980–83; chm: Tate and Lyle plc 1983–86, Br Steel Corporation 1983–86; dir Bank of England 1985–93, chm Br Coal 1986–90, advsy dir Unilever plc 1986–93; chm: Bechtel Ltd 1991–94, Wasserstein Perella & Co Ltd 1991–; Hon: DTech Brunel Univ 1987, DEng Birmingham Univ 1987; FIMinE; *Recreations* golf, travel; *Clubs* Brooks's, Wentworth; *Style*— The Rt Hon Lord Haslam; ✉ c/o House of Lords, London SW1A 0PW

HASLAM, Simon Mark; s of Peter Haigh Haslam, of Allestree, Derby, and Elizabeth Anne, *née* Gallimore; *b* 29 May 1957; *Educ* Ecclesbourne Sch Duffield Derbys, Magdalen Coll Oxford (MA); *m* 15 May 1982, Catherine (Kate) Nina (who retains her maiden name), da of Capt Robert Kenneth Alcock, CBE, RN, of The Court House, Brantham Court, Manningtree, Essex; 2 s (Thomas b 9 July 1987, Richard Matthew b 21 July 1993), 1 da (Eleanor b (twin) 9 July 1987); *Career* Touche Ross (now Deloitte & Touche): articled clerk 1978–81, mangr 1984–86, ptnr 1986–95; currently chief fin offr Fidelity International Ltd; dist councillor Welwyn Hatfield 1990–; memb: Ward Ctee Welwyn and Hatfield Cons Assoc; FCA 1991 (ACA 1981); *Books* The London Securities Markets (1990); *Recreations* choral societies, walking, reading; *Style*— Simon Haslam, Esq; ✉ Badgers End, 76 Brockswood Lane, Welwyn Garden City, Herts AL8 7BQ (☎ 01707 325117); Fidelity International Ltd, Oakhill House, 130 Tonbridge Road, Hildenborough, Kent TN11 9DZ (☎ 01732 777436, fax 01732 777145)

HASLEHURST, Peter Joseph Kinder; s of Col Arthur Kinder Haslehurst, TD (d 1987), and Beatrice Elizabeth, *née* Birkinshaw; *b* 4 March 1941; *Educ* Repton, Loughborough Univ (DLC); *m* 29 Oct 1977, Susan Marilyn, da of Geoffrey W Y Heath; 1 s (Thomas William Kinder b 22 May 1983); *Career* md Wellman Mechanical Engineering Ltd 1969–81, chm Flexibox International Ltd 1986– (chief exec 1981–86), currently dep chm and chief exec EIS Group plc; dir M&G Income Investment Trust plc 1995–; current chairmanships incl: Francis Shaw plc, Northampton Machinery Co Ltd, Aerostructures Hamble Ltd, Aerocontracts Ltd, AIT Ltd, Hick Hargreaves & Co Ltd, Beagle Aircraft Co Ltd, Zwicky Engineering Ltd, Plenty Ltd, Flightspares Ltd, The Mollart Engineering Co Ltd, Airpel Filtration Ltd; currently pres: Flexibox SA France, Flexibox Spa Italy, Hibon International SA; vice pres Bd of Companions Inst of Mgmnt 1996– (memb Bd 1994–); memb Anglo-Soviet Econ Conf 1978–88, ldr Indust Missions to E Europe and Latin America, chm Br Metalworking Plant Makers Assoc 1974 and 1980, memb Jt Trade Cmmn with Czechoslovakia 1978–80, industl advsr to Min of State on official visit to Czechoslovakia 1978, ldr Metals Soc Team N E China 1979; memb: Materials Chemicals and Vehicles Requirement Bd Dept of Indust 1981–84, Br Hydromechanics Res Assoc 1984–89, Cncl Inst of Materials 1991–, MENSA; Eisenhower fell 1980; Freeman City of London 1992, Liveryman Worshipful Co of Engrs 1993; CEng, FIMechE, FIProdE, FIM, CIMgt, FRSA 1991; *Recreations* sailing and the countryside; *Clubs* Naval and Military, Royal Thames Yacht (Rear Commodore 1994–96); *Style*— Peter Haslehurst, Esq; ✉ EIS Group plc, 6 Sloane Square, London SW1W 8EE (☎ 0171 730 9187, fax 0171 730 2271, e-mail crow2@netcomuk.co.uk)

HASLETT, Prof Christopher; s of James Haslett, of Bebington, Wirral; *b* 2 April 1953; *Educ* Wirral GS, Univ of Edinburgh (BSc, MB ChB, Ettles scholar and Leslie Gold medal); *m* Jean Margaret, da of Thomas Hale; 1 da (Kate b 29 Jan 1983), 1 s (Andrew b 4 March 1990); *Career* house physician and surgn Edinburgh Royal Infirmary 1977–78, SHO Dept of Respiratory Med City Hosp Edinburgh 1978–79, res fell and hon med registrar Eastern General Hosp Edinburgh 1980 (SHO in general med 1979–80), general med registrar Ealing Hosp and Dept of Med RPMS 1980–82, res assoc F L Bryant Jr Research Lab for the Study of the Mechanisms of Lung Disease and instr Dept of Med Nat Jewish Hosp and Research Centre/Nat Asthma Centre Denver 1982–85, sr registrar in respiratory med Dept of Med RPMS Hammersmith Hosp 1982–85, sr lectr Respiratory Div Dept of Med RPMS and conslt physician Hammersmith Hosp 1985–90, prof of respiratory med and dir of The Rayne Laboratories Univ of Edinburgh 1990–, chm Dept of Med Royal Infirmary Edinburgh 1995–; visiting prof RPMS 1990–; sec Working Gp on Lung Injury Euro Respiratory Soc 1991–, memb Cell and Molecular Med Bd MRC 1992–, vice chm Res Ctee Nat Asthma Campaign; Dorothy Temple Cross Award MRC 1982, George Simon Meml Fell Award Fleischner Soc 1985, sr clinical fell MRC 1986; memb: Fleischner Soc, Assoc of Physicians (memb Cncl for Scotland 1993–), Assoc of Clinical Profs, Br Thoracic Soc, MRS, American Thoracic Soc, Int Soc for Leukocyte Biology; FRCP(Edin) 1988, FRCP(Lond) 1991; author of numerous medical pubns; *Style*— Prof Christopher Haslett; ✉ Respiratory Medicine Unit, Department of Medicine, The Royal Infirmary, 1 Lauriston Place, Edinburgh EH3 9YW (☎ 0131 536 2263)

HASSALL, Tom Grafton; s of William Owen Hassall (d 1994), of The Manor House, Wheatley, Oxford, and Averil Grafton, *née* Beaves; *b* 3 Dec 1943; *Educ* Dragon Sch, Lord Williams's GS Thame, Corpus Christi Coll Oxford (BA); *m* 2 Sept 1967, Angela Rosaleen, da of Capt Oliver Goldsmith (d 1944), of Thirsk; 3 s (Oliver b 28 Nov 1968, Nicholas b 30 April 1970, Edward b 10 July 1972); *Career* asst local ed Victoria County History of Oxford 1966–67, dir Oxford Archaeological Excavation Ctee 1967–73, dir Oxford (formerly Oxfordshire) Archaeological Unit 1973–85, fell St Cross Coll Oxford (emeritus fell 1988–), assoc staff tutor Dept for External Studies Univ of Oxford 1978–85, sec Royal Cmmn on the Historical Monuments of England 1986–; tstee Oxford Preservation Tst 1973–, chm Standing Conf of Archaeological Unit Mangrs 1980–83, pres Cncl for Br Archaeology 1983–86, chm Br Archaeological Awards 1983–87, pres Oxfordshire Architectural and Historical Soc 1984–92; Freeman City of Chester 1973; FSA 1971, MIFA 1985; *Books* Oxford, The Buried City (1987); *Recreations* gardening; *Style*— Tom Hassall, Esq, FSA; ✉ The Manor House, Wheatley, Oxford OX33 1XX (☎ 01865 874428); The Royal Commission on the Historical Monuments of England, The National Monuments Record Centre, Kemble Drive, Swindon SN2 2GZ (☎ 01793 414625, fax 01793 414771)

HASSAN, The Hon Sir Joshua Abraham; GBE (1987, CBE 1957), KCMG (1985), kt (1963), LVO (1954), QC (Gibraltar 1961), JP (Gibraltar 1949); s of late Abraham M Hassan; *b* 21 Aug 1915; *Educ* Line Wall Coll Gibraltar; *m* 1, 1945 (m dis 1969), Daniela, *née* Salazar; 2 da; m 2, 1969, Marcelle, *née* Bensimon; 2 da; *Career* called to the Bar Middle Temple 1939 (hon bencher 1983); dep coroner for Gibraltar 1941–64, mayor of Gibraltar 1945–50 and 1953–69, MEC and MLC Gibraltar 1950–64 (chief memb 1958–64), chief minister of Gibraltar 1964–69 and 1972–87, ldr of oppn House of Assembly 1969–72; chm Gen Cncl of the Bar Gibraltar 1992–; Hon LLD Univ of Hull; *Clubs* United Oxford and Cambridge Univ, Royal Gibraltar Yacht; *Style*— The Hon Sir Joshua Hassan, GBE, KCMG, LVO, QC, JP; ✉ 11–18 Europa Rd, Gibraltar (☎ 00 350 77295); 57 Line Wall Rd, Gibraltar (☎ 00 350 79000)

HASSELL, Barry Frank; s of Edgar Frank Hassell (d 1990), and Rosetta Ethel, *née* Townsend; *b* 26 Sept 1944; *Educ* Swanscombe Co Secdy Sch, London Business Sch (LEP); *m* 29 Dec 1971, Sylvia Booth (wid); 2 step s (Stephen, Richard); *Career* various accounting and mktg appts incl periods in Scandinavia and Africa 1959–73, mgmnt conslt 1973–85, special projects exec Scope (formerly The Spastics Soc) 1980–85, chief exec The Children's Trust (formerly Tadworth Court Tst) 1983–92 (memb 1992–), dir Project Bombay 1983–88, chief exec Independent Healthcare Assoc 1992–; hon sec Union of Euro Private Hosps (UEPH) 1993–; memb Tadworth Court Children's Hosp Appeal Fund 1984–; MInstD, FIMgt, FRGS; *Recreations* travel, photography, skiing; *Style*— Barry Hassell, Esq; ✉ Independent Healthcare Association, 22 Little Russell Street, London WC1A 2HT (☎ 0171 430 0537, fax 0171 242 2681)

HASSELL, Christopher Derek; s of Leonard Arthur Hassell (d 1954), and Evelyn Mary, *née* Pease; *b* 27 Nov 1942; *Educ* Ewell Boys Sch, Ewell Co Secdy Sch; *m* 19 June 1965, (Eleanor) Claire, da of Douglas Reid; 1 s (Richard Douglas b 12 April 1975), 2 da (Amanda Claire b 28 Sept 1968, Sandra Carole b 10 Dec 1969); *Career* articled clerk chartered accountants 1960; Crystal Palace FC: admin asst 1961, asst sec June 1963, sec Dec 1963; sec: Everton FC 1973–75, Preston North End FC 1975–77; asst sec Arsenal FC 1977–78; sec Lancashire CCC 1978–91, chief exec Yorkshire CCC 1991–; FA referee (class one) 1960, FA preliminary coach 1961; Surrey Combination Football League: press fixtures and bulletin sec, vice chm, currently vice pres; memb Surrey Football Assoc Cncl 1968–73, chm Town Green Boys FC 1973–80, hon treas Football League Secretaries and Mangrs Assoc 1968–78 (asst sec 1965–68); memb: Addiscombe & Shirley Round Table 1971–73, Maghull & District Round Table 1973–84; Area 8 Lancs and Manx Round Table Cncl: sports offr 1980–81, vice chm 1981–82, chm 1982–83; memb Lord's Taverners (NW); vice pres: Croydon Schs FA, Lancashire Schs Cricket Assoc; *Clubs* Rainford 41, MCC, The Forty; *Style*— Christopher Hassell, Esq; ✉ Yorkshire CCC, Headingley, Leeds LS6 3BU (☎ 0113 278 7394, fax 0113 278 4099)

HASSELL, Prof Michael Patrick; s of Maj Albert Marmaduke Hassell, MC, of Mayfield House, Clench, nr Marlborough, Wilts, and Gertrude, *née* Loeser (d 1973); *b* 2 Aug 1942; *Educ* Whitgift Sch, Clare Coll Camb (MA), Oriel Coll Oxford (DPhil); *m* 1, 7 Oct 1966 (m dis), Glynis Mary Ethel, da of John Everett; 2 s (Adrian Michael b 6 Feb 1971, David Charles b 2 April 1973); m 2, Victoria Anne, da of Reginald Taylor (d 1984); 1 s (James Mark b 10 June 1986), 1 da (Kate Helen b 18 April 1988); *Career* Imperial Coll London: lectr Dept of Zoology and Applied Entomology 1970–75, reader in insect ecology Dept of Zoology and Applied Entomology 1975–79, prof of insect ecology Dept of Pure and Applied Biology 1979–, dep head Dept of Biology 1984–93, dir Silwood Park 1988– (head Dept of Biology 1993–); FRS 1986; *Books* The Dynamics of Competition and Predation (1976), The Dynamics of Arthropod and Predator-Prey Systems (1978); *Recreations* walking, natural history, croquet; *Style—* Prof Michael Hassell, FRS; ✉ Silwood Lodge, Silwood Park, Ascot, Berks SL5 7PZ; Imperial Coll at Silwood Park, Dept of Biology, Ascot, Berks SL5 7PY (☎ 01344 294207, fax 01344 874957)

HASTE, Cate (Catherine Mary); da of Eric L Haste, of Almondsbury, Avon, and J Margaret, *née* Hodge; *b* 6 Aug 1945; *Educ* Thornbury GS Bristol, Univ of Sussex (BA), Univ of Manchester (cert adult ed); *m* 1973, Melvyn Bragg, *qv*; 1 da (Alice b 1977), 1 s (Tom b 1980); *Career* freelance television documentary producer and director, writer and broadcaster; memb Directors' Guild of GB 1988–, BAFTA 1995–; *Television* The Secret War (BBC), Just Sex (Channel Four), End of Empire (Granada), Writing on the Wall (Channel Four), Munich - The Peace of Paper (Thames), Secret History - Death of a Democrat (Channel Four), The Churchills (ITV), Coldwar (Jeremy Isaacs Prodn/TOP); *Books* Keep The Home Fires Burning - Propaganda in the First World War (1977), Rules of Desire - Sex in Britain WWI to the Present (1992); *Recreations* reading, walking, gardening; *Style—* Ms Cate Haste; ✉ 12 Hampstead Hill Gardens, London NW3 2PL (☎ 0171 794 0473, work 0171 240 9920)

HASTE, Norman David; s of Jack Haste (d 1959), of Cleethorpe, Lincs, and Edith Eleanor, *née* Jarvis (d 1961); *b* 4 Nov 1944; *Educ* Humberstone Fndn Sch Cleethorpes, N Lindsey Tech Coll (ONC Mechanical Engrg), Royal Coll of Advanced Technol (now Univ of Salford, Associate); *Career* graduate engr rising to project mangr John Laing Construction Ltd 1966–73, section mangr Humber Bridge 1973–75, marine works mangr Littlebrook 'D' Power Station Construction 1976–78, project mangr Long Sea Outfall Construction Gosport 1978–81, divnl chief engr Laing Civil Engineering 1981–82, contracts mangr McConnell Dowell South East Asia Singapore 1982–84; project dir: Civil Engrg Works Sizewell 'B' Power Station 1985–90, Second Severn Crossing 1990–95, Terminal 5 Heathrow 1996–; memb Cncl Instn of Civil Engrs 1994–97; MASCE 1983, MIE Aust 1983, FICE 1984 (MICE 1970), FEng 1996; *Awards* James Prescott Joule Medal Instn of Civil Engrs 1970 (Instn Gold Medal 1996), Highways and Transportation Award Instn of Highways and Transportation 1996; *Recreations* golf, music; *Style—* Norman Haste, Esq, FEng; ✉ 38 Chatsworth Park, Thornbury, South Gloucestershire BS12 1JF (☎ 01454 885529); BAA plc, Heathrow Point North, 234 Bath Road, Harlington, Middlesex (☎ 0181 745 1611, fax 0181 745 1640, mobile 0802 790691)

HASTIE-SMITH, Richard Maybury; CB (1984); s of Engr Cdr D Hastie-Smith, and H I Hastie-Smith; *b* 13 Oct 1931; *Educ* Cranleigh Sch, Magdalene Coll Cambridge (MA); *m* 1956, Bridget Noel Cox; 1 s, 2 da; *Career* entered Civil Service (War Office) 1955: private sec to Perm Under Sec 1957, asst private sec to Sec of State 1958, princ 1960, asst sec to Sec of State for Defence 1965, private sec to Min of Defence (Equipment) 1968 (asst sec 1969), RCDS 1974, under sec MOD 1975, Cabinet Office 1979–81, dep under sec of state MOD 1981–91, ret; current memb: Civil Service Appeal Bd, Cncl Roehampton Inst of HE; current chm: Cncl Cranleigh and Bramley Schs, Incorporated Froebel Educnl Inst; *Style—* Richard Hastie-Smith, Esq, CB; ✉ 18 York Ave, East Sheen, London SW14 7LG (☎ 0181 876 4597)

HASTINGS, Rev Prof Adrian Christopher; s of William George Warren Hastings (d 1952), and Mary Hazel, *née* Daunais (d 1993); *b* 23 June 1929; *Educ* Douai Abbey Sch Woolhampton, Worcester Coll Oxford (BA, MA), Univ of Cambridge (DipEd), Urban Univ of Rome (DTheol), Univ of Edinburgh (DD); *m* 31 March 1979, (Elizabeth) Ann, da of Mervyn Spence, of Bristol; *Career* priest Diocese of Masaka Uganda 1958–66, visiting prof of theol Univ of Lovanium Kinshasa Zaire 1963–64, editor Post Vatican II Tanzania 1966–68, ecumenical lectr Mindolo Ecumenical Fndn Kitwe Zambia 1968–70, res offr Sch of Oriental & African Studies London 1973–76, fell St Edmund's House Cambridge 1974–76, lectr in religious studies Univ of Aberdeen 1976–80 (reader 1980–82), prof of religious studies Univ of Zimbabwe Harare 1982–85, prof of theology Univ of Leeds 1985–94 (emeritus prof 1994); Prideaux lectr Univ of Exeter 1990, Wiles lectr Queen's Univ Belfast 1996; ed Journal of Religion in Africa; *Books include* Prophet and Witness in Jerusalem (1958), Church and Mission in Modern Africa (1967), A Concise Guide to the Documents of the Second Vatican Council (2 Vol 1968–69), Christian Marriage in Africa (1973), The Faces of God (1975), A History of African Christianity 1950–75 (1979), A History of English Christianity 1920–85 (1986), African Catholicism (1989), The Theology of a Protestant Catholic (1990), Robert Runcie (1991), Church and State, the English Experience (1991), S.O.S Bosnia (1993), The Church in Africa 1450–1950 (1994), The Shaping of Prophecy (1995); *Recreations* walking, cutting hedges; *Style—* The Rev Prof Adrian Hastings; ✉ 3 Hollin Hill House, 219 Oakwood Lane, Leeds LS8 2PE (☎ 0113 240 0154); The Dept of Theology and Religious Studies, The University of Leeds, Leeds LS2 9JT (☎ 0113 233 3640, fax 0113 233 3654, tlx 556473 UNILDS G)

HASTINGS, Christine Anne (Mrs John Gambles); da of Peter Edwards Hastings, and Anne Fauvel, *née* Picot; *b* 15 Feb 1956; *Educ* Whyteleafe GS; *m* 1, 5 May 1985 (m dis 1988), Lawrie Lewis; m 2, 7 June 1991, John Gambles; *Career* dir: Pact Ltd (PR Consultancy) 1980–86, Biss Lancaster plc 1986–88; founding dir (currently ptnr) Quadrangle Consulting Ltd 1988–; *Style—* Ms Christine Hastings; ✉ Quadrangle Consulting Ltd, The Butlers Wharf Building, 36 Shad Thames, London SE1 2YE (☎ 0171 357 9919, fax 0171 357 9773)

HASTINGS, 22 Baron (E 1290); Sir Edward Delaval Henry Astley; 12 Bt (E 1660); s of 21 Baron (d 1956), and Lady Marguerite Nevill (d 1975), da of 3 Marquess of Abergavenny; *b* 14 April 1912; *Educ* Eton, abroad; *m* 1954, Catherine, yr da of Capt Harold Virgo Hinton, and formerly w of Vernon Coats; 2 s, 1 da; *Heir* s, Hon Delaval Astley, *qv*; *Career* Maj Coldstream Gds, ret; patron of eight livings; lord-in-waiting to HM The Queen 1961–62, jt Parly sec Miny of Housing and Local Govt 1962–64; former farmer S Rhodesia (now Zimbabwe); pres: British-Italian Soc 1972–95, Br Epilepsy Assoc 1965–93; govr: Br Inst Florence 1959–, Royal Ballet 1971–93; chm: Royal Ballet Benevolent Fund 1966–84, Dance Teachers' Benevolent Fund 1983–, Epilepsy Research Fndn 1991–; patron Camphill Village Tst 1980–; Grand Offr Order of Merit (Italy); *Clubs* Brooks's, Army and Navy, Northern Counties (Newcastle), Norfolk (Norwich); *Style—* The Lord Hastings; ✉ Seaton Delaval Hall, Northumberland NE26 4QR (☎ 0191 237 0786)

HASTINGS, Hon Lady (Elizabeth Anne Marie Gabrielle); *née* Fitzalan-Howard; DL (Cambs 1994); yr da of 2 and last Viscount FitzAlan of Derwent, OBE (d 1962), and Joyce Elizabeth, later Countess Fitzwilliam (d 1995); *b* 26 Jan 1934; *Educ* MPhil (Egyptology); *m* 1, 17 Jan 1952 (m dis 1960), Sir Vivyan Naylor-Leyland, 3 Bt; 1 s; m 2, 1975, Sir Stephen Lewis Edmonstone Hastings, MC, *qv*; *Career* hon res fell Dept of Egyptology Inst of Archaeology Univ Coll London; High Sheriff Cambs 1993–94; jt master Fitzwilliam Hounds; chm Badminton Conservation Tst, E Midlands rep Christie's; *Style—* The Hon Lady Hastings, DL; ✉ Milton, Peterborough, Cambridgeshire (☎ 01733 380780)

HASTINGS, (Andrew) Gavin; OBE; s of Clifford N Hastings, of Edinburgh, and Isobel, *née* Adams; *b* 3 Jan 1962; *Educ* George Watsons Coll Edinburgh, Paisley Coll of Technol, Magdalene Coll Cambridge (Rugby blue); *Career* rugby union full back; clubs: Univ of Cambridge 1984–86 (capt 1985–86), London Scottish FC, Watsonian FC, Barbarian FC; rep Scotland: tour North America 1985, debut v France 1986, shared Five Nations Championship (with France) 1986, 4 appearances World Cup 1987, memb Grand Slam winning team 1990, tour NZ 1990, 5 appearances World Cup 1991 (semi-finalists), tour Australia 1992, 4 appearances World Cup 1995, total 61 caps; Scotland records: most points scored (56) in a Five Nations Championship 1994–95, most points in an international (44) v Ivory Coast 1995, most conversions in internationals, most conversions in an international (8) v Zimbabwe 1987 and v Romania 1987, most penalty goals in a Five Nations Championship (14) 1985–86; Br Lions: memb tour Aust 1989 (3 tests), with Scott Hastings, *qv*, first Scottish brothers to play together in a Lions Test, capt tour NZ 1993 (3 Tests); marketing exec Hastings International Edinburgh; *Recreations* golf (6 handicap), squash, travelling; *Style—* Gavin Hastings, Esq, OBE; ✉ c/o Scottish Rugby Union, Murrayfield, Edinburgh EH12 5PJ (☎ 0131 346 5000, fax 0131 346 5001)

HASTINGS, Max Macdonald; s of Douglas Macdonald Hastings (d 1982), and Anne Scott-James (Lady Lancaster); *b* 28 Dec 1945; *Educ* Charterhouse, Univ Coll Oxford; *m* 1972 (m dis 1994), Patricia Mary, da of Tom Edmondson, of Leics; 2 s (Charles b 1973, Harry b 1983), 1 da (Charlotte b 1977); *Career* author, journalist and broadcaster; reporter: London Evening Standard 1965–70, BBC TV 1970–73; ed Evening Standard Londoner's Diary 1976–77; columnist and contrib: Evening Standard, Daily Express, Sunday Times 1973–86; The Daily Telegraph: ed 1986–95, dir The Daily Telegraph plc 1989; ed The Evening Standard 1995–; fell World Press Inst St Paul USA 1967–68; *Books* The Fire This Time (1968), The Struggle for Civil Rights in Northern Ireland (1970), The King's Champion (1976), Hero of Entebbe (1979), Bomber Command (1979, Somerset Maugham Prize), The Battle of Britain (with Len Deighton, 1980), Das Reich (1981), The Battle for the Falklands (with Simon Jenkins 1983, Yorkshire Post Book of the Year Prize), Overlord: D-Day and The Battle for Normandy (1984, Yorkshire Post Book of the Year Prize), Victory in Europe (1985), The Oxford Book of Military Anecdotes (ed, 1985), The Korean War (1987), Outside Days (1989); *Recreations* shooting, fishing; *Clubs* Brooks's, Pratt's, Saintsbury; *Style—* Max Hastings, Esq; ✉ The Evening Standard, Northcliffe House, 2 Derry Street, London W8 5EE (☎ 0171 938 6000)

HASTINGS, Scott; s of Clifford Hastings, of Edinburgh, and Isobel, *née* Macallum; *b* 4 Dec 1964; *Educ* George Watson's Coll, Newcastle upon Tyne Poly (now Univ of Northumbria); *m* Sept 1990, Jenny; 1 s (Corey b 14 Jan 1993); *Career* rugby union centre; clubs: Newcastle Poly RFC, Northern FC 1982–85, Watsonians FC 1982– (capt 1987–88 and 1988–89), Barbarians FC, Scottish Sch 1983 (3 caps), Northumberland 1984, Anglo Scots 1984, Edinburgh 1985– (incl grand slam appearances 1986, 1987 and 1988), Scotland U21 (3 caps) 1984, Scotland B 1985; Scotland: debut v France 1986, memb World Cup squad (1 appearance) 1987, memb Grand Slam winning team 1990, tour NZ 1990 (2 test appearances), memb World Cup squad 1991, 62 caps (Scotland's most capped int rugby player); memb Br Lions tour Aust 1989 (2 test appearances) and tour NZ 1993; with Gavin Hastings, *qv*, became first Scottish brothers to play together in a Lions test and won their 50th int caps against France March 1994; captained Barbarian FC against NZ All Blacks Nov 1993, memb Scotland Rugby World Cup squad to SA 1995 and NZ 1996; advertising/PR account dir Barkers Scotland; *Recreations* golf, all sporting and leisure activities, underwater snooker, mixed mud wrestling; *Style—* Scott Hastings, Esq; ✉ Scottish Rugby Union, Murrayfield, Edinburgh, Lothian (☎ 0131 346 5000, fax 0131 346 5001); B Barkers Scotland, 18 Rutland Square, Edinburgh EH1 2BH (☎ 0131 229 7493, fax 0131 228 1644)

HASTINGS, Lady Selina Shirley; da of 15 Earl of Huntingdon (d 1990), and his 2 w, Margaret Lane (d 1994); *b* 5 March 1945; *Educ* St Paul's Girls' Sch, St Hugh's Coll Oxford (MA); *Career* writer and journalist; *Books* incl: Nancy Mitford, Evelyn Waugh; *Style—* The Lady Selina Hastings; ✉ c/o Rogers, Coleridge & White, 20 Powis Mews, London W11

HASTINGS, Sir Stephen Lewis Edmonstone; kt (1983), MC (1944); s of Lewis Aloysius Macdonald Hastings, MC (d 1966), and Meriel, *née* Edmonstone (d 1971); *b* 4 May 1921; *Educ* Eton, RMC Sandhurst; *m* 1, 1948 (m dis 1971), Harriet Mary Elizabeth, da of late Col Julian Latham Tomlin, CBE, DSO; 1 s (Neil), 1 da (Carola); m 2, 1975, Hon Elizabeth Anne Marie Gabrielle Naylor Leyland, *née* Fitzalan Howard, *qv*; *Career* served Scots Gds 1939–48: 2 Bn Western Desert 1941–43 (despatches), SAS Regt 1943, ADC to Rt Hon Richard Casey, as Min of State Middle East Cairo 1943–44; later served with: Special Forces in Italy, Br Troops in Austria; FO 1948, Br Legation Helsinki and Embassy Paris 1952–58, first sec Political Office ME Forces 1959–60; MP (C) Mid-Bedfordshire 1960–83; dir of various cos; chm: British Field Sports Soc 1982–88, Peterborough Cathedral Devpt and Preservation Tst 1995–; ptnr and mangr Milton Park Thoroughbred Stud; *Publications* The Murder of TSR2 (1966), The Drums of Memory (1994); *Recreations* country sports, skiing, painting; *Clubs* White's, Buck's, Pratt's; *Style—* Sir Stephen Hastings, MC; ✉ Milton Hall, Peterborough (☎ 01733 380 780); 12a Ennismore Gardens, London SW7 (☎ 0171 589 6494)

HASTINGS, Steven Alan; s of Thomas Alan Hastings, OBE, of Larchmont, Crab Hill, Beckenham, Kent, and Margaret Elizabeth, *née* Webber; *b* 18 Sept 1957; *Educ* Dulwich, Univ of Bristol (BSocSci); *m* 19 July 1987, Teresa Lynne Eugenie, da of John Wimbourne, of Esher, Surrey; 1 s (Thomas Magna b 1 April 1989), 2 da (Rosie Beatrice b 14 April 1991, Flora Isabella b 15 Dec 1993); *Career* jr planner Leagas Delaney 1980–83, planner D'Arcy McManus & Masius 1983–84, sr planner Lowe Howard-Spink 1984–88, planning dir BBDO UK Ltd 1988–91, dir The Planning Group 1991–92, ptnr Banks Hoggins O'Shea advtg 1992–; memb: MRS, Account Planning Gp, Euro Soc for Opinion and Market Res; *Recreations* running classic cars; *Style—* Steven Hastings, Esq; ✉ 97 Chesterton Rd, London W10 6ET (☎ 0181 960 3242, fax 0181 964 3242)

HATCH, David Edwin; CBE (1984), JP (1993); s of Rev Raymond Harold Hatch (d 1967), and Winifred Edith May, *née* Brookes (d 1987); *b* 7 May 1939; *Educ* St John's Leatherhead, Queens' Coll Cambridge (MA, DipEd); *m* 1964, Ann Elizabeth, da of Christopher Martin (d 1945); 2 s (Christopher b 1967, Richard b 1970), 1 da (Penelope b 1965); *Career* co starred with John Cleese, Graham Chapman, Bill Oddie and Tim Brooke Taylor in Cambridge Footlights Revue Cambridge Circus 1963; BBC: actor and writer I'm Sorry I'll Read That Again (Radio Light Entertainment) 1965, exec prodr Prog Devpt 1971, ed Radio Network Manchester 1978, head of Radio Light Entertainment 1978, controller Radio 2 1980, controller Radio 4 1983, dir of progs 1986–87, md Network Radio 1987–93, advsr to DG 1993–95, vice chm BBC Enterprises Ltd 1986–95; chm Nat Consumer Cncl 1996–; vice chm The Servs Sound and Vision Corp, vice pres Euro Bdcasting Union's Radio Prog Ctee; pres Television and Radio Industs Club 1990–91; awarded Radio Academy Creative Award Sony Radio Awards 1993; FRSA, CIMgt; *Recreations* Bruegel jigsaws, family, laughing; *Style—* David Hatch, Esq, CBE, JP; ✉ The Windmill, Ray's Hill, Chesham, Bucks HP5 2UJ; National Consumer Council, 20 Grosvenor Gardens, London SW1 (☎ 0171 730 3469, fax 0171 730 0191)

HATCH, Prof David John; s of James Frederick Hatch (d 1991), of Hutton, Essex, and late Marguerite Fanny, *née* Forge; *b* 11 April 1937; *Educ* Caterham Sch, UCL (MB BS, MRCS, LRCP); *m* 4 June 1960, Rita, da of William Henry Wilkins Goulter (d 1956); 2 s (Michael b 1963, Andrew b 1969), 2 da (Susan b 1964, Jane b 1967); *Career* fell in anaesthesiology Mayo Clinic Rochester Minnesota 1968–69, conslt in anaesthesia and respiratory measurement Hosp for Sick Children Gt Ormond St 1969–91 (chm Div of Anaesthesia 1984–87), sub dean Inst of Child Health Univ of London 1974–85, prof of paediatric anaesthesia Univ of London 1991–; Assoc of Paediatric Anaesthetists: hon sec 1979–86, pres 1993–95; memb Cncl: Assoc of Anaesthetists of GB and Ireland

1982–86, Coll of Anaesthetists 1986– (vice pres 1991–93); memb GMC 1994–97; FFARCS 1965, FCAnaes 1988, FRCA 1992; *Books* with Sumner: Neonatal Anaesthesia and Perioperative Care (1981, 2 edn 1986, 3 edn 1995), Clinics in Anaesthesiology - Paediatric Anaesthesia (1985), Textbook of Paediatric Anaesthetic Practice (1989); *Recreations* squash, sailing; *Clubs* RSM, Medical Soc of London; *Style*— Prof David Hatch; ✉ 6 Darnley Rd, Woodford Green, Essex IG8 9HU (☎ 0181 504 4134, fax 0181 504 1605); The Institute of Child Health, 30 Guilford Street, London WC1N 1EH (☎ 0171 242 9789, fax 0171 829 8634, e-mail DHatch@ICH.UCL.AC.UK)

HATCH, John Vaughan; s of Brian Hatch (d 1990), and Eileen Mabel, *née* Woodmansey (d 1990); *b* 25 May 1949; *Educ* Worksop Coll, Mansfield Coll Oxford (MA), St Antony's Coll Oxford (MPhil); *m* 1973 (m dis 1994), Sally Margaret, da of Geoffrey William Randle Brownscombe (d 1950), of Hove, Sussex; 2 da (Rebecca b 1978, Amber b 1982); *Career* mgmnt conslt Deloitte Haskins & Sells 1973–82, dep dir of Investmt Water Authorities Superannuation Fund 1982–84, md Venture Link (Hldgs) Ltd 1984–87; chm: Venture Link Investors Ltd 1987–92, Venture Link Investment Panel 1993–94, Uptonia Ltd 1994–; non-exec chm UniSoft Group Ltd 1990–93; non-exec dir: Century Publishing Co Ltd 1982–85, Century Hutchinson Ltd 1985–89, Boxtree Ltd 1990–, Nat Grid Co plc 1990–, Energis Ltd 1992–; chm Electricity Consumers' Cncl 1984–90; memb: Nat Consumer Cncl 1980–86, Gen Optical Cncl 1984–88; chm inaugural ICC Test match Umpires' Conf 1993, pres Blewbury and Upton Cricket Club; Freeman: City of London 1985, Worshipful Co of Info Technologists 1989; ACMA 1980; *Books* Controlling Nationalised Industries (with John Redwood, 1982), Value For Money Audits (with John Redwood, 1981), How to Watch Cricket (1994); *Recreations* cricket, photography, bridge; *Clubs* City of London, Lansdowne; *Style*— John Hatch, Esq; ✉ Rose Cottage, High Street, Upton, Nr Didcot, Oxfordshire (☎ 01235 850671)

HATCH, Marshall Davidson (Hal); s of Lloyd Davidson Hatch (d 1979), and Alice Endersby Hatch (d 1983); *b* 24 Dec 1932; *Educ* Newington Coll Sydney, Sydney Univ (BSc, PhD); *m* July 1983, Lyndall Patricia, *née* Clarke; 2 s (Marcus Davidson b 12 June 1959, Lachlan Davidson b 7 July 1962); *Career* res scientist CSIRO Sydney 1955–59, post-doctoral fell Univ of Calif 1959–61, res offr Colonial Sugar Refining Co Ltd Brisbane 1961–66 and 1968–69, reader Dept of Botany Univ of Qld Brisbane 1967, chief res scientist Div of Plant Indust CSIRO Canberra; FAA 1975, FRS 1980, foreign associate Nat Acad of Sci of the USA 1990; memb Order of Aust 1981; *Awards* Clarke Medal Royal Soc of NSW 1973, Lemberg Medal Aust Biochemical Soc 1974, Charles Kettering Award American Soc of Plant Physiologists 1980, Rank Award Rank Fndn 1981, Int Prize for Biology Japan Soc for the Promotion of Sci 1991; *Publications* author or co-author 160 research papers and other publications mostly on photosynthetic carbon metabolism; *Style*— Dr Hal Hatch, FRS; ✉ 34 Dugdale St, Cook, ACT, 2614 Australia (☎ 00 61 6 251 5159); Division of Plant Industry, CSIRO, PO Box 1600, Canberra City, ACT 2601, Australia (☎ 00 61 6 246 5264, fax 00 61 6 246500)

HATCHER, Prof (Melvyn) John; s of John Edward Hatcher (d 1960), and Lilian Florence, *née* Lepper (d 1981); *b* 1 Jan 1942; *Educ* Owens GS Islington London, LSE (BSc(Econ), PhD), Univ of Cambridge (LittD 1994); *m* 19 Dec 1967, Janice Miriam, da of Herbert John Ranson; 2 da (Melissa Ann b 12 Sept 1978, Zara Sophie b 29 June 1982); *Career* research fell Inst of Historical Research Univ of London 1966–67, sr lectr in history Univ of Kent at Canterbury 1973–75 (lectr 1967–73); Univ of Cambridge: lectr in history 1976–86, reader in economic and social history 1986–95, prof of economic and social history 1996–; fell Corpus Christi Coll Cambridge 1976–; visiting prof Univ of Colorado at Boulder USA 1975–76, visiting fell Huntington Library Calif USA 1986–87; memb SSRC Econ and Social History Ctee 1979–82; ESRC: vice-chm Econ Affrs Ctee 1982–84, memb (jtly with UGC) New Blood Ctee, dir research initiative on history of prices and incomes 1984–86, Postgrad Awards Ctee 1988–90; memb Cncl Economic History Soc 1980–; ed Economic History Review 1995–; FRHistS 1974; *Books* Rural Economy and Society in the Duchy of Cornwall, 1300–1500 (1970), English Tin Production and Trade before 1550 (1973), A History of British Pewter (with T C Barker, 1974), Plague, Population and the English Economy, 1348–1530 (1977), Medieval England: rural society and economic change 1086–1348 (with E Miller, 1978), The History of the British Coal Industry: Before 1700 (1993, Wadsworth Prize 1993), Medieval England: towns, commerce and crafts, 1086–1348 (with E Miller, 1995); also author of book chapters and articles in learned jls; *Recreations* football, jazz; *Style*— Prof John Hatcher; ✉ Longfield, 49 Madingley Road, Cambridge CB3 0EL; Corpus Christi College, Cambridge CB2 1RH (☎ 01223 338000, fax 01223 338061)

HATCHER, Mark; s of Peter Thomas Hatcher (d 1995), of Great Bookham, Surrey, and Joan Beatrice, *née* Crisp; *b* 16 Oct 1954; *Educ* Sutton Valence Sch Kent, Exeter Coll Oxford (Winter Williams Law prize, MA); *m* 9 July 1988, Clare Helen, eld da of Prof Hugh Lawrence, FSA, *qv*, of London; 1 da (Sophie b 13 Nov 1990); *Career* called to the Bar Middle Temple 1978 (Astbury scholar, ad eundem Lincoln's Inn), in private practice 1978–80, with Law Cmmn 1980–83, with Legislation Gp Lord Chancellor's Dept 1983–88, Cts and Legal Servs Gp 1988; mgmnt conslt Deloitte Haskins & Sells 1988–90, head Public Affrs Consultancy Coopers & Lybrand (following merger) 1990–, public affrs counsel Coopers & Lybrand (UK) 1996–; contrib to various jls; corp fell Indust and Parl Tst 1994; memb: Greenwich Soc (conservation), Bar Assoc for Commerce Finance and Industry, Gen Cncl of Bar; FRSA 1994; *Recreations* architecture, second-hand books, cooking; *Clubs* Reform; *Style*— Mark Hatcher, Esq; ✉ 41 Gloucester Circus, Greenwich, London SE10 8RY (☎ 0181 293 4969); Coopers & Lybrand, 1 Embankment Place, London WC2N 6NN (☎ 0171 583 5000/0171 213 4714, fax 0171 213 1893, telex 887470)

HATELEY, Linzi; da of Raymond William Hateley, and Margery, *née* Hammond; *b* 23 Oct 1970; *Educ* Wilnecote HS Tamworth, Italia Conti Acad of Theatre Arts London; *Career* actress; *Theatre* incl: title role in RSC's Carrie (Stratford & Broadway), Eponine in RSC's Les Miserables, Kolakola Bird in Cameron Mackintosh's Just So, narrator in Andrew Lloyd Webber's Joseph And The Amazing Technicolour Dreamcoat, Shakers - The Musical, Peter Pan, The Rise and Fall of Little Voice, Rizzo in Grease; *Television* The Day The Music Died (Channel 4 documentary film); *Awards* incl: Theatre World Award for Most Promising Newcomer on Broadway 1988, Olivier Award nomination for Best Actress in a Musical/Entertainment 1992; *Style*— Ms Linzi Hateley; ✉ c/o Barry Burnett Organisation Ltd, Suite 42–43, Grafton House, 2–3 Golden Square, London NW1 (☎ 0171 437 7048, 0171 734 6118, fax 0171 437 1098)

HATELY, Dr William; s of William Williamson Hately (d 1956), and Janet Favard, *née* Roxburgh (d 1983); *b* 19 Dec 1935; *Educ* George Heriot's Sch Edinburgh, Univ of Edinburgh (MB ChB, DMRD); *m* 19 Sept 1959, Gillian, da of Charles William Massot, of Farnham, Surrey; 2 da (Ruth b 12 Nov 1964, Diane b 16 April 1969); *Career* Nat Serv Med Branch RAF 1959–62; conslt radiologist The Royal London Hosp 1968–, dir X-Ray Dept The London Clinic; past pres Br Inst of Radiology; FRCR, FRCPEd; *Recreations* swimming, travel; *Clubs* RAC; *Style*— Dr William Hately; ✉ 4 Hitherwood Drive, London SE19 1XB (☎ 0181 670 7644, fax 0181 670 9071); Casa Jinty 15, Mijas La Nueva, Mijas, Malaga, Spain (☎ 00 34 52 486179); Alexandra Wing X-Ray Department, The Royal London Hospital, Whitechapel, London E1 1BB (☎ 0171 377 7103, fax 0171 377 7102); X-Ray Department, The London Clinic, 20 Devonshire Place, London W1 (☎ 0171 935 4444)

HATHERTON, 8 Baron (UK 1835); Edward Charles Littleton; only s of Mervyn Cecil Littleton (d 1970), gs of 3 Baron, by his w, Margaret Ann, da of Frank Sheehy; *b* 24 May 1950; *m* 1974, Hilda Maria, da of Rodolfo Robert, of San José, Costa Rica; 1 s (Hon Thomas), 2 da (Hon Melissa Ann b 1975, Hon Valerie Ann b 1981); *Heir* s, Hon Thomas Edward, b 7 March 1977; *Style*— The Rt Hon Lord Hatherton; ✉ PO Box 1341–2150, Moravia, Costa Rica (☎ 00 506 240 4324)

HATHORN, Eric Anthony; s of James Hathorn, of Edinburgh; *b* 18 June 1929; *Educ* Wellington, Merton Coll Oxford; *m* 1966, Hon Mrs (Jean Rosemary) Hathorn, da of Lord Evans, GCVO (d 1963); 2 s, 1 da; *Career* 2 Lt Grenadier Gds; with ICI 1952–68, joined L Messel and Co stockbrokers 1968; ptnr: Beardsley Bishop Escombe 1973–83, Henderson Crosthwaite 1983–86; dir Henderson Crosthwaite Ltd 1986–; *Recreations* travel, theatre, opera, gardening; *Style*— Eric Hathorn, Esq; ✉ 51 Netherhall Gardens, London NW3 5RJ (☎ 0171 794 6892); Henderson Crosthwaite Ltd, 32 St Mary-at-Hill, London EC3P 3AJ (☎ 0171 283 8577)

HATHORN, (Alexander) Michael; s of Douglas Stuart Hathorn, and Elizabeth, *née* Snowdon; *b* 5 June 1948; *Educ* Stranraer HS Sedbergh; *m* 14 Oct 1972, Deborah Christian, da of Hamish Gordon Farquhar; 2 s (Iain Fergus b 30 April 1977, Andrew Alexander b 4 Aug 1984), 1 da (Emma Louise b 4 Sept 1979); *Career* ptnr Scott-Moncrieff Thomson & Sheills CAs 1974– (apprentice 1967–72); dir: Scott-Moncrieff Life & Pensions Ltd 1993–, Scott-Moncrieff Consultancy Ltd 1993–, Baillie Gifford Shin Nippon plc 1994–; accountant to the Village XIII Commonwealth Games 1986; assoc dir (Fin) Edinburgh International Festival 1989–90; dir: Scottish Child Law Centre 1991–, Family Mediation Scotland 1992–; chm: Moore Stephens UK National Partnership 1989–, Local Authy (Scotland) Accounts Advsy Ctee 1991–93, LASAAC/CIPFA Jt Ctee 1992–94; memb ASB Public Sector and Not-for-Profit Ctee 1994–; hon treas and tstee Age Concern Scotland 1988–; memb: CIPFA 1993 (Capital Accounting Gp 1991–93), ICAS 1972 (chm Members Services Ctee 1990–); *Recreations* golf, curling, music, visual arts; *Clubs* New (Edinburgh), Lismore RFC; *Style*— Michael Hathorn, Esq; ✉ Moore Stephens, 17 Melville Street, Edinburgh, Scotland EH3 7PH (☎ 0131 473 3599)

HATOUM, Mona; da of Joseph Salim Hatoum, MBE (d 1986), of Beirut, and Claire Indrawes Eid; *b* 11 Feb 1952; *Educ* Beirut UC, The Byam Shaw Sch of Art (Leverhulme Tst Fund bursary), Slade Sch of Art London; *Career* artist; Gtr London Arts Assoc grant 1982, Arts Cncl of GB bursary 1985; artist-in-residence: Western Front Art Center Vancouver 1984 and 1988, Chisenhale Dance Space London 1986–87, Capp Street Project San Francisco 1996; pt/t lectr St Martin's Sch of Art 1986–89, visual arts advsr Gtr London Arts 1986–88, sr fell in fine art Cardiff Inst of HE 1989–92, pt/t lectr Jan Van Eyck Akademie Maastricht 1992–97; nominated for Turner Prize 1995; *Important Works* incl: The Light at the End (installation work with electric heating elements in the collection of Arts Cncl of GB) 1989, Light Sentence (installation work with wire-mesh lockers and moving lightbulb in the collection of FNAC Paris) 1993, Corps Étranger (video projection inside a cylindrical structure in the collection of Centre Georges Pompidou); *Exhibitions* incl: The British Art Show (McLellan Galleries Glasgow and tour) 1990, Pour la Suite du Monde (Musée d'Art Contemporair de Montréal) 1992, Arnolfini Gallery Bristol 1993, Centre Georges Pompidou (solo exhbn) 1994, Sense and Sensibility: Women Artists and Minimalism in the Nineties (Museum of Modern Art NY) 1994, Tenjin 94 (Fukuoka Japan), Cocido y Crudo (Centro de Arte Reina Sofia Madrid) 1994/95, Heart of Darkness (Kröller Müller Holland) 1994/95, Corps Étranger (Venice Biennale) 1995, Rites of Passage: Art for the End of the Century (Tate Art Gallery) 1995, 4th International Istanbul Biennial 1995, The British Sch at Rome (solo exhbn) 1995, Distemper: Dissonant Themes in the Art of the 1990s (Hirshhorn Museum and Sculpture Garden Washington) 1996, Life/Live la Scène artistique au Royaume-Uni en 1996, de nouvelles aventures (Musée d'art moderne de la Ville de Paris) 1996; *Style*— Ms Mona Hatoum; ✉ c/o White Cube, 44 Duke Street, St James's, London SW1Y 6DD (☎ 0171 930 5373)

HATT-COOK, Mark Edward; OBE (1996), RD (and Bar); s of Lt-Col John Edward Hatt-Cook, MC, of The Courtyard, Stoke Farthing, Broadchalke, Salisbury, Wilts, and Lavender Helen, *née* Coverton; *b* 18 Dec 1942; *Educ* Bradfield; *m* 18 Oct 1969, Susan Georgina, da of Lt-Col Ronald John Henry Kaulback, OBE (d 1995), of Altbough, Hoarwithy, Hereford; 2 da (Catherine Emma b 13 Aug 1974, Georgina Alice b 13 June 1977); *Career* cmmnd RMR 1963, 45 Commando S Arabia 1963 (active serv), 42 Commando Malaysia 1969, 41 Commando N Ireland 1970, qualified Arctic survival instr 1980, TAVR staff course Camberley 1981, USMC staff course Quantico 1984, Lt-Col CO RMR City of London 1990–92, RMR Col 1992–95; vice chm Eastern Wessex TAVRA 1991, vice chm Cncl TAVRA 1992–95, vice chm City TAVRA 1996; Lord Mayor's Marshal 1980–96; ADC to HM The Queen 1992–95; articled with Hunters and with Bischoffs, admitted slr 1970, asst slr Deacons Hong Kong, ptnr Wilsons Salisbury; memb regnl Br Olympic Ctee 1988, pres Salisbury Slrs Assoc 1989; Freeman City of London 1981, Liveryman Worshipful Company of Turners 1995; memb Law Soc; *Recreations* shooting, skiing, sailing, numismatics, deer management; *Clubs* Army & Navy; *Style*— Col Mark Hatt-Cook, OBE, RD; ✉ Mascalls, Broadchalke, Salisbury, Wilts (☎ 01722 780480); Steynings House, Salisbury, Wilts (☎ 01722 412412, fax 01722 411500)

HATTERSLEY, Prof (William) Martin; s of Col Sidney Martin Hattersley, MC, MD, late RAMC (ka 1943), and Vera, *née* Blackbourn (d 1962); *b* 31 March 1928; *Educ* Marlborough, Univ of London (BSc); *m* 1, 1 Sept 1951 (m dis 1982), Shena Mary, da of Sydney Drummond Anderson (d 1961); 3 da (Susan Mary (Mrs Boyce) b 13 Jan 1955, Clare Helen (Mrs Papavergos) b 6 June 1956, Diana Rosine (Mrs Warner) b 5 Nov 1957); m 2, 1 Oct 1982, May Ling, da of Wee Bin Chye (d 1949), of Singapore; *Career* probationary 2 Lt RM 1946, Lt RM 1948, resigned cmmn 1950, elected memb HAC 1988; Gerald Eve & Co (chartered surveyors): improver 1950–54, tech asst 1954–58, ptnr 1958, responsible for all overseas assignments 1962–86, responsible for Brussels Office 1975–83; chief resident valuation offr Kuala Lumpur Municipal Cncl 1959–61; City Univ: prof and head of Dept of Property Valuation and Mgmnt 1985–91, visiting prof 1991–95, prof emeritus 1996; memb: RNLI, Lavant Valley Decorative and Fine Arts Soc, Emsworth Maritime and Historical Tst, Solent Protection Soc, Chichester Canal Soc; friend of: Chichester Festival Theatre, National Maritime Museum, Redgrave Theatre, Yvonne Arnaud Theatre, National Library of Wales; pres: BSc Estate Mgmnt Club 1970, Rating Surveyors' Assoc 1978; Freeman: City of London 1950, Co of Waterman and Lighterman 1992; Liveryman: Worshipful Co of Skinners 1963, Worshipful Co of Chartered Surveyors 1977; FIABCI Medaille d'Honor for Leadership of Professional Standards Ctee (France 1986), hon fell of SBV Univ of Amsterdam 1991; FRICS 1963, FISM 1968, FSVA 1971, FIABCI 1973; memb: RNSA 1946, RYA, IRRV 1986, Charter Soc 1991; ACIArb 1990; *Books* Valuation: Principles into Practice (contrib 1992); *Recreations* sailing; *Clubs* Carlton, Army & Navy, Naval and Military, City Livery; *Style*— Prof Martin Hattersley; ✉ 4 Roundhouse Meadow, Emsworth, Hants PO10 8BD (☎ 01243 375664, fax 01243 378464)

HATTERSLEY, Rt Hon Roy Sydney George; PC (1975), MP (Lab) Birmingham Sparkbrook (majority 13,572); s of late Frederick Hattersley, and Enid Hattersley (Lord Mayor Sheffield 1981–82); *b* 28 Dec 1932; *Educ* Sheffield City GS, Univ of Hull (BScEcon); *m* 1956, Edith Mary (Molly), da of Michael Loughran; *Career* joined Lab Pty 1949, memb Sheffield City Cncl 1957–65, Parly candidate (Lab) Sutton Coldfield 1959; MP (Lab) Birmingham Sparkbrook 1964–, PPS to Min of Pensions and Nat Insurance 1964–67, jt Parly sec of state for employment and productivity 1967–69, min of defence for admin 1969–70; oppn spokesman on: defence 1972, educn and science 1972–74; min of state FCO 1974–76, sec of state for prices and consumer protection 1976–79; chief oppn spokesman on: environment 1979–80, home affairs 1981–83, Treasy and econ affairs 1983–87, home affairs 1987–; dep ldr Lab Pty Oct 1983–1992; journalist; named columnist of the year What the Papers Say (Granada TV) 1982; *Books* Nelson (1974), Goodbye to Yorkshire (essays, 1976), Politics Apart (1982), Press Gang (1983), A Yorkshire Boyhood (1983), Choose Freedom - The Future for Democratic Socialism (1987), Economic Priorities for a Labour Government (1987), The Maker's Mark (novel, 1990), In That Quiet Earth (novel, 1991), Skylark's Song (novel, 1993), Who Goes Home? Scenes from a Political Life (1995); *Recreations* writing, watching football and cricket; *Style—* The Rt Hon Roy Hattersley, MP

HATTON, Christopher John Bower; s of Alan Herbert Hatton (d 1960); *b* 5 March 1933; *Educ* Charterhouse; *m* 1, 1962, Alison Myfanwy, da of Robert Faulkner Armitage (d 1982); 2 s (William, John), 1 da (Sarah); m 2, 1991, Melanie Jane, da of Dennis Wood; 2 da (Faye, Liberty); *Career* slr 1956; sr ptnr Robert Davies & Co Warrington; former chm (now non-exec dir) Greenalls Group plc (brewers, formerly Greenall Whitley plc), dir North Western Bd Sun Alliance Assurance Co; *Style—* Christopher Hatton, Esq; ✉ Robert Davies & Co Solicitors, PO Box 1, 21 Bold St, Warrington, Cheshire WA1 1DF (☎ 01925 650161, fax 01925 414330)

HATTON, David William; QC (1996); s of Thomas William Hatton, of Bolton, and Margery, *née* Greenhalgh; *b* 29 May 1953; *Educ* Bolton Sch, Univ of Bristol (LLB); *m* 1994, Janet Elizabeth, da of Terence Bossons; 1 da (Charlotte Rose b 6 Nov 1995); *Career* called to the Bar Gray's Inn 1976, recorder of the Crown Court 1995–; *Recreations* music, history, cooking, dining; *Clubs* Bolton Wanderers FC; *Style—* David Hatton, Esq, QC; ✉ Park Court Chambers, 40 Park Cross Street, Leeds LS1 2QH (☎ 0113 243 3277, fax 0113 242 1285)

HATTY, Sir Cyril James; kt (1963); s of James Hatty; *b* 22 Dec 1908; *Educ* Westminster City Sch; *m* 1937, Doris Evelyn Stewart; 2 s; *Career* dep dir O and M Div UK Treasy to 1947; MP for Bulawayo S Rhodesia 1950–62 (min of Treasy 1954–62, min of Mines 1956–62); min of Fin Bophuthatswana 1979–82; tstee Zimbabwe Nat Conservation Tst; FCIS, FCMA; *Recreations* painting, writing on environmental subjects; *Clubs* Harare; *Style—* Sir Cyril Hatty; ✉ Merton Park, Norton, Zimbabwe

HAUGHEY, Senator Dr Edward; OBE (1987), JP (1986); s of Edward Haughey (d 1943), of Kilcurry House, Dundalk, Co Louth, and Rose, *née* Traynor (d 1992); *b* 5 Jan 1944; *Educ* Christian Brothers Secdy Sch Dundalk; *m* 5 Jan 1972, Mary Gordon, da of Alfred William Young (d 1977); 2 s (Edward, James), 1 da (Caroline); *Career* md then chm Norbrook Laboratories Ltd 1969–, chm Norbrook Holdings Ltd 1988–, dir Short Brothers plc 1989–; dir Advsy Bd Bank of Ireland 1987–; appointed to the Irish Senate 1994; memb: Cncl CBI (NI) 1983–89, Bd of S ITEC 1985–89; chm IOD (NI Branch) 1985–86 and 1986–87; memb NI Fire Authy 1986–89; memb Bd: Warrenpoint Harbour Authy 1986 and 1989, Industl Tbnls 1990–; hon consul for the Embassy of Chile, Gran Oficial of the Order of Bernardo O'Higgins (Chile) 1995; Hon DBA; fell Int Acad of Mgmnt, FInstD, FIMgt; *Recreations* study of architectural history; *Clubs* Savage (London); *Style—* Senator Dr Edward Haughey, OBE, JP; ✉ Ballyedmond Castle, Rostrevor, Co Down, N Ireland (business fax 01693 69981)

HAUGHTON, Simon James; s of Pamela Standen Haughton, *née* Mitchell; *b* 10 Nov 1975; *Educ* Parkside Middle Sch Bradford, Bingley GS Bradford; *Career* professional rugby league player; Bingley Amateur Rugby League, Dudley Hill Amateur Club, rugby union Bingley GS, selected to play for England at rugby union and rugby league, Wigan RLFC 1992–; 7 GB Academy test matches including tour to Australia in 1994, rep England 1995 World Cup; Mentioned in Guiness Book of Records for most tries scored in a season (under 14) 130; *Recreations* relaxing after training; *Style—* Simon Haughton, Esq; ✉ Wigan RLFC, Central Park, Wigan WN1 1XF (☎ 01942 231321)

HAVARD, Dr John David Jayne; CBE (1989); s of Dr Arthur William Havard (d 1964), of Lowestoft, and Ursula Jayne Vernon, *née* Humphrey (d 1990); *b* 5 May 1924; *Educ* Malvern, Jesus Coll Cambridge (MA, MD, LLM), Middx Hosp Med Sch (FRCP); *m* 1, Sept 1950 (m dis 1982), Margaret Lucy, da of Albert Lumsden Collis, OBE (d 1963), of Wimbledon; 2 s (Jeremy Michael Jayne b 18 April 1952, Richard William b 27 Jan 1954), 1 da (Amanda b 12 May 1956); m 2, July 1982, Audrey Anne, da of Rear Adm Laurence Boutwood, CB, OBE (d 1982), of Tideford, Cornwall; *Career* Nat Serv Actg Sqdn Ldr RAF Med Serv 1950–52; called to the Bar Middle Temple 1954; house physician Professorial Med Unit Middx Hosp 1950, GP Lowestoft 1952–58, sec E Suffolk LMC 1956–58; staff BMA 1958–89, sec BMA 1979–89; former dep chm Staff Side Whitley Cncl (Health Servs), chm Sci Ctee Int Driver Behaviour Res Assoc 1969–94, pres Br Acad of Forensic Sciences 1985, hon sec Cwlth Med Assoc 1986–; memb: Gen Medical Cncl 1989–94, President's Advsy Bd Med Protection Soc 1991–, Clinical Res Ethical Ctee RCGP 1991–; Stevens medal RSM 1989, Green Coll lectr Oxford 1989, Widmark award Int Ctee on Alcohol, Drugs and Traffic Safety Chicago 1989, Gold medal for Distinguished Merit BMA 1990; *Books* Detection of Secret Homicide (Cambridge Studies in Criminology Vol XI, 1960), Medical Negligence: The Mounting Dilemma (1989), author of chapters in text books on subjects incl legal med, alcohol and drugs; *Recreations* country walks; *Clubs* United Oxford and Cambridge University, Achilles; *Style—* Dr John Havard, CBE; ✉ 1 Wilton Sq, London N1 3DL (☎ 0171 359 2802, fax 0171 354 9690); Myrtle Cottage, Tideford, Saltash, Cornwall PL12 5HW; Commonwealth Medical Association, BMA House, Tavistock Square, London WC1H 9JP (☎ 0171 383 6095, fax 0171 383 6195, e-mail 72242.3544@compuserve.com)

HAVELOCK, (Robert) Gary; s of Robert Brian Havelock, of Yarm, Cleveland, and Marjorie Wynn, *née* Smith; *b* 4 Nov 1968; *Educ* Conyers Comp Sch Yarm; *partner* Jayne Amanda Cloney; *Career* professional speedway rider 1985–; over 100 appearances Middlesbrough Tigers 1985–86, over 400 appearances Bradford Keyline Dukes 1987–; 80 England caps (capt 1992, 1993, 1994, 1995 and 1996); major titles incl: Br under 21 champion 1986, Euro under 21 champion 1987, Br champion 1991 and 1992, overseas champion 1992, world champion 1992, riders champion Premier League 1995; *Recreations* snowboarding, jet skiing, snooker; *Style—* Gary Havelock, Esq; ✉ c/o Philip Lanning, 17 Whitcroft, Langdon Hills, Laindon, Essex SS16 6LR (☎ 01268 416286)

HAVELOCK, Sir Wilfrid Bowen; kt (1963); s of Rev E W Havelock (d 1916), and F H Bowen; *b* 14 April 1912; *Educ* ISC Windsor; *m* 1, 1938 (m dis 1967), Mrs Muriel Elizabeth Pershouse, *née* Vincent; 1 s; m 2, 1972, Mrs Patricia Mumford; *Career* served in 3/4 African Rifles 1940–42; MLC Kenya 1948–63 (min Local Govt, Health and Lands 1954–62, min Agric and Animal Husbandry 1962–63), dep chm Kenya Agriculture Finance Corporation 1964–84, memb Nat Irrigation Bd Kenya 1974–79; dir: Bamburi Portland Cement Co 1974–86, Baobab Farm Ltd Bamburi 1974–; chm African Fund for Endangered Wildlife Ltd (Kenya) 1986–93; chm Kenya Assoc of Hotelkeepers and Caterers 1973–76, memb Hotels and Restaurant Authy 1975–82; *Clubs* Muthaiga Country (Nairobi), Mount Kenya Safari (Nanyuki), Nairobi, Royal Commonwealth Soc (Fellow), Mombasa; *Style—* Sir Wilfrid Havelock; ✉ No 5 Moundsmere Estate, PO Box 30181, Nairobi, Kenya (☎ 00 25 42 762835)

HAVELOCK-ALLAN, Sir Anthony James Allan; 4 Bt (UK 1858), of Lucknow; s of Allan Havelock-Allan (2 s of Sir Henry Havelock-Allan, 1 Bt, VC, GCB, MP, DL and his w Lady Alice Moreton, da of 2 Earl of Ducie), and Annie Julia, da of Sir William Chaytor, 3 Bt; suc bro, Sir Henry Ralph Moreton Havelock-Allan, 3 Bt, 1975; *b* 28 Feb 1904; *Educ* Charterhouse, Switzerland; *m* 1, 12 April 1939 (m dis 1952), (Babette) Valerie Louise (the film actress Valerie Hobson, *qv*, who m 2, 1954, John Dennis Profumo, CBE, *qv*), da of late Cdr Robert Gordon Hobson, RN; 2 s (Simon Anthony Henry b 1944 d 1991, (Anthony) Mark David b 1951); m 2, 1979, Maria Theresa Consuela (Sara), da of late Don Carlos Ruiz de Villafranca (formerly Spanish ambass to Chile and Brazil); *Heir* s, (Anthony) Mark David Havelock-Allan, QC, *qv*, b 4 April 1951; *Career* film producer; formerly produced quota films for Paramount, produced for Pinebrook Ltd and Two Cities Films 1938–40, assoc producer to Noel Coward 1941, with David Lean and Ronald Neame formed Cineguild 1942, producer, assoc producer and in charge of production for Cineguild 1942–47, formed Constellation Films 1949, formed with Lord Brabourne and Maj Daniel Angel Br Home Entertainment (first co to attempt to introduce pay TV by cable) 1962; chm British Film Academy 1952, govr Br Film Inst (memb Inst's Production Ctee) 1958–65, chm Council of Soc of Film and Television Arts (now BAFTA) 1962 and 1963; *Clubs* Boodle's, RAC; *Style—* Sir Anthony Havelock-Allan, Bt; ✉ c/o Lloyds Bank, Berkeley Square, London W1

HAVELOCK-ALLAN, (Anthony) Mark David; QC (1993); s and h of Sir Anthony James Allan Havelock-Allan, 4 Bt, *qv*, and Valerie Babette Louise Hobson, *qv* (now married to John Dennis Profumo, CBE, *qv*); *b* 4 April 1951; *Educ* Eton, Univ of Durham (BA Hons Law), Trinity Coll Cambridge (LLB, Dip in Int Law); *m* 1, 1976 (m dis 1984), Lucy Clare; yr da of Alexander Plantagenet Mitchell-Innes; m 2, 1986, Alison Lee Caroline, da of Leslie Francis Foster; 1 s (Henry Caspar Francis (Harry) b 6 Oct 1994), 1 da (Miranda Antonia Louise b 29 July 1993); *Career* called to the Bar Inner Temple 1974, bencher 1995, asst recorder 1993–; FCIArb 1991; *Recreations* salmon fishing, foreign travel; *Clubs* RAC; *Style—* Mark Havelock-Allan, Esq, QC; ✉ 38 West Square, London SE11 4SP (☎ 0171 582 9009); 20 Essex Street, London WC2R 3AL (☎ 0171 583 9294, fax 0171 583 1341)

HAVERS, Christopher Antony Gore; s of Antony Cecil Oldfield Havers, of Berks, and Barbara Harrison Havers; *b* 30 April 1950; *Educ* Repton, Trinity Coll Dublin (BA); *m* 6 May 1978, Christine Mary, da of Kevin Patrick Moore, of Coventry; 2 s (Timothy b 1981, Patrick b 1984), 1 da (Rosie b 1988); *Career* called to the Bar Inner Temple 1975; dir: Through Transport Mutual Services Ltd 1985, West of England Ship Owners Insurance Services 1987; *Recreations* shooting, sailing, farming; *Style—* Christopher A G Havers, Esq; ✉ West of England Services, Tower Bridge Court, 224 Tower Bridge Road, London SE1 2UP

HAVERS, Hon Nigel Allan; yr s of Baron Havers, PC, QC (Life Peer, d 1992), and Carol Elizabeth, *née* Lay (now Mrs Charles Hughesdon); *b* 6 Nov 1951; *m* 1, 1974 (m dis 1989), Carolyn Gillian, da of Vincent Cox; 1 da (Katharine b 1977); m 2, 12 Dec 1989, Mrs Polly Bloomfield; *Career* actor; *Theatre* incl: The Glittering Prizes, Nicholas Nickleby, Horseman, Ricochet; *Television* incl: A Horseman Riding By, Upstairs Downstairs, Nancy Astor, Strangers and Brothers, Don't Wait Up, The Charmer, A Perfect Hero, Sleepers, The Good Guys; *Films* incl: Chariots of Fire, A Passage to India, Burke and Wills, The Whistle Blower, Empire of the Sun, Farewell to the King, Burning Season; *Recreations* keeping fit, reading, gardening; *Clubs* Garrick; *Style—* The Hon Nigel Havers; ✉ c/o Michael Whitehall Ltd, 125 Gloucester Road, London SW7 4TE (☎ 0171 244 8466, fax 0171 244 9060)

HAVERS, Hon Philip Nigel; QC (1995); er s of Baron Havers, PC, QC (Life Peer, d 1992), and Carol Elizabeth, *née* Lay (now Mrs Charles Hughesdon); *b* 16 June 1950; *Educ* Eton, CCC Cambridge; *m* 20 March 1976, Patricia Frances, *née* Searle; *Career* called to the Bar Inner Temple 1974; *Recreations* tennis, music; *Clubs* Garrick; *Style—* The Hon Philip Havers, QC; ✉ 75 Cadogan Place, London SW1; 1 Crown Office Row, Ground Floor, Temple, London EC4Y 7HH (☎ 0171 797 7500, fax 0171 797 7550)

HAVERY, His Hon Judge; Richard Orbell; QC (1980); s of Joseph Horton Havery (d 1994), of Blackheath, London, and West Chiltington, and Constance Eleanor, *née* Orbell (d 1987); *b* 7 Feb 1934; *Educ* St Paul's, Magdalen Coll Oxford (MA); *Career* called to the Bar Middle Temple 1962, recorder of Crown Ct 1986–93 (asst recorder 1982–86), circuit judge and official referee 1993–; bencher Middle Temple 1989; *Books* Kemp and Kemp The Quantum of Damages (jt ed 3 edn, 1967); *Recreations* music, croquet, steam locomotives; *Clubs* Garrick, Hurlingham, Athenaeum; *Style—* His Hon Judge Havery, QC; ✉ Official Referees' Court, St Dunstan's House, 133–137 Fetter Lane, London EC4A 1HD (☎ 0171 936 7429)

HAVILAND, Christopher Philip; s of late Col Philip Haviland Haviland, OBE, and Molly Gwendoline Parker, *née* Butt; *b* 9 Feb 1940; *Educ* Trinity Coll Dublin (MA, LLB); *m* 1970, Catherine Margaret Joan, da of George Ernest Swanson, of Colinton, Lothian; 2 s (Philip Julian Swanson b 27 Jan 1972, Adrian Christopher Clemow (twin) b 27 Jan 1972), 1 da (Fiona Mary Katharine b 30 June 1975); *Career* merchant banker; dir N M Rothschild & Sons (CI) Ltd 1975–81, dir N M Rothschild & Sons Ltd 1976–81; Barclays; dir Barclays Merchant Bank Ltd 1981–86, dir Barclays de Zoete Wedd Ltd 1986–, md overseas banking Barclays Bank plc 1992–, dep chm Banque du Caire Barclays International SAE 1992–, dir Barclays Bank of Zambia 1992–; *Recreations* swimming, tennis, walking; *Style—* Christopher Haviland, Esq; ✉ Barclays Bank plc, 54 Lombard Street, London EC3P 3AH (☎ 0171 699 5000)

HAVILL, Brian Bond; s of Arthur Ernest Havill (d 1971), and Violet May, *née* Williams; *b* 31 Aug 1939; *Educ* Hafod-y-Ddol GS, Univ of Sheffield (BSc), Harvard Business Sch (PMD); *m* 29 Nov 1969, Ann Jennifer, da of late Charles Rooke; 2 s (Gervase Bond b 2 April 1972, Giles Dominic b 3 Feb 1976); *Career* joined Alcan Group as graduate trainee 1961, mktg dir Haden Carrier 1974, vice pres of ops Thomas Tilling 1974, dir and vice pres Citicorp Inc 1983, md Investmt Banking Div PaineWebber International (UK) Ltd (and Main Bd dir) 1986–; memb: Harvard Business Sch Assoc, Br American C of C; *Recreations* golf, literature, music; *Clubs* Royal Wimbledon Golf; *Style—* Brian Havill, Esq; ✉ Court Lodge, Ewhurst Green, East Sussex TN32 5TD (☎ 01580 830213); Investment Banking Division, PaineWebber International (UK) Ltd, 1 Finsbury Avenue, London EC2M 2PA (☎ 0171 422 2000)

HAVILLE, Robert William; s of James Haville (d 1983), and Eileen Haville; *b* 27 July 1955; *Educ* Marlborough GS, Univ of Lancaster (BA), Univ of Bradford (MBA); *m* 18 Oct 1980, Hazel Dawn, da of George Burke, of London; 2 s (James b 1988, Ralph b 1995), 2 da (Rosalind b 1986, Sarah b 1990); *Career* fin analyst Kimberley Clark 1976–77; investmt analyst: McAnally Montgomery 1978–81, James Capel 1982–87, Morgan Stanley 1988–91, Smith New Court/Merrill Lynch 1991–; memb Assoc of Business Graduates; MSI; *Clubs* RAC; *Style—* Robert Haville, Esq; ✉ Merrill Lynch, Smith New Court House, 20 Farringdon Rd, London EC1M 3NH (☎ 0171 772 1000)

HAW, Brandon; s of Ken Haw, and Brenda, *née* Walters; *b* 7 Sept 1960; *Educ* Brighton, Hove & Sussex GS for Boys, Bartlett Sch of Arch and Environmental Studies UCL (BSc Arch), Sch of Arch Princeton Univ USA (MArch); *partner* Pritanjan Kaler; 2 c (Marlon b 17 Dec 1992, Bonner b 5 Dec 1994); *Career* architect; NYC USA 1982–87; completed works incl: office designs for Weeks & Toomey Advertising NYC, Metalstand Showroom Chicago Merchandise Mart; with HOK then Skidmore Owings and Merrill NYC 1985–87; projects incl: commercial office towers Fifth Avenue, St Lukes/Roosevelt Hosp; Foster and Partners London 1987–: assoc 1988–91, project dir 1991–95, dir 1995–; projects incl: Kings Cross urban masterplan, ITN News HQ London, project architect Canary Wharf office tower, London Wall office devpt City of London, Sagrera masterplan Barcelona, Napp Pharmaceuticals mfrg facilty extension Cambridge, Chek Lap Kok airport competition Hong Kong, resident dir Commerzbank Project Frankfurt, mixed use devpt Riyadh Saudi Arabia, Citibank HQ Canary Wharf; sponsor: WWF, Khairabad Eye Hosp India; RIBA 1990, ARCUK 1990; *Recreations* 20th Century art and design, painting; *Style—* Brandon Haw, Esq; ✉ Foster and Partners, 22 Hester Road, London SW11 4AN (☎ 0171 738 0455, fax 0171 738 8612/1107)

HAW, Jonathan Stopford; s of Denis Stopford Haw (d 1979), of Sidcup, Kent, and Elisabeth Mary Dorothy, *née* Mack; *b* 16 March 1945; *Educ* Radley, Keble Coll Oxford (MA); *m* 20 Dec 1969, Hélène Lucie, da of Louis Lacuve, Chevalier de l'Ordre National du Mérite, of Perpignan, France; 1 s (Alexander b 1973), 1 da (Katherine b 1976); *Career* slr; Slaughter and May: ptnr 1977–, first ptnr New York 1984–87, exec ptnr 1996–; memb Ctee Bassishaw Ward Club London, chm Bd of Dirs The Juvenile Diabetes Fndn (UK); Freeman City of London 1970, Liveryman Worshipful Co of Armourers and Brasiers; memb: City of London Slrs Co, Law Soc; *Recreations* gardening, reading, wine; *Clubs* Leander; *Style—* Jonathan S Haw, Esq; ✉ Slaughter and May, 35 Basinghall St, London EC2V 5DB (☎ 0171 600 1200, fax 0171 600 0289, 0171 726 0038, telex 883486/888926)

HAWARDEN, 9 Viscount (I 1793); Sir (Robert) Connan Wyndham Leslie Maude; 11 Bt (I 1705); also Baron de Montalt (I 1785); er s of 8 Viscount Hawarden (d 1991), and Susannah Caroline Hyde, *née* Gardner; *b* 23 May 1961; *Educ* St Edmund's Sch Canterbury, RAC Cirencester; *m* 8 April 1995, Judith Anne, yst da of John Bates, of Shepherdswell, Kent; *Heir* bro, Hon Thomas Patrick Cornwallis Maude b 1964; *Career* farming and interactive distribution; *Recreations* shooting, motorcycling, riding, skiing, animal husbandry; *Style—* The Rt Hon the Viscount Hawarden; ✉ Great Bossington Farm House, Adisham, nr Canterbury, Kent CT3 2LW

HAWES, Ven Arthur John; s of John Beadnell Hawes, of Cumnor, Oxford, and Sylvia Mary Lilian, *née* Taylor; *b* 31 Aug 1943; *Educ* City of Oxford HS for Boys, Chichester Theol Coll, Richmond Fellowship Coll (Cert in Human Rels), Univ of Birmingham (Dip in Pastoral Studies, Dip in Liturgy and Architecture), Univ of E Anglia (BA Philosophy); *m* 1969, Melanie Gay, da of John Harris; 1 da (Emma b 13 July 1971), 1 s (Luke John b 6 June 1973); *Career* curate St John the Baptist Kidderminster 1968–72, priest-in-charge St Richard Droitwich 1972–76, rector of Alderford with Attlebridge and Swannington 1976–92, chaplain Hellesdon and David Rice Hosps and Yare Clinic 1976–92, rural dean of Sparham 1981–91, canon of Norwich Cathedral 1988–95, chm Norwich Diocesan Bd for Social Responsibility 1990–95, rector St Faith's Gaywood King's Lynn 1992–95, archdeacon of Lincoln and canon and prebendary of Lincoln Cathedral 1995–; Mental Health Act cmmr for England and Wales 1986–94; patron Nat Assoc for Mental Health (MIND), pres Purfleet Tst; *Recreations* golf, theatre, music; *Clubs* Royal Norwich Golf, Sleaford Golf, Rotary; *Style—* The Ven the Archdeacon of Lincoln; ✉ Archdeacon's House, Northfield Road, Quarrington, Sleaford, Lincs NG34 8RT (☎ 01529 304348, fax 01529 304354, mobile 0589 469413)

HAWKE, 11 Baron (GB 1776); Edward George Hawke; TD; o s of 10 Baron Hawke (d 1992), and his 2 w, Georgette Margaret, *née* Davidson; *b* 25 Jan 1950; *Educ* Eton; *m* 4 Sept 1993, Bronwen M, da of William James, BVMS, MRCVS; 1 s (Hon William Martin Theodore b 1995); *Heir* s, Hon William Martin Theodore Hawke b 23 June 1995; *Career* served 1 Bn Coldstream Gds 1970–73, The Queen's Own Yeomanry 1973–93; FRICS; *Style—* The Rt Hon the Lord Hawke, TD

HAWKER, Eur Ing Geoffrey Fort; TD; *b* 20 Dec 1929; *Educ* Univ of London (BSc); *m*; 2 da; *Career* chartered civil engr 1956; called to the Bar Gray's Inn 1970; in practice as conslt and arbitrator, head of chambers; pres Soc of Construction Arbitrators 1986–89; Liveryman: Worshipful Co of Arbitrators, Worshipful Co of Engrs; FEng 1988, FICE, CEng, FIEI, FIStructE, MSocIS (France), MConsE, FCIArb; *Books* A Guide to Commercial Arbitration under the 1979 Act (with R Gibson-Jarvis, 1980), The ICE Arbitration Practice (with Uff and Timms, 1986), The ICE Conditions of Contract for Minor Works - A User's Guide and Commentary (with G Cottam, 1992); *Style—* Eur Ing Geoffrey Hawker, TD, FEng; ✉ 46 Essex Street, London WC2R 3GH (☎ 0171 583 8899, fax 0171 583 8800, dx 1014 Lond/Chancery Lane)

HAWKER, Graham Alfred; s of Alfred Hawker, of New Tredegar, Gwent, and Sarah Rebecca, *née* Bowen; *b* 12 May 1947; *Educ* Bedwellty GS; *m* April 1967, Sandra Ann, *née* Evans; 1 s (Simon b 15 Aug 1971), 1 da (Sally b 17 Jan 1974); *Career* various posts in local govt rising to dep treas Abercarn UDC 1964–70, moved into water industry 1970; Hyder plc (Welsh Water Authy, privatised to become Welsh Water PLC 1989): devpt 1986–88, fin dir 1988–92, gp md 1992–93, chief exec 1993–; pres Inst of Water Offrs 1993; chm Business in the Community Wales, memb CBI Cncl for Wales, memb Bd Welsh Devpt Authy; IPFA 1969, FCCA, CIMgt, FRSA; *Recreations* walking, good wine, family; *Clubs* Cardiff and County; *Style—* Graham Hawker, Esq; ✉ St Teilo House, Llantilio Pertholey, Abergavenny, Gwent NP7 6NY (☎ 01873 853468); Hyder plc, Plas y Ffynnon, Cambrian Way, Brecon, Powys LD3 7HP (☎ 01874 614424, fax 01874 614634)

HAWKER, Yvonne Isabel; da of Bentley Hawker, of Bledington, Gloucestershire, and Maria Teresa, *née* Milan; *b* 14 July 1956; *Educ* Sch of St Clare Penzance, Penzance Art Sch, Goldsmiths' Coll London, Ravensbourne Coll Kent (BA); *Career* artist; *Solo Exhibitions* Galerie Era Karlstad 1982, Galerie Trollhaltan Goteborg 1983, Galerie Olab Goteborg 1984, Barclay Lennie Fine Art Glasgow 1986 and 1994, Richard Demarco Gallery Edinburgh 1987–88, Bruton Gallery Bruton 1987–88, Galerie Arcade Carcassonne 1988, touring exhbn sponsered by French Embassy (Edinburgh Coll of Art for Edinburgh Festival, Institut Français London and Bruton Gallery) 1990, Redfern Gallery London 1993 and 1995, Br Cncl Hong Kong 1996; *Group Exhibitions* incl: RSWA, RBA, RA Summer Exhbns, Int Art Fair Stockholm, ICAF, Bath Art Fair, Scottish Art Cncl, Scottish Artists in Yugoslavia; winner Blackstone prize RA Summer Exhbn 1989, awarded scholarship by Conseiller Culturel French Embassy London 1988; *Public Collections* incl: W H Smith Collection, The William Bowmore Collection, Ayrshire Dist Cncl; tstee The Maclaurin Art Gallery Ayr 1989–; *Recreations* walking, numerology; *Style—* Miss Yvonne Hawker; ✉ Kilrenzie, Colmonell, by Girvan, Ayrshire, Scotland KA26 0SJ (☎ 01465 881218); Redfern Gallery, 20 Cork Street, London W1X 2HL (☎ 0171 734 1732/0578, fax 0171 494 2908)

HAWKES, Prof Donald Durston; s of Clifford George Durston Hawkes (d 1983), of Cardiff, and Mabel Sophia Stephens (d 1979); *b* 18 July 1934; *Educ* Canton GS, Univ of London (BSc), Univ of Birmingham (MSc, Phd); *m* 22 July 1958, Janet Beatrice, da of Enoch Francis Davies (d 1988), of Cardiff; 1 s (David b 1965), 1 da (Jane b 1960); *Career* geologist: Br Antarctic Survey 1956–59, Overseas Geological Survey 1959–62; lectr then sr lectr Fourah Bay Coll 1963–70; prof and head of geology: Univ of Sierra Leone 1970–72, Univ of Aston 1972–88; prof of geological scis Univ of Birmingham 1988–; author of numerous scientific pubns; FGS 1957, CGeol 1978, FRSA 1981; *Recreations* motorboat cruising, gardening; *Style—* Prof Donald Hawkes; ✉ School of Earth Sciences, The University of Birmingham, Edgbaston, Birmingham B15 2TT (☎ 0121 414 3344, e-mail d.d.hawkes@bham.ac.uk)

HAWKES, Prof John Gregory; OBE (1994); s of Charles William Hawkes (d 1964), and Gertrude Maude, *née* Chappell (d 1970); *b* 27 June 1915; *Educ* Cheltenham GS, Christ's Coll Cambridge (BA, MA, PhD, ScD); *m* 20 Dec 1941, Ellen Barbara, da of Charles Henry Leather (d 1954); 2 s (Anthony Christopher b 1950, Peter Geoffrey b 1950), 2 da (Phillada Daphne (Dr Collins) b 1944, Stephanie Katherine (Mrs Hazeldine) b 1946); *Career* Cwlth Bureau of Plant Breeding and Genetics 1939–48, dir Colombian Miny of Agric Res Station 1948–52; Univ of Birmingham: lectr and sr lectr in botany 1952–61, prof of plant taxonomy 1961–67, prof and head Plant Biology Dept 1967–82, emeritus prof plant biology 1982; plant collecting expdns in Mexico, Central and South America 1939, 1949–50, 1958, 1964, 1965, 1966, 1971, 1974, 1980 and 1981; hon life memb: Euro Assoc for Research in Plant Breeding 1989, Potato Assoc of America 1989; fell Linnean Soc 1945 (pres 1991–94); FInstBiol 1976; *Books* incl: Reproductive Biology and Taxonomy of Vascular Plants (ed, 1966), Chemotaxonomy and Serotaxonomy (ed, 1968), The Potatoes of Argentina, Brazil, Paraguay and Uruguay (jtly, 1969), A Computer-Mapped Flora (jtly, 1971), Crop Genetic Resources for Today and Tomorrow (jt ed, 1975), Conservation and Agriculture (ed, 1978), The Biology and Taxonomy of the Solanaceae (jt ed, 1979), The Diversity of Crop Plants (1983), A Bibliography of Crop Genetic Resources (jt ed, 1983), Revised Edition of Salaman's History and Social Influence of the Potato (ed, 1985), The Potatoes of Bolivia (jtly, 1989), The Potato-Evolution, Biodiversity and Genetic Resources (1990), Plant Genetic Resources of Ethiopia (jt ed, 1991), Genetic Conservation of World Crops (ed, 1991), Solanaceae III - Taxonomy, Chemistry, Evolution (jt ed, 1991), Vavilov Lectures, Collecta Clusiana 4 (ed A T Sabo, BioTar series, 1994); *Recreations* gardening, travel; *Clubs* Athenaeum; *Style—* Prof John Hawkes, OBE; ✉ School of Continuing Studies, University of Birmingham, Birmingham B15 2TT (☎ 0121 414 6170)

HAWKES, Michael John; s of Wilfred Arthur Hawkes (d 1968), and Anne Maria Hawkes (d 1966); *b* 7 May 1929; *Educ* Bedford Sch, New Coll Oxford (MA); *m* 1, 7 Dec 1957 (m dis 1973), Gillian Mary, *née* Watts; 2 s (James b 1964, Jason Michael b 1967), 2 da (Louise b 1963, Laura b 1966); m 2, 10 July 1973, Elizabeth Anne, *née* Gurton; *Career* banker; former chm: Kleinwort Benson Ltd 1983–87, Sharps Pixley Ltd; former dep chm Kleinwort Benson Gp 1988–90; *Recreations* walking, gardening; *Style—* Michael Hawkes, Esq; ✉ Brookfield House, Burghfield Common, Berks RG7 3BD (☎ 0118 983 2912); Whitebays, Trebetherick, Cornwall PL27 6SA

HAWKES, (Anthony) Paul; s of Reginald Ernest Hawkes, and Maria Campbell, *née* Straton-Ferrier; *b* 19 April 1951; *Educ* City of London Sch, Brighton Poly (BA), Harvard Business Sch; *m* 6 Oct 1984, Marjorie, da of Frederick Smith; 2 s (Lee b 13 May 1980, Benjamin b 26 July 1985); *Career* mgmnt trainee: Shlackman & Son 1969, Alders of Croydon 1971–72; area mangr EF Student Services 1974–75, mktg mangr American Express 1977–78 (mktg exec 1975–77); Time-Life Books (Europe) Inc: mail order mangr 1978–80, Eng area mangr 1980–82, Euro mktg vice pres 1982–86; dir: Abram, Hawkes plc 1987–, BDMA 1988–92, IMC Ltd 1989–92, The Campbell Stratton Group 1989–93; MIMgt 1987, MInstD 1987–89, MCIM 1984, MIMC 1992; *Style—* Paul Hawkes, Esq; ✉ 10 Stanton Rd, West Wimbledon, London SW20 8RL (☎ 0181 946 9353); Abram, Hawkes plc, Oakfield House, 35 Perrymount Rd, Haywards Heath, West Sussex RH16 3BW (☎ 01444 441176, fax 01444 441268)

HAWKES, (Henry) William; s of late William Neville Hawkes, of Honington, Warwicks, and Marjorie Elsie, *née* Jackson; *b* 4 Dec 1939; *Educ* Uppingham, Univ of Cambridge (MA, DipArch); *m* 22 Oct 1966, Hester Elizabeth, da of David Foster Gretton (d 1967); 3 da (Harriet b 1967, Polly b 1969, Olivia b 1972); *Career* architect, in practice Hawkes and Cave; dir Stoneleigh Abbey Preservation Tst 1980–, chm Coventry Diocesan Advsy Ctee 1986–, memb Georgian Gp Exec Ctee 1985–, tstee Coventry and Warwickshire Historic Churches Tst 1986–, memb Ctee Cncl for the Care of Churches 1991–, exec tstee The Shakespeare Birthplace Tst 1992–; author of various publications on 18th Century Gothic Revival; *Recreations* hand printing, cycling, architectural history; *Style—* William Hawkes, Esq; ✉ 20 Broad Street, Stratford upon Avon, Warwickshire (☎ 01789 266415); Hawkes and Cave, 1 Old Town, Stratford upon Avon, Warwickshire (☎ 01789 298877)

HAWKESBURY, Viscount; Luke Marmaduke Peter Savile Foljambe; s and h of 5 Earl of Liverpool, *qv*; *b* 25 March 1972; *Career* sales exec: Imperial Hotel (Forte plc) 1995–96, The Norbreck Castle Hotel (Principal Hotels Ltd) 1996–; *Clubs* Bembridge Sailing, British Sub-Aqua; *Style—* Viscount Hawkesbury; ✉ Scofton Farmhouse, Osberton, Worksop, Notts S81 0UG

HAWKESFORD, John Ernest; s of Ernest Hawkesford (d 1965), of Rushwick Grange, Rushwick, Worcestershire, and Sarah Elizabeth, *née* Jones (d 1992); *b* 29 Nov 1946; *Educ* Warwick Sch Warwick, Univ Coll Med Sch London; *m* 29 June 1974, Barbara, da of Alexander Howe, of Low Fell, Gateshead, Tyne and Wear; 3 da (Abigail Lisa b 1976, Julia Marie b 1979, Rachel Chloe b 1989); *Career* registrar in oral maxillofacial surgery Stoke Mandeville Hosp Bucks 1973–76, sr registrar in oral maxillofacial surgery W of Scotland Plastic Surgery Unit Canniesburn Hosp Bearsden Glasgow, hon clinical lectr in oral surgery and oral med Univ of Glasgow 1976–79, hon clinical teacher in oral and maxillofacial surgery Univ of Newcastle upon Tyne 1979–; conslt in oral maxillofacial surgery 1979–: Newcastle Health Authy (teaching), Northern RHA, (latterly) Royal Victoria Infirmary and Assoc Hosp Tsts (clinical dir of oral and maxillofacial surgery 1991–95); chm Specialist Subctee Dentistry Northern Regnl Med Ctee 1987–, chm Regnl Ctee for Hosp Dental Servs 1990–, memb Northern Regnl Med Ctee 1987–; pres Br Dental Assoc Hosp Gp 1993–94; memb: RSM, BDA, Br Assoc of Oral Maxillofacial Surgery, Oral Surgery Club of GB; *Books* Maxillofacial and Dental Emergencies (1994); *Recreations* squash, skiing, swimming; *Style—* Mr John Hawkesford; ✉ The Quarry, 31 Batt House Rd, Stocksfield, Northumberland NE43 7RA (☎ 01661 842338); Catherine Cookson Maxillo Facial Surgery Department, Newcastle General Hospital, Westgate Rd, Newcastle upon Tyne NE4 6BE (☎ 0191 273 8811 ext 22204)

HAWKESWORTH, John Stanley; s of Lt-Gen Sir John Ledlie Inglis Hawkesworth, KBE, CB, DSO (d 1945), and Helen Jane, *née* McNaughton (d 1966); *b* 7 Dec 1920; *Educ* Rugby, Queen's Coll Oxford (BA); *m* 10 April 1943, Hyacinthe Nairne Marteine, da of Maj-Gen Philip Saxon George Gregson-Ellis, CB (d 1956); 1 s (Philip b 1949); *Career* WWII Capt Grenadier Gds served France, Belgium, Holland, Germany 1941–46; entered film indust 1946 as asst to Vincent Korda (London Films); art dir: The Third Man 1949, Sound Barrier 1952, The Heart of the Matter 1953; writer/producer: Rowlandson's England 1956, Tiger Bay 1959; for TV (creator/producer/writer): The Goldrobbers (LWT) 1967, Upstairs Downstairs (LWT) 1970–75, The Duchess of Duke Street (BBC) 1976–77, Danger UXB (Euston Films) 1979, The Flame Trees of Thika (Euston Films) 1981, QED (CBS) 1982, The Tale of Beatrix Potter (BBC) 1983, Oscar (BBC) 1985, By The Sword Divided (BBC) 1983–85; for TV (writer/developer) The Adventures and the Return of Sherlock Holmes (Granada) 1984–88, Mrs 'Arris Goes to Paris (CBS) 1991; developer Campion (BBC) 1989, co-creator Chelworth (BBC) 1989; painter; exhibitions: one man show Watercolour Paintings (73 Glebe Place 1989 and 1995), Film Designs from the Fifties (Austin/Desmond Gallery 1991), Paintings of Pembrokeshire (Newport 1994); chm Rutland Branch Mental Health Fndn, pres Rutland and Leics Branch Grenadier Guards Assoc; awards incl: BAFTA, Writers' Guild GB, Emmy (US), Critics' Circle (US), Peabody Award Univ of Georgia; *Books* Upstairs, Downstairs (1972), In My Lady's Chamber (1973); *Recreations* hunting, tennis, golf; *Style—* John Hawkesworth, Esq; ✉ Fishponds House, Knossington, Oakham, Rutland LE15 8LX (☎ 01664 77339)

HAWKESWORTH, Rex; s of Christopher Gilbert Hawkesworth (d 1963), and Queenie Victoria Hawkesworth; *b* 8 Sept 1939; *Educ* Portsmouth Northern GS, Portsmouth Sch of Architecture; *m* 25 Oct 1961, Pauline Mary Hawkesworth (poet); 2 da (Ruth b 1962, Lee b 1965); *Career* architect; freelance 1972–, specialist in private houses and estates in S Hampshire; lectr Highbury Tech Coll Portsmouth 1976–80; RIBA; *Books* Housing in the Private Sector - an architect's view towards a design philosophy (1994); author of articles on building, architecture and environment in national and local magazines and newspapers; *Recreations* athletics coaching (incl int athletes at various levels and events); *Clubs* City of Portsmouth Athletic; *Style—* Rex Hawkesworth, Esq; ✉ 4 Rampart Gardens, Hilsea, Portsmouth, Hants (☎ 01705 662330)

HAWKESWORTH, (Thomas) Simon Ashwell; QC (1982); s of Charles Peter Elmhirst Hawkesworth (d 1990), and Felicity, *née* Ashwell; *b* 15 Nov 1943; *Educ* Rugby, Queen's Coll Oxford (MA); *m* 1970 (m dis 1989), Jennifer, da of Dr Thomas Lewis (d 1944); 2 s (Thomas b 1973, Edward b 1978); m 2, 1990, Dr May Bamber; 2 twin s (Henry and Charles b 1992); *Career* called to the Bar Gray's Inn 1967, bencher 1990, recorder of the Crown Ct 1982–, head of chambers; *Style*— Simon Hawkesworth, Esq, QC; ✉ Kirby Hill House, Boroughbridge, North Yorkshire YO5 9DS (☎ 01423 323581); 199 Strand, London WC2R 1DR; York Chambers, 14 Toft Green, York YO1 1JT (☎ 01904 620048, fax 01904 610056)

HAWKINS, Andrew John; s of Austen Ralph Hawkins, of Bournemouth, and May, *née* O'Donnell; *b* 24 Sept 1958; *Educ* Bedford Modern Sch, Univ of Lancaster (BA), Kellogg Graduate Sch of Mgmnt Northwestern Univ Evanston Illinois (MBA); *m* 16 Nov 1990, Karen, da of Gerald Edward Pursey; 2 s (Jack b 2 May 1992, Ned b 14 Sept 1994), 1 da (Martha (twin) b 14 Sept 1994); *Career* graduate trainee Ogilvy and Mather advtg 1982, account dir Publicis (formerly McCormick Publicis) 1985 (account mangr 1983); GGK London: joined Bd 1988, dep md Jan 1990, md Nov 1990–93, jt chm and chief exec offr 1993–95; md Doner Cardwell Hawkins 1995–; *Recreations* water-skiing, skiing, running, movies; *Style*— Andrew Hawkins, Esq; ✉ 23 Westmoreland Road, London SW13 9RZ (☎ 0181 748 4465); Doner Cardwell Hawkins, 76 Dean Street, London W1V 5AB (☎ 0171 734 0511, fax 0171 287 5310, car 0831 168533)

HAWKINS, Prof Anthony Donald; s of Kenneth St David Hawkins, and Marjorie, *née* Jackson; *b* 25 March 1942; *Educ* Poole GS, Univ of Bristol (BSc, PhD); *m* 31 July 1966, Susan Mary; 1 s (David Andrew b 23 Feb 1973); *Career* dir of Fisheries Res Scotland 1987–, chief scientific offr SO 1987–, hon prof Univ of Aberdeen 1987; FRSE 1988; *Recreations* whippet racing; *Style*— Prof Anthony Hawkins, FRSE; ✉ Kincraig, Blairs, nr Aberdeen (☎ 01224 868984); Marine Laboratory, PO Box 101, Victoria Rd, Torry, Aberdeen (☎ 01224 876544, fax 01224 295413)

HAWKINS, Sir Arthur Ernest; kt (1976); s of Rev Harry Robert Hawkins (d 1942); *b* 10 June 1913; *Educ* The Blue Sch Wells Somerset, Gt Yarmouth GS, London Univ (BScEng); *m* 1939, Laura Judith Tallent, da of Albert Draper (d 1956); 1 s, 2 da; *Career* memb CEGB 1970– (chm 1972–77), memb Nuclear Power Advsy Bd 1973–; *Recreations* fell walking, swimming; *Clubs* The Hurlingham; *Style*— Sir Arthur Hawkins; ✉ 61 Rowan Rd, Brook Green, London W6 7DT (☎ 0171 603 2849)

HAWKINS, Prof Denis Frank; s of Frank Reginald Hawkins (d 1970), and Elsie Anne May, *née* Sallis (d 1986); *b* 4 April 1929; *Educ* Alleyn's Sch Dulwich, UCL, UCH (BSc, MB BS, PhD, DSc); *m* 10 July 1957, Joan Dorothy Vera, da of Walter James Taynton (d 1949); 2 s (Robert James b and d 1960, Richard Frank b 1961), 2 da (Valerie Joan b 1958, Susan Pauline b 1966 d 1995); *Career* prof and chm of obstetrics and gynaecology Boston Univ 1965–68, conslt obstetrician and gynaecologist Hammersmith Hosp 1968–; emeritus prof of obstetric therapeutics Univ of London 1989– (lectr 1961–65, sr lectr 1968–74, reader 1974–79, prof 1979–89); ed Journal of Obstetrics and Gynaecology 1980–95; memb: Br Fertility Soc, BMA, Br Pharmacological Soc, Italian Soc for Perinatal Med, Renal Assoc; Freeman City of London 1985, Liveryman Worshipful Soc of Apothecaries 1987; FACOG 1966, MRCOG 1962, DObstRCOG 1957, FRCOG 1970; *Books* Obstetric Therapeutics (1974), The Intrauterine Device (1977), Human Fertility Control (1979), Gynaecological Therapeutics (1981), Drugs and Pregnancy (1983, 2 edn 1987), Drug Treatment in Obstetrics (1983, 2 edn 1991), Perinatal Medicine (1986), Advances in Perinatal Medicine (1988), Diabetes and Pregnancy (1989), Progress in Perinatal Medicine (1990), Recent Advances in Perinatal Medicine (1993); *Recreations* Arabian primitive rock carvings, Greek archaeology; *Clubs* Savage; *Style*— Prof Denis Hawkins; ✉ Department of Obstetrics and Gynaecology, Hammersmith Hospital, Ducane Road, London W12 0HS; (☎ 01372 843073, fax 01372 843884)

HAWKINS, Dr (Thomas) Desmond; s of Thomas Hawkins (d 1985), of Co Cork, and Helen, *née* Laing (d 1960); *b* 22 May 1923; *Educ* Alleyne's Sch Herts, St Mary's Hosp Med Sch (exhibitioner, MB BS, MRCS, LRCP), Manchester Univ Med Sch (DMRD), Univ of Cambridge (MA, MPhil), MRCP, FRCR, FRCP (Lond); *m* 26 April 1947, Margaret Frances, da of Kenneth Archibald Blair; 1 da (Bryony Jane b 22 Sept 1949 (decd)), 3 s (Martin Thomas b 18 Oct 1951, Patrick Francis b 14 June 1957, Richard Oliver b 11 July 1962); *Career* student house offr Park Prewett (Mil) Hospital June-Aug 1944, British Red Cross (famine relief) Belsen Germany 1945; med offr RAF 1946–49, med registrar St Mary's Hosp 1949–50, sr house offr (paediatrics) W Middx Hosp 1951–52, GP Brill Bucks 1952–54, sr house offr (diagnostic radiology) Radcliffe Infirmary Oxford 1955, registrar and sr registrar (diagnostic radiology) Manchester Royal Infirmary 1955–60, visiting fell Stockholm and Göteborg Sweden 1960–61, conslt radiologist (neuroradiology) Addenbrooke's Hosp Cambridge 1960–88, assoc lectr Univ of Cambridge and memb St John's Coll 1976–88, clinical dean Sch of Clinical Med 1979–84, president Hughes Hall Cambridge 1989–94 (hon fell 1994–); author of papers on patho-physiology of the cereral circulation, interventional neuroradiology and palaeopathology 1961–92; fndr memb: Euro Soc of Neuroradiology 1969–, Br Soc of Neuroradiology 1970– (pres 1986–88), Assoc of Med Deans in Europe 1980–84; FRSM; *Books* Roads to Radiology (jtly, 1983), Textbook of X-Ray Diagnosis (contrib, 1984), The Drainage of Wilbraham, Fulbourn and Teversham Fens (1990), The Wilbrahams 1894–1994 (jtly, 1994); *Recreations* landscape history, gardening, cycling; *Clubs* United Oxford and Cambridge Univ, Hawks'; *Style*— Dr Desmond Hawkins; ✉ Greyfriars, Church Green, Little Wilbraham, Cambridge CB1 5LE (☎ 01223 811219); Hughes Hall, Mortimer Road, Cambridge CB1 2EW (☎ 01223 334893, fax 01223 311179)

HAWKINS, Prof Eric William; CBE (1973); s of James Edward Hawkins (d 1958), of West Kirby, Wirral, and Agnes, *née* Clarie Hawkins (d 1973); *b* 8 Jan 1915; *Educ* Liverpool Inst, Trinity Hall Cambridge; *m* 12 Aug 1938, Ellen Marie Baunsgaard, da of Prof Peder Thygesen (d 1955), of Copenhagen; 1 s (John b 1947), 1 da (Anne b 1939); *Career* WWII 1940–46; Offr 1 Bn Loyal Regt served: N Africa (wounded), Anzio beachhead (despatches), Adj 1944–45; headmaster: Oldershaw GS Wallasey 1949–53, Calday Grange GS West Kirby Cheshire 1953–65; Univ of York: reader in educn 1965–67, prof of language educn and dir Lang Teaching Centre 1967–79, emeritus prof 1979–; hon prof UCW Aberystwyth 1985; memb: Plowden Ctee Nat Advsy Educn Cncl 1963–67, Nat Ctee for Cwlth Immigrants 1965–68, Ctee of Inquiry Educn of Children of Ethnic Minorities 1979–81; FIL 1973; Commandeur dans l'Ordre des Palmes Académiques France 1985; *Books* Modern Languages in the Curriculum (2 edn 1987), Awareness of Language - An Introduction (2 edn 1987); *Recreations* cello, walking; *Style*— Prof Eric Hawkins, CBE

HAWKINS, Sir Howard Caesar; 8 Bt (GB 1778), of Kelston, Somersetshire; s of Sir Humphry Villiers Caesar Hawkins, 7 Bt (d 1993), and Anita, *née* Funkey; *b* 17 Nov 1956; *Educ* Hilton Coll; *Heir* bro, Richard Caesar Hawkins b 29 Dec 1958; *Career* S African Air Force 1975; *Style*— Sir Howard Hawkins, Bt

HAWKINS, Keith John; *b* 19 Nov 1947; *m* 1 (m dis 1985), 23 April 1977, Linda Claire; 1 s (Richard b 1979), 1 da (Philippa b 1982); m 2, 30 Aug 1991, Anthea Frances Hedley; *Career* admitted slr 1974; ptnr Dutton Gregory & Williams; memb Law Soc 1974; *Style*— Keith Hawkins, Esq; ✉ St Just, Red Lane, West Tytherley, Salisbury, Wiltshire SP5 1NY (☎ 01794 340689); Dutton Gregory and Williams, 95 Leigh Road, Eastleigh, Hampshire (☎ 01703 620211, fax 01703 611812)

HAWKINS, Louis; s of Edgar Ernest Hawkins, of Harrow, Middlesex (d 1996), and Winifred Elizabeth, *née* Stevens; *b* 19 Aug 1945; *Educ* Chandos Secdy Mod Stanmore, Willesden Tech Coll, Poly of Central London (DipArch); *m* 20 Aug 1966, Patricia Anne, da of Douglas Herbert Jarvis (d 1976), of Godstone, Surrey; 1 s (Joseph b 1983), 1 da (Harriet b 1980); *Career* architect; chm: Devon Branch of the Assoc of Conslts, ACA Quality Assur Working Pty 1988; vice chm Bd of Govrs Upottery C P Sch 1986–88, chm RIBA S Western Region Practice Ctee 1991–92; ARIBA; *Recreations* photography, fell walking, music; *Style*— Louis Hawkins, Esq; ✉ Stoneburrow Cottage, Rawridge, Upottery, Honiton, Devon EX14 9PY (☎ 01404 861533); The Louis Hawkins Practice, Chartered Architects, Stoneburrow, Rawridge, Upottery, Honiton, Devon EX14 9PY (☎ and fax 01404 861533)

HAWKINS, Michael Richard; OBE (1987); s of William Hawkins, MM (d 1987), of Minehead, Somerset, and Winifred May, *née* Strawbridge (d 1985); *b* 27 Nov 1927; *Educ* Minehead GS; *m* 1, 20 May 1950 (m dis 1977), Doreen, *née* Went; 2 s (Malcolm b 1951, Lyndsay b 1953); m 2, 4 Feb 1978, Judith Carole, da of Leslie Fauxton Yelland, of Newquay; *Career* borough engr Torquay 1965–68, dir of tech servs Torbay 1968–74, co engr and planning offr Devon 1974–90; pres: Inst of Municipal Engrs 1982–83, Co Surveyors Soc 1987–88; chm Br Nat Ctee of PIARC 1987–91; pres Concrete Soc 1991–92; chm Exmoor Soc, vice chm South Devon Healthcare Trust; hon memb Dartmoor Rescue Serv; Freeman City of London, Liveryman Worshipful Co of Paviors; FICE 1981, FIStructE 1962, MRTPI 1963, FIHT 1969, FRS 1986; *Books* Devon Roads (1988); *Recreations* walking, collecting antique maps; *Clubs* RAC; *Style*— Michael Hawkins, Esq, OBE, FRS; ✉ 19 Mead Road, Livermead, Torquay TQ2 6TG (☎ 01803 607819)

HAWKINS, Nicholas John (Nick); MP (C) Blackpool South (majority 1,667); s of Dr A E Hawkins and Mrs P J Hawkins; *b* 27 March 1957; *Educ* Bedford Modern Sch, Lincoln Coll Oxford (MA), Inns of Court Sch of Law; *m* 21 July 1979, Angela Margaret Turner; 2 s, 1 da; *Career* called to the Bar Middle Temple 1979, in practice Birmingham and Northampton 1979–86, legal conslt 1986–87, door tenant 1986–91, co legal advsr Access (credit card co) 1987–89, gp legal advsr Lloyds Abbey Life plc 1989–92; MP (C) Blackpool S 1992–; PPS to Mins of State for Defence 1995–96, PPS to Sec of State for Nat Heritage 1996–; chm Commons All-Pty Railways Gp 1995– (sec 1992–95), chm Cons Backbench Sports Ctee 1995– (sec 1992–94), sec Cons Backbench Educn Ctee 1992–95, memb Cons Backbench Ctees on Home Affrs, Trade and Indust, Fin and Tourism 1992–, memb All-Pty Gps on Fin Servs and Tourism 1992– (vice chm Fin Servs Gp 1994–); Bow Gp: md Bow Publications Ltd 1989–90, res sec 1990–91, campaign dir 1991–92, chm 1992–93; chm Bar Assoc for Commerce, Fin and Indust 1993–94 (chm International Ctee 1989–92); memb: Bar Cncl 1988–95, Exec Ctee Soc of Cons Lawyers 1992– (memb Fin and Gen Purposes Ctee 1987–, memb Exec Ctee 1992–); vice chm Rochford Constituency Cons Assoc 1988–91; ACIArb 1989; *Recreations* cricket, rugby, swimming and other sports, theatre, music, transport history; *Clubs* Carlton; *Style*— Nick Hawkins, Esq, MP; ✉ House of Commons, London SW1A 0AA

HAWKINS, Sir Paul Lancelot; kt (1982), TD (1945); s of Lance G Hawkins (d 1947), and Mrs Hawkins, *née* Peile; *b* 7 Aug 1912; *Educ* Cheltenham; *m* 1, 1937, Joan Snow (d 1984); 2 s, 1 da; m 2, 1985, Christine M Daniels; *Career* served Royal Norfolk Regt (TA) 1933–45 (POW Germany 1940–45); chartered surveyor 1933 (having joined family firm 1930); co cncllr Norfolk 1949–70, alderman 1968–70, MP (C) SW Norfolk 1964–87, asst govt whip 1970–71, Lord Cmmr of Treasury (govt whip) 1971–73, vice-chamberlain of HM Household 1973–74; memb: Select Ctee House of Commons Servs 1976–87, Delgn to WEU and Cncl Europe 1976–87; chm Agric Ctee Cncl of Europe 1985–87; dir Gorham & Bateson Agricultural Seed Merchants Fordham; *Recreations* gardening, travel; *Style*— Sir Paul Hawkins, TD; ✉ Stables, Downham Market, Norfolk

HAWKINS, Peter John; s of Derek Gilbert, of Ariège, France, and Harriet Joanne, *née* Mercier; *b* 20 June 1944; *Educ* private tutors, Hawtreys, Eton, Univ of Oxford (MA); *Career* dir Christies 1973–, md Christies Monaco (Monte Carlo) sale room 1987–89; Freeman City of London, Liveryman Worshipful Co of Gunmakers; *Recreations* shooting, driving collectors' cars, skiing, travel; *Clubs* Turf, Carlton House Terrace; *Style*— Peter Hawkins, Esq; ✉ 20 Ennismore Gardens, London SW7; Caroline Cottages, Hull Farm, Chipping Norton, Oxon; Christies, 8 King St, St James's, London SW1 (☎ 0171 389 2020)

HAWKINS, His Hon Judge; Richard Graeme; QC (1984); s of late Denis William Hawkins, of Frinton-on-Sea, Essex, and Norah Mary Hawkins, *née* Beckingsale; *b* 23 Feb 1941; *Educ* Hendon County Sch, UCL (LLB); *m* 1969, Anne Elizabeth, da of Dr Glyn Charles Edwards, of Bournemouth, Dorset; 1 s (Benjamin b 1975), 1 da (Victoria b 1972); *Career* called to the Bar Gray's Inn 1963, in practice SE Circuit, recorder of Crown Ct 1985, circuit judge (SE Circuit) 1989–; Liveryman Worshipful Co of Curriers; *Recreations* sailing; *Clubs* Royal Thames Yacht; *Style*— His Hon Judge Hawkins, QC; ✉ Central Criminal Court, City of London, London EC4M 7EH

HAWKINS, Richard Ingpen Shayle; s of Vice Adm Sir Raymond Hawkins, KCB (d 1987), and Rosalind Constance Lucy, *née* Ingpen (d 1990); *b* 20 June 1944; *Educ* Bedford Sch; *m* 26 July 1969, Amanda Louise, da of Rear Adm E F Gueritz, CB, OBE, DSC, *qv*, of Salisbury, Wilts; 2 s (William b 1973, George b 1976); *Career* cmmnd 2 Lt RM 1962, Lt 42 Commando Far East 1964–65, 43 Commando UK 1965–66, 45 Commando Aden and UK 1967–69, Capt 40 Commando Far East 1970–71, GSO3 HQ Commando Forces 1971–73, Adj RMR Tyne 1973–75, Army Staff Coll Camberley 1976, Co Cdr 45 Commando UK 1977–78, Maj Instr Sch of Inf 1978–80, GSO2 Dept of Cmdt Gen RM MOD 1980–82, ret 1982; insurance broking 1982–, dir Bowring Marsh & McLennan Ltd 1994–; *Recreations* sailing, field sports, cross country skiing; *Clubs* Royal Yacht Sqdn; *Style*— Richard Hawkins, Esq; ✉ The Old Forge, Upton, Andover, Hants SP11 OJS (☎ 01264 736269)

HAWKINS, Rt Rev Richard Stephen; *see:* Crediton, Bishop of

HAWKINS, Dr Thomas James; TD; s of Douglas William Richard Hawkins (d 1995), of Street, Somerset, and Caroline Emily Maria, *née* Drury (d 1982); *b* 16 May 1937; *Educ* Colfe's GS, Royal Free Hosp Sch of Med Univ of London (MB BS, DA); *m* 19 Nov 1960, Sylvia Colleen, da of Alan Adrian Parsons (d 1971), of Dorchester, Dorset; 1 s (Simeon b 1966), 1 da (Sarah b 1964); *Career* Lt-Col RAMC (TA), CO 144 Parachute Field Ambulance RAMC (Vol) 1983–86, offr i/c Resuscitation and Anaesthesia 257 Gen Hosp RAMC (Vol) 1987–88, lectr BATLS specialist trg team 1988–, offr in cmd 363 Field Surgical Team RAMC (Vol) 1989–; house surgn Dreadnought Seamen's Hosp 1961, jr casualty offr and anaesthetist Royal Free Hosp 1962, house physician St Alfege's Hosp 1962–63, sr res anaesthetist and sr house offr Royal Free Hosp 1963–64; registrar in anaesthesia: Peace Meml Hosp 1964–66, London Chest Hosp 1966–68, Charing Cross Hosp 1968–69; sr registrar in anaesthesia and chief asst St Bartholomew's Hosp 1969–73, conslt anaesthetist Univ and City Hosps Nottingham 1973–, clinical dir Dept of Anaesthesia Queen's Medical Centre 1991–95; memb: Assoc of Anaesthetists of GB and I, Assoc of Cardio-thoracic Anaesthetists, Sheffield and E Midlands Soc of Anaesthetists, World Anaesthesia, Airborne Med Soc, BMA, Nottingham Medico-Chirurgical Soc, TA Med Offr Assoc; assoc memb Tri-Serv Anaesthetic Soc; FFARCS, FRCA; *Recreations* model railways, kit car building, gardening; *Style*— Dr Thomas Hawkins, TD; ✉ Weatherbury, 119 Main St, Willoughby on the Wolds, Loughborough, Leicestershire LE12 6SY (☎ 01509 9880912); Dept of Anaesthesia, University Hospital, Queen's Medical Centre, Nottingham NG7 2UH (☎ 0115 970 9195)

HAWKSEY, Brian Foran; s of Joseph Osmund Hawksey (d 1979), of Manchester, and Mary Susan, *née* Foran (d 1981); *b* 22 Aug 1932; *Educ* St Bede's Coll Manchester, Douai Sch Woolhampton; *m* 19 June 1965, (Patricia) Anne, da of Patrick Maginnis, of Bognor

Regis, W Sussex; *Career* materials mangr Smiths Industries Ltd 1973–77, dep dir of trg Purchasing Economics Ltd 1977–79, ptnr Brian Hawksey & Associates 1979–80, purchasing devpt and trg mangr Thorn-EMI plc 1981–86; dir PMMS Consulting Group Ltd 1986–; assoc fell Singapore Inst of Purchasing and Materials Mgmnt; FCIPS, MIMgt; *Recreations* music, cricket, photography, reading; *Style—* Brian Hawksey, Esq; ✉ 1 Wexham Place, Framewood Road, Wexham, Slough SL2 4QX (☎ and fax 01753 664378)

HAWKSLEY, John Richard; s of Richard Walter Benson Hawksley (d 1976), and Jean Lilley of Norwich; *b* 11 March 1942; *Educ* Haileybury; *m* 9 March 1968, Jane, da of Col Hugh Pettigrew; 2 s (Benjamin b 26 Nov 1968, David b 23 April 1971), 1 da (Victoria b 11 Dec 1973); *Career* qualified chartered accountant 1965; Coopers & Lybrand (formerly Deloitte Haskins & Sells): ptnr 1975–, ptnr i/c Reading 1981–85, ptnr i/c Birmingham 1986–90, regnl ptnr i/c Midland Region 1987–95, ptnr i/c Birmingham Coopers & Lybrand (following merger) 1990–95; dir Public Arts Cmmn Agency 1988– (chm 1988–93), pres Cncl Birmingham Chamber of Indust & Co 1995–96 (vice pres 1993–95), memb Cncl West Midlands CBI 1991–, govr City Technol Coll Kingshurst 1988–, dep chm DTI Business Action Team 1989–94; dir: Birmingham Hippodrome Theatre Tst 1993–, Newtown and S Aston City Challenge Ltd 1992–95; memb Business Link Accreditation Bd 1996–; FCA (ACA 1965), FRSA, MInstD; *Recreations* travel, cricket, golf, skiing, watching all sport, opera, theatre, music; *Clubs* MCC, Stratford Oaks Golf; *Style—* John Hawksley, Esq; ✉ Coopers & Lybrand, 35 Newhall St, Birmingham B3 3DX (☎ 0121 265 5065, fax 0121 265 5050)

HAWKSLEY, (Philip) Warren; MP (C) Halesowen and Stourbridge (majority 9,582); s of late Bradshaw Warren Hawksley; *b* 10 March 1943; *Educ* Denstone Coll Uttoxeter Staffs; *m* 1, 1967 (m dis), Cynthia Marie, da of late Frederick Higgins; 2 da; m 2, 1987, Evelyn Giles; *Career* with Lloyds Bank Ltd 1960–79, currently hotel and restaurant proprietor; cncllr Shropshire CC 1970–81, Parly candidate (C) Wolverhampton NE 1974 (both gen elections); MP (C): The Wrekin 1979–87, Halesowen and Stourbridge 1992–; memb Select Ctee on Employment 1986–87, memb Select Ctee on Home Affairs 1996–; fndr memb Cons Parly Euro Reform Gp; *Style—* Warren Hawksley, Esq, MP; ✉ House of Commons, London SW1A 0AA (☎ 0171 219 3524)

HAWKSWORTH, Prof David Leslie; CBE (1996); *b* 5 June 1946; *Educ* Univ of Leicester (BSc, PhD, DSc); *Career* mycologist Cwlth Mycological Inst Kew 1969–81 (princ taxonomist 1980–81), scientific asst to exec dir Cwlth Agric Bureaux Farnham Royal Slough 1981–83, dir Int Mycological Inst Kew and Egham 1983–; memb Cncl (Govt appointee) English Nature 1996–; visiting prof: Univ of Reading 1984–, Univ of Kent 1990–, Univ of London 1992–; chm Int Cmmn on the Taxonomy of Fungi 1982–, pres Br Lichen Soc 1986–87 (memb 1964–), pres Br Mycological Soc 1990 (memb 1969–), pres Int Union of Biological Sciences 1994–, hon pres Int Mycological Assoc 1994– (sec gen 1977–90, pres 1990–94); Int Assoc for Plant Taxonomy: memb 1967–, memb Ctee for Fungi 1981–93, memb Gen Ctee 1987–, memb Editorial Ctee 1987–, Admin Finances 1993–; Systematics Assoc: memb 1969–, treas 1972–81, ed-in-chief 1981–84 and 1986, memb Cncl 1970–72 and 1986–95; ed: The Lichenologist 1970–90, Mycopathologia 1984–87, Plant Systematics and Evolution 1986–, Systema Ascomycetum 1986–; memb Editorial Bd: Field Studies 1975–80, Nat History Book Reviews 1976–80, Plant Pathology 1985–91, Cryptogamic Botany 1988–90; memb: Field Studies Cncl 1965–, Int Assoc for Lichenology 1967–, Botany Sub-Ctee Royal Soc Nat Ctee for Biology 1975–82, Tropical Agric Assoc 1982–, Ct Univ of Surrey 1983–, Ruislip Woods Mgmnt Advsy Gp 1983–, American Phytopathological Soc 1986–, Exec Bd World Fedn of Culture Collections 1988–96, Standing Ctee on Nomenclature Int Union of Biological Scis 1988–94, Int Relations Ctee Royal Soc 1994–95; Dr (hc) Univ of Umeå 1996; hon memb: Società Lichenologica Italiana 1989–, Ukrainian Botanical Soc 1992–, Mycological Soc of America 1994–, Br Mycological Soc (Centenary fell) 1996; author of numerous books, articles, papers and book reviews in learned jls mainly on fungi (incl lichens), biological diversity and bionomenclature; FLS 1969 (Bicentenary Medal 1978, vice pres 1985–88), FIBiol 1982; *Recreations* lichenology, natural history, museums, walking, swimming, history of biology; *Style—* Prof David L Hawksworth, CBE; ✉ International Mycological Institute, Bakeham Lane, Egham, Surrey TW20 9TY (☎ 01784 470111, fax 01784 470909, e-mail imi@cabi.org)

HAWLEY, Prof Christine Elizabeth; da of John and Margaret Hawley; *b* 3 Aug 1949, Shrewsbury; *Educ* City of London Sch for Girls, Architectural Assoc Sch of Arch London (AADipl); *m* 1974, Clyde Watson; 1 da (Lucy b 1982), 2 s (Samuel b 1984, Joseph b 1991); *Career* asst R&D Unit Dept of the Environment 1972; asst architect: Renton Howard Wood and Levin Architects London 1972–73, De Soissons Partnership London 1974–77, YRM (Yorke Rosenberg and Madell) London 1977, Pearson International London 1978; ptnr Cook and Hawley Architects London 1974–; unit master AA Sch of Arch London 1980–88 (tutor 1979–80), head Univ of E London (formerly Poly of East London) Sch of Arch 1987–93, prof of architectural studies Bartlett Sch of Arch 1993–; visiting prof: Western Aust Inst of Technol Perth 1985, Oslo Sch of Arch Norway 1987, Tech Univ Vienna 1993 and 1996–97; Hyde prof Lincoln Univ Nebraska 1987; lectures at numerous instns at home and abroad incl: Rhode Island Sch of Design 1978, AA 1979–87, Berkeley USA 1980–91, Aarhus Sch of Arch 1985–93, UCLA 1993, Hong Kong Univ 1994, RIBA 1995, UCL (inaugural lecture) 1996; subject of numerous articles in architectural/design pubns; Br Cncl Award Rome 1977, Yamagiwa Art Fndn Award Tokyo 1979, Br Cncl Award Helsinki and Stockholm 1980; ARCUK 1978, RIBA 1982, FRSA 1983; *Recent Projects* incl: limited int competition for social housing and exhbn centre W Berlin 1991, Stadel Acad Frankfurt 1992, competition in Lower Austria for a museum, belvedere, external amphitheatre and gallery 1993, participation of urban devpt forum on int workshops and symposium Hamburg 1993, Strathclyde Visions Centre Glasgow 1993, Elbberg Offices Hamburg 1993, Kitagata social housing Gifu 1994–, Shanghai planning study for social housing 1996; *Recent Exhibitions* incl: Graham Fndn Chicago (Three Architects) 1982, Manspace London and NY 1982, Aedes Gallery Berlin 1994 and 1995, Venice Biennale 1996; *Recreations* swimming, reading, badminton; *Style—* Prof Christine Hawley; ✉ The Bartlett School of Architecture, University College London, 22 Gordon Street, London WC1H 0QB (☎ 0171 380 7504, fax 0171 380 7453, e-mail c.hawley@ucl.ac.uk)

HAWLEY, Sir Donald Frederick; KCMG (1978, CMG 1970), MBE (1955); s of Frederick George Hawley (d 1973), of Little Gaddesden, Herts; *b* 22 May 1921; *Educ* Radley, New Coll Oxford (MA); *m* 1964, Ruth Morwenna Graham, da of Rev Peter Graham Howes (d 1964), of Charmouth, Dorset; 1 s, 3 da; *Career* served WWII Capt RA; Sudan Govt and Sudan Judiciary 1944–55; called to the Bar Inner Temple 1951; Dip Serv 1956–81: ambass Muscat 1971–75, asst under sec of state 1975–77, Br high cmmr Malaysia 1977–81; dir Ewbank & Partners 1981–82, chm Ewbank Preece Ltd 1982–86 (special advsr 1986–); memb London Advsy Ctee Hong Kong and Shanghai Banking Corp 1981–91; chm: Br Malaysian Soc 1983–95, The Centre for Br Teachers 1987–91, Confedn of Br SE Asian Socs 1988–95, Sudan Govt Br Pensioners Assoc 1992–, Royal Soc for Asian Affairs 1994–; vice pres Anglo-Omani Soc 1981–, pres Cncl Univ of Reading 1987–94, govr ESU 1989–95; Hon DLitt Univ of Reading 1994; *Books* Handbook for Registrars of Marriage and Ministers of Religion (Sudan Govt, 1963), Courtesies in the Trucial States (1965), The Trucial States (1971), Oman and its Renaissance (1977, new edn 1995), Courtesies in the Gulf Area (1978), Manners and Correct Form in the Middle East (1984, 2 edn 1996), Sandtracks in the Sudan (1995); *Recreations* tennis, golf, gardening, travel; *Clubs* Travellers, Beefsteak; *Style—* Sir Donald Hawley, KCMG, MBE; ✉ Little Cheverell House, nr Devizes, Wilts SN10 4JJ (☎ 01380 813322)

HAWLEY, James Appleton; TD (1968), JP (Staffs 1969); s of John James Hawley (d 1968), of Longdon Green, Staffs, and Ethel Mary Hawley, JP; *b* 28 March 1937; *Educ* Uppingham, St Edmund Hall Oxford (MA); *m* 8 April 1961, Susan Anne Marie, da of Alan Edward Stott, JP, DL, of Armitage, Staffs; 1 s (Charles John b 1965), 2 da (Catherine Marie (Mrs Taylor) b 1963, Jane Rachel b 1968); *Career* 2 Lt S Staffs Regt 1955–57, Nat Serv Cyprus, TA 2 Lt to Maj Staffs Yeo 1957–69; called to the Bar Middle Temple 1961; chm and md: John James Hawley Ltd 1961–, J W Wilkinson & Co Ltd 1970–; dir Stafford Railway Bldg Soc 1985–; High Sheriff Staffs 1976–77, DL Staffs 1978–93, Lord Lt Staffs 1993–; vice pres Walsall Soc for Blind 1992– (chm 1977–92), patron, pres and tstee of many orgns in Staffs; Freeman City of London 1987, Liveryman Worshipful Co of Saddlers 1988; KStJ 1993; *Recreations* family and outdoor pursuits; *Style—* James Hawley, Esq, TD, JP; ✉ Lieutenancy Office, County Buildings, Stafford ST16 2LH (☎ 01785 223121, fax 01785 215153)

HAWLEY, Peter Edward; s of Albert Edward Hawley (d 1962), of Leicester, and Winifred, *née* Skinner; *b* 20 July 1938; *Educ* Wyggeston Sch, Magdalene Coll Cambridge (MA, LLB); *m* 19 Sept 1964, (Mary) Tanya, da of John Ounsted, of Appletree Cottage, Woodgreen Common, Fordingbridge, Hants; 1 da (Sasha Louise b 26 Aug 1967); *Career* Nat Serv, Sgt (RAEC) attached 99 Gurkha Inf Bde Johore Malaya 1957–59; admitted slr 1967; Walker Martineau: articled clerk 1964–67, asst slr 1967–69, ptnr 1970–, managing ptnr 1983–91; hon treas Magdalene Coll Assoc 1975–87 (hon sec 1970–75), hon treas Whitchurch-on-Thames Twinning Assoc 1980–89; Freeman City of London 1989, Freeman Worshipful Co of Slrs 1988; MIOD 1984; *Recreations* hogging shade in hot climates; *Clubs* Gresham; *Style—* Peter Hawley, Esq; ✉ Walker Martineau, 64 Queen Street, London EC4R 1AD (☎ 0171 236 4232, fax 0171 236 2525)

HAWLEY, Peter Robert; s of Robert Thomas Hawley (d 1992), of Tunbridge Wells, and Edna May, *née* Tadman; *b* 16 Aug 1933; *Educ* King's Coll Sch Wimbledon, UCL, UCH (MB MS); *m* 16 Sept 1960, Valerie Geraldine, da of Stanley Bernard Warder (d 1971), of Reigate, Surrey; 2 s (Graham Robert Warder b 1964, David Richard Thomas b 1966), 1 da (Alison Margaret b 1962); *Career* conslt surgn: St Mark's Hosp London, King Edward VII's Hosp for Offrs London; past pres Assoc of Coloproctology of GB and Ireland; hon conslt surgn to the Army; author of articles and chapters on gastrointestinal surgery incl large bowel cancer and inflammatory bowel disease; fell UCL, fell Assoc of Surgns of GB and Ireland, memb Br Soc of Gastroenterology: FRSM, FRCS 1960; *Recreations* sailing, sport, travel; *Clubs* Garrick; *Style—* Peter Hawley, Esq; ✉ 149 Harley St, London W1N 2DE

HAWLEY, Dr Robert; s of William Hawley (d 1960), and Eva, *née* Dawson; *b* 23 July 1936; *Educ* Wallasey GS, Wallasey Tech Coll, Birkenhead Tech Coll, King's Coll Durham (BSc, PhD), Univ of Newcastle upon Tyne (DSc); *m* 17 Jan 1962, Valerie, da of Colin Clarke; 1 s (Nicholas Richard b 30 July 1968), 1 da (Fiona Jane b 10 Dec 1966); *Career* C A Parsons: head of research team 1961–64, electrical designer Generators 1964–66, dep chief generator engr 1966–70, dir and chief electrical engr 1973–74 (chief electrical engr 1970–73), dir of prodn and engrg 1974–76; NEI plc: md NEI Parsons Ltd (following t/o of C A Parsons) 1976–84, md Power Engineering Gp 1984–88, dir 1984–88, md Ops 1989–90, md 1990–92; chief exec: Nuclear Electric plc 1992–96, British Energy plc 1996–; non-exec dir: W S Atkins plc 1994–, Rotork plc 1996–; conslt SEMA 1995–; chm Hawley Ctee on Corp Governance and Information Mgmnt 1993; pres Energy Industs Club 1989–91, pres IEE 1996–; memb: Cncl Fellowship of Engrg (now Royal Acad of Engrg) 1981–84, Ct Univ of Newcastle 1979–, Bd of Advsrs (Electrical Engrg) Univ of London 1982–, Boat and Shoreworks Ctee RNLI 1992–; C A Parsons meml lectr IEE and Royal Soc 1977, Hunter meml lectr IEE 1990, Blackadder lectr NE Coast Instn of Engrs and Shipbuilders 1992, Wilson Campbell meml lectr 1994, Bowden lectr 1994; Freeman City of London; IEE Achievement Medal 1989; Hon Fell Inst of Nuclear Engrs 1994; FIEE 1970, FInstP 1970, FEng 1979, FIMechE 1987; *Publications* author of numerous scientific papers; *Recreations* gardening, philately; *Clubs* Athenaeum; *Style—* Dr Robert Hawley, FEng; ✉ British Energy plc, 10 Lochside Place, Edinburgh EH12 9DF (☎ 0131 527 2200, fax 0131 527 2109)

HAWORTH, Lionel; OBE (1958); s of John Bertram Haworth (d 1953), of Trooilaps Pan, Via Upington, Cape Province, SA, and Anna Sophia, *née* Ackerman (d 1916); *b* 4 Aug 1912; *Educ* Rondebosch Boys' HS Cape Town SA, Univ of Cape Town (BSc); *m* 1 Dec 1956, Joan Irene, da of Wilfred Bertram Bradbury, of Whitchurch, Shrops; 1 s (John Andrew), 1 da (Erica Jane); *Career* graduate apprentice Assoc Equipment Co 1934; Rolls Royce Ltd: designer 1936, asst chief designer 1944, dep chief designer 1951, chief designer (civil engines) 1954, chief engr (turboprops) 1962; Bristol Siddeley Engines Ltd: chief design conslt 1963, chief designer 1964, dir of design Aero Div Rolls Royce Ltd 1968–77; Br Gold Medal for Aeronautics 1971; RDI 1976; fndr and sr ptnr Lionel Haworth & Assocs 1977; GIMechE 1936, FIMechE 1954, FRAeS 1959, FRS 1971, FEng 1976 (fndr fell); *Recreations* sailing, walking; *Clubs* Bristol Scientific, Trent Valley Sailing, Island Cruising (Salcombe); *Style—* Lionel Haworth, Esq, OBE, FRS, FEng; ✉ 10 Hazelwood Road, Sneyd Park, Bristol BS9 1PX (☎ 0117 968 3032)

HAWORTH, Sir Philip; 3 Bt (UK 1911), of Dunham Massey, Co Chester; s of Sir (Arthur) Geoffrey Haworth, 2 Bt (d 1987); *b* 17 Jan 1927; *Educ* Dauntseys, Univ of Reading (BSc); *m* 1951, Joan Helen, da of late Stanley Percival Clark, of Ipswich; 4 s (Christopher b 1951, Mark b 1956, Simon Nicholas b 1961, Adam Ewart b 1964), 1 da (Penelope Jane b 1953); *Heir* s, Christopher Haworth; *Career* agriculture; chm Bd Buxton Festival; *Recreations* music, ornothology, sculpture; *Clubs* Farmers'; *Style—* Sir Philip Haworth, Bt; ✉ Free Green Farm, Over Peover, Knutsford, Cheshire

HAWORTH, Richard Anthony; s of George Ralph Haworth (d 1995), and Joan Kershaw, *née* Taylor; *b* 3 Sept 1955; *Educ* Oundle, Univ of Leeds (LLB); *m* 18 March 1994, Sara Kay, da of Dr Ian Smith; 1 s (George Frederick b 1 Jan 1996); *Career* called to the Bar Inner Temple 1978, in practice Northern Circuit; *Recreations* shooting, salmon fishing, growing sweet peas, working gundogs; *Clubs* East India, Yorkshire Flyfishers'; *Style—* Richard Haworth, Esq; ✉ 15 Winckley Square, Preston, Lancashire (☎ 01772 252828, fax 01772 258520)

HAWS, Edward Thomas; s of Edward Haws (d 1983), of Southend-on-Sea, and Phyllis Annie, *née* Thomas (d 1994); *b* 19 Jan 1927; *Educ* Southend-on-Sea HS, St John's Coll Cambridge (MA); *m* 26 Aug 1950, Moira Jane, da of John Forbes (d 1958), of Moulin, Perthshire; 2 s (Gordon b 1951, Tony b 1958 d 1995), 1 da (Linda b 1954); *Career* Sir Alexander Gibb & Ptnrs 1947–63: res engr Meig Dam, res engr Atiamuri Power Project, engr i/c Tongariro River Power Devpt; John Mowlem & Co Ltd 1963–78: dir Soil Mechanics Ltd, md Engrg and Resources Conslts; Rendel Palmer & Tritton 1978–92: chm, md, dir of 4 assoc cos; consulting engr 1992–; project engr Mersey Tidal Power Barrage; memb Panel AR (All Reservoirs) under Reservoirs Act (for inspection and certification of reservoirs and dams) 1971–; chm: Br Nat Ctee on Large Dams 1986–89, Br Hydromechanics Res Assoc 1978–81, Ctee on the Environment of Int Cmmn on Large Dams 1981–94; vice pres Int Cmmn on Large Dams 1993–; Parsons lectr Royal Soc 1996; MICE 1952, FIPENZ 1959, FICE 1962, FEng 1989; *Publications* contrib Chapter 5 (Diaphragm Walls) in Civil Engineering for Underground Rail Transport (1990), author of 44 technical papers; *Recreations* golf, hill walking, photography, music; *Style—* Edward Haws, Esq, FEng; ✉ Horsham, West Sussex (fax 01403 270826)

HAWTHORN, Ven Christopher John; s of John Christopher Hawthorn (d 1992), and Susan Mary, *née* Morris (1987); *b* 29 April 1936; *Educ* King's Coll Choir Sch Cambridge, Marlborough, Queens' Coll Cambridge (MA), Ripon Hall Oxford; *m* 4 Jan 1964, Elizabeth Margaret, da of Albert Edgar Lowe; 3 s (James Christopher b 20 Aug 1965, Richard John (twin) b 20 Aug 1965, Andrew Mark b 4 May 1967), 1 da (Helen Margaret b 28 May 1969); *Career* asst curate St James's Sutton-in-Holderness 1962–66; vicar: St Nicholas's Hull 1966–72, Christ Church Coatham 1972–79, St Martin's-on-the-Hill Scarborough 1979–91; rural dean of Scarborough 1982–91, proctor in convocation 1987–90, canon and preb of York 1987–, archdeacon of Cleveland 1991–; memb Gen Synod C of E 1995–; *Recreations* gardening, sport, fell walking; *Style—* The Ven the Archdeacon of Cleveland; ✉ Park House, Rosehill, Great Ayton, Middlesbrough TS9 6BH (☎ 01642 723221, fax 01642 724137)

HAWTHORNE, James Burns; CBE (1982); s of Thomas Hawthorne (d 1980), of Belfast, and Florence Mary Kathleen, *née* Burns (d 1977); twin bro of Dr William McMullan Hawthorne; *b* 27 March 1930; *Educ* Methodist Coll Belfast, Queen's Univ, Stranmillis Coll Belfast (BA); *m* 1958, Sarah Patricia, da of Thomas Allan King (d 1975); 1 s (Patrick), 2 da (Fiona, Deirdre); *Career* joined BBC 1960, schools prodr i/c NI, chief asst BBC NI 1969–70, controller of television Hong Kong 1970–72, dir of broadcasting Hong Kong 1972–77, controller BBC NI 1978–87; media conslt James Hawthorne Assocs 1988–; gave 1988 Listener lecture; NI Cncl for Educnl Devpt 1980–85; memb: Fair Employment Agency NI 1987–89, Accreditation Panel Hong Kong Acad for Performing Arts 1988–; chm: Health Promotion Agency 1988–, Cultural Traditions Gp 1988–90, NI Community Relations Cncl 1989–96, Prison Arts Fndn 1996–; visiting prof Univ of Ulster 1993–; Winston Churchill fellowship 1968, Hon LLD Queen's Univ Belfast 1988; memb RTS (Cyril Bennett award 1986), FRTS 1988; *Books* Two Centuries of Irish History (ed, 1967), Reporting Violence from Northern Ireland (1981); *Recreations* music, angling; *Clubs* BBC; *Style—* Dr James Hawthorne, CBE; ✉ The Long Mill, Lissara, 67 Kilmore Road, Crossgar, Northern Ireland BT30 9HJ (☎ 01396 831830, fax 01396 831840)

HAWTHORNE, Prof John Nigel (Tim); s of Ralph William Hawthorne (d 1970), of Dudley, and Alice Maud, *née* Baker (d 1965); *b* 7 March 1926; *Educ* Dudley GS, Univ of Birmingham (BSc, PhD, DSc); *m* 1, 21 Aug 1954 (m dis 1984), Jennifer, da of Dr Samuel Noel Browne (d 1971), of Church Stretton, Salop; 1 s (Barnabas b 1958), 2 da (Deborah b 1956, Prudence b 1962); m 2, 1984, Valerie Wallace; *Career* reader Univ of Birmingham 1966–69 (lectr in med biochemistry 1956–62, sr lectr 1963–65); prof of biochemistry: Univ of Calgary Alberta Canada 1970–72, Univ of Nottingham 1986–91 (prof and head of biochemistry 1972–85, pro-vice chancellor 1982–86, emeritus prof 1991–); chm Int Soc for Neurochemistry Ltd 1987–89 (co sec 1987–); FIBiol 1973; *Books* Questions of Science and Faith (1960), Phospholipids (jtly, 1982), Windows On Science and Faith (1986); *Recreations* music, gardening; *Style—* Prof Tim Hawthorne; ✉ 5 Lucknow Ave, Mapperley Park, Nottingham NG3 5AZ (☎ 0115 962 1477); Dept of Biochemistry, Medical School, Queen's Medical Centre, Nottingham NG7 2UH (☎ 0115 970 9361, fax 0115 942 2225)

HAWTHORNE, Nigel Barnard; CBE (1987); s of Dr Charles Barnard Hawthorne (d 1969), of Coventry, and Agnes Rosemary Rice (d 1982); *b* 5 April 1929; *Educ* Christian Brothers' Coll Cape Town, Univ of Cape Town; *Career* actor and writer; Hon MA: Univ of Sheffield 1987, Univ of Leicester 1994; Hon LLD Univ of Hertfordshire 1993; *Theatre* incl: Privates on Parade 1976–77, Uncle Vanya (Hampstead), The Magistrate (NT) 1986, Hapgood 1988, Shadowlands (London 1989–90, NY 1990–91, Antoinette Perry Award (Tony) 1990/91), The Madness of George III (RNT) 1991–94 (US tour 1993); dir debut The Clandestine Marriage (Queen's) 1994; *Television* incl: Yes Minister, Yes Prime Minister, Barchester Chronicles, Mapp and Lucia, The Fragile Heart 1996; *Films* incl: Demolition Man 1993, The Madness of King George 1994 (Oscar nomination, BAFTA for Best Actor 1996), Richard III 1995, Twelfth Night 1995, Murder in Mind 1996; *Awards* for The Madness of George III incl: Actor of the Year Olivier Awards 1992, Best Actor Evening Standard Drama Awards 1992; Variety Club Best Film Actor 1995; *Recreations* writing, gardening; *Style—* Nigel Hawthorne, Esq, CBE; ✉ c/o Ken McReddie Ltd, 91 Regent St, London W1R 7TB (☎ 0171 439 1456, fax 0171 734 6530)

HAWTHORNE, Prof Sir William Rede; kt (1970), CBE (1959); s of William Hawthorne, and Elizabeth Hawthorne; *b* 22 May 1913; *Educ* Westminster, Trinity Coll Cambridge (MA, ScD), MIT (ScD); *m* 1939, Barbara Runkle, of Cambridge, Mass (d 1992); 1 s (Alexander), 2 da (Joanna, Elizabeth); *Career* devpt engr Babcock and Wilcox 1937–39, sci offr RAE 1940–44, seconded to Sir Frank Whittle Power Jets Ltd (developed combustion chambers for first jet engine) 1940–41, head Gas Turbine Div Engine Dept RAE 1941–44, Br Air Cmmn Washington USA 1944–45, dep dir Engine Res Miny of Supply London 1945–46; MIT: assoc prof 1946–48, George Westinghouse prof of mech engrg 1948–51, Jerome C Hunsaker prof of aeronautical engrg 1955–56, visiting inst prof 1962–68, sr lectr 1978; MIT Corp 1968–73; Hopkinson and ICI prof of applied thermodynamics Univ of Cambridge 1951–80 (head Engrg Dept 1968–73, master Churchill Coll 1968–83); dir: Dracone Developments 1958–87, Cummins Engine Co Inc 1974–86; chm: Home Office Sci Advsy Cncl 1967–76, Def Sci Advsy Cncl 1969–71, Advsy Cncl on Energy Conservation 1974–79; former memb: Electricity Supply Res Cncl, Energy Cmmn, Cmmn on Energy and Environment; tstee Winston Churchill Fndn of USA 1968–, govr Westminster Sch 1956–76 (fell 1991–); has published numerous papers on fluid mechanics, aero-engines, flames and energy in scientific and tech jls; Hon DEng Univ of Sheffield 1976; Hon DSc: Univ of Salford 1980, Univ of Strathclyde 1981, Univ of Bath 1981, Univ of Oxford 1982, Univ of Sussex 1984; Hon DEng Univ of Liverpool 1982; fell Imperial Coll of Sci and Technol 1983; FRS (vice pres 1969–70 and 1979–81), FEng 1976 (fndr fell), FIMechE, Hon FRAeS, Hon FAIAA, Hon FRSE 1983, foreign assoc US Nat Acad of Sciences and US Nat Acad of Engrg; *Clubs* Athenaeum, Pentacle (Cambridge); *Style—* Prof Sir William Hawthorne, CBE, FRS, FEng; ✉ Churchill College, Cambridge CB3 0DS (☎ 01223 336000, fax 01223 840450); 19 Chauncy St, Cambridge, Massachusetts 02138, USA (☎ 001 617 253 2479)

HAWTIN, Ven David Christopher; *b* 7 June 1943; *Educ* King Edward VII Sch Lytham St Anne's Lancs, Keble Coll Oxford (MA), William Temple Coll Rugby, Cuddesdon Coll Oxford; *m* 14 Sept 1968, Elizabeth Ann, *née* Uden; 1 s (Richard Jonathan b 19 March 1970), 2 da (Catherine Elizabeth b 3 Feb 1972, Judith Mary b 6 April 1976); *Career* curate: St Thomas Pennywell Sunderland 1967–71, St Peter's Stockton 1971–74; priest-in-charge St Andrew's Leam Lane Gateshead 1974–79, rector of Holy Trinity Washington (Dio of Durham) 1979–88, i/c local ecumenical partnership and gp min 1979–88 (chm Washington Cncl for Voluntary Serv); diocesan ecumenical offr Dio of Durham 1988–92 (co-ordinator Churches Project for the Nat Garden Festival Gateshead 1990), local unity advsr for the Churches of Durham Ecumencical Rels Gp 1988–92, archdeacon of Newark (Dio of Southwell) 1992–, chm: Diocesan Bd of Educn 1994–, East Midlands Training & Educn for Ministry Consortium 1996–; memb: Gen Synod 1983– (memb Bd for Mission and Unity 1986–90, conslt Cncl for Christian Unity 1991–96), British Cncl of Churches 1985–90, Churches Together In England 1990– (memb CTE Enabling Gp 1991–, dep moderator CTE Forum 1995–), Cncl of Churches for Britain and Ireland 1990–; *Recreations* trams, trains, films, music, gardening, walking; *Style—* The Ven the Archdeacon of Newark; ✉ Dunham House, Westgate, Southwell, Notts NG25 0JL (☎ 01636 814490, fax 01636 815882)

HAXBY, David Arthur; s of Arthur Nugent Haxby, of Filey, N Yorks, and Alice Jane Milner; *b* 16 June 1941; *Educ* Bridlington GS, Univ Coll London (LLB); *m* 27 April 1968, Eileen Margaret, da of James Gallagher; 1 s (Daniel James b 31 Aug 1971), 3 da (Jane Louise b 14 Dec 1969, Sarah Kate b 5 Nov 1972, Linda Claire b 5 April 1978); *Career* Whitehill Marsh Jackson London 1963–68; Arthur Andersen & Co: Manchester 1968–75, Leeds 1975–91, managing ptnr of regnl practice 1986–91, managing ptnr London 1991–95; FCA; *Recreations* geriatric squash, social tennis, walking; *Style—* David Haxby, Esq

HAY, *see:* Dalrymple-Hay

HAY, Alexander Douglas; s of Lt-Col George Harold Hay, DSO (d 1967), of Duns Castle, Duns, Berwickshire, and Patricia Mary, *née* Hugonin; *b* 2 Aug 1948; *Educ* Rugby, Univ of Edinburgh (BSc); *m* 20 Jan 1973, Aline Mary, da of Robert Rankine Macdougall; 1 s (Robert Alexander b 29 July 1976), 1 da (Caroline Laura b 9 July 1978); *Career* ptnr Greaves West & Ayre CAs Berwick upon Tweed 1978– (joined 1975); chm: Scottish Episcopal Church Widows & Orphans Fund Corp Ltd 1980–89, Roxburgh & Berwickshire Cons & Unionist Assoc 1989–92, Berwickshire Housing Assoc 1994–; MICAS 1975; *Recreations* golf; *Clubs* Hon Co Edinburgh Golfers; *Style—* Alexander Hay, Esq; ✉ Duns Castle, Duns, Berwickwshire (☎ 01361 883211); 1–3 Sandgate, Berwick upon Tweed TD15 1EW (☎ 01289 306688)

HAY, Andrew Mackenzie; CBE (1968); s of Ewen James Mackenzie Hay (d 1961), and Bertine Louise Vavasseur, *née* Buxton; *b* 9 April 1928; *Educ* Blundell's, St John's Coll Cambridge (MA); *m* 30 July 1977, Catherine, da of Cdr Horace Newman, US Navy (d 1975); *Career* Intelligence Corps and RAEC 1946–48, demobbed 1948; commodity exec London and Colombo Ceylon 1950–54, pres and chief exec offr Calvert Vavasseur Co Inc NYC 1962–78 (vice pres 1954–61), merchant banking exec NY 1979–81, int trade conslt Portland Oregon 1982– (also HM hon consul at Portland); pres: Br American C of C 1966–68, American Assoc of Exporters and Importers NYC 1977–79; memb Bd and tstee Winston Churchill Fndn of US 1970–75, exec dir Pacific NW Int Trade Assoc 1986–; memb Advsy Ctee of Tech Innovation US Nat Acad of Sci; dean Oregon Consular Corps; *Books* A Century of Coconuts (1972); *Recreations* photography, food and wine, books; *Clubs* Arlington, University; *Style—* Andrew Hay, Esq, CBE; ✉ 3515 SW Council Crest Drive, Portland, Oregon 97201, USA; 5595 Norwester, Oceanside, Oregon 97134, USA (☎ 00 1 503 224 5163, 00 1 503 227 5669)

HAY, David John MacKenzie; s of Ian Gordon McHattie Hay, of Inverness, and Ishbel Jean Hay, *née* MacKenzie; *b* 30 June 1952; *Educ* Inverness Royal Acad, Univ of Edinburgh (MA), Magdalene Coll Cambridge (MA, LLM); *Career* called to the Bar Inner Temple 1977, managing ed Atkin's Encyclopaedia of Court Forms 1984–85, ed R & D 1985–86, managing ed Electronic Forms Publishing 1986–88; gen ed: Halsbury's Laws of England (reissue) 1995–96 (ed 1989–96), Words and Phrases Legally Defined 1993–, Halsbury's Laws of Hong Kong 1995–, Major Works Butterworths Asia 1996–; *Recreations* music, enjoying the countryside, reading, travel; *Style—* David Hay, Esq; ✉ The Cottage, School Lane, Barley, nr Royston, Herts SG8 8JZ; E3–02–4 Pantai Hill Park Phase 1, Jalan Pantai Dalam, 59200 Kuala Lumpur Malaysia; Malayan Law Journal Sdn Bhd, 10 Floor, Wisma Hamzah Kwong Hing, No 1 Leboh Ampang, 50100 Kuala Lumpur, Malaysia (☎ 00 60 3 232 1218, fax 00 60 3 238 7073)

HAY, Prof Frank Charles; s of Edward Frank Hay, of London, and Doris Irene, *née* Webber; *b* 8 Oct 1944; *Educ* Sir George Monoux GS, Brunel Univ (BTech), Univ of London (PhD); *m* 2 Aug 1969, Frances Margaret, da of Prof George Baron; 1 da (Rebecca b 28 March 1974), 1 s (Thomas b 9 Feb 1977); *Career* Middx Hosp Med Sch: res assoc 1972–77, lectr in immunology 1977–78, sr lectr 1978–84, reader 1984–89; St George's Hosp Med Sch: prof and chm Div of Immunology 1989–, head Dept of Cellular and Molecular Scis 1991–, vice-princ 1993–; memb: Br Soc for Immunology 1970, RSM 1982, Biochemical Soc 1991; *Books* Practical Immunology (3 edn, 1989); *Recreations* swimming, mountain walking; *Style—* Prof Frank Hay; ✉ 82 Longlands Road, Sidcup, Kent DA15 7LR (☎ 0181 302 4521); Division of Immunology, St George's Hospital Medical School, Cranmer Terrace, Tooting, London SW17 0RE (☎ 0181 725 5751, fax 0181 725 3549)

HAY, Ian Wood; s of John William Hay (d 1977), of Harwich, Essex, and Winifred May, *née* Fox (d 1975); *b* 25 Jan 1940; *Educ* Colchester Sch of Art (NDD), RCA; *m* 26 March 1968, Teresa Mary, da of Stanislav Antoni Sliski, of Harwich, Essex; 2 s (James b 1978, Rupert b 1982); *Career* artist known for pastel paintings of London and The Thames; visiting lectr: St Martin's Sch of Art 1963–77, Norwich Sch of Art 1971–75; sr lectr in drawing Sch of Art Colchester Inst 1978–; RCA prize for landscape painting 1963; many one man and group shows in Essex and London in The Minories and Phoenix Art Gallery; works in private and public collections incl: Guildhall Art Gallery, Sheffield Art Gallery, Doncaster City Art Gallery, Univ of Essex; memb Colchester Art Soc; ARCA (1963); *Recreations* travel; *Style—* Ian Hay, Esq; ✉ 32 Tall Trees, Mile End, Colchester, Essex CO4 5DU (☎ 01206 852510)

HAY, (Elizabeth) Joyce (Jocelyn); *née* Board; da of William George Board (d 1951), and Olive Price Jones (d 1962); *b* 30 July 1927; *Educ* Open Univ (BA); *m* 26 Aug 1950, William Andrew Hunter Hay, TD, s of Sheriff J C E Hay, CBE, MC, TD, DL (d 1975); 2 da (Penelope Jill b 1960, Rosemary Anne b 1961); *Career* freelance writer and broadcaster 1954–83; work incl: Forces Broadcasting Serv, Woman's Hour BBC Radio 2 and 4; head of press and PR Dept Girl Guides Assoc, Cwlth HQ 1973–78, fndr London Media Workshops 1978–94, fndr and chm Voice of the Listener and Viewer 1983–; examiner CAM Dip in PR Exams; assoc advsr Br Cncl; memb: Soc of Authors, RTS; FIPR, FRSA; *Recreations* gardening, bee-keeping, ancient history, bird-watching, travel; *Style—* Mrs Jocelyn Hay; ✉ 101 Kings Drive, Gravesend, Kent (☎ 01474 564676)

HAY, Lady Olga; *see:* Maitland, Lady Olga

HAY, Peter Laurence; s of Norman Leslie Stephen Hay (d 1979); *b* 7 March 1950; *Educ* St Paul's, Brunel Univ; *m* 19 July 1985 (m dis 1992), Perdita Sarah Amanda Lucie Rogers; *Career* chm: Norman Hay plc 1977–, Norman Hay (Metal Finishers) plc 1987–, Plasticraft Ltd 1987–, Techniplate Ltd 1988–, Montgomery Plating Co Ltd 1988–, Norman Hay International Ltd 1988–, Plasplate Ltd 1988–, Armourcote East Kilbride Ltd 1988–, Armourcote Suface Treatments Ltd 1988–, Surface Technology plc 1989–; *Recreations* flying helicopters; *Clubs* Lamborghini UK (chm); *Style—* Peter Hay, Esq; ✉ Windlesham Grange, Kennel Lane, Windlesham, Surrey GU20 6AA (☎ 01276 472980, fax 01276 476139); Norman Hay plc, Godiva Place, Coventry CV1 5PN (☎ 01203 229373, fax 01203 224420)

HAY, Peter Rossant; s of Vincent Hay, and Marie Winifred, *née* Chase; *b* 11 Oct 1948; *Educ* Clifton Coll; *m* 14 April 1973, Christine Maria; 2 s (Alexander William Rossant b 11 Feb 1978, James Vincent Rossant b 10 Aug 1985), 1 da (Nicola Marie b 8 March 1975); *Career* admitted slr 1973; ptnr: Penningtons 1973–92, Peter Hay & Associates 1993–; hon slr The Royal Scot Corp 1985–; chm Richmond Athletic Association Ltd 1986–91; non-exec dir: Meat Trade Suppliers plc 1988–89, West London TEC 1996–; vice pres Richmond C of C 1994–; memb Law Soc, MInstD, FRSA; *Recreations* golf, skiing, swimming, ex-rugby and rowing; *Clubs* City of London, Caledonian, London Scottish FC, Sunningdale, British Sportsman's; *Style—* Peter R Hay, Esq; ✉ Peter Hay & Associates, 25 The Green, Richmond, Surrey TW9 1LY (☎ 0181 332 7532, fax 0181 948 8013)

HAY, Richard; CMG (1992); s of Prof Denys Hay (d 1994), of Edinburgh, and Sarah Gwyneth, *née* Morley (d 1996); *b* 4 May 1942; *Educ* George Watson's Coll Edinburgh, Balliol Coll Oxford; *m* 1969, Miriam Marguerite Alvin, da of Charles Arthur England (d 1977); 2 s (Jonathan b 1971, Timothy b 1973); *Career* HM Treasy 1963–72; Euro Cmmn: memb Cabinet Sir Christopher Soames, vice pres 1973–77, chef de Cabinet to Christopher

Tugendhat 1977–79, dir Economic Structures and Community Interventions Directorate-General for Economic and Fin Affrs 1979–81, dir gen Directorate-General for Personnel and Administration European Cmmn 1986–91 (dep dir gen 1981–86), advsr EC 1991–92; conslt Sharing of Ministeries Abroad 1992–94; ordinand Cranmer Coll Durham 1994–96, ordained deacon 1996, curate St Clements and All Saints Hastings 1996–; *Style*— The Rev Richard Hay, CMG

HAY, Sheriff Principal Robert Colquhoun; CBE (1988), WS; s of J B Hay (d 1971), of Stirling, and J Y Kirkland (d 1971); *b* 22 Sept 1933; *Educ* Univ of Edinburgh (MA, LLB); *m* 14 June 1958, Olive, da of J C Black; 2 s (Robin b 2 March 1959, Michael b 11 Oct 1967), 2 da (Penelope b 1 Jan 1961, Elizabeth b 28 Dec 1975); *Career* private legal practice 1959–63 and 1968–76, dep procurator fiscal Edinburgh 1963–68, pres Industl Tribunals (Scot) 1981–89 (chm 1976–81), temp Sheriff 1984–89, Sheriff Princ of N Strathclyde 1989–; Northern Lights: cmmr 1989–, vice chm 1991–92, chm 1992–93; Sheriff Ct Rules Cncl: memb 1990–92, chm 1993–96; cmmr Clan Hay 1995–; *Books* The Laws of Scotland: Stair Memorial Encyclopaedia (contrib); *Clubs* Royal Highland Yacht (Oban); *Style*— Sheriff Principal Robert Hay, CBE, WS; ✉ Sheriff Principal's Chambers, Sheriff Court House, 106 Renfrew Road, Paisley PA3 4DD (☎ 0141 887 5291, fax 0141 889 1748)

HAY, Robin William Patrick Hamilton; s of William Reginald Hay (d 1975), of Nottingham, and (Mary Constance) Dora, *née* Bray; *b* 1 Nov 1939; *Educ* Eltham, Selwyn Coll Cambridge (MA, LLB); *m* 18 April 1969, Lady Olga Maitland, MP, *qv*, er da of 17 Earl of Lauderdale; 2 s (Alastair b 18 Aug 1972, Fergus b 22 April 1981), 1 da (Camilla b 25 June 1975); *Career* called to the Bar Inner Temple 1964, recorder of Crown Ct 1985–; ILEA candidate (Cons) Islington S and Finsbury 1986, chm Young Musicians Symphony Orch; *Recreations* gastronomy, church tasting, choral singing; *Clubs* Garrick; *Style*— Robin Hay, Esq; ✉ Goldsmith Building, Temple, London EC4Y 7BL (☎ 0171 353 7881, fax 0171 353 5319)

HAY, Sir Ronald Frederick Hamilton; 12 Bt (NS 1703), of Alderston; o s of Sir Ronald Nelson Hay, 11 Bt (d 1988), and Rita, *née* Munyard; *b* 1941; *m* 1978, Kathleen, da of John Thake; 2 s (Alexander James b 1979, Anthony Ronald b 1984), 1 da (Sarah Jane b 1981); *Heir* s, Alexander James Hay b 1979; *Style*— Sir Ronald Hay, Bt

HAY OF PARK, Sir John Erroll Audley; 11 Bt (NS 1663), of Park, Wigtownshire; s of Sir Arthur Thomas Erroll Hay of Park, 10 Bt, ISO (d 1993), and his 1 w, Hertha Hedwig Paula Louise, *née* Stölzle; *b* 3 Dec 1935; *Educ* Gordonstoun, St Andrew's Univ (MA); *Heir* none; *Style*— Sir John Hay of Park, Bt

HAYCOCKS, Richard John; s of Roy Terence Haycocks (d 1988), of Wiltshire, and Barbara Alice, *née* Rons; *b* 8 June 1949; *Educ* City of Westminster Coll, Dartford GS; *m* 30 June 1986, Myra Anne, da of Alan Douglas Kinghorn; 2 s (Thomas Richard Henry b 20 May 1987, James Richard John b 20 Aug 1990); *Career* Allfields 1969–74, Deloitte Haskins & Sells 1974–80, dir Baker Energy Holdings Ltd (part of Baker International Corporation) 1981–83; Ernst & Young: joined 1984, ptnr 1989, ptnr i/c corp fin 1990–; FCA (ACA 1971), MSI; *Clubs* RAC; *Style*— Richard Haycocks, Esq; ✉ Ernst & Young, Becket House, London SE1 7EU (☎ 0171 928 2000, fax 0171 928 1345)

HAYCRAFT, Anna Margaret; da of John Richard Alfred Lindholm (d 1960), and Gladys Irene Alexandra, *née* Griffith; *b* 9 Sept 1932; *Educ* Bangor County GS for Girls, Liverpool Art Coll; *m* 1956, Colin Berry Haycraft (d 1994), s of Maj William Church Stacpoole Haycraft, MC (d 1929); 5 s (William, Joshua d 1978, Thomas, Oliver, Arthur), 2 da (Rosalind d 1970, Sarah); *Career* writer; dir G Duckworth and Co Ltd 1975; weekly columnist: Home Life in The Spectator 1985–89, The Universe 1989–91, The Catholic Herald 1991–96, The Oldie 1996–; *Books* as Anna Haycraft: Natural Baby Food (1977), Darling You Shouldn't Have Gone to So Much Trouble (with Caroline Blackwood, 1980); as Alice Thomas Ellis: The Sin Eater (Welsh Arts Cncl award, 1977), The Birds of the Air (1980), The 27th Kingdom (Booker prize nomination, 1982), The Other Side of the Fire (1983), Unexplained Laughter (1985, Yorkshire Post Novel of the Year), Home Life (1986), Secrets of Strangers (with Tom Pitt-Aikens, 1986), More Home Life (1987), The Clothes in The Wardrobe (1987), The Skeleton in the Cupboard (1988), Home Life III (1988), The Loss of the Good Authority (with Tom Pitt-Aikens, 1989), The Fly in the Ointment (1989), Home Life IV (1989), The Inn at the Edge of the World (1990, Writers' Guild award for Best Fiction 1991), A Welsh Childhood (1990), Wales: an Anthology (1991), Pillars of Gold (1992), Serpent on the Rock (1994), The Evening of Adam (1994), Cat Among the Pigeons (1994), Fairy Tale (1996); *Style*— Anna Haycraft; ✉ 22 Gloucester Crescent, London NW1 7DS

HAYCRAFT, John Bernard; s of Bernard Gottfried Haycraft, of Bucks, and Diana Margery, *née* Brockwell; *b* 1 Sept 1942; *Educ* Eversley Sch Southwold, Marlborough; *m* 1, 1 Oct 1966, Marie Luize, da of Bryan Hervey Talbot, of Runcorn, Cheshire; 3 s (Alexander Richard b 1969, Oliver Talbot b 1972, Simon Hervey b 1973); *m* 2, 7 May 1982, Paula Celeste, da of Franco C Vegnuti, of Rowington, Warks; 1 s (Thomas Julian b 1984), 1 da (Jessica Celeste b 1987); *Career* fine art auctioneer and valuer; operational dir Phillips 1994– (regnl dir 1991–94); cameo roles: Chancer (Central TV) 1991, Remains of the Day (Merchant Ivory film) 1994; FRICS, ASVA; *Recreations* gardening, tennis, hockey; *Clubs* Warwick Hockey, Bath and County; *Style*— John Haycraft, Esq; ✉ 4 Little Kineton Cottages, Little Kineton, Warwicks CV35 0DN (☎ 01926 641409); Phillips, Old King Street, Bath BA1 2JT (☎ 01225 310609)

HAYDAY, Terence John (Terry); s of John Alfred Hayday (d 1978), and Annie Dorothy, *née* Tebby; *b* 23 June 1947; *Educ* Hampton GS, Univ of Sussex (BA); *m* 9 June 1973, Susan Pamela, da of Gordon Grenville Dean; 2 s (Nicholas b 1977, Christopher b 1979), 1 da (Annabel b 1987); *Career* Lloyd's broker Leslie & Godwin Ltd 1965–67, Lloyd's underwriting asst R W Sturge & Co 1967–69, reinsur underwriter Slater Walker Insurance Co Ltd 1972–76; Holmes Hayday (Underwriting Agencies) Ltd (formerly Holmes Kingsley Carritt Ltd): dep Lloyd's underwriter and dir 1976–79, md 1980–88, chm 1988–; active underwriter Lloyd's Syndicate 694 1980–91, dir and chief exec Sturge Holdings plc (which acquired Holmes Hayday in 1990) 1991–94, currently co sec and dir Owen & Wilby Underwriting Agency Ltd; non-exec dir: Newman & Stuchbery Ltd 1988–93, LIMNET Bd 1992–94; dir: Highgate Managing Agencies Ltd 1994–, Mitchell McLure Ltd 1995–, Apex Professional Education Programme at Lloyd's 1995–; chm Optimum Consultants Ltd 1994–; vice pres Insur Inst of London; FCII 1976; *Recreations* sailing, rugby, theatre, literature; *Clubs* Lloyd's Yacht, Twickenham Yacht; *Style*— Terry Hayday, Esq; ✉ Owen & Wilby Underwriting Agency Ltd, 10 Heneage Lane, London EC3A 5DQ (☎ 0171 337 2702, fax 0171 283 7117)

HAYDEN, Dr Jacqueline (Jacky); da of Robert Leslie James Hayden, of Majorca, Spain, and Dorothy Blanche, *née* Cowell (d 1986); *b* 4 Dec 1950; *Educ* Croydon HS, King's Coll London, St George's Hosp Med Sch (MB BS, LRCP MRCS, FRCP, DCH, DRCOG, FRCGP); *m* 11 Dec 1976, Edward Milne Dunbar, s of David Milne Dunbar; 2 s (Alexander James b 10 July 1980, Benjamin David b 20 Jan 1984); *Career* pre-registration house offr: St James's Hosp Balham London 1974, Ashford Hosp Middx 1975; SHO in thoracic med Churchill Hosp Oxford 1975–76, gen practice trg scheme Oxford 1976–79, princ in gen practice Unsworth Med Centre Bury Lancs 1979–, regional advsr in gen practice Univ of Manchester 1991– (assoc advsr in gen practice 1990–91); memb: Cncl RCGP 1985– (chm NW England Bd 1994–), Jt Ctee on Postgraduate Trg for Gen Practice 1986–, Armed Servs Gen Practice Approval Bd 1992–, Chief Med Offr's Working Pty on Specialist Trg 1993–94; chm Ctee of Regional Advsrs in Gen Practice in England 1994–; *Books* A Guide for New Principals (1996); contrib: The Med Annual (1987), Practice Information Booklets (1987), The Practice Receptionist (1989), Change and Teamwork in Primary Care (1993), The Child Surveillance Handbook (1994), Professional Development in General Practice; series ed OUP 1990–; *Recreations* my family, the house and garden; *Style*— Dr Jacky Hayden; ✉ 12 Mercers Road, Heywood, Lancs OL10 2NP (☎ 01706 625470, fax 01706 627593); Department of Postgraduate Medicine, Gateway House, Piccadilly South, Manchester M60 7LP (☎ 0161 237 2104, fax 0161 237 2108)

HAYDEN, The Hon William George (Bill); AC; *b* 23 Jan 1933; *Educ* Brisbane State HS, Queensland Secdy Correspondence Sch, Univ of Queensland (BEcon); *Career* Queensland State Public Serv 1950–52, Queensland Police Force 1953–61, memb for Fed Div of Oxley Australian Nat Parl 1961–88 (min for social security 1972–75, treas 1975, ldr of the opposition 1977–83, min for foreign affairs 1983–87, min for foreign affairs and trade 1987–88), govr-gen of the Cwlth of Australia 1989–96; Hon DUniv Griffith Univ 1990, Hon LLD Univ of Queensland 1990, Hon DUniv Univ of Central Queensland 1992; hon fell Australasian Coll of Physicians 1995; Companion of the Order of Australia; Gwanghwa Medal of the Korean Order of Diplomatic Merit; KStJ (Prior Order of St John in Australia 1989); *Recreations* reading (particularly social and economic issues), music, golf, horse riding, fly-fishing, cross country skiing and bush walking; *Style*— The Hon Bill Hayden, AC; ✉ Box 7829, Waterfront Place, Brisbane 4001, Australia

HAYDON, Sir Walter Robert (Robin); KCMG (1980, CMG 1970); s of Walter Haydon (d 1946), and Evelyn Louise, *née* Thom; *b* 29 May 1920; *Educ* Dover GS; *m* 1941, Joan Elizabeth (d 1988), da of Col Reginald Tewson (d 1948); 1 da (and 1 da decd), 1 s (decd); *Career* WWII served: France, India, Burma; head News Dept FO 1967–71, high cmmr Malawi 1971–73, chief press sec 10 Downing Street 1973–74, high cmmr Malta 1974–76, ambass to Republic of Ireland 1976–80, ret; dir: Imperial Group 1980–84, Imperial Tobacco 1984–88; govr: ESU 1980–86 and 1987, Dover GS; memb: Reviewing Ctee on Export of Works of Art 1984–87, Tobacco Advsy Cncl 1984–90; *Recreations* walking, swimming; *Clubs* Travellers', Special Forces; *Style*— Sir Robin Haydon, KCMG; ✉ c/o Lloyds Bank, Cox's and King's Branch, 7 Pall Mall, London SW1

HAYES, Dr Alan; CBE (1992), DL (W Sussex 1994); s of Ernest Hayes, and Annie, *née* Draycott; *b* 12 June 1930; *Educ* Newton Heath Tech Sch Manchester, Royal Tech Coll Salford (BSc London) Univ of Cambridge (PhD); *m* 26 Dec 1955, Audrey, da of Henry Leach; 2 da (Alison b 30 Oct 1959, Wendy b 4 July 1961), 1 s (Stephen b 12 May 1966); *Career* Nat Serv RAF 1954–56; ICI plc Pharmaceuticals 1950–78 (res scientist, dir, dep chm); chief exec: ICI Agrochemicals 1979–92, ICI Seeds 1985–92; chm Euro Trade Ctee DTI, memb Bd BOTB 1985–94, chm Bd Exwold Technology Ltd 1992–, non-exec dir Whatman plc 1993–; chm: Exec Bd Weald and Downland Museum Singleton Chichester 1992–94, Bd of Tstees Chichester Inst of HE (formerly W Sussex Inst of HE) 1992–, Cncl King Edward VII Hosp Midhurst 1994– (chm Exec and Fin Ctee 1990–); memb Cncl Univ of Surrey 1992–, pres Soc for Chemical Industry 1994–96; FRSC 1984; *Recreations* music (opera), gardening; *Style*— Dr Alan Hayes, CBE, DL; ✉ Highlands, Fernhurst, Haslemere, Surrey GU27 3LL (☎ 01428 652232, fax 01428 658449)

HAYES, Brian; CBE (1992), QPM (1985); s of James Hayes (d 1984), and Jessie, *née* Spratt; *b* 25 Jan 1940; *Educ* Plaistow Co GS, Univ of Sheffield (BA); *m* 8 Oct 1960, Priscilla Rose, da of Thomas Bishop; 1 s (Stephen Mark b 1962), 3 da (Priscilla Dawn (twin) b 1962, Jacqueline Denise b 1963, Emma Lucy b 1975); *Career* Met Police 1959–77: seconded NI 1971–72, police advsr Mexico 1975–76 and Colombia 1977 and 1993, Br Police rep EEC 1976–77; Asst Chief Constable Surrey 1977–81, Dep Chief Constable Wilts 1981–82, Chief Constable Surrey 1982–91, HM Inspr of Constabulary 1991–95, Dep Cmmr Metropolitan Police 1995–; first vice pres Assoc of Chief Police Offrs 1990–91, chm Police Athletic Assoc 1989–91 (nat sec 1984–88), pres Union Sportive des Polices d'Europe 1990–92; Police Long Service and Good Conduct medal 1982; OStJ 1987; *Recreations* martial arts, running, windsurfing, golf; *Style*— Brian Hayes, Esq, CBE, QPM; ✉ Deputy Commissioner, Metropolitan Police, New Scotland Yard, London SW1H 0BG (☎ 0171 230 1212)

HAYES, (Francis) Brian; s of Col Pierse Francis Hayes, OBE, RE (d 1991), of Marlow, and Sheila Mary, *née* O'Brien; *b* 22 April 1942; *Educ* Downside, Worcester Coll Oxford (BA); *m* 18 May 1968, Lesley Anne, da of Oliver Roy Holcroft (d 1984), of Pershore, Worcs; 8 s (William b 1969, Alexander b 1970, Oliver b 1974, Toby b 1977, Benedict b 1979, Damian b 1981, Matthew b 1985, Theodore b 1987), 2 da (Rebecca b 1972, Decima b 1990); *Career* CA; memb Governing Bd Coopers & Lybrand 1988–90 (joined 1964, ptnr 1971); memb Partnership Bd Coopers & Lybrand 1990–; tstee Clyclotron Tst 1984–; memb Historic Houses Assoc; memb ICAEW 1967; *Books* UK Taxation Implications International Trade (1985); *Recreations* shooting, riding; *Style*— Brian Hayes, Esq; ✉ Coopers & Lybrand, Embankment Place, London WC2N 6NN (☎ 0171 583 5000, fax 0171 822 4652)

HAYES, Brian; *b* 17 Dec 1937; *m*, 1 s; *Career* announcer 6KG Kalgoorlie Australia 1955–60, presenter Breakfast Show Perth, fndr (prog controller and chief presenter) Local Radio Station 6TZ-CI Bunbury, prodr and presenter (phone-ins, news and documentaries) Morning Talk Radio 6IX Perth; Capital Radio London: prodr talk progs 1973–74, presenter Open Line 1974–75; presenter: morning phone-in show LBC Radio 1976–90, late night phone-in GLR 1990, Breakfast Show Radio 2 1992, Breakfast Show London News Talk 1994–95; currently presenter: Hayes Over Britain Radio 2, Weekend Breakfast Show BBC Radio Five Live; memb NUM; *Television* work incl: Sunday Sunday (LWT), Out of Order (ITV), VIP (BSB), For Greater Good (BBC), Prime Suspect (Granada), Between the Lines (BBC), The Chief (Anglia), Rules of Engagement (YTV), Pty Conf coverage (BBC) 1995; *Awards* incl: Independent Radio Personality of the Year Variety Club Award 1980, Best Phone-in Prog Rediffusion/Radio Month Award 1981, commendation Local Radio Personality category Sony Special Award 1985, Outstanding Contrib to the Devpt of Radio Sony Special Award 1987, memb Sony Roll of Honour Sony Radio Awards 1988, Best Phone-in Show (for Hayes Over Britain) Sony Radio Awards 1993, Service to the Community Award (jtly) Sony Radio Awards; *Recreations* theatre, opera, cinema, television, literature, holidaying in Australia and USA; *Style*— Brian Hayes, Esq; ✉ c/o Sue Freathy, Curtis Brown Group Ltd, 28–29 Haymarket, London SW1Y 4SP (☎ 0171 396 6600, fax 0171 396 0110)

HAYES, Sir Brian David; GCB (1988, KCB 1980, CB 1976); s of Charles Wilfred Hayes (d 1958); *b* 5 May 1929; *Educ* Norwich Sch, CCC Cambridge (MA, PhD); *m* 1958, Audrey, da of Edward Mortimer Jenkins (d 1973); 1 s (Edward b 1963), 1 da (Catherine b 1962); *Career* 2 Lt RASC Home Cmd 1948–49; civil servant; perm sec: MAFF 1979–83, Dept of Indust 1983, DTI 1985–89 (jt perm sec 1983–85); dir: Guardian Royal Exchange plc, Tate and Lyle plc 1989–; advsy dir Unilever plc 1990–; Lloyd's membs' ombudsman 1994–; *Recreations* reading, watching cricket; *Style*— Sir Brian Hayes, GCB; ✉ c/o Tate & Lyle plc, Sugar Quay, Lower Thames Street, London EC3R 6DQ

HAYES, Colin Graham Frederick; s of Gerald Ravenscourt Hayes (d 1955), of London, and Mary Winifred, *née* Yule (d 1980); *b* 17 Nov 1919; *Educ* Westminster Sch, ChCh Oxford (MA), Ruskin Sch of Drawing Univ of Oxford (Cert in Fine Art); *m* 1, 10 Aug 1949, Jean Westbrook (d 1988), da of Frank Law; 3 da (Ann Catherine b 13 June 1950, Emily Westbrook b 29 Oct 1952, Claire Patricia b 10 Aug 1955); *m* 2, 21 May 1992, Marjorie Lucille Marriott, da of Thomas Berry; *Career* served WWII RE Field Survey, cmmnd 1940, served Iceland and Libya, ret Capt 1945; artist; RCA 1949–84 (tutor, sr tutor, reader), formerly govr Central Sch of Arts and Crafts; work in collections of: Arts Cncl, Br Cncl, numerous public and private collections at home and abroad; De

Lazlo Medal RBA; pres Royal Soc of British Artists 1993–; RA 1970; hon fell RCA (Hon ARCA); *Exhibitions* solo and featured incl: Marlborough Fine Art, Agnews, Gallery 10, Jonleigh, New Grafton; also exhibited many private galleries and mixed exhibitions; *Books* incl: Renoir, Stanley Spencer, A Grammar of Drawing, Rembrandt - A Woman Taken in Adultery, Landscape Painting in Oil, Robert Buhler; *Recreations* travel; *Clubs* Arts; *Style*— Colin Hayes, Esq, RA; ✉ 26 Cleveland Avenue, Chiswick, London W4 1SN (☎ 0181 994 8762)

HAYES, Derek William; s of George Hayes (d 1985), and Marjorie, *née* Frodsham; *b* 8 June 1952; *Educ* Upholland GS, Manchester Poly Sch of Art, Sheffield Poly Sch of Art (DipAD), Nat Film and TV Sch; *m* 1, Lee Kellgren; 1 da (Jessica), 1 s Jonas; *Career* film and video producer; dir Albion (film BBC Bristol) 1978, animation and effects Great Rock and Roll Swindle 1979–80; co-fndr (with Phil Austin) Animation City 1979; commercials incl: Lego, Smarties, Halls Mentholyptus, Delight Margarine, Credito Predial Portugese, Our Price; pop videos incl: Dire Straits (Brothers In Arms), Madonna (Dear Jessie), Elton John (Club at the End of the Street), Rod Stewart (Motown Song); TV title sequences: Blott on the Landscape, Porterhouse Blue, Forever Green, Jeeves and Wooster, Head over Heels; TV station promotional graphics: Autumn on Four, New Year on Four, Spring on Anglia, MTV; various documentary, corp and instructional videos and graphics; films for Channel 4: Skywhales, The Victor, Binky & Boo, Arcadia, Prince Cinders 1993, Elijah 1995; Mari Kuttna Award 1985, Best Publicity Film Award Ottowa Festival 1992, Best Graphics BAFTA Award for Jeeves and Wooster 1993; chm Jury Br Animation Awards 1988; judge: Channel 4 MOMI Awards 1990, Br Assoc Film Animators Awards 1989, Br Animation Awards 1995; external assessor: Film Dept RCA 1991–93, Surrey Inst 1994–; memb Int Animation Festival Advsy Ctee 1981–; memb: BECTU, NFTS graduate soc; *Recreations* drawing, cycling, walking, reading everything, staring into space; *Style*— Derek Hayes, Esq; ✉ 2 The Old Inn, Kingsweston Road, Bristol BS11 0UW (☎ 0117 968 6662, fax 0117 968 3203)

HAYES, Prof (John) Desmond; s of William John Hayes (d 1947), and Annie Matilda, *née* Butler (d 1975); *b* 27 July 1931; *Educ* Narberth GS, Univ Coll of Wales (BSc), Univ of Wisconsin (MS), Univ of Wales (PhD); *m* 21 Aug 1959, Nansi, da of Daniel Jones Lewis (d 1963); 3 s (John Daniel b 1965, Michael Edward b 1970, Timothy Lewis b 1973), 1 da (Sharon Ann b 1963); *Career* King George VI Meml Fell 1954–55, head of Arable Crops Breeding Dept Welsh Plant Breeding Station 1955–77, sci advsr to Agric Res Cncl 1977–79, prof of agric Univ Coll Wales 1979–95, ret; memb Governing Body SCRI; memb IOB, AAB, AEA, Eucarpia; FInstBiol, fell Indian Soc of Genetics and Plant Breeding; *Recreations* family, rugby, gardening, rambling, travel, exploring villages; *Clubs* Farmers; *Style*— Prof Desmond Hayes; ✉ Dunstall, Borth, Dyfed SY24 5NN (☎ 01970 871255)

HAYES, Francis Edward Sutherland; DL; s of Raymond Stanley Hayes, JP (d 1956), of Bryngarw, Brynmenyn, Bridgend, and Gladys Vera, *née* Keating (d 1981); *b* 14 May 1930; *Educ* Wycliffe Coll Stonehouse Gloucester, Jesus Coll Cambridge; *m* 26 April 1958, (Nesta) Suzanne, da of Maj Sir William Reardon Reardon Smith, 3 Bt, RA (d 1995), of Rhode Farm, Romansleigh, South Molton, N Devon; 1 s (Patrick Neil Sutherland b 5 Nov 1961), 3 da (Thira Nesta (Mrs John Rudd) b 3 April 1960, Elizabeth Ann (Mrs Ian Mellett) b 27 July 1964, Philippa Vera (Mrs Vincent Brigode) b 21 Sept 1966); *Career* Nat Serv Sub Lt RNR 1950–52; chm Gresswell Valves Ltd 1977–, dir AB Electronic Products Group plc 1982–92, dep chm Wales Regnl Bd TSB Eng & Wales 1987–89 (dir 1984); gen cmmr Inland Revenue 1976–; High Sheriff S Glamorgan 1977–78; fell The Woodard Corp 1973–95; chm The Br Valve Mfrs' Assoc 1984, chm of govrs The Cathedral Sch Llandaff Cardiff 1985–95, chm CLA Game Fair 1990, Cardiff chm Sail Trg Assoc; Freeman City of London 1966, Liveryman Worshipful Co of Farriers 1966; *Recreations* music, sailing, shooting; *Clubs* Cardiff & County, Naval; *Style*— Francis Hayes, Esq, DL; ✉ Llansannor House, Cowbridge, South Glamorgan CF7 7RW (☎ 01446 775453); New Worcester Works, Elkington St, Birmingham B6 4SL (☎ 0121 359 2052, fax 0121 359 5938)

HAYES, George Leslie John; s of Leslie Jack Hayes (d 1985), of London, and Elsie May, *née* Shaffert; *b* 22 June 1948; *Educ* Willesden Co GS, Hatfield Poly (BA); *m* Christine Mary, da of Herbert Burchell; 1 s (Stephen b 18 Jan 1976), 1 da (Emma b 4 Aug 1979); *Career* Carreras-Rothmans Ltd 1970–71, Spar (UK) Ltd 1971–73, product mangr General Foods Ltd 1973–76, mktg mangr Wander Foods Ltd 1976–79, mktg dir Swift Butterball Ltd 1979–83, sales and mktg dir Bernard Matthews plc 1983–94, gp mktg dir Kitchen Range Foods 1994–; memb Mktg Soc, MCIM; *Recreations* sport, music, photography; *Style*— George Hayes, Esq; ✉ Beetley Lodge, Fakenham Road, Beetley, Norfolk NR20 4BT (☎ 01362 860922)

HAYES, Jeremy Joseph James (Jerry); MP (Cons) Harlow (majority 2,940); s of Joseph B Hayes, of Theydon Mount, Essex, and Daye Julia Hayes; *b* 20 April 1953; *Educ* Oratory Sch, Univ of London (LLB); *m* 22 Sept 1979, Alison Gail, da of Frederick John Mansfield (d 1985), of Epping, Essex; 1 s (Lawrence Frederick b 1986), 1 da (Francesca Julia b 1984); *Career* barr at law practising on SE Circuit; MP (C) Harlow 1983–; memb House of Commons Select Ctee on: Social Servs 1987–90, Health 1990–92; PPS to Min of State for: Northern Ireland 1992–94, the Environment and Countryside 1994–95; currently memb Nat Heritage Select Ctee; hon dir State Leadership Fndn; Freeman: City of London, Worshipful Co of Fletchers, Worshipful Co of Watermen and Lightermen; *Clubs* Carlton; *Style*— Jerry Hayes, Esq, MP; ✉ House of Commons, London SW1A 0AA (☎ 0171 219 5205)

HAYES, John Forbes Raymond; s of (George) Forbes Raymond Hayes (d 1995), of Brocastle, Bridgend, Mid Glamorgan, and Jean Hayes, OBE, *née* Cory; *b* 21 Oct 1948; *Educ* Harrow, Trinity Hall Cambridge (MA); *m* 1 May 1976, Nicola Anne, da of Brian Thomas Reilly (d 1988); 4 s (Charles, Hugh, Matthew, Benjamin); *Career* accountant; Coopers & Lybrand: articles 1971, conslt 1980, dir Nigerian firm 1982–84, ptnr UK firm 1986–, chm UK Investment Gp 1990; Freeman City of London 1970, memb Worshipful Co of Tin Plate Workers 1970 (Master 1992); FCA 1980 (ACA 1975); *Recreations* music, shooting, sailing; *Clubs* Leander, City Livery; *Style*— John Hayes, Esq; ✉ Claymore House, Village Road, Coleshill, Bucks HP7 0LQ (☎ 01494 432859); Coopers & Lybrand, 1 Embankment Place, London WC2N 6NN (☎ 0171 583 5000, 0171 212 4715, fax 0171 212 4652, telex 887470)

HAYES, Vice Adm Sir John Osler Chattock; KCB (1967, CB 1964), OBE (1945); s of Maj Lionel Chattock Hayes, RAMC (d 1962); *b* 9 May 1913; *Educ* RNC Dartmouth; *m* 1939, Hon Rosalind Mary, da of 2 and last Viscount Finlay; 2 s (Colin b 1943, Malcolm b 1951), 1 da (Griselda b 1954); *Career* entered RN 1927; served WWII Atlantic, Far East (HMS Repulse), Arctic Convoys, Malta; naval sec to First Lord of Admiralty 1962–64, Flag Offr 2 i/c Western Fleet 1964–66, flag offr Scotland and N Ireland 1966–68; pres King George's Fund for Sailors (Scotland) 1968–79; memb Queen's Body Guard for Scotland (Royal Co of Archers) 1969–93; dep chm Gordonstoun Sch 1970–86; chm Cromarty Firth Port Authy 1974–77; HM Lord-Lt of Ross and Cromarty, Skye and Lochalsh 1977–88; *Books* Face the Music: A Sailor's Story (autobiography, 1991); *Recreations* walking, music, writing; *Style*— Vice Adm Sir John Hayes, KCB, OBE; ✉ Wemyss House, Nigg, by Tain, Ross and Cromarty IV19 1QW (☎ 01862 851212)

HAYES, John Philip; CB (1984); s of late Harry Hayes, and late G E Hayes, *née* Hallsworth; *b* 1924; *Educ* Cranleigh, CCC Oxford; *m* 1956, Susan Elizabeth, da of late Sir Percivale Liesching, GCMG, KCB, KCVO; 1 s, 1 da; *Career* WWII RAFVR 1943–46; political and econ planning 1950–53, OEEC 1953–58, Int Bank For Reconstruction and Devpt 1958–64, head Econ Devpt Div OECD 1964–67, dir World Economy Div (Econ Planning Staff) Miny of Overseas Devpt 1967–69, dep dir gen Econ Planning Miny of Overseas Devpt and Overseas Devpt Admin 1969–71; dir: Econ Program Dept (later Econ Analysis and Projections Dept) Int Bank for Reconstruction and Devpt 1971–73, Trade and Fin Div Cwlth Secretariat 1973–75; asst under-sec of state (economics) FCO 1975–84; sr fell Trade Policy Res Centre 1984–89; *Books* Economic Effects of Sanctions on Southern Africa (1987), Making Trade Policy in the European Community (1993); *Recreations* music, travel; *Style*— J P Hayes, Esq, CB; ✉ 51 Enfield Rd, Brentford, Middx TW8 9PA (☎ 0181 568 7590)

HAYES, Dr John Trevor; CBE (1986); s of Leslie Thomas Hayes (d 1976), of London, and Gwendoline, *née* Griffiths (d 1976); *b* 21 Jan 1929; *Educ* Ardingly Coll Sussex, Keble Coll Oxford (MA), Courtauld Inst of Art Univ of London (academic dip, PhD), Inst of Fine Arts NY (Cwlth Fund fell); *Career* dir: London Museum 1970–74 (asst keeper 1954–70), Nat Portrait Gallery 1974–94; visiting prof in history of art Yale Univ 1969; chm Walpole Soc 1982–96; hon fell Keble Coll Oxford; FSA 1975; *Books* The Drawings of Thomas Gainsborough (1970), Gainsborough as Printmaker (1971), Rowlandson Watercolours and Drawings (1972), Gainsborough Paintings and Drawings (1975), The Art of Graham Sutherland (1980), The Landscape Paintings of Thomas Gainsborough (1982), The Portrait in British Art (1991), Catalogue of the British Paintings, National Gallery of Art, Washington (1992); *Recreations* music, walking, gardening, travel; *Clubs* Beefsteak, Garrick, Arts; *Style*— Dr John Hayes, CBE, FSA; ✉ 61 Grantham Road, Chiswick, London W4 2RT (☎ 0181 747 9768)

HAYES, John William; CBE (1995); s of Dick Hayes (d 1979), and Bridget Isobel Hayes; *b* 10 Feb 1945; *Educ* Nottingham HS, Morecambe GS, Univ of Manchester (Dauntesey jr legal scholar, LLB); *m* 5 Dec 1970, Jennifer, da of Leslie Harvey and Teddie Grant, 2 s (Robert James b 13 Oct 1971, William Andrew b 20 Jan 1975), 1 da (Lucy Charlotte b 24 May 1973); *Career* slr; articled to Thomas Foord Town Clerk of Worthing 1966–69, slr Worthing, Nottingham and Somerset Co Cncls 1966–74, asst clerk then dep clerk Nottinghamshire CC 1974–79, clerk and chief exec Warwickshire CC 1980–86 (also clerk Warwickshire Magistrates Cts Ctee and clerk Warwickshire Probation Ctee), sec-gen The Law Soc 1987–96; clerk to HM Lord Lt for Warwickshire 1980–86; memb Law Soc 1965; memb City of London Solicitor's Co; *Publications include* Report Into River Safety (1992); *Recreations* cricket, music, idleness; *Clubs* Athaneum; *Style*— John Hayes, Esq, CBE

HAYES, Malcolm Lionel Fitzroy; s of Vice Adm Sir John Hayes, KCB, OBE, *qv*, and The Hon Rosalind Mary Finlay; *b* 22 Aug 1951; *Educ* St George's Sch Windsor, Eton, Univ of St Andrews, Univ of Edinburgh (BMus, Tovey Prize for Composition); *Career* formerly involved in weaving indust Lewis Outer Hebrides until 1981; music critic: The Times 1985–86, The Sunday Telegraph 1986–89, The Daily Telegraph 1989–95; contrib 1982–: Tempo, The Independent, Musical Times, The Listener, Classical Music, Opera Now, BBC Music Magazine, Classic FM Magazine, BBC Radio 4 (Kaleidoscope), BBC Radio 3, BBC World Service, Classic FM; memb Critics' Circle 1988–; *Books* New Music 88 (co-ed, 1988), Anton von Webern (1995); *Recreations* skiing, photography; *Clubs* Surrey CCC; *Style*— Malcolm Hayes, Esq; ✉ Arts Department, The Sunday Telegraph, 1 Canada Square, Canary Wharf, London E14 5DT (☎ 0171 538 7391, fax 0171 513 2504)

HAYES, Michael Anthony; s of Brian George Gerard Hayes (d 1983), of Wimbledon and Dorking, Surrey, and June Louise, *née* Wenner (d 1967); *b* 10 Jan 1943; *Educ* Wimbledon Coll, Univ Coll Oxford (MA); *m* 5 June 1971, Jacqueline Mary, da of Peter Kenneth Judd; 2 s (Dominic b 11 Aug 1972, William b 13 Feb 1978), 1 da (Victoria b 25 April 1974); *Career* admitted slr 1968; ptnr Macfarlanes 1974– (articled clerk 1966–68, asst slr 1968–71, assoc 1971–74, currently head of tax and fin planning dept); memb City of London Law Soc: Ctee 1978–92 (Distinguished Service award 1987); memb Law Soc: Standing Ctee on Entry and Trg 1987–89, Wills and Equity Ctee 1989–92, Land Law and Succession Ctee 1992–; memb Advsy Ctee of City of London CAB 1988– (chm 1985–88), tstee Tower Hamlets Tst; Freeman Worshipful Co of Slrs 1978–; memb Law Soc; *Recreations* jazz, wine, windsurfing; *Clubs* Wig and Pen, RAC, Roehampton; *Style*— Michael Hayes, Esq; ✉ 10 Norwich St, London EC4A 1BD (☎ 0171 831 9222, fax 0171 831 9607)

HAYES, Patrick (Paddy); s of Arthur Henry Hayes, of Charing, Kent, and Eva May, *née* Bowerman; *b* 14 Feb 1947; *Educ* Ashford HS, Enfield Coll of Technol (BA); *m* 28 March 1971, Lai May Choy; 2 da (Michele May b 21 Feb 1973, Annette Li b 29 Aug 1975); *Career* Garland Compton 1969–71 (successively trainee, asst account exec, account exec), account mangr CPV Ltd 1971–72, conslt rising to sr conslt Lloyd Group of Companies 1972–74, account dir BBD&O Ltd 1974–75, gp account dir Masius Wynne Williams D'Arcy MacManus 1975–76, dep md Leo Burnett Singapore 1976–82, md Kenyon & Eckhardt Thailand 1982–84, int client servs dir DMB&B Ltd 1984–93, gen mangr (China) DMB&B 1993–; *Recreations* squash, travel, theatre; *Style*— Paddy Hayes, Esq; ✉ DMB&B, Unit 606–611, Devon House, 979 Kings Road, Quarry Bay, Hong Kong

HAYES, Peter Richard Downham; *b* 22 Sept 1939; *Educ* Liverpool Coll; *m* 2 Sept 1967, Margaret Mary, *née* Makin; 1 da (Sarah Louise b 7 Oct 1970), 1 s (Richard James b 5 April 1973); *Career* various positions Martins Bank (became Barclays Bank Trust Co Ltd) 1956–73 (asst to Regnl Investmt Mangr Manchester 1970–73), NW regnl tax planning mangr Antony Gibbs (Personal Financial Planning) Ltd 1973–74; chm Plan Invest Group plc 1988–92 (fndr 1974, md 1974–88); chm: Macclesfield Dist Health Authy 1990–93, E Cheshire NHS Tst 1993–; cncllr Macclesfield BC 1996–; memb Cheshire Probation Bd 1993–, practitioner advsr to SIB 1986, memb Bd FIMBRA 1991–92; numerous published articles in newspapers and financial periodicals; ACIB (tstee dip); *Recreations* writing, sailing, motor cruising, dinghy racing; *Style*— Peter Hayes, Esq; ✉ Heronsbrook, Chelford Road, Prestbury, Cheshire SK10 4AW (☎ and fax 01625 829471); East Cheshire NHS Trust, Macclesfield District General Hospital, Victoria Road, Macclesfield, Cheshire SK10 3BL (☎ 01625 661501)

HAYES, Roger Peter; s of Peter Hall, and Patricia Mary, *née* Lacey; *b* 15 Feb 1945; *Educ* Isleworth GS, Univ of London, Univ of Southern California (BSc, MA); *m* 15 Feb 1974, Margaret Jean Hayes; 1 s (Nicolas Alexander b 25 Nov 1983); *Career* corr Reuters Paris 1967–72, dir and vice pres Burson Marsteller 1972–79, PA Management Consultants 1979–83, dir of corporate communications Thorn EMI plc 1985–88, dir IT World 1985–, chm Hayes Macleod International and Investor Corporate Communications 1988–91, non-exec chm Carma International 1989–; pres Int Public Relations Assoc 1997; vice pres Public Affairs and Govt Relations Ford of Europe 1991–93; DG British Nuclear Industry Forum 1993–; dir Matrix Communications Consultancy 1993– FRSA 1987; memb Bd of Regents Potomac Inst Wahington DC; FIPR 1988; *Books* Corporate Revolution (jtly, 1986), Experts in Action (jtly, 1988), Systematic Networking (1996); *Recreations* tennis, travel, movies and music; *Clubs* Reform, Hurlingham; *Style*— Roger Hayes, Esq; ✉ 75 Ellerby Street, London SW6 6EL (☎ 0171 731 1255); British Nuclear Industry Forum, 22 Buckingham Gate, London SW1E 6LB (☎ 0171 828 0116)

HAYES, Prof Tom Morgan; s of Wilfred Bernard Hayes (d 1990), of Cardiff, and Blodwen, *née* Morgan (d 1988); *b* 6 June 1936; *Educ* Birkenhead Sch, Univ of Liverpool (MB ChB); *m* Eirlys; 1 s (Gareth Morgan b 3 Aug 1963), 2 da (Jane Sarah (Mrs Milner) b 16 Oct 1964, Emma Louise b 8 Oct 1968); *Career* formerly conslt physician South and Mid Glamorgan HAs, currently prof of medical educn and dir and dean of postgraduate medical and dental educn Univ of Wales Coll of Medicine, hon conslt physician Univ

Hosp of Wales, non-exec dir Clwyd HA; author of over 100 publications on medicine and medical educn; FRCP 1963; *Recreations* travel literature, typography, croquet; *Style*— Prof Tom Hayes; ✉ University of Wales College of Medicine, Heath Park, Cardiff CF4 4XN (☎ 01222 743927)

HAYES, Dr William; s of Robert Hayes (d 1986), and Eileen, *née* Tobin (d 1985); *b* 12 Nov 1930; *Educ* Univ Coll Dublin (BSc, PhD), Univ of Oxford (MA, DPhil); *m* 28 Aug 1962, Joan Mary (d 1996), da of John Ferriss (d 1986); 2 s (Robert b 1973, Stephen b 1974), 1 da (Julia b 1970); *Career* official fell and tutor in physics St John's Coll Oxford 1960–67, 1851 overseas scholar 1955–57, sr fell American Nat Sci Fndn Purdue Univ USA 1963–64, visiting prof Univ of Illinois USA 1971, princ bursar St John's Coll Oxford 1977–87, dir and head Clarendon Laboratory Oxford 1985–87, pres St John's Coll Oxford 1987–, pro vice chllr Univ of Oxford 1990–, delegate of Oxford Univ Press 1991–, chm of curators Oxford Univ Chest 1992–; Hon DSc: Nat Univ of Ireland 1988, Purdue Univ 1996; *Books* Scattering of Light by Crystals (with R Loudon, 1978), Defects and Defect Processes in Non-Metallic Solids (with A M Stoneham, 1985); *Recreations* walking, reading, listening to music; *Style*— Dr William Hayes; ✉ President's Lodgings, St John's College, Oxford (☎ 01865 277 424); St John's College, Oxford (☎ 01865 277 419)

HAYFIELD, Colin John; s of Reginald George Hayfield (d 1960), and Vera Jessie, *née* Dawes (d 1996); *b* 9 Nov 1955; *Educ* The John Hampden Sch, LSE (BSc(Econs)); *Career* qualified CA; Binder Hamlyn 1977–83, ptnr Hardcastle Burton 1987– (joined 1983); fin dir The Marlborough Stirling Group plc 1994–; chm Ruislip-Northwood Cons Assoc 1993–94 (treas 1990–93); treas: Bucks Co Cricket Club 1993–96, Life Opportunities Trust 1993–; Freeman City of London 1989, Liveryman Worshipful Company of Tin Plate Workers Alias Wire Workers (auditor 1994–); FCA; *Recreations* reading; *Clubs* City Livery, Wallbrook Ward; *Style*— Colin Hayfield, Esq; ✉ 1 Moss Way, Beaconsfield, Bucks HP9 1TG (☎ 01494 680128); Hardcastle Burton, 166 Northwood Way, Northwood, Middx HA6 1RB (☎ 01923 824161, fax 01923 827895)

HAYGARTH-JACKSON, Angela Ray; OBE (1984); da of Harold Haygarth-Jackson, MC (d 1972), and Frieda, *née* Barraclough (d 1979); *b* 25 July 1929; *Educ* Cheltenham Ladies' Coll, Univ of Manchester (BSc, MSc); *Career* mangr Info Servs Section ICI Pharmaceuticals (now Zeneca) 1956–86, info sci conslt 1986–; pres Inst of Info Scientists 1983–84; chm: Editorial Bd of Journal of Documentation 1984–, Royal Soc of Chemistry Pubns Info Bd 1988–96; memb: Royal Soc Sci Info Ctee 1978–86, Br Library Advsy Cncl 1981–86; external examiner Dept of Info Studies Univ of Sheffield 1983–87; memb UK delgn to advise the People's Republic of China on library and info matters 1984; author of many papers on info sci and lectures in UK and overseas; CChem, FRSC, FIInfSc; *Recreations* travel, bridge, gardening, DIY, photography, original tapestry; *Style*— Miss Angela R Haygarth-Jackson, OBE; ✉ Highwayside, Bowdon, Altrincham, Cheshire WA14 3JD

HAYHOE, Baron (Life Peer UK 1992), of Isleworth in the London Borough of Hounslow; Rt Hon Sir Bernard John (Barney) Hayhoe; kt (1987), PC (1985); s of late Frank Stanley Hayhoe and Catherine Hayhoe; *b* 8 Aug 1925; *Educ* Borough Poly; *m* 1962, Ann Gascoigne, da of late Bernard W Thornton; 2 s (Hon Crispin Bernard Gascoigne b 1963, Hon Dominic Adam Scott b 1965), 1 da (Hon Sarah Anne Sherwood b 1967); *Career* MP (C): Heston and Isleworth 1970–74, Hounslow Brentford and Isleworth 1974–83, Brentford and Isleworth 1983–92; CRD 1965–70, PPS to Lord Pres of the Cncl and Ldr of the Commons 1972–74, additional oppn spokesman on Employment 1974–79, Parly under sec Def (Army) 1979–81; min of state: CSD 1981, Treasy 1981–85, for Health 1985–86; chm Guy's and St Thomas's NHS Tst 1993–95; CEng, FIMechE; *Clubs* Garrick; *Style*— The Rt Hon Lord Hayhoe, PC; ✉ 20 Wool Rd, London SW20 0HW (☎ 0181 947 0037)

HAYHURST-FRANCE, Christopher; s of Capt George Frederick Hayhurst-France, DSO, MC (d 1940), and Joyce Lilian, *née* Le Fleming (d 1961); *b* 6 Feb 1927; *Educ* Durham Sch, Coll of Estate Mgmnt; *m* 6 Sept 1956, Suzanne, da of Howard Spackman Ferris (d 1973), of Swindon; 2 s (David b 1957, Jonathan b 1960), 2 da (Sarah b 1959, Rachel b 1965); *Career* RM 1945 (invalided out), Lt 3 Glos Bn HG 1952–56; chartered surveyor, auctioneer, valuer; ptnr Moore Allen & Innocent Lechlade 1954–87; pres Central Assoc Agric Valuers 1975–76, dir Stroud Building Society 1970–93, chm Stroud & Swindon Building Society 1986–91 (pres 1993–), sec Berners Estate Co Faringdon 1988–93; FRICS 1951, FAAV 1956; *Clubs* Faringdon Rotary; *Style*— Christopher Hayhurst-France, Esq; ✉ 9 Orchard Hill, Faringdon, Oxon SN7 7EH (☎ 01367 240433)

HAYLER, Clive Reginald; s of Reginald Hayler (d 1985), and Dorothy Edith Hayler; *b* 11 Aug 1955; *Educ* Steyning GS, Univ of Liverpool (BSc), Univ of Exeter; *m* Heather Jayne, da of Derek John Roberts; 2 s (Richard Mark b 1984, Christopher James b 1985); *Career* mktg mangr Beckman RIIC Ltd 1979–83 (UK Sales Person of the Year 1981); md: Hawksley & Sons Ltd 1985–91 (gen mangr 1983–85), Marco Scientific Ltd 1991–; memb Ctee BSI; FInstD, CBiol, MIBiol, MSEE, MPS, MSSCC, FInstSMM; *Recreations* running, swimming, karate, reading, theatre, skiing; *Clubs* IOD, SEKU; *Style*— Clive Hayler, Esq; ✉ Marco Scientific Ltd, Unit 9, Henfield Business Park, Shoreham Road, Henfield, West Sussex BN5 9SL (☎ 01273 495700, fax 01273 495711)

HAYLOCK, John Mervyn; s of Dr Sydney John Haylock, FRCS, LRCP (d 1939), of Southbourne, Bournemouth, and Winifred Margaret, *née* Baker (d 1955); *b* 22 Sept 1918; *Educ* Aldenham Sch, Institut de Touraine Tours (dipl), Grenoble Univ, Pembroke Coll Cambridge; *Career* WWII: cmmnd Hampshire Regt 1940, served ME and Greece; writer; English instructor: Primary Teachers Trg Coll Baghdad, Coll of Commerce & Economics Baghdad 1948–56, Waseda Univ Tokyo 1958–60 and 1962–65; prof of English Rikkyo Univ Tokyo 1975–84; Ordre de Leopold II 1947, Croix de Guerre (Belge) 1947; FRSL 1995; author of short stories in Blackwoods Magazine, London Magazine, Winter Tales and others; *Novels* See You Again (1963), It's All Your Fault (1964), One Hot Summer in Kyoto (1980), A Touch of the Orient (1990), Uneasy Relations (1993); *Non-Fiction* New Babylon - A Portrait of Iraq (with Desmond Stewart, 1956); *Translations from the French* Robert de Montesquiou - A Prince of the Nineties (with Francis King, by Philippe Jullian, 1967), Flight into Egypt (by Phillipe Jullian, 1968); *Recreations* travel, swimming, collecting Oriental porcelain, reading, listening to music; *Clubs* Oriental; *Style*— John Haylock, Esq, FRSL; ✉ Flat 28, 15 Grand Avenue, Hove, East Sussex BN3 2NG (☎ 01273 325472)

HAYMAN, Baroness (Life Peer UK 1995), of Dartmouth Park in the London Borough of Camden; Helene Valerie Hayman; da of Maurice Middleweek; *b* 26 March 1949; *Educ* Wolverhampton Girls' HS, Newnham Coll Cambridge (BA, pres Cambridge Union 1969); *m* 1974, Martin Hayman, *qv*, s of Ronald Hayman, of Cadgwith, Cornwall; 4 s (Hon Ben b 1976, Hon Joseph b 1980, Hon Jacob b 1982, Hon David b 1985); *Career* worked successively with SHELTER (nat campaign for homeless), Camden Social Servs Dept then Nat Cncl for One Parent Families (dep dir) 1969–74, MP (Lab) Welwyn and Hatfield 1974–79, fndr memb Maternity Alliance (now nat charity) and broadcaster (incl 2 yrs presenting 7 Days for Channel 4) 1979–85, memb/vice chm Bloomsbury (subsequently Bloomsbury and Islington) HA 1985–92, chm Bloomsbury and Islington DHA 1992, chm Whittington Hosp NHS Tst 1992–; lay memb UCL Cncl; former chair of govrs Brookfield Sch; *Style*— The Rt Hon Baroness Hayman; ✉ c/o House of Lords, London SW1A OPW

HAYMAN, Martin Heathcote; *b* 20 Dec 1942; *Educ* Highgate Sch, Univ of Cambridge (MA); *m* 1974, The Rt Hon Baroness Hayman, *qv*; 4 s (Hon Ben, Hon Joseph, Hon Jacob, Hon David); *Career* slr 1964–69; successively co slr: Plessey Co, ITT and Pullman Kellogg; sec and chief legal advsr Cadbury Schweppes 1985–88 (chief legal advsr 1978–85), gp sec and head of gp legal servs Standard Chartered Bank 1988–; memb Bd CEDR; public speaker: on alternative dispute resolution, at legal and secretarial confs; chair of govrs William Ellis Sch NW London; winner In-House Banking/Finance Lawyer of the Year Award 1995; *Recreations* family; *Style*— Martin Hayman, Esq; ✉ Standard Chartered Bank, 1 Aldermanbury Square, London EC2V 7SB (☎ 0171 280 7021, fax 0171 280 7112)

HAYMAN, Ronald; s of John Hayman (d 1954), of Bournemouth, and Sadie, *née* Morris (d 1989); *b* 4 May 1932; *Educ* St Paul's, Trinity Hall Cambridge; *m* 11 Nov 1969, Monica, da of Hew Lorimer; 2 da (Imogen Hayman b 9 Jan 1971, Sorrel Trenchard b 16 Dec 1981); *Career* author, theatre director and broadcaster since 1967; actor in repertory and TV, first play staged The End of an Uncle 1959, memb Royal Court Writers' Gp 1959, dir Arts Theatre and Stratford East, trainee dir Northampton Repertory Co (under Associated Rediffusion trainee dirs scheme); prodns as freelance dir incl: An Evening with GBS (Edinburgh Festival and West End), a Peter Handke play (Open Space), a Fassbinder play (Traverse Edinburgh); as playwright: Playing the Wife (Belfast Festival 1992, Chichester Festival 1995); *Books* Samuel Beckett (1968), Harold Pinter (1968), John Osborne (1968), John Arden (1968), Techniques of Acting (1969), John Whiting (1969), Robert Bolt (1969), Tolstoy (1970), Arthur Miller (1970), Arnold Wesker (1970), John Gielgud: A Biography (1971), Edward Albee (1971), Eugène Ionesco (1972), Playback (1973), The Set-Up: an Anatomy of English Theatre Today (1974), The First Thrust (1975), The German Theatre (ed, 1975), How to Read a Play (1976), Leavis (1976), The Novel Today 1967–75 (1976), Artaud and After (1979), Tom Stoppard (1977), My Cambridge (ed, 1977), De Sade: A Critical Biography (1978), British Theatre since 1955 (1975), Theatre and Anti-Theatre (1979), Nietzsche: A Critical Life (1980), K: A Biography of Kafka (1981), Brecht: A Biography (1983), Brecht: The Plays (1984), Fassbinder: Film-Maker (1984), Secrets: Boyhood in a Jewish Hotel (1985), Writing Against: A Biography of Sartre (1986), Proust: A Biography (1990), The Death and Life of Sylvia Plath (1991), Tennessee Williams: Everyone Else is an Audience (1993), Thomas Mann (1995), Hitler and Geli (1997); *Recreations* tennis; *Clubs* Globe Tennis; *Style*— Ronald Hayman, Esq; ✉ c/o Peters Fraser & Dunlop Ltd, 503 The Chambers, Chelsea Harbour, Lots Road, London SW10 0XF (☎ 0171 344 1000, fax 0171 352 7356)

HAYMAN, Prof Walter Kurt; s of Prof Franz Samuel Haymann (d 1947), of Oxford, and Ruth Matilde Therese, *née* Hensel (d 1979); *b* 6 Jan 1926; *Educ* Gordonstoun, St John's Coll Cambridge (BA, MA, ScD); *m* 1, 20 Sept 1947, Margaret Riley (d 1994), da of Thomas William Crann (d 1978), of New Earswick, York; 3 da (Daphne Ruth b 1949, Anne Carolyn b 1951, Gillian Sheila b 1956); m 2, 11 May 1995, Waficka Katifi; *Career* lectr Univ of Newcastle 1947, fell St John's Coll Cambridge 1947–50, reader in mathematics Univ of Exeter 1953–56 (lectr 1947–53), dean Royal Coll of Sci Imperial Coll London 1978–81 (first prof of pure mathematics 1956–85), pt/t prof Univ of York 1985–93 (prof emeritus 1993), sr research fell Imperial Coll London 1995–; fndr with Mrs Hayman Br Mathematic Olympiad; memb: Cncl of RS 1962–63, Finnish Acad of Arts and Scis 1978, Bavarian Acad 1982, Accademia Dei Lincei (Rome) 1985, London Mathematic Soc (de Morgan Medal 1995), Cambridge Philosophical Soc, Soc Protection of Sci and Learning (memb Cncl); Hon DSc: Exeter 1981, Birmingham 1985, Uppsala Sweden 1992, Giessen Germany 1992; FRS 1956, FIC 1989; *Books* Multivalent Functions (1958, 2nd edn 1994), Meromorphic Functions (1964), Research Problems in Function Theory (1967), Subharmonic Functions (vol 1 with P B Kennedy, 1976, vol 2 1989); *Recreations* music, travel, television; *Style*— Prof W K Hayman, FRS; ✉ Department of Mathematics, Imperial College, Huxley Building, 180 Queen's Gate, London SW7 2BZ (☎ 0171 589 5111, ext 58609, fax 0171 594 8517)

HAYMAN-JOYCE, James Leslie; s of Maj Thomas F Hayman-Joyce, RA (d 1946), and Betty Christine, *née* Bruford (d 1995); *b* 12 May 1945; *Educ* Radley, RAC; *m* 3 March 1973, Charlotte Alexandra Mary, da of J P Crump, DFC, of Cold Aston, Glos; 2 s (Thomas Leslie b 12 April 1981, Simon Patrick b 10 Nov 1983); *Career* chartered surveyor; ptnr Blinkhorn & Co 1983–88, dir Sandoes Nationwide Anglia Estate Agents 1988–91, princ Hayman-Joyce Chartered Surveyors 1991–; FRICS 1970, FSVA 1991; *Style*— James Hayman-Joyce, Esq; ✉ Bakers Farmhouse, Barton-on-the-Heath, Moreton-in-Marsh, Glos GL56 0PN (☎ 01608 674291); Compton House, High St, Moreton-in-Marsh, Glos GL56 0AX (☎ 01608 651188, fax 01608 650030)

HAYMAN-JOYCE, Lt Gen Sir Robert John; KCB (1996), CBE (1989, OBE 1979); s of Maj Thomas Fancourt Hayman-Joyce (d 1946), and Betty Christine, *née* Bruford; *b* 16 Oct 1940; *Educ* Radley, Magdalene Coll Cambridge (MA); *m* 19 Oct 1968, Diana, da of Maj Neil Livingstone-Bussell, of East House, Sydling St Nicholas, Dorchester, Dorset; 2 s (Richard Livingstone b 21 Oct 1973, Alexander Robert b 11 Dec 1976); *Career* cmmnd 11 Hussars (PAO) 1963, Cmd Royal Hussars (PWO) 1980–82, Cdr RAC BAOR 1983–85, Dep Cmdt RMCS 1987, Dir UK Tank Prog 1988, DG Fighting Vehicles MOD(PE) 1989, DG Land Fighting Systems MOD (PE) 1990–92, Dir Royal Armoured Corps 1992–94, Mil Sec 1994–95, Master Gen of the Ordnance 1995–, Col Cmdt Royal Armoured Corps 1995–; *Recreations* skiing, horses, reading, music; *Clubs* Cavalry and Guards', Leander (Henley-on-Thames); *Style*— Lt Gen Sir Robert Hayman-Joyce, KCB, CBE; ✉ c/o Barclays Bank, 5 High St, Andover, Hants; MOD (PE), Yew 2a, MOD Abbeywood No 24, PO Box 702, Bristol BS12 7DU

HAYNES, Derek Leslie; s of Frederick Leslie Haynes, North Walsham, Norfolk, and Doreen Florence, *née* Saville; *b* 13 June 1950; *Educ* Dagenham Co HS; *m* Julie Iris, da of Iris Maskell; 1 s (Kieren Stephen b 20 Jan 1992); *Career* qualified CA 1975; articled clerk Rowley, Pemberton, Roberts 1968–74, mangr Deloitte Haskins & Sells 1974–80; Clark Whitehill: sr audit mangr 1980–82, tech ptnr 1982–92; ptnr and head of audit Mazars & Guerard 1993–; memb ICAEW: Audit Faculty Ctee, Tech and Practical Auditing Ctee, Nat Tech Advsy Ctee; memb LSCA Tech Ctee; Freedom of The City of London 1985, memb Worshipful Co of Glass Sellers of London 1985; FCA; *Recreations* classic cars, steam railways, photography, cricket, rugby, motor racing, music; *Clubs* City Livery; *Style*— Derek L Haynes, Esq; ✉ Pine Lodge, Gimingham Road, Trimingham, Norfolk NR11 8HP (☎ 01263 833902); Mazars & Guerard, 12th Floor, New Zealand House, 80 Haymarket, London SW1Y 4TE (☎ 0171 925 2333, fax 0171 930 0225)

HAYNES, John Harold; OBE (1995); *b* 25 March 1938; *Educ* Sutton Valence Sch Kent; *m* Annette Constance; 3 s (John b 1967, Marc b 1968, Christopher b 1972); *Career* wrote and published first book 1956, ret from RAF as Flt-Lt 1967 to take up full-time publishing, having founded J H Haynes and Co 1960; chm and Haynes Publishing Group plc; dir: J H Haynes and Co Ltd 1960–, Haynes Publications Inc (USA) 1974, GT Foulis and Co Ltd 1977–, Haynes Developments Ltd 1979–, J H Haynes (Overseas) Ltd 1979–, John H Haynes Developments Inc (USA) 1979–, Oxford Illustrated Press Ltd 1981–, Gentry Books Ltd, Camway Autographics Ltd 1984–, Oxford Publishing Co 1988–, Patrick Stephens Ltd 1990–; *Recreations* cycling, walking, veteran and vintage cars, reading; *Clubs* Southern Milestone Motor (pres), Guild of Motoring Writers; *Style*— John H Haynes, Esq, OBE; ✉ Haynes Publishing Group plc, Sparkford, nr Yeovil, Somerset BA22 7JJ (☎ 01963 440635, telex 46212); 861 Lawrence Drive, Newbury Park, Ca 91320, USA (☎ 00 1 818 889 5400)

HAYNES, Keith Anthony; s of Ernest Haynes, and Mary, *née* McElroy (d 1980); *b* 2 March 1958; *Educ* St Peter's GS, Univ of Hull (LLB), Manchester Poly (MSc); *m* 3 Sept 1986, Louise Mary, *née* Jackson; *Career* gen mangr Booth Hall Children's Hosp 1984–87, gen mangr Maternity and Paediatric Servs Gtr Glasgow Health Bd 1988–90; chief exec:

Liverpool Obstetric and Gynaecology Servs NHS Tst 1990–94, Royal Liverpool Univ Hosp Tst 1994–95; gen mangr Clinical Negligence Scheme for NHS Tsts Med Protection Soc and Willis Coroon Ltd 1995–; MHSM; *Recreations* walking, political biography, fine wine; *Style*— Keith Haynes, Esq; ✉ CNST, c/o Medical Protection Society, Granary Wharf House, Leeds LS11 5PY (☎ 0113 241 0700)

HAYNES, Lawrence John (Lawrie); s of Donald H Haynes, of Eastoft, Lincs, and Irene, *née* Langford; *b* 6 Dec 1952; *Educ* North Ayholme Comp Sch Crowle, Stevenson Coll of Further Educn, Heriot Watt Univ Edinburgh (BA); *m* Carol Anne, *née* Nelson; 2 step da (Natasha Jane b 15 March 1969, Victoria Louise b 21 July 1970), 1 da (Liberty Rose b 26 Aug 1981); *Career* apprentice RAF (Halton) 1968–71, RAF Sqdn Serv 1971–78, Stevenson Coll 1978–79, Heriot Watt Univ 1979–83, contracts offr rising to contracts exec British Aerospace (Space Systems) Ltd 1983–88, legal dir then md Microtel Communications Ltd (now Orange) 1988–91, projects dir British Aerospace plc 1991–94, chief exec Highways Agency 1994–; FRSA 1994, FIHT 1995; *Recreations* sailing, cricket; *Style*— Lawrie Haynes, Esq; ✉ Chief Executive, The Highways Agency, St Christopher House, Southwark Street, London SE1 0TE (☎ 0171 921 4080)

HAYNES, Philip Edmund; s of Herbert Thomas Haynes (d 1992), of Hove, Sussex, and Hilda, *née* Buckle (d 1981); *b* 8 July 1938; *Educ* Reigate GS; *m* June 1965, Susan, da of Cecil Lewis Blackburne; 2 s (Stephen b 1968, Michael b 1970); *Career* Nat Serv RAF 1956–58; articled clerk Hughes & Allen 1958–63, qualified CA 1964, ptnr Halletts (later Kidsons then Kidsons Impey) 1969–; memb Tech (Accounts and Audit) Sub Ctee LSCA 1975–76, chm Auditing Discussion Gp LSCA 1974–78; treas Buckland PCC 1989–, memb Buckland Parish Cncl 1991–; FCA 1969 (ACA 1964); *Recreations* photography, reading, gardening, theatre, classical music; *Style*— Philip Haynes, Esq; ✉ Kidsons Impey, Spectrum House, 20–26 Cursitor St, London EC4A 1HY (☎ 0171 405 2088, fax 0171 831 2206)

HAYNES, Timothy Hugh Penzer; s of Denzil Barry Penzer Haynes (d 1992), of Hampton-in-Arden, and Felicia Ann, *née* Nettlefold; *b* 2 April 1955; *Educ* Shrewsbury, Univ of Reading (BA), Pembroke Coll Cambridge (PGCE); *m* 1987, Charlotte Geraldine Mary, *née* Southall; 2 s (Theo Robert Penzer b 12 May 1994, Joseph Edward Penzer b 4 Dec 1995); *Career* stockbroker 1979–80; teacher: Queen Elizabeth's GS Blackburn 1980, Hampton Sch 1980–82; St Paul's Sch: teacher 1982–88, undermaster 1988–92, surmaster 1992–95; headmaster Monmouth Sch 1995–; *Style*— Tim Haynes, Esq; ✉ Monmouth School, Monmouth NP5 3XP (☎ 01600 713143)

HAYNES-DIXON, *see:* Godden, Rumer

HAYR, Air Marshal Sir Kenneth William; KCB (1988, CB 1982), KBE (1991, CBE 1976), AFC (1963 and bar 1972); s of Kenneth James Maxwell Hayr (d 1990), and Jeannie Templeton Hayr, *née* Crozier (d 1996), of Auckland, NZ; *b* 13 April 1935; *Educ* Auckland GS, RAF Coll Cranwell; *m* 1961, Joyce (d 1987), da of T Gardner (d 1954); 3 s (Simon, James, Richard); *Career* RAF Offr, Fighter Pilot 1957–71, OC RAF Binbrook 1974–76, Inspr of Flight Safety 1976–79, Asst Chief of Air Staff (Ops) 1981–82, Air Offr Cmdg No 11 Gp 1982–85, Cdr Br Forces Cyprus and Admin of the Sovereign Base Areas 1985–88, Dep C-in-C Strike Cmd/COS UKAIR 1988–90, Dep Chief Def Staff (Commitments) 1989–92; chm NZ Aviation Heritage Tst 1993–; Kuwait Liberation Order 1st Grade 1991; *Recreations* flying, tennis, paragliding, windsurfing, skiing, parachuting; *Clubs* RAF, Colonels'; *Style*— Sir Kenneth Hayr

HAYTER, Dianne; da of Flt Lt Alec Bristow Hayter (d 1972), and Nancy, *née* Evans (d 1959); *b* 7 Sept 1949; *Educ* Penrhos Coll, Aylesbury HS, Trevelyan Coll Univ of Durham (BA); *m* Prof Antony David Caplin; *Career* res asst GMWU 1970–72; res offr: Euro Trade Union Confedn Brussels 1973, Trade Union Advsy Ctee to OECD Paris 1973–74; gen sec Fabian Soc 1976–82 (asst gen sec 1974–76), journalist Channel 4's A Week in Politics 1982–83, dir Alcohol Concern 1983–90, chief exec Euro Parly Lab Pty 1990–96, dir corp affrs Wellcome Trust 1996–; memb: London Lab Pty Exec 1976–82, Royal Cmmn on Criminal Procedure 1978–81, Exec Ctee Fabian Soc 1986–95 (chair 1992–93), Exec Ctee NCVO 1987–90, Lab Pty Nat Constitutional Ctee 1987–; JP Inner London 1976–90; *Style*— Ms Dianne Hayter; ✉ 80 Leverton Street, London NW5 2NY

HAYTER, 3 Baron (UK 1927); Sir George Charles Hayter Chubb; 3 Bt (UK 1909), KCVO (1977), CBE (1976); s of 2 Baron (d 1967), by his 1 w Mary; *b* 25 April 1911; *Educ* Leys Sch, Trinity Coll Cambridge; *m* 1940, Elizabeth Anne Hayter, MBE, da of Thomas Rumbold (ggs of Sir Thomas Rumbold, 1 Bt); 3 s, 1 da; *Heir* s, Hon George Chubb; *Career* chm Chubb and Son's Lock and Safe Co 1957–81 (md 1941–57), dir Charles Early and Marriott (Witney) Ltd 1952–83; pres Royal Warrant Holders Assoc 1967; dep chm House of Lords 1982–95; govr King Edward's Hosp Fund for London 1983–86 (chm Mgmnt Ctee 1965–82); chm RSA 1965–66; Upper Bailiff Worshipful Co of Weavers 1961–62; *Style*— The Rt Hon the Lord Hayter, KCVO, CBE; ✉ Ashtead House, Ashtead, Surrey (☎ 013722 73476)

HAYTER, Paul David Grenville; LVO (1992); s of Rev Canon Michael George Hayter, and Katherine Patricia, *née* Schofield; *b* 4 Nov 1942; *Educ* Eton (King's scholar), ChCh Oxford (MA); *m* 1973, Hon Deborah Gervaise, da of Baron Maude of Stratford-upon-Avon; 2 s, 1 da; *Career* House of Lords: clerk Parliament Office 1964, seconded as private sec to Ldr of the House and Chief Whip 1974–77, clerk of ctees 1977, princ clerk of ctees 1985–90, reading clerk 1991–97, princ fin offr 1991–94, princ clerk of public bills 1994–, clerk asst 1997–; sec Assoc of Lord-Lieuts 1977–91; *Recreations* music, gardening, botanising, archery, painting; *Style*— Paul Hayter, Esq, LVO; ✉ Walnut House, Charlton, Banbury, Oxon OX17 3DR; House of Lords, London SW1A 0PW

HAYTER, Peter Reginald; s of Reginald James Hayter (d 1994), of Bushey, Herts and Lucy Gertrude Gray; *b* 13 March 1959; *Educ* Aldenham Sch Elstree Herts, Goldsmiths' Coll London (BA); *m* 28 Nov 1987, Mary Ann, da of late Geoffrey William Hamlyn; 1 s (Maximilian Geoffrey Reginald Hamlyn b 28 Dec 1990), 1 da (Sophie Grace b 9 July 1995); *Career* journalist; Hayter's Sports Reporting Agency 1982–86 (office boy, jr reporter, reporter, managing ed), football corr Sportsweek Magazine 1986–87, freelance writer 1987–88 (football diarist, writer and cricket writer Independent, football writer Observer, features ed Allsport Photographic), editorial prodr Running Late (C4 sports discussion prog) 1988, cricket corr The Mail on Sunday 1989–; dir Hayter's Sports Agency; *Books* Visions of Sport (1988), The Ashes - Highlights since 1948 (with BBC Test Match Special Team, 1989), Cricket Heroes (1990), Great Tests Recalled (1991), England v West Indies - Highlights since 1948 (with BBC Test Match Special Team, 1991), Botham - My Autobiography (Don't Tell Kath) with Ian Botham (1994); *Video* Botham Hits Back (interview, 1992); *Recreations* cricket, theatre, cinema, hard liquor; *Clubs* MCC, The Cricketers Club of London, Stanmore Cricket, Elvino's Cricket, Incogniti Cricket, Fleet St Strollers Cricket, Bunbury's Cricket; *Style*— Peter Hayter, Esq; ✉ The Mail On Sunday, Northcliffe House, Derry Street, London W8 5TS

HAYTON, Brian John; s of John Edward Hayton, of Ardrossan, Ayrshire, and Williamina Boden Cairns, *née* Tipper; *b* 1 May 1953; *Educ* Ardrossan Acad, Univ of Glasgow (MA), Univ of London (dip); *m* 23 July 1976, Fiona Mary-Ellen, da of John Murray Innes; 1 da (Pamela Jane b 21 July 1979), 1 s (Ian Brian b 8 June 1981); *Career* volunteer N Ayrshire Mus 1967–74, trainee Glasgow Museums and Art Galls 1975–78, dist curator Moray Dist Cncl 1978–80, dep dir NW Museums and Art Gall Serv 1981–87 (asst dir 1980–81), county museum offr N Yorks Co Cncl 1987–95, dir Compton Verney House Tst 1996–; chm Soc of County Museum Officers 1994–95, pres NW Fedn of Museums and Art Galls 1987–88; FMA 1988, FRSA 1996; *Recreations* walking, swimming, exploring towns; *Style*— Brian J Hayton, Esq; ✉ Compton Verney House Trust, Compton Verney, Warwick CV35 9HJ

HAYTON, Prof David John; s of Flt Lt Arthur Hayton, of Beaumont Park, Whitley Bay, Tyne and Wear, and Beatrice, *née* Thompson; *b* 13 July 1944; *Educ* Royal GS Newcastle, Univ of Newcastle (LLB, LLD), Jesus Coll Cambridge (MA); *m* 17 March 1979, Linda Patricia, da of James David Rae (d 1974); 1 s (John James b 28 July 1990); *Career* called to the Bar Inner Temple 1968; in practice Lincoln's Inn 1970–, recorder Co Ct 1992–; lectr Univ of Sheffield 1968–69 (asst lectr 1966–68), fell Jesus Coll Cambridge 1973–87, prof of law King's Coll London 1987– (dean Faculty of Law 1988–90); head of UK delgn to Hague Conf On Private Int Law 1988 (1984), dep chm English Tst Law Ctee 1994–; coach Cambridge RFC I XV 1980–83; *Publications* books: Registered Land (3 edn, 1981), Cases and Commentary on Law of Trusts (10 edn, 1996), Law of Trusts and Trustees (15 edn, 1995), Law of Trusts (2 edn, 1993), European Succession Law (1991); author of Hayton Report on Financial Services and Trust Law for SIB and IMRO (1990); *Recreations* playing tennis and squash, watching rugby; *Clubs* Royal Cwlth, MCC; *Style*— Prof David Hayton; ✉ 5 Stone Buildings, Lincoln's Inn, London WC2A 3RU (☎ 0171 242 6201); School of Law, King's College, London University, London WC2R 2LS (☎ 0171 836 5454, fax 0171 873 2465)

HAYTON, Philip John; s of Rev Austin Hayton, of Mansfield, Notts, and Jennie Margaret Violet, *née* Errington; *b* 2 Nov 1947; *Educ* Fyling Hall Sch Robin Hood's Bay Yorks; *m* 22 Dec 1972, Thelma Susan, da of James Gant; 1 s (James b 1980), 1 da (Julia Elizabeth b 1988); *Career* various former posts incl: teacher in Jordan, foundry worker, lavatory assembler, valet, doughnut salesman; pirate radio disc jockey and advertising salesman 1967, reporter and prodr BBC Radio Leeds 1968–71; BBC TV 1971: reporter and presenter Look North Leeds 1971–74, nat news reporter (covering Belfast, Beirut, Iranian Revolution, Ugandan War, Cod War and Rhodesian War) 1974–80, S Africa corr (also covering Argentina during Falklands War) 1980–83, reporter and newscaster (One, Six and Nine O'Clock News) 1983–93, presenter NorthWest Tonight and Great British Quiz (BBC) 1993–95, newscaster BBC World TV 1995–; *Recreations* sailing, theatre, walking, restaurants; *Style*— Philip Hayton, Esq; ✉ BBC TV, Television Centre, Wood Lane, London W12 7RJ (☎ 0181 743 8000)

HAYWARD, Sir Anthony William Byrd; kt (1978); s of Eric Hayward (d 1964), of Dane St House, Chilham, nr Canterbury, and Barbara Olive, *née* Bird (d 1976); *b* 29 June 1927; *Educ* Stowe, ChCh Oxford; *m* 1955, Jenifer Susan, da of Dr Francis Howard McCay (d 1985); 2 s (Simon, Charles), 2 da (Charlotte, Emma); *Career* temp Sub-Lt RNVR 1945–48; family business in India 1948–57, dir Shaw Wallace and Co India 1957–78 (chm and md 1970–78), pres Associated Chambers of Commerce and Indust of India 1977–78, md Guthrie Berhad Singapore 1978–81, pres and chief exec offr Private Investment Co for Asia (PICA) SA 1982–84, co dir in UK and Far East; FRSA; *Recreations* shooting, golf, photography; *Clubs* Oriental, Royal St George's; *Style*— Sir Anthony Hayward; ✉ Manwood House, Strand Street, Sandwich, Kent CT13 9HX (☎ 01304 612244, fax 01304 620030)

HAYWARD, The Ven (John) Derek Risdon; s of Eric Hayward (d 1964), of Chilham, nr Canterbury, and Barbara Olive, *née* Bird (d 1976); *b* 13 Dec 1923; *Educ* Stowe, Trinity Coll Cambridge (exhibitioner, MA, capt Polo), Westcott House; *m* 15 Oct 1965, Teresa Jane (Tessa), da of Nicholas Astell Kaye, MBE (d 1991), and Mrs Kaye, of Maidensgrove, nr Henley; 1 s (Leo Nicholas Eric b 1966), 1 da (Natasha Jane Dacomb b 1969); *Career* WWII Lt 27 Lancers, served Italy 1944–45 (twice wounded); md Hayward Waldie Calcutta 1946–53; returned to full-time educn 1953–57; asst curate St Mary Bramall Lane Sheffield 1957–59; vicar: St Silas Sheffield 1959–63, All Saints Isleworth 1964–94; archdeacon of Middx 1974–75 (emeritus 1975), gen sec Diocese of London 1975–93; chm: St Luke's Hosp for the Clergy 1991–, SCM Press 1992–; tstee Bath Preservation Tst, hon treas William Herschel Museum; Bronze Star (US) 1945 (for service in Italy); *Recreations* skiing; *Style*— The Ven Derek Hayward; ✉ 5 Sion Hill Place, Bath BA1 5SJ (☎ 01225 336305, fax 01225 421862)

HAYWARD, Sir Jack Arnold; kt (1986), OBE (1968); s of late Sir Charles Hayward, CBE, and Hilda, *née* Arnold; *b* 14 June 1923; *Educ* Stowe; *m* 1948, Jean Mary, *née* Forder; 2 s, 1 da; *Career* RAF 1941–46 (flying trg in Florida, active service pilot in SE Asia, demobilized as Flt Lt); served S Africa Branch Rotary Hoes Ltd until 1950 (joined 1947), fndr USA ops Firth Cleveland gp of cos 1951, joined Grand Bahama Port Authority Ltd 1956, chm Grand Bahama Development Co Ltd and Freeport Commercial and Industrial Ltd 1976–; pres: Lundy Field Soc, Wolverhampton Wanderers FC; vice pres: SS Great Britain Project, Wildfowl & Wetlands Tst; hon life vice pres Maritime Tst 1971, Paul Harris fell (Rotary) 1983; Hon LLD Exeter 1971; William Booth award Salvation Army 1987; *Recreations* promoting British endeavours (mainly in sport), watching cricket, amateur dramatics, preserving the British landscape, keeping all things bright, beautiful and British; *Clubs* MCC, Pratt's, RAF, RAC; *Style*— Sir Jack Hayward, OBE; ✉ Seashell Lane, (PO Box F-40099), Freeport, Grand Bahama Island, Bahamas (☎ 00 242 352 5165)

HAYWARD, Prof Jack Ernest Shalom; s of Menachem Hayward (d 1961), of Vancouver, Canada, and Stella, *née* Isaac (d 1959); *Educ* Horsley Hall, LSE (BSc, PhD); *m* 10 Dec 1965, Margaret Joy, da of Harold Clow Glenn (d 1985), of Adelaide, Australia; 1 s (Alan b 1973), 1 da (Clare b 1971); *Career* Nat Serv flying offr RAF 1956–58; asst lectr and lectr Univ of Sheffield 1959–63, lectr and sr lectr Univ of Keele 1963–73, sr res fell Nuffield Coll Oxford 1968–69, prof of politics Univ of Hull 1973–92, dir Oxford Univ Euro Studies Inst and professorial fell St Antony's Coll 1993–; vice pres Political Studies Assoc of the UK 1981– (chm 1975–77, pres 1979–81); visiting prof: Univ of Paris III 1979–80, Inst d'Etudes Politiques Paris 1990–91; Chevalier de l'Ordre Nat du Mérite France 1980, Chevalier de la Légion d'Honneur; FBA 1990; *Books* Private Interests and Public Policy, The Experience of the French Economic and Social Council (1966), The One and Indivisible French Republic (1973), Planning Politics and Public Policy: The British French and Italian Experience (with M Watson, 1975), Planning in Europe (with O Narkiewicz, 1978), State and Society in Contemporary Europe (with R Berki, 1979), The Political Science of British Politics (with P Norton, 1986), The State and the Market Economy: Industrial Patriotism and Economic Intervention in France (1986), Developments in French Politics (with P Hall and H Machin 1990 and 1994), After the French Revolution: Six Critics of Democracy and Nationalism (1991), De Gaulle to Mitterrand (1993), Industrial Enterprise and European Integration (1995), Governing the New Europe (with E Page, 1995), The Crisis of Representation in Europe (1995), Elitism, Populism and European Politics (1996); *Recreations* music, books, walking; *Clubs* Royal Commonwealth Soc; *Style*— Prof Jack Hayward; ✉ Flat 3, 5 St Johns Street, Oxford OX1 2LG (☎ 01865 552695); St Antony's College, Oxford OX2 6JF (☎ 01865 278701, fax 01865 278725)

HAYWARD, Mark Reece; s of Brian Walter Hayward, of Redbourn, Herts, and Rosalie Gordon, *née* Richards; *b* 27 Nov 1959; *Educ* Ellesmere Coll Shropshire; *Career* Central Selling Organisation De Beers 1978–79, HM Dip Serv 1979, apptd to Lord Carrington's private office 1981–82; theatre mangr: Comedy Theatre London 1982–84, Queen's Theatre London 1984–87, Her Majesty's Theatre London (Phantom of the Opera) 1987–93; gen mangr Theatre Royal Drury Lane London 1993–; *Recreations* swimming, weight training; *Style*— Mark Hayward, Esq; ✉ 43 Grosvenor Rd, Twickenham, Middx TW1 4AD; Theatre Royal Drury Lane, Catherine Street, London WC2 (☎ 0171 240 0115, fax 0171 379 6836)

HAYWARD, Peter Allan; s of Peter Hayward (d 1953), and Anne, *née* Jackson (d 1975); *b* 27 March 1932; *Educ* Haileybury, Trinity Coll Cambridge (BA, MA); *m* 13 March 1954, Elizabeth Layton, da of John Layton Smith (d 1976); 1 da (Pandora b 1962); *Career* Nat Serv 2 Lt RA 1952; called to the Bar Lincoln's Inn 1958 (Cassell scholar), practised at Patent Bar 1958–68, lectr UCL 1959–60, fell and tutor in jurisprudence St Peter's Coll Oxford 1968– (vice master 1992–94), dir Intellectual Property Law Centre 1990–; memb: Gen Bd of Faculties Univ of Oxford 1980–85, Holborn Borough Cncl 1962–66; *Books* Halsbury's Laws of England (3 edn), Trade Marks and Designs (contrib, 1962), Annual Survey of Commonwealth Law (contrib, 1970–73), Reports of Patent Cases (ed, 1970–74), Hayward's Patent Cases 1600–1883 (11 vols, 1988); *Style*— Peter Hayward, Esq; ✉ St Peter's College, Oxford, OX1 2DL (☎ 01865 278885); Priorton, Vernon Ave, Harcourt Hill, Oxford OX2 9AU (☎ 01865 248102)

HAYWARD, His Hon Judge; Richard Michael; s of George Michael Hayward (d 1993), of Winchelsea, Sussex, and Esmè Mary Florence, *née* Howard (d 1985); *b* 12 July 1946; *Educ* Highgate Sch, Inns of Court Sch of Law; *m* 1969, Laura Louise, da of E M Buchan; 2 s (Nicholas Richard b 20 Feb 1971, Anthony Pascoe b 17 Oct 1972), 1 da (Emily Alexandra b 23 Sept 1977); *Career* called to the Bar Middle Temple 1969, recorder 1994–96 (asst recorder 1990), circuit judge (SE Circuit) 1996–; *Recreations* golf, painting, gardening, horses; *Clubs* Rye Golf; *Style*— His Hon Judge Hayward; ✉ Lewes Combined Court, High Street, Lewes, East Sussex BN7 1YB

HAYWARD, Robert Antony; OBE (1991); s of late Ralph Hayward, of Swinford Farm, Eynsham, Oxon, and Mary Patricia, *née* Franklin; *b* 11 March 1949; *Educ* Maidenhead GS, Univ of Rhodesia (BSc); *Career* vice chm Nat Young Cons 1976–77, cncllr Coventry City Cncl 1976–78, MP (C) Kingswood 1983–92; PPS: to Under Sec of State for Trade and Indust 1985–87, to Min for Indust 1986–87, to Sec of State for Transport 1987–92; memb Select Ctee on Energy 1983–85, jt sec Back Bench Aviation Ctee 1991–92; co-fndr and jt co-ordinator Gulf Support Gp 1990–91; dir gen Br Soft Drinks Assoc 1993–; *Recreations* former national level rugby official, psephology; *Style*— Robert Hayward, Esq, OBE; ✉ 11 Grosvenor Park, London SE5 0NQ; Director General, The British Soft Drinks Association Ltd, 20 Stukeley Street, London WC2B 5LR (☎ 0171 430 0356, fax 0171 831 6014)

HAYWARD, (Christopher) Timothy Esmond (Tim); s of Tom Christopher Hayward, CBE, DL (d 1975), and Sybil Lisette, *née* Grainger-Brunt (d 1994); *b* 13 Sept 1940; *Educ* Eton, CCC Cambridge (MA); *m* 9 June 1964 (m dis 1976), Charmian Rosalind, da of Derek Leaf (d 1943); 1 s (Derek Christopher b 1967), 1 da (Chloe Amanda b 1969); *Career* qualified CA 1965, ptnr Peat Marwick Mitchell and Co 1977 (joined 1962); KPMG: sr ptnr corp recovery 1987–95, head of new serv devpt 1996–; memb Cncl: Soc of Practitioners of Insolvency 1992–, ICAEW 1995–; FCA (ACA 1966); *Recreations* shooting, farming; *Clubs* Bucks, MCC; *Style*— Tim Hayward, Esq; ✉ Springhead House, Amberley Road, Parham, Pulborough, W Sussex RH20 4HN (☎ 01903 740876); KPMG, 8 Salisbury Square, London EC4Y 8BB (☎ 0171 311 1000, fax 0171 311 8735, telex 8811541 PMM LON G)

HAYWARD, Maj-Gen (George) Victor; s of George Harold Hayward (d 1971), of Stratford-on-Avon, and Daisy, *née* Ball (d 1975); *b* 21 June 1918; *Educ* Blundell's, Univ of Birmingham (BSc); *m* 18 July 1953, Gay Benson, da of Hamilton Barrett Goulding (d 1947), of Dublin; 1 s (Stephen George Hamilton b 1954), 1 da (Victoria Clare b 1956); *Career* served WWII 1939–45, cmmnd 1940, transf to REME 1942, GSO1 REME Training Centre 1958, Cdr REME 2nd Div 1960, asst mil sec WO 1962, Col RARDE, Fort Halstead 1963, CO 38 Central Workshop 1965, Dep Cmdt Technical Gp REME 1966, Cmdt REME Trg Centre 1969, Cmdt Technical Gp REME 1971–73, Col Cmdt REME 1973–78, planning inspr DOE 1973–88; CEng, FICE, FIMechE, FIMgt; *Recreations* sailing, skiing, shooting; *Clubs* Army and Navy; *Style*— Maj-Gen G V Hayward; ✉ Chart Cottage, Chartwell, Westerham, Kent TN16 1PT (☎ 01732 866253)

HAYWARD SMITH, Rodger; QC (1988); s of Frederick Ernest Smith, and late Heather Hayward, *née* Rodgers, of Ingatestone, Essex; *b* 25 Feb 1943; *Educ* Brentwood Sch Essex, St Edmund Hall Oxford (MA); *m* 4 Jan 1975, (Gillian) Sheila, *née* Johnson; 1 s (Richard b 1976), 1 da (Jane b 1978); *Career* called to the Bar Gray's Inn 1967, recorder 1986– (asst recorder 1981–86); *Publications* Jackson's Matrimonial Finance and Taxation (jt ed, 5 and 6 edns); jt ed Practitioners' Child Law Bulletin; *Style*— Rodger Hayward Smith, Esq, QC; ✉ 1 King's Bench Walk, Temple, London EC4Y 7DB (☎ 0171 583 6266)

HAYWOOD, Bryan; s of Arthur Haywood; *b* 1 May 1939; *Educ* King Edward VII Sch Leics; *m* (m dis); 1 s (Timothy); *Career* certified accountant; dir: Balfour Kilpatrick Ltd 1975–88, Balfour Kilpatrick International Ltd UK, Kilpatrick Group of Cos; chm Xianity Galore Investments 1988–; *Recreations* country life; *Style*— Bryan Haywood, Esq; ✉ Trewylan, Glanteifion, St Dogmaels, Cardigan, Dyfed (☎ 01239 621781)

HAYWOOD, Sir Harold; KCVO (1988), OBE (1974), DL (1983); s of Harold Haywood (d 1988), of Burton on Trent, and Lillian, *née* Barratt (d 1929); *b* 30 Sept 1923; *Educ* Guild Sch Burton on Trent Staffs, Westhill Coll Birmingham, Ecumenical Inst Geneva; *m* Jan 1944, Amy, da of Charles William Richardson (d 1955), of Burton on Trent; 3 s; *Career* RN 1943 med discharge; organiser St Johns Clubland Sheffield 1948–51, lectr Westhill Coll of Educn 1951–53, regnl organiser Methodist Youth Dept Birmingham and vice pres Methodist Assoc of Youth Clubs 1954–55, nat tutor King George VI leadership course 1955–57, educn offr Nat Assoc of Mixed Clubs and Girls Clubs 1957–77, dir of trg Nat Assoc of Youth Clubs 1966–74, gen sec Educn Interchange Cncl 1974–78, dir Royal Jubilee and Princes Tsts 1978–88, nat chm YMCA 1989–92 (vice pres 1992–); chm Gen and Liberal Studies Dept Dacorum Coll of Further Educn Herts and vice chm of govrs 1965–69, memb Univ of Leeds Inst of Educn res project on Carnegie Community Sch 1966–74, external examiner Roehampton Inst and Rolle and St Lukes Colls Univ of Exeter 1969–74, visiting fell Inst of Technol Melbourne Aust 1987, govr Bell Educational Tst Cambridge until 1990; gen sec Educational Interchange Cncl and memb Advsy Ctee on Exchange Br Cncl 1974–78, memb Bd Anglo Austrian Soc 1974–81; vice chm Br Nat Ctee World Assembly of Youth 1964–66, memb Sec of State for Educn's Nat Advsy Cncl for the Youth Serv 1985–88, memb Bd Nat Youth Theatre 1987–90; memb: Home Sec's Advsy Cncl on the Misuse of Drugs 1970–75, Peterborough Devpt Corporation, Cresset Neighbourhood Mgmnt Bd 1971–74; chm BBC IBA Central Appeals Advsy Ctee 1988–93, memb BBC Gen Advsy Cncl 1988–93; tstee and chm Advsy Cncl Charities All Fndn 1989–, tstee Children in Need Tst 1989–93; chm: Assoc of Charitable Fndns 1989–93, The Help Tst 1992–96, Action Aid 1994–96; FRSA 1985; *Books* A Role for Voluntary Work (1970), Partnership with the Young (1979); *Recreations* the garden, books; *Clubs* Athenaeum, Civil Service, Penn; *Style*— Sir Harold Haywood, KCVO, OBE, DL

HAYWOOD, Roger; s of Maj George Haywood, of Norwich, and Ethel Florence, *née* Reynolds; *b* 24 July 1939; *Educ* Westcliff Sch Westcliff-on-Sea; *m* 30 June 1962, Sandra Leonora, da of George Yenson (d 1972); 2 s (Ian b 1965, Mark b 1966), 2 da (Sarah b 1963, Laura b 1971); *Career* mktg positions with Dunlop, Dexion and in various advertising agencies, Euro PR mangr Air Products 1970–72; md: Haywood Hood & Associates Ltd 1972–75, Tibbenham Group 1975–82; chm: Roger Haywood Associates Ltd 1982–92, Worldcom Inc 1989–91, Kestrel Communications Ltd 1992–; pres Inst of PR 1991; chm: Chartered Inst of Mktg 1992, Worldcom Europe 1997; vice chm PR Conslts Assoc; Freeman City of London, memb Worshipful Co of Marketors; FCIM, ABC, FCAM, FIPR; *Books* All About Public Relations (1985, 3 edn 1994), Managing Your Reputation (1994), Public Relations for Marketing Professionals (1997); *Recreations* economics, the media, motoring, music, politics and sport; *Clubs* Reform, Agency; *Style*— Roger Haywood, Esq; ✉ 22 The Cloisters, Folgate Street, London E1 6EB (☎ and fax 0171 247 4670); Barron Lodge Farm, Happisburgh, Norfolk (☎ 01692 651494, fax 01692 651573); Kestrel Communications Ltd, Broadway House, The Broadway, Wimbledon, London SW19 1RL (☎ 0181 543 2299, fax 0181 543 2292)

HAYZELDEN, John Eastcott; CBE (1994); s of Allan Frederick George Hayzelden (d 1955), of Pinner, Middx, and Grace Winifred, *née* Hutton (d 1987); *b* 20 June 1936; *Educ* Merchant Taylors', St John's Coll Oxford (MA); *m* 8 June 1963, Susan Clare, da of Dr Robert Strang (d 1977), of The White House, Penn, Bucks; 2 da (Clare b 11 Nov 1964, Gillian b 17 Sept 1966); *Career* 2 Lt RA 1956–57; called to the Bar Middle Temple 1968; Home Office: princ 1966–73, asst sec 1973–88, head Passport Dept 1988–91, chief executive United Kingdom Passport Agency 1991–94; memb Thames Customer Service Ctee OFWAT 1996–; *Recreations* tennis, golf, reading; *Clubs* Tring Lawn Tennis (former chm); *Style*— John Hayzelden, Esq, CBE; ✉ Uplands, 39 Mortimer Hill, Tring, Herts (☎ 0144 282 3563)

HAZEEL, Francis Ida McCulloch; s of late Capt Harry Hazeel, of Dunoon, Argyllshire, and late Eliane, *née* Parascou, of Chelsea; *b* 13 Feb 1945; *Educ* George Watson's Coll Edinburgh, King's Sch Canterbury, Pembroke Coll Oxford (Cleobury Scholar); *m* 1985, Carolyn Robin, da of the Hon Robin Warrender; 2 s (Jamie, Geordie); *Career* successively asst mangr Charterhouse Japhet, mangr Spencer Thornton Brussels, mangr corp fin and export credits Nordic Bank, mangr property and project fin Banque Indosuex London, currently head of London Representative Office Deutsche Pfandbrief-und Hypothekenbank AG (DePfa-Bank); former chm Export Credits Ctee Foreign Banks Assoc, pres Assoc of Property Bankers 1994–95; dir: Carolyn Warrender Ltd, Thistle II Ltd; memb Advsy Bd: Royal Acad of Arts Tst, UK Real Estate Acad de Montfort Univ, Sadlers Wells Appeal Fund; *Recreations* art, opera, architecture; *Style*— Francis Hazeel, Esq; ✉ 54 Alderney St, London SW1; DePfa-Bank, Royex House, Aldermanbury Square, London EC2V 7HR (☎ 0171 606 0656, fax 0171 606 2352)

HAZELDINE, James Anthony; s of Samuel Joseph Hazeldine (d 1984), of Salford, Lancs, and Annie (d 1962); *Educ* St Alberts Secdy Sch Salford; *m* 17 Sept 1971, Rebecca, *née* Moore; 1 s (Sam b 29 March 1972), 1 da (Chloe Katherine b 16 May 1980); *Career* actor; student Salford Rep, repertories at St Anne's, Liverpool and Manchester Library Theatre; first London appearance as understudy in Look Back in Anger, then Bond Season (Royal Court); *Theatre* RSC: Troilus in Troilus and Cressida, Alcibiades in Timon of Athens, Rodian Nemov in The Love Girl and the Innocent; NT: Jim in Kick for Touch, Gerard in Small Change, Don Everley in Long Time Gone; Royal Court: Over Gardens Out, Small Change; The Foursome (Fortune Theatre), Luther Gasgoine in The Daughter in Law (Hampstead Theatre Club), Sam Evans in Strange Interlude (West End and Broadway); *Television* BBC: Omega Factor, Truckers, Close Relations; Thames: Chocky, A Small Dance; LWT: Kids, Bay Leaf in London's Burning; Frank Barraclough in Sam (Granada), Kidder in One Summer (Yorkshire); several Plays For Today; *Films* Nicholas and Alexandra, The National Health, The Medusa Touch, Business As Usual, Stardust, The Wall; *Recreations* writing, wind surfing, sailing, drawing, scuba diving; *Style*— James Hazeldine, Esq; ✉ c/o Conway van Gelder Robinson Ltd, 18–21 Jermyn Street, London SW1Y 6HP (☎ 0171 287 0077, fax 0171 287 1940)

HAZELL, Robert John Davidge; s of Peter Hazell, of Cheltenham, and Elizabeth Complin, *née* Fowler; *b* 30 April 1948; *Educ* Eton, Wadham Coll Oxford (MA); *m* 27 June 1981, Alison Sophia Mordaunt, da of Arthur Hubert Mordaunt Richards (d 1982); 2 s (Alexander Robert Mordaunt b 5 May 1982, Jonathan William Joshua b 4 Jan 1985); *Career* barr 1973–75; numerous depts of Home Office 1975–89, Nuffield and Leverhulme travelling fellowship to study freedom of info in Aust, Canada and NZ 1986–87, dir Nuffield Fndn 1989–95, dir Consitution Unit 1995–; magistrate 1978–96; vice chm Assoc of Charitable Fndns 1990–92, tstee Citizenship Fndn 1991, memb Cncl JUSTICE 1995; FRSA 1991; *Books* Conspiracy and Civil Liberties (1974), The Bar on Trial (1978); *Recreations* opera, badgers, bird watching, canoeing; *Style*— Robert Hazell, Esq; ✉ 94 Constantine Rd, London NW3 2LS (☎ 0171 267 4881); Constitution Unit, 4 Tavistock Place, London WC1H 9RA (☎ 0171 209 1162, fax 0171 209 1163)

HAZELWOOD, Maurice Harry; s of George William Hazelwood (d 1967), of Heckington, and Nellie Hazelwood; *b* 24 May 1933; *Educ* Carrington Sch; *m* 1955, Monica Ruth Marshall; 3 s (Mike b 1958, Tim b 1961, George b 1968), 1 da (Gillian b 1956); *Career* Nat Serv Army 1952–54; water skiing administrator; began water skiing 1964; memb Lincs Speed Boat Club 1966, chm Castle Water Ski Club 1970–83; Br Water Ski Assoc: joined 1967, team capt and mangr 1972–90, chm 1982–89, vice chm and hon memb 1989–; football referee 1951–65; lorry driver 1948–52 and 1954, potato merchant 1955; proprietor: Hazelwood Haulage Ltd 1960, Hazelwood Distribution Ltd 1982–, Hazelwood Ski World 1984–; *Recreations* Hazelwood Ski World; *Style*— Maurice Hazelwood, Esq; ✉ Hazelwood Ski World, Moor Lane, Thorpe-on-the-Hill, Lincoln LN6 9DA (☎ 01522 688245)

HAZLEHURST, Ronnie; s of late Herbert Hazlehurst, and late Lilian May, *née* Wraith; *b* 13 March 1928; *Educ* Hyde Co GS Cheshire; *m* 1, Georgina Rowbottam (decd); m 2, (m dis), Sita Davenport; 2 s (Clive Ronald b 13 Oct 1955, Neil Roger b 24 Aug 1956); *Career* professional trumpet player 1944–60, arranger 1960–66, freelance arranger, composer, musical dir 1996– (mostly for BBC TV and Radio); compositions for BBC incl: Last of the Summer Wine, Yes Minister, Yes Prime Minister, Some Mothers Do 'Ave 'Em, To The Manor Born, The Fall and Rise of Reginald Perrin; conductor numerous Royal Variety Performances and Eurovision Song Contests; music dir for The Two Ronnies, Cilla Black etc; Freeman City of London; memb: Grand Order of Water Rats, The Lord's Taverners, Sports Aid Fndn; *Books* Laurel & Hardy's Music Box (1996); *Clubs* Lancashire CC, Middx CC; *Style*— Ronnie Hazlehurst, Esq

HAZLEMAN, Dr Brian Leslie; s of Eric Edward Hazleman (d 1981), of Reading, Berks, and Gladys Marjorie, *née* Wells; *b* 4 March 1942; *Educ* Leighton Park Sch Reading, London Hosp Univ of London (MB BS), Univ of Cambridge (MA); *m* 29 Jan 1972, Ruth Margaret, da of Douglas Eynon, of Bristol; 3 da (Anna b 1973, Christina b 1976, Sarah b 1983); *Career* London Hosp 1966–71: house physician and surgn 1966–67, registrar rheumatology 1968–69, registrar med 1969–71; sr registrar med and rheumatology: Radcliffe Infirmary Oxford 1971–73, Nuffield Orthopaedic Hosp 1971–73; conslt physician: Addenbrooke's Hosp Cambridge 1973–, Newmarket Hosp 1973–; hon conslt Strangeways Res Laboratory Cambridge 1973–, dir Rheumatology Res Unit Cambridge 1975–, assoc lectr Univ of Cambridge 1975– (fell CCC 1982); memb Cncl Br Soc of Rheumatology 1995– (pres elect); memb Editorial Bd: Jl of Orthopaedic Rheumatology, Jl of Inflammo Pharmacology; winner: Begley prize RCS 1965, Margaret Holyrode prize Heberden Soc 1975; FRCP; *Books* The Sclera and Systemic Disorders (1976), Rheumatoid Arthritis Pathology and Pharmacology (1976), The Shoulder Joint (1989), Polymyalgia Rheumatica and Giant Cell Arteritis (1992), Rheumatology Examination and Injection Techniques (1992); *Recreations* sailing, photography, travel; *Clubs* Aldeburgh Yacht Club (Suffolk); *Style*— Dr Brian L Hazleman; ✉ Church End House, Weston Colville, Cambs CB1 5PE (☎ 01223 290 543); Department of Rheumatology, Addenbrooke's Hospital, Hills Road, Cambridge (☎ 01223 217457, fax 01223 217838)

HAZLERIGG, 2 Baron (UK 1945); Sir Arthur Grey; 14 Bt (E 1622), MC (1945), TD (1948), JP (Leics 1946), DL (1946); s of 1 Baron (d 1949); *b* 24 Feb 1910; *Educ* Eton, Trinity Coll Cambridge; *m* 1945, Patricia (d 1972), da of John Pullar, of Natal, S Africa;

1 s, 2 da; *Heir* s, Hon Arthur Hazlerigg; *Career* served WWII Maj RA (TA) and Leics Yeo; Liveryman Worshipful Co of Merchant Taylors; FRICS; *Recreations* golf; *Clubs* MCC; *Style—* The Rt Hon the Lord Hazlerigg, MC, TD, JP, DL; ✉ Noseley Hall, Billesdon, Leicester LE7 9EH (☎ 01533 596322)

HAZLERIGG, Hon Arthur Grey; s and h of 2 Baron Hazlerigg, MC; *b* 5 May 1951; *m* 1986, Laura, eld d of Sir William Dugdale, 2 Bt; 1 s (Arthur William Grey b 13 May 1987), 3 da (Eliza Patricia 21 April b 1989, Amelia Frances b (twin) 1989, Viola Camilla Alice b 1 July 1993); *Clubs* Leicester Tigers Old Players, White's, MCC; *Style—* The Hon Arthur Hazlerigg; ✉ Noseley Hall, Billesdon, Leics LE7 9EH (☎ 01162 596606)

HAZLEWOOD, Gerald Alan (Gerry); OBE (1986); s of Richard Hazlewood, of Okanagan Centre, BC, Canada, and Lilian May, *née* Lofts; *b* 25 July 1939; *Educ* Royal GS High Wycombe; *m* 6 Sept 1961, Toni Gay, da of Sqdn Ldr Edward John Lisle, of Mundaring, Western Australia; 1 s (Daniel b 1979), 2 da (Christina b 1967, Helen b 1965); *Career* chm: Westwood Engineering Ltd 1986–90 (dir 1967–86), Westwood Automation Ltd 1990–; *Recreations* golf; *Style—* Gerry Hazlewood, Esq, OBE; ✉ Westwood Automation Ltd, Bell Close, Newnham Industrial Estate, Plympton, Plymouth PL7 4JH (car 0850 337140)

HAZLITT, Capt Simon Charles; s of Denis Roy Hazlitt (d 1994), of Woking, Surrey, and Jennifer Anne Margaret, *née* Dick; *b* 16 Oct 1966; *Educ* Clifton Coll Bristol, Univ of Nottingham (BA); *m* 18 Sept 1993, Karen, *née* Jennings; *Career* entered Sandhurst 1988, cmmnd 2 Lt 2 Bn The Light Infantry 1989–; hockey player; capt Hounslow Club, 60 England caps 1987–, 13 GB caps 1987–, also played Co Combined Servs, Gold medal Sultan Azlan Shah Tournament Ipoh Malaysia 1989 (Bronze 1987), Gold medal Sultan Azlan Shah 1994; England Capt: Indira Ghandhi tournament Delhi 1995, Champions Trophy Berlin 1995; *Recreations* golf, cricket, reading, current affairs, politics; *Clubs* Oatlands Park Cricket, Hounslow Hockey; *Style—* Capt Simon Hazlitt; ✉ c/o The Hockey Association, Norfolk House, 102 Saxon Gate West, Milton Keynes MK9 2EP

HAZZARD, (Lawrence) Gordon; s of Frederick Hazzard, and Minnie; *b* 1925; *Educ* Waverley GS Birmingham; *m* 1, 1956 (m dis), Margery Elizabeth Charles; 1 da (Clare); m 2, 1985, Miyuki Sedohara; *Career* served WWII, RAF 1943–47; gp md MK Electric Holdings until 1980; dep chm then chm Grosvenor Group plc 1981–86; chm: Wigfalls plc 1981–88, Waingate Insurance Ltd 1985–88, HB Electronic Components plc 1983–85, Toby Lane Ltd 1984–89, Gordon Hazzard Ltd Anglo Japanese Business Advsrs 1980–, Green Park Health Care plc 1989–94, Opera Holdings Ltd 1992–, Fleet International Ltd 1994–, Fleet Electronics 1996–; former: memb Cncl CBI (former memb Industl Policy Ctee), memb Bd ASTA, vice chm EIEMA, dep pres Br Electric and Allied Mfrs Assoc; memb: Japan Soc, Japan-Br Soc of Hiroshima; FInstD, CIMgt; *Recreations* music; *Clubs* RAC, Wig & Pen; *Style—* Gordon Hazzard, Esq; ✉ 5 Balfour Place, Mayfair, London W1Y 5RG (☎ 0171 408 0626, fax 0171 629 8105)

HEAD, His Hon Adrian Herbert; s of His Honour Judge George Herbert Head (d 1927), of Acomb, York, and Geraldine Maria, *née* Pipon (d 1959); *b* 4 Dec 1923; *Educ* RNC Dartmouth (invalided polio), privately, Magdalen Coll Oxford (BA, MA); *m* 22 July 1947, Ann Pamela, da of John Stanning (d 1928), of Engoshura Farm, Nakuru, Kenya; 3 s (Henry b 1948, Christopher b 1954, David b 1955); *Career* called to the Bar Gray's Inn 1947 (Holker exhibitioner 1945, Arden scholar and Holker sr exhibitioner 1947), subs ad eundem Inner Temple; chm Norfolk Lavender Ltd and Chilvers & Son (1874) Ltd 1958–71 (dir 1953–58), chm Agricultural Land Tbnls (SE Region) 1971, dep chm Middx QS 1971, circuit judge (SE Circuit) 1972–96; memb Law Advsy Bd UEA 1979–, co-fndr and sr tstee Norfolk Family Conciliation Serv 1983–96, pres West Norfolk and Fenland Marriage Guidance Cncl (now Relate) 1984–94; reader C of E 1961–; Hon DCL UEA 1987; *Books* The Seven Words and the Civilian (1946, awarded the Tredegar Meml Lectureship RSL 1948), Essays by Divers Hands (contrib, 1953), Safety Afloat (trans from Dutch, 1965), Consumer Credit Act Supplement to McCleary's County Ct Forms (1979), Poems in Praise (1982), Butterworths County Ct Precedents and Pleadings (deviser and gen ed 1985, contrib 1985–, consulting ed 1987–), Poems in Praise (2 edn, 1987); *Recreations* writing, painting, messing about in boats, trees; *Clubs* Norfolk (pres 1995), RNSA, Cruising Assoc, Jersey Soc; *Style—* His Hon Adrian Head; ✉ Overy Staithe, King's Lynn, Norfolk PE31 8TG (☎ 01328 738312); 5 Raymond Buildings, Gray's Inn, London WC1 5BP (☎ 0171 405 7146)

HEAD, Maj Sir Francis David Somerville; 5 Bt (UK 1838), of Rochester, Kent; s of Sir Robert Pollock Somerville Head, 4 Bt (d 1924), and Grace Margaret, *née* Robertson (d 1967); *b* 17 Oct 1916; *Educ* Eton, Peterhouse Cambridge (BA 1937); *m* 1, 11 Feb 1950 (m dis 1965), Susan Patricia, da of late Arthur Douglas Ramsay, OBE; 1 s (Richard Douglas Somerville b 1951), 1 da (Diana Mary Frances (Mrs Michael R Parkin) b 1954); m 2, 25 Jan 1967, Penelope Marion Acheson, yr da of late Wilfrid Archibald Alexander; *Heir* s, Richard Douglas Somerville Head, *qv*; *Career* Maj (ret) Queen's Own Cameron Highlanders; served WWII (wounded, POW); *Clubs* Naval and Military; *Style—* Maj Sir Francis Head, Bt; ✉ 63 Chantry View Rd, Guildford, Surrey GU1 3XU

HEAD, Michael Edward; CVO (1991); s of Alexander Edward Head (d 1971), of Kingston upon Thames, Surrey, and Wilhelmina Head (d 1963); *b* 17 March 1936; *Educ* Leeds, Kingston and Woking Grammar Schs, UCL (BA), Univ of Michigan USA (MA); *m* 21 Sept 1963, Wendy Elizabeth, da of Richard Davies, of Hayes, Middlesex; 2 s (Andrew Justin Nicholas b 1965, Timothy Richard Alexander b 1972), 2 da (Gillian Lucy b 1967, Philippa Jane b 1970); *Career* Nat Serv 1958–60, 2 Lt RA 29th Field Regt; Home Office: asst princ 1960 (Immigration and Gen Depts 1960–64), private sec to Parly Under Sec of State 1964–66, princ Fire Dept and Gen Dept 1966–74, asst sec Probation and Aftercare Dept 1974–78, asst sec Equal Opportunities Dept 1978–81, asst sec Criminal Dept 1981–84, asst under sec of state and head of Gen Dept 1984–86, head of Criminal Justice and Constitutional Dept 1986–91, head of Bdcasting Dept 1991, head of Equal Opportunities and Gen Dept 1991–96; Registrar of Baronetage 1984–91; memb: European Cmmn against Racism and Intolerence 1996–, Bd Rehab UK 1996–, Cts and Community Supervision Ctee Surrey Probation Ctee 1996–; FRSA; *Recreations* theatre, reading, golf; *Clubs* Reform, Rotary (Woking); *Style—* Michael Head, Esq, CVO; ✉ Byways, The Ridge, Woking, Surrey GU22 7EE (☎ and fax 01483 772929)

HEAD, Peter; s of Cyril Robert Head (d 1974), and Vera Alice, *née* Kent; *b* 27 Feb 1947; *Educ* Tiffin Sch Kingston-upon-Thames, Imperial Coll London (BSc Civil Engrg (1st class)); *m* 1970, Susan, da of Edmund East; 1 s (Andre b 3 Feb 1975), 1 da (Melody b 30 Oct 1976); *Career* engr: Geo Wimpey & Co 1965–66, Freeman Fox & Partners 1969–80; G Maunsell & Partners Ltd: sr engr 1980–84, assoc 1985–89, tech dir 1989–93, dir 1993–95, md 1995–; also dir Maunsell Structural Plastics Ltd 1983–; major projects incl: Avonmouth Bridge Bristol 1970–74, Friarton Bridge Perth 1975–78, Myton Bridge Hull 1973–79, Aberfeldy Bridge 1992, Kap Shui Mun Bridge Hong Kong 1993–97, Second Severn Crossing 1984–96; memb: Periodicals Panel and Formal Papers Sub-ctee IStructE, Research Panel SCI, Advsy Gp on Steel Bridge Design SCI, Advanced Performance Composites Ctee BPF Reinforced Plastics Gp 1985–; author and deliverer of numerous papers UK and overseas; ACGI, FICE 1977, FIHT 1981, FIStructE 1983, FEng 1996; *Awards* John Howard Structural Challenge Award SE ICE 1984, Gold Medal BPF Congress 1986 and 1990, Premier Gold Award Plastics and Rubber Weekly Awards for Excellence in Design 1993, Personal Award for Best Presentation and Best Paper Euro Pultrusion Technol Assoc 1994, Royal Acad of Engrg Silver Medal for Outstanding Contrib to Br Engrg 1995, Prince Philip Award for Polymers in the Serv of Mankind 1996; *Recreations* gardening, painting, hill walking; *Style—* Peter Head, Esq, FEng; ✉ Maunsell Group, Maunsell House, 160 Croydon Road, Beckenham, Kent BR3 4DE (☎ 0181 663 6565, fax 0181 663 6723)

HEAD, 2 Viscount (UK 1960); Richard Antony Head; s of 1 Viscount Head, GCMG, CBE, MC, PC (d 1983), MP (C) for Carshalton 1945–60, Sec of State for War 1951–56, Minister of Def 1956–57, first high cmmr to Fedn of Nigeria 1960–63, high cmmr to Fedn of Malaysia 1963–66, and Lady Dorothea Louise (d 1987), da of 9 Earl of Shaftesbury; *b* 27 Feb 1937; *Educ* Eton, RMA Sandhurst; *m* 1974, Alicia Brigid, da of Julian John William Salmond, of 9 The Green, Tetbury, Glos; 2 s (Hon Henry Julian b 30 March 1980, Hon George Richard b 20 July 1982), 1 da (Hon Sarah Georgiana b 26 Nov 1984); *Heir* s, Hon Henry Head; *Career* served Life Guards 1957–66, ret Capt; trainer of racehorses 1968–83; *Recreations* sailing, golf; *Clubs* White's; *Style—* The Rt Hon the Viscount Head; ✉ Throope Manor, Bishopstone, Salisbury, Wilts SP5 4BA

HEAD, Richard Douglas Somerville; s and h of Sir Francis David Somerville Head, 5 Bt, *qv*; *b* 16 Jan 1951; *Educ* Eton, Magdalene Coll Cambridge, Bristol (Art Coll) Poly (BA), Univ of London (PGCE), Outward Bount Moray Sea Sch, Centro d'Arte Verrochio, Summer Sch of Painting Siena; *m* 1991, Edwina, da of late Edward Mansell, of Underwood, Notts; *Career* gardener The Royal Hort Soc Wisley Garden; exhibited paintings: Michael Parkin Gall, First Gall Bitterne, Peter Goodall Guildford; *Recreations* music, painting, drawing, skiing; *Style—* Richard Head, Esq; ✉ Christmas Cottage, 5 Providence Place, Pyrford Rd, Woking, Surrey GU22 8UN

HEAD, Sarah Daphne (Sally); da of Richard George Head, of Helston, Cornwall, and Daphne Grace, *née* Henderson; *b* 20 Feb 1951; *Educ* Ancaster House Sussex, St Maurs Convent Weybridge; *m* 25 Sept 1975 (m dis 1987), Francis Vincent Keating, s of Bryan Keating; *Career* Sally Head Poetry Corner Radio London 1969, story ed of Warner Bros (Europe) 1972–75, script ed BBC and Thames TV 1976–84; prodr BBC Drama 1984–88: First Born, Marksman, Life and Loves of a She Devil, Breaking Up, The Detective, Inside Out; head then controller of drama Granada TV 1988–95 (responsible for series and serials incl Prime Suspect, Cracker and Band of Gold), controller of drama London Weekend Television 1995–; *Recreations* gardening sailing, theatre, pubs; *Clubs* Helford River Sailing, Strand-on-the-Green Sailing; *Style—* Miss Sally Head; ✉ The Dutch House, 60 Strand-on-the-Green, Chiswick, London W4 3PE (☎ 0181 994 8650); London Weekend Television plc, The London Television Centre, Upper Ground, London SE1 9LT (☎ 0171 620 1620)

HEADFORT, 6 Marquess of (I 1800); Sir Thomas Geoffrey Charles Michael Taylour; 9 Bt (I 1704); also Baron Headfort (I 1760), Viscount Headfort (I 1762), Earl of Bective (I 1766), and Baron Kenlis (UK 1831, which sits as); s of 5 Marquess, TD (d 1960), by his w Elsie, widow of Sir Rupert Clarke, 2 Bt, and da of James Tucker; *b* 20 Jan 1932; *Educ* Stowe, Christ's Coll Cambridge (MA); *m* 1, 1958 (m dis 1969), Hon Elizabeth Nall-Cain, da of 2 Baron Brocket; 1 s, 2 da; m 2, 1972, Virginia, da of Justice Nable, of Manila; *Heir* s, Earl of Bective; *Career* 2 Lt Life Gds 1950, PO RAFVR 1952; Commercial Pilot's Licence 1967; Freeman Guild of Air Pilots and Air Navigators; dir Bective Electrical Co 1953, sales mangr and chief pilot Lancashire Aircraft Co 1959, piloted prospector aircraft around Africa 1960; Lloyd's underwriter (ret); Inspector Royal Hong Kong Aux Police 1977; Liveryman Guild of Air Pilots and Air Navigators; FRICS, FCIArb, MIAUI; *Style—* The Most Hon the Marquess of Headfort; ✉ 1425 Figueroa Street, Paco, Manila, Philippines

HEADY, Donald Edward (Don); s of Albert Edward Heady (d 1957), of London, and Edith, *née* Hunt (d 1984); *b* 28 Sept 1933; *Educ* Southend on Sea HS for Boys; *m* 22 Sept 1956, Doreen Joan, da of Arthur Sharpe (d 1969), of Essex; *Career* CA; conslt; pres South Essex Soc of CA's 1980–81; memb: Cncl ICAEW 1981–, Accounting Standards Ctee Consultative Ctee of Accountancy Bodies 1982–85, Cncl for Licensed Conveyancers 1993–96; Freeman City of London, Liveryman Worshipful Co of CAs 1978–; FCA 1958, ATII 1962; *Recreations* sometimes swimming, still learning to play the piano and organ, an active Rotarian; *Style—* Donald Heady, Esq; ✉ 2 Great Lawn, Ongar, Essex CM5 0AA (☎ and fax 01277 362905)

HEAL, Susan (Sue); da of Raymond Heal, of Bridgwater, Somerset, and Florence May Heal (d 1971); *b* 1 March 1951; *Educ* Westover Secdy Modern Sch Bridgwater, Bridgwater Girls' GS, Univ of Nottingham (BA); *partner* Stephen Fleming; 1 da (Molly Kathleen b 24 Sept 1993); *Career* res The Financial Times 1974–78, campaign organiser Abortion Law Reform Assoc 1978–80, freelance feature writer 1980–82, features writer then asst features ed Woman's Own 1982–84, The Six O'Clock Show LWT 1984–85, freelance feature writer for nat papers and magazines 1986–88, film critic Today 1988–94 (contrib to The Observer, Homes & Gardens, also various magazines UK and abroad), freelance writer and bdcaster 1994–; first Br journalist to expose The Moonies; memb Film Ctee Nat Critics' Circle 1989, Int Film Festival Judge for Fedn of Film Writers; *Recreations* Italy, taking driving tests; *Clubs* Groucho; *Style—* Sue Heal; ✉ c/o Henrietta House, 17–18 Henrietta Street, London WC2E 8QX (☎ 0181 568 6646)

HEALD, Lady; Daphne Constance; *née* Price; CBE (1976); da of Montague Price; *b* 1904; *Educ* privately; *m* 1929, as his 2 w, Rt Hon Sir Lionel Heald, PC, QC, JP, sometime MP Chertsey and attorney-gen (d 1981); 2 s, 1 da; *Career* connected with many voluntary organizations; DStJ; *Recreations* gardening; *Style—* Lady Heald, CBE; ✉ Chilworth Manor, Guildford, Surrey (☎ 01483 61414)

HEALD, Mervyn; QC (1970); s of Rt Hon Sir Lionel Frederick Heald, PC, QC, MP (d 1982), and Daphne Constance Heald, CBE; *b* 12 April 1930; *Educ* Eton, Magdalene Coll Cambridge; *m* 1954, Clarissa, da of Harold Bowen; 1 s (Robert), 3 da (Henrietta (Mrs Adam Curtis), Annabel (Mrs Timothy Smith), Julia (Mrs Charles Prescot)); *Career* called to the Bar Middle Temple 1954; bencher 1978, cmmr Social Security 1988–; *Recreations* country pursuits; *Style—* Mervyn Heald Esq, QC; ✉ Colhook Lodge, Ebernoe, Petworth, Sussex

HEALD, Nicholas Francis Barry; s of Maj Barry Harvey Heald, of Leamington Spa, Warwicks, and Jean Patricia, *née* Watts; *b* 12 Nov 1947; *Educ* Harrow Co Sch for Boys; *m* 4 Sept 1971, Mary Elizabeth, da of George Edward Goodhall; 2 da (Elizabeth b 1972, Katharine b 1974); *Career* admitted slr 1972; ptnr Simmons & Simmons 1977–; Freeman City of London 1977, Liveryman Worshipful Co of London Slrs 1977; memb Law Soc; *Recreations* travel (especially to Spain), gardening, golf; *Style—* Nicholas Heald, Esq; ✉ Heatherdale, 49A Copperkins Lane, Amersham, Bucks HP6 5QP (☎ 01494 721720); Simmons & Simmons, 21 Dominion Street, London EC2M 2TX (☎ 0171 628 2020, fax 0171 628 2070)

HEALD, Oliver; MP (C) Hertfordshire N (majority 16,531); s of John Anthony Heald, of Folkestone, and Joyce, *née* Pemberton; *b* 15 Dec 1954; *Educ* Reading Sch, Pembroke Coll Cambridge (MA); *m* 18 Aug 1979, Christine Janice, da of Eric Arthur Whittle (d 1980), of Eastbourne; 1 s (William b 1987), 2 da (Sarah b 1985, Victoria b 1989); *Career* called to the Bar Middle Temple 1977, in practice SE Circuit; MP (C) Herts N 1992–; memb Employment Select Ctee 1992–94, vice chm Backbench Employment Ctee 1992–94; PPS: to Rt Hon Peter Lloyd, MP 1994, to Rt Hon William Waldegrave 1994–95; Parly under-sec of state DSS 1995–; pres Southwark and Bermondsey Cons Assoc; *Recreations* travel, gardening, sports; *Style—* Oliver Heald, Esq, MP; ✉ House of Commons, London SW1A 0AA

HEALD, Richard John; s of late John Eric Heald, and late Muriel Heald; *b* 11 May 1936; *Educ* Berkhamsted Sch, Gonville and Caius Coll Cambridge, Guy's Hosp Med Sch (MA, MB MChir); *m* 3 da (Sara b 1970, Lucy b 1972, Anna b 1977); *Career* ships surgn Union Castle Line; conslt surgn Basingstoke Dist Hosp, author of books and papers on surgery of rectal cancer; vice pres Royal College of Surgeons, former pres Section of Surgery RSM, pres Assoc of Coloproctology of GB; FRCS, FRCSEd; *Recreations* sailing; *Style—* Richard Heald, Esq; ✉ The Hampshire Clinic, Basing Rd, Basingstoke, Hampshire RG24 0AL (☎ 0256 54747, fax 0256 818005)

HEALD, His Hon Thomas Routledge; *b* 19 Aug 1923; *m* 1950, Jean Campbell; 2 s, 2 da (1 decd); *Career* barr Middle Temple 1948; prosecuting cncl to Inland Revenue Midland Circuit 1965–70; dep chm: Lindsey QS 1965–71, Notts QS 1969–71; circuit judge 1970–95; memb Matrimonial Causes Rule Ctee to 1979–83; pres Cncl of HM's Circuit Judges 1988 (sec 1984–85); memb Cncl Nottingham Univ 1975–93; *Style—* His Hon Thomas Heald; ✉ Rebbur House, Nicker Hill, Keyworth, Nottingham NG12 5ED

HEALD, Timothy Villiers; s of Col Villiers Archer John Heald, CVO, DSO, MBE, MC (d 1972), of Wilts, and Catherine Eleanor Jean, *née* Vaughan; *b* 28 Jan 1944; *Educ* Sherborne, Balliol Coll Oxford (MA); *m* 1968, Alison Martina, da of Norman Alexander Leslie, of Bucks; 2 s (Alexander b 1971, Tristram b 1977), 2 da (Emma b 1970, Lucy b 1973); *Career* author; contrib to various newspapers and magazines, writer Atticus Column Sunday Times 1965–67; features ed: Town Magazine 1967, Daily Express 1967–72; assoc ed Weekend Magazine Toronto 1977–78, thriller reviewer The Times 1983–89, Pendennis (The Observer) 1990; *Books* Simon Bognor Mystery Novels (1973–, televised by Thames TV), Networks (1983), Class Distinctions (1984), Red Herrings (1985), The Character of Cricket (1986), Brought to Book (1988), The Newest London Spy (ed, 1988), The Rigby File (ed, 1989), Business Unusual (1989), 150 Years of The Royal Warrant and Its Holders (by appt, 1989), My Lord's (ed, 1990), A Classic English Crime (ed, 1990), The Duke: A Portrait of Prince Philip (1991), Honourable Estates: The English and Their Country Houses (1992), Barbara Cartland - A Life of Love (1994), Denis - The Authorised Biography of the Incomparable Compton (1994), Brian Johnston - The Authorised Biography, A Classic Christmas Crime (ed, 1995), Beating Retreat - Hong Kong under the Last Governor (1997); *Recreations* real tennis, spectator sports, lunch; *Clubs* MCC, Royal Tennis, Crime Writers' Assoc (chm 1987–88), PEN (int co-ordinator Writers-in-Prison Ctee 1986–89), Soc of Authors, Groucho; *Style—* Timothy Heald, Esq; ✉ 66 The Esplanade, Fowey, Cornwall PL23 1JA (☎ 01726 832781, fax 01726 833246)

HEALEY, Baron (Life Peer UK 1992), of Riddlesden in the County of West Yorkshire; Denis Winston Healey; CH (1979), MBE (1945), PC (1964); s of William Healey, of Keighley, Yorks; *b* 30 Aug 1917; *Educ* Bradford GS, Balliol Coll Oxford; *m* 1945, Edna May, da of Edward Edmunds, of Coleford, Glos; 1 s (Hon Timothy Blair b 5 June 1949), 2 da (Hon Jenifer Clare (Hon Mrs Copsey) b 12 April 1948, Hon Cressida b 27 July 1954); *Career* MP (Lab): Leeds SE 1952–55, Leeds E 1955–92; sec Int Dept Lab Pty 1946–52, memb shadow cabinet PLP 1959, sec of state for def 1964–70, oppn spokesman on foreign and Cwlth affrs 1971, shadow chllr 1972–74, chllr of the exchequer 1974–79, dep ldr Lab Pty 1981–83, shadow foreign sec 1981–87; memb Exec Fabian Soc 1954–61; Freeman City of Leeds 1991; hon fell Balliol Coll Oxford 1980, Hon DLitt Univ of Bradford 1983, Hon LLD Univ of Sussex 1989; pres Birkbeck Coll 1993; Grand Cross Order of Merit (Germany) 1979; *Books* The Curtain Falls (1951), New Fabian Essays (1952), Neutralism (1955), Fabian International Essays (1956), A Neutral Belt in Europe (1958), NATO and American Security (1959), The Race Against the H Bomb (1960), Labour Britain and the World (1963), Healey's Eye (photographs, 1980), Labour and a World Society (1985), Beyond Nuclear Deterrence (1986), The Time of My Life (autobiography, 1989), When Shrimps Learn to Whistle (1990), My Secret Planet (1992), Denis Healey's Yorkshire Dales (1995); *Style—* The Rt Hon Lord Healey, CH, MBE, PC; ✉ c/o House of Lords, London SW1A OPW

HEALEY, Prof Deryck John; s of Leonard Melvon Healey, of Natal, SA, and Irene Isabella, *née* Ferguson; *b* 30 Jan 1937; *Educ* Northlands HS Natal SA (DipAD), Manchester Poly (DipAD); *m* 30 Sept 1962, Mary Elizabeth Pitt (decd), da of Col Philip Booth (d 1978), of Hay-on-Wye; 2 s (Paul Melyvon b 29 Aug 1963, Timothy Mathew b 29 Jan 1966); *Career* designer, artist sculptor, poet; design mangr Good Hope Textiles SA 1959–66; chm: Deryck Healey Associates 1966–85, Deryck Healey International 1969–85; design mangr WPM Wallpaper Manufacturers 1966–68, mangr ICI Design Studio 1968–80; dir: MMI 1987–89, Comcorp 1988–90, Retail Detail 1988–90; visiting prof Royal Coll of Art London 1996–; conslt: Texfi Industries USA 1970–80, Marubeni Japan 1974–85, SA Nylon Spinners 1975–83; one man painting and sculpture exhibitions 1990–: Have I Got Your Number (London), Big Names (Venice), Silent Poems (London), Galerie Langer Fain (Paris) 1992, Musée de la Poste (Paris), Arizona State Museum (Phoenix), Beyond All Responsible Doubt (Glasgow) 1992, Meditation Works (Long & Ryle Gallery London) 1992, Koplin Gallery Santa Monica 1993, UK/LA Masterclass (Los Angeles) 1994, R Demarco Ursa Major Discovery Walk Site Specific Sculpture Traquair Scotland 1995, Traquair Artist Colour Palette Art Project 1995, Four Colour Works (107 Studio Shaw Wiltshire) 1995, Manchester (Bridgewater Hall) International Concert Hall Sculpture 1996; int art fair exhibitions: Cologne, Frankfurt, Chicago and Paris; work incl Art of Concern (installation in collaboration with Greenpeace); chm Textile and Fashion Bd CNAA 1971–81; memb: Art and Design Ctee CNAA 1971–81, Design Working Pty Clothing and Allied Products Trg Bd, Textile and Design Selection Ctee Design Cncl 1978–87; Crafts Cncl Bd: memb Textile Panel 1980–87, memb Fin and Gen Purposes Ctee 1983–85, chm Textile Devpt Gp 1982–84, memb Projects and Orgns Ctee 1983–85; patron New Art Tate Gallery 1983–, memb RSA Bursary Bd 1982–88, govr London Coll Fashion 1978, external examiner numerous CNAA BA and MA courses; COID Design Award 1964, Queen's Award to Indust for Export 1974, RSA Bicentenary Medal 1981, Textile Inst Design Medal 1982; FRSA 1978, FCSD, fell SIAD 1964; *Books* contrib Colour (1980), Living with Colour (1982), The New Art of Flower Design (1986); *Publications* Open Studio (USA, 1994); *Art Film* Passing Time (Los Angeles); *Recreations* travel, painting, sculpture; *Style—* Prof Deryck Healey

HEALEY, Dr Norman John; s of Dr Ronald Jack Healey, of Launceston, Cornwall, and Monica Mary Patricia Healey, JP, *née* Gibbins (d 1995); *b* 2 Sept 1940; *Educ* Mount House Sch Tavistock, Epsom Coll, Guy's Univ of London (Kitchener scholarship 1959, MRCS, LRCP, DA, DObstRCOG, 1st XV Rugby); *m* 24 June 1978, Maureen Anne, da of Clarence Meadows Brock; 3 da (Rebecca Jane b 10 Feb 1980, Alicia June b 13 Sept 1981, Nicola Joy (twin) b 13 Sept 1981); *Career* Surgn Lt RN 1965–71; RN Hosp Haslar: Dept of Orthopaedics 1966, Dept of Anaesthetics 1967, HMS Albion serv in Far East 1968–69, RM Depot Deal 1970–71; sr house offr Obstetrics and Gynaecology Royal Bucks Hosp Aylesbury 1972, London Coll of Osteopathic Med 1973–74; clinical asst Dept of Rheumatology and Rehabilitation St Mary's Hosp London 1975–82; full time private practice as osteopathic physician and specialist in musculo-skeletal med 1975–; hon conslt St Luke's Hosp London 1987–; hon sec Br Osteopathic Assoc 1976–82, memb Cncl Br Assoc of Manipulative Med 1980–83; MRO 1975, FLCOM 1979, FRSM 1985, ND 1994; memb: Br Soc for Rheumatology 1982, Br Inst of Musculoskeletal Med 1992, Br Naturopathic Assoc 1994; *Recreations* country walks, swimming; *Clubs* Royal Western Yacht, Incogniti and Cornish Choughs Cricket; *Style—* Dr Norman Healey; ✉ Osteopathic Physician, 16 Upper Wimpole Street, London W1M 7TB (☎ 0171 487 3162)

HEALEY, Prof Patsy; da of Prof C T Ingold, CMG, of Benson, Oxon, and L M Ingold, *née* Kemp; *b* 1 Jan 1940; *Educ* Walthamstow Hall Sevenoaks Kent, UCL (BA), LSE (PhD), Regents St Poly (DipTP), Univ of Wales (DipEd); *m* 1, 25 June 1961, Dr Ian Nevill Healey (d 1972), s of Douglas Healey (d 1978); m 2, 9 July 1977, David Reiach Hunter (d 1979), s of David Reiach (d 1919); *Career* sch teacher 1962–65, planning offr London Borough of Lewisham GLC 1965–69, sr res fell LSE 1970–72, lectr in planning Kingston Poly 1969–70 and 1972–74, lectr then head of dept and dean Oxford Poly 1974–87; Univ of Newcastle upon Tyne: prof and head of Dept of Town and Country Planning 1988–92, prof and rector Centre for Research in European Urban Environments 1992–; memb: various ctees CNAA 1976–81, Cncl and various ctees RTPI 1987–92, various ctees ESRC, bd of Tyne and Wear Devpt Corp; pres Assoc of European Schs of Planning 1994–96; *Books* Professional Ideals and Planning Practice (with J Underwood, 1979), Planning Theory - Prospects for the 1980s (ed with G McDougall and M Thomas, 1982), Local Plans in British Land Use Planning (1983), Land Policy: Problems and Alternatives (ed with S M Barrett, 1985), A Political Economy of Land (with A Gilbert, 1985), Land Use Planning and the Mediation of Urban Change (with P F McNamara, M J Elson and A J Doak, 1988), Land and Property Development in a Changing Context (ed with R Nabarro, 1990), Dilemmas of Planning Practice (with H Thomas, 1991), Rebuilding the City (with S Davoudi, M O'Toole, S Tavsanoglu and D Usher, 1992), Managing the City (with S Cameron, S Davoudi, S Graham, 1995); *Recreations* reading, walking, swimming, travelling; *Style—* Prof Patsy Healey; ✉ Department of Town and Country Planning, University of Newcastle upon Tyne, Newcastle upon Tyne NE1 7RU (☎ 0191 222 7634, fax 0191 261 1182, telex UNINEW 953654)

HEALEY, Dr Tim; s of Thomas Henry Healey, of N Skelton, Cleveland, and Evelyn, *née* Hamilton; *b* 23 April 1935; *Educ* Boys HS Middlesbrough, Univ of Sheffield (MB ChB); *m* 18 Aug 1958, Ruth, da of Albert Edward Stagg (d 1977), of Northwich, Cheshire; 1 s (Trevor b 13 Sept 1960), 2 da (Janet b 9 March 1963, Sandra b 27 April 1969); *Career* house surgn Sheffield Royal Infirmary 1960 (house physician 1959), sr house offr orthopaedics Royal Hosp Sheffield 1960 (sr house offr in radiology 1960–61), sr registrar Leicester Royal Infirmary 1964–65 (registrar 1961–64), sr registrar United Sheffield Hosps 1965–66, conslt radiologist Barnsley 1966–95, ret; author of numerous articles on subjects incl: med, sci, history, philology; Br Inst of Radiology: memb Cncl, memb N Branch 1987–, sec 1982–87, pres 1987–92, Distinguished Serv Medal 1995; hon doctorate in med history World Univ 1989; FFRRCS, FRCR, FRAI, FRSA, MINucE, FIDiagE, MSAE; *Recreations* writing, collecting; *Clubs* New (Edinburgh), Cavendish; *Style—* Dr Tim Healey; ✉ Northfield, Salisbury St, Barnsley, S Yorks S75 2TL (☎ 01226 205348)

HEALY, Prof John Francis; s of John Healy (d 1968), of Bishopsteignton, Devon, and Iris Maud, *née* Cutland (d 1994); *b* 27 Aug 1926; *Educ* Trinity Coll Cambridge (BA, MA, PhD); *m* 1, 5 Jan 1957 (m dis 1985), Carol A McEvoy; 1 s (John Matthew Charles b 18 Oct 1964); m 2, 21 Sept 1985, Barbara Edith, da of John Douglas Henshall (d 1988), of Macclesfield; *Career* War Serv Essex Regt and Intelligence Corps 1944, Capt Intelligence Corps JAG Dept Singapore 1946–48 (Lt 1945–46); lectr in classics and classical archaeology Univ of Manchester 1953–61 (hon curator of coins 1958–80); Univ of London: reader in Greek Bedford Coll 1961–66, head Classics Dept Royal Holloway Coll 1966–85, chm Classics Dept Royal Holloway and Bedford New Coll 1985–88, dean Faculty of Arts and Music Royal Holloway Coll 1978–81, chm Bd of Classical Studies 1979–81, emeritus prof of classics Univ of London 1990; chm Fin Sub Ctee Inst of Classical Studies 1966–88, former pres Windsor Art Soc; FRNS 1950, FRSA 1971, memb Royal Inst of GB 1979; *Books* Cyrenaican Expeditions of the Manchester University Museum (1955–57) (with A Rowe, 1959), Mining and Metallurgy in the Greek and Roman World (1978), Sylloge Nummorum Graecorum VII, Manchester University Museum: The Raby and Güterbock Collections (1986), Pliny the Elder, Natural History (1991), Miniere e Metallurgia nel Mondo greco e Romano (1993); *Recreations* music, travel, creative gardening (Alpines); *Clubs* Cambridge Union; *Style—* Prof John Healy; ✉ c/o Royal Holloway and Bedford New College (University of London), Egham, Surrey TW20 0EX (☎ 01784 434455, fax 01784 37520, telex 935504)

HEALY, Maurice Eugene; s of Thomas Shine Healy (d 1961), and Emily Mary, *née* O'Mahoney (d 1980); *b* 27 Nov 1933; *Educ* Downside, Peterhouse Cambridge (BA); *m* 20 Dec 1958, Jose Barbara Speller, da of John Edward Dewdney (d 1971); 3 da (Kate b 1961 d 1977, Lulu b 1963, Jessica b 1964); *Career* Nat Serv 2 Lt RA 1954–56; asst princ Bd of Trade 1956–60, Consumers' Assoc 1960–76; Which? magazine: ed-in-chief and head of Editorial Div 1973–76, project offr, dep ed, ed Motoring Which? and Handyman Which?; dir Nat Consumer Cncl 1987–91 (joined 1977); chm: Consumer Policy Ctee British Standards Inst 1993–, Insurance Ombudsman Bureau Cncl 1996– (memb 1991–), Consumer Policy Ctee Int Standards Orgn 1996–; memb: Banking Code of Practice Review Ctee 1992–, Optical Consumer Complaints Service Mgmnt Ctee 1992–, consumer panel Personal Investment Authy 1993–; vice pres Nat Fedn of Consumer Gps 1992–; dir Jazz Services Ltd 1992–; chm Patients' Assoc 1991–93; memb: Highgate Primary Sch Soc, Highgate Wood Sch Soc (govr 1976–86, chm 1982–86); FRSA; *Recreations* jazz, Zimbabwean sculpture, Irish music, gardening, walking; *Style—* Maurice Healy, Esq; ✉ 15 Onslow Gardens, Muswell Hill, London N10 3JT (☎ 0181 883 8955)

HEALY, Noel Patrick; *b* 25 Nov 1954; *Educ* Xaverian Coll Manchester, Hertford Coll Oxford; *Career* private sec to chm National Coal Bd 1976–82, exec dir County Bank Ltd 1982–90, dir Financière Indosuez Ltd 1992–93, md Sunset + Vine plc (television prodn and distribution co) 1993–95; *Recreations* reading, cinema- and theatre-going, walking, Manchester United FC; *Clubs* National Liberal, Harlequins FC; *Style—* Noel Healy, Esq; ✉ 6 Billing Street, London SW10 9UR

HEALY, Prof Thomas Edward John; s of Thomas Healy (d 1977), and Gladys May, *née* Paulger; *b* 11 Dec 1935; *Educ* Guy's Hosp Univ of London; *m* 3 Nov 1966, Lesley Edwina; 3 da (Maria b 23 March 1968, Michaela b 8 Dec 1970, Laura b 28 Jan 1975), 1 s (Thomas b 19 April 1979); *Career* prof Dept of Anaesthesia and chm Sch of Surgical Scis Univ of Manchester 1992–94; visiting prof Univs of Arizona, Michigan, Philadelphia and Vancouver; memb S Manchester DHA 1981–87; ed Monographs in Anaesthesiology, ed-in-chief The European Jl of Anaesthesiology and author of over 200 published papers; memb Cncl: Assoc of Anaesthetists 1973–76, Anaesthetic Res Soc Cncl 1978–80, RSM 1985–92 (hon sec Editorial Representative Jl Bd, pres Section of Anaesthetics 1996), Royal Coll of Anaesthetists 1989– (chm Quality of Practice Ctee 1994–96, Professional Standards Ctee 1996–), Postgrad Medical Fellowship 1990–94; memb Stanton-on-the-Wolds PC; Freeman: Worshipful Soc of Apothecaries, City of London; academician and memb of Senate and Exec Ctee Euro Acad of Anaesthesiology, hon memb Romanian Soc of Anaesthesiology; FRCA; *Books* Aids to Anaesthesia Book 1: Basic Science, Aids to Anaesthesia Book 2: Clinical Practice, Anaesthesia for Day Case Surgery, A Practice of Anaesthesia (VI edn); *Recreations* walking, reading; *Style—* Prof Thomas Healy; ✉ Department of Anaesthesia, The University of Manchester, Manchester Royal Infirmary, Manchester (☎ 0161 276 1234)

HEANEY, Henry Joseph; OBE (1996); s of Michael Heaney (d 1951), of Newry, Co Down, and late Sarah, *née* Fox; *b* 2 Jan 1935; *Educ* Abbey GS Newry Ireland, Queen's Univ Belfast (BA, MA); *m* 19 March 1976, Mary Elizabeth, da of Desmond Moloney, of Dublin; *Career* asst librarian Queen's Univ Belfast 1959–63, librarian Magee Univ Coll Londonderry 1963–69, dep librarian New Univ of Ulster Coleraine 1967–69, asst sec Standing Conf of Nat and Univ Libraries 1969–72, librarian Queen's Univ Belfast 1972–74, librarian and dir Sch of Librarianship Univ Coll Dublin 1975–78, librarian and keeper of the Hunterian Books and Manuscripts Univ of Glasgow 1978–; chm Consortium of Univ Res Libraries 1995–; memb: Br Library Bd, Cncl Standing Conf of Nat and Univ Libraries 1989–95; tstee: Nat Library of Scotland 1980–91, Nat Manuscripts Conservation Tst 1992–95; pres Scottish Library Assoc 1990, dir Company of Biologists 1993–; FLA 1967 (ALA 1962), FRSE 1992, FRSA 1996; *Books* World Guide to Abbreviations of International Organisations (9 edn, 1991); *Clubs* XIII (Glasgow); *Style—* Henry Heaney, Esq, OBE, FRSE; ✉ 21 Whittinghame Court, Glasgow G12 0BG (☎ 0141 357 0162); Glasgow University Library, Hillhead Street, Glasgow G12 8QE (☎ 0141 330 5634, fax 0141 330 5633, e-mail h.heaney@lib.gla.ac.uk)

HEANEY, Prof Seamus Justin; *b* 13 April 1939; *Educ* St Columb's Coll Derry, Queen's Univ Belfast (BA); *m* 1965, Marie, *née* Devlin; 3 c; *Career* formerly on staff St Joseph's Coll of Educn, lectr English Dept Queen's Univ 1966–72, freelance writer for BBC and various jls 1972–75, teacher Carysfort Coll 1975, Boylston prof of rhetoric Harvard Univ 1985–, prof of poetry Univ of Oxford 1989–94; visiting prof Univ of California 1970–71; Somerset Maugham Award 1968, Denis Devlin Award 1973, American Irish Fndn Literary Award 1973, Duff Cooper Meml Prize 1975, W H Smith Annual Award 1976, Whitbread Award (for The Haw Lantern) 1987, winner Nobel Prize for Literature 1995; memb: Irish Acad of Letters, Aosdana; CLit 1991; *Books* Eleven Poems (1965), Death of a Naturalist (1966), Door into the Dark (1969), Wintering Out (1972), North (1975), Field Work (1979), Preoccupations: Selected Prose 1968–1978 (1980), Selected Poems 1965–1975 (1980), The Rattle Bag (ed with Ted Hughes, 1982), Sweeney Astray (1984), Station Island (1984), The Haw Lantern (1987), The Government of the Tongue (1988), New Selected Poems 1966–1987 (1990), The Cure at Troy - A Version of Sophocles' Philoctetes (1990), Seeing Things (1991), Sweeney's Flight (1992), The Redress of Poetry (1995), Laments (ed with Stanislaw Baranczak, 1995), The Spirit Level (1996); also Faber Poetry Cassette (with Tom Paulin, 1983); *Style—* Prof Seamus Heaney; ✉ c/o Publicity Department, Faber & Faber, 3 Queen Square, London WC1N 3AU (☎ 0171 465 0045, fax 0171 465 0034)

HEAP, Sir Desmond; kt (1970); s of William and Minnie Heap, of Burnley, Lancs; *b* 17 Sept 1907; *Educ* Burnley GS, Univ of Manchester (LLB, LLM); *m* 27 Oct 1945, Adelene Mai, da of Frederick Lacey, of Harrogate; 1 s (John Nicholas Desmond b 5 July 1951), 2 da (Sally Elizabeth Adelene b 10 Aug 1946, Joanna Mary Alison b 29 April 1948); *Career* admitted slr 1933; chief asst slr City of Leeds 1938–40 (prosecuting slr 1935–38), dep town clerk Leeds 1940–47, comptroller and city slr to Corporation of London 1947–73; lectr Leeds Sch of Architecture 1935–47; RTPI: legal memb 1935–, memb Cncl 1947–77, pres 1955–56; assoc memb RICS 1953– (memb Cncl 1957–84); memb: Colonial Office Housing and Town Planning Advsy Panel 1953–65, Editorial Bd of Planning and Environment Law 1948–, Cncl on Tbnls 1971–77; vice pres Statute Law Soc 1982–94, dep pres City of London Branch BRCS 1956–76, chm govrs Hurstpierpoint Coll 1975–82; elected hon assoc Worshipful Co of Solicitors of City of London 1987, Liveryman and Hon Asst Worshipful Co of Carpenters, hon memb Ct Worshipful Co of Chartered Surveyors; Law Soc: memb Cncl 1954–78, chm Law Reform Ctee 1955–60, chm Town Planning Ctee 1964–70, pres 1972–73; Hon LLD Univ of Manchester 1973; FRSA (memb Cncl 1974–78); *Books* Planning Law for Town and Country (1938), Planning and the Law of Interim Development (1944), An Outline of Planning Law (1949, 11 edn 1996), Encyclopaedia of Planning Law and Practice (6 vols, 1960), Encyclopaedia of Betterment Levy (1967), How to Control Land Development (1974, 2 edn 1981), The Hamlyn Lectures (1975), The Marvellous Years - Pages from a Scrapbook (1993); *Recreations* formerly swimming, pedal biking, stage and theatre; now theatre, writing, taking things gently and observing the injunction to 'consider the lilies of the field' because although they neither toil nor spin yet Soloman in all his glory 'was not arrayed like one of these'; *Clubs* Athenaeum, City Livery, Guildhall; *Style—* Sir Desmond Heap; ✉ c/o The Athenaeum, Pall Mall, London SW1Y 5ER

HEAP, Sir Peter William; KCMG (1995, CMG 1987); s of Roger Heap (d 1966), and Dora Heap, *née* Hosier; *b* 13 April 1935; *Educ* Bristol Cathedral Sch, Merton Coll Oxford (MA); *m* 1, 1960; 2 s (Alan, Derek d 1989), 2 da (Angela, Jane); *m* 2, 1986, Ann, *née* Johnson; 1 step s (Christopher), 1 step da (Sabrina); *Career* former posts HM Dip Serv in Dublin, Ottawa, Colombo, NY, Caracas, FCO London; high cmmr Nassau Bahamas 1983–86, min Lagos 1986–89, Br sr trade cmmr Hong Kong 1989–92, ambass to Brazil 1992–95, ret 1995; advsr to Bd HSBC Investment Bank Ltd 1995–, advsr Amerada Hess (Brazil) Ltd, chm Brazilian C of C in GB; *Clubs* Reform, Royal Cwlth Soc; *Style—* Sir Peter Heap, KCMG; ✉ 6 Carlisle Mansions, Carlisle Place, London SW1; c/o HSBC Investment Bank Ltd, 10 Queen Street Place, London EC4R 1BL

HEAPS, Christopher Seymour; s of Capt Christopher Robert Milner Heaps, TD (d 1962), and Peggy Margaret Catherine, *née* Mill (d 1984); *b* 15 Nov 1942; *Educ* Dorking GS, Univ of Exeter (LLB); *m* 14 March 1970, Ann Mary, da of Capt Peter Frederick Dudley Mays (d 1994), of Dorking; 2 da (Grace b 1973, Elizabeth b 1975); *Career* admitted slr 1967; ptnr Eversheds (formerly Jaques & Lewis) 1971–96, conslt 1996–; pres Holborn Law Soc 1983–84, memb Cncl Law Soc 1985–, memb Cncl on Tbnls 1991–; chm Law Soc: Planning & Environmental Law Ctee 1988–91 and 1995–96, Adjudication and Appeals Ctee (Slrs' Complaint Bureau) 1992–95; memb: Transport Users' Consultative Ctee for London 1981–84, London Regnl Passengers Ctee 1984–92 (dep chm 1985–92), Advsy Panel Railway Heritage Tst 1985–; chm Dorking Round Table 1978–79, pres Dorking Deepdene Rotary Club 1986–87; memb Cncl of Mgmnt PDSA 1996–; tstee Harrowlands Appeal (Dorking Hosp), govr Parson's Mead Sch Ashtead, hon steward Helston Furry Dance 1996–; Upper Warden Worshipful Co of Curriers (Liveryman 1976), Liveryman Worshipful Co of Coachmakers and Coach Harness Makers 1985; MCIT 1988; *Books* London Transport Railways Album (1978), Western Region in the 1960's (1981), This is Southern Region Central Division (1982), BR Diary 1968–1977 (1988); *Recreations* transport and transport history; *Style—* Christopher Heaps, Esq; ✉ Pinecroft, Ridgeway Rd, Dorking, Surrey RH4 3AP (☎ and fax 01306 881752); 33 Wendron St, Helston, Cornwall TR13 8PT; Eversheds, Senator House, 85 Queen Victoria Street, London EC4V 4JL (☎ 0171 919 4500, fax 0171 919 4919)

HEARD, Peter Graham; CB (1987); s of Sidney Horwood Heard (d 1959), of Devon, and Doris Winifred Heard, *née* Gale, MBE (d 1982); *b* 22 Dec 1929; *Educ* Exmouth GS, Coll of Estate Mgmnt; *m* 1953, Ethne Jean, da of Denys Stanley Thomas (d 1956), of Devon; 2 da (Tessa Jane b 1956, Julie Ann b 1957); *Career* chartered surveyor; Inland Revenue Valuation Office: joined 1950, served in Exeter, Kidderminster, Dudley and Leeds, district valuer Croydon 1971, superintending valuer Head Office 1973, asst sec Somerset House 1975, superintending valuer Midlands 1978, asst chief valuer Head Office 1978, dep chief valuer Head Office 1983–89, ret 1989; FRICS; *Recreations* cricket, golf, theatre, countryside, walking the dog; *Clubs* MCC, Civil Serv; *Style—* Peter Heard, Esq, CB; ✉ Romany Cottage, High St, Lindfield, Sussex (☎ 01444 482095)

HEARLEY, Timothy Michael; s of Maurice James Goodwin Hearley, CBE (d 1975); *b* 10 March 1942; *Educ* Malvern, Lincoln Coll Oxford (MA); *m* 1966, Pauline Muriel, *née* Dunn; 3 s (Philip Michael b 1967, James Paul b 1970, Richard Matthew b 1973); *Career* currently chm: Rolfe & Nolan plc, Ultimate Perspective Management Consultancy Ltd, Valcast Holdings Ltd, Securitex Investments Ltd, Vail Corporation Ltd, Bessa Lincoln College plc, Bessa II Lincoln College plc; currently dir: Interbrand Group plc, Moorepay Group plc, MPT (Healthcare) Ltd, Hoskins Healthcare Ltd, Hay Group Holdings Ltd; AIIMR, MSI; *Recreations* tennis, piano, ballet, theatre; *Clubs* Reform; *Style—* Timothy Hearley, Esq; ✉ Rush Leys, 4 Birds Hill Rise, Oxshott, Surrey KT22 0SW (☎ 01372 842506); Vail Corporation Ltd, 40 Long Acre, Covent Garden, London WC2F 9JT (☎ 0171 240 6090, fax 0171 240 6091)

HEARN, Andrew; *b* 23 July 1957; *Educ* Univ Coll Sch London, St John's Coll Oxford (BA Jurisprudence); *m* Sarah; 3 s (Luke, Adam, Matthew); *Career* Titmuss Sainer Dechert: articled clerk (qualified 1982), ptnr 1986–, currently head Litigation Dept (specialising in intellectual property, competition, defamation and gen commercial litigation); accredited mediator CEDR, mediator World Intellectual Property Orgn and patents county court; former memb Litigation Sub-ctee City of London Law Soc; author of various pubns and articles in the press; memb: City of London Law Co, Law Soc; *Recreations* skiing, the arts, trying to keep fit; *Clubs* Paddington Lawn Tennis, Old Gowers; *Style—* Andrew Hearn, Esq; ✉ Titmuss Sainer Dechert, 2 Serjeants' Inn, London EC4Y 1LT (☎ 0171 583 5353, fax 0171 353 3683)

HEARN, Barry Maurice William; *m* Susan; 1 da (Katie), 1 s (Edward); *Career* sports promoter; qualified CA 1970, spent several years at int accountancy firm before becoming fin dir Kensal House Investments, chm Lucania Snooker Clubs 1974–82, currently proprietor and dir Matchroom Ltd; clients incl: Herbie Hide, Eamonn Loughran, Steve Davis, Jimmy White and Ronnie O'Sullivan; owner and chm Leyton Orient FC 1995–; *Recreations* boxing, snooker, cricket, athletics; *Style—* Barry Hearn, Esq; ✉ Matchroom Ltd, 10 Western Road, Romford, Essex RM1 3JT (☎ 01708 730480, fax 01708 723425)

HEARN, Donald Peter; s of Lt-Col Peter James Hearn, and Anita Margaret Hearn; *b* 2 Nov 1947; *Educ* Clifton, Selwyn Coll Cambridge; *m* 21 July 1973, Rachel Mary Arnold; 2 da (Emma b 1975, Sarah b 1977); *Career* Ernst & Young 1969–79, gp fin controller Saga Holidays 1979–83, chief fin offr Lee Valley Water Co 1983–86, sec Royal Horticultural Soc 1989– (fin dir 1986); Gen Cmmr of Taxes, memb Fin Gen Purposes Ctee Royal Postgrad Med Sch; *Style—* Donald Hearn, Esq; ✉ The Royal Horticultural Society, 80 Vincent Square, London SW1P 2PE

HEARN, Prof John Patrick; s of Lt-Col Hugh Patrick Hearn, and Cynthia Ellen, *née* Nicholson; *b* 24 Feb 1943; *Educ* Crusaders Sch Headley Hampshire, St Mary's Sch Nairobi Kenya, Univ Coll Dublin (MSc, BSc), Australian Nat Univ Canberra (PhD); *m* 30 Sept 1967, Margaret Ruth Patricia, *née* McNair; 4 s (Shaun Robin b 1968, Bruce Edward b 1973, Adrian Hugh b 1975, Nicholas Gordon b 1984), 1 da (Karina Anne b 1970); *Career* lectr in zoology Strathmore Coll Nairobi 1967–69 (head of biology and dean of sci 1968–69), res scholar Dept of Zoology Australian Nat Univ Canberra 1969–72, scientist Med Res Cncl Reproductive Biology Unit Univ of Edinburgh 1972–79 (hon fell 1974–79), conslt scientist WHO Geneva (special programme of res, devpt and res trg in human reproduction, seconded by MRC) 1978–79, visiting prof in reproductive biology Dept of Biology UCL 1979–; Zoological Soc of London: dir Wellcome Laboratories of Comparative Physiology 1979–80, dir of sci 1980–87, dir Inst of Zoology 1980–87; dir MRC/AFRC Comparative Physiology Res Gp 1983–89, dep sec AFRC 1987–90, prof Dept of Physiology Univ of Wisconsin Med Sch 1990–, dir Wisconsin Regnl Primate Res Center (with special interest in the devpt and reproductive physiology of primates) 1990–; author of scientific res papers/articles; Bolliger Award Australian Mammal Soc 1972, Scientific Medal Zoological Soc of London 1983, Osman Hill Medal Primate Soc of GB 1986; memb: American Soc of Primatology, Brazilian Soc of Primatology, Soc for the Study of Fertility, Soc for the Study of Reproduction, Primate Soc of GB, Int Primatological Soc (pres 1984–88); FIBiol, scientific fell Zoological Soc of London; *Publications* ed: Immunological Aspects of Reproduction and Fertility Control (1980), Reproduction in New World Primates (1983), Advances in Animal Conservation (1985), Reproduction and Disease in Captive and Wild Animals (1988), Conservation of Primate Species Studied in Biomedical Research (1994); *Recreations* squash, swimming, running, conservation; *Clubs* Zoological Soc of London Sports and Social (past pres), Athenaeum; *Style—* Prof John Hearn; ✉ Wisconsin Regional Primate Research Center, University of Wisconsin, 1220 Capitol Court, Madison, Wisconsin 53715 1299, USA (☎ 00 1 608 263 3500, fax 00 1 608 263 4031)

HEARNE, Graham James; CBE; s of Frank Hearne, and Emily, *née* Shakespeare; *b* 23 Nov 1937; *Educ* George Dixon GS Birmingham; *m* 1961, Carol Jean, *née* Brown; 1 s, 3 da; *Career* admitted slr 1959, Pinsent & Co Slrs 1959–63, attorney NYC Fried Frank Harris Shriver & Jacobson 1963–66, Herbert Smith & Co Slrs 1966–67, Industrial Reorganisation Ctee 1967–68, N M Rothschild & Sons Ltd 1968–77, fin dir Courtaulds Ltd 1977–81, chief exec Tricentrol plc 1981–83, gp md Carless Capel & Leonard plc 1983–84, chief exec Enterprise Oil plc 1984–91 (chm 1991–); non-exec dir: N M Rothschild & Sons Ltd 1977–, Reckitt & Colman plc 1990–, Courtaulds plc 1991–; High Sheriff for Greater London 1995; *Clubs* Reform, MCC; *Style—* Graham Hearne, Esq, CBE; ✉ 5 Crescent Place, London SW3 2EA (☎ 0171 460 0296); One Hook Lane, Bosham, Chichester, W Sussex PO18 8EY (☎ 01243 572351); Enterprise Oil plc, Grand Buildings, Trafalgar Square, London WC2N 5EJ (☎ 0171 925 4000, fax 0171 925 4617, telex 8950611 EPRISE G)

HEARNE, John Michael; s of Reginald Hearne (d 1974), of Ipplepen, Devon, and Mary Rachel, *née* Rees; *b* 19 Sept 1937; *Educ* Torquay GS, St Luke's Coll Exeter, Univ Coll of Wales Aberystwyth (BMus, MMus); *m* 6 July 1974, Margaret Gillespie, da of Archibald Jarvie, of Glasgow; *Career* teacher Tónlistarskóli Borgarfjardar (Rural Music Sch) Iceland 1968–69, lectr Aberdeen Coll of Educn 1970–87; composer, singer (bass-baritone) and conductor; compositions incl: Piano Sonata 1968, Piano Trio 1981, Songs and Choral Music, String Quartet 1971, Triduum (Festival Oratorio) 1982, Channel Firing 1979, The Four Horsemen (brass, percussion) 1985, Trumpet Concerto (BBC Cmmn) 1990, Laetatus Sum for chorus (jt winner Gregynog Composers Award of Wales 1992), De Profundis for wind band (Aberdeen University Quincentenary Cmmn) 1995; self publishing Longship Music; performances incl: reader in Sincerely Edvard Grieg (compilation of Grieg's letters, songs, piano music), regular concert appearances in Scotland, conductor Stonehaven and Dist Choral Soc; chm: Gordon Forum for the Arts 1991–94, Aberdeen Branch ISM, Aberdeen Scandinavian Soc, Scot Music Advsy Ctee BBC 1986–90; memb Exec Ctee Composers' Guild of GB 1994–; DC (E Scotland) Inc Soc Musicians; memb Lions Club Garioch; *Recreations* classic motoring - 1954 Daimler Conquest Roadster; *Style—* John Hearne, Esq; ✉ Longship Music, Smidskot, Fawells, Keithhall, Inverurie AB51 0LN (☎ and fax 01651 882274)

HEARNE, Peter Ambrose; s of Dr Arthur Ambrose Hearne (d 1976), of Sunderland, Tyne and Wear, and Helen Mackay, *née* Noble (d 1981); *b* 14 Nov 1927; *Educ* Tunstall Sch Sunderland, Sherborne, Loughborough Coll (DLC), Coll of Aeronautics Cranfield (MSc), MIT USA; *m* 19 April 1952, Georgina Gordon; da of Alexander Gordon Guthrie (d 1986), of Farningham, Kent; 3 s (Patrick Gordon b 7 June 1956, Mark Alexander b 3 Feb 1958, Charles Peter Garrett b 24 May 1962); *Career* aerodynamicist Saunders Roe IOW 1946–47, ops devpt engr BOAC 1949–54, helicopter project engr BEA 1954–58, asst gen mangr Guided Flight Group Elliott Bros 1960–65 (mangr Guided Weapons Div 1959), dir and gen mangr Elliot Flight Automation (subsequently GEC Avionics) 1965–86, md GEC Avionics 1986–87; GEC Marconi: asst md 1987–90, pres US Ops 1990–92; chm GEC Marconi Avionics 1992–93, dir of civil aviation GEC Marconi 1993–94; aerospace conslt 1994–; pres: Royal Aeronautical Soc 1980, Cranfield Soc 1979–87; FEng 1984, Hon FRAeS 1990; *Recreations* mountain soaring, multi-hull sailing, model railways; *Clubs* Surrey & Hants Gliding, Aero Club Alpin, Southwold Sailing; *Style—* Peter Hearne, Esq, FEng; ✉ The Limes, Wateringbury, Kent ME18 5NY (☎ 01622 812385, fax 01622 813073)

HEARSE, Prof David James; s of James Read Hearse (d 1974), of Holt, Wilts, and Irene Annetta, *née* Nokes (d 1982); *b* 3 July 1943; *Educ* John Willmott GS, Univ of Wales (BSc, PhD, DSc); *Career* instr in pharmacology New York Univ Med Centre 1968–70, res fell Br Heart Fndn Imperial Coll London 1970–76, hon sr lectr St Thomas' Hosp

Med Sch 1976–86, prof of cardiovascular biochemistry United Med and Dental Schs Guy's Hosp and St Thomas' Hosp, currently dir cardiovascular research The Rayne Inst St Thomas's Hosp; author of 8 books and over 500 scientific papers in areas of res into heart disease; fell American Coll of Cardiology 1980; memb: RSM, Br Cardiac Soc; *Recreations* furniture, house restoration, photography, carpentry; *Clubs* RSM; *Style*— Prof David Hearse; ✉ Director Cardiovascular Research, The Rayne Institute, St Thomas's Hospital, London SE1 7EH (☎ 0171 928 9292)

HEARSEY, David Glen; s of Leonard Walter Hearsey (d 1985), of London, and Gwenda Kathleen, *née* Taylor; *b* 7 Feb 1948; *Educ* Willesden Coll of Technol; *m* 23 Dec 1972 (m dis 1987); 1 s (Lee James b 26 Sept 1979), 1 da (Sophie Jane b 28 Sept 1976); *Career* David Glen Assocs (consulting engrs): fndr 1969, ptnr 1970, sr ptnr 1980–; sr ptnr Glen Leasing 1981–86; conslt engr in respect of over 300 major construction projects worldwide; memb Cons Assoc; Freeman City of London 1973, Liveryman Worshipful Co of Plumbers; MRSH 1970, MIP 1972, TEngCEI 1972, AMIMunBM 1979, MSAME 1980; *Recreations* offshore sailing, skiing, shooting, golf, squash, tennis, chess, fishing; *Clubs* City Livery; *Style*— David Hearsey, Esq; ✉ David Glen Assocs Consulting Engineers, 19 Chiltern Court Business Park, Asheridge Road, Chesham, Bucks HP5 2PY (☎ 01494 793371, fax 01494 793372)

HEARST, Stephen; CBE (1979); s of Dr Emanuel Hirschtritt (d 1962), of Harley St, London, and Claire Hearst (d 1980); *b* 6 Oct 1919; *Educ* Rainer Gymnasium Vienna, Vienna Univ Med Faculty, Univ of Reading, Brasenose Coll Oxford (MA); *m* 17 July 1948, Lisbeth Edith, da of Dr Ludwig Neumann (d 1979), of Haifa, Israel; 1 s (David Andrew b 1954), 1 da (Daniela Carol (Mrs Pountney) b 1951); *Career* joined Pioneer Corps 1940, Corpl Home Serv 1940–42, cmmnd 1943, served N Africa 1943, Beach Landing Bde 5 Army Salerno Landing 1943, posted Allied Mil Govt 1944 (served Florence, Bologna and Piacenza), Capt 1945, camp cmdt POW Camps Palestine 1945, demobbed 1946; BBC TV: newsreel writer 1952, trainee prodr 1952–53, writer for Richard Dimbleby documentaries 1953–55, documentary writer and prodr 1955–64, exec prodr arts programmes 1965–67, head of arts features 1967–71; controller BBC Radio 3 1972–78, controller Future Policy Gp BBC 1978–82, dir Orsino Productions 1980–, special advsr to Dir-Gen BBC 1982–86; visiting fell Inst for the Advanced Study of the Humanities Univ of Edinburgh 1988; memb BAFTA; FRSA 1980; *Books* 2000 Million Poor (1965), The Third Age of Broadcasting (jtly, 1984), Television and the Public Interests (jtly, 1991); *Recreations* reading, gardening, swimming, golf; *Style*— Stephen Hearst, Esq, CBE; ✉ c/o The British Academy of Film and Television Arts, 195 Piccadilly, London SW1

HEARTH, John Dennis Miles; CBE (1983); s of Cyril Howard Hearth, MC (d 1973), of Leicester, and Dr Pauline Kathleen, *née* O'Flanagan (d 1989); *b* 8 April 1929; *Educ* The King's Sch Canterbury, Brasenose Coll Oxford (MA); *m* 1959, Pamela Anne, da of Arthur Gilbert Bryant, MC (d 1966), of Speldhurst, Kent; 2 s (Jonathan, Dominic), and 1 da decd; *Career* Nat Serv Intelligence Corps 1947–49; admin offr Overseas Civil Serv Br Solomon Islands Protectorate 1953–60, ed Fairplay Shipping Journal Fairplay Pubns Ltd 1961–66; called to the Bar Gray's Inn 1962; The Cunard Steamship Co Ltd: special asst 1966–67, gp planning advsr 1967–68, jt ventures dir 1969–71; chief exec Royal Agric Soc of Eng 1972–89 and 1991–92; dep chm: Rural Housing Tst (Village Homes for Village People) 1992– (tstee 1988–), Ctee English Rural Housing Assoc 1993–; chm: Nat Rural Enterprise Centre 1988–94, BBC Rural and Agric Affrs Advsy Ctee 1990–96, British Food and Farming Ltd 1990–, Bd of Mgmnt Nat Fedn Young Farmers Clubs 1989–95, English Villages Housing Assoc 1994– (memb Ctee 1990–); pres Nat Pig Breeders' Assoc 1990–93; treas Univ of Warwick 1989– (memb Cncl 1985–), govr Royal Agric Coll 1980–92; CIMgt 1982, hon fell Royal Agric Soc of Eng 1989; FRSA 1989; *Recreations* golf, theatre, travel, history; *Clubs* Anglo-Belgian; *Style*— John D M Hearth, Esq, CBE; ✉ Bayard's, Fenny Compton, nr Leamington Spa, Warwicks CV33 0XY (☎ and fax 01295 770849)

HEASLIP, Rear Adm Richard George; CB (1987); s of Eric Arthur Heaslip, and Vera Margaret Heaslip, *née* Bailey (d 1986); *b* 30 April 1932; *Educ* Chichester HS, RN Coll Dartmouth; *m* 1959, Lorna Jean, da of Alfred D Grayston (d 1976), of Canada; 3 s (Edmund b 1960, Christopher b 1964, Paul b 1966), 1 da (Lorna b 1960); *Career* Capt second submarine sqdn 1975–76, CO HMS Conqueror 1971–72, exec offr of first RN nuclear submarine HMS Dreadnought 1965–67, CO HMS Sea Devil 1961–62; NATO Defence Coll Rome 1979–80; dir of Defence Policy MOD 1982–84; asst Chief of Staff Operations SHAPE 1984; ADC 1984; Flag Offr Submarines and NATO and Cdr Submarine Forces Eastern Atlantic 1984–87; dir gen English Speaking Union 1987–90; chm RN Football Assoc 1977–84; pres London Submarine Old Comrades Assoc 1987; *Recreations* walking, music; *Style*— Rear Adm Richard Heaslip, CB; ✉ South Winds, Wallis Rd, Waterlooville, Hants (☎ 01705 241679); Dartmouth House, Charles St, London W1 (☎ 0171 493 3328)

HEATH, Prof Anthony Francis; s of Ronald John Heath, of Bampton, Oxon, and Cicely Florence, *née* Roberts; *b* 15 Dec 1942; *Educ* Merchant Taylors', Crosby, Trinity Coll Cambridge (sr scholar, BA, cross-country half blue); *m* Mary-Jane, da of David Lionel Pearce; 2 s (Oliver Francis b 17 Oct 1975, Ralph Francis b 18 April 1987), 1 da (Eleanor b 13 Nov 1984); *Career* asst lectr Univ of Cambridge 1968–70; Univ of Oxford: lectr and fell Jesus Coll 1970–87, fell Nuffield Coll 1987–; jt dir Centre for Research into Elections and Social Trends 1994–; FRSS, FBA 1992; *Books* Rational Choice and Social Exchange (1976), Origins and Destinations (with A Halsey and J Ridge, 1980), Social Mobility (1981), How Britain Votes (with R Jowell and J Curtice, 1985), Understanding Political Change (jtly, 1991), Labour's Last Chance? (with Jowell and Curtice, 1994); *Recreations* running, climbing, piano; *Clubs* Achilles; *Style*— Prof Anthony Heath, FBA; ✉ Nuffield College, Oxford OX1 1NF (☎ 01865 278543, fax 01865 278557)

HEATH, Christopher John; s of Lt-Gen Sir Lewis Macclesfield Heath (d 1954), of Bath, and Katherine Margaret, *née* Lonergan (d 1984); *b* 26 Sept 1946; *Educ* Ampleforth; *m* 14 June 1979, Margaret Joan, da of Col Richard Arthur Wiggin, TD, JP, DL (d 1977), of Ombersley, Worcs; 1 s (William Henry Christopher b 29 April 1983); *Career* commercial asst ICI 1964–69; sales exec George Henderson & Co 1969–75; ptnr Henderson Crosthwaite & Co 1975–84; chief exec offr Baring Securities Ltd 1984–93, dir Baring Bros & Co Ltd 1986–93, dir Barings Plc 1992–93; fndr investmt bank Caspian Securities Ltd 1995; memb Joy to the World (Save the Children Fund); MSI, memb SFA; *Recreations* fishing; *Clubs* Boodle's, Pratt's, Turf; *Style*— Christopher Heath, Esq; ✉ 7 Bloomfield Terrace, London SW1W 8PG

HEATH, David Arthur; s of Richard Arthur Heath, of Chesterfield, and Gladys Heath; *b* 6 Sept 1946; *Educ* Chesterfield Boys' GS, Glos Coll of Art and Design (DipArch), RIBA; *m* 27 June 1973, Angela Mary, da of James Joseph Niall Hardy (d 1988), and Una, *née* Hanley (d 1993); 2 s (Richard b 1978, John b 1980); *Career* architect; ptnr Heath Avery Partnership 1980–, tstee Heath Family Properties 1986, memb Cotswold Dist Cncl Architects Panel 1988–; Cheltenham Civic award 1987, 1989 and 1992 (commendations 1986 and 1987); *Books* Accommodating Technology in Schools (co-author, 1990); *Recreations* motor racing, music, walking, reading; *Clubs* Alfa Romeo Owners; *Style*— David Heath, Esq; ✉ 11A The Verneys, Old Bath Rd, Cheltenham, Glos (☎ 01242 242066); 3 Bath Mews, Bath Parade, Cheltenham, Glos (☎ 01242 529169, fax 224069)

HEATH, David William St John; CBE (1989); s of Eric William Heath, of Street, Somerset, and Pamela Joan, *née* Bennett; *b* 16 March 1954; *Educ* Millfield Sch, St John's Coll Oxford (MA), The City Univ; *m* 15 May 1987, Caroline Marie Therese, da of Harry Page Netherton, of Alicante, Spain; 1 s (Thomas b 2 May 1991), 1 da (Bethany b 31 March 1988); *Career* optician; memb: Somerset CC 1985– (ldr 1985–89), Nat Exec Lib Pty 1986–87, Fed Exec Lib Democrats 1989–92 and 1994–, Audit Cmmn 1995–; vice chm and ldr Lib Democrats Assoc of CCs 1994–, Parly conslt to Worldwide Fund for Nature 1990, chm Avon & Somerset Police Authy 1993–96 (dep chm 1996–), vice chm Ctee of Local Police Authorities 1995–; head of fund raising Nat Meningitis Tst 1992–93; *Recreations* rugby football, cricket, pig-breeding; *Clubs* Nat Lib; *Style*— David Heath, Esq, CBE; ✉ 34, The Yard, Witham Friary, nr Frome, Somerset (☎ 0174 985 458); County Hall, Taunton, Somerset (☎ 01823 255065, fax 01823 255 258, telex 46682)

HEATH, Rt Hon Sir Edward Richard George; KG (1992), PC (1955), MBE (1946), MP (C) Old Bexley and Sidcup (majority 15,699); s of late William George Heath and his 1 w Edith Annie, *née* Pantony; the family has been traced back in a continuous male line to one William Heath, of Cliston in Blackawton, Devon (d 1546); Sir Edward's f was a builder, his gf a railwayman, his ggf a merchant seaman, his gggf a coastguard, his ggggf a mariner; *b* 9 July 1916; *Educ* Chatham House Sch Ramsgate, Balliol Coll Oxford; *Career* served WWII RA (Maj 1945, despatches); Lt-Col cmdg 2 Regt HAC (TA) 1947–51; Master Gunner within the Tower of London 1951–54; admin Civil Service 1946–47, worked in journalism and merchant banking 1947–50; MP (C): Bexley 1950–74, Bexley, Sidcup 1974–83, Old Bexley and Sidcup 1983–; oppn leader 1965–70 and 1974–75, PM 1970–74; asst oppn whip 1951, Lord Cmmr of the Treasury 1951, jt dep chief whip 1952, dep chief whip 1953–55, Parly sec to the Treasy and govt chief whip 1955–59, min of labour 1959–60, Lord Privy Seal with FO responsibilities (negotiating UK entry into EEC) 1960–63, sec of state for indust, trade and regnl devpt and pres BOT 1963–64; Father of the House of Commons 1992–; memb of Ind Cmmn on Int Devpt Issues (the Brandt Cmmn 1977–80 Advsy Ctee), chm IRIS 1981–83; chm LSO Tst 1963–70 (memb 1974–92), vice pres Bach Choir 1970–, pres EU Youth Orch 1977–, hon memb LSO 1974–; visiting Chubb fell Yale 1975, Montgomery fell Dartmouth Coll 1980, Deroy prof Univ of Michigan 1990; Charlemagne prize 1963, Estes J Kefauver prize 1971, Stresseman Gold medal 1971, Freiherr Von Stein Fndn prize 1972, Gold medal of City of Paris 1978, World Humanity award 1980, Gold medal European Parl 1981; Hon DCL Oxford, Hon DTech Bradford, Hon DCL Kent, Hon Doctorate Sorbonne, Hon DL Westminster Coll Fulton Missouri, Hon LLD Univ of Calgary, Hon Degree Southampton Inst of HE; hon fell: Balliol Coll Oxford, Queen Mary and Westfield Coll, Nuffield Coll Oxford, Inst of Devpt Studies at Univ of Sussex; Hon FRCM, Hon FRCO, hon fell Royal Canadian Coll of Organists; Liveryman Worshipful Co of Goldsmiths, Hon Freeman Worshipful Co of Musicians; *Lectures* recent lectures incl: Fells Lecture at Queen Mary and Westfield Coll 1990, Ball Lecture Princeton 1991, Dong-A Ilbo Lecture Korea 1991, Lothian European Lecture Edinburgh 1992, Franco-British Cncl 20th Anniversary Lecture 1992, Disraeli Lecture St Stephens Constitutional Club 1993, Prince Frederick of Prussia Lecture Anglo-German Assoc 1993, Andrew John Williamson Meml Lecture Univ of Stirling 1993, Beethoven Memorial Lecture Bonn 1995, Churchill Lecture London 1996, RAB Butler Memorial Cambridge 1996; *Music* chm London Symphony Orch Tst 1963–70, conducted LSO in Elgar's Cockaigne Overture at its gala concert in the Royal Festival Hall London 1971; has since conducted LSO in London, Cologne and Bonn, and orchs at the World Festival of Youth Orchs Aberdeen 1977 and 1978; has conducted numerous orchs incl: Royal Philharmonic, Philharmonia, London Sinfonia, Liverpool Philharmonic, Bournemouth Symphony, Bournemouth Sinfonia, English Chamber Orch, Thames Chamber Orch, Sarum Chamber Orch, Berlin Philharmonic, Chicago Symphony, Philadelphia Symphony, Cleveland Symphony, Minneapolis Symphony, Grand Teton Festival, Jerusalem Symphony, Shanghai Philharmonic, Beijing Central Symphony, Swiss-Italian Radio Television Symphony, Zurich Chamber Orch, Singapore Symphony, Leningrad Conservatoire Orch, City of Oxford Orchestra, BBC Big Band Orch, Manchester Camerata Orch, English Sinfonia; was instrumental in founding the European Union Youth Orch of which he is pres, and conducted it on its 1978 Easter tour and 1978, 1979 and 1980 Summer tours of Europe; *Sailing* bought ocean racer 'Morning Cloud' 1969, won Sydney to Hobart race 1969, capt British team Admiral's Cup 1971 and 1979, capt British team Sardinia Cup 1980; *Books* One Nation: A Tory Approach to Social Problems (co-author 1950), Old World, New Horizons (1970), Sailing - A Course of My Life (1975), Music - A Joy for Life (1976), Travels - People and Places in My Life (1977), Carols - The Joy of Christmas (1977), Music (rev edn, 1997); CDs on EMI, Carlton Classics; *Recreations* music, sailing; *Clubs* Royal Yacht Sqdn, Buck's, Pratt's, Carlton, St Stephen's; *Style*— The Rt Hon Sir Edward Heath, KG, MBE, MP; ✉ House of Commons, London SW1A 0AA

HEATH, Sir Mark Evelyn; KCVO (1980), CMG (1980); s of Capt John Moore Heath, RN and Hilary Grace Stuart, *née* Salter; *b* 22 May 1927; *Educ* Marlborough, Queens' Coll Cambridge; *m* 1954, Margaret Alice, da of Sir Lawrence Bragg, CH, OBE, MC (d 1971); 2 s (Nicholas, William), 1 da (Clare (m Dr Richard Staughton, *qv*)); *Career* RNV(S)R 1945–48; HM Dip Serv 1950–85: formerly served Jakarta, Copenhagen, Sofia and Ottawa, dep head UK Delgn to OECD 1971–74, on secondment to Cabinet Office 1974–75, head W African Dept FCO and ambass Chad 1975–78, inspr FCO 1978–80, Br ambass to Holy See 1982–85 (upgraded from representation as min which rank held from 1980); dir protocol Hong Kong Govt 1985–88; chm Friends of the Anglican Centre Rome 1984–90; *Clubs* Nikaean; *Style*— Sir Mark Heath, KCVO, CMG; ✉ St Lawrence, Lansdown Road, Bath BA1 5TD (☎ 01225 428272)

HEATH, Air Marshal Sir Maurice Lionel; KBE (1962, OBE 1946), CB (1957), CVO (1978); s of late H Lionel Heath (miniature painter and princ Mayo Sch of Arts, Lahore, India), and Maggie, *née* Forsyth; *b* 12 Aug 1909; *Educ* Sutton Valence Sch, RAF Coll Cranwell; *m* 1, 1938, Kathleen Mary (d 1988), da of Boaler Gibson, of Bourne, Lincs; 1 s (James), 1 da (Julia); m 2, 7 Dec 1989, Lisa (d 1996), wid of Col J M B Cooke, MC; *Career* joined RAF 1927, served in Nos 16 and 28 Sqdns 1929–32, specialist armament duties 1933–43, OC Bomber Station 5 Gp Bomber Cmd 1944–45 (despatches), dep to Dir Gen Armament Air Miny 1946–48, CO Central Gunnery Sch 1948–49, sr air liaison offr Wellington NZ 1950–52, CO Bomber Cmd Bombing Sch 1952–53, Air Cdre 1953, idc 1954, dir plans Air Miny 1955, dep air sec 1955–57, Air Vice-Marshal 1956, Cdr Br Forces Arabian Peninsula 1957–59, Cmdt RAF Staff Coll Bracknell 1959–62, Air Marshal 1962, COS Allied Air Forces Central Europe 1962–65, ret 1965; dir Boyd and Boyd Estate Agents 1971–76; memb Cncl Offrs Pension Soc 1974–83, KCH appeal dir 1977–79, appeal conslt Voluntary Res Tst KCH 1979–84, private agent Henderson Fin Mgmnt 1980–88; chief hon steward Westminster Abbey 1964–74, Gentleman Usher to HM The Queen 1966–79 (Extra Gentleman Usher 1979–); DL W Sussex 1977–84 (non-active 1984–); *Recreations* reading, gardening, travel; *Clubs* RAF; *Style*— Air Marshal Sir Maurice Heath, KBE, CB, CVO, DL; ✉ Heronscroft, Rambledown Lane, W Chiltington, Pulborough, W Sussex RH20 2NW

HEATH, (Bryan) Michael; s of late (George) Bryan Stevens Heath, of Buckingham, and late Euphemia, *née* Wilson; *b* 16 June 1944; *Educ* Keswick Sch, Univ of Manchester (BSc); *m* 4 Dec 1976, Patricia Jane Margaret, da of late Francis Johnston; 1 da (Jane Mary Felicity b 1979); *Career* ptnr Arthur Andersen 1977– (joined 1967); *Style*— Michael Heath, Esq; ✉ Arthur Andersen & Co, 1 Surrey Street, London WC2R 2PS (☎ 0171 438 3316, fax 0171 438 5775, telex 8812711)

HEATH, Michael Stuart (Mike); CBE (1991), CB (1993); s of Col Bernard Stuart Heath (d 1995), of Bickley, Kent, and Blanche Dorothy Ellen, *née* Fairey (d 1991); *b* 7 Sept

1940; *Educ* St Albans, Welbeck Coll, RMCS (BSc(Eng)); *m* 4 Sept 1965, Frances Margaret, da of Robert Anderson Wood; 1 da (Victoria Clare Stuart b 8 Feb 1967), 1 s (Rupert Guy Stuart b 4 Sept 1968); *Career* cmmnd REME 1961, served Malaya, BAOR and Edinburgh until 1971, RMCS and Staff Coll 1972–73, Armour Sch Bovington 1974–75, cmd 7 Field Workshop BAOR 1976–77, Nat Defence Coll 1978, Berlin Field Force 1978–80, cmd MAINT HQ 2 Armoured Div BAOR 1981–82, MOD 1982–85, RCDS 1986, Dir Support Planning (Army) MOD 1987–89, cmd MAINT HQ BAOR 1990–91, DG Electrical and Mech Engrg 1991–92, DG Equipment Support (Army) HQ QMG (on reorganisation) 1992–93, Defence Costs Study Exec Gp 1993–94, ret Army as Maj-Gen; DG Engrg Cncl 1995–; CEng 1976, FIEE 1988, FIMgt 1988; *Recreations* walking, music; *Clubs* Army and Navy; *Style*— Mike Heath, CB, CBE; ✉ Director General, The Engineering Council, 10 Maltravers Street, London WC2R 3EE (☎ 0171 240 7891, fax 0171 240 6014)

HEATH, Samuel Bonython; s of Denis William Heath (d 1983), and Ada Bray, *née* Bonython (d 1988); *b* 11 Feb 1938; *Educ* Rugby; *m* 1, 11 Feb 1961 (m dis 1978), Jill, da of Philip Brandon Angas Parsons; 2 s (Guy Samuel b 12 Dec 1961, Christopher Angas b 24 June 1963), 1 da (Stephanie Ann b 17 Jan 1965); m 2, 1981, Bobbi, da of Thomas Cruickshanks; 2 step da (Bobbi b 29 Nov 1972, Shona b 24 May 1974); *Career* Nat Service cmmn RAF 1956–58; chm and md Samuel Heath & Sons plc 1970– (dir 1961, jt md 1963–70); *Recreations* travel, languages, jazz; *Style*— Samuel Heath, Esq; ✉ c/o Samuel Heath & Sons plc, Leopold St, Birmingham B12 OUJ (☎ 0121 772 2303, fax 0121 772 3334, telex 336908)

HEATH, Stephen Christopher; s of George Albert Heath, of Knottingley, W Yorks, and Patricia Anne, *née* Miller (d 1989); *b* 18 April 1959; *Educ* Knottingley HS, Wakefield Coll of Art, Teesside Poly (BA), Leicester Poly (MA); *Career* commerical interior designer; site mangr Space Planning and Coordinated Environmental Services Ltd (Spaces) 1985–86 (designer/planner 1983–85), assoc David Leon Partnership 1989–94 (joined 1986, design team ldr 1988–94), design assoc BDG/McColl 1994–96, dir and princ conslt Special Projects Bureau 1996–; work covers the professions, professional instns, healthcare, sci & technol, financial instns; clients incl: Unilever Research Ltd, Borax Consolidated Ltd, National Trust, V & A Museum, Russell Reynolds Associates Inc, BMW (GB) Ltd; FCSD 1993; *Recreations* fitness training, travelling, writing; *Style*— Stephen Heath, Esq; ✉ 24 Derby Lodge, East End Road, Finchley, London N3 3QG (☎ and fax 0181 349 3750)

HEATH-BROWN, Dr David Rodney (Roger); s of Basil Heath-Brown, of Welwyn Garden City, Herts, and Phyllis Joan, *née* Watson; *b* 12 Oct 1952; *Educ* Welwyn Garden City GS, Trinity Coll Cambridge (BA, PhD, Smith's essay prize); *m* 11 July 1992, Ann Louise, da of William Sharpley; 1 da (Jennifer Louisa b 5 Oct 1993); *Career* res fell Trinity Coll Cambridge 1977–79; tutor in pure mathematics Magdalen Coll Oxford 1979–; reader in pure mathematics Univ of Oxford 1990–; memb London Mathematical Soc 1979 (Jr Berwick Prize 1981, Sr Berwick Prize 1996); FRS 1993; *Recreations* British field botany, gardening, practical nature conservation; *Style*— Dr Roger Heath-Brown, FRS; ✉ Magdalen College, Oxford OX1 4AU (☎ 01865 276026)

HEATH-STUBBS, John Francis Alexander; OBE (1989); s of Francis Heath-Stubbs (d 1938), and Edith Louise Sara, *née* Marr (d 1972); *b* 9 July 1918; *Educ* Bembridge Sch, Worcester Coll for the Blind, Queen's Coll Oxford (BA, MA); *Career* English master The Hall Sch Hampstead 1944, editorial asst Hutchinsons 1944–45, Gregory fell in poetry Univ of Leeds 1952–55, visiting prof of English Ann Arbor Univ Michigan 1960–61, lectr in English Coll of St Mark & St John Chelsea 1962–72, non-stipendiary lectr Merton Coll Oxford 1972–, pres Poetry Soc 1992–94; Queen's Medal for Poetry 1973; hon vice pres Omar Khayyam Soc (pres 1989–90); conslt memb English Assoc; memb: Kathreen Briggs Soc, Folklore Soc, Charles Williams Soc, George MacDonald Soc; FRSL; *Style*— John Heath-Stubbs, Esq, OBE, FRSL; ✉ 22 Artesian Road, London W2

HEATHCOAT-AMORY, Rt Hon David Philip; PC (1996), MP (C) Wells (majority 6,649); s of Brig Roderick Heathcoat-Amory, and Sonia, da of Capt Edward Conyngham Denison, MVO, RN; half-bro of Michael Heathcoat-Amory, *qv*; *b* 21 March 1949; *Educ* Eton, ChCh Oxford (MA); *m* 1978, Linda Adams; 2 s, 1 da; *Career* CA, asst fin dir Br Technol Gp 1980–83; Parly candidate (C) Brent S 1979, MP (C) Wells 1983–, PPS to Home Sec 1987–88, asst whip 1988–89; Parly under sec of state: DOE 1989–90, Dept of Energy 1990–92; treasurer HM Household (dep chief whip) 1992–93, min of state Foreign Office 1993–94, Paymaster Gen 1994–96 (resigned); FCA; *Recreations* walking, talking; *Style*— The Rt Hon David Heathcoat-Amory, MP; ✉ House of Commons, London SW1

HEATHCOAT AMORY, Sir Ian; 6 Bt (UK 1874), of Knightshayes Court, Tiverton, Devon; DL (Devon 1981); s of Lt-Col Sir William Heathcoat-Amory, 5 Bt, DSO (d 1982), and Margaret, da of Col Sir Arthur Doyle, 4 Bt, JP (d 1948); *b* 3 Feb 1942; *Educ* Eton; *m* 1972, (Frances) Louise, da of late (Jocelyn Francis) Brian Pomeroy (gggs of 4 Viscount Harberton); 4 s (William Francis b 1975, Harry James b 1977, Patrick Thomas b 1979, Benjamin David b 1983); *Heir* s, William Francis Heathcoat-Amory b 19 July 1975; *Style*— Sir Ian Heathcoat Amory, Bt, DL; ✉ Calverleigh Court, Tiverton, Devon

HEATHCOAT-AMORY, Michael FitzGerald; only s of Maj Edgar Heathcoat-Amory, by his w Sonia, da of Capt Edward Conyngham Denison, MVO, RN; half-bro of David Heathcoat-Amory, MP, *qv*; *b* 2 Oct 1941; *Educ* Eton, Christ Church Oxford; *m* 1, 1965 (m dis 1970), Harriet Mary Sheila, da of Lt-Gen Sir Archibald Nye, GCSI, GCMG, GCIE, KCB, KBE, MC (d 1967); 1 s (Edward b 1969); m 2, 1975, Arabella, da of late Raimund von Hofmannstahl, and formerly w of Piers von Westenholz; 2 da (Lucy b 1977, Jessica b 1979); *Career* chm: London & Devonshire Trust Ltd, Jupiter International Green Investment Trust PLC; md Jupiter Asset Management Ltd; dir: PWS PLC, River Plate & General Investment Trust PLC, Exmoor Dual Investment Trust PLC, Masthead Insurance Underwriting PLC, China Investment Trust PLC, CST Emering Asia Trust PLC, The Hong Kong Investment Trust PLC, Jupiter Split Investment Trust PLC; High Sheriff of Devon 1985–86; farmer; *Recreations* field sports, collecting oak trees, talking politics; *Clubs* White's, Pratt's; *Style*— Michael Heathcoat-Amory, Esq; ✉ Chevithorne Barton, Tiverton, Devon EX16 7QB; 2 Montrose Court, London SW7

HEATHCOTE, Brig Sir Gilbert Simon; 9 Bt (GB 1733), of London, CBE (Mil 1964, MBE 1945); s of Lt-Col Robert Evelyn Manners Heathcote, DSO (d 1969), of Manton Hall, Rutland (gggs of Sir Gilbert Heathcote, 3 Bt, MP, who was gs of Sir Gilbert Heathcote, 1 Bt, one of the originators of the Bank of England and Lord Mayor of London 1711, also bro of Samuel, ancestor of Heathcote, Bt of Hursley), and Edith Millicent Heathcote (d 1977); suc kinsman, 3 Earl of Ancaster, 8 Bt, KCVO, TD, JP, DL, who d 1983; *b* 21 Sept 1913; *Educ* Eton; *m* 1, 1939 (m dis 1984), Patricia Margaret, da of Brig James Leslie, MC, of Sway, Hants; 1 s (Mark Simon Robert b 1941), 1 da (Joanna b 1947); m 2, 1984, Ann, da of Wing Cdr J A Hatton, and widow of Brig James Frederick Charles Mellor, DSO, OBE; *Heir* s, Mark Simon Robert Heathcote, *qv*; *Career* 2 Lt RA 1933, served WWII NW Europe, Lt-Col 1953, Brig 1960, COS Mid E Cmd 1962–64, Brig RA Scottish Cmd 1964–66, ret 1966; vice pres Royal Star and Garter Home; *Recreations* equitation, writing; *Clubs* Garrick, Army and Navy; *Style*— Brig Sir Gilbert S Heathcote, Bt, CBE; ✉ The Coach House, Tillington, nr Petworth, W Sussex GU28 0RA

HEATHCOTE, Mark Simon Robert; OBE (1988); s and h of Brig Sir Gilbert Simon Heathcote, 9 Bt, CBE, *qv*, and Patricia Margaret, *née* Leslie; *b* 1 March 1941; *Educ* Eton, Magdalene Coll Cambridge (BA); *m* 1975, Susan, da of Lt-Col George Ashley (d 1963), of Torquay; 2 s (Alastair Robert b 1977, Nicholas Alexander b 1979); *Career* Peninsular and Oriental Steamship Co 1963–70; HM Dip Serv: second later first sec FCO 1971, on loan to Home Civil Serv 1974, language student 1975, first sec (info) Athens 1976, FCO 1979, Buenos Aires 1980, FCO 1982, first sec Islamabad 1987, cnsllr FCO 1991–94; British Petroleum 1994–; *Recreations* water sports; *Style*— M S R Heathcote, Esq, OBE; ✉ c/o Lloyds Bank plc, 13 Cornhill, Ipswich, Suffolk IP1 1DG; BP International PLC, Britannic House, 1 Finsbury Circus, London EC2M 7BA (☎ 0171 496 4000)

HEATHCOTE, Sir Michael Perryman; 11 Bt (GB 1733), of Hursley, Hampshire; s of Sir Leonard Vyvyan Heathcote, 10 Bt (d 1963); in remainder to the Earldom of Macclesfield; *b* 7 Aug 1927; *Educ* Winchester, Clare Coll Cambridge; *m* 2 June 1956, Victoria, da of Cdr James Edward Rickards Wilford, RD, RNR, of Ackland Cottage, Shirley Holms, Lymington, Hants; 2 s (Timothy Gilbert b 1957, George Benjamin b 1965), 1 da ((Harriet) Louise (Mrs Richard J Rouse) b 1962); *Heir* s, Timothy Gilbert Heathcote, *qv*; *Career* 2 Lt 9 Lancers; farmer 1951–; *Style*— Sir Michael Heathcote, Bt; ✉ Warborne Farm, Boldre, Lymington, Hants SO41 5QD (☎ 01590 673478)

HEATHCOTE, Paul; s of Ken Heathcote, of Bolton, Lancs, and Brenda, *née* Walsh; *b* 3 Oct 1960; *Educ* Turton HS Bromley Cross Bolton, Bolton Catering Coll; *Career* chef/restaurateur; apprenticeship Holdsworth House Halifax 1979–80, Hotel Sternen Bern Switzerland 1980–81, Sharrow Bay Hotel Ullswater 1981–83, The Connaught Mayfair London 1983–85, Le Manoir aux Quat'Saison Oxford 1985–87, Broughton Park Hotel Preston 1987–90, chef/proprietor Paul Heathcote's Restaurant Preston 1990–, proprietor Heathcote's Brasserie 1995–; 1 Egon Ronay star 1990, 1 Michelin star 1990, Good Food Guide Co Restaurant of Yr 1990, Catey Newcomer of Yr 1992, 2 Michelin stars 1994, Egon Ronay Chef of Yr 1994, 2 Egon Ronay stars 1994, 4/5 Good Food Guide (Paul Heathcote's Restaurant) 1996, Good Food Guide Lancashire Newcomer Restaurant of the Year (Heathcote's Brasserie) 1996; hon fell Univ of Lancs 1995; *Style*— Paul Heathcote, Esq; ✉ Paul Heathcote's Restaurant, Higher Road, Longridge, Preston, Lancashire PR3 3SY (☎ 01772 784969, fax 01772 785713)

HEATHCOTE, Dr (Frederic) Roger; s of Frederic William Trevor Heathcote, of 6 Adrian Croft, Moseley, Birmingham, and late Kathleen Annie, *née* Muckley; *b* 19 March 1944; *Educ* Bromsgrove, Univ of Birmingham (BSc, PhD); *m* 1, 26 Sept 1970 (m dis 1986), Geraldine Nixon; m 2, 20 Dec 1986, Mary Campbell Syme Dickson; 1 s (David Frederic b 9 Jan 1988), 1 step da (Sarah Louise Campbell Cragg b 21 Feb 1984); *Career* res assoc Univ of Birmingham 1969–70; civil servant; Miny of Technol and DTI: joined 1970 as asst princ Oil Div 4, admin trainee 1971, Tariff Div 2 (a) 1971, higher exec offr (a) 1972, private sec to Sec (Industl Devpt) 1973; Dept of Energy: private sec to Perm Under Sec of State 1974, princ 1974, Offshore Technol Branch 1975 (sec Offshore Energy Technol Bd), asst sec Offshore Technol Unit 1978, Branch 1 Petroleum Engrg Div 1981, Branch 2 Gas Div 1982, Branch 1 Electricity Div 1984, Branch 3 Estab and Fin Div 1987, dir of resource mgmnt Estab and Fin Div 1988, head Coal Div 1989, princ estab and fin offr 1991–92; DTI: head Services Mgmnt Div 1992–96, dir Export Control and Non-Proliferation 1996–; *Recreations* reading, gardening, painting; *Style*— Dr Roger Heathcote; ✉ Department of Trade and Industry, Kingsgate House, 66–74 Victoria Street, London SW1E 6SW (☎ 0171 215 4321, fax 0171 215 4379)

HEATHCOTE, Timothy Gilbert; s and h of Sir Michael Perryman Heathcote, 11 Bt, *qv*; *b* 25 May 1957; *Style*— Timothy Heathcote, Esq

HEATHER, Charles; s of Norman Heather, of Uckfield, E Sussex, and Joan Alma Peggy, *née* Salmon; *b* 24 Sept 1955; *Educ* Green Grove Zimbabwe, Oriel Boys' Sch Zimbabwe; *m* 29 July 1978, Emma Patricia, da of Robin Spencer Dier; 2 s (Samuel b 25 October 1983, Jonathan b 20 September 1992), 2 da (Amy b 21 March 1981, Kate b 12 May 1994); *Career* with Baine Dawes 1972, Tradewinds Airways 1973–78, owner and md World Aviation Group 1978–; with brothers John, Neil and Lea writers of music and lyrics and co-prodrs musicals incl: Big Sin City (1976, nat tour 1977), The Comeback (1981, nat tour 1985), Whisper in the Wind (1984), Lust...circa 1674 (1987, West End 1993), A Slice of Saturday Night (West End 1988 and 1993, nat tour 1991, Charringtons LFA Best Musical 1989/90); *Recreations* mycology, music, social and economic development of Africa, Ancient British history; *Style*— Charles Heather, Esq; ✉ Heather Brothers Entertainment Group, 2 Horsted Square, Bellbrook Business Park, Uckfield, East Sussex TN22 1QW (☎ 01825 765055, fax 01825 768440)

HEATHER, John; s of Norman Heather, of Uckfield, Sussex, and Joan Alma Peggy, *née* Salmon; bro of Lea Heather, *qv*, and Neil Heather, *qv*; *b* 7 June 1947; *Educ* Courteney Selous Zimbabwe, Churchill Sch Zimbabwe; *m* 1 Sept 1973, Deirdre Anthea, da of Col Thomas Arthur Kingsley Howe; 1 s (Jacob b 11 Dec 1984), 2 da (Jessica b 21 Jan 1979, Anna b 10 Aug 1980); *Career* Chequers Group 1960–65, Delyse Record Company 1965–68, Pye Records Company 1969–71; with brothers Neil Lea and Charles wrote music and lyrics and co-produced musicals incl: Big Sin City (1976, nat tour 1977), The Comeback (1981, nat tour 1985), Whisper in the Wind (1984), Lust...circa 1674 (1987, Theatre Royal Haymarket 1993), A Slice of Saturday Night (West End 1988, nat tour 1991, Strand Theatre 1993), Blood Money (1993, USA 1995), Lust (Broadway, 1995); An Oz, a Yank and a Pom (1996, film); Charrington's LFA award Best Musical 1989/90 for A Slice of Saturday Night; memb: Performing Rights Soc, Br & American Dramatist Guild; *Books* co-wrote with brothers: Big Sin City (1976), The Comeback (1981), A Slice of Saturday Night (1988); *Style*— John Heather, Esq; ✉ Heather Brothers Entertainments Group, 2 Horsted Square, Bellbrook Business Park, Uckfield, East Sussex TN22 1QW (☎ 01825 765055, fax 01825 768440)

HEATHER, Lea; s of Norman Heather, of Uckfield, Sussex, and Joan Alma Peggy, *née* Salmon; bro of John Heather, *qv*, and Neil Heather, *qv*; *b* 2 Aug 1945; *Educ* Courteney Selous Zimbabwe, Churchill Sch Zimbabwe; *m* Nina, da of Tom Heaton; 2 s (Tarin Lea b 23 Aug 1979, Kim Arron b 13 Jan 1982), 1 da (Skye Mian b 30 June 1984); *Career* Chequers Group 1960–65, Delyse Record Company 1965–68, Pye Record Company 1969–71; with brothers John Neil and Charles wrote music and lyrics and co-produced musicals incl: Big Sin City (1976, nat tour 1977), The Comeback (1981, nat tour 1985), Whisper in the Wind (1984), Lust...circa 1674 (1987, West End 1993), A Slice of Saturday Night (West End 1988, nat tour 1991, West End 1993), Blood Money (1993, USA 1995), Lust (Broadway, 1995); An Oz, a Yank and a Pom (1996, film); Charrington's LFA award Best Musical 1989/90 for A Slice of Saturday Night; memb: Performing Rights Soc, Br & American Dramatist Guild; *Books* co-wrote with brothers: Big Sin City (1976), The Comeback (1981), A Slice of Saturday Night (1988); *Recreations* sailing; *Clubs* Sussex Yacht, Newhaven and Seaford Sailing; *Style*— Lea Heather, Esq; ✉ Heather Brothers Entertainments Group, 2 Horsted Square, Bellbrook Business Park, Uckfield, East Sussex TN22 1QW (☎ 01825 765055, fax 01825 768440)

HEATHER, Neil; s of Norman Heather, of Uckfield, Sussex, and Joan Alma Peggy, *née* Salmon; bro of John Heather, *qv*, and Lea Heather, *qv*; *b* 16 Aug 1942; *m* 19 Aug 1971, Edith, da of Walter Aubert; 1 da (Nadine Alice b 4 Nov 1985); *Career* Pye Record Company 1969–71; with brothers John Lea and Charles wrote music and lyrics and co-produced musicals incl: Big Sin City (1976, nat tour 1977), The Comeback (1981, nat tour 1985), Whisper in the Wind (1984), Lust...circa 1674 (1987), A Slice of Saturday Night (West End 1988, nat tours 1991 and 1992), Blood Money (1993, USA 1995), Lust (Broadway 1995); An Oz, a Yank and a Pom (1996, film); Charrington's LFA award Best Musical 1989/90 for A Slice of Saturday Night; memb: Performing Rights Soc, Br & American Dramatist Guild; *Books* co-wrote with brothers: Big Sin City (1976), The Comeback (1981), A Slice of Saturday Night (1988); *Style*— Neil Heather, Esq;

✉ Heather Brothers Entertainments Group, 2 Horsted Square, Bellbrook Business Park, Uckfield, East Sussex TN22 1QW (☎ 01825 765055, fax 01825 768440)

HEATHER, Stanley Frank; CBE (1980); s of Charles Heather (d 1954), of Ilford, Essex, and Jessie, *née* Powney (d 1953); *b* 8 Jan 1917; *Educ* privately, Downhills Sch, Univ of London; *m* 11 March 1946, Janet Roxburgh (Bunty) (d 1989), da of William Adams (d 1951), of Perth, Scotland; 1 s (Gerald Roxburgh b Jan 1949), 1 da (Gillean Alison Elsie b Aug 1951); *Career* WWII 1939–45, cmmnd RAC 1941, served Burma and India; admitted slr 1959; in private practice Horsham 1959–63, legal advsr City of London Police Force 1974–80, comptroller and city slr Corp of London 1974–80 (dep comptroller 1968–74, asst slr 1963–68); as comptroller was hon slr to: Museum of London, City Arts Tst, City Educnl Tsts Fund, City Archaeological Tst Fund, Sir W M Coxon Tst Fund, William Lambe Charity (also tstee), Sir John Langham Tst Fund, The Wilson Tst, Leonidas Alcibiades Oldfield Charity, The City Almshouse Charities; attorney and gen counsel: to City of London (Arizona) Corp, to Ironbridge Gorge Museum Devpt Tst; Freeman City of London 1964, Liveryman Worshipful Co of Slrs 1965; Hon Liveryman: Worshipful Co of Clothworkers, Worshipful Co of Engrs 1983, Worshipful Co of Scriveners 1993; Hon Freeman Co of Water Conservators 1995; FRSA 1981; *Recreations* golf, fishing; *Clubs* City Livery, Guildhall; *Style*— S F Heather, Esq, CBE; ✉ 71 Rosehill, Arun Court, Billingshurst, West Sussex RH14 9QQ (☎ 01403 783981)

HEATLEY, Dr (Richard) Val; s of Walter Russell Heatley, of Bridport, Dorset, and Constance Marjorie, *née* Davis; *b* 11 Oct 1947; *Educ* Latymer Upper Sch, Welsh Nat Sch of Med (MB BCh, MD); *m* 5 May 1979, Ruth Mary, da of William Elderkin, of Leics; 2 s (Richard Piers b 1986, Matthew Connel b 1988), 2 da (Kirsteen Ruth b 1980, Francine Mary b 1982); *Career* clinical fell Sr Res Dept of Med Univ of McMaster Hamilton Ontario 1978–80, sr lectr in med Welsh Nat Sch of Med and conslt physician Univ Hosp of Wales 1981–82, sr lectr in med Univ of Leeds 1982–, conslt physician St James's Univ Hosp Leeds 1982–; ed Int Jl of Gastroenterology; memb: Br Soc of Gastroenterology and Immunology, Bd Aliment Pharmacology and Therapeutics, Ctee on Gastroenterology RCP; FRCP; *Books* Helicobacter pylori and Gastroduodenal Disease (1992), Consensus in Clinical Nutrition (1994), The Helicobacter pylori Handbook (1995); *Recreations* children, music, travel, walking; *Style*— Dr Val Heatley; ✉ Department of Medicine, St James's University Hospital, Leeds LS9 7TF (☎ 0113 243 3144)

HEATLY, Sir Peter; kt (1990), CBE (1971), DL (1984); s of Robert Heatly (d 1968), of Edinburgh, and Margaret Ann, *née* Sproull (d 1955); *b* 9 June 1924; *Educ* Leith Acad, Univ of Edinburgh (BSc); *m* 1, 3 April 1948, (Jean) Robertha Johnston (d 1979), da of William Brown Hermiston (d 1995); 2 s (Peter Hermiston b 20 Aug 1955, Robert Johnston b 31 Aug 1958), 2 da (Ann May b 27 May 1949, Jane Margaret b 9 May 1951); m 2, 7 Dec 1984, Mae Calder Cochrane, OBE; *Career* lectr in civil engrg Univ of Edinburgh 1947–50; md Peter Heatly & Co Ltd 1950–; chm: Scottish Sports Cncl 1975–87, Cwlth Games Fedn 1982–90 (Cwlth Diving Champion 1950, 1954 and 1958); govr Scottish Sports Aid Fndn; Master Merchant Co of Edinburgh 1988–90; convener of trades of Edinburgh 1971–75; Liveryman Worshipful Co of Engrs 1991; Dr honoris causa Univ of Edinburgh 1992, Hon DLitt Queen Margaret Coll 1994; FICE; *Recreations* swimming, gardening, travel; *Clubs* New (Edinburgh); *Style*— Sir Peter Heatly, CBE, DL; ✉ Lanrig, Balerno, Edinburgh EH14 7AJ (☎ 0131 449 3998); 1 Fidra Court, North Berwick, East Lothian; Peter Heatly & Co Ltd, 17 Elbe St, Leith, Edinburgh (☎ 0131 554 3226, fax 0131 555 3193)

HEATON, *see:* Henniker-Heaton

HEATON, Anne (Mrs John Field); da of Guy Heaton, of Ilkley, Yorks, and Ellen Jane, *née* Beckett (d 1985); *b* 19 Nov 1930; *Educ* Edgbaston HS Birmingham, Sadler's Wells Ballet Sch; *m* 31 March 1956, John Field, CBE (d 1991), former ballet dancer and dir, s of William Greenfield; *Career* fndr memb Sadler's Wells Theatre Ballet 1946, soloist and princ Covent Garden 1947–56, ballerina Sadler's Wells Theatre Ballet 1956–59 (left co after injury), guest artist Covent Garden 1960, subsequently teacher, prodr and choreographer, artistic dir Br Ballet Orgn until 1992, currently freelance prodr and teacher; danced all leading classical roles, cr main roles in ballets by Ashton Macmillan, Roland Petit and Peter Wright; danced in partnership with: Donald MacLeary (1957–60), John Field, Robert Helpmann, Léonide Massine; *Style*— Ms Anne Heaton Field; ✉ Cynara, The Moorings, Willows Riverside Park, Windsor, Berks SL4 5TR (☎ 01753 864 288)

HEATON, Frances Anne; da of John Ferris Whidborne (d 1985), and Marjorie Annie, *née* Maltby (d 1989); *b* 11 Aug 1944; *Educ* Queen Anne's Sch Caversham, Trinity Coll Dublin (BA, LLB); *m* 26 April 1969, Martin Christopher Crispin Heaton; 2 s (Mark Christopher Francis b 14 April 1972, Andrew John Ralph b 9 Nov 1974); *Career* called to the Bar Inner Temple 1967; Dept of Econ Affrs 1967–70, HM Treasy 1970–80 (seconded S G Warburg & Co Ltd 1977–79), dir of corporate finance Lazard Brothers & Co Ltd 1986– (joined 1980), dir gen Panel of Takeovers and Mergers March 1992–94; non-exec dir: W S Atkins 1990–, Commercial Union 1994–, Harrisons & Crosfield 1994–; memb Ct Bank of England 1993–; *Recreations* riding, gardening, bridge; *Style*— Mrs Frances Heaton; ✉ Lazard Brothers & Co Ltd, 21 Moorfields, London EC2P 2HT (☎ 0171 588 2721)

HEATON, Dr Kenneth Willoughby; s of Philip John Heaton (d 1971), of Salisbury, and Anna Stenberg (d 1963); *b* 3 Aug 1936; *Educ* Marlborough, Univ of Cambridge, Middx Hosp Med Sch (MD); *m* 15 July 1961, Susan Tandy, da of Dr Brian Victor O'Connor (d 1968), of Jersey; 2 s (Philip b 1964, John b 1975), 1 da (Jenny b 1962); *Career* res fell Duke Univ Med Center N Carolina 1966–67, reader in med Univ of Bristol 1979– (lectr 1968–72, conslt sr lectr 1972–79), author of numerous pubns on intestinal and gallbladder physiology, disease and nutrition; hon treas RSM, former hon sec RCP Working Party on Dietary Fibre, former chm RSM Forum on Food and Health; former memb: Cncl Br Soc of Gastroenterology, Editorial Bd of Gut, COMA Panel on Dietary Sugars and Human Disease; memb: Nutrition Soc, Assoc of Physicians of GB and I; FRCP 1973; *Books* Bile Salts in Health and Disease (1972), Dietary Fibre, Fibre-depleted Foods and Disease (contrib, 1985), Understanding Your Bowels (1995); *Recreations* music, walking; *Style*— Dr Kenneth Heaton; ✉ University Department of Medicine, Bristol Royal Infirmary, Bristol BS2 8HW (☎ 0117 928 2313, fax 0117 927 3631)

HEATON, Mark Frederick; s of Peter Heaton (d 1965), and Rachael, *née* Frampton; *b* 20 Dec 1951; *m* 1, 24 July 1976 (m dis 1986), Lorna, da of Col Ralph Stewart-Wilson, MC; 2 s (Henry Peter Frederick b 14 April 1980, Oliver James Stewart b 12 Jan 1983); m 2, 18 March 1988, Naomi Claire Helen, *qv*, da of Dr Antony Jarrett; *Career* farmer in Gloucs; dep chm Leo Burnett Advertising Ltd (joined 1972); memb: CLA, Br Field Sports Soc, Racehorse Owners' Assoc, Lloyd's, BASC, Mktg Soc, Game Conservancy Tst; *Recreations* horse racing, skiing, shooting; *Clubs* White's, MCC, Turf; *Style*— Mark Heaton, Esq; ✉ Ampney St Mary Manor, Cirencester, Gloucestershire GL7 5SP (☎ 0128585 1321); 32 Bryanston Square, London W1H 7LS (☎ 0171 262 0665); Leo Burnett Ltd, The Leo Burnett Building, 60 Sloane Avenue, London SW3 3XB (☎ 0171 591 9111, fax 0171 591 9457)

HEATON, Naomi Claire Helen; *née* Jarrett; da of Dr Boaz Antony Jarrett, of Chiswick, London, and Patricia Evelyn, *née* White; *b* 11 Sept 1955; *Educ* Walthamstow Hall Sch for Girls, St Hilda's Coll Oxford (BA); *m* 18 March 1988, Mark Frederick Heaton, *qv*; *Career* Leo Burnett Advertising 1977–82; main bd dir: Saatchi & Saatchi Advertising 1984 (joined 1982), Young & Rubicam 1985–86; md London Central Portfolio Services Ltd (acquisition, refurbishment and mgmnt of residential investment property) 1994– (estab 1989); *Recreations* skiing, horse racing, interior design; *Clubs* Boodle's; *Style*— Mrs Mark Heaton; ✉ 32 Bryanston Square, London W1H 7LS; Ampney St Mary Manor, Cirencester, Glos GL7 5SP (office ☎ 0171 723 1733)

HEATON-ARMSTRONG, Anthony Eustace John; s of William Henry Dunamace Heaton-Armstrong, of Berks, and Idonea, *née* Chance; *b* 27 Sept 1950; *Educ* Ampleforth, Univ of Bristol (LLB); *m* 1, 10 Feb 1973 (m dis 1977), Susan, *née* Allnutt; m 2, 20 May 1982, Anne Frances, da of late Ethel Robigo; 1 s (John William b 15 Feb 1983), 2 da (Eleanor b 8 May 1985, Celestine b 3 Sept 1988); *Career* called to the Bar Gray's Inn 1973, in practice 1973–; expert on police evidence, Int Cmmn of Jurists' observer at trials overseas involving alleged human rights abuses, asst sec gen (meetings) Br Acad of Forensic Scis; tstee Aldo Tst; *Books* Confession Evidence (with David Wolchover, 1996); also author of numerous legal articles in learned jls; *Recreations* prisoners' welfare, gardening, wildlife and the countryside; *Clubs* Garrick; *Style*— Anthony Heaton-Armstrong, Esq; ✉ 9–12 Bell Yard, London WC2A 2LF (☎ 0171 400 1800, fax 0171 404 1405)

HEATON-WARD, Dr (William) Alan; s of 2 Lt Ralph Heaton-Ward (d 1921), of Durham City, and Mabel, *née* Orton (d 1963); *b* 19 Dec 1919; *Educ* Sefton Bristol, Queen Elizabeth's Hosp Clifton Bristol, Univ of Bristol (MB ChB, DPM); *m* 28 March 1945, Christine Edith, da of Maj David Fraser, DSO, MC, RHA (d 1943), of Nairn, Scotland; 2 da (Nicola (Mrs Kennedy), Lindsay (Mrs Maldini)); *Career* jr clerk Messrs W D & H O Wills Bristol 1936–38; Local Def Vols and HG 1940–41, Surgn Lt-Cdr and neuropsychiatrist Nore Cmd RNVR 1946–48; sr psychiatric registrar St James' Hosp Portsmouth 1948–50, dep med supt Hortham/Brentry Hosp Gp Bristol 1950–54, clinical teacher in mental health Univ of Bristol 1954–78; Stoke Park Hosp Gp Bristol: med supt 1954–61, conslt psychiatrist in charge 1961–78, hon conslt 1978–; memb S Western Mental Health Review Tbnl 1960–78 and 1985–92, Lord Chllr's med visitor Ct of Protection 1978–89, Blake Marsh lectr RCPsych 1976, Burden Res Gold medal and prize 1978; Br Cncl visiting lectr Portugal 1971; vice pres RCPsych 1976–78, pres Br Soc for Study of Mental Subnormality 1978–79; vice pres: Fortune Centre of Riding Therapy 1980–, Rescare 1995–; memb: Advsy Cncl Radio Bristol 1985–88, Police Liaison Ctee 1988–90, Bristol Medico-Legal Soc, Bristol Medico-Chirurgical Soc, BMA; FRCPsych 1971; hon memb American Assoc of Physician Analysts 1978–; *Books* Notes on Mental Deficiency (3 edn, 1955), Mental Subnormality (4 edn, 1975), Left Behind (1978), Mental Handicap (jtly, 1984); *Recreations* following all forms of sport, asking 'Why', gardening; *Clubs* Bristol Savages; *Style*— Dr Alan Heaton-Ward; ✉ Flat 2, 38 Apsley Rd, Clifton, Bristol BS8 2SS (☎ 0117 973 8971)

HEATON-WARD, Patrick Francis; s of Kenneth Pearce Heaton-Ward (d 1985), and Joan Moria Stuart, *née* Wilson-Steele; *b* 3 Oct 1939; *Educ* Bristol GS, Brasenose Coll Oxford (sr scholar, MA); *m* 18 June 1966, Danielle Paulette Michele, da of Hubert Mussot; 2 da (Anne Christine b 13 April 1971, Alice Mary b 24 June 1977); *Career* Bowater Paper Corporation 1962–64; Ogilvy & Mather 1964–: account dir 1970, on secondment to Ogilvy & Mather Milan as client serv dir 1976–77, on secondment to Livraghi Ogilvy & Mather Milan as dir 1982–88, dir Ogilvy Adams & Rinehart Ltd 1988–91, dir Primary Contract Ltd 1992–; MIPA 1990; *Recreations* skiing, opera, ballet; *Style*— Patrick Heaton-Ward, Esq; ✉ Primary Contact Ltd, 20 Soho Square, London W1V 6AU (☎ 0171 437 4947, fax 0171 437 5057)

HEATON WATSON, Richard Barrie; s of Kenneth Walter Heaton Watson (d 1981), of Albufeira, Portugal, and Jean Alexandra, *née* Harvey (d 1958); *b* 29 April 1945; *Educ* Harrow, Queen's Univ Belfast (BA), Cambridge (PGCE); *m* 29 July 1978, Caroline Ann, da of Leonard Cyril McKane, MBE, of Lingfield, Surrey; 1 s (Dominic b 1982), 2 da (Lucy b 1979, Fenella b 1987); *Career* head of dept Charterhouse 1975–84, housemaster Weekites 1985–97, dir of PR 1997–; memb GA 1971; FRGS 1989; *Recreations* antiques, theatre, skiing; *Clubs* 1900, Golf Soc of GB; *Style*— Richard Heaton Watson, Esq; ✉ 20 Bywater St, London SW3 4XD; Brooke Hall, Charterhouse, Godalming, Surrey GU7 2DX (☎ 01483 291671)

HEAVEN, HE Derick Roy; *b* 19 Dec 1940; *Educ* Cornwall Coll, Jamaica Sch of Agriculture (DipAg); *m*; 3 c; *Career* Jamaican diplomat; MP (People's Nat Pty) S St Catherine 1976, Parly sec Miny of Foreign Affrs with special responsiblity for foreign trade 1976, min of trade and commerce 1980, consul gen NY 1989–92, ambass Japan (concurrently non resident ambass to People's Republic of China and to Republic of Korea) 1992–94, Jamaican high cmmr to Ct of St James's 1994–; chm/rapporteur at numerous meetings of Caribbean Community and Common Market, African Caribbean and Pacific/EEC Talks and Econ Cmmn for Latin America and the Caribbean; formerly: extension offr Citrus Growers' Assoc, field offr Agricultural Mktg Conf, mangr Cecil-de-Cordova Ltd; involved in farming and dir of various cos 1980–; *Recreations* reading, travelling, sports; *Style*— HE Mr Derick Heaven; ✉ Jamaican High Commission, 1–2 Prince Consort Road, London SW7 2BZ (☎ 0171 823 9911)

HEBBLETHWAITE, (Richard) Jeremy; TD; s of Lt-Col Roger Vavasour Hebblethwaite, MC (d 1976), and Susan, *née* Hawkins (d 1994); *b* 5 Dec 1933; *Educ* Wellington, Univ of Nottingham; *m* 1, 1966 (m dis 1988), Sara Elisabeth, da of James Stucker Offutt (d 1985); 2 s (Richard Alexander Vavasour b 1968, James Andrew Lewis b 1971); m 2, 1988, Josceline Mary, da of late Rt Hon Lord Justice (Sir Harry) Phillimore, OBE; *Career* Nat Serv 2 Lt 2 RHA, Capt TA; dir Save & Prosper Group 1969–87, fin and mktg advsr 1987–92, chm Optimist Investments Ltd 1993–; memb: Organising Ctee Mktg Investmt Bd 1985–86, Sir Norman Fowler's Pension Advsy Gp 1986–87, Occupational Pensions Bd 1987–93; vice chm Authorisation Ctee ICAEW 1987–92; FCA 1969 (ACA 1959); *Recreations* sailing, ice yachting, opera, horticulture, golf; *Clubs* City; *Style*— Jeremy Hebblethwaite, Esq, TD; ✉ 2 The Green, Evenley, Brackley, Northants NN13 5SQ

HEBDITCH, Maxwell Graham (Max); CBE (1994); s of Harold Oliver Hebditch (d 1975), of Yeovil, Somerset, and Lily, *née* Bartle; *b* 22 Aug 1937; *Educ* Yeovil Sch, Magdalene Coll Cambridge (MA); *m* 1 June 1963, Felicity Margaret, da of William Brinley Davies (d 1982); 2 s, 1 da; *Career* Nat Serv pilot offr (Secretarial Branch) RAF 1956–58; field archaeologist Leicester Museum 1961–64, asst curator Archaeology City Museum Bristol 1965–71 (latterly curator Social History); dir: Guildhall Museum London 1971–75, Museum of London 1977– (dep dir 1975–77); pres Museum Assoc 1990–92, chm UK Ctee Int Cncl of Museums 1981–87; Hon DLitt City Univ 1992; FSA, FMA; *Publications* contribs to specialist and academic jls; *Style*— Max Hebditch, Esq, CBE, FSA; ✉ Museum of London, London Wall, London EC2Y 5HN (☎ 0171 600 3699, fax 0171 600 1058)

HECKS, Malcolm; s of Ronald Frederick Hecks, of Chippenham, Wilts, and Ivy, *née* Rose (d 1962); *b* 5 Dec 1942; *Educ* Chippenham GS, Univ of Bath (BSc, BArch); *m* 12 Aug 1967, Donna Leslie, da of Robert Leslie Pratt, of Cape Town, SA; 1 s (Oliver Lewis Ledoux b 1978), 1 da (Alexandra Sophie Ivy b 1975); *Career* conslt architect; sr ptnr Malcolm Hecks Assocs Surrey 1970–; designed World Wildlife HQ Bldg Godalming 1982; RIBA 1971, MBIM 1978, FFAS 1985; *Recreations* music, theatre, travel, films, history of art and architecture, ecology; *Style*— Malcolm Hecks, Esq; ✉ Priors Glade, Priorswood, Compton, Guildford GU3 1DR

HECTOR, Gordon Matthews; CMG (1966), CBE (1961, OBE 1955); s of George Pittendrigh Hector (d 1962), of Aberdeen, and Helen Elizabeth, *née* Matthews (d 1963); *b* 9 June 1918; *Educ* St Mary's Sch Melrose, Edinburgh Acad, Lincoln Coll Oxford (MA); *m* 28 Aug 1954, Mary Forrest, da of Robert Gray (d 1933); 1 s (Alistair b 5 Oct 1955),

2 da (Jean b 30 April 1957, Katy b 12 Oct 1961); *Career* cmmnd RASC 1939, served with E Africa Forces 1940–45; dist offr Kenya 1946, dist cmmr 1948, asst sec 1950, sec to Road Authy 1951, sec to Govt of Seychelles 1952, actg govr 1953, dep res cmmr and govt sec Basutoland 1956, dep Br Govt rep Lesotho 1965; dep sec Univ of Aberdeen 1976 (clerk to Univ Ct 1967–76), sec Assembly Cncl of Gen Assembly Church of Scot 1980–85; chm: Victoria League for Cwlth Friendship Scot 1983–89, W End Community Cncl Edinburgh Dist 1986–89, Gt North of Scotland Railway Assoc 1990–92; hon vice pres The St Andrew Soc Edinburgh; Burgess of Guild City of Aberdeen 1979; fell Cwlth Fund 1939; *Recreations* town and country walking, railways, grandchildren; *Clubs* Royal Over-Seas League, Vincent's (Oxford); *Style*— Gordon Hector, Esq, CMG, CBE; ✉ 4 Montgomery Court, 110 Hepburns Gardens, St Andrews KY16 9LT

HEDDEN, Robert; s of Frederick Hedden (d 1982), of Okehampton, Devon, and Winifred Elizabeth, *née* Trenaman; *b* 22 Feb 1948; *Educ* Okehampton GS, King's Coll London (LLB, AKC); *m* 10 Sept 1977 (m dis 1996), Jean Mary, da of Walter John Worboyes (d 1982), of London; 1 s (Oliver Michael Ward), 1 da (Rachel Louise); *Career* admitted slr 1972 (Clifford's Inn prizeman), ptnr Herbert Smith 1980–93 (conslt 1993–94), gp slr Freshwater Group of Companies 1993–; Liveryman Worshipful Co of Slrs, Freeman City of London; memb Planning and Environmental Law Sub-Ctee City of London Law Soc 1991–93; memb Ctee Br-Polish Legal Assoc 1989–93, assoc memb The Dirs' Guild of GB 1990–96; memb: Law Soc, Int Bar Assoc; *Recreations* theatre (making and watching), music (making and listening), tennis, skiing, swimming, travel; *Clubs* Athenaeum, Croydon Stagers; *Style*— Robert Hedden, Esq; ✉ 25 Lewin Rd, London SW16 6JZ; Casa Veleta, Puig Redo, Santa Eulalia, Ibiza, Balearics; Freshwater House, 158–162 Shaftesbury Avenue, London WC2H 8HR (☎ 0171 836 1555, fax 0171 240 9770)

HEDGECOE, Prof John; s of William Alec Hedgecoe (d 1983), of Gt Dunmow, Essex, and Kathleen Alice, *née* Don (d 1981); *b* 24 March 1937; *Educ* Gulval Village Sch, Guildford Sch of Art, Epsom Sch of Art, Ruskin Coll Oxford, RCA (Dr RCA); *m* 3 Oct 1959 (m dis 1994), Julia, da of Sidney Mardon (d 1971), of Bishop's Stortford, Herts; 2 s (Sebastian John b 1961, Auberon Henry b 1968), 1 da (Imogen Dolly Alice b 1964); *Career* photographer; Nat Serv RAF SAC 1955–56; staff photographer Queen magazine 1957–72; freelance for most int magazines 1958– (Sunday Times and Observer 1960–70); RCA: fndr Photography Sch 1965, reader and head Photography Dept 1965–74, fell 1973, prof of Photography 1975, fndr Audio/Visual Dept 1980, fndr Holography Unit 1982, managing tstee 1983, pro-rector until 1993, sr fell 1992, prof emeritus 1995; advsr English Heritage 1995; portrait of HM The Queen for Br and Aust postage stamps 1966, photographer The Arts Multi-Projection Br Exhibition Expo Japan Show 1970, visiting prof Norwegian Nat TV Sch Oslo 1985; dir: John Hedgecoe Ltd 1965–95, Perennial Pictures Ltd 1980–90; md Lion & Unicorn Press Ltd 1986–94; illustrator of numerous books 1958–, contributor to numerous radio broadcasts; TV: Tonight (Aust) 1967, Folio (Anglia TV) 1980, eight programmes on photography (C4) 1983 (repeated 1984), Winners (C4) 1984, Light and Form (US Cable TV) 1985; exhibitions: London, Sydney, Toronto, Detroit, Edinburgh, Venice and Prague; work in collections incl: V & A, Museum Art Gallery of Ontario, Nat Portrait Gallery, Citibank London, Henry Moore Fndn, Museum of Modern Art NY, Leeds City Art Gallery; govr W Surrey Coll of Art 1975–80 (memb Acad Advsy Bd 1975–80), memb Photographic Bd CNAA 1976–78, acad govr Richmond Coll London; laureate and medal for achievement in photography (Czechoslovakian Govt) 1989; fell Indian International Photographic Soc, FRSA; *Books* Henry Moore (1968, prize best art book world-wide 1969), Kevin Crossley-Holland Book of Norfolk Poems (jtly 1970), Photography, Material and Methods (jtly 1971–74 edns), Henry Moore Energy in Space (1973), The Book of Photography (1976), Handbook of Photographic Techniques (1977, 2 edn 1982), The Art of Colour Photography (1978, Kodak Book Prize), Possession (1978), The Pocket Book of Photography (1979), Introductory Photography Course (1979), Master Classes in Photography: Children and Child Portraiture (1980), Poems of Thomas Hardy (illustrated 1981), Poems of Robert Burns (illustrated), The Book of Advanced Photography (1982), What a Picture! (1983), The Photographer's Work Book (1983), Aesthetics of Nude Photography (1984), The Workbook of Photo Techniques (1984), The Workbook of Darkroom Techniques (1984), Pocket Book of Travel and Holiday Photography (1986), Henry Moore: His Ideas, Inspirations and Life as an Artist (1986), The Three Dimensional Pop-up Photography Book (with A L Rowse, 1986), Shakespeare's Land (1986), Photographers Manual of Creative Ideas (1986), Portrait Photography (with A L Rowse, 1987), Rowse's Cornwall (1987), Practical Book of Landscape Photography (1988), Hedgecoe on Photography (1988), Hedgecoe on Video (1989), The Complete Guide to Photography (1990), The Complete Guide to Video Photography (1992), The Art of Ceramics and Zillage (1992), The New Book of Photography (1994), The Complete Guide to Black and White Photography (1994), John Hedgecoe's New Book of Photography (1995), John Hedgecoe's Video Basics (1995), Breakfast with Dolly (1996), John Hedgecoe's Figure and Form (1996), Hedgecoe on Photography (CD-Rom); *Recreations* sculpture, building, gardening; *Clubs* Arts; *Style*— Prof John Hedgecoe; ✉ Oxmead Hall, Oxmead, Nr Norwich, Norfolk NR10 5HP

HEDGER, John Clive; s of Leslie John Keith Hedger, and Iris, *née* Freidlos; *b* 17 Dec 1942; *Educ* Victoria Coll Jersey, Univ of Sussex (MA); *m* 1966, Jean Ann, *née* Felstead; 2 s, 1 da; *Career* Department for Educn and Employment (formerly DES then Dept for Educn): joined 1966, asst private sec 1970–74, sec Ctee of Enquiry on Educn of the Handicapped 1974–76, head of schs and under sec 1988–92, dep sec 1992–95; dir of operations Dept for Educn and Employment 1995–; *Recreations* coarse sailing, coarse acting, walking; *Clubs* Odney (Cookham); *Style*— John Hedger, Esq; ✉ Department for Education and Employment, Sanctuary Buildings, Great Smith Street, London SW1P 3BT (☎ 0171 925 6211, fax 0171 925 6309); Moorfoot, Sheffield S1 4PQ (fax 0114 275 1479)

HEDGES, Dr Anthony John; s of Sidney George Hedges (d 1974), and Mary, *née* Dixon; *b* 5 March 1931; *Educ* Bicester GS, Keble Coll Oxford (BA, BMus, DipEd, MA); *m* 28 Aug 1957, (Delia) Joy, da of Maj Albert Marsden (d 1971); 2 s (Nicholas b 28 Oct 1964, Simon b 10 May 1966), 2 da (Fiona b 25 Feb 1959, Deborah b 4 March 1961); *Career* Nat Serv Royal Signals Band 1955–57; teacher and lectr Royal Scottish Acad of Music 1957–63; Univ of Hull: lectr 1963, sr lectr 1968, reader in composition 1978–95; princ compositions incl; orchestral: Comedy Overture 1962 (revised 1967), Overture Oct '62 1962 (revised 1968), Variations on a Theme of Rameau 1969, Festival Dances 1976, Four Breton Sketches 1980, Sinfonia Concertante 1980, Scenes from the Humber 1981, Symphony 1972–73, A Cleveland Overture 1984, Concertino for Horn and String Orchestra 1987, Sinfonia Giovanile 1991; choral: Epithalamium 1969, Psalm 104 1973, The Temple of Solomon 1979, I Sing the Birth (Canticles for Christmas) 1985, I'll Make Me a World 1990; chamber music: String Quartets 1970 and 1990, Piano Trio 1977, Flute Trios 1985 and 1989, Clarinet Quintet 1988; Sonatas for Piano 1974, Flute 1989, Cello 1982, Viola 1982, Wind Quintet 1984, Bassoon Quintet 1991, Piano Quartet 1992, Piano Duets 1993, Cello Suite 1993; opera: Shadows in the Sun 1976; musical: Minotaur 1978; miscellaneous: anthems, partsongs music for TV, film and stage, complete archive in Hull Central Library; memb Cncl The Composers' Guild of GB (memb Exec Ctee 1969–73 and 1977–81, chm 1972–73); memb: Cncl Central Music Library Westminster 1970–91, SPNM Cncl 1974–81; memb Music Panels: Yorkshire Arts 1974–75, Lincs and Humberside Arts 1975–78; memb Music Bd CNAA 1974–77; Hon DMus Univ of Hull 1977; LRAM; *Books* Basic Tonal Harmony (1988), An Introduction to Counterpoint (1988); *Recreations* reading, playing chamber music; *Style*— Dr Anthony Hedges; ✉ Malt Shovel Cottage, 76 Walkergate, Beverley, East Yorkshire HU17 9ER (☎ 01482 860580)

HEDGES, Neil Francis; s of Kenneth Francis Chevalier, of Walmer, Kent, and Peggy, *née* Best; *b* 12 Dec 1956; *Educ* Watford Boys' GS, Univ of Sheffield (BA); *m* 19 Sept 1981, Katherine Anne, da of Trevor Noel Louis, of Bushey Heath, Herts; 2 da (Frances b 13 Feb 1986, Alexandra b 18 March 1989); *Career* md Valin Pollen Ltd 1988–90 (asst md 1985, account exec 1980), co-fndr and chief exec Fishburn Hedges (formerly Fishburn Hedges Boys Williams); *Recreations* music, cinema, walking, family; *Style*— Neil Hedges, Esq; ✉ Fishburn Hedges, 1 Northumberland Avenue, Trafalgar Square, London WC2N 5BW (☎ 0171 839 4321, fax 0171 839 2858)

HEDLEY, His Hon Judge; Mark; s of Peter Hedley, of Windsor, and Eve, *née* Morley; *b* 23 Aug 1946; *Educ* Framlingham Coll, Univ of Liverpool (LLB); *m* 14 April 1973, Erica Rosemary, da of late John Capel Britton, of Ashbourne; 3 s (Michael b 1975, Steven b 1981, Peter b 1982), 1 da (Anna b 1978); *Career* called to the Bar Gray's Inn 1969; recorder of Crown Ct 1988; circuit judge (Northern Circuit) 1992–; reader C of E; *Recreations* cricket, railways; *Style*— His Hon Judge Hedley; ✉ 55 Everton Road, Liverpool L6 2EH (☎ and fax 0151 260 6266)

HEDLEY, Dr Ronald Henderson; CB (1986); s of Henry Armstrong Hedley (d 1970), of Scarborough, Yorks, and Margaret, *née* Hopper (d 1950); *b* 2 Nov 1928; *Educ* Durham Johnston Sch, Univ of Durham (BSc, PhD), Univ of Newcastle Upon Tyne (DSc); *m* 28 Feb 1957, Valmai Mary, da of Roy Griffith (d 1971), of Taihape, NZ; 1 s (Iain b 18 June 1960); *Career* cmmnd RA 1953–55; Br Museum Natural History: sr and princ scientific offr, dep keeper of zoology 1955–71, dep dir 1971–76, dir 1976–88; nat res fell NZ 1960–61; author of tech papers on biology and cytology of protozoa; memb Cncl Fresh Water Biol Assoc 1972–76, tstee Percy Sladen Meml Fund 1972–77, pres Br Soc of Protozoa 1975–78, memb Cncl and govr Marine Biology Assoc 1976–92, vice pres Zoological Soc of London 1980–85 (hon sec 1977–80); memb Cncl: Royal Albert Hall 1982–88, Nat Tst 1986–88; FIBiol 1970; *Books* Foraminifera Vols 1–3 (1974–78), Atlas of Testate Amoebae (1980); *Recreations* horology, horticulture, humour; *Style*— Dr Ronald Hedley, CB; ✉ Pineways, Halley Rd, Broad Oak, Heathfield, E Sussex TN21 8TG

HEDLEY LEWIS, Vincent Richard; s of John Hedley Lewis (d 1976), of Birkholme Manor, Corby Glen, and Sheelagh Alice Valentine, *née* De Paravicini; *b* 24 May 1941; *Educ* Wellesley House, Harrow; *m* 17 June 1978, Penelope Ann, da of A C Hobson, MC; 3 da (Selena Priscilla b 27 Sept 1980, Melissa Sheelagh b 12 Sept 1982, Amanda Jane b 28 Jan 1985); *Career* articled to H R Crouch, Crouch Chapman & Co 1960–56, CA 1966; ptnr i/c Agribusiness Div Deloitte & Touche 1975–; memb: Lincolnshire Jt Devpt Ctee 1981–, Econ Advsy Panel Rural Devpt Cmmn 1989–, Country Landowners' Cncl 1994–; dir Peterborough Devpt Agency 1987–94, farmer of 700 acres Corby Glen Lincs; memb SCGB (Gold medallist), ran London Marathon 1989; *Books* Contract Farming (1990); *Recreations* cricket, skiing, tennis, golf, shooting; *Clubs* Farmers', Marylebone Cricket, Free Foresters Cricket, Luffenham Heath Golf, Lincolnshire; *Style*— Vincent Hedley Lewis, Esq; ✉ Birkholme Manor, Corby Glen, Grantham, Lincolnshire NG33 4LF (☎ 01476 550255); Deloitte & Touche, Leda House, Station Rd, Cambridge CB1 2RN (☎ 01223 460222, car 0836 759553)

HEDLEY-MILLER, Dame Mary Elizabeth; DCVO (1989), CB (1983); da of late J W Ashe; *b* 5 Sept 1923; *Educ* Queen's Sch Chester, St Hugh's Coll Oxford (MA); *m* 1950, Roger Latham Hedley-Miller; 1 s, 2 da (1 of whom Rosalind Hedley-Miller, *qv*); *Career* under sec HM Treasy 1973–83, ceremonial offr Cabinet Office 1983–88; *Style*— Dame Mary Hedley-Miller, DCVO, CB; ✉ 108 Higher Drive, Purley, Surrey

HEDLEY-MILLER, Rosalind; da of Roger Latham Hedley-Miller, and Dame Mary Elizabeth Hedley-Miller, DCVO, CB, *qv*; *b* 25 Nov 1954; *Educ* St Paul's Girls' Sch, St Hugh's Coll Oxford (MA), Harvard Univ; *Career* Investmt Dept J Henry Schroder Wagg & Co Ltd 1977–79; Kleinwort Benson Ltd: Corp Fin Dept 1979–, dir 1987–, jt head Corp Fin Dept 1994–96, gp dir 1996–; non-exec dir: Bejam Group plc 1987–88, TV-am plc 1990–93; memb Fin Ctee Oxford University Press 1995–; *Recreations* chamber music, singing, bridge, tennis, golf; *Style*— Miss Rosalind Hedley-Miller; ✉ 11 Manchuria Rd, London SW11 6AF; 20 Fenchurch St, London EC3P 3DB (☎ 0171 623 8000, fax 0171 623 5535)

HEDWORTH, (Alan) Toby; QC (1996); s of John William Swaddle Hedworth, and Margaret Ena, *née* Dodds; *b* 23 April 1952; *Educ* King's Sch Tynemouth, Royal GS Newcastle upon Tyne, St Catharine's Coll Cambridge (MA); *m* 12 Dec 1987, Kathleen Mary, da of Gordon Luke; 2 da (Anna Charlotte Pettinger b 2 July 1979, Alice Lucinda Marie b 6 May 1989); *Career* called to the Bar Inner Temple 1975, recorder 1995– (asst recorder 1991); memb Tyneside Ctee Northumberland & Newcastle Soc; memb Criminal Bar Assoc; *Recreations* Newcastle Utd FC, English Lake District, motoring, the built environment; *Style*— Toby Hedworth, Esq, QC; ✉ Trinity Chambers, 9–12 Trinity Chare, Quayside, Newcastle upon Tyne NE1 3DF (☎ 0191 232 1927, fax 0191 232 7975)

HEEKS, Alan David; s of Leonard Frank Heeks, and Peggy Eileen, *née* Lawless; *b* 20 Aug 1948; *Educ* Reading Sch, Balliol Coll Oxford, Harvard Business Sch (MBA); *m* 7 Aug 1971, Ruth Frances, da of Arthur Stone; 2 da (Elinor b 1977, Frances b 1979); *Career* brand mangr Procter & Gamble 1969–73, mangr mktg and new prods Hygena Kitchens 1976–78; dir mktg and sales: Chloride Standby Systems 1978–81, Redland Roof Tiles 1981–83; md: Redland Prismo 1983–86, Caradon Twyfords Ltd 1986–89 (exec dir Caradon plc); dir Nat Home Improvement Cncl 1986–90, md Working Vision Consultancy 1989–; fndr and tstee Wessex Fndn 1990–; FInstM; *Recreations* music, nature, philosophy; *Style*— Alan Heeks, Esq; ✉ Working Vision, Well House, 13 St Thomas Street, Winchester, Hants SO23 9HE (☎ 01962 852900, fax 01962 853900)

HEELIS, Robert McRae; s of Robert Loraine Heelis (d 1971), of Mickledore, West Bridgford, Notts, and Susannah Heelis; *b* 20 June 1930; *Educ* Repton, Nottingham Univ (LLB); *m* 1, 23 July 1955 (m dis 1965), Elizabeth Isobelle, *née* Radford; m 2, 20 Dec 1968, Patricia Margaret, *née* Fletcher; 2 s (Robert Alexander Piers b 2 Dec 1970, Toby Edward Loraine b 12 May 1973), 1 da (Sarah Caroline Nesbitt); *Career* Nat Serv 2 Lt 1953–55, Capt Leics and Derbys Yeo 1955–68; memb E Midland TA & VRA Cncl; slr 1953; local chm Rent Tbnls 1978–; cncllr Derby Borough Cncl 1967–70; dir Burton on Trent Hospitals Tst; Under Sheriff Derbyshire 1980–95; *Recreations* shooting, vintage car racing; *Clubs* County, Derby, Army & Navy, VSCC, BOC; *Style*— Robert Heelis, Esq; ✉ Shaw House, Melbourne, Derby DE73 1DJ (☎ 01332 863827)

HEFFER, Simon James; s of James Heffer (d 1971), of Woodham Ferrers, Essex, and Joyce Mary, *née* Clements; *b* 18 July 1960; *Educ* King Edward VI Sch Chelmsford, Corpus Christi Coll Cambridge (MA); *m* 31 July 1987, Diana Caroline, da of Sqdn Ldr P A Clee, of Marlow, Buckinghamshire; 2 s (James William Frederick b 3 Sept 1993, Charles Hubert John b 5 July 1996); *Career* med journalist 1983–85, freelance journalist 1985–86; Daily Telegraph: leader writer 1986–91, dep political corr 1987–88, political sketch writer 1988–91, political columnist 1990–91; dep ed: The Spectator 1991–94, The Daily Telegraph 1994–95; columnist: Evening Standard 1991–93, Daily Mail 1993–94 and 1995–; *Books* A Century of County Cricket (ed, 1990), A Tory Seer (jt ed with C Moore, 1989), Moral Desperado: a Life of Thomas Carlyle (1995); *Recreations* cricket, music, ecclesiology, bibliophily, my wife; *Clubs* Beefsteak, Essex County Cricket; *Style*— Simon Heffer, Esq; ✉ The Daily Mail, 2 Derry Street, London W8 5TT (☎ 0171 938 6000)

HEFFERNAN, John Francis; *b* 1 Sept 1927; *Educ* Gunnersbury GS, Univ of London (BCom); *m* 19 July 1952, Veronica, da of Dr John Laing; 2 da (Maureen, Catherine); *Career*

called to the Bar Inner Temple 1954; fin journalist Daily Express then Evening Standard, chm and princ shareholder City Press newspaper 1965–75, city ed United Provincial Newspapers Ltd 1965–93 (incl Yorkshire Post 1985–94); memb Cncl City Livery Club; Worshipful Co of Basketmakers: Liveryman 1965, Jr Warden 1995, Prime Warden 1996; memb Assoc of Regional City Eds (currently hon sec); *Style*— John Heffernan, Esq; ✉ 1 Fern Dene, top of Templewood, off Cleveland Road, Ealing, London W13 8AN (☎ 0181 997 6868)

HEFFERNAN, Patrick Benedict; s of Dr Daniel Anthony Heffernan, of Reading, Berks, and Margaret, *née* Donovan (d 1996); *b* 17 March 1948; *Educ* Wimbledon Coll, Jesus Coll Cambridge (MA); *m* 5 May 1973, Elizabeth, da of Robert Essery (d 1966), of Huddersfield and Melbourne; 2 s (Thomas b 1984, Rory Patrick b 1993), 1 da (Miranda b 1987); *Career* slr 1974, ptnr Clyde & Co 1988–; Liveryman Worshipful Company of Farriers (1994); *Recreations* Times crossword, sport, reading; *Style*— Patrick Heffernan, Esq; ✉ 3 Cholmeley Crescent, Highgate, London N6 5EZ; Clyde & Co, 51 Eastcheap, London EC3M 1JP (☎ 0171 623 1244, fax 0171 623 5427, telex 884886)

HEFFLER, Lady Tara Francesca; *née* Fitz-Clarence; er da of 7 Earl of Munster, and his 1 w, Louise Marguerite Diane Delvigne; descended from William, Duke of Clarence (later King William IV) and Dorothy Jordan; *b* 6 Aug 1952; *m* 1979, Ross Jean Heffler, s of Dr Leon Heffler (d 1983); 1 s (Leo Edward Michael b 1985); 1 da (Alexandra Louise b 1982); *Career* dir Sotheby Fine Art Auctioneers; memb Advsy Bd of Paintings in Hosp; *Recreations* family, travelling, the arts; *Style*— The Lady Tara Heffler; ✉ 146 Ramsden Rd, London SW12 8RE (☎ 0181 673 4017)

HEGGARTY, Hugh J; s of John Heggarty (d 1957), and Cecilia, *née* McGuire; *b* 28 Feb 1938; *Educ* St Aloysius Coll Glasgow, Univ of Glasgow (MB ChB); *m* 4 Jan 1964, Ann, da of late JS Hudson; 3 s (Kevin John b 6 Dec 1964, Paul Andrew b 15 July 1967, James Michael b 19 Sept 1970), 2 da (Marie Clare b 29 Feb 1972, Catherine Anne 15 April 1977); *Career* med registrar Univ of Zimbabwe 1964, res fell Iowa and Baltimore 1974, visiting prof Univ of Grenada W Indies 1987, currently conslt paediatrician York Dist Hosp; lectr: Canada, USA, Zimbabwe, Saudi Arabia, Iran, Libya, India; author of numerous med pubns on paediatric topics; memb: Br Paediatric Assoc, Life, SPUC; MRCP, MRCP (Glasgow), FRCPGlas, FRCPS; *Recreations* soccer, golf; *Clubs* York Golf; *Style*— Hugh Heggarty, Esq; ✉ 8 Hobgate, Acomb Rd, York YO2 4HF (☎ 01904 791240); York District Hospital, Wigginton Rd, York YO3 7HE (☎ 01904 31313)

HEGGS, Geoffrey Ellis; s of George Heggs, MBE (d 1972), of Guernsey, and Winifred Grace Ellis (d 1974); *b* 23 Oct 1928; *Educ* Elizabeth Coll Guernsey, Univ of London (LLB), Yale Univ (LLM); *m* 28 March 1953, (Renée Fanny) Madeleine, da of Emilio Calderan (d 1940), of London; 2 s (Christopher b 1957, Oliver b 1963), 1 da (Caroline b 1960); *Career* admitted slr 1952; asst sec to The Law Soc 1956–58, practised as a slr in London 1958–77, chm of Industl Tbnls 1977–, recorder Crown Ct SE Circuit 1983–, regnl chm of London North Region Industl Tbnls 1990–; Freeman City of London; memb: City of London Slrs' Co, Law Soc; *Recreations* military history, music, painting; *Style*— Geoffrey Heggs, Esq; ✉ 19–29 Woburn Place, London WC1H 0LU (☎ 0171 273 8579)

HEGINBOTHAM, Prof Wilfred Brooks; OBE (1978); s of Fred Heginbotham (d 1958), of Bardsley, Ashton-under-Lyne, Lancs, and Alice, *née* Brooks (d 1986); *b* 9 April 1924; *Educ* pt/t student (ONC-HNC), UMIST (BSc, MSc, PhD, DSc); *m* 1957, Marjorie, *née* Pixton; 3 da (Janet Anne b 9 Oct 1958, Judith Rose b 11 Dec 1960, Robina Alice b 29 Jan 1963); *Career* jr clerk 1938–40, apprentice wood pattern maker 1940–45, textile machine designer 1945–46, prodn engr Textile Machinery 1950–51, lectr in prodn engrg subjects UMIST 1951–58; Univ of Nottingham: sr lectr in prodn engrg Dept of Mechanical Engrg 1958–61, fndr BSc course in prodn engrg (first in UK) 1961, head Dept of Prodn Engrg and Prodn Mgmnt 1961–64, Cripps prof of prodn engrg 1964–79, dean Faculty of Applied Science 1968–1971, special prof 1982–85, emeritus prof of prodn engrg 1990–; DG Prodn Engrg Res Assoc 1979–84; visiting prof: Univ of Warwick 1979–89, Dept of Electrical and Electronic Engrg Queen's Univ Belfast 1986–89, Univ of Rhode Island Sept-Dec 1987; visiting res fell Univ of Birmingham 1989–, freelance author lectr and conslt 1984–89; fndr Wolfson Industl Automation Gp Univ of Nottingham 1965; developed with Dept of Electronic and Electrical Engrg Univ of Nottingham: first programmable assembly machine in Europe 1967, first potentially practical assembly robot with artificial vision 1971; Robot Inst of America Joseph Engelburger award 1983; Hon DSc Aston Univ, Hon DTech Univ of Eindhoven (Holland); British Robot Assoc: fndr chm 1977–81, pres 1981–84, hon memb 1984–; memb ACARD 1980–83, emeritus memb Int Coll for Prodn Engrg Res 1990– (memb 1965–89); CEng, FEng 1985, FIEE, MIMechE; *Books* Programmable Assembly (ed, 1984), Robot Grippers (ed with Dr D T Pham, 1986); *Recreations* gliding, remotely controlled model aircraft, microcomputing; *Clubs* University of Nottingham Gliding, Long Eaton Model Aircraft, Rolls Royce Model Aircraft, Ten Ton (1000 mph); *Style*— Prof Wilfred B Heginbotham, OBE, FEng; ✉ Bardsley Brow, 7 Paddocks View, Eaton Grange, Long Eaton, Notts NG10 3QF (☎ 0115 946 3250, e-mail FAMoth@aol.com)

HEHIR, Peter Noel; s of Valentine Hehir, MBE (d 1977), and Hazel Florence Hehir (d 1989); *b* 22 Dec 1944; *Educ* Paisley GS; *m* (m dis); 3 s (Alexander John b 23 May 1972, Stuart Michael b 11 Feb 1974, Christopher Valentine b 2 Dec 1981); *Career* journalist Paisley and Renfrewshire Gazette 1963–65, PR asst rising to PR exec then chief press offr Milk Marketing Bd 1965–68, news ed The Grocer 1969–73, gp md rising to gp chm Countrywide Porter Novelli (formerly Countrywide Communications) 1973–; former pres N Oxfordshire Sports Advsy Cncl, pres ICO (worldwide body for PR consultancy assocs), vice chm Public Relations Consultants Assoc; Oxfordshire Service to Sport Award 1987, Consultancy of the Year 1989–90, 1990–91 and 1994–95; memb Inst of Grocery Distribution 1973, MInstD 1975, FIPR 1987, FRSA 1993; *Recreations* reading, sport; *Clubs* Reform, West Bromwich Albion; *Style*— Peter Hehir, Esq; ✉ Countrywide Porter Novelli Ltd, 39 High Street, Banbury, Oxon OX16 8ET (☎ 01295 272288)

HEIGHTON, Martyn; *b* 28 Feb 1947; *Educ* City of Leicester Boys GS, St John's Coll Cambridge (MA), Univ of Leeds (Dip in Educn), Dip in Museum Studies; *Career* history teacher Harrogate GS 1969–72, asst educn offr then sr educn offr Oxfordshire Museum Education Service 1972–75, curator Museum of Oxford 1975–77, project dir Cogges Manor Museum 1977–78, project dir (latterly dir) Merseyside Maritime Museum 1978–85, dir of arts Bristol City Council 1985–91, dir of leisure servs City of Bristol 1991–; advsr Bristol Old Vic, visiting lectr Ironbridge Inst of Heritage Management; memb: Bd Bristol 97, Bd Business Sch Univ of the West of England, Bd Bristol Cultural Development Partnership, Leisure Advsy Ctee Assoc of District Councils, Ct Univ of Bristol; advsr Bristol 2000 Co Ltd; chm Public Art Ctee European Culture Cmmn, vocational bd memb Filton Coll; *Recreations* sailing, caravanning, horse riding, music, theatre and classic cars; *Style*— Martyn Heighton; ✉ Bristol City Council, Colston House, Colston Street, Bristol BS1 5AQ (☎ 0117 922 2634, fax 0117 922 3991)

HEILBRON, Hilary Nora Burstein; QC (1987); da of Dr Nathaniel Burstein, and Dame Rose Heilbron, DBE, *qv*; *b* 2 Jan 1949; *Educ* Huyton Coll, LMH Oxford (MA); *Career* called to the Bar: Gray's Inn 1971 (bencher 1995), NSW Aust 1996; dir City Disputes Panel, DTI inspr into the affairs of Blue Arrow plc 1989; chm: Jt Ctee on Civil Cts Gen Cncl of the Bar and Law Soc, London Common Law and Commercial Bar Assoc 1992–93; memb: Commercial Ct Ctee, Gen Cncl of the Bar 1991–, Advsy Cncl CEDR, Marshall Aid Commemoration Cmmn 1996–; *Style*— Hilary Heilbron, QC; ✉ Brick Court Chambers, 15/19 Devereux Court, London WC2R 3JJ (☎ 0171 583 0777, fax 0171 583 9401)

HEILBRON, Dame Rose; DBE (1974); da of late Max Heilbron, and Nellie Heilbron; *b* 19 Aug 1914; *Educ* Belvedere Sch, Univ of Liverpool (LLM); *m* 1945, Dr Nathaniel Burstein; 1 da (Hilary Heilbron, QC, *qv*); *Career* Lord Justice Holker scholar Gray's Inn 1936, called to the Bar Gray's Inn 1939, QC 1949, bencher 1968, recorder and hon rec of Burnley 1972–74, memb Bar Cncl 1973–74, joined Northern Circuit (ldr 1973–74), judge of the High Court of Justice Family Div 1974–88, chm Home Sec's Advsy Gp on Law of Rape 1975–, presiding judge Northern Circuit 1979–82; treas Gray's Inn 1985; hon fell: Lady Margaret Hall Oxford 1976, UMIST 1986; Hon LLD: Univ of Liverpool 1975, Univ of Warwick 1978, Univ of Manchester 1980, CNAA 1988; Hon Col WRAC(TA) (disbanded 1992); *Style*— Dame Rose Heilbron, DBE

HEIM, Paul Emil; CMG (1988); s of George Heim, of London, and Hedy, *née* Herz; *b* 23 May 1932; *Educ* Prince of Wales Sch Nairobi, Univ of Durham (LLB); *m* 31 Aug 1962, Elizabeth, da of Lt-Col Geoffrey Morris Allen, MBE (d 1962), of Karen, Kenya; 1 s (Mathew Jacques b 1968), 2 da ((Elizabeth) Andrea b 1964, (Susan) Dominique b 1965); *Career* called to the Bar Lincoln's Inn 1955 (bencher); magistrate, dep registrar and actg registrar HM Supreme Ct Kenya (HMOCS) 1955–65, admin and princ admin Cncl of Europe 1965–73, head div and dir Euro Parl 1973–82, registrar Euro Ct of Justice 1982–88; chm: Fin Servs Tribunal, VAT Tribunal; pres FIMBRA Appeal Tribunals; visiting prof Univ of Leicester; hon res fell Univ of Exeter; *Style*— Paul Heim, Esq, CMG; ✉ Wearne Wych, Picts Hill, Langport, Somerset TA10 9AA

HEINDORFF, Michael; *b* 1949; *Educ* Art Coll and Univ of Braunschweig, Royal Coll of Art London; *Career* artist; teacher Royal Coll of Art London 1980–; work in the collections of: Royal Coll of Art, Univ of Liverpool, V&A, Vicaria di Santiago de Chile, Herzog Anton Ulrich-Museum Braunschweig, State of Niedersachsen Germany, Arts Cncl of GB, The Br Cncl, Bank of America LA, Security Pacific Bank LA, The Museum of Modern Art NY, The Bank of Montreal London, Bradford Municipal Museum, Green Coll Oxford, Imperial War Museum, Nat Gallery Washington USA; awards: German Nat Scholarship Fndn scholar 1972–76, DAAD scholarship for London 1976–77, John Moore's Liverpool award 10 1976, State of Niedersachsen scholarship 1980, Schmidt-Rotluff prize 1981, Rome prize Villa Massimo 1981; fell Royal Coll of Art; *Solo Exhibitions* Galerie Axiom Cologne 1977, Bernard Jacobson Gallery London 1978, 1981–83, Bernard Jacobson Gallery NY 1983, Middendorf-Lane Washington 1983, Stadia Graphics Sydney 1983, Bernard Jacobson Gallery LA 1981, 1982 and 1984, Jacobson/Hochman Gallery NY 1981 and 1982, Mathildenhoehe Darmstadt Germany 1983, Villa Massimo Rome 1984, Bernard Jacobson Gallery NY and London 1985–87, Northern Centre for Contemporary Art Sunderland 1987, Royal Coll of Art 1995; *Group Exhibitions* incl: John Moore's Liverpool Exhibition 1976, Air Gallery 1977, Royal Coll of Art London (Annual Exhibitions) 1977, Whitechapel Art Gallery London 1979, Serpentine Gallery London (Summer show 1) 1980, Anne Berthand Gallery London 1981, Herzog Anton Ulrich-Museum Braunschweig 1981, Bradford Print Biennale 1982, Paton Gallery London (Alternative Tate) 1982, Ashmolean Museum Oxford (Innovations in Contemporary Printmaking) 1982, Third Biennale of European Graphic Art Baden-Baden 1983, Bruecke Museum Berlin 1984, Museum of Modern Art NY 1984, Univ of Maryland USA 1985, Bank of America San Francisco 1985, V&A Museum London 1986, Sunderland Arts Centre & Laing Art Gallery Newcastle 1987, Royal Acad of Art London 1988, Royal Coll of Art 150th Anniversary Show 1988, Imperial War Museum London (On Commission) 1989, Nat Gallery Washington USA 1989, Bernard Jacobson Gallery London 1990; *Clubs* Chelsea Arts (life memb); *Style*— Michael Heindorff, Esq

HEISER, Sir Terence Michael (Terry); GCB (1992, KCB 1987, CB 1984); s of David and Daisy Heiser; *b* 24 May 1932; *Educ* Windsor Co Boys' Sch Berks, Birkbeck Coll London (BA); *m* 1957, Kathleen Mary Waddle; 1 s, 2 da; *Career* served RAF 1950–52; joined Civil Serv 1949, served with Colonial Office, Miny of Works, Miny of Housing and Local Govt; princ private sec to Sec of State for the Environment 1975–76, under sec Housing Directory 1976–79, under sec Local Govt Fin Directorate 1979–81, perm sec DOE 1985–92 (dep sec 1981–85); dir: Abbey National plc 1992–, J Sainsbury plc 1992–, Wessex Water plc 1993–, McDonnell Information Systems Group until 1996; chm BBC Advsy Cncl 1992–, memb Bd Personal Investment Authy 1994–, tstee Victoria and Albert Museum 1993–, memb Exec Ctee Nat Tst 1993–; govr and fell Birkbeck Coll London; Freeman City of London 1990; Hon DLitt Univ of Bradford 1988; *Clubs* Garrick; *Style*— Sir Terry Heiser, GCB

HELAL, Basil; s of Ibrahim Helal, CBE (d 1972), of Cairo, and Helena, *née* Sommerville (d 1942); *b* 28 Oct 1927; *Educ* English Sch Cairo, Univ of London (MB BS), Univ of Liverpool (MCh); *m* 1, 10 Oct 1954, Stella, *née* Feldman (d 1987); 1 s (Adam b 1965), 2 da (Dina b 1956, Manda b 1958); m 2, 30 Jan 1988, Susan Carolyn, *née* Livett; 2 s (Matthew b 1974, Simon b 1978); *Career* sr registrar St George's Hosp London 1962–65; orthopaedic conslt: London Hosp 1965–88, Royal Nat Orthopaedic Hosp and Enfield Gp of Hosps 1965–88; now emeritus hon conslt; orthopaedic advsr Br Olympic Assoc 1972–, pres Coll Internationale du Chirurgie Medecin du Pied 1996–, memb Cncl Br Orthopaedic Assoc 1980–82, co fndr Rheumatoid Arthritis Surgical Soc 1983 (former pres), first pres Egyptian Med Soc UK 1984; pres: Br Orthopaedic Foot Surgery Soc 1983 (fndr 1975), Br Soc for Surgery of the Hand 1985, Br Assoc of Sport and Med 1987–, Orthopaedic Div RSM 1991–92, Hunterian Soc 1991–92; fndr and chm ed bd The Foot - Jl of Foot Science (publ Churchill Livingstone); former vice pres and chm BASM; memb: BMA 1951, BOA 1957, BSSH; FRCS, FRCSEd; *Books* Surgical Repair and Reconstruction in Rheumatoid Disease (1980), Sports Injuries (1986), The Foot (1988); *Recreations* squash, scuba diving, golf, swimming; *Clubs* Savage, Blizzard; *Style*— Basil Helal, Esq; ✉ The Corner House, 23 St Catharines Rd, Broxbourne, Herts EN10 7LD (☎ 01992 466688); Wellington Hospital, Wellington Place, London NW8 9LE (☎ and fax 01992 477791, car 0976 727595)

HELE, (James) Warwick; CBE (1986); s of John Warwick Hele (Capt Border Regt, d 1954), of Cumbria, and Elizabeth, *née* Gibb (d 1966); *b* 24 July 1926; *Educ* Sedbergh, Hertford Coll Oxford, Trinity Hall Cambridge (MA); *m* 3 April 1948, Audrey, da of Thomas Davenport Whalley (d 1969), of Bournemouth; 4 da (Elizabeth Ann b 1949, Jane Mary (twin) b 1949, Sarah Catherine b 1956, Rachel Shirley b 1964); *Career* Royal Armoured Corps 1944–48, Lt 5 Royal Inniskilling Dragoon Guards 1946–48; schoolmaster King's Coll Sch Wimbledon 1951–55; Rugby Sch: schoolmaster 1955–73, housemaster Kilbracken 1965–73, second master 1970–73; high master St Paul's Sch 1973–86; chm: Headmasters' Conf 1982 (memb 1973–86), Advsy Ctee Ind Schs Jt Cncl 1983–89, Sherborne Sch 1989–96, Westminster Centre for Educn 1992–, History Ctees Secondary Examinations Cncl 1986–88, Combined Trusts Scholarship Trust 1986–, Clouds House East Knoyle Wilts 1992–; govr: Port Regis Sch Shaftesbury 1986–, Rossall Sch 1986–89, Uppingham Sch 1986–93, Sherborne Sch 1986–96; memb Exec Ctee GBA 1988–97; conslt Depart of Education and Science (City Technol Colls) 1986–89, non-exec dir Dorset Family Health Serv Authy 1990–92; *Recreations* gardening, hill-walking; *Clubs* East India and Public Schools; *Style*— Warwick Hele, Esq, CBE; ✉ Hillside, Hawkesdene Lane, Shaftesbury, Dorset SP7 8EX (☎ 01747 854205)

HELEY, Richard William; s of Wilfred Charles Heley, of Shaw, Newbury, Berks, and Joyce, *née* Chalker; *b* 9 Oct 1948; *Educ* Forest Sch, Univ of Wales (BA), Univ of Sussex; *m* 7 Sept 1974, Barbara Alessandra, da of Alexander Kirk Kidd, of Banbury Rd, Oxford; 1 s (Adam Frederick Peter b 1983), 1 da (Lara Alessandra Cornelia Constantina b 1985); *Career* Int Fin Dept Phillips & Drew 1969–74, dir Corporate Fin Dept Hill Samuel &

Co Ltd 1974–86, head of corporate fin Barclays de Zoete Wedd Ltd 1986–89, md UK corp fin Citibank NA 1989–90, vice chm Hill Samuel Bank Ltd 1990–95, currently dir Charterhouse Bank Limited; *Books* Profit Forecasting (1981); *Recreations* riding; *Style—* Richard Heley, Esq; ✉ c/o Charterhouse Bank Limited, 1 Paternoster Row, St Paul's, London EC4M 7DH (☎ 0171 248 4000, fax 0171 248 6522)

HELLAWELL, Keith; QPM (1990); s of Douglas Hellawell (d 1986), and Ada Alice, *née* Battye; *b* 18 May 1942; *Educ* Kirkburton Secdy Modern Sch, Dewsbury Tech Coll, Barnsley Col of Mining, Univ of London (LLB 1972), Cranfield Inst of Technol (MSc 1982); *m* 1963, Brenda, da of late Percy Hey; 2 da (Samantha Louise b 26 Sept 1965, Alexandra Jane b 18 May 1967), 1 s (Charles Justin Spencer b 17 May 1970); *Career* Huddersfield Borough Police: joined 1962, Sgt 1965, Inspr 1967; W Yorks Police (later W Yorks Metropolitan Police): joined 1968, Chief Inspr 1972, Supt 1975, Chief Supt 1979, Asst Chief Constable 1983; Dep Chief Constable Humberside 1985–90, Chief Constable Cleveland Constabulary 1990–93, Chief Constable W Yorks Police 1993–; memb Bd of Tstees NSPCC, memb Bd Northern Counties Housing Assoc; SBStJ; *Recreations* reading, design, gardening, sport; *Style—* Keith Hellawell, Esq, QPM; ✉ Chief Constable, West Yorkshire Police, PO Box 9, Wakefield, West Yorkshire WF1 3QP (☎ 01924 292002, fax 01924 292180)

HELLER, Lawrance (Laurie); *b* 14 April 1934; *Educ* Battersea GS, Sidney Sussex Coll Cambridge (scholar, MA); *m* Lilian Patricia Heller; 1 da (Charlotte b 9 April 1964); *Career* articled Silkin & Silkin 1956–59, jr ptnr Titmuss Sainer & Webb 1962–63 (asst slr 1959–62), ptnr Leighton & Co 1964–70, a fndr and sr ptnr Berwin Leighton 1970–; *Books* Practical Commercial Precedents (contrib, 1987), Commercial Property Development Precedents (gen ed and maj contrib, 1993); *Recreations* teaching law, writing articles, skiing, gardening; *Style—* Laurie Heller, Esq; ✉ Berwin Leighton, Adelaide House, London Bridge, London EC4R 9HA (☎ 0171 623 3144, fax 0171 623 4416)

HELLER, Michael Aron; s of Simon Heller (d 1989), of Harrogate, Yorks, and Nettie, *née* Gordon; *b* 15 July 1936; *Educ* Harrogate GS, St Catharine's Coll Cambridge (MA); *m* 1965, Morven, da of Dr Julius Livingstone; 2 s (John b 1966, Andrew b 1968), 1 da (Nicola b 1981); *Career* chm: London & Associated Properties plc, Bisichi Mining plc, Electronic Data Processing plc; dep chm Centre for Policy Studies; FCA; *Recreations* opera, walking, collecting modern British paintings; *Clubs* RAC; *Style—* Michael Heller, Esq; ✉ London & Associated Properties plc, 8–10 New Fetter Lane, London EC4A 1NQ (☎ 0171 415 5000)

HELLER, Robert Gordon Barry; s of late Norman Joseph Heller, and Helen, *née* Flatto; *b* 10 June 1932; *Educ* Christ's Hosp, Jesus Coll Cambridge (BA); *m* 8 Jan 1955, Lois Ruth, da of Michael Malnick; 1 s (Matthew Jonathan b 1960), 2 da (Jane Charlotte b 1962, Kate Elizabeth b 1965); *partner* Angela Mary Flowers, *qv*; 1 da (Rachel Pearl b 1973); *Career* 2 Lt RASC 1950–52; industl corr (later diary ed and US corr) Financial Times 1955–63, business ed Observer 1963–65, ed (later ed-in-chief and editorial dir) Management Today 1965–87, editorial dir Haymarket Publishing 1978–85; chm: Graduate Gp, Heller Arts; dir: Angela Flowers Gallery plc 1970–, Sterling Publishing Group plc 1985–, Rebus Group plc 1996–; *Books* Superman, Can you Trust your Bank? (with Norris Willatt), The European Revenge (with Norris Willatt), The Naked Investor, The Common Millionaire, The Once and Future Manager, The Business of Winning, The Business of Success, The Naked Market, The Pocket Manager, The New Naked Manager, The State of Industry, The Supermanagers, The Supermarketers, The Age of the Common Millionaire, Unique Success Proposition, The Decision Makers, The Best of Robert Heller, Culture Shock, The Super Chiefs, The Quality Makers, The Fate of IBM, The Leadership Imperative, The Naked Manager for the 90s, The Way to Win (with Will Carling); *Recreations* art, food and wine, books, music, exercise; *Style—* Mr Robert Heller; ✉ Sterling Publishing Group plc, 86/88 Edgware Rd, London W2 2YW (☎ 0171 258 0066)

HELLICAR, Michael William; s of Jonathan Ernest Hellicar (d 1991), of London, and Eileen May, *née* Williams (d 1983); *b* 3 April 1941; *m* 1962, June Betty, da of Charles Edward Pitcher; 3 da (Nicola Jane b 24 May 1965, Justine Louise b 28 July 1966, Charlotte Laura b 18 April 1979); *Career* journalist; apprentice reporter South London Observer 1956–60, asst news ed and feature writer New Musical Express 1960–63, news ed Rave Magazine 1963–64, feature writer Daily Sketch 1964–67; Daily Mirror: feature and leader writer 1967–72, ed Inside Page 1972–73, features ed 1973–76, sr writer 1976–81; asst ed Daily Star 1989– (chief feature writer 1982–89); chief critic: World's Greatest Restaurants Monthly 1991–, First Class Air Travel Monthly 1993–; *Recreations* causing trouble, whingeing; *Style—* Michael Hellicar, Esq; ✉ 13 Charlecote Grove, London SE26 4BW (☎ 0181 699 8289); Daily Star, Express Newspapers plc, Ludgate House, 245 Blackfriars Rd, London SE1 9UX (☎ 0171 928 8000, fax 0171 922 7962)

HELLIKER, Adam Andrew Alexander; s of Maurice William Helliker, DFC, AFC (d 1984), and Jane Olivia, *née* Blunt; *b* 13 Sept 1958; *Educ* King's Sch Bruton, Somerset Coll of Arts and Technol; *Career* reporter: Western Times Co Ltd 1978–81, Daily Mail 1981–86; dep diary ed: Daily Mail 1986–, Mail on Sunday 1988–; contrib to several nat magazines; vice chm London Diarists' Club; Freeman: City of London 1989, Worshipful Co of Wheelwrights 1989; FRGS, FRSA, memb Royal Soc of Lit; *Books* The Debrett Season (ed, 1981), The English Season (contrib, 1988); *Recreations* shooting, collecting leather luggage; *Clubs* Carlton, St James's, Mosimann's, Mortons, RAC, Hurlingham; *Style—* Adam Helliker, Esq; ✉ 27 Cranbury Road, London SW6 2NS (☎ 0171 384 1367); Coombe Hill House, Keinton Mandeville, Somerset; Daily Mail, Northcliffe House, 2 Derry St, London W8 5TT (☎ 0171 938 6154, fax 0171 937 3957)

HELLINGA, Dr Lotte; da of Arie Querido (d 1983), and Catharina Geertruida, *née* Nagtegaal (d 1976); *b* 9 Sept 1932; *Educ* Barlaeus Gymnasium Amsterdam, Univ of Amsterdam (PhD); *m* Wytze Hellinga (d 1985); 1 s (Homme Wytzes b 1960); *Career* trainee Dept of Printed Books British Library 1959–60, res Netherlands Organisation for Pure Research 1965–67, sr lectr Univ of Amsterdam 1970–76 (lectr 1967–70), dep keeper British Library 1986–95 (asst keeper 1976–86); sec Consortium of European Research Libraries 1994–, memb Cncl Bibliographical Soc 1978–81 and 1990–93 (memb 1978–); Menno Hertzberger prize 1968, Int League of Antiquarian Bookdealers prize 1970, Gutenberg prize Gutenberg Gesellschaft and City of Mainz 1989; correspondent Royal Netherlands Acad 1986, FBA 1990 (memb Cncl 1991–94); *Books* The Fifteenth-Century Printing Types of the Low Countries (with W Hellinga, 1966), Henry Bradshaw's Correspondence (jtly, 1968, 2 edn 1978), Caxton in Focus (1982); numerous contribs to scholarly collections and periodicals; *Style—* Dr Lotte Hellinga, FBA; ✉ The British Library, Great Russell Street, London WC1B 3DG (☎ 0171 412 7581, fax 0171 412 7762)

HELLINGS, Brian Aliol; s of Robert Aliol Hellings (d 1984), of Falmouth, Cornwall, and Phyllis Selena, *née* Ferris (d 1987); *b* 12 Jan 1936; *Educ* Truro Cathedral Sch; *m* 23 May 1959, Ann, da of Edward Robert Rule (d 1961); 3 s (Mark Robert Aliol b 6 Oct 1962, James Edward Aliol b 16 May 1970, Charles Matthew Aliol b 9 Sept 1978), 3 da (Caroline Gail b 21 June 1961, Joanne Elizabeth b 24 April 1964, Sarah Victoria b 9 Sept 1978); *Career* articled Lodge & Winter 1953–59, audit clerk Deloitte Plender Griffiths & Co 1959–61, dir PB Cow & Co Ltd 1967–68 (fin comptroller and co sec 1961–68); sr dir responsible for fin Hanson plc 1988– (fin comptroller 1968, fin dir 1973); FCA 1959; *Recreations* fishing, gardening, reading; *Style—* Brian Hellings, Esq; ✉ 2 Third Street, Rumson, NJ, USA (☎ 00 1 908 549 7058, fax 00 1 908 549 7058, telex 132222, car tel 00 1 908 715 9742)

HELLMAN, Louis Mario; MBE (1993); s of late Mario Biselli, and Monalda, *née* Caraffi; *b* 19 March 1936; *Educ* William Ellis GS, UCL, Ecole des Beaux-Arts Paris (BArch); *m*, Maria Anna, da of late Sabin Popkiewicz; 1 da (Katherine Monalda b 31 Aug 1963), 1 s (Nicholas Sabin b 5 Sept 1964); *Career* architect; work incl: Spastics Soc (now Scope), GLC, YRM; cartoonist Architects Jl 1967–92, Building Design 1992–; cartoons published in: Observer, Sunday Times, Guardian, Architectural Review, Punch, Private Eye, Spectator; lectr: UK, USA, Australia; portrait painter; Exhibitions incl: AA 1979, Interbuild 1991, RIBA 1989–; subject of biography - Seven Ages of the Architect: The Very Best of Louis Hellman 1967–92 (1991); memb: Assoc of Architect Artists, ARCUK; *Books* A Is for Architect (1974), All Hellman Breaks Loose (1980), Architecture for Beginners (1986); author of numerous articles in architectural magazines; *Recreations* music, cinema, travel, art; *Style—* Louis Hellman, Esq, MBE

HELLNER, Rabbi Dr Frank; s of Louis B Hellner (d 1961), of Philadelphia, Pa, and Mildred, *née* Rosen (d 1994); *b* 1 Jan 1935; *Educ* Yeshiva Univ NY (BA), Hebrew Teachers' Coll NY, Inst for Leaders Jerusalem, Hebrew Union Coll NY (MA, BHL, DD); *m* 1, 1964 (m dis 1986), Faye Lynne, da of Prof Dr Maxwell Kettner; 3 da (Marni Lynne b 30 April 1965, Rachel Deborah b 8 July 1968, Katherine Rebecca b 29 May 1970); m 2, 28 July 1988, Valerie Boyd; 2 step s (Elliot Simon, Jonathan Daniel), 1 step da (Antonia Victoria); *Career* co-ordinator and supr Israel Youth Prog Jerusalem 1960–61, ordained rabbi 1964; rabbi: Temple Shalom Monticello NY 1964–66, Finchley Progressive Synagogue London 1966–; ed ULPS News London 1978–86, chm Rabbinic Conf 1969–71, exec Barnet Community Rels Cncl 1980–84; currently: govr Akiva Sch, hon vice pres Finchley Cncl of Christians and Jews, memb Leo Baeck Coll Co, pt/t lectr Birkbeck Coll Univ of London and Leo Baeck Coll; chaplain to the Mayor of London Borough of Barnet 1993–94; memb Central Conf of American Rabbis 1964, Rabbinic Conf of Union of Liberal and Progressive Synagogues 1966; *Books* I Promise I Will Try Not To Kick My Sister (1977); articles in Bible Today, Jewish Chronicle, The Times, etc; *Style—* Rabbi Dr Frank Hellner; ✉ Finchley Progressive Synagogue, 54 Hutton Grove, London N12 8DR (☎ 0181 446 4063, fax 0181 446 9599)

HELLYER, Robert Charles Orlando; s of Graham Hellyer, of North Humberside, and Lois Anness, *née* Anderton; *b* 8 Sept 1952; *Educ* Shrewsbury, Trinity Coll Dublin (BBS); *m* 14 June 1980, Elizabeth Ann, da of William Alan Rutherford; 3 da (Georgina b 9 April 1983, Chloë b 25 March 1987, Alexandra b 10 March 1989); *Career* CA 1980; KPMG (formerly Peat Marwick Mitchell) 1976–82, co sec Charterhall plc 1982–86, fin dir J O Hambro & Co Ltd 1986–; *Recreations* shooting, fishing; *Style—* Robert Hellyer, Esq; ✉ J O Hambro & Co Ltd, 10 Park Place, London SW1A 1LP (☎ 0171 222 2020, fax 0171 222 1823)

HELM, Michael Thomas; s of Rev Thomas Helm (d 1978), of Tunbridge Wells, and Kathleen, *née* Hall (d 1976); *b* 17 May 1939; *Educ* Tonbridge; *m* 17 Oct 1973, Christine Jennifer, da of Stanley Alfred Henry Slattery, of Chislehurst, Kent; 1 s (Sebastian b 1974), 1 da (Alexandra b 1976); *Career* co sec Nitrate Corporation of Chile Ltd 1969–78; fin dir: Croom-Helm Ltd 1978–86, WH Allen and Co Plc 1986–90; fin controller Granta Publications Ltd 1990; fin sec Glass & Glazing Federation 1991; chm Woodlands Art Gallery Ltd 1996; Lord of the Manor of Fitzjohns Co of Suffolk; FCA 1963; *Recreations* Napoleonic studies, opera, art; *Style—* Michael Helm, Esq

HELMS, Prof Peter Joseph; s of Joseph Helms (d 1966), and Eileen Dorothea, *née* Macfarlane, of Birmingham; *b* 26 June 1947; *Educ* Wimbledon Coll, Royal Free Hosp Sch of Med London (MB BS), PhD (London); *m* 7 Nov 1970, Kathleen Mary, da of Reginald Woodward; 3 da (Rachel Anne b 19 March 1973, Joanna Catherine b 23 April 1974, Laura Jane b 1 Oct 1980), 1 s (Matthew John b 12 May 1977); *Career* house offr posts Royal Free Hosp, London Hosp, Royal Brompton Hosp, Hammersmith Hosp and Hosp for Sick Children Great Ormond St 1973–76, lectr Charing Cross Hosp 1977–78, research fell Inst of Child Health and Cardiothoracic Inst Univ of London 1978–83, sr lectr Inst of Child Health London 1983–92, prof of child health and head of dept Univ of Aberdeen 1992–; Donald Patterson Prize Br Paediatric Assoc 1983; FRCP 1991, FRCPEd 1992; *Recreations* hill walking, music; *Style—* Prof Peter Helms; ✉ Department of Child Health, University of Aberdeen, Foresterhill, Aberdeen AB9 2ZD (☎ 01224 404461, fax 01224 663658)

HELSBY, Richard John Stephens (Rick); s of John Michael Helsby (d 1972), and Margaret Stella, *née* Andrews; *b* 10 Jan 1949; *Educ* Magdalen Coll Sch Oxford, Warwick Univ (BA), Oxford Univ (Dip Ed); *children* 4 s (James b 1968, Nathan b 1972, William b 1986, Joseph 1993); *Career* HM inspr of Taxes Oxford 1972–78, sr inspr of Taxes Inland Revenue Enquiry Branch 1978–84, sr tax mangr Deloitte Haskins & Sells 1984–87, nat ptnr Fraud and Investigations Gp Coopers & Lybrand 1987–; *Books* Trouble with the Taxman (1985), Offshore Survival (with Jim McMahon, Bernard McCarthy 1988); *Recreations* squash, football, theatre, cinema, snooker; *Style—* Rick Helsby, Esq; ✉ Coopers & Lybrand, Plumtree Court, London EC4A 4HT (☎ 0171 583 5000)

HELVIN, Marie; da of Hugh Lee Helvin, of Honolulu, Hawaii, USA, and Linda S Helvin; *b* 13 Aug 1952; *m* 1975 (m dis 1985), David Bailey, *qv*; *Career* model; Vogue 12 covers; modelled for: (designers) St Laurent, Armani, Valentino, Chanel, Calvin Klein, (photographers) Lartique, Helmut Newton, David Bailey; presenter Frocks on the Box (ITV series); appeared in the film The Children (dir Tony Palmer 1990); fashion designer (own label collections of body and swimwear); author of articles for: The Independent, The Sunday Telegraph, Time Out; dep chm Aids Crisis Tst; patron: Foster Parents Plan, Frontliners, Zoo Check; *Books* Catwalk - The Art of Model Style (1985), Body Pure - Your Complete Detox Programme for Health and Beauty (1995); *Fitness Video* Body and Soul (1994); *Style—* Miss Marie Helvin; ✉ Storm, 5 Jubilee Place, London SW3 3TD (fax 0171 376 5146)

HELY HUTCHINSON, Hon Timothy Mark; 2 s of 8 Earl of Donoughmore, *qv*; *b* 26 Oct 1953; *Educ* Eton, Oxford; *Career* md: Macdonald & Co (Publishers) Ltd 1982–86, Headline Book Publishing PLC 1986–93; gp chief exec Hodder Headline PLC 1993–; *Clubs* Groucho; *Style—* The Hon Timothy Hely Hutchinson; ✉ 25 Royal Crescent, Holland Park, London W11 4SN

HEMANS, HE Simon Nicholas Peter; CMG (1992), CVO (1983); s of Brig Peter Rupert Hemans, CBE (d 1993), and Margaret Estelle, *née* Melsome; *b* 19 Sept 1940; *Educ* Sherborne, LSE (BSc); *m* 1970, Ursula Martha, da of Herr Werner Naef (d 1972); 3 s (Alexander b 1967, Oliver b 1974, Anthony (twin) b 1974), 1 da (Jennifer b 1972); *Career* HM Dip Sev: FO 1964, Br Embassy Moscow 1966–68, dep cmmr Anguilla 1969, FCO 1969–71, UK Mission to UN NY 1971–75, Br Embassy Budapest 1975–79, asst head Southern African Dept FCO 1979–81, dep high cmmr Nairobi 1981–84, cnsllr and head of chancery Moscow 1985–87, appt head of Soviet Dept FCO 1987–90, asst under sec of state (Africa) FCO 1990–92; ambass: Kiev 1992–95, Nairobi 1995–; *Recreations* travel, ballet, opera; *Style—* HE Mr Simon Hemans, CMG, CVO; ✉ c/o FCO (Nairobi), King Charles St, London SW1A 2AH

HEMERY, David Peter; MBE (1969); s of Peter Ronald Bentley Hemery, of London, and Eileen Beatrice, *née* Price (d 1985); *b* 18 July 1944; *Educ* Endsleigh Sch Colchester, Thayer Acad USA, Boston Univ USA (BSc, DEd) St Catherine's Coll Oxford (CertEd), Harvard (MEd); *m* 31 July 1981, Vivian Mary, da of Alan Patrick William Bruford; 2 s (Adrian David b 6 Aug 1982, Peter Robert b 28 Oct 1984); *Career* former international athlete; achievements incl: Gold medal 120 yards high hurdles Cwlth Games 1966, Gold medal 400m hurdles Olympic Games 1968, American Nat Collegiate 400m hurdles champion 1968, Silver medal 110m high hurdles Euro Championships 1969, Gold medal 110m high hurdles World Student Games 1970, Gold medal 110m high hurdles Cwlth Games 1970, Silver medal 4 x 400m relay Olympic Games 1972, Bronze medal 400m hurdles Olympic Games 1972; records: UK indoor 60 yards high hurdles 1966, Euro indoor 600 yards 1966, UK 120 yards high hurdles 1966 and 1969, UK 400m hurdles 1968, Olympic and world 400m hurdles 1968, world 300m hurdles 1972; winner Br Superstars 1973 and 1976, winner Br Past Masters Superstars 1983; gen clerk National Westminster Bank London 1962–63, computer and settlement clerk National Shawmut Bank Boston 1963–64, res Rank Audio-Visual London 1968–69, teacher and housemaster Millfield Sch 1970–71 and 1972–73, dir Sobell Sports Centre 1974–75, head track coach and lectr Boston Univ 1976–83, coach educn, team building and mgmnt training courses 1984–, dir Performance Consultants 1992–; chm Int Athletics Club 1973–75; memb: Grants Ctee Sports Aid Fndn 1986–90, Educn Ctee BOA 1986–91; govr St Francis Sch 1990– (chm 1993–); *Books* Another Hurdle (autobiography, 1976), Sporting Excellence (1986, 2 edn 1991), Athletic in Action (1988), Winning Without Drugs (1990); *Recreations* sport, family, new age developments; *Style*— David Hemery, Esq, MBE; ✉ White Acre, Fyfield, Marlborough, Wiltshire SN8 1PX (☎ 01672 861645, fax 01672 861135)

HEMINGFORD, 3 Baron (UK 1943), of Watford, Co Hertford; (Dennis) Nicholas Herbert; s of 2 Baron Hemingford (d 1982), and Elizabeth McClare, *née* Clark (d 1979); *b* 25 July 1934; *Educ* Oundle, Clare Coll Cambridge (MA); *m* 8 Nov 1958, Jennifer Mary Toresen, DL (Cambs 1996), o da of Frederick William Bailey (d 1986), of Harrogate; 1 s (Hon Christopher Dennis Charles b 1973), 3 da (Hon Elizabeth Frances Toresen (Hon Mrs Witt) b 1963, Hon Caroline Mary Louise b 1964, Hon Alice Christine Emma (Hon Mrs McManus) b 1968); *Heir* s, Hon Christopher Dennis Charles Herbert b 1973; *Career* known professionally as Nicholas Herbert; journalist Reuters Ltd London and Washington DC 1956–61; joined The Times 1961: asst Washington correspondent 1961–65, Middle East correspondent 1965–69, dep features ed 1969–70; ed Cambridge Evening News 1970–74, dep chief exec Westminster Press 1992–95 (editorial dir 1974–92), pres Guild of Br Newspaper Editors 1980–81 (vice pres 1979–80); hon sec Assoc of British Editors 1985–94; chm East Anglia Regnl Ctee Nat Tst 1990–; pres Huntingdonshire Family History Soc 1985; dir and tstee Arts 2000 East 1996–; Liveryman Worshipful Co of Grocers 1975–; FRSA; *Recreations* genealogy, Victorian military history, destructive gardening; *Clubs* Commonwealth Trust, City Livery; *Style*— The Rt Hon the Lord Hemingford; ✉ The Old Rectory, Hemingford Abbots, Huntingdon, Cambs PE18 9AN (☎ 01480 466234, fax 01480 380275)

HEMINGWAY, Michael Patrick; s of John Allman Hemingway, and Helen Bridget Barbara, *née* Prowse; *b* 28 Aug 1951; *Educ* Oundle; *m* 17 Dec 1977, Annamaria, da of John David Fitness; 2 s (Jay Matthew John Allman b 15 May 1980, Toby Michael Christopher Allman b 28 May 1983); *Career* account mangr Leo Burnett advtg agency 1976 (joined Invoice Control Dept 1975), account dir Michael Bungey and Partners 1977–82, Collett Dickenson Pearce 1982–85; bd dir: Boase Massimi Pollitt 1985–88, DDB Needham 1989; Grey Communications Group: joined as bd dir 1989, vice chm Grey London 1991, subsequently sr vice pres Grey Europe, currently exec vice pres Grey International; *Recreations* watching sport, travel, popular music; *Clubs* Tramp; *Style*— Michael Hemingway, Esq; ✉ Grey International, Wells Point, 79 Wells Street, London W1P 3RE (☎ 0171 453 7777)

HEMINGWAY, Wayne Andrew; s of Chief Billy Two Rivers (chief of Khanawake Tribe (Mohawk) Quebec), and Maureen, *née* Hemingway; *b* 19 Jan 1961; *Educ* Queen Elizabeth's GS Blackburn, UCL (BSC); *m* Gerardine Mary, da of Ken Astin; 1 s (Jack b 22 June 1986), 2 da (Tilly b 23 July 1987, Corey b Aug 1990); *Career* fashion designer; Red or Dead: founded as design co retailing from Camden Market Stall 1982, entered jt venture with Pentland Gp Plc 1996, currently chm and head of design, winners of Street Style Categroy British Fashion Awards 1995 and 1996; md Dr Martens Clothing 1992–94; regular speaker to fashion colls and footwear assocs on shoe, clothing and interior design; res presenter fashion section Big Breakfast (Channel 4); work shown in numerous exhibitions of Br design incl: Boymans Museum Rotterdam, Orange County California, V & A London; second place Young Business Person of the Year 1990; *Recreations* football, cricket, tennis; *Style*— Wayne Hemingway, Esq; ✉ Red or Dead, Building 201, Courtenay Road, GEC East Lane Estate, Wembley, Middlesex HA9 7PP (☎ 0181 904 4774/1133, fax 0181 908 4659)

HEMMING, Dr John Henry; CMG (1994); s of Lt-Col Henry Harold Hemming, OBE, MC (d 1977), of London, and Alice Louisa, OBE, *née* Weaver (d 1994); *b* 5 Jan 1935; *Educ* Eton, McGill Univ, Univ of Oxford (MA, DLitt); *m* 19 Jan 1979, Sukie Mary, da of Brig Michael J Babington-Smith, CBE (d 1984); 1 s (Henry Sebastian b 1979), 1 da (Beatrice Margaret Louisa b 1981); *Career* charity dir Royal Geographical Soc 1975–96; publisher; jt chm: Hemming Publishing Ltd (formerly Municipal Jl Ltd) 1976– (dir 1962, dep chm 1967–76), Hemming Group Ltd 1976–; chm: Brintex Ltd 1979– (md 1962–71), Newman Books Ltd 1979–; ldr Maracá Rainforest Project Brazil 1987–89; fndr tstee and sponsor Survival International; memb Cncl/Ctee: Br Cncl, Anglo-Brazilian Soc, Geographical Club, L S B Leakey Tst, Gilchrist Educnl Tst, Beefsteak Club, Pro Natura Int, Gren Card Tst, Hakluyt Soc; chm: Museum of Empire & Cwlth Tst, Anglo-Peruvian Soc; Hon DLitt: Univ of Warwick 1989, Univ of Stirling 1991; Founders medal RGS 1990, Mungo Park medal Royal Scottish Geographical Soc 1988, Washburn medal Boston Museum of Sci 1990; Orden de Mérito (Peru) 1987, hon corresponding memb Academia Nacional de Historia Venezuela; *Books* The Conquest of the Incas (1970), Tribes of the Amazon Basin in Brazil (1973), Red Gold (1978), The Search for El Dorado (1978), Machu Picchu (1981), Monuments of the Incas (1982), Change in the Amazon Basin (1985), Amazon Frontier (1987), Maracá (1988), Roraima, Brazil's northernmost frontier (1990), The Rainforest Edge (1993); *Recreations* writing, travel; *Clubs* Beefsteak, Boodle's, Geographical; *Style*— Dr John Hemming, CMG; ✉ 10 Edwardes Square, London W8 6HE (☎ 0171 602 6697); Hemming Publishing Ltd, 32 Vauxhall Bridge Rd, London SW1V 2SS (☎ 0171 973 6404, fax 0171 233 5049, telex 262568 MUNBEX G)

HEMMING, Lindy; da of Alan Hemming (d 1983), of Crug-y-Bar, Llanwrda, Dyfed, and Jean, *née* Alexander; *b* 21 Aug 1948; *Educ* RADA; *m* Bob Starrett; 1 s (Daniel Grace b 16 Nov 1974), 1 da (Alexandra Grace b 30 Jan 1969); *Career* costume designer for theatre, television and film 1972–; memb Soc Br Theatre Designers; *Theatre* Hampstead Theatre Club 1974–79: Abigail's Party, Ecstasy, The Elephant Man, Uncle Vanya, Clouds; RSC 1978–84: Juno and the Paycock, Mother Courage, All's Well That Ends Well; NT: Death of a Salesman, Schweyk in the Second World War, Pravda, A View from the Bridge, A Small Family Business, Waiting for Godot; West End theatre: Donkeys Years, Brighton Beach Memoirs, Steel Magnolias, Clouds, Chorus of Disapproval, King (musical) 1990, Revengers Comedies 1991; *Film and Television* incl: Wetherby, 84 Charing Cross Rd, Abigail's Party, My Beautiful Laundrette, High Hopes, Meantime, Porterhouse Blue, Queen of Hearts, The Kray's, Life is Sweet, Hear My Song; most recently: Blame it on the Bellboy 1991, Waterland 1992, Running Late 1992, Naked (dir Mike Leigh) 1993, Four Weddings and a Funeral 1993, Dancing Queen 1993, Funnybones (dir P Chelsom) 1994, Goldeneye (Bond film, dir Martin Cambell) 1995, Blood and Wine (dir Bob Rafelson) 1995, The Brave (dir Johnny Depp) 1996, 18th Bond Film (untitled, dir Roger Spottiswode) 1996; *Recreations* cycling, walking, eating, drinking coffee, watching people; *Style*— Ms Lindy Hemming; ✉ 8 Bewdley St, London N1 1HB (☎ 0171 607 6107, fax 0171 700 3738)

HEMMINK, Wilhelmus Hubertus Matheus Maria (Wim); s of late Matheus Hemmink, and late Maria Hemmink Van Den Brink; *Educ* Fashion Dept Koninklijke Academie voor Beeldende Kunst S'Gravenhage Holland, Rotterdamse Snijschool, Rundshau Germany, Constance Wilbaut's Sch Amsterdam Holland, Chambre Syndicale de la Couture Parisienne France; *Career* fashion designer; recipient Cotton Inst award Holland, subsequent experience with Madeleine de Rauch (haute couture house) Paris, Kay Selig Inc NY, Michael of Carlos Place (couture house) London; latterly estab own label Wim Hemmink (retailed worldwide and with extensive private clientele); *Style*— Wim Hemmink, Esq; ✉ 106 Crawford Street, London W1 (☎ 0171 935 1755, fax 0171 224 0573)

HEMPHILL, Dr Barry Francis; s of Robert John Hemphill (d 1963), and Dorothy Mary, *née* Witherdin (d 1982); *b* 30 March 1934; *Educ* De la Salle Coll Armidale NSW (state bursar), Univ of Sydney (Cwlth scholarship and univ exhibition, BDS, MDS), FDS RCS Eng 1962, St Bartholomew's Hosp (LRCP, MRCS, MB BS); *m* 17 Oct 1964, Shelagh Veronica, Hemphill, JP, da of Oscar Ronald Gilbey (d 1994); 1 s (Guy Francis b 22 March 1966), 2 da (Beth Frances b 15 Jan 1969, Sophia Frances b 15 Sept 1970); *Career* sr teaching fell Faculty of Dentistry Univ of Sydney, studying and practising 1956–59, in specialised dental practice Harley St 1970–; Capt Royal Australian Army Dental Corps; formerly: pres Br Endodontic Soc, former memb Cncl Odontological Soc of RSM; Freeman City of London 1981, Liveryman Worshipful Co of Barbers 1982; memb Pierre Fauchard Acad; FRACDS 1964, FRSM 1972, fell Int Coll of Dental Surgeons 1976; memb: BDA 1959, BMA 1970, Br Endodontic Soc 1974; *Books* Preservation of Pulpal Vitality (Master's thesis, 1959); *Recreations* art, music, theatre, swimming, rugby football; *Clubs* Athenaeum, Harlequins, Lansdowne; *Style*— Dr Barry Hemphill; ✉ 40 Harley Street, London W1N 1AB (☎ 0171 580 3299); 10 Sandy Lane, Petersham, Richmond, Surrey TW10 7EL (☎ 0181 940 4700)

HEMPHILL, 5 Baron (UK 1906); Peter Patrick Fitzroy Martyn Martyn-Hemphill; assumed the additional surname of Martyn by deed poll of 1959; s of 4 Baron (d 1957); *b* 5 Sept 1928; *Educ* Downside, Brasenose Coll Oxford (MA Jurisprudence); *m* 1952, Olivia, da of Major Robert Ruttledge, MC, of Co Mayo, and sis of Lady Edward FitzRoy (herself da-in-law of 10 Duke of Grafton); 1 s, 2 da; *Heir* s, Hon Charles Martyn-Hemphill; *Career* memb Turf Club and former sr steward; memb Irish Nat Hunt Steeplechase Ctee and former sr steward, chm Galway Race Ctee 1990–; Cross of Order of Merit, Order of Malta; *Clubs* White's, Irish Cruising, RIAC; *Style*— The Rt Hon the Lord Hemphill; ✉ Raford House, Kiltulla, Co Galway, Ireland (☎ 00 353 91848002, fax 00 353 91848174)

HEMSLEY, Henry Neville (Harry); DL (Leics); s of Neville Hemsley (d 1948), of Jersey, CI, and Mary Florence Eliza, *née* Farran (d 1968); *b* 27 Nov 1922; *Educ* Sherborne, Univ of Cambridge (MA); *m* 26 Feb 1949, Margaret Ruth, da of Hon William Borthwick (d 1956); 2 s (John Neville b 1956, Oliver Charles b 1960), 2 da (Patricia Mary b 1964, Clare Margaret b 1953); *Career* Lt (E) Temp RN 1942–46; engr 1946–60, farmer 1961–; dep chm Rutland Magistrates' Ct 1990–92 (chm 1987–90); memb Bd of Vistors Ashwell Prison 1969–92, chm LRC Ashwell Prison 1990–92, former chm local NAVSS, memb Nat Mgmnt Ctee NAVSS 1982–87, former cdre Rutland Sailing Club; *Recreations* shooting, bridge; *Style*— Harry Hemsley, Esq, DL; ✉ Langham Lodge, Oakham, Rutland LE15 7HZ (☎ 01572 722912)

HEMSLEY, Michael Stuart; s of Alan Fraser Hemsley, of Totton, Southampton, Hants, and Janet Enid, *née* Taylor; *b* 13 July 1957; *Educ* Beverley Boys' Sch New Malden Surrey, Salisbury Coll of Art; *m* 30 May 1981, Catherine Bernadette Hemsley, da of Thomas Oswald O'Keeffe; 2 s (Thomas Joseph b 26 Sept 1986, Robert Michael b 19 Oct 1988); *Career* professional photographer; Colt International Ltd Havant: trainee Photographic Dept 1974, photographed industl sites for advtg and promotional use until 1981; industl and commercial photographer Walter Gardiner Photography Worthing 1981–; photographic assignments in UK and abroad incl: submarines, toothpaste, sewage works and dead bodies in coffins; winner Bausch and Lomb Young Photographer of the Year 1982, Ilford Photographer of the Year 1985 and 1989 (Highly Commended 1992), winner Peter Grudgeon award for best fellowship application 1986; FBIPP 1986; *Style*— Michael Hemsley, Esq; ✉ Walter Gardiner Photography, Southdownview Rd, Worthing, W Sussex BN14 8NL (☎ 01903 200528, fax 01903 820830)

HEMSLEY, Thomas Jeffrey; s of Sydney William Hemsley (d 1986), of Little Eversden, Cambs, and Kathleen Annie, *née* Deacon (d 1976); *b* 12 April 1927; *Educ* Ashby-de-la-Zouch Boys GS, Brasenose Coll Oxford (MA); *m* 9 Nov 1960, Hon Gwenllian Ellen James, s of Walter Ernest Christopher James, 4 Baron Northbourne (d 1982), of Northbourne Ct, Deal, Kent; 3 s (William b 1962, Matthew b 1963, Michael b 1965); *Career* PO RAF 1948–50; vicar choral St Paul's Cathedral 1950–51, opera debut Mermaid Theatre 1951, Glyndebourne Festival Opera debut 1953 (first of many appearances until 1983); princ baritone: Stadttheater Aachen 1953–56, Deutsche Oper am Rhein 1957–63, Opernhaus Zurich 1963–67; freelance singer 1967–: Covent Garden, ENO, Scottish Opera, WNO, Kent Opera, Glyndebourne Festival, Edinburgh Festival, Bayreuth Festival (1968–70); soloist for many orchs throughout Europe; teaching incl: RNCM, Guildhall Sch of Music of Drama, Royal Danish Acad of Music, Britten-Pears Sch, Trinity Coll of Music, Dartington Int Summer Sch (dir opera prog); TV masterclasses: Denmark 1971, BBC TV 1976; opera prodr: RNCM, Dallas Public Opera, Kent Opera; jury memb at many singing competitions, Cramm lectr Univ of Glasgow 1976; Hon RAM (1974), Hon FTCL 1988; memb: ISM 1953, Equity 1953; *Recreations* gardening, mountain walking; *Clubs* Garrick; *Style*— Thomas Hemsley, Esq; ✉ 10 Denewood Rd, London N6 4AJ (☎ 0181 348 3397)

HENCKE, David Robert; s of late Charles Ewald Hencke, of London, and Enid, *née* Rose; *b* 26 April 1947; *Educ* Tulse Hill Comp Sch, Univ of Warwick (BA); *m* 5 July 1969, Margaret Mary, da of late Laurie Langrick; 1 da (Anne Margaret b 14 Aug 1979); *Career* jr reporter Northamptonshire Evening Telegraph 1968–71; reporter: Western Mail 1971–73, Times Higher Educational Supplement 1973–76; The Guardian: reporter 1976–79, planning corr 1979–81, social servs corr 1981–86, Westminster corr 1986–; Reporter of the Year: E Midlands Allied Press 1971, Br Press awards 1989 (specialist writer of the year 1981) and 1993 (reporter of the year), Journalist of the Year What the Papers Say 1994; *Books* Colleges in Crisis (1976); *Recreations* theatre, walking, gardening, cooking, riding; *Style*— David Hencke, Esq; ✉ The Guardian, 119 Farringdon Rd, London EC1R 3ER (☎ 0171 278 2332 or 0171 219 6769 (Westminster office), fax 0171 222 1321)

HENDER, John Derrik; CBE (1986), DL (W Midlands 1973); s of Jesse Peter Hender (d 1944), and Jennie, *née* Williams (d 1965); *b* 15 Nov 1926; *Educ* Great Yarmouth GS; *m* 29 Oct 1949, Kathleen Nora, da of Frederick William Brown (d 1945); 1 da (Annette b 6 May 1955); *Career* RN 1944–47; chief exec Coventry City 1969–73 (city treas 1964–69), chief exec W Midlands CC 1973–86, public sector conslt 1986–; hon fell Inst of Local Govt Studies Univ of Birmingham; FCA, IPFA; *Style*— John Hender, Esq, CBE, DL; ✉ 16 South Avenue, Thorpe St Andrew, Norwich, Norfolk NR7 0EZ (☎ 01603 35548)

HENDERSON, Alan Brodie; yr s of Neil Brodie Henderson (d 1982), of Buntingford, Herts, and Conn, *née* Madden (d 1979); *b* 30 July 1933; *Educ* Eton; *m* 1, 25 April 1956 (m dis), Antonia, only da of James McMullen, of 63 Eaton Square, London; 2 s (Bryan

Brodie b 1960, Gavin Brodie b 1963), 1 da (Kerena Brodie b 1958); m 2, 9 June 1969, Fiona Douglas, er da of Maj Thomas Douglas Pilkington of Reay; 2 s (David Brodie b 1970, Thomas Brodie b 1976); m 3, 30 Sept 1992, Hon Diana Cara, da of 3 Baron Fairhaven, *qv*; *Career* Capt Welsh Gds 1952–59; with James Capel stockbrokers 1959–63, md Henderson Administration Ltd 1965–77 (joined 1963), chm Henderson Unit Trust Co Ltd 1974–77; dir: Mackay Shields Financial Corporation NY 1974–77, Schlesinger Investment Management Services Ltd 1977–81; md Schlesinger Trust Managers Ltd 1979–81; non-exec chm: Newmarket Venture Capital plc 1972–, Ranger Oil (UK) Ltd 1995– (chm 1994–95), Abtrust New Thai Investment Trust Plc, Abtrust Emerging Economies Investment Trust Plc; non-exec dir: ADT Ltd, Abtrust New Dawn Investment Trust Plc, Greenfriar Investment Co Plc, Herring Baker Harris Group plc, Energy Capital Investment Company plc; *Clubs* White's, City of London; *Style*— Alan Henderson, Esq; ✉ Ranger Oil (UK) Ltd, Ranger House, Walnut Tree Close, Guildford, Surrey GU1 4US (☎ 01483 401503, fax 01483 401407)

HENDERSON, Bernard Vere; CBE (1988); s of Col Percy C Henderson, OBE (d 1961), and Ruth Elizabeth, *née* Morphew (d 1995); *b* 8 June 1928; *Educ* Ampleforth; *m* Valerie Jane, da of Capt Charles Cairns (d 1931); 2 s (Mark, Paul), 1 da (Annabel); *Career* md PC Henderson Group 1956–79; dir: Water Training International 1983–, Water Aid 1989–, Water Research plc 1989–, Shirescot 1992–; chm: Anglian Water plc 1981–94, British Waterways 1994–; memb Essex County Cncl 1970–74, magistrate 1974–80; *Recreations* countryside, narrow boat cruising and music; *Style*— Bernard Henderson, Esq, CBE; ✉ British Waterways, Willow Grange, Church Road, Watford WD1 3QA (☎ 01923 201346, fax 01923 201455)

HENDERSON, Prof Brian; s of George Henderson (d 1965), of Rossington, Yorkshire, and Mary Jane, *née* Oliver (d 1980); *b* 26 March 1936; *Educ* Maltby GS Yorkshire (Co Minor scholar), Univ of Birmingham (Co Major scholar, BSc, PhD), Trinity Coll Dublin (MA, ScD); *m* 9 Feb 1958, Sheila Yvonne, da of Edward Vernon Slack; 3 s (Michael John b 14 April 1959, Nigel Brian David b 18 Nov 1960, Richard Vernon b 18 April 1964); *Career* Austin res fell in metallurgy Univ of Birmingham 1958–60, sr scientific offr AERE (Harwell) 1960–66, reader in physics Univ of Keele 1966–74; Trinity Coll Dublin: Erasmus Smiths prof of natural and experimental philosophy 1974–84, head Dept of Physics 1974–84, fell 1976–84; Univ of Strathclyde: Freeland prof of natural philosophy 1984–, head Dept of Physics 1984–88, dean Faculty of Science 1988–92, vice principal 1992–95; FInstP 1972, CPhys 1982, FRSE 1986; *Books* Defects in Crystalline Solids (1972), Defects and their Structures in Non-Metallic Solids (1975), Defects in the Alkaline Earth Oxides (1977), Optical Spectroscopy of Inorganic Solids (1989); *Recreations* golf, theatre, wine; *Style*— Prof Brian Henderson, FRSE; ✉ University of Strathclyde, Colville Building (4.26), North Portland Street, Glasgow G1 1XN (☎ 0141 548 3165, fax 0141 553 4162)

HENDERSON, Charles Edward; CB (1992); s of David Henderson (d 1972), and Georgiana Leggatt, *née* Mackie; *b* 19 Sept 1939; *Educ* Charterhouse, Univ of Cambridge; *m* 1966, Rachel, da of Dr A S Hall, of Bucks; 1 da (Catherine b 1970), 1 s (Luke b 1971); *Career* asst investmt sec Equity and Law Life Assurance Soc Ltd 1966–70, princ Export Credits Guarantee Dept DTI 1971–73; Dept of Energy: princ 1971–75, asst sec 1976–82, head Atomic Energy Div 1982–84, head Oil Div 1984–85, princ estab and fin offr 1985–88; head Office of Arts and Libraries 1989–92, dep sec DTI 1992–96; FIA; *Recreations* music (listening and playing), golf, reading, mountain walking; *Style*— Charles Henderson, Esq, CB; ✉ 33 Fairfax Rd, London W4 1EN (☎ 0181 994 1345)

HENDERSON, Rt Rev Charles Joseph; s of Charles Stuart Henderson (d 1977), and Hanora, *née* Walsh (d 1970); *b* 14 April 1924; *Educ* Mount Sion Schs Waterford, St John's Seminary Waterford; *Career* curate: St Stephen's Welling Kent 1948–55, English Martyrs Streatham 1955–58; chllr RC Dio of Southwark 1958–70; vicar gen: RC Dio of Arundel and Brighton 1965–66, RC Archdiocese of Southwark 1969–; episcopal vicar for religious 1968–73, parish priest St Mary's Blackheath 1969–82, canon Cathedral Chapter 1972– (provost 1973–), auxiliary bishop of Southwark and titular bishop of Tricala 1972–, area bishop SE Southwark 1980–; memb: Ecumenical Cmmn for England and Wales 1976–83, Nat Ctee for Racial Justice 1978–81, English Anglican/RC Ctee 1982–92 (co-chm 1983–92), Methodist/RC Nat Ecumenical Ctee 1983–92 (co-chm 1984–92), Pontifical Cncl for Inter Religious Dialogue 1990–; chm RC Ctee for Dialogue with other Faiths 1984–, memb Exec Ctee Inter-Faith Network for the UK 1987–, chm RC Ctee for Catholic-Jewish Rels 1992–, vice chm Nat Cncl for Christians and Jews 1992–, memb Churches' Ctee for Inter Faith Rels 1994–; RC consultor-observer BCC 1982–86, Papal Chamberlain 1960, prelate Papal Household 1965; Freeman City of Waterford 1973; Canon Law Soc of GB and Ireland 1959; Knight Cdr with Star of the Equestrian Order of the Holy Sepulchre of Jerusalem 1973; *Recreations* special interest in sports and in art; *Style*— The Rt Rev Charles Henderson; ✉ Park House, 6A Cresswell Park, Blackheath, London SE3 9RD (☎ 0181 318 1094, fax 0181 318 9470)

HENDERSON, (George) Clifford McLaren; s of Robert McLaren Henderson (d 1962), and Stella, *née* Walter (d 1996); *b* 7 Feb 1938; *Educ* Bembridge Sch IOW; *Career* dir: Frank Partridge 1973–77, Stair and Co New York 1977–79; antiques conslt 1979–88, exec dir Partridge Fine Arts PLC 1988–; *Recreations* music, swimming, theatre, bridge; *Style*— Clifford Henderson, Esq; ✉ 18 Lochmore House, Ebury St, London SW1W 9JX (☎ 0171 730 2725); The Vine House, 38 Roedean Crescent, Roedean, East Sussex BN2 5RH (☎ 01273 685809)

HENDERSON, David Alexander; s of George Alexander Henderson (d 1973), of Edinburgh, and Jessie, *née* Wilson; *b* 16 Sept 1944; *Educ* Broughton HS; *m* 5 April 1970, (Constance) Mary, da of Adam Renton (d 1986), of Edinburgh; 1 s (Bryan b 1973), 1 da (Dayle b 1977); *Career* audit mangr Scott Moncrieff Thomson-Sheills 1969–71; Scottish Equitable Life & Pensions: asst accountant 1917–74, accountant 1974–79, chief accountant 1979–84, asst gen mangr 1984–87, md Life and Pensions Div 1988–92; Scottish Equitable plc: md UK Ops 1993–95, md and dep chief exec 1995–; FCCA 1968; *Recreations* golf, rugby; *Clubs* Watsonian, Mortonhall Golf; *Style*— David A Henderson, Esq; ✉ Scottish Equitable plc, Edinburgh Park, Edinburgh EH12 9SE (☎ 0131 339 9191, fax 0131 549 4234)

HENDERSON, Sir Denys Hartley; *b* 11 Oct 1932; *Educ* Univ of Aberdeen (MA, LLB); *m*; 2 da; *Career* admitted slr; chm: Imperial Chemical Industries PLC 1987–95, Zeneca Group plc (following demerger from ICI) 1993–95, The Rank Organisation plc 1995– (non-exec dir 1994–); non-exec dir: Dalgety plc 1981–87 and 1996– (chm Jan 1997–), Barclays Bank plc 1983–, The RTZ Corporation plc 1990–96 (non-exec dir CRA Ltd Dec 1995–96), Spencer Stuart & Associates 1995–, Schlumberger Ltd 1995–, Market and Opinion Research International Ltd (MORI) 1995–; First Crown Estate Cmmr 1995–; memb Advsy Cncl of The Prince's Youth Business Tst; pres and chm Bd British Quality Fndn 1993–97, tstee Natural History Museum; chllr Univ of Bath 1993–; chm Quincentenary Appeal Ctee Univ of Aberdeen 1993–96; Hon DUniv: Brunel 1987, Strathclyde 1993; Hon DSc: Cranfield Inst of Technol 1989, Univ of Teesside 1993; Hon LLD: Univ of Nottingham 1990, Univ of Manchester 1991, Univ of Bath 1993; memb Law Soc of Scot; hon memb Worshipful Co of Salters; Hon FCGI, FCIM, FRSA, CIMgt; *Recreations* family life, swimming, reading, travel, minimal gardening, unskilled but enjoyable golf; *Clubs* Athenaeum, RAC; *Style*— Sir Denys Henderson; ✉ The Rank Organisation plc, 6 Connaught Place, London W2 2EZ (☎ 0171 873 7211)

HENDERSON, Douglas John (Doug); MP (Lab) Newcastle upon Tyne North (majority 8,946); s of John Henderson, and Joan, *née* Bryson; *b* 9 May 1949; *Educ* Waid Acad, Central Coll Glasgow, Univ of Strathclyde (BA); *m* 1974, Janet Margaret, da of Robert Graham (d 1984), of Scotland; 1 s (Keir John b 1986); *Career* apprentice Rolls Royce Glasgow 1966–68, Trade Union organiser (GMWU later GMB) 1973–87, MP (Lab) Newcastle upon Tyne North 1978–, memb Exec Scottish Cncl Lab Pty 1979–87 (chm 1984–85), memb NEDO Sector Working Pty 1981–84; oppn spokesman on: indust 1988–92, local govt 1992–94, public servs 1994–95, home affairs 1995–; *Recreations* athletics, mountaineering; *Clubs* Lemington Labour, Newburn Memorial, Dinnington, Cambuslang Harriers, Elswick Harriers, Desperados Climbing; *Style*— Doug Henderson, Esq, MP; ✉ House of Commons, London SW1A OAA (☎ 0171 219 5017, home 0191 267 2427)

HENDERSON, Douglas Lindsay; s of Capt Arthur Henderson, of Sydney, Australia, and Sheila Lindsay, *née* Russel; *b* 17 Dec 1947; *Educ* Univ of New England (BA), Univ of NSW Australia (MBA, PhD); *m* 20 Jan 1970, Marilyn Gail, da of Ronald Clifford (d 1982), of Sydney, Australia; 3 s (Angus Arthur Lindsay b 1975, Duncan Ronald Alan b 1978, Stuart b 1987); *Career* lectr Univ of NSW Aust 1972–74; vice pres Bank of America NT & SA 1974–83, first vice pres and dir Swiss Bank Corporation 1983–89, dir Europacific Corporate Finance Ltd 1991–; memb Graduate Business Assoc; ACIB, MSI; *Clubs* Royal Over-Seas League; *Style*— Douglas Henderson, Esq; ✉ Europacific Corporate Finance Ltd, 2 Burgon Street, London EC4B 5DR (☎ 0171 329 3515)

HENDERSON, Gavin Douglas; s of Magnus Reginald Henderson (d 1975), and Sybil Nancy, *née* Horton, of Brighton; *b* 3 Feb 1948; *Educ* Brighton Coll (music and art scholar), Brighton Coll of Art, Kingston Coll of Art (BA), Slade Sch of Fine Art (Goldsmith's travelling scholarship to USA); *m* 1, 1973, Jane Williams; 1 s (Piers b 1980); m 2, 1984, Carole Becker; 1 s (Caspar b 1985); m 3, 1992, Mary Jane Walsh; *Career* fndr dir Crawley Festival 1972–73, artistic dir York Festival and Mystery Plays 1973–76, chief exec Philharmonia Orch 1975–79, dir South Hill Park Arts Centre and fndr Wilde Theatre Bracknell 1979–85, artistic dir Brighton Festival 1984–94, princ Trinity Coll of Music 1994–; dir Dartington Int Summer Sch 1985–; chm: Br Arts Festivals Assoc 1992–, Music Panel Arts Cncl of England 1994–; pres Nat Piers Soc, pres Bournemouth Festival, vice pres Euro Festivals Assoc; patron: Chiddingly Festival, A Very Moving Festival; chm World Circuit Arts; memb Musicians' Union 1964, ISM 1994, memb RSM 1996; Freeman City of London 1996, Liveryman Worshipful Co of Musicians 1996; FRSA; *Recreations* cooking seafood, baroque trumpet, vintage motoring; *Clubs* Garrick, Savile; *Style*— Gavin Henderson, Esq; ✉ Trinity College of Music, 11–13 Mandeville Place, London W1M 6AQ (☎ 0171 935 5773, fax 0171 935 5069)

HENDERSON, Geoffrey; s of James Thomas Henderson (d 1981), of Benfleet, Essex, and Hannah, *née* O'Callaghan; *b* 19 April 1955; *Educ* Univ of Sussex (BA); *Career* BBC News: trainee 1978–79, sub ed and scriptwriter 1979–81, chief sub ed 1981–82, organiser 1982–83, asst ed home news 1985–88, sr prodr 1988–89; ITN: programme ed Into the Night 1989–91, ed World News 1995– (programme ed 1991–95); *Recreations* travel, reading, cookery, music, gardening; *Style*— Geoffrey Henderson, Esq; ✉ ITN World News, Room G 326, 200 Gray's Inn Road, London WC1X 8XZ (☎ 0171 430 4664/4688, fax 0171 430 4138)

HENDERSON, George Poland; s of George James Henderson (d 1963), and Emma Rouse Wilson (d 1949); *b* 24 April 1920; *Educ* Westminster City, Univ of London; *m* 27 April 1953, (Shirley) Prudence Ann Cotton, da of Kenneth W Cotton, librarian of Bank of England (d 1942); 2 s (Crispin Alastair Poland b 1955, Antony James Willis b 1957); *Career* Capt RA 1940–46; commercial reference librarian Guildhall Library London 1946–63, dir Kellys Directories Ltd 1963–66, dir CBD Research Ltd 1966–; pres: Assoc of Br Directory Publishers 1974–75, Euro Assoc of Directory Publishers 1976–78; Freeman City of London 1961; memb Royal Instn of GB 1975, FInstD 1970; *Books* Current British Directories (6 edns, 1953–71), European Companies, A Guide to Sources of Information (3 edns, 1961–72), Directory of British Associations (11 edns, jtly, 1965–92); *Recreations* travel, gardening, postal history; *Style*— George Henderson, Esq; ✉ CBD Research Ltd, 15 Wickham Rd, Beckenham, Kent BR3 5JS (☎ 0181 650 7745, fax 0181 650 0768)

HENDERSON, Giles Ian; CBE (1992); s of Charles David Henderson (d 1980), of Henfield, Sussex, and Joan, *née* Firmin (d 1994); *b* 20 April 1942; *Educ* Michaelhouse Natal SA, Witwatersrand Univ SA (BA), Magdalen Coll Oxford (MA, BCL); *m* 21 Aug 1971, Lynne, da of Charles William Fyfield, OBE, of Alnmouth, Northumberland; 2 s (Mark b 1974, Simon b 1975), 1 da (Clare b 1978); *Career* admitted slr 1970, sr ptnr Slaughter and May 1993– (ptnr 1975–); memb Hampel Ctte on Corp Governance; *Recreations* sport, music; *Clubs* Wildernesse Golf, City Law; *Style*— Giles Henderson, Esq, CBE; ✉ Slaughter and May, 35 Basinghall St, London EC2V 5DB (☎ 0171 600 1200, fax 0171 726 0038, 0171 600 0289)

HENDERSON, Henry Merton (Harry); s of John Ronald Henderson, CVO, OBE, *qv*, and Katherine Sarah, *née* Beckwith-Smith (d 1972); *b* 25 April 1952; *Educ* Eton; *m* 4 Feb 1977, Sarah Charlotte Margaret, *née* Lowther; 1 s (Harry Oliver b 24 March 1979), 1 da (Katie Sarah Henderson b 7 April 1981); *Career* ptnr Cazenove & Co 1982–, md Cazenove Unit Trust Management Ltd; dir: Updown Investment Co plc 1984–, Witan Investment Co plc 1988–, Hotspur Investments plc 1990–; MSI; *Recreations* skiing, shooting, squash, golf; *Clubs* White's; *Style*— Harry Henderson, Esq; ✉ West Woodhay House, Newbury, Berkshire RG20 0BS (☎ 01488 668233); Cazenove & Co, 3 Copthall Avenue, London EC2R 7BH (☎ 0171 606 0708, fax 0171 606 9205)

HENDERSON, Hugh Peter; s of Dr Peter Wallace Henderson (d 1984), and Dr Stella Dolores Henderson of Langport, Somerset; *b* 23 Oct 1945; *Educ* Radley, St Catharine's Coll Cambridge, St Thomas's Hosp (MB BChir); *m* 11 Dec 1971, Elizabeth Anne Lynette, da of The Hon Mr Justice Arthur Douglas Davidson (d 1977), of Johannesburg, SA; 1 da (Fiona Elizabeth b 1984); *Career* trg as plastic surgn 1975–82, conslt plastic surgn 1982–; author of articles in plastic surgery on subjects incl: thermography, hypospadias, palate fistulae, anti-drooling operation, use of turbinates as graft material; chm: Res and Educn Sub-Ctee Br Assoc of Plastic Surgns, Leicester Royal Infirmary Pressure Sore Working Party; memb Br Assoc of Aesthetic Plastic Surgns; FRCS 1975; *Books* Questions and Answers in General Surgery, Questions and Answers in Surgery for Students; *Style*— Hugh Henderson, Esq; ✉ Nether Hall, Snows Lane, Keyham, Leics LE7 9JS (☎ 01162 595214); Leicester Royal Infirmary, Leicester LE1 5WW (☎ 0116 254 1414, fax 0116 272 0666, office 0116 2 718 994); The Bupa Hospital, Gartree Rd, Oadby, Leicester

HENDERSON, Ian James Sinclair; s of James Muirhead Henderson (d 1978), and Constance Jessie, *née* Sinclair; *b* 7 Jan 1933; *Educ* Chigwell Sch, Wadham Coll Oxford; *m* 1956, Jean, da of Ernest Thomas Fryer; 2 s (Mark Jeremy b 1959, d 1981, Philip James b 1962), 1 da (Judith Claire b 1969); *Career* Instr Lt RN 1954–60; Norwich Union Life Insurance Society 1960–63, asst actuary Scottish Union & National Insurance Company 1963–68; Scottish Equitable Life Assurance Society: asst actuary 1968, investmt mangr 1972, dep gen mangr 1977–80; dir London and Manchester Group plc 1981–86 (gen mangr (investmt) 1980–81), dir Gartmore American Securities plc 1983–; chm 1986–: Ian Henderson Associates Ltd, Sinclair Henderson Ltd, Exeter Fund Managers Ltd, Exeter Investment Group Ltd; FIA 1962; *Style*— Ian Henderson, Esq

HENDERSON, Ian Ramsay; s of David Hope Henderson (d 1977), of Achie Farm, New Galloway, Kirkcudbrightshire, and Eleanora A Henderson, *née* Spence; *Educ* Eton, Univ of Edinburgh (MA, LLB); *m* 28 Oct 1978, Virginia Theresa, da of Lt-Col John E B Freeman (d 1986), and Lady Winefride Freeman, of Buxhall Vale, Buxhall, Stowmarket,

Suffolk; 3 s (Alexander b 1982, Charles b 1984, George b 1987); *Career* Peat Marwick Mitchell & Co 1972–76, Morgan Grenfell & Co 1977–82; md Wardley Marine Int Investmt Mgmnt Ltd 1985 (dir 1982), dir Wardley Investment Servs Int Ltd 1987–91, dir Fleming Investment Management Ltd 1991–; FCA 1980 (ACA 1975); *Recreations* golf, tennis; *Clubs* Brooks's, St James's; *Style*— Ian Henderson, Esq; ✉ 20 Westbourne Park Rd, London W2 5PH; Fleming Investment Management Ltd, 25 Copthall Avenue, London EC2R 7DR

HENDERSON, (William) James Carlaw; s of James Henderson, of Kelso, Roxburghshire, and Nan Stark, *née* Fergusson (d 1984); *b* 26 Sept 1948; *Educ* George Heriot's Sch Edinburgh, Univ of Edinburgh (LLB); *Career* apprentice Patrick & James WS Edinburgh 1971–73, asst Wallace & Guthrie WS Edinburgh 1973–74; ptnr: Allan McDougall & Co SSC Edinburgh 1976–83 (asst 1974–76), Brodies WS Edinburgh 1983–; govr Edinburgh Coll of Art 1996–; memb: Soc of Scottish Artists 1983 (sec 1980–83), Soc of Writers to the Signet 1981; FRGS 1992; *Recreations* sailing, mountaineering, skiing, the arts; *Clubs* Royal Highland Yacht, Edinburgh Sports, Scottish Arts; *Style*— James Henderson, Esq; ✉ 11 Inverleith Place, Edinburgh EH3 5QE (☎ 0131 552 7518); Drimmie Cottage, Bridge of Cally, Perthshire PH10 7JS; Brodies WS, 15 Atholl Crescent, Edinburgh EH3 8HA (☎ 0131 228 3777)

HENDERSON, Dr James Ewart; CVO; s of Rev James Ewart Henderson (d 1968), of Trinity Manse, Beith, Ayrshire, and Agnes Mary, *née* Crawford (d 1957); *b* 29 May 1923; *Educ* Univ of Glasgow, Univ of Edinburgh (MA, DSc); *m* 1, 20 Aug 1949, Alice Joan, da of Horace James Hewlitt (d 1958), of Herts; 1 da (Joanna b 1956); m 2, 17 Jan 1966, Nancy Maude, da of Henry Tothill Dominy (d 1958), of Cornwall; 2 s (Jamie b 1966, Crawford b 1969); *Career* scientist, operational res (air rockets and guns) MAP 1943–44, hon cmmn RAFVR 1944–46, operational res air attacks in Belgium, Holland and Germany, 2 TAF 1944–45; experimental res: fighter armament RAF APC Germany 1945–46, fighter and bomber capability and use of radar and radio aids Fighter Cmd 1946–49 and Central Fighter Estab 1949–52, weapons effects and capability Air Miny 1952–54; AWRE 1955, Air Miny 1955–58, asst scientific advsr (ops) Air Miny 1958–63, dep chief scientist (RAF) MOD 1963–69, chief scientist (RAF) and memb Air Force Bd 1969–73; aviation conslt Hawker Siddeley Aviation Ltd 1973–77, fin conslt Charles Stapleton and Co Ltd 1973–78, freelance operational res and mgmnt conslt 1974–78, dir Lewis Security Systems Ltd 1976–77, sci advsr Br Aerospace 1978–82, chm TIB Netherlands 1982–86, pres and chief exec Mastiff Systems (US) Inc 1982–88, pres Mastiff Electronic Systems Ltd 1995– (dir 1977–82, md 1982–90, chm 1985–95); life vice pres Air League 1994 (memb Cncl 1979–80, chm 1981–87, pres 1987–94); chm Air League Educnl Tst 1983–87; *Publications* author of tech papers on operational capability of aircraft and weapons 1949–73, UK Manual on Blast Effects of Nuclear Weapons (1955); *Recreations* sailing, golf, opera; *Clubs* Naval and Military, Royal Scottish Automobile, Royal Western Yacht, Moor Park Golf, New Zealand Golf; *Style*— Dr James E Henderson, CVO; ✉ Mastiff Electronic Systems Ltd, Little Mead, Cranleigh, Surrey (☎ 01483 272097, telex 859307 MASTIF G, fax 01483 276728)

HENDERSON, John Crombie; s of Maj Morrice Pitcairn Henderson, TD; *b* 8 April 1939; *Educ* Uppingham; *m* 1968, Marylou Susan, da of Maj-Gen Sir Francis de Guingand, KBE, CB, DSO (d 1979); 2 da; *Career* Lt Black Watch 1959–63; chief exec Capel-Cure Myers Capital Management Ltd 1988– (joined 1964); MSI (memb Stock Exchange 1969); *Recreations* shooting, fishing, golf; *Clubs* Turf, Berkshire Golf; *Style*— John Henderson, Esq; ✉ 125 Abbotsbury Rd, London W14 8EP; Capel-Cure Myers Capital Management Ltd, The Registry, Royal Mint Court, London EC3

HENDERSON, John Ronald; CVO (1986), OBE (1985, MBE 1944); s of late Maj R H W Henderson, and Marjorie, *née* Garrard; *b* 6 May 1920; *Educ* Eton, Univ of Cambridge; *m* 1, 1949, Katherine Sarah (d 1972), yr da of Maj-Gen Merton Beckwith-Smith, DSO, MC (d 1942); 2 s (Nicholas John Henderson, *qv* b 1950, Henry Merton Henderson, *qv* b 1952), 1 da (Joanna b 1955); m 2, 1976, Catherine, da of Geoffrey William Barford, JP, and wid of Lt-Col John Monsell Christian, MC; 1 step s, 2 step da; *Career* former chm: Henderson Administration, Witan Investment Tst; dir Barclays Bank 1971–87; tstee Winston Churchill Tst; Lord Lt Berks 1989 (Vice Lord Lt 1979, formerly DL); *Recreations* racing, shooting, hunting; *Clubs* White's; *Style*— John Henderson, Esq, CVO, OBE; ✉ West Woodhay House, Newbury, Berks (☎ 01488 668271)

HENDERSON, Hon Launcelot Dinadan James; QC (1995); er s of Baron Henderson of Brompton (Life Peer), and Susan Mary, *née* Dartford; *b* 20 Nov 1951; *Educ* Westminster, Balliol Coll Oxford; *m* 1989, Elaine Elizabeth, er da of Kenneth Frank Webb, of Dringhouses, York; 2 s (Peter George Galahad b 12 Aug 1990, Arthur Frank Gabriel b 18 Feb 1994), 1 da (Matilda Jane b 29 Aug 1992); *Career* called to the Bar Lincoln's Inn 1977; appointed standing jr counsel Chancery to the Inland Revenue 1987, standing jr counsel to Inland Revenue 1991–95; fell All Souls Coll Oxford 1974–81 and 1982–89; *Recreations* botany, art, music; *Style*— The Hon Launcelot Henderson, QC; ✉ 17 Carlisle Road, London NW6 6TL; 5 Stone Buildings, Lincoln's Inn, London WC2A 3XT (☎ 0171 242 6201, fax 0171 831 8102)

HENDERSON, Lucinda Mary (Lucy); da of late James Henderson, of Winchester, Hants, and Mary Anne, *née* O'Hanlon (d 1993); *b* 25 April 1934; *Educ* privately; *partner* Henry Patterson; *Career* former interior designer (numerous projects both in Europe and USA); currently freelance journalist specialising in design; *Recreations* painting, reading, sailing; *Style*— Ms Lucy Henderson; ✉ Redhurst, Knowle Lane, Cranleigh, Surrey GU6 8JN

HENDERSON, Mark; s of Gordon Henderson, of Mansfield, and Margaret Eileen, *née* Moakes; *b* 26 Sept 1957; *Educ* Sherwood Hall Tech GS Mansfield; *partner* Caroline Mary Mander; 2 s (Sam b 8 Nov 1993, Charlie b 1 Aug 1995); *Career* lighting designer; started career as lighting technician Newark Notts 1975; subsequently chief electrician for: Kent Opera, English Music Theatre, London Contemporary Dance, Sadler's Wells, Opera North; *Theatre* has lit over 50 West End shows incl: Grease, Follies, Girlfriends, Mutiny, Kiss me Kate, Carmen Jones, Becket, The Merchant of Venice, A Patriot for Me, The Dresser, Gasping, Heartbreak House, No Man's Land, The Deep Blue Sea, Rowan Atkinson in Revue, Home, St Joan, Neville's Island, Indian Ink, Design for Living, Passion; RNT prodns incl: The Shaugraun, Cat on a Hot Tin Roof (also Broadway), Hamlet, The Changeling, Racing Demon, Long Day's Journey into Night, Napoli Millionaria, Murmuring Judges, Pygmalion, The Absence of War, The Birthday Party, Les Parent Terribles (Indescretions, Broadway) Sweet Bird of Youth, Le Cid, Absolute Hell, La Grande Magia, A Little Night Music, John Gabriel Borkman, Oedipus Plays; RSC prodns incl: Macbeth, The Tempest, Kiss Me Kate, Measure for Measure, General from America; Almeida prodns incl: The Deep Blue Sea, Rules of the Game, No Man's Land, Life of Galileo, Hamlet, Tartuffe; other prodns incl: Hamlet (Broadway), Rowan Atkinson Tours (Aust, NZ, USA); *Opera* numerous prodns incl: The Merry Widow (New Sadler's Wells), Werther (Opera de Nancy), The Flying Dutchman (Royal Opera), The Makropulos Case (Glyndebourne Festival Opera), Tosca (Welsh Nat Opera), Anna Karenina (ENO); *Dance* prodns incl: Agora, Shadows in the Sun (both London Contemporary Dance Theatre), Swan of Tuonela (Sadler's Wells Royal Ballet), Quicksilver (Rambert Dance Co); for Royal Ballet: The Tales of Beatrix Potter, The Planets, Don Quixote, The Judas Tree, Daphnis and Chloe; *Films* incl: The Tall Guy (Working Title Prodn), Under Milk Wood (Imagination Entertainment), Rowan Atkinson in Boston USA; *Other Work* Madame Tussaud's: 200 Years Exhibition, Garden Party Exhibition, Spirit of London Dark Ride, Rock Circus Entrance, Planetarium Foyer, Royal Court redevelopment; *Awards* incl: Olivier Award for Lighting Designer of the Year 1992, Olivier Award for Best Lighting Designer 1995, Tony Award nomination Best Lighting Designer 1995, Olivier Award nomination for Best Lighting Designer 1996; *Style*— Mark Henderson, Esq; ✉ c/o PBJ Management Ltd, 5 Soho Square, London W1V 5DE (☎ 0171 287 1112, fax 0171 287 1448)

HENDERSON, Mark Ian; s of Ian Sidney Campbell Henderson (d 1954), and Patricia Joyce, *née* Muers; *b* 10 April 1947; *Educ* Stowe, CLP (BA); *m* 1970, Ann, da of Albert Edwin Reed (d 1982); 1 s (James b 1978), 1 da (Johanna b 1976); *Career* md RCB International Ltd 1987–89; dir: Hill Samuel Pensions Investment Management 1981–87 (md 1986–87), Mpalanganga Estates (Malawi) 1983–, Hill Samuel Asset Management 1984–87, Hill Samuel Investment Management 1985–87, Touche Remnant 1989–93, Clerical Medical Investment Group 1993–96, Solutions in Investment 1996–; memb Worshipful Co of Curriers; memb Lloyd's, assoc London Oil Analysts Gp; AMIIMR, MSI; *Publications* numerous articles on investmt mgmnt; *Recreations* running, music, bonsai trees, scuba diving; *Clubs* Carlton; *Style*— Mark Henderson, Esq; ✉ 39 Winsham Grove, London SW11 6NB; Solutions in Investment, 6 Kinghorn Street, London EC1A 7HT (☎ 0171 600 9270)

HENDERSON, Michael John Glidden; s of William Glidden Henderson (d 1946), and Aileen Judith, *née* Malloy (d 1996); *b* 19 Aug 1938; *Educ* St Benedict's Sch Ealing; *m* 29 Sept 1965, Stephanie Maria, da of John Dyer, of Hampton Court, Surrey; 4 s (Nicholas b 1966, Simon b 1968, Angus b 1972, Giles b 1976); *Career* formerly chm and chief exec Cookson Group plc; chm Henderson Crossthwaite Ltd; dir: Guinness Mahon Holdings plc, Ronar Services Ltd, Three Counties Ltd, Pennymead Sports Ground Ltd, Centrocen Projects (Pty) Ltd S Africa; memb DTI Innovation Advsy Bd, tstee Natural History Museum Devpt Tst; govr: St George's Coll Weybridge, Cranmore Sch W Horsley; FCA 1961, FRSA; *Recreations* tennis, golf; *Clubs* MCC, The Wisley Golf, Horsley Sports; *Style*— Michael Henderson, Esq; ✉ Langdale, Woodland Drive, East Horsley, Surrey KT24 5AN (☎ 01483 283844); Ronar Services Ltd, 79 Knightsbridge, London SW1X 7RB (☎ 0171 235 6969, fax 0171 823 1235, telex 8813248)

HENDERSON, Sir (John) Nicholas; GCMG (1977, KCMG 1972, CMG 1965), KCVO (1991); s of Prof Sir Hubert Henderson; *b* 1 April 1919; *Educ* Stowe, Hertford Coll Oxford; *m* 1951, Mary Barber, *née* Cawadias; 1 da (Alexandra (Countess of Drogheda)); *Career* private sec to Foreign Sec 1963–65, min Madrid 1965–69; ambass: Poland 1969–72, W Germany 1972–75, France 1975–79, USA (Washington) 1979–82; dir: M and G Reinsurance 1982–89, Foreign and Colonial Investment Trust plc 1982–89, Hambros plc 1983–89, Tarmac plc 1983–92, F and C Eurotrust plc 1984–, Sotheby's 1989–; chm: Channel Tunnel Gp 1985–86, Fuel Tech NV; Lord Warden of the Stannaries, Keeper of the Privy Seal of the Duchy of Cornwall, vice chm of the Prince of Wales Cncl 1985–90; tstee Nat Gallery 1985–89; hon fell Hertford Coll Oxford 1975, Hon DCL Oxford; *Books* Prince Eugen of Savoy (biography), The Birth of NATO (1982), The Private Office (1984), Channels and Tunnels (1987), Mandarin (1994); *Recreations* gardening; *Clubs* Brooks's, Garrick, Pratt's; *Style*— Sir Nicholas Henderson, GCMG, KCVO; ✉ 6 Fairholt St, London SW7 1EG (☎ 0171 589 4291)

HENDERSON, Nicholas John; s of John Ronald Henderson, CVO, OBE, *qv*, of West Woodhay House, Newbury, Berks, and Katherine Sarah, *née* Beckwith-Smith (d 1972); *b* 10 Dec 1950; *Educ* Eton; *m* 10 June 1978, Diana Amanda, da of John Thorne; 3 da (Sarah Lucy b 5 Dec 1981, Tessa Jane b 8 Dec 1983, Camilla Penny b 3 Nov 1987); *Career* national hunt racehorse trainer; asst trainer to Fred Winter 1973–78, amateur rider 1970–78 (rode 75 winners incl The Imperial Cup Sandown and Liverpool Foxhunters); trainer 1978–; trained over 500 winners incl See You Then (3 Champion Hurdles 1985, 1986, 1987), Brown Windsor (Whitbread Gold Cup), The Tsarevich (16 races and 2nd place in Grand National), Zongalero (won Mandarin Chase and 2nd place in Grand National), First Bout, Alone Success (Daily Express Triumph Hurdle), Remittance Man (Champion Chase); leading nat hunt trainer 1986–87 and 1987–88, Piper Heidsieck trainer of the Year 1986, 1987 and 1988; dir Berkeley Hotel; *Recreations* golf, shooting; *Style*— Nicholas Henderson, Esq; ✉ Seven Barrows, Lambourn, Newbury, Berks RG17 8UH (☎ 01488 72259, fax 01488 72596)

HENDERSON, Paul; s of Gen Frederick Paul Henderson, of New Jersey, USA, and Eva Holland Henderson (d 1990); *b* 2 Dec 1938; *Educ* Purdue Univ USA (BA), Wharton Sch Univ of Pennsylvania USA (MBA); *m* 1963, Kay Carathers; *Career* served US Marine Corps 1962–66; McKinsey & Co 1968–74, World Wildlife Fund 1974–77; proprietor Gidleigh Park Devon; *Awards* Egon Ronay Guide: Wine Cellar of the Year 1982, Hotel of the Year 1990; Country House Hotel of the Year (Good Food Guide) 1983; Good Hotel Guide Ceasar Awards: Hauteur of Cuisine 1984, Most Sumptuous Country House Hotel 1989; Grand award (The Wine Spectator, USA) 1984, 1987 and 1990, Hotel Restaurant of the Year (The Times) 1989, English Country Hotel of the Year (The Hideaway Report, USA) 1990, 3 Red Stars and Rosette for restaurant (AA Guide) 1991, Blue Ribbon award (RAC Guide) 1991, Four Leaf Clover symbol Ackerman Guide, 4 out of 5 rating (Good Food Guide) 1996; *Recreations* walking, travel; *Clubs* Stockey Furzen Cricket & Croquet; *Style*— Paul Henderson, Esq; ✉ Gidleigh Park Hotel, Chagford, Devon TQ13 8HH (☎ 01647 432367, fax 01647 432574)

HENDERSON, Prof Paul; s of Thomas William Henderson (d 1988), and Dorothy Violet, *née* Marriner; *b* 7 Nov 1940; *Educ* King's Coll Sch Wimbledon, Univ of London (BSc), Univ of Oxford (DPhil); *m* Aug 1966, Elizabeth Kathryn, da of William Albert Ankerson; 1 s (Gideon Mark b 29 July 1968), 1 da (Laura Kate b 19 Jan 1972); *Career* asst lectr in chemistry Univ of Glasgow 1966–67, lectr in geochemistry Chelsea Coll London 1968–76; Br Museum (Natural History): head Rock and Mineral Chemistry Div 1977–87, dep keeper of Mineralogy Natural History Museum (name change) 1987–89, keeper of Mineralogy 1989–95, also assoc dir for Earth Scis 1992–95, dir of Sci 1995–; visiting prof in mineral scis UCL 1990–; pres Mineralogical Soc of GB and Ireland 1989–91; winner Fourmarier Medal Belgian Geological Soc 1989; FGS 1990, chartered geologist; *Books* Inorganic Geochemistry (1982), Rare Earth Element Geochemistry (1984); *Recreations* music, Paris, skiing, wine; *Style*— Prof Paul Henderson; ✉ Science Directorate, The Natural History Museum, Cromwell Road, London SW7 5BD (☎ 0171 938 9010, fax 0171 938 9506)

HENDERSON, Dr Richard; *b* 19 July 1945; *Educ* Hawick HS and Boroughmuir Secondary Sch, Univ of Edinburgh (Isaac Newton Scholar, Neil Arnott Scholar, BSc), Univ of Cambridge (MRC Scholar, PhD); *Career* research staff MRC Lab of Molecular Biology Cambridge 1969–70, Helen Hay Whitney postdoctoral fell Yale Univ 1970–73; MRC Lab of Molecular Biology Cambridge: research staff 1973–79, sr research staff 1979–84, special appts grade research staff 1984–86, jt head Div of Structural Studies 1986–95, dep dir 1995–96, dir 1996–; fell Darwin Coll Cambridge 1982–; memb EMBO 1981; William Bate Hardy Prize Cambridge Philosophical Soc 1978, Ernst-Ruska Prize for electron microscopy 1980, Rosenstiel Award 1991, Louis Jeantet Award 1993; FRS 1983; *Style*— Dr Richard Henderson, FRS; ✉ MRC Laboratory of Molecular Biology, Hills Road, Cambridge CB2 2QH (☎ 01223 402215, fax 01223 249565, e-mail rh15@mrc-lmb.cam.ac.uk)

HENDERSON, Maj Richard Yates; TD (1966), JP; s of late John Wishart Henderson, and late Dorothy, *née* Yates; *b* 7 July 1931; *Educ* Rugby, Hertford Coll Oxford (BA), Univ of Glasgow (LLB); *m* 1957, Frances Elizabeth Chrystal; 2 s, 1 da; *Career* Nat Serv: Royal Scots Greys 1950–52, Ayrshire Yeomanry 1953–69; conslt Mitchells Roberton Slrs 1990–92 (ptnr 1958–90); tstee TSB Glasgow 1966–74, dir West of Scotland TSB 1974–83;

Lord-Lt for Ayrshire and Arran 1991– (DL 1970–90); Brig Queen's Body Guard for Scotland (Royal Co of Archers), Hon Col Ayrshire Yeomanry Sqdn Scottish Yeomanry 1992–, pres Lowlands TAVRA 1996–; *Recreations* shooting, tennis, golf; *Clubs* Western (Glasgow); *Style*— Maj Richard Henderson, TD, JP; ✉ Blairston, by Ayr KA7 4EF (☎ 01292 441601)

HENDERSON, Robert Brumwell; CBE (1979); s of Cdr Oscar Henderson, CVO, CBE, DSO (d 1969); bro of Oscar W J Henderson; *b* 28 July 1929; *Educ* Brackenber House Sch Belfast, Bradfield, Trinity Coll Dublin (MA); *m* 1970, Patricia Ann, da of Mathew Davison (d 1993), of Belfast; 2 da (from previous m); *Career* journalist 1951–59; dir: ITN 1964–68, Ind TV Pubns 1968–87, Airtronics International 1990–94; chm: Ulster TV 1983–90 (md 1959–84, dep chm 1977–83), Laganside Corp 1987–92; dep chm Powerscreen International plc 1989–92, vice pres Co-Operation North 1985–; chm: Royal TV Soc 1982–84 (also fell and vice pres), NI Millennium Fund Bid Ctee 1994–95; pres: Assoc of Ulster Drama Festivals 1983–, Northern Ireland C of C and Indust 1979–80, NI Chartered Inst of Mktg 1984–92; memb Cncl IOD 1972–93 (chm NI Div 1972–78); DLitt Ulster 1982; *Books* Midnight Oil (1961), A Television First (1977), Amusing (1984); *Recreations* reading and golf; *Clubs* Royal County Down Golf, Malone Golf; *Style*— Robert Brumwell Henderson, Esq, CBE; ✉ 8 Crabtree Rd, Ballynahinch, Co Down, N Ireland BT24 8RH

HENDERSON, Roger Anthony; QC (1980); s of Dr Peter Wallace Henderson (d 1984), and Dr Stella Dolores, *née* Morton; *b* 21 April 1943; *Educ* Radley, St Catharines Coll Cambridge; *m* 1968, Catherine Margaret; 3 da (Camilla (Mrs Andrew Roberts), Antonia, Venetia); *Career* called to the Bar 1964, recorder 1983–, dep High Ct judge 1987–, bencher Inner Temple 1985, head of chambers; pres Br Acad of Forensic Sci 1986, memb Cncl Legal Educn 1986–90; chm: Public Affrs Ctee of the Bar 1989 and 1990, Special Ctee of St Peter's Hosps Gp 1989–92, Civil Serv Arbitration Tbnl 1994–; chm London Hosp Med Coll 1993– (govr 1989–), govr Queen Mary & Westfield Coll 1993–; *Recreations* fly-fishing, gardening, shooting; *Style*— R A Henderson, Esq, QC; ✉ 9 Brunswick Gardens, London W8 (☎ 0171 727 3980); 2 Harcourt Buildings, Temple, London EC4 (☎ 0171 583 9020, fax 0171 583 2686); Holbury Mill, Lockerley, Hants; Upper Round Rd, St John's Parish, Nevis, West Indies

HENDERSON, Ronald Andrew; *b* 2 Feb 1946; *Educ* Kirkcaldy HS, Univ of Edinburgh; *m* Nancy; *Career* articled clerk then CA Arthur Andersen & Co 1968–72, with Brown & Root plc (UK, USA, Norway) 1972–87, fin dir Balfour Beatty plc 1987–90, fin dir BICC plc 1990–; *Style*— Ronald Henderson, Esq; ✉ BICC plc, Devonshire House, Mayfair Place, London W1X 5FH (☎ 0171 629 6622)

HENDERSON, Sir William MacGregor; kt (1976); s of William Simpson Henderson (d 1948); *b* 17 July 1913; *Educ* George Watson's Coll Edinburgh, Univ of Edinburgh (BSc, DSc), Royal (Dick) Veterinary Coll Edinburgh; *m* 1941, Alys Beryl, da of Owen Cyril Goodridge (d 1932); 4 s; *Career* asst Dept of Med Royal (Dick) Veterinary Coll Edinburgh 1936–38, dep dir sci Animal Virus Res Inst Pirbright 1955–56 (memb Sci Staff 1939–55); dir: Pan-American Foot and Mouth Disease Centre Rio de Janeiro 1957–65, ARC Inst for Res on Animal Diseases Compton 1967–72 (dep dir 1966–67); sec Agric Res Cncl 1972–78, chm Genetic Manipulation Advsy Gp 1979–81; memb: Sci Cncl Celltech Ltd 1980–82 (Bd of Dirs 1982–84), Bd Wellcome Biotechnology Ltd 1983–89; pres: Zoological Soc of London 1984–89, Royal Assoc of Br Dairy Farmers 1985–87; FRS, FRSE 1977; *Clubs* Athenaeum; *Style*— Sir William Henderson, FRS, FRSE; ✉ Culvers, Croft Road, Goring-on-Thames, Reading, Berks RG8 9ES (☎ 01491 872162)

HENDERSON-STEWART, Sir David James; 2 Bt (UK 1957), of Callumshill, Co Perth; s of Sir James Henderson-Stewart, 1 Bt, MP (d 1961); *b* 3 July 1941; *Educ* Eton, Trinity Coll Oxford; *m* 1972, Anne, da of Count Serge de Pahlen; 3 s (David b 1973, Nicolas b 1974, André b 1976), 1 da (Nathalie b 1981); *Heir* s, David Henderson-Stewart b 2 Feb 1973; *Clubs* Travellers'; *Style*— Sir David Henderson-Stewart, Bt; ✉ 90 Oxford Gardens, London W10 (☎ 0181 960 1278)

HENDRICK, Mark; MEP (Lab) Lancashire Central (majority 12,191); *b* 2 Nov 1958; *Educ* Univ of Manchester (MSc, CertEd); *Career* design engr for six years SERC; Lab Pty: memb 1982–, memb (and former branch sec) Salford Co-op Pty 1984–, chm Weaste and Seedley Branch 1987–94, chm Eccles Constituency 1990–94; MEP (Lab Co-op) Lancashire Central 1994–; Euro Parly Lab Pty spokesperson on economic and monetary affrs, memb Euro Parl Economic and Monetary Affrs Ctee, substitute memb Foreign Affrs and Temp Employment Ctees, sec NW Gp of Lab MEPs, memb Euro Parly Delgn to Japan; memb Salford City 1987– (served on Policy, Planning, Educn Ctees and Management Services Ctee (vice-chm)); alternate dir representing City of Salford Manchester Airport plc; memb NATFHE; *Style*— Mark Hendrick, Esq, MEP; ✉ Constituency Office: 260–262 Church Street, Blackpool FY1 3PZ (☎ 01253 292491, fax 01253 292493)

HENDRIE, Prof Gerald Mills; s of James Harold Hendrie (d 1981), and Florence Mary, *née* MacPherson (d 1968); *b* 28 Oct 1935; *Educ* Framlingham Coll Suffolk, RCM, Selwyn Coll Cambridge (MA, MusB, PhD); *m* 1, 11 July 1962, Dr Dinah Florence Barsham (d 1985); 2 s (Piers Edward b 13 May 1968, Dorian Mills b 15 Sept 1969); m 2, 15 Feb 1986, Dr Lynette (Lynne) Anne Maddern; *Career* dir of music Homerton Coll Cambridge 1962–63, lectr in history of music Univ of Manchester 1963–67, founding prof and chm Dept of Music Univ of Victoria Canada 1967–69, reader in music then founding prof Open Univ 1969–90, dir of studies in music St John's Coll Cambridge 1981–84, visiting fell in music Univ of Western Australia 1985; active as scholar, organist and composer; founding memb Cncl Handel Inst; FRSA 1981, FRCO, ARCM; *Recreations* windsurfing, cycling, rambling, reading; *Style*— Prof Gerald Hendrie

HENDRIE, HE Robert Andrew Michie; s of John Hendrie (d 1978), of Edinburgh, and Effie Campbell, *née* Mackay; *b* 4 May 1938; *Educ* Bradford GS, Trinity Hall Cambridge (MA); *m* 4 May 1964, Consuelo Liaño Solórzano, da of Ismael Liaño Fernández (d 1956), of Torrelavega, Spain; 2 da (Jessica Elena b 11 July 1967, Olivia Caroline b 24 Nov 1973); *Career* HM Dip Serv: MECAS 1961, Political Residency Bahrain 1962–65, HM Embassy Tehran Iran 1965–68, HM Embassy Tripoli Libya 1968–69, Latin-American Dept FCO 1969–73, HM Embassy Lima Peru 1973–75, HM Embassy Buenos Aires Argentina 1975–80, asst head Central African Dept, ME Dept and Info Dept FCO 1980–86, HM consul gen Lille France 1986–90, HM consul gen Dubai UAE 1990–94, HM ambass Uruguay 1994–; MIMgt 1985, MIL 1988; *Recreations* reading, walking, rugby, languages; *Style*— HE Mr Robert Hendrie; ✉ c/o FCO (Montevideo), King Charles St, London SW1A 2AH

HENDRY, Prof Arnold William; s of George Hendry (d 1952), of Buckie, and Mary, *née* Grassick (d 1921); *b* 10 Sept 1921; *Educ* Buckie HS, Univ of Aberdeen (BSc, PhD, DSc); *m* 1, 27 June 1946, Sheila Mary Cameron (d 1966), da of William Nicol Roberts (d 1962); 2 s (George b 1953, Eric b 1958, d 1978), 1 da (Margaret b 1949); m 2, 28 Dec 1968, Elizabeth Lois Alice, da of Harry R G Inglis (d 1939); *Career* civil engr Sir William Arrol & Co 1941–43, lectr Univ of Aberdeen 1943–49, reader King's Coll London 1949–51, prof of civil engrg Univ of Khartoum 1951–57, prof of bldg sci Univ of Liverpool 1957–63, prof of civil engrg Univ of Edinburgh 1964–88 (now prof emeritus); past pres, hon ed and hon memb Br Masonry Soc, memb Cncl The Cockburn Assoc Edinburgh 1978–87, pres Scottish Assoc for Public Tport; FICE, FIStructE, FRSA, FRSE 1961; *Recreations* reading, walking, travel, DIY; *Style*— Professor Arnold Hendry, FRSE; ✉ 146/6 Whitehouse Loan, Edinburgh EH9 2AN (☎ 0131 447 0368, fax 0131 447 8433)

HENDRY, Charles; MP (C) High Peak (majority 4,819); s of late Charles W R Hendry, and Peggy Hendry; *b* 6 May 1959; *Educ* Rugby, Univ of Edinburgh (BComm); *m* 20 July 1995, Mrs Sallie A Moores, yr da of Stuart Smith; 1 s (Charles Stuart Benjamin b 3 Sept 1996); *Career* account dir Ogilvy & Mather PR Ltd then assoc dir Burson-Marsteller Ltd PR conslts 1982–88; political advsr: to Rt Hon John Moore, MP as Sec of State for Social Servs 1988, to Rt Hon Tony Newton, MP as Sec of State for Social Servs then Trade and Indust 1988–90; Parly candidate (C): Clackmannan 1983, Mansfield 1987; MP (C) High Peak 1992–; PPS: to William Hague, MP as Min for Disabled People 1994–95, to Rt Hon Gillian Shephard, MP as Sec of State for Educn Feb-July 1995; vice chm Cons Pty July 1995–; chm All-Pty Parly Gp on Homelessness 1992–95; sec Cons Backbench: Social Security Ctee 1992–94, Inner Cities and Urban Affairs Ctee 1994–95; sec E Midlands Cons MPs 1992–; hon pres Br Youth Cncl 1992–; pres Edinburgh Univ Cons Assoc 1979–80, vice chm Scot Fedn of Cons Students 1980–81, vice chm Battersea Cons Assoc 1981–83, tstee Drive for Youth 1989–, tstee The Big Issue Fndn 1996–; *Recreations* tennis, skiing; *Style*— Charles Hendry, Esq, MP; ✉ House of Commons, London SW1A 0AA (☎ 0171 219 3000, fax 0171 219 2643)

HENDRY, (Edward) Colin James; s of Edward Alexander James Hendry, of Keith, Grampian, Scotland, and Anne, *née* Mackie; *b* 7 Dec 1965; *Educ* Keith GS; *m* Denise, da of David Duff; 1 da (Rheagan b 21 Aug 1989); *Career* professional footballer; 44 appearances Dundee 1984–87, 99 appearances Blackburn Rovers 1987–89, Manchester City 1989–91, rejoined Blackburn Rovers FC 1991–; Scotland B cap v E Germany 1990, memb full Scottish squad European Championship 1996; honours with Blackburn Rovers: Full Members' Cup 1987 (scored winning goal), promotion to Premier League 1992, winner FA Premier League 1994/95; Young Player of the Year Dundee 1985; Player of the Year: Blackburn Rovers 1988, Manchester City 1990; *Recreations* family, music; *Style*— Colin Hendry, Esq; ✉ c/o Blackburn Rovers FC, Ewood Park, Blackburn BB2 4JF

HENDRY, Prof David Forbes; s of Robert Ernest Hendry, of Fortrose, and Catherine Elizabeth, *née* Mackenzie; *b* 6 March 1944; *Educ* Glasgow HS, Univ of Aberdeen (MA), LSE (MSc, PhD); *m* 7 Oct 1966, Evelyn Rosemary, da of Rev John Vass (d 1974), of Aberdeen; 1 da (Vivien Louise b 1977); *Career* prof of econs LSE 1977–81 (lectr 1969–73, reader 1973–77), prof of econs Univ of Oxford and fell Nuffield Coll 1982–95, Leverhulme personal research prof 1995–; visiting prof: Yale Univ 1975, Univ of California Berkeley 1976, Catholic Univ of Louvain-la-Neuve 1980, Univ of California San Diego 1981 and 1989–90; special advsr House of Commons Select Ctee on the Treasy and Civil Serv 1979–80 and 1991, memb Academic Panel of HM Treasy 1976–89, chm Research Assessment Panel in Economics 1995–; Royal Economic Soc: pres 1992–95, hon vice-pres 1995–; foreign hon memb: American Econ Assoc 1991, American Acad of Arts and Sciences 1994; Guy medal in Bronze of the Royal Statistical Soc 1986; Hon LLD Univ of Aberdeen 1987; fell Econometric Soc 1976, FBA 1987; *Books* Econometrics and Quantitative Economics (with K F Wallis, 1984), PC-Give: An Interactive Econometric Modelling System (1989, and with J A Doornik 1992 and 1994), PC-Naive: An Interactive Program for Monte Carlo Experimentation in Econometrics (with A J Neale and N R Ericsson, 1991), Econometrics: Alchemy or Science (1993), Cointegration, Error Correction and the Econometric Analysis of Non-stationary Data (with A Banerjee, J J Dolado and J W Galbraith, 1993), Dynamic Econometrics (1995), The Foundations of Econometric Analysis (with M S Morgan, 1995); *Recreations* squash, golf; *Style*— Prof David F Hendry, FBA; ✉ 26 Northmoor Rd, Oxford OX2 6UR (☎ 01865 515588); Nuffield College, Oxford OX1 1NF (☎ 01865 278587, fax 01865 278557)

HENDRY, Diana Lois; da of Leslie Gordon McConomy (d 1964), and Amelia, *née* Kesler (d 1993); *b* 2 Oct 1941; *Educ* W Kirby Co GS for Girls, Filton Tech Coll, Univ of Bristol (BA, MLitt), privately (LLCM); *m* 1965 (m dis 1981), George Alexander Forbes Hendry; 1 s (Hamish b 1966), 1 da (Kate b 1970); *Career* reporter/feature writer The Western Mail Cardiff 1960–65, freelance journalist and writer 1965–; Eng teacher Clifton Coll 1987–90, tutor Bristol Poly 1987–93, tutor in lit Open Univ 1990–91, tutor in creative writing Univ of Bristol 1995–; first prize Stroud Int Poetry Competition 1976, second prize Peterloo Poetry Competition 1993 (third prize 1991), Whitbread Award (for children's novel) 1991, first prize Housman Soc Poetry Competition 1996; memb Soc of Authors 1987, memb PEN 1993; *Books* incl: Fiona Finds Her Tongue (1985, short-listed Smartie Award), Double Vision (1990), Harvey Angell (1991), Peterloo Preview 3 (1993), Making Blue (Peterloo Poets) (1995), The Awesome Bird (1995); numerous poems published in leading jls and anthologies; *Recreations* playing the piano; *Style*— Diana Hendry; ✉ c/o Julia MacRae Books, Random Century House, 20 Vauxhall Bridge Rd, London SW1V 2SA (☎ 0171 973 9750, fax 0171 233 8791)

HENDRY, James David (Jim); s of Alexander Hendry (d 1986), of Perth, and Ethel, *née* Stephen (d 1990); *b* 10 Oct 1939; *Educ* Perth Sr Acad; *m* 1 Sept 1969, Georgina, da of Edwin John Adkins (d 1989), of Wibarston, Leics; *Career* housing offr: Perth Town Cncl 1955–61, Glenrothes Devpt Corp 1961–65; dist housing offr Corby Devpt Corp 1965–76, sr housing offr Corby Town Cncl 1976–79; Br Cycling Fedn: offr and coach nat team mangr 1969–79, dir of racing 1979–85, dir of coaching devpt 1985–87, chief exec 1987–; club div and nat offr Scottish Cyclists' Union 1956–62; memb: Nat Assoc of Sports Coaches 1979, Soc of Assoc Execs 1988; *Books* BCF Training Manual (1987), Take Up Cycle Racing (1989); *Recreations* cycling, sea fishing; *Style*— Jim Hendry, Esq; ✉ British Cycling Federation, Stuart Street, Manchester M11 4DQ (☎ 0161 230 2301, fax 0161 231 0591)

HENDRY, John Alexander; s of Alexander Gore Hendry, of Upminster, Essex, and Joan Frances, *née* Davis; *b* 26 Nov 1955; *Educ* Campion Sch Hornchurch, Univ of Sussex (BA), Cranfield Sch of Mgmnt (MBA, Dirs' prize); *m* 16 April 1994, Susan, da of Dr B Q Scruggs, Jr, of Birmingham, Alabama, USA; *Career* grad trainee Ford Motor Co 1977–79, planner Milton Keynes Devpt Corp 1979–82, planning conslt Conran Roche 1982–88, chief exec Butlers Wharf 1988–91, dir The Design Museum 1991–94, mgmnt conslt 1994–; *Recreations* watching Millwall FC, cycling, listening to and playing country music; *Style*— John Hendry, Esq; ✉ 46 The Lane, London SE3 9SL (☎ and fax 0181 318 7315)

HENDRY, Stephen Gordon; MBE (1993); s of Gordon John Hendry, of Edinburgh, and Irene Agnes, *née* Anthony; *b* 13 Jan 1969; *Educ* Inverkeithing HS; *m* 30 June 1995, Amanda Elizabeth; 1 s (Blaine Thomas b 2 Oct 1996); *Career* professional snooker player 1985–; winner Rothmans Grand Prix 1987, 1991 and 1992, world doubles champion 1987 and 1991, Australian Masters champion 1987, Br Open champion 1988 and 1991, NZ Masters champion 1988, Scottish champion 1986, 1987 and 1988, Benson & Hedges Masters champion 1989, 1990, 1991, 1992, 1993 and 1996, Asian champion 1989 and 1990, Regal Masters champion 1989, 1990 and 1995, Dubai Classic champion 1989 and 1990, UK champion 1990, 1991, 1994, 1995 and 1996, Matchroom League champion 1991–92, 1993–94 and 1994–95, Hong Kong 555 Classic 1991, India Masters 1991, Benson & Hedges Irish Masters 1992, Canal+ Challenge 1992, Embassy world champion 1990, 1992, 1993, 1994, 1995 and 1996 (equalling record); holds record for most major titles won in a season (9 in 1991–92), holder of 62 major titles worldwide; memb Lord's Taverners Scotland; *Recreations* golf, music; *Style*— Stephen Hendry, Esq, MBE; ✉ Stephen Hendry Snooker Ltd, Kerse Rd, Stirling FK7 7SG (☎ 01786 462634, fax 01786 450068)

HENDRY, William Forbes (Bill); s of Duncan William Hendry, and Edna Beatrice, *née* Woodley; *b* 15 June 1938; *Educ* Uppingham, Univ of Glasgow (MD ChM); *m* 1961,

Christina Marie (Chirsty), da of Donald Macdonald (d 1990), of Brue Barvas, Isle-of-Lewis; 2 s (Duncan Forbes b 1962, Alexander Donald (Sandy) b 1968), 1 da ((Catherine) Louise b 1965); *Career* Univ of Glasgow Air Sqdn 1957–60; conslt urologist St Bartholomew's Hosp and Royal Marsden Hosp London, civilian conslt in urology to the RN, Hunterian prof and Sir Arthur Sims Cwlth travelling prof RCS 1989–90; co-ed British Jl of Urology; pres Section of Urology RSM 1994–95, pres Br Assoc of Urological Surgns 1996–; FRCS; *Books* Recent Advances in Urology/Andrology (6 edn 1993); *Recreations* gardening, fishing, cycling, skiing; *Clubs* RSM, RAC; *Style*— Bill Hendry, Esq; ✉ Dene Cottage, 6 Fulford Rd, Ewell, Epsom Surrey KT19 9QX (☎ 0181 786 8170); 149 Harley St, London W1N 2DE (☎ 0171 636 7426, fax 0171 935 5765)

HENDY, John; QC (1987); s of Jack Hendy, of Penzance, and Mary, *née* Best; *b* 11 April 1948; *Educ* Univ of London (LLB), Queen's Univ Belfast (LLM); *Career* called to the Bar 1972, bencher 1995; chm Inst Employment Rights 1989–; visiting fell Univ of Kent; memb Hon Soc of Gray's Inn 1966; ACIArb 1989; *Books* A Law unto themselves (3 edn 1993), Personal Injury Practice (co-author, 2 edn 1994), Redgrave's Health and Safety (co-author, 2 edn 1994), Munkman's Employers' Liability (co-author, 12 edn 1995); *Style*— John Hendy, Esq, QC; ✉ 1 Verulam Buildings, Gray's Inn, London WC1R 5LQ (☎ 0171 831 0801, fax 0171 405 1387)

HENDY, John; *Career* keyboardist; memb East 17 with Brian Harvey, *qv*, Anthony Mortimer, *qv*, Terry Coldwell, *qv*; 14 top twenty singles; singles incl: House Of Love 1992, Gold, Slow It Down, Deep 1993, West End Girls 1993, It's Alright 1993, Around the World 1994, Steam 1994, Stay Another Day (UK no 1) 1994, Let It Rain 1995, Do U Still 1996, Someone to Love 1996, Hey Child 1997; albums: Walthamstow (1992, UK no 1, platinum disc), Steam (UK no 4, 1994), Up All Night (UK no 7, 1995); *Style*—John Hendy, Esq; ✉ c/o London Records 90 Ltd, PO Box 1422, Chancellor's House, Chancellor's Road, London W6 9RS (☎ 0181 910 5111, fax 0181 741 2600)

HENHAM, His Hon John Alfred Henham; s of Alfred Henham, and Daisy Henham; *b* 8 Sept 1924; *m* 1946, Suzanne Jeanne Octavie Ghislaine, *née* Pinchart (d 1972); 2 s; *Career* stipendiary magistrate 1975–83, recorder 1979–83, circuit judge (NE Circuit) 1983–95; *Style*— His Hon J A Henham; ✉ 7 Middlefield Croft, Dore, Sheffield S17 3AS

HENIG, Prof Stanley; s of Sir Mark Henig (d 1978), of Leicester, and Grace, *née* Cohen; *b* 7 July 1939; *Educ* Wyggeston Sch Leicester, CCC Oxford (BA), Nuffield Coll Oxford (MA); *m* 27 March 1966, Ruth Beatrice, da of Kurt Munzer, of Leicester; 2 s (Simon Antony b 10 June 1969, Harold David b 27 May 1972); *Career* MP Lancaster 1966–70; lectr Civil Serv Coll 1972–75; Univ of Central Lancashire (formerly Lancashire Poly): lectr 1976–82, prof 1982–, dean Faculty of Health and Social Studies 1985–90, head Centre of European Studies 1990–95, head Dept of Politics and European Studies 1995–; govr Br Inst Recorded Sound 1975–80, chm Ct Royal Northern Coll of Music 1986–89 (hon memb 1989), ldr Lab Group Lancaster Cncl 1989– (ldr Cncl 1991–), memb Univ Assoc Contemporary Euro Studies 1970–; sec: Historic Masters Ltd 1984–, Historic Singers Tst 1985–; *Books* European Political Parties (1969), External Relations of European Community (1971), Political Parties in the European Community (1979), Power and Decision In Europe (1980), The Uniting of Europe (1997); *Recreations* listening to opera, collecting records; *Style*— Prof Stanley Henig; ✉ 10 Yealand Drive, Lancaster LA1 4EW (☎ 01524 69624); University of Central Lancashire, Corporation St, Preston (☎ 01772 893921, fax 01772 892919)

HENKEL, Dr David John; *b* 13 Jan 1921; *Educ* Univ of Natal (BSc), Univ of London (PhD), Imp Coll London (DIC); *Career* served WWII SACS 1941–45; head Soil Mechanics section Nat Bldg Res Inst Pretoria 1945–49, lectr then sr lectr in civil engrg Imp Coll of Sci and Technol and conslt on foundations dams landslides and harbours 1949–63, prof of soil mechanics Indian Inst of Technol and conslt to Indian Govt 1963–65, prof of civil engrg and head Dept of Geotechnical Engrg Cornell Univ NY 1965–70; Ove Arup & Partners: geotechnical conslt and advsr 1970–77, dir 1977–85, conslt concerned with foundation stability of offshore oil platforms and major bldgs worldwide, problems of ground subsidence in Nigeria, Das Island and S Africa, design and construction of Dubai dry docks and underground stations for the Hong Kong Mass Transit Railway and slope stability problems in Hong Kong 1986–94; chm Geotechnique Advsy Panel 1976–79; geotechnical advsr: Dept of Energy, Singapore Mass Rapid Transit Railway; advsr: DOE, CEGB; ret 1987; FICE, FEng 1986, FGS; *Publications* The Measurement of Soil Properties in the Triaxial Test (with A W Bishop, 1957), The Shear Strength of Saturated Remoulded Clays (1960), Local Geology and the Stability of Natural Slopes (1967), Geology and Foundation Problems in Urban Areas (1969), The Role of Waves in Causing Submarine Landslides (1970) The 22nd Rankine Lecture, Geology Geomorphology and Geotechnical Engineering (1982); *Style*— Dr D J Henkel, FEng

HENLEY, Sir Douglas Owen; KCB (1973, CB 1970); *b* 5 April 1919; *Educ* Beckenham Co Sch, LSE (BScEcon); *m* 1942, June Muriel, da of Thomas Ibbetson; 4 da; *Career* served WWII Queen's Own Royal W Kent Regt and HQ 12 Inf Bde N Africa Italy Greece (despatches twice); joined Treasy 1946; asst then dep under sec Dept of Econ Affrs 1964–69, second perm sec Treasy 1972–76, Comptroller and Auditor Gen 1976–81, advsr Deloitte Haskins and Sells (accountants) 1982–90; memb Cncl GPDST 1981–, govr Alleyn's Coll of God's Gift Dulwich 1981–90; hon fell LSE, Hon LLD Univ of Bath 1981; *Style*— Sir Douglas Henley, KCB; ✉ Walwood House, Park Rd, Banstead, Surrey SM7 3ER (☎ 01737 352626)

HENLEY, 8 Baron (I 1799); Oliver Michael Robert Eden; also (and sits as) Baron Northington (UK 1885); s of 7 Baron (d 1977) by his 2 w Nancy, da of late S Walton, of Gilsland, Cumbria; *b* 22 Nov 1953; *Educ* Clifton, Univ of Durham; *m* 11 Oct 1984, Caroline Patricia, da of late A G Sharp, of Mackney, Oxon; 3 s (Hon John Michael Oliver b 30 June 1988, Hon Patrick Francis b 23 Nov 1993, Hon Edward Andrew b 16 July 1996), 1 da (Hon Elizabeth Caroline b 26 Feb 1991); *Heir* s, Hon John Michael Oliver Eden b 30 June 1988; *Career* sits as Cons in House of Lords; called to the Bar Middle Temple 1977; memb Cumbria CC 1986–89, chm Penrith and The Border Cons Assoc 1987–89 (pres 1989–94); Lord in Waiting Feb-July 1989; Parly under sec of state: Dept of Social Security 1989–93, Dept of Employment 1993–94, MOD 1994–95; min of state Dept for Education and Employment 1995–; *Clubs* Brooks's, Pratt's; *Style*— The Rt Hon the Lord Henley; ✉ Scaleby Castle, Carlisle, Cumbria

HENMAN, Tim; *b* 6 Sept 1974; *Career* tennis player; turned professional 1993; ATP Tour ranking: 434 in 1993, 161 in 1994; results 1995: winner Br Nat Championships, winner (singles and doubles) Seoul ATP Challenger, winner Reunion ATP Challenger, semi-finalist Beijing ATP Challenger, semi-finalist Newcastle ATP Challenger, quarter-finalist Nottingham ATP Tour Event, winner both Davis Cup matches against Monaco, ATP Tour ranking 95; results 1996: winner Br Nat Championships, semi-finalist Compaq Grand Slam Cup Munich, semi-finalist ATP Tour Events Ostrava, Lyon, Seoul, Rotterdam, Copenhagen and Shanghai, quarter-finalist Wimbledon Championships, 4th round US Open, 2nd round Lipton Championships and Australian Open, winner Silver Medal men's doubles (with Neil Broad) Olympic Games Atlanta, ATP Tour ranking (as at Dec) 25, British Number 1; currently memb Br Davis Cup Team; *Style*— Tim Henman, Esq; ✉ c/o IMG, The Pier House, Strand on the Green, Chiswick, London W4 3NN (☎ 0181 233 5000)

HENNESSY, Sir James Patrick Ivan; KBE (1982, OBE 1968, MBE 1959), CMG (1975); s of Richard Hennessy, DSO, MC; *b* 26 Sept 1923; *Educ* Bedford Sch, Sidney Sussex Coll Cambridge, LSE; *m* 1947, Patricia, da of Wing Cdr F Unwin, OBE; 1 s (decd), 5 da; *Career* served RA 1942, seconded to IA (Adj) 1944, Battery Cdr 6 Indian FD Regt 1945; entered Colonial Admin Serv 1948; appts incl: dist offr Basutoland 1948, judicial cmmr 1953, jt sec Constitutional Cmmn 1957–59, sec to Exec Cncl 1960, seconded to Br High Cmmr's Office Pretoria 1961–63, electoral cmmr 1963; perm sec: Miny of Local Govt 1964, Home Affrs and Internal Security 1965, External Affrs and PM's Office 1966, ret; entered Dip Serv 1968; appts incl: chargé d'affaires Montevideo 1971–72, high cmmr to Uganda and non resident ambass to Rwanda 1973–76, consul-gen Cape Town 1977–79, govr and C-in-C Belize 1980–81, ret 1982; HM Chief Inspr of Prisons for Eng and Wales 1982–87; memb Parole Bd 1988–91; tstee Butler Tst 1988–; *Clubs* Naval and Military, Royal Cwlth Soc; *Style*— Sir James Hennessy, KBE, CMG

HENNESSY, Prof Peter John; s of William Gerald Hennessy, and Edith, *née* Wood-Johnson (d 1986); *b* 28 March 1947; *Educ* Marling Sch Stroud, St John's Cambridge (BA, PhD), LSE, Harvard Univ USA; *m* 14 June 1969, Enid Mary, *née* Candler; 2 da (Cecily b 1976, Polly b 1979); *Career* lobby corr Financial Times 1976, reporter Br Section The Economist 1982; The Times: reporter Higher Educn Supplement 1972–74, reporter 1974–76, Whitehall corr 1976–82, ldr writer 1982–84; columnist: New Statesman 1986–87, Whitehall Watch The Independent 1987–91; presenter Analysis BBC Radio Four 1986–92, columnist Director Magazine 1989–93; co fndr and co dir Inst of Contemporary Br History 1986–89 (bd memb 1989–, hon fell 1995–), ptnr Intellectual R & D 1990–, prof of contemporary history Queen Mary and Westfield Coll London 1992–, Gresham prof of rhetoric Gresham Coll 1994–97; visiting prof of govt Univ of Strathclyde 1989–, visiting scholar Giffith Univ Brisbane 1991; memb Cncl Policy Studies Inst 1992–; visiting fell: Policy Studies Inst 1986–92, Dept of Politics Univ of Reading 1988–94, Politics Dept Univ of Nottingham 1989–94, RIPA 1989–92; hon res fell Birkbeck Coll London 1990–91, tstee Attlee Fndn 1986–; chm Kennedy Meml Tst 1995–; Hon DLitt: Univ of the West of England 1995, Univ of Westminster 1996; FRSA 1992, FRHistS 1993; *Books* States of Emergency (jtly, 1983), Sources Close to the Prime Minister (jtly, 1984), What the Papers Never Said (1985), Cabinet (1986), Ruling Performance (jt ed, 1987), Whitehall (1989), Never Again - Britain 1945–51 (1992, Duff Cooper prize 1993, NCR award for non-fiction 1993), The Hidden Wiring - Unearthing the British Constitution (1995), Muddling Through - Power, Politics and the Quality of Government in Post War Britain (1996); *Recreations* running, listening to music; *Clubs* Savile, Attlee Mem Runners; *Style*— Prof Peter Hennessy; ✉ Department of History, Queen Mary and Westfield College, Mile End Road, London E1 4NS (☎ 0171 975 5555)

HENNIG, HE Dr Georg; LVO (1963); s of late Max Hennig, and late Eva, *née* Weinberger; *b* 3 Sept 1937; *Educ* Schottengymnasium Vienna, Univ of Vienna (Dr jur), Sch of Advanced Int Studies Johns Hopkins Univ (dip); *m* 1968, Ilona, *née* Esterhazy; 1 s (Maximilian b 1974); *Career* Austrian diplomat; Legal Dept Protocol Div Fed Miny for Foreign Affrs Vienna 1961–63, Perm Mission to UN NY 1963–66, PA to Foreign Min 1966–70, first sec Madrid 1970–71, sr dir Office of the Sec Gen of the UN 1972–75, min/head Office of the Sec Gen for Foreign Affrs Vienna 1976–79, ambass to India and accredited to Bangladesh, Sri Lanka and Nepal 1979–83, ambass to Japan and accredited to Repub of Korea 1983–86, special advsr to Fed Pres of Austria 1987–92, ambass Fed Miny for Foreign Affrs Vienna 1992–93, Austrian ambass to Ct of St James's 1993–96, dir Office of Federal Pres of Austria 1996–; Chev House Order of Orange (Netherlands) 1962; Kt Cdr: Francisco de Miranda (Venezuela) 1977, Adolphe of Nassau (Luxembourg) 1978, Merito Civil (Spain) 1979, Order of Omayeden (Syria) 1990, Order of Makarios III (Cyprus) 1991; Grand Cross: Rising Sun (Japan) 1986, Order of Independence (Jordan) 1987, Order of Merit (Malta) 1988, Order of Merit (Liechtenstein); *Recreations* reading, shooting; *Clubs* Travellers', St Johann's (Vienna); *Style*— Dr Georg Hennig, LVO; ✉ Office of the Federal President of Austria, Hofburg, 1010 Wien, Austria (☎ 00 43 1 534 220, fax 00 43 1 535 6512)

HENNIKER, Sir Adrian Chandos; 9 Bt (UK 1813), of Newton Hall, Essex; s of Brig Sir Mark Chandos Auberon Henniker, 8 Bt, CBE, DSO, MC (d 1991), and Kathleen Denys, *née* Anderson; *b* 18 Oct 1946; *Educ* Marlborough; *m* 1971, Ann, da of Stuart Britton, of Malvern House, Fairwater Rd, Llandaff, Cardiff; 2 da (Victoria Louise b 1976, Holly Georgina b (twin) 1976); *Heir* kinsman, Richard Frederick Henniker b 1906; *Style*— Sir Adrian Henniker, Bt; ✉ Llwyndu Court, Abergavenny, Gwent

HENNIKER, 8 Baron (I 1800); Sir John Patrick Edward Chandos Henniker; 9 Bt (GB 1765), KCMG (1965, CMG 1956), CVO (1960), MC (1945), DL (Suffolk 1994); also Baron Hartismere (UK 1866); s of 7 Baron Henniker (d 1980), and Molly (d 1953), da of Sir Robert Burnet, KCVO, MD; *b* 19 Feb 1916; *Educ* Stowe, Trinity Coll Cambridge (MA); *m* 1, 18 Dec 1946, (Margaret) Osla (d 1974), da of James Benning, of Montreal; 2 s (Hon Mark Henniker-Major, *qv*, Hon Charles Henniker-Major), 1 da (Hon Jane, *see* Richard Spring, MP); m 2, 1976, Mrs Julia Poland, da of George Mason, of Kew; *Heir* s, Hon Mark Henniker-Major, *qv*; *Career* served WWII Rifle Bde, Maj, Western Desert and mil mission to Yugoslav Partisans; Foreign Serv 1938–68: ambass Jordan 1960–62, ambass Denmark 1962–66, asst under sec FO 1966–68; dir-gen Br Cncl 1968–72, dir Wates Fndn 1972–78; tstee City Parochial Fndn 1973–90, govr Cripplegate Fndn 1979–90; memb: Parole Bd 1979–83, Mental Health Review Tbnl (Broadmoor), Cncl UEA 1974–86; dep chm Toynbee Hall 1980–87 (memb Cncl 1978–87); vice pres Nat Assoc Victims Support Schemes 1986–90; pres Rainer Fndn (chm Intermediate Treatment Fund 1985–90); chm: Suffolk Rural Housing Assoc 1985–91, Suffolk Community Alcohol Servs 1983–90; pres Community Cncl for Suffolk 1986–93, vice pres Suffolk Tst for Nature Conservation, pres Suffolk and N Essex Br Inst of Mgmnt 1985–88, govr Stowe Sch 1982–90; lay canon St Edmundsbury Cathedral 1986–92; DL (Suffolk 1988), pres Suffolk Agric Assoc 1989; Hon DCL UEA 1989, Hon LLD New England Coll Henniker New Hampshire 1993; *Clubs* Special Forces; *Style*— The Rt Hon the Lord Henniker, KCMG, CVO, MC, DL; ✉ The Red House, Thornham Magna, Eye, Suffolk (☎ 01379 783336)

HENNIKER-HEATON, Sir Yvo Robert; 4 Bt (UK 1912), of Mundarrah Towers, Sydney, Aust; s of Wing Cdr Sir (John Victor) Peregrine Henniker-Heaton, 3 Bt (d 1971); *b* 24 April 1954; *m* 1978, Freda, da of Brian Jones, of The Hollies, Broughton Astley, Leics; 1 s (Alastair John b 1990), 1 da (Julia Sermonda b 1987); *Heir* s, Alastair John Henniker-Heaton b 1990; *Career* memb NW Leics DC 1987–95; chm Kegworth Conservative Assoc 1986–89 and 1991–94; govr Ashby Willesley Sch 1995–; chm CEA Computer Security Technical Ctee 1993–95; MIIA; *Recreations* walking, writing, public speaking, travel; *Style*— Sir Yvo Henniker-Heaton, Bt; ✉ 7 Brendon Way, Ashby de la Zouch, Leics LE6 5EW

HENNIKER-MAJOR, Hon Mark Ian Philip Chandos; s and h of 8 Baron Henniker, KCMG, CVO, MC, *qv*, by his w, Margaret Osla Benning (d 1974); *b* 29 Sept 1947; *Educ* Eton, Trinity Coll Cambridge (MA), UCL (LLM); *m* 1973, Mrs Lesley Antoinette Masterton-Smith, da of Wing Cdr G W Foskett, of Spitchwick Farm, Poundsgate, Newton Abbot, Devon; 2 s (Frederick John Chandos b 1983, Edward George Major b 1985), 3 da (Jessica b 1977, Josephine b 1979, Harriet b 1981); *Career* slr and farming ptnr; co-fndr (1982) and ptnr Henniker-Major & Co of Ipswich, Felixstowe, Needham Market (as Crossman Henniker-Major & Co) and Cambridge; dir: Foxwest Ltd, Anglia Business Consultants Ltd, East Anglian Management Services; memb: Royal Aeronautical Soc, Br Insur Law Assoc, Law Soc, CLA, Lloyd's, East Anglian Marine Insur Assoc; FCIArb; *Recreations* squash, chess, bridge; *Clubs* Ipswich and Suffolk, MCC; *Style*— The Hon Mark Henniker-Major; ✉ Henniker-Major & Co, 1 & 3 Upper Brook Street, Ipswich, Suffolk IP4 1EG (☎ 01473 212681, fax 01473 215118)

HENNING, Claus Christian; OBE (1996); s of H G E Henning (d 1994), and Susanne, *née* Görtz (d 1993); *b* 16 Nov 1940; *Educ* Roan GS for Boys, Camberwell Sch of Arts and Crafts, Slade Sch of Art (Dip); *m* 1963, Maisie, *née* Tschang; 2 da; *Career* art asst and display offr Reading Museum 1963–69; British Council: exhbn designer 1969–73, asst regnl dir Sao Paulo 1973–79, dir Gen Exhbns Dept 1979–82, regnl dir Berlin 1982–86, dir Visiting Arts 1986–91, dir and cultural attaché Romania 1991–; *Recreations* driving, walking, DIY; *Style*— Claus Henning, Esq, OBE; ✉ The British Council, 10 Spring Gardens, London SW1A 2BN

HENNING, Matthew Clive Cunningham; s of Matthew Henning (d 1982), of Co Londonderry, and Olivia Mary, *née* Cunningham (d 1990); *b* 4 Jan 1934; *Educ* St Andrew's Coll Dublin, Coll of Architecture Oxford (DipArch); *m* 27 Sept 1972, Vivien Margaret, da of David Ernest Walker (d 1971), of Armagh; 1 s (Daniel Clive Walker b 1978), 1 da (Kate Louise b 1982); *Career* conslt architect in private practice; princ architect for the Southern Educn and Library Bd 1966–78; ARIBA, memb Royal Soc of Ulster Architects; *Recreations* Golf; *Clubs* Portadown Golf, Tandragee Golf, Bushfoot Golf, County (Armagh), City (Armagh); *Style*— Matthew C C Henning, Esq; ✉ Carraboo, Upper Church Lane, Portadown, Craigavon, County Armagh, Northern Ireland BT63 5JE (☎ 01762 333066); Bawnmore, Castlerock, Coleraine, Co Londonderry; Clive Henning Architects, Progressive House, Market St, Portadown, Co Armagh BT62 3JY (☎ 01762 338811, fax 01762 330567)

HENRI, Adrian Maurice; s of Arthur Maurice Henri (d 1970), and Emma, *née* Johnson (d 1970); *b* 10 April 1932; *Educ* St Asaph GS N Wales, Dept of Fine Art King's Coll Newcastle, Univ of Durham (BA); *m* 28 Oct 1959 (m dis 1974), Joyce (d 1987), da of Inspr Joseph Wilson; *Career* lectr in art: Manchester Coll of Art 1961–64, Liverpool Coll of Art 1964–67; led poetry-rock gp Liverpool Scene 1967–70, freelance poet, painter, singer songwriter and playwright 1970–; writer in residence: The Tatterhall Centre Cheshire 1981–82, Dept of Educn Univ of Liverpool 1989; pres: Merseyside Arts Assoc 1978–80, Liverpool Acad of Arts 1972–81; Hon DLitt Liverpool 1990; *Exhibitions* princ one-man shows: John Moores Liverpool Exhibitions 1962, 1963 and 1967 (second prizewinner 1972, 1974, 1978, 1980, 1989 and 1993), ICA London 1968, Art Net London 1975, Williamson Art Gallery Birkenhead 1976, Retrospective 1960–76, Wolverhampton City Art Gallery 1976, Demarco Gallery Edinburgh 1978, The Art of Adrian Henri 1933–85, South Hill Park Bracknell and touring 1986–87, Acorn Gallery Liverpool 1992, Southport Arts Centre 1993, Storey Inst Lancaster 1994, Merkmal Gallery Liverpool 1994, Whitford Gallery London 1997; *TV Plays* Yesterday's Girl 1973, The Husband, The Wife and The Stranger 1986; *Lyrics* Lowlands Away (music by Richard Gordon-Smith for Royal Liverpool Orch) 1996; *Books* Collected Poems (1986), Wish You were Here (poems 1990), Not Fade Away (poems 1994); for children: The Phantom Lollipop Lady (poems 1986), Rhinestone Rhino (poems 1989), Dinner with The Spratts (1993), Eric the Punk Cat (1980), Eric and Frankie in Las Vegas (1987), The Postman's Palace (1990); for teenagers: Box and Other Poems (1990), The Mersey Sound (with Roger McGough and Brian Patten, 1967, 3 edn, 1983), New Volume (1983), Playscript - The Wakefield Mysteries (1991); *Plays* I Wonder (with Michael Kustow, 1968), I Want (with Nell Dunn, 1983), The Wakefield Mysteries (1988), Fears and Miseries of the Third Term (1989); *Recreations* watching Liverpool FC, food and wine, travel, crime and Gothic novels and films; *Clubs* Chelsea Arts; *Style*— Adrian Henri, Esq

HENRIQUES, Richard Henry Quixano; QC (1986); s of Cecil Quixano Henriques, of Thornton, Cleveleys, and Doreen Mary Henriques (d 1965); *b* 27 Oct 1943; *Educ* Bradfield, Worcester Coll Oxford (BA); *m* 14 July 1979, Joan Hilary (Toni), da of Maj Percy Sheard Senior (d 1947); 1 s (Daniel b 1981), 1 step s (David b 1970); *Career* called to the Bar Inner Temple 1967 (bencher 1994); recorder of the Crown Ct 1983, memb Gen Cncl of the Bar 1993–, memb Northern Circuit Exec Ctee 1993–, ldr of Northern Circuit 1996–; memb Cncl Rossall Sch 1986–96; *Style*— Richard Henriques, Esq, QC; ✉ Ilex House, Woodhouse Rd, Little Thornton, Lancashire FY5 5LQ (☎ 01253 826199); Deans Court Chambers, Crown Sq, Manchester (☎ 0161 834 4097)

HENRY, Anthony Patrick Joseph; s of Patrick Joseph Henry (d 1944), of Nottingham, and Helen Alethea, *née* Green; *b* 19 April 1939; *Educ* Epsom Coll Surrey, St Thomas' Hosp Med Sch London (MB BS); *m* 1973, Patricia Mary, da of Kenneth Spiby, of Packington, nr Ashby De La Zouch, Leics; 2 s (Joseph Patrick b 1974, George Michael b 1981), 1 da (Sarah Louise b 1977); *Career* TA Artists Rifles 21 SAS 1959–61; lectr in anatomy Univ of Alberta Canada 1966–67, res in surgery Durban S Africa 1968–70, sr registrar in orthopaedics Nottingham 1972–76, conslt orthopaedic surgn Derby 1976–; lectr in anatomy Derby Sch of Occupational Therapy 1974–; examiner in surgery Br Assoc of Occupational Therapists 1976–88, pres Naughton-Dunn Club (orthopaedic club of the Midlands) 1993–94; govr St Wynstans Sch Repton 1980–86; memb BMA 1963, FRCS 1971, fell Br Orthopaedic Assoc 1976; *Recreations* sailing, tennis, cricket; *Style*— Anthony Henry, Esq; ✉ Four Winds, Wagon Lane, Bretby, Derbys DE15 0QF (☎ 01283 217358); Orthopaedic Department, Derbyshire Royal Infirmary, Derby DE1 2QY (☎ 01332 347141)

HENRY, Clare; da of Walter Price Jenkinson (d 1989), and Marjorie Amy, *née* Bratley; *b* 21 Feb 1947; *Educ* Queen Elizabeth GS, Univ of Reading (BA); *children* 1 s (Damian b 25 Dec 1969), 1 da (Zara b 29 Nov 1976); *Career* researcher Paul Mellon Fndn of Br Art 1968–70, art critic The Herald 1980–; Scot ed: Artline 1984–90, Arts Review 1984–93, Scottish TV 1984–87; currently arts contrib to BBC radio and TV, contrib to various magazines and exhibition catalogues; exhibition curator: New Scottish Prints (NY) 1983, London's Serpentine Summer Show 1985, Artists at Work (Edinburgh Festival) 1986, The Vigorous Imagination (Nat Gallery of Scot, Edinburgh Festival) 1987, Scotland at the Venice Biennale 1990, Critics Choice London 1992, Critics Choice Glasgow 1994, Glasgow Sch of Art Choice 1994; memb: Glasgow Print Studio 1973–80 (also chm), NUJ, AICA, Visiting Arts Br Cncl; fndr memb: SALVO, Glasgow Print Studio; FRSA; *Clubs* Chelsea Arts; *Style*— Clare Henry; ✉ c/o The Herald, 195 Albion Street, Glasgow G1 1QP (☎ 0141 552 6255)

HENRY, Dorothy Sarah; da of John Morris (d 1963), of Anglesey, and Margaret Gladys, *née* McLeod (d 1973); *b* 27 Sept 1918; *Educ* Liverpool Inst for Girls (scholar); *m* 4 Sept 1953, Samuel Alexander Campbell Henry; 1 da (Katherine Mary Campbell (Mrs Orme) b 19 April 1956); *Career* sec and dir Instn of British Engrs 1963–; *Books* Golden Age of Concrete (1964), Modern British Bridges (1966); *Style*— Mrs Dorothy Henry; ✉ Institution of British Engineers, 6 Hampton Place, Brighton BN1 3DD (☎ 01273 734274)

HENRY, Sir James Holmes; 2 Bt (UK 1923), of Cahore, Co Londonderry, CMG (1960), MC (1944), TD (1950), QC (Tanganyika 1953, Cyprus 1957); s of Rt Hon Sir Denis Stanislaus Henry, 1 Bt (d 1925), 1 Lord Chief Justice of NI, and Violet (d 1966), da of Rt Hon Hugh Holmes (former Lord Justice, Court of Appeal Ireland); *b* 22 Sept 1911; *Educ* Mount St Mary's Coll Chesterfield, Downside, UCL (BA); *m* 1, 1941 (m dis 1948), Susan Mary, da of Arthur G Blackwell; m 2, 1949, Christina Hilary, da of Sir Hugh Oliver Holmes, KBE, CMG, MC, QC, and wid of Lt-Cdr Christopher Hayward Wells, RN; 3 da (Teresa Violet (Mrs Gordon Stewart) b 1949, Christina Mary (Mrs Peter W I Ingram) b 1951, Rosemary Jane (Mrs Peter Winckley) b 1955); *Heir* nephew, Patrick Denis Henry b 20 Dec 1957; *Career* served WW II (wounded), Capt London Irish Rifles (Royal Ulster Rifles); called to the bar Inner Temple 1934, crown counsel Tanganyika 1946, legal draftsman 1949, slr-gen 1952, attorney-gen Cyprus 1956; memb Foreign Compensation Cmmn 1960–83 (chm 1977–83), ret; *Clubs* Travellers'; *Style*— Sir James Henry, Bt, CMG, MC, TD, QC; ✉ Kandy Lodge, 18 Ormond Ave, Hampton-on-Thames, Middx TW12 2RU

HENRY, Dr John Anthony; s of John Aloysius Henry, and Emma Susanna, *née* Elphick; *b* 11 March 1939; *Educ* St Joseph's Acad Blackheath, King's Coll and King's Coll Hosp London (MB BS); *Career* conslt physician Guy's Hosp 1982–, conslt physician Nat Poisons Information Serv 1982–; FRCP 1986; *Books* ABC of Poisoning (jtly, 1984), BMA Guide to Medicines and Drugs (1988, 3 edn 1994); *Recreations* walking; *Style*— Dr John Henry; ✉ Guy's Hospital, St Thomas Street, London SE1 9RT (☎ 0171 433 1160, fax 0171 433 1276)

HENRY, Keith Nicholas; s of Kenneth George Henry, of 108 Montrose Ave, Luton, Beds, and Barbara, *née* Benns (d 1989); *b* 3 March 1945; *Educ* Bedford Sch, Univ of London (BSc), Univ of Birmingham (MSc); *m* 1974, Susan Mary, da of Roy Horsburgh; 2 da (Lucy Elizabeth b 1976, Claire Suzanne b 1978); *Career* engr mangr Brown & Root de France SA 1975–77, md Far East area Brown & Root (Singapore) Ltd 1977–80; Brown & Root (UK) Ltd: sr mangr 1980–83, chief engr 1983–85, commercial dir 1985–87; md: Brown & Root Vickers Ltd 1987–89, Brown & Root Marine 1989–90; chief exec Brown & Root Ltd 1990–95; chief exec National Power PLC 1995–; non-exec dir Enterprise Oil plc 1995–; memb Cncl Defence Evaluation & Research Agency; FEng, FICE, MInstD, FRSA, FIMgt; *Recreations* shooting, sailing, golf; *Clubs* RAC, IOD, Mark's; *Style*— Keith Henry, Esq, FEng; ✉ National Power PLC, Senator House, 85 Queen Victoria Street, London EC4V 4DP (direct ☎ 0171 615 3030, fax 0171 615 3031)

HENRY, Lenny; *b* 29 Aug 1958; *m* Dawn French; *Career* comedian and actor; numerous tours incl Loud! 1994, Australia 1995; *Television* incl: New Faces (debut), Tiswas, Three of a Kind (BBC) 1981–83, The Lenny Henry Show, Alive and Kicking (BBC) 1991, Bernard & the Genie (BBC) 1991, In Dreams (BBC) 1992, The Real McCoy (BBC) 1992, Gareth Blackstock in Chef (3 series, BBC), Lenny Hunts the Funk (South Bank Special), New Soul Nation (Channel 4), White Goods (ITV) 1994, Funky Black Shorts 1994, The Lenny Henry Show (6 episodes, BBC) 1995, Comic Relief; *Films* incl: True Identity (Touchstone/Disney) 1991; *Video* Lenny Henry Live and Unleashed 1989, Lenny Henry Live and Loud 1994; *Awards* incl: Monaco Red Cross Award, The Golden Nymph Award (for Alive and Kicking) 1992, Radio & Television Industry Club Award for BBC Personality of the Year 1993; *Books* The Quest for the Big Woof (autobiographical, 1991), Charlie and the Big Chill (children's book, pub Victor Gollancz 1995); *Style*— Lenny Henry, Esq; ✉ c/o PBJ Management Ltd, 5 Soho Square, London W1V 5DE (☎ 0171 287 1112, fax 0171 287 1448)

HENRY, Maxwell Delvin (Max); s of Ernist William Henry (d 1981), of Devon, and Eunice Constance, *née* Powell (d 1975); *b* 6 June 1941; *Educ* Addison Garden Secdy Modern, Christopher Wren Art Coll; *m* (m dis); 4 s (Saul b 1968, Aaran b 1969, Rufus b 1982, Barnaby b 1985), 1 da (Tracy b 1963); *Career* dispatch Pritchard Wood & Partners 1961–62, paste up Holmwood Advertising 1962–65, art dir McKay & Partners 1965–68, creative group head Horniblow Cox Freeman 1968–70, art dir FCB Ltd 1970–74, bd dir Doyle Dane Bernbach 1974–80, head of art and creative dir J Walter Thompson 1980–87; exec creative dir: Ted Bates & Partners 1987–88, Laing Henry Ltd 1988–95 (merged with Saatchi & Saatchi Advertising 1995); recipient awards from: D&AD, Creative Circle, Campaign Press, Cannes Film Festival, London TV Awards, One Show NY, BTA; *Clubs* Groucho, Harry's Bar; *Style*— Max Henry, Esq; ✉ The Tannery, Eyhorne Street, Hollingbourne, Kent (☎ 01622 880544, car 0589 141135)

HENRY, Michael Meldrum; s of Cdre J M Henry, of Prinsted, Hants, and Helen Muriel, *née* Davies (d 1971); *b* 19 Aug 1946; *Educ* Steyning GS, Univ of London (MB BS); *m* 3 Aug 1981, Christine Mary, da of Alfred Douglas Parkyn (d 1985); *Career* lector to Trinity Coll Cambridge and lectr in surgery Cambridge Univ 1976–78, Hunterian prof RCS 1980, conslt surgn Royal Marsden Hosp and Chelsea and Westminster Hosp, sr lectr Academic Surgical Unit UCL; hon conslt surgn: St Mark's Hosp for Diseases of Colon and Rectum London, Nat Hosp for Nervous Diseases London; Freeman Worshipful Soc of Apothecaries; memb: BMA, RSM; FRCS; *Books* Coloproctology & The Pelvic Floor (1985), Surgery of Prolapse & Incontinence (1988); *Recreations* modern history, opera; *Clubs* Athenaeum; *Style*— Michael Henry, Esq; ✉ 26 Langham Mansions, Earls Court Square, London SW5 9UJ (☎ 0171 370 7551); 106 Harley St, London W1N 1AF (☎ 0171 935 3889)

HENRY, Richard Charles; TD (1976); s of John Richard Henry, OBE, JP (d 1993), and Blanche Catherine, *née* Barrett; *b* 26 Feb 1941; *Educ* Sherborne; *m* 15 April 1976, Judy Ann Massey; 1 s (Charles b 1977), 3 da (Belinda b 1979, Jane b 1979, Margaret b 1983); *Career* articled Deloittes 1960; Coopers & Lybrand 1978–84; fin dir and sec Press Association 1984–96; gp fin dir Nation Printers and Publishers 1996–; Capt HAC (TA) 1961–76; memb Ct of Assts HAC 1975 (treas 1990–93, vice pres 1994–96), Freeman City of London 1986, Liveryman Worshipful Co of Barbers 1989; FCA 1966; *Recreations* TA, bridge, fishing; *Clubs* Army and Navy, Muthaiga; *Style*— Richard Henry, Esq, TD; ✉ c/o Nation House, PO Box 49010, Kimathi Street, Nairobi, Kenya

HENRY, Stephen James Bartholomew (Steve); s of John Keith Maxwell Henry (d 1979), and Jose Isobel Prendergast, *née* Bartholomew (d 1975); *b* 21 Sept 1955; *Educ* Cranleigh Sch, St Catherine's Coll Oxford (BA, Shelley-Mills prize); *m* 18 Oct 1986, Angela Marie, da of Michael Coates; 2 da (Sophia Dominique Marie b 19 Nov 1989, Bryony Christabel b 24 Dec 1992); *Career* copywriter: Crawfords 1979–81, Gold Greenlees Trott 1981–85; copywriter and creative gp head Wight Collins Rutherford Scott 1985–87, fndr and creative ptnr HHCL and Partners (formerly Howell Henry Chaldecott Lury) 1987–; agency of year Campaign magazine 1989, winner of awards for various advertising campaigns; FIPA; *Recreations* swimming, reading, writing, being with my daughters; *Style*— Steve Henry, Esq; ✉ HHCL and Partners, Kent House, 14–17 Market Place, Great Titchfield Street, London W1N 7AJ (☎ 0171 436 3333, fax 0171 436 2677)

HENRY, Susie Elizabeth Jane; da of Brian Glynn Henry, of Bere House, Pangbourne, Berks, and Elizabeth Jean, *née* Craig; *b* 24 June 1951; *Educ* Wycombe Abbey Sch, Winchester Coll of Art, Goldsmiths' Coll of Art (DipAD); *m* 1 1975 (m dis 1988), Michael Richard Graham Gilmore, s of Richard Gilmore; m 2 1989, Alexander Denis Field, s of late Denis Alfred Field; 2 s (Rory Alexander Ernest Field b 1984, Angus James Alfred Field b 1990), 1 da (Sarah-Rose Elizabeth Mathilde Gilmore b 1979); *Career* copywriter: Maisey Mukerjee Russell 1972–74, French Gold Abbott Kenyon and Eckhart 1974–76, Cogent Elliott London 1976–78; sr writer Doyle Dane Bernbach 1978–80; Waldron Allen Henry & Thompson: founding ptnr 1980, jt creative dir 1980, dir Miller & Leeves WAHT and BST Ltd since mergers 1990 and 1992; sr copywriter and memb Bd K Advertising (formerly KHBB) 1993–; best known campaign 'We won't make a drama out of a crisis' for Commercial Union; other award winning campaigns incl: COI drink-drive and child safety, Bob Martin's, Welsh Devpt Agency; major awards: 5 Silver D&AD Awards, 3 Gold and 5 Silver BTA Awards, Best Financial Advertisement Campaign Press Awards 1980, 1988 and 1994, Cannes Silver Lion, Clio Gold Award, etc; memb D&AD Assoc; *Recreations* family, cooking, Italian opera, walking, Scotland; *Clubs* Academy; *Style*— Ms Susie Henry; ✉ K Advertising, 89 Whitfield Street, London WC1 (☎ 0171 462 7777, fax 0171 462 7766)

HENSHALL, John Mark; s of John Henshall (d 1996), of Stockport, and Margaret Winifred, *née* Passmore (d 1989); *b* 6 Jan 1942; *Educ* Queen Elizabeth GS Wakefield, Stockport GS; *m* 21 Sept 1979, Paulien, da of Dr Pieter Roorda (d 1991), of Haarlem, Netherlands, and Jeanette Pauline, *née* Volkmaars; 1 s (John Pieter b 12 May 1987), 2 da (Annelies b 11 Jan 1981, Martien b 13 July 1984); *Career* BBC cameraman and lighting 1961–76; dir of photography and lighting in film and TV 1978–, dir EPI Centre of Electronic Photo-Imaging 1993–; conslt, writer and lectr on electronic and digital imaging - photography without film 1991–; memb Ctee Soc of TV Lighting Dirs 1986–93; Guild of TV Cameramen: vice chm 1974–78, hon life memb 1978, hon fell 1984; memb Cncl RPS 1988–94 (chm Film and Video Associateship and Fellowship Distinctions Ctee 1992–); BIPP: chm Admissions and Qualifications in motion picture, TV, video and electronic imaging, memb Cncl 1986–94, pres 1991–92; memb Cncl and chm Digital Imaging Ctee Br Photographic Assoc; FRGS 1967, FRPS 1985, FBIPP 1985; *Books* Dealers in Coins (1969), Sir H George Fordham, Cartobibliographer (1969), Photographic Qualifications for Professionals (1992); ed Digital Imaging Plus; contributing ed: electronic and digital imaging, The Photographer; author of numerous articles on digital imaging, photography, film and TV; *Recreations* philogyny, philately, philomathy; *Style*— John Henshall, Esq; ✉ Electronic Photo-Imaging, 68 High Street, Stanford in the Vale, Oxfordshire SN7 8NL (☎ 01367 710191, fax 01367 710192, cellphone 0836 263000, e-mail henshall@epicentre.co.uk, website http://www.epicentre.co.uk)

HENSHALL, Keith Rodney; s of Bernard Henry Henshall, and Doris Lilian Henshall, of London; *b* 15 Aug 1947; *Educ* Henry Thornton Sch London, Univ of Manchester (LLB, MBA); *m* 9 Dec 1967, Maureen, da of George Pascoe; 1 s (Carl Matthew b 10 July 1968), 1 da (Sharon Marie b 9 Sept 1970); *Career* md Charles Barker Public Relations Ltd 1985–88; chm: The Henshall Centre Ltd 1988–, Cutting Edge Software Ltd 1988–; IPR: memb Nat Cncl 1984–89, nat educn chm 1988 and 1989, pres-elect 1994, pres 1995; founding external examiner to PR degrees Bournemouth and Stirling Univs, fndr chm Professional Advsy Ctee to PR masters degree Manchester Metropolitan Univ; MIPR 1984, FInstD 1986; *Recreations* basketball; *Style*— Keith Henshall, Esq; ✉ Bridge Mount, Jacksons Lane, Hazel Grove, Stockport, Cheshire SK7 5JP (☎ 0161 439 4448); The Henshall Centre Ltd, Victoria Station House, 191 Victoria Street, London SW1E 5NE (☎ 0171 592 0900, fax 0171 828 3626)

HENSHALL, Ruthie; da of David Henshall, of Stulton, Suffolk, and Gloria Diana, *née* Wilson; *b* 7 March 1967; *Educ* Bullswood GS Chislehurst Kent, Laine Theatre Arts Coll Epsom Surrey; *Career* actress and singer; *Theatre* work incl: Mitzi in the Pied Piper of Hamlyn (Churchill Theatre Bromley) 1985, Ethel Dobbs in Fainettes (Bromley) 1985, lead role in Celluloid City Dandini in Cinderella (Aldershot) 1986, Maggie in A Chorus Line (nat tour) 1987, Jemima/Demeter/Grizabella/Griddlebone in Cats (New London Theatre) 1987–89, Ellen in Miss Saigon (Theatre Royal London) 1989–90, Aphra in Children of Eden (The Prince Edward Theatre) 1990–91, season at Chichester Festival Theatre 1991, Mary in Follow the Star (Chichester); singer and dancer: Mack and Mabel (charity performance for Theatre Royal), Fantine in Les Miserables, Polly Baker in Crazy for You (Prince Edward) 1993, Amalia Balash in She Loves Me (Savoy Theatre) 1995, Oliver (Palladium) 1996; other credits incl: singer in Andrew Lloyd Webber's concert in Spain for Expo 92, Ruthie Henshall in Concert (Royal Festival Hall), opening solo performance Olivier Awards 1994, debut album Love is Here to Stay; contribs to numerous recording sessions; *Television* incl: Wogan (BBC), Friday Live (Central), Children in Need (BBC), Secrets Out (BBC), Save The Children (Thames); *Awards* Olivier Awards for Best Actress: Crazy for you 1993, She Loves Me 1995; *Recreations* water skiing, snow skiing, keeping fit, swimming; *Style*— Ms Ruthie Henshall; ✉ Hilary Gagan, Daly Gagan Associates, 68 Old Brompton Rd, London SW7 3LQ (☎ 0171 581 0121, fax 0171 589 2922)

HENSHAW, Brig Clinton Lionel Grant; CBE (1985), ADC (1988); s of Col C F G Henshaw, OBE, TD (d 1972), and Joan Aymer, *née* Ainslie; *b* 27 June 1936; *Educ* Wellington, RMA Sandhurst; *m* 15 Feb 1964, Suzanne Elliot, da of Cdr J A Philips (d 1986); 2 da (Caroline Emma Grant b 24 Sept 1965, Nichola Elizabeth b 25 July 1967); *Career* cmmnd King's Royal Rifle Corps 1956; served: BAOR, Berlin, Guiana, Zimbabwe, France, Canada, NI; CDS staff MOD 1975–77, CO Rifle Depot 1977–79, DA Zimbabwe 1980–82, head DI ROW MOD 1982–85, cabinet office 1985–87, MA Paris 1988–91; sec The Beit Tst; FIMgt; *Recreations* fishing, shooting, golf, gardening; *Clubs* Army and Navy; *Style*— Brig Clinton Henshaw, CBE

HENSHAW, Hugh Nigel; s of Harold Henshaw (d 1955), of Rottingdean, Sussex, and Evelyn Louise, *née* Henshaw; *b* 28 Sept 1935; *Educ* Sherborne; *m* 29 March 1980, Anne Victoria Helen, da of Henry Thomas Hamilton Foley, MBE, JP (d 1959), of Stoke Edith Park, Hereford; 1 s (Thomas b 1983), 1 da (Katharine b 1981); *Career* Nat Serv 2 Lt 2 RHA 1954–55, TA Capt HAC 1956–60; admitted slr 1961; Clifford Turner, Freshfields; ptnr: Lovell White & King 1968–88 (former memb), Lovell White Durrant 1988–96, conslt Farrer & Co 1996–; chm Will Charitable Tst 1989–, exec chm Will Woodlands 1994–; memb Law Soc 1961; *Recreations* conservation, travel, opera; *Clubs* Bucks, HAC; *Style*— Hugh Henshaw, Esq; ✉ Farrer & Co, 66 Lincolns Inn Fields, London WC2A 3LH (☎ 0171 242 2022, fax 0171 831 6301)

HENSLOWE, Philip Francis Armitage; s of Lt-Col Francis Arthur Henslowe, MBE, (late RA, d 1985), of Bournville, and Mercy Eleanor, *née* Robertson (d 1993); *b* 27 April 1934; *Educ* Cheltenham Coll, RMA Sandhurst; *m* 1960, Elizabeth Moira, da of Herbert Millar Allely, of Tralee, Co Kerry; 1 da (Anyon Elizabeth Deloraine b 1961); 2 s (James Philip Robert b 1964, Peter Ross Barthelemon b 1968); *Career* cmmnd RA 1953, served Korea, Hong Kong, Malaya, Borneo, Germany, UK and various UN appts, ret as Maj 1973; area mangr (Cornwall) Celtic Cross Insurance & Investment Brokers 1973–75, mangr private health care homes Cornwall 1975–79; Bournville Village Trust Birmingham: community and public affrs offr 1979–89, head of PR servs 1989–91, gp dir of public affrs 1991–97; IPR: chm Midland Region 1986–88, chm Educn and Trg Ctee 1989–91, memb Nat Cncl 1989–91 and 1996–98, chm Professional Practice Ctee 1996; tstee PR Educn Tst 1989–93; chm: Mktg Standards Bd, Bd of Tstees Zillwood Tst 1990–93; co-opted govr CAM Fndn, chm of govrs Kings Norton Girls' GM Sch Birmingham 1990–94; memb Indust Advsy Panel of Business Sch: Napier Univ Edinburgh, Coll of St Mark & St John Plymouth; occasional lectr in PR: Univ of Sheffield, Holborn Law Coll London; PR advsr on Communication Studies Course: Univ of Central England Birmingham, Univ of Central Lancashire Preston; visiting tutor in PR Matthew Boulton Coll Birmingham, tutor in PR numerous other bodies/instns; MIMgt 1981, FIPR 1991 (MIPR 1980), MIPRA 1993 (memb UK Ctee), FCAM 1995; *Publications* PR for Housing Associations (NFHA, 1983), Help (NFHA, 1986), Ninety Years On (Bournville Village Tst, 1984), Practitioners Guide to Implementing Public Relations (1996); *Recreations* music, photography, reading (novels and history), gardening, travel; *Clubs* Birmingham Publicity; *Style*— Philip Henslowe, Esq

HENSMAN, Hon Mrs ((Mary) Sheila); *née* Wakefield; OBE (1992); da of 1 Baron Wakefield of Kendal (d 1983), and Rowena Doris, *née* Lewis (d 1981); *b* 29 April 1922; *Educ* Francis Holland Sch, Downe House Newbury; *m* 6 July 1945, Brig Richard Frank Bradshaw Hensman, CBE (d 1988), s of Capt Melvill Hensman, DSO, RN (d 1967), of South Hay House, Bordon, Hants; 1 s (Peter Richard Wavell b 30 Aug 1948), 1 da (Suzannah Mary b 9 Feb 1953); *Career* dir: Battlefields (Holdings) Ltd, Lake District Estates Co Ltd, Ullswater Navigation & Transit Co Ltd, Ravenglass & Eskdale Railway Co Ltd; pres DHO Ski Club 1975–80, Ladies Ski Club 1987–90, Cumbria Tourist Bd 1996– (chm 1990–96); *Recreations* skiing, walking, gardening; *Clubs* Lansdowne, Ski Club of Great Britain; *Style*— The Hon Mrs Hensman, OBE; ✉ Lindum Holme, Stricklandgate, Kendal, Cumbria LA9 4QG (☎ 01539 725093)

HENSON, Brian David; s of late James Maury (Jim) Henson, of New York and London, and Jane Anne Nebel Henson; *b* 3 Nov 1963; *Educ* Phillips Acad Andover Mass, Univ of Colorado; *m* Nov 1990, Ellis Flyte, *qv*; *Career* film and TV prodr, dir and puppeteer; pres Jim Henson Productions; special effects technician and performer The Great Muppet Caper 1981 and The Muppets Take Manhattan 1983, performer of Jack Pumpkinhead in Return to Oz 1984, princ performer and performer co-ordinator Labyrinth 1984–85, princ performer Little Shop of Horrors 1986, princ performance co-ordinator Storyteller (TV series) 1987, dir Mother Goose Stories (TV) 1988, exec prodr Dinosaurs (TV series) 1991–93, dir and prodr The Muppet Christmas Carol 1993; memb: SAG, AFTRA, Equity (UK), ACTT; *Recreations* skiing, squash, cars, dogs, travelling; *Style*— Brian Henson, Esq; ✉ 18 Parliament Hill, Hampstead, London NW3

HENSON, Michael Brian; s of Patrick Henson, and Irene Henson; *b* 3 May 1961; *Educ* Collyers Sch Horsham, Univ of Sheffield (BMus), Univ of Leicester (MPhil, scholarship to study in Vienna); *m* 1993, Helen; *Career* research fell Huddersfield Poly 1985–88, educn and community dir Bournemouth Orchestras 1988–92, chief exec Ulster Orch 1992–; memb Bd of Sonorities Contemporary Music Festival of NI; *Books* Musical Awareness (with G Pratt, OUP), Proceedings of Musical Awareness (ed); also author of 20 articles; *Style*— Michael Henson, Esq; ✉ Ulster Orchestra, Elmwood Hall at Queen's, 89 University Road, Belfast BT7 1NF (☎ 01232 664535, fax 01232 662761)

HENSON, Nicholas Victor Leslie (Nicky); s of Leslie Lincoln Henson, and Billie Dell, *née* Collins; *b* 12 May 1945; *Educ* St Bedes Eastbourne, Charterhouse, RADA; *m* 1, 1968 (m dis 1975), Una Stubbs; 2 s (Christian b 25 Dec 1971, Joe b 18 Sept 1973); m 2, 1 Aug 1986, Marquerite Ann Porter; 1 s (Keaton b 24 March 1988); *Career* actor; former popular song writer incl 3 year writing contract with The Shadows and Cliff Richard, fndr memb Young Vic Co 1970; *Theatre* incl: All Square (Vaudeville) 1963, Camelot (Drury Lane) 1964, Passion Flower Hotel (Prince of Wales) 1965, London Laughs (Palladium) 1966, Canterbury Tales (Phoenix) 1968, The Ride Across Lake Constance (Hampstead and Mayfair) 1973, Hamlet (Greenwich) 1973, Mind Your Head (Shaw) 1973, A Midsummer Night's Dream (Open Air) 1973, Taming of the Shrew (Shaw) 1973, Cinderella (Casino) 1973, Mardi Gras (Prince of Wales) 1976, Rookery Nook (Her Majesty's) 1979, Noises Off (Lyric and Savoy) 1982, The Relapse (Lyric) 1983, Sufficient Carbohydrate (Hampstead and Albery) 1983, Journeys End (Whitehall) 1988, Ivanov (Strand) 1989, Much Ado About Nothing (Strand) 1989, Three Sisters (Royal Court) 1990, Reflected Glory (Vaudeville) 1992, An Ideal Husband (Globe) 1993, Rage (Bush) 1994; Young Vic incl: Waiting for Godot, Scapino, The Soldier's Tale, She Stoops to Conquer, Measure for Measure, Oedipus, Wakefield Nativity Plays, Romeo and Juliet, The Maids, Deathwatch, Look Back in Anger, Rosencrantz and Guildenstern are Dead, Charley's Aunt; NT incl: The Cherry Orchard, Macbeth, The Women, The Double Dealer, A Fair Quarrel, The Browning Version, Harlequinade, The Provok'd Wife, The Elephant Man, Mandragola, Long Time Gone; RSC incl: Man and Superman 1977, As You Like It 1985–86, The Merry Wives of Windsor 1985–86; *Television* incl: A Midsummer Night's Dream, Absurd Person Singular, Seasons Greetings, Love After Lunch, Thin Air, Startrap 1988, Inspector Morse 1988, Boon 1989, After Henry 1990, The Upper Hand 1990; The Green Man 1990, The Healer 1994, Preston Front 1994, Shine On Harvey Moon 1994; *Films* appearances in over 25 incl: There's A Girl in My Soup, Witch Finder General, Tom Jones, Number One of The Street Service; *Recreations* snooker; *Style*— Nicky Henson, Esq; ✉ c/o Richard Stone Partnership, 25 Whitehall, London SW1 2BS (☎ 0171 839 6421, fax 0171 839 5002)

HENTON, Roger Gordon; s of (William) Gordon Henton (d 1990), of Lincoln, and Pamela, *née* Evans (d 1983); *b* 2 Aug 1940; *Educ* Bedford Sch; *m* 25 June 1966 (sep 1990), Susan Eleanor, da of John Richmond Edwards; 1 s (Thomas b 1972), 1 da (Isabel b 1970); *Career* Streets & Co CAs Lincoln 1959–64, Coopers & Lybrand Geneva 1965–67, pa to md AAH plc Lincoln 1968–72, dir Camamile Assocs Lincoln 1973–77, fndr and sr ptnr Henton & Peycke CAs Leeds 1978–93, princ Roger Henton & Co CAs 1993–, fin dir LD Group plc 1993–, mangr Euro Defi EEIG accountants network 1994–, chm Todds of Lincoln Ltd 1995–; FCA (ACA 1964); *Recreations* golf; *Clubs* RAC, Scarcroft Golf; *Style*— Roger Henton, Esq; ✉ 12 York Place, Leeds, West Yorks (☎ 0113 245 7553, fax 0113 242 0474, mobile 0836 742200)

HENTY, Jonathan Maurice; s of Richard Iltid Henty (d 1954), of Fairy Hill, Chichester, Sussex, and Lettice Ellen, *née* Moore-Gwyn (d 1987); *b* 22 Dec 1933; *Educ* Eton, New Coll Oxford (MA); *m* 1, 15 July, Margaret Louise (d 1972), da of David Sadler (d 1954), of Biggar; 2 s (Richard Edward Jonathan b 9 March 1959 d 1993, Charles James Christian b 4 July 1963), 1 da (Julia Rose b 7 April 1961); m 2, 26 March 1977, Veronica Mary Francis, da of Lt-Col Miller, of Camberley, Surrey; 2 da (Josephine Frances Veronica b 4 Aug 1978, Clemency Margaret Anne b 1 April 1983); *Career* called to the Bar Lincoln's Inn 1957, bencher Lincoln's Inn 1989; chllr Diocese of Hereford 1977; social security commr and child support commr 1993–; *Recreations* shooting, fishing, architecture; *Clubs* Athenaeum; *Style*— Jonathan Henty, Esq; ✉ Fisher Hill House, Northchapel, Petworth, Sussex GU28 9EJ (☎ 01428 707659)

HENWOOD, John Philip; s of Snowdon William Henwood (d 1980), and Amy Doris, *née* Stickley (d 1979); *b* 27 Aug 1945; *Educ* St Lawrence Sch Jersey, Victoria Coll Jersey; *Career* Channel Television: joined as trainee 1962, cameraman, studio mangr, ops supervisor and head of prog planning and presentation, dep ops mangr, estab Commercial Prodn Unit, head of news and features 1977, prog controller, dir of progs, md 1987–; chief exec: Channel Islands Communications (Television) Ltd, Channel Television Group; dir Guild of Local Television; chm Jersey Young Enterprise Bd, memb Training and Employment Partnership; memb Horserace Writers' Assoc, MInstD; *Recreations* horseracing and thoroughbreds, writing, painting, reading, skiing; *Clubs* Channel Islands Racing and Hunt; *Style*— John Henwood, Esq; ✉ Channel Television Ltd, La Pouquelaye, St Helier, Jersey, CI (☎ 01534 816803, fax 01534 816801)

HENWOOD, Roderick Waldemar Lisle; s of Noel Gordon Lisle Henwood (d 1972), and Daphne Muirhead, *née* Schroeder; *b* 29 Nov 1963; *Educ* Dollar Acad, Univ of Geneva, New Coll Oxford (BA); *m* 22 June 1996, Amanda Penelope, da of Michael Stacey, of Blakedown, Worcs; *Career* controller of prog business affrs Central Independent TV plc 1988–90; Central Broadcasting: dir of legal and business affrs 1990–93, dir of bdcasting 1993–94, md 1995–; *Recreations* tennis, running; *Style*— Roderick Henwood, Esq; ✉ Central Broadcasting, Central House, Broad St, Birmingham B1 2JP (☎ 0121 643 9898, fax 0121 643 4897, telex 338966)

HENZE, Hans Werner; *b* 1926; *Career* composer; studied under Wolfgang Fortner 1946–48 then Rene Leibowitz; fndr Montepulciano Cantiere 1976, composition teacher Cologne Acad of Music 1980–, artistic dir Accademia Filarmonica Romana 1981–83, fndr Munich Int Festival of New Music Theatre 1988, dir Gütersloh Henze Summer Acad 1989, first int chair of composition RAM, composer-in-residence Aldeburgh Festival 1996; subject of major festival by BBC Barbican 1991; compositions incl: Boulevard Solitude 1953, König Hirsch 1952–55, Der Prinz von Homburg 1958, Elegy for Young Lovers 1959–61, Novae de Infinito Laudes 1962, Los Caprichos 1963, Der Junge Lord 1964, The Bassarids 1965, The Raft of the Medusa 1968, El Cimarron 1970, Voices 1973, Orpheus 1978, The English Cat 1980–83, Le Miracle de la Rose 1981, Seventh Symphony 1983–84, Das Verratene Meer 1986–90, Requiem 1990–92, Eighth Symphony 1993 (performed by CBSO under Sir Simon Rattle BBC Proms 1995), Ninth Symphony (premiered by Berlin Philharmonic Orchestra 1996), Venus and Adonis 1995, Three Pieces for Orchestra (UK premiere BBC Proms 1996); hon memb: Deutsche Oper Berlin, American Acad and Inst of Arts and Letters; *Awards* incl: Siemens Prize 1990,

Apollo d'Oro 1990; *Style*— Hans Werner Henze, Esq; ✉ c/o Schott & Co Ltd, 48 Great Marlborough Street, London W1V 2BN (☎ 0171 437 1246, fax 0171 437 0263)

HEPBURN, Jack William; *b* 8 Sept 1938; *Career* MAFF: joined 1961, seconded as memb UK Delgn to EC Brussels 1969–71, princ private sec to Lord Prior and late Lord Godber 1971–73, asst sec 1973–82, under sec 1982–87, dir of Establishments 1987–90, under sec Food Drink and Mktg Policy 1990–96, dir of Establishments 1996–; *Style*— Jack Hepburn, Esq; ✉ Ministry of Agriculture, Fisheries and Food, Whitehall Place, London SW1A 2HH (☎ 0171 270 8529, fax 0171 270 8934)

HEPBURN, Prof Ronald William; s of William George Hepburn (d 1961), of Aberdeen, and Grace Ann, *née* Fraser (d 1974); *b* 16 March 1927; *Educ* Aberdeen GS, Univ of Aberdeen (MA, PhD); *m* 16 July 1953, Agnes Forbes, da of Rev William Anderson, of Edinburgh (d 1969); 2 s (David W b 1954, Antony R b 1957), 1 da (Catriona M b 1972); *Career* Nat Serv Army 1944–48; asst then lectr Dept of Moral Philosophy Univ of Aberdeen 1952–60, visiting assoc prof Univ of NY 1959–60, prof of philosophy Univ of Nottingham 1960–64, prof of moral philosophy Univ of Edinburgh 1975–96 (prof of philosophy 1964–75); various contribs to books, articles and broadcasts; *Books* Christianity & Paradox (1958, 2 edn 1966, 3 edn 1968), 'Wonder' and Other Essays (1984); *Recreations* music, hill-walking, photography; *Style*— Prof Ronald Hepburn; ✉ 8 Albert Terrace, Edinburgh EH10 5EA

HEPBURNE-SCOTT, Hon Andrew Walter; *see:* Polwarth, Master of

HEPHER, Michael Leslie; s of Leslie Hepher, and Edna Hepher; *b* 17 Jan 1944; *Educ* Kingston GS; *m* 1971, Janice Morton; 1 s (Daniel b 1980), 2 da (Kelly b 1973, Erin b 1975); *Career* former chm and chief exec Lloyds Abbey Life plc, former dir Lloyds Bank, former pres and chief exec Maritime Life Assurance Co of Canada; gp md British Telecommunications plc until 1995, chief exec Charterhouse plc 1996–; currently also: non-exec dir Grand Metropolitan plc, chm Concert Communications Co, dir MCI (USA); Liveryman Worshipful Co of Actuaries; FIA, FCIA, ASA, FLIA; *Recreations* reading; *Style*— Michael Hepher, Esq; ✉ Charterhouse plc, 1 Paternoster Row, St Paul's, London EC4M 7DH (☎ 0171 248 4000, fax 0171 248 6522)

HEPPEL, Peter John Merrick; QC (1992); s of John Edward Thomas Heppel (d 1964), of Romford, Essex, and Ida Florence, *née* Ford (d 1983); *b* 31 March 1948; *Educ* Royal Liberty Sch Romford Essex, Univ of Hull (LLB), UCL (LLM); *m* 20 Sept 1980 (m dis 1995), Janice, da of John Coulton, of Southport, Merseyside; 2 s (Edward b 1981, William b 1986), 2 da (Charlotte b 1979, Indea b 1982); *Career* called to the Bar Middle Temple 1970, in practice NE Circuit 1972–, recorder 1988–, head of chambers; *Recreations* family, music, reading; *Clubs* Sloane; *Style*— Peter Heppel, Esq, QC; ✉ Warriston, Parkfield Ave, N Ferriby, Humberside HU14 3AL (☎ 01482 631657); Paradise Chambers, 12 Paradise Square, Sheffield S1 2DE (☎ 0114 273 8951); 4 King's Bench Walk, Temple, London EC4Y 7DL (☎ 0171 353 0478); Wilberforce Chambers, 171 High Street, Hull HU1 1NE (☎ 01482 23264)

HEPPELL, John; MP (Lab) Nottingham East (majority 7,680); s of Robert Heppell, and late Helen Heppell; *b* 3 Nov 1948; *Educ* Rutherford GS, SE Northumberland Tech Coll, Ashington Tech Coll; *m* Eileen Golding; 2 s, 1 da; *Career* fitter NCB 1964–70, with various cos Nottingham 1970–75, workshop supervisor BR 1978–89 (diesel fitter 1975–78); Notts CC: cncllr 1981–92, asst Lab whip 1982, vice chm Environment Ctee 1983, chm Resources Ctee 1986, chm Equal Opportunities Ctee, dep ldr 1989–92; MP (Lab) Nottingham E 1992–; vice chm Lab Pty Tport Ctee 1992–; sec All Pty Gp Kashmir 1992–; chm All Pty Gp: Head Injuries 1995–, Home Safety 1995–; treas All Pty Gp Breast Cancer 1995–; chm: East Midlands Airport 1985, Greater Nottingham LRT Bd 1990–92; *Recreations* walking, reading; *Style*— John Heppell, Esq, MP; ✉ House of Commons, London SW1A 0AA; 1 Talbot Street, Nottingham NG1 5GQ (☎ 0115 956 0450, fax 0115 956 0445)

HEPPELL, (Thomas) Strachan; CB (1986); s of Leslie Thomas Davidson Heppell, and Doris Abbey, *née* Potts; *b* 15 Aug 1935; *Educ* Acklam Hall GS Middlesbrough, The Queen's Coll Oxford (BA); *m* 1963, Felicity Ann, da of Lt-Col Richard Bernard Rice (ka 1943); 2 s (Jeremy Strachan b 1965, Martin Richard b 1967); *Career* princ Nat Assistance Bd 1963 (asst princ 1958); DHSS: asst sec 1973, under sec 1979, dep sec 1983, conslt 1995–; chm Mgmnt Bd Euro Medicines Evaluation Agency, vice chm Family Fund Tst; *Recreations* gardening, travelling; *Style*— Strachan Heppell, CB; ✉ Department of Health, Richmond House, Whitehall, London SW1

HEPPER, Anthony Evelyn; s of Lt-Col John E Hepper (d 1967), and Rosalind, *née* Bowker; *b* 16 Jan 1923; *Educ* Wellington, Loughborough Coll; *m* 1970, Jonquil Francesca; *Career* served RE (N Africa, Sicily, Italy, France, Belgium, Holland, Norway, Palestine, Egypt), Maj; dir Cape plc 1968–93, chm Hyde Sails Ltd 1984–; CEng, FIMechE; *Recreations* golf; *Clubs* Boodle's; *Style*— A E Hepper, Esq; ✉ 70 Eaton Place, London SW1X 8AT (☎ 0171 235 7518)

HEPPLE, Prof Bob Alexander; Hon QC (1996); s of Alexander Hepple (d 1983), of Canterbury, and Josephine, *née* Zwarenstein (d 1992); *b* 11 Aug 1934; *Educ* Univ of Witwatersrand (BA, LLB), Univ of Cambridge (LLD, MA); *m* 1, 1960 (m dis 1993), Shirley Rona, da of Morris Goldsmith (d 1972), of London; 1 s (Paul Alexander b 11 Dec 1962), 1 da (Brenda (Mrs Henson) b 7 July 1961); m 2, 1994, Mary Coussey, da of Rev Stanley Dowding; *Career* practising attorney Johannesburg 1958, lectr in law Univ of Witwatersrand 1959–62, practising advocate Johannesburg 1962–63, called to the Bar Gray's Inn 1966 (bencher 1996), practising barr 1972–; lectr in law Univ of Nottingham 1966–68, fell Clare Coll and lectr law Cambridge 1968–76, prof of comparative social and labour law Univ of Kent 1976–77, chm Industl Tbnls England and Wales 1977–82 (pt/t chm 1974–77 and 1982–93); UCL: prof of Eng law 1982–93, dean Faculty of Laws and head Dept of Laws 1989–93, visiting prof 1993–; master of Clare Coll Cambridge 1993–, prof of law Univ of Cambridge 1995–; chm Univ of Cambridge: Local Exams Syndicate 1994–, Septemviri 1995–; chm Managers Smuts Meml Fund 1994–; memb: Cmmn for Racial Equality 1986–90, Tbnls Ctee Judicial Studies Bd 1988–93, Lord Chllr's Advsy Ctee on Legal Educn and Conduct 1994–; tstee Canon Collins Educnl Tst for S Africa 1990–; Hon LLD Univ of Witwatersrand 1996; *Publications* numerous books and articles on labour law and industl relations, race relations and discrimination and legal obligations in general; *Recreations* theatre, music, reading, walking, gardening; *Clubs* Reform; *Style*— Prof Bob Hepple, QC; ✉ The Master's Lodge, Clare College, Cambridge CB2 1TL (☎ 01223 333241, fax 01223 333249)

HEPPLEWHITE, Rosalind Mary Joy (Ros); da of Anthony Gordon Phillips, of Yeovil, Somerset, and Annie Maud, *née* Smith; *b* 20 Dec 1952; *Educ* Portsmouth Northern GS, UCL (BA); *m* 4 Sept 1971, Julian Hepplewhite, s of William Hepplewhite, of Southsea, Hampshire; 1 s (Sebastian b 1978), 1 da (Charlotte b 1976); *Career* postgrad res Somerville Coll Oxford 1974–75, dean's asst and admissions offr Inns of Ct Sch of Law 1975–76, gen administrative asst Herts AHA 1978–80, asst house govr Bethlem Royal & Maudsley Hosp 1980–82, hosp sec Bethlem Royal & Maudsley Special Health Authy 1982–83, unit admin Mental Health Servs Unit Hammersmith & Fulham Health Authy 1983–84; Brighton Health Authy: unit admin Mental Handicap Unit 1984–85, unit gen mangr Mental Health & Mental Handicap Unit 1985–88, dir of corp devpt 1988–89; nat dir Nat Assoc for Mental Health (MIND) 1989–91, chief exec DSS Child Support Agency 1992–94, chief exec and registrar Gen Dental Cncl 1996–; *Recreations* home and family; *Style*— Mrs R Hepplewhite; ✉ General Dental Council, 37 Walpole Street, London W1M 8DQ (☎ 0171 486 2171, fax 0171 224 3294)

HEPWORTH, David; s of Ernest Hepworth (d 1981), of Ossett, Yorkshire, and Sarah Marjorie, *née* Rollinson; *b* 27 July 1950; *Educ* Queen Elizabeth GS Wakefield, Trent Park Coll of Educn Barnet Herts (BEd); *m* 5 Sept 1979, Alyson, da of Ronald Elliott, of Hove, Sussex; 1 s (Henry b 1987), 2 da (Clare b 1982, Imogen b 1992); *Career* freelance journalist 1975–79; presenter: The Old Grey Whistle Test (later just Whistle Test, BBC TV) 1980–86, BBC Radio GLR; ed: Smash Hits 1980–82, Just Seventeen 1983–85; editorial dir: Emap Metro 1984–94, Emap Consumer Magazines 1994–; Periodical Publishers' Assoc: Ed of the Year 1985, Writer of the Year 1988; British Soc of Magazine Editors Mark Boxer Award 1993; *Recreations* books, tennis, music; *Style*— David Hepworth, Esq; ✉ Emap Metro Publications, Mappin House, Winsley Street, London W1 (☎ 0171 436 1515)

HEPWORTH, Brig Nicholas George Rispin; OBE (1985); s of Lt-Col Alfred Geoffrey Edwards Hepworth (d 1992), and Mary Rispin, *née* Humble, of N Yorks; *b* 16 Aug 1941; *Educ* Daniel Stewart's Coll Edinburgh, RMA Sandhurst; *m* 6 April 1974, Teresa Jane, da of John Guy Henderson Huntley (d 1953); 1 s (Charles David Huntley b 15 May 1976), 1 da (Virginia Mary Louise b 26 May 1978); *Career* cmmnd 2 Lt King's Regt 1961; served 1961–74: England, Berlin, Br Guiana, seconded Sultan's Armed Forces Oman Dhofar War 1968–70, BAOR, Ulster, MOD; successively 1975–79: Maj, Army Staff Coll, Rifle Company Cdr 1 Bn King's Regt (Ulster, UN Forces Cyprus, England), Bde Maj BAOR; successively 1980–85: Lt-Col, DS Army Staff Coll Camberley, CO 1 Bn King's Regt BAOR and Ulster, MOD; Col PSO Sultan's Land Forces Oman 1985–86; successively 1987–96: Brig, Cdr Br Forces Belize, Indian NDC New Delhi, Cdr Br Mil Mission to the Saudi Arabian Nat Guard, ret 1996; currently sec North of England TAVR Assoc; *Recreations* walking, travelling, reading; *Clubs* Army and Navy; *Style*— Brig Nicholas Hepworth, OBE; ✉ c/o ANZ Grindlays Bank, 13 St James's Square, London SW1Y 4LF

HEPWORTH, Vivien; da of William Cecil Hepworth, OBE (d 1993), of Leigh, Kent, and Emmie, *née* Hepworth; *b* 9 March 1953; *Educ* Beaverwood Girls' Sch Kent, Univ of Manchester (BA Politics and Modern History); *m* 29 May 1976, Ian Michael Jones, s of Derek Jones; 2 s (Samuel Martin b 16 Aug 1983, William Max b 4 Aug 1986); *Career* reporter Croydon Advertiser Series 1974–76; Northcliffe Newspapers: gen news and features writer 1976–78, lobby corr 1978–87; maternity leave 1987–88; Grayling Group of Companies: dir Westminster Strategy (public affrs subsid) 1989– (joined 1988), dir Grayling Holding Bd 1991–, dir Grayling (PR consultancy) 1994–; fndr Nystagmus Action Gp (visual impairment charity) 1984; *Recreations* politics; *Style*— Miss Vivien Hepworth; ✉ Grayling, 4 Bedford Square, London WC1B 3RA (☎ 0171 255 1100, fax 0171 580 5216)

HERBECQ, Sir John Edward; KCB (1977); s of Joseph Edward, and Rosina Elizabeth Herbecq; *b* 29 May 1922; *Educ* Chichester HS for Boys; *m* 1947, Pamela Filby; 1 da; *Career* joined Colonial Office 1939; Treasy 1950, private sec to chm UKAEA 1960–62, 2 perm sec Civil Serv Dept 1975–81; church cmmr 1982–96, chm Chichester Diocesan Bd of Fin 1989–; *Style*— Sir John Herbecq, KCB; ✉ Maryland, 10 Ledgers Meadow, Cuckfield, Haywards Heath, W Sussex RH17 5EW (☎ 01444 413387)

HERBERT, Anthony James; s of Maj Kenneth Faulkner Herbert, MBE (d 1993), and Kathleen Ellis, *née* Robertson; *b* 28 March 1940; *Educ* Eton, King's Coll Cambridge (MA); *children* 2 s (Dominic b 9 April 1971, Daniel b 21 Feb 1973), 1 da (Julia b 21 March 1978); *Career* admitted slr 1965, ptnr Allen & Overy 1970– (asst slr 1965–69); memb: Law Soc, Int Bar Assoc, City of London Law Soc; *Recreations* painting, tennis, skiing; *Clubs* City of London; *Style*— Anthony Herbert, Esq; ✉ c/o Allen & Overy, One New Change, London EC4M 9QQ (☎ 0171 330 3000, Fax 330 9999)

HERBERT, Arthur James (Jim); CBE (1982); s of Arthur Stephens Herbert (d 1959), of Middx, and Ethel Mary Ferguson (d 1954), of Tasmania; *b* 24 Oct 1918; *Educ* Sydney C of E GS, Merchant Taylors', Pembroke Coll Cambridge (MA); *m* 1948, Pamela Mary, da of Capt John Gyde Heaven (d 1923), of Bristol; 1 s (Richard b 1949), 3 da (Caroline b 1951, Nicola b 1955, Linda b 1958); *Career* served WWII Maj RE (Gibraltar, N Africa and Italy), granted rank of Hon Maj on demob (despatches); dir: Herbert & Sons Ltd (chm 1958–93), Foodex/Meatex Ltd; pres: Nat Fedn Scale and Weighing Machine Mfrs 1966–68 and 1982–84, E Anglian Engr Employers' Assoc 1980–82 and 1986–88; memb Engr Employers' Fedn: Policy Ctee 1982–89, Mgmnt Bd 1981–90; chm: Bury St Edmunds Constituency Cons Assoc 1972–80 (pres 1980–86), Suffolk & SE Cambs Euro Constituency Cons Assoc 1987–89 (pres 1989–94); pres S Suffolk Constituency Cons Assoc 1987–90; Freeman City of London; *Recreations* gardening; *Clubs* Hawks' (Cambridge), East India and Sports, MCC; *Style*— Jim Herbert, Esq, CBE; ✉ Herbert & Sons Ltd, 18 Rookwood Way, Haverhill, Suffolk CB9 8PD (☎ 01440 703551, fax 01440 62048)

HERBERT, Hon Christopher Dennis Charles; only s and h of 3 Baron Hemingford, *qv*; *b* 4 July 1973; *Educ* King's Coll Choir Sch Cambridge, Oundle, Univ of Manchester (BA); *Recreations* cricket, fives; *Style*— The Hon Christopher Herbert

HERBERT, Rt Rev Christopher William; *see:* St Albans, Bishop of

HERBERT, Prof David Thomas; s of Trevor John Herbert (d 1992), of Rhondda, and (Winifred) Megan, *née* Pearce (d 1990); *b* 24 Dec 1935; *Educ* Rhondda Co GS, Univ of Wales (BA, DipEd, DLitt), Univ of Birmingham (PhD); *m* 30 Dec 1968, Tonwen, da of Thomas Maddock (d 1953); 1 s (David Aled b 1971), 1 da (Nia Wyn b 1973); *Career* Nat Serv RAF 1954–56; lectr Univ of Keele 1963–65; Univ of Wales Swansea: lectr 1965–73, sr lectr 1973–77, reader 1977–80, prof of geography 1980–, dean 1981–84, vice princ 1986–89, pro vice-chllr 1995–; visiting prof: Univ of Toronto 1965, Univ of Manitoba 1967, Univ of York Ontario 1969, Univ of Leuven 1973, Univ of Colorado 1979, Univ of Oklahoma 1980, Univ of Sudan 1982, Univ of Warsaw 1987 (1985), Univ of Calgary 1989; Killam visiting scholar Calgary 1992; memb: Inst of Br Geographers (formerly on Cncl), Geographical Assoc, Gen Dental Cncl, Sports Cncl for Wales, Pembrokeshire Coast Nat Park, Welsh Jt Educn Ctee; former memb SSRC, chm Swansea Crime Prevention Panel, pres Br Assoc for the Advancement of Science (Section E) 1994; *Books* incl: Urban Geography - A Social Perspective (1972), Geography of Urban Crime (1982), Cities in Space - City as Place (with C J Thomas, 1990), Heritage Sites - Strategies for Marketing and Development (jtly, 1989), Geography and the Urban Environment (ed with R J Johnston), Social Problems and the City (ed with D M Smith), Communities Within Cities (with W K D Davies, 1993), Crime, Policing and Place (ed, 1993), Heritage, Tourism and Society (ed, 1995); *Recreations* tennis, fishing, skiing, reading, music; *Style*— Prof David Herbert; ✉ Department of Geography, University of Wales, Swansea SA2 8PD (☎ 01792 295229, telex 48358 UCSWAN G, fax 01792 205556)

HERBERT, Ivor; s of Sir Edward Herbert, OBE (d 1963), and Lady Sybil, *née* Davis (d 1989); *b* 20 Aug 1925; *Educ* Eton, Trinity Coll Cambridge (MA); *m* 1, 1950 (m dis), Jennifer, da of D R McBean, MC; 1 s (Nicholas b 1954; m Serena, da of Maj Sir Hamish Forbes, Bt, MBE, MC, *qv*); m 2 (m dis), Gilly, da of Dr Peter Steele-Perkins; 2 da (Kate b 20 Sept 1970, Jane b 11 March 1972); *Career* served Capt Coldstream Gds 1944–47 (seconded to Intelligence Germany 1945–47); PA to Chm then asst md Charterhouse Finance Corporation 1949–54, columnist Evening News Associated Newspapers 1954–70, racing corr and features columnist Sunday Express 1970–80, racing ed and main travel writer Mail on Sunday 1980–; ptnr: Bradenham Wines 1970–, Equus Productions 1974–; trained Nat Hunt racehorses 1947–62 (winner Cheltenham Gold Cup with Linwell 1957); scriptwriter and playwright: The Great St Trinian's Train Robbery, Night of the Blue Demands; TV documentaries incl: Odds Against, Stewards' Enquiry,

Classic Touch and The Queen's Horses; chm Bradenham Parish Cncl 1966–; memb: Soc of Authors, Writers' Guild; *Books* 26 incl: Arkle, Red Rum, The Winter Kings, Winter's Tale, The Diamond Diggers, Riding Through My Life (with HRH The Princess Royal); novels incl: The Filly, Revolting Behaviour; *Recreations* tennis, travel; *Clubs* Turf; *Style—* Ivor Herbert, Esq; ✉ The Old Rectory, Bradenham, nr High Wycombe, Bucks HP14 4HD (☎ 01494 563310, fax 01494 564504)

HERBERT, James; s of H Herbert, of London, and Catherine, *née* Riley; *b* 8 April 1943; *Educ* Our Lady of the Assumption Sch Bethnal Green, St Aloysius Coll Highgate, Hornsey Coll of Art Highgate; *m* August 1967, Eileen; 3 da (Kerry Jo b 22 July 1968, Emma Jane b 21 April 1972, Casey Lee b 31 Oct 1983); *Career* author; typographer John Collings Advertising 1962, successively art dir, gp head then assoc dir Charles Barker Advertising 1965–77; *Films* The Rats, The Survivor, Fluke (1995), Haunted (1995); *Books* The Rats (1974), The Fog (1975), The Survivor (1976, Avoriaz Grand Prix for Literature Fantastique 1977), Fluke (1977), The Spear (1978), Lair (1979), The Dark (1980), The Jonah (1981), Shrine (1983), Domain (1984), Moon (1985), The Magic Cottage (1986), Sepulchre (1987), Haunted (1988), Creed (1990), Portent (1992), James Herbert: by Horror Haunted (ed by Stephen Jones, 1992), James Herbert's Dark Places (photographs by Paul Barkshire, 1993), The City (graphic novel, illustrated by Ian Miller, 1993), The Ghosts of Sleath (1993), '48 (1996); *Recreations* guitar, piano, painting, book design, swimming, small firearms shooting, wildlife conservation; *Style—* James Herbert, Esq; ✉ c/o David Higham Associates, 5–8 Lower John St, Golden Square, London W1R 4HA (☎ 0171 437 7888, fax 0171 437 1072)

HERBERT, (Elizabeth) Jane; da of Reginald John Herbert, of Bridgwater, Somerset, and Elsa, *née* Drake; *b* 17 July 1956; *Educ* Surrey Co GS for Girls, Bridgwater GS for Girls, Collingwood Coll Univ of Durham (BSc), Univ of Bath (MBA); *Career* Clarks International 1977–91: various positions UK and Eire 1977–85, factory mangr Exmouth 1985–88, factory mangr Shepton Mallet 1988–91; Gtr Glasgow Health Bd 1991–94: unit gen mangr Care for the Elderly 1991–92, unit gen mangr W Glasgow Hosps 1992–94; chief exec W Glasgow Hosps Univ NHS Tst 1994–; *Recreations* sailing, ornithology, gardening; *Style—* Ms Jane Herbert; ✉ West Glasgow Hospitals University NHS Trust, Administration Building, Western Infirmary, Dumbarton Road, Glasgow G11 6NT (☎ 0141 211 2276, fax 0141 211 1920)

HERBERT, Eur Ing Jeffrey William; *b* 21 July 1942; *Educ* Loughborough Univ, Cranfield Business Sch; *m*; 2 da, 1 s; *Career* graduate trainee rising to mfrg dir Perkins Engines Ltd/Massey Ferguson Group Ltd 1965–76, md Rover Triumph Cars Ltd 1976–81, md GEC Diesels Ltd 1981–85, chm Charter plc 1996– (exec dir industry 1985–89, chief exec 1990–96); chm: Cape plc until 1996, Anderson Group plc until 1995; non-exec dir: Vickers plc, M&G Recovery Investment Trust plc, ESAB AB 1994–; memb Worshipful Co of Wheelwrights; CEng, FIMechE, MIEE, MIMfgE, MInstD, MIMgt, FEng 1993; *Style—* Eur Ing Jeffrey Herbert, FEng; ✉ Charter plc, 7 Hobart Place, London SW1W 0HH (☎ 0171 838 7000)

HERBERT, Jocelyn; da of A P Herbert, and Gwendolen Quilter; *b* 22 Feb 1917; *Educ* St Paul's Girls' Sch Paris and Vienna; *m* 1937, Anthony Lousada (m dis 1960); 1 s, 3 da; *Career* theatre designer, film production designer; memb Eng Stage Co Royal Court Theatre 1956, freelance designer 1958–; retrospective exhibition RNT 1993; Hon FRCA, Hon FRA, RDI; *Theatre* Royal Court designs incl: The Chairs (Ionesco) 1957, Purgatory (W B Yeats) 1957, Sport of my Mad Mother (Jellico) 1958, Krapps' Last Tape (Beckett) 1958, Roots (Wesker) 1959, Serjeant Musgrave's Dance (Arden) 1959, Chicken Soup with Barley 1960, I'm Talking about Jerusalem (Wesker) 1960, Trials by Logue, Antigone, The Trial of Cob and Leach (Logue) 1960, The Changeling 1961, The Kitchen (Wesker) 1961, Luther (Osborne) 1961, A Midsummer Night's Dream 1962, Chips With Everything (Wesker) 1962, Happy Days (Beckett) 1962, Skyvers (Reckford) 1963, Exit the King (Ionesco) 1963, Inadmissible Evidence (Osborne) 1964, A Patriot for Me (Osborne) 1965, The Lion and the Jewel (Soyinka) 1966, Life Price (O'Neil & Seabrook) 1969, Three Months Gone (Donald Howarth) 1970, The Changing Room (Storey) 1971, Krapps Last Tape and Not 1 (Beckett) 1973, Savages (Hampton) 1973, Life Class (Storey) 1974, What the Butler Saw (Orton) 1975; RNT incl: Othello 1964, A Women Killed by Kindness 1966, Mother Courage 1965, Tyger 1967, Early Day's 1980, Gallileo 1980, The Oresteia 1981, March on Russia 1988, Trackers 1989–91, Square Rounds 1992, Stages 1992; other theatre prodns incl: Richard III (RSC), Baal (Phoenix) 1963, The Seagull (Chekov) 1964, Saint Joan of the Stock Yards (Brecht) 1964, Home (Storey) 1970, Cromwell (Storey) 1973, The Merchant (NY) 1977, Ghosts (Aldwych) 1967, Hamlet (Roundhouse) 1967, Pygmalion (Majesty's) 1967, Portage to San Christabel of Adolf Hitler (Mermaid) 1982, Heartbreak House (Shaw) 1983, The Devil and the Good Lord (Lyric Hammersmith) 1984, Gigi (Lyric) 1985, J J Fahr (Phoenix) 1987, Timon of Athens (Haymarket Leicester) 1988, Julius Caeser (Haymarket Leicester) 1988, Creon (Haymarket Leicester) 1988, The Threepenny Opera (NY) 1989, Krapps Last Tape (Haymarket Leicester), Riverside (Paris), The Kaiser of Carnumtum (roman arena Austria) 1995, The Labourers of Herakles (New Theatre ECCD Delphi) 1995; *Opera* incl: Orpheus and Euridice (Sadler's Wells) 1967, The Force of Destiny (Paris Opera) 1975, Lulu (Metropolitan NY) 1977, The Entfuhrung aus dem Serail (Metropolitan NY) 1979, The Rise and Fall of Mahagonny (Brecht & Weil, Metropolitan NY) 1979, The Mask of Orpheus (Coliseum) 1986; *Films* colour and costume conslt film Tom Jones 1961; prodn designer incl: Isadora 1968, If... 1969, Ned Kelly 1970, Hamlet 1969, O Lucky Man 1972, Hotel New Hampshire 1983, The Whales of August 1986; *Books* Jocelyn Herbert - a theatre workbook (ed Cathy Courtney, 1993); *Style—* Ms Jocelyn Herbert; ✉ 45 Pottery Lane, London W11 4LY

HERBERT, John Anthony; s of Rev Canon Frank Selwood Herbert (d 1978), of Nuneaton, Warks, and Joan Mary Walcot Herbert, *née* Burton (d 1976); *b* 10 Sept 1939; *Educ* Dean Close Sch, Cheltenham, Exeter Univ; *m* 2 Aug 1962, Michelle, da of Nigel Forbes Dennis, of Malta; 2 da (Rebecca b 1964, Tamsin b 1968); *Career* over 250 films and documentaries to credit, on archaeological, mil trg and historical subjects (clients incl Saudi Arabian TV, MOD, oil indust); ed: Qaryat Al Fau (1981), Al Rabadhah (1984), books of archaeological excavations; contrib Illustrated London News on Arabian archaeology; photo exhibitions London and Paris 1986; Gold Award for Excellence Int Video and Cinema Awards Festival for Film for Fighting the Good Fight 1990; *Recreations* France, sailing; *Clubs* The Anglo-Arab Assoc, The Georgian Gp; *Style—* John A Herbert, Esq; ✉ 1 Ovington Gardens, London SW3 1LS (☎ 0171 225 2234)

HERBERT, John Paul (Johnny); s of Robert Ernest Trevor Herbert, and Georgina Jane Herbert; *b* 25 June 1964; *Educ* Forest Lodge Comp Sch; *m* 10 Dec 1990, Rebecca May, da of Michael Francis Cross; 2 da (Chloe Ann b 31 Jan 1990, Aimelia Jane b 21 July 1992); *Career* motor racing driver; go-karts: began racing aged 10, memb Br team 1978–82, Br jr champion 1979, Br sr champion 1982; Formula Ford 1600 1983–85 (Formula Ford Festival winner 1985), Formula Ford 2000 and Formula 3 1986, Br Formula 3 champion 1987, Formula 3000 1988 (won first race then injured in crash at Brands Hatch), Formula 1 with Benetton 1989 (fourth in debut race Brazil), Formula 3000 Japan 1990–91 (winner Le Mans with Mazda 1991); Formula 1 with Lotus 1991–94, rejoined Benetton 1995 season, joined Sauber team 1996; (winner British Grand Prix 1995 and Italian Grand Prix 1995); Formula One career: 81 races, 2 wins; Cellnet Award 1986; *Recreations* golf; *Style—* Johnny Herbert, Esq; ✉ John Paul Herbert Ltd, Pier House, Strand on the Green, Chiswick, London W4 3NN (☎ 0181 233 5039, fax 0181 233 5001)

HERBERT, Mark Jeremy; QC (1995); s of Kenneth Falkner Herbert (d 1993), of Winchester, and Kathleen Ellis, *née* Robertson; *b* 12 Nov 1948; *Educ* Lancing Coll, King's Coll London (BA); *m* 1977, Shulanjini Shiranikha, da of Dr Sefton Pullenayegum (decd); *Career* called to the Bar Lincoln's Inn 1974, in practice Chancery Bar 1975–; *Books* Whiteman on Capital Gains Tax (contrib, 1988), Drafting and Variation of Wills (1989); *Recreations* bell-ringing, theatre, travel; *Style—* Mark Herbert, Esq, QC; ✉ 5 Stone Buildings, Lincoln's Inn, London WC2A 3XT (☎ 0171 242 6201, fax 0171 831 8102)

HERBERT, Maxwell Glyn (Max); *b* 3 Oct 1946; *Educ* BSc; *m* (Catherine) Jane; 1 s (Alexander (Alex) b 29 May 1982); *Career* asst slr London Borough of Merton 1973–75, sr slr Surrey CC 1975–78, sr legal asst Central Electricity Generating Bd 1979–85, ptnr Herbert Lord & Co 1985–89, co sec and slr National Power PLC 1989–95, dir int business devpt Asia Pacific National Power PLC 1995–; memb Law Soc; *Recreations* golf, football, racing, family; *Style—* Max Herbert, Esq; ✉ National Power PLC, Windmill Hill Business Park, Whitehill Way, Swindon, Wilts SN5 6PB (☎ 01793 893200, fax 01793 893208, mobile 0860 891455)

HERBERT, Michael; CBE (1991); s of W R Herbert (d 1982), of Kent, and Eileen, *née* McKee (d 1995); *b* 16 Aug 1933; *Educ* The King's Sch Canterbury, St Edmund Hall Oxford (MA); *m* 1967, Anna Vibeke, da of Christian Madsen (d 1971), of Denmark; *Career* Nat Serv in RHA Germany 1956–58, 2 Lt; non-exec dir Royal Armouries (International) plc; memb: Advsy Bd Historic Royal Palaces, Ctee Bethnal Green Museum of Childhood, Cncl Europa Nostra/IBI, Cultural Tourism Ctee Icomos UK; dir Bristol 2000; tstee and hon treas Dian Fossey Gorilla Fund Europe; memb Ct of Assts Worshipful Co of Wax Chandlers (Liveryman, Master 1992–93); FCA, FRSA; *Recreations* walking, cricket, speaking Danish; *Clubs* Travellers', Hurlingham, Royal Anglo-Belgian, MCC (memb Fin Ctee), Kent CC, Buccaneers CC (pres); *Style—* Michael Herbert, Esq, CBE; ✉ 14 Eaton Place, London SW1X 8AE (☎ and fax 0171 235 3986); Knudsеje, 9352 Dybvad, Denmark (☎ and fax 00 45 98 86 40 56)

HERBERT, Adm Sir Peter Geoffrey Marshall; KCB (1982), OBE (1969); s of A G S Herbert, and P K M Herbert; *b* 28 Feb 1929; *Educ* Dunchurch Hall, RN Coll Dartmouth; *m* 1953, Ann Maureen, *née* McKeown; 1 s, 1 da; *Career* served in submarines 1949–63, Cdr Nuclear Submarine HMS Valiant 1963–68, Capt appts 1966–78, cmd HMS Blake 1974–75, dep chief Polaris Exec 1976–78, Flag Offr Carriers and Amphibious Ships 1978–79, DG Naval Manpower and Trg 1980–81, Flag Offr Submarines and Cdr Sub Area E Atlantic 1981–83, Adm 1983, Vice Chief of Def Staff (Personnel and Logistics) 1983–85; def conslt; non-exec dir Radamec Group 1985–; nat chm SSAFA 1985–94, chm Central Cncl Royal Soc of St George 1985–; pres: Glos KGFS, Evesham Sea Cadets, N Cotswold RNLI; memb Exec Ctee: White Ensign Assoc, Royal Patriotic Fund; chm Bd of Govrs Cheam Sch, govr Cheltenham Ladies' Coll; CIMgt, MINucE; *Recreations* swimming, woodwork, gardening; *Clubs* Naval; *Style—* Adm Sir Peter Herbert, KCB, OBE; ✉ Dolphin Sq, London SW1

HERBERT, Peter George; s of George Frederick Herbert (d 1974), of London, and Ellen Alice, *née* Reed (d 1980); *b* 11 June 1926; *Educ* Dulwich and Rossall, Royal College of Music (scholarship); *m* 1, 1951, (m dis 1977), Pip, *née* Harkell; 2 s (Leigh Seaton b 1953, Robin Harkell Seaton b 1960), 1 da (Jennifer Reed b 1958); m 2, 1978, Susan Alison, da of Dr Gilbert Edward Hicks; 2 da (Joanna Kate b 1980, Nicola Jane b 1982); *Career* served Royal Fusiliers & Royal Sussex Regt 1944–48; trg in family hotel business then Austria & France 1948–50; md: Gore Hotel & Elizabethan Rooms London 1950–67, The Yard Arm Club Westminster 1963–67; chm Gravetye Manor Hotel East Grinstead W Sussex 1957–; Chevalier du Tastevin 1958, fell HCIMA 1960; *Recreations* sailing, game fishing, opera (Glyndebourne), gardening; *Style—* Peter Herbert, Esq; ✉ Gravetye Manor, nr East Grinstead, W Sussex RH19 4LJ (☎ 01342 810567); Gravetye Manor Hotel and Country Club Ltd, nr East Grinstead, W Sussex RH19 4LJ (☎ 01342 810567, fax 01342 810080)

HERBERT, Russell; *m*; 2 s; *Career* trained as mechanical engr; British Gas: joined 1966, various appts SE Gas and North Thames Gas, dir of engrg Northern then E Midlands Gas, dir of engrg Gas Business Div British Gas HQ 1989, md Corp Servs (incl secretariat, safety and environment, personnel, property, R&D and technol), md Global Gas Div 1992–94, exec dir British Gas plc 1994–; chm British Gas Corporate Ventures Ltd, dir NGC Coproration (Texas USA), pres Gas de Chile Ltd (Santiago Chile); Freeman City of London 1983; CEng, MIMechE, MIGasE, FIPD, CIMgt; *Style—* Russell Herbert, Esq; ✉ British Gas plc, The Adelphi, John Adam Street, London WC2N 6JT (☎ 0171 821 1444)

HERBERT, Wally; s of Capt Walter William Herbert, RAPC (d 1972), and Helen, *née* Manton (d 1982); *b* 24 Oct 1934; *m* 24 Dec 1969, Marie Rita, da of Prof Charles McGaughey (d 1982); 2 da (Kari b 17 Sept 1970, Pascale b 30 March 1978 d 1993); *Career* RE 1950–54; trained as surveyor Sch of Mil Survey, serv in Egypt 1953–54; surveyor Falklands Islands Dependencies Survey based at Hope Bay Antarctica 1955–58, hitch hiked 15,000 miles from Montevideo Uruguay to UK 1958–59, expeditions to Lapland and Spitzbergen 1960, surveyor with NZ Antarctic Expdn based at Scott Base McMurdo Sound 1960–62; ldr: expdn to NW Greenland (retracing route of Dr Frederick Cook) 1967–68, Br Trans-Arctic Expdn (first surface crossing of Arctic Ocean from Alaska via N Pole to Spitzbergen, a 3,800 mile journey with dog teams which took 16 months to complete) 1968–69, expdn to NW Greenland (travelling over 4,000 miles with Eskimos) 1971–73, winter expdn to Lapland 1974, Br N Polar Expdn (attempting to circumnavigate Greenland with dog teams and Eskimo skin boat) 1977–80, expdn to NW Greenland 1980; conducted feasibility study for an Explorers Museum at Sir Francis Drake's house (Buckland Abbey) 1981–84; writing and filming biog of Adm Robert E Peary 1985–88, filming in NW Greenland 1987 with second visit to N Pole 1987 and third visit 1991; total time spent in polar regions 13 yrs, total distance travelled by dog sledges and in open boats in polar regions over 25,000 miles; one-man exhibitions of paintings: QE2 1994, Explorers Club NY 1994, Jamestown Community Coll NY 1994, Australian Geographic Soc 1995; Polar medal (1962, Clasp 1969) awarded for Antarctic and Arctic exploration, Livingstone Gold Medal RGS (Scot) 1969, Founders Gold Medal RGS 1970, City of Paris Medal 1983, French Geog Soc Medal 1983, Explorers Medal 1985, Finn Ronne Award 1985; hon memb Br Schs Exploring Soc, hon pres World Expeditionary Assoc; FRGS; *Books* A World of Men (1968), Across the Top of the World (1969), The Last Great Journey on Earth (1971), Polar Deserts (1971), Eskimos (1976), North Pole (1978), Hunters of the Polar North (1982), The Noose of Laurels (1989); *Recreations* painting; *Clubs* Lansdowne, Explorers; *Style—* Wally Herbert, Esq; ✉ c/o Royal Geographical Society, 1 Kensington Gore, London SW7 2AR

HERBERT-JONES, Hugo Jarrett; CMG (1973), OBE (1963); s of Capt H Herbert-Jones (d 1923), of Llanrwst, Denbighshire, and Dora Jarrett, *née* Rowlands, MBE (d 1974); *b* 11 March 1922; *Educ* Bryanston, Worcester Coll Oxford (MA); *m* 1954, Margaret (d 1996), da of Rev J P Veall, of Eastbourne; 1 s (Nicholas), 2 da (Sarah, Siân); *Career* served Welsh Gds 1941–46 (wounded NW Europe 1944), Maj; HM Foreign later Dip Serv 1947–79; dir int affrs CBI 1979–87, chm The Aldeburgh Soc 1988–93; *Recreations* sailing, golf, shooting, music, spectator sports; *Clubs* Garrick, MCC, London Welsh Rugby Football, Aldeburgh Yacht, Aldeburgh Golf; *Style—* Hugo Herbert-Jones, Esq, CMG, OBE; ✉ Priors Hill, Aldeburgh, Suffolk IP15 5ET (☎ 01728 453335)

HERBERTSON, (Robert) Ian; yr s of Robert Hopkirk Herbertson (d 1969), and Winifred Rose, *née* Rawlinson (d 1994); *b* 30 Dec 1953; *Educ* Selhurst GS, Birkbeck Coll London (BA); *m* 22 March 1985, Joanna Hazel, da of Reginald Bernard North, of Gwent;

3 da (Rebecca Elizabeth b 1987, Emma Louise b 1990, Amy Ellen b 1992); *Career* Bank of England: joined 1985, an audit mangr 1990–92, official Banking Supervision 1992–93, Legal Unit 1993, Monetary and Fin Statistics Div 1994–96, Business Fin Div 1996–; dir Claridge Press 1987–88; memb: Convocation Univ of London 1984, Ctee Ct of Electors Birkbeck Coll London 1987–90; Freeman of City of London, Liveryman Worshipful Co of Chartered Secs and Admins; memb: Aristotelian Soc, Cambridge Antiquarian Soc, Prehistoric Soc; CDipAF 1985, FIAP 1986–92, FCIS 1995 (ACIS 1991), fell Royal Statistical Soc 1995; *Recreations* philosophy, prehistoric archaeology, literature; *Clubs* Royal Over-Seas League, Lansdowne, City Livery; *Style*— Ian Herbertson, Esq; ✉ 7 Falcon Way, Buckden, Cambridgeshire PE18 9UU (☎ 01480 811430); Bank of England, Threadneedle Street, London EC2R 8AH (☎ 0171 601 4276)

HERDMAN, Dr John Macmillan; s of William Morrison Herdman (d 1975), of Edinburgh, and Catherine, *née* Macmillan (d 1991); *b* 20 July 1941; *Educ* Merchiston Castle Sch, Magdalene Coll Cambridge (MA, PhD); *m* 30 July 1983 (m dis 1993), Dolina, da of Angus Maclennan (d 1950), of Marvig, Isle of Lewis; *Career* writer; awarded Scottish Arts Cncl bursaries 1976 and 1982, creative writing fell Univ of Edinburgh 1977–79, winner book awards 1978 and 1993, Hawthornden Writer's fellowship 1989 and 1995, William Soutar Writer's fellowship 1990–91; *Books* Descent (1968), A Truth Lover (1973), Clapperton (1974), Pagan's Pilgrimage (1978), Stories Short and Tall (1979), Voice without Restraint: Bob Dylan's Lyrics and their Background (1982), Three Novellas (1987), The Double in Nineteenth Century Fiction (1990), Imelda and Other Stories (1993), Ghostwriting (1996); *Recreations* reading, walking, listening to music, medieval church history; *Style*— Dr John Herdman; ✉ Roselea, Bridge of Tilt, Pitlochry PH18 5SX

HERDMAN, (John) Mark Ambrose; CBE (1990), LVO (1979); s of Cdr Claudius Alexander Herdman, DL, RN (d 1993), of Co Tyrone, and Joan Dalrymple, *née* Tennant (d 1937); *b* 26 April 1932; *Educ* St Edward's Sch Oxford, Univ of Dublin (BA, MA), Queen's Coll Oxford; *m* 29 June 1963, Elizabeth Anne, da of Rupert McLintock Dillon (d 1972), of Dublin; 1 s (Patrick b 1969), 2 da (Deirdre b 1966, Bridget b 1970); *Career* HMOCS Kenya 1954–64; FCO (formerly CRO) London 1964–65, MECAS Lebanon 1965–66, Amman 1966–68, FCO 1969–71, Lusaka 1971–74, Jedda 1974–76, FCO 1976–78, Lilongwe 1978–81, FCO 1981–83, dep govr Bermuda 1983–86, govr Br Virgin Is 1986–91, head Br Deln to EC Monitoring Mission in Yugoslavia 1991–92, FCO 1992–93; *Recreations* fishing, philately, gardening; *Clubs* Royal Cwlth Soc, Ebury Court; *Style*— Mark Herdman, Esq, CBE, LVO; ✉ Tullywhisker House, Berry Lane, Fox Corner, Guildford, Surrey GU3 3PU

HEREFORD, Dean of; *see:* Willis, Very Rev Robert Andrew

HEREFORD, 103 Bishop of (cr 676) 1990–; Rt Rev John Keith Oliver; s of Walter Keith Oliver (d 1977), of Danehill, Sussex, and Ivy, *née* Nightingale (d 1981); *b* 14 April 1935; *Educ* Westminster, Gonville and Caius Coll Cambridge (BA, MA, MLitt); *m* 16 Sept 1961, Meriel, da of Sir Alan Moore, Bt (d 1959), of Battle, Sussex; 2 s (Thomas b 1964, Henry b 1968), 1 da (Mary b 1971); *Career* curate Hilborough Gp of Parishes Norfolk 1964–68, chaplain and asst master Eton Coll 1968–72; team rector: S Molton Gp 1973–82 (rural dean 1974–80), Central Exeter 1982–85; archdeacon of Sherborne, canon of Salisbury and priest-in-charge W Stafford 1985–90; chm C of E's Advsy Bd of Min 1993–; *Recreations* railways, music, architecture, walking, motorcycling; *Clubs* United Oxford and Cambridge, Worcestershire CCC, Herefordshire CCC; *Style*— The Rt Rev the Bishop of Hereford; ✉ The Bishop's House, The Palace, Hereford (☎ 01432 271355)

HEREFORD, 18 Viscount (E 1550); Sir Robert Milo Leicester Devereux; 15 Bt (E 1611); Premier Viscount in the Peerage of England; s of Hon Robert Godfrey de Bohun Devereux (d 1934, s of 17 Viscount) and Audrey (d 1978), who m, as her 2 husb, 7 Earl of Lisburne; suc gf 1952; *b* 4 Nov 1932; *Educ* Eton; *m* 1969 (m dis 1982), Susan Mary, only child of Maj Maurice Godley, of Sevenoaks; 2 s (Hon Charles, Hon Edward Mark de Breteuil b 1977); *Heir* s, Hon Charles Robin de Bohun Devereux b 11 Aug 1975; *Style*— The Rt Hon the Viscount Hereford

HERFORD, (Richard) Henry; s of Philip Henry Herford (d 1982), of Glasgow, and Elisabeth Jean, *née* Hawkins; *b* 24 Feb 1947; *Educ* Trinity Coll Glenalmond, King's Coll Cambridge, Univ of York, Royal Manchester Coll of Music; *m* 14 Feb 1982, Jane Lindsay, da of Peter John; 2 s (Thomas Hal b 31 Oct 1982, John Peter b 19 Jan 1985), 1 da (Alice Jane b 5 March 1988); *Career* opera and concert singer; performances incl operas with Covent Garden, Glyndebourne, Scottish Opera and throughout Europe, concerts, recitals, broadcasts and recordings throughout Britain, Europe and the USA, and in Canada, S America and Hong Kong; tutor Sch of Vocal Studies Royal Northern Coll of Music 1994; Curtis Gold medal for singing RNCM 1976, Benson and Hedges Gold award 1980, first prize Int American Music Competition 1982; *Recordings* incl: Rameau Castor et Pollux (Erato), Bridge The Christmas Rose (Pearl), Handel Messiah (excerpts, Contour), Peter Dickinson Dylan Thomas Song Cycle (Conifer), Britten A Midsummer Night's Dream (Virgin) Charles Ives Song Recital I and II (Unicorn-Kanchana, Music Retailers' Assoc Record of the Year), Charles Ives songs with instrumental ensemble (Ensemble Modern, EMI), George Lloyd Iernin (Albany), Stravinsky Pulcinella (Naxos), Edward Gregson Missa Brevis Pacem, Handel Israel in Egypt (Decca); *Recreations* family, house restoration, chamber music (cello), reading, walking; *Style*— Henry Herford; ✉ Pencots, Northmoor, Oxon OX8 1AX (☎ 01865 300884)

HERFORD, Mark John; s of John Rogers Herford, of Adelaide, Aust, and Helen May Lambert, of Bowral, NSW, Aust; *b* 11 March 1952; *Educ* Univ of Sydney Aust (BA), Univ of New England Aust (BLitt); *m* 22 July 1988, Stephanie Kay, da of Reginald Wilkes; 1 s (Christopher Mark b 11 Sept 1989), 1 da (Amy b 22 Oct 1991); *Career* ed: Butterworths 1972–74, NSW Inst of Technol 1974–77; internal communications mangr Esso Australia Ltd 1977–79, gen mangr Hill & Knowlton International Brisbane 1980–85, fndr dir Macro Communications Sydney 1985–92, chm Business Software Alliance Sydney 1990–92, devpt dir Shandwick Communications London 1992–; memb: PR Inst of Aust 1984 (Oustanding Achievement Award 1987), Int Assoc of Business Communicators 1988; *Recreations* tennis, swimming, sailing, skiing, property restoration; *Style*— Mark Herford, Esq; ✉ Shandwick Communications Ltd, 114 Cromwell Road, London SW7 4ES (☎ 0171 835 1001, fax 0171 373 4311, e-mail mherford@shandwick.com)

HERHOLDT, Frank Devilliers; s of Albrecht Johan Devilliers Herholdt, of St James, Cape Town, SA, and Frances, *née* Robberts (d 1992); *b* 6 Oct 1945; *Educ* Parktown Boys' HS, Johannesburg Sch of Art; *m* (m dis 1981), Verona Somers; *partner* Susan Rowlands; *Career* photographer; asst to Lynton Stephenson Johannesburg SA 1967–68, in-house photographer Forsyth Advertising 1969–71, in own studio Johannesburg 1971–75, freelance photographer in London and Europe assisting various photographers incl Art Kane 1976–83, in own studio London 1983–; memb: Assoc of Photographers, Dirs' Guild of GB; *Awards* Assoc of Photographers: Silver 1988, Merit 1989 and 1994; NY Advtg Festival finalist 1987, Communication Arts Magazine Award of Excellence 1993 and (3 awards) 1995; *Recreations* cooking, eating and travelling; *Style*— Frank Herholdt, Esq; ✉ 49 Eagle Wharf Road, London N1 7ED (☎ 0171 490 7857, fax 0171 490 3034)

HERINCX, (Raymond Frederick) Raimund; s of Florent Herincx (d 1974), and Marie Therese Lucia, *née* Cheal; *b* 23 Aug 1927; *Educ* St Mary Abbot's Kensington, Thames Valley GS Twickenham, Univ of London; *m* 27 March 1954, Margaret Jean, aka Astra Blair, da of Lt-Col Douglas Waugh; 1 s (Gareth James) 2 da (Nicole Elaine, Gemma Marelen); *Career* Educn Offr Household Cavalry 1946–48; memb Royal Opera House Chorus 1949–53, joined Welsh Nat Opera 1956, joined Sadler's Wells Opera (now English Nat Opera) 1957 and Royal Opera House Covent Garden 1968, joined Met Opera House (NY) 1976; prof of voice RAM 1970–77, sr voice teacher NE of Scotland Music Sch 1979–, lectr Univ Coll Cardiff 1984–87, voice teacher Trinity Coll of Music London 1993–; voice therapist 1979–, music critic 1987–; many commercial recordings incl creators' recordings and first recordings; fndr: Quinville Tst (for Handicapped Children), Sadler's Wells Soc; fndr memb Assoc of Artists Against Aids; world record for no of operatic roles and concert works sung (468); int music awards opera medal 1968, Hon RAM 1971; fndr Monks' Vineyard 1987, co-owner Wraxall Vineyard 1991–, fndr Fosse Way Vineyard (for vine growing res) 1991; *Recreations* wine and its history, vine and plant breeding; *Style*— Raimund Herincx, Esq; ✉ Monks' Vineyard, Larkbarrow, East Compton, Pilton, Shepton Mallet, Somerset (☎ and fax 01749 344462)

HERITAGE, John Langdon; CB (1990); s of Francis John Heritage, OBE, ISO (d 1967), and Elizabeth, *née* Langdon (d 1960); *b* 31 Dec 1931; *Educ* Berkhamsted Sch, Exeter Coll Oxford; *m* 3 April 1956, Elizabeth Faulkner, da of Charles Jamieson Robertson (d 1957); 2 s (Charles Francis b 1957, Edward John b 1965), 1 da (Rebecca Jane b 1960); *Career* Nat Serv Royal Hants Regt and RWAFF; called to the Bar Middle Temple 1956; sr legal asst Treasy Slr's Office 1964 (legal asst 1957), asst slr Lord Chllr's Dept 1973, sec Royal Cmmn on Legal Servs 1976–79; under sec circuit admin SE Circuit 1983–88, head of judicial appts 1989–92; chm Chesham Building Society 1992– (dir 1989–, vice chm 1991–92); author of articles in legal jls and reference books; *Recreations* painting, making things; *Clubs* Utd Oxford and Cambridge Univ; *Style*— John Heritage, Esq, CB; ✉ Chesham Building Society, 12 Market Square, Chesham, Bucks HP5 1ER

HERITAGE, Robert Charles; CBE (1980); s of Charles John Heritage, and Daisy May, *née* Clay; *b* 2 Nov 1927; *Educ* King Edward's GS Birmingham, Birmingham Coll of Art and Industl Design, RCA Furniture Sch (MDes); *m* 4 April 1953, Dorothy, da of William Shaw; 2 s (Paul Robert b 1956, Michael Justin Lawrence b 1965), 1 da (Rachael Francesca b 1958); *Career* design conslt in private practice 1953–; prof of furniture design RCA 1974–85; Br Aluminium Design award 1966; Cncl of Industl Design awards for: Hamilton Sideboard 1958, Wall Units 1963, Oregon Dining Chair 1963, Memory Master Clock 1964, Quartet Major 1965, Silverspan Fluroescent Fitting 1968, Restaurant Chair 1969, Superjet 1969, Powerflood 1971, Pan Parabolic 1971, Effect Lighting Lumiere Projector 1972, Lytespan 7 Track 1973, Eurospot 1973; Bundespreise for Powerflood, Litespan 7, Eurospot and Parabolic 1972; Liveryman Worshipful Co of Furniture Makers 1962; RDI 1963, hon fell RCA, FRSA, FCSD; *Recreations* salmon fishing, tennis; *Style*— Robert Heritage, Esq, CBE

HERMAN, Josef; OBE (1980); s of David and Sarah Herman (k ca 1941), of Warsaw; *b* 3 Jan 1911; *Educ* Warsaw Sch of Art and Decoration; *m* 1955, Eleanor, *née* Ettlinger; 1 s, 1 da (decd); *Career* painter and draughtsman; *Exhibitions* incl: Warsaw 1932, Glasgow 1942, Edinburgh 1942, London 1943, Roland, Browse and Delbanco Gall 1946–, Whitechapel Art Gall (retrospective, 1956), Camden Arts Centre (retrospective, 1980); *Work in collections* Tate Gall, V & A, Contemporary Art Soc, Arts Cncl, Br Cncl, Br Museum, Cardiff Nat Museum, Bezalel Nat Museum, Ottawa Nat Gall, Wellington Nat Gall, Melbourne Nat Gall, Johannesburg Nat Gall; *Awards* Contemporary Art Soc prize 1952 and 1953, John Moore Exhbn 1956, Gold medal Royal Nat Eisteddfod 1962, Trust House award 1962, Silver medal Arts Cncl for Wales; RA 1990; *Publications* Related Twilights (autobiog, 1975), Reflections on Drawing (1985), Notes from a Welsh Diary (1988); *Style*— Josef Herman, Esq, OBE, RA; ✉ 120 Edith Road, London W14 9AP (☎ 0171 603 5091)

HERMAN, Dr Stephen Sydney; s of Maurice Herman (d 1975), and Deborah, *née* Dutkevitch (d 1980); *b* 7 July 1942; *Educ* Central Foundation Boys GS, King's Coll London, St George's Hosp Med Sch (MB BS); *m* 21 June 1966, Yvette Hannah, da of Isaac Solomons (d 1964); 1 s (Simon b 13 March 1969), 2 da (Rachel b 31 July 1970, Ruth b 5 May 1973); *Career* conslt paediatrician Royal National Orthopaedic Hosp 1974, hon clinical sr lectr Inst of Orthopaedics Univ of London, conslt paediatrician Central Middx Hosp 1974–93; memb: Br Paediatric Assoc 1974, Neonatal Soc 1972; FRCP 1981; *Recreations* short wave and vintage radio; *Style*— Dr Stephen Herman; ✉ Barbary House, California Lane, Bushey Heath, Herts WD2 1EX (☎ 0181 950 1006); 25 Wimpole St, London W1M 7AD (☎ 0171 323 4959, fax 0171 636 3500)

HERMAN-SMITH, Robert; s of Herman Geldert Smith (d 1985), of Carver House, Norton Rd, Stourbridge, W Midlands, and Alice, *née* Power (d 1989); *b* 12 Jan 1940; *Educ* Sebright Sch, Univ of Birmingham (BSc, Postgrad Dip); *m* 17 Sept 1964, (Florence) Jennifer Elizabeth, da of Gerald Whitmore Munday, of Church Farm, Swindon, W Midlands; 2 da (Mary Louise b 23 July 1965, Suzanne b 12 June 1967); *Career* jt md and dep chm Herman Smith plc 1961–85; mktg and business conslt 1985–; dir: Darchem Engineering Ltd 1985–, Soc of Br Aerospace Companies 1992–; memb Charitable Tst Pedmore Sporting Club; *Recreations* fishing, shooting; *Style*— Robert Herman-Smith, Esq; ✉ Halfpenny Manor, Bobbington, Stourbridge, W Midlands DY7 5EG (☎ 01384 241177, fax 01384 234141)

HERMON-TAYLOR, Prof John; s of Hermon Taylor, of Bosham, W Sussex, and Marie Amelie, *née* Pearson (d 1981); *b* 16 Oct 1936; *Educ* Harrow, St John's Coll Cambridge (BA, MB BChir, MChir), The London Hosp Med Coll; *m* 18 Sept 1971, Eleanor Ann, da of Dr Willard S Pheteplace (d 1985), of Davenport, Iowa; 1 s (Peter Maxwell b 1979), 1 da (Amy Caroline b 1975); *Career* various NHS and Univ trg posts in surgery 1963–68, MRC travelling fell in gastrointestinal physiology Mayo Clinic USA 1968–69, reader in surgery The London Hosp Med Coll 1971–76 (sr lectr 1970–71), prof and chm of surgery St George's Hosp Med Sch 1976–, conslt in gen surgery RN 1989, author of numerous scientific and med res articles; memb: Cncl Assoc of Surgeons of GB and Ireland 1980–83, Clinical Panel The Wellcome Tst 1985–88, Cncl Action Research 1988, Scientific Ctee Br Digestive Fndn 1991; winner: The Times Newspaper/Barclays Bank Innovator of the Year award 1988, Hallet prize; FRCS 1963, memb Biochem Soc; *Recreations* sailing, shooting; *Style*— Prof John Hermon-Taylor; ✉ 11 Parkside Avenue, Wimbledon, London SW19 5ES; Dept of Surgery, St George's Hosp Medical Sch, London SW17 ORE (☎ 0181 767 7631, fax 0181 725 3594)

HERMSEN, (Adriaan) John; s of Adriaan Marinus Christiaan Hermsen (d 1982), of Broadway, Worcestershire, and Margaret, *née* Stanley (d 1989); *b* 20 Aug 1933; *Educ* Salvatorian Sch, Royal West of England Acad Sch of Architecture, MSc (CL&A) 1992; *m* 23 March 1963, Jean Russell, da of Charles Herbert Simmonds (d 1971), of Durban, S Africa; 2 s ((Adriaan) Keir b 1968, Mark Christian Piers b 1971); *Career* Howard Lobb & Partners 1956–57, Richard Sheppard Robson & Partners 1957–59, R D Russell & Partners 1961–62, Douglas Stephen & Partners 1962–64, Nat Building Agency 1964–71, ptnr and dir Ahrends Burton & Koralek 1974– (joined 1971); rep Miny Housing & Local Govt on Br Standard Ctee 3921 1969–71; chair Architects' Law Forum RIBA 1995–; FRIBA 1969 (ARIBA 1962), FCIArb 1993 (ACIArb 1984), MAE 1992; *Recreations* construction law, walking and sailing; *Style*— John Hermsen, Esq; ✉ 18 Frogmore Close, Hughenden Valley, High Wycombe, Buckinghamshire HP14 4LN (☎ 01494 562260); Ahrends Burton & Koralek, Unit 1, 7 Chalcot Rd, London NW1 8LH (☎ 0171 586 3311, fax 0171 722 5445)

HERON, (John) Brian; s of John Henry Heron (d 1944), of Leeds, and Dorothy, *née* Hinton; *b* 22 Jan 1933; *Educ* Manchester GS, St Catharine's Coll Cambridge (MA); *m* 7 Sept 1968, Margaret, da of Harvey Jessop (d 1965), of Heywood; 1 s (John Michael b 16

Nov 1972), 1 da (Joanne Elizabeth b 29 July 1970); *Career* dir: TBA Indust Products Ltd 1969, Deeglass Fibres 1969; chief exec and dep chm TBA 1968–89; chm: TBA (Pty) Aust 1986–89, Moor Plastics Ltd 1988–89, Telford Rubber Processors Ltd 1986–89, Fratherm GmbH 1987–89; vice pres Bentley-Harris Inc 1988–89; chm Textilver SA 1988–89; dir Manchester Sci Park; UMIST: chm Cncl, pro-chllr 1990–; chm: Rochdale Healthcare NHS Trust, Asbestosis Research Council Ltd; dir: Rochdale TEC 1989–, Hopwood Hall Coll of Further Educn 1993–; *Recreations* sailing, motoring; *Clubs* Hawks, Cambridge Univ Cruising, Oxford and Cambridge Sailing Soc, Royal Yachting Assoc, Hollingworth Lake Sailing; *Style*— Brian Heron, Esq; ✉ Cleggswood Heys Farm, Hollingworth Lake, Littleborough, Lancs (☎ and fax 01706 373292)

HERON, Sir Conrad Frederick; KCB (1974, CB 1969), OBE (1953); s of Richard Foster Heron, of South Shields, and Ida Fredrika Heron; *b* 21 Feb 1916; *Educ* South Shields HS, Trinity Hall Cambridge; *m* 1948, Envye Linnéa, da of Hermann Gustafsson, of Sweden; 2 da; *Career* entered Miny of Labour 1938, dep chm Cmmn on Industl Relations 1971–72, perm sec Dept of Employment 1973–76, ret; *Style*— Sir Conrad Heron, KCB, OBE; ✉ Old Orchards, West Lydford, Somerton, Somerset (☎ 0196 240 387)

HERON, David Leslie Norton; s of Edward Wallace Heron, of the Isle of Wight, and Eunice Cecilia, *née* Mott; *b* 5 Oct 1941; *Educ* Christs Coll Finchley; *m* 25 July 1965, Margaret Ann, *née* Berry, da of Leonard Kenneth Berry; 3 s (Simon Alexander b 6 Sept 1968, Daniel Mark b 17 April 1970, Luke Nicholas b 20 Sept 1978), 1 da (Kathryn Alice b 29 Dec 1973); *Career* trainee CA 1957–59; James Capel & Co: accountant asst 1959–61, investmt analyst asst 1961–66, stockbroker 1966–, fund mgmnt 1966–68, institutional sales 1968–72 and 1976–83, head of Far East sales 1972–76, head of derivatives 1983–94, dir 1987–94; head of derivatives Smith New Court 1994, dep chm LIFFE 1992–94; dir Premier Radio Ltd (parent co of London Christian Radio) 1995–; *Recreations* tennis, active church member; *Style*— David L N Heron, Esq; ✉ 71 Grasmere Road, Muswell Hill, London N10 2DH; Premier Radio Ltd, Glen House, Stag Place, London SW1E 5AG (☎ 0171 233 6705, fax 0171 233 6706)

HERON, Prof James Riddick; s of James Riddick Heron (d 1959), of Birmingham, and Sophia, *née* Leatham (d 1956); *b* 21 Jan 1932; *Educ* King Edward's Sch Birmingham, Univ of Birmingham (MB ChB); *m* 27 May 1961, Ann Fionnuala, da of Dr Richard Raphael Gamble (d 1955); 2 s (Richard b 31 May 1962, Robert b 24 Oct 1973), 3 da (Fiona b 27 April 1963, Elizabeth b 8 July 1964, Caroline b 15 Dec 1969); *Career* registrar: in neurology Royal Free Hosp London 1963–65, Nat Hosp For Nervous Diseases 1965–66; sr registrar Queen Elizabeth Hosp and United Birmingham Hosps 1966–67, clinical tutor in neurology Univ of Birmingham 1966–67, conslt neurologist N Staffs Royal Infirmary and N Staffs Hosp Centre 1967–94; visiting neurologist: Burton-on-Trent Hosps 1967–94, Robert Jones and Agnes Hunt Orthopaedic Hosp 1967–94; Univ of Keele: hon res fell Dept of Communication and Neuroscience 1969, sr res fell Dept of Postgraduate Med 1978, sr lectr in neurology 1980, prof of neurology Sch of Post-Graduate Med 1994–; Wellcome res travelling fell Univ of Oslo 1967, Med Gilliand travelling fell to Centres in the United States of America 1982, assoc examiner ophthalmology RCS 1987–90; ed N Staffs Med Inst Journal 1971–85; author of numerous articles and papers on neurological sci; memb Cncl Assoc of Br Neurologists 1984–87 and 1991–94 (pres 1993–94), pres elect West Midlands Physicians' Assoc 1994–95, former sec and pres Midland Neurological Soc, former chm W Midlands Regnl Advsy Ctee in Neurosurgery and Neurology; chm Stoke-on-Trent and N Staffs Theatre Tst, pres Bedford Singers; Mayor The Ancient Corp of Hanley 1995; FRCP, FRCPE, FRSA; *Books* Metamorphoses (1985), Trees (1988), Improvisations (1990), Constants (1991); *Recreations* poetry and literature, music, history of medicine, natural phenomena; *Clubs* Osler; *Style*— Prof James Heron; ✉ Willowbrake, 6 Granville Ave, Newcastle, Staffordshire ST5 1JH (☎ 01782 617766)

HERON, Sir Michael Gilbert (Mike); kt (1996); s of Gilbert Thwaites Heron (d 1962), and Olive Lilian, *née* Steele; *b* 22 Oct 1934; *Educ* St Joseph's Acad Blackheath, New Coll Oxford (MA); *m* 16 Aug 1958, Celia Veronica Mary, da of Capt Clarence Hunter (d 1960); 2 s (Jonathan, Damian), 2 da (Louise, Annette); *Career* Lt RA 1953–55; dir BOCM Silcock 1971–76, chm Batchelors Foods Ltd 1976–82, dep co-ordinator Food and Drinks Co-ordination Unilever 1982–86, dir Main Bd Unilever plc and NV 1986–92, chm The Post Office 1993–; chm Cncl of St George's Hosp Med Sch 1992; memb Armed Forces Pay Review Bd 1981 and 1982; dep chm Business in the Community 1990– (chm Educn Business Ptnrships), chm NCVQ 1993–, patron Nat Trg Awards 1993 and 1994; *Recreations* very keen sportsman in the past, now a viewer; *Style*— Sir Mike Heron; ✉ Smithincott, The Avenue, Bucklebury Common, Berks RG6 7NP (☎ 0118 974 4387); Garden Flat, 19 Kensington Court, London W8 5DW (☎ 0171 460 0314); The Post Office, 148 Old Street, London EC1V 9HQ (☎ 0171 250 2524, fax 0171 250 2960)

HERON, Patrick; CBE (1977); s of Thomas Milner Heron (d 1983), and Eulalie Mabel, *née* Davies (d 1986); *b* 30 Jan 1920; *Educ* St Ives Cornwall, Welwyn Garden City HS, St George's Sch Harpenden; *m* 17 April 1945, Delia (d 1979), da of Richard Leopold Reiss; 2 da (Katharine Bride b 13 March 1947, Susanna b 22 September 1949); *Career* painter; *Exhibitions* incl: Redfern Gallery London 1947, 1948, 1950, 1951, 1954, 1956 and 1958, II Bienal de Sao Paul Brazil 1953 and VIII Bienal (touring to Rio de Janeiro, Buenos Aires, Santiago, Lima, Caracas, awarded Silver medal) 1965, John Moores Liverpool Exhibition II (awarded Grand prize) 1959, Waddington Galleries London 1959, 1960, 1963, 1964, 1967, 1969, 1970, 1973, 1975, 1977, 1979, 1983, 1987, 1989, 1991 and 1992, Bertha Schaefer Gallery NY 1960, 1962 and 1965, Galerie Charles Lienhard (Zurich) 1963, Richard Demarco Gallery Edinburgh 1967, Museum of Modern Art Oxford 1968, Whitechapel Art Gallery London 1972, Bonython Art Gallery Sydney 1973, Galerie le Balcon des Arts Paris 1977, Univ of Texas at Austin Art Museum 1978, Riverside Studios London 1981, Barbican Art Gallery London 1985, Setagaya Art Museum Tokyo Japan 1989, Art Gallery of NSW Sydney 1990, Anthony Hepworth Fine Art Bath 1993; cmmns incl stained-glass foyer wall Tate Gallery St Ives 1992; art critic: New English Weekly 1945–47, New Statesman and Nation 1947–50; London corr Arts NY 1955–58; subject of monograph (ed by Vivien Knight) 1988; subject of TV films: Omnibus 1983, South Bank Show (LWT) 1986; Power Lecture in Contemporary Art (The Shape of Colour) Aust 1973, E William Doty Lectures in Fine Arts (The Colour of Colour) Univ of Texas at Austin 1979; tstee Tate Gallery 1980–87, artist in residence Art Gallery of NSW Sydney 1989–90; Hon Texas Citizen at Austin Texas 1978; Hon DLitt: Univ of Exeter 1982, Univ of Kent 1986; Hon Dr RCA 1987, Hon DPhil CNAA 1989; Hon FRIBA 1991; *Publications* The Changing Forms of Art (1955), Braque (1958), Paintings by Patrick Heron: 1965–1977 (1978), The Shapes of Colour (1978), The Colour of Colour (1979), Barbican Catalogue (1985); *Style*— Patrick Heron, Esq, CBE; ✉ c/o Waddington Galleries Ltd, 11 Cork St, London W1X 1PD (☎ 0171 437 8611, fax 0171 734 4146)

HERON, Robert; CVO (1988); s of James Riddick Heron (d 1959), and Sophie Lockhart, *née* Leathem (d 1956); *b* 12 Oct 1927; *Educ* King Edward's Sch Birmingham, St Catharine's Coll Cambridge (MA); *m* 8 Aug 1953, Patricia Mary, da of Frank Robert Pennell (d 1945); 2 s (Andrew, Neil), 1 da (Susan); *Career* housemaster: Strathallan Sch Perthshire 1953–59, Christ Coll Brecon 1959–62; headmaster King James I Sch IOW 1962–66, head of educnl bdcasting ATV London 1967 (responsible for TV series incl sciences and social documentaries), del Euro Broadcsting Union (Paris, Rome, Stockholm, Basle), prog dir EVR Partnership (CBS USA, ICI UK, Ciba-Geigy UK) 1970, md EVR Enterprises Nippon EVR 1976–78, dir Duke of Edinburgh's Award 1978–87; formerly 6/7 Bn The Black Watch RHR TA; Freeman City of London 1981; *Recreations* sports and travel; *Clubs* Hawks (Cambridge), Achilles (Oxford and Cambridge); *Style*— Robert Heron, Esq, CVO; ✉ The Oast House, Ingleden Park, Tenterden, Kent

HERON-MAXWELL, Sir Nigel Mellor; 10 Bt (NS 1683), of Springkell, Dumfriesshire; s of Sir Patrick Ivor Heron-Maxwell, 9 Bt (d 1982), sr male rep of the Maxwells of Pollock and the Clydesdale Maxwells, and (Dorothy) Geraldine Emma, *née* Mellor; *b* 30 Jan 1944; *Educ* Milton Abbey; *m* 1972, Mary Elizabeth Angela, o da of William Ewing, of Co Donegal; 1 s, 1 da (Claire Louise b 1977); *Heir* s, David Mellor Heron-Maxwell b 22 May 1975; *Career* navigation apprentice London and Overseas Freighters Ltd 1961–65, navigation offr Royal Fleet Aux Service 1966–76, flying instr 1976–80; commercial pilot 1980–83; asst data controller SmithKline & French Research Ltd 1983–85, analyst/programmer SmithKline & French Laboratories Ltd 1985–89; SmithKline Beecham Pharmaceuticals: analyst/programmer 1989–94, planning and scheduling co-ordinator 1994–96; *Style*— Sir Nigel Heron-Maxwell, Bt; ✉ 50 Watlington Road, Old Harlow, Essex CM17 0DY (☎ 01279 301669); 50 Watlington Road, Old Harlow, Essex CM17 0DY

HERRIES OF TERREGLES, Lady (14 holder of S Lordship 1490); Lady Anne Elizabeth; *née* Fitzalan-Howard; eldest da of 16 Duke of Norfolk, KG, GCVO, GBE, TD, PC (d 1975, when the Dukedom and all other honours save the Lordship passed to his kinsman, 17 Duke of Norfolk, *qv*; the late Duke's mother was Lady Herries of Terregles *suo jure* following the death of her f, the 11 Lord), and Lavinia, Duchess of Norfolk, LG, CBE (d 1995); *b* 12 June 1938; *m* 1985, as his 2 w, Sir (Michael) Colin Cowdrey, CBE, *qv*; *Heir* sis, Lady Mary Mumford, *qv*; *Career* racehorse trainer; *Style*— The Rt Hon the Lady Herries of Terregles; ✉ Angmering Park, Littlehampton, West Sussex BN16 4EX (☎ 01903 871421)

HERRIN, John Edward; CBE (1985); s of Harold John Herrin (d 1974), of Humecourt, Hythe, Kent, and Gertrude Mary, *née* MacDermot (d 1989); *b* 15 Sept 1930; *Educ* Bancrofts Sch, Rugby Coll of Technol; *m* 4 April 1959, Heather Yeoman, da of Leslie Kirkpatrick Reid, JP (d 1980), of Mill House, Hale, Cheshire; 1 s (Jeremy b 1970), 2 da (Johanna b 1961, Caroline b 1962); *Career* Lt Cdr RNR 1953–55; chm Welwyn Electronics Ltd 1972; md: Royal Worcester plc 1975–83, Crystalate Holdings plc 1983–88; dir: Queensgate Instruments Ltd 1989–, Croster Electronics Ltd 1990–, Mion Electronics plc 1994–96, Hybrid Memory Products Ltd 1994–; chm: Yeoman Technology 1989–, Powerpike Ltd 1991–, PRP Optoelectronics Ltd 1991–; pres Euro Electronic Component Mfrs Assoc 1986–88; chm: Electronic Component Indust Fedn 1981–82, N Regnl Cncl for Sport and Recreation 1982–84; Freeman City of London, memb Ct of Assts Worshipful Co of Scientific Instrument Makers (Master 1990–91); CEng, FIEE, FRSA; *Recreations* sailing, fishing; *Clubs* MCC, East India; *Style*— John Herrin, Esq, CBE; ✉ Petteridge Oast, Matfield, Tonbridge, Kent TN12 7LX

HERRING, Timothy Stephen; s of Cdr Philip Maurice Herring, RNVR (d 1982), and Flora Pepita Herring (d 1985); *b* 25 May 1936; *Educ* Bishop's Stortford Coll; *m* 22 April 1960, Cathleen Elizabeth, da of Thomas Stephen Nevin (d 1972); 2 s (Stephen Ashley b 26 Nov 1960, Andrew Philip b 15 March 1963); *Career* Lamson Engineering 1956–66; proprietor: Julie's Restaurant 1969–, Portobello Hotel 1970–, Ark Restaurant USA 1983–; yachtsman; winner: Britannia Cup, Queen's Cup, Queen Victoria Cup; Freeman City of London 1961, Renter Warden Worshipful Co of Blacksmiths (memb 1961), Liveryman Worshipful Co of Turners; *Recreations* yachting; *Clubs* Royal Burnham Yacht, Royal Thames Yacht; *Style*— Timothy Herring, Esq; ✉ 127 Elgin Crescent, London W11 (☎ 0171 727 2776); Quaycote, Burnham-on-Crouch, Essex

HERRINGTON, Timothy John; s of John Herrington, of Basingstoke, Hants, and Barbara Jean Margaret, *née* Toon; *b* 22 April 1954; *Educ* Queen Mary's GS Basingstoke Hants, Univ of Bristol (LLB); *m* 20 Feb 1982, Kathleen Mary, da of Peter Loy Chetwynd Pigott, of Bulawayo, Zimbabwe; 1 s (James b 1987); *Career* admitted slr 1978; ptnr: Coward Chance 1985–87 (joined 1976), Clifford Chance 1987–; memb Law Soc Standing Ctee on Co Law 1988– (chm 1996–); Freeman: City of London 1977, Worshipful Co of Solicitors 1985; memb Law Soc; *Books* Life After Big Bang (contrib, 1987), Insider Dealing in Europe (contrib, 1994); *Recreations* cricket, travel, walking, gardening, wine; *Clubs* Hampshire CCC; *Style*— Timothy Herrington, Esq; ✉ Clifford Chance, 200 Aldersgate St, London EC1A 4JJ (☎ 0171 600 1000, fax 0171 600 5555)

HERROD, His Hon Donald; QC (1972); s of Wilfred Herrod (d 1988), and Phyllis Herrod (d 1974); *b* 7 Aug 1930; *Educ* grammar schs in Doncaster and Leeds; *m* 9 May 1959, Dr (Kathleen) Elaine Herrod, da of Dr Harold Douglas Merrington (d 1982); 2 da (Dr Philippa Ann Groves b 1960), Mrs Rosanne Louise Logan-Green b 1962); *Career* Nat Serv entered Army 1948, cmmnd 1949; called the the Bar 1956, recorder 1972–78, appointed to Bench 1978, circuit judge (NE Circuit) 1978–95; memb: Parole Bd 1978–81, Judicial Studies Bd 1982–86; *Recreations* golf; *Style*— His Hon Donald Herrod, QC; ✉ c/o North Eastern Circuit Office, 17th Floor, West Riding House, Albion Street, Leeds LS1 5AA (☎ 0113 244 1841)

HERRON, Anthony Gavin (Tony); TD (1972); s of Gavin Bessell Herron (d 1990), of The Wilderness, Maresfield Park, Sussex, and Irene Dorothy, *née* Peel (d 1986); *b* 10 April 1934; *Educ* Canford Sch, LSE (BSc); *m* 5 July 1958, Gray, da of Henry Francis Gray (d 1987); 1 s (Angus b 1966), 1 da (Tracy b 1964); *Career* ptnr Touche Ross and Co 1966–94 (latterly Corporate Fin Gp, seconded to Postal Servs as dir of postal fin and corp planning 1973–75); chm Highbury House Communications plc 1994–; dir: Expamet International plc 1974–, Fletcher Newspapers Ltd 1994–, Premier Fund Managers Ltd 1995–; fin dir CAA 1996–; past treas and vice pres HAC; Liveryman Worshipful Co of Chartered Accountants; FCA, FRSA; *Recreations* golf, swimming, walking, antiques; *Clubs* RAC; *Style*— Anthony Herron, Esq, TD; ✉ 12a Charterhouse Square, London EC1M 6AX (☎ 0171 608 0888, fax 0171 608 2648)

HERSCHELL, 3 Baron (UK 1886); Rognvald Richard Farrer; s of 2 Baron, GCVO (d 1929), and Vera (d 1961), da of Sir Arthur Nicolson, 10 Bt; *b* 13 Sept 1923; *Educ* Eton; *m* 1 May 1948, Lady Heather Mary Margaret Legge, o da of 8th Earl of Dartmouth; 1 da; *Heir* none; *Career* page of hon to King George V, King Edward VIII and King George VI; Capt Coldstream Gds (ret), served WWII 1942–45; *Style*— The Rt Hon the Lord Herschell; ✉ Westfield House, Ardington, Wantage, Oxfordshire OX12 8PN (☎ 01235 833224)

HERSEY, David Kenneth; s of Charles Kenneth Hersey, and Ella, *née* Morgan; *b* 30 Nov 1939; *Educ* Oberlin Coll; *m* 1, 1962 (m dis 1967), Ellen Diamond; m 2, 1967 (m dis 1972), Juliet Case; 1 da (Miranda Louise b 1969); m 3, 25 Sept 1976, Demetra, da of Demetrius Maraslis; 1 s (Demetri Alexander b 1978), 1 da (Ellen Katherine b 1980); *Career* lighting designer; fndr DHA Lighting, lighting conslt NT 1974–84, chm Assoc of Lighting Designers 1984–86; West End and Broadway prodns incl: Oliver, Piaf, Cyrano, Miss Saigon, Baker's Wife, Les Miserables, Cats, Starlight Express, Chess, Metropolis, Song and Dance, The Little Shop of Horrors, Evita, Nicholas Nickleby, Merrily We Roll Along, Burning Blue, The Glass Menagerie, Martin Guerre; NT prodns incl: Bartholomew Fair, Ghetto and many others; various prodns for RSC incl: Twelfth Night 1995; numerous operas and ballets incl: Royal Opera House, ENO, Ballet Rambert, London Contemporary Dance, Scot Ballet, Glyndebourne, Birmingham Royal Ballet; *Awards* for Miss Saigon: Drama Desk Award 1991; for Les Miserables: Tony Award 1987, Los Angeles Drama Critics' Circle Award 1988, Dora Mavor Moore Award 1989; for Cats Tony Award 1983, Drama Desk Award 1983, Dora Mavor Moore Award 1984; for Evita: Los Angeles Drama Critics' Circle Award 1979, Tony Award 1980; Olivier Award for Best Lighting Designer 1996; *Recreations* sailing; *Style*— David Hersey, Esq;

✉ DHA Lighting Ltd, 289–302 Waterloo Road, London SE1 8RQ (☎ 0171 582 3200, fax 0171 582 4779)

HERTFORD, 8 Marquess of (GB 1793); Hugh Edward Conway Seymour; DL (Warwicks 1959); also Lord Conway, Baron Conway of Ragley (E 1703), Baron Conway of Killultagh (I 1712), Viscount Beauchamp, Earl of Hertford (both GB 1750), and Earl of Yarmouth (GB 1793); patron of 3 livings; s of Brig-Gen Lord Henry Seymour, DSO (2 s of 6 Marquess), and Lady Helen Grosvenor, da of 1 Duke of Westminster; *b* 29 March 1930; *Educ* Eton, Royal Agricultural Coll Cirencester; *m* 1956, Comtesse Pamela Thérèse Louise de Caraman-Chimay, da of Lt-Col Prince Alphonse de Chimay, TD (d 1973), by his w, Brenda (d 1985), da of Lord Ernest Hamilton (7 s of 1 Duke of Abercorn); 1 s, 3 da; *Heir* s, Earl of Yarmouth, *qv*; *Career* late Lt Grenadier Gds; Hertford PRs Ltd 1962–73; estate mangr and prop of Ragley Hall 1940–91; *Clubs* White's, Pratt's, Turf; *Style*— The Most Hon the Marquess of Hertford; ✉ North Wing, Ragley Hall, Alcester, Warwicks B49 5NJ (☎ 01789 762455)

HERTFORD, Bishop of 1990–; Rt Rev Robin Jonathan Norman Smith; *b* 1936; *Educ* Worcester Coll Oxford (BA, MA), Ridley Hall Cambridge; *m* 1961, Hon Lois Jean, da of Baron Pearson, CBE, PC (Life Peer, d 1980); *Career* ordained: deacon 1962, priest 1963; curate St Margaret's Barking 1962–67, chaplain Lee Abbey Lynton 1967–72, vicar St Mary's Chesham Bucks 1972–80, rural dean Amersham 1979–82, rector Great Chesham 1980–90, hon canon Christ Church 1988–90; *Recreations* walking, travel, gardening; *Style*— The Rt Rev the Bishop of Hertford; ✉ Hertford House, Abbey Mill Lane, St Albans, Herts AL3 4HE (☎ 01727 866420)

HERVEY, Rear Adm John Bethell; CB (1982), OBE (1970); s of Capt Maurice William Bethell Hervey, RN (d 1965), of Lee Common Bucks, and Joan Hanbury (d 1975); f served in both World Wars and was in HMS Ocean at the Dardanelles and in HMS Colossus at Jutland; *b* 14 May 1928; *Educ* Marlborough; *m* 1950, Audrey Elizabeth, da of Leonard Mallett Mote (d 1947), of Colombo; 2 s (Nicholas, Jonathan), 1 da (Katrina); *Career* RN 1946, specialized in submarines 1950, nuclear submarines 1968; cmd appts: HMS Miner VI 1956, HMS Aeneas 1956–57, HMS Ambush 1959–62, HMS Oracle 1962–64, Sixth Submarine Div 1964–66, HMS Cavalier 1966–67, HMS Warspite 1968–69, Second Submarine Sqdn 1973–75, HMS Kent 1975–76; staff appts: Course Offr RN Petty Offrs Leadership Sch 1957–59, Submarine Staff Offr to Canadian Maritime Cdr Halifax Nova Scotia 1964–66, Flotilla Ops Offr to Flag Offr Submarines 1970–71, Def Operational Requirements Staff 1971–73, Dep Chief Allied Staff to C-in-C Channel, C-in-C E Atlantic 1976–80, Hon ADC to HM The Queen 1979, Cdr Br Navy Staff and Br Naval Attaché Washington; UK Nat Liaison Rep to SACLANT 1980–82, Rear Adm 1980, ret; mktg vice pres Western Hemisphere MEL 1982–86, ind naval conslt 1986–; *Recreations* walking, talking, reading; *Clubs* Army and Navy, Royal Navy of 1765 and 1785, Anchorites (pres 1988); *Style*— Rear Adm John Hervey, CB, OBE; ✉ c/o National Westminster Bank, 208 Piccadilly, London W1A 2DG

HERVEY, Lord (Frederick William Charles) Nicholas Wentworth; s of 6 Marquess of Bristol (d 1985), and his 2 w, Lady Anne Juliet Dorothea Maud Fitzwilliam da of 8 Earl Fitzwilliam; hp of half-bro, 7 Marquess of Bristol; *b* 26 Nov 1961; *Educ* Eton, Yale Univ; *Career* pres and fndr: Rockingham Club, Woodhouse Ltd; fndr and pres of Youth Assoc of the Nonarchist League; vice pres ESU Eastern Regn; *Recreations* skiing, swimming; *Clubs* The Pundits Soc of Yale Univ; *Style*— The Lord Nicholas Hervey; ✉ 26 Redburn Street, London SW3 4BX (☎ 0171 352 0830)

HERVEY-BATHURST, Sir (Frederick) John Charles Gordon; 7 Bt (UK 1818), of Lainston, Hants; s of Sir Frederick Peter Methuen Hervey-Bathurst, 6 Bt (d 1995), and his 1 w, Maureen Gladys Diana, *née* Gordon; *b* 23 April 1934; *Educ* Eton, Trinity Coll Cambridge (MA); *m* 1957, Caroline Myrtle, da of Sir William Randle Starkey, 2 Bt; 1 s (Frederick William John b 1965), 2 da (Louisa Caroline (Lady Portal) b 1959, Sophia Selina Irene (Mrs Henry Colthurst) b 1961); *Heir* s, Frederick William John Hervey-Bathurst b 1965; *Career* Lt Grenadier Gds (Reserve); former dir Lazard Bros and Co Ltd, ret; Liveryman Worshipful Co of Skinners; *Style*— Sir John Hervey-Bathurst, Bt; ✉ Somborne Park, King's Somborne, Hants SO20 6QT (☎ and fax 01794 388322)

HERXHEIMER, Dr Andrew; s of Herbert G J Herxheimer (d 1985), of London, and Ilse M, *née* König (d 1980); *b* 4 Nov 1925; *Educ* Highgate Sch, St Thomas' Hosp Med Sch (MB, BS); *m* 1, 4 March 1960 (m dis 1974), Susan Jane, da of Harry Collier (d 1983), of London; 2 da (Charlotte b 1961, Sophie b 1963); m 2, 24 March 1983, Dr Christine Herxheimer, da of Willrecht Bernecker (d 1942), of Stuttgart, Germany; *Career* lectr and sr lectr in pharmacology London Hosp Med Coll 1959–76, sr lectr in clinical pharmacology Charing Cross and Westminster Med Sch 1976–91, extraordinary prof of clinical pharmacology Univ of Groningen Netherlands 1968–77; ed Drug and Therapeutics Bulletin 1963–92; conslt UK Cochrane Centre NHS R&D Prog Oxford 1992–95, chm Int Soc of Drug Bulletins 1986–96, vice pres Coll of Health, dir Language Line, emeritus fell UK Cochrane Centre 1996–; memb Br Pharmacological Soc 1960; FRCP 1977; *Books* Drugs and Sensory Functions (ed, 1968), Pharmaceuticals and Health Policy (jt ed, 1981); *Recreations* reading, travel; *Style*— Dr Andrew Herxheimer; ✉ 9 Park Crescent, London N3 2NL (☎ 0181 346 5470, fax 0181 346 0407, e-mail 101364.2017@compuserve.com)

HERZBERG, Henry Joseph; s of Georges Herzberg (d 1989), and Nancibel, *née* Joseph; *b* 7 Oct 1943; *Educ* Ashburton Secdy Sch, Selhurst GS, Architectural Assoc London, RIBA (AADipl); *m* 6 Aug 1976, Kate, da of Thomas Bampton, 1 s (Joseph Daniel b 4 July 1977), 3 da (Chloe Zylpha b 18 Feb 1972, Anna Zimena b 12 Sept 1973, Rachel Henrietta b 4 April 1982); *Career* architect; in professional practice Ahrends, Burton and Koralek 1966–67; site architect: Sir Robert McAlpine Ltd 1969–71, Wates Ltd 1971–72; Lethaby and Bannister Fletcher scholar Soc for the Protection of Ancient Buildings 1972; project architect Wimpey Ltd 1973–75, Ahrends Burton Koralek 1975; bldg ed Architects Journal 1975–77; architect (work includes: Colin St John Wilson & Ptnrs (The Br Library Euston) 1977–79, YRM (Central Med Stores and Laundry Bahrain) 1979–80; Chapman Taylor Partners: architect 1980– (Ridings Wakefield), assoc 1983– (The Poplars Supermarket and District Centre Stevenage, Orchard Square Fargate Sheffield), ptnr 1986– (refurbishment of The Octagon High Wycombe, Lakeside Thurrock, Priory Park Merton, Vicarage Field Barking, Peacocks Woking, Royal Victoria Place Tunbridge Wells, South Terminal Departure Lounge Gatwick, refurbishment of Brunel Centre Swindon); ARIBA 1970; memb: AA 1970, Soc for the Protection of Ancient Buildings 1971, Victorian Soc, Georgian Soc, Wind and Windmill Soc; *Style*— Henry Herzberg, Esq; ✉ Chapman Taylor Partners, 364 Kensington High Street, London W14 8NS (☎ 0171 371 3000, fax 0171 371 1949)

HERZBERG, Dr Joseph Larry; s of Adolf Heinrich Herzberg, of London, and Pearl, *née* Mesh; *b* 10 May 1953; *Educ* Carmel Coll Berks, Hasmonean Sch London, The London Hosp Med Coll (BSc, MB BS, MPhil); *m* 13 Feb 1977, Helene Ruth, da of Harry Gordon, of London; 1 s (Laurence b 1982); *Career* sr house offr and registrar in pyschiatry London Hosp 1980–84 (house physician 1979–80); sr registrar in psychiatry: St Mary's Hosp London 1984–85, The Bethlem Royal and Maudsley Hosps London 1986–87; conslt psychogeriatrician Lewisham & Guy's Mental Health and NHS Trust (formerly Guy's Hosp) and sr lectr sr lectr UMDS Guy's Campus 1987–96; conslt old age psychiatrist The Royal London Hosp (St Clements), assoc dean of postgrad med (mental health) N Thames Region and TPMDE Univ of London 1996–; author of various scientific papers on: social psychiatry, neuropsychiatry, psychogeriatrics, audit and psychiatric educn; memb Cncl: Section of Geriatrics and Gerontology RSM, Assoc for the Study of Medical Education (RCPsych representative); FRSM, FRCPsych 1995 (MRCPsych 1983); *Recreations* music (particularly opera), theatre, travel; *Style*— Dr Joseph Herzberg; ✉ 82b Ashley Gardens, Thirleby Rd, Westminster, London SW1P 1HG; Guy's Hospital, St Thomas St, London SE1 9RT (☎ 0171 955 5000)

HESELTINE, Rt Hon Michael Ray Dibdin; PC (1979), MP (C) Henley (majority 18,392); s of late Col R D Heseltine, of Swansea, Glamorgan; *b* 21 March 1933; *Educ* Shrewsbury, Pembroke Coll Oxford (BA, pres Oxford Union); *m* 1962, Anne Harding Williams; 1 s, 2 da; *Career* Nat Serv cmmnd Welsh Gds 1959; Parly candidate (C): Gower 1959, Coventry North 1964; MP (C): Tavistock 1966–74, Henley 1974–; dir Bow Publications 1961–65, chm Haymarket Press 1966–70; vice chm Cons Parly Tport Ctee 1968, oppn spokesman on Tport 1969, Parly sec Miny of Tport June-Oct 1970, Parly under-sec for the Environment 1970–72, min for Aerospace and Shipping DTI 1972–74, oppn spokesman on Indust 1974–76, oppn spokesman on the Environment 1976–79, sec of state for the Environment 1979–83, sec of state for Defence 1983–86 (resigned over Westland affair), contested leadership of Cons Party Nov 1990, sec of state for the Environment Nov 1990–92, pres Bd of Trade (sec of state for Trade and Industry) 1992–95, dep PM 1995–; pres: Assoc of Cons Clubs 1978, Nat Young Conservatives 1982–84 (vice pres 1978); memb Cncl Zoological Soc of London 1987–; hon fell Pembroke Coll Oxford 1986; Hon LLD Univ of Liverpool 1990; *Publications* Reviving the Inner Cities (1983), Where There's A Will (1987), The Challenge of Europe, Can Britain Win? (1989); *Clubs* Carlton; *Style*— The Rt Hon Michael Heseltine, MP; ✉ House of Commons, London SW1A 0AA (☎ 0171 219 3000)

HESELTINE, Richard Mark Horsley; s of late Edwin Oswald Heseltine, and Penelope Horsley, *née* Robinson; *b* 3 Oct 1945; *Educ* Winchester, New Coll Oxford (MA), Wharton Sch Univ of Pennsylvania (MBA); *m* 1976, Joanna Elisabeth, da of Ronald C Symonds, CB, of London; 2 da (Catherine b 1978, Emma b 1981); *Career* Corp Fin Dept Morgan Grenfell 1969–71, dir Croda International plc 1981– (exec 1971–80); non-exec dir: The Smaller Companies Investment Trust plc, Overseas Investment Trust plc; cncllr London Borough of Islington (SDP) 1986–90; *Recreations* yacht racing; *Clubs* Reform, Oxford and Cambridge Sailing Soc; *Style*— Richard Heseltine, Esq; ✉ 29 Gibson Square, London N1 (☎ 0171 359 0702); Passage House, The Quay, Dittisham, nr Dartmouth, S Devon; Croda International plc, 168 High Holborn, London WC1 (☎ 0171 836 7777)

HESELTINE, Rt Hon Sir William Frederick Payne; GCB (1990, KCB 1986, CB 1978), GCVO (1988, KCVO 1981, CVO 1969, MVO 1961), AC (1988), QSO (1990), PC (1986); s of Henry William Heseltine (d 1984), of Fremantle, WA, and Louise Mary Gwythyr, *née* Payne (d 1966); *b* 17 July 1930; *Educ* Christ Church GS Claremont, Univ of Western Aust (BA); *m* 1, Ann (d 1957), da of late L Turner, of Melbourne; m 2, 1959, Audrey Margaret, da of late Stanley Nolan, of Sydney; 1 s (John b 1964), 1 da (Sophy b 1961); *Career* Aust Civil Serv: PM's Dept Canberra 1951–62, private sec to PM of Aust (Sir Robert Menzies) 1955–59; asst fed dir Lib Pty of Aust 1962–64; press sec to HM The Queen 1967–72 (asst press sec 1960–61 and 1965–67), private sec to HM The Queen 1986–90 (asst private sec 1972–77, dep private sec 1977–86); chm NZI Australia (dep chm 1990–92), dir P&O Australia Ltd, formerly dir West Coast Telecasters Ltd 1992–96; *Clubs* Weld (Perth WA), Press, BAFTA; *Style*— The Rt Hon Sir William Heseltine, GCB, GCVO, AC, QSO; ✉ PO Box 35, York, Western Australia 6302

HESFORD, Stephen; s of Bernard Hesford, of Lymm, Cheshire, and Nellie, *née* Haworth; *b* 27 May 1957; *Educ* Univ of Bradford (BSc), Poly of Central London (Postgrad Dip Law); *m* 21 July 1984, Elizabeth Anne, da of Dudley Henshall, of Bramhall, Cheshire; 2 s (John b 1986, David b 1988); *Career* called to the Bar Gray's Inn 1981; memb: Fabian Soc, Lab Pty; Parly candidate 1992; *Recreations* cricket, politics, antiquarian books, biographies; *Clubs* Lancashire CCC (life memb); *Style*— Stephen Hesford, Esq; ✉ 56 The Downs, Altrincham, Cheshire WA14 2QJ (☎ 0161 928 1046); 38 Young Street, Manchester (☎ 0161 833 0489, fax 0161 835 3938)

HESKETH, (Claude Robert) Blair; s of Maj Claude Walter Hesketh (d 1964), and Antoinette Roberta, *née* Bull; *b* 15 Jan 1939; *Educ* Stowe; *m* 10 April 1974, Margaret Isabel, da of Col Hubert Bromley Watkins, DSO (d 1984); 1 s (Rollo b 1975), 1 da (Arabella b 1977); *Career* dir Hill Samuel Aust Ltd 1969–78, md Hill Samuel Pacific Ltd 1978–84, dir Hill Samuel Bank Ltd 1984–95, md C G Hacking & Sons Ltd 1996–; govr Cheam Sch; FCA 1962; *Recreations* music, gardening, golf; *Clubs* Turf, Berkshire Golf; *Style*— Blair Hesketh, Esq; ✉ Plastow Farm, Plastow Green, nr Newbury, Berkshire RG19 8LP (☎ 01635 268230); C G Hacking & Sons Ltd, 50 Borough High Street, London SE1 1XN (☎ 0171 407 6451, fax 0171 407 3001)

HESKETH, Dowager Baroness; Christian Mary; OBE (1984), DL (Northants); da of Sir John McEwen, 1 Bt, JP, DL, and Bridget, da of Rt Hon Sir Francis Lindley, GCMG, CB, CBE, and Hon Etheldreda Fraser, 3 da of 13 Lord Lovat; *b* 17 July 1929; *Educ* John Watson's Sch, St Mary's Convent Ascot; *m* 22 Nov 1949, 2 Baron Hesketh, DL (d 1955); 3 s (incl 3 Baron); *Career* county organiser WRVS 1952–83; chm Daventry Cons Assoc 1964–74; memb Arts Cncl 1960–63; High Sheriff Northants 1981, cncllr Northants CC 1989–93, vice chm Royal Theatre Northampton 1980–90, memb Roxburghe Club 1991; Hon LLD Univ of Leicester 1982; *Books* Tartans (1961), The Country House Cookery Book (with Elisabeth Luard and Laura Blond, 1985), For King and Conscience: John Graham of Claverhouse, Viscount Dundee (with Magnus Linklater, 1989); *Style*— The Rt Hon the Dowager Lady Hesketh, OBE, DL; ✉ 20a Tregunter Rd, London SW10 (☎ 0171 373 9821); Pomfret Lodge, Towcester, Northants (☎ 01327 50526)

HESKETH, Baroness; Hon Claire Georgina; *née* Watson; eldest da of 3 Baron Manton; *b* 7 Feb 1952; *m* 1977, 3 Baron Hesketh, *qv*; 1 s, 2 da; *Style*— The Lady Hesketh; ✉ Easton Neston, Towcester, Northants NN12 7HS (☎ 01327 350969)

HESKETH, 3 Baron (UK 1935); Sir Thomas Alexander Fermor-Hesketh; 10 Bt (GB 1761), KBE (1997), PC (1991); s of 2 Baron Hesketh (d 1955), and Dowager Lady Hesketh; *b* 28 Oct 1950; *Educ* Ampleforth; *m* 1977, Hon Claire, *qv*, da of 3 Baron Manton; 1 s, 2 da; *Heir* s, Hon Frederick Hatton Fermor-Hesketh b 13 Oct 1988; *Career* a govt whip House of Lords 1986–91, Parly under sec of state DOE 1989–90, Min of State DTI 1990–91, Capt Hon Corps Gentlemen-at-Arms (govt chief whip House of Lords) 1991–93; non-exec dir: Babcock International plc 1993–, British Aerospace plc 1993–; chm British Mediterranean Airways 1994–; pres British Racing Drivers' Club; hon fell Soc of Engrs 1979; *Clubs* Turf, White's, Beefeater; *Style*— The Rt Hon the Lord Hesketh, KBE, PC; ✉ Easton Neston, Towcester, Northants NN12 7HS (☎ 01327 350969, fax 01327 351751); office: 33 Cork Street, London W1X 1HB (☎ 0171 437 4760, fax 0171 494 3854)

HESLOP, Martin Sydney; QC (1995); s of Sydney Heslop, and Patricia Mary, *née* Day; *b* 6 Aug 1948; *Educ* St George's Coll Weybridge, Univ of Bristol; *Career* called to the Bar Lincoln's Inn 1972, first jr Treasy counsel Central Criminal Court 1992 (jr Treasy counsel 1987), sr Treasy counsel Central Criminal Court and recorder of the Crown Court 1993– (asst recorder 1989–93); *Recreations* sailing, travel, photography, swimming; *Clubs* Royal London Yacht, Bar Yacht; *Style*— Martin Heslop, Esq, QC; ✉ 1 Hare Court, Ground Floor, Temple, London EC4Y 7BE (☎ 0171 353 5324)

HESLOP, Richard William; s of Richard Basil Heslop (d 1962), of Nottingham, and Edith Margaret, *née* Butler (d 1994); *b* 12 May 1931; *Educ* Nottingham HS, Univ of Birmingham (BSc, MB ChB); *m* 12 Sept 1959, Jean Elizabeth, da of A J N Gammond (d 1977), of Rudhall, Ross on Wye, Herefordshire; 1 s (Richard b 1962), 2 da (Janet b 1960, Elizabeth b 1964); *Career* Capt RAMC Hong Kong 1956–58; registrar and sr registrar Utd Birmingham Hosps 1960–66, hon conslt urologist Hull and E Riding of Yorks 1967–92; surgn to Corp of Hull Trinity House, former memb Hull Health Authy; memb:

BMA, Br Assoc of Urological Surgns; FRCS; *Recreations* freemasonry, motor sport, photography; *Style*— Richard Heslop, Esq; ✉ Eata House, Etton, East Riding of Yorkshire HU17 7PQ (☎ 01430 810488); The Nuffield Hospital, 81 Westbourne Ave, Hull (☎ 01482 342327)

HESS, Nigel John; s of John Hess, of Weston-Super-Mare, Somerset, and Sheila, *née* Merrick; *b* 22 July 1953; *Educ* Weston-Super-Mare GS for Boys, St Catharine's Coll Cambridge (MA); *m* 1996, Lisa Claire, da of Raymond Telford; 1 da (Alice Elizabeth b 31 Aug 1990); *Career* composer and conductor in TV theatre and film; music scores for TV incl: A Woman of Substance, Deceptions, Anna of the Five Towns, All Passion Spent, Vanity Fair, Campion, Summer's Lease (TV and Radio Industs Club Award for Best TV Theme), The London Embassy, The One Game, Testament (Novello Award for Best TV Theme), Chimera, Titmuss Regained, Maigret, Growing Pains, Screen Play (nominated for Oscar), Wycliffe, Just William, Dangerfield, Hetty Wainthropp Investigates; co-music dir and house composer RSC 1981–85; contrib music scores to 20 RSC prodns incl: Troilus and Cressida, Much Ado About Nothing, Julius Caesar, Cyrano de Bergerac (NY Drama Desk Award for Outstanding Music in a Play on Broadway), Comedy of Errors, Hamlet, Love's Labour's Lost, Othello, The Winter's Tale, The Swan Down Gloves, A Christmas Carol, Twelfth Night; West End prodns incl The Secret of Sherlock Holmes; composer many chamber vocal and orchestral pieces; commercial recordings incl: The Swan Down Gloves (London Cast Album), Much Ado About Nothing (RSC original score), Chameleon (MRA Award for Best MOR Album), Screens and Stages, Maigret and other TV themes, East Coast Pictures; *Recreations* travel and photography; *Clubs* Assoc of Professional Composers; *Style*— Nigel Hess, Esq; ✉ c/o Bucks Music Ltd, 1a Farm Place, London W8 7SX (☎ 0171 221 4275, fax 0171 229 6893)

HESSAYON, Dr David Gerald; s of Jack Hessayon (d 1958), and Lena Hessayon (d 1933); *b* 13 Feb 1928; *Educ* Univ of Leeds, Univ of Manchester; *m* 1951, Joan Parker, da of Weeden T Gray, of USA; 2 da; *Career* chm: Pan Britannica Industries Ltd 1972–93, Turbair 1970–93, Expert Publications 1988–, pbi Publications 1988–93, Hessayon Books Ltd 1993–; dir Orion Publishing Group 1992–93; chm Br Agrochemicals Assoc 1980–81; vice patron Royal National Rose Soc, hon vice pres Capel Manor; Freeman City of London, memb Worshipful Co of Gardeners; *Books* The Tree and Shrub Expert, The Armchair Book of the Garden, The Flower Expert, The Indoor Plant Spotter, The Garden Expert, The Home Expert, The Gold Plated House Plant Expert, Rose Jotter, House Plant Jotter, Vegetable Jotter, Be Your Own Greenhouse Expert, The Bio Friendly Gardening Guide, The Fruit Expert, The House Plant Expert, The Garden DIY Expert, The Rock & Water Garden Expert, The Greenhouse Expert, The Flowering Shrub Expert, The Flower Arranging Expert, The Container Expert, The Bulb Expert, The Easy-care Gardening Expert, The New Bedding Plant Expert, The New Rose Expert, The New Lawn Expert, The New Vegetable & Herb Expert; *Recreations* Times crossword, American folk music; *Clubs* London Press; *Style*— Dr David Hessayon; ✉ Expert Publications Ltd, Sloe House, Halstead, Essex CO9 1PA (☎ 01787 474744, fax 01787 474700)

HESTER, Rev Canon John Frear; s of William Hester (d 1978), and Frances Mary, *née* Frear (d 1964); *b* 21 Jan 1927; *Educ* West Hartlepool GS, St Edmund Hall Oxford (MA), Cuddesdon Coll Oxford; *m* 1959, Elizabeth Margaret, da of late Sir Eric Riches, of Rutland Gate, London; 3 s (Robert b 1963, James b 1965, Alexander b 1971); *Career* clerk in holy orders, chaplain Actors' Church Union 1958–, rector of Soho 1963–75, priest-in-charge St Paul's Covent Garden 1969–75, vicar of Brighton 1975–85, rural dean of Brighton 1976–85, hon chaplain Brighton & Hove Albion FC 1979–, chaplain to HM The Queen 1984–97, canon residentiary and precentor Chichester Cathedral 1985–97 (canon and prebendary 1976–85, canon emeritus 1997–); chm: Chichester Diocesan Overseas Cncl 1985–94, Tstees Chichester Centre of Arts 1990–; pres Forum Soc 1985–; vice pres: Royal Theatrical Fund 1979–, Guild of Sussex Craftsmen 1991–; chm of Govrs Lavant House Rosemead Sch 1995–; *Books* Soho Is My Parish (1970); *Recreations* travel (real and imaginary), theatre, soccer; *Style*— The Rev Canon John Hester; ✉ The Hovel, Oving, Chichester, West Sussex PO20 6DE (☎ 01243 782071)

HESTER, Prof Ronald Ernest; s of Ernest Hester, of Heworth Place, York, and Rhoda Pennington, *née* Lennox (d 1985); *b* 8 March 1936; *Educ* Royal GS High Wycombe, Univ of London (BSc, DSc), Cornell Univ (PhD); *m* 30 Aug 1958, Bridget Ann, da of Sqdn Ldr Ernest Francis Maddin (d 1988); 2 s (Stephen b 1960, David b 1965), 2 da (Alison b 1962, Catherine b 1968); *Career* res fell Univ of Cambridge 1962–63, asst prof Cornell Univ USA 1963–65, prof Univ of York 1965– (former lectr, sr lectr, reader); approx 300 pubns in sci jls; ed jls: Issues in Environmental Science and Technol, Biospectroscopy; chm: SERC Chemistry Ctee 1988–90, Euro Res Cncls Chemistry Ctee 1990–93; memb: UGC Equipment Ctee 1987–89, SERC Sci Bd 1988–90, SERC Cncl 1990–94, SERC Astronomy and Planetary Scis Bd 1991–93, RSC Scientific Affrs Bd 1992–94, RSA; FRSC 1970, CChem 1970; *Books* Physical-Inorganic Chemistry (1965), Understanding our Environment (1985), Advances in Spectroscopy vols 1–26 (1975–96); *Recreations* squash, tennis, skiing, travel; *Style*— Prof Ronald E Hester; ✉ The Old Rectory, Crayke, York YO6 4TA; Dept of Chemistry, University of York, York YO1 5DD (☎ 01904 432557, fax 01904 432562, e-mail REH1@york.ac.uk)

HESTER, Stephen A M; *b* 14 Dec 1960; *Educ* Univ of Oxford (MA); *m*; *Career* CS First Boston: joined 1982, dir 1987–, an md 1988–, currently co-head Euro Investment Banking Dept; *Style*— Stephen Hester, Esq; ✉ CS First Boston Ltd, One Cabot Square, London E14 4QJ (☎ 0171 516 1616, fax 0171 513 1600)

HETHERINGTON, Prof (Hector) Alastair; s of Sir Hector J W Hetherington, KCB (d 1965), and Alison, *née* Reid (d 1966); *b* 31 Oct 1919; *Educ* Gresham's, Corpus Christi Coll Oxford (BA, MA); *m* 1, 27 June 1957 (m dis 1977), (Helen) Miranda, da of Prof Richard Oliver, of Manchester; 2 s (Thomas b 1959, Alexander b 1961), 2 da (Lucy b 1963, Mary b 1965); m 2, 26 Oct 1979, Sheila Janet Cameron, wid of Hamish Cameron; *Career* served WWII Maj RAC 1940–46; reporter Glasgow Herald 1946–50; Manchester Guardian (later The Guardian): joined 1950, foreign ed 1953–56, ed 1956–75; controller BBC Scotland 1976–79, res prof in media studies Univ of Stirling 1982–87 (emeritus prof 1987), hon fell Corpus Christi Coll Oxford; FRIAS 1987; Dr hc Univ of Lille III 1989, Freeman City of Lille 1989; *Books* Guardian Years (1981), News Newspapers and Television (1985), Perthshire in Trust (1988), News in the Regions (1989), Highlands and Islands - A Generation of Progress (1990), Cameras in the Commons (1990), Inside BBC Scotland 1975–1980 (1991), A Walker's Guide to Arran (1995); *Recreations* hill walking, golf; *Clubs* Athenaeum; *Style*— Prof Alastair Hetherington; ✉ High Corrie, Isle of Arran KA27 8JB (☎ 01770 810652)

HETHERINGTON, Anthony Richard; s of Richard Ernest Hetherington, of Hants, and late Charlotte Alice Annie, *née* Miller; *b* 6 Nov 1940; *Educ* Preston Manor Sch, Law Soc Sch of Law; *m* 1, 19 June 1965, Jacqueline, da of Auguste Théophile Duteil, of Paris; 2 s (David Anthony St Clare b 1967, Julian Anthony St John b 1968); m 2, 14 Feb 1977, Hazel Mary, da of late George Gorman, of Hampshire; 2 da (Sarah Jane and Joanna Mary b 1967); *Career* service Inns of Ct Regt (later Inns of Ct and City Yeomanry 1959–65); slr; cmmr for Oaths; dep dist judge of the High Ct and Co Ct 1975–; Freeman City of London, Liveryman Worshipful Co of Arbitrators 1981; sec The Palmerston Forts Soc 1986–; FCIArb; *Recreations* music, fly fishing, shooting, military history, travel, books, dogs; *Clubs* Fly Fishers', Fareham and County; *Style*— Anthony Hetherington, Esq; ✉ La Huronnière, 61210 Champcerie par Putanges, Pont-Ecrepin; 12 Ambleside Court, Crescent Road, Alverstoke, Hampshire

HETHERINGTON, Sir Arthur Ford; kt (1974), DSC (1944); s of Sir Roger Gaskell Hetherington, CB, OBE (d 1952), and Honoria, *née* Ford; *b* 12 July 1911; *Educ* Highgate Sch, Trinity Coll Cambridge (BA); *m* 1937, Margaret Lacey; 1 s, 1 da; *Career* serv WWII RNVR; chm: Southern Gas Bd 1961–64 (dep chm 1956–61), E Midlands Gas Bd 1964–66, Br Gas Corp (formerly Gas Cncl) 1972–76 (memb 1961, dep chm 1967–72); Hon DSc Univ of London 1974; FEng 1976 (fndr fell); *Clubs* Athenaeum; *Style*— Sir Arthur Hetherington, DSC, FEng; ✉ 32 Connaught Sq, London W2 2HL (☎ 0171 723 3128)

HETHERINGTON, Lt-Col John David; s of Howard Walklett Hetherington (d 1977), of Berks, and Doris Amy, *née* Dowling; *b* 28 Feb 1934; *Educ* Haileybury and ISC, Eaton Hall, Def Serv Staff Coll India; *Career* 2 Lt The Sherwood Foresters 1953; served: BAOR, Far E, India, Cyprus; Lt-Col OIC The Worcestershire and Sherwood Foresters Regt 1972–74, ret 1979; memb Co Ctee TA & VRA Derbyshire 1984–, memb Ctee ABF Derbyshire 1984–; chm The Midlands Driving Trials Gp 1993–94 (vice chm and tech del 1984–92), dep pres The Sherwood Foresters Assoc 1985–90, vice pres The Worcs and Sherwood Foresters Regtl Assoc 1990–; memb: Ctee Royal Windsor Horse Show 1986– (Exec Ctee 1994–), Burton Dist Ctee Staffs Agric Soc 1988–93, Ctee Br Horse Soc Horse Driving Trials 1990–94, Safety Policy Ctee Br Horse Soc 1990–94; dir Windsor Equestrian Promotions Ltd 1994–; chm BBC Radio Derby Advsy Cncl 1990–94, memb BBC Midlands and East Regnl Advsy Cncl 1990–94; govr Repton Sch 1994–; OStJ 1987; Derbyshire St John Ambulance: cdr 1986–88, cmmr 1987–88; land owner; *Recreations* competition carriage driving, ornithology; *Style*— Lt-Col John D Hetherington; ✉ The Stud Farm, Byrkley, Rangemore, Burton upon Trent, Staffordshire DE13 9RF (☎ 01283 712368)

HETHERINGTON, Sir Thomas Chalmers; KCB (1979), CBE (1970), TD, QC (1978); s of W Hetherington; *b* 1926; *Educ* Rugby, ChCh Oxford; *m* 1953, June Catliff; 4 da; *Career* called to the Bar Inner Temple 1952, bencher 1978; former dep Treasy slr; dir of Public Prosecutions 1977–87, War Crimes Inquiry 1988–89; *Books* Prosecution and the Public Interest (1989); *Style*— Sir Thomas Hetherington, KCB, CBE, TD, QC; ✉ Rosemount, Mount Pleasant Road, Lingfield, Surrey RH7 6BH

HETTIARATCHY, Dr Pearl Daisy Jebaranee; da of Solomon Vinnasitamby Muttiah (d 1952), and Grace Constance Manonmanie, *née* Sittampalam (d 1977); *b* 4 Feb 1942; *Educ* Holy Family Convent Bambalipittya Sri Lanka, Univ of Colombo Sri Lanka (MB BS), Univ of London (Dip in Psychological Med, MRCPsych 1972, FRCPsych 1986); *m* 2 Jan 1967, Dr Sidney Walter Hettiaratchy, s of Cornelius Peter Hettiaratchy; 2 da (Ashanti Suvendrini (Mrs Dickson) b 25 Jan 1968, Chemaine Natasha b 25 May 1975), 1 s (Dr Shehan Peter Hettiaratchy b 5 Nov 1969); *Career* pre-registration Kandy Gen Hosp Sri Lanka 1965–66, women's med offr Akurana Sri Lanka 1966–68; conslt psychiatrist (old age psychiatry): St James' Hosp Portsmouth 1975–84 (trg in psychiatry 1968–75), Winchester and Eastleigh Healthcare NHS Tst (formerly Winchester DHA) 1984–; clinical teacher Univ of Southampton 1985–, memb Exec Ctee Age Concern Hampshire 1985–93, Mental Health Act cmmr (Sec of State appt) 1989–, hon conslt St Luke's Hosp for the Clergy London 1990–, selector Med Faculty Univ of Southampton 1990–94, conslt advsr Samaritans Winchester and Dist Branch 1990–; RCPsych: memb Special Ctee on Unethical Psychiatric Practice 1990–94, vice-pres 1995–97; memb: GMC 1994–, Mental Health Review Tbnl (Lord Chllr's appt) 1994–; memb: BMA, Med Protection Soc, Alzheimer's Disease Soc; Care in the Community (contrib chapter, 1982), Psychotherapy Supporting the Carers of Mentally Ill People (contrib chapter, 1992), International Review of Psychiatry (contrib chapter, 1993); *Recreations* gardening, religious music, spending time with my children and grandchildren; *Style*— Dr Pearl Hettiaratchy; ✉ Department of Old Age Psychiatry, Melbury Lodge, Royal Hampshire County Hospital, Queen's Road, Winchester Hampshire SO22 5DG (☎ 01962 825542)

HEUMANN, Andreas Carl Manuel; s of Rainer Heumann, and Renate Fischer; *b* 17 April 1946, Germany; *Educ* Switzerland; *m* Philippa Ramsay; 1 da (Marina b 11 Aug 1992); *Career* photographer; early career as apprentice block-maker and printer, subsquent fashion assignments for Stern, Vogue, Twen, Harpers, etc London, currently serving advtg indust; one-man exhbns incl: Photographers Gallery London, Hamiltons Gallery London, Special Photographers Co London, Assoc of Photographers Gallery London, K61 Gallerie Amsterdam, Royal Photographic Soc Bath; awards incl: Gold (Art Dirs Club of NY) 1988, Silver (Art Dirs Club of Switzerland) 1990, Silver (Art Dirs Club of France) 1990, Gold and 5 Silvers (Campaign Press Awards) 1991, 6 Golds, 6 Silvers and 14 Merits (Assoc of Photographers) since 1983 (judge 1990 Awards), Fine Art Photography category winner (World Image Awards USA) 1992, Gold for best advtg picture (Art Dir Club Italy) 1993, merit award (New York Art Directors Club) 1994, Agfa Picture of the Year award 1994, finalist (John Kobal portrait award) 1995; work in the collections of V&A, Kodak's Museum of Photography Rochester USA, and in numerous private collections; *Style*— Andreas Heumann, Esq; ✉ 35 Larkhall Rise, London SW4 6HU (☎ 0171 622 3979, fax 0171 720 1738)

HEWARD, Edmund Rawlings; CB (1984); s of late Rev Thomas Brown Heward, and Kathleen Amy Rachel Rawlings; *b* 19 Aug 1912; *Educ* Repton, Trinity Coll Cambridge; *m* 1945, Constance Mary Sandiford, da of late George Bertram Crossley, OBE; *Career* served WWII 1940–46 RA, Maj; admitted slr 1937, ptnr Rose, Johnson and Hicks 1946; chief master of the Supreme Ct (Chancery Div) 1980–85 (master 1959–79); *Books* incl: Guide to Chancery Practice (1962), Matthew Hale (1972), Lord Mansfield (1979), Chancery Practice (1983), Chancery Orders (1986), Lord Denning, A Biography (1990), Masters in Ordinary (1991), The Great and the Good, A Life of Lord Radcliffe (1995); *Style*— Edmund Heward, Esq, CB; ✉ 36a Dartmouth Row, Greenwich SE10 8AW (☎ 0181 692 3525)

HEWER, Prof Richard Langton; s of Dr Christopher Langton Hewer (d 1986), of London, and Doris Phoebe, *née* Champney (d 1978); *b* 29 March 1930; *Educ* St Lawrence Coll Ramsgate, Bart's Univ of London (MB BS); *m* 21 June 1958, Jane Ann, da of Robert Wotherspoon, of St Helens, Lancs; 1 s (Simon Christopher b 9 Nov 1962), 2 da (Marian Jane b 19 April 1961, Sarah Ann b 21 Jan 1965); *Career* Nat Serv, RAF; chief asst Professorial Neurology Unit Oxford 1965–68, conslt neurologist Bristol 1968–95; Univ of Bristol: prof of neurology 1990–95, sr research fell Dept of Social Med 1995–; fndr chm: Friedreich's Ataxia Gp 1963–75, Bristol Stroke Fndn 1983–; fndr and dir Experimental Stroke Res Unit 1975, sec and chm RCP Disability Ctee 1978–92, chm Bristol Stroke Fndn 1981–, memb Cncl Assoc of Br Neurologists 1987–91 (1981–84), chm Assoc of Br Neurologists' Serv (Policy) Ctee 1983–, sec Working Gp on Physical Disability RCP 1986, chm Med Disability Soc 1986–88, pres Bristol Medico-Chirurgical Soc 1990–91; memb: World Fedn of Neurology, Med Disability Soc, Soc for Res in Rehabilitation, Chest Heart and Stroke Assoc; FRSM, FRCP; *Books* Stroke - A Critical Approach to Diagnosis Treatment and Management (jtly, 1985), Stroke - A Guide to Recovery (with D T Wade, 1986), Modern Medicine (ed, 1975, 1979, 1983), The Oxford Companion to the Mind (1987), Rehabilitation of the Physically Disabled Adults (1988), More Dilemmas in the Management of the Neurological Patient (1987), The Management of Motor Neurone Disease (1987), The Stroke Recovery Plan (with D T Wade, 1996); *Recreations* sailing, walking; *Style*— Prof Richard Langton Hewer; ✉ home (☎ 0117 973 2110, fax 0117 973 0071)

HEWES, Robin Anthony Charles (Bob); s of Leslie Augustus Hewes (d 1991), of Colchester, Essex, and Lily Violet, *née* Norfolk (d 1979); *b* 15 April 1945; *Educ* Colchester

Royal GS, Univ of Bristol (LLB); *m* 23 Sept 1967, Christine Diane, da of Geoffrey William Gosnell Stonebridge (d 1983), and Irene Constance Stonebridge; 1 s (Stephen b 24 Dec 1969) 2 da (Kirstie b 11 March 1972, Rachel b 26 Jan 1977); *Career* HM Inspr of Taxes Inland Revenue 1966–74, princ Dept of Indust 1974–80 (asst sec 1980–85), non-exec dir Comfort-Vickers 1983–88, Machinery of Govt Div Cabinet Office (MPO) 1985–87, dir Enterprise and Deregulation Unit DTI 1987–88, dir of fin Lloyd's of London 1994– (head of regulatory services 1988–94, memb Cncl of Lloyd's and Lloyd's Regulatory Bd 1993–94), memb Lloyd's Mkt Bd 1995–; vice pres and past chm Brentwood Swimming Club; hereditary Freeman Borough of Colchester 1966–; *Recreations* swimming; *Style*— Bob Hewes, Esq; ✉ 38 Plovers Mead, Wyatts Green, Brentwood, Essex CM15 0PS (☎ 01277 822891); Lloyd's of London, One Lime St, London EC3M 7HA (☎ 0171 327 6711, fax 0171 327 6604, telex 8950741C Lloyd G)

HEWETSON, Ven Christopher; s of Edward Pearson Hewetson (d 1975), of Oxford, and Mary, *née* Snow (d 1991); *b* 1 June 1937; *Educ* Shrewsbury, Trinity Coll Oxford (MA), Chichester Theol Coll; *m* 16 April 1963, Alison Mary, da of William Alan Croft; 4 da (Lucy Ann b 5 Feb 1964, Emma Mary b 3 April 1966, Martha Jane b 2 Dec 1971, Hannah Frances b 6 Aug 1977); *Career* asst master: Dragon Sch Oxford 1960–64 and 1966–67, The Craig Windermere 1964–66; ordained: deacon 1969, priest 1970; asst curate: St Peter and St Paul Leckhampton 1969–71, All Saints Wokingham 1971–73; vicar of St Peter Didcot 1973–82, rector of Ascot Heath 1982–90, chaplain St George Sch for Girls Ascot 1985–89, rural dean of Bracknell 1986–90, priest i/c Headington Quarry Oxford 1990–94, hon canon of Christ Church 1992–94, rural dean of Cowley 1994, archdeacon of Chester 1994–; *Recreations* fell walking, opera, restoring old paintings; *Style*— The Ven the Archdeacon of Chester; ✉ 25 Bartholomew Way, Westminster Park, Chester CH4 7RJ (☎ 01244 675417, fax 01244 383835)

HEWETSON, Sir Christopher Raynor; kt (1984), TD (1967), DL (1986); s of Harry Raynor Hewetson, MRCVS (d 1976), of Southport, and Emma, *née* Seed (d 1989); *b* 26 Dec 1929; *Educ* Sedbergh, Peterhouse Cambridge (MA); *m* 5 May 1962, Alison May, da of Prof Allan Watt Downie, FRS (d 1988); 2 s (Charles b 1964, Richard b 1970), 1 da (Jane b 1966); *Career* Nat Serv 2 Lt 4 RHA 1951–53, 359 Medium Regt RA (TA) 1953–68 (Lt-Col cmdg 1965–68); admitted slr 1956; ptnr Lace Mawer Slrs 1961–95; memb Cncl Law Soc 1966–87, pres Liverpool Law Soc 1976, pres Law Soc 1983 (vice pres 1982); Hon Col 33 Signal Regt (V) 1992–94; *Recreations* golf, walking; *Clubs* Army and Navy, Athenaeum (Liverpool), Royal Birkdale Golf; *Style*— Sir Christopher Hewetson, TD, DL; ✉ 24c Westcliffe Rd, Birkdale, Southport, Merseyside PR8 2BU (☎ 01704 567179)

HEWETT, Sir Peter John Smithson; 6 Bt (UK 1813), of Nether Seale, Leics; MM; s of Sir John George Hewett, 5 Bt, MC (d 1990), and Yuilleen Maude, *née* Smithson (d 1980); *b* 27 June 1931; *Educ* Bradfield, Jesus Coll Cambridge (BA); *m* 1958, Jennifer Ann Cooper, da of E T Jones, OBE, of Nairobi, Kenya; 2 s (Richard Mark John b 1958, David Patrick John b 1968), 1 da (Joanna Yuilleen b 1960); *Heir* s, Richard Mark John Hewett b 1958; *Career* called to the Bar Gray's Inn 1954; practising advocate Kenya; *Recreations* windsurfing, birdwatching; *Clubs* Muthaiga Country, Karen Country, Naivasha Yacht; *Style*— Sir Peter Hewett, Bt, MM; ✉ PO Box 15669, Nairobi, Kenya

HEWETT, Roy Scrymgeour Graham; GSM (1949), JP (Somerset 1972); s of Graham Scott Hewett, DSC (d 1969), of Essex, and Dorothy, *née* Sanders (d 1950); *b* 29 Dec 1929; *Educ* Charterhouse, Wye Coll London (BSc); *m* 1956, Shirley, da of Langton Highton, DL (d 1972), of Cumberland; 2 da (Catherine Susan (Mrs Harwood) b 1958, Elizabeth Bridget (Mrs Watkins) b 1960), 1 s (Nicholas Langton Scrymgeour b 1961); *Career* Mil Serv cmmnd RA, served 1 Singapore Artillery Regt Malaya 1948–49; farm mangr Wilts 1953–63, tenant farmer Somerset 1963–; dir: Fresh Wharf Estates Barking, Fresh Wharf Management Barking, Cuckolds' Island Ltd Barking; memb Mendip Dist Cncl 1973–95 (chm 1986–88); chm Frome Magistrates' Bench 1989, first chm Mendip Petty Sessional Div 1990–93, memb Somerset Magistrates' Ctee 1990–95, chm Trg Sub-ctee 1993–95, fndr memb Regional Justices Trg Bd, chm Regional Staff Trg and Devpt Bd 1994–95; memb Mells Parish Cncl 1975–96; High Sheriff of Somerset 1995–96; Freeman City of London, Master Worshipful Co of Fletchers 1973–74; memb: NFU 1963 (branch chm 1972–73), Magistrates' Assoc 1972 (county chm 1982–84); *Recreations* sailing (completed trans world voyage), visiting different parts of the world; *Clubs* Royal Corinthian Yacht, Agricola; *Style*— Roy Hewett, Esq, JP; ✉ Claveys Farm, Mells, Frome, Somerset BA11 3QP (☎ and fax 01373 812209)

HEWINS, John Francis; s of late John Hewins, and Gladys Maud, *née* Van Mierlo; *b* 19 March 1936; *Educ* Mount St Mary's Coll; *m* 20 Oct 1964, Valerie, da of late John Fife Mortimer; 1 s (Dominic John b 12 July 1969), 2 da (Natalie Brigid b 2 May 1966, Frances Camille b 2 Jan 1968); *Career* Nat Serv; student apprentice Davy Utd 1953, md Davy McKee Sheffield 1988 (sales dir 1977, gen mangr 1983, md 1983–90); exec vice chm S York Supertram 1992–94; dir Hallamshire Investments 1990–95, chm Mechtech International 1992–95, dir Eurolube AB; chm and md: Ernest H Hill Ltd, Watsons, Name Plates Ltd; Freeman Cutlers' Co in Hallamshire; FRSA; *Recreations* garden, mediocre tennis, remote trekking, walking, sailing; *Style*— John Hewins, Esq; ✉ The Homestead, Nether Shatton, Bamford, Hope Valley, Derbyshire S30 2BG (☎ 01433 651201)

HEWISH, Prof Antony; s of Ernest William Hewish (d 1975), and Francis Grace Lanyon, *née* Pinch (d 1970); *b* 11 May 1924; *Educ* King's Coll Taunton, Gonville and Caius Coll Cambridge (MA, PhD); *m* 19 Aug 1950, Marjorie Elizabeth Catherine, da of Edgar Richards (d 1954); 1 s (Nicholas b 1956), 1 da (Jennifer b 1954); *Career* RAE Farnborough 1943–46; Univ of Cambridge: res fell Gonville and Caius Coll 1952–54 (hon fell 1976–), asst dir of res 1954–62, fell Churchill Coll 1962–, lectr in physics 1962–69, reader 1969–71, prof of radioastronomy 1971–89; discovered pulsars (with S J Bell-Burnell) 1967; Nobel Prize for Physics (with M Ryle) 1974, Hughes medal Royal Soc 1974; prof of astronomy Royal Instn 1977–81, dir Mullard Radio Astronomy Observatory 1982–87; churchwarden Kingston Parish Church Cambridge; Hon DSc: Leicester 1976, Exeter 1977, Manchester 1989, Santa Maria Brazil 1989, Cambridge 1996; FRS 1968, foreign hon memb American Acad of Arts and Scis, foreign fell Indian Nat Sci Acad 1982, hon fell Tata Inst of Fundamental Sci Bombay 1996, hon citizen Kwangju S Korea 1995; memb: Belgian Royal Acad 1990, Academia Europaea 1993; *Recreations* music, sailing, gardening; *Style*— Prof Antony Hewish, FRS; ✉ Pryor's Cottage, Field Rd, Kingston, Cambridge CB3 7NQ (☎ 01223 262657); Cavendish Laboratory, Madingley Road, Cambridge CB3 0HE (☎ 01223 337296, fax 01223 354599)

HEWITT, Anthony Ronald; s of Ronald Berwick Hewitt (d 1995), and Phyllis Lavina, *née* Tammadge (d 1992); *b* 9 May 1949; *Educ* St Albans GS, BRNC Dartmouth, RNC Greenwich, Open University (BA); *m* 11 Nov 1978, Felicity Heather, da of Roy Chalice Orford, CBE, of Budleigh Salterton, Devon; 2 s (Richard b 1980, Edward b 1987), 2 da (Penelope b 1981, Deborah b 1984); *Career* cmmnd serv RN 1968–88: Robert Roxburgh prize 1971, Ronald Megaw prize 1972, submarine cmdg offr's course 1979, submarine tactics and weapons gp 1981–83, exec offr HMS Churchill 1980, HMS Revenge 1983–86, Directorate of Naval Warfare MOD 1986–88; sec Cable Authy 1989–90, dep sec Ind TV Cmmn 1991–96, dep dir Cable Ind TV Cmmn 1996–; ICSA Ralph Bell prize 1989; Freeman City of London 1992, Liveryman Worshipful Co of Chartered Secs and Administrators; MIMgt 1988, FCIS 1990; *Recreations* music, gardening, kite flying; *Style*— Anthony Hewitt, Esq; ✉ 4 Orchard Drive, Ashtead, Surrey KT21 2PD (☎ 01372 276745); Independent Television Commission, 33 Foley Street, London W1P 7LB (☎ 0171 255 3000, fax 0171 306 7800)

HEWITT, David Stuart; s of Geoffrey Walter Hewitt, of Hoylake, Merseyside, and Margery Jessie, *née* Stuart (d 1984); *b* 30 Oct 1932; *Educ* Calday Grange GS, Wrekin Coll; *m* 24 June 1961, Susan, da of Sidney Milton Heathcote Caddick (d 1984); 2 s (Nicholas Michael b 19 April 1968, Richard David (twin) b 1968), 2 da (Jennifer Mary (Mrs Kevin Owens) b 22 July 1962, Helen Judith (Mrs Christopher Lee) b 20 Feb 1965); *Career* Nat Serv cmmnd RA 1951–53; articled clerk Dawson Graves & Co Liverpool 1953–58, qualified chartered accountant 1958, joined Whinney Smith & Whinney 1959 (which became Whinney Murray & Co 1965, Ernst & Whinney 1979, Ernst & Young 1989), ret 1993; non-exec dir: Cheshire Building Society 1987–, Wrights Engineering (UK) Ltd 1995–, Wrights Engineering (South Wales) Ltd 1995–; govr Wrekin Coll 1991–; FCA (ACA 1958); *Recreations* golf, family, bridge; *Clubs* Heswall Golf; *Style*— David Hewitt, Esq; ✉ Ridgewood, 41 Quarry Road East, Heswall, Merseyside L60 6RB (☎ 0151 342 3440)

HEWITT, Ewan Christian; s of Dr Rupert Conrad Hewitt (d 1981), of Glenbeigh, Frinton-on-Sea, Essex, and Gladys Muriel, *née* Christian (d 1967); *b* 13 April 1928; *Educ* Wellington, Gonville and Caius Coll Cambridge (MA), Manchester Business Sch; *m* 1, 25 July 1959 (m dis 1973), Gaylor Margaret Joyce, da of Henry Fraeke, of Westerham, Kent; m 2, 14 Dec 1973, Susan Mary, da of Donald James Maclachlan, of Hull, Yorkshire; 2 da (Annabel Elizabeth Christina b 16 Sept 1974, Lucinda Katherine Mary b 11 March 1977); *Career* Nat Serv Royal Engrs 1946–48; apprentice Davy Paxman & Co Ltd Colchester 1949; Davy & United Engineering Co Ltd Sheffield: apprentice 1952–54, sales engr 1954–56, contract mangr Durgapur Steelworks Project 1956–57, sr sales engr 1957–59, liaison engr Pittsburgh Pennsylvania 1959–60, asst chief engr Proposals 1961–64, tech sales mangr 1964–67, tech asst to MD 1967–68; tech dir: Davy Construction Co Sheffield 1971–72 (mangr tech services 1968–71), Davy Ashmore Ltd Stockton-on-Tees 1972–73, Davy-Loewy Ltd 1973–80, Davy McKee Ltd 1980–88 (dir tech mktg 1988–93); engrg conslt 1993–; Metals Soc Ablett prize; Metals Soc/Inst of Metals: memb Engrg Ctee 1974–85, memb Iron and Steel Ctee 1975–, memb Cncl 1981–87; memb Rolling Gp Inst of Metals 1989–, memb Bd Manufacturing Industs Div IMechE 1981–87; memb: Assoc of Iron and Steel Engrs USA 1959, Iron and Steel Soc of AIME USA 1982, Iron and Steel Inst (Metals Soc) Inst of Metals 1973, Sheffield Metallurgical and Engrg Assoc 1976; FIMechE 1976 (MIMechE 1954), FEng 1989; *Recreations* photography, fly-fishing, bridge, gardening, walking, riding, jazz record collection; *Style*— Ewan Hewitt, Esq, FEng; ✉ Ash Cottage, Clarendon Rd, Fulwood, Sheffield S10 3TQ (☎ 0114 230 3197)

HEWITT, Gavin James; s of Rev Thomas Hewitt (d 1964), and Daffodil Anne, *née* Thorne; *b* 13 Jan 1951; *Educ* St John's Sch Leatherhead, Univ of Durham (BA); *m* 1972, Sally Jane, da of Norman Lacey; 1 s (Daniel James b 1980), 1 da (Rebecca Jane b 1978); *Career* reporter BBC TV News 1976–81, corr The Journal (CBC Canada) and documentary maker McNeil-Lehrer Newshour USA 1981–84, reporter Newsnight (BBC2) 1985–92, corr Panorama (BBC1) 1992–; *Books* Terry Waite and Oliver North (1991); *Style*— Gavin Hewitt, Esq; ✉ BBC White City, London W12 7TS (☎ 0181 752 7162)

HEWITT, HE Gavin Wallace; CMG (1995); s of Rev George Burrill Hewitt, TD, FEIS (d 1976), and Elisabeth Murray, *née* Wallace (d 1976); *b* 19 Oct 1944; *Educ* George Watson's Coll Edinburgh, Univ of Edinburgh (MA); *m* 6 Oct 1973, Heather Mary, da of Trevor Shaw Clayton, of Whaley Bridge, Derbyshire; 2 s (Alexander Francis Reid b 3 Nov 1977, Peter James Clayton b 26 Jan 1982), 2 da (Claire Rebecca b 20 March 1975, Mary Elisabeth Courtney b 29 Sept 1979); *Career* asst princ Miny of Tport 1967–70, second sec UK delegation to the Euro Communities Brussels 1970–72, first sec Br High Cmmn Canberra 1973–78, first sec and head of chancery Br Embassy Belgrade 1981–84, dep permanent rep UK mission UN Geneva 1987–92, cnsllr FCO 1992–94, ambass to Republic of Croatia 1994–; vice chm Bd of Govrs Geneva English Sch 1989–92; *Style*— HE Mr Gavin Hewitt, CMG; ✉ Foreign and Commonwealth Office (Zagreb), King Charles St, London SW1A 2AH (☎ 0171 270 3000)

HEWITT, Prof Geoffrey Frederick (Geoff); s of Frederick Hewitt (d 1961), and Elaine, *née* Ellam (d 1975); *b* 3 Jan 1934; *Educ* Boteler GS, UMIST (BScTech, PhD); *m* 11 Aug 1956, Shirley Hodges, da of Stanley Foulds; 2 da (Karen Louise b 4 April 1958, Alison Jane b 29 Oct 1959); *Career* scientist UKAEA Harwell 1957–90 (div head 1976); fndr and head Heat Transfer and Fluid Flow Service 1968–92; pres: Heat Transfer Soc 1977, Inst of Chem Engrs 1989; Courtaulds prof of chem engrg Imperial Coll London 1985–; Hon DSc Univ of Louvain, Hon DEng Heriot Watt Univ 1995; FIChemE, FRSC, FIMechE, FEng 1985, FRS 1989; *Awards* Donald Q Kern award American Inst of Chem Engrs 1981, fellowship award Int Centre for Heat and Mass Transfer 1982, Max Jacob award American Soc of Mechanical Engrs 1994; *Books* Annular Two-Phase Flow (with N S Hall Taylor, 1970), Measurement of Two-Phase Flow Parameters (1978), Two-Phase Flow and Heat Transfer in the Power and Process Industries (with J G Collier, A E Bergles, J M Delhaye and F Mayinger, 1981), Introduction to Nuclear Power (with J G Collier, 1987), Process Heat Transfer (with G L Shires and T R Bott, 1994); *Recreations* music, bridge; *Style*— Prof Geoffrey Hewitt, FRS, FEng; ✉ Department of Chemical Engineering and Clinical Technology, Imperial College of Science, Technology & Medicine, Prince Consort Road, London SW7 2BY (☎ 0171 594 5562, fax 0171 594 5564)

HEWITT, Prof Godfrey Matthew; s of Horace John Hewitt, of Hereford and Worcester, and Violet May, *née* Hann (d 1989); *b* 10 Jan 1940; *Educ* Worcester Cathedral King's Sch, Univ of Birmingham (BSc, PhD, DSc); *m* 23 June 1963 (m dis 1982), Elizabeth June, da of Ivor Cecil Shattock, of Taunton, Somerset; 3 s (Daniel John b 14 July 1965, Matthew Alexander b 27 March 1967, James Justin b 20 May 1968); *Career* Fulbright fell Univ of California 1965–66; visiting fell: Gulbenkian Fndn Lisbon 1970, Aust Nat Univ Canberra 1973–74, Univ of Hawaii 1979; prof UEA 1988– (lectr 1966–75, reader 1975–88); numerous pubns in learned sci jls; memb: SERC Ctee, NERC Ctee, Genetical Soc, Soc Study of Evolution, Euro Soc of Evolution; FIBiol 1975, FRES 1980, FLS 1987; *Books* Animal Cytogenetics-Grasshoppers and Crickets (1979), Molecular Techniques in Taxonomy (1991), Genes in Ecology (1991); *Recreations* alpine hiking, jazz, running, cooking; *Style*— Prof Godfrey Hewitt; ✉ 25 Camberley Rd, Norwich NR4 6SJ (☎ 01603 458142); School of Biological Sciences, University of East Anglia, Norwich NR4 7TJ (☎ 01603 456161, fax 01603 592250)

HEWITT, Jamie Neil Terry; s of Peart Derek Hewitt, and Leanne, *née* Vallely; *b* 3 Jan 1959; *Educ* Rugby, City of London Poly (BA); *m* Roslyn Joyce, da of Thomas Russell Lennon; 1 s (Harry Moutray b 6 March 1992), 1 da (Eleanor Joy b 21 July 1990); *Career* articled clerk Peat Marwick Mitchell CAs 1980–83, co sec Zetland Advertising Ltd 1983–86, chief accountant Conran Design Group Ltd 1986–88; fin dir: Brewer Jones Ltd 1988–89, Butterfield Day Devito Hockney Ltd 1989–95, Collett Dickenson Pearce & Partners Ltd advtg agency 1995–; ACA 1983; *Recreations* rugby, running, dogs; *Style*— Jamie Hewitt, Esq; ✉ Collett Dickenson Pearce & Partners Ltd, 33–34 Soho Square, London W1V 6DP (☎ 0171 292 4000)

HEWITT, Michael Earling; s of Herbert Erland Hewitt (d 1938), and Dorothy Amelia, *née* Morris; *b* 28 March 1936; *Educ* Christ's Hosp, Merton Coll Oxford (MA), Univ of London (BSc); *m* 10 Aug 1961, Elizabeth Mary Hughes, da of Maj Arnold James Batchelor (d 1956); 1 s (Thomas b 1970), 1 da (Joanna b 1974); *Career* Gunner RA 1955–57; Bank of England: joined 1961, seconded as econ advsr to Govt of Bermuda 1970–74, asst advsr on oil 1974–76, financial forecaster 1976–78, advsr financial instns 1981–83 (asst advsr 1979–81), head of financial supervision Gen Div 1984–87, head Finance and Industry Area 1987–88, sr advsr finance and industry 1988–90, dir of central banking studies 1990–94; IMF trg advsr for Bank of Russia 1994–; memb: EEC Central Bank Gp of Experts on Money Supply 1976–78, Br Invisible Exports Cncl 1987–90, Dearing Ctee on Making of Accounting Standards 1988, City Advsy Panel City Univ Business Sch 1988–91; chm: City EEC Ctee 1987–90, OECD Gp of Experts on Securities Mkts 1988–90; AMIIMR 1979; *Recreations* chess, travel, wine; *Style*— Michael Hewitt, Esq; ✉ c/o Centre for Central Banking Studies, Bank of England, New change, London EC4M 9AA (☎ 0171 601 4657, fax 0171 601 5860, telex 885001)

HEWITT, Michael Geoffrey; s of Geoffrey Hewitt, of Bradmore, Wolverhampton, and Edna, *née* Sharples; *b* 6 Sept 1962; *Educ* Wolverhampton Sch, Univ of Stirling (BA); *m* 21 April 1990, Sara da of Ian Bryant; 1 s (Max b 17 April 1994), 1 da (Susanna b 21 May 1996); *Career* ed The Publisher 1987–89, ed Journalist's Week 1989–91; Haymarket Publishing: ed Marketing 1993–96, gp ed Marketing, Marketing Direct 1996–; memb: Inst of Printing 1992–, Br Soc of Magazine Eds; Freeman City of London 1993, Liveryman Worshipful Co of Stationers and Newspapermakers 1994; *Recreations* travel, books, military history, food; *Style*— Michael Hewitt, Esq; ✉ Marketing Magazine, Haymarket Business Publications Ltd, 174 Hammersmith Road, London W6 7JP (☎ 0171 413 4270, fax 0171 413 4504)

HEWITT, Sir Nicholas Charles Joseph; 3 Bt (UK 1921), of Barnsley, West Riding, Co York; s of Maj Sir Joseph Hewitt, 2 Bt (d 1973), and Marguerite, *née* Burgess; *b* 12 Nov 1947; *m* 1969, Pamela Margaret, da of Geoffrey J M Hunt, TD, of Scalby, Scarborough; 2 s (Charles Edward James b 1970, Michael Joseph b 1973), 1 da (Victoria Alexandra Margaret b 1978); *Heir* s, Charles Edward James Hewitt b 15 Nov 1970; *Style*— Sir Nicholas Hewitt, Bt; ✉ Colswayn House, Huttons Ambo, York YO6 7HJ

HEWITT, Patricia Hope; da of Sir (Cyrus) Lenox Simson Hewitt, OBE, of Sydney, Aust, and (Alison) Hope Hewitt; *b* 2 Dec 1948; *Educ* Girls' GS Canberra, Aust Nat Univ Canberra, Newnham Coll Cambridge (MA), Univ of Sydney (AMusA); *m* 1, 8 Aug 1970 (m dis 1978), (David) Julian Gibson Watt, s of Baron Gibson-Watt, *qv*; m 2, 17 Dec 1981, William Jack Birtles, s of William George Birtles (d 1976), of Shepperton, Middx; 1 da (Alexandra b 1986), 1 s (Nicholas b 1988); *Career* gen sec NCCL 1974–83, policy coordinator to Ldr of the Opposition 1988–89 (press and broadcasting sec 1983–88), dep dir and sr res fell Inst for Public Policy Res 1989–94, dir of research Andersen Consulting 1994–; prospective Parly candidate (Lab) Leicester West 1996–, assoc Newnham Coll Cambridge, visiting fell Nuffield Coll Oxford; tstee Inst for Public Policy Research; memb: Bd Int League for Human Rights, Sec of State's Advsy Ctee on the Employment of Women 1977–83; dep chair Cmmn for Social Justice 1992–94; Parly candidate Leicester East 1983; FRSA; *Books* The Abuse of Power: Civil Liberties in the United Kingdom (1983); Your Second Baby (with Wendy Rose-Neil, 1990), About Time: The Revolution in Work and Family Life (1993); *Recreations* gardening, music, theatre, cooking; *Style*— Ms Patricia Hewitt; ✉ 21 Rochester Square, London NW1 9SA (☎ 0171 267 2567); Andersen Consulting, 2 Arundel Street, London WC2R 3LT (☎ 0171 438 5000, fax 0171 831 1133)

HEWITT, Dr Penelope Boulton; da of Leslie Frank Hewitt (d 1967), of Belmont, Surrey, and Beryl Boulton (d 1978); *b* 23 July 1938; *Educ* Sutton HS GPDST, Guy's Hosp, Univ of London (MB BS, LRCP, MRCS); *Career* res anaesthetist Guy's Hosp 1962–63; registrar in anaesthetics 1963–67: Nat Hosp for Nervous Diseases Queen Square London, St Mary's Hosp, Guy's Hosp; conslt anaesthetist Guy's Hosp 1972– (sr registrar 1967–72, hon sr lectr in anaesthetics 1992–), recognised teacher in anaesthetics Univ of London 1974–; approved lectr: Central Midwives Bd 1979–83, English Nat Bd 1983–, combined Guy's and St Thomas' Hosp Schs of Midwifery, King's Coll 1994–; anaesthetics tutor Faculty of Anaesthetists RCS Guy's Hosp 1980–87, regnl assessor in anaesthetics for confidential enquiries into maternal deaths SE Thames Region Dept of Health 1981–, hon sec and treas SE Thames Soc of Anaesthetists 1984–87 (pres 1991–93), anaesthetic assessor confidential enquiry into perioperative deaths Nuffield Prov Hosp Tst 1985–87, examiner for fellowship examination of the Royal Coll of Anaesthetists 1986–, examiner for European Dip in Anaesthesia and Intensive Care 1992–, chm OSCE Working Pty Royal Coll of Anaesthetists 1994–96, memb Cncl Anaesthetics Section RSM (hon sec 1987–89, pres elect 1996–), pres Assoc of Dental Anaesthetists 1995– (hon asst sec and ed of proceedings 1989–92, hon sec 1992–95); FFARCS 1966; *Books* Emergency Anaesthesia (1986); *Recreations* golf, gardening; *Clubs* The Addington Golf; *Style*— Dr Penelope B Hewitt; ✉ Department of Anaesthetics, Guy's Hospital, St Thomas's St, London SE1 9RT (☎ 0171 955 4051/5000, fax 0171 955 8844)

HEWITT, Peter John; s of Charles Rowland Hewitt (d 1993), and Eunice, *née* Nixon; *b* 17 Nov 1951; *Educ* Barnard Castle Sch Co Durham, Univ of Leeds (BA, MA); *m* (sep), Joan, *née* Coventry; 3 da (Laura b 26 March 1978, Anna b 29 July 1980, Kate b 23 Jan 1984); *Career* Inter-Action Trust 1976–77, arts offr N Tyneside BC 1977–82; Northern Arts 1982–: community arts and gen arts offr, asst dir Local Devpt, dep dir, chief exec 1992–; *Recreations* the arts, squash, walking, Middlesbrough FC; *Style*— Peter Hewitt, Esq; ✉ Northern Arts, 9/10 Osborne Terrace, Jesmond, Newcastle upon Tyne NE2 1NZ (☎ 0191 281 6334, fax 0191 281 3276)

HEWLETT, Hon Thomas Anthony; s of Baron Hewlett, CBE (Life Peer, d 1979), and Millicent, *née* Taylor (d 1991); *b* 31 March 1952; *Educ* Oundle, Magdalene Coll Cambridge (BA, MA); *m* 2 Oct 1980, Jane Elizabeth, da of Brian A Dawson, of Aldeburgh, Suffolk; 2 s (Harry b 30 Dec 1986, Charles b (twin) 30 Dec 1986), 2 da (Emily b 14 Feb 1983, Georgina b 24 July 1984); *Career* dir: Anchor Chemical Gp plc 1976–83, V Berg & Sons Ltd 1986–91; vice pres Morgan Guaranty Tst 1974–84; owner Portland Gallery 1985–; Freeman City of London, Liveryman Worshipful Co of Tin Plate Workers; *Books* Cadell - A Scottish Colourist (1988); *Recreations* golf, tennis; *Clubs* Aldeburgh Golf, Royal St Georges Golf; *Style*— The Hon Thomas Hewlett; ✉ Kyson House, Woodbridge, Suffolk IP12 4DN (☎ 0139438 3441); Portland Gallery, 9 Bury St, St James's, London SW1 (☎ 0171 321 0422)

HEWSON, Paul; *see:* Bono

HEXHAM AND NEWCASTLE, Bishop of (RC) 1992–; Rt Rev Dom (Michael) Ambrose Griffiths; OSB; s of Henry John Martin Griffiths (d 1970), and Hilda Kathleen, *née* Griffiths (d 1989); *b* 4 Dec 1928; *Educ* Ampleforth, Balliol Coll Oxford (MA, BSc), Collegio S'Anselmo Rome; *Career* entered Ampleforth Abbey 1950, ordained priest 1957; Ampleforth Coll and Abbey: asst master sci, RE and woodwork 1957–65, sr sci master 1965–71, theol teacher 1963–71, procurator (bursar) 1971–76, abbot 1976–84; parish priest St Mary's Leyland 1984–92; *Recreations* walking; *Style*— The Rt Rev Ambrose Griffiths, OSB; ✉ Bishop of Hexham and Newcastle, Bishop's House, East Denton Hall, 800 West Road, Newcastle upon Tyne NE5 2BJ (☎ 0191 228 0003/4, fax 0191 274 0432)

HEY, Prof John Denis; s of George Brian Hey (d 1991), of Adlington, Cheshire, and Elizabeth Hamilton, *née* Burns; *b* 26 Sept 1944; *Educ* Manchester GS, Univ of Cambridge (BA), Univ of Edinburgh (MSc); *m* 18 Oct 1968, Marlene Robertson, da of Thomas Bissett (d 1958), of Perth; 1 s (Thomas b 1981), 2 da (Clare b 1979, Rebecca b 1984); *Career* econometrician Hoare & Co Stockbrokers 1968–69; lectr in econs: Univ of Durham 1969–73, Univ of St Andrews 1974–75; prof of econs and statistics Univ of York 1984– (lectr in social and econ statistics 1975–81, sr lectr 1981–84), ed Economic Journal 1986–96, co-dir Centre for Experimental Econs 1986–, author of articles for numerous jls; memb: RES, AEA; *Books* Statistics in Economics (1974), Uncertainty in Microeconomics (1979), Britain in Context (1979), Economics in Disequilibrium (1981), Data in Doubt (1984), A Century of Economics (ed, 1990), Experiments in Economics (1991), Recent Developments in Experimental Economics (ed, 1993); *Recreations* squash, walking, eating; *Style*— Prof John Hey; ✉ 49 Monkgate, York, N Yorks (☎ 01904 621333); Dept of Economics and Related Studies, University of York, Heslington, York, N Yorks YO1 5DD (☎ 01904 433786, fax 01904 433759, telex 57933)

HEYDERMAN, Dr Eadie; da of Reuben Kirstein (d 1969), of London, and Sarah, *née* Haskell (d 1967); *b* 8 Oct 1931; *Educ* Central Foundation Sch for Girls London, UCH Dental Sch (BDS LDS RCS), UCH Med Sch (MB BS), St Thomas's Hosp Med Sch London (MD); *m* 29 April 1956, Dennis Manfred Heyderman, s of Leopold Heyderman (d 1966), of London; 2 s (Robert Simon b 16 July 1960, John Bernard b 23 Sept 1962), 2 da (Emma Louise b 21 March 1966, Laura Jane b 8 Sept 1967); *Career* pt/t dental practice 1953; UCH: dental house surgn 1953, hon clinical asst (Dental Sch) 1958–59, house surgn 1959; house physician N Middx Hosp 1959–60; fndr (with husband) John Dobbie Educational Toy Stores 1963–73 (memb Ctee and lectr in design Design Centre); John Marshall fell (later Grahame scholar in morbid anatomy) UCH 1974–75, clinical scientist and hon pathologist Ludwig Inst for Cancer Res Royal Marsden Hosp Sutton 1975–79, locum res asst (clinical) and hon sr registrar in pathology St Mary's Hosp 1979, sr lectr and hon sr registrar Dept of Histopathology St Thomas's Hosp Med Sch 1979–80 (sr lectr and hon conslt 1980–86), reader in histopathology and hon conslt UMDS St Thomas's Hosp 1986–92 (emeritus reader in histopathology St Thomas's Hosp 1992–), distinguished visitor Royal Free Hosp Sch of Med 1993–; memb Editorial Bd: Jl of Clinical Pathology 1979–84, Jl of Immunological Methods 1989–88; Bristol Myers Travelling Fellowship 1986; former examiner at various univs incl: Cambridge, London, Bristol and Surrey; papers presented in many countries incl: USA, Sweden, W Germany, Brazil, Holland and Switzerland; author of numerous papers and chapters in books and lectr on main res field of immunocytochemistry in cancer; memb: Cncl Assoc of Clinical Pathologists 1984–89 (pres SE branch 1989–92), Pathological Soc of GB and Ireland, Int Acad of Pathology, Assoc of Clinical Pathologists, Br Assoc for Cancer Res, Br Soc of Endocrine Pathologists, American Assoc for Cancer Res, RSM; FRCPath; *Books* Coping with Breast Cancer (1996); *Recreations* theatre, reading, visual arts; *Style*— Dr Eadie Heyderman

HEYER, Elizabeth Anne; da of Aubrey Thomas Heyer, of Reigate, Surrey, and Anne, *née* Arnott; *b* 3 June 1956; *Educ* Bishop Simpson Girls' Sch, Poly of Central London (BA), Inst of Health Serv Mangrs (Dip), Cranfield Univ (MBA); *ptnr* Martin Stewart Clyne Hunter; *Career* clerical offr Guy's Hosp London 1974–75, mgmnt trainee SW Thames RHA 1975–78, asst hosp admin Queen Mary's Hosp Sidcup 1978–81, asst hosp sec The London Hosp Whitechapel 1981–84, planning admin The Middx and UC Hosps London 1984–86, unit gen mangr of mental health and mental handicap servs Harrow Health Authy 1986–88, unit gen mangr then chief exec Harrow Community Health Servs NHS Tst 1988–94, chief exec Harrow and Hillingdon Healthcare NHS Tst 1994–; MHSM (prizewinner 1976), memb Stategic Planning Soc, Cranfield Mgmnt Assoc; *Recreations* Austin Healey cars, swimming, foreign travel; *Style*— Ms Elizabeth Heyer; ✉ 62 Ruskin Walk, Herne Hill, London SE24 9LZ (☎ and fax 0171 274 1251); Harrow and Hillingdon Healthcare NHS Trust, Malt House, 285 Field End Road, Eastcote, Middx HA4 9NJ (☎ 0181 956 2301)

HEYGATE, Sir Richard John Gage; 6 Bt (UK 1831), of Southend, Essex; s of Sir John Edward Nourse Heygate, 4 Bt (d 1976), suc bro, Sir George Lloyd Heygate, 5 Bt (d 1991); *b* 30 Jan 1940; *Educ* Repton, Balliol Coll Oxford; *m* 1, 1968 (m dis 1972), Carol Rosemary, da of late Cdr Richard Michell, RN, of Leith House, Amberley, Sussex; m 2, 1974 (m dis 1988), Jong-Ja Hyun, da of In Suk, of Seoul; 1 da (Eun-Hee Isobella Gage b 1977); m 3, 1988, Susan Fiona, da of late Robert Buckley, of Cobblers Cottage, Peasmarsh, E Sussex; 2 s (Frederick Carysfort Gage b 1988, Robert George Liam b 1991); *Heir* s, Frederick Carysfort Gage Heygate b 28 June 1988; *Career* IBM (United Kingdom) Ltd 1967–70, McKinsey & Co Inc 1970–77; dir: Olaf Foods Ltd 1977–85, Index Group 1985–87; princ McKinsey & Co Inc 1992–; memb Fin Ctee Cancer Res Campaign 1992–; *Style*— Sir Richard Heygate, Bt; ✉ 29 Rossetti Gardens Mansions, Flood Street, London SW3 5QX

HEYHOE FLINT, Rachael; *née* Heyhoe; MBE (1971); da of Geoffrey Heyhoe (d 1972), of Penn, Wolverhampton, and Roma Kathleen, *née* Crocker (d 1978); Heyhoe is an Anglo-Saxon farming name derived from Hey Mow; *b* 11 June 1939; *Educ* Wolverhampton Girls' HS, Dartford Coll of Physical Educn (DipPhysEd); *m* 1 Nov 1971, Derrick Flint, s of Benjamin Flint, of Underwood, Notts; 1 s (Benjamin b 8 June 1974); *Career* Women's Cricket Int England 1960–83, Capt 1966–77, scored 179 v Aust (Oval) 1976 (world record score for England, world's fourth highest score by woman in tests); Women's Hockey Int England 1964; journalist; PR conslt: La Manga Club, Patshull Park Hotel, Wolverhampton Wanderers FC; memb Bd Family Assurance Friendly Soc; Best After Dinner Speaker Guild of Professional Toastmasters 1972; *Books* Fair Play, History of Women's Cricket (1976), Heyhoe (autobiography 1978); *Recreations* golf; *Clubs* South Staffs Golf (Wolverhampton), La Manga Club Resort (Spain), Patshull Park Golf and Country (Wolverhampton); *Style*— Mrs Rachael Heyhoe Flint, MBE; ✉ Danescroft, Wergs Rd, Tettenhall, Wolverhampton, W Mids (☎ 01902 752103)

HEYLIN, Angela Christine Mary (Mrs Maurice Minzly); da of Bernard Heylin (d 1985), and Ruth Victoria Heylin; *b* 17 Sept 1943; *Educ* Apsley GS, Watford Coll; *m* 13 March 1971, Maurice Minzly, s of Solomon Minzly (d 1974); 1 s (James b 1982); *Career* chief exec Charles Barker Lyons 1984 (formerly dir F J Lyons, dir 1976, jt md 1980), chm and chief exec Charles Barker Gp 1988 (dir 1984), chm Charles Barker plc 1996– (chief exec 1992–96); tstee Int Fndn for PR Studies 1987, chm PRCA 1990–92; memb Citizen's Charter Advsy Panel 1993–; FInstM 1987, FIPR 1987; *Recreations* theatre, entertaining; *Style*— Ms Angela Heylin; ✉ 46 St Augustine's Rd, London NW1 9RN (☎ 0171 485 4815); Charles Barker plc, 56 Dean Street, London W1V 6HX (☎ 0171 494 1331, fax 0171 439 1071)

HEYMAN, Sir Horace William; kt (1976); *b* 13 March 1912; *Educ* Ackworth Sch, Technische Hochschule Darmstadt, Univ of Birmingham (BSc); *m* 1, 1939; 1 s (Timothy), 1 da (Helen Thompson); m 2, 1966, Dorothy Forster Atkinson; *Career* chm English Industrial Estates Corporation 1970–77, pres Northumbria Tourist Bd 1983–86, govr Newcastle-on-Tyne Poly 1974–86 (vice-chm 1983–86, hon fell 1985), dir various UK and European engrg and travel cos; FIEE, FRSA, CEng; *Style*— Sir Horace Heyman; ✉ 20 Whitburn Hall, Whitburn, Sunderland SR6 7JQ

HEYMANN, Bernard; s of Joseph Heymann (d 1954) and Luise Irene Heymann (d 1977); *b* 19 Jan 1937; *Educ* Quintin Sch London, Univ of Durham (BA); *m* 10 Sept 1966, Anne Catherine Valentine, da of Melville Elphinstone Thomson; 1 s (dec'd), 1 da (Anne Belinda b 29 July 1968); *Career* dir: Leopold Joseph & Sons Ltd 1985–88 (conslt 1976–85), Highland Forest Products plc 1986–88, Location of Indust Bureau Ltd 1986–90; FCA, FIMgt; *Recreations* gardening; *Style*— Bernard Heymann, Esq; ✉ 5 Ranulf Rd, London NW2 2BT; 2 Scott House, Sekforde St, London EC1R OHH (☎ 0171 490 3464, fax 0171 490 4202)

HEYNES, David Gordon; s of Gordon Albert Arthur Heynes; *b* 17 April 1945; *Educ* Charterhouse; *m* 1968, Jennifer Jane, *née* Dreyer; 2 s, 1 da; *Career* CA, Hill Samuel and Co Ltd 1969–71, chief exec Park Place Group plc 198l (dir 1972–86); chm: The Cleveland Trust plc (dir 1987–), Flare Group plc (formerly Hewitt Group plc) 1990–; non-exec dir UPF Group plc 1994–; *Recreations* shooting and motor racing; *Clubs* Boodle's; *Style*— David Heynes, Esq; ✉ Newton House, Buckland, Faringdon, Oxon SN7 8PY

HEYWOOD, Eur Ing John Edwin; s of George Edwin Heywood (d 1971), of Tring, Hertfordshire, and Vera, *née* Heron (d 1967); *b* 8 April 1938; *Educ* Lower Sch of John Lyon Harrow; *m* 2 June 1962, Ann Patricia, da of William Hiram Wootton (d 1987), of West Bridgford, Nottingham; 4 da (Susan b 1964, Wendy b 1966, Helen b 1967, Katherine b 1971); *Career* Nat Serv REME attached to Army Air Corps 1960–62; D Napier and Son Ltd Acton 1955–60, Mission Aviation Fellowship in UK Kenya and Ethiopia 1963–68, chief engr Rogers Aviation Ltd Cranfield 1968–69, dep chief engr Safari Air Services Nairobi Kenya 1969–73, airworthiness surveyor CAA in Eng and Scot 1973–84, md J E Heywood Ltd Glenrothes 1984–89, dir of engrg Air Service Training Ltd 1989–90, conslt aeronautical engr 1990–; chm Nairobi branch Soc of Licensed Aircraft Engrs and Technologists 1971–73; CEng 1974, FRAeS 1987, MBAC 1990, Eur Ing 1990; *Books* Light Aircraft Inspection (1977), Light Aircraft Maintenance (1983); *Recreations* photography, hillwalking; *Style—* Eur Ing John Heywood; ✉ 257 Widney Road, Bentley Heath, Solihull, Birmingham B93 9BJ (☎ 01564 773892, fax 01564 773180)

HEYWOOD, John Kenneth; s of Samuel George Heywood (d 1987), of Devon, and Hilda Kathleen, *née* Lamey (d 1985); *b* 29 Jan 1947; *Educ* Shebbear Coll, UCL (LLB), INSEAD Fontainebleau (Advanced Mgmnt Course); *m* 1976, Susan Ann Heywood; 2 s (James Samuel b 15 Nov 1981, William John b 22 Oct 1984), 1 da (Sophie Elizabeth b 4 May 1990); *Career* Price Waterhouse: joined 1968, ptnr 1980–, dir London office and memb UK Exec 1991–95, chm E European firm 1993–, memb Euro Mgmnt Bd 1993–, sr ptnr London 1995–, dir Price Waterhouse China 1995–; FCA; *Recreations* golf, tennis; *Style—* John Heywood, Esq; ✉ Price Waterhouse, Southwark Towers, 32 London Bridge St, London SE1 9SY (☎ 0171 939 3000)

HEYWOOD, Keith Alban; s of John Alban Heywood (d 1955), and Kittie Elizabeth, *née* Rennie (d 1993); *b* 7 Oct 1948; *Educ* The Royal Masonic Sch; *m* 26 Aug 1968, Vivien, da of Alan Irwin (d 1979); 1 s (Jason b 1972), 1 da (Kirsten b 1970); *Career* CA; Crane Christmas & Co 1965, ptnr Jeffreys Ubysz and Co 1975, slr practitioner Heywood & Co 1982, ptnr Brett Jenkins & Ptnrs 1987, fin conslt 1988, sole practitioner Keith A Heywood FCA 1990; Royal Soc of St George: memb Cncl 1991–, hon treas 1992–; Freeman and Liveryman Worshipful Co of Scriveners 1993; FCA; *Recreations* painting, reading, classics; *Style—* Keith Heywood, Esq; ✉ 10 Green End St, Aston Clinton, Aylesbury, Bucks HP22 5JE (☎ 01296 630114)

HEYWOOD, Sir Peter; 6 Bt (UK 1838), of Claremont, Lancashire; s of Sir Oliver Kerr Heywood, 5 Bt (d 1992), and Denise, *née* Godefroi; *b* 10 Dec 1947; *Educ* Bryanston, Keble Coll Oxford (MA); *m* 1970, Jacqueline Anne, da of Sir Robert Frederick Hunt, CBE, *qv*; 2 da (Vanessa Jane b 1975, Annabel Sarah b 1976); *Heir* bro, Michael Heywood b (twin) 10 Dec 1947; *Career* company director; *Style—* Sir Peter Heywood, Bt; ✉ 64 Newbridge Rd, Weston, Bath BA1 3LA

HEYWORTH, John; s of Lt-Col Reginald Francis Heyworth (ka 1941), and Hon Moyra, *née* Marjoribanks, da of 3 Baron Tweedmouth; *b* 21 Aug 1925; *Educ* Eton; *m* 10 June 1950, Susan Elizabeth, da of Sir John Henry Burder, ED, of Burford, Oxford; 1 s (Reginald b 1961), 3 da (Caroline b 1952, Jane b 1953, Joanna b 1957); *Career* Royal Dragoons NW Europe 1943–47; farmer and owner of Wild Life Park; High Sheriff Oxon 1962; *Style—* John Heyworth, Esq; ✉ Bradwell Grove, Burford, Oxford (☎ 01993 823154)

HEZLET, Vice Adm Sir Arthur Richard; KBE (1964), CB (1961), DSO (and Bar 1944, 1945), DSC (1941), DL (Co Londonderry); s of Maj-Gen Robert Knox Hezlet, CB, CBE, DSO (d 1963); *b* 7 April 1914; *Educ* RNC Dartmouth, RNC Greenwich; *m* 1948, Anne Joan Patricia, *née* Clark; 2 adopted da; *Career* served WWII submarines, dir RN Staff Coll Greenwich 1956–57, Rear Adm 1959, Flag Offr Submarines 1959–61, Flag Offr Scotland and NI 1961–64, Vice Adm 1962, ret 1964; area pres Royal Br Legion NI, a vice pres RNLI; *Books* The Submarine and Sea Power (1967), Aircraft and Sea Power (1970), Electron and Sea Power (1975), The B Specials (1972); *Clubs* Army and Navy, Royal Ocean Racing; *Style—* Vice Adm Sir Arthur Hezlet, KBE, CB, DSO, DSC, DL; ✉ Bovagh House, Aghadowey, Co Londonderry, N Ireland BT51 4AU (☎ 01265 868 206)

HIBBARD, Prof Bryan Montague; s of Montague Reginald Hibbard (d 1972), of Norfolk, and Muriel Irene, *née* Wilson (d 1989); *b* 24 April 1926; *Educ* Queen Elizabeth's Sch Barnet, St Bartholomew's Hosp Med Coll and Univ of London (MB BS, MD), Univ of Liverpool (PhD); *m* 30 July 1955, Elizabeth Donald, da of Dr James Campbell Grassie (d 1976), of Aberdeen; *Career* sr lectr Univ of Liverpool 1963–73, prof and head of Dept of Obstetrics and Gynaecology Univ of Wales Coll of Med 1973–91; memb Advsy Sub Ctee in Obstetrics and Gynaecology Welsh Office 1974–91, central assessor and memb Editorial Bd Confidential Enquiries into Maternal Deaths DHSS 1988– (chm Clinical Sub-Gp 1991–); memb: Ctee on Safety of Meds 1980–84, Maternity Servs Advsy Ctee DHSS 1980–85, Gynaecological Cytology Ctee DHSS 1983–89, S Glamorgan Health Authy 1983–88, Cncl RCOG 1982–88 and 1989–91 (curator of instruments 1986–90, chm Library Ctee 1987–92, curator of museum 1990–, hon librarian 1992–94); pres: Welsh Obstetric and Gynaecological Soc 1985–86, Medicines Cmmn 1986–89, History of Med Soc of Wales 1995–96; chm Jt Standing Advsy Ctee on Obstetric Anaesthesia RCOG and Royal Coll of Midwives 1988–91; FRCOG 1965 (MRCOG 1956); *Books* Principles of Obstetrics (1988), The Obstetric Forceps (1988, 2 edn 1992); *Recreations* 18th century glass, fell walking, coarse gardening; *Clubs* RSM; *Style—* Prof Bryan Hibbard; ✉ The Clock House, Cathedral Close, Llandaff, Cardiff CF5 2ED

HIBBERD, Dr Alan Ronald; s of George Peter Hibberd (d 1946), of Bendigo, Victoria, Aust, and Flora Gertrude, *née* Dainty (d 1973); *b* 25 Oct 1931; *Educ* High Sch Bendigo (Alexander Rushall scholarship), Ridley Coll Melbourne, Victorian Coll of Pharmacy Melbourne (PhC), Chelsea Coll Univ of London (DCC, PhD); *m* 1, 1954, Doreen Imilda, da of James Collier; 2 s (David b 1954, Andrew b 1957), 2 da (Wendy b 1959, Christine b 1962); m 2, 1974, Lois, da of Howard Kenneth Stratton; *Career* specialist in clinical ecology/clinical biochemistry; community pharmacy practice Melbourne 1953–73; dir: ARH Pharmaceuticals 1959–74, Pressels Laboratories 1959–74; pt/t demonstrator in practical pharmaceutics Victorian Coll of Pharmacy 1961–64; Victorian Branch Aust Dental Assoc 1966–74: lectr to postgrads in pharmacology and therapeutics, conslt in dental therapeutics and prescribing; i/c of Drug Info Dept and Ward Pharmacy Services Hackney Hosp London 1975, res fell Pharmacy Dept Chelsea Coll Univ of London 1976–79, lectr Sch of Pharmacy Univ of London 1980–81, tutor in clinical pharmacy Northwick Park Hosp Harrow 1980–81, first course organiser and supervisor MSc course in clinical pharmacy Univ of London (first clinical pharmacy degree course in SE England) 1980–81, dir Hibbro Research Hereford 1981–84, private practice in clinical ecology London 1985–, conslt in clinical pharmacology Biocare Ltd 1989–, conslt in clinical biochem/pharmacology to Soc for Promotion of Nutritional Therapy (UK) 1992–, scientific advsr to Register of Nutritional Therapists (UK) 1993–; author of numerous articles and scientific papers on drug metabolism and relating to specialist field and contrib to many learned pubns; vice pres The Int Acad of Oral Med and Toxicology (UK) 1994–; memb: Pharmaceutical Soc of Victoria 1953 (fell (by examination) 1961), Royal Soc of Victoria 1968, Br Dental Soc for Clinical Nutrition 1985, Nutrition Assoc 1987, Environmental Dental Association USA 1991, British Soc for Allergy and Environmental Med with The British Soc for Nutritional Med 1993; FRSH 1971, MRPharmS 1974, fell Pharmaceutical Soc of Aust 1983 (life fell 1991); *Recreations* golf, flying light aircraft, bridge, travelling, languages, music; *Clubs* Ross-on-Wye Golf, Herefordshire Flying, Herefordshire Conservative; *Style—* Dr Alan Hibberd; ✉ Bayswater Clinic, 25B Clanricarde Gardens, London W2 4JL (☎ and fax 0171 229 9078)

HIBBERD, Dr Joan Louise; da of Peter Nalty (d 1943), of Queensland, Aust, and Jean, *née* Byrne (d 1987); *b* 28 Nov 1930; *Educ* Sacre Coeur Sch Melbourne, Univ of Melbourne (BDSc, LDS), Univ of Toronto (LDS), Dept of Oral Med and Periodontology Royal London Hosp Med Coll Univ of London (PhD); *m* 1, 1953, Prof John Hunt Hibberd (d 1972); 6 s (Peter Hunt b 1954, Michael John b 1955, Graeme Robert b 1957, John Anthony b 1965, Christopher Richard b 1966, Robert James b 1970), 2 da (Jennifer Ann b 1959, Catherine Mary b 1969); m 2, 1984, Geoffrey Edwards (d 1990); *Career* conslt Queen Elizabeth Centre for Handicapped 1964–67, in gen practice 1964–67 then practice with Medical Arts Bd Toronto, assoc in dentistry Univ of Toronto Ontario 1975–77; Royal London Hosp Med Coll: lectr and clinical teacher in periodontology 1978–81, hon lectr 1981–83, dep dir Sch of Dental Hygiene 1981–82; in practice in periodontics Harley St 1983–; Specialist in Periodontics awarded by RCDS Canada 1981; memb: Canadian Dental Assoc 1975, FDI 1975, Int Assoc for Dental Res 1980, BDA 1981, Br Soc of Periodontology 1981, Canadian Acad of Periodontology 1981; fell Int Coll of Dentistry 1985, FRSM 1983; *Recreations* family, fishing, swimming, reading; *Style—* Dr Joan Hibberd; ✉ 70 Harley Street, London W1 (☎ 0171 580 4082)

HIBBERT, Christopher; MC (1945); s of Canon H V Hibbert (d 1980); *b* 5 March 1924; *Educ* Radley, Oriel Coll Oxford (MA); *m* 1948, Susan, da of Rayner Piggford (d 1978); 2 s (James, Tom), 1 da (Kate); *Career* Capt London Irish Rifles Italy 1944–45; ptnr firm of land agents and auctioneers 1948–59; author 1959–; Heinemann Award for Lit 1962, McColvin Medal 1989; Hon DLitt Univ of Leicester; FRSL, FRGS; *Books* incl: The Destruction of Lord Raglan (1961), Corunna (1961), Benito Mussolini (1962), The Battle of Arnhem (1962), The Court at Windsor (1964), The Roots of Evil (1964), Agincourt (1965), Garibaldi and his Enemies (1966), The Making of Charles Dickens (1967), London: Biography of a City (1969), The Dragon Wakes: China and the West (1970), The Personal History of Samuel Johnson (1971), George IV (2 vols 1972, 1973), The Rise and Fall of the House of Medici (1974), Edward VII (1976), The Great Mutiny: India 1857 (1978), The French Revolution (1980), The London Encyclopaedia (ed, 1983), Rome: Biography of a City (1985), The English: A Social History (1986), The Grand Tour (1987), Venice: The Biography of a City (1988), The Encyclopaedia of Oxford (ed, 1988), The Virgin Queen: The Personal History of Elizabeth I (1990), Redcoats and Rebels: The War for America, 1770–1781 (1990), The Story of England (1992), Cavaliers and Roundheads: The Civil War in England 1642–49 (1993), Florence: The Biography of A City (1993), Nelson: A Personal History (1994), Soldier of the Seventy-first: The Journal of a Soldier in the Peninsular War (ed, 1996), No Ordinary Place: Radley College and the Public School System (1997), Wellington: A Personal History (1997); *Recreations* cooking, crosswords, gardening, travel; *Clubs* Army and Navy, Garrick; *Style—* Christopher Hibbert, Esq, MC; ✉ 6 Albion Place, West Street, Henley-on-Thames, Oxfordshire

HIBBERT, Sir Reginald Alfred; GCMG (1981, KCMG 1979, CMG 1966); s of Alfred Hibbert, of Sawbridgeworth; *b* 21 Feb 1922; *Educ* Queen Elizabeth's Sch Barnet, Worcester Coll Oxford; *m* 1949, Ann Alun, da of His Honour Sir Alan Pugh (d 1971), of Dunsfold, Surrey; 2 s, 1 da; *Career* served WWII, SOE and 4 Hussars (Albania and Italy); joined FO 1946; served: Bucharest, Vienna, Guatemala, Ankara, Brussels; chargé d'affaires Ulaan Bator (Mongolian People's Republic) 1964–66, res fell Univ of Leeds 1966–67, Political Advsr's Office Singapore 1967–69, political advsr to C-in-C Far East 1970–71, min Bonn 1972–75, asst under-sec of state FCO 1975–76, dep under-sec 1976–79, ambass France 1979–82, ret 1982; dir Ditchley Fndn 1982–87, chm Franco-Br Soc 1990–95; pres Albania Soc of Br 1995–; visiting fell Nuffield Coll Oxford 1984–88; hon res fell Univ Coll Swansea 1988–, hon fell Worcester Coll Oxford 1991–; Albanian Order of Liberty (1 Class) 1994, Légion d'Honneur (commandeur) 1995; *Publications* The Albanian National Liberation Struggle: The Bitter Victory (1991); *Clubs* Reform; *Style—* Sir Reginald Hibbert, GCMG; ✉ Frondeg, Pennal, Machynlleth, Powys SY20 9JX (☎ 01654 791220)

HIBBERT, William John; s of Sir Reginald Hibbert, GCMG, *qv*, of Machynlleth, Powys, and Ann Alun, *née* Pugh; *b* 23 Feb 1957; *Educ* Charterhouse, Worcester Coll Oxford (BA); *m* 19 April 1980, (Caroline) Maria Hibbert, da of Sir John Lucas-Tooth, 2 Bt, *qv*, of East Hagbourne, Oxon; 2 da (Cosima Mary b 1984, Clover Frances b 1988); *Career* called to the Bar Inner Temple 1979; *Style—* William Hibbert, Esq; ✉ 41 Lancaster Rd, London W11 1QJ; Gough Square Chambers, 6/7 Gough Square, London EC4 (☎ 0171 353 0924, fax 0171 353 2221)

HIBBITT, Brian Leslie; s of Edgar Bennett Hibbitt (d 1977), and Kathleen Marion, *née* Groom (d 1965); *b* 15 July 1938; *Educ* SW Essex County Tech Sch, London Coll of Printing; *m* 1963, Jill Mavis, da of Albert Henry Oakley (d 1983); 2 s (Timothy John b 1964, Andrew James b 1968); *Career* md: Greenaway Harrison Ltd 1984–89, Turnergraphic Ltd 1989–; chm: Br Printing Industs Fedn Industl Rels Ctee SE Region 1986–90, SE Regn Br Printing Industs Fedn 1990–92, International Printers Network 1993–; FIOP, FInstDS; *Recreations* local affairs, gardening, theatre; *Style—* Brian L Hibbitt, Esq; ✉ Priors Lodge, Priors Wood, Crowthorne, Berkshire RG45 6BZ (☎ 01344 772215); Turnergraphic Ltd, Communications House, Winchester Rd, Basingstoke, Hants RG22 4AA (☎ 01256 59252, fax 01256 51501)

HIBBITT, Tari; da of Suwondo Budiardjo, of London, and Carmel, *née* Brickman; *b* 18 June 1951; *m* 1971 (m dis 1996), Roger Hibbitt, s of John A Hibbitt; 1 da (Claire b 28 June 1976), 1 s (Laurence b 9 June 1978); *Career* fndr dir Clasma Software Ltd 1980–86, jt md UK The Rowland Co 1988–95, dep md UK and md European Business and Technol Edelman Public Relations Worldwide 1995–; MIPR 1989, MInstD 1990, memb AWPR (Assoc of Women in PR); FRSA; *Recreations* theatre, cinema, opera; *Style—* Ms Tari Hibbitt; ✉ Edelman Public Relations Worldwide, 28 Haymarket, London SW1Y 4SP (☎ 0171 344 1289, fax 0171 344 1222, mobile 0385 307933, e-mail thibbitt@edeluk.com)

HICHENS, Antony Peverell; RD (1969); s of Lt Cdr Robert Peverell Hichens, DSO and bar, DSC and two bars, RNVR, and Catherine Gilbert Enys; *b* 10 Sept 1936; *Educ* Stowe, Magdalen Coll Oxford, Univ of Pennsylvania; *m* 1963, Sczerina Neomi, da of Dr F T J Hobday; 1 da (Tamsin (Hon Mrs Edward Lennox-Boyd)); *Career* Nat Serv Midshipman RNVR 1954–56, ret as Lt Cdr RNR 1969; called to the Bar Inner Temple, dep md Redland Ltd 1979 (fin dir 1972), md fin Consolidated Gold Fields plc 1981–89; chm: Caradon plc 1987–89, Y J Lovell (Holdings) plc 1990–93, Caradon plc (non-exec) 1990–; dir: Greenfriar Investment Co plc 1985–, Candover Investments plc (dep chm) 1989–, South Western Electricity plc 1990–95, Courtaulds Textiles plc (dep chm) 1990–, British Coal Corporation 1992–96, Fleming Income & Capital Investment Trust 1992–, London Insurance Market Investment Trust 1993–, Global Stone Corp 1994–, LASMO plc (dep chm) 1995–; Waynflete fell Magdalen Coll Oxford 1996; *Recreations* travel, shooting, wine; *Clubs* City of London, Brooks's; *Style—* Antony Hichens, Esq; ✉ Slape Manor, Netherbury, Nr Bridport, Dorset (☎ 01308 488232); 93 Eaton Place, London SW1 (☎ 0171 245 9933)

HICK, Graeme Ashley; s of John Douglas Baskerville Hick, of Trelawney, Zimbabwe, and Eva Francis Lister, *née* Noble; *b* 23 May 1966; *Educ* Prince Edward Boys' HS Harare Zimbabwe; *Career* professional cricketer Worcestershire CCC 1984– (awarded county cap 1986); represented Zimbabwe 1983–86; England: debut v W Indies 1991, memb tour NZ 1992, memb World Cup squad Aust 1992, memb team touring India and Sri Lanka

1992/93, W Indies 1993/94, Australia 1994/95 and S Africa 1995/96, memb World Cup squad India, Pakistan and Sri Lanka 1996, 37 test matches, memb tour India and Sri Lanka 1992/93, over 46 one day ints, scorer fastest 50 in one day ints (off 34 balls); honours with Worcs: Refuge Assurance League 1987 and 1988, Co Championship 1988 and 1989, Benson & Hedges Cup 1991 (Gold award for Man of the Match, runners-up 1990), Refuge Cup 1991, NatWest Trophy 1994 (runners-up 1988); achievements incl: youngest player to score 2,000 runs 1986, scored 1,000 runs before end of May 1989, highest individual innings 405 not out, shared in 4 record stands for Worcs, youngest player to play in World Cup (for Zimbabwe); *Style—* Graeme Hick, Esq; ✉ Worcestershire CCC, County Ground, New Road, Worcester WR2 4QQ (☎ 01905 748474)

HICKEY, (James) Kevin; MBE (1987); s of James Francis Hickey (d 1972), of Blackpool, and Mary Veronica, *née* Queenan; *b* 25 July 1941; *Educ* St Joseph's Coll Blackpool, De La Salle Coll Middleton, St Mary's Coll Twickenham; *m* Kyra Marjorie, da of George C Collen; 2 s (Sean Francis b 11 May 1965, Adrian Kevin b 12 April 1966), 1 da (Katherine Kyra b 24 Nov 1969); *Career* sports coach and administrator; teacher 1962–69, nat coach ABA 1969–89 (dir of coaching 1973–89), tech dir Br Olympic Assoc 1989–; dep chef de mission (technical) to GB Olympic teams: Barcelona 1992, Albertville 1992, Lillehammer 1994, Atlanta 1996; vice chm Euro Coaches Fedn 1982–89, chm Br Assoc of Nat Coaches 1986–89; memb: Grants Ctee Sports Aid Fndn, Cncl Br Inst of Sports Coaches 1989–92, World Safety Cmmn 1986–89; lectured worldwide, contrib to various coaching gps incl Coaching Review Panel 1989–90; conceived and implemented: Schs' ABA Standards Scheme, Golden Gloves Award; sporting achievements: co youth player rugby, represented London Colls at rugby, nat amateur boxing champion 1955–57; coaching achievements: coached GB Boxing Team Olympic Games 1972, 1976, 1980, 1984 and 1988 (total 7 medals), coached England Boxing Team Cwlth Games 1970, 1974, 1978, 1982 and 1986 (total 33 medals, every English boxer won medals 1984 and 1988); fell Br Inst of Sports Coaches 1989, Sports Writers' J L Manning Award 1987, UK Coach of the Year Br Assoc of Nat Coaches 1989; *Books* ABA Coaching Manual; *Recreations* keep fit activities including running and weight training, outdoor pursuits, fell walking, squash, golf; *Style—* Kevin Hickey, Esq, MBE; ✉ 180 West Park Drive, Blackpool, Lancs FY3 9LW (☎ 01253 64900); British Olympic Association, 1 Wandsworth Plain, London SW18 1EH (☎ 0181 871 2677, fax 0181 871 9104)

HICKEY, Dr Stephen Harald Frederick; s of Rev Dr James Peter Hickinbotham (d 1990), and Ingeborg Alice Lydia, *née* Manger; *b* 10 July 1949; *Educ* St Lawrence Coll, Corpus Christi Coll Oxford (BA), St Antony's Coll Oxford (DPhil); *m* 1976, Janet Elizabeth, *née* Hunter; 3 s (James b 1979, Thomas b 1982, Edward b 1985); *Career* DHSS (now DSS): admin trainee and higher exec offr (admin) 1974–79, asst private sec to Sec of State 1978–79 and 1984–85, princ 1979–85, asst sec 1985–89, seconded to Rank Xerox (UK) Ltd 1989–90, asst sec Benefits Agency 1990–92, Fin Div 1992–94; under sec and chief exec Civil Service Coll 1994–; *Books* Workers in Imperial Germany: The Miners of the Ruhr (1985); *Recreations* music, walking, swimming; *Style—* Dr Stephen Hickey; ✉ Civil Service College, Sunningdale Park, Larch Avenue, Ascot, Berks SL5 0QE (☎ 01344 634000, fax 01344 634233)

HICKLING, Rev Colin John Anderson; s of Charles Frederick Hickling, ScD, CMG (d 1977), of Totteridge, and Marjorie Ellerington, *née* Blamey (d 1978); *b* 10 July 1931; *Educ* Haverfordwest GS, Taunton Sch, Epsom Coll, King's Coll Cambridge (BA, MA), Chichester Theological Coll; *Career* Nat Serv E Surreys and Royal W Sussex 1949–50; ordained: deacon 1957, priest 1958; asst curate St Luke's Pallion Sunderland 1957–61, asst tutor in Old Testament Chichester Theol Coll 1961–65, asst priest vicar Chichester Cathedral 1963–65, lectr in New Testament studies King's Coll London 1968–84 (asst lectr 1965–68), hon asst curate St Mary Magdalene's Munster Square 1965–68, dep minor canon St Paul's Cathedral 1969–78, (subwarden King's Coll Hall 1969–78), warden King's Coll Hostel 1978–81, hon asst curate St John's E Dulwich 1970–84, Priest in Ordinary to HM The Queen 1974–84 (dep Priest in Ordinary 1971–74), Canon Theologian Leicester Cathedral 1982–96, tutor Queen's Coll Birmingham 1984–85, EW Benson fell Lincoln Theol Coll 1985–86, vicar All Saints Arksey by Doncaster 1986–, hon lectr in Biblical studies Univ of Sheffield 1986–; memb: Soc for Old Testament Study 1963–, Studiorum Novi Testamenti Societas 1974–, Soc for the Study of Theology 1964–; Queen's Jubilee Medal 1977; *Books* contribs include: Church Without Walls (1968), Bible Bibliography 1967–73 (1974), What About the New Testament? (jt ed, 1975), L'Evangile de Jean (1977), The Ministry of the Word (1979), This is the Word of the Lord (1980), Logia - Sayings of Jesus (1982), The Bible in Three Dimensions (1990), A Dictionary of Biblical Interpretation (1990), Mneme Ioannou Anastasiou (1992), Resurrection (1994), The Corinthian Correspondence (1996); *Recreations* music; *Clubs* Nikaean, Arksey Victoria Social, Danum Social and Literary; *Style—* The Rev Colin Hickling; ✉ All Saints' Vicarage, Station Road, Arksey by Doncaster, S Yorks DN5 0SP (☎ 01302 874445)

HICKMAN, Anthony Stanley Franklin; JP (1984); s of Franklin Hickman (d 1981), of Wargrave, Berks, and Kathleen Irene, *née* Hancock (d 1955); *b* 12 April 1931; *Educ* Edward VI Royal GS Guildford, Kingston Sch of Art (DipArch); *m* 6 Jan 1962, Brenda Valerie, da of Gp Capt Eric Passmore, CBE (d 1982), of Seychelles; 1 s (Christopher John b 3 June 1965), 1 da (Charlotte Sarah b 20 May 1963); *Career* Nat Serv RAF, cmmn PO 1956, qualified navigator, ret 1958, appointed flying offr in res; John R Harris 1955–56 and 1958–64, gp architect BPB Industs plc 1964–71, assoc ptnr Adams Holden and Pearson 1971–74, ptnr Stevens Scanlan and ptnrs 1974–; commendation: Financial Times Ind Architecture Award 1971, Civic Tst; author of various articles in Architects Journal, sec gen Franco-Br Union of Architects London and Paris 1963–; Freeman City of London 1983; Chevalier dans l'Ordre des Palmes Académiques (France) 1990; FRIBA; *Recreations* architecture, gardening, making things, music; *Style—* Anthony Hickman, Esq, JP; ✉ Stevens Scanlan & Partners, 56 Buckingham Gate, London SW1E 6AH (☎ 0171 834 4806, fax 0171 630 8246)

HICKMAN, Sir (Richard) Glenn; 4 Bt (UK 1903), of Wightwick, Tettenhall, Staffordshire; s of Sir (Alfred) Howard Whitby Hickman, 3 Bt (d 1979), and Margaret Doris, *née* Kempson (d 1996); *b* 12 April 1949; *Educ* Eton; *m* 1981, Heather Mary Elizabeth, er da of Dr James Moffett (d 1982), of Swindon, and Dr Gwendoline Moffett (d 1975); 2 s (Charles Patrick Alfred b 1983, Edward William George b 1990), 1 da (Elizabeth Margaret Ruth b 1985); *Heir* s, Charles Patrick Alfred Hickman b 5 May 1983; *Clubs* Turf; *Style—* Sir Glenn Hickman, Bt; ✉ Stocks Close, Badbury, Wilts SN4 0EU

HICKMAN, John Kyrle; CMG (1977); s of John Barlow Hickman (d 1932), and Joan Hickman (d 1995), of Cirencester, Glos; *b* 3 July 1927; *Educ* Tonbridge, Trinity Hall Cambridge (BA); *m* 1956, Jennifer, da of Reginald Kendall Love (d 1976); 2 s (Matthew, Andrew), 1 da (Catherine); *Career* HM Forces 1948–50 2 Lt RA, WO 1950; transferred to CRO 1958 then to FO 1964, first sec Wellington 1959, first sec Madrid 1966, cnsllr and consul gen Bilbao 1967, dep high cmmr Singapore 1969, head SW Pacific Dept FCO 1971, cnsllr Dublin 1974 (chargé d'affaires 1976), ambass to Ecuador 1977–80, chm Belize Independence Conf and foreign affrs advsr to Inchape Group plc 1981–82, ambass to Chile 1982–87; dir Anaconda (S America) Inc 1988–; conslt to World Fedn of Engrg Orgns and others 1988–; chm: Anglo-Ecuadorean Soc 1988–91, Anglo-Chilean Soc 1991–95; tstee New Theatre Royal Portsmouth; Grand Cross Order of Merit (Chile) 1992; FRGS; *Books* The Enchanted Islands: The Galapagos Discovered (1985); *Recreations* reading, golf, tennis, history; *Clubs* Garrick, Los Leones Golf (Santiago); *Style—* J K Hickman, Esq, CMG; ✉ Ivy Bank, Oare, nr Marlborough, Wiltshire SN8 4JA (☎ 01672 563462)

HICKMAN, His Hon Michael Ranulf; s of John Owen Hickman (d 1949), and Nancy Viola, *née* Barlow (d 1963); *b* 2 Oct 1922; *Educ* Wellington, Trinity Hall Cambridge (MA); *m* 1943, Diana, da of Col Derek Charles Houghton Richardson (d 1975); 1 s (Peter), 1 da (Susan); *Career* Flt Lt RAFVR 1940–46, served in Atlantic and SE Asia Coastal Cmd; called to the Bar Middle Temple 1949; dep chm Hertfordshire Quarter Sessions 1965–72, recorder 1972–74, circuit judge 1974–93; *Recreations* shooting, fishing, gun dog training; *Style—* His Hon Michael Hickman; ✉ The Acorn, Bovingdon, Herts (☎ 01442 832226)

HICKOX, Richard Sidney; s of Sidney Edwin Hickox (d 1988), and Jean MacGregor, *née* Millar; *b* 5 March 1948; *Educ* Royal GS High Wycombe, Royal Acad of Music (LRAM), Queens' Coll Cambridge (organ scholar, MA, ChM); *m* 1, 1970 (m dis), Julia Margaret, *née* Smith; m 2, 1976 (m dis) Frances Ina, *née* Sheldon-Williams; 1 s (Thomas Richard Campbell b 1981); m 3, 1995, Pamela, *née* Helen Stephen; 1 s (Adam b 1996); *Career* organist and master of music St Margaret's Westminster 1972–82, Promenade debut 1973; artistic dir: Woburn Festival 1967–89 (now pres), St Endellion Festival 1974–, London Symphony Chorus 1976–, ChCh Spitalfields Festival 1978–, Truro Festival 1981–, Northern Sinfonia 1982–90 (conductor emeritus 1996–), Chester Summer Music Festival 1989–; conductor and musical dir: City of London Sinfonia (fndr 1971), Richard Hickox Singers; co-fndr (with Simon Standage) Collegium Musicum '90 1990; princ guest conductor Bournemouth Symphony Orch 1992–95, assoc conductor LSO 1985–; regular conductor: RPO, Bournemouth Symphony Orch and Sinfonietta, Royal Liverpool Philharmonic Orch, BBC Symphony and Welsh orchs; conductor for many int orchestras; conducted anniversary performance of Mendelssohn's Elijah (BBC Proms) 1996; FRCO (cncl memb), ARAM; *Opera* recent performances incl: Walton's Troilus and Cressida (Opera North) 1995, Rusalka (Rome Opera) 1995, Gluck's Armide (Spitalfields Festival), A Midsummer Night's Dream (Opera London), Handel's Julius Caesar (Komische Oper Berlin and Australian Opera Sydney), Seraglio (Scottish Chamber Orch at Istanbul Festival), Cunning Little Vixen (ENO) 1996, Fidelio (Australian Opera Sydney), Ariadne auf Naxos (Australian Opera) 1997, Vaughan Williams' Pilgrim's Progress (Royal Opera House) 1997, Vaughan Williams' Riders to the Sea and Purcell's Dido and Aeneas (Royal Opera House), Lohengrin (Spoleto Festival Italy); *Recordings* over 150 recordings incl: Britten War Requiem, Delius Sea Drift (with Bournemouth Symphony Orch), works by Bach, Handel and Telemann (with Collegium Musicum '90), Troilus and Cressida (Opera North), Walton The Bear, Vaughan Williams Riders to the Sea, Holst The Wandering Scholar (with Northern Sinfonia), complete Haydn masses (with Collegium Musicum '90), Peter Grimes (with City of London Sinfonia and London Symphony Chorus); *Television* incl: South Bank Show (Ken Russell film with Bournemouth Symphony), Dido and Aeneas with Collegium Musicum '90 and Maria Ewing (BBC); *Awards* Gramophone Award for best choral recording (Britten's War Requiem) 1992, Gramophone Award for best choral recording (Delius' Sea Drift) 1994, Nat Fedn of Music Socs' first Sir Charles Groves Prize for Services to Br Music, Royal Philharmonic Soc Music Award 1995 (for Opera North's Troilus and Cressida and first ever complete cycle of Vaughan Williams' symphonies with Bournemouth Symphony Orch), Gramophone Opera Award 1995 (for Walton's Troilus and Cressida), Deutsche Schallplattenpreis, Diapason d'Or; *Recreations* watching football and tennis, surfing, politics; *Style—* Richard Hickox, Esq; ✉ c/o Intermusica Artists' Management, 16 Duncan Terrace, London N1 8BZ (☎ 0171 278 5455, fax 0171 278 8434)

HICKS, Air Cdre Alan George; CBE (1990); s of William John Hicks, TD, of Verwood, Dorset, and Ellen Rose, *née* Packer; *b* 18 Feb 1936; *Educ* Fosters Sch Sherborne, St Catharine's Coll Cambridge (MA); *m* 30 Oct 1961, Jessie Elizabeth, da of James Hutchison, of Perth, Scotland; 1 s (Jeremy b 8 Aug 1962), 3 da (Cressida b 22 Aug 1963, Gemma b 10 June 1965, Clare b 27 March 1967); *Career* cmmnd RAF 1957, 42 Sqdn 1962–65, 204 Sqdn 1965–67, Avionics Spec RAF Coll Manby 1969–71, Flt Cdr 203 Sqdn Malta 1973–76, OC 42 Sqdn 1976–78, Directing Staff RAF Staff Coll 1978–80, Central Tactics and Trials Orgn 1981, Station Cdr RAF Turnhouse 1982–84, MOD Concepts Staff 1985–87, MOD Dir of Def Commitments 1987–90, head Gulf War Report Team 1990–91 (ret 1991); sec gen UK Industl Space Ctee 1993–; chm United Servs Catholic Assoc 1984–90 (vice pres 1990–); CEng, MRAeS, MIERE 1971; *Recreations* music, books, local history; *Clubs* RAF; *Style—* Air Commodore Alan Hicks, CBE; ✉ c/o National Westminster Bank, 50 Cheap Street, Sherborne, Dorset

HICKS, Dr Brendan Hamilton; s of Bryan Hamilton Hicks (d 1968), of London, and Winefrede, *née* O'Leary; *b* 22 Feb 1942; *Educ* St Brendan's Coll Bristol, Univ of London (BSc, MB BS, MD); *m* 8 Oct 1966, Jacqueline Ann, da of William R Box, of Reading; 1 s (Benjamin John Hamilton b 18 June 1974), 1 da (Amelia Clare Hamilton b 10 Oct 1970); *Career* lectr in med Guys Hosp Med Sch 1969–72, NIH int fell of the US Public Health Serv 1972–73, postgrad dean to United Med and Dental Schs of Guys and St Thomas' Hosps Univ of London 1985–95 (sr lectr in med and conslt physician and endocrinologist 1974–95), regnl dean dir of postgrad med and dental educn Univ of London and S Thames Regnl Office of NHS Exec 1996–; Freeman City of London, Freeman Worshipful Soc of Apothecaries 1985 (memb Ct of Examiners); FRCP 1982; *Books* contrib Priciples of Clinical Medicine (1995); *Recreations* good books, theatre & films, cocker spaniels, narrow boats, sailing and walking; *Style—* Dr Brendan Hicks; ✉ Pembury House, 3 Brewery Rd, Bromley Common, Kent BR2 8LG (☎ 0181 462 3244, fax 0181 462 2756); South Thames PGMDE, 33 Millman Street, London WC1 3EJ (☎ 0171 831 6222, fax 0171 831 1925)

HICKS, Dr Colin Peter; s of George Stephen Frederick Hicks (d 1976), and Irene Maud, *née* Hargrave; *b* 1 May 1946; *Educ* Rutlish Sch Merton, Univ of Bristol (BSc, PhD); *m* Elizabeth Joan, da of Rev Sidney Eric Escourt Payne, of Birmingham; 2 da (Rachel Heather b 1970, Joanna Katharine b 1972); *Career* lectr in chemistry Univ of the West Indies 1970–73, ICI research fell Univ of Exeter 1973–75, researcher Nat Physical Laboratory 1975–80, various research positions DTI 1980–83, tech advsr Barclays Bank 1983–84, dep dir Laboratory of the Govt Chemist 1984–87, sec Industl Devpt Advsy Bd 1988–90, under sec i/c res and technol policy DTI 1990–94, under sec i/c environment and energy technologies DTI 1994–96, dir Environment Directorate DTI 1996–; sec Teddington Baptist Church 1979–1990, memb London Baptist Assoc Cncl 1986–, FRSC 1985; *Recreations* computing; *Style—* Dr Colin Hicks; ✉ Environment Directorate, Department of Trade and Industry, 151 Buckingham Palace Road, London SW1W 9SS (☎ 0171 215 5815, fax 0171 215 1504)

HICKS, David Nightingale; s of Herbert Hicks (d 1940), of Coggeshall, Essex, and Iris Elsie, *née* Platten; *b* 25 March 1929; *Educ* Charterhouse, Central Sch of Art and Design; *m* 1960, Lady Pamela Carmen Louise, *qv*, yr da of 1 Earl Mountbatten of Burma, KG, OM, DSO, FRS (d 1979); 1 s (Ashley Louis David b 1963), 2 da (Edwina Victoria Louise (Mrs Jeremy Brudenell) b 1961, India Amanda Caroline, b 1967, bridesmaid to Lady Diana Spencer at her marriage to HRH The Prince of Wales 1981); *Career* interior, product, garden and jewellery designer; author; FRSA; *Books* David Hicks on Decoration (1966), David Hicks on Living ... With Taste (1968), David Hicks on Bathrooms (1970), David Hicks on Decoration With Fabrics (1971), David Hicks on Decoration - 5 (1975), David Hicks on Flower Arranging (1976), David Hicks Living With Design (1979), David Hicks Garden Design (1982), David Hicks Style & Design (1987), Cotswold Gardens (1995); *Recreations* gardening and talking; *Clubs* Pratt's; *Style—* David Hicks, Esq;

✉ The Grove, Brightwell Baldwin, Oxon OX9 5PF (fax 01491 836844); Albany, Piccadilly, London W1V 9RP (☎ 0171 437 2499)

HICKS, His Hon Judge John Charles; QC (1980); s of Charles Hicks (d 1963), and Marjorie Jane, *née* Bazeley (d 1980); *b* 4 March 1928; *Educ* King Edward VI GS Chelmsford, King Edward VI GS Totnes, Univ of London (LLB, LLM); *m* 1957, (Elizabeth) Mary, da of Rev John Barnabas Jennings (d 1979); 1 s (David, decd), 1 da (Elizabeth (Mrs Geraint Wyn Edwards)); *Career* Nat Serv RA (Gunner) 1946–48; slr 1952–66, ptnr Messrs Burchells 1954–65; Methodist Missionary Soc (Caribbean) 1965–66; barr 1966–88, recorder Western Circuit 1978–88, circuit judge (SE Circuit) 1988–, official referee 1993–; jl sec Methodist Conference 1989–; *Recreations* music, theatre, opera, squash racquets, the Methodist constitution; *Style*— His Hon Judge John Hicks, QC; ✉ Flat 3, 17 Montagu Square, London W1H 1RD (☎ and fax 0171 935 6008)

HICKS, John Geoffrey; s of John Albert Hicks (d 1971), of Redhill, Surrey, and Blanche Christian, *née* Arnot (d 1979); *b* 7 April 1936; *Educ* The Perse Sch for Boys Cambridge, Downing Coll Cambridge (MA); *m* 1, 1967 (m dis 1976), Janice Marilyn Denson; 1 s (David Markham John b 1971); m 2, 1983, Janet Florence Morrison; 1 s (Peter John Cameron b 1985); *Career* Vickers Armstrongs (Aircraft) Ltd/British Aircraft Corp 1954–64 (apprentice, stressman, section ldr), The Welding Inst 1964–75 (investigator, head of Design Advsy Serv, mangr UK Offshore Steels Res Project), conslt Sir William Halcrow and Partners 1976 (former project engr), advsr Standards and Quality HM Treas 1987–90, sec gen Int Inst of Welding 1990–96; Freeman City of London 1990, Liveryman Worshipful Co of Engineers 1991; MRAes 1963; fell: Welding Inst 1973, Welding Technol Inst of Aust 1980, Inst of Quality Assurance 1985, Assoc of Quality Mgmnt Conslts; ACIArb 1987, FEng 1990; *Books* Welded Joint Design (1979, 2 edn 1987), A Guide to Designing Welds (1989); *Recreations* church organ playing, creative gardening; *Style*— John Hicks, Esq, FEng; ✉ 35 Boxworth Road, Elsworth, Cambridgeshire CB3 8JQ (☎ 01954 267320, fax 01954 267063)

HICKS, Prof (Ruth) Marian; OBE (1992); da of Joe Ridgway Handforth (d 1973), and Gladys, *née* Entwistle (d 1960); *b* 27 Feb 1932; *Educ* St Paul's Girls' Sch London (state scholarship, leaving exhibitioner), UCL (BSc, PhD), Middx Hosp Med Sch (DSc, MRCPath, FRCPath); *m* 1954, Anthony Hicks, s of William Rooke Hicks (d 1933); 1 s (Nicholas Rooke b 1958); *Career* MRC postgrad scholar 1953–56, lectr in biochemistry and ICI res fell Biochemistry Dept UCL 1956–59, prof of experimental pathology Middx Hosp Med Sch 1979–86 (lectr then reader in pathology 1959–79); Group R & D Centre United Biscuits (UK) Ltd: sci dir 1986–93, dir (Food Issues) 1993–94, conslt (Food Issues) 1994–; chm SW Thames RHA 1992–94, chm Berkshire Family Health Sevs Authy 1994–96; non-exec dir: Anglia and Oxford RHA 1994–96, Royal Berkshire & Battle Hospitals NHS Trust 1996–; chm British Assoc for Cancer Res 1979–81, pres Oncology Cncl RSM 1981–82, vice chm BNF Industl Scientists Ctee 1989–92; chm Food Res Ctee AFRC 1993–94; memb Cncl and scientific advsr Campden Food and Drink Research Assoc; memb: Food Advsy Ctee 1988–94, Priorities Bd MAFF and AFRC 1993–94, Stratgegy Bd and Cncl AFRC 1991–94, Cncl St George's Sch 1992–94, Med Advsy Ctee and Res Advsy Gp HEFCE, Cncl and Exec Bd Br Nutrition Fndn, Parly and Scientific Ctee, Supervisory Bd Brunel Inst of Bioengineering, BBSRC Food Directorate Mgmnt Ctee, Innovative Manufacturing Initiative (IMI) Mgmnt Ctee, NHS Advsy Ctee on Breast Cancer Screening, Cncl UCL; occasional external examiner MSc, PhD and DSc awards at various univs, author of numerous scientific pubns in refereed jls; fell UCL 1986; FRSA 1989, FIFST 1990–96; *Recreations* gardening; *Clubs* RSM, RSA; *Style*— Prof Marian Hicks, OBE; ✉ Wood End, Shirvell's Hill, Goring Heath, nr Reading, Berks RG8 7SP (☎ 01491 680227, fax 01491 682145); United Biscuits (UK) Ltd, Group Research and Development Centre, Lane End Road, Sands, High Wycombe, Bucks HP12 4JX (☎ 01494 463388, fax 01494 465996)

HICKS, Maj-Gen (William) Michael Ellis; CB (1983), OBE (1969); s of Gp Capt William Charles Hicks, AFC (d 1939), and Nellie Kilbourne Kay (d 1970); *b* 2 June 1928; *Educ* Eton, RMA Sandhurst; *m* 1950, Jean Hilary, da of Brig William Edmonstone Duncan, CVO, DSO, MC (d 1970); 3 s (William Hicks, *qv*, Peter, Alistair); *Career* Army Offr, cmmnd 1948, attended Staff Coll 1958; GSO1 MOI 1967–70, CO 1 Bn Coldstream Guards 1970–72, attended RCDS 1973, cmd 4 Guards Armd Bde 1974–75, BGS Trg HQ UKLF 1976–78, GOC NW Dist 1980–83, ret 1983; sec RCDS 1983–93; *Recreations* gardening; *Style*— Maj-Gen Michael Hicks, CB, OBE

HICKS, Michael Frank; s of Frank Henry Hicks (d 1985), and Annie Elizabeth Lydia, *née* Beeson (d 1988); *b* 11 March 1935; *Educ* Fairlop Secdy HS Hainault, Dane Secdy Modern Ilford; *m* 19 Sept 1959, Veronica Constance, da of Frederick Edwin Martin; 2 da (Corinne Veronica b 14 May 1962, Anne Christine b 15 April 1964); *Career* Nat Serv RAF 1953–55, serv Aden; stockbroker: HE Goodison 1948–56, Blount 1956–59; ptnr Simon and Coates 1959–80, equity ptnr Statham Duff Stoop 1980–86; dir: Prudential Bache Capital Funding 1986–89, Société Générale Strauss Turnbull Securities Ltd 1989–; *Recreations* tennis and walking; *Style*— Michael F Hicks, Esq; ✉ Spring Hill, Stoke by Nayland, Suffolk (☎ 01206 337327); Société Générale Strauss Turnbull Securities Ltd, Exchange House, Primrose St, Broadgate, London EC2A 2DD (☎ 0171 638 5699)

HICKS, Nicola Katherine; MBE (1995); da of Philip Lionel Shalto Hicks, of Radcot House Bampton Oxfordshire, and Jill Tweed; *b* 3 May 1960; *Educ* Frensham Heights Sch, Chelsea Sch of Art (BA), RCA (MA); *m* 1 (m dis); m 2, 28 Feb 1992, Daniel Flowers; 1 s (William Gabriel Sholto b 31 March 1992); *Career* artist; *Solo Exhibitions* incl: Angela Flowers Gallery London 1985 and 1986, Angela Flowers Co Cork 1986, Beaux Arts Gallery Bath 1987, Flowers East London 1988, 1989, 1992 and 1994, Tegnerforbundet Oslo Norway 1991, Fire and Brimstone (Flowers East and Watermans Art Centre Brentford) 1991, Peter Scott Gallery Univ of Lancaster 1993, Castlefield Gallery Manchester 1993; *Gp Exhibitions* incl: Christie's Inaugural Graduate Exhibition London 1982, Mixed Christmas Show (New Grafton Gallery) 1982, Current Issues (RCA London) 1982, Portland Clifftops Sculpture Park 1983, Sculptural Drawings (Ruskin Coll Oxford) 1983, Int Garden Festival Liverpool: Sculpture Garden 1984, Hayward Annual (Hayward Gallery London) 1985, Basel Art Fair Switzerland 1985 and 1986, '85 Show (Serpentine Gallery London) 1985, Opening Exhibition (Damon Brandt Gallery NY) 1985, Sixteen (Angela Flowers Gallery London) 1986, The Living Art Pavillion (The Ideal Home Exhibition London) 1986, Beaux Arts Summer Exhibition Bath 1986, Antithesis (Angela Flowers Gallery) 1986, Chicago Art Fair 1987 and 1988, The Scottish Gallery Edinburgh 1987, Art In The City (Lloyds Building London) 1987, Rocket 6–1 (installed at the Economist Building Piccadilly London) 1988, Hakone Open Air Museum 1988, Veksolund Udstilling For Sculptor Copenhagen 1988, Out of Clay (Manchester) 1988, Daley Hicks Jeffries Jones Kirby Lewis (Flowers East London) 1989, Los Angeles Art Fair 1990, Sculptors Drawings (Cleveland Bridge Gallery Bath) 1990, The Drawings Show (Thumb Gallery) 1990, Bryan Kneale's Choice (Dover Street Arts Club) 1990, The Discerning Eye (Mall Galleries) 1990, Inaugural Exhibition (Lannon Cole Gallery Chicago) 1991, Millfield British 20th Century Sculpture Exhibition 1992, RA Summer Exhibition 1993, New Grafton Gallery 1993, Beaux Arts Gallery Bath 1993, first RWA Open Sculpture Exhibition 1993 (Morris Singer Award), Norrkopings Museum Sweden 1993, Dialogue with the Other (Kunsthallen Brandts) 1993, Flowers East 1993–94; work in various collections incl: Contemporary Arts Soc, Chase Manhattan Bank, Castle Museum Norwich, Huddersfield Art Gall, Hakone Open Air Museum, Arthur Andersen; cmmn for monument in Battersea Park; artist in residence Brentwood HS; *Recreations* poker, backgammon, dice, dog and horse racing, travelling, searching for horned rhino on elephantback and white water surfing; *Clubs* Chelsea Arts; *Style*— Ms Nicola Hicks, MBE; ✉ c/o Flowers East, 199/205 Richmond Rd, Hackney, London E8 3NJ (☎ 0181 985 3333)

HICKS, Lady Pamela Carmen Louise; *née* Mountbatten; yr da of 1 Earl Mountbatten of Burma, KG, GCB, OM, GCSI, GCIE, GCVO, DSO, PC, FRS (assas 1979); sister of Countess Mountbatten of Burma, *qv*; *b* 19 April 1929; *m* 13 Jan 1960, David Nightingale Hicks, *qv*; 1 s, 2 da; *Career* bridesmaid to HRH The Princess Elizabeth at her marriage 1947; lady-in-waiting to HM The Queen on her tour of Aust and NZ 1953–54; patron The Leukaemia Care Soc; vice-pres SSAFA; pres King Edward VII British-German Fndn; memb Inst King Edward VII Hosp Midhurst; patron The Girls' Nautical Trg Corps 1955–79; pres: Royal London Soc for the Blind 1960–82, The Embroiderers' Guild 1970–80; govr United World Coll of the Atlantic 1970–91; *Style*— The Lady Pamela Hicks; ✉ Albany, Piccadilly, London W1V 9RP (☎ 0171 734 3183); The Grove, Brightwell Baldwin, Oxon OX9 5PF (☎ 01491 824555)

HICKS, Philip; s of Brig Philip Hugh Whitby Hicks, CBE, DSO, MC (d 1967), and Patty, *née* Fanshawe (d 1985); *b* 11 Oct 1928; *Educ* Winchester, RMA Sandhurst, Royal Acad Schs (Dip RAS); *m* 22 July 1952, Jill, da of Maj Jack Tweed (d 1979); 1 s (David b 1971), 1 da (Nicola b 1960); *Career* Irish Gds 1946–47, 2 Lt Royal Warwicks Regt 1948–49; pt/t teacher various art schs 1960–85, concentrated full time on painting 1986–; solo exhibitions incl: Camden Arts Centre 1971, Richard Demarco Gallery Edinburgh 1971, Robert Self Gallery London 1971, Imperial War Museum 1975, Galerie VFCU Antwerp 1977–79, Battersea Arts Centre 1977, Gallery 22 Dublin 1980, New Art Centre (London) 1980–82, Galleri Engstrom Stockholm 1985, Gallery 10 London 1986–91, Bohun Gall Henley 1986–90, Heffer Gallery Cambridge 1992, Courcoux and Courcoux Fine Art Salisbury 1992, David Messum Fine Art London 1996; mixed exhibitions incl: Tate Gallery London 1976, Mall Galleries London 1980, Israel Israel Museum Jerusalem 1980–81, Serpentine Gallery London 1982, Angela Flowers Gallery 1985, Art '89 London 1989; works in public collections incl: Tate Gallery, Comtemporary Art Soc, V & A, Imperial War Museum; Br Cncl award 1977; also performs professionally as a jazz pianist; chm and memb Cncl Artists Gen Benevolent Inst; *Recreations* music; *Clubs* Cheslea Arts, Arts; *Style*— Philip Hicks, Esq; ✉ Radcot House, Buckland Rd, Bampton, Oxford OX18 2AA (☎ 01993 850347, fax 01993 851733)

HICKS, Sir Robert Adrian; kt (1996), MP (C) Cornwall SE (majority 7,704); s of W H Hicks of Horrabridge, Devon; *b* 18 Jan 1938; *Educ* Queen Elizabeth GS, Univ Coll London, Exeter Univ; *m* 1, 1962 (m dis 1987), Maria, da of Robert Gwyther of Plympton, Devon; 2 da; m 2, 1991, Mrs Glenys Foote; *Career* nat vice chm Young Cons 1964–66, tech coll lectr 1964–70, Parly candidate (C) Aberavon 1966; MP (C): Bodmin 1970–74 and 1974–83, Cornwall SE 1983–; chm Horticultural Ctee 1971–73, asst govt whip 1973–74, memb Select Ctee on European Secdy Legislation 1973–; vice chm: Cons Pty Agric Ctee 1971–73 and 1974–81, Cons Pty European Affrs Ctee 1979–81; chm: Westcountry Cons Membs Ctee 1977–78 (sec 1970–73), UK branch Parly Assoc for Euro-Arab Co-operation 1983–, Cons Pty Agric Ctee 1988–90; vice chm Cons Pty Middle East Cncl 1992–96 (treas 1979–92), memb Speaker's Panel of Chairmen 1992–; Parly advsr: Br Hotels Restaurants and Caterers Assoc 1974–, Milk Mktg Bd 1985–; pres Plymouth Albion RFC 1991–96; *Recreations* cricket, golf, walking, gardening; *Clubs* MCC; *Style*— Sir Robert Hicks, MP; ✉ Burndoo, Luckett, Callington, Cornwall; House of Commons, London SW1A 0AA (☎ 0171 219 3000)

HICKS, Robin Edgcumbe; s of late Ronald Eric Edgcumbe Hicks, of Clifton, Bristol, and late Freddy Hicks; *b* 6 Dec 1942; *Educ* Bancrofts' Sch, Seale Hayne Coll (NDA, Dip Farm Mgmnt), Univ of Reading (DipAg extension); *m* 19 Sept 1970, Sue, da of Peter Dalton, of Downton, Salisbury, Wiltshire; 1 s (Robert b 1977), 1 da (Sarah b 1976); *Career* agric advsr Ministry of Agriculture Fisheries & Food 1966–68, prodr BBC 1968–77 (London, Norwich, Birmingham, Edinburgh), head of mktg and devpt RASE Stoneleigh 1977–79, head Network Radio South & West BBC Bristol 1979–88, chief exec RASE 1989–91 (chief exec designate 1988–89); dir; P & O Events Ltd 1992–, Royal Smithfield Show 1992–; former memb: Bristol & Weston Health Authy, SW Concerts Bd, Cncl The Radio Academy; former tstee: St George's Music Tst, Rural Housing Tst, Head Injury Recovery Tst; Freeman City of London 1979, Liveryman Worshipful Co of Drapers 1981; assoc fell Royal Agric Socs 1995; *Recreations* boats, gardening, motorbiking, family; *Clubs* Farmers'; *Style*— Robin Hicks, Esq; ✉ 271 Lauderdale Mansions, London W9 1LZ (☎ 0171 266 0405); P & O Events Ltd, Earls Court Exhibition Centre, Warwick Road, London SW5 9TA (☎ 0171 370 8224, fax 0171 370 8230)

HICKS, William David Anthony; QC (1995); s of Maj-Gen (William) Michael Ellis Hicks, *qv*, of Wiltshire, Jean Hillary, *née* Duncan; *b* 11 June 1951; *Educ* Eton, Magdalene Coll Cambridge (MA Economics); *m* 1982, Jennifer Caroline, da of Dr Louis Ross; 2 da (Julia Rebecca b 6 June 1986, Olivia Clare b 4 May 1988), 1 s (George David Alexander b 1 March 1990); *Career* called to the Bar Inner Temple 1975; *Recreations* tennis, fishing, skiing; *Clubs* Vanderbilt Racquets; *Style*— William Hicks, Esq, QC; ✉ 1 Serjeants' Inn, 4th Floor, Inner Temple, London EC4Y 1NH (☎ 0171 583 1355, fax 0171 583 1672)

HICKS BEACH, Hon David Seymour; yst s of 2 Earl St Aldwyn, PC, GBE, TD, JP, DL (d 1992); hp to bro, 3 Earl of St Aldwyn; *b* 1955; *Educ* Eton, Royal Agricultural Coll Cirencester; *m* 17 July 1993, Katrina Louise Susannah, da of Michael Henriques, of Winson Manor, Cirencester, Glos; 1 da (Lucy Susan b 31 Oct 1996); *Career* a page of honour to HM The Queen 1969–71, agriculture, corp entertainment, pet mail order catalogue business; *Recreations* natural history, greyhound racing, fishing, shooting, travel; *Clubs* Royal Agricultural Soc of England, Royal Geographical Soc, Pratt's; *Style*— The Hon David Hicks Beach; ✉ The Upper Mill, Coln St Aldwyns, Glos GL7 5AJ

HICKSON, Joan Bogle (Mrs Eric Butler); OBE (1987); da of Harold Alfred Squire Hickson, and Edith Mary, *née* Bogle; *b* 5 Aug 1906; *Educ* Castle Hall Sch Northampton, Castle Bar Sch London, Oldfeld Sch Swanage, RADA; *m* 29 Oct 1932, Eric Norman Butler, s of Thomas Harrison Butler (d 1944), of Hampton-in-Arden, Warwickshire; 1 s (Nicholas Andrew Mark b 24 May 1936), 1 da (Caroline Margaret Julia b 3 May 1939); *Career* actress, debut His Wife's Children 1927, first London appearance The Tragic Muse 1928; Hon MA Univ of Leicester 1988; *Theatre* appeared in numerous plays incl: Appointment with Death, See How They Run, The Guinea Pig, A Day in the Life of Joe Egg, Forget-me-not-Lane, Bedroom Farce Tony Award); *Television* numerous TV appearances incl adaptations of Agatha Christie novels in which she played Miss Marple 1984–92; *Films* incl: The Guinea Pig, The Magic Box, Seven Days to Noon; *Recreations* reading; *Clubs* New Cavendish; *Style*— Miss Joan Hickson, OBE; ✉ c/o Plunket Green Ltd, 21 Golden Green, London W1R 3PA (☎ 0171 434 3801, fax 0171 494 1547)

HICKSON, Peter Charles Fletcher; s of Geoffrey Fletcher Hickson (d 1978), of Cambridge, and Jane Margaret Amy, *née* Cazenove (d 1993); *b* 30 May 1945; *Educ* Uppingham Sch, Fitzwilliam Coll Cambridge (MA); *m* Rosemary, da of Hugh Dawson, of Newport, Gwent; 1 da (Sally b 1978), 3 s (Richard b 1979, David b 1981, James b 1983); *Career* articled clerk Chalmers Impey 1967–71, chief accountant Doulton Glass Industries 1971–78, fin dir Wimpey Asphalt 1978–80, fin dir Tarmac Building Products 1980–85, dep chief exec United Scientific Holdings 1986–89, fin dir MAI plc 1991–96, fin dir PowerGen plc 1996–; non-exec dir: Meridian Broadcasting 1991–95, Intrum Justitia NV 1993–, Anglia Television 1993–95, Lex Service plc 1994–; FCA 1970; *Recreations* cricket, squash, golf, music; *Clubs* United Oxford and Cambridge University, MCC, Royal Wimbledon Golf, Wimbledon Park Golf; *Style*— Peter Hickson, Esq;

✉ PowerGen plc, 53 New Broad Street, London EC2M 1JJ (☎ 0171 826 2727, fax 0171 826 2894)

HIDALGO, Alexander; s of Alexander Hidalgo, of Moca, Puerto Rico, and Estebania Hidalgo; *b* 31 Dec 1938; *Educ* Brooklyn Tech HS New York, Brooklyn Coll Univ of the City of New York (BA, academic honour roll), Queen's Univ Belfast; *m* 27 Nov 1973, June Anne, da of Edward Arnold Davies (d 1964); 1 da (Theodora Juana Alexandra b 23 Dec 1972); *Career* conservator Royal Albert Memorial Museums Exeter 1969–72, curator Kirkaldy Museums & Art Gallery Fife 1972–75, dep dir Aberdeen Art Gallery & Museums 1975–89, head of Arts & Museums Servs Aberdeen City Cncl 1989–; memb Br Cactus and Succulent Soc; FSA Scot 1973, memb ICOM 1978, MIMgt 1989, FMA 1992 (AMA 1969); *Style*— Alexander Hidalgo, Esq; ✉ Head of Arts & Museums Services, City Arts & Recreation Department, Aberdeen City Council, Schoolhill, Aberdeen AB9 1FQ (☎ 01224 646333, fax 01224 632133)

HIDE, Prof Raymond; CBE (1989); s of Stephen Hide (d 1940), and Rose Edna, *née* Cartlidge (later Mrs Thomas Leonard, d 1995); *b* 17 May 1929; *Educ* Percy Jackson GS, Univ of Manchester (BSc), Univ of Cambridge (PhD, ScD); *m* 1958, (Phyllis) Ann, da of Gerald James William Licence (d 1949), and Margaret, *née* Davis; 1 s (Stephen), 2 da (Julia, Kathryn); *Career* res assoc in astrophysics Univ of Chicago 1953–54, sr res fell Gen Physics Div AERE Harwell 1954–57, lectr in physics Univ of Durham 1957–61, prof of geophysics and physics MIT 1961–67, head Geophysical Fluid Dynamics Laboratory UK Meteorological Office 1967–90, dir Robert Hooke Inst and visiting prof of physics Univ of Oxford 1990–92, research prof Dept of Physics and Earth Scis Univ of Oxford 1992–94 (emeritus prof 1994–); visiting prof: Dept of Meteorology Univ of Reading 1970–90, Dept of Mathematics UCL 1970–82, Depts of Earth Scis and Maths Univ of Leeds; Adrian fell Univ of Leicester 1980–83 (Hon DSc 1985), fell Jesus Coll Oxford 1983–, Gresham prof of astronomy Gresham Coll City of London 1985–90, hon sr res fell Inst of Oceanographic Scis Deacon Laboratory 1990–, hon scientist Rutherford Appleton Lab 1992–; author of numerous scientific papers in learned jls; pres: RMS 1975–76 (hon fell 1989), Euro Geophysical Soc 1982–84 (hon fell 1988), RAS 1983–85; Charles Chree medal and prize Inst of Physics 1974, Holweck medal and prize Société Française de Physique and Inst of Physics 1982, Gold medal Royal Astronomical Soc 1989; Hon DSc: Univ of Leicester 1985, UMIST 1994, Paris 1995; fell American Acad of Arts and Scis 1964, FRS 1971, memb: Academia Europaea 1988, Pontifical Acad of Scis 1996; *Style*— Prof Raymond Hide, CBE, FRS; ✉ Department of Physics (Atmospheric, Oceanic and Planetary Physics), Clarendon Lab, Parks Road, Oxford OX1 3PU (☎ 01865 272084, fax 01865 272924)

HIDER, (Kenneth) Mark; s of Maj Kenneth George Hider, RA, of Hampstead, London, and Marian, *née* Richards; *b* 18 Sept 1953; *Educ* Sir William Borlase's Sch Marlow, Trinity Coll Oxford (MA); *m* 20 June 1981, Nicola Louise, da of John Haigh; 3 s (Tom, Ben, George); *Career* former media res controller Scottish Television, subsequently analyst rising to a sr planner Masius advtg; Ogilvy & Mather advtg: initially sr planner, estab Strategic Analysis Unit, planning dir 1988–91, business devpt dir 1991–92, worldwide dir of strategy 1992–; memb: Mktg Soc, Market Res Soc; MIPA; *Recreations* cricket, soccer, theatre, walking the dog, supporting Manchester United FC, travel; *Style*— Mark Hider, Esq; ✉ Ogilvy & Mather Worldwide, 10 Cabot Square, Canary Wharf, London E14 4QB (☎ 0171 345 3180, fax 0171 345 9001, mobile 0374 809289)

HIGGIN, Capt William Bendyshe; s of Maj Walter Wynnefield Higgin, DL (d 1971), of Cheshire, and Olive, *née* Earle (d 1978); *b* 14 Feb 1922; *Educ* Hawtreys, Gresham's Sch Holt, Royal Agric Coll; *m* 26 March 1947, Mary Patricia, da of Capt George Lee-Morris, RNVR (d 1983), of Cheshire; 2 s (Mark b 1954, Jonathan b 1956), 1 da (Gail b 1947); *Career* WWII co cdr 5/10 Baluch Regt IA 1941, ADC to GOC N India 1943–44, invalided out 1946, Hon Adm Nebraskan Navy 1962; landowner in Clwyd, Cheshire and Anglesey; *Recreations* game shooting, gardening, cricket; *Clubs* Sind, Shropshire; *Style*— Capt William Higgin; ✉ Melus Manaw, Bodedern, Anglesey LL65 3UN

HIGGINS, Dr Andrew James; s of Edward James Higgins (d 1966), and Gabrielle Joy, da of Sir John Kelland; *b* 7 Dec 1948; *Educ* St Michael's Coll Leeds, RVC, Univ of London (BVetMed, PhD), Centre for Tropical Veterinary Med Univ of Edinburgh (MSc); *m* 19 Dec 1981, Nicola Lynn, da of Peter Rex Eliot (d 1980); 1 s (Benjamin b 1982), 3 da (Amelia b 1984, Joanna b 1986, Venetia b 1993); *Career* cmmnd RAVC 1973, Capt, served Dhofar War 1974; veterinary offr HM The Sultan of Oman 1975–76, vet advsr The Wellcome Fndn 1977–82, conslt Food and Agric Orgn of the UN 1981–, dir Animal Health Tst 1988–; memb Cncl Soc for the Protection of Animals in N Africa (vice chm 1987–89); memb: Conservation & Welfare and Ethics Ctee Zoological Soc of London 1987–, Cncl Br Equine Vet Assoc 1984– (hon sec 1984–88); ed British Veterinary Journal 1991– (dep ed 1990–91), memb Advsy Bd Equine Veterinary Journal; hon vet advsr to Jockey Club 1988–, hon scientific advsr Fédération Equestre Internationale 1991–; winner Equine Veterinary Journal Open Award 1986, Ciba-Geigy prize for res in animal health 1985, awarded Univ of London Laurel 1971; Liveryman Worshipful Co of Farriers; MRCVS, FIBiol; *Books* An Anatomy of Veterinary Europe (contrib, 1972), The Camel in Health and Disease (ed and contrib, 1986), Proceedings of the First International Council Conference Dublin (co-ed and contrib, 1992), The Equine Manual (ed, 1995); papers in scientific and general pubns and communications to learned societies; *Recreations* skiing, riding, opera, camels; *Clubs* Buck's; *Style*— Dr Andrew Higgins; ✉ Animal Health Trust, PO Box 5, Newmarket, Suffolk CB8 7DW (☎ 01638 661111, fax 01638 665789)

HIGGINS, Prof (John) Christopher; s of Sidney James Higgins (d 1958), of Surbiton, Surrey, and Margaret Eileen, *née* Dealtrey (d 1973); *b* 9 July 1932; *Educ* King George V Sch Southport, Gonville and Caius Coll Cambridge (BA, MA), Bedford Coll London (MSc), Birkbeck Coll London (BSc), Univ of Bradford (PhD); *m* 24 Sept 1960, Margaret Edna, da of William John Howells, of Llandaff, Cardiff; 3 s (Peter John b 1962, David Richard b 1964, Mark Robert b 1969); *Career* short serv cmmn RAF 1953–56; conslt Metra Gp 1964–67, dir of econ planning and res IPC Newspapers Ltd 1967–70, prof of mgmnt sci 1970–89, dir Mgmnt Centre Univ of Bradford 1972–89, non-exec dir Amos Hinton & Sons plc 1980–84, visiting prof Open Univ 1991–; tstee Wool Fndn; memb: DTI Regnl Industl Devpt Bd 1988–91, CS Scientific Advsrs Branch Air Miny 1962–64, various govt ctees 1976–; FIEE 1981, CBIM 1982; *Books* Last Two Strategic and Operational Planning Systems, Computer Based Planning Systems; *Recreations* music, fell walking, bridge; *Clubs* Royal Over-Seas League; *Style*— Prof Christopher Higgins; ✉ 36 Station Rd, Baildon, Shipley, W Yorks (☎ 01274 592836); Univ of Bradford, Richmond Rd, Bradford BD7 1DP (☎ 01274 733466)

HIGGINS, Prof Christopher Francis; s of Prof Philip John Higgins, of Durham, and Betty Ann, *née* Edmonds; *b* 24 June 1955; *Educ* Raynes Park Grammar/Comp Sch, Univ of Durham (scholar, BSc, PhD, W E Foster prize), Royal Coll of Music (exhibitioner, Hugh Bean prize), Univ of Oxford (MA); *m* 1, 1978 (m dis), Elizabeth Mary Joy; 2 da (Alison Elizabeth b 1982, Julia Katherine b 1984); m 2, 1994, Suzanne, *née* Wilson; 3 da (Katherine Ann b 1989, Jennifer Dorothy b 1992, Emily Frances b 1995); *Career* SERC/NATO fell Univ of California Berkeley 1979–81, prof of molecular genetics Univ of Dundee 1988–89 (lectr 1981–87, reader 1987–88); Univ of Oxford: princ scientist Imperial Cancer Res Fund 1989–93, fell Keble Coll 1989–93, dep dir Inst of Molecular Med 1989–93, prof and head Dept of Clinical Biochemistry 1993–, fell Hertford Coll 1993–; res fell Lister Inst 1983–89, Howard Hughes int res scholar 1993; Fleming award Soc for General Microbiology 1987, CIBA medal and prize Biochemical Soc 1994; fell Euro Molecular Biology Orgn 1989; FRSE 1990; *Recreations* science, music; *Style*— Prof Christopher Higgins, FRSE; ✉ Nuffield Department of Clinical Biology, University of Oxford, John Radcliffe Hospital, Oxford OX3 9DU (☎ 01865 222423, fax 01865 222431)

HIGGINS, Sir Christopher Thomas; kt (1977); s of Thomas Higgins (d 1964), and Florence Maud, *née* Wilkinson (d 1966); *b* 14 Jan 1914; *Educ* West Kensington Central Sch, Univ of London; *m* 1936, Constance Joan, da of Walter Herbert Beck (d 1951); 1 s (Geoffrey b 1944), 1 da (Jacqueline b 1939); *Career* served WWII Lt RA; memb: Acton Borough Cncl 1945–64 (mayor 1957), Middx Co Cncl 1952–55 and 1958–64, GLC 1964–67, Hemel Hempstead Devpt Corp 1947–52, Bracknell Devpt Corp 1965–68; chm: Peterborough Devpt Corp 1968–81, North Thames Gas Consumers' Cncl 1969–79; *Style*— Sir Christopher Higgins; ✉ 2 North Lodge, Bicester House, King's End, Bicester, Oxon OX6 7HZ (☎ 01869 241982)

HIGGINS, Clare Frances Elizabeth; da of James Stephen Higgins, and Paula Cecilia, *née* Murphy; *Educ* St Philomena's Convent Sch Derbyshire, Ecclesbourne Sch Derbyshire, LAMDA; *Career* actress; *Theatre* Royal Exchange: Isabella in Measure for Measure, Alexis in Rollo, Judith in Blood Black and Gold, The Deep Man; Greenwich: Kay in Time and the Conways, Julie in The Rivals, Stella in A Street Car Named Desire; RSC: Titania in A Midsummers Night's Dream 1989–90, Gertrude in Hamlet 1989–90, Cleopatra in Antony and Cleopatra 1992–93; RNT: Lili Brik in The Futurists 1986, Katherine in The Secret Rapture 1988, Queen Elizabeth in Richard III 1990–91, Regan in King Lear 1990–91, Amelia in Napoli Milionaria 1991, Lyndsey Fontaine in The Absence of War 1993–94, Princess Kosmanopolis in Sweet Bird of Youth 1995 (Best Actress: Olivier Award, Critics' Circle Award and Time Out Reader's Award 1995), Martha Dobie in The Children's Hour 1995 (Critics' Circle Best Actress Award 1995); other roles incl: A View from the Bridge (Harrogate), The White Devil (Oxford Playhouse), Beethoven's Tenth (Vaudeville), Jenkin's Ear (Royal Court), The Ride Down Mt Morgan (Wyndhams, world premiere); *Television* incl: Pride and Prejudice, Unity, Byron, The Concubine, Mitch, The Citadel, Cover Her Face, Foreign Body, Beautiful Lies, After the War, Downtown Lagos, Boon, Inspector Alleyn, Circle of Deceit, Men of the Month, Absence of War, Kavanagh QC, Silent Witness; *Films* incl: 1919, Hellraiser, Hellbound, The Fruit Machine, Bad Behaviour, Let it Come Down 1995, Small Faces 1996; *Recreations* yoga, being in the country, reading, theatre-going, seeing friends, cats; *Style*— Miss Clare Higgins; ✉ c/o Pippa Markham, Markham & Froggatt Ltd, Julian House, 4 Windmill Street, London W1P 1HF (☎ 0171 636 4412, fax 0171 637 5233)

HIGGINS, John Andrew; s of George Henry Higgins, of 80 Elphinstone Rd, Hastings, Sussex, and Mildred Maud, *née* Ullmer (d 1985); *b* 19 Feb 1940; *m* 18 Sept 1965, Susan Jennifer, da of George Alfred Mathis (d 1964); 1 s (Simon David b 1966); *Career* Exchequer and Audit Dept: asst auditor 1958, auditor 1968, sr auditor 1971, chief auditor 1977, dep dir 1981; Office of the Auditor Gen of Canada 1983–84; asst auditor gen National Audit Office 1988– (dir 1984); treas Crawley and Horsham Organists' Assoc; ARCO 1988; *Recreations* golf, bridge, classical organ playing, supporting Crystal Palace; *Clubs* Ifield Golf and Country; *Style*— John Higgins, Esq; ✉ Zaria, 65 Milton Mount Avenue, Pound Hill, Crawley, Sussex RH10 3DP (☎ 01293 417075); National Audit Office, Buckingham Palace Road, London SW1W 9SP (☎ 0171 798 7380, fax 0171 828 3774)

HIGGINS, John Dalby; s of Frank Edward John Higgins (d 1991), and Edith Florence, *née* Dalby (d 1986); *b* 7 Jan 1934; *Educ* KCS Wimbledon, Worcester Coll Oxford (BA); *m* 3 Sept 1977, Linda Irene, da of Edward Sidney Christmas (d 1983); *Career* Nat Serv PO RAF; Financial Times: features ed 1962–64, arts ed 1963–69, literary ed 1966–69; The Times: arts ed 1970–88, chief opera critic 1988–92, obituaries ed 1988–92; Royal Literary Fund: memb Ctee 1969–, registrar 1993–; BP Special Award for Services to Arts Journalism 1992, Royal Opera House Medal for Distiguished Services to Opera 1992; Ehrenkreuz für Kunst und Wissenschaft (First Class) Austria 1977, Goldene Verdienstzeichen des Landes Salzburg Austria 1985, Officier de L'Ordre des Arts et des Lettres France 1989; *Books* Travels in the Balkans (1970), The Making of An Opera (1977), Glyndebourne: A Celebration (ed, 1984), British Theatre Design 1978–88 (contrib, 1989); *Recreations* claret, Chelsea FC; *Clubs* Garrick; *Style*— John Higgins, Esq; ✉ 47 Thornhill Square, London N1 1BE (☎ and fax 0171 607 3217)

HIGGINS, Very Rev Dr Michael John; s of Claud John Higgins (d 1984), of Wells, Somerset, and Elsie, *née* Howarth (d 1986); *b* 31 Dec 1935; *Educ* The GS Whitchurch Cardiff, Univ of Birmingham (LLB), Gonville and Caius Coll Cambridge (LLB, PhD, Yorke univ prize), Harvard Univ, Ridley Hall Cambridge; *m* 24 July 1976, Margaret Beryl, *née* Stringer; 1 da (Gabrielle Margaret b 27 Feb 1978); *Career* Choate fell Harvard Univ and tutor in law Winthrop Coll Harvard 1959–60, tutor in law Gonville & Caius and Clare Colls Cambridge 1958–59 and 1960–61, lectr in law Univ of Birmingham 1961–63 (memb Faculty Bd/examiner), Ridley Hall 1963–65, ordained deacon and priest 1965, curate of Ormskirk PC (Dio of Liverpool) 1965–68, selection sec Advsy Cncl for the Churches' Miny Church House Westminster 1968–74, non-stipendiary priest St Mark's Marylebone (Dio of London) 1968–74 (in-charge 1973–74), vicar of Frome and priest-in-charge of Woodlands (Dio of Bath and Wells) 1974–80, rector of Preston and of Preston Town Centre Team Miny (Dio of Blackburn) 1980–91, dean of Ely 1991–; *Publications* Specialised Miny (1972), The Vicar's House (1986); articles in professional legal periodicals; *Style*— The Very Rev the Dean of Ely; ✉ The Deanery, Ely, Cambridgeshire CB7 4DN (☎ 01353 662432)

HIGGINS, Prof Peter Matthew; OBE (1986); s of Peter Joseph Higgins (d 1952), of Stamford Hill, London, and Margaret, *née* De Lacey (d 1981); *b* 18 June 1923; *Educ* St Ignatius Coll London, UCL, UCH (MB BS); *m* 27 Sept 1952, Jean Margaret Lindsay, da of Capt Dr John Currie, DSO (d 1932), of Darlington; 3 s (Nicholas b 1954, Anthony b 1956, David b 1958), 1 da (Jane b 1959); *Career* Capt RAMC 1948–49; asst med registrar UCH (house physician med unit 1947 and 1950, res med offr 1951–52); princ in gen practice: Rugeley Staffs 1954–65, Castle Vale Birmingham 1966–67, Thamesmead London 1968–88; prof in gen practice Guy's Hosp Med Sch 1974–88 (sr lectr 1968–73); vice chm SE Thames RHA 1976–92 (memb 1974–92); chm: Thamesmead Family Serv Unit 1983–91, Kent Family Health Servs Authy 1990–92, Inquiry into A & E Dept King's Coll Hosp 1992, Review (into emergency admission arrangements) Ealing Hosp 1994, Nurse Practitioner Project Steering Ctee 1992–94; memb: Attendance Allowance Bd 1971–74, Standing Med Advsy Ctee DHSS 1970–74, Nat Cncl of Family Serv Units 1983–95 (memb Nat Exec 1991–95), London Health Partnership 1994–; tstee: Thamesmead Community Assoc, Tst Thamesmead; formerly vice chm of govrs Linacre Centre for Study of Med Ethics; memb Court Univ of Kent 1979–; FRSM 1950, FRCP, FRCGP; *Recreations* reading, music; *Style*— Prof Peter Higgins, OBE; ✉ Wallings, Heathfield Lane, Chislehurst, Kent BR7 6AH (☎ 0181 467 2756)

HIGGINS, Rodney Michael; s of Ronald George Platten Higgins (d 1952), and Mina Emily, *née* Botterill (d 1993); *b* 24 Oct 1927; *Educ* Hurstpierpoint Coll, Univ of Durham (BSc); *m* (Lilian) Joyce, da of late Thomas Bookless (d 1956); 1 s (Michael), 3 da (Lesley, Frances, Nicola); *Career* RE 1946–50; engr; designer and estimator British Reinforced Concrete 1952–54, designer Clarke Nichols & Marcel Bristol 1954–55, Kellogg International Corporation 1955–56, in private practice London 1958–64; princ: Cooper Higgins & Ptnrs Newcastle 1964–76, RM Higgins Associates 1976–91, Higgins RTJ 1992–95, Higgins-WSP 1995–; FRSA 1960, FIStructE 1966, MConsE 1966; *Recreations* industrial archaeology, folklore traditions of wild flowers, genealogy, local history; *Style*— Rodney Higgins, Esq; ✉ Newsteads, Causey Hill, Hexham, Northumberland

NE46 2DN (☎ 01434 602941); Higgins-WSP, Lakeside Court, Team Valley, Gateshead NE11 0NL (☎ 0191 491 5700)

HIGGINS, HE Judge; Dame Rosalyn; DBE (1995), QC (1986); da of Lewis Cohen, and Fay, *née* Inberg; *b* 2 June 1937; *Educ* Burlington GS London, Girton Coll Cambridge (Minor and Major scholar, Campbell scholar, Bryce-Tebbs scholar, BA, MA, LLB, Montefiore award), Yale (JSD); *m* 1961, Rt Hon Sir Terence Higgins, KBE, DL, MP, *qv*; 1 s, 1 da; *Career* UK intern Office of Legal Affairs UN 1958, Cwlth Fund fell 1959, visiting fell Brooking's Inst Washington DC 1960, jr fell in int studies LSE 1961–63, staff specialist in int law RIIA 1963–74, visiting lectr in law Yale Law Sch 1966 and 1975, visiting fell LSE 1974–78; visiting prof of law: Stanford Law Sch 1975, Yale Law Sch 1977; prof of int law: Univ of Kent Canterbury 1978–81, Univ of London 1981–95; judge Int Ct of Justice 1995–; bencher Inner Temple 1989; memb: UN Ctee on Human Rights 1984–, Gen Course in Public Int Law Hague Acad of Int Law 1991, Advsy Cncl British Inst of Int and Comparative Law; guest lectr at numerous univs in Europe and America, memb Bd of Eds American Jl of Int Law 1975–85; lectr for HM Govt on variety of int law matters; former vice pres American Soc Int Law 1972–74 (former memb Exec Cncl); memb: Energy Law Ctee Int Bar Assoc, Int Law Assoc; hon life memb American Soc of Int Law, hon vice pres American Soc of Int Law; memb Institut de Droit International 1991 (assoc 1987); Hon Doctorate: Univ of Paris 1980, Univ of Dundee 1992, Univ of Durham 1995, Univ of London 1995, Univ of Cambridge 1996, Univ of Kent 1996, Univ of Sussex 1996; Ordre des Palmes Académiques; *Books* The Development of International Law Through the Political Organs of the United Nations (1963), Conflict of Interests: International Law in a Divided World (1965), The Administration of the United Kingdom Foreign Policy Through the United Nations (1966), UN Peacekeeping: Documents and Commentary (Vol I ME 1969, Vol II Asia 1970, Vol III Africa 1980, Vol IV Europe 1981), Law in Movement-Essays in Memory of John McMahon (jt ed with James Fawcett, 1974), The Taking of Property by the State (1983), International Law and the Avoidance, Containment and Resolution of Disputes (General Course on Public International Law), Vol 230 Recueil des cours (Martinus Nijhoff, 1991), Problems and Process: International Law and How We Use It (1994); author of numerous articles for law jls and jls of int relations; *Recreations* golf, cooking, eating; *Style—* HE Judge Rosalyn Higgins, DBE, QC; ✉ International Court of Justice, Peace Palace, The Hague 2517 KJ, Netherlands

HIGGINS, Stuart James; *b* 26 April 1956; *m* Jennifer; 1 da (Katharine), 1 s (Robert); *Career* The Sun: joined as district reporter Bristol 1979, subsequently dep then exec news ed, dep ed 1991–Dec 1993; actg ed News of the World Dec 1993–Jan 1994, ed The Sun 1994–; Scoop of the Year 1995: What the Papers Say, London Press Club; *Style—* Stuart Higgins, Esq; ✉ The Sun, 1 Virginia Street, London E1 9XP (☎ 0171 782 4001, fax 0171 782 4095)

HIGGINS, Rt Hon Sir Terence Langley; PC (1979), KBE (1993), DL (W Sussex 1988), MP (Cons) Worthing (majority 16,533); s of Reginald Higgins; *b* 18 Jan 1928; *Educ* Alleyn's Sch Dulwich, Gonville and Caius Coll Cambridge (MA); *m* 1961, HE Judge Rosalyn Higgins, DBE, QC, *qv*, *née* Cohen; 1 s, 1 da; *Career* NZ Shipping Co 1948–55, lectr in econ principles Yale Univ 1958–59, economist Unilever 1959–64; MP (C) Worthing 1964–; Min of State Treasy 1970–72, fin sec to Treasy 1972–74; oppn spokesman: on Treasy and Econ Affrs 1966–70 and 1974, on Trade 1974–76; chm: Cons Parly Sports Ctee 1979–81, Cons Parly Tport Ctee 1979–90, House of Commons Liaison Ctee 1983–, Treasy and Civil Serv Select Ctee 1983–91 (memb 1980–91); memb: Public Accounts Cmmn 1983–, Cncl Inst of Advanced Motorists; govr: Dulwich Coll 1978–, Alleyns Sch 1995–; memb Cncl: NIESR 1989–, Policy Studies Inst 1988–95; tstee Indust and Parly Tst 1987–91; dir: Warne Wright Group 1976–84, Lex Service Group 1980–92, First Choice Holidays plc (formerly Owners Abroad Group plc) 1991–; memb Br Olympic Athletics Team 1948 and 1952, pres Cambridge Union Soc 1958; *Style—* The Rt Hon Sir Terence Higgins, KBE, DL, MP; ✉ House of Commons, London SW1A 0AA

HIGGINS, Rear Adm William Alleyne; CB (1985), CBE (1980); s of Cdr Henry Gray Higgins, DSO, RN (d 1977), of Salisbury, and Lilian Anne, *née* Leete (d 1980); *b* 18 May 1928; *Educ* Wellington; *m* 1963, Wiltraud, da of Josef Hiebaum (d 1968), of Innsbruck, Austria; 2 s (Charles, David), 1 da (Selina); *Career* joined RN 1945, Rear Adm 1982, Last Flag Offr Medway and Port Adm Chatham 1982–83, dir gen Naval Personal Servs 1983–86, sec Defence Press and Bdcasting Ctee 1986–92; *Recreations* skiing, hill walking; *Style—* Rear Adm William Higgins, CB, CBE

HIGGINSON, Sir Gordon Robert; kt (1992); *b* 8 Nov 1929; *Educ* Univ of Leeds (BSc, PhD); *m* 1954, Marjorie Forbes, *née* Rannie (d 1996); 3 s (James, Simon, John), 2 da (Jill, Catherine); *Career* Miny of Supply 1953–56; lectr in mechanical engrg Univ of Leeds 1956–62, assoc prof and head Materials Branch Royal Military Coll of Science Shrivenham 1962–65, prof of engrg Univ of Durham 1965–85, dean Faculty of Science Univ of Durham 1972–75, vice-chllr Univ of Southampton 1985–94; chm: A-Level Ctee 1987–88, Engrg Bd SERC 1989–94, Clinical Standards Advsy Gp Dept of Health 1991–96, Steering Ctee Interdisciplinary Res Centre in Biomedical Materials (IRC) 1992–96, Educn Ctee Royal Acad of Engrg; memb Engrg Cncl 1986–92, fndr memb Planning Ctee and Cncl Hong Kong Univ of Sci and Technol 1986–95; non-exec dir: Rolls-Royce plc 1988–, British Maritime Technology Ltd 1992–, Pirelli General plc 1995–; Hon DSc: Univ of Durham 1991, Univ of Southampton 1995, Univ of Bournemouth 1996; Hon DEng Univ of Portsmouth 1993, Hon LLD Univ of Leeds 1994; Hon FRCP; FIMechE, FICE, FEng 1991; *Style—* Sir Gordon Higginson, FEng; ✉ 29 Oak Vale, West End, Southampton SO30 3SE (☎ 01703 470837)

HIGGINSON, John Sydney; CBE (1962, OBE (Mil) 1949), JP (Belfast 1948, Co Down 1974), DL (Co Down 1969); s of John Higginson (d 1948), of Glenmakeiran, Co Down, and Margaret, *née* Black (d 1975); *b* 17 Dec 1909; *Educ* Campbell, Greenmount Agric Coll; *Career* RAF Regt Armd Cars 1940–46 (despatches), raised and cmd No 2502 (Ulster) Sqdn RAF Regt 1948–52, Wing Cdr RAFVR; chm John Higginson & Co Ltd 1948–69, Hon ADC to successive Govrs of NI (Earl Granville, Lord Wakehurst, Lord Erskine of Rerrick, Lord Grey of Naunton) 1952–75; fndr Manor St Boys' Club Belfast; Youth Ctee Miny of Educn: memb 1949, vice chm 1951, chm 1952–61; chm NI Youth & Sports Cncl 1962–65; fndr memb and chm NI Branch RAF Benevolent Fund 1948–79, fndr Outward Bound Tst NI 1952, rural dist cncllr 1967–73, reserve constable RUC 1972–75; High Sheriff of Co Down 1972; parochial nominator, sch govr; Hon MA Queen's Univ of Belfast; *Books* Thoughts on Leadership (1948); *Recreations* fishing, gardening; *Clubs* Brooks's; *Style—* John Higginson, Esq, CBE, JP, DL; ✉ Ballyward Lodge, Ballyward, Co Down, N Ireland BT31 9PP (☎ 0182 065 0225)

HIGGS, Air Vice-Marshal Barry; CBE (1981); s of Percy Harold Higgs (d 1973), of Hitcham, Ipswich, Suffolk, and Ethel Eliza (d 1994), *née* Elliot; *b* 22 Aug 1934; *Educ* Finchley Co GS; *m* 30 March 1957, Sylvia May, da of Harry Wilks; 2 s (David Stanford b 1958, Andrew Barry b 1959); *Career* 1955–70 served with Sqdn nos: 207, 115, 138, 49, 51; RAF Staff Coll 1968, Directorate of Forward Policy RAF 1971–73, Nat Def Coll 1974, cmd 39 (PR) Sqdn 1975–77, Asst Dir of Def Policy 1978–79, cmd RAF Finningley 1979–81, Royal Coll of Def Studies 1982, Dep Dir of Intelligence 1983–85, Asst Chief of Def Staff (overseas) 1985–87; dir gen Fertiliser Mfrs Assoc 1987–; *Recreations* sailing (cruising), bridge, gardening, theatre; *Clubs* RAF, Farmers; *Style—* Air Vice-Marshal Barry Higgs, CBE; ✉ 33 Parsonage St, Cambridge CB5 8DN (☎ 01223 369062; FMA, Greenhill House, Thorpe Road, Peterborough PE3 6GF (☎ 01733 331303, fax 01733 333617)

HIGGS, Brian James; QC (1974); s of James Percival Higgs (d 1984), of Brentwood, and Kathleen Anne, *née* Sullivan (d 1993); *b* 24 Feb 1930; *Educ* Wrekin Coll, Univ of London; *m* 1, 1953 (m dis), Jean Cameron Dumerton; 2 s (Jeremy b 1953, Jonathan b 1963), 3 da (Antonia b 1955, Nicola b 1962, Juliet b 1969); m 2, Vivienne Mary, da of Vivian Oliver Johnson, of Essex; 1 s (Julian b 1982); *Career* cmmnd RA, served 1948–50; called to the Bar Gray's Inn 1955, bencher 1986, recorder of the Crown Ct 1974–, head of chambers; *Recreations* gardening, golf, wine, chess, bridge; *Clubs* Thorndon Park Golf; *Style—* Brian Higgs, Esq, QC; ✉ 5 Paper Buildings, Temple, London EC4 (☎ 0171 353 5638)

HIGGS, Derek Alan; s of Alan Edward Higgs (d 1979), and Freda Gwendoline, *née* Hope (d 1984); *b* 3 April 1944; *Educ* Solihull Sch, Univ of Bristol (BA); *m* 1970, Julia Mary, da of Robert T Arguile, of Leics; 2 s (Oliver b 1975, Rowley b 1980), 1 da (Josephine b 1976); *Career* former chm S G Warburg & Co Ltd, former UK country head SBC Warburg; chm Prudential Portfolio Managers and Main Bd dir Prudential Corporation plc Feb 1996–; memb: City Arts Tst Bd 1995–, Bd Coventry City FC 1996–, Cncl Fin Reporting Cncl 1996–; FCA; *Style—* Derek Higgs, Esq; ✉ 41 Upper Addison Gardens, London W14 8AJ; The Prudential Corporation plc, 142 Holborn Bars, London EC1N 2NH (☎ 0171 405 9222, fax 0171 548 3802)

HIGGS, Prof Roger Hubert; MBE (1987); s of Rt Rev Hubert Lawrence Higgs, Bishop of Hull (d 1991), and Elizabeth Higgs, of Chediston, Suffolk; *b* 10 Dec 1943; *Educ* Marlborough (fndn scholar), Christ's Coll Cambridge (Classics and Tancred scholar, MA, MB BChir, pres Jr Common Room, Coll 1st VIII Boat), Westminster Med Sch (Hart prize); *m* 9 Jan 1971, Susan, da of Prof Tom Hewer, and Anne Hewer, of Vine House, Henbury, Bristol; 1 s (Ben b 18 Dec 1971), 1 da (Jessie b 2 July 1975); *Career* VSO Starehe Boys' Centre Nairobi Kenya 1961–62; house offr posts: Westminster Hosp 1969–70, W Middx Hosp 1970, Whittington Hosp 1970–71; resident med offr Whittington Hosp 1971–72, med registrar St George's Hosp 1972–74, gen practice trainee Dr McEwan and Partners 1974–75, currently princ in gen practice partnership Drs Higgs, Haigh, Mackay, Dale and Herzmark Walworth London (founded as solo practice 1975); ldr Lambeth Community Care Centre Devpt Gp 1979–85; King's Coll Sch of Med: lectr in gen practice 1978–81, sr lectr and head of dept 1981–89, chair Dept of Gen Practice and Primary Care 1989–; fndr Jl of Med Ethics and ed Case Conference 1974–96; memb Worshipul Soc of Apothecaries 1978; FRCGP 1986, FRCP 1993; memb: Lab Pty, CND; *Books* In That Case (with Alastair Campbell, 1982), A Case Study in Developing Primary Care: The Camberwell Report (1991), Mental Health and Primary Care: A Changing Agenda (1993), Medical Ethics in General Practice, Dictionary of Medical Ethics; *Recreations* playing oboe, planting trees, listening to classical music and jazz; *Style—* Prof Roger Higgs, MBE; ✉ Department of General Practice and Primary Care, King's College School of Medicine, Bessemer Road, London SE5 9PJ (☎ 0171 346 3016, fax 0171 737 3556)

HIGHAM, Geoffrey Arthur; s of late Arthur Higham, and late Elsie Higham; *b* 17 April 1927; *Educ* King Williams Coll Isle of Man, St Catharine's Coll Cambridge (MA); *m* 1951, Audrey, da of Charles W Hill; 1 s (Nicholas b 1 June 1954), 1 da (Susan b 20 Sept 1957); *Career* served RE 1945–48, Metal Box Co 1950–64, Montague Burton 1964–65; Cape Industries: joined 1965, md 1971–80, chm 1980–85; industl dir Charter Consolidated plc 1980–87, non-exec chm The Rugby Group plc 1986– (dir 1979–); non-exec dir: Pirelli General plc 1987–, Travers Morgan Ltd 1988–91, Try Group plc 1989–; vice chm Cncl BIM 1984–88 (chm BIM fndn 1981–83); memb United Kingdom South Africa Trade Assoc; CIMgt 1975, FRSA 1989; *Recreations* music, cricket, gardening; *Clubs* Army & Navy, Middlesex Cricket; *Style—* Geoffrey Higham, Esq; ✉ 32 East St Helen St, Abingdon, Oxfordshire OX14 5EB; The Rugby Group plc, Crown House, Rugby, Warwickshire (☎ 01788 542666, fax 01788 546726, telex 31523)

HIGHAM, John Arthur; QC (1992); s of Frank Greenhouse Higham (d 1988), and Muriel, *née* King; *b* 11 Aug 1952; *Educ* Shrewsbury, Churchill Coll Cambridge (MA, LLM, scholar); *m* 1, 1982, Francesca Mary Antonietta, *née* Ronan (d 1988); 2 da (Miranda Elizabeth Francesca b 9 April 1983, Charlotte Daisy Emilia b 14 August 1984), 1 s (John) Christian Alexander b 3 March 1987); m 2, 1988, Catherine Ennis, *qv*; 2 s (Patrick Rupert James b 14 Sept 1989, Edmund George Christopher b 24 March 1992), 1 da (Cecily Mary Catherine b 17 Jan 1994); *Career* called to the Bar Lincoln's Inn 1976; *Books* Loose on Liquidators (jt ed, 1981), A Practitioner's Guide to Corporate Insolvency and Corporate Rescues (contrib, 1991), The Law and Practice of Corporate Administrations (jt ed, 1994); *Recreations* opera, gardening, cricket; *Style—* John Higham, Esq, QC; ✉ 3/4 South Square, Gray's Inn, London WC1R 5HP (☎ 0171 696 9900, fax 0171 696 9911)

HIGHAM, John R; *Career* Fisher and Ludlow Div Br Motor Corp 1950–71 (successively tech apprentice, tool designer, mangr of body and chassis engrg, mangr of facilities planning, md Domestic Appliance Div), md Delco Electronics Overseas Corp (div of General Motors Corporation) 1971–88 (concurrently vice chm General Motors Public Affrs Cncl and memb Opel Supervisory Bd); chm: St Helens and Knowsley HA 1988–91, St Helens & Knowsley Hosps NHS Tst 1991–; CEng, memb Soc of Automotive Engrs USA, licensed engr State of Michigan; *Recreations* designing and building large-scale passenger hauling steam locomotives and traction engines, fly casting; *Style—* John R Higham, Esq; ✉ St Helens and Knowsley Hospitals NHS Trust, Whiston Hospital, Warrington Road, Prescot, Merseyside L35 5DR

HIGHAM, Martin Pownall; s of Denis Higham, of Grayshott, Surrey, and Winifred Mary, *née* Bussey (d 1994); *b* 3 May 1949; *Educ* Reigate GS; *m* 1974, Ann, da of Edward McMullen (d 1967); 1 s (Daniel Edward b 1978), 1 da (Emma Lucy b 1980); *Career* cashier and supervisor Barclays Bank Ltd 1969–71; Dexion International Ltd 1971–74 (asst press offr, press offr); account exec: James Mills & Associates 1974–75, Bastable Public Relations 1975–77; dir Kestrel Communications Ltd 1977–93; ptnr: Kestrel Services 1981–93, Broadway Partnership 1987–93, Chisnell and Higham 1994–; dir: Loo of the Year Awards Ltd 1994–; proprietor The Last Word 1994–; memb winning team Queen Mother's Birthday award (environment servs) 1990; MIPR; *Recreations* squash, travel, theatre; *Style—* Martin Higham, Esq; ✉ Lynsted, Kiln Way, Grayshott, Surrey GU26 6JF (☎ and fax 01428 712138, mobile 0831 774729)

HIGHAM, Nicholas Geoffrey (Nick); s of Geoffrey Arthur Higham, of Abingdon, Berks, Audrey Mary, *née* Hill; *b* 1 June 1954; *Educ* Bradfield, St Catharine's Coll Cambridge (BA); *m* 1981, Deborah Joan, da of Brig J G Starling, CBE, MC; 1 s (William b 12 May 1987), 1 da (Catherine b 10 July 1989); *Career* freelance journalist 1978–88; contrib to: The Times, The Listener, Sunday Times, Observer, Guardian, London Daily News, Time Out, Elle, World Broadcast News; ed Radio Month 1979–81, radio ed Broadcast 1981–83 and 1986–88, arts and media correspondent BBC News and Current Affairs 1993– (media corr 1988–93), columnist Marketing Week 1989–; presenter The Technophobes Guide to the Future (BBC2) 1996; *Style—* Nick Higham, Esq; ✉ Arts and Media Correspondent, BBC News and Current Affairs, Television Centre, Wood Lane, London W12 7RJ (☎ 0181 225 8231, fax 0181 749 9016)

HIGHE, Jackie; da of John Barraclough (d 1988), and Lily, *née* Senior (d 1989); *b* 17 Sept 1947; *Educ* Univ of Leeds; *m* 5 April 1968, Brian Highe, s of Philip Highe, of Yorkshire; 1 s (Philip b 1971), 1 da (Jane b 1969); *Career* assoc ed Living Magazine 1984–86, ed Parents Magazine 1986–88; ed in chief: Bella Magazine 1988–90, First For Women (USA) 1990–92, Bella Magazine 1993–; memb: UK Women's Forum, Br Soc of Magazine Eds; *Recreations* music, riding, walking, reading; *Style—* Mrs Jackie Highe

HIGHFIELD, Dr Roger; s of Ronald Albert Highfield, of Enfield, Middx, and Dorothea Helena, *née* Depta; *b* 11 July 1958; *Educ* Christ's Hosp Horsham Sussex, Pembroke Coll Oxford (Domus scholar, MA, DPhil), Queen Elizabeth House Oxford (Leverhulme fell), Balliol Coll Oxford (Sabbatical fell); *m* Julia Brookes; *Career* news/clinical reporter Pulse 1983–84 (dep features ed), news ed Nuclear Engineering International 1984–86; The Daily Telegraph: technol corr 1986, technol ed 1987, science ed 1988–; memb: Ctee on the Public Understanding of Sci, Pembroke Coll Ctee; organiser of Megalab nat experiments; *Awards* Med Journalist of the Year 1987, Science Writer of the Year 1988 and 1995, Br Press Awards Specialist Corr of the Year 1989 (commended 1991), cited by Save British Science as Campaigning Journalist of the Year, Cwlth Media Award 1994; *Books* The Arrow of Time (1990), The Private Lives of Albert Einstein (1993), Frontiers of Complexity (1995); *Recreations* swimming, drinking; *Style—* Dr Roger Highfield; ✉ Daily Telegraph, 1 Canada Square, Canary Wharf, London E14 5DT (☎ 0171 538 5000, fax 0171 538 6883)

HIGHMORE, Neil Sinclair; s of John Sinclair Highmore (Maj ret), of Rookdykes, Corse, by Huntly, Aberdeenshire, and Margaret Boyes Highmore, *née* Sinclair (d 1974); *b* 27 May 1948; *Educ* Broughton Secdy Sch, Edinburgh Art Coll, Heriot-Watt Univ (BArch); *Career* ptnr in architectural practice Patience and Highmore, former chm of Borders Architectural Gp; RIBA, ARIAS; *Recreations* squash, gardening, angling; *Style—* Neil Highmore, Esq; ✉ Tighcarr, St Ronan's Terrace, Innerleithen, Peeblesshire (☎ 01896 830128); Quadrant, 17 Bernard St, Edinburgh EH6 6PW (☎ 0131 555 0644)

HIGHTON, David Peter; s of Allan Peter Highton, of Hartlip, nr Sittingbourne, Kent, and May Highton; *b* 22 May 1954; *Educ* Borden GS Kent, Univ of Bristol (BSc); *partner* Wendy Ann Attree; 1 da (Emily Katherine Highton b 7 May 1990); *Career* Turquands Barton Mayhew (now Ernst & Young): articled clerk 1975–78, qualified CA 1978, audit sr 1978–79, audit supr 1979; fin accountant Tunnel Avebe Starches Ltd 1979–81, London controller R P Martin plc 1981–83, fin planning and analysis mangr Watney Mann & Truman Ltd 1986–87 (fin controller (central staffs and Cos) 1983–86), regnl fin dir SE Region Prudential Property Services 1987–89, md Property Mail (pt of Prudential Group until 1990) 1989–90, chief exec Ealing Health Authy 1991–92 (dir of fin and purchasing 1990–92), dir of fin and business devpt Riverside Hosps 1992–94, tst project mangr Chelsea and Westminster Hosp 1993–94, chief exec Chelsea and Westminster Healthcare NHS Tst 1994–; chm Sittingbourne RUFC 1991–94 (treas 1976–90), fin sec Gore Court Cricket Club 1994–; FCA 1989; *Recreations* rugby, cricket; *Style—* David Highton, Esq; ✉ Chelsea and Westminster Healthcare NHS Trust, 369 Fulham Road, Chelsea, London SW10 9NH

HIGLETT, Simon Ian; s of John Higlett, of Allesley, Coventry, and Patricia Anne, *née* Such; *b* 30 May 1959; *Educ* Wimbledon Sch of Art (BA), Slade Sch of Fine Art (Higher Dip in Fine Art, Leslie Hurry Prize for Theatre Design); *m* 21 Aug 1988, Isobel, da of Alan Arnett, of Tuffley, Gloucester; 1 da (Charlotte Hope b 27 Sept 1994); *Career* theatre designer; asst to Tim Goodchild 1982–84; prodns incl: Rosenkavalier (Marseilles Opera) 1984, A Midsummer Night's Dream and Ring Round the Moon (New Shakespeare Co) 1985, Night and Day and See How They Run (Theatr Clwyd) 1985, Medea (Young Vic) 1985, Taming of the Shrew and Antony and Cleopatra (Haymarket) 1986, Daughter in Law and School for Scandal (Birmingham Repertory) 1987, Hobson's Choice, Plotters of Cabbage Patch Corner, Mrs Warren's Profession, Gingerbread Man (all at Leeds Playhouse) 1988, A Midsummer Night's Dream, The Contractor, The Railway Children (all at Birmingham Repertory) 1988, A Midsummer Night's Dream and Babes in Arms (New Shakespeare Co) 1988, Winnie (Victoria Palace) 1988, Last Waltz (Greenwich) 1989, A Month in the Country (Leeds Playhouse) 1989, A Midsummer Night's Dream, Twelfth Night, Swaggerer (all at New Shakespeare Co) 1989, An Inspector Calls (Plymouth Theatre Royal) 1989, Boys from Syracuse (Crucible Theatre Sheffield) 1989, Singer (RSC Barbican) 1990, Kean (Old Vic London and Canada) 1990, Scenes from a Marriage (Chichester) 1990, Some Like it Hot (West Yorkshire Playhouse) 1990, Don Giovanni and The Marriage of Figaro (Jugendstil Theater Vienna) 1991, The Sisterhood (Chichester) 1991, Broadway Bound (Greenwich) 1991, The Cabinet Minister (Haymarket) 1991, Jamaica Inn (Plymouth Theatre Royal) 1991, The Miser (Manchester Royal Exchange) 1992, Talking Heads (Comedy Theatre) 1992, La Cenerentola (Vienna Festival) 1992, Mother Tongue (Greenwich) 1992, Il Seraglio (Scottish Opera) 1992, King Lear in New York (Chichester Festival Theatre) 1992, The Marriage Of Figaro (Hamburg) 1993, Making It Better (Criterion) 1993, Ricochet (tour) 1993, The Brothers Karamazov (Manchester Royal Exchange) 1993, The Crucible (Crucible Sheffield) 1993, Rope (Chichester Festival Theatre) 1993, Cosi Fan Tutte (Hamburg) 1993, The Barber of Seville (Essen State Opera) 1994, The Count of Monte Cristo (Manchester Royal Exchange) 1994, La Traviata (Covent Garden Opera Festival) 1994, Dangerous Corner (Chichester) 1994, The Miser (Chichester), The Magic Flute (Hamburg), Tartuffe (Royal Exchange), Julius Casear (Essen State Opera), Miss Julie (Royal Exchange), Tempest (New Shakespeare Co) 1996, Mansfield Park, Beethoven's Tenth, Talking Heads (all Chichester) 1996, The Rakes Progress (Essen State Opera) 1997, Der Rosenkavalier (Gelsenkirchen Germany) 1997, Lady Windermere's Fan, The Philadelphia Story (Manchester Royal Exchange) 1997; *Recreations* reading, drawing, theatre; *Style—* Simon Higlett, Esq; ✉ 29 Maltravers Street, Arundel, West Sussex BN18 9BU (☎ 01903 882586)

HIGNETT, John Mulock; s of Reginald Arthur Hignett (d 1975), and Marjorie Sarah Louise, *née* Mulock (d 1992); *b* 9 March 1934; *Educ* Harrow, Magdalene Coll Cambridge (boxing blue 1955, team capt 1956); *m* 5 Aug 1961, Marijke Inge, da of Rudolf-Jeorje de Boer (d 1988), of Amsterdam; 1 s (Martin b 26 Nov 1962), 1 da (Karin b 4 March 1965); *Career* Lazard Bros: joined 1963, mangr Issues Dept 1971, dir 1972, head of corporate finance 1980–81, on secondment 1981–84, md 1984–88; fin dir Glaxo Holdings plc 1988–94; non-exec dir: TI Group plc 1989– (dep chm 1993–), Sedgwick Group plc, Schroders Income Growth Fund plc, Alfred McAlpine plc 1994–; dir gen Panel on Takeovers and Mergers 1981–84 and CSI 1983–84 (first time these two posts have been held by one person); Liveryman Worshipful Co of Chartered Accountants; FCA 1961; *Recreations* growing orchids; *Clubs* MCC, Hawks (Cambridge), Roehampton; *Style—* John M Hignett, Esq; ✉ TI Group plc, 50 Curzon Street, London W1Y 7PN (☎ 0171 499 9131)

HILDESLEY, Michael Edmund; s of Paul Francis Glynn Hildesley, and Mary, *née* Morgan; *b* 16 Oct 1948; *Educ* Sherborne, Trinity Coll Oxford (MA); *m* 1972, Judith Carol, da of George Michael Pistor, of USA; 3 s (Robert b 1980, David b 1982, Charles b 1982); *Career* merchant banker; dir Morgan Grenfell & Co Ltd 1984–; *Style—* Michael Hildesley, Esq; ✉ Morgan Grenfell & Co Ltd, 23 Great Winchester Street, London EC2P 2AX (☎ 0171 545 8000, fax 0171 545 7900)

HILDYARD, Sir David Henry Thoroton; KCMG (1975, CMG 1966), DFC (1943); s of His Hon Gerard Moresby Thoroton Hildyard, QC, DL (d 1956), of Flintham Hall, Newark, and Sybil Hamilton Hoare (d 1978); *b* 4 May 1916; *Educ* Eton, ChCh Oxford; *m* 1947, Millicent, da of Sir Edward Baron (d 1962), and widow of Wing Cdr R M Longmore; 1 s (Robert b 1952), 1 da (Marianna b 1955); *Career* served WWII RAF; joined Foreign Serv 1948, cnsllr Mexico 1960–65, head of Econ Rels Dept FO 1965–68, min and alternate UK delegate to UN 1968–70, ambass Chile 1970–73, ambass and perm rep to UN (Geneva) 1973–76, head UK Delgn to CSCE 1974–75; dir Lombard Odier International Portfolio Management 1980–92; *Clubs* Brooks's, Garrick, Reform, Hurlingham; *Style—* Sir David Hildyard, KCMG, DFC; ✉ 97 Onslow Square, London SW7 (☎ 0171 584 2110)

HILDYARD, Robert Henry Thoroton; QC (1994); s of Sir David Hildyard, KCMG, DFC, of London, and Millicent, *née* Baron; *b* 10 Oct 1952; *Educ* Eton, ChCh Oxford (BA); *m* 9 Aug 1980, Isabella Jane, da of James Rennie (d 1964); 3 da (Catherine b 31 Oct 1983, Camilla b 15 May 1985, d 1987, Alexandra b 15 Sept 1988); *Career* called to the Bar Inner Temple 1977, jr counsel to the Crown (Chancery) 1992–94; *Books* contrib to: Butterworths Forms and Precedents: Company Law, Tolleys Company Law; *Recreations* tennis, shooting; *Clubs* Hurlingham; *Style—* Robert Hildyard, Esq, QC; ✉ 4 Stone Buildings, Lincoln's Inn, London WC2A 3XT (☎ 0171 242 5524, fax 0171 831 7907)

HILEY, Peter Haviland; s of Sir (Ernest) Haviland Hiley, KBE (d 1943), of Cambridge, and Brenda Lee, *née* Lord (d 1961); *b* 19 Feb 1921; *Educ* Eton, Grenoble Univ; *m* 21 May 1955, (Isabel) Susan, da of Herbert George Hope, MBE (d 1956), of Blackmoor, Hants; 1 s (William b 1960); *Career* WWII Intelligence Corps 1941–45; Br Cncl 1945–49, joined Laurence Olivier Productions Ltd 1949; currently dir: Wheelshare Ltd (formerly Laurence Olivier Productions Ltd), The Olivier Fndn, Old Vic Trust Ltd, Royal Victoria Hall Fndn; gen cmmr of income tax 1966–92; govr Petersfield Comprehensive Sch 1965–92; *Recreations* theatre, sightseeing; *Style—* Peter Hiley, Esq; ✉ Byways, Steep, Petersfield, Hants GU32 1AD; 102 Valiant House, Vicarage Crescent, London SW11 3LX

HILHORST, Rosemary; da of Raymond Bowditch, of Portesham, Dorset, and June, *née* Ebdon; *b* 10 April 1954; *Educ* Woodroffe Sch Lyme Regis, UCL (BSc), Chelsea Coll (PGCE); *m* 10 April 1981, Francis Hilhorst, s of Henk Hilhorst (d 1991); 1 da (Malaika b 5 April 1982), 1 s (Sean b 6 Jan 1985); *Career* physics/integrated science teacher: Portslade Community Coll 1976–80, Int Sch of Tanganyika Dar es Salaam 1980–82, American Cultural Assoc Turin 1982–83, Portesham CE Primary Sch (pt/t) 1983–84; British Council: science advsr 1985–86, asst rep Khartoum 1986–88, head Exchanges Unit Khartoum 1988–89, head Project Devpt Dept (asst dir 1989–90), dir Bratislava 1991–93, dir Slovakia 1993–; *Recreations* family, literature, walking, running and cycling; *Style—* Mrs Rosemary Hilhorst

HILL, Alastair Malcolm; QC (1982); s of Sir Ian George Wilson Hill, CBE, TD (d 1982); *b* 12 May 1936; *Educ* Trinity Coll Glenalmond, Keble Coll Oxford (BA); *m* 1969 (m dis 1977), Elizabeth Maria Innes; 2 children; *Career* called to the Bar Gray's Inn 1961; recorder Crown Ct SE Circuit 1982, currently lawyer for the Crown Prosecution Serv; *Recreations* fly-fishing, collecting watercolours and prints, opera; *Style—* Alastair Hill, Esq, QC; ✉ Crown Prosecution Service, 50 Ludgate Hill, London EC4M 7EX

HILL, Alfred Edward; s of Mervyn Ewart Phillips Hill, of Gozo, and Betty Deborah Jane Matilda, *née* Bennett; *b* 29 Aug 1945; *Educ* Clifton Coll, IMEDE (MBA); *m* 14 July 1973, Rosemary Scarth, da of John William Chandos Lloyd-Kirk; 2 c (Charlotte Rosina b 13 Aug 1975, Rupert Alfred b 23 Dec 1977); *Career* articled clerk: Monahans Swindon 1964–66, Grace Ryland (formerly CJ Ryland & Co) 1966–69; qualified CA 1969, seconded to Spafax SA 1972; ptnr: Thomson McLintock 1974–87, KPMG 1987–95 (conslt 1995–); underwriting memb Lloyd's 1979; govr Clifton Coll 1989–; FCA 1979 (ACA 1969); *Clubs* Clifton, Bristol Savages; *Style—* Alfred Hill, Esq; ✉ Campfield, Church Rd, Abbots Leigh, nr Bristol BS8 3QU (☎ 01275 372104); KPMG, 15 Pembroke Rd, Clifton, Bristol BS8 3BG (☎ 0117 946 4000, fax 0117 946 4065)

HILL, Prof (Hugh) Allen Oliver; s of Hugh Rankin Stewart Hill (d 1974), and Elizabeth, *née* Burns; *b* 23 May 1937; *Educ* Royal Belfast Academical Inst, Queen's Univ Belfast (BSc, DPh, Hon DSc), Univ of Oxford (MA, DSc); *m* 29 June 1967, Dr Boglarka Anna, da of Pal Pinter (d 1945); 2 s (Alister Pal Stewart b 1969, Roderick Ferenc Allen b 1972), 1 da (Natalie Elizabeth Margit b 1974); *Career* Univ of Oxford: DSIR res fell Inorganic Chemistry Lab 1962–64, Turner and Newall res fell 1964–65, Weir jr res fell Univ Coll 1964, fell and tutor in chemistry Queen's Coll 1965–, departmental demonstrator in inorganic chemistry 1965–67, lectr in inorganic chemistry 1967–90, sr proctor 1976–77, reader in bioinorganic chemistry 1990–92, prof of bioinorganic chemistry 1992–; visiting lectr Dept of Biological Chemistry Harvard Univ 1970–71, assoc Dept of Med Peter Bent Brigham Hosp Boston 1970–71, Cwlth visiting fell Univ of Sydney Aust 1973, inorganic lectr W Coast USA 1981, visiting prof Univ of California 1982; FRSC 1978 (Interdisciplinary award 1987, Chemistry and Electrochemistry of Transition Metals medal 1990), Breyer medal Royal Aust Chemical Inst, Robinson award 1994; FRS 1990 (Mullard medal 1993); *Publications* Physical Methods in Advanced Inorganic Chemistry (Interscience London, ed with P Day, 1968), Inorganic Biochemistry Vol 1 2 & 3 (specialist periodical report RSC London, 1979), Chemical and Biochemical Aspects of Superoxide Dismutases (Elsevier/North-Holland NY, ed with J V Bannister, 1980); *Recreations* opera, theatre, film, gardening; *Style—* Prof Allen Hill, FRS; ✉ Queen's College, Oxford OX1 4AW (☎ 01865 279177); New Chemistry Laboratory, South Parks Rd, Oxford OX1 3QT (☎ and fax 01865 275900)

HILL, 8 Viscount (UK 1842); Sir Antony Rowland Clegg-Hill; 10 Bt (GB 1727); also Baron Hill of Almarez and of Hardwick (UK 1814); the full title of the Viscountcy is Viscount Hill of Hawkstone and of Hardwick; s of 7 Viscount Hill (d 1974, fourth in descent from John, er bro of 1 Viscount, who commanded Adam's Brigade in the Battle of Waterloo, was second in command of the Army of Occupation (of France) 1815–18 and was C-in-C 1828–42) by his 1 w Elisabeth, *née* Smyth-Osbourne (d 1967); *b* 19 March 1931; *Educ* Kelly Coll, RMA Sandhurst; *m* 1, 1963 (m dis 1976), Juanita Phyllis, da of John W Pertwee, of Salford, Surrey; m 2, 11 May 1989, Elizabeth Harriett, da of Ronald Offer, of Salisbury, Wilts; *Heir* cous, Peter Clegg-Hill, *qv*; *Career* late Capt RA; Freeman of Shrewsbury 1957; *Style—* The Rt Hon Viscount Hill; ✉ c/o House of Lords, SW1A 0PW

HILL, Bernard; *b* 17 Dec 1944; *Career* actor; *Theatre* incl: John Lennon in John, Paul, George, Ringo... and Bert (West End), Toby Belch in Twelfth Night, title role in Macbeth (Leicester Haymarket), Lophakhin in The Cherry Orchard (Aldwych), Eddie in A View From the Bridge (Bristol Old Vic and Strand Theatres) 1995; *Television* for BBC: Boys from the Blackstuff, John Lennon - A Journey in the Life, The Burston Rebellion, New World, The Gospel According to St Luke, Permanent Red, The Lawlord, Mike in Olly's Prison - Edward Bond Trilogy Once Upon a Time in the North; for Channel 4: Squaring the Circle, Lipstick on your Collar 1993, Without Walls - The Art of Tripping 1993; also Telltale (HTV); *Film* incl: The Bounty, Ghandi, The Chain, Restless Natives, No Surrender, Bellman and True (and TV series), Drowning By Numbers, Shirley Valentine, Mountains of the Moon, Double X, Skallagrigg (also TV release), The Wind in the Willows, The Ghost of Darkness; *Recreations* skiing, squash, tennis, swimming, fishing, Apple Macintosh; *Style—* Bernard Hill, Esq; ✉ c/o Harriet Robinson, Conway van Gelder Robinson Ltd, 18–21 Jermyn Street, London SW1Y 6HP (☎ 0171 287 0077, fax 0171 287 1940)

HILL, Sir Brian John; s of Gerald A Hill, OBE (d 1974); *b* 19 Dec 1932; *Educ* Stowe, Univ of Cambridge (MA); *m* 1959, Janet Joyce, da of Alfred S Newman, OBE; 3 children; *Career* Nat Serv Army; gp md Higgs and Hill Ltd 1972–83, exec chm Higgs and Hill plc 1989–92 (chm and chief exec 1983–89); dir Building Centre 1981–85; memb Advsy Bd Property Services Agency 1981–86; dir: Lazard Property Unit Trust 1982–, Lancs and Yorks Property Management Ltd 1985–93, Etonbrook Property plc 1985–93, Property Services Agency 1986–88, Southern Regnl Bd National Westminster Bank 1990–92, London Docklands Development Corp 1994–; chm Goldsborough Holdings 1994–; pres: Bldg Employers' Confedn 1992–95 (pres London Region 1981–82, chm Nat Contractors Gp 1983–84), Chartered Inst of Building 1987–88; chm: Vauxhall Coll of Bldg and Further Educn 1976–86, Gt Ormond Street Hosp for Children NHS Tst 1992–; govr Aberdour Sch Tadworth 1987–, external examiner Univ of Reading 1993–; Hon

DSc, Hon LLB; memb Ct of Assts Worshipful Company of Chartered Surveyors (Master 1994–95); FRICS, FCIOB, Hon FIStructE; *Recreations* travelling, tennis, gardening, amateur dramatics; *Clubs* RAC; *Style*— Sir Brian Hill; ✉ Barrow House, The Warren, Kingswood, Surrey; Higgs and Hill plc, Crown House, Kingston Rd, New Malden, Surrey KT3 3ST (☎ 0181 942 8921)

HILL, (Robert) Charles; QC (1974 NI); s of Benjamin Morrison Hill (d 1968), of Belfast, and Mary, *née* Roche (d 1980); *b* 22 March 1936; *Educ* St Paul's Sch Belfast, St Malachy's Coll Belfast, Queen's Univ Belfast (LLB), Trinity Coll Dublin (MA); *m* 1961, Kathleen, *née* Allen, da of Robert Wilson Allen; 1 da (Kathryn Elizabeth b 18 Nov 1962), 3 s (Robert Charles Michael b 30 Dec 1963, Niall Benjamin Morrison b 19 March 1969, Alan Lawther Roche b 13 March 1974); *Career* called to the Bar: N Ireland 1959, Gray's Inn 1971, King's Inn Dublin 1986; referee under Finance Act 1976; chm: Statutory Ctee of Pharmaceutical Soc of NI 1977–92, Poisons Bd of NI 1982–92, Standing Advsy Cmmn on Human Rights in NI 1992–95 (memb 1990–95); sr counsel Ireland 1987, bencher Inn of Ct of NI 1988; *Recreations* farming, forestry; *Style*— Charles Hill, Esq, QC

HILL, Dr Christina Bernadette Thérèse; da of Howard E Hill (d 1971), and Elsie, *née* Punnett-Beale (now Mrs Robert L Hall); *Educ* Univ of Wales (BA), Univ of Birmingham (MA, PhD); *partner* (David) Clive Harries Williams; 1 step da (Rebecca b 1975), 1 step s (Robert b 1977); *Career* Tidy Britain Gp: field offr 1977, dir Midlands 1977–81, dir Devpt and Trg 1981–88, head of research and legislation 1988; dir of public affairs Aviation Environment Fedn & Tst 1988–89, nat dir Sch & Gp Travel Assoc (SAGTA) 1988–94; environmental and educnl conslt 1988–; UK Environmental Law Assoc (UKELA): hon dir of conferences and hon annual conference organiser 1989–93, memb Noise Working Party 1989–, memb Cncl of Mgmnt 1989–95, co sec 1995–96, gen sec 1996–; co sec TecKnow Ltd 1995–; vice chm Berkshire Environment Tst 1990–92 (memb Exec Ctee 1989–92); YWCA: chair Steering Gp for Major Appeal Ctee 1993, acting chair Appeal Ctee 1994, chair Open The Door Appeal Ctee 1994–95, chair Special Events Ctee 1996; advsr Bd of Tstees Prisoners Abroad 1990–95 (vice chair Fundraising Ctee 1988, memb Fundraising Working Gp 1990–93), memb Exec Ctee SPISE (Sane Planning in the SE) 1989– (memb Working Gp 1989–91, memb Policy Gp 1991–93); author various pubns for Tidy Britain Gp and SAGTA, ed SAGTA News 1989–92; assoc memb Inst of Wastes Mgmnt 1981–, assoc memb Inst of Environmental Health Offrs 1988; FIPD 1985, FRGS 1989, FRSA 1989; *Recreations* reading, theatre, music, walking, skiing, gardening, keeping ducks; *Style*— Dr Christina Hill; ✉ The United Kingdom Environmental Law Association, Honeycroft House, Pangbourne Road, Upper Basildon, Berkshire RG8 8LP (☎ 01491 671631)

HILL, (John Edward) Christopher; s of Edward Harold Hill (d 1965), and Janet Augusta, *née* Dickenson (d 1964); *b* 6 Feb 1912; *Educ* St Peter's Sch York, Balliol Coll Oxford (BA, MA, DLitt); *m* 1, 1944 (m dis), Inez Bartlett; 1 da (Fanny Catherine d 1989); m 2, 1956, Bridget Irene, da of the Rev Harry Sutton; 1 s (Andrew Oliver b 16 June 1958), 1 da (Dinah Jane b 8 June 1960); *Career* Army and FO 1940–45; fell All Souls Coll Oxford 1934–38, asst lectr in modern history UCW Cardiff 1936–38, master Balliol Coll Oxford 1965–78 (fell and tutor in modern history 1938–65); Ford lectr Univ of Oxford 1962, visiting prof Open Univ 1978–80; Milton Soc of America award 1978, WH Smith literary award 1989; FRHistS 1948, FBA 1965; foreign hon memb: American Acad of Sciences 1973, Hungarian Acad of Sciences 1982; *Books* The English Revolution 1640 (1940), Lenin and the Russian Revolution (1947), Economic Problems of the Church (1956), Puritanism and Revolution (1958), The Century of Revolution (1961), Society and Puritanism (1984), Intellectual Origins of the English Revolution (1965), Reformation to Industrial Revolution (1967), God's Englishman - Oliver Cromwell (1970), Antichrist in 17th Century England (1971), The World Turned Upside Down (1972), Change and Continuity in 17th Century England (1974), Milton and the English Revolution (1977), Some Intellectual Consequences of the English Revolution (1980), The Experience of Defeat - Milton and Some Contemporaries (1984), Writing and Revolution in 17th Century England (1985), Religion and Politics in 17th Century England (1986), People and Ideas in 17th Century England (1986), A Turbulent, Seditious and Factious People - John Bunyan and His Church (1988), A Nation of Change and Novelty - Radical Politics, Religion and Literature in 17th Century England (1990), The English Bible and the Seventeeth-Century Revolution (1993), Liberty Against the Law: Some Seventeenth-Century Controversies (1996); *Style*— Christopher Hill, Esq; ✉ Woodway House, Sibford Ferris, Banbury, Oxon OX15 5RA

HILL, Rt Rev Christopher; *see:* Stafford, Bishop of

HILL, Christopher Richard; s of Horace Rowland Hill (d 1966), of Trotton Place, near Petersfield, Hants, and Gwendolen Edith, *née* Smith (d 1987); *b* 4 March 1935; *Educ* Radley, Trinity Coll Cambridge (MA); *Career* HM Foreign Serv 1958–62, asst dir Inst of Race Rels London 1962–65, lectr in govt Univ Coll of Rhodesia 1965–66, sr lectr in politics Univ of York 1982–93 (lectr 1966–82), dir Centre for S African Studies 1972–82, visiting fell Cranleigh Sch 1988–90, sr conslt Jockey Club Educn Tst (later Br Horseracing Bd educn conslt) 1991–96, visiting fell Chichester Inst of Higher Educn 1995–; hon offr Youth Clubs UK 1993–95; tstee: Southern African Studies Tst 1984–94, UK Forum on Young People and Gambling 1992–93; Liveryman Worshipful Co of Leathersellers 1956; *Books* Bantustans: The Fragmentation of South Africa (1964), Rights and Wrongs: Some Essays on Human Rights (contrib ed, 1969), European Business and South Africa: An Appraisal of the EC Code of Conduct (contrib ed, 1981), The West and South Africa (jtly, 1982), Change in South Africa: Blind Alleys or New Directions (1983), Horse Power: The Politics of the Turf (1988), Olympic Politics (1992, revised edn 1996); *Recreations* gardening, cooking, travel, writing; *Clubs* Athenaeum, Travellers'; *Style*— Christopher Hill, Esq; ✉ Rother Cottage, Dodsley Grove, Midhurst, West Sussex GU29 9AB

HILL, Rev Colin Arnold Clifford; OBE (1996); s of William Hill (d 1934), of Lillteport, Cambs, and May Anne Clifford, *née* Simpson (d 1961); *b* 13 Feb 1929; *Educ* Reading Sch, Univ of Bristol, Ripon Hall Theol Coll Oxford; *m* 1, 1958, Shirley (d 1960), da of Frank Randall (d 1960); 1 s (Simon Timothy); m 2, 1971, Irene Florence Chamberlain (wid); 1 step s (Michael); *Career* former mgmnt trainee GEC Ltd; Nat Serv RAF Malaya 1947–49; ordained Sheffield Cathedral 1957; curate Rotherham Sheffield 1957–60, vicar of Brightside 1960, rector of Easthampstead Bracknell 1964–73, chaplain RAF Staff Coll Bracknell 1964–73, proctor in convocation Canterbury/memb Gen Synod C of E 1970–73, vicar of Croydon 1973–94 (Dio of Canterbury until 1985, Southwark thereafter), proctor in convocation Canterbury/memb Gen Synod C of E 1980–84; hon canon: Canterbury Cathedral 1975–84, Southwark Cathedral 1985–94; former religious advsr to London Borough of Croydon and Mayor's chaplain; chaplain to The Queen 1990–; *Recreations* walking, reading, films; *Clubs* Naval and Military; *Style*— The Rev Canon Colin Hill, OBE; ✉ Silver Birches, Preston Crowmarsh, Wallingford, Oxon OX10 6SL (☎ 01491 836102)

HILL, Damon Graham Devereux; OBE (1997); s of (Norman) Graham Hill (d 1975, twice Formula 1 world champion 1962 and 1968), and Bette Hill; *b* 17 Sept 1960; *Educ* Haberdashers' Aske's; *m* 21 Oct 1988, Georgie; 2 s, 1 da; *Career* Formula 1 racing driver; Williams test driver 1991 and 1992, first Grand Prix (Silverstone) 1992 (driving for Brabham team); driver with: Canon Williams team 1993, Rothmans Williams Renault team 1994, 1995 and 1996, Danka Arrows Yamaha team 1997; winner: Hungarian Grand Prix 1993 and 1995, Belgian Grand Prix 1993 and 1994, Italian Grand Prix 1993 and 1994, Spanish Grand Prix 1994, British Grand Prix 1994, Portuguese Grand Prix 1994, Japanese Grand Prix 1994 and 1996, Argentinian Grand Prix 1995 and 1996, San Marino Grand Prix 1995 and 1996, Australian Grand Prix 1995 and 1996, Brazilian Grand Prix 1996, Canadian Grand Prix 1996, French Grand Prix 1996, German Grand Prix 1996; Formula 1 World Drivers' Championship: third place 1993, second place 1994 and 1995, world champion 1996; 67 Grand Prix starts, 21 wins, 20 pole positions, 19 fastest laps, 40 podium finishes; *Awards* Sportsman of the Year Daily Express 1993, International Racing Driver of the Year Autosport Awards 1994 and 1996, British Competition Driver of the Year Autosport Awards 1995 and 1996, Driver of the Year Guild of Motoring Writers 1994, BBC Sports Personality of the Year 1994 and 1996, sixteen awards (incl Gold Stars 1993, 1994, 1995 and 1996) British Racing Drivers' Club 1993, 1994, 1995 and 1996, Abbey National RADAR People of the Year Award 1996, Autosprint Golden Helmet Award 1996, l'Automobile Magazine Trophy 1996, Daily Mirror Sports Personality of the Year 1996, Barclaycard Daily Telegraph Champion of British Sport 1996; *Books* Damon Hill Grand Prix Year (1994), Damon Hill My Championship Year (1996); *Video* Damon Hill The Fight for Victory (1996); *Recreations* golf, music, cinema, current affairs; *Style*— Damon Hill, Esq, OBE; ✉ c/o Arrows Grand Prix, Leafield Technical Centre, Leafield, Witney, Oxfordshire OX8 5PF

HILL, David Roderick; s of Desmond D'Artrey Hill, of Beaconsfield, Bucks, and Margaret Angela Ellis, *née* Hughes; *b* 28 Feb 1952; *Educ* Merchant Taylors'; *m* 6 April 1988, Jane Frances, da of Jack Collins, of Canterbury, Kent; 1 s (Henry Orlando b 7 April 1989), 1 da (Annabel Lucy b 15 May 1991); *Career* violin maker; Freeman City of London, Liveryman Worshipful Co of Musicians 1973 (memb Ct of Assts 1994); *Recreations* fishing, shooting, art, music; *Clubs* MCC; *Style*— David Hill, Esq; ✉ Granary Barn, Little Missenden, Buckinghamshire (☎ 01494 862660, fax 01494 862663)

HILL, Air Cdre Dame Felicity Barbara; DBE (1966, OBE 1954); da of late Edwin Frederick Hill, and Frances Ada Barbara, *née* Cocke; *b* 12 Dec 1915; *Educ* St Margaret's Sch Folkestone; *Career* joined WAAF 1939, cmmnd 1940, Inspr of WRAF 1956–59, OC RAF Hawkinge 1959–60, OC RAF Spitalgate 1960–63, dir of the WRAF 1966–69; Hon ADC to HM The Queen 1966–69; *Clubs* RAF; *Style*— Air Cdre Dame Felicity Hill, DBE; ✉ Worcester Cottage, Mews Lane, Winchester, Hants SO22 4PS

HILL, George Raymond; s of George Mark Hill, and Jill Hill; *b* 25 Sept 1925; *Educ* St Dunstan's Coll London; *m* 1948, Sophie, *née* Gilbert; 2 da; *Career* Lt RM 1943–46; Distillers Co Ltd (Industl Gp) 1952–66, BP Chems Ltd 1967–69, chief exec Br Transport Hotels Ltd 1970–76 (chm 1974–76), dir Bass plc 1976–84 (memb Exec Ctee); chm: Bass UK Ltd 1978–80, Crest Hotels Investment Ltd 1982–89, Howard Machinery plc 1984–85, Sims Catering plc 1984–87, Channel Tunnel Nat Tourism Working Pty 1986–89, Liquor Licensing Ctee (Br Tourist Authy), Regal Hotel Group plc 1989–92; dir: Chester International Hotel plc 1987–92, Ashford International Hotel plc 1988–; memb Br Tourist Authy Bd 1982–89; memb Hon Artillery Co 1942–; fell Br Hospitality Assoc 1992, FCA, FCIT, FHCIMA, FRSA 1980; *Recreations* music, theatre, works of art, country life; *Style*— George Hill, Esq; ✉ 23 Sheffield Terrace, London W8 7NQ (☎ 0171 727 3986); The Paddocks, Chedworth, Gloucestershire

HILL, Gillian (Mrs Gillian Miller); da of Roger John Wright (d 1979), of Biggleswade, Beds, and Vera Florence, *née* Camp; *b* 18 Feb 1947; *Educ* Sacred Heart Convent Hitchin; *m* 1, 15 Aug 1968, George Hill; 1 da (Samantha Julia b 1973); m 2, 20 July 1978, Royston Miller, s of William Miller (d 1958); *Career* Lloyds Bank 1964–69, md Windscreens (Biggleswade) Ltd 1968–73, exec offr Br Water Ski Fedn 1974–; memb and sec Biggleswade Water Ski Club 1970–73; Int Water Ski Fedn: chair Barefoot Cncl 1980–94, memb Tournament Cncl 1994–; memb Br Assoc of Nat Sports Administrators 1980; *Recreations* water skiing, tennis, squash, reading; *Style*— Ms Gillian Hill; ✉ 390 City Rd, London EC1V 2QA (☎ 0171 833 2855, fax 0171 837 5879)

HILL, Graham Starforth; s of Capt Harold Victor John Hill (d 1955), of Alresford, Hants; *b* 22 June 1927; *Educ* Dragon Sch Oxford, Winchester, St John's Coll Oxford; *m* 1952 (m dis), Margaret Elise, da of Charles Ambler (d 1952), of Itchen Abbas, Hants; 1 s, 1 da; *Career* Flying Offr RAF Fighter Cmd UK 1948–50; called to the Bar Gray's Inn 1951, admitted slr 1961; crown counsel Colonial Legal Serv Singapore 1953–56, ptnr (later sr ptnr) Rodyk and Davidson Advocates and Slrs Singapore 1957–76, chm Guinness Mahon & Co Ltd 1979–83 (dir 1977–79); conslt to Rodyk & Davidson (Singapore) 1985–, resident conslt to Frere Cholmeley (subsequently Frere Cholmeley Bischoff) Rome and Milan 1991–94; chm London City Ballet Tst 1981–82; tstee: Southwark Cathedral Devpt Tst Fund 1980–84, Royal Opera House Tst 1982–85; pres Law Soc of Singapore 1970–74; Cavaliere della Solidarieta 1975, Commendatore al Merito 1977; *Recreations* music, Italy; *Clubs* Garrick, Hampshire; *Style*— Graham Hill, Esq; ✉ 10 St Thomas St, Winchester, Hants SO23 9HE (☎ 01962 854146, fax 01962 867674); Le Terrazze del Porto, 07020 Porto Cervo, Italy (☎ 00 39 789 92626, fax 00 39 789 9215)

HILL, Harry Douglas; s of Jack Hill, of S Yorks, and Katheline Francis, *née* Curran; *b* 4 April 1948; *Educ* Holgate GS Barnsley; *m* 1 (m dis 1979), Glenis Margaret, *née* Brown; 2 s (Jonathan b 1973, Matthew b 1975); m 2, 23 Nov 1985, Mandy Elizabeth, da of Frederick Aldred, of Downham Market, Norfolk; 3 s (William b 1986, Joshua b 1987, Rupert b 1992); *Career* surveyor; articles A E Wilby & Son Barnsley 1964–67, various surveying appts 1967–74; ptnr: David Bedford Norfolk 1974–82, Hill Nash Pointen 1982–84, James Abbott Ptnrship 1984–86; dir Mann & Co 1986–87, md Hambro Countrywide plc 1988– (dir 1987–88); *Style*— Harry Hill, Esq; ✉ Hambro Countrywide Plc, Queensgate, 1 Myrtle Rd, Brentwood, Essex CM14 5EG (☎ 01277 264466, fax 01277 217916)

HILL, (Michael) Hedley; s of late Kenneth Wilson Hill, and Dorothy, *née* Etchells (d 1984); *b* 3 Feb 1945; *Educ* Rydal Sch Colwyn Bay, St John's Coll Cambridge; *Career* admitted slr 1969; NP; ptnr Weightman Rutherfords Liverpool 1971–95 (conslt 1995–); gen cmmr for Income Tax 1996–; pres Liverpool Law Soc 1992–93 (vice pres 1991–92), former chm Liverpool Young Slrs Gp; former pres Old Rydalian Club; memb: Law Soc, Liverpool Law Soc; *Recreations* canal boating, oenology; *Clubs* Liverpool Racquet, Union Soc Cambridge; *Style*— Hedley Hill, Esq; ✉ Fulwood Park Lodge, Liverpool L17 5AA (☎ 0151 727 3411); Weightman Rutherfords, Richmond House, 1 Rumford Place, Liverpool L3 9QW (☎ 0151 227 2601, fax 0151 227 3223, telex 627538)

HILL, Ian Canning; s of Hamilton Erskine Hill (d 1985), of Barnton, Edinburgh, and Janet MacColl, *née* Canning; *b* 20 Feb 1943; *Educ* Blackburn Tech and GS, George Heriot's Edinburgh, Univ of Strathclyde (Stenhouse scholar, MBA); *m* Aug 1973, Helen Taylor; 3 da (Fiona b Sept 1974, Kirstie b June 1976, Catriona b Nov 1979); *Career* inspr Royal Exchange Assurance 1960–66, mgmnt asst Northern Assurance Co Ltd 1966–67; Royal Insurance Holdings plc 1968–: head of mktg 1968–70, Mgmnt Res Unit 1970–72, asst agency mangr 1972–75, asst mktg mangr 1975–78, gp staff pensions mangr Royal Insurance plc 1978–; FCII; *Recreations* golf; *Style*— Ian Hill, Esq; ✉ Schiehallion, 7 Links Close, Raby Mere, Wirral, Merseyside (☎ 0151 334 5519); Group Staff Pensions Manager, Royal Insurance plc, PO Box 144, New Hall Place, Liverpool L69 3EN (☎ 0151 224 3443, fax 0151 224 4490)

HILL, Ian Frederick Donald; JP (1978); s of Frederick Donald Banks Hill (d 1952); *b* 14 May 1928; *Educ* Shrewsbury; *m* 1955, Marlene Elizabeth, da of Norman Vincent Rushton (d 1971); 2 c; *Career* ptnr Arthur Young 1958–88, chm Kwik Save Group plc 1973–94, dir Park Food Group plc 1983–; chm Royal Liverpool Children's Hosp NHS Tst 1990–94; FCA; *Recreations* golf; *Clubs* Royal Birkdale Golf; *Style*— Ian Hill, Esq, JP; ✉ 22 Hastings Rd, Southport, Merseyside PR8 2LW (☎ 01704 568398)

HILL, Sir (Stanley) James Allen; kt (1996), MP (C) Southampton Test (majority 585); s of James Hill, and Florence Cynthia Hill, of Southampton; *b* 21 Dec 1926; *Educ* Regent's Park Sch, N Wales Trainging Coll, Univ of Southampton; *m* 1958, Ruby Evelyn, da of Ross Albert Ralph, of Clanfield Farm, Basingstoke; 2 s, 3 da; *Career* Signals Offr Royal Fleet Aux 1941–46, served 11 yrs on BOAC flying staff, seconded to UN flying staff Kashmir; sr ptnr firm of Estate Agents; cncllr: Southampton City Cncl 1966–70 and 1976–79 (chm Housing Ctee 1968–70 and 1976–79, memb Ctee S Hampshire Plan); MP (C) Southampton Test 1970–Oct 1974 and 1979–; memb House of Commons Select Ctees on: Expenditure 1972–73, Euro Legislation 1979–83, Indust and Trade 1979–83; memb Mr Speaker's Panel of Chairmen 1990–, chm Cons Backbench Ctee on Housing and Construction 1971–73, chm Cons Constitutional Affairs Ctee, chm Housing Improvements Ctee, vice chm All Party Anglo-Singapore Gp, chm All Party Anglo-Sri Lankan Gp; UK memb Euro Parl Strasbourg 1972–75 (chm Tport Ctee for Europe and chm Ctee for Regnl Dept Policy 1973–75, govt whip to Cncl of Europe and Western European Defence 1979–90); memb: Cwlth Parly Assoc, Inter-Parly Union, British-American Parly Gp, Conservative Gp of Europe, Anglo-Hong Kong Gp, Anglo-Greek Gp, UN Assoc; Fell Indust and Parliament Tst; *Recreations* private aviation, farming; *Clubs* St Stephen's Constitutional; *Style*— Sir James Hill, MP; ✉ Gunfield Lodge, Melchet Park, Plaitford, Hants; House of Commons, London SW1A 0AA (☎ 0171 219 3000)

HILL, Sir James Frederick; 4 Bt (UK 1916), of Bradford; DL (W Yorks 1994); s of Sir James Hill, 3 Bt (d 1976), and Marjory, *née* Croft; *b* 5 Dec 1943; *Educ* Wrekin Coll, Univ of Bradford; *m* 1966, Sandra Elizabeth, da of late J C Ingram, of Ilkley; 1 s (James Laurence Ingram b 1973), 3 da (Juliet Clare (Mrs Richard Morton) b 1969, Georgina Margaret b 1971, Josephine Valerie b 1976); *Heir* s, James Laurence Ingram Hill b 22 Sept 1973; *Career* exec chm Sir James Hill Wool Ltd; dir: MGM (Int) Ltd, Airedale NHS Trust; chm Bradford Kirklees Calderdale CEPD; pres Keighley Business Forum; *Recreations* tennis, sailing, golf; *Clubs* RAC, Bradford, Ilkley, St Enodoc; *Style*— Sir James F Hill, Bt, DL; ✉ Roseville, Moor Lane, Menston, Ilkley, W Yorks LS29 6AP (☎ 01943 874624)

HILL, Jeremy Adrian; s of Lt-Col Cecil Vivian Hill (d 1978); *b* 16 Jan 1940; *Educ* Eton, Ch Ch Oxford; *m* 1965, Virginia Ann, da of Maj Gordon Darwin Wilmot; 3 s; *Career* dir: J Henry Schroder and Co, Schroder Investment Management Ltd, Korea Europe Fund plc; chm: Schroder Korea Fund plc, Schroder Japan Growth Fund plc, Schroder Indian Communications Fund Ltd, Schroder Asiapacific fund plc; *Recreations* tennis, shooting, tree planting; *Style*— Jeremy Hill, Esq; ✉ Peyton Hall, Bures, Suffolk; J Henry Schroder Wagg and Co Ltd, 120 Cheapside, London EC2V 6DS (☎ 0171 382 6000, telex 885029)

HILL, John Andrew Patrick; CBE (1978); s of Henry Wilfred Hill and Beatrice Rose, *née* Smith; *b* 8 Feb 1936; *Educ* Ealing Tech Coll, MECAS; *m* 1960, Barbara Anne, da of Maj Frederick Joseph Knifton (d 1965); 2 s (Andrew, Timothy), 1 da (Philippa); *Career* served RAF 1954–56; banker; British Bank of the ME 1956–78, Hongkong and Shanghai Banking Corporation Hong Kong 1979–89; dir 1990–: British Bank of the ME, Egyptian British Bank, Cyprus Popular Bank; chm British Arab Commercial Bank London; chm Ctee for Middle E Trade; *Recreations* organ playing, travel, photography, fishing; *Style*— J A P Hill, Esq, CBE; ✉ 30 Gresham Street, London EC2V 7LP

HILL, John Edward Bernard; s of Capt Robert William Hill (ka 1917), and Marjorie Jane Lloyd-Jones, *née* Scott-Miller (d 1981); *b* 13 Nov 1912; *Educ* Charterhouse, Merton Coll Oxford (MA); *m* 7 July 1944, Edith (d 1995), wid of Cdr R A E Luard, RNVR, and da of John Maxwell (d 1940), of Cove, Dumbartonshire; 1 adopted da (Linda (Mrs Jackson) b 7 March 1943); *Career* cmmnd RA (TA) 1938, air observation post pilot RA WO 1942 (wounded Tunisia 1943), specially employed WO 1944, invalided out 1945; called to the Bar Inner Temple 1938; farmer in Suffolk 1946–; memb CLA Exec 1957–59 and 1977–82; MP (C) South Norfolk 1955–74, govt whip and lord cmmr of Treasy 1959–64, memb Cncl of Europe and WEU 1970–72, MEP 1973–74; memb: E Suffolk and Suffolk Rivers Bd 1952–62, Governing Body Charterhouse Sch 1957–90, Exec Ctee GBA 1966–83, Bd of Govrs Suttons Hosp in Charterhouse 1966–, Cncl UEA 1975–82; *Clubs* Garrick, Farmers'; *Style*— J E B Hill, Esq; ✉ Watermill Farm, Wenhaston, Halesworth, Suffolk IP19 9BY (☎ 01502 478207, fax 01502 478777)

HILL, John Lawrence; s of Sidney Hill (d 1978), and Hilda Wardle, *née* Sutcliffe (d 1991); *b* 21 July 1934; *Educ* Abbotsholme Sch, Sidney Sussex Coll Cambridge (MA); *m* 1960, Elizabeth, da of Robert Hamilton Godfrey; 1 s (Timothy b 1961), 3 da (Jane b 1962, Rebecca (twin) b 1962, Lucy b 1966); *Career* Nat Serv RCS 1953–55; with Royal Dutch Shell Group 1959–67, PA Consulting Group 1967–86, chief exec Loss Prevention Cncl 1986–, chm Britannia Building Society 1990–94 (dir 1984–94); dir: Loss Prevention Certification Bd 1986–, Britannia Life 1989–94, Nat Approval Cncl for Security Systems 1990–; govr Inst of Risk Mgmnt 1987–93; CEng, MIMechE 1965, FIRM 1987, CIMgt 1992; *Recreations* golf, music, opera; *Clubs* Royal and Ancient (Golf); *Style*— John Hill, Esq; ✉ Warwick Lodge, Warwicks Bench, Guildford, Surrey GU1 3TG (☎ 01483 566413)

HILL, Sir John McGregor; kt (1969); s of John Campbell Hill (d 1982); *b* 21 Feb 1921; *Educ* King's Coll London, St John's Coll Cambridge; *m* 1947, Nora Eileen, *née* Hellett; 2 s, 1 da; *Career* Flt Lt RAF 1941; UKAEA: joined 1950, memb of prodn 1964–67, chm 1967–81; chm: Br Nuclear Fuels Ltd 1971–83 (hon pres 1983–86), Amersham International plc 1975–88, Aurora Holdings 1984–88, Rea Bros plc 1987–95; memb: Advsy Cncl on Technol 1968–70, Nuclear Power Advsy Bd 1973–81, Energy Cmmn 1977–79; FRS, FInstP, FIChemE, FInstE, FEng 1982; Chevalier de la Légion d'Honneur; *Recreations* golf, gardening; *Clubs* East India; *Style*— Sir John Hill, FRS, FEng; ✉ Dominic House, Sudbrook Lane, Richmond, Surrey TW10 7AT (☎ 0181 940 7221)

HILL, Sir John Maxwell; kt (1974), CBE (1969), DFC (1945), QPM; s of late L S M Hill, of Plymouth; *b* 25 March 1914; *Educ* Plymouth Coll; *m* 1939, Marjorie Louisa Reynolds (d 1992); 1 s (John), 1 da (Monica); *Career* served WW II Flying Offr Bomber Cmd RAFVR; HM Inspr of Constabulary 1965–66; asst cmmr: Admin and Ops 1966–68, Personnel and Trg Met Police 1968–71; dep cmmr 1971–72, Chief Inspr of Constabulary Home Office 1972–75; *Recreations* golf, walking; *Clubs* RAC, RAF; *Style*— Sir John Hill, CBE, DFC, QPM; ✉ 4 The Kingsway, Epsom, Surrey KT17 1LT

HILL, John Michael; s of Stanley Hill, of Mychett, Surrey, and Ellen May, *née* Rose; *b* 28 Aug 1944; *Educ* St Dunstan's Coll Catford, Jesus Coll Cambridge (MA); *m* 25 Jan 1973, (Jean) Shirley, da of Jan Jakub Spyra (d 1979), of Cheadle; 1 s (Jeffrey), 1 da (Nicola); *Career* ptnr Watson Wyatt Partners (formerly R Watson & Sons) Consulting Actuaries 1974– (joined 1970); FIA 1971, FPMI 1981; *Recreations* music, keeping fit; *Style*— John Hill, Esq; ✉ 4 Underhill Park Rd, Reigate, Surrey RH2 9LX (☎ 01737 249473); Watson Wyatt Partners, Watson House, Reigate, Surrey RH2 9PQ (☎ 01737 241144, fax 01737 241496, telex 946070)

HILL, Jonathan Hopkin; CBE (1995); s of Rowland Louis Hill, and Paddy Marguerite, *née* Henwood; *b* 24 July 1960; *Educ* Highgate Sch, Trinity Coll Cambridge (MA History); *m* 3 Sept 1988, Alexandra Jane, da of John Nettlefield, MC; 2 da (Georgia Elizabeth b 9 Oct 1991, Harriet Victoria b 10 Jan 1993), 1 s (Archie William Augustus b 1 June 1995); *Career* RIT & Northern 1983, Hamish Hamilton 1984–85, Cons Research Dept 1985–86, special advsr to Rt Hon Kenneth Clarke at Dept of Employment, DTI and Dept of Health 1986–89, Lowe Bell Communications 1989–91, No 10 Policy Unit 1991–92, political sec to PM 1992–94, sr conslt Lowe Bell Communications 1994–; memb: Cncl Nat Literacy Tst, Bd Crime Concern; govr Highgate Sch; *Books* Too Close to Call (with Sarah Hogg, 1995); *Style*— Jonathan Hill, Esq, CBE; ✉ Lowe Bell Communications Ltd, 7 Hertford Street, London W1Y 8LP (☎ 0171 495 4044)

HILL, Judith Lynne; LVO (1995); da of Dr Michael James Raymond (d 1996), and Joan, *née* Chivers; *b* 8 Oct 1949; *Educ* Brighton and Hove HS, Univ of Cambridge (MA); *m* 1, 9 Oct 1976 (m dis 1986), Brent Arthur Hill; 1 da (Olivia b 1981); m 2, 6 March 1987, Edward Richard Regenye, s of Edward Joseph Regenye (d 1987), of New Jersey, USA; *Career* admitted slr 1975, ptnr Farrer and Co 1986; dir: Melloward Ltd, WRVS Office Premises Ltd, GSN Ltd; vice-chm Ctee 20 Int Bar Assoc; memb: Law Soc, Ctee Charity Law Assoc; *Recreations* travel, gardening; *Clubs* Reform; *Style*— Mrs Judith Hill, LVO; ✉ Messrs Farrer & Co, 66 Lincoln's Inn Fields, London WC2A 3LH (☎ 0171 242 2022, telex 24318, fax 0171 831 9748)

HILL, Julian; s of Harold Brian Cunningham Hill (d 1980), and Elise Magdalen, *née* Jeppe (d 1971); *b* 9 Aug 1932; *Educ* Rottingdean Sch, Eastbourne Coll; *m* 20 March 1956, (Ruth) Monica, da of late Paul Sekvens Toll, of Stockholm; 2 s (Rowland b 1956, Michael b 1960), 1 da (Anne-Louise b 1963); *Career* Nat Serv 2 Lt 22 Cheshire Regt 1952–54 (served in Egypt); dir various cos operating UK and overseas for Unilever plc 1954–77; chm and md: Scanhill Ltd 1977–94, Julian Hill Ltd 1977–95; commercial advsr UN 1977–93; Freeman City of London 1982, Liveryman Worshipful Co of Marketors 1984; FIMgt, FInstD, MCIM; *Recreations* skiing, watching cricket, opera; *Clubs* MCC, Naval & Military; *Style*— Julian Hill, Esq; ✉ Huntsland Cottage, Huntsland Lane, Crawley Down, Sussex RH10 4HB (☎ and fax 01342 712286)

HILL, (Trevor) Keith; MP (Lab) Streatham (majority 2,317); s of George Ernest Hill, of Birstall, Leics, and Ena Ida, *née* Dakin; *b* 28 July 1943; *Educ* City of Leicester Boys' GS, CCC Oxford (MA), Univ Coll of Wales Aberystwyth (DipEd); *m* 19 May 1972, Lesley Ann Sheppard, da of Heinz Doktor; *Career* tutorial asst in politics Univ of Leicester 1966–68, Belgian Govt scholar Brussels 1968–69, lectr in politics Univ of Strathclyde 1970–73 (res asst 1969–70), res offr Lab Pty International Dept 1974–76, political offr RMT (formerly NUR) 1976–92; MP (Lab) Streatham 1992–; *Books* European Political Parties (contrib, 1969), Electoral Behaviour (contrib, 1974); *Recreations* films, books, music, walks; *Style*— Keith Hill, Esq, MP; ✉ 110 Wavertree Road, London SW2 3SN (☎ 0181 674 0434); House of Commons, London SW1A 0AA (☎ 0171 219 6980)

HILL, Kenneth Leslie (Ken); s of William Leslie Hill (d 1965), of Great Barr, Birmingham, and Doris Agnes, *née* Clarke (d 1975); *b* 13 May 1941; *Educ* W Bromwich Tech HS, W Bromwich Tech Coll, Wolverhampton Poly, Alban & Lamb Coll, Harvard Business Sch; *m* 2 Sept 1964, Wendy, da of George Somerville; 2 s (Christopher David and Richard Anthony (twins) b 28 July 1966), 2 da (Suzanne Marie b 8 Aug 1965, Lisa Joanne b 28 Nov 1971); *Career* accountant West Bromwich CBC 1957–62, sr accountant Walsall CBC 1962–67, chief accountant Harlow Development Corp 1967–69, chief financial offr Essex River Authy 1969–72, chief financial offr Glamorgan River Authy 1972–73, dir of fin Severn Trent Water 1973–89, gp dir of fin South West Water plc 1989–; CIPFA 1963; *Recreations* golf, cricket, squash, tennis; *Clubs* Harvard Business, Exeter Golf and Country; *Style*— Ken Hill, Esq; ✉ South West Water plc, Peninsula House, Rydon Lane, Exeter EX2 7HR (☎ 01392 446688, fax 01392 443778, car 0831 414873)

HILL, (Eliot) Michael; QC (1979); s of late Cecil Charles Hill, and late Rebecca Betty Hill; *b* 22 May 1935; *Educ* Bancroft's Sch Woodford Green Essex, BNC Oxford (MA); *m* 27 April 1965, Kathleen Irene (Kitty), da of late Rev Tom Venables Hordern; 1 s (Jonathan Edward Venables b 3 Oct 1970), 2 da (Penelope Gillian b 8 Dec 1968, Carolyn Patricia b 24 Nov 1972); *Career* called to the Bar Gray's Inn 1958, bencher 1986, head of chambers 1982–95; admitted to the Bar of NSW 1991, QC (NSW) 1991; recorder of the Crown Ct 1977–; Treasy counsel: Inner London Sessions/Inner London Crown Court 1969–74, Central Criminal Court 1974–79; memb: Senate of the Inns of Ct and the Bar and Gen Cncl of the Bar 1976–79 and 1982–90, Cncl of Legal Educn 1977–86, Criminal Law Revision Ctee 1983–; Criminal Bar Assoc: fndr memb 1969, memb Ctee 1970–86, sec 1972–75, vice chm 1979–82, chm 1982–86; chm: Gray's Inn Continuing Educn Ctee 1991–94, Mgmnt Ctee Soc for the Reform of Criminal Law 1992–96 (dir 1988–), Inns of Ct Advocacy Trg Ctee 1995–; dir Bar Mutual Indemnity Fund 1987– (chm Investment Ctee 1992–); memb Wine Ctee SE Circuit 1972–89; *Clubs* Garrick; *Style*— Mr Michael Hill, QC; ✉ 36 Essex St, London WC2R 3AS (☎ 0171 413 0353, fax 0171 413 0374, home ☎ and fax 0181 287 9005)

HILL, Ven Michael Arthur; s of Arthur Hill, of Congleton, Cheshire, and Hilda, *née* Fisher; *b* 17 April 1949; *Educ* Wilmslow Co GS, N Cheshire Coll of FE (dip in business studies), Ridley Hall Cambridge, Fitzwilliam Coll Cambridge (CertTheol); *m* Anthea Jean, da of Michael Longridge (d 1958); 4 da (Naomi Annabel, Charis Rebeccah, Alexa Helen, Eleanor Fay), 1 s (Nicholas Michael); *Career* mgmnt trainee/jr exec in printing indust 1969–72, memb Scargill House Community 1972–73; theol educn 1973–77 (ordained 1977); asst curate St Mary Magdalene Croydon Surrey (then Dio of Canterbury) 1977–80, curate-in-charge Christ Church Slough (Dio of Oxford) 1980–83, priest-in-charge St Leonard Chesham Bois (Dio of Oxford) 1983–90, rector of Chesham Bois 1990–92, archdeacon of Berkshire 1992–; *Recreations* sport, reading, civil aircraft; *Style*— The Ven the Archdeacon of Berkshire; ✉ Foxglove House, Love Lane, Donnington, Newbury RG13 2JG (☎ 01635 552820, fax 01635 522165)

HILL, Michael William; s of Geoffrey William Hill (d 1961), of Cadewell Park, Torquay, and Dorothy, *née* Ursell (d 1973); *b* 27 July 1928; *Educ* King Henry VIII Sch Coventry, Nottingham HS, Lincoln Coll Oxford (MA, MSc); *m* 1, 1957, Elma Jack, *née* Forrest (d 1967); 1 s (Alastair Geoffrey Frank b 1961), 1 da (Sally Ann b 1959); m 2, 1969, Barbara Joy, *née* Youngman; *Career* Sgt Instr RAEC 1947–49; res scientist Laporte Chemicals Ltd 1953–56, res and prodn mangr Morgan Crucible Group 1956–64, asst keeper Br Museum 1964–68; dir: Nat Reference Library of Sci and Invention 1968–73, Sci Reference Library Br Library 1973–86; assoc dir sci technol and industry Br Library 1986–88, jt series ed Bowker-Saur Guides to Information Sources; memb: UK Delgn to CEC Working Parties on Patents and on Info for Indust 1973–78, UK Chemical Info Serv Bd 1974–77, Advsy Ctee for Scot Sci Reference Library 1983–88; vice pres IATUL (Int Assoc of Technol Univ Libraries) 1976–81; chm: Circle of State Librarians 1977–79, Cncl ASLIB 1979–81, Mgmnt Bd UDC 1990–91; fndr Western European Round Table on Information (later renamed European Cncl of Information Assocs) 1981, pres Int Fedn for Info and Documentation 1984–90; FRSA, MRSC, FIInfSci; *Books* Patent Documentation (with Wittmann and Schiffels, 1979), Michael Hill on Science Invention and Information (1988), National Surveys of Library & Information Services: Yugoslavia (with Tudor-Silovic, 1990), National Information Policies and Strategies (1994); *Recreations* golf; *Clubs* United Oxford & Cambridge Univ; *Style*— Michael Hill, Esq; ✉ Jesters, 137 Burdon Lane, Cheam, Surrey SM2 7DB (☎ 0181 642 2418)

HILL, Peter; s of Percy Hill (d 1964), and Mary Anne, *née* Coffey (d 1982); *b* 22 Sept 1934; *Educ* Univ of Cambridge; *m* 2 Aug 1969, Sandra; 1 s (Ben b 1977); *Career* surgical registrar Royal Melbourne Hosp 1964–67, orthopaedic registrar and sr registrar Bristol Royal Infirmary 1969–73, conslt orthopaedic surgn N Staffs Hosp Centre 1973–; FRCS, FBOA; *Recreations* golf, gardening; *Style*— Peter Hill, Esq; ✉ private consulting rooms: MIC House, 8 Queen St, Newcastle, Stoke-on-Trent, Staffs ST5 1EB (☎ 01782 620201)

HILL, Prof Peter David; s of Derryck Albert Hill (d 1988), and Phyllis Mary, *née* Carn; *b* 16 March 1945; *Educ* Leighton Park Sch, Univ of Cambridge and St Bartholomew's Hosp London (MA, MB BChir); *m* 10 June 1972, Christine Margaret, da of Stanley

William Seed, of Seaton, Devon; 2 s (Gulliver b 1974, Luke b 1976), 1 da (Jessica b 1981); *Career* registrar then sr registrar Maudsley Hosp 1972–79, currently prof of child mental health, head of section and conslt in child and adolescent psychiatry St George's Hosp and Med Sch Univ of London 1992– (sr lectr 1979–92), hon conslt St Thomas' Hosp 1981–, conslt Tadworth Court Children's Hosp 1987–, conslt advsr British Army; chm Child and Adolescent Specialist Section RCPsych 1993–, advsr Select Ctee on Health 1996–; FRCP 1994 (MRCP 1972), FRCPsych 1987 (MRCPsych 1975), MCPCH 1996; *Books* Essentials of Postgraduate Psychiatry (with R Murray and A Thorley, 1979 and 1986), A Manual of Practical Psychiatry (with P Bebbington, 1986), Adolescent Psychiatry (1989), The Child Surveillance Handbook (with D Hall and D Elliman, 1990 and 1994), The Child with a Disability (with D Hall, 1996), Essentials of Psychiatry (with R Murray and P McGuffin, 1996); *Recreations* jazz trumpet, house restoration; *Style*— Prof Peter Hill; ✉ Strand End, 78 Grove Park Rd, London W4 3QA (☎ 0181 994 4349, fax 0181 742 8609); Department of Mental Health Sciences, St George's Hospital Medical School, Cranmer Terrace, London SW17 0RE (☎ 0181 725 5531, fax 0181 725 3592)

HILL, Reginald Charles; s of Reginald Hill (d 1961), and Isabel, *née* Dickson; *b* 3 April 1936; *Educ* Carlisle GS, St Catherine's Coll Oxford (BA); *m* 1960, Patricia, da of Leslie Ruell; *Career* worked for Br Cncl Edinburgh 1960–61; Eng teacher: Royal Liberty Romford Essex 1962–64, Fryerns Sch Basildon Essex 1964–67; Eng lectr Doncaster Coll of Educn 1967–81; author; Crimewriters' Assoc Gold Dagger award (for the best crime novel) 1990 and Diamond Dagger award 1995; memb: Crime Writers' Assoc 1971, The Detection Club 1978, Soc of Authors 1984; *Books* A Killing Kindness (1980), Who Guards A Prince (1982), Traitor's Blood (1983), Deadheads (1983), Exit Lines (1984), No Man's Land (1985), Child's Play (1987), The Collaborators (1987), Under World (1988), Bones and Silence (1990), Recalled to Life (1992), Blood Sympathy (1993), Pictures of Perfection (1994), The Wood Beyond (1996); novels under the pseudonym of Patrick Ruell incl: The Long Kill (1986), Death of a Dormouse (1987), Dream of Darkness (1989), The Only Game (1991); novels under the pseudonym of Dick Morland: Heart Clock (1973), Albion! Albion! (1974); novels under the pseudonym of Charles Underhill: Captain Fantom (1978); short story collections: Pascoe's Ghost (1979), There are No Ghosts in the Soviet Union (1987); plays: An Affair of Honour (BBC, 1972), Ordinary Levels (Radio 4, 1982); *Recreations* fell walking, listening to classical music, watching rugby, Siamese cats; *Style*— Reginald Hill, Esq; ✉ Caradoc King, A P Watt Ltd, Literary Agents, 20 John St, London WC1N 2DR (☎ 0171 405 6774, fax 0171 831 2154)

HILL, Rear Adm (John) Richard; s of Stanley Hill (d 1963), of Standlake, Oxon, and May, *née* Henshaw (d 1969); *b* 25 March 1929; *Educ* RNC Dartmouth, King's Coll London; *m* 21 July 1956, Patricia Anne, da of (Leslie) Edward Sales, of Upwey, Dorset; 1 s (Nigel b 1959), 2 da (Anna b 1960, Penelope b 1960); *Career* Naval Offr (Navigation Specialist) HM ships until 1962, MOD, Flag Offr Admty Interview Bd 1981–83, ret 1983; under treas The Hon Soc of The Middle Temple 1983–94, hon bencher 1994, sec Cncl of the Inns of Ct 1987–93; ed The Naval Review 1983–; memb: Navy Records Soc (memb Cncl 1993–), Soc for Nautical Res (memb Cncl 1993–, chm 1994–); *Books* The Royal Navy Today and Tomorrow (1981), Anti-Submarine Warfare (1984), British Seapower in the 1980s (1985), Maritime Strategy for Medium Powers (1986), Air Defence at Sea (1988), Arms Control at Sea (1989), Oxford Illustrated History of the Royal Navy (gen ed, 1995); author articles in jls incl: Survival, Navy Int, Naval Forces, NATO's 16 Nations, Brassey's Annual, Defence and Diplomacy, World Survey, The Naval Review; *Recreations* amateur theatre, crumbly cricket; *Clubs* Royal Cwlth Soc; *Style*— Rear Adm Richard Hill; ✉ Cornhill House, Bishop's Waltham, Southampton SO32 1EF (☎ 01489 892656)

HILL, Richard; s of Charles Loraine Hill, JP (d 1976), of Alveston, nr Bristol, and Mary Amabel, *née* Harford (d 1966); *b* 25 July 1921; *Educ* Eton; *m* 17 April 1948, (Jean) Mary Vernon, da of Sir George Vernon Proctor Wills, Bt (d 1931), of Blagdon, nr Bristol; 1 s (Charles Peter Loraine b 1954), 3 da (Angela Mary Loraine (Mrs Stone) b 1949, Caryll Loraine (Mrs Ingerslev) b 1951, Sarah Loraine b 1957); *Career* RE 1944–46, demobbed as Capt; Charles Hill of Bristol Ltd 1939–81 (chm 1968–81), chm Bristol City Line of Steamships 1968–81; memb: Exec Cncl Shipbuilding Conf 1955–68, SW Regnl Bd for Indust 1961–66; chm Dry Dock Owners and Repairers Central Cncl 1962–63; memb: SW Region Econ Planning Cncl 1965–66, Shipbuilding and Shiprepairing Cncl 1966–68; chm Statistics Working Pty 1967–68, memb Grand Cncl CBI 1967–82; chm: Maritime Tport Res Steering Panel 1967–77, SW Regnl Cncl CBI 1968–70, Dart Containerline Bermuda Ltd 1969–72, memb Gen Ctee Lloyd's Register of Shipping 1973–77; directorships incl: Heenan Gp Ltd, Prince of Wales Dry Dock Co Ltd, Lovells Shipping and Tport Ltd, Dart Containerline Inc; nat and local involvement incl: memb Lloyd's Underwriters 1951–, pro chllr Univ of Bristol 1986– (memb Cncl 1959–, chm of Cncl 1972–86), tstee Bristol Municipal Charities 1962–, memb Nat Assoc of Youth Clubs (now Youth Clubs UK) 1964– (chm Exec Ctee 1964–70, later vice pres), chm W of England Branch IOD 1967–69 and 1972–75, memb SW Electricity Bd 1972–77, memb Appeal Ctee Wells Cathedral Appeal 1976–84, memb Ctee AA 1979–89, memb St George's House Assoc 1982– chm Bristol Local Ctee Br Assoc for Advancement of Sci 1984–87; Freeman: City of London 1954, City of Bristol 1957, Soc of Merchant Venturers (Master 1975–76), Worshipful Co of Shipwrights (Prime Warden 1976–77); JP: Somerset 1962–74, Avon 1974–91; High Sheriff of Somerset 1964; Hon LLD Univ of Bristol 1976; CEng, FRINA 1967 (assoc memb 1955); *Recreations* fishing, chess, painting; *Style*— Richard Hill, Esq, JP

HILL, Richard John; s of John Lewin Hill, of Keynsham, nr Bristol, and Audrey, *née* Chatterton; *b* 4 May 1961; *Educ* Bishop Wordsworth's GS Salisbury, Sch of Educn Univ of Exeter; *m* 3 Aug 1985, Karen Jane, da of Terry Shrapnell; 1 s (Joshua b 17 March 1987), 1 da (Natalie b 20 April 1988); *Career* rugby union scrum-half Bath RFC and England (29 caps); Salisbury RFC 1979–84, Exeter Univ RFC 1980–83 (capt 1982–83), replacement England Colts (under 19) v Wales and France 1980, English Univs and England Students 1982; Bath RFC: debut v Maesteg 1983, 265 appearances (incl 8 Cup Final victories) 1983–94; England: debut v South Africa Port Elizabeth 1984, NZ 1985, capt for 3 matches 1987, played in World Cup 1987, first try v Wales Twickenham 1990, toured Argentina 1990, played in World Cup 1991 (runners-up); record as England's most capped scrum-half; physical educn teacher 1984–86, fin conslt Sedgwick Noble Lowndes Ltd 1988–96, dir of coaching Gloucester Rugby Club 1996–; *Recreations* family, travel; *Style*— Richard Hill, Esq; ✉ 117 Newbridge Road, Bath BA1 3HG (☎ 01225 312057)

HILL, Richard Kenneth; TD (1972), DL (1993 Cambs); s of Lt-Col Peter Kenneth Hill, TD (d 1988), of Peterborough, and Sylvia Mary Jephson, *née* Widdowson (d 1996); *b* 20 April 1941; *Educ* Oakham Sch; *m* 29 April 1967, Pip Mary, da of Bernard Shipman (d 1995), of Belton, nr Grantham, Lincolnshire; 1 s (Timothy Kenneth b 6 Sept 1969), 1 da (Zoë Louise b 31 Dec 1971); *Career* TA served: 8 Bn Sherwood Foresters, 5/8 Bn Sherwood Foresters, 4/5 Bn Northamptonshire Regt, 5 (volunteer) Bn Royal Anglian Regt, Maj 1970 (served as OC HQ at Peterborough); admitted slr 1964, sr ptnr Wyman & Abbott Peterborough; fndr vice pres of Rotary Club of Peterborough Ortons, chm Cambridgeshire TAVR Assoc 1989–95, pres Peterborough Branch of Northants Regtl Comrades Assoc; Freeman City of London 1994, memb Worshipful Co of Pattenmakers; memb Law Soc; *Recreations* gardening, field sports; *Clubs* Royal Over-Seas League; *Style*— Richard Hill, Esq, TD, DL; ✉ Cherry Orton Farm, Orton Waterville, Peterborough PE2 5EQ (☎ 01733 231495); 35 Priestgate, Peterborough PE1 1JR (☎ 01733 64131)

HILL, Prof Robert Mount; s of Arthur Hardie Hill (d 1963), and Georgina Victoria Alexandra, *née* Gibson (d 1976); *b* 8 June 1933; *Educ* Hillhead HS, Royal Coll of Science and Technol (ARCST), Univ of Glasgow (PhD, DSc); *m* Morag, da of Ian Aberigh Mackay; 3 s (Nicholas Andrew Mackay b 13 March 1960, Robert Ian Arthur b 7 Aug 1961, Colin William Gibson b 20 Nov 1964), 1 da (Elizabeth Janette Alexandra b 31 Aug 1966); *Career* res fell Nat Standards Laboratory Sydney 1958–61, ICI res fell Clarendon Laboratory 1961–62, Electrical Research Assoc 1962–69; Univ of London: prof in physics Chelsea Coll 1982–85 (reader 1969–82), prof in physics KCL 1985–, head Sch of Physical Sciences and Engrg KCL 1994– (dep head 1990–94); FInstP 1974, FIEE 1981, FRSE 1992; *Style*— Prof Robert Hill, FRSE; ✉ School of Physical Sciences and Engineering, King's College London, The Strand, London WC2R 2LS (☎ and fax 0171 873 2881)

HILL, District Judge Robert Nicholas; s of Edward Hill, and Sylvia Grace, *née* Kingham; *b* 19 Oct 1947; *Educ* Salford GS, Manchester Coll of Commerce, Coll of Law Lancaster Gate; *m* 30 Sept 1967, Ann Elizabeth, da of Bernard Frost, and Lily Frost; 1 s (Giles Robert b 20 Aug 1976), 1 da (Shona Ann b 1 Jan 1980); *Career* jr clerk Messrs Hall Brydon & Co Slrs Manchester 1964–67, articled to Michael Bowman Bowman's Slrs Minehead Somerset 1968–73, admitted slr 1974 (John Mackrell Prize); Coll of Law Chester: lectr 1974–78, sr lectr 1978–83, princ lectr 1983–88, Bd of Mgmnt 1988–92; princ Coll of Law York 1988–92, district judge 1992–, asst recorder 1996–; memb: Law Soc 1974–, Assoc of District Judges 1992–; fell Inst of Legal Execs 1972 (associate 1967); TA: joined 1978, trg RMA Sandhurst 1980, cmmd 33 Signal Regt, RARO York 1988–; *Books* Civil Litigation (with John O'Hare, 1 edn 1980, 7 edn 1995), How To Survive Your Articles (1987); author of numerous articles; *Style*— District Judge Robert Hill; ✉ Kingston Upon Hull Combined Court, Lowgate, Kingston Upon Hull HU1 2EZ (☎ 01482 586161, fax 01482 588527)

HILL, Robin Murray; s of Albert Edward Hill, of Bramshot Dr, Fleet, Hampshire, and Phyllis, *née* Edgeler; *b* 13 Nov 1942; *Educ* Lancing; *m* Susan Margaret, da of Dr Gordon Carter (d 1994), of Sheephatch Farm, Tilford, Farnham, Surrey; 2 da (Victoria b 1968, Vanessa b 1972); *Career* chartered surveyor Jones Lang Wootton 1972–79, ptnr Clifford Tee and Gale (architects and surveyors) 1979–; FRICS 1967; *Recreations* equestrian and country pursuits, skiing, rough gardening; *Clubs* Athenaeum; *Style*— Robin Hill, Esq; ✉ Southdown House, Lower Froyle, Alton, Hampshire GU34 4NA (☎ 01420 22187); Clifford Tee & Gale, 5 Eccleston St, London SW1W 9LY (☎ 0171 730 9633)

HILL, Dr Ronald David; s of David Josiah Hill (d 1974), and Theresa, *née* Handy; *b* 20 June 1932; *Educ* Coventry Tech Coll, Guy's Hospital (MB BS); *m* 27 June 1957, Juliet Dorothea, da of Charles William Webb; 1 s (Simon Peter b 1966), 1 da (Sarah Louise b 1968); *Career* Nat Serv, NCO RAMC 1952–54; sr registrar Guy's Hosp 1967–70 (res fell 1967), conslt physician Wessex RHA 1970–; memb Br Diabetic Assoc, fndr chm Wessex Diabetes and Endocrine Assoc; FRCP 1978, MRCS, fell Assurance Med Soc 1989; *Books* contrib: Essentials Clinical Medicine (1984), Compendium of Anaesthetic and Resuscitative Data (1984), Microalbuminuria (1988); Diabetes Health Care (1987), Diabetes and Primary Eye Care (1993); *Recreations* sailing, walking, gardening; *Clubs* Royal Motor Yacht; *Style*— Dr Ronald Hill; ✉ Marlow Grange, 20 Martello Road, Poole, Dorset BH13 7DH (☎ 01202 708917); Department of Diabetes, Poole General Hospital, Poole, Dorset (☎ 01202 665511)

HILL, Rosalind Margaret; da of Brian Percival Hill (d 1992), and Joan Barbara Warren, *née* Rollinson; *b* 18 April 1955; *Educ* St Margaret's Convent Sussex, Univ of Exeter (BA); *Career* ACA; Ernst & Young 1977, J Henry Schroder Wagg & Co Ltd 1986, dir corporate fin P&P plc 1988–92 dir Capita Corporate Finance Ltd 1992–93, independent corp advsr Warren Hill & Co 1992–; memb: The Pilgrims, London Friends of The Home Farm Tst, The Lady Taverners; MInstD, ACA 1981; *Recreations* travel, entertaining, the arts; *Style*— Miss Rosalind Hill; ✉ Warren Hill and Co, 10 Westmoreland Terrace, London SW1V 4AF (☎ 0171 828 8460)

HILL, Selima; da of James Wood, and Elisabeth, *née* Robertson (d 1991); *b* 13 Oct 1945; *Educ* New Hall Cambridge; *m* 1968, Roderic Hill; 2 s (Moby b 1972, Albert b 1977), 1 da (Maisie b 1970); *Career* author; writer in residence Royal Festival Hall 1992–; winner: Cholmondeley Award for Lit 1989, Arvon Observer Int Poetry Competition 1989, Arts Cncl writers bursary 1993; writing fell UEA 1991, tutor Exeter and Devon Arts Centre 1990–96; exhibitor Imperial War Museum 1996; memb Assoc Faculty Schumacher Coll 1992, cultural exchange visit to Mongolia 1993 and 1994; *Books* Saying Hello at the Station (1984), My Darling Camel (1987), The Accumulation of Small Acts of Kindness (1988), Point of Entry (Multimedia work Imperial War Museum, 1990), A Little Book of Meat (1993), Trembling Hearts in the Bodies of Dogs (1994), Violet (1996); *Recreations* swimming, learning Mongolian; *Style*— Ms Selima Hill; ✉ c/o Bloodaxe Books, PO Box 1SN, Newcastle upon Tyne NE99 1SN (☎ 0191 232 5988, fax 0191 222 0020)

HILL, Shaun Donovan; s of George Herbert Hill (d 1969), and Molly, *née* Cunningham, of London; *b* 11 April 1947; *Educ* The London Oratory, St Marylebone GS; *m* 11 June 1966, Anja Irmeli, da of Martti Toivonen, of Lahti, Finland; 1 s ((Kim) Dominic b 18 Jan 1967), 2 da (Maija b 9 April 1972, Minna b 10 June 1975); *Career* cook: Carrier's Restaurant London 1968–71, The Gay Hussar London 1972–74, Intercontinental Hotel London 1975–76; head chef: Capital Hotel Knightsbridge 1976–77, Blakes Chelsea 1978–80, Lygon Arms Broadway Worcs 1981–82; chef and patron Hill's Stratford upon Avon 1983–85, chef and md Gidleigh Park Chagford Devon 1985–94 (currently dir), chef and proprietor Merchant House Ludlow Shropshire 1995–; memb Academie Culinaire de France 1982, elected master chef by Master Chef's Inst 1983, Egon Ronay Guide Chef of the Yr 1992, Catey Chef Award 1993; research fell Dept of Classics Univ of Exeter; *Books* Shaun Hill's Gidleigh Park Cookery Book, Quick and Easy Vegetables, Masterclass; *Recreations* eating and drinking (not necessarily in that order); *Style*— Shaun Hill, Esq; ✉ The Merchant House, Lower Corve Street, Ludlow, Shropshire SY8 1DU (☎ 01584 875438)

HILL, Stanley Arthur; s of John Henry Hill (d 1976), and Edith Muriel, *née* Mathews (d 1985); *b* 22 May 1935; *Educ* Townsend C of E Sch St Albans; *m* 9 July 1960, Elizabeth Scott (Betty), da of James McKay, of Forsyte Shades, Canford Cliffs, Poole, Dorset; 2 da (Elizabeth Scott b 19 Feb 1962, Catherine McKay b 11 Nov 1963); *Career* Nat Serv RMP 1953–55, served ME; gp md Coopers Holdings Ltd until 1994; Queen's Award for Export 1982 and 1986; pres Br Scrap Fedn 1993–94; Br vice pres Bureau Int de la Recuperation (BIR) 1989–94; memb Ctee: 1986 Indust Yr, Lechlade Soc; FInstD 1968; *Recreations* cricket, golf; *Clubs* Burford Golf (pres 1996–), IOD; *Style*— Stanley Hill, Esq; ✉ The Butts, Bryworth Lane, Lechlade, Gloucestershire GL7 3DY (☎ 01367 252598, fax 01367 253232)

HILL, His Hon (Ian) Starforth; QC (1969); s of Capt Harold Victor John Hill (d 1967), and Helen Dora, *née* Starforth; *b* 30 Sept 1921; *Educ* Dragon Sch Shrewsbury, BNC Oxford (MA); *m* 1, 1950 (m dis), Bridget Mary Footner; 1 s (David b 1951), 2 da (Jane b 1953, Juliet b 1956); *m* 2, 1982 (m dis), Greta Grimshaw; *m* 3, Wendy Elizabeth Stavert; *Career* Capt Indian Army 1940–45, India, Africa, Italy (despatches); called to the Bar 1949; dep chm IOW Quarter Sessions 1968–71, recorder Crown Ct 1972–74, circuit judge 1974, memb Parole Bd 1983–84, resident judge Winchester Combined Court Centre 1990–94, ret; *Recreations* gardening, games, amateur theatre; *Clubs* Hampshire; *Style*—

His Hon Starforth Hill, QC; ✉ Ladywell House, Ladywell Lane, Alresford, Hampshire SO24 9DF

HILL, Susan Elizabeth (Mrs Stanley Wells); da of R H Hill, and Doris, *née* Bailey; *b* 5 Feb 1942; *Educ* Scarborough Convent, Barr's Hill Sch Coventry, King's Coll London (BA); *m* Prof Stanley Wells, *qv*; 3 da (Jessica b 1977, Imogen b 1984 d 1984, Clemency b 1985); *Career* novelist, playwright, book reviewer; novels: The Enclosure (1961), Do Me A Favour (1963), Gentleman and Ladies (1968), A Change for the Better (1969), I'm the King of the Castle 1970, The Albatross (1971), Strange Meeting (1971), The Bird of Night (1972), A Bit of Singing and Dancing (collected short stories, 1973), In the Springtime of the Year (1974), Air and Angels (1991), Mrs de Winter (1993); ghost stories: The Woman in Black (1983), The Mist in the Mirror (1992); autobiography: The Magic Apple Tree (1982), Family (1989); children's books: One Night at a Time, Mother's Magic, Can it be true?, Suzy's Shoes, Pirate Poll, Septimus Honeydew, I won't go There Again, Stories of Codling Village, The Glass Angels, I've Forgotten Edward; ed: The Distracted Preacher and other stories (Thomas Hardy), The Walker Book of Ghost Stories, The Penguin Book of Modern Women's Short Stories; plays: The Cold Country, and other plays for radio; *Style*— Miss Susan Hill; ✉ Longmoor Farmhouse, Ebrington, Chipping Campden, Glos GL55 6NW (☎ 01386 593352, fax 01386 593443)

HILL, Vince; s of late William Hill, and late Lillian Hill; *b* 16 April 1937; *Educ* Coventry; *m* 4 June 1959, Annie; 1 s (Athol Vincent William b 19 Oct 1971); *Career* Nat Serv Band of Royal Corps of Signals; former baker and miner Keresley Colliery Coventry; singer; operatic baritone touring and appearing at prestigious venues, fndr of vocal gps: Four Others, The Raindrops; solo performer 1962–; singles incl: The Rivers Run Dry, Edelweiss 1967, Roses of Picardy, Look Around; Cabaret Performer of the Year; composer of musicals: Tolpuddle (played the lead role in BBC Radio 4 broadcast), Zodiac (with Alan Plater and Johnny Worth); radio series incl: Vince Hill's Solid Gold Music Show, Simply Vince (1991), The Joint is Jumping (BBC) 1994; TV series: The Musical Time Machine, They Sold a Million; stage acting debut as Ivor Novello in My Dearest Ivor (1990); successes in int song festivals as singer and composer, winner of many awards and recognised as one of Britain's top male vocalists, appeared as guest on numerous TV and radio shows in Britain and Europe, toured overseas, featured as subject of This is Your Life; *Style*— Vince Hill, Esq; ✉ Representative: Robert Holmes, GBA, Sherborne Wharf, 27–28 Sherborne Street, Birmingham B16 8DZ (☎ 0121 608 6000, fax 0121 608 2223)

HILL, Prof William George; s of William Hill (d 1984), of Hemel Hempstead, Herts, and Margaret Paterson, *née* Hamilton (d 1987); *b* 7 Aug 1940; *Educ* St Albans Sch, Wye Coll Univ of London (BSc), Univ of California Davis (MS), Iowa State Univ, Univ of Edinburgh (PhD, DSc); *m* 1 July 1971, (Christine) Rosemary, da of John Walter Austin, of Kingskerswell, Devon; 1 s (Alastair b 1977), 2 da (Louise b 1973, Rachel b 1974); *Career* Univ of Edinburgh: prof of animal genetics 1983– (lectr 1965–74, reader 1974–83), head Inst of Cell, Animal and Population Biology 1990–93, head Div of Biological Sciences 1993–; visiting prof and visiting res assoc: Univ of Minnesota 1966, Iowa State Univ 1967–78, N Carolina State Univ 1979, 1985 and 1988–; ed: Animal Production 1971–78, Livestock Production Science 1994–95, Genetical Research 1996–; memb: Sci Study Gp Meat and Livestock Cmmn 1969–72, AFRC Animals Res Grant Bd 1986–92, Dir's Advsy Gp AFRC Animal Breeding Res Orgn 1983–87, AFRC Inst of Animal Physiology and Genetics Res 1987–93, Bd of Govrs Roslin Inst 1994–, Cncl Royal Soc 1993–94, RAE Biological Scis Panel 1995–96; FRSE 1979, FRS 1985; *Books* Benchmark Papers on Quantitative Genetics (1984), Evolution and Animal Breeding (1989); *Recreations* farming, bridge; *Clubs* Farmers'; *Style*— Prof William Hill, FRS, FRSE; ✉ 4 Gordon Terrace, Edinburgh EH16 5QH (☎ 0131 667 3680); Institute of Cell, Animal and Population Biology, University of Edinburgh, West Mains Rd, Edinburgh EH9 3JT (☎ 0131 650 5705, fax 0131 650 6564)

HILL-ARCHER, Clive; s of Malcolm Hill-Archer, of Menorca, Spain, and Agnes Keech, *née* Harrison, of Hampton, Middx; *b* 23 March 1946; *Educ* Duke of York Sch Nairobi Kenya, Dulwich Coll, SW London Tech Coll (HND Business Studies), DipM (CIM), Univ of Strathclyde (MSc); *m* 2 April 1966, Valerie Frances, *née* Balchin; 2 da (Maxine Louise b 6 Feb 1969, Naomi Angelina b 29 Aug 1970); *Career* account mangr/dir with several advtg agencies incl Garland Compton, Dorland (Paris), Grey (Paris) and Allen Brady & Marsh 1967–80, Univ of Strathclyde 1980–82, new technol mangr Thames Television Ltd 1982–84, mktg dir Thorn EMI Cable Television Ltd 1984–86, mktg devpt dir Tupperware UK and Ireland 1986–87, mangr mktg consultancy Pennell Kerr Forster Associates 1987–, non-exec dir International Weather Productions 1990–93, owner/managing conslt Niche Marketing & Communications 1992–; interim exec mktg mangr The Wine Soc Jan-July 1996; memb Nat Cncl CIM (Pres's Award 1993); visiting lectr in mktg London Guildhall Univ 1988–95, external examiner Univ of East London 1995–; memb: Wine Soc, Clay Pigeon Shooting Assoc; Freeman City of London 1991, Liveryman Worshipful Co of Marketors 1991; memb: RTS 1982, Assoc of MBAs 1986; FCIM 1990 (MCIM 1969), MInstTT 1994, memb Int Consulting Economists' Assoc 1995, MIDM 1996; *Recreations* keeping fit (running, squash and tennis), rambling, driving (follower of motor sport), shooting, wine, the Arts (ballet, music, theatre and art); *Style*— Clive Hill-Archer, Esq; ✉ Niche Marketing & Communications, 127 Turney Road, Dulwich Village, London SE21 7JB (☎ 0171 274 5235, fax 0171 274 4482, e-mail niche.mktg@btinternet.com)

HILL-NORTON, Vice Adm the Hon Sir Nicholas John; KCB (1991); s of Adm of the Fleet Baron Hill-Norton, GCB (Life Peer); *b* 1939; *Educ* Marlborough Coll, RNC Dartmouth; *m* 1966, Ann Jennifer, da of Vice Adm Dennis Mason, CB, CVO (d 1996); 2 s (Simon b 1967, Tom b 1975), 1 da (Claudia b 1969); *Career* RN: Capt HMS Invincible 1983–84, Flag Offr Gibraltar 1987–90, Flag Offr Flotilla Three and Cdr Anti-Submarine Warfare Striking Force 1990, Flag Offr Surface Flotilla 1992, Dep Chief of Defence Staff 1992; defence advsr GEC-Marconi Ltd 1995–; dir: Matra Marconi Space 1996–, Lear Astronics USA 1996–, GM Electronic Systems Corp and Hazeltine USA 1996–; memb Cncl RUSI; *Clubs* Farmers', Valderrama Golf (Spain, hon memb); *Style*— Vice Admiral the Hon Sir Nicholas Hill-Norton, KCB; ✉ GEC-Marconi Ltd, The Grove, Stanmore, Middlesex HA7 4LY (☎ 0181 954 2311, fax 0181 954 7808)

HILL-NORTON, Adm of the Fleet Baron (Life Peer UK 1978); Peter John; GCB (1970, KCB 1967, CB 1964); s of Capt Martin John Norton (d 1928); *b* 8 Feb 1915; *Educ* RNCs Dartmouth and Greenwich; *m* 1936, Eileen, da of Carl Adolph Linstow (d 1947); 1 s, 1 da; *Career* Independent peer in House of Lords; RN 1932, served WWII Arctic Convoys and NW Approaches, Capt 1953, Rear Adm 1962, ACNS 1962–64, Flag Offr 2 in cmd Far East Fleet 1964–66, Vice Adm 1965, dep CDS (Personnel and Logistics) 1966–67, Second Sea Lord 1967, vice CNS 1967–68, Adm 1968, C-in-C UK Forces Far East 1969–70, CNS and First Sea Lord 1970–71, Adm of the Fleet 1971, CDS 1971–74, chm NATO Mil Ctee 1974–77; pres Sea Cadet Assoc 1978–84, chm Steering Ctee for Volunteer Home Def Force 1983, fndr pres Br Maritime League, pres Friends of Osborne House 1980–; Freeman City of London 1974, Liveryman Worshipful Co of Shipwrights 1974; *Books* No Soft Options (1978), Sea Power (1982); *Recreations* gardening, shooting; *Clubs* Army and Navy, Royal Navy of 1765; *Style*— Adm of the Fleet the Rt Hon the Lord Hill-Norton, GCB; ✉ Cass Cottage, Hyde, Fordingbridge, Hants (☎ 01425 652392)

HILL SMITH, Marilyn; da of George Francis Smith, and Irene Charlotte, *née* Clarke; *b* 9 Feb 1952; *Educ* Nonsuch HS For Girls Ewell Surrey, Guildhall Sch of Music & Drama; *Career* opera singer; soprano soloist: Viennese Gala Performances Southbank and touring 1975–80, Gilbert & Sullivan For All touring England Australasia (1974) USA/Canada (1975–76) 1969–75; debut: BBC Radio 1975, princ soprano ENO 1978 (memb co 1978–84), Royal Opera House 1981, New Sadler's Wells Opera 1981, Canadian Opera 1984, Welsh Nat Opera 1987, Scottish Opera 1988, New D'Oyly Carte Opera 1990, Singapore Opera 1992 and 1993; festivals incl: Aldeburgh, Henley, Versailles, Nurenburg, Cologne, Athens, Granada, Bologna, Siena, Rome, Hong Kong; TV incl: Top C's and Tiaras (C4) 1983, Queen Mother's 90 Birthday Celebration 1990; recordings incl: Dixit Dominus (CBS Masterworks) 1977, The Songwriters (BBC) 1978, Christopher Columbus (Opera Rara) 1978, La Princesse de Navarre (Erato) 1980, Dinorah (Opera Rara) 1980, Robinson Crusoe (Opera Rara) 1981, Count of Luxembourg and Countess Maritza (New Sadler's Wells Opera) 1983, Vienna Premiere Vol I (Chandos, Music Retailers Assoc award 1984) 1983, Friday Night is Music Night (BBC Records) 1985, Treasures of Operetta Vol I (Chandos Retailers Assoc award 1985) 1985, Vienna Premiere Vol II (Chandos) 1987, Ruddigore (New Sadler's Wells) 1987, Candide (Bernstein, Scottish Opera) 1988, Treasures of Operetta Vol III (Chandos) 1989, Pirates of Penzance (New D'Oyly Carte, Music Retailers Assoc) 1990, Student Prince (TER) 1990, Marilyn Hill Smith sings Kálmán and Lehár (Chandos) 1991, Is It Really Me? (TER) 1991, Edwardian Echoes (Chandos) 1992, Novello Centenary (Chandos) 1992; *Recreations* cooking, reading, sleeping; *Style*— Ms Marilyn Hill Smith; ✉ c/o Music International, 13 Ardilaun Rd, Highbury, London N5 2QR (☎ 0171 359 5183, fax 0171 226 9792)

HILL-WOOD, Sir David Basil; 3 Bt (UK 1921), of Moorfield, Glossop, Co Derby; s of Sir Basil Samuel Hill Hill-Wood, 2 Bt (d 1954), by his w, Hon Joan Louisa Brand (d 1996), da of 3 Viscount Hampden; *b* 12 Nov 1926; *Educ* Eton; *m* 1970, Jennifer Anne McKenzie Stratmann (assumed surname, Stratmann, by deed poll 1960), da of Peter McKenzie Strang (Japanese POW, presumed d 1943); 2 s, 1 da; *Heir* s, Samuel Thomas Hill-Wood b 24 Aug 1971; *Career* Lt Grenadier Gds (Palestine) 1945–48; Morgan Grenfell 1948–55; Myers and Co stockbrokers 1955–74 (ptnr 1955–77, sr ptnr 1971–74); dir: Capel Cure Myers 1974–77, Guinness Mahon and Co 1977–; High Sheriff Berks 1982–83; former pres Victoria FA (Aust), Aust rep on FA 1977; *Recreations* tennis, farming; *Clubs* White's, Melbourne (Australia); *Style*— Sir David Hill-Wood, Bt; ✉ Dacre Farm, Farley Hill, Reading, Berks (☎ 0118 973 3185); 58 Cathcart Rd, London SW10 (☎ 0171 352 0389); Guinness Mahon and Co Ltd, 32 St Mary at Hill, London EC3P 3AJ (☎ 0171 623 9333)

HILL-WOOD, Peter Denis; s of Denis John Charles Hill Hill-Wood, MC (d 1982), of Hartley Wintney, Hants, and Mary Cecilia, *née* Martin Smith; *b* 25 Feb 1936; *Educ* Eton; *m* 1971, Sarah, *née* Andrews; 1 da (Sarah Frances b 5 July 1972), 2 s (Julian Peter b 16 Jan 1974, Charles Denis b 21 April 1976); *Career* with David A Bevan Simpson & Co (later de Zoete & Bevan) stockbrokers 1956–60; Hambros Bank Ltd: joined 1960, exec dir i/c fund mgmnt 1968, vice chm 1987, non-exec dir 1994–96, ret; chm: Arsenal Football Club plc, River Plate and General Investment Trust plc, Berkeley Hambro Property Co Ltd, Top Technology Ltd, Hambro International Venture Company Ltd, Royal National Pension Fund for Nurses, Masthead Insurance Underwriting plc 1993–, Corney and Barrow Group plc 1994–; non-exec dir Delphi Group plc 1996–; *Recreations* association football, golf, country pursuits; *Clubs* White's, Pratt's; *Style*— Peter Hill-Wood, Esq; ✉ office: 41 Tower Hill, London EC3N 4HA (☎ 0171 480 5000, fax 0171 702 9262)

HILLARY, Sir Edmund Percival; KG (1995), KBE (1953); s of Percival Augustus Hillary, of Remuera, Auckland, NZ; *b* 20 July 1919; *Educ* Auckland GS, Auckland Univ Coll; *m* 1, 1953, Louise Mary Rose (d 1975); 1 s (Peter), 2 da (Sarah, Belinda (d 1975)); m 2, 21 Dec 1989, June Mulgrew, wid of Peter Mulgrew; *Career* mountaineer, explorer, author, lectr; served navigator RNZAF Pacific Theatre WWII; first person to reach summit of Mt Everest (with Sherpa Tensing) Br Mount Everest Expdn 1953; leader: NZ section Br Trans Antarctic Expdn 1957–58 (supervised building of Scott Base in McMurdo Sound), various Himalayan expdns 1960–66, Antarctic Expdn 1967 (first ascent of Mt Herschel); other expdns incl: river journey E Nepal 1968, river journey up the Ganges from ocean to source in Himalayas 1977, American expdn to China and Tibet 1981, twin engined ski plane landing at North Pole (with Neil Armstrong) 1985; NZ High Cmmr to India, Nepal and Bangladesh 1985–89, formerly pres NZ Voluntary Service Abroad, int dir WWF, dir Field Educn Enterprises of Australasia Pty Ltd, advsr on camping activities to Sears Roebuck and Co Chicago and Toronto, appointed UNICEF special rep for children of the Himalayas 1991–; involved with extensive fund raising and aid activities in Himalayas 1960– (incl construction of schs, hosps, bridges, airfields, pipelines, etc), honoured by UN Environmental Prog for conservation work; Founders medal RGS, Hubbard medal Nat Geographical Soc, Polar medal, Cdr Merite et Sportif, Star of Nepal (1st Class), ONZ; *Books* incl: High Adventure (1956), East of Everest (with George Lowe, 1956), No Latitude for Error (1961), High in the Thin Cold Air (with Desmond Doig, 1963), Schoolhouse in the Clouds (1965), Nothing Venture Nothing Win (autobiography, 1975), From the Ocean to the Sky (1979), Two Generations (with Peter Hillary, 1983); *Recreations* skiing, camping, mountaineering; *Clubs* Explorers (NY, hon pres), New Zealand Alpine (hon memb); *Style*— Sir Edmund Hillary, KG, KBE; ✉ 278a Remuera Rd, Auckland, New Zealand

HILLER, Robin John Cecil; s of Cecil Bernard Hiller (d 1966), and Esmé Leonora Patience, *née* Hughes (d 1991); *b* 31 Oct 1933; *Educ* Epsom Coll; *m* 17 June 1961, Ann Margaret, da of Edwin Walter Booth, of Limpsfield, Surrey; 1 s (Mark Andrew Robin b 1962), 1 da (Alison Claire b 1963); *Career* Lt (X) RNR Nat Serv; CA Annan Dexter & Co to BDO Binder Hamlyn 1951–87, Lloyd's underwriter 1972–; fin dir and conslt; memb: Royal Surgical Aid Soc 1979–89, King's Fund Grants Ctee 1982–85; Liveryman Worshipful Co of Glovers; *Recreations* charitable work, walking, skiing, golf, bridge; *Clubs* City Livery, Naval; *Style*— Robin J C Hiller, Esq; ✉ Bydown, 73 Blue House Lane, Limpsfield, Surrey RH8 0AP (☎ 01883 714658, fax 01883 730685)

HILLER, Susan; *b* 1942; *Educ* Smith Coll US (AB), Tulane Univ (MA); *Career* artist; lectr Maidstone Coll of Art and tutor St Martin's Sch of Art 1975–80, post grad tutor Slade Sch of Art UCL 1980–91, assoc prof of art Dept of Fine and Applied Arts Univ of Ulster 1991–, distinguished visiting prof Dept of Art Calif State Univ Long Beach 1988, visiting prof of new genres Univ of Calif LA 1991, visiting Art Cncl chair Dept of Fine Art UCLA 1992; external examiner CNAA (various BA and MA Fine Art courses); memb Visual Arts Panel Greater London Arts Assoc 1976–81; Arts Cncl of GB: memb Sub-ctee Support Schemes for Artists 1978–82, judge Student Film and Video Awards 1986, memb Purchasing Panel South Bank Exhibition Centre 1990–92; artist in residence Univ of Sussex 1975, Visual Artist's Award GB (Gulbenkian Fndn) 1976 and 1977, Nat Endowment for the Arts fell (USA) 1982, Visual Arts Bd travelling fell (Aust) 1982; work in public collections incl: Arts Cncl of GB, Tate Gallery, V & A Museum, Contemporary Arts Soc; *Works* incl: Belshazzar's Feast (video installation), Monument (photography and audio), Midnight, Baker Street (self-portrait), An Entertainment (video installation); *Exhibitions* solo incl: Gallery House 1973, Hester van Royen 1976 and 1978, Serpentine Gallery 1976, Museum of Modern Art Oxford 1978, Gimpel Fils London (various 1980–95), A Space Toronto 1981, Akumulatory Warsaw 1982, Roslyn Oxley Gallery Sydney 1982, Interim Art 1984, ICA 1986, Pat Hearn NY 1988–90, Kettle's Yard Cambridge 1989, Mappin Gallery Sheffield 1990, Matt's Gallery London 1991, Pat Hearn Gallery NY 1991, Nicole Klagsbrun NY 1991, Third Eye Centre Glasgow 1991, Tate Gallery Liverpool 1996; group incl: From Britain '75 (Taidehall Helsinki) 1975, Hayward

Annual 1978, The British Art Show (Arts Cncl of GB) 1984, Kunst mit Eigen-Sinn (Museum Moderner Kunst Vienna) 1985, Staging the Self (Nat Portrait Gallery) 1986, Towards a Bigger Picture (V & A) 1987, 100 Years of Art in Britain (Leeds City Museum) 1988, Lifelines (Br Cncl, BASF, Tate, Ludwigshafen and Liverpool) 1989–90, Great British Art (Maclellon Galleries Glasgow) 1990, Ten Artists (Ceibu Caison Tokyo) 1990, Now for the Future (Hayward Gallery London) 1990, At One/At War with Nature (Pratt Inst Galleries NY) 1991, In Vitro (Joan Miro Fndn Barcelona), Rites of Passage (Tate Gallery London) 1995, Sydney Biennale 1996, Indside the Visual (ICA Boston) 1996; *Books* Dreams - Visions of the Night (co-author), The Myth of Primitivism (ed), various artists books and monographs; *Style*— Ms Susan Hiller; ✉ 83 Loudoun Rd, London NW8 ODL (☎ 0171 372 0438)

HILLER, Dame Wendy; DBE (1975, OBE 1971); da of Frank Watkin, and Marie Hiller; *b* 15 Aug 1912; *Educ* Winceby House Bexhill; *m* 1937, Ronald Gow (d 1993); 1 s (Anthony), 1 da (Ann); *Career* actress; *Theatre* incl: Love on the Dole (Garrick London and Shubert NY), Twelfth Night (war factory tour), Tess of the d'Urbervilles (Piccadilly), The Heiress (Biltmore NY 1948 and Haymarket London 1949), Aspern Papers (NY) 1962, The Wings of the Dove (Lyric) 1963, The Sacred Flame 1967, Crown Matrimonial (Haymarket), John Gabriel Borkman (NT) 1975, The Importance of Being Earnest (Royalty) 1987, Driving Miss Daisy (Apollo) 1988; *Films* incl: Pygmalion, Major Barbara, I Know Where I'm Going, Sons and Lovers, A Man for all Seasons, David Copperfield, Separate Tables (Oscar winner), Murder on the Orient Express, The Elephant Man, The Lonely Passion of Judith Hearne; *Style*— Dame Wendy Hiller, DBE; ✉ ICM Ltd, Oxford House, 76 Oxford Street, London W1N 0AX (☎ 0171 636 6565, fax 0171 323 0101)

HILLHOUSE, Sir (Robert) Russell; KCB (1991); s of Robert Hillhouse, of Newton Mearns, Glasgow, and Jean Russell; *b* 23 April 1938; *Educ* Hutchesons' GS Glasgow, Univ of Glasgow (MA); *m* 4 June 1966, Alison Janet, da of Barclay Stewart Fraser, of Edinburgh; 2 da (Catriona b 1967, Susanna b 1969); *Career* entered Home Civil Serv; Scottish Office: asst princ Educn Dept 1962, princ 1966, Treasy 1971, asst sec 1974, Home and Health Dept 1977, princ fin offr 1980, sec Educn Dept 1987 (under sec 1985), perm under-sec of state Scottish Office 1988–; CIMgt 1990, FRSA 1992, FRSE 1995; *Recreations* making music; *Style*— Sir Russell Hillhouse, KCB, FRSE; ✉ c/o Scottish Office, St Andrew's House, Regent Rd, Edinburgh EH1 3DG (☎ 0131 556 8400)

HILLIARD, Spenser Rodney; s of Alfred Hilliard (d 1982), of London, and Kathleen Claribelle Hilliard; *b* 14 March 1952; *Educ* City of London Sch, QMC, Univ of London (LLB); *m* 1 May 1993, Rachel Frances, *née* Hindle; 2 da (Daisy Isobel b 2 April 1994, Chloe Valentine b 14 Feb 1996); *Career* called to the Bar Middle Temple 1975, practising barr; memb Hon Soc of Middle Temple; non-exec dir N Middx Hosp 1990–; *Recreations* wine; *Clubs* Bar Yacht, Academy; *Style*— Spenser Hilliard, Esq; ✉ Lamb Building, Temple, London EC4Y 7AS (☎ 0171 797 7788, fax 0171 353 0535)

HILLIER, John Michael; s of Clifford Henry Hillier (d 1952), and Alice Jane, *née* Lane; *b* 8 Oct 1941; *Educ* Royal Masonic Sch Bushey, Wycliffe Coll Glos, Univ of Sheffield (BA); *m* 1994, Lesley Patricia, *née* Forrest; 2 s from previous m; *Career* HM inspr of taxes Inland Revenue 1963–64, educn officer and prodn mangr Pilkington Bros 1964–67, gp trg advsr Warrington Gp Trg Assoc 1967–68, sr conslt Industl Trg Serv 1968–73, successively trg mangr, salary systems mangr, employee rels mangr then personnel mangr W D and H O Wills 1973–86, chief exec Tobacco Indust Trg Orgn 1986–90; Nat Cncl for Vocational Qualifications: dir accreditation 1990–91, chief exec 1991–; chm Nat Cncl Indust Trg Orgns 1988–90; dir: NFMED 1992–, International Training Service Ltd 1992–; CIMgt; *Recreations* music, drama, tennis; *Style*— John Hillier, Esq; ✉ National Council for Vocational Qualifications, 222 Euston Road, London NW1 2BZ (☎ 0171 728 1800, fax 0171 916 6573, car 0385 924858)

HILLIER, Prof Sheila Mary Bernadette; da of John Francis Kelleher, of Penwortham, Lancs, and Bridget Cecilia, *née* O'Riordan; *b* 5 Oct 1944; *Educ* Convent of the Holy Child Jesus Preston, LSE (BSc), Bedford Coll London (MSc(Econ)), Univ of London (PhD), Renmin Daxue (People's Univ) Beijing (Dip in Chinese), London Hospital Medical Coll (certified bereavement cnsllr); *m* William Robert George Hillier, s of late Reginald Hillier; 1 da (Martha Tamar Riordan b 6 Sept 1975); *Career* res asst Dept of Social Admin LSE 1965–66, researcher Dept of Social Med Guy's Med Sch 1966–68, res asst Statistical Research Unit DHSS 1968–70; Bedford Coll London: res asst Social Research Unit 1971–73, lectr in med sociology 1973–74; Bart's/The London Hosp Med Colls: lectr in med sociology 1974–86, sr lectr 1986–94, prof 1994–; memb: Br Sociological Assoc 1984, Royal Society of Medicine 1987; *Books* Health-Care and Traditional Medicine in China 1800–1982 (with J A Jewell, 1983), Researching Cultural Differences in Health (with D Kelleher, 1995); *Recreations* early music, Westminster parents choir, cookery, gardening; *Style*— Prof Sheila Hillier; ✉ 166 Richmond Road, London E8 3HN (☎ 0171 254 2228); Department of Human Science & Medical Ethics, St Bartholomew's and the Royal Hospital School of Medicine and Dentistry, Turner Street, London E1 2AD (☎ 0171 377 7167)

HILLIER, William Edward; s of William Edward Hillier (d 1976), and Ivy, *née* Elliott; *b* 11 April 1936; *Educ* Acton Co GS, Luton Tech Coll (HNC, DMS), Open Univ (BA); *m* 12 April 1958, Barbara Mary, da of William Victor Thorpe (d 1980); 1 s (William Edward b 1963), 1 da (Joy Marie b 1961); *Career* Nat Serv 1955–57; missile electronic systems De Havilland Propellors Ltd 1957, semiconductor mfrg Texas Instruments Ltd 1960, tech dir Racal-Redac Ltd 1974 (involved with computer aided engrg systems 1970), computer integrated mfrg Racal Group Services 1984; EPSRC: dir of Application of Computers and Manufacturing-Engineering Directorate 1985–94, dir Information Technology 1991–94, head of Marketing and Industl Policy 1994–96; visiting industl fell Engrg Dept Univ of Cambridge 1996–; IEE: chm Computing and Control Bd Oct 1993–Oct 1994, memb Cncl 1992–94, memb membership Ctee 1995–, memb Mfrg Bd 1996–; CEng, FIEE, FIMgt; *Recreations* railway preservation (dir and company sec Gloucestershire & Warwickshire Steam Railway plc); *Style*— William Hillier, Esq; ✉ 19 Simon de Montfort Drive, Evesham, Worcs WR11 4NR (☎ 01386 443449)

HILLMAN, David; s of Leslie Hillman (d 1969), and Margery Joan, *née* Nash (d 1988); *b* 12 Feb 1943; *Educ* Aristotle Central Sch, London Sch of Printing (Graphic Art NDD); *m* 1, 27 Oct 1963 (m dis 1983), Eileen Margaret, *née* Griffin; 1 s (Stephen b 1968), 1 da (Jane b 1965); m 2, 2 July 1983, Jennie Diana, da of Max David Keith Burns, of Burley, Hants; 2 s (James Daniel b 3 July 1992, Thomas David b 3 July 1995); *Career* asst Sunday Times Magazine 1962–65; art ed: London Life 1965–66, Sunday Times 1966–68; ed Design for Living Section Sunday Times Magazine 1968–75, art dir and dep ed Nova Magazine 1968–75, freelance practice London 1975–76; art dir: Wolff Olins Ltd 1976–77, Le Matin de Paris 1977–78; ptnr Pentagram Design 1978–; Designers and Art Dirs Assoc: Gold Award for Design 1973, Silver Award 1972–73, 1975, 1983, 1984, 1989 and 1994; NY Art Dirs Int Silver Award 1992; memb AGI (UK pres), FCSD; *Books* Ideas on Design (co ed 1986), Puzzlegrams (1989), Pentagames (1990), Phantasmagrams (1992), Pentagram, The Compendium (co ed 1993), Nova 1965–75 (co author, 1993), Puzzlegrams Too! (1994); *Style*— David Hillman, Esq; ✉ 12 Dungarvan Avenue, London SW15 5QU (☎ 0181 876 4476); Pentagram Design Ltd, 11 Needham Rd, London W11 2RP (☎ 0171 229 3477, fax 0171 727 9932)

HILLMAN, Ellis Simon; s of David Hillman (d 1974), of London NW6, and Annie, *née* Roland (d 1967); *b* 17 Nov 1928; *Educ* York House Sch, Univ Coll Sch, Chelsea Coll of Science and Technol (BSc); *m* 10 Dec 1967, Louise, da of Jack Shalom (d 1971), of Manchester; 1 s (Eli Yaakov b May 1974); *Career* ground wireless mechanic RAF 1947–49, instr Empire Radio Sch RAF Debden 1948–49; scientific tech offr: Soil Mechanics Ltd 1955, NCB Field of Investigation Gp 1956–59; secondary sch teacher 1960–64, admin offr Architectural Assoc 1964–69, lectr Kilburn Poly 1969–70; Univ of E London (formerly Poly of E London): sr lectr 1970–73, princ lectr in environmental studies 1973–, head of Int Office 1981–85; princ lectr Sch of Architecture Sch of Ind Studies 1985–; cncllr: LCC Norwood 1958, GLC (chm Arts and Recreation Ctee 1977–81) and ILEA Hackney 1964–80 (vice chm 1980–81, chm Further and Higher Educn Ctee 1977–81), Colindale Ward London Borough of Barnet 1986–; mayor London Borough of Barnet 1994–95; chm London Subterranean Survey Assoc 1968–, govr Imperial Coll of Science and Technol 1969–90; memb: ARCUK Bd of Educn 1973–82 and 1986– (memb GP Ctee 1991–), Lee Valley Regnl Park Authy 1973–81, Sports Cncl 1975–81, Water Space Amenity Cmmn 1977–80, Inland Waterways Amenity Advsy Cncl 1977–80; govr: Museum of London 1973–82, Archaeology Ctee Museum of London 1980–92; pres Lewis Carroll Soc; FRSA; *Books* Essays in Local Government Enterprise (3 vols 1964–67), Towards a Wider Use (1976), London Under London (with Richard Trench, 1985); *Recreations* walking, classical music, reading, writing poetry; *Style*— Ellis S Hillman, Esq; ✉ University of East London (☎ 0181 590 7722 ext 3239/3229)

HILLMAN, Prof John Richard; s of Robert Hillman (d 1990), of Farnborough, Orpington, Kent, and Emily Irene, *née* Barrett; *b* 21 July 1944; *Educ* Chislehurst and Sidcup GS, Univ Coll of Wales (BSc, PhD); *m* 23 Sept 1967, Sandra Kathleen, da of George Palmer, of Luton; 2 s (Robert George b 1968, Edmund John b 1969); *Career* lectr in physiology and environmental studies Univ of Nottingham 1969–71 (asst lectr 1968–69); Univ of Glasgow: lectr in botany 1971–77, sr lectr 1977–80, reader 1980–82, prof 1982–86; dir Scottish Crop Research Inst 1986–; visiting prof: Univ of Dundee 1986–, Univ of Strathclyde 1986–, Univ of Edinburgh 1988–, Univ of Glasgow 1991–; author of papers in scientific jls and books on plant physiology and plant biochemistry; Bawden lectr 1993; chm Technology Foresight Panel on Agric, Natural Resources and Environment 1994–95, and Panel on Agric, Horticulture and Forestry 1995–; Hon DSc Univ of Strathclyde 1994; FIBiol, CBiol 1985, FLS 1982, FBIM 1987, FRSE 1985; *Books* ed: Isolation of Plant Growth Substances (1978), Biosynthesis and Metabolism of Plant Hormones (with A Crozier, 1984), Biochemistry of Plant Cell Walls (with C T Brett, 1985), Opportunities and Problems in Plant Biotechnology (with W Powell, 1992); *Recreations* landscaping, building renovations, horology, reading; *Clubs* Farmers; *Style*— Prof John Hillman, FRSE; ✉ Scottish Crop Research Institute, Invergowrie, Dundee DD2 5DA (☎ 01382 562731, fax 01382 561412, telex 265871 MONREF G Quote Ref NQQOO3)

HILLS, Andrew Worth; s of Roland Frederick Hills, of Newbury, Berks, and Margaret Eunice, *née* Johnson; *b* 1 Sept 1949; *Educ* Abingdon Sch, Corpus Christi Coll Cambridge (exhibitioner, Manners scholar, MA); *m* 1, 1974 (m dis 1992), Frances Mary, da of Victor Hargreaves Ralston; 3 s (Robert John b 28 May 1979, David Richard b 5 May 1981, Nicholas Anthony b 17 Dec 1983); m 2, 1992, Mary Sandra, da of Arnolfo John Caraffi; *Career* UKAEA: joined 1971, princ fin and progs offr 1984–86, authy personnel offr 1986–89, exec dir fin and personnel 1989–91, md sites and personnel 1991–92, md corp servs 1992–94, md Servs Div 1994–95; dir special projects BBC 1995–96, dir BBC Monitoring 1996–; participant Duke of Edinburgh's Commonwealth Study Conf 1980; CIMgt 1993, FRSA 1995; *Recreations* historic churches, music, reading, gardening; *Style*— Andrew Hills, Esq; ✉ Director BBC Monitoring, Caversham Park, Reading, Berks RG4 8TZ (☎ 01734 469209, fax 01734 461105)

HILLS, Barrington William (Barry); s of William George (d 1967), of Upton on Severn, Worcs, and Phyllis, *née* Biddle; *b* 2 April 1937; *Educ* Ribston Hall Gloucester, St Mary's Convent Newmarket, Mr Whittaker's Worcester; *m* 1, 21 Nov 1959 (m dis 1977), Maureen, da of late Patrick Newson; 3 s (John b 1960, Michael b 1963, Richard b 1963); m 2, 1 Sept 1977, Penelope Elizabeth May, da of John Richard Woodhouse, of Widmerpool, Notts; 2 s (Charles b 1978, George b 1983); *Career* Nat Serv King's Troop RHA, racehorse trainer 1969–; won: Prix de L'Arc de Triomphe, Budweiser Irish Derby, Irish 1000 Guineas, Irish Oaks, Prix Royal-Oak, 2000 Guineas Newmarket, 1000 Guineas Newmarket; second place Epsom Derby three times; *Recreations* hunting, shooting, golf; *Clubs* Turf; *Style*— Barry W Hills, Esq; ✉ B W Hills Southbank Ltd, Southbank, Newbury Road, Lambourn, Berks RG17 7LL (☎ 01488 71548)

HILLS, David Henry; CBE (1993); s of Henry Stanford Hills (d 1945), and Marjorie Vera Lily, *née* Constable; *b* 9 July 1933; *Educ* Varndean Sch Brighton, Univ of Nottingham (BA); *m* 1957, Jean Helen, *née* Nichols; 1 s (Simon b 1962); 2 da (Susan b 1959, Jacqueline b 1960); *Career* MOD: entered 1956, dir of mktg Defence Sales Orgn 1979–82, dir of econ and logistic intelligence 1982–88, dir gen of intelligence 1988–93; memb: NBPI 1967–70, Nat Indust Rels Ct 1971–73; *Recreations* gardening; *Clubs* Royal Cwlth Soc; *Style*— David Hills, Esq, CBE

HILLS, Prof Peter John; OBE (1995); s of Maj Neville Morris Hills, TD, of Ashtead, Surrey, and Geraldine Yvonne, *née* Cazalet; *b* 17 Aug 1938; *Educ* Sutton Valence Sch Maidstone Kent, Imperial Coll London (BSc), Univ of Birmingham (MSc); *m* 26 July 1968, Lesley Edna, da of Albert Edward Slater (d 1957); 2 da (Karin Elizabeth b 1970, Fiona Suzanne b 1972); *Career* asst engr Miny of Transport 1962–63 (Buchanan Report working gp), lectr and conslt Imperial Coll London 1964–72, asst res dir Inst for Transport Studies Univ of Leeds 1972–77; Univ of Newcastle upon Tyne: prof of transport engrg 1977–, dir Transport Ops Res Group 1977–96, dean Faculty of Engrg 1996–; pres Instn of Highways and Transportation 1992–93, memb Transportation Bd Instn of Civil Engrs 1989; FCGI 1993 (ACGI 1961), CEng, MICE 1967, FIHT 1976, MIHE 1963, FCIT 1978 (MCIT 1971); *Books* Traffic In Towns (jtly, 1963), Motorways in London (jtly, 1969), Urban Transportation Planning Techniques (jtly, 1976), Roads and Traffic in Urban Areas (jtly, 1987); *Recreations* jazz, 20th century history; *Clubs* National Liberal; *Style*— Prof Peter Hills, OBE; ✉ 5 Rectory Terrace, Gosforth, Newcastle upon Tyne, Tyne and Wear NE3 1XY (☎ 0191 285 5157); Division of Transport Engineering, The University, Claremont Tower, Newcastle upon Tyne, Tyne and Wear NE1 7RU (☎ 0191 222 7997, fax 0191 222 6822)

HILLSBOROUGH, Earl of; Arthur Francis Nicholas Wills Hill; s and h of 8 Marquess of Downshire, *qv*; *b* 4 Feb 1959; *m* 28 April 1990, Diana Jane (Janey), o da of Gerald Leeson Bunting, of Otterington House, Northallerton, N Yorkshire; 1 s (Edmund Robin Arthur, Viscount Kilwarlin b 21 May 1996), 2 da (Lady Isabella Diana Juliet b 3 April 1991, Lady Beatrice Hannah Georgina b 10 Feb 1994); *Career* ACA; *Style*— Earl of Hillsborough; ✉ High Burton, Masham, nr Ripon, N Yorkshire HG4 4BS

HILLYER, John Selby; OBE (1975); s of Stanley Gordon Hillyer, OBE (d 1965), and Margaret, *née* Selby (d 1990); *b* 14 Feb 1925; *Educ* Stowe, Trinity Coll Oxford (MA); *m* 2 June 1951, Elizabeth Ann, da of Sinclair Jeavons Thyne, CBE, of Tasmania; 1 s (James b 1952), 2 da (Sarah b 1955, Caroline b 1958); *Career* Lt Coldstream Gds; called to the Bar Inner Temple 1949; ptnr Hill Vellacott CA 1954–88, sr ptnr Chantrey Vellacott 1988–89; dir: T H White Ltd 1954–94, Capel-Cure Myers Unit Trust Management Ltd 1983–; memb Cncl Barnardo's 1962–92 (chm 1970); Master Worshipful Co of Fanmakers 1969 (memb Ct of Assts); *Recreations* gardening, keeping ornamental ducks, genealogy; *Clubs* Royal Automobile; *Style*— John S Hillyer, Esq, OBE; ✉ Copden House, Biddenden, Kent TN27 8HE

HILSUM, Prof Cyril; CBE (1990); s of Benjamin Hilsum, and Ada Hilsum; *b* 17 May 1925; *Educ* Raines GS, UCL (BSc, PhD); *m* 16 Aug 1947, Betty (d 1987), da of Herbert Cooper; 2 da (Karen b 1954, Lindsey b 1958); *Career* Admty HQ 1945–47, Admty Res Laboratory 1947–50, Servs Electronics Res Laboratory 1950–64, RSRE 1964–83, dir of research GEC plc 1983–92; visiting prof of physics UCL; foreign assoc US Nat Acad, FRS, FEng 1978, FInstP, FIEE; *Books* Semiconducting III - V Compounds (1961), Handbook of Semiconductors (1993); *Recreations* tennis, chess; *Style*— Prof Cyril Hilsum, CBE, FRS, FEng; ✉ 12 Eastglade, Moss Lane, Pinner, Middx HA5 3AN (☎ 0181 866 8323, fax 0181 933 6114)

HILTON, Anthony Victor; s of Dr Raymond W Hilton (d 1975), and Miriam Eileen Norah, *née* Kydd; *b* 26 Aug 1946; *Educ* Woodhouse Grove Sch Bradford Yorks, Aberdeen Univ (MA); *m* 1, 30 March 1969 (m dis 1973); 1 s (Steven b 1969); m 2, Cyndy Miles; 2 s (Michael b 1985, Peter b 1987), 1 da (Emily b 1991); *Career* city ed The Times 1982–83, city ed Evening Standard 1984–89 and 1996– (md 1989–95); dir: Associated Newspapers plc 1989–95, London Forum 1993–, London First 1993–, St John's Ambulance Nat Fundraising Appeal 1993–95; vice pres Children's Film Unit 1993–95; memb Stock Exchange Ctee on Private Share Ownership (Weinberg Ctee) 1995–96; *Books* Employee Reports (1978), City within a State (1987); *Recreations* after dinner speaking; *Clubs* Lansdowne; *Style*— Anthony Hilton, Esq; ✉ Evening Standard, Northcliffe House, Derry St, London W8 5EE (☎ 0171 938 6000)

HILTON, Brian James George; CB (1992); s of Percival William Hilton, and Gladys, *née* Haylett; *b* 21 April 1940; *Educ* St Marylebone GS London; *m* 1965, Mary Margaret, *née* Kirkpatrick; 1 s, 2 da; *Career* joined Civil Serv 1958, Export Credits Guarantee Dept 1958–68, Bd of Trade 1968–71, first sec UK Delgn to OECD Paris 1971–74, asst sec DOI 1976–84, RCDS 1981, head Fin Servs Div DTI 1984–87, under sec and head Central Unit DTI 1987–89, dep sec MAFF 1989–91, dir Citizen's Charter Unit Cabinet Office 1991–94, dep sec DTI 1994–; fndn govr Hampden Gurney Primary Sch London 1976–; *Recreations* cricket, rugby, music, gardening, opera; *Style*— Brian Hilton, Esq, CB; ✉ Department of Trade and Industry, 1 Victoria Street, London SW1H 0ET (☎ 0171 215 5589, fax 0171 215 5500)

HILTON, Colin John; s of Herbert Jackson Mason Hilton, of Boston, Lincs, and Marjorie, *née* Wray (d 1975); *b* 17 Aug 1945; *Educ* Boston GS, Univ of Newcastle Med Sch (MB BS); *m* 15 Feb 1969, Helen, da of Flt Lt Joseph William Atkinson, DFC, of Newcastle upon Tyne; 1 da (Nicola b 27 Sept 1972); *Career* locum registrar in thoracic and gen surgery Queen Elizabeth Hosp Birmingham and Wolverhampton Royal Infirmary 1973, locum sr registrar in cardiothoracic surgery Harefield Hosp 1975–76 (registrar 1973–75), registrar in cardiac surgery Nat Heart Hosp 1976, sr registrar in cardiothoracic surgery Papworth Hosp Cambridge 1976–77, res fell Brown Univ Providence Rhode Is 1978, sr registrar St Bartholomew's Hosp 1979, conslt cardiothoracic surgn Freeman Hosp Newcastle 1979–; postgrad dean Soc of Cardiothoracic Surgns 1991–95; chm Specialist Advsy Ctee in Cardiothoracic Surgery RCS 1995–98; memb Ctee Soc of Cardiothoracic Surgns of GB and NI; FRCS 1973; *Recreations* golf, skiing; *Clubs* Northumberland Golf; *Style*— Colin Hilton, Esq; ✉ Rodborough, 8 Westfield Grove, Gosforth, Newcastle upon Tyne NE3 4YA (☎ 0191 284 7394); Regional Cardiothoracic Centre, Freeman Hospital, Freeman Rd, High Heaton, Newcastle upon Tyne NE7 7DN (☎ 0191 284 3111 ext 26587, fax 0191 213 1968)

HILTON, Isabel N; da of Dr Raymond W Hilton (d 1975), and Miriam Evelyn, *née* Kydd; *b* 25 Nov 1947; *Educ* Bradford Girls' GS, Walnut Hills HS Ohio USA, Univ of Edinburgh (MA), Peking Languages Inst, Univ of Fudan Shanghai (scholar); *m* 1, 1970 (m dis 1975), John Armstrong Black; m 2, Charles Neal Ascherson; 1 s (Alexander Stephen Thomas b 5 March 1985), 1 da (Iona Susan b 23 May 1988); *Career* journalist; teaching asst Chinese Dept Univ of Edinburgh 1972–73, Scottish TV 1976–77, Sunday Times 1977–86 (special corr China, feature writer, news reporter, Latin America ed, asst foreign ed); The Independent: Latin America ed 1986, Euro Affrs ed 1989, chief feature writer 1991–95; presenter The World Tonight (BBC radio) 1995–; memb: Chatham House (RIIA) 1977, Br Assoc of China Studies 1978, IISS 1989; *Books* The Falklands War (jtly, 1982), The Fourth Reich (jtly, 1984), Betrayed (contrib, 1988), The General (1990); *Recreations* family, gardening; *Clubs* Groucho; *Style*— Ms Isabel Hilton; ✉ BBC, The World Tonight, Broadcasting House, London W1A 1AA (☎ 0171 580 4468)

HILTON, Jane Elizabeth Anne; s of Derek George Ernest Hilton, and Anne Kathleen, *née* Stacy; *b* 3 Nov 1962; *Educ* Beaconsfield HS, Lancaster Univ (BA); *Career* photographic asst to various photographers incl Clive Arrowsmith, Gill Campbell and Koo Stark 1984–89, freelance photographer 1989–; clients incl: Next, Marks & Spencer, Austin Reed, Daily Telegraph, Valentino; Assoc of Photographers award 1994 and 1996; memb Assoc of Photographers; *Recreations* travel and music; *Style*— Miss Jane Hilton; ✉ Wingate House, 1–5 Corsham Street, London N1 6DR (☎ 0171 865 6020, fax 0171 490 0888)

HILTON, (Alan) John Howard; QC (1990); s of Alan Howard Hilton, (d 1986), of Bowdon, and Barbara Mary Campbell, *née* Chambers, (d 1958); *b* 21 Aug 1942; *Educ* Haileybury, Univ of Manchester (LLB); *m* 21 Dec 1978, Nicola Mary, da of Percy Harold Bayley (d 1977), of Brighton; 1 s (Felix b 24 Dec 1983); *Career* called to the Bar Middle Temple 1964, in practice 1964–, recorder 1985–; *Books* Fish Cookery (1981), Opera Today (1985); *Recreations* opera, conjuring, 19th century females in oils, cooking; *Clubs* Garrick, Les Six; *Style*— John Hilton, Esq, QC; ✉ Queen Elizabeth Building, Temple EC4 (☎ 0171 583 5766, fax 0171 353 0339)

HILTON, Rear Adm John Millard Thomas; s of Edward Thomas Hilton (d 1962), and Margaret Norah, *née* Millard (d 1994); *b* 24 Dec 1934; *Educ* Wyggeston GS Leicester, Clacton Co HS Essex, RNC Dartmouth (Civil Serv open scholarship), City Univ (MSc), Imperial Coll London (DIC); *m* 1, 1957 (m dis 1984), Patricia Anne, da of Rev Percy George Kirby; 1 s (Paul Christopher Michael b 24 May 1960), 1 da (Karen Deborah Lois b 8 Oct 1962); m 2, 28 May 1985, (Cynthia Mary) Caroline Seddon-Brown, da of Ian Edward Hargreave; 1 step da; *Career* Royal Navy: various Weapons Offr and other appts 1956–72, base engr and Princ Tech Offr Hong Kong 1973–76, Dir of Naval Engrg RNEC Manadon 1976–78, research and compliance appts Admty Surface Weapons Estab 1979–81, Asst Dir (Operational Requirements) and Dep Chief Naval Signal Offr 1983–85, project dir MOD Procurement Exec 1985–87, Pres of the Ordnance Bd Procurement Exec 1987–90, Rear Adm 1988, ret 1990; independent IT design conslt 1990–, also advsr to P-E International plc; visiting sr fell City Univ 1992; Freeman City of London, memb Ct of Assts Worshipful Co of Scientific Instrument Makers; FIEE 1977, FIMechE 1977; *Recreations* software engineering, Christian apologetics, DIY, photography, gardening, travel; *Style*— Rear Adm John Hilton; ✉ Pennyfold, Church Road, Steep, nr Petersfield, Hants GU32 2DF (☎ and fax 01730 263460, e-mail 100042.121@compuserve.com)

HILTON, Prof Julian; s of R K Hilton; *b* 11 Sept 1952; *Educ* Canford, BNC Oxford, Univ of Grenoble, Munich and Salamanca (MA, D Phil); *m* 1, 10 July 1976, Hanne, da of H J Boenisch; 1 da (Ruth b 18 Feb 1978); m 2, 29 Aug 1996, Malika, da of B Moussaid; *Career* res fell Alexander van Humboldt Stiftung 1976, fell Stiftung Maximilianeum Munich 1977, prof of drama and communications UEA 1988–91 (lectr 1977, sr lectr 1987, dir audio-visual centre 1987–91); fndr and ptnr Technol Arts Info 1985–, project mangr AIM prog EC 1989–91, dir AVC Multimedia Ltd 1991–93, md Telos Consulting Ltd 1993–95, pres Telos Grp 1995–; bd memb Theatre Royal Norwich, vice chm Norfolk Arts Forum, chm Artificial Intelligence and Interactive Systems Gp; fell Swedish Center for Working Life, jt project mangr COMETT proj EC 1991–, dir Value Project EC DGXIII; visiting prof Tech Univ Vienna conslt WHO 1991–; *Books* Georg Buchner (1982), Performance (1987), New Directions in Theatre (1992); Plays incl: The Enchanted Bird's Nest (1985), Broken Ground (1986), The Marriage of Panurge (1986), Courage (1989); *Recreations* opera, walking, shopping; *Style*— Prof Julian Hilton; ✉ Telos Bioinformatics Ltd, Suite 38, Beaufort Court, Admiral's Way, Waterside, London E14 9XL (☎ 0171 987 1773, fax 0171 537 9022)

HILTON, Mark William; s of Peter Entwistle Hilton, of Ripley, N Yorks, and Monica, *née* Smith; *b* 15 July 1958; *Educ* Wrekin Coll Wellington Shropshire, Univ of Leeds (LLB); *m* 25 April 1987, Catharine, da of George Canavan, of Ripon; 1 s (Thomas b 26 March 1994), 1 da (Camilla b 21 July 1991); *Career* slr; Last Suddards Bradford 1980–82, Barlow Lyde & Gilbert London 1982–85, ptnr Last Suddards Leeds 1986–88 (joined 1982, rejoined 1985), ptnr Hammond Suddards Leeds 1988–; memb Law Soc 1980–, FCIArb; *Recreations* skiing, scuba diving, tennis; *Clubs* RAC; *Style*— Mark Hilton, Esq; ✉ Birthwaite House, Birthwaite Lane, Ripley, Harrogate, N Yorks (☎ 01432 770136, fax 01423 772517); Hammond Suddards, 2 Park Lane, Leeds LS31 1ES (☎ 0113 284 7000, fax 0113 284 7001)

HILTON, Nicholas David; s of John David Hilton, and Dorothy Gwendoline, *née* Eastham; *b* 27 June 1952; *Educ* Marlborough; *m* 14 July 1984, Vanessa Jane, da of late Brig W John Reed; 2 da (Lucy Vanessa b 1989, Emma Rachel b 1992); *Career* CA 1974; ptnr Moore Stephens 1979–, nat exec dir Moore Stephens (UK) Ltd 1990–; FCA 1979, MCIM 1996; *Recreations* golf, skiing, mah-jong, entertaining; *Clubs* Richmond Golf; *Style*— Nicholas Hilton, Esq; ✉ Moore Stephens, St Paul's House, Warwick Lane, London EC4P 4BN (☎ 0171 334 9191, fax 0171 248 3408, telex 884610)

HILTON, Prof Rodney Howard; *b* 17 Nov 1916; *Educ* Manchester GS, Balliol Coll Oxford, Merton Coll Oxford (BA, DPhil); *Career* served WWII 46 Bn RTR 1940–45 (served Middle East and Italy), served Indian Army 1945–46; lectr, reader and prof of medieval social history Sch of History Univ of Birmingham 1946–84, dir Inst for Advanced Res in the Humanities Univ of Birmingham 1984–87; memb Editorial Bd jl Past and Present 1952–87; memb Past and Present Soc 1952–; FBA 1977; *Books* The Economic Development of Some Leicestershire Estates in the 14th and 15th Centuries (1947), The English Rising of 1381 (with H Fagan, 1950), A Medieval Society: the West Midlands at the End of the 13th Century (1966), Bond Men Made Free: Medieval Peasant Movements and the English Rising of 1381 (1973), The English Peasantry in the Later Middle Ages (Ford lectures, 1975), Class Conflict and the Crisis of Feudalism: Essays in Medieval Social History (1985), English and French Towns in Feudal Society (1992); *Style*— Prof Rodney Hilton, FBA

HILTON, Ronnie; s of John William Goodfellow Hill (d 1943), and Sarah Elizabeth, *née* Morgan (d 1965); *b* 26 Jan 1926; *Educ* Paisley Street Boys' Sch Hull, Ainthorpe Grove Mixed Sch Hull; *m* 1, 24 April 1948, Joan Lilian, *née* Conyer (d 1986); 1 s (Derry Richard b 10 April 1962), 2 da (Geraldine b 6 Aug 1949, Jane Lesley b 16 Nov 1960); m 2, 21 Jan 1989, Christine Kay, *née* Westoll; 1 s (Simon Matthew b 7 Dec 1966); *Career* began recording and broadcasting in 1954, 24 records in the charts incl No Other Love (number 1 for 6 weeks 1956); appeared in three Royal Command Performances; made numerous radio broadcasts and TV appearances incl two series of Hilton's Half Hour (STV) and Sounds of the 50's (BBC Radio 2), appeared in numerous summer shows and pantomines in many major theatrical venues in GB, entertained abroad and for HM Forces in Cyprus and Germany; Fellow Brother Grand Order of Water Rats 1993; *Awards* Daily Mirror Disc Festival Award of Merit 1956, Ivor Novello Award (for A Windmill in Old Amsterdam), Br Authors Songwriters and Composers Award 1990 (for contrib to Br music); *Recreations* my work is my pleasure, golf (mostly for charities); *Style*— Ronnie Hilton, Esq; ✉ Beaters Court, Harebeating Lane, Hailsham, East Sussex BN27 1EP (☎ 01323 844829)

HIME, Martin; CBE (1987); s of Percy Joseph Hime (d 1966), and Esther Greta, *née* Howe (d 1974); *b* 18 Feb 1928; *Educ* King's Coll Sch Wimbledon, Trinity Hall Cambridge (MA, Lawn Tennis blue); *m* 1, 1960 (m dis 1971), Henrietta Mary Elisabeth, *née* Fehling; 1 s (Martin b 1962), 3 da (Marigold b 1964, Juliet b 1966, Jessica b 1967); m 2, 1971, Janina Christine, *née* Majcher; 1 da (Cordelia b 1973); *Career* RA 1946–48; called to the Bar Inner Temple 1951; Marks & Spencer 1952–58; HM Dip Serv: entered 1960, HM consul gen Houston Texas 1985–88, assessor FCO 1988–93; admin NHS Network 1996–; Freeman: Louisville Kentucky 1982, State of Texas 1985; *Recreations* golf, lawn tennis, table games, reading; *Clubs* All England Lawn Tennis, Royal Wimbledon Golf, Hawks (Cambridge); *Style*— Martin Hime, Esq, CBE; ✉ Field House, 248 Dover House Road, Roehampton, London SW15 5DA

HINCHCLIFFE, Peter Robert Mossom; CMG (1987), CVO (1979); s of Herbert Peter Hinchcliffe (d 1978), and Jeannie, *née* Wilson (d 1973); *b* 9 April 1937; *Educ* Radley, Trinity Coll Dublin (MA); *m* 1965, Archbold Harriet Hinchcliffe, MBE, da of Hugh Edward Siddall, of Dublin; 3 da (Fiona b 1967, Sally b 1969, Clare b 1972); *Career* Military Serv W Yorks Regt 1955–57, 2 Lt (Suez Campaign 1956), HMOCS Aden, political offr 1961–67, acting dep high cmmr 1967; joined FCO 1969, first sec UK mission to UN 1971–74, first sec and head of chancery Kuwait 1974–76, asst head of Sci and Tech Dept and Central and Southern African Dept 1976–78, counsellor and dep high cmmr Dar es Salaam 1978–81, consul gen Dubai UAE 1981–85, head Info Dept FCO 1985–87, HM ambass Kuwait 1987–90, Br high cmmr Lusaka 1990–93, ambass Jordan 1993–April 1997, ret; *Recreations* writing poetry, golf, tennis; *Clubs* East India, Royal Co Down Golf; *Style*— Peter Hinchcliffe, Esq, CMG, CVO; ✉ c/o Foreign and Commonwealth Office, King Charles St, London SW1A 2AH

HINCHCLIFFE, Prof Ronald; s of Charles Hinchcliffe, and Fenella, *née* Pearce; *b* 20 Feb 1926; *Educ* Bolton Sch, Univ of Manchester, Harvard, Univ of London; *m* 4 July 1953 (m dis 1980), Doreen, *née* Lord; *Career* Sqdn Ldr and RAF med servs offr i/c RAF Acoustics Laboratory 1951–55; hon conslt neuro-otologist Royal Nat ENT Hosp London 1967–91, prof of audiological med Univ of London 1977–91, conslt to Hearing and Balance Centre Portland Hosp London 1991–; immediate past pres Int Soc of Audiology; memb Collegium Otorhinolaryngologicum Amicitiae Sacrum 1969; *Books* Scientific Foundations of Otolaryngology (jt ed, 1976), Hearing and Balance in the Elderly (ed, 1983); *Recreations* skiing, sailing; *Clubs* Athenaeum; *Style*— Prof Ronald Hinchcliffe; ✉ Institute of Laryngology and Otology, 330 Gray's Inn Rd, London WC1X 8EE (☎ 0171 580 4400, fax 01462 454394)

HINCHLIFFE, David Martin; MP (Lab) Wakefield (majority 6,590); s of Robert Victor Hinchliffe (d 1982), of Wakefield, and Muriel, *née* Preston (d 1987); *b* 14 Oct 1948; *Educ* Cathedral Secdy Mod Sch Wakefield, Wakefield Tech and Art Coll, Leeds Poly, Univ of Bradford (MA), Huddersfield Poly (CertEd); *m* 17 July 1982, Julia, da of Harry North, of Mold, Clwyd; 1 s (Robert b 10 Oct 1985), 1 da (Rebecca b 24 May 1988); *Career* princ social worker Leeds Social Servs Dept 1974–79, social work tutor Kirklees Cncl 1980–87; cncllr: Wakefield City Cncl 1971–74, Wakefield DC 1978–88; MP (Lab) Wakefield 1987–; Lab spokesman for personal social servs and community care; former vice pres: Wakefield and Dist Trades Cncl, Wakefield Constituency Lab Pty; *Recreations* rugby league; *Clubs* Wakefield Trinity RLFC (vice pres); *Style*— David Hinchliffe, Esq, MP; ✉ 18 King Street, Wakefield, W Yorks WF1 2SR (☎ 01924 305722); House of Commons, London SW1A 0AA (☎ 0171 219 3000)

HINCHLIFFE, Stephen Leonard; s of William Leonard (d 1974), and Ilse, *née* Sparer; *b* 2 Jan 1950; *m* 14 July 1973, Marjorie, da of Eric Wood (d 1971); 1 s (James b 1975), 1 da (Julia b 1978); *Career* formerly accountant with Sheffield Twist Drill and Trent Regnl Hosp Bd; chm and chief exec Facia Ltd (parent co of retailers Sock Shop, Salisburys and Freeman Hardy Willis) until 1996; also former chm and chief exec: Wade Group of Cos Ltd, James Wilkes plc, Lynx Holdings plc, En-tout-cas plc; ACIM, AFA, FIMgt,

FSMM; *Recreations* helicopter flying, golf, motoring, shooting; *Clubs* Dore and Totley Golf; *Style—* Stephen L Hinchliffe, Esq; ✉ c/o Chase Montagu Ltd, Parkhead Hall, Eccleshall Road South, Sheffield S11 9PX (☎ 0114 262 0062)

HINCKLEY, Gilbert Clive; OBE (1988); s of Capt Gilbert Percy (d 1972), of Hinckley, and Dorothy Kate, *née* Bown; *b* 6 July 1937; *Educ* The Leys Sch, Clare Coll Cambridge (MA); *m* 1 (m dis 1977), Jane Susan, *née* Bourne; 1 da (Hannah Jane b 1969); m 2, 21 Aug 1981, Karen Ann, da of Gerald Wilson; *Career* 2 Lt Pack Tport RASC 1957–58, TA 1959–64 Lt Queen's Own Yorks Yeo; Hinckley Group of Assoc Cos: gp dir 1962–, jt chief exec 1976–82, chm Flogates Div, dep chm KSR Int Div, gp chm and md 1982–; chm Derbyshire Cncl Order of St John 1980–95, memb London Cncl and Chapter Gen Order of St John 1996–; Founders Medal Ostrava Univ Czech Republic 1994; Freeman Cutlers' Co of Hallamshire; fell Inst of Foundrymen 1973, fell Inst of Materials 1994, FRSA 1996; *Recreations* field sports, walking; *Clubs* Cavalry & Guards; *Style—* Gilbert Hinckley, Esq, OBE; ✉ Amber House, Kelstedge, Amber Valley, Derbyshire S45 0EA; Hinckley Group of Companies, Sandiron House, Beauchief, Sheffield S7 2RA (☎ 0114 262 1162, fax 0114 262 2222)

HIND, Andrew Charles; s of John William Hind (d 1986), of Grayshott, and Evelyn May, *née* Sidford (d 1986); *b* 10 July 1943; *Educ* Sutton County GS; *m* 27 Dec 1969, Janet Margaret, da of Norman William George Scullard (d 1983), of Hove; 1 s (Duncan William b 1976), 3 da (Joanna Scullard b 1973, Annalee Scullard b 1975, Suzanne Catherine b 1985); *Career* Lovell and Rupert Curtis Ltd (advertising): joined 1966, dir 1974, md 1984, chm and md 1987; chm The Garrick Gp 1988; dir Butler Borg Millest Fraser LRC Ltd 1990; business devpt mangr European Marketing Communication Organisation 1992; MIPA, FInstD; *Clubs* Milford Golf; *Style—* Andrew Hind, Esq; ✉ Churchlee, 2 New Inn Lane, Guildford, Surrey GU4 7HW (☎ 01483 450515, fax 01483 450212)

HIND, Dr Charles Robert Keith; s of Col (Robert) Keith Hind, of Kegworth House, Derby, and Dorothy, *née* Kinsey; *b* 7 June 1953; *Educ* King's Coll Taunton, Univ of London Med Sch (BSc, MB, BS, MD, FRCP); *m* 21 July 1985, Fiona, da of Maj Alexander Hugh Fraser, of Calduthel, Cradley, Worcs; 2 s (James b 1986, Alexander b 1992), 1 da (Eleanor b 1989); *Career* conslt physician gen and respiratory med Royal Liverpool Hosp and The Cardiothoracic Centre Liverpool 1987–; ed Postgraduate Medical Jl; *Books* X-Ray Interpretation for the MRCP (1983), Short Cases for the MRCP (1984), Amyloidosis and Amyloid P Component (1986); *Style—* Dr Charles Hind; ✉ 45 Rodney St, Liverpool L1 9EW (☎ 0151 708 0842, fax 0151 709 5679); Royal Liverpool Liverpool Hospital, University of Liverpool, Liverpool L7 8XP (☎ 0151 706 3571, fax 0151 706 5833); The Cardiothoracic Centre, Liverpool L14 3LB (☎ 0151 228 1616 ext 5390, fax 0151 220 8573)

HIND, Rt Rev John William; *see:* Gibraltar in Europe, Bishop of

HIND, Kenneth Harvard; CBE (1995); *b* 15 Sept 1949; *Educ* Woodhouse Grove Sch Bradford Yorks, Univ of Leeds; *m* Patricia Anne, *née* Millar; 1 s, 1 da; *Career* called to the Bar Gray's Inn 1973, practising barr Leeds until 1983, in practice Temple 1992–; MP (C) Lancs W 1983–92; PPS to: Lord Trefgarne MOD 1986–87, John Cope as Min of State DOE 1987–90, Rt Hon Peter Brooke as Sec of State for NI 1990–92; chm De Keyser Europe Ltd; vice pres: Central & W Lancs C of C, Merseyside C of C; chm W Lancs Employers' Assoc; MInstD; *Recreations* sailing, skiing; *Clubs* Headingley Rugby Union Football (vice pres); *Style—* Kenneth Hind, Esq, CBE; ✉ 2 King's Bench Walk, First Floor, Temple, London EC4Y 7DE (☎ 0171 353 9276, fax 0171 353 9949)

HINDE, David Richard; s of Walter Stanley Hinde (d 1952), and Marjorie Jewell Grieg, *née* Butcher (d 1970); *b* 16 Aug 1938; *Educ* Marlborough, Univ of Cambridge; *m* 1963, Rosemary Jill, da of Malcolm Hartree Young (d 1965); 3 da (Sasha Karen b 1966, Rachel Olivia b 1968, Anna-Louise b 1972); *Career* asst slr Slaughter and May 1961–69; exec dir: Wallace Bros Group 1969–77, Wardley Ltd 1977–81, Samuel Montagu and Co Ltd 1981–95, Dah Sing Financial Holdings Ltd Hong Kong 1995–; Liveryman Emeritus Worshipful Co of Woolmen; *Recreations* skiing, tennis, golf, gardening, travel; *Clubs* MCC, City of London, Hong Kong; *Style—* David Hinde, Esq; ✉ Flat 2, 17 Clarendon Rd, London W11 4JB; The Glebe House, Great Gaddesden, Hemel Hempstead, Hertfordshire HP1 3BY; Dah Sing Financial Holdings Ltd, 108 Gloucester Road, Hong Kong (☎ 00 852 2507 8608, fax 00 852 2598 8170)

HINDE, Keith Stevens Gleave; TD (1969); s of Wing Cdr Sydney Arthur Hinde, OBE, DL (d 1977), of W Mersea, Essex, and Guinevere Waneeta Ashore, *née* Gleave (d 1974); *b* 4 Oct 1934; *Educ* Colchester Royal GS, CCC Cambridge (MA); *m* 8 May 1965, Gillian Myfanwy, da of William Godfrey Morgan (d 1955), of Coventry; 1 s (Edward Morgan Stevens b 1976); *Career* 2 Lt RA 1953–55, Battery Capt Suffolk & Norfolk Yeo 1955–67, Maj Suffolk/Cambs Regt (S and NY) 1967–69; admitted slr 1961; conslt (former ptnr) Pothecary & Barratt; chm Stretham Engine Tst, tstee Suffolk & Norfolk Yeo Tst; cncl memb and hon slr King George's Fund for Sailors; Master Worshipful Co of Slrs 1988–89 (Liveryman 1966, Clerk 1969–76), Clerk Worshipful Co of Cutlers 1975–; *Books* Steam in the Fens (1974), History of The City of London Solicitors Company (1994); *Recreations* history (local and general), country pursuits; *Clubs* United Oxford and Cambridge; *Style—* Keith Hinde, Esq; ✉ Denny House, Waterbeach, Cambs (☎ 01223 860895); Pothecary & Barratt, Talbot House, Talbot Court, Gracechurch St, London EC3 (☎ 0171 623 7520)

HINDE, Prof Robert Aubrey; CBE (1988); *b* 26 Oct 1923; *Educ* Oundle, St John's Coll Cambridge (BA), Univ of London (BSc), Univ of Oxford (DPhil), Univ of Cambridge (ScD); *Career* res asst Edward Grey Inst Dept of Zoology Univ of Oxford 1948–50, curator Ornithological Field Station Dept of Zoology Univ of Cambridge 1950–63; St John's Coll Cambridge: res fell 1951–54, steward 1956–58, tutor 1958–63, fell 1958–89, master 1989–94; res prof Royal Soc 1963–89, Hitchcock prof Univ of Calif 1979, Green visiting scholar Univ of Texas 1983, Croonian lectr Royal Soc 1990; vice pres Ex-Servicemen's Campaign for Nuclear Disarmament; FRS 1974 (memb Cncl 1985–87); hon fell: American Ornithologists Union 1976, British Psychological Soc 1981, Balliol Coll Oxford 1986, Royal Coll of Psychiatry 1988, Trinity Coll Dublin 1990; hon dir Medical Res Cncl Unit on the Devpt and Integration of Behaviour 1970–89; Docteur honoris causa: dans la faculté des Sciènces Psychologiques et Pedagogiques Université Libre Bruxelles 1974, Université de Paris Nanterre 1978, Univ of Stirling 1991, Univ of Göteborg 1991, Univ of Edinburgh 1992, Univ of Western Ontario 1996; foreign hon memb American Acad of Arts and Scis 1974, hon foreign assoc US Nat Acad of Sciences 1978; hon memb: Assoc for Study of Animal Behaviour 1987, Deutsche Ornithologische Gesellschaft 1988; memb Academia Europeae 1990; Zoological Soc's Scientific medal 1961, Osman Hill medal Primate Soc of GB 1980, Leonard Cammer award NY Psychiatric Inst Columbia Univ 1980, Albert Einstein Award for Psychiatry Albert Einstein Coll of Medicine NY 1987, Huxley medal Royal Anthropological Inst 1990, Frink medal Zoological Soc of London 1992, G Stanley Hall Medal American Psychological Assoc 1993; *Books* Animal Behaviour: A Synthesis of Ethology and Comparative Psychology (1966, 2 edn 1970), Biological Bases of Human Social Behaviour (1974), Towards Understanding Relationships (1979), Ethology: Its Nature and Relations with Other Sciences (1982), Individuals, Relationships and Culture: Links between Ethology and the Social Sciences (1987), Relationships: a dialectical perspective (1997); also edited various books and numerous scientific papers; *Style—* Prof Robert Hinde, CBE, FRS; ✉ St John's College, Cambridge (☎ 01223 338635)

HINDE, Stephen Victor Cecil; s of Eric Stanley Hinde (d 1972), and Joyce, *née* Ball (d 1994); *b* 31 Aug 1948; *Educ* Plymouth Coll; *m* 1 July 1978, Mary Elizabeth Margaret, da of Basil Wilfred Mulligan; 2 da (Clare Venetia b 26 June 1980, Laura Mary b 7 March 1982); *Career* articled clerk Grace Darbyshire & Todd (now KPMG) 1966–71, audit sr Arthur Young McClelland Moores (now Ernst & Young) 1972, computer audit mangr Rediffusion Group 1972–78, audit servs mangr Brooke Bond Foods 1978–88, sr gp mangr computers Unilever plc 1988–90, gp mangr Courage Internal Audit Fosters Brewing Group 1990–95, gp info protection mangr BUPA 1995–; Faculty of Info Technol ICAEW: memb 1988–, chm Communications Ctee 1991–94, chm Professional Educn and Qualifications Ctee 1994–; Inst of Internal Auditors UK & Ireland: memb 1976–, jt fndr of qualification in computer auditing and chm QiCA Ctee 1981–88, jt fndr and chm Int Conf on Computer Audit Control and Security (COMPACS) 1981–91, chm Educn Co-ordinating Ctee 1983–85 (memb 1981–86), memb Cncl 1982–88, memb Res Co-ordinating Ctee 1983–85, chm EDP Res Ctee 1982–85 (memb 1980–), chm EDP Educn Ctee 1982–84 (memb 1981–86), memb Editorial Bd 1982–88, dir 1984–88, pres 1986–87, chm Disciplinary Ctee 1988–; memb Advanced Technol Ctee Inst of Internal Auditors Inc USA 1983–87, UK rep of Admin Cncl Euro Confedn of Inst of Internal Auditors 1986–88; fndr ed Computer Audit Update jl 1987–; chm Int Food & Wine Soc - Young Membs 1981–85 (hon treas 1979–82); govr St James's C of E First and Middle Sch Weybridge 1992–93; capt 4 XV Old Redcliffians RFC (Bristol); FCA 1971, MIIA 1981, FIIA 1986; *Books* Control & Audit of Mini Computer Systems (contrib, 1981), Use of Generalized Audit Software (contrib, 1983), Comparison of Access Control Software (ed, 1983), Internal Auditing (co-author, 1990, 2 edn 1996), Manual of Internal Audit Practice (1990), Information Security Guide (1990), Computer Auditing (co-author, 1991), Computer Audit and Control Handbook (contrib, 1995); *Recreations* assisting wife to run Christian Drama Youth Club, wine and food, history, literature; *Style—* Stephen Hinde, Esq; ✉ 80 Dudley Road, Walton-on-Thames, Surrey KT12 2JX (☎ 01932 242159)

HINDE, Thomas; *see:* Chitty, Sir Thomas

HINDLE, Timothy Simon; s of Edwin Frederick Branwell Hindle (d 1969), and Joan Marjorie, *née* Pearson (d 1995); *b* 7 June 1946; *Educ* Shrewsbury, Worcester Coll Oxford (MA), Heriot Watt Univ Edinburgh (Postgrad Dip Fin Studies); *m* 11 June 1975, Ellian Lea, da of Eli Aciman, of Istanbul; 1 s (Alexis b 1982), 1 da (Alara b 1979); *Career* dep ed The Banker 1978; The Economist: banking corr 1980, fin ed 1983, world business ed 1985; fndr ed: EuroBusiness 1988–91 and 1994–96, The Guide Istanbul; VSO Dacca Bangladesh 1968–69; *Books* Pocket Banker (1984), The Sultan of Berkeley Square (1991), Pocket Manager (1992), Pocket MBA (1992), Living in Istanbul (1993); *Recreations* reading, cinema; *Style—* Timothy Hindle, Esq; ✉ 22 Royal Crescent, Holland Park, London W11 4SL (☎ 0171 602 2601)

HINDLEY, Estella Jacqueline; QC (1992); da of Arthur John Hindley, of Sutton Coldfield, and Olive Maud, *née* Stanley; *b* 11 Oct 1948; *Educ* Sutton Coldfield Girls GS, Univ of Hull (LLB); *m* John Gilbert Harvey; 1 s (Andrew Timothy Hindley Harvey b 14 May 1977); *Career* called to the Bar Gray's Inn 1971, memb Midland and Oxford Circuit, recorder of the Crown Ct 1989–; non-exec dir Birmingham Children's Hosp NHS Tst; *Recreations* book collecting, theatre, the fine arts; *Style—* Estella Hindley, QC; ✉ 5 Fountain Court, Steelhouse Lane, Birmingham B4 6DR (☎ 0121 606 0500)

HINDLEY, Michael John; MEP (Lab) Lancashire South (majority 41,404); *Career* MEP (Lab): Lancashire E 1984–94, Lancashire S 1994–; *Style—* Michael Hindley, Esq, MEP; ✉ Transport House, 40–42 Abbey Street, Accrington, Lancashire BB5 1EB (☎ 01254 393103, fax 01254 393379)

HINDLIP, 6 Baron (UK 1886); Sir Charles Henry Allsopp; 6 Bt (UK 1880); s of 5 Baron Hindlip, JP, DL (d 1993), and Cecily Valentine Jane, *née* Borwick; *b* 5 Aug 1940; *Educ* Eton; *m* 18 April 1968, Fiona Victoria Jean Atherley, da of late Hon William Johnston McGowan, 2 s of 1 Baron McGowan; 1 s (Hon Henry William b 1973), 3 da (Hon Kirstie Mary b 1971, Hon Sophia Atherley b 1980, Hon Natasha Fiona b 1986); *Heir* s, Hon Henry William Allsopp b 8 June 1973; *Career* Coldstream Gds 1959–62, Lt; Christie's: joined 1962, gen mangr NY 1965–70; Christie Manson & Wood: dir 1970, dep chm 1985, chm 1986; *Recreations* painting, shooting; *Clubs* White's, Pratt's; *Style—* The Rt Hon the Lord Hindlip; ✉ The Cedar House, Inkpen, Berks; 55 Campden Hill Rd, London W8; Christies, 8 King Street, St James's, London SW1Y 6QT (☎ 0171 839 9060)

HINDMARSH, Irene; JP (Durham 1974); da of Albert Hindmarsh, and Elizabeth, *née* White; *b* 22 Oct 1923; *Educ* Heaton HS, Lady Margaret Hall Oxford (MA), Univ of Durham (PGCE); *Career* teacher: St Paul's Girls' Sch London 1947–49, Rutherford HS Newcastle-upon-Tyne 1949–59 (interchange teacher Lycée de Jeunes Filles Dax Landes France 1954–55); lectr in educn and French King's Coll Durham 1959–64, headmistress Birkenhead HS GPDST 1964–70, princ St Aidan's Coll Durham 1970–88, second pro vice-chllr Univ of Durham 1982–85; visiting prof: NY State, Syracuse, Cornell and Harvard Univs 1962, Fu-Dan Univ Shanghai 1979, 1980 and 1986, SW China Teachers' Univ Beibei Sichuan 1986; del Int Fedn of Univ Women UNO NY to Cmmns on Human Rights and Status of Women 1962, del and translator int conf FIPESO 1963–70; chm: Int Ctee Headmistresses' Assoc 1966–70, Int Panel of Jt Four 1967–70; JP Birkenhead 1966; FRSA 1989; *Books* History of Durham from the Air (contrib, St Aidan's Coll), numerous articles and seminar papers; *Recreations* travel, music, fine art, architecture, theatre and films; *Style—* Miss Irene Hindmarsh, JP; ✉ 8 Dickens Wynd, Merryoaks, Elvet Moor, Durham DH1 3QR (☎ 0191 386 1881)

HINDMARSH, John Reed; s of Maj Frederick Denis Hindmarsh, TD, (d 1984), of Newcastle on Tyne, and Frances Myrtle Reed; *b* 28 Aug 1944; *Educ* Sedbergh Sch, Univ of Newcastle (MB BS, MD); *m* 29 June 1974, Katharine Rosemary, da of Maj Charles Henry Anthony Howe (d 1978), of Saltburn by the Sea, North Yorks; 1 s (Richard b 1978), 1 da (Rachel b 1977); *Career* clinical tutor Univ of Edinburgh 1978–81, sr lectr Univ of London 1981–84; conslt urologist: St Peter's Hosp London 1981–84, South Tees Acute NHS Tst 1984–; FRCS, FRCSEd 1975, memb Br Assoc of Urological Surgns 1977; *Recreations* fishing, music, tennis, wine, philately; *Clubs* RSM, Army & Navy; *Style—* John Hindmarsh, Esq; ✉ Croft House, Hurworth Place, Croft on Tees, nr Darlington (☎ 01325 720684)

HINE, Dame Deirdre Joan; DBE (1997); da of David Alban Curran (d 1987), and Noreen Mary, *née* Cliffe; *b* 16 Sept 1937; *Educ* Charlton Park Sch Cheltenham, WNSM (DPH, MB Bch); *m* 12 Sept 1963, Raymond Hine; 2 s (Jonathan David b 2 Feb 1966, Andrew James b 17 Sept 1967); *Career* house physician and surgn Cardiff Royal Infirmary 1961–62; MO Glamorgan CC 1964–74 (asst MO 1962–64); specialist in community med S Glamorgan Health Authy 1974–82, sr lectr in geriatric med Univ of Wales Coll of Med 1982–84, dep chief MO Welsh Office 1984–87, dir Breast Cancer Screening Serv Breast Test Wales 1987–90, chief MO Welsh Office 1990–; FRCP, FFPHM; *Recreations* reading, walking, canal cruising, classical music; *Style—* Dame Deirdre Hine, DBE; ✉ Health Professional Group, Welsh Office, Cathays Park, Cardiff CF1 3NQ (☎ 01222 823911, fax 01222 825242)

HINE, John; s of late Leonard John Hine, and Elizabeth Jane, *née* Jenkins; *b* 21 Jan 1946; *Educ* Taunton Sch, Univ of Bristol (LLB); *m* 14 Dec 1974, Margaret Alice Stuart, *née* Morton; 3 c (Louise b 10 Jan 1977, Alice b 29 Sept 1978, William b 30 June 1981); *Career* articled clerk Dodson & Pulman Taunton 1968–70; asst slr: Wragge & Co Birmingham 1970–73, Lovell White & King 1974–80; ptnr Slaughter and May 1983– (joined 1980); Freeman Worshipful Co of Slrs 1974; memb Law Soc; *Recreations* theatre, architecture; *Style—* John Hine, Esq; ✉ Slaughter and May, 35 Basinghall St, London EC2V 5DB (☎ 0171 600 1200)

HINE, Air Chief Marshal Sir Patrick Bardon (Paddy); GCB (1989, KCB 1983), GBE (1991); s of Eric Graham Hine (d 1971) and Cecile Grace, *née* Philippe (d 1971); *b* 14 July 1932; *Educ* Peter Symonds Sch Winchester; *m* 1956, Jill Adèle, da of James Charles Gardner (d 1984); 3 s (Nicholas b 1962, Andrew b 1966, Jeremy b 1969); *Career* joined RAF 1950, memb Black Arrows aerobatic team 1957–59, cmd RAF Wildenrath 1974–75, dir P/R RAF 1975–77, SASO HQ RAF Germany 1979, ACAS rank of Air Vice Marshal (Policy) MOD 1979–83, Air Marshal 1983, C-in-C RAF Germany and Cdr Second Allied Tactical Air Force 1983–85, Vice CDS 1985–87, Air Memb for Supply and Organisation 1987–88, AOC-in-C Strike Cmd and C in C UK Air Forces 1988–91, Jt Cdr of Br Forces during Gulf War 1990–91; Air ADC to The Queen 1989–91; mil advsr to British Aerospace 1992–; Liveryman Guild of Air Pilots and Air Navigators; FRAeS, CIMgt; *Recreations* golf, skiing, fell walking, photography, military history; *Clubs* RAF, Royal and Ancient, Brokenhurst Manor Golf; *Style*— Air Chief Marshal Sir Patrick Hine, GCB, GBE

HINES, (Melvin) Barry; s of Richard Lawrence Hines (d 1963), and Annie Westerman; *b* 30 June 1939; *Educ* Ecclesfield GS, Loughborough Coll of Educn (Teaching Cert); *m* (m dis), Margaret; 1 s (Thomas b 1969), 1 da (Sally b 1967); *Career* writer; teacher in various schs: London 1960–62, S Yorkshire 1963–72; hon fell Sheffield City Poly 1985; FRSL 1977; *Films* Kes 1970, Looks and Smiles 1981; *TV* Billy's Last Stand 1970, Speech Day 1973, Two Men From Derby 1976, The Price of Coal (two films, 1977), The Gamekeeper 1979, A Question of Leadership 1981, Threads 1984, Shooting Stars 1990, Born Kicking 1992; *Books* The Blinder (1966), A Kestrel for a Knave (1968), First Signs (1972), The Gamekeeper (1975), The Price of Coal (1979), Looks and Smiles (1981), Unfinished Business (1983), The Heart of It (1994); *Style*— Barry Hines, Esq, FRSL; ✉ c/o The Agency, 24 Pottery Lane, Holland Park, London W11 4LZ (☎ 0171 229 9216)

HINGLEY, Gerald Bryan Grosvenor; s of Martin Ward Hingley, of White House Farm, S Broughton, Middlesbrough, Cleveland, and Mary Hingley; *b* 2 July 1943; *Educ* Shrewsbury, Univ of Nottingham (BA); *m* 28 July 1978, Veronica Mary, da of John Hird (d 1972), of York; 2 s (John b 1981, David b 1986), 1 da (Helen b 1979); *Career* admitted slr 1970; ptnr Wragge & Co 1974–; memb advsy bd of W Midlands Salvation Army; tstee Kilcuppes Charity; memb: Law Soc, Assoc of Pension Lawyers; *Recreations* sailing; *Clubs* Edgbaston Priory, English Speaking Union; *Style*— Gerald Hingley, Esq; ✉ Wragge & Co, 55 Colmore Row, Birmingham B2 3AS (☎ 0121 233 1000, fax 0121 214 1099)

HINKS, Frank Peter; s of Henry John Hinks, and Patricia May, *née* Adams; *b* 8 July 1950; *Educ* Bromley GS, St Catherine's Coll Oxford (MA, BCL); *m* 31 July 1982, Susan Mary, da of Col John Arthur Haire; 3 s (Julius b 1984, Alexander b 1985, Benjamin b 1987); *Career* called to the Bar Lincoln's Inn 1973, Chancery Bar 1974–; churchwarden Shoreham PC 1995–; Liveryman Worshipful Co of Innholders 1991; *Recreations* poetry, gardening, collecting jugs; *Style*— Frank Hinks, Esq; ✉ The Old Vicarage, Shoreham, Sevenoaks, Kent (☎ 0195 952 4480); 13 Old Square, Lincoln's Inn, London WC2 (☎ 0171 242 6105, fax 0171 405 4004)

HINNELLS, Prof John Russell; s of William Hinnells (d 1978), and Lilian, *née* Jackson; *b* 27 Aug 1941; *Educ* Derby Coll of Art, King's Coll London (BD, AKC), Sch of Oriental and African Studies London; *m* 24 June 1965, Marianne Grace, da of William Bushell (d 1973); 2 s (Mark b 11 June 1966, Duncan b 9 Oct 1968); *Career* lectr Univ of Newcastle 1967–70; Univ of Manchester: joined 1970, prof 1985–93, dean Faculty of Theology 1987–88; prof of comparative religion Sch of Oriental & African Studies Univ of London 1993–; visiting appts: sr lectr Open Univ 1975–77, govt res fellowship lectr Bombay 1975, Shann lectr Univ of Hong Kong 1986, Ratanbai Katrak lectr Univ of Oxford 1986; author of numerous articles on religious and theological topics published in books and jls; series ed: Library of Religious Beliefs and Practices, Sources for the Study of Religion, Religion and the Arts, Sherman Studies on Judaism in Modern Times; sec gen Soc for Mithraic Studies, fndr and first sec Shap Working Pty on world Religions in Educn 1968–75, memb Governing Cncl Br Inst of Persian Studies 1982–86, convenor Int Congress of Mithraic Studies Manchester (first) 1971, Tehran (second) 1975, Rome (Fourth) 1990, chm UNESCO Int Symposium on the Conception of Human Rights in World Religions Inter-Univ Centre Dubrovnik 1985, chief speaker American Acad of Religious Conference LA USA 1985, office bearer of Assoc of Univ Depts of Theology and Religious Studies 1986–87 and 1992–; FSA, FRAS; *Books* incl: Comparative Religion in Education (1970), Hinduism (ed, 1972), Persian Mythology (1974), Mithraic Studies (2 vols, ed 1975), Spanning East and West (1978), Zoroastrianism and Parsis (1981), Penguin Dictionary of Religions (ed, 1984), Handbook of Living Religions (ed, 1985), Who's Who of World Religions (1991), Studies in Mithraism (1993), New Dictionary of Religions (ed, 1995), Zoroastrians in Britain (1996); *Recreations* drawing, painting, photography; *Style*— Prof John Hinnells, FSA; ✉ School of Oriental & African Studies, University of London, Thornhaugh Street, Russell Square, London WC1H 0XG (☎ 0171 637 2388, fax 0171 436 3844)

HINSLEY, Prof Sir (Francis) Harry; kt (1985), OBE (1946); s of Thomas Henry Hinsley (d 1956), and Emma, *née* Adey (d 1980); *b* 26 Nov 1918; *Educ* Queen Mary's GS Walsall, St John's Coll Cambridge (MA); *m* 1946, Hilary Brett, da of Herbert Francis Brett Smith (d 1952); 2 s (Charles b 1947, Hugo b 1950), 1 da (Clarissa b 1954); *Career* HM FO (war serv) 1939–46; Univ of Cambridge: res fell St John's Coll 1944–50, tutor St John's Coll 1956–63, lectr of history 1949–65, reader in history of int relations 1965–69, prof of history of int relations 1969–83, chm Faculty Bd of History 1970–72, master 1979–89, vice chancellor 1981–83; FBA 1981; *Style*— Prof Sir Harry Hinsley, OBE, FBA; ✉ St John's College, Cambridge CB2 1TP (☎ 01223 355075)

HINSON, Kenneth Jack (Ken); s of Thomas Walter Hinson (d 1980), of Leicester, and Doris Elizabeth, *née* Stuart (d 1967); *b* 19 Sept 1943; *Educ* Wandsworth GS; *m* 1, 1962 (m dis 1989), Janet Taylor 1 s (Gary Thomas b 1962), 1 da (Lorna Elizabeth Bland b 1963); m 2, 12 April 1989, Christina Page Holt, da of George Christopher Anderson (d 1988), of Nottingham; *Career* Harvey Preen & Co London: articled 1961, audit mangr 1968, qualified CA 1970, ptnr 1972–77; md Böttcher UK Ltd 1977–92; sr ptnr Hinson & Co 1992–; FCS 1970, FIAA 1975, FIMgt 1977; *Recreations* game shooting and fishing, vintage cars; *Clubs* IOD; *Style*— Ken Hinson, Esq; ✉ Onen House, The Onen, Monmouth, Gwent NP5 4EN (☎ 01600 780570); Hinson & Co (☎ and fax 01600 780543)

HINTON, Graham Peter Henry; s of Anthony Henry Hinton (d 1989), and Gwendoline Mary, *née* Coleman; *b* 27 Jan 1946; *Educ* Epsom Coll, LSE, Kingston Poly, Univ of London (BSc); *m* 9 May 1970, Deborah Poland, da of Dr John Anthony Poland Bowen; 3 s (Tom Henry b 15 Oct 1978, Dudley John b 17 Oct 1980, Joshua James b 18 Oct 1985), 2 da (Kirsty Miranda b 21 Oct 1976, Abigail Liesel b 5 March 1984); *Career* graduate trainee then account supervisor SSCB Lintas 1969–74, exec dir then head of account mgmnt McCann-Erickson 1974–81; DMB&B: joined 1981, subsequently jt chm chief exec and regnl md Europe, chm until 1995; chm Bates Dorland 1996–; *Recreations* children, squash, tennis, theatre, classical guitar; *Clubs* RAC, St James, Champneys; *Style*— Graham Hinton, Esq; ✉ Bates Dorland Ltd, 121–141 Westbourne Terrace, London W2 6JR (☎ 0171 262 5077)

HINTON, Jennifer (Jennie); da of William Francis Young (d 1949), of Surrey, and Mary Louisa, *née* Siddall (d 1978); *b* 26 Nov 1934; *Educ* Crouch End HS for Girls London; *m* 15 July 1959, Dr (John) Michael Hinton, s of Robert Joseph Hinton (d 1985); 2 s (Mark b 1961, Timothy b 1962), 1 da (Kate b 1965); *Career* memb: SE Regnl Ctee Rural Devpt Cmmn, Mgmnt Ctee Sussex Heritage Tst, Rail Users' Consultative Ctee for Southern England 1993–, Southern Regn Ctee RSA 1993–; chm: Chichester Civic Soc 1980–84, Bd of Tstees Opera 70 1984–90, Bd of Govrs Fordwater Special Sch Chichester 1989–93; memb: Exec Sussex Rural Community Cncl 1987–93, Exec Chichester Festivities 1988–96, Ct Univ of Sussex 1989–95; FRSA 1976; *Recreations* listening to music, admiring gardens; *Clubs* Royal Over-Seas League; *Style*— Mrs Michael Hinton; ✉ Stoke Dorothy, West Burton, Pulborough, W Sussex RH20 1HD (☎ 01798 831237)

HINTON, Kevin Leslie; s of Ernest Leslie Hinton, of Oxford, and Diana, *née* Churchill; *b* 27 Nov 1955; *Educ* Oxford Sch, Newcastle upon Tyne Poly (BA); *m* 7 May 1988, Carolyn, da of Robert Ian Tricker; 1 da (Lauren Kay b 12 Nov 1990), 1 s (Jack Samuel b 16 May 1993); *Career* design asst Hancock Museum Newcastle upon Tyne 1977–78, graphic designer VAP Kidlington Oxford 1978–80, sr designer The Medicine Group Abingdon Oxford 1980–89, fndr ptnr The Hinton Chaundy Design Partnership 1989–; MCSD 1988 (chm S of England Region 1994–97); *Recreations* reading, drawing, enjoying my family; *Style*— Kevin Hinton, Esq; ✉ Hinton Chaundy Design Partnership, 6a St Andrews Court, Wellington Street, Thame, Oxfordshire OX9 3WT (☎ 01844 260770, fax 01844 260771)

HINTON, Michael Herbert; JP; s of Walter Leonard Hinton (d 1979), of Thorpe Bay, Essex, and Freda Millicent Lillian, *née* Crowe; *b* 10 Nov 1934; *Educ* Ardingly; *m* 1, 4 April 1955 (m dis 1982), Sarah, da of Oliver Gordon Sunderland, DL (d 1967); 1 s (Timothy b 1964), 2 da (Catherine b 1956, Jennifer b 1960); m 2, 5 Nov 1984, Jane Margaret, da of Arthur Crichton Howell; *Career* CA; currently ptnr C Jacobs & Co; Alderman City of London 1970–81 (Sheriff 1977–78, memb Ct of Common Cncl 1968–70); Freeman: City of London, Worshipful Co of Watermen & Lightermen of the River Thames; Liveryman: Worshipful Co of Farmers (Master 1981–82), Worshipful Co of Wheelwrights, Worshipful Co of Arbitrators; FCA, FRSA, FICM, FFA, ACIArb; *Recreations* cricket, association football, travel, theatre, collecting; *Clubs* Farmers', MCC, City Livery (pres 1976); *Style*— Michael Hinton, Esq, JP; ✉ Quags, Lower Oddington, Gloucestershire GL56 OUP (☎ 01451 831692); C Jacobs & Co, 66 Churchway, London NW1 1LT (☎ 0171 383 7525)

HINTON, Nicholas John; CBE (1985); s of the Rev Canon John Percy Hinton (d 1990), of Wiltshire, and Josephine Eleanor Hinton (d 1971); *b* 15 March 1942; *Educ* Marlborough, Selwyn Coll Cambridge (MA); *m* 1971, Deborah Mary, da of The Hon Douglas Vivian (d 1973); 1 da (Josephine Mary b 1984); *Career* dir: Nat Assoc for the Care and Resettlement of Offenders 1973–77, Nat Cncl for Voluntary Orgns 1977–84; dir gen The Save the Children Fund 1984–95, pres The International Crisis Group 1995–; *Recreations* music; *Style*— Nicholas J Hinton, Esq, CBE; ✉ 22 Westmoreland Place, London SW1V 4AE (☎ 0171 828 3965)

HINTON, Wendy Pamela; da of Norman George Hinton (d 1991), and Jean Clarise, *née* Swain; *b* 14 July 1962; *Educ* Benedictine Convent Sch Dumfries, Emerson Park Sch Hornchurch, Havering Tech Coll Hornchurch, London C of C and Indust; *m* 18 Sept 1987, Paul Doherty, s of Llewellyn Patrick John Doherty; 1 da (Jasmine Anne b 4 July 1991), 1 s (Jordan Llewellyn George b 13 Nov 1996); *Career* Woman's Journal Magazine 1981–86, Signature Magazine 1986–87, pictures ed ES Magazine 1987–; freelance projects incl Veuve Cliquot Guide to Season; judge 1995 Assoc of Photographers Twelfth Awards; interviewed for Image Magazine on commissioning photography; *Recreations* photography exhibitions, being a mother; *Style*— Mrs Wendy Hinton; ✉ ES Magazine, Associated Newspapers, Northcliffe House, 2 Derry Street, London W8 5EE (☎ 0171 938 7669, fax 0171 937 9302)

HINTON COOK, Gavin; s of Ronald Edward William Cook, and Gwendolin Bessie Hinton; *b* 9 April 1947; *Educ* Kingsbury GS, Architectural Assoc Sch of Architecture (AA Dipl); *m* 11 Sept 1971, Janine Dewar, da of Wing Cdr William Charles Ramsay (d 1979); *Career* chartered architect: WF Johnson and Assoc, Melvin and Lansley, London Borough of Lambeth, Philip Mercer RIBA; project architect Milton Keynes Devpt Corp 1976–79 (chief architect 1979–85, completed 2400 houses and co-ordinated Energy World at MK); md Orchard Design 1985– (39 current design projects, complete site development, engrg and total integration managed); lectr architectural studies Univ of Birmingham; awards: Arch Design Magazines, Best of Br Architecture Design Award Commendation, RIBA S Regn Energy Award; ARIBA; *Recreations* sailing, squash, cycling; *Style*— Gavin Hinton Cook, Esq; ✉ Orchard Design Studio, Mentmore, Leighton Buzzard, Beds LU7 0QF (☎ 01296 662189)

HIORNS, Brennan Martin; s of Hubert Hiorns (d 1986), of Pengam, Gwent, and Catherine Mary, *née* Brennan; *b* 21 Sept 1943; *Educ* The Lewis Sch Pengam, Univ of Birmingham (BSc, PhD), Univ of London (Dip in Arch); *m* 1969, Mary Diana, da of Ernest Long; 1 s (Christopher Brennan b 1972), 1 da (Catherine Victoria b 1970); *Career* res engr Plastics Div ICI 1970–74; Kleinwort Benson Securities (Grieveson Grant until taken over): investment analyst Chemicals, Paper and Textiles 1974–77, fund mangr 1977–79, equity salesman 1979–87, ptnr (Grieveson Grant) 1983–84, head of res 1987–90, dep md 1990–95, chief Investment offr Kleinwort Benson Investment Management 1995–; AMIIMR 1976, memb Prehistoric Soc 1978, memb Stock Exchange 1983; *Recreations* archaeology, military and naval history, English literature; *Style*— Brennan Hiorns, Esq; ✉ Kleinwort Benson Investment Management Ltd, 10 Fenchurch Street, London EC3M 3LB

HIPKIN, Dr Leslie John; TD (1987); *b* 10 July 1935; *Educ* Birkenhead Sch, Univ of Liverpool (MB ChB, MD, PhD); *m* 5 July 1958, Marjorie June; 1 s (John b 1966), 1 da (Sally 1972); *Career* cmmnd RAMC Vols 1974 (CO 208(m) Gen Hosp 1987–90), Col; Widnes cancer res fell Liverpool 1959–61; sr lectr in endocrine pathology Univ of Liverpool 1971–89 (lectr 1963–71), sr lectr in clinical chemistry 1989–; Carlsberg-Wellcome fell Copenhagen 1969–70, hon conslt in endocrinology Liverpool DHA and Mersey RHA 1972–; memb: Endocrine Soc, RSM, NW Endocrine Soc, Br Assoc of Sport and Med, Liverpool Medical Inst; MRCS, LRCP 1958, FRCPath 1982, FRCPEdin 1992; *Books* Clinical Endocrine Pathology (with J C Davis); *Style*— Dr Leslie Hipkin, TD; ✉ 3 Poplar Rd, Oxton, Birkenhead, Merseyside L43 5TB (☎ 0151 652 2021); University Department of Clinical Chemistry (Endocrine Section), Duncan Building, Royal Liverpool University Hospital, Prescot Street, Liverpool L7 8XP (☎ 0151 706 4303)

HIPWOOD, Julian Brian; s of Brian John Hipwood, of Thame, Oxon and Marion Barbara Sharpe, *née* Brice; *b* 23 July 1946; *Educ* Kohat Sch Pakistan, St George's Sch Amberley, Tech Coll Stroud; *m* 1, 11 Oct 1969 (m dis 1980), Zofia Krystina, da of Col Przemyflaw Kazimerz Kaminski, Polish Army (d 1985); 1 s (Tristan Julian b 28 Feb 1976), 1 da (Accalia Colette b 14 March 1971); m 2, 1 April 1980, Patricia Anne Secunda, da of Maj Neal Lane McRoberts, US Army (d 1966), of The Old Hall, Ashwell, Rutland; *Career* became professional polo player 1964, England capt 1971–76 and 1978–91; captained England to win the Coronation Cup against: Mexico 1979, USA 1988 and 1989, France 1990; captained England II in 1992 to beat Spain for Silver Jubilee Cup; first player to have won World Cup in five consecutive years 1980–84, twice Br Open Winner, twice French Open winner, once US Open winner; memb Ctee Cowdray Park Polo Club; *Recreations* racing and breeding of thoroughbreds; *Style*— Julian Hipwood, Esq; ✉ Lychgate Cottage, Easebourne, Midhurst, West Sussex (☎ 0173 081 3293); 12665 Shady Pines Ct, West Palm Beach, Florida 33414 USA (☎ 00 1 407 793 1327)

HIRD, David Forbes; s of late James William Hird, and Violet Catherine Hird, of Aberdeen; *b* 11 May 1943; *Educ* Robert Gordon's Coll Aberdeen, Univ of Aberdeen (academic yr for CA student apprenticeship); *m* 3 Aug 1968, Irene Margaret, da of George Mason Guild; 1 s (Derek John b 13 April 1970), 2 da (Susan Elaine b 4 March

1972, Alison Fiona b 8 Oct 1974); *Career* apprentice CA 1961–66, mgmnt accountant Aberdeen Special Hosps 1966–67, asst treas SE Regional Hosp Bd Edinburgh 1970–74 (fin accountant 1967–70); dist fin offr: E Fife Dist 1974–79, N Lothian Dist 1979–84; Forth Valley Health Bd: treas 1984–91, dir of fin and contracts 1991–93, gen mangr 1993–; MICAS 1966; *Recreations* curling, walking; *Style—* David Hird, Esq; ✉ Forth Valley Health Board, 33 Spittal Street, Stirling FK8 1DX (☎ 01786 457249, fax 01786 451474)

HIRD, Dame Thora; DBE (1993, OBE 1983); da of James Henry Hird (d 1946), and Mary Jane, *née* Mayor (d 1942); *b* 28 May 1911; *m* 3 May 1937, James Scott (d 1994), s of James Scott (d 1942); 1 da (Janette (Mrs Rademaekers) b 14 Dec 1938); *Career* actress of stage and screen; has appeared in numerous Br films; fndr The Thora Hird Charitable Tst; Pye Female Comedy Star Award 1984; Hon DLitt Univ of Lancaster 1990; *Theatre* credits incl: The Queen Came By (Duke of York's) 1949, Tobacco Road (Playhouse) 1951, The Happy Family (Duchess) 1951, The Same Sky (Duke of York's) 1952, The Troublemakers (The Strand) 1952, The Love Match (Palace) 1953; *Television* comedy series: Meet the Wife, In Loving Memory, Hallelujah, Last of the Summer Wine; drama series: First Lady, Flesh and Blood; plays: Romeo and Juliet, A Cream Cracker Under The Settee (BAFTA Award), Pat and Margaret 1994; presenter Praise Be (BBC), Straight and Narrow (BBC) 1993; *Books* Scene and Hird (autobiography, 1976), Thora Hird's Praise Be Notebook (1990), Thora Hird's Praise Be Year Book (1991), Thora Hird's Praise Be Christmas Book (1991), Thora Hird's Praise Be Prayer Book, Thora Hird's 2nd Autobiography (1996); *Style—* Dame Thora Hird, DBE; ✉ c/o Felix de Wolfe, Manfield House, 376/379 The Strand, London WC2R OLR (☎ 0171 379 5767, fax 0171 836 0337)

HIRSCH, Prof Sir Peter Bernhard; kt (1975); s of Ismar Hirsch; *b* 16 Jan 1925; *Educ* Sloane Sch Chelsea, St Catharine's Coll Cambridge (MA, PhD); *m* 1959, Mabel Anne, *née* Stephens, wid of James Noel Kellar; 1 step s, 1 step da; *Career* reader in physics Univ of Cambridge 1964–66, fell St Edmund Hall Oxford 1966–92 (emeritus fell 1992), Isaac Wolfson prof of metallurgy Univ of Oxford 1966–92 (emeritus prof 1992); chm Isis Innovation Ltd 1989–96, dir Rolls-Royce Associates 1994–; chm Tech Advsy Gp on Structural Integrity 1993–; pt/t chm Atomic Energy Authy 1982–84 (pt/t memb 1982–94), chm Materials and Processes Advsy Bd Rolls Royce plc 1996–; hon fell: RMS, Christ's Coll Cambridge 1978 (fell 1960–66), St Catharine's Coll Cambridge 1983, Imperial Coll 1988; Hon DSc: Univ of Newcastle upon Tyne, City Univ, Northwestern Univ, Univ of E Anglia; Hon DEng: Univ of Liverpool, Univ of Birmingham; FRS; *Style—* Prof Sir Peter Hirsch, FRS; ✉ 104A Lonsdale Rd, Oxford OX2 7ET; Department of Materials, University of Oxford, Parks Rd, Oxford OX1 3PH (☎ 01865 273773, fax 01865 273764)

HIRSCH, Prof Steven Richard; *b* 12 March 1937; *Educ* Amherst Coll Mass USA (BA), Johns Hopkins Univ USA (MD); *m* Teresa; 1 s (Phineas), 3 da (Georgina, Collette, Eleanor); *Career* attached res worker MRC social psychiatry Maudsley Hosp 1971–73 (sr registrar and lectr 1967–71), sr lectr and hon conslt Westminster and Queen Mary's Hosp 1973–75, prof of psychiatry and head Dept of Psychiatry Charing Cross and Westminster Med Sch and hon conslt Charing Cross Hosp 1975–; former pres of Psychiatry Section RSM, former chm Assoc of Univ Teachers of Psychiatry, former dep chm Mental Health Cmmn BMA, currently chm Psychopharmocology Sub-Ctee RCPsych, convenor of Psychiatry Subject Panel Faculty of Med Univ of London; FRCPsych 1979, FRCP 1983; *Books* Themes and Variations in European Psychiatry: An anthology (ed with M Shepherd, 1974), Abnormalities in Parents of Schizophrenics: Review of the Literature and an Investigation of Communication Defects and Deviances (with J Leff, 1975), The Suicide Syndrome (ed with R Farmer, 1980), Social Behaviour Assessment Schedule. Training Manual and Rating Guide (with S Platt and A Weyman, 1983), The Psychopharmacology and Treatment of Schizophrenia (ed with P B Bradley, 1986), Consent and the Incompetent Patient: Ethics, Law and Medicines (ed with J Harris, 1988), Learning Psychiatry through MCQ: a comprehensive text (with T E Sensky, C Thompson et al, 1988), Schizophrenia (ed with D Weinberger, 1995); author of reports incl: Psychiatric Beds and Resources: Factors Influencing Bed Use and Service Planning RCPsych 1988, Services for Patients with Chronic Disabilities Resulting from Mental Illness RCPsych 1993; *Recreations* sport; *Style—* Prof Steven Hirsch; ✉ Department of Psychiatry, Charing Cross & Westminster Medical School, St Dunstan's Rd, London W6 8RP (☎ 0181 846 7390, fax 0181 846 7372)

HIRST, Christopher Halliwell; s of John Kenneth Hirst, of Hutton Buscel, nr Scarborough, Yorks, and Marian Harrison, *née* Smith; *b* 27 May 1947; *Educ* Merchant Taylors', Trinity Hall Cambridge (MA); *m* 1, 12 Aug 1972 (m dis 1985), (Moira) Cecilia, da of Arthur Tienken, of Minneapolis, USA; 1 s (William b 1974), 1 da (Elizabeth b 1976); m 2, 28 March 1987, Sara Louise, da of Arthur James Petherick, of Bodmin, Cornwall; 3 da (Victoria b 1988, Catherine b 1989, Emily b 1991); *Career* trainee exec Bank of London & S America Chile 1969–71; housemaster Radley Coll 1978–85 (asst master 1972–85), headmaster Kelly Coll Tavistock 1985–95, headmaster Sedbergh Sch 1995–; chm Sports Sub-Ctee HMC 1995–; *Recreations* antiquarian, literary, sporting; *Clubs* East India, Free Foresters, Jesters, MCC; *Style—* Christopher Hirst, Esq; ✉ Birksholme, Sedbergh, Cumbria LA10 5HQ (☎ 01539 620491); Sedbergh School, Sedbergh, Cumbria LA10 5HG (☎ 01539 620535)

HIRST, Damien; *b* 1965; *Educ* Goldsmith's Coll; *Career* artist; winner: Prix Eliette von Karajan 1995, Turner Prize 1995; *Solo Exhibitions* In & Out of Love (Woodstock Street) 1991, When Logics Die (Emmanuel Perrotin) 1991, Internal Affairs (ICA) 1991, Where's God Now? (Jay & Donatella Chiat) 1992, Marianne, Hildegard (Unfair) 1992, Pharmacy (Cohen Gall) 1992, Visual Candy (Regen Projects) 1993, Damien Hirst (Galerie Jablonka) 1993, Making Beautiful Drawings (Bruno Brunnet) 1994, Currents 23 (Milwaukee Art Museum) 1994, A Bad Environment for White Monochrome Paintings (Mattress Factory) 1994, A Good Environment for Coloured Monochrome Paintings (DAAD Gall) 1994, Pharmacy (Dallas Museum) 1994, Pharmacy (Kukje Gall Seoul) 1995, Still (White Cube/Jay Jopling London) 1995; *Group Exhibitions* Freeze (Surrey Docks) 1988, New Contemporaries (ICA) 1989, Third Eye Centre 1989, Modern Medicine (Building One) 1990, Gambler (Building One) 1990, Louder Than Words (The Cornerhouse) 1991, Broken English (Serpentine Gall) 1991, Young British Artists (Saatchi Collection) 1992, Made for Arolsen (Arolsen) 1992, Moltiplici/Cultura (Rome) 1992, London Portfolio (Karsten Schubert) 1992, Post Human (Fondation Asher Edelman) 1992, Group Show (Lois Campana Gall) 1992, Strange Developments (Anthony d'Offay Gall) 1992, British Art (Barbara Gladstone Gall) 1992, Avantgarde & Kampagne (Stadtische Kunsthalle, Düsselldorf) 1992, Turkish Biennial (Istanbul) 1992, Turner Prize Exhibition (Tate Gall) 1992, Under Thirty (Galerie Metropol) 1992, The 21st Century (Kunsthalle, Basel) 1993, The Nightshade Family (Museum Friedericianum) 1993, Venice Biennial (Aperto Section) 1993, Displace (Cohen Gall) 1993, A Wonderful Life (Lisson Gall) 1993, Some Went Mad, Some Ran Away (Serpentine Gall) 1994, Domestic Violence (Gio Marconi) 1994, Virtual Reality (Nat Gall of Australia Canberra) 1994, Cocido y Crudo (Reina Sofia Madrid) 1994, Nature Morte (Tanya Bonakdar Gall NY) 1994, Art Unlimited (Centre for Contemporary Art Glasgow and South Bank Centre London) 1994, From Beyond the Pale (Irish Museum of Modern Art Dublin) 1994, Drawing the Line (Southampton City Art Gall, Manchester City Art Gall, Ferens Art Gall Hull, Whitechapel Art Gall London) 1995, Signs and Wonders (Kunsthaus Zurich) 1995, Minky Manky (South London Gall, Arnolfini Gall Bristol) 1995, From Here (Waddington Galls London, Karsten Schubert London) 1995, Spellbound (Art and Film, Hayward Gall) 1996; *Style—* Damien Hirst, Esq; ✉ c/o Julia Royse, The White Cube Gallery, 44 Duke Street, St James's, London SW1Y 6DD (☎ 0171 930 5373, fax 0171 930 9973)

HIRST, David Brian Addis; JP (1992); s of Harold Rupert Hirst, CBE (d 1990), and Maureen, *née* Doherty; *b* 31 Aug 1938; *Educ* St George's Coll Weybridge; *m* 20 Dec 1969, Honoria (Nora) Bernadette, da of Dr P W Kent, OBE, of Orlingbury, Northants; 2 s (Richard b 15 June 1973, Michael b 28 Nov 1977), 2 da (Patricia b 30 Sept 1971, Anthea b 4 May 1976); *Career* with Coopers & Lybrand 1956–91 (ptnr 1970–91), ret; sec Lieutenancy of England and Wales Equestrian Order of the Holy Sepulchre of Jerusalem 1993–; KSG 1984, Knight Cdr with Star Equestrian Order of the Holy Sepulchre of Jersualem (Knight 1985, Knight Cdr 1991); FCA 1972 (ACA 1962); *Recreations* golf, music; *Clubs* Royal Cwlth Soc, Wellingborough Golf; *Style—* David Hirst, Esq, JP; ✉ Home Farm House, Rectory Lane, Orlingbury, Kettering, Northants NN14 1JH (☎ 01933 678250)

HIRST, Rt Hon Lord Justice; Rt Hon Sir David Cozens-Hardy; kt (1982), PC (1992); er s of Thomas William Hirst (d 1965), of West Lodge, Aylsham, Norfolk, and Margaret Joy, *née* Cozens-Hardy (niece of 1 Baron Cozens-Hardy) (d 1984); *b* 31 July 1925; *Educ* Eton, Trinity Coll Cambridge; *m* 1951, Pamela Elizabeth Molesworth, da of Col Temple Percy Molesworth Bevan, MC, of London (s of Hon Charlotte Molesworth, 2 da of 8 Viscount Molesworth); 3 s (one of whom Jonathan William Hirst, QC, *qv*), 2 da (one of whom Rachel Joy Hirst, *qv*); *Career* served WWII, RA and Intelligence Corps, Capt 1946; called to the Bar Inner Temple 1951, reader 1994, treas 1995, QC 1965, judge of the High Court of Justice (Queen's Bench Div) 1982–92, Lord Justice of Appeal 1992–, treas Inner Temple 1995; memb: Lord Chllr's Law Reform Ctee 1966–80, Cncl on Tbnls 1966–80, Ctee to Review Defamation Act, Supreme Ct Rule Ctee 1984; chm of the Bar 1978–79 (vice chm 1977–78); *Recreations* shooting, theatre and opera, growing vegetables; *Clubs* Boodle's, MCC; *Style—* The Rt Hon Lord Justice Hirst; ✉ Royal Courts of Justice, Strand, London WC2A 2LL

HIRST, Derek; *b* 11 April 1930; *Educ* Doncaster Sch of Art, Royal Coll of Art (ARCA); *m* 13 July 1951, Ellen Birgitte, *née* Hempel; *Career* artist; fndr studio London 1951, first artist in res Univ of Sussex 1966, visiting prof Faculty of Fine Arts York Univ Canada 1971–73, fndr studio Sidlesham nr Chichester 1977–; guest artist and lectr: Detroit Print Symposium Cranbrooke Acad of Art 1980, Faculty of Fine Arts Arizona State Univ 1980; guest artist: Victorian Coll of the Arts Melbourne 1981, APADEC Symposium Portugal 1988; *Solo Exhibitions* Drian Galleries London 1961, Tooth's Gallery London 1962, Stone Galleries Newcastle upon Tyne 1962, Univ of Sussex 1966, Towner Art Gallery Eastbourne 1966, Angela Flowers Gallery London 1970, 1972, 1975, 1979, 1984, 1987, 1989, 1991 and 1993, Victorian Centre for the Arts Melbourne 1980, Pallant House Gallery Chichester 1987 and 1991, Flowers East Gallery London 1991 and 1995; *Gp Exhibitions* incl: Pittsburgh Int (Carnegie Inst Pittsburgh) 1961 and 1964, John Moores Exhbn (Walker Gallery Liverpool) 1963 and 1974, New Painting: 1961–1964 (Arts Cncl tour) 1964, Modern British Painting (Sydney) 1964, Five British Painters (Gallerie Aujourd'hui Brussels) 1966, London Under Forty (Gallerie Milano Italy) 1966, Select Twentieth Century Drawings (JPL Fine Arts London) 1974, Recent Acquisitions: 1972–1975 (Tate Gallery) 1975, British Painting (Genesis Gallery NY) 1976, Int Print Exhbn (Cranbrooke Acad Gallery Detroit) 1980, Pintura Británica Contemporáne (Museo Municipal Madrid) 1983, Exhbn Road: Painters at the RCA (Gulbenkian Gall RCA) 1988; works incl in numerous public collections; *Style—* Derek Hirst, Esq; ✉ 3 The Terrace, Mill Lane, Sidlesham, nr Chichester, W Sussex PO20 7NA

HIRST, Jonathan William; QC (1990); s of Rt Hon Lord Justice Hirst, *qv*, and Pamela Elizabeth Molesworth, *née* Bevan; *b* 2 July 1953; *Educ* Eton, Trinity Coll Cambridge (MA); *m* 20 July 1974, Fiona Christine Mary, da of Dr Peter Anthony Tyser; 2 s (Thomas James b and d 1991, Charles John b 11 June 1993); *Career* called to the Bar Inner Temple 1975 (bencher 1994), in practice SE Circuit, asst recorder 1993–; memb Gen Cncl of Bar 1986–; chm: Law Reform Ctee 1992–94, Professional Standards Ctee 1996–; govr Taverham Hall Sch Norfolk 1990–95; *Recreations* shooting, gardening, music; *Clubs* Boodle's; *Style—* Jonathan Hirst, Esq, QC; ✉ Brickcourt Chambers, 15–19 Devereux Court, Temple, London WC2R 3JJ (☎ 0171 583 0777, fax 0171 583 9401)

HIRST, Sir Michael William; kt (1992); s of John Melville Hirst (d 1969), and Christina Binning, *née* Torrance; *b* 2 Jan 1946; *Educ* Glasgow Acad, Univ of Glasgow (LLB), Univ of Iceland (exchange student); *m* 1, 21 Sept 1972, Naomi Ferguson, da of Robert Morgan Wilson (d 1977); 1 s (John b 1976), 2 da (Sarah b 1974, Kate b 1979); *Career* qualified CA 1970, ptnr Peat Marwick Mitchell & Co 1977–83, conslt KPMG Peat Marwick 1983–92, Michael Hirst Assocs 1987–; MP (C) Strathkelvin and Bearsden 1983–87, PPS Dept of Energy 1985–87; company director; pres Scottish Cons and Unionist Assoc 1989–92, chm Scottish Cons and Unionist Pty 1993– (vice chm 1987–89); hon sec Br Diabetic Assoc 1993–, chm The Park Sch Educn Tst; memb: Exec Ctee Princess Louise Scottish Hosp 1979–, Ct of Glasgow Caledonian Univ (chm Audit Ctee); dir Weavers Soc of Anderston 1981–, dir Childrens Hospice Assoc Scotland 1993–; Elder Kelvinside Hillhead Parish Church 1975–; FRSA 1993; *Recreations* golf, hill walking, theatre, skiing; *Clubs* Carlton, Western (Glasgow); *Style—* Sir Michael Hirst; ✉ Enderley, Milngavie, Glasgow G62 8DU

HIRST, Neil Alexander Carr; s of Theodore James Hirst, and Valerie Adamson Hirst; *b* 16 May 1946; *Educ* Canford Sch, Lincoln Coll Oxford (BA), Cornell Univ (Telluride scholar, MBA); *m* 1984, Caroline Rokeby, da of Peter Blumfeld Collins; 2 da (Emily Clare Collins b 10 Dec 1987, Alice Lydia Collins b 25 March 1993); *Career* jr reporter Eastborne Gazette 1964–65; civil service: asst princ Fin and Econ Appraisal then Coal Div 1970–73, asst private sec to Min for Indust then two Mins for Energy and Sec of State for Trade 1973–75, princ Dept of Energy 1975–78, Atomic Energy Div Dept of Energy 1978–81, seconded to Goldman Sachs NY 1981, public flotation of Britoil 1982, asst sec Br Nuclear Fuels plc 1983–85, energy cnsllr FCO Washington DC 1985–88, DTI (projects incl legislation for privatisation of coal indust) 1992–95, dir Nuclear Industries 1995–; sec Curriculum Ctee Reay Primary Sch; *Recreations* gardening, music, theatre, walking; *Style—* Neil Hirst, Esq; ✉ Department of Trade and Industry, 1 Victoria Street, London SW1H 0ET (☎ 0171 215 0242, fax 0171 215 2897)

HIRST, Prof Paul Heywood; s of Herbert Hirst (d 1971), of Huddersfield, and Winifred, *née* Michelbacher; *b* 10 Nov 1927; *Educ* Huddersfield Coll, Trinity Coll Cambridge (BA, MA), Univ of London (Dip), ChCh Oxford (MA); *Career* lectr and tutor Dept of Educn Univ of Oxford 1955–59, lectr in philosophy of educn Univ of London Inst of Educn 1959–65; prof of educn: King's Coll London 1965–71, Univ of Cambridge 1971–88 (emeritus prof 1988–); fell Wolfson Coll Cambridge 1971–; visiting prof Univs of: Br Columbia, Malawi, Otago, Melbourne, Puerto Rico, Sydney, Alberta, London; CNAA: vice chm Ctee for Educn 1975–81, chm Res Ctee 1988–92; memb: Cncl Royal Inst of Philosophy 1972–89, Educn Sub Ctee UGC 1974–80, Ctee for Enquiry into the Educn of Children from Ethnic Minorities (Lord Swann Ctee) 1981–85; Hon DEd CNAA 1992; elected memb Royal Norwegian Soc of Scis and Letters 1995; *Books* Knowledge and the Curriculum (1974), Moral Education in a Secular Society (1974), Education and its Foundation Disciplines (jtly, 1983), Initial Teacher Training and the Role of the School (jtly, 1988); *Recreations* music (especially opera); *Clubs* Athenaeum; *Style—* Prof Paul H Hirst; ✉ Flat 3, 6 Royal Crescent, Brighton BN2 1AL (☎ 01273 684118)

HIRST, Prof Paul Quentin; s of Henry Hirst, of Plymouth, and Joyce Evelyn, *née* Schaeffer; *b* 20 May 1946; *Educ* Public Secdy Sch for Boys Plymouth, Univ of Leicester (BA), Univ of Sussex (MA); *m* 16 Feb 1981, Penelope Ann Franklin, da of Alexander J

Woolley, of Elsted, W Sussex; 1 s (James Alexander Henry b 26 Feb 1981); *Career* Birkbeck Coll Univ of London: lectr 1969–74, reader in social theory 1978–85, prof 1985–95, academic dir The London Consortium 1995–; memb: Lab Pty, Charter 88 Exec, Fabian Soc, Editorial Bd of The Political Quarterly; *Books* incl: Durkheim Bernard and Epistemology (1975), Mode of Production and Social Formation (with B Hindess, 1977), On Law and Ideology (1979), Social Relations and Human Attributes (with P Woolley, 1982), Marxism and Historical Writing (1985), After Thatcher (1989), Representative Democracy and its Limits (1990), Associative Democracy (1994), Globalisation in Question (with G Thompson, 1996); *Style—* Prof Paul Hirst; ✉ Dept of Politics, Birkbeck College, Malet St, London WC1E 7HX (☎ 0171 631 6782, fax 0171 631 6787)

HIRST, Rachel Joy; da of Rt Hon Lord Justice Hirst, *qv*, and Pamela Elizabeth Molesworth, *née* Bevan; *b* 14 Nov 1960; *Educ* Cranborne Chase Sch; *Career* PR exec; with Good Relations 1982–85, dir Gavin Anderson & Co 1990–94 (joined 1985), dir Shandwick Consultants 1994–; memb UK Ctee of Br-American C of C 1990–; dir and memb Cncl Benenden Sch 1993–; *Style—* Ms Rachel Hirst; ✉ Shandwick Consultants Ltd, Aldermary House, 10–15 Queen Street, London EC4N 1TX (☎ 0171 329 0096, fax 0171 329 6009)

HISCOCK, David Miles; s of Jeffrey Hiscock, of Coombe Bissett, nr Salisbury, Wilts and Rosalind Mary, *née* Marshall; *b* 20 Sept 1956; *Educ* Bishop Wordsworths GS, Salisbury Art Sch, St Martin's Sch of Art (BA), RCA (MA); *m* Anna Maria Russell; *Career* freelance photographic asst London 1979–82; freelance photographer: magazine work 1982–, advertising cmmns and commercials dir 1985–; currently pt/t lectr in photography RCA; Pentax bursaries 1983–85, Vogue Award for photography 1985, Madame Tussaud's Award for figurative work 1985, official VISA Olympic artist 1992; FRCA 1996; *Solo Exhibitions* incl: RPS Bath 1987, Pomeroy Purdey Gallery London 1988 and 1990, Parco Gallery Tokyo 1990, Norwich Arts Centre Norwich 1990, The Chateau D'Eau Gallery Toulouse France 1991, Pomeroy Purdy Gallery London 1992, Olympic Works (Zelda Cheatle Gallery London) 1992, Zelda Cheatle Gallery London 1993 and 1995, Transmutations (Purdy Hicks Gallery London) 1994; *Selected Gp Exhibitions* 1990: Identities (Philadephia Art Alliance USA), Rencontres Photographiques (Carcassonne France), Face On (Zelda Cheatle Gallery London), David Hiscock and Calum Colvin (Seagate Gallery), Dundee and Theatre Clwyd (Mold), Works by 54 Master Printers (John Jones Gallery London) 1992, The Figure Laid Bare (Pomeroy Purdy Gallery London) 1992, Print Center Editions (Pomeroy Purdy Gallery London) 1992, Fictions of the Self (Weatherspoon Art Gallery USA and tour) 1993, Time Machine (British Museum London) 1994; *Work in Collections* incl: Madame Tussauds's London, Nat Portrait Gallery, Haggerty Museum USA, Chateau D'Eau, Toulouse; *Books* David Hiscock - Work from 1982–90 (SKOOB Books, 1992), David Hiscock (Zelda Cheatle Press, 1994); *Style—* David Hiscock, Esq; ✉ c/o Purdy Hicks Gallery, 65 Hopton Street, London SE1 9GZ (☎ 0171 237 6062)

HISCOX, Robert Ralph Scrymgeour; s of Ralph Hiscox, CBE (d 1970), and Louisa Jeanie, *née* Boal; *b* 4 Jan 1943; *Educ* Rugby, Corpus Christi Coll Cambridge (MA); *m* 1, 1966 (m dis 1978), Lucy, da of Charles Henry Mills (d 1996); 2 s (Renshaw b 5 June 1968, Frederick b 5 June 1972); m 2, 1985, Lady Julia Elizabeth, da of 6 Earl of Clanwilliam (d 1989); 3 s (Milo Edmund b 4 Jan 1987, Henry Charles b 23 Sept 1989, Sidney John b 24 Jan 1993); *Career* memb Lloyd's 1967–; chm Hiscox plc, Hiscox Harrison Ltd, Hiscox Syndicates Ltd, Roberts & Hiscox Ltd, R K Harrison Holdings and other cos in the Hiscox Group; dir Hiscox Select Insurance Fund plc; dep chm Lloyd's of London 1993–95; memb: Cncl Friends of the Tate Gallery 1986–94, Museums and Galleries Cmmn 1996–; govr St Francis Sch Pewsey 1994–; *Recreations* family life, country life, the arts; *Clubs* City of London; *Style—* Robert Hiscox, Esq; ✉ Rainscombe Park, Oare, Marlborough, Wilts SN8 4HZ (☎ 01672 563491, fax 01672 564120); Hiscox plc, 52 Leadenhall Street, London EC3A 2BJ (☎ 0171 423 4000, fax 0171 626 2222)

HISKEY, Rex Arthur; s of Harry Charles Hiskey, and Gwynneth, *née* Bush; *b* 9 March 1947; *Educ* Univ of Birmingham (LLB); *m* 2 Oct 1971, Christine Elizabeth, da of Maurice Henry Cobbold; 1 s (Thomas b 1981), 2 da (Florence b 1986, Clara b 1990); *Career* slr; in private practice holding various local appts, ptnr Hayes & Storr; *Recreations* reading, sailing; *Style—* Rex Hiskey, Esq; ✉ Chancery Lane, Wells-next-the-Sea, Norfolk (☎ 01328 710210, fax 01328 711261)

HISLOP, Ian; s of late David Atholl Hislop, and Helen Hislop; *b* 13 July 1960; *Educ* Ardingly Coll Sussex, Magdalen Coll Oxford (BA); *m* 16 April 1988, Victoria, *née* Hamson; 1 s (William David b 26 June 1993), 1 da (Emily Helen b 3 Oct 1990); *Career* ed Private Eye 1986–; scriptwriter Spitting Image 1984–89, columnist The Listener 1985–89; regular book reviewer and contrib to various newspapers and magazines; writer and broadcaster for radio (incl comedy series GUSH! for Radio 4 1995) and TV (presenter series The Canterbury Tales for Channel 4 1996); team capt Have I Got News For You (BBC 2) 1991–; TV plays (all co-written with Nick Newman): The Stone Age (BBC 2) 1990, Briefcase Encounter (ITV) 1991, He Died a Death (BBC 2) 1991, The Case of the Missing (BBC 2) 1991, Mangez Merveillac (BBC 2) 1993, Dead on Time (BBC 2) 1995, Gobble (BBC 2) 1996; *Publications* incl various Private Eye compilations; *Style—* Ian Hislop, Esq; ✉ Private Eye, 6 Carlisle St, London W1V 5RG (☎ 0171 437 4017, fax 0171 437 0705)

HITCH, Brian; CMG (1985), CVO (1980); s of Richard Souter Hitch (d 1986), of Wisbech, Cambridge, and Gladys Evelyn, *née* Harley (d 1989); *b* 2 June 1932; *Educ* Wisbech GS, Magdalene Coll Cambridge (MA); *m* 4 Sept 1954, Margaret (Margot) Kathleen Wooler; 2 da (Susan Jennifer Magdalene b 1956, Caroline Margaret b 1959); *Career* joined FO 1955, language student second (formerly third) sec Tokyo 1955–61, Far Eastern Dept FO 1961–62, first (formerly second) sec Havana 1962–64, language student first sec Athens 1965–68, head of Chancery Tokyo 1968–72, asst head Southern European Dept FCO 1972–73, head (formerly dep head) Marine and Transport Dept FCO 1973–75, cnsllr (Bonn Gp) Bonn 1975–77, cnsllr and consul gen Algiers 1977–80, consul gen Munich 1980–84, min Tokyo 1984–87, high cmmr Malta 1988–91; dir Univ of Oxford Dip Course in Euro Studies and fell Kellogg Coll 1991–96 (fell emeritus 1996–); LRAM 1949, FRCO 1950; *Recreations* music; *Style—* Brian Hitch, Esq, CMG, CVO; ✉ 19 Moreton Road, Oxford OX2 7AX (☎ 01865 556764)

HITCHCOCK, Robert Edward (Robin); s of Edward Hitchcock (d 1976), of Clavering, Essex, and Isobel Mary, *née* Balch; *b* 1 May 1936; *Educ* Gresham's, Emmanuel Coll Cambridge (BSc); *m* 27 Feb 1965, Vera Eileen, da of Gilbert Thomas Boyce (d 1977); 2 da (Vanessa b 20 May 1967, Christina b 18 March 1969); *Career* md various subsids RTZ 1960–69; dir: McKechnie plc 1970–88, Lilleshall plc 1988–96, ret; non-exec dir Philip Harris Holdings plc 1986–95; Liveryman Worshipful Co of Farmers 1960; MInstM 1962, CEng 1970; *Style—* Robin Hitchcock, Esq; ✉ The Barn House, Barley Lands, Aldeburgh, Suffolk IP15 5LW (☎ 01728 453867)

HITCHING, His Hon Judge Alan Norman; s of Norman Henry Samuel Hitching (d 1987), and Grace Ellen, *née* Bellchamber (d 1992); *b* 5 Jan 1941; *Educ* Forest Sch Snaresbrook, ChCh Oxford (MA, BCL); *m* 1967, Hilda Muriel, da of Arthur William King (d 1984); 2 s (Malcolm b 1972, Robert b 1977), 1 da (Isabel b 1969); *Career* called to the Bar Middle Temple 1964, recorder 1985–87, circuit judge (SE Circuit) 1987–; *Style—* His Hon Judge Alan Hitching; ✉ 9 Monkhams Drive, Woodford Green, Essex IG8 0LG; Snaresbrook Crown Court, Hollybush Hill, Snaresbrook, London E11 1QW

HITCHINGS, Russell Walter; s of Walter Hitchings (d 1956), and Gladys Magdelin, *née* Bell; *b* 22 March 1922; *Educ* Rutlish Sch, RMC Sandhurst; *m* 1, 1941 (m dis 1956), Joan Kathleen Hughes (d 1980); 1 s (Derek Russell b 1947 d 1979); 2 da (Janet Kathleen b 1943, Ann Kathleen b 1948); m 2, 1956 (m dis 1961), Olga Dubska (d 1975); m 3, 24 Jan 1963, Betty Jean, JP, da of Keith Robinson (d 1978); 1 da (Julia Betty b 1964); *Career* TA Middx Yeo 1939, Cadet RMC Sandhurst 1942–43, Royal Tank Regt 1943–46; organiser Liberal Pty Orgn 1946–50, gen mangr Pilot Travel Ltd 1950–51, exec Eldridge and Co Ltd 1951–53; H J Symons (agencies) Ltd: dir 1953–55, md 1955, managing ptnr; H J Symons Gp of Cos: chm and chief exec 1960, pres 1987, ret 1988; forestry owner in Argyllshire and Cumbria, underwriting memb Lloyd's; memb Liberal Pty; Freeman City of London 1969, Freeman Worshipful Co of Blacksmiths; FCIB 1955; *Recreations* sailing, gardening; *Clubs* Royal Thames Yacht, Lloyd's Yacht, City Livery; *Style—* Russell Hitchings, Esq; ✉ The Mount, South Godstone, Surrey RH9 8JD (☎ 01342 892176, fax 01342 893488)

HITCHINSON, David Anthony; s of The Rev Prebendary William Henry Hitchinson, of 66 Waller Drive, Northwood, Middx, and Joan Lucretia, *née* Blakeley; *b* 8 July 1948; *Educ* Merchant Taylors', Rose Bruford Coll of Speech and Drama (RBC Dip), Univ of Kent (BA); *m* Jean, *née* Braithwaite; 1 step da (Sarah Bell); *Career* BBC: radio drama 1972–80, Radio 4 newsreader 1980–85, sr prodr drama World Serv 1985–; *Recreations* music, swimming, theatre; *Clubs* BBC; *Style—* David Hitchinson, Esq; ✉ BBC World Service Drama, Bush House, London WC2B 4PH (☎ 0171 257 2419, fax 0171 497 0287)

HITCHMAN, Frank Hendrick; s of Sir (Edwin) Alan Hitchman, KCB (d 1980), of London, and Katharine Mumford, *née* Hendrick (d 1996); *b* 21 July 1941; *Educ* Westminster, Univ of St Andrews (BSc); *Career* Coopers & Lybrand 1964–69, Samuel Montagu & Co Ltd 1970–73, Sedgwick Group plc 1973–89 (sec 1980–85), dir E W Payne Co Ltd 1985–89; Greig Fester Group Ltd: gp sec 1989–, dep gp fin dir 1989–91, gp fin dir 1992–; FCA 1978; *Recreations* opera, travel, collecting; *Clubs* Savile, City of London; *Style—* Frank Hitchman, Esq; ✉ 226 Cranmer Court, London SW3 3HD (☎ 0171 581 4705); 12 Darnaway Street, Edinburgh EH3 6BG (☎ 0131 225 4130); Greig Fester Group Ltd, Devon House, 58–60 Katharine's Way, London E1 9LB (☎ 0171 488 2828, fax 0171 816 1600)

HITCHMAN, Prof Michael L; s of Leslie S Hitchman (d 1993), of Bearsden, and Grace H Hitchman, *née* Callaghan (d 1991); *b* 17 Aug 1941; *Educ* Stratton GS Biggleswade, QMC London (BSc), King's Coll London (PGCE), Univ Coll Oxford (DPhil); *m* 8 Aug 1964, Pauline J, da of George V Thompson (d 1990), of Benfleet; 1 s (Timothy b 8 Feb 1973), 2 da (Natasha b 8 July 1971, Fiona E b 17 May 1977); *Career* asst lectr in chemistry Leicester Regnl Coll of Technol 1963–65, jr res fell Wolfson Coll Oxford 1968–70, ICI Postdoctoral Res fell Physical Chemistry Laboratory Oxford 1968–70, chief scientist Orbisphere Corpn Geneva 1970–73, staff scientist Laboratories RCA Ltd Zurich 1973–79, lectr then sr lectr Univ of Salford 1979–84; Univ of Strathclyde: Young prof of chemical technol 1984–, chm of Dept of Pure and Applied Chemistry 1986–89, vice dean Faculty of Sci 1989–92; treas Electrochemistry Gp RSC 1984–90, chm Electroanalytical Gp RSC 1985–88; memb Advsy Bd EUROCVD 1985– (chm 1989–92); memb SERC Ctees on: chemistry 1987–90, semiconductors 1988–90, non-metallic materials 1986–88; co-chm of W Scotland Sci Park Advsy Ctee 1988–92; memb: Electrochemical Soc, Int Soc of Electrochemistry, Br Assoc of Crystal Growth, Br Assoc, Materials Research Soc; British Vacuum Cncl medal and prize 1992; CChem, FRSC, FRSA, FRSE; *Books* Ring Disk Electrodes (jtly, 1971), Measurement of Dissolved Oxygen (1978), Proceedings of the Eighth European Conference on Chemical Vapour Deposition (ed, 1991), Chemical Vapour Deposition (ed, 1992); *Recreations* humour, cooking, eating, walking, losing weight; *Style—* Prof Michael Hitchman; ✉ Dept of Pure and Applied Chemistry, University of Strathclyde, 295 Cathedral St, Glasgow G1 1XL (☎ 0141 552 4400, 0141 553 4189, telex 77472 UNSLIB G, fax 0141 552 5664, e-mail m.l.hitchman@strath.ac.uk)

HITCHON, George Michael; s of Alfred Clifford Hitchon (d 1987), and Beatrice Helen, *née* Daniels (d 1982); *b* 26 Nov 1944; *Educ* King Edward's Five Ways Sch, Newent Sch, Univ of Nottingham (MSc); *Career* horticulturist at Scot Agric Coll 1969–; treas Ayr Arts Guild 1982–, dir Ayr Arts Festival 1983– (co sec 1991–), pres Kyle and Carrick Civic Soc 1981–, sec Int Soc of Horticultural Science's First Int Conf on Educn and Trg in Horticulture at Scottish Agric Coll 1992, treas Fort and Seafield CC 1992–, Churchill fell 1973; MIHort (chm Scottish Branch 1996–); *Books* Growing in Perlite (1991), Education and Training for Horticulture (1993); *Recreations* music, conservation, architectural history, curling; *Clubs* Auchincruive Curling, Ayr Curling; *Style—* George M Hitchon, Esq; ✉ The Scottish Agricultural College, Auchincruive, Ayr KA6 5HN (☎ 01292 520331, fax 01292 525389)

HITMAN, Prof Graham Alec; s of Maxwell Hitman (d 1987), and Annette Hitman (d 1976); *b* 19 Jan 1953; *Educ* Bromley GS, Univ Coll Hosp Med Sch (MB BS); *m* Avril Frona, da of Ivor Sevitt, of 63 Court Rd, Eltham; 1 s (Oliver b 1980), 1 da (Nadia b 1978); *Career* sr house offr and registrar King's Coll Hosp London, RD Lawrence res fell St Bartholomew's Hosp; London Hosp: successively lectr Med Unit, asst dir, then reader, currently prof of molecular med, hon conslt, and clinical dir Diabetes and Metabolism; memb: Br Diabetic Assoc, American Soc of Human Genetics; FRCP; *Recreations* windsurfing, tennis; *Style—* Prof Graham Hitman; ✉ 7 Toynbec Close, Chislehurst, Kent BR6 7TH (☎ 0181 467 3331); Medical Unit, The Royal London Hospital, Whitechapel, London E1 1BB (☎ 0171 377 7111, fax 0171 377 7636)

HITNER, Stella Annette; da of Alfred Wright, of Thame, Oxfordshire, and Esmé Ada Lillian, *née* Lovell; *b* 5 Nov 1946; *Educ* Holton Park Girls' GS Oxford, Oxford Poly; *m* 1, 27 March 1967 (m dis); m 2, 20 April 1985, Robert Ian Hitner, s of Laurence Hitner; 1 s (Philip Robert b 20 Nov 1984), 1 da (Claudia Elizabeth b 25 April 1974); *Career* Warren Cook & Partners (PR consultancy) London: sec and PA 1965–68, asst PR offr 1968–69, jr ptnr 1969–74; freelance PR conslt 1974–79, account dir Datanews Ltd (PR consultancy) Luton 1979–83; md: Media Communications and Marketing 1983–85, The Reputation Managers (formerly TRM Datanews Ltd, strategic mktg communications & PR consultancy) 1985–; dist cncllr Aylesbury Vale Dist Cncl 1970–74, dir and organiser Bedfordshire Country Festival 1979–83, dir Milton Keynes and North Bucks C of C Trg and Enterprise 1994; MIPR 1983, MInstD 1989, corporate memb PR Conslts Assoc 1989; *Recreations* golf, family, working; *Clubs* IOD; *Style—* Mrs Stella Hitner; ✉ Village House, 17 Bradwell Road, Loughton, Milton Keynes MK5 8AP (☎ 01908 608792); The Reputation Managers Ltd, Chancery House, 199 Silbury Boulevard, Central Milton Keynes MK9 1LN (☎ 01908 696169, fax 01908 690766, car 0802 264210)

HO-YEN, Dr Darrel Orlando; s of Basil Orlando Ho-Yen, and Cicely Ho-Yen; *b* 1 May 1948; *Educ* Univ of Dundee (BMSc, MB ChB, MD); *m* 18 July 1975, Jennifer, da of Arthur Maxwell Nicholls; 2 s (Gregory Orlando b 9 Aug 1977, Colan Maxwell b 2 Oct 1979); *Career* dir S Toxoplasma Reference Laboratory 1987–, conslt microbiologist Raigmore Hosp Inverness 1987–, hon clinical sr lectr Univ of Aberdeen 1987–; memb: Br Soc for Study of Infection, Assoc of Clinical Pathologists, Pathology Soc of GB & Ireland, Soc of Authors; MRCPath 1986; *Books* Better Recovery From Viral Illness (2 edn, 1987, 3 edn 1993), Diseases of Infection (jtly, 1987, 2 edn 1993), Unwind! Understand and Control Life, Be Better!! (1991), Human Toxoplasmosis (jtly, 1992), Climbing Out (1995); *Style—* Dr Darrel Ho-Yen; ✉ Microbiology Department, Raigmore Hospital, Inverness (☎ 01463 704207)

HOARE, Rev Brian Richard; s of Williams Charles Hoare, of Southwell, Notts, and Kathleen Nora, *née* Thwaites; *b* 9 Dec 1935; *Educ* Southwell Minster GS, Westminster Coll London (Teacher's Cert, Cert in Religious Educn), Richmond Coll Univ of London

(BD); *m* 24 March 1962, Joyce Eleanor, da of late Edwin Eli Davidson; 1 da (Karen Judith (Mrs Lomas) b 16 July 1965), 1 s (Andrew Richard b 21 May 1967); *Career* Nat Serv Ops Clerk RAF (Middleton St George and Cranwell) 1954–56; teacher Col Frank Seeley Secdy Sch Calverton Notts 1959–62, travelling sec and subsequently nat sec Colls of Educn Christian Union Inter-Varsity Fellowship London 1962–68; undergraduate Univ of London 1968–71, chaplain Hunmanby Hall Sch Filey and min of three churches Filey Circuit 1971–74, min Endike Hall and Thornton Hall Hull Mission Circuit 1974–77, New Testatment tutor Cliff Coll Sheffield 1977–86, superintendent min Longton Central Hall Stoke-on-Trent 1986–88, Methodist Home Mission Div 1988–95 (dep gen sec 1989–95), pres Methodist Conf 1995–96, Methodist sec for evangelism 1996–; represented Br Methodism Ghana Methodist Conf 1984, memb World Methodist Cncl Nairobi Kenya 1986, Singapore 1991 and Rio de Janeiro Brazil 1996, regional sec UK and Ireland World Methodist Evangelism Ctee 1992–; memb numerous Methodist ctees; vice chm Pratt Green Tst; memb: Cncl Royal Sch of Church Music, Enabling Gp Churches Together in England, Co-ordinating Gp for Evangelisation CTE; author of various Methodist pubns, composer of hymns/songs published in a variety of books (winner BBC TV Songs of Praise Festival of New Hymns 1991) and of New Creation (full-length musical); *Recreations* music, literature, travel, walking; *Style*— The Rev Brian Hoare; ✉ 1 St Peter's Close, Staines, Middlesex TW18 2ED (☎ and fax 01784 461340); Methodist Church, 1 Central Buildings, London SW1H 9NH (☎ 0171 222 8010, fax 0171 233 0323)

HOARE, Prof Charles Antony Richard; s of late Henry Samuel Malortie Hoare, of Beckenham, Kent, and Marjorie Francis, *née* Villiers; *b* 11 Jan 1934; *Educ* King's Sch Canterbury, Merton Coll Oxford (MA), Moscow State Univ; *m* 13 Jan 1962, Jill, da of late John Pym, of Foxwold, Brasted Chart, Westerham, Kent; 2 s (Thomas b 1964, Matthew b 1967, d 1981), 1 da (Joanna b 1965); *Career* Nat Serv RN 1956–58, Lt RNR 1958; Elliot Bros Ltd 1960–68: programmer, chief engr, tech mangr, chief scientist; prof of computer sci Queen's Univ Belfast 1968–77, prof of computation Univ of Oxford 1977–93, James Martin prof of computing Univ of Oxford 1993–; Turing award 1980, Faraday medal 1985; Hon DSc: Univ of Southern Calif (1979), Univ of Warwick (1985), Univ of Pennsylvania (1986), Queen's Univ Belfast (1987), Univ of York (1989); Hon DUniv: Essex 1991, Bath 1993; Soc Stran Accad dei Lincei 1988; Distinguished FBCS 1978, FRS 1982; *Books* Structured Programming (1972), Communicating Sequential Processes (1985), Essays in Computing Science (1988); *Recreations* reading, walking, swimming, music; *Style*— Prof C A R Hoare, FRS; ✉ 22 Chalfont Rd, Oxford OX2 6TH (☎ 01865 558933); Computing Laboratory, Wolfson Building, South Parks Road, Oxford OX1 3QD (☎ 01865 273841, fax 01865 273839)

HOARE, Christopher Henry St John (Toby); s of J Michael Hoare, and Ann St John, *née* Kingham; *b* 2 Feb 1960; *Educ* Harrow; *m* 2 Aug 1986, Hon Sarah Jane, da of Baron Dixon-Smith (Life Peer), *qv*; 2 s (Oscar b 16 July 1988, Giles b 22 June 1990); 1 da (Camilla b 17 Nov 1994); *Career* mgmnt trainee Distillers Co Ltd 1979–80, Express Newspapers 1980–84, Centaur Communications 1984–85, Dorland Advertising Ltd 1985–87; Young & Rubicam Ltd: joined 1987, dir 1989, business devpt dir 1991–94, md 1994–96, chief exec 1996–; Freeman City of London 1987, Liveryman Worshipful Co of Distillers 1982; *Recreations* shooting, golf, music, wine; *Clubs* Garrick, Royal Worlington Golf; *Style*— Toby Hoare, Esq; ✉ 130 Kensington Park Road, London W11 2EP (☎ 0171 221 5159, fax 0171 727 7214); Young & Rubicam Ltd, Greater London House, Hampstead Road, London NW1 7QP (☎ 0171 611 6431, car 0836 277578, fax 0171 611 6915)

HOARE, David John; s of Sir Peter William Hoare, 7 Bt (d 1973), and hp of bro, Sir Peter Richard David Hoare, 8 Bt, *qv*; *b* 8 Oct 1935; *Educ* Eton; *m* 1, 1965, Mary Vanessa, yr da of Peter Cardew, of Westhanger, Cleeve, Bristol; 1 s (Simon Merrick b 1967); m 2, 1984, Virginia Victoria Labes, da of Michael Menzies, of Long Island, NY; *Career* banker and farmer; dep chm and managing ptnr C Hoare & Co; *Recreations* fishing, shooting, golf, skiing; *Clubs* White's, Royal St George's Golf, Swinley, Sunningdale; *Style*— David Hoare, Esq; ✉ Luscombe Castle, Dawlish, Devon; C Hoare and Co, 37 Fleet St, London EC4P 4DQ (☎ 0171 353 4522)

HOARE, Henry Cadogan; s of Henry Peregrine Rennie Hoare (d 1981), and Lady Beatrix Lilian Ethel Cadogan (*see* Lady Beatrix Fanshawe); *b* 23 Nov 1931; *Educ* Eton, Trinity Coll Cambridge (MA); *m* 1, 30 May 1959 (m dis 1970), Pamela Saxon, da of late Col G F Bunbury, OBE; 2 s (Timothy b 1960, Nicholas b 1964), 1 da (Arabella b 1968); m 2, 16 June 1977, Caromy Maxwell Macdonald, da of Robert Jenkins, CBE, JP; *Career* banker; chm C Hoare & Co 1988– (managing ptnr 1959–); *Style*— Henry Hoare, Esq

HOARE, Jonathan Michael Douro; s of Capt Michael Douro Hoare, of Downsland Court, Ditchling, Sussex, and Valerie Ann, *née* James; *b* 21 Oct 1953; *Educ* Eton, Oriel Coll Oxford (BA, MA); *m* 7 Aug 1982, Clare Elizabeth, da of Peter Parsons, of The Grove, Stocklinch, Somerset; 2 s (Timothy Jonathan b 4 Oct 1986, Sebastian Michael b 18 Dec 1989), 1 da (Natasha Ruth b 1 June 1984); *Career* advertising mangr The Economist 1977–83, business devpt mangr Valin Pollen 1983–85, chief exec BMP Business 1985–91, chief exec Hoare Wilkins Advertising Ltd 1991–94; TBWA: md (following merger) 1994–96, chm 1996–; Freeman City of London, Liveryman Worshipful Co of Marketors; memb: IAA, IPA, Inst of Mktg, Mktg Soc; *Books* Racial Tension in the Twelfth Century in the Holylands (1975), The Third Crusade (1974); *Recreations* tennis, cricket, real tennis, golf, shooting; *Clubs* RAC, Queen's, Chelsea Harbour, White's, MCC, Wentworth Golf, Piltdown Golf; *Style*— Jonathan Hoare, Esq; ✉ TBWA, 8 Crinan Street, Battle Bridge Basin, London N1 9UF (☎ 0171 833 5544)

HOARE, Joseph Andrew Christopher; o s of Sir Reginald Hervey Hoare, KCMG (d 1954), and Lucy Joan (d 1971), da of William George Frederick Cavendish-Bentinck, JP, and sis of 8 and 9 Dukes of Portland; *b* 23 March 1925; *Educ* Le Rosey, Eton, Univ of Southampton, Balliol Coll Oxford (MA); *m* 23 Jan 1963, Lady Christina Alice McDonnell (d 1991), o da of 13 Earl of Antrim, KBE, DL (d 1977); 1 s, 2 da; *Career* Flying Offr: RAF Regt BAOR Bonn and Gütersloh 1946–47, 604 Sqdn (Co of Essex Fighter Sqdn, flying Vampires and Meteors) RAF North Weald 1951–57; dir Canadian Overseas Packaging Industries 1962–, farmer 1972–, property developer 1986–91; memb Stock Exchange 1957–77, chm Assoc of Chartered and Tech Analysts 1970–73, underwriting memb Lloyd's 1985–; memb: Secretan Names Assoc, Janson Green Action Gp, Merrett No 2 Gp, Wellington Names Assoc; *Recreations* studying religion and ethics of ancient Egypt and lives of Thothmes III and Rameses II, forecasting 13 leading currencies and gold bullion prices, keeping black cats, editing memoirs of Sir James Campbell (1745–1832), formerly flying Oerlinghausen German sailplanes (1946–47); *Clubs* Brooks's; *Style*— J Hoare; ✉ Hartridge Manor Farm, Cranbrook, Kent TN17 2NA (☎ 01580 891414)

HOARE, Michael Rollo; s of Rollo Hoare (d 1983), of Dogmersfield, and Elizabeth, *née* Charrington; *b* 8 March 1944; *Educ* Eton, New Coll Oxford; *m* 1, 1965 (m dis 1978), Penelope, da of Sir Charles Mander, 3 Bt, *qv*; 2 da (Venetia b 1965, Fiona b 1969); m 2, 1981 (m dis 1985), Caroline Jane, da of Derek Abele; 1 s (Rollo b 1987), 1 da (Isabella b 1985); *Career* memb Stock Exchange 1977–81, managing ptnr C Hoare & Co 1982–; RAM: govr 1984–, hon treas 1994–; Hon FRAM 1993; *Recreations* hunting, skiing, singing, gardening; *Clubs* Brooks's; *Style*— Michael Hoare, Esq; ✉ C Hoare & Co, 37 Fleet St, London EC4P 4DQ

HOARE, Penelope Mary (Nell); da of Alan Riley Maynard (d 1970), and Elizabeth Mary Hall, *née* Wells; *b* 17 Nov 1957; *Educ* St Helen's Sch Middx, Univ of Southampton (BA Hons), Museums' Assoc/Univ of Leicester (Museums Dip), Oxford Poly (DMS); *m* 18 May 1985, Simon Hoare, s of Sam Hoare (d 1970); *Career* asst keeper then acting keeper Livesey Museum Southwark 1980–84; Area Museum Serv for SE England: museum advsr 1984–86, museum devpt offr 1986–89, asst dir 1989–91, jt acting dir 1989–90 and 1990–91; dir Textile Conservation Centre 1991–; ICOM: memb Exec Bd 1989–, hon sec UK Nat Ctee 1991–; memb UK Inst of Conservation; FMA, FRSA; *Books* Exploring Museums - The Home Counties (jt author, 1990, HMSO); *Recreations* literature (esp the 19th century English novel), garden history and plants, collecting 19th and early 20th century watercolours, visiting museums and historic houses; *Style*— Mrs Nell Hoare; ✉ Textile Conservation Centre, Apartment 22, Hampton Court Palace, East Molesey, Surrey KT8 9AU (☎ 0181 977 4943, fax 0181 977 9081)

HOARE, Sir Peter Richard David; 8 Bt (GB 1786), of Barn Elms, Surrey; s of Sir Peter William Hoare, 7 Bt (d 1973), of Luscombe Castle, Dawlish, Devon, and Laura Ray, *née* Esplen (d 1992); *b* 22 March 1932; *Educ* Eton; *m* 1961 (m dis 1967), Jane, o da of late Daniel Orme; m 2, 1978 (m dis 1982), Katrin Alexa, da of late Erwin Bernstiel; m 3, 1983, Angela Francesca de la Sierra, da of late Fidel Fernando Ayarza, of Santiago, Chile; *Heir* bro, David John Hoare b 8 Oct 1935; *Career* co dir; *Recreations* travel, skiing; *Clubs* Royal Automobile; *Style*— Sir Peter Hoare, Bt; ✉ c/o Crèdit Andorrà, Avinguda Princep Benlloch 25, Andorra La Vella, Principality of Andorra

HOARE, Richard John; s of Wing Cdr Charles Frederick Hoare, of Farnham, Surrey, and Joyce Mary, *née* Stamp; *b* 5 Oct 1952; *Educ* Mill Hill Sch; *m* 1993, Jennifer Grace Agnes, da of William Thomas Patrick Donohue, of Marlborough, Wilts; 1 da (Héloïse Trafalgar Agnès Archer b 30 Nov 1996); *Career* ptnr: Barlow Lyde and Gilbert 1983–93 (joined 1973), Wilkinson Maughan 1993–95; slr to Hinduja Group 1995–; govr Surrey Inst of Art and Design; Freeman: City of London 1984, City of London Slrs Co; memb Law Soc 1978; *Recreations* gardening, sport, fine arts; *Style*— Richard Hoare, Esq; ✉ 18 Woodseer Street, London E1 5HD (☎ 0171 375 2856); Le Chateau de Villeneuve Les Montreal, Villeneuve Les Montreal, 11290, Aude, France; Richard Hoare, 13 Floor, New Zealand House, 80 Haymarket, London SW1Y 4TQ (☎ 0171 839 4661, fax 0171 930 7102)

HOARE, Richard Quintin; s of Quintin Vincent Hoare, OBE, and Lucy Florence, *née* Selwyn; *b* 30 Jan 1943; *Educ* Eton; *m* 19 Oct 1970, Hon Frances Evelyn Hogg, da of Lord Hailsham of St Marylebone, KG, CH, PC, *qv*; 2 s (Alexander b 1973, Charles b 1976), 1 da (Elizabeth b 1978); *Career* HAC 1963–68, Home Serv Force HAC Detachment 1985–88; managing ptnr C Hoare & Co Bankers 1969–; chm: Bulldog Holdings Ltd 1986– (dir 1964), The Bulldog Trust 1983–, Vaudeville Enterprises Ltd 1996–, Vaudeville Theatre 1996–; dir: Placehill Ltd 1992–, Thompson Clive (Jersey No 2) Ltd 1994–, S R Pan European Investment Trust 1995–, Finsbury Technology Tst plc 1995–; govr Westminster Med Sch 1972–76, treas Old Etonian Assoc 1984–95, hon tstee African Med Research Fndn (memb Cncl 1977–84), pres Interbank Athletics Assoc 1980; *Recreations* travel, walking, stalking, reading, collecting antiques; *Clubs* White's, Boodle's, HAC; *Style*— Richard Hoare, Esq; ✉ Tangier House, Wootton St Lawrence, Basingstoke, Hants RG23 8PH (☎ 01256 780240); Flat 7, 3–7 Walpole St, London SW3 4QP (☎ 0171 730 7705); C Hoare & Co, 37 Fleet St, London EC4P 4DQ (☎ 0171 353 4522, fax 0171 353 4521, telex 24622)

HOARE, Rt Rev Dr Rupert William Noel; *see:* Dudley, Bishop of

HOARE, SaraJane; da of Jeff Hoare, of 53 Strand on the Green, London, and Elizabeth Jane Hoare; *b* 27 June 1955; *Educ* Univ of Warwick (BA); *Career* fashion ed Observer newspaper 1985–87, sr fashion ed Vogue 1987–; fashion dir British Vogue 1989–92 (fashion ed 1987–89), fashion dir Harpers Bazaar NYC 1992–; *Style*— Miss SaraJane Hoare; ✉ Harpers Bazaar, New York (☎ 00 1 212 903 5300, fax 00 1 212 262 7101)

HOARE, Sir Timothy Edward Charles; 8 Bt (I 1784), of Annabella, Co Cork, OBE (1996); s of Maj Sir Edward O'Bryen Hoare, 7 Bt (d 1969), and Nina Mary, *née* Hope-Wallace (d 1995); *b* 11 Nov 1934; *Educ* Radley, Worcester Coll Oxford (MA), Birkbeck Coll Univ of London (MA); *m* 1969, Felicity Anne, da of late Peter Boddington, JP, of Stratford-upon-Avon; 1 s (Charles James b 1971), 2 da (Louisa Hope b 1972, Kate Annabella b (twin) 1972); *Heir* s Charles James Hoare b 15 March 1971; *Career* dir: Career Plan Ltd, New Metals and Chemicals Ltd; memb: Church Assembly 1960–70, C of E 1970–, Chadwick Cmmn on Church and State, Crown Appointments 1987–92, Cncl of St John's Coll Durham Univ; chm: Law of Marriage Gp 1984–88, Clergy Condition of Service Group 1991–; delegate WCC Conference 1991; dir World Vision of Britain 1984–95, govr Canford Sch; fell Linnean Soc, FZS; *Recreations* music, literature, natural history, the creative works of God in nature and of man in art; *Clubs* MCC, National; *Style*— Sir Timothy Hoare, Bt, OBE; ✉ 10 Belitha Villas, London N1 1PD (☎ 0171 607 7359)

HOBAN, Russell Conwell; s of Abram Hoban, and Jenny, *née* Dimmerman; *b* 4 Feb 1925; *Educ* Lansdale HS Pennsylvania, Philadelphia Museum Sch of Industl Art; *m* 1, 1944 (m dis 1975), Lillian Aberman; 1 s, 3 da; m 2, 1975, Gundula Ahl; 3 s; *Career* Army, served 339 Infantry 85 Div 5 Army Italian Campaign (Bronze Star Medal); various jobs 1946–56 incl TV art dir Batten Barton Durstine & Osborn; freelance illustrator 1956–65; assignments incl: Sports Illustrated, Fortune, Time; copywriter Doyle Dane Bernbach NY 1965–67; full-time author 1967–; FRSL 1988; *Books* novels: The Mouse and His Child (1967, made into film 1977, The Lion of Boaz-Jachin and Jachin-Boaz (1973), Kleinzeit (1974), Turtle Diary (1975, made into film 1984), Riddley Walker (1980, John W Campbell Meml award 1982, Aust Sci Fiction Achievement award 1983), Pilgermann (1983), The Medusa Frequency (1987), Fremder (1996), The Trokeville Way (1996); The Moment Under the Moment (stories, essays and a libretto, 1992), The Second Mrs Kong (opera, music by Sir Harrison Birtwistle, Glyndebourne 1994); 58 children's picture books incl: Charlie the Tramp (1966, Boys' Club Junior Book Award 1968), Emmet Otter's Jug-Band Christmas (1971, Lewis Carroll Looking-Glass Shelf award and Christopher award 1972), How Tom Beat Captain Najork and His Hired Sportsmen (1974, Whitbread award 1974); also author of essays and fragments, short stories, verse for children, and theatre pieces; *Style*— Russell Hoban, Esq, FRSL; ✉ c/o David Higham Associates, 5–8 Lower John Street, Golden Square, London W1R 4HA (☎ 0171 437 7888, fax 0171 437 1072)

HOBART, Sir John Vere; 4 Bt (UK 1914), of Langdown, Co Southampton; s of Sir Robert Hampden Hobart, 3 Bt (d 1988), and his 1 w Sylvia, *née* Argo (d 1965); gggs of 3 Earl of Buckinghamshire and hp to kinsman 10 Earl; *b* 9 April 1945; *m* 1980, Kate, o da of late George Henry Iddles, of Cowes, Isle of Wight; 2 s (George Hampden b 1982, James Henry Miles b 1986); *Heir* s, George Hampden Hobart b 10 June 1982; *Style*— Sir John Hobart, Bt; ✉ Shore End, Queen's Road, Cowes, Isle of Wight

HOBBS, Anne Elizabeth; da of John William Hobbs, of Alderley Edge, Cheshire, and (Patricia Mary) Josephine, *née* Doherty; *b* 21 Aug 1959; *Educ* Hollies Convent FCJ GS West Didsbury, Empire State Coll NY (BSc in Psychological Studies 1994); *Career* former professional tennis player; *Singles record* winner: Virginia Slims Indianapolis 1983, NZ Open 1985, UK Nat Championship 1985; reached last 16: Wimbledon 1981 and 1984, French Open 1983, US Open 1987, Aust Open 1987; *Doubles record* winner: UK Nat Championships 7 times (with Jo Durie) 1981–89, Birmingham 1982, Canadian Open 1983, Sydney 1983, Brisbane 1983, German Open 1983 and 1984, Virginia Slims Denver 1984, NZ Open 1985; finalist: Aust Open 1983, Eastbourne 1983, US Open 1984, Hilton Head 1984, WITA Championships 1984, Newport 1987, Mawah 1987; semi-finalist Wimbledon (with Jo Durie) 1984; GB rep Wightman Cup and Federation Cup 1978–89; Br rankings: jr number 1 1977, sr number 1 1988; highest world ranking number 34 (singles) and 7 (doubles); memb Tournament Ctee Women's Tennis Assoc 1983–84; has directed numerous children's tennis clinics for LTA, currently teaches in private lessons and clinics East River Tennis Club Long Island City NY; winner Ladies Superstars (BBC TV) 1979, researcher A Question of Sport (BBC TV) 1988 (dir Mystery Personality feature 1988–89), presenter Children in Need (BBC NW Region) 1988, numerous TV and radio appearances incl The New Tennis Magazine Show 'A Tip from the Pro' segment (Sports Channel America) 1992 and 1993 and Tennis TV with Brad Holbrook (Prime Network USA) Jan-May 1994, tennis commentator various TV and radio stations, author of articles in Serve and Volley magazine 1988; *Recreations* music, art, theatre, hockey, netball, squash, table tennis, athletics, skiing, watching sport (soccer, rugby, golf and cricket); *Clubs* All England (Wimbledon), East River Tennis (Long Island City); *Style*— Miss Anne Hobbs; ✉ c/o Fred Sharf, Sharf Marketing Group, 822 Boylston St, Suite 203, PO Box 67197, Chesnut Hill, Mass 02167, USA (☎ 00 1 617 566 7070); East River Tennis Club, 44–02 Vernon Boulevard, Long Island City, NY 11101 (☎ 00 1 718 937 2381)

HOBBS, Grete; da of Oscar V Fogh (d 1956), and Elly, *née* Petersen (d 1982); *b* 9 Dec 1927; *Educ* Ballerup Private Real Skole; *m* 15 Sept 1950, Joseph Hobbs (d 1984), s of late J W Hobbs; 1 s (Peter b 23 Nov 1955), 1 da (Annemarie b 28 March 1953); *Career* hotelier of 25 years; awards: Hotel of the Year 1971, Hotelier of the Year 1989, Scottish Free Enterprise award 1987, numerous hotel awards from different countries; *Recreations* golf, bridge; *Style*— Mrs Grete Hobbs; ✉ Inverlochy Castle, Fort William, Scotland PH33 6SN (☎ 01397 702177, fax 01397 702953, car 0860 332319)

HOBBS, Prof Kenneth Edward Frederick; s of Thomas Edward Ernest Hobbs (d 1951), of Suffolk, and Gladys May, *née* Neave (d 1986); *b* 28 Dec 1936; *Educ* W Suffolk Co GS Bury St Edmunds, Guy's Hosp Med Sch Univ of London (MB BS), Univ of Bristol (ChM); *Career* surgical res fell Harvard Univ 1968–69, sr lectr in surgery Univ of Bristol 1970–73 (lectr 1966–70), prof of surgery Royal Free Hosp Sch of Med 1973–, conslt surgn Royal Free Hosp Hampstead (now Royal Free Hampstead NHS Tst) 1973–, dean Faculty of Med Univ of London 1994–, (elected memb of Senate 1985–, vice dean 1986–90); memb MRC Ctee Systems Bd 1982–86, chm MRC Grants Ctee A 1984–86; memb: UGC Med Sub Ctee (now Univ Funding Cncl) 1986–89, UFC Med Ctee 1991–93; chm Mason Medical Fndn 1993–; Int Master Surgeon Int Coll of Surgeons 1994; hon fell The Sri Lanka Coll of Surgeons 1995; FRCS 1964; *Books* contrib: Surgical Techniques Illustrated (1985), Operative Surgery and Management (1987), Surgery of the Liver and Biliary Tract (1988), Oxford Textbook of Hepatology (1991), Liver and Biliary Disease (1992), General Surgical Operations (1994); *Recreations* gourmet dining, the countryside; *Clubs* Athenaeum; *Style*— Prof Kenneth Hobbs; ✉ The Rookery, New Buckenham, Norfolk NR16 2AE (☎ 01953 860558); University Department of Surgery, Royal Free Hospital, Pond St, London NW3 2QG (☎ 0171 435 6121, fax 0171 431 4528)

HOBBS, Maj Gen Michael Frederick; CBE (1982, OBE 1979, MBE 1975); s of Brig Godfrey Pennington Hobbs (d 1985), and Elizabeth Constance Mary, *née* Gathorne Hardy (d 1952); *b* 28 Feb 1937; *Educ* Eton; *m* 1967, Tessa Mary, da of Gerald Innes Churchill, of Oxon; 1 s (William b 1978), 2 da (Elizabeth b 1969, Victoria b 1970); *Career* served Grenadier Gds 1956–80, DS Staff Coll 1974–77; MOD 1980–82; cdr 39 Inf Bde 1982–84; dir PR Army 1984–85; GOC 4 Armd Div 1985–87 (ret 1987); dir Duke of Edinburgh's Award Scheme 1988–; *Recreations* field sports, horticulture; *Style*— Maj Gen Michael Hobbs, CBE; ✉ The Duke of Edinburgh's Award, Gulliver House, Madeira Walk, Windsor, Berks SL4 1EU (☎ 01753 810753, fax 01753 810666)

HOBBS, Peter Thomas Goddard; s of Reginald Stanley Hobbs, BEM (d 1970), of Gloucester, and Phyllis Gwendoline, *née* Goddard; *b* 19 March 1938; *Educ* Crypt Sch Gloucester, Exeter Coll Oxford (MA); *m* Victoria Christabel, da of Rev Alan Matheson (d 1988), of Clifton Campville, Staffs; 1 da (Katharine b 1971); *Career* Nat Serv 2 Lt RASC 1957–59, Capt RCT TA 1959–68; ICI Ltd 1962–79 (rising to jt personnel mangr Mond Div), gp personnel dir Wellcome Fndn and Wellcome plc 1979–92; HM Inspector of Constabulary 1993–; Chemical Industs Assoc: dep chm Pharmaceuticals and Fine Chems Jt Industl Cncl 1979–89, chm Trg Ctee 1985–89, chm Employment Affr Bd 1989–91, memb Cncl 1989–92, chm Chemical Indust Educn Centre Univ of York 1992–94; dir Employment Conditions Abroad Ltd 1984–91 and 1993, vice pres Int Inst of Personnel Mgmnt 1987–89 and 1990–91, dir and dep chm Roffey Park Inst 1989–93, dir London Business Sch Centre for Enterprise 1989–92; CBI: memb Task Force on Vocational Educn and Trg 1989–90, memb Educn and Trg Policy Ctee 1990–94; Business in The Community: memb Target Team for Indust/Educn Partnerships 1988–90, memb Target Team for Priority Hiring 1988–91; chm Learning from Experience Tst 1992–93 (tstee 1988–); memb Advsy Cncl Mgmnt Centre Europe Brussels 1989–, fndr chm Employers' Forum for Disability 1990–93; memb: Employment Ctee IOD 1989–, Nat Advsy Cncl on Employment of People with Disabilities 1991–93, Cncl Contemporary Applied Arts 1990–92, Indust Advsy Gp Nat Curriculum Cncl 1990–92, Personnel Standards Lead Body 1992–94, Cncl BTEC (now EDEXCEL Fndn) 1994–; CIPM, FInstD, FRSA; *Recreations* history, topography, theatre, opera; *Clubs* United Oxford and Cambridge; *Style*— Peter Hobbs, Esq; ✉ HM Inspector of Constabulary, White Rose Court, Oriental Road, Woking, Surrey GU22 7LG (☎ 01483 729337, fax 01483 756812)

HOBBS, Philip John; s of Anthony Lewis Hobbs, and Barbara, *née* Thomas; *b* 26 July 1955; *Educ* King's Coll Taunton, Univ of Reading (BSc); *m* 12 June 1982, Sarah Louise, da of Albert Edwin Hill; 3 da (Caroline Elizabeth, Katherine Louise, Diana Margaret); *Career* professional jockey for 10 years (160 winners); racehorse trainer 1985–: currently trg 80 horses, over 400 winners incl County Hurdle and Mackenson Gold Cup; *Recreations* shooting; *Clubs* Sportsman; *Style*— Philip Hobbs, Esq; ✉ Sandhill, Bilbrook, Minehead, Somerset (☎ 01984 40366)

HOBBS, Ronald William; s of William Matthew Hobbs (d 1976), of Nailsea, Somerset, and Florence Harriet Martha, *née* Holder (d 1988); *b* 18 Oct 1923; *Educ* Cotham GS, Univ of Bristol (BSc); *m* 5 June 1948, (Beatrice) May, da of Albert Hilling (d 1966), of Broadstairs, Kent; 1 s (Malcolm b 20 Nov 1951), 1 da (Marilyn b 9 May 1954); *Career* Royal Aircraft Estab 1943–46; jr engr Oscar Faber & ptnrs 1946–48, Ove Arup & Partners 1948–93 (ptnr 1961), Arup Associates 1963–89 (fndr ptnr, chm 1981–84), Ove Arup Partnership 1969–93 (fndr dir, co chm 1984–89, conslt 1989–93); visiting prof Univ of Reading 1991–; memb Awards Panel ARCUK 1970–91, rep of ACE on Jt Contracts Tbnl 1979–, memb Cncl of Assoc of Consulting Engrs 1982–83 and 1985–87; past chm: S Bucks Lib Party, Iver Parish Cncl; Hon DEng: Heriot Watt 1990, Univ of Bristol 1996; FICE 1985, FIStructE 1981, FEng 1990, Hon FRIBA 1990; *Recreations* bridge, gardening, history, 18th century porcelain; *Style*— Ronald Hobbs, Esq, FEng; ✉ Dobbins, Low Ham, Langport, Somerset TA10 9DR (☎ 01458 250433)

HOBDAY, Sir Gordon Ivan; kt (1979); s of Alexander Thomas Hobday (d 1971), and Frances Cassandra, *née* Meads; *b* 1 Feb 1916; *Educ* Long Eaton GS, Univ Coll Nottingham (BSc, PhD, LLD); *m* 1940, Margaret Jean Joule; 1 da; *Career* chm: Boots Co Ltd 1972–82, Central Independent TV 1981–85; dir Lloyds Bank 1981–86 (also chm N and E Regnl Bd); DL 1981–83, Lord-Lt Notts 1983–91; chllr Univ of Nottingham 1979–92 (pres Cncl 1973–82); FRSC; *Style*— Sir Gordon Hobday; ✉ c/o Lloyds Bank, St James's St, Nottingham NG1 6FD (☎ 0115 942 501)

HOBDAY, Peter; *b* 16 Feb 1937; *Educ* St Chad's Coll Wolverhampton, Univ of Leicester; *Career* journalist, broadcaster; Wolverhampton Express and Star & Chronicle 1960–61; formerly with BBC World Service, progs incl The Financial World Tonight (Radio 4), The Money Programme (BBC2) 1979–81, Newsnight (BBC2) 1980–82, Today (Radio 4) 1981–96; other work for TV incl: The Business Programme (Channel 4), Pebble Mill Midlands at Westminster, European Business Weekly (satellite TV); *Books* Saudi Arabia Today (1979), In the Valley of the Fireflies; *Style*— Peter Hobday, Esq; ✉ (home fax 0171 371 1002)

HOBHOUSE, Sir Charles John Spinney; 7 Bt (UK 1812), of Broughton-Gifford, Bradford-on-Avon, and of Monkton Farleigh, Wiltshire; o s of Sir Charles Chisholm Hobhouse, 6 Bt, TD (d 1991), and his 2 w Elspeth Jean, *née* Spinney; *b* 27 Oct 1962; *Educ* Eton; *m* 5 June 1993, Katrina, da of Maj-Gen Sir Denzil Macarthur-Onslow, CBE, DSO, ED (d 1984); *Heir* uncle, John Spencer Hobhouse, AFC b 1910; *Style*— Sir Charles Hobhouse, Bt; ✉ The Manor, Monkton Farleigh, Bradford-on-Avon, Wilts (☎ 01225 858558)

HOBHOUSE, (Mary) Hermione; MBE (1981); da of Sir Arthur Lawrence Hobhouse, JP (d 1965), of Somerset, and Konradin Huth Jackson (d 1965); *b* 2 Feb 1934; *Educ* Cheltenham Ladies' Coll, Lady Margaret Hall Oxford (MA); *m* 1958 (m dis 1988), Henry Trevenen Davidson Graham, s of W Murray Graham (d 1956), of Cairo; 1 s (Francis Henry b 1960), 1 da (Harriet Konradin b 1964); *Career* writer, conservationist, freelance journalist 1960–76, sec Victorian Soc 1976–82, gen ed Survey of London RCHM(E) 1983–94; memb: Cncl Nat Tst 1983–, Royal Cmmn for 1851 Exhibition 1984–, Cncl Br Sch at Rome 1990–95; FSA 1980; *Books* Thomas Cubitt: Master Builder (1971, republished 1995), Lost London (1971), Prince Albert - His Life and Work (1983), Southern Kensington - Kensington Square to Earl's Court (ed, 1986), County Hall (ed, 1991), Poplar, Blackwall and the Isle of Dogs (ed, 1994), London Survey'd, The Work of the Survey of London 1894–1994 (1994); *Recreations* gardening, looking at buildings of all periods; *Clubs* Reform; *Style*— Miss Hermione Hobhouse, MBE, FSA; ✉ 61 St Dunstan's Road, Hammersmith, London W6 8RE (☎ 0181 741 2575)

HOBHOUSE, Rt Hon Lord Justice; Rt Hon Sir John Stewart; kt (1982), PC (1993); 2 s of Sir John Hobhouse, MC, JP (d 1961), and Catherine (d 1991), yr da of Henry Stewart-Brown; *b* 31 Jan 1932; *Educ* Eton, ChCh Oxford (BA, BCL); *m* 1959, Susannah Sybil Caroline, o da of Sir Ashton Wentworth Roskill, QC (d 1991); 2 s (William b 1963, Sebastian s b 1964), 1 da (Charlotte (Mrs Edward Farquharson) b 1961); *Career* called to the Bar 1955, practised at Commercial Bar until 1982, QC 1973, judge of the High Court of Justice (Queen's Bench Div and Commercial Ct) 1982–93, Lord Justice of Appeal 1993–; chm Cncl of Legal Educn 1986–89; *Style*— The Rt Hon Lord Justice Hobhouse; ✉ Royal Courts of Justice, Strand, London WC2A 2LL (☎ 0171 936 6000)

HOBHOUSE, Penelope (Mrs Malins); da of Capt James Jackson Lenox-Conyngham Chichester-Clark, DSO, RN (d 1933), and Marion Caroline Dehra, *née* Chichester (d 1976); *b* 20 Nov 1929; *Educ* North Foreland Lodge Sch, Girton Coll Cambridge (BA); *m* 1, 17 May 1952 (m dis 1983), Paul Rodbard Hobhouse (d 1994), s of Sir Arthur Hobhouse (d 1965), of Hadspen House, Castle Cary, Somerset; 2 s (Niall Alexander b 29 Aug 1954, David Paul b 9 Sept 1957), 1 da (Georgina Dehra Catherine b 9 March 1953); m 2, 1983, Prof John Melville Malins (d 1992); *Career* writer and garden designer; *Books* incl: The Country Gardener (1976), The Smaller Garden (1981), Gertrude Jekyll on Gardening (1983), Colour in Your Garden (1985), The National Trust: A Book of Gardening (1986), Private Gardens of England (1986), Garden Style (1988), Borders (1989), The Gardens of Europe (1990), Flower Gardens (1991), Plants in Garden History (1992), Penelope Hobhouse on Gardening (1994); *Style*— Ms Penelope Hobhouse; ✉ The Coach House, Bettiscombe, Bridport, Dorset DT6 5NT (☎ 01308 868560, fax 01308 867560)

HOBLEY, Brian; s of William Hobley (d 1959), and Harriet Hodgson (d 1976); *b* 25 June 1930; *Educ* Univ of Leicester (BA), Univ of Oxford (MSt); *m* 1953 (m dis 1992); 1 s (Paul), 1 da (Toni); partner since 1992, Dr Liz Greene; *Career* head of field archaeology Coventry Museum 1965–73, chief urban archaeologist City of London 1973–89, dir Hobley Archaeological Consultancy Services Ltd 1989–92; research student Univ of Oxford 1992–; FSA, AMA, MIFA; *Books* Waterfront Archaeology in Britain and Northern Europe (jt ed, 1981), Roman Urban Defences in the West (jt ed, 1983), Roman Urban Topography in Britain and the Western Empire (jt ed, 1985), The Rebirth of Towns in the West AD 700–1050 (jt ed 1988), Roman and Saxon London: a Reappraisal (1986); reports in many learned jls; *Recreations* music, gardening, visiting Italy; *Style*— Brian Hobley, Esq, FSA; ✉ 4 Farm Court, Church Road, Weston-on-the-Green, Oxford OX6 8QP (☎ 01869 351263, fax 01869 351190)

HOBLEY, Denis Harry; s of John Wilson Hobley, of Olney, and Ethel Anne, *née* Dixon (d 1995); *b* 6 Feb 1931; *Educ* King George V GS Southport; *m* 1 April 1957, June, da of Barnard Windle (d 1982); 3 s (Philip b 12 Jan 1961, David b 11 Oct 1962, Keith b 25 Oct 1964); *Career* Nat Serv RAPC 1953–55; qualified CA 1953, sr ptnr Lithgow Nelson and Co 1985–94 (joined 1948); pres Liverpool Soc of CAs 1986–87; memb Cncl ICAEW 1992–; fin dir Birkdale Sch for Hearing Impaired Children Ltd; memb: ctee many local charities, Methodist Church (memb fin bd and dist, circuit and local ctees); FCA; *Style*— Denis Hobley, Esq; ✉ 11 Silverthorne Drive, Southport, Lancs (☎ 01704 25274)

HOBMAN, David Burton; CBE (1983); s of Joseph Burton Hobman (d 1953), and Daisy Lucy, *née* Adler (d 1961); *b* 8 June 1927; *Educ* Univ Coll Sch, Blundell's; *m* 1954, Erica, da of Hugh Irwin (d 1954); 1 s (Anthony), 1 da (Lucy Ann); *Career* community work Forest of Dean 1954–56, Br Cncl for Aid to Refugees 1957, Nat Cncl of Social Services 1958–67, visiting lectr in social admin Nat Inst for Social Work 1967, dir Social Work Advsy Service 1968–70, dir Age Concern England 1970–87 (vice pres 1988–); visiting prof Sch of Social Work McGill Univ Montreal 1977, visiting research fell Univ of Sussex 1993–; memb: BBC/ITA Appeals Advsy Cncl 1965–69, Steering Ctee Enquiry into Homelessness Nat Assistance Bd 1967–68, Advsy Cncl Nat Corp for Care of Old People 1970–74, Metrication Bd 1974–80, Lord Goodman's Ctee Reviewing Law and Charity 1975–76, Family Housing Assoc 1969–70; conslt UN Div of Social Affairs 1968–69; observer White House Congress on Ageing 1971–; pres Int Fedn on Ageing 1977–80 and 1983–87 (vice-pres 1974–77); memb: Personal Social Services Cncl 1978–80, Exec Ctee Nat Cncl of Vol Orgns 1981–83, Anchor Housing 1982–85; special advsr Br Delgn to World Assembly on Ageing 1982, prodr Getting On (Central TV) 1987–88, exec sec Charities Effectiveness Review Tst 1986–92; chm: Ctee for Elderly Disabled People, Office of Telecommunications (OFTEL) 1987–92; chm Bd of Govrs Newman Comprehensive Sch Hove 1971–76, govr Volunteer Centre 1975–79; dir Cinetel Ltd 1988–; conciliator The Sheltered Housing Advsy and Conciliation Service 1990–94, cnsllr The Helen Hamlyn Fndn 1991–, co ombudsman Peverel Sheltered Housing Ltd 1995–; KSG 1977; *Books* A Guide to Voluntary Service (1964, 2 edn 1967), Who Cares (1971), The Social Challenge of Ageing (1978), The Impact of Ageing (1981), The Coming of Age (ed 1987), Planning Your Retirement (1990), Uniting Generations (ed 1993), The More We Are Together (1995); and numerous papers and broadcasts; *Recreations* writing, garden watching, grandchildren; *Clubs* Reform; *Style*— David Hobman, Esq, CBE; ✉ Robinswood, George's Lane, Storrington, Pulborough, W Sussex RH20 3JH (☎ 01903 742987)

HOBSBAUM, Prof Philip Dennis; s of Joseph Hobsbaum (d 1970), and Rachel, *née* Sapera (d 1992); *b* 29 June 1932; *Educ* Belle Vue GS Bradford, Downing Coll Cambridge (MA), Univ of Sheffield (PhD), Univ of Glasgow (DLitt), Royal Academy of Music (LRAM), Guildhall Sch of Music (LGSM); *m* 1, 7 Aug 1957 (m dis 1968), Hannah Kelly, da of Khedourie Baruch Chaim (d 1945); m 2, 20 July 1976, Rosemary, *née* Phillips; *Career* asst master English Tulse Hill Sch 1956–58, dir Philip Hobsbaum Studio London 1958–59, lectr in English Queen's Univ Belfast 1962; Univ of Glasgow: sr lectr (formerly lectr) in English lit 1966–79, reader 1979–85, titular prof in English lit 1985–; memb: Soc of Teachers of Speech and Drama 1957–59, N Kelvin Community Cncl 1978–80; chm Schs-Univs Liaison Ctee for the Teaching of English 1979–88; ed The Glasgow Review 1993–94, judge Whitbread Book of the Yr 1994; *Books* A Group Anthology (ed, with Edward Lucie-Smith, 1963), The Place's Fault and Other Poems (1964), In Retreat: poems (1966), Coming Out Fighting: poems (1969), A Theory of Communication (1970), Women and Animals: poems (1972), A Reader's Guide to Charles Dickens (1972), Tradition and Experiment in English Poetry (1979), A Reader's Guide to D H Lawrence (1981), Essentials of Literary Criticism (1983), A Reader's Guide to Robert Lowell (1988), William Wordsworth: Poetry and Prose (ed, 1989), Channels of Communication (ed with Paddy Lyons and Jim McGhee, 1992), Metre, Rhythm and Verse Form (1996); *Recreations* dog-walking, piano-playing; *Style*— Prof Philip Hobsbaum; ✉ Department of English Literature, University of Glasgow, Glasgow G12 8QQ (☎ 0141 339 8855, fax 0141 330 4601, telex 777070 UNIGLA)

HOBSLEY, Prof Michael; TD (1969); s of Henry Hobsley (d 1950), and Sarah Lily, *née* Blanchfield (d 1959); *b* 18 Jan 1929; *Educ* La Martinière Coll Calcutta, St Xavier's Coll Univ of Calcutta, Sidney Sussex Coll Cambridge (BA, MA, MB MChir), Middx Hosp Med Sch (PhD); *m* 28 July 1953, Jane Fairlie, *née* Cambell, da of Neville Cambell (d 1963); 1 s (James Campbell b 1960), 3 da (Alison Fairlie b 1954, Clare Gillian b 1956, Katherine Sarah b 1963); *Career* Nat Serv Lt RAMC 1952–54 (Capt 1953), TA 1954–72 (Maj 1962); house offr, registrar and lectr The Middx Hosp, The Whittington Hosp and Chase Farm Hosp London 1951–64; The Middx Hosp and Med Sch: sr lectr Dept of Surgical Studies 1967–70 (lectr 1964–67), hon conslt surgn 1969–94, reader in surgical sci 1970–75, prof of surgical sci 1975–83, prof of surgery and dir Dept of Surgical Studies 1983–88; prof of surgery and head Dept of Surgery Univ Coll and Middx Sch of Med 1988–92, David Patey prof 1984–94, emeritus prof 1994–; memb Enfield Health Authy 1990–93; currently conslt in distance learning UCL, chm Acad Cncl Inst of Sports Med and vice chm Professional Linguistic Assessment Bd; RCS: Hunterian prof 1962–63, examiner in applied physiology in Primary Examination for Fellowship of RCS 1968–74, Penrose-May tutor 1973–78, Sir Gordon Gordon-Taylor lectr 1980; Comyns Berkeley fell Gonville and Caius Coll Cambridge and The Middx Hosp 1965–66, Howard C Naffziger surgical res fell Univ of California San Francisco Med Center and univ examiner in surgery 1966, visiting prof Harvard Med Sch Beth Israel Hosp Boston Mass USA 1966; examiner: in nursing studies Univ of London Dip of Nursing 1976–79, in MS Univ of London, in BS Univ of Nigeria 1977–79, in BS Univ of West Indies 1978 and 1980, in MB ChB Univ of Bristol 1986–88, in MB BChir Univs of Cambridge 1986–, Newcastle 1992–95 and Birmingham 1992–95, Dip of Sports Med The London Hosp 1987–, in surgery MB BS St Mary's Hosp Univ of London 1989; Windemere Fndn travelling prof of surgery and visiting prof Monash Univ of Melbourne Aust 1984, guest American Surgical Assoc San Francisco 1988, visiting prof Dept of Surgery Univ of Louisville 1988 and 1995; hon sec Br Soc of Gastroenterology 1976–82 (pres 1992–93); hon fell: Assoc of Surgeons of India 1983, American Surgical Assoc 1989; past pres Section of Measurement in Med RSM, past pres Assoc of Professors of Surgery; memb: Soc of Authors (former chm Med Writers' Gp), Assoc of Surgeons (former chm Educn and Trg Ctee), Br Assoc of Clinical Anatomists, Br Assoc of Surgical Oncology, North East Metropolitan Surgical Soc, Société Internationale de Chirurgiae, Collegium Internationale Chirurgiae Digestivae (past Br del), Enfield Health Authy 1990–93; Freeman: Worshipful Soc of Apothecaries 1981, City of London 1983; *Books* Pathways in Surgical Management (1979, 2 edn 1986), Physiological Principles in Medicine: Disorders of the Digestive System (1982), A Colour Atlas of Parotidectomy (1984), MCQ Tutor for Primary FRCS: Basic Science for the Surgeon (with P Abrahams and B Cardell, 1980), Current Surgical Practice Vols 1 - VII (ed), Pathology in Surgical Practice (ed 1985, 2 edn 1988), Physiology in Surgical Practice (1992), numerous med pubns; *Recreations* cricket; *Clubs* MCC, Athenaeum; *Style*— Prof Michael Hobsley, TD; ✉ Fieldside, Barnet Lane, Totteridge, London N20 8AS (☎ 0181 445 6507); Dept of Surgery, University College London; Charles Bell House, 67–73 Riding street, London W1P 7LD (☎ 0171 380 9312, fax 0171 636 5176)

HOBSON, Anthony Robert Alwyn; s of Geoffrey Dudley Hobson, MVO (d 1949), of London, and Gertrude Adelaide, *née* Vaughan; *b* 5 Sept 1921; *Educ* Eton, New Coll Oxford (MA, DLitt); *m* 4 Dec 1959, (Elena Pauline) Tanya (d 1988), da of Igor Pavlovich Vinogradoff (d 1987), of London; 1 s (William b 1963), 2 da (Emma b 1960, Charlotte b 1970); *Career* WWII Scots Gds 1941–46, Capt Italy 1943–46 (despatches); dir Sotheby & Co 1949–71 (assoc 1971–77), Sandars reader in bibliography Univ of Cambridge 1974–75, Franklin Jasper Walls lectr Pierpont Morgan Library NY 1979 (hon fell 1983–), visiting fell All Souls Coll Oxford 1982–83, Rosenbach lectr Univ of Pennsylvania 1990, Lyell reader in bibliography Univ of Oxford 1990–91; pres: Assoc Internationale de Bibliophilie 1985–, Bibliographical Soc 1977–79; hon pres Edinburgh Bibliographical Soc 1971–; tstee: Eton Coll Collections Tst 1977–, Lambeth Palace Library 1984–90, Socio Straniero Accademia Veneta 1987–; awarded Gold medal of The Bibliographical Soc 1992; Freeman City of London, Liveryman Worshipful Co of Clothworkers; Cavaliere Al Merito della Repubblica Italiana; FBA 1992; *Books* French and Italian Collectors and their Bindings (1953), Great Libraries (1970), Apollo and Pegasus (1975), Humanists and Bookbinders (1989, awarded Premio Felice Feliciano 1991 and 10th Triennial Prize Int League of Antiquarian Booksellers); *Recreations* travel, opera, visiting libraries founded before 1800; *Clubs* Brooks's, Roxburghe, Beefsteak, Grolier (NY, hon foreign corresponding memb); *Style*— Anthony Hobson, Esq, FBA; ✉ The Glebe House, Whitsbury, Fordingbridge, Hampshire SP6 3QB (☎ 01725 518221)

HOBSON, Peter; *b* 2 Oct 1944; *Educ* Rossall Sch Fleetwood Lancs, Queen's Coll Oxford (Fletcher exhibitioner), Univ of Oxford (MA, DipEd); *m* 1976, Amanda Rosemary, da of Michael Thomas Emilius Clayton, CB, OBE (d 1995); *Career* Wellington Coll Berks: Dept of Classics 1968–86, housemaster 1971–86, industl liaison offr 1978–86; headmaster: Giggleswick Sch 1986–93, Charterhouse Sch 1993–95; HMC: memb 1986–95, rep Business and Educn Initiative DTI 1989–90, memb Professional Devpt Sub-Ctee 1990–91, memb Boarding Sub-Ctee 1991–93, dir HMC course for new housemasters and housemistresses 1991–95; chm ISIS North 1991–93, memb London and SE Ctee ISIS 1994–95; govr: Sindlesham Special Sch 1978–83, Lady Lane Park Sch (chm) 1990–93, Edgeborough, Haslemere and St Edmund's Prep Schs 1994–95; Schoolmaster fell Queen's Coll Oxford 1982; MInstD 1989, FRSA 1991; *Clubs* East India; *Style*— Peter Hobson, Esq; ✉ c/o The Headmaster's Office, Charterhouse, Godalming, Surrey GU7 2DE (☎ 01483 291600)

HOBSON, Valerie Babette Louise; da of late Capt Robert Gordon Hobson, RN, and late Violet, *née* Hamilton-Willoughby; *b* 14 April 1917; *Educ* St Augustine's Priory London, RADA; *m* 1, 1939 (m dis 1952), Anthony James Allan Havelock-Allan, now Sir Anthony Havelock-Allan, 4 Bt; 2 s (Simon (decd), (Anthony) Mark David, *qv*); m 2, 1954, John Profumo, CBE, *qv*; 1 s (David); *Career* stage, television and film actress; *Recreations* painting, reading, writing; *Style*— Miss Valerie Hobson

HOCKADAY, Sir Arthur Patrick; KCB (1978, CB 1975), CMG (1969); s of (William) Ronald Hockaday (d 1974), of Plymouth, and Marian Camilla Hockaday (d 1988); *b* 17 March 1926; *Educ* Merchant Taylors', St John's Coll Oxford; *m* 1955, Peggy, da of Hector Wilfred Prince, of Portsmouth; *Career* private sec to successive Mins and Secs of State MOD 1962–65, NATO Int Staff 1965–69, asst sec gen Def Planning and Policy 1967–69, asst under sec of state MOD 1969–72, under sec Cabinet Office 1972–73, dep under sec of state MOD 1973–76, second perm under sec of state MOD 1976–82; sec and DG Cwlth War Graves Cmmn 1982–89; *Books* The Strategic Defence Initiative: New Hope or New Peril? (1985); contrib: Ethics and Nuclear Deterrence (1982), Ethics and European Security (1986), Ethics and International Relations (1986), Just Deterrence (1990); *Recreations* fell-walking; *Clubs* Naval and Military, Civil Service; *Style*— Sir Arthur Hockaday, KCB, CMG; ✉ 11 Hitherwood Court, Hitherwood Drive, London SE19 1UX (☎ 0181 670 7940)

HOCKLEY, Rev Canon Raymond Alan; s of Henry Hockley (d 1957), and Doris, *née* Stonehouse (d 1987); *b* 18 Sept 1929; *Educ* Firth Park Sch, Royal Acad of Music (BMus, RAM), Westcott House Cambridge (MA); *Career* curate St Augustine's Sheffield 1958–61, priest i/c Holy Trinity Wicker Sheffield 1961–63, chaplain Westcott House Cambridge 1963–68, fell chaplain and dir of music Emmanuel Coll Cambridge 1968–76, canon residentiary precentor and chamberlain York Minster 1976–95, canon emeritus 1995–; Prize for Best Piece of Br Chamber Music (String Quartet) 1954, Oratorio, Suite for Orchestra, Piano Pieces etc; intercessions, articles for learned journals; *Recreations* cooking; *Style*— The Rev Canon Raymond Hockley; ✉ 2a Sycamore Terrace, York (☎ 01904 646702)

HOCKMAN, Stephen Alexander; QC (1990); s of Dr Nathaniel Hockman, of Bromley, Kent, and Trude, *née* Schlossman; *b* 4 Jan 1947; *Educ* Eltham Coll London, Jesus Coll Cambridge; *Career* called to the Bar Middle Temple 1970; recorder Crown Court 1987; *Clubs* RAC; *Style*— Stephen Hockman, Esq, QC; ✉ 6 Pump Court, Temple, London EC4Y 7AR (☎ 0171 797 8400, fax 0171 797 8401)

HOCKNEY, David; s of Kenneth and Laura Hockney; *b* 9 July 1937; *Educ* Bradford GS, Bradford Sch of Art, RCA; *Career* artist, photographer, costume and set designer (opera); Hon Dr RCA; winner Smithsonian Award of Achievement 1993; RA 1991 (ARA 1985); *Solo Exhibitions* incl: Kasmin Ltd London 1963, 1965, 1966, 1968, 1969, 1970, 1972, Alan Gallery New York 1964–67, Louvre Paris 1974, Knoedler Gallery 1979, 1981, 1982, 1986, Tate 1986, Hayward Gallery 1983, 1985, Tate Gallery Liverpool 1993, A Drawing Retrospective (Royal Academy) 1995–96, Annely Juda Fine Art 1996; exhibition of photographs Hayward Gall 1983; *Stage Design* incl: The Rake's Progress (Glyndebourne) 1975, The Magic Flute (Glyndebourne) 1978, costumes and sets for Met Opera N York 1980, Die Frau Ohne Schatten (Royal Opera House) 1992; *Books* The Blue Guitar (1977), China Diary (with Stephen Spender, 1982, reissued 1993), Hockney Paints the Stage (1983); *Style*— David Hockney, RA; ✉ 7508 Santa Monica Boulevard, Los Angeles, California 90046, USA

HOCKNEY, Michael Brett; s of Stanley Waller Hockney, of St Annes-on-the-Sea, Lancs, and Jean, *née* Duston; *b* 29 July 1949; *Educ* King Edward VII Sch Lytham, Univ of Manchester, LSE; *m* 30 July 1983, Dr Elizabeth Anne Hockney, da of Bruce Cryer, of Richmond, Surrey; *Career* dir and memb Exec Ctee of Boase Massimi Pollitt 1980–87, gp md BDDH Group plc 1987–93, gp mktg dir Christie's International and memb Christie's International Mgmnt Bd 1994–95; memb Cncl: Royal Sch of Church Music 1986–, Inst of Practitioners in Advtg 1981–93, Advtg Assoc 1989–93; vice chm Berkeley Square Ball Charitable Trust 1986–90; organist and choir master All Saints Church London 1976–; FCIM, FIMgt, FIPA; *Recreations* church music, Worcester porcelain; *Clubs* Athenaeum, IOD; *Style*— Michael B Hockney, Esq

HODDER, Prof Ian Richard; s of Bramwell William (Dick) Hodder, and Noreen Victoria Hodder; *b* 23 Nov 1948; *Educ* Magdalen Coll Sch Oxford, Inst of Archaeology Univ of London (BA), Univ of Cambridge (PhD); *m* 1, (m dis), Françoise Hivernel; 2 s (Christophe b 1976, Gregoire b 1979); m 2, Christine Hastorf; 2 s (Kyle and Nicholas (twins) b 1991); *Career* lectr Dept of Archaeology Univ of Leeds 1974–77; Univ of Cambridge: asst lectr Dept of Archaeology 1977–81, lectr Dept of Archaeology 1981–90, reader in prehistory 1990–96, prof of archaeology 1996–; fell Darwin Coll Cambridge 1990–; adjunct asst prof of anthropology State Univ of NY USA 1984–89, adjunct prof and visiting prof Dept of Anthropology Univ of Minnesota USA 1986–; visiting prof: Van Giffen Inst for Pre- and Proto-history Amsterdam 1980, Univ of Paris I Sorbonne 1985; fell Center for Advanced Study in the Behavioural Scis Stanford Calif USA 1987; dir gen Cambridge Archaeological Unit 1990–; memb Ed Bd: New Directions in Archaeology 1978–89, Anthropology Today, Archeologia e Calcolatori, Cambridge Archaeological Jl, Jl of European Archaeology; memb Advsy Bd: Rural History: Economy, Society, Culture, Jl of Material Culture; Gordon Childe prize Inst of Archaeology; memb Founding Ctee Euro Assoc of Archaeologists 1991–95; memb Prehistoric Soc, Associate Inst of Field Archaeologists (memb Cncl 1986–89); FRAI (memb Cncl 1985–88), FSA, FBA 1996; *Publications* authored volumes: Spatial analysis in archaeology (with C Orton, 1976), Symbols in action. Ethnoarchaeological studies of material culture (1982), The Present Past. An Introduction to anthropology for archaeologists (1982), Reading the Past. Current approaches to interpretation in archaeology (1986, revised edn, 1991), The domestication of Europe: structure and contingency in Neolithic societies (1990), Theory and practice in archaeology (1992), The archaeological process (1997); edited volumes incl: The Archaeology of contextual meanings (1987), Archaeology as long term history (1987), The meanings of things: material culture and symbolic expression (1989), Archaeological Theory in Europe. The last three decades (1991), Interpreting Archaeology (with M Shanks, 1994), Archaeology in Theory. A Reader (with R Preucel, 1996); also author of numerous articles and reviews in learned jls; *Recreations* playing piano and violin, sports especially tennis and golf; *Style*— Prof Ian Hodder, FBA, FSA; ✉ University of Cambridge, Department of Archaeology, Downing Street, Cambridge CB2 3DZ (☎ 01223 333520, fax 01223 333503, e-mail IH13@cus.cam.ac.uk)

HODDER-WILLIAMS, Mark; s of Paul Hodder-Williams, OBE, TD, of Somerset, and Felicity Blagden (d 1986); *b* 24 March 1939; *Educ* Rugby, Univ of Oxford (MA); *m* 1961, Janette Elspeth, da of Harry Archibald Cochran, OBE (d 1980), of Kent; 3 s (Andrew b 1963, James b 1964, Peter b 1968), 1 da (Susanna b 1969); *Career* book publisher; formerly dir Hodder and Stoughton Holdings Ltd, md First Edition EDI Services Ltd; FRSA 1990; *Recreations* golf, skiing, gardening, music; *Clubs* Vincent's (Oxford), Wildernesse (Sevenoaks); *Style*— Mark Hodder-Williams, Esq; ✉ 38 Greenhill Rd, Otford, Sevenoaks, Kent TN14 5RS

HODDINOTT, Prof Alun; CBE (1983); s of Thomas Ivor Hoddinott, MM (d 1974), and Gertrude Jones (d 1964); *b* 11 Aug 1929; *Educ* Gowenton GS, Univ Coll Cardiff (Glamorgan music scholar, BMus, DMus, Walford Davies prize, Arnold Bax medal); *m* (Beti) Rhiannon, da of Rev Llewellyn C Huws (d 1982); 1 s (Huw Ceri); *Career* lectr: Welsh Coll of Music and Drama 1951–59, Univ Coll Cardiff 1959–66; reader Univ of Wales 1966–67, prof and head Dept of Music Univ Coll Cardiff 1967–87 (now prof emeritus); fndr and artistic dir Cardiff Festival of Music 1967–90 (currently pres), fndr and chm Oriana Records 1983–91, govr St John's Coll Cardiff, patron Live Music Now; Hopkins medal St David's Soc of NY 1981; Hon DMus Univ of Sheffield 1993, hon memb Royal Acad of Music; fell: RNCM, UCW, Welsh Coll of Music and Drama; *Works* incl: String Trio (Cardiff) 1949, Concerto for Harp and Orchestra (Cheltenham Festival) 1957, concerto for piano, wind and percussion (London) 1960, Carol for SSA (Cardiff) 1961, Sinfonia for string orchestra (Bromsgrove Festival) 1964, Fioriture for orchestra (Aberdeen) 1968, Suite for orchestra (Southampton) 1970, The Sun The Great Luminary music for orchestra (Swansea Festival) 1970, Sonata for horn and piano (St Donats) 1971, The Silver Swimmer (Manchip White) for mixed voices and piano duet (Austin Texas) 1973, Sinfonia fidei for soprano, tenor, chorus and orchestra (Llandaff Festival)

1977, Scena for String Quartet (Portsmouth) 1979, Six Welsh Folk Songs (Cardiff Festival) 1982, Ingravescentum Aetatem (Manhattan Kansas) 1983, Piano Sonata No 7 (London) 1984, Passacaglia and Fugue (St Davids) 1985, Concerto for Clarinet and Orchestra (Manchester) 1987, Piano Sonata No 9 (Cheltenham Festival) 1989, Star Children for orchestra (London Proms) 1989, Noctis Equi for cello and orchestra (Rostropovitch London) 1989, Emynau Pantycelyn (Rhymni) 1990, Sonata for flute and piano (Harrogate Festival) 1991, Advent Carols (St John's Coll Cambridge) 1991, Sonata no 5 for violin and piano (NY) 1992, A May Song (Wales Garden Festival) 1992, Symphony for brass and percussion (Cardiff Festival) 1992, Chorales, Variants and Fanfares for organ and brass quintet (Swansea Festival) 1992, Gloria for chorus and organ (Tenby Festival) 1992, A Vision of Eternity symphony for soprano and orch (Gwyneth Jones) 1993, Three Motets for chorus and organ (Atlanta Georgia) 1993, Wind Quintet (Gower Festival) 1993, Piano Sonata II (Griccieth Festival) 1993, Piano Sonata 12 (London) 1994, Missa Sancti David (Fishguard Festival) 1994, Six Bagatelles for Quartet (Lower Machen Festival) 1994, Three Hymns for Mixed Chorus and Organ (N Wales Festival) 1994, Shakespeare Songs for Mixed Voices (Swansea Festival) 1994, Five Poems of G A Becquer for baritone and piano (Manchester) 1994, One Must Always Have Love songs for high voice and piano (Atlanta Georgia) 1994, Concerto for violin and orchestra (BBC) 1995, Concerto for trumpet and orchestra (Hallé) 1995, Sonata for Oboe and Harp (Cardiff) 1995, Magnificat and Nunc Dimittis (St David's Festival) 1996, String Quartet No 4 (Mach Ynlleth Festival) 1996, Piano Trio No 3 (Fishguard Festival) 1996; *Style*— Prof Alun Hoddinott, CBE

HODDINOTT, Rear Adm (Anthony) Paul; CB (1994), OBE (1979); s of Cdr Peter Frost Hoddinott, RN, of Southbourne-on-Sea, Bournemouth, Dorset, and Florence Marjorie, *née* Kent; *b* 28 Jan 1942; *Educ* St Michael's Sch Otford nr Sevenoaks Kent, Bloxham Sch nr Banbury Oxon, Brittania RNC Dartmouth; *m* 23 Oct 1965, Ellen Ruby (Rue), da of Henry Cassibilian Burton (d 1983), of Nambour, Queensland, Aust; 1 s (Charles Peter b 1968), 2 da (Kimberley Angela b 1970, Giselle Nicole b 1972); *Career* RN: cmd HMS Andrew 1973–75, Cdr 1976, cmd HMS Revenge 1976–79, Cdr Submarine Tactics and Weapons Gp 1979–81, Capt 1981, cmd HMS Glasgow S Atlantic 1981–83, Asst Dir of Naval Warfare MOD 1983–85, NATO Def Coll Rome 1985–86, Cdre 1986, Dep UK Mil Rep to NATO Brussels 1986–88, Chief of Staff (Submarines) 1988–90, Rear Adm 1990, Naval Attaché and Cdr Br Naval Staff Washington 1990–94; dir Warship Preservation Tst 1994–, exec dir Int Bar Assoc 1995–; *Recreations* theatre, swimming, travel, kitchen bridge; *Clubs* Naval; *Style*— Rear Adm Paul Hoddinott, CB, OBE; ✉ 45 Oaklands Road, Petersfield, Hampshire GU32 2EY (☎ 01730 300375, fax 01730 300372)

HODDLE, Glenn; s of Derek Hoddle, and Teressa, *née* Roberts; *b* 27 Oct 1957; *Educ* Burnt Mill Sch Harlow; *m* Christine Anne, da of Raymond Stirling; 2 da (Zoe Anne b 14 Jan 1983, Zara Marie b 28 Jan 1986), 1 s (Jamie Glenn b 6 Jan 1991); *Career* professional football manager (former player); debut Tottenham Hotspur (v Stoke City) 1976, transferred for £800,000 to AS Monaco France 1986, player/manager Swindon Town 1991–93 (promoted to FA Premier League 1993); player/manager Chelsea 1993–96; coach English National Team 1996–; England: 12 under 21 caps, 53 full caps 1980–88, 8 goals, played World Cup Spain 1982 and Mexico 1986; honours: FA Cup winners' medal (Tottenham Hotspur) 1981 and 1982, UEFA Cup winners' medal (Tottenham Hotspur) 1984, French Championship winners' medal (Monaco) 1988, play-off winners (Swindon) 1992–93, runners-up FA Cup (Chelsea) 1994; *Books* Spurred to Success (autobiography); *Recreations* tennis, golf, reading; *Style*— Glenn Hoddle, Esq; ✉ c/o The Football Association, 16 Lancaster Gate, London W2 3LW (☎ 0171 262 4542)

HODGART, Alan William; s of William George Hodgart, of Australia, and Hilda Murial Herschel, *née* Hester; *b* 19 July 1940; *Educ* Univ of Melbourne (MA), Univ of Cambridge; *Career* mgmnt conslt Cortis Powell Ltd (UK) 1967–76; Deloitte Haskins and Sells: md DHS Consultants Ltd 1976–83, dep managing ptnr Deloitte Haskins & Sells Australia 1983–84, dir int strategy NY 1984–88; md Spicers Consultants Group Ltd (UK) 1988–90, chm Hodgart Temporal & Co 1990–, chm Carey Howells, Jeans & Spiro Ltd 1993–; *Books* The Economics of European Imperialism (1978); *Recreations* literature, 19th century music, walking; *Clubs* Athenaeum, Princeton Univ; *Style*— Alan Hodgart, Esq; ✉ 29 Micklethwaite Road, London SW6 1QD (☎ 0171 385 4548, fax 0171 386 0081); Hodgart Temporal & Company, 30 St James's Street, London SW1A 1HB (☎ 0171 460 4160, fax 0171 460 4161)

HODGE, HE Sir James William; KCVO (1996), CMG (1996); s of William Hodge (d 1994), of Edinburgh, and Catherine, *née* Carden (d 1977); *b* 24 Dec 1943; *Educ* Holy Cross Acad Edinburgh, Univ of Edinburgh (MA); *m* 20 June 1970, Frances Margaret, da of Michael Coyne (d 1995), of Liverpool; 3 da (Catherine b 1973, Fiona b 1975, Claire b 1979); *Career* Cwlth Office 1966, second sec Br Embassy Tokyo 1970–72 (third sec 1967–69), FCO 1972–75, first sec High Cmmn Lagos 1975–78, FCO 1978–81, cnsllr (commercial) Tokyo 1982–86 (first sec 1981–82), cnsllr and head of Chancery Br Embassy Copenhagen 1986–90, cnsllr FCO 1990–93, RCDS 1994, min Peking 1995–96, HM ambass Thailand 1996– (concurrently non-resident ambass to Laos); MIL 1990; *Recreations* books, music; *Clubs* MCC; *Style*— HE Sir James Hodge, KCVO, CMG; ✉ c/o Foreign & Commonwealth Office (Bangkok), King Charles Street, London SW1A 2AH

HODGE, Jane Aiken; da of Conrad Potter Aiken, and Jessie McDonald; *b* 4 Dec 1917; *Educ* Hayes Court Hayes Kent, Somerville Coll Oxford (BA), Radcliffe Coll Cambridge Mass (AM); *m* 3 Jan 1948, Alan Hodge; 2 da; *Career* author; asst: Br Bd of Trade Washington DC 1942–44, Br Supply Cncl 1944–45; res: Time Inc NY 1945–47, Life Magazine London 1947–48; memb: Soc of Authors, Authors' Lending and Copyright Soc, Lewes Monday Literary Club; *Fiction* Maulever Hall, The Adventurers, Watch The Wall, My Darling, Here Comes a Candle, The Winding Stair, Marry in Haste, Greek Wedding, Savannah Purchase, Strangers in Company, Shadow of a Lady, One Way to Venice, Rebel Heiress, Runaway Bride, Judas Flowering, Red Sky at Night, Last Act, Wide is the Water, The Lost Garden, Secret Island, Polonaise, First Night, Leading Lady, Windover, Escapade and Whispering; *Non-Fiction* The Double Life of Jane Austen, The Private World of Georgette Heyer, Passion and Principle: The Loves and Lives of Regency Women; *Style*— Mrs Jane Hodge; ✉ 23 Eastport Lane, Lewes, East Sussex BN7 1TL; c/o David Higham, 5–8 Lower John St, Golden Square, London W1R 4HA

HODGE, Sir Julian Stephen Alfred; kt (1970); s of Alfred Hodge, and Jane, *née* Simcocks; *b* 15 Oct 1904; *Educ* Cardiff Tech Coll; *m* 31 Dec 1951, Moira, da of John Oswald Thomas (d 1983); 2 s (Robert b 24 April 1955, Jonathan b 3 April 1958), 1 da (Jane b 2 June 1953); *Career* former chm: Julian S Hodge & Co Ltd, Gwent Enterprises Ltd, Hodge Fin Ltd, Hodge Life Assur Ltd, Carlyle Tst Ltd; fndr Hodge & Co Accountants 1941; dir: Channel Islands Conslts Ltd 1968–89, Standard Chartered Bank 1973–75, Bank of Wales (IOM) Ltd 1974–85; chm: Avana Group Ltd 1973–81, Bank of Wales (Jersey) Ltd 1974–87, Carlyle Trust (Jersey) Ltd 1977–, St Aubins Investment Co Ltd 1986–; fndr and chm Bank of Wales 1971–85, exec chm Hodge Group 1975–78 (chm and md 1963–75); fndr: Jane Hodge Fndn 1962, Sir Julian Hodge Charitable Tst 1964; UWIST: treas 1968–76, dep pres 1976–81, pres 1981–85, memb Cncl; treas Welsh Centre for Int Affrs 1973–84; memb: Industl Project Sub-Ctee Welsh Econ Cncl 1965–68, Welsh Cncl 1968–79, Duke of Edinburgh Conf 1974, Prince of Wales Ctee, Fndn Fund Ctee Univ of Surrey; former govr All Hallows (Cranmore Hall) Sch Tst Ltd, tstee Welsh Sports Tst, chm Aberfan Disaster Fund, pres S Glamorgan Dist St John Ambulance Bde; Hon LLD Univ of Wales 1971; FCCA 1930, FTII 1941, FRSA; KSG 1978, KStJ 1977 (CStJ 1972); *Books* Paradox of Financial Preservation (1959); *Recreations* golf, gardening, reading, walking; *Clubs* Victoria (St Helier), La Moye Golf (Jersey); *Style*— Sir Julian Hodge; ✉ Clos Des Suex, Mont du Coin, St Aubin, St Brelade, Jersey, Channel Islands

HODGE, Margaret Eve; MBE (1978), MP (Lab) Barking (majority 11,414); da of Hans and Lisbeth Oppenheimer; *b* 8 Sept 1944; *Educ* Bromley HS, Oxford HS, LSE (BSc(Econ)); *m* 1, 1968 (m dis 1978), Andrew Watson; 1 s (Nick), 1 da (Lizzi); m 2, 1978, Henry Hodge; 2 da (Anna and Amy); *Career* teacher and int market research 1966–73; London Borough of Islington: cncllr 1973–94, chm Housing Ctee 1975–79, dep ldr 1981, ldr 1982–92; sr conslt Price Waterhouse 1992–94, MP (Lab) Barking 1994–; chm: Lab Pty's inquiry team on early years educn 1994–, London Gp of Lab MPs; memb Educn & Employment Select Ctee; fndr and chm Assoc of London Authys 1984–92, vice-chm AMA 1991–92, chm Circle 33 Housing Assoc 1993–96; dir CILNTEC 1990–92, non-exec dir London First 1992–, memb Cncl Univ of London 1993–; govr LSE 1990–; memb Exec Ctee Fabian Soc 1990–; visiting fell Inst of Public Policy Research 1992–, hon fell Univ of North London, Hon DCL City Univ; *Publications* Quality, Equality and Democracy: Improving Public Services (1991), Beyond the Town Hall - Reinventing Local Democracy (1994); contrib chapters to: Reinventing the Left (ed David Miliband), Making Gender Work (ed Jenny Shaw); *Recreations* family, cooking, cycling, theatre and opera; *Style*— Mrs Margaret Hodge, MBE, MP; ✉ House of Commons, London SW1A 0AA (☎ 0171 219 6666, fax 0171 219 3640)

HODGE, Patricia Ann; da of Eric Hodge (d 1988), and Marion, *née* Phillips; *b* 29 Sept 1946; *Educ* Grimsby Wintringham Girls' GS Lincs, St Helen's Sch for Girls Northwood Middx, Maria Grey Teachers' Training Coll Isleworth Middx, LAMDA (Eveline Evans Award for Best Actress on graduating); *m* 31 July 1976, Peter Douglas Owen; 2 s (Alexander Richard Charles b 18 Feb 1989, Edward Frederick James b 27 Dec 1991); *Career* actress; *Theatre* incl: All My Sons, Say Who You Are, The Birthday Party, The Anniversary (dir Peter Farago, Gateway Theatre Chester) 1971, Two Gentlemen of Verona (Musical, dir Mel Shapiro, Phoenix) 1993, Hair (dir Rufus Collins, Queen's) 1974, The Beggar's Opera (dir Max Stafford-Clarke, Nottingham Playhouse) 1975, Pal Joey, Look Back In Anger (dir Phillip Hedley, Oxford Playhouse) 1976, Then and Now (Hampstead) 1979, The Mitford Girls (Chichester Festival Theatre) 1981, Noel and Gertie (Comedy Theatre) 1989/90, Seperate Tables 1993, A Talent to Amuse 1993, The Prime of Miss Jean Brodie (Strand) 1994, A Little Night Music (RNT) 1995; *Television* for BBC incl: Valentine (series) 1973, The Girls of Slender of Means 1975, Jackanory Playhouse 1977, Act of Rape 1977, Crimewriters 1978, Hotel du Lac 1985, The Life and Loves of a She Devil 1986, The Legacy of Reginald Perrin 1996, The Moonstone 1996; for Thames incl: The Naked Civil Servant 1975, Rumpole of the Bailey 1978/79/86/88/90, Edward and Mrs Simpson 1978, Rumpole's Return 1980, Jemima Shore Investigates 1982, Rumpole and the Female Species 1983; other credits incl: The Professionals (Mark 1 Productions) 1979, Holding the Fort (LWT, 3 series) 1979/81/82, Robin of Sherwood (HTV) 1985, Time for Murder (Granada) 1985, Inspector Morse (Central) 1988, The Shell Seekers (ABC/Central) 1989, The Secret Life of Ian Fleming (Turner Entertainment) 1989, Rich Tea and Sympathy (Yorkshire) 1991, The Cloning of Joanna May (Granada) 1991; *Films incl* The Disappearance (dir Stuart Cooper) 1977, The Elephant Man 1979, Betrayal (dir Sam Spiegel) 1982, Sunset (dir Blake Edwards) 1987, Just Ask for Diamond (dir Stephen Bayly) 1988, The Leading Man 1996; *Awards* nominations for: 2 Olivier Awards, 1 Br Acad Award, 1 Ace Award (USA); *Style*— Miss Patricia Hodge; ✉ c/o ICM Ltd, Oxford House, 76 Oxford Street, London W1N 0AX (☎ 0171 636 6565, fax 0171 323 0101)

HODGE, Ralph Noel; s of Ralph Hodge, of Ardbrecknish, Argyll, and Helena Florence, *née* Mason; *b* 1 Nov 1934; *Educ* Culford Sch, Univ of Liverpool (BEng); *m* 11 Sept 1954, Jean Margaret, *née* Rowlands; 2 s (David Ralph b 13 July 1956, Ian William b 5 May 1962), 2 da (Jackie Ann b 28 April 1959, Andrea Jane b 29 June 1966); *Career* cadet pilot RAFVR; ICI 1956–92: joined as graduate trainee 1956, division dir 1976, division dep chm 1978, gen mangr personnel 1981, chm Petrochemicals and Plastics Div 1985, chm ICI Chemicals and Polymers 1990–92 (dep chm 1987–90); dir: Halifax Building Society 1992–, Coal Investments plc 1993–96, BTP plc 1995–; chm: Enron Europe Ltd 1992–, Tech Board Ltd 1993–, WRC plc 1994–; Melchett Medal for services to UK energy industries 1991; memb British Standards Bd 1992; FIPM; *Recreations* farming; *Style*— Ralph Hodge, Esq; ✉ Enron Europe Ltd, 4 Millbank, London SW1P 3ET (☎ 0171 316 5300, fax 0171 316 5322); Halifax Building Society, Trinity Road, Halifax, W Yorks HX1 2RG

HODGES, Anthony; s of John Humphrey Hodges (d 1950), and Emma, *née* Fadil (d 1984); *b* 3 Oct 1947; *Educ* Harrow, Oriel Coll Oxford; *m* 4 Oct 1975, Deborah June, da of Maj Arthur Wright, REME, of Cheam, Surrey; *Career* dir Benton & Bowles Advertising Agency 1978–83 (joined 1970), fndr The Hodges Consultancy (formerly Tony Hodges & Ptnrs) 1983; MIPA; *Recreations* tennis, fly-fishing, wine collecting; *Style*— Anthony Hodges, Esq; ✉ The Hodges Consultancy, 77a Walton Street, London SW3 2HT (☎ 0171 351 4477, fax 0171 351 2231)

HODGES, David Reginald Eyles; s of Edward Reginald George Hodges, of Dolphin Square, London, and Irene Muriel, *née* Turner; *b* 26 Aug 1942; *Educ* Mickleburgh; *m* 1, 19 Dec 1969, Yolande Wadih (d 1988), da of Joseph Yuja (d 1975), of San Pedro Sula, Honduras; 1 s (Crispin James David b 1973), 1 da (Patricia Marie b 1964); m 2, 22 July 1989, Patricia Emma, da of Cesar Augusto Pancorvo Noriega Del Valle (d 1983), of Lima, Peru; *Career* dir Cayzer Steel Bowater International Ltd 1975–86, dir and chm Ridgelawn Associates Ltd 1986–; *Recreations* sailing, travel; *Clubs* Turf; *Style*— David Hodges, Esq; ✉ c/o Messrs C Hoare and Co, 37 Fleet St, London EC4 (☎ 0171 821 0179 or 01227 721224)

HODGES, Air Chief Marshal Sir Lewis MacDonald; KCB (1968, CB 1963), CBE (1958), DSO (1944 and Bar 1945), DFC (1942 and Bar 1943), DL (Kent, 1991); s of Arthur MacDonald Hodges (d 1940); *b* 1 March 1918; *Educ* St Paul's, RAF Coll Cranwell; *m* 1950, Elisabeth Mary, da of Geoffrey Blackett, MC (d 1977); 2 s; *Career* joined RAF 1937, served WWII Bomber Cmd, SE Asia, Gp Capt 1957, Air Cdre 1961, Air Vice-Marshal 1963, ACAS (Ops) MOD 1965–68, AOC-in-C Air Support Cmd 1968–70, air memb Personnel Air Force Bd 1970–73, Air Chief Marshal 1971, dep C-in-C AFCENT 1973–76, Air ADC to HM The Queen 1973–76, ret; dir Pilkington Bros plc (Optical Div) 1979–83; govr British United Provident Assoc 1973–85, chm Govrs Duke of Kent Sch 1979–86, chm RAF Benevolent Fund Educn Ctee 1979–86; govr BUPA Med Foundation Ltd 1987–95; pres: RAF Escaping Soc 1979–, RAF Assoc 1981–84, Special Forces Club 1982–86, Old Pauline Club 1985–87, RAF Club 1985–93; Liveryman: Worshipful Co of Fruiterers, Guild of Air Pilots and Air Navigators; Croix de Guerre France 1944, Cdr Légion d'Honneur France 1948 (Grand Offr 1988); *Clubs* RAF, Special Forces; *Style*— Air Chief Marshal Sir Lewis Hodges, KCB, CBE, DSO, DFC, DL; ✉ c/o Lloyds Bank, 121 High Street, Tonbridge, Kent

HODGES, Mark Willie; s of William Henry Hodges (d 1924), of Newport, Monmouthshire, and Eva, *née* Smith (d 1964); *b* 20 Oct 1923; *Educ* Cowbridge GS, Jesus Coll Oxford (MA); *m* 11 May 1948, Glenna Marion, da of Alfred Leopold Peacock (d 1979), of Oxford; 1 s (Timothy b 1965), 1 da (Tessa b 1957); *Career* WWII Sub Lt RNVR 1942–45; lectr Univ of Sheffield 1950–54, Dept of Scientific and Industl Res 1954–56, asst scientific attaché Br Embassy Washington 1956–61, Office of the Min for Sci 1961–64, sec Royal Cmmn on Med Educn 1965–68; asst sec Dept of Educn and Sci 1968–79 (Arts and Libraries branch 1977–79), head Office of Arts and Libraries 1982–84 (joined 1979, under sec 1982, dep sec 1983); chm South Bank Theatre Bd 1984–93 (memb 1982–93), memb: Cncl Royal Albert Hall 1983–93, Cncl and Mgmnt Ctee Eastern Arts Assoc 1986–89; *Recreations* woodwork, computer programming, listening to music; *Style—* Mark Hodges, Esq; ✉ The Corner Cottage, Church Way, Little Stukeley, Cambs PE17 5BQ (☎ 01480 459266)

HODGES, Mike; s of Graham Hodges (d 1987), and Norah, *née* Cotterel (d 1994); *b* 29 July 1932; *Educ* Prior Park Coll Bath, ACA; *m* 1964 (m dis 1982), Jean Alexandrov (d 1990); 2 s (Ben b 22 Dec 1964, Jake b 23 July 1966); *Career* writer, film producer and director; memb: Amnesty, Charter 88, Intermediate Technology, VES; *Television* World in Action (prodr/dir) 1963–65, Tempo (exec prodr/dir, ABC arts programme) 1965–68; *Theatre* Soft Shoe Shuffle (writer, Hammersmith Lyric) 1985; *Films* as writer/dir incl: Get Carter 1970, Pulp 1972, Missing Pieces 1982, Black Rainbow 1991; as writer/dir/prodr incl: Suspect 1968, Rumour 1969, The Terminal Man 1974; as dir incl: Flash Gordon 1979, Squaring the Circle 1984, Morons from Outer Space 1986, Florida Straits 1987, A Prayer for the Dying 1988, Dandelion Dead 1993, The Healer 1994, Croupier 1996; *Recreations* drawing, painting, playing clarinet, walking, gardening; *Style—* Mike Hodges, Esq; ✉ c/o Stephen Durbridge, The Agency, 24 Pottery Lane, London W11 4LZ (☎ 0171 727 1346, fax 0171 727 9037)

HODGES, Peter Lewis (Lew); *b* 29 Feb 1956; *Educ* Peter Symmonds GS Winchester, UCL (BA), London Business Sch (MBA); *Career* asst fin dir Arts Council 1985–87, head of fin and personnel CNAA 1987–89, dir of fin and resources Arts Council 1989–96, fin dir Sports Council 1996–; FCA; *Style—* Lew Hodges, Esq; ✉ Sports Council, 16 Upper Woburn Place, London WC1H 0QP

HODGES, Prof Richard Andrew; OBE (1995); s of Roy Clarence Hodges, of Box, Wiltshire, and Joan Mary, *née* Hartnell; *b* 29 Sept 1952; *Educ* City of Bath Boys' Sch, Univ of Southampton (BA, PhD); *m* Deborah, da of F C P Peters; 1 s (William b 15 March 1984), 1 da (Charlotte b 25 Oct 1986); *Career* archaeologist; Univ of Sheffield: lectr 1976–86, sr lectr 1986–88, prof 1993–95; prof Univ of E Anglia 1995–; visiting prof: Suny-Binghamton 1983, Univ of Siena 1984–87, Univ of Copenhagen 1987–88; dir Br Sch at Rome 1988–95, dir Prince of Wales' Inst of Architecture; maj archaeological excavations: Roystone Grange Derbyshire 1978–88, San Vincenzo al Volturno 1980–, Montarrenti Siena 1982–87, Butrint Albania 1994–; FSA 1984; *Books* The Hamwih Pottery (1981), Dark Age Economics (1982), Mohammed, Charlemagne and Origins of Europe (1983), Primitive and Peasant Markets (1988), The Anglo-Saxon Achievement (1989), Wall-to-Wall History (1991), San Vincenzo al Volturno I (1993), San Vincenzo al Volturno 2 (1995); *Recreations* hill walking, listening to classical music, tennis; *Style—* Prof Richard Hodges, OBE, FSA; ✉ University of East Anglia, Norwich, Norfolk NR4 7TJ (☎ 01603 456161)

HODGKIN, Sir Alan Lloyd; OM (1973), KBE (1972); s of George Lloyd Hodgkin (d 1918); *b* 5 Feb 1914; *Educ* Gresham's Sch Holt, Trinity Coll Cambridge (MA, ScD); *m* 1944, Marion de Kay, da of Francis Peyton Rous (d 1970); 1 s, 3 da; *Career* scientific offr working on radar for Air Miny and Miny of Aircraft Prodn 1939–45, lectr then asst dir of res Cambridge Univ 1945–52, Foulerton res prof Royal Soc 1952–69, J F Plummer prof of biophysics Cambridge Univ 1970–81, pres Royal Soc 1970–75, chllr Leicester Univ 1971–85, master Trinity Coll Cambridge 1978–84 (fell 1936–78 and 1984–); jt winner Nobel Prize for Medicine or Physiology 1963; FRS; *Recreations* travel, ornithology, fishing; *Style—* Sir Alan Hodgkin, OM, KBE, FRS; ✉ 18 Panton St, Cambridge CB2 1HP (☎ 01223 352707); Physiological Laboratory, Cambridge (☎ 01223 64131)

HODGKIN, Sir (Gordon) Howard Eliot; kt (1992), CBE (1977); s of Eliot Hodgkin, and the Hon Katherine Mary Hodgkin, *née* Hewart; *b* 6 Aug 1932, London; *Educ* Camberwell Sch of Art London, Bath Acad of Art Corsham; *m* 16 April 1955, Julia Hazel Ann, da of Albert Ernest Lane; 2 s (Louis b 23 Oct 1957, Sam b 20 Feb 1960); *Career* artist (represented by Anthony d'Offay Gallery London, Gagosian Gallery NY and Galerie Lawrence Rubin Zurich); teacher: Charterhouse 1954–56, Bath Acad of Art Corsham 1956–66, Chelsea Sch of Art 1966–72; visiting lectr Slade and Chelsea Schs of Art London 1976–77, artist in residence Brasenose Coll Oxford 1976–77; tstee: Tate Gallery London 1970–76, Nat Gallery London 1978–85; memb Exec Ctee Nat Art Collections Fund 1988–; recipient: second prize John Moore's Liverpool Exhibition 1976 and 1980, Turner Prize Tate Gallery London 1985, Shakespeare Prize 1997; Hon DLitt Univ of London 1985; hon fell Brasenose Coll Oxford 1988; *Collections* incl: Arts Cncl of GB, Br Cncl London, Govt Picture Collection London, Contemporary Art Soc London, Tate Gallery London, V&A London, The Br Museum London, Saatchi Collection London, Museum of Modern Art Edinburgh, Museum of Modern Art NY, Met Museum of Art NY, Museum of Art Carnegie Inst, Nat Gallery of Washington, Fogg Art Museum Cambridge Mass, Louisiana Museum Denmark, Oldham Art Gallery, Sao Paulo Museum Brazil, Walker Art Center Minneapolis, Nat Museum of S Aust Adelaide; *One Man Exhibitions* incl: Arthur Tooth and Sons London 1962, 1964 and 1967, Kasmin Gallery London 1969 and 1971, Arnolfini Gallery Bristol 1970, Galerie Muller Cologne 1971, Kornblee Gallery New York 1973, Museum of Modern Art Oxford 1976 and 1977, Serpentine Gallery London 1976, Waddington/Kasmin Galleries London 1976, Andre Emmerich New York and Zurich 1977, Br Cncl exhbn touring India 1978 (graphics), Waddington Galleries London 1980, 1988 and 1991 (graphics), M Knoedler & Co New York 1981, 1982, 1984, 1986, 1988, 1990 and Dec 1993–Jan 1994, Bernard Jacobson NY 1980 and 1981, Los Angeles 1981 and London 1982 (graphics), Macquarie Galleries Sydney 1981, Tate Gallery London 1982, Br Pavilion Venice Biennale 1984, Phillips Collection Washington DC 1984, Yale Center for Br Art Connecticut 1985, Kestner-Gesellschaft Hanover 1985, Whitechapel Art Gallery London 1985, Tate Gallery London 1985 (graphics), Michael Werner Gallery Cologne 1990, Anthony d'Offay Gallery London 1993, retrospective exhbn Metropolitan Museum of Art NY to Modern Art Museum Fort Worth then Der Kunstverein Dusseldorf and Hayward Gallery 1995–96; *Style—* Sir Howard Hodgkin, CBE; ✉ c/o Anthony d'Offay Gallery, 9, 21, 23 and 24 Dering Street, London W1R 9AA (☎ 0171 499 4100, fax 0171 493 4443)

HODGKINS, David John; CB (1993); s of late Rev Harold Hodgkins, and Elsie Hodgkins, of Rhos-on-Sea, Clwyd; *b* 13 March 1934; *Educ* Buxton Coll, Peterhouse Cambridge (MA); *m* 6 July 1963, Sheila; 2 s (James b 1964, Andrew b 1967); *Career* Miny of Labour: asst princ 1956, princ 1956–65; Treasy 1965–68, Dept of Employment 1969–84 (under sec 1976), Health & Safety Exec 1984 (memb Exec 1988–92), dir Resources and Planning 1992–94; memb Employment Appeal Tbnl 1996–; *Clubs* Royal Cwlth Soc; *Style—* David Hodgkins, Esq, CB; ✉ Four Winds, Batchelors Way, Amersham, Bucks HP7 9AJ (☎ 01494 725207)

HODGKINSON, (James) Andrew; s of Peter George Hodgkinson (d 1986), of Lincoln, and Gwyneth Anne, *née* Evans (d 1984); *b* 22 Jan 1952; *Educ* City Sch Lincoln, Brighton Poly (BA); *m* 6 Sept 1996, Mariann Halkjaer; *Career* dir John Michael Design Consultants 1975–80, fndr and md Simons Design 1980–94, Main Bd dir and shareholder of The Simons Gp, fndr and md Hodgkinson & Co 1994; MInstD, MCSD 1989; *Recreations* design, art, polo and numerous sports, ethnography, natural history; *Clubs* Guards' Polo; *Style—* Andrew Hodgkinson, Esq; ✉ Hodgkinson & Co, 29 Alexander Street, London W2 5NU (☎ 0171 221 7557, fax 0171 221 6336)

HODGKINSON, (Anne) Catherine; da of Richard Hodgkinson, of Ledbury, Herefordshire, and (Joyce) Marten, *née* Green (d 1990); *b* 19 Dec 1946; *Educ* New Hall Chelmsford Essex, Institut D'Art et D'Archeologie Paris (LèsL); *m* 19 Dec 1975 (m dis 1985), John Louis Rishad Zinkin, s of Maurice Zinkin, OBE, of Kensington, London; 1 da (Kate b 1977); *Career* art dealer; md Lumley Cazalet Ltd 1973–; *Recreations* theatre, art, travel; *Clubs* The Arts; *Style—* Miss Catherine Hodgkinson; ✉ Lumley Cazalet Ltd, 4 New Burlington Street, London W1X 1FE (☎ 0171 491 4767, fax 0171 493 8644)

HODGKINSON, Air Chief Marshal Sir (William) Derek; KCB (1971, CB 1969), CBE (1960), DFC (1941), AFC (1942); s of late Ernest Nicholls Hodgkinson; *b* 27 Dec 1917; *Educ* Repton; *m* 1939, Nancy Heather Goodwin; 1 s, 1 da; *Career* joined RAF 1936, serv WWII (POW 1942–45), OC 210 and 240 (GR) Sqdns, DS Aust Jt Anti Sub Sch and Jt Serv Staff Coll 1946–58, Gp Capt 1958, OC RAF St Mawgan 1958–61, on Staff of CDS and ADC to HM The Queen 1959–63, Air Cdre 1963, IDC 1964, cmdt RAF Staff Coll Andover 1965, Air Vice-Marshal 1966, Asst Chief of Air Staff (Ops Req) 1966–69, report on RAF Offr Career Structure 1969, SASO RAF Trg Cmd 1969, Air Marshal 1970, C-in-C NEAF, Cdr Br Force NE and Admin Sovereign Base Areas Cyprus 1970–73, Air Sec 1973–76, Air Chief Marshal 1974, ret 1976; pres Regular Forces Employment Assoc 1982–86 (vice chm 1977–80, chm 1980–82); *Recreations* fishing, cricket; *Clubs* RAF, MCC; *Style—* Air Chief Marshal Sir Derek Hodgkinson, KCB, CBE, DFC, AFC

HODGKINSON, George Howard; s of Frank Howard Hodgkinson (d 1975), of Boxford, Colchester, Essex, and Dorothy Georgina, *née* Levis (d 1983); *b* 4 March 1945; *Educ* Rugby, St John's Coll Oxford (MA); *m* 12 July 1975, Sarah, da of Maj John Bruce Robertson, OBE (d 1973), of Fernden Hill, Haslemere; 2 s (Mark b 1980, Robert b 1984), 1 da (Katie b 1977); *Career* admitted slr 1970; asst slr: Coward Chance 1970–71 (articled clerk 1967), Legal and Claims Div B P Tanker Co Ltd 1971–73; ptnr: Sinclair Roche & Temperley 1975– (asst slr 1973), Sinclair Roche Hong Kong 1978–; taught English Simla Hills India with VSO 1962; Freeman: Worshipful Co of Slrs, Worshipful Co of Shipwrights; memb: Law Soc, Baltic Exchange 1988 (currently non-trading memb); *Recreations* dinghy racing (Wayfarers), tennis, golf; *Clubs* Aldeburgh Yacht; *Style—* George Hodgkinson, Esq; ✉ Sinclair Roche & Temperley, Royex House, Aldermanbury Square, London EC2V 7LE

HODGKINSON, Michael S (Mike); *Career* gp airports dir BAA plc; non-exec dir Molins plc, dir W London Trg and Enterprise Cncl; *Style—* Mike Hodgkinson, Esq; ✉ BAA plc, 130 Wilton Road, London SW1V 1LQ (☎ 0171 834 9449)

HODGKINSON, Neville John; s of John Robert Hodgkinson, of Minehead, Somerset, and Joan Evelyn, *née* Tye; *b* 3 Feb 1944; *Educ* Whitgift Sch S Croydon, Univ of Durham; *m* 1965 (m dis 1990), Liz, *née* Garrett; 2 s (Tom b 10 April 1968, Will b 9 Dec 1969); *Career* journalist; Chronicle & Journal Newcastle upon Tyne (reporter, sub ed, leader writer) 1965–70, sub ed Daily Telegraph 1970–72, The Times (sub ed, reporter, social policy corr) 1972–77, medical corr Daily Mail 1977–80, freelance writer 1981–85, ed Best of Health Magazine 1985–86, medical corr Sunday Times 1986–89, medical ed Sunday Express 1989–91, science corr Sunday Times 1991–94, freelance science writer 1994–; runner up Reporter of the Year IPC Press Awards 1976; memb Guild of Health Writers; student and lectr in meditation Brahma Kumaris World Spiritual Univ 1981–; *Books* Will to be Well, The Real Alternative Medicine (1984, Spectator Book of the Year), AIDS: The Failure of Contemporary Science (1996); *Recreations* spiritual study, walking; *Style—* Neville Hodgkinson, Esq; ✉ Global Retreat Centre, Nuneham Park, Nuneham Courtenay, Oxford OX44 9PG (☎ 01865 340650, fax 01865 343576)

HODGKINSON, Paul Richard; s of Peter George Hodgkinson, DL (d 1986), of St Georges House, Lincoln, and Gwyneth Anne, *née* Evans (d 1984); *b* 9 March 1956; *Educ* Lincoln GS, Oxford Poly (BA, DipArch); *m* 13 Oct 1984, Catherine Ann, da of George Giangrande, of New Vernon, New Jersey, USA; 2 s (Christopher Peter, Alexander George); *Career* Shepherd Ipstein & Hunter 1975–76, Capital and Counties plc 1979–81, Simons Design Consits 1981–86, chm and chief exec Simons Group Ltd 1986–; chm E Midlands Regional Ctee CBI 1997–, chm Lincolnshire Training and Enterprise Cncl 1989–94; RIBA 1980, ARCUK, MInstD, RSA 1986; *Recreations* squash, cricket, reading, golf, walking, food, opera, skiing; *Style—* Paul Hodgkinson, Esq; ✉ Simons Group Ltd, 401 Monks Road, Lincoln LN3 4NU (☎ 01522 510000)

HODGKINSON, (Claude) Peter; s of Claude Harold Hodgkinson, of Stoke-on-Trent, and Gweneth Mary, *née* Cupit; *b* 26 June 1943; *Educ* Ratcliffe Coll Leicester, Univ of Manchester (BA); *m* 27 Nov 1974, Julie Margaret Wesley Thompson, of Birmingham; 1 s (Oliver b 1976), 1 da (Sophie b 1982); *Career* dir: Hanley Economic Building Society 1972– (chm), A G (Plaster) Ltd 1978–, Reece plc 1983–; memb Br Pottery Mfrs Fedn; FCA 1968; *Recreations* golf; *Clubs* Trentham Golf; *Style—* Peter Hodgkinson, Esq; ✉ Holly Cottage, Maer, Newcastle, Staffs ST5 5EF (☎ 01782 680255); A G (Plaster) Ltd, Unit 19, Reddicap Trading Estate, Coleshill Rd, Sutton Coldfield, W Midlands B75 7BU (☎ 0121 329 2874, fax 0121 311 1883)

HODGKISS, Christopher Ian; s of William Morris Hodgkiss, of York, and Sylvia, *née* Dorn; *b* 18 Sept 1961; *Educ* King's Sch Pontefract, York Coll of Art and Design, Liverpool Poly (BA); *Career* advertising exec; art dir Cogent (Cogent Elliott Group) London 1984–91, principal accounts worked on incl: Cuprinol Ltd, Milton Keynes Development Corp, Thorntons plc, Vauxhall Motors (Network Q), ICI (Garden Div), Polycell, Pioneer Hi-Fi, Epson (UK) Ltd; art dir Hoare Wilkins 1991–94; principal clients incl: Royal London Insurance, British Aerospace, AXA Equity and Law, Direct Line, Kall Kwik, Nissan, Nivea, ICL; art dir TBWA 1994–; *Awards* Creative Circle Silver award 1986, D & AD commendation (for Cuprinol TV commercial) 1988, Silver award and commendation Campaign Poster awards (for Milton Keynes poster) 1990, various DIY awards (for Cuprinol), Silver Creative Circle Awards 1993, finalist Cannes Lion Awards (for Royal London TV commercial) 1993; *Recreations* films, books, theatre, collecting; *Style—* Christopher Hodgkiss, Esq; ✉ TBWA Ltd, 8 Crinan Street, London N1 9UF (☎ 0171 833 5544)

HODGSON, Allan Ferguson; s of Allan Ferguson Hodgson (d 1965), and Catherine, *née* Archibald; *b* 19 May 1945; *Educ* George Heriot's Sch, Univ of Edinburgh (MA); *m* 2 July 1969, Irene Devine Finlay, da of John Rennie, of Falkirk; 2 da (Sara Margaret b June 1972, Amanda Catherine (twin) b June 1972); *Career* economist: Edinburgh Investment Trust 1967–70, Ivory & Sime 1970–76; jt investmt sec Scottish Widows' Fund 1976–80, md Hodgson Martin Ltd 1980–; dir: Imperial College Residences plc, Balliol and Magdalen Cos; FRSA; *Recreations* golf, jogging, opera, travel, antiquarian books; *Style—* Allan Hodgson, Esq; ✉ Hodgson Martin Ltd, 36 George Street, Edinburgh EH2 2LE (☎ 0131 226 7644, fax 0131 226 7647)

HODGSON, (Arthur) Brian; CMG (1962); s of Maj Arthur Hammond Francis Hodgson (d 1952), and Annie Isabel Wallace, *née* Kidston (d 1973); *b* 24 Aug 1916; *Educ* Eton, Oriel Coll Oxford (MA), Trinity Coll Cambridge; *m* 6 May 1945, Anne Patricia Halse, da of Lt-Col Edward Marlborough Ley, DSO, KRRC (d 1948), and Marjorie, *née* Broadbridge (d 1954); 2 s (William Francis Halse b 1 Sept 1947, Paul Edward Brian (twin) b 1 Sept 1947), 2 da (Isabel Ann Ley b 1 March 1951, Odeyne Alison Patricia b 21 Jan 1958); *Career* HM Colonial Serv Tanganyika Territory: dist offr 1939, dist cmmr 1949, sr dist cmmr 1956, perm sec PM Office 1958–62, princ Dept of Tech Co-operation (now ODA) London 1963; Br Red Cross Soc: sec 1964, asst dir gen 1967, dir gen 1970–75, conslt 1976–81; conslt League of Red Cross Socs Geneva 1981–90; memb: Br Refugee Cncl 1967–81 (life memb 1982), Appeals Ctee IBA and BBC 1971–75, Cncl Impact Fndn 1986–; tstee Rebecca Hussey Tst 1985–; steward Henley Royal Regatta; Henry Dunant medal Int Red Cross 1993; FRGS; *Recreations* walking, gardening, boating; *Clubs* Leander, Naval; *Style—* Brian Hodgson, Esq, CMG; ✉ Chandlers, Furners Green, nr Uckfield, Sussex TN22 3RH (☎ 01825 790310)

HODGSON, Carole; *b* 1940, London; *Educ* Wimbledon Sch of Art, Slade Sch of Fine Art; *Career* artist; visiting prof of sculpture and painting Univ of Wisconsin USA 1968 and 1980; pt/t lectr: Univ of Reading 1964–71, Phillipa Fawcett Coll of Educn 1971–75; lectr in art Univ of London Inst of Educn 1975–79, visiting lectr Norwich Sch of Art 1979–87, visiting tutor RCA Painting Sch 1981–86; currently: sr lectr BA Hons Fine Art Kingston Univ, visiting lectr Christie's Educn; memb RBS 1994; *Solo Exhibitions* Angela Flowers Gallery London 1973, 1977, 1979, 1984, 1989, 1994 and Flowers East London 1992, UCW 1973, Royal Shakespeare Theatre Stratford 1975, Welsh Arts Cncl 1976, The Fine Arts Galleries Univ of Wisconsin USA 1980, The Wustum Museum Racine USA 1981, Lawrence Univ Appleton USA 1981, The Bedford Way Gallery Univ of London 1981, Llanelli Festival 1984, Christie's Fine Arts Courses London 1986, Whitefriars Museum Coventry 1991, New Ashgate Gallery Farnham 1991, Centro Cultural Recoleta Buenos Aires Argentina 1995, GEC Mgmnt Coll Rugby 1995, Sudbury bronzes in garden Gainsborough's house 1996; *Group Exhibitions* incl: Br Art Show (Arts Cncl of GB touring Sheffield, Newcastle and Bristol) 1979, Probity of Art (Welsh Arts Cncl touring Wales, Eng, Spain and Turkey) 1980–82, RCA Painting Staff Exhibition 1981, City Gallery Arts Tst Milton Keynes 1984, Int Contemporary Art Fair London 1986, The Artist Day Book (Smiths Gallery London) 1987, Chicago Art Fair Chicago USA 1989, Bath Contemporary Print Fair 1990, Royal Acad Summer Exhibition 1990, Print of the Month (Flowers East London) 1990, Royal Acad Print Fair 1991, Islington Business Centre Art Fair 1991, Chelsea Harbour Sculpture 1993, Downeen Decade (Angela Flowers Ireland) 1994, Instituto Chileno-Britancio de Cultura Santiago Chile 1995, Grafica International Museo de Arte Contemporaneo Santiago Chile 1995, The Gallery Garden Broughton Stockbridge 1996; *Commissions* incl: bronze sculpture for British Aerospace Kingston upon Thames 1986–87, medal for Br Medal Soc (commemorating' Bogman' exhibition Br Museum) 1987, bronze 'River Celebration' cmmnd by Royal Borough of Kingston upon Thames 1988–90, Still Life bronze cmmnd by Knee Surgery Unit Wellington Hosp 1996; *Work in Collections* Arts Cncl of GB, Dept of the Environment, Br Cncl, Contemporary Arts Soc, Univ of London, Unilever House, Welsh Contemporary Arts Soc, Pontevedra Museum Spain, Bello Piñeiro Museum Ferrol Spain, La Escuelo Nacional de Bellas Artes Buenos Aires Argentina, Universidad Catolica Santiago Chile, Manpower, private collections in Europe, USA, Mexico and Aust; *Awards* Univ of Reading res grant to travel Mexico 1968, Arts Cncl of GB Award 1973, Br Cncl Award 1978 and 1980, The Elephant Tst Award 1979 and 1986, Grocers' Co bursary Br Sch at Rome 1982, Univ of Kingston res grant to travel to China 1993 and to Chile and Argentina 1995, Humanity Medal (Honorarium Prize) RBS/Worshipful Co of Goldsmiths 1993, Purchase Prize X Premio de Grabado Maximo Ramos Ferrol Spain; *Publications* contrib TES: Women Artist (1978), Sculpture a Missing Dimension in School Art (1980); From the Sea to the Wall (Kingston Univ Press, 1995); *Style*— Ms Carole Hodgson; ✉ c/o Flowers East, 199–205 Richmond Rd, London E8 3NJ

HODGSON, Dr Courtney; s of Lt-Col Gordon Lothian Hodgson (d 1966), and Constance Emily, *née* Catcheside (d 1976); *b* 20 Jan 1929; *Educ* King Edward VI Sch Five Ways Birmingham, Univ of Birmingham (MB ChB, MD); *m* 21 Sept 1957, Thelma Royle, da of Dr John Newton Friend (d 1966); 1 s (Peter John Gordon b 3 May 1970), 1 da (Joy Margaret b 4 Nov 1967); *Career* Capt RAMC 1953–55, RMO 15/19 King's Royal Hussars 1954–55; res assoc Univ of Pennsylvania USA 1960–61, pt/t memb Med Res Unit for the Experimental Pathology of the Skin Birmingham 1966–76, conslt dermatologist Birmingham RHA 1966–; MRCS, LRCP 1951, MRCP 1959; memb: RSM 1960, Br Assoc of Dermatologists 1976, BMA; FRCP 1978; *Recreations* tennis, golf; *Clubs* Priory (Edgbaston); *Style*— Dr Courtney Hodgson; ✉ 134 Church Rd, Moseley, Birmingham B13 9AA (☎ 0121 449 1908); 6 Northumberland St, Alnmouth, Northumbria; Priory Hospital, Priory Rd, Edgbaston, Birmingham B5 7UG (☎ 0121 440 2323, fax 0121 440 0804, telex 267335 AMILDN 6)

HODGSON, Godfrey Michael Talbot; s of Arthur Benjamin Hodgson (d 1961), of Southampton, and Jessica, *née* Hill (d 1947); *Educ* Winchester (open scholar, Goddard Leaving Scholarship, first cricket XI), Magdalen Coll Oxford (demy open scholar, MA Modern History), Univ of Pennsylvania (MA); *m* 1, 1958 (m dis 1970), Alice Anne Simone, da of Jacques Vidal, Légion d'Honneur, MM; 2 s (Pierre Thomas Godfrey b 1959, Francis James Samuel b 1960); m 2, 1970, Hilary Mary, da of Brian F C Lamb; 2 da (Jessica b 1971, Laura b 1974); *Career* reporter TES 1956, reporter The Times 1958; The Observer: wrote Mammon column 1960, Washington corr 1962–65; reporter This Week (ITV) 1965, ed Insight Sunday Times 1968, foreign features ed 1971, freelance 1972–90, presenter The London Programme (LWT) 1976–81, presenter of progs incl The Great Depression (ITV) 1981 and Reagan on Reagan (Channel 4) 1988, foreign ed The Independent and The Independent on Sunday 1990–92, dir Reuter Fndn Prog Univ of Oxford 1992–; fell Green Coll Oxford; contrib articles and reviews to numerous pubns incl: Sunday Times, New Statesman, New York Times, Financial Times, Washington Post, The Independent; memb Soc of American Historians; *Books* incl: Carpetbaggers et Ku-Klux Klan (in French, 1965), An American Melodrama (with L Chester and B Page, 1969), Do You Sincerely Want to Be Rich? (with B Page and C Raw), In Our Time (1976), All Things to All Men (1980), Lloyd's of London (1986), The Colonel (1990), A New Grand Tour (1995), People's Century (1995), The World Turned Right Side Up (1996); *Recreations* travelling, walking, reading, listening to classical music, watching cricket; *Clubs* Beefsteak, Groucho; *Style*— Godfrey Hodgson, Esq; ✉ 41 Southmoor Road, Oxford OX2 6RF (☎ 01865 512542, fax 01865 513576)

HODGSON, Gordon Hewett; s of John Lawrence Hodgson (d 1936), and Alice Joan, *née* Wickham (d 1966); *b* 21 Jan 1929; *Educ* Oundle, UCL (LLB); *m* 1958, Pauline Audrey, da of William George Gray (d 1979), of Pinner; 2 s (John, William); *Career* Nat Serv RAEC 1947–49; called to the Bar Middle Temple 1953, in private practice SE circuit 1954–83, asst boundary cmmr 1976–83, asst recorder 1979–83; Master of the Supreme Court 1983–; jt ed Supreme Court Practice 1991, chm Ctee Bentham Club 1990–94 (memb Ctee 1987); *Recreations* sailing, enjoying Tuscany; *Clubs* East India, Royal Corinthian, Bar Yacht; *Style*— Gordon Hodgson, Esq; ✉ Royal Courts of Justice, Strand, London WC1A 2LL (☎ 0171 936 6031, fax 0171 936 7339)

HODGSON, Guy Richard; s of Derek Hodgson, of 8 Lansdowne House, Wilmslow Rd, Manchester, and Doreen, *née* Fish; *b* 15 Dec 1955; *Educ* William Hulme's GS Manchester; *m* 1, 1981 (m dis 1987), Patricia Anne, *née* Sumner; 1 da (Josie Amber b 31 March 1982); m 2, Jennifer Nan Louise, *née* Roberts; 2 da (Charlotte b 20 Jan 1989 d 1989, Alexandra Fleur b Jan 1992); *Career* sports reporter; Cadishead and Irlam Guardian 1974–76, Sale Guardian 1976–78, Birmingham Post 1978–80, BBC 1980–86, The Independent 1986–89, currently football writer The Independent on Sunday; *Recreations* reading, playing golf, football, badminton, music; *Clubs* MCC; *Style*— Guy Hodgson, Esq; ✉ The Independent on Sunday, 1 Canada Square, Canary Wharf, London EC14 5AP (☎ 0171 293 2000, fax 0171 293 2435)

HODGSON, Howard Osmond Paul; s of Osmond Paul Charles Hodgson (d 1985), and Sheila Mary, *née* Ward (now Mrs Baker); *b* 22 Feb 1950; *Educ* Aiglon Coll Villars Switzerland, MBIFD, DipEd, AFFIL, RSH; *m* 12 Aug 1972, Marianne Denise Yvonne, da of Samuel Kaitibien (d 1995), of Aix-en-Provence; 3 s (Howard James Paul b 20 Dec 1973, Charles Alexandre Howard b 11 Jan 1979 d 1982, Jamieson Charles Alexandre Howard b 30 May 1983), 1 da (Davinia Clementine Marianne b 27 June 1990); *Career* asst mangr Hodgson & Sons Ltd 1969–71, life assur exec 1971–75; acquired: Hodgson & Sons 1975 (floated USM 1986), Ingalls 1987 (from House of Fraser); launched Dignity in Destiny Ltd 1989; merger of Pompes Funèbres Générales of France, Kenyon Securities and Hodgson Holdings plc to form PFG Hodgson Kenyon International plc 1989; formed: Hodgson & Partners (with John Gunn and others) 1990, Hodgson Securities plc 1990; chief exec Hoskins Brewery plc 1993; launched: Bereavement Support Serv 1990, PHKI Nat Trg Sch 1990; co Halkin Holdings plc acquired Ronson plc and LGW plc 1994, acquired Home Shopping Marketing, DCK and Smiths Packaging 1995, changed name to Ronson plc 1995; Business Magazine top 40 under 40 1986, Sunday Times top dozen 1987, USM Entrepreneur of the Year 1987; presented How Euro Are You? (BBC TV series) 1990; hon vice pres Royal Soc of St George; *Books* How To Get Dead Rich (1992); *Recreations* cricket, yachting, skiing, riding, history; *Clubs* Carlton, RMYC; *Style*— Howard Hodgson, Esq; ✉ Ronson plc, 16 Grosvenor Place, London SW1X 7HH (☎ 0171 245 6009)

HODGSON, Prof Humphrey Julian Francis; s of Harold Robinson Hodgson (d 1985), and Celia Frances Hodgson; *b* 5 May 1945; *Educ* Westminster (Queen's scholar), ChCh Oxford (scholar, MA, BSc, Martin Wronker Prize), St Thomas' Hosp Med Sch London (BM BCh, DM, Charles Box Prize in Med); *m* Shirley Victoria, da of Prof Lionel Penrose; 1 s (Julian b 1973), 1 da (Anna b 1974); *Career* research fell Massachusetts Gen Hosp Boston 1976–77, conslt physician Hammersmith Hosp 1978–, jt med dir Hammersmith Hosps Tst 1994–; Royal Postgraduate Med Sch: vice dean 1989–, prof of gastroenterology 1990–95, prof of med 1995–; Radcliffe travelling fell UC Oxford 1976, Humphrey Davy Rolleston lectr RCP London 1991, Fitzgerald Peel lectr Scot Soc of Physicians 1993; academic registrar RCP London 1993–; author of books and original articles on gastrointestinal and liver disease; chm: Liver Group Charity 1993–, Scientific Co-ordinating Ctee Arthritis and Rheumatism Cncl 1996–; FRCP 1982 (MRCP 1972); *Recreations* walking, reading; *Style*— Prof Humphrey Hodgson; ✉ 40 Onslow Gardens, London N10 3JU (☎ 0181 883 8297); Royal Postgraduate Medical School, London W12 0HS (☎ 0181 383 3266, fax 0181 749 3436, e-mail hhodgson@rpms.ac.uk)

HODGSON, Jonathan James; s of John Hodgson, of Sutton Coldfield, and Barbara, *née* Middlemiss; *b* 6 May 1960; *Educ* Park Hall Comp, Solihull Coll of Technol, Liverpool Poly (BA), RCA (MA); *m* Sept 1990, Emma Mary, da of Brian Hubble; *Career* film and video director, musician and soundtrack composer; co fndr Unicorn Productions 1985, fndr Sherbet Films 1996; freelance dir: Barry Joll Associates 1985–88, Practical Pictures 1985–88, Felix Films 1988–90, Bermuda Shorts 1991–93, Mojo Working 1993–4, Speedy Films 1995; commercials, title sequences and pop videos for clients incl: UN, Brooke Bond, McVities, MTV, BBC, Channel 4, Lambie-Nairn, English-Markell-Pockett, Thames TV, SAAB USA, Prince Matchabelli, Initial TV; films credits incl: An Unseen Flight 1980, Dogs (first prize Stuttgart Trickfilmtage) 1981, Experiments In Movement and Line 1981, Night Club (6 int awards) 1983, Menagerie 1984, Train of Thought 1985, The Doomsday Clock (cmmnd by UN) 1987; art work published in European Illustration 1981–; *Recreations* digging; *Style*— Jonathan Hodgson, Esq; ✉ 4 Percy Place, Grosvenor, Bath BA1 6AR (☎ and fax 01225 315079)

HODGSON, Sir Maurice Arthur Eric; kt (1979); s of late Walter Hodgson, and Amy, *née* Walker; *b* 21 Oct 1919; *Educ* Bradford GS, Merton Coll Oxford (MA, BSc); *m* 20 March 1945, Norma, da of late Tom Fawcett; 1 s (Howard b 1953), 1 da (Vivien (Mrs Webster) b 1949); *Career* chm: ICI 1978–82 (joined 1942, dep chm 1972–78), BhS 1982–87; non-exec dir Storehouse plc 1985–89; nominated memb Cncl of Lloyd's 1987–94; chm: Civil Justice Review Advsy Ctee 1985–88, Dunlop Holdings plc 1984 (resigned 1984, non-exec dir 1982–83), Imperial Chemicals Insurance Ltd 1972–78; memb: Int Cncl Salk Inst 1978–, Cncl CBI 1978–82, Court Univ of Bradford 1979–94, Int Advsy Ctee Chase Manhattan Bank 1980–83, President's Ctee The Advertising Assoc 1978–90, Euro Advsy Cncl Air Products and Chemicals Inc 1982–84, Int Advsy Bd AMAX Inc 1982–85; govr London Graduate Sch of Business Studies 1978–87; visiting fell Sch of Business and Organisational Studies Univ of Lancaster 1970–; hon fell Merton Coll Oxford 1979, hon fell UMIST; pres Merton Soc 1986–89; Hon DTech Univ of Bradford, Hon DUniv Heriot-Watt, Hon DSc Loughborough Univ; Messel medal Soc of Chemical Indust 1980, George E Davis medal IChemE 1982; FEng 1979, FIChemE 1964, CChem 1978, FRSC 1978; *Recreations* racing, swimming; *Clubs* RAC; *Style*— Sir Maurice Hodgson; ✉ Suite 75/76, Kent House, 87 Regent Street, London W1R 7HF (☎ 0171 734 7777)

HODGSON, Patricia Anne; CBE (1995); da of Harold Hodgson, of Brentwood, Essex, and Lilian Mary, *née* Smith; *b* 19 Jan 1947; *Educ* Brentwood Co High, Newnham Coll Cambridge (MA); *m* 23 July 1979, George Edward Donaldson, s of Edward George Donaldson, of Donington-le-Heath, Leics; 1 s; *Career* Cons Res Dept 1968–70, prodr for BBC Open Univ (specialising in history and philosophy) 1970–82, freelance journalist and broadcaster in UK and USA; BBC: dep sec 1982–83, the sec 1985–87, head of Policy and Planning Unit 1987–, dir of policy and planning 1993–; TV series incl: English Urban History 1978, Conflict in Modern Europe 1980, Rome in the Age of Augustus 1981; chm Bow Group 1975–76, ed Crossbow 1976–80; assoc fell Newnham Coll Cambridge 1994; memb: Monopolies & Mergers Cmmn, London Arts Bd 1991–; dir BARB 1987–; FRSA; *Recreations* quietness; *Clubs* The Reform; *Style*— Miss Patricia Hodgson, CBE; ✉ BBC, Broadcasting House, Portland Place, London W1 (☎ 0171 765 4974, fax 0171 436 0393, telex 265 781)

HODGSON, Peter Barrie; s of Clive Ward (d 1980), and Gladys Stewart, *née* Ross (d 1983); *b* 12 March 1942; *Educ* Clayesmore Sch, St Peter's Coll Oxford (BA); *m* 10 Feb 1973, Audrone Ona, da of Jonas Grudzinskas (d 1992), formerly of Kretinga, Lithuania; 1 s (Lindsay Matthew Oliver b 3 Aug 1977); *Career* dir: Opinion Res Centre 1973–75, Professional Studies Ltd 1975–77; md: Professional Studies Ireland 1977, Action Research Ltd 1977–78; chm and md Travel and Tourism Research Ltd 1978–, dir City Research Associates Ltd 1981–89; chm Assoc of Br Market Res Cos 1987–89, chm Assoc of Euro Market Res Insts 1991–94; memb: Cncl Market Res Soc 1978–81, Tourism Soc 1981–84, Market Res Society, Euro Soc for Opinion & Marketing Res; fndr memb Social Res Assoc; fell: Tourism Soc 1980, Inst of Travel and Tourism 1989; *Publications* author of articles in: Espaces (Paris), Marketing, Jl of the Market Res Soc, Jl of the Professional Market Res Soc of Canada, Research Plus, Jl of Travel Research (US), Survey, Tourism Management; *Recreations* opera, wine, travel; *Style*— Peter Hodgson, Esq; ✉ Travel and Tourism Research Ltd, 4 Cochrane House, Admirals Way, London E14 9UD (☎ 0171 538 5300, fax 0171 538 3299)

HODGSON, Peter Gerald Pearson; s of Thomas William Hodgson, of Elloughton, N Humberside, and Edna, *née* Pearson; *b* 13 July 1934; *Educ* Reade Sch Yorks, Univ of Hull (BSc), Imperial Coll London (DIC); *m* 30 Sept 1956, Noreen, da of Albert James Warnes, of Byfleet, Surrey; 2 s (Michael Charles Peter b 1966, John Paul Richard b 1967); *Career* chm: Petrocon Group plc 1963–89 (chief exec 1963–88), Richards Group plc 1987–93, Loma Group plc 1990–95, HAT Property Services Ltd 1994–, Service Team Ltd 1995–; MIChemE 1965, FInstPet (1968); *Recreations* golf, horse racing (owner), watching cricket; *Clubs* MCC, RAC; *Style*— Peter Hodgson, Esq; ✉ Arlington, Ashtead Park, Ashtead, Surrey KT21 1EG (☎ 01372 277579, fax 01372 277509)

HODGSON, Peter John Dixon; CBE (1992, OBE 1979); s of John Dixon Hodgson, of Manaton, Launceston, Cornwall, and Dorothy Blanche, *née* Saunders (d 1991); *b* 21 March 1947; *Educ* Charterhouse; *m* 18 July 1970, Cecilia Anne, da of Brig Arnold de Lerisson Cazenove, CBE, DSO, MVO (d 1969); 2 s (James b 1973, Timothy b 1975), 1 da (Charlotte b 1977); *Career* CA; chm: Fin Ctee Red Cross Cornwall 1988–95, Western Area Nat Union of Cons and Unionist Assocs 1991–94; currently chm SRC Nat Union of Cons and Unionists Assocs; FCA 1970; *Recreations* gardening, fishing; *Style*— Peter

Hodgson, Esq, CBE; ✉ Manaton, Launceston, Cornwall PL15 9JE (☎ 01566 772880); John D Hodgson, 12 Southgate St, Launceston, Cornwall PL15 9DP (☎ 01566 772177)

HODGSON, (Adam) Robin; s of Thomas Edward Highton Hodgson, CB (d 1985), and Emily Catherine Hodgson; *b* 20 March 1937; *Educ* William Ellis Sch London, Worcester Coll Oxford (MA); *m* 14 April 1962, (Elizabeth Maureen) Linda, da of Vernon Gordon Fitzell Bovenizer, CMG, of Cambridge; 1 s (Harvey James b 1971), 2 da (Emily Kate b 1968, Amy Elizabeth b 1972); *Career* admitted slr 1964; asst slr: LCC and GLC 1964–66, Oxfordshire CC 1966–71; asst clerk Northamptonshire CC 1972–74, dep co sec East Sussex CC 1974–77, dep chief exec and clerk Essex CC 1977–85, chief exec Hampshire CC 1985–; pres Winchester Dist Scouts Assoc; memb Law Soc; *Recreations* music, drama, geology; *Clubs* Hampshire; *Style—* Robin Hodgson, Esq; ✉ Hampshire CC, The Castle, Winchester, Hants SO23 8UJ (☎ 01962 847375, fax 01962 844024, telex 477729)

HODGSON, Robin Granville; CBE (1992); s of Henry Edward Hodgson, of Astley Abbotts, Bridgnorth, Shropshire, and Natalie Beatrice, *née* Davidson; *b* 25 April 1942; *Educ* Shrewsbury, Univ of Oxford (BA), Wharton Sch Univ of Pennsylvania (MBA); *m* 8 May 1982, Fiona Ferelith, da of Keith Storr Allom; 4 s (Barnaby Peter Granville b 1986, James Maxwell Gower (twin) b and d 1986, Toby Henry Storr b 1988, Hugo Edward Valentine b 1992), 1 da (Poppy Ferelith Alice b 1990); *Career* Lt 4 Bn Kings Shrops LI TA 1960–64; chm and gp chief exec Granville & Co (investmt bankers) 1972–; chm Nasdim 1979–85; non-exec chm: Spotlaunch plc, Walter Alexander plc 1990–92; dir: Dominic Hunter plc, Staffordshire Building Society 1995–, Community Hospital plc 1995–; memb West Midland Industl Devpt Bd 1988–96; dir: Securities and Investmt Bd 1985–89, Securities and Futures Authy 1991–; MP (C) Walsall North 1976–79, chm Cons Party West Midlands Area 1991–94 (treas 1985–91); Nat Union of Cons Assocs: memb Exec Ctee 1988–, vice pres 1995–96, chm 1996–; tstee Shrewsbury Sch Fndn; Liveryman Worshipful Co of Goldsmiths; *Style—* Robin Hodgson, Esq, CBE; ✉ Nash Court, Nash, Ludlow, Shropshire SY8 3DF (☎ and fax 01584 811677); 15 Scarsdale Villas, London W8 (☎ and fax 0171 937 2964); Granville Holdings plc, Mint House, 77 Mansell Street, London E1 8AF (☎ 0171 488 1212, fax 0171 481 3911, telex 8814 884 GVILCO G)

HODKINSON, James Clifford; s of John Eric Thomas Hodkinson (d 1985), of Ferndown, Dorset, and Edith Lilian, *née* Lord; *b* 21 April 1944; *Educ* Salesian Coll Farnborough Hants; *m* 8 Feb 1968, Janet Patricia, da of George William Lee (d 1941); 1 da (Justine b 30 April 1970); *Career* trainee mangr F W Woolworth 1962–71; B & Q plc: mangr Bournemouth Store 1971–74, sales mangr in South 1974–79, ops dir 1979–84, ops and personnel dir 1984–86, chief exec 1986–92, int devpt dir 1992–94, chm and chief exec 1994–; chief exec (DIY) Kingfisher plc 1994–; non-exec dir Hamleys Plc; memb Bd Nat Steering Ctee to Advsy Cncl Prince's Youth Business Tst; FInstD, CIMgt; *Recreations* golf, shooting; *Style—* James Hodkinson, Esq; ✉ B & Q plc, Portswood House, 1 Hampshire Corporate Park, Chandlers Ford, Eastleigh, Hampshire SO53 3YX (☎ 01703 256256, fax 01703 257480)

HODKINSON, Prof (Henry) Malcolm; s of Charles Hodkinson (d 1986), of Mossley, Lancs, and Olive, *née* Kennerley (d 1988); *b* 28 April 1931; *Educ* Manchester GS, Brasenose Coll Oxford (BA, BM BCh, MA, DM), Middx Hosp Med Sch (MRCP); *m* 1, 2 Jan 1956 (m dis 1980), Elaine Margaret, *née* Harris; 4 da (Sarah b 1958, Isabel b 1960, Ruth b 1965, Naomi b 1967); m 2, 22 Nov 1986, Judith Bryant, *qv*; *Career* conslt geriatrician N Middx and St Ann's Gen Hosps London 1962–70, conslt geriatrician and memb MRC scientific staff Northwick Park Hosp and Clinical Res Centre Harrow Middx 1970–78, sr lectr in geriatric med Royal Postgrad Med Sch Hammersmith Hosp 1978–79 (prof of geriatric med 1979–84), Barlow prof of geriatric med Univ Coll and Middx Sch of Med UCL 1985–91 (emeritus prof 1991); vice pres Res into Ageing; Liveryman Worshipful Soc of Apothecaries; FRCP 1974; *Books* An Outline of Geriatrics (several edns, 1975–84), Common Symptoms of Disease in the Elderly (several edns, 1976–83), Biochemical Diagnosis in the Elderly (1977), Clinical Biochemistry of the Elderly (1984), Sherratt? A natural family of Staffordshire figures (1991); *Recreations* British glass and ceramics; *Style—* Prof Malcolm Hodkinson; ✉ 8 Chiswick Square, Burlington Lane, Chiswick, London W4 2QG (☎ and fax 0181 747 0239)

HODKINSON, Paul James; s of Francis Raymond Hodkinson, of Northwood, Kirkby, Merseyside, and Patricia Ann, *née* Fergus; *b* 14 Sept 1965; *Educ* St Kevin's Comp; *m*; 3 s (Kevin James, Jason, Lewis b 3 April 1995); *Career* professional boxer (featherweight); Br Champion 18 May 1988 (defended 14 Dec 1988), Euro Champion 12 April 1989 (defended 13 Dec 1989 and 13 Oct 1990), won Lonsdale Belt outright 6 Sept 1989 (for defence of Br and Euro Championships); World Boxing Cncl title: unsuccessful challenge 2 June 1990, won 13 Nov 1991, first defence 25 April 1992, second defence 12 Sept 1992, defeated 1993; record to date: fights 25, won 22, drawn 1, lost 2; Boxer of the Year award 1990, Dave Crawley Belt, Fight of the Year Lonsdale Int Sporting Club BBB of C boxing awards; *Style—* Paul Hodkinson, Esq; ✉ 4 Mintor Rd, Northwood, Kirkby, Merseyside (☎ 0151 546 8280)

HODKINSON, Philip Andrew (Phil); s of Bernard Joseph Hodkinson, of Poulton-le-Fylde, Lancs, and Edith, *née* Stevenson; *b* 26 April 1958; *Educ* Wimbledon Coll, St John's Coll Cambridge (Baylis scholar, MA); *m* 1987, Julia Jane, da of Norman Dennis; 1 s (Robert Andrew b 16 Aug 1991), 1 da (Sarah Jane b 8 Feb 1996); *Career* actuarial trainee Duncan C Fraser & Co 1980–84, product devpt actuary Hambro Life Assurance Ltd 1984–88, exec dir Allied Dunbar Assurance plc 1988–92, md Dunbar Bank plc 1993–, dir Allied Dunbar Assurance plc 1995–; winner Burns Prize Worshipful Co of Actuaries; FIA 1985; *Recreations* running, walking, tennis, railways; *Style—* Phil Hodkinson, Esq; ✉ Managing Director, Dunbar Bank plc, 9–15 Sackville Street, London W1A 2JP (☎ 0171 437 7844)

HODSON, Clive; CBE (1992); s of Stanley Louis Hodson (d 1993), and Elsie May, *née* Stratford; *b* 9 March 1942; *Educ* Erith GS; *m* 18 Sept 1976, Fiona Mary, *née* Pybus; 1 s (James Andrew b 12 Feb 1983), 1 da (Kate Alexis b 19 Jan 1985); *Career* Fin Dept London Transport 1960–69, asst co sec and accountant London Country Bus Services Ltd 1970–74, mgmnt accountant London Transport 1974–78, fin dir London Buses 1978–89, md London Buses Ltd 1989–95, project dir (bus privatisation) London Transport 1993–95, md London Transport Buses 1994–, project dir Croydon Tramlink 1995–, chm Victoria Coach Station Ltd 1995–; memb Bd London Transport 1995–; Freeman City of London 1995, Liveryman Worshipful Co of Carmen 1995; ATII 1968; FCCA 1967, FCIT 1969; *Recreations* travel, walking, reading; *Style—* Clive Hodson, Esq, CBE; ✉ London Transport Buses, 172 Buckingham Palace Road, Westminster, London SW1W 9TN (☎ 0171 918 3873, fax 0171 918 3880)

HODSON, Daniel Houghton; s of Henry Vincent Hodson, of London, and Margaret Elizabeth, *née* Honey; *b* 11 March 1944; *Educ* Eton, Merton Coll Oxford (MA); *m* 22 Feb 1979, Diana Mary, da of Christopher Breen Ryde, of Middleton-on-Sea, W Sussex; 2 da (Susannah Fleur b 1980, Emma Katharine b 1982); *Career* Chase Manhattan Bank NA 1965–73, dir Edward Bates & Sons Ltd 1974–76 (joined 1973), gp fin dir Unigate plc 1981–87 (gp treas 1976–81), pres Unigate Inc 1986–87, dir Girobank plc 1986–89, chm Davidson Pearce Group plc 1988 (chief exec 1987–88), dep chief exec and gp fin dir Nationwide Building Society 1989–92, chief exec LIFFE 1993–; non-exec dir: The Post Office 1984–95, Ransomes plc 1993–, Independent Insurance Group plc 1995–; chm Euro Ctee of Options and Futures Exchanges (ECOFEX) 1996–; pres Assoc of Corporate Treasurers 1992–93 (chm 1984–86); chm Fulham Carnival 1979–81, govr The Yehudi Menuhin Sch 1984–; memb Worshipful Co of Mercers 1965–; FCT 1979; *Books* Businessman's Guide to the Foreign Exchange Market (jtly), Corporate Finance and Treasury Management (founding ed 1984–); *Recreations* music, travel, skiing, gardening; *Clubs* Brooks's, City of London; *Style—* Daniel Hodson, Esq; ✉ Treyford Manor, Midhurst, W Sussex GU29 0LD (☎ 01730 825436); London International Financial Futures and Options Exchange (LIFFE), Cannon Bridge, London EC4R 3XX (☎ 0171 623 0444, fax 0171 588 3624)

HODSON, His Hon Judge; (Thomas) David Tattersall; s of Thomas Norman Hodson (d 1987), and Elsie Nuttall Hodson (d 1987); *b* 24 Sept 1942; *Educ* Sedbergh, Univ of Manchester (LLB); *m* 9 Aug 1969, Patricia Ann, da of Robert Arthur Vint (d 1967); 2 s (Nicholas b 1970, Benjamin b 1979), 1 da (Philippa b 1972); *Career* leader writer The Yorkshire Post 1964–65, called to the Bar Inner Temple 1966, in practice Northern Circuit 1966–87 (jr 1968), recorder Crown Court 1983–87, circuit judge (Northern Circuit) 1987–; memb Parole Bd 1996–; pres S Lancashire Branch Magistrates' Assoc 1994; *Books* One Week in August: The Kaiser at Lowther Castle 1895 (1995); *Recreations* music, fell-walking, family history; *Clubs* Lancashire CCC; *Style—* His Hon Judge Hodson; ✉ c/o The Crown Court, Courts of Justice, Crown Square, Manchester (☎ 0161 954 1800)

HODSON, Denys Fraser; CBE (1982); s of Rev Harold Victor Hodson, MC (d 1977), of Gloucestershire, and Marguerite Edmée (Madge), *née* Ritchie (d 1996); *b* 23 May 1928; *Educ* Marlborough, Trinity Coll Oxford (MA); *m* 1954, Julie Compton, da of Harold Goodwin (d 1984), of Warwicks; 1 s (Nicolas b 1965), 1 da (Lucy b 1963); *Career* dir arts and recreation Thamesdown Borough Cncl 1970–92; dir Arts Research Ltd 1994–; chm: Southern Arts Assoc 1975–81 and 1985–87, Cncl Regnl Arts Assoc 1976–81; dir Oxford Playhouse Co 1974–86, govr Br Film Inst 1976–87, memb Arts Cncl GB 1987–94 (vice chm 1989–94), dir Brewery Arts 1991– (chm 1994–), vice chm Voluntary Arts Network (VAN) 1991– (chm 1994), chm Public Arts Cmmns Agency 1993–; *Recreations* arts, fishing, bird watching; *Style—* Denys Hodson, Esq, CBE; ✉ Manor Farm House, Fairford, Gloucestershire GL7 4AR (☎ and fax 01285 712462)

HODSON, John; s of late Arthur Hodson, of Stoke-on-Trent, Staffs, and Olga, *née* Vernon; *b* 19 May 1946; *Educ* Hanley HS Stoke-on-Trent, Worcester Coll Oxford (BA); *m* 1970, Christina, *née* McLeod; 1 s (Jonathan b 13 Feb 1973), 2 da (Sarah b 3 Jan 1972, Lucinda b 7 Oct 1978); *Career* graduate trainee Fin Div Bowater Paper Corp 1967–68, Burroughs Machines 1968–70; Singer & Friedlander: joined 1970, asst dir 1974–83, dir 1983–, head of investments 1985–90, memb Bd Singer & Friedlander Group 1987–, chief exec Singer & Friedlander Holdings 1990– (dir 1986–), chief exec Singer & Friedlander Group 1992–; non-exec dir Associated Nursing Services 1994–; *Recreations* tennis, family; *Style—* John Hodson, Esq; ✉ Singer & Friedlander Ltd, 21 New Street, Bishopsgate, London EC2M 4HR (☎ 0171 623 3000)

HODSON, Sir Michael Robin Adderley; 6 Bt (I 1787), of Holybrooke House, Wicklow; s of Maj Sir Edmond Adair Hodson, 5 Bt, DSO (d 1972); *b* 5 March 1932; *Educ* Eton; *m* 1, 16 Dec 1963 (m dis 1978), Katrin Alexa, da of late Erwin Bernstiel, of St Andrew's House, St Andrew's Major, Dinas Powis, Glam; 3 da (Tania Elizabeth (Mrs Guy Deacon) b 1965, Alexa Adderley (Mrs Christopher M Chambers) b 1966, Jane Katrina b 1970); m 2, 1978, Catherine, da of John Henry Seymour, of Wimpole Street, London; *Heir* bro, Patrick Richard Hodson, *qv* b 27 Nov 1934; *Career* Capt (ret) Scots Gds; *Style—* Sir Michael Hodson, Bt; ✉ The White House, Awbridge, Romsey, Hants

HODSON, Patrick Richard; s of Maj Sir Edmond Adair Hodson, 5 Bt, DSO (d 1972), and hp of bro, Sir Michael Robin Adderley Hodson, 6 Bt, *qv*; *b* 27 Nov 1934; *Educ* Eton; *m* 1961, June, o da of late H M Shepherd-Cross, of The Manor, Skewsby, Yorks; 3 s (Mark Adair b 1964, James Patrick b 1966, Rupert Edward b 1972); *Career* Capt (ret) Rifle Bde; *Style—* Patrick Hodson, Esq; ✉ Shipton Slade Farm, Woodstock, Oxford

HODSON, Philip; s of Kenneth David Hodson, of Peterborough, and Freda Margaret, *née* Reedman; *b* 2 Oct 1944; *Educ* Oundle, St Edmund Hall Oxford (MA); *m* 3 Aug 1968, Diane Elizabeth, da of Sydney Farrar Stansfield, of Peterborough; *Career* admitted slr 1969; slr Manchester CC 1969–73, ptnr Cobbett Leak Almond 1974–; chm Manchester Young Slrs' Assoc 1980, treas S Manchester Law Centre Mgmnt Ctee 1982–88 (chm 1988–89); pres Manchester Law Soc 1988–89; memb: Slr Disciplinary Tbnl 1989–, Salford Playhouse Mgmnt Ctee 1989–91; FCIArb; *Recreations* squash, golf, theatre; *Clubs* St James's; *Style—* Philip Hodson, Esq; ✉ Cobbett Leak Almond, Ship Canal House, King St, Manchester M2 4WB (☎ 0161 833 3333, fax 0161 833 3030)

HODSON, Phillip I; *b* 1946; *Educ* Univ of Oxford; *partner* Anne Hooper; 1 s (Alexander), 2 step s (Barnaby, Joel); *Career* psychotherapist, broadcaster, lecturer and writer; ed Forum (int jl of human rels) 1972–79; columnist: Psychology Today, SHE Magazine (columnist of the year 1984), Woman's World, Family Circle, TV Quick, Today newspaper (Sex Talk), Daily Star (Heartline), OK Weekly; contributing ed Cosmopolitan Magazine 1994–96; host LBC Radio problem phone-in 1976–91, agony columnist News of the World 1992–94, counsellor BBC Radio 2 1995–, counsellor Talk Radio 1996–; numerous appearances on TV incl own shows for TVS, LWT, and as presenter of BBC1's Daytime UK and Going Live!, prodr-presenter of award winning films on counselling skills; author of numerous books on related subjects and also on opera; memb: British Assoc for Counselling, British Assoc of Sexual and Marital Therapists; tstee Impotence Assoc; *Books* Cosmopolitan Guide to Love, Sex and Relationships (1997); *Recreations* playing cricket, opera; *Clubs* Groucho; *Style—* Phillip Hodson, Esq

HOEHLER, Prof Gertrud; *Educ* Academic Fndn of the German People, Univ of Mannheim (DPhil); *Career* prof of gen literary studies and German studies Univ of Paderborn 1976– (lectr 1972–76), PR conslt Deutsche Bank AG 1987–90, non-exec dir Grand Metropolitan plc 1992–; freelance mgmnt conslt 1987–; memb: Advsy Cncl Rowohlt-Verlage, Advsy Cncl Styria Verlag, Fed Defence Min's Internal Leadership Advsy Cncl, Fed Educn and Sci Min's Advsy Cncl, Fed Research and Technol Min's Advsy Cncl, Bd of Dirs Ancient Monuments and Historic Bldgs Fndn, Bd of Govrs Univ of Witten-Herdecke, Senate Fraunhofer-Gesellschaft, Bd of Govrs Forum for Germany, Bd of Govrs Fndn for Beautiful Old Trees in Germany; *Awards* Culture Prize of City of Wuppertal for Lyrical Poetry 1964, Anti-Deadly-Seriousness Award 1988, Konrad Adenauer Prize for Literature 1988; *Books* incl: Die Anspruchsgesellschaft/The Aspiration Society (1979), Das Glück/Happiness (1981), Die Kinder der Freiheit/The Children of Liberty (1983), Die Bäume des Lebens/The Trees of Life (1985), Die Zukunftsgesellschaft/The Society of the Future (1986), Spielregeln des Glücks/Rules of the Game of Happiness (1988), Offener Horizont/Open Horizon (1989), Spielregeln für Sieger/Rules of the Game for Winners (1991); *Style—* Prof Gertrud Hoehler; ✉ c/o Sekretariat Inge Matthiae, Auf dem Dudel 35, 45468 Mülheim an der Ruhr, Germany (☎ and fax 00 49 208 35208); Grand Metropolitan plc, 20 St James's Square, London SW1Y 4RR

HOERNER, John Lee; s of Robert Lee Hoerner (d 1990), and Lulu Alice, *née* Stone, of St Louis, Missouri; *b* 23 Sept 1939; *Educ* Univ of Nebraska (BS, BA); *m* 1, 9 Aug 1959 (m dis 1971), Susan Kay, da of Fred W Morgan, of Lincoln, Nebraska; 1 s (John Scott b 30 May 1960), 1 da (Joanne Lynne b 21 Sept 1962); m 2, 16 Feb 1973, Anna Lea, da of Leonard O Thomas, of Kansas City, Missouri; *Career* with Hovland-Swanson Lincoln Nebraska 1959–68, Woolf Brothers Kansas City Missouri 1968–72, Hahnes New Jersey 1972–73, pres and chief exec offr First 21st Century Corporation McLean Virginia, with Hahnes NJ 1974–81; Associated Dry Goods Corporation/May Company: chm and chief exec H & S Pogue Co Cincinnati Ohio 1981–82, chm and chief exec L S Ayres & Co Indianapolis Indiana 1982–87; The Burton Group plc: chm Debenhams 1987–92, chm Harvey Nichols 1988–91, chief exec stores 1989–92, gp chief exec 1992–; tstee:

Crimestoppers Tst, Indust in Educn; vice chm The Dogs' Home Battersea; *Books* Ayres Adages (1983), The Director's Handbook (1991); *Recreations* dogs, riding, flying; *Clubs* Indianapolis University, The Groucho; *Style*— John Hoerner, Esq; ✉ The Burton Group plc, 10 Great Castle St, London W1N 7AD (☎ 0171 927 0501, fax 0171 631 0400)

HOEY, Catharine Letitia (Kate); MP (Lab) Vauxhall (majority 10,488); da of Thomas Hoey, and Letitia Hoey; *b* 21 June 1946; *Educ* Belfast Royal Acad, Ulster Coll of Physical Educn, City of London Coll (BSc); *Career* lectr Southwark Coll 1972–76, sr lectr Kingsway Coll 1976–85, educnl advsr to London Football Clubs 1985–89; memb Hackney Borough Cncl 1978–82, Parly candidate (Lab) Dulwich 1987, MP (Lab) Vauxhall June 1989–, shadow min for Citizens Rights and Equality 1992–93; memb: Select Ctee on Broadcasting, Political Ctee South East CWS 1984–, Select Ctee on Social Security 1994–, League for Introduction of Canine Control; author of various articles on sport; *Recreations* watching soccer, keeping fit; *Clubs* Barbican Health and Fitness Centre; *Style*— Kate Hoey, MP; ✉ House of Commons, London SW1A 0AA

HOFFBRAND, Dr Barry Ian; *b* 18 March 1934; *Educ* Bradford GS, Univ of Oxford (MA, BM BCh, DM), UCH Med Sch London (Goldsmid entrance scholar, Luke silver medal in clinical pathology), Cardiovascular Research Inst Univ of California San Francisco; *m* Marina; 3 da; *Career* med trg Bradford, London (UCH) and San Francisco (Bay Area sr research fell), conslt physician Whittington Hosp London 1970–; hon conslt physician: The Italian Hosp 1975–89, Hosp of St John and St Elizabeth 1994–; hon sr clinical lectr Faculty of Clinical Scis UCH; ed Postgraduate Med Jl 1980–94; examiner: Univ of London, Univ of Malta, Royal Coll of Physicians, Royal Coll of Surgns; Royal Soc of Med: hon sec 1976–82, hon librarian 1983–85, vice pres 1990–92, pres Clinical Section 1982–83, fndr sr sec Section of Nephrology 1994–95; pres London Jewish Med Soc 1985–86, memb Cncl RCP 1992–95; TMA Pai Gold Medal for contribs to postgraduate med educn 1991; memb Worshipful Soc of Apothecaries; memb: BMA, Int Hypertension Soc, Br Hypertension Soc, Renal Assoc; FRCP 1976; *Books* MRCP Part 1 Review Book (1981); *Recreations* looking at pictures, opera; *Clubs* RSM; *Style*— Dr Barry Hoffbrand; ✉ Wellington Hospital, Wellington Place, London NW8 9LE (☎ 0171 586 5959)

HOFFBRAND, Prof (Allan) Victor; s of Philip Hoffbrand (d 1959), of Bradford, Yorks, and Minnie, *née* Freedman; *b* 14 Oct 1935; *Educ* Bradford GS, The Queen's Coll Oxford (MA, DM), London Hosp (BM BCh); *m* 3 Nov 1963, (Irene) Jill, da of Michael Mellows, of Wembley Park, Middx; 2 s (Philip b 11 May 1967, David b 12 July 1970), 1 da (Caroline b 21 March 1966); *Career* jr hosp doctor London Hosp 1960–62, lectr in haematology St Bart's Hosp 1966–67, MRC res scholar Tufts Univ Boston 1967–68, lectr and sr lectr in haematology Royal Postgrad Med Sch 1968–74 (registrar and res fell 1962–66), prof of haematology Royal Free Sch of Med 1974–; DSc 1987; hon FRCP (Ed) 1986, FRCP 1976, FRCPath 1980; *Books* Essential Haematology (jtly 1980, 3 edn 1993), Clinics in Haematology (ed Vol 5.3 1976, Vol 15.3 1986), Clinical Haematology Illustrated (jtly, 1988), Recent Advances in Haematology (ed, 8 edn 1996), Sandoz Atlas: Clinical Haematology (jtly, 1988, 2 edn 1994), Postgraduate Haematology (jt ed, 3 edn 1989); *Recreations* chess, bridge, antiques, music; *Style*— Prof Victor Hoffbrand; ✉ 57 Camden Square, London NW1 9XE (☎ 0171 485 6984); Department of Haematology, Royal Free Hospital, London NW3 2QG (☎ 0171 794 0500 ext 3258)

HOFFMAN, Anthony Edward; o s of late Geoffrey and Jean Hoffman; *b* 21 Feb 1937; *Educ* City of London Sch; *m* 1992, Dr Christine Ann Facer; 3 da from prev m (Anna b 1968, Sofie b 1969, Kate b 1971), 1 step s (Oliver b 1978); *Career* admitted slr 1960; jr ptnr Joelson & Co (now Joelson Wilson) 1960, sole practioner 1960–62, currently sr ptnr Hamlin Slowe (after various mergers); dep High Ct taxing master; memb Law Soc; *Recreations* walking, shooting, fishing, horticulture; *Style*— Anthony E Hoffman, Esq; ✉ Hamlin Slowe, Roxburghe House, 273–287 Regent Street, London W1A 4SQ (☎ 0171 629 1209)

HOFFMAN, George Henry; s of George Hoffman (d 1993), of USA, and Anna Cecilia, *née* Hojnowski; *b* 30 Oct 1939; *Educ* Cornell Univ (BA), Columbia Univ (MA); *m* 1961, Pauline Margaret, da of Gilbert R Lewis; 1 s (Philip b 1968), 2 da (Erika b 1962, Bridgit b 1965); *Career* banker 1962–88, chm and chief exec Hoffman Associates 1988–; dir: Lithuanian Development Bank 1994–, Investment Bank of Latvia 1996–; memb Ad Hoc Cncl Euro Govt Business Relations Cncl 1979–; former dir American C of C UK; *Recreations* tennis, scuba diving, reading; *Clubs* Gravetye; *Style*— George Hoffman; ✉ c/o Hoffman Associates, PO Box 71, Guildford, Surrey GU3 3YZ (☎ 01483 306820, fax 01483 306828)

HOFFMAN, Mark; s of Dr Mark Hoffman (d 1975), of USA; *b* 14 Dec 1938; *Educ* Harvard Coll (AB), Trinity Coll Cambridge (MA), Harvard Business Sch (MBA); *m* 1968, Mary Jo, da of John C Pyles, of Washington DC, USA; 3 s (Nicholas b 1969, John b 1972, James b 1978); *Career* East African Common Services Orgn/MIT (Africa/USA) 1964–66, World Banks Int Finance Corp (Washington) 1966–68, Olympic Investmt Gp (Paris) 1968–69; dir: Hambros Bank (UK) 1970–74, Millipore Corpn (USA) 1975–, George Weston Ltd (Canada) 1975– (fin dir 1975–80, pres Weston Resources 1980–82), Guinness Peat Group plc (UK) 1982–84 (gp md 1982–83), LAC Minerals (Canada) 1984–86, Advent International Inc (Boston) 1989–, Guinness Flight Global Asset Management Ltd (UK) 1989–; chm: Int Financial Markets Trading Ltd (UK) 1984–93, Cambridge Research Group Ltd, Cambridge Capital Group Ltd 1990–, Hamilton Lunn Holdings Ltd 1990–; int dir Harvard Alumni Assoc 1989–92; chm: Oxford and Cambridge Rowing Fndn 1990–94, Harvard Club of UK 1993– (pres 1988–93), United World Colleges Int and Exec Bds 1993–; *Clubs* Boodle's, Leander (Henley-on-Thames, chm 1989–93), Utd Oxford and Cambridge Univ, Hawks' (Cambridge), Guards' Polo, Toronto, Royal Canadian Yacht; *Style*— Mark Hoffman, Esq; ✉ 21 Campden Hill Square, London W8; Hugh Cargill Road, Estabrook Woods, Concord, Mass, USA; Cambridge Research Group Ltd, 13 Station Road, Cambridge CB1 2JB

HOFFMAN, Eur Ing Michael Richard; s of Sydney William Hoffman (d 1987), of Letchworth, Herts, and Ethel Margaret Hoffman (d 1978); *b* 31 Oct 1939; *Educ* Hitchin GS, Univ of Bristol (BSc(Eng)); *m* 1, 1963, Margaret Edith; 1 da (Rachel); m 2, 1982, Helen Judith; *Career* Rolls Royce 1961, AE Ltd 1973; Perkins Engines Group: md 1976, chm 1977; Massey Ferguson Ltd: vice pres 1980, pres Farm Machinery Div 1981; chief exec and md Babcock International 1983–87; Airship Industries Ltd: chief exec 1987–88, dep chm 1988–90; Thames Water plc: gp chief exec 1989–96, dep chm 1993–96; dep chm Cosworth Engineering Ltd 1988–91; dir: Cray Electronics Holdings plc 1990–, PowerGen plc 1993–; pres IProdE 1987–88 (vice pres 1985–87), chm UK S African Trade Assoc 1987, vice pres Engrg Employers Fedn 1985–87; memb: Technol Requirements Bd 1985–88, Engrg Cncl 1991–96, Monopolies and Mergers Cmmn 1988–94, BOTB 1986–89, Cncl Brunel Univ 1984– (chm 1991–); Watts Meml Prize 1961; Freeman City of London 1984, Liveryman Worshipful Co of Engrs 1984; FIMechE, FIEE, FEng 1989; *Recreations* shooting, sailing, real tennis; *Clubs* RAC, Reform, MCC, Royal Thames YC; *Style*— Eur Ing Michael Hoffman, FEng; ✉ 43 De Vere Gardens, London W8 5AW (☎ 0171 581 4612, fax 0171 823 7816)

HOFFMAN, Tom; s of Dirk Hoffman (d 1986), of Cambridge, and Marie-Luise, *née* Leyser; *b* 9 Aug 1945; *Educ* The Leys Sch Cambridge, Univ of Exeter (LLB); *m* June 1971, Verena; 1 s (Alexander b 1975); *Career* chartered accountant Spicer & Oppenheim 1963–70, Arthur Andersen & Co 1970–71, Williams & Glyn's Bank 1971–76, Hill Samuel & Co 1976–78, dir of capital mkts Lloyds Bank International 1978–84, dep md Fuji International Finance 1984–89, head of corporate banking in UK Algemene Bank Nederland NV 1989–91, UK gen mangr Banco Espirito Santo 1991–; dir: Tower Bridge Square Management, London Festival Orchestra 1996–; tstee and dir Maryport Heritage Tst Cumbria 1990–; tstee and hon treas Anglo-Portuguese Fndn 1993–, vice chm UK-Portuguese C of C 1995– (memb Cncl 1993–); govr Corp of the Sons of the Clergy 1990–; hon treas Ward of Cordwainer Club London 1985– (chm 1993–94); Liveryman Worshipful Co of Tylers and Bricklayers (memb Livery Ctee 1995–); fell Royal Cwlth Soc 1964, memb Royal Soc for Asian Affrs 1989; FCA 1971, FRSA 1990, MSI 1993; various articles in banking, finance and accountancy journals; *Recreations* gardening, ballet, opera, 17th and 18th century choral music, travel; *Clubs* City Livery, Bankers, Royal Cwlth; *Style*— Tom Hoffman; ✉ Old Curteis, Biddenden, Kent TN27 8JN; 72 Gainsford St, London SE1 2NB; Banco Espirito Santo, 33 Queen St, London EC4R 1ES

HOFFMAN, Walter Max; s of Bernard Hoffman (d 1944), and Paula Kirschberger (d 1944); *b* 27 Sept 1929; *Educ* Manchester GS, Univ of Manchester (BA); *m* (Renate) Shoshanah, da of Dr Max Plaut; *Career* trained as chartered accountant, qualified taking first place ICAEW final examination 1953, former ptnr with Baker Tilly (currently conslt), chm BKR International (accounting gp) 1992–94, inspector under Companies Act to investigate Barlow Clowes affair; FCA (ACA 1953); *Recreations* theatre, music and travel; *Clubs* Athenaeum; *Style*— Walter M Hoffman, Esq; ✉ Baker Tilly, Chartered Accountants, 2 Bloomsbury St, London WC1B 3ST (☎ 0171 413 5100, fax 0171 413 5101)

HOFMEYR, Stephen Murray; s of late Jan Murray Hofmeyr, of Cape Town, and Stella Mary, *née* Mills; *b* 10 Feb 1956; *Educ* Diocesan Coll Rondesbosch, Univ of Cape Town (BCom, LLB), Univ Coll Oxford (MA); *m* 28 June 1980, Audrey Frances, da of late James Murray Cannan, of Cape Town; 2 s (Timothy b 6 July 1986, Paul (triplet) b 6 July 1986), 1 da (Rebecca (triplet) b 6 July 1986); *Career* called to the Bar Gray's Inn 1982; *Recreations* photography, bird watching; *Clubs* Vincents; *Style*— Stephen Hofmeyr, Esq; ✉ The Gables, Midway, Walton on Thames, Surrey KT12 3HY (☎ 01932 253614); 7 King's Bench Walk, Temple, London EC4Y 7DS (☎ 0171 583 0404, fax 0171 583 0950, telex 887491–KBLAW)

HOGAN, Desmond; s of William Hogan (d 1979), of Ballinasloe, and Christina, *née* Connolly; *b* 10 Dec 1950; *Educ* Garbally Coll Ballinasloe, Univ Coll Dublin (BA, MA); *Career* author; hon chair Dept of English Univ of Alabama 1989; *Awards* Hennessy Award 1971, Rooney Prize 1977, John Llewelyn Rhys Meml Prize 1981, Irish Post Award 1985, DAAD Award Deutsch Acad 1991; *Work incl* Jimmy (radio play) 1978, The Mourning Thief (TV play) 1984, Through Other Eyes (TV documentary) 1987; *Books include* The Ikon Maker (1976), The Diamonds at the Bottom of the Sea (stories, 1979), The Leaves on Grey (1980), Children of Lir (stories, 1981), Stories (1982), A Curious Street (1984), A New Shirt (1986), Lebanon Lodge (stories, 1988), A Link with the River (collected stories, 1989), The Edge of the City (a scrap-book 1976–91, 1993), A Farewell to Prague (1995); *Style*— Desmond Hogan, Esq; ✉ c/o Faber and Faber, 3 Queen Square, London WC1N 3AU

HOGAN, Prof Eileen Mary; da of Thomas Matthew Hogan, of Woking, Surrey, and Marjorie Coyle (d 1982); *b* 1 March 1946; *Educ* Streatham Hill and Clapham HS, Camberwell Sch of Arts and Crafts, Royal Acad Schs, Br Sch of Archaeology Athens, Royal Coll of Art (BA, MA); *m* Kenneth Ersser; *Career* artist; princ lectr and course ldr in illustration and dir Camberwell Press 1985, dean Sch of Applied and Graphic Arts 1989; represented by The Fine Art Soc 1979; *Solo Exhibitions* incl: Br Cncl Athens 1971 and 1983, New Grafton Gallery 1972, RCA 1974 and 1977, The Fine Art Soc London 1980, 1982, 1984, 1985, 1986, 1988, 1992 and 1997, The Fine Art Soc Glasgow 1980, The Alden Library Ohio Univ 1982, The King Library Univ of Kentucky 1982, The Imperial War Museum 1984, Morehead Univ Kentucky 1986, Graduate Sch of Library Servs Univ of Alabama 1988; *Group Exhibitions* incl: Hayward Gallery London 1969, Royal Acad Summer Show 1969, 1974, 1976–94, ICA London 1973, Serpentine Gallery London 1973, The English Landscape (Usher Gallery) 1975, Draw the Line (V & A Museum London) 1977, Open and Shut (V & A Museum London) 1979, British Fine Printing (London) 1984, London Ecology Centre 1987, The President's Choice (Royal Acad) 1989; *Commissions* incl: Women at Work in the Royal Navy (for Artistic Records Ctee of Imperial War Museum) 1983–84, The Queen presenting Colours to the Portsmouth Fleet (for HMS Nelson) 1986, stamps for Royal Mail 1989, 1990 and 1993; numerous work in public collections; *Awards* Reeves purchase prize 1968, David Murray scholarship 1968, Br Inst fund 1968, Gtr London award for Young Artists 1969, Landseer scholarship 1970 and 1971, Royal Over-Seas League award 1970 and 1972, Walter Neurath prize 1970, Greek Govt scholarship 1971, Arts Cncl of GB award 1974, Gtr London Arts Assoc award 1975, Crafts Cncl Advsy Ctee grant 1978, Spirit of London award 1982; *Publications* Oedipus and Iocaste (1972), Fragments from Sappho (1973), Variations (1974), Dream of Gerontius (1976), Ogham (1977), Morning Sea (1978), Haiku (1978), 500 Points of Good Husbandry by Thomas Tusser (1981), A Selection of Poems by C P Cavafy (1985), On Common Ground (1987), Anaskaphes (1989), All Over the Place (1993); *Clubs* Chelsea Arts, Double Crown; *Style*— Prof Eileen Hogan; ✉ 102 Coleherne Court, Old Brompton Road, London SW5 0ED

HOGAN, James V J; *b* 12 Sept 1951; *Educ* Univ of Lancaster (BA Political Sci), Univ of Oxford (MLitt Social Sci); *m* Jane Eveline; 1 da (Cassandra Jane Eveline b 1983), 1 s (Alexander James William b 1987); *Career* BBC TV News and Current Affrs 1978–91: asst prodr/researcher Nationwide, Westminster, and Tonight 1978–80, prodr Newsweek, The Pursuit of Power, and 20th Century Remembered 1980–84, sr prodr Panorama and Newsnight 1984–88, ed This Week Next Week 1987–88, ed BBC News Event Unit (exec prodr of Gen Election progs, Party Political Confs and major current affrs documentaries on domestic and foreign topics) 1988–90, ed BBC Question Time 1990–91; md Broadstone Productions (Current Affrs and Factual Progs Div of Zenith Group) 1992–94, bdcast policy and devpt conslt SelectTV plc (team ldr on Channel 5 bid) 1994–96; ptnr Brunswick Public Relations 1996–; Robert McKenzie fell LSE (with special reference to TV indust) 1993 and 1994; speaker at LSE and Univ of Oxford, author of articles for The Times and elsewhere; memb: Inst of Dirs, Royal TV Soc, Inst of Jewish Affairs Cmmn on Racist Movements in Western Europe 1993–96; fell LSE; *Publications* BBC Review of the Year (ed, 1990 and 1991), From Demigods to Democrats? the Television Revolution (1997) and various LSE working papers on TV indust 1996 and 1997; *Recreations* writing, music, gardening, theatre, sport; *Style*— James Hogan, Esq; ✉ Brunswick Public Relations Ltd, 16 Lincoln's Inn Fields, London WC2A 3ED (☎ 0171 404 5959, fax 0171 831 2823)

HOGAN, William Patrick (Bill); s of William Daniel Hogan (d 1983), of Laindon, Essex, and Lilian, *née* Morley; *b* 7 Sept 1943; *Educ* Christ's Hospital; *m* 20 March 1971, Audrey Margaret, da of Arthur Willber; 2 c (Neil b 28 May 1975, Natalie b 15 Dec 1982); *Career* qualified chartered accountant 1966, ptnr Baker Tilly Chartered Accountants; int tax specialist; writer and lectr; FCA 1976 (ACA 1966); *Recreations* theatre, golf, travel; *Clubs* Christ's Hospital; *Style*— Bill Hogan, Esq; ✉ Baker Tilly, 2 Bloomsbury St, London WC1B 3ST (☎ 0171 413 5100, fax 0171 413 5101)

HOGARTH, Prof Cyril Alfred; s of Alfred Hogarth (d 1975), of Chaston, Clacton-on-Sea, and Florence Mary, *née* Farrow (d 1981); *b* 22 Jan 1924; *Educ* Tottenham Co Sch, Queen Mary Coll London (BSc, PhD, DSc); *m* 4 Sept 1951, Audrey, da of Frederick Percy Jones (d 1975), of Thorpe-le-Soken; 1 s (Adrian b 1960), 2 da (Celia (Mrs Stuart-Lee) b 1954, Yvonne (Mrs Goyder) b 1954 d 1994); *Career* pt/t Lt (Sp) RNVR 1944–46; experimental offr Admty 1943–46, lectr Chelsea Coll 1948–49, res fell Univ of

Reading 1949–51, sr sci offr Royal Radar Estab 1951–58; Brunel Univ: head Physics Dept 1958–82 and 1984–85, prof 1964–89, emeritus prof 1989–; visiting prof: S Bank Univ 1987–, Univ of Keele 1989–; Leverhulme emeritus fellowship 1991–93; consit to Westcode Semiconductors 1958–; examiner and conslt to many orgns, author of numerous sci pubns; S Bucks DC: memb 1983–, vice chm 1991–93, chm 1993–95; memb Nat Housing and Town Planning Cncl, chm Local Authorities M25 Consortium 1992–; parish cncllr Gerrards Cross 1975–; FInstP 1958, FRSA 1972, FIEE 1985, CEng, CPhys; *Books* Techniques of Non-Destructive Testing (with J Blitz, 1960), Materials used in Semi-Conductor Devices (1965); *Recreations* gardening, foreign travel; *Clubs* Royal Over-Seas League; *Style*— Prof Cyril Hogarth; ✉ Shepherds Hey, Orchehill Ave, Gerrards Cross, Bucks SL9 8QG (☎ 01753 884217); Department of Physics, Brunel University, Uxbridge, Middlesex UB8 3PH (☎ 01895 274000, fax 01895 272391)

HOGARTH, (Arthur) Paul; OBE (1989); s of Arthur Hogarth (d 1966), of Kendal, Cumbria, and Janet, *née* Bownass (d 1992); *b* 4 Oct 1917; *Educ* St Agnes Sch, Manchester Coll of Art, St Martin's Sch of Art London, RCA (PhD); *m* 1, 1940, Doreen (d 1948), da of Albert Courtman, of Alderley Edge, Cheshire; m 2, 1949, Phyllis, *née* Pamplin (d 1962); 1 s (Toby Graham b 1 Aug 1960); m 3, 2 Feb 1963, Patricia Morgan Graham, *née* Douthwaite (d 1981); m 4, 1989, Diana Marjorie, *née* Cochran; *Career* painter in watercolours, illustrator, author and printmaker; sr tutor Faculty of Graphic Art RCA 1964–71, cmmnd by Imperial War Museum to depict Berlin Wall 1981; drawings, watercolours and prints in permanent collections: Br Museum, Fitzwilliam Museum, Whitworth Gallery, Univ of Manchester, City Art Gallery Manchester, V & A Museum, Library of Congress (Washington USA), Boston Public Library (USA), Yale Centre of Br Art (USA); regular exhibitions Francis Kyle Gallery London; Francis Williams Award for Best Literary Illustration 1982, Yorkshire Post Award for Best Art Book 1986; memb: Library Ctee Royal Acad of Arts (memb Cncl 1979–80 and 1986–88), Advsy Ctee Royal Acad Enterprises; hon pres Assoc of Illustrators; ARA 1974, RA 1984, RDI 1979, RE 1988, FCSD 1964; *Books* Looking at China (1955), Creative Pencil Drawing (1964, 2 edn 1981), Artists on Horseback (1972, USA only), Drawing Architecture (1973, 2 edn 1980), Arthur Boyd Houghton (1982), Artist as Reporter (1986), Drawing on Life: Memoirs and Travels (1997); illustrated books in collaboration with authors notably: Brendan Behan's Island (with Brendan Behan, 1962), Majorca Observed (with Robert Graves, 1965), Graham Greene Country (with Graham Greene, 1986), The Mediterranean Shore (with Lawrence Durrell, 1988), The Illustrated A Year in Provence (with Peter Mayle, 1992), In Praise of Churches (with John Betejan, 1996); *Clubs* Arts; *Style*— Paul Hogarth, Esq, OBE, RA; ✉ c/o Tessa Sayle, 11 Jubilee Place, London SW3 3TE (☎ 0171 823 3883, fax 0171 823 3363)

HOGARTH, Peter Laurence; s of Michael Hogarth, of Perranaworthal, and Joyce, *née* Ponder; *b* 10 July 1949; *Educ* Haileybury; *m* 15 July 1972, Margaret Rosemary, da of Alexander Sidney Alison; 1 s (Ian b 30 Jan 1982), 2 da (Rosemary b 6 June 1983, Juliet b 25 April 1988); *Career* CA 1972; KPMG Peat Marwick 1967–88, Société Générale Strauss Turnbull Securities 1988–90, exec dir London Stock Exchange 1991–92, fndr and dir The Change Partnership Ltd 1994–; memb Cncl Toynbee Hall 1995–; Master Worshipful Co Joiners and Ceilers 1995–96; MSI 1992, FRSA 1992; *Recreations* golf, bridge, chess, cooking; *Style*— Peter Hogarth, Esq; ✉ 6 Frank Dixon Way, Dulwich, London SE21 7BB (☎ 0181 693 8881)

HOGBEN, Dr Neil; s of Eric O'Neill Hogben (d 1984), and Alma, *née* Ault (d 1986); *b* 23 March 1923; *Educ* St Paul's, Univ of Durham (1851 exhibition postgrad res scholarship in naval architecture, BSc, PhD); *m* 1958, Edith Cornelia, da of Wilhelm Leister (d 1971); 1 s (Giles Dominic b 1971), 2 da (Anita Ruth b 1959, Kim Frances b 1960); *Career* history scholarship Magdalene Coll Cambridge (declined due to War Serv) 1941; served WWII: gunner RA 1942–47, 72 Anti Tank Regt N Africa Italy Austria; mgmnt trainee J L Thompson Shipbuilders 1947–51, tech asst Rotol Propeller Co 1951–52; National Physical Laboratory (Ship Div merged to National Maritime Institute 1976 became NMI Ltd 1982): princ scientific offr 1956, sr princ scientific offr (individual merit) 1967, dep chief scientific offr (individual merit) 1979, sr res advsr to NMI Ltd 1983–85; pt/t conslt BMT (British Maritime Technology) Fluid Mechanics Ltd 1985–; RINA: Silver medal (Experience in Computing Wave Loads on Large Bodies) 1974, Bronze medal (Wave Climate Synthesis Worldwide) 1984, Bronze medal (Increases in Wave Heights over the N Atlantic) 1996; ICE George Stephenson medal (Estimation of Fluid Loading on Offshore Structures) 1977, MOD award for Oceanography 1989 (from Soc for Underwater Technol); chm: Environmental Conditions Ctee of Int Ship Structures Congress 1964–70 and 1973–79, Working Gp on Surface Waves for Engrg Ctee on Oceanic Resources 1972–76; FRINA 1967, assoc memb NE Coast Instn of Engrs and Shipbuilders 1956, FEng 1988; *Books* Ocean Wave Statistics (jtly, 1967), Global Wave Statistics (jtly, 1986); contrib to: Advances in Hydroscience Vol 4 (1967), The Sea Vol 9 pt A (1990), Encyclopaedia of Fluid Mechanics Vol 10 (1990); *Recreations* music (piano playing of a sort); *Style*— Dr Neil Hogben, FEng; ✉ 60 Foley Rd, Claygate, Surrey KT10 0ND (☎ 01372 462966); BMT (British Maritime Technology) Fluid Mechanics Ltd, Orlando House, 1 Waldegrave Rd, Teddington, Middlesex TW11 8LZ

HOGBIN, Walter; CBE (1990); s of Walter Clifford John Hogbin (d 1969), and Mary, *née* Roberts; *b* 21 Dec 1937; *Educ* Kent Coll Canterbury, Queens' Coll Cambridge (MA); *m* 1968, Geraldine Anne-Marie, da of Gerald Castley; 2 s (Justin Walter b 1970, Mark Walter b 1972); *Career* dir Taylor Woodrow plc, chm Taylor Woodrow International Ltd; dep chm Overseas Projects Bd 1989–91; European International Contractors: memb Bd 1989–, vice pres 1992–94, pres 1994–; memb Cncl: Export Gp Construction Indust 1980– (chm 1988–90), ICE 1989–92; memb: Advsy Cncl ECGD 1983–88, Overseas Project Bd 1986–88; Col Engr and Tport Staff Corps RE 1986–; CEng, FEng 1994; *Recreations* golf, tennis, gardening; *Style*— Walter Hogbin, Esq, CBE, FEng; ✉ Taylor Woodrow International Ltd, 345 Ruislip Road, Southall, Middx UB1 2QP (☎ 0181 813 0813, fax 0181 231 1000)

HOGG, Sir Christopher; kt (1985); *b* 2 Aug 1936; *Educ* Marlborough, Trinity Coll Oxford (MA), Harvard (MBA); *m* (sep); 2 da; *Career* Nat Serv 1956; IMEDE Business Sch Lausanne 1962, Philip Hill Higginson Erlangers Ltd (now Hill Samuel & Co Ltd) 1963–66, Industrial Reorganisation Corporation 1966–68; Courtaulds plc: joined 1968, dir 1973–, dep chm 1978, chief exec and chm designate 1979, chm and chief exec 1980–91, non-exec chm until July 1996; non-exec chm: Reuters Holdings plc 1985– (non-exec dir 1984–), Courtaulds Textiles plc 1990–95, Allied Domecq plc 1996– (dep chm 1995–96); non-exec dir Bank of England 1992–96, memb International Council of J P Morgan 1988–, memb Bd Smithkline Beecham 1993–; memb: Bd of Tstees Ford Fndn 1987–, Dept of Industry's Industl Advsy Bd 1976–80; chm Royal National Theatre 1995–; hon fell Trinity Coll Oxford 1982; Hon DSc Cranfield Inst of Technol 1986, Hon DSc Aston Univ 1988; Centenary medal Soc Chem Indust 1989, Alumni Achievement award Harvard Business Sch 1989, Gold medal BIM 1986; hon fell Chartered Soc of Designers 1987–; *Recreations* theatre, reading, skiing, walking; *Style*— Sir Christopher Hogg; ✉ Reuters Holdings PLC, 85 Fleet Street, London EC4P 4AJ (☎ 0171 542 7029, fax 0171 542 5874)

HOGG, Rt Hon Douglas Martin; PC (1992), QC (1990), MP (C) Grantham (majority 19,588); s of Baron Hailsham of St Marylebone, KG, PC, *qv* (Life Peer 1970; suc as 2 Visc Hailsham 1950, disclaimed Viscountcy 1963); h to Viscountcy of Hailsham; *b* 5 Feb 1945; *Educ* Eton, Ch Ch Oxford; *m* 6 June 1968, Hon Sarah Elizabeth Mary Hogg (Baroness Hogg, *qv*); 1 s (Quintin b 12 Oct 1973), 1 da (Charlotte b 26 Aug 1970); *Career* pres Oxford Union 1965; called to the Bar Lincoln's Inn 1968; MP (C) Grantham 1979–, PPS to Leon Brittan as chief sec to Treasury 1982–83, asst govt whip 1983–84, Parly under sec Home Office 1986–89, Min of State for Indust and Enterprise 1989–90, Min of State Foreign Office 1990–95, Min for Agriculture Fisheries and Food 1995–; *Style*— The Rt Hon Douglas Hogg, QC, MP; ✉ House of Commons, London SW1A 0AA (☎ 0171 219 3000)

HOGG, Gilbert Charles; s of Charles Hogg and Ivy Ellen Hogg; *b* 11 Feb 1933; *Educ* Victoria Univ Coll Wellington NZ (LLB); *m* 1, Jeanne, *née* Whiteside; 1 s, 1 da; m 2, 1979, Angela Christina, *née* Wallace; *Career* served as Lt RNZAC (TF) 1955–62; called to the NZ Bar and admitted slr NZ 1957, ptnr Phillips Shayle-George and Co slrs Wellington 1960–66, sr crown counsel Hong Kong 1966–70, ed Business Law Summary 1970–72, admitted slr GB 1971, divnl legal advsr British Steel Corp 1974–79; British Gas plc (formerly British Gas Corp): dir of legal servs 1979–84, sec 1984–90, dir of regulatory ops 1990–95; slr and regulatory conslt 1995–; cncl memb Energy Law Section Int Bar Assoc 1991–, memb Professional Ethics Ctee IBA 1994–; chm Pheonix House charity; dir and tstee: Community Housing and Therapy, Charterhouse-in-Southwark charities; *Style*— Gilbert Hogg, Esq; ✉ 73 Ellerby Street, London SW6 6EU (☎ and fax 0171 736 8903)

HOGG, Vice Adm Sir Ian Leslie Trower; KCB (1968, CB 1964), DSC (1941, and Bar 1944); s of Col John M T Hogg (d 1955); *b* 30 May 1911; *Educ* Cheltenham; *m* 1945, Mary Gwynneth Jean, da of Col Cecil W Marsden, MC (d 1973); 2 s (Anthony, Jeremy); *Career* joined RN 1929, served WWII Atlantic, Med, Far E and Normandy, Capt 1953, Cdre Cyprus 1960–62, Rear Adm 1963, Flag Offr Medway and Adm Supt HM Dockyard Chatham 1963–66, Vice Adm 1966, Def Servs Sec 1966–67, Vice Chief of Def Staff 1967–70, ret; Comptroller Royal Soc of St George 1971–74; dir Richard Unwin International Ltd 1975–87; Queen's Award for export achievement 1982; *Recreations* enjoying my grandchildren; *Style*— Vice Adm Sir Ian Hogg, KCB, DSC; ✉ 21 Chapelside, Titchfield, Hampshire PO14 4AP (☎ 01329 847515)

HOGG, James Dalby; s of Sir James Cecil Hogg, KCVO (d 1973), of London, and Lady Hogg; *b* 9 July 1937; *Educ* Eton; *m* 19 Aug 1964, Joan, da of Richard Blackledge; 2 s (James b 1965, Samuel b 1966); *Career* reporter: Bolton Evening News 1960–64, Morning Telegraph Sheffield 1964–65, BBC Manchester 1965–66, BBC Leeds 1967–69, 24 Hours BBC London 1970–72, Nationwide 1972–83, Newsnight 1983–88; writer and presenter of numerous documentaries; *Books* Lord Emsworth's Annotated Whiffle (1991); *Recreations* keeping animals, reading, jazz, trying to play the piano; *Clubs* Drones (NY); *Style*— James Hogg, Esq; ✉ Noon's Folly Cottage, nr Melbourn, Cambs SG8 7NG (☎ 01763 246096); BBC TV, Television Centre, London W12 7RJ (☎ 0181 743 8000)

HOGG, Sir John Nicholson; kt (1963), TD (1946); s of Sir Malcolm Hogg (d 1948, yr bro of 1 Viscount Hailsham and sometime dep chm Bombay Chamber of Commerce, banker and memb Viceroy's Legislative Cncl in India), and Lorna, da of Sir Frank Beaman, sometime High Court Judge Bombay; 1 cous of Lord Hailsham of St Marylebone, *qv*; *b* 4 Oct 1912; *Educ* Eton, Balliol Coll Oxford; *m* 1948, Barbara Elisabeth, yr da of Capt Henry Arden Franklyn (d 1960), of Shedfield, Hants, and wid of Brig Viscount Garmoyle (who d 1942, of wounds received in action); 1 s (Malcolm b 1949), 1 da (Susan b 1954); *Career* served WWII KRRC (Greece, Crete, Western Desert, Tunisia, NW Europe); joined Glyn Mills and Co (later Williams and Glyn's Bank) 1934, md Glyn Mills and Co 1950–70 (dep chm 1963–68, chm 1968–70), dep chm Gallaher Ltd 1964–78, dir Royal Bank of Scotland Group 1970–82, dep chm Williams and Glyn's Bank plc 1970–83, chm Banque Francaise de Crédit Int 1972–83, dir Prudential Corporation Ltd 1964–85; fell Eton Coll 1951–70, memb Cwlth War Graves Cmmn 1958–64, Sheriff County of London 1960, chm ECGD's Advsy Cncl 1962–67, tstee Imperial War Graves Endowment Fund 1965–87, chm Abu Dhabi Investmt Bd 1967–75, pres Eton Ramblers 1976–91; Inst of Child Health: hon treas 1974–87, hon fell 1987; *Style*— Sir John Hogg, TD; ✉ Red House, Botley Road, Shedfield, Southampton SO32 2HN (☎ 01329 832121)

HOGG, Hon Mrs Justice; Hon Dame Mary Claire; DBE (1995); eld da of Baron Hailsham of St Marylebone, KG, CH, PC, *qv*, and Mary Evelyn, *née* Martin (d 1978); *b* 15 Jan 1947; *Educ* St Paul's Girls' Sch; *m* 11 Sept 1987, Eric Koops, *qv*, s of late Lendeert Koops; 1 da (Katharine Mary b 17 March 1989), 1 s (William Quintin Eric b 21 Dec 1991); *Career* called to the Bar: Lincoln's Inn 1968 (bencher 1995), NI 1993; QC 1989, recorder of the Crown Court 1990–95 (asst recorder 1986–90), judge of the High Court of Justice (Family Div) 1995–; govr Univ of Westminster 1992– (govr Poly of Central London 1982–92), tstee The Harrison Homes 1983–; memb Cncl Church of England's Children's Soc 1990–95; Hon LLD Univ of Westminster 1995; Freeman City of London 1981; FRSA; *Style*— The Hon Mrs Justice Hogg, DBE; ✉ c/o Royal Courts of Justice, Strand, London WC2A 2LL

HOGG, Sir Michael David; 8 Bt (UK 1846), of Upper Grosvenor Street, Co Middlesex; s of Sir Arthur Ramsay Hogg, 7 Bt, MBE (d 1995), and Mary Aileen Hester Lee (d 1980), da of late Philip Herbert Lee Evans; *b* 19 Aug 1925; *Educ* Sherborne, Ch Ch Oxford (BA 1950, MA 1953); *m* 21 Jan 1956, Elizabeth Anne Thérèse, da of Sir Terence Edmond Patrick Falkiner, 8 Bt (d 1987); 3 s (Piers Michael James b 25 April 1957, Adam Charles b 1958, Oliver John b 1961); *Heir* s, Piers Michael James Hogg b 25 April 1957; *Career* WWII 1943–45, Capt Grenadier Guards; journalist; The Daily Telegraph 1951–87: ed Peterborough 1971–79, asst ed 1976, arts ed 1979–86, letters ed 1986–87; *Style*— Sir Michael Hogg, Bt; ✉ 19 Woodlands Rd, Barnes, London SW13

HOGG, Min Georgina Rose; MBE (1994); da of Sir Cecil Hogg, KCVO (d 1973), of Harley Street, London, and Pollie Victoria, *née* Dalby; *b* 28 Sept 1938; *Educ* Benenden Sch, Central Sch of Art; *Career* Queen magazine 1960–62, The Observer 1962–67, photographers' and cartoonists' agent 1967–74; fashion ed: Harpers & Queen magazine 1974–79, Sheba magazine 1979–81; ed in chief The World of Interiors magazine 1981–; Magazine Ed of the Year 1984; *Books* The World of Interiors Decororation Book (1988); *Recreations* exploring, the decorative arts, other people's houses; *Style*— Ms Min Hogg, MBE; ✉ 10 Brompton Square, London SW3 2AA

HOGG, Norman; MP (Lab) Cumbernauld and Kilsyth (majority 9,215); *b* 12 March 1938; *Educ* Ruthrieston Secdy Sch; *m* 1964, Elizabeth McCall Christie; *Career* dist offr Nat and Local Govt Offrs Assoc 1967–69, memb Tport Users' Consultative Ctee for Scotland 1977–79; non-exec dir Kelvin Central Buses Ltd 1990–; MP (Lab): E Dunbartonshire 1979–83, Cumbernauld and Kilsyth 1983–; memb Select Ctee: Scottish Affrs 1979–82, Public Accounts 1991–92; Scottish Lab whip 1982–83, Lab dep chief whip 1983–87; oppn front bench spokesman for Scottish Affrs 1987–88, memb Chairman's Panel 1989–; chm Labour Friends of Israel 1993–; *Style*— Norman Hogg, Esq, MP; ✉ House of Commons, London SW1A 0AA (☎ 0171 219 5095)

HOGG, Rear Adm Peter Beauchamp; CB (1980); s of Beauchamp Hogg (d 1964), of Hungerford, Berks, and Sybil, *née* Medley (d 1967); *b* 9 Nov 1924; *Educ* Bradfield; *m* 1951, Gabriel Argentine, da of Argentine Francis Alington (d 1977), of Dorset; 2 s (Christopher b 1954, Gavin b 1960), 2 da (Catherine b 1956, Annabel b 1962); *Career* RN Engrg Branch 1943–80: various appts rising to head Br Def Liaison Staff and def advsr Br High Cmmn Canberra 1977–80, ret as Rear Adm; appeal sec and bursar i/c bldg modernisation Winchester Coll 1980–88, chm Hereford Cathedral Fabric Advsy Ctee 1991–; *Style*— Rear Adm Peter Hogg, CB; ✉ c/o National Westminster Bank, 14 Old Town St, Plymouth PL1 1DG

HOGG, Rear Adm Robin Ivor Trower; CB (1987); s of Dudley William Bruce Trower Hogg, and Lillian Nancy Hogg; *b* 25 Sept 1932; *Educ* New Beacon Sevenoaks, Bedford

Sch; *m* 1, 1958, Susan Bridget Beryl, da of Adm Sir Guy Grantham, GCB, CBE, DSO; 2 s, 2 da; m 2, 1970, Angela Sarah Patricia, da of Brig Rudolph Kirwan, CBE, DSO; *Career* RCDS 1977, RN Presentation Team 1978, Capt First Frigate Sqdn 1979–81, dir Naval Operational Requirements 1981–84, Rear Adm 1984, Flag Offr First Flotilla 1984–86, COS to C-in-C Fleet 1986–88, resigned RN; chief exec and dir Colebrand Ltd 1988, md Raidfleet Ltd; FNI, FIMgt; *Recreations* private life; *Style—* Rear Adm Robin Hogg, CB; ✉ c/o Barclays Premier Banking, PO Box 104, 22/24 Upper Marlborough Road, St Albans AL1 3AL

HOGG, Baroness (Life Peer UK 1995), of Kettlethorpe in the County of Lincolnshire; Sarah Elizabeth Mary Hogg; *née* Boyd-Carpenter; yr da of Baron Boyd-Carpenter, PC, DL (Life Peer), *qv*; *b* 14 May 1946; *Educ* St Mary's Convent Ascot, Lady Margaret Hall Oxford; *m* 6 June 1968, Rt Hon Douglas Hogg, QC, MP, *qv*; 1 s, 1 da; *Career* Economist Newspaper 1968–82; economics ed: Sunday Times 1981–82, The Times 1983–86; presenter and economics ed Channel 4 News 1982–83, dir London Broadcasting Co 1985–90, govr Centre for Economic Policy Research 1985–90, asst ed, business and fin ed The Independent 1986–89, dir National Theatre 1987–90, economics ed The Daily Telegraph and The Sunday Telegraph 1989–90, head of Policy Unit No 10 Downing St with rank of second permanent sec 1990–95; chm London Economics 1997– (dir 1995–); dir: Foreign and Colonial Small Companies 1995–, National Provident Institution 1996–, GKN 1996–; memb: Int Advsy Bd National Westminster Bank 1995–, Cncl Hansard Soc 1995–, Inst of Fiscal Studies 1996–, House of Lords Select Ctee on Sci and Technol 1996–; advsr Bankinter 1995–; Wincott Fndn Fin Journalist of the Year 1985; Hon MA Open Univ 1987, Hon DLitt Loughborough Univ 1992; *Books* Too Close to Call (with Jonathan Hill, 1995); *Style—* The Rt Hon Baroness Hogg; ✉ London Economics, 66 Chiltern Street, London W1M 1PR

HOGGART, (Herbert) Richard; s of Tom Longfellow Hoggart, and Adeline Hoggart; *b* 24 Sept 1918; *Educ* schs in Leeds, Univ of Leeds (MA, LittD); *m* 1942, Mary Holt France; 2 s (one of whom, Simon Hoggart, *qv*), 1 da; *Career* served WWII RA; staff tutor and sr staff tutor Univ Coll Hull 1946–59, sr lectr in English Univ of Leicester 1959–62, prof of English Univ of Birmingham 1962–73 (dir Centre for Contemporary Cultural Studies 1964–73), visiting fell Inst of Devpt Studies Univ of Sussex 1975, warden Goldsmiths' Coll London 1976–84; visiting prof Rochester Univ (NY) 1956–57; hon prof Univ of E Anglia 1984–, Reith lectr 1971; memb: British Cncl Br Books Overseas Ctee 1959–64, BBC Gen Advsy Cncl 1959–60 and 1964–, Pilkington Ctee on Broadcasting 1960–62, Culture Advsr Ctee of UK Nat Cmmn for UNESCO (asst dir gen UNESCO 1970–75), Arts Cncl 1976–81 (chm Drama Panel 1977–80, vice-chm 1980–81), Editorial Bd New Univs Quarterly, Cncl Soc of Authors 1991–; chm: Advsy Cncl for Adult and Continuing Educn 1977–83, Euro Museum of the Year Award Ctee 1977–95, Statesman and Nation Publishing Co 1978–81 (publishers New Statesman), Nat Broadcasting Res Unit 1981–91, The Book Trust 1996–; govr Royal Shakespeare Theatre until 1988; pres Br Assoc Former UN Civil Servants 1979–86; Liveryman Worshipful Co of Goldsmiths; Hon Dès Lettres Univ Bordeaux 1975, Hon DUniv Surrey 1981, Hon LLD Cncl for Nat Academic Awards 1982, Hon LLD York Univ Toronto, Hon DLitt: Open Univ 1973, Univ of Leicester, Univ of Hull, Poly Univ of Leeds 1995, Univ of Keele 1995; hon fell Sheffield Poly 1983, hon fell Goldsmiths' Coll 1985, Hon DUniv East Anglia 1986, Hon Dès Lettres Paris 1987; *Books* The Uses of Literacy (1957), various works on W H Auden, Speaking to Each Other (1970), Only Connect (1972), An Idea and Its Servants (1978), An English Temper (1982), An Idea of Europe (with Douglas Johnson, 1987), A Local Habitation (1988), A Sort of Clowning (1990), An Imagined Life (1992), Townscape with Figures (1994), The Way We Live Now (1995); *Style—* Richard Hoggart, Esq; ✉ Mortonsfield, Beaver's Hill, Farnham, Surrey GU9 7DF (☎ and fax 01252 715740)

HOGGART, Simon David; s of (Herbert) Richard Hoggart, *qv*, of Farnham, Surrey, and Mary Holt, *née* France; *b* 26 May 1946; *Educ* Hymers Coll Hull, Wyggeston GS Leicester, King's Coll Cambridge (MA); *m* 9 July 1983, Alyson Clare, da of Cdr Donald Louis Corner, RN, of Rusper, Sussex; 1 s (Richard b 1988), 1 da (Amy b 1986); *Career* political corr: The Guardian 1973–81 (reporter 1968–71, NI corr 1971–73), Punch 1979–85; The Observer: reporter 1981–85, US corr 1985–89, columnist 1989–93, political ed 1992–93; Parly corr The Guardian 1993–; *Books* incl: The Pact (with Alistair Michie, 1978), Michael Foot: A Portrait (with David Leigh, 1981), On The House (1981), Back On The House (1982), House of Ill Fame (1985), House of Cards (ed, 1988), America - A User's Guide (1990), House of Correction (1994), Bizarre Beliefs (with Mike Hutchinson, 1995), Live Briefs (with Steve Bell, 1996); *Recreations* reading, writing, travel; *Style—* Simon Hoggart, Esq; ✉ The Guardian, 119 Farringdon Road, London EC1R 3ER (☎ 0171 278 2332)

HOGGE, Philip Arthur Fountain; s of Arthur Henry Hogge (d 1952), and Margaret Julia, *née* Large (d 1994); *b* 2 Sept 1941; *Educ* Blundell's Sch Devon, CAT Hamble; *m* 3 Oct 1964, Joyce Ann, da of Herbert Vassall Southby, of Vancouver, Canada; 2 s (Gavin b 1965, Giles b 1972), 1 da (Alice b 1968); *Career* British Airways (formerly BOAC): pilot 1962, Capt 1975, flt trg mangr 707 1978, flt trg mangr 747 1981, mangr flt crew 747 1986, chief pilot 747 1988, gen mangr Op Servs 1991–95; dir Infrastructure Europe Int Air Transport Assoc (IATA) 1995–; Liveryman Guild of Air Pilots and Air Navigators, Freeman City of London; *Recreations* gardening, sailing, steam boating; *Style—* P A F Hogge, Esq; ✉ The Moorings, Wharfe Lane, Henley-on-Thames, Oxon RG9 2LL; International Air Transport Association, Avenue Louise 350, B-1050 Bruxelles, Belgium

HOGGER, Henry George; s of Rear Adm Henry Charles Hogger, CB, DSC (d 1982), and Ethel Mary, *née* Kreiner (d 1973); *b* 9 Nov 1948; *Educ* Winchester, Univ of Cambridge (MA); *m* 21 Oct 1972, Fiona Jane, da of Alexander Patrick McNabb (d 1971); 2 s (Charles b 1984, Harry b 1984), 2 da (Rosalind b 1979, Eleanor b 1982); *Career* joined FCO 1969; third sec Aden 1972, second sec Caracas 1972–75, first sec Kuwait 1975–78, first sec and head of chancery Abu Dhabi 1982–86, dep head of mission and consul gen Amman 1989–92 (cnsllr), high cmmr to Namibia 1992–96; memb Inst of Advanced Motorists; *Recreations* sailing, golf, guitar; *Style—* Henry Hogger, Esq; ✉ Shop Farm House, Briantspuddle, Dorchester, Dorset DT2 7HY (☎ 01929 471491); c/o Foreign and Commonwealth Office, King Charles Street, London SW1A 2AH

HOGGETT, Brenda Marjorie; *see:* Hale, Hon Mrs Justice Brenda Marjorie

HOGGETT, Dr (Anthony) John Christopher; QC (1986); s of Christopher Hoggett (d 1989), and Annie Marie, *née* Barker (d 1991); *b* 20 Aug 1940; *Educ* Leeds GS, Hymers Coll Hull, Clare Coll Cambridge (scholar, MA, LLB), Univ of Manchester (PhD); *m* 1968 (m dis 1992), Brenda Marjorie (Hon Mrs Justice Hale), *qv*, da of Cecil Frederick Hale (d 1958); 1 da (Julia Anne b 1973); *Career* lectr in law Univ of Manchester 1963–69, res fell Univ of Michigan 1965–66; called to the Bar 1969; head of Chambers 1985–, recorder of the Crown Ct 1988–; memb: DOE's Final Selection Bd for Planning Insprs, Editorial Bd Environmental Law Reports; *Recreations* swimming, walking; *Style—* Dr John Hoggett, QC; ✉ 40 King Street, Manchester M2 6BA (☎ 0161 832 9082, fax 0161 835 2139)

HOGWOOD, Christopher Jarvis Haley; CBE (1989); s of Haley Evelyn Hogwood (d 1982), of Saffron Walden, Essex, and Marion Constance, *née* Higgott; *b* 10 Sept 1941; *Educ* Nottingham HS, Skinners' Sch Tunbridge Wells, Univ of Cambridge (MA), Charles Univ Prague; *Career* harpsichordist, conductor, musicologist; fndr memb Early Music Consort of London 1965–76, fndr dir Acad of Ancient Music 1973–, memb Music Faculty Univ of Cambridge 1975–, artistic dir Handel & Haydn Soc Boston USA 1986–, hon prof of music Univ of Keele 1986–90, princ guest conductor Saint Paul Chamber Orch Minnesota USA 1992– (dir of music 1987–92), int prof of early music performance Royal Acad of Music London 1992–, visiting prof Dept of Music King's Coll London 1992–, NSO artistic dir Summer Mozart Festival 1993–; various pubns in jls; Freeman Worshipful Co of Musicians 1989 (Willson Cobbett Medal 1986); Hon DMus Univ of Keele; hon fell: Jesus Coll Cambridge 1989, Pembroke Coll Cambridge 1992; FRSA; *Books* Music at Court (1977), The Trio Sonata (1979), Haydn's Visits to England (1980), Music in Eighteenth-Century England (jtly, 1983), Handel (1984), New Grove Dictionary of Music and Musicians (contrib), The Life of Mozart by Edward Holmes (ed, 1991); *Style—* Christopher Hogwood, Esq, CBE; ✉ 10 Brookside, Cambridge CB2 1JE (☎ 01223 363975, fax 01223 327377)

HOGWOOD, Paul Arthur; s of Robert Thomas Hogwood, of Forest Hill, and Hilda Jesse, *née* Marshall; *b* 18 July 1949; *Educ* Haberdashers' Aske's, Univ of Hull (BSc); *m* 30 Oct 1971, Sylvia Ann, da of Gordon McCulloch (d 1971); 2 s (James b 1978, Christopher b 1980); *Career* CA; audit mangr Coopers & Lybrand 1970–78, project fin asst dir Morgan Grenfell & Co Ltd 1983–86 (chief internal auditor 1978–83), dir Morgan Grenfell Investment Funds Ltd 1993–; co sec: Morgan Grenfell Securities Holdings Ltd 1986–88, Morgan Grenfell Asset Management Ltd 1989–93, Anglo & Overseas Trust plc 1989–, The Overseas Investment Trust plc 1989–, Morgan Grenfell Equity Income Trust plc 1991–, Morgan Grenfell Latin American Companies Trust plc 1994–; FCA 1974; *Recreations* travel; *Style—* Paul Hogwood, Esq; ✉ 15 Ambleside, Epping, Essex CM16 4PT (☎ 01992 570264); Morgan Grenfell Asset Management Ltd, 20 Finsbury Circus, London EC2M 1NB (☎ 0171 545 0036, fax 0171 545 0331, telex 920286 MGAM G, car 0860 257895)

HOHNEN, David Leslie; *b* 19 Jan 1935; *Educ* Merchant Taylors'; *Career* CA 1958; ptnr Somerset Cowper & Co (now Saffery Champness) 1963–; Freeman City of London 1972, Liveryman Worshipful Co of Fruiterers 1972 (Master 1991); FCA 1968; *Style—* David Hohnen, Esq; ✉ Saffery Champness, Fairfax House, Fulwood Place, Gray's Inn, London WC1V 6UB (☎ 0171 405 2828, fax 0171 405 7887)

HOLBEN, Terence Henry Seymour; s of Henry George Seymour Holben (d 1991), and Ivy Blanche, *née* Blomfield; *b* 4 March 1937; *Educ* Mark House Sch, S W Essex Technical Coll, London Coll of Printing; *m* 7 Oct 1961, June Elizabeth, da of Alan John Elliot, of Uckfield, Sussex; 2 s (Matthew Seymour b 1966, Simon Lee b 1969); *Career* Royal Navy 1955–57; advtg art dir: J Walter Thompson 1958–60, McCann Erickson 1960–66, Graham and Gillies 1967–77; Ogilvy and Mather: creative dir 1977–91, dir 1983–91, Euro creative dir 1991–; *Recreations* rowing, wife and two sons; *Style—* Terence H S Holben, Esq; ✉ Oakwood, 19 London Road, Stanford Rivers, Ongar, Essex CM5 9PH; Ogilvy & Mather, 10 Cabot Square, Canary Wharf, London E14 4QB (☎ 0171 345 3000)

HOLBOROW, Christopher Adrian; OBE (1989), TD (1969); s of Rev Canon George Holborow (d 1966), of Northants, and Barbara Stella, *née* Watson (d 1971); 11 in female descent from Sir Richard Gresham, Lord Mayor of London 1537 and father of Sir Thomas Gresham, fndr of The Royal Exchange; *b* 24 Dec 1926; *Educ* Repton, Gonville and Caius Coll Cambridge (MA, MD), Middx Hosp; *m* 1, 1960, Wanda Margaret (d 1982), da of John Douglas Nickels (d 1963), of Bridgnorth; 1 s (John b 1967), 2 da (Caroline (Mrs Simon Beale) b 1961, Emma b 1963); m 2, 1984, Caroline Ann, da of The Rev Edward Percy Woollcombe, OBE (d 1975), of Somerset; *Career* Maj RAMC (RARO) City of London Field Regt RA TA 1955–80, served Germany 1953–55; conslt surgn Westminster Hosp and Westminster Children's Hosp 1964–85; hon consulting surgn Westminster Hosp 1985–; JP 1978–82; chm Cwlth Soc for the Deaf 1984–95 (med advsr 1964–84), pres SW Regnl Assoc for the Deaf 1983–; memb Ct of Assts Worshipful Co of Tallow Chandlers 1988– (Master 1996); Cdr Order of The Republic of The Gambia 1984 (offr 1978); FRCS, FRCSEd; *Recreations* fishing, shooting, travel; *Clubs* Army and Navy; *Style—* Christopher Holborow, Esq, OBE, TD; ✉ Witham House, Witham Friary, Frome, Somerset (☎ 01749 850340, fax 01749 850340); 2/129 Fentiman Rd, London SW8 1JZ (☎ 0171 735 5609)

HOLBOROW, Jonathan; s of Eric John Holborow, of Fingest, Oxon, and Cicely Mary, *née* Foister; *b* 12 Oct 1943; *Educ* Charterhouse; *m* 1, 12 June 1965, Susan, *née* Ridings (d 1993); 1 da (Rachel Katherine b 16 Sept 1971), 1 s (Matthew Daniel b 12 May 1974); m 2, 21 Oct 1994, Mrs Vivien Claire Ferguson; *Career* jr reporter Maidenhead Advertiser 1961–65; reporter: Lincolnshire Echo 1965–66, Lincoln Chronicle 1966–67, Daily Mail Manchester 1967–69; Scottish news ed Daily Mail Glasgow 1969–70; Daily Mail Manchester: northern picture ed 1970–72, northern news ed 1972–74; Daily Mail London: dep news ed 1974–75, news ed 1975–80; ed Cambrian News 1980–82, asst ed then assoc ed The Mail on Sunday 1982–86; dep ed Today 1986–87, dep ed Daily Mail 1988–92 (asst ed then assoc ed 1987–88), ed The Mail on Sunday 1992–, dir Associated Newspapers Ltd; *Recreations* golf, reading, historical churches in SE England; *Style—* Jonathan Holborow, Esq; ✉ The Mail on Sunday, Northcliffe House, 2 Derry Street, Kensington, London W8 5TS (☎ 0171 938 6000)

HOLBOROW, Lady Mary Christina; *née* Stopford; JP (1970); da (by 1 m) of 8 Earl of Courtown, OBE, DL, TD (d 1976); *b* 19 Sept 1936; *m* 8 Aug 1959, Geoffrey Jermyn Holborow, OBE; 1 s, 1 da; *Career* memb Regnl Bd Trustee Savings Bank 1981–89, dir South West Water plc 1989–95; Lord-Lt of Cornwall 1994–; dir Devon and Cornwall Trg and Enterprise Cncl, vice chm Cornwall & Isles of Scilly Health Authy; chm: Cornwall Ctee Rural Devpt Cmmn, Cornwall Macmillan Serv; cmmr St John Ambulance Cornwall 1982–87; DStJ 1987; *Style—* The Lady Mary Holborow, JP; ✉ Ladock House, Ladock, Truro, Cornwall (☎ 01726 882274)

HOLBROOK, David Kenneth; s of Kenneth Redvers Holbrook (d 1968), of Norwich, and Elsie Eleanor Holbrook (d 1956); *b* 9 Jan 1923; *Educ* City of Norwich Sch, Downing Coll Cambridge (BA, MA); *m* 23 April 1949, (Frances Margaret) Margot, da of Charles Davies-Jones (d 1938), of Bedwas, Wales; 2 s (Jonathan b 1956, Thomas b 1966), 2 da (Susan (Suki) b 1950, Kate b 1953); *Career* Lt E Riding Yeomanry RAC 1942–45, serv Normandy Invasion and NW Europe; asst ed Bureau of Current Affrs 1947–52, tutor Bassingbourn Village Coll Cambridge 1954–61, fell King's Coll Cambridge 1961–65, sr Leverhulme res fell 1965, writer in residence Dartington Hall Cambridge 1971–73; Downing Coll Cambridge: asst dir 1973–75, fell and dir of Eng studies 1981–88, emeritus fell 1988; Hooker visiting prof MacMaster Univ Hamilton Ontario 1984, sr Leverhulme res fell 1988–90; Arts Cncl Writers' Grant 1968, 1976 and 1980; memb Editorial Bd Universities Quarterly 1978–86; *Books* Imaginings (1961), English for Maturity (1961), English for the Rejected (1964), The Quest for Love (1965), Flesh Wounds (1966), The Exploring Word (1967), Object Relations (1969), Human Hope and the Death Instinct (1971), The Pseudo-Revolution (1972), Gustav Mahler and the Courage to be (1974), A Play of Passion (1977), Selected Poems (1980), English for Meaning (1980), Nothing Larger than Life (1987), The Novel and Authenticity (1987), Worlds Apart (1988), Images of Woman in Literature (1990), A Little Athens (1990), Jennifer (1990), The Skeleton in the Wardrobe: the Fantasies of C S Lewis (1991), Edith Wharton and the Unsatisfactory Man (1991), The Gold in Father's Heart (1992), Where D H Lawrence Was Wrong About Woman (1992), Charles Dickens and the Image of Woman (1993), Even if They Fail (1994), Creativity and Popular Culture (1994), Tolstoy, Women and Death (1997); *Recreations* oil painting, foreign travel, cooking, gardening; *Style—* David Holbrook,

Esq; ✉ Denmore Lodge, Brunswick Gardens, Cambridge CB5 8DQ (☎ 01223 328341); Downing College, Cambridge (☎ 01223 334800)

HOLCROFT, Charles Anthony Culcheth; s and h of Sir Peter George Culcheth Holcroft, 3 Bt, *qv*; *b* 22 Oct 1959; *m* 28 June 1986, Mrs Elizabeth Carter, yr da of late John Raper, of Four Crosses, Powys; 1 s (Toby David Culcheth b 5 Feb 1990), 1 da (Samara Elisabeth b 29 Aug 1988), 1 step s (Jamie); *Style*— Charles Holcroft, Esq

HOLCROFT, Sir Peter George Culcheth; 3 Bt (UK 1921), of Eaton Mascott, Berrington, Shropshire, JP (Shropshire 1976); s of Sir Reginald Culcheth Holcroft, 2 Bt, TD (d 1978), and his 1 w, Mary Frances, *née* Swire (d 1963); *b* 29 April 1931; *Educ* Eton; *m* 21 July 1956 (m dis 1987), Rosemary Rachel, yr da of late Capt George Nevill Deas, 8 Hussars; 3 s (Charles Anthony Culcheth b 1959, Thomas Marcus Culcheth b 1967, Alexander James Culcheth b 1969), 1 da (Tania Melanie b 1961); *Heir* s, Charles Anthony Culcheth Holcroft, *qv*; *Career* High Sheriff of Shropshire 1969–70; *Style*— Sir Peter Holcroft, Bt, JP; ✉ Berrington House, Berrington, Shrewsbury, Shropshire

HOLDEN, Anthony Ivan; s of John Holden (d 1985), of Southport, Lancs, and Margaret Lois, *née* Sharpe (d 1985); *b* 22 May 1947; *Educ* Oundle, Merton Coll Oxford (MA); *m* 1 May 1971 (m dis 1988), Amanda Juliet, da of Sir Brian Warren; 3 s (Sam b 1975, Joe b 1977, Ben b 1979); m 2, 21 July 1990, Cynthia Blake, da of Mrs Rosemary Blake, of Brookline, Mass, USA; *Career* trainee reporter Evening Echo Hemel Hempstead 1970–73; The Sunday Times: home and foreign corr 1973–77, Atticus column 1977–79; Washington and chief US corr The Observer 1979–81, Transatlantic Cables columnist Punch 1979–81, features ed and asst ed The Times 1981–82, exec ed Sunday Today 1985–86; Br Press Awards: Young Journalist of the Year 1972, Reporter of the Year 1976, Columnist of the Year 1977; freelance journalist and author: Holden At Large column Sunday Express magazine 1982–85, presenter In the Air BBC Radio 4 1982–83; TV documentaries: The Men who Would be King 1982, Charles at Forty 1988, Anthony Holden on Poker 1992, Who Killed Tchaikovsky? 1993; opera translations (with Amanda Holden): Don Giovanni ENO 1985, La Boheme Opera North 1986, The Barber of Seville ENO 1987; *Books* Aeschylus' Agamemnon (translated and ed, 1969), The Greek Anthology (contrib, 1973), Greek Pastoral Poetry (translated and ed, 1974), The St Albans Poisoner (1974), Charles, Prince of Wales (1979), Their Royal Highnesses (1981), Anthony Holden's Royal Quiz - The Penguin Masterquiz (1983), Of Presidents, Prime Ministers and Princes (1984), The Queen Mother (1985, revised edns 1990 and 1993), Don Giovanni (1987), Olivier, A Biography (1988), Charles, A Biography (1989), Big Deal: A Year as a Professional Poker Player (1990), The Last Paragraph: The Journalism of David Blundy (ed, 1990), The Oscars: A Secret History of Hollywood's Academy Awards (1993), The Tarnished Crown: Crisis in the House of Windsor (1993), Power and the Throne (contrib, 1994), Tchaikovsky (1995); *Recreations* music, poker, Arsenal FC, Lancashire CCC; *Clubs* Barracuda, Victoria Casino; *Style*— Anthony Holden, Esq; ✉ Rogers Coleridge & White Ltd, Literary Agents, 20 Powis Mews, London W11 1JN (☎ 0171 221 3717, fax 0171 229 9084)

HOLDEN, Brian Peter John; s of Sir George Holden, 3 Bt (d 1976), and hp of n, Sir John Holden, 4 Bt, *qv*; *b* 12 April 1944; *m* 1984, Bernadette Anne Lopez, da of George Gerard O'Malley; *Style*— Brian Holden, Esq

HOLDEN, Sir David Charles Beresford; KBE (1972), CB (1963), ERD (1954); s of Oswald Addenbrooke Holden (ka 1917), and Ella Mary Beresford (d 1960); *b* 26 July 1915; *Educ* Rossall, King's Coll Cambridge (MA); *m* 1948, Elizabeth Jean, da of Arthur Norman Odling, OBE (d 1975); 1 da, 1 s; *Career* served WWII RA, BEF 1939–40, India, Burma 1942–45; temp Maj; NI Civil Serv 1937–76: sec Miny of Fin 1970–76, head Civil Serv 1970–76, dir Ulster Office London 1976–77; *Style*— Sir David Holden, KBE, CB, ERD; ✉ Falcons, Wilsford Cum Lake, Amesbury, Salisbury, Wilts SP4 7BL (☎ 01980 622493)

HOLDEN, His Hon Judge Derek; s of Frederic Holden, of Sussex, and Audrey Lilian Holden (d 1985); *b* 7 July 1935; *Educ* Cromwell House, Staines GS; *m* 1961, Dorien Elizabeth, da of Henry Douglas Bell, of Sunningdale; 2 s (Derek Grant b 1968, Derek Clark b 1970); *Career* Lt East Surrey Regt 1953–56, ptnr Derek Holden and Co (slrs) 1966–82, recorder 1980–84, circuit judge (SE Circuit) 1984–; pres 1990–92: Social Security Appeal Tbnls, Med Appeal Tbnls, Vaccine Damage Tbnls, Disability Appeal Tbnls; chm Tbnls Ctee of Judicial Studies Bd 1990–92; *Recreations* sailing, rowing, photography, music; *Clubs* Leander, Royal Solent Yacht, Remenham, Staines Boat, Burway Rowing, Eton Excelsior Rowing, Western (Glasgow), Sonata Assoc; *Style*— His Hon Judge Derek Holden; ✉ Kingston Courts Administrator's Office, 10 Sundial Court, Tolworth Rise, South Tolworth, Surbiton, Surrey KT5 9NN

HOLDEN, Sir Edward; 6 Bt (UK 1893), of Oakworth House, Keighley, Yorks; s of Sir Isaac Holden, 5 Bt (d 1962); *b* 8 Oct 1916; *Educ* Leys Sch, Christ's Coll Cambridge, St Thomas's Hosp (MRCS, LRCP); *m* 17 Oct 1942, Frances Joan, da of John Spark, JP, of Ludlow, Stockton-on-Tees; 2 adopted s; *Heir* bro, Paul Holden b 3 March 1923; *Career* conslt anaesthetist Darlington and Northallerton Gp Hosps 1957–74; FFARCS; *Clubs* Farmers'; *Style*— Sir Edward Holden, Bt; ✉ 50 South End, Osmotherley, Northallerton, N Yorkshire DL6 3BL

HOLDEN, Harold Benjamin; s of Reginald Holden (d 1979), and Frances Hilda, *née* Haslett (d 1983); Haslett family built and manned the first lifeboats on the Sussex coast (circa 1880–1910); *b* 2 June 1930; *Educ* Highgate, Charing Cross Hosp Med Sch Univ of London (MB BS); *m* 1, Nov 1963, Ann, da of Archibald Sinclair, of Cardiff; 2 s (Andrew b 1964, Michael b 1970), 1 da (Sarah b 1966); m 2, March 1978, Lydia, da of Dr Ronald James, of Toronto, Canada; 2 s (Benjamin b 1978, Robin b 1979); *Career* surgn; formerly: postgraduate dean Charing Cross Hosp Med Sch, dir ENT Unit Charing Cross and Westminster Hosp Med Sch London (currently hon conslt and sr lectr); fell Harvard Univ; FRCS; *Recreations* yachting, flying, golf; *Clubs* Royal Southampton YC, British Med Pilots Assoc, St Georges Hill GC; *Style*— Harold B Holden, Esq; ✉ ENT Unit, Cromwell Hospital, London SW5 0TU (☎ 0171 460 5784)

HOLDEN, Sir John David; 4 Bt (UK 1919), of The Firs, Leigh, Co Lancaster; s of David George Holden (d 1971, eldest s of Sir George Holden, 3 Bt), and Nancy, *née* Marwood; suc gf 1976; *b* 16 Dec 1967; *m* 29 Aug 1987, Suzanne, *née* Cummings; 3 da; *Heir* unc, Brian Peter John Holden b 12 April 1944; *Style*— Sir John Holden, Bt

HOLDEN, Dr Michael Preston; s of Capt Malcolm Holden (d 1971), and Mary Agnes, *née* Preston (d 1985); *b* 10 May 1939; *Educ* Friends Sch Lancaster, Univ of Leeds (MB ChB); *m* 1 April 1963, Susan Margaret, da of Raymond Ashton, of Wilsden; 1 s (David Mark b 1970), 1 da (Helen Jane b 1967); *Career* lectr in anatomy Univ of Glasgow 1964, first asst cardiovascular surgery Auckland NZ 1973, sr registrar cardiothoracic surgery Leeds 1966, sr conslt cardiothoracic surgn Univ of Newcastle 1974–; sr examiner RCS; FRCS 1967, DObst RCOG 1966, FACN 1982; *Books* Towards Safer Cardiac Surgery (1980), Cardiothoracic Surgery (1981); *Recreations* gardening, horse riding, wood turning, dogs; *Style*— Dr Michael Holden; ✉ Cardiothoracic Department, Freeman Hospital, Newcastle upon Tyne NE7 7DN (☎ 0191 284 3111)

HOLDEN, Patrick Brian; s of Reginald John Holden, of East Hampshire, and Winifred Isabel Holden; *b* 16 June 1937; *Educ* All Hallows Sch, St Catharine's Coll Cambridge (MA); *m* 1972, Dr Jennifer Ruth, da of Francis Meddings (d 1985); *Career* served Royal Hampshire Regt 1955–57, seconded 1 Ghana Regt RWAFF; Fine Fare Group 1960–69 (legal and property dir 1965–69), Pye of Cambridge 1969–74, sec New Towns Assoc 1974–75, dir and sec Oriel Foods Group 1975–81, gp sec Fisons plc 1981–83; chm: Steak Away Foods Ltd 1982–, Ainsfield plc 1991–; non-exec Mortimer Growth plc 1993–; FCIS, FIMgt; *Publications* Map of Tewin and its Rights of Way; *Recreations* bridge, walking, dog training; *Clubs* Naval and Military; *Style*— Patrick Holden, Esq; ✉ The Old School House, Lower Green, Tewin, Welwyn, Herts AL6 0LD (☎ 01438 717573)

HOLDEN, Paul; s of Sir Isaac Holden, 5 Bt (d 1962), and hp of bro, Sir Edward Holden, 6 Bt; *b* 1923; *m* 1950, Vivien Mary, da of late Hedley Broxholme Oldham, of Allesley, Coventry; 1 s (Michael Peter b 1956), 2 da (Judith Margaret (Mrs Tumelty) b 1952, Susan Diana (Mrs Aked) b 1953); *Career* software and quality mgmnt, ret; former chm: Understanding Disability Educnl Tst, Friends of Wey Valley House (Abbeyfield Extra Care Unit); *Recreations* cine and video photography; *Clubs* Lions, Surrey Border Film and Video Makers; *Style*— Paul Holden, Esq; ✉ Glenside, Rowhills, Heath End, Farnham, Surrey GU9 9AU (☎ 01252 24116)

HOLDEN, Robert David; s of Major Hubert Robert Holden, MC (d 1987), of Sibdon Castle Craven Arms, Shropshire, and Lady Elizabeth, *née* Herbert; *b* 14 Jan 1956; *Educ* Eton; *m* 18 June 1988, Susan Emily Frances, da of Sir Joshua Rowley, 7 Bt, *qv*; *Career* chm Robert Holden Ltd 1978–, dir Fine Arts Courses Ltd 1985–; patron of the living of Sibdon; *Clubs* Army & Navy; *Style*— Robert Holden, Esq; ✉ Sibdon Castle, Craven Arms, Salop; 34 Nevern Place, London SW5; Robert Holden Ltd, 15 Savile Row, London W1 (☎ 0171 437 6010)

HOLDEN, Robin John; s of John Holden (d 1985), of Southport, and Margaret Lois, *née* Sharpe (d 1985); *b* 22 May 1942; *Educ* Oundle; *m* 19 Sept 1964, (Margaret) Susan, da of George Ingham Rushton (d 1984); 2 s (Richard Ingham b 10 Dec 1966, Jonathan Robin b 26 April 1969); *Career* Coopers & Lybrand (formerly Cooper Brothers & Co): joined 1959, qualified CA 1964, ptnr 1974–95; non-exec dir The Open Coll; freelance writer; treas and dir Manchester C of C and Indust 1982–95; memb Cncl: ICAEW 1989–95, AAT 1992–95; pres Manchester Soc of CAs 1984–85; FCA 1974 (ACA 1964); *Recreations* travel, theatre, photography, collecting historic bank notes and matchbooks, golf, snooker; *Clubs* Royal Over-Seas League, Manchester Literary & Philosophical Soc, Manchester Luncheon, Manchester Tennis and Racquets, Royal Birkdale Golf, Hale Golf; *Style*— Robin J Holden, Esq; ✉ Tall Trees, Barry Rise, Bowdon, Cheshire WA14 3JS (☎ 0161 928 8700)

HOLDEN-BROWN, Sir Derrick; kt (1979); *b* 14 Feb 1923; *Educ* Westcliff; *m* 1950, Patricia Mary Ross Mackenzie; 1 s, 1 da; *Career* WWII Lt RNVR; CA 1948; vice chm Allied Breweries 1975–82 (dir 1967, fin dir 1972), dep chm Sun Alliance and London Insurance Co 1977–92; chm: Allied-Lyons 1982–91, White Ensign Assoc Ltd 1987–90; chm: Brewers Soc 1978–80, Portsmouth Naval Heritage Tst 1989–; memb Alcohol Educn and Res Cncl 1982–85; memb Ct of Assts Worshipful Co of Brewers; *Recreations* sailing (yacht Aqualeo); *Clubs* Boodle's, Royal Yacht Squadron; *Style*— Sir Derrick Holden-Brown; ✉ Copse House, De La Warr Rd, Milford-on-Sea, Hants (☎ 01590 642247)

HOLDER, Derek Alfred; s of Jesse Alfred Holder, of Isleworth, Middx, and Vera Helen, *née* Haynes; *b* 7 Sept 1951; *Educ* Isleworth GS, Univ of Manchester (BSc); *Career* mgmnt trainee BOAC 1970–71, marketing graduate Ford Motor Company 1974–75, sales mangr then marketing mangr McGraw-Hill Book Company 1975–79, marketing mangr Readers Digest Assoc 1979–80, sr lectr then princ lectr Kingston Poly Business Sch 1980–87, fndr md The Inst of Direct Mktg (IDM) 1987–; creator IDM Dip in Direct Marketing 1981; govr CAM Fndn, chm Educn Cncl Euro Direct Mktg Assoc (EDMA); memb: DMA 1981, Direct Marketing Assoc (USA) 1983; FInstD 1985; *Recreations* squash, running, snooker, world travel; *Style*— Derek Holder, Esq; ✉ The Institute of Direct Marketing, 1 Park Road, Teddington, Middx TW11 0AR (☎ 0181 977 5705, fax 0181 943 2535)

HOLDER, Sir (John) Henry; 4 Bt (UK 1898), of Pitmaston, Moseley, Worcs; s of Sir John Eric Duncan Holder, 3 Bt (d 1986), and his 1 w, Evelyn Josephine, *née* Blain; *b* 12 March 1928; *Educ* Eton, Univ of Birmingham (Dip Malting and Brewing); *m* 1, 10 Sept 1960, Catharine Harrison (d 1994), da of Leonard Baker (d 1973); 2 s (Nigel John Charles b 1962, Hugo Richard b (twin) 1962), 1 da (Bridget Georgina b 1964); m 2, 14 Sept 1996, Josephine Mary Rivett, da of Alfred Ellicott (d 1937); *Heir* s, Nigel John Charles Holder b 6 May 1962; *Career* prodn dir and head brewer Elgood and Son Ltd (Wisbech) 1975–93, ret 1993; chm E Anglian Section Incorporated Brewers' Guild 1981–83; dip memb Inst of Brewing; *Recreations* sailing; *Clubs* Brancaster Staithe Sailing; *Style*— Sir Henry Holder, Bt; ✉ Rosemary Cottage, The Street, Aylmerton, Cromer, Norfolk NR11 8AA

HOLDER, John Wakefield; s of Charles Holder (d 1969), of Superlatine, St George, Barbados, and Carnetta, *née* Blackman (d 1984); *b* 19 March 1945; *Educ* Combermere HS Barbados, Rochdale Coll; *m* Glenda Ann; 2 s (Christopher Paul b 1968, Nigel Anthony John b 1970); *Career* cricket umpire 1983–; playing career: Combermere HS 1959–63, Central CC Barbados 1964, Caribbean CC London 1965, BBC Motspur Park 1965–66, Hampshire CCC 1966–72; professional: Rawtenstall 1974, Norden 1975, Slaithwaite 1976, Royton 1977–78 and 1980–82, Austerlands 1979; test match umpire: debut England v Sri Lanka (Lords) 1988, England v Aust (Edgbaston) 1989, England v Aust (Headingley) 1989, Pakistan v India series (Karachi, Faisalabad, Lahore, Sialkot) 1989, England v NZ (Edgbaston) 1990, England v India (Old Trafford) 1990, England v West Indies (Oval) 1991; Texaco Trophy One Day Int umpire: England v Sri Lanka (Oval) 1988, England v Aust (Old Trafford) 1989, England v India (Headingley) 1990; umpire India Nehru Cup (Delhi, Bombay, Calcutta, Madras, Jullunder) 1989, umpire CBFS Pepsi Champions Trophy 1993; first English umpire with John Hampshire to officiate in a test match series abroad Pakistan 1989; *Recreations* keep fit, supporting Manchester Utd FC; *Style*— John Holder, Esq; ✉ 1 Heald Close, Shawclough, Rochdale OL12 7HJ (☎ 01706 39554); Test & County Cricket Board, Lords Cricket Ground, London NW8 8QZ (☎ 0171 286 4405/6)

HOLDER, Maj Nicholas Paul; TD (1982); s of Air Marshal Sir Paul Holder, KBE, CB, DSO, DFC, *qv*, of Hindhead, Surrey, and Mary Elizabeth, *née* Kidd; *b* 10 Nov 1942; *Educ* Sherborne; *Career* Royal Scots Greys (2 Dragoons) 1963–71, Royal Scots Dragoon Gds Reserve of Offrs 1971–82; cmmnd Inns of Ct and City Yeo Home Service Force 1987–91; assoc dir Kleinwort Benson Ltd 1984–87, dir Fuji International Finance (merchant banking subsid of Fuji Bank Tokyo) 1987–94, dir Silverdale Investment Management Ltd 1994–; memb: Br Jostedhals Glacier Expedition 1967, Br White Nile Hovercraft Expedition 1969; treas Br Ski Mountaineering Assoc; *Recreations* mountaineering, skiing, gardening, tennis; *Clubs* Boodles, Alpine, Lloyd's; *Style*— Maj Nicholas Holder, TD; ✉ 92 Settrington Rd, London SW6 3BA (☎ 0171 736 0072); Siverdale Investment Management Ltd, 137 Station Road, Hampton, Middlesex TW12 2AL

HOLDER, Nigel John Charles; s and h of Sir (John) Henry Holder, 4 Bt, *qv*; *b* 6 May 1962; *Career* open water scuba instructor 1989, master scuba diver trainer 1990, IDC course dir 1993 (staff instructor 1990, master instructor 1992), medic first aid instructor trainer 1993 (instructor 1990), Nitrox instructor 1993; dir Fathom & Blues Ltd 1995–; memb: EATD (European Assoc of Technical Divers), IANTD (Int Assoc of Nitrox and Technical Divers), PADI (Professional Assoc of Diving Instructors); *Recreations* scuba diving, motorcycling; *Style*— Nigel Holder, Esq; ✉ Ashlar Court, 270 Creighton Avenue, East Finchley, London N2 9BQ; Fathom & Blues Ltd (☎ 0181 883 4640, fax 0181 883 2851)

HOLDER, Air Marshal Sir Paul Davie; KBE (1965), CB (1964), DSO (1942), DFC (1941); s of Hugh John Holder (d 1961); *b* 2 Sept 1911; *Educ* Bristol Univ (MSc, PhD), Univ of Illinois USA (Robert Blair Fell); *m* 1941, Mary Elizabeth Kidd; 2 s; *Career* cmmnd RAF 1936, Flt Cdr No 84 Sqdn Shaibah 1937–38, CO No 218 Sqdn Bomber

Cmd 1942, Admin Staff Coll Henley-on-Thames 1949, IDC 1956, AOC Singapore 1957, AOC Hong Kong 1958–59, ACAS (Trg) Air Miny 1960–63, AOC No 25 Gp Flying Trg Cmd 1963–64, AOC-in-C Coastal Cmd, Cdr Maritime Air E Atlantic and Cdr Maritime Air Channel Cmd NATO 1965–68, ret 1968; memb Waverley Dist Cncl 1976–83; FRAeS; *Clubs* RAF; *Style*— Air Marshal Sir Paul Holder, KBE, CB, DSO, DFC; ✉ Innisfree, Bramshott Chase, Hindhead, Surrey GU26 6DG (☎ 01428 604579)

HOLDER, Robert Woollard; s of Frank Douglas Holder, OBE, MC, JP, DL (d 1978), and Cynthia Olive Woollard, *née* Hart (d 1956); *b* 4 Dec 1924; *Educ* Charterhouse, Peterhouse Cambridge (MA); *m* 10 Sept 1949, Margaret Helen, da of Hubert Charles Baker (d 1948); 4 s (Robert George b 26 Sept 1950, Simon Edward b 18 July 1952, James Douglas b 22 June 1954, Benjamin William b 9 Jan 1969), 1 da (Charlotte Helen Cynthia (Mrs Crossley) b 16 July 1956); *Career* War Serv Lt Royal Devon Yeo RA 1943–46; admitted slr 1949; ptnr Dodson and Pulman Taunton 1951–60, md and chm Fairey Co Ltd Heston 1970–77 (Avimo Ltd Taunton 1960–71); chm: Bridport Gundry plc 1975–88, Longclose Ltd Leeds 1983–96, Delta Communications plc 1984–89, Langdon Industries Ltd Taunton 1986–, Bridport-Gundry Ireland Ltd 1988–90, Slades Countrywise Ltd 1996–; dir: Webb Group Ltd 1988–96, Tellabs Ltd (Republic of Ireland) 1988–, Gundrys Ltd (Republic of Ireland) 1994–; memb Ctee on the Intermediate Areas (the Hunt Ctee) 1968–70, chm SW Regnl Cncl CBI 1968–71, memb Cncl CBI 1968–78, memb Eng Industl Estates Corpn 1970–75, chm Industl Ctee SW Regnl Economic Cncl 1972–74; Univ of Bath: treas 1974–84, chm cncl 1984–86, pro chllr 1985–96; chm Ctee for Investmt Lead Times 1977–78, dir Cncl for Small Businesses in Rural Areas 1981–85, memb Wessex Water Authy 1981–86; Hon LLD Univ of Bath 1986; FBIM; *Books* A Dictionary of American and British Euphemisms (1987), The Faber Dictionary of Euphemisms (1989), Thinking About Management (1991), A Dictionary of Euphemisms (1995); *Style*— Robert Holder, Esq; ✉ Langdon Industries Ltd, Walford Cross, Taunton, Somerset

HOLDERNESS, Martin William; s and h of Sir Richard William Holderness, 3 Bt, *qv*; *b* 24 May 1957; *m* 1984, Elizabeth D, da of Dr R Thornton, of 5 Bristow Park, Belfast; 1 s (Matthew William Thornton b 23 May 1990), 1 da (Tessa Elizabeth Mary b 8 Sept 1992); *Style*— Martin Holderness, Esq; ✉ 12 Chapel Road, Worthing, W Sussex BN11 1BJ

HOLDERNESS, Baron (Life Peer UK 1979); Hon Richard Frederick Wood; PC (1959), DL (Yorks E Riding 1967); 3 s of 1 Earl of Halifax, KG, OM, GCSI, GCMG, GCIE, TD, PC, sometime Viceroy of India and Foreign Sec (d 1959), and Lady Dorothy Onslow, CI, DCVO, JP, DGStJ, yr da of 4 Earl of Onslow; unc of present (3) Earl of Halifax, 1 cous of 6 Earl of Onslow; *b* 5 Oct 1920; *Educ* Eton, New Coll Oxford; *m* 15 April 1947, Diana, o da of late Col Edward Orlando Kellett, DSO, MP (ka 1943; whose widow, Myrtle, m as her 2 husb Hon William McGowan, 2 s of 1 Baron McGowan); 1 s (Edward), 1 da (Emma, m Sir Nicholas Brooksbank, 3 Bt, *qv*); *Career* sits as Cons Peer in House of Lords; serv WWII, ME, Lt KRRC 1943, ret severely wounded, Hon Col 4 Bn Royal Green Jackets TAVR 1967–89; MP (C) Bridlington 1950–79; Parly sec to: Min of Pensions and Nat Insur 1955–58, Min of Labour 1958–59, Min of Power 1959–63, Min of Pensions and Nat Insur 1963–64, Min for Overseas Devpt 1970–74; chm Disablement Servs Authy 1987–91, chm Advsy Gp on Rehabilitation 1991–96; dir Hargreaves Group 1974–86; regnl dir Lloyds Bank 1980–89; Hon LLD: Sheffield 1962, Leeds 1978, Hull 1982; *Recreations* gardening, travel; *Style*— The Rt Hon Lord Holderness, PC, DL; ✉ House of Lords, London SW1; Flat Top House, Bishop Wilton, York YO4 1RY (☎ 01759 6266); 43 Lennox Gardens, London SW1X 0DF (☎ 0171 225 2151)

HOLDERNESS, Sir Richard William; 3 Bt (UK 1920), of Tadworth, Surrey; s of Sir Ernest William Elsmie Holderness, 2 Bt, CBE (d 1968); *b* 30 Nov 1927; *Educ* Corpus Christi Coll Oxford (MA); *m* 1953, Pamela, da of Eric Chapman, CBE (d 1985); 2 s (Martin William b 1957, Andrew James b 1962), 1 da (Jane Carleton (Mrs Richard D B Pailthorpe) b 1955); *Heir* s, Martin William Holderness b 24 May 1957; *Career* ret as dist offr HM Overseas Civil Serv 1954; dir Whiteheads (estate agents and surveyors) 1967–86, ret; FRICS 1976; *Recreations* golf, gardening; *Clubs* West Sussex Golf; *Style*— Sir Richard Holderness, Bt; ✉ 1 Tollhouse Close, Chichester, W Sussex PO19 1SE

HOLDGATE, Sir Martin Wyatt; kt (1994), CB (1978); s of Francis Wyatt Holdgate, JP (d 1981), of Lancs, and Lois Marjorie, *née* Bebbington (d 1990); *b* 14 Jan 1931; *Educ* Arnold Sch Blackpool, Queens' Coll Cambridge (BA, MA, PhD); *m* 2 April 1963, Elizabeth Mary, *née* Dickason; 1 s (Nicholas Michael David b 1965); 1 step s (Martin Robert Arnold Weil b 1956); *Career* res fell Queens' Coll Cambridge 1953–56, sr scientist and jt ldr Gough Island Sci Survey 1955–56; lectr in zoology: Univ of Manchester 1956–57, Univ of Durham 1957–60; ldr Royal Soc expdn to Southern Chile 1958–59, asst dir of res Scott Polar Res Inst Cambridge 1960–63, sr biologist Br Antarctic Survey 1963–66, dep dir The Nature Conservancy 1966–70, dir Central Unit on Environmental Pollution DOE 1970–74, Inst of Terrestrial Ecology Natural Environment Res Cncl 1974–76, dir gen of res (and dep sec) DOE and Dept of Tport 1976–83, dep sec (environment protection) and chief environment scientist DOE 1983–88, chief sci advsr Dept of Tport 1983–88, dir gen Int Union for Conservation of Nature and Natural Resources (The World Conservation Union) 1988–94 (chm UK Energy Advsy Panel 1993–96), pres Zoological Soc of London 1994–; jt chm Intergovernmental Panel on Forests 1995–; *Awards* UNEP 500 award 1988, UNEP Silver medal 1983, Bruce medal Royal Soc Edinburgh 1964, Cdr Order of the Golden Ark (Netherlands) 1991, Patron's medal Royal Geographical Soc 1992, Livingstone medal RSGS 1993; Hon DSc: Univ of Durham 1991, Univ of Sussex 1993, Univ of Lancaster 1995; CBiol, FIBiol; *Books* Mountains in the Sea (1958), Antarctic Ecology (ed, 1970), A Perspective of Environmental Pollution (1979), The World Environment 1972–82 (jt ed, 1982), From Care to Action (1996); numerous papers in biological and environmental journals and works on Antarctic; *Recreations* hill walking, local history, natural history; *Clubs* Athenaeum; *Style*— Sir Martin Holdgate, CB; ✉ 35 Wingate Way, Trumpington, Cambridge CB2 2HD (☎ 01223 840086, fax 01223 512131)

HOLDING, Capt Alan Oswald; RN; s of James William Holding (d 1964), and Dorothy Florence, *née* Corney (d 1990); *b* 15 Feb 1935; *Educ* Outram House Sch, Univ of Durham (BSc); *m* 1, 13 Sept 1958, Pauline Frances (d 1989), da of Frederick James Eugene (d 1968); 1 s (Clive b 1962), 1 da (Paula b 1965); m 2, 26 Jan 1995, Dione Morie Hobbs, da of Reginald Herman Willmot (d 1993); *Career* joined RN 1958; promoted: Cdr 1972, Capt 1981; dean RNEC Manadon 1982 (dep dean 1980), chief staff offr to C in C Naval Home Cmd 1984, dir naval educn and training support 1987, chief naval instr offr 1989–; CEng, MRINA; *Recreations* golf, gardening; *Style*— Capt Alan Holding, RN; ✉ Ciboney, 8 Worsley Road, Southsea, Hants (☎ 01705 814224); Ministry of Defence, Whitehall, London SW1

HOLDING, John Francis; s of Francis George Holding (d 1968), and Gwendoline Elizabeth, *née* Jenkins (d 1985); *b* 12 Aug 1936; *Educ* Colwyn Bay GS, LSE (external); *m* 1, 7 Feb 1970 (m dis 1984), Pamela Margaret Straker-Nesbit; 2 da (Sarah Frances b 1971, Julia Ashley b 1974); m 2, 10 July 1993, Susan Ann Clark; *Career* Nat Serv 1955–57; Miny of Housing 1957–63; HM Dip Serv 1964–: Pakistan 1964–66, vice consul Zaire 1970–73, first sec economic Australia 1973–78, The Gambia 1978–80, Barbados and East Caribbean 1984–87, dep high cmmr Bangladesh 1987–90, consul-gen Auckland and dir of UK trade promotion New Zealand 1990–; *Recreations* tennis, sailing, photography, pianoforte; *Style*— John Holding, Esq; ✉ British Consulate-General, 151 Queen St, Auckland, New Zealand (☎ 00 64 9 303 2973, fax 00 64 9 303 1836, telex 2412 BRITN); c/o FCO, King Charles St, London SW1A 2AH

HOLDRIDGE, Ven Bernard Lee; s of Geoffrey Holdridge, of Doncaster (d 1971), and Lucy Medlow, *née* Lee (d 1952); *b* 24 July 1935; *Educ* The GS Thorne, Bernard Gilpin Soc Durham, Theol Coll Lichfield; *Career* ordained: deacon 1967, priest 1968; curate of Swinton 1967–71, vicar of St Jude Doncaster 1971–81, rector of St Mary Rawmarsh with Parkgate 1981–88, rural dean of Rotherham 1986–88, vicar of Worksop Priory with St Mary the Virgin Clumber Park and St Giles Carburton 1988–91, chm Southwell Diocesan Advsy Ctee for the Care of Churches 1991–94, chm Bassetlaw Community and Vol Servs 1991–94, archdeacon of Doncaster 1994–; *Recreations* travel, theatre, a glass of wine with friends; *Style*— The Ven the Archdeacon of Doncaster; ✉ Diocesan Church House, 95–99 Effingham St, Rotherham, S Yorks S65 1BL (☎ 01709 837547, fax 01719 837556)

HOLDSWORTH, Brian John; s of Reginald Hugh Holdsworth (d 1996), of Long Eaton, and Dorothy, *née* Ellis; *b* 27 Jan 1950; *Educ* Southwell Minster GS, Guy's Hosp Med Sch (BSc, MB BS); *m* 21 Sept 1974, Ursula Jean, da of Victor Robert Lees (d 1974), of Roehampton; 3 s (Matthew b 1978, Thomas b 1982, Christopher b 1989); *Career* house jobs Guy's Gp of Hosps 1973–76, registrar in surgery Royal Infirmary Sheffield 1976–78, sr orthopaedic registrar Nottingham Hosps 1981–86 (orthopaedic registrar 1978–81); conslt orthopaedic surgn: Harlow Wood Orthopaedic Hosp nr Mansfield 1986–95, Univ Hosp Nottingham 1986–; FRCS 1978, fell Br Orthopaedic Assoc 1987; *Publications* Frontiers of Fracture Management (contrib, 1989); author various papers on traumatic conditions of the elbow joint; *Recreations* photography, picture framing, growing cacti; *Style*— Brian Holdsworth, Esq; ✉ 32 Victoria Cres, Sherwood, Nottingham NG5 4DA (☎ and fax 0115 960 4142)

HOLDSWORTH, Lt Cdr (Arthur) John Arundell; CVO (1980), OBE (1962), DL (Devon 1973), RN (ret); eld s of Frederick John Cropper Holdsworth, JP, DL, sometime Mayor of Totnes and Master of the Dart Vale Harriers (whose maternal grandmother was Hon Margaret, da of 1 Baron Denman); *b* 31 March 1915; *Educ* RNC Dartmouth; *m* 1940, Barbara Lucy Ussher (d 1996), da of Lt-Col William Acton, DSO; 1 s (Nicholas Holdsworth, *qv*, b 1942), 1 da (Jane b 1945); *Career* served WWII at sea (despatches), Asst naval attaché Warsaw 1947–49; Br Jt Servs Mission Washington DC 1950–51, Naval Staff Germany 1954–56, Flag Lt to Admty Bd 1956–65; gentleman usher to HM The Queen 1967–85 (extra gentleman usher 1985–); steward Newton Abbot Racecourse 1967–85; dep pres Devon Branch BRCS 1971–85 (patron 1985–); High Sheriff Devon 1976–77, Vice Lord Lt Devon 1982–90; *Recreations* gardening, fishing; *Style*— Lt Cdr John Holdsworth, CVO, OBE, DL, RN; ✉ Holbeam Mill, Ogwell, nr Newton Abbot, Devon TX12 6LX (☎ 01626 65547)

HOLDSWORTH, Nicholas John William Arthur; s of Lt Cdr (Arthur) John Arundell Holdsworth, CVO, OBE, DL, RN, *qv*, of Newton Abbot, S Devon, and Barbara Lucy Ussher, *née* Acton (d 1996); *b* 10 May 1942; *Educ* Winchester; *m* 17 Sept 1966, Susan Antonia, da of Charles Anthony Fradgley, of Hill Hay, Combe Florey, Somerset; 2 s (Ben b 7 May 1968, Sam b 5 July 1970); *Career* Rifle Bde 1961–64, Lt; account exec Charles Hobson and Grey 1964–69, account mangr Lintas Ltd 1969–70, account dir Charles Barker Group 1970–84 (dir Charles Barker City 1981–84), dir Dewe Rogerson 1984–; *Recreations* cricket, national hunt racing; *Clubs* MCC, Hurlingham; *Style*— Nicholas Holdsworth, Esq; ✉ 32 Carmalt Gardens, Putney, London SW15 6NE (☎ 0181 788 1240); Dewe Rogerson Ltd, 3 1/2 London Wall Buildings, London Wall, London EC2M 5SY (☎ 0171 638 9571, fax 0171 628 3444, telex 883610)

HOLDSWORTH, Sir (George) Trevor; kt (1981), CVO (1997); s of William Holdsworth; *b* 29 May 1927; *Educ* Hanson GS Bradford, Keighley GS Yorkshire; *m* 1, 1951, Patricia June Ridler (d 1993); 3 s (Anthony, Peter, Nicholas); m 2, 1995, Jenny Watson; *Career* Rawlinson Greaves and Mitchell 1944–51, Bowater Corporation Ltd 1952–63; GKN plc (formerly Guest Keen and Nettlefolds): joined as dep chief accountant 1963, dep chm 1974, md and dep chm 1977, gp chm 1980–88; chm: Allied Colloids Group plc 1983–96, British Satellite Broadcasting 1987–90, National Power plc 1990–95, Beauford plc 1991–, Lambert Howarth Group plc 1993–; dir: Thorn-EMI plc 1977–87, Midland Bank plc 1979–88, Prudential Corporation plc 1986–96 (dep chm 1988–92), Owen-Corning Inc 1994–; CBI: memb Cncl 1974–, memb Steering Gp on Unemployment 1982–83, memb Special Programmes Unit 1982–83, chm Tax Reform Working Party 1984–85, dep pres 1987, pres 1988–90; vice pres: Engrg Employers' Fedn 1980–87, Ironbridge Gorge Museum Devpt Tst 1981–, BIM (now Inst of Mgmnt) 1982– (vice chm 1978–80, chm 1980–82); Fndn for Mfrg and Industry: chm Governing Cncl 1993–, chm of Tstees 1995–; chm: Brighton Festival Tst 1982 (tstee 1980–90), Wigmore Hall Tst 1992–; dep chm Advsy Bd of Inst of Occupational Health 1980; tstee: Anglo-German Fndn for the Study of Industl Soc 1980–92, Royal Opera House Tst 1981–86, Outward Bound Tst 1995–, Br Neurological Research Tst 1987– (chm 1995–); memb: Bd of Govrs Ashridge Mgmnt Coll 1978–92, Engrg Industries Cncl 1980–87 (chm 1985–87), Ct Br Shippers' Cncl 1981–87, British-N America Ctee 1981–85, Cncl Royal Inst of Int Affrs 1983–85, Int Cncl INSEAD 1985–91, Euro Advsy Ctee NY Stock Exchange 1985–; tstee: Overseas Panel Duke of Edinburgh's Award 1988–95 (memb 1980), Duke of Edinburgh's Award UK 1988–; chllr Univ of Bradford 1992–; Freeman City of London 1977, Liveryman Worshipful Co of CAs 1977; Hon DTech Loughborough 1981, Hon DSc Aston 1982, Hon DEng Bradford 1983, Hon DSc Sussex 1988, Hon DSc Birmingham 1992; CAs Founding Socs' Centenary Award 1983, BIM Gold Medal 1987; hon fell City & Guilds of London Inst 1991; FCA, FRSA 1988; *Recreations* music, theatre; *Style*— Sir Trevor Holdsworth, CVO; ✉ Foundation for Manufacturing and Industry, 134 Buckingham Palace Road, London SW1W 9SA (☎ 0171 823 5360, fax 0171 823 5361)

HOLDSWORTH HUNT, Christopher; s of Peter Holdsworth Hunt (d 1996), of London, and Monica, *née* Neville (d 1971); *b* 2 Aug 1942; *Educ* Eton, Univ of Tours; *m* 1, 24 Feb 1969 (m dis), Charlotte Folin; m 2, 24 June 1976, Joanne Lesley Starr Minoprio, *née* Reynolds; 2 s (Rupert Daniel b 10 Sept 1976, Piers Richard b 4 July 1980); *Career* cmmnd Coldstream Gds 1961–64; joined Murton & Adams Stockjobbers 1964 (firm acquired by Pinchin Denny 1969), memb Mgmnt Ctee Pinchin Denny 1985 (ptnr 1971, firm acquired by Morgan Grenfell 1986), dir Morgan Grenfell Securities 1987, fndr Peel Hunt & Company Ltd 1989–; Freeman City of London 1970; memb Ct of Grocers Co 1988 (master 1994–95); *Recreations* opera, ballet, theatre, golf, tennis, walking; *Clubs* White's, City of London, Vanderbilt, Berkshire Golf; *Style*— Christopher Holdsworth Hunt, Esq; ✉ 105 Elgin Crescent, London W11 2JF (☎ 0171 221 5755); Peel, Hunt & Co Ltd, 62 Threadneedle St, London EC2R 8HP (☎ 0171 418 8900, fax 0171 972 0112)

HOLE, The Very Rev Derek Norman; s of Frank Edwin Hole (d 1987), of Crownhill, Plymouth, Devon, and Ella Evelyn, *née* Thomas; *b* 5 Dec 1933; *Educ* Public Central Sch Plymouth, Lincoln Theol Coll; *Career* ordained Leicester Cath: deacon 1960, priest 1961; asst curate St Mary Magdalen Knighton Leicester 1960–62, domestic chaplain to Archbishop of Cape Town 1962–64, asst curate St Nicholas Kenilworth Warwicks 1964–67, rector St Mary the Virgin Burton Latimer Kettering Northants 1967–73, vicar St James the Greater Leicester 1973–92, hon canon Leicester Cathedral 1983–92, rural dean Christianity South 1983–92, provost of Leicester 1992–; chaplain: to the Lord Mayor of Leicester 1976–77, 1994–95 and 1996–97, to Leicester Branch RAFA 1978–92 Leicester HS 1983–92 (govr and tstee 1992–), to HM The Queen 1985–92, to the High Sheriffs of Leicestershire 1980–85 and 1987, to the Master of the Merchant Taylors' Co 1995–96; chm: House of Clergy 1986–94, Leicester Diocesan Redundent Churches Uses Ctee 1985–; vice pres: Diocesan Synod 1986–94, The English Clergy Assoc 1993–; memb Bishop's Cncl 1986–; govr: Alderman Newton's Sch Leicester 1976–82, Alderman Newton's

Educnl Fndn 1992–, Leicester GS 1992–; tstee Leicester Church Charities 1983–, pres Leicester Rotary Club 1987–88; memb: Leicester Charity Orgn Soc 1983–, Victorian Soc 1986–, Actors' Church Union (priest assoc 1995–) and chaplain to Haymarket Theatre 1980–83 and 1993–95; hon life memb Leicestershire Branch Br Red Cross Soc 1995–; *Recreations* music, walking, reading biographies and Victorian history; *Clubs* The Leicestershire, The Royal Western Yacht Club of England; *Style*— The Very Reverend Derek Hole; ✉ The Provost's House, 1 St Martin's East, Leicester LE1 5FX (☎ 0116 262 5294, fax 0116 262 5295)

HOLE, Max; s of Anthony Frederick Hole (d 1975), of London, and Barbara Mary Hole; *b* 26 May 1951; *Educ* Haileybury, Univ of Kent at Canterbury; *m* (m dis) Cynthia; 2 s (Jamie b 23 June 1979, Mark b 24 Jan 1984); partner Jan Ravens (actress); *Career* fndr (with Geoff Jukes): Gemini Artists (clients incl Camel, Mungo Jerry, Arthur Brown), Criminal Records 1976 (signings incl Bram Tchaikovsky, Robin Williamson, Susan Fassbender); mangr: Chris Hughes, Ross Cullum; WEA: A&R mangr 1982–83, dir of A&R 1983–87, md UK div 1987–90; md East West Records (following splitting of WEA into 2 cos) 1990–; *Recreations* walking and boating at my house in Cornwall, watching cricket; *Clubs* MCC, Groucho; *Style*— Max Hole, Esq; ✉ East West Records, Electric Lighting Station, 46 Kensington Court, London W8 5DP (☎ 0171 938 2181, fax 0171 938 5545)

HOLGATE, Peter Alan; s of Harold Holgate, of Leeds, and Ivy, *née* Instrell; *b* 8 Feb 1953; *Educ* West Leeds Boys HS, Univ of Bradford (MSc); *m* 1980, Dr Nelda Elizabeth Frater; 1 s (Andrew b 25 Nov 1985); *Career* articled clerk John Gordon Walton & Co CAs Leeds 1970–74, audit sr and asst mangr Coopers & Lybrand London and Nairobi 1975–78, fin controller Mitchell Cotts Kenya Ltd 1978–79, business planning mangr Hertz Europe Ltd London 1979–81; under sec then sec Accounting Standards Ctee 1981–86; sr tech mangr Deloitte Haskins & Sells 1986–90, accounting tech ptnr Coopers & Lybrand 1990–; author of numerous articles in professional jls, frequent speaker at accounting confs; memb: Fin Reporting Ctee and Res Bd ICAEW 1990–, Main Ctee and Tech Ctee LSCA 1990–93 (chm Tech Ctee 1991–93); memb Accounting Standards Bd's Urgent Issues Task Force; FCA; *Books* A Guide to Accounting Standards - Accounting For Goodwill (1985, updated 1990), A Guide To Accounting Standards - SSAP 23 Accounting For Acquisitions and Mergers (1986), A Guide to Accounting Standards - SSAP 12 revised Accounting for Depreciation (1987), Goodwill, Acquisitions & Mergers (1990), Operating and Financial Review (1994), The Coopers & Lybrand Manual of Accounting (princ author, 1995); *Recreations* music, visiting second hand bookshops, reading; *Style*— Peter Holgate, Esq; ✉ Coopers & Lybrand, 1 Embankment Place, London WC2N 6NN (☎ 0171 583 5000)

HOLGATE, Peter Roy; s of Leonard George Holgate (d 1984), of Sussex, and Phyllis Evelyn, *née* Haynes (d 1995); *b* 24 March 1942; *Educ* Eltham Coll London; *m* 28 June 1969, Carol Priscilla, da of Edward Charles Thewlis; 1 da (Charlotte Amanda b 20 Sept 1972), 1 s (Matthew James b 20 Sept 1974); *Career* chartered accountant; sr ptnr Callingham Crane until 1991, ptnr Kingston Smith (following merger with Callingham Crane) 1991–; memb Cncl ICAEW 1993–; Freeman City of London, Liveryman Worshipful Co of Needlemakers; FCA (ACA 1965), assoc MSI 1994; *Recreations* cricket, gardening, forestry; *Style*— Peter Holgate, Esq; ✉ Kingston Smith, Chartered Accountants, Devonshire House, 60 Goswell Road, London EC1M 7AD (☎ 0171 566 4000, fax 0171 566 4010, mobile 0468 222964)

HOLL-ALLEN, Dr Robert Thomas James; s of Robert Thomas James Allen (d 1988), and Florence Janet Rachel (d 1972); *b* 3 Dec 1934; *Educ* Warwick Sch, Univ of London, Harvard Med Sch (BSc, MD, MS, DLO); *m* 1, 2 June 1962 (m dis 1972), Barbara Mary, da of Leslie Thomas Holl (d 1971); 1 s (Jonathan Guy b 7 April 1966); m 2, 2 March 1974 (m dis 1989), Diana Elisabeth Tootill; 1 s (Robert (Robin) Gerald b 10 Jan 1975), 1 da (Amanda Jane b 23 Nov 1976); m 3, 2 Sept 1992, Julia Anne Gollance, *née* Rush; *Career* house physician UCH 1959, registrar Radcliffe Infirmary Oxford 1963–65, res fell Harvard Med Sch 1968–69, sr surgical registrar W Midland RHA 1966–72, conslt surgn Birmingham Heartlands and Solihull Hosp 1972–96; hon sr clinical lectr Univ of Birmingham; visiting overseas professorships; FRSM 1964, FRCS 1963, FACS 1974, fell Int Coll of Surgeons 1974, memb NY Acad of Scis; *Recreations* golf, travel, good food; *Clubs* Squire, Tennessee; *Style*— Dr Robert Holl-Allen; ✉ 1 Avenbury Drive, Solihull, West Midlands B91 2QZ (☎ 0121 704 4488, fax 0121 704 4488)

HOLLAMBY, Edward Ernest; OBE (1970); s of Edward Thomas Hollamby (d 1979), of Kent, and Ethel May Kingdom; *b* 8 Jan 1921; *Educ* Sch of Building and Arts and Crafts Hammersmith, Univ of London (Dip in Town Planning and Civic Design); *m* 1941, Doris Isabel, da of William John Parker, of London; 1 s (Andrew b 1953), 2 da (Marsha b 1946, Jillian b 1948); *Career* Royal Marine Engrs Far East 1941–46; architect, designer and town planner; sr architect London CC 1949–62, dir of architecture and town planning London Borough of Lambeth 1969–81 (borough architect 1962–69), conslt London Docklands Development Corporation 1985–88 (chief architect and planner 1981–85); town planning projects incl: Erith Township Kent (Thamesmead prototype), Brixton Town Centre, relocation of Covent Garden Market, Isle of Dogs, London Docklands, Wapping and Limehouse, Royal Docks, Becton; works incl conservation of historic bldgs: Brandon Est, Kennington, offices, housing and shops Elephant and Castle, offices and recreation centre Brixton, major and minor housing devpts Lambeth, Christopher Wren and Burlington Schs Hammersmith, special schs for handicapped children Brixton and Kennington, holiday home for disabled Netley, public library and civic hall W Norwood; numerous design awards including 2 DOE Bronze medals; RIBA: memb Cncl 1961–72, hon treas 1967–70, memb NW Kent Branch SE Region; vice pres London Forum of Civic and Amenity Socs; memb: Historic Bldgs Cncl for Eng 1971–83, London Advsy Ctee Eng Heritage 1986–90, London Borough of Bexley Cons Consultative Ctee; fndr memb: William Morris Soc, Bexley Civic Soc; FRIBA, FRTPI, FCSD, FRSA; hon assoc Landscape Institute; *Books* Docklands Heritage - A Study in Conservation and Regeneration in London Docklands (1987), London Docklands - Backyard into Frontyard (pamphlet, 1990), Red House Bexleyheath 1859 - The Home of William Morris (1990); *Recreations* travel, music, theatre, opera, gardening; *Clubs* Arts; *Style*— Edward Hollamby, OBE; ✉ Red House, Red House Lane, Upton, Bexleyheath, Kent (☎ 0181 303 8808)

HOLLAND, (John) Anthony; s of Maj John Holland, of Cornerways, Southella Rd, Yelverton, Devon, and Dorothy Rita, *née* George; *b* 9 Nov 1938; *Educ* Ratcliffe Coll Leics, Univ of Nottingham (LLB); *m* 1 June 1963, Kathleen Margaret (Kay), da of John Smellie Anderson (d 1978); 3 s (Andrew John, Christopher Iain, Nicholas Alexander); *Career* admitted slr 1962, currently ptnr Foot & Bowden Plymouth; chm: Social Security Appeals Tbnl, Regnl Advsy Cncl BBC SW 1984–87, Plymouth C of C and Indust 1994–96; a chm Securities and Futures Authy 1993–; govr Coll of Law 1991–; hon slr and memb Cncl Howard League for Penal Reform, memb Cncl of Justice 1991–, memb Marre Ctee; pres: Plymouth Law Soc 1986, Cornwall Law Soc 1988; hon memb Soc of Public Teachers of Law 1992; memb Law Soc 1962 (elected to Cncl 1976, vice pres 1989, pres 1990); *Books* Principles of Registered Land Conveyancing (1968), Landlord and Tenant (1970), Mines and Quarries Section Butterworths Encyclopedia of Forms and Precedents (jt consulting ed, 1989–), Cordery on Solicitors (gen ed, 9 edn); *Recreations* opera, travel, sailing; *Clubs* Royal Western Yacht of England; *Style*— Anthony Holland, Esq; ✉ 46 Thornhill Way, Mannamead, Plymouth PL3 5NP (☎ 01752 220529); 66 Andrewes House, Barbican, London EC2Y 8AY (☎ 0171 638 5044); Foot & Bowden, 21 Derrys Cross, Plymouth PL1 2SW (☎ 01752 675000, fax 01752 671802, telex 45223)

HOLLAND, Ashley James Mainwaring; s of Barrie Holland, and Jayne, *née* Stracey; *b* 2 April 1968; *Educ* Univ of Warwick (BA), RNCM (Sybil Tutton Award, Curtis Gold Medal); *Career* baritone; studies with Robert Alderson; Scottish Opera 1989–92, RNCM 1993–95, co princ ENO 1995–; winner Frederick Cox competition 1993, winner Webster-Booth/ESSO competition 1994, Eng entrant Cardiff Singer of the World 1995, finalist Placido Domingo World Opera Contest Madrid 1995, finalist Leonard Bernstein Int Oratorio and Song Competition Jerusalem 1996 *Performances* roles at Scottish Opera incl: Benze in Madama Butterfly, Yamadori in Madama Butterfly, Bosun in Billy Budd, Benoit in La Bohème, Dunois in The Maid of Orleans, Don Carlo in Ernani; roles at ENO incl: Morales in Carmen, Mandarin in Turandot, Sciarrone in Tosca, 2 Nazarene in Salome, Baron Douphol in La Traviata, Zurga in Pearl Fishers, Sharpless in Madama Butterfly; other roles incl: Smirnov in The Bear (UKLA Festival) 1994, Marcello in La Bohème (LaTour Festival France), Zurga in Pearl Fishers (Kenwood House); concert repertoire incl: The Messiah, Verdi Requiem, Brahms Requiem, Mahler Symphony No 8, Beethoven Symphony No 9, the Dream of Gerontius, Belshazzar's Feast, Mahler Ruckert-Lieder, Stanford Songs of the Fleet, Delius Sea Drift; *Recreations* watching films, reading, listening to music; *Style*— Ashley Holland, Esq; ✉ c/o Susannah MacAlpine, IMG Artists, Media House, 3 Burlington Lane, Chiswick, London W4 2TH (☎ 0181 747 9977, fax 0181 233 5801)

HOLLAND, Barry K; s of Frank Hope Holland, of Wallasey, Merseyside, and Mary, *née* Kay; *b* 6 Feb 1947; *Educ* Wallasy GS, Univ of Nottingham (LLB); *m* 1 Dec 1973, Lois Bradley, da of Dr T H H Green, of Wallasey, Merseyside; 2 s (James b 7 Aug 1974, Benjamin b 13 Nov 1975), 2 da (Samantha b 15 Aug 1969, Nathalie b 25 Feb 1972); *Career* admitted slr 1970, NP 1980; ptnr Percy Hughes & Roberts 1972–85, sole princ Hollands 1985–86; ptnr: Davies Wallis 1986–91, Elliott & Co 1991–; fndr chm The Caldy Soc 1985–; memb Law Soc 1970; *Style*— Barry K Holland, Esq; ✉ Butts Mead, East Farm Mews, Caldy, Wirral L48 1QB (☎ 0151 625 7413); Elliott & Co, Centurion House, Deansgate, Manchester M3 3WT (☎ 0161 834 9933, fax 0161 832 3693, car 0831 835360)

HOLLAND, Hon Mr Justice; Hon Sir Christopher John Holland; kt (1992); s of Frank Holland (d 1979), of Leeds, and Winifred Mary, *née* Pigott (d 1984); *b* 1 June 1937; *Educ* Leeds GS, Emmanuel Coll Cambridge (MA, LLB); *m* 11 Feb 1967, Jill Iona; 1 s (Charles Christopher b 20 May 1969), 1 da (Victoria Joanna b 1 June 1971); *Career* Nat Serv 3 Royal Tank Regt 1956–58; called to the Bar Inner Temple 1963, practised NE Circuit, QC 1978, bencher Inner Temple 1985; vice chm Ctee of Inquiry into the Outbreak of Legionnaires' Disease at Stafford 1985; chm Lower Washburn Parish Cncl 1976–91; recorder NE Circuit 1992, judge of the High Court of Justice (Queen's Bench Div) 1992–, presiding judge NE Circuit 1993–97; memb Criminal Injuries Compensation Bd 1992, judge Employment Appeal Tbnl 1994–; *Style*— The Hon Mr Justice Holland; ✉ Royal Courts of Justice, London WC2A 2LL

HOLLAND, Rt Rev Edward; *see:* Colchester, Bishop of

HOLLAND, (Robert) Einion; s of Robert Ellis Holland, and Bene, *née* Williams; *b* 23 April 1927; *Educ* Univ Coll N Wales Bangor (BSc); *m* 1955, Eryl Haf (d 1988); 1 s (Gareth), 2 da (Sian, Eluned); *Career* Pearl Assurance plc: joined 1953, chief mangr 1977–83, dir and chm 1983–89; dir: Aviation and General Insurance Co Ltd 1973–89, Pearl Assurance (Unit Funds) Ltd 1975–89, Crawley Warren Group plc, New London Properties Ltd 1984–89, Queens Ice Skating Ltd 1984–89, Pearl Group plc 1986–90 (chm 1986–89), BR Property Board 1987–90; memb Cncl Univ of Wales 1990–; FIA; *Recreations* golf, Welsh lit; *Style*— Einion Holland, Esq

HOLLAND, Sir Geoffrey; KCB (1989, CB 1984); s of late Frank Holland, CBE, and Elsie Freda, *née* Smith; *b* 9 May 1938; *Educ* Merchant Taylors', St John's Coll Oxford (MA); *m* 1964, Carol Ann, da of Sidney Challen (d 1982); *Career* joined Miny of Labour 1961, asst private sec 1964–65, princ private sec to Sec of State for Employment 1971–72; Manpower Servs Cmmn: head of Planning 1973, dir of Special Programmes 1977, dep sec 1981, dir 1981, second perm sec 1986; conslt Industrial Ctee C of E Bd of Social Responsibility 1985–, perm sec Employment Dept Group (formerly Dept of Employment) 1988–93, perm sec DFE 1993–94, vice chllr Univ of Exeter 1994–; hon fell: Polytechnic of Wales 1986, Inst of Training Devpt 1986, St John's Coll Oxford 1991; Liveryman Merchant Taylors' Co 1967–; CIMgt 1987; *Publications* Young People and Work (1977); author of many articles on manpower, education and training; *Recreations* journeying, opera, exercising the dog; *Clubs* East India; *Style*— Sir Geoffrey Holland, KCB; ✉ The University, Exeter EX4 4QJ (☎ 01392 263263)

HOLLAND, Sir Guy Hope; 3 Bt (UK 1917), of Westwell Manor, Co Oxford; yr s of Sir (Alfred Reginald) Sothern Holland, 1 Bt, JP (d 1948), and Stretta Aimee, *née* Price (d 1949); suc er bro, Sir Jim Sothern Holland, 2 Bt, TD, 1981; descended from the Holland family of Pendleton, Lancashire, as recorded at the College of Arms; *b* 19 July 1918; *Educ* privately, ChCh Oxford; *m* 12 May 1945, Joan Marianne, da of late Capt Herbert Edmund Street, 20 Hussars; 2 da (Davina Huntly (Mrs Guy T G Conant) b 1946, Georgiana (Mrs Nicholas A N S Robertson) b 1951); *Heir* none; *Career* late Capt Royal Scots Greys; farmer; art dealer; *Recreations* hunting, shooting, gardening, travel; *Clubs* Boodle's, Pratt's; *Style*— Sir Guy Holland, Bt; ✉ Sheepbridge Barn, Eastleach, Cirencester, Glos GL7 3PS (☎ 01367 850296)

HOLLAND, John Lewis; s of George James Holland (d 1988), of Notts, and Esther, *née* Swindell (d 1993); *b* 23 May 1937; *Educ* Nottingham Tech GS; *m* 1958, Maureen Ann, da of Leonard Adams (d 1973), of Notts; 1 s (Jeremy b 1965), 1 da (Lesley b 1959); *Career* reporter Nottingham Evening News 1954, sports ed Aldershot News Group 1956, sub ed Bristol Evening Post 1964, ed West Bridgford and Clifton Standard 1966, dep sports ed Birmingham Evening Mail 1972; ed: Sandwell Evening Mail 1979 (gen mangr 1981), The Birmingham Post 1984–90, Birmingham Post and Evening Mail 1986–90 (promotions dir); md Herts and Essex Newspapers Ltd 1990–; pres Chiltern Newspaper Proprietors Assoc 1995–; *Recreations* sport (playing golf), gardening, DIY, horses; *Clubs* Hertford Club, Heydon Grange Golf and Country Club; *Style*— John Holland, Esq; ✉ Malting House, Malting Lane, Litlington, nr Royston, Herts; 5 Maistrali II, Protaras, Cyprus; Herts and Essex Newspapers Ltd, 1 Fore Street, Hertford SG14 1DB

HOLLAND, Julian Miles (Jools); s of Derek Holland, of London, and June Rose, *née* Lane; *b* 24 Jan 1958; *Educ* Park Walk Sch, Invicta Sherington Sch, Shooters' Hill Sch; *partner* 1 (until 1986), Mary Leahy; 2 c (George Soloman b 14 April 1984, Rosie Areatha Mae b 1 Oct 1985; *partner* 2, Christabel Durham; 1 da (Mabel Ray Brittania b 22 Nov 1990); *Career* pianist 1975–78; keyboard player Squeeze 1978– (hits incl Take Me I'm Yours, Cool for Cats, Up The Junction, Hourglass, Annie Get Your Gun, Pulling Mussels from a Shell, Tempted, Slap and Tickle), regularly tours UK and US, concerts at Madison Square Garden and Royal Albert Hall; solo albums: A World of His Own 1990, Full Compliment 1991, A-Z Of Piano 1993, Live Performance 1995, Solo Piano 1995; guest performances with numerous artists incl: Elvis Costello, Sting, Al Green, Dr John, The The, Fine Young Cannibals, George Harrison; TV Presenter: The Tube (Channel 4) 1981–86, Juke Box Jury (BBC 2) 1989, Sunday Night (with David Sanborn, NBC) 1990, The Happening (BSB) 1990, Later With Jools Holland (series, BBC 2) 1993–; actor and writer The Groovy Fellers (Channel 4) 1988, wrote and produced films Walking To New Orleans 1985 and Mr Roadrunner (Channel 4) 1991; *Recreations* sketching, giving advice; *Style*— Jools Holland, Esq; ✉ Helicon Mountain Ltd, Helicon Mountain, Station Terrace Mews, London SE3 7LP (☎ 0181 858 0984, fax 0181 293 4555)

HOLLAND, Sir Kenneth Lawrence; kt (1981), CBE (1971), QFSM (1974); s of Percy Lawrence Holland (d 1966), of Colwyn Bay, Wales; *b* 20 Sept 1918; *Educ* Whitcliffe Mount GS Yorks; *m* 1941, Pauline Keith, da of George Mansfield (d 1925), of Oldham; 2 s, 1 da; *Career* entered fire serv Lancs 1937; chief fire offr: Bristol 1960–67, W Riding Yorks 1967–72; HM chief inspr of Fire Servs 1972–80; dir Gent Ltd Leicester 1981–, chm Loss Prevention Certification Bd Ltd 1984–; chm: Fire Services Central Examinations Bd 1978–84, Loss Prevention Certification Bd 1984–, Firelaw Ltd 1988–; tstee Fire Services Res and Trg Tst 1983–; hon treas Poole Arts Fedn (Friends of the Poole Arts Centre 1985–); OStJ 1964; pres Assoc Structure Fire Protection Contractors and Manufacturers; memb BS2 Bd, chm BSI Multitechnics cncl 1984–; *Recreations* motor sport, the arts (especially theatre); *Clubs* St John House, Royal Over-Seas League; *Style*— Sir Kenneth Holland, CBE, QFSM

HOLLAND, Nigel; s of Beatrice Marjorie Diana Holland; *b* 28 April 1954; *Educ* Tong Comp Bradford, Bradford Regnl Coll of Art (Fndn Course), Hull Regnl Coll of Art (BA), Richmond Coll Sheffield and Wednesbury (press photography cert); *m* (m dis); 1 s (Jason Carl b 1 Jan 1982); 2 da (Carly Jane b 15 July 1984, Jodie Lynn b 8 May 1986); *Career* photographer; trainee Hull Daily Mail 1977–80, Jack Hickes Press Agency Leeds 1980–81, Evening Argus Brighton 1981–85, The Yorkshire Evening Press 1985–; *Exhibitions* Land of Green Ginger (Rotterdam) 1977, 50 from 82 (Brighton Poly) 1983, Our Henry (30–page supplement Yorkshire Evening Press and exhbn 1993), Henry - Next World Champ (Barbican) 1993; *Awards* winner Southern Press Awards 1982, winner Sports Cncl Theme Section Yorkshire & Humberside 1986, winner Yorkshire TV Press & Publicity Awards 1986, Yorkshire Press Photographer of the Year 1987 and 1996, Yorkshire Press Journalist of the Year 1996, shortlisted UKPG Sports Photographer of the Year 1996, UK Picture Editors Guild Regnl Photographer of the Year 1996; *Books* Wembley Wonders (1996); *Recreations* football, furniture restoration, carpentry, art; *Style*— Nigel Holland, Esq; ✉ c/o Picture Desk, Yorkshire Evening Press, PO Box 29, 76–86 Walmgate, York YO1 1YN (☎ 01904 653051, mobile 0585 661025)

HOLLAND, Peter Rodney James; s of Arthur Giles Stewart Holland (d 1981), and Elizabeth Hamilton, *née* Simpson; *b* 31 July 1944; *Educ* St Edmund's Canterbury, Univ Coll Oxford (MA); *m* 16 May 1975, Susan Elizabeth, da of Frederick Roger Okeby (d 1987); 1 s (William), 1 da (Philippa); *Career* admitted slr 1968, ptnr Allen & Overy 1972–; chm Co Law Ctee Law Soc 1983–87, memb Clergy Orphan Corporation 1993–; govr: St Edmund's Canterbury 1993–, St Margaret's Bushey 1993–96; *Recreations* skiing, outdoor activities; *Style*— Peter Holland, Esq; ✉ Long Sutton, Hook, Hants, RG29 1SS; Allen & Overy, One New Change, London EC4M 9QQ (☎ 0171 330 3000, fax 0171 330 9999)

HOLLAND, Sir Philip Welsby; kt (1983); s of late John Holland, of Middlewich, Cheshire; *b* 14 March 1917; *Educ* Sir John Deane's Sch Northwich; *m* 1943, Josephine Alma, da of Arthur Hudson, of Plymouth; 1 s; *Career* RAF 1936–46, cmmnd Electrical Engrg Branch 1943; memb Cncl Kensington 1955–59, fndr memb Cons Cwlth Cncl; MP (C): Acton 1959–64, Nottinghamshire (Carlton) 1966–83, Gedling 1983–87; PPS to: Min of Pensions and Nat Insur 1961–62, Chief Sec to Treasy 1962–64, Min for Aerospace 1970–72, Min for Trade and Indust 1972–74; chm Ctee of Selection 1979–84, memb Mr Speaker's Panel of Chairmen 1983–87; personnel mangr ULTRA Electronics Gp of Cos 1964–66, personnel conslt Standard Telephones and Cables 1969–81; rector's warden St Margaret's Church Westminster Abbey 1990–95; *Books* The Quango Explosion (1978), Quango Quango Quango (1979), The Governance of Quango (1981), Quelling the Quango (1982), Lobby Fodder (1988), St Margaret's, Westminster (1993), The Hunting of the Quango (1994); *Style*— Sir Philip Holland; ✉ 53 Pymers Mead, West Dulwich, London SE21 8NH

HOLLAND, Robert Matthew Crowder; s of Maj Charles Matthew Holland (d 1959), and Roberta Violet Holland, JP, *née* Crowder; *b* 18 May 1948; *Educ* St Philip's GS Birmingham, Birmingham Art Coll, Oxford Poly Sch of Architecture; *m* 22 Sept 1973, Philippa Madeleine, da of Wilfred Tracy (d 1980); 2 s (Matthew, Thomas), 1 da (Elizabeth); *Career* bd dir CG Smedley & Assocs Ltd Advertising Agency 1978–89, prop The Holland Owen Partnership 1989–95, bd dir The Birmingham Media Devpt Agency Ltd 1989–; memb Cncl Birmingham Publicity Assoc (chm 1987–88) 1982–94; hon sec Edgbaston Archery and Lawn Tennis Soc (the oldest lawn tennis club in the world) 1987– (chm 1991–93), hon trophies sec Warwicks Lawn Tennis Assoc 1989–, fndr and managing ed Network tennis magazine 1995–; *Recreations* tennis, swimming, walking, photography, reading; *Style*— Robert Holland, Esq; ✉ c/o Edgbaston Archery and Lawn Tennis Society, 14A Westbourne Road, Edgbaston, Birmingham B15 3TR (☎ 0121 454 2846)

HOLLAND, Thelma; da of William Gordon Holland, of Biddulph, Staffs, and Dorothy Mary, *née* Stoddard (d 1977); *b* 9 Oct 1949; *Educ* Biddulph GS, Univ of Southampton/St Thomas' Hosp London (RGN, RHV Cert in Community Care), Open Univ (MBA); *partner* Colin Walker; *Career* VSO Madras Tamil Nadu S India 1973–75, nursing offr 1975–77, SNO 1977–82, dir of nursing servs S Nottingham Health District 1982–85, change mgmnt conslt NHS Trg Authy 1985–87, independent mgmnt conslt 1987–90, gen mangr/chief exec Nottingham City Hosp NHS Tst 1990–; dir Gtr Nottingham TEC 1995–, govr Clarendon Coll Nottingham 1995–; *Recreations* sailing, amateur theatre; *Style*— Ms Thelma Holland; ✉ Nottingham City Hospital NHS Trust, Hucknall Road, Nottingham NG5 1PB (☎ 0115 969 1169, fax 0115 962 7788, mobile 0850 707067)

HOLLAND, Prof Walter Werner; CBE (1992); s of Henry H Holland (d 1959), of London, and Hertha, *née* Zentner; *b* 5 March 1929; *Educ* Rugby, Univ of London, St Thomas' Hospital Med Sch (BSc, MB BS, MD); *m* 29 Oct 1964, Fiona, da of Douglas C Love (d 1976), of Bristol; 3 s (Peter b 1965, Richard b 1967, Michael b 1970); *Career* Flying Offr and Flt Lt RAF 1956–58; res fell: MRC 1959–61, Johns Hopkins Univ Baltimore USA 1961–62; prof (former sr lectr and reader) St Thomas's Hosp 1962–94 (casualty offr 1955–56), visiting professorial fell LSE Health London Sch of Economics 1995–, chm Euro Health Policy Network 1996–; author of over 315 articles and books; inaugural lectr Johns Hopkins Univ 1977 (elected lifetime memb Soc of Scholars 1970), Fogarty Scholar-in-Residence NIH Bethesda USA 1984–85, Theodore Badger visiting prof Harvard Univ Cambridge USA 1984, first Sawyer Scholar in Res Case Western Reserve Med Sch Cleveland USA 1985, Europe et Médecine Prize Institut des Sciences de la Santé 1994, Queen Elizabeth The Queen Mother lectr Faculty of Public Health Med RCP 1995, Harben lectr Royal Inst of Public Health 1995, Cruickshank lectr Int Epidemiological Assoc 1996, Rock Carling lectr Nuffield Provincial Hosps Tst 1996/97; pres Int Epidemiological Assoc 1987–90, pres Faculty of Public Health Med 1989–92, vice chm W Lambeth Health Authy 1983–86, hon memb American Epidemiological Soc 1985; Hon DUniv Bordeaux Univ 1981, Hon DUniv Free Univ of Berlin 1990; memb: RSM, Soc for Social Med, Royal Statistical Soc, Int Union Against Tuberculosis, Int Epidemiological Assoc; FFPHM, FRCPE, FRCPath, FRCP, FRCGP, FFPHMI; *Clubs* Athenaeum; *Style*— Prof Walter Holland, CBE; ✉ 11 Ennerdale Rd, Kew, Richmond, Surrey TW9 3PG

HOLLAND, Wright Henry (Harry); s of Joseph Holland (d 1942), of Glasgow, and Joan Rose, *née* Goddard; *b* 11 April 1941; *Educ* Rutlish Sch Merton, St Martin's Sch of Art (DipAD); *m* Maureen, da of Lucien Coulson; 2 da (Samantha Joan b 18 June 1964, Emma Corinna b 6 May 1967); *Career* artist; lectr 1969–78 (Coventry, Hull, Stourbridge, Cardiff); *Solo Exhibitions* Roundhouse Gallery 1979, Oriel Gallery Cardiff 1979, Welsh Arts Cncl Touring Exhibition 1980, Mineta Move Gallery Brussels 1981, Robin Garton Gallery London 1982 and 1983, Arnold Katzen Gallery NY 1982, FIAC Paris (Mineta Move) 1983 and 1984, Ian Birksted Gallery 1984, Artiste Gallery Bath 1985, Edinburgh Demarcations (Garton & Cooke) 1985, Chicago Art Fair (Ian Birksted Gallery) 1986, New Drawings (Birksted Gallery) 1986, Andrew Knight Gallery Cardiff 1987, Bohun Gallery Henley 1987, 1989, Thumb Gallery 1988, 1990, Garton & Co 1988, Forum Art Fair Hamburg (Thumb Gallery) 1989, Beaux Arts Bath 1993; *Gp Exhibitions* incl: Aspects of Realism 1976–78, From Wales 1977, Fruitmarket Gallery Edinburgh 1977, Nat Eisteddfod of Wales (prizewinner) 1978, Grandes et Jeunes d'Aujourd'hui (Grand Palais Paris) 1979, Probity of Art (Welsh Arts Cncl touring exhibition) 1980, Br Art Show (Arts Cncl of GB) 1980, Art of the Eighties (Walker Art Gallery) 1981, Euro Print Biennale Heidelberg 1983, The Male Nude (Ebury Gallery) 1983, Bradford Print Biennale 1984, second Int Contemporary Art Fair 1985, Int Contemporary Art Fair LA (Thumb Gallery) 1986, 1987 and 1988, Bruton Gallery 1987, Self Portrait - A Modern View (touring) 1987, The Drawing Show (Thumb Gallery) 1988, Ways of Telling (Mostyn Gallery Wales) 1989, Fourth Int Contemporary Art Fair LA (Thumb Gallery) 1989; *Collections* Contemporary Art Soc, Tate Gallery, Newport Museum and Art Gallery, Glynn Yivian Art Gallery and Museum Swansea, Nat Museum of Wales Cardiff, Welsh Arts Cncl, Contemporary Arts Soc for Wales, Metropolitan Museum of Art NYc, Heineken Collection Amsterdam, Euro Parl Collection, Belgian Nat Collection; *Clubs* Chelsea Arts; *Style*— Harry Holland, Esq; ✉ c/o Jill George, 38 Lexington St, London W1R 3HR (☎ 0171 439 7319, fax 0171 287 0478)

HOLLAND-HIBBERT, Hon Henry Thurstan; er s and h of 6 Viscount Knutsford, *qv*; *b* 6 April 1959; *Educ* Eton, RAC Cirencester; *m* 1988, Katherine, da of Sir John Bruce Woolacott Ropner, 2 Bt; 1 s (Thomas Arthur b 15 Dec 1992), 2 da (Rosie Sarah b 12 Dec 1990, Isabel Katherine b 11 May 1995); *Career* Coldstream Guards 1979–83; dir Lane Fox (Residential) Ltd; *Clubs* Boodle's; *Style*— The Hon Henry Holland-Hibbert; ✉ Munden, Watford, Hertfordshire WD2 7PZ (☎ 01923 672002)

HOLLAND-MARTIN, Robert George (Robin); s of Cyril Holland-Martin (d 1983), and Rosa, *née* Chadwyck-Healey; *b* 6 July 1939; *Educ* Eton; *m* 1976, Dominique, da of Maurice Fromaget; 2 da; *Career* Cazenove & Co 1960–74 (ptnr 1968–74), fin dir Paterson Products Ltd 1976–86, conslt Newmarket Venture Capital plc 1982–94, dir Henderson Administration Group plc 1983–; memb: Cncl Met Hosp-Sunday Fund 1964– (chm 1977–), Homoeopathic Tst 1970–90 (vice-chm 1975–90), Advsy Cncl V & A Museum 1972–83, Assocs of V & A Ctee 1976–85 (chm 1981–85), Visiting Ctee RCA 1982–93 (chm 1984–93); tstee V & A 1983–85 (dep chm); hon dep treas Cons and Unionist Pty 1979–82; tstee Blackie Fndn Tst 1971–96 (chm 1987–96); Liveryman Worshipful Co of Fishmongers; *Clubs* White's, RAC; *Style*— Robin Holland-Martin, Esq; ✉ 18 Tite St, London SW3 4HZ (☎ 0171 352 7871)

HOLLAND-MARTIN, Lady; Dame Rosamund Mary; DBE (1983, OBE 1948), DL (Hereford & Worcester); da of Charles Harry St John Hornby (d 1946), and Cicely Rachel Emily, *née* Barclay (d 1971); *b* 26 June 1914; *m* 1951, Adm Sir Deric (Douglas Eric) Holland-Martin, GCB, DSO, DSC (d 1977), s of Robert Holland-Martin (d 1944), of Overbury Ct, Tewkesbury; 1 s (Benjamin b 1955), 1 da (Emma (Mrs Timothy Cobb) b 1953); *Career* regnl admin WVS 1946–51; memb CEC NSPCC 1947–93, chm NSPCC 1969–88; pres: Sea Cadets, Friends of Worcester Cathedral; *Recreations* photography, needlework, collecting; *Style*— Lady Holland-Martin, DBE, DL; ✉ Bell's Castle, Kemerton, Tewkesbury, Glos GL20 7JW

HOLLEDGE, Richard Antony; *b* 25 Oct 1946; *Educ* Hurstpierpoint Coll, Univ of Bristol; *Career* Mirror Group Training Scheme 1968–71, People Newspaper 1971–76, features ed Reveille 1976–77, dep chief sub Daily Mirror 1978–80; Sunday Mirror: dep chief sub ed 1977–78, chief sub ed 1980–82, asst ed 1982–87; night ed Today 1987–89, ed Wales on Sunday 1989–91; asst ed The European 1991–92 (ed elan section), features ed Sunday Express 1992, ed Hilton Guest Magazine 1992, features ed Daily Mirror (exec features ed 1993) until 1995, with The Independent 1995–; *Recreations* skiing, gardening, opera; *Style*— Richard Holledge, Esq; ✉ The Independent, 1 Canada Square, Canary Wharf, London E14 5DL (☎ 0171 293 2000)

HOLLENDEN, 3 Baron (UK 1912); Gordon Hope Hope-Morley; o s of Hon Claude Hope-Morley (d 1968, yr s of 1 Baron), and Lady Dorothy Edith Isabel Hobart-Hampden-Mercer-Henderson (d 1972), da of 7 Earl of Buckinghamshire; suc unc 1977; *b* 8 Jan 1914; *Educ* Eton; *m* 27 Oct 1945, Sonja, da of late Thorolf Sundt, of Bergen, Norway; 3 s; *Heir* s, Hon Ian Hampden Hope-Morley, *qv*; *Career* served Black Watch 1939–45, Maj; alderman City of London 1954–58, former chm I and R Morley Ltd, ret; Liveryman Worshipful Co of Fishmongers; *Clubs* Brooks's, Beefsteak; *Style*— The Rt Hon the Lord Hollenden; ✉ Hall Place, Leigh, Tonbridge, Kent (☎ 01732 832255)

HOLLEY, Rear Adm Ronald Victor; CB (1987); s of Lt Victor Edward Holley, BEM (d 1986), and Queenie Marion, *née* Watts (d 1989); *b* 13 July 1931; *Educ* Rondebosch SA, Portsmouth GS, RN Engrg Coll, RAF Tech Coll, NATO Def Coll, RCDS; *m* 21 Aug 1954, Dorothy Brierley, da of Lt James Brierley, MBE; 2 s (Jonathan b 1956, Matthew b 1957), 2 da (Rachel b 1959, Amanda b 1959); *Career* joined RN 1949, Cdr 1968, Capt and naval asst to Controller of the Navy 1975, Cdre and dir of helicopter projects Procurement Exec, Capt HMS Thunderer, Rear Adm staff RCDS 1984, DG aircraft, ret 1987; ADC 1984; tech dir Shell Aircraft 1987–92, memb: Lord Chancellor's Panel of Independent Inspectors 1992–, Parly Group for Engrg Devpt 1993–; vice chm aerospace IMechE until 1991, sec Euro helicopter Operators' Ctee until 1991; MIMechE 1958, MIEE 1978, FRAeS 1988; *Recreations* the bassoon, sailing, rowing; *Style*— Rear Adm Ronald Holley, CB

HOLLICK, Baron (Life Peer UK 1991), of Notting Hill in the Royal Borough of Kensington and Chelsea; Clive Richard Hollick; s of Leslie George Hollick, of Southampton, and Olive Mary, *née* Scruton; *b* 20 May 1945; *Educ* Taunton's Sch Southampton, Univ of Nottingham (BA); *m* 1977, Ms Susan Mary Woodford, da of His Excellency P L U Cross, of Trinidad and Tobago; 3 da (Caroline Daniela b 1975, Georgina Louise b 1979, Abigail Miranda b 1981); *Career* md MAI plc, chm Meridian Broadcasting plc, dir various other MAI subsids, chief exec United News & Media plc; non-exec dir: Hambros Bank Ltd 1973–96, British Aerospace plc 1992–; founding tstee Inst for Public Policy Research, memb Financial Law Panel 1993–; memb Cmmn on British Business and Public Policy 1995–; *Recreations* reading, theatre, cinema, tennis, countryside; *Style*— The Rt Hon Lord Hollick; ✉ House of Lords, London SW1A 0PW

HOLLICK, Peter Nugent; JP (Dunstable 1991); s of Dr Cyril Leslie Hollick, of Seaton, Devon, and Grace Helena, *née* Gibbins; *b* 23 Feb 1949; *Educ* Wycliffe Coll, Univ of Birmingham (LLB), Inns of Court Sch of Law, Brunel Univ (MEd); *Career* called to the Bar Middle Temple 1969; princ lectr Windsor and Maidenhead Coll 1983–85, head of Dept of Business Studies and Humanities Dunstable Coll 1985–91, bursar and estate mangr Cannock Sch Chelsfield Kent 1993–95; ed and author; cncllr Beds CC 1993–; past chm: Beds Fedn Professional Assoc of Teachers, Tertiary Educn Ctee Professional Assoc of Teachers; former moderator Business and Technician Educn Cncl, sr examiner AEB, examiner Coll of Preceptors, examiner Inst of Data Processing Mgmnt; chm SW Beds Cons Assoc; memb: Coll of Preceptors (fell 1985), Hon Soc of the Middle Temple 1969, Magistrates' Assoc 1991–, Beds Police Authy; *Recreations* tennis, squash, cycling, photography, travel and transport systems; *Style*— Peter Hollick, Esq, JP; ✉ 1 Carlisle Close, Dunstable, Beds LU6 3PH (☎ 01582 665133)

HOLLIDAY, (Peter) David; s of Leslie John Holliday, *qv*, of Berkhamsted, and Kathleen Joan Marjorie, *née* Stacey; *b* 20 July 1947; *Educ* Brixton Sch of Bldg, London Business Sch; *m* 1972, Diana Patricia, da of Philip Shirley Christian Aldred, of Surrey;

1 s (Michael Stuart b 1978), 2 da (Rebecca Louise b 1976, Amanda Alice b 1982); *Career* chm: Laing Homes 1983–88, Super-Homes 1983–88, John Laing Homes Inc (California) 1985–88; dir John Laing plc 1984–88, chief exec Admiral Homes Ltd 1988–; dir National House Building Cncl 1994–, pres House Builders' Fedn 1991–92 (vice pres 1988–91); Freeman: City of London 1987, Worshipful Co of Plaisterers, Worshipful Co of Constructors; MCIOB, FInstD; *Recreations* sailing, golf; *Clubs* Royal Southern Yacht, Woburn Golf; *Style—* David Holliday, Esq; ✉ Dundry, Water End Rd, Potten End, Berkhamsted, Herts HP4 2SG (☎ 01442 865556)

HOLLIDAY, Prof Sir Frederick George Thomas; kt (1990), CBE (1975); s of Alfred Charles Holliday, of Scotland, and Margaret, *née* Reynolds; *b* 22 Sept 1935; *Educ* Bromsgrove Co HS, Univ of Sheffield (BSc, DSc); *m* 1957, Philippa Mary, da of Charles Davidson (d 1985), of Dunning, Scotland; 1 s (Richard John b 1964), 1 da (Helen Kirstin b 1961); *Career* Devpt Cmmn fisheries res student Aberdeen 1956–58, sci offr Marine Lab Aberdeen 1958–61, acting princ and vice-chllr Univ of Stirling 1973–75 (prof and head Dept of Biology 1967–75, dep princ 1972–73), prof of zoology Univ of Aberdeen 1975–79 (lectr in zoology 1961–66), vice-chllr and warden Univ of Durham 1980–90; non-exec dir: Shell UK Ltd 1980–, BR Eastern Region Bd 1983–90 (chm 1986–90), BR Main Bd 1990–93, Bd Union Railways 1993–; non-exec chm Northumbrian Water Group plc 1993– (non-exec dir 1991–); dir: Northern Investors Ltd 1984–89, Lloyds Bank Northern Regnl Bd 1985–90 (chm 1986–89, dep chm 1989–90); chm: Nature Conservancy Cncl 1977–80 (memb 1975–80), Joint Nature Conservation Ctee 1990–91, Northern Venture Tst Plc 1996–; pres Freshwater Biological Assoc 1995–; vice-pres Scottish Wildlife Tst 1980–, chm indep review of Disposal of Radioactive Waste at Sea 1984; memb: Leverhulme Tst Res Awards Advsy Ctee 1978–95 (chm 1987–95), Environment Ctee CBI 1994, Bd Lyonnaise des Eaux 1996–, Lyonnaise Europe 1996; tstee: The Scottish Civic Tst 1984–87, The Nat Heritage Meml Fund 1980–91, Water Aid Cncl 1995–; DL Co Durham 1985–90; FRSE 1971; *Recreations* hill walking, vegetable gardening; *Clubs* Cwlth Tst, Fettercairn Farmers'; *Style—* Prof Sir Frederick Holliday, CBE, FRSE; ✉ Regent Centre, Gosforth, Newcastle upon Tyne NE3 3PX (☎ 0191 284 3151, fax 0191 213 0648)

HOLLIDAY, Leslie John; s of John Holliday (d 1976), and Elsie May, *née* Hutchinson (d 1985); *b* 9 Jan 1921; *Educ* St John's Whitby; *m* 1943, Kathleen Joan Marjorie, da of Ernest Stacey (d 1963); 2 s ((Peter) David Holliday, *qv*, b 1947, Philip b 1950); *Career* radio offr Merchant Navy 1940–45, Atlantic, Mediterranean and Indian Ocean; mgmnt conslt 1985–; non-exec dir: Decan Kelly Group plc 1985–89, Robert M Douglas Holdings plc 1986–89; chm and chief exec John Laing plc 1982–85; chm: Nat Contractors Gp, Nat Fedn of Bldg Trades Employers 1976–77, Laing Homes Ltd 1978–81, Super Homes Ltd 1979–81, Laing Mgmnt Contracting Ltd 1980–81, John Laing Construction Ltd 1980–84, John Laing Int Ltd 1981–82; non-exec dir and chm Admiral Homes Ltd 1989–96; dir Redrow Gp Ltd 1989–92; Prince Philip Medal 1982; Freeman City of London 1982, memb Worshipful Company of Plaisterers 1982; FCIOB, CIMgt; *Recreations* golf; *Clubs* Berkhamsted; *Style—* Leslie Holliday, Esq; ✉ The White House, Frithsden Copse, Berkhamsted, Herts HP4 2RQ (☎ and fax 01442 872563)

HOLLIDAY, Raymond (Ray); s of Ronald Holliday (d 1992), and Mary Louisa, *née* Cowen; *b* 30 May 1949; *Educ* Boteler GS Warrington, Univ of Newcastle upon Tyne (BA, PGCE, MEd), Newcastle upon Tyne Poly (TEFL Dip (RSA)); *m* 1975, Régine, da of Gérard Leclerc; 4 da (Kristelle b 6 May 1981, Chloé b 13 April 1985, Loriane b 19 April 1987, Géraldine b 8 Aug 1992), 1 s (Marc Alexandre b 20 Feb 1988); *Career* teacher of French and English Seaton Sluice Middle Sch Northumberland 1975–80, year leader and teacher of French and English Blyth Wensleydale Middle Sch Northumberland 1980–82 (dep head 1982–87); British Council School of Madrid: dep head 1987–93, actg head 1993–94, head 1994–; *Recreations* reading, music, cycling, a wide variety of sports with no great level in any; *Style—* Ray Holliday, Esq; ✉ British Council School of Madrid, c/o Solano 5–7, Prado de Somosaguas, 28023 Pozuelo de Alarcon, Madrid, Spain (☎ 00 34 1 337 36 08, fax 00 34 1 337 36 34)

HOLLIHEAD, Garry Stephen; s of Brian Clifford Hollihead, and Barbara Margaret, *née* Bodinnar; *b* 22 Feb 1960; *Educ* Ash Green HS Exhall Warwicks, Henley Coll Warwicks; *Career* chef; commis saucier Belfry Golf and Country Club 1980–81, commis saucier rising to sous chef 90 Park Lane 1981–84, chef L'Oasis La Napoule France 1984, saucier/larder Fourways Washington and premier sous chef Savoy (involved in promotional work for Savoy Group Florida) 1986–87; head chef: Sutherlands Restaurant 1987–93, L'Escargot 1993–; *Awards* Mouton Cadet Menu of the Year 1987, Good Food Guide Newcomer of the Year award 1989, Egon Ronay rosette 1989, 1990 and 1991, Ackerman Guide White Clover award 1989, Ackerman Guide Black Clover award 1990, Michelin Guide one star award; *Style—* Garry Hollihead, Esq; ✉ L'Escargot, 48 Greek Street, London W1V 5LQ (☎ 0171 437 2679)

HOLLINGBERY, Michael John; s of George Henry Hollingbery (d 1958), and Mary Orovida Hammond (d 1984); *b* 16 April 1933; *Educ* Rossall; *m* 1962, Karen Jane, da of Edward Wells (d 1971); 2 s, 1 da; *Career* chm Comet Group plc 1972–86 (dir 1958–86); former dir: Kingfisher plc (formerly Woolworth Holdings plc) 1984–96, Wilson (Connolly) Holdings plc, Hewetson plc; Hon LLD; Liveryman: Worshipful Co of Painter-Stainers 1980, Worshipful Co of Merchant Adventurers of City of York 1984; CIMgt 1975; *Recreations* fishing, shooting; *Clubs* Brooks; *Style—* Michael Hollingbery, Esq

HOLLINGDALE, John Patrick; s of William George Hollingdale, of Chigwell, Essex, and Mary Patricia, *née* Macmillan; *b* 20 April 1952; *Educ* Campion Sch Hornchurch Essex, King's Coll London, Westminster Med Sch (MB BS); *m* 3 July 1976, Jane Susan, da of late Dr Alwyn Kinsey, of Dorset; *Career* conslt orthopaedic surgn: Kettering Gen Hosp 1988–89, Central Middx Hosp 1989–; FBOA, FRCS, FRSM; *Books* contrib: Short Textbook of Surgery, Airds Companion to Surgical Studies; *Recreations* golf, skiing; *Clubs* Lambourne Golf, Windsor Med Soc; *Style—* John Hollingdale, Esq; ✉ Central Middlesex Hospital, Acton Lane, Park Royal, London NW10 7NS (☎ 0181 453 2416, 0171 629 3763)

HOLLINGS, Sir (Alfred) Kenneth; kt (1971), MC (1944); s of Alfred Holdsworth Hollings (d 1941); *b* 12 June 1918; *Educ* Leys Sch Cambridge, Clare Coll Cambridge (MA); *m* 1949, Harriet Evelyn Isabella, da of W J C Fishbourne, OBE, of Brussels; 1 s, 1 da; *Career* served WWII, Africa, Sicily and Italy, Maj RA (Shropshire Yeo); called to the Bar Middle Temple 1947; QC 1966, recorder of Bolton 1968, Co Ct judge (Circuit 5) 1968–71, master of the Bench Middle Temple 1971, judge of the High Ct of Justice (Family Div) 1971–93, presiding judge of the Northern Circuit 1975–78; *Clubs* Garrick, Hurlingham, Tennis and Racquets (Manchester); *Style—* Sir Kenneth Hollings, MC; ✉ Royal Courts of Justice, Strand, London WC2

HOLLINGS, Rev Michael Richard; MBE (1993), MC (1943); s of Lt Cdr Richard Eustace Hollings, RN, and Agnes Mary, *née* Hamilton-Dalrymple; *b* 30 Dec 1921; *Educ* Beaumont Coll, St Catherine's Soc Oxford (MA), St Catherine's Sandhurst, Beda Coll Rome; *Career* Maj Coldstream Guards 1942–45, trained for priesthood Beda Coll Rome 1946–50, ordained Rome 1950, asst priest St Patrick's Soho Square London 1950–54, chaplain Westminster Cathedral 1954–58, asst chaplain London Univ 1958–59, chaplain to RCs at Oxford Univ 1959–70; parish priest: St Anselm's Southall Middx 1970–78, St Mary of the Angels Bayswater London 1978–; dean of North Kensington 1980–; religious advsr: ATV 1958–59, Rediffusion 1958–68, Thames Television 1968; advsr Prison Christian Fellowship 1983–; lay memb Press Cncl 1969–75; memb: Nat Catholic Radio and TV Cmmn 1968, Westminster Diocesan Schs Cmmn 1970–, Southall C of C 1971–78, Oxford and Cambridge Catholic Educn Bd 1971–78, Exec Cncl of Christians and Jews 1971–79 and 1984–, Nat Conf of Priests Standing Ctee 1974–76, Rampton Ctee 1979–81, Swann Ctee 1981–84; exec: Ealing Community Relations Cncl 1973–76, Notting Hill Social Cncl 1980–; chm N Kensington Action Gp 1980–81; memb: W London Family Service Unit 1981–, Portobello Tst 1987, Bd Christian Aid 1984–87; chaplain: SMOM 1957, Nat Cncl of Lay Apostolate 1970–74, Catholic Inst of Int Relations 1971–80; govr: St Charles Catholic VIth Form Coll 1990, Sion Manning Sch 1990 (chm); *Books* Hey, You! (1955), Purple Times (1957), Chaplaincraft (1963), The One Who Listens (1971), The Pastoral Care of Homosexuals (1971), It's Me, O Lord (1972), Day by Day (1972), The Shade of his Hand (1973), Restoring the Streets (1974), I Will be There (1975), You Must Be Joking, Lord (1975), The Catholic Prayer Book (1976), Alive to Death (1976), Living Priesthood (1977), His People's Way of Talking (1978), As Was His Custom (1979), St Thérèse of Lisieux (1981), Hearts not Garments (1982), Chaplet of Mary (1982), Path to Contemplation (1983), Go in Peace (1984), Christ Died at Notting Hill (1985), Athirst for God (1985), Prayers Before and after Bereavement (1986), By Love Alone (1986), Prayers for the Depressed (1986), You are not Alone (1988), Dying to Live (1990), Thoughts of Peace (1991), Love Heals (1993), Praying with the New Catechism (1994); *Recreations* reading, walking, people; *Style—* The Rev Michael Hollings, MBE, MC; ✉ St Mary of the Angels, Moorhouse Rd, Bayswater, London W2 5DJ (☎ 0171 229 0487)

HOLLINGSWORTH, Michael Charles (Mike); s of Albert George Hollingsworth, of Petersfield, Hampshire, and Gwendolen Marjorie; *b* 22 Feb 1946; *Educ* Reading Sch, Carlisle Sch; *m* 1, 10 Aug 1968 (m dis 1988), Patricia Margaret Jefferson Winn; 1 da (Rebecca b 7 Oct 1974); m 2, 1 Jan 1989, Anne Margaret Diamond; 5 s (Oliver b 12 July 1987, Jamie b 21 Dec 1988, Sebastian b and d 1991, Jacob b 21 May 1993, Conor b 17 March 1995); *Career* prodr radio and TV BBC 1967–75; editor news and current affairs: Southern TV Ltd 1975–79, ATV Network Ltd/Central TV 1979–82; sr prodr current affairs BBC 1982–84, dir of progs TV-am Ltd 1984–85, md Music Box Ltd 1985–88, chief exec Venture Television and md Venture Artistes 1988–, fndr Daytime TV 1990, ed Good Morning with Anne and Nick (BBC1) until 1994, conslt on daytime programming to Sky TV until 1994, md Liberty Broadcasting 1996–; presenters' agent 1994–; dir: TV Production and Management Ltd, Good Morning Britain Ltd; former dir TV-am Ltd and TV-am News Ltd (resigned 1986); memb Campaign for Freedom from the Press; *Recreations* polo, house renovation; *Clubs* RAC, Guards' Polo; *Style—* Mike Hollingsworth, Esq; ✉ Managing Director, Venture Artistes and Liberty Broadcasting, Cuddesdon House, Cuddesdon, Oxford OX44 9HB (☎ 07000 402001)

HOLLINGTON, Geoffrey Arnold (Geoff); s of Henry Cecil Hollington (d 1983), of West Wickham, Kent, and Eileen Caroline, *née* Fletcher; *b* 5 Feb 1949; *Educ* Beckenham GS Kent, Central Sch of Art and Design London (BA), RCA London (MA); *m* 1, 1971 (m dis 1984) Judith Ann, da of Dennis Frederick Leonard Fox; 1 s (Simon James b 7 Feb 1979); m 2, 1984, Elizabeth Ann Beecham, da of Clement Joseph Lawton; 1 s (James Henry b 23 Sept 1986), 3 da (Gemma Beecham (adopted 1987) b 27 Oct 1977, Emily b and d 29 Feb 1985, Sophy Imogen b 18 July 1989); *Career* industl designer; Milton Keynes Devpt Corp 1976–78, ptnr Glickman & Hollington 1978–80, princ Hollington Associates 1980–; clients incl: Herman Miller Inc USA, Parker Pen, Ever Ready; regular contrib Blueprint magazine; memb: Industl Design Soc of America 1991; FRSA 1988, FCSD 1994; *Publications* Hollington: Industrial Design (1990); *Recreations* family, theatre, music, opera, reading, writing; *Style—* Geoff Hollington, Esq; ✉ Hollington Associates, The Old School House, 66 Leonard Street, London EC2A 4QX (☎ 0171 739 3501, fax 0171 739 3549)

HOLLINGWORTH, Corinne Ann; da of George Hollingworth, and Dorothy, *née* Grice; *b* 25 May 1952; *Educ* Sherwood Hall GS, Drama Dept Univ of Bristol (BA), Webber Douglas Acad of Dramatic Art; *m* 1983, Robert Gabriel; 1 s (Jonathan William Hamilton b 1985); *Career* BBC TV: prodr Eastenders 1988–91, prodr Elderado 1992–93, prodr Casualty 1993–96, exec prodr Eastenders 1994–96; controller of drama Channel 5 1996–; memb: BAFTA 1996, RTS 1996; *Style—* Ms Corinne Hollingworth; ✉ Channel 5 Broadcasting Ltd, 22 Long Acre, London WC2E 9LY (☎ 0171 421 7115, fax 0171 421 7111)

HOLLINGWORTH, John Harold; s of Harold Hollingworth (d 1978), of Birmingham, and Lilian Mary, *née* Harris (d 1982); *b* 11 July 1930; *Educ* King Edward's Sch Birmingham; *m* 1967 (m dis 1986), Susan Barbara, da of J H Walters (d 1984), of Isle of Man; *Career* MP (C) Birmingham All Saints 1959–64; govr Cambridge Symphony Orchestra Tst Ltd 1982–92 (dir and gen mangr 1979–82), dir Cambridge Connection Ltd (support for young musicians), dir Thaxted Festival Fndn Ltd (Music Festival) 1987–92; dir and sec Newport Investments 1993–; tstee Br Performing Arts Medicine Tst 1985– (hon chief exec 1992–93, treas 1993–); *Recreations* walking, map reading, talking; *Clubs* Lansdowne; *Style—* John Hollingworth, Esq; ✉ Home Farm Lodge, Clavering, Saffron Walden, Essex CB11 4QR (☎ 01799 550600)

HOLLINS, Rear Adm Hubert Walter Elphinstone; CB (1974); s of Lt-Col Walter Thorne Hollins (d 1956), and Ellen Murray, *née* Rigg (d 1974); *b* 8 June 1923; *Educ* Stubbington House, RNC Dartmouth; *m* 11 May 1963, Jillian Mary, da of Donald McAlpin, of Victoria, Australia; 1 s (Rupert Patrick b 1964), 1 da (Rachel Jane b 1965); *Career* RN 1940–76; in cmd HM Ships: Petard, Dundas, Caesar (Capt (D) 26), Antrim; Flag Offr Gibraltar; cmd Gibraltar Med and Port Admiral Gibraltar 1972–74, Adm cmdg Reserves 1974–76; gen mangr Middle East Navigation Aids Serv 1977–84; marine conslt 1984–; younger brother Trinity House, memb Trinity House Lighthouse Bd and assoc memb Corp of the Trinity House 1985–91; vice patron The Gallantry Medallists' League; FIMgt; *Recreations* fishing, gardening; *Clubs* Naval; *Style—* Rear Adm Hubert W E Hollins, CB; ✉ Waunllan, Llandyfriog, Newcastle Emlyn, Cardiganshire SA38 9HB (☎ and fax 01239 710456)

HOLLINS, Prof Sheila Clare; da of Capt Adrian M Kelly, of Bristol, and Monica Dallas, *née* Edwards; *b* 22 June 1946; *Educ* Notre Dame HS Sheffield, St Thomas's Hosp Med Sch London (MB BS); *m* 7 June 1969, Martin Prior Hollins, s of Harry Pryor Hollins (d 1985), of Cheadle Hulme; 1 s (Nigel b 1973), 3 da (Kathryn b 1971, Emily b 1976, Abigail b 1978); *Career* sr registrar in child psychiatry Earls Court Child Guidance Unit and Westminster Children's Hosp 1979–81, sr lectr in the psychiatry of learning disability St George's Hosp Med Sch (prof 1990–), hon conslt Wandsworth Community Health Tst and Richmond Twickenham and Roehampton Healthcare Tst 1981–, head Div of Psychiatry of Disability 1986–, seconded to Policy Div Dept of Health 1993; chair: Exec Ctee Mental Handicap Section RCPsych, Community Care and Disability Sub-Ctee Joseph Rowntree Fndn, C of E Bd for Social Responsibility; memb lay community Worth Abbey; Winston Churchill fell 1993; FRCPsych 1988 (MRCPsych 1978); *Books* Mental Handicap: A Multi Disciplinary Approach (ed with M Craft, J Bicknell, 1985), Going Somewhere - Pastoral Care for People with Mental Handicap (with M Grimer, 1988), When Dad Died and When Mum Died (2 books with L Sireling, 1990), Working Through Loss with People Who Have Learning Disabilities (with L Sireling, 1991), Jenny Speaks Out (with V Sinason, 1992), Bob Tells All (with V Sinason, 1992), Hug Me, Touch Me (Best author Read Easy Awards Book Tst and Joseph Rowntree Fndn 1994); *Recreations* family and music; *Style—* Prof Sheila Hollins; ✉ Department of Psychiatry and Disability, St Georges Hospital Medical School, Cranmer Terrace, London SW17 0RE (☎ 0181 725 5501)

HOLLIS, Hon Mr Justice; Hon Sir Anthony Barnard; kt (1982); s of Henry Lewis Hollis; *b* 11 May 1927; *Educ* Tonbridge, St Peter's Hall Oxford (hon fell 1992); *m* 1956, Pauline Mary, *née* Skuce; 1 step da; *Career* called to the Bar Gray's Inn 1951, bencher 1979; QC 1969, chm Family Law Bar Assoc 1974–76, Crown Court recorder 1976–82, High Court judge 1982–; *Style—* The Hon Mr Justice Hollis; ✉ Royal Courts of Justice, Strand, London WC2

HOLLIS, Anthony John; s of Henry Clifford Hollis (d 1946), of Finchley, London, and Dora Elizabeth, *née* Mason (d 1957); *b* 31 Oct 1930; *Educ* King Edward VI GS Totnes; *m* 22 Oct 1960, Margaret Joyce, da of Percy Herbert Dennis (d 1979), of Radlett, Herts; 2 s (Richard b 1962, David b 1964), 2 da (Elizabeth b 1966, Catherine b 1969); *Career* Nat Serv 1953–55 RAPC, 2 Lt 1954, Lt; CA; ptnr: Hope Agar 1961–88 and 1990–93 (joined 1947), Kidsons 1988–90; tstee Finchley Charities, govr Penrhos Coll 1993–95, govr Rydal Penrhos Sch 1995–; Freeman City of London 1966, Liveryman Worshipful Co of Fanmakers 1976; FCA 1964 (ACA 1953); *Recreations* gardening; *Style—* Anthony Hollis, Esq; ✉ Foxbrooke House, 25 The Green, Evenley, Northamptonshire NN13 5SQ (☎ 01280 700597)

HOLLIS, Arthur Norman; OBE (1985), DFC (1943); s of Egerton Clark Hollis (d 1967), of Eastbourne, Sussex, and Vera Lina, *née* Leigh (d 1944); *b* 11 Aug 1922; *Educ* Dulwich; *m* 2 Dec 1944, Elizabeth, da of Reginald Chase Edmunds (d 1986), of Westwell, nr Ashford, Kent; 1 s (Richard b 1953), 2 da (Jennifer b 1945, Sylvia b 1949); *Career* RAFVR 1941–46, Sqdn Ldr 1945–46; memb HAC 1978; CA; ptnr: Limebeer & Co 1953–75, Russell Limebeer 1975–88; sr ptnr based in City of London specialising in countries of W Europe; dir various cos; memb Mgmnt Ctee Yehudi Menuhin Sch 1964–88 (vice pres 1989), govr Live Music Now 1977–90, offr of various Cons Assocs; chm: Ashford Constituency 1980–83 (vice pres 1991), Kent East Euro Constituency 1985–88 (pres 1991–96), Westwell Parish Cncl 1976–79; Master Worshipful Co of Woolmen 1982–83; FCA 1958, FRSA 1983; *Recreations* travel, shooting, country pursuits; *Clubs* Travellers, City of London, United and Cecil; *Style—* Arthur Hollis, Esq, OBE, DFC; ✉ Court Lodge, Westwell, nr Ashford, Kent TN25 4JX (☎ 01233 712555)

HOLLIS, Rt Rev Crispian; *see:* Portsmouth, Bishop of (RC)

HOLLIS, Daniel Ayrton; QC (1968), VRD; *b* 30 April 1925; *Educ* Geelong GS Aust, Brasenose Coll Oxford; *m* 1, 1950 (m dis 1960), Gillian Mary Turner; 2 twin c (Sarah Elizabeth b 1955 and Simon Ayrton (d 1992)); m 2, 1963, Stella Hydleman, *née* Gergel; 1 s (Gideon James b 1967), 2 step c (Jean and Marc Hydleman); *Career* served RNVR 1943–46 (Lt Cdr 1955); called to the Bar Middle Temple 1949 (bencher 1975, treas 1994), head of chambers 1967–95, recorder of the Crown Ct 1972–96, memb Home Sec's Advsy Bd on Restricted Patients 1986–92, memb Criminal Injuries Compensation Bd 1995–; *Style—* Daniel Hollis, Esq, VRD, QC; ✉ 33 Peartree Lane, London E1 9SR (☎ and fax 0171 481 0012); 13 Rue du Fer a Cheval, Port Grimaud 83310, France (☎ 00 33 494 43 44 63)

HOLLIS, John Charles; s of Charles Henry Hollis, and Audrey Cynthia, *née* Davis; *b* 16 June 1953; *Educ* Latymer Upper Sch, Univ of Bristol (BSc); *children* 5 da (Emma b 1980, Lisa b 1981, Amy b 1983, Hannah b 1993, Emily b 1995), 1 s (Thomas b 1991); *Career* Arthur Andersen: joined 1974, ptnr Andersen Consulting 1985, i/c Worldwide Financial Planning and Reporting Consulting Function 1985, i/c UK Consumer Prods Consulting Gp 1988, i/c Euro Consumer Prods Sector 1992, i/c Smart Store Europe 1993; memb IMA, FCA; *Books* Disappearing Financial Systems (1988), The Torturing and Dismembering of the Finance Function (1988); *Recreations* music, sports, interior design; *Clubs* RAC; *Style—* John Hollis, Esq; ✉ Andersen Consulting, SMART STORE Europe, Riverside House, Riverside Walk, Windsor, Berkshire SL4 1NA

HOLLIS, Prof Malcolm Richard Arthur; s of Arthur Edwin Hollis (d 1970), of Southport, Merseyside, and Esmé Muriel, *née* Pettit; *b* 17 March 1944; *Educ* King George V GS Southport, Univ of South Wales and Monmouth, Univ of London (BSc); *m* 11 Sept 1965, Andrea Joan, da of Sqdn Ldr John Edward Fuller (d 1989), of Challows, The Martlets, W Chiltington; 2 s (Richard b 1969, Gavin b 1976), 1 da (Tricia b 1970); *Career* chartered building surveyor; ptnr Best Gapp & Ptnrs 1969, princ Malcolm Hollis Associates 1972–80, ptnr Baxter Payne & Lepper (incl Malcolm Hollis Associates) 1980–91 (dep chm 1986–88), sr ptnr Malcolm Hollis & Partners 1991–95; chm Acutec UK 1995–; Surveyor to the Fabric Worshipful Co of Skinners 1982–, mangr professional servs Nationwide Anglia Estate Agents 1987–91, memb Cncl RICS Bldg Surveyors 1988–92; cncllr London Borough of Lambeth 1977–81; govr Woodmansterne Sch 1978–81 (chm 1979–81); over 100 appearances on TV and radio 1984–; hon prof Univ of Reading 1989; Freeman City of London 1983, Freeman Worshipful Co of Chartered Surveyors 1982; FSVA 1969, FBEng 1969, FRICS 1970, ACIArb 1974; *Books* Surveying Buildings (1983, 2 edn 1986, 3 edn 1989, 4 edn 1991), Householders Action Guide (1984), Model Survey Reports (1985, 2 edn 1989), Surveying for Dilapidations (1988), Cavity Wall Tie Failure (1990), Surveyors Fact Book (1990), Dilapidations (1992); *Recreations* writing, photography, skiing, thinking; *Clubs* Hurlingham, Ski Club of GB; *Style—* Prof Malcolm Hollis; ✉ 6 Rydal Rd, London SW16 1QN (☎ 0181 769 9927)

HOLLIS, Prof (James) Martin; s of Hugh Marcus Noel Hollis, and Ruth Margaret Hollis; *b* 14 March 1938; *Educ* Winchester, New Coll Oxford (MA); *m* 1965, Baroness Hollis of Heigham, *qv*, da of (Harry) Lesley George Wells; 2 s; *Career* Harkness Cwlth Fund fell Univs of Berkeley and Harvard 1961–63, FCO 1964, extraordinary lectr New Coll Oxford 1964, lectr Balliol Coll Oxford 1965–67; UEA: lectr 1967–72, sr lectr 1972–82, prof of philosophy 1982–, pro-vice chllr 1992–95; distinguished visitor and lectr: Univ of Br Columbia 1980, Queen's Univ Ontario 1982, Univ of Bayreuth 1988, Wake Forest Univ 1995; pres Aristotelian Soc 1986; memb Cncl: Univ of Bayreuth 1989–, Royal Inst of Philosophy 1991–; JP (Norwich) 1972–82, govr Eaton (CNS) Sch 1972–75, ed Ratio magazine 1980–87; FBA 1990; *Books* incl: The Light of Reason (1971), Models of Man (1977), Philosophy and Economic Theory (jtly, 1979), Rationality and Relativism (jtly, 1982), Invitation to Philosophy (1985), The Cunning of Reason (1988), Explaining and Understanding International Relations (jtly, 1990), Rationalität and soziales Verstehen (1991) The Theory of Choice (jtly, 1992), The Philosophy of Social Science (1994), Reason in Action (1996); *Recreations* puzzles; *Style—* Prof Martin Hollis, FBA; ✉ School of Economic and Social Studies, University of East Anglia, Norwich NR4 7TJ (☎ 01603 456161, fax 01603 250434)

HOLLIS OF HEIGHAM, Baroness (Life Peer UK 1990), of Heigham in the City of Norwich; Patricia Lesley Hollis; DL (Norfolk 1994); da of H L G Wells, of Norwich, and (Queenie) Rosalyn, *née* Clayforth; *b* 24 May 1941; *Educ* Plympton GS, Univ of Cambridge (BA, MA), Univ of California Berkeley, Columbia Univ NY, Nuffield Coll Oxford (MA, DPhil); *m* 18 Sept 1965, Prof (James) Martin Hollis, *qv*, s of (Hugh) Mark Noel Hollis, of Oxted, Surrey; 2 s (Hon Simon b 1969, Hon Matthew b 1971); *Career* Harkness fell 1962–64, Nuffield scholar 1964–67, reader (formerly sr lectr and lectr) modern history UEA 1967–, dean Sch of English and American Studies UEA 1988–90; councillor Norwich City 1968–91 (ldr 1983–88); memb: E Anglia Economic Planning Cncl 1975–79, Regnl Health Authy 1979–83, BBC Regnl Advsy Ctee 1979–83, Norfolk CC 1981–85; dir Radio Broadland 1983; Parly candidate Gt Yarmouth 1974 and 1979; nat cmmr English Heritage 1988–91, memb Press Cncl 1989–91; FRHistS; *Books* The Pauper Press (1970), Class and Class Conflict 1815–50 (1973), Women in Public 1850–1900 (1979), Pressure from Without (1974), Ladies Elect: Women in English Local Govt 1865–1914 (1987); *Recreations* singing, boating on the broads, domesticity; *Style—* The Rt Hon Baroness Hollis of Heigham, DL; ✉ School of English and American Studies, University of East Anglia, Norwich NR4 7TJ (☎ 01603 56161); c/o House of Lords, London SW1A 0PW (☎ 0171 219 3000)

HOLLOM, Sir Jasper Quintus; KBE (1975); s of Arthur Hollom (d 1954); *b* 16 Dec 1917; *Educ* King's Sch Bruton Somerset; *m* 1954, Patricia Elizabeth Mary Ellis; *Career* Bank of England: joined 1936, dep chief cashier 1956–62, chief cashier 1962–66, exec dir 1966–70, non-exec dir 1980–84, dep govr 1970–80; non-exec dir: BAT Industries plc 1980–87, Portals Holdings 1980–88; chm: Eagle Star Group 1985–87; chm: Cncl for Securities Industs 1985–86, Panel on Takeovers and Mergers 1980–87; memb Ct of Assts Worshipful Co of Needlemakers; *Style—* Sir Jasper Hollom, KBE; ✉ The Long Barn, Alexanders Lane, Privett, Alton, Hants GU34 3PW (☎ 01730 828419)

HOLLOWAY, His Hon Judge (Frederick Reginald) Bryn; s of William Herbert Holloway, of Alberbury, Shrewsbury, and Audrey Eileen, *née* Hull-Brown; *b* 8 Jan 1947; *Educ* Wrekin Coll Wellington, Holborn Coll of Law London; *m* 6 Aug 1974, Barbara, da of William Archie Bradley; 2 s (Christopher Reginald Bradley b 11 Sept 1978, William Benjamin b 30 Oct 1979); *Career* called to the Bar Lincoln's Inn 1971, pupillage with His Hon Judge Henry Lachs 1972, recorder 1989–92 (asst recorder 1984–89), circuit judge (Northern Circuit) 1992–; *Recreations* gardening, Shrewsbury Town FC, cricket, rugby; *Style—* His Hon Judge Holloway; ✉ Queen Elizabeth II Law Courts, Derby Square, Liverpool (☎ 0151 473 7373)

HOLLOWAY, Charles Henry Warner; s of Adrian George Warner Holloway, of Boscobel, Burleigh, Glos, and Helen Pendrill, *née* Charles; *b* 2 Nov 1950; *Educ* Winchester, Univ Coll Oxford (BA, MA); *m* 20 Sept 1975, Georgina Alice, da of Maj Hon George Nathaniel Rous (d 1982), of Dennington Hall, Woodbridge, Suffolk; 2 s (George Henry Rous b 1983, Edward Charles b 1986), 2 da (Alice Victoria Pendrill b 1978, Lucinda Rose b 1980); *Career* articled clerk to Sir John Pendrill Charles, KCVO, MC (Allen & Overy), admitted slr 1975; ptnr Eversheds Norwich 1981–; area cmmr for Breckland St John Ambulance 1983–86, under sheriff of Norfolk 1995–; memb: Law Soc, Slrs Euro Gp, St John Cncl for Norfolk, Anglo-Spanish Soc; ACIArb; *Recreations* shooting, skiing, tennis; *Clubs* Boodle's, Norfolk, Vincent's; *Style—* Charles Holloway, Esq; ✉ The Old Rectory, Whissonsett, Dereham, Norfolk NR20 5TF (☎ 01328 700514, fax 01328 700722); Eversheds, Holland Court, The Close, Norwich NR1 4DX (☎ 01603 272727, fax 01603 610535); Eversheds, Senator House, 85 Queen Victoria Street, London EC4V 4JL (☎ 0171 919 4500, fax 0171 919 4919)

HOLLOWAY, Edgar Christopher; s of William Henry Holloway (d 1964), of Doncaster, and Ethel Harriet, *née* Allison (d 1982); *b* 6 May 1914; *Educ* Doncaster GS, Slade Sch of Fine Art Univ of London; *m* 1, 5 July 1943, Daisy Monica (d 1979), da of David Hawkins; 1 da (Elisabeth Mary b 17 June 1945), 3 s (Peter Michael b 3 Sept 1946, Timothy William b 4 March 1949, Kevin Joseph b 26 March 1951); m 2, 12 May 1984, Jennifer Marion Boxall, *née* Squire; *Career* artist; work incl portraits of: T S Eliot, Herbert Read and Stephen Spender; sr memb RBA 1947, sr fell RE 1991; *Exhibitions* solo exhbns: Twenty-One Gallery London 1931 and 1934, Greatorex Gallery London 1933, USA 1972–75, Ditchling 1977, Robin Garton Gallery London 1979, Brighton Coll 1980 and 1986, Studio One Oxford 1980, Doncaster 1982, Edinburgh 1986, Ashmolean 1991–92, Michael Parkin Gallery London 1993, Edgar Holloway at 80 (touring exhbn) 1994; *Collections* work in numerous incl: British Museum, British Council, V&A, Ashmolean Museum Oxford, Fitzwilliam Museum Cambridge, NY Public Library, Scottish National Gallery of Modern Art, Scottish National Portrait Gallery, National Museum of Wales, National Library of Wales, Oxford and Cambridge colls, Guildhall Library, Harvard Univ, Rensselaer Poly Inst NY, Birmingham City Art Gallery, Univ Coll of Wales Aberystwyth; *Style—* Edgar Holloway, Esq; ✉ Woodbarton, Ditchling Common, Hassocks, West Sussex BN6 8TP (☎ 01444 244356)

HOLLOWAY, Gordon Passmore; *b* 10 Jan 1933; *Educ* Christ's Coll Cambridge (MA); *m* Valerie, *née* Little; 3 c; *Career* began working for RTZ (latterly commercial dir of its largest UK subsid); chief exec The Shaftesbury Society 1978–95 (joined 1975); *Recreations* most sports, theatre, ballet, reading; *Style—* Gordon Holloway, Esq; ✉ c/o The Shaftesbury Society, 18–20 Kingston Road, London SW19 1JZ (☎ 0181 542 5550, fax 0181 545 0605)

HOLLOWAY, Prof John Henry; s of William Henry Holloway (d 1983), of Coalville, and Ivy May, *née* Sarson; *b* 20 Dec 1938; *Educ* Ashby-de-la-Zouch Boys' GS, Univ of Birmingham (BSc, PhD, DSc); *m* 14 April 1962, Jennifer, da of Albert Burne, of Coalville; 1 s (Mark b 1969), 2 da (Sarah b 1964, Amanda b 1965); *Career* Univ of Aberdeen: asst lectr 1963–64, lectr 1964–70; Univ of Leicester: lectr 1971–78, sr lectr 1978–87, prof and head of chemistry 1987–96, prof 1996–; memb Technol Foresight Chemicals Panel Office of Science and Technology; Royal Soc of Chemistry: chm Professional Affrs and Membership Bd, memb Finance Ctee, memb Cncl, memb Strategic Planning Ctee, memb Steering and Co-ordinating Ctee, memb Parly Affrs Ctee; author of over 200 papers on fluorine chemistry; reviser for Oxford and Cambridge Schs Examination Bd; chm HE Chemistry Conf; CChem, FRSC; *Books* Noble Gas Chemistry (1968); *Recreations* painting, drawing, sailing, classic car restoration; *Style—* Prof John Holloway; ✉ 43 Morland Ave, Stoneygate, Leicester LE2 2PF (☎ 0116 270 4701); Chemistry Department, The University, Leicester LE1 7RH (☎ 0116 252 2106, fax 0116 252 3789, telex LEICUL 347250)

HOLLOWAY, Julian Pendrill Warner; s of Adrian George Warner Holloway, JP, of Boscobel, Minchinhampton, Glos, and Helen Pendrill, *née* Charles; *b* 6 May 1954; *Educ* Winchester, Univ of Durham (BA); *m* 4 Oct 1980, Emma Jane Caroline, da of Col Peter Charles Ormrod, MC, JP, DL, of Pen-y-Lan Ruabon, Wrexham, Clwyd; 3 s (James b 29 June 1986, Thomas b 14 March 1988, Alexander b 29 Aug 1991), 1 da (Lavinia b 28 April 1984); *Career* articled clerk Denton Hall & Burgin 1979–81, admitted slr to the Supreme Ct 1981, asst slr Brecher & Co 1981–83, ptnr McKenna & Co 1988–92 (asst slr 1984–88), ptnr Greenwoods 1993–; dir Centre for Dispute Resolution, case-notes ed Construction Law Jl; memb Law Soc; *Recreations* tennis, skiing, shooting; *Clubs* Hurlingham; *Style—* Julian Holloway, Esq; ✉ 64 Alderbrook Rd, London SW12 8AB (☎ 0181 675 0308); Greenwoods, 20 Bedford Square, London WC1B 3HL (☎ 0171 323 4632, fax 0171 631 3142)

HOLLOWAY, Julian Robert Stanley; s of Stanley Augustus Holloway, OBE, the celebrated actor (d 1982), and Violet Marion, *née* Lane; *b* 24 June 1944; *Educ* Harrow, Royal Acad of Dramatic Art; *m* 1, (m dis 1977), Zena Cecilia Walker; 1 da (Sophie b 15 Sept 1977); m 2, Deborah Jane Wheeler; *Career* actor; *Theatre* incl: When Did You Last See My Mother, Spitting Image, The Norman Conquests, Arsenic And Old Lace, Charley's Aunt, Pygmalion, My Fair Lady (Broadway); as director: Play It Again Sam, When Did You Last See My Mother; *Television* incl: The Importance of Being Earnest, An Adventure In Bed, Rebecca, The Scarlet And The Black, Ellis Island, The Endless Game, Michelangelo, Grass Roots, Torch Song; *Films* actor/prodr incl: Carry On Films, The Spy's Wife, The Chairman's Wife, Loophole; *Recreations* golf, cricket, racing; *Style—* Julian Holloway, Esq; ✉ c/o Barry Burnett Organisation Ltd, Suite 42–43, Grafton House, 2–3 Golden Square, London W1R 3AD (☎ 0171 437 7048/9, fax 0171 734 6118)

HOLLOWAY, Laurence (Laurie); s of Marcus Holloway (d 1978), of Oldham, Lancs, and Annie, *née* Gillespie (d 1992); *b* 31 March 1938; *Educ* Oldham GS; *m* 1, 31 March 1956, Julia Planck, da of Rufus Macdonald (d 1975), of Rothesay, Isle of Bute; 1 da (Karon Julie b 9 Jan 1957); m 2, 16 June 1965, Marian Montgomery, singer, da of Forrest Marion Runnels (d 1966), of Atlanta, Georgia; 1 da (Abigail Ann Montgomery b 31 Jan

1967); *Career* pianist, composer, arranger; studio musician 1959–69; compositions incl: A Dream of Alice (BBC TV), pop preludes, About Time (C5 Records); musical dir: Engelbert Humperdinck 1969–74, Dame Edna Everage 1980– (currently md), Elaine Paige 1992–, Piaf (musical) 1992, Bob Monkhouse, Lily Savage TV Special, Bob Downe TV Special, Bob Holness radio series; pianist for Judy Garland and Liza Minnelli London Paladium 1964; composer TV signature tunes incl Blind Date, occasional guest conductor London Symphony Orch; *Recreations* golf, music; *Clubs* Wig and Pen, Temple Golf; *Style*— Laurie Holloway, Esq; ✉ Elgin, Fishery Rd, Bray-on-Thames, Berkshire (☎ 01628 37715, fax 01628 776232)

HOLLOWAY, Most Rev Richard Frederick; *see:* Edinburgh, Bishop of

HOLLOWAY, Dr Robin Greville; s of Robert Charles Holloway (d 1986), and Pamela Mary, *née* Jacob; *b* 19 Oct 1943; *Educ* St Paul's Cathedral Choir Sch, King's Coll Sch Wimbledon, King's Coll Cambridge, New Coll Oxford; *Career* composer; lectr in music Univ of Cambridge 1975–; compositions incl: Scenes from Schumann (Cheltenham) 1970, Domination of Black (London) 1974, Second Concerto for Orchestra (Glasgow) 1979, Seascape and Harvest (Birmingham) 1986, Clarissa (Eng Nat Opera) 1990, The Spacious Firmament (Birmingham) 1992, Violin Concerto (Manchester) 1992, Frost at Midnight (Bournemouth) 1994, Concerto No 3 (London) 1996; *Books* Debussy and Wagner (1978); *Style*— Dr Robin Holloway; ✉ Gonville and Caius Coll, Cambridge CB2 1TA (☎ 01223 335424); 531 Caledonian Rd, London N7 9RH (☎ 0171 607 2550)

HOLM, Ian; CBE (1990); *b* 12 Sept 1931; *Educ* RADA; *m* 3, 1990, Penelope Wilton, *qv*; *Career* actor; *Theatre* debut in Othello (Shakespeare Memorial Theatre) 1954, Worthing Rep 1956, at Stratford 1957–60 (roles incl Verges, Puck, The Fool in King Lear, Lorenzio and Gremio); with RSC (Aldwych) until 1967: Ondine, The Devils, Becket, The Taming of the Shrew, The Cherry Orchard; other RSC prodns until 1967: Troilus and Cressida (Stratford), The Tempest, Edward IV, Richard III, Henry IV and V 1964, Edward IV 1964, Richard III 1964, The Homecoming (Aldwych 1965, Music Box NY 1967), Henry IV (I and II) 1966, Henry V 1966, Twelfth Night 1966, Romeo and Juliet 1967; other prodns incl: The Friends (Roundhouse) 1970, A Bequest to the Nation (Haymarket) 1970, Caravaggio Buddy (Traverse Theatre, Edinburgh) 1972, Hatch in the Sea (Royal Court), Other People (Hampstead) 1974, The Iceman Cometh (Aldwych) 1976, The Devil's Disciple (Aldwych) 1976, Uncle Vanya (Hampstead) 1979, The Room (Pinter benefit, Haymarket) 1989, Moonlight (Almeida) 1993, Moonlight and Landscape (Pinter Festival Gate Theatre Dublin) 1994, Landscape (NT) 1994; *Television* for BBC: Flayed, The Lost Boys, The Misanthrope, Lloyd George, We The Accused, The Bell, After The Party, The Browning Version, Mr and Mrs Edgehill, Uncle Vanya, The Last Romantics, The Borrowers, Landscape; for Granada: Night School, Strike, Game Set and Match, Mirage; other credits incl: Napoleon in Love, Jesus of Nazareth, The Road From Mandalay, SOS Titanic, All Quiet on the Western Front, Inside The Third Reich, Death Can Add (Anglia TV), The Endless Game (HTV), Taylor of Gloucester (Thames); *Film* A Midsummer Night's Dream, The Fixer, The Bofers Gun, The Homecoming, Juggernaut, Shout at the Devil, The Man in the Iron Mask, March or Die, Thief of Baghdad, Alien, Chariots of Fire, The Time Bandits, The Return of the Soldier, Dead as they Come, Greystoke, Brazil, Laughterhouse, Dance with a Stranger, Wetherby, Dreamchild, Another Woman, Henry V, Michaelangelo, Hamlet, Kafka, The Naked Lunch, Blue Ice, The Hour of the Pig, Frankenstein; more recently: Dr Willis in The Madness of King George 1994, Loch Ness 1995, Big Night 1995, The Fifth Element 1996, A Life Less Ordinary 1996, The Sweet Hereafter 1996; *Awards* Evening Standard for Best Actor (Henry V) 1964, Tony for Best Supporting Actor in a Drama (The Homecoming) 1967, BAFTA for Best Supporting Actor (The Bofers Gun) 1968; for Chariots of Fire: BAFTA for Best Supporting Actor 1981, Cannes Film Festival Best Supporting Actor 1981, Oscar nomination 1982; Evening Standard Award for Best Actor (Moonlight) 1993; BAFTA nomination for The Madness of King George 1995; *Style*— Ian Holm, Esq, CBE; ✉ c/o Julian Belfrage Associates, 46 Albemarle Street, London W1X 4PP (☎ 0171 491 4400, fax 0171 493 5460)

HOLM, Dr Jessica Lynn; da of Ian Holm, CBE, *qv*, and Lynn Mary, *née* Shaw; *b* 29 March 1960; *Educ* Putney HS for Girls, Royal Holloway Coll Univ of London (BSc, PhD); *m* 27 Feb 1988, Gavin Bernard Chappell, s of Lt-Col Robin Chappell, OBE; *Career* zoologist and broadcaster BBC Natural History Unit and others, presenter Radio 4 Natural History Progamme 1988–93; BBC Natural History Unit films: The Case of the Vanishing Squirrel 1987, Daylight Robbery 1988, Badger Watch 1990, Daylight Robbery II 1991, Nightshift 1993; presenter: Wild about the West (TSW) 1988, Up Country (Tyne Tees TV) 1990, 1991, 1992 and 1993, Crufts 1993, 1994, 1995 and 1996, Wild West Country (WCTV) 1994, 1995 and 1996; painter; Slipper Thief (first limited edition print, Greenwich Workshop) 1996; *Books* Squirrels (1987), The Red Squirrel (1989); contrib various articles to wildlife and conservation magazines; *Recreations* dogs, natural history, riding; *Style*— Dr Jessica Holm; ✉ c/o Rachel Daniels, London Management, 2–4 Noel Street, London W1V 3RB (☎ 0171 287 9000); Greenwich Workshop, One Greenwich Place, PO Box 875, Shelton, Connecticut 06484–4675, USA (☎ 00 1 203 925 0131)

HOLMAN, Barry William; s of Ronald Cecil Holman, of Loughton, Essex, and Irene Winifred Holman; *b* 7 July 1949; *Educ* Coopers' Co GS; *m* 17 Aug 1974, Christine, da of Norman Thomas Richards; *Career* CA: B W Holman & Co (own practice), Newman Harris & Co, Silver Altman & Co, Lewis Bloom, Macnair Mason; FCA; *Recreations* golf, horse riding, clay pigeon shooting, music, chess; *Clubs* Abridge Golf and Country, Beldlam Golf Soc (past capt); *Style*— Barry W Holman, Esq; ✉ Brook House, Ongar Rd, Abridge, Essex RM4 1UH (☎ 01992 813079); B W Holman & Co, 309 High Rd, Loughton, Essex IG10 1AH (☎ 0181 508 9228)

HOLMAN, Hon Mr Justice; Hon Sir (Edward) James; kt (1995); s of Edward Theodore Holman, formerly of Ringwood, Hants and Manaccan, Cornwall, and Mary Megan, *née* Morris, MBE; *b* 21 Aug 1947; *Educ* Dauntsey's, Exeter Coll Oxford (BA, MA); *m* 14 July 1979, Fiona Elisabeth, da of Dr Ronald Cathcart Roxburgh, of Wiggenhall St Mary, King's Lynn, Norfolk; 2 s (Edward b 1988, Henry b 1991), 1 da (Charlotte b 1984); *Career* called to the Bar Middle Temple 1971, bencher 1995; memb Western Circuit, QC 1991, recorder of the Crown Court 1993–95, judge of the High Court of Justice (Family Div) 1995–, Family Div liaison judge for Western Circuit 1995–; standing counsel to the Treasury (Queen's Proctor) 1980–91, legal assessor UK Central Cncl for Nursing Midwifery and Health Visiting 1983–95; Family Law Bar Assoc: sec 1988–92, chm 1992–95; ex officio memb Gen Cncl of the Bar 1992–95; memb: Family Proceedings Rules Ctee 1991–95, Supreme Ct Procedure Ctee 1992–95; memb: Cncl RYA 1980–83, 1984–87 and 1988–91, Ctee Royal Ocean Racing Club 1984–87; *Recreations* sailing, skiing, music; *Clubs* Royal Yacht Sqdn, Royal Ocean Racing; *Style*— The Hon Mr Justice Holman; ✉ Royal Courts of Justice, Strand, London WC2A 2LL

HOLMAN, His Hon Judge Richard Christopher; s of Frank Harold Holman (d 1984), and Joan, *née* Attrill (d 1988); *b* 16 June 1946; *Educ* Eton, Gonville and Caius Coll Cambridge (BA, MA); *m* 9 Aug 1969, Susan Holman, MBE, da of George Amos Whittaker, of Wilmslow; 2 s (Nicholas b 12 Jan 1973, Simon b 26 May 1977); *Career* admitted slr 1971, dep dist registrar of High Court and dep registrar County Court 1982–88, asst recorder 1988–92, recorder Northern Circuit 1992–94, circuit judge (Northern Circuit) 1994–; managing ptnr Davies Wallis Foyster 1988–89 (ptnr 1973); memb Cncl Manchester Law Soc until 1990, memb Area Ctee NW Legal Aid until 1994; chm Pownall Hall Sch 1993– (govr 1990–); *Recreations* golf, gardening, theatre, wine; *Clubs* Wilmslow Golf; *Style*— His Hon Judge R C Holman; ✉ Courts of Justice, Crown Square, Manchester M3 3FL

HOLME OF CHELTENHAM, Baron (Life Peer UK 1990), of Cheltenham in the County of Gloucestershire; Richard Gordon Holme; CBE (1983); s of J R Holme (d 1940), and E M Holme, *née* Eggleton; *b* 27 May 1936; *Educ* St John's Coll Oxford (MA); *m* 1958, Kay Mary, da of Vincent Powell; 2 s (Hon Richard Vincent b 1966, Hon John Gordon b (twin) 1966), 2 da (Hon Nicola Ann b 1959, Hon Penelope Jane b 1962); *Career* chm: Constitutional Reform Centre 1984–94, Threadneedle Publishing Group 1988–, Prima Europe Ltd 1991–95; dir: RTZ Corporation plc 1995–, CRA Ltd Dec 1995–; sec Parly Democracy Tst 1979–, pres Lib Pty 1981, Lib Dem Parly spokesman on N Ireland 1990–; chm English Coll in Prague 1991–; *Recreations* reading, walking, opera; *Clubs* Reform, Brooks's; *Style*— The Rt Hon Lord Holme of Cheltenham, CBE; ✉ House of Lords, London SW1A OPW

HOLMES, Alan Wilson Jackson; s of Luke Jackson Holmes (d 1979); *b* 13 Sept 1945; *Educ* Portora Royal Sch Enniskillen, Univ of Cambridge; *m* 1970, Frances-Maria, *née* Kadwell; 3 s, 1 da; *Career* dir Courage (Central) Ltd 1973–81, chm Courage (Scotland) Ltd 1979–81, dir Courage Ltd 1982–96, dir Scottish Courage Ltd 1996–; memb Ct of Assts Worshipful Co of Brewers; *Recreations* golf, theatre; *Clubs* Royal and Ancient Golf, Huntercombe Golf; *Style*— Alan Holmes, Esq; ✉ 25 Carlton Terrace Mews, Edinburgh EH7 5DA (☎ 0131 557 9788); Scottish Courage Ltd, Fountain House, Dundee Street, Edinburgh (☎ 0131 656 5000, fax 0131 221 1772)

HOLMES, Andrea; da of Peter Douglas, of Dunstable, Beds, and Loraine Brenda, *née* Triscott; *b* 2 Jan 1970; *Educ* Brewers Hill Middle Sch, Northfields Upper Sch; *Career* trampolinist; nat age gp champion 1979–88, winner of over 250 nat competitions with Dunstable Trampoline Club; honours: Gold medal Euro Sr Championships 1983, 1985 and 1991, Euro jr champion 1984 and 1986, Silver medal World Championships 1986, 1988, 1990 and 1994, winner World Games 1985 and 1989, winner World Cup Birmingham 1991, Denmark 1992, France 1993, Germany 1993, Switzerland 1994 and Russia 1995, World Synchro champion 1992, Br sr champion 1994 (7 times); youngest int to represent GB aged 12 World Championships 1982; Champion Child of the Year for Sport 1983; material control clerk 1987–89, receptionist radio station 1989–90; performer at trampoline shows 1990–; *Recreations* skiing, travel; *Style*— Miss Andrea Holmes; ✉ 36 Douglas Crescent, Duntable, Beds LU5 5AT (☎ 01582 662230)

HOLMES, Christopher John (Chris); s of Gordon Holmes, and Doris, *née* Waite; *b* 13 July 1942; *Educ* Clare Coll Cambridge (MA), Univ of Bradford (Dip in Industl Admin); *m* 1969 (m dis 1989); 1 s, 1 da; partner, Hattie Llewelyn-Davies; 1 s, 1 da; *Career* John Laing Construction 1966–68, NE Islington Community project then N Islington Housing Assoc Rights Project 1969–74, dep dir Shelter 1974–76; dir: Soc for Co-operative Dwellings 1976–79, E London Housing Assoc 1979–82, CHAR (Housing Campaign for Single People) 1982–87; conslt Priory Estates Project 1988–89, dir of housing London Borough of Camden 1990–95, dir Shelter 1995–; memb Nat Consumer Cncl 1975–80; *Recreations* family, reading, walking, theatre, cricket; *Style*— Chris Holmes, Esq; ✉ 2 Carpenters Yard, Park Street, Tring, Herts HP23 6AR (☎ 01442 822366); Director, Shelter, 88 Old Street, London EC1V 9HU (☎ 0171 505 2124, fax 0171 505 2169, mobile 0385 307212)

HOLMES, David; CB (1985); s of George Archibald Holmes (d 1962), of Doncaster, and Annie, *née* Hill (d 1979); *b* 6 March 1935; *Educ* Doncaster GS, Christ Church Oxford (MA); *m* 1963, Ann, da of late John Chillingworth, of London; 1 s (Matthew b 1970), 2 da (Joanne b 1965, Elise b 1972); *Career* asst princ Miny of Tport and Civil Aviation 1957, princ HM Treasy 1965–68, princ private sec to Min of Tport 1968–70, asst sec DOE 1970, under sec 1976, dep sec Dept of Tport 1982–91; British Airways plc: dir Government and Industry Affairs 1991–95, dir Corp Resources 1996–; *Clubs* United Oxford and Cambridge University, Royal Automobile; *Style*— David Holmes, Esq, CB; ✉ British Airways plc, PO Box 10, Heathrow Airport (London), Hounslow TW6 2JA (☎ 0181 759 5511)

HOLMES, David Frederick Cecil; s of Norman Holmes (d 1995), and Kathleen Alice, *née* Bennett (d 1983); *b* 10 Sept 1933; *Educ* Little Ealing Sr Boys' Sch, Ealing Coll of Art, Shrewsbury Coll of Art, Central Sch of Art (pt/t); *m* 16 April 1960, Marie Lily Theresa, da of James Frederick Wilkinson; 2 s (Toby John b 20 Oct 1962, Rupert James b 20 May 1964), 1 da (Polly Victoria b 18 Nov 1967); *Career* joined Colman Prentis & Varley as junior 1950–52; Nat Serv RAOC 1952–54; junior creative Colman Prentis & Varley 1954–55, junior art dir W S Crawford Advertising 1955–58, art dir Mather & Crowther 1958–63, gp head of art Colman Prentis & Varley 1963–65, sr art dir (later ptnr and head of art) Kingsley Manton & Palmer Partnership 1965–71, dir and art dir The Television Department Ltd 1971–75, proprietor David Holmes & Partners (creative consultants) 1975–77, jt fndr dir and creative dir Holmes Knight Keeley Ltd (later Holmes Knight Ritchie WRG Ltd) 1977–92, exec creative dir TBWA/Holmes Knight Ritchie Ltd 1990–92, freelance artist, art dir and film maker 1992–; winner: numerous D & AD awards 1966–, Campaign Poster award for The Macallan 1986, Clio award for the Macallan poster 1988, D & AD Silver medal for Singapore Brochure design 1988 (also Gold award Aust Art Dirs' and Writers' Club 1988), shortlist certificate for The Long Sleep (The Macallan Malt Whisky cinema commercial) 1990 (also winner The One Show merit award 1990, Clio award 1990 and Oscar Br Animation awards 1990), 4 Gold awards Scotmedia Advertising Awards 1991; memb: D & AD 1968– (memb Ctee 1971–72), The Advertising Creative Circle 1967– (memb Cncl and sec 1979–81); *Publications* created books for Pan Books: My First Watch (Timex), My First Torch (Duracell), My First Toothbrush (Wisdom), My First Fountain Pen (Platignum), My First Crayons (Platignum); *Recreations* painting, illustrating, film making, walking; *Style*— David Holmes, Esq; ✉ Studio, 5 Calvert Street, Primrose Hill, London NW1 8NE (☎ 0171 586 0363)

HOLMES, Dr Geoffrey Kenneth Towndrow; s of Kenneth Geoffrey Holmes (d 1974), and Majorie, *née* Towndrow; *b* 15 Feb 1942; *Educ* Tupton Hall GS, Univ of Birmingham (BSc, MB ChB, MD), DRCOG, MRCP, FRCP, PhD; *m* 4 May 1970, Rosemary, da of Stanley Alfred Guy, MBE, of Derby; 1 s (Simon b 1973), 2 da (Rachel b 1971, Emma b 1976); *Career* res fell Birmingham Gen Hosp and Dept of Experimental Pathology Univ of Birmingham 1971–74, sr med registrar United Birmingham Hosps 1974–78, conslt physician and gastroenterologist Derbyshire Royal Infirmary 1978–, clinical teacher Univ of Nottingham 1980–; author various res papers on gastrointestinal disorders; memb Br Soc of Gastroenterology 1973, med advsr Derby and Dist Coeliac Soc 1980–, pres Derby and Burton Ileostomy Assoc 1986; memb BMA 1966; *Books* Coeliac Disease Inflammatory Bowel Disease and Food Intolerance in Clinical Reactions to Food (1983), Coeliac Disease (1984), Coeliac Disease in Bockus Gastroenterology (1985); *Recreations* gardening, reading, theology; *Style*— Dr Geoffrey Holmes; ✉ Derbyshire Royal Infirmary, London Road, Derby, Derbyshire (☎ 01332 347141)

HOLMES, Prof George Arthur; s of John Holmes (d 1949), of Aberystwyth, and Margaret, *née* Thomas (d 1977); *b* 22 April 1927; *Educ* Ardwyn Co Sch Aberystwyth, Univ Coll of Wales, St John's Coll Cambridge (MA, PhD); *m* 19 Dec 1953, (Evelyn) Anne, da of Dr John William Klein (d 1973), of Wimbledon; 2 s (Peter b 1955 d 1968, Nicholas b 1963), 2 da (Susan b 1957, Catherine (twin) b 1957); *Career* fell St John's Coll Cambridge 1951–54, tutor St Catherine's Soc Oxford 1954–62, fell and tutor St Catherine's Coll Oxford 1962–89 (vice-master 1969–71), Chichele prof of medieval history and fell All Souls' Coll Oxford 1989–94; visiting prof Harvard Univ Center for Italian

Renaissance Studies Florence 1995; memb Inst for Advanced Study Princeton 1967–68, delegate Oxford Univ Press 1982–92, jt ed English Historical Review 1974–81, chm Victoria Co History Ctee of Inst of Historical Res 1978–89; FBA 1985 (Serena medal 1993); *Books* The Estates of the Higher Nobility in 14th Century England (1957), The Later Middle Ages (1962), The Florentine Enlightenment 1400–50 (1969), Europe: Hierarchy and Revolt 1320–1450 (1975), The Good Parliament (1975), Dante (1980), Florence, Rome and the Origins of the Renaissance (1986), The Oxford Illustrated History of Medieval Europe (ed, 1988), The First Age of the European City 1300–1500 (1990), Art and Politics in Renaissance Italy (ed, 1993); *Style—* Prof George Holmes, FBA; ✉ Highmoor House, Bampton, Oxon (☎ 01993 850408)

HOLMES, George Dennis; CB (1979); s of James Henry Holmes (d 1960), of Gwynedd, N Wales, and Florence Jones (d 1978); *b* 9 Nov 1926; *Educ* John Bright's Sch Llandudno, Univ of Wales (BSc, DSc); *m* 1953, Sheila Rosemary, da of George Henry Woodger (d 1949), of Surrey; 3 da (Carolyn, Deborah, Nicola); *Career* dir gen Forestry Cmmn 1977–86; chm Capability Scotland 1986–; FRSE 1982; *Recreations* golf, fishing; *Style—* George Holmes, Esq, CB, FRSE; ✉ 7 Cammo Rd, Edinburgh EH4 8EF (☎ 0131 339 7474)

HOLMES, James Christopher (Jim); s of Herbert Frederick Holmes (d 1978), and Dorothy Gladys, *née* Thomas; *b* 21 Nov 1948; *Educ* Tottenham Co GS, Univ of Sheffield (BA), London Opera Centre (repetiteurs dip); *m* 1981, Jean, da of William J Wilkinson; 2 s (Edward b 1983, Robert b 1985); *Career* conductor; ENO: chorus master 1973–78, princ coach 1978–96, res conductor 1985–96; head of music/asst music dir Opera North 1996–; princ coach Glyndebourne Festival 1986–94; memb: Editorial Advsy Bd Kurt Weill Edn 1994–, Reading Panel Contemporary Opera Studio 1995–; *Repertoire* incl: Orpheus in the Underworld, The Magic Flute, Mikado, Princess Ida, Die Fledermaus, Hansel and Gretel, Peter Grimes, Turn of the Screw, Falstaff, Oedipus Rex, Pacific Overtures, La Belle Vivette, Fidelio, Porgy and Bess, Marriage of Figaro, Cosi Fan Tutte, Don Giovanni; other prodns incl: assoc music dir Carousel RNT 1993, I'm A Stranger Here Myself - Kurt Weill in America (BBC Television/Hessicher Rundfunk, Street Scene (Theater des Westens Berlin, Theater im Pfalzbau Ludwigshafen) 1994–95, debut Montreal Symphony Orch 1995; *Recordings* Pacific Overtures (Grammy Award nomination 1989), Soprano in Red (with Lesley Garrett, Silver Disc) 1996, Porgy and Bess (musical asst to Sir Simon Rattle); *Recreations* reading, crosswords, logic puzzles, fine art (sketching), cinema, model railways, tennis, swimming, soccer (lifelong Spurs fan); *Style—* Jim Holmes, Esq; ✉ c/o Opera North, Grand Theatre, New Briggate, Leeds LS1 6NU (☎ 0113 243 9999, fax 0113 244 0418)

HOLMES, Dr Jeremy Alan; s of Robin Holmes (d 1985), of Oare, Wilts, and Marjorie, *née* Brown (d 1988); *b* 21 Feb 1943; *Educ* Westminster, King's Coll Cambridge (MA, MB BCh), UCH London (MRCP, MRCPsych); *m* 1978, Rosamund, da of Erroll Bruce; 3 s (Jacob b 1967, Matthew b 1969, Joshua b 1983), 1 da (Lydia b 1971); *Career* house physician London 1968–71, lectr in med Tanzania 1971–73, registrar then sr registrar in psychiatry Maudsley Hosp London 1973–77, conslt psychiatrist and hon sr lectr UCH London 1977–86, conslt psychiatrist N Devon, conslt psychotherapist and sr clinical lectr Univ of Bristol 1986–; Wellcome sr research fell 1992; FRCPsych 1986 (memb Cncl); *Books* Textbook of Psychotherapy in Psychiatric Practice (ed, 1971), The Values of Psychotherapy (jtly, 1989), Between Art and Science - Essays in Psychiatry and Psychotherapy (1992), John Bowlby and Attachment Theory (1993), The Good Mood Guide (jtly, 1993), Introduction to Psychoanalysis (jtly, 1995); *Recreations* family, literature and the Arts; *Style—* Dr Jeremy Holmes; ✉ North Devon District Hospital, Barnstaple, Devon EX31 4JB (☎ 01271 22666)

HOLMES, Kelly; da of D Constantine Holmes, and Pamela, *née* Norman; *b* 19 April 1970; *Educ* Hugh Christie Comp Sch; *Career* athlete; rep GB 6 times; memb Ealing Southall and Middx Athletics Club; English Schs winner 1,500m 1983 and 1987, Gold medal 800m Mini Youth Olympics 1987, Gold medal 1,500m GB Int Germany and Ipswich 1987, semi-finalist World Championships Stuttgart 1993, Silver medal 1,500m Euro Championships Helsinki 1994, Gold medal 1,500m Cwlth Games Victoria 1994, Silver medal 1,500m and Bronze medal 800m World Championships Gothenburg 1995; English, Br and Cwlth record holder 800m, Br and Cwlth record holder 1000m; Army Athlete of the Yr 1989–, Combined Servs Sports Woman of the Yr 1993 and 1994, Middx County Sports Woman of the Yr 1994 and 1995, Athlete of the Year Sports Writers' Assoc 1995, nominated Mover & Shakers Award Company Magazine 1995, Br Athletics Female Athlete of the Year 1995; non-sporting career: recreation asst 1986–87, nursing asst 1987–88, Sergeant (army physical trg instr) HM Forces 1988–; *Style—* Miss Kelly Holmes; ✉ c/o Barry Nevill, Premier Marketing and Management, 4th Floor, CTS House, 7 Upper St Martin's Lane, London WC2H 9DL

HOLMES, Mark Jason; s of John Brian Holmes, of Nantwich, Cheshire, and Mavis Evelyn, *née* Hobson; *b* 24 March 1969; *Educ* Malbank Sch Nantwich, S Cheshire Coll Crewe; *m* Helen Louise, *née* Dix; *Career* chef: The Mayfair Intercontinental (under Michael Coaker) 1987–90, The Naval and Military Club (under Gerry Hazelgrove) May-Sept 1990, The Ivy (under Tony Howarth and Nigel Davis) Sept 1990–Jan 1992, The Greenhouse (under Gary Rhodes) Jan 1992–May 1992, The Square (under Philip Howard) May 1992–Aug 1993; head chef and dir The Lexington 1993–95, head chef Scotts Restaurant, Oyster Terrace and Cocktail Bar 1995–; Young Student Chef of the Yr 1987, Taste of Britain regional and nat winner 1987; *Recreations* participating in all sports (former U18 Crewe and Dist badminton champion and nat U19 men's doubles champion), gym; *Style—* Mark Holmes, Esq; ✉ Scotts Restaurant, Oyster Terrace and Cocktail Bar, 20 Mount Street, London W1Y 6HE (☎ 0171 629 5248 (restaurant), 0171 514 2808 (chef's office), fax 0171 499 8246)

HOLMES, Sir Maurice Andrew; kt (1969); s of Rev A T Holmes (d 1942); *b* 28 July 1911; *Educ* Felsted; *m* 1935, Joyce Esther Hicks; *Career* WWII serv RASC (despatches); called to the Bar Gray's Inn 1948; chm: Tilling Gp 1960–65, London Tport Bd 1965–69; circuit admin SE Circuit 1969–74; *Style—* Sir Maurice Holmes; ✉ The Limes, Felsted, nr Dunmow, Essex (☎ 01371 820352)

HOLMES, Sir Peter Fenwick; kt (1988), MC (1952); s of Gerald Hugh Holmes (d 1950), and Caroline Elizabeth, *née* Morris (d 1989); *b* 27 Sept 1932; *Educ* Malvern, Trinity Coll Cambridge (MA); *m* 19 March 1955, Judith Millicent, da of Brig Robert Fowler Walker, CBE, MC (d 1976); 3 da (Hermione b 1957, Josephine b 1958, Martha b 1961); *Career* Nat Serv Royal Leicestershire Regt 1950–52 (served Korea 1951–52); Royal Dutch/Shell Group of Companies 1956–; gen mangr Shell Markets ME 1965–68, chief rep Libya 1970–72, md Shell-BP Nigeria 1977–81, pres Shell International Trading 1981–83, md Royal Dutch/Shell Group 1982–93, dir Shell Transport and Trading Co plc 1982– (chm 1985–93); tstee WWF UK 1989–96; Hon DSc Cranfield Univ 1993; RIIA, FRGS; *Books* Mountains and a Monastery (1958), Nigeria, Giant of Africa (1985), Turkey, A Timeless Bridge (1988); *Recreations* mountaineering, skiing, travel to remote areas, photography, golf, 19th century travel books; *Clubs* Climbers', Himalayan, Alpine, Athenaeum, Sunningdale, Kandahar; *Style—* Sir Peter Holmes, MC; ✉ The Shell Transport and Trading Co plc, Shell Centre, London SE1 7NA (☎ 0171 934 5611)

HOLMES, HE Peter Rodney; *b* 29 July 1938; *m* Anne Cecilia, *née* Tarrant; 1 s, 3 da; *Career* HM Dip Serv: joined Foreign Office 1956, vice-consul Strasbourg 1959–63, third sec Belgrade 1963–66, second sec Paris 1966–69, asst economic sec Central Treaty Orgn Ankara 1969–71, FCO 1971–74 first sec Stockholm 1974–78, HM consul Douala 1978–80, FCO 1980–83, dep head of mission Bahrain 1983–86, commercial cnsllr Santiago 1987–90, FCO 1990–95, HM ambass Honduras 1995–; *Style—* HE Mr Peter Holmes; ✉ c/o Foreign & Commonwealth Office (Tegucigalpa), King Charles Street, London SW1A 2AH; British Embassy, Edificio Palmira, Colonia Palmira, Tegucigalpa, Honduras (☎ 00 504 32 5429, fax 99 504 32 5480)

HOLMES, Peter Sloan; s of George Horner Gaffikin Holmes (d 1971), of Newcastle, Co Down, and Anne Sloan, *née* Reid (d 1987); *b* 8 Dec 1942; *Educ* Rossall Sch Lancashire, Magdalen Coll Oxford (BA); *m* 14 April 1966, Patricia, da of Frederick Alexander McMahon (d 1984), of Belfast; 2 s ((Christopher) Paul b 25 Jan 1967, Patrick Michael b 4 June 1969); *Career* Lt RNR 1965–68; teacher Eastbourne Coll 1965–68, head of English Grosvenor HS Belfast 1968–71, lectr and sr lectr Stranmillis Coll of Educn Belfast 1971–75; Dept of Educn: joined 1975, sr inspector 1980–82, staff inspector 1982–83, asst sec 1983–87, under sec 1987–96, dep sec 1996–; *Recreations* singing, sailing, gliding; *Clubs* United Oxford & Cambridge University; *Style—* Peter Holmes, Esq; ✉ Department of Education for Northern Ireland, Rathgael House, Bangor, Co Down BT19 2PR (☎ 01247 279317)

HOLMES, Prof (Edward) Richard; OBE, TD, JP (NE Hampshire); s of Edward William Holmes (d 1965), and Helen, *née* Jacques (d 1990); *b* 29 March 1946; *Educ* Forest Sch Snaresbrook, Emmanuel Coll Cambridge (History scholar, MA), Northern Illinois Univ (travelling fell), Univ of Reading (PhD); *m* 1975, Katharine Elizabeth, da of William Richard Dawson Saxton (sr princ surveyor Lloyd's Register of Shipping); 2 da (Jessica Helen b 1980, Sara Corinna b 1983); *Career* military historian, author and broadcaster; RMA Sandhurst 1969–85 (lectr in war studies, sr lectr, dep head of dept), Lt-Col cmdg 2 Bn The Wessex Regt (Vol) 1985–88, co-dir Cranfield Security Studies Inst 1990–; conslt historian Army Staff Coll 1988–, prof of military and security studies Cranfield Univ 1995–; TA: enlisted 1964, cmmnd 1965, currently Brig TA; TV credits (writer/presenter) incl: Comrades in Arms (ITV) 1980, Soldiers (BBC) 1985, The War Within (ITV) 1990, Tales from the Map Room: Burma (BBC) 1995, War Walks (BBC) 1996; memb: Royal United Servs Inst, Br Cmmn for Mil History; *Books* incl: The English Civil War (with Brig Peter Young, 1974), The Little Field-Marshal - Sir John French (1981), The Road to Sedan (1984), Firing Line (1985, US title Acts of War), Soldiers (jtly, 1985), Nuclear Warriors (1991), Fatal Avenue (1992), Riding the Retreat: Mons to the Marne 1914 Revisited (1995), War Walks (1996); *Clubs* Army and Navy; *Style—* Prof Richard Holmes, OBE, TD, JP; ✉ Cranfield Security Studies Institute, Royal Military College of Science, Shrivenham, Swindon, Wilts SN6 8LA (☎ 01793 785474, fax 01793 785459)

HOLMES, (Cecil) Robert; LVO (1988); s of Cecil Edward Holmes (d 1993), of Donaghadee, NI, and Martha, *née* Fry; *b* 29 May 1940; *Educ* Grosvenor HS Belfast; *m* 10 Nov 1962, Margaret Jean (d 1995), da of William Arthur Laing (d 1950); 1 s (Stephen Robert Charles b 30 May 1971), 2 da (Brenda Jean b 26 May 1964, Christine Margaret b 18 February 1967); *Career* FCO (formerly FO): Fin Dept 1957–61, Br Embassy Moscow 1961–62, Br Embassy Santiago Chile 1963–65, Br Embassy Budapest 1965–66, Br Embassy Bonn 1967–70, head of ops room Personnel Ops Dept FCO 1970–73, dep to High Cmmr Br High Cmmn Nuku'Alofa Tonga 1973–75, second sec (mgmnt) Br Embassy Oslo 1975–79, vice consul (commercial) Br Consulate Gen Chicago 1979–81, int auditor Int Audit Unit FCO 1982–83, computer audit mangr and dep head of int audit FCO 1983–86, first sec (mgmnt) Br Embassy Madrid 1986–90, seconded to Purchasing Gps ICI Engineering 1991, dep dir of purchasing FCO 1991–94; dir of procurement Univ of Glasgow 1994–; hon memb Spanish Order of Merit 1988; MIIA 1985, MIMgt 1986, MCIPS 1993; *Recreations* sailing, driving, road running (Chicago Marathon 1980, Madrid Marathon 1989 and 1990, London Marathon 1992 and 1994, Belfast Marathon 1993), DIY, Rotarian; *Clubs* Royal Over-Seas League; *Style—* Robert Holmes, Esq, LVO; ✉ 21 Glencairn Road, Langbank, Port Glasgow PA14 6XL; University of Glasgow, Glasgow G12 8QQ (☎ 0141 330 4114, fax 0141 330 4614)

HOLMES, Robert George; s of George Holmes (d 1981), of Birmingham, and Violet, *née* Keightley; *b* 4 June 1947; *Educ* Paget Road Secdy Sch Pype Hayes Birmingham; *m* 22 Feb 1969, Sylvia, da of James Barley; 1 s (Paul Robert Francis b 15 March 1973), 3 da (Lisa Jayne b 25 Nov 1969, Sarah Louise b 3 March 1971, Gemma b 26 Dec 1980); *Career* British Homing World (specialist newspaper for racing pigeon fanciers) 1962–70 (office jr, journalist, supervisor, asst ed), md George Bartram Associates (showbusiness PR and promotion) 1988– (joined 1970); clients incl: Ken Dodd, Cannon & Ball, Don Maclean, Vince Hill, Brian Conley, Jimmy Bowen; Barker Variety Club of GB; *Recreations* golf, snooker, writing, relaxing with family, definitely not DIY; *Clubs* Variety Club of GB; *Style—* Robert Holmes, Esq; ✉ George Bartram Associates, Sherborne Wharf, 27–28 Sherborne Street, Birmingham B16 8DE (☎ 0121 608 6000, fax 0121 608 2223)

HOLMES, Robin Edmond Kendall; s of R F G Holmes, and K Holmes; *b* 14 July 1938; *Educ* Wolverhampton GS, Clare Coll Cambridge (BA), Univ of Birmingham (LLM); m, Karin, *née* Kutter; 2 s (Stephen b 1966, Nicholas b 1969); *Career* articled clerk to Town Clerk Wolverhampton 1961–64, Miny of Housing and Local Govt (now DOE) 1965–73, Colonial Secretariat Hong Kong 1973–75, DOE 1976–82; Lord Chancellor's Dept: under sec 1983–, circuit admin 1986–92, head Judicial Appointments 1992–; *Recreations* travelling; *Style—* Robin Holmes, Esq; ✉ Lord Chancellor's Department, Selbourne House, 54/60 Victoria Street, London SW1R 6QB

HOLMES, Dr William Francis (Bill); s of William Francis Holmes (d 1970), and Margaret Mary, *née* Carty; *b* 7 May 1954; *Educ* St Mary's Coll Crosby Liverpool, Univ of Nottingham (BM BS, MRCGP); *m* Dr Sheelagh Littlewood; *Career* GP 1980–; ptnr Health at Work 1987–, dir Clinic Systems Ltd 1990–; special lectr Dept of Respiratory Med Univ of Nottingham 1992–; memb GMC 1994–; *Recreations* golf; *Clubs* Savage, Royal and Ancient Golf; *Style—* Dr Bill Holmes; ✉ Sherrington Park Medical Practice, 402 Mansfield Road, Nottingham NG5 2EJ (0115 985 8552, fax 015 985 8553)

HOLMES-WALKER, Dr (William) Anthony; ERD (1971), TD (1991); s of Lt-Col William Roger Holmes Walker, TD (d 1967), of South Corner, Duncton, nr Petworth, Sussex, and Katharine Grace, *née* Foote (d 1988); *b* 26 Jan 1926; *Educ* Westminster, Queen's Univ Belfast (BSc, PhD), Imperial Coll London (DIC); *m* 26 July 1952, Marie-Anne, da of Willy Eugene Russ (d 1959), of Neuchâtel, Switzerland; 2 da (Antonia b 1954, Katharine b 1957); *Career* RE: Belfast 1944, Lt 1945, Capt 1946, served ME; Lt-Col AER/TAVR 1960 (Maj 1956); tech offr ICI Ltd 1954–59, head of plastics R & D Metal Box Co Ltd 1959–66, prof of polymer sci & technol Brunel Univ 1966–74, dir Br Plastics Fedn 1974–81, visiting prof City Univ 1981–83, sec gen Euro Brewers Trade Assoc 1983–88, dir of industl liaison Univ of Reading 1988–90, chm BioInteractions Ltd 1991–, chm TEC 20 The Executive Committee Ltd 1995–; memb Round Table Hemel Hempstead 1955–66, pres Villars Visitors Ski Club 1955–74, churchwarden St John's Boxmoor 1966–72; Freeman: City of London 1951, Worshipful Co of Skinners (Master 1980–81 and memb Ct); FRSC 1966, FPRI 1969, FIM 1972; *Books* Polymer Conversion (1975), Best Foote Forward (1995); *Recreations* music, genealogy; *Style—* Dr Anthony Holmes-Walker, TD, ERD; ✉ Blue Cedars, Sheethanger Lane, Felden, Boxmoor, Herts HP3 0BG (☎ 01442 253117)

HOLMPATRICK, 4 Baron (UK 1897), of HolmPatrick, Co Dublin; Hans James David Hamilton; eldest s of 3 Baron HolmPatrick (d 1991), and Anne Loys Roche, *née* Brass; *b* 15 March 1955; *Educ* Harrow; *m* 19 July 1984, Mrs Gill Francesca Anne du Feu, eldest da of Kenneth James Harding (d 1990), of Binisafua, Minorca; 1 s (Hon James Hans Stephen b 6 Oct 1982), 1 step s (Dominic Mark du Feu b 15 Jan 1975); *Heir* bro, Hon Ion Henry James Hamilton b 12 June 1956; *Style—* The Rt Hon Lord HolmPatrick;

✉ Horse Shoe Cottage, 67 Vicarage Road, St Agnes, Cornwall TR5 0TH (☎ 01872 552813)

HOLNESS, Robert Wentworth John (Bob); s of Charles John Holness (d 1973), of Herne Bay, Kent, and Ethel Eileen Holness (d 1972); *b* 12 Nov 1928; *Educ* Ashford GS Kent, Maidstone Coll of Art; *m* 16 April 1955, Mary Rose, da of Thomas Vernon Clifford; 1 s (Jonathan Clifford b 9 April 1966), 2 da (Carol Ann (Mrs Gibson) b 2 Feb 1956, Rosalind Mary b 23 Sept 1957); *Career* Nat Serv RAF 1947–49; apprentice in printing trade, memb repertory co Intimate Theatre (where met wife) S Africa 1953–55, radio actor, interviewer and presenter of music and magazine progs S Africa 1955–61, Granada TV Eng 1961–64 (host of quiz progs Take a Letter and Junior Criss Cross Quiz, worked on World in Action, What the Papers Say and Breakthrough, reporter, newsreader, interviewer and announcer), freelance 1964–68 (mainly with BBC in London), Thames TV 1968 (reporter and co presenter of Today news magazine prog), Radio 4 (presenter Top of the Form), Radio 2 (presenter Late Night Extra 1967–74), LBC (co-presenter AM Show 1974–84), freelance work incl voice-over commentary work and radio and tv tutoring, presenter Blockbusters (ITV until 1993, Sky One 1994–) 1982–, Bob Holness and Friends BBC Radio 2, presenter Raise the Roof (Action Time/Yorkshire TV for ITV) 1995, chairman Call my Bluff (BBC1) 1996–; Freeman City of London 1981, Liveryman Worshipful Co of Glaziers & Painters of Glass, Grand Order of Water Rats; *Awards* (jtly) Top News Presenter Nat Radio and Record Industs 1978, (for AM Show) Best Current Affairs Programming Local Radio awards 1979, Jt Ind Radio Personality Variety Club of GB 1979 and 1984, (for Blockbusters) Favourite Game Show on TV award TV Times 1985 and 1986 and five BAFTA nominations; *Recreations* walking, gardening, listening to every type of music; *Style*— Bob Holness, Esq; ✉ c/o The Spotlight, 7 Leicester Place, London WC2H 7BP (☎ 0171 437 7631, fax 0171 437 5881)

HOLROYD, (William) Andrew Myers; s of William Holroyd (d 1992), of Bradford, and Joan, *née* Myers (d 1993); *b* 13 April 1948; *Educ* Bradford GS, Univ of Nottingham (BA Law); *m* 26 July 1975, Caroline Irene, da of Jack Skerry, of Southport; 2 da (Emma b 1 Feb 1977, Clare b 3 Dec 1979); *Career* VSO Indonesia 1970–72, articled clerk Alsop Wilkinson 1972–74, managing ptnr Jackson & Canter Liverpool (ptnr 1977–); memb Cncl Law Soc 1996–; Liverpool Law Soc: memb Ctee 1983–95, chm Legal Aid and Advice Ctee 1986–92, vice pres 1993, pres 1994; circuit steward Liverpool South Circuit, involved with Liverpool Vol Soc for the Blind and Vauxhall Law Centre Liverpool; Methodist local preacher; memb Law Soc 1974; *Recreations* music, walking, sailing; *Clubs* Athenaeum (Liverpool); *Style*— Andrew Holroyd, Esq; ✉ Jackson & Canter, 32 Princes Road, Liverpool, Merseyside L8 1TH (☎ 0151 708 6593, fax 0151 708 5850)

HOLROYD, Air Marshal Sir Frank Martyn; KBE (1989), CB (1985); s of George Lumb Holroyd (d 1987), and Winifred Hetty, *née* Ford; *b* 30 Aug 1935; *Educ* Southend-on-Sea GS, Cranfield Univ (MSc); *m* 1 Feb 1958, Veronica Christine, da of Arthur George Booth (d 1984); 2 s (Martyn Paul b 26 Jan 1959, Myles Justin b 9 Nov 1966), 1 da (Bryony Jane b 4 June 1961); *Career* joined RAF 1956, appt Fighter Stations RAF Leconfield and RAF Leeming, Blind Landing Experimental Unit RAE Bedford 1960–63, HQ Fighter Cmd 1965–67, OC Electrical Engrg Sqdn RAF Changi Singapore 1967–69, Wing Cdr Staff Coll RAF Bracknell 1970, MOD 1970–72, OC Engrg Wing RAF Brize Norton 1972, Gp Capt 1974, Station Cdr No 1 Radio Sch RAF Locking 1974–76, sr engrg offr HQ 38 Gp 1976, Air Cdre dir Aircraft Engrg MOD 1977, RCDS 1981, dir Weapons and Support Engrg 1982, Air Vice Marshal dir gen Strategic Electronic Engrg MOD (PE) 1982, air offr engrg HQ Strike Cmd 1986, Air Marshal chief engr RAF 1988–91, chief Logistics Support RAF 1989–91; chm: AVR Communications Ltd 1991–95, Composite Technology Ltd 1992–, Electronica (UK) Ltd 1992–95; dir: Admiral plc 1992–, Ultra Electronics Ltd 1995–, REW Communications Services plc 1995–, Airinmar Ltd 1996–; memb: BBC Engrg Advsy Bd 1984–90, Advsy Cncl RMCS 1988–91, Cncl Cranfield Univ 1990– (memb Ct 1988–), Cncl (now Senate) Engrg Cncl 1990–; pres RAeS 1992–93; MacRobert Award tstee Royal Acad of Engrg; FEng 1992, FRAeS, FIEE, CIMgt; *Recreations* gardening, maintaining 14th century house, travel; *Clubs* RAF; *Style*— Air Marshal Sir Frank Holroyd, KBE, CB, FEng; ✉ c/o RAF Club, 128 Piccadilly, London W1V 0PY

HOLROYD, John Hepworth; CB (1993); s of Rev Harry Holroyd (d 1971), and Annie Dodgshun, *née* Hepworth; *b* 10 April 1935; *Educ* Kingswood Sch Bath, Worcester Coll Oxford (Open scholar, MA); *m* 30 Nov 1963, Judith Mary, da of John Mitchell Hudson; 1 s (Stephen Charles b 10 Dec 1966), 1 da (Sarah Ann b 9 Oct 1969); *Career* MAFF: joined 1959, asst private sec to Minister 1961–63, princ 1963–69, asst sec 1969–78, under sec 1978, chm Civil Service Selection Bd 1978–80, dir of Establishments 1981–85; Cabinet Office: European Secretariat 1985–89, first Civil Service cmmr and dep sec 1989–93, sec for appointments to the Prime Minister and ecclesiastical sec to the Lord Chancellor 1993–; sr fell European Inst of Public Admin; tstee: St Albans Cathedral Tst, Elmore Abbey; reader and staff memb Cathedral and Abbey Church of St Albans; treas to Govrs Kingswood Sch 1985–; *Recreations* music, travel, beekeeping, gardening; *Style*— John Holroyd, Esq, CB; ✉ c/o Cabinet Office, 70 Whitehall, London SW1A 2AS

HOLROYD, Michael de Courcy Fraser; CBE (1989); s of Basil de Courcy Fraser Holroyd, of Surrey, and Ulla, *née* Hall; *b* 27 Aug 1935; *Educ* Eton; *m* 1982, Margaret Drabble, *qv*, da of John Frederick Drabble, QC (d 1983), of Suffolk; *Career* biographer; chm: Soc of Authors 1973–74, Nat Book League 1976–78; pres English PEN 1985–88, chm Arts Cncl Literature Panel 1992–95; memb Arts Cncl of GB 1992–95; Hon DLitt: Univ of Ulster 1992, Univ of Sheffield 1993, Univ of Warwick 1993, Univ of East Anglia 1994; *Books* Lytton Strachey (1967–68 and 1994), Augustus John (1974–75 and 1996), Bernard Shaw (1988–92); *Recreations* listening to music and stories, watching people dance; *Style*— Michael Holroyd, Esq, CBE; ✉ 85 St Mark's Rd, London W10 6JS (☎ 0181 960 4891)

HOLROYDE, Geoffrey Vernon; s of Harold Vincent Holroyde (d 1978), and Kathleen Olive, *née* Glover (d 1990); *b* 18 Sept 1928; *Educ* Wrekin Coll, Univ of Birmingham (BSc), Royal Coll of Organists (ARCO), Birmingham Conservatoire (BMus); *m* 20 Feb 1960, Elizabeth Mary, da of Rev Canon Ernest Oldham Connell (d 1986), of Edinburgh; 2 s (Nicholas b 22 Sept 1963, Timothy b 7 Nov 1968), 2 da (Jacqueline b 6 May 1962, Penelope b 5 May 1966); *Career* RN short serv cmmn 1949–54 and 1956–61; sch master and house tutor Welbeck Coll 1954–56, dir of studies and princ Eng Electric Staff Coll 1961–70, Br Leyland Central Trg staff 1970–71, head master Sidney Stringer Community Sch Coventry 1971–75, dir Coventry Poly 1975–87, advsr on higher educn Manpower Servs Cmmn 1987–88, dir GEC Mgmnt Coll 1988–91 (GEC mgmnt devpt advsr 1991–92); dir of music Collegiate Church of St Mary Warwick 1962–72; dir: Oken Singers 1972–78, Coventry Cathedral Chapter House Choir 1982–, Coventry and Warwickshire Young Organists Project 1978–84; hon life memb Royal Sch of Church Music 1970–, govr Mid Warwickshire Coll of Further Educn 1976–87; chm: Industl Links Advsy Gp of the CDP 1981–87, W Midlands RHA Non-Clinical Res Ctee 1986–90, Nat Forum for Performing Arts in Higher Educn 1987–90, Steering Ctee LET JMRT YTS Project 1988–90, Governing Body Brathay Hall 1983–89; memb: W Midlands Advsy Cncl for Further Educn 1975–86, Cncl of Upper Avon Navigational Tst 1980–, W Midlands RHA 1986–90, RSA Educn Indust Forum 1986–91; FRSA; *Books* Managing People (1968), Delegation (1968), Communications (1969), The Organs of St Mary's Warwick (1969), Enterprise in Higher Education (1988); *Recreations* outdoors, travel, music making, narrowboating; *Style*— Geoffrey Holroyde, Esq; ✉ 38 Coten End, Warwick CV34 4NP (☎ 01926 492329)

HOLROYDE, Timothy Victor (Tim); QC (1996); s of Frank Holroyde, and Doreen, *née* Bell; *b* 18 Aug 1955; *Educ* Bristol GS, Wadham Coll Oxford (BA Jurisprudence); *m* 1980, Miranda Elisabeth, da of Alex Stone; 2 da (Caroline Louise b 26 Dec 1986, Imogen Sarah b 15 Sept 1989); *Career* called to the Bar Middle Temple 1977, in practice Northern Circuit; *Recreations* squash, tennis; *Style*— Tim Holroyde, Esq, QC; ✉ Exchange Chambers, Pearl Assurance House, Derby Square, Liverpool L2 9XX (☎ 0151 236 7747, fax 0151 236 3433)

HOLT, Andrea Mary; da of Wilton Eric Holt, of 72 Victoria St, Ramsbottom, Bury, Lancs, and Maureen Margaret, *née* Rogers; *b* 11 Nov 1970; *Educ* St Gabriel's RC HS Bury, Bury Coll of Further Educn (BTEC in Sports Sci); *Career* professional table tennis player; nat jr champion 3 times, English nat champion 1991 (runner-up 1990 and 1992), semi-finalist Italian Open 1990; England: first appearance aged 13, rep World and Euro Championships, over 100 appearances, English nat champion in singles 1991, 1993 and 1995, doubles 1993; rep GB Olympic Games: Barcelona 1992, Atlanta 1996; finalist English Open 1995; Euro Bronze medallist 1994 and 1996, Cwlth Silver team and doubles 1994 and 1995, Bronze women's doubles 1995; Manchester Evening News Sports Personality of the Month Jan 1995; currently ranked second in England; *Recreations* tennis, golf, watching football, listening to music; *Style*— Miss Andrea Holt; ✉ 72 Victoria St, Ramsbottom, nr Bury, Lancashire (☎ 01706 825197); 21 Hunter Drive, Radcliffe, Manchester M26 4NL (☎ 0161 724 0196)

HOLT, (Roma) Hazel Kathryn; da of Charles Douglas Young (d 1986), of Clearwell, Glos, and Roma, *née* Simpson; *b* 3 Sept 1928; *Educ* King Edward VI HS Birmingham, Newnham Coll Cambridge (BA); *m* Geoffrey Louis Holt; 1 s (Thomas Charles Louis Holt, *qv* b 13 Sept 1961); *Career* editorial asst International African Institute 1950–79, feature writer and reviewer Stage and Television Today 1979–82; *Books* edited for posthumous publication the novels of Barbara Pym (literary executor); A Very Private Eye (with Hilary Pym, 1984), Gone Away (1989), A Lot to Ask: A Life of Barbara Pym (1990), The Cruellest Month (1991), The Shortest Journey (1992), Uncertain Death (1993), Death on Campus (1994), Superfluous Death (1995), Death of a Dean (1996); *Recreations* reading, writing and watching cats; *Clubs* Univ Women's; *Style*— Mrs Hazel Holt; ✉ Tivington Knowle, nr Minehead, Somerset TA24 8SX (☎ 01643 704707)

HOLT, Prof Sir James Clarke; kt (1990); s of Herbert Holt (d 1980), of Bradford, Yorks, and Eunice Holt, BEM, *née* Clarke (d 1974); *b* 26 April 1922; *Educ* Bradford GS, Queen's Coll Oxford, Merton Coll Oxford (MA, DPhil); *m* 3 July 1950, (Alice Catherine) Elizabeth, da of David Suley (d 1962), of Bingley, Yorks; 1 s (Edmund b 7 Oct 1954); *Career* RA 1942–45, Capt 1943; prof of medieval history Univ of Nottingham 1962–66 (lectr 1949–62), dean Faculty of Letters and Social Sciences Univ of Reading 1972–76 (prof of history 1966–78); Univ of Cambridge: prof of medieval history 1978–88, professorial fell Emmanuel Coll 1978–81, master Fitzwilliam Coll 1981–88; memb Advsy Cncl on Public Records 1974–81, chm Cncl Pipe Roll Soc 1976–; vice pres: Selden Soc 1978–, Br Acad 1987–89; pres: Royal Historical Soc 1980–84, Lincoln Record Soc 1987–; Hon DLitt: Univ of Reading 1984, Univ of Nottingham 1996; Comendador de la Orden del Merito Civil 1988; FRHistS 1954, FBA 1978; *Recreations* music, mountaineering, fly-fishing; *Clubs* Utd Oxford and Cambridge, Nat Lib, MCC, Wayfarers (Liverpool); *Style*— Prof Sir James Holt, FBA; ✉ 5 Holben Close, Barton, Cambridge CB3 7AQ; Fitzwilliam College, Cambridge CB3 0DG (☎ 01223 332041)

HOLT, (Stanley) John; s of Frederick Holt (d 1949), of Toot-Hill, nr Chipping Ongar, Essex, and May, *née* Abblett (d 1984); *b* 27 Sept 1931; *Educ* Chipping Ongar, Walthamstow; *m* 6 Aug 1959, Anne, da of Richard Catherall (d 1942); 3 da (Sarah b 30 May 1960, Ruth b 15 July 1962, Rachel b 13 April 1966); *Career* Nat Serv RAMC 1953–55; chm Isodan UK Ltd 1975–; formerly with: Rentokil Laboratories, Pilkington's Tiles, Bayer AG W Germany; ed The Liveryman; past master and former sec Portsoken Ward Club; memb: Utd Wards Club, Royal Soc of St George, Cncl City Livery Club, Fellowship of Clerks; former chm Lunchtime Comment Club; memb Guild of Freemen, Freeman City of London 1983, Liveryman Worshipful Co of Marketors 1983; clerk: Worshipful Co of Environmental Cleaners 1986, Worshipful Co of Horners 1989, Worshipful Co of Tin Plate Workers alias Wire Workers 1991; MCIM, MIMgt, MIEx, FInstD; *Recreations* showering, being horrid to wife; *Clubs* Wig and Pen, City Livery, Thunderers; *Style*— John Holt, Esq; ✉ Whitethorns, Rannoch Rd, Crowborough, E Sussex TN6 1RA (☎ 01892 655780); 102 Marlyn Lodge, Portsoken St, London E1 8RB (☎ 0171 265 0753); A3 Los Olivos, Avd de Torrox, 29754 Competa (Malaga), Spain (☎ 00 34 5 2553542)

HOLT, John Antony; *b* 31 March 1938; *Educ* Imperial Coll London (BSc(Eng), ACGI, Dip Imperial Coll, MSc), Henley Mgmnt Centre; *m*; 2 c; *Career* sr industl fell Univ of Leeds 1969–71, chief systems engr (Space) and head of New Space Technol Electronic and Space Systems Guided Weapons Div British Aircraft Corporation 1971–76 (joined 1960), gen mgmnt course Henley Mgmnt Centre 1976; British Aerospace: head of Guided Weapons New Projects Br Aerospace Dynamics Gp (Bristol) 1976–80, engrg dir 1980–82, tech dir Br Aerospace Dynamics Gp 1982–85, md Br Aerospace Space and Communications Ltd 1985–92; fndg dir McLaurin-Holt Associates Ltd 1993–; visiting prof RMCS 1985; non-exec dir: Orion Network Systems Inc 1989–92, Surrey Satellite Technology Ltd 1994–, Esys Ltd 1995–; chm: Euro MESH consortium for collaboration on space projects 1987–92, UK Electronic Industry Component Policy Cncl 1987–91, UK Industl Space Ctee 1988–90, UK Electronic Components Policy Cncl 1993–; memb Advsy Bd: Inst of Engrg Survey and Space Geodesy Univ of Nottingham 1990–94, Centre for Space Engrg Research Univ of Surrey 1991–; memb Ct Cranfield Inst of Technol; Hon DSc Capitol Coll Maryland 1992; MInstD, FRAeS, FEng 1985; *Style*— John Holt, Esq, FEng; ✉ McLaurin-Holt Associates Ltd (☎ 01462 436626, fax 01462 452885)

HOLT, John Frederick; s of Edward Basil Holt (d 1984), and Monica, *née* Taylor; *b* 7 Oct 1947; *Educ* Ampleforth, Univ of Bristol (LLB); *m* 26 Sept 1970, Stephanie Ann, da of Peter Watson, of Belaugh, Norfolk; 3 s (Samuel John b 16 June 1973, Benjamin Alexander b 2 Sept 1974, Edward Daniel b 11 Oct 1980); *Career* called to the Bar Lincoln's Inn 1970, asst recorder 1988–92, recorder of the Crown Ct 1992–, head of chambers; memb Co Ct Rules Ctee 1981–85; *Recreations* cricket, restoring vintage motor cars; *Clubs* Twinstead Cricket; *Style*— John Holt, Esq; ✉ East Anglian Chambers, 57 London St, Norwich NR3 1HR (☎ 01603 617351, fax 01603 633589)

HOLT, Dr John Michael; s of Frank Holt (d 1977), and Constance Cora, *née* Walton (d 1991); *b* 8 March 1935; *Educ* St Peter's Sch York, Univ of St Andrews (MB ChB, MD), Queen's Univ Ontario Canada (MSc), Univ of Oxford (MA); *m* 27 June 1959, Sheila Margaret, da of William Hood Morton (d 1968), of Harrogate; 1 s (Timothy b 8 May 1964), 3 da (Jane b 27 May 1960, Sally b 13 July 1962, Lucy b 30 July 1968); *Career* res fell Dept of Med and Biochemistry Queen's Univ Ontario Canada 1961–63, registrar lectr and med tutor Nuffield Dept of Med Radcliffe Infirmary Oxford 1963–74, conslt physician Oxford 1969–, dir of clinical studies Univ of Oxford 1972–77, civil conslt in med to RAF 1994–; fell Linacre Coll Oxford 1970–, chm med staff Oxford 1983–85 and 1994–96; memb: Ctee on Safety of Med 1978–86, Oxford RHA 1984–88, Gen Bd of Faculties Univ of Oxford 1987–91; examiner Univs of Oxford, London, Glasgow, Hong Kong, Dublin; Liveryman Worshipful Soc of Apothecaries, Freeman City of London; FRCP London 1974 (memb Cncl 1990–93, censor 1995–); *Recreations* sailing; *Clubs* Royal Cornwall Yacht; *Style*— Dr John Holt; ✉ Old Whitehill, Tackley, Oxon OX5 3AB; 23 Banbury Road, Oxford OX2 6NX; John Radcliffe Hospital, Headington, Oxford OX3 9DU (☎ 01865 220975, 01865 404142)

HOLT, Her Hon Mary; da of late Henry James Holt, and Sarah, *née* Chapman (d 1987); *Educ* Park Sch Preston, Girton Coll Cambridge (MA, LLB); *Career* called to the Bar Gray's Inn 1949 (Atkin Scholar 1949); practised at Chancery Bar on Northern Circuit 1949–77; MP (C) Preston N 1970–74, Parly candidate (C) Preston N Feb and Oct 1974; circuit judge (Northern Circuit) 1977–95; BRCS: vice pres Lancashire Branch 1976–95, Badge of Hon 1989–; Freeman: City of Dallas Texas 1987, City of Denton Texas 1987; *Books* Benas and Essenhigh's Precedents of Pleading (ed 2 edn, 1956); *Recreations* walking; *Clubs* Royal Commonwealth Soc, Royal Over-Seas League; *Style*— Her Hon Mary Holt; ✉ c/o The Sessions House, Preston, Lancs

HOLT, Nicholas John; s of Eric Holt and Eileen Patricia, *née* Macritchee; *b* 2 April 1958; *Educ* Manchester GS, Fitzwilliam Coll Cambridge (BA, MA); *m* 14 April 1984, Georgina Mary, da of Dr William Mann; 2 s (William James Edward b 1987, Frederick Nicholas Jack b 1993), 1 da (Alexandra Olivia b 1989); *Career* articled clerk then asst slr Coward Chance 1980–84, asst slr then mangr Corp Legal Dept Jardine Matheson & Co Hong Kong 1984–87, legal and compliance dir Smith New Court plc 1989–92 (gp legal advsr 1987–89), chief exec Smith New Court Far East Ltd 1992–94, dir Merrill Lynch International Ltd 1994–; memb Law Soc; *Recreations* football, squash, cricket; *Clubs* Reform; *Style*— Nicholas Holt, Esq; ✉ Merrill Lynch International Ltd, Ropemaker Place, 25 Ropemaker Street, London EC2Y 9LY (☎ 0171 867 2000, fax 0171 867 4818)

HOLT, (James) Richard Trist; s of George Richard Holt (d 1954), and Gladys Floyd, *née* Bennetts (d 1971); *b* 17 Aug 1924; *Educ* Giggleswick Sch Settle Yorks, Queen's Coll Oxford (MA Jurisprudence), Univ of London (LLB (external)); *m* 1, 1952 (m dis 1973), Helen, da of Cyril Worswick; 1 da (Caroline Frances (Mrs Jones) b 29 Sept 1953), 1 s (Richard Nigel b 17 Nov 1955); m 2, 1977, Patricia Mary Hartley, da of Fred Bennell; *Career* served in HG 1941–42; Royal Signals: joined 1942, wireless/line operator 1943–45, cmmnd 1945, demobbed 1947; articled clerk G R Holt Rossendale Lancs 1941–42, admitted slr 1951, ptnr Holt and Longworth Slrs Rawtenstall Lancs 1952–73; called to the Bar Gray's Inn 1973, in practice NW Circuit; pt/t legal chm Med Appeals Tbnls and Vaccine Damage Tbnls 1979–, adjudicator Immigration Appeals 1982–90, memb Mental Health Act Cmmn 1985–86; Pensions Appeal Tbnls: pt/t legal chm 1985, dep pres 1989, pres 1993–; pt/t chm Disability Appeal Tbnls 1993; memb Rawtenstall BC 1951–57, Parly candidate (C) Rossendale 1959; *Recreations* military and local history, travel, building dry-stone walls; *Clubs* Army & Navy; *Style*— Richard Holt, Esq; ✉ The Hey Farm, Newton in Bowland, Nr Clitheroe, Lancashire BB7 3EE (☎ 01200 446213); Pensions Appeal Tribunals (England and Wales), 48–49 Chancery Lane, London WC2A 1JR (direct ☎ 0171 936 7031, gen ☎ 0171 936 7033/7034)

HOLT, Thelma Mary Bernadette; CBE (1994); da of David Holt (d 1941), and Ellan, *née* Finnagh Doyle (d 1969); *b* 4 Jan 1933; *Educ* St Anne's Coll for Girls, RADA; *m* 1, 31 March 1957 (m dis), Patrick Graucob; m 2, 6 Oct 1968 (m dis), David Pressman; *Career* producer; actress 1955–68; jt art dir Open Space Theatre 1968–77, art dir Round House Theatre 1977–83, exec prodr Theatre of Comedy 1983–85, head of touring and commercial exploitation Nat Theatre 1985–88, exec prodr Peter Hall Co 1988; prod Int Theatre, Nat Theatre 1989–; dir: Thelma Holt Ltd, Infinite Space Ltd, Theatre Investment Fund Ltd, Citizens' Theatre Glasgow; Observer Award for Special Achievement in Theatre 1987; memb Cncl: RADA, Arts Cncl of England 1993 (chm Drama Advisory Panel); Hon DUniv Middlesex 1994; *Style*— Miss Thelma Holt, CBE; ✉ Thelma Holt Ltd, Waldorf Chambers, 11 The Aldwych, London WC2B 4DA (☎ 0171 379 0438, fax 0171 836 9832)

HOLT, Thomas Charles Louis; s of Geoffrey Louis Holt, and (Roma) Hazel Kathryn Holt, *qv*, *née* Young; *b* 13 Sept 1961; *Educ* Westminster, Wadham Coll Oxford, Coll of Law Chancery Lane; *m* 6 Aug 1988, Kim Nicola, da of John Clifford Foster; 1 da (Natalie Alicia Alexandria b 12 Mar 1992); *Career* author; *Publications* incl: Poems by Tom Holt 1973, Lucia in Wartime (1985, US 1986), Lucia Triumphant (1986, US 1986), Expecting Someone Taller (1987, US 1988), Who's Afraid of Beowulf? (1988, US 1989), Goatsong (1989, US 1990), I Margaret (with Steve Nallon, 1989), The Walled Orchard 1990, Flying Dutch (1991, US 1992), Ye Gods! (1992), Overtime (1993), Here Comes The Sun (1993), Grailblazers (1994), Faust Among Equals (1994), Odds and Gods (1995), Djinn Rummy (1995), My Hero (1996), Paint Your Dragon (1996); *Recreations* engineering; *Style*— Thomas Holt, Esq; ✉ c/o James Hale, 47 Peckham Rye, London SE15 3NX (☎ and fax 0171 732 6338)

HOLT, Prof (David) Tim; s of Ernest Frederick Holt (d 1989), and Catherine Rose, *née* Finn; *b* 29 Oct 1943; *Educ* Coopers' Company's Sch, Univ of Exeter (BSc, PhD); *m* 1966, Jill, *née* Blake; 1 s (Dickon Stuart b 6 Nov 1969), 1 da (Sarah Helen Rachel b 9 Sept 1972); *Career* research fell Univ of Exeter 1969–70, survey statistician Statistics Canada 1970–73; Univ of Southampton: lectr in social statistics 1973–80, Leverhulme prof of social statistics 1980–, dean Faculty of Social Science 1981–83, dep vice-chllr 1990–95; dir Office for National Statistics, Registrar General for England and Wales and head Govt Statistical Service 1996–; scientific advsr to Chief Scientist DHSS 1983–88; conslt: Statistics Canada 1974–75, Statistics NZ 1981, OPCS 1983, 1987 and 1991, ESRC 1990, Australian Bureau of Statistics 1990; ed Jl of RSS A (Statistics and Society) 1991–94; assoc ed: Jl of RSS B 1983–88, Survey Methodology 1988–; vice pres Int Assoc of Survey Statisticians 1989–91 (memb 1973–, scientific sec 1985–87), elected memb Int Statistical Inst 1985–; tstee Newitt Tst; FRSS 1973, fell American Statistical Assoc 1990, FRSA 1995; *Books* Analysis of Complex Surveys (with C J Skinner and T M F Smith, 1989); also author of numerous articles in learned jls; *Recreations* orienteering, theatre, walking, food; *Style*— Prof Tim Holt; ✉ Office for National Statistics, 1 Drummond Gate, London SW1V 2QQ

HOLT, Vesey Martin Edward; DL (Shropshire 1986); s of Martin Drummond Vesey Holt (d 1956), of Mount Mascal, Bexley, Kent, and Lady Phyllis Hedworth Camilla Herbert, sis of 5 and 6 Earls of Powis (d 1972); direct decendant of Lord Clive (Clive of India); *b* 28 March 1927; *Educ* Radley, RAC Cirencester; *m* 1955, Elizabeth Jane, da of John Geoffrey Sanger (d 1991), of Prattenden, Bury, West Sussex; 1 s (Peter), 1 da (Amanda); *Career* farmer; memb Shropshire CC 1968–74 and 1977–, govr Wrekin Coll 1970–; Shropshire Valuation Panel: memb 1970–, dep chm 1984–90, chm 1990–95, vice pres 1995–; pres: Shropshire CCC 1973–, Minor Counties Cricket Assoc 1983–; memb Agric Land Tbnl 1975–; pres Wrekin Cons Assoc 1983–92; High Sheriff Shropshire 1981; Liveryman Worshipful Co of Grocers; *Recreations* shooting, cricket; *Clubs* Brooks's, MCC; *Style*— Vesey Holt, Esq, DL; ✉ Orleton Hall, Wellington, Telford, Shropshire (☎ 01952 242780); 42 Stanford Road, London W8 (☎ 0171 937 4970)

HOLTAM, Rev Nicholas Roderick; s of Sydney Roderick Holtam, and Kathleen, *née* Freeberne; *b* 8 Aug 1954; *Educ* Latymer GS Edmonton London, Collingwood Coll Durham (BA Geography), KCL (BD, AKC, Tinniswood prize), Westcott House Cambridge, MA (Dunelm); *m* 1981, Helen, da of Esmond (Ted) Harris; 3 s (David b 1983, Timothy b 1984, Philip b 1989), 1 da (Sarah b 1986); *Career* asst curate St Dunstan and All Saints Stepney London 1979–82, lectr Lincoln Theol Coll 1983–87, vicar Christ and St John with St Luke Isle of Dogs London 1988–95, vicar St Martin in the Fields 1995–; *Style*— The Rev Nicholas Holtam; ✉ 6 St Martin's Place, London WC2N 4JJ; St Martin in the Fields, Trafalgar Square, London WC2N 4JJ (☎ 0171 930 0089, fax 0171 839 5163)

HOLTBY, Very Rev Robert Tinsley; s of William Holtby (d 1972), of Dalton, Thirsk, N Yorks, and Elsie, *née* Horsfield (d 1959); *b* 25 Feb 1921; *Educ* Scarborough Coll, St Edmund Hall Oxford (MA, BD), King's Coll Cambridge (MA); *m* 22 Nov 1947, Mary, da of Rt Rev Eric Graham, Bishop of Brechin (d 1964), of Forbes Court, Broughty Ferry, Dundee; 1 s (David b 1953), 2 da (Veronica b 1948, Caroline b 1951); *Career* ordained 1946, curate Pocklington Yorks 1946–48, chaplain to the Forces Catterick and Singapore 1948–52; chaplain and asst master: Malvern Coll 1952–54, St Edward's Sch Oxford 1954–59; canon residentiary Carlisle Cathedral and diocesan dir of educn 1959–67, gen sec Nat Soc for Religious Educn 1967–77, sec Schools Cncl C of E 1967–74, gen sec C of E Bd of Educn 1974–77, dean Chichester 1977–89 (dean emeritus 1989–); select preacher Oxford and Cambridge Univs, visiting fell W Sussex Inst of Higher Educn; chm Cumberland Cncl of Social Servs 1962–67, memb Cumberland and Carlisle Educn Ctees, chaplain to High Sheriff of Cumberland; author of biographies, educnl and historical works; FSA; *Recreations* music, historical work; *Clubs* United Oxford and Cambridge Univ; *Style*— The Very Rev R T Holtby, FSA; ✉ 4 Hutton Hall, Huttons Ambo, York, N Yorks YO6 7HW (☎ 01653 696366)

HOLTHAM, Gerald Hubert; s of Denis Arthur Holtham (d 1995), of Quinton, Birmingham, and Dilys Maud, *née* Bull; *b* 28 June 1944, Aberdare, Glamorgan; *Educ* King Edward's Sch Birmingham, Jesus Coll Oxford (BA), Nuffield Coll Oxford (MPhil); *m* 1, 1969 (m dis), Patricia Mary, *née* Blythin; 1 da (Clare Miriam b 1971); m 2, 1979, Edith, *née* Hodgkinson; 1 da (Sophie Maud b 1976), 1 s (Rhodri Huw b 1982); *Career* journalist 1962–66 and 1969–70, at Oxford 1967–69 and 1971–73, research offr Overseas Devpt Inst London 1973–75, head Gen Economics Div Economics Dept Orgn for Econ Co-operation and Devpt (OECD) Paris 1982–85 (economist 1975–78), visiting fell Brookings Instn Washington DC 1985–87, chief international economist Credit Suisse First Boston London 1987–88, chief international economist Shearson Lehman Hutton London 1988–91, fell and tutor in economics Magdalen Coll Oxford 1991–92, chief economist Europe Lehman Brothers London 1992–94, dir Inst for Public Policy Research 1994–; visiting prof Univ of Strathclyde 1990–, affiliated prof London Business Sch 1993–; *Books* Aid and Inequality in Kenya (with A Hazlewood, 1976), Deficits and the Dollar (with R Bryant and P Hooper, 1988), Empirical Macroeconomics for Interdependent Economies (jtly, 1988); also author of numerous articles in learned jls; *Recreations* gardening, windsurfing, listening to jazz; *Style*— Gerald Holtham, Esq; ✉ 13 Lansdowne Gardens, London SW8 2EQ (☎ 0171 622 8673); The Institute for Public Policy Research, 30–32 Southampton Street, London WC2E 7RA (☎ 0171 470 6100, fax 0171 470 6111)

HOLWELL, Peter; s of Frank Holwell (decd), and Helen, *née* Howe (decd); *b* 28 March 1936; *Educ* Palmers Endowed Sch Grays Essex, Hendon GS, LSE (BSc(Econ)); *m* 1959, Jean Patricia Ashman; 1 s (William b 22 June 1967), 1 da (Felicity b 18 May 1964); *Career* mgmnt conslt Arthur Andersen & Co 1961–64 (articled clerk 1958–61); Univ of London: head of computing Sch Exams Bd 1964–67, head of Univ Computing and O & M Unit 1966–67, sec for accounting and admin computing 1977–82, clerk of the Ct 1982–85, princ 1985–; memb CVCP 1985–94, dir Univ of London Examinations and Assessment Cncl 1991–, dir Sch Exams Cncl 1988–94; tstee Samuel Courtauld Tst (formerly Home House Tst) 1985–; non-exec dir: NE Thames Regnl Health Authy 1989–94, Edexcel Fndn 1996–; chm: City and E London FSHA 1994–96, St Mark's Research Tst and Educn Fndn 1995–; memb: Governing Body Wye Coll 1996–, Cncl Sch of Pharmacy 1996–; FCA 1972, MBCS 1974, FZS 1988; *Recreations* walking, music, horology; *Clubs* Athenaeum, Royal Soc of Medicine; *Style*— Peter Holwell, Esq; ✉ University of London, Malet Street, London WC1E 7HU (☎ 0171 636 8000)

HOMA, Peter Michael; *b* 1957; *Educ* Ernest Bevin Sch Tooting, Univ of Sussex (BA), Univ of Hull (MBA), IHSM (DipHSM); *m*; 1 s (b 1988), 1 da (b 1990); *Career* health service manager; self-employed 1979–81, national admin trainee SW Thames RHA 1981–82, operational servs administrator St George's Hosp London 1982–84, dep unit administrator Bristol Children's and Maternity Hosps 1984–86, dep unit gen mangr Acute Servs Unit Bromsgrove and Redditch Health Authy 1986–89; The Leicester Royal Infirmary: assoc gen mangr 1989–90, unit gen mangr 1990–93, chief exec The Leicester Royal Infirmary NHS Trust 1993–; pres Infirmary Drama and Operative and Literary Soc (IDOLS); memb Strategic Planning Soc; MHSM (vice chm 1996–97); *Recreations* rock climbing, windsurfing, running, cycling, squash, picture framing, car mechanics, photography, writing, reading and research for doctorate; *Style*— Peter Homa, Esq; ✉ The Leicester Royal Infirmary NHS Trust, Leicester LE1 5WW (☎ 0116 254 1414, direct line 0116 258 6311, fax 0116 258 6868)

HOMAN, Lawrence Hugh Adair; s of Lawrence William Nicholson Homan (d 1981), of Harpenden, Herts, and Mary Graves, *née* Adair; *b* 26 June 1945; *Educ* Sherborne, Worcester Coll Oxford (MA); *children* 1 s (Alexander b 1973), 1 da (Olivia b 1976); *Career* admitted slr 1970; asst slr Allen & Overy 1968–73, ptnr Berwin Leighton 1975–; memb Law Soc; *Recreations* sailing, golf; *Style*— Hugh Homan, Esq; ✉ 2 Montrose Villas, Hammersmith Terrace, London W6 9TT; Berwin Leighton, Adelaide House, London Bridge, London EC4R 9HA (☎ 0171 623 3144, fax 0171 623 4416, telex 88642)

HOMAN, (Andrew) Mark; s of Philip John Lindsay Homan (d 1988), of Stokenham, Devon, and Elisabeth Clemency, *née* Hobson; *b* 27 June 1942; *Educ* Maidstone GS, Univ of Nottingham (BA); *m* 3 Oct 1970, Pamela Joan, da of George Lawson Robertson; 1 s (Andrew Thomas b 17 Sept 1977), 1 da (Sally Ann b 4 Aug 1974); *Career* Price Waterhouse: joined 1963, ptnr 1975, sr corp recovery ptnr; pres Soc of Practitioners of Insolvency 1993–94; memb Accountants Advsy Panel Insolvency Law Review Ctee (Cork Ctee) 1979–81, chm Jt Insolvency Examination Bd 1988–92; FCA (ACA 1966); *Recreations* cricket, gardening, chess, opera, croquet; *Clubs* MCC; *Style*— Mark Homan, Esq; ✉ Price Waterhouse, 1 London Bridge, London SE1 9QL (☎ 0171 939 5620, fax 0171 939 5566)

HOMAN, (John) Richard Seymour; CBE (1985); s of Capt Charles Edward Homan (d 1936), of London and Hants, and Mary Muriel, *née* Hewetson (d 1979); *b* 7 Jan 1925; *Educ* Radley, ChCh Oxford (MA); *m* 7 April 1961, Hon Mrs (Mary Graham) Homan, da of 2 Baron Wrenbury (d 1940), of E Sussex and London; 1 s (Robert b 1964), 2 da (Frances b 1967, Rosalind b 1969); *Career* RNVR 1943, Sub Lt RNVR 1944–46; Second Sea Lord's Dept Admiralty London 1944, HMS Tracker 1944–45, Underwater Weapons Div 1945–46; corp internal mgmnt conslt Head Office ICI 1950–57, corp planner and export sales mangr ICI Metals/IMI 1957–64, head Computing and Mgmnt Servs Agric Div ICI 1964–68; NEDO: Br head Industl Div 1968–72, head Assessment Div 1972–74, asst industl dir 1974–77, actg industl dir 1977–79, dep industl dir 1979–83, industl dir 1984–85, chm Speciality Chemicals Sector Gp 1986–90; author of various NEDO reports on Industrial Policies and Issues 1977–85, conslt CEGB and successor companies 1986–, memb Advsy Ctee on Hazardous Substances 1991–94; chm: Govrs Uplands Community Coll Wadhurst 1989–94 and 1996–, E Sussex Strategic Forum 1995–, Salters Inst of Industl Chemistry 1995–; memb Ct of Assts Worshipful Co of Salters (Master 1994–95), Freeman City of London (Liveryman 1957); *Recreations* walking, music, reading; *Style*— Richard Homan, Esq, CBE; ✉ 30 High St, Ticehurst, Wadhurst, E Sussex TN5 7AS (☎ 01580 200651)

HOMAN, Dr Roger Edward; s of Edward Alfred Homan, of Brighton, and Olive Florence, *née* Dent (d 1988); *b* 25 June 1944; *Educ* Varndean GS Brighton, Univ of Sussex (BA), Univ of Lancaster (PhD), LSE (MSc); *Career* Brighton Coll of Educn: lectr in religious studies 1971–73, lectr in educn 1973–76; University of Brighton (formerly Brighton Poly): lectr in educn 1976–85, princ lectr in educn 1985–; memb: Prayer Book Soc (former nat vice chm), Victorian Soc, RHS; *Recreations* sweet peas and auriculas, church music, chapel hunting, poetry; *Style—* Dr Roger Homan; ✉ University of Brighton, Falmer, East Sussex (☎ 01273 643405)

HOME, Anna Margaret; OBE (1993); da of James Douglas Home (d 1989), and Janet Mary, *née* Wheeler (d 1974); *b* 13 Jan 1938; *Educ* Convent of Our Lady St Leonards-on-Sea Sussex, St Anne's Coll Oxford (MA); *Career* joined: BBC Radio 1961, BBC TV 1964; researcher, dir and prodr Children's Programmes 1964–70, exec prodr Children's Drama 1970–81; controller of programmes (later dep dir programmes) TVS 1981–86, head of Children's Programmes BBC TV 1986–; Women in Film and Television Lifetime Achievement Award 1996; FRTS; *Recreations* reading, theatre, gardening; *Style—* Miss Anna Home, OBE; ✉ BBC Television, Television Centre, Wood Lane, London W12 7RJ (☎ 0181 576 1875)

HOME, 15 Earl of (S 1605); David Alexander Cospatrick Douglas-Home; CBE (1991); also Lord Dunglass (S 1605), Lord Home (S 1473), and Baron Douglas (UK 1875); only s of Baron Home of the Hirsel, KT, PC, who disclaimed the Earldom of Home for life 1963 (d 1995), and Elizabeth Hester, *née* Alington (d 1990); *b* 20 Nov 1943; *Educ* Eton, Christ Church Oxford; *m* 1972, Jane Margaret, yr da of Col John Williams-Wynne, *qv*; 1 s (Lord Dunglass b 1987), 2 da (Lady Iona Katherine b 1980, Lady Mary Elizabeth b 1982); *Heir* s, Michael David Alexander, Lord Dunglass b 30 Nov 1987; *Career* dir: Morgan Grenfell & Co Ltd 1974–, Morgan Grenfell Group plc 1996–; chm: Morgan Grenfell Export Services Ltd 1984–, Morgan Grenfell (Scotland) Ltd 1986– (dir 1978–), Morgan Grenfell International Ltd 1987–; dir: Deutsche Morgan Grenfell Hong Kong Ltd (formely Morgan Grenfell Asia (Hong Kong) Ltd until 1996) 1989–, Deutsche Morgan Grenfell Asia Pacific Holdings Pte Ltd (formerly Morgan Grenfell Asia Holdings Pte Ltd until 1996) 1989–; pres cmmr Bd of Pres Cmmrs P T Morgan Grenfell Asia Indonesia 1993–; dir: Douglas and Angus Estates 1966–, Agricultural Mortgage Corporation 1979–93, Credit for Exports PLC 1984–94, K & N Kenanga Holdings Bhd (formerly K & N Kenanga Sdn Bhd until 1996) 1993–, Kenanga DMG Futures Sdn Bhd 1995–; non-exec dir Grosvenor Estate Holdings 1993–; tstee Grosvenor Estate 1993–; chm: Tandem Group plc (formerly EFG plc) 1991– (dir 1981–96), Cegelec Controls Ltd 1991–94; The Ditchley Fndn: govr and memb Cncl of Mgmnt 1976–; chm Ctee for ME Trade 1986–92, memb Export Guarantee Advsy Cncl ECGD 1988–93, govr Cwlth Inst 1988–; memb: Offshore Industry Export Advsy Gp 1989–93, Cncl RASE 1990–; *Recreations* outdoor sports; *Clubs* Turf; *Style—* The Rt Hon the Earl of Home, CBE; ✉ 99 Dovehouse Street, London SW3 6JZ (☎ 0171 352 9060); The Hirsel, Coldstream, Berwicks (☎ 01890 882345); Castlemains, Douglas, Lanarks (☎ 01555 851241)

HOME, Prof Philip David; s of Philip Henry Home, and Kathleen Margaret, *née* Young; *b* 11 Jan 1948; *Educ* Birkenhead Sch, Univ of Oxford (BA, MA, DM, DPhil), Guy's Hosp (BM BCh); *m* 28 Aug 1971, Elizabeth Mary, da of Sidney Thomas Broad; 1 s (Jonathan Paul b 1979), 1 da (Deborah Mary b 1976); *Career* Wellcome Tst sr res fell in clinical sci 1982–86, prof Univ of Newcastle upon Tyne 1993– (reader 1986–93); conslt physician Freeman Hosp Newcastle 1986–, ed Diabetic Medicine 1987–91; author of over 200 articles on aspects of diabetes med; chm Int Diabetes Fedn (Euro), jt chm and chief exec WHO/Int Diabetes Fedn St Vincent Declaration Initiative; memb Assoc of Physicians of GB 1989–; FRCP 1989–; *Recreations* gardening, travel, work; *Style—* Prof Philip Home; ✉ Department of Medicine, Framlington Place, Newcastle upon Tyne NE2 4HH (☎ 0191 222 7019, fax 0191 222 0723)

HOME, Sir William Dundas; 14 Bt (NS 1671), of Blackadder, Co Berwick; o s of John Home (d 1988, er s of Sir David George Home, 13 Bt), and Nancy Helen, *née* Elliott (now Lady Gorton); suc gf 1992; *b* 19 Feb 1968; *Educ* Cranbrook Sch Sydney; *m* 30 Sept 1995, Dominique Meryl, da of Sydney Fischer, OBE; *Heir* uncle, Patrick Home b 4 July 1941; *Career* horticulturalist and arboriculturalist; memb: Int Soc of Arboriculture, Aust Inst of Horticulture, Nat Arborist Assoc; *Recreations* tennis, golf; *Clubs* Royal Sydney Golf; *Style—* Sir William Home, Bt

HOME ROBERTSON, John David; MP (Lab) East Lothian (majority 10,036); s of Lt-Col John Wallace Robertson, TD, JP, DL (d 1979), and Helen Margaret (d 1987), eld da of Lt-Col David Milne-Home (assumed additional name of Home by Scottish licence 1933); *b* 5 Dec 1948; *Educ* Ampleforth, West of Scotland Agric Coll; *m* 1977, Catherine Jean, da of Alex Brewster, of Glamis, Angus; 2 s (Alexander b 1979, Patrick b 1981); *Career* farmer; memb: NUPE, TSSA, Berwickshire Dist Cncl 1974–78, Borders Health Bd 1975–78; MP (Lab): Berwick and East Lothian Oct 1978–1983, E Lothian 1983–; memb Select Ctee Scottish Affrs 1979–83, chm Scottish Gp of Lab MPs 1983, Scottish Labour whip 1983–84; oppn spokesman: on Agric 1984–87 and 89–90 in Scotland 1987–89, Select Ctee on Defence 1990–; *Clubs* Prestonpans Labour, East Lothian Labour, Haddington Labour; *Style—* John Home Robertson, Esq, MP; ✉ House of Commons, London SW1 (☎ 0171 219 4135)

HOMER, Peter Norman; s of Norman Homer, and Majorie Betty, *née* Sale; *b* 7 June 1939; *Educ* Moseley GS, Univ of Manchester (BSc, MSc); *m* 23 Aug 1961, Valerie Anne; 3 s (Mark b 1962, James b 1964, Michael b 1967); *Career* res scientist and corp planner 1961–73; dir: Simpson Lawrence Ltd 1973–74, subsids of Grampian Holdings plc 1974–79; asst dir Scottish Devpt Agency 1979–84, chief exec IMD Holdings Ltd 1984–86, dir James Finlay Bank Ltd 1986–94, md Mercantile Securities (Scotland) Ltd 1995–; chm local Cons branch 1980–82; MIMgt 1973; *Recreations* sailing, reading, wine, books; *Clubs* Royal Northern & Clyde Yacht (past Commodore), IOD; *Style—* Peter Homer, Esq; ✉ Mercantile Securities (Scotland) Ltd, 10–14 West Nile St, Glasgow G1 2PP (☎ 0141 204 1321, telex 777844, fax 0141 204 4254)

HOMER, Dr Ronald Frederick; s of George Frederick Alexander Homer (d 1976), and Evelyn Partridge, *née* Chillington (d 1984); *b* 15 April 1926; *Educ* Dudley GS, Univ of Birmingham (BSc, PhD); *m* 1950, Audrey, *née* Adcock; 2 s (Richard b 1954, Peter b 1956); *Career* res chemist ICI 1948–59, gp mangr Nat Res Devpt Corp 1959–81, divnl dir Br Technol Gp 1981–82; conslt and writer on pewter and pewtering, ed Journal of the Pewter Society 1984–95; numerous articles and part works on pewter; pres The Pewter Soc 1975–77; Leverhulme Tst grant for res on pewtering 1983–85; Freeman of the City of London 1981, Liveryman Worshipful Co of Pewterers 1982 (archivist 1988–); FSA 1989; *Books* Five Centuries of Base Metal Spoons (1975), Provincial Pewterers (with D W Hall, 1985); *Recreations* gardening, DIY; *Style—* Dr Ronald Homer, FSA; ✉ Gorse Croft, West Hill Rd, West Hill, Ottery St Mary, Devon EX11 1TU

HON, Prof (Kwok Keung) Bernard; s of Chung Ki Hon, and Yuet Seen, *née* Shaw; *b* 16 Jan 1950; *Educ* Hong Kong Tech Coll, Univ of Birmingham (MSc, PhD); *m* 18 Dec 1976, Yuk Ching Metis, da of late Yat Chow Hui; 2 s (Chen Yue (Daniel) b 1979, Wai Yue (Adrian) b 1982); *Career* lectr: Univ of Bath 1979–81, Univ of Birmingham 1981–87; prof of mfrg systems: Univ of Dundee 1987–1990, Univ of Liverpool 1990–; head Dept of Industrial Studies Univ of Liverpool 1990–; dir: Merseyside Innovation Centre 1992–, CIRP(UK) Ltd 1993–, Rapid Prototyping Centre 1994–, Product Innovation and Development Centre 1995–; memb Technology Foresight Manufacturing Production and Business Processes Panel 1994–; FIMfgE 1990; *Recreations* badminton, music; *Style—* Prof Bernard Hon; ✉ Department of Industrial Studies, University of Liverpool, PO Box 147, Liverpool L69 3BX (☎ 0151 794 4681)

HONAN, Corinna Jeannette; da of Prof Park Honan, of Burley, Leeds, and Jeannette, *née* Colin; *b* 7 May 1953; *Educ* Classical HS Rhode Is USA, King Edward VI HS for Girls Birmingham UK, St Hugh's Coll Oxford (BA), NCTJ; *m* 21 July 1984, Nicholas Inge, s of Edward Inge; 2 da (Anabel India Kitty b 20 June 1985, Sophie Georgia Rachelle b 12 April 1989); *Career* news reporter Newcastle Journal 1975–78, staff feature writer Woman magazine 1978–81; Daily Mail: news reporter 1981–83, TV and foreign correspondent 1984–87, showbusiness ed 1987–91, feature writer and personality interviewer 1991–95; features ed Daily Telegraph 1995–; *Recreations* nineteenth-century novels, antiques; *Style—* Ms Corinna Honan; ✉ The Daily Telegraph, 1 Canada Square, Canary Wharf, London E14 5DT (☎ 0171 538 6392)

HONDERICH, Prof Edgar Dawn Ross (Ted); s of John William Honderich (d 1956), and Rae Laura, *née* Armstrong (d 1952); *b* 30 Jan 1933; *Educ* Univ of Toronto (BA), Univ of London (PhD); *m* 1, 22 Aug 1964 (m dis 1976), Pauline da of Paul Goodwin (d 1976), of Dunlavin; 1 s (John Ruan b 1962), 1 da (Kiaran Aeveen b 1960); m 2, 8 Dec 1989, Jane, da of Maj Robert O'Grady, MC, of Midford Place, Bath; *Career* lectr in philosophy Univ of Sussex 1962–64, ed International Library of Philosophy And Scientific Method 1965–, advsy ed Penguin Philosophy 1965–, ed The Arguments of the Philosophers 1970–; visiting prof: Yale Univ 1970, City Univ of NY 1971; ed The Problems of Philosophy 1983–, Grote prof of philosophy of mind and logic UCL 1988– (lectr 1964–72, reader 1972–83, prof 1983–88); memb Lab Pty; memb: Mind Assoc, Aristotelian Soc; *Books* Punishment: The Supposed Justifications (1969), Essays on Freedom of Action (ed, 1973), Social Ends and Political Means (ed, 1976), Philosophy As It Is (ed with M Burnyeat, 1979), Violence for Equality: Inquiries in Political Philosophy (1980), Philosophy Through its Past (ed, 1984), Morality and Objectivity (ed, 1985), A Theory of Determinism: The Mind, Neuroscience and Life-Hopes (1988), Conservatism (1990), How Free are You? The Determinism Problem (1993), The Oxford Companion to Philosophy (ed, 1995); *Recreations* wine, music, cycling; *Clubs* Garrick; *Style—* Prof Ted Honderich; ✉ 4 Keats Grove, London NW3 (☎ 0171 435 2687); Department of Philosophy, University College London, Gower St, London WC1 (☎ 0171 380 7115)

HONE, Richard Michael; s of Maj-Gen Sir (Herbert) Ralph Hone, KCMG, KBE, GCStJ, MC, TD, QC (d 1992), and Sybil Mary, *née* Collins; *b* 15 Feb 1947; *Educ* St Paul's (scholar), University Coll Oxford (MA); *m* 29 March 1980, Sarah, da of Col J W A Nicholl-Carne, of Guildford, Surrey; 2 s (Nathaniel b 1987, Rufus b 1989); *Career* called to the Bar Middle Temple 1970, master of the bench 1994; recorder of the Crown Court 1991; Cocks' referee 1988–94; chm Jt Regulations Ctee 1995– (vice chm 1993–95); memb Professional Conduct Ctee of the Bar 1993–; CStJ 1993 (OStJ 1972); *Recreations* reading, travel, wine, photography; *Clubs* Boodle's, Pratt's, 151; *Style—* Richard Hone, Esq; ✉ 4 Astaire House, 89 Sloane Street, London SW1X 9PB; 1 Paper Buildings, Temple, London EC4Y 7EP (☎ 0171 583 7355, fax 0171 353 2144)

HONER, Julian Anthony; s of John David Honer, of London, and Shirley, *née* Gerrish; *b* 19 Feb 1961; *Educ* Lewes Priory Sch, Univ of Stirling (BA), Univ of Birmingham, Barber Inst of Fine Arts (MPhil); *Career* researcher and cataloguer Dept of Modern Br Pictures Bonhams Fine Art Auctioneers Knightsbridge London 1986–88, fine art insur underwriter Eagle Star (Star Assurance Soc Ltd) 1988–89, account exec Frizzell Fine Art Insurance 1989–90, ed The Art Directory 1990–, ed The Dictionary of Art 1992–95, managing ed Macmillan 1995–; author of a number of articles; friend Royal Acad of Arts, memb Nat Tst; *Recreations* travel, art, music; *Style—* Julian Honer, Esq; ✉ Macmillan, 25 Eccleston Place, London SW1W 9NF (☎ 0171 881 8069)

HONEYBORNE, Dr Christopher Henry Bruce; s of Henry Thomas Honeyborne, of Romsey, Hants, and Lily Margaret, *née* Fox (d 1991); *b* 5 Dec 1940; *Educ* Cambridgeshire HS for Boys, St Catharine's Coll Cambridge (MA, DipAgSci), Univ of Reading (PhD); *m* 12 Oct 1968, (Anne) Veronica, da of Stephen Sullivan, of Guernsey; 1 s (James b 1970), 2 da (Clare b 1975, Katharine b 1986); *Career* res demonstrator Univ of Reading 1964–68, res scientist ARC Univ of Bristol 1968–70, mangr Cuprinol Ltd 1971–72, sr mangr Lazard Bros & Co Ltd 1972–77 (seconded to Dalgety Ltd 1976–77), Banque Paribas 1977–89 (dep gen mangr London Branch 1977–86, chief exec Quilter Goodison Co Ltd 1986–88); chief exec Bank of N T Butterfield & Son Ltd London Branch and Seymour Pierce Butterfield Ltd 1993–94; dir: Cartier Ltd 1979–, Secure Retirement plc 1991–93, Yorkshire Water plc 1994–, Kunick plc 1995–; chm: Finotel plc 1989– (dir 1983), Cameron Richard and Smith (Holdings) Ltd 1989–; MIBiol, MSI; *Recreations* gardening, shooting, viewing art; *Clubs* City of London, The Arts, United & Cecil; *Style—* Dr Christopher Honeyborne; ✉ Scawton Croft, Rievaulx, York YO6 5LE (☎ 01439 770392); c/o Yorkshire Water plc, 2 The Embankment, Sovereign Street, Leeds LS1 4BG (☎ 0113 234 3234)

HONEYBOURNE, Dr David; s of Gerald George Honeybourne (d 1986), and Jean Beatrice, *née* Mapp; *b* 26 March 1951; *Educ* Redditch HS, Univ of Bristol Med Sch (MB ChB, MD); *m* 30 Aug 1980, Jane Elizabeth, da of Dr David John Rudman, of Whitton, London; 2 da (Laura Ann b 1982, Clare Louise b 1985); *Career* house physician Bristol Gen Hosp 1974; sr house offr: Southmead Hosp Bristol 1975–76 (house surgn 1975), Brook Hosp London 1976–77; registrar in med King's Coll Hosp London 1977–78, res fell King's Coll Hosp Med Sch London 1978–80, sr registrar in med Manchester 1980–85, conslt physician specialising in chest diseases City Hosp Birmingham 1985–, RCP college tutor, sr clinical lectr in med Univ of Birmingham; author of books and pubns on chest diseases; memb: Br Thoracic Soc, Euro Respiratory Soc, American Thoracic Soc; FRCP 1993 (MRCP 1977); *Recreations* golf, photography; *Style—* Dr David Honeybourne; ✉ Priory Hospital, Priory Rd, Edgbaston, Birmingham B5 7UG (☎ 0121 440 2323); Department of Thoracic Medicine, City Hospital, Birmingham B18 7QH (☎ 0121 507 4586, fax 0121 507 5581)

HONEYCOMBE, (Ronald) Gordon; s of Gordon Samuel Honeycombe (d 1957), and Dorothy Louise Reid, *née* Fraser (d 1965); all the Honeycombes in the world (approx 300) are related, being descended from Matthew Honeycombe, of St Cleer, Cornwall, who died in 1728; the earliest Honeycombe is documented as John de Honyacombe of Calstock, Cornwall 1326; *b* 27 Sept 1936; *Educ* Edinburgh Acad, Univ Coll Oxford (MA); *Career* announcer, actor, author and playwright; Radio Hong Kong 1956–57, Scottish Home Serv 1958; newscaster: ITN 1965–77, TV-am 1984–89; TV presenter: A Family Tree, Brass-Rubbing 1973, Something Special 1978, Family History 1979; TV narrator Arthur C Clarke's Mysterious World 1980 and others; actor: Tomorrow's Audience 1961–62, RSC 1962–63, That Was The Week That Was 1964, Playback 625 1970, Paradise Lost 1975, Noye's Fludde 1978, Suspects 1989, Aladdin 1989, Run For Your Wife 1990, Aladdin 1990; has also appeared in films, TV series and plays and in TV, charity and variety shows; *Plays* for TV incl: The Golden Vision (1968), Time and Again (1974), The Thirteenth Day of Christmas (1985); for stage: The Miracles (1960), The Redemption (1970), Paradise Lost (1975), Lancelot and Guinevere (1980); musicals incl: The Princess and the Goblins (1976), Waltz of my Heart (1980); for radio: Paradise Lost (1975), Lancelot and Guinevere (1976); Royal Gala performances: God Save the Queen! (1977), A King Shall Have a Kingdom (1977); *Books* Neither the Sea Nor the Sand (1969), Dragon under the Hill (1972), Adam's Tale (1974), Red Watch (1976), Nagasaki 1945 (1981), The Edge of Heaven (1981), Royal Wedding (1981), The Murders of the Black Museum (1982), The Year of the Princess (1982), Selfridges (1984), TV-am Official Celebration of the Royal Wedding (1986), Siren Song (1992), More Murders of the Black Museum (1993); *Recreations* brass-rubbing, bridge, crosswords; *Style—* Gordon Honeycombe, Esq; ✉ c/o Jules Bennett, 19 Lainson Street, Southfields, London SW18 5RS (☎ 0181 265 5491)

HONEYCOMBE, Prof Sir Robert William Kerr; kt (1990); s of William Honeycombe (d 1962), of Geelong, Victoria, Australia, and Rachel Annie (Rae), *née* Kerr (d 1952); *b* 2 May 1921; *Educ* Geelong Coll Australia, Univ of Melbourne (BSc, MSc, DSc), Univ of

Cambridge (PhD); *m* 8 Dec 1947, June, da of Leslie Wilton Collins (d 1969); 2 da (Juliet Rae (Mrs Wilson) b 24 March 1950, Celia Alice b 1 Dec 1953); *Career* res offr Cwlth Scientific and Indust Res Orgn Aust 1942–47, ICI res fell Cavendish Laboratory Cambridge 1948–49, Royal Soc Armourers and Brasiers' res fell Cambridge 1949–51; Univ of Sheffield: sr lectr 1951–55, prof of physical metallurgy 1955–66; Univ of Cambridge: Goldsmiths prof of metallurgy 1966–84 (emeritus prof 1984–), fell Trinity Hall 1966–73 (hon fell 1973–), pres Clare Hall 1973–80 (emeritus fell 1985–); pres: Inst of Metallurgists 1977–78, Metals Soc 1980–81; treas and vice pres The Royal Soc 1986–92, memb Court Worshipful Co of Goldsmiths 1977– (prime warden 1986–87); Hon DApplied Sci Univ of Melbourne 1974, Hon DMet Univ of Sheffield 1983, Hon DMontan Wiss Leoben Univ 1990; FEng 1980, FRS 1981; *Books* The Plastic Deformation of Metals (1968, 2 edn 1984), Steels: Microstructure and Properties (1981, 2 edn with H K D A Bhadeshia 1995); *Recreations* gardening, photography, walking; *Style*— Prof Sir Robert Honeycombe, FRS, FEng; ✉ 46 Main Street, Hardwick, Cambridge CB3 7QS (☎ 01954 210501); Department of Materials Science & Metallurgy, University of Cambridge, Pembroke St, Cambridge CB2 3QZ (☎ 01223 334300, fax 01223 334567, telex 81240 CAMSPL G)

HONEYMAN, Stanley Holmes; *Career* chief exec English Property Corporation (EPC) 1978–86 (dir 1970–86), dir various subsids of Olympia & York following its purchase of EPC 1979, conslt to Olympia & York and dir Canary Wharf devpt 1987–93, chm Stanhope Properties plc 1994–95 (dir 1989–); chm Stanhope PLC 1995–; non-exec dir: Trizec Corp Canada 1975–85, MEPC plc 1985–86, W H Smith Group PLC until 1992; FRICS; *Style*— Stanley Honeyman, Esq; ✉ Stanhope PLC, 11 Brunton Street, London W1X 7AG (☎ 0171 495 7575, fax 0171 409 7209)

HONEYMAN BROWN, Christopher; s of Edward Honeyman Brown (d 1981), of St Mawes, and Nancy Elisabeth Ellen Odgers, *née* Hall (d 1991); *b* 2 June 1948; *Educ* Stowe; *m* 7 Sept 1973, Rosamund, da of late Peter Bluett Winch; 1 da (Emma b 15 Sept 1976), 1 s (Thomas b 2 Nov 1978); *Career* ptnr: Croydon & Co (chartered accountants) 1977–85, Binder Hamlyn (chartered accountants) 1986–96; chief exec Alsop Wilkinson (slrs) 1996, dir of ops Dibb Lupton Alsop (following merger) 1996–; govr Stowe Sch; Liveryman Worshipful Co of Fletchers; FCA 1979 (ACA 1973); *Recreations* gardening, cars; *Style*— Christopher Honeyman Brown, Esq; ✉ Dibb Lupton Alsop, 125 London Wall, London EC2Y 5AE (☎ 0171 814 6128, fax 0171 814 6424)

HONIGSBERGER, Dr Leo Max; TD (1975); s of Max Honigsberger (d 1991), of Chessetts Wood, West Midlands, and Lorna, *née* Mayell; *b* 20 Dec 1928; *Educ* Oundle, Univ of Capetown (MB ChB); *m* 21 Jan 1945, Joy, da of Melt de Kock (d 1968), of Paarl, Cape Province, SA; 2 da (Laura b 1957, Julia b 1959); *Career* conslt electroencephalographer Midland Centre for Neurosurgery 1964–71, conslt clinical neurophysiologist United Birmingham Hosps 1971–93, visiting conslt electroencephalographer HM Prison Birmingham 1970–, visiting conslt clinical neurophysiologist HM Prison Blakenhurst 1993–, hon conslt clinical neurophysiologist Ronkswood Hosp Worcester 1994–; chm Bromsgrove and Redditch DHA 1982–86, cncllr Bromsgrove DC 1980–82; FRPsych 1979; *Recreations* food and drink, sports cars; *Style*— Dr Leo Honigsberger, TD; ✉ 1 School Lane, Alvechurch, Worcestershire B48 7SA (☎ and fax 0121 445 2047)

HONORÉ, Prof Antony Maurice (Tony); QC (1987); s of Frédéric Maurice Honoré (d 1977), and Marjorie Erskine, *née* Gilbert (d 1991); *b* 30 March 1921; *m* 1, 10 July 1948 (m dis), Martine Marie-Odette, da of Col Pierre Genouville (d 1976); 1 s (Frank Martin b 1952), 1 da (Véronique Martine b 1949); m 2, 28 June 1980, Deborah Mary, da of Sir Patrick Duncan; *Career* Union Def Forces 1940–45: cmmnd 1941, Lt Rand Light Infantry 1942, Mil Coll Voortrekkerhoogte 1943–45; asst lectr Univ of Nottingham 1948–49; Univ of Oxford: lectr Queen's Coll 1948–49, fell and praelector in law Queen's Coll 1949–64, Rhodes reader in Roman Dutch law 1958–70, fell New Coll 1964–70, regius prof of civil law 1971–88 (emeritus 1988), fell All Souls Coll 1971–89 (emeritus 1989), acting warden All Souls Coll 1987–89; Hon LLD: Univ of Edinburgh 1977, Univ of SA 1984, Univ of Stellenbosch 1988, Univ of Cape Town 1990; hon bencher Lincoln's Inn 1971; corresponding memb Bavarian Acad 1992; memb: Accademia Costantiniana 1994, Int Acad of Comparative Law 1994; FBA 1972; *Books* Gaius (1962), Tribonian (1978), Sex Law (1978), Ulpian (1982), Causation in The Law (2 edn with H L A Hart, 1985), Making Law Bind (1987), The South African Law of Trusts (4 edn with E Cameron, 1992), Emperors and Lawyers (2 edn 1994), About Law (1996); *Style*— Prof Tony Honoré, QC, FBA; ✉ 94C Banbury Rd, Oxford OX2 6JT (☎ 01865 559684, fax 01865 279299)

HONYWOOD, Sir Filmer Courtenay William; 11 Bt (E 1660), of Evington, Kent; s of Col Sir William Wynne Honywood, 10 Bt, MC (d 1982), and Maud, yr da of William Hodgson-Wilson, of Hexgrave Park, Southwell, Notts; *b* 20 May 1930; *Educ* Downside, RMA Sandhurst, RAC Cirencester (MRAC Dip); *m* 1956, Elizabeth Margaret Mary Cynthia, 2 da of late Sir Alastair George Lionel Joseph Miller, 6 Bt; 2 s (Rupert Anthony b 1957, Simon Joseph b 1958), 2 da (Mary Caroline (Mrs C Bear) b 1961, Judith Mary Frances b 1964); *Heir* s, Rupert Anthony Honywood b 2 March 1957; *Career* 3 Carabiniers (Prince of Wales's Dragoon Gds); farmed 1954–64 (Suffolk Co Dairy Herd Production awards 1955 and 1956); Agricultural Land Serv MAFF Maidstone 1964, asst land cmmr 1966, surveyor Cockermouth Cumbria 1973–74; sr lands offr SE Region CEGB 1974–78, Regnl Surveyor and Valuer 1978–88, conslt on agric restoration and compensation to UK Nirex Ltd 1989–90, pt/t sr valuer Inland Revenue Folkestone 1989–90; land agency conslt Nuclear Electric plc 1993–94; examiner in agriculture: Incorporated Soc of Estates & Wayleaves Offrs 1988–, Soc of Surveying Technicians 1996–; FRICS; *Style*— Sir Filmer Honywood, Bt; ✉ Greenway Forstal Farmhouse, Hollingbourne, Maidstone, Kent ME17 1QA (☎ 01622 880418)

HONYWOOD, Rupert Anthony; s and h of Sir Filmer Courtenay William Honywood, 11 Bt, *qv*; *b* 2 March 1957; *Educ* Downside; *Career* systems and software designer and owner of Professional Systems; *Style*— Rupert Honywood, Esq; ✉ Greenway Forstal, Hollingbourne, Maidstone, Kent ME17 1QA (☎ 01622 880418)

HOOD, 7 Viscount (GB 1796); Sir Alexander Lambert Hood; 7 Bt (GB 1778); also Baron Hood (I 1782 and GB 1795); s of Rear Adm Hon Horace Hood, KCB (never invested due to death at Jutland 1916), MVO, DSO; suc bro, 6 Viscount 1981; Lord Hood is sixth in descent from 1 Viscount, the naval hero who captured Corsica 1793; *b* 11 March 1914; *Educ* RNC Dartmouth, Trinity Coll Cambridge (MA), Harvard Business Sch (MBA); *m* 1957, Diana Maud, CVO (1957, MVO 1952); *b* 1920; asst press sec to George VI 1947–52 (HM The Queen 1952–57), eldest da of Hon George Lyttelton (sometime asst master at Eton, 2 s of 8 Viscount Cobham, and yr bro of 9 Viscount), sister-in-law of two former house masters at Eton (Peter Lawrence and Robert Bourne), and sis of Humphrey Lyttelton, the jazz musician and journalist; 3 s; *Heir* s, Hon Henry Hood, *qv*; *Career* Lt Cdr RNVR WWII; former chm: Continental and Industl Tst, Tanganyika Concessions Ltd; chm Petrofina (UK) 1982–89 (dir 1958–89); dir: J Henry Schroder Wagg 1957–75, George Wimpey 1957–90, Elbar (chm until 1983), Tanks Consolidated Investments (chm 1976–83), Union Minière SA Belgium, Abbott Laboratories Inc; former part time memb Br Waterways Bd; memb Ct of Assts Worshipful Co of Grocers; *Clubs* Brooks's; *Style*— The Rt Hon Viscount Hood; ✉ 67 Chelsea Square, London SW3 6LE (☎ 0171 352 4952); Loders Court, Bridport, Dorset (☎ 01308 422983)

HOOD, Prof Christopher Cropper; s of David White Hood, and Margaret, *née* Cropper (d 1985); *b* 5 March 1947; *Educ* Univ of York (BA, DLitt), Univ of Glasgow (BLitt); *m* 1979, Gillian Thackwray White; 2 da; *Career* jr research fell Carnegie Corporation Project 1970–72, lectr Dept of Politics Univ of Glasgow 1972–77, research fell SSRC Machinery of Govt Project Univ of York 1977–79, lectr Dept of Politics Univ of Glasgow 1979–86, sr teaching fell Faculty of Law Nat Univ of Singapore 1984–85, prof of govt and public admin Univ of Sydney 1986–89, prof of public admin and public policy LSE 1989–; visiting research fell Univ of Bielefeld Mar-Aug 1982 and Jan-Feb 1989, Simon Senior Research fell Univ of Manchester autumn term 1994, Leverhulme Tst Research fell Jan-March 1995, D N Chester Senior Research fell Nuffield Coll Oxford April-July 1995; memb Ed Bd: Governance, Jl of Theoretical Politics, Administration and Society; article referee: Jl of Public Policy, Political Studies Public Administration, Government and Policy; memb Public Admin Panel Public Finance Fndn 1995–; FBA 1996; *Books* The Limits of Administration (1976), Bureaumetrics (with Prof A Dunsire, 1981), Big Government in Hard Times (ed with Prof M Wright, 1981), The Tools of Government (1983), Administrative Analysis: An Introduction to Rules, Enforcement and Organization (1986), Delivering Public Services: Sharing Western European Experience (1988), Cutback Management in Public Bureaucracies (with Prof A Dunsire, 1989), Administrative Argument (with Prof M W Jackson, 1991), Rewards at the Top (ed with Prof Guy Peters, 1994), Explaining Economic Policy Reversals (1994); also author of numerous book chapters and articles in learned jls; *Style*— Prof Christopher Hood, FBA; ✉ Department of Government, London School of Economics and Political Science, Houghton Street, London WC2A 2AE (☎ 0171 955 7203, e-mail C.HOOD@LSE.ac.uk)

HOOD, (Hilary) David Richard; s of Maj Hilary Ollyett Dupuis Hood, RA (d 1982), and Mrs Patrick Reid, *née* Sampson; *b* 6 Feb 1955; *Educ* Dragon Sch Oxford, Radley, Millfield, King's Coll London (LLB); *Career* called to the Bar Inner Temple 1980; *Style*— David Hood, Esq; ✉ 90 Overstrand Mansions, Prince of Wales Drive, London SW11 4EU (☎ 0171 622 7415, fax 0171 622 6929)

HOOD, Sir Harold Joseph; 2 Bt (UK 1922), of Wimbledon, Co Surrey, TD; s of Sir Joseph Hood, 1 Bt (d 1931); *b* 23 Jan 1916; *Educ* Downside; *m* 1946, Hon Ferelith Rosemary Florence Kenworthy, da of 10 Baron Strabolgi; 2 s (John Joseph Harold b 1952, Basil Gervase Francis Gerard b 1955), 2 da (Josepha Ferelith Emma Margaret-Mary (Mrs Ian Murray) b 1953, Margaret Marie Elizabeth Felicia (Mrs Michael Gresslin) b 1965), and 1 s decd; *Heir* s, John Joseph Harold Hood b 27 Aug 1952; *Career* 2 Lt 58 Middx Bn RE (AA) (TA) 1939, Lt RA 1941; ed The Catholic Who's Who 1952 edn, circulation dir Universe 1953–60, managing ed The Catholic Directory 1959–60, circulation dir Catholic Herald 1961–87; KCSG 1979, GCSG 1986, Kt of Sovereign Mil Order of Malta; *Clubs* RAC, MCC; *Style*— Sir Harold Hood, Bt, TD; ✉ 31 Avenue Rd, St John's Wood, London NW8 6BS (☎ 0171 722 9088)

HOOD, Hon Henry Lyttelton Alexander; s and h of 7 Viscount Hood, *qv*; *b* 16 March 1958; *m* 5 Oct 1991, Flora Susan, yr da of Cdr Michael Bernard Casement, OBE, RN, of Dene Cottage, West Harting, Petersfield, Hants; 2 s (Archibald Lyttelton Samuel b 16 May 1993, Atticus Michael Alexander b 20 Oct 1995); *Career* Liveryman Worshipful Co of Grocers; *Style*— The Hon Henry Hood; ✉ 4 Alexander Street, London W2 5NT

HOOD, James; MP (Lab) Clydesdale (majority 10,187); *Career* MP (Lab) Clydesdale 1987–; *Style*— Jimmy Hood, Esq, MP; ✉ House of Commons, London SW1A 0AA (☎ 0171 219 3000)

HOOD, Prof Neil; s of Andrew Hood (d 1984), of Wishaw, Lanarks, and Elizabeth Taylor, *née* Carruthers; *b* 10 Aug 1943; *Educ* Wishaw HS, Univ of Glasgow (MA, MLitt); *m* 24 Aug 1966, Anna Watson, da of Alexander Clark, of Lesmahagow, Lanarks; 1 s (Cameron b 1970), 1 da (Annette b 1967); *Career* res fell and lectr Scottish Coll of Textiles 1966–68, lectr and sr lectr Paisley Coll of Technol 1968–78, prof of business policy Univ of Strathclyde 1979–, assoc dean then dean Strathclyde Business Sch Univ of Strathclyde 1982–87, dir Locate in Scotland Scottish Devpt Agency Scotland and Scottish Office 1987–89, dir of employment and special initiatives Scottish Devpt Agency 1989–90, dep princ/special advsr (devpt) Univ of Strathclyde 1991–94, dir Strathclyde Int Business Univ 1992–; visiting appts: Univ of Texas Dallas 1981, Stockholm Sch of Economics 1982–87, Euro Inst for Advanced Study in Mgmnt Brussels 1986; non-exec dir: Euroscot Meat (Holdings) Ltd 1981–86, Prestwick Holdings plc 1986–87, Lamberton (Holdings) Ltd 1989–92, GA (Holdings) Ltd 1990–92, Shanks and McEwan Group PLC 1990–94, First Charlotte Assets Trust plc 1990–92, Charlotte Marketing Services Ltd 1991–94, Kwik-Fit plc 1991–, I & S Smaller Companies Trust plc 1992–, Grampian Holdings plc 1993–, I & S Trustlink Ltd 1994–, John Dickie Group Ltd 1995–; investmt advsr Castleforth Fund Managers Ltd 1984–88, dir Scottish Development Finance Ltd 1984–90 and 1993–; advsr and conslt to: Scottish Devpt Agency 1977–87, Sec of State for Scotland 1980–87, DTI 1981–83 and 1991–, Indust and Employment Ctee ESRC 1985–87; corp advsr S Scot Electricity Bd (Scottish Power plc) 1989–, memb Bd Irvine Devpt Corp 1985–87, dir Lanarks Industrial Field Exec Ltd 1984–86; conslt to: International Finance Corp Worldbank 1981–83 and 1990, UN Centre of Transnational Corps 1982–83, ILO 1984–85; FRSE 1987; *Books* Chrysler UK - A Corporation in Transition (with S Young, 1977), The Economics of Multinational Enterprise (with S Young, 1979), Multinationals in Retreat: The Scottish Experience (with S Young, 1982), Multinational Investment Strategies in the British Isles (with S Young, 1983), Industry Policy and the Scottish Economy (co-ed with S Young, 1984), Foreign Multinationals and the British Economy (with S Young and J Hamill, 1988), Strategies in Global Competition (co-ed with J E Vahlne, 1988), The Scottish Financial Sector (with P Draper, I Smith and W Stewart, 1988), Marketing in Evolution (with S Shaw, 1996), Baltics in Transition - Microlevel Studies (with J E Vahlne and R Killis, 1997); *Recreations* gardening, walking, reading, golf, writing; *Clubs* RAC, Glasgow; *Style*— Prof Neil Hood, FRSE; ✉ 95 Mote Hill, The Park, Hamilton ML3 6EA (☎ 01698 424870, fax 01698 422629); Strathclyde Business Sch, University of Strathclyde, 173 Cathedral St, Glasgow G4 0RQ (☎ 0141 552 4400, fax 0141 552 2802, car 0831 503671)

HOOD, Prof Roger Grahame; CBE (1995); s of Ronald Hugo Frederick Hood, of Aldridge, W Midlands, and Phyllis Eileen, *née* Murphy (d 1991); *b* 12 June 1936; *Educ* King Edward's Sch Five Ways Birmingham, LSE (BSc), Downing Coll Cambridge (PhD); *m* 1, 15 June 1963 (m dis 1985), Barbara, da of Donald Waldo Smith (d 1979), of Washington, Illinois; 1 da (Catharine b 1964); m 2, 5 Oct 1985, Nancy Colquitt, da of Maj John Heyward Lynah (d 1984), of Charleston, S Carolina; 2 step da (Clare b 1964, Zoe b 1969); *Career* res offr LSE 1961–63, lectr in social admin Univ of Durham 1963–67, asst dir of res Inst of Criminology Univ of Cambridge 1967–73, fell Clare Hall Cambridge 1969–73; Univ of Oxford: fell All Souls Coll 1973– (sub-warden 1994–96), reader in criminology 1973–96, prof of criminology 1996–, dir Centre for Criminological Res; Sellin-Glueck Award for Int Contribs to Criminology 1986; memb: Parole Bd 1973, SSRC Ctee on Social Sci and Law 1975–79, Judicial Studies Bd 1979–85, Dept Ctee to Review the Parole System 1987–88; expert conslt UN Ctee on Crime Prevention and Control 1988, pres Br Soc of Criminology 1986–89; FBA 1992; *Books* Sentencing in Magistrates Courts (1962), Borstal Re-Assessed (1965), Key Issues in Criminology (with Richard Sparks, 1970), Sentencing the Motoring Offender (1972), Crime, Criminology and Public Policy - Essays in Honour of Sir Leon Radzinowicz (ed, 1974), A History of English Criminal Law - Vol 5, The Emergence of Penal Policy (with Sir Leon Radzinowicz, 1986), The Death Penalty - A Worldwide Perspective (1989, 2 edn 1996), Race and Sentencing (1992); *Recreations* cooking; *Style*— Prof Roger Hood, CBE, FBA; ✉ 63 Iffley Rd, Oxford OX4 1EF (☎ 01865 246084); Centre for Criminological Research, University of Oxford,

12 Bevington Road, Oxford OX2 6LH (☎ 01865 274448/279347, fax 01865 274445, e-mail roger.hood@crim.ox.ac.uk)

HOOD, Stephen John; s of Leslie Gilbert Hood, of Australia, and Margaret, *née* Vinnicombe; *b* 12 Feb 1947; *Educ* Brisbane Boys Coll, Univ of Queensland, Univ of London (LLM); *m* 1 Oct 1971, Maya, da of Leon Togonal (d 1984), of Paris; 4 s (Ludovic b 1973, William b 1974, Roderick b 1978, Frederick b 1980), 1 da (Victoria b 1985); *Career* ptnr Clifford Chance (formerly Coward Chance) 1978–; chm: Royal Cwlth Soc in Hong Kong 1983–86, Exec Ctee Sir Robert Menzies Meml Tst 1988–; Freeman City of London 1987, Liveryman City of London Solicitors' Co; *Books* Equity Joint Ventures in The People's Republic of China, Technology Transfer in The People's Republic of China; *Recreations* fly fishing, bow hunting; *Clubs* Oriental, MCC, Hong Kong; *Style*— Stephen Hood, Esq; ✉ Clifford Chance, 200 Aldersgate Street, London EC1A 4JJ (☎ 0171 600 1000, fax 0171 600 5555)

HOOD, William Nicholas (Nick); CBE; s of Sir Tom Hood, KBE, CB, TD, and Joan, *née* Hellyar; *b* 3 Dec 1935; *Educ* Clifton; *m* 1, 1963 (m dis 1990), Angela, *née* Robinson; 1 s, 1 da; m 2, 1994, Ann E H Reynolds; *Career* served DCLI 1955–57; NEM General Insurance Association Ltd and Credit Insurance Association Ltd 1958–64, G B Britton UK Ltd 1964–70 (rising to sales and mktg dir); UBM Group Plc: various positions rising to dir Central Region 1970–84, md UBM Overseas Ltd 1972–82; dir HAT Group Ltd 1984–86; chm: Wessex Water Authy 1987–89, Wessex Water Plc 1989–, Wessex Water Services Ltd, Wessex Water Commercial Ltd, Wessex Waste Management Ltd; non-exec dir: Bremhill Industries Plc 1987–93, Provident Life Association Ltd 1988–, Commercial Union Environmental Trust plc 1992–, APV plc 1994–; memb Cncl: Water Trg Cncl 1987–, Fndn for Water Res 1989–, Water Servs Assoc (vice chm 1994, chm 1995); chm WaterAid 1990–95 (memb Cncl 1989–); memb The Prince of Wales Cncl 1993–, dep chm Business in the Community 1993–, vice pres Int Water Supply Assoc 1993–, chm Bristol 2000 1994–, dir Centre for Performing Arts 1995–; Liveryman Worshipful Co of Plumbers; *Recreations* music, fishing, cricket, painting; *Clubs* Army & Navy, MCC; *Style*— Nick Hood, Esq, CBE; ✉ Wessex Water Plc, Wessex House, Passage Street, Bristol BS2 0JQ

HOODLESS, Elisabeth Ann Marion Frost; CBE (1992); da of Maj Raymond Evelyn Plummer, TD, of Shoreham House, Shoreham, Sevenoaks, Kent, and late Maureen Grace, *née* Frost; *b* 11 Feb 1941; *Educ* Redland HS Bristol, Univ of Durham (BA), LSE (Dip); *m* 28 Aug 1965, Donald Bentley Hoodless, s of Ernest William Hoodless, of Weald Ridge, Ticehurst, E Sussex; 2 s (Christopher, Mark); *Career* Community Service Volunteers: asst dir 1963, dep dir 1972, exec dir 1975–; cncllr London Borough of Islington 1964–68, JP Inner London 1969; chm Juvenile Court: Westminster 1985, Islington 1988, Hackney 1992; memb Inst of Med Social Work 1963, Churchill fellowship 1966, Sec of State's nominee to Personal Social Services Cncl 1972–79, Cwlth Youth fellowship to Jamaica 1974, pres Volonteurope 1988, dep chm Speaker's Cmmn on Citizenship 1988–90; memb: Home Sec's Ctee on Volunteering 1994–, Dept of Health Task Force on Volunteering 1995–; govr: Reeves Fndn 1981, Elizabeth Garrett Anderson Sch 1985–, Sevenoaks Sch 1991–; chm of Govrs Barnsbury Sch 1969–85; *Recreations* ballet, gardening and travel; *Style*— Mrs Donald Hoodless, CBE; ✉ 17 Cross St, London N1 (☎ and fax 0171 359 0231); Weald Ridge, Ticehurst, E Sussex (☎ 01580 200256); Community Service Volunteers, 237 Pentonville Rd, London N1 9NJ (☎ 0171 278 6601, fax 0171 837 9621)

HOOK, Prof Andrew; s of Wilfred Thomas Hook (d 1964), and Jessie, *née* Dunnett (d 1984); *b* 21 Dec 1932; *Educ* Wick HS, Daniel Stewart's Coll Edinburgh, Univ of Edinburgh (MA), Princeton Univ New Jersey (PhD); *m* 18 July 1966, Judith Ann (d 1984), da of George Hibberd, of Comberton, Cambridge; 2 s (Caspar b 1968, Nathaniel b 1975), 1 da (Sarah b 1964 d 1995); *Career* Nat Serv NCO Intelligence Corps 1954–56; lectr in American lit Univ of Edinburgh 1961–70, sr lectr in English Univ of Aberdeen 1970–79, Bradley prof of English lit Univ of Glasgow 1979–; CNAA: chm Ctee on Humanities, memb Ctee on Academic Affrs 1986–92; chm English Panel Scottish Univ Cncl on Entrance, chm English Panel (Scotland) UCAS 1994–, memb Scottish Exam Bd 1986–92, pres Eighteenth Century Scottish Studies Soc 1990–92; *Books* ed: Scott's Waverley (1972), Charlotte Brontë's Shirley (with Judith Hook, 1974), John Dos Passos Twentieth Century Views (1974); Scotland and America - A Study of Cultural Relations 1750–1835 (1975), American Literature in Context 1865–1900 (1983), History of Scottish Literature Vol II 1660–1800 (1987), Scott Fitzgerald (1992), The Glasgow Enlightenment (with Richard Sher, 1995); *Recreations* theatre, opera, reading; *Style*— Prof Andrew Hook; ✉ 5 Rosslyn Terrace, Glasgow G12 9NB (☎ 0141 334 0113); Department of English Literature, University of Glasgow, Glasgow G12 8QQ (☎ 0141 339 8855 ext 4226, fax 0141 330 4601, telex 777070 UNIGLA)

HOOK, Brian Laurence; s of Laurence Hook, and Joan Brookes, *née* Read; *b* 31 Dec 1934; *Educ* Christ's Hosp Horsham, Oxford Sch of Architecture (DipArch), Oxford Brookes Univ (MSc); *m* 26 March 1960, (Thelma) Jill, da of Morton Griffiths Mathias (d 1974), of Deddington, Oxford; 3 da (Caroline Sanderson, Dr Sarah Hall, Philippa Rothwell); *Career* Nat Serv 2 Lt RE served Malta and N Africa 1958–60, Lt RE (TA) 1961–64; architect; assoc Peter Bosanquet & Partners Oxford 1966–70, princ in own practice Brian Hook & Partners Abingdon and Oxford 1970–; co cncllr: Berks 1971–74, Oxfordshire 1973–81 and 1989–; chm: Oxfordshire Environmental Ctee 1979–81, govrs Sch of St Helen and St Katharine Abingdon 1985–90, Wantage Constituency Cons Assoc 1987–91; chm Wilts Cons European Constituency Cncl 1991–93; ARIBA 1959, FRSA 1995; *Recreations* sailing, travel, water colour painting; *Clubs* Frewen (Oxford); *Style*— Brian Hook, Esq; ✉ Green Farm, 1 The Green, Charney Bassett, Wantage, Oxfordshire OX12 0EU; St Simeon, Gorron, N Loire, France

HOOK, Colin Peter; *b* 30 March 1942; *Educ* Windsor Sch Germany, Welbeck Coll, RMA Sandhurst, Emmanuel Coll Cambridge (BSc), King's Coll London, INSEAD; *Career* served HM Armed Forces 1960–70 (cmmnd RE 1962), devpt programmer IBM UK Ltd 1970–71, founding md Joseph Sebag & Co (Far East) Ltd Hong Kong 1971–78, mangr Corp Devpt Neptunia Corporation Ltd Hong Kong 1978–82, md San Miguel International Ltd Hong Kong 1982–84; founding md and shareholder: J Rothschild Charterhouse Management Ltd Hong Kong 1984–86, Global Asset Management (Asia) Ltd Hong Kong 1986–89; chm Feltrim Names' Association London 1990–94, jt md Clan Asset Management London July - Oct 1994, md Ivory & Sime plc Edinburgh 1994–; *Recreations* military history, photography, skiing, sailing, rowing, shooting; *Style*— Colin Hook, Esq; ✉ Ivory & Sime plc, One Charlotte Square, Edinburgh EH2 4DZ (☎ 0131 225 1357, fax 0131 225 2375)

HOOK, Harry; s of Hilary Hook (d 1991); *b* 27 March 1959; *Educ* London Coll of Printing (BA), Nat Film Sch Beaconsfield; *Career* writer and director; short films incl: Do Not go Gently 1978, Art and Madness 1979, Unknown Region 1980, Sins of the Father 1982, Snakes and Ladders 1983, Before I Die for Ever 1986; feature films incl: The Kitchen Toto 1987, Lord of the Flies (dir only) 1989, The Last of his Tribe (dir only) 1992; *Awards* Thames TV Bursary 1979, Evening Standard Film Award (for The Kitchen Toto) 1987, Sakwa Gold Prize Tokyo Film Festival (for The Kitchen Toto) 1987, First Prize Brussels Film Festival (for Before I Die Forever) 1988; *Publications* The Kitchen Toto (screenplay, 1987); *Style*— Harry Hook, Esq; ✉ c/o Rochelle Stevens & Co Ltd, 2 Terrett's Place, Upper Street, London N1 1QZ (☎ 0171 359 3900, fax 0171 354 5729)

HOOK, Michael John; s of Frederick John Hook, and Eileen Naomi Louise, *née* Cox; *b* 3 July 1934; *Educ* Harrow GS; *m* 23 Aug 1958, Hazel, da of Geoffrey Rowling; 1 s (Philip Douglas b 12 Nov 1959), 1 da (Christine Vivien b 23 Dec 1961); *Career* Nat Serv 1952–54; Spottiswoode Advertising 1950–62, CPV International 1962–66, Ogilvy & Mather 1966–87 (md Ogilvy & Mather International Media 1981–87), Yershon Media Management 1987, fndr Media Mondiale 1989– (current clients incl Marks & Spencer, BASF Health and Nutrition, IFAW, Lladro Porcelain, Sheaffer Pens, Vatry Europort, Benvenuto, Pattaya Orphanage Trust); writes for leading trade pubns and has spoken at seminars worldwide on topics related to int advtg, raised £12 million worth of donated space in int media for World Wildlife Fund 1978–87; memb Int Advtg Assoc (former dir UK Chapter), FIPA 1974 (MIPA 1960), chm IPA Soc 1971–72; *Recreations* umpiring hockey and cricket, morris dancing, gardening, francophile; *Style*— Michael Hook, Esq; ✉ Media Mondiale, PO Box 1564, Andover, Hampshire SP11 7TQ (☎ 01264 334419, fax 01264 357847)

HOOKE, Robert Lowe, Jr; s of Robert Lowe Hooke, of Sag Harbour, NY, and Elizabeth, *née* Salter; *b* 12 Sept 1942; *Educ* Millburn HS, Bowdoin Coll Maine (BA), Columbia Univ NYC (MBA), NY Sch of Visual Arts; *Career* investment advsr and sculptor; Lt USN 1966–70, Vietnam Patrol Boat Cmd, Bronze Star and Navy Commendation Medal; account exec Merrill Lynch 1970–73, md London Donaldson Lufkin & Jenrette Inc 1979–86 (account exec NYC and md London 1979–86), dir Euro-equities Paribas Capital Markets London 1986–90, md Research Vision Ltd 1993–, dir Blains Fine Art Ltd 1996–; md Art Scene Ltd 1986–93; exhbns of sculpture 1982–94: London, Paris, Geneva, Basel, Zürich, Baden Baden, Amsterdam, Sydney, Johannesburg, Capetown; sculpture in public collections: Compton Gardens Poole, Oppenheimer Collection Durban; solo Atlantic yacht crossings 1986 and 1990, BOC singlehanded around the world race 1990–91; *Recreations* sky diving, polo, tennis, sailing, heli-skiing; *Clubs* Hurlingham, Annabel's, Clermont; *Style*— Robert Hooke, Jr; ✉ 61 Holland Park, London W11 3SJ (☎ 0171 229 8063); Northampton Shores, Sag Harbor, New York, NY 11963, USA (☎ 00 1 516 725 1673); Research Vision Ltd, 43 Upper Grosvenor Street, London W1X 9PG (☎ 0171 495 6009, fax 0171 495 6011)

HOOKER, David Symonds; s of Cdr John Joseph Symonds Hooker, RN, and Pamela Bowring, *née* Toms; *b* 9 Oct 1942; *Educ* Radley, Magdalene Coll Cambridge (MA), Royal Sch of Mines (MSc); *m* 16 Jan 1965, (Catharine) Sandra, da of Maurice Hilary Thornely Hodgson (d 1986); 2 s (Benjamin b 1969, Joshua b 1979), 1 da (Samantha b 1966); *Career* Pennzoil Co 1965–73, Edward Bates & Sons Ltd 1973–75; md: Candecca Resources plc 1978–82, Plascom Ltd 1982–85, Hurricane International Ltd 1985–87, Aberdeen Petroleum plc 1987–93, Bakyrchic Gold plc 1993–96, Gammell Kershaw & Co Ltd 1996–; *Style*— David Hooker, Esq; ✉ 12 Lindsay Square, London SW1V 3SB; Ardura, Isle of Mull; Gammell Kershaw & Co Ltd, 38 St Mary Axe, London EC3A 8EX

HOOKER, Dr Michael Ayerst; s of late Albert Ayerst Hooker (d 1989), of Broomsleigh Park, Seal Chart, Kent, and Marjorie Mitchell, *née* Gunson (d 1981); *b* 22 Jan 1923; *Educ* Marlborough, St Edmund Hall Oxford (MA), Univ of the Witwatersrand (PhD); *Career* HG 1940, Univ of Oxford Sr Trg Corps 1941, ACF TARO 1942–48; memb Br Cncl 1945–47, sch master 1947–51, WELLS Orgns in NZ and UK 1951–53, involved with visual aids and PR 1953–59; md: Hooker Craigmyle & Co Ltd 1959–72 (first UK institutional fund-raising conslts), Michael Hooker and Associates Ltd 1972–79 (has helped to raise some £70 million for good causes); chief exec govr Truman and Knightley Educnl Tst 1981–87, exec dir the Jerwood Award 1987–91; sr educnl advsr The Jerwood Award 1991–93, cultural dir Shi-tennoji International 1991–; chm Fedn of Cons Students 1944, Parly candidate (C) Coventry E 1955, various offices Cons Cwlth Cncl 1955–60; memb: Advsy Ctee on Charitable Fund Raising Nat Cncl of Social Serv 1971–73, Working Pty on Methodist Boarding Schs 1971–72; tstee: Ross McWhirter Fndn 1976–, Dicey Tst 1978–92, Jerwood Oakham Fndn 1981–92, Police Convalescence and Rehabilitation Tst 1985–92, All Hallows House Tst 1990–; chm Dame Flora Robson Meml Ctee 1994–96, jt fndr Donnington Grove Soc (for Anglo-Japanese cultural exchange); govr Oakham Sch 1971–83, govr Shi-Tennoji Sch Suffolk 1985–, memb Cncl Newton Prep Sch 1991–92 (chm Exec), jt chm Routledge Soc 1986–90, a patron Elton John AIDS Fndn; FRSA 1990; *Books* The Charitable Status of Independent Schools (with C P Hill, 1969), School Development Programmes (1969), Counter Measures to Guard Against Loss of Charitable Status (1977), Uncrowned Queen of Brighton: Portrait of Dame Flora (with Canon Michael Butler, 1996); *Recreations* food and drink, inter-faith relations; *Style*— Dr Michael Hooker; ✉ Flat 8, 85 Marine Parade, Brighton, East Sussex BN2 1AJ (☎ 01273 624265, fax 01273 624304)

HOOKER, Prof Morna Dorothy; da of Percy Francis Hooker (d 1975), of High Salvington, Sussex, and Lily, *née* Riley (d 1988); *b* 19 May 1931; *Educ* Univ of Bristol (BA, MA), Univ of Manchester (PhD), Univ of Cambridge (DD); *m* 30 March 1978, Rev Dr (Walter) David Stacey (d 1993), s of Walter Stacey (d 1957); *Career* res fell Univ of Durham 1959–61, lectr in New Testament King's Coll London 1961–70; Univ of Oxford: lectr in theology 1970–76, fell Linacre Coll 1970–76, lectr in theology Keble Coll 1972–76; Lady Margaret's prof of divinity Univ of Cambridge 1976–; visiting prof: McGill Univ Canada 1968, Duke Univ N Carolina 1987 and 1989; visiting fell Clare Hall Cambridge 1974; jt ed Jl of Theological Studies 1985–; fell: Robinson Coll Cambridge 1977–, King's Coll 1979–, hon fell Linacre Coll Oxford 1980–; pres Studiorum Novi Testamenti Societas 1988–89 (memb 1959–); Hon DLitt Bristol; *Books* Jesus and The Servant (1959), The Son of Man in Mark (1967), What about The New Testament? (ed, 1975), Pauline Pieces (1979), Studying The New Testament (1979), Paul and Paulinism (ed, 1982), The Message of Mark (1983), Continuity and Discontinuity (1986), From Adam to Christ (1990), A Commentary on the Gospel According to St Mark (1991), Not Ashamed of the Gospel (1994); *Recreations* molinology, music, walking; *Style*— Prof Morna Hooker; ✉ The Divinity School, St John's Street, Cambridge CB2 1TW (☎ 01223 332598, fax 01223 332582)

HOOKER, Ronald George; CBE (1985); s of Alfred George Hooker (d 1956), and Gertrude, *née* Lane (d 1950); *b* 6 Aug 1921; *Educ* Mitcham GS, Wimbledon Tech Coll, Univ of London; *m* 26 June 1954, Eve, *née* Pigott; 1 s (Jonathan), 1 da (Jane); *Career* Philips Electrical Ltd 1938–50, special asst to Sir Norman Kipping Fedn of Br Indust 1948–50, Brush Group 1950–60, 600 Group 1960–65, Rolls Royce (1971) 1971–73; chm: Creston plc, Management and Business Services Ltd, Thos Storey (Engrs) Ltd, Warner Howard Group plc, London Ventures Ltd, EAC Ltd; dir: The Top Management Partnership Ltd; industrial advsr Hambros Bank; fndr memb Engrg Cncl, former pres Engrg Employers' Fedn; Freeman City of London, memb Worshipful Co of Coachmakers and Coach Harness Makers; FEng 1984, hon fell Mfrg Engr (USA), Hon Life FIEE (former pres), CIMgt, FRSA; *Recreations* gardening, music, reading, travel; *Clubs* Athenaeum, Lansdowne; *Style*— Ronald G Hooker, Esq, CBE, FEng; ✉ Loxborough House, Bledlow Ridge, nr High Wycombe, Bucks HP14 4AA; Hambros Bank, 41 Tower Hill, London EC3N 4HA (☎ 0171 480 5000)

HOOKS, Kenneth John (Kenny); s of Norman Henry Hooks, of Bangor, Co Down, N Ireland, and Florence Mary, *née* Wilson; *b* 1 Jan 1960; *Educ* Bangor GS, Queen's Univ Belfast; *m* 9 Aug 1984, Lesley-Ann, da of Randal Young Black; 2 s (Gareth John b 3 Jan 1989, Stuart David b 4 Nov 1994); *Career* rugby union wing three quarter RFC and Ireland (6 caps); capt Bangor GS (winners Ulster Schs Cup 1978); memb: Irish Schs Athletics team 1976, Ulster Schs Rugby XV 1976–78, Irish Schs XV 1976–78; clubs: Queen's Univ RFC 1978–83 (capt 1982–83), Ards RFC 1985–90 (capt 1989–90), Bangor RFC 1983–85 and 1990–93, Armagh RFC 1993–; rep: Irish Univs 1979, Ulster 1979–91, Ireland B (debut 1979, 2 caps); debut for Ireland v Scotland 1981; mathematics teacher Royal Sch Armagh 1983–; *Recreations* farming, gardening, hill walking, church youth work; *Style*— Kenny Hooks, Esq; ✉ 34 Annareagh Road, Richhill, Co Armagh, Northern Ireland (☎ 01762 870253)

HOOKWAY, Sir Harry Thurston; kt (1978); s of William Hookway (d 1982); *b* 23 July 1921; *Educ* Trinity Sch of John Whitgift, Univ of London (BSc, PhD); *m* 1956, Barbara (d 1991), da of Oliver Butler; 1 s, 1 da; *Career* head Info Div Dept of Scientific and Industl Res 1964–65 (joined 1949), asst under sec DES 1969–73, dep chm and chief exec Br Library Bd 1973–84, pres Inst Info Scientists 1973–76; dir Arundel Castle Tstees 1976–89, chm UNESCO Int Advsy Ctee on Documentation Libraries and Archives, govr Br Inst of Recorded Sound 1981–83, memb Royal Cmmn on Historical Monuments (Eng) 1981–88, pres Library Assoc 1985, chm LA Publishing Ltd 1986–89; pro chllr Loughborough Univ 1987–; hon fell: Inst of Info Science, Library Assoc; Hon LLD Sheffield 1976, DLitt Loughborough 1980; *Style*— Sir Harry Hookway; ✉ 3 St James Green, Thirsk, North Yorkshire YO7 1AF

HOOLAHAN, Anthony Terence; QC (1973); s of Gerald Hoolahan (d 1961), and Doris Miriam Valentina, *née* Jackson (d 1990); *b* 26 July 1925; *Educ* Dorset House Sussex, Framlingham Coll Suffolk, Lincoln Coll Oxford (MA); *m* 1949, Dorothy Veronica, da of Osmund Connochie (d 1963); 1 s (Mark b 1956), 1 da (Catriona b 1961); *Career* Sub Lt RNVR 1944, called to the Bar Inner Temple 1949, bencher 1980; recorder of the Crown Ct 1976–, Social Security cmmr 1986, barr NI 1980, QC NI 1980; chm: Richmond Soc 1976–80, Tstees Richmond Museum 1983–96; govr St Elizabeth's Sch Richmond 1989; *Recreations* swimming; *Clubs* RAC; *Style*— Anthony Hoolahan, Esq, QC; ✉ 83–86 Farringdon St, London EC4A 4BC (☎ 0171 353 5145)

HOOLE, HE Alan Norman; OBE (1991); s of Walter Norman Hoole, of Chesterfield, Derbys, and Elsie, *née* Lomas (d 1986); *b* 25 April 1942; *Educ* Chesterfield GS, Lady Manners GS Bakewell, Univ of Sheffield, Coll of Law London; *m* 1, 1962, Pauline Claire, da of Herbert Gordon Bettison; 1 s (John Edward b 26 March 1969), 1 da (Claire Louise b 18 Nov 1970); m 2, Delia Rose, da of Herbert Donald Clingham; *Career* admitted slr 1964, ptnr Blakesley & Rooth Slrs Chesterfield 1965–78; attorney-gen: St Helena 1978–83, Anguilla 1983–85; chief sec Turks & Caicos Islands 1986–88, attorney-gen Anguilla 1989–90, dep govr Anguilla 1990–91, govr and C-in-C St Helena and its Dependencies 1991–95, govr Anguilla 1995–; memb Law Soc 1964 (S H Clay prize 1963); *Recreations* fishing and walking; *Clubs* Commonwealth Tst; *Style*— HE Mr Alan Hoole, OBE; ✉ Government House, Anguilla (☎ 00 1 809 497 2621/2622)

HOOLE, Sir Arthur Hugh; KB (1985); s of Hugh Francis Hoole (d 1947), of Surrey, and Gladys Emily, *née* Baker (d 1975); *b* 14 Jan 1924; *Educ* Sutton Co Sch, Emmanuel Coll Cambridge (MA, LLM); *m* 1945, Eleanor Mary, da of Frank Washington Hobbs (d 1931), of Sutton; 2 s (Philip b 1955, John b 1957), 2 da (Margaret b 1957, Elizabeth b 1961); *Career* Flying Offr RAFVR; admitted slr 1951; ptnr Tuck & Mann 1951–88, conslt 1989–; chm Govrs Coll of Law 1983–90, pres Law Soc 1984–85, memb Criminal Injuries Compensation Bd 1985–; govr: St Johns Sch Leatherhead 1987–94, Sutton GS 1987–; pres Epsom Sports Club 1991–; *Recreations* cricket, reading, music; *Clubs* RAC; *Style*— Sir Arthur Hoole; ✉ Yew Tree House, St Nicholas Hill, Leatherhead, Surrey; Sweech House, Gravel Hill, Leatherhead, Surrey

HOOLE, Christopher John; s of Terence Kevin Hoole, of Chorley, Lancs, and Lilian, *née* Hall; *b* 15 Feb 1948; *Educ* John Rigby GS, Orrel-Univ of Hull (BSc); *m* 21 Aug 1971, Jaqueline Francis Theresa, da of Joseph Smith, of Preston, Lancs; 2 s (James Benedict b 9 Nov 1978, Dominic John b 6 Aug 1990), 1 da (Caroline Anne b 26 Aug 1980); *Career* md Cafe Inns PLC 1986–; memb Subscription Club; *Recreations* art and design, food and drink, garden design; *Style*— Christopher Hoole, Esq; ✉ Holm Lea Farm, Sandy Lane, Brindle, Preston, Lancs PR6 8NA (☎ 01772 313589); Cafe Inns PLC, George House, 3 St Thomas' Rd, Chorley, Lancs PR7 1HP (☎ 01257 262424, fax 01257 260497, car 0836 379792)

HOOLE, John George Aldick; s of John Aldick Hoole (d 1992), and Pamela Betty, *née* Coleman; *b* 3 Feb 1951; *Educ* Canford Sch Wimborne, Lawrenceville Sch New Jersey, Southampton Coll of Technol, Univ of E Anglia (BA); *m* 1975, Lindsey Gladstone, *née* Rushworth; 1 da (Poppy Imogen b 9 Nov 1983), 1 s (Theodore Edmund Inigo b 23 June 1990); *Career* asst keeper of art Southampton Art Gall 1974–78, asst dir Museum of Modern Art Oxford 1978–82, curator Barbican Art Gall 1982–; *Exhibitions curated* James Dickson Innes (Southampton Art Gall) 1977, John Piper (Museum of Modern Art) 1980; Barbican Art Gall: Matthew Smith 1983, Patrick Heron 1985, The Edwardian Era 1987, Stanley Spencer 1991, The Cutting Edge 1992, Alphonse Mucha 1993; *Recreations* collecting books and art; *Style*— John Hoole, Esq; ✉ Barbican Art Gallery, Barbican Centre, Silk Street, London EC2Y 8DS (☎ 0171 382 7105, fax 0171 628 0364)

HOOLEY, Peter; *b* 13 June 1946; *Educ* Rishworth Sch, Univ of Bradford (MSc); *m* 1978, Marianne Patricia; 1 s (James), 1 da (Rebecca); *Career* assoc fin dir Matthew Hall plc 1977–85, gp fin controller BICC plc 1985–91, gp fin dir Smith & Nephew plc 1991–; FCA; *Recreations* shooting, horse racing, rugby, theatre, holidays; *Style*— Peter Hooley, Esq; ✉ Smith & Nephew plc, 2 Temple Place, Victoria Embankment, London WC2R 3BP (☎ 0171 836 7922, fax 0171 836 0007)

HOON, Geoffrey William; MP (Lab) Ashfield (majority 12,987); s of Ernest Hoon, and June, *née* Collett; *b* 6 Dec 1953; *Educ* Nottingham HS, Jesus Coll Cambridge (MA); *m* 4 April 1981, Elaine Ann Dumelow; 1 s (Christopher b 15 May 1985), 2 da (Julia b 4 Nov 1987, Nathalie b 21 May 1990); *Career* lectr Univ of Leeds 1976–79, visiting prof of law Univ of Louisville 1979–80, barr 1982–84; MEP (Lab) Derbyshire 1984–94, MP (Lab) Ashfield 1992–, Treasy whip 1994–95, shadow min for indust 1995–; vice chm Bd of Govrs Westminster Fndn for Democracy; *Recreations* sport, cinema, music; *Style*— Geoffrey Hoon, Esq, MP; ✉ House of Commons, London SW1A 0AA (☎ 0171 219 3477, fax 0171 219 2428); c/o 8 Station Street, Kirkby-in-Ashfield, Notts NG17 7AR (☎ 01623 720399, fax 01623 720398)

HOOPER, Hon Mr Justice; Hon Sir Anthony; kt (1995); *Educ* Univ of Cambridge (MA, LLB); *Career* called to the Bar Inner Temple 1965, QC 1987, recorder of the Crown Court until 1995, judge of the High Court of Justice (Queen's Bench Div) 1995–, presiding judge NE Circuit 1997–; bencher Inner Temple 1993; chm Inns of Court Sch of Law 1996–; former prof of law Osgoode Hall Law Sch Toronto; memb Bar Br Columbia; *Style*— The Hon Mr Justice Hooper; ✉ Royal Courts of Justice, Strand, London WC2A 2LL (☎ 0171 936 7177)

HOOPER, Baroness (Life Peeress UK 1985); Gloria Hooper; da of Frederick Hooper, of Sparrow Grove, Shawford, Hants (d 1977), and Frances, *née* Maloney (d 1984); *b* 25 May 1939; *Educ* Univ of Southampton (BA); *Career* slr 1973, ptnr Taylor & Humbert 1974–85; MEP (C) Liverpool 1979–84; govt whip House of Lords 1985–87; Parly under sec of state: Dept Educn and Science 1987–88, Dept of Energy 1988–89, Dept of Health 1989–92; memb Parly Delgn to Cncl of Europe and WEU 1992–; dep speaker House of Lords 1993–; non-exec dir: SmithKline Beecham plc 1994–, General Healthcare Group plc, Winterthur Life UK Ltd; ind dir Med Defence Union; govr Centre for Global Energy Studies; *Style*— The Rt Hon Baroness Hooper; ✉ House of Lords, Westminster, London SW1A 0PW

HOOPER, Dr (J) Harry; CBE (1981), TD (1978); *b* 6 Dec 1920; *Educ* King Henry VIII Coventry, Coventry Tech Coll; *m* Jean Hooper; 2 s (Mark, Paul); *Career* REME Burma 1946–48, Parachute Bde TA 1948–62; chief metallurgist and chemist The Rootes Group 1954–56, head of laboratories Body Div Ford Motor Co 1957–61, prodn mangr Halewood startup Ford Motor Co 1962–64, global dir of manufacturing Perkins Diesel Group 1964–66, chm and md Armstrong Equipment PLC 1973–86 (md and chief exec 1966–73), chllr Univ of Humberside 1994– (pro-chllr and chm Bd Univ of Humberside 1991–93, chm Bd of Govrs Humberside Poly and Humberside Coll of Higher Educn 1976–91); chm: Cncl Prodn Engrg Res Assoc (PERA) 1975–77, CBI Cncl Yorks and Humberside 1977–79, Industry Devpt Bd DTI for Yorks and Humberside 1981–83, E Yorkshire Health Authy 1985–90; pres SMMT 1984–86 (also chm Exec Ctee) 1984–86; Hon DSc (CNAA) 1986; *Style*— Dr Harry Hooper, CBE, TD; ✉ Jalna, 12 Welton Old Road, Welton, Brough, East Yorkshire HU15 1NU; The University of Humberside, Cottingham Road, Hull HU6 7RT (☎ 01482 440550, fax 01482 440846)

HOOPER, John Charles; *b* 18 Nov 1940; *Educ* Wallington Co GS, Univ of Leeds (BA); *m* three times; 2 c, 4 step c; *Career* Procter & Gamble Ltd 1962–68 (copy supervisor, sr brand mangr), Glendinning Companies Inc 1968–72 (mktg conslt, head of manufacturer promotions, retail promotion conslt Westport Connecticut, head of promotions Frankfurt Germany, md Danbury Mint), fin dir Scott International Marketing 1972–73, md Clarke Hooper plc 1974–91, managing ptnr Scorpion promotional mktg consultancy 1991–94, DG Incorporated Soc of British Advertisers (ISBA) 1995–; vice pres Sales Promotion Conslts Assoc, past chm Ctee of Advtg Practice; fell Mktg Soc (past chm), fell Inst of Sales Promotion, FRSA, FInstD; *Style*— John Hooper; ✉ Cedar House, 7 Hethersett Close, Reigate, Surrey RH2 0HQ (☎ 01737 241771, fax 01737 246101); ISBA, 44 Hertford Street, London W1Y 8AE (☎ 0171 499 7502, fax 0171 629 5355)

HOOPER, John Edward; s of William John Henry Hooper (d 1996), and Noëlle Patricia Thérèse, *née* Lang (d 1979); *b* 17 July 1950; *Educ* St Benedict's Abbey London, St Catharine's Coll Cambridge (BA); *m* 19 July 1980, Hon Lucinda Mary Evans, da of 2 Baron Mountevans (d 1974); *Career* reporter BBC Current Affrs 1971–73, dip corr Independent Radio News 1973–74, corr Cyprus BBC, Guardian and Economist 1974–76; Guardian: corr Spain and Portugal 1976–79, London staff 1979–88; presenter Twenty Four Hours BBC World Service 1984–88, corr Spain, Portugal and N Africa Guardian and Observer 1988–94, corr Southern Europe Guardian 1994–; winner Allen Lane award best first work of history or lit 1987; memb Soc of Authors; *Books* The Spaniards: a portrait of the new Spain (1986 and 1987), The New Spaniards (1995); *Recreations* reading, travelling without having to write about it afterwards; *Style*— John Hooper, Esq; ✉ c/o La Stampa, Via Barberini 50, 00187, Roma, Italy (☎ 00 396 482 8901)

HOOSON, Baron (Life Peer UK 1979); (Hugh) Emlyn Hooson; QC (1960); s of Hugh Hooson, of Denbigh; *b* 26 March 1925; *Educ* Denbigh GS, Univ Coll of Wales Aberystwyth; *m* 1950, Shirley Margaret Wynne, da of Sir George Hamer, CBE, of Powys; *Career* sits as Lib peer in House of Lords; called to the Bar Gray's Inn 1949, dep chm Merioneth QS 1960–67 (chm 1967–71), dep chm Flintshire QS 1960–71, recorder Merthyr Tydfil 1971 and Swansea 1971, recorder Crown Court 1972–93, ldr Wales & Chester circuit 1971–74, bencher Gray's Inn 1968 (vice-treas 1985, treas 1986); MP (Lib) Montgomeryshire 1962–79, ldr Welsh Lib Pty 1966–79, vice chm Political Ctee Atlantic Assembly 1976–79, non-exec chm: Severn River Crossing PLC 1991–, Laura Ashley Holdings Ltd 1995–96 (non-exec dir 1985–96); vice pres Peace Through NATO 1985–; pres Llangollen Int Eisteddfod 1987–93; memb Governing Body Inst of Grass and Environmental Research 1989–93; hon professorial fell Univ Coll of Wales 1971–; farmer; *Style*— The Rt Hon the Lord Hooson, QC; ✉ Summerfield, Llanidloes, Powys (☎ and fax 01686 412298); House of Lords, London SW1A 0PW (☎ and fax 0171 219 5226)

HOPCROFT, George William; s of Frederick Hopcroft (d 1952), and Dorothy Gertrude, *née* Bourne (d 1972); *b* 30 Sept 1927; *Educ* Chiswick GS, Univ of London (BCom), BNC Oxford, INSEAD Fontainebleau; *m* 31 March 1951, Audrey Joan, da of James Rodd (d 1963); 3 s (Terry b 1954, David b 1956, Martin b 1960), 1 da (Geraldine b 1958); *Career* sr underwriter Export Credits Guarantee Dept 1946–53 and 1957–65, asst UK trade cmmr Madras 1953–57, FCO 1965; first sec: (commercial) Amman 1965–69, (econ) Bonn 1969–71, (commercial) Kuala Lumpur 1971–75, FCO London 1975–77; cnsllr Br Embassy Bangkok 1977–81, fndr memb Export and Overseas Trade Advsy Panel (EOTAP) 1982, advsr Govt of Belize 1982–83, conslt on int affrs 1981–; *Recreations* leisure and circumnavigation, sports (former Civil Serv 880 yds champion) and serendipity; *Clubs* Hoe Bridge Golf; *Style*— George Hopcroft, Esq; ✉ Ffrogs, Pond Rd, Hook Heath, Woking, Surrey GU22 0JT (☎ 01483 715121)

HOPE, Christopher David Tully; s of Dudley Mitford Hope, and Kathleen Mary, *née* McKenna; *b* 26 Feb 1944; *Educ* Christian Brothers Coll Pretoria SA, Univ of Witwatersrand (BA, MA), Univ of Natal (BA); *m* 18 Feb 1967, Eleanor Marilyn Margaret, da of Hans Richard Klein (d 1977); 2 s (Jasper Antony b 1969, Daniel Clement b 1973); *Career* author and poet; *Publications* A Separate Development (1981), The King, the Cat and the Fiddle (with Yehudi Menuhin, 1983), Kruger's Alp (1984), The Dragon Wore Pink (1985), The Hottentot Room (1986), Black Swan (1987), White Boy Running (1988), My Chocolate Redeemer (1989), Learning to Fly and Other Tales (1990; originally published as Private Parts, 1982), Moscow! Moscow! (1990), Serenity House (1992, shortlisted for Booker Prize 1992), The Love Songs of Nathan J Swirsky (1993), Darkest England (1996); *Poetry* Cape Drives (1974), In the Country of the Black Pig (1981), Englishmen (1985); *Awards* Cholmondeley award 1972, David Higham award 1981, Whitbread Prize for Fiction for Kruger's Alp 1985, CNA Literary award (S Africa) 1989; FRSL 1990; *Recreations* getting lost; *Style*— Christopher Hope, Esq; ✉ Rogers, Coleridge & White, 20 Powis Mews, London W11 1JN (☎ 0171 221 3717, fax 0171 229 9084)

HOPE, Most Rev and Rt Hon Dr David Michael; *see:* York, Archbishop of

HOPE, Emma Mary Constance; da of Capt John David Hope, RN, of Poundhill Cottage, Bletchingly, Surrey, and Margaret Daphne, *née* Boutwood; *b* 11 July 1962; *Educ* Reigate Co Sch for Girls, Sevenoaks Sch, Cordwainers Coll (SIAD Dip); *Career* shoe designer; fndr own business 1984, opened shop 1987; designer for: Laura Ashley, Betty Jackson, Jean Muir, Nicole Farhi, Anna Sui; FRSA 1993; *Awards* 5 Design Cncl Awards for Footwear 1987–88, Martini Style Award 1988, Harpers and Queens Award for Excellence 1988, DTI/Clothes Show Award for Best Accessories 1996; articles for Design magazine: Salvatore Ferragamo (review of his exhibition at the V & A, 1988), Shoe Design: Tiptoeing into Industry (review of college shows, 1988); *Recreations* exploring, riding, golf, shopping; *Style*— Miss Emma Hope; ✉ Emma Hope's Shoes, 33 Amwell St, London EC1R 1UR (☎ 0171 833 2367, fax 0171 833 2353)

HOPE, Sir John Carl Alexander; 18 Bt (NS 1628), of Craighall, Co Fife; s of Gp Capt Sir Archibald Philip Hope, OBE, DFC, AE (d 1987), and Ruth (d 1986), da of Carl R Davis; *b* 10 June 1939; *Educ* Eton; *m* 1968, Merle Pringle, da of late Robert Douglas, of Holbrook, Suffolk; 1 s, 1 da (Natasha Anne b 1971); *Heir* s, Alexander Archibald Douglas Hope b 16 March 1969; *Style*— Sir John Hope, Bt; ✉ 9 Westleigh Ave, London SW15 6RF (☎ 0181 785 7997)

HOPE, HE Marcus Laurence Hulbert; s of Laurence Frank Hope, OBE, of Exmouth, Devon, and Doris Phyllis Rosa, *née* Hulbert; *b* 2 Feb 1942; *Educ* City of London Sch, Sydney C of E GS, Univ of Sydney (BA), King's Coll London (BA); *m* 20 Feb 1980, Uta Maria Luise, da of Hans Müller (d 1989); 1 s (Alexander Marcus John b 1985); *Career* HM Dip Serv: joined 1965, MECAS 1966–68, second sec Tripoli 1968–70, FCO 1970–74 (first sec 1972), head of chancery Dubai 1974–76, first sec commercial Bonn 1976–80, FCO 1980–84, cnsllr NATO Def Coll Rome 1984, cnsllr Beirut 1984–85, head of chancery Berne 1985–89, dep head of mission and cnsllr commercial and aid Jakarta 1989–92, head of Western Euro Dept FCO 1992–95, ambass Zaire (concurrently non-resident ambass to Republic of Congo) 1996–; *Recreations* astronomy, scuba diving, classical guitar; *Style*— HE Mr Marcus Hope; ✉ c/o Foreign & Commonwealth Office (Kinshasa), King Charles Street, London SW1A 2AH

HOPE, Sir (Charles) Peter; KCMG (1972, CMG 1956), TD (1945); s of George Leonard Nelson Hope (d 1973); *b* 29 May 1912; *Educ* Oratory Sch Reading, Univ of London, Univ of Cambridge (BSc, DSc); *m* 1936, Hazel Mary, da of George Turner (d 1920); 3 s; *Career* WWII RA (TA), Maj; entered WO 1938, transferred FO 1946, first sec Br Embassy Paris, asst head UN Dept FO 1950, cnsllr Bonn 1953–56, head News Dept FO 1956–59, min Madrid 1959–62, consul gen Houston USA 1963–64, alternate del to UN 1965–68, ambass Mexico 1968–72, ret; memb Acad Int Law 1970, pres Br Assoc SMOM 1983–89, bailiff Grand Cross SMOM, chm Graffham Branch Cons Pty, vice chm Cncl for the Protection of Rural England; Grand Cross of the Aztec Eagle (Mexico), Grand Offr Merito Melitense, KStJ 1985; *Recreations* shooting, fishing; *Clubs* White's, Army and Navy; *Style*— Sir Peter Hope, KCMG, TD; ✉ Guillards Oak House, Midhurst, Sussex (☎ 0173 081 3877)

HOPE, (David) Terence; s of George Charles Oswald Hope (d 1988), and Lucy, *née* Bollom (d 1970); *b* 2 April 1946; *Educ* Rutherford GS Newcastle upon Tyne, Univ of Liverpool (MB ChB, ChM); *m* 28 Oct 1975, Vanessa Mary, da of Edwin Richardson, of W Sussex; 1 s ((Charles) Benjamin b 1976), 2 da (Lucy Alexandra b 1979, Victoria Mary b 1983); *Career* served in RNR; conslt neurosurgeon: Aberdeen 1982, Univ Hosp of Nottingham 1985; author of chapters in books on vascular neurosurgery; examiner: RCS, Intercollegiate Bd of Examiners in Neurosurgery; memb: Soc of British Neurological Surgeons, Ct of Examiners RCS; FRCS 1975; *Recreations* fishing, shooting, gardening; *Style*— Terence Hope, Esq; ✉ The Nunnery, Hemington, Derby DE7 2RB (☎ 01332 811724); Department of Neurosurgery, University Hospital, Queen's Medical Centre, Nottingham NG7 2UH (☎ 0115 970 9102)

HOPE-DUNBAR, Sir David; 8 Bt (NS 1664), of Baldoon; o s of Maj Sir Basil Douglas Hope-Dunbar, 7 Bt (d 1961), and Edith Maude Maclaren, *née* Cross; *b* 13 July 1941; *Educ* Eton, RAC Cirencester; *m* 1971, Kathleen Ruth, yr da of late J Timothy Kenrick, of Birmingham; 1 s (Charles b 1975), 2 da (Philippa b 1973, Juliet Antonia b 1976); *Heir* s, Charles Hope-Dunbar b 11 March 1975; *Career* founded Dunbar & Co (now Allied Dunbar) 1962, chartered surveyor; ARICS; *Recreations* fishing, tennis, shooting; *Style*— Sir David Hope-Dunbar, Bt; ✉ Banks House, Kirkcudbright (☎ and fax 01557 330424)

HOPE-FALKNER, Patrick Miles; s of Robert E Hope-Falkner (d 1991), and Diana, *née* Hazlerigg (d 1977); *b* 1 Dec 1949; *Educ* Wellington; *m* 1972 (sep 1993), Wendy Margaret, *née* Mallinson; 2 s (Timothy Douglas b 1980, James Edward b 1982); *Career* articles 1968–73, admitted slr 1973, Freshfields 1973–84, Lazard Brothers & Co Ltd 1985–90; dir: Lazard Investors Ltd 1985–90, Lazard Brothers & Co (Jersey) Ltd 1985–89; ptnr Crossman Block 1991–94; sr dir American Express Bank 1995–; memb Law Soc; *Clubs* Brooks's, Cowdray Polo; *Style*— Patrick Hope-Falkner, Esq; ✉ American Express Bank, 60 Buckingham Palace Road, London SW1W 0RR (☎ 0171 824 6000)

HOPE-MASON, David Gordon; s of Gordon Nisbett Hope-Mason (d 1987), and Gunnel Anna, *née* Schele; *b* 11 June 1940; *Educ* Haileybury, ISC; *m* 1, 15 June 1962 (m dis 1981), Maralyn Florence, da of Royce Gordon Martland, of St Brelades, Jersey, CI; 1 s (Justin b 1969), 1 da (Amanda (Mrs Thierry Haziza) b 1966); m 2, 9 May 1981; *Career* exec chm Lockwood Press Ltd, jt md Market Intelligence Ltd; past chm Fresh Produce Consortium; Liveryman Worshipful Co of Fruiterers 1973 (Master 1989); *Recreations* music, golf; *Clubs* RAC; *Style*— David Hope-Mason, Esq; ✉ Bounty House, Ropley, Hants SO24 0BY (☎ 01962 773601); Lockwood Press Ltd, Market Towers, London SW8 5NN (☎ 0171 622 6677, fax 0171 720 2047)

HOPE-MORLEY, Hon Ian Hampden; s and h of 3 Baron Hollenden, *qv*; *b* 23 Oct 1946; *Educ* Eton; *m* 1, 1972 (m dis), Beatrice Saulnier, da of Baron Pierre d'Anchald, of Paris; 1 s (Edward b 9 April 1981), 1 da (Juliette b 1974); m 2, 10 Oct 1988, Caroline N, o da of Kim Ash, of Johannesburg, S Africa; 2 s (Alastair Kim b 1990, Henry (Harry) Gordon b 1993); *Career* Liveryman Worshipful Co of Fishmongers; *Style*— The Hon Ian Hope-Morley; ✉ c/o The Hampden Estate Office, Great Hampden, Bucks

HOPE OF CRAIGHEAD, Baron (Life Peer UK 1995), of Bamff in the District of Perth and Kinross; (James Arthur) David Hope; PC (1989); s of Arthur Henry Cecil Hope OBE, TD, WS (d 1986), of Edinburgh, and Muriel Ann Neilson, *née* Collie; *b* 27 June 1938; *Educ* Edinburgh Acad, Rugby, St John's Coll Cambridge (MA), Univ of Edinburgh (LLB); *m* 11 April 1966, (Katharine) Mary, da of William Mark Kerr, WS (d 1985), of Edinburgh; 2 s (Hon William Thomas Arthur b 1969, Hon James David Louis b (twin) 1969), 1 da (Hon Lucy Charlotte Mary b 1971); *Career* Nat Serv cmmnd Seaforth Highlanders 1957, Lt 1959; admitted Faculty of Advocates 1965, standing jr counsel in Scotland to Bd of Inland Revenue 1974–78, QC (Scotland 1978), advocate depute 1978–82, chm Med Appeal Tbnls 1985–86, legal chm Pensions Appeal Tbnl 1985–86; memb Scottish Ctee on Law of Arbitration 1986–89; elected dean of Faculty of Advocates 1986; senator of the Coll of Justice, a Lord of Session with the title of Lord Hope, Lord Justice General of Scotland and Lord President of the Court of Session 1989–96, a Lord of Appeal in Ordinary 1996–; hon prof of law Univ of Aberdeen 1994–, hon fell St John's Coll Cambridge 1995; hon memb: Canadian Bar Assoc 1987, Soc of Public Teachers of Law 1991; hon bencher: Gray's Inn 1989, Inn of Court of N Ireland 1995; pres The Stair Soc; Hon LLD: Univ of Aberdeen 1991, Univ of Strathclyde 1993, Univ of Edinburgh 1995; *Books* Gloag and Henderson's Introduction to the Law of Scotland (jt ed 7 edn 1968, asst ed 8 edn 1980 and 9 edn 1987), Armour on Valuation for Rating (jt ed 4 edn 1971, 5 edn 1985); *Recreations* walking, music, ornithology; *Clubs* New (Edinburgh); *Style*— The Rt Hon Lord Hope of Craighead, PC; ✉ 34 India Street, Edinburgh EH3 6HB (0131 225 8245); Law Lords Corridor, House of Lords, London SW1A 0PW (☎ 0171 219 3202, fax 0171 219 6156)

HOPE-STONE, Dr Harold Francis; s of Sidney Hope-Stone (d 1933), of Liverpool, and Doris, *née* Cohen (d 1943); *b* 20 Aug 1926; *Educ* The Liverpool Inst GS for Boys, Strathcona Acad Montreal, The London Hosp Medical Coll (MB BS, LRCP, MRCS); *m* 20 Aug 1954, Shelagh, da of Harold William Gallimore; 2 s (Rodney Alan b 5 July 1957, Hugh William b 10 Dec 1960), 1 da (Laura Doris b 16 Feb 1963); *Career* Capt RAMC RMO 13/18 Royal Hussars and King's African Rifles 1952–54; house surgn Poplar Hosp 1951; The London Hosp: house physician 1952, registrar Whitechapel Clinic 1955, registrar Radio Therapy Dept 1956–63, sr registrar Radio Therapy Dept 1963, conslt radiotherapist and oncologist 1963–, conslt in admin charge Dept of Radiotherapy and Oncology 1975–91; hon conslt radiotherapist and oncologist: Whipps Cross Hosp 1965–91, Harold Wood Hosp Romford 1968–, The Royal London Hosp 1991–, Cromwell Hosp 1991–, London Independent Hosp 1991–; lectr in radiotherapy and oncology Univ of London 1968–, advsr in radiation protection Queen Mary Coll London 1973–; chm: Medical Advsy Ctee The London Ind Hosp 1985–89, Regnl Advsy Ctee on Radiotherapy and Oncology NE Thames RHA 1970–79, Working Party Radiotherapy Servs NE Thames Region 1977–79; memb London Univ Bd Studies in Medicine 1970–, examiner RCR 1978–81, vice pres Section of Radiology RSM 1979–82 and 1986–88 (hon sec 1985–86), examiner for MD in radiotherapy Colombo Sri Lanka 1986–, examiner Royal Coll of Radiologists 1976–79; The London Hosp: memb Academic Bd 1971–74 and 1990–91, chm Ctee Sch of Radiology and Radiotherapy 1976–80, chm Medical Records Sub Ctee Medical Cncl 1972–77, chm Div of Surgery 1980–84, chm Private Practice Sub Ctee of Medical Cncl 1977–85, Medical Cncl rep Final Medical Ctee 1978–80, memb Exec Ctee Scanner Appeal 1984–85, chm Medical Cncl 1988–91 (vice chm 1985–89); DMRT 1957, FRCR 1959; memb: BIR, Section of Radiology RSM, Section of Oncology RSM, Assoc Br Head and Neck Oncologists, Euro Soc of Therapeutic Radiology and Oncology, Br Oncological Soc; *Books* Tumours of the Testicle (jtly, 1970), Malignant Diseases in Children (contrib, 1975), Bladder Cancer (contrib, 1981), Urology I - Bladder Cancer (contrib, 1984), Radiotherapy in Clinical Practice (ed, 1986), Urological and Genital Cancer (co-ed, 1989); *Recreations* gardening, tennis, skiing, sailing, opera, ballet, theatre, travelling; *Style*— Dr Harold F Hope-Stone; ✉ The London Independent Hospital, Beumont Square, London E1 4NL (☎ 0171 790 0990); The Cromwell Hospital, Cromwell Road, London SW5 6TU (☎ 0171 370 4233)

HOPETOUN, Earl of; Andrew Victor Arthur Charles Hope; eldest s and h of 4 Marquess of Linlithgow, *qv*; *b* 22 May 1969; *Educ* Eton, Exeter Coll Oxford; *m* 10 July 1993, Skye, er da of Maj Bristow Charles Bovill, 5th Royal Inniskilling Dragoon Gds, of Shipston-on-Stour, Warwicks; *Career* Page of Honour to HM Queen Elizabeth The Queen Mother 1985–87; styled Viscount Aithrie 1969–87; *Style*— Earl of Hopetoun; ✉ c/o Hopetoun House, South Queensferry, West Lothian EH30 9SL

HOPKIN, Sir (William Aylsham) Bryan; kt (1971), CBE (1961); s of William Hopkin; *b* 7 Dec 1914; *Educ* Barry Co Sch, St John's Coll Cambridge, Univ of Manchester; *m* 1938, Renée Ricour; 2 s (Edward b 1940, Richard b 1944); *Career* joined Miny of Health 1938; dir Nat Inst of Econ and Social Res 1952–57, sec Cncl on Prices Productivity and Incomes 1957–58, dep dir Econ Section Treasy 1958–65, Mauritius 1965, ODM 1966, dir-gen econ planning 1967–69, dir-gen Dept of Econ Affrs 1969; HM Treasy: dep chief econ advsr 1970–72, chief econ advsr and head Govt Econ Serv 1974–77; prof of econs Univ Coll Cardiff 1972–82; memb Cwlth Devpt Corp 1972–74, chm MSC Wales 1978–79; hon fell St John's Coll Cambridge 1982, hon prof fell Univ Coll Swansea 1988; *Style*— Sir Bryan Hopkin; ✉ 15 St John's Close, Cowbridge, S Glamorgan CF71 7HL (☎ and fax 01446 772303)

HOPKIN, Nicholas Buxton; s of Dr Geoffry Buxton Hopkin, of Littleton, Winchester, and Harriet, *née* Moxon; *b* 31 March 1944; *Educ* George Watson's Coll Edinburgh, Univ of Edinburgh (MB ChB), FRCS; *m* 30 Sept 1966, Jennifer Margaret Bruce, da of Lt John MacPherson Ainslie, RN (ka 1944); 1 s (Tobias b 1976), 3 da (Lucy b 1967, Rosalind b 1970, Penelope b 1972); *Career* RN 1965–82, ret in rank of Surgn Cdr; conslt in otorhinolaryngology; hon registrar Head and Neck Unit Royal Marsden Hosp 1979–80, currently conslt ENT Surgn West Dorset Gen Hosps NHS Tst and East Somerset NHS Tst; *Style*— Mr Nicholas Hopkin; ✉ The Old Vicarage, Sydling St Nicholas, Dorchester, Dorset DT2 9PB; West Dorset Hospital, Dorchester (☎ 01305 251150 ext 4205)

HOPKIN, Raymond John (Ray); s of Hywel Raymond Hopkin (d 1970), of Farnborough, Hants, and Violette Madge Lorraine, *née* Lethaby; *b* 13 July 1944; *Educ* Farnborough GS, Imperial Coll London (BSc, ARCS); *m* 24 Nov 1967, Jeanette Graham, da of Robert William Clark (d 1990), of Sanquhar, Dumfriesshire; *Career* AXA Equity & Law: joined 1966, projects mangr 1992–, md Trg and and Competence Office 1995–; dep gen mangr AXA Equity & Law Assocs 1988–92; chm Insur Servs Devpt Ctee BT 1988–89; *Recreations* bridge, golf, all music, Paradores, working; *Clubs* Phyllis Court (Henley-on-Thames), Henley Golf, Harlequin FC; *Style*— Ray Hopkin, Esq; ✉ Crawfordjohn, Upper Warren Ave, Caversham Heights, Reading RG4 7EB (☎ 0118 946 1403); AXA Equity & Law House, Amersham Rd, High Wycombe, Bucks HP13 5AL (☎ 01494 463 463, fax 01494 461 989, car 0850 653537, telex 83385)

HOPKINS, Sir (Philip) Anthony; kt (1993), CBE (1987); s of Richard Arthur Hopkins (d 1981), and Muriel Annie Yeates; *b* 31 Dec 1937; *Educ* Cowbridge GS, Welsh Coll of Music and Drama, RADA; *m* 1, 1968 (m dis 1972), Petronella; 1 da (Abigail b 1968); m 2, 1973, Jennifer Ann, da of Ronald Arthur Lynton; *Career* actor and director; first joined Nat Theatre 1965, Broadway debut Equus 1974; lived and worked in USA 1975–84, returned to England 1984; Hon DLitt Univ of Wales 1988, hon fell St David's Coll Lampeter Wales; Commandeur dans l'Ordre National des Arts et des Lettres (France, 1996); *Theatre* incl: Julius Caesar (debut) 1964, A Flea in Her Ear (NT) 1966, The Three Sisters, Dance of Death (NT) 1967, As You Like It 1967, The Architect and The Emperor of Assyria, A Woman Killed with Kindness, Coriolanus (NT) 1971, The Taming of the Shrew (Chichester) 1972, Macbeth (NT) 1972, Equus (Plymouth Theatre NY 1974 and 1975, Huntington Hartford Theatre LA 1977), The Tempest (The Mark Taper Forum Theatre LA) 1979, Old Times (Roundabout Theatre NY) 1983, The Lonely Road (Old Vic) 1985, Pravda (NT) 1985, King Lear 1986, Antony and Cleopatra 1987, M Butterfly (Shaftesbury) 1989, August (also dir) 1994; *Television* incl: A Heritage and Its History (ATV) 1968, A Company of Five (ATV) 1968, The Three Sisters (BBC) 1969, The Peasants Revolt (ITV) 1969, Dickens (BBC) 1970, Danton (BBC) 1970, The Poet Game (BBC) 1970, Uncle Vanya (BBC), Hearts and Flowers (BBC), Decision to Burn (Yorkshire) 1970, War and Peace (BBC) 1971 & 1972, Cuculus Canorus (BBC) 1972, Lloyd George (BBC) 1972, QB VII (ABC) 1973, Find Me (BBC) 1973, A Childhood Friend (BBC) 1974, Possessions (Granada) 1974, All Creatures Great and Small (NBC) 1974, The Arcata Promise (Yorkshire) 1974, Dark Victory (NBC) 1975, The Lindbergh Kidnapping Case (NBC) 1975, Victory at Entebbe (ABC) 1976, Kean (BBC) 1978, The Voyage of the Mayflower (CBS) 1979, The Bunker (CBS) 1980, Peter and Paul (CBS) 1980, Othello (BBC) 1981, Little Eyolf (BBC) 1981, The Hunchback of Notre Dame (CBS) 1981, A Married Man (LWT/ Channel 4) 1982, Strangers and Brothers (BBC) 1983, The Arch of Triumph (CBS) 1984, Mussolini and I (RAI Italy) 1984, Hollywood Wives (ABC) 1984, Guilty Conscience (CBS) 1984, Blunt (BBC) 1985, Across the Lake (BBC) 1988, Heartland (BBC) 1988, The Tenth Man (CBS) 1988, Magwitch in Great Expectations (Disney Primetime TV USA) 1988, To Be The Best (USA mini series) 1990, Big Cats (wildlife documentary) 1993; *Films* The Lion in Winter (debut) 1967, The Looking Glass War 1968, Hamlet 1969, When Eight Bells Toll 1969, Young Winston 1971, A Doll's House 1972, The Girl from Petrovka 1973, Juggernaut 1974, A Bridge Too Far 1976, Audrey Rose 1976, International Velvet 1977, Magic 1978, The Elephant Man 1979, A Change of Seasons 1980, The Bounty (Captain Bligh) 1983, The Good Father 1985, 84 Charing Cross Road 1986, The Dawning 1987, A Chorus of Disapproval 1988, The Desperate Hours 1989, The Silence of the Lambs 1990, Spotswood 1990, One Man's War 1990, Howard's End 1991, Freejack 1992, Chaplin 1992, Bram Stoker's Dracula 1993, The Trial 1993, Remains of the Day 1993, Shadowlands 1993, Legends of the Fall 1994, The Road to Welville 1994, August (also dir) 1994, Nixon 1995, Surviving Picasso 1995; *Awards* for War and Peace BAFTA Best Television Actor Award 1973; for Equus 1975: NY Drama Desk Award for Best Actor, Outer Critics' Circle Award, American Authors and Celebrities Forum Award, LA Drama Critics' Award); for The Lindbergh Kidnapping Case Emmy Award for Best Actor 1976, for The Bunker Emmy Award for Best Actor 1981, for The Bounty Variety Club Film Actor of 1983 Award 1984; for Pravda 1985: Variety Club Stage Actor Award, Br Theatre Assoc Best Actor Award, The Observer Award for Outstanding Achievement (Olivier Awards); for Mussolini & I Ace Award 1985, for Charing Cross Road Moscow Film Festival Best Actor Award 1987, Award for Career Excellence (Montreal Film Festival) 1991; for Silence of The Lambs 1992: Academy Award for Best Actor in a Leading Role, BAFTA Award for Best Film Actor, NY Film Critics' Circle Award for Best Actor, Chicago Film Critics' Award for Best Actor, Boston Film Critic's Award for Best Actor; for Remains of the Day 1994: BAFTA Award for Best Film Actor, Guild of Regnl Film Writers Award for Best Actor, LA Film Critics' Assoc Award for Best Actor, Variety Club Film Actor of 1993 Award; for Shadowlands 1994: US Nat Bd of Review Best Actor Award, LA Film Critic's Assoc Best Actor Award; other awards incl: Evening Standard Film Awards' Special Award for UK Body of Work 1994, The US Film Advisory Bd Special Career

Achievement Award for US Body of Work 1994, US BAFTA The Britannia Award for Outstanding Contribution to the Int Film and TV Industry 1995, Japan Critics' Awards Best Actor in a Foreign Film for Remains of the Day 1995, Mexican Int Film Festival Best Actor Award for Shadowlands 1995, Spencer Tracy Award for Excellence on Stage and Screen 1996; *Recreations* piano, reading; *Style*— Sir Anthony Hopkins, CBE; ✉ 25 St George's Court, 258 Brompton Road, London SW3 2AT (☎ 0171 589 2827, fax 0171 589 9770)

HOPKINS, Dr Anthony Philip; s of Gerald Hopkins (d 1985), of London, and Barbara Isobel, *née* Summers (d 1986); *b* 15 Oct 1937; *Educ* Sherborne, Guy's Hosp Med Sch (MB), Univ of London, (MD); *m* 14 Aug 1965, Elizabeth Ann, da of Edward Wood; 3 s (Felix b 1968, Nicholas b 1971, Edward b 1973); *Career* physician i/c Dept of Neurological Sciences St Bartholomew's Hosp 1976–88 (conslt neurologist 1972–76 and 1988–), dir Res Unit Royal Coll of Physicians 1988–; FRCP 1976; *Books* Measuring the quality of medical care (1990), Clinical neurology: a modern approach (1993); *Recreations* reading, walking, theatre; *Clubs* Garrick; *Style*— Dr Anthony Hopkins; ✉ 149 Harley St, London W1N 2DE (☎ 0171 935 4444)

HOPKINS, Anthony Strother; CBE (1996); *b* 1940; *Educ* Queen's Univ Belfast (BSc(Econ)); *Career* sr mangr Audit Dept Thomson McLintock & Co (now KPMG Peat Marwick), CA Industrial Development Organisation Dept of Commerce 1971–76; chief exec: Northern Ireland Development Agency 1979–82 (joined 1976, subsequently head of corp fin, dep chief exec), Industrial Development Bd for NI 1988–92 (joined as dep chief exec Inward Investment 1982, dep chief exec Home Indust 1984); managing ptnr NI Touche Ross (now Deloitte & Touche) 1992–; chm: Milk Marketing Bd for NI 1995–, Laganside Corp 1996– (dep chm 1995–96); visiting prof Univ of Ulster (memb Advsy Bd Ulster Business Sch); memb NI Tourist Bd 1992–; FCA, CIMgt (chm NI region 1992–); *Style*— Anthony Hopkins, Esq, CBE; ✉ Deloitte & Touche, 19 Bedford Street, Belfast, Northern Ireland BT2 7EJ (☎ 01232 322861)

HOPKINS, Antony; CBE (1976); *b* 21 March 1921; *Educ* Berkhamsted Sch, RCM (Chappell Gold medal, Cobbett prize); *m* Feb 1947, Alison Purves (d 1991); *Career* freelance composer of incidental music incl: Oedipus Rex (Old Vic 1945), Antony and Cleopatra (1945, 1953), Moby Dick (BBC 1947), The Oresteia (BBC 1956), twelve programmes on insects (BBC); films incl: Pickwick Papers, Decameron Nights, Billy Budd; operas incl: Lady Rohesia (1948), Three's Company (1953), Dr Musikus (1971); other works incl John and the Magic Music Man (1975, which won Grand Prix at Besançon Film Festival 1976); conductor of most maj orchestras UK, also Hong Kong, Adelaide, Belgrade and Tokyo; pres numerous music clubs; Medal of Hon City of Tokyo 1973; DUniv Stirling 1980, hon fell Robinson Coll Cambridge 1980; Hon RAM 1964, Hon FRCM 1979; *Books* Talking About Symphonies (1961), Talking About Concertos (1964), Music All Around Me (1967), Lucy and Peterkin (1968), Music Face to Face (with André Previn, 1971), Talking About Sonatas (1971), Downbeat Music Guide (1977), Understanding Music (1979), The Nine Symphonies of Beethoven (1981, reprinted 1996), Songs for Swinging Golfers (1981), Sounds of Music (1982), Beating Time (1982), Pathway to Music (1983), Musicamusings (1983), The Concertgoer's Companion (Vol I 1984, Vol II 1986, reprinted as 1 Vol 1993), The Seven Concertos of Beethoven (1996); *Recreations* golf, motor sport; *Style*— Antony Hopkins, Esq, CBE; ✉ Woodyard, Ashridge, Berkhamsted, Herts (☎ 01442 842257)

HOPKINS, Clyde David Frederick; s of (Frederick) Paul Hopkins (d 1978), and Ivy May, *née* Hill (d 1994); *b* 24 Sept 1946, Bexhill, Sussex; *Educ* Barrow-in-Furness GS, Univ of Reading (BA); *m* 1969, Marilyn, da of Flt Lt James Ronald Hallam, of Wetherby, Yorks; *Career* painter (studios in London and Hastings Sussex); various occupations 1969–73 (incl printmaking demonstrator, gardener, visiting lectr and chief examiner); visiting pt/t and sessional lectr 1973–82 (incl Hull Coll of Art, Manchester Poly, Univ of Reading, Canterbury Coll of Art, Slade Sch, Chelsea Sch of Art, Cyprus Coll of Art); head of fine art Winchester Sch of Art 1987–90 (head of painting 1982–87), head of painting Chelsea Coll of Art 1990–; numerous solo and gp exhbns in GB, Europe and N America 1972–96; Gtr London Arts Assoc award 1979, Arts Cncl of GB purchase award 1980, Mark Rothko Scholarship (USA) 1980–81; memb: Painting Faculty Br Sch at Rome 1985–90, The Edwin Austen Abbey Scholarship Cncl 1987–; *Clubs* Chelsea Arts; *Style*— Clyde Hopkins; ✉ c/o Francis Graham-Dixon Gallery, 17–18 Great Sutton St, London EC1V ODN (☎ 0171 250 1962, fax 0171 490 1069); Chelsea College of Art, Manresa Rd, London SW3 6LS (☎ 0171 514 7750, fax 0171 514 7777)

HOPKINS, Prof Colin Russell; s of Bleddyn Hopkins (d 1939), and Vivienne, *née* Jenkins; *b* 4 June 1939; *Educ* Pontypridd Boys GS, Univ of Wales (BSc, PhD); *m* Aug 1964, Hilary, da of Fredrick Floyd (d 1973); 1 s (Laurence b 1973), 1 da (Sally b 1970); *Career* dir MRC Inst for Molecular Cell Biology, prof of molecular biology Univ Coll London, Rank prof of physiological biochemistry Imperial Coll London, prof of med cell biology Univ of Liverpool Med Sch, assoc prof Rockefeller Univ New York; *Recreations* music; *Style*— Prof Colin Hopkins; ✉ Department of Biology, University College, Gower St, London WC1B 3AE

HOPKINS, (Richard) Julian; s of Richard Robert Hopkins, CBE, of Harpenden, Herts, and Grace Hilda, *née* Hatfield (d 1973); *b* 12 Oct 1940; *Educ* Bedford Sch; *m* 1, 1961 (m dis 1969), Jennifer, *née* Hawkesworth; 1 s (Justin b 1962), 1 da (Julia b 1963); m 2, 6 Aug 1971, Maureen Mary, da of Norman George Hoye (d 1977), of London; 1 s (Benjamin b 1976); *Career* asst mangr London Palladium 1964–66, central servs mangr BBC 1966–70, exec dir RSPCA 1978–82 (admin and fin offr 1972–78), gen mangr Charity Christmas Card Cncl 1982–83, fin dir War on Want 1984–88, nat dir CARE 1988–94, dir ORBIS USA 1994–; dir and exec memb Ctee World Soc for Protection of Animals 1977–83; memb: Farm Animal Welfare Cncl Miny of Agric 1979–83, Nat Soc of Fundraising Execs 1994–; dir and memb Bd The Humane Soc of the US 1995–; FIMgt 1976; *Recreations* music (particularly opera), theatre, travel; *Style*— J Hopkins, Esq; ✉ 560 West 43rd Street, Apt 41b, New York, NY 10036, USA (☎ 00 1 212 714 9113); ORBIS, 330 West 42nd Street, Suite 1900, New York, NY 10036, USA (☎ 00 1 212 244 2525, fax 00 1 212 244 2744)

HOPKINS, Justine Tracy; da of John Richard Hopkins, of Los Angeles, and Prudence Anne, *née* Balchin; *b* 1 Oct 1960; *Educ* Univ of Bristol (Eric Pendry prize, Tucker-Cruze prize, Thomas David Taylor prize, BA), Courtauld Inst (Br Acad state studentship, MA), Birkbeck Coll London (Br Acad state studentship, PhD); *Career* exhbn offr for Michael Ayrton and the Maze exhbn Victoria Art Gallery Bath 1983, gallery invigilator and exhbns guide Arnolfini Gallery Bristol 1984, asst restorer W of England Restoration Studios Bristol 1984, excavations illustrator (ceramics) Cuello Archaeological Project Belize 1987 and 1990–93; pt/t lectr: Sch of Humanities Leicester Poly 1988–89 and 1991, Birkbeck Coll London 1993–94, History of Arts Dept Univ of the West of England 1994–97, Dept of Continuing Educn Univ of Bristol 1995–97; visiting lectr: Sotheby's Fine Arts Educn Dept 1989, Birkbeck Coll London 1989 and 1990, City of London Poly 1990, Tate Gallery, V&A; Harold Hyam Wingate scholar 1993/94; *Publications* A Way Through the Maze - Michael Ayrton's Labyrinths (exhbn catalogue, 1983), Michael Ayrton (1921–75) - Paintings, Drawings, Sculpture and Graphics (1990), Wright of Derby (slide pack with commentary, 1990), Samuel Palmer: Visionary Printmaker (exhbn review, Apollo Magazine, 1991), Ben Nicholson (exhbn guide, 1993), Michael Ayrton: a biography (1994), Drawing on these Shores (exhbn review, 1994), Good Company: Diaries of Frances Partridge (book review, Charleston Magazine, 1995), The Enemy as Mentor: Michael Ayrton and Wyndham Lewis (Wyndham Lewis Annual, 1995); pottery illustrations in various archaeological jls incl Antiquity and National Geographic; *Recreations* travel, theatre and the performing arts, art conservation and restoration, photography, walking, reading; *Style*— Dr Justine Hopkins; ✉ The Maze House, Rockhampton, Berkeley, Glos GL13 9DS (☎ 01454 260285, fax 01454 261776)

HOPKINS, Keith Barrie; s of Clement Lawrence Hopkins (d 1979), of Coventry, and Beatrice Anne Roberts (d 1987); *b* 27 Oct 1929; *Educ* King Henry VIII Coventry, St John's Coll Oxford (MA); *m* April 1955, Madeline Ann, da of William George Gilbert; 3 s (Nicholas John b 26 Jan 1956, Rupert William b 1 July 1958, Matthew Thomas b 19 March 1963); *Career* trainee accountant Coventry Corp 1953, PR trainee Standard Motor Co 1955–58, overseas PR offr Standard Triumph 1958–62 (PR exec 1962–64), PR mangr Leyland Motor Corp 1964–68, dir PR British Leyland 1968–74, md Austin Morris Div British Leyland 1974–75, dir of sales and mktg Leyland Cars 1975–78, fndr Opus Public Relations Ltd (in partnership with Shandwick) 1978, sold shares in Opus to Shandwick 1984, fndr and chm KBH Communications Ltd 1985–95, dep chm Lowe Bell Good Relations Ltd (following takeover) 1995–; Hon FRBS; MIPR, FRSA; *Recreations* rugby, swimming, walking, reading, writing; *Clubs* RAC, Academy; *Style*— Keith Hopkins, Esq; ✉ 13 Carroll House, Elms Mews, Lancaster Gate, London W2 3PP (☎ 0171 723 0779); Redberry Cottage, 15 Market Square, Lower Heyford, Oxon (☎ 01869 340419); Lowe Bell Good Relations Ltd, 59 Russell Square, London WC1B 4HJ (☎ 0171 631 3434)

HOPKINS, Rowland Rhys; s of David Verdun Hopkins, of Ammanford, Carmarthenshire, and Phyllis, *née* Dyson; *b* 19 Dec 1948; *Educ* Lawrence Sheriff Sch Rugby, UCL (LLB); *m* 12 Dec 1987, Elizabeth Ann, da of Ronald Williams (d 1980), of Church Stretton, Shrops; 1 da (Sarah Elizabeth b 24 Oct 1989); *Career* called to the Bar Inner Temple 1970; memb Gen Synod C of E 1985–90, chm House of Laity of Birmingham Diocesan Synod C of E 1988–94; *Recreations* skiing, fell walking; *Style*— Rowland Hopkins, Esq; ✉ 108 Stanmore Rd, Edgbaston, Birmingham B16 0SX (☎ 0121 429 8793); Rowchester Chambers, 4 Rowchester Court, Whittall St, Birmingham B4 6DH (☎ 0121 233 2327)

HOPKINS, Russell; OBE (1989); s of Charles Albert Hopkins (d 1948), of Sunderland, Co Durham, and Frances Doris, *née* Baldwin (d 1980); *b* 30 April 1932; *Educ* Barnard Castle Sch, Univ of Durham (BDS), Univ of London (MRCS, LRCP); *m* 24 April 1970, Jill Margaret, da of Dudley Frederick Pexton (d 1961); 2 s (Richard Jonathon b 6 May 1971, Robert Geoffrey Russell b 24 April 1979), 1 da (Claire Louise b 31 May 1972); *Career* gen dental practice Salisbury Rhodesia 1957–58 (Cambridge 1956–57), sr house offr (oral surgery) Nottingham Gen Hosp 1959, registrar (oral surgery) St Peter's Hosp Chertsey 1959–61, house surgeon (surgery) Bolingbroke Hosp Wandsworth 1964, house physician (medicine) Mayday Hosp 1964, surgeon Union Castleline 1965, sr registrar (oral surgery) Royal Victoria Infirmary Newcastle upon Tyne 1965–68, gen mangr University Hosp of Wales 1985–91 (conslt in oral maxillo and facial surgery 1968–95), dir Med Audit S Glam Health Authy 1991–95; chm Hosp Dental Staff Ctee 1976–78, Hosp Med Staff Ctee and Med Bd 1980–82, chm Welsh Conslts and Specialists Ctee 1990–94, chm Gen Mangrs Gp BMA 1987–90, chm Glan-Y-Môr NHS Tst 1995–; chm Welsh Cncl BMA 1990–94, memb Cncl BMA 1990–95; memb Joint Conslts Ctee 1980–93, Central Ctee Hosp Med Services 1975–90; pres BAOMS 1992–93 (hon treas 1978–80); external examiner Univ of Hong Kong 1991–93; Llandudno Vase BAOMFS 1980, Down Surgical Prize 1993; memb: BMA, EAOMS, BDS 1956; MRCS 1964, LRCP 1964, FDSRCS 1961; *Books* Atlas of Oral Preprosthetic Surgery (1986), Farbatlas Der Präprothelischen Chirurgie (1990), Mandibular Fractures in Maxillo Facial Injuries (1985), Preprosthetic Surgery in Surgery of Mouth & Jaws (1986), Bone Dysplasias in Clinical Dentistry (1986); *Recreations* golf, sea fishing, photography, walking North Pembrokeshire, work; *Style*— Russell Hopkins, Esq, OBE; ✉ 179 Cyncoed Rd, Cyncoed, Cardiff, South Glamorgan CF2 6AH (☎ 01222 752319); Glamorgan House BUPA Hospital, Pentwyn, Cardiff CF2 7XL (☎ 01222 736011)

HOPKINSON, Ven Barnabas John (Barney); s of Preb Alfred Stephan Hopkinson, of South Harting, Hampshire, and Anne Cicely, *née* Fletcher (d 1988); *b* 11 May 1939; *Educ* Emanuel Sch, Trinity Coll Cambridge (MA), Geneva Univ (Certificat d'Etudes Oecumeniques), Lincoln Theol Coll; *m* 27 July 1968, Esme Faith, da of Rev Cecil Wilson Gibbons (d 1985), of Cambridge; 3 da (Rachel b 1969, Sarah b 1971, Clare b 1974); *Career* asst curate: Langley 1965–67, Great St Mary's Cambridge 1967–70; asst chaplain Charterhouse 1970–75, rural dean Marlborough 1977–81 (team vicar 1976–81), rector Wimborne Minster 1981–86, canon Salisbury Cathedral 1983–, rural dean Wimborne 1985–86, archdeacon of Sarum 1986–, priest i/c Stratford-sub-Castle 1987–; memb General Synod 1995–; *Recreations* walking, climbing, gardening; *Style*— The Ven the Archdeacon of Sarum; ✉ Russell House, Stratford-sub-Castle, Salisbury, Wilts SP1 3LG (☎ 01722 328756, fax 01722 329894)

HOPKINSON, Prof Brian Ridley; s of Rev E A E Hopkinson (d 1982), of Cheltenham, and May Olive, *née* Redding (d 1986); *b* 26 Feb 1938; *Educ* Univ of Birmingham (MB ChB, ChM); *m* 4 July 1962, Margaret Ruth, da of Percival Bull (d 1945), of Burton-on-Trent; 3 s (Nicholas b 1967, Adrian b 1968, Jonathan b 1969), 1 da (Susannah b 1971); *Career* RSO West Bromwich Hosp 1964 (house surgn 1962), lectr in surgery Queen Elizabeth Hosp Birmingham 1968–73, conslt surgn Nottingham Gen Hosp 1973–, prof of vascular surgery Univ of Nottingham 1996–; Hunterian prof RCS 1970; dep chm Annual Representatives Meeting BMA 1995–; memb: Exec Ctee Vascular Surgical Soc of GB and Ireland, Cncl BMA; licensed lay reader C of E 1961–; FRCS 1964; *Recreations* steam boating and motor caravanning at home & abroad; *Clubs* BMA; *Style*— Prof Brian Hopkinson; ✉ Lincolnsfield, 18 Victoria Crescent, Private Rd, Sherwood, Nottingham NG5 4DA (☎ 0115 960 4167); Consulting Rooms, 32 Regent St, Nottingham NG1 5BT (☎ 0115 947 2860)

HOPKINSON, David Hugh Laing; CBE (1986), RD (1975), DL (1987); *b* 14 Aug 1926; *Educ* Wellington, Merton Coll Oxford (BA); *m* 1951, Prudence Margaret Holmes; 2 s (Adrian b 1953, Christopher b 1957), 2 da (Rosalind b 1955, Katherine b 1961); *Career* Lt Cdr RNVR 1944–65; clerk House of Commons 1949–59, chief exec M & G Group 1963–87; chm: Harrisons and Crosfield plc 1988–91, BR (Southern) 1979–86; dep chm English China Clays plc 1986–92; dir: Merchants Trust 1976–, Charities Investment Managers 1972–, Wolverhampton and Dudley Breweries 1987–96; church cmmr 1973–94; High Sheriff of W Sussex 1988–89; govr: Sherborne Sch, Wellington Coll; hon fell St Anne's Coll Oxford; dir Chichester Diocesan Bd of Fin 1970–; tstee: West Dean Fndn, Pallant House Gallery Chichester, Royal Pavilion Brighton, Chichester Cathedral Devpt Tst, Nat Assoc of Almshouses, Weald and Downland Museum, Royal Acad of Music Fndn; *Recreations* travel, opera; *Clubs* Brooks's; *Style*— David Hopkinson, Esq, CBE, RD, DL; ✉ St John's Priory, Poling, Arundel, W Sussex BN18 9PS (☎ 01903 882393)

HOPKINSON, Jeremy Stephen Frederick; s of John Gordon Hopkinson, of Crown House, Common Road, Kensworth, Dunstable, and Edith, *née* Lord; *b* 28 Aug 1943; *Educ* Berkhamsted Sch; *m* 14 Sept 1968, Helle, da of Alfred Holter, of Brevik, Norway; 1 s (Peter John b 18 Nov 1969), 2 da (Cecilia Ann b 22 Feb 1972, Theresa Janet b 19 July 1974); *Career* articled clerk Robert H Marsh & Co CA 1961–68, Hillier Hills Frary & Co 1968–70; ptnr Marsh Wood Drew & Co 1972–78 (joined 1970), ptnr Dearden Farrow 1978– (chm Tax Ctee 1983–86), currently ptnr (following merger) Binder Hamlyn (part of Arther Andersen Worldwide Organisation from Oct 1994); memb local church and Deanery Synod; FCA 1976 (ACA 1966); *Recreations* golf, choir singing, marquetry; *Clubs* Woburn Golf & Country; *Style*— Jeremy Hopkinson, Esq; ✉ Lynghouse, 12 Heath Road,

Great Brickhill, Milton Keynes, Buckinghamshire MK17 9AL (☎ and fax 01525 261674); Binder Hamlyn, 20 Old Bailey, London EC4M 7BH (☎ 0171 489 6100, fax 0171 489 6286)

HOPKINSON, Maj-Gen John Charles Oswald Rooke; CB (1984); s of late Lt-Col John Oliver Hopkinson, DSO, MC, and Aileen Disney, *née* Rooke (d 1994); *b* 31 July 1931; *Educ* Stonyhurst, RMA Sandhurst; *m* 1956, Sarah Elizabeth, da of Maj-Gen (Matthew Herbert) Patrick Sayers, OBE; 3 s, 1 da; *Career* CO 1 Bn Queen's Own Highlanders 1972–74 (despatches), Col GS D Inf 1975–77, Dep Cdr 2 Armd Div and Cdr Osnabrück Garrison 1977–78, student RCDS 1979, dir Operational Requirements 3 (Army) 1980–82, COS HQ Allied Forces Northern Europe 1982–84, Col Queen's Own Highlanders 1983–94; dir Br Field Sports Soc 1984–93, chm Wye Salmon Fishery Owners Assoc; *Recreations* shooting, fishing, sailing; *Clubs* Army and Navy; *Style—* Maj-Gen John Hopkinson, CB; ✉ Bigsweir, Gloucestershire; Craigroy, Ballindalloch, Morayshire

HOPKINSON, Martin James; *b* 6 Aug 1946; *Career* Walker Art Gallery Liverpool: asst keeper Br art 1973–74, asst keeper foreign art 1974–77; curator of prints and non-Scottish art Hunterian Art Gallery Univ of Glasgow 1977–, dep dir The Centre for Whistler Studies Univ of Glasgow Library; *Publications* Foreign Schools catalogue 2 vols (with Edward Morris for Walker Art Gallery, 1977); Exhibition Catalogues: The Macfie Collection (1980), Whistler in Europe 1990 (and James McNeill Whistler at the Hunterian Art Gallery - An Illustrated Guide), James McNeill Whistler (with Denys Sutton, Isetan Museum of Art Tokyo, 1987), Printmaking in Paris 1900–1940 (1991), The Italian Renaissance Print (Hunterian Art Gallery, 1994), Colours and Time: Five Centuries of Colour Woodcuts (Hunterian Art Gallery, 1994); Alexander Mann 1853–1908 - sketches and correspondence with his wife and family (Fine Art Soc, 1985); *Style—* Martin Hopkinson, Esq; ✉ Hunterian Art Gallery, University of Glasgow, Hillhead Street, Glasgow G12 8QQ (☎ 0141 339 8855 ext 5430, fax 0141 307 8017)

HOPKINSON, Nicola Gillian (Nicki); da of John Remington, of Leicester, and Marian Daphne, *née* Purnell; *b* 30 Oct 1958; *Educ* Loughborough HS, Univ of Bradford (BA); *m* 1 Sept 1984, Nigel Geoffrey Hopkinson, s of Geoffrey Hopkinson; 2 da (Miranda Lucy b 31 Dec 1991, Rebecca Sophie b 15 Aug 1993); *Career* trainee accountant Ernst & Whinney 1981–85, gp accountant The Ogilvy Group (UK) Ltd 1985–87; fin dir: Ogilvy & Mather Partners Ltd 1987–92, London Media Group Ltd 1992–93; with Mosseri Associates Ltd 1994–; ACA 1984; *Style—* Mrs Nicki Hopkinson

HOPKINSON, Simon Charles; s of Frederick Bruce Hopkinson, of Pembrokeshire, and Anne Dorothie Mary, *née* Whitworth; *b* 5 June 1954; *Educ* St John's Coll Cambridge (chorister), Trent Coll Derbyshire; *Career* Normandie Hotel Birtle 1970–71, Hat & Feather Knutsford 1971–72, St Non's Hotel St Davids 1972–74, Druidstone Hotel Little Haven 1974–75; chef and proprietor: Shed Restaurant Dinas 1975–77, Hoppy's Restaurant 1977–78; inspr Egon Ronay 1978–80; chef: private house 1980–83, Hilaire London 1983–87; founding chef and co-proprietor Bibendum 1987–; *Books* Roast Chicken and Other Stories (1994); also cookery writer The Independent; *Recreations* dining; *Clubs* The Groucho, Colony Room; *Style—* Simon Hopkinson, Esq; ✉ Bibendum Restaurant Ltd, 81 Fulham Rd, London SW3 6RD (☎ 0171 581 5817, fax 0171 823 7925)

HOPKINSON, (George) William; s of William Hartley Hopkinson (d 1971), and Mary, *née* Ashmore; *b* 13 Sept 1943; *Educ* Tupton Hall GS, Pembroke Coll Cambridge (MA); *m* Mary Agnes, *née* Coverdale; 1 s (William St John b 9 Nov 1974); *Career* Inland Revenue: joined 1965, Civil Serv Dept 1973–76, private sec to Min of State 1976–78, asst sec 1978–81; HM Treasy 1981–86; MOD: head Defence Arms Control Unit 1988–92, head Defence Lands Serv 1992–93, asst under sec of state (Policy) 1993–; visiting fell Global Security Prog Univ of Cambridge 1991; contrib to pubns on security policy; *Recreations* walking, reading; *Clubs* United Oxford and Cambridge; *Style—* William Hopkinson, Esq; ✉ Ministry of Defence, Main Building, Whitehall, London SW1A 2HB (☎ 0171 218 2533, fax 0171 218 8292)

HOPKIRK, (Margaret) Joyce; *née* Nicholson; da of late Walter Nicholson, of Newcastle, and late Veronica, *née* Keelan; *Educ* Middle St Secdy Sch Newcastle; *m* 1, 1964, Peter Hopkirk; 1 da (Victoria b 11 April 1966); m 2, 9 Aug 1974, William James (Bill) Lear, s of Maj Cyril James Lear (d 1988), of Newick, Sussex; 1 s (Nicholas b 22 Nov 1975); *Career* women's ed (launch) Sun Newspapers 1969, ed (launch) Br Cosmopolitan 1970, asst ed Daily Mirror 1972–78, women's ed Sunday Times 1986, ed dir (launch) Br Elle 1987, ed She Magazine 1987–89, ed Chic Magazine 1993–94, conslt ed TV Plus 1991–, conslt to ed Sunday Express 1992–, fndr ed Chic magazine 1994–; FRSA; *Books* Splash (co-author, 1995), Best of Enemies (1996); *Style—* Mrs Joyce Hopkirk; ✉ Gadespring, Piccotts End, Hemel Hempstead, Herts (☎ 01442 245608)

HOPLEY, Damian Paul; *b* 12 April 1970; *Educ* Harrow, Univ of St Andrews, Univ of Cambridge (Rugby blue 1992); *Career* professional Rugby Union player Wasps RFC; England: full Eng tours to Australia and Fiji 1991 and S Africa 1994, memb World Cup squad S Africa 1995, 3 full caps 1995, World Cup 7–a-side champion 1993, capt 7–a-side team 1996; *Recreations* blues piano, skiing, golf, extensive travel and dangerous sports; *Clubs* Hawks, Ferretz, Gilston Golf (vice capt); *Style—* Damian Hopley, Esq; ✉ Thorncote, Edgehill Rd, Ealing, London W13 8HW (☎ 0181 998 9882); Wasps FC, Rangers Stadium, South Africa Road, Shepherd's Bush, London W12 7PA

HOPMEIER, George Alan Richard; JP (Inner London); s of Dr Lucian Hopmeier (d 1981), and Yolanda Hopmeier; *b* 23 Sept 1948; *Educ* Dulwich, UCL (BA); 1 da (Charlotte b 29 March 1981); *Career* chief exec CEBA Ltd 1991–; memb: Inner London Juvenile Cts Panel and W Central Div, Inst for the Study and Treatment of Delinquency 1988, ISBA 1980; *Recreations* boating, reading, flying; *Clubs* RAC; *Style—* George Hopmeier, Esq, JP; ✉ 31 Blenheim Gardens, London SW2 5EU (☎ 0181 678 6060, fax 0181 671 5134)

HOPPER, Ian; s of John Frederick Hopper (d 1989), and Dora, *née* Lambert (d 1970); *b* 19 May 1938; *Educ* Dame Allans Sch Newcastle on Tyne, High Storrs GS Sheffield, Univ of Sheffield (MB ChB); *m* 19 Aug 1961, Christine Margaret, da of Tom Raymond Holroyd Wadsworth (d 1978); 1 s (Andrew b 1964), 1 da (Penny b 1962); *Career* sr ENT registrar Royal Infirmary Sheffield 1967–69, conslt ENT surgn City Hosps Sunderland 1969–; hon conslt in otorhinolaryngology The Duchess of Kent's Military Hosp Catterick 1991–; memb Cncl Br Assoc of Otolaryngologists; FRCSEd 1967, FRCS 1991; *Recreations* travel, bowling; *Clubs* Sunderland; *Style—* Ian Hopper, Esq; ✉ 3 Corby Hall Drive, Sunderland, Tyne & Wear SR2 7HZ (☎ 0191 522 7313); District General Hospital, Kayll Road, Sunderland SR4 7TP (☎ 0191 565 6256)

HOPPER, Col Patrick Desmond Leo (Pat); DL (Essex 1990); s of Brig Charles Reginald Leo Hopper (d 1959), and Daphne Elise, *née* Williams (d 1987); *b* 22 Nov 1930; *Educ* Monkton Combe Sch, RMA Sandhurst; *m* 28 March 1959, Gemma Felicity Bevan, da of Brig James Bevan Brown (d 1962); 1 s (Jonathan b 1962), 1 da (Joanna b 1960); *Career* cmmnd Suffolk Regt 1951, Platoon Cdr Malaya (despatches) 1951–53, served 3 Para 1953–57 (took part in Suez Op), Adj 1 Suffolk 1958–59, cmd 5 Bn Royal Anglian Regt 1973–75, Asst Adj-Gen Rhine Army 1975–78; ret from Regular Army 1978; sec East Anglia TA and VR Assoc 1986–95 (dep sec 1979–86), Dep Hon Col TA (Essex) Royal Anglian Regt 1987–92; memb Ct Univ of Essex 1990–; *Recreations* fly fishing, sailing; *Clubs* Army and Navy; *Style—* Col Pat Hopper, DL; ✉ Rose Lodge, Stetchworth, Newmarket, Suffolk CB8 9TP (☎ 01638 507608)

HOPPER, Robert Thomas Cort; s of late John Ronald Thomas Hopper, of Langham, Rutland, and Joan Rosemary, *née* Thompson; *b* 26 June 1946; *Educ* Sedbergh, Univ of Manchester (BA); *m* 24 Aug 1972, Christine Anne, da of Bryan Christopher Ball; 1 s (Henry b 25 April 1984), 2 da (Rebecca b 19 Jan 1980, Sophie b 21 Oct 1982); *Career* articled clerk Messrs Pearless de Rougement (solicitors) Sussex 1964–68, dep princ keeper The Whitworth Art Gallery Univ of Manchester 1980–81 (asst keeper fine art 1973–80), dir Art Galleries and Museums City of Bradford Metropolitan DC 1981–88, dir Henry Moore Sculpture Tst 1988–, chm Ctee of Mgmnt Yorkshire Sculpture Park Bretton Hall Wakefield 1981–; memb:. Faculty of Art Br Sch at Rome 1994–, Tstees' Advsy Ctee Tate Gallery Liverpool 1993–, Ct Univ of Leeds 1993–, Govrs' Ctee Whitworth Art Gallery Univ of Manchester 1994–, Ctee Contemporary Art Soc, Advsy Bd Hayward Gallery 1994–; chm Art Projects Ctee Arts Cncl of England 1994– (memb 1993–), tstee Yorks Dance Centre 1994–, govr Bretton Hall Coll 1994–, patron Little Sparta Tst 1995–, dir Art Transpennine 1996–; Hon MA Univ of Bradford 1988, Hon DA Manchester Metropolitan Univ 1995–; professional memb Museums Assoc 1981, FRSA 1982; *Style—* Robert Hopper, Esq; ✉ The Henry Moore Sculpture Trust, The Henry Moore Institute, 74 The Headrow, Leeds

HOPPER, William Joseph; s of late Isaac Vance Hopper, and late Jennie Josephine Black; *b* 9 Aug 1929; *Educ* Queen's Park Secdy Sch, Univ of Glasgow (MA); *m* 1 (m dis); 1 da (Catherine b 1971); m 2, 1987 (m dis), Marjorie; *Career* Flying Offr RAF 1952–55; fin analyst W R Grace and Co New York 1956–59, London office mangr H Hentz and Co (memb NY Stock Exchange) 1960–66, gen mangr S G Warburg and Co Ltd 1966–69; dir: Hill Samuel and Co Ltd 1969–74, Morgan Grenfell and Co Ltd 1975–79 (advsr 1979–86), Wharf Resources Ltd (Calgary) 1984–87, Manchester Ship Canal Co 1985–87; exec chm Shire Trust Ltd 1986–91, chm Robust Mouldings Ltd 1986–90, exec chm W J Hopper & Co Ltd 1992–; fndr chm (now memb Exec Ctee) Inst for Fiscal Studies 1969–, treas Action Resource Centre 1985–94, tstee Nat Hosp for Nervous Diseases Devpt Fndn 1986–90, tstee Hampstead Wells and Campden Trust 1989–, chm Rosslyn Hill Unitarian Chapel Hampstead 1990–; MEP (C) Greater Manchester W 1979–84; *Recreations* listening to music, gardening; *Clubs* Garrick; *Style—* W J Hopper, Esq; ✉ 43 Flask Walk, London NW3 1HH (☎ 0171 435 6414, fax 0171 431 5568)

HOPPS, Stuart Gary; s of Alec Hopps (d 1973), of London, and Lucie, *née* Dombek; *b* 2 Dec 1942; *Educ* Stratford GS, King's Coll London (BA), MFA Sarah Lawrence Coll; *Career* choreographer; Dance Dept Dartington Coll of Art 1970–71, assoc dir Scottish Ballet 1971–76, fndr dir SB's movable Workshop, fndr chm Dance Panel Gr London Arts, chm Br Assoc of Choreographers, memb Dance Panel Arts Cncl of GB 1976–80, dir MA Studies Laban Centre 1986–89, memb Accreditation Ctee Cncl for Dance Educn & Training; dir: Diversion Dance Co, Janet Smith Dancers; *Theatre* incl: Elizabeth (Ginza Saison Theatre Tokyo), Medea (Barcelona Cultural Olympics), A Midsummer Night's Dream, Salome, Candide (Edinburgh Festival), The Oresteia, Animal Farm (NT), Henry VIII and As You Like it (RSC), Oliver (Nat Youth Music Theatre); theatre in West End: Pal Joey, Girl Friends, The Rocky Horror Show, Carmen Jones; *Opera* incl: The Cunning Little Vixen, Queen of Spades and Christmas Eve (ENO), Orfeo ed Euridice (Glyndebourne), Carmen, Idomeneo and Onegin (WNO), HMS Pinafore and The Merry Widow (Sadler's Wells), The Cunning Little Vixen and Carmen (Royal Opera), Macbeth (Metropoloitan Opera), Peter Grimes (Kent Opera); *Films* incl: Sense and Sensibility, Twelfth Night, Kenneth Branagh's Much Ado About Nothing and Hamlet; *Style—* Stuart Hopps, Esq; ✉ c/o Marina Martin Associates, 12–13 Poland Street, London W1V 3DE (☎ 0171 734 4818, fax 0171 734 4832)

HOPSON, David Joseph; s of Geoffrey Paul Hopson (d 1980), of Merryways, Newbury, and Nora Winifred, *née* Camp (d 1968); *b* 26 Feb 1929; *Educ* St Bartholomew's GS Newbury; *m* 1 June 1957, Susan, da of Horace Caleb George Buckingham (d 1965); 2 s (Jonathan Joseph b 13 March 1960, Christopher Ian b 9 April 1963); *Career* RN 1946–49; chm: Camp Hopson & Co Ltd 1966– (dir 1961), Newbury Building Society 1986– (dir 1963); pres Newbury and Dist Agric Show 1991; *Recreations* fly-fishing; *Clubs* Fly Fishers'; *Style—* David Hopson, Esq; ✉ Camp Hopson & Co Ltd, 6–12 Northbrook Street, Newbury, Berks RG13 1DN (☎ 01635 523 523, fax 01635 529 009)

HOPWOOD, Prof Anthony George; s of George Hopwood (d 1986), of Stoke-on-Trent, and Violet, *née* Simpson (d 1986); *b* 18 May 1944; *Educ* Hanley HS, LSE (BSc), Univ of Chicago (MBA, PhD); *m* 31 Aug 1967, Caryl, da of John H Davies (d 1981), of Ton Pentre, Mid Glam; 2 s (Mark b 1971, Justin b 1974); *Career* lectr in mgmnt accounting Manchester Business Sch 1970–73, sr staff Admin Staff Coll Henley-on-Thames 1973–75, professorial fell Oxford Centre for Mgmnt Studies 1976–78, ICA prof of accounting and fin reporting London Business Sch 1978–85, Ernst and Young prof of int accounting and fin mgmnt LSE 1985–95, prof of mgmnt studies and dep dir of mgmnt studies Univ of Oxford 1995–, fell Templeton Coll Oxford 1995–; visiting prof of mgmnt European Inst for Advanced Studies Mgmnt Brussels 1972– (pres of Bd 1995–), visiting distinguished prof of accounting Pennsylvania State Univ 1983–88; pres Euro Accounting Assoc 1977–79 and 1987–88, distinguished int lectr American Accounting Assoc 1981, John V Ratcliffe Meml lectr Univ of NSW 1988; accounting advsr to: Euro Cmmn 1989–90, OECD 1990–91; memb: Mgmnt and Industl Rels Ctee SSRC 1975–79; Hon DEcon Turku Sch of Econs Finland 1989, Hon DEcon Univ of Gothenburg Sweden 1992; *Books* An Accounting System and Managerial Behaviour (1973), Accounting and Human Behaviour (1974), Essays in British Accounting Research (with M Bromwich, 1981), Auditing Research (with M Bromwich and J Shaw, 1982), Accounting Standard Setting - An International Perspective (with M Bromwich, 1983), European Contributions to Accounting Research (with H Schreuder, 1984), Issues in Public Sector Accounting (with C Tomkins, 1984), Research and Current Issues in Management Accounting (with M Bromwich, 1986), Acccounting from the Outside (1989), International Pressures for Accounting Change (1989), Understanding Accounting in a Changing Environment (with M Page and S Turley, 1990), Accounting and the Law (with M Bromwich, 1992), Accounting as Social and Institutional Practice (with P Miller, 1994); *Style—* Prof Anthony Hopwood; ✉ School of Management Studies, University of Oxford, The Radcliffe Infirmary, Woodstock Road, Oxford OX2 6HE (☎ 01865 228470, fax 01865 228471)

HOPWOOD, Prof Sir David Alan; kt (1994); s of Herbert Hopwood (d 1963), of Lymm, Cheshire, and Dora, *née* Grant (d 1972); *b* 19 Aug 1933; *Educ* Purbrook Park Co HS Hants, Lymm GS Cheshire, Univ of Cambridge (MA, PhD), Univ of Glasgow (DSc); *m* 15 Sept 1962, Joyce Lilian, da of Isaac Bloom (d 1964), of Hove, Sussex; 2 s (Nicholas Duncan b 1964, John Andrew b 1965), 1 da (Rebecca Jane b 1967); *Career* John Stothert bye-fell Magdalene Coll Cambridge 1956–58, univ demonstrator and asst lectr in botany Univ of Cambridge 1957–61, res fell St John's Coll Cambridge 1958–61, lectr in genetics Univ of Glasgow 1961–68, John Innes prof of genetics UEA and head Genetics Dept John Innes Centre 1968–; hon prof: Chinese Acad Med Sciences 1987, Chinese Acad of Sciences (Insts of Microbiology and Plant Physiology) 1987, Huazhong Agric Univ Wuhan China 1989; hon fell: UMIST 1990, Magdalene Coll Cambridge 1992; memb: Genetical Soc of GB 1957 (pres 1984–87), Euro Molecular Biology Orgn 1984, Academia Europaea 1988; hon memb: Spanish Microbiological Soc 1985, Hungarian Acad of Sciences 1990, Soc Gen Microbiology; foreign fell Indian Nat Sci Acad 1987; Hon Dr of Sci ETH Zürich 1989; FIBiol 1968, FRS 1979; *Recreations* cooking, gardening; *Style—* Prof Sir David Hopwood, FRS; ✉ John Innes Centre, Norwich Research Park, Colney, Norwich NR4 7UH (☎ 01603 452571, fax 01603 456844); 244 Unthank Rd, Norwich NR2 2AH (☎ 01603 53488)

HORAM, John Rhodes; MP (C) Orpington (majority 12,935); s of Sydney Horam, of Preston, Lancs; *b* 7 March 1939; *Educ* Silcoates Sch Wakefield, St Catharine's Coll

Cambridge; *m* 1, 1977, Iris Crawley; m 2, 1987, Judith Margaret Jackson, *qv*; *Career* former fin journalist: Financial Times, The Economist; MP (Lab 1970–81, SDP 1981–83) Gateshead West 1970–83, joined Cons Pty Feb 1987, MP (C) Orpington 1992–; Parly under sec for tport 1976–79, memb Public Accounts Ctee 1992–95, Parly sec Office of Public Service March-Nov 1995, Parly under sec Dept of Health Nov 1995–; CRU International Ltd: md 1968–70 and 1983–92, dep chm 1992–95; *Style*— John Horam, Esq, MP; ✉ 6 Bovingdon Rd, London SW6 2AP; House of Commons, London SW1A 0AA

HORAN, Francis Thomas (Frank); s of Leo Patrick Horan (d 1979), and Rose, *née* Finch (d 1983); *b* 24 July 1933; *Educ* Torquay GS, St Mary's Hosp Med Sch, RCS, McGill Univ Montreal (MSc); *m* 17 Feb 1962, Cynthia Anne, da of Percy John Reginald Bambury (d 1988), of Bournemouth; 2 s (Thomas Charles b 1965, John Patrick b 1968), 1 da (Julia Anne b 1968); *Career* med dir and hon conslt orthopaedic surgn Princess Royal Hosp Haywards Heath W Sussex; hon med advsr: English Basketball Assoc, Br and Irish Basketball Fedn, TCCB; memb Med Ctee BOA; hon orthopaedic surgn: Lord's Cricket Ground, Middlesex CCC, Sussex CCC (memb Ctee); chm Editorial Bd and English language ed Int Orthopaedics, ed Br Orthopaedic News, dep ed Jl of Bone and Joint Surgery; pres Br Orthopaedic Sports Trauma Assoc (BOSTA), memb Int Ctee Societé International de Chirugie Orthopedie et Traumatologie (Br nat delegate); LRCP, MRCS 1959, FRCS 1966, fell Br Orthopaedic Assoc (memb Cncl 1987–89 and 1991–96, Robert Jones Gold Medal); *Books* Orthopaedic Problems in Inherited Skeletal Disorders (1982), Harris's Orthopaedics (contrib), Medicine Sport and the Law (contrib), Modern Trauma Management (contrib); *Recreations* sport, travel, food; *Clubs* MCC, Sussex CCC; *Style*— Frank Horan, Esq; ✉ Providence, Plumpton, E Sussex BN7 3AJ (☎ 01273 890316, fax 01273 890482); Consulting Rooms, 40 Wilbury Rd, Hove, E Sussex (☎ 01273 206206); 71 Park St, London W1 (☎ 0171 629 3763)

HORBERRY, Andrew William; s of John Alexander Horberry, of Portpatrick, Wigtownshire, and Moya Rita, *née* Reid; *b* 30 June 1962; *Educ* Stranraer Acad, Univ of Edinburgh (MA); *Career* account exec/supervisor Grandfield Rork Collins advtg agency 1984–86, account dir Saatchi & Saatchi 1986–90; The Leith Agency gp account dir 1990–93, business devpt dir 1993–95; account dir M&C Saatchi 1995–; assoc memb Market Res Soc 1990 (Scottish Ctee sec); memb Account Planning Gp 1991; dir: Youth & Music 1988–90, Traverse Theatre 1994–; memb: Perrier Awards Panel Edinburgh Fringe Festival 1984, Olivier Awards Panel 1988; *Recreations* theatre, travel, architecture; *Style*— Andrew Horberry, Esq; ✉ M&C Saatchi Ltd, 34–36 Golden Square, London W1R 4EE (☎ 0171 543 4500, fax 0171 543 4501)

HORDEN, Prof John Robert Backhouse; s of Henry Robert Horden (d 1950), of Warwicks, and Ethel Edith, *née* Backhouse (d 1970); *Educ* ChCh Oxford, Pembroke Coll Cambridge, Heidelberg, Sorbonne, Lincoln's Inn; *m* 10 Jan 1948, Aileen Mary (d 1984), da of Col Walter John Douglas, TD (d 1949), of Warwicks and S Wales; 1 s (Peregrine b 1955); *Career* formerly: tutor and lectr ChCh Oxford; dir: Inst of Bibliography and Textual Criticism Univ of Leeds, Centre for Bibliographical Studies Univ of Stirling; Cecil Oldman Meml lectr 1971, Marc Fitch prize 1979, devised new academic discipline of Publishing Studies Univ of Leeds 1972, initiated first Br degree in PR Stirling Univ 1987; visiting prof: Pa State, Saskatchewan, Erlangen-Nürnberg, Texas at Austin, Münster; Golf: represented England, capt for Warwicks, Oxford, Cambridge and Br Univs; Doctor of Humane Letters honoris causa Indiana State Univ 1974; FSA, FRSL; *Books* Francis Quarles: a Bibliography (1953), Quarles' Hosanna and Threnodes (1960, 2 edn 1965), Art of the Drama (1969), English and Continental Emblem Books (22 vols 1968–74), Everyday Life in Seventeenth-Century England (1974), Techniques of Bibliography (1977), John Freeth (1985, 2 edn 1993), Bibliographia (1992); *Recreations* golf, music, painting; *Clubs* Athenaeum, Hawks', Vincent's; *Style*— Prof John Horden, FSA, FRSL; ✉ Department of English Studies, University of Stirling, Stirling FK9 4LA (☎ 01786 467495)

HORDER, Dr John Plaistowe; CBE (1980, OBE 1971); s of Gerald Morley Horder (d 1939), and Emma Ruth, *née* Plaistowe (d 1971); *b* 9 Dec 1919; *Educ* Lancing, Univ Coll Oxford (BA, MA), London Hosp Med Coll (BM BCh); *m* 20 June 1940, Elizabeth June, da of Maurice Wilson (d 1924); 2 s (Timothy John b 1943, William Morley b 1950), 2 da (Annabelle Mary b 1945, Josephine Elizabeth b 1953); *Career* GP London 1951–81, conslt to Expert Ctee WHO 1960–61, travelling fell 1964 and 1984, Jephcott visiting prof Univ of Nottingham 1977; RCGP: chm Educn Ctee 1967–70, John Hunt fell 1973–76, pres 1979–82, Wolfson prof France and Belgium 1978; RSM: pres section of gp, hon fell 1982, vice pres 1987–89; visiting fell King Edward's Hosp Fund 1983–86, visiting prof Royal Free Hosp Med Sch 1983–91; pres: Centre for the Advancement of Inter-Professional Educn 1987–, Med Art Soc 1989–92; hon fell Green Coll Oxford 1988; Hon MD Free Univ Amsterdam 1985; hon memb The Canadian Coll of Family Practice 1981, visiting prof Univ of Zagreb Med Sch 1990–; FRCGP 1970, FRCP 1972 (Samuel Gee lectr 1991), FRCPsych 1980, FRCP (Ed) 1981; *Books* The Future General Practitioner (jtly and ed, 1972), 14 Prince's Gate (jtly, 1987); *Recreations* playing the piano, painting water-colours; *Style*— Dr John Horder, CBE; ✉ 98 Regent's Park Rd, London NW1 8UG (☎ 0171 722 3804)

HORDER, 2 Baron (UK 1933); Sir Thomas Mervyn Horder; 2 Bt (UK 1923); s of 1 Baron Horder, GCVO, DL, MD, FRCP (d 1955); *b* 8 Dec 1910; *Educ* Winchester, Trinity Coll Cambridge; *m* 6 July 1946 (m dis 1957), Mary Ross, yr da of Dr William Scott McDougall, of Wallington, Surrey; *Heir* none; *Career* served WWII, RAF Fighter Cmd, Air HQ India and SEAC, Wing Cdr RAFVR; chm Gerald Duckworth and Co 1948–70; *Books* The Little Genius - a Memoir of the First Lord Horder (1966), Six Betjeman Songs (1967), A Shropshire Lad - Five Housman Songs (1980), On Their Own - Shipwrecks and Survivals (1988), Seven Shakespeare Songs (1988), Black Diamonds - Six Dorothy Parker Songs (1990), Five Burns Songs (1995), Dorset Delight - Five William Barnes Songs (1996); *Style*— The Rt Hon Lord Horder; ✉ 4 Hamilton Close, London NW8 8QY

HORDERN, (Anthony) Christopher Shubra; s of Anthony Arthur Shubra Hordern (d 1981), of Jersey, and Alison Mary, *née* Bigwood (d 1984); *b* 7 July 1936; *Educ* Malvern; *m* 1, 12 Sept 1959, Lucy (d 1988), da of Michael Pemberton Green; 1 s (Anthony Miles Shubra b 18 March 1965), 2 da (Catherine Anne b 2 June 1961, Josephine Alex b 21 Oct 1962); m 2, 7 Oct 1989, Jane, da of David Moore Barlow; *Career* CA; articled clerk C Herbert Smith & Russell; Price Waterhouse: joined 1963 (on amalgamation with Howard Smith Thompson & Co), ptnr 1967–91; dir: TI Pensions Ltd 1991–, Univ Hosp Birmingham NHS Tst 1995–; pres: Birmingham CAs Students Soc 1976, Birmingham and W Midlands Soc of CAs 1983–84; memb Cncl ICAEW 1985–94, chm Worcester Gp of CAs 1995–; govr: Alice Ottley Sch Worcester, Malvern Coll; tstee: Baron Davenport Charity Tst, Joseph Hopkins Charity (also chm); hon treas Hereford & Worcester Branch British Red Cross Soc; Freeman City of London, memb Worshipful Co of Chartered Accountants 1987; FCA; *Recreations* walking, fly-fishing; *Clubs* RAC; *Style*— Christopher Hordern, Esq; ✉ Church House, North Piddle, Worcestershire WR7 4PR (☎ and fax 01905 381438)

HORDERN, Rt Hon Sir Peter Maudslay; kt (1985), PC (1993), DL (Horsham 1983), MP (C) Horsham (majority 25,072); s of C H Hordern, MBE; *b* 18 April 1929; *Educ* Geelong GS Aust, ChCh Oxford (MA); *m* 1964, Susan Chataway; 2 s, 1 da; *Career* memb London Stock Exchange 1957–74, dir Touche Remnant Technology 1975–; chm: Fina plc 1987–, F & C Smaller Cos 1976–; MP (C): Horsham 1964–74 and 1983–, Horsham and Crawley 1974–83; jt sec 1922 Ctee 1988– (memb Exec 1968–), chm Public Accounts Cmmn 1988– (memb 1984–), chm Cons Backbench Ctee on Europe 1992–; memb Ct of Assts Worshipful Co of Salters; *Style*— The Rt Hon Sir Peter Hordern, DL, MP; ✉ House of Commons, London SW1A 0AA

HORE, Dr Brian David; s of William Harold Banks Hore, and Gladys Hilda, *née* Preedy; *b* 21 Sept 1937; *Educ* Lower Sch of John Lyon Harrow Middx, Bart's Med Coll London, Maudsley Hosp London (BSc, MB BS, MPhil); *m* Eva Elliot, da of George Elliot Shepherd (d 1955); 2 s (Ian b 19 March 1968, Andrew b 29 Jan 1971); *Career* house offr Bart's London 1963–65, registrar in psychiatry Maudsley Hosp 1967–70, sr registrar in psychological med Hammersmith Hosp 1970–71; conslt psychiatrist: Withington Hosp Manchester 1972–, Univ Hosp of S Manchester 1972–; hon lectr in psychiatry Univ of Manchester 1972– (lectr and hon conslt 1971–72); memb: Bd of Dirs ICAA Lausanne Switzerland, Exec Ctee and Jt Ctee Med Cncl on Alcoholism; temp advsr WHO regnl Euro office; vice chm Turning Point; memb BMA 1963, FRCPsych 1981, FRCP 1983; *Books* Alcohol Dependence (1976), Alcohol Problems in Employment (jt ed and contrib, 1981), Alcohol and Health (jtly), Alcohol Our Favourite Drug (jtly, 1986); *Recreations* theatre, cinema, soccer (Manchester City FC); *Style*— Dr Brian Hore; ✉ 17 St John St, Manchester M3 4DR (☎ 0161 834 5775)

HORLICK, Vice Adm Sir Edwin John (Ted); KBE (1981); s of late Edwin William Horlick; *b* 1925; *Educ* Bedford Modern Sch, RN Engrg Coll; *m* 1953, Jean Margaret, da of Herbert Covington; 4 s; *Career* Vice Adm 1979, Chief Naval Engr Offr 1981–83, dir-gen ships MOD (Navy) 1979–83, ret; FEng 1983, FIMechE, MIMarE; *Recreations* golf, gardening; *Clubs* Army and Navy; *Style*— Vice Adm Sir Ted Horlick, KBE, FEng; ✉ Garden Apartment, 74 Gt Pulteney St, Bath BA2 4DL

HORLICK, Sir James Cunliffe William; 6 Bt (UK 1914), of Cowley Manor, Co Gloucester; s of Sir John James Macdonald Horlick, 5 Bt (d 1995), and June, *née* Cory-Wright; *b* 19 Nov 1956; *Educ* Eton; *m* 1985, Fiona Rosalie, eldest da of Andrew Mclaren, of Alcester, Warwicks; 3 s (Alexander b 8 April 1987, Jack b 1989, Hugo b 1991); *Heir* s, Alexander Horlick b 8 April 1987; *Career* 2 Lt Coldstream Guards; co dir; *Clubs* Beefsteak; *Style*— Sir James Horlick, Bt; ✉ Braelangwell House, Balblair, Dingwall, Ross-shire IV7 8LQ

HORLICK, Nicola Karina Christina; da of Michael Robert Dudley Gayford, of Chichester, and Suzanna Christina Victoria, *née* Czyzewska; *b* 28 Dec 1960; *Educ* Cheltenham Ladies' Coll, Birkenhead HS GPDST, Phillips Exeter Acad (USA), Balliol Coll Oxford (BA Jurisprudence); *m* 23 June 1984, Timothy Piers Horlick, s of Vice-Adm Sir Ted Horlick, KBE, FEng, *qv*; 4 da (Georgina b 19 Oct 1986, Alice b 17 Nov 1988, Serena b 2 Nov 1990, Antonia b 10 June 1996), 1 s (Rupert b 1 Dec 1993); *Career* Mercury Asset Management 1983–91, md Morgan Grenfell Investment Management (UK Institutional Business) Morgan Grenfell Asset Management 1991–; *Recreations* music, theatre, skiing; *Style*— Mrs Nicola Horlick; ✉ Morgan Grenfell Asset Management, 20 Finsbury Circus, London EC2M 1NB (☎ 0171 256 7500)

HORLOCK, Very Rev Brian William Horlock; OBE (1977); s of Albert Peace Horlock (d 1978), of Winsor, nr Totton, Hants, and Celia, *née* Smith (d 1969); *b* 16 Oct 1931; *Educ* Ealing Co GS, St David's Coll Lampeter (BA), Chichester Theol Coll; *m* 27 Oct 1962, Rosemary Christine, da of Rev Preb George Arthur Lewis Lloyd (d 1989); 2 s (Nicolas John b 7 Oct 1963, Michael David b 30 July 1968); *Career* ordained (St Paul's Cathedral): deacon 1957, priest 1958; curate St Nicolas with St Mary Magdalene Chiswick 1957–61, priest-in-charge Holy Trinity Witney 1961–62, vicar St Gabriel N Acton London 1962–68, Anglican chaplain in Norway and chaplain St Edmund's Church Oslo 1968–89, rural dean in Scandinavia 1975–79, archdeacon of Scandinavia 1979–89, dean of Gibraltar 1989–; *Recreations* DIY, travel, painting; *Style*— The Very Rev Brian Horlock, OBE; ✉ The Deanery, Bomb House Lane, Gibraltar (☎ 00 350 78377); Cathedral of the Holy Trinity, Cathedral Square, Gibraltar (fax 00 350 78463)

HORLOCK, Prof Sir John Harold; kt (1996); s of Harold Edgar Horlock (d 1971), of Tonbridge, Kent, and Olive Margaret Horlock (d 1989); *b* 19 April 1928; *Educ* Edmonton Latymer Sch, St John's Coll Cambridge (MA, PhD, ScD); *m* 8 June 1953, Sheila Joy, da of Percy Kendolph Stutely (d 1980), of Hordle, Hants; 1 s (Timothy John b 4 Jan 1958), 2 da (Alison Ruth (Mrs Heap) b 20 April 1955, Jane Margaret (Mrs Spencer) b 28 Nov 1961); *Career* design engr Rolls Royce 1949–51; res fell St John's Coll Cambridge 1954–57, prof of mechanical engrg Univ of Liverpool 1958–67, prof of engrg Univ of Cambridge 1967–74; vice chllr: Univ of Salford 1974–80, Open Univ 1981–90 (fell 1990–); hon prof Univ of Warwick 1990–, pro chllr UMIST 1995–; dir: British Engine Insurance Ltd 1979–86, BL Technology Ltd 1979–87, National Grid Co plc 1989–94; memb: SRC 1974–77, Engrg Cncl 1982–84; chm: ARC 1979–80, Advsy Ctee on Safety of Nuclear Installations 1984–93; vice pres Royal Soc 1982–84 and 1992– (treas 1992–); hon fell: St John's Coll Cambridge 1989–, UMIST 1991; Hon DSc: Heriot-Watt 1980, Salford 1981, Univ of E Asia 1985, CNAA 1991, de Montfort 1995; Hon DEng Liverpool 1987, Hon DUniv Open Univ 1991; foreign assoc Nat Ac Eng (USA); FRS 1976, FEng 1977, FIMechE; *Books* Axial Flow Compressors (1958), Axial Flow Turbines (1967), Actuator Disc Theory (1978), Cogeneration (1987), Combined Heat and Power (1992); *Recreations* music, golf; *Clubs* Athenaeum, MCC; *Style*— Prof Sir John Horlock, FEng, FRS; ✉ 2 The Ave, Ampthill, Bedford MK45 2NR (☎ 01525 841307)

HORLOCK, (Henry) Wimburn Sudell; s of Rev Dr Henry Darrell Sudell Horlock (d 1953), and Mary Haliburton, *née* Laurie (d 1953); *b* 19 July 1915; *Educ* Pembroke Coll Oxford (MA); *m* 21 July 1960, Jeannetta Robin, da of Frederick Wilfred Tanner, JP (d 1958), of The Towers, Farnham Royal, Bucks; *Career* serv WWII Army 1939–42; civil serv 1942–60; fndr and dir Stepping Stone Sch 1962–87; memb Ct of Common Cncl City of London 1969–, Sheriff City of London 1972–73, dep Ward of Farringdon Within (North Side) 1978–; chm: City of London Sheriffs' Soc 1985–, West Ham Park Ctee 1979–82, Police Ctee 1987–90; memb: City Livery Club 1969– (pres 1981–82), Farringdon Ward Club 1970– (pres 1978–79), United Wards Club 1972– (pres 1980–81), Guild of Freemen 1972– (Master 1986–87), Royal Soc of St George (City of London Branch) 1972– (chm 1989–90); Freeman City of London 1937; Liveryman Worshipful Co of: Saddlers 1937 (Master 1976–77), Parish Clerks 1966 (Master 1981–82), Plaisterers 1975, Fletchers 1977, Gardeners 1980; hon memb Soc of Young Freeman 1994; Cdr Order of Merit Federal Repub of Germany 1972, Cdr Nat Order of Aztec Eagle of Mexico 1973, Cdr Du Wissam Alouite of Morocco 1987; *Recreations* travel, country pursuits; *Clubs* Athenaeum, Guildhall, City Livery; *Style*— Wimburn Horlock, Esq; ✉ Copse Hill House, Lower Slaughter, Glos GL54 2HZ (☎ 01451 820276); 97 Defoe House, Barbican, London EC2Y 8DN (☎ 0171 588 1602)

HORN, Bernard P; *Educ* Catholic College Preston, Harvard Business Sch (Exec Prog); *m*; *Career* National Westminster Bank plc: joined 1965, in retail banking in N of England 1965–70, mgmnt studies course Manchester 1970–72, joined International Div 1972, dir of corp and institutional fin 1988–89, gen mangr Gp Chief Exec's Office 1989–90, gen mangr i/c gp strategy and communications 1990–91, chief exec NatWest Group International Businesses 1991–96, gp main bd dir 1995–, chief exec Gp Ops 1996–; dir: Coutts & Co Group, Lombard North Central plc, Ulster Bank Ltd; FCIB, FRSA; *Recreations* keeping fit, theatre, ballet, opera, playing the piano; *Style*— Bernard P Horn, Esq; ✉ NatWest Group, 41 Lothbury, London EC2P 2BP (☎ 0171 726 1000, fax 0171 726 1920)

HORN, Dr David Bowes; s of David Horn (d 1952), of Edinburgh, and Joan, *née* Milne (d 1989); *b* 18 Aug 1928; *Educ* Daniel Stewart's Coll Edinburgh, Heriot-Watt Univ (BSc), Univ of Edinburgh (PhD); *m* 5 Oct 1963, Shirley Kay, da of John Henry Riddell (d 1974), of Newcastle upon Tyne; 2 da (Kathryn b 1964, Jane b 1967); *Career* sr grade biochemist Western Infirmary Glasgow 1956–59 (with secondment to equip, open and run new clinical chemical laboratory, Vale of Leven Hosp, Dunbartonshire), top grade biochemist Royal Victoria Infirmary Newcastle upon Tyne 1964–66 (princ grade 1959–64), hon lectr in clinical biochemistry Univ of Newcastle 1963–66, head of Dept of Clinical Chemistry Edinburgh Northern Hosps Gp at Western Gen Hosp Edinburgh 1966–87, hon sr lectr in clinical chem Univ of Edinburgh 1966–87; memb Panel of Assessors for Top Grade Biochemist Appts Scot Home and Health Dept 1972–87; Lothian Health Bd: memb Area Scientific Servs Advsy Ctee 1974–79, Hepatitis Advsy Gp 1982–84, Advsy Gp on Genetic Servs 1985–87; CSTI: chm Registration Ctee of Scientists in Health Care 1981–86 (memb 1979–86), memb Health Care Advsy Ctee 1985–88; memb: Dist Med Records Ctee 1975–83, Nat Consultative Ctee of Scientists in Professions Allied to Med 1975–79 (chm 1976–79), Computer Res Ctee of Chief Scientist Orgn 1976–83, Scientific Servs Advsy Gp 1977–79 (memb Sub Ctee in Clinical Chemistry 1973–79, chm Sub Ctee in Clinical Chemistry 1978–80), Assoc of Clinical Biochemists Cncl 1963–68 and 1978–80 (chm Scottish region 1978–80, hon treas 1964–68), Exam and Inst Ctee Royal Soc of Chemistry 1980–88 (rep on Jt Exam Bd for Mastership in Biochemistry 1973–88), Ethic Ctee Scottish Nat Blood Transfusion Serv 1984–87; chm Div of Laboratory and Scientific Med N Lothian Dist 1975–79; FRSC 1961, FRCPath 1976, FRSE 1978, FIBiol 1989; *Recreations* walking, gardening; *Style*— Dr David B Horn, FRSE; ✉ 2 Barnton Park, Edinburgh EH4 6JF (☎ 0131 336 3444)

HORN, Prof Gabriel; s of Abraham Horn (d 1946), of Birmingham, and Anne, *née* Grill (d 1976); *b* 9 Dec 1927; *Educ* Univ of Birmingham (BSc, MB ChB, MD), Univ of Cambridge (MA, ScD); *m* 1, 29 Nov 1952 (m dis 1979), Hon Ann Loveday Dean, da of Baron Soper (Life Peer), *qv*, of London, and Marie Soper, *née* Dean; 2 s (Nigel b 1954, Andrew b 1960), 2 da (Amanda b 1953, Melissa b 1962); m 2, 30 Aug 1980, Priscilla, da of Edwin Victor Barrett (d 1976), of Cape Town, and Sarah Eliza, *née* McMaster (d 1989); *Career* Educn Branch RAF 1947–49; house appts Birmingham Children's and Birmingham and Midland Eye Hosps 1955–56; Univ of Cambridge: demonstrator and lectr in anatomy 1956–72, reader in neurobiology 1972–74, prof of zoology 1978–95, head Dept of Zoology 1979–94, fell King's Coll 1962–74 and 1978–92, Master of Sidney Sussex Coll 1992–, dep vice-chllr 1994–; sr res fell in neurophysiology Montreal Inst McGill Univ 1957–58, Kenneth Craik Award in Physiological Psychology 1962, visiting prof Univ of California Berkeley USA 1963, visiting res pres Ohio State Univ 1965, visiting prof of zoology Makerere Univ Coll Uganda 1966, Leverhulme res fell Laboratoire de Neurophysiologie Cellulaire France 1970–71, prof of anatomy and head of dept Univ of Bristol 1974–77, distinguished visiting prof Univ of Alberta 1988, visiting Miller prof Univ of California Berkeley 1989, visiting prof Chinese Univ of Hong Kong 1995; Charnock Bradley lectr Univ of Edinburgh 1988, Crisp lectr Univ of Leeds 1990; memb: Biological Scis Advsy Panel and Ctee Scientific Res Cncl 1970–75, Res Ctee Mental Health Fndn 1973–78, Advsy Bd Inst of Animal Physiology Babraham Cambridge 1980–85, Cncl AFRC 1991–94; chm: BBSRC Working Party on Biology of Spongiform Encephalonpathies 1991–94, Animal Sciences and Psychology Research Ctee Biotechnology and Biological Sciences Research Cncl 1994–96 (memb Sci and Engrg Bd 1994–); dir Co of Biologists 1980–93; pubns in various scientific journals; FRS 1986; *Books* Memory, Imprinting and the Brain (1985), Short-term Changes in Neural Activity and Behaviour (jt ed, 1970), Behavioural and Neural Aspects of Learning and Memory (jt ed, 1991); *Recreations* riding, cycling, walking, listening to music, wine and conversation; *Style*— Prof Gabriel Horn, FRS; ✉ The Master's Lodge, Sidney Sussex College, Cambridge CB2 3HU (☎ 01223 330868, fax 01223 338884); Univ of Cambridge, Department of Zoology, Downing St, Cambridge CB2 3EJ (☎ 01223 336601, fax 01223 336676, telex 81240 CAMSPL G)

HORN, Eur Ing Dr George; s of George Horn, MM (d 1937), of Sheffield, and Theodora, *née* Mason (d 1977); *b* 10 April 1928; *Educ* King Edward VII Sheffield, Univ of Sheffield (BSc, PhD, DSc); *m* 28 July 1951, Doreen, da of Edward Nash (d 1971), of Sheffield; 2 s (Christopher b 30 Oct 1954, Nicholas b 18 Jan 1957); *Career* 2 Lt 19 Air Formation Signal Regt Royal Signals 1948–49; res engr GEC Atomic Energy Div 1955–58, head of Thermodynamics Section CEGB Marchwood Engineering Laboratories 1958–65, head of Engrg Div GEGB Berkeley Nuclear Laboratories 1965–70, dep chm Ireland Alloys (Holdings) Ltd 1983–91 (gp tech dir 1970–89), engrg conslt 1991–; author of over 40 scientific and tech papers; chm Advsy Ctee Dept of Chemical Engrg and Fuel Technol Univ of Sheffield 1989–91; FInstE 1963, CEng 1968, MInstMet 1975, AIME 1984, FIMechE 1990 (MIMechE 1968), Eur Ing 1990, FRSA 1990, MSTA (memb Soc of Tech Analysts) 1996; *Recreations* charting and technical analysis, swimming, skiing; *Style*— Dr George Horn; ✉ 10 Fountain Craig, 1010 Gt Western Rd, Glasgow G12 0NR (☎ 0141 334 1635)

HORN, Trevor; s of Robert Horn, of Durham, and Elizabeth, *née* Lambton; *b* 15 July 1949; *Educ* Johnson GS; *m* 1980, Jill, da of David Sinclair; 1 s (Aaron b 15 Dec 1983), 3 da (Alexandra b 24 April 1982, Rebecca b 25 March 1990, Gabriella b 17 April 1995); *Career* record prodr; formerly vocalist of pop bands Buggles and Yes, fndr memb and innovator The Art of Noise, fndr ZTT records, dir SPZ Group; past prodn credits incl: Buggles' The Age of Plastic (1980, gold disc), ABC's Lexicon of Love (1982, platinum), Malcolm McClaren's Duck Rock (1983, gold), Yes' 90125 (multi platinum), Frankie Goes To Hollywood's Welcome To The Pleasure Dome (multi platinum), Simple Minds' Street Fighting Years (platinum), Seal (multi platinum), Mike Oldfield's Tubular Bells II; prodr of many other artists incl: Grace Jones, Spandau Ballet, Foreigner, Godley and Creme, Paul McCartney, Rod Stewart, Pet Shop Boys, Propaganda, Dollar, Tina Turner, Tom Jones; BPI Br Prodr of the Year 1983, 1985 and 1991 (nominated 1983, 1984, 1985, 1986, 1987, 1988 and 1994), Radio 1 Award for contribution to pop music 1984; Ivor Novello Awards: best recorded record for Owner of a Lonely Heart 1983, best contemporary song for Relax 1984, most performed work for Two Tribes 1984; BMI Award for Owner of A Lonely Heart 1984, Grammy Award for best instrumental Cinema 90125, Q Magazine Best Prodr Award 1991, Music Week Best Prodr Award 1991, Grammy Award nomination for Best Prodr 1994; *Style*— Trevor Horn, Esq; ✉ Sarm Productions, 42–46 St Luke's Mews, London W11 1DG (☎ 0171 221 5101, fax 0171 221 3374)

HORNBY, Sir Derek Peter; kt (1990); s of F N Hornby (d 1942), of Bournemouth, and Violet May, *née* Pardy; *b* 10 Oct 1930; *Educ* Canford; *m* 1, 1953 (m dis), Margaret Withers; 1 s (Nicholas Peter John b 1957), 1 da (Gillian Margaret b 1959); m 2, 20 Feb 1971, Sonia Margaret (*see* Lady Hornby), da of Sidney Beesley (d 1985), of Birmingham; 1 s (Jonathan Peter b 1967), 1 da (Victoria Jane b 1968); *Career* Mars Ltd 1960–64, Texas Instruments 1964–73, dir international operations Xerox Corp USA 1973–80, md Rank Xerox Services Ltd 1980–84, chm Rank Xerox UK Ltd 1984–90; memb Br Overseas Trade Bd 1987– (chm 1990–95), pres European Cncl of Management 1992–94; chm: Video Arts Ltd 1993–96, London and Continental Railways 1994–, Morgan Sindall plc 1995–; dir: Dixons Group plc 1990–, Sedgewick Group 1993–, AMP Asset Management 1994–, Pillar Properties Investments plc; Liveryman Worshipful Co of Loriners; Hon DSc Aston; CIMgt, FRSA, FInstD; *Recreations* cricket, real tennis, theatre; *Clubs* Garrick, MCC, Leamington Real Tennis; *Style*— Sir Derek Hornby; ✉ Badgers Farm, Idlicote, Shipston on Stour, Warwickshire CV36 5DT (☎ 01608 661890); Flat 2, 48 Thurloe Square, London SW7 2PX (☎ 0171 581 5701)

HORNBY, John Fleet; s of John Fleet Hornby, of Cumbria, and Marion, *née* Charnley (d 1981); *b* 23 Dec 1945; *Educ* Dowdales Co Sch Cumbria; *m* 1976, Elizabeth, da of John Chorley, of Cumbria; 1 s (Paul b 1978); *Career* CA; audit mangr R F Miller & Co 1968–69 (articled clerk 1963–68); James Fisher & Sons plc (shipowners and port operators): accountant special duties 1969, asst co sec 1969–70, PA to md 1970–71, group accountant 1971–78, divnl dir of fin 1978–81, fin dir 1981–86, commercial dir 1986–88, md 1988–89, chm and md 1989–93; princ J F Hornby CAs 1994–, business conslt 1994–, assoc conslt Armstrong Watson & Co CAs 1994–; former dir/chm numerous other companies; dir Chamber of Shipping 1991–94, memb Gen Ctee Lloyd's Register of Shipping 1992–94; memb: Mgmnt Ctee The Sea Cadet Corps Barrow-in-Furness Unit 23 TS Sovereign, Citizens' Advice Bureau Barrow-in-Furness; chm Cumbria Christian Crusade Tst, pres Barrow Chrysanthemum Soc, dep chm Governing Body Dowdales Sch; hon consul of Norway at Barrow-in-Furness; Freeman City of London, Liveryman Worshipful Co of Shipwrights; FCA 1968, FInstD, FRSA; *Recreations* fell walking, fitness, travelling, reading; *Style*— John Hornby, Esq; ✉ Hillside, Guards Road, Lindal, Ulverston, Cumbria LA12 0TN (☎ 01229 465614, fax 01229 588061)

HORNBY, John Hugh; s of Richard Phipps Hornby, of Bowerchalke, Wilts, and Stella, *née* Hichens; *b* 23 Jan 1954; *Educ* Winchester, Univ of Exeter (BSc); *m* 18 June 1983, Anne Elizabeth Meredydd, da of George Hugh Kenefick Rae (d 1989); 3 s (David Hugh b 1988, Edward John b 1990, Julian Patrick b 1992); *Career* admitted slr 1980, Macfarlanes: joined 1977, ptnr 1987–, currently specialising in property (housing, leisure and agric); *Recreations* ball game sports, vocal classical music; *Clubs* Hurlingham; *Style*— John Hornby, Esq; ✉ Macfarlanes, 10 Norwich St, London EC4A 1BD (☎ 0171 831 9222, fax 0171 831 9607, telex 296381)

HORNBY, His Hon Judge; Keith Anthony Delgado; s of James Lawrence Hornby (d 1993), of Heathfield, Sussex, and Naomi Ruth, *née* Delgado; *b* 18 Feb 1947; *Educ* Oratory Sch, Trinity Coll Dublin (BA Hons); *m* 14 Feb 1970, Judith Constance, da of Patrick Yelverton Fairbairn; 1 da (Katya Eugenie b 13 Dec 1973), 2 s (Jamie Alexander Fairbairn b 11 Oct 1976, Nicholas Thomas Fairbairn b 13 May 1980); *Career* lectr in commercial law 1969–70, called to the Bar Gray's Inn 1970, recorder of the Crown Court 1992–95 (asst recorder 1988–92), circuit judge (SE Circuit) 1995–; *Recreations* art, theatre, music, golf, tennis, squash; *Clubs* Hurlingham; *Style*— His Hon Judge Hornby; ✉ Bow County Court, 96 Romford Road, Stratford, London E15 4EG (☎ 0181 555 3421)

HORNBY, Sir Simon Michael; kt (1988); er s of Michael Charles St John Hornby (d 1987), of Pusey House, Faringdon, and Nicolette Joan, *née* Ward (d 1988); *b* 29 Dec 1934; *Educ* Eton, New Coll Oxford; *m* 15 June 1968, (Ann) Sheran, da of Peter Victor Ferdinand Cazalet, of Fairlawne, Tonbridge, Kent; *Career* 2 Lt Grenadier Gds 1953–55; W H Smith Group plc: joined 1958, merchandise dir 1968, retail dir 1974, retail md 1977, gp chief exec 1978, chm 1982–94; non-exec chm Lloyds Abbey Life plc 1992– (dir 1991–); non-exec dir: Pearson plc 1978–, Lloyds Bank plc (now Lloyds TSB Group plc) 1988–; tstee Br Museum 1975–85, chm Nat Book League 1978–80; memb Cncl: Nat Tst 1978– (memb Exec Ctee 1966–93), RSA 1985–90, Royal Horticultural Soc 1992–; chm: Design Cncl 1986–92, Assoc of Business Sponsorship of the Arts 1988–, Nat Literary Tst 1993–; pres: Newsvendors' Benevolent Inst 1989–94, The Book Tst 1990–96, RHS 1994–; Hon DUniv: Stirling 1993, Reading 1996; Hon DLitt Hull 1994; FIMgt, FRSA; *Recreations* golf, gardening, music; *Style*— Sir Simon Hornby; ✉ The Ham, Wantage, Oxon OX12 9JA; 8 Ennismore Gardens, London SW7 1NL; Lloyds Abbey Life plc, 205 Brooklands Road, Weybridge, Surrey KT13 0PE (☎ 01932 850888)

HORNBY, Lady; Sonia Margaret; *née* Beesley; da of Sidney Beesley (d 1985), of Birmingham; *b* 1936; *Educ* King Edward VI HS for Girls Birmingham, Univ of Bristol (BA); *m* Sir Derek Peter Hornby, *qv*; 1 s (Jonathan Peter b 1967), 1 da (Victoria Jane b 1968); *Career* Fulbright scholar Harvard 1959–60, personnel offr ICI Birmingham 1960–62, personnel mangr Mars Ltd Slough 1962–65; news reporter BBC Midlands 1966–69, freelance reporter France 1969–73, freelance reporter USA 1973–80, writer and presenter (as Sonia Beesley) of features and documentaries BBC Radio 4 1980–; chm Gloucestershire Royal NHS Trust 1992–; dir Compass Theatre Co 1991–92; memb: Higginson Ctee on A-levels 1987–88, Advsy Cncl to Public Records Office 1988–92; tstee: Ellen Badger Hosp Devpt Tst Warwickshire 1989–91, Knowle Hill Fund Educnl Tst Warwickshire 1989–; *Style*— Lady Hornby; ✉ Badgers Farm, Idlicote, Shipston on Stour, Warwickshire CV36 5DT (☎ 01608 661890); Flat 2, 48 Thurloe Square, London SW7 2PX (☎ 0171 581 5701)

HORNBY PRIESTNALL, Cdr (Thomas) Keith; VRD (1963 and Clasp 1975); s of Rev Thomas Hornby Priestnall (d 1956), and Norah Hayward (d 1961); *b* 22 June 1925; *Educ* Burton Sch, Univ of Nottingham; *m* 2 Sept 1982, Gillian Christine, da of Police Supt William Edward Thomas Hinckley (d 1977), of Staffordshire; 1 da (Daniella b 1959); *Career* served WWII Midget Subs (X Craft); chm and md Salesprint and Display Ltd and Salesprint Temple Group Ltd 1963–83, chm Peel House Publicity 1983–; vice pres E Midland Areas C of C; dir: Brewery Traders Publications Ltd, Brewing and Distilling International; tstee and former chm Allied Brewery Traders' Assoc, chm Burton upon Trent & Uttoxeter SSAFA, pres Trg Ship Modwena Sea Cadet Corps, vice pres Burton Cons Assoc; memb: Inst of Brewing, Equity; *Recreations* riding, bird watching, sailing; *Clubs* Naval and Military, Army and Navy, The Burton; *Style*— Cdr Keith Hornby Priestnall, VRD; ✉ The Old Rectory, Kedleston, Derbyshire (☎ 01332 841515); Southbound House, Burton upon Trent, Staffordshire (☎ 01283 561163)

HORNE, Alistair Allan; CBE (1992); s of late Sir (James) Allan Horne, and Auriol Camilla, *née* Hay; *b* 9 Nov 1925; *Educ* Jesus Coll Cambridge (MA, LittD 1993), Le Rosey Switzerland, Millbrook USA; *m* 1, 1953 (m dis 1982), Renira Margaret, da of Adm Sir Geoffrey Hawkins, KBE, CB, MVO, DSC; 3 da; m 2, 1987, Sheelin Ryan Eccles; *Career* served RAF 1943–44, Coldstream Gds 1944–47, Capt attached to Intelligence Serv (ME); foreign corr Daily Telegraph 1952–55; founded Alistair Horne Res Fellowship in Modern History St Antony's Coll Oxford 1969 (supernumerary fell 1978–88, hon fell 1988–), fell Woodrow Wilson Centre Washington DC 1980–81; lectr, journalist and contrib to a number of books and various periodicals; memb: Mgmnt Ctee Royal Literary Fund 1969–90, Franco-Br Cncl 1979–, Ctee of Mgmnt Soc of Authors 1979–81; tstee Imperial War Museum 1975–82; Chevalier Légion d'Honneur 1993; FRSL; *Publications*Back into Power (1955), The Land is Bright (1958), Canada and the Canadians (1961), The Price of Glory: Verdun 1916 (1962, Hawthornden Prize 1963), The Fall of Paris: The Siege and the Commune 1870–71 (1965), To Lose a Battle: France 1940 (1969), Death of a Generation (1970), The Terrible Year: The Paris Commune (1971), Small Earthquake in Chile (1972), A Savage War of Peace: Algeria 1954–62 (1972, Yorkshire Post Book of the Year Prize 1978, Wolfson Literary Award 1978), Napoleon Master of Europe 1805–07 (1979), The French Army and Politics 1870–1970 (1984, Enid Macleod Prize), Macmillan 1894–1956, Vol I (1988), Macmillan 1957–86, Vol II (1989), A Bundle from Britain (1993), The Lonely Leader: Monty 1944–45 (1994), How far from Austerlitz? Napoleon 1805–1815 (1996); *Recreations* skiing, gardening, painting, travel; *Clubs* Garrick, Beefsteak; *Style*— Alistair Horne, Esq, CBE; ✉ The Old Vicarage, Turville, nr Henley-on-Thames, Oxon RG9 6QU

HORNE, Christopher Malcolm; CVO (1996); s of Gerald Fitzlait Horne (d 1970), and Dora, *née* Hartley; *b* 14 June 1941; *Educ* King Edward VI Chelmsford; *m* 12 Sept 1964, Christine Ann, da of Reginald Arthur Fradley (d 1985); 2 s (Darren James b 7 Feb 1968, Alec Gerald b 20 Jan 1970); *Career* Coutts & Co 1958–: head of personnel 1980–88, assoc dir 1980–89, sec of Bank 1988–, sr assoc dir 1989–, co sec Coutts & Co Group 1991–; memb Vines Rochester United Reformed Church; *Recreations* golf, gardening, interest in most sports; *Clubs* Rochester & Cobham Park Golf; *Style*— Christopher

Horne, Esq, CVO; ✉ Silver Birches, 151 Maidstone Rd, Chatham, Kent ME4 6JE (☎ 01634 847594); Coutts & Co, 440 Strand, London WC2R 0QS (☎ 0171 753 1000)

HORNE, Geoffrey Norman; s of Albert Edward Horne (d 1982), of Berks, and Doris Irene, *née* Blackman; *b* 7 Feb 1941; *Educ* Slough GS, Open Univ (BA); *m* 1, 1967 (m dis 1977), Barbara Ann Mary; 1 s (Rupert b 1971); m 2, 1980, Davina Dorothy, da of David Lockwood London, of Dyfed; 2 s (Edward b 1984, Richard b 1986); *Career* advertising exec; sr writer: CDP 1973–74, Davidson Pearce Berry and Spottiswoode 1974–77, Saatchi and Saatchi 1985–88; bd dir: KMP Partnership 1978–84 (creative dir 1977–84), Grandfield Rork Collins 1984–85 (creative gp head 1984–85), Saatchi and Saatchi 1985–88, Freeland 1988–; over 70 advtg awards incl: Br Advertising Press awards, D & AD Assoc awards, NY One Show, Br Advertising TV awards, The Creative Circle; MIPA, MCAM; *Recreations* cooking, reading, travel; *Clubs* Phyllis Court; *Style—* Geoffrey Horne, Esq; ✉ Pine Ridge, 46 Altwood Rd, Maidenhead, Berks

HORNE, Sir (Alan) Gray Antony; 3 Bt (UK 1929), of Shackleford, Surrey; s of Antony Edgar Alan Horne (d 1954; only s of 2 Bt, Sir Alan Edgar Horne, MC, who died 1984), and Valentine Antonia (d 1981), da of Valentine Dudensing, of Thenon, Dordogne, France and 55 East 57th St, New York City; *b* 11 July 1948; *m* 1980, Cecile Rose, da of Jacques Desplanche, of 5 rue de Cheverny, Romorantin, France; *Heir* none; *Style—* Sir Gray Horne, Bt; ✉ Château du Basty, Thenon, Dordogne, France

HORNE, Prof Michael Rex; OBE (1980); s of Rev Ernest Horne (d 1959), and Katie, *née* Smeeton (d 1976); *b* 29 Dec 1921; *Educ* Boston GS Lincs, Leeds GS, St John's Coll Cambridge (MA, PhD, ScD, Archibald Denny prize, John Winbolt prize); *m* 14 Aug 1947, Dorcas Mary, da of Mark Hewett; 1 da (Sara Josephine b 7 April 1949), 2 s (John Gregory b 4 Oct 1952, Barnabas Robert b 7 June 1955), 1 adopted da (Shanti Margaret b 29 Dec 1966); *Career* asst engr River Great Ouse Catchment Bd 1941–45, res offr British Welding Research Assoc 1945–51, lectr Dept of Engrg Univ of Cambridge 1957–60 (asst dir of res 1951–57), prof of engrg Univ of Manchester 1960–83 (Beyer prof 1978–83), ret; memb Merrison Ctee on Box Girders 1970–73, chm Ctee Review of Public Utilities Streetworks Act 1983–85, pres Inst of Structural Engrs 1980–81; IStructE: Henry Adams Award 1970–71, Oscar Faber Bronze medal 1972–73, Gold medal 1986; Baker Gold medal ICE 1977; Hon DSc Univ of Salford 1981; hon fell Inst of Works and Highways Mgmnt 1986; FICE, FIStructE, FEng 1978, FRS 1981; *Books* The Steel Skeleton (jtly, 1956), The Stability of Frames (with W Merchant, 1965), Plastic Theory of Structures (1971), Plastic Design of Low-Rise Frames (with L J Morris, 1981); *Recreations* hill walking, photography; *Style—* Prof Michael Horne, OBE, FRS, FEng; ✉ 19 Park Road, Hale, Altrincham, Cheshire WA15 9NW (☎ 0161 941 2223)

HORNE, Dr Nigel William; s of Eric Charles Henry Horne (d 1963), and late Edith Margaret, *née* Boyd; *b* 13 Sept 1940; *Educ* Lower Sch of John Lyon Harrow, Univ of Bristol (BSc), Univ of Cambridge (PhD); *m* 30 Oct 1965, Jennifer Ann, da of William Henry Holton (d 1988); 1 s (Peter b 1970), 2 da (Catherine b 1967, Joanna b 1973); *Career* dir and gen mangr GEC Telecommunications Ltd 1976–81, md GEC Information Systems Ltd 1981–83; dir: Tech and Corp Devpt STC plc 1983–89, Abingworth plc 1985–90; IT ptnr KPMG Peat Marwick 1989–92 (special advsr 1992–); non-exec chm: Alcatel Ltd 1992–, STC Submarine Systems 1994–; non-exec dir: FI Group plc 1993–, Abingworth Management Ltd 1993–; chm Info Technol Advsy Bd DTI 1988–91, memb Strategy Advsy Gp DGIII Euro Cmmn 1994– (chm Software and Multimedia Advsy Gp); visiting prof Univ of Bristol 1990–; memb: ACOST Cabinet Office 1990–93, Esprit Advsy Bd Euro Cmmn 1986–93; Hon DEng Univ of Bristol 1993; Hon DSc: Univ of Hull 1993, City Univ London 1994; Caballeros del Monasteria de Yuste (Spain) 1993; Freeman City of London; memb Worshipful Co of Info Technologists; FIIM 1979, FEng 1982, FRSA 1983, FIEE 1984, CIMgt 1992; *Recreations* piano, music, gardening; *Clubs* Athenaeum, United Oxford and Cambridge; *Style—* Dr Nigel Horne, FEng; ✉ KPMG Management Consulting, 8 Salisbury Square, London EC4Y 8BB (☎ 0171 311 1000, fax 0171 311 8697)

HORNE, Robert Drake; s of Capt Harold Metcalfe Horne, RN (d 1960), and Dorothy Katharine, *née* Drake (d 1992); *b* 23 April 1945; *Educ* Mill Hill Sch, Oriel Coll Oxford (BA); *m* 20 May 1972, Jennifer Mary, da of Raymond Harold Gill; 3 da (Annabel Mary b 1974, Rachel Dorothy b 1977, Octavia Jane b 1981); *Career* DFEE: entered 1968, princ in Cabinet Office 1979–80, asst sec 1980–88, under sec 1988–95; dir of fin and planning Employment Service 1995–; *Recreations* entertaining Australians, running, gardening; *Style—* Robert Horne, Esq; ✉ Employment Service, St Vincent House, 30 Orange Street, London WC2H 7HT (☎ 0171 389 1538, fax 0171 389 1399)

HORNE, Prof (Charles Hugh) Wilson; MBE; s of Charles Hugh Wilson Horne (d 1977), and Jean, *née* Wells; *b* 13 Sept 1938; *Educ* Ardrossan Acad, Univ of Glasgow (MB ChB, MD), Univ of Aberdeen (DSc), FRCPath, FRCP(Ed); *m* 5 Sept 1964, Agnes Irvine, da of Joseph Scott (d 1977); 1 s ((Charles Hugh) Wilson b 25 Oct 1969), 1 da (Glenda May b 16 Nov 1966); *Career* lectr in pathology Univ of Glasgow 1966–73, prof of immunopathology Univ of Aberdeen 1980–84 (sr lectr in pathology 1973–80), head of Sch of Pathological Sciences Univ of Newcastle upon Tyne 1988–95 (prof 1984–), chm and md Novocastra Laboratories Newcastle upon Tyne 1989–; author of numerous pubns on immunology and pathology; regnl advsr Northern Region RCPath 1985–95; *Recreations* philately, golf; *Style—* Prof Wilson Horne, MBE; ✉ 7 Elmtree Grove, Gosforth, Newcastle upon Tyne NE3 4BG (☎ 0191 284 8803); University Department of Pathology, Royal Victoria Infirmary, Queen Victoria Rd, Newcastle upon Tyne NE1 4LP (☎ 0191 222 7144, fax 0191 222 8100, e-mail C.H.W.Horne@ncl.ac.uk.

HORNE-ROBERTS, Jennifer; da of Frederick William Horne (d 1969), and Daisy Jessie Elizabeth, *née* Norman; *b* 15 Feb 1949; *Educ* State Schs NW London, Univ of Perugia (Dip Italian), Univ of London (BA); *m* 29 April 1987, Keith Michael Peter Roberts, s of Gerald Roberts (d 1962); 1 s (Harry Alexander b 29 June 1989), 1 da (Francesca Elizabeth b 24 July 1990); *Career* called to the Bar Middle Temple 1976, ad eundem memb Inner Temple; dir of family co; contrib pubns on: political issues, family law, employment law, human rights, literature; Parly candidate: (Lab) Fareham 1974, (Alliance) Medway 1987; cncllr Camden 1971–74; memb Bar Assocs: admin law, common law, family law; first chair Assoc of Women Barristers; memb: Bar Euro Gp Justice and Amnesty Lawyers, Lib Democrats Lawyers Exec Ctee; former memb Young Bar Ctee, Parly candidate (Lib Democrats) Holborn and St Pancras 1992; fndr Alliance for Govt of National Unity 1994; *Books* Trade Unionists and the Law (1984), Justice for Children (1992); *Recreations* writing, visual and literary arts, politics, travel; *Clubs* National Liberal, Highgate Golf, Arts; *Style—* Mrs Jennifer Horne-Roberts; ✉ c/o 1 Dr Johnson's Buildings, Temple, London EC4Y 7AX

HORNER, Damian Ryan; *b* 5 Nov 1965; *Educ* Boston Spa Comp Sch, Univ of Sussex (BA); *m* 15 May 1993, Joanne Elizabeth, da of David Anthony Sayer; *Career* account dir WCRS 1988–91, new business dir Lowe Howard-Spink 1991–93, business devpt dir Mustoe Merriman Herring Levy 1993–; *Recreations* classic cars, windsurfing, wooden boats, sailing; *Style—* Damian Horner, Esq; ✉ Mustoe Merriman Herring Levy, 133 Long Acre, Covent Garden, London WC2E 9AG (☎ 0171 379 9999, fax 0171 379 8487, e-mail mustoe@easynet.co.uk)

HORNER, Prof (Robert) Malcolm Wigglesworth; s of James William Horner (d 1986), and Emma Mary, *née* Wigglesworth (d 1977); *b* 27 July 1942; *Educ* Bolton Sch, UCL (BSc, PhD); *m* 21 March 1970, Beverley Anne, *née* Wesley, da of Ewart Alexander (d 1986); 1 s (Jonathan b 3 Oct 1980), 1 da (Victoria b 10 Sept 1977); *Career* Taylor Woodrow Construction Ltd: civil engr 1966–72, engrg rep W Germany 1972–74, site agent 1974–77; Univ of Dundee: lectr Dept of Civil Engrg 1977–83, sr lectr 1983–86, head of dept 1985–91, prof of engrg mgmnt 1986–; dir R & D Atlantic Power and Gas Ltd 1993–, dir Dundee Repertory Theatre Ltd 1991–; fndr chm Tayside branch Opening Windows on Engrg 1980–85, chm Winton Caledonian Ltd 1995–; memb: ICE Working Pty on Strategy Construction Mgmnt Res 1987–89, Technol Foresight Construction Sector Panel 1994–, Science and Engrg Advsy Ctee Br Cncl 1992–, Editorial Bd Construction Mgmnt and Economics 1991–94; govr Duncan of Jordanstone Coll of Art 1990–92; chm: Educn Ctee Engrg Cncl Regnl Orgn Mgmnt Ctee (E Scotland) 1988–91, Scottish Int Resource Project Steering Gp 1993–, Friends of St Paul's Cathedral 1993–95; memb Cncl Nat Conf of Univ Profs 1989–93; CEng, MICE, MIMgt; *Recreations* gardening, amateur dramatics; *Clubs* Rotary; *Style—* Prof Malcolm Horner; ✉ Westfield Cottage, 11 Westfield Place, Dundee DD1 4JU (☎ 01382 225933); Department of Civil Engineering, The University, Dundee DD1 4HN (☎ 01382 344350, fax 01382 334816, telex 76293)

HORNER, (William) Noel Arthur; s of William Arthur Horner, MBE (d 1984), of Derbys, and Kitty Barbara, *née* Tonkin; *b* 25 Dec 1942; *Educ* various GSs, Univ of Manchester (LLB); *m* 25 March 1967, Margaret Jean, da of Wilfred Teed Tayler (d 1978), of Exeter, Devon; 1 s (Julian b 1970), 3 da (Sally b 1968, Anna b 1978, Natasha b 1980); *Career* admitted slr 1969; ptnr: Amery Parkes and Co London 1969–72, Chellews St Ives 1973–77; princ Noel Horner 1977–; chllr Diocese of Damaraland-in-exile 1977–81; represented families of 2 decd lifeboatmen at Penlee Lifeboat Enquiry 1983; Ind Parly candidate St Ives 1983; *Recreations* music, history; *Clubs* Wig and Pen; *Style—* Noel Horner, Esq; ✉ c/o 73 Lemon St, Truro, Cornwall TR1 2PN (☎ 01872 71305)

HORNIBROOK, John Nevill; OBE (1992); *b* 25 Oct 1928; *Educ* Wellington Coll Berks, Univ of Birmingham (BSc); *m*; 2 da; *Career* cmmnd RN 1949–51, RNVR 1951–74, ret Lt Cdr RNR (VRD); various indust appts at home and overseas 1951–72; Roche Products Ltd: asst to works mangr 1972–73, works mangr 1973–81, divnl dir and memb Bd 1981–93; tstee dir Roche Pension Fund 1974–94; memb Scot Regnl Cncl CBI 1974–80 and 1983–89 (memb Educn and Trg Affrs Ctee 1990–94); Chem Industs Assoc Ltd: memb Scot Regnl Cncl 1975–93, memb Cncl 1991–93; dir Scotvec Ltd 1993–; non-exec dir Renfrewshire Healthcare NHS Tst 1993–; vice chm Garnock Valley Devpt Exec Ltd 1988–96 (dir 1986–96), chm Enterprise Ayrshire (div of Scot Enterprise) 1989–95, chm Vocational Qualification Awarding Body Chemical Pharmaceutical and Allied Industries 1993–, memb Ct Univ of Paisley 1989–; FEng 1991, FIChemE, FInstD; *Style—* John Hornibrook, Esq, OBE, FEng; ✉ Cruachan, West Glen Road, Kilmacolm, Renfrewshire PA13 4PN (☎ and fax 01505 873265)

HORNSBY, Dr Bevé; da of Lt Leonard William Hodges, RNAS (d 1917); *b* 13 Sept 1915; *Educ* St Felix Sch Southwold Suffolk, Univ of London (MSc, PhD), Univ Coll N Wales (MEd); *m* 1, 14 July 1939, Capt Jack Myddleton Hornsby (d 1975), s of Maj Frederick Myddleton Hornsby, CBE (d 1931), of Millfield, Stoke D'Abernon, Surrey; 3 s (Michael b 1942, Peter b 1943, Christopher b 1948), 1 da (Julie b 1947); m 2, 21 Dec 1976 (m dis 1986), John Hillyard Tennyson Barley; *Career* ambulance driver FANY and Mechanised Tport Corps 1939–42, Pilot Civil Air Gd 1938–39; head of Speech Therapy Clinic Kingston 1969–71, head of remedial teaching St Thomas's Hosp 1970–71, teacher World Blind Clinic Bart's 1969–71, head Dyslexia Dept Bart's 1971–80, dir Hornsby International Centre for Learning Difficulties 1980–, princ Hornsby House Sch 1987–; govr All Farthing Primary Sch Wandsworth; hon fell: Coll of Speech Therapists 1988, Br Dyslexia Assoc 1987; memb Rodin Remediation Soc, AFBPsS 1983, Chartered Psychologist, FRSA; *Books* Alpha to Omega - The A to Z of Teaching Reading, Writing and Spelling (1974), Alpha to Omega Flash Cards (1975), Overcoming Dyslexia (1984), Before Alpha - A Pre-Reading Programme for the Under-Fives (1989), Alpha to Omega Activity Packs (1990 and 1992); *Recreations* riding, sailing, golf, reading, walking, theatre, music; *Clubs* Lansdowne; *Style—* Dr Bevé Hornsby; ✉ The Hornsby International Dyslexia Centre, Glenshee Lodge, 261 Trinity Rd, Wandsworth, London SW18 3SN (☎ 0181 874 1844, fax 0181 877 9737)

HORNSBY, Guy Philip; s of Norman Dalton Hornsby (d 1970), and Yvonne Betty Hornsby, of Twickenham, Middx; *b* 24 March 1958; *Educ* Emanuel Sch Wandsworth; *Career* computer programmer and company liaison supervisor Head Office Honda (UK) Ltd 1978–79; BBC Radio London: joined 1979 as reporter and prodn asst on daily arts prog, variously asst prodr Robbie Vincent Prog, prodr Tony Blackburn Show, presenter/prodr London Weekend and London This Week, exec prodr Radio London Unemployment Festival of Music, prodr BBC Children in Need prog, prodr daily afternoon music prog; outside bdcast presenter Saturday Superstore BBC TV 1984, prodr Popular Music Unit BBC World Service 1984–85, continuity announcer TVS Southampton 1986–90; Southern Radio plc (formerly Ocean Sound plc): presenter breakfast show then prodr and presenter afternoon prog 1986–90, prog mangr Ocean Sound and South Coast Radio 1990–92, gp prog controller Southern Radio plc 1992–94; md Kiss 102 Manchester 1994–96, gp chief exec Kiss 102 Manchester and Kiss 105 Yorkshire 1996–; International Radio Award for Sweet Soul Music series BBC World Service 1985 (prodr and writer); memb: Equity 1988, Br Film Inst; *Recreations* music, cinema, computers, working out; *Clubs* Y (Manchester); *Style—* Guy Hornsby, Esq; ✉ 9 Manor Bridge Court, Tidworth, Hampshire SP9 7NH (☎ 01980 842425); 12 Irwell House, Slate Wharf, Manchester M15 5AW (☎ 0161 835 2225); Kiss 102, Kiss House, PO Box 102, Manchester M60 1GJ (☎ 0161 228 0102, fax 0161 228 1020)

HORNSBY, Timothy Richard; s of Harker William Hornsby (d 1973), and Agnes Nora Phillips (d 1992); *b* 22 Sept 1940; *Educ* Bradfield, ChCh Oxford (MA); *m* 1971, Charmian Rosemary, da of Frederick Cleland Newton, of Weybridge; 1 s (Adrian b 1977), 1 da (Gabrielle b 1975); *Career* res lectr ChCh Oxford 1964–65, HM Treasy 1971–73, dir ancient monuments historic bldgs and rural affrs DoE 1983–88, DG Nature Conservancy Cncl 1988–91; chief exec: Royal Borough of Kingston upon Thames 1991–95, National Lottery Charities Board 1995–; *Recreations* conservation, skiing; *Clubs* Athenaeum; *Style—* Timothy Hornsby, Esq; ✉ The National Lottery Charities Board, 7th Floor, St Vincent House, 30 Orange Street, London WC2H 7HH (☎ 0171 747 5201, fax 0171 747 5213)

HORNTVEDT, Kristoffer Charles (Kit); s of late Lt Cdr Kjell Horntvedt, RNorN, of Bergen, Norway, and Yvonne, *née* Carter; *b* 29 June 1946; *Educ* Barnstaple GS, Univ of Sussex (BA), Brandeis Univ Mass USA (Wien International Scholar); *m* 1970, Sally Ann, da of late Shepherd Mead; *Career* Lintas London 1969–76, Ayer Barker (part of Charles Barker Group) 1976–84, McAvoy Wreford Bayley (part of Valin Pollen Group) 1984–86, fndr Horntvedt Associates 1986–95, non-exec dir Taylor Made Solutions 1995–; MIPR 1990; *Recreations* reading, church, gardening, mountain biking; *Clubs* Arts, Hurlingham; *Style—* Kit Horntvedt, Esq; ✉ Homecroft, Longparish, nr Andover, Hants SP11 6QE (☎ 01264 720338); 52 South Prado, Atlanta, GA 30309, USA (☎ 00 1 404 881 6425)

HORNYOLD, Antony Frederick; Marchese (of the Habsburg cr, and of the Papal cr) di Gandolfi (Emperor Charles V 1529, Pope Leo XIII 1895), Duca di Gandolfi (Pope Leo XIII 1899); s of Ralph Gandolfi-Hornyold (d 1938), s of Thomas Gandolfi-Hornyold, cr Marchese Gandolfi by Pope Leo XIII 1895 and Duca 1899, Thomas being in his turn s of John Vincent Gandolfi-Hornyold (12 Marchese di Gandolfi, of the cr of Emperor Charles V of 1529, according to Ruvigny), whose mother Teresa was sis of Thomas Hornyold, then sr male rep of the old Hornyold recusant family (Teresa and Thomas's aunt by marriage was Mrs Fitzherbert, whom George IV, when Prince of Wales, m in contravention of the Royal Marriages Act); *b* 20 June 1931; *Educ* Ampleforth, Trinity

Coll Cambridge; *m* 14 July 1993, Caroline Mary Katherine, MVO, da of Maj Patrick Dudley Crichton-Stuart (d 1978); *Heir* bro, Simon Hornyold (b 11 Feb 1933); *Career* FO 1957–67 (1 sec Rawalpindi 1966–67), MOD 1967–90; Kt of SMOM; *Style*— Antony Hornyold, Esq; ✉ Blackmore House, Hanley Swan, Worcester WR8 0ES (☎ 01684 310389)

HORNYOLD-STRICKLAND, Angela Mary; *née* Engleheart; OBE (1994), DL (Cumbria 1988); da of Francis Henry Arnold Engleheart (d 1963), and Filumena Mary, *née* Mayne (d 1983); *b* 31 May 1928; *Educ* New Hall Convent, St Mary's Convent Ascot; *m* 20 Jan 1951, Lt Cdr Thomas Henry Hornyold-Strickland, DSC, RN, 7 Count della Catena (d 1983), s of Henry Hornyold-Strickland (d 1975), of Sizergh, Cumbria; 4 s (Henry b 1951, Robert b 1954, John b 1956, Edward b 1960), 2 da (Clare b 1953, Alice b 1959); *Career* pres: Br Red Cross Soc Westmorland 1972–74, Cumbria 1974–91; memb Bd Catholic Caring Servs (Diocese of Lancaster) until 1995; *Style*— Mrs Thomas Hornyold-Strickland (Dowager Countess della Catena), OBE, DL; ✉ Sizergh Castle, Kendal, Cumbria LA8 8AE (☎ 015395 60285, fax 105395 61481)

HORNYOLD-STRICKLAND, 8 Count Della Catena (Malta 1745); Henry Charles; s of Lt Cdr Thomas Henry Hornyold-Strickland, DSC, RN, 7 Count della Catena (d 1983), of Sizergh Castle, Kendal, Cumbria, and Angela Mary, *née* Engleheart; *b* 15 Dec 1951; *Educ* Ampleforth, Exeter Coll Oxford (BA), INSEAD Fontainebleau (MBA); *m* 1979, Claudine Thérèse, da of Clovis Poumirau, of Etche Churia, Av Des Piballes, Hossegor 40200, France; 2 s (Hugo b 1979, Thomas b 1985); *Career* product support planning engr Rolls Royce Ltd 1973–76, mgmnt conslt Arthur D Little Ltd 1977–84, ind mgmnt conslt 1984–; dir: Allied Newspapers Ltd (Malta) 1988–, Progress Press (Malta) 1988–, Allied Insurance Services (Malta) 1991–; Knight of Honour and Devotion SMOM 1977; *Style*— Henry Hornyold-Strickland, Esq (Count della Catena); ✉ 56 Ladbroke Rd, London W11 3NW (☎ 0171 229 1949, fax 0171 229 6217); Sizergh Castle, Kendal, Cumbria LA8 8AE (☎ 015395 60285)

HOROVITZ, Joseph; s of Dr Bela Horovitz (d 1955), and Lotte, *née* Beller; *b* 26 May 1926; *Educ* City of Oxford HS, New Coll Oxford (MA, BMus); *m* 16 Aug 1956, Anna Naomi, da of Frederic Moses Landau, of London; 2 da; *Career* WWII Army Educn Corps 1943–44; music dir Bristol Old Vic 1949–51, conductor Ballets Russes 1952, music staff Glyndebourne Opera 1956, prof of composition RCM 1961–, dir Performing Rights Soc 1969–96, pres Conseil International des Auteurs de Musique 1981–89; winner: Cwlth Medal for Composition 1959, Ivor Novello Award 1976 and 1979; Gold Order of Merit of Vienna 1996; compositions incl: 16 ballets incl Alice in Wonderland, two one act operas, five string quartets, eleven concertos, works for orchestra, brass band, wind band and choirs incl Capt Noah and his Floating Zoo; Son et Lumière incl: St Paul's Cathedral, Canterbury Cathedral, Royal Pavilion Brighton, Chartwell; numerous TV scores incl: Search for the Nile, Lillie, The Tempest, Twelfth Night, Agatha Christie Series, Dorothy L Sayers series, Rumpole of the Bailey; memb: Royal Soc of Musicians 1968, Cncl Composers Guild of GB 1970; FRCM 1981; *Recreations* books; *Style*— Joseph Horovitz, Esq; ✉ The Royal College of Music, Prince Consort Rd, London SW7

HORRELL, John Ray; CBE (1979), TD (1960), DL (Hunts and Peterborough 1973); s of Harry Ray Horrell (d 1963), of Westwood, Peterborough, and Phyllis Mary, *née* Whittome; *b* 8 March 1929; *Educ* Wellingborough Sch; *m* 26 March 1951, Mary Elizabeth (Betty) Noëlle, da of Arthur Thomas Dickinson (d 1984), of Northorpe Hall, nr Gainsborough; 1 s (Peter Geoffrey Ray b 23 Feb 1952), 1 da (Judith Carolyn (Mrs Drewer) b 23 April 1954); *Career* Maj TA (ret); farmer; dir: Horrell's Farmers Ltd; memb: Cambridgeshire (formerly Huntingdon and Peterborough) CC 1963– (chm 1971–77), Peterborough City DC 1996–; chm: ACC 1981–83, E Anglia TA & VR Assoc 1986–91, E of England Agric Soc 1984–87; memb Peterborough New Town Devpt Corp 1969–88, md East Anglia RHA 1986–90; Hon MCGI (memb Cncl), FRSA; *Recreations* country pursuits; *Clubs* Farmers'; *Style*— John Horrell, Esq, CBE, TD, DL; ✉ The Grove, Longthorpe, Peterborough, Cambs PE3 6LZ (☎ 01733 262618)

HORRELL, Roger William; CMG (1988), OBE (1974); s of William John Horrell (d 1980), and Dorice Enid, *née* Young (d 1994); *b* 9 July 1935; *Educ* Shebbear Coll, Exeter Coll Oxford (MA); *m* 1970 (m dis 1975), Patricia Mildred Eileen Smith, *née* Binns; 1 s (Oliver b 1972), 1 da (Melissa b 1973); *Career* Nat Serv Devonshire Regt 1953–55; Overseas Civil Serv Kenya 1959–64; Dip Serv: FCO 1964, econ offr Dubai 1965–67, FCO 1967–70, Kampala 1970–73, FCO 1973–76, Lusaka 1976–80, cnsllr FCO 1980–93; ret 1993; *Recreations* walking, bridge, reading, cricket spectator; *Clubs* Reform; *Style*— Roger Horrell, Esq, CMG, OBE; ✉ 51 Oatlands Drive, Weybridge, Surrey KT13 9LU (☎ 01932 220509)

HORROCKS, (Barbara) Jane; da of John Horrocks, of Rossendale, Lancs, and Barbara, *née* Ashworth; *b* 18 Jan 1964; *Educ* Fearns Co Secdy Sch, Oldham Coll of Technol, RADA (Bronze medal); *Career* actress; RSC (joined 1985) incl: Hetty in The Dillen, Flo in Mary After the Queen, Phoebe in As You Like It; other roles incl: Fanny in Ask For The Moon (Hampstead) 1986, various parts in Road (Royal Court) 1987, Beatrice in A Colliers Friday Night (Greenwich) 1987, Sherry in Valued Friends (Hampstead) 1989, Teddy in The Debutante Ball (Hampstead) 1989, Sylvie in Our Own Kind (Bush) 1991, Little Voice in The Rise and Fall of Little Voice (RNT and Aldwych) 1992, Sally Bowles in Cabaret (Donmar) 1994, Lady Macbeth in Macbeth (Greenwich) 1995; *Television* BBC incl: Road 1987, Heartland 1988, Nona 1990, Alive and Kicking 1991, Came Out, It Rained, Went Back In Again 1991, Roots 1991, Absolutely Fabulous (3 series) 1992–94, Bad Girl 1992, Suffer the Little Children 1994, Nightlife (BBC Scotland) 1995, Henry IV (parts I & II) 1995; Channel Four incl: Storyteller 1988, Self Catering (TV film) 1993, Never Mind the Horrocks 1996; other credits incl: Cabaret (Carlton) 1994, Some Kind of Life (Granada) 1995, Tales from the Crypt (HBO) 1996; *Films* incl: The Dressmaker 1987, The Wolves of Willoughby Chase 1988, Witches 1988, Getting It Right 1988, Memphis Belle 1989, Life Is Sweet 1990, Deadly Advice 1993, Second Best 1993; *Awards* LA Film Critics' Award and American Nat Soc of Film Critics' Award for Best Supporting Actress 1991 (for Life Is Sweet); Royal Television Soc Award for Best Actress and Banff Television Festival Special Jury Award (for Suffer the Little Children); *Style*— Ms Jane Horrocks; ✉ c/o Peters Fraser & Dunlop Ltd, 503 The Chambers, Chelsea Harbour, Lots Road, London SW10 0XF (☎ 0171 352 4446, fax 0171 352 7356)

HORROCKS, Peter Leslie; s of (Arthur Edward) Leslie Horrocks, of Beaconsfield, Bucks, and Phillis Margaret Chiene, *née* Bartholomew; *b* 31 Jan 1955; *Educ* Winchester, Trinity Hall Cambridge (MA); *m* 15 Sept 1995, Catherine Alicia Brinsley, er da of Dr (Moryd) Brinsley Sheridan; *Career* called to the Bar Middle Temple 1977 and Lincoln's Inn 1987, in private practice 1978–; memb Cncl: Sherlock Holmes Soc of London 1984–87, 1990–93 and 1996–, Royal Stuart Soc 1987–; Freeman City of London 1982; FRAS 1984; *Recreations* travel, real tennis, cricket, Sherlock Holmes, opera, collecting books, dancing the minuet; *Clubs* MCC, Royal Tennis Court; *Style*— Peter Horrocks, Esq; ✉ 1 Garden Court, Temple, London EC4Y 9BJ (☎ 0171 797 7900, fax 0171 797 7927)

HORROCKS, Raymond (Ray); CBE (1983); s of Cecil Horrocks (d 1933), and Elsie Horrocks; *b* 9 Jan 1930; *Educ* Bolton Municipal Secdy Sch, Wigan Technical Coll, Univ of Liverpool; *m* 1953, Pamela Florence, *née* Russell; 3 da (Susan, Lynn, Raina); *Career* HM Forces Army Intelligence Corps 1948–50; mgmnt trainee Textile Indust (Bolton and Manchester) 1950–51, sales rep Proctor and Gamble 1951–52, merchandiser Marks and Spencer 1953–58, buying controller Littlewoods Mail Order Stores 1958–63; Ford Motor Co 1963–72: depot mangr replacement parts 1963, mangr warranty and customer rels 1964, mangr car supply 1965, divnl mangr engine and special equipment operations 1966, mktg mangr 1967–69, mangr Advanced Vehicle Ops 1970–72; regnl dir (Europe and ME) Materials Handling Group Eaton Corporation Inc 1972–77; BL Cars Ltd: dep md 1977–78, chm and md Austin Morris Ltd 1978–80, md BL Cars Ltd 1980–81, memb bd of dirs BL Cars Ltd 1981–86, chm and chief exec BL Cars Ltd 1981–82; chm: Unipart Group Ltd 1981–86, Jaguar Cars Holdings Ltd 1982–84, Chloride Group PLC 1988– (dir 1986–, chm and chief exec 1989, chm 1992), Owenbell Ltd 1987–, Kay Consultancy Group plc 1989–91; chm and chief exec ARG Holdings Ltd 1981–86, dir Nuffield Services Ltd 1982–86, dep chm Applied Chemicals Ltd 1988–94; non-exec dir: The Caravan Club 1983–87, Jaguar plc 1984–85, Image Interiors (Wessex) Ltd 1985–86, Electrocomponents plc 1986–, Lookers plc 1986–, Lookers South East Ltd (formerly SMAC Group plc) 1989–94 (chm 1988–89); memb: CBI Cncl 1981–86, CBI Europe Ctee 1985–86; tstee Br Motor Ind Heritage Tst 1983–86; chm: Exide Europe 1986–88; Liveryman Worshipful Co of Coachmakers & Coach Harness Makers; FIMI, CIMgt, FRSA; *Recreations* fly fishing, steam trains, gardening; *Style*— Ray Horrocks, Esq, CBE; ✉ Far End, Riverview Rd, Pangbourne, Reading, Berks RG8 7AU; Chloride Group PLC, Abford House, 15 Wilton Road, London SW1V 1LT (☎ 0171 834 5500, fax 0171 630 0563/1646, telex 262038)

HORROX, Alan Stuart; s of Stanley Horrox, and Gudrun Horrox; *b* 3 Jan 1947; *Educ* St John's Leatherhead, Christ's Coll Cambridge; *m* Viveka Britt Inger, da of Torsten Nyberg, of Föllinge, Sweden; 2 da (Anna Helga b 1981, Katarina b 1983); *Career* prodr-dir of children's progs BBC, educn progs, dramas and documentaries Thames TV (controller children's and educn dept 1986–92), md Tetra Films 1992–; televised work incl: Our People, Small World, Accidental Death of an Anarchist, A Foreign Body, Voices in the Dark, The Belle of Amherst, Rose, The Gemini Factor, Catherine, Ingmar Bergman-The Magic Lantern, The Thief, Young Charlie Chaplin, The Green Eyed Monster, Brief Lives, Rosie The Great, Somewhere to Run, Handle with Care, Spatz, Lorna Doone, Forget About Me, Long Way Home, The Strangers, Sea Dragon, A Small Dance, Time Riders, Pirate Prince, Romeo and Juliet, Tomorrow People, The Merchant of Venice, Delta Wave; London Film Festival Screenings: Forget About Me 1990, A Small Dance 1991, Under The Sun 1992, Faith 1996; *Awards* Int Emmy 1987, Special Jury Award at the San Francisco Film Festival 1988, Valladolid Int Film Festival Award 1988 (for best documentary), Special Prize for fiction at the Prix Europa 1988, 1989 and 1991, Prime Time Emmy Nomination 1989, BAFTA Nominations 1989, 1990, 1991, 1995 & 1996, Chicago Int Film Festival Special Live Action Award 1990, RTS Enid Love Award Nomination 1990 and 1991, Writers' Guild Award B&B 1992 (nomination 1995), Japan Prize Award nomination 1995, runner up BFI Children's Award 1995, Special FX Monitor Award for Tomorrow People 1996, RTS Award for Ourselves 1996; *Style*— Alan S Horrox, Esq; ✉ Tetra Films Ltd, 175 Tottenham Court Road, London W1P 9LG (☎ 0171 580 7141, fax 0171 580 7125)

HORSBRUGH, Ian Robert; s of Walter Horsbrugh (d 1973), and Sheila May, *née* Beckett-Overy; *b* 16 Sept 1941; *Educ* St Paul's, Guildhall Sch of Music and Drama, RCM; *m* 10 July 1965, Caroline Wakeling, da of Dr Alan Everett (d 1987); 2 s (Benedict b 1967, Matthew b 1972), 2 da (Lucy b 1968, Candida b 1970); *Career* head of music: St Mary's Sch Hendon 1969–72, Villiers HS Southall 1972–79; dep warden ILEA Music Centre 1979–85, vice dir RCM 1985–88, princ Guildhall Sch of Music and Drama 1988–; memb: Music Advsy Panel Arts Cncl of GB 1981–86, Music Ctee Br Cncl 1988–, Ctee of Principals of Conservatoires Music Coll 1988–; dep chm London Arts Bd 1991–94; Freeman City of London 1989, Liveryman Worshipful Co of Musicians; FRCM 1988, FGSM 1988, FRSAMD, FRNCM 1993; Hon RAM 1993, Hon DMus 1995; *Books* Leoš Janáček - The Field that Prospered (1981); *Recreations* watching sports, drawing, walking, reading; *Clubs* MCC; *Style*— Ian Horsbrugh, Esq; ✉ Guildhall School of Music and Drama, Barbican, London EC2Y 8DT (☎ 0171 382 7141)

HORSBRUGH, Oliver Bethune; s of Archibald Walter Bethune Horsbrugh (d 1973), of London, and Sheila May, *née* Beckett-Overy; *b* 13 Nov 1937; *Educ* St Pauls; *m* 6 Oct 1962, Josephine Elsa, *née* Hall; 1 s (Edward b 8 Feb 1966), 1 da (Rebecca b 1 Feb 1969); *Career* Nat Serv RN 1956–58; TV 1958–: BBC TV staff dir 30 minute theatres Newcomers and Boy Meets Girl 1968–71; freelance TV dir 1971– incl: Z Cars, The Brothers, Crown Court, Coronation Street, Emmerdale, A Kind of Loving, Cribb, Fallen Hero, Bergerac, Juliet Bravo, The Gibraltar Inquest, Birmingham 6 Appeal; dir: various corp videos, trg films, ITN bulletins; memb Dir's Guild of GB, BAFTA, GSM 1957; *Recreations* sport, photography, enjoying food and wine, visiting the cinema and theatre, history of cinema buildings; *Style*— Oliver Horsbrugh, Esq; ✉ 21 Harbledown Road, Fulham, London SW6 5TW (☎ 0171 731 8325)

HORSBRUGH-PORTER, Sir John Simon; 4 Bt (UK 1902), of Merrion Sq, City and Co of Dublin; s of Col Sir Andrew Marshall Horsbrugh-Porter, 3 Bt, DSO and Bar (d 1986), and (Annette) Mary, *née* Browne-Clayton (d 1992); *b* 18 Dec 1938; *Educ* Winchester, Trinity Coll Cambridge; *m* 18 July 1964, Lavinia Rose, 2 da of Ralph Meredyth Turton, of Kildale Hall, Whitby; 1 s (Andrew), 2 da (Anna (Mrs Nicholas McNulty) b 1965, Zoë (Mrs Nicholas Curtis) b 1967); *Heir* s, Andrew Alexander Marshall b 1971; *Career* Nat Serv 2 Lt 12 Lancers (Germany and Cyprus) 1957–59; schoolmaster; *Recreations* hunting, gliding, music, literature; *Style*— Sir John Horsbrugh-Porter, Bt; ✉ Bowers Croft, Coleshill, Amersham, Bucks HP7 0LS (☎ 01494 724596)

HORSEY, John Sebastian Norman James; s of Rev Frank Bokenham Horsey (d 1970), of Broadwindsor, Dorset, and Maria Luisa de Montezuma (d 1973); *b* 26 Nov 1938; *Educ* St John's Sch Leatherhead, City Univ London (Dip in Horology and Instrument Technol); *m* 1 (m dis); 3 s (Jonathan Charles b 25 Dec 1964, Guy Anthony b 29 July 1966, Mark Edward b 14 Sept 1968), 1 da (Charlotte Rosemary Louise b 23 June 1973), 1 step s (Thomas Duncan Stewart b 20 Feb 1972); m 2, 28 Oct 1978 (Eveline) Theresa Paton, slr, da of Dr Edward Harry Stewart Weston (d 1968), of Charter Alley, Hampshire; 1 s (Oliver George Sebastian b 10 Dec 1979), 1 da (Natasha Annabel Clare b 13 April 1985); *Career* admitted slr 1966; memb Bd Sovereign Housing Assoc, memb Parochial Church Cncl St Katharine's Savernake Forest; memb Law Soc 1966, memb IOD; *Recreations* music, skiing, tennis, motorcycling, shooting; *Style*— John Horsey, Esq; ✉ Durley House, Savernake, Marlborough, Wiltshire SN8 3AZ (☎ 01672 810217); Horsey Bomer & Partners, 20 West Mills, Newbury, Berkshire (☎ 01635 580858, fax 01635 582813, car 0836 773251)

HORSFALL, Edward John Wright; s and h of Sir John Musgrave Horsfall, 3 Bt, MC, TD, *qv*; *b* 17 Dec 1940; *Educ* Uppingham; *m* 1965, Rosemary, da of Frank N King, of East Morton, Keighley; 3 s (David Edward b 1966, Robert Ian b 1968, James Christopher b 1971); *Style*— Edward Horsfall, Esq; ✉ Long Thatch, Uffington, Faringdon, Oxon SN7 7RP

HORSFALL, Sir John Musgrave; 3 Bt (UK 1909), of Hayfield, Glusburn, West Riding of Yorkshire, MC (1946), TD (1949, and clasp 1951), JP (N Yorks 1959); s of Sir (John) Donald Horsfall, 2 Bt (d 1975); *b* 26 Aug 1915; *Educ* Uppingham; *m* 1940, Cassandra Nora Bernardine, da of late George Wright, of Brinkworth Hall, Elvington, York; 2 s (Edward John Wright b 1940, Donald James Linton b 1942), 1 da (Henrietta Nora (Mrs Arthur Eubank) b 1947); *Heir* s, Edward John Wright Horsfall b 17 Dec 1940; *Career* late Maj Duke of Wellington's (W Riding) Regt, served 1939–45 war in Burma; Lloyd's underwriter; gen cmmr of Taxes 1964–90; former dir: Skipton Building Society, John C Horsfall and Sons Ltd, Bradford Wool Exchange; dir Worsted Spinners Fedn 1954–80; memb: Bradford A Gp Hosp Mgmnt Ctee 1952–69, Skipton Rural DC 1952–74, Wool and Allied Textile Employer Cncl 1957–75, Wool Textile Delgn 1957–75; pres Skipton Div Cons Assoc 1966–79; *Style—* Sir John Horsfall Bt, MC, TD, JP; ✉ Greenfield House, Embsay, Skipton, N Yorks BD23 6SD (☎ 01756 794560)

HORSFALL TURNER, Jonathan; s of Harold Horsfall Turner, CBE (d 1981), and Eileen Mary, *née* Jenkins; *b* 27 Nov 1945; *Educ* The King's Sch Canterbury, Gonville and Caius Coll Cambridge (MA); *m* 25 Aug 1973, Yvonne Roberts, da of Angus Munro Thomson (d 1971); 1 da (Olivia Jane b 1980); *Career* admitted slr 1970; ptnr Allen and Overy 1973–; carried out res on Eng Medieval Graffiti of Canterbury Cathedral 1963–67 (manuscripts in cathedral library and results published by Canterbury Cathedral Chronicles); Freeman Worshipful Co of Slrs 1973; memb Law Soc 1970; *Recreations* architecture, antiques, opera, canals; *Clubs* Garrick; *Style—* Jonathan Horsfall Turner, Esq; ✉ Greenwich, London; Palace St, Canterbury; Allen & Overy, One New Change, London EC4M 9QQ (☎ 0171 330 3000, fax 0171 330 9999)

HORSFIELD, Maj-Gen David Ralph; OBE; s of Maj Ralph Beecroft Horsfield (d 1966), and Morah Susan Stuart, *née* Baynes (d 1980); *b* 17 Dec 1916; *Educ* Oundle, RMA Woolwich, Univ of Cambridge (MA); *m* 1948, Sheelah Patricia Royal, da of Thomas George Royal Eagan (d 1970); 2 s (Crispin b 1952, Hugo b 1955), 2 da (Antonia b 1954, Claudia b 1957); *Career* cmmnd Royal Signals 1936, WWII served in Egypt, Burma, Assam, India; cmd Burma Corps Signals 1942, instr Staff Coll Quetta 1944–45, cmd 2 Indian Airborne Div Signals 1946–47, instr RMA Sandhurst 1950–53 (co cmd to HM King Hussein of Jordan), cmd 2 Div Signal Regt 1956–59, princ Army Staff Offr MOD Malaya 1959–61, dir Telecommunications (Army) 1966–68, ADC to HM The Queen 1968–69, dep Communications and Electronics SHAPE 1968–69, Maj-Gen 1969, chief Signal Offr BAOR 1969–72 (ret); dir Rollalong Ltd 1965–76, assoc conslt PA Management Consultants 1972–87; vice pres Nat Ski Fedn; MInstD; *Recreations* house and garden, skiing (Br Champion 1949); *Clubs* Ski Club of Great Britain, Hawks; *Style—* Maj-Gen David Horsfield, OBE; ✉ Preybrook Farm, Preywater Road, Wookey, Wells, Somerset BA5 1LE (☎ 01749 673241)

HORSFIELD, Dr Dorothy; da of Cyril Gordon Horsfield (d 1968), and Mabel, *née* Berry (d 1981); *b* 24 Nov 1932; *Educ* Crossley and Porter Sch Halifax, Royal Free Hosp Sch of Med London (MB BS); *Career* house surgn Royal Free Hosp London 1958, house physician Royal Northern Infirmary Inverness 1958–59; SHO: in chests and geriatrics St Luke's Hosp Bradford 1959–60, in pathology Royal Free Hosp 1960–61; registrar in clinical pathology Guy's Hosp 1963–66, lectr in chemical pathology Nat Hosp for Nervous Diseases 1966–72, sr registrar in chemical pathology Hammersmith Hosp 1975–76, conslt chemical pathologist Barnsley Dist Gen Hosp 1977–94, emeritus conslt chemical pathologist Barnsley Dist Gen Hosp NHS Tst 1994–; memb CLA; conservation projects with: Countryside Cmmn, York Co Stand, York Racecourse, Yorks Agric Soc, NFU; FRSM 1961, memb BMA 1979, FRCPath 1984; *Recreations* organic and compassionate farming, races, needlework, music; *Style—* Dr Dorothy Horsfield; ✉ Holly Farm, New Brighton, Birdsedge, Huddersfield HD8 8XP

HORSFIELD, Peter Muir Francis; QC (1978); s of Henry Taylor Horsfield, AFC, and Florence Lily, *née* Muir; *b* 15 Feb 1932; *Educ* Beaumont Sch, Trinity Coll Oxford (BA); *m* 1962, Anne Charlotte, da of late Sir Piers Debenham, 2 Bt; 3 s; *Career* RNR 1955–57 (Lt 1960); called to the Bar Middle Temple 1958, in practice at Chancery Bar 1958–94, bencher 1984–; pt/t chm VAT Tbnls and dep cmmr Income Tax 1993–; *Recreations* portrait and landscape painting; *Clubs* Garrick; *Style—* Peter Horsfield, Esq, QC; ✉ Chambers, 8 Stone Buildings, Lincoln's Inn, London WC2A 3TA

HORSFORD, Cyril Edward Sheehan; CVO (1984); s of Dr Cyril Arthur Bennett Horsford (d 1953), of 24 Harley St, London W1, and Edith Louise, *née* Sayers (d 1987); *b* 13 March 1929; *Educ* Marlborough, Clare Coll Cambridge (MA); *m* 31 Aug 1957, Susan Frances, da of Francis Randall Hugh Bolton (d 1937), of London; 1 s (Simon b 1958); *Career* 2 Lt RA 1948–49; called to the Bar Inner Temple 1953, clerk of arraigns Central Criminal Ct Old Bailey 1954–56, sr asst Inner London Sessions 1956–68, dep asst registrar of Criminal Appeals 1968–74, dep clerk Privy Cncl 1974–89, clerk Bar Disciplinary Tribunal 1990–; vice pres Medico Legal Soc of London 1988, hon registrar Royal Soc of St George 1994–; dir Int Inst of Space Law 1961–72; Andrew G Haley Award for contrib to space law (Warsaw) 1964; Freeman City of London 1970; FBIS 1973; *Books* Assize and Quarter Sessions Handbook (1958); contrib: Halsbury's Laws of England (4 edn), Journal of Criminal Law, Criminal Law Review, Solicitors Journal; *Recreations* amateur theatre, flyfishing; *Style—* Cyril Horsford, Esq, CVO; ✉ 32 Prairie St, London SW8 3PP (☎ 0171 622 5984)

HORSFORD, Maj-Gen Derek Gordon Thomond; CBE (1962, MBE 1953), DSO (1944, and bar 1945); s of Capt Harry Thomond Horsford (d 1963), of Crowborough, and Violet Edith, *née* Inglis (d 1989); *b* 7 Feb 1917; *Educ* Clifton, RMC Sandhurst; *m* 1, 1948, Sheila Louise Russell Crawford (d 1995); 1 s (Ian b 1948), 1 step s (George b 1939), 2 step da (Joanna b 1942, Gail b 1945); m 2, 1996, Gillian Patricia Moorhouse, da of K O'B Horsford; *Career* cmmnd 8 Gurkha Rifles 1937, Cdr 4/1 Gurkha Rifles Burma 1944–45 (Lt-Col), instr Staff Coll 1950–52, GSO1 2 Inf Div 1955–56, Cdr 1 Bn The Kings Regt 1957–59, AAG AG2 MOD 1959–60 (Col), Cdr 24 Inf Bde Gp 1960–62 (Brig), IDC 1963, BGS HQ BAOR 1964–66, GOC 50 (Northumbrian) Div/Dist 1966–67 (Maj-Gen), GOC Yorks Dist 1967–68, GOC 17 Div Malaya Dist 1969–70, Dep Cdr Land Forces Hong Kong 1970–71, Col The Kings Regt 1965–70, Col The Gurkha Tport Regt 1973–78; ret 1972 (Maj-Gen); dir RCN Devpt Tst 1972–75, sec League of Remembrance 1978–90; *Recreations* travel; *Style—* Maj-Gen Derek Horsford, CBE, DSO

HORSHAM, Archdeacon of; *see:* Filby, The Ven William Charles Leonard

HORSHAM, Bishop of 1993–; Rt Rev Lindsay Goodall Urwin; s of William Edward Urwin, and Beryl Jesse, *née* Towler; *b* 13 March 1956, Melbourne, Australia; *Educ* Camberwell C of E Boys' GS Canterbury Victoria Aust, Trinity Coll Melbourne, Ripon Coll Cuddeson Oxford (CertTheol (Oxon)), KCL (ongoing); *Career* clerk Dept of Social Servs Australian Govt 1973 and 1975–76, on staff Double M Club community and social centre St Mary Magdalen Munster Square London 1976–77; ordained 1980; asst curate St Peter Walworth Southwark Dio 1980–83, vicar St Faith Red Post Hill Southwark Dio 1983–88, diocesan missioner Chichester Dio 1988–93; memb: Southwark Diocesan Synod 1982 and 1986–88, Archdeaconry Pastoral Ctee 1986–88; chm Southwark Diocesan Church Union 1985–88, diocesan dir Cursillo spiritual renewal movement Southwark Dio 1985–88; nat chm Church Union 1995–; memb: At Home Ctee Gen Synod Bd of Mission, Renewal and Evangelism 1992–95, Diocesan Ctee for Social Responsibility Chichester Dio 1991–94; tstee Cuthbert Bardsley Evangelism Award; OGS 1991 (UK Provincial 1996–); *Publications* Before We Go (audio study course, 1989), Prayer Together for the New Evangelisation (study course, 1991), Food for the Journey (study course, 1993); *Style—* The Rt Rev the Bishop of Horsham; ✉ Bishop's House, 21 Guildford Road, Horsham, West Sussex RH12 1LU (☎ 01403 211139)

HORSLEY, Adrian Mark; JP; s of (Ian) Mark Horsley, of Hayton, York, and Patricia Horsley, JP, *née* Farrell (d 1994); *b* 12 April 1949; *Educ* Ampleforth, Leicester Sch of Architecture (DipArch); *m* 28 Sept 1974, Louise Jane, da of Peter Bentham Oughtred, JP, *qv*, of Raby Lodge, Brough; 2 s (Adam b 1979, Luke b 1982); *Career* architect; managing ptnr Gelder and Kitchen 1994– (joined 1974, ptnr 1978–); former pres N Humberside Soc of Architects, former chm Yorks Region RIBA; memb: Magistrates' Assoc of E Yorks, Hull Civic Soc, Georgian Soc of E Yorks, The Company of Merchant Adventurers of the City of York 1978; tstee: Hull and E Riding Charitable Tst, Joseph Rank Meml Tst; RIBA 1976, ACIArb 1980, memb Assoc of Project Mangrs 1994, FRSA 1984; *Recreations* shooting, tennis, croquet, gardening; *Style—* Adrian Horsley, Esq, JP; ✉ Gelder & Kitchen, Architects, Maister House, High St, Hull HU1 1NL (☎ 01482 324114, fax 01482 227003, mobile 0410 919873)

HORSLEY, Very Rev Dr Alan Avery; s of Reginald James Horsley, of Staffs, and Edith Irene, *née* Allen; *b* 13 May 1936; *Educ* Worcester Royal GS, Northampton GS, St Chad's Coll Durham (BA), The Queen's Coll at Birmingham Univ of Birmingham, Pacific Western Univ (MA, PhD); *Career* curate: Daventry 1960–63, St Giles Reading 1963–64, St Paul Wokingham 1964–66; vicar St Andrew Yeadon 1966–71, rector Heyford with Stowe-Nine-Churches 1971–78, rural dean Daventry 1976–78, vicar Oakham with Hambleton and Egleton 1978–86 (with Braunston and Brooke from 1980–), non-residentiary canon Peterborough 1979–86, canon emeritus 1986–, vicar Lanteglos-by-Fowey 1986–88, provost of St Andrew's Cathedral Inverness 1988–91; priest i/c: St Mary-in-the Fields Culloden 1988–91, St Paul Strathnairn 1988–91; vicar Mill End Heronsgate and W Hyde 1991–; *Style—* The Very Rev Dr Alan Avery; ✉ St Peter's Vicarage, Berry Lane, Rickmansworth WD3 2HQ (☎ 01923 772785)

HORSLEY, Air Marshal Sir (Beresford) Peter Torrington; KCB (1974), CBE (1964), LVO (1956), AFC (1945); s of late Capt Arthur Beresford Horsley, CBE; *b* 26 March 1921; *Educ* Wellington; *m* 1, 1943 (m dis 1976), Phyllis Conrad Phinney; 1 s, 1 da; m 2, 1976, Ann MacKinnon, da of Gareth Crwys-Williams; 2 step s, 2 step da; *Career* joined RAF 1940, serv 2 TAF and Fighter Cmds; Equerry: to Princess Elizabeth and to the Duke of Edinburgh 1949–52, to HM The Queen 1952–53, to the Duke of Edinburgh 1953–56; Asst CAS (Ops) 1968–70, AOC No 1 Bomber Gp 1971–73, Dep C-in-C Strike Cmd 1973–75, ret 1975; chm: National Printing Ink Co Ltd, Osprey Aviation; dir RCR International Ltd; *Books* Journal of a Stamp Collector; *Style—* Air Marshal Sir Peter Horsley, KCB, CBE, LVO, AFC; ✉ c/o Barclays Bank Ltd, High Street, Newmarket

HORSLEY, William Frederick Moreton; *b* 28 Jan 1949, Macau; *Educ* St Edward's Sch Oxford, Pembroke Coll Oxford (BA, exhbner); *m* 1979, Noriko, *née* Makuuchi; *Career* prodr BBC Far Eastern Serv External Servs 1971–74, BBC secondee to Radio Japan (Japan Broadcasting Co Tokyo 1974–76, freelance writer and journalist Tokyo 1976–77, prodr Special Current Affairs unit BBC and The World Tonight 1977–80, prodr and news presenter Newsnight BBC TV 1981, reporter The World Tonight and BBC Radio News 1981–83, Tokyo corr and bureau chief BBC Tokyo 1983–90, corr for radio and TV Bonn and other parts of Europe BBC Bonn 1991–; chm Foreign Press 1984–88, dir Foreign Corrs Club of Japan 1985–87 and 1988–89, memb Advsy Ctee on Internationalisation Cncl on Local Govt Tokyo 1985–89, memb Ctee on Internationalisation of Local Govt Bodies Cncl of Local Authys for Int Relations Tokyo 1989–90; *Books* Newspapers and Democracy (contrib, 1980), Is Japan Really Rich? (1986), Nippon - New Superpower (with Roger Buckley, 1990); author of numerous articles on Japan, Germany and int affairs in The Listener, Millenium and other jls; *Style—* William Horsley, Esq; ✉ BBC, Pressehaus 1/428, Heussallee 2–10, 53113 Bonn, Germany (☎ 00 49 228 215652, fax 00 49 228 215969)

HORSMAN, Greg; *Educ* Victorian College of the Arts Melbourne; *m* Lisa Pavane, sr princ with English National Ballet; 1 da (Cassandra b 1992); *Career* ballet dancer; studied with Peter Dickinson, Anne Woolliams; The Australian Ballet: joined 1982, soloist 1985–87, princ artist 1987–94; roles incl: Lensky in Onegin, Benvolio and Romeo in Romeo and Juliet, Bluebird and the Prince in The Sleeping Beauty, peasant pas de deux and Albrecht in Giselle, Colas in La Fille Mal Gardée, Franz in Coppelia, Siegfied in Swan Lake, James in La Sylphide, Spartacus and Crassus in Spartacus, Solor in La Bayadère, the Prince in The Nutcracker, Lucentio in The Taming of the Shrew, Red Knight in Checkmate, Des Grieux and Lescaut in Manon and Apollo, Gemini, Voluntaries, Aureole, Forgotten Land, Sinfonietta, In the Night, Etudes, Paquita, Song of a Wayfarer, Four Last Songs, The Leaves are Fading; sr princ English National Ballet 1994–; roles incl: Romeo and Mercutio in Nureyev's Romeo and Juliet, Albrecht in Derek Deane's Giselle, Lichine's Graduation Ball, Balanchine's Square Dance, The Mad Hatter in Derek Deane's Alice in Wonderland, the Prince in Michael Corder's Cinderella; guest appearances with Boston Ballet, Houston Ballet, Kirov Ballet, Royal Danish Ballet, Tokyo Ballet, Rudolf Nureyev's Farewell Tour of Australia and sixth and seventh World Ballet Festivals Japan (with Lisa Pavane); *Style—* Greg Horsman, Esq; ✉ English National Ballet, Markova House, 39 Jay Mews, London SW7 2ES (☎ 0171 581 1245, fax 0171 225 0827)

HORSMAN, Michael John; s of Graham Joseph Vivian Horsman, of Dollar, Scotland, and Ruth, *née* Guest; *b* 3 March 1949; *Educ* Dollar Acad, Univ of Glasgow (MA(Hons)), Balliol Coll Oxford (Snell exhibitioner, Brackenbury scholar); *m* 1977, Anne Margaret, da of late John Marley; 3 s (Graham John b 10 Dec 1979, Ian Michael b 17 Feb 1982, William David b 27 April 1986); *Career* Dept of Employment: joined 1974, sec to Chm of Manpower Services Cmmn 1978–79, area mangr 1982–84, dir Professional and Exec Recruitment 1984–85, head of MSC Fin Policy and resource controller 1985–87, head of Employment Serv Ops Branch 1987–89, regnl dir Employment Serv London and SE 1989–92, dir Office of Manpower Economics 1992–; *Recreations* reading, historical research, cycling; *Clubs* Cyclist Touring; *Style—* Michael Horsman, Esq; ✉ Oxford House, 9th Floor, 76 Oxford Street, London W1N 9FD (☎ 0171 467 7200, fax 0171 467 7208)

HORSMAN, Peter James; s of Markham Henry Horsman, of Pinner, Middlesex, and Barabara, *née* Blow; *b* 11 Jan 1956; *Educ* Harrow County Sch; *m* 5 April 1980, Ruth Margaret, da of Rev Kenneth Thomas Jarvis; 1 s (James Edward b 2 Feb 1985), 1 da (Julia Katherine b 22 Feb 1988); *Career* articled clerk Allfields (now Stoy Hayward) 1976–80, lectr Financial Training Co 1980–85, ptnr Armitage & Norton CAs 1987 (joined 1985); Saffery Champness: ptnr 1987–, nat tax ptnr 1990–, mktg ptnr 1992–; memb: Chartered Inst of Taxation 1985 (memb Cncl 1995–), Assoc of Taxation Technicians 1994 (memb Cncl 1994–); FCA 1990 (ACA 1980); *Recreations* country pursuits, motor racing; *Style—* Peter Horsman, Esq; ✉ Hockley Threshing Barn, Latimer, Bucks; Saffery Champness, Fairfax House, Fulwood Place, London (☎ 0171 405 2828, fax 0171 405 7887, mobile 0860 436495)

HORT, Sir Andrew Edwin Fenton; 9 Bt (GB 1767), of Castle Strange, Middlesex; s of Sir James Fenton Hort, 8 Bt (d 1995), and Joan Mary, *née* Peat; *b* 15 Nov 1954; *m* 15 Nov 1986, Mary, da of Jack Whibley, of Spalding, Lincs; 1 s (James John Fenton b 1989), 1 da (Jennifer Briony b 1987); *Heir* s, James John Fenton Hort b 1989; *Clubs* Muswell Hill Golf; *Style—* Sir Andrew Hort, Bt; ✉ Westerlee, 77 Fortis Green, East Finchley, London N2 9JD

HORTON, Brian; s of Richard Horton (d 1990), of Cannock, Staffs, and Irene, *née* Russell; *b* 4 Feb 1949; *Educ* Blake Secdy Modern; *m* Denise Andrea, da of John William Callaghan; 1 s (Matthew Brian b 27 April 1987), 1 da (Lucy Andrea (twin) b 27 April 1987); *Career* professional football manager; player (midfielder): Walsall 1964–66, Hednesford Town 1966–70, Port Vale 1970–76 (236 appearances), Brighton & Hove Albion 1976–81 (218 appearances), Luton Town 1981–84 (118 appearances), Hull City 1984–88 (player/manager, 38 appearances); manager Oxford Utd 1988–93 (joined as asst manager), manager Manchester City FC 1993–95 (sacked), manager Huddersfield Town FC 1995–; *Recreations* golf, badminton; *Style—* Brian Horton, Esq; ✉ c/o Huddersfield Town FC, Leeds Road, Huddersfield, West Yorkshire HD1 6PE

HORTON, Gavin Tobias Alexander Winterbottom (Toby); s of Alistair Winterbottom (bro of late Lord Winterbottom), of Crawley Grange, N Crawley, Newport Pagnell, Bucks and formerly of Horton House, Northants, and Maria Kersti; *b* 18 Feb

1947; *Educ* Westminster, ChCh Oxford (MA); *m* 1977, Hon Fiona Catherine Peake, da of 2 Viscount Ingleby; 2 s (George William Arthur b 1983, Thomas Henry Ralph b 1985), 2 da (Alice Emily Rose b 1978, Violet Constance Lily b 1980); *Career* md Sound Broadcasting (Teesside) 1979–83, dir and head Corp Fin Dept Minster Trust Ltd 1984–90; dir: Minster Sound Radio plc 1991–, Yorkshire Coast Radio Ltd 1993–, Heritage Media Ltd 1993–, Sun City FM 1995–; Parly candidate (C) Sedgefield 1983, Parly agent (C) Bethnal Green and Stepney 1987, Euro Parly candidate (C) Yorkshire SW 1989, Parly candidate (C) Rother Valley 1992; chm: Fndn for Defence Studies, Yorkshire & NE Bow Gp, Richmond Cons Assoc 1996–; *Books* Going to Market: New Policy for the Farming Industry (1985), Programme for Reform: a New Agenda for Broadcasting (1987); *Recreations* radio, country pursuits; *Clubs* Northern Counties (Newcastle); *Style*— Toby Horton, Esq; ✉ Whorlton Cottage, Swainby, Northallerton, N Yorkshire DL6 3ER (☎ 01642 700213, fax 01642 701615)

HORTON, Geoffrey; s of Leonard Horton (d 1987), and Joan, *née* Bissell; *b* 23 July 1951; *Educ* Bristol GS, Exeter Coll Oxford (BA, MA), UCL (MSc Econ); *m* 1991, Dianne Alexandra (Alex), da of Dr Eric Craker; 2 da (Camilla b 1993, Beatrice b 1996); *Career* econ asst HM Treasy 1974–76, lectr in econ Univ Coll Swansea 1976–78, econ advsr HM Treasy 1978–85, chief economist DRI (Europe) Ltd 1985–88, sr econ advsr Dept of Energy 1988–90, pt/t sr conslt Nat Economic Research Associates 1990–92, pt/t dir of regulation and business affairs Office of Electricity Regulation (GB) 1990–95, pt/t DG Electricity Supply Office of Electricity Regulation (NI) 1992–95, dir of consumer affairs OFT 1995–; *Publications* Working papers: Modelling the World Economy (1984), The Economic Effects of Lower Oil Prices (with Stephen Powell, 1984); Links between Environmental and International Trade Policies: A Study on the Implications of Greenhouse Gas Emissions Control Policies for Trade (with James Rollo and Alistair Ulph, 1992), British Electricity Privatisation: The Customer's Standpoint (proceedings of Br Inst of Energy Economics conf, 1995); contrib various reports for EC, articles in economic magazines and seminar papers; *Recreations* sailing, reading, cooking; *Style*— Geoffrey Horton, Esq; ✉ Office of Fair Trading, 15–25 Breams Buildings, London EC4A 1PR (☎ 0171 269 8821, fax 0171 269 8819)

HORTON, Matthew Bethell; QC; s of Albert Leslie Horton, of Tunbridge Wells, Kent, and Gladys Rose Ellen, *née* Harding; *b* 23 Sept 1946; *Educ* Sevenoaks, Trinity Hall Cambridge (MA, LLM); *m* 1, 22 May 1972 (m dis 1983), Liliane, da of Henri Boleslawski, of Nice, France; 1 s (Jerome b 1971), 1 da (Vanessa b 1973); *Career* called to the Bar Middle Temple 1969; in private practice specialising in: commercial property law, planning, environmental and local govt law, admin law, Parly law; memb: Admin Law Ctee of Justice, Euro Sub-Ctee of Environmental Law Ctee Int Bar Assoc, Ctee Jt Planning Law Conf; *Recreations* tennis, skiing, windsurfing; *Clubs* Tramp; *Style*— Matthew Horton, Esq, QC; ✉ 2 Mitre Court Buildings, Temple, London EC4Y 7BX (☎ 0171 583 1380, fax 0171 353 7772, DX LDE 0032)

HORTON, Prof Michael Anthony; s of Dr (John Anthony) Guy Horton, of Newcastle upon Tyne, and Margaret Louisa, *née* Jenkins; *b* 6 May 1948; *Educ* Oundle, St Bartholomew's Hosp Med Coll Univ of London (BSc, MB BS); *m* 10 Aug 1968, Susan Geraldine Horton, JP, da of Capt Gerald Taylor, MBE (d 1973); 1 s (Benjamin b 1977), 1 da (Rachel b 1971); *Career* MRC fell UCL 1976–79; St Bartholomew's Hosp: sr lectr and conslt haematologist 1979–94, Wellcome Tst clinical res fell 1979–84, princ scientist Imperial Cancer Res Fund 1984–94; head Bone and Mineral Centre Dept of Medicine and prof in medicine UCL Med Sch 1995–; visiting scientist MRC Lab of Molecular Biology Cambridge 1991, visiting prof Meikai Univ Japan 1992; memb: Br Soc of Haematology, Br Soc of Immunology; pres Bone and Tooth Soc; author of various publications on haematology, immunology and bone biology and diseases; memb Lib Democrats; FRCP, FRCPath; *Recreations* gardening, archaeology, family history; *Style*— Prof Michael Horton; ✉ The Priory, Quendon, Essex CB11 3XJ (☎ 01799 543255); Department of Medicine, UCL Medical School, Sir Jules Thorn Institute, The Middlesex Hospital, Mortimer Street, London W1N 8AA (☎ 0171 380 9152, fax 0171 636 3151, e-mail horton@medicine.ucl.ac.uk)

HORTON, (John) Philip (Phil); s of Frank Horton (d 1982), and Elsie, *née* Gill; *b* 19 Jan 1956; *Educ* Bournemouth Boys' Sch, Univ of Southampton (BA); *m* 26 July 1979 (m dis); *Career* various positions in sales and mktg Ford of Britain 1977–85, Mktg Dept Ford of Europe 1985–90, dir of communications (i/c advtg, promotions and PR activities) Renault UK 1990–; *Recreations* motorcycling, skiing, tennis; *Style*— Phil Horton, Esq; ✉ Renault UK Ltd, Denham Lock, Widewater Place, Moorhall Road, Harefield, Middx UB9 6RT (☎ 01793 486001)

HORTON, Sir Robert Baynes; kt (1997); s of W H Horton (d 1969), of Pangbourne; *b* 18 Aug 1939; *Educ* Kings Sch Canterbury, Univ of St Andrews (BSc), MIT (SM); *m* 1962, Sally Doreen, da of Edward Wells (d 1971), of Beverley, E Yorks; 1 s, 1 da; *Career* joined BP Co Ltd 1957, gen mangr BP Tanker Co 1975–76 and corp planning BP 1976–79, md and chief exec BP Chemicals International 1980–83, chm and chief exec offr Standard Oil (Ohio) 1986–88; British Petroleum plc: a managing dir 1983–86 and 1988–92, dep chm 1989–90, chm and chief exec 1990–92; vice chm British Railways Bd 1992–94; chm: Railtrack plc 1993–; chm JKX Oil & Gas plc 1995–; non-exec dir: ICL plc 1982–84, Pilkington Bros plc 1985–86, Emerson Electric Co 1987–, Partner Re 1993–, Farnell Electronics plc 1995–; chllr Univ of Kent at Canterbury 1990–95; pres: Chemical Industs Assoc 1982–84, BESO 1993–; memb: SERC 1985–86, Bd of MIT 1987– (chm Sloan Visiting Ctee 1991–), UFC 1989–92; tstee: Case Western Reserve Univ 1987–92, Cleveland Orchestra 1987–93; govr King's Sch Canterbury 1983–, vice chm ABSA 1992–; Hon LLD: Dundee 1988, Aberdeen 1992; Hon DSc: Cranfield 1992, Kingston 1993; Hon DCL Kent 1990, Hon DBA North London 1991, Hon DUniv Open Univ 1993; Hon FCGI, FIChemE, CIMgt; *Recreations* music, country pursuits; *Clubs* Leander, Athenaeum; *Style*— Sir Robert Horton; ✉ Railtrack plc, 40 Bernard Street, London WC1N 1BY (☎ 0171 344 7100)

HORWICH, Prof Alan; s of late William Horwich, and Audrey Miriam Lindley, *née* Rigby; *b* 1 June 1948; *Educ* William Hulme's GS, UCL, UCH Med Sch (MB BS, PhD), FRCR, FRCP; *m* 1981, Pauline Amanda, da of A R Barnes; 2 s (Oscar Samuel b 18 May 1985, Barnaby James b 24 March 1987), 1 da (Florence Harriet b 27 April 1989); *Career* house physician/surgn UCH 1972–73, house physician Royal N Hosp London 1973, SHO Hammersmith Hosp 1974, fell in oncology Harvard Med Sch Boston 1974–75, res fell Imperial Cancer Res Fund 1975–78, registrar The Royal Marsden Hosp 1979–81, lectr Inst of Cancer Res 1981–83, MRC sr grade scientist MRC Radiobiology Unit 1983–84; Inst of Cancer Res and Royal Marsden Hosp: sr lectr 1984–86, prof of radiotherapy 1986– (head of section), dean 1994–, dir of clinical res 1994–; memb: RSM, RCR, RCP; *Books* Testicular Cancer (1991), Combined Radiotherapy and Chemotherapy in Clinical Oncology (1992), Oncology: A Multidisciplinary Textbook (1995); *Style*— Prof Alan Horwich; ✉ The Royal Marsden Hospital, Downs Road, Sutton, Surrey (☎ 0181 642 6011 ext 3274, fax 0181 643 8809)

HORWOOD-SMART, Rosamund; QC (1996); da of John Horwood-Smart, of Cheveley, nr Newmarket, Suffolk, and Sylvia, *née* Nutt; *b* 21 Sept 1951; *Educ* Felixstowe Coll, Cambridgeshire HS for Girls, Inns of Court Sch of Law; *m* 1, 16 July 1983 (m dis 1994), Richard Clive Blackford; 1 s (Frederick John b 3 Sept 1986), 1 da (Eleanor Kate b 30 Aug 1989); m 2, 22 Feb 1996, Richard Bernays, *qv*; *Career* called to the Bar Inner Temple 1974, recorder 1995– (asst recorder 1990–95); memb: S Eastern Circuit, Criminal Bar Assoc, Bar European Gp; govr Int Students House London; chm of tstees Prisoners of Conscience Fund, tstee National Music Day; *Recreations* music, gardening, theatre; *Style*— Miss Rosamund Horwood-Smart, QC; ✉ 5 King's Bench Walk, Temple EC4Y 7DN (☎ 0171 797 7600, fax 0171 797 7648)

HOSEASON, James William Nicholson; OBE (1990); s of William Ballantyne Hoseason (d 1950), of Lowestoft, and Jessie Mary Hoseason (d 1972); *b* 6 Nov 1928; *Educ* Lowestoft GS; *m* 20 March 1965, Lesley Jean, da of Leslie Charles Edmonds (d 1964), of Chedgrave, nr Norwich; 1 s (James Charles William b 6 Feb 1967); *Career* articled pupil then chartered civil engr and chartered structural engr Sir Owen Williams & Partners 1945–50; Hoseasons Holidays Ltd: trainee 1950, md 1952–64, chm and jt md 1964–90, chm 1990–96; memb Inland Waterways Amenity Advsy Cncl 1972–80, govt appointed memb Anglian Water 1973–76, river cmmr Norfolk Broads 1982–88, past chm Br Hire Cruiser Fedn; Bd memb English Tourist Bd 1982–93, memb Broads Authy (memb Navigation Ctee); FTS 1973, FIMgt 1974, FCIM 1976; *Books* The Thousand Day Battle (1979, 3 edn 1990); *Recreations* sailing, writing, flying light aircraft, gardening; *Clubs* RAC, Royal Norfolk & Suffolk Yacht; *Style*— James Hoseason, Esq, OBE; ✉ Hoseasons Holidays Ltd, Sunway House, Lowestoft, Suffolk NR32 2LW (☎ 01502 500505)

HOSEGOOD, Charles Thomas Dennehy; s of Capt Thomas William Harold Hosegood (d 1939), and Nora Marie, *née* Dennehy (d 1946); *b* 4 Jan 1921; *Educ* King George V Hong Kong, Prior Park Coll Bath; *m* 9 Dec 1950, Jane, da of Norman Ernest Jacob (d 1969), of Grimsby; 2 s (Nigel b 7 March 1953, Ian b 14 Jan 1958); *Career* WWII, Pilot Fleet Air Arm 1939–47; HMS Alcantara 1941–43, US Coast Guards Floyd Bennett Field NY 1944, RN memb jt servs Helicopter Experimental Unit AFEE RAF Beaulieu 1945–46; test pilot Br Aeroplane Co 1948–51 (chief helicopter test pilot 1951–60), chief test pilot Bristol Div Westlands Aircraft Ltd 1960–63, introduced helicopters to Electricity Indust 1963, offr-in-charge Jt Electricity Helicopter Unit 1963–83, ret 1983; maiden flights Bristol Helicopters: Bristol 173 tandem and first twin engine, Bristol 191, Bristol 192 (Belvedere); official air speed helicopter record 30 May 1961 and 2 June 1961 London-Paris-London; memb: Test Pilots Ctee SBAC, Flying Ctee SBAC Farnborough Flying Display, Air Legislation Ctee for Helicopter Advsy Bd; GAPAN Master Pilot Certificate 1960; Freeman Worshipful Co of Air Pilots and Air Navigators 1964; Alan Marsh medal 1962; FRAeS 1976; Scroll of Bd of Fndn Flakkeese Gemeenschap 1953; *Recreations* cricket, squash, sailing, golf; *Clubs* Burnham and Berrow Somerset Golf, The Forty Cricket, Aero Golfing Soc; *Style*— Charles Hosegood, Esq; ✉ The Hyall, Lye Hole, Wrington, Somerset BS18 7RN (☎ 01934 862416)

HOSFORD-TANNER, (Joseph) Michael; s of late Dr Hubert Hosford-Tanner, of London, and Betty, *née* Bryce; *b* 8 Aug 1951; *Educ* Midleton Coll, Trinity Coll Dublin (BA, LLB); *Career* called to the Bar Inner Temple 1974; legal assessor: Farriers Registration Cncl 1985–, UK Central Cncl for Nursing, Midwifery and Health Visiting 1991–; *Recreations* horses, cricket, travel; *Clubs* Chelsea Arts, Kildare Street and Univ; *Style*— Michael Hosford-Tanner, Esq; ✉ Queen Elizabeth Building, Temple, London EC4Y 9BS (☎ 0171 797 7837, fax 0171 353 5422)

HOSKER, Sir Gerald Albery; KCB (1995, CB 1987), QC (1991); s of Leslie Reece Hosker (d 1971), and Constance, *née* Hubbard; *b* 28 July 1933; *Educ* Berkhamsted Sch; *m* 1956, Rachel Victoria Beatrice, da of Cdr Clifford Victor Middleton, RINVR (ret); 1 s (Jonathan Edward George b 1961), 1 da (Helen Bridget b 1958); *Career* admitted slr 1956, assoc Faculty of Secretaries and Admins 1964, legal asst Treasy Slr's Dept 1960; Treasy: sr legal asst 1966, asst slr 1973, princ asst slr 1980, dep Treasy slr 1982, slr DTI 1987–92, HM procurator gen and Treasy slr 1992–95; Queen's proctor 1992–95; FRSA 1964; *Clubs* Royal Over-Seas League; *Style*— Sir Gerald Hosker, KCB, QC

HOSKING, Barbara Nancy; OBE (1985); da of William Henry Hosking (d 1963), and Ada Kathleen, *née* Murrish (d 1951); *b* 4 Nov 1926; *Educ* West Cornwall Sch for Girls, Hillcroft Coll; *Career* Civil Serv 1965–77, press offr 10 Downing St 1970–72, private sec to Parly Secs Cabinet Office 1973–75; controller of info servs IBA 1977–86; occasional broadcaster and writer, conslt Yorkshire TV, non-exec dir Westcountry TV 1991–; former: pres Media Soc, jt vice chm Nat Cncl of Voluntary Orgns; former tstee: Charities Aid Fndn, 300 Gp, ITV Telethon; memb Cncl: RSA 1991–96, Literary Tst 1993–, Family Policy Studies Centre 1994–; Hon DUniv Ulster 1996; FRSA 1984, FRTS 1988; *Recreations* opera, lieder, watching politics; *Clubs* Reform; *Style*— Ms Barbara Hosking, OBE; ✉ 9 Highgate Spinney, Crescent Rd, London N8 8AR (☎ 0181 340 1853, fax 0181 347 9107)

HOSKING, Prof Geoffrey Alan; s of late Stuart William Steggall Hosking, of Maidstone, Kent, and Jean Ross, *née* Smillie; *b* 28 April 1942; *Educ* Maidstone GS, King's Coll Cambridge (BA), Moscow State Univ, St Antony's Coll Oxford, Univ of Cambridge (MA, PhD); *m* 19 Dec 1970, Anne Lloyd Hirst; 2 da (Katya b 1974, Janet b 1978); *Career* Univ of Essex: lectr Dept of Govt 1966–71, lectr Dept of History 1972–76, reader Dept of History 1976–80 and 1981–84; Sch of Slavonic and E European Studies Univ of London: prof of Russian history 1984–, dep dir 1996–; visiting prof: Dept of Political Sci Univ of Wisconsin USA 1971–72, Slavisches Inst Univ of Cologne 1980–81; Reith lectr BBC 1988, memb jury Booker Prize for Russian Fiction 1993; memb: Cncl of Writers and Scholars Int 1985–, Cncl Keston Coll 1987–89, Bd of Govrs Camden Sch for Girls 1988–94, Br Univs Assoc for Soviet and E Euro Studies, Royal Inst for Int Affrs; FBA 1993, FRHistS 1995; *Books* The Russian Constitutional Experiment: Government & Duma 1907–14 (1973), Beyond Socialist Realism: Soviet Fiction since Ivan Denisovich (1980), A History of The Soviet Union (1985, 3 edn 1992, Los Angeles Times History Book Prize 1986), The Awakening of The Soviet Union (1990, 2 edn 1991), The Road to Post-Communism: independent political movements in the Soviet Union 1985–91 (with J Aves and P Duncan, 1992), Russia: People and Empire 1552–1917 (1997); *Recreations* walking, music, chess; *Style*— Prof Geoffrey Hosking, FBA; ✉ School of Slavonic & East European Studies, University of London, Senate House, Malet St, London WC1E 7HU (☎ 0171 637 4934 ext 4064, fax 0171 436 8916, e-mail g.hosking@ssees.ac.uk)

HOSKING, John Everard; CBE, JP, DL; s of J Everard Hosking, OBE (d 1978), and Eveline Margaret, *née* Shaxson (d 1994); *b* 23 Oct 1929; *Educ* Marlborough, Wye Coll London (BSc); *m* 16 Sept 1953, Joan Cecily, da of Dr John Wilfrid Whitaker, OBE, FRS (d 1980); 2 s (Julian Bernard b 1957, Bruce Adrian b 1960); *Career* farmer and landowner in Kent 1953–69; md Eastes and Loud Ltd 1965–69; dir: Ashford Corn Exchange Co 1965–69, Newgrain-Kent 1969–74, Agroup Ltd 1987–94, Bureau Europeen de Recherche SA 1987–90, European Intelligence Ltd 1987–94; chm Agra Europe (London) Ltd 1989–94 (chief exec 1974–89); chm: Ashford Magistrates' Court 1975–84, Centre for Euro Agric Studies Assoc 1977–83, Kent Magistrates' Courts Ctee 1984–88; vice pres Magistrates' Assoc (chm Cncl 1987–90); memb: Lord Chllr's Advsy Ctee on the appointment of Magistrates 1977–89, Kent Police Authy 1970–74, Central Cncl Magistrates' Cts Ctees 1980–83, Bar Cncl Professional Conduct Ctee 1983–86, Senate of Inns of Ct and the Bar Disciplinary Tbnl 1983–86, Cncl Cwlth Magistrates and Judges Assoc 1989–92, Lord Chief Justice's Working Party on Mode of Trial 1989, Lord Chllr's Advsy Ctee on Legal Educn and Conduct 1991–94; tax cmmr 1980–; govr Ashford Sch 1976– (chm); Wye Coll: govr 1995–, pres Agricola Club (former students) 1995–; memb Royal Agric Soc 1960; *Books* Rural Response to the Resource Crisis in Europe (ed, 1981), The Agricultural Industry of West Germany (1990); *Recreations* the arts, the countryside; *Clubs* Farmers'; *Style*— John Hosking, Esq, CBE, JP, DL

HOSKING, Patrick Anthony James; s of Roger Michael Hosking, and Mollie June, *née* Allen; *b* 8 Feb 1960; *Educ* Rugby, Pembroke Coll Cambridge; *m* Amanda Clare, *née*

Lindsay; *Career* asst ed Inst for Int Research 1981–83, newsletter ed Stonehart Publications 1983–86, business reporter then banking corr The Independent 1986–90; business corr: The Age Melbourne Australia 1990–91, The Independent 1991–93; The Independent on Sunday: sr business writer 1993–94, dep City ed then City ed 1994–; *Style*— Patrick Hosking, Esq; ✉ The Independent on Sunday, 1 Canada Square, Canary Wharf, London E14 5DL (☎ 0171 293 2050, fax 0171 293 2096)

HOSKINS, Arthur Henry James; CBE; s of Alfred George Hoskins; *b* 14 Jan 1923; *m* 1949, Margaret Lilian Rose, da of Albert Davis (d 1959); 1 child; *Career* certified accountant, chartered sec; md and dep chm Matthew Hall plc 1939–86, chm Abbeyfield SE London Extra Care Society Ltd, dir Barbados Management (Bexhill) Ltd; *Recreations* reading, walking; *Style*— Arthur Hoskins, Esq, CBE; ✉ 2 Acorn Close, Chislehurst, Kent BR7 6LD (☎ 0181 467 0755)

HOSKINS, Prof Brian John; s of George Frederick Hoskins (d 1979), and Kathleen Matilda Louise, *née* Rattue; *b* 17 May 1945; *Educ* Bristol GS, Trinity Hall Cambridge (MA, PhD); *m* 25 May 1968, Jacqueline, *née* Holmes; 2 da (Brooke b 22 Sept 1972, Bryony b 7 Oct 1974); *Career* prof of meteorology Univ of Reading 1981– (reader in atmospheric modelling 1976–81, head of dept 1990–96); Rothschild visiting prof Isaac Newton Math Inst Cambridge 1996; special advsr to Sec of State for Tport 1989–90; memb Cncl Natural Environment Res Cncl 1988–94, pres Int Assoc for Meteorology and Atmospheric Physics 1991–95; Starr Meml lectr MIT 1989, Br Geological Survey distinguished lectr 1992, Haurwitz lectr American Meteorological Soc 1995; Royal Meteorological Soc: Symons Meml lecture 1982, L F Richardson prize 1972, Buchan prize 1976; Charles Chree Silver medal Inst of Physics 1987, Carl-Gustaf Rossby Res medal American Meteorological Soc 1988; FRMetS 1970, FRS 1988, fell Academia Europaea 1990; *Books* Large-Scale Dynamical Processes in the Atmosphere (1982), author of 95 papers in learned jls; *Recreations* singing, gardening; *Style*— Prof Brian Hoskins, FRS; ✉ 32 Reading Rd, Wokingham, Berks RG41 1EH (☎ 0118 979 1015); Department of Meteorology, University of Reading, Whiteknights, Reading RG6 2AU (☎ 0118 931 8953, fax 0118 935 2604)

HOSKINS, Malcolm Geoffrey Ronald; s of Ronald Arthur Hoskins (d 1986), of Bath, and (Edith) Marjorie, *née* Caseley; *b* 19 Dec 1941; *Educ* Felixstowe Acad; *m* 21 Sept 1974, (Dorothy) Christine Naden; *Career* articled clerk Paterson & Thompson 1958–64, ptnr Touche Ross (now Deloitte & Touche) 1971– (joined 1964, Exec Office 1992–); pres Manchester Soc of Chartered Accountants 1986–87, memb Cncl ICAEW 1988–93 and 1996–; ACA 1963; *Recreations* cricket, racing, theatre; *Clubs* Lancashire CCC, Somerset CCC, Racegoers'; *Style*— Malcolm Hoskins, Esq; ✉ Deloitte & Touche, Hill House, 1 Little New Street, London EC4A 3TR

HOSKINS, Robert (Bob); s of Robert Hoskins, and Elsie Lilian Hopkins; *b* 26 Oct 1942; *Educ* Stroud Green Sch; *m* 1, Jane Livesey; 1 s (Alexander b 8 Aug 1968), 1 da (Sarah b 30 Dec 1972); m 2, June 1982, Linda Banwell; 1 da (Rosa Louise b 27 May 1983), 1 s (Jack Anthony b 5 March 1985); *Career* actor; previously held numerous jobs incl accountant; theatre debut Unity Theatre London, early experience on tour with Ken Campbell's Road Show; *Theatre* Victoria Theatre Stoke-on-Trent 1968: Romeo and Juliet, Toad of Toad Hall, Christopher Pee in Heartbreak House; Century Theatre 1969: Marker in A View From the Bridge, Pinchwife in The Country Wife, Hiring in The Anniversary, Meneleus in The Trojan Women; Lenny in the Homecoming 1969 and Richard in Richard III 1970 (Hull Arts Theatre), Azdac in The Caucasian Chalk Circle and Lear (Royal Court) 1970–71, Bernie the Volt in Veterans (Royal Court) 1972, Sextus Pompeius in Antony and Cleopatra (Globe) 1973, Lear in Lear (Dartington Hall) 1973, Mr Doolittle in Pygmalion (Albery) 1974, Common Man in A Man For All Seasons (Sixty Nine Theatre Co) 1974, Geography of a Horse Dreamer (Royal Court) 1974, Touchstone in As You Like It (Oxford Playhouse) 1975, Biu Cracker in Happy End (Lyric) 1975–76; RSC 1976 incl: Rocky in The Iceman Cometh, Seargeant in The Devil's Disciple; other roles incl: The Bystander (also writer, Soho Poly Theatre) 1977, The World Turned Upside Down and Has Washington Legs? 1978, Lee in True West 1981, Nathan Detroit in Guys and Dolls 1982, Bosola in The Duchess of Malfi 1983; most recently Professor Mashkan in Old Wicked Songs (Gielgud Theatre) 1996; *Television* 1971–1984 incl: Joe Gramaldi in Omnibus - It Must Be Something in the Water, Knocker in Villains, Woodbine in Her Majesty's Pleasure, All Who Sail Around Her. On the Road, Crown Court, New Scotland Yard, Sexton in If there Weren't Any Blacks..., Doobs in Thick as Thieves, Schmoedius, Shoulder to Shoulder, Thriller - To Kill Two Birds, Omnibus on Brecht, Three Piece Suite, In The Looking Glass, Napoleon in Peninsular, Arthur Parker in Pennies From Heaven (nominated BAFTA Best Actor), Chorus in Mycenae and Men, Sheppey in Sheppey, Arnie Cole in Flickers, Iago in Othello, Eddie Reed in You Don't Have to Walk to Fly, The Beggars Opera; most recently incl: The Changeling (BBC) 1993, World War II: And then there were Giants (NBC) 1994; *Films* incl: Foster in The National Health 1973, Royal Flash 1974, Big Mac in Inserts 1975, Colour Sergeant Major Williams in Zulu Dawn 1979, Harold Shand in The Long Good Friday 1980 (Evening Standard Award for Best Actor, nominated for Best Actor Award British Acad of Film & Television Arts), Rock and Roll Manager in The Wall 1982, Colonel Perez in The Honorary Consul (titled Beyond The Limit in USA) 1983, Owney Madden in The Cotton Club 1984, Spoor in Brazil 1985, Stanley in Sweet Liberty 1986, George in The Woman Who Married Clark Gable 1986, George in Mona Lisa (nominated for Oscar Award for Best Actor, won New York Critics and Golden Globe Awards, Best Actor Award Cannes Film Festival, also numerous English awards) 1986, The Priest in A Prayer For The Dying 1987, Madden in The Lonely Passion of Judith Hearne 1987, Eddie Valiant in Who Framed Roger Rabbit? 1988, Darky in The Raggedy Rawney (also writer, dir) 1988, Lou Landsky in Mermaids 1989, Jack Moony in Heart Condition 1990, Shattered 1990, The Favour The Watch and The Very Big Fish 1990, The Projectionist 1990, Hook 1991, Passed Away 1992, Mario in Mario Bros 1993, Super Mario Brothers 1992, Balto (animation) 1995, Rainbow (also dir) 1995, Nixon 1995; *Style*— Bob Hoskins, Esq; ✉ c/o Hutton Management Ltd, 200 Fulham Rd, London SW10 9PN (☎ 0171 352 4825, fax 0171 352 8579)

HOSKYNS, Sir Benedict Leigh; 16 Bt (E 1676), of Harewood, Herefordshire; 3 s of Rev Sir Edwyn Clement Hoskyns, 13 Bt, MC, DD (d 1937), and Mary Trym, *née* Budden (d 1994); suc bro, Sir John Chevallier Hoskyns, 15 Bt, 1956; *b* 27 May 1928; *Educ* Haileybury, Corpus Christi Coll Cambridge (MB BChir 1952), London Hosp; *m* 19 Sept 1953, Ann, da of Harry Wilkinson, of London; 2 s (Edwyn Wren b 1956, John Chandos b 1961), 2 da (Janet Mary (Mrs Christopher Harris) b 1954, Sarah Leigh (Mrs Julian P C Raphael) b 1959); *Heir* s, Dr Edwyn Wren Hoskyns b 4 Feb 1956; *Career* Capt RAMC (ret); in general med practice 1958–93, ret; DObstRCOG 1958; *Style*— Sir Benedict Hoskyns, Bt; ✉ Russell House, Wherry Corner, High Street, Manningtree, Essex CO11 1AP (☎ 01206 396432)

HOSKYNS, Dr Edwyn Wren; s and h of Sir Benedict Leigh Hoskyns, 16 Bt, *qv*; *b* 4 Feb 1956; *Educ* Nottingham Univ Med Sch (BM BS); *m* 1981, Jane, da of John Sellers; 1 s (Robin Chevallier b 5 July 1989), 1 da (Lucy Mary b 1993); *Career* conslt paediatrician Leicester General Hosp 1993; MRCP 1984; *Style*— Dr Edwyn Hoskyns; ✉ Brook's Edge, 62 Main Street, Cosby, Leicester LE9 5UU

HOSKYNS, Sir John Austin Hungerford Leigh; kt (1982); s of Lt-Col Chandos Benedict Arden Hoskyns (d of wounds after defence of Calais 1940; gs of Rev Sir John Hoskyns, 9 Bt, JP), and Joyce Austin, *née* Taylor; *b* 23 Aug 1927; *Educ* Winchester; *m* 1956, Miranda Jane Marie, o da of late Tom Mott, of Onslow Square, London SW7; 2 s (Barnaby b 1959, Benedict b 1963), 1 da (Tamasine b 1961); *Career* Capt Rifle Bde; IBM (UK) 1957–64, fndr John Hoskyns and Co (later part of Hoskyns Gp, of which chm and md 1964–75, co later called Hoskyns Group plc), head of PM's Policy Unit 1979–82; non-exec dir: ICL 1982–84, Ferranti International plc 1986–94; dir-gen IOD 1984–89; dir: AGB Research plc 1983–88, Pergamon-AGB plc 1988–89, Clerical Medical and General Life Assurance Society 1983–, McKechnie plc 1983–93; non-exec chm The Burton Group plc 1990–, chm EMAP plc 1994–; *Style*— Sir John Hoskyns; ✉ c/o Child & Co, 1 Fleet St, London EC4Y 1BD

HOSKYNS-ABRAHALL, (Anthony David) Wren; s of Rt Rev Anthony Leigh Egerton-Hoskyns-Abrahall (former Bishop of Lancaster, d 1982), and Margaret Ada, *née* Storey; *b* 19 May 1943; *Educ* St John's Sch Leatherhead, Britannia RNC Dartmouth, London Graduate Sch of Business Studies; *m* 23 April 1965, Phyllis Penrose, da of Rear Adm Willian Penrose Mark-Wardlaw, DSO, DSC, ADC; 1 s (Mark b 22 July 1966) 1 da (Sarah b 18 April 1971); *Career* RNC Dartmouth 1961–63, HMS Tiger 1962–63, RN Trg then Staff Offr Ops Kenya Navy 1966–68, HMS Chichester 1969–70, HMS Rapid 1970, HMS Malcolm 1970–71, Flag Lt to FOSNI 1972–72; dir: Portsmouth & Sunderland Newspapers plc 1973–77, Debenhams plc 1978–82, Prontaprint 1982–; memb Gen Synod C of E 1994–95; ed Barnes In Common; cncllr Fareham BC 1974–76; HCIM 1979; *Recreations* fishing; *Style*— Wren Hoskyns-Abrahall, Esq; ✉ 20 Grange Rd, Barnes, London SW13 9RE (☎ 0181 748 8455); Prontaprint, 60 Wandsworth High St, London SW18 4LD (☎ 0181 870 7672, fax 0181 870 0056)

HOSTOMBE, Roger Eric; s of late Eric Rudolf Hostombe, of Sheffield, and Irene, *née* Baxter; *b* 22 Dec 1942; *Educ* Sedbergh; *m* 20 Sept 1975, Susan Mary, da of late Frank Ian Cobb, of Sheffield; 5 da (Clare b 1976, Natalie b 1979, Annabel b 1982, Lucinda b 1982, Sophie b 1989); *Career* CA 1968, exec chm Hostombe Group Ltd 1975–; underwriter Lloyd's 1975–; regnl cncllr CBI Yorkshire and Humberside branch 1981–87; *Recreations* tennis, squash, skiing, gardening; *Clubs* The Sheffield, Annabel's; *Style*— Roger E Hostombe, Esq; ✉ Fullwood Hall, Sheffield, Yorks S10 4PA (☎ 0114 230 2148); Hostombe Group Ltd, Minalloy House, Regent St, Sheffield S1 3NJ (☎ 0114 272 4324, fax 0114 272 9550)

HOTHAM, Anthony; TD (1969); s of Edward Hotham (d 1985), and Freda Elizabeth, *née* Smith (d 1988); *b* 30 May 1933; *Educ* Warwick Sch; *m* 6 Nov 1954, Patricia Margaret, da of George Henry Day (d 1956); 2 s (Charles Anthony b 7 Sept 1959, Timothy Edward b 9 Oct 1961); *Career* Nat Serv 1952, cmmnd RASC 1953, TA 1954, Capt 1957, Maj 7 Bn Worcs Regt TA 1967, ret 1969; md Starr Roadways Ltd 1968–72; called to the Bar Middle Temple 1971, in practice 1973–91; pt/t pres Mental Health Review Tbnl 1987–; chm Starr Roadways Ltd 1985–; cncllr Wychavon DC 1991–; memb CIT (until 1982); *Recreations* squash, golf, skiing; *Style*— Anthony Hotham, Esq, TD; ✉ 5 Fountain Court, Steelhouse Lane, Birmingham B4 6DR (☎ 0121 606 0500, fax 0121 606 1501)

HOTHAM, 8 Baron (I 1797); Sir Henry Durand Hotham; 18 Bt (E 1622), DL (Humberside 1981); 3 s of 7 Baron Hotham, CBE (d 1967), and Lady (Letitia Sibell) Winifred Cecil (d 1992), da of 5 Marquess of Exeter, KG, CMG, TD; *b* 3 May 1940; *Educ* Eton; *m* 1972, Alexandra Mary, 2 da of Maj Andrew Charles Stirling Home Drummond Moray; 2 s (Hon William Beaumont, Hon George Andrew b 1974), 1 da (Hon Elizabeth Henrietta Alexandra b 1976); *Heir* s, Hon William Beaumont Hotham b 13 Oct 1972; *Career* former Lt Grenadier Gds; patron of 1 living; ADC to Govr of Tasmania 1963–66; *Style*— The Rt Hon Lord Hotham, DL; ✉ Scorborough Hall, Driffield, Yorks; Dalton Hall, Dalton Holme, Beverley, Yorks

HOTHERSALL, Dr (Thomas) Edward; s of Thomas Hothersall (d 1971), of Accrington, Lancashire, and Mary Alice, *née* O'Connor (d 1985); *b* 23 Sept 1939; *Educ* Thornleigh Coll Bolton, Univ of Edinburgh (MB ChB); *m* 4 April 1964, Pauline Ann, da of James Hepburn Waterston McMartin (d 1941); 4 s (Martin, James, Thomas, Duncan); *Career* res fell (diabetes) Royal Infirmary Edinburgh 1964–65, registrar Northern Gen Hosp Edinburgh 1966–69; conslt physician: Devonshire Royal Hosp 1969–79, N Staffs Health Authy 1969–; sr clinical lectr Postgraduate Medical Dept Univ of Keele 1993–; Midlands Rheumatology Soc: fndr sec 1972, pres 1979–82; chm Regnl Rheumatology Servs Ctee 1977–80 and 1983–85, pres Br Med Assoc N & Mid-Staff div 1978–79, dir of Depts of Rheumatology & Remedial Servs Staffs Rheumatology Centre 1981–; Br Soc of Rheumatology: memb Cncl 1985–87, chm Clinical Affairs Ctee 1988–91; Speciality Advsy Ctee (rheumatology) of Jt Ctee on Higher Med Trg: memb 1985–88, chm 1988–91; regnl advsr RCP of Edinburgh (W Midlands) 1982–, chm NW Rheumatology Club 1989–91, pres N Staffs Med Soc 1989–90, fndr chm Haywood Rheumatism Res & Devpt Fndn, pres Arthritis & Rheumatism Cncl (Potteries branch), chm N Staffs & Dist Cricket League; chm: Med Advsy Ctee North Staffs Health Dist 1991–94, District Med Staff Cncl 1994–96; memb: Ctee and hon med offr Staffordshire CCC, Stoke-on-Trent Rotary (pres 1992–93); *Style*— Dr Edward Hothersall; ✉ 540 Etruria Rd, Basford, Newcastle-under-Lyme, Staffs ST5 05X (☎ 01782 614419, fax 01782 630270)

HOTHFIELD, 6 Baron (UK 1881), of Hothfield, Co Kent; Sir Anthony Charles Sackville Tufton; 7 Bt (UK 1851); s of 5 Baron Hothfield, TD, DL (d 1991), and Evelyn Margarette, *née* Mordaunt (d 1989); *b* 21 Oct 1939; *Educ* Eton, Magdalene Coll Cambridge (MA); *m* 1975, Lucinda Marjorie, da of Capt Timothy John Gurney, and formerly w of Capt Graham Morison Vere Nicoll; 1 s (Hon William Sackville b 1977), 1 da (Hon Emma b 1976); *Heir* s, Hon William Sackville Tufton b 14 Nov 1977; *Career* civil engrg; CEng, MICE; *Recreations* real tennis (champion 1964, doubles 1962, 1963 and 1964), lawn tennis, bridge, shooting; *Style*— The Rt Hon Lord Hothfield; ✉ Drybeck Hall, Appleby-in-Westmorland, Cumbria CA16 6TF

HOTUNG, Eric Edward; s of Edward Sai Kim Hotung (d 1957), and Mordia Alice, *née* O'Shea (d 1992); gs of Sir Robert Hotung; *b* 8 June 1926; dual Anglo-Chinese nationality; *Educ* Mt Francis Xavier Coll Shanghai, Georgetown Univ Washington DC (BSS), NY Inst of Finance NYC; *m* 17 Jan 1959, Patricia Anne, da of Michael Shea (d 1938); 5 s (Michael Eric b 8 Jan 1960, Robert Eric b 28 Jan 1961, Eric Shea-Kim b 11 Aug 1963, Sean Eric McLean b 17 Jan 1965, Anthony Eric Ryan b 14 March 1966), 3 da (Mara Tegwen b 20 July 1967, Gabrielle Marie b 3 Jan 1971, Sheridan Patricia b 27 March 1972); *Career* security analyst Henry Hentz & Co NY 1951, admin asst to dir Pacific Area Foreign Distributors Div General Motors 1953–58, dir Hong Kong & Kowloon Entertainment Co 1958, chm Hotung International Ltd 1960, fndr chm Hong Kong Development Ltd and Cosmopolitan Properties & Securities Ltd 1970–; memb Hong Kong Stock Exchange and Hong Kong Gold and Silver Exchange 1958; special advsr on Chinese affrs Centre for Strategic and Int Studies Washington DC 1975, dir US Nat Ctee on US-China Relations 1986, econ and fin advsr to Tianjin Govt of China 1990; fndr Hotung Institute; fndr/sponsor numerous philanthropical, charitable and other projects incl: Convent of Santa Rosa de Lima Macau 1962, Low Cost Home Ownership and Financing Schemes Hong Kong 1964–93, Eric Hotung Tst Fund for Secdy Educn 1965, radio stns for marginados (underprivileged youth) Costa Rica 1975, Georgetown Univ Trauma Team for Vietnamese refugees in Cambodia and other projects 1978, Intercultural Centre Georgetown Univ (jt sponsor with US Govt) 1980, Brathay Expdn and Operation Drake 1980, visit of Cardinal Sin of the Philippines to China 1984, US-China Trade Confs at US Senate (advocating unconditional renewal of China's Most Favoured Nation trading status) 1987, SES Expdn to Mt Xixibangma Tibet 1987, co-sponsor (with US-China Business Cncl) conf on Reassessing US-China Ties: Economic Policy and the Role of Business at US State Dept 1990, co-host (with US Nat Ctee on US-China Relations) to Chinese Mayors' Delgn at US Senate and State Dept 1990; tstee

Marine Mil Acad Harlingen Texas 1978, vice pres Operation Drake 1979, vice pres Operation Raleigh 1984, dir Soong Ching Ling Fndn for Children 1987, patron Hotung Tech Sch for Girls 1988, chm Non-Combatants Pacific War 1937–45 Assoc Inc 1994, tstee Spirit of Normandy Int Appeal 1994; hon memb Scientific Exploration Soc 1980, life memb Hong Kong Arts Centre 1984, life memb Royal Philharmonic Orch 1984, friend of St George's Chapel Windsor 1984; Freeman City of San Francisco 1972, Hon Dr Georgetown Univ 1984; Knight of Malta 1974, Caballero do la Ordennde Isabella Catholica 1974, Knight of St Sylvester 1984, CStJ 1995 (OStJ 1966); *Recreations* game fishing, calligraphy; *Clubs* Carlton, Wig and Pen, Metropolitan (Washington DC), Chinese (Hong Kong); *Style—* Eric Hotung, Esq; ✉ Cosmopolitan International Holdings Ltd, 1219 Princes Building, Chater Road, Central, Hong Kong (☎ 00 852 2526 2271, fax 00 852 2810 5216)

HOUGH, George Hubert; CBE (1965); s of late Wilfrid Hough; *b* 21 Oct 1921; *Educ* Winsford Verdin GS Cheshire, King's Coll London (PhD); *m* 1943, Hazel Ayrton, da of late Kenneth Russell; 1 s, 2 da; *Career* md Hawker Siddeley Dynamics Ltd 1977–78; memb: British Aerospace Bd, BAC Guided Weapons Div Bd 1977–78; chm and chief exec Br Smelter Constructions Ltd 1978–80, dir Programmed Neuro Cybernetics (UK) Ltd 1979–84, chm Forthstar Ltd 1980–; dir: Landis & Gyr UK 1978–84, Leigh Instruments Ltd (Canada) 1987–88; chm: Magnetic Components Ltd 1986–89, Abasec Ltd 1988–, Fernau Holdings Ltd 1989–94; *Books* The Anatomy of Major Projects (with P Morris); *Recreations* shooting, golf; *Style—* George H Hough, Esq, CBE; ✉ Trelyon, Rock, Wadebridge, Cornwall (☎ 01208 863454)

HOUGH, Prof James Richard; s of George Hough (d 1993), of Brighton, Sussex, and Eileen Isobel, *née* Donovan (d 1993); *b* 2 Aug 1937; *Educ* Xaverian Coll Brighton, Brighton GS, Univ of Keele (BA), Univ of London (MSc), Univ of Leicester (PhD); *m* 31 Aug 1968, Jane Louise, da of Vernon Blake Vincent (d 1982); 2 s (Steven David b 1972, Richard Martin b 1974), 1 da (Catherine Theresa b 1978); *Career* exec Lloyd's Underwriters 1953–65, sr lectr in econs Huddersfield Poly 1971–72; Loughborough Univ: lectr 1972–77, sr lectr 1977–84, reader 1984–85, dean of educn and humanities 1985–88, prof 1988–93, prof emeritus and conslt in educn and economics 1993–; conslt on econs of educn for: World Bank, UNESCO, IIEP, The Br Cncl, ODA, TETOC; *Books* A Study of School Costs (1981), The French Economy (1982), Educational Policy (1984), Education and the National Economy (1987); *Recreations* walking, tennis, cycling, golf, historical biography; *Style—* Prof James R Hough; ✉ Loughborough University, Loughborough, Leics LE11 3TU (☎ and fax 01509 261021)

HOUGH, Richard; s of G S Hough (d 1970), of Brighton, and Margaret, *née* Esilman (d 1974); *b* 15 May 1922; *Educ* Frensham Heights; *m* 1, 17 July 1943 (m dis 1980), Helen Charlotte Woodyatt; 4 da (Sarah, Alexandra, Deborah, Bryony); m 2, 7 June 1980, Julie Marie (Judy) Taylor, MBE; *Career* Flt Lt RAF Pilot Fighter Cmd 1941–46; book publishing: mangr Bodley Head 1947–55, dir Hamish Hamilton 1955–70 (dir, fndr and md Hamish Hamilton Children's Books Ltd and Elm Tree Books); freelance writer 1955–; cncl memb and vice pres Navy Records Soc 1970–82, chm Auxiliary Hosps Ctee King Edward VII's Hosp Fund 1975–80 (cncl memb 1970–84); *Books* The Fleet That Had to Die (1958), Admirals in Collision (1959), The Potemkin Mutiny (1960), The Hunting of Force Z (1963), Dreadnought (1964), The Big Battleship (1966), First Sea Lord: an authorised life of Admiral Lord Fisher (1969), The Blind Horn's Hate (1971), Captain Bligh and Mr Christian (1972, Daily Express Best Book of the Sea Award), Louis and Victoria - The First Mountbattens (1974), One Boy's War - Per Astra ad Ardua (1975), Advice to a Grand-daughter (Queen Victoria's letters, ed, 1975), The Great Admirals (1977), The Murder of Captain James Cook (1979), Man o' War (1979), Nelson (1980), Mountbatten - Hero of Our Time (1980), The Great War at Sea - 1914–1918 (1983), Edwina, Countess Mountbatten of Burma (1983), Former Naval Person - Churchill and the Wars at Sea (1985), The Ace of Clubs - A History of the Garrick (1986), The Longest Battle - The War at Sea 1939–45 (1986), Born Royal - The Lives and Loves of the Windsors (1988), The Battle of Britain - The Jubilee History (with Denis Richards, 1989), Winston and Clementine, The Triumph of the Churchills (1990), Bless our Ship, Mountbatten & the Kelly (1991), Other Days Around Me, a Memoir (1992), Edward and Alexandra - Their Private and Public Lives (1992), Captain James Cook: A Biography (1994), Victoria and Albert: their love and their tragedies (1996); *Clubs* Garrick, MCC; *Style—* Richard Hough, Esq; ✉ 31 Meadowbank, Primrose Hill Road, London NW3 3AY (☎ 0171 722 5663)

HOUGH, Robert Eric; s of Gordon Hough, and Joyce, *née* Davies; *b* 18 July 1945; *Educ* William Hulme's GS Manchester, Univ of Bristol (LLB); *m* 14 June 1975, Pauline Elizabeth, da of Austin David Gilbert Arch, and Amy Jean, *née* Watt; 2 s (Mark Ian b 11 Oct 1979, Christopher James b 21 Feb 1985); *Career* admitted slr 1970, Notary Public; ptnr Slater Heelis (slrs) Manchester 1974–89; exec dep chm Peel Holdings plc 1989– (dir 1986–), exec chm The Manchester Ship Canal Co 1989– (chm 1987–); non-exec dir Brammer plc 1993–; memb Bd of Mgmnt Manchester Business Sch 1993–, past pres Manchester C of C, memb Ct Univ of Manchester, chm Manchester Commonwealth Games 2002, govr William Hulme's GS; memb Law Soc; Hon DBA Manchester Metropolitan Univ 1996, Hon DLitt Univ of Salford 1996; *Recreations* golf, gardening; *Clubs* St James's (Manchester), Hale Golf; *Style—* Robert Hough, Esq; ✉ Peel Holdings plc, Quay West, Trafford Wharf Road, Manchester M17 1PL (☎ 0161 877 4714, fax 0161 877 4720)

HOUGH, Stephen; *b* 1961, Cheshire; *Educ* RNCM, Juilliard Sch NY; *Career* concert pianist; performed with orchs incl: Philharmonia, Royal Philharmonic, LSO, London Philharmonic, BBC Symphony, Eng Chamber, City of Birmingham Symphony, Cleveland, Chicago Symphony, Detroit Symphony, Hong Kong Philharmonic, Toronto Symphony, Monte Carlo Philharmonic, Philadelphia, LA Philharmonic, Lausanne Chamber, Orch of St Cecilia Rome; worked with conductors incl: Claudio Abbado, Klaus Tennstedt, Mstislav Rostropovich, James Levine, Simon Rattle, Esa-Pekka Salonen, Christoph von Dohnányi, Yuri Temirkanov, Jeffrey Tate; performed at festivals incl: Ravinia, Blossom, Spoleto, NY Mostly Mozart, Sorrento, Tivoli, Bath, Cheltenham, La Grange de Meslay, BBC Promenade Concerts; Terence Judd award 1982, first prize Naumburg Int Piano Competition 1983; FRNCM 1996; *Recordings* incl: Hummel Piano Concertos (with the Eng Chamber Orch, Gramophone Magazine best concerto record 1987), The Piano Album (collection of favourite encores), Brahms Piano Concerto No 2 (with the BBC Symphony Orch and Andrew Davis, various works by Britten, Schumann and Liszt (awarded Deutsche Schallplattenpreis), Scharwenka and Sauer piano concertos (Gramophone Record of the Year 1996), York Bowen piano music; *Style—* Stephen Hough, Esq; ✉ c/o Harrison/Parrott, 12 Penzance Place, London W11 4PA (☎ 0171 229 9166, fax 0171 221 5042)

HOUGHAM, John William; CBE (1996); s of William George Hougham, of Ash, Canterbury, Kent, and Emily Jane, *née* Smith; *b* 18 Jan 1937; *Educ* Sir Roger Manwood's Sch Sandwich Kent, Univ of Leeds (BA); *m* 26 Aug 1961, Peggy Edith, da of Ernest Grove (d 1972), of Halesowen, Worcs; 1 s (Simon b 1967), 1 da (Elizabeth b 1965); *Career* Royal Regt of Artillery 1955–57 (2 Lt 1956), TA 1957–60 (Lt 1959); dir industl rels Ford Espana SA Valencia Spain 1976–80, dir industl relations mfrg Ford of Europe Inc 1982–86, exec dir for personnel Ford Motor Co Ltd 1986–93, chm Advisory, Conciliation and Arbitration Serv (ACAS) 1993–; visiting fell City Univ 1991–, visiting prof Univ of E London 1991–; vice pres Involvement and Participation Assoc 1994–; chm Employment Occupational Standards Cncl 1994–; memb: Cncl CRAC 1986–, CBI Employment Policy Ctee 1987–93, Engrg Indust Trg Bd 1987–91, IPM Ctee on Equal Opportunities 1987–92, Bd Personnel Management Services Ltd 1989–93, Cncl Engineering Training Authority Ltd 1990–93, Trg and Employment Agency Bd NI 1990–93, Editorial Advsy Bd Human Resource Mgmnt Jl 1991–, Editorial Advsy Bd Personnel Mgmnt Magazine 1993–, Review Body on Doctors' and Dentists' Remuneration 1992–93, Advsy Bd Civil Serv Occupational Health Serv 1992–, Employment Appeal Tribunal 1992–93, Cncl of Reference Ridley Hall Fndn Cambridge 1993–; Freeman City of London 1995; CIPM 1991, CIMgt 1986; *Recreations* walking, collecting books on Kent; *Clubs* Harlequin FC; *Style—* John Hougham, Esq, CBE; ✉ Advisory, Conciliation and Arbitration Service, Brandon House, 180 Borough High Street, London SE1 1LW (☎ 0171 210 3670, fax 0171 210 3664)

HOUGHTON, Sir John Theodore; kt (1991), CBE (1983); s of Sidney Maurice Houghton (d 1987), of Abingdon, and Miriam, *née* Yarwood (d 1974); *b* 30 Dec 1931; *Educ* Rhyl GS, Jesus Coll Oxford (MA, DPhil); *m* 1, 1962, Margaret Edith (d 1986), da of Neville Broughton, of Colne, Lancs; 1 s (Peter b 1966), 1 da (Janet b 1964); m 2, 1988, Sheila, da of Sydney Thompson, of Bradford, Yorks; *Career* res fell Royal Aircraft Estab, lectr in atmospheric physics Oxford 1958 (reader 1962, prof 1976), official fell and tutor in physics Jesus Coll Oxford 1960–73 (prof fell 1973, hon fell 1983), visiting prof Univ of California LA 1969; dir Appleton Sci and Engrg Res Cncl 1979–83, dir gen (later chief exec) Meteorological Office 1983–91, hon scientist Rutherford Appleton Lab 1991–; developed: Selective Chopper Radiometer (for the Nimbus 4 and 5 satellites), Pressure Modulator Radiometer (flown on Nimbus 6) 1975, Stratospheric and Mesopheric Sounder (flown on Nimbus 7) 1978; chm: Jt Scientific Ctee for World Climate Res Programmes 1981–84, Scientific Assessment Intergovernmental Panel on Climate Change 1988–, Royal Cmmn on Environmental Pollution 1992–, Jt Scientific and Technical Ctee Global Climate Observing System 1992–95; vice pres World Meteorological Orgn 1987–91; fell Optical Soc of America; memb American Meteorological Soc; Darton Prize (RMS) 1954, Buchan Prize (RMS) 1966, Charles Chree medal of the Inst of Physics 1979, Glazebrook medal Inst of Physics 1989, jt winner Rank prize for opto electronics 1989, Symons Gold medal Royal Meteorological Soc 1991, Bakerian lectr Royal Soc 1991, Global 500 Award UN Environment Prog 1994, Gold medal Royal Astronomical Society 1995; Hon DSc Univ of Wales 1991, Hon DUniv Stirling 1992, Hon DSc UEA 1993, Hon DSc Univ of Leeds 1995; FRS, FInstP, FRMetS (pres 1976–78); *Books* Infra Red Physics (with S D Smith, 1966), The Physics of Atmospheres (1977, ed 1986), Remote Sensing of Atmospheres (with F W Taylor and C D Rodgers, 1984), The Global Climate (ed, 1984), Does God Play Dice? (1988), Global Warming: The Complete Briefing (1994), The Search for God: can science help (1995); *Style—* Sir John Houghton, CBE, FRS; ✉ Royal Commission on Environmental Pollution, Church House, Great Smith Street, London SW1P 3BL (☎ 0171 276 2098)

HOUGHTON, Raymond J (Ray); *b* 9 Jan 1962; *Career* professional footballer; 1 appearance West Ham Utd 1979–82, 129 league appearances Fulham 1982–85, 83 league appearances (10 goals) Oxford Utd 1985–87, over 200 appearances Liverpool 1987–92, joined Aston Villa 1992–95, transferred to Crystal Palace 1995–; Republic of Ireland: 43 full caps 1986–, rep in Euro Championships W Germany 1988 and World Cup Italy 1990, memb World Cup squad 1994; honours: League Cup 1986 (Oxford Utd), League Championship 1988 and 1990 (Liverpool), FA Cup 1989 and 1992 (Liverpool, runners up 1988); honours with Aston Villa: runners up inaugural FA Premier League Championship 1992/93, winners Coca Cola Cup 1994; *Style—* Ray Houghton, Esq; ✉ c/o Crystal Palace FC, Selhurst Park, London SE25 6PU

HOUGHTON, Maj-Gen Robert Dyer; CB (1962), OBE (1947), MC (1942), DL (1977); s of John Mayo Houghton, of Sarum, Dawlish, Devon (d 1947), and Lucy Evelyn, *née* Trotman (d 1973); *b* 7 March 1912; *Educ* Haileybury; *m* 1940, Dorothy Uladh (d 1995), da of late Maj-Gen R W S Lyons, IMS; 2 s (Adam, Neill), 1 da (Lucy); *Career* RM Offr 1930–64, Maj-Gen 1961, Chief of Amphibious Warfare 1961, ADC to HM The Queen 1959–64; Col Cmdt RM 1973–75; gen sec Royal UK Beneficent Assoc 1968–78; *Recreations* gardening, model engineering; *Clubs* Army and Navy; *Style—* Maj-Gen Robert Houghton, CB, OBE, MC, DL; ✉ Vert House, Whitesmith, nr Lewes (☎ 01825 872451)

HOULDER, Bruce Fiddes; QC (1994); s of Dr Charles Alexander Houlder (d 1993), and Jessie, *née* Fiddes; *b* 27 Sept 1947; *Educ* Felsted; *m* 1974, Stella Catherine, da of Dr Michael Mattinson, and Barbara, *née* Wilkins; 2 da (Diana Elizabeth b 3 March 1981, Francesca Maria b 20 Aug 1983); *Career* called to the Bar Gray's Inn 1969, recorder 1991–; memb: Criminal Bar Assoc, General Cncl of the Bar 1995–; vice chm Professional Standards Ctee 1995–, vice chm Public Affairs Ctee Bar Cncl 1996–; *Recreations* painting, sailing, theatre; *Style—* Bruce Houlder, Esq, QC; ✉ 6 King's Bench Walk, Temple, London EC4Y 7DR (☎ 0171 583 0410, fax 0171 353 8791, DX 26 Chancery Lane)

HOULDSWORTH, Philippa Caroline (Pippy); da of Maj Ian George Henry Houldsworth, TD, JP (d 1963), of Dallas, Moray, and Clodagh, *née* Murray, JP; *b* 17 Aug 1957; *m* 18 Aug 1995, Matthew Julius Radford; 2 s (Frederick b 1994, Marcus b 1996); *Career* head buyer Children's Book Centre 1978–80, ed Children's Book News 1981–82, mktg and PR conslt 1983–85, New Art Centre 1986–87, proprietor Houldsworth Fine Art 1987–; patron of new art Tate Gallery 1992–, memb Soc of London Art Dealers 1994–; *Recreations* reading, visiting galleries, photography; *Style—* Pippy Houldsworth; ✉ Houldsworth Fine Art, Pall Mall Deposit, 124 Barlby Road, London W10 6BL (☎ 0181 969 8197, fax 0181 964 3595)

HOULDSWORTH, Sir Richard Thomas Reginald; 5 Bt (UK 1887), of Reddish, Manchester, Co Lancaster, and Coodham, Symington, Ayrshire; s of Sir Reginald Douglas Henry Houldsworth, 4 Bt, OBE, TD (d 1989), and Margaret May, *née* Laurie (d 1995); *b* 2 Aug 1947; *Educ* Bredon Sch Tewkesbury; *m* 1, 1970 (m dis 1979), Jane, o da of Alistair Orr, of Sydehead, Beith, Ayrshire; 2 s (Simon Richard Henry b 1971, Nicolas Peter George b 1975); m 2, 2 May 1992, Ann Catherine, da of late Capt Jean Jacques Tremayne, and Mrs Stella Mary Tremayne; 1 s (Matthew James b 12 Nov 1992); *Heir* s, Simon Richard Henry Houldsworth b 6 Oct 1971; *Style—* Sir Richard Houldsworth, Bt; ✉ Kirkbride, Glenburn, Crosshill, Maybole, Ayrshire

HOULSBY, Prof Guy Tinmouth; s of Thomas Tinmouth Houlsby, of South Shields, and Vivienne May, *née* Ford; *b* 28 March 1954; *Educ* Trinity Coll Glenalmond (War Meml scholar), St John's Coll Cambridge (Whytehead open scholar, MA, PhD, Rex Moir prize, Roscoe prize, Archibald Denny prize); *m* 28 March 1985, Jenny Lucy Damaris, da of Dr Ronald M Nedderman; 2 s (Neil Matthew Tinmouth b 16 Oct 1987, Ian Thomas Tinmouth b 13 Oct 1990); *Career* civil engr: Binnie & Partners 1975–76, Babtie Shaw & Morton 1976–77; Univ of Oxford: jr res fell Balliol Coll 1980–83, lectr in engrg and fell Keble Coll 1983–91, prof of civil engrg and fell Brasenose Coll 1991–; Br Geotechnical Soc prize 1985, Geotechnical Res medal ICE 1989; CEng 1983, MICE 1983; *Books* Basic Soil Mechanics (with G W E Milligan, 1984), Predictive Soil Mechanics - Proceedings of the Wroth Memorial Symposium (ed); *Recreations* ornithology, woodwork, Northumbrian small pipes; *Style—* Prof Guy Houlsby; ✉ 25 Purcell Road, Marston, Oxford OX3 0HB (☎ 01865 722128); Department of Engineering Science, Parks Road, Oxford OX1 3PJ (☎ 01865 273138, fax 01865 283301, e-mail Guy.Houlsby@eng.ox.ac.uk)

HOUNSFIELD, Sir Godfrey Newbold; kt (1981), CBE (1976); s of Thomas Hounsfield; *b* 28 Aug 1919; *Educ* Magnus GS Newark, Farady House Coll, City Coll London; *Career* served RAF 1939–46; joined EMI Ltd 1951 (working on radar systems, computers, computed tomography (CT); conslt scientist Central Res Laboratories of EMI 1986– (head of Medical Systems Section 1972–76, chief staff scientist 1976–77, sr staff scientist 1977–85); magnetic resonance imaging advsr Nat Heart Hosp and Brompton Hosp, professorial fell in imaging sciences Univ of Manchester 1978–; Nobel Prize for Physiology or Medicine (jtly) 1979; Dr Medicine (hc) Universität Basel; Hon DSc: City 1976, London 1976; Hon DTech Loughborough 1976; Hon FRCP, Hon FRCR 1976; FRS, Hon FEng 1994; *Style*— Sir Godfrey Hounsfield, CBE, FRS, FEng; ✉ EMI Central Research Laboratories, Dawley Road, Hayes, Middx UB3 1HH (☎ 0181 848 6404, home ☎ 0181 894 1746)

HOURAHINE, Lyn; *b* 17 Oct 1947, Newport, Gwent; *Educ* Newport Coll of Art and Design (SIAD graphic design vocational course, Gold Star Starpacks Awards 1967); *m*; 2 c; *Career* graphic designer: Alcan Polyfoil 1968–70, Rank Hovis McDougall 1970–73, Siebert/Head Packaging Design Consultants 1973–77, McCann Design Associates 1977–79; fndr Lyn Hourahine Design Associates 1979–85: packaging design for clients incl Milton Bradley Europe, Van Den Berghs, The Boots Company and Hoechst; estab Paper Power 1985–: designing paper products from the devpt of paper engrg skills for clients incl Second Nature of the UK and Popshots of the USA (greetings cards), Clarks shoes (display), British Airways (cabin organiser), various advertising agencies (direct mail) and design consultancies (effects and self promotion); category and overall Card of the Year winner (USA Greeting Card Assoc Awards) 1989, 1992 and 1995; variously lectr Canterbury/Kent Inst, Hounslow Borough Coll, Epsom, Kingston Univ, Richmond and the American Coll, has conducted several portfolio surgeries for the CSD, assessor for membership of CSD; memb DBA, FCSD; *Recreations* percussion, cinema and theatre, the outdoors, Welsh Rugby Union, golf, watercolour painting; *Style*— Lyn Hourahine, Esq; ✉ Paper Power, 53 Warwick Road, London W5 5PZ (☎ 0181 579 6631, fax 0181 840 1990)

HOUSE, Lt-Gen Sir David George; GCB (1977, KCB 1975), KCVO (1985), CBE (1967, OBE 1964), MC (1944); s of Arthur George House, of Wimpole Street, London; *b* 8 Aug 1922; *Educ* Regent's Park Sch London; *m* 25 Oct 1947, Sheila Betty Germaine, o da of Capt Robert Henry Darwin, Green Howards (d 1944); 2 da (Jennifer Rosamund b 18 July 1948, Elizabeth Mary b 2 Sept 1953); *Career* served WWII Italy KRRC, dep mil sec MOD 1969–71, Maj-Gen 1971, COS HQ BAOR 1971–73, Lt-Gen 1975, dir of inf MOD 1973–75, GOC and Dir (Ops) NI 1975–77, ret; Col Cmdt: Small Arms Sch Corps 1974–77, The Light Div 1974–77; Gentleman Usher of the Black Rod House of Lords 1978–85; regnl dir Lloyds Bank Yorks and Humberside Region 1985–91; *Style*— Lt-Gen Sir David House, GCB, KCVO, CBE, MC; ✉ Dormer Lodge, Aldborough, nr Boroughbridge, N Yorks YO5 9EP

HOUSE, Prof John Peter Humphry; s of (Arthur) Humphry House (d 1955), and Madeline Edith, *née* Church (d 1978); *b* 19 April 1945; *Educ* Westminster, New Coll Oxford (BA), Courtauld Inst of Art Univ of London (MA), Univ of London (PhD); *m* 31 Aug 1968, Jill Elaine, da of Ernest Sackville Turner, OBE, of Kew, Surrey; 2 s (Adam b 1973, Joseph b 1975); *Career* lectr: UEA 1969–76, UCL 1976–80, Courtauld Inst of Art Univ of London 1980–87; Slade prof of fine art Univ of Oxford 1986–87, prof Courtauld Inst of Art Univ of London 1995– (reader 1987–95), awarded Br Acad Res Readership 1988–90; organiser Impressionism exhibition Royal Acad of Arts 1974, co-organiser Post-Impressionism exhibition Royal Acad of Arts 1979–80, co-organiser Renoir exhibition Arts Cncl of GB 1985, curator Landscapes of France: Impressionism and its Rivals (Hayward Gallery) 1995; *Books* Monet (1976, enlarged edn 1981), Monet: Nature into Art (1986), Impressionist and Post-Impressionist Masterpieces: The Courtauld Collection (co-author, 1987), Impressionism for England: Samuel Courtauld as Patron and Collector (co-author, 1994); *Recreations* second-hand bookshops; *Style*— Prof John House; ✉ Courtauld Institute of Art, University of London, Somerset House, The Strand, London WC2R ORN (☎ 0171 872 0220, fax 0171 873 2410)

HOUSE, Keren Ruth (Mrs John Hookway); da of Alan Sidney House, of Purley, Surrey, and Maureen Elizabeth Evelyn, *née* Atkinson; *b* 1 June 1951; *Educ* Purley Co GS for Girls, London Coll of Printing (BA), RCA (MA); *m* 9 Feb 1980, John Hookway, s of Leslie Hookway; 3 da (Jessica Rose b 27 Aug 1984, Eleanor Kate b 22 Oct 1987, Meredith Anne b 17 June 1992); *Career* lectr in graphic design Pennsylvania State Univ USA 1976–78; graphic designer: Bloomfield/Travis London 1978–79, Pentagram London 1979–81; pt/t lectr in graphic design Harrow Sch of Art 1981–82, fndr ptnr (with David Stuart) The Partnership London 1981–83, fndr ptnr and dir The Partners London 1983–87, art dir Glenn Travis Associates London 1988–90, creative dir the Design Bridge London 1990–; external assessor BA course in graphic design: Bath Coll of Higher Educn 1988–91, London Coll of Printing (London Inst) 1991–94, Univ of Brighton 1994–; work accepted: D&AD Annual and exhibition 1979, 1981, 1983, 1985, 1987 and 1989, Communication Arts Annual (USA) 1982, 1986 and 1989; memb Jury Design & Art Direction: graphics 1986, 1990 and 1992, Illustration 1989; memb: D&AD 1978, CSD 1982; *Recreations* children, husband and home; *Style*— Ms Keren House; ✉ Design Bridge, 18 Clerkenwell Close, London EC1R 0AA (☎ 0171 814 9922, fax 0171 814 9024)

HOUSEGO-WOOLGAR, William Michael; s of George Arthur Housego (d 1992), of Brighton, and Irene Maureen, *née* Newman; *b* 3 July 1944; *Educ* Brighton Sch of Architecture, Leeds Sch of Town Planning, Brighton Mgmnt Coll (DipArch, DipTP, DMS); *m* 13 July 1968, Diana Lilian, da of William Woolgar (d 1971); 1 s (Alexis William b 24 Nov 1970), 1 da (Isabella Jane b 1 Oct 1972); *Career* architect Warr and King Hove 1966–67, architect and planner Leeds City Cncl 1969–72, asst borough planning offr and gp leader Brighton Cncl 1972–76, asst cmmr Sultanate Brunei Perangchan Bandar Dan Negara 1976–79, advsr Miny of Foreign Affrs Riyadh Dip Quartar Saudi Arabia 1980–83, sr architectural and planning advsr ODA 1983–94, head Engrg Admin ODA 1994–95; UK rep UN cmmn of human settlements 1984–95, Euro Bank for Reconstruction and Devpt 1991–93; treas Int Devpt Forum 1990–94; chm Preston Lawn Lawn Tennis and Croquet Club, memb Sussex LTA Cncl; Lord of the Manor of St Giles in the Wood; RIBA 1972, MIMgt 1975, FRSA 1976, RIPA 1976, FRTPI 1988 (MRTPI 1975); *Recreations* tennis, philately, squash, porches, ESP planning; *Clubs* Savage; *Style*— William M Housego-Woolgar, Esq; ✉ Tabora, London Road, Brighton BN1 8QA (☎ and fax 01273 509695)

HOUSEMAN, Alexander Randolph; CBE (1984); s of Capt Alexander William Houseman (d 1962), and Elizabeth Maud, *née* Randolph (d 1986); *b* 9 May 1920; *Educ* Stockport GS, Stockport Coll; *m* 1942, Betty Edith (d 1990), da of Alfred G Norrington (d 1976); 1 da; *Career* apprenticed Crossley Motors Ltd and Fairey Aviation, prodn engr Ford Motor Co (aero engines) Ltd 1940–43, Saunders-Roe Ltd 1943–48, gen works mangr 1948–54, conslt (later dir, md and dep chm) P-E International plc 1954–81; chm: W Canning plc 1975–80, NEDO EDC Gauge and Tool Indust 1978–85; dir: P-E Consulting Gp Ltd 1968–81, Record Ridgway Ltd 1978–81; dir and dep chm British Rail Engrg Ltd 1979–89; memb: Cncl Inst of Mgmnt Conslts 1968–80, Industl Advsy Panel and Membership Panel of Fellowship of Engrg 1980–85; FEng 1980, FIMechE, FIEE, FIMC, CIMgt, life memb SME (USA), Hon Memb IIE (USA); various awards incl Nat Soc of Professional Engrs Distinguished Engrg Mgmnt Award (USA); *Recreations* DIY, walking, sailing, photography; *Clubs* Caledonian; *Style*— Alexander Houseman, Esq, CBE, FEng; ✉ 11 Kings Ave, Ealing, London W5 2SJ (☎ 0181 997 3936)

HOUSHIARY, Shirazeh; *b* 10 Jan 1955, Iran; *Educ* Chelsea Sch of Art London; *Career* artist/sculptor; *Solo Exhibitions*: Chapter Arts Centre 1980, Kettle's Yard Gallery Cambridge 1982, Centro d'Arte Contemporanea Siracusa Italy 1983, Galleria Massimo Minini Milan 1983, Galerie Grita Insam Vienna 1983, Lisson Gallery London 1984, Galerie Paul Andriesse Amsterdam 1986, Breath (Lisson Gallery London) 1987, Centre d'Art Contemporain Musée Rath Geneva (travelling to The Museum of Modern Art Oxford) 1988–89, Valentina Moncada Rome 1992, Lisson Gallery London 1992, Camden Arts Centre London (travelling to Douglas Hyde Gallery Dublin), Fine Arts Centre Univ of Massachusetts (travelling to Art Gallery of York Univ Canada) 1993–94; *Gp Exhibitions* incl: London/New York 1982 (Lisson Gallery London) 1982, The Sculpture Show (Arts Cncl of GB, Hayward Gallery and Serpentine Gallery London) 1983, New Art (Tate Gallery London) 1983, British Art Show - Old Allegiances and New Directions 1979–84 (Arts Cncl of GB, travelling to Birmingham Museum and Art Gallery, Ikon Gallery Birmingham, Royal Scottish Acad Edinburgh, Mappin Art Gallery Sheffield and Southampton Art Gallery) 1984, Galerie Montenay-Delsol Paris 1985, The British Show (Art Gallery of NSW Sydney and Br Cncl, travelling to Art Gallery of Western Aust Perth, Art Gallery of NSW Sydney, Queensland Art Gallery Brisbane, The Exhibition Hall Melbourne and Nat Art Gallery Wellington NZ) 1985, Jack Shainman Gallery NY 1987, Walk out to Winter (Bess Cutler Gallery NY) 1988, Magiciens de la Terre (Centre Georges Pompidou Paris) 1989, Terskel II/Threshold II (Museet for samtidskunst Oslo Norway) 1990, Studies on Paper - Contemporary British Sculptors (Connaught Brown London) 1990, Now for the Future (Arts Cncl of GB, Hayward Gallery London) 1990, Dujourie, Fortuyn/O'Brien, Kapoor, Houshiary (Rijksmuseum Kröller-Müller Otterlo Holland) 1990, Rhizome (Haags Gemeentemuseum Netherlands) 1991, Misure e Misurazioni (Naples) 1992, Bruges La Morte Gallery Belgium 1992, II Tyne Int Newcastle 1993, Venic Biennale 1993, Travellers Treasures (Mechitarist Monastery Venice) 1993, Int Biennale of Obidos Portugal 1993, Sculptors' Drawings The Body of Drawing (Univ of Warwick Coventry and The Mead Gallery) 1993; work subject of numerous exhibition catalogues, articles and reviews; jr fell Cardiff Coll of Art 1979–80; *Style*— Ms Shirazeh Houshiary; ✉ Lisson Gallery London Ltd, 67 Lisson St, London NW1 5DA (☎ 0171 724 2739, fax 0171 724 7124)

HOUSLAY, Prof Miles Douglas; s of (Edwin) Douglas Houslay, of Wolverhampton, and Georgina Marie (Molly), *née* Jeffs; *b* 25 June 1950; *Educ* The Grammar Sch Brewood Staffs, UC Cardiff (BSc), King's Coll Cambridge (PhD); *m* 29 July 1972, Rhian Mair, da of Charles Henry Gee, of Aberystwyth, Wales; 1 da (Emma b 14 Feb 1978), 2 s (Thomas b 29 March 1981, Daniel b 21 Feb 1988); *Career* res fell Queens' Coll Cambridge 1975–76 (ICI postdoctoral res fell Dept of Biochemistry 1974–76), reader in biochemistry UMIST 1982–84 (lectr 1976–82), Gardiner prof of biochemistry Univ of Glasgow 1984–; memb: Res Ctee British Diabetic Assoc 1986–91, MRC Cell Biology & Disorders Bd 1990–94 (memb Grant Ctee A 1989–93 (chm 1990–93)), Clinical Biomedical Res Ctee Scottish Office Home & Health Dept 1991–93, AFRC Cell Signalling Initiative Grant Ctee 1992–, HEFC Res Assessment Panel (Basic Medical and Dental Sciences) 1992 and 1996, Cell and Biochemistry Grant Panel Wellcome Trust, Advsy Bd for External Appts Univ of London 1990–, Ctee of the Biochemical Soc of GB 1983–86; external assessor Univ of Malaysia 1991–; ed-in-chief Cellular Signalling 1987–; memb Editorial Bd: Biochemical Jl 1981–88 (dep chm 1985–88), Biochem Biophys Acta 1982–93, Biochemical Pharmacology 1988–90, Progress in Growth Factor Res 1988–93; hon sr res fell: California Metabolic Res Fndn 1982–94, Hannah Res Inst 1988–; Selby Fell Aust Acad of Sci 1984; Colworth Medal Biochemical Soc GB 1985, Most Cited Scientist in Scotland 1992 (period 1986–91); FRSE 1986, FIBiol, CBiol, FRSA; *Books* Dynamics of Biological Membranes (with K K Stanley, 1983); author of over 350 res pubns; *Recreations* reading, hill walking, travel, sailing, driving, cooking; *Style*— Prof Miles Houslay, FRSE; ✉ Molecular Pharmacology Group, Division of Biochemistry & Molecular Biology, IBLS, Wolfson Building, University of Glasgow, Glasgow G12 8QQ (☎ 0141 330 5903, fax 0141 330 4365, e-mail gbca29@udcf.gla.ac.uk)

HOUSLEY, Dr Edward; s of Albert Edward Housley (d 1980), and Minnie, *née* Davis (d 1934); *b* 10 Jan 1934; *Educ* Mundella GS, Univ of Birmingham (MB ChB); *m* 8 July 1956, Alma Mary, da of Harold Ferris (d 1968); 1 da (Lucy Elizabeth b 1962); *Career* short serv cmmn RAMC 1960–63; conslt physician Royal Infirmary Edinburgh 1970–, hon sr lectr in med Univ of Edinburgh 1970–, med specialist Armed Forces Scotland 1975–, dir Murrayfield plc 1982–92; chm MRCP (UK) Part I Examining Bd 1990–95; FRCPEd 1975, FRCP 1979, FRSM 1986; *Recreations* tennis, skiing, crossword puzzles; *Style*— Dr Edward Housley; ✉ 16 Sunbury Place, Edinburgh EH4 3BY (☎ 0131 225 2040, fax 0131 225 2040); Murrayfield Hospital, Edinburgh EH12 6UD (☎ 0131 334 0363)

HOUSLEY, Michael John Vernon; s of Ronald Housley, of Chigwell, Essex, and Josephine Milne Housley (d 1988); *b* 15 March 1934; *Educ* Coopers' Company's Sch, King's Coll London; *m* 10 Sept 1960, Helen Russell, da of Rex Ransom (d 1970), of London; 3 s (Russell b 15 March 1964 d 1996, Richard b 12 March 1967, Matthew b 8 Oct 1970), 1 da (Catherine b 30 May 1962 d 1991); *Career* Nat Serv RN 1954–56; dir Scott North & Co Ltd 1964–66 (joined as trainee 1956), sr ptnr Housley Heath & Co 1966–76; md: Hambro Housley Heath Ltd 1977–79, Michael Housley Ltd (insur broker) 1980–92 (taken over by Thompson Heath & Bond Ltd 1992); memb Lloyd's; gp scout ldr 1956, asst co cmmr (int) Essex 1984–88; govr: Coopers' Co and Coborn Educn Fndn, Coopers' Co Sch; Freeman City of London, Liveryman Worshipful Co of Coopers (Master 1995–96), Liveryman Worshipful Co of Insurers; ACII 1960; *Recreations* walking, sailing, music; *Clubs* City of London East India; *Style*— M J V Housley, Esq; ✉ 4 Burnt House, Pudding Lane, Chigwell, Essex 1G7 6BY (☎ 0181 500 3544); Thompson Heath & Bond Ltd, 20/22 Curtain Road, London EC2A 3NQ (☎ 0171 377 5060)

HOUSSEMAYNE DU BOULAY, Sir Roger William; KCVO (1982, CVO 1972), CMG (1975); s of Capt Charles Houssemayne du Boulay, RN; *b* 30 March 1922; *Educ* Winchester, Univ of Oxford; *m* 1957, Elizabeth, da of late Brig Francis Wyville Home, and Molly, Lady Pile (d 1988); 1 da, 2 step s; *Career* serv WWII, RAFVR Flt Lt, Pilot; Colonial Serv in Nigeria, joined FO 1959, Washington 1960–64, FO 1964–67, cnsllr Manila 1967–71, dir Asian Devpt Bank 1969–71 (alternate dir 1967–69), cnsllr and head chancery Paris 1971–73, resident cmmr New Hebrides 1973–75, vice-marshal Dip Corps 1975–82; advsr: Solomon Islands Govt 1986, Swaziland Govt 1992; *Recreations* bellringing, riding, gardening; *Clubs* Boodle's; *Style*— Sir Roger Houssemayne du Boulay, KCVO, CMG; ✉ Anstey House, nr Buntingford, Herts SG9 0BJ

HOUSTON, Maj-Gen David; CBE (1975, OBE 1972), JP (1991); s of late David Houston, and Christina Charleson, *née* Dunnett; *b* 24 Feb 1929; *Educ* Latymer Upper Sch; *m* 1959, Jancis Veronica Burn; 2 s; *Career* cmmnd Royal Irish Fus 1949; cmd 1 Loyals then 1 QLR 1969–71, 8 Inf Bde 1974–75, Br Mil Attaché Washington 1977–79, BGS HQ UKLF 1979–80; pres Regular Cmmns Bd 1980–83, Col Queen's Lancs Regt 1983–92; Hon Col Manchester and Salford Univ OTC 1985–90; Lord-Lt Highland Region (Dist of Sutherland) 1991–96 (DL 1990), Lord-Lt Area of Sutherland 1996–; *Style*— Maj-Gen David Houston, CBE; ✉ c/o Bank of Scotland, Bonar Bridge, Sutherland IV24 3EB

HOUSTON, Prof Ian Briercliffe; s of Dr Walter Houston, and Nancy, *née* Briercliffe; *b* 11 Sept 1932; *Educ* Baines GS Poulton le Fylde, Univ of Manchester (MB ChB, MD); *m* 12 May 1956, Pamela Beryl, da of Leslie Rushton; 1 s (Andrew Ian b 9 Aug 1960), 2 da (Jacqueline Pamela b 7 Oct 1958, Fiona Elizabeth b 9 July 1963); *Career* Nuffield res fell Albert Einstein Coll of Med NY USA 1965–67, prof of child health Univ of Manchester 1974– (lectr 1963–69, sr lectr 1969–74), hon conslt in paediatrics Royal Manchester Children's Hosp, dean of postgrad med studies N West Region (East); former pres Assoc Of Clinical Profs of Paediatrics, former pres Euro Soc For Paediatric

Nephrology; memb: Br Paediatric Assoc 1968, Euro Soc For Paediatric Nephrology 1967, Assoc Of Clinical Profs and Heads Of Depts Of Paediatrics 1975; FRCP 1974; *Recreations* squash, gardening, walking; *Clubs* Northern Lawn Tennis; *Style*— Prof Ian Houston; ✉ University Department of Postgraduate Medicine and Dentistry, University of Manchester, Gateway House, Piccadilly South, Manchester M60 7LP

HOUSTON, John; OBE (1990); s of Alexander Anderson Houston (d 1947), of Windygates, Fife, Scotland, and Alison Crichton, *née* McKelvie; *b* 1 April 1930; *Educ* Buckhaven HS Fife, Edinburgh Coll of Art (Dip Drawing and Painting, Postgrad Dip, Andrew Grant travelling scholarship), Moray House Teachers Trg Coll (Teachers Trg Cert); *m* 1958, Elizabeth Violet Blackadder, OBE, RA, *qv*, da of Thomas Blackadder; *Career* artist; dep head Sch of Drawing and Painting Edinburgh Coll of Art 1982–89 (teacher 1955–89); memb: SSA, RGI, RSW; RSA 1972; *Works* incl: Dusk (Scot Arts Cncl) 1971, Bathers (Carlsberg Breweries Copenhagen) 1966, Wisconsin Landscape 1969, Dune Sounds 1971, Lake Owen Wisconsin 1970–71, Summer In Fife (private collection Sweden) 1968, Low Tide, North Berwick 1982, Winter Walk 1985, Beach Party 1986–90, A Day By The Sea, Summer 1990; exhibits regularly with: Scot Gallery Edinburgh, Mercury Gallery London, Royal Scot Acad, Royal Acad, RGI; *Awards* incl: Guthrie Award (Royal Scot Acad, 1964), Cargill Prize (RGI, 1965 and 1988), Sir William Gillies Prize (RSW, 1990); *Recreations* golf; *Clubs* Gullane Golf; *Style*— John Houston, Esq, OBE; ✉ 57 Fountainhall Road, Edinburgh EH9 2LH (☎ 0131 667 3687)

HOUSTON, John McLellan; *b* 18 July 1944; *Career* fin dir Kwik-Fit Holdings plc 1988–; formerly dir: Coats Viyella plc, Coats Patons plc, J & P Coats Ltd, Textile Pensions Trust Ltd; FCCA; *Style*— John Houston, Esq; ✉ Kwik-Fit Holdings plc, 17 Corstorphine Rd, Murrayfield, Edinburgh, Lothian EH12 6DD (☎ 0131 337 9200, fax 0131 346 7386)

HOUSTON, Robert Ian; s of Ivan Thomas Houston (d 1985), of Gloucester, and Joy, *née* Meehan (d 1987); *b* 18 Oct 1950; *Educ* Sebright Sch Worcs, Nottingham Trent Univ (BSc); *m* Gillian Duret, da of Frederick John Floyd; 2 s (Ian David b 8 July 1979, Andrew Robert b 6 May 1983), 1 da (Claire Alexandra b 10 March 1981); *Career* chartered surveyor; Richard Ellis 1972–80, chief exec Rowe & Pitman Property Services 1980–84, chm Baring, Houston & Saunders 1984–; chm Governing Body Busbridge County Infant Sch; Liveryman Worshipful Co of Chartered Surveyors; FRICS; *Recreations* rugby, cricket; *Style*— Robert Houston, Esq; ✉ Winkford Lodge, Church Lane, Witley, nr Godalming, Surrey GU8 5PR (☎ 01428 683016); Baring, Houston & Saunders, 9 Devonshire Square, London EC2M 4YL (☎ 0171 621 1433, fax 0171 623 8177)

HOUSTOUN-BOSWALL, Sir (Thomas) Alford; 8 Bt (UK 1836); s of Sir Thomas Houstoun-Boswall, 7 Bt (d 1982), by his 1 w (*see* Houstoun-Boswall, Margaret, Lady); *b* 23 May 1947; *m* 1971, Eliana Michele, da of Dr John Pearse, of New York; 1 s Alexander Alford b 1972), 1 da (Julia Glencora b 1979); *Heir* s, Alexander Alford Houstoun-Boswall b 16 Sept 1972; *Style*— Sir Alford Houstoun-Boswall, Bt; ✉ 18 Rue Basse, Biot 06410, France (☎ 00 33 93 65 7244); 11 East 73rd St, New York City, NY 10021, USA (☎ 212 517 8057); c/o The Harrodian School, Lonsdale Road, London SW13 9QN (☎ 0181 748 6117)

HOVELL-THURLOW-CUMMING-BRUCE, Hon Roualeyn Robert; s and h of 8 Baron Thurlow, KCMG, *qv*; *b* 13 April 1952; *Educ* Milton Abbey; *m* 5 May 1980, Bridget Anne Julia, o da of (Hugh) Bruce Ismay Cheape, TD, of South Lodge, Craignure, Isle of Mull, Argyll; 2 s (Nicholas Edward b 1986, George Patrick Ranelagh b 1990), 2 da (Tessa Iona Bridget b 1987, Lorna Belinda Diana b 1991); *Career* with Jones Lang Wootton chartered surveyors; *Clubs* Pratt's, White's; *Style*— The Hon Roualeyn Hovell-Thurlow-Cumming-Bruce; ✉ 22 Hanover Square, London W1A 2BN (☎ 0171 413 1377, telex 23858)

HOW, Peter Cecil; s of Cecil P How (d 1995, aged 100), of Rugeley, Staffs, and Dora, *née* Marshall (d 1960); *b* 27 June 1931; *Educ* Oundle, Open Univ (BA); *m* 21 Sept 1951, Jane, da of Thomas Erickson (d 1936); 2 s (Neil b 1952, Adam b 1954); *Career* dir Froggatt & Prior Ltd 1955–63; chm: How Group Ltd and assoc cos 1974–86 (dir 1963), How Group plc 1986–, Hansgross Estates plc 1986–, H & V Welfare Ltd 1974–90; pres Genie Climatique International 1986–88 (hon pres 1994–); memb W Midlands Regnl Cncl CBI 1979–85; pres Heating and Ventilating Contractors' Assoc 1975–76; Liveryman Worshipful Co of Fan Makers 1975; *Recreations* travel, theatre, opera, music; *Clubs* East India, City Livery; *Style*— Peter How, Esq; ✉ 11 The Regents, Norfolk Road, Edgbaston, Birmingham B15 3PP (☎ 0121 454 4777); 7412 Mayfair Court, University Park, Florida 34201, USA (☎ 00 1 941 358 9512, fax 00 1 941 358 9402); How Group plc, Intersection House, West Bromwich, W Midlands B70 6RX (☎ 0121 500 5000, fax 0121 500 5159)

HOW, Ronald Mervyn; s of Mervyn Darvell How (d 1973), of Bucks, and Kathleen Dorothy, *née* Honour (d 1990); *b* 24 Dec 1927; *Educ* general schooling; *m* 30 June 1951, Brenda (d 1989), da of Harold Brown (d 1976), of Herts; 1 s (David b 1953), 1 da (Margaret b 1956); *Career* RAF AC1 1946–47; farmer; Br Turkey Fedn: fndr memb, dir 1978–, treas 1984–88; dir Br Poultry Meat Fedn 1978–, Central Region turkey del NFU HQ Poultry Ctee 1992–; Rotary Club: memb 1973–, pres Chesham branch 1981, treas Chesham branch 1983–92; memb Ctee Hawridge Commons Pres Soc 1970–, pres League of Friends Amersham and Chesham Hosps (memb Ctee 1979–, former chm), memb Ctee Chesham Town Cncl Environmental Sub-Gp Ctee 1992–, treas Friends of St Mary's Church 1994–; Goodchild Trophy for Service to Turkey Indust 1987; *Recreations* tennis, computer programming, photography; *Clubs* Chesham Rotary, Amersham Photographic Soc; *Style*— Ronald How, Esq; ✉ Woodlands Cottage, The Vale, Chesham, Bucks HP5 3NT (☎ 01494 782434); Woodlands Farm, The Vale, Chesham, Bucks HP5 3NS (☎ 01494 783737)

HOWARD, *see:* Fitzalan Howard

HOWARD, Hon (Donald) Alexander Euan; s (by 1 m) and h of 4 Baron Strathcona and Mount Royal; *b* 24 June 1961; *Educ* Gordonstoun, London Business Sch (MBA); *m* 6 June 1992, Jane Maree, da of Shaun and Ruth Gibb, of Sydney, Australia; 1 s (Donald Angus Ruairidh b 29 Sept 1994), 1 da (Amelia Alexandra b 4 May 1996); *Career* cmmnd RN 1980–88; N M Rothschild & Sons Ltd 1991–93; Liveryman Worshipful Co of Fishmongers; *Recreations* classic cars, steam boats, sailing, shooting; *Clubs* Fishmongers; *Style*— The Hon D Alex Howard

HOWARD, Anthony John; s of Peter Dunsmore Howard (d 1965, former Capt Eng Rugby Team), of Sudbury, Suffolk, and Doris Emily, *née* Metaxas (former winner Wimbledon Ladies Doubles); *b* 31 Dec 1937; *Educ* Cheam Sch, Eton, Trinity Coll Oxford; *m* 12 Oct 1963, Elisabeth Ann, da of Capt Roddie Casement, OBE, RN (d 1987); 1 s (Tom), 2 da (Katie, Emma); *Career* film researcher, producer, dir and writer for TV; 2000 films and progs for TV incl: Greece - The Hidden War, A Passage to Britain, A Full Life, Dick Barton - Special Agent, Country Ways (13 series), Every Night Something Awful, The Missa Luba, The Cathedrals of Britain, Country Faces, Great House Cookery, Pub People, Land Girls, Michael Barry's Undiscovered Cooks; fndr chief exec Countrywide Films Ltd 1989–; *Books* ten books published on the English countryside; *Recreations* walking, talking, reading, wood clearing; *Style*— Anthony Howard, Esq; ✉ Drove Cottage, Newbridge, nr Cadnam, Southampton, Hants SO40 2NW (☎ 01703 813233); Countrywide Films Ltd, Production Office, TV Centre, Northam, Southampton, Hants S014 0PZ (☎ 01703 230286/712270)

HOWARD, Dr Anthony John; *b* 14 April 1949; *Educ* Surbiton GS for Boys, King's Coll London (AKC, MB BS, MSc), St George's Hosp Med Sch London (Brackenbury prize in surgery); *m*; 2 c; *Career* St George's Hosp London: house physician 1972–73, house surgn 1973, SHO in pathology 1972–74, registrar in med microbiology 1974–76; sr lectr in med microbiology London Hosp Med Coll 1979–81 (lectr 1976–79), conslt in med microbiology Gwynedd Dist Hosp Bangor 1981–93, dir Bangor Public Health Lab 1993–95, chm R&D Ctee and asst med dir Gwynedd Hosps NHS Tst 1994–95, gp dir Public Health Lab Serv Wales 1995–; memb: Welsh Microbiology Standing Specialist Advsy Ctee 1981– (chm 1989–94), Dept of Health Infection Working Gp 1992–94; Assoc of Med Microbiologists: Welsh rep Clinical Servs Sub-ctee 1985–93, memb Educn Sub-ctee 1986–89; Welsh Microbiology Assoc: sec 1984–87, vice pres 1987–90, pres 1990–93; memb Cncl: Hosp Infection Soc 1985–90 (gen sec 1986–89), Br Soc for the Study of Infection 1989–91 (memb Ctee English Branch 1987–90), Br Soc for Antimicrobial Chemotherapy 1992–94 (memb Antimicrobial Susceptibility Testing Working Pty 1994–), RCPath 1994– (Welsh regional rep 1992–94); Gillson scholar in pathology Soc of Apothecaries London 1979, Br Cncl travelling fell Turkey 1993; memb: American Soc for Microbiology, Med Scis Historical Soc, NW Epidemiology Club, Y Gymdeithas Feddygol; contrib various book chapters and author of numerous papers in scientific jls; asst ed Jl of Hosp Infection 1987–93, section ed Current Opinions in Infectious Diseases 1991; FRCPath 1990 (MRCPath 1978); *Recreations* book collecting, history, cricket, music, food and wine; *Style*— Dr Anthony Howard; ✉ Public Health Laboratory Service, University Hospital of Wales, Heath Park, Cardiff CF4 4XW (☎ 01222 744515)

HOWARD, Anthony Michell; s of late Canon Guy Howard, and Janet Rymer Howard; *b* 12 Feb 1934; *Educ* Westminster, Ch Ch Oxford; *m* 1965, Carol Anne Gaynor; *Career* political journalist; called to the Bar Inner Temple 1956; Nat Serv 2 Lt Royal Fus 1956–58; political corr Reynolds News 1958–59, Editorial Staff Manchester Guardian 1959–61 (Harkness fell USA 1960), political corr New Statesman 1961–64, Whitehall corr Sunday Times 1965, Washington corr Observer 1966–69 (political columnist 1971–72), ed The New Statesman 1972–78 (asst ed 1970–72), ed The Listener 1979–81, dep ed The Observer 1981–88, reporter BBC TV 1989–92, Obituaries ed The Times 1993–; presenter: Face the Press (Channel 4) 1982–85, The Editors (Sky) 1989–90; *Books* The Baldwin Age (contrib, 1960), Age of Austerity (contrib, 1963), The Making of the Prime Minister (with Richard West, 1965), The Crossman Diaries (ed, 1979), RAB: The Life of R A Butler (1987), Crossman: The Pursuit of Power (1990); *Clubs* Garrick; *Style*— Anthony Howard, Esq; ✉ 17 Addison Avenue, London W11 4QS (☎ 0171 603 3749); Dinham Lodge, Ludlow, Shropshire SY8 1EH (☎ 01584 878457)

HOWARD, (Thomas) Charles Francis; LVO (1968); s of Brig Thomas Farquharson Ker Howard, DSO (d 1962), of Southampton, and Anne Cuningham, *née* Scott (d 1996); *b* 5 March 1937; *Educ* Winchester, Sandhurst; *m* 16 July 1969, Mary Henrietta, da of Capt Hugh Dixon, DSC, RN (d 1960), of S Devon; 2 da (Jane b 1970, Philippa b 1971); *Career* Queen's Dragoon Gds 1957–68, equerry to HM The Queen 1965–68, ret Hon Maj 1968; trainee in insur indust 1968–73; dir: HA Outhwaite 1973–95, A & B Outhwaite Ltd 1995–; *Recreations* gardening, silviculture, shooting; *Clubs* Army and Navy; *Style*— Charles Howard, Esq, LVO; ✉ Brunton House, Collingbourne Kingston, Marlborough, Wilts SN8 3SE (☎ 01264 850243); A & B Outhwaite Ltd, 40–43 Chancery Lane, London WC2A 1JB (☎ 0171 405 8535, fax 0171 831 8950)

HOWARD, David Howarth Seymour; s and h of Sir (Hamilton) Edward de Coucey Howard, 2 Bt, GBE, *qv*; *b* 29 Dec 1945; *Educ* Radley, Worcester Coll Oxford (MA); *m* 16 June 1968, Valerie Picton, o da of late Derek Weatherly Crosse, of Chase House, Callis Court Rd, Broadstairs; 2 s (Robert Picton Seymour b 1971, James Picton Seymour b 1979), 2 da (Caroline Picton Seymour b 1970, Victoria Picton Seymour b 1975); *Career* Alderman City of London 1986–, Common Councilman City of London 1972–86; councillor London Borough of Sutton 1974–78; Master Worshipful Co of Gardeners 1990–91; memb cncl City Univ 1995–; chm London Gardens Soc 1996–; MSI; *Style*— D H S Howard, Esq; ✉ 25 Luke St, London EC2A 4AR

HOWARD, David John; *b* 1 June 1941; *Educ* Whitgift Sch Croydon; *m* 1969, Anne Westmore; 2 s, 2 da; *Career* civil servant; Exchequer and Audit Dept 1960–69, princ HM Customs and Excise 1969–72, private sec to Chief Sec to Treasy 1972–74; HM Customs & Excise: asst sec 1976–84, dir VAT control 1985–87, dir personnel 1987–90, dir organisation 1990–91; dep dir of savings and princ estab and fin offr Dept for Nat Savings 1991–94; dir excise and central policy HM Customs and Excise 1994–; chm of govrs Coulsdon HS Old Coulsdon Surrey 1993–; *Recreations* vintage films, walking; *Style*— David J Howard, Esq; ✉ Director Excise and Central Policy, HM Customs and Excise, New King's Beam House, 22 Upper Ground, London SE1 9PJ (☎ 0171 865 5019, fax 0171 865 4841)

HOWARD, Prof David Martin; s of Jack Bruere Howard, of Rochester, Kent, and Philis Joan, *née* Probert; *b* 13 April 1956; *Educ* King's Sch Rochester, UCL (BSc(Eng), Clinton prize, PhD); *m* 3 October 1981, Clare, da of Robert Hilton Wake; 1 s (Joseph Leo b 11 March 1993); *Career* trainee offr RN Britannia Royal Naval Coll 1974–78; lectr in experimental phonetics UCL 1979–90; Univ of York: lectr in music technol 1990–93, sr lectr 1993–96, prof 1996–, head Dept of Electronics 1996–; fndr ed Voice 1992–; memb: Br Assoc of Academic Phoneticians 1988–, Br Voice Assoc 1990–, Int Assoc of Forensic Phoneticians 1991–; Ferens Inst of Otolaryngology Prize 1989, Br Aerospace Engrg Design Award 1992, Ken Brodie Award 1993, Thorn EMI Prize 1994; fell Inst of Acoustics 1993 (memb 1990), CEng 1995; *Recreations* organist, keyboard playing, choral direction, choir singing, sailing, model flying (fixed wing), skiing, walking; *Clubs* York Model Flying Assoc, Br Model Flying Assoc; *Style*— Prof David Howard; ✉ Head Department of Electronics, University of York, Heslington, York YO1 5DD (☎ 01904 432405, fax 01904 432335)

HOWARD, David Sanctuary; s of H Howard (d 1979), and Gemma, *née* Sanctuary (d 1966); *b* 22 Jan 1928; *Educ* Stowe; *m* 1, 1952, Elizabeth, da of late Adm Sir Dudley North, GCVO; 1 s (Thomas), 3 da (Philippa, Sophie, Joanna); m 2, 1974, Anna-Maria, da of late Dante Bocci; m 3, 1989, Angela Mary, da of Robin Postlethwaite; *Career* Coldstream Guards 1946–48; co dir 1960–73, dir Heirloom and Howard Ltd 1973–; FSA; *Books* Chinese Armorial Porcelain (1974), China for the West (1978), New York and the China Trade (1984), The Choice of the Private Trader (1994); *Clubs* Oriental; *Style*— David Howard, Esq, FSA; ✉ Manor Farm, West Yatton, Chippenham, Wilts SN14 7EU (☎ 01249 783038, fax 01249 783039)

HOWARD, Dr Deborah Janet; da of Thomas Were Howard, of Loughton, Essex, and Isobel, *née* Brewer (d 1990); *b* 26 Feb 1946; *Educ* Loughton HS for Girls, Newnham Coll Cambridge (MA), Courtauld Inst of Art (MA, PhD); *m* 26 Sept 1975, Prof Malcolm Sim Longair, s of James Longair; 1 s (Mark Howard b 13 Sept 1976), 1 da (Sarah Charlotte b 7 March 1979); *Career* Leverhulme fell in history of art Clare Hall Cambridge 1972–73, lectr in history of art UCL 1973–76, visiting lectr Yale Univ 1977 and 1980, pt/t lectr, sr lectr then reader Dept of Architecture Univ of Edinburgh 1982–91, pt/t lectr Courtauld Inst of Art 1991–92; Univ of Cambridge: librarian to Faculty of Architecture & History of Art 1992–96, fell St John's Coll 1992–, reader in architectural history 1996–; cmmr: Royal Fine Art Cmmn for Scotland 1985–95, Royal Cmmn on Ancient and Historic Monuments of Scotland 1989–; FSA 1984, FSA(Scot) 1991, Hon FRIAS 1996; *Books* Jacopo Sansovino: Architecture & Patronage in Renaissance Venice (1975, 2 edn 1987), The Architectural History of Venice (1980, 2 edn 1987), William Adam (Architectural Heritage I, ed 1990), Scottish Architects Abroad (Architectural Heritage II, ed 1991, winner Glenfiddich Award), Scottish Architecture from the Reformation to the Restoration (1995); *Recreations* music (especially playing and listening to chamber music), hill-walking, skiing, gardening; *Style*— Dr Deborah Howard, FSA; ✉ Faculty of Architecture & History of Art, University of Cambridge, 1 Scroope Terrace, Cambridge CB2 1PX (☎ 01223 332977, fax 01223 332960); St John's College, Cambridge CB2 1TP (☎ 01223 339360)

HOWARD, Hon Edmund Bernard Carlo; CMG (1969), LVO (1961); s of 1 Baron Howard of Penrith, GCB, GCMG, CVO (d 1939); *b* 8 Sept 1909; *Educ* Downside, Newman Sch USA, New Coll Oxford; *m* 1936, Cécile Henriette, da of Charles Geoffroy-Dechaume, of Valmondois, France; 3 s, 1 da (and 1 da decd); *Career* served WWII KRRC (Italy), ret Maj; called to the Bar Middle Temple 1932, sec to tstees and mangrs of Stock Exchange 1937–39; Dip Serv: second sec (info) Rome 1947–51, FO 1951–53, first sec Madrid 1953–57, head of Chancery Bogota 1957–59, FO 1960, consul gen San Marino and consul Florence 1960–61, cnsllr Rome 1961–65, consul gen Genoa 1965–69, ret; Cdr Order of Merit Italy 1973; *Books* Genoa - History and Art in an Old Seaport (1971), Italia - The Art of Living Italian Style (1996); *Recreations* travel, gardening, walking; *Style*— The Hon Edmund Howard, CMG, LVO; ✉ Jerome Cottage, Marlow Common, Bucks SL7 2QR (☎ 01628 482129)

HOWARD, Sir (Hamilton) Edward de Coucey; 2 Bt (UK 1955), of Great Rissington, Co Gloucester; GBE (1971); s of Sir (Harold Walter) Seymour Howard, 1 Bt, Lord Mayor of London 1954 (d 1967); *b* 29 Oct 1915; *Educ* Le Rosey, Radley, Worcester Coll Oxford; *m* 1943, Elizabeth Howarth, da of Maj Percy H Ludlow (d 1968); 2 s (David Howarth Seymour b 1945, John Ludlow Seymour b 1948); *Heir* s, David Howarth Seymour Howard b 29 Dec 1945; *Career* serv WWII Flt Lt RAF (despatches); memb of Stock Exchange London 1946, sr ptnr Charles Stanley and Co (stockbrokers); chm: Eucryl 1946–71, LRC Int Ltd 1971–82; alderman City of London 1963–85, Sheriff City of London 1966, Lord Mayor of London 1971–72, HM Lt City of London 1976; Master Worshipful Co of Gardeners 1961; KStJ 1972; *Recreations* gardening; *Clubs* City Livery, United Wards; *Style*— Sir Edward Howard, Bt, GBE; ✉ Courtlands, Bishops Walk, Shirley Hills, Surrey CR0 5BA (☎ 0181 656 4444); Charles Stanley and Co Ltd, Stockbrokers, 25 Luke St, London EC2A 4AR (☎ 0171 739 8200)

HOWARD, Elizabeth Jane; da of David Liddon Howard (d 1962), and Katharine Margaret Somervell (d 1975); *b* 26 March 1923; *m* 1941 (m dis 1951), Peter Markham Scott (later Sir Peter Scott, CH, CBE, DSC, FRS, d 1989), s of Capt Robert Falcon Scott; 1 da (Nicola); m 2, James Douglas-Henry; m 3, 1965 (m dis 1983), Sir Kingsley William Amis, CBE (d 1995); *Career* novelist, playwright of 14 TV plays; FRSL; *Books* The Beautiful Visit (1950), The Long View (1956), The Sea Change (1959), After Julius (1965), Something in Disguise (1969), Odd Girl Out (1972), Mr Wrong (short stories, 1975), Lovers' Companion (ed, 1978), Getting It Right (1982), The Light Years (1990), Green Shades (1991), Marking Time (1991), Confusion (1993), Casting Off (1995); *Recreations* gardening, cooking, reading, music; *Style*— Miss Elizabeth Jane Howard, FRSL; ✉ c/o Jonathan Clowes, 10 Iron Bridge House, Bridge Approach, London NW1 8BD (☎ 0171 722 7674)

HOWARD, Dr Frances Marianne (Mrs D Howard-Pearce); da of Vincent Joseph Howard, of South Norwood, Surrey, and Dorothy Mary, *née* Newling; *b* 21 Aug 1946; *Educ* Coloma Convent, Royal Free Hosp Sch of Med (MB BS, FRCP, DCH, DRCOG); *m* 5 June 1982, David Ivan, s of Leonard Samuel Pearce, of Weir Quay, Devon; 1 da (Tamar Anne b 1984); *Career* RMO Middx Hosp 1973–74, hon sr registrar Hosp for Sick Children Gt Ormond St 1978–80; Frimley Park Hosp: conslt paediatrician and geneticist 1981–, clinical dir paediatrics Frimley Park Hosp 1992–96; memb Academic Bd BPA 1989–92; Dreamflight Doctor 1987–90; *Books* Catalogue of Unbalanced Translocations in Man (translation, 1984); *Recreations* gardening, hedging and ditching; *Style*— Dr Frances Howard; ✉ Orchard House, Glaziers Lane, Normandy, Guildford, Surrey GU3 2DE (☎ 01483 810972); Frimley Park Hospital Trust, Camberley, Surrey (☎ 01276 692777)

HOWARD, Francis John Adrian; s of Ewen Storrs Howard (d 1979), of Cape Town, S Africa, and Cynthia Beatrice, *née* Wallace; *b* 11 July 1935; *Educ* Michaelhouse Sch SA, Univ of Natal (BCom); *m* 30 Sept 1961, Lynette, da of John Ashford Mader (d 1988), of S Africa; 2 s (Gregory Andrew b 1964 d 1996, Philip Ewen b 1966); *Career* dir: The Diamond Trading Co 1973–75, Beralt Tin and Wolfram Ltd 1977–86, Cape Industries plc 1977–86, Charter Consolidated plc 1978–87, Anderson Strathclyde Ltd 1980–87, Howard Perry Assocs Ltd 1987–, Nestor-BNA plc 1987–, Hawtal Whiting Holdings PLC 1988–95, Consolidated Communications Management Ltd (non-exec chm) 1989–, I Hennig and Co Ltd 1990–, International Training Equipment Conference Ltd (chm) 1991–96; hon chm African Medical and Research Fndn 1990–; *Recreations* gardening, painting, shooting, skiing; *Clubs* Boodle's, Rand (Johannesburg), Johannesburg Country; *Style*— Francis Howard, Esq; ✉ 11 Cadogan Square, London SW1X 0HT (☎ 0171 245 6905, fax 0171 259 6839); Howard Perry Associates Ltd, 1–5 Poland St, London W1V 3DG (☎ 0171 287 2087, fax 0171 734 0772)

HOWARD, Greville Patrick Charles; s of Col Henry Redvers Greville Howard (d 1978), and Patience Nichol (d 1987); *b* 22 April 1941; *Educ* Eton; *m* 1, 4 March 1978 (wife decd); m 2, 20 Nov 1981, Mary Cortlandt, da of Robert Veitch Culverwell, of Chippenham, Wilts; 2 s (Thomas b 1983, Charles b 1986), 1 da (Annabel b 1984); *Career* landowner; Liveryman Worshipful Co of Mercers; *Recreations* hunting; *Style*— Greville P C Howard, Esq; ✉ Castle Rising, Kings Lynn, Norfolk

HOWARD, Ian; s of Harold Geoffrey Howard, of Aberdeen, and Violet, *née* Kelly; *b* 7 Nov 1952; *Educ* Aberdeen GS, Univ of Edinburgh, Edinburgh Coll of Art; *m* 1977, Ruth, da of Henry D'Arcy; 2 da (Francesca b 21 April 1982, Annabelle b 25 Jan 1986); *Career* artist; travelling scholarship Italy 1976, lectr in painting Grays Sch of Art Aberdeen 1977–86, head of painting Duncan of Jordanstone Coll of Art Dundee 1986–95, prof of fine art Univ of Dundee 1995–; William Gillies Bequest Scholarship 1990 (travelled in India and Thailand); over 40 exhibitions incl: Different Realists (Talbot-Rice Art Centre Edinburgh) 1973, Edinburgh Int Film Festival 1976, Recent Acquisitions Scot Arts Cncl Gallery 1979 and 1981, Grease & Water (Scot Arts Cncl touring) 1982, Dunbar & Howard (Glasgow Arts Centre) 1984, Contemporary Scottish Printmakers (Mercury Gallery London) 1984, Sculptors' Drawings (Arts Cncl touring) 1984–85, Ian Howard - New Drawings (Compass Gallery Glasgow) 1985, The Human Touch (Fischer Fine Art London) 1986, Br Cncl British/Malaysian Exhibition Kuala Lumpur 1986, Br Cncl touring exhibition (Bangkok, Singapore, Hong Kong) 1987, Scottish Contemporary Art (Clare Hall Cambridge) 1987, Royal Over-Seas League London 1987, Scottish Art in Yugoslavia (Richard Demarco Gallery touring, Yugoslavia) 1988, London Art Fair 1989, Fine Art Soc (Edinburgh and Glasgow) 1990, Jordanstone Folio Kindred Spirits (Ancrum Gallery, Duncan of Jordanstone) 1990, Royal Scot Acad Summer Exhibition 1990; work in collections incl: Fife Region, Lothian Region and Leicestershire Educ Authorities, Edinburgh Coll of Art, Scot Arts Cncl, Contemporary Arts Soc, Hunterian Gallery Glasgow, Unilever plc, Arts Cncl of GB, ICI plc, Clare Coll Cambridge, City Arts Centre Edinburgh, Aberdeen Hosps Art Project; awards incl: Guthrie award Royal Scot Acad 1978, Scot Arts Cncl award 1979, Scot Arts Cncl major bursary 1984–85, first prize Scot Open Drawing competition 1985, Shell Premier award 1985, prizewinner Tolly-Cobbold Eastern Arts nat competition 1985; Royal Scot Acad: associate 1984–, memb John Kinross Ctee 1989–; dir ALBA magazine 1989–, memb Scot Arts Cncl Awards Panel and Purchasing Ctee 1990–, memb Faculty of Fine Art Br Sch at Rome 1995–; *Style*— Ian Howard, Esq; ✉ Duncan of Jordanstone College of Art, University of Dundee, 12 Perth Road, Dundee (☎ 01382 345227, fax 01382 200983, e-mail i.g.howard@dundee.ac.uk)

HOWARD, Dr James Griffiths; s of Joseph Griffiths Howard (d 1973), and Kathleen Mildred (d 1984); *b* 25 Sept 1927; *Educ* Raynes Park GS, Middx Hosp Med Sch, Univ of London (MB BS, PhD, MD); *m* 14 July 1951, Opal St Clair, da of John Harman Echalaz (d 1947); 1 s (Roger St Clair b 1956 d 1984), 2 da (Flavia Rosamund b 1954, Charmian Isabel b 1958); *Career* reader Depts of Zoology and Surgical Sci Univ of Edinburgh 1958–69; The Wellcome Research Laboratories 1969–86: dir Biomedical Res, head of Biological Res Div and head of Experimental Immunobiology; asst dir The Wellcome Tst 1986–90; FRS 1984; *Recreations* fine arts, music, hillwalking, cooking; *Style*— Dr James Howard, FRS; ✉ Sarnesfield Grange, Sarnesfield, Herefordshire HR4 8RG (☎ 01544 318302)

HOWARD, Jane Alison; da of Eric George Bullough, of Blackpool, Lancs, and Doreen Ruth, *née* Towers, of Thornton Cleveleys, Lancs; *b* 6 Feb 1956; *Educ* Blackpool Collegiate GS, LSE (BScEcon), Leeds Univ (Postgrad Mgmnt Dip); *Career* mgmnt trainee NHS 1978–79, dir Hospitality Servs AMI 1979–80, exec dir (later business devpt dir) The Rowland Co (Saatchi & Saatchi Gp PR Agency) 1982–91, md Leedex Ltd 1992–; won HCITB Travelling Scholarship 1979; memb London Region CBI; MHCIMA, MCFA, MIPR; *Recreations* riding; *Style*— Mrs Jane Howard; ✉ Leedex Ltd, 52–54 Broadwick St, London W1V 1FF (☎ 0171 734 9681, fax 0171 734 4913)

HOWARD, Jane Mary; da of Gilbert Edward Howard, of Yaxley, Suffolk, and Mary Teresa Howard, *née* Slater; *b* 20 Dec 1959; *Educ* Catherine McAuley Upper Sch Doncaster, Girton Coll Cambridge (BA); *m* May 1992, Laurens Jolles, of UNHCR, s of Adriaan Jolles, of Rome; 2 s (Alexander b 16 April 1994, Thomas b 11 March 1996); *Career* journalist: Thomson Regnl Newspapers 1982–84, Evening Gazette Middlesbrough Cleveland; Journalists in Europe fellowship Paris 1985–86, chief sub-ed BBC World Serv 1986–88, Ankara corr for The Guardian and the BBC 1988–91, Belgrade corr BBC World Serv 1991–93, duty ed World Serv 1993–96; memb NUJ 1981–; *Recreations* reading, theatre, TV, swimming, riding; *Style*— Ms Jane Howard; ✉ Tehran (☎ 00 9821 200 6885)

HOWARD, John; s of Henry Vivian Howard, and Florence Elizabeth, *née* Pulley; *b* 11 Feb 1951; *Educ* Strode's Sch Egham Surrey; *m* Angela Margaret; *Career* admitted slr 1979; presenter: You and Yours (Radio 4) 1980–95, Nature (BBC TV) 1988–89, The Leading Edge (Radio 5), An Unfortunate Turn of Events (Radio 4) 1995, presenter BBC World TV 1996–; winner: Soc of Authors/Pye Radio award Best Light Entertainment Programme Radio 1979, RICS Radio award Best Investigative Programme Radio 1983, Argus Consumer Journalist award Radio 1985, Sony award for Best Social Affairs Programme Radio 1989; *Style*— John Howard, Esq; ✉ 28 Royal Crescent, Holland Park, London W11 4SN

HOWARD, (James) Ken; s of Frank Howard (d 1974), of Mousehole, Cornwall, and Elizabeth Crawford, *née* Meikle (d 1987); *b* 26 Dec 1932; *Educ* Kilburn GS, Hornsey Coll of Art, Royal Coll of Art (ARCA); *m* 1, 1961 (m dis 1974), Margaret Ann, da of Philip Popham, of Ickenham, Middx; m 2, 13 Oct 1991, Christa Gaa, *née* Koehler, ARWS (d 1992), formerly wife of Hartmut Gaa; 2 step da; *Career* Nat Serv RM 1953–55; artist; Br Cncl scholarship Florence 1958–59, taught at various London art schs 1959–73, official artist Imperial War Museum NI 1978; painted for Br Army: NI, Germany, Cyprus, Hong Kong, Brunei, Nepal, Belize, Norway, Lebanon; Hon RBA 1988, Hon ROI 1988; NEAC 1962, RWA 1981, RWS 1983, RBSA 1991, RA 1992 (ARA 1983); *Solo Exhibitions* Plymouth Art Centre 1955, John Whibley Gallery 1966–68, New Grafton Gallery 1971–, Hong Kong 1979, Jersey 1980, Nicosia 1982, Delhi 1983, Oscar J Peter Johnson 1986–, Duncalfe Gallery Harrogate 1987–, Sinfield Gallery 1991, 1993 and 1995, Hollis Taggart Inc Washington DC 1993, *Work in Collections* Plymouth Art Gallery, Imperial War Museum, Guildhall Art Gallery, Ulster Museum, Nat Army Museum, Southend Art Gallery, HNC Art Gallery, Sheffield Art Gallery, Bankside Gallery; *Portraits* incl: Gerald Durrell, Gen Sir Martin Farndale; *Commissions* Drapers' Co, Haberdashers' Co, States of Jersey, HQ Br Army of the Rhine, HM Forces in Cyprus, The Stock Exchange, Lloyd's of London, Royal Hosp Chelsea, Banque Paribas; *Books* The War Artists (1986), Art Class (1989), Venice - The Artist's Vision (1990), Visions of Venice (1990), The Paintings of Ken Howard (1992); Inspired by Light (video, 1996); *Style*— Ken Howard, Esq, RA; ✉ 8 South Bolton Gardens, London SW5 0DH (☎ 0171 373 2912, fax 0171 244 6246); St Clements Hall, Paul Lane, Mousehole, Cornwall TR19 6TR (☎ 01736 731596)

HOWARD, Margaret; da of John Bernard Howard (d 1969), and Ellen Corwenna, *née* Roberts; *b* 29 March 1938; *Educ* St Mary's Convent Rhyl, St Teresa's Convent Sunbury-On-Thames, Guildhall Sch of Music and Drama (LGSM), Univ of Indiana USA; *Career* BBC announcer 1966–69, reporter World This Weekend 1971–74, presenter Pick of the Week 1974–91, radio columnist Sunday Express 1991–92; Classic FM: presenter Classic Reports 1992–94, ed and presenter Howard's Week 1994–, presenter Masterclass 1994–; radio critic The Tablet 1991–, columnist The Universe 1991–93, classical CD reviewer Chic Magazine 1995–; female UK Personality of the Year Sony Awards 1984, Sony Radio Awards Roll of Honour 1988, Voice of the Listener Award for Excellence 1991, Radio Personality of the Year Television and Radio Industries Club Awards 1996; memb: LRAM, LGSM; *Books* Margaret Howard's Pick of the Week (1984), Court Jesting (1986); *Recreations* riding, walking Jack Russell terrier, wine tasting; *Style*— Miss Margaret Howard; ✉ 215 Cavendish Rd, London SW12 0BP (☎ 0181 673 7336)

HOWARD, Dr Mary Elizabeth; da of William Joseph Howard (d 1974), and Mary, *née* Breaden (d 1979); *b* 17 April 1953; *Educ* Notre Dame HS Glasgow, Univ of Glasgow (MB ChB); *m* 14 July 1976, John Hilary Higgins, s of John Joseph Higgins, MBE (d 1972); 1 da (Louise Mary Anne b 1985); *Career* sr registrar in histopathology Gtr Glasgow Health Bd 1980–83 (house surgn and house physician 1976–77, registrar 1977–80), conslt histopathologist Law Hosp NHS Tst 1983–; memb: BMA, Assoc of Clinical Pathologists, Mensa; FRCPath 1994 (MRCPath 1982); *Recreations* music, arts and crafts, reading; *Style*— Dr Mary Howard; ✉ Department of Histopathology, Law Hospital, Carluke, Lanarkshire ML8 5ER (☎ 01698 361100)

HOWARD, Rt Hon Michael; PC (1990), QC (1982), MP (C) Folkestone and Hythe (majority 8,910); s of late Bernard Howard, and Hilda Howard; *b* 7 July 1941; *Educ* Llanelli GS, Peterhouse Cambridge; *m* 1975, Sandra Clare, da of Wing Cdr Saville Paul; 1 s, 1 da, 1 step s; *Career* pres Cambridge Union 1962, called to the Bar Inner Temple 1964, chm Bow Group 1970; Parly candidate (C) Liverpool Edge Hill 1966 and 1970, MP (C) Folkestone and Hythe 1983–; memb: Cons Gp for Europe, Euro Movement Exec Ctee 1970–73; PPS to Slr-Gen 1984–85, Parly under-sec of state for Consumer and Corporate Affrs 1985–87, min for Local Govt 1987–88, min for Water and Planning 1988–90, sec of state for Employment 1990–92, sec of state for the Environment 1992–93, Home Sec 1993–; chm Coningsby Club 1972–73; *Recreations* watching sport, reading; *Clubs* Carlton; *Style*— The Rt Hon Michael Howard, QC, MP; ✉ House of Commons, London SW1

HOWARD, Sir Michael Eliot; kt (1986), CBE (1977), MC (1943); s of Geoffrey Eliot Howard (d 1956), of Dorset, and Edith Julia Emma Edinger (d 1977); *b* 29 Nov 1922; *Educ* Wellington, Christ Church Oxford (MA, DLitt); *Career* served Italian Theatre with 2 & 3 Bns Coldstream Gds (Capt) 1943–45; prof of war studies King's Coll London 1963–68, Chichele prof of history of war Oxford 1977–80, pres Int Inst of Strategic Studies, Regius prof of modern history Univ of Oxford 1980–89, prof of history Yale

Univ 1989–93; FRHistS, FBA; *Books* The Franco-Prussian War (1961), Grand Strategy, Vol IV in UK Official History of World War II (1972), The Continental Commitment (1972), War in European History (1976), The Causes of Wars (1983), Strategic Deception in World War II (1990), The Lessons of History (1991); *Recreations* music; *Clubs* Athenaeum, Garrick; *Style*— Sir Michael Howard, CBE, MC; ✉ The Old Farm, Eastbury, Hungerford, Berks RG17 7JN

HOWARD, Michael Newman; QC; s of Henry Ian Howard, and Tilly Celia, *née* Newman; *b* 10 June 1947; *Educ* Clifton Coll, Magdalen Coll Oxford (BA, MA, BCL); *Career* called to the Bar Gray's Inn 1974, bencher 1995; lectr in law LSE 1970–74, in practice at the Bar 1972–, visiting prof of law Univ of Essex 1987–92, panel memb Lloyds Salvage Arbitrators 1988–, recorder of the Crown Ct 1993– (asst recorder 1989–93); *Books* Phipson on Evidence (jt ed, 12 edn 1976, 13 edn 1982, 14 edn 1990), Force Majeure and Frustration of Contract (contrib, 1991, 2 edn 1994), Consensus ad idem: Essays on Contract in Honour of Guenter Treitel (contrib, 1996); *Recreations* books, music, sport; *Clubs* Oxford and Cambridge, RAC; *Style*— M N Howard, Esq, QC; ✉ 4 Essex Court, Temple, London EC4Y 9AJ (☎ 0171 797 7970, fax 0171 353 0998, telex 8812528 ADROIT G)

HOWARD, Michael Stockwin; s of Frank Henry Howard (d 1934), and Florence Mable, *née* Jones (d 1957); *b* 14 Sept 1922; *Educ* Ellesmere Coll, RAM; *Career* post war study with Marcel Dupré, organist and choirmaster Tewkesbury Abbey 1943–44, dir The Renaissance Singers 1944–64, organist and magister choristarum Ely Cathedral 1953–59, dir Cantores in Ecclesia 1964–83, asst BBC music presentation 1968–78, organist and rector chori St Michael's Benedictine Abbey Farnborough 1984–86; int tours as recitalist and conductor Europe and Scandinavia; Prix Musical de Radio Brno 1967, Charpentier Academie Nationale Prix du Disque 1975; reg broadcasts BBC 1945– (incl BBC promenade concerts and other princ festivals); recordings incl work for: HMV, Argo, Oiseau Lyre, Time Life, Wealden and Herald; published various vocal and organ compositions; contribs incl: The Musical Times, The Monthly Musical Record, EMG Jl, The Organists' Review; *Books* The Private Inferno (autobiography, 1975), A Tribute to Aristide Cavaillé-Coll (1986); *Recreations* steam railway traction and village fairgrounds; *Style*— Michael Howard, Esq; ✉ 9 Wallis Field, Groombridge, Sussex TN3 9SE

HOWARD, Dr Norman; s of Philip Howard (d 1987), and Deborah Howard (d 1952); *b* 25 Nov 1926; *Educ* Haberdashers' Aske's, Wadham Coll Oxford (MA, DM), UCH London; *m* 26 June 1955, Anita, da of H Selby; 2 s (Anthony b 1956, David b 1959); *Career* registrar and sr registrar Royal Marsden Hosp 1956–63; conslt radiotherapy and oncology: Charing Cross Hosp 1963–91 (dir 1980–91), Wembley Hosp 1965–91 (hon conslt 1991–), Royal Marsden Hosp 1970–; conslt in clinical oncology Cromwell Hosp 1982–; chm: Royal Coll of Radiologists Research Appeal 1995–; Final Fellowship Bd RCR 1986–91, Gunnar Nilsson Cancer Res Tst Fund, Med Staff Ctee Charing Cross Hosp 1974–79; memb Cncl Medical Insurance Agency Ltd; DMRT 1956, FFR 1958, FRCR 1975; memb: BMA, RSM, BIR; Commendatore Order of Merit Republic of Italy 1976; *Books* Mediastinal Obstruction in Lung Cancer (1967); author of numerous chapters and papers on cancer; *Recreations* reading, theatre; *Style*— Dr Norman Howard; ✉ 5A Clarendon Rd, London W11 4JA (☎ 0171 229 6704); Old Malthouse Cottage, Shurlock Row, Reading RG10 0PL (☎ 0118 934 3368); Cromwell Hospital, Cromwell Rd, London SW5 (☎ 0171 460 5626/7, fax 0171 460 5622); Princess Margaret Hospital, Osborne Road, Windsor, Berks SL4 3SJ (☎ 01753 868292)

HOWARD, Peter Milner; s of Thomas Roland Howard (d 1984), of Filey, Yorkshire, and Margaret Annie, *née* Potter (d 1974); *b* 27 June 1937; *Educ* Dialstone Lane Secdy Mod, Woodseats Co Sheffield, Sheffield Coll of Commerce and Technol, Nat Cncl for Trg of Journalists (proficiency cert); *m* 3 April 1965, Janet, da of Kenneth William Crownshaw; 1 s (Andrew b 6 Sept 1966), 1 da (Fiona Catherine b 15 April 1969); *Career* Nat Serv Army 1958–60; The Star Sheffield: copy boy 1952–54, trainee reporter 1954–56, sports reporter/sub-ed 1956–58 and 1960–73 (mainly covering Sheffield United FC, also Euro and int football), sports ed 1973–75; MOD: information offr 1975–83 (with RN, RAF and Army, served in FDR and Falkland Is), ed Soldier (Army magazine) 1983–85; Jane's Defence Weekly: features ed 1985–87, managing ed 1987–89, ed 1989–95; managing ed Military Gp Jane's Information Group Ltd 1995–; *Recreations* golf, walking, military history, military music; *Clubs* Hindhead British Legion, Petersfield Golf; *Style*— Peter Howard, Esq; ✉ New Product Development, Jane's Information Group, Sentinel House, 163 Brighton Road, Coulsdon, Surrey CR5 2NH (☎ 0181 700 3793, 3830, fax 0181 700 3788)

HOWARD, Hon Philip Esme; s and h of 2 Baron Howard of Penrith, *qv*; *b* 1 May 1945; *Educ* Ampleforth, Ch Ch Oxford; *m* 1969, Sarah, da of late Barclay Walker; 2 s (Thomas Philip b 1974, Michael Barclay b 1984), 2 da (Natasha Mary b 1970, Laura Isabella b 1976); *Style*— The Hon Philip Howard; ✉ 45 Erpingham Rd, London SW15

HOWARD, Philip Ewen; s of Francis John Adrian Howard, of London, and Lynnette, *née* Maider; *b* 5 June 1966; *Educ* Bradfield Coll Berks, Kent Univ at Canterbury (BSc); *m* 15 Dec 1990, Jennifer Elizabeth, da of Robert Collier; 1 da (Amelia May b 7 July 1995); *Career* trg/apprenticeship: with Roux Restaurants Ltd 1988–89, under Marco Pierre White Harvey's Restaurant 1989–90, under Simon Hopkinson Bibendum 1990–91; head chef/jt patron The Square 1991–; Michelin star 1994; *Style*— Philip Howard, Esq; ✉ 58 Chaldon Road, London SW6 7NJ; The Square, 6–10 Bruton Street, Mayfair, London W1X 7AG (☎ 0171 495 7100, fax 0171 495 7500)

HOWARD, Philip Nicholas Charles; s of Peter Dunsmore Howard (d 1965), and Doris Emily Metaxa; *b* 2 Nov 1933; *Educ* Eton, Trinity Coll Oxford (MA); *m* 1959, Myrtle Janet Mary, da of Sir Reginald Houldsworth, *qv*; 2 s, 1 da; *Career* Nat Serv Lt Black Watch; newspaper reporter, columnist and author; Glasgow Herald 1959–64, columnist, ldr writer and composer of Word Watching The Times 1990– (joined 1964, literary ed 1978–90), London ed Verbatim 1977–; fndr patron Friends of the Classics; Liveryman Worshipful Co of Wheelwrights; FRSL; *Books* The Black Watch (1968), The Royal Palaces (1970), London's River (1975), New Words for Old (1977), The British Monarchy (1977), Weasel Words (1978), Words Fail Me (1980), A Word in Your Ear (1983), The State of the Language (1984), We Thundered Out, 200 Years of The Times 1785–1985 (1985), Winged Words (1988), Word-Watching (1988), A Word in Time (1990), The Times Bedside Book (ed, 1990 and 1992); *Recreations* reading, walking, talking; *Style*— Philip Howard, Esq; ✉ Flat 1, 47 Ladbroke Grove, London W11 3AR (☎ 0171 727 1077)

HOWARD, Ronald John Frederick; s of Frederick Perceval Howard (d 1947), and Lydia Mary Howard (d 1976); *b* 1 Sept 1921; *Educ* Whitgift Middle Sch; *m* 1, 1944, (Sylvia) Betty (d 1974); m 2, 25 Sept 1976 (m dis 1991), (Ann) Veronica, da of Ward Turner Nicholson (d 1967); *Career* Metal Industries Ltd 1947–67 (dir 1959–67), dep gen mangr AEI/GEC Controls Group 1967–68; chief exec dir: Plantation Holdings Ltd 1969–78, Phicom plc 1978–81 (chm 1981–84); non-exec dir: Graseby plc (formerly Cambridge Electronic Industries plc) 1980–92, Fothergill and Harvey plc 1973–87; dir: Cynamanid-Fothergill Ltd 1981–87, Infrared Associates Incorporated 1985–88; fndr bd dir and dep chm Chiltern Radio plc 1980–95; chm: The Rank Phicom Video Group Ltd 1981–84, Technology Management Services Ltd 1981–, Baird UK Holdings Ltd 1982–89, Silver Chalice Productions International Ltd (Bermuda) and Silver Chalice Productions Ltd 1983–86, Reflex Holdings Ltd 1986–88, Commtel Consumer Electronics plc 1987–88, Synoptics Ltd 1988–, Universal Machine Intelligence Group Ltd 1989–90, SyFA Data Systems plc 1990–93, Solix Systems Ltd 1993–94; dir: Kratos Group plc (formerly Spectros International plc) 1984– (vice chm 1984–91), Myriad Solutions Ltd 1995–; memb Ct of Assts Worshipful Co of Scientific Instrument Makers (Master 1987); CIMgt 1984, FInstM 1986; *Recreations* sailing, photography; *Clubs* City of London, Savile, Royal Thames Yacht; *Style*— Ronald Howard, Esq; ✉ Springwood House, Ickwell Green, Beds SG18 9EE (☎ 01767 627348, fax 01767 627647); 5 Ordnance Mews, St Johns Wood, London NW8 6PF (☎ 0171 586 8693); Technology Management Services Ltd, PO Box 1775, London NW8 6PQ (☎ 0171 722 2521, fax 0171 483 0396, car 0831 178861)

HOWARD, Hon Simon Bartholomew Geoffrey; 3 s of Baron Howard of Henderskelfe (Life Peer; d 1984); *b* 26 Jan 1956; *Educ* Eton, RAC Cirencester, Study Centre for Fine and Decorative Arts; *m* 1983, Annette Marie, Countess Compton, er da of Charles Antony Russell Smallwood, and formerly 2 w (m dis 1977), of Earl Compton (now 7 Marquess of Northampton); *Career* chm of estate co 1984–; landowner (10,000 acres); chm Yorkshire Regnl HHA 1986–; High Sheriff North Yorks 1995–96; *Recreations* photography, wine, country sports; *Style*— The Hon Simon Howard; ✉ Castle Howard, York YO6 7DA (☎ 01653 648444)

HOWARD, Timothy Charles Maxwell (Tim); s of Edward Maxwell Howard (d 1970), and Eleanor Monica Newsum; *b* 29 July 1947; *Educ* Uppingham, Univ of Dundee (LLB), Coll of Law; *m* 1, 1970 (m dis 1993), Elizabeth Marion; 3 s (Andrew Oliver Maxwell b 30 April 1976, Edward William b 25 May 1978, Thomas Timothy b 26 May 1982); m 2, 1994, Gillian Lesley; *Career* Norton Rose: joined 1970, asst slr 1973–78, ptnr 1978–, recruitment ptnr 1988–90, memb Mgmnt Ctee 1988–91, sr conslt Norton Rose Consultants OE Greece 1995–; memb Editorial Bd: European Transport Law, Charterparty International, Maritime Focus, Jl of Maritime Law and Commerce; Liveryman City of London Slrs Co 1978; memb: Law Soc 1970, Baltic Exchange London, Maritime Arbitrators Assoc 1978; *Recreations* theatre, golf, DIY, travel; *Style*— Tim Howard, Esq; ✉ Norton Rose, Kempson House, Camomile Street, London EC3A 7AN (☎ 0171 283 6000, fax 0171 283 6500); Norton Rose Consultants OE, 126 Kolokotroni Street, 185 35 Piraeus, Greece (☎ 00 301 428 0202, fax 00 301 428 2427)

HOWARD, Wilfred Patterson; *b* 13 Sept 1922; *Educ* City of London Sch, Exeter Coll Oxford (MA); *m* 1, Juliette Ann, *née* Leathart (d 1991); m 2, 1993, Valerie Stirling; *Career* press offr Bakelite Ltd 1949–51, dep to Chief Press Offr GEC Ltd 1951–55, publicity mangr Ferodo Ltd 1956–60, gp PR advsr Turner & Newall Ltd 1971–82 (PRO 1961–70), PR conslt 1982–; pres IPR 1974–75 (pres's award 1971); memb CAM Soc 1972; FIPR 1969 (MIPR 1960); *Books* Practice of Public Relations (ed); *Recreations* walking, music, theatre; *Clubs* United Oxford and Cambridge Univ; *Style*— Wilfred Howard, Esq; ✉ 64 Park Road, Buxton, Derbys SK17 6SN (☎ 01298 24697)

HOWARD DE WALDEN, 9 Baron (E 1597); John Osmael Scott-Ellis; TD; also Baron Seaford (UK 1826); s of 8 Baron Howard de Walden (d 1946, gs of 1 Baron Seaford, whose w Elizabeth was gda of 4 Earl of Bristol (Lord Bristol's f's mother was maternal gda of 3 Earl of Suffolk, who also held the Barony of Howard de Walden), and Margherita Van Raalte, CBE, da of Charles Van Raalte, JP; *b* 27 Nov 1912; *Educ* Eton, Magdalene Coll Cambridge; *m* 1, 1934, Countess Irene Harrach (d 1975), yst da of Count Hans Albrecht Harrach, of Munich (of a Mediatised Sovereign House of the Holy Roman Empire; the title of Baron Harrach was conferred by Ferdinand I 1552 (and under the Hungarian crown 1563) and the title of Count Harrach was cr by Emperor Ferdinand II 1627); 4 da; m 2, 1978, Gillian Margaret, da of Cyril Francis Stuart Buckley and formerly w of 17 Viscount Mountgarret; *Heir* all 4 da as co-heiresses: Hon Mrs Czernin, Hon Mrs Buchan of Auchmacoy, Hon Mrs White, Hon Mrs Acloque; *Career* Maj Westminster Dragoons (TA); *Clubs* Jockey (sr steward 1957, 1964, 1976), Turf, Whites; *Style*— The Rt Hon the Lord Howard de Walden, TD; ✉ Avington Manor, Hungerford, Berks (☎ 01488 658229); Flat K, 90 Eaton Sq, London SW1 (☎ 0171 235 7127)

HOWARD-DOBSON, Gen Sir Patrick John; GCB (1979, KCB 1974, CB 1973); s of Canon Howard Dobson; *b* 12 Aug 1921; *Educ* King's Coll Choir Sch, Framlingham Coll; *m* 1946, Barbara Mills; 2 s, 1 da; *Career* joined 7 QOH 1941, served Egypt, Burma, ME, Italy, Germany, CO QOH 1963–65, CO 20 Armd Bde 1965–67, COS Far East Cmd 1969–71, Cmdt Staff Coll Camberley 1972–74, MS 1974–76, QMG 1977–79, Vice CDS (personnel and logistics) 1979–81, ret; ADC Gen to HM The Queen 1978–81, Col Cmdt Army Catering Corps 1976–82; Nat Pres Royal Br Legion 1981–87; Liveryman Worshipful Co of Cooks; *Recreations* sailing, golf; *Clubs* Royal Cruising, Senior Golfers Soc; *Style*— Gen Sir Patrick Howard-Dobson, GCB; ✉ 1 Drury Park, Snape, Saxmundham, Suffolk IP17 1TA

HOWARD-LAWSON, Sir John Philip; 6 Bt (UK 1841), of Brough Hall, Yorkshire; s of Sir William Howard Lawson, 5 Bt (d 1990); assumed by Royal Licence surname and arms of Howard 1962; *b* 6 June 1934; *m* 1960, Jean Veronica, da of late Col John Evelyn Marsh, DSO, OBE; 2 s (Philip William b 1961, Thomas John b 1963), 1 da (Julia Frances b 1964); *Heir* s, Philip William Howard b 28 June 1961; *Style*— Sir John Howard-Lawson, Bt; ✉ Hunter Hall, Great Salkeld, Penrith, Cumbria CA11 9NA

HOWARD OF PENRITH, 2 Baron (UK 1930); Francis Philip Howard; DL (Glos 1960); 2 s of 1 Baron Howard of Penrith, GCB, GCMG, CVO (d 1939, 4 s of Henry Howard, n of 12 Duke of Norfolk), by his w Lady Isabella Giustiniani-Bandini, da of 8 Earl of Newburgh, Duca di Mondragone and Prince Giustiniani Bandini; *b* 5 Oct 1905; *Educ* Downside, Trinity Coll Cambridge; *m* 1 July 1944, Anne, da of John Beaumont Hotham (fifth in descent from Sir Beaumont Hotham, 7 Bt and f of 8, 9, 11 & 12 Bts, the last two being also 1 & 2 Barons Hotham); 4 s; *Heir* s, Hon Philip Howard, *qv*; *Career* serv WWII, Capt RA (wounded); called to the Bar Middle Temple 1931; *Style*— The Rt Hon the Lord Howard of Penrith; ✉ Dean Farm, Coln St Aldwyns, Glos

HOWARD-WILLIAMS, Peter; *b* 13 Nov 1947; *m* 29 May 1971, Sheilagh Elizabeth, *née* Scandrett; 2 s (Edward Alexander b 2 April 1973, Adam Henry b 28 May 1979); *Career* Adamsez Ltd 1966–67, Uddeholm Ltd 1967–69, Thomson Publications 1969–73, md Rank Screen Advertising 1990–92 (joined as sales exec 1974), md Pearl and Dean 1993–, DG Distel (Spanish cinema advtg co) 1996–; chm Publicity Club of London 1995–97; memb: Variety Club of GB, BAFTA, Cinema Advtg Assoc; MIAA, MInstD, MCIM; *Recreations* cinema, rugby, military history; *Clubs* Solus, Swigs; *Style*— Peter Howard-Williams, Esq; ✉ Pearl and Dean, Woolverstone House, 61–62 Berners Street, London W1P 3AE (☎ 0171 636 5252, fax 0171 637 3191)

HOWARTH, Alan Thomas; CBE (1982), MP (C until 1995 whereafter Lab) Stratford-on-Avon (majority 22,892); *b* 11 June 1944; *Educ* Rugby, King's Coll Cambridge; *m* 1967, Gillian Martha, da of Arthur Chance, of Dublin; 2 s, 2 da; *Career* former head Chm's Office CCO (private sec to Rt Hon William Whitelaw and Rt Hon Lord Thorneycroft as Pty Chm), dir Cons Res Dept 1979–81, vice chm Cons Pty Orgn 1980–81, MP Stratford-on-Avon 1983– (resigned Cons Pty 1995, memb Lab Pty 1995–), PPS to Dr Rhodes Boyson 1985–87, asst Govt whip 1987, a Lord Cmmr of the Treasy (Govt whip) 1988, Parly under sec of state Dept of Educn and Sci June 1989–92, memb Nat Heritage Select Ctee 1992–93, memb Social Security Select Ctee 1995–; *Books* Changing Charity (jtly, 1984), Monty At Close Quarters (1985), Save Our Schools (1987), Arts: The Way Ahead, Cities of Pride (jtly, 1994); *Recreations* books, arts, running; *Style*— Alan Howarth, Esq, CBE, MP; ✉ House of Commons, London SW1A 0AA

HOWARTH, Elgar; s of Oliver Howarth (d 1976), and Emma, *née* Wall (d 1979); *b* 4 Nov 1935; *Educ* Eccles GS Manchester, Univ of Manchester (BMus), Royal Manchester Coll of Music; *m* 22 May 1958, Mary Bridget, da of John Francis Neary (d 1953); 1 s (Patrick b 1962), 2 da (Theresa b 1960, Maria b 1963); *Career* trumpeter and conductor; trumpeter: Royal Opera House Orch 1958–63, Royal Philharmonic Orch 1963–70,

London Sinfonietta and Nash Ensemble 1968–74, Philip Jones Brass Ensemble 1965–75; freelance conductor 1969–, princ guest conductor Opera North 1985–90; musical advs to Grimethorpe Colliery Band 1972–; various compositions and arrangements published by Novello, Chester and Rosehill; Hon DUniv Central England Birmingham Univ Conservatoire of Music 1993, Hon DMus Keele Univ 1995; fell Royal Manchester Coll of Music, Hon FRAM 1990, hon fell UC Salford 1992, FRNCM 1994; *Books* What a Performance (jtly with son Patrick Howarth); *Recreations* cycling; *Style—* Elgar Howarth, Esq; ✉ c/o Allied Artists, 42 Montpelier Square, London SW7 1JZ (☎ 0171 589 6243, fax 0171 581 5269)

HOWARTH, George; MP (Lab) Knowsley North (majority 22,403); *Career* MP (Lab) Knowsley N 1986–; *Style—* George Howarth, Esq, MP; ✉ House of Commons, London SW1A 0AA (☎ 0171 219 3000)

HOWARTH, (James) Gerald Douglas; s of late James Howarth, of Berks, and Mary Howarth; *b* 12 Sept 1947; *Educ* Bloxham Sch Banbury, Univ of Southampton; *m* 1973, Elizabeth; 2 s, 1 da; *Career* gen sec Soc for Individual Freedom 1969–71, Bank of America International 1971–76, European Arab Bank 1976–81, Standard Chartered Bank plc 1981–83 (loan syndication mangr); MP (C) Cannock and Burntwood 1983–92, prospective Cons Parly candidate for Aldershot; PPS to: Michael Spicer at the Dept of Energy 1987–90, Sir George Young at the DOE 1990–91, Rt Hon Margaret Thatcher 1991–92; hon sec Cons Parly Aviation Ctee 1983–87; jt md Taskforce Communications Ltd 1993–95, currently independent consIt in public affrs; non-exec dir Military and Aerospace Museums (Aldershot) Tst; cncllr London Borough of Hounslow 1982–83; fell Indust and Parly Tst; *Publications* No Turning Back (1985) and other publications of the No Turning Back Group; *Recreations* flying (Britannia Airways Parly Pilot of the Year 1988), walking, DIY; *Style—* Gerald Howarth, Esq; ✉ 35 Grantham Road, Chiswick, London W4 (☎ and fax 0181 995 6386); 37 Southampton Street, Farnborough, Hants (☎ 01252 518078)

HOWARTH, Prof (Charles) Ian; s of Charles William Howarth (d 1972), of Jersey, and Violet, *née* Moore (d 1982); *b* 12 Nov 1928; *Educ* Manchester GS, Balliol Coll Oxford (MA, DPhil); *m* 11 July 1951, (Sonia) Patricia (d 1981), da of William Young (d 1964), of Isle of Man; 3 s (Bill b 1954, James b 1956, Robert b 1972), 1 da (Kitty b 1958); *Career* pilot offr RAF Inst of Aviation Med 1954–56; research fell Miny of Aviation Univ of Oxford 1956–58, lectr Univ of Hull 1958–64, fell in psychiatry Stanford Univ Med Sch 1961–62; Univ of Nottingham: prof of psychology and head of dept 1964–94 (emeritus prof 1994–), dir Accident Research Unit and Blind Mobility Research Unit 1970–94, dir Inst Applied Cognitive Sci 1986–; pres Br Psychological Soc 1984–85; advsr Higher Educn Quality Cncl 1995–; at various times chm or memb of research ctees and working parties: MRC, SERC, ESRC, MOD, DHSS; FBPsS 1987, CPsychol 1987; *Books* Structure of Psychology (with W E C Gillham, 1981), Studies of Selection Validation in British Industry (with C B T Cox, J Watts and Lazzerini, 1981), Teaching and Talking with Deaf Children (with D Wood, H Wood, A Griffiths, 1986); *Recreations* walking, reading, conversation; *Style—* Prof Ian Howarth; ✉ Department of Psychology, University of Nottingham, University Park, Nottingham NG7 2RD (☎ 0115 951 5390)

HOWARTH, His Hon Judge; Nigel John Graham; s of Vernon Howarth (d 1960), of Sale, Cheshire, and Irene, *née* Lomas (d 1962); *b* 12 Dec 1936; *Educ* Manchester GS, Univ of Manchester (LLB, LLM); *m* 9 June 1962, Janice Mary, da of Francis Harry Hooper; 1 da (Rosamond Irene b 19 June 1963), 2 s (Charles Vernon b 12 Oct 1965, Laurence Francis b 19 Jan 1973); *Career* called to the Bar Gray's Inn 1960 (Macaskie scholar 1960, Atkin scholar 1962), in practice Chancery Bar Manchester 1961–92, recorder of the Crown Court 1989–92 (asst recorder 1983–89), circuit judge (Northern Circuit) 1992–; chm Northern Chancery Bar Assoc 1990–92, former pres Inc Law Library Soc Manchester, actg deemster Isle of Man 1985 and 1989, vice pres Disabled Living; *Recreations* music, theatre, fell walking, keen supporter Altrincham FC; *Clubs* Northern Counties (Newcastle-upon-Tyne); *Style—* His Hon Judge Howarth; ✉ c/o Circuit Administrator, Northern Circuit Office, 15 Quay Street, Manchester M60 9FD

HOWAT, John Michael Taylor; s of Henry Taylor Howat, CBE, of Bramhall, Cheshire, and Rosaline, *née* Green; *b* 18 April 1945; *Educ* Manchester Warehousemen and Clerks Orphan Sch Cheadle Hulme, Victoria Univ of Manchester (MB ChB, MD); *m* 16 July 1988, Dr Trudie Elizabeth Roberts, da of John Roberts, of Millbrook, Stalybridge; 2 da (Fiona Katherine b 17 Oct 1989, Alexandra Helen b 19 June 1992); *Career* consIt surgn N Manchester gp of hosps 1982–, clinical dir of surgery N Manchester Gen Hosp; FRCS 1973; *Recreations* industrial archaeology, photography, clock restoration; *Style—* John Howat, Esq; ✉ Department of Surgery, North Manchester General Hospital, Delauneys Rd, Manchester M8 6RB (☎ 0161 795 4567 ext 2608)

HOWATCH, Susan; da of George Stanford Sturt (d 1944), and Ann, *née* Watney; *b* 14 July 1940; *Educ* Sutton HS GPDST, King's Coll London (LLB); *m* 1964 (sep), Joseph Howatch; 1 da (Antonia b 1970); *Career* author; memb: Soc of Authors, PEN, C of E; *Books* The Dark Shore (1965), The Waiting Sands (1966), Call in the Night (1967), The Shrouded Walls (1968), April's Grave (1969), The Devil on Lammas Night (1970), Penmarric (1971), Cashelmara (1974), The Rich are Different (1977), Sins of the Fathers (1980), The Wheel of Fortune (1984); series on C of E in 20th Century: Glittering Images (1987), Glamorous Powers (1988), Ultimate Prizes (1989), Scandalous Risks (1991), Mystical Paths (1992), Absolute Truths (1994); *Recreations* reading theology; *Clubs* Royal Over-Seas League; *Style—* Mrs Susan Howatch; ✉ c/o Brian Stone, Aitken & Stone, 29 Fernshaw Rd, London SW10 0TG (☎ 0171 351 7561, fax 0171 376 3594)

HOWDEN, Timothy Simon (Tim); s of Phillip Alexander Howden (d 1970), and Irene Maud, *née* Thomas (d 1985); *b* 2 April 1937; *Educ* Tonbridge; *m* 20 Sept 1958 (m dis), Penelope Mary, *née* Wilmott; 2 s (Charles b 6 April 1959, Dominic b 12 Oct 1965), 1 da (Joanna b 4 April 1961); *Career* Nat Serv 2 Lt RA 1955–57; Reckitt and Colman: sales mangr Industl Floor Care UK 1959–62, gen mangr Industl Floor Care France 1962–64, mktg mangr then dep md Germany 1964–70, dir Euro Div 1970–73; Ranks Hovis McDougall plc: dir Cereals Div 1973–75, md RHM Foods 1975–81, chm Bakery Div 1981–85, gp planning dir 1985–86, dep md 1987–89, md 1989–92; gp chief exec Europe Albert Fisher Group plc 1992–; non-exec dir: Scholl plc 1994–, Saltire plc 1996–; *Recreations* tennis, skiing, diving; *Clubs* Annabel's, Naval and Military; *Style—* Tim Howden, Esq; ✉ Albert Fisher Group plc, C Sefton Park, Stoke Poges, Bucks SL2 4HS (☎ 01753 677877, fax 01753 664011); home (☎ 01628 484121, fax 01628 478838)

HOWE, Prof Christopher Barry; s of Charles Roderick Howe, and Patricia, *née* Creeden; *b* 3 Nov 1937; *Educ* William Ellis Sch Highgate London, St Catharine's Coll Cambridge (MA), Univ of London (PhD); *m* 2 Dec 1967, Patricia Anne, da of L G Giles; 1 s (Roderick Giles b 1972), 1 da (Emma Claire (Mrs Dominic Soares) b 1968); *Career* Econ Directorate Fedn Br Industs 1961–63, res fell and lectr SOAS, reader in the economics of Asia Univ of London 1972– (prof 1979–), head Contemporary China Inst 1972–78; memb: Hong Kong Univ and Poly Grants Ctee 1974–93, UGC 1979–84, Hong Kong RGC 1991–; *Books* Employment and Economic Growth in Urban China (1971), Wage Patterns and Wage Policies in Modern China (1973), China's Economy: A Basic Guide (1978), Shanghai (1980), Foundations of the Chinese Planned Economy (1989), The Origins of Japanese Trade Supremacy (1995); *Recreations* walking, swimming, cycling, antiquarian books, France, music, photography; *Style—* Prof Christopher Howe; ✉ School of Oriental & African Studies, Thornaugh St, Russell Sq, London WC14 0XG (☎ 0171 637 2388)

HOWE, Prof Daniel Walker; s of Maurice Langdon Howe (d 1945), and Lucie, *née* Walker; *b* 10 Jan 1937; *Educ* East HS Denver, Harvard Univ (Phi Beta Kappa), Magdalen Coll Oxford (MA), Univ of California at Berkeley (PhD); *m* 3 Sept 1961, Sandra Fay, da of Gaylord David Shumway; 1 da (Rebecca b 1964), 2 s (Christopher Shumway b 1967, Stephen Walker b 1971); *Career* Lt US Army 1959–60; Yale Univ: instr 1966–68, asst prof 1968–72, assoc prof 1972–73; Univ of California at Los Angeles: assoc prof 1973–77, prof 1977–92, chm Dept of History 1983–87; Harmsworth prof of American history and fell Queen's Coll Univ of Oxford 1989–90, Rhodes prof of American history and fell St Catherine's Coll 1992–; fell: Charles Warren Center for Studies in American History Harvard Univ 1970–71, Nat Endowment for the Humanities 1975–76, John Simon Guggenheim Meml Fndn 1984–85; res fell Henry E Huntington Library San Marino 1991–92 and 1994–; memb: American Historical Assoc, Inst of Early American History and Culture, Br Assoc for American Studies, Soc of American Historians; The Unitarian Conscience (1970, 2 edn 1988), Victorian America (1976), The Political Culture of the American Whigs (1980); *Recreations* music; *Style—* Prof Daniel Howe; ✉ St Catherine's College, Oxford OX1 3UJ (☎ 01865 271700, fax 01865 271768); 3814 Cody Road, Sherman Oaks, California, 91403 USA

HOWE, Prof Denis; s of Alfred Howe (d 1979), of Chesham, Watford and Bedford, and Alice, *née* Tomkins (d 1985); *b* 3 Sept 1927; *Educ* Watford GS, Southall Tech Coll (Hele Shaw prize), Coll of Aeronautics (Dip, PhD), MIT (SM); *m* 29 Dec 1954, Audrey Marion (d 1980), da of Joseph Dawson Wilkinson (d 1977), of Rickmansworth and Avon; 2 s (Lawrence John b 1956, Adrian James b 1959), 1 da (Elaine Joy b 1961), 2 step da (Penelope Ann b 1966, Denise b 1969); *Career* tech advsr to Project Office Fairey Aviation Co Ltd 1952–54, Coll of Aeronautics Cranfield 1954–72 (lectr, sr lectr, reader); Cranfield Inst of Technol: prof of aircraft design 1972–92, dir of aircraft projects 1977–92, head Coll of Aeronautics 1986–90, dean of engrg 1988–91; currently aircraft design consIt; FRAeS 1967, FIMechE 1970; *Recreations* gardening, church administration; *Style—* Prof Denis Howe; ✉ 57 Brecon Way, Bedford MK41 8DE (☎ 01234 356747); College of Aeronautics, Cranfield University, Bedford MK43 0AL (☎ 01234 752741, fax 01234 751550)

HOWE, Eric James; CBE (1990); s of Albert Henry Howe, and Florence Beatrice, *née* Hale; *b* 4 Oct 1931; *Educ* Stretford GS, Univ of Liverpool (BA); *m* 1967, Patricia Enid, *née* Schollick; 2 da; *Career* NCB 1954–59, Br Cotton Indust Res Assoc 1959–61, English Electric Computer Co 1961–66, memb Bd of Dirs Nat Computing Centre 1976–84 (joined 1966, dep dir 1975–84), Data Protection Registrar (responsible for implementing the Provisions of the Data Protection Act 1984) 1984–94; chm: Nat Computer Users Forum 1977–84, Focus Ctee for Private Sector Users DOI 1982–84; memb: Cncl Br Computer Soc 1971–74 and 1980–83, NW Regnl Cncl CBI 1977–83, User Panel NEDO 1983–84; UK rep Confedn of Euro Computer Users Assocs 1980–83; FBCS 1972, FIDPM 1990 (MIDPM 1981); *Recreations* gardening, golf; *Style—* Eric Howe, Esq, CBE

HOWE, 7 Earl (UK 1821); Frederick Richard Penn Curzon; also Baron Howe of Langar (GB 1788), Baron Curzon of Penn (GB 1794) and Viscount Curzon of Penn (UK 1802); s of Cdr (Chambré) George William Penn Curzon, RN (d 1976), and Enid Jane Victoria, da of late Malcolm Mackenzie Fergusson; suc cous, 6 Earl Howe, CBE (d 1984); *b* 29 Jan 1951; *Educ* Rugby, Christ Church Oxford (MA); *m* 1983, Elizabeth Helen (DL Bucks 1995), elder da of Capt Burleigh Edward St Lawrence Stuart, of Ickford, Bucks; 1 s (Thomas, Viscount Curzon b 22 Oct 1994), 3 da (Lady Anna Elizabeth b 19 Jan 1987, Lady Flora Grace b 12 June 1989, Lady Lucinda Rose b 12 Oct 1991); *Heir* s, Viscount Curzon b 22 Oct 1994; *Career* banker and farmer; dir: Adam & Co plc 1987–90, Provident Life Assoc Ltd 1988–91; Lord-in-Waiting to HM The Queen (Govt Whip) 1991–92; Govt spokesman: on Employment and Transport 1991, on Environment and Def 1992; Parly sec: MAFF 1992–95, MOD 1995–; pres: Nat Soc for Epilepsy, RNLI (Chilterns Branch), South Bucks Assoc for The Disabled; govr: King William IV Naval Fndn, Milton's Cottage Tst; hon treas The Trident Tst; ACIB 1976; *Recreations* musical composition; *Style—* The Rt Hon the Earl Howe; ✉ c/o House of Lords, London SW1

HOWE, Prof Geoffrey Leslie; TD 1962 (and Bars 1969, 1974); s of Leo Leslie John Howe (d 1934), of Maidenhead, Berks, and Ada Blanche, *née* Partridge (d 1973); *b* 22 April 1924; *Educ* Royal Dental Hosp, Middx Hosps; *m* 8 April 1948, Heather Patricia Joan, *née* Hambly; 1 s (Timothy John b 31 May 1958); *Career* dental offr RADC 1946–49, Col RADC (V) 1972–75, Col RARO 1973–89 (Hon Col Cmdt RADC 1975–90); prof of oral surgery Univs of Durham and Newcastle upon Tyne 1959–67, dean Royal Dental Hosp London Sch of Dental Surgery 1973–78 (prof of oral surgery 1967–78), prof Univ of Hong Kong 1978–84 (fndr dean of dentistry 1978–83), dean Faculty of Dentistry Jordan Univ of Sci and Technol 1988–90 and 1993–96 (prof of oral surgery 1986–90, prof of oral surgery and med 1993–96); memb Cncl RCS 1977–78, vice pres Br Dental Assoc 1979– (vice chm 1971–73, chm Cncl 1973–78); Liveryman Worshipful Soc of Apothecaries, Int Freeman New Orleans USA, Freeman Louisville USA; hon fell: Philippine Coll of Oral and Maxillo-Facial Surgns 1979, Acad of Dentistry Int (USA) 1982; fell Int Coll of Dentists, hon memb American Dental Assoc; LRCP, MRCS 1954, FDSRCS 1955 (LDSRCS 1946), MDS 1961, FFD RCSI 1964; OStJ; *Books* Extraction of Teeth (2 edn, 1980), Local Anaesthesia in Dentistry (with F I H Whitehead, 3 edn, 1990), Minor Oral Surgery (3 edn, 1989); *Recreations* sailing, reading, music, club life; *Clubs* Gents, Hong Kong, Royal Hong Kong Yacht; *Style—* Prof Geoffrey Howe, TD; ✉ 70 Croham Manor Rd, S Croydon, Surrey CR2 7BF (☎ 0181 686 0941); Villa 2-1, Marina de Casares, Km 146 Cts Cadiz/Malaga; Sabinillas, Manilva, Andalucia, Spain

HOWE, Geoffrey Michael Thomas; s of Michael Edward Howe, and Susan Dorothy, *née* Allan; *b* 3 Sept 1949; *Educ* The Manchester GS, St John's Coll Cambridge (MA); *Career* admitted slr 1973; ptnr Co Dept Clifford-Turner 1980 (joined 1975), managing ptnr Clifford Chance 1989–; Freeman Worshipful Co of Slrs; memb Law Soc 1973; *Recreations* golf, squash, wine, antiques, opera; *Clubs* Oxford & Cambridge; *Style—* Geoffrey Howe, Esq; ✉ Clifford Chance, 200 Aldersgate St, London EC1A 4JJ (☎ 0171 600 1000, fax 0171 600 5555)

HOWE, Gordon James; s of Frank Ernest Howe (d 1979), of Colchester, Essex, and Jessie Smith, *née* Withycombe (d 1953); *b* 6 Jan 1932; *Educ* Royal Liberty Sch Romford Essex; *m* 28 April 1957, Dawn Angela, da of Albert Edward Diver (d 1969), of Banstead, Surrey; 1 s (Duncan b 1962, d 1964), 1 da (Fiona b 1966); *Career* RA 1954–56, Lt 1955; qualified CA 1954; Arthur Young/Ernst & Young: ptnr 1961, memb Exec Ctee 1977, chm Arthur Young Europe 1984, memb Int Cncl 1984, memb Exec Ctee 1990–92, ret 1992; non-exec dir various private cos and Debenham Tewson Chinnocks plc 1993–; dir Investment Management Regulatory Organisation 1993–; non-exec dir: SW Thames Regnl Health Authy 1990–94, Kiln Capital plc 1994–; treas Young Minds Charity, chm S Thames Blood Transfusion Service 1990–94; FCA 1964; *Recreations* swimming, travel, philately; *Clubs* RAC; *Style—* Gordon Howe, Esq; ✉ 19 Evelyn Gardens, London SW7 3BE (☎ 0171 370 6475)

HOWE, John Francis; CB (1996), OBE (1974); s of late Frank Howe, OBE, of Devon, and Marjorie Alice, *née* Hubball; *b* 29 Jan 1944; *Educ* Shrewsbury, Balliol Coll Oxford (MA); *m* 1981, Angela Ephrosini, da of Charalambos Nicolaides (d 1973), of Alicante and London; 1 da (Alexandra b 1983), 1 step da (Caroline b 1973); *Career* civil serv: princ MOD 1972 (asst princ 1967), civil advsr GOC NI 1972–73, private sec to Perm Under Sec 1975–78, asst sec MOD 1979, seconded FCO, cnsllr UK Delgn to NATO 1981–84, head Def Arms Control Unit 1985–86, private sec to Sec of State for Def 1986–87, asst under sec of state (personnel and logistics) 1988–91, dep under sec of state (civilian mgmnt) 1992–96, dep chief of defence procurement (support) 1996–; FRSA; *Books* International Security and Arms Control (contrib); *Recreations* travel, gardening; *Clubs* Athenaeum; *Style*— John Howe, Esq, CB, OBE; ✉ Ministry of Defence, Main Building, Whitehall SW1 (☎ 0171 218 6833)

HOWE, Air Vice-Marshal John Frederick George; CB (1985), CBE (1980), AFC (1961); *b* 26 March 1930; *Educ* St Andrew's Coll Grahamstown S Africa; *m* 1961, Annabelle Gowing; 3 da; *Career* Cmdt-Gen RAF Regt and dir gen Security (RAF) 1983–85, ret; Hon Col Field Sqdns (South)/77 Engrg Regt (TA) (V) 1988–93; American DFC 1951, Air Medal 1951; *Style*— Air Vice-Marshal J F G Howe, CB, CBE, AFC

HOWE, Rt Rev John William Alexander; s of Frederic Arthur (d 1979), and Elsie, *née* Garner (d 1975); *b* 14 July 1920; *Educ* Westcliff HS (Essex), St Chad's Coll, Durham Univ (BA, MA, BD); *Career* ordained Dio of York 1943, curate All Saints' Scarborough 1943–46, chaplain Adisadel Coll Ghana 1946–50, vice princ Edinburgh Theological Coll Scotland 1950–55, consecrated bishop of Dio of St Andrews, Dunkeld and Dunblane 1955, bishop 1955–69, exec offr Anglican Communion 1969; first sec gen Anglican Consultative Cncl 1971–82 (first research fell 1983–85, ret 1985); asst bishop Dio of Ripon 1985–91; sec Lambeth Conf 1978; hon degrees: STD General Theological Seminary New York USA 1974, DD Lambeth 1978; *Books* Highways and Hedges: Anglicanism and the Universal Church (1985), various articles; presentation essays: Authy in The Anglican Communion; *Clubs* Royal Cwlth Soc; *Style*— The Rt Rev John Howe; ✉ Stuart Court, High Street, Kibworth Beauchamp, Leicester LE8 0LE (☎ 0116 279 6205)

HOWE, Leslie Clive; s of Alexander Leslie Howe, of Cheshunt, Herts, and Patricia Ann, *née* Lord; *b* 21 April 1955; *Educ* Cheshunt GS, Royal Dental Hosp Univ of London (BDS); *Career* house surgn Royal Dental Hosp 1979, sr house surgn London Hosp 1979–80; lectr in conservative dentistry: Royal Dental Hosp 1980–85, Guy's Dental Sch 1985–; conslt in restorative dentistry Guy's Hospital 1993–; Lunt prize, Sounders scholar, Baron Cornelius ver Heyden de Lancey award; memb: Br Soc for Restorative Dentistry, Br Soc for Dental Res; Accreditation in Restorative Denistry 1989; FDSRCS 1983; *Books* Inlays, Crowns and Bridges (1993); *Style*— Leslie Howe, Esq; ✉ Conservation Department, Guy's Hospital Dental School, London Bridge, London SE1 9RT (☎ 0171 955 4533); 21 Wimpole St, London W1M 7AD (☎ 0171 636 3101)

HOWE, Dr Martin; CB (1995); s of Leslie Wistow Howe (d 1979), and Dorothy Vernon, *née* Taylor-Farrell (d 1994); *b* 9 Dec 1936; *Educ* High Storrs GS, Univ of Leeds (BCom), Univ of Sheffield (PhD); *m* 1959, Anne Cicely, da of Ernest Lawrenson, of Parbold; 3 s (Graeme Neil b 1963, Andrew Keith b 1965, Robert Anthony b 1968); *Career* sr lectr Univ of Sheffield 1965–72 (formerly asst lectr and lectr), sr econ advsr MMC 1973–77, asst sec DTI 1983–84; OFT: sr economic advsr 1977–80, asst sec 1980–83, under sec dir Competition Policy Div 1984–97; *Books* Equity Issues and The London Capital Market (with A J Merrett and G D Newbould, 1967); *Recreations* theatre, amateur dramatics, cricket, gardening; *Style*— Dr Martin Howe, CB; ✉ c/o Office of Fair Trading, Field House, Breams Buildings, London EC4A 1PR

HOWE, Martin Russell Thomson; QC (1996); s of Colin Thomson Howe, FRCS (d 1988), of Kenley, Surrey, and Dr Angela Mary, *née* Brock (d 1977), da of Lord Brock (life peer d 1979); *b* 26 June 1955; *Educ* Winchester, Trinity Hall Cambridge (MA); *m* 30 Dec 1989, Lynda, *née* Barnett; 1 s (Philip Anthony b 19 Oct 1990), 2 da (Julia Angela b 13 Nov 1992, Jennifer Rosalind b 19 Feb 1996); *Career* called to the Bar Middle Temple 1978; specialising in patents, copyright, trade marks and EC law; jt ed Halsbury's Laws of England section on Trade Marks, Trade Names and Designs; Parly candidate (Cons) Neath 1987, memb Hammersmith and Fulham Borough Cncl 1982–86 (chm Planning Ctee); *Publications* Europe and the Constitution after Maastricht, author of other pubns on EC Constitutional Law; *Recreations* flying gliders; *Style*— Martin Howe, Esq, QC; ✉ 8 New Square, Lincoln's Inn, London WC2A 3QP (☎ 0171 405 4321)

HOWE, His Hon Judge; Ronald William; s of William Arthur Howe (d 1979), and Lilian Mary, *née* Marsh (d 1987), of London; *b* 19 June 1932; *Educ* Morpeth Sch, Coll of Law; *m* 24 March 1956, Jean Emily Howe; 3 s (Mark b 6 Dec 1960, Kevin b 5 Sept 1962, Nigel b 11 Nov 1973), 1 da (Karen b 19 Oct 1965); *Career* admitted slr 1966, registrar 1975–91, circuit judge (SE Circuit) 1991–; memb Law Soc; past memb: Judicial Studies Bd, Civil and Family Law Ctee JSB; former tutor and course dir for refresher courses for district judges and induction courses for dep district judges; *Recreations* badminton, golf (when time permits), gardening, relaxing; *Style*— His Hon Judge Howe; ✉ Chelmsford County Court, London House, New London Road, Chelmsford, Essex CM2 0QR

HOWE OF ABERAVON, Baroness; Elspeth Rosamund Howe; *née* Morton Shand; JP (Inner London 1964); da of late Philip Morton Shand and Sybil Mary, *née* Sissons; *b* 8 Feb 1932; *Educ* Bath HS, Wycombe Abbey Sch, LSE (BSc 1985); *m* Aug 1953, Baron Howe of Aberavon (Life Peer), *qv*; 1 s (Hon Alexander b 1959), 2 da (Hon Caroline b 1955, Hon Amanda b (twin) 1959); *Career* sec to princ of Architectural Assoc's Sch of Architecture 1952–55, dep chm Equal Opportunities Cmmn Manchester (chm Legal Ctee) 1975–79; chm Inner London Juvenile Cts: Southwark 1970–80, Greenwich 1980–83, Lambeth 1983–86, Wandsworth 1987–90; non-exec dir: Kingfisher (Holdings) plc (formerly Woolworth Holdings plc) 1986–, United Biscuits (Holdings) Ltd 1988–94, Legal and General Group plc 1989–; chm BOC Foundation 1990–; pres: Peckham Settlement 1976–94, Fedn of Recruitment and Employment Servs 1980–94, UNICEF UK 1993–; chm: Business in the Community Opportunity 2000 Initiative 1988–, NACRO Working Pty on Fine Enforcement 1980–81, NACRO Drugs Advsy Gp 1988–92, Local Govt Mgmnt Bd Inquiry and Report 'The Quality of Care' 1991–92, The Archbishops' Cmmn on Cathedrals 1992–94, Broadcasting Standards Cncl 1993–; vice pres Pre-School Playgroups Assoc 1978–83; memb: Lord Chllr's Advsy Ctee on Legal Aid 1971–75, Parole Bd For England and Wales 1972–75, The Justice Ctee on the English Judiciary 1992; tstee The Westminster Fndn for Democracy 1992–96; govr LSE 1985–; memb Cncl St George's House Windsor 1989–93; contrib articles to: The Times, Financial Times, Guardian, New Society; Hon LLD London 1990, Hon DUniv Open Univ 1993; Hon DLitt: Bradford 1993, Aberdeen 1994, Liverpool 1994, Sunderland 1995, South Bank 1995; *Style*— The Lady Howe of Aberavon, JP; ✉ c/o The Broadcasting Standards Council, 5–8 The Sanctuary, London SW1P 3JS (☎ 0171 233 0544, fax 0171 233 0397)

HOWE OF ABERAVON, Baron (Life Peer UK 1992), of Tandridge in the County of Surrey; Sir (Richard Edward) Geoffrey Howe; kt (1970), CH (1996) PC (1972), QC (1965); er s of late B Edward Howe, of Port Talbot, Glamorgan, and Mrs E F Howe, JP, *née* Thomson; *b* 20 Dec 1926; *Educ* Winchester, Trinity Hall Cambridge; *m* 1953, Elspeth Rosamund, JP, *see* Lady Howe of Aberavon, da of late Philip Morton Shand; 1 s (Hon Alexander Edward Thomson b 1959), 2 da (Hon Caroline (Hon Mrs Ralph) b 1955, Hon Amanda (Hon Mrs Glanvill) b (twin) 1959); *Career* called to the Bar 1952; memb Gen Cncl of the Bar 1957–61, memb Cncl of Justice 1963–70, dep chm Glamorgan QS 1966–70, Parly candidate (C) Aberavon 1955 and 1959; chm Bow Gp 1955, ed Crossbow 1960–62 (md 1957–60); MP (C): Bebington 1964–66, Reigate 1970–74, Surrey E 1974–92; oppn front bench spokesman on labour and social servs 1965–66, SG 1970–72, min for trade and consumer affrs 1972–74; oppn front bench spokesman: on social servs 1974–75, on Treasy and econ affrs 1975–79; Chllr of the Exchequer and Lord Cmmr of the Treasy 1979–83, chm IMF Policy-Making Interim Ctee 1982–83, ldr team of Policy Gps preparing Cons Gen Election Manifesto 1982–83, sec of state for foreign and Cwlth affrs 1983–July 1989, Leader of the Commons and Lord Pres of the Cncl July 1989–Nov 1990, dep PM July 1989–Nov 1990; non-exec dir: Glaxo Wellcome plc (formerly Glaxo Holdings plc) 1991–96, BICC plc 1991–97; chm Framlington Russian Investment Fund 1994–, special advsr on Euro and international affrs Jones Day Reavis and Pogue 1991–, memb J P Morgan Int Advsy Cncl 1992–, memb Bertelsmann Fndn Int Advsy Cncl 1992–; patron Enterprise Europe 1990–, memb Steering Ctee Project Liberty 1991–, memb Advsy Cncl Presidium of the Supreme Rada of Ukraine 1991–, jt pres Wealth of Nations Fndn 1991–; pres: Assoc of Consumer Res 1992–, GB-China Centre 1992–, Academy of Experts 1996–; vice pres Royal United Servs Inst for Def Studies 1992–; visitor to Sch of Oriental and African Studies of Univ of London 1991–, visiting fell John F Kennedy Sch of Government Harvard Univ 1991–92, Herman Phleger visiting prof Stanford Law Sch 1992–93, hon fell Trinity Hall 1992–; Joseph Bech prize FVS Stiftung of Hamburg 1993; Hon Fell Univ Coll of Wales Swansea 1996, Hon LLD Wales 1988, Hon DCL City of London; Hon Freeman Port Talbot 1992; Grand Cross Order of Merit Germany 1992; *Style*— The Rt Hon the Lord Howe of Aberavon, CH, PC, QC; ✉ House of Lords, London SW1A 0PW

HOWELL, Rt Hon David Arthur Russell; PC (1979), MP (C) Guildford (majority 13,404); s of Col Arthur Howard Eckford Howell, DSO, TD, DL (d 1980), and Beryl Stuart, *née* Bowater; *b* 18 Jan 1936; *Educ* Eton, King's Coll Cambridge (MA); *m* 1967, (Cary) Davina, da of Maj David Wallace (ka 1944); 1 s (Toby David b 1975), 2 da (Frances Victoria b 1969, Kate Davina b 1970); *Career* serv Coldstream Gds 1954–56, 2 Lt; worked in Econ Section Treasy 1959–60, ldr writer Daily Telegraph 1960–64, chm Bow Gp 1961–62, ed Crossbow 1962–64, Parly candidate (C) Dudley 1964, dir Cons Political Centre 1964–66, MP (C) Guildford 1966–, lord cmmr Treasy 1970–71, Parly sec CSD 1970–72; Parly under sec: Employment 1971–72, NI March-Nov 1972; min of state: NI 1972–74, Energy 1974; sec of state for: Energy 1979–81, Transport 1981–83; chm House of Commons Foreign Affrs Ctee 1987–, chm UK Japan 2000 Gp; former dir Trafalgar House plc; dir: Jardine Insurance Brokers plc, Monks Investment Trust; memb Int Advsy Bd Swiss Bank Corporation 1988–, sr advsr to Bd SBC-Warburg 1996–; Liveryman Worshipful Co of Clothworkers; *Publications* A New Style of Government (1970), Time to Move On (1976), Freedom and Capital (1981), Blind Victory (1986); *Recreations* tennis, golf, writing, DIY; *Clubs* Buck's; *Style*— The Rt Hon David Howell, MP; ✉ House of Commons, London SW1A 0AA

HOWELL, Baron (Life Peer UK 1992), of Aston Manor in the City of Birmingham; Denis Herbert Howell; PC (1976); s of Herbert and Bertha Howell, of Birmingham; *b* 4 Sept 1923; *Educ* Gower St Sch, Handsworth GS; *m* 1955, Brenda Marjorie, da of Stephen Willson; 2 s (Hon Andrew b 16 April 1957, Hon Michael b 8 March 1959) (and 1 s decd), 1 da (Hon Kathryn (Hon Mrs Molloy) b 24 July 1962); *Career* memb Birmingham City Cncl 1946–56; MP (Lab): Birmingham All Saints 1955–59, Birmingham Small Heath 1961–92; jt Parly under sec DES and min for Sport 1964–70, min of state Housing and Local Govt and Min for Sport 1969–70, oppn spokesman Local Govt and Sport 1970–74, min of state for the Environment and min for Sport 1974–79; oppn front bench spokesman: Environment and Sport 1979–83, Home Affrs 1983–84, Sport 1984–92; oppn front bench spokesman (Lords) Defence 1992–; pres: Labour Movement for Europe, European Movement, APEX 1971–83; memb Nat Exec 1982–83; former football league referee and memb Birmingham City Cncl 1946–56, Silver medal Olympic Order 1981, sr vice-pres Aston Villa FC 1994–97, vice-pres: Central Ctee of Physical Recreation, Warwicks CCC; dir: Wembley Stadium Ltd, Birmingham Cable Authy, Denis Howell PR; Hon Freeman City of Birmingham 1990; Hon LLD Univ of Birmingham Univ 1993; FIPR 1986; *Books* Soccer Referee Pelham (1969), Made in Birmingham (autobiography, 1990); *Recreations* sport, music, theatre; *Clubs* Reform, MCC, Warwickshire Cricket, Birmingham Press; *Style*— The Rt Hon Lord Howell, PC; ✉ 33 Moor Green Lane, Moseley, Birmingham B13 8NE (☎ 0121 449 7124, fax 0121 442 4814)

HOWELL, Air Vice-Marshal Evelyn Michael Thomas; CBE (1961); s of Sir Evelyn Berkeley Howell (d 1971), of Cambridge, and Laetitia Cecilia Campbell (d 1978); *b* 11 Sept 1913; *Educ* Downside, RAF Coll Cranwell; *m* 1, 1937, Helen Joan, da of Brig William Moring Hayes (d 1960); 1 s (Michael William Davis Howell, *qv*), 3 da (Jennifer, Mary, Philippa); m 2, 1972, Rosemary, da of Ian Alexander Cram (d 1996), of Warwick; 1 s (Rupert b 1975), 1 da (Caroline b 1977); *Career* cmmnd RAF 1934, dir Air Armament Res & Devpt 1960–62, Cmdt RAF Tech Coll Henlow 1962–65, sr air staff offr Tech Trg Cmd 1966–67, ret 1967; Aircraft Indust 1967–79; Liveryman Worshipful Co of Clothworkers; FRAeS 1963; *Recreations* gardening, conservation; *Clubs* RAF; *Style*— Air Vice-Marshal E M T Howell, CBE; ✉ 47 Captain French Lane, Kendal, Cumbria LA9 4HP (☎ 01539 730336)

HOWELL, Geoffrey Colston; s of Leonard Colston Howell (d 1968), and Leah Emily, *née* Probert (d 1971); *b* 17 July 1932; *Educ* Latymer Upper Sch Hammersmith, St John's Coll Cambridge (MA, MSc); *m* 23 April 1957 (m dis 1992), Elizabeth Mary, *née* Dutton; 2 s (Martin Colston b 29 May 1960, Antony Gerald b 17 June 1961), 2 da (Jacqueline Mary b 18 July 1958, Philippa Joan b 16 Feb 1964); m 2, 16 May 1992, Margaret Anne, *née* Worger; *Career* RAE Farnborough: scientific offr 1955–60, sr scientific offr 1960–64, princ scientific offr 1964–71, supt Controls & Displays Div 1971–72; chief supt RAE Bedford 1977–80 (head Blind Landing Experimental Unit 1972–77), head Flight Systems Dept RAE Farnborough 1980–82, dir of aircraft equipment & systems (MOD) PE 1982–84, chief scientist CAA 1988–92 (dir of res 1984–88), self employed aviation conslt 1992–; pres RAeS 1990–91; FRAeS 1974, FRSA 1988, FEng 1992; *Recreations* music, reading; *Style*— Geoffrey Howell, Esq, FEng; ✉ Thenon, Razac de Saussignac, Dordogne 24240, France (☎ 00 33 53 05 27 9974, fax 00 33 53 05 22 9049

HOWELL, Gwynne Richard; s of Gilbert Lewis Howell (d 1991), and Ellaline, *née* Richards (d 1986); *b* 13 June 1938; *Educ* Pontardawe GS, Univ Coll Swansea (BSc), Univ of Manchester (DipTP); *m* 26 Oct 1968, Mary Edwina, da of Edward Morris (d 1988); 2 s (Richard b 23 May 1970, Peter b 31 May 1972); *Career* bass; sr planning offr Corporation of Manchester 1965–68, commenced professional music career 1968; with Sadler's Wells Opera (now ENO) 1968–72, Royal Opera 1972; given concerts with numerous leading conductors incl: Claudio Abbado, Daniel Barenboim, Pierre Boulez, Leonard Bernstein, Sir Colin Davis, Sir Bernard Haitink, James Levine, Zubin Mehta, Riccardo Muti, Tadaaki Ozawa and Sir Georg Solti; *Performances* notable operatic roles incl: First Nazarene in Salome (Covent Garden debut) 1969, Arkell in Pelleas and Melisande (Glyndebourne and Covent Garden 1969 and 1982), Otello (Met Opera NY debut) 1985, Hans Sachs in Die Meistersinger (ENO), Bluebeard in Bluebeard's Castle (ENO) 1991, Phillip II in Don Carlos (ENO) 1992, Boris Godunov (San Francisco Opera) 1992, Iolanta (Opera North) 1993, Fidelio (ENO) 1996, King Marke in Tristan und Isolde (ENO) 1996, King in Ariodante (ENO) 1996; concert performances incl: St Matthew Passion (US debut, with Chicago Symphony Orch) 1974, Oedipus Rex (with Chicago Symphony Orch under Solti and with NY Philharmonic), numerous others at festivals incl Salzburg and Edinburgh; *Recordings* incl: Mahler's 8th Symphony (with Boston Symphony Orch under Ozawa), Un Ballo in Maschera, Luisa Miller and Rossini's Stabat Mater (all under Muti), Handel's Messiah (under Solti), Beethoven's 9th Symphony (under Kurt Masur); fell Welsh Coll of Music and Drama 1994; *Recreations* tennis, golf, gardening, good wine, walking; *Style*— Gwynne Howell, Esq; ✉ 197 Fox Lane, London N13 4BB

HOWELL, Prof John Bernard Lloyd (Jack); CBE (1991); s of David John Howell (d 1978), of Ynystawe, Swansea, and Hilda Mary, *née* Hill (d 1943); *b* 1 Aug 1926; *Educ* Swansea GS, Middx Hosp Med Sch and Univ of London (BSc, MB BS, PhD); *m* 12 July

1952, Heather Joan, da of Lawrence Victor Rolfe (d 1939); 2 s (David b 1955, Peter b 1959), 1 da (Gillian b 1953); *Career* Nat Serv RAMC 1952–54; lectr in physiological med Middx Hosp Med Sch 1954–56, MRC travelling fell Johns Hopkins Hosp 1957–58; Univ of Manchester: sr lectr and hon physician 1960–66, conslt physician and sr lectr 1966–69; Goulstonian lectr RCP 1966; Univ of Southampton: fndn prof of med 1969–91, emeritus prof 1991–, dean Faculty of Med 1978–83; memb GMC 1978–83, pres Thoracic Soc 1988–89, pres BMA 1989–90; chm: Southampton & SW Hampshire Dist Health Authy 1983–, Bd of Sci and Educn BMA 1991–; memb Advtg Advsy Ctee ITC 1993–; hon life memb Canadian Thoracic Soc 1978; Hon DSc Univ of Southampton; FRCP 1966, Hon FACP 1982; *Books* Breathlessness (1966); *Recreations* DIY, wine; *Style*— Prof Jack Howell, CBE; ✉ The Coach House, Bassett Wood Drive, Southampton SO16 3PT (☎ and fax 01703 768878)

HOWELL, Dr John Frederick; s of Frederick John Howell (d 1996), and Glenys Griffiths (d 1990); *b* 16 July 1941; *Educ* Welwyn Garden GS, Univ Coll Swansea (BA), Univ of Manchester (MA), Univ of Reading (PhD); *m* 1993, Paula Wade; 2 s, 1 step s; *Career* lectr Univ of Khartoum 1966–73, sr lectr Univ of Zambia 1973–77, dir ODI 1987– (res fell 1977–87), visiting prof Wye Coll Univ of London 1988–96; pres UK Chapter Soc for Int Devpt, advsr All Pty Parly Gp on Overseas Devpt; *Style*— Dr John Howell; ✉ Overseas Development Institute, Portland House, Stage Place, London SW1E 5DP (☎ 0171 393 1600, fax 0171 393 1699, e-mail director@odi.org.uk)

HOWELL, Lisbeth Edna (Lis); da of Frederick Baynes, and Jessica Edna Baynes; *b* 23 March 1951; *Educ* Liverpool Inst HS for Girls, Univ of Bristol (BA); *partner* Ian Prowiewicz; 1 da (Alexandra b 19 Sept 1984); *Career* reporter BBC local radio 1973–77; reporter/presenter: Border TV 1977–79, Granada TV 1978–80, Tyne Tees TV 1981–84; Border TV: head of news 1986–88, dep dir of progs 1988–89; managing ed Sky News 1990–91, dir of progs GMTV 1991–93, conslt United Artists Programming 1993, dir of progs UK Living satellite and cable channel 1993–; *Books* After the Break (novel, 1995), The Director's Cut (novel, 1996), A Job to Die For (novel, 1997); *Style*— Ms Lis Howell; ✉ The Quadrangle, 180 Wardour Street, London W1V 4AE (☎ 0171 306 6100)

HOWELL, Maj-Gen Lloyd; CBE (1972); s of Thomas Idris Howell (d 1987), and Anne Howell (d 1964); *b* 28 Dec 1923; *Educ* Barry GS, UC Cardiff (BSc); *m* 1, 14 Feb 1945, Hazel (d 1974), da of Frank Edward Barker (d 1963); 5 s (Rhodri b 1945, d 1979, Geraint b 1948, Ceri b 1952, Dewi b 1956, Alwyn b 1959), 3 da (Carys b 1949, Eirlys b 1951, Sara b 1954); m 2, 19 April 1975, Elizabeth June Buchanan Husband, da of Archibald John Buchanan Atkinson (d 1966); *Career* Capt: regtl and staff appts RA 1943–47, instr RMA Sandhurst RAEC 1949–53, staff course RMCS 1953–54; Maj: TSO 2 Trials Estab RA 1954–57, SO 2 Educn Div HQ BAOR 1957–59, long GW course RMCS 1959–60; Lt-Col: DS RMCS 1960–64, SEO Army Apprentices Coll 1964–67, headmaster and Cmdt Duke of York's Royal Mil Sch 1967–72 (Col 1970); Col (educn) MOD 1972–74, Brig chief educn offr UK Land Forces 1974–76; Maj-Gen: dir of Army Educn 1976–80, Col Cmdt RAEC 1982–86; conslt on tech educn devpt UCW 1980–86; dir Bldg Trades Exhibitions Ltd 1980–93; memb: Cncl City and Guilds of London Inst 1976–89, Ct of Govrs Univ of Wales Coll Cardiff 1980–; govr of several schs 1980–93; fell Univ of Wales Coll Cardiff 1981; Hon MA Open Univ 1980; CEng 1963, MRAeS 1963–80; *Recreations* golf, gardening; *Style*— Maj-Gen Lloyd Howell, CBE

HOWELL, Margaret; *b* 5 Sept 1946; *Educ* Goldsmiths' Coll London; *children* 2; *Career* first of new Br fashion designers to modernise the classics of Br clothing using traditional fabrics; postgrad experience mfrg accessories 1969, expanded to produce clothing collections (wholesaled internationally) from own studio 1970–76, concession shops opened London 1977 and Paris 1978, flagship shop opened St Christopher's Place 1980 (Beauchamp Place from 1987), second London shop opened Brook St 1992, currently produces mens and womenswear (often interchangeable) with 50 retail outlets worldwide incl UK, Japan, USA, Italy, France, Germany and Holland; outfits on display Costume Museum Bath and Costume Dept V & A London; *Recreations* walking, gardening, visiting houses and gardens, art exhibitions, films and photography; *Style*— Ms Margaret Howell; ✉ Margaret Howell (87) Ltd, 5 Garden House, 8 Battersea Park Road, London SW8 4BG

HOWELL, Michael John; s of Jack Howell, and Emmie Mary Elizabeth Howell; *b* 9 June 1939; *Educ* Strodes, King's Coll London (LLB), Chigaco Univ (JD), Cape Town Univ; *m* 14 May 1966, Caroline Sarah Eifiona, da of Charles Herbert Gray; 2 da (Juliet b 1967, Lucy b 1973); *Career* admitted slr 1966; ptnr Clifford Chance (formerly Clifford-Turner) 1969– (joined 1964); Asst Worshipful Co of Coopers (Under Warden 1988–89, Upper Warden 1989–90), Freeman Worshipful Co of Slrs; memb: Law Soc, Int Bar Assoc; assoc memb Chartered Inst of Patent Agents; *Clubs* City Livery; *Style*— Michael Howell, Esq; ✉ Wood Cottage, Dome Hill Park, London SE26 6SP (☎ 0181 778 9763); Clifford Chance, 200 Aldersgate Street, London EC1A 4JJ (☎ 0171 600 1000, fax 0171 600 5555, telex 887 847 LEGIS G)

HOWELL, Michael William Davis; s of Air Vice-Marshal Evelyn Michael Thomas Howell, CBE, *qv*, and Helen Joan, *née* Hayes (d 1976); *b* 11 June 1947; *Educ* Charterhouse, Trinity Coll Cambridge, INSEAD and Harvard Business Sch (MBA); *m* 1975, Susan Wanda, da of Andrew Adie (d 1986); 2 s (William b 1982, Andrew b 1988), 1 da (Anna b 1990); *Career* gen mangr Gen Electric Co (US) Inc 1988–91; dir: Arlington Capital Management Ltd 1991–, Fenner plc 1993–; vice pres: Cummins Engine Co Inc 1976–88, BL Truck & Bus Div 1969–74; *Recreations* aviation, walking; *Clubs* Royal Scottish Automobile, United Oxford and Cambridge Univ; *Style*— Michael Howell, Esq; ✉ 40 St James's Place, London SW1A 1NS (☎ 0171 493 8111, fax 0171 629 3244)

HOWELL, Patrick Leonard; QC (1990); *Educ* Univ of Oxford (MA), Univ of London (LLM); *Career* called to the Bar: Inner Temple 1966, Lincoln's Inn; social security cmmr 1994–; *Style*— Patrick Howell, Esq, QC; ✉ Office of the Social Security Commissioners, Harp House, 83 Farringdon Street, London EC4 (☎ 0171 353 5145)

HOWELL, Paul Frederic; s of Sir Ralph Frederic Howell, MP, *qv*, of Wendling Grange, Dereham, Norfolk, by his w Margaret Ellene; *b* 17 Jan 1951; *Educ* Gresham's, St Edmund Hall Oxford; *m* 23 May 1987, Johanna, *née* Turnbull; 2 s; *Career* MEP (EDG) Norfolk 1979–94; *Recreations* sport, adventures; *Clubs* Farmers', Carlton; *Style*— Paul Howell, Esq; ✉ The White House Farm, Bradenham Rd, Scarning, E Dereham, Norfolk NR19 2LA (☎ 01362 687239)

HOWELL, Peter Adrian; s of Lt Col Harry Alfred Adrian Howell, MBE (d 1985), of Chester, and Madge Maud Mary, *née* Thompson (d 1992); *b* 29 July 1941; *Educ* Downside, Balliol Coll Oxford (BA, MA, MPhil); *Career* Univ of London: asst lectr then lectr Dept of Latin Bedford Coll 1964–85, sr lectr Dept of Classics Royal Holloway and Bedford New Coll 1994– (lectr 1985–); memb: Westminster Cathedral Art Ctee 1974–91, Dept of Art and Architecture Liturgy Cmmn Roman Catholic Bishops' Conf for Eng and Wales 1977–84, Churches Ctee English Heritage 1984–88, Westminster Cathedral Art and Architecture Ctee 1993–, Archdiocese of Westminster Historic Churches Ctee 1995–, RC Historic Churches Ctee for Wales and Herefordshire 1995–; chm Victorian Soc 1987–93 (memb Ctee 1968–), dep chm Jt Ctee Nat Amenity Socs 1991–93; *Books* Victorian Churches (1968), Companion Guide to North Wales (with Elisabeth Beazley, 1975), Companion Guide to South Wales (with Elisabeth Beazley, 1977), A Commentary on Book I of the Epigrams of Martial (1980), The Faber Guide to Victorian Churches (ed with Ian Sutton, 1989), Martial: The Epigrams, Book V (1996); *Style*— Peter Howell, Esq; ✉ Department of Classics, Royal Holloway, University of London, Egham Hill, Egham, Surrey TW20 0EX (☎ 01784 443211)

HOWELL, Sir Ralph Frederic; kt (1993), MP (C) Norfolk North (majority 12,545); s of Walter Howell, of Dereham, Norfolk; *b* 25 May 1923; *Educ* Diss GS; *m* 1950, Margaret, da of Walter Bone, of Gressenhall; 2 s, 1 da; *Career* RAF 1941–46; farmer; cnllr Mitford and Launditch RDC 1961–74; former local chm NFU, MP (C) Norfolk N 1970– (also contested 1966), memb Euro Parl 1974–79, former chm Cons Backbench Ctee Agric and Employment, memb Select Ctee on the Treasy and Civil Serv 1981–87, memb Employment Ctee 1994–96, memb Cncl of Europe and WEU 1981–84 and 1987–, memb Select Ctee on Employment 1996–; sometime vice chm Cons Backbench Ctee on Social Security, chm Br-Polish Parly Gp; memb Lloyd's; *Clubs* RAF, Farmers'; *Style*— Sir Ralph Howell, MP; ✉ Wendling Grange, Wendling, Dereham, Norfolk

HOWELL, Dr Richard Stanley Charles; s of Rev Herbert Stanley Howell (d 1978), of Braceborough Rectory, Stamford, Lincs, and Gwendolen Eleanor, *née* Davies; *b* 13 Aug 1945; *Educ* Stamford Sch, St Mary's Hosp Med Sch London (MB BS); *m* 3 Jan 1976, Susan Katherine Veronica; *Career* res anaesthetist Mount Sinai Sch of Med NY 1971–72, sr registrar Addenbrooke's Hosp Cambridge 1973–76; conslt anaesthetist: Walsgrave Hosp Coventry 1976–, Warwickshire Nuffield Hosp Leamington Spa 1980–; sr clinical lectr Univ of Birmingham 1991–; Royal Coll of Anaesthetists regnl advsr for W Midlands 1989–96; author of scientific papers on med gases and med gas systems; DObstRCOG 1970, FFARCS 1973, FRSM 1984; *Recreations* church organist, aviation; *Style*— Dr Richard Howell; ✉ Keppel Gate Cottage, Frankton, Rugby; Department of Anaesthetics, Walsgrave Hospital, Coventry CV2 2DX (☎ 01203 602020)

HOWELL, Robert; s of Jim Howell, of Chesterfield, Derbys, and Gladys Mary, *née* Clayworth; *b* 18 April 1950; *Educ* Brunts' GS Mansfield, Univ of Manchester (BA); *m* 21 Sept 1984, Kathleen Mary, da of Richard John Rabey (d 1990); 1 s (Richard b 1987), 1 da (Nicola b 1984); *Career* asst treas Blue Circle Industries plc 1979–85, treas Tesco plc 1986–; ACMA 1979, MCT 1984; *Recreations* squash, various sports, fine wine; *Clubs* Lingfield Health; *Style*— Robert Howell, Esq; ✉ Tesco plc, New Tesco House, Delamare Rd, Cheshunt, Herts EN8 9SL (☎ 01992 644137, fax 01992 635883)

HOWELL, Rupert Cortlandt Spencer; s of Lt-Col F R Howell, of Ascot, Berkshire, and Sheila Dorothy Lorne McCallum; *b* 6 Feb 1957; *Educ* Wellington, Univ of Warwick (BSc); *m* 4 Sept 1987, Claire Jane, da of Dr Nigel Ashworth; 1 da (Amy Jane b 8 Aug 1991), 1 s (Dominic James Spencer b 4 Feb 1995); *Career* account exec Mathers Advertising (now Ogilvy and Mather Partners) 1979–80, account supervisor Grey Advertising 1982–83 (account mangr 1981); Young and Rubicam: account dir 1983–84, dir 1984–87, jt head of Account Mgmnt 1987; fndr ptnr HHCL and Partners (formerly Howell Henry Chaldecott Lury) 1987–; FIPA 1995 (MIPA 1989); *Recreations* cricket, golf, tennis (playing and spectating), rugby and soccer (spectating only!); *Clubs* MCC, London Rugby, Wentworth; *Style*— Rupert Howell, Esq; ✉ HHCL and Partners, Kent House, 14–17 Market Place, Great Titchfield St, London W1N 7AJ (☎ 0171 436 3333, fax 0171 436 2677, e-mail ruperth@hhcl.com)

HOWELL-DAVIES, Peter; *b* Glasgow; *m* (wife decd); 2 da; *Career* Cable & Wireless plc: joined 1962, various tech appts overseas 1960s and 1970s (latterly project mangr Middle E), gen mangr Yemen Arab Republic 1984–86; Mercury Communications Ltd (subsid of Cable & Wireless): dir of ops 1986–87, chief operating offr 1987–88, dep md 1988–90, md 1990–92, dep chief exec 1992–93; dep chief exec Hong Kong Telecommunications Ltd (also subsid of C&W) 1993–95, chief exec Mercury Communications Ltd 1995–; *Recreations* tennis, golf, France; *Style*— Peter Howell-Davies, Esq; ✉ Mercury Communications Ltd, New Mercury House, 26 Red Lion Square, London WC1R 4HQ (☎ 0171 528 2000, fax 0171 528 2181)

HOWELLS, David John; s of Ivor Mervyn Howells, of Shrewsbury, and Veronica Carey, *née* Jones; *b* 14 March 1953; *Educ* London Hosp Med Coll (BDS), Univ Hosp of Wales (MScD); *m* 18 Feb 1978, Lisa Pauline, da of Peter Noble, of Esher, Surrey; 2 da (Lowri b 1989, Ffion b 1991); *Career* postgrad training in orthodontics Welsh Nat Sch of Med, registrar Queen Alexandra Hosp Portsmouth 1982–84, sr registrar Birmingham Dental Hosp 1984–87, conslt orthodontist to Morriston Hosp Swansea and Prince Phillip Hosp Llanelli 1987–, clinical dir Morriston Hosp 1990–95, chm W Glam Dist Dental Ctee 1991–96, chm Lechyd Morgannwg Dist Dental Ctee 1996–; also in private orthodontic practice; author of several academic papers in specialist jls; LDS, DOrth, MOrth, FDSRCS (Eng); *Recreations* scuba diving, hiking, photography, nature conservation; *Style*— David Howells, Esq; ✉ Maxillofacial Unit, Morriston Hospital, Swansea (☎ 01792 703101, fax 01792 703632, e-mail 100305.341@compuserve.com)

HOWELLS, Dr Kim Scott; MP (Lab) Pontypridd (majority 19,797); s of Glanville James Howells, of Aberdare, Mid-Glamorgan, and Glenys Joan, *née* Edwards; *b* 27 Nov 1946; *Educ* Mountain Ash GS, Hornsey Coll of Art, Cambridge Coll of Advanced Technol (BA), Univ of Warwick (PhD); *m* 22 Oct 1983, Eirlys, da of William Elfed Davies, of Neath, West Glamorgan; 2 s (Cai James b 26 April 1984, Scott Aled b 20 Feb 1988), 1 da (Seren Rachel Morgans b 23 Dec 1976); *Career* steel worker 1969–70, coal miner 1970–71, lectr 1975–79; res offr: Univ of Wales 1979–82, NUM S Wales 1982–89 (also ed); TV presenter and writer 1986–89; MP (Lab) Pontypridd 1989–, memb House of Commons: Select Ctee on Welsh Affairs, Select Ctee on the Environment, Public Accounts Ctee; oppn front bench spokesman on: Overseas Cooperation and Devpt 1993, Foreign Affairs 1994, Home Affairs 1994–95, Trade and Industry 1995–; *Publications* various essays in collections dealing mainly with mining history, trade unionism, literature and the environment; *Recreations* mountaineering, jazz, cinema; *Clubs* Llantwit Fadre CC, Pontypridd CC, Hopkinstown CC; *Style*— Dr Kim Howells, MP; ✉ 30 Berw Road, Pontypridd, Mid-Glamorgan CF37 2AA (☎ 01443 402551, fax 01443 485628); House of Commons, Westminster, London SW1A 0AA (☎ 0171 219 5813, fax 0171 219 5526)

HOWELLS, Michael Sandbrook; s of Benjamin George Howells (d 1971), of Pembroke Dock, and Blodwen, *née* Francis (d 1978); *b* 29 May 1939; *Educ* Dean Close Sch, Cheltenham, Univ Coll London; *m* 18 June 1966, Pamela Vivian, da of Gordon Harry Francis, of Clandon, Surrey; 2 s (Luke b 1970, Toby b 1972); *Career* admitted slr 1966; sr ptnr Price and Kelway Slrs 1980–95 (ptnr 1971), princ Michael S Howells Slrs 1995–; HM coroner Pembrokeshire 1980; memb: Cncl Law Soc 1983– (dep treas 1992–95, treas 1995–96), Supreme Ct Rules Ctee 1985–88, Cncl of Coroners' Soc of England and Wales 1986–; pres Pembrokeshire C of C 1995–96; *Recreations* theatre, bee keeping, messing about in boats; *Clubs* RAC, Waterloo, Milford Haven, Neyland Yacht; *Style*— Michael Howells, Esq; ✉ Glenowen, Mastlebridge, Milford Haven, Dyfed SA73 1QS (☎ 01646 600 208); Michael S Howells, Hamilton Terrace, Milford Haven, Dyfed SA73 3JJ (☎ 01646 690929, fax 016462 690607)

HOWELLS, Col (William) Peter; CBE (1988), OBE (Mil, 1976), TD (1964, 2 clasps 1970 and 1976), DL (Pembrokeshire (later Dyfed) 1973); s of Lt-Col Percy Rotherham Howells (d 1961), and Maggie May, *née* Jones, MBE, JP; *b* 17 Oct 1931; *Educ* Ellesmere Coll Shropshire; *m* 29 Aug 1956, Marlene Jane, da of Richard Stanley Scourfield (d 1966); 2 s (Paul b 1958, Philip b 1960); *Career* 1 Bn The Welch Regt 1950–52, 4 (V) Bn The Welch Regt 1952–69; Pembroke Yeomanry 1967–69, 224 Sqdn RCT(V) 1969–71; CO 157 (Tport) Regt RCT (V) 1973–76, Col TA Wales 1977–80, Hon Col 4 (V) Bn Royal Regt of Wales 1982–93; md and chm Howells (Jewellers) Ltd 1961–; ADC to HM The Queen 1978–82, High Sheriff of Dyfed 1980–81, OStJ (1988, SBStJ 1980); Wales Territorial Army Assoc: memb West Wales Ctee 1969–, memb 1973–, chm 1985, memb Cncl Reserve Forces 1985– (vice chm 1992–); vice chm Tax Cmmrs for Haverfordwest Dist 1984– (tax cmmr 1977–); Nat Assoc of Round Tables: chm Tenby Branch 1955 (fndr vice chm

1954), pres Haverfordwest Branch 1979 (fndr chm 1957); pres: Haverfordwest Rotary Club 1969, Little and Broad Haven Lifeboat Ctee RNLI 1978–, St John Ambulance Bde Haverfordwest 1980–, Boys Bde Co Haverfordwest 1982–83, Dyfed Ctee Duke of Edinburgh Award Scheme 1988–; Broad and Little Haven Branch Royal Br Legion: memb 1977–, vice pres 1978–81, pres 1981–, memb Ctee 1981–; chm Pembroke Yeomanry Dinner Club 1979–; Royal Br Legion: patron of Pembrokeshire Co Branch 1980–, vice pres for Wales 1988 (pres 1992–); Freeman Haverfordwest 1975; *Recreations* motoring, shooting, walking, music; *Clubs* Cardiff and County, Naval and Military, Army & Navy; *Style*— Col Peter Howells, CBE, TD, DL; ✉ Howells Jewellers Ltd, 2 Quay St, Haverfordwest, Pembrokeshire, Dyfed SA61 1BG (☎ 01437 762050, car 0860 845445)

HOWELLS, Roger Alan; s of Lt-Col George Edward Howells, OBE, late RAMC (d 1991), of Fleet, Hampshire, and Cecilia Doris May, *née* Pope; *b* 30 Oct 1943; *Educ* Farnborough GS; *m* 18 June 1982, (Edome) Rowena, da of late John Raymund Sharpe, of Earl Soham, Suffolk; 1 s (Christian Peter George b 1985), 1 da (Lucinda Chloe b 1983); *Career* Lt HAC 1968–74; dir: Howells Rawlings & Ward Ltd (independent fin advsrs) 1972–, Howells & Bingham Ltd (registered insur brokers) 1980–; memb Lloyd's; Freeman City of London 1978, Liveryman Worshipful Co of Makers of Playing Cards 1979 (Master 1995–96); ACII 1969; *Recreations* tennis, golf, shooting, fishing; *Clubs* HAC, Hurlingham, Berkshire Golf, Royal Wimbledon Golf; *Style*— R A Howells, Esq; ✉ 17 Nicosia Rd, London SW18 3RN (☎ 0181 874 0299); Howells Rawlings & Ward Ltd, 29 Bunhill Row, London EC1Y 8LP (☎ 0171 638 8693, fax 0171 638 1177)

HOWELLS, Roger Godfrey; s of Godfrey Frank Howells, of Bridgend, and Hilda, *née* Rogers; *b* 21 Oct 1954; *Educ* Bridgend Boys GS; *m* (m dis); m 2, 29 Dec 1994, Judith Wendy; *Career* CA; ptnr Caulfield Cavells 1994; dir: Mutual Accountants Professional Indemnity Co Ltd, Inpact (UK) Ltd, QTac Solutions Ltd, Caulfield Cavells Limited, Caulfield Cavells Consulting Limited; *Recreations* fishing, swimming, golf; *Style*— Roger Howells, Esq; ✉ Ross Cottage, Northwick Rd, Pilning, Bristol (☎ 01454 632438); Caulfield Cavells, Barley House, Oakfield Grove, Clifton, Bristol (☎ 0117 923 8226, fax 0117 923 8488)

HOWES, Prof Christopher Kingston; CB (1993); s of Leonard Arthur Howes, OBE, of Norfolk, and Marion Amy, *née* Bussey; *b* 30 Jan 1942; *Educ* Gresham's, LSE, Coll of Estate Mgmnt (BSc), Univ of Reading (MPhil); *m* 1967, Clare, da of Gordon Edward Cunliffe (d 1987), of Sussex; 2 s (Robert b 1976, Michael b 1977), 2 da (Catherine b 1973, Rosalind b 1975 (decd)); *Career* GLC Planning & Valuation Depts 1965–67; ptnr (later sr ptnr) Chartered Surveyors & Planning Consits 1967–79, dep dir Land Economy Directorate DOE 1979–80 (dir Land Economy 1981–84), dir Land and Property 1985–89, second Crown Estate cmmr and chief exec Crown Estate 1989–; visiting lectr Univs of London, E Anglia (sr visiting fell 1973), Cambridge, Reading and Aberdeen 1966–; visiting prof UCL 1985–; memb Norwich Cncl 1970–74, magistrate for Norfolk 1973–79, memb Ct of Advsrs St Paul's Cathedral 1980–, steward and hon surveyor to Dean and Chapter Norwich Cathedral 1972–79; RICS: memb Policy Review Ctee 1979–81, memb Planning & Devpt Divnl Cncl 1984–92; memb Cncl Duchy of Lancaster 1993–, memb Sec of State for the Environment's Thames Advsy Gp 1995–; hon memb Cambridge Univ Land Soc 1989; memb: HRH Prince of Wales's Cncl 1990–, Cncl Br Property Fedn 1992–, Ct Univ of E Anglia 1992–; tstee HRH Prince of Wales's Inst of Architecture 1991–; first hon fell Local Authy Valuers' Assoc 1990, Hon FRIBA 1995; *Books* Value Maps: Aspects of Land and Property Values (1980), Economic Regeneration (1988), Urban Revitalization (1988); contributor to many books and articles in learned journals; *Recreations* music, art, architecture, sailing; *Clubs* Athenaeum, Norfolk (Norwich), Aldeburgh Yacht; *Style*— Prof Christopher Howes, CB; ✉ Highfield House, Woldingham, Surrey; 305 High Street, Aldeburgh, Suffolk; The Crown Estate, 16 Carlton House Terrace, London SW1Y 5AH (☎ 0171 210 4231)

HOWES, Jacqueline Frances (Jaki); da of Frank Bernard Allen (d 1974), of Hardingstone, Northants, and Hilda Evelyn, *née* Bull; *b* 5 April 1943; *Educ* Northampton HS, Univ of Manchester (BA); *m* (m dis 1982), (Anthony) Mark Howes, s of Anthony Cecil George Howes (d 1974); 1 da (Josephine); *Career* Guardian and Manchester Evening News Manchester 1969–71, Leach Rhodes and Walker 1971–72, sr lectr Sch of Architecture Huddersfield Poly 1972–89, conslt to Geoffrey Alsop Practice Manchester 1983–85, princ lectr in architecture Leeds Metropolitan Univ (formerly Leeds Poly) 1990–; chair IT Working Gp RIBA, memb Cncl RIBA Yorks region; convenor IT Gp, CIC IT Forum, tstee Huddersfield Poly Fund for Students with Disabilities; Liveryman Worshipful Co of Chartered Architects 1992, Freeman City of London 1993; ARCUK 1970, RIBA 1976; *Books* The Technology of Suspended Cable Net Structures (with Chaplin and Calderbank, 1984), Computers Count (1989); numerous contrib to learned jls incl: Architects Journal, RIBA Journal, Yorkshire Architect; *Recreations* sailing, music, cartoons; *Style*— Mrs Jaki Howes; ✉ School of Art, Architecture and Design, Leeds Metropolitan University, Brunswick Building, Leeds LS2 9BU (☎ 0113 283 2600)

HOWES, Prof Michael John; s of Lt Cdr Ernest Stanley George Howes (d 1984), of Lowestoft, Suffolk, and Louisa Anne, *née* Hart (d 1976); *b* 19 Jan 1941; *Educ* Lowestoft GS, Univ of Leeds (BSc, PhD); *m* 8 Oct 1960, Dianne Lucie, da of Rex Crutchfield, of Stevenage, Herts; 1 da (Emma); *Career* scientific offr MAFF 1957–62; Univ of Leeds: lectr 1967–78, sr lectr 1978–80, head of dept and prof of electronic engrg 1984–95; visiting prof Cornell Univ USA 1980–81, tech dir MM Microwave Yorks 1981–84; author of numerous engrg and scientific pubns; MInstP, FIEE, FIEEE, FRSA; *Books* incl: Solid State Electronics (with D V Morgan, 1973), Microwave Devices (ed with D V Morgan, 1976), Optical Fibre Communications (ed with D V Morgan, 1980), Reliability and Degradation (ed with D V Morgan, 1982), Worked Examples in Microwave Subsystem Design (jtly, 1984), Reliability and Degradation (ed with D V Morgan, 1985); *Recreations* golf; *Clubs* Moortown Golf; *Style*— Prof Michael Howes; ✉ 32 West Park Drive, Leeds LS16 5BL (☎ 0113 275 2156); Department of Electronic and Electrical Engineering, The University, Leeds LS2 9JT (☎ 0113 233 2014, fax 0113 233 2032, e-mail m.j.howes@elec.eng.leeds.ac.uk)

HOWEY, Kate Louise; da of David Michael Howey, and Sharon Kathleen, *née* Tipping; *b* 31 May 1973; *Educ* Winton Sch; *Career* judoist; took up judo aged 7; clubs: Chalkhill, Brighton Hill, Kent Invicta JudoKwai; honours incl (under 66kg category): Gold medal Jr Euro Championships Greece 1989, Turkey 1990 and Finland 1991, Gold medal Jr World Championships France 1990, Silver medal Sr Euro Championships Germany 1990 and Prague 1991, Bronze medal Sr World Championships Spain 1991, Bronze medal Olympic Games Barcelona 1992 (first Br woman to win Olympic judo medal), Silver medal World Championships Canada 1993; VDU operator; *Recreations* music, sport in general; *Style*— Miss Kate Howey; ✉ 6 Linton Drive, Andover, Hants SP10 3TT (☎ 01264 358285)

HOWGRAVE-GRAHAM, Christopher Michael; s of Hamilton Stuart Howgrave-Graham, of Salisbury, Wilts, and Joyce Mary, *née* Rowlatt; *b* 18 Feb 1949; *Educ* Ardingly Coll, UEA (BA), Institut d'Etudes Politiques; *m* 5 Aug 1972, Rossana, da of Giliande Mastroddi; 2 s (Jonathan b 7 Dec 1977, Matthew b 28 March 1981); *Career* NHS trainee (Winchester, Portsmouth, Kings Fund Coll London) 1971–73; planner: East Birmingham HMC 1973–74, South Birmingham Health Authy 1974–75; house governor St Stephen's Hosp 1975–80 (latterly sector admin Chelsea & Kensington), dep dist admin and acute servs mangr Redbridge Health Authy 1980–85, gen mangr Community & Mental Health Servs Barking Havering and Brentwood Health Authy 1986–88, dir of acute servs Bloomsbury and Islington Health Authy 1989–90, mangr Middlesex Hosp, UCH and associated hosps, Whittington Hosp and Royal Northern Hosps 1990–92, London review co-ordinator NE Thames RHA 1992–; chief exec Coventry Health Authy 1993–, sec Special Tstees of Middx Hosp 1990–92; MIHSM 1976; *Books* The Hospital in Little Chelsea (with Dr L Martin, 1978); *Recreations* keeping fit, gardening, seeing the family; *Style*— Christopher Howgrave-Graham, Esq; ✉ Coventry Health Authority, Christchurch House, Greyfriars Lane, Coventry CV1 2GQ (☎ 01203 844001, fax 01203 226280)

HOWICK OF GLENDALE, 2 Baron (UK 1960); Charles Evelyn Baring; s of 1 Baron Howick of Glendale, KG, GCMG, KCVO (d 1973; formerly Hon Sir Evelyn Baring, sometime govr Kenya and yst s of 1 Earl of Cromer), and Lady Mary Grey, da of 5 Earl Grey; *b* 30 Dec 1937; *Educ* Eton, New Coll Oxford; *m* 1964, Clare, yr da of Col Cyril Darby, MC, of Kemerton Court, Tewkesbury; 1 s, 3 da (Hon Rachel Monica (Hon Mrs Lane Fox) b 1967, Hon Jessica Mary Clare (Hon Mrs Laithwaite) b 1969, Hon Alice Olivia b 1971); *Heir* s, Hon David Evelyn Charles Baring b 26 March 1975; *Career* md Baring Bros & Co 1969–82, dir London Life Assoc 1972–82, dir Northern Rock Building Society 1988–; memb Exec Ctee Nat Art Collections Fund 1973–88; *Style*— The Lord Howick of Glendale; ✉ Howick, Alnwick, Northumberland NE66 3LB (☎ 01665 577624); 42 Bedford Gardens, London W8 (☎ 0171 221 0880)

HOWIE, Prof Archibald; s of Robert Howie (d 1992), of Grange, Kirkcaldy, Fife, and Margaret Marshall, *née* McDonald (d 1971); *b* 8 March 1934; *Educ* Kirkcaldy HS, Univ of Edinburgh (BSc), California Inst of Technol (MS), Univ of Cambridge (PhD); *m* 15 Aug 1964, Melva Jean, da of Ernest Scott (d 1959), of Tynemouth, Northumberland; 1 s (David Robert b 9 Oct 1965, d 1986), 1 da (Helena Margaret b 14 July 1971); *Career* Univ of Cambridge: ICI fell 1960–61, demonstrator in physics 1962–65, lectr 1965–78, reader 1978–86, prof 1986–, head Dept of Physics 1989–; Churchill Coll Cambridge: fell 1960–, res fell 1960–61, teaching fell in physics 1962–86; visiting prof of physics: Aarhus 1974, Bologna 1984; pres Royal Microscopical Soc 1984–86; Hughes medal Royal Soc (with Dr M J Whelan) 1988; Hon Dr of Physics: Bologna 1989, Thessaloniki 1995; FRS 1978, FInstP 1978, Hon FRMS 1978, Hon FRSE 1995; *Books* Electron Microscopy of Thin Crystals (jtly 1965, revised 1977), Electron Optical Imaging of Surfaces (jtly); *Recreations* winemaking; *Style*— Prof Archibald Howie, FRS; ✉ 194 Huntingdon Rd, Cambridge CB3 0LB (☎ 01223 570977); Cavendish Laboratory, Madingley Rd, Cambridge CB3 0HE (☎ 01223 337334, fax 01223 363263)

HOWIE, Prof John Garvie Robertson; CBE (1996); s of Sir James William Howie (d 1995), of Edinburgh, and Lady Winifred Howie, *née* Mitchell; *b* 23 Jan 1937; *Educ* Univ of Glasgow (MD), Univ of Aberdeen (PhD); *m* 27 Dec 1962, Elizabeth Margaret (Margot), da of William Lochhead Donald, of Craigleith Rd, Edinburgh; 2 s (Alastair b 1963, Brian b 1965), 1 da (Claire b 1969); *Career* GP Glasgow 1966–70, sr lectr in gen practice (formerly lectr) Univ of Aberdeen 1970–80, prof of gen practice Univ of Edinburgh 1980–; FRCGP 1980, FRCPE 1989; *Books* Research in General Practice (2 edn, 1989); *Recreations* gardening, music, sport; *Style*— Prof John Howie, CBE; ✉ 4 Ravelrig Park, Balerno, Midlothian, Scotland EH14 7DL (☎ 0131 449 6305); University of Edinburgh, Department of General Practice, 20 West Richmond St, Edinburgh EH8 9DX (☎ 0131 650 2675, fax 0131 650 2681)

HOWIE, Prof John Mackintosh; CBE (1993); s of Rev David Yuille Howie, of Aberdeen, and Janet Macdonald, *née* Mackintosh (d 1989); *b* 23 May 1936; *Educ* Robert Gordon's Coll Aberdeen, Univ of Aberdeen (MA, DSc), Balliol Coll Oxford (DPhil); *m* 5 Aug 1960, Dorothy Joyce Mitchell, da of Alfred James Miller, OBE (d 1980), of Aberdeen; 2 da (Anne b 1961, Katharine b 1963); *Career* asst in maths Univ of Aberdeen 1958–59, asst then lectr in maths Univ of Glasgow 1961–67, sr lectr in maths Univ of Stirling 1967–70, regius prof of maths Univ of St Andrews 1970– (dean Faculty of Sci 1976–79); visiting appts: Tulane Univ 1964–65, Univ of Western Aust 1968, State Univ of NY at Buffalo 1969 & 1970, Monash Univ 1979, Northern Illinois Univ 1988, Univ of Lisbon 1996; chm: Scot Central Ctee on Mathematics 1975–81, Dundee Coll of Educn 1983–87, Ctee to Review Fifth and Sixth Years (The Howie Ctee) 1990–; memb Ctee to Review Examinations (The Dunning Ctee) 1975–77, vice pres London Mathematical Soc 1984–86 and 1990–92; FRSE 1971; *Books* An Introduction to Semigroup Theory (1976), Automata and Languages (1991), Fundamentals of Semigroup Theory (1995), and author of articles for various mathematical jls; *Recreations* music, gardening; *Style*— Prof John M Howie, CBE, FRSE; ✉ Longacre, 19 Strathkinness High Road, St Andrews, Fife KY16 9UA (☎ 01334 474103); Mathematical Institute, University of St Andrews, North Haugh, St Andrews, Fife KY16 9SS (☎ 01334 463746, fax 01334 463748, e-mail jmh@st-andrews.ac.uk)

HOWIE, Prof Peter William; s of Sir James William Howie (d 1995), of Edinburgh, and Isabella Winifred, *née* Mitchell; *b* 21 Nov 1939; *Educ* Aberdeen GS, Glasgow HS, Univ of Glasgow (MB ChB, MD); *m* 25 March 1965, Anne Jardine, da of William Jardine Quigg; 1 da (Lesley Anne b 21 Nov 1967), 1 s (Andrew Goodwin b 29 April 1971); *Career* house offr and SHO positions in med, surgery, obstetrics and gynaecology 1963–67, registrar in obstetrics and gynaecology Queen Mother's Hosp Glasgow 1967–69, Astor Fndn res fell RCPath and Univ Dept of Med Royal Infirmary Glasgow 1970–71, sr lectr Univ Dept of Obstetrics and Gynaecology Glasgow Royal Infirmary and Glasgow Royal Maternity Hosp 1974–78 (lectr 1971–74), clinical conslt Reproductive Biology Unit MRC 1978–81; Univ of Dundee: prof of obstetrics and gynaecology 1981–, dean Faculty of Med and Dentistry 1990–93, vice princ 1996–; Blair Bell Meml lectr RCOG 1978, Sims Black prof 1995; memb GMC 1994–96; chm: WHO Task Force on Natural Methods of Fertility Regulation 1988–96, Scottish Cncl of Postgrad Med and Dental Educn 1996–; memb: Assoc of Clinical Profs of Obstetrics and Gynaecology, Blair-Bell Res Soc, Glasgow Obstetrical and Gynaecological Soc, Gynaecological Visiting Soc, Munro-Kerr Res Soc, Royal Medico-Chirurgical Soc of Glasgow, Scottish Soc of Experimental Med, Edinburgh Obstetrical Soc, BMA; FRCOG 1981 (MRCOG 1968), FRSE 1992, FRCP 1994; author of numerous articles in refereed jls; *Books* The Small Baby (jt ed), Volume of Clinics in Obstetrics and Gynaecology (ed, 1984); *Recreations* golf, music; *Clubs* Panmure Golf; *Style*— Prof Peter Howie, FRSE; ✉ 8 Travebank Gardens, Monifieth, Angus DD5 4ET (☎ 01382 534802); Department of Obstetrics and Gynaecology, University of Dundee, Ninewells Hospital and Medical School, Dundee DD1 9SY (☎ 01382 632147, fax 01382 566617)

HOWIE OF TROON, Baron (Life Peer UK 1978); William Howie; s of Peter Howie; *b* 2 March 1924; *Educ* Marr Coll Troon, Royal Tech Coll Glasgow; *m* 1951, Mairi, da of John Sanderson; 2 da, 2 s; *Career* civil engr, journalist and publisher; MP (Lab) Luton 1963–70, asst whip 1964–66, lord cmmr Treasy 1966–67, comptroller HM Household 1967–68, vice-chm PLP 1968–70, dir of internal rels Thos Telford Ltd 1976–95; pro-chllr City Univ 1984–91 (memb Cncl 1968–91); MSocIS (France), FICE; *Style*— Rt Hon Lord Howie of Troon; ✉ 34 Temple Fortune Lane, London NW11 (☎ 0181 455 0492)

HOWITT, Miriam; *née* Cooper; da of Charles Brodie Cooper (d 1978), of Broad Howe, Cumbria, and Lydia, *née* Peltzer (d 1984); *b* 1 Feb 1929; *Educ* St Leonard's Sch, St Andrews, AA Sch of Architecture (DipArch); *m* 8 Oct 1958, David Alan Howitt, s of Claude Elborne Howitt (d 1964), of Nottingham; 3 s (Nicholas b 1960, Mark b 1962, Paul b 1963), 1 da (Philipa b 1959); *Career* architect and designer; in private practice with husband, work incl airports, hotels, showrooms, offices, schools, clubs, convents and facilities for the disabled; winner: Crown Inn Hotel Ampney Crucis Design competition 1975, Br Design in Japan Lighting competition 1988; former govr London Coll of

Furniture; freedom to trade as citizen of City of London by virtue of birth on island of St Helena; RIBA 1953, FCSD 1976 (formerly vice pres, memb Cncl, examiner, chm of Examiners); *Books* One Room Living (1972, Japanese edn, 1979); *Recreations* pottery, skiing, fell walking; *Style*— Mrs David Howitt; ✉ 33 Roehampton Gate, London SW15 5JR (☎ 0181 878 0520, fax 0181 878 0054)

HOWITT, Richard; MEP (Lab) Essex South (majority 21,367); *Educ* Lady Margaret Hall Oxford (MA), Univ of Hertfordshire (Dip in Mgmnt Studies); *Partner* Wendy Fitzgibbon; *Career* co-ordinator Harlow Cncl for Voluntary Service 1982–86, specialist in community care for the disabled Waltham Forest Social Services 1986–94; chm South-East Economic Devpt Strategy (SEEDS) 1986–94, memb Bd Centre for Local Economic Strategies (CLES) 1988–91, UK rep Helios Prog 1988–91; Harlow DC: cncllr 1984–94, chm Planning and Economic Devpt Ctee 1985–91, leader 1991–94; MEP (Lab) Essex South 1994–; memb: Regional Affrs Ctee, Devpt Ctee; sec Lab Gp of MEPs in South East, vice pres All Pty Disability Gp of MEPs; *Recreations* photography, travel, opera and cricket; *Style*— Richard Howitt, Esq, MEP; ✉ Suite 3 Top Floor, Tudor Chambers, Station Lane, Pitsea, Basildon, Essex SS13 3BQ (☎ 01268 550600, fax 01268 550700)

HOWITT, Victor Charles; s of Sqdn Ldr Ronald Charles Howitt, DFC, of Bognor Regis, Sussex, and Ruby Frances Howitt (d 1976); *b* 13 July 1935; *m* 1, Dec 1956 (m dis 1977), Mary, da of Charles Langridge (d 1955); 2 s (Peter Charles b 28 Sept 1961, Stephen Jarvis Boughton b 7 Nov 1965), 1 da (Allison Mary b 13 Sept 1958); m 2, 17 June 1978, Elizabeth Anne (Betty), da of Charles Anthony Reghelini (d 1966); *Career* Nat Serv drill instr RAF 1953–55; articled CA 1951, trainee mangr 1952, locum dispensing optician R W Bradshaw 1960 (trainee 1956); dir Wigmores 1968, regnl md London and Home Counties, D & A International 1974 (memb Devpt Team 1973); md 1982: Wigmores Ltd, Theodore Hamblin Ltd, Hamblin Wigmores Ltd; observer to Bd D & A Group Ltd 1983, dir of trg and chm Hamblin Wigmores 1983–85, dir D & A Group UK 1985–95, md D & A Group Operations (gp ops dir 1985–89), main bd dir Dollond Aitchison Group plc 1989–94 (UK gp dir of retail devpt 1989–93), UK gp franchise dir 1993–95, ret; franchise and retail conslt 1995–; sr ptnr Victor and Betty Howitt Associates; memb Cncl: Companies Ctee Gen Optical Cncl 1985–93, Guild of Br Dispensing Opticians 1981–84, Fedn of Ophthalmic and Dispensing Opticians 1984–86; vice chm Abbey Park Residents Assoc 1986–87; Freeman: City of London 1988, Worshipful Co of Spectacle Makers 1988; FBDO 1961; *Recreations* photography, reading, gardening, old houses, travel, collecting cranberry glass and stamps; *Style*— Victor Howitt, Esq; ✉ The Penthouse, Baronscroft, 4 Milner Road, West Cliff, Bournemouth, Dorset BH4 8AD (☎ and fax 01202 385971, mobile 0385 922237)

HOWKER, Janni; da of Malcolm John Cookson Walker, of Kendal, Cumbria, and Mavis Nancy, *née* Bond; *b* 6 July 1957; *Educ* Monk's Dyke HS Louth Lincs, Kendal HS Cumbria, Univ of Lancaster (BA, MA); *m* 1 (m dis 1986), Ian Howker; m 2, 15 Oct 1988, Mick North, s of Tom North; 1 s (John Edward b 26 Jan 1990); *Career* author; various jobs 1976–84 (pt/t care asst hostel for mentally ill, invigilator for Open Univ, res asst, park attendant for Lancaster City Cncl, landlady for long distance lorry drivers), freelance author 1984–; memb: Soc of Authors, Royal Soc of Literature, Arvon Fndn Cncl; *Awards* Int Reading Assoc Award 1985, Tom Gallon Award Soc of Authors 1985, Burnley Express Children's Book of the Year 1985, Young Observer Teenage Fiction Prize 1985, Whitbread Award for Children's Fiction 1985, highly commended for Carnegie Medal 1986 and 1987, Silver Pencil Award (Holland) 1987 and 1993, Somerset Maugham Award 1987, Boston Globe Horn Book Award 1987; *Television Work* incl: Janni Howker-Storyteller (Thames TV) 1985, Dramarama (ITV) 1987, The Nature of the Beast (Channel 4) 1988; *Books* Badger on the Barge (1984), The Nature of the Beast (1985), Isaac Campion (1986), The Topiary Garden (1993), Martin Farrell (1994); *Recreations* fell walking, silence, fishing, mending things, writing letters to friends; *Style*— Ms Janni Howker; ✉ The Cottage, Cumwhitton, Carlisle, Cumbria CA4 9EX (☎ 01228 560926)

HOWKINS, Ben Walter; s of Col Walter Ashby (Tim) Howkins (d 1977), and Lesley, *née* Stops, of Olney, Bucks; *b* 19 Aug 1942; *Educ* Rugby, Amherst Coll Mass USA; *m* 6 Nov 1976, Clarissa Jane, da of Thomas John Fairbank, of Cambridge; 1 s (James b 1980), 1 da (Lucy b 1981); *Career* Vintners scholar 1963, Lt Northants Yeo TA 1964–69; brand mangr IDV UK 1968–70, int sales and mktg dir Croft & Co 1970–80, md Morgan Furze 1980–89, dir Taylor Fladgate & Yeatman 1989–90, chm Wine Promotion Bd 1990–93, wine conslt Waddesdon Manor 1991–; dir: Château de Landiras 1993–, Royal Tokay Wine Co 1993–; memb Cncl Wine Guild of UK; Freeman City of London 1986, Liveryman Worshipful Co of Vintners 1986; *Books* Rich, Rare and Red - A Guide to Port (1982, paperbook edn 1987); *Recreations* skiing, tennis, shooting; *Clubs* Brooks's; *Style*— Ben Howkins, Esq; ✉ Staverton Manor, Staverton, Northamptonshire NN11 6JD (☎ 01327 703600); 3 St James's Place, London SW1A 1NP (☎ 0171 495 3010, fax 0171 493 3973)

HOWKINS, John Anthony; s of Col Ashby (Tim) Howkins (d 1977), and Lesley, *née* Stops; *b* 3 Aug 1945; *Educ* Rugby, Univ of Keele (BA), Architectural Assoc (AADipl); *m* 1, 1971, Jill, da of Ian Liddington; m 2, 1977, Annabel, da of John Whittet; *Career* mktg mangr Lever Bros 1968–70, TV ed Time Out 1971–74, jt fndr TV4 Conf 1971, dir Whittet Books 1976–84, chm Pool Video Graz Austria 1976, ed Vision 1977–79, chm London Int Film Sch 1979–84, TV columnist Illustrated London News 1981–83, exec ed Nat Electronics Review 1981–90, exec dir Int Inst of Communications 1984–89, conslt and dir ETR & Co 1989–, assoc Coopers & Lybrand Deloitte 1990–91; specialist advsr Select Ctee on Euro Communities House of Lords 1985; advsr: Polish Radio and TV 1989–, Minister for Film Poland 1991–; dep chm Br Screen Advsy Cncl 1991– (memb 1985–); chm Createc 1996–; memb: Interim Action Ctee on the Film Indust DTI 1980–85, Exec Ctee Broadcasting Res Unit 1981–90, vice chm Assoc of Ind Producers 1984–85; *Books* Understanding Television (1977), Mass Communications in China (1982), New Technologies, New Policies (1982), Satellites International (1987); *Style*—John Howkins, Esq; ✉ E6 Albany, Piccadilly, London W1V 9RH (☎ 0171 434 1400, fax 0171 439 3241)

HOWKINS, John David; s of Gordon Arthur Howkins, and Olga Annie, *née* King; *b* 4 Feb 1955; *Educ* Crossfields Prep Sch, Windsor GS, Univ of Exeter (BSc); *m* 14 April 1984, Susan, da of Richard Andreas Oakley; 2 da (Lily May b 23 May 1988, Scarlett Hannah b 20 Feb 1991); *Career* media trainee rising to dep media dir D'Arcy McManus Masius advtg agency 1976–82, assoc dir of planning DMB&B 1982–84, planning dir Lowe Howard-Spink 1984–88, ptnr Elgie Stewart Smith 1988–90, md Planning Consultancy 1990–91, md DDM Advertising 1991–93, strategic planning dir McCann-Erickson 1993–; memb Market Res Soc 1982; *Recreations* media journalism, campanology; *Clubs* Royal Scottish Automobile; *Style*— John Howkins, Esq; ✉ Hermongers Barn, Rudgwick, West Sussex RH12 3AL (☎ 01403 822476); McCann-Erickson Ltd, 36 Howland Street, London W1A 1AT (☎ 0171 580 6690, fax 0171 915 2191)

HOWLAND, Lord; Andrew Ian Henry Russell; s and h of Marquess of Tavistock, *qv*; *b* 30 March 1962; *Educ* Harrow, Harvard Univ (BA); *Recreations* racing, shooting; *Style*— Lord Howland; ✉ 6 Fairlawns, Dullingham Rd, Newmarket, Suffolk CB8 9JS; Tattersalls Ltd, Terrace House, Newmarket, Suffolk CB8 9BT

HOWLAND JACKSON, Anthony Geoffrey Clive; s of Arthur Geoffrey Howland Jackson, MBE (d 1996), and Pamela Foote, *née* Wauton; *b* 25 May 1941; *Educ* Sherborne; *m* 15 June 1963, Susan Ellen, da of Geoffrey Hickson (d 1984); 1 s (James Geoffrey b 10 Feb 1965), 2 da (Anna Kate b 10 July 1968, Louisa Jane b 13 May 1971); *Career* md: Clarkson Puckle 1979–87, Bain Clarksons 1987; exec dir Gill & Duffus plc 1983–87; chm and chief exec Hogg Group PLC 1987–94, chm Bain Hogg PLC 1994–; memb Lloyd's Regulatory Bd 1993–, chm Lloyd's Insurance Brokers' Ctee (LIBC) 1996–; Freeman City of London, Liveryman Worshipful Co of Insurers; *Recreations* shooting, cricket, racing; *Clubs* Turf, City of London; *Style*— A G C Howland Jackson, Esq; ✉ Marks Gate, Fordham, Colchester, Essex CO6 3NR (☎ 01206 240420); Bain Hogg PLC, Lloyd's Chambers, No 1 Portsoken St, London E1 8DF (☎ 0171 301 4212, fax 0171 301 4388)

HOWLETT, Gen Sir Geoffrey Hugh Whitby; KBE (1984, OBE 1972), MC (1952); s of Brig Bernard Howlett, DSO (ka 1943), and Joan, *née* Whitby; *b* 5 Feb 1930; *Educ* Wellington, RMA Sandhurst; *m* 1955, Elizabeth Anne, da of Sqdn Ldr Leonard Aspinal, of Speldhurst; 1 s (Nigel b 1957), 2 da (Diana b 1958, Alexandra b 1963); *Career* cmmnd Queen's Own Royal West Kent Regt 1950, transfd Parachute Regt 1959, cmd 2 Para 1971–73, RCDS 1973–75, cmd 16 Para Bde 1975–77, dir Army Recruiting 1977–79, GOC 1 Armoured Div (Lower Saxony, W Germany) 1979–82, Cmdt RMA Sandhurst 1982–83, GOC SE Dist 1983–85; C-in-C Allied Forces Northern Europe (Oslo) 1986–89; Col Cmdt: Army Catering Corps 1981–89, The Parachute Regt 1983–90; chm: Services Sound and Vision Corp 1990– (vice chm 1989), Leonard Cheshire Fndn 1990–95 (tstee 1988–95); pres: CCF 1989–, Stragglers of Asia Cricket Club 1989–94, Regular Forces Employment Assoc 1993– (chm 1990–93), Dorset Army Benevolent Fund 1993–; cmmr Royal Hosp Chelsea 1989–95, chm Milton Abbey Sch Cncl 1994–; Liveryman Worshipful Co of Cooks 1991; *Recreations* cricket, shooting; *Clubs* Naval & Military, MCC; *Style*— Gen Sir Geoffrey Howlett, KBE, MC; ✉ c/o Lloyds Bank, Tonbridge, Kent TN12 0QQ

HOWLETT, Neil Baillie; s of Terence Howlett (d 1975), of Storrington, W Sussex, and Margaret Marshall, *née* Baillie (d 1983); *b* 24 July 1934; *Educ* Trent Coll, King's Coll Cambridge (MA), Hochschule Für Musik Darstellende Kunst Stuttgart; *m* 1, 1962 (m dis 1988); 2 da (Alexandra b 1971, Olivia b 1974); m 2, 1988, Carolyn Margaret, *née* Hawthorn; *Career* opera singer; Eng Opera Gp (Aldeburgh Festival, Soviet Union Tour) 1964; Glyndebourne tour: L'Ormindo 1967, Idem 1968, Macbeth; Aix-en-Provence Festival: Don Giovanni 1970, Falstaff 1971; ENO 1972–89; guest appearances in: Cologne, Frankfurt, Hamburg, Royal Opera House Covent Garden, Athens Festival, Buenos Aires, Vichy Festival, Trieste, Netherlands Opera, Trondheim, Catania, ENO; concerts with: LPO, LSO, CBSO, SNO, Oslo Philharmonic, Orquesta Nacional Madrid, Orquesta de Cataluna Barcelona, Radio Orch Katowice and Warsaw, Slovenian Philharmonic, Maggio Musicale Firenze; recording Otello (with ENO 1984 and 1990); prof Guildhall Sch of Music 1974–92, head of Sch of Vocal Studies Royal Northen Coll of Music 1992–; Kathleen Ferrier Meml Scholarship 1957; *Recreations* sport, history, philosophy, piano, gardening, theatre, reading; *Style*— Neil Howlett, Esq; ✉ Ingpen and Williams Ltd, 14 Kensington Court, London W8 (☎ 0171 937 5158, fax 0171 938 4175); Royal Northern College of Music, 124 Oxford Road, Manchester M13 9RD (☎ 0161 273 6283, fax 0161 273 7611)

HOWLETT, Air Vice-Marshal Neville Stanley; CB (1982); s of Stanley Herbert Howlett (d 1981), and Ethel Shirley, *née* Pritchard (d 1934); *b* 17 April 1927; *Educ* Liverpool Inst HS, Peterhouse Cambridge; *m* 1952, Sylvia, da of James Foster (d 1982), of Lincs; 1 s (Michael), 1 da (Gillian); *Career* RAF pilot trg 1945–47, 32 and 64 (Fighter) Sqdns 1948–56, RAF Staff Coll Course 1957, Sqdn Cdr 229 (Fighter) OCU 1958–59, took part in London-Paris Air Race 1959, SO HQ Fighter Cmd 1959–61, OC Flying Wing RAF Coltishall 1961–63, RAF Coll of Air Warfare Course 1963, SO HQ Allied Forces Northern Europe 1964–66, OC Admin Wing RAF St Mawgan 1966–67, DS RAF Staff Coll 1967–69, Station Cdr RAF Leuchars 1970–72, RCDS Course 1972, Dir of Ops (Air Def and Overseas) MOD 1973–74, Air Attaché Washington DC 1975–77, Dir Mgmnt Support of Intelligence MOD 1978–80, DG RAF Personal Servs MOD 1980–82, ret; memb Lord Chllr's Panel of Ind Inquiry Insprs 1982–95; vice pres RAF Assoc 1984– (chm Exec Ctee 1990–); memb: Offrs' Assoc Cncl 1982–, Pensions Appeal Tbnl 1988–; *Recreations* golf, fishing; *Clubs* RAF, Phyllis Court (Henley-on-Thames), Huntercombe Golf; *Style*— Air Vice-Marshal Neville Howlett, CB; ✉ Milverton, Bolney Trevor Drive, Lower Shiplake, Oxon RG9 3PG

HOWLETT, Dr Trevor Anthony; s of Ivan William Howlett, of Cambridge, and Daphne May, *née* Long; *b* 20 July 1952; *Educ* Perse Sch Cambridge, Gonville and Caius Coll Cambridge (BA, MA, MB BChir, MD, FRCP), King's Coll Hosp Med Sch London; *Career* house physician King's Coll Hosp 1977–78, sr house offr Central Middx Hosp London 1978–79, med registrar Frimley Park Hosp Surrey 1980–81, lectr in endocrinology Dept of Endocrinology Bart's 1985–88 (MRC trg fell 1981–85), conslt physician and endocrinologist Leicester Royal Infirmary Leicester 1988–; sec Endocrine Section RSM 1992–96, UK rep Euro Bd Endocrinology 1994–; chair Specialist Working Gp in Endocrinology to the Clinical Terms Project (NHS Mgmnt Exec Info Mgmnt Gp); numerous scientific articles on clinical endocrinology and endogenous opioid peptides; FRSM, memb Soc for Endocrinology; *Recreations* gardening, skiing; *Style*— Dr Trevor Howlett; ✉ Leicester Royal Infirmary, Leicester LE1 5WW (☎ 0116 254 1414)

HOWLING, Richard John; s of Cecil Baden Howling (d 1990), of Dorset, and Florence Irene Crowther, *née* Firth (d 1993); *b* 22 Aug 1932; *Educ* Repton; *m* 4 April 1959, Shirley Maureen, da of Clifford Jackson (d 1964), of Lancs; 2 s (Rex b 1961, Philip b 1962), 1 da (Sally b 1964); *Career* Sub Lt RNVR 1956–58, served Pacific, Malaya; ptnr Bird Potter & Co CAs 1961–68, dir Peter Robinson Ltd 1968–71, asst to Fin Dir Carreras Rothmans 1971–72, dir Rednor Ltd (and other subsids) 1972–74, chm Mediscus International Ltd and Mediscus Products Ltd 1977–91, dir Mediscus Group Inc (USA) 1987–90; chm: Actus Holdings Ltd 1988–90, The Schubert Group Ltd 1989–90, Activity & Leisure Products (International) Ltd; dir Sandcastles (Poole) Management Ltd 1994–, ptnr Richley Properties 1994–; Royal Warrant Holder as Organ Blower Manufacturer to HM The Queen (Watkins & Watson Ltd, a subsid of the Lingard Group) 1981–87; chm: Wessex Export Club 1985–87, Dorset Indust Year Educn/Indust Ctee 1986, Dorset Co Gp CBI 1989–92; memb: Engrg Industs Assoc Nat Cncl 1985–87, Dorset Indust Matters Ctee 1987–91, S West Regnl Cncl CBI 1985–91, Fin and Econ Ctee (small firms) CBI 1985–87, Mktg and Consumer Affrs Ctee CBI 1987–91; dir Dorset C of C 1991–96, vice pres Dorset C of C and Indust 1995–96; vice chm Environmental Forum for Dorset Indust 1994–96, memb Nat Cncl ABCC 1994–96; advsr Prince's Youth Business Tst 1989–96; govr The Purbeck Sch 1988–93, external examiner Bournemouth Univ (Dorset Business Sch) 1994–96; FCA, FRSA; *Recreations* sailing, tennis, golf, flying, reading, photography, travel, walking; *Clubs* Royal Motor Yacht, Royal Over-Seas League; *Style*— Richard Howling, Esq; ✉ Roakham, Old Coastguard Rd, Sandbanks, Poole (☎ and fax 01202 708976); Puerto Calero, Lanzarote, Canary Islands

HOWORTH, Prof Jolyon Michael; s of Joseph Alfred Howorth (d 1966), and Constance, *née* Styles; *b* 4 May 1945; *Educ* Rossall and Henry Box Schs, Univ of Manchester (BA), Univ of Reading (PhD), Univs of Lausanne and Geneva; *m* 1, 27 Aug 1966 (m dis 1982), Pauline, *née* Macqueen; 1 da (Stephanie Jeanne b 1974); m 2, 4 Jan 1985 (m dis 1987), Laura, *née* Levine; m 3, 5 Sept 1988 (m dis 1994), Dr (Kirstine) Mairi Maclean, da of Alexander Gordon Maclean, of Glasgow; 1 s (Alexander Boris b 1989), 1 da (Emily Kirstine b 1988); *Career* lectr: Univ of Paris III (Sorbonne Nouvelle) 1969–76, Ecole des Hautes Etudes Commerciales Paris 1970–76; visiting prof Univ of Wisconsin Madison USA 1974–75, sr lectr Univ of Aston 1979–85 (lectr 1976–79); visiting scholar Harvard Univ 1981–82, 1984 and 1985; prof of French civilisation Univ of Bath 1985–, Jean Monnet prof of European Political Union 1993–; dir: EU/US Transatlantic Studies Prog, Language Conslts for Indust Bath 1986–91; conslt: Univs Funding Cncl, FCO, RIIA, EU; fndr memb Assoc for Study of Modern and Contemporary France, pres Br

Assoc for the Study of European Languages and Socs 1993–; memb: Royal Inst of Int Affrs, Int Inst for Strategic Studies, Soc for French Hist Studies, Institut Français d'Histoire Sociale; *Books* Elites in France: Origins, Reproduction and Power (with P Cerny, 1981), Edouard Vaillant et La Création de l'Unité Socialiste en France (1982), France: The Politics of Peace (1984), Defence and Dissent in Contemporary France (with P Chilton, 1984), Contemporary France: A Review of Interdisciplinary Studies (with George Ross, vol 1 1987, vol 2 1988, vol 3 1989), Europeans on Europe: Transnational Visions of a New Continent (with M Maclean, 1992); *Recreations* numismatics, skiing, swimming, travel; *Style*— Prof Jolyon Howorth; ✉ School of Modern Languages and International Studies, University of Bath, Bath BA2 7AY (☎ 01225 826490, fax 01225 826987 (gp 3), telex 449097, e-mail JM Howorth@bath.ac.uk)

HOWSON, Peter John; s of Tom William Howson, of Prestwick, Scotland, and Janet Rosemary, *née* Smith; *b* 27 March 1958; *Educ* Prestwick Acad, Glasgow Sch of Art (BA); *m* 1, 1983 (m dis 1984), Francis, *née* Nevay; m 2, 1989, Terry Jane, da of James Peter Cullen; 1 da (Lucie Elizabeth b 19 May 1986); *Career* artist; RHF 1977, warehouseman Tesco Stores Ltd 1978, bouncer Caledonian Hotel 1978, shelf filler Safeway plc 1983, labourer 1983; official Br war artist Bosnia 1993; recent exhbns incl: Flowers East London 1993 and 1994, McLellan Galleries Glasgow 1993, Imperial War Museum (series of paintings of Bosnia) 1994; painter: mural for Feltham Community Centre London (voluntary), The Boxer (series of etchings) 1985, Lowland Hero Spurns the Cynics 1986, Regimental Bath 1986, Saracen Heads (series of paintings), The Heroic Dosser 1987, The Noble Dosser 1987, Just Another Bloody Saturday 1987, A Wing and a Prayer 1987, The Fools of God 1989, The Wild Hunt 1989, The Sisters of Mercy 1989, Stairway to Heaven 1990, The Wrestlers 1990, Riding The Gauntlet 1990, Patriots 1991, The Road to Zenica Bosnia 1994, Plum Grove Bosnia 1994; public collections: Tate Gallery, Museum of Modern Art NY, Metropolitan Museum of Art NY, V & A, Oslo Museum of Modern Art, Scottish Nat Gallery of Modern Art, Glasgow Art Galleries and Museum; Scottish Drawing Prize 1985, Edwin Morgan Prize 1987, First Prize European Painters Sofia Bulgaria 1989, Henry Moore Prize Bradford International Print Biennial; Hon Doctorate Strathclyde 1996; *Recreations* walking, reading; *Style*— Peter Howson, Esq; ✉ c/o Matthew Flowers, Flowers East, 199 Richmond Rd, London E8 3NJ (☎ 0181 985 3333)

HOY, David Forrest; s of Peter Harold Hoy, of Bromley, Kent, and Helena Muriel, *née* Blackshaw; *b* 7 April 1946; *Educ* Leeds GS Yorks, Merchant Taylors' Sch Crosby Lancs; *m* 11 Sept 1971, Angela, da of John Piddock; 1 da (Susanne Mary b 4 April 1976); *Career* asst internal auditor Dunlop Co Ltd 1964–67, accountant Redwood Press Ltd 1967–68, gen mangr Guinness Superlatives Ltd 1974–76 (co accountant 1968–74), md Guinness Publishing Ltd 1976–88, project dir Guinness Enterprises Ltd 1989–90; vice pres: Gleneagles Group Inc, Champneys Group Inc 1991–92; commercial dir Guinness Nigeria plc 1992–95, fin dir Guinness Brewing Worldwide Ltd (Africa) 1995–; *Recreations* skiing, tennis, powerboating, sailing, photography, philately; *Style*— David Hoy, Esq; ✉ 71 The Park, St Albans, Hertfordshire AL1 4RX

HOYER MILLAR, Gurth Christian; s of Edward George Hoyer Millar, and Phyllis Edith Amy Wace (d 1956); *b* 13 Dec 1929; *Educ* Harrow, Oxford (boxing blue), Michigan Univ (LLM); *m* 17 March 1956, Jane Taylor, da of Harold John Aldington; 2 s (Christian b 1959, Luke b 1962), 1 da (Eliza b 1965); *Career* cmmnd Malaya 1949–50, cmmnd Reserve Bn SAS 1950–58; called to the Bar Middle Temple; exec dir J Sainsbury plc 1967–91; chm: J Sainsbury (Properties) Ltd until 1991, Homebase Ltd 1979–91, Bonham's Fine Art Auctioneers 1988–; non-exec dir: Hudson's Bay Co of Canada 1976–, P&O Steam Navigation Co 1980–89, London & Edinburgh Trust plc 1988–91; dir H W Park Place Ltd 1993–; dir Br Property Fedn until 1989; played rugby Oxford and Scotland 1952; *Clubs* MCC; *Style*— Gurth Hoyer Millar, Esq; ✉ 27 Trevor Place, London SW7 1LD (☎ 0171 584 3883)

HOYER MILLAR, Hon (Christian) James Charles; o s and h of 2 Baron Inchyra, *qv*; *b* 12 Aug 1962; *m* 3 Oct 1992, Caroline J, da of late Robin Swan, of Lower Wield, Hants; 1 s (Jake b 10 July 1996), 1 da (Eleanor b 23 Aug 1994); *Style*— The Hon James Hoyer Millar

HOYES, Dr Thomas; s of Fred Hoyes, and Margaret Elizabeth Hoyes; *b* 19 Nov 1935; *Educ* Queen Elizabeth's GS Alford Lincs, Downing Coll Cambridge (BA, MA, PhD); *m* 27 Aug 1960, Amy Joan, da of Harry Bew Wood (d 1973), of Skegness, Lincolnshire; 2 da (Rebecca b 1963, Charlotte b 1966); *Career* conslt Hallam Brackett chartered surveyors Nottingham 1983–88 (ptnr 1963–83), prof of land mgmnt Univ of Reading 1983–88 (head of dept 1986–88); memb Lands Tbnl 1989–; pres: Cambridge Univ Land Soc 1973, Land Inst 1991–; govr Nottingham HS for Girls 1976–82; tstee Centre for Studies in Property Valuation City Univ 1989; memb: Rating Surveyors Assoc 1968, Gen Cncl RICS 1982–85 (pres Planning and Devpt Div 1983–84); Liveryman Worshipful Co of Chartered Surveyors 1980; Hon FSVA 1996; FRICS 1969 (ARICS 1964); *Recreations* adapting houses, gardening; *Clubs* Farmers'; *Style*— Dr Thomas Hoyes; ✉ c/o The Lands Tribunal, 48–49 Chancery Lane, London WC2A 1JR (☎ 0171 936 7200)

HOYLAND, John; *b* 12 Oct 1934; *Educ* Sheffield Coll of Art, Royal Acad Schs London; *m* 1958 (m dis 1968), Airi; 1 s (Jeremy b 1958); *Career* artist and sculptor; taught at Hornsey, Oxford, Croydon, Luton and Chelsea Schs of Art 1960s, taught at St Martin's Sch of Art 1970s and The Slade Sch of Fine Art 1970s until resigned 1989; set designs for Zansa Sadler's Wells; memb Rome Scholarship Ctee (printmaking) 1975; *Solo Exhibitions* incl: Marlborough New London Gallery London 1964, Whitechapel Art Gallery London 1967, Waddington Galleries London 1970, Andre Emmerich Gallery NY 1972, Kingpitcher Contemporary Art Gallery Pittsburgh 1975, Waddington Galleries London (paintings 1966–68) 1976, Galeria Modulo Lisbon 1976–77, Serpentine Gallery London (retrospective) touring to Birmingham City Art Gallery and Mappin Art Gallery Sheffield 1979–80, Univ Gallery Univ of Melbourne touring to Art Gallery of S Aust Adelaide and Macquarie Galleries Sydney 1980, Gump's Gallery San Francisco 1981, Castlefield Gallery Manchester 1984, Erika Meyerovich Gallery San Francisco 1988, Waddington Galleries London 1990, Eva Cohen Gallery Chicago 1991, Galerie Josine Bokhoven Amsterdam 1992, Graham Modern Gallery NYC 1992, CCA Gallery London (ceramic sculptures) 1994, Murano Italy (glass sculptures) 1994, Sydney Australia 1994, Theo Waddington Gallery London (Bali Paintings) 1994; *Two-Man Exhibitions* incl: Biennial de Sao Paulo Brazil 1969, Leslie Waddington Prints London 1972, Waddington Graphics London 1979, Van Straaten Gallery Chicago 1980, Hokin Gallery Miami 1981; *Group Exhibitions* incl: Royal Acad Summer Exhibition 1956, 1957, 1958 and 1993, 7th Tokyo Biennial Tokyo 1963, 4th Biennial Exhibition of Young Artists Musée d'Art Moderne de la Ville de Paris 1965, Documenta IV Kassel W Germany 1968Affinities in Paint (Crane Gallery) 1991, Peter Stuyvesant Fndn Kunst Werkt Artworks touring Holland, Spain and France 1992, Painting of the Sixties (Arts Cncl Collection Royal Festival Hall and on tour) 1992, Redfern Gallery 1992 and summer exhbn 1992, Galerie zur alten Deutschen Schule Switzerland 1992, New Realities: Art From Post-War Europe 1945–1968 (Tate Liverpool) 1993, New Prints (CCA Galleries London) 1993, New Prints (Curwen Gallery London) 1993, RA Collection (Sackler Galleries RA) 1993, The Sixties Art Scene in London (Barbican) 1993; *Awards* prizewinner John Moores Liverpool Exhibition 1965 and Open Paintings Exhibition Belfast 1966; first prize: (with Robyn Denny) Edinburgh Open 100 Exhibition 1969, Chichester Nat Art Exhibition 1975, John Moores Liverpool Exhibition 1982, Korn Ferry Int Award Exhibition (with William Scott) 1986, Athena Art Awards Exhibition 1987; RA 1991 (ARA 1983); *Style*— John Hoyland, Esq, RA; ✉ c/o Royal Academy of Arts, Piccadilly, London W1V 0DS

HOYLE, (Eric) Douglas Harvey; JP (1958), MP (Lab) Warrington North (majority 12,622); s of late William Hoyle, and Leah Ellen Hoyle; *b* 17 Feb 1930; *Educ* Adlington Sch, Horwich and Bolton Tech Colls; *m* 1953, Pauline (d 1991), da of William Spencer; 1 s (Lindsay); *Career* sales engr; Parly candidate (Lab) Clitheroe 1964; MP (Lab): Nelson and Colne 1974–79 (contested same 1970 and 1974), Warrington (by-election) July 1981–1987, Warrington N 1987–; chm Lab Parly Pty 1992–, memb shadow cabinet 1992–; memb Manchester Regnl Hosp Bd 1968–74, pres ASTMS 1985–88 (memb 1958, vice pres 1981–85), pres MSF 1990–91 (jt pres 1988–90), memb Lab Pty NEC 1978–82 and 1983–85 (chm Home Policy Ctee 1983), chm Lab Parly Pty Trade and Indust Ctee 1987–92, memb House of Commons Trade and Indust Select Ctee 1985–92; *Style*— Douglas Hoyle, Esq, JP, MP; ✉ House of Commons, London SW1A 0AA

HOYLE, Prof Sir Fred; kt (1972); s of Benjamin Hoyle; *b* 24 June 1915; *Educ* Bingley GS, Emmanuel Coll Cambridge (MA); *m* 1939, Barbara Clark; 1 s, 1 da; *Career* fell St John's Coll Cambridge 1939–72, res in RADAR Admty 1940–45, Plumian prof of astronomy and experimental philosophy Univ of Cambridge 1958–72, prof of astronomy Royal Inst 1969–72, Andrew D White prof-at-large Cornell Univ USA 1972–78, hon res prof Univ of Manchester 1972–; fndr and dir Inst of Theoretical Astronomy Univ of Cambridge 1967–72; foreign assoc US Nat Acad of Scis 1969, foreign memb American Philosophical Soc 1980; hon memb: American Acad of Arts and Scis 1964, Mark Twain Soc 1978, Royal Irish Acad in the Section of Sci 1977; hon life memb Astron Soc of India 1996; hon fell: St John's Coll Cambridge 1973, Emmanuel Coll Cambridge 1983; FRS 1957; *Publications* incl Some Recent Researches in Solar Physics (1949), The Nature of the Universe (1950), A Decade of Decision (1953), Frontiers of Astronomy (1955), Man and Materialism (1956), Astronomy (1962), Galaxies, Nuclei and Quasars (1963), Of Men and Galaxies (1964), Man in the Universe (1966), From Stonehenge to Modern Cosmology (1973), Nicholas Copernicus (1973), The Relation of Physics and Cosmology (1973), Astronomy and Cosmology (1975), Ten Faces of the Universe (1977), On Stonehenge (1977), Energy or Extinction (1977), The Intelligent Universe (1983); with N C Wickramasinghe: Lifecloud (1978), Diseases from Space (1979), Space Travellers: The Bringers of Life (1981), Cosmic Life Force (1988), Cosmology and Action at a Distance Electrodynamics (with J V Narlikar); *Novels incl:* The Black Cloud (1957), Ossian's Ride (1959), October the First is Too Late (1966), Element 79 (1967); with G Hoyle: Fifth Planet (1963), Rockets in Ursa Major (1969), Seven Steps to the Sun (1970), The Molecule Men (1971), The Inferno (1973), Into Deepest Space (1974), The Incandescent Ones (1977), The Westminster Disaster (1978); Comet Halley (1985), The Small World of Fred Hoyle (1986), Home is Where The Wind Blows (autobiography, 1994); *Style*— Prof Sir Fred Hoyle, FRS; ✉ c/o The Royal Society, 6 Carlton House Terrace, London SW1Y 5AG (fax 01202 299550)

HOYLE, Rupert Felix; s of Stephen Thomas Hoyle (d 1971), of Bath, Avon, and Joan *née* Asher (d 1956); *b* 23 May 1939; *Educ* Ridge Sch Johannesburg, Hilton Coll, Univ of Cape Town (BComm); *m* 1, 5 Sept 1964, Catherine, da of Reginald Albert Rawlings; 4 c (Caroline Joan b 20 January 1966, Audrey Lilian b 5 August 1967, Roger Stephen b 25 March 1970, Susan Olive b 24 March 1972); m 2, 11 Sept 1980, Janice Marie, da of A Herman Hutto; 1 s (Robert Herman b 11 Feb 1981); *Career* articled clerk Salisbury Rhodesia 1956–61, audit sr Turquand Young & Co London 1961–63, ptnr Deloitte Plender Griffiths Annan & Co Rhodesia 1969–77 (audit sr then mangr 1963–69); ptnr Deloitte Haskins & Sells: Johannesburg 1977–79, Cape Town 1979–86; audit ptnr Coopers & Lybrand London 1986–; FCA 1975 (ACA 1964), ACII 1988; *Recreations* golf, running; *Clubs* Leatherhead Golf; *Style*— Rupert Hoyle, Esq; ✉ Greycote, 4 Prince's Drive, Oxshott, Surrey KT22 0UF (☎ 01372 842884); Coopers & Lybrand, 1 Embankment Place, London WC2N 6NN (☎ 0171 583 5000, fax 0171 822 4652)

HOYLE, Susan (Sue); da of Roland Hoyle, and Joan, *née* Dickson; *b* 7 April 1953; *Educ* Nottingham HS for Girls, Univ of Bristol; *Career* educn offr Eng Nat Ballet (formerly London Festival Ballet) 1980–83, admin Extemporary Dance Theatre 1983–86, dance dir Arts Cncl 1989–94 (dance and mime offr 1986–89), dep sec-gen Arts Cncl 1994–; *Style*— Ms Sue Hoyle; ✉ Arts Council of Great Britain, 14 Great Peter St, London SW1P 3NQ (☎ 0171 333 0100, 0171 973 6579, fax 0171 973 6584)

HOYLES, Prof Celia Mary; da of Harold Gainsford French, of 17 The Heights, Loughton, Essex, and Elsie Florence, *née* Last; *b* 18 May 1946; *Educ* Univ of Manchester (BSc), Univ of London (MEd, PhD); *m* (m dis); *Career* mathematics teacher in secdy schs 1967–72, sr lectr then princ lectr Poly of N London 1972–84, prof of mathematics educn Univ of London 1984–; presenter: Fun and Games YTV 1987–, several TV shows on gender and computing; *Books* Girls and Computing (1988), Logo Mathematics in the Classroom (with R Sutherland, 1989), Learning Mathematics and Logo (with R Noss, 1992), Windows on Mathematical Meanings: Learning Cultures and Computers (with R Ross, 1996); *Recreations* tennis, swimming; *Style*— Prof Celia Hoyles; ✉ Institute of Education, University of London, 20 Bedford Way, London WC1 0AL (☎ 0171 612 6659)

HOYOS, Hon Sir (Fabriciano) Alexander; kt (1979); s of Emigdio and Adelina Hoyos, of Peru; *b* 5 July 1912; *Educ* Harrison Coll, Codrington Coll, Durham Univ (MA); *m* 1, 1940, Kathleen Carmen (d 1970); 3 s, 1 da; m 2, 1973, Gladys Louise; *Career* leader-writer of Daily Advocate 1937–43, correspondent The Times London 1937–65; history teacher Barbados and Trinidad 1943–72; moderator and lectr Caribbean History Survey Course Cave Hill University WI 1963–70; memb: Barbados Christian Cncl 1976–79, Constitution Review Cmmn 1977–78, Privy Cncl for Barbados 1977–84; Queen's Silver Jubilee Medal 1977; *Style*— Hon Sir Alexander Hoyos

HUBAND, Neil; *b* 22 April 1948; *Career* journalist 1967–82 (initially with regnl newspapers, latterly as Parly corr for BBC TV and Radio), account dir Shearwater Communications 1982–83, dir O&M PR Ltd and dep chief exec offr O&M Corporate Financial Ltd 1983–87; dir: Gresham Financial 1987–, Shandwick Network 1987–, Shandwick Consultants Ltd 1988– (currently sr dir); MIPR; *Style*— Neil Huband, Esq; ✉ Shandwick Consultants Ltd, Aldermary House, 10–15 Queen Street, London EC4N 1TX (☎ 0171 329 0096)

HUBBARD, (Richard) David Cairns; OBE (1995); s of John Cairns Hubbard, of Esher, Surrey, and Gertrude Emilie, *née* Faure (d 1967); *b* 14 May 1936; *Educ* Tonbridge, Harvard Business Sch; *m* 7 Feb 1964, Hannah Neale, da of Arthur Gilbert Dennison (d 1987); 3 da (Katy-Jane b 1966, Juliet b 1970, Nicola b 1973); *Career* Nat Serv RA 1955–57; Peat Marwick Mitchell & Co London 1957–64, sec and gp fin dir Cape Asbestos plc 1965–73, dir of fin and admin Bache & Co London 1974–76; chm Exco plc 1996–; former chm: Powell Duffryn plc 1986–96 (gp fin dir 1976), London & Manchester Assurance plc 1993; non-exec dir: Blue Circle Industries plc 1986–96, Southern Advsy Bd National Westminster Bank plc 1988–91, TR City of London Trust PLC 1989–, Shandwick plc 1991–, Slough Estates plc 1995–; memb Bd of Crown Agents 1986–89, alternate memb Takeover Panel, memb Cncl IOD; chm Cncl Cancer Res Campaign, treas Berkshire Golf Club 1980–93; Freeman City of London, Liveryman Worshipful Co of Skinners, Liveryman Worshipful Co of Chartered Accountants; FCA; *Recreations* golf, skiing, family; *Style*— David Hubbard, Esq, OBE; ✉ Meadowcroft, Windlesham, Surrey GU20 6BJ (☎ 01276 473667)

HUBBARD, Gp Capt Kenneth Gilbert; OBE (1952), DFC (1944), AFC (1957); s of Gilbert Claud Hubbard (d 1978), of Norwich, and Florence, *née* Dack (d 1980); *b* 26 Feb 1920; *Educ* Norwich Tech Coll (Nat Cert, HNC); *m* 1, 1946 (m dis 1953), Daphne, da of

Richard Taylor, of Norwich; m 2, Margaret Julia, *née* Grubbe; *Career* joined RAF 1940, Pilot 205 Gp ME and Italy, qualified flying instr A2; RAF Flying Coll: directing staff awarded PFC 1950–51, awarded PSA 1954; Wing Cdr and CO 49 Sqdn 1956–58, Capt Valiant XD818 dropped Britain's first hydrogen bomb at Christmas Island tests 1957, Gp Capt 1961, CO RAF E L Adam Libya 1961–62, CO RAF Scampton 1963–64, Gp Capt trg Transport Cmd 1964–66, ret 1966; memb Bd Hubbard Reader Group 1975–82; exec chm of all ATC Sqdn Civilian Ctees in S Suffolk 1979–94, chm Local Review Ctee for Parole HM Prison Blundeston 1982–94; *Books* Operation Grapple (1984); *Recreations* horse riding, golf, writing; *Clubs* RAF, RAF Inominate; *Style*— Gp Capt Kenneth Hubbard, OBE, DFC, AFC; ✉ The Priory, Blythburgh, Suffolk IP19 9LR (☎ 01502 478232)

HUBBARD, Michael Joseph; QC (1985); s of Joseph Thomas Hubbard, of Sussex, and Gwendoline Phyllis, *née* Bird (d 1957); *b* 16 June 1942; *Educ* Lancing; *m* 1967, Ruth Ann, *née* Logan; 5 s (Mark b 1968, Duncan b 1970, Lucian b 1972, Angus b 1974, Quinten b 1976); *Career* slr 1966–72, called to the Bar Gray's Inn 1972, initially in practice Western Circuit; prosecuting counsel to Inland Revenue Western Circuit 1983–85; recorder of the Crown Ct 1984–; *Recreations* sailing; *Style*— Michael Hubbard, QC; ✉ 1 Paper Buildings, 1st Floor, Temple, London EC4Y 7EP (☎ 0171 353 3728, fax 0171 353 2911)

HUBBARD, Hon Michael Walter Leslie; s of 5 Baron Addington (d 1982); hp of bro, 6 Baron Addington, *qv*; *b* 7 July 1965; *Educ* Hewett Sch Norwich, Univ of Manchester (BA), Leicester Polytechnic (PGD, MA); *Style*— The Hon Michael Hubbard

HUBER, Peter John; s of James Huber (d 1989), and Doris, *née* Fickling (d 1960); *b* 1 April 1940; *Educ* St Benedict's London, Columbia Univ NY USA; *m* Evelyn, da of William Hayhow; 2 da (Belinda b 13 Sept 1971, Gillian b 21 Jan 1974); *Career* advtg exec; J Walter Thompson: joined 1960, NY 1961–62, Amsterdam 1962–63, assoc dir London 1963–73, account dir 1973–79, Bd dir 1979– (currently conslt); MIPA 1985; *Clubs* MCC, Surrey CCC, Ealing Squash (chm 1976–); *Style*— Peter Huber, Esq; ✉ J Walter Thompson, 40 Berkeley Square, London W1X 6AD (☎ 0171 499 4040, fax 0171 493 8432)

HUCKER, His Hon Judge Michael; s of Lt-Col Ernest George Hucker, CBE (d 1986), of Willingdon, Sussex, and Mary Louise, *née* Jowett (d 1991); *b* 25 Oct 1937; *Educ* St Dunstans Coll, LSE; *m* 7 Jan 1961, Hazel Zoë, JP, da of Alfred Roy Drake (d 1940), of Hampstead; 2 s (Nicholas b 1963 d 1992, Rupert b 1967), 1 da (Sally (Mrs Ducker) b 1961); *Career* cmmnd RE 1957, ret 1976; called to the Bar: Lincoln's Inn 1974, Gibraltar 1988; in practice London 1976–94, head of chambers 1978–91, appointed by AG Counsel to Army Bd 1979, recorder 1992–94, circuit judge (SE Circuit) 1994–; Freeman City of London 1978; *Recreations* music, English history, biography; *Style*— His Hon Judge Hucker; ✉ Kingston Crown Court, Canbury Park Road, Kingston upon Thames, Surrey KT2 6JU

HUCKER, Rev Michael Frederick; MBE (1970); s of William John Hucker (d 1981), and Lucy Sophia, *née* Ashley (d 1991); *b* 1 May 1933; *Educ* City of Bath Boys' Sch, Didsbury Coll Bristol, Univ of Bristol (MA), Univ of London (BD); *m* 13 May 1961, (Katherine) Rosemary, da of Sidney Cyril Parsons (d 1992); 1 s (Martin William b 1963), 1 da (Rachel Mary b 1964); *Career* cmmnd chaplain RAF 1962, asst princ chaplain 1983, QHC 1987, princ chaplain Church of Scotland and Free Churches 1987–90, sec Forces Bd of the Methodist Church 1990–96, ret; *Recreations* gardening, reading; *Style*— The Rev Michael Hucker, MBE; ✉ 1 Central Buildings, Westminster, London SW1H 9NU

HUCKFIELD, Leslie John; s of Ernest Leslie Huckfield, and Suvla Huckfield; *b* 7 April 1942; *Educ* Prince Henry's GS Evesham, Keble Coll Oxford, Univ of Birmingham; *Career* contested (Lab) Warwick and Leamington 1966, MP (Lab) Nuneaton March 1967–83, PPS to Min of Public Bldgs and Works 1968–70, Parly under-sec for Industry 1976–79, oppn front bench spokesman on Industry 1979–81; memb: Lab NEC 1978–82, Lab W Midlands Regnl Exec Ctee 1978–82; political sec Nat Union Lab and Socialist Clubs 1979–82; former chm Lab Tport Gp 1974–76, ind advsr Cmmn of Tport Gp 1975–76; MEP (Lab) for Merseyside East 1984–89; pres Worcs Fedn of Young Socialists 1962–64; memb: Birmingham Regnl Hosp Bd 1970–72, Political Ctee Co-op Retail Soc 1981–; advertising mangr Tribune Pubns Ltd; princ offr of external resources St Helen's Coll Mersyside, currently Euro offr Merseyside Colleges, Euro funding mangr Wirral Metropolitan Coll 1995–; *publications* various newspaper and periodical articles; *Recreations* running marathons; *Style*— Leslie Huckfield; ✉ PO Box 200, Northwich, Cheshire CW9 6RL (☎ and fax 01606 352225)

HUCKIN, (Peter) Hugh; s of Albert Edward Huckin, OBE (d 1983), and Margaret, *née* Harris (d 1991); *b* 17 Oct 1930; *Educ* Harrisons Coll Barbados, Haileybury & ISC, Royal Sch of Mines London Univ (BSc); *m* 10 Sept 1955, Anne Margaret, da of James Duncan Webster (d 1964); 2 da (Jennifer b 1960, Elizabeth b 1963); *Career* Lt RCS 1950–53; petroleum engr: Shell International Holland and Columbia 1956–62, Texaco Trinidad 1962–63; chief petroleum engr: Iraq Petroleum Co 1964–73, ARCO 1973–75; md REMI (UK) Ltd 1975–76, chm Welldrill Group Ltd 1977–93; chm Geopec Ltd 1988–93, chief exec Oil and Gas (BVI) Ltd 1993–, md Ogden Energy Ltd; ARSM, AIME; *Recreations* work, garden, boats; *Style*— P Hugh Huckin, Esq; ✉ Haywards, Headley Fields, Headley, Bordon, Hants GU35 8PX (☎ 01428 712224, fax 01428 717365)

HUCKNALL, Mick; *b* 8 June 1960; *Career* singer and songwriter; formerly with own punk band Frantic Elevators, fndr/lead singer Simply Red 1984–; tours incl: support on James Brown's UK tour 1984, world tours 1989–90 and 1992; albums: Picture Book (1985), Men and Women (1987), A New Flame (1989), Stars (1991, nominated Mercury Music Award 1992), Life (1995); singles incl: Money's Too Tight To Mention, Holding Back the Years (reached number 1 USA 1985), The Right Thing, A New Flame, Something Got Me Started, Stars; Best Group BRIT Awards (BPI) 1992 (jtly) and 1993; *Style*— Mick Hucknall, Esq; ✉ c/o East West Records, Electric Lighting Station, 46 Kensington Court, London W8 5DA (☎ 0171 938 2181, fax 0171 937 6645, telex 261425)

HUCKS, Edwin (Ed); s of Frederick Albert Hucks (d 1983), of Dudley, Worcs, and Winnifred, *née* Shaw; *b* 7 June 1944; *Educ* Univ of Aston (BSc), Univ of Birmingham (MSc); *m* 7 August 1971, Lucia, da of Isaac Stamper; 2 da (Sasha b 6 Oct 1975, Emma Victoria b 9 March 1978), 1 s (Mark Edward b 25 Oct 1979); *Career* in operational research with Cadbury-Schweppes then Birmingham RHA 1968–72; Mars Group Services: joined as sr business analyst 1972, internal projects mangr then regnl systems mangr until 1979; head of info systems Fisons Pharmaceuticals 1979–83, vice pres European info systems Dun & Bradstreet 1983–85, gp IT dir BPCC plc 1985–87, md PCT Ltd 1987–88, IT dir AGB Research plc 1988–89; National & Provincial Building Society: dir of process systems and servs 1989–93, dir of savings and personal credit 1994, dir customer service 1995–96; md Bradford Ops Abbey National plc (following takeover of N & P Building Soc) 1996–; *Recreations* squash, tennis, gardening, walking; *Style*— Ed Hucks, Esq; ✉ Abbey National plc, Provincial House, Bradford, W Yorks BD1 1NL (☎ 01274 842468)

HUDD, Dr Nicholas Payne (Nick); s of Harold Payne Hudd (d 1977), of Essex, and Marguerita Eva, *née* Clarke; *b* 11 Oct 1945; *Educ* Palmer's Sch Essex, Sidney Sussex Coll Cambridge (MA, MB BChir, first boat colour), Westminster Hosp; *m* 11 Oct 1969, Gwendeleen Mary, da of John Johnstone, of Cardonald, Glasgow; 2 s (Alastair Payne b 28 Dec 1973, Robert Nicholas Harold b 23 June 1984), 1 da (Anne Marguerita Jane b 10 Dec 1976); *Career* house surgn Westminster Children's Hosp 1970, house physician Princess Alexandra Hosp Harlow 1971, sr house offr Orsett Hosp 1972, med registrar St Andrew's Hosp Billericay and Basildon Hosp 1972–74, haematology registrar Orsett Hosp 1974–76; sr med registrar: Withington Hosp & Manchester Royal Infirmary 1976–78, Benenden Hosp 1978–79; conslt physician Benenden Hosp 1980–; memb: BMA, Br Diabetic Assoc, Historical Assoc, Royal Nat Rose Soc; chm Romney Marsh Historic Churches Tst 1988–96 (vice chm 1982–88), pres The Rising Mercury Soc (Benenden Ex-Patients); conductor Benenden Hosp Choir; FRCP 1995; *Recreations* golf music (singing and conducting), rose-growing, cricket, history, talking; *Clubs* Tenterden Golf, Kent CCC, Royal Society of Medicine; *Style*— Dr N P Hudd; ✉ 13 Elmfield, Tenterden, Kent TN30 6RE (☎ 01580 763704, fax 01580 240021); 54 Wimpole St, London W1M 7DF (☎ 0171 935 6863, e-mail 100423.2254@COMPUSERVE.COM)

HUDD, Roy; s of Harold Hudd, of London, and Evelyn, *née* Barham; *b* 16 May 1936; *Educ* Croydon Secdy Tech Sch; *m* 25 Sept 1988, Deborah Ruth, da of Gordon Flitcroft (d 1986), of Lytham, Lancashire; *Career* comedian, playwright, author and actor; commercial artist 1952–55, Nat Serv RAF 1955–57, entered show business 1958; Centenary King Rat of The Grand Order of Water Rats 1989; monthly column Yours magazine; *Theatre* incl: seasons at Richmond Theatre and The Young Vic, pantomime at Theatre Royal Bath, the clown in The Birth of Merlin (Theatr Clwyd), Fagin in Oliver!, Stanley Gardner in Run For Your Wife (Whitehall and Criterion), The Fantasticks (Open Air Theatre) 1990, Babes in the Wood (Ashcroft Theatre Croydon 1990, Theatre Royal Plymouth 1991, New Theatre Cardiff 1992, Pavilion Theatre Bournemouth 1993, Sadler's Wells 1994), Midsummer Night's Dream (Open Air Theatre) 1991, George Pigden in Two into One 1993; writer of stage prodns: The Victorian Christmas, Roy Hudd's very own Music Hall, Just a Verse and Chorus, Beautiful Dreamer, While London Sleeps, Underneath the Arches (winner Best Actor in a Musical from Soc of West End Theatre), numerous pantomimes; *Radio* incl: Workers' Playtime, The News Huddlines, disc jockey Radio 2; *Television* incl: Not So Much a Programme More a Way of Life, The Maladjusted Busker (winner Montreaux Press Prize), Hudd, The Illustrated Weekly Hudd, Comedy Tonight, The 607080 Show, Movie Memories, Halls of Fame, The Puppet Man, Hometown, regular panelist on What's My Line?, Lipstick on Your Collar, Common as Muck, Karaoke, Common as Muck 2; *Awards* incl: Sony Gold Award 1990 for outstanding contrib to radio, LWT Lifetime Achievement for Radio Comedy award 1990, Variety Club BBC Radio Personality 1979 and 1993, Columnist of the Year EMAP 1994; *Books* Music Hall (1970), Roy Hudd's Book of Music Hall, Variety and Showbiz Anecdotes (1993); *Recreations* walking, singing, napping; *Clubs* Green Room; *Style*— Roy Hudd, Esq; ✉ PO Box 8923, London SW4 0ZD

HUDDIE, Sir David Patrick; kt (1968); s of James Huddie (d 1936); *b* 12 March 1916; *Educ* Mountjoy Sch Dublin, Trinity Coll Dublin (MA); *m* 1941, Wilhelmina Betty, da of Dr John Booth (d 1940), of Cork; 3 s; *Career* engr; md Aero Engine Div Rolls-Royce Ltd 1965–70, chm Rolls-Royce Aero Engines Inc 1968–70; sr res fell Imp Coll London 1971–80 (hon fell 1981); Hon ScD Dublin; FIQA, FIMechE, FEng 1981; *Recreations* music, reading, gardening; *Style*— Sir David Huddie, FEng; ✉ The Croft, Butts Rd, Bakewell, Derbys DE45 1EB (☎ 01629 813330)

HUDDLESTON, The Most Reverend (Ernest Urban) Trevor; *b* 15 June 1913; *Educ* Lancing, ChCh Oxford (MA), Wells Theological Coll; *Career* ordained priest 1937; Community of Resurrection: joined 1939, priest i/c Sophiatown and Orlando Anglican Mission Dio of Johannesburg 1943, provincial in SA and supt St Peter's Sch 1949, guardian of novices Mirfield 1956, prior of London House 1958, bishop Dio of Masasi Tanganiyka 1960, suffragan bishop Stepney 1968, bishop of Mauritius 1978, archbishop of Anglican Province of Indian Ocean until 1983; Anti-Apartheid Movement: addressed founding meeting London 1959, vice pres 1961, pres 1981–94; founding patron Action for Southern Africa 1994–; chm Tstees Int Def and Aid Fund for SA 1983; addressed: UN Gen Assembly 1982, UN Special Ctee Against Apartheid 1984; initiated Nelson Mandela Int Reception Ctee 1990; provost emeritus Selly Oak Colls, patron Fair Play for Children, pres Nat Peace Cncl; Hon DLit Lancaster 1972; Hon DD: Univ of Aberdeen 1956, City of London 1987, Univ of Oxford 1993, Univ of Birmingham 1993, Whittier Coll California USA 1994, Dundee 1994; Hon LLD: Univ of Warwick 1989, City of London Poly 1990, Univ of Leeds 1991, Univ of Exeter 1992, Univ of Natal S Africa 1995; Hon Dr of Humane Letters Denison Univ Ohio USA 1989; fell Queen Mary and Westfield Coll London 1991, hon fell Christ Church Oxford 1993; UN Gold medal 1982; ANC Isitwalandwe 1955; Zambian Order of Freedom (first class) 1984, Dag Hammerskjold award for peace 1984, Grand Cdr Nigerian Order of the Niger 1989, Indira Gandhi prize 1994; *Books* Naught for your Comfort (1956), The True and Living God (1964), God's World (1966), I Belive (1986), Return to South Africa (1991); *Style*— The Most Rev Trevor Huddleston, CR; ✉ House of the Resurrection, Mirfield, West Yorkshire WF14 0BN

HUDLICKA, Prof Olga; da of Jaroslav Hudlicky (d 1956), and Marie Hudlicka, *née* Babackova (d 1986); *b* 11 July 1926; *Educ* Charles Univ (MD), Czechoslovak Acad of Scis (PhD, DSc); *m* 24 June 1950, Dr Andrej Klein (d 1980), s of Majer Klein (d 1922); 1 s (Pavel b 1 Aug 1954), 1 da (Olga (Mrs Barochovsky) b 26 July 1951); *Career* scientist Inst of Physiology Czechoslovak Acad of Sciences Prague 1950–69, visiting prof Goethe's Univ Frankfurt 1969, prof Dept of Physiology Med Sch 1969–; prof of physiology Univ of Birmingham 1987–93 (prof emeritus 1993–); memb: Br Physiological Soc 1972–, American Microcirculation Soc 1978, American Physiological Soc 1979–; hon sec Br Microcirculation Soc 1985–91 (hon memb 1993–); pres Br Microcirculation Soc 1996–; *Books* Circulation in Skeletal Muscle (1968), Muscle Blood Flow (1973), Angiogenesis (1986), Muscle Ischaemia (1988); *Recreations* swimming, skiing; *Style*— Prof Olga Hudlicka; ✉ Department of Physiology, The University of Birmingham Medical School, Vincent Drive, Birmingham B15 2TJ (☎ 0121 414 6908, fax 0121 414 6919)

HUDSON, Prof Anthony Hugh; s of Dr Thomas Albert Gibbs Hudson (d 1959), and Bridget, *née* Quinn (d 1979); *b* 21 Jan 1928; *Educ* St Joseph's Coll Blackpool, Pembroke Coll Cambridge, Univ of Manchester (PhD); *m* 10 Jan 1962, Joan Bernadette, da of Anthony O'Malley (d 1953); 1 s (Michael Hugh b 1963), 3 da (Mary Bridget b 1962, Margaret Mary Theresa b 1964, Catherine Agnes b 1965); *Career* called to the Bar Lincoln's Inn 1954, lectr Univ of Hull 1954–57 (asst lectr 1951–54), lectr in common Law Univ of Birmingham 1957–62, lectr Univ of Manchester 1962–64; Univ of Liverpool: sr lectr 1964–71, prof of law 1971–77, dean Faculty of Law 1971–78 and 1984–91, prof of common law 1977–92, prof emeritus and sr fell 1992–; *Books* jtly: Hood Phillips First Book of English Law (1977 and 1988), Pennington, Hudson & Mann Commercial Banking Law (1978), Stevens and Borrie Mercantile Law (1978); *Recreations* history, gardening, walking; *Style*— Prof Anthony Hudson; ✉ University of Liverpool, Faculty of Law, PO Box 147, Liverpool L69 3BX (☎ 0151 794 2000, fax 0151 794 2829, telex 627095 UNILPL G)

HUDSON, (Norman) Barrie; CB (1996); s of William Hudson (d 1994), of Coventry, and Lottie Mary, *née* Taylor; *b* 21 June 1937; *Educ* King Henry VIII Sch Coventry, Univ of Sheffield (BA), UCL (MSc); *m* 5 Oct 1963, Hazel, da of Capt Frederick Cotterill (d 1965); 2 s (Richard Jonathan b 12 March 1965, Mark William b 22 Jan 1974), 1 da (Catherine Jane b 13 Nov 1966); *Career* economist: Tube Investments Ltd 1960–62, Economist Intelligence Unit 1962–63; nat accounts advsr Govt of Jordan 1963–65, econ advsr Br Devpt Div Beirut 1967–72, sr econ advsr ODA 1973, head Br Devpt Div Bangkok 1974–76, under sec (principal estabs offr) ODA 1981–85, under sec ODA (Africa) 1986–93, under sec ODA (Int Div) 1993–; *Recreations* theatre, reading, watching football and cricket; *Style*— Barrie Hudson, Esq, CB; ✉ The Galleons, Sallows Shaw,

Sole Street, Cobham, Kent DA13 9BP (☎ 01474 814419); Overseas Development Administration, 94 Victoria St, London SW1E 5JL (☎ 0171 917 0156)

HUDSON, Christopher John; s of John Augustus Hudson, of The Holt, Benenden, Kent, and Margaret Gwendolen, *née* Hunt; *b* 29 Sept 1946; *Educ* The King's Sch Canterbury, Jesus Coll Cambridge (MA); *m* 10 March 1978, (Margaret) Kirsty, da of Alexander Drummond McLeod, of Ticehurst, Sussex; 1 s (Rowland Alexander b 1983); *Career* ed Faber & Faber 1968–70, literary ed The Spectator 1971–73, Harkness fell 1975–77, columnist The Evening Standard 1985–91 (leader writer 1978–81, literary ed 1982–85), leader page ed The Daily Telegraph 1991–94; memb: Soc of Authors, PEN; *Books* Overlord (filmed 1975), The Final Act (1979), Insider Out (1981), The Killing Fields (1984), Colombo Heat (1986), Playing in the Sand (1989), Spring Street Summer - A Journey of Rediscovery (1992); *Style*— Christopher Hudson, Esq; ✉ Little Dane, Biddenden, Kent TN27 8JT (☎ 01580 291101)

HUDSON, David Charles; *b* 10 April 1950, Leeds; *Educ* King's Sch Pontefract Yorks, Queen's Coll Oxford (MA); *m*; 3 c; *Career* asst brand mangr rising to brand mangr (petfoods) Spillers Foods 1971–74, gen mktg mangr (milks, healthcare, petfoods) Nestlé UK 1985–88 (successively brand mangr, brand gp mangr, mktg mangr 1977–85), gen mktg mangr (retail products) Nestlé Japan 1988–92, dir of mktg Nestlé Food Div 1992–95, dir of communication and corporate affrs Nestlé UK 1995–; *Style*— David Hudson, Esq; ✉ Nestlé UK, St George's House, Croydon, Surrey CR9 1NR (☎ 0181 667 5416, fax 0181 681 1218)

HUDSON, David Norman; s of Sir Edmund Peder Hudson (d 1978), of Edinburgh; *b* 29 May 1945; *Educ* Marlborough, Balliol Coll Oxford; *m* 1, 1967 (m dis 1993), Rosemary McMahon, *née* Turner; 1 s (Stephen b 1969), 2 da (Isobel b 1971, Sarah b 1976); m 2, 1993, Carole Annis, *née* Williams; 1 s (Christopher b 1995); *Career* merchant banker, dir Samuel Montagu & Co Ltd 1974–81, asst gen mangr Arlabank 1981–84, ptnr and head of corporate fin James Capel & Co 1984–87, dep chm and chief exec Henry Ansbacher & Co Ltd 1987–89, dir and shareholder Campbell Lutyens Hudson & Co Ltd 1989–93, chm David Hudson & Co 1992–, dir MacArthur & Co 1993–; *Recreations* natural history, bridge, opera; *Style*— David Hudson, Esq; ✉ David Hudson & Co Ltd, 30 City Road, London EC1Y 2AY (☎ 0171 638 5677)

HUDSON, Gaye; da of Rt Hon Sir Peter Emery, and Elizabeth, *née* Nicholson; *b* 14 Feb 1957; *Educ* Westonbirt Sch, Eastbourne Coll, Coll of Distributive Trade; *m* 2 Oct 1982, Jonathan Michael Hudson; 1 s (Charles Peter Meadows b 22 Dec 1989), 1 da (Holly Elizabeth b 13 Feb 1988); *Career* formerly with Young and Rubicam advertising agency; dir Burson-Marsteller, main bd dir and head of marketing Hill and Knowlton int PR consultancy, currently PR and mktg conslt; *Recreations* total love of skiing; *Style*—Mrs Gaye Hudson; ✉ 21 Gorst Road, London SW11 6JB (☎ 0171 228 3189)

HUDSON, Prof George; s of George Hudson (d 1956), of Edenfield, and Edith Hannah, *née* Bennett (d 1956); *b* 10 Aug 1924; *Educ* Edenfield C of E Sch, Bury GS, Univ of Manchester (BSc, MB ChB, MSc), Univ of Bristol (MD, DSc); *m* 14 April 1955, Mary Patricia (d 1977), da of Frank Hibbert (d 1929), of Chester; 1 da (Elisabeth b 1961); *Career* Capt RAMC 1951–53, unit MO Green Howards, Army Operational Res Gp; house offr Manchester Royal Infirmary 1949–50; Univ of Bristol: demonstrator in anatomy 1950–51, lectr then reader in anatomy 1953–68, pre-clinical dean 1963–68; visiting prof (Fulbright award) Univ of Minnesota 1959–60; Univ of Sheffield: admin dean 1968–83, hon clinical lectr in haematology 1968–75, prof of experimental haematology 1975–89, head Dept of Haematology 1981–89, postgrad dean 1984–88, regnl postgrad dean 1988–91, emeritus prof of haematology 1989–; hon conslt in haematology Sheffield Health Authy 1969–89, chm Conf of Deans of Prov Med Schs 1980–82, lay reader C of E 1953–; memb: Sheffield Regnl Hosp Bd 1970–74, Sheffield Health Authy 1974–84, Cncl for Med Postgrad Educn for England and Wales 1980–83; chm Ethical Ctee Northern Gen Hosp 1986–89; Hon LLD Univ of Sheffield 1993; FRCPath 1975 (MRCPath 1970), FRCP 1988 (MRCP 1984); *Recreations* history of medicine, cavies, garden; *Style*— Prof George Hudson; ✉ 275 Ringinglow Road, Sheffield S11 7PZ (☎ 0114 236 8004)

HUDSON, Gillian Grace (Gill); da of Brian Hudson (d 1985), of E Grinstead, Sussex, and Grace Iris, *née* Hill; *b* 23 March 1955; *Educ* Univ of Sussex (BA); *children* 1 da (Alexia b 15 Jan 1994); *Career* press offr Eng Tourist Bd 1978–81, ed Home and Country Magazine 1981–83, dep ed then ed Fitness Magazine 1984–85, ed Cook's Weekly 1986, dep ed then ed Company Magazine 1987–92, ed New Woman 1992–95; ed-in-chief: Maxim 1995–, Stuff 1996–; winner PPA Campaign of the Year award 1991 and 1993; chm British Soc of Magazine Editors 1993 (memb Ctee 1993–), memb BSME 1981; *Recreations* cycling, reading, windsurfing, travel, walking, swimming; *Clubs* Groucho's; *Style*— Ms Gill Hudson; ✉ Editor-in-Chief, 19 Bolsover Street, London W1P 7HJ (☎ 0171 631 1433)

HUDSON, Hugh; s of Michael Donaldson-Hudson (d 1965), and Jacynth Mary, *née* Ellerton (later Lady Lawrence, d 1987); *b* 25 Aug 1936; *Educ* Eton; *m* 25 Aug 1977, Susan Caroline, *née* Michie; 1 s (Thomas John b 8 Aug 1978); *Career* director and film maker; memb: Exec Ctee Cinema 100, 2nd Decade Cncl of AFI, BAFTA, Acad of Motion Picture, Arts and Sci (USA); Liveryman Worshipful Co of Haberdashers; *Films* incl: Chariots of Fire 1980 (5 BAFTA Awards, 4 Oscars, Golden Globe Award for Best Foreign Film, Best Picture UK & USA 1982), Greystoke - Legend of Tarzan 1983 (6 BAFTA & 5 Oscar nominations, BFI Technical Achievement Award), Revolution 1985 (BFI Anthony Asquith Award for Music), Lost Angels 1989, Son of Adam 1996; *Documentary* incl: A is for Apple (BAFTA nomination for Best Short Film 1963, Screenwriters' Guild Award), Tortoise & Hare (BAFTA nomination, Venice Festival Documentary Award), Fangio; *Political Films* Labour Party Election Broadcasts 1987–92 (incl Kinnock the Movie); *Advertising* over 600 commercials produced 1968–92 for clients incl: Levis, Coty, Benson & Hedges, Fiat Strada, Courage (Gercha), British Airways (Island and Face); *Awards* incl: 3 times D&AD Gold & Best Dir Awards, 5 Gold and 6 Silver Cannes Awards 1975–85, Cannes Grand Prix, Venice Grand Prix; *Recreations* reading, travel; *Style*— Hugh Hudson, Esq; ✉ Hudson Film Ltd, 11 Queensgate Place Mews, London SW7 5BG (☎ 0171 581 3133, fax 0171 584 6834)

HUDSON, James Ralph; CBE (1976); s of William Shand Hudson (d 1967), and Ethel, *née* Summerskill (d 1953); *b* 15 Feb 1916; *Educ* King's Sch Canterbury, Middx Hosp Med Sch (MB BS, LRCP); *m* 29 June 1946, Margaret May Hunter, da of Paul Eugene Oulpe (d 1986); 2 s (James b 1949, Andrew b 1956), 2 da (Ann b 1948, Sarah b 1953); *Career* WWII RAFVR 1942–46: Flying Offr 1942–43, Flt Lt 1943–44, Sqdn Ldr 1944–46; civil conslt in ophthalmology to RAF 1970–82; res MO Tindal House Hosp Aylesbury 1939–42, house surgn and sr res offr Moorfields Eye Hosp; conslt ophthalmic surgn: W Middx Hosp 1950–56, Mount Vernon Hosp 1953–59, Moorfields Eye Hosp 1956–81, Guy's 1963–76; hon ophthalmic surgn: Hosp of St John and St Elizabeth 1953–86, King Edward VII Hosp for Offrs 1970–86; hon consulting surgn Moorfields Eye Hosp 1981–, conslt advsr in ophthalmology DHSS 1969–82; teacher: Inst of Ophthalmology Univ of London 1961–81, Guy's 1964–76; examiner Dip Ophthalmology Exam Bd of England 1960–65, memb Ct of Examiners RCS 1966–72; memb Soc Française d'Ophtal 1950–; membre déLégué Étranger 1970–93, UK rep Union Européene des Médecins Spécialistes Ophthalmology Section 1973–91 (pres 1982–86); hon steward Westminster Abbey 1972–88 (non-active list 1988–); Freeman City of London, Liveryman Worshipful Soc of Apothecaries 1953; DOMS, FRCS, Hon FRCOphth 1990 (FCOphth 1988), Hon FRACO, FRSM; Ophthal Soc UK: memb 1948–88, hon sec 1956–58, vice-pres 1969–71, pres 1982–84; Faculty Ophthalmologists: memb 1950–88, memb Cncl 1960–81, hon sec 1960–70, vice pres 1970–74, pres 1974–77; Pilgrims of GB; *Recreations* motoring, travel; *Clubs* Garrick; *Style*— James Hudson, Esq, CBE; ✉ Flat 2, 17 Montagu Square, London W1H 1RD (☎ 0171 487 2680)

HUDSON, John; s of Don Hudson, of Barnsley, and Joyce, *née* Winterbottom (d 1995); *b* 16 Feb 1961; *Educ* Worsborough HS Barnsley, Gravnille Art Coll Sheffield, GSM; *m* Claire Elizabeth Olwen, da of Richard John Foulkes Taylor; *Career* tenor; memb chorus Welsh Nat Opera 1992–93, co princ ENO 1993–; performances incl: Paris, Auckland, Ireland, Canada, Barbican, Kenwood, Birmingham Symphony Orch, Royal Albert Hall; appeared with Lesley Garratt Viva La Diva (BBC 2) 1996; subject of various articles in magazines and newspapers; *Recreations* tennis, painting, cooking, playing cricket; *Clubs* Savage, London Sketch; *Style*— John Hudson, Esq; ✉ c/o Ingpen & Williams Ltd, 14 Kensington Court, London W8 5DN (☎ 0171 937 5158)

HUDSON, John Lewis; s of Wilfred Hudson, and Edith Hudson; *Educ* Univ of Aston (MSc), Birmingham Poly; *m* 22 Sept 1973, Eileen Cornelia; 1 s (Mark Standring b 7 Feb 1975), 1 da (Vicki Samantha b 24 Sept 1977); *Career* BSA Motorcycles Ltd 1960–71, Chrysler (UK) Ltd 1971–72, GEC Ltd 1971–72; md: Morphy Richards Ltd 1972–78, Sperryn & Co Ltd 1978–82; Delta Group plc: joined 1978, divnl dir and gen mangr Gas Controls and Engrg Div 1982–84, divnl md Fluid Controls Div 1984–86, md 1986–; gp chief exec Wagon Industrial Holdings 1986–; non-exec dir: Senior Engineering Group PLC 1991, Temple Bar Investment Trust PLC 1991; regnl cncllr CBI, memb Cncl Univ of Aston in Birmingham; CEng, FIEE, FIMechE, FIMgt, FRSA; *Recreations* walking, chess; *Style*— John Hudson, Esq; ✉ Wagon Industrial Holdings plc, 3100 Solihull Parkway, Birmingham Business Park, Birmingham B37 7YN (☎ 0121 717 2000, fax 0121 717 2050, private fax 0121 717 2052)

HUDSON, John Richard; s of Arthur Richard Hudson (d 1978), and Beryl Dorothy, *née* Brett; *b* 3 Sept 1944; *Educ* Ryde GS Ryde IOW, Thames Poly (HNC); *m* 12 Aug 1976, Kathleen Mary (Kate) Hudson, *qv*, da of David Thomas Heckscher (d 1950), of Aust; *Career* recording engr and md Mayfair Recording Studios London, recorded more than 159 top ten records (studio voted top Br Recording Studio 1986); Grammy Award (USA) 1984, nominated for Br Acad Award 1985, Grammy Award Certificate for work on Tina Turner Live in Europe 1988; Ultrastate Genetics Ltd (pedigree cattle breeders, home of the Ultragen herd of Holsteins); ARPS; *Recreations* skiing, video filming and editing; *Style*— John Hudson, Esq; ✉ Mayfair Recording Studios, 11A Sharpleshall Street, Primrose Hill, London NW1 8YN (☎ 0171 586 7746, fax 0171 586 9721)

HUDSON, Kathleen Mary (Kate); da of David Thomas Hecksher (d 1950), of Ipswich, Queensland, Aust, and Eileen Mary, *née* Downs; *b* 16 Aug 1944; *Educ* St Brigidine's Coll Scarborough, Queensland Aust; *m* 1 (m dis 1969), Raymond Douglas Geitz; m 2, 12 Aug 1976, John Richard Hudson, *qv*; *Career* telephonist Queensland Newspapers 1966–68, sec Leeds Music Sydney Aust 1968–73, PA Martin Coulter Music 1974–76, sec to Fin Dir Chrysalis Records London 1976–77, owner and md Mayfair Recording Studios 1977– (winner Top Br Recording Studio award 1986), advsrs to Ultrastate Genetics Ltd; pedigree cattle breeders (noted Holstein herd) Lodge Farm Snitterfield Warwicks; APRS; *Recreations* skiing; *Style*— Mrs Kate Hudson; ✉ Mayfair Recording Studios, 11A Sharpleshall Street, Primrose Hill, London NW1 8YN (☎ 0171 586 7746, fax 0171 586 9721)

HUDSON, Prof Liam; s of Cyril Hudson (d 1985), and Kathleen Maud, *née* Shesgreen; *b* 20 July 1933; *Educ* Whitgift Sch, Univ of Oxford (MA), Univ of Cambridge (PhD); *m* 1, 8 Aug 1955 (m dis 1965), (Wendy) Elizabeth, da of Douglas Ward (d 1955); m 2, July 1965 (Claribel Violet) Bernadine, da of Bernard Louis Jacot de Boinod (d 1977); 3 s (Dominic b 1958, William b 1966, George b 1967), 2 da (Lucie b 1960, d 1965, Annabel b 1967); *Career* Nat Serv 2 Lt RA 1952–54; fell King's Coll Cambridge 1966–68, prof of educnl sciences Univ of Edinburgh 1968–77, prof of psychology Brunel Univ 1977–87; memb Inst of Advanced Study Princeton NJ 1974–75; visiting prof Tavistock and Portman Clinics 1987–; Tanner lectr Yale Univ 1997; memb Br Psychological Soc; *Books* Contrary Imaginations (1967), Frames of Mind (1968), The Cult of the Fact (1972), Human Beings (1975), The Nympholepts (1977), Bodies of Knowledge (1982), Night Life (1985), The Way Men Think (1991), Intimate Relations (1995); *Recreations* painting, photography, making things; *Style*— Prof Liam Hudson; ✉ Balas Copartnership, 34 North Park, Gerrards Cross, Bucks (☎ and fax 01753 886281)

HUDSON, Manley O (Jr); s of Judge Manley O Hudson (d 1960), of Cambridge, Mass, and Janet A Hudson, *née* Aldrich; *b* 25 June 1932; *Educ* Middx Sch Concord Mass, Harvard (AB), Harvard Law Sch (LLB); *m* 1 July 1971, Olivia, da of Count Olivier d'Ormesson, of Ormesson-sur-Marne, France; 1 s (Nicholas b 1989), 1 da (Antonia b 1992); *Career* sec to Justice Reed Supreme Ct of the US 1956–57, ptnr Cleary Gottlieb Steen & Hamilton 1968– (assoc 1958–68); memb Cncl on Foreign Relations; *Clubs* Century Assoc (NY), Knickerbocker (NY), Turf; *Style*— Manley O Hudson, Jr; ✉ Cleary, Gottlieb, Steen & Hamilton, Level 5, City Place House, 55 Basinghall Street, London EC2V 5EH (☎ 0171 614 2200, fax 0171 600 1698)

HUDSON, (Anthony) Maxwell; s of Peter John Hudson, CB, of Haslemere, and Joan Howard Hudson, *née* Fitzgerald; *b* 12 April 1955; *Educ* St Paul's, New Coll Oxford (MA); *m* 14 Sept 1991, Cordelia Jennifer, da of Nigel Roberts, of Haslemere; 1 s (James Nicholas Maxwell b 10 Sept 1994); *Career* admitted slr 1980; ptnr: Frere Cholmeley 1987–95, Payne Hicks Beach 1995–; *Recreations* wine, military history; *Clubs* United Oxford and Cambridge Univ; *Style*— Maxwell Hudson, Esq; ✉ Payne Hicks Beach, 10 New Square, Lincoln's Inn, London WC2A 3QG (☎ 0171 465 4300, fax 0171 465 4400)

HUDSON, Lt-Gen Sir Peter; KCB (1977), CBE (1970, MBE 1965), DL (Berks 1984); s of Capt William Hudson (d 1964); *b* 14 Sept 1923; *Educ* Wellingborough Sch, Jesus Coll Cambridge; *m* 1949, Susan Anne, da of Maj Vernon Cyprian Knollys (d 1973); 1 da, 1 adopted s, 1 adopted da; *Career* cmmnd Rifle Bde 1944, served Mau Mau and Malaya Campaigns (despatches 2), CO 3 Royal Green Jackets 1966–67, Cdr 39 Inf Bde NI 1968–70, GOC E Dist 1973–74, COS Allied Forces N Europe 1975–77, Dep C-in-C UKLF 1977–80, Col Cmdt Light Div 1977–80, Inspr-Gen TAVR 1978–80; sec gen Order of St John 1981–88; Lt HM Tower of London 1986–89; chm: Green Jackets Club 1977–85, Rifle Brigade Museum Tstees 1979–85, Royal Sch Bath 1981–88 (govr 1976–96), Rifle Bde Club and Assoc 1979–85, Eastern Wessex TAVRA 1980–, TAVR Cncl 1981–90; memb: Gen Advsy Cncl BBC 1981–84, Cncl Bradfield Coll 1983–93; Hon Col: Southampton UOTC 1979–85, 5 Royal Green Jackets 1985–93; pres: RFA 1984–91, Frilsham PC 1989–; Freeman City of London 1966; KStJ 1981 (sec gen 1981–88, memb Cncl Royal Berkshire 1988–96), vice chm St John Fellowship 1993–; FIMgt, fell RSPB 1987; *Recreations* travel, wildlife, watching most games and sports; *Clubs* Naval and Military, MCC, IZ, Greenjackets; *Style*— Lt-Gen Sir Peter Hudson, KCB, CBE, DL; ✉ Little Orchard, Frilsham, Newbury, Berks (☎ 01635 201266)

HUDSON, Prof Richard Anthony; s of Prof John Pilkington Hudson, and Mary Greta, *née* Heath (d 1989); *b* 18 Sept 1939; *Educ* Loughborough GS, CCC Cambridge (open major scholar, BA), SOAS London (PhD); *m*; 2 c; *Career* UCL: research asst to Prof M Halliday 1964–70, lectr in linguistics 1970–80, reader 1980–89, prof of linguistics 1989–, admissions tutor BA linguistics and combinations 1990–94, memb Language Centre Mgmnt Ctee 1991–, memb Faculty Teaching Ctee 1993–, vice-dean Faculty of Arts 1993–96; formerly fndr memb Ctee for Linguistics in Educn (CLIE); conslt ed Linguistics and also Cognitive Linguistics; FBA 1993; *Books* Arguments for a Non-transformational Grammar (1976), Sociolinguistics (1980), Word Grammar (1984), English Word Grammar (1990), Teaching Grammar: A Guide for the National Curriculum (1992), Word Meaning

(1995); Linguistic Theory Guides (initiator and ed), Routledge Language Workbooks (initiator and ed, 1994–); also author of numerous articles in learned jls; *Style—* Prof Richard Hudson, FBA; ✉ Phonetics and Linguistics Department, University College London, Gower Street, London WC1E 6BT

HUDSON, Richard Lawrence; s of Charles Percy Hudson, CBE (d 1982), of Hessle, E Yorks, and Ethel Maud, *née* Howell (d 1991); *b* 24 March 1944; *Educ* Sedbergh, Grenoble Univ; *m* 1, Judith Bernadette Heaney; 2 s (Dominic William b 6 March 1972, Oliver Charles b 7 Jan 1974), 1 da (Emma Jane b 2 Oct 1969); m 2, 2 Dec 1978, Carol Sandra, da of Alan Megginson, of Beechwood, Driffield, E Yorks; 2 da (Annabel Juliet b 15 Dec 1979, Jennie Deborah b 21 Jan 1982); *Career* CA; Peat Marwick Mitchell & Co London 1963–70 (qualified 1968); ptnr: Hodgson Harris Hull 1975 (joined 1970), Price Waterhouse (following its merger with Hodgson Impey) 1990–; underwriting memb Lloyd's 1973–90; rugby formerly played for the 1st XV of Grenoble RFC and for Rosslyn Park RFC as well as playing cricket for numerous clubs; Freeman City of London 1979, memb Worshipful Co of CAs in England and Wales 1979; FCA 1973 (ACA 1968); *Recreations* shooting, golf, cricket, tennis; *Clubs* Ganton Golf, Yorkshire Gentlemen's Cricket, Yorkshire County Cricket, Army and Navy; *Style—* R L Hudson, Esq; ✉ 29 North Bar Without, Beverley, East Yorkshire HU17 7AG (☎ 01482 861382); Price Waterhouse, Queen Victoria House, Guildhall Road, Hull HU1 1HH (☎ 01482 224111, fax 01482 327479)

HUDSON, Prof Robert Francis; s of John Frederick Hudson (d 1966), and Ethel Lizzie, *née* Oldfield (d 1968); *b* 15 Dec 1922; *Educ* Brigg GS Lincolnshire, Imperial Coll London (BSc, PhD, ARCS, DIC); *m* 3 Aug 1945, Monica Ashton, da of Charles Ashton Stray; 1 s (John Martin Edward b 1949), 2 da (Sarah Elizabeth b 1952, Mary Alexandra b 1952); *Career* asst lectr Imperial Coll 1945–47, conslt Wolsey Leicester 1945–50, lectr QMC London 1947–59, gp dir CERI Geneva 1960–66, prof of organic chemistry Univ of Kent 1966–85 (emeritus 1985–); visiting prof: Rochester USA 1970, Bergen 1971, CNRS Thiais Paris 1973, Calgary 1975, Mainz 1979, Queen's Ontario 1983; memb: Chem Soc Cncl 1967–71; RSC: Dalton Cncl 1973–71, Perkin Cncl 1980–83; FRSC, FRS; *Clubs* Athenaeum; *Style—* Prof Robert Hudson, FRS; ✉ 37 Puckle Lane, Canterbury, Kent CT1 3LA (☎ 01227 761340)

HUDSON, Robert L F; s of Lionel Derek Hudson (d 1985), of Kidderminster, and Moreen, *née* Glarvey; *b* 18 Feb 1952; *Educ* King Charles I GS, Univ of Nottingham (BSc); *m* 1974, Katrina Susan, da of Charles Peter Poulsen; 1 da (Coralie Kate b 12 May 1978), 1 s (Alexander Robert b 23 Sept 1980); *Career* Arthur Andersen & Co: articled clerk 1973–76, audit sr 1976–80, audit mangr 1980–84; audit ptnr Pannell Kerr Forster 1987– (audit mangr 1984–87); dir of Audit and Accountancy 1990 and 1991; memb: Nat Audit and Accounting Standards Ctee 1989–95, Nat Audit and Accounting Tech Bd 1994–; pres The Three Counties C of C and Indust 1994–96, vice chm Worcester Gp of CAs 1994–96; Scout Assoc: medal of merit and bar, asst Co Cmmn for activities (Hereford and Worcester); FCA 1976; *Recreations* caravanning, scouting and hillwalking; *Style—* Robert Hudson, Esq; ✉ Pannell Kerr Forster, Virginia House, The Butts, Worcs WR1 3PA (☎ 01905 24437, fax 01905 29006, mobile 0378 412390)

HUDSON, Prof Robin Lyth; s of Frederick Lyth Hudson, of Kidderminster, Worcs, and Enid, *née* Wright (d 1982); *b* 4 May 1940; *Educ* King Edward VI GS Stourbridge, Stockport GS, Univ of Oxford (BA, DPhil); *m* 22 July 1962, Geraldine Olga Margaret, da of Percival George Beak, MBE (d 1995), of Dorchester on Thames; 3 s (Daniel b 1965, Hugh b 1966, Michael b 1975), 1 da (Lucy b 1968); *Career* applied mathematics Univ of Nottingham: asst lectr 1964–66, lectr 1966–76, reader 1976–85, prof 1985–; head of Mathematics Dept Univ of Nottingham 1987–90; visiting prof Univ of: Heidelberg 1978, Denver 1980, Texas 1983, Colorado 1996; visiting prof Indian Statistical Inst 1987 and 1996; memb: Amnesty Int, CND, London Mathematical Soc, American Mathematical Soc; *Recreations* music, literature, walking; *Style—* Prof Robin Hudson; ✉ Mathematics Department, University of Nottingham, Nottingham NG7 2RO (☎ 0115 951 4930, fax 0115 951 4951, telex 37346 UNINOT G, e-mail rlh@maths.nott.ac.uk)

HUDSON, Tom; s of Michael John Hudson, and Jean Mary, *née* Overton; *b* 18 June 1963; *Educ* Dulwich, Univ of Oxford; *Career* formerly copywriter: Bartle Bogle Hegarty, Leagas Delaney; creative dir BST-BDDP 1996–; *Clubs* Crystal Palace FC; *Style—* Tom Hudson, Esq; ✉ BST-BDDP, 4–6 Soho Square, London W1V 5DE (☎ 0171 287 7778)

HUE WILLIAMS, Charles James; s of Charles Anthony Hue Williams (d 1969), and Joan, *née* Winfindale (d 1991); *b* 28 Sept 1942; *Educ* Harrow; *m* 14 March 1964, Joey Oriel Marie-Lou, da of Charles George Clover, of Fishponds, S Stoke, Goring on Thames, Oxon; 1 s (Mark b 29 Oct 1968), 1 da (Sarah (Mrs Timothy Haslam) b 27 June 1966); *Career* ptnr Wedd Durlacher Mordaunt & Co 1970–85; dir: Kleinwort Benson Ltd 1986–90, Kleinwort Benson Securities 1986–90 (md 1989–90), Kleinwort Benson Holdings plc 1989–90, dir Henderson Crosthwaite Institutional Brokers Ltd 1992–; *Recreations* rackets, lawn tennis, real tennis, golf; *Clubs* Tennis and Rackets Assoc, Queen's, Swinley, Prestwick, Royal St George's Sandwich, Royal and Ancient, Berkshire, MCC; *Style—* Charles Hue Williams, Esq; ✉ Headley Meadows, The Hanger, Headley, Hants (☎ 01428 713970); Henderson Crosthwaite Institutional Brokers Ltd, 32 St Mary's Hill, London EC3 (☎ 0171 623 9992)

HUEBNER, Michael Denis; CB (1994); s of Dr Denis William Huebner (d 1994), of Yarm, Cleveland, and Mary Irene Hargraves, *née* Jackson (d 1971); *b* 3 Sept 1941; *Educ* Rugby, St John's Coll Oxford (BA); *m* 18 Sept 1965, Wendy Ann, da of Brig Peter Crosthwaite, of Hove, Sussex; 1 s (Robin b 1971), 1 da (Clare b 1975); *Career* called to the Bar Gray's Inn 1965, bencher 1994; Lord Chllr's Dept 1966: seconded Law Offrs' Dept 1968–70, asst slr 1978, under sec 1985, circuit admin N Eastern Circuit 1985–88, princ estab and fin offr 1988–89, dep sec 1989–, dep clerk of the Crown in Chancery 1993–, chief exec Ct Serv 1995– (head Ct Serv 1993–95); *Recreations* looking at pictures, architecture; *Style—* Michael Huebner, Esq, CB; ✉ The Court Service, Southside, 105 Victoria Street, London SW1E 6QT

HUERTAS, Dr Thomas F; *b* 11 April 1949; *Educ* Fordham Univ, Univ of Chicago (MA, PhD); *m* Edith Rigler-Huertas; 1 s (Michael Huertas b 5 Oct 1983); *Career* gp head Public Sector Europe Citibank London; chm: EU Ctee of Bankers' Assoc for Foreign Trade, Financial Servs Sub-Ctee of EC Ctee of American C of C; memb EC Payment System Tech Devpt Gp, memb Conf Bd Europe Cncl of Bank Chief Financial Officers; author of various articles in professional banking jls; *Books* Citibank 1812–1970 (1985); *Style—* Dr Thomas F Huertas; ✉ Citibank NA, PO Box 200, Cottons Centre, Hays Lane, London SE1 2QT (☎ 0171 234 2917, fax 0171 234 2588)

HUGGETT, Brian George Charles; MBE (1978); s of George William Huggett (d 1983), and Annie May, *née* Flower (d 1990); *b* 18 Nov 1936; *m* 1961, Winifred, da of Griffith Hughes (d 1979); 2 da (Yvonne b 1968, Sandra b 1973); *Career* int professional golfer; 33 tournament wins incl: Dunlop Masters, PGA Match Play Champion, PGA Stroke Champion, Vardon Trophy winner, Welsh Nat Champion, second and third Br Open, Dutch Open, German Open, Portuguese Open, Algarve Open, Singapore Int; Ryder Cup player (6 appearances, former capt), capt GB twice, World Cup player (9 appearances); golf course designer, dir; memb PGA, memb Professional Golfers Architects' Assoc; *Recreations* following sport generally; *Clubs* MCC, Royal Porthcawl Golf, Lord's Taverners; *Style—* Brian Huggett, Esq, MBE; ✉ Cherry Orchard, Weston-under-Penyard, Ross-on-Wye, Herefordshire HR9 7PH (☎ 01989 562634)

HUGGETT, Monica Elizabeth; da of Victor Lewis Huggett (d 1983), of Epsom, and Monica Germaine, *née* May; *b* 16 May 1953; *Educ* Green Sch for Girls, Isleworth, Royal Acad of Music London; *Career* violinist; ldr Amsterdam Baroque Orchestra 1979–87, ldr/dir The Hanover Bond 1983–86 (recordings incl Beethoven Symphonies), memb Trio Sonnerie with Sarah Cunningham and Gary Cooper, first violin of Hansmusik (romantic chamber ensemble); other recordings incl Bach sonatas with Ton Koopman, Vivaldi concertos with The Academy of Ancient Music, Mozart concertos, Beethoven concerto and Mendelssohn concerto with the Orchestra of the Age of Enlightenment; prof of baroque and classical violin Höchschule für Kunste Bremen 1993; memb Musicians' Union; *Recreations* gardening, cycling, non-business travel; *Style—* Ms Monica Huggett; ✉ c/o Francesca McManus, 71 Priory Rd, Kew Gardens, Surrey TW9 3DH (☎ 0181 940 7086, fax 0181 332 0879)

HUGGINS, Sir Alan Armstrong; kt (1980); s of William Armstrong Huggins (d 1938); *b* 15 May 1921; *Educ* Radley, Sidney Sussex Coll Cambridge (MA); *m* 1, 1950 (m dis), Catherine Davidson, da of David Dick (d 1929); 2 s, 1 da; m 2, 1985, Elizabeth Low, da of Dr Christopher William Lumley Dodd (d 1973); *Career* serv WWII Admty; called to the Bar Lincoln's Inn 1947; resident magistrate Uganda 1951–53; Hong Kong: stipendiary magistrate 1953–58, dist judge 1958–65, puisne judge 1965–76, justice of appeal 1976–80, vice pres Ct of Appeal 1980–87; judicial cmmr Brunei 1966–87 and 1991–; justice of appeal: Gibraltar 1988–96, Br Antarctica 1988–, Br Indian Ocean Territory 1991– (pres), Falkland Islands 1988– (pres 1991), Bermuda 1989–; hon life govr Br and Foreign Bible Soc, hon life memb American Bible Soc, Anglican reader; *Recreations* boating, archery, amateur theatre, tapestry, forestry; *Clubs* Royal Over-Seas League; *Style—* Sir Alan Huggins; ✉ Widdicombe Lodge, Widdicombe, Kingsbridge, Devon TQ7 2EF

HUGGINS, Rodney Philip; s of Maj Rowland Huggins (d 1961), of Reading, Berks, and Barbara Joan Trowbridge, *née* Hayter; *b* 26 Nov 1935; *Educ* Reading Sch, Lycée Lakanal Sceaux Paris; *m* 30 March 1959, José Rhoda, da of Charles Hatch; 1 s (Jeremy b 1963); *Career* Kenya advocate 1960, fndr and sr ptnr RP Huggins and Co Slrs Reading 1961–85; chm: Nat Insur Local Tbnl 1975–84, Indust Tbnls 1981–84, Vaccine Damage Tbnl 1984–, VAT Tbnls 1988–; nat chm Independent Tbnl Service 1992–; regnl chm Social Security Appeals Tbnls 1984–92; gen tax cmmr 1983–; pres Nat Assoc of Round Tables of GB and I 1975–76, govr Dist 1090 Rotary Int 1987–88, vice pres Rotary Int in GB and Ireland 1996–97; hon slr Nat Assoc Ex Tablers Clubs 1984–; Freeman City of London 1981, Liveryman Worshipful Co of Arbitrators 1981; FCIArb; *Books* Guide to Procedure in Social Security Appeal Tribunals (1985), Guide to Procedure in Medical Appeal Tribunals; *Recreations* golf, singing, swimming, bridge; *Clubs* MCC, Leander, Royal Over-Seas League, RAC, Sonning Golf; *Style—* Rodney Huggins, Esq; ✉ The Quarries, 10 West Drive, Sonning-on-Thames, Berkshire RG4 6GD (☎ 0118 969 3096); 22 Cerro Grande, Albufeira 8200, Algarve, Portugal; Independent Tribunal Service, City Gate House, 39–45 Finsbury Square, London EC2A 1DX (☎ 0171 814 6502)

HUGH-JONES, Sir Wynn Normington (Sir Hugh Jones); kt (1984), LVO (1961); s of Huw Hugh-Jones (d 1937), and May, *née* Normington (d 1979); *b* 1 Nov 1923; *Educ* Ludlow, Selwyn Coll Cambridge (MA); *m* 1 (m dis); 1 s, 2 da; m 2, 1987, Oswynne, *née* Buchanan; *Career* RAF 1943–46; HM Dip Serv 1947–73: FO, Jeddah, Paris, Conakry, Rome (head of chancery), FCO, Elizabethville, Ottawa (cnsllr and head of chancery) 1968–70, FCO 1971, Lord President's Office 1971, Cabinet Office 1972–73; dir gen English Speaking Union 1973–77; sec gen Lib Pty 1977–83, hon jt treas Lib Pty 1984–87; chm Avebury in Danger 1988–89; govr Queen Elizabeth Fndn for the Disabled 1985–, vice chm Euro-Atlantic Gp 1986–92, tstee Wilts Community Fndn 1991–93, vice-pres Lib International (Br Gp) 1995–; FIMgt; *Recreations* golf, gardening; *Style—* Sir Hugh Jones, LVO; ✉ Fosse House, Avebury, Wilts SN8 1RF

HUGH SMITH, Sir Andrew Colin; kt (1992); s of Lt-Cdr Colin Hugh Smith, RN (d 1975); *b* 6 Sept 1931; *Educ* Ampleforth, Trinity Coll Cambridge; *m* 1964, Venetia, da of Lt-Col Peter Flower (d 1993); 2 s; *Career* called to the Bar Inner Temple 1956, sr ptnr Capel-Cure Myers 1979–85, chm London Stock Exchange 1988–94; chm: Holland & Holland plc 1987–95, Penna plc 1995–; dir: J Bibby & Sons plc, Matheson Lloyds Investment Trust plc; MSI (memb Stock Exchange 1970); *Recreations* reading, shooting, fishing, gardening; *Clubs* Brooks's, Pratt's; *Style—* Sir Andrew Hugh Smith; ✉ c/o National Westminster Bank plc, 21 Lombard Street, London EC3P 3AB

HUGHES, Allan Berkeley Valentine; *b* 27 Feb 1933; *Educ* Wellington Coll; *m* 24 April 1964, (Gina) Ann Stephen; 2 s (Rupert b 18 April 1966, Oliver b 8 Aug 1968); *Career* QOH 1952–53, Queen's Own Worcs Hussars 1953–57; admitted slr 1959; Payne Hicks Beach: ptnr 1960–94, sr ptnr 1989–94, conslt 1994–; chm: UK Bd Colonial Mutual Life Assurance 1994–, Iris Fund for Prevention of Blindness, Cncl of Govrs Heathfield Sch; memb Law Soc; *Recreations* art, golf, gardening; *Clubs* Buck's, Cavalry & Guards', MCC, The Justinians; *Style—* Allan Hughes, Esq; ✉ The Glebe House, Sapperton, Cirencester, Glos GL7 6LE; Payne Hicks Beach, 10 New Square, Lincoln's Inn, London WC2A 3QG (☎ 0171 465 4301, fax 0171 465 4465)

HUGHES, Aneurin Rhys; s of William Hughes, of Swansea, and Hilda Hughes; *b* 11 Feb 1937; *Educ* Swansea GS, Oregon City HS USA, UCW Aberystwyth (BA); *m* 1964, Jill Salisbury; 2 s; *Career* pres NUS 1962–64, research on HE in South America; HM Dip Serv: FO London 1966–68, first sec Political Advsr's Office (later Br High Cmmn) Singapore 1968–70, first sec Br Embassy Rome 1971–73; Secretariat General of the Euro Community: head Div for Internal Coordination 1973–76, advsr to Spokesman and DG for Info 1977–80, chef de cabinet of Ivor Richard (memb Euro Cmmn) 1981–85, chm Selection Bd for Candidates from Spain and Portugal 1985–87, organiser Conf on Culture Econ New Technol (Florence) 1986–87; ambass and head of Delgn of the Euro Cmmn: to Oslo Norway 1987–95, to Aust and NZ 1995–; *Recreations* squash, golf, music, hashing; *Style—* Aneurin Hughes, Esq; ✉ European Commission Delegation, 18 Arakana Street, Yarralumla ACT 2600, Canberra, Australia (☎ 00 61 62 71 27 77, fax 00 61 62 73 44 45)

HUGHES, Anthony; s of Francis James Hughes (d 1983), and Mabel, *née* Hall (d 1995); *b* 23 June 1938; *Educ* King Edward's Sch Birmingham; *m* 22 Sept 1973, Gillian Rose, da of Roger Hamilton Aitken, TD, of Birmingham; *Career* sr ptnr J W Scrivens & Co CA's 1967–; champion: Br Eton Fives nine times 1968–75, Br Rugby Fives Veterans 1986 and 1987, Br Rugby Fives Vintage 1995 and 1996; FCA (ACA 1962); *Recreations* Eton Fives, Rugby Fives, handball, travel; *Clubs* Edgbaston Priory; *Style—* Anthony Hughes, Esq; ✉ J W Scrivens & Co, Imperial House, 350 Bournville Lane, Bournville, Birmingham, B30 1QZ (☎ 0121 478 1431)

HUGHES, Anthony Philip Gilson; QC (1990); *Educ* Univ of Durham (BA); *Career* called to the Bar Inner Temple 1970, recorder of the Crown Court, head of chambers; *Style—* Anthony Hughes, Esq, QC; ✉ 1 Fountain Court, Steelhouse Lane, Birmingham B4 6DR

HUGHES, Anthony (Tony); s of Richard Hughes (d 1944), and Lucy Cotton, *née* Sproule (d 1989); *b* 24 Sept 1944; *Educ* Blackfriars Sch, UCL, Univ of Edinburgh (MA); *m* 1975, Marie-Estelle, da of Jean Dufournier; 1 da (Chantal Madeleine Lucy b 26 Sept 1980), 2 s (Timothy Anthony Jean b 16 March 1983, Christopher François Wilfrid b 27 Aug 1986); *Career* film ed BBC 1970–74; called to the Bar Inner Temple 1975 (scholar 1973), barr 1975–77; tax mangr Peat Marwick Mitchell 1978–82; Deloitte Haskins & Sells (merged with Coopers & Lybrand 1990): tax mangr 1982–86, ptnr 1986–; memb Dell Ctee 1982; contrib to Financial Times and professional jls; ATII 1979; *Books* International Tax Planning for UK Companies (1984, 1990 and 1994); *Recreations* squash, tennis; *Clubs* Wimbledon Lakeside; *Style—* Tony Hughes, Esq; ✉ Coopers &

Lybrand, 1 Embankment Place, London WC2N 6NN (☎ 0171 213 5466, fax 0171 213 2418)

HUGHES, Dr Antony Elwyn; s of Ifor Elwyn Hughes, and Anna Betty, *née* Ambler; *b* 9 Sept 1941; *Educ* Newport HS Gwent, Jesus College Oxford (Scott Prize in Physics); *m* 1963, Margaret Mary, da of Arthur James Lewis (d 1978); 2 s, 2 da; *Career* Harkness fell Cornell Univ USA 1967–69; UKAEA: scientific offr 1963–67, sr scientific offr 1969–72, princ scientific offr 1972–75, individual merit appt 1975–81, sr personal appt 1981–83, ldr Defects in Solids Gp 1973–78, ldr Solid State Scis Gp 1978–83, head Materials Physics Div 1983–86, dir Underlying Res and Non-Nuclear Energy Res 1986–87, chief scientist and dir Nuclear Res 1987–88; dir Laboratories SERC 1988–91, dir Progs and dep chm SERC 1991–94, dir of engrg and science and dep chief exec EPSRC 1994–96; memb NI HE Cncl 1993–, memb Cncl CRAC 1994–, memb Cncl Royal Instn GB 1995–; chm Winterbrook Youth Club Harwell 1980–93, govr Didcot Girls' Sch 1981–88; CPhyS, FInstP 1972, CPhys; *Books* Real Solids and Radiation (1975), Defects and Their Structure in Non-Metallic Solids (ed 1976); *Recreations* walking, watching rugby & cricket, music, playing the trumpet, gardening; *Style—* Dr Antony E Hughes; ✉ Kingswood, King's Lane, Harwell, Didcot, Oxon OX11 0EJ (☎ 01235 835301, fax 01235 832667)

HUGHES, Prof Barry Peter; s of John Frederick Hughes (d 1987), of Wolverhampton, and Dorothy, *née* Elwell; *b* 29 Aug 1932; *Educ* Wolverhampton GS, Univ of Birmingham (BSc, PhD, DSc, DEng); *m* 21 Sept 1957, (Pamela) Anne, da of Joseph Sydney Barker (d 1979), of Prestatyn; 1 s (Rowan b 29 Aug 1958), 2 da (Hilary b 6 Feb 1962, Sara b 8 March 1963); *Career* concrete engr in charge of site laboratory and concrete quality control Berkeley Nuclear Power Station 1956–58; Univ of Birmingham: lectr 1963–68, sr lectr 1968–71, reader 1971–73, prof of civil engrg 1974–95, emeritus prof 1995–; private conslt 1995–; author of numerous res and tech pubns on concrete and concrete structures; chm: W Mids Region Concrete Soc 1974–75, Mids Branch Inst of Structural Engrs 1976–77; memb: BSI Ctee CVCP7, Rilem, Concrete Soc; FICE (MICE 1961), FIStructE (memb 1969); *Books* Handbook for BS 5337 (1976, 2 edn 1983), Limit State Theory for Reinforced Concrete Design (3 edn 1980); *Recreations* sailing, music, walking; *Clubs* Dale Sailing; *Style—* Prof Barry P Hughes; ✉ Long Barn, 8 Parkfields, Arden Drive, Dorridge, Solihull B93 8LL (☎ and fax 01564 776584); Veronica Cottage, St Anne's Head, Dale, Pembrokeshire, Dyfed SA62 3RS; School of Civil Engineering, University of Birmingham, Edgbaston, Birmingham B15 2TT (☎ 0121 414 5065, fax 0121 414 3675)

HUGHES, Catherine Eva; CMG (1984); da of Edmund Ernest Pestell (d 1965), and Isabella Cummine, *née* Sangster (d 1987); sister of John Edmund Pestell, *qv*; *b* 24 Sept 1933; *Educ* Leeds Girls' HS, St Hilda's Coll Oxford (MA); *m* 1991, Dr John Trevor Hughes; *Career* HM Dip Serv: 3 sec The Hague 1958, 2 sec Bangkok 1961, FO 1964, 1 sec UK Delgn to OECD Paris 1969, FCO 1971, St Antony's Coll Oxford 1974, cnsllr E Berlin 1975–78, Cabinet Office 1978–80, Dip Serv inspr 1980–82, min (econ) HM Embassy Bonn 1983–87, asst under sec (public depts) FCO 1987–89; princ Somerville Coll Oxford 1989–96; *Style—* Mrs Catherine Hughes, CMG; ✉ 2 Bishop Kirk Place, Oxford OX2 7HJ

HUGHES, Christopher Carl; s of Norman Alfred Hughes (d 1983), of Sheffield, and Betty, *née* Roebuck; *b* 19 Aug 1950; *Educ* Harrow Weald Co GS, Univ of Sheffield (BSc); *m* 26 Aug 1972, Julia Clare, da of Dr Maxwell Chapman Pennington, of Caerphilly; 1 s (Daniel Andrew b 13 Feb 1983); *Career* BBC: studio mangr World Serv 1971–73, prodr Radio Sheffield 1975–79 (station asst 1973–75), prodr Special Current Affrs Unit Radio 4 1979–80; Radio Trent Ltd: prog controller 1980–89, md 1989–94, station dir 1994–; memb Radio Acad; *Recreations* birdwatching, gardening; *Style—* Christopher Hughes, Esq; ✉ Radio Trent Ltd, 29–31 Castlegate, Nottingham NG1 7AP (☎ 0115 958 1731, fax 0115 952 7003)

HUGHES, Christopher Wyndham; s of Dr John Philip Wyndham Hughes (d 1981), of Marsh Lock House, Henley-on-Thames, Oxfordshire, and Christine, *née* Jolley (d 1947); *b* 22 Nov 1941; *Educ* Manchester GS, King Edward's Sch Birmingham, UCL (LLB); *m* 31 Dec 1966, Gail, da of Percival Eric Ward (d 1957), of Cricklewood, London; 3 s (Christian Wyndham b 29 Feb 1968, Marcus Wyndham (twin) b 1968, Dominic Wyndham b 20 June 1974); *Career* admitted slr 1966; Wragge & Co Birmingham: articled clerk and slr until 1970, ptnr 1970–, managing ptnr 1994–95; Notary Public; non-exec chm Newman Tonks Group plc 1995–; Birmingham Law Soc: memb 1966, memb Cncl 1977–91, jt hon sec 1977–84, vice pres 1988–89, pres 1989–90; memb and later chm of Solihull Ctee of Cancer Res Campaign 1972–85, memb Bd Severn Trent Water Authy 1982–84; govr of The Schs of King Edward VI Birmingham 1984–; memb: Law Soc 1966, The Notaries Soc 1979; *Recreations* travel, theatre, sport, languages, old buildings; *Clubs* Warwickshire CCC; *Style—* Christopher Hughes, Esq; ✉ Cuttle Pool Farm, Cuttle Pool Lane, Knowle, Solihull, W Midlands B93 0AP (☎ 01564 772611); Wragge & Co, 55 Colmore Row, Birmingham B3 2AS (☎ 0121 233 1000, fax 0121 214 1099)

HUGHES, Colin; s of Gerald Arthur Hughes, and Edith Anna-Lina, *née* Welsch; *b* 17 March 1958; *Educ* The Bulmershe Sch Reading, Hertford Coll Oxford (BA); *m* 1, 1981 (m dis 1990), Nicola Gerrard; 1 s (Edgar b 6 Sept 1987), 1 da (Anna-Lena b 16 Dec 1988); m 2, 1992, Alexandra Smith; 1 da (Harriet Agnes b 9 April 1994), 1 s (William Alfred b 18 Aug 1996); *Career* municipal corr Sheffield Star 1979–81, reporter Press Assoc 1982; The Times: educn and local govt reporter 1983–85, Whitehall reporter 1986; The Independent: political corr 1986–89, US corr 1990, policy corr 1990–91, educn ed 1991–93, asst ed 1993–95, managing ed 1995–96, dep ed 1996–; commended Young Journalist of the Year Br Press Awards 1982; *Books* Labour Rebuilt: The New Model Party (with Patrick Wintour, 1990); *Recreations* piano playing, sailing, tennis, walking, being with my children; *Style—* Colin Hughes, Esq; ✉ The Independent, Newspaper Publishing, 1 Canada Tower, Canary Wharf, London E14 5DL (☎ 0171 293 2559, fax 0171 293 2022)

HUGHES, David Campbell; yr s of Trevor George Hughes (d 1988), of Herefordshire, and Flora Jean, *née* Britton; *b* 13 Dec 1953; *Educ* Millfield, King's College London (LLB, Pres of Union 1975–76); *m* 1992, Claire Margaret, da of Ian Mitchell Bennet (d 1990), and Doreen Margaret, *née* Wilson, of Cheshire; *Career* admitted slr 1979, admitted slr Hong Kong 1992; ptnr Allen & Overy 1985–; Parly candidate (C) Bow and Poplar 1987; vice pres City of London Solicitors' Co; memb Law Soc, MInstD; *Recreations* golf, chess, cricket; *Clubs* Oriental, Men of Principle, Lyneham Golf; *Style—* David C Hughes, Esq; ✉ Allen & Overy, One New Change, London EC4M 9QQ (☎ 0171 330 3000, fax 0171 330 9999)

HUGHES, David Clewin; s of Harry Alfred Hughes of West Sussex, and Margaret Eileen; *b* 14 Oct 1953; *Educ* Whitgift Sch, Univ of Oxford (MA); *m* 16 July 1977, Rosanne Margaret, da of Ian Brunton Graham; 3 da (Katherine Rosanne b 26 March 1982, Victoria Louise b 25 June 1985, Emily Charlotte b 13 May 1988); *Career* Arthur Andersen: joined 1976–, ptnr 1987–; pres Croydon and District Soc of CA'S 1989–90; FCA; *Recreations* sport, theatre, travel, gardening, wine; *Clubs* RAC, Old Whitgiftians; *Style—* David Hughes, Esq; ✉ Arthur Andersen, 1 Surrey Street, London WC2R 2PS (☎ 0171 438 3522)

HUGHES, Sir David Collingwood; 14 Bt (GB 1773), of East Bergholt, Suffolk; s of Sir Richard Edgar Hughes, 13 Bt (d 1970), and Angela Lilian Adelaide, *née* Pell (d 1967); *b* 29 Dec 1936; *Educ* Oundle, Magdalene Coll Cambridge (MA); *m* 14 March 1964, Rosemary Ann, da of Rev John Pain, of Framfield Vicarage, Uckfield, Sussex; 4 s (Thomas Collingwood b 1966, Timothy John Pell b 1968, Benjamin Richard b 1969, Anthony George David b 1972, d 1991); *Heir* s, Thomas Collingwood Hughes b 16 Feb 1966; *Career* heraldic sculptor, md Louis Lejeune Ltd 1978–; Liveryman Worshipful Co of Grocers; *Recreations* fishing; *Clubs* Flyfishers, Cambridge County; *Style—* Sir David Hughes, Bt; ✉ The Berristead, Wilburton, Ely, Cambs CB6 3RP (☎ 01353 740770)

HUGHES, David John; s of Glynn Hughes (d 1985), and Gwyneth Mary, *née* Jenkins; *b* 19 March 1955; *Educ* Wolverhampton GS, Jesus Coll Oxford (MA); *m* 4 Sept 1987, Linda Anne, da of Thomas Hunt (d 1991), of Wolverhampton; 1 s (Richard b 1987), 1 da (Lisa b 1990); *Career* asst slr: Nabarro Nathanson 1980–82, Slaughter and May 1982–85; ptnr Pinsent Curtis (formerly Pinsent & Co) 1987– (asst slr 1985–87); memb Law Soc; *Recreations* music, theatre; *Style—* David Hughes, Esq; ✉ Pinsent Curtis, 3 Colmore Circus, Birmingham B4 6BH (☎ 0121 200 1050, fax 0121 626 1040)

HUGHES, David John; s of Gwilym Fielden Hughes (d 1989), and Edna Frances, *née* Cochrane (d 1996); *b* 27 July 1930; *Educ* Eggar's GS, King's Coll Sch Wimbledon, ChCh Oxford (MA); *m* 1, April 1958 (m dis 1977), Mai Elisabeth, *née* Zetterling (the actress and director Mai Zetterling; d 1994), formerly wife of Isak Lemkow; m 2, Nov 1980, Elizabeth Jane, da of James Westoll, DL; 1 s (Merlin b 1984), 1 da (Anna Rose b 1981); *Career* Nat Serv RAF 1949–50, cmmnd PO 1949, Flying Offr (Res) 1951; editorial asst London Magazine 1953–55, lit advsr Elek Books 1956, reader Rupert Hart-Davis Ltd 1957–60, screen writer of documentary and feature films 1960–, ed Town Magazine 1960–61, film critic The Sunday Times 1983–84, fiction critic The Mail On Sunday 1983–, theatre critic Night & Day 1996–; ed Letters (jl of RSL) 1992–; FRSL 1986; *Books* A Feeling in the Air (1957), Sealed With a Loving Kiss (1958), J B Priestley: An Informal Study (1958), The Horsehair Sofa (1961), The Major (1964), The Road to Stockholm (1964), The Seven Ages of England (1967), The Man Who Invented Tomorrow (1968), The Rosewater Revolution (1971), Evergreens (1976), Memories of Dying (1976), A Genoese Fancy (1979), The Imperial German Dinner Service (1983), The Pork Butcher (1984), But For Bunter (1985), Winter's Tales: New Series I (ed 1985), Best Short Stories (ed 1986, 10 edn 1995), The Little Book (1996), Himself and Other Animals, a portrait of Gerald Durrell (1997); *Clubs* Savile, Academy; *Style—* David Hughes, Esq; ✉ 163 Kennington Road, London SE11 6SF

HUGHES, David John; s of John David Hughes (d 1994), of Wendover, Bucks, and Mary Deirdre, *née* Lowen; *Educ* St Paul's, Univ of Southampton (BA, pres Students' Union 1975–76); *m* 21 Oct 1995, Jane Katherine Wynsome, *née* Anstiss; 1 da (Alice b 1 Aug 1996); *Career* mktg exec Express Newspapers 1979–82, Parly and external affrs offr Fedn of Civil Engrg Contractors 1982–85, exec sec Cncl for Environmental Conservation 1985–88, sr conslt then bd dir Shandwick Public Affairs 1988–93, dir of govt rels and public affrs The Communication Group plc 1993–95, jt md The Rowland Company and md Rowland Sallingbury Casey 1995–; nat chm Lib Students 1976–77; Parly candidate: (Lib) Southampton Test 1979, (Lib-SDP Alliance) Westbury 1983 and 1987; nat chm Parly Candidates Assoc 1984–87, vice chm Lib Pty 1985–88; memb: Hansard Soc for Parly Govt 1991, Assoc of Professional Political Conslts 1995; MInstD 1996; *Books* Liberals and Social Democrats: the Case for an Alliance (1981), Guide to Westminster and Whitehall (1994); various articles in New Statesman, PR Week and other pubns; *Recreations* historical and political biography, theatre and cinema; *Clubs* National Liberal; *Style—* David Hughes, Esq; ✉ 4 Rosenau Crescent, Battersea, London SW11 4RZ (☎ 0171 924 1400); The Rowland Company, 67–69 Whitfield Street, London W1P 5RL (☎ 0171 323 0221, fax 0171 255 2131)

HUGHES, His Hon Judge; David Morgan; s of Rev John Edward Hughes (d 1959), of Brynsiencyn, Anglesey, and Margaret Ellen Hughes, MBE, *née* Jones (d 1978); *b* 20 Jan 1926; *Educ* Beaumaris GS, Bangor Univ Coll, LSE (LLB), McGill Univ Montreal (Rockefeller Fndn Fellowship in Int Air Law); *m* 1 Sept 1956, Elizabeth Jane, da of Richard Thomas Roberts; 2 da (Janet Mary b 29 Aug 1958, Karen Elizabeth b 26 April 1961), 1 s (David Richard Morgan b 28 June 1967); *Career* served Royal Welch Fus 1944–48 (Capt, attached to 2 Bn Welch Regt Burma), Univ of London 1948–51, McGill Univ 1951–52; called to the Bar Middle Temple 1953, in practice Wales and Chester Circuit 1953–72, recorder Jan-Nov 1972, circuit judge (Wales and Chester Circuit) 1972–; dep chm Caernarvonshire Quarter Sessions 1970–71, chm Agric Lands Tbnl Wales 1970–72; pres: Mental Health Review Tbnl 1990–, HM Circuit Judges' Assoc 1995; *Recreations* gardening, tennis, watching cricket and football, fell walking, reading, theatre; *Style—* His Hon Judge Hughes; ✉ Chester Crown Court, The Castle, Chester (☎ 01244 317606)

HUGHES, Dr David Treharne Dillon; s of Maj-Gen W D Hughes, CB, CBE, of Farnham, Surrey, and Kathleen Linda Elizabeth, *née* Thomas (d 1976); *b* 31 Oct 1931; *Educ* Cheltenham, Trinity Coll Oxford (BSc, MA), London Hosp Med Coll (BM BCh); *m* 11 Nov 1959, Gloria Anna; 1 s (David Edward Treharne b 29 April 1974), 2 da (Carly Anna b 22 Sept 1960, Mandy Lou b 19 Oct 1962); *Career* Capt RAMC 1959–61 (jr med specialist BMH Hong Kong); jr res fell MRC Univ of Oxford 1953–54, res fell Univ of California 1963–64, conslt physician Royal London Hosp 1970–96 (jr appts 1957–68), head Dept of Clinical Investigation Wellcome Res Laboratories 1978–93; tstee Hunterian Soc (former pres); memb Int Soc of Internal Med (former pres), memb General Medical Cncl 1993–96; chm Bd of Govrs Moving Theatre Tst; Freeman City of London, past Master Worshipful Soc of Apothecaries (memb Court of Assts 1981); memb RSM, FRCP; *Books* Tropical Health Science (1967), Human Biology and Hygiene (1969), Lung Function for the Clinician (1981); *Recreations* cricket, horseracing; *Clubs* Savage; *Style—* Dr David Hughes; ✉ 94 Overbury Avenue, Beckenham, Kent BR3 2PY (☎ 0181 650 3983)

HUGHES, (Edward) Emyr Byron; s of Rev Thomas Byron Hughes (d 1979), of Beaumaris, Anglesey, and Jennie Gwladys, *née* Richards (d 1992); *b* 22 June 1951; *Educ* David Hughes Sch Menai Bridge Anglesey, UCW Aberystwyth (LLB); *m* 20 Aug 1977, Eleanor Mair Eluned Hughes; *Career* slr in private practice Anglesey 1975–78, slr Gwynedd CC 1978–81; S4C: contracts offr 1981–82, head of legal servs 1982–85, head of financial planning 1984–85, controller of finance 1985–89, sec to The Welsh Fourth Channel Authority 1985–, dir of corp policy 1989–; dir Cyngor Ffilm Cymru (Film Cncl for Wales) 1988–, tstee Welsh Bdcasting Tst 1988–; *Style—* Emyr Byron Hughes, Esq; ✉ S4C, Parc Ty Glas, Llanishen, Cardiff CF4 5DU (☎ 01222 747444, fax 01222 741417)

HUGHES, Gary William; s of William Muir Hughes, of Paisley, and Frances, *née* Carruthers; *b* 23 April 1962; *Educ* Castlehead HS Paisley, Univ of Strathclyde (BA Econ); *m* July 1990, Margaret Frances, da of Frank Swallow; 1 s (Gavin Andrew b June 1996); *Career* accountant Ernst & Whinney 1987–89 (articled clerk 1984–87); Guinness plc/United Distillers: gp accountant 1989–90, controller mergers and acquisitions Guinness plc 1990–92, vice pres fin United Distillers N America 1992–94; dir of fin control Forte plc 1994–96, commercial dir Forte Hotels Div Granada plc Feb-May 1996, fin dir Scottish Television plc 1996–; ACA 1987; *Recreations* golf, tennis, cooking, cinema, reading, football; *Style—* Gary Hughes, Esq; ✉ Scottish Television plc, Cowcaddens, Glasgow G2 3PR (☎ 0141 300 3111, fax 0141 300 3753, mobile 0468 506470)

HUGHES, George (aka John Campbell); s of Peter Hughes; *b* 4 May 1937; *Educ* Liverpool Collegiate, Gonville and Caius Coll Cambridge (MA), Harvard Business Sch (MBA); *m* 1963, Janet; 2 s (David b 1964, Edward b 1966); *Career* ski instr 1959, lead role in J Arthur Rank film Holiday 1959–60; banker Paris 1960, with IBM London 1960–69 (strategy unit mangr 1968–69), merchant banking London 1969–70, vice chm and gp md Duple Group Ltd 1970–71; chm and chief exec: Hughes International Ltd 1970–85, Willowbrook World Wide Ltd 1971–83, Willowbrook International 1970–83, Castle Hughes Group Ltd 1975–87, Hughes Truck and Bus Ltd 1976–84, Hughes Technology Ltd 1987–; landowner, author; chm Derbyshire CCC 1976–77, memb Test and County Cricket Bd 1976–77; *Books* The Effective Use of Computers (1968), Strategy in Business and War (1968), New Towns (1974), Economic Development as Strategic Choice (1978), Mobility: a basic human need (1979), Traffic Congestion in Capital Cities (1979), Getting Action and Making Things Happen (1979), Integrated Cattle Development (1980), Choosing the Best Way (1980), Control (1980), Scenario for the President (1981), Spare Parts Management (1981), Strategy for Survival (1982), Road to Recovery (1982), New Patterns in World Trade (1983), All the Meat and Milk China Needs (1984), Speed Thinking Kaleidoscope (1990), Scenarios into Strategy (1992), Galatea gAIa galactica - the Samsara of AI for Design of Industries (1994); *Recreations* travel, perception of visual patterns in thinking, 'imagineering', esoterica, artificial intelligence, historic buildings, shooting, cattle, soccer, tennis, squash, 'dolche far niente'; *Clubs* Carlton; *Style*— George Hughes, Esq; ✉ Xanadu, Matthews Green, Wokingham, Berks RG41 1JU

HUGHES, Glyn Tegai; s of Rev John Hughes (d 1985), and Ketura, *née* Evans (d 1946); *b* 18 Jan 1923; *Educ* Newtown and Towyn Co Schs, Liverpool Inst, Manchester GS, Corpus Christi Coll Cambridge (MA, PhD); *m* 21 Aug 1957, Margaret Vera (d 1996), da of Desmond Andrew Herbert, CMG (d 1976), of Brisbane, Queensland; 2 s (Alun b 1960, David b 1961); *Career* RWF 1942–46, temp Maj DAAG HQ Alfsea; lectr in Eng Univ of Basel 1951–53, tutor to Faculty of Arts Univ of Manchester 1961–64 (lectr in comparative literary studies 1953–64), warden of Gregynog Univ of Wales 1964–89, BBC nat govr for Wales and chm Bdcasting Cncl for Wales 1971–79; memb Bd Channel 4 TV 1980–87, authy of S4C 1981–87; Lib Pty candidate W Denbigh: 1950, 1955, 1959; memb Welsh Arts Cncl 1967–76, chm Undeb Cymru Fydd 1968–70, vice pres N Wales Arts Assoc 1977–94, pres Private Libraries Assoc 1980–82, chm Welsh Bdcasting Tst 1988–96, Methodist local preacher; *Books* Eichendorff's Taugenichts (1961), Romantic German Literature (1979), Thomas Olivers (ed, 1979), Williams Pantycelyn (1983), Gwasg Gregynog: A Descriptive Catalogue (with David Esslemont, 1990); *Recreations* book collecting, shrub propagation; *Style*— Glyn Tegai Hughes, Esq; ✉ Rhyd-Y-Gro, Tregynon, Newtown, Powys SY16 3PR (☎ 01686 650609)

HUGHES, (George) Graham McKenny; s of George Hughes (d 1982), of London, and Peggy, *née* Graham (d 1965); *b* 17 April 1926; *Educ* Eton, Trinity Coll Cambridge (exhibitioner); *m* 1951, Serena, da of Sir Stanley Robinson (d 1976); 1 s (Benjamin b 1960), 3 da (Emma b 1953, Clare b 1955, Harriot b 1957); *Career* exhibition sec then art dir Goldsmiths' Hall (Worshipful Co of Goldsmiths) 1951–80, head of design Royal Mint 1973–77; owner and ed Arts Review magazine 1980–92; currently head Starcity Ltd (Publishers); hon chm Crafts Centre of GB 1966–75; organiser of exhibitions of modern silver, jewellery and crafts throughout the world incl: Br Fair NY 1960 (consequently estab perm showrooms for artists' products in NY and Tokyo), Int Exhibition of 20th Century Artists' Jewellery (Goldsmiths' Hall) 1961; RSA Gold Medal 1966; hon memb: Soc of Antiquaries, Royal Soc of Arts, RCA, Sheffield Hallam Univ, Dusseldorf Goldsmiths' Guild, German Goldsmiths' Soc, Art Workers' Guild; Liveryman Worshipful Co of Goldsmiths; FSA; *Publications* Sven Boltenstern (biog), Marit Guinness Aschan (biog), Rural Barns of Britain; also author of numerous books on silver, jewellery and crafts; *Recreations* playing clarinet; *Style*— Graham Hughes, Esq, FSA; ✉ Burnt House Cottage, Dukes Green, Alfriston, Polegate, E Sussex BN26 5TS (☎ 01323 870 231); 69 Faroe Rd, London W14 0EL (☎ 0171 603 6563)

HUGHES, Dr Graham Robert Vivian; s of Robert Arthur Hughes, and Emily Elizabeth Hughes (d 1989); *b* 26 Nov 1940; *Educ* Cardiff HS For Boys, London Hosp Med Coll (MD); *m* 2 March 1966, Monica Ann; 1 s (Richard John Vivian b 7 July 1971), 1 da (Sarah Imogen b 19 Oct 1967); *Career* rheumatologist; trained London Hosp, res fell Columbia Presbyterian Hosp, reader in med and head of Dept of Rheumatology Royal Postgrad Med Sch London, conslt rheumatologist and head of the Lupus Arthritis Res Unit St Thomas' Hosp London, conslt rheumatologist RAF 1987, 700 pubns on arthritis res; Ciba Geigy ILAR int res prize for rheumatology res 1993; ed LUPUS, life pres LUPUS UK, tstee St Thomas' Lupus Tst; hon memb: Aust Rheumatology Soc, Scandinavian Rheumatology Soc, Hong Kong Rheumatology Soc, Portugese Rheumatology Soc, Turkish Rheumatology Soc, memb: American Lupus Hall of Fame, Assoc of Physicians of GB & I; FRCP; *Books* Modern Topics in Rheumatology (1978), Systemic Lupus Erythematosus (1982), Connective Tissue Diseases (4 edn, 1994), Lecture Notes in Rheumatology (1987), Problems in The Rheumatic Diseases (1988), SLE: A Guide for Patients (1988), Phospholipid Binding Antibodies (1991); *Recreations* tennis, piano; *Style*— Dr Graham Hughes; ✉ Lupus Arthritis Research Unit, Rayne Institute, St Thomas' Hospital, London SE1 (☎ 0171 928 9292 ext 2888, fax 0171 633 9422)

HUGHES, Gwen; *Career* editor Opera BBC Radio 3 1995–; *Style*— Ms Gwen Hughes; ✉ BBC Radio 3, Broadcasting House, London W1A 1AA (☎ 0171 765 4434, fax 0171 765 4363)

HUGHES, Howard; s of Charles William Hughes (d 1969), of W Kirby, Cheshire, and Ethel May, *née* Howard (d 1994); *b* 4 March 1938; *Educ* Rydal Sch; *m* 1, 20 June 1964, Joy Margaret (d 1984), da of Charles Francis Pilmore-Bedford (d 1966), of Keston, Kent; 2 s (Quentin b 1969, Edward b 1971), 1 da (Charlotte b 1974); m 2, 2 April 1988, Christine Margaret, da of Walter George Miles, of Tunbridge Wells, Kent; 1 s (Andrew b 1982); *Career* CA; articled clerk Bryce Hammer & Co Liverpool 1955–60; Price Waterhouse London: joined 1960, ptnr 1970–, memb Policy Ctee 1979–, dir London Office 1982–85, managing ptnr UK 1985–88, memb World Bd 1988–, managing ptnr Europe 1988–91, dep chm Europe 1991–92, world managing ptnr 1992–; hon treas and memb Cncl Royal London Soc for the Blind, memb Agric Wages Bd for England and Wales; Liveryman Worshipful Co of Chartered Accountants; FCA 1960; *Recreations* golf, music; *Clubs* Carlton, MCC, Wildernesse Golf; *Style*— Howard Hughes, Esq; ✉ Witham, Woodland Rise, Seal, nr Sevenoaks, Kent TN15 0HZ (☎ 01732 761161), Price Waterhouse, 32 London Bridge, London SE1 9QL (direct ☎ 0171 939 2022, fax 0171 939 2155);

HUGHES, Prof Ieuan Arwel; s of Arwel Hughes, OBE (d 1988), of Cardiff, and Enid Phillips, *née* Thomas (d 1995); bro of Owain Arwel Hughes, the conductor, *qv*; *b* 9 Nov 1944; *Educ* Univ of Wales Coll of Med (MB BCh, MD), MA Cantab; *m* 27 July 1969, Margaret Maureen (Mac), da of William Edgar Davies; 2 s (Gareth Arwel, Wiliam Arwel), 1 da (Mari Arwel); *Career* reader in child health Univ of Wales Coll of Med 1985–89 (sr lectr 1979–85), prof of paediatrics Univ of Cambridge 1989–; fell Clare Hall Cambridge; pres: Euro Soc of Paediatric Endocrinology 1993 (sec 1987–92), Assoc of Clinical Professors of Paediatrics 1995–97; memb: Br Paediatric Assoc, RCP; FRCP(C) 1975, FRCP 1984; *Books* Handbook of Endocrine Tests In Children (1989); also author of papers on genetic endocrine disorders; *Recreations* music (memb Ralph Vaughan Williams Soc), travel, squash, cycling, hill-walking; *Style*— Prof Ieuan Hughes; ✉ University of Cambridge, Department of Paediatrics, Addenbrooke's Hospital, Hills Rd, Cambridge CB2 2QQ (☎ 01223 336885, fax 01223 336996)

HUGHES, Sir Jack William; kt (1980); s of George William Hughes, of Maidstone, Kent, and Isabel Hughes; *b* 26 Sept 1916; *Educ* Maidstone GS, Univ of London (BSc), Open Univ (BA); *m* 1, 1939, Marie-Theresa (d 1987), da of Graham Parmley Thompson; m 2, 1994, Helena Hughes, da of Franciszek Kanik; *Career* local authy municipal and county engrg work 1933–40, Special Duties Branch RAF 1940–46, demobilised Sqdn Ldr; chartered surveyor; jt sr ptnr Jones Lang Wootton 1949–76, conslt Jones Lang Wootton Int Real Estate Advsrs 1976–; chm Bracknell Devpt Corpn 1971–82; dir: South Bank Estates 1960–, URPT 1961–86, MEPC 1971–86, Housing Corporation (1974) Ltd 1974–78, TR Property Investment Trust 1982–91, Property and Reversionary Investments 1982–86, Brighton Marina Co (representing interests of Brighton Corp) 1974–86, BR Property Bd 1976–86; chm Property Advsy Gp DOE 1978–82; memb: Property Div Mercantile Credit Bank, Ctee of Mgmnt Charities Property Unit Tst 1967–74, Advsy Gp to DOE on Commercial Property 1974–78, DOE Working Pty on Housing Tenure 1976–77; chm and co-fndr South Hill Park Arts Centre Tst 1972–79, vice pres Pestalozzi Children's Village Tst 1994–; tstee New Towns Pensions Fund 1975–82; fndr memb Continuing Professional Devpt Fndn 1980–, fndr memb Estates Golf Soc; Freeman City of London, Liveryman Worshipful Co of Painter Stainers Guild 1960–; FRSA, FRICS, FRIPHH; *Publications*(jtly) Town and Country Planning Act 1949 (RICS), Glossary of Property Terms (1990), The Land Problem: a fresh approach (chm RICS ctee); also author of articles in the technical press on property devpt, investment and funding; *Recreations* Open University studying, golf, travel, reading; *Clubs* Carlton, Bucks, RAF; *Style*— Sir Jack Hughes; ✉ Challoners, The Green, Rottingdean, East Sussex

HUGHES, John; s of Evan John Hughes, and Dellis, *née* Williams; *b* 28 April 1930; *Educ* Stationers' and Newspapermakers' Sch London, Colby Coll; *m* 1, 20 Aug 1955 (m dis 1987), Vera Elizabeth Pockman; 1 s (Mark Evan), 1 da (Wendy Elizabeth); m 2, 1988, Peggy Janeane Chu; 1 s (Evan Jordan); *Career* Natal Mercury Durban SA 1946–49 and 1952–54, Daily Mirror then Reuters London 1949–52; Christian Science Monitor Boston: joined 1954, corr Africa 1955–61, asst foreign ed 1962–64, corr Far East 1964–70, managing ed 1970, ed 1970–76, ed and mangr 1976–79; broadcaster Westinghouse Broadcasting Co Boston 1962–70 (based Far East 1964–70), dir News Journal Co Wilmington 1975–78, pres and publisher Hughes Newspapers Inc Orleans Mass 1977–81, assoc dir USIA Washington 1981–82, dir Voice of America 1982, asst sec of state Department of State 1982–84, syndicated columnist 1985–, pres Concord Communications Inc Rockland Maine 1989–91, dir Int Media Studies Program Brigham Young Univ 1991–95, asst sec gen/dir of communications UN 1995–; memb: American Soc of Newspaper Editors (dir 1972–80, pres 1978–79), Pulitzer Prize Bd 1975–81; Nieman fell Harvard 1961–62; Pulitzer Prize for Int Reporting 1967, Overseas Press Club Award 1970, Yankee Quill Award (Sigma Delta Chi) 1977; The New Face of Africa (1961), Indonesian Upheaval (1967); *Clubs* Overseas Press, Hong Kong Country, Harvard; *Style*— John Hughes, Esq; ✉ 1579 Willow Lane, Provo, Utah 84604, USA

HUGHES, Dr John Martel; TD (1968); s of Morris Hughes (d 1964), of Newport, Gwent, and Catherine Ann, *née* Morgan (d 1968); *b* 12 April 1923; *Educ* Newport HS, Quakers Yard Secdy Sch, Hereford Cathedral Sch, Univ of Wales (BSc, MB BCh, DPM); *m* 6 May 1950, Sarah Ruth, da of Rhys Williams; 1 s (David Martel b 16 Sept 1961), 5 da (Olwen Rhiannon b 16 May 1951, Catrin Llinos b 12 Nov 1953, Sara Martel b 24 June 1957, Elen Mari b 22 Dec 1958, Sioned Ruth b 9 Dec 1964); *Career* short serv cmmn RAMC 1947–50, CO Mil Hosp Mogadiscio Somalia 1949–50, MO TA 1956–73, Col (late RAMC), CO 203(W) Gen Hosp RAMC(V) 1967–73 (Hon Col 1977–82), Hon Col 382 Field Co RAMC 1987–; trg in gen med Cardiff Royal Infirmary 1946–47 and 1950–53, trg in psychiatry Whitchurch Hosp Cardiff 1953–61; St Cadoc's Hosp Newport: conslt psychiatrist 1961–64, physician supt 1964–89; conslt psychiatrist Health Advsy Serv DHSS 1974–87, gen mangr Gwent Mental Health Unit 1986–88; hon physician to HM The Queen 1973–75; chm: Gwent Div BMA 1970, Welsh Div RCPsych 1982–86, RAMC Assoc S Wales and W of Eng 1987–; National Eisteddfod of Wales: chm Exec Ctee Newport 1985–88, memb Gorsedd of Bards 1989; gen sec Cambrian Archaeological Soc 1991– (memb 1959–), memb Friends of Friendless Churches 1988–; memb BMA 1946, FRCPEd 1970 (MRCPEd 1958), FRCPsych 1970 (MRCPsych 1969); OStJ 1973; *Publications* Pelvic Pain in Women (jtly, 1990), Criminal Law and Psychiatry (jtly, 1991); *Recreations* archaeology, foreign languages, gardening; *Style*— Dr J M Hughes, TD; ✉ The Laurels, Westfield Road, Newport, Gwent NP9 4ND (☎ 01633 262449); St Cadoc's Hospital, Caerleon, Newport, Gwent NP6 1XQ (☎ 01633 421121)

HUGHES, Prof John Pinnington; s of Joseph Henry Hughes (d 1956), and Edith Annie Hughes; *b* 6 Jan 1942; *Educ* Mitcham Co GS, Chelsea Coll London (BSc), King's Coll London (PhD), Univ of Cambridge (MA); *m* (m dis 1981), Madeleine Carol; 1 da (Katherine b 1967); *partner* Julie; 3 s (Joseph Francis b 1986, John Stephen b 1988, Tomas James b 1990), 1 da (Georgina Anne b 1984); *Career* sr lectr and dep dir Unit for Res on Addictive Drugs Univ of Aberdeen 1973–77 (lectr in pharmacology 1969–73), prof in pharmacological biochemistry Imperial Coll London 1979–83 (reader in biochemistry 1977–79), dir Parke-Davis Res Centre Cambridge 1983–, fell Wolfson Coll Cambridge 1983–, vice pres of res Parke-Davis (Warner-Lambert Corp) 1988–, hon prof of neuropharmacology Univ of Cambridge 1989–; jt chief ed Neuropeptides 1980–; chm Persistent Viral Disease Res Fndn; memb Substance Abuse Ctee Mental Health Fndn; sch govr Local Educn Authy Swaffham Prior Community Sch; Hon Dr of Med Univ of Liége 1978; memb of honour Romanian Acad of Sciences, memb Biochemical Soc, MPS, FRS 1993; *Books* Centrally Acting Peptides (1978), Opioid Peptides (1983), Opioids Past Present and Future (1984), The Neuropeptide Cholecystokinin (1989); *Recreations* gardening, dogs; *Style*— Prof John Hughes, FRS; ✉ Parke-Davis Neuroscience Research Centre, Cambridge University Forvie Site, Robinson Way, Cambridge CB2 2QB (☎ 01223 210929, fax 01223 214534)

HUGHES, Judith Caroline Anne; QC (1994); 3 da of William Frank Hughes, and Eva-Ruth, *née* Meier; *b* 13 Oct 1950; *Educ* Woodhouse GS Finchley, Univ of Leeds (LLB); *m* 27 Aug 1977, Mark G Warwick; 2 da (Sarah b 1981, Lucy b 1985); *Career* called to the Bar Inner Temple 1974, bencher 1994; recorder of the Crown Court 1995– (asst recorder 1991–95), dep judge of the High Court of Justice 1997–; tstee: Gilbert Place Centre 1995–, The Children's Soc 1996–; memb: South Eastern Circuit, Family Bar Assoc; *Recreations* reading, theatre, swimming, philately, gardening; *Style*— Miss Judith Hughes, QC; ✉ 1 Mitre Court Buildings, Temple, London EC4Y 7HE

HUGHES, Katherine; da of William Frank Hughes, of Carinthia, Austria, and Eva Ruth, *née* Meier; *b* 24 July 1949; *Educ* Woodhouse GS, Bethesda Chevy Chase HS Maryland, Univ of E Anglia (BA), Univ of Wales (MSc); *Career* res assoc Univ of Wales 1973–75, asst planning offr Mid Glamorgan CC 1975–77, dir Welsh Consumer Cncl 1978–94 (res offr 1977–78); Wales office Nat Fedn of Women's Institutes: acting head 1994–95, policy offr 1995–; MRTPI, FRSA; *Style*— Miss Katherine Hughes; ✉ K H Associates, 26 Bryn Gwyn, Caerphilly CF8 1ET (☎ 01222 886569)

HUGHES, Kerrie Lynn; da of William Hughes, of Wellington, NZ, and Beverley, *née* Masterton; *b* 11 Oct 1959; *Educ* Taita Coll, Wellingotn Poly, St Martin's Sch of Art (dip in fashion, MA); *partner* Hugo Alexander Wilmar; *Career* fashion designer; apprentice dressmaker 1976–78, Wellington Poly 1979–81, costume design for NZ Ballet and Opera 1981, own label Svelt retailed Wellington 1981–83 then Auckland 1983–85, new label Siren (womenswear) retailed Wellington 1985–86, travelled internationally to research costume (NZ Arts Cncl Award) 1986, St Martins Sch of Art London 1986–88, asst designer to Murray Arbeid 1988–89, private cmmns 1989–90, fndr ptnr Idol (wholesaling internationally) 1990–; *Recreations* reading, travel; *Style*— Ms Kerrie Hughes; ✉ Idol, 15 Ingestre Place, Soho, London W1R 3LP (☎ and fax 0171 439 8537)

HUGHES, Kevin; MP (Lab) Doncaster North (majority 19,813); s of Leonard Hughes, and Annie Hughes; *b* 15 Dec 1952; *Educ* Univ of Sheffield; *m* 26 Aug 1972, Lynda, *née*

Saunders; 1 s, 1 da; *Career* former coal miner, branch del Brodsworth NUM 1981–90, memb Exec Ctee Yorks NUM 1983–87; sec and agent: Don Valley Constituency Lab Pty 1980–83, Doncaster N Constituency Lab Pty 1983–89; cncllr Doncaster BC 1986–92 (chm Social Servs Ctee 1987–92); MP (Lab) Doncaster N 1992–, pty whip 1996–; fell Industry and Parliamentary Trust 1995; *Recreations* golf, walking, opera; *Style*— Kevin Hughes, Esq, MP; ✉ House of Commons, London SW1A 0AA

HUGHES, Prof Leslie Ernest; s of Charles Joseph Hughes (d 1975), of Parramatta, NSW, and Vera Dorothy, *née* Raines (d 1984); *b* 12 Aug 1932; *Educ* Parramatta HS, Univ of Sydney (MB BS); *m* 19 Dec 1955, Marian, da of James Edwin Castle (d 1956), of Sydney, NSW; 2 s (Graeme b 1964, Stephen James b 1971, d 1995), 2 da (Bronwyn b 1957, Gillian b 1960); *Career* reader in surgery Univ of Queensland 1964–71, Eleanor Roosevelt int cancer fell Roswell Park Meml Inst Buffalo NY 1969–70, prof of surgery Univ of Wales Coll of Med 1971–92; visiting prof Albany Univ NY, Hong Kong, Benares, Sydney, Melbourne and Brisbane; pres: Surgical Res Soc 1992–94, Welsh Surgical Soc 1991–92; chm Editorial Bd European Jl of Surgical Oncology 1993–96; FRCS 1959, FRACS 1959, DS (Queensland) 1974; *Books* Benign Disorders of the Breast (1988); *Recreations* music, walking; *Style*— Prof Leslie Hughes; ✉ 14 Millwood, Lisvane, Cardiff CF4 5TL

HUGHES, Lewis Harry (Lew); CB (1996); s of Reginald Hughes (d 1975), and Gladys Hughes; *b* 6 March 1945; *Educ* Devonport HS, City of London Coll; *m* July 1975, Irene, *née* Nash; 1 s (Robert David b 27 May 1977); *Career* Nat Audit Office: asst auditor then sr auditor 1963–79, audit mangr then dep dir 1979–88, dir 1988–89, asst auditor gen 1990–; memb CIPFA; *Recreations* golf, music, family life; *Clubs* Tavistock Golf; *Style*— Lew Hughes, Esq, CB; ✉ 1 Wood End Road, Harpenden, Herts AL5 3EB (☎ 01582 764992); Assistant Auditor General, Unit E, National Audit Office, 157–197 Buckingham Palace Road, London SW1W 9SP (☎ 0171 798 7678, fax 0171 931 8874)

HUGHES, Dr Louis; s of Richard Hughes (d 1962), and Anne, *née* Green (d 1958); *b* 10 March 1932; *Educ* Holyhead County Sch, Univ Coll Cardiff, Welsh Nat Sch of Med (MB BCh, DObst); *m* 26 June 1959, Margaret Caroline Mary, da of Thomas Cyril Wootton (d 1992), of Newport, Gwent; 1 s (Christopher b 1964), 1 da (Deborah b 1960); *Career* Capt RAMC (TA) 1964; pt/t MO (infertility) Queen Charlotte and Chelsea Hosp 1979–; conslt (infertility) Margaret Pyke Centre 1979–; author numerous papers on fertility; chm: Childless Tst 1980–83, Int Wine and Food Soc 1982–86 (memb Mgmnt Ctee); memb: Br Fertility Soc, Br Andrology Soc, American Fertility Soc; Freeman: City of London 1975, Worshipful Soc of Apothecaries 1974; DRCOG, MBMA, FRSM; *Books* Monographs on Wine; *Recreations* golf, wine and food, cricket, book collecting; *Clubs* MCC, Savile, Saintsbury, Denham Golf; *Style*— Dr Louis Hughes; ✉ Beechwood, Burton's Lane, Chalfont St Giles, Bucks HP8 4BA (☎ 01494 762297); 99 Harley St, London W1 (☎ 0171 935 9004)

HUGHES, Malcolm Edward; *b* 22 July 1920; *Educ* Regional Coll of Art Manchester, RCA; *Career* artist; tutor: Sch of Architecture Polytechnic of Central London, Bath Acad, Chelsea Sch of Art; reader in fine art Sch of Postgraduate Studies The Slade Sch of Fine Art; co-fndr: The Systems Group 1969, Exhibiting Space 1984; hon res fell Univ Coll London 1982, emeritus reader in fine art Univ of London 1982, hon fell Univ Coll London 1991; memb Edwin Austin Abbey Scholarship Ctee; *Exhibitions* numerous solo exhibitions; gp exhibitions incl: Looking Forward (Whitechapel Art Gallery London) 1952, Four Artists: Reliefs, Constructions and Drawings (V&A) 1971, Systems (Whitechapel Art Gallery and on tour with Arts Council) 1972, Basically White (ICA) 1974, Art as Thought Process (for Arts Council, Serpentine Gallery) 1974, New Work 2 (Hayward Gallery London) 1975, Sculpture for the Blind (Tate Gallery) 1976, British Artists of the Sixties (Tate Gallery) 1977, British Painting 1952–77 (Royal Acad) 1977, Constructive Context (Warehouse Gallery London, Arts Cncl Tour) 1978, Arts Council Collection (Hayward Gallery) 1980, British Council Collection (Serpentine Gallery London) 1980, Systematic Constructive Work (Ruskin Sch of Drawing and Fine Art Oxford) 1987, Modern British Sculpture (Tate Gallery) 1988, Painting Space, Gallery Space (Annely Juda Fine Art) 1989, Britisch-Systematisch - Stiftung für Konstruktive und Konkrete Kunst (Zurich) 1990, Repères Paris (Reuttingen) 1992/3 (Centre d'Art Contemporain de Saint-Priest 1994), Glaerie Art In Nürnberg 1993/94, Testing the System (Kettles Yard Univ of Cambridge) 1996; also numerous works in US, Euro and Br exhibitions; *Awards* Arts Council award 1966, John Moores Exhibition prize 1967, Edwin Abbey premier scholarship 1973; *Style*— Malcolm Hughes, Esq; ✉ Annely Juda Fine Art, 23 Dering Street, London W1R 9AA (☎ 0171 629 7578, fax 0171 491 2139)

HUGHES, Melvyn; s of Evan Llewellyn Hughes, of Newcastle upon Tyne, and Irene Kathleen, *née* Spires; *b* 18 Nov 1950; *Educ* Royal GS Newcastle upon Tyne, St Catherine's Coll Oxford (MA); *m* 6 July 1974, Diane, da of Percival Moffett (d 1987); 2 s (Richard b 2 Nov 1983, David b 9 March 1990), 1 da (Alexandra b 28 Oct 1980); *Career* Slaughter and May: articled clerk 1974–76, asst slr 1976–83, ptnr 1983–, personnel ptnr 1989–; Freeman City of London; memb: City of London Slrs' Co, Law Soc; *Recreations* reading, cars, sport; *Clubs* RAC; *Style*— Melvyn Hughes, Esq; ✉ Slaughter and May, 35 Basinghall St, London EC2V 5DB (☎ 0171 600 1200, fax 0171 726 0038/071 600 0289/071 600 1455)

HUGHES, (Thomas) Merfyn; QC (1994); s of John Medwyn Hughes, of Beaumaris, Anglesey, and Jane Blodwen, *née* Roberts; *b* 8 April 1949; *Educ* Rydal Sch Colwyn Bay, Liverpool Univ (LLB); *m* 16 April 1977, Patricia Joan, da of John Edmund Talbot (d 1982), of Brentwood, Essex; 2 s (Thomas Jenkin Edmund b 14 Sep 1982, Joshua Edward Talbot b 7 Dec 1987), 1 da (Caitlin Mary b 19 Feb 1980); *Career* called to the Bar Inner Temple 1971, practising Wales and Chester circuit, recorder 1991– (asst recorder 1987–91); former Lab Pty candidate Caernarfon; *Recreations* sailing, rugby; *Clubs* Royal Anglesey Yacht; *Style*— Merfyn Hughes, Esq, QC; ✉ Plas Llanfaes, Beaumaris, Anglesey LL58 8RH (fax 01248 810228); 3 Stamford Court, Vicars Cross, Chester (☎ 01244 323886); Goldsmith Building, Temple, London EC4Y 7BL (☎ 0171 353 7881); 40 King Street, Chester CH1 2AH

HUGHES, Michael; s of Leonard Hughes, of Clwyd and Gwyneth Mair, *née* Edwards; *b* 26 Feb 1951; *Educ* Rhyl GS, Univ of Manchester (BA), LSE (MSc); *m* 11 Feb 1978, Jane Ann, da of Percival Frederick Gosham (d 1977), of Ipswich; 2 da (Sophie b 1979, Harriet b 1981); *Career* economist BP Pension Fund 1973–75, chief economist and ptnr de Zoete and Bevan 1976–86, dir Barclays de Zoete Wedd Securities Ltd; BZW: Capital Markets 1986, exec dir Gilts Ltd 1986–89, md Economics and Strategy 1989–, chm BZW Pensions Ltd 1996–; memb ESRC, chm Fin Ctee Cncl for Advancement of Communication with Deaf People; AMSIA 1977, MSI(Dip); *Recreations* horses; *Clubs* National Liberal; *Style*— Michael Hughes, Esq; ✉ Barclays de Zoete Wedd Ltd, Ebbgate House, 2 Swan Lane, London EC4R 3TS (☎ 0171 956 3511, fax 0171 956 3488, telex 888221)

HUGHES, Prof (John) Michael Barton; s of Dr Stanley Barton Hughes (d 1963), of Helen's Bay, Co Down, and Dorothy Jane Augusta, *née* Tornblad (d 1990); *Educ* Lancing, Trinity Coll Oxford (BM BCh, MA, DM); *m* 22 Feb 1963, Shirley Ann, da of Hedley Frank Stenning (d 1977); 2 da (Penelope Barton b 1971, Caroline Barton b 1975); *Career* house physician med unit London Hosp 1963–64, house physician and res fell Hammersmith Hosp 1965–68, MRC travelling fell Harvard Sch of Public Health 1968, prof of thoracic med Royal Postgrad Med Sch 1993– (lectr, sr lectr then reader 1969–93), conslt physician Hammersmith Hosp 1974– (Cournand lectr 1975, Fleischner lectr 1989–); author of chapters on lung gas exchange, pulmonary circulation, radioisotopes and lung function, over 150 sci articles on pulmonary physiology, pharmacology and lung disease; memb: Med Res Soc, Assoc Physicians, Physiological Soc, American Physiological Soc, British Thoracic Soc, Euro Resp Soc; FRCP 1979; *Recreations* golf, ornithology; *Clubs* Royal West Norfolk Golf; *Style*— Prof Michael Hughes; ✉ Dept of Medicine, Royal Postgraduate Medical School, Hammersmith Hospital, London W12 0HS (☎ 0181 383 3269, fax 0181 743 9733, e-mail j.hughes@rpms.ac.uk)

HUGHES, Michael James Hamilton; s of George Hamilton Hughes, of S Queensferry, Scotland, and Beatrice, *née* Bartlett; *b* 1 Oct 1948; *Educ* George Watson's Coll, Univ of Edinburgh (BCom); *m* 1974, Tytti, *née* Marttila; 4 s (Andrew Hamilton b 1979, Simon Tapio b 1981, Eric Michael b 1986, Alexander Peter b 1989); *Career* KPMG: joined 1970, CA 1973, mangr 1975, ptnr 1977–, memb Bd 1991, memb Urgent Issues Task Force Accounting Standards; *Recreations* sailing, travel; *Style*— Michael Hughes, Esq; ✉ KPMG, 8 Salisbury Square, London EC4Y 8BB (☎ 0171 311 5048)

HUGHES, Michael John; s of Frank Miller Hughes, of Denmead, Hants, and Jean Mary Hughes, MBE, *née* Allford; *b* 20 Nov 1949; *Educ* Collyer's GS Horsham, Oxford Poly, Univ of London (BEcon); *m* 10 Sept 1977, Elizabeth Charlotte Margaret Mary Antoinette Marie-Thérèse, da of Maj Leslie William Hutchins (d 1968), of Norwich; 2 da (Sophie b 1979, Caroline b 1982); *Career* media conslt; gen mangr Anglia TV Ltd 1984–88 (dir 1986); Anglia TV Group plc: dir 1986, asst gp chief exec 1988–90, dep gp chief exec 1990–94; resource and devpt dir MAI Media 1994–95; non-exec dir: East Anglian Radio plc 1991–94, Meridian Broadcasting Ltd 1994–95; exec dir: Three on Four Ltd 1993–95 (chm), Televirtual Ltd 1993–95; currently project co-ordination dir Channel 5 Broadcasting Ltd; dir Anglia TV Telethon Tst 1987–95; chm Cinema and Television Benevolent Fund (CTBF) East of England Ctee; *Recreations* tennis, squash, skiing, saxophone; *Clubs* East Anglian Lawn Tennis; *Style*— Michael Hughes, Esq; ✉ Hall Farmhouse, Stanfield, nr Wymondham, Norfolk NR18 9RL (☎ and fax 01953 606199); Channel 5 Broadcasting Ltd, 22 Long Acre, London WC2E 9LY (☎ 0171 550 5555, fax 0171 497 5618)

HUGHES, Nerys (Mrs Turley); da of Roger Edward Kerfoot Hughes (d 1974), of Rhyl, N Wales, and Annie Myfanwy, *née* Roberts; *b* 8 Nov 1941; *Educ* Howells Sch Denbigh, Rose Bruford Coll; *m* 13 May 1972, (James) Patrick Turley, s of James Turley (d 1983), of Wednesbury, Staffs; 1 s (Ben b 1974), 1 da (Mari-Claire b 1978); *Career* actress; vice pres Nat Children's Home; *Theatre* work incl: BBC Rep Co, RSC, English Stage Co Royal Court Theatre, RNT (Under Milk Wood 1995); *Television* series incl: Diary of a Young Man, The Liver Birds (revival 1996), The District Nurse, How Green was my Valley, Alphabet Zoo (children's TV), Bazaar (BBC) 1990, With A Little Help (BBC Wales) 1995, Capital Woman 1996, Molly; *Film* Second Best 1993, Handmade Moon (for TV) 1993; *Awards* incl: Pye Female Comedy Star Award 1974, Variety Club TV Actress of the Year 1984; *Recreations* gardening, reading; *Style*— Miss Nerys Hughes; ✉ c/o Barry Burnett Organisation Ltd, Suite 42–43, Grafton House, 2–3 Golden Square, London W1R 3AD (☎ 0171 437 7048/9, fax 0171 734 6118)

HUGHES, Nicholas Maxwell Lloyd; s of late Glyn Hughes, of Brighton, and late (Muriel) Joyce, *née* Hardaker; *b* 10 Oct 1955; *Educ* Univ of Sheffield (BA); *m* 8 June 1986, (Margaret) Ruth, da of Prof David Cornelius Morley, CBE, of Harpenden; 2 da (Olivia Emily b 3 July 1990, Eleanor Joyce b 27 July 1993); *Career* admitted slr 1981; ptnr Barlow Lyde & Gilbert 1984–; dir AIRMIC 1992–; consulting ed Transport Law and Policy Jl 1993–, author of articles on aviation and environmental law; Freeman City of London, Liveryman City of London Slrs Co; memb: Royal Aeronautical Soc, Law Soc; *Publications* Contracts for the Carriage of Goods by Land, Sea and Air (gen ed, 1993); *Recreations* wine, antique furniture, golf, opera; *Clubs* City of London; *Style*— Nicholas Hughes, Esq; ✉ Beaufort House, 15 St Botolph St, London EC3A 7NJ (☎ 0171 782 8459, fax 0171 782 8505, telex 913281 G)

HUGHES, Norman; s of Walter Hughes (d 1975), of Minshull Vernon, Crewe, and Edith Marjorie Hughes (d 1988); *b* 30 Sept 1952; *Educ* Crewe GS, Leeds Poly (BA); *m* Pamela, da of Joseph Holmes Newsome; 1 s (Richard Thomas b 1985, d 1987), 1 da (Amy Rebecca b 1979); *Career* former hockey player; Euro Bronze medal 1978, Champions Trophy Bronze medal 1979 and 1984, Olympic Bronze Los Angeles 1984, World Cup Silver London 1986; currently hockey coach; coach: England Team Euro Bronze 1991, GB Olympic Squad Barcelona 1992; sports centre mangr Wakefield Sports Club 1974–76, sales coordinator St Peter Sporting Goods 1976–79, sales office controller Slazenger Ltd 1979–83; Dunlop Slazenger International Ltd: product mangr (hockey) 1984–89, mktg mangr (cricket, hockey and table tennis) 1989–; *Books* Take Up Hockey (1990); *Recreations* hockey, walking, golf, travelling, making people laugh; *Clubs* Wakefield Hockey; *Style*— Norman Hughes, Esq; ✉ Dunlop Slazenger International Ltd, Shire Hall Industrial Estate, Saffron Walden, Essex CB11 3BY

HUGHES, Owain Arwel; s of Arwel Hughes, OBE (d 1988), of Cardiff, and Enid Phillips, *née* Thomas (d 1995); bro of Prof Ieuan Hughes, *qv*; *b* 21 March 1942; *Educ* Howardian HS Cardiff, Univ Coll Cardiff, RCM London; *m* 23 July 1966, Jean Bowen, da of William Emlyn Lewis; 1 s (Geraint John b 15 Feb 1974), 1 da (Lisa Margaret b 25 Dec 1970); *Career* conductor; since 1970 has conducted all the UK symphony orchs and their respective choirs, in particular The Hallé, London Philharmonic and The Royal Philharmonic; assoc conductor: BBC Welsh Symphony Orch 1980–86, Philharmonia Orch London 1985–90; musical dir Huddersfield Choral Soc 1980–86, fndr, artistic dir and conductor the Annual Welsh Proms 1986–, creator and musical dir The World Choir (10,000 male voices) 1992; princ conductor Aalborg Symphony Orch Denmark 1995–; performances in Norway, Sweden, Finland, Iceland, Luxembourg, France, Germany, Portugal, Hong Kong, Japan and NZ; many TV appearances in concert or special projects incl Mahler Symphony No 8, Requiem series, Holy Week series, Much Loved Music series, 40 anniversary concert of Granada TV (with Hallé and Royal Liverpool Philharmonic Orchs); memb Inst of Advanced Motorists, vice pres Nat Children's Home; hon bard Royal Nat Eisteddfod of Wales; Hon DMus: CNAA London, Univ of Wales; *Recordings* incl: Music of Delius (Philharmonia Orch, ASV), London Symphony by Vaughan Williams (Philharmonia Orch, ASV), Music of Paul Patterson (London Philharmonic, EMI), Much Loved Music Vols I and II (Hallé Orch, EMI), Carols Album and Hymns Album (Huddersfield Choral Soc, EMI), St David by Arwel Hughes (BBC Welsh Orch and Choir, Chandos), African Sanctus by David Fanshawe (Ambrosian Chorus and Instrumentalists, Phillips), complete cycle of Holmboe twelve symphonies (with Aarhus Symphony Orch, Grammophon BIS), Handel Messiah (with RPO and Royal Choral Soc, Pickwick), Verdi Requiem (with RPO, Royal Choral Soc and Brighton Festival Chorus, EMI), Sullivan Irish Symphony (with BBC Concert Orch, CPO), Holmboe Symphony No 13 & Koepell Oratorio Moses da Capo (with Danish Radio Symhony Orch); *Awards* Gold medal Welsh Tourist Bd, Communicator of the Year, 2 Gold Discs BPI; *Recreations* rugby, cricket, golf, motoring, travel; *Clubs* Rugby Club of London, London Welsh Assoc, London Welsh Rugby; *Style*— Owain Arwel Hughes, Esq; ✉ Rod Gunner Organisation, Argyll House, 1a All Saints Passage, London SW18 1EP (☎ 0181 874 3900, fax 0181 877 9050)

HUGHES, Paul; s of James Henry Hughes (d 1986), of Dublin, and Mary, *née* O'Hanlon; *b* 22 June 1956; *m* 24 June 1983, Liliane Niederer; 1 s (Kean b 11 Sept 1990); *Career* knitwear designer for Cachaca shop King's Road 1976–70; own galleries: Textile Gallery NY 1979–81, Gallery of Ethnographic Textiles San Francisco 1981–82, Gallery of Antique and Ancient Textiles London 1983–; organiser of numerous historical, African and South American textile exhibitions; author of exhibition catalogues; conductor of ecological tours of Amazon, builder of Mississippi-style steamer boat from scratch to act as local field hosp for indigenous Indians of Bolivian/Brazilian Amazon; *Style*— Paul Hughes, Esq; ✉ The Gallery, 3A Pembridge Square, London W2 4EW (☎ 0171 243 8598, fax 0171 221 8785)

HUGHES, Peter Thomas; QC (1993); s of Peter Hughes, JP (d 1991), and Jane Blakemore, *née* Woodward; *b* 16 June 1949; *Educ* Bolton Sch, Univ of Bristol; *m* 20 July 1974, Christine Stuart, da of Rex Taylor, of West Kirby, Wirral; 1 s (Richard b 12 July 1985), 1 da (Rosemary b 27 May 1982); *Career* called to the Bar Gray's Inn 1971, practising Wales and Chester Circuit, asst recorder Wales and Chester Circuit 1988–92, recorder 1992–, memb Gen Cncl of the Bar 1993–, chm Med Appeal Tbnl 1988–93, chm Registered Homes Tbnl 1993–; circuit junior 1991; chm: City of Chester Cons Assoc 1983–86, Euro Constituency Cncl 1984–87; memb Gray's Inn 1967–; *Recreations* fell walking, sailing, creative gardening, islands; *Clubs* Army and Navy, Lancashire County Cricket; *Style*— Peter Hughes, Esq, QC; ✉ 3 Paper Buildings, Temple, London EC4Y 7EU (☎ 0171 583 8055, fax 0171 353 6271); 40 King St, Chester CH1 2AH (☎ 01244 323886, fax 01244 347732)

HUGHES, Peter Travers; OBE (1993); *b* 24 Dec 1946; *Educ* Wishaw HS Lanarkshire, Tech Coll Coatbridge (HNC Metallurgy), Univ of Strathclyde (DMS), Univ of Dundee (MBA); *m* Patricia; 1 da (Laurie), 2 s (Robbie, Alexander); 2 s by prev m (Alan, William); *Career* trainee metallurgist Clyde Alloy (latterly British Steel), foundry metallurgist rising to foundry mangr North British Steel Group 1968–76, gen mangr Lake & Elliot Essex 1976–80 (also dir 1977–80), md National Steel Foundry (1914) Ltd (subsid of Lake & Elliot) 1980–83, initiated MBO forming Glencast Ltd 1983, co sold to NACO Inc Illinois USA 1994, currently md Glencast Ltd (winners Queen's Award for Technological Achievement 1990); current related appts: memb Exec Ctee Scottish Engrg (immediate past pres), memb Gen Cncl Engrg Employers' Fedn (EEF) London (memb Strategy Review Gp 1995), memb DTI/EPSRC LINK Prog Mgmnt Ctee for Enhanced Engrg Materials London, memb Cncl Castings Technology Int, memb Scottish Action Gp DTI sponsored team on Action for Engrg Initiatives 1995, chm Scottish Steel Founders' Assoc; guest lectr at various confs UK and abroad; former appts: chm Steel Castings Research and Trade Assoc 1988–92 (chm Research Ctee 1985–88), memb Materials Advsy Ctee Mfrg Technol Div DTI 1987–93, chm DTI Steering Ctee on UK Devpt of Solidification Simulation Prog for Castings 1988–89, chm Steering Ctee Scottish Employers' Assoc (leading to formation of Scottish Engrg), UK pres Inst of Br Foundrymen 1994–95; pres Scottish Branch Inst of Br Foundrymen 1984–85, pres Scottish Engrg 1993 (also former treas); former govr and memb Ct Univ of Abertay (formerly Dundee Inst of Technol); elder Church of Scotland 1976 (currently memb Kirk Session Elie Parish Church); FIMgt 1986, FIBF 1988, FRSA 1992, FIM 1993, CEng 1994, FEng 1995; *Recreations* soccer, golf, tennis, curling, music, church; *Clubs* Lundin Golf, Elie Tennis, Hercules Curling; *Style*— Peter Hughes, Esq, OBE, FEng; ✉ Glencast Ltd, Kirkland Works, Leven, Fife KY8 2LE (☎ 01333 423641, fax 01333 425734)

HUGHES, Philip Arthur Booley; CBE (1982); s of Leslie Booley Hughes, and Elizabeth Alice, *née* Whyte; *b* 30 Jan 1936; *Educ* Bedford Sch, Univ of Cambridge (BA); *m* 21 Aug 1964, Psiche Maria Anna Claudia, da of Bertino Bertini (d 1971); 2 da (Francesca b 1966, Simona b 1968), 2 step da (Pauline b 1952, Carole b 1954); *Career* engr Shell International Petroleum Co 1957–61, computer conslt Scicon (formerly CEIR) 1961–69, dir Logica plc 1990–95 (co-fndr, chm and md 1969–72, chm 1972–90); artist; gp exhibitions: Monks Gallery Sussex (with Beryl Bainbridge) 1972, Contemporary Br Painting (Madrid) 1983, Contemporary Painters (Ridgeway Gallery Swindon) 1986; one man exhibitions: Parkway Focus Gallery London 1976, Angela Flowers Gallery London 1977, Gallery Cance Manguin Vaucluse 1979 and 1985, Francis Kyle Gallery London 1979, 1982, 1984, 1987, 1989, 1992 and 1994, Inverness Museum 1990, Lesley Craze Gallery London 1992, Galerie Le Tour des Cardinaux Vaucluse France 1993, L'Ambassade de l'Australie Paris 1995; chm Bd of Tstees National Gallery London; dir Thames & Hudson Ltd, tstee Inst for Public Policy Res; *Style*— Philip Hughes, Esq, CBE; ✉ c/o The National Gallery, Trafalgar Square, London WC2N 5DN

HUGHES, Richard; s of Lt Walter Cyril Hughes, RA (d 1947), of Cardiff, and Emily, *née* Palfrey (d 1941); *b* 15 April 1938; *Educ* Cardiff HS, Eaton Hall Offr Cadet Sch, Mons Offr Cadet Sch, Queens' Coll Cambridge (MA, LLM), Coll of Law Guildford Surrey; *m* 11 June 1963, Marie Elizabeth, da of William Rieb (d 1972), of Somerset West, Cape, SA; 1 s (David b 31 March 1964); *Career* cmmnd 2 Lt The Welch Regt 1958, serving Cyprus (GSM) and Libya 1958–59; legal advsr: Royal Insurance Group 1963–65, S African Mutual Life Assurance Society 1965–66; slr of the Supreme Ct 1969, sr ptnr Sprake and Hughes 1982–91 (ptnr in private practice 1969–91); literary critic and reviewer The Cape Times 1964–66; memb Law Soc; *Recreations* travel, walking, reading, music; *Style*— Richard Hughes, Esq; ✉ Apple Acre, Low Rd, Norton Subcourse, nr Norwich, Norfolk NR14 6SA (☎ 01508 548316); 70 Queenswood Gardens, Blake Hall Road, Wanstead, London

HUGHES, Prof Richard Anthony Cranmer; s of late Dr Anthony Chester Cranmer Hughes, of Chester, and Lilian Mildred, *née* Crisp; *b* 11 Nov 1942; *Educ* Marlborough Coll, Clare Coll Cambridge, Guy's Hosp Med Sch; *m* 17 Feb 1968, Coral Stephanie, da of James Albert Whittaker (d 1983); 1 s (Henry b 1975), 2 da (Polly b 1970, Romany b 1971); *Career* conslt neurologist Guy's Hosp 1975, prof of neurology United Med and Dental Schs 1987, ed Journal of Neurology, Neurosurgery and Psychiatry 1979; chm Neurology Ctee RCP; govr Highgate Sch 1990–95; FRCP 1980; *Books* Immunology of The Nervous System (1983), Guillain-Barré Syndrome (1990), The Neurofibromatoses (1994); *Recreations* tennis, dinghy sailing, mountaineering, theatre; *Clubs* Royal Society of Medicine; *Style*— Prof Richard Hughes; ✉ c/o UMDS Guy's Hospital, St Thomas Street, London SE1 9RT

HUGHES, Robert; MP (Lab) Aberdeen N (majority 9,237); *b* 3 Jan 1932; *Educ* Robert Gordon's Coll Aberdeen, Benoni HS Transvaal, Pietermaritzburg Tech Coll; *m* 1957, Ina, *née* Miller; 2 s, 3 da; *Career* formerly engrg apprentice in SA, chief draughtsman C F Wilson & Co 1932 Ltd (Aberdeen until 1970); Parly candidate N Angus and Mearns 1959, memb Aberdeen Town Cncl 1962–70 (convenor of Health and Welfare Ctee 1963–68 and Social Work Ctee 1969–70), MP (Lab) Aberdeen N 1970–; memb: Standing Ctee on Immigration Bill 1971, Scot Affairs Select Ctee 1971 and 1992–; Parly under sec of state Scot Office 1974–75, jr oppn spokesman 1981–83; princ oppn spokesman: agriculture 1983–84, transport 1985–88; memb PLP Shadow Cabinet 1985–88; chm: Aberdeen City Lab Party 1961–69, Anti-Apartheid Movement (vice chm 1975–76) 1976–, Aberdeen CND (founder memb); memb AEU 1952–, Gen Med Cncl 1976–79, Scot Poverty Action Gp; *Recreations* fishing, golf; *Style*— Robert Hughes, Esq, MP; ✉ House of Commons, London SW1A 0AA

HUGHES, Robert Charles; s of Clifford Gibson Hughes, of Walton-On-The-Hill, Surrey, and Elizabeth Joan, *née* Goodwin; *b* 20 Jan 1949; *Educ* Westminster, Emmanuel Coll Cambridge (MA); *m* 23 June 1973, Cynthia Rosemary (Cindy), da of Lionel Edward Charles Kirby-Turner (d 1986), of Guildford, Surrey; 3 da (Zoe b 1975, Emma b 1976, Sophie b 1980); *Career* Ernst & Young (formerly Barton Mayhew & Co): joined 1970, ptnr London 1978–81, ptnr Dubai UAE 1981–86, London 1986–; FCA; *Recreations* golf, puzzles; *Clubs* Royal Automobile, Sutton Tennis and Squash, Cuddington Golf; *Style*— Robert Hughes, Esq; ✉ Crazes, Heather Close, Kingswood, Surrey KT20 6NY (☎ 01737 832 256); Ernst & Young, Becket House, 1 Lambeth Palace Rd, London, SE1 7EU (☎ 0171 928 2000, fax 0171 928 1345, telex 885224)

HUGHES, Robert Gurth (Bob); MP (C) Harrow West (majority 17,897); s of Gurth Martin Hughes, and Rosemary Dorothy, *née* Brown; *b* 14 July 1951; *Educ* Spring Grove GS, Harrow Coll of Technol; *m* 1986, Sandra Kathleen, da of James Vaughan; 4 da (Catherine b 1987, Elizabeth b 1988, Victoria b 1990, Alexandra b 1996); *Career* BBC TV News picture ed until 1987, MP (C) Harrow W 1987–; PPS to: Rt Hon Edward Heath MP 1988–90, Rt Hon Nicholas Scott 1990–92; asst whip 1992–94, Parly sec Office of Public Service and Science 1994–95 (resigned); *Recreations* watching cricket, listening to music, photography; *Clubs* St Stephen's & Constitutional; *Style*— Bob Hughes, Esq, MP; ✉ House of Commons, London SW1A 0AA (☎ 0171 219 6854)

HUGHES, Rodger Grant; s of Eric Hughes, of Rhyl, Clwyd, and Doreen, *née* Barnes; *b* 24 Aug 1948; *Educ* Rhyl GS, Queens' Coll Cambridge (MA); *m* 9 June 1973, Joan Clare, da of James Barker; 2 s (Marcus b 9 July 1979, Oliver b 2 Feb 1983); *Career* Price Waterhouse: joined 1970, ptnr 1982–, ptnr i/c Ind Business Gp 1988–91, ptnr i/c NW Region 1991–95, memb Supervisory Ctee 1991–95, UK dir Audit and Business Advisory Services 1995–; FCA 1973; *Style*— Rodger Hughes, Esq; ✉ Price Waterhouse, Southwark Towers, 32 London Bridge Street, London SE1 9SY (☎ 0171 939 3000, fax 0171 378 0647, telex 884657)

HUGHES, Dr Roger Llewellyn; s of Flt-Lt Clifford John Silke Hughes (d 1963), and Jean Christine Roger, *née* Stewart; *b* 2 June 1947; *Educ* The HS of Glasgow, Univ of Glasgow (MB ChB, MD); *m* 14 Oct 1971, Pamela Jane, da of Dr Finlay Finlayson (d 1983); 4 da (Vivienne b 1972, Caroline b 1974, Zoe b 1979, Jennifer b 1981); *Career* sr registrar Glasgow Royal Infirmary 1975 (sr house offr 1971–72, registrar of anaesthesia 1972–75), conslt in anaesthesia Stobhill Hosp Glasgow 1980–, currently hon clinical sr lectr Univ of Glasgow (lectr in anaesthesia 1975–80); author of papers on liver blood flow and baroreceptor reflex; chm of jr gp Assoc of Anaesthetists of GB and I 1977–79; memb: BMA, Intensive Care Soc; FRCP, FRCA; *Recreations* gardening, walking; *Style*— Dr Roger Hughes; ✉ 7 Ballaig Ave, Bearsden, Glasgow G61 4HA (☎ 0141 942 5626); Stobhill Hospital, Glasgow G21 (☎ 0141 201 3005); Glasgow Nuffield Hospital, Glasgow G12

HUGHES, Ronald Frederick (Ron); s of Harry Frederick James Hughes (d 1964), of Beccles, Suffolk, and Violet Kate, *née* Terry; *b* 21 Oct 1927; *Educ* Birmingham Central Tech Coll, Bradford Coll of Technol; *m* 21 Dec 1957, Cecilia Patricia, da of Maurice Nunis (d 1957), of Seremban, Malaysia; 2 s (Anthony b 1959, John b 1968), 1 da (Lesley-Ann b 1958); *Career* engrg cadet RE 1946, cmmnd RE 1950, SORE 3 Design HQ Malaya Cmd 1950, garrison engr Centl Malaya 1951, engr offr 22 SAS (Malayan Scouts) 1952, Adj CRE S Malaya 1953, SORE 3 Resources HQ Northern Cmd (UK) 1954; res asst BISRA 1954–55, civil engr (later md) HW Evans & Co Malaya 1955–59, civil engr WO Chessington 1959–63, works Gp Singapore 1963–66, area offr MPBW Malaya 1966–69, princ civil engr PO works MPBW 1969–76, area offr PSA Birmingham 1977–79, asst dir (later dir) civil engrg PSA 1979–87, dir and quality systems mangr Mott MacDonald Conslt Engrs 1987–91, systems mgmnt conslt London Underground Ltd 1992, project mgmnt and systems conslt 1993–; memb: Standing Ctee for Structural Safety 1983–87, Cncl Construction Indust Res and Info Assoc 1983–87, Parly Maritime Gp 1986–, Cncl Steel Construction Inst 1986–88; govt del Permanent Int Assoc of Navigation Congresses 1983–, dir Construction Indust Computing Assoc 1982–87; FICE 1962 (memb Bd Maritime Gp 1983), FIStructE 1987, MSIS (Fr) 1987; *Recreations* golf, squash, music, photography; *Clubs* Naval, Effingham (Surrey); *Style*— Ron Hughes, Esq; ✉ 9A The Street, West Horsley, Leatherhead, Surrey KT24 6AY (☎ 01483 282182)

HUGHES, Royston John (Roy); DL (Gwent 1992), MP (Lab) Newport East (majority 9,899); s of late John Hughes (coal miner), of Pontllanfraith; *b* 9 June 1925; *Educ* Pontllanfraith County GS, Ruskin Coll Oxford; *m* 1957, Florence Marion, da of John Appleyard, of Scarborough; 3 da; *Career* official TGWU 1959–66, memb Coventry City Cncl and sec Coventry Borough Lab Pty 1962–66; MP (Lab): Newport 1966–83, Newport E 1983–; chm: PLP Sports Gp 1974–84, Welsh Lab Gp 1975–76, PLP Steel Gp 1975–86 and 1992–, Welsh Grand Ctee 1982–84 and 1991–, Speaker's Panel 1982–84 and 1990–, Ctee of Selection 1982–84; memb Speaker's Panel of Chairmen 1991–; front bench spokesman Welsh Affairs 1984–88, memb Exec Inter-Parly Union 1987–92 (treas 1990–92), memb Cncl of Europe and WEU 1990–, jt chm All Party Motor Gp 1987, jt chm All Party Rugby Union Gp 1993–; *Recreations* rugby, cricket; *Clubs* United Services Mess (Cardiff), Pontllanfraith Working Men's, Caldicot Labour, Newport Athletic (life memb), Crawshay's Welsh RFC (vice pres), Glamorgan CCC (vice pres); *Style*— Roy Hughes, Esq, MP, DL; ✉ Chapel Field, Chapel Lane, Abergavenny, Gwent NP7 7BT; House of Commons, London SW1A 0AA (☎ 0171 219 3000)

HUGHES, Sean; *Career* comedian, writer and actor; stand up comic London clubs 1987; performances incl: Edinburgh Fringe, A One Night Stand with Sean Hughes (Int tour, Perrier Award 1990), Patrick's Day (Edinburgh Critics' Award 1991), nat UK and Eire tour 1994, Melbourne Comedy Festival 1994, live tour Aust 1995, Thirtysomehow (nat tour, also TV) 1995; *Television* incl: Sean's Show (Channel Four), Sean's Shorts (BBC), Aaaah Sean (Channel Four), The Signal Box (Parallel Films) 1995; *Film* incl: The Commitments (debut), Snakes and Ladders (Livia Films) 1995; *Video* Sean Hughes Live and Seriously Funny; *Books* Sean's Book (1993), The Grey Area (1995); *Style*— Sean Hughes, Esq; ✉ c/o PBJ Management Ltd, 5 Soho Square, London W1V 5DE (☎ 0171 287 1112, fax 0171 287 1448)

HUGHES, Prof Sean Patrick Francis; s of Dr Patrick Hughes (d 1995), and Kathleen Ethel, *née* Biggs; *b* 2 Dec 1941; *Educ* Downside, St Mary's Hosp Med Sch Univ of London (MB BS, MS); *m* 22 Jan 1972, Dr Felicity Mary Anderson; 1 s (John Patrick b 3 Feb 1977), 2 da (Sarah Jane b 28 Nov 1972, Emily Anne b 25 July 1974); *Career* MO Save the Children Fund Nigeria, sr registrar in orthopaedics The Middx Hosp and Royal Nat Orthopaedic Hosp London, res fell Mayo Clinic USA, sr lectr/hon conslt orthopaedic surgn Royal Postgraduate Med Sch Hammersmith Hosp London, prof and head Dept of Orthopaedic Surgery Univ of Edinburgh, hon conslt orthopaedic surgn Royal Infirmary Edinburgh and Princess Margaret Rose Orthopaedic Hosp Edinburgh, prof and head of orthopaedic surgery Royal Postgrad Med Sch Univ of London, hon conslt orthopaedic surgn Hammersmith and Ealing Hosps, hon conslt Nat Hosp for Nervous Diseases Queen's Square, hon civilian orthopaedic conslt to RN; vice pres: RCS Edinburgh, ARCO; pres Br Orthopaedic Res Soc; fell Br Orthopaedic Assoc; FRSM; *Books* Musculoskeletal Infections, Short Textbook of Orthopaedics and Traumatology (4 ed), Orthopaedics: The Principles and Practice of Musculoskeletal Surgery; *Recreations* walking, diving, music; *Clubs* Athenaeum, Naval; *Style*— Prof Sean Hughes; ✉ 24 Fairfax Road, London W4 8EP (☎ 0181 995 2039); Orthopaedic Surgery, Hammersmith Hospital, London W12 0NN (☎ 0181 740 3215, fax 0181 742 9202)

HUGHES, Simon; *b* 1949; *Educ* Univ of London, LSE; *m*; 2 da; *Career* formerly with British Rail, C & J Clark Ltd, Chaussures Ravel; Storehouse plc: joined British Home Stores as merchandise controller 1985, dir BhS 1990–94 (latterly logistics dir), chief exec Mothercare (UK) Ltd 1994–; *Clubs* Brentwood Hockey (chm); *Style*— Simon Hughes, Esq; ✉ Mothercare (UK) Ltd, Cherry Tree Road, Watford, Herts WD2 5SH (☎ 01923 206000, fax 01923 255782)

HUGHES, Simon Henry Ward; MP (Lib Dem) Southwark and Bermondsey (majority 9,845); s of James Henry Annesley Hughes (d 1976), and Sylvia, *née* Ward; *b* 17 May 1951; *Educ* Christ Coll Brecon Wales, Selwyn Coll Cambridge (MA), Inns of Court Sch of Law, Coll of Europe Bruges (Cert in Higher Euro Studies); *Career* called to the Bar Inner Temple 1974, trainee EEC Brussels 1975–76, trainee and memb Secretariat,

Directorate and Cmmn on Human Rights Cncl of Europe Strasbourg 1976–77, in practice as barr 1978–; MP (Lib 1983–88, Lib Dem 1988–) Southwark and Bermondsey 1983–; Parly spokesman: (Lib) on Environment 1983–Jan 1987 and June 1987–March 1988, (Alliance) on Health Jan-June 1987, (Lib Dem) on Environment March-Oct 1988, on Educn, Sci and Trg Oct 1988–90, on Environment, Natural Resources and Food 1990–94, on Community & Urban Affrs and Young People and on the C of E 1994–95, on Health & Social Welfare 1995–; Lib Dem dep whip 1989–; memb: Accommodation and Works Select Ctee 1992–, Ecclesiastical Ctee 1987–; memb All-Pty: Bangladesh Gp, South Africa Gp, Asthma Gp, Northern Line Gp, Christian Fellowship, Housing Co-ops Gp; pres: Southwark C of C, Lib Dem Youth and Students, Redriff Club; chair of govrs St James C of E Sch Bermondsey; jt Parly chair: Cncl for Educn in the Cwlth, Save Guy's Hosp Campaign; tstee: Salmon Youth Centre Bermondsey, Rose Theatre Tst; conslt Assoc of Teachers and Lectrs; hon fell South Bank Univ; *Publications* jtly: Human Rights in Western Europe - The Next Thirty Years (1981), The Prosecutorial Process in England and Wales (1981), Across the Divide - Liberal Values for Defence and Disarmament (1986), Pathways to Power (1992); *Recreations* music, theatre, sport (Millwall and Hereford FC, Glamorgan CCC and Wales RFU), the open air; *Style*— Simon Hughes, Esq, MP; ✉ 6 Lynton Rd, Bermondsey, London SE1; House of Commons, London SW1A OAA (☎ 0171 219 6256)

HUGHES, Simon Peter; s of Peter Clowe Hughes, and Erica Christine, *née* Brace; *b* 20 Dec 1959; *Educ* Latymer Upper Sch Hammersmith, Coll of St Hild & St Bede Durham Univ; *m* 1, 1990 (m dis); m 2, 10 June 1994, Tanya Rimmer; *Career* former professional cricketer; Middlesex CCC: debut 1980, awarded county cap 1981, benefit 1991; Durham CCC 1992–93; rep: England Young Cricketers 1979, England A team v Sri Lanka 1981, Northern Transvaal SA 1982–83 (25 appearances); honours with Middlesex CCC: County Championship winners 1980, 1982, 1985 and 1990, NatWest Trophy 1980, 1984 and 1988, Benson & Hedges Cup 1983 and 1986, Refuge League Cup 1990; columnist: From the Inside (Cricketer International) 1982–88, Cricketers' Diary (The Independent) 1987–94, The Daily Telegraph 1994–; presenter County Talk Test Match Special (BBC Radio 3) 1990–93, BBC TV commentator 1991–; *Books* A Lot of Hard Yakka (1997); *Recreations* India & Indian food, people, current affairs; *Style*— Simon Hughes, Esq

HUGHES, Stephen Skipsey; MEP (Lab) Durham (majority 111,638); *b* 19 Aug 1952; *Educ* St Bede's Sch Lanchester, Newcastle Poly; *m* (m dis), Cynthia, 1 s, 2 da (twins); *Career* local govt offr; memb: TGWU, GMBU; MEP (Lab) Durham 1984–, dep ldr Euro Parly Lab Pty 1991–93, health and safety spokesperson for Socialist Gp of Euro Parliament, memb Delgn for Rels with Japan, chair Social Affairs and Employment Ctee 1994–, substitute memb Legal Affrs and Citizens' Rights Ctee; memb Advsy Ctee Roebens Inst 1994–; *Style*— S S Hughes, Esq, MEP; ✉ Room 1/76, County Hall, Durham DH1 5UR (☎ 0191 384 9371, fax 0191 384 6100 and 01325 384107)

HUGHES, Sir Trevor Poulton; KCB (1982, CB 1974); s of late Rev John Evan Hughes, and Mary Grace, *née* Hughes; *b* 28 Sept 1925; *Educ* Ruthin Sch; *m* 1, 1950 (m dis), Mary Walwyn; 2 s; m 2, 1978, Barbara June Davison; *Career* serv RE, Capt 1945–48; former local govt engr; Miny of Transport 1961–62, Miny of Housing and Local Govt Engrg Inspectorate 1962–70; DOE: dep chief engr 1970–71, dir 1971–72, dir gen water engrg 1972–74, dep sec 1974–77; dep sec Dept of Tport 1977–80, perm sec Welsh Office 1980–85; chm Public Works and Municipal Servs Congress Cncl 1989–90 (vice chm 1975–89); a vice pres ICE 1984–86, memb Br Waterways Bd 1985–88, chm B & C E H Management Co 1987–; Hon FCIWEM, CEng, FICE; *Style*— Sir Trevor Hughes, KCB; ✉ Clearwell, 13 Brambleton Ave, Farnham, Surrey GU9 8RA (☎ 01252 714246)

HUGHES, Baron (Life Peer UK 1961); William Hughes; CBE (1965, OBE 1942), PC (1970), DL (Dundee 1960); s of Joseph Hughes (d 1962), and Margaret Ann, *née* Stott (d 1971); *b* 22 Jan 1911; *Educ* Balfour Street Public Sch Dundee, Dundee Tech Coll; *m* 1951, Christian Clacher (d 1994), da of James Gordon; 2 da (Hon (Christian) Alison (Hon Mrs Henry) b 1952, Hon Janet Margaret b 1956); *Career* ARP controller Dundee 1939–43, Armed Forces 1943–46, cmmnd RAOC 1944, demob Capt 1946; contested (Lab) E Perthshire 1945 and 1950, jt Parly under sec of state for Scot 1964–69, min of state for Scot 1969–70 and 1974–75; co dir; pres: Scot Fedn of Housing Assocs 1975–93, Scot Assoc for Mental Health 1975–; JP Dundee 1943–76; Hon LLD Univ of St Andrews 1960; Chevalier Légion d'Honneur 1958; *Recreations* gardening, travel; *Style*— The Rt Hon the Lord Hughes, CBE, PC, DL; ✉ The Stables, Ross, Comrie, Perthshire PH6 2JU (☎ 01764 670557); House of Lords, SW1A OPW (☎ 0171 219 3207)

HUGHES, William Young; CBE (1987); s of Hugh Prentice Hughes, and Mary Henderson Hughes; *b* 12 April 1940; *Educ* Firth Park GS Sheffield, Univ of Glasgow (BSc), Univ of Strathclyde; *m* 1964, Anne MacDonald Richardson; 2 s, 1 da; *Career* lectr in Dept of Pharmacy Heriot-Watt Univ 1964–66, ptnr R Gordon Drummond Retail Chemists 1966–70, md MSJ Securities Ltd 1970–76, chm and chief exec Grampian Holdings plc 1976–; chm Aberforth Smaller Companies Trust plc 1990–; dir Royal Scottish Nat Hosp & Community NHS Tst 1992–; dep chm Scottish Conservative Party 1989–92 (treas 1993–), chm Euro Summer Special Olympic Games 1990, former chm CBI Scotland 1987–89; memb: Governing Cncl SCOTBIC, St Andrews Church Falkirk; *Recreations* golf; *Clubs* Glenbervie Golf; *Style*— William Hughes, Esq, CBE; ✉ The Elms, 12 Camelon Rd, Falkirk FK1 5RX; Grampian Hldgs plc, Stag House, Castlebank St, Glasgow G11 6DY (☎ 0141 357 2000)

HUGHES-GAMES, Dr John Stephen; s of Guy Stephen Hughes-Games (d 1985), of Congresbury, nr Bristol, and Doris, *née* Munro-Smith (d 1989); *b* 26 May 1927; *Educ* King William's Coll Isle of Man, Univ of Bristol (MB ChB), Faculty of Homoeopathy London (FF Hom); *m* 1, (m dis 1966), Hilary Cove; 1 s (Martin John b 16 April 1956), 1 da (Philippa b 3 May 1958); m 2, 26 July 1975, Susan Elizabeth, da of Tom Driver (d 1988), of Worthing; 2 s (Ben b 7 Oct 1977, Guy b 20 June 1982); *Career* Nat Serv Lt RA (Field) 1945–48; GP Knowle West Bristol 1959–; pres: Faculty of Homoeopathy Royal London Homoeopathic Hosp 1984–87, W Country Branch Faculty of Homeopathy 1986–92; med advsr to Blackie Fndn Tst 1991–96; chm Bristol Med Homoeopathic Gp 1987, chm and fndr memb W Country Flyfishers; *Recreations* broadcasting, fly fishing, sketching, family; *Clubs* Clifton (Bristol); *Style*— Dr John Hughes-Games; ✉ 22 Duchess Rd, Clifton, Bristol BS8 2LA (☎ 0117 973 5966); The Whitchurch Health Centre, Whitchurch, Bristol, BS14 0SU (☎ 01275 839421, car tel 0831 486222)

HUGHES HALLETT, Prof Andrew Jonathan; s of Vice Adm Sir Charles Hughes Hallett, KCB, CBE (d 1985), of Salisbury, Wilts, and Joyce Plumer, *née* Cobbold (d 1996); *b* 1 Nov 1947; *Educ* Radley, Univ of Warwick (BA), LSE (MSc), Nuffield Coll Oxford Univ (DPhil); *m* 22 July 1982, Claudia Ilse Luise, da of Karl Becker (d 1988), of Kassel, W Germany; 2 s (David b 1983, James b 1986), 1 da (Nicola b 1990); *Career* lectr in economics Univ of Bristol 1973–77, assoc prof of economics Erasmus Univ Rotterdam 1977–85, David Dale prof of economics Univ of Newcastle upon Tyne 1985–89, Jean Monnet prof of economics Univ of Strathclyde 1989–; visiting prof: Princeton Univ, Univ of Rome; author of papers on: theory of economic policy, int economic policy, (european) economic integration, commodity markets and economic devpt, game theory, numerical analysis; reg bdcasting on economic affairs; conslt to: IMF, UN, World Bank, EEC Cmmn, OECD, UNESCO, various govts; memb: Royal Econ Soc 1975, Euro Econ Assoc 1985; fell Centre for Econ Policy Res, FRSA; *Books* Quantitative Economic Policies and Interactive Planning (1983), Applied Decision Analysis and Economic Behaviour (1984), Stabilising Speculative Commodity Markets (1987), Optimal Control, Expectations and Uncertainty (1989); *Recreations* hill walking, beer, jazz from the 30s, 40s and 50s, history; *Style*— Prof Andrew Hughes Hallett; ✉ Department of Economics, University of Strathclyde, 100 Cathedral Street, Glasgow G4 0LN (☎ 0141 552 4400, fax 0141 552 5589, e-mail economics@Strath.ac.uk)

HUGHES-HALLETT, Lucy Angela; da of Michael Hughes-Hallett, of Gloucs, and Penelope, *née* Fairbairn; *b* 7 Dec 1951; *Educ* St Mary's Calne, Bedford Coll London (BA); *m* 1985, Dan J Franklin, s of Michael Franklin, of Much Hadham, Herts; 2 da (Lettice b 1 March 1990, Mary b (twin) 1 March 1990); *Career* freelance writer and critic 1973–; *Books* Cleopatra: Histories, Dreams and Distortions (1990); *Awards* Catherine Pakenham Award 1980, Emily Toth Award 1990, Fawcett Book Prize 1992; *Style*— Lucy Hughes-Hallett; ✉ c/o Lutyens & Rubinstein, 231 Westbourne Park Road, London W11 1EB (☎ 0171 792 4855)

HUGHES-MORGAN, His Hon Judge; Sir David John; 3 Bt (UK 1925), of Penally, Pembroke; CB (Mil 1983), CBE (Mil 1973, MBE Mil 1959); s of Sir John Vernon Hughes-Morgan, 2 Bt (d 1969); *b* 11 Oct 1925; *Educ* RNC Dartmouth; *m* 1959, (Isabel) Jean Blacklock Gellatly Milne (d 1994), da of John Milne Lindsay (d 1969), of Annan, Dumfriesshire; 3 s; *Heir* s, (Ian) Parry David Hughes-Morgan b 22 Feb 1960; *Career* Sub Lt RN, ret 1946; admitted slr 1950; cmmnd Army Legal Servs 1955, Brig Legal HQ UKLF 1976–78, dir Army Legal Servs BAOR 1978–80, dir Army Legal Servs (Maj Gen) MOD 1980–84; recorder SE Circuit 1983–86, circuit judge (SE Circuit) 1986–; *Style*— His Hon Judge Sir David Hughes-Morgan, Bt, CB, CBE; ✉ Croydon Combined Court Centre, The Law Courts, Altyre Road, Croydon CRO 3NE (☎ 0181 681 2533, fax 0181 681 5048)

HUGHES-MORGAN, (Ian) Parry David; s and h of Sir David John Hughes-Morgan, 3 Bt, CB, CBE; *b* 22 Feb 1960; *Career* dir of business devpt Kingfisher Plc 1995–; *Style*— Parry Hughes-Morgan, Esq; ✉ Kingfisher Plc, North West House, 119 Marylebone Road, London NW1 5PX

HUGHES-ONSLOW, James Andrew; s of Andrew Hughes-Onslow (d 1979), and Betty Lee (now Mrs David Crichton), half-sister of Lord Rossmore; gs of Capt Oliver Hughes-Onslow (d 1972), of Ayrshire; *b* 27 Aug 1945; *Educ* Castle Park Dublin, Eton; *m* 1982, Christina Louise, da of Peter Henry Hay, bro of Sir David Hay, of Aust; 1 s (Andrew b 1985), 3 da (Flora b 1988, Marina b 1990, Harriet b 1993); *Career* sub ed and feature writer The Field 1968–70; reporter: Sunday Telegraph 1970–71, Daily Express 1971–73; columnist: The Spectator 1974–75, What's On in London 1976–82; columnist and feature writer: London Evening Standard 1983–96, Daily Express 1996–; articles and reviews in: Punch, The Times, The Field, Books and Bookmen, Business Traveller, The Spectator, Tatler, Country Times, Southside, The Illustrated London News, Country Living, The Melbourne Age, Sydney Morning Herald; *Recreations* travel; *Clubs* Boodle's; *Style*— James Hughes-Onslow, Esq; ✉ 42 Knatchbull Rd, Camberwell, London SE5 9QY (☎ 0171 274 9347); Daily Express, 245 Blackfriars Road, London SE1 9UX (☎ 0171 928 8000)

HUGHES-PARRY, Thomas Antony; s of Maj Thomas Garrard Hughes-Parry, of Llangollen, Clwyd (d 1987), and Rachael Constance Luz, *née* Boger; *b* 9 Feb 1949; *Educ* Canford, Univ of Exeter (BSc); *m* 1 May 1976, Rosemary Constance, da of Robert James Foster; 2 s (Thomas David b 9 Sept 1981, Philip John b 19 Sept 1983); *Career* articled clerk Harmood Banner 1969–73, chartered accountant Investigation Dept Deloitte Haskins & Sells 1974–78, ptnr Beer Aplin 1979–; memb SW Soc Chartered Accountants: Tech Advsy Ctee 1979–91 (del to London Ctee 1988–91), GP Bd 1991– (del to London Ctee); Exeter District Soc of Chartered Accountants: careers advsr 1980–84, vice chm 1989–90, chm 1990–91; vice treas Exeter Cncl for Voluntary Service 1980–88, various offices Dawlish Round Table 1980–89, clerk to Govrs Maynard's Girls' Sch 1981–, sec to Govrs Royal West of England Residential Sch for the Deaf 1986–, adult educn lectr 1986–, chm Exeter Voluntary Trading Enterprizes 1988–; FCA, ACIArb; *Recreations* squash, walking, gardening, dancing, yoga, windsurfing, classical music, reading; *Clubs* Musgrave; *Style*— Thomas Hughes-Parry, Esq; ✉ Beer Aplin, 23 Longbrook Street, Exeter, Devon EX4 6AD (☎ 01392 77325, fax 01392 420927)

HUGHES-WAKE-WALKER, *see:* Wake-Walker

HUGHESDON, Charles Frederick; AFC (1943); *b* 10 Dec 1909; *Educ* Raine's GS; *m* 1, 1937, Florence Elizabeth (the actress Florence Desmond; d 1993), *née* Dawson, wid of Capt Tom Campbell Black; 1 s (Michael); m 2, 10 May 1993, Carol Elizabeth, widow of Baron Havers, PC, QC (Life Peer, d 1992), and da of Stuart Lay, of London; *Career* chm: Stewart Smith Group of Companies, Stewart Wrightson Group of Companies (until ret 1976), Tradewinds Helicopters Ltd, Charles Street Co; formerly chm and dir Tradewinds Airways Ltd, dir Aeronautical Trust Ltd; memb: Guild of Air Pilots and Air Navigators, Gunmakers' Guild; Upper Freeman City of London; FRAeS (hon treas 1969–85); Knight of the Order of the Cedar (Lebanese Republic) 1972; *Recreations* horse riding, shooting, water skiing, yachting, flying helicopters; *Clubs* RAF, Royal Thames Yacht, Garrick; *Style*— Charles Hughesdon, Esq, AFC; ✉ 5 Grosvenor Square, London W1X 9LA; Leckhampstead House, Leckhampstead, Newbury, Berkshire RG20 8QH (☎ 01488 638229)

HUGHESDON, John Stephen; s of Eric Hughesdon (d 1994), of Crowborough, Sussex, and Olive Mona, *née* Quirk (d 1980); *b* 9 Jan 1944; *Educ* Eltham Coll; *m* Mavis June, da of Charles Henry George Eburne, OBE; 1 s (Simon Charles b 18 Aug 1978), 1 da (Fiona Louise b 22 Nov 1975); *Career* Peat Marwick Mitchell 1962–73 (articled 1962–66), ptnr Neville Russell 1977– (mangr 1973–76); hon treas: Girls' Bde Nat Cncl Eng & W 1979–91, TEAR Fund 1992–; govr Bishopsgate Fndn 1993–, almoner Christ's Hosp Fndn 1993–; Freeman City of London, Liveryman Worshipful Co of Coopers; memb: Guild of Freemen of City of London, Ct of Common Cncl City of London 1991–; FCA 1977 (ACA 1967), FRSA 1990; *Recreations* church, golf; *Clubs* City Livery, Bishopsgate Ward, Broad Street Ward; *Style*— John Hughesdon, Esq; ✉ 44 Christchurch Rd, Sidcup, Kent DA15 7HQ (☎ 0181 300 6648); Neville Russell, 24 Bevis Marks, London EC3A 7NR (☎ 0171 377 1000, fax 0171 377 8931)

HUGHFF, Victor William; s of William Scott Hughff (d 1974), and Alice Doris, *née* Kerry (d 1988); *b* 30 May 1931; *Educ* City of Norwich; *m* 1955, Grace Margaret; 1 s (David), 1 da (Joanna); *Career* insur exec; chief gen mangr Norwich Union Insurance Group 1984–89; dir 1981–89: Norwich Union Life Insurance Society, Norwich Union Fire Insurance Society Ltd, Scottish Union & National Insurance Co, Maritime Insurance Co Ltd, Norwich Union Holdings plc, Norwich General Trust Ltd, Castle Finance Ltd, Norwich Union (Services) Ltd; dir: Norwich Winterthur Holdings Ltd 1984–89, Stalwart Assurance Group plc 1989–93, Congregational & General Insurance plc 1989–, URC Ministers' Pension Trust Ltd 1994–; memb Cncl Nat Assoc of Victim Support Schemes 1989–91, elder United Reformed Church; Liveryman Worshipful Co of Actuaries; FIA, CIMgt; *Recreations* tennis, badminton, bowls; *Clubs* Royal Over-Seas League; *Style*— Victor Hughff, Esq; ✉ 18 Hilly Plantation, Thorpe St Andrew, Norwich NR7 0JN (☎ 01603 434517)

HUGILL, John; QC (1976); s of John Alfred Hugill (d 1950), and Alice, *née* Clarke (d 1982); *b* 11 Aug 1930; *Educ* Fettes, Trinity Hall Cambridge (MA); *m* 1956, Patricia Elizabeth, da of Stanley Welton (d 1966), of Cheshire; 2 da (Gail b 1962, Rebecca b 1968); *Career* RA 1949–50 2 Lt, Capt RA (T); called to the Bar Middle Temple 1954, asst recorder Bolton 1971, recorder 1972, bencher Middle Temple 1984; memb: Senate of the Inns of Ct and the Bar 1984–86, Gen Cncl of the Bar 1987–89; chm: Darryn Clarke Inquiry 1979, Stanley Royd Inquiry 1985; hon legal advsr Clay Pigeon Shooting Assoc

(CPSA); *Style*— John Hugill, Esq, QC; ✉ 45 Hardman St, Manchester M3 3HA (☎ 0161 832 3791, fax 0161 835 3054)

HUGO, Lt-Col Sir John Mandeville; KCVO (1969, CVO 1959), OBE (1947); s of R M Hugo (d 1921), and Marion, *née* Dickins (d 1942); *b* 1 July 1899; *Educ* Marlborough, RMA Woolwich; *m* 1952, Joan Winifred Hill; 2 da (Nicola-Jane, Tessa); *Career* WWI 2 Lt RFA 1917, appointed to RHA 1922, served WWII with 7 Light Cavalry (India), Lt-Col; cmd: Bombay Body Guard 1937–38, Bengal Body Guard 1938–39; mil sec to Govr Bengal 1939–40 and 1946–47; asst ceremonial sec CRO 1948–52, ceremonial and protocol sec 1952–69; gentleman usher to HM The Queen 1952–69 (extra gentleman usher 1969–); *Style*— Lt-Col Sir John Hugo, KCVO, OBE; ✉ Hilltop House, Vines Cross, Heathfield, E Sussex TN21 9EN (☎ 01435 812562)

HUHNE, Christopher Murray Paul; s of Peter Ivor Paul Huhne, and Margaret Ann Gladstone, *née* Murray; *b* 2 July 1954; *Educ* Westminster, Sorbonne, Magdalen Coll Oxford (BA); *m* 19 May 1984, Vicky, da of Nicholas Courmouzis (d 1987); 2 s (Nicholas b 1985, Peter b 1992), 1 da (Lydia b 1989), 2 step da (Georgia b 1976, Alexandra b 1979); *Career* freelance journalist 1975–76, graduate trainee Liverpool Daily Post 1976–77, Brussels corr The Economist 1977–80, economics leader writer The Guardian 1980–84, economics ed 1984–90, business and economics ed The Independent on Sunday 1990–91, business and city ed The Independent and The Independent on Sunday 1991–94, md of sovereign ratings and economics dir IBCA Ltd 1994–; Financial Journalist of the Year (Wincott award) 1990; memb Cncl Royal Econ Soc 1993; *Books* Debt and Danger - The World Financial Crisis (with Lord Lever, 1985), Real World Economics (1990), The Ecu Report (with Michael Emerson, 1991); *Recreations* cinema, family; *Clubs* Hurlingham, Broadgate; *Style*— Christopher Huhne, Esq; ✉ 8 Crescent Grove, London SW4 7AH (☎ 0171 498 2618, fax 0171 498 5242)

HUISMANS, Sipko; s of Jouka Huismans, and Roeloffina Huismans; *b* 28 Dec 1940; *Educ* Stellenbosch Univ SA (BA); *m* 1969, Janet, *née* Durston; 2 s (Jake, Nicholas), 1 da (Emma); *Career* Usutu Pulp Co Swaziland 1961–68; Courtaulds plc: sales mangr 1968, gen mangr Springwood Cellulose Co Ltd 1968, md Courtaulds Central Trading (formerly Lustre Fibres Ltd) 1973, md Fibres Bd 1982, main bd dir 1984–96, non-exec dir BCL 1985–86, ldr Chem and Indust Task Force 1986–88, chm International Paint 1986–96, chm Chemical and Industrial Executive 1988–90, group md 1990, chief exec 1991–July 1996; non-exec dir: Vickers plc 1994–, Imperial Tobacco plc; *Recreations* motor racing, sailing; *Style*— Sipko Huismans, Esq; ✉ Latchmoore House, Brockenhurst, Hants SO42 7UE (☎ 01590 624419, fax 01590 624453)

HULBERT, (Evelyn) Gervase Carson; OBE (1993); s of Lt Col John Harvey Hulbert (d 1981), and Elisabeth, *née* Lovett (d 1985); *b* 1 April 1942; *Educ* Winchester Coll, Univ of Paris; *m* 23 March 1968, Susannah Mary, da of Lt Cdr Ralph Henry Hood Laurence Oliphant, RN (ret) (d 1995); 2 s (George Gervase b 24 Nov 1970, William Laurence b 12 June 1972); *Career* Moore Stephens: articled clerk 1962–67, Moore Stephens & Butterfield Bermuda 1968–69, ptnr 1970, chm Moore Stephens International 1989–; co-chm Polish British Accountancy Assoc 1990–94; FCA; *Recreations* collecting antiques, pictures, classic cars; *Style*— Gervase Hulbert, Esq, OBE; ✉ Moore Stephens, 1 Snow Hill, London EC1A 2EN (☎ 0171 334 9191, fax 0171 334 7976)

HULL, Prof Derek; s of William Hull (d 1974), of Blackpool, and Nellie, *née* Hayes (d 1958); *b* 8 Aug 1931; *Educ* Baines GS Poulton-Le-Fylde, Univ of Wales (BSc, PhD, DSc); *m* 5 Aug 1953, Pauline, da of Norman Scott (d 1950), of Halifax; 1 s (Andrew b 1956), 4 da (Sian b 1958, Karen b 1961, Beverley b 1965, Alison b 1967); *Career* section ldr AERE Harwell 1956–60; Univ of Liverpool: lectr 1960–62, sr lectr 1962–64, prof 1964–84, dean of engrg 1971–74, pro vice chllr 1983–84; Goldsmiths prof Univ of Cambridge 1984–91, emeritus prof Univ of Cambridge and sr fell Univ of Liverpool 1991–; Hon DTech Tampere Univ Finland 1987; Liveryman Worshipful Co of Goldsmiths; FIM 1966, FPRI 1978, FEng 1986, FRS 1989; *Books* Introduction to Dislocations, An Introduction to Composite Materials; *Recreations* golf, fell walking, music; *Clubs* Heswall Golf; *Style*— Prof Derek Hull, FRS, FEng; ✉ Department of Materials Science and Engineering, University of Liverpool, PO Box 147, Liverpool L69 3BX (☎ 0151 794 4669, fax 0151 794 4675)

HULL, Bishop of 1994–; Rt Rev James Stuart Jones; s of Maj James Stuart Anthony Jones (d 1990), and Helen Deans Dick Telfer, *née* McIntyre; *b* 18 Aug 1948; *Educ* Duke of York's RMS Dover, Univ of Exeter (Kitchener scholar, BA), Univ of Keele (PGCE); *m* 19 April 1980, Sarah Caroline Rosalind, da of Rev Canon Peter Marrow; 3 da (Harriet Emma b 26 May 1982, Jemima Charlotte b 13 Aug 1984, Tabitha Rose b 14 Feb 1987); *Career* asst master Sevenoaks Sch 1971–75, prodr Scripture Union 1975–81, assoc vicar Christ Church Clifton 1984–90 (asst curate 1982–84), vicar Emmanuel Church Croydon 1990–94; author and broadcaster; *Books* incl: Following Jesus (1984), Finding God (1987), Why do People Suffer? (1993), The Power and The Glory (1994); *Recreations* swimming, reading and planning family holidays; *Style*— The Rt Rev the Bishop of Hull; ✉ Hullen House, Woodfield Lane, Hessle, East Riding HU13 0ES (☎ 01482 649019)

HULL, Janet Elizabeth; da of Thomas Edward Lacy (d 1989), of Southport, and Marjorie, *née* Forster; *b* 20 March 1955; *Educ* Southport HS for Girls, St Anne's Coll Oxford (MA), Napier Coll Edinburgh (DEML), Inst of Direct Mktg (DipIDM); *m* 1977 (m dis 1988), Howard Anthony Hull; 1 s (Archibald Campbell b 19 Dec 1991); *Career* Ted Bates Ltd 1979–80, Abbott Mead Vickers SMS Ltd 1980–85, Geer Gross Ltd 1985–86, Young & Rubicam Ltd 1986–93, md Y & R Capital Image (Corporate Communications) 1991, creative dir Burson-Marsteller 1991–93, first dir of advtg effectiveness IPA 1993–; conslt to The Mktg Cncl 1995–; memb: Women of the Year Luncheon Ctee 1990–, Women's Advtg Club of London 1990–; MIPR 1995, FRSA 1995; *Recreations* food and wine, classic cars, video film-making; *Clubs* Reform, RSA, Arts; *Style*— Ms Janet Hull; ✉ 4 Edith Grove, London SW10 0NW (☎ 0171 376 7541)

HULL, John Folliott Charles; CBE (1993); s of Sir Hubert Hull, CBE (d 1976), and Judith, *née* Stokes (d 1937); *b* 21 Oct 1925; *Educ* Downside, Jesus Coll Cambridge (MA); *m* 1951, Rosemarie Kathleen, da of Col Herbert Waring (d 1961); 1 s (Jonathan), 3 da (Judith-Rose, Charlotte, Victoria); *Career* Capt RA 1944–48, served with RIA 1945–48; called to the Bar Inner Temple 1952; dir: J Henry Schroder Wagg & Co Ltd 1961–72 and 1974–85 (md 1961–72, dep chm 1974–77, chm 1977–83), Schroders plc 1969–72 and 1974–85 (dep chm 1977–85), Lucas Industries plc 1975–90, Legal & General Assurance Society 1976–79, Legal & General Group plc 1979–90, Goodwood Racecourse Limited 1987–92; dep chm Land Securities plc 1976–; memb Cncl Manchester Business Sch 1974–86, chm City Co Law Ctee 1976–79, lay memb Stock Exchange 1983–84, dep chm City Panel on Takeovers and Mergers 1987– (dir-gen 1972–74); *Recreations* reading political history, 19th century novelists; *Clubs* MCC; *Style*— John Hull, Esq, CBE; ✉ 33 Edwardes Square, London W8 6HH (☎ 0171 603 0715); Little Norton, Norton sub Hamdon, Stoke sub Hamdon, Somerset (☎ 01935 88465); J Henry Schroder Wagg & Co Ltd, 120 Cheapside, London EC2V 6DS (☎ 0171 382 6000, telex 885029)

HULL, His Hon Judge; John Grove; QC (1983); s of Tom Edward Orridge Hull (d 1957), and Marjorie Ethel Whitaker, *née* Dinsley; *b* 21 Aug 1931; *Educ* Rugby, King's Coll Cambridge (MA, LLB); *m* 1961, Gillian Ann, da of Leslie Fawcett Stemp (d 1968); 2 da (Katharine (Mrs Richard Stephens) b 1965, Caroline b 1968); *Career* Nat Serv RE 1954–56, 2 Lt; called to the Bar 1958, recorder 1983, circuit judge (SE Circuit) 1991–; *Recreations* gardening, English literature; *Style*— His Hon Judge Hull, QC; ✉ 33 Essex Street, London WC2R 3AR (☎ 0171 353 6381/2)

HULL, Prof Michael George Raworth; s of Leslie George Raworth Hull, of Doncaster, and Beryl Theresa, *née* Everett; *b* 2 July 1939; *Educ* Ratcliffe Coll Leicester, Univ of London (MB BS, MD); *m* 3 April 1976, Griselda Frances Clare, da of Antony Clive Goodden; 3 da (Natalie b 18 Dec 1978, Sophie b 28 April 1980, Emily b 14 July 1984); *Career* Women's Hosp Liverpool 1964–65, Queen Charlotte's Maternity Hosp London 1965–66, St Mary's Hosp Manchester 1966–67, Charing Cross Hosp 1967–69, St Mary's Hosp London 1969–76, prof of reproductive med and surgery Univ of Bristol 1989– (sr lectr 1976–84, reader 1984–89); Green-Armytage Anglo-American lectr RCOG 1982; memb Ctee: Br Fertility Soc 1985–92, Soc for the Study of Fertility 1988–91, Euro Soc for Human Reproduction and Embryology 1987–90, Human Reproduction (jl) 1986–92, Fertility & Sterility (jl) 1994–96; FRCOG; *Books* Undergraduate Obstetrics and Gynaecology (1980, 3 edn 1996), Developments in Infertility Practice (1981); author of over 130 scientific papers and 25 book chapters on human fertility and infertility; *Recreations* children, tennis, food and wine, theatre and opera, international travel; *Style*— Prof Michael Hull; ✉ University of Bristol, Department of Obstetrics and Gynaecology, St Michael's Hospital, Bristol BS2 8EG (☎ 0117 928 5293, fax 0117 927 2792)

HULL, Paul Anthony; s of Cordell Benjamin Hull, and Eula Elizabeth, *née* Cargill; *b* 17 May 1968; *Educ* The Gordon Boy's Sch West End, Woking Surrey; *m* 27 July 1991 (m dis), Lesley Ann Green; *Career* rugby union full back; formerly with RAF XV, currently professional with Bristol FC (capt 1995–96); rep: Bucks Colts, RAF Colts and under 21, Combined Servs Colts and under 21, S and SW under 21, S and SW Div, London Div, Eng Colts (3 caps at centre), Eng under 21, Eng B (debut v Fiji 1990); memb England tour Argentina 1990, selected for England Sevens 1992, memb England tour S Africa (first cap first test) 1994; former corpl and physical training instructor RAF; *Recreations* all sports (youth footballer Belmont Utd Harrow, triallist Southampton FC), music (soul), good time (night life); *Style*— Paul Hull, Esq; ✉ Flat 6, Alma House, 25 Alma Road, Clifton, Bristol BS8 2BZ

HULME, Geoffrey Gordon; CB (1984); s of Alfred Hulme, and Jessie Hulme; *b* 8 March 1931; *Educ* King's Sch Macclesfield, CCC Oxford (MA); *m* 1951, Shirley Leigh, da of Herbert and Doris Cumberlidge; 1 s (Andrew), 1 da (Alison); *Career* DHSS: joined min 1953, under sec 1974, dep sec and princ fin offr 1981–86; dir Public Expenditure Policy Unit 1986–91; conslt Public Fin Fndn 1991–; memb Editorial Bd Office of Health Economics 1990–; *Recreations* the usual things, collecting edible fungi; *Clubs* Royal Automobile; *Style*— Geoffrey Hulme, Esq, CB; ✉ 163A Kennington Park Rd, London SE11; Stone Farm, Little Cornard, Sudbury, Suffolk (☎ 01787 312728); Public Finance Foundation, 3 Robert St, London WC2 (☎ 0171 543 5600)

HULME, Rev Paul; s of Harry Hulme, and Elizabeth, *née* Deakin; *b* 14 May 1942; *Educ* Hatfield House Sch Yorks, Didsbury Theol Coll Bristol; *m* 1 May 1976, Hilary Frances, da of Leonard John Martin; 3 s (Giles Martin b 7 Feb 1977, James Marcus b 29 Dec 1978, Alexander Paul b 22 March 1985); *Career* chaplain Univ of Sussex 1970–75; methodist minister: Bungay 1968–70, Newquay Wesley Church 1975–79, The Temple Church Taunton 1979–86, Trinity Church Enfield 1986–88; superintendent minister Wesley's Chapel City Rd London 1988–; memb Senate City of London Univ, memb London Churches Bdcasting Gp, free church chaplain Moorfields Eye Hosp London, borough dean Islington; Freeman City of London 1990; *Books* Personal Evangelism (1978); *Recreations* music, walking; *Clubs* National Liberal; *Style*— The Rev Paul Hulme; ✉ 5 Colebrooke Row, Islington, London N1 (☎ 0171 278 5980); Wesley's Chapel, 49 City Road, London EC1Y 1AU (☎ 0171 253 2262)

HULSE, Sir Edward Jeremy Westrow; 10 Bt (GB 1739), of Lincoln's Inn Fields; DL (Hants 1989); s of Sir (Hamilton) Westrow Hulse, 9 Bt (d 1996), and his 1 w, Philippa Mabel, *née* Taylor; *b* 22 Nov 1932; *Educ* Eton; *m* 1957, Verity Ann, da of William Pilkington, of Bournemouth; 1 s ((Edward) Michael Westrow b 1959), 1 da (Camilla Ann (Mrs Luca C Corona) b 1962); *Heir* s, (Edward) Michael Westrow Hulse b 1959; *Career* late Capt Scots Gds, High Sheriff of Hants 1978; *Style*— Sir Edward Hulse, Bt, DL; ✉ Breamore House, nr Fordingbridge, Hants (☎ 01725 512233)

HULSE, Graham; s of Robert Hulse (d 1980), of Chirk, Clwyd, and Linda Constance, *née* Cooper; *b* 14 Nov 1926; *Educ* Llangollen GS, UCNW Bangor (BSc, MSc, DipEd, Soccer colours); *m* 4 Sept 1953, Laura Glenys, da of Josiah Jones (d 1987), of Pwllheli, Gwynedd; *Career* Monsanto gp: mktg mangr Monsanto Chemicals Ltd UK 1962–64 (res physicist 1951–53, tech serv engr rising to mangr 1953–60, sales mangr 1960–62), mktg dir plastics Monsanto Europe SA Belgium 1968–74 (mktg mangr plastics 1964–68), dir Monsanto Chemicals Intermediates Co 1974–78, admin dir 1978–82, dir (Monsanto) Eastern Europe 1982–84, bd dir 1978–84, ret 1984; conslt: NHS Wales 1986–87, Univ of Wales 1987; chm Gwynedd Health Authy 1992 (non-exec memb 1988–92); treas Criccieth Branch British Heart Fndn 1991–; assoc memb Inst of Physics 1950–60; *Recreations* golf, walking, reading (science and history), foreign travel; *Clubs* Rotary, Probus; *Style*— Graham Hulse, Esq

HUM, HE Christopher Owen; CMG (1996); s of Norman Charles Hum (d 1950), and Muriel Kathleen, *née* Hines; *b* 27 Jan 1946; *Educ* Berkhamsted Sch, Pembroke Coll Cambridge (MA), Univ of Hong Kong; *m* 31 Oct 1970, Julia Mary, da of Hon Sir Hugh Park, *qv*, of London and Cornwall; 1 s (Jonathan b 1976), 1 da (Olivia b 1974); *Career* FCO: joined 1967, Hong Kong 1968–70, Peking 1971–73, office of UK Perm Rep to the EEC Brussels 1973–75, FCO 1975–79, Peking 1979–81, Paris 1981–83, head Hong Kong Dept 1986–89 (asst head 1983, cnsllr 1985), dep head Falkland Islands Dept 1985–86, cnsllr and head of Chancery UK Mission to the UN NYC 1989–92, asst under sec of state (Northern Asia) 1992–94, asst under sec of state (Northern Asia and Pacific) 1994–95, ambass Poland 1996–; *Recreations* music (piano, viola), walking; *Style*— HE Mr Christopher Hum, CMG; ✉ c/o Foreign and Commonwealth Office (Warsaw), King Charles Street, London SW1A 2AH

HUMAN, (Henry) Robin John; s of Roger Henry Charles Human (d 1942), and Rosalind Mary, *née* Gepp (d 1991); *b* 5 Oct 1937; *Educ* Repton Sch Derbyshire, Clare Coll Cambridge (BA); *m* 4 Nov 1961, Alison Phyllida, da of Dr Oliver Frederick Thompson; 1 s (Charles Robin Graham b 21 June 1963), 1 da (Joanna Alison b 7 April 1965); *Career* admitted slr 1965; Linklaters & Paines 1962–95: ptnr 1969–95, conslt 1995–; memb: City of London Solicitors Co, Bd of Crown Agents 1986–92; *Recreations* golf, shooting, painting; *Clubs* MCC; *Style*— Robin Human, Esq; ✉ Perrymans, Boxted, Colchester, Essex C04 5SL (☎ and fax 01206 271344)

HUMBLE, James Kenneth; OBE (1996); s of Joseph Humble (d 1993), and Alice, *née* Rhodes (d 1992); *b* 8 May 1936; *m* 1962, Freda, da of George Frederick Holden, OBE (d 1964); 3 da (Josephine Clare b 1964, Rebecca Jane b 1965, Sarah Louise b 1966); *Career* Nat Serv RN 1954–56; Weights and Measures Oldham 1956–62, supt metrology Nigeria 1962–66, chief trading standards offr Croydon 1966–73, asst dir of consumer affrs Office of Fair Trading 1973–78, dir of Metrication Bd 1978–80, chief exec Local Authorities Co-ordinating Body on Food and Trading Standards (LACOTS) 1980–; dir Nat Metrological Co-ordinating Unit 1980–88; memb: Methven Ctee 1976, Eden Ctee 1987, Forum of Euro Food Law Enforcement Practitioners (FLEP) 1990–, Western Euro Legal Metrologists Cooperative (WELMEC) 1989–, Euro Product Safety Enforcement Gp (PROSAFE) 1991–, Cars Ctee 1984–; chm Euro Ctee of Experts 1976–; sport: capt Oldham RU 1957–59, professional rugby league Leigh RFC 1959–65; chm Addiscombe and Shirley Round Table 1980–81; DMS, DCA, FITSA; *Recreations* golf, bridge, opera; *Style*— James K Humble, Esq, OBE; ✉ 153 Upper Selsdon Rd, Croydon, Surrey (☎ 0181

657 6170); LACOTS, PO Box 6, Token House, Robert Street, Croydon, Surrey CR9 1LG (☎ 0181 688 1996)

HUME, Sir Alan Blyth; kt (1973), CB (1963); s of Walter Alan Hume (d 1937); *b* 5 Jan 1913; *Educ* George Heriot's Sch Edinburgh, Univ of Edinburgh (MA); *m* 1943, Marion Morton, da of William Garrett, QC; 1 s, 1 da; *Career* Scottish Office: entered 1936, asst under sec of state 1959–62, under sec Miny of Public Bldg and Works 1963–64, sec Scottish Devpt Dept 1965–73; chm: Ancient Monuments Bd Scotland 1973–81, Edinburgh New Town Conservation Ctee 1975–90; *Recreations* golf, fishing; *Clubs* New (Edinburgh), English Speaking Union; *Style*— Sir Alan Hume, CB; ✉ 12 Oswald Rd, Edinburgh, Scotland EH9 2HJ (☎ 0131 667 2440)

HUME, Cardinal (George) Basil; *see:* Westminster, Archbishop (RC) of

HUME, James Douglas Howden; CBE (1983); s of James Howden Hume (d 1981), and Kathleen Douglas, *née* Macfarlane (d 1973); *b* 4 May 1928; *Educ* Loretto, Royal Tech Coll, Univ of Glasgow (BSc), Univ of Strathclyde (LLD); *m* 1950, June Katharine, da of Sir Frank Spencer Spriggs, KBE (d 1969); 1 s (Duncan), 2 da (Evelyn (d 1989), Clare); *Career* chm: Howden Group 1987 (dir 1957, md 1963, dep chm and md 1973), Drimard Ltd 1988; non-exec dir and chm Magnum Power PLC 1992; FIMechE; *Recreations* sailing; *Clubs* Royal Northern and Clyde Yacht; *Style*— J D H Hume, CBE; ✉ Drimard Ltd, 22 East Lennox Drive, Helensburgh, Dunbartonshire G84 9JD (☎ 01436 75132)

HUME, John; MP (SDLP) Foyle (majority 13,005), MEP Socialist Group (SDLP) N Ireland (SDLP vote 136,335); *b* 18 Jan 1937; *Educ* St Columb's Coll, Nat Univ of Ireland; *m* 1951, Patricia Hone, 2 s, 3 da; *Career* pres Irish League of Credit Unions 1964–69, Derry civil rights leader 1968–70, Ind Stormont MP 1969–72, elected NI Assembly 1973, NI Convention 1975–76, special advsr to EEC Cmmr Burke 1977–79, MEP (SDLP) Northern Ireland (one of three) 1979–, MP (SDLP) Foyle 1983–; memb: New Ireland Forum 1983–84, Irish TGWU (now SIPTU); fndr memb SDLP (dep ldr 1970–79, ldr 1979–), min for Commerce (in power-sharing exec) 1974; sponsor: Irish Anti-Apartheid Movement, Europeans for Nuclear Disarmament; memb Advsy Ctee on Protection of the Sea 1988–; Hon DUniv: Univ of Massachusetts 1985, Catholic Univ of America 1986, St Joseph's University Philadelphia 1986, Tusculum Coll Tennessee 1988; assoc fell Center for Int Affrs Harvard 1976, res fell European Studies Trinity Coll Dublin 1976–77; winner St Thomas More award Univ of San Francisco 1991; *Books* Personal Views: Politics, Peace and Reconciliation in Ireland (1996); *Style*— John Hume, Esq, MP, MEP; ✉ House of Commons, London SW1A 0AA

HUME, Brig Richard Trevor Pierce; s of Capt Trevor Hume (d 1968), of Ongar, Essex, and Sybil Clare, *née* Lacy (d 1960); *b* 5 May 1934; *Educ* Ampleforth, RMA Sandhurst; *m* 1, 25 April 1962 (m dis), Gillian, da of Cdr Hodson, RN (d 1962); 1 da (Deirdre b 1963); m 2, 29 April 1971, Jane, da of Sir Eric Tansley, CMG, of London; 2 step s, 1 step da; *Career* cmmnd Irish Gds 1954, served ME, Far East, Europe, USA, Canada, Falklands, UK and NI; cmd: 1 Bn Irish Gds 1974–77, Irish Gds Regt 1979–81, 2 Inf Bde 1982–84, Fortress Gibraltar 1984–86; ret 1987; bursar St Catherine's Sch 1987–; res govr and dep constable Dover Castle, Dep Lord Warden Cinque Ports 1981–84; *Clubs* Army and Navy; *Style*— Brig Richard Hume; ✉ Little Orchard, Blackheath, Guildford, Surrey GU4 8QY (☎ 01483 892216); St Catherine's School, Bramley, Guildford, Surrey GU5 0DF (☎ 01483 892562)

HUME, Dr Robert; *b* 6 Jan 1928; *Educ* Ayr Acad, Bellahouston Acad, Univ of Glasgow (MB ChB, MD, DSc); *m* 1 June 1959, Kathleen Ann Ogilvie; 2 s (Robert, David), 1 da (Morag); *Career* Nat Serv Intelligence Corps, cmmnd Gordon Highlanders India and Germany 1946–48; Univ of Glasgow: Hutcheson res scholar 1955–56, Hall fellowship 1956–59, hon clinical lectr 1965, hon sub dean Faculty of Med 1988; conslt physician Southern Gen Hosp Glasgow 1965–93, ret 1993; memb Bd Health Care International 1995–; author of numerous pubns on haematological and vascular disorders; memb BMA 1954, memb Scot Soc for Experimental Med 1955–, memb Br Soc for Haematology 1960, memb Res Support Gp Gtr Glasgow Health Bd 1978–90, memb Intercollegiate Standing Ctee on Nuclear Med UK 1980–83, memb Scot Cncl BMA 1980–83, chm Sub Ctee in Med Gtr Glasgow Health Bd 1985–90; RCPS: hon registrar for examinations 1971–83, visitor and pres elect 1988, pres 1990–92; chm: Conf of Scot Royal Colls and Faculties 1991–92, Jt Ctee on Higher Med Trg of Royal Colls of UK 1990–93; memb Scot Soc of Physicians 1965, FRCPS 1968, FRCPE 1969, hon memb Assoc of Physicians of GB and Ireland 1971, Hon FACP 1991, Hon RACP 1991, memb Acad of Med of Malaysia 1991, Hon FCM (SA), Hon FRCPS (Canada), FRCPath, FRCPI 1993; *Recreations* hillwalking, reading, opera, TV; *Clubs* Scott Royal Automobile, Cwlth Tst; *Style*— Dr Robert Hume; ✉ 6 Rubislaw Drive, Bearsden, Glasgow G61 1PR (☎ 0141 942 5331)

HUMER, Dr Franz Bernhard; *Career* Glaxo Holdings plc: main bd dir 1989–94, dir i/c technical and commercial policies 1989–93, chief operating dir 1993–94, resigned Dec 1994; non-exec dir Cadbury Schweppes plc 1994–; *Style*— Dr Franz Humer; ✉ c/o Cadbury Schweppes plc, 25 Berkeley Square, London W1X 6HT (☎ 0171 409 1313, fax 0171 830 5200)

HUMFREY, Charles Thomas William; s of Brian Humfrey (d 1976), of St James, Barbados, and Marjorie Humfrey; *b* 1 Dec 1947; *Educ* The Lodge Sch Barbados, St Edmund Hall Oxford (BA); *m* 1971, Enid, *née* Thomas; 2 s (James b 2 May 1975, Nicholas b 15 May 1983), 1 da (Susannah b 7 July 1977); *Career* HM Dip Serv: joined FCO 1969, Br Embassy Tokyo 1971–76, SE Asian Dept FCO 1976–79, private sec to Min of State FCO 1979–81, UK Mission NY 1981–85, Southern African Dept FCO 1985–87, cnsllr Br Embassy Ankara 1988–90, cnsllr (economic) Br Embassy Tokyo 1990–94, head Southern African Dept FCO 1994–95, min Br Embassy Tokyo 1995–; *Style*— Charles Humfrey, Esq; ✉ c/o Foreign & Commonwealth Office (Tokyo), King Charles Street, London SW1A 2AH

HUMM, Roger Frederick; s of Leonard Edward Humm, MBE (d 1964), and Gladys, *née* Prevotat (d 1986); *b* 7 March 1937; *Educ* Hampton Sch, Univ of Sheffield (BA(Hons)Econ); *m* 1966 (m dis), Marion Frances, *née* Czechman; *Career* md Ford Motor Co Ltd 1986–90 (dir 1980–90); dir: Ford Motor Credit Company Ltd 1980–90, Imperial Hospitals Ltd 1991–; vice chm and chief exec Alexanders Holdings plc 1992–; Liveryman Worshipful Co of Carmen; FIMI, CIMgt, FInstD, FRSA; *Recreations* golf, scuba diving, writing, Harlequins; *Clubs* RAC, Variety of GB, Lord's Taverners; *Style*— Roger F Humm, Esq; ✉ c/o The Clock House, Kelvedon, Essex CO5 9DG

HUMPHERY-SMITH, Cecil Raymond Julian; s of Frederick Humphery-Smith, MBE (d 1979), and Violet Agnes Humphery-Smith (d 1990); *b* 29 Oct 1928; *Educ* St John's Hurstpierpoint, Univ of London Sch of Hygiene and Tropical Med, Parma, Univ of Kent (BSc, LCh, DLet &c); *m* 1951, Alice Elizabeth Gwendoline, da of late Charles Thomas Cogle; 1 s, 5 da; *Career* mangr Consumer Servs Dept H J Heinz Co 1955–60, conslt De Rica Spa 1961–72, md Achievements Ltd 1961–81 (chm 1981–91); fndr, princ and tstee Inst of Heraldic and Genealogical Studies 1961– (chm of Ct 1961–77 and 1990–); dir Tabard Press 1959–94 (managing ed 1991–94), ed Family History 1962–; co-fndr Fedn Family History Societies 1974; lectr in extra mural studies: Univ of London 1951–91, Univ of Oxford Delegacy 1960–65, Univ of Kent 1964–; visiting prof: Univ of Minho 1970–72, Univ of Bologna 1996; memb Governing Cncl Rutherford Coll 1992–; sec gen: XIII Int Congress of Heraldry and Genealogy 1976, VIII Colloquium Internationale d'Héraldique 1993; designer of coats of arms; vice pres Heraldry Soc 1993– (memb Cncl 1953–93); memb Cncl: Manorial Soc of GB 1979–, Sub-Priory B Adrian Fortescue 1981–87, Domesday Nat Ctee 1984–85; vice pres Cambridge Univ Heraldic and Genealogical Soc 1954–, sec gen Bureau Permanent des Congrès Internationaux des Sciences Généalogique et Héraldiques 1994–, vice pres Assoc of Genealogists and Record Agents 1994–; UNESCO, ISSC, corr Int Archives Cncl; Arvid Bergman Lauriat 1961, D'Altenstein Prize 1961, Academician l'Académie Internationale d'Héraldique 1976 (memb Cncl 1986–), Julian Bickersteth Meml Medal 1986, Prix Delenda 1995, Gustaf von Numers Prize 1996; hon memb Florida Bar 1980, hon citizen of Caldarola 1996; Freeman and Liveryman Worshipful Cos of Broderers and Scriveners (hon historian); memb Confédération Internationale des Sciences Généalogique et Héraldique (vice pres 1980–86, pres 1986–90, pres emeritus 1991), fell Heraldry Society, FSA, FSG, FGSU etc; Knight of Obedience SMOM; *Publications* books incl: The Colour of Heraldry (jtly), General Armory Two, Heraldry in Canterbury Cathedral, Chronicles of Thomas Chough, Anglo-Norman Armory (2 volumes), An Atlas and Index of Parish Registers (2 edn as The Phillimore Atlas, 1995), A Genealogist's Bibliography, Our Family History, Introducing Family History, Sonnets of Life, Hugh Revel, Master of the Hospital, 1258–1277, Visitation Records, The Book of Irish Arms; author of numerous articles and lectures on subjects auxiliary to history, heraldry and family history; *Recreations* writing sonnets, walking, listening to good music, enjoying the company of grandchildren; *Clubs* Athenaeum, Royal British (Lisbon); *Style*— Cecil Humphery-Smith, Esq, FSA; ✉ Saint Michael's, Allan Road, Seasalter, Kent CT5 4AH (☎ 01227 275791, fax 01227 765617)

HUMPHREY, Albert S; s of Prof Albert Swartsindruver Humphrey, and Margaret Elizabeth Tomlinson, *née* Benton; *b* 2 June 1926; *Educ* Univ of Illinois (BSc), MIT (MSc), Harvard Sch of Business Admin (MBA); *m* 1, 6 Oct 1957 (m dis 1970), Virginia, da of Norman Potter (d 1976), of Cambridge, Mass; 2 s (Albert b 9 July 1959, Jonathon Benton Cantwell b 29 May 1962), 2 da (Virginia b 13 Sept 1960, Heidi b 10 Oct 1963); m 2, 20 Oct 1983, Myriam Alice Octaaf, da of Willy Petrus de Baere, of Lokeren, Belgium; 1 da (Stephania b 22 Sept 1986), 1 step s (Jonas Willems b 29 Aug 1974), 1 step da (Roosje Willems b 27 April 1972); *Career* staff engr Esso Standard Oil Co New Jersey 1948, chief of chemical and protective gp Office of the Chief Chemical Offr US Army Chemical Corp Washington DC 1952, asst to the Pres Penberthy Instrument Co Seattle 1955, chief of product planning Boeing Airplane Co Seattle 1956, mangr of value analysis Small Aircraft Div GE Boston 1960, mangr of R & D planning P R Mallory & Co Inc Indianapolis 1961, head of mgmnt audit General Dynamics San Diego 1963, dir Int Exec Seminar in Business Planning Stanford Res Inst California and conslt NASA Office of Advanced Res and Technol Washington 1965, chief exec Business Planning and Development Kansas City 1969, currently chm and chief exec Business Planning and Development Inc (London); dir: Visual Enterprises Ltd (London), Sanbros Ltd (London), Tower Lysprodukter a/s (Oslo Norway), Petrochemische Anwendungssysteme GmbH (Nurnberg Germany), East West Herbs Ltd (Kingham Oxon), Webb Industries Ltd (Derby), Friborg Instruments Ltd (London), The Bank Consultancy Group Ltd (London), GP Bank Advisory Services Ltd (London), Hidden Valley Ltd (Staverton Northants); conslt Retaina Group Ltd (London); faculty memb: Extension Sch for Adult Educn Univ of Washington, US Naval Res Offrs Trg Sch; visiting prof Sch of Business and Mgmnt Newcastle Poly, assoc Blackwood Hodge Mgmnt Centre Nene Coll Northampton, memb Exec Advsy Bd Nat Bureau of Professional Mgmnt Conslts; frequent contrib to various business and mgmnt pubns; memb: ESU, American Inst of Chemical Engrs, Harvard Alumni, MIT Alumni Assoc, Univ of Illinois Alumni Assoc; MCIM, MInstD; *Recreations* public service, seminars, lectures, writing, skiing, windsurfing, water skiing; *Clubs* East India, Devonshire Sports and Public Schools, Harvard (Boston); *Style*— Albert Humphrey, Esq; ✉ 1D Randolph Crescent, Little Venice, Maida Vale, London NW9 1DP (☎ 0171 266 0395, fax 0171 266 0039, e-mail humph@bpdev.demon.co.uk); 4030 Charlotte St, Kansas City, Missouri 64110, USA (☎ 00 1 816 753 0495); Sportlaan 6 W 22, 9100 Lokeren, Belgium (☎ 00 32 91 488 666)

HUMPHREY, Ann Louise; da of John Frederick Wood (d 1989), of Selby, Yorkshire, and Brenda Elizabeth, *née* Simpson; *b* 24 July 1952; *Educ* Selby Girls' HS, Univ of Durham (BA), King's Coll London (LLM); *m* 23 July 1977, Anthony Humphrey, *qv*, s of Idwal Robert Humphrey, of Bosworth House, Woodbridge, Suffolk; *Career* stage Euro Cmmn 1974, admitted slr 1977, memb VAT Practitioners Gp 1982–93, corp tax ptnr Richards Butler 1988–93, tax and business conslt 1993–; memb Worshipful Co of Solicitors, memb Law Soc; *Books* Advanced Value Added Tax Planning (1988), Fiscal Frontiers: Tax Changes for the Internal Market (1993); *Recreations* golf, tennis, theatre, dance; *Style*— Ann L Humphrey; ✉ 279 Camberwell New Road, London SE5 0TF (☎ and fax 0171 701 3939)

HUMPHREY, Anthony Robert; s of Idwal Robert Humphrey, of Suffolk, and Mary Agnes, *née* Richards; *b* 12 Jan 1951; *Educ* Douai Sch, Univ of Durham (BA); *m* 24 July 1977, Ann Louise Humphrey, *qv*, da of John Frederick Wood (d 1989), of Yorkshire; *Career* ptnr (specialising in fin and corp law) Allen & Overy 1981– (joined 1973); memb: Law Soc, Int Bar Assoc; *Recreations* golf, hunting, tennis, skiing; *Clubs* RAC; *Style*— Anthony Humphrey, Esq; ✉ Allen & Overy, One New Change, London EC4M 9QQ (☎ 0171 330 3000, fax 0171 330 9999)

HUMPHREY, Raymond John; s of Thomas Geoffrey Humphrey, and Mary Irene, *née* Warwick; *b* 4 Oct 1951; *Educ* St Joseph's GS Blackpool, Blackpool Sch of Technol & Art; *m* 1, 16 Aug 1975 (m dis); 1 s (Liam Jason b 4 Nov 1976); m 2, 26 May 1990, Lynne Roberta, da of Robert Fraser Andrews; 1 da (Charlotte Elizabeth b 30 Oct 1992); *Career* professional photographer; formerly: industl photographer Winter & Kidson Preston, retinal photographer RPMS, commercial and advertising photographer Gordon Hammonds Photography Co Southampton, dir of own co The Picture House Eastleigh 1982–; awards: Kitchenham Trophy (Industrial) 1979–80, Wessex Colour Plaque (Industl and Commercial) 1980–81, 1982–83 and 1984–86, Master Photographers Industl Award 1981–82, Master Photographers Pictorial Photography Gold Certificate, 3M Award for Best Use of Colour in Industl and Commercial Photography 1981, Inst of Incorporated Photographers Industl and Commercial Photographer of the Year 1981–82, World Cncl of Professional Photographers Gold Certificate 1988; FBIPP; *Recreations* archery, pool, jogging; *Style*— Raymond Humphrey, Esq; ✉ The Picture House, 117 Leigh Road, Eastleigh, Hants SO50 9DS (☎ 01703 641237, fax 01703 650286)

HUMPHREY OF DINNET, (James Malcolm) Marcus; CBE (1993), DL (Aberdeenshire 1989); s of Lt Col James McGivern Humphrey, MC (d 1979), and Violet Joan, da of Col Sir Malcolm Barclay-Harvey of Dinnet, Govr of S Aust 1939–44 and for many years MP for Kincardine and W Aberdeenshire; *b* 1 May 1938; *Educ* Eton, ChCh Oxford (MA); *m* 15 Oct 1963, Sabrina Margaret, da of Lt Cdr Thomas Edward Pooley, RN (ret); 2 s (Edward b 1965, Simon b 1978), 2 da (Tania b 1966, Natasha b 1972); *Career* chartered surveyor; landowner; chm N of Scotland Bd Eagle Star Group 1971–91; memb: NFU of Scotland HQ Cncl 1968–73, Grampian Regnl Cncl 1974–94 (chm of fin 1974–78); non-exec dir Grampian Healthcare NHS Tst 1993–; alternate memb UK Delegation Euro Ctee of the Regions 1994–; Parly candidate (C): N Aberdeen 1966, Kincardine and Deeside By-election 1991; chm of fin Aberdeen CC 1973–75, memb Aberdeenshire Cncl 1995–; Grand Master Mason of Scotland 1983–88, memb Queen's Body Guard for Scotland (Royal Co of Archers) 1969–; FRICS; OStJ 1970; *Recreations* fishing, shooting, photography, philately; *Clubs* Boodle's, Royal Northern and Univ (Aberdeen); *Style*— Marcus Humphrey of Dinnet, CBE, DL; ✉ Dinnet, Aboyne, Aberdeenshire; Estate Office, Dinnet, Aboyne AB34 5LL (☎ 013398 85341, fax 013398 85319)

HUMPHREYS, Prof Colin John; s of Arthur William Humphreys (d 1994), of Syston, Leicestershire; and Olive Annie Harton (d 1965); *b* 24 May 1941; *Educ* Luton GS, Imperial Coll London (BSc), Churchill Coll Cambridge (PhD), Jesus Coll Oxford (MA); *m* 30 July 1966, Sarah Jane, da of Henry Matthews, of Cottingham, N Humberside; 2 da (Katherine Jane b 1968, Elizabeth Mary Louise b 1971); *Career* Univ of Oxford: sr res offr 1971–80, lectr in metallurgy and science of materials 1980–85, sr res fell Jesus Coll 1974–85; Henry Bell Wortley prof of materials engrg and head Dept of Materials Sci and Engrg Univ of Liverpool 1985–89; visiting prof: Arizona State Univ 1979, Univ of Illinois 1982–86; Univ of Cambridge: prof of materials science 1990–92, head Dept of Materials Sci and Metallurgy 1991–95, professorial fell Selwyn Coll 1990–, Goldsmiths' prof of materials science 1992–; hon pres Canadian Coll for Chinese Studies 1996–; chm: Cmmn on Electron Diffraction Int Union of Crystallography 1984–87 (memb Cmmn on Int Tables), Materials Science and Engrg Cmmn SERC 1988–92; vice pres Inst of Metals 1993–96 (memb Cncl 1992–96); memb Cncl: SERC 1988–92, Inst of Metals 1989–92; vice chm Technol Foresight Ctee on Materials DTI 1994–; RSA Medal 1963, Reginald Mitchell Medal 1989, Rosenhain Medal and Prize 1989, D K C MacDonald Meml lectr Canada 1993, Templeton Award 1994, Elgant Work Prize Inst of Materials 1996; memb: Ct Univ of Bradford 1990–, John Templeton Fndn 1994–, BBC Panel on Engrg and Technol progs 1995–; tstee Link House 1994–; Freeman City of London 1994, Freeman Worshipful Co of Goldsmiths 1994; CEng 1980, FIM 1985, FInstP 1985, Academia Europaea 1991, FEng 1996; *Books* High Voltage Electron Microscopy (ed, 1974), Electron Diffraction 1927–77 (ed, 1978), Creation and Evolution (1985, translated into Chinese 1988); *Recreations* chronology of biblical events, contemplating gardening; *Style*— Prof Colin Humphreys, FEng; ✉ 8 Diamond Close, Cambridge CB2 2AU; Department of Materials Science and Metallurgy, University of Cambridge, Pembroke St, Cambridge CB2 3QZ (☎ 01223 334457, fax 01223 334437, telex 81240 CAMSPL G)

HUMPHREYS, Emyr Owen; s of William Humphreys, of Prestatyn, Flints, and Sarah Rosina Humphreys; *b* 15 April 1919; *Educ* Univ Coll Aberystwyth, Univ Coll Bangor; *m* 1946, Elinor Myfanwy, da of Rev Griffith Jones, of Bontnewydd, Carns; 3 s, 1 da; *Career* author; Somerset Maugham award 1953, Hawthornden prize 1959, Welsh Arts Cncl prize 1972, Soc of Authors Travelling award 1979, Welsh Arts Cncl Non Fiction prize 1984, Book of the Year Welsh Arts Cncl 1992; hon prof of English Univ Coll of N Wales Bangor; hon fell: Univ of Wales Aberystwyth, Univ Coll Swansea; Gregynog Arts fell 1974–75; Hon DLitt Univ of Wales; FRSL; *Books* The Little Kingdom (1946), The Voice of a Stranger (1949), A Change of Heart (1951), Hear and Forgive (1952), A Man's Estate (1955), The Italian Wife (1957), Y Tri Llais (1958), A Toy Epic (1958), The Gift (1963), Outside the House of Baal (1965), Natives (1968), Ancestor Worship (1970), National Winner (1971), Flesh and Blood (1974), Landscapes (1976), The Best of Friends (1978), Penguin Modern Poets number 27 (1978), The Kingdom of Brân (1979), The Anchor Tree (1980), Pwyll a Riannon (1980), Miscellany Two (1981), The Taliesin Tradition (1983), Jones (1984), Salt of the Earth (1985), An Absolute Hero (1986), Darn o Dir (1986), Open Secrets (1988), The Triple Net (1988), Bonds of Attachment (1991), Outside Time (1991), Unconditional Surrender (1996); *Recreations* rural pursuits; *Style*— Emyr Humphreys, Esq, FRSL; ✉ Llinon, Penyberth, Llanfairpwll, Ynys Môn, Gwynedd LL61 5YT (☎ 01248 714540)

HUMPHREYS, Sir (Raymond Evelyn) Myles; kt (1977), JP, DL (Belfast); s of Raymond and May Humphreys; *b* 24 March 1925; *Educ* Skegoneil Primary Sch, Londonderry HS, Belfast Royal Acad; *m* 1, 1963, Joan Tate (d 1979); 2 s (Ian, Mark); m 2, 1987, Sheila Clements-McFarland; *Career* res engr NI Road Tport Bd 1946–48, Ulster Tport Authy 1948–55, tport mangr Nestle's Food Prodn (NI) Ltd 1955–59, dist tport offr St John Ambulance Bde 1946–66; memb: Belfast City Cncl 1964–81, NI Tport Hldg Co 1968–74, Nat Planning and Town Planning Cncl 1970–81 (chm 1976–77), NI Tourist Bd 1973–80, May Ctee of Inquiry into UK Prison Servs 1978–79, Bd Abbey Nat Building Soc 1981–91 (chm Advsy Bd NI 1981–92); chm City Cncl Town Planning and Environmental Health Ctee 1973–75, dep chm NI Housing Exec 1975–78; dir: Walter Alexander (Belfast) Ltd 1959–92, Quick Service Stations Ltd 1971–86, Bowring Martin 1978–88; chm: Belfast Corp Housing Ctee 1966–69, NI Railways Co Ltd 1967–90, Ulster Tourist Devpt Assoc 1968–78, City Cncl Planning Ctee 1973–75, Fin and Gen Purposes Ctee Belfast 1978–80, NI Police Authy 1976–86, Belfast Marathon Ltd 1981–85, NI Tport Holding Co 1988–93; Belfast Harbour cmmr 1979–88; High Sheriff Belfast 1969, Lord Mayor 1975–77 (dep Lord Mayor 1970); sen Jr Chamber Int, NI rep Motability Int; pres: NI Polio Fellowship 1977–, City of Belfast Youth Orchestra 1980–; memb Exec and former pres NI C of C and Indust 1970–, pres BIM (Belfast branch) 1983–96; pres Belfast Junior C of C 1964; past chm: Bd of Mgmnt Dunlambert Secdy Sch, Bd of Visitors to HM Prison Belfast 1960–76; memb: Senate Queen's Univ Belfast 1975–77, Ct Univ of Ulster 1985–; tstee Ulster Folk and Tport Museum 1976–81; memb Cncl Queen's Silver Jubilee Appeal, dir Ulster Orchestra Soc 1980–82; life memb and vice pres Railway Preservation Soc of Ireland 1970–; vice pres NI Branch Royal Scottish Pipe Band Assoc 1977–, pres Belfast Tport Officials' Club 1996–; patron Model Engineers Soc NI 1974–; Freeman City of London 1976; OStJ; FCIT; *Clubs* Reform, Belfast; *Style*— Sir Myles Humphreys, JP, DL; ✉ Mylestone, 23 Massey Ave, Belfast BT4 2JT

HUMPHREYS, Nigel Craven; s of Gordon Stephen Humphreys (d 1985), of Godalming, Surrey, and Joan Olive, *née* Mudditt; *b* 15 March 1938; *Educ* Sherborne, New Coll Oxford (MA); *m* 29 Sept 1962, Jennifer Nan, da of Maj Adrian Hugh Lovegrove, TD (d 1993), of West End House, Over Stratton, Somerset; 2 da (Julia Jane Craven (Mrs Michael Parker) b 1964, Annabella Claire Gough b 1966); *Career* RB 1956–58, cmmnd 1957, seconded to 3 Bn King's African Rifles Kenya; Courtaulds Ltd 1961–65, Andrews & Partners 1965–68, Chaucer Estates Ltd 1968–71, md Mitropa Group Brussels 1971–77; Tyzack & Partners Ltd: conslt 1977, ptnr 1978–84, managing ptnr 1984–95, ptnr Accord Group Tyzack Ltd (after name change) 1995–; chm Accord Group 1995–; memb: Vol Serv Housing Soc 1966–68, Cherwell Housing Tst 1968–71; chm of govrs The Old Ride Sch 1989–91; Freeman City of London 1984, Liveryman Worshipful Co of Glovers 1984 (memb Ct of Assts 1990–94); *Recreations* opera, country sports, uninhabited places; *Clubs* Boodle's, Royal Green Jackets; *Style*— Nigel Humphreys, Esq; ✉ Meadow House, Smannell, Andover, Hants SP11 6JJ (☎ 01264 352628, fax 01264 323488); Accord Group Ltd, Smannell, Andover, Hants SP11 6JJ (☎ 01264 337175, fax 01264 323488, e-mail 106047.40@COMPUSERVE.COM)

HUMPHREYS, Col (Thomas) Victor; OBE (1958); s of Cdr Thomas Victor Humphreys (ka 1942), of Ballycastle, Co Antrim (family lived there for six generations), and Anne Breakey, *née* Douglas (d 1967); *b* 26 May 1922; *Educ* Ballycastle HS Antrim, The Queen's Univ of Belfast (MB BCh, BAO); *m* 18 Oct 1969, Elisabeth Penrose, da of Rev John Alfred Clarence Rogers (d 1984), vicar of Hindhead, Surrey; *Career* res hosp appts in med and surgery 1946–52, MO and second sec of legation HBM Legation Bucharest 1952–55, MO and first sec HBM Embassy Moscow 1955–57, surgn Royal Mail Line 1958–62; RAMC: entered 1963, Lt-Col 1969, Local Col 1977, Actg Col 1979, Col Staff 1980; sr specialist Army Community and Occupational Med 1980, regtl MO 2 Coldstream Gds and later Queen's Dragoon Gds; SMO: (UK) SHAPE Belgium 1971–74, Chief MO HQ Allied Forces N Europe Oslo Norway 1974–77; CO Br Mil Hosp: Munster BAOR 1977–79, acting Garrison Cdr two periods 1977, ADMS Berlin and CO BMH 1979–82; Cdr Army Med Servs: HQ Western Dist UK 1982–86, HQ London Dist Horse Gds 1986–87, ret from Army 1987; med case advsr to MOD 1987–; pres emeritus Berlin Int Med Soc 1981–, fell (former pres) SHAPE Int Med Soc Belgium; a vice pres Coldstream Gds Assoc (Exeter) 1989–, memb The Exeter Flotilla 1988–; Cdr Order of Polonia Restituta (govt in exile); OStJ 1981 (SBStJ 1962); Lord of the Manor of Postcombe; *Publications*: author of articles in various professional med jls on medicine and surgery in Eastern Europe, various historical articles on European Monarchies (particularly the Habsburgs); *Recreations* European history, languages, genealogy, research into Wild Geese O'Brien kinsmen, Counts of the Holy Roman Empire in the military service of the House of Austria, heraldry and all the vanished pomps of yesterday; *Style*— Col Victor Humphreys, OBE; ✉ Powderham House, Powderham, nr Exeter EX6 8JJ (☎ 01626 890536)

HUMPHRIES, (John) Barry; AO (1982); *b* 17 Feb 1934; *Career* actor and writer; stage characters incl: Dame Edna Everage, Sir Les Patterson, Sandy Stone; Hon DUniv Griffith Aust 1994; *Theatre* incl: Estragon in Waiting for Godot (Melbourne), Fagin in Oliver (Piccadilly), Maggie May (Aldephi), Bed-Sitting Room (Comedy Theatre), Long John Silver in Treasure Island (Mermaid), Just A Show (one man show, Australia and Fortune Theatre), Housewife Superstar (Apollo and Globe), A Night with Dame Edna (Piccadilly), An Evening's Intercourse (Drury Lane), Song for Australia (Albert Hall), Back with A Vengeance (Strand, Royal and tour), numerous one man shows in Aust; *Television* incl: The Bunyip (Channel 7), The Barry Humphries Scandals (BBC), The Dame Edna Experience (LWT), Audience With Dame Edna (LWT), Another Audience with Dame Edna (LWT), A Profile of Barry Humphries (LWT), Single Voices (BBC), Selling Hitler (Euston Films), Dame Edna's Hollywood (NBC), Dame Edna's Neighbourhood Watch (series of 12, LWT); *Film* incl: Bedazzled, Bliss of Mrs Blossom, The Adventures of Barry McKenzie, Barry McKenzie Holds His Own, Sir Les Saves the World, The Getting of Wisdom; *Awards* SWET Award Best Comedy of the Year (for A Night with Dame Edna) 1979, BAFTA Award nomination Best Arts Programme (for A Profile of Barry Humphries), TV Personality of the Year 1990, Golden Rose of Montreux Award (for A Night with Dame Edna) 1991, JR Ackerley Prize 1994 (for More Please); *Books* incl: Bizarre, The Wonderful World of Barry McKenzie (1970), Dame Edna's Coffee Table Book (1976), Les Patterson's Australia (1979), The Traveller's Tool (1985), My Gorgeous Life: the autobiography of Dame Edna Everage (1989), More Please (autobiog, 1992), Women in the Background (debut novel, 1995); *Style*— Barry Humphries, Esq, AO; ✉ c/o Megastar Productions Ltd, 113 Canalot Studios, 222 Kensal Road, London W10 5BN

HUMPHRIES, His Hon Judge; Gerard William; s of John Alfred Humphries (d 1980), and Marie Frances, *née* Whitwell (d 1980); *b* 13 Dec 1928; *Educ* St Bede's Coll Manchester, Univ of Manchester (LLB); *m* 1957, Margaret Valerie, da of William Woodburn Gelderd (d 1975), of Cumbria; 4 s (Stephen b 1961, Paul b 1962, David b 1966, Bernard b 1971), 1 da (Frances b 1967); *Career* Flying Offr RAF 1951–53; barr 1954–80, circuit judge (Northern Circuit) 1980–; charter memb Serra International N Cheshire 1963– (pres 1968, 1973 and 1995–96); Knight of the Holy Sepulchre (Vatican) 1986; *Books* Stations of the cross - a meditation; *Recreations* tennis, gardening, sail-boarding, bad golf, computers, caravanning, fell-walking, dining and wining with family and friends; *Clubs* Lansdowne, Northern LT (Manchester); *Style*— His Hon Judge Humphries; ✉ Crown Court, Crown Square, Manchester

HUMPHRIES, John Anthony Charles; OBE (1980); s of Charles Humphries; *b* 15 June 1925; *Educ* Fettes, Peterhouse Cambridge (LLB); *m* 1951, Olga June, da of Dr Geoffrey Duckworth; 4 da; *Career* served WWII RNVR 1943–46; admitted slr 1951, sr ptnr Travers Smith Braithwaite 1982–95; chm Evans of Leeds plc 1982–, memb London Bd Halifax Building Society 1985–92; chm Water Space Amenity Cmmn 1973–83, vice pres Inland Waterways Assoc 1973– (chm 1970–73), memb Inland Waterways Amenity Advsy Cncl 1971–88, advsr to HM Govt on amenity use of water space 1972; memb: Nat Water Cncl 1973–83, Thames Water Authy 1983–87, Sports Cncl 1987–88; dep chm Environment Cncl 1985–94; chm: Southern Cncl for Sport and Recreation 1986–92, Lothbury Property Tst 1996–; vice chm Cncl Univ of Surrey 1994–; *Recreations* inland waters, gardening; *Clubs* Naval, City; *Style*— John Humphries, Esq, OBE; ✉ 21 Parkside, Wimbledon, London SW19 (☎ 0181 946 3764)

HUMPHRYS, John Desmond; s of Edward George Humphrys, and Winifred May Humphrys (d 1988); *b* 17 Aug 1943; *Educ* Cardiff HS; *m* 5 Sept 1964 (m dis), Edna Wilding; 1 s (Christopher b 30 April 1967), 1 da (Catherine b 21 July 1969); *Career* BBC TV: foreign corr in USA and SA 1970–80, dip corr 1980–81, presenter 9 O'Clock News 1981–86; presenter: Today Programme (BBC Radio 4) 1987–, On the Record (BBC TV), BBC TV News; memb Cncl Save the Children Fund; *Recreations* music, farming; *Style*— John Humphrys, Esq; ✉ BBC, Broadcasting House, Langham Place, London W1A 1AA (☎ 0171 927 5566)

HUNGERFORD, John Leonard; s of Leonard Harold Hungerford (d 1979), and Violet Miriam, *née* Bickerstaff; *b* 12 Oct 1944; *Educ* The Glyn Sch Epsom, Gonville and Caius Coll Cambridge, Charing Cross Hosp Med Sch (MA, MB BChir, DO); *m* 16 July 1987, Yvonne Carole, da of Sydney George Rayment (d 1962); 1 da (Miranda b 1988); *Career* conslt surgn Moorfields Eye Hosp 1983–, conslt ophthalmic surgn St Bartholomew's Hosp 1983–; author of pubns on ocular cancer; FRCS 1978, FRCOphth 1988; *Recreations* travel, gardening, architecture; *Style*— John Hungerford, Esq; ✉ 114 Harley St, London W1N 1AG (☎ 0171 935 1565, fax 0171 224 1752)

HUNNICUTT, (Virginia) Gayle; da of Col S L Hunnicutt, of Fort Worth, Texas, and Mary Virginia, *née* Dickenson; *b* 6 Feb 1943; *Educ* Pascal HS, Texas Christian Univ, UCLA (Regent scholar, BA); *m* 1, 1968 (m dis 1974), David H Hemmings; 1 s (Nolan); m 2, 1 Sept 1978, Simon David Jenkins, *qv*, s of Rev Daniel Jenkins, of London; 1 s (Edward); *Career* actress; memb Bd of Tstees The Theatre Tst, hon memb BFI 1980; memb: Acad of Motion Pictures Arts and Scis 1979, Br Theatre Assoc 1982, Bd English Shakespeare Co 1992; *Theatre* incl: A Ride Across Lake Constance 1974, Twelfth Night 1975, The Tempest 1976, The Admiral Crichton 1977, A Woman of No Importance 1978, Hedda Gabler 1978, Peter Pan 1979, Macbeth 1980, Uncle Vanya 1980, The Philadelphia Story 1981, The Miss Firecracker Contest 1982, Exit The King 1983, The Doctor's Dilemma 1984, So Long On Lonely Street 1985, The Big Knife 1987, The Little Foxes 1991, Edith Wharton at Home 1993, Dangerous Corner 1994, Edith Wharton at Home 1995; *Television* incl: Man and Boy 1971, Humbolt's Gift 1971, The Golden Bowl 1972, The Ripening Seed 1973, Fall of Eagles 1974, The Ambassadors 1975, The Martian Chronicles 1978, A Man Called Intrepid 1979, Fantomas 1980, Tales of the Unexpected 1987, Taxi 1982, Dylan Thomas 1983, The First Modern Olympics 1984, Phillip Marlow 1984, Sherlock Holmes 1985, Privilege 1986, Strong Medicine 1986, Dream West 1987, Dallas 1989–91, Voices in the Garden 1991; *Films* incl: New Face in Hell 1967, Eye of the Cat and The Little Sisters 1968, Fragment of Fear 1969, Running Scared 1971, Scorpio 1972, Legend of Hell House 1973, L'Homme Sans Visage 1974, The Spiral Staircase 1976, Once in Paris 1977, Dream Lovers 1985, Target 1986, Silence Like Glass 1988; *Books* Health and Beauty in Motherhood (1984); *Recreations* travel, reading, music; *Style*— Miss Gayle Hunnicutt; ✉ c/o William Morris Agency (UK) Ltd, 31/32 Soho Square, London W1V 6DG (☎ 0171 434 2191, fax 0171 437 0238)

HUNNIFORD, Gloria; *b* 10 April 1940; *Career* TV and radio personality; started singing at age of 9 in NI (appearing on all 3 TV networks and releasing 4 records), own weekly TV and radio music request show Ontario Canada 1969, worked on own 2 1/2 hour daily radio programme and weekly World Serv programme on Irish music for BBC NI, appeared on TV programmes such as Songs of Praise, Big Band specials and Queen's Jubilee Celebrations culminating in own daily one hour TV programme for Ulster TV, weekly broadcast for Br Forces Broadcasting to Germany 1969–81; host own daily radio show for BBC Radio 2 (first woman to do so) 1982–95, host chat show Sunday Sunday (LWT) 1982–91, host Gloria Live (Monday to Friday, BBC) 1990–93, stand in for Terry Wogan 1991, co-hosted (with Kenny Everett) That's Showbusiness (BBC), family affairs prog (with da Caron Keating, BBC) 1992–, reports for Holiday (BBC) 1993; other TV shows hosted: We Love TV (LWT), The Newly Wed Game (LWT), Gloria Plus (Saturday night chat show, UTV), Saturday Night Live (BBC), 6 O'Clock Show (LWT), BBC Pebble Mill Lunchtime Show, Good Fortune (BBC 1) 1994, Sunday Live (Yorkshire TV), Sunday (LWT); other TV credits (as singer): ten Royal Variety Performances, Val Doonican Show, Les Dawson Show, Children in Need Appeal, Paul Daniels Magic Show, Des O'Connor Show, Cannon & Ball Show, Bruce Forsyth's Show, Noel Edmonds' Saturday Night Live Show, Freddie Starr Show; *Awards* incl: Variety Club Radio Personality of the Year 1982 and 1992, TV and Radio Indust Club Radio Personality of the Year 1983 and 1992, Panavista Britain's Best Dressed Woman 1985, TV Times TV Personality of the Year 1987, Spectacle Wearer of the Year 1991, Top Radio Personality (voted by readers of Chat magazine) 1991, Neighbour of the Year 1993; *Books* Gloria (autobiography, 1994), Gloria Hunniford's Family Cookbook (1995); *Style—* Miss Gloria Hunniford; ✉ c/o Simpson Fox Associates Ltd, 52 Shaftesbury Avenue, London W1V 7DE (☎ 0171 439 9167)

HUNSDON OF HUNSDON, *see:* Aldenham (and Hunsdon of Hunsdon), Rt Hon Lord

HUNT, Alan Charles; CMG (1990); s of John Henry Hunt (d 1990), of Hounslow, and Nelly Elizabeth Hunt (d 1978); *b* 5 March 1941; *Educ* Latymer Upper Sch, UEA (BA); *m* 6 May 1978, Meredith Margaret, da of Reginald Claydon, of Sydney, Australia; 2 da (Charlotte Louise b 1980, Victoria Clare b 1982); *Career* clerical offr Miny of Power 1958; HM Dip Serv 1959–; vice consul Tehran 1962–63, third sec Jedda 1964–65, floating duties Latin America 1965–67, second later first sec FCO 1970–73; first sec: Panama 1973–76, (commercial) Madrid 1977–81, FCO 1981–83; cnsllr (economic) Oslo 1983–87, head Br Interests Section (later Chargé d'Affaires) Buenos Aires 1987–90, cnsllr FCO 1990–91, consul gen Düsseldorf 1991–95, seconded to RCDS 1995, dir Trade and Investment Promotion FCO 1996; *Recreations* tennis, music, reading; *Style—* Alan Hunt, Esq, CMG; ✉ c/o Foreign and Commonwealth Office, King Charles St, London SW1

HUNT, Alannah Elizabeth; da of Humphrey Cecil Hunt (d 1965), of Curry Rivel, Somerset, and Molly Daphne Albury, *née* Hill (d 1979); *b* 22 March 1949; *Educ* Millfield, Taunton Tech Coll Somerset; *Career* selection conslt Webb Whitley Associates Ltd 1975–82, dir Overseas Link Ltd 1982–84; Price Waterhouse: head of exec search and selection 1984–, ptnr 1990–; author of various articles on recruitment and selection; FIPD 1986, FIMC 1987; *Recreations* opera, theatre, gardening; *Style—* Miss Alannah Hunt; ✉ Price Waterhouse Managment Consultants, Southwark Towers, 32 London Bridge Street, London SE1 9SY (☎ 0171 939 3000, fax 0171 939 3454)

HUNT, Dr Albert Charles (Bill); s of Albert Edward Hunt (d 1944), of Bromley, Kent, and Ethel Olivia, *née* Sherborne (d 1984); *b* 26 Dec 1927; *Educ* Bromley GS, The London Hosp (MD, BS); *m* 1, 1950 (m dis 1974), Enid Watkins; 3 s (Matthew Sherborne b 1952, Paul Sherborne b 1954, Benjamin Sherborne b 1958); m 2, Josephine Carol, da of Arthur Harold Whitney (d 1970), of W Mersea; *Career* pathologist to Home Office 1957–; reader in histopathology Univ of Bristol 1969–71 (reader in forensic pathology 1965–69), conslt histopathologist Plymouth 1971–92; former vice-pres: RCP, World Assoc of Socs of Pathology; former chm Cncl and pres Assoc of Clinical Pathologists; FRCPath 1969; *Books* Pathology of Injury (1972); *Recreations* collecting all sorts of things; *Style—* Dr A C Hunt; ✉ 29 The Cooperage, Commercial Wharf, Leith, Edinburgh EH6 6LF (☎ and fax 0131 555 0162)

HUNT, Andrew; s of Bernard Hunt (d 1976), and Lena, *née* Bloor; *b* 26 Feb 1948; *Educ* Redcliffe Endowed Boys Sch Bristol, Bath Tech Coll (City & Guilds); *m* 1967, Anne; 1 s (Kevin), 2 da (Karen, Kerry); *Career* head chef Mill Hotel Kingham Oxon 1968–70, exec chef Mendip Hotel and Restaurant Blagdon 1970–72, exec chef Harvey's Restaurant Bristol 1976–81 (chef saucier 1972–74), lectr Brunel Tech Coll Bristol 1981–88, ptnr Markwick & Hunt Bristol 1988–90, chef/patron Hunt's Restaurant Bristol 1990–; winner various Gold Medals Salon Culinaires; rep West Country Schs Swimming Championships 1960–63, swam in 4 British Championships, various swimming records Glos & Western Counties Championships 1964–66; *Recreations* clay pigeon shooting; *Clubs* Mendip Shooting; *Style—* Andrew Hunt, Esq; ✉ Hunt's, 26 Broad Street, Bristol BS1 2HG (☎ 0117 926 5580, fax 0117 926 5580)

HUNT, Anthony James (Tony); s of James Edward Hunt (d 1976), and Joan Margaret, *née* Cassidy; *b* 22 June 1932; *Educ* Salesian Coll Farnborough, Westminster Tech Coll; *m* 1, 1957 (m dis 1972), Patricia, *née* Daniels; 1 s (Julian b 12 Sept 1959), 1 da (Polly Leah b 27 July 1961); m 2, 1975 (m dis 1982), Patricia, *née* Daniels; m 3, 1985, Diana Joyce, *née* Collett; *Career* articled pupil Worshipful Co of Founders 1948–51, engr F J Samuely & Ptnrs 1951–59, engr Morton Lupton Architects 1960–62; Anthony Hunt Assocs Conslt Engrs (now subsid of Kendell plc): fndr 1962, chm 1988–, chm 1988–, chm YRM plc 1993–94; Graham Willis visiting prof Sch of Architecture Sheffield 1993–; recent projects incl: Hilton Hotel Heathrow, Waterloo Int Station, The Law Faculty Cambridge, West India Quay Bridge; current projects incl: New HQ for Lloyds Register of Shipping, city devpt Malaysia, competition entry for Olympic stadium Stockholm; Gold medal IStructE 1995; CEng, Hon Fell RIBA 1989, FIStructE, FRSA; *Awards* for: The Reliance Controls Factory Swindon, Willis Faber HQ Ipswich, Sainsbury Centre for the Visual Arts Norwich, Inmos Micro-electronics Factory Newport, Schlumberger Research Facility Cambridge, Don Valley Athletics Stadium Sheffield; *Recreations* music, sailing, food, wine; *Clubs* Chelsea Arts; *Style—* Tony Hunt, Esq; ✉ Overley House, Daglingworth, Cirencester, Glos GL7 7HX (☎ 01285 653605, fax 01285 641648)

HUNT, Bernard Andrew Paul; s of Sir Joseph (Anthony) Hunt (d 1982), and Hilde, *née* Pollitzer; *b* 24 March 1944; *Educ* Oundle, Magdalene Coll Cambridge (MA); *m* 1973, Florence, da of Alan White, of W Sussex; 1 s (Andrew b 1977), 1 da (Susanna b 1975); *Career* architect; ptnr Hunt Thompson Assocs 1969–; chm Housing Gp RIBA 1995–, dir Nat House Building Cncl 1995–; FRSA; *Recreations* cinema, theatre, reading, skiing, swimming, scuba diving; *Clubs* Reform; *Style—* Bernard Hunt, Esq; ✉ 34 Fitzroy Road, London NW1; 79 Parkway, London NW1 (☎ 0171 485 8555, fax 0171 485 1232)

HUNT, Dr Bernard Peter; s of William Branson Hunt, of Lincoln, and Ivy, *née* Hammond; *b* 30 July 1948; *Educ* Southend HS for Boys, St Catharine's Coll Cambridge (MA, MB); *m* 30 Sept 1972, June Elizabeth (Linda), da of George Syrnicki, of Buxton, Derbyshire; 2 s (Richard b 1976, Gareth b 1978), 1 da (Elizabeth b 1983); *Career* conslt rheumatologist Pilgrim Hosp Boston and Lincoln Acute Hosps 1982–; treas Lincolnshire Amateur Swimming Assoc, pres Lincoln Branch Arthritis and Rheumatism Cncl; FRCP 1993 (MRCP 1976); *Recreations* swimming; *Style—* Dr Bernard Hunt; ✉ Saddlers Mead, Northlands, Sibsey, Boston, Lincs (☎ 01205 750165)

HUNT, Brian Norman; s of Norman Frederick Hunt (d 1970), and Irene Olive, *née* Brimble; *b* 1 July 1936; *Educ* Yeovil Tech Sch Somerset; *m* 20 Feb 1960, Norah Ann, da of Edward William Haynes (d 1972); 2 s (Timothy Andrew b 1962, Stephen Christopher b 1965); *Career* Nat Serv photographer RAF 1956–58, apprenticed to H Tilzey (photographer) 1952–56, chief photographer Cranfield Inst of Technol (now Cranfield University) 1962–92 (joined as asst photographer 1958), mktg mangr Cranfield Press Cranfield Univ 1992–; pres Br Inst of Professional Photography 1979–80 (chm Industrial Ctee 1982–90); govr Salisbury Coll of Art 1984–; FRPS 1970 (memb 1967), FBIPP 1971 (memb 1958); *Recreations* charity work (chm church restoration appeal), caravanning, walking; *Style—* Brian Hunt, Esq; ✉ 16 Richmond Way, Newport Pagnell, Buckinghamshire MK16 0LF (☎ 01908 612875); Photography Department, Cranfield University, Cranfield, Bedford MK43 OAL (☎ 01234 754115, fax 01234 750875)

HUNT, Rt Hon David James Fletcher; PC (1990), MBE (1973), MP (C) Wirral W (majority 11,064); s of late Alan Hunt, OBE; *b* 21 May 1942; *Educ* Liverpool Coll, Montpellier Univ, Univ of Bristol, Guildford Coll of Law; *m* 1973, Patricia Margery (Paddy), *née* Orchard; 2 s, 2 da; *Career* slr; ptnr Stanley Wasbrough and Co 1965–77, ptnr Beachcroft Stanleys 1977– (sr ptnr 1996–); Parly candidate: Bristol S 1970, Kingswood 1974; chm YC Nat Advsy Ctee 1972–73, vice chm Nat Union of Cons and Unionist Assocs 1974–76, oppn spokesman on shipping 1977–79, vice chm Parly Youth Lobby 1978–80, pres Br Youth Cncl 1978–81 (chm 1971–74), chm Cons Gp for Europe 1981–82; MP (C) Wirral 1976–83, MP (C) Wirral W 1983–; PPS to: Trade Sec 1979–81, Def Sec 1981; jr Cons whip 1981–83, a Lord Cmmr of the Treasy (govt whip) 1983–84, vice chm Cons Party 1983–85, Parly under sec of state Dept of Energy 1984–87, treas HM Household (dep Govt chief whip) 1987–89, minister for Local Govt and InnerCities 1989–90, sec of state for Wales 1990–93, sec of state for Employment 1993–94, Chancellor of the Duchy of Lancaster (with responsibility for Science and the Citizen's Charter) 1994–95; pres Tory Reform Gp 1991–; *Clubs* Hurlingham; *Style—* The Rt Hon David Hunt, MBE, MP; ✉ Beachcroft Stanleys, 20 Furnival Street, London EC4A 1BN (☎ 0171 242 1011, fax 0171 430 1532)

HUNT, David Maitland; s of Bernard Wallis Hunt, and Doreen Margeret, *née* Shipp (d 1985); *b* 8 Aug 1948; *Educ* Radley, Guy's Hosp Med Sch London (MB BS); *m*; 2 s, 2 da; *Career* conslt orthopaedic surgn St Mary's Hosp 1983–; Oppenheimer travel award 1969, St Mary's Hosp short paper prize 1981 and 1982; memb: Orthopaedic Section RSM, BMA, Hunterian Soc, Br Orthopaedic Res Soc, Br Assoc for Surgery of the Knee, Br Children's Orthopaedic Soc, Med Defence Union; FRCS 1978, FRCSEd 1978, fell Br Orthopaedic Assoc; *Publications* Minimal Access Surgery (contrib chapters, ed R Rosin), Minimal Access Orthopaedics (ed), author of papers in various learned jls; *Recreations* fishing, sailing; *Clubs* RSM; *Style—* David M Hunt, Esq; ✉ 106 Harley St, London W1N 1AF (☎ 0171 935 6347, fax 0171 935 2788)

HUNT, David Malcolm; s of Albert Francis Hunt (d 1990) of Southgate, London, and Winifred Helena, *née* Pearce (d 1992); *b* 22 Dec 1941; *Educ* Owen's Sch, Univ of Warwick (MSc); *m* 24 Aug 1968, Betty, da of Maurice John Gifford Upchurch (d 1992), of Huntingdon; 3 s ((Jonathan) Mark b 5 Nov 1969, Patrick Simon b 26 March 1975, Wesley Paul (twin) b 26 March 1975); *Career* articled clerk Baker Sutton & Co 1961–68, auditor Arthur Andersen & Co 1968–70, Baker Sutton & Co 1971–75, ptnr and dir of communication Pannell Kerr Forster 1975–; visiting prof Nottingham Trent Univ; memb Cncl Univ of Warwick; non-exec memb Central Notts Healthcare (NHS) Tst; dir and tstee Family First Ltd; memb Cncl ICAEW; FCA (ACA 1966), FIPD 1979, FRSA 1992; *Publications* On-The-Job Training (ICAEW, 1980), Business Briefing: Doctors Accounts (ICAEW, with G Littlewood, 1984); *Recreations* squash, music, theatre, working for charities, watching cricket; *Style—* David Hunt, Esq; ✉ Pannell Kerr Forster Chartered Accountants, Regent House, Clinton Avenue, Nottingham NG5 1AZ (☎ 0115 960 8171, fax 0115 962 2229, car 0973 253578)

HUNT, David Roderic Notley; QC (1987); s of Dr Geoffrey Notley Hunt (d 1982), of Pembury, Kent, and Deborah Katharine Rosamund, *née* Clapham; *b* 22 June 1947; *Educ* Charterhouse, Trinity Coll Cambridge (MA); *m* 27 April 1974, Alison Connell, da of Lt-Col Arthur George Jelf (d 1958); 2 s (Thomas b 8 Feb 1976, Robert b 20 Feb 1979); *Career* called to the Bar Gray's Inn 1969, bencher Gray's Inn 1995; recorder 1991–; *Recreations* sailing, golf, skiing; *Clubs* Bewl Valley Sailing, Nevill Golf; *Style—* David Hunt, Esq, QC; ✉ 2 Hare Court, Temple, London EC4Y 7BH (☎ 0171 583 1770, fax 0171 583 9269)

HUNT, Sir David Wathen Stather; KCMG (1963, CMG 1959), OBE (1943); s of Rev Canon Bernard Hunt (d 1967), of Norwich, and Elizabeth, *née* Milner; *b* 25 Sept 1913; *Educ* St Lawrence Coll Ramsgate, Wadham Coll Oxford; *m* 1, 1948 (m dis 1967), Pamela Muriel, da of late Nicholas Medawar; 2 s; m 2, 1968, Iro, da of late John Myrianthousis; *Career* fell Magdalen Coll Oxford 1937; served WWII Welch Regt ME, Balkans, N Africa, Sicily and Italy; Col Gen Staff Allied Force HQ 1945–46, Hon Col 1947; joined CRO 1947, private sec to PM 1950–52, dep UK high cmmr Pakistan 1954–56 (asst under sec 1959), dep UK high cmmr Lagos 1960–62; high cmmr: Kampala 1962–65, Cyprus 1965–66, Nigeria 1967–69; ambass Brazil 1969–73; chm Govrs Cwlth Inst 1974–84; memb Appts Cmmn Press Cncl 1977–82, dir Observer Newspapers 1982–93, visiting prof of int rels Univ of Edinburgh 1980; winner TV Mastermind 1977 and Mastermind of Masterminds 1982; pres: Soc for Promotion of Hellenic Studies 1986–90, Soc for Preservation of Lindfield 1987–; DHum hc Ball State Univ Indiana 1991; US Bronze Star 1945, Grand Cross Order of Southern Cross Brazil 1985; *Publications* A Don at War (1966, revised edn 1990), On The Spot (1975), Footprints in Cyprus (ed 1982, revised and augmented edn 1990), Gothic Art and the Renaissance in Cyprus (1987), Caterina Cornaro, Queen of Cyprus (ed with Iro Hunt, 1989); *Clubs* Athenaeum, Beefsteak; *Style—* Sir David Hunt, KCMG, OBE; ✉ Old Place, Lindfield, W Sussex RH16 2HU (☎ 01444 482298, fax 01444 482742)

HUNT, Dr Donald Frederick; OBE (1993); s of Albert Edward Hunt (d 1964), of Gloucester, and Dorothy, *née* Dixon (d 1959); *b* 26 July 1930; *Educ* King's Sch Gloucester; *m* 24 July 1954, Josephine Ann, da of Jack Benbow (d 1977), of Gloucester; 2 s (Thomas Christopher b 1957, Nicolas William b 1960), 2 da (Jacqueline Ann b 1955, Jane Elizabeth b 1958); *Career* asst organist Gloucester Cathedral 1948–53; dir of music: St John's Torquay 1953–56, Leeds Parish Church 1956–75; conductor: Halifax Choral Soc 1956–88, Leeds Philharmonic Soc 1962–75; chorus dir Leeds Festival 1962–75, Leeds City organist 1972–75, organist and master of the choristers Worcester Cathedral 1975–96; conductor Worcester Festival Choral Soc 1975–, conductor and artistic dir Worcester Three Choirs Festival 1975–96, artistic dir Bromsgrove Festival 1981–91; tstee and dir The Elgar Fndn; Hon DMus Univ of Leeds 1975; ARCM 1950, FRCO 1951; *Books* S S Wesley - Cathedral Musician (1990); *Recreations* literature, travel, sport (especially cricket); *Style—* Dr Donald Hunt, OBE; ✉ c/o 43 Park Avenue, Worcester WR3 7AJ (☎ 01905 24067)

HUNT, Dr Eric Millman; s of Arthur Millman Hunt (d 1951), and Irene Olive Cordwell (d 1981); *b* 30 April 1923; *Educ* Marling Sch Stroud, Univ of Leeds (BSc, PhD), UCL (Dip Chem Eng); *m* 1, 14 Dec 1957 (m dis 1971), Eve Sangster; 1 s (Trevor b 1959), 1 da (Cynthia b 1962); m 2, 15 July 1974, Phyllis Mary Charteris, da of Capt James Charteris Burleigh (d 1954); 1 s (Andrew b 1975), 1 da (Katrina b 1977); *Career* chief exec Akzo Chemicals Ltd 1967–81, chm Thomas Swan & Co Ltd 1982–, memb Merton and Sutton Health Authy 1990–94; treas Plastics and Rubber Inst 1983–91 (chm 1981–83); chm N W Wimbledon Res Assoc 1982–88, vice chm Wimbledon Union of Res Assocs 1989–, vice chm Wimbledon Guild of Social Welfare 1992–; memb Ct Univ of Surrey 1984–92, memb Cncl Inst of Materials 1992–93; Freeman City of London 1965, Master Worshipful Co of Horners 1994 (Liveryman 1965, Clerk 1982–91); FRSC, FIChemE, FIM, FInstD; *Style—* Dr Eric M Hunt; ✉ 37 Drax Avenue, Wimbledon, London SW20 0EQ (☎ 0181 946 9767)

HUNT, (Henry) Holman; CBE (1988); s of Henry Hunt (d 1951); *b* 13 May 1924; *Educ* Queen's Park Sch Glasgow, Univ of Glasgow (MA); *m* 1954, Sonja, *née* Blom; 1 s, 2 da; *Career* bd dir PA Consulting Group (formerly PA Management Consultants Ltd) 1970–83, md PA Computers and Telecommunications 1976–83; dep chm MMC 1985–91 (memb 1980–91), pres Inst of Mgmnt Consits 1974–75; *Recreations* music, reading, walking, travel, photography; *Clubs* Caledonian; *Style*— Holman Hunt, Esq, CBE; ✉ 28 The Ridings, Epsom, Surrey KT18 5JJ (☎ 01372 720974)

HUNT, (Patrick) James; QC (1987); s of Thomas Ronald Clifford Hunt, and Doreen Gwyneth Katarina, *née* Granville-George; *b* 26 Jan 1943; *Educ* Ashby de la Zouch Boys GS, Keble Coll Oxford (MA); *m* 20 July 1969, Susan Jennifer Goodhead, JP, da of Noel Allen Goodhead, of Swadlincote; 1 s (Thomas Miles Benjamin b 1973), 3 da (Victoria Katharine b 1971, Suzanna Elisabeth b 1980, Alexandra Emily b 1982); *Career* called to the Bar Gray's Inn 1968, Master of the Bench 1994–; recorder of the Crown Ct 1982–, head of chambers 36 Bedford Row 1991–; memb Gen Cncl of the Bar 1989–92, legal assessor to Disciplinary Ctee Royal Coll of Vet Surgns 1990–, ldr Midland & Oxford Circuit 1996– (dep ldr 1992–96), dep judge of the High Ct 1995–; defence counsel in Matrix Churchill case 1992 and R v Beverley Allitt 1993; *Recreations* singing, tennis, stonework; *Clubs* RAC, Northants County, Notts United Services; *Style*— James Hunt, QC; ✉ Easton Hall, Easton on the Hill, Stamford, Lincs PE9 3LL; 36 Bedford Row, London WC1R 4JH (☎ 0171 421 8000, fax 0171 421 8080)

HUNT, John Brian; s of Peter Douglas Hunt, of Croxley Green, Herts, and Cynthia Mary, *née* Weatherilt; *b* 19 April 1951; *Educ* Rickmansworth GS, Harlow Tech Coll, Open Univ (BA); *m* 7 Feb 1986, Christine Elizabeth, da of Ronald Arthur Curl; 1 step s (Dean Keith Halls b 18 Feb 1970), 1 step da (Candice Margaret Halls b 30 Nov 1971); *Career* trainee journalist Doncaster Newspapers 1970–73, Sheffield Morning Telegraph 1973–79, dep chief sub ed Oracle Teletext 1979–84, scriptwriter and dep news ed 1984–89, sr news ed Channel Four News 1989–95, resource mangr ITN 1995–; memb NUJ Nat Exec 1979, vice chm NUJ Broadcasting Industl Cncl 1988–89, chm ITN Jt Shops' Ctee 1989–93, tstee ITN Pension Fund 1989–95; *Recreations* cricket, football, photography, travel; *Clubs* Watford FC; *Style*— John Hunt, Esq; ✉ Derlee House, East Lane, Bedmond, Herts WD5 0QG; ITN, 200 Gray's Inn Rd, London WC1X 8XZ (☎ 0171 833 3000)

HUNT, Baron (Life Peer UK 1966), of Llanfairwaterdine, Co Salop; Sir (Henry Cecil) John Hunt; KG (1979), kt (1953), CBE (1945), DSO (1944); s of Capt Cecil Edwin Hunt, MC (d 1914), and Ethel Helen, *née* Crookshank; *b* 22 June 1910; *Educ* Marlborough, Sandhurst; *m* 3 Sept 1936, Joy, da of Dr Mowbray-Green; 4 da (Sally, Susan, Prudence, Jennifer); *Career* Sits as Lib Dem Peer in House of Lords; ldr Br Expedition to Mt Everest 1952–53; cmd 11 KRRC in Italy and Middle East 1943–44 and 11 Indian Inf Brigade in Italy and Greece 1944–46, Indian Police Medal 1940; post-war as GSOI ME Land Forces and as GSOI Col GS ALF Central Europe, HQ (1) Br Corps, Asst Cmdt Staff Coll 1953–55, Cdr 168 Inf Bde TA 1955–56; rector Aberdeen Univ 1963–66; advsr to PM during Nigerian Civil War 1968–70; memb Royal Cmmn on Press 1973–77; chm: Inquiry into Police in NI 1969, Parole Bd England and Wales 1967–73, Intermediate Treatment Ctee 1980–85; past pres: Alpine Club, Climbers' Club, Br Mountaineering Cncl, Nat Ski Fedn, Nat Assoc of Probation Offrs, Cncl for Volunteers Overseas, Rainer Fndn; pres: RGS 1977–80, Cncl Nat Parks 1980–86; Hon DCL Univ of Durham 1954; Hon LLD: Univ of Aberdeen 1954, Univ of London 1954, City Univ 1976, Univ of Leeds 1979; Hon DSc Univ of Sheffield 1989; *Style*— The Rt Hon the Lord Hunt, KG, CBE, DSO; ✉ Highway Cottage, Aston, Henley-on-Thames, Oxon

HUNT, Sir John Leonard; kt (1989), MP (C) Ravensbourne (majority 19,714); s of William John Hunt (d 1968), of Keston, Kent, and Dora Maud Hunt (d 1991); *b* 27 Oct 1929; *Educ* Dulwich; *Career* Bromley Borough Cncl: memb 1953–65, alderman 1961–65, mayor 1963–64; memb London Stock Exchange 1958–69; Parly candidate (C) Lewisham South 1959; MP (C): Bromley 1964–74, Ravensbourne 1974–; memb: Gen Advsy Cncl BBC 1975–87, Select Ctee on Home Affrs 1979–87 (memb Chm's Panel 1980–); jt pres Indo-British Parly Gp, memb UK Delgn to Cncl of Europe and Western Euro Union 1974–77 and 1988–; *Style*— Sir John Hunt, MP; ✉ House of Commons, London, SW1A 0AA

HUNT, John Michael Graham; s of Robert Graham Hunt, and Patricia Hunt (d 1989); *b* 5 Feb 1942, Torquay, Devon; *Educ* Mill Hill Sch London, Guy's Hosp Dental Sch Univ of London (BDS, LDS RCSEng); *m* Jill Mason, *née* Williams; 2 da (Jemma Lucy b 1 Oct 1969, Annabel Jane b 15 Sept 1971), 1 s (Edward Oliver Graham b 12 Aug 1976); *Career* resident dental house surgn Guy's Hosp 1965–66, clinical dental fell Eastman Dental Center Rochester NY (awarded Fulbright travelling scholarship) 1966–67, registrar in conservative dentistry London Hosp Dental Inst 1967–68, pt/t lectr in oral surgery London Hosp and pt/t in practice S London 1968–70, gen dental practice Torquay Devon 1970–80, clinical dental surgn The Prince Philip Dental Hosp Univ of Hong Kong 1980–84, dental reference offr DHSS 1984–88, dental offr Dept of Health (on secondment from Dental Reference Serv to Dental Div) 1988–89, sr dental offr Dental Div Dept of Health 1989, hon lectr Dept of Child Dental Health London Hosp Med Coll 1989; chief exec BDA (former chm and sec Torquay Section, former sec Western Counties Branch, memb Gen Dental Servs Ctee); memb: Br Assoc for the Study of Community Dentistry, Br Soc of Paediatric Dentistry, Br Soc for Restorative Dentistry; *Recreations* squash, sailing, hill walking, skiing; *Clubs* RSM; *Style*— John Hunt, Esq; ✉ Chief Executive, British Dental Association, 64 Wimpole Street, London W1M 8AL (☎ 0171 935 0875, fax 0171 487 5232)

HUNT, Jonathan Charles Vivian; OBE (1983), TD (1977, 3 clasps 1983, 1990 and 1994), DL (S Yorks 1981); s of Col George Vivian Hunt, OBE, TD (d 1979), and Sylvia Ann, *née* Tyzack (d 1985); *b* 6 March 1943; *Educ* Stowe; *m* 17 July 1971, Susan Aline, eld da of Francis Rawdon Crozier, of Thorpell House, Wickham Market, Woodbridge, Suffolk; 2 s (James b 14 Sept 1973, Edward 6 June 1976); *Career* TA: cmmnd Queen's Own Yorks Yeo 1963, transfd B (Sherwood Rangers Yeo) Sqdn Royal Yeo (OC 1975–78), cmd Royal Yeo 1979–82, Dep Cdr 49 Inf Bde 1983–87, Project Offr Fast Track (new TA compact commissioning course) 1987–91; TA Col RMA Sandhurst 1988–91, TA Col Ind Units MOD 1991–92, TA Col (Combat Arms) HQ UKLF 1992–95, Hon Col Sherwood Rangers Yeo 1994–; sr ptnr Wake Smith & Co Slrs Sheffield 1988– (ptnr 1967), dir Sheffield Training and Enterprise Cncl 1990–; chm: Sheffield Enterprise Agency Ltd 1986–, Rotherham Rural Div SSAFA; memb Law Soc 1966; *Recreations* sailing, walking, golf, TA; *Clubs* Sheffield, Lindrick Golf, Cavalry and Guards'; *Style*— Jonathan C V Hunt, Esq, OBE, TD, DL; ✉ Wake Smith & Co, 68 Clarkehouse Road, Sheffield S10 2LJ (☎ 0114 266 6660)

HUNT, Prof Julian Charles Roland; s of Roland Charles Colin Hunt, CMG, of London SE11, and Pauline, *née* Garnett (d 1989); *b* 5 Sept 1941; *Educ* Westminster, Trinity Coll Cambridge (BA, PhD); *Career* res offr Fluid Dynamics Section Central Electricity Res Laboratories 1968–70; Univ of Cambridge: lectr in applied mathematics and engrg 1970–78, reader in fluid mechanics 1978, prof of fluid mechanics 1980–; chief exec Meteorological Office 1992–; pt/t lectr in fluid mechanics Lanchester Coll of Technol 1965, visiting lectr Univ of Cape Town SA 1967, res assoc Dept of Theoretical and Applied Mechanics Cornell Univ Ithaca NY 1967, teaching fell Trinity Coll Cambridge 1970 (res fell 1966), visiting prof Dept of Civil Engrg Colorado State Univ 1975, visiting assoc prof Dept of Geosciences N Carolina State Univ 1977–79, asst (later assoc) ed Jl of Fluid Mechanics 1978, visiting scientist CIRES Univ of Colarado Boulder Colorado 1980–86, memb UK Atmospheric Dispersion Working Gp 1980, visiting scientist Nat Center for Atmospheric Res Boulder Colorado 1983; Inst of Mathematics and its Applications: chm Environmental Mathematics Gp 1978, hon sec and chm Prog Ctee and memb Cncl Fin and Gen Purposes Ctees 1983–, memb Prog Ctee of Int Congress of Industl and Applied Mathematics 1986–, pres 1993–95; visiting lectr and res advsr Indian Inst of Technol Delhi 1984 and 1986, chm Turbulence Sub-Ctee Euro Mechanics Ctee 1984–92, memb Advsy Panel on Environmental Res Central Electricity Generating Bd 1985–91, visiting scientist Stanford Univ and NASA Ames 1987–90, gen sec Euro Res Community for Flow Turbulence and Combustion 1988 (chm Steering Ctee 1987–88), visiting scientist Japanese Soc for Visiting Scholars 1988; cncllr Cambridge City Cncl 1971–74 (ldr Lab Gp 1972–73); govr Chesterton Secdy Sch 1971–85 (chm 1979–85); dir Cambridge Environmental Resource Consultants Ltd 1986–91; FRS 1989; *Style*— Prof Julian Hunt, FRS; ✉ Meteorological Office, London Road, Bracknell, Berkshire RG12 2SZ (☎ 01344 854600)

HUNT, Brig Kenneth; OBE (1955), MC (1943); s of John Hunt (d 1952), and Elizabeth, *née* Sills (d 1974); *b* 26 May 1914; *Educ* Chatham House Sch Ramsgate, Army Staff Coll Camberley, IDC; *m* 28 Jan 1939, Mary Mabel (d 1995), da of Charles Crickett (d 1962); 2 s (Timothy John Leigh b 30 July 1949, Jeremy Peter b 25 Sept 1950), 1 da (Sarah Elizabeth b and d 1948); *Career* cmmnd RA 1940, Africa, Italy, Austria with HAC, 1 RHA and 2 RHA 1942–46, Brevet Lt-Col 1955, CO 40 FD Regt 1958–60, Brig and CRA 51 Highland Div 1961–63, dep standing gp rep NATO Cncl 1964–66, resigned from Army 1967; specialist advsr House of Commons Defence Ctee 1971–84, dir Br Atlantic Ctee 1978–81; visiting prof: Fletcher Sch of Law Cambridge Mass 1975, Univ of Surrey 1978–86, Univ of Southern Calif 1979; res assoc Inst for Peace and Security Tokyo 1979–88, vice pres Int Inst for Strategic Studies 1988 (dep dir 1967–77); Freeman City of London 1977; Hon Dr political sci Korea Univ S Korea 1977; Order of the Rising Sun Japan 1984; *Books* The Third World War (jtly, 1978), Europe in the Western Alliance (ed, 1988); *Recreations* fly fishing; *Clubs* Army and Navy; *Style*— Brig Kenneth Hunt, OBE, MC; ✉ 6 Canal Walk, Hungerford, Berkshire RG17 0EQ (☎ 01488 683996); International Institute for Strategic Studies, 23 Tavistock Street, London WC2E 7NQ (☎ 0171 379 7676)

HUNT, Maj-Gen Malcolm Peter John; OBE (1984); s of Peter Gordon Hunt, of Putney, London, and Rachel Margaret, *née* Owston; *b* 19 Nov 1938; *Educ* St John's Sch Leatherhead Surrey; *m* 22 Dec 1962, Margaret (d 1996), da of Samuel Beadman Peat (d 1966); 2 s (James b 3 Dec 1964, John b 14 Dec 1966); *Career* joined RM 1957, 45 Commando RM 1960–61 Malta, Aden, HMS Nubian 1966–68, Army Staff Coll Camberley 1971, Staff HQ 3 Commando Bde 1971–74, instr Army Staff Coll 1979–81, CO 40 Commando RM 1981–83 Falklands and NI, HQ NATO 1984–87, MOD 1987–90, Cdr British Forces Falkland Islands 1990–91; exec dir National Back Pain Assoc 1993–94, gen sec Assoc of British Dispensing Opticians 1995–; memb Metropolitan Police Ctee 1995–; govr St John's Sch Leatherhead 1993–; FRSA 1993; *Recreations* reading, theatre, politics, all sport; *Style*— Maj-Gen Malcolm Hunt, OBE; ✉ 20 Kent Road, East Molesey, Surrey KT8 9JZ

HUNT, Maurice William; s of Maurice Hunt (d 1987), of London, and Helen, *née* Andrews; *b* 30 Aug 1936; *Educ* Selhurst GS Croydon Surrey, LSE (BSc); *m* 27 Aug 1960, Jean Mary, da of Herbert Ellis (d 1940); 1 s (Neil b 1965), 1 da (Claire b 1966); *Career* Nat Serv RAF 1955–57; ANZ Bank London 1953–66, Jt Iron Cncl 1967, Bd of Trade DTI 1968–84, RCDS 1982; CBI: dir of membership 1984, sec 1986–, exec dir (ops) 1987, dep dir gen 1989–; dir Pool Reinsurance Co Ltd; *Style*— Maurice Hunt, Esq; ✉ 24 Fairford Close, Haywards Heath, W Sussex RH16 3EF (☎ 01444 452916); Centre Point, New Oxford St, London WC1A IDU (☎ 0171 379 7400, fax 0171 240 1578, telex 21332)

HUNT, Adm Sir Nicholas John Streynsham; GCB (1987, KCB 1985), LVO (1961), DL (Surrey 1996); s of Brig John Montgomerie Hunt (d 1980), of Godalming, Surrey, and Elizabeth, *née* Yates; *b* 7 Nov 1930; *Educ* RNC Dartmouth; *m* 1966, Meriel Eve, da of Maj and Mrs Henry Cooke Givan; 2 s, 1 da; *Career* exec offr HMS Ark Royal 1969–71, RCDS 1974, dir of Naval Plans 1976–78, Flag Offr 2 Flotilla 1980–81, DG Naval Manpower and Trg 1981–83, Flag Offr Scot and NI 1983–85, C-in-C Fleet, Allied C-in-C Channel, C-in-C East Atlantic Area 1985–87; Rear Admiral of the United Kingdom; sometime asst private sec to HRH Princess Marina, Duchess of Kent; dep md (orgn and devpt) Eurotunnel 1987–89; dir-gen Chamber of Shipping 1991–; pres The Royal Naval Benevolent Soc 1995–; vice pres English Speaking Union of Malta; Liveryman Worshipful Co of Shipwrights; CIMgt; *Clubs* Boodle's; *Style*— Adm Sir Nicholas Hunt, GCB, LVO, DL; ✉ Chamber of Shipping, Carthusian Court, 12 Carthusian Street, London EC1M 6EB (☎ 0171 417 8400)

HUNT, (David) Peter; *b* 25 April 1951; *Educ* Grangefield GS Stockton, Keble Coll Oxford (MA); *m* 1 June 1984, Cherryl Janet, da of Alexander Hubert Nicholson, of Pinner, Middx; 2 s (James b 1985, Nicholas b 1987); *Career* called to the Bar Gray's Inn 1974; memb Bar Cncl 1981–84, jr NE circuit 1982, recorder 1993–; *Books* Distribution of Matrimonial Assets on Divorce (1990); *Style*— Peter Hunt, Esq; ✉ 25 Park Square, Leeds LS1 2PW (fax 0113 242 0194)

HUNT, Peter Roland; s of Roland George Hunt (d 1974), and Violet Hunt; *Educ* Taunton's Sch Southampton; *m* 1955, Mary Elizabeth, da of late Arthur Douglas Davis; 1 s (Roger Ian b 1958); *Career* successively reporter, feature writer then air reporter Southern Daily Echo Southampton 1944–53; Nat Serv RAF India/UK 1945–48; account exec John Webb Press Services London 1954–55, PR mangr Downtons Ltd Fleet St 1955–58; The Coca-Cola Company: joined Coca-Cola Export Corp London as PR mangr UK and Ireland 1958, subsequently head of PR Coca-Cola Northern Europe, dir of PR Coca-Cola Europe, dir of public affrs Coca-Cola Northwest Europe, exec asst to the Pres and dir of Govt and indust affrs, external affrs advsr Coca-Cola Great Britain and Ireland 1988–; co-fndr Dolphin Trophy Learn to Swim Awards Scheme (sponsored by Coca-Cola GB) 1963, author of first research paper on sports sponsorship for IPR 1966, recipient Olympic medal (awarded by Pres of Austria for originating The Coca-Cola Co's film Olympic Harmony) 1976, memb Ctee of Enquiry into Sports Sponsorship for CCPR (The Howell Report) 1981–83; IPR: chm Int Ctee 1974–77, pres IPR 1978, chm Benevolent Fund Tstees 1992–, chm Fellows' Forum Working Pty 1994–, memb Govt Affrs Gp and Mind Link; BSDA: memb Exec Cncl and Bd 1987–95, chm PR Ctee 1987–, pres BSDA 1988–90, chm Publishing Panel 1993–, memb Europe Gp until 1995, hon life memb 1996; tstee The Soft Drinks Indust Benevolent Soc 1987–; Union of Euro Soft Drinks Assocs (UNESDA) Brussels: memb Nominations Ctee 1990, vice chm Communications Ctee 1991–95; fndr and chm Civil Serv/Indust Network Dinner Prog (sponsored by Coca-Cola GB) 1982–; memb: Mgmnt Ctee and Cncl Indust Cncl for Packaging and the Environment 1983–88, Food and Drink Fedn Key Issues Forum 1992–96; Tree Cncl: memb Fin and Gen Purposes Ctee 1990–, memb Funding Review Ctee 1992–; memb: Charing Cross Club 1975–, Caxton Gp (co-fndr 1984), Strategic Planning Soc (Govt affrs gp); MCAM (dipCAM), FIPR 1977 (MIPR 1959); *Recreations* family, home, garden, photography, sketching, social history of writing and writing equipment; *Clubs* Travellers'; *Style*— Peter R Hunt, Esq; ✉ Quarr Cottage, 14 Woodside Road, New Malden, Surrey KT3 3AH (☎ 0181 942 7430)

HUNT, Philip Alexander; OBE; *b* 19 May 1949; *Educ* City of Oxford HS, Univ of Leeds (BA); *m* 1, 1974 (m dis); 1 da; m 2, 1988, Selina Ruth Helen, *née* Stewart; 3 s, 1 da; *Career* catering asst Mount Newman W Aust 1971–72, work study offr Oxford RHB 1972–74, hosp admin Nuffield Orthopaedic Centre 1974–75, sec Edgware/Hendon Community Health Centre 1975–78; National Association of Health Authorities: asst sec 1978–79, asst dir 1979–84, dir 1984–90; dir National Association of Health Authorities and Trusts 1990–; co-chair Assoc for Public Health 1994– (memb Cncl 1992–94); memb: Oxford City Cncl 1973–79, Oxon area Health Authy 1975–77, Bd Volunteer Centre

1979–83, Birmingham City Cncl 1980–82, Home Office Devpt Gp on Voluntary Action 1980–82, Cncl Flouridation Soc 1981–93, Nat Advsy Ctee World Assembly on Ageing 1981–83, Cncl Int Hosp Fedn 1986–91, NHS Exec Advsy Gp on Patient's Charter 1992–93, Working Gp on Induction and Devpt of Chm and Bd Dirs NHS Exec 1993–94, Rail Users' Consultative Ctee (Midlands) 1994, External Advsy Study of Probity in the NHS Audit Cmmn 1994, Public Policy Advsy Bd Queen Mary & Westfield Coll London 1996–; MHSM; *Publications* The Authority Member (with W E Hall, 1978), various articles in Health Service pubns, The Quango Debate (contrib); *Recreations* City of Birmingham Symphony Orchestra, cycling, swimming and football (Birmingham City); *Style—* Philip Hunt, Esq; ✉ National Association of Health Authorities and Trusts, Birmingham Research Park, Vincent Drive, Birmingham B15 2SQ (☎ 0121 471 4444, fax 0121 414 1120)

HUNT, Sir Rex Masterman; kt (1982), CMG (1980); s of Henry William Hunt (d 1982), of Burnham, Bucks, and Ivy, *née* Masterman; *b* 29 June 1926; *Educ* Coatham Sch, St Peter's Coll Oxford (BA); *m* 22 Sept 1951, Mavis Amanda, da of George Arthur Buckland, MM, of Chingford, Essex; 1 s (Antony Paul Masterman b 29 June 1964), 1 da (Diana Molly Amanda (Mrs Thurman) b 2 May 1962); *Career* RAF 1944–48, Fighter Pilot Nos 5 and 26 Sqdns, Flt Lt; Hon Air Cdre RAuxAF No 2729 (City of Lincoln) Sqdn; Overseas Civil Service 1951: dist cmmr Uganda 1962, CRO 1963–64, first sec Kuching (Sarawak) 1964–65, Jesselton (Sabah) 1965–67, Brunei 1967, first sec (economic) Ankara 1968–70, first sec and head of Chancery Jakarta 1970–72, M East Dept FCO 1972–74, cnsllr Saigon 1974–75, cnsllr Kuala Lumpur 1976–77, dep high cmmr 1977–79, high cmmr Br Antarctic Territory 1980–85, govr and C-in-C Falkland Islands 1980–82, temporarily forced to evacuate Islands owing to Argentinian invasion in April 1982, returned June 1982 as civil cmmr (govr 1985); chm Falkland Islands Assoc, vice pres Falkland Conservation; chm Shackleton Scholarship Fund, dep chm Desire Petroleum; Freeman of City of London 1979, Freedom of Stanley (Falkland Islands) 1985; *Books* My Falkland Days (1992); *Recreations* golf, gardening; *Clubs* Wentworth; *Style—* Sir Rex Hunt, CMG; ✉ Old Woodside, Broomfield Park, Sunningdale, Berks SL5 0JS

HUNT, Richard Bruce; s of late Percy Thompson Hunt; *b* 15 Dec 1927; *Educ* Christ's Hosp; *m* 1972, Ulrike Dorothea, *née* Schmidt; 2 da; *Career* md R B Hunt and Ptnrs Ltd 1966–95, dir Baltic Exchange 1977–80 (re-elected 1981, chm 1985–87), dep chm Howe Robinson & Co Ltd 1990–, chm B and K Topfit Ltd 1992–95; govr Christ's Hosp 1980–; Liveryman Worshipful Co of Shipwrights 1980; FICS 1955; *Recreations* golf, skiing; *Clubs* Royal Lymington Yacht, Royal Wimbledon Golf; *Style—* Richard Hunt, Esq; ✉ 77 Mansell Street, London E1 8AF

HUNT, Robert Alan; OBE (1984), QPM (1991); s of Peter Hunt (d 1972), and Minnie Hunt (d 1979); *b* 6 July 1935; *Educ* Dulwich Coll, Univ of London (LLB (external)); *m* Feb 1956, Jean Kathleen, da of John White (ka 1945); 3 da (Gay b 29 Jan 1957, Sharon b 31 July 1959, Tracey b 10 Aug 1962), 1 s (Murray b 29 Sept 1965); *Career* Nat Serv RA 1953–55; Met Police: joined 1955, subsequently 5 years at Brixton, then Sergeant and Inspr at Balham, Lewisham, Tooting and Wandsworth Common Police Stations, Chief Inspr Brixton and Streatham, Chief Inspr then Supt Community Rels Branch New Scotland Yard, Supt Peckham then Chief Supt Marylebone Lane and Paddington Green, Cdr M (Southwark), L (Lambeth), and H (Tower Hamlets) Districts for 5 years 1976–81 (also i/c Public Order Branch and Force Inspectorate), Dep Asst Cmmr 1981, took charge Serv Trg then 4 Area 1982–87, Met Police Serv Inspectorate 1987–89, Territorial (Ops) Dept 1989–95, Asst Cmmr Police Territorial (Ops) Dept 1990–95, ret; *Recreations* family, reading, music, walking; *Style—* Robert Hunt, Esq, OBE, QPM; ✉ c/o Metropolitan Police Service, New Scotland Yard, The Broadway, London SW1H 0BG

HUNT, Sir Robert Frederick; kt (1979), CBE (1974), DL (Glos 1977); s of Arthur Hunt, of Cheltenham; *b* 11 May 1918; *Educ* Pates GS Cheltenham, N Glos Tech Coll; *m* 1947, Joy (d 1984), da of Charles Harding; 4 da (of whom Jacqueline m Peter Heywood, *qv*); m 2, 1987, Joyce Baigent, da of Otto Leiske; *Career* WWII RAF Trg Cmd; joined Dowty Equipment as apprentice 1935; Dowty Gp: dir 1956–86, dep chm 1959–75, chief exec 1975–83, chm 1975–86; dir: Dowty Equipment of Canada 1949–86 (pres 1954–76, chm 1973–86), BL 1980–88 (dep chm 1982–88), Eagle Star Insur 1980–88, Dellfield Ltd 1983–86, Charter Consolidated 1983–; chm: Gp Mgmnt Ctee Cheltenham Hosp 1959–74, Glos AHA 1974–81; Liveryman Worshipful Co of Coachmakers & Coach Harness Makers; Hon DSc Bath, Hon FRAeS; FEng 1982, FCASI; *Style—* Sir Robert Hunt, CBE, DL, FEng; ✉ Maple House, Withington, Glos GL54 4DA (☎ 01242 890344)

HUNT, Simon Hugh d'Aquilar; s of Prof Hugh Hunt, CBE, of Criccieth, Gwynedd, and Janet Mary, *née* Gordon; *b* 4 Jan 1948; *Educ* Cranbrook Sch Australia, Abbotsholme Sch Staffs, Univ of Manchester (BA, post grad dip); *m* Anne, *née* Please; *Career* asst keeper Salford Museum and Art Gall 1972–73, sr curator Royal Albert Meml Museum Exeter 1975–78 (curator of decorative art 1973–75), curator Bath Museum Serv 1978–83, curator and asst dir of leisure Bath 1983–88, dir Area Museum Cncl for the SW 1988–; sec Bath Archaeological Trust 1978–88; memb Somerset Archaeology and Natural History Soc, memb Wessex Regnl Ctee Nat Trust, memb Bd Museum Documentation Assoc, dir Morwellham Quay and Tamar Valley Trust; FMA; *Books* Bath Camera (1987), West Country Silversmiths (1977); *Recreations* fly fishing, sketching, walking; *Style—* Simon Hunt, Esq; ✉ Longstone, Holford, Somerset TA5 1RZ (☎ 01278 741345); Area Museum Council for the South West, Hestercombe House, Cheddon Fitzpaine, Taunton, Somerset TA2 8LQ (☎ 01823 259696, fax 01823 413114)

HUNT, Terence William (Terry); s of William Herbert Hunt, (d 1983), and Audrey, *née* Austen; *b* 8 June 1955; *Educ* Royal Liberty GS, UEA (BA); *Career* teacher N Africa 1977–78, graduate trainee Macmillan Publishers 1978–79, copywriter Smith Bundy Partners 1979–83, bd dir DDM Advertising 1986 (creative dir 1983–86), chm Evans Hunt Scott 1990 (founding ptnr 1986); Ctee Memb Direct Mktg Assoc (UK); winner: over 43 creative and mktg awards, Most Creative Direct Marketer Campaign Poll 1989, Direct Marketer of the Year nomination 1996; *Books* Nationwide Book of Literary Quizzes (1979); *Recreations* family, sailing, running, collecting books; *Clubs* Groucho, Colony Rooms, Blacks; *Style—* Terry Hunt, Esq; ✉ 11 Granard Rd, London SW12 8UJ; Evans Hunt Scott, 7 Soho Square, W1V 6EH (☎ 0171 878 2600, fax 0171 439 0096)

HUNT, Terry; CBE (1996); s of Thomas John Hunt (d 1976), of Taunton, Somerset, and Marie Louise, *née* Potter; *b* 8 Aug 1943; *Educ* Huish's GS Taunton; *m* 7 Jan 1967, Wendy Graeme, da of Dr Aldwyn Morgan George, MC, of Perranwell Cornwall; 1 s (Philip Benjamin (Ben) b 1968), 1 da (Nicola Jane b 1969); *Career* hosp admin: Tone Vale Hosp 1963–65, NE Somerset Hosps 1965–67, Winchester Hosps 1967–69, Lincoln Co Hosp 1969–70; hosp sec Wycombe Gen Hosp 1970–73, dep gp sec Hillingdon Hosps 1973–74, area gen admin Kensington & Chelsea and Westminster AHA (T) 1974–76, dist admin NW Kensington & Chelsea and Westminster 1976–82, dist admin Paddington & N Kensington Health Authy 1982–84; gen mangr NE Thames RHA 1984–91; nat dir NHS Supplies Authy 1991– (chief exec 1996–); memb: Cncl of Govrs The London Hosp Med Coll 1985–91, Cncl UCL 1985–91, Steering Gp on Undergraduate Med and Dental Educn and Res 1987–91, Med Ctee Universities Funding Cncl 1989–93, Hosp Ctee of the EEC 1991–93, NHS Central R & D Ctee 1991–; memb: Twyford & Dist Round Table 1975–84 (chm 1980–81, pres 1988), Ctee Reading Town Regatta 1983– (treas 1984–86, chm 1989–); memb Inst of Health Serv Mgmnt; CIMgt; *Recreations* sculling, rowing, cycling; *Style—* Terry Hunt, Esq, CBE; ✉ NHS Supplies Authority, Apex Plaza, Forbury Road, Reading, Berks RG1 1AX (☎ 0118 959 5085, fax 0118 956 7667)

HUNT, Dr (Richard) Timothy (Tim); s of Richard Hunt (d 1979), and Kit, *née* Rowland (d 1977); *b* 19 Feb 1943; *Educ* Dragon Sch Oxford, Magdalen Coll Sch Oxford, Clare Coll Cambridge (MA, PhD); *m* Dr Mary Collins; 1 da (Celia Daisy b 27 Nov 1994); *Career* postdoctoral fell Dept of Med Albert Einstein Coll of Med 1968–70; Dept of Biochemistry Univ of Cambridge: joined as research fell 1971, Beit meml fell 1972–75, MRC sr asst in research 1975–76, Royal Soc research fell 1976–81, univ lectr 1981–90; Clare Hall Cambridge: research fell 1967–74, official fell 1975–, princ scientist ICRF Clare Hall Labs South Mimms 1991–; jr proctor Univ of Cambridge 1982–83; summer course instr Marine Biological Lab Woods Hole USA: in embryology 1977 and 1979, in physiology 1980–83; memb: EMBO Fund Ctee 1990–94, Cncl John Innes Inst 1991–93, BBSRC Cell and Molecular Biology Panel 1995–, Scientific Advsy Bd IMP Vienna 1995–, Cncl Royal Soc 1996–; author of numerous articles in learned jls; memb Editorial Bds: Trends in Biochemical Scis (ed-in-chief), Cell, Jl of Cell Sci, Molecular Biology of the Cell, Genes to Cells; Abraham White Scientific Achievement Award George Washington Univ Dept of Biochemistry and Molecular Biology Washington DC 1993, Nina C Werblow lecture Cornell Univ Med Coll NY 1993; memb EMBO 1979, FRS 1991; *Style—* Dr Tim Hunt, FRS; ✉ ICRF Clare Hall Laboratories, South Mimms, Herts EN6 3LD (☎ 0171 269 3981, fax 0171 269 3804, e-mail tim.hunt@icrf.icnet.uk)

HUNT-DAVIS, Brig Miles Garth; CBE (1990, MBE 1977); s of Lt-Col Eric Hunt Davis, OBE, ED (d 1977), of Johannesburg, SA, and Mary Eleanor, *née* Boyce (d 1964); *b* 7 Nov 1938; *Educ* St Andrew's Coll Grahamstown SA; *m* 11 Jan 1965, (Anita) Gay, da of Francis James Ridsdale, of SA; 2 s (Justin b 11 Sept 1970, Benedict b 15 March 1972), 1 da (Joanna b 2 Jun 1968); *Career* cmmnd 6 Queen Elizabeth's Own Gurkha Rifles 1962, active serv Borneo and Malaya 1964–66, student Canadian Land Forces Cmd and Staff Coll 1969–70, Brig Maj 48 Gurkha Infantry Brigade 1974–76, Cmdt 7 Duke of Edinburgh's Own Gurkha Rifles 1976–79, Instr Staff Coll Camberley 1982–83; Cdr: Br Gurkhas Nepal 1985–87, Bde of Gurkhas 1987–90 (ret 1991); private sec to HRH The Prince Philip, Duke of Edinburgh 1993– (asst private sec 1991–92), Col 7 Duke of Edinburgh's Own Gurkha Rifles 1991–94; chm Gurkha Brigade Assoc 1991–; *Recreations* golf, Gurkha war medals; *Clubs* Army and Navy, Royal Hong Kong Golf, West Wilts Golf; *Style—* Brig Miles Hunt-Davis, CBE; ✉ 5b The Old Barracks, Kensington Palace, London W8 4PU

HUNT OF TANWORTH, Baron (Life Peer UK 1980), of Stratford-upon-Avon; John Joseph Benedict; GCB (1977, KCB 1973, CB 1968); s of Maj Arthur L Hunt, MC (d 1959), of Hale House, Churt, Surrey, and Daphne Hunt (d 1956); *b* 23 Oct 1919; *Educ* Downside, Magdalene Coll Cambridge; *m* 1, 1941, Hon Magdalen Mary (d 1971), da of 1 Baron Robinson (d 1952); 2 s (Hon Michael b 1942, Hon Martin b 1962), 1 da (Hon Charlotte (Hon Mrs Gill) b 1947, d 1995); m 2, 1973, Madeleine Frances, da of Sir William Hume, CMG, and wid of Sir John Charles, KCB; *Career* RNVR 1940; Dominions Office 1946, attached Office of High Cmmr for UK in Ceylon 1948–50, memb directing staff IDC 1951–52, Office of High Cmmr for UK in Canada 1953–56, private sec to Sec of Cabinet 1956–58, private sec to Perm Sec to Treasy and Head of Civil Serv 1957–58, CRO 1958–60, Cabinet Office 1960–62, HM Treasy 1962, under-sec 1965–67, dep-sec 1968, first Civil Serv cmmr and dep sec CSD 1968–71, HM Treasy 1971, second perm sec Cabinet Office 1972, sec Cabinet 1973–79; chm Banque Nationale de Paris plc 1980–, dir IBM UK 1980–90, advsy dir Unilever 1980–90; chm: Disaster Emergency Ctee 1981–89, Govt Inquiry into Cable Expansion and Broadcasting Policy 1982, Ditchley Fndn 1983–91, Tablet Publishing Co 1984–, Prudential Corp 1985–90 (dir 1980–, dep chm 1982–85), European Policy Forum 1992–; hon fell Magdalene Coll Cambridge; Officier Légion d'Honneur (France) 1987–; *Style—* The Rt Hon the Lord Hunt of Tanworth, GCB; ✉ 8 Wool Rd, Wimbledon, London SW20 (☎ 0181 947 7640, fax 0181 947 4879)

HUNTER, Alan James Herbert; s of Herbert Ernest Hunter (d 1955), and Isabella, *née* Andrew (d 1933); *b* 25 June 1922; *Educ* Wroxham Sch Norfolk; *m* 1944, Adelaide Elizabeth Cecily, da of Charles Cecil Cubitt; 1 da (Helen Adelaide Isabella b 1963); *Career* poultry farmer 1936–40, served RAF 1940–46, bookseller/author 1946–57, author 1957–; memb: Soc of Authors, CWA; *Books* The Norwich Poems (1945); 43 crime novels featuring Chief Supt Gently incl: Gently Does It (1955), Gently in the Sun (1959), Gently Go Man (1961), Gently Floating (1963), Gently North-West (1967), Gently With The Innocents (1970), Vivienne - Gently Where She Lay (1972), Gently Where The Birds Are (1976), The Honfleur Decision (1980), Gabrielle's Way (1981), The Unhung Man (1984), Traitor's End (1988), Gently Scandalous (1990), Gently to a Kill (1992), Gently Tragic (1992), Gently in the Glens (1993), Bomber's Moon (1994), Jackpot! (1995), The Love of Gods (1997); *Recreations* nature, ex-yachtsman, camper and motor-caravanner; *Style—* Alan Hunter, Esq; ✉ c/o Constable & Co Ltd, 3 The Lanchesters, 162 Fulham Palace Road, London W6 9ER (☎ 0181 741 3663, fax 0181 748 7562)

HUNTER, Sir Alexander Albert; KBE (1976); s of Alexander Hunter, KSG; *b* 21 May 1920; *Educ* St John's Coll Belize, Regis Coll Denver USA, Queen's Univ Kingston Canada; *m* 1947, Araceli; 1 s, 2 da; *Career* served WWII RAF; joined James Brodie and Co 1947; co sec 1948, dir 1952–61, conslt 1975–82; Belize: MLA (PUP) 1961, min of Natural Resources Commerce and Industry 1961, MHR (PUP) 1965, min of Natural Resources and Trade 1965–69, min of Trade and Industry 1969–74; speaker of the House of Representatives of Belize 1974–79; rep of and conslt to: Auschutz Overseas Corp (Petroleum) Denver Colorado 1975–82, Pecten Belize Co (Shell Oil) Houston Texas 1982–; *Style—* Sir Alexander Hunter, KBE; ✉ 6 St Matthew Street, Caribbean Shores, Belize City, Belize (☎ 00 501 2 44482)

HUNTER, Air Vice-Marshal Alexander Freeland Cairns (Sandy); CBE (1982, OBE 1981), AFC (1978), DL (Northumberland 1994); s of Herbert Andrew Cairns Hunter (d 1948), and Lillian Edith Middleton, *née* Trail (d 1991); *b* 8 March 1939; *Educ* Aberdeen GS, Univ of Aberdeen (MA, LLB); *m* 7 Nov 1964, Wilma Elizabeth, da of Howard Bruce-Wilson (d 1958); *Career* RAFVR 1957–62, RAF 1962–93, 81 (PR) Sqdn FEAF 1964–67, Central Flying Sch 1967–68, Northumbrian Univs Air Sqdn 1968–69, Asst Air Attaché Moscow 1971–75, RAF Staff Coll 1974, Flt Cdr 230 Sqdn 1975–77, OC 18 Sqdn RAF Germany 1978–80, Air Warfare Course 1981, MOD (Air) Policy Div 1981, OC RAF Odiham 1981–83, Gp Capt Plans HQ Strike Cmd 1983–85, RCDS 1986, Dir of PR for RAF 1987–88, Cmdt RAF Staff Coll 1989–90, Adminstrator of Sovereign Base Areas of Akrotiri and Dhekelia and Cdr Br Forces Cyprus 1990–93; dir: Newcastle Building Society 1993–, Clyde Helicopters Ltd 1993–95, Newcastle Bank (Gibraltar) 1994–; dep chm Annington Homes 1996–; vice chm North Housing Association 1994–95, chm Home Housing Association Ltd 1995–; OStJ 1994; *Recreations* shooting, fishing, hill walking, military history; *Style—* Air Vice-Marshal Sandy Hunter, CBE, AFC, DL; ✉ c/o Clydesdale Bank, Queen's Cross, Aberdeen

HUNTER, Sir Alistair John; KCMG (1994, CMG 1985); s of Kenneth Clarke Hunter (d 1987), of Spratton Hall School, Northampton, and Joan, *née* Tunks (d 1993); *b* 9 Aug 1936; *Educ* Felsted Sch Essex, Magdalen Coll Oxford (BA); *m* 1, July 1963 (m dis 1977), Gillian Mary Bradbury; 1 s (Matthew Edmund b 1970), 2 da (Natalie Charlotte b 1966, Sophie Olivia b 1970); m 2, 30 Jan 1978, Helge Elfriede Elsbeth Milton, *née* Kahle; *Career* Nat Serv RAF 1955–57; with BP 1960; CRO (later HM Dip Serv): private sec to Permanent Under Sec 1961–63, 2 sec Kuala Lumpur 1963–65, 1 sec (Commercial) Peking 1965–68, seconded to Cabinet Office 1969–70, FCO 1970–73, 1 sec Rome 1973–75, FCO 1975–80, head of Chancery Bonn 1980–85, seconded to DTI as under sec overseas trade 1985–88, Br consul-gen Düsseldorf and DG of trade and investmt promotion in Germany

1988–91, Br consul-gen NY and DG of trade and investmt in USA 1991–96; exec chm Br American Chamber of Commerce 1996–; external dir The Performing Right Society Ltd 1996–; vice chm Locate in Kent 1996–; tstee Horniman Museum and Gardens 1996–; *Style*— Sir Alistair Hunter, KCMG; ✉ Bay View House, 2A Bay View Road, Broadstairs, Kent CT10 2EA

HUNTER, Andrew Lorimer; s of Eric Newton Hunter (d 1982), of Gairloch, Wester Ross, Scotland, and Elizabeth Mary Anne, *née* Lorimer (d 1996); *b* 27 July 1946; *Educ* George Watson's Coll Edinburgh, Edinburgh Sch of Art; *m* 1, 1970 (m dis 1988), Patricia Thérèse O'Rourke; 1 s (Daniel b 1973), 1 da (Harriet b 1976); m 2, Alison Janet, da of Prof Ian Adair Silver, *qv*; 1 da (Emily b 1991), 1 s (Freddie b 1993); *Career* packaging designer trainee William Thyne Ltd 1966–70, dir Forth Studios 1973–79 (designer 1970–73), fndr and jt md Tayburn Design 1979–87; design dir: McIlroy Coates Design Consultants (now Tayburn McIlroy Coates) 1987–96 (md 1990–96), Redpath Design 1996–; maj design projects incl: corporate indentity Design Cncl (UK), identity and literature Edinburgh Int Festival, corporate literature NCR Corp; external assessor Scotvec Graphic Design courses 1987–; chm: Design Business Assoc (Scotland), CSD (Scotland) 1991–; memb Advsy Bd Napier Univ Inst of Design Mgmnt; fndr memb Creative Forum, memb D & AD 1980, FCSD 1985 (MCSD 1966); *Recreations* skiing, hill walking, fishing, tennis, travel, gardening; *Style*— Andrew Hunter, Esq; ✉ Redpath Design Ltd, 110b St Stephen Street, Edinburgh EH3 5AQ (☎ 0131 226 1441, fax 0131 226 1551)

HUNTER, Andrew Robert Frederick; MP (C) Basingstoke (majority 21,198); s of late Sqdn Ldr Roger Edward Hunter, DFC, of Winchester, and Winifred Mary, *née* Nelson; *b* 8 Jan 1943; *Educ* St George's Sch Harpenden, Univ of Durham, Jesus Coll Cambridge, Westcott House Cambridge; *m* 1972, Janet, da of late Samuel Bourne, of Gloucester; 1 s, 1 da; *Career* Maj TAVR 1973 (resigned 1984); in indust 1969; asst master: St Martin's Sch Northwood 1970–71, Harrow Sch 1971–83; Parly candidate (C) Southampton Itchen 1979, MP (C) Basingstoke 1983–; memb Agric Select Ctee 1985, PPS to Lord Elton Min of State Dept of the Environment 1985–86, memb Environment Select Ctee 1986–91, memb Agric Select Ctee 1992–93, memb N Ireland Affairs Select Ctee 1994–; chm Cons NI Ctee 1992–; vice pres Nat Prayer Book Soc 1987–; memb: NFU, Br Field Sports Soc; Order of Polonia Restituta 1980; hon memb Soc of the Sealed Knot; *Recreations* horse riding, watching cricket and rugby football; *Clubs* St Stephen's Constitutional, Pratt's, Carlton; *Style*— Andrew Hunter, Esq, MP; ✉ House of Commons, London SW1A OAA (☎ 0171 219 5216)

HUNTER, Dr Anthony Rex (Tony); s of Ranulph Rex Hunter, of Bucksford Lodge, Great Chart, Ashford, Kent, and Nellie Ruby Elsie, *née* Hitchcock; *b* 23 Aug 1943; *Educ* Felsted, Gonville and Caius Coll Cambridge (BA, MD, PhD); *m* 1, 1969 (m dis 1974), Philippa Charlotte Marrack; m 2, 1992, Jennifer Ann Maureen Price; 1 s (Sean Alexander Brocas Price-Hunter b 17 Dec 1990); *Career* research fell Christ's Coll Cambridge 1968–71 and 1973–75; Salk Inst La Jolla San Diego: research assoc 1971–73, asst prof 1975–78, assoc prof 1978–82, prof 1982–; adjunct prof Univ of California San Diego 1983– (adjunct assoc prof 1979–83), research prof American Cancer Soc 1992–; memb Editorial Bd: Molecular and Cellular Biology 1982–88 (ed 1989–93), Jl of Virology 1982–, Molecular Endocrinology 1987–91, Cancer Cells 1989–91, Current Biology 1991–; assoc ed: Cell 1980–, Virology 1982–93; author of over 300 scientific pubns; chm: Melbourne Branch Ludwig Inst for Cancer Research Scientific Review Ctee 1987– (memb 1983–), Sci Advsy Bd La Jolla Cancer Research Fndn 1991– (memb 1984–); vice chm Animal Cells and Viruses Gordon Conf 1988; dir Fndn for Advanced Cancer Studies 1989–; memb: Advsy Ctee Frederick Cancer Research Facility 1985–89, Scientific Review Bd Howard Hughes Med Inst 1989–, Biology Panel AAAS Project 2061, Ciba Fndn Scientific Advsy Panel; assoc memb European Molecular Biology Orgn 1992; American Business Fndn for Cancer Research Award 1988, Katharine Berkan Judd Award, Meml Sloan-Kettering Cancer Center 1992, General Motors Cancer Research Fndn Mott Prize 1994, Gairdner Fndn International Award 1994, Biochemical Soc Hopkins Meml Medal 1994; FRS 1987, FRSA 1989, FAAAS 1992; *Recreations* white water rafting, exploring Baja peninsula; *Style*— Dr Tony Hunter, FRS; ✉ Molecular Biology and Virology Laboratory, The Salk Institute, PO Box 85800, San Diego, California 92186, USA (☎ 00 1 619 453 4100, fax 00 1 619 457 4765, e-mail Hunter@sc2.salk.edu)

HUNTER, Brig (John) Antony; DSO (1944), OBE (1955, MBE 1943), MC (1942); s of Maj-Gen Sir Alan Hunter, KCVO, CB, CMG, DSO, MC (d 1942), and Hon Joan, *née* Adderley (d 1988), da of 5 Baron Norton; *b* 12 Sept 1914; *Educ* Stowe, RMC Sandhurst; *m* 1, 14 Feb 1944 (m dis 1971), Dauphine Laetitia Janet Colquhoun (d 1979), da of Nicholas Conyngham Simons Bosanquet (d 1955); 1 s (Antony b 1945), 1 da (Sarah (Mrs Ellson) b 1947); m 2, 1971, Carole, da of Dr David Reid Milligan (d 1985); *Career* cmmnd 60 Rifles 1934; regtl serv 1934–39: Ireland, Burma, Egypt; GSO3 (later GSO2) intelligence GHQ ME 1940–41, Co Cdr 1 KRRC Western Desert and Libya 1941–42, Bde Maj 4 Armd Bde El Alamein 1942, Staff Coll Haifa 1942–43, GSO2 ops HQ 13 Corps invasion of Sicily 1943, DSD Staff Coll Camberley 1943–44, CO 8 Bn The Rifle Bde Normandy to Germany 1944–45, GSO1 HQ 21 Army Gp Germany 1945–46, chief instr New Coll Sandhurst 1947–50, Jt Servs Staff Coll 1951, GSO1 6 Armd Div Germany 1952–55, CO 1 Bn Beds and Herts Regt 1955–57, Col GS ME ops WO Whitehall 1957–59, Cdr 11 Inf Bde Gp Germany 1960, ret 1960; Union Castle Line: 2 i/c Southampton 1960–63, dir staff Admin Staff Coll Henley 1963–64, area dir Southampton 1964–77 (also dir: Union Castle Line, Cayzer Irvine & Co, London & Southampton Stevedoring Co); regnl dir Lloyds Bank Salisbury region 1974–85, dir Red Funnel Gp 1977–85 (chm Vectis Tport Co), pres Ocean Sound Hldgs plc (dir 1984–90), dir Southampton C of C 1966–75 (pres 1972–73); dir and dep chm Southern Radio Hldgs 1989–90; Freeman: City of London 1983, Worshipful Co of Bowyers 1983; FInstD 1966–85, MIMgt 1966–77, MCIT 1966–77; *Recreations* fishing, shooting, archery, skiing; *Style*— Brig Antony Hunter, DSO, OBE, MC; ✉ The Wheelwrights, Warmington, Banbury OX17 1DB

HUNTER, Archibald Sinclair (Archie); DL (Renfrewshire, 1995); s of John Lockhart Hunter (d 1986), and Elizabeth Hastings, *née* Sinclair; *b* 20 Aug 1943; *Educ* Queens' Park Sch Glasgow; *m* 6 March 1969, Patricia Ann; 1 da (Claire Patricia b 4 Feb 1973), 2 s (Stephen John b 4 July 1974, Craig Robertson b 25 Oct 1977); *Career* CA Mackie & Clark Glasgow 1966; Thomson McLintock: joined 1966, ptnr 1974, managing ptnr Glasgow Office 1983; KPMG Peat Marwick: managing ptnr 1987, Scottish sr ptnr 1992–, memb Ctee UK Ops; memb Cncl Scotbic, vice pres ICAS; *Recreations* golf, swimming, hill walking; *Clubs* Williamwood Golf (former capt), Western Gailes Golf, RSAC; *Style*— Archie Hunter, Esq; ✉ KPMG, 24 Blythswood Square, Glasgow, Scotland G2 4QS (☎ 0141 226 5511, fax 0141 204 1584)

HUNTER, Dr (Charles) Christopher; s of Charles William Hunter (d 1972), of Nottingham, and Dorothy Mary, *née* Ward; *b* 2 Feb 1950; *Educ* High Pavement GS Nottingham, Guy's Hosp Univ of London (MB BS, MRCS, LRCP, Dip in Psychological Med); *Career* Surgn Lt RN 1974–79 (med offr HMS Glamorgan 1974–76); conslt forensic psychiatrist and dep med dir Park Lane Hosp Liverpool 1982–89, conslt forensic psychiatrist and co-ordinator of the All Wales Forensic Psychiatric Service 1989–, advsr in forensic psychiatry to the Welsh Office 1989–, conslt forensic psychiatrist and clinical dir S Wales Forensic Psychiatric Serv 1992–; clinical teacher in forensic psychiatry Univ of Wales Coll of Med; memb: Nat Advsy Ctee on Mentally Disordered Offenders, Mental Health Review Tbnl, Exec Ctee Forensic Section RCPsych, Parole Bd; memb BMA, FRCPsych 1994 (MRCPsych 1980); *Recreations* reading, theatre, travel; *Style*— Dr Christopher Hunter; ✉ South Wales Forensic Psychiatric Service, Caswell Clinic, Glanrhyd Hospital, Bridgend, Mid-Glamorgan CF31 4LN (☎ 01656 662179, fax 01656 662157)

HUNTER, Doreen Eleanor Maude; da of James Wylie Hunter, of Craigavad, Holywood, Co Down, and Maude Elizabeth, *née* Warnock; *b* 14 Feb 1940; *Educ* Richmond Lodge Sch Belfast, Queen's Univ Belfast (BA), Univ of Reading (Dip Ed); *Career* headmistress: Princess Gardens Sch Belfast 1982–87, Hunterhouse Coll Belfast 1987–; govr Rockport Prep Sch Co Down 1987–, chm ptnrship NI Boarding Schs and Colls 1987–90, dir NI Railways 1987–92; memb: SHA 1982–, Cncl of Queen's Univ and Schs 1987–, Educn Ctee IOD 1996–; *Recreations* gardening, golf; *Clubs* Royal Belfast Golf, Malone Golf; *Style*— Miss Doreen Hunter; ✉ Hunterhouse Coll, Finaghy, Belfast BT10 0LE (☎ 01232 612293/612 588)

HUNTER, Ian; s of Malcolm Robert Hunter, of Cranbourne, and Sheila, *née* Tadd; *b* 15 Feb 1968; *Educ* Lake Sch Windermere, Cumbria Coll of Art and Design, Leicester Poly (BA Prod Design); *Career* rugby union player (full-back and wing); former clubs: Windermere, Carlisle; current club Northampton; rep: North Div 1990–91, Barbarians 1990–91; England: students 1989–91, 4 B caps 1990–91, England XV 3 caps tour Aust and Fiji 1991, 7 full caps, memb British Lions' team touring NZ 1993; *Recreations* reading, outdoor sports; *Style*— Ian Hunter, Esq; ✉ Northampton Rugby Club, Sturidge Pavilion, Weedon Lane, Northampton (☎ 01604 755149)

HUNTER, Sir Ian Bruce Hope; kt (1983), MBE (1945); s of William O Hunter; *b* 2 April 1919; *Educ* Fettes; *m* 1, 1949, Susan (d 1977), da of late Brig Alec Gaudie Russell; 4 da (Eugenie, Josephine, Serena, Catherine); m 2, 1984, Marie Sadie, da of Charles Golden, and wid of Sir Keith Showering (d 1982); 4 step s, 2 step da; *Career* dir numerous music festivals in UK and abroad incl: Bath 1948–68, Edinburgh 1950–55, City of London 1962–80, Brighton 1967–83, Hong Kong 1973–75; dir gen Cwlth Arts Festival 1965, pres and dir Harold Holt Ltd; chm: London Festival Ballet Tst (English National Ballet) 1984–89, Musicians Benevolent Fund 1987–95; dir Euro Arts Fndn 1989–, vice chm Japan Festival Soc 1991–; Liveryman Worshipful Co of Musicians; FRCM 1991, FRSA (chm 1981–83); *Clubs* Garrick; *Style*— Sir Ian Hunter, MBE; ✉ Harold Holt Ltd, 31 Sinclair Road, London W14 0NS

HUNTER, Ian Gerald Adamson; QC (1980); s of Gerald Oliver Hunter (d 1995), and June, *née* Brown (d 1979); *b* 3 Oct 1944; *Educ* Reading Sch, Pembroke Coll Cambridge (open scholar, Squire Univ law scholar, Trevelyan scholar, BA, MA, LLB), Harvard Law Sch (Kennedy Meml scholar, LLM); *m* 22 March 1975, Maggie, da of Herbert Reed (d 1984); 2 s (James Elyot b 1977, Edward Iain b 1981); *Career* called to the Bar Inner Temple 1967, bencher Inner Temple 1986–; sr counsel New South Wales 1994, avocat au barreau de Paris 1995; Bar Cncl: memb Int Rels Ctee 1982–90, memb Exec Ctee 1985–86; chm Consolidated Regulations and Transfer Ctee Senate of the Inns of Ct 1986–87; Union Internationale des Avocats: pres 1989–90, dir of studies 1990–91; hon memb Canadian Bar Assoc 1990, treas Bar Pro Bono Unit 1995; *Recreations* be-bop, French cuisine; *Style*— Ian Hunter, Esq, QC; ✉ Essex Court Chambers, 24 Lincoln's Inn Fields, London WC2A 3ED (☎ 0171 813 8000, fax 0171 813 8080)

HUNTER, Ian William; s of William Gurnham Hunter, and Anna-Marie, *née* Faliescewska; *b* 17 March 1955; *Educ* Alleyn's Sch Dulwich, Univ of Surrey; *m* 8 Nov 1986, Susan, da of James Edward Morris; *Career* economist Bank of England 1975–79, fund mangr Swiss Bank Corp 1979–81, sr investmt mangr Lazard Bros 1981–87, dir Far E div Midland Montagu Asset Mgmnt 1987–92, dir Hambros Investment Management 1992–94, dep md Daishin International (Europe) Ltd 1994–; MSI, ACA; *Recreations* skiing, motor racing; *Clubs* 190, AMOC; *Style*— Ian Hunter, Esq; ✉ 24 Beaufort Close, London SW15 3TL; Daishin International (Europe) Ltd, 35 Moorgate, London EC2R 6DS (☎ 0171 638 6438, fax 0171 256 9190)

HUNTER, Prof John Angus Alexander; s of Dr John Craig Alexander Hunter (d 1992), of Holbeach, Lincolnshire, and Alison Hay Shand, *née* Alexander, MBE; *b* 16 June 1939; *Educ* Loretto, Pembroke Coll Cambridge (BA), Univ of Edinburgh (MB ChB, MD); *m* 26 Oct 1968, Ruth Mary, da of Douglas Verdun Farrow, of Spalding, Lincolnshire; 1 s (Hamish John Alexander b 2 July 1973), 2 da (Rebecca Jean Alexander b 13 Sept 1970, Abigail Ruth Alexander b 24 Jan 1972); *Career* med posts: Royal Infirmary Edinburgh, Inst of Dermatology London 1967, Univ of Minnesota USA 1968–69; Grant prof of dermatology Univ of Edinburgh 1981–; author dermatological papers in scientific jls; memb Med Appeal Tbnl; memb: BMA, Assoc of Physicians of GB and Ireland, Br Assoc of Dermatologists, Scottish Dermatological Soc, RSM; FRCPE 1978; *Books* Common Diseases of the Skin (with J A Savin, 1983), Clinical Dermatology (with J A Savin and M V Dahl, 1989 and 1994), Skin Signs in Clinical Medicine (with J A Savin and N C Hepburn, 1996); *Recreations* gardening, music, golf; *Clubs* Hon Co of Edinburgh Golfers, Hawks; *Style*— Prof John Hunter; ✉ Department of Dermatology, University of Edinburgh, The Royal Infirmary, Edinburgh EH3 9YW (☎ 0131 536 2042)

HUNTER, John Foster Bray; s of late Jack Holmes Hunter, and Joyce Eileen Hunter; *b* 25 Jan 1937; *m* 14 May 1966, Diane Frances Hunter; 1 s (Jeffrey Jonathan b 6 June 1970), 1 da (Karen Frances b 26 Aug 1968); *Career* Nat Serv pilot offr RAF 1955–57 (later Reserve flying offr); SmithKline Beecham: gp mgmnt trainee Co Laboratories 1957–59, sr mktg mangr Beecham Toiletry Div (previously brand asst) 1959–65, mktg mangr Beecham Clifton (USA) 1965–67, mktg gp mangr UK Toiletries 1967–69, md Beecham Drinks (previously gen mangr) 1969–73, md Beecham SA 1973–76, md Beecham Proprietaries UK June-Sept 1976, regnl dir Proprietaries Div (Euro responsibilities) 1976–80, md Proprietaries Europe Western Div 1980–84, chm Food and Drink Div 1984, chm Int Div 1986, chm Beecham Italia 1987, Manetti Roberts 1987, chm Beecham Products Europe and International 1987, chm Beecham Products Worldwide Operations, chm SmithKline Beecham Consumer Brands, left SmithKline Beecham 1993; currently dep chm The Hartstone Group plc; also non-exec dir: Blue Circle Industries PLC 1991–, Wace Group plc, More O'Ferrall plc; memb various trade assocs incl: Proprietary Assoc of GB, Cosmetic Toiletry and Perfumery Assoc and Food Mfrs' Fedn; non-exec memb Nat Devpt Bd LTA; memb various govt sponsored activities incl: Consumer Goods Study Gp, Single Euro Market Consumer Gp; *Recreations* reading, theatre, cinema, tennis; *Clubs* St George's Hill Lawn Tennis, Roehampton; *Style*— J F B Hunter, Esq; ✉ The Hartstone Group plc, 4 Brent Cross Gardens, London NW4 3RJ (☎ 0181 359 1000, fax 0181 359 1010)

HUNTER, John Garvin; s of Garvin Hunter (d 1970), and Martha, *née* McCracken (d 1976); *b* 9 Aug 1947; *Educ* Merchant Taylors' Crosby, Queen's Univ (BA), Cornell Univ (MBA); *m* 20 March 1976, Rosemary Alison, *née* Haire; 2 da (Laurie Helen b 8 July 1979, Fiona Aileen b 14 May 1983), 1 s (Michael Garvin b 18 June 1981); *Career* asst princ N Ireland Office 1970–72, dep princ DHSS 1972–77, Harkness fell Cornell Univ 1977–79; asst sec: DHSS 1982–86 (princ offr 1979–82), Dept of Fin and Personnel 1986–89; dir General International Fund for Ireland 1987–89, under sec DHSS 1989–90, chief exec Health and Personal Social Servs Mgmnt Exec 1990–94; MIHSM; *Recreations* tennis, camping, hillwalking, swimming; *Style*— John Hunter, Esq

HUNTER, Dr Judith Marylyn; da of Leslie Edward Palmer (d 1984), and Dorothy Edith, *née* Neave (d 1974); *b* 26 Jan 1938; *Educ* Blyth Sch Norwich, UCL (BSc); *m* 1 April 1961, Roy Leslie Hunter, s of William Henry Hunter (d 1951); 2 da (Fiona Louise Jane b 21 Jan 1961, Karen Teresa b 25 Dec 1963); *Career* adult educn tutor Univ of Oxford ESD and other educnl instns 1969–; hon curator Royal Borough Collection Windsor 1977–, memb various cmmns for historical res 1981–95; vice chm and former jl ed Berks

Local History Assoc; *Books* The Changing Face of Windsor (1977), The Story of a Village, Eton Wick 1217–1977 (1977), A Town in the Making: Slough 1851 (ed, 1980), The Story of Slough (1983), From Tudor Inn to Trusthouse Hotel (1984), Tough Assignment: A History of the Eton Wick Methodist Chapel 1886–1986 (1986), The George Inn, Southwark (1989), Victorian Childhood in Windsor (schools pack 1990), Slough: A Pictorial History (1991), Ye Olde George Inn at Colnbrook (1991), Around Slough in Old Photographs (1992), Victuallers Licences: Records for Family and Local Historians (co-author, 1994), The Inns and Public Houses of Wokingham (co-author, 1994), A History of Berkshire (1995); *Recreations* walking, gardening, theatre going; *Style*— Dr Judith Hunter; ✉ 26 Wood Lane, Cippenham, Slough SL1 9EA (☎ 01753 525547)

HUNTER, Keith Robert; OBE (1981); s of Robert Ernest Williamson Hunter (d 1967), of Hull, and Winifred Mary, *née* Bradshaw (d 1987); *b* 29 May 1936; *Educ* Hymers Coll Hull, Magdalen Coll Oxford (MA), SOAS, Inst of Educn Univ of London; *m* 1, 21 Dec 1959 (m dis 1989), Ann Patricia, da of Frederick Fuller, of Eastbourne; 1 s (James b 1965), 2 da (Alisoun b 1961, Euphan b 1963); m 2, 16 Feb 1991, Victoria, da of George Solomonidis, of Athens; *Career* Nat Serv RAEC 1954–56; Br Cncl 1960–96: Cambodia 1960–64, London 1964–66, Hong Kong 1967–69, Malaysia 1970–74, Algeria 1975–78, China 1979–82, controller Arts Div London 1985–90, dir Italy 1990–96; *Recreations* music; *Style*— Keith Hunter, Esq, OBE; ✉ 15 Queensdale Road, London W11 4SB

HUNTER, Dr Kenneth Ross; s of Frank Church Hunter (d 1993), of Edinburgh, and Jessie Hill, *née* Adam (d 1971); *b* 31 May 1939; *Educ* Workington GS, Strathallan Sch, St John's Coll Cambridge (MA, MB BChir, MD), UCH Med Sch London (Fellowes gold medal); *m* 1, 18 July 1964, Diana (d 1988), da of Emrys Newton John; 1 s (Kenneth Andrew b 22 Sept 1965), 2 da (Eleanor Jane b 26 Sept 1968, Clare Christina b 17 May 1972); m 2, 19 Jan 1991, Penelope Ann Robinson, da of Charles Joseph Cooper; *Career* house offr: UCH London 1964–65, Whittington Hosp London April-Sept 1965; SHO Westminster Hosp London 1965–66, med registrar Queen Mary's Hosp Roehampton 1967–68, med registrar/research asst UCH London 1968–71; sr med registrar: Plymouth Gen Hosp 1971–73, Bristol Royal Infirmary 1973–77; hon sr med registrar Dept of Clinical Pharmacology Hammersmith Hosp 1975–76, conslt physician Plymouth Hosps 1977–; memb Cncl RCP 1994– (regnl advsr 1991–94); chm Governing Body Penlee Sch 1986–89; hon fell Soc of Chiropodists 1992; memb Br Pharmacological Soc 1974, FRCP 1983; *Recreations* golf; *Clubs* RSM, Royal Western Yacht Club of England (Plymouth); *Style*— Dr Kenneth Hunter; ✉ 104 Molesworth Road, Plymouth PL3 4AQ (☎ 01752 568985); Derriford Hospital, Plymouth PL6 8DH (☎ 01752 792752, fax 01752 768976)

HUNTER, Prof Sir Laurence Colvin; kt (1995), CBE (1987); s of late Laurence O Hunter, and late Jessie P, *née* Colvin; *b* 8 Aug 1934; *Educ* Hillhead HS Glasgow, Univ of Glasgow (MA), Univ Coll Oxford (DPhil); *m* 1958, Evelyn Margaret, *née* Green; 3 s (David Stuart b 1962, Niall Laurence b 1964, Martin Alan b 1967), 1 da (Jennifer Ann b 1973); *Career* asst lectr Univ of Manchester 1958–59; 2 Lt Rifle Bde Nat Serv 1959–61; Walgreen post doctoral fell Univ of Chicago 1961–62; Univ of Glasgow: lectr 1962–66, sr lectr 1966–70, prof of applied economics 1970–, vice princ 1982–86, dir of external relations 1987–92, dir Business Sch 1996–; visiting prof Indust and Labour Relations Sch Cornell Univ 1973; memb: Cncl ACAS 1974–86, Royal Economic Soc, Scottish Economic Soc (pres 1993–96); chm Police Negotiating Bd 1986– (dep chm 1979–86), ed Scottish Jl of Political Economy 1966–; FRSE, FRSA; *Recreations* golf, curling, painting; *Style*— Prof Sir Laurence Hunter, CBE, FRSE; ✉ University of Glasgow Business School, University of Glasgow, Glasgow G12 8LF (☎ 0141 339 8855)

HUNTER, Margaret Steele; da of Thomas Hunter, of Irvine, Ayrshire, and Norma, *née* Botley (d 1986); *b* 20 Jan 1948; *Educ* Irvine Royal Acad, James Watt Coll, Glasgow Sch of Art (1981–85), Hochschule der Künste Berlin (1985–87); *m* 1969 (m dis 1982); 1 s (Thomas b 1969), 1 da (Alana b 1970); partner since 1985, Joachim Gross; *Career* artist; drawing office tracer/jr draughtswoman Skefko Ball Bearing Co 1964–68; *Solo Exhibitions* Galerie IX Atelier Berlin 1986, Rozelle House Gallery Ayr 1986, Berlin-Scotland-Transfer (Galerie IX Atelier) 1988, 369 Gallery Edinburgh 1988, Vanessa Devereux Gallery London 1988, Galerie Werkstatt Berlin 1988, Kunstraum Klapperhof Cologne 1989, Petrus Kirche Berlin 1990, touring exhbn (Maclaurin Gallery Ayr, 369 Gallery, Vanessa Devereux Gallery) 1990, Deutsche Industriebank Berlin 1990, Paintings and Drawings (Galerie IX Atelier) 1992, touring exhbn Changing Places (Collins Gallery Univ of Strathclyde, Galerie M Berlin, Talbot Rice Gallery Univ of Edinburgh, Kunstverein Weinheim Germany, Vanessa Devereux London, Darlington Art Centre) 1992–93, Archaische Zeichen (Galerie Dr Ch Muller Berlin) 1994, Scratching the Surface (Rebecca Hossack Gallery) 1994, Portal Gallery Bremen 1995, Skulpturen und Malerei (Galerie Krafünf Berlin) 1995; *Group Exhibitions* incl: Art in Exile (Mackintosh Museum Glasgow Sch of Art) 1987, Chicago Int Art Exposition 1988, The Franciscan Monastery Przemysl Poland 1988, New Directions (St Andrews Festival) 1989, Scottish Art Since 1900 (Scottish Nat Gallery of Modern Art and Barbican London) 1989–90, EAST Nat Open Art Expdn Norwich 1991, Festival Fourteen - Scottish Women Artists Exhbn (Dunfermline Museum) 1992, Through Women's Eyes (City Art Centre Edinburgh) 1992–93, Europa in Berlin (Verborgenes Museum Berlin) 1993, Buchinstallation (Fragile Gesellschaft Berlin) 1993, Pendant Perdu (Gallery Dr Christiane Muller Berlin), Thursday's Child (Roger Billcliffe Gallery Glasgow) 1994, Paths of the Spirit The Artist as Shaman (Isis Gallery Leigh-on-Sea) 1995, The continuing tradition 75 Years of Painting at Glasgow Sch of Art 1920–95 (GSA Glasgow) 1995; *Public Collections* Scottish Nat Gallery of Modern Art Edinburgh, Graphothek Kunstamt Charlottenburg Berlin, Scottish Arts Cncl, Städtische Kunstsammlung Görlitz Germany, Niederschlesische Sparkasse Görlitz Germany, Univ of Strathclyde, Robert Fleming plc London; *Awards* Cargill Travel Scholarship 1985, Scottish Int Educn Tst 1985, Wilforge Fndn 1985, American Express Travel Prize 1985, Artists Bursary Scottish Arts Cncl 1987, prizewinner for painting exhbn Franciscan Monastery Przemysl Poland 1988, scholarship The Karl Hofer Gesellschaft Berlin 1993; *Style*— Ms Margaret Hunter; ✉ Haeseler Strasse 23, 14050 - Berlin, Germany; The Craig Cottage, 60 Main Road, Fairlie, Ayrshire KA29 0DL, Scotland

HUNTER, Prof (James) Martin Hugh; s of Colin Boorer Garrett Hunter (d 1958), of IOW, and Barbara Anne Crawford, *née* Cavendish (d 1962); *b* 23 March 1937; *Educ* Shrewsbury, Pembroke Coll Cambridge (MA); *m* 21 Jan 1972, Linda Mary, da of Francis Kenneth Ernest Gamble (d 1971); *Career* admitted slr 1964, ptnr Freshfields 1967–94 (asst slr 1964); called to the Bar Lincoln's Inn 1994, barr in private practice Essex Court Chambers 1994–; Sweet and Maxwell prof of int dispute resolution Nottingham Law Sch 1995–; sr visiting fell Queen Mary and Westfield Coll London 1987–, hon dean of postgraduate studies Asser Inst The Hague 1991–, hon visiting fell Faculty of Law Univ of Edinburgh 1992–; vice chm DTI Ctee on Arbitration Law 1990–; memb Editorial Bd: Arbitration International 1985–, American Review of International Arbitration 1989–; memb: Cncl Int Cncl for Commercial Arbitration 1988–, Ct of London Ct of Int Arbitration 1985–, Int C of C Ct of Arbitration 1988–90; Freeman: City of London, Worshipful Co of Arbitrators, Worshipful Co of Slrs, Worshipful Co of Spectacle Makers; FCIArb; *Books* Law & Practice of International Commercial Arbitration (with Alan Redfern, 2 edn 1991), The Freshfields Guide to Arbitration and ADR Clauses in International Contracts (with others, 1991), Arbitration Title, Butterworths Encyclopedia of Forms & Precedents (ed), The Internationalisation of International Arbitration (ed with others, 1995); *Recreations* cruising under sail, golf; *Clubs* Royal Cruising, Sunningdale Golf; *Style*— Prof Martin Hunter; ✉ Essex Court Chambers, 24 Lincoln's Inn Fields, London WC2A 3ED (☎ 0171 813 8000, fax 0171 813 8080); Nottingham Law School, Belgrave Centre, Chancer Street, Nottingham NG1 5LP (☎ 0115 948 6874, fax 0115 948 6989)

HUNTER, Muir Vane Skerrett; QC (1965); s of Hugh Stewart Hunter (d 1960), and Bluebell Matilda, *née* Williams (d 1960); *b* 19 Aug 1913; *Educ* Westminster, ChCh Oxford (MA); *m* 1, 29 July 1939, Dorothea Verstone (d 1986), 1 da (Camilla b 7 April 1947); m 2, 4 July 1986, Gillian Victoria Joyce Petrie; *Career* WWII service enlisted RTR 1940, cmmnd 2 Lt RMA Sandhurst 1941, 2 Royal Gloucestershire Hussars, transferred 7 KOYLI (renamed 149 Regt RAC) 1941, Capt (Bde IO) 50 Indian Tank Bde India 1941, Staff Capt (GSO 3) Gen Staff Intelligence GHQ New Delhi 1942, Lt-Col (GSO 1) War and Legislative Depts Govt of India New Delhi (judge of Anti-Corruption Tbnl Lahore and Karachi) 1943, ret 1945, demobbed with rank of Hon Lt-Col 1946; called to the Bar Gray's Inn 1938 (Master of Bench 1975), advsr to Kenya Law Reform Cmmn Nairobi; memb: Exec and Cncl Justice 1961–88, Cncl Royal Shakespeare Theatre Tst 1970– (govr RSC 1980–), Advsy Ctee on Draft EEC Bankruptcy Convention DTI 1973–76, Insolvency Law Review Ctee DTI 1977–82; memb and int observer Amnesty Int, int observer Int Cmmn of Jurists; fndr chm N Kensington Neighbourhood Law Centre 1970; memb Exec Br-Polish Legal Assoc, fndr chm Polish Hospices Fund (formerly Gdansk Hospices Fund), hon memb Polish Soc for Palliative Care; memb Gen Cncl of the Bar; MRI; *Books* Williams on Bankruptcy (later Williams & Muir Hunter on Bankruptcy, ed 1948, 1958, 1968, 1979), Butterworths County Court Practice & Precedents (part ed, 1980–), Muir Hunter on Personal Insolvency (sr author, 1988), Kerr on Receivers and Administrators (supervising ed, 1989, ed 1992–); *Recreations* travel, poetry (pres E Street Poets), theatre; *Clubs* Hurlingham, Union (Oxford); *Style*— Muir Hunter, Esq, QC; ✉ Hunterston, Donhead St Andrew, Shaftesbury, Dorset SP7 9EB (☎ 01747 828779, fax 01747 828045); 3–4 South Square, Gray's Inn, London WC1R 5HP (☎ 0171 696 9900, fax 0171 696 9911)

HUNTER, (John) Murray; CB (1980), MC (1943); s of Rev John Mercer Hunter (d 1968), of Fife, and Frances Margaret, *née* Martin (d 1953); *b* 10 Nov 1920; *Educ* Kirkcaldy HS, Fettes, Clare Coll Cambridge (BA); *m* 1948, Margaret Mary Phyllis, da of Stanley Cursiter, CBE (d 1976); 2 s (Andrew, David), 3 da (Frances, Sunniva, Caroline); *Career* served Army 1941–45 W Desert, N Africa, Italy, Capt The Rifle Brigade; played rugby football Cambridge 1946, Scotland 1947; Dip Serv: consul gen Buenos Aires 1969–71, head of Latin America Dept FCO 1971–73; cmmr for admin and fin Forestry Cmmn 1976–81; Scottish tourist guide; chm Edinburgh W End Community Cncl 1983–86; *Recreations* music, curling; *Clubs* Scottish Tourist Guides Assoc, Nat Tst for Scotland, Hawks, Saltire Soc; *Style*— Murray Hunter, Esq, CB, MC; ✉ 21 Glencairn Cres, Edinburgh EH12 5BT (☎ 0131 337 8785)

HUNTER, Dame Pamela; *née* Greenwell; DBE (1981); da of Col Thomas George Greenwell, TD, JP, DL (d 1967), of Whitburn Hall, Co Durham, and Mabel Winifred, *née* Catcheside (d 1967); *b* 3 Oct 1919; *Educ* Westonbirt Sch, Eastbourne Sch of Domestic Economy; *m* 1942, Gordon Lovegrove Hunter, s of Sir Summers Hunter, JP (d 1963), of Jesmond, Newcastle upon Tyne; 1 s (Mark), 1 da (Victoria); *Career* served WRNS 1942–45; memb: Northumbrian Water Authy 1973–77, Berwick-upon-Tweed Borough Cncl 1973–83; chm: Northern Area Cons Women's Advsy Ctee 1972–75 (vice-chm 1969–72), Cons Women's Nat Advsy Ctee 1978–81 (vice-chm 1974–75); vice-pres Nat Union of Cons and Unionist Assocs 1985– (memb Exec Ctee 1971–88, vice chm 1981–84, chm 1984–85, chm Brighton Conf 1984), memb Cons Party Policy Ctee 1978–85; memb Chatton Parish Cncl 1987–95 (chm 1993–95), lay chm PCC and churchwarden, active in RNLI, NSPCC and Save the Children Fund, formerly govr of first and middle schs; *Recreations* politics, antiques, the garden, crosswords; *Clubs* Lansdowne; *Style*— Dame Pamela Hunter, DBE; ✉ The Coach House, Chatton, Alnwick, Northumberland NE66 5PY (☎ 01668 215259)

HUNTER, Paul Anthony; s of Gordon Nicholson Hunter (d 1985), of Leeds, and Kathleen Margaret, *née* Tyldesley (d 1991); *b* 22 Nov 1944; *Educ* The Leys Sch Cambridge, Univ of Cambridge (MA, MB BChir), Middx Hosp Med Sch; *m* 10 July 1971, Elizabeth Alex, da of Wing Cdr Jack Granville Pearse, of Harston, Cambridgeshire; 1 s (Adam b 1978), 1 da (Rebecca b 1975); *Career* res surgical offr Moorfields Eye Hosp 1976–80, conslt ophthalmic surgn King's Coll Hosp 1982–, hon lectr King's Coll Hosp Med Sch Univ of London 1982–; hon sec: Ophthalmological Soc of the UK 1987–88, Royal Coll of Ophthalmologists 1991–; FRCS 1977, FCOphth 1988; *Books* Atlas of Clinical Ophthalmology (jt ed 1985); *Recreations* gardening, travel, photography; *Style*— Paul Hunter, Esq; ✉ 94 Harley St, London W1N 1AF (☎ 0171 935 0777)

HUNTER, Peter Basil; s of Harry Norman Hunter, and Martha Rose, *née* Lloyd-Jones; *b* 19 Oct 1938; *Educ* Kingswood Sch Bath, Oxford Sch of Arch (Dip Arch); *Career* architect, ptnr Shepheard Epstein and Hunter 1962; independent conslt 1990–; involvement with: Univ of Lancaster, local authy housing, inner city devpts incl Salford Quays, Piccadilly Manchester and Laganside Belfast, Manningham Mills Bradford, Commonwealth Univ London, Ramsgate and Crewe; former Civic Tst assessor; RIBA, FSAI; *Recreations* music; *Style*— Peter Hunter, Esq; ✉ County Mark House, 50 Regent Street, London W1R 6LP (☎ 0171 470 7121, fax 0171 470 7122)

HUNTER, Rita Nellie; CBE (1980); da of Charles Newton Hunter (d 1965), of Cheshire, and Lucy, *née* Parkinson-Davies (d 1973); *b* 15 Aug 1933; *Educ* Secdy Modern Sch; *m* 9 Dec 1960, John Darnley Thomas (d 1994), s of Richard Thomas (d 1977), of Aberdare, S Wales; 1 da (Mairwyn Sarita b 30 Nov 1967); *Career* soprano; debut: Berlin 1970, Covent Garden 1972, Met NY 1972, Munich 1973; sang first complete performance of Ring Cycle Sadler's Wells 1973; leading roles in: Aida, Norma, Il Trovatore, Masked Ball, Don Giovanni, Cavalleria Rusticana, Lohengrin, Flying Dutchman, Idomeneo, Don Carlos, Isolda, Elektra, Sieglinda; recordings incl: complete Siegfried and Götterdamerung, Walküre, Macbeth and solo CD Ritorna Vincitor, complete Euryanthe and solo CD Rita Hunter in Concert; currently teaches voice in USA and UK and runs late husband's singing sch in Sydney Australia, has inaugurated and runs the John Darnley Thomas singing scholarship in Australia; Hon DLitt Univ of Warwick 1978, Hon DMus Univ of Liverpool 1983, Hon RAM 1978; *Books* Wait Till The Sun Shines Nellie (autobiography, 1986); *Recreations* swimming, sewing, tapestry, cooking, oil painting; *Clubs* White Elephant, Royal Nat Rose Soc; *Style*— Miss Rita Hunter, CBE; ✉ 305 Bobbin Head Rd, North Turramurra, Sydney, NSW, Australia 2074 (☎ 00 61 2 9144 5062, fax 00 61 2 9488 7526)

HUNTER, Sally Elizabeth; da of Edward Ison Andrews (d 1986), of Woodbridge, Suffolk, and Elizabeth Margaret, *née* Hutchison (d 1992); *b* 20 March 1947; *Educ* Queenswood Sch, Cambridge Coll of Arts & Technol; *m* 1, 1970 (m dis 1978), Ian Hunter; m 2, 1990, Ian Richard Rosgate; *Career* ptnr Wills Lane Gallery St Ives Cornwall 1971–74, with Patrick Seale Gallery London 1978–83, fndr Sally Hunter Fine Art London (specialising in mid 20th Century Br paintings) 1984; *Recreations* theatre; *Style*— Ms Sally Hunter; ✉ Sally Hunter Fine Art, 11 Halkin Arcade, Motcomb Street, London SW1X 8JU (☎ 0171 235 0934)

HUNTER, William Hill; CBE (1971), JP (1970), DL (1987); s of Robert Dalglish Hunter (d 1942), of Ayrshire, and Margaret Walker, *née* Hill (d 1977); *b* 5 Nov 1916; *Educ* Cumnock Acad; *m* 22 March 1947, Kathleen, da of William Alfred Cole (d 1966), of Cardiff; 2 s (John b 1950, Robert b 1953 d 1994); *Career* Private RASC 1940, cmmnd RA 1941, Severn Fixed Defences 1941–44, Staff Capt Middle East with Br Mil Govt Cyrenaica 1944–46; CA 1940; ptnr McLay McAlister and McGibbon Glasgow 1946–91 (currently pt/t consIt); Parly candidate (Unionist) S Ayrshire 1959 and 1964; pres: Scot Young Unionist Assoc 1958–60, Scot Unionist Assoc 1964–65, Renfrew West and Inverclyde Cons and Unionist Assoc 1972–; dir: Abbey Nat Building Society Scot Advsy Bd 1966–86, J and G Grant Glenfarclas Distillery 1966–92; Quarrier's Homes: hon treas 1972–95, acting chm 1989–92; dir CBI Scot Cncl 1978–84, pres Scottish Friendly Assurance Soc 1980–88 (dir 1966–88), chm Salvation Army Advsy Bd in W Scotland 1982–93 (chm Housing Association Scotland Ltd 1985–91), deacon convenor The Trades House of Glasgow 1986–87, hon vice pres The Royal Scottish Agricultural Benevolent Instn, hon pres The Friends of Glasgow Botanic Gardens; *Recreations* gardening, golf, swimming, music; *Clubs* The Western (Glasgow), The Royal Scot Automobile (Glasgow); *Style*— William Hill Hunter, Esq, CBE, JP, DL; ✉ Armitage, Kilmacolm (☎ 01505 872444); McLay McAlister and McGibbon CA, 53 Bothwell St, Glasgow G2 6TF (☎ 0141 221 6516, fax 0141 204 1008)

HUNTER, Dr William John; *b* 5 April 1937; *Educ* Westminster Hosp Med Sch London (MB BS, LRCP, MRCS); *Career* Commission of the European Union: princ admin 1974–83, head Div of Industl Med and Hygiene 1983–88, dir Public Health and Safety at Work Directorate 1988–; serving brother order of St John; FRCP (FFOM); *Books* ed of several books and author of numerous articles on occupational safety and health and public health; *Style*— Dr William Hunter; ✉ Commission of the European Union, Public Health and Safety at Work Directorate, Jean Monnet Building - Office EUFO 4270, Plateau du Kirchberg-L-2920, Luxembourg (☎ 00 352 430 132719, fax 00 352 430 134511, telex COMEUR LU 3423 3446)

HUNTER BLAIR, Sir Edward Thomas; 8 Bt (GB 1786), of Dunskey; s of Sir James Hunter Blair, 7 Bt (d 1985), and Jean Galloway MacIntyre (d 1953); *b* 15 Dec 1920; *Educ* Eton, Univ of Paris, Balliol Coll Oxford (BA); *m* 21 April 1956, Norma (d 1972), er da of Walter S Harris (d 1983), of Bradford, Yorks; 1 adopted s (Alan Walter b 1961), 1 adopted da (Helen Cecilia (Mrs Watson) b 1963); *Heir* bro, James Hunter Blair b 18 March 1926; *Career* served WWII 1939–41 with KOYLI, discharged; temp civil servant Miny of Info 1941–43; journalist London Evening News (asst foreign ed) 1944–49; mangr and dir own co in Yorks 1950–63, landowner and forester SW Scotland 1964–; memb: Kirkcudbright CC 1970–71, Scottish Countryside Activities Cncl, Timber Growers UK SW Scotland Ctee until 1996, Cncl Wyndham's Tst 1992–; *Books* Scotland Sings, A Story of Me (poems and autobiog, 1981), A Future Time, With An Earlier Life (poems, autobiog and prophecy), A Mission in Life (philosophy, religion, autobiog, poems, 1987), Nearing The Year 2000 (1990), Our Troubled Future (1993); *Recreations* gardening, hill walking; *Clubs* Western Meeting (Ayr), Royal Overseas League; *Style*— Sir Edward T Hunter Blair, Bt; ✉ Parton House, Castle Douglas, Kirkcudbrightshire DG7 3NB (☎ 01644 470234)

HUNTER BLAIR, James; DL (Ayrshire 1975); s of Sir James Hunter Blair, 7 Bt (d 1985), and Jean, *née* McIntyre (d 1953); *b* 18 March 1926; *Educ* Eton, Balliol Coll Oxford (BA); *Career* Lt Scots Guards 1944–48; merchant banker London 1951–53, currently landowner family estate Ayrshire; former pres Royal Scot Forestry Soc, tstee National Galleries of Scotland; *Recreations* shooting, fishing, curling, going to the opera; *Style*— James Hunter Blair, Esq, DL; ✉ Blairquhan, Maybole, Ayrshire (☎ 01655 770239, fax 01655 770278)

HUNTER GORDON, Christopher Neil (Kit); s of Maj Patrick Hunter Gordon, CBE, MC, JP, DL (d 1978), of Ballindoun, Beauly, Inverness, and Valerie Margaret Frances, *née* Ziani de Ferranti; *b* 8 June 1958; *Educ* Ampleforth, Trinity Hall Cambridge (MA); *m* 29 Sept 1984, Georgina Mary, da of Capt Owen Varney, of Hill House, Dedham, Essex; 2 s (Sam William b 5 March 1988, Ivan b 20 Sept 1989), 2 da (Ione Mary b 18 July 1992, Hebe Elizabeth b 9 Aug 1996); *Career* J Rothschild Holdings plc, md Aurit Serv 1983–85, md and co fndr The Summit Group plc 1985–, dir Comcap plc 1986–89, chief exec Anglo Leasing Holdings 1993–95; *Recreations* painting, architectural design, skiing; *Clubs* Brooks's, Chelsea Arts, United Oxford and Cambridge Univ; *Style*— Kit Hunter Gordon, Esq; ✉ The Summit Group plc, 84 St Katharine's Way, London E1 9YS (☎ 0171 480 5588, fax 0171 480 5577)

HUNTER GORDON, Nigel; s of Maj Patrick Hunter Gordon, CBE, MC, JP (d 1978), of Ballindoun House, Beauly, Inverness-shire, and Valerie Margaret Frances, *née* Ziani de Ferranti; *b* 2 Sept 1947; *Educ* Ampleforth, Univ of St Andrews (MA); *m* 16 April 1977, Linda Anne, da of Brendan Robert Magill, of Eastbourne; 2 s (Kim b 23 March 1981, Bret b 19 March 1983); *Career* trained as CA Coopers & Lybrand 1970–76, James C Pringle & Co CA Inverness 1977–79; Ernst & Young: joined 1979, tax ptnr 1983–92, managing ptnr Highland & Island 1992–; Highland Area rep on Tax Practices Ctee, chm Highland Area Tax Ctee 1985–91 (memb Tech Sub Ctee); sec CBI Highland Area Gp; FCA 1975 (ACA 1973), ATII 1979; *Recreations* skiing, windsurfing; *Clubs* Highland; *Style*— Nigel Hunter Gordon, Esq; ✉ Killearnan House, Muir of Ord, Ross-shire (☎ 01463 870002); Ernst & Young, Moray House, 16 Bank St, Inverness (☎ 01463 237581, fax 01463 226098)

HUNTER JONES, Col Hugh Edward; CBE (1980), MC (1942), TD (1946), JP (Essex 1965), DL (1961); s of Stanley Hunter Jones, of Ongar, Essex (d 1961); *b* 20 July 1915; *Educ* Rugby, Corpus Christi Coll Cambridge (MA); *m* 1947, Sheila Kathleen, OBE (1994), chm Essex branch Soldiers', Sailors' and Airmen's Families Assoc, da of Alfred Dickinson (d 1952), of Lanchester; 3 s (Nigel, Patrick, Nicholas), 1 da (Sarah); *Career* served Essex Yeo (CO 1959–62) 1938–43, MEF Staff Coll Haifa 1943, despatches 1943, staff appts in Italy and Germany 1944–46, dep cdr RA 54 Div 1964–67 (cdr 1967), actg Brig; dir Charrington & Co until 1976, chm Hotel and Catering Indust Trg Bd 1973–85; pres: Br Inst of Innkeeping 1981–85, Friends of Essex Churches 1987–; chm E Anglian TAVR Assoc 1976–80; ADC to HM The Queen 1966–70; High Sheriff Essex 1963–64; memb Ct of Assts Worshipful Co of Merchant Taylors (Master 1976–77); *Recreations* country pursuits; *Clubs* Army & Navy; *Style*— Col Hugh Hunter Jones, CBE, MC, TD, JP, DL; ✉ Church Farm, Langham, Colchester, Essex CO4 5PS (☎ 01206 322181)

HUNTER-PEASE, Charles E; *b* 1946; *m* 1984, Susan; 1 da (Alison b 1986), 1 s (Henry b 1988); *Career* articled clerk 1964–68, asst accountant in bldg industry 1968–69, branch mangr Autohall (later Godfrey Davis) 1969–70 (successively in Edinburgh, Glasgow, Manchester and London), operational auditor, agency mangr then dist mangr (NW) Avis Ltd 1970–72, auditing position with Continental Oil 1972–73; Volvo: business mgmnt conslt Scotland 1973–75, dist planning mangr 1975, dealer representation mangr 1976–78, regnl mangr Harrogate then Nottingham 1978–83, nat sales mangr 1983, field ops mangr 1984–86, UK bd dir 1986–, dir of dealer ops 1986, sales and mktg dir 1987–92, concurrently dep chief exec 1990–92, chm VOCS Finance Ltd 1991–, md Volvo Car UK Ltd 1992–96, sr vice pres Volvo Car Corp Sweden 1993–, chief exec Volvo Car UK Ltd 1996–, vice pres Network Volvo Cars Europe Mktg 1996–; tstee RNLI 1996–; memb Swedish C of C 1995–; *Recreations* sailing, antiques; *Style*— Charles Hunter-Pease, Esq; ✉ Volvo Car UK Ltd, Globe Park, Marlow, Bucks SL7 1YQ (☎ 01628 477977, fax 01628 476173)

HUNTER SMART, (William) Norman; s of William Hunter Smart (d 1960), and Margaret Thorburn, *née* Inglis (d 1966); *b* 25 May 1921; *Educ* George Watson's Coll Edinburgh; *m* 1, 9 Feb 1948, Bridget Beryl (d 1974), da of Dr Edward Philip Andreae (d 1975); 4 s (Alastair (d 1992), Charles, James, Ian); m 2, 3 Dec 1977, Sheila Smith Stewart, da of Graham Mushet Speirs (d 1965), 1 step s (Robin); *Career* RAC Trg Centre 1941–42, cmmnd 1 Lothians and Border Horse 1943, 2 Lt Warks Yeo, Capt (Adj) 1944 (despatches), served ME 1943–44, UK 1945, Germany 1946; CA 1948; ptnr Hays Akers and Hays 1950–84, sr ptnr Hays Allan 1984–86 (ret); chm: C J Sims Ltd 1963–, Charterhouse Development Capital Fund Ltd 1987–95; memb: Gaming Bd of GB 1985–90, Scottish Legal Aid Bd 1987–89; pres Inst of CAs of Scotland 1978–79, chm Assoc of CAs London 1970–72, pres London Watsonian Club 1975–; *Recreations* gardening; *Clubs* Caledonian; *Style*— Norman Hunter Smart, Esq; ✉ Flat 1, Imperial Court, 12 Ravine Road, Canford Cliffs, Poole, Dorset BH13 7HX (☎ 01202 701433)

HUNTER-TOD, Air Marshal Sir John Hunter; KBE (1971, OBE 1956), CB (1969); s of Hunter Finlay Tod (d 1923), of London, and Yvonne Grace, *née* Rendall (who m 2, Cdr A P N Thorowgood, DSO, and d 1981); *b* 21 April 1917; *Educ* Marlborough, Trinity Coll Cambridge (MA), Coll of Aeronautics Cranfield (DCAe); *m* 12 Dec 1959, (Gwenith Ruth) Anne, da of late Thomas Chaffer Howard; 1 s (James Fredrik b 3 Dec 1960); *Career* cmmnd RAF 1940; served in night fighters Fighter Cmd and ME, HQME staff 1942, Actg Wing Cdr 1944, Air Miny 1945–46, Coll of Aeronautics Cranfield 1946–48, Guided Weapons Dept Royal Aircraft Estab 1949–55, HQ Fighter Cmd 1955–57, Br Jt Servs Mission Washington DC (as Gp Capt) 1957–60, dep dir radio Air Miny 1960–62, Air Cdre 1963, dir guided weapons (Air) Min of Aviation 1962–65, Air Offr Engrg RAF Germany 1965–67, AOC No 24 Gp RAF 1967–70, Air Vice-Marshal 1968, head of engrg and dir gen of Engrg RAF 1970–73, Air Marshal 1971, ret 1973; Hon DSc Cranfield Inst of Technol 1974; CEng; *Recreations* gardening; *Clubs* RAF; *Style*— Air Marshal Sir John Hunter-Tod, KBE, CB; ✉ 21 Ridge Hill, Dartmouth, Devon TQ6 9PE (☎ 01803 833130)

HUNTING, (Lindsay) Clive; s of Gerald Lindsay Hunting (d 1966), and Ruth, *née* Pyman (d 1972); *b* 22 Dec 1925; *Educ* Loretto, Trinity Hall Cambridge (MA); *m* 4 Oct 1952, Shelagh Mary Pamela, da of Capt A N V Hill-Lowe; 1 s (Peter), 1 da (Deborah); *Career* RN 1944–47; Hunting plc (formerly Hunting Group of Companies): joined 1950, dir 1952–, vice chm 1962, chm 1975–91; pres: Br Independent Air Tport Assoc 1960–62, Fedn Internationale de Transporte Aerien Privée 1961–63, Air Educn and Recreation Orgn 1970–90, Society of British Aerospace Companies Ltd 1985–86; chm Air League 1968–71, vice chm Battle of Britain Meml Tst 1992–, fndr and first pres Air League Educational Tst 1969–83, memb Cncl Cranfield Inst of Technol 1989– (memb Ct 1980–), former cdre Royal London YC; Nile Gold Medal for Aerospace Educn 1982; Freeman City of London 1982, former Master Worshipful Co of Coachmakers and Coach Harness Makers; CIMgt 1980, CRAeS 1983, FRSA 1984; *Recreations* fishing, yachting, bird watching; *Clubs* Royal Yacht Sqdn, Royal London Yacht; *Style*— Clive Hunting, Esq; ✉ April Cottage, Alderbourne Lane, Fulmer, Slough SL3 6JB; Hunting plc, 3 Cockspur Street, London SW1Y 5BQ (☎ 0171 321 0123, fax 0171 839 2072)

HUNTING, Richard Hugh; s of Charles Patrick Maule Hunting, CBE (d 1993), and Diana Margaret, *née* Pereira (d 1995); *b* 30 July 1946; *Educ* Rugby, Univ of Sheffield (BEng), Univ of Manchester (MBA); *m* 31 Oct 1970, Penelope Susan, da of Col L L Fleming, MBE, MC; 1 s (Rupert b 1974), 2 da (Joanna b 1976, Chloë b 1979); *Career* Hunting Group 1972–: Hunting Surveys and Consultants, Field Aviation, E A Gibson Shipbrokers, Hunting Oilfield Services, Hunting Engineering, chm Hunting Associated Industries 1989 (dir 1986–89), chm Hunting plc 1991– (dir 1989–); memb Ct of Assts Worshipful Co of Ironmongers (Master 1996–97); *Recreations* skiing, board sailing, computing; *Clubs* Travellers'; *Style*— Richard Hunting, Esq; ✉ Hunting plc, 3 Cockspur Street, London SW1Y 5BQ; (☎ 0171 321 0123, fax 0171 839 2072)

HUNTINGDON, Bishop of 1997–; Rt Rev John Robert Flack; s of Edwin John Flack, of Hoddesdon, Herts, and Joan Annie, *née* Stevens; *b* 30 May 1942; *Educ* Hertford GS, Univ of Leeds (BA), Coll of the Resurrection Mirfield; *m* 5 Oct 1968, Julia Clare, da of Rev Canon Maurice Basil Slaughter; 1 da (Alison Clare b 13 Oct 1969) 1 s (Robert Alban b 22 June 1972); *Career* ordained (Ripon Cathedral): deacon 1966, priest 1967; curate: St Bartholomew Armley Leeds 1966–69, St Mary's Northampton 1969–72; vicar of Chapelthorpe 1972–81, vicar of Ripponden with Rishworth and of Barkisland with W Scammonden, concurrently chaplain of Rishworth Sch 1981–85, vicar of Brighouse 1985–92 (team rector 1988–92), rural dean of Brighouse and Elland 1986–92, hon canon of Wakefield Cathedral 1989–97, archdeacon of Pontefract 1992–97; chm: Wakefield Bd of Mission 1980–94, House of Clergy Wakefield 1988–93; selector: C of E Advsy Bd of Miny 1992–, Gen Synod 1994–, C of E Central Bd of Fin 1994–; church cmmr 1995–; memb: Crigglestone CC 1973–80, Ripponden Stones CC 1981–84, Brighouse CC 1985–91; Capt Wakefield Clergy CC 1978–88; *Recreations* cricket (still playing), Mozart (writing about and speaking on); *Style*— The Rt Rev the Bishop of Huntingdon; ✉ c/o Bishop Woodford House, Barton Road, Ely, Cambs CB7 4DX (☎ 01353 663579)

HUNTINGDON, 16 Earl of (E 1529); William Edward Robin Hood Hastings-Bass; s of Capt Peter Hastings-Bass (assumed additional name Bass 1954, d 1964), and Priscilla (b 1920, m 1947, dir Newbury Race Course, memb Jockey Club), da of Capt Sir Malcolm Bullock, 1 Bt, MBE, and Lady Victoria Stanley, da of 17 Earl of Derby; suc kinsman, 15 Earl of Huntingdon 1990; *b* 30 Jan 1948; *Educ* Winchester, Trinity Coll Cambridge; *m* 1989, Susan Mary Gavin, da of John Jellico Pelham Francis Warner, and gda of Sir Pelham Warner, MBE; *Heir* bro, Simon Aubrey Robin Hood Hastings-Bass b 1950; *Style*— The Rt Hon the Earl of Huntingdon; ✉ Hodcott House, West Ilsley, nr Newbury, Berks

HUNTINGFIELD, 7 Baron (I 1796); Sir Joshua Charles Vanneck; 9 Bt (GB 1751); s of 6 Baron Huntingfield (d 1994), and Janetta Lois, *née* Errington; *b* 10 Aug 1954; *Educ* Eton, Magdalene Coll Cambridge (MA); *m* 1982, Arabella Mary, da of Maj Alastair Hugh Joseph Fraser, MC (d 1986), of Moniack Castle, Kirkhill, Inverness; 1 da (Hon Vanessa Clare b 1983), 4 s (Hon Gerard Charles Alastair b 1985, Hon John Errington b 1988, Hon Richard Fraser b 1990, Hon David Guise b (twin) 1990); *Heir* s, Hon Gerard Charles Alastair Vanneck b 12 March 1985; *Career* Royal Scots Dragoon Guards; accountant: Deloitte Haskins & Sells Cambridge, NFU Cambridge; *Clubs* Pratt's; *Style*— The Lord Huntingfield; ✉ 69 Barrons Way, Comberton, Cambridge CB3 7EQ

HUNTINGTON-WHITELEY, Sir Hugo Baldwin; 3 Bt (UK 1918), of Grimley, Worcester; DL (Worcs 1972); s of Capt Sir Maurice Huntington-Whiteley, 2 Bt, RN (d 1975), and Lady (Pamela) Margaret (d 1976), 3 da of 1 Earl Baldwin of Bewdley, KG, PC; *b* 31 March 1924; *Educ* Eton; *m* 1959, Jean Marie Ramsay, DStJ, JP, da of late Arthur Francis Ramsay Bock; 2 da (Sophie Elizabeth (Mrs Zdatny) b 1964, Charlotte Anne (Mrs McAuliffe) b 1965); *Heir* bro, (John) Miles Huntington-Whiteley, *qv*; *Career* RN 1942–47; ptnr Price Waterhouse 1963–83; High Sheriff of Worcs 1971; memb Ct of Assts Worshipful Co Goldsmiths (Prime Warden 1989–90); FCA; *Recreations* music and travel; *Clubs* Brooks's; *Style*— Sir Hugo Huntington-Whiteley, Bt, DL; ✉ Ripple Hall, Tewkesbury, Glos GL20 6EY (☎ 0168 459 2431)

HUNTINGTON-WHITELEY, (John) Miles; VRD (two clasps); s of Capt Sir Maurice Huntington-Whiteley, 2 Bt, RN (d 1975), and Lady (Pamela) Margaret (d 1976), 3 da of 1 Earl Baldwin of Bewdley, KG, PC; hp of bro, Sir Hugo Huntington-Whiteley, 3 Bt, DL, *qv*; *b* 18 July 1929; *Educ* Eton, Trinity Coll Cambridge; *m* 1960, HIllH Countess Victoria Adelheid Clementine Luise, da of late HIllH Count Friedrich Wolfgang zu Castell-Rüdenhausen (ka 1940) *see* Debrett's Peerage, Royal Family section; 1 s (Leopold Maurice b 1965), 2 da (Alice Louise Esther Margot b 1961, m 1985, Charles Percy Sewell, 3 s of the late Maj Geoffrey Richard Michael Sewell by his wife Joan, 3 da of Sir Watkin Williams-Wynn, 8 Bt; Beatrice Irene Helen Victoria b 1962, m 1995, Andrew William Grant, of Bransford Manor, nr Worcester); *Career* Writer RN 1947–49, cmmnd RNVR 1949, recalled for Korean War and served Far East 1951–53, Lt Cdr RNR 1960; int investment portfolio mangr, ret; *Recreations* applied and fine arts, music, the paranormal; *Clubs* Naval; *Style*— Miles Huntington-Whiteley, Esq, VRD; ✉ 6 Matheson Rd, London W14 8SW (☎ and fax 0171 602 8484)

HUNTLY, 13 Marquess of (S 1599); Granville Charles Gomer Gordon; Premier Marquis of Scotland, also Earl of Aboyne, Lord Gordon of Strathavon and Glenlivet (both S 1660), and Baron Meldrum of Morven (UK 1815); s of 12 Marquess of Huntly (d 1987), and his 1 w, Hon Pamela, *née* Berry, da of 1 Viscount Kemsley; *b* 4 Feb 1944; *Educ* Gordonstoun; *m* 1, 1972 (m dis 1990), Jane Elizabeth Angela, da of late Lt-Col Alistair Monteith Gibb and Hon Yoskyl, *née* Pearson, da of 2 Viscount Cowdray, DL; 1 s, 2 da (Lady Amy b 1975, Lady Lucy b 1979); m 2, 15 Feb 1991, Catheryn, da of Gay Kindersley, *qv*, and formerly w of Robert Lennon Millbourn; 1 da (Lady Rose Marie-Louise b 24 June 1993); *Heir* s, Alistair Granville Gordon, Earl of Aboyne b 26 July 1973; *Career* patron Inst of Commercial Mgmnt, pres Inst of Financial Accountants, chm Vin Services Ltd, dir Ampton Investments Ltd; *Style*— The Most Hon the Marquess of Huntly; ✉ Aboyne Castle, Aberdeenshire

HUNWICKS, Trevor Alec; s of Alec Alfred Hunwicks, of Maldon, Essex, and Jean, *née* Brazier; *b* 22 Sept 1943; *Educ* Chislehurst and Sidcup GS, Univ of Greenwich (MA); *m* 14 Dec 1968, Zara, da of Peter John Harris, of IOW; 1 s (William George b 7 Oct 1974), 1 da (Victoria Louise b 21 August 1971); *Career* Nationwide Anglia Building Soc (formerly Anglia Building Soc) 1968–90: branch mangr 1968, London mangr 1971, London regnl mangr 1975, gen mangr mktg 1985, gen mangr corp devpt 1987; dir Benton International (retail banking conslts) 1991–95, managing ptnr (UK) Strategic Futures International 1995–; chm of govrs Northampton Coll 1990–; FCIM 1981, FCIB 1977, FIMgt 1986, FRSA 1992; *Recreations* theatre, music, painting, tennis; *Clubs* RAC, Wig and Pen; *Style*— Trevor Hunwicks, Esq; ✉ The Old Barn, Ecton, Northampton NN6 0QB (☎ 01604 406203); Strategic Futures International, St Alphage House, Fore Street, London EC2Y 5DA (☎ 0171 628 1304, fax 0171 256 6930)

HUPPERT, Prof Herbert Eric; s of Leo Huppert (d 1957), and Alice, *née* Neuman (d 1967); *b* 26 Nov 1943; *Educ* Sydney Boys' HS, Univ of Sydney (BSc), ANU (MSc), Univ of California San Diego (MS, PhD), Univ of Cambridge (MA, ScD); *m* 20 April 1966, Felicia Adina, da of Bernard David Ferster (d 1993), of Bellevue Hill, NSW, Aust; 2 s (Julian b 1978, Rowan b 1982); *Career* Univ of Cambridge: fell King's Coll 1970–, asst dir of res 1970–81, lectr 1981–88, reader in geophysical dynamics 1988–89, prof of theoretical geophysics and dir Inst of Geophysics 1989–; prof of mathematics Univ of NSW 1991–95; memb Ed Bd Philosophical Transactions of the Royal Soc 1994–, assoc ed Jl of Fluid Mechanics 1970–90, sr res fell BP Venture Unit 1983–89; co-chm Scientists for the Release of Soviet Refusniks 1987–91, memb Cncl NERC 1993–, memb Scientific Cncl The Earth Centre 1995–; FRS 1987; *Recreations* my children, playing squash and tennis, walking, dreaming of a less hassled life; *Style*— Prof Herbert Huppert, FRS; ✉ 46 De Freville Ave, Cambridge CB4 1HT (☎ 01223 356071); Institute of Theoretical Geophysics, Dept of Applied Mathematics & Theoretical Physics and Dept of Earth Sciences, 20 Silver St, Cambridge CB3 9EW (☎ 01223 337853, fax 01223 337918, telex 81240 CAMSPL G, e-mail hehl@esc.cam.ac.uk)

HURD, Rt Hon Douglas Richard; CH (1996), CBE (1974), PC (1982), MP (C) Witney (majority 22,568); eldest s of Baron Hurd, sometime MP Newbury and agric corr The Times (Life Peer, d 1966; himself er s of Sir Percy Angier Hurd, sometime MP Frome and Devizes, ed Canadian Gazette and London ed Montreal Star; Sir Percy was er bro of Sir Archibald Hurd, also a journalist (Daily Telegraph) and formerly chm Shipping World Co), and Stephanie Frances, *née* Corner (d 1985); *b* 8 March 1930; *Educ* Eton, Trinity Coll Cambridge (BA 1952, MA 1957); *m* 1, 10 Nov 1960 (m dis 1982), Tatiana Elizabeth Michelle, o da of (Arthur Charles) Benedict Eyre, MBE, of Bury, Sussex; 3 s (Nicholas Richard b 13 May 1962, Thomas Robert Benedict b 20 Sept 1964, Alexander Paul Anthony b 7 June 1969); m 2, 1982, Judy J, 2 da of Sidney Smart, of Chaddleworth, Berks; 1 s (Philip Arthur b 1983), 1 da (Jessica Stephanie b 1985); *Career* Dip Serv 1952–66 (Peking, UK Mission to UN, Rome, also private sec to perm under sec FO); CRD 1966–68 (head Foreign Affrs Section 1968); MP (C): Mid Oxon Feb 1974–1983, Witney 1983–; private sec to Rt Hon Edward Heath as ldr of Oppn 1968–70, political sec to PM 1970–74, oppn spokesman on foreign affrs (with special responsibility for EEC) 1976–79; min of state: FCO 1979–83, Home Office 1983–84; sec of state for NI 1984–85, home secretary 1985–89, sec of state for foreign and Cwlth affrs 1989–95; dir National Westminster Bank plc 1995–; dep chm: NatWest Markets 1995–, British Invisibles 1996–; visiting fell Nuffield Coll Oxford 1978; *Books* The Arrow War (1967), Truth Game (1972), Vote to Kill (1975), An End to Promises (1979); with Andrew Osmond: Send Him Victorious (1968), The Smile on The Face of the Tiger (1969), Scotch on the Rocks (1971), War Without Frontiers (1982); Palace of Enchantments (with Stephen Lamport, 1985); *Clubs* Beefsteak, Travellers'; *Style*— The Rt Hon Douglas Hurd, CH, CBE, MP; ✉ NatWest Markets, 135 Bishopsgate, London EC2M 3UR

HURD, Martyn Roy; s of (Bernard) Roy Hurd, and Marjorie Sheila, *née* Burton; *b* 28 Sept 1948; *Educ* Blatchington Court Seaford Sussex, Open Univ (BA); *m* 31 Aug 1976, Philippa Helen, da of late (John) Angus Beckett, CB, CMG; 2 da (Jane b 6 May 1979, Helen b 21 July 1981); *Career* planning offr W Midlands Central Independent TV until 1983; ITN: mangr of prodn planning 1983–91, head of studios programme and resource planning 1991–94, dir of human resources 1994–; chm nat educational registered charity Norsuch (History and Dance) Ltd; memb: Cncl Nat Cncl for the Trg of Broadcast Journalists (NCTBJ), TV Ctee Br Kinematograph Sound and Television Soc, RTS; *Recreations* walking, swimming, reading; *Style*— Martyn Hurd, Esq; ✉ 7 Roy Rd, Northwood, Middx HA6 1EQ (☎ 01923 826868); Independent Television News, 200 Gray's Inn Road, London WC1X 8XZ (☎ 0171 430 4495, fax 0171 430 4131)

HURD, Mick; s of Norman Frank Hurd, of Hitchin, Herts, and Irene May, *née* Cook; *b* 18 Sept 1956; *Educ* Hitchin Boys' GS, Herts Coll of Art and Design St Albans, Central Sch of Art (BA); *Career* design asst Palace Theatre Westcliff-on-Sea 1980–81; freelance designer of window displays and PR sets 1981–; window displays for shops incl: Barneys NY (5 sets incl Christmas 1988), Katherine Hamnett (temp shops and showroom), North Beach Leather Sloane St, Simpsons of Piccadilly, Browns South Molton St, Moschino at Italian Trade Centre, Hyper Hyper Kensington High St; PR Cos worked with incl: Lynne Franks (Ratners, Lamb's Rum, New York Seltzer, Cable & Co, Swatch Watches, Brylcream and Littlewoods), Shilland & Co (Levis), Marysia Woroniecka (Benetton), Caroline Neville Assocs (Lycra); video art dir on various pop promos incl Dreams and Going Nowhere (Gabrielle); photographic backdrop designer for: Correspondent, BR, Independent on Sunday, Eurax; prodn designer The Attendant, co-designer Blow Your Mind (C4), art dir Don't Forget Your Toothbrush (Channel 4); designer: New Big Breakfast (Channel 4), The Sunday Show (BBC 2), Gaytime TV (BBC 2), Love Is (Channel 4), Capital Holidays (Carlton), Street-Porter's Men (Channel 4), Life's A Bitch (BBC 2), Belinda Lang Fitness Video, Janet Thompson Fitness Video; *Style*— Mick Hurd, Esq; ✉ 15 Gibraltar Walk, London E2 7LH (☎ 0171 729 3624, mobile 0831 362919)

HURD, Hon Stephen Anthony; JP (Wilts 1969); yr s of Baron Hurd (Life Peer, d 1966), and Stephanie Frances, *née* Corner (d 1985); bro of Rt Hon Douglas Hurd, *qv*; *b* 6 April 1933; *Educ* Winchester, Magdalene Coll Cambridge (BA, Dip Agric, MA); *m* 30 June 1973, Pepita Lilian, da of late Lt-Col Walter Hingston, OBE; 2 s (William b 1976, Christopher b 1977); *Career* farmer; dir: North Wilts Cereals Ltd 1970–85, Group Cereals Ltd 1970–84, West of England Farmers Ltd 1968–89 (chm 1988–89), West of England Building Society (formerly Ramsbury Building Society) 1973–90, Portman Building Society 1990, West Midland Farmers' Assoc Ltd 1989– (chm 1992–95); tstee Duchess of Somerset Hosp Froxfield Wilts, chm Marlborough Petty Sessional Div 1987–91; *Style*— The Hon Stephen Hurd, JP; ✉ The Oxyard, Oare, Marlborough, Wilts SN8 4JA

HURDLE, Michael William Frederick; s of Maurice Frederick Hurdle (d 1994), of Burton-on-Trent, and Mary Murielle Morton Wilson; *b* 3 June 1941; *Educ* Uppingham, Univ of Keele (BA); *Career* chm Marston Thompson and Evershed plc (Brewers); Liveryman Worshipful Co of Brewers; *Recreations* shooting, fishing, golf, tennis, horseracing; *Clubs* The Burton, The Oriental, Lloyds; *Style*— Michael Hurdle, Esq; ✉ Marston Thompson & Evershed plc, PO Box 26, Shobnall Rd, Burton-on-Trent, Staffs DE14 2BW

HURFORD, Prof James Raymond (Jim); *b* 16 July 1941; *Educ* Exeter Sch, St John's Coll Cambridge (BA), UCL (PhD); *Career* assoc Dept of Germanic Languages UCLA 1963–64, postdoctoral res fell System Development Corporation California 1967–68, asst prof Dept of English Univ of California Davis 1968–71, sr lectr Dept of Linguistics Univ of Lancaster 1976–79 (lectr 1972–76), prof of general linguistics Univ of Edinburgh 1979–; visiting res fell Univ of Melbourne 1989–90; visiting prof: Cairo Univ 1976, Univ of California 1982; memb of Faculty Linguistic Inst Linguistic Soc of America 1995; *Books* The Linguistic Theory of Numerals (1975), Semantics: a Coursebook (with B Heasley, 1983), Language and Number: the emergence of a cognitive system (1987), Grammar: a Student's Guide (1994); *Style*— Prof Jim Hurford; ✉ Department of Linguistics, University of Edinburgh, Adam Ferguson Building, Edinburgh EH8 9LL (☎ 0131 650 3959/3960)

HURFORD, Peter John; OBE (1984); *b* 22 Nov 1930; *Educ* Blundell's Sch, RCM, Jesus Coll Cambridge (MA, MusB); *m* 6 Aug 1955, Patricia Mary, da of Prof Sir Bryan Matthews, of Cambridge; 2 s, 1 da; *Career* organist; Master of the Music St Albans Cathedral 1958–78; fndr Int Organ Festival 1963; visiting prof: Univ of Cincinnati USA 1967–68, Univ of W Ontario 1976–77; visiting artist-in-residence Sydney Opera House 1980–82, memb Cncl Royal Coll of Organists 1964– (pres 1980–82), prof RAM 1982–88, memb Hon Cncl of Mgmnt Royal Philharmonic Soc 1983–87, John Betts fell Univ of Oxford 1992–93; frequent recital tours 1960– (America, Canada, Australia, New Zealand, E and W Europe, Japan and Far E); over 70 recordings incl: complete organ works of J S Bach, Couperin, Handel, Hindemith; radio appearances incl: 34 progs of Bach's complete organ music 1980 and 1982, 7 progs 1990; TV appearances incl Music in Time 1983; Hon DMus Baldwin-Wallace Coll Ohio 1981, Hon DMus Univ of Bristol 1992; Hon RAM 1981, HonFRSCM 1977, Hon FRCM 1987; *Books* Making Music on the Organ (1988), contrib to many Musical Magazines; *Recreations* walking, wine, silence; *Style*— Peter Hurford, Esq, OBE; ✉ Broom House, St Bernard's Rd, St Albans, Herts AL3 5RA

HURFORD, Sam; s of Alister Edwin Hurford, of Moorlands, East Winch Road, Ashwicken, Kings Lynn, Norfolk, and June Mary, *née* Kenny; *b* 9 Sept 1956; *Educ* Stanground Sch Peterborough, Peterborough Tech Coll, Trent Poly Nottingham (DipAD); *m* 5 Sept 1981, Christina Helen, da of Alojzy Brunon Gdaniec; 1 s (Max Michael b 28 April 1988), 1 da (Rosie Louise b 5 June 1990); *Career* typographer Boase Massimi Pollitt advtg agency 1979–81; art dir: Saatchi & Saatchi 1981–82, Gold Greenlees Trott 1982–85; art dir/gp head: Yellowhammer 1985–88, Publicis 1988–92; head of art/dep creative dir TBWA Holmes Knight Ritchie 1992–93, freelance creative (ptnr Mike Cozens) 1993–94, sr creative Young & Rubicam 1994–; awards incl: Creative Circle Gold, Silver and Bronze, Campaign Poster Silver and Bronze, D&AD Silver, Clio Gold, Euro Gold, Kinsale Grand Prix and 4 Golds, Cannes Silver 1992; memb 1991–92: D&AD, Creative Circle; *Recreations* skiing, sailing, windsurfing, running, football, gym; *Style*— Sam Hurford, Esq; ✉ Young & Rubicam Ltd, Greater London House, Hampstead Road, London NW1 7QP (☎ 0171 387 9366)

HURLEY, Elizabeth Jane; da of Roy Leonard Hurley, and Angela Mary Hurley; *b* 10 June 1965; *Career* actress and model; spokeswoman and model for Estée Lauder; head devpt Simian Films; *Theatre* incl: The Cherry Orchard - A Jubilee (Russian & Soviet Arts Festival), The Man Most Likely To (Middle East tour); *Television* incl: title role in Christabel (BBC), The Orchid House (Channel 4), Act of Will (Portman Prodns), The Resurrector (Fox TV), Rumpole (Thames), Inspector Morse (Zenith), The Good Guys (Havahall Pictures), The Young Indiana Jones Chronicles (Lucas Films Ltd), Sharpe's Enemy (Sharpe Films), Cry of the City (Universal TV); *Films* incl: Aria - Rowing in the Wind (Ditirambo Films), The Skipper (Rialto Films), The Long Winter of 39 (Tibidabo Films), Passenger 57 (Warner Bros), Bedlam (Bedlam Films), Mad Dogs and Englishmen (Moor Street Films), The Spear (New Line Cinema); *Recreations* gardening, toxicology, angling, embroidery; *Style*— Ms Elizabeth Hurley; ✉ c/o ICM Ltd, Oxford House, 76 Oxford Street, London W1N 0AX (☎ 0171 636 6565, fax 0171 323 0101); c/o Simian Films, 3 Cromwell Place, London SW7 2JE (☎ 0171 589 6822, fax 0171 589 9405)

HURLEY, (Ronald) John; s of Harold Hurley (d 1989), and (Margaret) Olga, *née* Fisher; *b* 29 Jan 1937; *Educ* Bridgend Boys' GS, Sch of Architecture UWIST (Dip Arch, ARIBA); *m* 14 July 1962, Yvonne Mary, da of Dr Robert James Phillips, MBE; 1 da (Sian Gillian b 1965), 1 s (David Rhys b 1966); *Career* architect: Thomas & Morgan & Partners (Pontypridd) 1960–62, Sir Frederick Gibberd & Partners Harlow 1962–66; sr ptnr Denys Lasdun Peter Softley & Associates (joined Sir Denys Lasdun & Partners 1966), dir Hurley, Robertson and Associates Architects; chm Harlow Sports Cncl; *Recreations* rugby, sailing; *Style*— John Hurley, Esq; ✉ Denys Lasdun Peter Softley & Associates, 146 Grosvenor Road, London SW1V 3JY (☎ 0171 630 8211, fax 0171 821 6191); Hurley, Robertson and Associates Architects, 146 Grosvenor Road, London SW1V 3JY (☎ 0171 932 0599, fax 0171 821 6191)

HURN, Sir (Francis) Roger; kt (1996); s of Francis James Hurn, and Joyce Elsa, *née* Bennett; *b* 9 June 1938; *Educ* Marlborough; *m* 1980, Rosalind Jackson; 1 da; *Career* Nat Serv 1959–61; engrg appentice Rolls-Royce Motors 1956–58; Smiths Industries plc: export rep Automotive Business Europe and N America 1958–59 and 1961–65, export dir Motor Accessory Div 1969 (export mangr 1965–69), corp staff dir Overseas Ops 1969–74, md Int Ops 1974–76, exec dir 1976–78, md 1978–81, chief exec and md 1981–91, chm and chief exec 1991–96, chm 1991–; non-exec dir: ICI plc 1993–, Glaxo Wellcome PLC; vice pres Engineering Employers' Fedn; chm of govr Henley Management Coll; Liveryman Worshipful Co of Coachmakers and Coach Harness Makers 1979; Young Business of the Year (The Guardian) 1980; *Style*— Sir Roger Hurn; ✉ Smiths Industries plc, 765 Finchley Road, London NW11 8DS (☎ 0181 458 3232)

HURN, Stanley Noel; s of Leonard Frederick Hurn (d 1973), of Colchester, and Kathleen Alice, *née* Frost (d 1984); *b* 24 Dec 1943; *Educ* Colchester Royal GS, Univ of Hull (BSc); *Career* mangr Standard Chartered Bank 1968–78, asst dir Orion Royal Bank Ltd 1978–82, dir Samuel Montagu & Co Ltd 1982–96, dir and head Loan Syndication HSBC 1996–; FCIB 1995; *Books* Syndicated Loans - A Handbook for Banker and Borrower (1990); *Clubs* Bankers, Royal Automobile; *Style*— Stanley Hurn, Esq; ✉ 301 Shakespeare Tower, Barbican, London EC2Y 8NJ; HSBC Investment Bank plc, 10 Queen Street Place, London EC4R 1BL (☎ 0171 336 9200, fax 0171 336 9609)

HURRELL, Sir Anthony Gerald; KCVO (1986), CMG (1984); s of late William Hurrell, and Florence Hurrell; *b* 18 Feb 1927; *Educ* Norwich Sch, St Catharine's Coll Cambridge; *m* 1951, Jean, *née* Wyatt; 2 da; *Career* RAEC 1948–50, Miny of Lab 1950–53, Miny of Educn 1953–64, Miny of Overseas Devpt 1964, fell Center for Int Affrs Harvard 1969–70, head of SE Asia Devpt Div Bangkok 1972–74; under sec: Int Div ODM 1974–75, Central Policy Review Staff Cabinet Office 1976, Duchy of Lancaster 1977, Asia and Oceans

Div ODA 1978–83, Int Div ODA 1983; ambass to Nepal 1983–86; *Style*— Sir Anthony Hurrell, KCVO, CMG; ✉ Lapwings, Dunwich, Saxmundham, Suffolk IP17 3DR

HURRELL, Air Vice-Marshal Frederick Charles; CB (1986), OBE (1970); s of Alexander John Hurrell (Lt, d 1933), and Maria Del Carmen, *née* Di Biedma (d 1968); *b* 24 April 1928; *Educ* Royal Masonic Schs Bushey, St Mary's Hosp Med Sch and Univ of London (MB BS, MRCS, LRCP, Dip Av Med (RCP), FFOM); *m* 7 Oct 1950, Jay Ruby, da of Hugh Gordon Jarvis (d 1975); 5 da (Caroline b 1951, Rosemary b 1953, Katherine b 1956, Alexandra b 1959, Anne b 1960); *Career* cmmd RAF (Med Branch): flying offr 1953, sr med offr on flying stations in UK Aust and Far East 1954–67, Flt Lt 1954, Actg Sqdn Ldr 1954, Sqdn Ldr 1959, Wing Cdr 1965, various jr staff appts 1967–74, Gp Capt and dep dir of aviation med 1974–77, staff offr (aerospace med) Br Def Staff Washington 1978–80, Air Cdre and OC Princess Alexandra Hosp RAF Wroughton 1980–82, dir of health and res 1982–84, Air Vice-Marshal and princ med offr RAF Strike Cmd 1984–86, DG of RAF med servs 1986–88, ret 1988; dir of appeals RAF Benevolent Fund 1988–95; FRSM 1986, FRAeS 1987; CStJ 1986; *Recreations* photography, gardening, golf; *Clubs* RAF, Sports Club of London; *Style*— Air Vice-Marshal Frederick Hurrell, CB, OBE; ✉ Hale House, 4 Upper Hale Rd, Farnham, Surrey GU9 0NJ (☎ 01252 714190)

HURST, Lady Barbara; *née* Lindsay; 6 da of 27 Earl of Crawford and 10 of Balcarres, KT, PC (d 1940), and Constance (d 1947), da of Sir Henry Carstairs Pelly, 3 Bt, MP; *b* 31 Dec 1915; *m* 23 May 1939, Col Richard Lumley Hurst, Royal Sussex Regt TA, barr (d 1962), s of Sir Cecil James Barrington Hurst, GCMG, KCB; 1 s (Robert b 1945), 3 da (Elizabeth (Mrs Gilroy) b 1940, Cecilia (Mrs Goodlad) b 1944, Katharine (Mrs Gibbs) b 1948); *Style*— The Lady Barbara Hurst; ✉ Powers Wood, Elkstone, Cheltenham, Glos GL59 9PT (☎ 01285 821 869)

HURST, Geoffrey Charles (Geoff); MBE (1977); s of Charles Hurst, of Chelmsford, Essex, and Evelyn May, *née* Hopkins; *b* 8 Dec 1941; *Educ* Rainsford Secdy Modern, Chelmsford, Essex; *m* 13 Oct 1964, Judith Helen, da of Jack Henry Harries; 3 da (Claire Helen b 30 Oct 1965, Joanne Louise b 16 March 1969, Charlotte Jane b 13 Feb 1977); *Career* former professional footballer and mangr; clubs: West Ham (500 appearances, 250 goals scored), Stoke City 1972–75 (128 appearances, 37 goals scored), West Bromwich Albion 1975–76 (12 appearances, 2 goals scored); player mangr Telford Utd 1976–79; mangr: Chelsea 1979–81, Kuwait 1982–84; England: debut v W Germany 1966, scored hat-trick in World Cup final 4–2 defeat of W Germany Wembley 1966, 49 caps, 24 goals, coach 1977–82; sales dir Motor-Plan Limited 1984–90, new business support mangr Ryan Insurance Group Europe 1992–93, md Appliance Warranty Div London General Insurance 1993–; *Books* World Game (1967); *Recreations* golf; *Style*— Geoff Hurst, Esq, MBE; ✉ London General Holdings, Combined House, 15 Wheatfield Way, Kingston-upon-Thames, Surrey KT1 2PA (direct ☎ 0181 541 6405, 0181 541 6233, fax 0181 541 4027)

HURST, George; *b* Edinburgh; *Educ* Sr Sch of the Royal Conservatory Canada (first graduate in composition); *Career* conductor and composer; prof of composition Peabody Inst Baltimore aged 21, conductor Peabody Conservatory Orch and Symphony Orch of York Pennsylvania 1950–55, London debut with London Philharmonic Orch 1953 (asst conductor 1955–57), princ conductor BBC Northern Symphony Orch (now BBC Philharmonic Orch) 1958–68; co-fndr Bournemouth Sinfonietta 1968, staff conductor Western Orchestral Soc (parent orgn of Bournemouth Sinfonietta and Bournemouth Symphony Orch) 1974– (artistic advsr 1969–74), princ guest conductor BBC Scot Symphony Orch 1986–89, first princ conductor RTE Nat Symphony Orch of Ireland 1990–93; conducted numerous other orchs incl: all major Br and Irish orchs, Nord Deutsch Rundfunk Symphony Orch, Orchestre National Paris, Orchestre Lamoureux Paris, Orchestre de la Suisse Romande, Royal Danish Orch, Hamburg Orch, Israel Philharmonic Orch; *Style*— George Hurst, Esq; ✉ c/o Transart (UK) Ltd, 8 Bristol Gardens, London W9 2JG (☎ 0171 286 7526)

HURST, John Edward; s of Edward Gostling Hurst (d 1964), of Weston Longville, Norwich, and Grace, *née* Holder; *b* 10 Oct 1947; *Educ* Gresham's, Univ of London (LLB), Univ of Amsterdam (Post Grad Dip); *m* 19 Dec 1972, Julia, da of Hendrik Jan Engelbert van Beuningen, of Cothen (U), The Netherlands; 1 s (Robert Adriaan b 13 April 1979), 2 da (Olivia b 8 Sept 1974, Annette b 16 April 1977); *Career* admitted slr 1976; ptnr: Hurst van Beuningen (Farms) 1982–, Daynes Hill & Perks 1987–92, Eversheds Daynes Hill & Perks 1992–95, Eversheds 1995–; Law Soc's Slr's Euro Gp 1987–88, lay chm Sparham Deanery Synod C of E 1987–96; memb: Law Soc 1976, NFU 1982; govr Taverham Hall Prep Sch 1996–; *Books* Legal Issues of European Integration: Harmonisation of Company Law in the EEC (1974); *Recreations* swimming, stalking and country pursuits; *Clubs* Norfolk; *Style*— John Hurst, Esq; ✉ Eversheds, Holland Court, The Close, Norwich NR1 4DX (☎ 01603 272727, fax 01603 630588)

HURST, Kim Barbara; da of Norman Campbell Hurst, of Sheffield, and Elsie, *née* Hands; *b* 8 Aug 1956; *Educ* Ecclesfield Sch, Univ of Leicester (BA); *Career* trainee Grant Thornton 1978–81, Griffin Stone Moscrop 1982–83, under sec to the Auditing Practices Ctee ICAEW 1983–85, nat tech ptnr Neville Russell 1990– (joined 1985); FCA 1992 (ACA 1982); *Books* Tolley's Charities Manual (3rd edn, 1991), Business Briefing Charities (3rd edn, 1993); *Recreations* theatre, charity work, swimming; *Clubs* Broadgate; *Style*— Ms Kim Hurst; ✉ Neville Russell, 24 Bevis Marks, London EC3A 7NR (☎ 0171 377 1000, fax 0171 377 8931)

HURST, Peter Thomas; s of Thomas Lyon Hurst (d 1981), of Cheshire, and Norah Mary, *née* Delaney (d 1977); *b* 27 Oct 1942; *Educ* Stonyhurst, Univ of London (LLB); *m* 1968, Diane, da of Ian George Irvine, of Cheshire; 1 s (Charles b 1975), 2 da (Elizabeth b 1970, Catherine b 1972); *Career* slr of Supreme Court 1967; ptnr: Hurst and Walker Slrs Liverpool 1967–77, Gair Roberts Hurst and Walker Slrs Liverpool 1977–81; Supreme Court Taxing Office: Master 1981–90, Chief Master 1991–; *Books* Butterworths Costs Service (1986–): Costs in Criminal Cases, Solicitors' Remuneration, Order 62; Cordery on Solicitors (contrib 8 edn, 1988); Legal Aid Practice (1996); Halsbury's Laws of England (Legal Aid, 1994, Solicitor's Remuneration 1995), Civil Costs (1995), Supreme Court Practice (1997),; *Style*— Peter Hurst, Esq; ✉ Supreme Court Taxing Office, Royal Courts of Justice, Cliffords Inn, Fetter Lane, London EC4A 1DQ

HURST-BROWN, (Christopher) Nigel; s of Alan Dudley Hurst-Brown, of Hants, and June Marcella, *née* Wood; *b* 11 July 1951; *Educ* Wellington, Univ of Bristol (BSc); *m* 1976, Candida Madeleine, da of Arthur George Bernard Drabble, of Surrey; 2 da (Annabella, Tania); *Career* dir Hill Samuel Investment Management 1984–86, md Lloyds Merchant Bank Ltd 1986–90, chm Lloyds Investment Managers Ltd 1986–90, dep chm Mercury Asset Management plc 1990–96; *Recreations* golf, tennis, shooting, fishing; *Clubs* Berks GC; *Style*— Nigel Hurst-Brown, Esq; ✉ School Farm, Heckfield, nr Basingstoke, Hants (☎ 0118 932 6633); Mercury Asset Management plc, 33 King William St, London EC4R 9AS (☎ 0171 280 2800, fax 0171 280 2820)

HURSTHOUSE, Roger Stephen; *b* 20 June 1941; *Educ* Henry Mellish GS; *m* 1, (m dis), Janet; 2 s (James Roger b 1969, Andrew Stephen b 1972); m 2, 29 Feb 1996, Julia Gunn; *Career* articled Clerk Harold T Hooley & Co Nottingham 1957–62; Pannell Kerr Forster Nottingham: mangr 1962–68, ptnr 1968–, chm Nottingham Office; pres: Nottingham Soc of CAs 1980–81, Nottinghamshire C of C and Indust 1988–90; memb: Bd Business Link Gtr Nottingham, Bd Nottingham Devpt Enterprise, Ct Univ of Nottingham; chm Nottinghamshire Business Venture, chm Binns Organ Restoration Appeal Fund; serving offr brother Order pf St John, dep chm Cncl for Nottinghamshire; memb IOD; *Recreations* golf, cricket, music; *Clubs* 41; *Style*— Roger S Hursthouse, Esq; ✉ 3 Elm Park, Gonalston Lane, Epperstone, Nottinghamshire NG14 6BE

HURT, John Vincent; s of Rev Father Arnould Herbert Hurt, and Phyllis, *née* Massey (d 1975); *b* 22 Jan 1940; *Educ* Lincoln Sch, St Martin's Sch of Art, RADA; *m* 1, 1984 (m dis 1990), Donna Lynn Peacock, da of Don Wesley Laurence (d 1986), of Texas USA; m 2, 1990, Jo Dalton; 2 s; *Career* actor; debut Arts Theatre London 1962; *Theatre* incl: Chips with Everything (Vaudeville) 1962, The Dwarfs (Arts, Critics Award for Most Promising Actor 1963) 1962, Inadmissable Evidence (Wyndhams) 1965, Little Malcolm and His Struggle Against The Eunuchs (Garrick) 1966, Belcher's Luck (Aldwych, RSC) 1966, The Caretaker (Mermaid) 1971, Travesties (Aldwych, RSC) 1973, The Shadow of a Gunman (Nottingham Playhouse) 1978, The Seagull (Lyric Hammersmith) 1985, London Vertigo (Gate Dublin) 1991, A Month in the Country (Albery) 1994; *Television* incl: The Playboy of the Western World (BBC) 1971, The Naked Civil Servant (Thames TV) 1975 (Br Acad Award for Best Actor 1978), I Claudius (BBC) 1976, Treats (YTV) 1977, Crime and Punishment (BBC) 1978, Fool in King Lear (with Olivier) 1982, The Storyteller (35 episodes) 1986, Poison Candy (BBC) 1987, Deadline 1988, Who Bombed Birmingham? (Granada) 1989, Journey to Knock 1991, Red Fox (LWT) 1991, Six Characters in Search of an Author (BBC) 1992, Enemy Within (BBC) 1995, Prisoner in Time (BBC) 1995; *Films* incl: A Man for All Seasons 1966, 10 Rillington Place 1970, East of Elephant Rock 1976, Spectre 1977, The Disappearance 1977, The Shout 1977, Watership Down 1977, Midnight Express 1977 (Oscar nomination 1978, Br Acad Award 1978, Golden Globe Award 1978, Variety Club Award 1978), Alien 1978, Heaven's Gate 1979, The Elephant Man 1980 (Oscar nomination, Br Acad Award, Variety Club Award), Night Crossing 1980, History of the World Part I 1982, Champions 1983 (Evening Standard Award for Best Actor 1984), Nineteen Eighty-Four 1984, The Hit 1984, Jake Speed 1986, Rocinante 1986, Aria 1987, White Mischief 1987, Bengali Night 1988, Scandal 1988, La Dame aux Chats 1988, Windprints 1989, Frankenstein Unbound 1989, The Field 1990, King Ralph 1990, Memory 1990, Dark at Noon 1991, Lapse of Memory 1991, Even Cowgirls get the Blues 1992, Great Moments in Aviation 1992, Crime & Punishment 1993, Wild Bill 1994, Rob Roy 1995, Saigon Baby 1995; *Recreations* cricket, conservation activity; *Clubs* MCC, TVRF; *Style*— John Hurt, Esq; ✉ c/o Julian Belfrage Associates, 46 Albemarle Street, London W1X 4PP (☎ 0171 491 4400, fax 0171 493 5460)

HURWITZ, Emanuel Henry; CBE (1978); s of Isaac Hurwitz (d 1951), of London, and Sarah Gabrilowitz (d 1966); *b* 7 May 1919; *Educ* RAM; *m* 3 Aug 1948, Kathleen Ethel, da of Reginald Samuel Crome, of Slough, Bucks; 1 s (Michael b 1949), 1 da (Jacqueline b 1942); *Career* musician band RAMC; concerts in: Eng, Ireland, Egypt, Palestine, Syria, Lebanon, Iraq, Iran, Germany, Italy; leader: Hurwitz String Quartet 1946–52, Goldsborough Orch 1947–57, London String Trio 1952–68, London Pianoforte Quartet 1952–68, Melos Ensemble of London 1956–74, English Chamber Orch 1957–69, New Philharmonia Orch 1969–71, Aeolian String Quartet 1970–81; prof RAM 1968–; visiting lectr: RSAMD 1987–, Univ of Michigan State USA 1995; recordings incl: Brandenburg Concerti, Handel Concerto Grossi, Schubert Octet, Beethoven Septet, Trout Quintet, Mozart and Brahms Clarinet Quintets, Complete Haydn String Quartets, Ravel, Debussy, Beethoven, etc; memb: Inc Soc of Musicians 1958 (pres 1995–96), Euro String Teachers Assoc 1982; Gold Medal Worshipful Co of Musicians 1967; FRAM 1961, FRSAMD 1990; *Recreations* old violins and bows, swimming, walking, music of other instruments; *Style*— Emanuel Hurwitz, Esq, CBE; ✉ 25 Dollis Avenue, London N3 1DA (☎ 0181 346 3936)

HUSBAND, John; s of John Husband (d 1986), of Edgware, and Bridget Agnes Leahy; *b* 21 April 1945; *Educ* St Vincent's RC Sch Mill Hill, St James' RC HS Edgware, Univ of Hull (BSc); *Career* Daily Mirror: trainee reporter 1966–68, fin reporter 1968–74, dep City ed 1974–90 (and Sunday Mirror 1975–90), City ed 1990–93, City ed and personal finance ed 1993–; memb ABI Code Monitoring Ctee 1990–; Personal Fin Journalist of The Year 1990, Wincott Business Jl of the Year (for Sunday Mirror City column) 1991; memb NUJ 1966; *Books* Money Mirror (1980), Daily Mirror Guide to Money (1993); *Recreations* music, record collecting, walking, history; *Style*— John Husband, Esq; ✉ Mirror Group Newspapers, 1 Canada Square, Canary Wharf, London E14 5AP (☎ 0171 293 3323)

HUSBAND, Prof Thomas Mutrie (Tom); s of Thomas Mutrie Husband, and Janet, *née* Clark; *b* 7 July 1936; *Educ* Shawlands Acad Glasgow, Univ of Strathclyde (BSc, MA, PhD); *m* 1962, Pat Caldwell; 2 s; *Career* Weir Ltd Glasgow: apprentice fitter 1953–58, engr/jr mangr 1958–62, Sandwich degree student of mech engrg 1958–61; various engrg and mgmnt positions ASEA Ltd (Denmark, UK, S Africa) 1962–65, teaching fell Univ of Chicago 1966–67, lectr Univ of Strathclyde 1969–70, sr lectr Univ of Glasgow 1970–73, prof of mfrg orgn Univ of Loughborough 1973–81; Imperial Coll London: prof of engrg manufacture 1981–90, dir Centre for Robotics 1982–90, head Dept of Mech Engrg 1983–90; vice-chllr Univ of Salford 1990–; chm Univ of Salford Holdings PLC 1990–; non-exec dir: Royal Exchange Theatre Manchester 1994–, Univs and Colls Employers Assoc 1994–; memb Engrg Cncl 1992–96; FEng 1988, FIEE, FIMechE; *Publications* Work Analysis and Pay Structure (1976), Maintenance and Terotechnology (1977), Education and Training in Robotics (1986), author of articles in various jls; *Recreations* watching Arsenal FC, music, theatre; *Style*— Prof Tom Husband, FEng; ✉ 34 Hawthorn Lane, Wilmslow SK9 5DG (☎ 01625 520519); University of Salford, Salford M5 4WT (☎ 0161 745 5000, fax 0161 745 5999)

HUSKINSON, (George) Nicholas Nevil; s of Thomas Leonard Bousfield Huskinson (d 1974), of Triscombe House, Triscombe, Taunton, Somerset, and Helen Margaret, *née* Hales (d 1983); *b* 7 Dec 1948; *Educ* Eton, King's Coll Cambridge (MA); *m* 20 Dec 1972, Pennant Elfrida Lascelles, da of Thomas Lascelles Isa Shandon Valiant Iremonger, of Milbourne Manor, Malmesbury, Wilts; 2 s (Thomas b 1978, Charles b 1981); *Career* called to the Bar Gray's Inn 1971, in practice 1971–; memb Local Govt and Planning Bar Assoc; *Books* Woodfall's Law of Landlord and Tenant (asst ed 28 edn, 1978); *Recreations* cooking, family life, wine and food; *Clubs* Beefsteak, MCC; *Style*— Nicholas Huskinson, Esq; ✉ 34 Cheyne Row, Chelsea, London SW3 5HL (☎ 0171 352 6866); 4–5 Gray's Inn Square, Gray's Inn, London WC1R 5AY (☎ 0171 404 5252, fax 0171 242 7803, telex GRALAW 8953743)

HUSKISSON, Dr Edward Cameron; s of Edward William Huskisson, of Northwood, Middx, and Elinor Margot, *née* Gibson; *b* 7 April 1939; *Educ* Eastbourne Coll, King's Coll London and Westminster Hosp (BSc, MB BS, MD); *m*; 3 s (Ian b 1971, Robert b 1990, Alexander b 1994), 1 da (Anna b 1974); *Career* rheumatologist in private practice; chm Charterhouse Conference and Communication Co Ltd; conslt physician St Bartholomew's Hosp London until 1993, conslt rheumatologist King Edward VII Hosp for Offrs London; memb: BMA, RSM; MRCS, FRCP 1980 (MRCP 1967); *Books* Joint Disease All The Arthropathies (fourth edn 1988), Repetitive Strain Injury (1992); *Style*— Dr Edward Huskisson; ✉ 14A Milford House, 7 Queen Anne St, London W1M 9FD (☎ 0171 636 4278, fax 0171 323 6829)

HUSKISSON, Robert Andrews; CBE (1979); s of Edward Huskisson (d 1964), and Catherine Mary, *née* Downing (d 1964), of Buckhurst Hill; *b* 2 April 1923; *Educ* Merchant Taylors', St Edmund Hall Oxford; *m* 1969, Alice Marian Swaffin, da of William John Tuck; 2 step da; *Career* dep chief exec Shaw Savill and Albion Co Ltd 1971–72; pres: Br Shipping Fedn 1971–72, Int Shipping Fedn 1969–73; chm: Lloyd's Register of Shipping 1973–83 (dep chm and treas 1972–73), Hotel and Catering Ctee 1975–79,

Marine Technol Mgmnt Ctee SRC; dir: Smit International Group (UK) Ltd 1973–87, Lloyd's of London Press Ltd 1983–89, Harland and Wolff 1983–87, Chatham Historic Dockyard Tst 1984–91; *Recreations* golf; *Clubs* Thorndon Park Golf, Vincent's (Oxford); *Style*— Robert Huskisson, Esq, CBE; ✉ Lanterns, 3 Luppitt Close, Hutton Mount, Brentwood, Essex CM13 2JU

HUSSAIN, Mukhtar; QC (1992); s of Karam Dad (d 1991), and Rehmi Bi (d 1955); *b* 22 March 1950; *Educ* William Temple Secdy Sch Preston; *m* 1972, Shamim Akhtar, *née* Ali; 3 da (Rukhshanda Jabeen b 30 March 1974, Farakhanda Jabeen b 12 Dec 1975, Mariam Sophia Rahmi b 20 May 1985); *Career* called to the Bar Middle Temple 1971, asst recorder 1987–90, recorder 1990–, head of chambers 1992–; *Recreations* reading, cricket, squash, bridge; *Style*— Mukhtar Hussain, Esq, QC; ✉ Lincoln House, 5th Floor, 1 Brazennose Street, Manchester M2 5EL (☎ 0161 832 5701)

HUSSAIN, Nasser; s of Joe Hussain, of Brentwood, Essex, and Shireen, *née* Price; *b* 28 March 1968; *Educ* Highlands Sch Ilford, Forest Sch Snaresbrook, Univ of Durham (BSc); *m* Karen, *née* Birch; *Career* professional cricketer; former player Ilford Cricket Club, represented England Schs under 15 (capt 1 year) and Essex Schs; first class debut Essex CCC 1987 (awarded county cap 1989, vice capt 1995–); Young England: tour Sri Lanka 1987, Youth World Cup Aust 1988; England: memb tour India and W Indies 1990, 4 test matches, 3 one day ints, A tour Sri Lanka 1991 (West Indies 1992), played Ashes series 1993, memb team touring W Indies 1993/94, capt A tour to Pakistan 1995, memb team touring Zimbabwe and New Zealand 1996–97; Gold Awards: Combined Univs v Somerset in Benson & Hedges Cup, Young England v Aust, Natwest Gold Award versus Cumberland; *Recreations* golf, football; *Style*— Nasser Hussain, Esq; ✉ c/o Essex CCC, County Ground, New Writtle Street, Chelmsford CM2 OPG (☎ 01245 252420)

HUSSELBY, William Eric (Bill); DL (W Midlands 1991); s of Eric Shaw Husselby, of Sandbanks, Dorset, and Betty, *née* Oubridge; *b* 7 July 1939; *Educ* Oundle; *m* 1968, Jillian Lyndon, da of Lyndon B Mills; 1 s (Marcus b 10 Dec 1971), 2 da (Francesca b 5 Aug 1969, Tania b 10 Dec 1971); *Career* md Cogent Elliott Limited 1967, chm Cogent Group 1973–; memb Cncl IPA 1990–; chm Birmingham NSPCC Centenary Appeal 1987–88, pres Birmingham NSPCC 1989; vice chm Industry 96; govr Lady Katherine Leveson Tst 1989, High Sheriff West Midlands 1986–87; FIPA 1990; *Style*— William Husselby, Esq, DL; ✉ Cogent Elliott Limited, Heath Farm, Meriden, West Midlands CV7 7LL (☎ 01676 522808)

HUSSEY, Richard Alban; s of Sydney Frederick George Hussey (d 1949), and Doris Catherine Ellen, *née* Baker (d 1983); *b* 20 March 1940; *Educ* Colfe's GS; *m* 1967, Kay Frances, da of Albert Edward Povey England; 1 s (Paul Nicholas b 1977), 1 da (Erin Elizabeth b 1970); *Career* dir: Weidenfeld and Nicolson Ltd 1970, Weidenfeld (Publishers) Ltd 1986, Orion Publishing Group Ltd 1992; *Recreations* cricket and rugby football (played rugby for Kent on 5 occasions); *Clubs* Old Colfeians Rugby and Cricket; *Style*— Richard Hussey, Esq; ✉ Orion Publishing Group, Orion House, 5 Upper St Martin's Lane, London WC2H 9EA (☎ 0171 240 3444)

HUSSEY, Lady Susan Katharine; *née* Waldegrave; DCVO (1984, CVO 1971); 5 da of 12 Earl Waldegrave, KG, GCVO, TD (d 1995); *b* 1 May 1939; *m* 25 April 1959, Baron Hussey of North Bradley, *qv*; 1 s (Hon James Arthur b 1961, Page of Honour to HM The Queen 1975–76), 1 da (Hon Katharine Elizabeth (Hon Lady Brooke) b 1964); *Career* woman of the bedchamber to HM The Queen 1960–; *Style*— Lady Susan Hussey, DCVO; ✉ Flat 15, 45–47 Courtfield Rd, London SW7 4DB (☎ 0171 370 1414); Waldegrave House, Chewton Mendip, nr Bath, Somerset (☎ 01761 241289)

HUSSEY OF NORTH BRADLEY, Baron (Life Peer UK 1996), of North Bradley in the County of Wiltshire; Marmaduke James Hussey; s of Eric Robert James Hussey, CMG (d 1958), and Christine Elizabeth Justice, *née* Morley; *b* 29 Aug 1923; *Educ* Rugby, Trinity Coll Oxford (scholar, MA); *m* 25 April 1959, Lady Susan Katharine Hussey, DCVO, *qv*, *née* Waldegrave; 1 s (Hon James Arthur b 1961), 1 da (Hon Katharine Elizabeth (Hon Lady Brooke) b 1964); *Career* Lt Grenadier Gds N942–45; dir Associated Newspapers 1964 (joined 1949), md Harmsworth Publications 1967–70, md and chief exec Times Newspapers Ltd 1971–80 (when owned by Lord Thomson); dir: Thomson Organisation 1971–80, Times Newspapers Ltd 1982–86, Colonial Mutual Group (British Bd) 1982–, MK Electric Group 1982–88, William Collins plc 1985–89, Maid plc 1996–; chm Ruffer Investment Management Ltd 1995–; Rhodes tstee 1972–92, tstee Royal Acad Tst 1988–; chm: Royal Marsden NHS Tst 1985–, Bd of Govrs BBC 1986–96, King's Fund London Cmmn 1991–92 and 1995–; memb: Br Cncl 1982–, Govt Working Pty on Artificial Limbs and Appliance Centres in England 1984–86, Mgmnt Ctee King Edward's Hosp Fund for London 1987–; hon fell Trinity Coll Oxford 1989; cr a life peer 1996; *Clubs* Brooks's; *Style*— The Rt Hon Lord Hussey of North Bradley; ✉ Flat 15, 45–47 Courtfield Road, London SW7 4DB (☎ 0171 370 1414); BBC Broadcasting House, Portland Place, London W1A 1AA (☎ 0171 580 4468)

HUSTLER, John Randolph; s of William Mostyn Collingwood Hustler (d 1976), and Angela Joan, *née* Hanson (d 1983); *b* 21 Aug 1946; *Educ* Eton; *m* 23 Sept 1978, Elizabeth Mary, da of Andrew George Hughes-Onslow (d 1979); 2 s (Charles b 1982, Frederick b 1986), 1 da (Willa b 1983); *Career* CA; ptnr KPMG Peat Marwick 1983–93 (joined 1965), chm Hustler Venture Partners Ltd 1993–; FCA 1975; *Recreations* golf, tennis, gardening; *Clubs* Boodle's; *Style*— John Hustler, Esq; ✉ Ripsley House, Liphook, Hants GU30 7JH (☎ 01428 722 223); Hustler Venture Partners, 2 Queen Anne's Gate Buildings, Dartmouth Street, London SW1H 9BP (☎ 0171 222 5472, fax 0171 222 5250)

HUTCHEON, Dr Andrew William; s of George Hutcheon (d 1989), of 5 Devanha Gardens, E Aberdeen, and Elsie Sophia, *née* Murison (d 1983); *b* 21 May 1943; *Educ* Robert Gordon's Coll, Univ of Aberdeen (MB ChB, MD); *m* 14 July 1966, Christine Gray, da of Francis Gray Cusiter, of Kiama, Berstane Rd, Kirkwall, Orkney; 1 s (Barry b 1970), 2 da (Louise b 1967, Wendy b 1973); *Career* house offr med and surgery Aberdeen Royal Infirmary 1968–69, sr house offr and registrar gen med Glasgow Western 1969–72, res fell Western Infirmary Glasgow 1972–75, sr registrar Western Infirmary Glasgow and Royal Marsden London 1975–78, conslt physician and conslt med oncologist Aberdeen Hosps 1978–, sr lectr in med Univ of Aberdeen 1978–; memb: Cancer Res Campaign, Imperial Cancer Res Fund, Br Assoc for Cancer Res; FRCP, FRCPEd, MRCP; *Books* Textbook of Medical Treatment (contrib 1987); *Recreations* skiing, curling; *Clubs* Rubislaw Curling, Aberdeen; *Style*— Dr Andrew Hutcheon; ✉ Moreseat, 159 Midstocket Rd, Aberdeen AB2 4LU (☎ 01224 637204); Ward 46, Aberdeen Royal Infirmary, Foresterhill, Aberdeen AB9 2ZB (☎ 01224 681818)

HUTCHESON, Robert Bennett; s of John Holden Hutcheson (d 1981), of Montreal, and Alice Bernadette, *née* Kinchsular (d 1985); *b* 23 July 1933; *Educ* Lower Canada Coll Montreal, McGill Univ Montreal (BA); *m* 30 Sept 1972 (m dis 1985), Nichola Caroline Pumphrey, da of Edward Laird, of Topsham, Devon; 4 da (Venetia b 1973, Sacha b 1974, Suki b 1976, Alice b 1977); *Career* sr registrar Hammersmith Hosp 1974–75, sr obstetrician and gynaecologist Gloucester Royal Hosp 1975–; FRCOG 1983; *Recreations* travel, photography, tennis; *Style*— Robert Hutcheson, Esq; ✉ 1 Burnet Close, Robinswood, Gloucester, Glos GL4 9YS (☎ 01452 305841); The Winfield Hospital, Tewkesbury Road, Gloucester GL2 9EE; Gloucester Maternity Hospital, Great Western Rd, Gloucester, Glos (☎ 01452 855292)

HUTCHINGS, Graham Derek; s of William Hutchings, of Upper Beeding, Sussex, and Beryl, *née* Bedwell; *b* 2 Nov 1951; *Educ* Imberhorne Co Secdy Modern Sch, Hatfield Poly, Ealing Coll of Higher Educn, SOAS London; *m* Elisabeth Marion, da of Cyril Leslie Judd (d 1987); 1 s (Nicholas Graham b 1978), 1 da (Anna Elisabeth b 1981); *Career* journalist; office jr JLP Denny Ltd fruit importers 1968–69, shop asst Forrest Stores 1969–70, telephone engr 1970–76, lectr in modern history Hatfield Poly 1983–85, research ed China Business Report 1985–86, dep ed Asian Electricity 1986–87; The Daily Telegraph: China specialist 1987–89, Peking corr 1989–93, China corr 1993–; memb NUJ; *Recreations* motor cycling, music; *Style*— Graham Hutchings, Esq; ✉ China Correspondent, The Daily Telegraph, 1 Canada Square, Canary Wharf, London E14 5DT

HUTCHINGS, Gregory Frederick; s of Capt Frederick Garside Hutchings, and Edna May, *née* McQueen; *b* 22 Jan 1947; *Educ* Uppingham, Univ of Aston (BSc), Aston Mgmnt Centre (MBA); *m* 14 June 1980, Caroline Jane; *Career* Hanson plc 1981–83, exec chm Tomkins plc 1995– (dir 1983–, chief exec 1984–94); *Recreations* sport, music, literature; *Style*— Gregory Hutchings, Esq; ✉ Tomkins PLC, East Putney House, 84 Upper Richmond Rd, London SW15 2ST (☎ 0181 871 4544)

HUTCHINGS, Michael Balfour; s of Benjamin Legh Balfour Hutchings (d 1981), and Ann, *née* Carter; *b* 8 Nov 1948; *Educ* Marlborough, Coll of William and Mary Virginia USA (BA); *m* 8 April 1992, Victoria, da of Arthur Trollope; 1 da (Anna b 4 July 1978), 1 s (William b 9 Jan 1981), 3 step s (Robin b 6 March 1979, Sholto b 16 Nov 1981, Dominic b 11 Aug 1985); *Career* articled clerk McKenna & Co 1970–72, admitted slr 1973, ptnr Lovell White Durrant 1981–95 (asst slr 1974–81); Euro law conslt 1996–; Liveryman Worshipful Co of Drapers; memb: Law Soc, Br Inst of Int and Comparative Law; *Recreations* woodturning, golf; *Clubs* Woking Golf; *Style*— Michael Hutchings, Esq; (fax 0181 767 9457)

HUTCHINS, Brig Peter Edward; s of Edward Stanley Hutchins (d 1976), and Afreda Beryl, *née* Newton-Davey (d 1985); *b* 11 Feb 1919; *Educ* St Dunstan's Coll London, UCL; *m* 1, 15 July 1944 (m dis), Cynthia Margaret, da of Gilbert Gaul Gross (d 1944), of Essex; 2 s (Jeremy b 1946, Miles b 1948), 1 da (Georgina b 1958); m 2, 28 July 1984, Barbara Patience, da of Frederick Dillon-Edwards (d 1958), of Bucks; *Career* WWII cmmnd RCS 1940, eventually Brig GS MOD, ret 1970; attended Slade Sch of Fine Art 1937–39 (Alfred Rich Open Scholarship 1937, Slade scholar 1938–39), princ CS 1970–71, md London Press Centre 1971–88, memb and dir Int Press Centre 1971–88; chm and dir Greston Sch 1968–75, chm Armed Forces Art Soc 1976–90; FRSA, FIMgt; *Recreations* painting, boats, gardening; *Clubs* Army and Navy, Press; *Style*— Brig Peter E Hutchins; ✉ 6 Yew Tree Court, Goring-on-Thames, Oxfordshire RG8 9HF (☎ 01491 874091)

HUTCHINSON, Gillian Mary; JP (1977); da of late (Alpheus) John Robotham, of Quarndon, Derby, and Gwendolyn Constance, *née* Bromet; *b* 3 June 1935; *Educ* Lowther Coll Abergele; *m* 14 March 1956, Maj Frederick Alan (Bill) Hutchinson, s of Edward Thomas Hutchinson; 1 s ((Jeremy) Mark b 29 July 1957), 1 da ((Jane) Nicola b 29 May 1960); *Career* sec in family slrs 1954–56, proprietor fine china and gift ware business 1974–93; memb Ctee Children Soc (S Derbys) 1990– (former treas); High Sheriff for Co of Derbyshire 1994–95; govr Repton Sch 1994–, memb Ct Univ of Derby 1995–; vice pres Derbyshire Community Fndn 1995–, assoc memb Appeal Ctee Mencap (Derbyshire) 1996–; *Recreations* county tennis (plays for Derbyshire Super Veterans); *Style*— Mrs Gillian Hutchinson, JP; ✉ Somersal House, Somersal Herbert, Ashbourne, Derbys DE6 5PD (☎ 01283 585257)

HUTCHINSON, (Edward) Graham; OBE (1997); s of Roger Hutchinson (d 1971), of Southport, Merseyside, and Katharine Norma, *née* Robinson (d 1984); *b* 11 Jan 1940; *Educ* Bryanston, King's Coll Cambridge (MA), Euro Inst of Business Admin Fontainebleau France (MBA); *m* 7 Nov 1970, Diana Fair, da of William Fair Milligan, of Heswall, Wirral, Merseyside; 1 s (Mark b 1974), 2 da (Camilla b 1972, Christina b 1977); *Career* dir and chief exec Neptun International Holding AG Basle 1972–80, md Dan-Air Servs Ltd 1981–91; dir: Davies and Newman Holdings plc 1980–90, Bowater Europe 1977–80, Air Scandinavia Ltd 1991–94, Ashford Hosp Trust 1991–, Trusts in Partnership Ltd 1992–; chm: Yeldall Christian Centres Ltd 1979–, The Safe Tst 1995–; dir Agapé Ministries Ltd 1991–96 (chm 1980–91); proprietor Thames Business Group 1993–; memb CBI London Regional Cncl 1983–89; *Recreations* leisure travel, music, family; *Clubs* Leander; *Style*— Graham Hutchinson, Esq, OBE; ✉ Silver Birches, Startins Lane, Cookham Dean, Berks SL6 9TS (☎ and fax 01628 481719)

HUTCHINSON, John; s of John Hutchinson, and Beatrice Hutchinson; *b* 5 Aug 1944; *Educ* King Charles I GS Kidderminster, Harvard Business Sch (Prog for Mgmnt Devpt, Managing Info System Resource course); *m* 1 April 1967, Elspeth Nanette; 1 da (Abigail Lucy b 5 November 1974); *Career* Lloyds Bank: various branch and Head Office positions 1960–80, corp devpt mangr 1980–82, dir and dep gen mangr Black Horse Agencies 1982–84, divnl mangr UK Retail Banking 1984–87, head of personal banking UK Retail Banking 1987–89, gen mangr support and devpt 1989–90; Nationwide Building Society: main bd dir 1990–92, retail ops dir 1990–92, corp strategy dir 1992, exec chm Nationwide Property Services 1992; md Visa UK Ltd 1993–95; chief exec The Performing Right Soc Ltd 1995–; FCIB, CIMgt; *Recreations* skiing, swimming, travel, reading, theatre, ballet; *Style*— John Hutchinson, Esq; ✉ The Performing Right Society Ltd, 29/33 Berners Street, London W1P 4AA (☎ 0171 580 5544, fax 0171 306 4040)

HUTCHINSON, Prof John Neville; s of Frank Hutchinson (d 1978), and Elizabeth Helen, *née* Booth (d 1978); *b* 27 Dec 1926; *Educ* Bablake Sch Coventry, Univ of Birmingham (BSc), Univ of Cambridge (PhD), Univ of London (DSc Eng); *m* 29 July 1961, Patricia, da of Frederick Hilton (d 1943); 1 s (Thomas b 8 April 1974), 2 da (Kristin b 15 Aug 1965, Julia b 23 Nov 1970); *Career* civil engr: Robert M Douglas (contractors) Ltd Birmingham 1947–50, Rendel Palmer & Tritton conslt engrs London 1950–57, Swedish Geotechnical Inst Stockholm 1957–58, Norwegian Geotechnical Inst Oslo 1958–61, Soil Mechanics Div Bldg Res Station Watford 1961–65; Dept of Civil Engrg Imperial Coll London: sr lectr 1965–70, reader in soil mechanics 1970–76, prof of engrg geomorphology 1977–92, prof emeritus and sr research fell 1992; chm Working Cmmn on landslides and other mass movements Int Assoc of Engrg Geology 1982–88, pres Quaternary Research Assoc 1985–88; FGS 1966, FICE 1983, CGeol 1991; *Recreations* gardening, music, painting, reading, mountaineering; *Style*— Prof John Hutchinson; ✉ Dept of Civil Engineering, Imperial College, Imperial College Rd, London SW7 2BU (☎ 0171 594 6034, fax 0171 225 2716, e-mail j.n.hutchinson@ic.ac.uk)

HUTCHINSON, (John) Maxwell; s of Frank Maxwell Hutchinson (d 1977), and Elizabeth Ross Muir, *née* Wright (d 1987); *b* 3 Dec 1948; *Educ* Oundle, Scott Sutherland Sch of Architecture Aberdeen, Architectural Assoc Sch of Architecture London (AADipl); *Career* chm: The Permarock Group Loughborough 1985–95, Hutchinson and Ptnrs Architects Ltd 1972–92, The Hutchinson Studio Architects 1992–; RIBA: memb Cncl 1978–93, sr vice pres 1988–89, pres 1989–91; visiting prof of architecture Queen's Univ Belfast 1989–93, special prof of architectural design Univ of Nottingham 1992–96; chm: Industrial Building Bureau 1986–88, Br Architectural Library Tst 1991–, Schools of Architecture Validation Panel 1991–96, E Midlands Arts Bd 1991–94; vice chm Construction Industry Cncl 1989–91, hon fell Royal Soc of Ulster Architects, fell Univ of Greenwich; Freeman City of London 1980, Worshipful Co of Chartered Architects 1988; radio and TV broadcaster, compositions incl: The Kibbo Kift (Edinburgh Festival) 1976, The Ascent of Wilberforce III (Lyric Hammersmith) 1982, Requiem 1988, Christmas Cantata 1990; assoc memb PRS 1988; *Books* The Prince of Wales Right or Wrong? (1989); *Recreations* composing, recording, playing the guitar loudly, the music of Edward Elgar, cooking; *Clubs* Athenaeum; *Style*— Prof Maxwell Hutchinson; ✉ Flat 61, Cavendish Mansions, Clerkenwell Road, London EC1R 5DH

HUTCHINSON, Dr (Robert) Michael; s of Vivien Roy Owen Hutchinson (d 1969), and Iris May, *née* Moseley (d 1979); *b* 11 Sept 1939; *Educ* King Edward VI Sch Birmingham, Univ of Oxford (MA, BSc), St Mary's Hosp Med Sch (BM BCh); *m* 23 Sept 1967, Ann, da of Geoffrey Edward Milner (d 1979), of Hailsham, Sussex; 3 s (Jonathan Mark b 26 Aug 1970, Nicholas Paul b 19 May 1972, Andrew Simon James b 13 Dec 1976); *Career* registrar in clinical med and haematology Royal Postgrad Med Sch Hammersmith Hosp 1971–73, sr registrar in haematology United Bristol Hosps 1973–75; Leicester Royal Infirmary NHS Tst: conslt haematologist, head of dept, dir of blood and bone marrow transplantation 1976–; author of numerous scientific pubns on related haematological disorders; memb: Br Soc of Haematology, MRC Working Party on Adult Leukaemia and Related Disorders, Govt Working Party on Bone Marrow Transplantation; tstee The Cope Childhood Oncology Fund, is actively involved in the church's miny of healing; FRCPath 1987, FRCP 1989; *Recreations* clarinet player in local orchestra and music group; *Style*— Dr Michael Hutchinson; ✉ Department of Haematology, Leicester Royal Infirmary, Leicester LE1 5WW (☎ 0116 258 6615, fax 0116 258 5093)

HUTCHINSON, (George) Peter; CBE (1984); s of late Robert Hutchinson, and late Eleanor Heath, *née* Moffitt; *b* 12 Dec 1926; *Educ* St Bees Sch Cumbria, Univ of Durham (BSc); *m* 7 June 1958, Audrey, da of late W O A Dodds; 1 s (Robert b 1959), 1 da (Katherine b 1962); *Career* chartered surveyor and land agent; sr ptnr J M Clark & Partners until 1992; currently dir Northumbrian Water Group plc; memb Northumberland CC 1973–93, ldr Cons Gp 1985–93, chm Educ Ctee 1988–89; chm: Northern Area Cons Cncl 1981–84, Northgate and Prudhoe NHS Tst 1991–; FRICS; *Recreations* gardening, travel; *Clubs* Farmers'; *Style*— Peter Hutchinson, Esq, CBE; ✉ Low House, Hexham, Northumberland (☎ 01434 673237)

HUTCHINSON, Prof Philip; s of George Hutchinson, of Tayport, Fife, and Edna Hutchinson; *b* 26 July 1938; *Educ* King James I GS Bishop Auckland Co Durham, King's Coll Durham (BSc), Univ of Newcastle upon Tyne (PhD); *m* 1960, Joyce Harrison, da of Fred Harrison, of Bishop Auckland, Co Durham; 1 s (John Paul b 1973), 1 da (Barbara Helen b 1967); *Career* AERE Harwell: scientific offr rising to princ scientific offr Theoretical Physics Div 1962–69 and 1970–75, head Thermodynamics and Fluid Mechanics Gp Engrg Scis Div 1975–80, head Combustion Centre 1980–87, head Engrg Physics Branch Engrg Scis Div 1980–85, head Engrg Scis Div 1985–87; Cranfield Univ: head Sch of Mech Engrg 1987–, dep vice chllr 1996–, pro-vice chllr 1996–; princ Royal Mil Coll of Sci 1996–; visiting fell Dept of Chem Engrg Univ of Houston Texas 1969–70; visiting prof: Imperial Coll London 1980–85, Univ of Leeds 1985–; formerly chm: Exec Ctee on Fundamental Res in Combustion Int Energy Agency (1977–81), Combustion Physics Gp Inst of Physics (1985–89), Computational Fluid Dynamics Advsy Gp SERC; chm Bd Euro Res Community on Flow Turbulence and Combustion (fndr memb); formerly Inst of Physics rep then Combustion Inst (Br Section) rep on Watt Ctee Inst of Energy, memb Energy Panel Forsight Survey, UK memb COST (Co-operation in Sci and Technol) F1 Gp of CEC, Editorial Advsy Bd Experiments in Fluids jl; MRI 1989, CPhys, CEng, FInstP; *Publications* author of numerous articles in learned jls on statistical mechanics, fluid mechanics, spray and particle cloud disperson and combustion; *Recreations* squash, music, reading, Go, gadgets; *Style*— Prof Philip Hutchinson; ✉ School of Mechanical Engineering, Cranfield University, Cranfield, Beds MK43 0AL (☎ 01234 754769, fax 01234 751204)

HUTCHINSON, His Hon Judge Richard Hampson; s of John Riley Hutchinson (d 1958), and May, *née* Hampson (d 1959); *b* 31 Aug 1927; *Educ* Hull Univ Coll (LLB), St Bede's GS Bradford; *m* 1954, Nancy Mary, da of John William Jones (d 1983); 2 s (Christopher, Damian), 3 da (Paula, Hilary, Marie-Louise); *Career* Nat Serv 1949–51, Flying Offr RAF; called to the Bar Gray's Inn 1949, practised NE Circuit 1951–74; recorder: Rotherham 1971, Crown Ct 1972–74; circuit judge (Midland and Oxford Circuit) 1974–; tech advsr Central Cncl of Probation Ctees 1989–, memb County Ct Rules Ctee 1990–94, hon recorder Lincoln 1991–; *Recreations* reading, conversation; *Style*— His Hon Judge Hutchinson; ✉ Crown Court, Lincoln

HUTCHINSON, Thomas (Tom); s of Thomas Charles Hutchinson, of Sheffield, and Gladys, *née* Unsworth; *b* 22 May 1930; *Educ* Longley Cncl Sch Sheffield, City GS Sheffield, Univ of Sheffield (extra-mural dept); *m* Patricia; 2 s (Michael, Stephen), 1 da (Janetta); *Career* journalist and broadcaster; Sheffield Telegraph, Kinematograph Weekly, Picturegoer, Daily Cinema, ABC TV, Daily Express, Tyne Tees TV, ITN, Nova Magazine, Reveille, Evening Standard, Battle of Britain Film-Unit, Guardian; film critic: Sunday Telegraph, Now! Magazine, Scottish Sunday Standard, Mail On Sunday, The Movie Quiz (BBC Radio 2), Hampstead and Highgate Express, Film Review Magazine, Film Guide Magazine; dep film critic Today newspaper, science fiction critic The Times; question setter Mastermind; Hon DUniv Sheffield; sec and past chm Film Critics' Circle, memb BAFTA; *Books* Horror and Fantasy in the Cinema, Marilyn Monroe, Elizabeth Taylor, Goddesses of the Cinema, Niven's Hollywood; *Recreations* walking to the cinema, worrying about my family, wondering why my wife puts up with me, books, crosswords, entertaining cats; *Clubs* Groucho; *Style*— Tom Hutchinson, Esq; ✉ 64 Southwood Lane, Highgate Village, London N6 5DY (☎ 0181 340 8822, fax 0181 341 9217)

HUTCHINSON OF LULLINGTON, Baron (Life Peer UK 1978); Jeremy Nicolas Hutchinson; QC (1961); o s of St John Hutchinson, KC (d 1943), and Mary, o da of Sir Hugh Barnes, KCSI, KCVO; *b* 28 March 1915; *Educ* Stowe, Magdalen Coll Oxford (MA); *m* 1, 1940 (m dis 1966), Dame Peggy Ashcroft, DBE (d 1991); 1 s (Hon Nicholas St John Hutchinson), 1 da (Hon Eliza b 14 June 1941); m 2, 1966, June, yr da of Capt Arthur Edward Capel, CBE (d 1919), and formerly wife of Franz Osborn; *Career* served RNVR 1939–46; called to the Bar Middle Temple 1939; recorder: Bath 1962–72, Crown Court 1972–76; sits as Lib Dem Peer in House of Lords (sat as Lab Peer until joining SDP 1981); vice chm Arts Cncl 1977–79; tstee: Tate Gallery 1977–84 (chm 1980–84), Chantrey Bequest 1977–; prof of law RA 1988; *Clubs* MCC; *Style*— The Rt Hon Lord Hutchinson of Lullington, QC; ✉ House of Lords, London SW1A 0PW

HUTCHISON, David Alan; MBE (1976); s of Hector Donald Hutchison (d 1948), of Amberley Gardens, Bush Hill Park, Enfield, Middx, and Winifred, *née* Middlehurst (d 1986); *b* 13 Jan 1937; *Educ* Royal Masonic Sch Bushey Herts, Bartlett Sch of Architecture Univ Coll London (BA); *m* 3 April 1961 (m dis 1989), Helen Elizabeth, da of Arthur George Penn (d 1981), of High St Pembury, Tunbridge Wells, Kent; 2 s (Michael b 1 Nov 1963, Peter b 24 Dec 1966), 2 da (Gillian b 21 Jan 1962, Christine b 9 Aug 1965); m 2, 18 May 1990, Audrey, da of Horace Scott, of Tolworth, Surrey; *Career* architect; worked with Powell & Moya 1960–64: chm: HLM (formerly Hutchison Locke & Monk) 1988–92 (fndr ptnr 1964), HLM Architects Ltd, HLM Planning Ltd, HLM Landscape Ltd; fndr and dir Moloney O'Beirne Hutchison Partnership Dublin 1977–, fndr and sr ptnr David Hutchison Partnership 1992– (architect St James Hosp Dublin, Royal London Hosp redevpt, Barry Hosp, Chepstow Hosp, 6th Form Coll Farnborough, Royal Marsden Hosp, Princess Alexandra Hosp Harlow); architect for major public sector cmmns in health and civic authys 1964–88; health projects (hosps) incl: Bournemouth, Cheltenham, Ealing, Whipps Cross, Lister, Northern Gen Sheffield, Medway, Dunfermline West Fife, Liverpool Maternity, Royal Brompton London; civic projects: Surrey Heath Borough Cncl, Broxbourne Borough Cncl, Daventry Dist Cncl, Colchester Borough Cncl, Waltham Forest Cncl, Macclesfield Cncl, Epsom and Ewell Cncl, Reigate and Banstead Cncl, Stoke-on-Trent Cncl; cmmns: Univs of Reading and Surrey, Smithfield Market Corp of London; winner: int competition (architecture) Paisley Civic Centre 1964, 7 Civic Tst awards DOE Good Housing award, RIBA Architecture commendation, Redland Roof Tile award, RIBA Energy award, Concrete Soc architecture award; nat seat on Cncl RIBA 1987–93, assessor Civic Tst; Freeman: City of London 1977 (Liveryman 1990), Worshipful Co of Constructors 1977, Worshipful Co of Arbitrators 1987; RIBA, ARIAS, FIA, FFB, AInst(Hosp)E, FIE, FRSA 1989; *Recreations* amateur theatre, local amenity soc; *Clubs* Arts Club (London), Camberley Soc (chm), Farnborough and RAE Operatic Soc, Camus Productions, Bath Light Operatic Gp, Avon Light Operatic Company; *Style*— David Hutchison, Esq, MBE; ✉ High Paddock, Wilkes Farm, Doynton, nr Bristol BS15 5TJ (☎ 0117 937 3771)

HUTCHISON, Donald Colin Trevor; s of Brig Colin Ross Marshall Hutchison, DSO, MC (ka 1943), and Jovine Helen Trevor, *née* Williams (d 1957); *b* 12 March 1934; *Educ* Eton, Magdalene Coll Cambridge (MA); *Career* landowner; 2 Lt Oxon and Bucks LI 1952, served in Korean War 1953 and Egypt 1954 Durham LI; dir H C Stephens Ltd 1960–63, dir various property cos London, Paris and Nice 1964–79; *Recreations* landscaping, shooting, art collecting; *Clubs* Brooks's; *Style*— D C T Hutchison, Esq; ✉ Heath House, Stockbridge, Hampshire SO20 6BX (☎ 01264 810556)

HUTCHISON, Lt Cdr Sir (George) Ian Clark; kt (1954), DL (Edinburgh 1958); s of Sir George A Clark Hutchison, KC, MP (d 1928); *b* 4 Jan 1903; *Educ* Edinburgh Acad, RNC Osborne, RNC Dartmouth; *m* 1926, Sheena Campbell (d 1966); 1 da; *Career* joined RN 1916, ret 1931, recalled 1939, served Naval Ordnance Inspection Dept 1939–43; MP (U) Edinburgh (West) 1941–59; memb Royal Co of Archers (Queen's Body Guard for Scotland); *Style*— Lt Cdr Sir Ian Hutchison, DL; ✉ 16 Wester Coates Gdns, Edinburgh, Scotland EH12 5LT (☎ 0131 337 4888)

HUTCHISON, Rt Hon Lord Justice; Rt Hon Sir Michael; kt (1983); s of Ernest Hutchison (d 1959), and Frances Barron, *née* Spiers (d 1989); *b* 13 Oct 1933; *Educ* Lancing, Clare Coll Cambridge (MA, Athletic blue); *m* 1957, Mary, da of Ralph Hayden Spettigue; 2 s (Andrew b 25 Feb 1960, John b 26 April 1964), 3 da (Elizabeth b 13 May 1961, Clare b 5 Oct 1962, Jane b 30 Oct 1967); *Career* called to the Bar Gray's Inn 1958, recorder of the Crown Court 1975–83, QC 1976, bencher Gray's Inn 1983, judge of the High Court of Justice (Queen's Bench Div) 1983–95, a Lord Justice of Appeal 1995–; memb: Judicial Studies Bd 1985–87, Parole Bd 1988–90; *Recreations* music, carpentry, grandchildren; *Style*— The Rt Hon Lord Justice Hutchison; ✉ c/o Royal Courts of Justice, Strand, London WC2A 2LL (☎ 0171 936 6000)

HUTCHISON, Sir Peter; 2 Bt (UK 1939), of Thurle, Streatley, Co Berks; s of Sir Robert Hutchison, 1 Bt (d 1960), of Thurle Grange, Streatley-on-Thames, nr Reading, and Laetitia Norah, *née* Ede (d 1963); *b* 27 Sept 1907; *Educ* Marlborough, Lincoln Coll Oxford (MA); *m* 16 July 1949, Mary-Grace, da of Very Rev Algernon Giles Seymour (d 1933, Rector and Provost of St Mary's Cathedral Glasgow); 2 s (Robert b 1954, Mark b 1960), 2 da (Elspeth b 1950, Alison b 1951); *Heir* s, Robert Hutchison, *qv*; *Career* Flt Lt RAFVR 1941–45, intelligence offr photographic reconaissance unit (PRU); admitted slr 1932; asst slr: Warwicks CC 1934–36, E Suffolk CC 1936–47; dep clerk of the peace of the CC E Suffolk 1947–70, clerk of the peace and county slr E Suffolk CC 1970–72; memb Suffolk Coastal Dist Cncl 1973–83; chm govrs Orwell Park Prep Sch Nacton nr Ipswich 1974–86; *Recreations* gardening, reading; *Style*— Sir Peter Hutchison, Bt

HUTCHISON, Sir Peter Craft; 2 Bt (UK 1956), of Rossie, Co Perth, CBE (1992); s of Sir James Riley Holt Hutchison, 1 Bt, DSO, TD (d 1979), and Winefryde Eleanor Mary (Anne) (d 1988); *b* 5 June 1935; *Educ* Eton, Magdalene Coll Cambridge (BA); *m* 1966, Virginia, da of John Millar Colville, of Gribloch, Kippen, Stirlingshire; 1 s; *Heir* s, James Colville Hutchison b 7 Oct 1967; *Career* former Lt Royal Scots Greys; chm Hutchison and Craft Ltd, former dir Stakis plc and other cos; memb Bd: Scottish Tourist Bd 1981–87, Deacon Incorporation of Hammermen 1984–85; Scottish National Heritage June-Dec 1994; chm Forestry Cmmn Dec 1994–; vice chm Bd Br Waterways Bd (memb 1987–); chm of Tstees Royal Botanic Garden Edinburgh 1985–94, chm Loch Lomond and Trossachs Working Pty 1991–93; *Style*— Sir Peter Hutchison, Bt, CBE; ✉ Broich, Kippen, Stirlingshire FK8 3EN

HUTCHISON, Robert; s and h of Sir Peter Hutchison, 2 Bt, *qv*; *b* 25 May 1954; *Educ* Orwell Park Ipswich, Marlborough; *m* 7 Feb 1987, Anne Margaret, er da of Sir (Godfrey) Michael David Thomas, 11 Bt, *qv*; 2 s (Hugo Thomas Alexander b 16 April 1988, Guy Piers Giles b 30 April 1990); *Career* with J & A Scrimgeour Ltd 1973–78, financial adviser 1978–; *Recreations* tennis, watching association football, travelling, golf; *Clubs* Woodbridge Golf; *Style*— Robert Hutchison, Esq; ✉ Hawthorn Cottage, Lower Road, Grundisburgh, Nr Woodbridge, Suffolk IP13 6UQ (☎ 01473 738199)

HUTCHISON, Sidney Charles; CVO (1977, LVO 1967); s of Henry Hutchison (d 1979), and Augusta Rose, *née* Timmons (d 1912); *b* 26 March 1912; *Educ* Holloway Sch London, Univ of London (Dip History of Art); *m* 24 July 1937, Nancy Arnold (d 1985), da of Alfred Brindley (d 1962); *Career* joined staff Royal Acad of Arts 1929; served WWII Lt Cdr RNVR 1939–45; Royal Acad of Arts: librarian 1949–68, sec 1968–82, hon archivist 1982–, hon memb (Antiquary) 1992–; lectr in history of art Univ of London 1957–67; gen cmmr of Taxes 1972–87; govr Holloway Sch 1969–81; sec: E A Abbey Meml Tst Fndn 1960–87, Chantrey Bequest 1968–82 (tstee 1982–), Inc E A Abbey Scholarships 1965–92, E Vincent Harris Fndn 1970–87, Br Inst Fndn 1968–82, Richard Ford Award Fndn 1977–82; pres Southgate Soc of Arts 1983–; organist and choirmaster St Matthew's Westminster 1933–37; memb ICOM, FRSA, FSA, FMA, FAA; Offr Polonia Restituta 1971, Chevalier Belgian Order of the Crown 1972, Grand Decoration of Honour (silver) Austria 1972, Cavaliere Ufficiale al Merito della Repubblica Italiana 1980; *Books* The Homes of the Royal Academy (1956), The History of the Royal Academy 1768–1968 (1968; enlarged, updated edn 1768–1986, 1986); *Recreations* music, travel; *Clubs* Athenaeum, Arts; *Style*— Sidney Hutchison, Esq, CVO; ✉ 60 Belmont Close, Mount Pleasant, Cockfosters, Barnet, Herts EN4 9LT (☎ 0181 449 9821); Royal Academy of Arts, Piccadilly, London W1V 0DS (☎ 0171 439 7438)

HUTCHISON, Thomas Oliver; s of late James Hutchison, and Thomasina, *née* Oliver; *b* 3 Jan 1931; *Educ* Hawick HS, Univ of St Andrews (BSc); *m* 1955, Frances Mary Ada; 3 s; *Career* dir: Océ Finance Ltd 1977–79, Phillips-Imperial Petroleum Ltd 1981–85 (chm 1982–85), ICI plc 1985–91, ICI Australia 1985–91, Impkemix Investments Pty 1985–91, Hammerson plc 1991–, AMP Asset Management plc 1991–; dep govr Bank of Scotland 1991– (dir 1985–), dep chm Cadbury Schweppes plc 1992– (dir 1986–), dir Bank of Wales 1993–96; pres Assoc of Plastic Mfrs Europe 1980–82, chm Euro Ctee CBI 1989–91; FRSE 1991; *Recreations* tennis, music, opera, golf; *Clubs* Athenaeum, RAC; *Style*— T O Hutchison, Esq, FRSE; ✉ c/o Bank of Scotland, 38 Threadneedle Street, London EC2P 2EH (☎ 0171 601 6521, fax 0171 601 6310)

HUTCHISON, Prof William McPhee; s of William Hutchison (d 1956), of Giffnock, Glasgow, and Anne, *née* McPhee (d 1962); *b* 2 July 1924; *Educ* Eastwood HS, Univ of Glasgow (BSc, PhD), Univ of Strathclyde (DSc); *m* 15 March 1963, Rev Ella Duncan, da of James McLaughland, of Bearsden, Glasgow; 2 s (Bruce b 1964, Leslie b 1966); *Career* Univ of Strathclyde: asst lectr 1952–53, lectr 1953–68, sr lectr 1969–71, prof of parasitology 1971–86, res prof 1986–89 emeritus prof of parasitology 1989–; Fencing blue Glasgow Univ Athletic Club 1949, Scottish Epée Open Champion 1949, Ford Epée Cup 1949, Capt and Champion Glasgow Univ Fencing Club 1949–51; elder Church of Scotland; Robert Koch Fndn medal and prize 1970; FIBiol 1971, CBiol 1971, FRSE 1973, FLS 1974; *Recreations* gardening, woodwork, writing, music; *Style*— Prof William M

Hutchison, FRSE; ✉ 597 Kilmarnock Rd, Newlands, Glasgow G43 2TH (☎ 0141 637 4882)

HUTCHON, Dr David James Riddell; s of James Hutchon (d 1971), of Edinburgh, and Alice Mary, *née* McIntosh; *b* 17 April 1945; *Educ* George Watson's Boys Coll Edinburgh, Univ of Edinburgh (BSc, MB ChB); *m* 12 June 1971, Rosemary Elizabeth, da of Dr Ronald Caile (d 1978), of Southport, Lancs; 1 s (Christopher b 1978), 1 da (Fiona b 1979); *Career* govt med offr Grand Cayman BWI 1972–74, sr house offr Simpson Memorial Hosp Edinburgh 1974–76, registrar in obstetrics and gynaecology Ninewells Hosp Dundee 1976–78, res registrar Northwick Park Hosp London 1978–79, sr registrar in obstetrics and gynaecology Eastern Gen Hosp Edinburgh and clinical tutor Univ of Edinburgh 1979–81, conslt obstetrician and gynaecologist Darlington Health Authy 1981–; clinical dir women and children's health; FRCOG, fell Edinburgh Obstetrical Soc; *Recreations* golf, skiing, sailing; *Clubs* Blackwell Grange Golf; *Style—* Dr David Hutchon; ✉ 9 Farr Holme, Blackwell, Darlington, Co Durham DL3 8QZ (☎ 01325 358134); Dept of Obstetrics and Gynaecology, Memorial Hospital, Darlington, Co Durham (☎ 01325 380100)

HUTH, Angela Maureen; da of Harold Edward Strachan Huth (d 1967), and Bridget, *née* Nickols; *Educ* Guilsborough Lodge Sch Northants, Lawnside Great Malvern Worcs, Beaux Arts Sch of Art Paris, Annigoni's Sch of Art Florence, Byam Shaw Art Sch London; *m* 1, 1961 (m dis 1970), Quentin Crewe, *qv*; 1 da (Candida Crewe, *qv*); m 2, 1978, Dr James Howard-Johnston, s of late Rear Adm C D Howard-Johnston, CB, DSO, DSC; 1 da (Eugenie b 1981); *Career* memb Art Dept J Walter Thompson Advertising 1958–59, travel ed Queen Magazine 1959–61, woman's page Sunday Express 1962–63, reporter Man Alive (BBC) 1965–68, presenter How It Is (BBC) 1969–70, freelance journalist and reviewer 1965– (incl The Times, Sunday Times, Telegraph, Sunday Telegraph, Spectator, Guardian, Observer); FRSL 1975; *Publications* novels: Nowhere Girl (1970), Virginia Fly is Drowning (1972), Sun Child (1975), South of the Lights (1977), Monday Lunch in Fairyland and Other Stories (1978), Wanting (1984), Such Visitors (1989), Invitation to the Married Life (1991), Land Girls (1994), Another Kind of Cinderella and other stories (1996); non fiction: The English Woman's Wardrobe (1987), Island of the Children (poetry anthology, ed, 1987), Casting a Spell (poetry anthology, ed, 1991); stage plays: The Understanding (first performed 1981), The Trouble with Old Lovers (first performed 1995); TV plays incl: The Summer House (BBC, 1969), The Emperor's New Hat (BBC, 1971), Virginia Fly is Drowning (adaptation, BBC, 1975), Sun Child (YTV, 1988), The Understanding (YTV, 1987); *Recreations* dancing, buying and selling paste jewellery; *Style—* Ms Angela Huth; ✉ c/o Felicity Bryan, 2A North Parade, Banbury Rd, Oxford OX2 6PE (☎ 01865 513816, fax 01865 310055)

HUTSON, Maurice Arthur; s of William Arthur Hutson (d 1980), of S Yorkshire, and Ivy, *née* Roberts (d 1989); *b* 27 Jan 1934; *Educ* Gainsborough Tech Coll, Leeds Coll of Technol; *m* 1959, Janet, da of Arthur Edward Parkin, of S Yorkshire; 2 s (Mark Andrew b 1961, Jonathan Peter b 1970), 1 da (Helen Claire b 1963); *Career* chartered engr; devpt engr Tarmac Roadstone Ltd 1963–71 (prodn and engrg mangr 1965, staff offr 1970); chm and md: Seaham Harbour Dock Co 1971–81 (dir 1981–87), Mahcon Construction (Services) Ltd 1972–, Transport and Aggregates Ltd 1972–81, Wath Quarries Ltd 1977–, Allerton Engineering Ltd 1983–, Naylor Sportscars Ltd 1986–93, Hutson Motor Company Ltd 1986–; chm and chief exec Parker Plant Ltd 1990–; dir: Neocast Ltd 1980–90, The Sundial Hotel Ltd Northallerton until 1996, The Seaham Harbour Dock Co 1981–86, Modern Air Systems Ltd 1992–, Leicestershire Engineering Trg Gp 1996–; memb: Cncl and vice pres Fedn of Mfrs of Construction Equipment and Cranes (FMCEC) 1992–, Lighthouse Club 1990–, Br Thai Business Gp; advsr Prince's Tst; CEng, MIMechE, MIEE, FIQ; *Recreations* motor sport, travel and walking, gardening; *Clubs* Rotary (Stokesley), 41 Club (Guisborough); *Style—* Maurice Hutson, Esq; ✉ West Acre, 25 The Ridgeway, Rothley, Leicestershire LE7 7LE (☎ 0116 230 3230); Parker Plant Limited, PO Box 146, Canon Street, Leicester LE4 6HD (☎ 0116 266 5999, fax 0116 261 0745)

HUTSON, Robin; s of Derek Charles Hutson, of Whitsbury, Wilts, and Eileen Hilda, *née* Juniper; *b* 9 Jan 1957; *Educ* Haberdasher Askes Boys Sch Hatcham, Godalming GS, Brookland Tech Coll (OND); *m* 25 June 1983, Judith Alison, da of Douglas Hill; 2 s (Oliver Charles Westley b 10 Oct 1985, William Charles Westley b 3 Nov 1988); *Career* trainee Savoy Hotels Ltd 1975–81, front office mangr The Berkeley Hotel 1981–84, ops mangr Elbow Beach Hotel Bermuda 1984–86, md Chewton Glen Hotel Ltd 1990–94 (gen mangr 1986–90), md and chm Hotel du Vin Ltd 1994–; dir Richmond FC 1986–; memb: Bd of Friends Univ of Food & Wine Soc, Advsy Bd Eastleigh Coll of FE, Champagne Acad Pillar de Chablis; benefactor Theatre Royal Winchester; Egon Ronay Newcomer of the Year 1995, Newcomer of the Year Caterer & Hotelkeeper 1996; MHCIMA 1990; *Style—* Robin Hutson, Esq; ✉ Hotel du Vin & Bistro, 14 Southgate Street, Winchester, Hampshire SO23 9EF (☎ 01962 841414, fax 01962 842458)

HUTSON, Thomas Guybon; TD (1966); s of Guybon John Hutson (d 1963), of London, and Diana Chisholm, *née* Davidson (d 1972); *b* 17 April 1931; *Educ* Morrison's Acad Crieff, St Paul's Sch Hammersmith; *m* 9 May 1959, (Ann) Rosemary, da of Arthur Cranfield Coltman (d 1981), of Hampstead; 1 s (Charles b 1960), 3 da (Catherine b 1962, Anna b 1964, Fiona b 1970); *Career* Nat Serv: Private Gordon Highlanders 1949, cmmnd 2 Lt 1950; served Highland Bde Trg Centre, Fort George and Cameron Barracks Inverness 1951, 2 Lt 1 Bn London Scottish (TA) 1951, ret as Maj 1967; joined Bank of England 1948, seconded Libya to establish Central Bank Tripoli 1957, mangr Exchange Control Dept Nat Bank Libya 1958, returned Bank of England 1959, joined Tozer Kemsley & Millbourn 1960 (who founded International Factors), md International Factors Ltd 1978–93 (dir 1967–, vice chm 1992–), gp chm International Factors Group Brussels 1994– (gp dir 1991–); chm Assoc of Br Factors 1987–89, memb Cncl CBI 1993–96; FICM, FRPSL, memb Caledonian Soc London; *Books* Management of Trade Credit (1968); *Recreations* tennis, bridge, chess, opera, hill walking, philately, travel; *Style—* Thomas Hutson, Esq, TD; ✉ Ditchling Court, Ditchling, Sussex BN6 8SP (☎ 01273 843558); International Factors Ltd, Sovereign House, Church Street, Brighton, Sussex (☎ 01273 321211, fax 01273 771501, telex 87382)

HUTT, Peter Morrice; s of late Sqdn Ldr Harry Morrice Hutt, of Caversham, Reading, Berks, and Joan Ethel Ludlow, *née* Whitmore; *b* 15 April 1945; *Educ* Leighton Park Sch, Univ of Southampton (LLB); *m* 23 March 1974, Cynthia Anne, da of John Gauntlett Gubb (d 1988), of Uitenhage, SA; 1 s (Stephen b 1977); *Career* admitted slr 1969; ptnr Brain & Brain 1973–, Notary Public 1978, dep master Supreme Ct Queen's Bench Div 1992–; Rotherfield Peppard: chm Parish Cncl 1987–90, lay chm All Saints Parochial Church Cncl 1986–90; tstee Relief in Need Charity, tstee Mem/Hall, clerk Polehampton Charities Twyford, former memb Caversham Round Table; memb: Law Soc 1967, Slr Benevolent Assoc 1969, Notaries Soc 1978; *Recreations* music, walking, gardening, tennis; *Style—* Peter Hutt, Esq; ✉ Rushton House, Church Lane, Rotherfield Peppard, Henley-on-Thames RG9 5JR (☎ 01491 628335); Brain & Brain, Addington House, 73 London St, Reading RG1 4QB (☎ 0118 958 1441, fax 0118 959 7875, telex 847645)

HUTTON, Alasdair Henry; OBE (1989, MBE 1986), TD (1977); s of Alexander Hutton (d 1954), and Margaret Elizabeth Hutton (1990); *b* 19 May 1940; *Educ* Gatehouse of Fleet Sch, Dollar Acad, Brisbane State HS Australia; *m* 1975, Deirdre Mary Hutton, *qv*, da of Kenneth Alexander Home Cassels, of Wimbish Green, Essex; 2 s (Thomas b 1978, Nicholas b 1982); *Career* sr conslt Coutts Career Consultants Edinburgh, chm Calchou Electronics Kelso; writer, broadcaster and public events commentator, Euro political conslt; MEP (EDG) S Scot 1979–89; 2 i/c 15 Scot (Vol) Bn The Parachute Regt 1979–87, Watchkeepers Pool 1987–96; narrator: Edinburgh Military Tattoo 1992–, Berwick Military Tattoo 1994–; chm: Scot Cons Ctees on Environment and Europe 1989–93, Crime Concern Scot 1990–95, Disease Prevention Orgn 1990–; memb Kelso/Jedburgh Advsy Gp Scottish Borders Enterprise 1990–, dir Scot Agric Coll 1990–95, vice pres Kelso Branch Royal Br Legion 1987–; hon pres: Scottish Assoc of CB Clubs 1984–, Clydesdale Cons and Unionist Assoc 1991–95; vice chm John Buchan Soc 1995– (life memb 1985); vice chm Scottish Cons Christian Forum 1990–, tstee Community Serv Vols 1985–, elder Church of Scotland 1985–; memb: Border Area Ctee Lowland TAVRA 1990–, Int Rels Ctee Law Soc of Scot 1991–, Bd UK 2000 Scotland 1991–, Church & Nation Ctee Church of Scot 1992–96, Devonshire House Mgmnt Club 1996, Social Security Advsy Ctee 1996–; memb Queen's Body Guard for Scotland (Royal Co of Archers) 1988; fell Indust and Parl Tst, memb IACMP 1995; *Style—* Alasdair Hutton, Esq, OBE, TD; ✉ Rosebank, Shedden Park Rd, Kelso, Roxburghshire TD5 7PX (☎ and fax 01573 224369)

HUTTON, Anthony Charles; CB (1995); s of Charles James Hutton, and Athene Mary, *née* Hastie; *b* 4 April 1941; *Educ* Brentwood Sch, Trinity Coll Oxford (MA); *m* Sara, *née* Flemming; 2 s (Simon James b 1966, Nicholas Henry Coit b 1970), 1 da (Katharine Mary b 1968); *Career* civil servant; HM inspr of taxes 1962–64, princ Bd of Trade 1968–74 (asst princ 1964–68), PPS to Sec of State for Trade 1974–77; DTI: asst sec 1977–84, under sec 1984–91, dep sec and princ estab and fin offr 1991–96, DG Resources and Services 1996–; *Clubs* Athenaeum; *Style—* Anthony Hutton, Esq, CB; ✉ Department of Trade and Industry, 1 Victoria Street, London SW1H 0ET (☎ 0171 215 6911)

HUTTON, Baron (Life Peer UK 1997), of Bresagh in the County of Down; Sir (James) Brian Edward Hutton; kt (1988), PC (1988); s of late James and Mabel Hutton, of Belfast; *b* 29 June 1931; *Educ* Shrewsbury Sch, Balliol Coll Oxford (BA Jurisprudence), Queen's Univ Belfast; *m*; 2 da; *Career* called to the Bar NI 1954, jr counsel to Attorney Gen NI 1969, QC (NI) 1970, sr crown counsel NI 1973–79, judge of the High Court of Justice (NI) 1979–88, Lord Chief Justice of NI 1988–97, a Lord of Appeal in Ordinary 1997–; memb Jt Law Enforcement Cmmn 1974, dep chm Boundary Cmmn for NI 1985–88, pres NI Assoc for Mental Health 1983–; author of various articles in Modern Law Review; *Style—* The Rt Hon Lord Hutton; ✉ The Royal Courts of Justice, Belfast BT1 3JF (☎ 01232 235111, fax 01232 236838)

HUTTON, Deirdre Mary; da of Kenneth Alexander Home Cassels, of Wimbish Green, Essex, and Barbara Kathleen, *née* Alington; *b* 15 March 1949; *Educ* Sherborne Girls, Hartwell House; *m* 1 Nov 1975, Alasdair Henry Hutton, *qv*, s of late Alexander Hutton; 2 s (Thomas Kennedy b 28 June 1978, Nicholas Alasdair b 27 Feb 1982); *Career* Anchor Housing Assoc Oxford 1973–75, res asst Glasgow C of C 1975–82, memb, treas and chm Broomlands Sch Bd 1984–91, memb Music Ctee Scot Arts Cncl 1985–91, hon sec Kelso Music Soc 1985–95; chm Scot Consumer Cncl 1991– (memb 1986–90, vice chm 1990–91); memb: Scot Consultative Cncl on the Curriculum 1987–91, Ctee on Reporting 1989–91, Parole Bd for Scot 1993–, Bd Borders Health Bd 1996–; dep chm Ombudsman Cncl Personal Investment Authy 1994–, vice chm Nat Consumer Cncl 1997– (memb Cncl 1991–); lay memb for Scot of Gen Dental Cncl and memb Professional Misconduct Ctee 1988–94, memb Ctee to Review Curriculum Examinations in Fifth and Sixth Years of Scot Educn (Howie Ctee) 1990–92; chm: Rural Forum (Scotland) Ltd 1992–, Enterprise Music Scotland Ltd 1993–95; vice chm Borders Local Health Cncl 1991–95; *Recreations* gardening, music (particularly singing); *Style—* Mrs Deirdre Hutton; ✉ Scottish Consumer Council, Royal Exchange House, 100 Queen Street, Glasgow G1 3DN (☎ 0141 226 5261, fax 0141 221 0731)

HUTTON, His Hon Judge Gabriel Bruce; s of late Robert Crompton Hutton, of Gloucs, and late Elfreda, *née* Bruce; fourth successive generation of judges living in Gloucs; *b* 27 Aug 1932; *Educ* Marlborough, Trinity Coll Cambridge (BA); *m* 1965, Deborah Leigh, da of Vivian Leigh Windus (d 1950), of Sussex; 1 s (Alexander b 1972), 2 da (Joanna b 1966, Tamsin b 1968); *Career* called to the Bar Inner Temple 1956, dep chm Gloucs Quarter Sessions 1971, recorder Crown Ct 1972–78, circuit judge (Western Circuit) 1978–, liaison judge for Glos and res judge for Gloucester Crown Ct 1987–; chm Criminal Justice Liaison Ctee for Glos and Wilts 1992–; chm Glos Branch CPRE 1992; *Recreations* hunting (chm Berkeley), boating, shooting; *Style—* His Hon Judge Hutton; ✉ Chestal, Dursley, Gloucs (☎ 01453 543285)

HUTTON, Graeme; s of Harry Hutton, of Malvern, Worcs, and Ellen, *née* Graham (now Mrs Morton), of New Ash Green, Kent; *b* 6 Feb 1954; *Educ* Worcester Royal GS, Communication Advtg & Mktg Dip; *Career* Ogilvy & Mather advtg agency: press buyer 1974–75, TV buyer 1975–76, media planner 1976–79, media gp head 1979–83; media dir Billett & Co 1983–89, Euro devpt dir CIA Medianetwork UK Ltd 1995 (planning dir 1989–95), Euro media dir Ammirati Puris Lintas 1996–; chm: Audit Bureau of Circulations Ltd 1994–96 (memb Cncl), Verified Free Distribution Ltd 1994–96; Jt Admap/Media Res Gp Media Planning Award 1981, IPA Media Award for Research 1996; *Recreations* horse racing, riding, skiing; *Style—* Graeme Hutton, Esq; ✉ Ammirati Puris Lintas, 84 Eccleston Square, Victoria, London SW1V 1PX (☎ 0171 932 8888)

HUTTON, Ian; s of John Noel Locke Hutton, of Dublin, and Marguerite, *née* Barry; *b* 9 Nov 1942; *Educ* Christian Brothers Coll Cork, St Mary's Coll Dublin; *m* 1, 1975 (m dis 1983), Bodil, da of O Tvergrov; 1 da (Tara Mari b 1977); m 2, 26 Aug 1986, Charity, da of Patrick Hugh Coghlan Hamilton; 1 s (Patrick Hugo b 1987), 1 da (Trinity Ann b 1989); *Career* sports reporter Irish Press 1963–65; advtg copywriter: Kenny's Dublin 1966, McConnell's Dublin 1967, S H Benson London 1968–69, London Press Exchange 1969–71; J Walter Thompson: joined 1971, assoc dir 1979, sr assoc dir 1983, bd dir 1985–; winner numerous professional awards incl: 5 Silvers Br TV Awards, 4 Silvers and 1 Gold Cannes Film Festival, 2 Golds and the Grand Prix Irish Film Festival, The Euro Grand Prix 1990; work exhibited by Metropolitan Museum of Modern Art NY; memb D&AD 1973–91; winner numerous prizes as amateur boxer Dublin 1961–63; *Recreations* chess, boxing, rugby and Murphy's Stout; *Clubs* Mortons; *Style—* Ian Hutton, Esq; ✉ J Walter Thompson, 40 Berkeley Square, London W1X 6AD (☎ 0171 499 4040, fax 0171 493 8342/8418)

HUTTON, John; MP (Lab) Barrow and Furness (majority 3,578); s of late George Hutton, and Rosemary Hutton; *b* 6 May 1955; *Educ* Westcliff HS Southend, Magdalen Coll Oxford (BA, BCL); *m* 28 April 1978 (m dis 1993), Rosemary Caroline, *née* Little; 3 s (and 1 s decd), 1 da; *Career* legal asst CBI 1978–80, res assoc Templeton Coll Oxford 1980–81, sr lectr in law Newcastle Poly 1981–92; Parly candidate (Lab) Penrith and the Border 1987, Euro Parly candidate Cumbria and N Lancs 1989, MP (Lab) Barrow and Furness 1992–; *Clubs* Cemetary Cottages Working Men's (Barrow-in-Furness); *Style—* John Hutton, Esq, MP; ✉ House of Commons, London SW1A 0AA

HUTTON, John Christopher; s of John Francis Hutton, of Cranmer Ct, Llandaff, Cardiff, and Elizabeth Margery Ethel, *née* Pugh; *b* 7 June 1937; *Educ* Kingswood Sch Bath, ChCh Oxford (MA); *m* 5 Aug 1963, Elizabeth Ann, da of Prof Eric Evans (d 1967); 2 da (Catrin b 1965, Bethan b 1968); *Career* Nat Serv RA Cyprus 1956–58; methods engr Tube Investmts 1963–64 (graduate trainee 1961–63); Bristol and West Building Society: PA to Gen Mangr 1964–67, res mangr 1967–76, asst gen mangr 1976–88 (mktg and res 1976–86, corporate info and analysis 1986–88); fin mktg conslt 1988–; dir: Bristol & West Personal Pensions Ltd 1988–89, Wildscreen Trading Ltd 1991–94; conslt Money Which? 1971–; chm Housing Fin Panel Bldg Socs Assoc 1973–84 (memb 1967–), co-chm Tech Sub Ctee of Jt Advsy Ctee on Mortgage Fin 1973–82; memb: Construction Industs

Jt Forecasting Ctee NEDO 1978–89 (Housing Strategy Ctee 1975–77), Cncl Sub Ctee on Reserves and Liquidity BSA 1981, Fin Advertising Sub Ctee Advertising Standards Authy 1982–92; ldr BSA Netherlands Res Gp 1979; dir: Bristol Bldgs Preservation Tst Ltd 1984–, The Wildscreen Tst 1987–94; chm Kingsweston Preservation Soc 1993–; FSS 1968, assoc IMS 1968, MCIB; author of many articles for the nat press; *Recreations* antiques, wine, countryside, journalism; *Style*— John Hutton, Esq; ✉ Ferns Hill, Kingsweston Rd, Bristol BS11 0UX (☎ 0117 982 4324); Wyevern, Aberedw, Builth Wells, Powys LD2 3UN (☎ 01982 560439)

HUTTON, Matthew Charles Arthur; s of Capt Ronald David Hutton, MC (d 1984), of Langley Grange, Loddon, Norfolk, and Rhodanthe Winnaretta, *née* Leeds (now Mrs Gerald Selous); *b* 10 Sept 1953; *Educ* Eton, ChCh Oxford (BA, MA); *m* 6 Oct 1984, Anne Elizabeth Caroline, da of Leslie James Leppard, DFC, of Cobb Cottage, Dalwood, Axminster, Devon; 1 s (David b 1988), 2 da (Victoria b 1986, Alexandra b 1990); *Career* tax conslt, ptnr Daynes Hill & Perks (Slrs) Norwich 1987–89; FCInstT 1992 (ACInstT 1980); ptnr in family farming business 1977–; govr St Felix Sch Southwold 1987–94, lay reader Church of England 1992; *Publications* Tax Planning for Private Residences (2 edn, 1994), Post-death Rearrangements: Practice and Precedents (5 edn, 1995); *Recreations* family life, country pursuits; *Clubs* Athenaeum, MCC, Norfolk (Norwich); *Style*— Matthew Hutton, Esq; ✉ Broom Farm, Chedgrave, Norwich NR14 6BQ (☎ 01508 520775, fax 01508 528096)

HUTTON, (Hubert) Robin; OBE; s of Kenneth Douglas Hutton, and Dorothy, *née* de Wilde; *b* 22 April 1933; *Educ* Merchant Taylors', Peterhouse Cambridge (MA); *m* 1, 25 June 1956 (m dis 1967), Valerie, *née* Riseborough; 1 s (Andrew b 1958), 1 da (Sarah b 1960); m 2, 3 May 1969, Deborah, *née* Berkeley; 2 step da (Susan b 1957, Linda b 1959); *Career* Royal Tank Regt 1951–53; asst gen mangr Finance Corporation for Industry Ltd 1956–61, dir Hambros Bank Ltd 1961–70, special advsr HM Govt 1970–73, dir Fin Instns Commission of Euro Communities 1973–78, dir SG Warburg and Co Ltd 1978–82; dir gen: Accepting Houses Ctee, Issuing Houses Assoc 1982–87, Br Merchant Banking and Securities Houses Assoc 1988–92; non-exec dir: Singer & Friedlander Holdings Ltd, Northern Rock Building Soc; dir Investment Management Regulatory Organisation Ltd; memb Exec Ctee Br Bankers' Assoc 1982–92, chm English Nat Advsy Ctee on Telecoms 1984–93; *Recreations* cricket, gardening, travel; *Clubs* MCC; *Style*— Robin Hutton, Esq, OBE; ✉ Church Farm, Athelington, nr Eye, Suffolk IP21 5EJ (☎ 01728 628 361)

HUTTON, Will; s of William Thomas Hutton, and Dorothy Anne, *née* Haynes; *b* 21 May 1950; *Educ* Chislehurst & Sidcup GS, Univ of Bristol (BSocSci), INSEAD Fontainebleau (MBA); *Career* institutional account exec Phillips and Drew 1971–77; BBC: presenter various Panoramas, BBC2 series and radio documentaries, sr prodr The Financial World Tonight (Radio 4) 1978–81, prodr and dir The Money Programme (BBC 2) 1981–83, economics corr Newsnight (BBC2) 1983–88; ed-in-chief European Business Channel Zurich 1988–90, economics ed The Guardian 1990–96 (asst ed 1995–96), ed The Observer 1996–; presenter: series on the City (Radio 4) 1995, series on The State We're In (Channel 4) 1996; chm Employment Policy Inst; memb Cncl: Policy Studies Inst, Inst of Political Economy Univ of Sheffield; memb: Ed Bd New Economy, Bd LSE; dir London Int Festival of Theatre; sr assoc memb St Antony's Coll Oxford summer 1993, visiting fell Nuffield Coll Oxford; Political Journalist of the Year What the Papers Say Awards 1993; Hon DLitt: Kingston Univ 1995, De Montfort Univ 1996; *Books* A Revolution That Never Was (1986), The State We're In (1994); *Style*— Will Hutton, Esq; ✉ The Observer, 119 Farringdon Road, London EC1R 3ER (☎ 0171 713 4284, fax 0171 713 4437)

HUXLEY, Sir Andrew Fielding; OM (1983), kt (1974); s of Leonard Huxley (d 1933; 2 s of T H Huxley, the scientist and humanist), and his 2 w Rosalind, *née* Bruce (d 1994, aged 104); half-bro of Sir Julian Huxley, the biologist, and Aldous Huxley, the novelist; *b* 22 Nov 1917; *Educ* University Coll Sch, Westminster, Trinity Coll Cambridge; *m* 1947, Jocelyn Richenda Gammell, JP, da of Michael Pease (whose paternal grandmother was Susanna, da of Joseph Fry, of the Bristol Quaker family of cocoa manufacturers, and 1 cous of Sir Theodore Fry, 1 Bt), and his w Hon Helen, *née* Wedgwood, JP, eldest da of 1 Baron Wedgwood; 1 s (Stewart Leonard b 1949), 5 da (Janet b 1948, Camilla b 1952, Eleanor b 1959, Henrietta b 1960, Clare b 1962); *Career* operational research for Anti-Aircraft Cmd and Admty WWII; Trinity Coll Cambridge: fell 1941–60, dir of studies 1952–60, hon fell 1967–90, master 1984–90, fell 1990–; Univ of Cambridge: demonstrator Physiology Dept 1946–50, asst dir of research 1951–59, reader in experimental biophysics 1959–60; Jodrell prof of physiology and head of dept UCL 1960–69, Fullerian prof of physiology and comparative anatomy Royal Inst 1967–73, Royal Soc research prof Univ of London 1969–83 (emeritus prof of physiology 1983); Cecil H and Ida Green visiting prof Univ of BC 1980; memb ARC 1977–81; pres: British Assoc for Advancement of Science 1976–77, Bath Inst of Med Engrg 1994–; tstee: British Museum of Natural History 1981–91, Science Museum 1984–88; memb Nature Conservancy Cncl 1985–87, Animal Procedures Ctee (Home Office) 1987–95; hon memb: Royal Inst 1981, Royal Irish Acad 1986, Japan Acad of Science 1988; hon fell: Inst of Biology, Darwin Coll Cambridge, Royal Soc of Canada, Royal Soc of Edinburgh, Univ Coll London, Imperial Coll, Royal Acad of Engineering, Queen Mary and Westfield Coll; foreign assoc Nat Acad Sci USA, pres Int Union of Physiological Sciences 1986–93; Nobel Laureate in Physiology or Medicine 1963, Copley Medal Royal Society 1973; Dr (hc) of 24 Univs; FRS 1955 (memb Cncl 1960–62 and 1977–79, pres 1980–85), Hon FEng 1986; Grand Cordon of the Sacred Treasure (Japan) 1995; *Books* Reflections on Muscle (1980); *Recreations* walking, designing scientific instruments; *Style*— Sir Andrew Huxley, OM, FRS, Hon FEng; ✉ Manor Field, 1 Vicarage Drive, Grantchester, Cambridge CB3 9NG (☎ and fax 01223 840207)

HUXLEY, Elspeth Josceline; *née* Grant; CBE (1962); da of Maj Josceline Grant (d 1947), of Njoro, Kenya, and Hon Eleanor, *née* Grosvenor (d 1977); *b* 23 July 1907; *Educ* Univ of Reading; *m* 12 Dec 1931, Gervas Huxley, CMG, MC (d 1971), s of Dr Henry Huxley; 1 s (Charles b 1944); *Career* writer; author of 40 books incl: biography, autobiography, fiction, crime, travel; most of these books relate to Africa and many to Kenya (her childhood home); two were semi-fictional autobiographical: The Flame Trees of Thika (TV Series) and The Mottled Lizard; Out in The Midday Sun (semi-travel, semi-autobiographical), Biography of Peter Scott (1993); *Recreations* resting, gossip; *Style*— Mrs Elspeth Huxley, CBE; ✉ Green End, Oaksey, Malmesbury, Wiltshire (☎ 01666 577252)

HUXLEY, Prof George Leonard; s of late Sir Leonard G H Huxley, and late Lady Molly Huxley; *b* 23 Sept 1932; *Educ* Blundell's Sch, Magdalen Coll Oxford (BA); *m* 1957, Davina Best; 3 da; *Career* Mil Serv cmmnd RE 1951; fell All Souls Coll Oxford 1955–61, asst dir Br Sch at Athens 1956–58, visiting lectr Harvard Univ 1958–59 and 1961–62, prof of Greek Queen's Univ of Belfast 1962–83, temp asst lectr St Patrick's Coll Maynooth 1984–85, hon res assoc Trinity Coll Dublin 1984–89, dir Gennadius Library American Sch of Classical Studies Athens 1986–89; hon prof of Greek Trinity Coll Dublin 1989–; memb: Exec NI Civil Rights Assoc 1971–72, Royal Irish Acad Dublin (sec for polite literature and antiquities 1979–86, sr vice pres 1984–85, hon librarian 1990–94, special envoy 1994–97), Irish Advsy Bd Inst of Irish Studies Univ of Liverpool 1996–; chm Organising Ctee 8th Int Congress of Classical Studies Dublin 1984, sr vice pres Fédération Internationale des Sociétés d'Études Classiques 1984–89, Irish memb Standing Ctee for the Humanities Euro Sci Fndn Strasbourg 1978–86; visiting prof of history Univ of Calif San Diego 1990; Cromer Greek Prize 1963; Hon LittD Dublin, Hon DLitt Belfast; memb Academia Europaea 1990 (chm Classics subject gp 1995–96); FSA, MRIA; author of various articles on Hellenic and Byzantine subjects; *Books* Achaeans and Hittites (1960), Early Sparta (1962), The Early Ionians (1966), Greek Epic Poetry from Eumelos to Panyassis (1969), Kythera, Excavations and Studies (ed with J N Coldstream, 1972), Pindar's Vision of the Past (1975), On Aristotle and Greek Society (1979), Homer and the Travellers (1988); *Recreations* siderodromophilia; *Clubs* Athenaeum; *Style*— Prof George Huxley; ✉ c/o School of Classics, Trinity College, Dublin 2, Ireland

HUXLEY, Dr Hugh Esmor; MBE (Mil 1948); s of Thomas Hugh Huxley (d 1967), and Olwen, *née* Roberts (d 1963); *b* 25 Feb 1924; *Educ* Park HS Birkenhead, Christ's Coll Cambridge (BA, MA, PhD, ScD); *m* 12 Feb 1966, Frances, da of Glenway Maxon; 1 da (Olwen b 1970); *Career* radar offr RAF 1943–47; res student Laboratory of Molecular Biology Cambridge 1948–52, postdoctoral fell Mass Inst of Technol 1952–54; MRC: Molecular Biology Unit Cambridge 1954–56, res assoc Dept of Biophysics London 1956–62, Laboratory of Molecular Biology Cambridge 1962–87 (jt head Structural Studies Div 1975–87, dep dir 1978–87); sr visiting instructor Physiology Course Marine Biol Laboratory Woods Hole Mass 1966–71; Brandeis Univ Waltham Mass: Ziskind visiting prof of biol 1971, Lucille P Markey distinguished prof of biol 1987–, dir Rosenstiel Basic Med Scis Res Center 1988–94 (memb External Advsy Bd 1971–77); fell: Christ's Coll Cambridge 1953–56, King's Coll Cambridge 1961–67, Churchill Coll Cambridge 1967–87; Euro Molecular Biol Laboratory: convenor Working Gp of Techniques and Instrumentation 1969–70, memb Scientific Advsy Cncl 1975–81, memb Instrumentation Policy Planning Ctee 1978–81; jt ed Progress In Biophysics and Molecular Biology 1964–67; memb Editorial Bd: Jl of Cell Biology 1961–64, Jl of Molecular Biology 1962–70, 1978–87 and 1990–94, Jl of Ultra-structure Research 1958–67, Jl of Cell Science 1966–70, Proceedings of the Royal Soc (B) 1969–71, Jl of Cell Motility and Muscle Research 1980–; tstee Associated Univs Inc 1987–90; awards: Feldberg prize for Experimental Med Res 1963, Hardy prize for Biological Research 1965, Louisa Gross Horwitz prize 1971, Feltrinelli Int prize for Med 1974, Gairdner award 1975, Baly medal RCP 1975, E B Wilson award 1983, Albert Einstein World Award of Sci 1987, Franklin medal 1990, Distinguished Scientist award Electron Microscope Soc America 1991; hon foreign memb: Leopoldina Acad 1964, American Acad of Arts and Scis 1965, Danish Acad of Scis 1971; hon memb: American Soc of Biological Chemists 1976, American Assoc of Anatomists 1981, American Physiological Soc 1981, Br Biophysical Soc 1992; Hon DSc: Harvard Univ 1969, Univ of Chicago 1974, Univ of Pennsylvania 1976; hon fell Christ's Coll Cambridge 1981, foreign assoc US Nat Acad of Scis 1978, FRS 1960 (memb Cncl 1973–75 and 1984–85); *Publications* numerous pubns in scientific jls; *Recreations* skiing, sailing; *Clubs* United Oxford and Cambridge Univ; *Style*— Dr Hugh Huxley, MBE, FRS; ✉ 349 Nashawtuc Rd, Concord, MA 01742, USA (☎ 00 1 508 369 4603); Rosenstiel Center, Brandeis Univ, 214 South St, Waltham, MA 02254, USA (☎ 00 1 617 736 2490, fax 00 1 617 736 2405)

HUXLEY, Rev Keith; s of George Frederick Huxley (d 1984), of Heswall, and Eluned Elizabeth, *née* Owen (d 1986); *b* 17 Sept 1933; *Educ* Birkenhead Sch, ChCh Cambridge (Tancred student, MA), Cuddesdon Theol Coll Oxford; *Career* Nat Serv Royal Army Educn Corps 1952–54; student Cambridge 1954–57; curate: St Mary's Bowdon 1959–61, Christ Church Crewe 1961–62; Chester diocesan youth chaplain and asst chaplain Chester Cathedral 1962–68, vicar of St Andrew's Runcorn 1968–73, ldr Runcorn Ecumenical Team Miny 1968–76, team rector E Runcorn with Halton 1973–77, home sec Bd for Mission and Unity Gen Synod and sec English Ptnrs in Mission Consultation 1977–83, team rector of Gateshead 1983–, rural dean of Gateshead 1988–92; chaplain to the Queen 1981; Medal of Merit The Scout Assoc 1982; *Recreations* ornithology; *Style*— The Rev Keith Huxley; ✉ Gateshead Rectory, 91 Old Durham Road, Gateshead, Tyne & Wear NE8 4BS (☎ 0191 477 3990)

HUXLEY, Prof Paul; s of late Ernest William Huxley, of London, and Winifred Mary, *née* Hunt; *b* 12 May 1938; *Educ* Harrow Sch of Art, Royal Acad Sch; *m* 1, Sept 1957 (m dis 1972), Margaret Doris, *née* Perryman; 2 s (Mark b 1961, Nelson b 1963); m 2, May 1990, Susan Jennifer, da of late Henry Francis Metcalfe; *Career* artist; Harkness fell 1965–67, Lindbury Tst award 1977, Athena Arts award 1985, Nat Arts Collections Fund award 1989; prof of painting RCA 1986–; *Group Exhibitions* incl: Whitechapel Gallery London 1964, Marlborough Gerson NY 1965, Galerie Milano Milan 1965, Pittsburgh Int Carnegie Inst Pittsburgh 1967, UCLA Art Galleries Los Angeles 1968, Tate Gallery London 1968, Museum of Modern Art NY 1968, Museum am Ostwall Hanover 1969, Walker Art Gallery Liverpool 1973, Hayward Gallery London 1974, Royal Acad London 1977, Museo Municipal Madrid 1983, RCA London 1988, Mappin Art Gallery Sheffield 1988; *Solo Exhibitions* Rowan Gallery London, Gillian Jason Gallery London, Galerie zur Alten Deutchen Schule Switzerland, Kornblee Gallery NY, Galleria da Emenda Lisbon, Forum Kunst Rotweil, Gardner Arts Centre Univ of Sussex; *Commisions* incl: London Tport to design 22 ceramic murals for King's Cross Underground Station 1984, Rambert Dance Co to design sets and costumes for Cats Eye 1992; *Work in Public Collections* incl: Albright-Knox Gallery Buffalo NY, Art Gallery of NSW Aust, Leeds City Art Gallery, Museum of Modern Art NY, Tate Gallery, V & A Museum, Whitworth Art Gallery Manchester, Stuyvesant Fndn Holland, Ulster Museum Belfast, Art Gallery of Ontario Toronto, Centro Cultural Arte Contemporanes Mexico; memb: Ctee Serpentine Gallery 1971–74, Arts Panel Arts Cncl GB 1972–76, Exhibitions Ctee Royal Acad 1988–; tstee Tate Gallery 1975–82; RA 1991 (ARA 1987); *Books* Exhibition Road - Painters at The Royal College of Art (1988); *Style*— Prof Paul Huxley, RA; ✉ Royal College of Art, Kensington Gore, London SW7 2EU (☎ 0171 590 4444)

HUXTABLE, Gen Sir Charles Richard; KCB (1984, CB 1982), CBE (1976, OBE 1972, MBE 1961), DL (N Yorkshire 1994); s of Capt W R Huxtable; *b* 22 July 1931; *Educ* Wellington, RMA Sandhurst; *m* 31 March 1959, Mary, da of late Brig J H C Lawlor; 3 da; *Career* Col Cmdt The King's Div 1982–87, Col Duke of Wellington's Regt 1982–90; Dir Army Staff Duties MOD 1982–83, Cdr Trg and Arms Directors 1983–86, Quartermaster Gen 1986–88, Cdr in Chief UK Land Forces 1988–90; ADC Gen 1988–90; Col Royal Irish Regt 1992–96; pres Ex-Servs Mental Welfare Soc 1991–, govr Giggleswick Sch 1991–; *Clubs* Army and Navy; *Style*— Gen Sir Charles Huxtable, KCB, CBE, DL; ✉ c/o Lloyds Bank, 23 High St, Teddington, Middx TW11 8EX

HYAM, His Hon Judge Michael Joshua; s of Isaac Joseph Hyam (d 1972), of Sussex, and Rachel Hyam (d 1992); *b* 18 April 1938; *Educ* Westminster, Univ of Cambridge (MA); *m* 1968, Diana, da of Rupert Vernon Mortimer, of Yorks; 3 s; *Career* barr SE circuit 1962–84, rec Crown Ct 1983–84, circuit judge (SE Circuit) 1984–, resident judge Norwich 1991–, designated care judge Norfolk 1991–; memb: Cncl of Legal Educn 1980–85, Ethical Ctee Cromwell Hosp 1983–92; govr Dulwich Coll Prep Sch 1986–92; *Publications* Advocacy Skills (1990, 3 edn 1995); *Recreations* book collecting, cricket, gardening; *Clubs* Garrick, Norfolk, MCC; *Style*— His Hon Judge Hyam; ✉ Norwich Crown Court, The Law Courts, Bishopgate, Norwich NR3 1UR (☎ 01603 761776)

HYATT, Derek James; s of Albert James Hyatt (d 1972), of Ilkley, W Yorks, and Dorothy, *née* Sproat; *b* 21 Feb 1931; *Educ* Ilkley GS, Leeds Coll of Art (NDD), Norwich Coll of Art, RCA (ARCA); *m* 20 Feb 1960, Rosamond Joy, da of Sidney Rockey (d 1983), of Torquay; 1 da (Sally Jane b 27 June 1962); *Career* Nat Serv RAF Fighter Cmd 1952–54; artist, writer and teacher; visiting lectr Kingston Sch of Art 1959–64, lectr Leeds Coll of Art 1964–68, sr lectr Leeds Poly 1968–84 (head of illustration studies), visiting prof Cincinnati Univ 1980; *Solo Exhibitions* incl: New Art Centre London 1960,

1961, 1963 and 1966, Univ of York 1966, Goosewell Gallery Menston 1967, Arthur Gallery Tampa USA 1967, Scottish Gallery Edinburgh 1969, Compass Gallery Glasgow 1970, Waddington Gallery London 1975, Waddington and Tooths Gallery London 1977, Northern Arts Gallery 1980, Gillan Jason Gallery London 1988, Austin Desmond Gallery London 1989, Ruskin Gallery Sheffield 1990, Univ of Leeds 1990, Art Space Gallery London 1993, Mappin Gallery Sheffield 1995; *Work in Public Collections* incl: Carlisle Art Gallery, Nuffield Fndn London, Balliol Coll Oxford, Yale Univ USA; life memb Nat Soc of Art Educn; *Books* The Challenge of Landscape Painting (1990), Ark Journal of RCA (ed nos 21, 22 and 23); various pubns in jls incl: Modern Painters, Contemporary Art, Green book, Arts Review; *Recreations* tennis, badminton, walking, looking, drawing; *Style*— Derek Hyatt, Esq; ✉ Rectory Farm House, Collingham, Wetherby, Yorkshire LS22 5AS (☎ 01937 572265)

HYATT, Peter Robin; s of Maj Arthur John Roach Hyatt (d 1987), of Send, nr Woking, Surrey, and Molly, *née* Newman (d 1983); *b* 12 May 1947; *Educ* Cheltenham; *m* 1 (m dis 1984), Julie Ann, *née* Cox; 1 s (Rafe James Roach b 1978), 1 da (Gabriella Rosa b 1975); m 2, 15 Jan 1988, Jenny Courtenay, da of Rt Rev John Bernard Taylor, *qv*; *Career* gp mangr Coopers and Lybrand 1964–80; Neville Russell: sr mangr 1980–82, ptnr 1983–, seconded as asst dir to the Serious Fraud Office 1991–94; FCA 1978 (ACA 1971); *Recreations* leading a bible study group, cycling, watching cricket and rugby; *Clubs* National; *Style*— Peter Hyatt, Esq; ✉ 3 Alderley Court, Chesham Rd, Berkhamsted, Herts HP4 3AD (☎ 01442 873191); Neville Russell, 24 Bevis Marks, London EC3A 7NR (☎ 0171 220 3462)

HYDE, Margaret Elizabeth; da of William Hyde (d 1972), of Bexley, Kent, and Betty Gwendolen Mary, *née* Haynes; *b* 5 March 1947; *Educ* Bexley HS Kent; *m* 18 April 1970, Stephen Geoffrey Noël, s of (Harry) Gordon Noël (d 1987), of Orpington, Kent; 1 da (Louisa b 1977); *Career* journalist Liverpool Echo and Daily Post 1970–73; BBC Radio Merseyside 1973–83: presenter and prodr, first woman news ed in English local radio 1979; BBC Radio Newsroom London 1983, head of progs Radio Lancashire 1984–86, chief asst BBC NW Region TV and Radio 1986–87; managing ed: BBC Radio Cambridgeshire 1987–95, BBC Essex 1995–; memb: Assoc of Br Eds, Radio Acad; *Recreations* music, theatre, criminology, naval history and talking!; *Style*— Miss Margaret Hyde; ✉ Staccato, 34 Hicks Lane, Girton, Cambridge CB3 0JS (☎ 01223 276886); BBC Essex, PO Box 765, Chelmsford CM2 9XB (☎ 01245 262393, fax 01245 490703)

HYDE, Peter John; s of late Arthur Albert Hyde, of Harpenden, Herts, and Eileen, *née* Smith; *b* 21 July 1941; *Educ* Aldenham; *m* 19 Feb 1971, Jennifer Anne, da of Anne Gavina Venables, of Maresfield Park, Uckfield, E Sussex; 1 s (Nicholas b 5 Jan 1976), 2 da (Henrietta b 24 May 1973, Gemma b 7 Nov 1979); *Career* WS Crawford Ltd 1960–64; Hyde and Partners Ltd: dir 1966, md 1971, chm and chief exec 1976; md Hyde Marketing Services Ltd 1995–; memb: Cncl Inst of Practitioners in Advertising 1974, Membership Ctee Inst of Dirs 1977–88; pres Solus Club 1989 (hon treas 1983–), chm Bd of Govrs Epsom Sch of Art and Design 1989–94 (govr 1980), govr Surrey Inst of Art and Design 1994–; MCAM 1966, MIPA 1966, FIPA 1977; *Recreations* golf, offshore sailing, skiing, tennis, swimming; *Style*— Peter Hyde, Esq; ✉ Elmet House, Brimpton, Berks RG7 4TB (☎ 0118 971 2977); Hyde Marketing Services Ltd, 195 Euston Road, London NW1 2BN (☎ 0171 753 8683, fax 0171 753 8689, e-mail hyde@corporate.nethead.co.uk)

HYDE PARKER, Sir Richard William; 12 Bt (E 1681), DL (Suffolk 1995); s of Sir William Stephen Hyde Parker, 11 Bt (d 1951); *b* 5 April 1937; *Educ* Millfield, RAC Cirencester; *m* 1972, Jean, da of late Sir Lindores Leslie, 9 Bt; 1 s (William), 3 da (twins Beata and Margaret b 1973, Lucy b 1975); *Heir* s, William John b 10 June 1983; *Career* High Sheriff of Suffolk 1995–96; *Style*— Sir Richard Hyde Parker, Bt, DL; ✉ Melford Hall, Long Melford, Suffolk CO10 9AA

HYDE-THOMSON, Paul Cater; CBE, DL (Leicestershire 1986); s of Robert Hyde Hyde-Thomson (d 1970), of London, and Joan Perronet, *née* Sells (d 1972); *b* 17 March 1927; *Educ* Harrow, ChCh Oxford (MA); *m* 26 Oct 1950, Zoë Caroline Georgia, da of Robin Regis d'Erlanger, MC (d 1934); 1 s (Henry b 1954), 4 da (Catherine b 1952, Philippa b 1956, Eleanor b 1960, Lucy b 1971); *Career* Capt Oxon and Bucks LI; chm: Ibstock Johnsen plc 1961–92 (dir 1951–92), TR Property Investment Trust plc 1991–; dir: Simons Group Ltd, Kilworth Group Ltd; High Sheriff Leics 1965; pres Nat Cncl of Bldg Material Producers 1981–83, chm Blaby Cons Assoc 1986–89, memb Leics CC 1961–70; FCA 1954; *Recreations* music, art, travel, gardening; *Style*— Paul Hyde-Thomson, Esq, CBE, DL; ✉ The Stable House, North Kilworth, Lutterworth, Leics LE17 6JE (☎ 01858 880581); Flat 91, 55 Ebury Street, London SW1 (☎ 0171 730 5270)

HYDON, Kenneth John; s of John Thomas Hydon (d 1966), and Vera, *née* Cheaney (d 1972); *b* 3 Nov 1944; *m* 1966, Sylvia Sheila; 2 c; *Career* fin dir: Racal SES Ltd 1979–81, Racal Defence and Avionics Group 1981–85, Racal Millicom Ltd 1985–88, Racal Telecommunications Group Ltd 1985–88, Orbitel Mobile Communications (Holdings) Ltd 1987–96, Racal Telecom plc 1988–91, Vodafone Group plc 1991–, Vodafone Europe Holdings BV 1992–, Vodafone Australasia Pty 1993–96; FCMA, FCCA; *Recreations* badminton, sailing, rugby, cricket; *Style*— Kenneth Hydon, Esq; ✉ Vodafone Group plc, The Courtyard, 2–4 London Rd, Newbury, Berks RG13 1JL (☎ 01635 33251, fax 01635 35237)

HYETT, Paul David Etheridge; s of Derek James Hyett, of Breinton Common, Hereford, and Josephine Mable, *née* Sparks (d 1990); *b* 18 March 1952; *Educ* Hereford Cathedral Sch, Architectural Association (AADipl), Bartlett Sch of Planning (MPhil); *m* 1976, Susan Margaret, da of Richard Harry Beavan; 3 s (James b 1981, Benjamin b 1983, Peter b 1986); *Career* asst: Cedric Price Architects 1974–78, Alan Baxter Assocs 1978–80; ptnr: Arno Jobst and Paul Hyett Architects 1981–82, Nicholas Lacey Jobst and Hyett Architects 1982–87, Paul Hyett Architects 1987–; teacher: Canterbury Sch of Architecture 1986–87, Dusseldorf Sch of Architecture 1987–89, Bartlett Sch of Architecture and Planning 1994–; memb Governing Body and hon treas Architectural Assoc Sch, chm Urban Design Gp Educn Ctee 1994–96, cncl memb Architects' Registration Cncl UK 1979–; RIBA 1979; memb: Architectural Assoc 1972, RTPI 1992; MAE; *Recreations* hill trekking, sailing, classical music, writing, chess; *Style*— Paul Hyett, Esq; ✉ Paul Hyett Architects, 36/37 Featherstone Street, London EC1Y 8QX (☎ 0171 251 0783, fax 0171 251 1691)

HYLAND, Paul Robert; s of Kenneth George Hyland (d 1979), and Hetta Grace, *née* Tilsley, of Boscombe, Dorset; *b* 15 Sept 1947; *Educ* Canford, Univ of Bristol (BSc); *m* 1, 21 Aug 1971 (m dis 1988), Noëlle Jean, da of James Houston Angus; m 2, 8 Dec 1990, Margaret Ann, da of Thomas William Ware; *Career* writer; teacher of creative writing Arvon Fndn and other centres; memb: Dorset Natural History and Archaeological Soc, Poetry Soc, Soc of Authors; broadcast work incl: plays, drama-documentaries, features, poetry; *Books* Purbeck: The Ingrained Island (1978), Poems of Z (1982), Wight: Biography of an Island (1984), The Stubborn Forest (1984), The Black Heart: A Voyage into Central Africa (1988), Getting Into Poetry (1992), Indian Balm: Travels in the Southern Subcontinent (1994), Kicking Sawdust (1995), Backwards out of the Big World: a Voyage into Portugal (1996); *Style*— Paul Hyland, Esq; ✉ David Higham Associates Ltd, 5–8 Lower John St, Golden Square, London W1R 4HA (☎ 0171 437 7888, fax 0171 437 1072)

HYLSON-SMITH, Gillian Jean; da of Gilbert Walter Kirby, of Pinner, Middx, and Joan, *née* McGaw (d 1943); *b* 17 July 1939; *Educ* Wycombe Abbey, Univ of Leicester (BA), Hatfield Poly (Dip Careers Educn and Guidance); *m* 1961, Dr Kenneth Hylson-Smith, bursar St Cross Coll Oxford; 2 s (Simon Charles b 16 March 1963, Luke Gilbert b 10 Oct 1970), 1 da (Clare Joanna 18 Feb 1965); *Career* Downe House Sch 1960–61, Dore & Totley HS Sheffield 1961–62, St Crispins Prep Sch Leicester 1966–70, St Marylebone GS For Boys 1973–79, Haberdashers' Aske's Sch For Girls Elstree 1980–86, headmistress Westonbirt Sch 1986–; *Recreations* family life, dogs, antique collecting (esp blue and white egg cups); *Style*— Mrs Gillian Hylson-Smith; ✉ Westonbirt School, Tetbury, Gloucs GL8 8QT (☎ 01666 880333, fax 01666 880364)

HYLTON, 5 Baron (UK 1866); Sir Raymond Hervey Jolliffe; 5 Bt (UK 1821); s of Lt-Col 4 Baron Hylton (d 1967, whose mother was Lady Alice Hervey, da of 3 Marquess of Bristol), and Lady Perdita Asquith (d 1996), sis of 2 Earl of Oxford and Asquith and gda of 1 Earl, better known as HH Asquith, the Lib PM, by his 1 w); *b* 13 June 1932; *Educ* Eton, Trinity Coll Oxford (MA); *m* 1966, Joanna, da of Andrew de Bertodano, himself eldest s of 8 Marques de Moral (cr by King Charles III of Spain 1765), by Andrew's m to Lady Sylvia Savile (3 da of late 6 Earl of Mexborough, and sis of late Lady Agnes Eyston and late Lady Sarah Cumming-Bruce); 4 s (Hon William b 1967, Hon Andrew b 1969, Hon Alexander b 1973, Hon John b 1977), 1 da (Hon Emily b 1975); *Heir* s, Hon William Jolliffe; *Career* Lt Coldstream Gds Reserve; asst private sec to Govr-Gen Canada 1960–62; sits as independent peer in House of Lords, memb All-Pty Parly Gps on Human Rights and Penal Affairs; chm: St Francis and St Sergius Trust Fund re Russia, MICOM re Moldova; former chm: Catholic Housing Aid Soc, Nat Federation of Housing Associations, Housing Assoc Charitable Tst, Help the Aged Housing Tst; pres: NIACRO, Hugh of Witham Foundation; govr Ammerdown Study Center; tstee: Acorn Christian Healing Tst, ABCD (a tst for Palestinian children with disabilities); Hon Dr of Soc Sciences, Univ of Southampton 1994; ARICS; *Style*— The Rt Hon the Lord Hylton; ✉ Ammerdown, Radstock, Bath BA3 5SH (☎ 0171 219 5353, fax 0171 219 5979)

HYLTON-FOSTER, Baroness (Life Peer UK 1965); Hon Audrey Pellew Hylton-Foster; *née* Clifton-Brown; DBE (1990); da of 1 and last Viscount Ruffside, PC, DL, speaker House of Commons 1943–51 (d 1958); *b* 19 May 1908; *Educ* St George's Ascot; *m* 1931, Rt Hon Sir Harry Hylton-Foster, QC, MP, speaker House of Commons 1959–65 (d 1965), s of Harry Braustyn Hylton-Foster; *Career* Br Red Cross Soc: dir Chelsea Div London Branch 1950–60, pres London Branch 1960–83, memb Cncl 1967–80, appointed to Nat HQ consultative panel 1984–86; pres Prevention of Blindness Research Fund 1965–76, convenor Cross Bench Peers 1974–95 (cross bencher 1965); *Recreations* fishing, gardening; *Style*— The Rt Hon the Baroness Hylton-Foster, DBE; ✉ 54 Cranmer Court, Whitehead Grove, London SW3 3HW (☎ 0171 584 2889); The Coach House, Tanhurst, Leith Hill, Holmbury St Mary, Dorking, Surrey RH5 6LU (☎ 01306 711975)

HYMAN, (Robert) Anthony; s of Alexander Hyman (d 1967), and Fanny, *née* Robinson (d 1961); *b* 5 April 1928; *Educ* Dartington Hall Sch, Trinity Coll Cambridge (MA, PhD); *m* 11 Jan 1962, Hon Laura Alice, da of late Gilbert Allan Rowland Boyd, Baron Kilmarnock; 2 s (Anthony Arie b 1962, Merlin Michael b 1969), 1 da (Francesca Maona Doon b 1966); *Career* sr physicist Standard Telecommunications Res Lab 1950–56 and 1958–62 (made first diffused transistor in GB 1951), memb scientific staff Medical Res Cncl 1956–58, sr res fell Technion 1962–63, computer technology res mangr English-Electric-Leo Computers 1964–71, freelance computer conslt and historian of science 1971–96, Alastair Horne fell in modern history St Antony's Coll Oxford 1977–78, hon research fell Dept of Economic & Social History Univ of Exeter 1996–; *Books* The Computer in Design (1973), Computing - A Dictionary of Terms, Concepts & Ideas (1976), The Coming of the Chip (1980), Charles Babbage - Pioneer of the Computer (1982), Memoir of the Life and Labours of the Late Charles Babbage, FRS (ed and intro, 1987), Science and Reform (1988); *Recreations* sculpture, walking, gardening; *Style*— Anthony Hyman, Esq

HYMAN, Howard Jonathan; s of Joe Hyman, of London, and Corrine Irene, *née* Abrahams; *b* 23 Oct 1949; *Educ* Bedales Sch, Univ of Manchester (BA); *m* 21 Sept 1972, Anne Moira, da of Capt Harry Sowden, of Ilkley, Yorks; 2 s (Daniel b 1977, Sam b 1979), 1 da (Hannah b 1982); *Career* Price Waterhouse: ptnr 1984–94, specialist advsr on privatisation HM Treasy 1984–87, ptnr i/c Privatisation Servs Dept 1987–90, head corporate fin Europe 1990–94, memb E European Jt Venture Bd 1990–94, memb China Bd 1991–94, memb Euro Mgmnt Bd 1991–94, world head corporate fin 1994; dep chm Charterhouse Bank 1994–, an md Charterhouse plc 1994–; FCA; *Recreations* walking, classical music, cricket, gardening; *Clubs* Reform, MCC; *Style*— Howard Hyman, Esq; ✉ Deputy Chairman, Charterhouse Bank, 1 Paternoster Row, London EC4M 7DH (direct ☎ 0171 246 2424)

HYMAN, Robin Philip; s of Leonard Albert Hyman (d 1964), of London, and Helen Josephine, *née* Mautner (d 1991); *b* 9 Sept 1931; *Educ* Henley GS, Univ of Birmingham (BA); *m* 17 April 1966, Inge, *née* Neufeld; 2 s (James b 29 May 1967, Peter b 23 Nov 1968), 1 da (Philippa 13 March 1971); *Career* Nat Serv RAF 1949–51; ed Mermaid 1953–54, md Evans Bros Ltd 1972–77 (dep md 1967, dir 1964), chm Bell and Hyman Ltd 1977–86, chm and chief exec Unwin Hyman Ltd 1989–90 (md 1986–88), chm Calmann & King Ltd 1991–, conslt Hambro Group Investments Ltd 1991–, memb BBC Gen Advsy Cncl 1992–; memb Editorial Bd World Yearbook of Educn 1969–73, treas Educnl Publishers' Cncl 1972–75 (memb Exec Ctee 1971–76), memb first Br Publishers' Delegn to China 1978, pres Publishers' Assoc 1989–91 (memb Cncl 1975–92, treas 1982–84, vice pres 1988–89 and 1991–92); FRSA; *Books* A Dictionary of Famous Quotations (1962), Boys and Girls First Dictionary (with John Trevaskis 1967); 11 children's books with Inge Hyman incl: Barnabas Ball at the Circus (1967), Runaway James and the Night Owl (1968), The Hippo Who Wanted to Fly (1973), The Greatest Explorers in the World (1978), The Treasure Box (1980); *Clubs* Garrick, MCC; *Style*— Robin Hyman, Esq; ✉ 101 Hampstead Way, London NW11 7LR (☎ 0181 455 7055)

HYMAS, Charles Southern Albert; s of Peter David Hymas, of Northampton, and Margaret, *née* Southern; *b* 7 Jan 1961; *Educ* Harrow, Univ of Durham (BA), Univ Coll Cardiff (Postgrad Dip in Journalism); *m* Sarah Elizabeth, da of Prof Michael Barbour; 1 da (Katharine Anna); *Career* trainee journalist South Wales Argus Newport 1983–84 (educn corr 1984–85); Western Mail Cardiff: gen news reporter 1985–86, educn corr 1986–87, political corr 1987–88; political reporter Yorkshire Post 1988–90; The Sunday Times: educn corr 1990–95, dep ed Insight 1995–; *Recreations* swimming, tennis and cooking; *Style*— Charles Hymas, Esq; ✉ The Sunday Times, 1 Pennington Street, London E1 9XW (☎ 0171 782 5685, fax 0171 782 5732)

HYMAS, Roger; s of William Frederick, of Southend-on-Sea, and Stella, *née* Cardy; *b* 21 April 1946; *Educ* Southend-on-Sea HS for Boys, City of London Poly (Dip); *m* 29 March 1969, Yvonne Ann, *née* Levett; 2 s (Simon David b 9 Aug 1972, Christopher Andrew (twin)); *Career* various positions incl head of market planning, chief business economist and head of retail travel AA 1962–79; American Express: mktg dir Travel Div Europe 1979–82, vice pres Mktg and Sales Travel Div New York 1982–84, vice pres mktg Card Div Europe 1984–86, vice pres and gen mangr Fin Servs Div 1986–87; exec dir Burton Group Financial Services 1987–91, exec dir Retailer Fin Servs GE Capital Co USA 1991–92; BUPA: gp mktg dir 1992–94, md/chief strategy offr 1994–; CDipAF, assoc MIPM, FCIM; *Recreations* travel, reading, current affairs, opera; *Style*— Roger Hymas, Esq; ✉ BUPA Ltd, Provident House, 15 Essex Street, London WC2R 3AU (☎ 0171 353 5212)

HYND, Ronald; s of William John Hens (d 1991), of London, and Alice Louisa, *née* Griffiths (d 1994); *b* 22 April 1931; *Educ* Holloway Co Sch, Rambert Sch of Ballet; *m* 24

June 1957, Annette Page, *qv*, da of James Lees Page (d 1979); 1 da (Louise b 20 April 1968); *Career* former ballet dancer, now dir and choreographer; Ballet Rambert 1949–51, Royal Ballet 1951–70 (princ dancer 1959), danced all major classical roles and many dramatic and romantic ballets; dir Bavarian State Ballet 1970–73 and 1984–86; choreographed full length ballets: The Nutcracker (London Festival Ballet, L'Opera de Nice) 1976, Rosalinda (Johannesburg Ballet, Festival Ballet, Houston, Ljubljana, Santiago, Cincinnati, Bonn, Salt Lake City) 1978, Papillon (Houston, Sadlers Wells Royal Ballet, Johannesburg, Munich, Santiago) 1979, Le Diable a Quatre (Johannesburg, Santiago) 1984, Coppelia (Festival Ballet) 1985, The Merry Widow (Aust 1975 and Canada 1986, Johannesburg 1993, Vienna 1994, Santiago and Houston 1995, La Scala Milan 1996), Ludwig II (Munich) 1986, Hunchback of Notre Dame (Houston) 1988, The Sleeping Beauty (English Nat Ballet 1993); one act ballets incl: Dvorak Variations, Le Baiser de la Fee, Mozartiana, Pasiphaë, La Chatte, Wendekreise, Das Telefon, Charlotte Bronte, Liaisons Amoureuses, Marco Polo, Scherzo Capriccioso, The Seasons, The Sanguine Fan, Les Valses, In a Summer Garden, Fanfare, Valse Glacé and Winter 1850 for John Curry; *Recreations* music, travel, gardens; *Style*— Ronald Hynd, Esq

HYNES, Catherine Wyn (Kate); da of Arthur Wyn Pugh, of Dolgellau, Gwynedd, and Olwen Mair, *née* Seaman; *b* 31 Oct 1945; *Educ* Dr Williams Sch Dolgellau (capt N Wales schoolgirls hockey team 1962), Univ of Liverpool (BA French); *m* 1968, Kenneth Hynes, s of Herbert Hynes; 2 s (Llewelyn Wyn b 12 Dec 1975, Ossian Wyn b 19 Feb 1986), 1 da (Elinor Wyn b 18 May 1984); *Career* London Weekend Television: admin asst Engrg Planning Dept 1968–74, mangr of wages 1974–79, mangr studio and location servs 1979–87, head of schedules 1987–90, controller of prodn planning The London Studios (subsid of LWT) 1990–92, dir of staff relations and studio ops The London Studios 1992–95, dir of operations 1995–; *Recreations* bridge, children; *Style*— Mrs Kate Hynes; ✉ The London Studios, The London Television Centre, Upper Ground, London SE1 9LT (☎ 0171 261 3423, fax 0171 261 3437)

HYNES, Prof Richard Olding; *b* 29 Nov 1944; *Career* res fell Imperial Cancer Res Fund Laboratories London 1971–74; Massachusetts Inst of Technol: asst prof 1975–78, assoc prof 1978–83, prof of biology 1983–, assoc head of biology 1985–89, head of biology 1989–91, dir Center for Cancer Res 1991–; investigator, Howard Hughes Med Inst 1988–; memb: American Soc for Cell Biology, Soc for Developmental Biology, Inst of Med 1995, US Nat Acad of Scis 1996; fell AAAS, FRS 1989, fell American Acad of Arts and Sci 1994; *Books* Surfaces of Normal and Malignant Cells (ed, 1979), Fibronectins (1990); *Recreations* music, reading, gardening, skiing; *Style*— Prof Richard Hynes, FRS; ✉ E17–227, Center for Cancer Research, Massachusetts Inst of Technolgy, Cambridge, Mass 02139, USA (☎ 00 1 617 253 6422, fax 00 1 617 253 8357, e-mail rohynes@mit.edu)

HYPHER, David Charles; s of Harold Eldric Hypher, MBE (d 1971), of Byfleet, Surrey, and Marcia Evelyn, *née* Spalding (d 1992); *b* 24 July 1941; *Educ* Weybridge Tech Coll; *m* 1, March 1966 (m dis 1971), Jenifer da of Robert Ingle; m 2, 17 July 1978, Pamela Alison, da of Peter Rowland Craddock; 2 da (Nicola, Emma); *Career* stockbroker 1958–82; dir: INVESCO Asset Management Ltd (Britannia Asset Mgmnt) 1983–, INVESCO Fund Managers Ltd 1984–, various INVESCO International (offshore) Jersey and Luxembourg fund cos 1985–, INVESCO Luxembourg SA 1993–, MIM International Management 1987–92, London Wall Britannia 1989–; tstee Rydes Hill Prep Sch Guildford; memb IIMR 1965, memb Stock Exchange 1972–83; *Recreations* collecting antiques and cars; *Style*— David Hypher, Esq; ✉ The Forge, Wood Street Village Green, nr Guildford, Surrey GU3 3DY (☎ 01483 234938); 8 La Fustera, Benisa, Alicante, Spain; c/o INVESCO Asset Management Ltd, 11 Devonshire Sq, London EC2M 4YR (☎ 0171 454 3150)

HYTNER, Benet Alan; QC (1970); s of Maurice Hytner (d 1978), of Manchester, and Sarah, *née* Goldberg (d 1988); *b* 29 Dec 1927; *Educ* Manchester GS, Trinity Hall Cambridge (MA); *m* 19 Dec 1954 (m dis 1980), Joyce Hytner, *qv*, da of Maj Bernard Myers (d 1979), of Cheshire; 3 s (Nicholas Hytner b 1956, *qv*, Richard b 1959, James b 1964), 1 da (Jennifer b 1958); *Career* Nat Serv Lt RASC 1949–51; called to the Bar Middle Temple 1952, recorder of the Crown Ct 1970–96, bencher 1977–, judge of appeal Isle of Man 1980–, ldr Northern Circuit 1984–88; memb: Gen Cncl of the Bar 1969–73 and 1984–88, Senate of Inns of Ct and Bar 1977–81; *Recreations* walking, reading, theatre; *Clubs* MCC; *Style*— Benet Hytner, Esq, QC; ✉ Byrom Chambers, 61 Fleet Street, London EC4Y 1JU (☎ 0171 353 4363); 25 Byrom St, Manchester M3 4PF

HYTNER, Joyce Anita; da of Bernard Myers (d 1979), of Altrincham, Cheshire, and Vera Myers, *née* Classick (d 1974); *b* 9 Dec 1935; *Educ* Withington Girls' Sch Manchester; *m* 19 Dec 1954 (m dis 1980), Benet Hytner, QC, *qv*; 3 s (Nicholas Hytner b 1956, *qv*, Richard b 1959, James b 1964), 1 da (Jennifer b 1958); *Career* head of devpt Royal Court Theatre; memb Bd Manchester Royal Exchange Theatre 1989–; non-exec memb Oxfordshire Health Authy 1996–, memb Cncl London Acad of Music and Dramatic Arts (LAMDA) 1993–; tstee: Lowry Centre Salford, Performing Arts Laboratories (PAL), International House; *Recreations* theatre, music; *Style*— Mrs Joyce Hytner; ✉ 20 Portsea Place, London W2 2BL

HYTNER, Nicholas Robert; s of Benet Alan Hytner, QC, *qv*, of London, and Joyce Hytner, *qv*, *née* Myers; *b* 7 May 1956; *Educ* Manchester GS, Trinity Hall Cambridge (MA); *Career* theatre, opera and film dir; prodns at Northcott Theatre Exeter and Leeds Playhouse; assoc dir Royal Exchange Theatre Manchester 1985–88, assoc dir Royal NT 1989–; *Theatre* dir: Measure for Measure (RSC) 1987, The Tempest (RSC) 1988, King Lear (RSC) 1990, Miss Saigon (Drury Lane Theatre and Broadway) 1989–91, The Importance of Being Earnest (Aldwych) 1993; prodns for Royal NT incl: Ghetto 1989, Wind in the Willows 1990, The Madness of George III 1991, Carousel 1993 (winner Best Musical Direction Olivier Award 1993); *Opera* prodns incl: King Priam (Kent Opera) 1984, Rienzi (ENO) 1983, Xerxes (ENO) 1985, The Magic Flute (ENO) 1988, Julius Caesar (Paris Opéra) 1987, Le Nozze di Figaro (Opéra de Genève) 1989, La Clemenza di Tito (Glyndebourne) 1991, The Force of Destiny 1992; *Film* dir The Madness of King George 1995, The Crucible 1995; *Awards* incl: Olivier Award for Best Opera Prodn (Xerxes), Evening Standard Opera Award (Xerxes), Evening Standard Best Director Award, Critics' Circle Best Director Award 1989, Best Director of a Musical Tony Awards 1994 for Carousel; *Style*— Nicholas Hytner, Esq; ✉ National Theatre, Upper Ground, South Bank, London SE1 9PX (☎ 0171 928 2033)

I

IBBOTSON, Eva Maria Charlotte Michele; da of Berthold Wiesner (d 1973), of London and Anna, *née* Gmeyner (d 1991); *b* 21 Jan 1925; *Educ* Dartington Hall Devon, Bedford Coll London (BSc); *m* 1948, Alan Ibbotson; 3 s (Tobias b 1951, Piers b 1954, Justin b 1959), 1 da (Lalage b 1949); *Career* lectr Univ of London 1945–48; author 1953–; *Awards* Carnegie Commendation (for Which Witch) 1979, Romantic Novel of the Year award 1983; *Books* for children: The Great Ghost Rescue (1975), Which Witch (1979), The Haunting of Hiram (1987), The Worm and The Toffee Nosed Princess (1989), Not Just a Witch (1989), The Secret of Platform Thirteen (1994); for adults: Countess Below Stairs (1981), Magic Flutes (1983), A Glove Shop in Vienna (1984), A Company of Swans (1985), Madensky Square (1988), The Morning Gift (1993); *Recreations* travel, music; *Style*— Mrs Eva Ibbotson; ✉ c/o Curtis Brown, 4th Floor, Haymarket House, 28–29 Haymarket, London SW1Y 4SP (☎ 0171 396 6600)

IBBOTSON, Peter Stamford; s of Capt Arthur Ibbotson, of Cranleigh, Surrey, and Ivy Elizabeth, *née* Acton (d 1988); *b* 13 Dec 1943; *Educ* Manchester GS, St Catherine's Coll Oxford (BA); *m* 13 Dec 1975, Susan Mary, da of Capt Peter Eric Fyers Crewdson, of Summerhow, Kendal, Cumbria; 2 s (John William Stamford b 1977, James Francis Peter b 1978), 1 da (Jane Elizabeth Phillippa b 1980); *Career* ed: Panorama 1983–85, Newsweek 1978–82; dep dir of progs BBC TV 1987–89, corp conslt Channel 4 TV 1989–91 and 1994–, dir of corp affairs Carlton Television Ltd 1991–94; dir FTC plc; FRTS; *Books* The Third Age of Broadcasting (co-author, 1978); *Recreations* silviculture, photography; *Clubs* RAC; *Style*— Peter Ibbotson, Esq; ✉ Newnham Farm House, Wallingford, Oxon OX10 8BW (☎ 01491 833111, fax 01491 833584)

IBBOTT, Alec; CBE (1988); s of Francis Joseph Ibbott (d 1976), of Croydon, Surrey, and Madge Winifred, *née* Graham (d 1976); *b* 14 Oct 1930; *Educ* Selhurst GS Croydon; *m* 4 April 1964, Margaret Elizabeth, da of Rev Ernest Alfred Brown (d 1968), of Sompting, Sussex; 1 s (Jonathan b 1971), 1 da (Elizabeth b 1969); *Career* Nat Serv Intelligence Corps 1949–51; joined FO 1949, ed FO list 1951, studied at MECAS 1955–56, second sec and vice consul Br Embassy Rabat 1956, FO 1960, second sec (info) Br Embassy Tripoli 1961, second sec Br Embassy Benghazi 1961, first sec (info) Br Embassy Khartoum 1965, FCO 1967, asst political agent Dubai 1971, first sec, head of chancery and consul Br Embassy Dubai 1971 and Abu Dhabi 1972, first sec and head of chancery Br High Cmmn Nicosia 1973, first sec FCO 1975, first sec and head of chancery Br Embassy Caracas 1977, cnsllr and head of chancery Br Embassy Khartoum 1979, seconded to Int Mil Serv Ltd 1982, HM ambass and consul gen Monrovia 1985, Br high cmmr Banjul 1988–90; chief exec Southern Africa Assoc 1992–95, gen mangr UK Southern Africa Business Assoc 1994–95, memb Cncl Anglo-Arab Assoc 1992–, tstee Charlton Community Devpt Tst 1995–; *Books* Professionalism: Problems and Prospects in Liberia (1986), One Hundred Years of English Law in the Gambia: Whither Gambian Law (1988); *Recreations* reading, walking, bird watching, Scottish dancing; *Style*— Alec Ibbott, Esq, CBE

IBBS, Sir Robin John; KBE (1988), kt (1982); o s of late Prof T L Ibbs, MC, and Marjorie, *née* Bell; *b* 21 April 1926; *Educ* Univ of Toronto, Trinity Coll Cambridge (MA mech scis); *m* 1952, Iris Barbara, da of late S Hall; 1 da; *Career* called to the Bar Lincoln's Inn; ICI: joined 1952, dir 1976–80 and 1982–88, seconded as head CPRS Cabinet Office 1980–82; Lloyds Bank plc: dir 1985–, dep chm 1988–93, chm 1993–; chm Lloyds TSB Group PLC 1995–; dep chm Lloyds Bank Canada 1989–90, chm Lloyds Merchant Bank Holdings 1989–92; Prime Minister's advsr on efficiency in govt 1983–88, leader Review of House of Commons Services 1990; chm Cncl UCL 1989–95; Hon DSc Univ of Bradford 1986, Hon LLD Univ of Bath 1993; *Style*— Sir Robin Ibbs, KBE; ✉ Lloyds TSB Group plc, 71 Lombard Street, London EC3P 3BS (☎ 0171 626 1500)

IDDESLEIGH, 4 Earl of (UK 1885); Sir Stafford Henry Northcote; 11 Bt (E 1641), DL (Devon 1979); also Viscount St Cyres (UK 1885); s of 3 Earl of Iddesleigh (d 1970, gs of 1 Earl, better known as Sir Stafford Northcote, a confidant of Gladstone in his youth and of Disraeli in maturity), and Elizabeth, *née* Lowndes (d 1991); *b* 14 July 1932; *Educ* Downside; *m* 1955, Maria Luisa (Mima) Alvarez-Builla y Urquijo, Condesa del Real Agrado (Spain CR of 1771), OBE, DL, da of Don Gonzalo Alvarez-Builla y Alvera and Maria Luisa, Viscountess Exmouth; 1 s, 1 da; *Heir* s, Viscount St Cyres; *Career* late 2 Lt Irish Gds; chm SW TSB 1981–83, trustee of England and Wales TSB 1983–86, chm SW region TSB 1983–88; dir: Westward TV 1981–82, Television South West 1982–92, TSB Group plc 1987–88, United Dominions Trust Ltd 1983–87, TSB Commercial Holdings Ltd 1987–88, Gemini Radio Ltd 1994–, Devon & Exeter Steeplechases Ltd; *Recreations* shooting; *Clubs* Army & Navy; *Style*— The Rt Hon the Earl of Iddesleigh, DL; ✉ Shillands House, Upton-Pyne-Hill, Exeter, Devon EX5 5EB (☎ 01392 58916)

IDDON, Michael Ian; s of Harold Edgar (d 1971), and Edna Iddon, *née* McTear (d 1981); *b* 18 Oct 1938; *Educ* Arnold Sch Blackpool, Harris Technical Coll Preston; *m* 1963, Rhona, da of Robert Paul (d 1972), of Chorley; 2 s (Michael James b 1965, David Robert b 1966), 1 da (Katherine Michelle b 1971); *Career* chm and md Iddon Bros Ltd 1971–, dir Engineer and Marine Applications Ltd 1980–, non-exec dir RAPRA Technology Ltd 1985–; vice pres Engrg Employers Fedn NW; holder of The Plastics and Rubber Inst Nelton Award Gold Medal 1985, Hancock Medal 1988; CEng, MIMechE, FPRI; *Recreations* fishing, golf, classic cars, stamps; *Clubs* Shaw Hill Golf and Country (Chorley); *Style*— Michael Iddon, Esq; ✉ The Crest, 2 Kingsway, Penwortham, Preston, Lancs PR1 0AP (☎ 01772 742416); Iddon Bros Ltd, Quin Street, Leyland PR5 1TB (☎ 01772 421258)

IDE, Christopher George; s of George Frederick Ide, of West Wickham, Kent, and Edith Harty, *née* Good; *b* 25 Sept 1950; *Educ* Howard Sch Croydon, Heath Clark GS, Imperial Coll London (BSc); *m* 21 Oct 1978 (m dis 1989), Elizabeth Mary Miller; 1 s (Edward Christopher b 30 Nov 1983); *Career* actuarial student The English Insurance Company Ltd 1972–73; The Swiss Life Group: joined 1973, asst actuary 1975–81, dep actuary 1982–86, UK actuary (incl responsibility of appointed actuary) 1987–89, md Swiss Life (UK) Group plc 1989–, chm Swiss Life Investment Management Ltd Dublin 1991–; memb Glyndebourne Festival Opera; Freeman City of London 1982, memb Court Worshipful Co of Actuaries 1993 (Liveryman 1982); FIA 1975, ASA 1985; *Recreations* hockey, opera, the works of Anthony Trollope; *Clubs* Reform, Fellowship, City Livery; *Style*— Christopher Ide, Esq; ✉ Swiss Life (UK) Group plc, Swiss Life House, South Park, Sevenoaks, Kent TN13 1BG (☎ 01732 582000, fax 01732 582001, car 0831 546912)

IDLE, Eric; *b* 29 March 1943, South Shields, Co Durham; *Educ* Royal Sch Wolverhampton, Pembroke Coll Cambridge (BA, pres Footlights); *m* 1 (m dis), Lyn Ashley; 1 s (Carey b 1973); m 2, Tania Kosevich; 1 da (Lily b 1990); *Career* actor, writer and film director; pres Prominent Features film co; *Stage* performances incl: Footlights '63 and '64 (Edinburgh Festival), I'm Just Wild About Harry (Edinburgh Festival) 1963, One For the Pot (Leicester Phoenix) 1965, First Farewell Tour (UK and Canada) 1973, Monty Python Live at Drury Lane 1974, Monty Python Live at City Centre 1976, Monty Python Live at the Hollywood Bowl 1980; writing incl Pass the Butler (Globe) 1981, The Frog Prince (also dir, Faerie Tale Theatre); *Opera* Ko-Ko in Jonathan Miller's prodn of The Mikado (ENO 1987, Houston Opera House 1989); *Television* acting/performing incl: We Have Ways of Making You Laugh (LWT) 1968, Do Not Adjust Your Set (two series, BBC) 1968–69, Monty Python's Flying Circus (also writer, four series, BBC, winner Silver Rose Montreux) 1969–74, Monty Python's Fliegende Zirkus (Bavaria TV) 1971–72, Rutland Weekend Television (also writer, two series, BBC) 1975–76, Laverne and Shirley (ABC), Saturday Night Live (guest star twice, host four times, NBC), The Mikado (Thames TV) 1987, Nearly Departed (Lorimar Productions for NBC) 1989, Parrot Sketch Not Included (BBC) 1989; writing also incl: Twice a Fortnight (BBC) 1967, The Frost Report (BBC, winner Golden Rose Montreux) 1967, The Two Ronnies (BBC), Marty Feldman (BBC) 1968–69; *Radio* performing incl: Radio Five (also writer, two series, BBC Radio 1) 1975, Behind the Crease (also writer, musical, BBC) 1990; writing also incl I'm Sorry I'll Read That Again (BBC); *Films* acting incl: Isadora The Biggest Dancer in the World (dir Ken Russell, BBC TV film) 1966, Alice in Wonderland (dir Jonathan Miller, BBC TV film) 1966, And Now For Something Completely Different (also writer) 1971, Monty Python and the Holy Grail (also writer) 1974, The Rutles - All You Need is Cash (also writer and dir, NBC TV film) 1978, Monty Python's Life of Brian (also writer) 1979, Monty Python Live at the Hollywood Bowl (also writer) 1980, Monty Python's The Meaning of Life (also writer, winner Cannes Jury Prize) 1983, Yellowbeard 1983, The Adventures of Baron Munchausen 1988, Nuns on the Run 1990, Too Much Sun 1990, Missing Pieces 1991, Splitting Heirs (also writer and prodr) 1993, Casper 1995; *Recordings* incl: Monty Python's Flying Circus (1970), Another Monty Python Record (1970), Monty Python's Previous Record (1972), Matching Tie and Handkerchief (1973), Live at Drury Lane (1974), Monty Python's Instant Record Collection (1977), Monty Python's Contractual Obligation Album (prodr, 1980), The Final Ripoff Album (1987), Monty Python Sings (1989), Nearly Departed (theme song for TV series, 1989), One Foot in the Grave (theme song for TV series, 1990), Always Look on the Bright Side of Life (single, reached Number Two 1991); *Books* Monty Python's Big Red Book (contrib and ed, 1971), The Brand New Monty Python Bok (contrib and ed, 1973), The Monty Python Paperbok (1974), Hello Sailor (novel, 1975), The Rutland Dirty Weekend Book (1976), Monty Python and the Holy Grail (1977), Monty Python's Scrapbook/Life of Brian (contrib and ed, 1979), Pass the Butler (1981), Monty Python's Flying Circus - Just the Words (1989); *Style*— Eric Idle, Esq; ✉ c/o ICM Ltd, Oxford House, 76 Oxford Street, London W1N 0AX (☎ 0171 636 6565, fax 0171 323 0101)

IGGLESDEN, Alan Paul; s of Alan Trevor Igglesden, of Westerham, and Gillian Catherine, *née* Relf; *b* 8 Oct 1964; *Educ* Churchill Sch Westerham; *m* 20 Jan 1990, Hilary Moira, da of William Henry Middleton; *Career* professional cricket player; cricket coach in townships of Cape Town SA 1985–89, represented Western Province and Avendale CC Cape Town SA 1985–89; Kent CCC 1984– (awarded county cap 1989); England: 3 tests and 4 one day ints, memb A team to Zimbabwe and Kenya 1990, memb team touring W Indies 1993/94; leading wicket-taker CCC 1989 and 1993; memb Boland Cricket Union 1992–93; *Recreations* Crystal Palace FC, golf, music, most sports; *Style*— Alan Igglesden, Esq; ✉ Kent CCC, St Lawrence Ground, Old Dover Rd, Canterbury CT1 3NZ (☎ 01227 456886, fax 01227 76168)

ILCHESTER, 9 Earl of (GB 1756), Maurice Vivian de Touffreville Fox-Strangways; Lord Ilchester of Ilchester, Somerset, and Baron Strangways of Woodford Strangways, Dorset (GB 1741), and Lord Ilchester and Stavordale, Baron of Redlynch, Somerset (GB 1747); s of 8 Earl of Ilchester (d 1970), and Laure Georgine Emilie, *née* Mazaraki; the 1 Earl was unc of Charles James Fox and brother of 1 Lord Holland; from 1889 Holland House reverted to the Earls of Ilchester before being bombed in WWII; it is now a Youth Hostel; *b* 1 April 1920; *Educ* Kingsbridge Sch, RAF; *m* 29 Nov 1941, Diana Mary Elizabeth (pres WAAF Assoc), da of George Frederick Simpson, of Cassington, Oxford; *Heir* bro, Hon Raymond Fox-Strangways, *qv*; *Career* RAF 1936–76 (ret Gp Capt); vice chm Nottingham Building Society 1985–87 (dir 1982–90); md: Biggin Hill News Ltd, Bromley Borough News Ltd, County Border News Ltd 1983–95 (vice chm 1995–); pres: Soc of Engrs 1974–75, Edenbridge Town Band 1976–, Biggin Hill Branch RAFA 1976–, 285 (Coulsdon) Sqdn ATC 1973–, 2427 (Biggin Hill) Sqdn ATC 1977–, SE Area RAFA 1978–; pres: Inst Nuclear Engrs 1982–84, Grant-Maintained Schs Fndn 1989–, Govrs Cannock Sch 1992–95 (chm 1978–92), Darent River Preservation Soc 1993–, Kent and Downs Region Newspaper Soc 1994–95; vice chm Biggin Hill Airport Consultative Ctee 1976–86 and 1989–95, memb House of Lords Select Ctee on Sci and Technol 1984–89; Freeman City of London, Liveryman Guild of Air Pilots and Air Navigators; CEng, MRAeS, FINucE, Hon FSE, FIMgt, Hon FCP; *Recreations* outdoor activities, passive enjoyment of the arts; *Clubs* RAF; *Style*— The Rt Hon the Earl of Ilchester; ✉ Farley Mill, Westerham, Kent TN16 1UB (☎ 01959 562314); Biggin Hill News Ltd, Winterton House, Westerham, Kent TN16 1AJ (☎ 01959 564766)

ILES, Adrian; s of Arthur Henry Iles, of Loughton, Essex, and Joan, *née* Williams; *b* 19 Sept 1958; *Educ* Buckhurst Hill Co HS Essex, Jesus Coll Cambridge (MA); *m* 16 March 1985, Helen Marie, da of Frederick James Singleton, of Chelmsford, Essex; 2 da (Rosemary b 30 Aug 1989, Nancy b 13 July 1991); *Career* called to the Bar Inner Temple 1980, memb: SE Circuit, London Common Law and Commercial Bar Assoc, Professional Negligence Bar Assoc Panel of Chairmen Disciplinary Ctee Milk Marketing Bd 1990–94; *Recreations* cricket; *Clubs* High Beach Cricket, Henley Royal Regatta; *Style*— Adrian Iles, Esq; ✉ 5 Paper Buildings, Temple, London EC4Y 7HB (☎ 0171 583 9275, fax 0171 583 1926, telex 8956431 ANTON G)

ILES, Ronald Alfred; s of George Iles (d 1966), of London, and Marie Elizabeth, *née* Kohl (d 1955); *b* 16 Dec 1935; *Educ* Raine's Fndn GS London; *m* Patricia Maud, da of John Alfred Hayes; 2 da (Sandra Gail (Mrs Delve) b 12 Sept 1962, Carol Ann (Mrs

Markowski) b 18 Sept 1966); *Career* trainee surveyor British Rail 1952, finance position Metropolitan Water Bd 1952–53, Nat Serv RAF 1954–56; Alexander Howden: joined 1957, dir 1970, dep chm 1979, chm Alexander Howden Reinsurance Brokers Ltd 1981, sr vice pres Alexander & Alexander Services Inc (US parent co) 1985, chm Alexander & Alexander Services (UK) 1992–, memb Mgmnt Exec Ctee Alexander & Alexander Services Inc 1992–; memb Lloyd's, assoc Corpn of Insurance Brokers, FCII; *Style*— Ronald Iles, Esq; ✉ Alexander & Alexander Services (UK) Ltd, 8 Devonshire Square, London EC2M 4PL (☎ 0171 623 5000, fax 0171 972 9872)

ILEY, Geoffrey Norman; s of (Henry) Norman Iley (d 1975), of Stratford-upon-Avon, and Winifred Lalla, *née* Bowman (d 1988); *b* 24 Sept 1928; *Educ* Oakham Sch, Univ of London (BSc), Univ of Birmingham; *Career* asst gen mangr MG Car Co Abingdon 1955–58, prodn mangr Morris Motors Ltd Cowley 1958–61, dep to dir of supplies British Motor Corporation 1961–65, dir prodn, paint, trim, assembly British Motor Corporation 1965–68; md: Triplex Safety Glass Co Birmingham 1968–72, Pilkington ACI Ltd Aust 1972–77; dir Pilkington plc 1977–90, non-exec chm Wellman plc 1990–; Freeman City of London 1984, Liveryman Worshipful Co of Spectacle Makers 1986; FIMgt, CEng, MIMechE, MIEE; *Recreations* golf, walking, motoring, theatre, reading; *Clubs* East India; *Style*— Geoffrey Iley, Esq; ✉ Ivy Bank, Mill Lane, Grimscote, Towcester, Northants NN12 8LJ (☎ 01327 830937)

ILIFFE, 3 Baron (UK 1933); Robert Peter Richard Iliffe; s of Hon William Henry Richard Iliffe (d 1959; yr s of 1 Baron Iliffe, GBE); suc uncle, 2 Baron Iliffe (d 1996); *b* 22 Nov 1944; *Educ* Eton, Ch Ch Oxford; *m* 1966, Rosemary Anne, da of Cdr Arthur Grey Skipwith, RN; 3 s (Hon Edward Richard b 1968, Hon George Langton b 1970, Hon Thomas Arthur b 1973), 1 da (Hon Florence Clare b (twin) 1973); *Heir* s, Hon Edward Richard Iliffe b 1968; *Career* chm Yattendon Investment Trust PLC (parent co of Marina Developments Ltd, Cambridge Newspapers Ltd, The Burton Daily Mail Ltd, Herts and Essex Newspapers Ltd); dir British Air Transport (Holdings) Ltd, Scottish Provincial Press Ltd; High Sheriff of Warks 1983–84, chm Cncl Royal Agric Soc of England; *Style*— The Rt Hon the Lord Iliffe; ✉ Yattendon Park, Yattendon, Berkshire RG18 0UT

ILLINGWORTH, Dr David Gordon; CVO (1987, LVO 1980); s of Sir Cyril Gordon Illingworth (d 1959), and Grace Margaret Illingworth (d 1992); *b* 22 Dec 1921; *Educ* George Watson's Coll, Univ of Edinburgh (MD (with commendation), MB ChB); *m* 1946, Lesley Anderson, da of George Beagrie (d 1937), of Peterhead; 2 s (Lawrence, Stephen), 1 da (Susan); *Career* Surgn Lieut RNVR 1944–46, served in Atlantic and Northern Waters (2 Escort Group); various medical appts Edinburgh Northern Hosps 1947–80, travelling fell Nuffield Fndn 1966, surgn apothecary HM Household Palace of Holyrood House 1970–87, sr lectr Dept of Rehabilitation Studies Univ of Edinburgh 1975–80; life govr Imperial Cancer Research Fund 1975; FRCP; *Publications* papers in learned jls on cancer diagnosis and preventive medicine; *Recreations* golf, gardening; *Clubs* Univ of Edinburgh Staff, Bruntsfield Links Golfing Society; *Style*— Dr David Illingworth, CVO; ✉ 19 Napier Rd, Edinburgh EH10 5AZ (☎ 0131 229 8102)

ILLINGWORTH, Richard Keith; s of Keith Illingworth, of Bradford, W Yorkshire, and Margaret, *née* Hill; *b* 23 Aug 1963; *Educ* Salts GS Saltaire Bradford; *m* Anne Louise, da of George Bentley; 2 s (Miles Jonathan b 28 Aug 1987, Thomas Lynden b 20 April 1989); *Career* professional cricketer Worcestershire CCC 1982– (awarded county cap 1986, Benefit Year 1997); close seasons: Whitbread Scholarship with Colts CC Brisbane 1982–83, Wisden Cricket XI to Barbados 1983, St Heliers Univ Auckland 1986–87 and 1987–88, Zingari CC Pietermaritzburg and Natal 1988–89; England: memb A tour Zimbabwe 1990 and Pakistan/Sri Lanka 1991, full debut v W Indies Trent Bridge 1991, played 9 test matches and 25 one day ints, memb tour NZ 1992, memb World Cup squad Aust 1992, and Pakistan, India and Sri Lanka 1996, memb MCC tour to W Africa incl Ghana, Gambia, Sierra Leone and Nigeria 1994, 4 test matches v W Indies 1995, selected for tour to S Africa 1995–96; took a wicket with first ball bowled in test cricket (only eleventh person to do so); civil servant 1981, buyer Golding Pipework Services close season 1989–90; *Recreations* playing golf and soccer, watching Leeds Utd FC; *Style*— Richard Illingworth, Esq; ✉ Worcestershire CCC, New Rd, Worcester WR2 4QQ

ILLIS, Dr Léon Sebastian (Lee); s of Sacha Illis (d 1933), of London, and Rebecca Magyar (d 1976); *b* 4 March 1930; *Educ* UCH London (BSc, MB BS, MD, FRCP); *m* 14 Oct 1967, Oonagh Mary, da of Lt-Col Derek Lewton-Brain, of Sevenoaks, Kent; 3 s (Max b 13 Jan 1970, Ben b 11 Apr 1973, Sebastian b 30 Dec 1974); *Career* RAC and RA 1948–50; RMO Nat Hosp Queen Square London 1963–67 (registrar, sr registrar), conslt neurologist Wessex Neurological Centre Southampton 1967–95, clinical sr lectr in neurology Univ of Southampton Med Sch 1967–95; visiting prof: Univ of Sri Lanka 1972 and 1977, Univ of Wisconsin Madison 1984; tstee Int Spinal Res Tst, chm Scientific Ctee Int Spinal Res Tst; pres: Int Neuromodulation Soc, S of Eng Neuroscience Assoc; asst ed Spinal Cord; *Books* Rehabilitation of the Neurological Patient (ed, 1982), Herpes Simplex Encephalitis (1973), Viral Diseases of the Central Nervous System (1976), Spinal Cord Dysfunction (I 1988, II 1991, III 1992), Disorders of the Spinal Cord in Current Opinion (ed, 1988–89), Neurological Rehabilitation (1994); numerous papers in scientific journals; *Recreations* skiing, sailing, walking; *Clubs* Athenaeum, RSM, Royal Lymington Yacht; *Style*— Dr Lee Illis; ✉ Pond House, Sowley, Lymington, Hampshire SO41 5SQ (☎ 01590 626351); Wessex Nuffield Hospital, Chandlers Ford, Southampton, Hampshire (☎ 01703 737929)

ILLMAN, (Charles) John; s of Henry Alfred Charles Illman, of Kirkby Fleetham, Northallerton, Yorks, and Margaret Moorhouse (d 1975); *b* 22 Sept 1944; *Educ* King's Sch Ely; *m* 1975, Elizabeth Mary, da of Ronald Stamp; 2 s (James David Charles b 21 Dec 1979, Christopher George John b 12 June 1982); *Career* student actor Nottingham Playhouse 1963, asst stage mangr Southwold Repertory Company 1963; trainee reporter Hertfordshire Express 1964, reporter The Journal Newcastle upon Tyne 1968, features ed General Practitioner 1971; ed: New Psychiatry 1974, General Practitioner 1975; freelance journalist 1976–83, med corr Daily Mail 1983–88, health ed The Guardian 1989–96, med corr The Observer 1996–; chm Medical Journalists Assoc 1996–; Family Planning Assoc Award for reporting on women's health 1993, first prize Norwich Union Healthcare/Med Journalists' Assoc Awards 1994; memb RSM 1987; *Books* Body Machine (jtly, 1981); *Recreations* family, cricket, running, reading, scuba diving; *Style*— John Illman, Esq; ✉ The Observer, 119 Farringdon Road, London EC1R 3ER (☎ 0171 278 2332)

ILLMAN, HE John; s of Reginald Thomas Illman (d 1973), and Hilda Kathleen, *née* Targett (d 1986); *b* 26 Oct 1940; *Educ* Reading Sch, Univ of St Andrews; *m* 1962, Elizabeth Hunter, da of William Robert Owen Frame (d 1994), and Margaret Hunter Frame; 2 da (Sarah Jane Hunter b 25 Nov 1964, Claire Louise Elizabeth b 2 Feb 1967), 1 s (Jonathan Robin b 31 March 1972); *Career* HM Dip Serv; FO 1961, third sec (Chancery) Leopoldville later Kinshasa 1963–66, second sec (commercial) Dublin 1967–71, second sec (economic) Paris 1971–73, first sec FCO 1973–75, first sec and head of Chancery Buenos Aires 1975–79, first sec (commercial) Lagos 1979–82, first sec FCO 1982–86, cnsllr, dep head of mission and consul-gen Algiers 1986–90, consul-gen Marseille 1990–95, ambass Peru 1995–; *Recreations* squash, cricket, rugby, tennis, amateur dramatics, photography; *Clubs* Royal Commonwealth Soc; *Style*— HE Mr John Illman; ✉ c/o Foreign and Commonwealth Office (Lima), King Charles Street, London SW1A 2AH

ILLSLEY, Eric; MP (Lab) Barnsley Central (majority 19,361); s of John Illsley, of S Yorks, and Maud, *née* Bassett; *b* 9 April 1955; *Educ* Barnsley Holgate GS, Univ of Leeds (LLB); *m* 1978, Dawn, da of Robert Charles Webb, of Barnsley; 2 da (Alexandra b 1980, Rebecca b 1982); *Career* chief offr Yorks Area NUM 1985–87; MP (Lab) Barnsley Central 1987–; memb Select Ctee: on Energy 1988–91, on Televising Proceedings of the House of Commons 1988–91, on Procedure 1991–; Lab Pty whip 1991–94, oppn spokesperson on health 1994–95, shadow min for local govt 1995, oppn spokesperson on NI 1995–; dep chm Parly and Scientific Ctee, jt chm All Party Parly Glass Gp, treas Yorks Gp of Labour MPs; *Style*— Eric Illsley, Esq, MP; ✉ House of Commons, Westminster, London SW1A 0AA (☎ 0171 219 3501, fax 0171 219 4863); 18B Regent St, Barnsley S75 1DY (☎ 01226 730692, fax 01226 779429)

ILOTT, Mark Christopher; s of John Ilott, of Watford, and Glenys Barbara, *née* Shardlow; *b* 27 Aug 1970; *Educ* Francis Combe Sch Garston; *m* 14 Oct 1994, Sandra Bishop; *Career* professional cricketer; former minor cos player Hertfordshire; Essex CCC: debut 1988, over 300 first class wickets, Co Championship winners 1992, Natwest Trophy runner-up 1996; England: former under 19 schs rep, memb England A tour Sri Lanka 1990–91 (2 unofficial test caps), full memb England A tour Australia 1992–93, debut sr team Ashes series 1993 (3 test caps), memb England A tour to SA 1993–94, to India 1994–95, memb full England Tour to S Africa 1995–96 (2 test caps); *Recreations* listening to music, keeping fit, playing guitar, reading, playing golf and snooker; *Style*— Mark Ilott, Esq; ✉ c/o Essex CCC, County Cricket Ground, New Writtle Street, Chelmsford, Essex CM2 0PG (☎ 01245 252420)

IMAI, Nobuko; *b* 18 March 1943; *Educ* Toho Sch of Music Tokyo, Juilliard Sch of Music NY, Yale Univ; *m* 1981, Aart von Bochove; 1 s (Ayumu Mori), 1 da (Kiyoko); *Career* viola player; memb Vermeer Quartet 1974–79, solo artist 1980–; performed with numerous major orchs incl: LSO, RPO, LPO, Chicago Symphony, Royal Concertgebouw, Vienna Symphony, Boston Symphony, Orchestre de Paris; prof of viola High Sch of Music Detmold; winner first prize Geneva and Munich Int Music Competitions; *Recordings* incl: Berlioz' Harold in Italy (with LSO under Sir Colin Davis, Philips), Takemitsu's A String Around Autumn (with Saito Kinen Orch under Seiji Ozawa, Philips), Walton Viola Concerto (with LPO under Jan Latham-Koenig, Chandos), Schnittke and Peterson Viola Concerti (with Malmo Symphony Orch under Lev Markiz, BIS), various recital discs; *Recreations* golf, cookery; *Style*— Nobuko Imai; ✉ c/o Terry Harrison Artists' Management, The Orchard, Market Street, Charlbury, Oxon OX7 3PJ (☎ 01608 810330, fax 01608 811331)

IMBERT, Sir Peter Michael; QPM (1980), DL (Greater London 1994); s of William Henry Imbert, and Frances May, *née* Hodge (d 1985); *b* 27 April 1933; *Educ* Harvey GS Folkestone Kent; *m* 1956, Iris Rosina, da of Christopher Thomas Charles Dove (d 1984), of London; 1 s (Simon), 2 da (Elaine, Sally); *Career* asst then dep Chief Constable Surrey Constabulary 1976–79, Chief Constable Thames Valley Police 1979–85; Met Police: joined 1953, Detective Chief Supt until 1976, dep Cmmr 1985–87, Cmmr 1987–93; *Recreations* golf, bridge; *Style*— Sir Peter Imbert, QPM, DL; ✉ c/o New Scotland Yard, London SW1H 0BG (☎ 0171 230 2345)

IMBERT-TERRY, Sir Michael Edward Stanley; 5 Bt (UK 1917); s of Maj Sir Edward Henry Bouhier Imbert-Terry, MC, 3 Bt (d 1978), and Lady Sackville, *née* Garton, of Knole, Kent; suc bro, Sir Andrew Imbert-Terry, 4 Bt (d 1985); *b* 18 April 1950; *Educ* Cranleigh; *m* 1975, Frances Dorothy, 3 da of Peter Scott (d 1978), of Ealing; 2 s (Brychan Edward b 1975, Jack b 1985), 2 da (Song b 1973, Bryony Jean b 1980); *Heir* s, Brychan Edward; *Style*— Sir Michael Imbert-Terry, Bt; ✉ Little Hennowe, St Ewe, St Austell, Cornwall (☎ 01726 843893)

IMESON, Michael David; s of Terence Imeson, of Bradford, W Yorks, and Marian, *née* Glasby; *b* 26 Oct 1955; *Educ* Hanson GS Bradford, Univ of Bradford (BSc), LSE (MPhil); *m* 14 May 1988, Joanne Edwina, da of John Edward Simpson; 1 da (Sophia Rose b 8 June 1992); *Career* ed Export Times 1983–84 (reporter 1980–83); reporter: The Times Diary 1986, London Daily News 1987; ed Maxwell Consumer Publishing and Communications 1987–92, dir Financial and Business Publications 1992–, ed Chartered Banker magazine (Chartered Inst of Bankers magazine) 1995–; *Books* Finance for Growth (ed, 1989); *Recreations* running, cycling, photography, travel; *Style*— Michael Imeson, Esq; ✉ 15 Portsea Place, London W2 2BL (☎ 0171 262 3253); Financial and Business Publications Ltd, 4 Cavendish Square, London W1M 9HA (☎ 0171 637 1115, fax 0171 637 1117)

IMISON, Tamsyn; da of Dr Joseph Trenaman (d 1961), and Margaret, *née* Shaw (d 1979); *b* 1 May 1937; *Educ* Hitchin Girls' GS, Milham Ford Sch Oxford, Somerville Coll Oxford, Queen Mary Coll London (BSc); *m* 1958, Michael Imison; 2 da (Candace b 1959, Katherine b 1965), 1 s (Thomas b 1966 d 1984); *Career* scientific, exhbn and illustration work Oxford Museum and British Museum of Natural History; teacher: Brentford Sch for Girls 1972–76, Pimlico Sch 1976–79, Abbey Wood Sch 1979–84; headteacher Hampstead Sch 1984–; memb: Secdy Educn Cncl 1986–88 (chaired A level and GCSE Biology and Music Ctees), Cncl and Exec Secdy Heads Assoc 1993–; chair IT and EO Ctees SHA; tstee 300 Gp Educnl Trust (now Menerva Educnl Trust); memb Cncl: Univ Coll Sch, Inst of Educn Univ of London 1993–, Univ of London 1995–, CRAC 1996–; educnl conslt Women's Playhouse Trust, dir Int Literary Agency for Playwrights; memb: British Educnl Mgmnt & Admin Soc, The Assoc for Science Educn; scientific fell Royal Zoological Soc, FRSA; *Recreations* fun, theatre, painting, gardening, walking, swimming, sailing; *Style*— Mrs Tamsyn Imison; ✉ 28 Almeida Street, London N1 1TD (☎ 0171 359 6273, fax 0171 359 6273); Hampstead School, Westbere Road, London NW2 3RT (☎ 0171 794 8133, fax 0171 435 8260)

IMPALLOMENI, Dr Mario Giuseppe; s of Prof Col Rosario Impallomeni (d 1983), and Ada, *née* Ascarelli (d 1994); *b* 19 July 1937; *Educ* Scuole Pie Fiorentine Florence Italy, Faculty of Med Univ of Florence Italy (MD); *m* 10 March 1973, Madeleine Clare, da of Hugh Edward Blackburn (d 1964); 1 s (Tommaso Fergus b 11 Oct 1979), 1 da (Laura Chiara b 18 July 1982); *Career* jr lectr Dept of Clinical Med Univ of Florence Italy 1961–66, registrar Queen's Hosp Croydon 1966–69, conslt physician Italian Hospital London 1969–90, sr registrar Central Middlesex Hosp & St Thomas' Hosp 1969–71, conslt geriatrician N Middlesex Hosp & St Anne's Hosp 1972–78, conslt gen and geriatric med and sr lectr Hammersmith Hosp 1978–, hon physician Saracens RUFC 1992–; contrib to several books on geriatric med, memb editorial bd of several med jls; chm NW branch Br Geriatrics Soc 1985–89; MRCP 1969, FRCP 1985; *Recreations* history, chess, cycling, fell walking, classic music; *Style*— Dr Mario Impallomeni; ✉ Head Geriatric Services Unit, Geriatric Division, Department of Medicine, Royal Postgraduate Medical School, Hammersmith Hospital, Du Cane Road, London W12 0HS (☎ 0181 740 3056, fax 0181 743 0798)

IMRAY, Sir Colin Henry; KBE (1992), CMG (1983); s of Henry Gibbon Imray (d 1936), and Frances Olive, *née* Badman (d 1992); *b* 21 Sept 1933; *Educ* Highgate and Hotchkiss USA, Balliol Coll Oxford; *m* 1957, Shirley Margaret, da of Ernest Matthews (d 1972); 1 s (Christopher), 3 da (Frances, Elizabeth, Alison); *Career* Nat Serv 2 Lt Seaforth Highlanders (Royal W African Force) 1952–54; CRO 1957, third (later second) sec UK High Cmmn Canberra 1958–61, first sec Nairobi 1963–66, Br Trade Cmmn Montreal 1970–73, cnsllr, head of chancery and consul gen Islamabad 1973–77, RCDS 1977, commercial cnsllr Tel Aviv 1977–80, dep high cmmr Bombay 1980–84, dep chief clerk and chief inspr FCO 1984–85, Br high cmmr to the Utd Republic of Tanzania 1986–89, Br high cmmr to the People's Republic of Bangladesh 1989–93; Freeman City of London 1994; sec gen The Order of St John 1993–; KStJ 1993; *Clubs* Travellers', Commonwealth

Trust; *Style—* Sir Colin Imray, KBE, CMG; ✉ c/o Chancery, Order of St John, St John's Gate, Clerkenwell, London EC1M 4DA (☎ 0171 253 6644, fax 0171 235 0796)

IMRIE, Prof Derek Charles; s of Charles Imrie (d 1970), of Montrose, Angus, and Margaret Ellen, *née* Patching (d 1955); *b* 22 Jan 1939; *Educ* RGS Guildford, Bishophalt Sch Hillingdon, UCL (BSc, PhD); *m* 24 Aug 1963, Sandra Veronica, da of Albert Best, BEM (d 1977), of Ruislip; 2 da (Alison b 1968, Claire b 1970); *Career* res fell Harvard Univ 1966–68, lectr UCL 1968–81, reader in physics Univ of London 1981–84 (ICI res fell 1963–66), Brunel Univ: prof of physics 1984–, head of physics 1985–, dean of sci 1988–91 and 1993–96, pro-vice-chllr 1996–; Royal Soc Leverhulme Tst sr res fell 1991–92; FInstP 1973, CPhys, FRSA 1989; *Recreations* travel, DIY; *Style—* Prof Derek Imrie; ✉ Brunel University, Department of Physics, Uxbridge, Middx UB8 3PH (☎ 01895 203204, fax 01895 272391, telex 261173 G)

IMRIE, Frazer Keith Elliott; s of William Alexander Richie Imrie (d 1941), and Lily Patience, *née* Taylor (d 1988); *b* 4 Dec 1932; *m* 17 Aug 1957, Janice Margaret, da of Albert Edward Molloy (d 1975); 1 s (Andrew Keith Elliott b 1961), 3 da (Judith Meryl b 1964, Elizabeth Anne b 1964, Sarah Jane b 1964); *Career* private conslt microbiologist and food technologist 1956–59 (public analyst for Watford and St Albans), dir of res Manbre & Garton UK Ltd 1959–68, head Fermentation Dept Philip Lyle Memorial Res Laboratory Univ of Reading 1968–71, fell Leverhulme Indust Res Univ of Aston-in-Birmingham 1971–73, gp devpt mangr and div md of New Ventures Tate & Lyle plc 1973–82; Sempernova plc 1982–91 (fndr, exec chm, chief exec), fndr and md PPRD Ltd 1982–, dir CWA Consultants Ltd, CWA (ESR) Ltd 1992–; author of 30 scientific papers, contrib to scientific text books, sometime broadcaster on biological topics; former chm Microbiology Panel Food Res Assoc, advsr on Codex Alimentarius Miny of Agric; former memb UK Govt Advsy Ctee on Energy; memb Tech Ctee Int Sugar Res Fndn, assoc referee Int Cmmn for Unification of Methods of Sugar Analysis, past chm OECD Ctee on Energy Resources, memb CENTO Travelling Working Gp on Res and Devpt in Developing Countries, conslt OECD on Molasses Utilisation in Greek Sugar Indust; co organiser and princ lectr on industl fermentation, UNESCO, UNEP, ICRO Regional Trg Course 1976, memb Br Govt Tech Mission to USSR 1974, former tech conslt Nat Fedn of Fruit and Potato Trades; guest lectr: Conference on Post-Harvest Physiology of Pineapples Institut de Recherches sur Les Fruits et Agrumes Montpellier France 1986, Guangdong Acad of Agric Sci Guangzhou China 1986, South China Agric Univ 1985, Miny of Agric Trg Course on Post-Harvest Technol Beijing China 1989 and 1990; FRSA, FInstD; *Recreations* travel, reading, gardening; *Style—* Frazer Imrie, Esq; ✉ PPRD Ltd, 44 Alexandra Road, Reading, Berks RG1 5PF (☎ 0118 926 1454, fax 0118 935 3450)

INCE, Paul; *b* 21 Oct 1967; *Career* professional footballer (midfielder); with West Ham Utd 1982–89, transferred to Manchester Utd (for £1.9m) 1989, transferred to Inter Milan 1995–; honours with Manchester Utd: FA Cup 1990, League Cup 1992, European Cup Winners' Cup 1991, winners inaugural FA Premier League Championship 1992/93, winners League and FA Cup double 1994, Charity Shield 1994; England: former Youth, under-21 and B team memb, 26 full caps and 2 goals (as at Jan 1997) (2 as capt), memb squad Euro 96; *Style—* Paul Ince, Esq; ✉ Internazionale FC, 20122 Milano, Piazza Duse 1, Milan, Italy

INCH, Dr Thomas David; s of Thomas Alexander Inch (d 1990), and Sarah Lang Graves, *née* Brown (d 1991); *b* 25 Sept 1938; *Educ* St Austell GS, Univ of Birmingham (BSc, PhD, DSc); *m* 1964, Jacqueline Vivienne, *née* Pudner; 1 da (Vivienne Nicola b 1967); *Career* Salters res fell Univ of Birmingham 1963–64, post doctoral fell NIH 1964–65; Chemical Defence Estab Porton Down: joined as sr scientific offr 1965, princ scientific offr 1969–73, sr princ scientific offr 1973–80, dep chief scientific offr 1980–85; RCDS 1985–86, gen mangr Res Business Devpt BP Research 1986–90, vice-pres R & D BP in USA 1990–93, sec gen RSC 1993–; author of over 100 pubns on chemistry in various jls; CChem, FRSC 1976; *Recreations* golf; *Clubs* Athenaeum, High Post Golf; *Style—* Dr Thomas Inch; ✉ Royal Society of Chemistry, Burlington House, Piccadilly, London W1V 0BN (☎ 0171 437 8658, fax 0171 437 8883)

INCHBALD, Denis John Elliot; s of Rev Christopher Chantrey Elliot Inchbald, CF (d 1976), and Olivia Jane, *née* Mills (d 1975); *b* 9 May 1923; *Educ* Oswestry Sch, Jesus Coll Cambridge; *m* 1955, Jacqueline Hazel, *née* Jones; *Career* Lt RNVR; Daily Telegraph 1950–52, head of publicity Br Industs Fair 1954–56, dir PR Foote Cone & Belding Ltd 1959–68 (memb Bd 1977–79), chm and md Welbeck PR Ltd 1968–84, chm Welbeck PR 1985–88; independent PR conslt 1988–94; pres Inst of PR 1969–70, govr CAM 1970–72, chm PRCA 1975–78, memb Cncl Int PR Assoc 1988–92, memb Cncl of Mgmnt PDSA 1991–; Stephen Tallents medal for exceptional achievement in PR practice 1988; FIPR 1967, FIPA 1974, MCAM 1979, Hon FIPR 1988; *Recreations* reading, gardening, photography, travel; *Clubs* Reform, Naval, MCC; *Style—* Denis Inchbald, Esq; ✉ 10 Shardeloes, Amersham, Bucks HP7 0RL (☎ 01494 726781)

INCHBALD, Michael John Chantrey; s of Geoffrey Herbert Elliot Inchbald (sr ptnr City law firm Bischoff & Co, d 1982), and Rosemary Evelyn (d 1958), da of Arthur Ilbert, and niece of Sir Courtenay Peregrine Ilbert (President of the Viceroy's Cncl and actg Viceroy of India, Clerk of the House of Commons for 18 years, he declined a peerage); *b* 8 March 1920; *Educ* Sherborne, Architectural Assoc Sch of Architecture; *m* 1, 31 Jan 1955 (m dis 1964), Jacqueline Bromley; 1 s (Courtenay Charles Ilbert b Dec 1958), 1 da (Charlotte Amanda b Feb 1960); m 2, June 1964 (m dis 1970), Eunice Haymes; *Career* architectural and interior designer; dir Michael Inchbald Ltd 1953–83, design conslt 1983–; co fndr Inchbald Sch of Design 1960; design projects for clients incl: Bank of America, Cncl of Industl Design, Crown Estate Cmmrs, Cunard, Dunhill worldwide, Ferragamo, Forte (Post House, London Airport and several restaurants), Imperial Group, Justerini & Brooks, Law Soc, John Lewis, Manufacturers Hanover Bank, Manufacturers Hanover Trust Bank, John Player, Plessey Co, Pratt Bernard Engineering, Savoy Group (Berkeley, Claridges and Savoy Hotels, Stones Chop House complex), Scottish Highland Industries, Wolsey; other projects incl: ships (QE2, Carmania, Franconia, Windsor Castle), royal and private yachts and houses, projects for The Duc de la Rochefoucauld, 13 Duke of St Albans, 8 Marquess of Ailesbury, 6 Marquess of Bristol, 17 Earl of Perth, 9 Earl of Dartmouth, 2 Earl St Aldwyn, Lords Gisborough, Kilmarnock, Latymer and St Levan; conslt to furniture and carpet manufacturers, consulted re changes at Buckingham Palace; work exhibited at: Triennale Milan, V&A Museum, design centres in London, NY and Helsinki; winner of four out of four design competitions entered incl: Shapes of Things to Come 1946, National Chair Design Competition 1955; contrib: Architectural Review, Architectural Digest, Connaissance des Arts, Connoisseur, Country Life, Harpers/Queen, House & Garden, International Lighting Review, Tatler, Vogue, etc; Freeman Worshipful Co of Clockmakers 1984; FCSD; *Recreations* arts, travel, antiques, reading, music, walking; *Style—* Michael Inchbald, Esq; ✉ Stanley House, 10 Milner St, London SW3 2PU (☎ 0171 584 8832)

INCHBALD, Stephen Charles Elliot; s of Ralph Mordaunt Elliot Inchbald (d 1991), and Gertrude Elizabeth, *née* Ferres; *b* 16 Dec 1940; *Educ* Downside; *m* 16 Dec 1968, Elizabeth Mary, da of Bryan Frank Pocock (d 1979); 2 s (Charles b 1972, Alexander b 1974), 1 da (Louise b 1978); *Career* chartered surveyor; md TSB Property Services Ltd 1988–94; chm Wickham Rye & Co Ltd, devpt land conslt (t/a Elliot Consultancy); FInstD, FRICS; *Recreations* shooting, gardening, travel; *Clubs* IOD, Beaconsfield Golf; *Style—* Stephen Inchbald, Esq; ✉ Elliot Consultancy, West Riding, Bottom Lane, Seer Green, Beaconsfield, Bucks HP9 2RH (☎ and fax 01494 677477)

INCHCAPE, 4 Earl of (UK 1929); (Kenneth) Peter Lyle Mackay; also Baron Inchcape (UK 1911), Viscount Inchcape (UK 1924), and Viscount Glenapp (UK 1929); s of 3 Earl of Inchcape (d 1994), and his 1 w, Aline Thorn, *née* Pease; *b* 23 Jan 1943; *Educ* Eton; *m* 7 June 1966, Georgina, da of Sydney Cresswell Nisbet; 1 s (Viscount Glenapp), 2 da (Lady Elspeth Pease b 1972, Lady Ailsa Fiona b 1977); *Heir* s, Fergus James Kenneth Mackay, Viscount Glenapp b 9 July 1979; *Career* Lt 9/12 Royal Lancers served: Aden, Arabian Gulf, BAOR; formerly with Inchcape plc (20 years); dir: Duncan MacNeill Holdings Ltd, The Assam Company Ltd, Inchcape Family Investments Ltd, Glenapp Estate Co Ltd; asst to Ct Worshipful Co of Grocers (Master 1993–94), Warden Worshipful Co of Shipwrights, Liveryman Worshipful Co of Fishmongers; AIB; *Recreations* shooting, fishing, golf, skiing, travel, farming; *Clubs* White's, Oriental, Pratt's, New, Royal Sydney Golf; *Style—* The Rt Hon the Earl of Inchcape; ✉ Manor Farm, Clyffe Pypard, nr Swindon, Wilts; 63E Pont St, London SW1; office: Duncan MacNeill Group, 32 St James's Street, London SW1A 1HT

INCHIQUIN, 18 Baron (I 1543); Sir Conor Myles John O'Brien; 10 Bt (I 1686); The O'Brien, Chief of the name and the O'Brien Clan (one of the 20 recognised Irish bloodline Chiefs and Chieftains); s of Hon (Fionn) Myles Maryons O'Brien (yst s of 15 Baron Inchiquin); suc unc, 17 Baron Inchiquin, 1982; Lord Inchiquin is 13 in descent from the 3 s of 1 Baron Inchiquin, the latter being cr Earl of Thomond for life; the descendants of the eldest s of the 1 Baron held the Marquessate of Thomond 1800–55; The O'Briens descend from Brian Boroimhe, Prince of Thomond and High King of Ireland in 1002, who was k at the moment of victory against the Danes in the Battle of Clontarf 1014; *b* 17 July 1943; *Educ* Eton; *m* 1988, Helen O'Farrell, da of Gerald Fitzgerald Farrell, of Newtown Forbes, Co Longford; 2 da (Hon Slaney Alexandra Anne b 7 July 1989, Hon Lucia Josephine Mary b 27 May 1991); *Heir* father's 1 cous, Maj Murrough O'Brien; *Career* late Capt 14/20 King's Hussars; *Clubs* Kildare Street and University (Dublin); *Style—* The Rt Hon the Lord Inchiquin; ✉ Thomond House, Dromoland, Newmarket-on-Fergus, Co Clare, Republic of Ireland (☎ 061 368304)

INCHYRA, 2 Baron (UK 1962), of St Madoes, Co Perth; Robert Charles Reneke Hoyer Millar; er s of 1 Baron Inchyra, GCMG, CVO (d 1989), and (Anna Judith) Elizabeth, da of Jonkheer Reneke de Marees van Swinderen, sometime Netherlands Min in London; *b* 4 April 1935; *Educ* Eton, New Coll Oxford; *m* 1 Aug 1961, Fiona Mary, yr da of Edmund Charles Reginald Sheffield (d 1977), of Normanby Park, Scunthorpe, Lincs; 1 s (Hon (Christian) James Charles Hoyer), 2 da (Hon Henrietta Julia Hoyer (Hon Mrs Villanueva Brandt) b 21 Sept 1964, Hon Louisa Mary Hoyer b 26 April 1968); *Heir* s, Hon (Christian) James Charles Hoyer Millar b 12 Aug 1962; *Career* late Scots Gds; banker; local dir Barclays Bank Newcastle upon Tyne 1967–75, regnl gen mangr Barclays Bank 1976–81, dep chm Barclays Bank Tst Co Ltd 1982–85, gen mangr Barclays Bank plc 1985–87, dir UK Fin Services 1987–88, dir gen British Bankers Assoc 1988–94; dir Witan Investment Co plc 1979–, chm Johnson Fry European Utilities Tst plc 1994–; memb Queen's Body Guard for Scotland (Royal Co of Archers); *Clubs* White's, Pratt's; *Style—* The Rt Hon the Lord Inchyra; ✉ Rookley Manor, King's Somborne, Stockbridge, Hants SO20 6QX (☎ 01794 388319)

IND, Dr Philip Waterloo; s of John Waterloo Ind, of San Juan, Spain, and Marjorie, *née* Hesketh; *b* 17 Feb 1950; *Educ* Haberdashers' Aske's, Gonville and Caius Coll Cambridge (BA, MA), UCH (MB BChir, MRCP); *m* 30 June 1973, Dr Sally Ind, da of Dr Charles Hutcheon Thomson (d 1962), of Low Fell, Co Durham; 1 s (Robert b 3 Oct 1977), 2 da (Sarah b 25 April 1980, Kathryn b 28 Oct 1982); *Career* med registrar Edgware Gen Hosp 1975, hon sr registrar Hammersmith Hosp 1981 (registrar 1977), hon sr lectr and conslt physician Hammersmith and Ealing Hosp 1985–; multiple academic papers and book chapters; FRCP 1991; *Recreations* reading, windsurfing, bridge, squash, tennis; *Style—* Dr Philip Ind; ✉ Respiratory Medicine, Clinical Investigation Unit, Royal Postgraduate Medical School, Hammersmith Hospital, Du Cane Rd, London W12 0HS (☎ 0181 740 3077)

INESON, Dr Nigel Richard; s of Jeffrey Ineson, of Milton Keynes, and late Eileen, *née* Wood; *Educ* Watford GS, Guy's Hosp Med Sch London (MB BS, FRCGP, DRCOG, DFFP); *children* 2 s (James Richard Mannakee b 8 Dec 1984, Andrew Nicholas Mannakee b 23 July 1986); *Career* various house jobs Hillingdon Hosp (med) and Wycombe Gen Hosp (surgical), subsequently on staff A&E Dept Hillingdon Hosp then SHO (gen surgical and orthopaedics rotation) Medway Hosp Gp Kent, SHO posts in med/geriatrics, psychiatry, paediatrics & obstetrics and gynaecology then gen practice trainee (vocational trg scheme) Watford 1981–84, ptnr in teaching practice Watford 1984–; princ Herts FHSA, company med offr DDD Ltd (mfr of ethical pharmaceuticals); memb Acad of Experts; *Style—* Dr Nigel Ineson; ✉ Wentworth, 30 Green Lane, Oxhey, Herts WD1 4NH (☎ 01923 233992); The Callowland Surgery, 141a Leavesden Road, Watford, Herts WD2 5EP (fax 01923 443143, mobile 0831 686531)

INFIELD, Paul Louis; s of Gordon Mark Infield, and Roda Molca, *née* Lincoln; *b* 1 July 1957; *Educ* Haberdashers' Aske's, The Peddie Sch Hightstown New Jersey USA, Univ of Sheffield (LLB); *m* 6 Feb 1987, Catharine Grace, da of Ancrum Francis Evans, of Clifton on Teme, Worcs, 1 s (Samuel b 1988), 1 da (Margery b 1991); *Career* called to the Bar Inner Temple 1980; chm Bd of Visitors HM Prison Wandsworth 1996–, memb Exec Ctee Assoc of Membs of Bds of Visitors; Freeman City of London 1979, Liveryman Worshipful Co of Plaisterers 1979; *Recreations* family, running; *Style—* Paul Infield, Esq; ✉ 34 Hillier Rd, London SW11 6AU; 5 Paper Buildings, Temple, London EC4Y 7HB (☎ 0171 583 9275/4555, 0171 353 8494, fax 0171 583 1926/2031, e-mail P_Infield@Link.org)

ING, David Newson; MBE (1986); s of Gilbert Newson Ing (d 1975), of Hull, E Yorks, and Edith Mary, *née* Adamson (d 1982); *b* 30 May 1934; *Educ* Pocklington Sch York; *m* 15 Sept 1962, Penelope Ann, da of Basil Charles William Hart, of Cranleigh, Surrey; 2 s (Richard b 1965, William b 1967); *Career* Nat Serv cmmnd RAF 1957–59 (Sword of Honour); admitted slr 1957; Downs Solicitors Dorking: joined 1961, ptnr 1963–95, sr ptnr 1985–94, conslt 1996–; lay chm Dorking Deanery Synod 1970–73; chm: Mgmnt Ctee Dorking and Dist CAB 1966–85, Surrey Building Society 1981–93 (dir 1969–93); hon slr: Fire Servs Nat Benevolent Fund 1975–, The Lutyens Tst 1984–; Master Worshipful Co of Woolmen 1988–89 (Liveryman 1967–); memb Law Soc; *Recreations* reading, walking, gardening, cricket, theatre, opera; *Clubs* Law Soc, MCC; *Style—* David N Ing, Esq, MBE; ✉ Ravenspur, Sutton Place, Abinger Hammer, Dorking, Surrey RH5 6RN (☎ and fax 01306 730260)

INGAMELLS, John Anderson Stuart; s of George Harry Ingamells (d 1988), and Gladys Lucy, *née* Rollett (d 1979); *b* 12 Nov 1934; *Educ* Hastings and Eastbourne GS, Univ of Cambridge (BA); *m* 30 May 1964, Hazel, da of George William Wilson (d 1985); 2 da (Ann b 1965, Clare b 1969); *Career* 2 Lt RASC 1956–58, served Cyprus; art asst York City Art Gallery 1959–63, asst keeper Nat Museum of Wales Cardiff 1963–67, curator York City Art Gallery 1967–77, dir Wallace Collection 1978–92 (asst to Dir 1977–78), memb Exec Ctee Nat Art Collections Fund 1992–; tstee Dulwich Picture Gallery 1988–92; *Books* Dictionary of British and Irish Visitors to Italy in the 18th Century (ed, 1997); *Catalogues of Pictures Produced incl* The Davies Collection of French Art 1967, The English Episcopal Portrait 1981, The Wallace Collection (Vol 1 1985, Vol II 1986, Vol III 1989, Vol IV 1992); author of articles in: The Burlington Magazine, Apollo, The Walpole Soc, Journal of Aesthetics, La Revue du Louvre, etc; *Style—* John Ingamells, Esq; ✉ c/o Paul Mellon Centre for Studies in British Art, 16 Bedford Square, London WC1B 3JA (☎ 0171 580 0311)

INGE, Field Marshal Sir Peter Anthony; GCB (1992, KCB 1988), DL (N Yorkshire 1994); s of Raymond Inge (d 1995), and Grace Maud Caroline, *née* Du Rose (d 1962); *b* 5 Aug 1935; *Educ* Wrekin Coll, RMA Sandhurst; *m* 26 Nov 1960, Letitia Marion, da of Trevor Thornton Berry (d 1967); 2 da (Antonia b 17 May 1962, Verity b 12 Oct 1965); *Career* cmmnd Green Howards 1954; served: HK, Malaya, Germany, Libya and N Ireland, ADC to GOC 4 Div 1960–61, Adj 1 Green Howards 1963–64, student Staff Coll 1966, MOD 1967–69, Co Comd 1 Green Howards 1969–70, student JSSC 1971, BM 11 Armd Bde 1972, instr Staff Coll 1973–74, CO 1 Green Howards 1974–77, Comdt Jr Div Staff Coll 1977–79, Comd 4 Armd Bde 1979–81, Chief of Staff HQ 1 (BR) Corps 1982–83, GOC NE Dist and Comd 2 Inf Div 1984–86, DGLP (A) MOD 1986–87, Comd 1 (BR) Corps 1987–89, C-in-C BAOR and Comd NORTHAG 1989–91, Col Comdt RMP 1987–92, ADC (Gen) to HM The Queen 1991–94; CGS 1992–94, CDS 1994–97, Field Marshal 1994; Constable HM Tower of London 1996–; Col The Green Howards 1982–94, Col Comdt APTC 1988–; Hon DCL Univ of Newcastle 1995; CIMgt 1993, FRSA 1995; *Recreations* cricket, walking, music, reading (especially military history); *Clubs* Army & Navy, MCC, Boodle's, Beefsteak; *Style*— Field Marshal Sir Peter Inge, GCB, DL; ✉ c/o Barclays Bank, Leyburn, N Yorks

INGE-INNES-LILLINGSTON, George David; CVO (1993), CBE (1986), DL (Staffs 1969); s of Cdr Hugh William Innes-Lillingston, RN (d 1953); *b* 13 Nov 1923; *Educ* Stowe, Merton Coll Oxford (MA); *m* 1, 1946, Alison Mary (d 1947), da of late Rev Canon Frederick Green; 1 da; m 2, 1955, Elizabeth Violet Grizel Thomson-Inge, yr da of Lt-Gen Sir William Montgomerie Thomson, KCMG, CB, MC (d 1963); 2 s, 1 da; *Career* WWII served Lt RNVR 1942–45; Lt Cdr RNR 1966; memb Agric Land Tbnl 1962–72; chm: N Birmingham & Dist Hosps 1968–74, Agric and Horticultural Ctee BSI 1980–86, Sail Trg Assoc (Midland Region) 1983–94; dir Lands Improvement Group of Cos 1983–91; Crown Estate Cmmr 1974–93; pres: Staffs Agric Soc 1970–71, CLA 1979–81 (chm 1977–79, pres Staffs Branch 1983–94); awarded RASE Bledisloe Gold medal for Landowners 1991; tstee Lichfield Cathedral 1980–; High Sheriff Staffs 1966; JP 1967–75; FRAgS 1986; *Recreations* growing trees; *Clubs* Boodle's, Royal Thames Yacht, Royal Highland Yacht (Oban), Farmers'; *Style*— George Inge-Innes-Lillingston, Esq, CVO, CBE, DL; ✉ The Old Kennels, Thorpe Constantine, Tamworth, Staffs B79 0LH (☎ 01827 830224)

INGHAM, Barrie Stanton; s of Harold Ellis Stead Ingham (d 1975), and Irene, *née* Bolton (d 1977); *b* 10 Feb 1932; *Educ* Heath GS Halifax; *m* 15 July 1957, Tarne, da of David Watkin Phillips, of Aust; 4 da (Catrin Marie b 7 March 1961, Liâne Jane b 12 March 1963, Francesca Shelley b 8 June 1964, Mali Terez b 5 Sept 1976); *Career* actor; 2 Lt RA 1951, TA offr 1953–; UK conslt to Int Theatre Arts Forum 1976, visiting prof Univ of Texas at Austin 1979, drama conslt to Baylor Univ 1980, hon assoc artist RSC 1989 (assoc artist 1974); *Theatre* debut London in 12 classical plays, Sganarelle, Tartuffe and The Magistrate (Old Vic) 1957–59; West End: Joie de Vivre 1959, The Happy Haven 1960, England Our England 1962, Virtue in Danger 1963, The Possessed 1963, The Bacchae 1964, Pickwick 1964, On the Level, Love, Love, Love 1972, Gypsy 1973, Snap 1974, Aspects of Love 1990; RSC Stratford, London and world tours: Lalo in Criminals, Brutus in Julius Caesar, Leontes in Winter's Tale, Sir Andrew in Twelfth Night, Lord Foppington in the Relapse, Dazzle in London Assurance, Buffalo Bill in Indians, Pleasure and Repentance (all 1967–71), the Duke in Measure for Measure 1974, Beverly Carlton in the Man Who Came to Dinner 1989; National Theatre: The American Clock and the Bay at Nice 1986–87; Broadway: Claudio in Much Ado About Nothing 1959, Uriah Heep in Copperfield 1981, Pellimore in Camelot 1982, George in Aspects of Love 1991, Col Fickering in My Fair Lady 1994; US Nat tours: Camelot 1982, Me and My Girl 1987, Aspects of Love 1992; *Television* over 100 TV plays in USA and UK incl: The Victorians 1962, Ann Veronica 1965, The Caesars 1968, The Power Game 1970, title role in Hine 1971, Beyond a Joke 1972, Funny Man 1979, George Washington 1983, Time Warrior 1994; *Films* incl: title role in A Challenge for Robin Hood 1966, Day of the Jackal 1973; *Awards* Aust Theatre Most Distinguished Actor Award 1975, Freedom of City of Austin 1980, Drama Logue Award Best Performance in a Broadway Musical 1981, Southern Calif Motion Picture Cncl Award 1983; *Clubs* Groucho; *Style*— Barrie Ingham, Esq; ✉ c/o London Management, 2–4 Noel Street, London W1V 3RB (☎ 0171 287 9000, fax 0171 287 3036); Artists' Group West, 1930 Century Park West, Suite 303, Los Angeles, Calif 90067, USA (☎ 00 1 310 552 1100)

INGHAM, Sir Bernard; kt (1990); s of Garnet Ingham (d 1974), of Hebden Bridge, W Yorks; *b* 21 June 1932; *Educ* Hebden Bridge GS; *m* 1956, Nancy Hilda, da of Ernest Hoyle (d 1944), of Halifax, W Yorks; 1 s (Dr John Bernard Ingham, *qv* b 16 Feb 1958); *Career* journalist: Hebden Bridge Times 1948–52, The Yorkshire Post and Yorkshire Evening Post 1952–59, The Yorkshire Post (northern industl corr) 1959–62, The Guardian 1962–67 (Leeds 1962–65, Lab Staff London 1965–67); press advsr Nat Bd for Prices and Incomes 1967–68, head of info Dept of Employment and Productivity 1968–72; dir of info: Dept of Employment 1973, Dept of Energy 1974–78; under sec (Energy Conservation Div) Dept of Energy 1978–79, chief press sec to Prime Minister 1979–90; chm Bernard Ingham Communications 1991–; columnist: Daily Express 1991–, PR Week (winner Business and Professional Magazines Columnist of the Year PPA Awards 1995); non-exec dir: McDonald's Restaurants Ltd, Hill and Knowlton; pres Br Franchise Assoc 1993–; visiting fell Dept of Politics Univ of Newcastle upon Tyne; memb Cncl Univ of Huddersfield 1994–; *Books* Kill the Messenger (1991); *Recreations* walking, gardening, reading; *Clubs* Reform; *Style*— Sir Bernard Ingham; ✉ 9 Monahan Ave, Purley, Surrey CR8 3BB (☎ 0181 660 8970, fax 0181 668 4357)

INGHAM, (George) Bryan; s of George William Ingham (d 1990), of Sowerby Bridge, and Alice May, *née* Mitchell (d 1989), of Elland, W Yorks; *b* 11 June 1936; *Educ* St Martin's Sch of Art, Royal Coll of Art, Academmia Britannica Rome; *Career* artist; *Two-Person Exhibitions* Lords Gallery London (with David Hall) 1963, Ashgate Gallery (with Elizabeth Frink) 1965, Ashgate Gallery (with Anthony Gross) 1968, Wills Lane Gallery St Ives (with Anthony Gross) 1970; *Solo Exhibitions* Kunsthalle Bremen, Kunsthalle Wordspede Germany, Francis Graham Dixon Gallery 1989, 1990, 1991, 1993, 1995 and 1996; working on restoration programme of Stobhall by Perth for The Earl of Perth 1966–; John Murray travelling scholarship, Italian Govt travelling scholarship, Leverhulme post graduate res award; former memb: Penwith Soc St Ives, Royal Soc of Painter-Etchers and Engravers; *Clubs* Blue Anchor (Helston); *Style*— Bryan Ingham, Esq; ✉ c/o Francis Graham-Dixon Gallery, 17/18 Great Sutton Street, London EC1V 0DN (☎ 0171 250 1962)

INGHAM, Prof Derek Binns; s of George Arthur Ingham (d 1967), and Fanny Walton, *née* Binns (d 1965); *b* 7 Aug 1942; *Educ* Univ of Leeds (BSc, PhD, DSc); *m* 22 Aug 1964, Jean, da of Tom Hirst (d 1963); 1 s (Mark Andrew b 10 July 1967), 1 da (Catherine Gail b 30 Dec 1965); *Career* Univ of Leeds: lectr in mathematics 1968–78 (1964–66), sr lectr 1978–83, reader 1983–86, prof 1986–, head of Dept of Applied Mathematical Studies 1988–91; CLE Moore instr Mass Inst of Technol Boston Mass USA 1966–68, FIMA 1988; *Books* Boundary Integral Equation Analyses of Singular, Potential and Biharmonic Problems (1984), The Mathematics of Blunt Body Sampling (1988), The Boundary Element Method for Solving Improperly Posed Problems (with Y Yuan, 1994); *Recreations* all forms of sport; *Style*— Prof Derek Ingham; ✉ 3 Fairfax Ave, Menston, Ilkley, W Yorks LS29 6EP (☎ 01943 875810); Dept of Applied Mathematical Studies, University of Leeds, Leeds, W Yorks LS2 9JT (☎ 0113 233 5113, fax 0113 242 9925, tlx 0113 255 6473)

INGHAM, Graham; s of Alan Ingham, of Stacksteads, Bacup, Lancs, and Marjorie, *née* White; *b* 30 Sept 1953; *Educ* Bacup and Rawtenstall GS, Thames Poly (BA), LSE (MSc); *Career* HM Treasy 1975–84: private sec to Sir Kenneth Couzens 1978–80, princ monetary policy 1980–81, princ Euro monetary affrs 1982–84; visiting fell and Fulbright scholar Princeton Univ 1981–82, economics specialist BBC World Serv 1984–88, economics corr BBC TV News and Current Affrs 1988–96, Guardian research fell Nuffield Coll Oxford 1995–96 (on leave from BBC), freelance broadcaster and journalist 1996–; head of public affairs Centre for Economic Performance LSE 1995–; visiting prof of economics Univ of Greenwich 1992–93, visiting reader in economics Royal Holloway Univ of London 1995–; *Books* Romance of the Three Empires (contrib, 1988); *Recreations* opera, travel, reading; *Clubs* Reform; *Style*— Graham Ingham, Esq; ✉ 34A Horsell Road, London N5 1XP (☎ and fax 0171 609 8366)

INGHAM, Dr John Bernard; s of Sir Bernard Ingham, *qv*, of Purley, Surrey, and Lady Nancy Ingham, *née* Hoyle; *b* 16 Feb 1958; *Educ* Univ of Durham (BA, Fulbright scholar, PhD), Bowling Green State Univ of Ohio USA (MA); *m* 7 Sept 1985, Christine, da of James Yendley; 1 da (b 21 Sept 1991), 1 s (b 16 Sept 1994); *Career* visiting researcher Georgetown Univ Washington DC USA 1982–83, dep ed BNFL News 1984–87, ed Sellascene 1986–87, freelance sports reporter Sunday Express 1986–89; Northern Correspondent, Building Magazine, Chartered Surveyor Weekly 1987–89; news reporter Daily Express Manchester 1989–90; Daily Express London: def and dip corr 1990–94, political corr 1994–96, environment corr 1996–; *Recreations* travel, birdwatching, following cricket and soccer; *Clubs* Travellers; *Style*— Dr John Ingham; ✉ Environment Correspondent, The Daily Express, Ludgate House, 245 Blackfriars Rd, London SE1 9UX (☎ 0171 922 7108, fax 0171 620 1654)

INGHAM, Stuart Edward; s of Edward Ingham (d 1978), and Dorothy Mary, *née* Pollard (d 1983); *b* 9 Oct 1942; *Educ* Canon Slade GS Bolton; *m* 30 June 1969, Jane Stella, da of Donald Wilkinson; 1 s (David Edward b 6 March 1979), 1 da (Helen Jane b 4 Jan 1982); *Career* chief exec United Leeds Teaching Hosps NHS Trust; MHS, DipHSM; *Recreations* equestrian sports; *Style*— Stuart Ingham, Esq; ✉ The Turnings, Woodacre Crescent, Bardsey, Leeds LS17 9DQ (☎ 01937 572673); United Leeds Teaching Hospitals NHS Trust, Trust Headquarters, Leeds General Infirmary, Great George Street, Leeds LS1 3EX (☎ 0113 292 6624, fax 0113 292 6282)

INGILBY, Sir Thomas Colvin William; 6 Bt (UK 1866), of Ripley Castle, Yorkshire; s of Maj Sir Joslan William Vivian Ingilby, 5 Bt, JP, DL (d 1974), and Diana, *née* Colvin; *b* 17 July 1955; *Educ* Eton, RAC Cirencester (MRAC); *m* 25 Feb 1984, Emma Clare Roebuck, da of Maj Richard R Thompson, of Whinfield, Strensall, York; 4 s (James William Francis b 1985, Joslan Richard Ryland b 1986, Jack Henry Thomas b 1990, Richard Joseph Frederick b 1994), 1 da (Eleanor Jane Pamela b 1989); *Heir* s, James William Francis Ingilby b 15 June 1985; *Career* teacher Springvale Sch Rhodesia 1973–74; asst land agent: Stephenson & Son York 1978–80, Strutt and Parker Harrogate 1981–83; mangr Ripley Castle Estates 1983–; lecture tours USA 1978 and 1979; pres: Harrogate and Dist Talking Newspaper 1978–, Harrogate Gilbert and Sullivan Soc 1987–, Nidderdale Amateur Cricket League 1979–, Cncl for the Prevention of Art Theft 1991–; fndr and coordinator Nat Stately Home Hotline (a stately home and museum neighbourhood watch scheme) 1988–; dir N York TEC 1989–93, chm Action Harrogate Ltd 1992–, chm Harrogate Management Centre Ltd 1992–; landowner (750 acres); int hon citizen New Orleans 1979; ARICS, FAAV, FRSA 1992; *Recreations* squash, tennis, cricket; *Style*— Sir Thomas Ingilby, Bt; ✉ Ripley Castle, Ripley, nr Harrogate, N Yorks HG3 3AY (☎ 01423 770152, fax 01423 771745)

INGLE, Prof Stephen James; s of James Ingle (d 1991), of London, and Violet Grace, *née* Stephenson; *b* 6 Nov 1940; *Educ* The Roan Sch, Univ of Sheffield (BA, MA Econ, DipEd), Victoria Univ of Wellington NZ (PhD); *m* 5 Aug 1964, Margaret Anne, da of Henry James Hubert Farmer (d 1979), of Sutton Bridge, Lincs; 2 s (Jonathan James Stuart b 11 Oct 1970, Benedict John Stephen b 13 April 1972), 1 da (Cassie Louise b 8 June 1979); *Career* Cwlth scholar in NZ 1964–67, head of Dept Univ of Hull 1985–90 (lectr in politics 1967–80, sr lectr 1980); prof and head of Dept of Politics Univ of Stirling 1991–; visiting research fell Victoria Univ of Wellington 1993; memb E Yorkshire Health Authy 1985–90, sec Political Studies Assoc UK 1987–88, chief examiner in politics Univ of Oxford delegacy 1987–; *Books* Socialist Thought in Imaginative Literature (1979), Parliament and Health Policy (1981), British Party System (2 edn 1989), George Orwell - A Political Life (1993); *Recreations* music, theatre, hill walking; *Style*— Prof Stephen Ingle; ✉ The Ridings, Perth Road, Dunblane FK15 0HA (☎ 01786 823372); University of Stirling, Stirling FK9 4LA (☎ 01786 67593)

INGLEBY, 2 Viscount (UK 1956); Martin Raymond Peake; s of 1 Viscount Ingleby (d 1966), and Lady Joan Rachel de Vere Capell (d 1979), da of 7 Earl of Essex; *b* 31 May 1926; *Educ* Eton, Trinity Coll Oxford; *m* 1952, Susan (d 1996), da of Capt Henderson Russell Landale, of Ewell Manor, W Farleigh, Kent; 1 s (decd), 4 da; *Heir* none; *Career* late Lt Coldstream Gds; called to the Bar Inner Temple 1956; dir Hargreaves Gp Ltd 1960–80, CC N Riding Yorks 1964–67; landowner; *Recreations* forestry; *Style*— The Rt Hon the Viscount Ingleby; ✉ Snilesworth, Northallerton, N Yorks DL6 3QD; Flat 1, 61 Onslow Square, London SW7 3LS

INGLEFIELD, David Gilbert Charles; s of Sir Gilbert Samuel Inglefield, GBE, TD (d 1991), Lord Mayor of London 1967–68, and (Laura) Barbara Frances, *née* Thompson; *b* 19 Nov 1934; *Educ* Eton, Trinity Coll Cambridge (MA); *m* 31 Oct 1970, Jean Mary, MBE, da of Col Sir Alan Gomme-Duncan, MC (d 1963), and Lady Gomme-Duncan (d 1970), of Dunbarney, Bridge of Earn, Perthshire; 1 s (Charles b 1977), 1 da (Mary b 1974); *Career* Nat Serv 1953–55, 2 Lt 12 Royal Lancers; advsr to the Tstees of the Police Fndn; memb Overseas Ctee Save the Children Fund 1969–80, chm Prevention of Blindness Res Fund 1969–72, tstee Order of Malta Homes Tst 1975–94; memb Chapter-Gen OstJ 1979–96, Sheriff City of London 1980–81, memb Ct of Assts Worshipful Co of Haberdashers; CStJ 1995 (OStJ 1973); SMOM 1978; *Recreations* travel, shooting, military history; *Clubs* Boodle's; *Style*— David Inglefield, Esq; ✉ The Old Rectory, Staunton-in-the-Vale, Orston, Notts NG13 9PE

INGLEFIELD-WATSON, Lt-Col Sir John Forbes; 5 Bt (UK 1895); s of Sir Derrick William Inglefield-Watson, 4 Bt (d 1987), by his 1 w, Margrett Georgina (later Mrs Savill; d 1995), da of Col Thomas Stokes George Hugh Robertson Aikman, CB; *b* 16 May 1926; *Educ* Eton; *Heir* 2 cous Simon Conran Hamilton Watson b 11 Aug 1939; *Career* RE 1945–81: cmmnd 1946, ret as Lt-Col 1981; *Recreations* philately, football refereeing (FA staff referee instr 1978–); *Style*— Lt-Col Sir John Inglefield-Watson, Bt; ✉ The Ross, Hamilton, Lanarkshire, ML3 7UF (☎ 01698 283734)

INGLESE, Anthony Michael Christopher; s of Angelo Inglese, and Dora, *née* Di Paola; *b* 19 Dec 1951; *Educ* Salvatorian Coll Harrow Weald, Fitzwilliam Coll Cambridge (MA, LLB); *m* 1974, Jane Elizabeth Kerry, *née* Bailes; 1 s, 1 da; *Career* called to the Bar Gray's Inn 1976, Legal Adviser's Branch Home Office 1975–86, legal secretariat to Law Offrs 1986–88, Legal Adviser's Branch Home Office 1988–91, legal dir Office of Fair Trading 1991–95, legal advsr Treasy Slr's Dept Min of Defence 1995–; *Recreations* organising theatricals; *Clubs* ICA; *Style*— Anthony Inglese, Esq; ✉ Ministry of Defence, Metropole Building, Northumberland Avenue, London WC2N 5BL (☎ 0171 218 9000)

INGLETON, Diana Margaret; da of John Harston (d 1980), of Norfolk, and Freda Mary, *née* Boulton; *b* 7 Dec 1957; *Educ* Havant GS, Havant Sixth Form Coll, Winchester Sch of Art, Norwich Sch of Art (BA); *m* 17 May 1986, William Simon Luke Ingleton, s of Richard William John Ingleton; *Career* graphic designer; formed design consultancy

Design Motive Ltd specialising in brand identity and mgmnt (clients incl: Hertz, Hasbro, British Airways, Mazda and Whitbread) 1993; *Recreations* horse riding, conservation, sailing, walking; *Style*— Ms Diana Ingleton; ✉ The Hayloft, Rose Lane, Ripley, Surrey GU23 6NE

INGLEWOOD, 2 Baron (UK 1964); (William) Richard (Fletcher-) Vane; DL (Cumbria); s of 1 Baron Inglewood, TD, DL (d 1989); *b* 31 July 1951; *Educ* Eton, Trinity Coll Cambridge (MA), Cumbria Coll of Agric and Forestry; *m* 29 Aug 1986, Cressida Rosa, yst da of late (Alan) Desmond Frederick Pemberton-Pigott, CMG, of Fawe Park, Keswick; 1 s (Henry William Frederick b 24 Dec 1990), 2 da (Miranda Mary b 19 May 1987, Rosa Katharine b 25 July 1989); *Heir* s, Hon Henry William Frederick (Fletcher-)Vane b 24 Dec 1990; *Career* called to the Bar Lincoln's Inn 1975; contested (C): Houghton and Washington Gen Election 1983, Durham Euro-Election 1984; MEP (C) Cumbria and Lancashire N 1989–94; Cons spokesman legal affrs Euro Parliament 1989–94, Cons dep whip Euro Parliament 1992–94, chief whip 1994, Lord in Waiting 1994–95; Capt Yeomen of the Guard 1995, Parly under-sec of state Dept of National Heritage 1995–; memb: Lake Dist Special Planning Bd 1984–90, Regnl Land Drainage Ctee NWWA 1985–89, Ct Univ of Lancaster 1985, NWWA 1987–89; Liveryman Worshipful Co of Skinners; ARICS; *Clubs* Travellers', Pratt's; *Style*— The Rt Hon Lord Inglewood, DL; ✉ Hutton-in-the-Forest, Penrith, Cumbria CA11 9TH (☎ 017684 84500, fax 017684 84571)

INGLIS, Prof (James) Alistair Macfarlane; CBE (1984); s of Alexander Inglis (d 1948), and Dr Edith Marion Douglas, *née* Smith (d 1960); *b* 24 Dec 1928; *Educ* Fettes, Univ of St Andrews (MA), Univ of Glasgow (LLB); *m* 18 April 1959, (Mary) Elizabeth, da of John Ronald Howie, JP, (d 1982); 2 s (Alexander b 1960, Ronald b 1973), 3 da (Elspeth b 1962, Morag b 1963, Marion b 1966); *Career* Nat Serv RCS 1952–54, ret Capt TA; ptnr McClure Naismith Anderson and Gardiner Glasgow 1956–93; Univ of Glasgow: prof of conveyancing 1979–93, prof of professional legal practice 1984–93, now emeritus prof; contrib to various jls incl Stair Meml Encyclopaedia: Laws of Scotland; pres Rent Assessment Panel Scotland 1976–87, memb Gtr Glasgow Health Bd 1975–83, dean Royal Faculty of Procurators Glasgow 1989–92, memb Ct of Patrons Royal Coll of Physicians and Surgns of Glasgow 1995–; gen tstee Church of Scotland 1994–; memb Law Soc Scotland 1952; *Recreations* golf, gardening; *Clubs* Western (Glasgow), Royal Scottish Automobile (Glasgow); *Style*— Prof Alistair Inglis, CBE; ✉ Crioch, Uplawmoor, Glasgow G78 4DE (☎ and fax 01505 850315)

INGLIS, George Harrison; CBE (1991); *b* 25 Nov 1927; *Educ* Univ of Durham (BSc); *Career* apprentice CA Parsons & Co Ltd; nuclear indust 1952–92 (initially on design of Calder Hall reactors), chief mechanical engr NPPC 1955–60 (consortium constructing power stations Bradwell, Latina and Dungeness A), chief engr fuel Prodn Gp UKAEA 1960; transferred to BNFL: divnl chief engr 1973, dir Fuel Div 1976, memb Bd 1976–84; md and memb Bd Urenco Ltd 1984–91, chm Bd of Dirs Urenco Inc USA 1985–92, chm Mgmnt Centec GmbH Germany 1984–91; Offr of the Order of Orange Nassau (Netherlands) 1991; FIMechE, FEng 1983; *Style*— George Inglis, Esq, CBE, FEng; ✉ Oakdean, Dean Lane, Cookham, Berks SL6 9BQ

INGLIS, Ian Brownlie; WS (1971); s of Charles Inglis (d 1971), and Margaret Boyes, *née* Brownlie (d 1984); *b* 6 Feb 1941; *Educ* Lanark GS, Chartered Inst of Bankers in Scotland (John Dallas Prize), Univ of Edinburgh (Sir John Robertson Prize, LLB); *m* 31 July 1965, Eleanor McLuckie, da of Richard Mitchell Taylor; 2 da (Carol Margaret b 19 July 1971, Joanne Helen b 26 Nov 1974); *Career* Royal Bank of Scotland: bank apprentice 1957–60, bank clerk 1960–65, apprentice slr 1965–66; Shepherd & Wedderburn WS: apprentice slr 1966–67, asst slr 1967–68, ptnr 1968–92, sr ptnr 1992–95, sr ptnr Corp Dept 1995–; memb: Chartered Inst of Bankers in Scotland 1960, Law Soc of Scotland 1967; *Recreations* golf; *Clubs* New (Edinburgh), Polmont Rotary, Glenbervie Golf; *Style*— Ian B Inglis, Esq, WS; ✉ Shepherd & Wedderburn WS, Level 2, Saltire Court, 20 Castle Terrace, Edinburgh EH1 2ET (☎ 0131 228 9900, fax 0131 228 1222)

INGLIS, (James Craufuird) Roger; WS; s of Lt-Col John Inglis (d 1967); *b* 21 June 1925; *Educ* Winchester, Univ of Cambridge, Univ of Edinburgh; *m* 1952, Phoebe Aeonie, da of Edward Mackenzie Murray-Buchanan; 2 s, 4 da; *Career* dir: Scottish Provident Institution for Mutual Life Assurance 1962–95, Royal Bank of Scotland plc 1967–89, Selective Assets Trust plc 1988–95; ptnr: Dundas & Wilson CS 1953–73, Ivory & Sime 1973–75, Shepherd & Wedderburn WS 1976–89; chm: Br Assets Tst plc 1978–95 (dir 1957–78), Investors Capital Tst plc 1985–94, Ivory & Sime Optimum Income Tst plc 1989–95, European Assets Tst NV 1972–95; *Recreations* golf; *Clubs* Royal and Ancient, Army and Navy, New (Edinburgh), Hon Co of Edinburgh Golfers; *Style*— Roger Inglis, Esq, WS; ✉ Inglisfield, Gifford, East Lothian EH41 4JH (☎ 01620 810339)

INGLIS-JONES, Nigel John; QC (1982); s of Maj John Alfred Inglis-Jones (d 1977), and Hermione, *née* Vivian (d 1958); *b* 7 May 1935; *Educ* Eton, Trinity Coll Oxford (BA); *m* 1, 1965, Lenette (d 1986), o da of Lt-Col Sir Walter Bromley-Davenport, of Cheshire; 2 s (James b 1968, Valentine b 1972), 2 da (Imogen b 1966, Cressida b 1967); m 2, 1987, Ursula Jane Drury, y da of the late Captain G D and Mrs Culverwell (now Lady Pile), of Sussex; 1 s (Sebastian b 1991); *Career* served as Ensign (Nat Serv) with Grenadier Gds 1953–55; called to the Bar Inner Temple 1954, recorder of the Crown Ct 1977–92, gen cmmr for Income Tax 1992, dep social security cmmr 1993–, bencher Inner Temple 1981; *Books* The Law of Occupational Pension Schemes; *Recreations* fishing, gardening, collecting early English glass; *Clubs* MCC; *Style*— Nigel Inglis-Jones, Esq, QC; ✉ 21 Elms Crescent, London SW4 8QE (☎ 0171 622 3043); 35 Essex Street, Temple, London WC2R 3AR (☎ 0171 353 6381)

INGLIS OF GLENCORSE, Sir Roderick John; 10 Bt (NS 1703), of Glencorse, Midlothian (formerly Mackenzie of Gairloch, Ross-shire); s of Sir Maxwell Ian Hector Inglis, 9 Bt (d 1974); *b* 25 Jan 1936; *Educ* Winchester, Edinburgh Univ (MB ChB); *m* 1, 1960 (m dis 1975), Rachel Evelyn, da of Lt-Col N M Morris, of Dowdstown, Ardee, Co Louth; 2 s (Ian Richard b 1965, Alexander Colin (twin) b 1965), and 1 s decd, 1 da (Amanda Fiona b 1963); m 2, 1975 (m dis 1977), Geraldine, yr da of R H Kirk, of Thaxted, Essex; 1 da (Harriet b 1977); m 3, 1986, Marilyn, da of A L Irwin, of Glasgow; 1 s (Harry Mackenzie b 1987); *Heir* s, Ian Richard Inglis of Glencorse, yr, b 1965; *Clubs* Country (Pietermaritzburg); *Style*— Sir Roderick Inglis of Glencorse, Bt; ✉ 18 Cordwalles Rd, Pietermaritzburg, Natal, S Africa

INGMAN, David Charles; CBE (1993); s of Charles Ingman (d 1983), of Torquay, and Muriel, *née* Bevan (d 1974); *b* 22 March 1928; *Educ* Univ of London (BSc), Univ of Durham (MSc); *m* 29 Dec 1951, Joan Elizabeth Walker; 2 da (Heather b 26 Dec 1953, Suzanne b 20 July 1957); *Career* ICI 1949–85: works mangr Polyolefines Wilton 1972–75, div dir for Prodn and Engrg 1975–78, div res dir 1978, dep chm Plastics Div 1978, gp dir Plastics and Petrochemical Div 1981–85; dir Engrg Servs Ltd 1975–78, alternate dir ACCI Ltd SA 1978–82, non-exec dir Negretti-Zambra 1979–81, chm and chief exec Bestobell plc 1985–86, chm Br Waterways Bd 1987–93; memb Nationalised Industs Chairmen's Gp 1987–93; *Recreations* golf, painting, gardening, travel; *Style*— David Ingman, Esq, CBE; ✉ Old Trees, Letchworth Lane, Letchworth, Herts SG6 3ND

INGMIRE, David Richard Bonner; s of Gordon Ingmire, and Dorothy Edith, *née* Bonner; *b* 29 Sept 1940; *Educ* Chatham House Sch, King's Coll London (BA); *m* (dis); 2 s (James b 20 June 1968, Charles b 29 Sept 1971); *Career* articled clerk Blackburns Robson Coates & Co 1962–65, qualified CA 1965, Neville Russell 1967–69, corp tax offr Binder Hamlyn 1970–72, corp tax mangr Arthur Young McClelland Moores & Co 1972–74, corp tax ptnr Neville Russell 1974–; Freeman City of London, memb Worshipful Co of Glaziers and Painters of Glass; FCA, ATII; *Recreations* music, theatre, travel, golf, long distance walking; *Style*— David Ingmire, Esq; ✉ Neville Russell, 24 Bevis Marks, London EC3A 7NR (☎ 0171 377 1000, fax 0171 377 8931)

INGRAM, Adam Paterson; MP (Lab) East Kilbride (majority 11,992); s of Bert Ingram, of Glasgow, and Louisa, *née* Paterson; *b* 1 Feb 1947; *Educ* Cranhill Secdy Sch; *m* 20 March 1970, Maureen, da of Leo and Flora McMahon, of Glasgow; *Career* systems analyst SSEB 1970–77, trade union official NALGO 1977–87; MP (Lab) E Kilbride 1987–, PPS to the Leader of the Oppn Rt Hon Neil Kinnock 1988–92, memb Select Ctee on Trade and Industry 1992–93, front bench spokesman (Lab) on Social Security matters 1993–95, shadow min for Sci & Technol 1995–; memb: Lab Pty, Co-op Pty; *Recreations* fishing, cooking, reading; *Style*— Adam Ingram, Esq, MP; ✉ 17 Weaver Place, East Kilbride G75 8SH (☎ 01355 235343); House of Commons, Westminster, London SW1A 0AA (☎ 0171 219 4093, fax 0171 219 4929)

INGRAM, Alexander Henry (Alex); s of Richard Irvine Ingram, of Kings Nympton, N Devon, and Peggy, *née* Ayers; *b* 25 Sept 1955; *Educ* St Paul's, Trinity Coll Cambridge (MA); *m* 19 Aug 1979, Caroline Rebecca, da of Dr Arnold Levene; 2 da (Zoë Abigail b 16 April 1984, Naomi Rose b 19 Dec 1986); *Career* conductor; Guildhall Sch of Music 1976–78, Nat Opera Studio 1978–79, Welsh Nat Opera 1979–80, ENO 1980–83, asst md then md State Opera of S Australia 1983–85, Kiel Germany 1986–87, ENO 1987–; *Style*— Alex Ingram, Esq; ✉ c/o English National Opera, London Coliseum, St Martin's Lane, London WC2N 4ES (☎ 0171 836 0111, fax 0171 836 8379)

INGRAM, Christopher John (Chris); s of late Thomas Frank Ingram, of Southwick, Sussex, and late Gladys Agnes, *née* Louttid; *b* 9 June 1943; *Educ* Woking GS Surrey; *m* 10 Oct 1964, Janet Elizabeth, da of late Charles Rye; 1 da (Kathryn Elizabeth b 30 March 1967), 1 s (Jonathan Devereux b 25 June 1969); *Career* messenger Collett Dickenson Pearce 1960–62, media planner/buyer Greenlys 1962–64, planner/buyer Grey Advertising 1964–65, media gp head KMP 1965–68, media gp head Dorland 1969–70, media mangr then media dir KMP 1970–72, md TMD 1972–76, fndr Chris Ingram Associates 1976–, chm and chief exec CIA Group PLC 1989–; non-exec dir: Interactive News Network Ltd, JSB Restaurants; vice chm Assoc of Media Communications Specialists, govr MENCAP City Fndn 1991–; *Recreations* jogging, watching football, art, theatre, eating out; *Clubs* Carlton, Solus, Marketing Group; *Style*— Chris Ingram, Esq; ✉ CIA Group PLC, 1 Paris Garden, Stamford St, London SE1 8NU (☎ 0171 633 9999, fax 0171 261 1226)

INGRAM, Prof David John Edward; CBE (1991), DL (1992); s of John Evans Ingram (d 1967), of Bexhill-on-Sea, and Marie Florence, *née* Weller (d 1965); *b* 6 April 1927; *Educ* King's Coll Sch Wimbledon, New Coll Oxford, Clarendon Lab Oxford (MA, DPhil, DSc); *m* 4 July 1952, (Ruth) Geraldine Grace, da of Donald McNair (d 1975), of Cirencester, Glos; 2 s (Jonathan b 1953, Bruce b 1960), 1 da (Marion b 1956); *Career* lectr and reader Dept of Electronics Univ of Southampton 1952–59, dep vice chllr Univ of Keele 1964 and 1968–71 (prof and head of physics 1959–73), princ Chelsea Coll Univ of London 1973–80, vice chllr Univ of Kent 1980–94; memb Governing Body: King's Coll Med Sch 1984–94, SPCK 1985–93, South Bank Univ 1988–96, Br Cncl Bd 1991–95; treas Ctee of Vice Chllrs and Princs 1988–94; chm UCCA 1991–94; memb: Carnegie UK Tst 1982–, Enterprise Agency of E Kent, Kent CC Educn Ctee; vice chm Canterbury-Reims Twinning Assoc, pres Kent Fedn of Amenity Socs 1986–87; chm: Chaucer Hosp Community Advsy Bd, Kent Co Consultative Ctee for Industry Year 1986, Nat Unit on Staff Devpt for Univs 1988–93, Br Cncl Ctee on Europe 1989–94; non-exec dir Taunton and Somerset NHS Tst 1995–; tstee Canterbury Cathedral Appeal Tst; memb Bd of Govrs: King's Sch Canterbury, West Heath Sch; memb Bd British Cncl 1991–95; Hon DSc: Univ of Clermont-Ferrand 1960, Univ of Keele 1983; Hon DCL Univ of Kent 1994; fell: Roehampton Inst 1988, King's Coll London 1986; FInstP; *Books* Spectroscopy at Radio and Microwave Frequencies (1955, 2 edn 1967), Free Radicals as Studied by Electron Spin Resonance (1958), Biological and Biochemical Applications of Electron Spin Resonance (1969), Radiation and Quantum Physics (1973), Radio and Microwave Spectroscopy (1976); *Recreations* sailing, DIY; *Clubs* Athenaeum; *Style*— Prof David Ingram, CBE; ✉ Cordwainers Cottage, Maundown, Wiveliscombe, Somerset TA4 2BU (☎ 01984 623761)

INGRAM, Prof David Stanley; s of Stanley Arthur Ingram, of Berrow, Somerset, and Vera May, *née* Mansfield (d 1973); *b* 10 Oct 1941; *Educ* Yardley GS Birmingham, Univ of Hull (BSc, PhD), Univ of Cambridge (MA, ScD); *m* 28 July 1965, Alison Winifred, da of Spencer Thomas Graham (d 1975); 2 s (Michael b 27 Aug 1967, Jonathan b 14 Aug 1969); *Career* res fell: Univ of Glasgow 1966–68, Univ of Cambridge 1968–69; sr scientific offr Agric Res Cncl Cambridge 1969–74; Univ of Cambridge: lectr in botany 1974–88, fell of Downing Coll 1974–90 (dean, tutor and dir of studies in biology), reader in plant pathology 1988–90; regius keeper (dir) Royal Botanic Garden Edinburgh 1990–, hon prof Univ of Edinburgh 1991–, visiting prof Univ of Glasgow 1991–, hon prof of horticulture RHS 1995–; vice pres: Linnean Soc, Br Soc of Plant Pathology 1996 (pres elect 1997, pres 1998); memb: Sci Ctee RHS, Scotland's Garden Scheme Ctee, Scot Nat Heritage SSSI Advsy Ctee, Int Editorial Bd for Flora of China Project, Advsy Ctee Univ of Edinburgh Div of Biol Sci; chm Sci and Plants for Schools Tst; hon vice pres Royal Caledonian Hort Soc 1990, hon pres Int Congress of Plant Pathology 1998; memb editorial bds: Biology Reviews, Annals of Botany and Advances in Plant Pathology; scientific advsr Gatsby Charitable Fndn; tstee: Botanic Gardens Conservation Int, various other gardens and charities; CBiol, FIBiol 1988, FRSE 1993; *Books* Plant Tissue Culture (1974), Tissue Culture Methods for Plant Pathologists (1980), Cambridge Encyclopaedia of Life Sciences (1985), Advances in Plant Pathology (vols I-IX, 1982–93), Shape and Form in Plants and Fungi (1994); *Recreations* literature, music, art, ceramics, gardening, travel, strolling around capital cities; *Clubs* Caledonian, New (Edinburgh); *Style*— Prof David Ingram, FRSE; ✉ Royal Botanic Garden, Edinburgh EH3 5LR (☎ 0131 552 7171, fax 0131 552 0382)

INGRAM, David Vernon; s of (Harold) Vernon Ingram, OBE, TD (Col RAMC, d 1980), of Ferndown, Dorset, and Bessie Mary, *née* Montauban; *b* 13 Nov 1939; *Educ* Rugby, St Johns Coll Cambridge, Middx Hosp Med Sch (MA, MB BChir), Royal Coll of Surgns London; *m* 13 May 1967, Stella Mary, da of (Alan) Howard Cornes (d 1974), of Stockton Brook, Staffs; 1 s (Matthew b 1969), 2 da (Harriet b 1970, Catherine b 1972); *Career* sr resident offr Moorfields Eye Hosp London 1969–70, sr ophthalmic registrar St George's Hosp London 1970–73; conslt ophthalmic surgn: Sussex Eye Hosp Brighton 1973–, Cuckfield and Crawley Health Dist 1973–92; pres Brighton and Sussex Medico Chirurgical Soc 1988; memb Gen Optical Cncl 1990–; Liveryman Worshipful Soc of Apothecaries of London 1970, Freeman City of London 1971; FRCS 1969, FRSM 1971, FRCOphth 1988 (memb Cncl 1994–); *Recreations* yacht cruising, photography, DIY; *Clubs* Cruising Assoc; *Style*— David Ingram, Esq; ✉ 4 Tongdean Rd, Hove, E Sussex BN3 6QB (☎ 01273 552 305); Sussex Eye Hospital, Eastern Rd, Brighton (☎ 01273 606 124)

INGRAM, Sir James Herbert Charles; 4 Bt (UK 1893), of Swineshead Abbey, Lincolnshire; s of (Herbert) Robin Ingram (d 1979, only s of Sir Herbert Ingram, 3 Bt, who d 1980), by his first w, Shiela, only da of late Charles Peczenik; *b* 6 May 1966; *Educ* Eton, Cardiff Univ; *Heir* half-bro, Nicholas David Ingram b 12 June 1975; *Recreations* golf, skiing, tennis; *Style*— Sir James Ingram, Bt; ✉ 8 Lochaline Street, London W6 9SH

INGRAM, Julian Andrew; s of Ernest Alfred Ingram, of Worthing, W Sussex, and June Jamieson, *née* Ralph; *b* 17 April 1956; *Educ* Worthing GS for Boys, Worthing Sixth Form Coll, LSE (BSc(Econ), London Univ laurel); *m* 1, 19 July 1980 (m dis 1987), Jane, *née* Brockliss; m 2, 1 Oct 1994, Jennifer Lorraine, *née* Smith; 1 da (Alicia Imogen b 1 Sept 1995); *Career* bd dir and chm London Student Travel Ltd 1978–80; Saatchi & Saatchi Advertising: trainee account exec 1980–81, account exec 1981–83, account supr 1983–85, account dir 1985–86; Abbott Mead Vickers BBDO: account dir 1986–89, bd account dir 1989–91, dept head 1991–94, dir 1994–96, Euro Directorate 1996–; Party candidate (Lib Dem) 1983 and 1987 gen elections; memb: Lib Dems 1974, LSE Soc 1982, Mensa 1992, IPA 1992, Mktg Soc 1994; *Recreations* films, military history, cooking, gym; *Style—* Julian Ingram, Esq; ✉ Abbott Mead Vickers BBDO Ltd, 191 Old Marylebone Road, London NW1 5DW (☎ 0171 402 4100, fax 0171 723 1451, mobile 0850 741834)

INGRAM, Dame Kathleen Annie; *see:* Raven, Dame Kathleen Annie

INGRAM, Prof Malcolm David; s of Arthur Ingram (d 1959), and Elisie May, *née* Cross (d 1993); *b* 18 Jan 1939; *Educ* Oldershaw GS, Univ of Liverpool (Sir W H Tate open scholar, BSc, PhD), Univ of Aberdeen (DSc); *m* 1967, Lorna, da of late Thomas Hardman; 1 da (Fiona Catherine b 1969), 1 s (Richard David b 1972); *Career* res assoc Rensselaer Poly Inst 1964–65; Univ of Aberdeen: lectr in physical chemistry 1965–78, sr lectr 1978–90, reader 1990–93, prof of chemistry 1993–; visiting prof: Univ of Franche Comté 1992, Univ of Bordeaux 1994; chm RSC (Aberdeen) 1990–93; FRSC 1982; author of over 125 scientific papers on solid state electrochemistry and glass science; *Recreations* foreign travel, swimming in warm seas, playing tennis (badly); *Style—* Prof Malcolm Ingram; ✉ Kenmore, 40 Manor Place, Cults, Aberdeen AB1 9QN (☎ 01224 861183); Department of Chemistry, University of Aberdeen, Meston Walk, Aberdeen AB9 2UE (☎ 01224 272905, fax 01224 272921)

INGRAM, Martin Alexander; s of late George Ingram, of Folkington, Sussex, and late Joyce Mercia, *née* Jones; *b* 1 July 1945; *Educ* Charterhouse, King's Coll London (LLB); *m* 28 Feb 1970, Amanda Susanna, da of Stephen Alexander Lockhart, CMG, OBE (d 1989), of Milton Lockhart, Lanarks; 1 s (Bruce Richard b 14 July 1972), 1 da (Antonia Mary b 11 Aug 1976); *Career* ptnr Heseltine Moss & Co 1976–88, chm and md Brown Shipley Stockbroking Ltd 1988–91 (conslt 1991–92), chm Ruegg Ingram & Co 1991–, conslt J M Finn & Co 1992–; memb Int Stock Exchange; MSI (Dip), AIIMR; *Recreations* painting, tennis; *Clubs* Brooks's, St Moritz Tobogganing, Rye Golf; *Style—* Martin Ingram, Esq; ✉ Cralle Place, Vines Cross, Heathfield, East Sussex TN21 9HF; J M Finn & Co, Salisbury House, London EC2M 5TA

INGRAM, Nicholas David; s of (Herbert) Robin Ingram (d 1979, only s of Sir Herbert Ingram, 3 Bt, who d 1980), by his 2 w, Sallie Willoughby, da of Frank Hilary Minoprio; hp of half-bro, Sir James Ingram, 4 Bt; *b* 12 June 1975; *Educ* Stowe, RAC Cirencester; *Style—* Nicholas Ingram Esq; ✉ Southridge House, nr Streatley, Berks RG8 9SJ

INGRAM, Simon Jonathan Joseph; s of Jack Arthur Malcolm Ingram (d 1978), and Eileen Louise Ingram; *b* 20 Feb 1955; *Educ* St Benedict's Sch Ealing; *m* Marisa Maria, da of Paul Oddi; 1 da (Charlotte Joanne b 15 Nov 1983), 2 s (Oliver Simon b 7 April 1986, Tobias Paul b 13 July 1988); *Career* own import/export business Simon Ingram Exports Ltd until 1979, trainee rising to branch mangr Berkeley Walbrook 1979–81; The Porchester Group Ltd: fndr memb 1981, gp branch mangr 1981–84, sr gp mangr 1984–87; The MI Group Ltd (life assurance and financial services): sales dir 1987–89, gp sales dir 1989–90, dep md (life sales) 1990–91, chief exec 1991–92; chief exec City Financial Partners Ltd 1992–; ALIA, MDRT; *Recreations* rugby, golf, tennis, keeping fit, art; *Style—* Simon Ingram, Esq; ✉ City Financial Partners Ltd, Russell Square House, 10–12 Russell Square, London WC1B 5EH (☎ 0171 493 9090, fax 0171 629 0213)

INGRAM, Tamara; da of John Ingram, and Sonia, *née* Bolson; *b* 1 Oct 1960; *Educ* Queen's Coll Harley St London, Univ of East Anglia (BA); *m* Andrew Millington; 1 s (Max b 4 April 1991), 1 da (Anya Eve b 31 Dec 1992); *Career* prodr's asst working on various films incl A Private Function (with Dame Maggie Smith and Michael Palin, *qqv*) 1982–85; Saatchi & Saatchi Advertising: estab computer presentation dept 1985, account exec 1985–87, account supr 1987–88, account dir 1988–89, bd account dir 1989, gp account dir and memb Exec Bd 1990–95, jt chief exec offr 1995–; memb The Ad-Women 1995, MIPA 1995; *Recreations* theatre, opera, family and friends; *Clubs* Women's Advertising Club of London; *Style—* Ms Tamara Ingram; ✉ Saatchi & Saatchi Advertising, 80 Charlotte Street, London W1A 1AQ (☎ 0171 636 5060, fax 0171 637 8489, mobile 0836 766225)

INGRAMS, Hon Caspar David; s and h of Baroness Darcy de Knayth, DBE, *qv*, and Rupert George Ingrams (k in a motor accident 1964); *b* 5 Jan 1962; *Educ* Eton, Reading Univ (BSc); *m* 14 Sept 1996, Catherine Ann, eldest da of Bryan Baker; *Style—* The Hon Caspar Ingrams

INGRAMS, Leonard Victor; OBE (1980); s of Leonard St Clair Ingrams, OBE (d 1953), and Victoria Susan Beatrice, *née* Reid; *b* 1 Sept 1941; *Educ* Stonyhurst, Munich Univ, CCC Oxford (MA, BLitt); *m* 19 Sept 1964, Rosalind Ann, da of Antony Ross Moore, CMG, of Touchbridge, Brill; 1 s (Rupert b 23 Aug 1967), 3 da (Lucy b 3 Dec 1965, Elizabeth b 9 Feb 1971, Catherine b 30 Nov 1976); *Career* Baring Bros 1967, Eurofinance 1968–69, mangr and dir London Multinat Bank 1970–73, md Baring Bros 1975–81 (mangr 1973–74), chief advsr to the Govr Saudi Arabian Monetary Agency 1981–84 (sr advsr 1975–79); dir: Robert Fleming Holdings Ltd, Robert Fleming & Co Ltd, Robert Fleming Investment Management 1985–96; sr vice pres Arab Banking Corporation 1996–; chm: Deutschland Investment Corp 1990–96 (dir 1996–), Czechoslovakia Investment Corp 1992–96 (dir 1996–), Garsington Opera Ltd 1990–; *Publications* author of contribs to the Oxyrhynchus Papyri (various vols), Bond Portfolio Mgmnt (1989); *Recreations* music, gardening; *Clubs* Beefsteak; *Style—* Leonard Ingrams, Esq, OBE; ✉ Garsington Manor, Garsington, Oxford OX9 9DH; Arab Banking Corporation, PO Box 5698, Manama, Bahrain

INGRAMS, Richard Reid; s of Leonard St Clair Ingrams (s of Rev William Smith Ingrams, MA), and Victoria Susan Beatrice, da of Sir James Reid, 1 Bt, GCVO, KCB, MD, LLD; *b* 19 Aug 1937; *Educ* Shrewsbury, Univ Coll Oxford; *m* 1962 (sep), Mary Joan Morgan; 1 s, 1 da (and 1 s decd); *Career* ed Private Eye 1963–86 (chm 1974–), columnist The Observer 1988–, fndr and ed The Oldie magazine 1992–; *Books* Muggeridge - the biography (1995); *Style—* Richard Ingrams, Esq; ✉ The Oldie Magazine, 45/46 Poland Street, London W1V 4AU (☎ 0171 734 2225, fax 0171 734 2226)

INGROW, Baron (Life Peer UK 1982), of Keighley, W Yorkshire; John Aked Taylor; kt (1972), OBE (1960), TD (1951); s of Percy Taylor, of Knowle Spring House, Keighley, and Gladys, *née* Broster (who m 2, Sir Donald Horsfall, 2 Bt); *b* 15 Aug 1917; *Educ* Shrewsbury; *m* 1949, Barbara Mary, da of Percy Wright Stirk, of Crestmead, Keighley; 2 da (Hon Anne Elizabeth (Hon Mrs Dent) b 1951, Hon Diana Mary (Hon Mrs Dent) b 1953); *Career* served WWII Duke of Wellington's Regt and Royal Signals (Norway, Middle East, Sicily, NW Europe, Far East), Maj; chm and md Timothy Taylor and Co Ltd, Mayor Keighley 1956–57; Keighley Town Cncl: chm Educn Ctee 1949–61, chm Fin Ctee 1961–67, memb 1946–67; memb: Keighley Cons Assoc 1952–56 and 1957–67; gen cmmr Income Tax 1965–92; chm Yorks Area Nat Union Cons and Unionist Assocs 1966–71, pres Nat Union Cons and Unionist Assocs 1982–83 (memb Exec Ctee 1964–83, chm 1971–76); JP Keighley Yorks 1949–87, formerly DL W Riding, Lord-Lieut W Yorks 1985–92 (DL 1971, Vice Lord-Lieut 1976–85); chm Yorks W Cons Euro Constituency Cncl 1978–84, hon treas Magistrates' Assoc 1976–86 (memb Cncl 1957–86); *Style—* The Rt Hon Lord Ingrow, OBE, TD; ✉ Fieldhead, Keighley, W Yorks (☎ 01535 603895)

INKIN, Sir Geoffrey David; kt (1993), OBE (1974, MBE 1971); s of Noel David Inkin (d 1983), of Cardiff, and Evelyn Margaret Inkin; *b* 2 Oct 1934; *Educ* Dean Close Sch, RMA Sandhurst, Army Staff Coll, RAC Cirencester; *m* 1961, Susan Elizabeth, da of Lt-Col Laurence Stewart Sheldon (d 1988), of East Coker, Somerset; 3 s (Piers b 1965, Charles b 1967, Edmund b 1971); *Career* cmmnd Royal Welch Fusiliers 1955–74, Malaya 1956–57, Cyprus 1958–59 (despatches), cmd 1 Bn 1972–74; Parly candidate (Cons) Ebbw Vale 1977–79, memb Gwent CC 1977–83, chm Cwmbran Devpt Corpn 1983–87 (memb Bd 1980–83), memb Bd Welsh Devpt Agency 1984–87; High Sheriff of Gwent 1987; chm: Land Authy for Wales 1986–, Cardiff Bay Devpt Corp 1987–; memb: Cncl UWIST 1987–88, Ct Univ Coll of Wales of Cardiff 1988–; hon memb RICS (by election) 1994; hon doctorate Univ of Glamorgan 1996 FRSA; *Clubs* Brooks's, Cardiff and County, Ebbw Vale Cons; *Style—* Sir Geoffrey Inkin, OBE; ✉ The Old Rectory, St George's Super Ely, South Glamorgan CF5 6EP

INKSON, Prof John Christopher; s of George William Inkson, and Catherine Cynthia, *née* Laing (d 1988); *b* 18 Feb 1946; *Educ* Gateshead GS, Univ of Manchester (BSc), Univ of Cambridge (MA, PhD, ScD); *m* Pamela, da of William Henry Hepworth (d 1971); 1 s (Jonathan Allen), 2 da (Andrea Louisa, Beverley Jane); *Career* res physicist English Electric 1966–69, res fell Jesus Coll Cambridge 1972–85, demonstrator and lectr Univ of Cambridge 1975–85; Univ of Essex: prof of theoretical physics 1985–, head Dept of Physics 1989–, dep vice-chllr 1994–; conslt to MOD; FInstP; *Publications* over 150 articles published on the theory of semiconductor physics; *Recreations* reading, walking; *Style—* Prof John Inkson; ✉ Department of Physics, University of Exeter, Exeter EX4 4QL (☎ 01392 264148, tlx 42894 EXUNIV G, fax 01392 264111)

INMAN, His Hon Judge; Derek Arthur; s of Arthur William Inman (d 1978), and Majorie, *née* Knowles; *b* 1 Aug 1937; *Educ* Roundhay Sch Leeds, RNC Dartmouth (Queen's Sword of Honour, Queen's Telescope); *m* 1 (m dis 1979), Sarah, *née* Cahn; 2 da (Rachel b 20 Dec 1963, Chloe b 6 Oct 1968), 1 s (Benedick b 26 Dec 1965); m 2, June 1983, Elizabeth, *née* Dickenson, wid of Lt Col Colin Thomson, OBE; *Career* served RN 1957–73 (retired as Lt Cdr); called to the Bar Middle Temple 1968, in practice SE Circuit 1973–93, circuit judge (SE Circuit) 1993–; *Recreations* watching rugby and cricket, compulsory gardening; *Style—* His Hon Judge Inman; ✉ Middlesex Guildhall, Broad Sanctuary, London SW1P 3BB

INMAN, Edward Oliver; s of John Inman, of Cumnor, Oxford, and Peggy Florence, *née* Beard; *b* 12 Aug 1948; *Educ* King's Coll Sch Wimbledon, Gonville and Caius Coll Cambridge (MA), Sch of Slavonic and E European Studies London (MA); *m* 1, 1971 (m dis 1982); 1 s, 1 da; m 2, 1984, Sherida Lesley, *née* Sturton; 1 da, 2 step da; *Career* Imperial War Museum: joined as res asst 1972, asst keeper 1974, dir Duxford Airfield 1978–; govr 2nd Air Div Meml Library Norwich; *Recreations* the family, tennis, travel; *Style—* Edward Inman, Esq; ✉ Director, Imperial War Museum, Duxford Airfield, Cambridge CB2 4QR (☎ 01223 835000, fax 01223 836750)

INMAN, Karen Valerie; MBE (1990); da of Albert Briggs, and Elsie May, *née* Coult (d 1989); 4 bros, 1 sister; *b* 11 April 1963; *Educ* Winifred Holtby Sch, Hull Coll of Further Educn; *m* 6 August 1994, Peter Roy Inman; 1 da (Jade Chantelle, b 14 Dec 1995); *Career* judoist (under 48kg category); took up judo aged 12, gained black belt first dan aged 17, currently black belt sixth dan; memb GB jr team 1979–80, individual GB sr number 1 1981–92; achievements incl: Br Open champion 1981, 1982, 1986, 1987, 1989, 1990 and 1992, world champion 1982, 1984, 1986 and 1989, Euro champion 1982, 1983, 1984, 1986 and 1987, Dutch Open champion 1981 and 1982, Gold medal Canada Cup 1981, German Open champion 1982, 1983 and 1985, Austrian Open champion 1982, 1983, 1985, 1986, 1989 and 1992, Japanese Open champion 1983, 1984, 1985, 1986 and 1988, Swiss Open champion 1984, Belgium Open champion 1984 and 1989, Gold medal Cwlth Games 1990, Gold medal Euro Teams 1990, Norwegian Open champion 1990, American Open champion 1991, winner Paris Tournament 1992, GB rep Olympic Games Barcelona 1992 (dislocated shoulder in semi-final); *Recreations* embroidery, all sports, shopping; *Style—* Mrs Karen Inman, MBE

INMAN, Stephen Eric; s of John Eric Inman (d 1978), and Vera Alice, *née* Willis (d 1985); *b* 14 Oct 1935; *Educ* All Saints Sch Bloxham, St Thomas's Hosp Med Sch Univ of London (MB BS); *m* 1 July 1961, Ione Elizabeth Jill, da of Maurice Scott Murdoch (d 1963); 2 s (Paul b 1966, Dominic b 1973), 1 da (Nicola b 1962); *Career* resident med offr: Queen Charlotte's Hosp 1965–66, Chelsea Hosp for Women 1966–67; lectr St Thomas's Hosp 1968–70, sr registrar St Thomas's Hosp 1970–74, conslt obstetrician and gynaecologist W Surrey/NE Hants Health Dist 1974, chm Div of Obstetrics, Gynaecology and Paedriatrics at Frimley Park Hosp; memb Hosp Conslts and Specialists' Assoc 1974; FRCOG 1981; *Recreations* sailing, swimming, squash, tennis; *Clubs* Royal Aldershot Officers'; *Style—* Stephen E Inman, Esq; ✉ Folly Hill House, Farnham, Surrey (☎ 01252 713389)

INMAN, Prof William Howard Wallace (Bill); s of Wallace Mills Inman (d 1971), and Maude Mary, *née* Andrews (d 1973); *b* 1 Aug 1929; *Educ* Ampleforth, Gonville and Caius Coll Cambridge (MA, MB BChir, FRCP); *m* 21 July 1962, June Evelyn, da of Stewart Arthur Maggs (d 1970), of Doncaster; 3 da (Stella b 1955 (adopted), Rosemary b 1963, Charlotte b 1966); *Career* med advsr ICI Ltd Pharmaceuticals Div 1959–64, princ med offr DHSS Ctee on Safety of Medicines 1964–80, fndr Drug Safety Research Unit (dir 1980–94), prof of pharmacoepidemiology Univ of Southampton 1985; tstee Drug Safety Research Tst 1986–95; author of Monitoring for Drug Safety (1980); *Recreations* fishing, gardening; *Style—* Prof Bill Inman; ✉ South Croft House, Winchester Road, Botley, Hampshire S032 2BX (☎ 01703 695181); Drug Safety Research Unit, Bursledon Hall, Southampton

INNES, Callum; s of Donald Innes, of Edinburgh, and Christina Dow, *née* Charmichael (d 1968); *b* 5 March 1962; *m* 20 Sept 1990, Hyjdla Jadwiga Paula Kosaniuk; *Career* artist; *Solo Exhibitions* Artspace Gallery 1986, 369 Gallery Edinburgh 1988, Frith St Gallery London 1990, Jan Turner Gallery LA 1990, Frith St Gallery 1991, Patrick de Brock Antwerpen 1991, ICA London 1992, Galerie Nachst St Stephan Vienna 1992, Scottish Nat Gallery of Modern Art 1992, Bob Van Orsouw Galerie Zurich 1993, Patrick De Brock Antwerp 1993, Jan Turner Gallery Los Angeles 1993, Frith Street Gallery London 1994, Mackintosh Museum Glasgow Sch of Art 1995, Gilbert Brownstone and CIE Paris 1995, M & R Fricke Dusseldorf 1995, Bob Van Orsouw Galerie Zurich 1995, Angel Row Gallery Nottingham 1995, Gentili Arte Contemporanea Florence 1995, The Turner Prize Tate Gallery 1995, Frith Street Gallery 1996, Patrick De Brock Gallery Knokke 1996, Callum Innes (1990–1996) Inverleith House Royal Botanic Garden Edinburgh 50 Edinburgh Int Festival 1996, Galerie Slewe Amsterdam 1996; *Group Exhibitions* incl: Scottish Young Contemporaries 1985, Smith Biennial Stirling 1985 and 1989, Greenock Biennial Scotland 1988, 369 Gallery 1988 and 1989, Scatter (Third Eye Centre Glasgow) 1989, The Fruitmarket Gallery Edinburgh 1989, The Br Art Show 1990, Hayward Gallery London 1990, Resumé (Frith Street Gallery London) 1990, Painting Alone (The Pace Gallery NY) 1990, Kunst Europa (Br Cncl) 1991, Artisti Invitati Al Premio Internazionale (first prize) Milan, London, Rome and USA 1992, Abstrakte Malerei Zwischen Analyse und Synthese Galerie Nachst St Stephan Vienna, Galleria L'Attico Rome, Johnen & Scholte Cologne, Prospect 93 Frankfurt 1993, New Voices Br Cncl Touring Exhbn 1993, Callum Innes/Perry Roberts Frith Street Gallery 1993, John Moores 18 1993, Galerie Nachst St Stephen Vienna 1993, Wonderful Life Lisson Gallery London

1993, Coalition C C A Glasgow 1993, New Voices (Centre d'Art Santa Monica Barcelona, Museo de Bellos Artes Bilbao, touring to Murcia and Madrid) 1994, Delit d'inities (Gilbert Brownstone and Cie Paris) 1994, The Curator's Egg (Anthony Reynolds Gallery London) 1994, Lead and Follow: The Continuity of Abstraction (Robert Loader collection, Atlantis Gallery London) 1994, Paintmarks (Kettles Yard Cambridge, Southampton City Art Gallery, The Mead Gallery Univ of Warwick) 1994, Seeing and The Unseen (Peter Fleissig Collection, nvisible Museum) 1994, (Collezione Agostino e Patrizia Re Rebaudengo Turin, La Galleria Civice di Modena Italy) 1994, Idea Europe (Palazza Publico Sienna Italy) 1994, The Mutated Painting (Galerie Martina Detterer Frankfurt) 1995, From Here (Waddington Galleries London) 1995, Architecture of the Mind (Galerie Barbara Farber Amsterdam) 1995, Busche Galerie Berlin 1995, Swarm (Scottish Arts Cncl travelling summer exhbn) 1995, New Paintings (Arts Cncl Collection travelling exhbn) 1995, New Voices (Br Cncl travelling exhbn) 1995, Jerwood Award for Painting (Royal Scottish Acad and RA) 1995, New Abstraction (Kohn Turner Gallery LA) 1995, The Punter's Art Show (The Orchard Gallery Derry) 1995, Kleine Welten (Galerie M & R Fricke Dusseldorf) 1996, Leoncavallo (Milan) 1996, Museum of Modern Art (Oxford) 1996; *Style*— Callum Innes, Esq; ✉ c/o Frith Street Gallery, 60 Frith St, London W1V 5TA (☎ 0171 494 1550, fax 0171 287 3733)

INNES, David Archibald; s of Lt-Col J A Innes, DSO (d 1948), of Horringer Manor, Bury St Edmunds, Suffolk, and Evelyn Adelaide, *née* Dawnay (d 1985); *b* 1 May 1931; *Educ* Eton, Magdalene Coll Cambridge (MA); *m* 10 June 1955, Philippa, da of Maj Sir Alastair Penrose Gordon Cumming, MC (d 1939); 2 s (Guy b 1956, John b 1959), 1 da (Davina b 1957); *Career* Nat Serv Royal Scots Greys 1950–52; ptnr Rowe and Pitman 1958–84, memb Stock Exchange Cncl 1979–83; farmer 1976– (breeder of Limpsfield Herd of Pedigree Holstein-Friesians); memb: Bd of Tstees Chevening Estate 1983–, Kent Ctee CLA 1989– (chm 1994–96), Kent and E Sussex Ctee Nat Tst 1989–; tstee Kent Gdns Tst 1987–93; *Recreations* shooting, golf, gardening; *Clubs* Boodle's, Cavalry and Guards', Rye Golf; *Style*— David Innes, Esq; ✉ Hensill House, Hawkhurst, Kent TN18 4QH (☎ 01580 752162); Titsey Place, Oxted, Surrey RH8 0SD (☎ 01883 712124, fax 01883 717607)

INNES, (Alexander) Guy Berowald; s and h of Sir Peter Innes of Balvenie, 17 Bt, *qv*; *b* 4 May 1960; *Educ* Queen Mary's Coll Basingstoke; *m* 1986 (m dis 1990), Sara-Jane, da of late Dennis Busher, of Moraira, Spain; *partner* Susan da of late Peter Barwick, of Coringham, Swindon, Wilts; *Career* branch mangr with W H Smith & Virgin Retail 1978–87; fin conslt and training offr Prudential Property Services 1987–90; branch mangr Cheltenham & Gloucester Building Soc 1990–95; area mangr Skipton Building Soc 1995–96; residential property and mortgage conslt (Alexander Residential, Alexander Mortgage Services) 1996–; *Style*— Guy Innes, Esq; ✉ Rosebank, Church Road, Longhope, Glos GL17 0LG

INNES, Hammond; *see:* Hammond Innes, Ralph

INNES, Lt-Col James; s of Lt-Col James Archibald Innes, DSO (d 1948), and Lady Barbara Lowther (d 1979, da of 6 Earl of Lonsdale, OBE, JP, DL); *b* 7 June 1915; *Educ* Eton; *m* 14 Jan 1941, Hon (Veronica Wenefryde) Nefertari, da of Capt the Hon Richard Bethell (d 1929); 2 s (James R, Peter D), 1 da (Elizabeth M (Mrs Nicholl)); *Career* 2 Lt Coldstream Gds 1935, served France and Germany 1939–45 (despatches twice), Capt 1945 (temp Lt-Col), ret as Hon Lt-Col 1949; tstee John Innes Fndn 1948–90 (chm 1961–90), vice chm John Innes Inst 1967–90, dir Univ Life Assur Soc 1951–80 (chm 1968–80), memb Ct UEA 1969–, vice pres BOA 1980– (treas 1964–80); memb: Royal Inst of GB, London Stock Exchange 1955–80; JP: Berks 1955–73, Inner London 1973–74; Liveryman Worshipful Co of Clothworkers 1936 (memb Ct 1971, Master (excused serv) 1983–84); Hon DCL UEA 1989; *Recreations* gardening, game shooting; *Clubs* Turf, All England Lawn Tennis and Croquet; *Style*— Lt-Col James Innes; ✉ 25 Beaufort Close, London SW15 3TL (☎ 0181 785 6614)

INNES, Dr (Norman) Lindsay; OBE (1994); s of Norman James Mackay Innes (d 1945), and Catherine Mitchell, *née* Porter (d 1992); *b* 3 May 1934; *Educ* Webster's Seminary Kirriemuir, Univ of Aberdeen (BSc, PhD), Univ of Cambridge, Univ of Birmingham (DSc); *m* 18 April (1960), Marjory Niven, da of William Farquhar (d 1938); 1 s (Neil b 1962), 1 da (Helen b 1964); *Career* sr cotton breeder Cotton Res Corpn: Sudan 1958–66, Uganda 1966–71; head Cotton Res Unit Uganda 1972, head Plant Breeding Section Nat Vegetable Res Station 1973–84 (dep dir 1977–84), hon prof Univ of Birmingham 1973–84 (former hon lectr), head Plant Breeding Div Scot Crop Res Inst 1984–89 (dep dir 1986–94), agricultural conslt 1994–; hon prof Univ of Dundee 1988–; memb Governing Bd Int Crop Res Inst for Semi-Arid Tropics India 1982–88 (chm Prog Ctee 1984–88), chm Governing Bd Int Potato Centre Peru 1991–95 (memb 1988–95), memb Governing Bd Int Centre Insect Physiology and Ecology Kenya 1996–; author of numerous pubns in sci jls on agriculture, horticulture, plant breeding and genetics; chm Br Assoc of Plant Breeders 1982–84; memb: Oxfam Cncl of Tstees 1982–84, Bd of Euro Assoc of Plant Breeders 1981–86; pres Assoc of Applied Biologists 1993–94 (vice pres 1990–92); Freeman City of Antigua (Guatemala) 1989; FBiol 1979, FIHort 1986, FRSE 1989; *Recreations* golf, photography, travel; *Clubs* Downfield Golf; *Style*— Dr Lindsay Innes, OBE, FRSE; ✉ 14 Hazel Drive, Dundee DD2 1QQ (☎ 01382 660064, fax 01382 562426)

INNES, Sheila Miriam; da of late Dr James McGregor Innes, of Farnham Royal, Bucks, and Nora Elizabeth Amelia, *née* Wacks; *b* 25 Jan 1931; *Educ* Talbot Heath Sch Bournemouth, Lady Margaret Hall Oxford (MA); *Career* prodr BBC Radio World Serv 1955–61; BBC TV: prodr family programmes 1961–65, exec prodr Further Educn TV 1973–77, head BBC Continuing Educn TV 1977–84, controller BBC Educnl Broadcasting 1984–87; chief exec and dep chm The Open College 1987–91; memb: Gen Bd Alcoholics Anonymous 1980–83, Bd of Govrs Centre for Info on Language Teaching and Res 1981–84, Cncl for Educnl Technol 1984–86, Cncl Open Univ 1984–87, City & Guilds of London Inst, Educn Ctee RSA 1989–95, Women's Advsy Ctee RSA 1991–94, Editorial Panel Inst of Mgmnt 1991–; chm: Br Gas Trg Awards 1989–92, BTEC Product Devpt Ctee 1989–91; vice pres: (Educn Section) Br Assoc for the Advancement of Sci 1991–, Inst of Mgmnt Res Bd - Mgmnt Devpt to the Millennium; non-exec dir Brighton Health Care NHS Tst 1993–96; Govrs Talbot Heath Sch Bournemouth 1989–95; hon memb Cncl Standing Conf on Schools Sci and Technol; Hon DLitt S Bank Univ 1992; memb RTS 1984, CIMgt 1987, FRSA 1987, FITD 1987; *Books* author of numerous articles in educn jls; *Recreations* music (classical & jazz), swimming, photography, travel, languages, country pursuits; *Clubs* Reform, Forum UK, Oxford Soc; *Style*— Miss Sheila Innes; ✉ Wychwood, Barcombe, nr Lewes, E Sussex BN8 5TP (☎ 01273 400268)

INNES OF BALVENIE, Sir Peter Alexander Berowald; 17 Bt (NS 1628), of Balvenie, Banffshire; s of Lt-Col Sir Berowald Innes of Balvenie, 16 Bt (d 1988), and his 1 w Elizabeth Haughton, *née* Fayle (d 1958); *b* 6 Jan 1937; *Educ* Prince of Wales Sch Nairobi, Univ of Bristol (BSc); *m* 18 July 1959, Julia Mary, yr da of late Alfred Stoyell Levesley; 2 s ((Alexander) Guy Berowald b 1960, Alastair John Peter b 1965), 1 da (Fiona Julie b 1963); *Heir* s, (Alexander) Guy Berowald Innes, *qv*; *Career* conslt civil engr; dir Scott Wilson Kirkpatrick & Co Ltd; FICE, MConsE, MAPM; *Recreations* travel, pointers; *Clubs* Naval & Military, Dummer Golf; *Style*— Sir Peter Innes of Balvenie, Bt; ✉ The Wheel House, Nations Hill, Kings Worthy, Winchester SO23 7QY

INNES OF COXTON, Sir David Charles Kenneth Gordon; 12 Bt (NS 1686), of Coxton, Co Moray; o s of Sir Charles Kenneth Gordon Innes of Coxton, 11 Bt (d 1990), and Margaret Colquhoun Lockhart, *née* Robertson (d 1992); *b* 17 April 1940; *Educ* Haileybury, London Univ (BSc Eng); *m* 1969, Marjorie Alison, da of Ernest Walter Parker; 1 s (Alastair Charles Deverell b 1970), 1 da (Dione Elizabeth Colquhoun b 1974); *Heir* s, Alastair Charles Deverell Innes b 17 Sept 1970; *Career* tech dir Peak Technologies 1972–78, md Peak Combustion Controls 1978–80, chief engr Combustion Controls Peabody Hamworthy 1983–92, conslt 1992–; ACGI; *Style*— Sir David Innes of Coxton, Bt; ✉ 28 Wadham Close, Shepperton, Middx TW17 9HT

INNES OF EDINGIGHT, Sir Malcolm Rognvald; KCVO (1990, CVO 1981), WS (1964); s of Sir Thomas Innes of Learney, GCVO, LLD (d 1971), and Lady Lucy Buchan, 3 da of 18 Earl of Caithness; *b* 25 May 1938; *Educ* The Edinburgh Acad, Univ of Edinburgh (MA, LLB); *m* 19 Oct 1963, Joan, da of Thomas D Hay, CA, of Edinburgh; 3 s (John Berowald Innes of Edingight, yr b 1965, Colin William Innes of Kinnairdy b 1967, Michael Thomas Innes of Crommey b 1970); *Career* Lord Lyon King of Arms 1981– (Falkland Pursuivant Extraordinary 1957–58, Carrick Pursuivant 1958–71, Marchmont Herald 1971–81, Lyon Clerk and Keeper of the Records 1966–81); sec to Order of Thistle 1981–; pres Heraldry Soc Scotland; KStJ 1981, Grand Offr of Merit SMO Malta; memb Royal Co of Archers (Queen's Body Guard for Scotland); *Recreations* reading; *Clubs* New (Edinburgh); *Style*— Sir Malcolm Innes of Edingight, KCVO, WS, Lord Lyon King of Arms; ✉ Court of the Lord Lyon, HM New Register House, Edinburgh EH1 3YT (☎ 0131 556 7255, fax 0131 557 2148)

INNES-SMITH, Robert Stuart; s of Stuart William Innes-Smith, MM, MRCS, LRCP (d 1953), of Bedmonton Manor, Sittingbourne, Kent, and Florence Constance, *née* Green (d 1977); *b* 10 March 1928; *Educ* abroad, Univ of Sheffield (LLB) Lincoln's Inn; *m* 5 June 1954, Elizabeth Greta, da of Bertram John Lamb (d 1938), of Chestfield, Kent; 1 s (James Stuart Tenison b 1966), 2 da (Victoria (Mrs Simon Keeble) b 1957, Augusta Sibyl (Mrs Derek Wreay) b 1961); *Career* asst Burke's Peerage 1953–54, sr asst librarian Reuters News Agency 1954–56, ed-in-chief then editorial dir Illustrated County Magazine Gp 1960–69, ed Edinburgh Tatler and Glasgow Illustrated 1961–67, dir and ed Tatler and Bystander 1968–69, in charge of publications for English Life Publications Ltd, Pilgrim Press Ltd and Derbyshire Countryside Ltd 1969–93; FSA(Scot) 1963; *Books and Monographs* An Outline of Heraldry in England and Scotland (1973, 6 edn 1990), Notable Derbyshire Houses (1972), The Dukeries (1953), The Dukeries and Sherwood Forest (1974, 3 edn 1984), Windsor Castle, St George's Chapel and Parks (with foreword by Sir Sacheverell Sitwell, Bt, CH, 7 edn 1993, with French, German, Japanese, Spanish and Dutch edns), Notable Derbyshire Churches (1976, 3 edn 1991), Castleton and its Caves (1976, 2 edn 1986), Wellington (1970, 3 edn 1980), Marlborough (1974, 2 edn 1992), The Derbyshire Guide (1 ed, 1982, 2 edn 1991), Glamis Castle (1983, 3 edn 1993, with French, German, Spanish, Italian and Japanese edns), Jervaulx Abbey (1972), Whitehall (1978), Naworth Castle (1984), Pembroke Castle (1990), Matlock Bath (1978, 2 edn 1993), Bakewell (1977, 3 edn 1993), St Mary on the Bridge (1987), St Mildred's, Whippingham (with foreword by Countess Mountbatten of Burma, 1989), The House of Innes (1990), Clovelly (1990), Tissington (3 edn, 1990), St Martin's in the Bullring (1991), A Derbyshire Christmas (ed, 1992), Historic Houses of Pembrokeshire and their Families (ed author's notes, 1996); contributor to: The Sunday Telegraph, Country Life, The Lady, Derbyshire Life, Burke's Peerage, Debrett's Best of Britain, Dictionary of National Biography; *Recreations* playing the harpsichord, doing nothing; *Clubs* Beefsteak; *Style*— Robert Innes-Smith, Esq; ✉ The Old Vicarage, Swinburne Street, Derby DE1 2HL (☎ 01332 383510)

INNES-WILKIN, David; s of Charles Wilkin (d 1978), and Louisa Jane, *née* Innes; *b* 1 May 1946; *Educ* Lowestoft GS, Liverpool Univ Sch of Architecture (BArch, MCD); *m* 1, 10 April 1968, Beryl; 2 s (Dylan b 1972, Matthew b 1974), 1 da (Thomasine b 1971); m 2, 25 April 1987, Sarah, da of Rev Prof Peter Runham Ackroyd, *qv*; 1 da (Emma Jane b 1989), 1 s (James Ackroyd b 1991); *Career* chartered architect; princ Innes-Wilkin Architecture; chm SW Housing Assoc 1986–87, pioneered tenant participation in new housing estates designed 1979 ; memb: RIBA Regnl Ctee, Community Architecture Gp 1983–84; visiting lectr Univs of Liverpool, Cardiff, Manchester and Bristol; memb Int Congress of Architects; design awards: RTPI Commendation 1983, Housing Centre Tst Jubilee award for Good Design in Housing 1983, Times/RIBA Community Enterprise awards 1986/87 (three), Energy Action award 1990, Civic Soc 1991; RIBA, MRTPI, MFB; *Publications include* A Common Language (The Architects Jl, 1984), Among The Grass-Roots (RIBA Jl, 1983), Cuba: Universal Home Ownership (Roof, 1987), Shelter and Cities (Int Congress of Architects, 1987), Community Schools (Educn Res Unit, 1972); *Recreations* offshore sailing, music, writing, the Renaissance; *Style*— David Innes-Wilkin; ✉ Park Road House, 7 Park Road, Stapleton, Bristol BS16 1AZ

INNISS, Sir Clifford de Lisle; kt (1961); s of Archibald de Lisle Inniss (d 1957), and Lelia Emmaline, *née* Springer (d 1963); *b* 26 Oct 1910; *Educ* Harrison Coll Barbados, Queen's Coll Oxford (BA, BCL); *Career* called to the Bar Middle Temple 1935, KC Tanganyika 1950, QC Trinidad and Tobago 1953; legal draftsman: Barbados 1938, Tanganyika 1947; slr gen Tanganyika 1949, attorney gen Trinidad and Tobago 1953, chief justice Br Honduras (now Belize) 1957–72, judge of the Cts of Appeal of Bermuda, the Bahamas and the Turks and Caicos Islands 1974–75, judge of the Ct of Appeal of Belize 1974–81; chm of Integrity Cmmn of Nat Assembly of Belize 1981–87, memb of Belize Advsy Cncl 1985; *Recreations* tennis, gardening, music, cricket; *Clubs* Barbados Yacht, Pickwick Sports (Barbados); *Style*— Sir Clifford Inniss; ✉ 11/13 Oriole Ave, Belmopan, Belize, Central America

INNS, Michael Godfrey; s of George Alfred Inns, and Gwedeline Inns; *b* 4 Aug 1943; *Educ* Brookside GS; *m* 1972, Gillian; 3 s (Dominic, Nathan, Adam); *Career* London mangr Keystone Reinsurance 1969–76, mktg mangr Domestic & General Insurance Ltd 1976–80, md Charterhouse Insurance Services plc 1980–90, md Mercantile Insurance Services plc 1990–95, sales and mltg mangr Sun Alliance Insurance Co 1995–; MCIM 1980; *Recreations* tennis, cricket, swimming; *Clubs* Wellington; *Style*— Michael Inns, Esq; ✉ Chatswood, Llangar Grove, Crowthorne, Berks RG11 6EA (☎ 01344 776287)

INSALL, Donald William; CBE (1995, OBE 1981); s of William R Insall (d 1966), of Bristol, and Phyllis Irene, *née* Hill (d 1987); *b* 7 Feb 1926; *Educ* Univ of Bristol, Royal Acad Sch of Architecture; *m* 13 June 1964, Libby, da of Malcolm H Moss, of Nanpantan, Loughborough, Leics; 2 s (Robert b 1965, Christopher b 1968), 1 da (Hilary b 1972); *Career* WWII Coldstream Gds (Regtl HQ Staff); dir (princ since 1958) Donald W Insall & Assocs Ltd (architects and planning conslts specialising in architectural conservation and new bldg in sensitive sites); conservation conslts to City of Chester 1970–87, and to Admin Tstees for reconstruction of Chevening House 1970–75, responsible to PSA for restoration of ceiling of Lords' Chamber in The Palace of Westminster 1981–84, appointed co-ordinating architects for post-fire restoration at Windsor Castle (phases 3 and 4) 1993–; awards incl: Europa Nostra medals, Euro Architectural Heritage awards, Queen's Jubilee medal 1977; visiting lectr RCA 1964–69, adjunct prof Univ of Syracuse 1971–81, visiting prof Coll of Europe Bruges and Catholic Univ of Leuven Belgium 1980–; conslt architect and Freeman Worshipful Co of Goldsmiths; academician Royal West of England Acad; memb: UK Cncl Int Cncl of Monuments and Sites 1968–, Cncl RSA 1976–78, Historic Bldgs Cncl for England 1971–83, Ancient Monuments Bd for England 1980–83, Fabric Advsy Ctee Southwark Cathedral 1992–, Architectural Advsy Ctee Westminster Abbey 1993; fndr cmmr Historic Bldgs and Monuments Cmmn for England (English Heritage) 1984–89; fndn memb: Advsy Ctee Getty Grants Programme 1988–92, Architectural Advsy Ctee World Monuments Fund UK 1996–; life memb: SPAB (and memb Cncl), Georgian Gp, Victorian Soc, Royal Photographic Soc, Nat Tst; hon memb Bath Preservation Tst, vice chm Conf on Trg in Architectural Conservation

1989– (hon sec 1959–89), vice pres Bldg Crafts and Conservation Tst 1993–; pres Assoc for Studies in the Conservation of Historic Buildings 1995 (currently memb); FSA, FRSA 1948, FRIBA 1948, FRTPI 1973, RWA 1985; *Books* The Care of Old Buildings Today (1973), Chester: A Study in Conservation (1968), Conservation in Action (1982), Historic Buildings: Action to Maintain the Expertise for their Care & Repair (1974); contrib Encyclopaedia Britannica, contrib Buildings - Who Cares? (Arts Council Film for ITV); *Recreations* visiting, photographing, enjoying places, appreciating craftsmanship; *Clubs* Athenaeum; *Style*— Donald Insall, Esq, CBE, FSA; ✉ 73 Kew Green, Richmond, Surrey TW9 3AH; Donald W Insall & Associates Ltd, 19 West Eaton Place, Eaton Square London SW1X 8LT (☎ 0171 245 9888, fax 0171 235 4370)

INSCH, Brian Douglas; s of James Ferguson Insch, CBE (d 1994), of Barnt Green, nr Birmingham, and Jean, *née* Cunningham; *b* 2 Feb 1942; *Educ* Fettes Coll, Aston Univ; *m* 1 June 1968, Susan Jane, da of Kenneth Hal Harper, of East Bridgford, Notts; 2 s (Mark Harper b 1975, Andrew Ferguson b 1977); *Career* GKN plc: joined 1963, commercial dir Salisbury Transmission (subsid co) 1972 (md 1974), sales dir Hardy Spicer Ltd (subsid co) 1973, gen mangr Commercial 1979, corporate mgmnt dir 1982, dir 1986–, human resources dir 1987–; FCIS 1966; *Recreations* golf; *Style*— Brian Insch, Esq; ✉ GKN plc, PO Box 55, Redditch, Worcs B98 0TL (☎ 01527 517715, fax 01527 517763, telex 3366321)

INSKIP, Henry Thurston; JP; s of Geoffrey May Inskip, JP (d 1959), and Lily Ethel, *née* Thurston (d 1979); *b* 2 April 1934; *Educ* Bedford Sch; *m* 9 May 1959, Margaret Vera, da of William James Topping, of Saffron Walden, Essex; 1 s (Charles b 1962), 2 da (Elizabeth b 1963, Amanda b 1963); *Career* chartered surveyor; sr ptnr E H C Inskip & Son architects and surveyors (founded by gf in 1900) 1959–94; FRICS; *Recreations* history, photography, genealogy; *Style*— Henry Inskip, Esq, JP; ✉ 8 Rothsay Gardens, Bedford MK40 3QB (☎ 01234 266784)

INSKIP, Hon Piers James Hampden; s and h of 2 Viscount Caldecote, KBE, DSC, *qv*; *b* 20 May 1947; *Educ* Eton, Magdalene Coll Cambridge; *m* 1, 1970 (m dis 1981), Susan Bridget, da of late W P Mellen, of Hill Farm, Gt Sampford, Essex; m 2, 1984, Kristine Elizabeth, da of Harvey Holbrooke-Jackson, of 12 Abbots Close, Ramsey, Cambs; 1 s (Thomas James b 22 March 1985); *Career* associate dir Carlton Communications; *Recreations* golf, tennis; *Style*— The Hon Piers Inskip

INSOLE, Douglas John; CBE (1979); s of John Herbert Insole (d 1975), and Margaret Rose, *née* Moore (d 1988); *b* 18 April 1926; *Educ* Sir George Monoux GS, St Catharine's Coll Cambridge (MA); *m* 18 Sept 1948, Barbara Hazel (d 1982), da of James Ridgway (d 1981); 3 da (Susan Carole b 1950 d 1979, Anne Barbara b 1953, Gwenda Elizabeth b 1958); *Career* Special Communications Unit Royal Signals 1944–46; capt: Univ of Cambridge CC 1949, Essex CCC 1950–60, England (9 appearances), vice capt S African tour 1956; chm England Selectors 1964–68, mangr England tour to Australia 1978–79 and 1982–83; chm: Essex CCC 1973–93, TCCB 1975–78; tstee MCC 1988–94; JP Chingford Bench 1962–74; Town & City Properties 1970–75, Fosroc Int 1975–85, Trollope & Colls Ltd 1975–93, memb FA Cncl; Freeman City of London; *Recreations* cricket, soccer, jazz; *Clubs* MCC, Essex CCC, East India & Sports; *Style*— Douglas Insole, Esq, CBE; ✉ 8 Hadleigh Court, Crescent Rd, Chingford, London E4 6AX (☎ 0181 529 6546)

INSTONE, Peter Duncan; s of Geoffrey Charles Instone, of Plaistow, W Sussex, and Kathleen Marjorie, *née* Hawkeswood (d 1960); *b* 31 Oct 1942; *Educ* Uppingham; *m* 6 May 1966, Anne Mary Instone, JP, da of Maurice Dennis Pannell, of Hove, East Sussex; 1 da (Amanda b 1966), 1 s (Dominic b 1969); *Career* slr; ptnr Masons; sec St Bride's Fleet St Worldwide Media Tst, tstee St Bride's Restoration Fund Tst, dep chm Bd of Govrs St Bride's Fndn; memb Law Soc; *Recreations* travel, gardening, visiting battlefields; *Clubs* Army and Navy, Athenaeum; *Style*— Peter Instone, Esq; ✉ Little Coopers, Hermongers, Rudgwick, West Sussex RH12 3AL; Masons, 30 Aylesbury St, London EC1R 0ER (☎ 0171 490 4000, fax 0171 490 2545, telex 8811117)

INVERARITY, James Alexander (Sandy); OBE; s of William Inverarity (d 1978), and Alexina, *née* Davidson (d 1978); *b* 17 Sept 1935; *Educ* Loretto; *m* 8 March 1960, Jean Stewart, da of James Rae Gellatly (d 1979); 1 s (Graeme b 1964), 2 da (Catherine b 1960, Alison b 1962); *Career* farmer, CA and co dir; pres NFU of Scot 1970–71; memb: Eggs Authy 1971–74, Farm Animal Welfare Cncl 1978–88, Panel of Agric Arbiters 1983–, Governing Body Scot Crop Res Inst 1984– (chm 1989–90), Dairy Produce Quota Tbnl for Scot 1984–85; dir: Scottish Agricultural Securities Corporation plc 1983– (chm 1987–), United Oilseeds Producers Ltd 1985– (chm 1987–); chm Scottish Agric Coll 1990– (dir 1990–); FRAgS, FInstD, FRSA; *Recreations* shooting, curling; *Clubs* Farmers', Royal Scottish Automobile; *Style*— Sandy Inverarity, Esq, OBE; ✉ Cransley Liff, by Dundee DD2 5NP (☎ 01382 580327)

INVERFORTH, 4 Baron (UK 1919); Andrew Peter Weir; only s of 3 Baron Inverforth (d 1982), and Jill Elizabeth Inverforth, *née* Thornycroft; *b* 16 Nov 1966; *Style*— The Rt Hon the Lord Inverforth; ✉ House of Lords, London SW1A 0PW

INVERURIE, Lord; James William Falconer Keith; Master of Kintore; s and h of 13 Earl of Kintore, *qv*; *b* 15 April 1976; *Educ* Gordonstoun; *Style*— Lord Inverurie

INVEST, Clive Frederick; s of Frederick Arthur Invest (d 1987), of Toddington, Beds, and Daphne Mary, *née* Bice; *b* 6 Oct 1940; *Educ* Southgate County GS, Royal Dental Hosp London (BDS, LDS RCS), DGDP (UK) 1993; *m* 19 March 1966, Kirsten Elisabeth, da of Alfin Isaksen (d 1986), of Oslo; 2 s (James Clive Frederick b 27 Feb 1972, Robin Julian b 21 March 1975); *Career* pilot offr RAF 1963, qualified as dental surgn 1965, Flt Lt RAF Dental Branch 1965–70; in private practice: Geelong Aust 1970–71, Chichester Sussex 1971–74, Harley St London 1974–; teacher and clinical asst Guy's 1978–83; memb: BDA, Br Soc of Restorative Dentistry, Br Endodontic Soc; former memb Cncl Endo Soc; *Books* contrib one chapter in General Dental Practitioner's Handbook; *Recreations* skiing, waterskiing, swimming, photography, art, reading; *Clubs* Royal Air Force; *Style*— Clive Invest, Esq; ✉ 21 Hill Road, Haslemere, Surrey GU27 2JN (☎ 01428 653457); 90 Harley St, London W1N 1AF (☎ 0171 935 5400, fax 0171 935 4185)

INWOOD, Ven Richard Neil; s of Cyril Edward Inwood, of Westbury, Wilts, and Frances Sylvia, *née* Burbridge; *b* 4 March 1946; *Educ* Burton-on-Trent GS, UC Oxford (MA, BSc Chemistry), Univ of Nottingham (BA Theol), St John's Coll Nottingham (Dip in Pastoral Studies); *m* 27 Dec 1969, Elizabeth Joan, da of Robert Abram; 3 da (Hilary Rachel b 11 Aug 1976, Ruth Elizabeth b 1 Jan 1978, Alison Mary b 9 Nov 1980); *Career* teacher Mvara Secdy Sch Uganda 1969, R&D chemist ICI Dyestuffs Div 1970–71, trg for Anglican miny St John's Coll Nottingham 1971–74, asst curate Christ Church Fulwood Sheffield 1974–78, dir of pastoring All Souls Langham Place London 1978–81, vicar St Luke's Bath 1981–89, hon chaplain Dorothy House Fndn Bath 1984–89, rector Yeovil with Kingston Pitney 1989–95, prebendary Wells Cathedral 1990–95, church cmmr 1991–95, archdeacon of Halifax 1995–; tstee: Simeon's Tstees, Hyndman Tst; *Books* Biblical Perspectives on Counselling (1980), The Church (contrib, 1987); *Recreations* fell walking, music, family, essential gardening, films; *Style*— The Ven the Archdeacon of Halifax; ✉ 2 Vicarage Gardens, Rastrick, Brighouse, W Yorks HD6 3HD (☎ 01484 714553, fax 01484 711897)

ION, Dr Susan Elizabeth (Sue); da of Lawrence James Burrows, of Longton, Preston, and Doris, *née* Cherry; *b* 3 Feb 1955; *Educ* Penwortham Girls' GS, Imperial Coll London (BSc, PhD, Matthey Prize); *m* 7 July 1980, John Albert Ion; *Career* dir of research and technology devpt BNFL 1992– (head of Research & Devpt Fuel Div 1990–92); non-exec dir: Insys Ltd 1992–95, Viridian Bioprocessing Ltd 1993–95, Westlakes Trading Ltd 1993–; memb Cncl PPARC 1994–; winner Hinton Medal for outstanding contrib to nuclear engrg Inst of Nuclear Engrs 1993; govr Kirkham GS Preston; FIM 1993, FINucE 1996, FEng 1996; *Publications* Process Development in Nuclear Fuel Fabrication (1990), Nuclear Fuel Cycle Needs for the Year 2020 (1993), Alternatives for the Treatment and Management of Radwaste (1996); *Recreations* skiing, walking, sailing, playing the violin; *Style*— Dr Sue Ion, FEng; ✉ British Nuclear Fuels, Hilton House, Risley, Warrington (☎ 01925 832152, fax 01925 833576)

IONS, William Westbrook; s of William Westbrook Ions (d 1958), and Ethel Maud, *née* Skillen; *b* 4 Sept 1941; *Educ* Rutherford GS Newcastle upon Tyne; *m* 19 Nov 1964, Patricia Loquain; 1 s (Adrian William b 30 Aug 1971), 1 da (Fiona Rosalind b 19 May 1973); *Career* fin controller: Dunlop Ltd, Rank Organisation, Wilkinson Sword; md Brown Bros (Polystyrene) Ltd; currently chm and md: Lumsden Machine Co Ltd, Lumsden Services Ltd; currently memb Cncl ICAEW; ACA 1964; *Recreations* all forms of sport (as a spectator); *Style*— William Ions, Esq; ✉ Lumsden Services Ltd, Hawks Road, Gateshead NE8 3BT (☎ 0191 478 3838, fax 0191 490 0282)

IPSWICH, Archdeacon of; *see:* Gibson, Ven Terence Allen

IRANI, Dr Mehernoosh Sheriar; s of Sheriar Ardeshir Irani, of London, and Banoo Sheriar; *b* 24 Aug 1949; *Educ* Chiswick County GS for Boys, KCH (BSc, LRCP, MRCS, MB BS, FRCP); *m* 19 Sept 1987, Susan Clare, da of Air Cdre Philip David Mallilieu Moore, of Fowey, Cornwall; 1 da (Jasmine b 1989), 2 s (Matthew b 1991, Beyrom b 1993); *Career* house physician KCH 1974, house surgn Kent and Sussex Hosp Tunbridge Wells 1974, registrar in nephrology and gen med Canterbury Hosp Kent 1977 (sr house offr 1975–76), registrar in rheumatology and gen med Radcliffe Infirmary Oxford 1977–79, hon sr registrar and res fell Dept of Rheumatology and Biochemical Pharmacology KCH 1979–81, sr registrar Westminster and Charing Cross Hosp 1981–85, currently conslt rheumatologist Ashford Hosp Middx; visiting physician: Princess Margaret Hosp Windsor, Royal Masonic Hosp, Lister Hosp; MO Br Olympic team: Los Angeles 1984, Calgary 1988, Seoul 1988, Barcelona 1992; Int Weightlifting Fedn duty Dr Olympic Games Atlanta 1996; MO Br Cwlth games team: Edinburgh 1986, Auckland NZ 1990, Victoria Canada 1994; MO: Br Amateur Weightlifters Assoc 1986–, BCU 1986–, English Badminton Team World Championships Beijing China 1987, Br Dragon Boat Racing Assoc 1988–; sec gen Int Assoc of Olympic Med Offrs 1988–; pres Med Ctee EWF; memb: Med Ctee IWF, Medical Cmmn on Accident Prevention RCS, Br Soc for Rheumatology, BOA; vice chm Ethics Ctee NW Surrey and Royal Masonic Hosp, med advsr Ind Tbnl Service; hon lectr Charing Cross & Westminster Hospital Med Schs (recognised teacher in med Univ of London), lectr in basic sciences Royal Coll of Surgeons; *Books* contrib to Rheumatology and Rehabilitation (1984); *Recreations* family, cricket; *Clubs* Riverside; *Style*— Dr Mehernoosh S Irani; ✉ 20 Devonshire Gardens, Chiswick, London W4 3TN (☎ 0181 994 0119); Dept of Rheumatology, Ashford Hospital, London Rd, Ashford, Middlesex TW15 3AA (☎ 01784 884488, fax 01784 884240)

IRANI, Ronnie; *b* 26 Oct 1971; *Career* professional cricketer; Lancashire CCC 1989–93, debut Essex CCC 1994; England: U19 v Aust 1991, A team v Pakistan 1995, memb squad touring Zimbabwe and New Zealand 1996–97; *Style*— Ronnie Irani, Esq; ✉ c/o Essex CCC, County Ground, New Writtle Street, Chelmsford, Essex CM2 0PG (☎ 01245 252420)

IRBY, Charles Leonard Anthony; s of The Hon Anthony P Irby (d 1986), and Mary, *née* Apponyi (d 1952); *b* 5 June 1945; *Educ* Eton; *m* 23 Sept 1971, Sarah Jane, da of Col David G Sutherland, MC, of London; 1 s (Nicholas Charles Anthony b 10 July 1975), 1 da (Caroline Sarah b 21 May 1977); *Career* dir: Baring Brothers & Co Ltd 1984–95, Baring Brothers International 1995–, ING Baring Group Holdings Ltd 1995–; FCA; *Recreations* travel, photography, skiing; *Clubs* City of London; *Style*— Charles L A Irby, Esq; ✉ 125 Blenheim Crescent, London W11 2EQ (☎ 0171 221 2979); The Old Vicarage, Chieveley, Newbury, Berks, RG20 8UX (☎ 01635 248 117); ING Barings, 60 London Wall, London EC2M 5TQ (☎ 0171 767 1000)

IREDALE, (John) Martin; s of John Leslie Iredale (d 1988), of Woodcote, Reading, and Hilda, *née* Palfry; *b* 10 June 1939; *Educ* Abingdon Sch; *m* 14 Sept 1963, (Margaret) Anne, da of Reginald Walter Jewell (d 1968), of Reading; 3 s (Edward b 1 May 1965, Mathew b 3 Oct 1966, William b 18 May 1976), 1 da (Hannah b 30 March 1973); *Career* CA and licensed insolvency practitioner; ptnr: Cork Gully 1971–, Coopers & Lybrand 1983–; sec Royal Shakespeare Theatre Tst 1970–91, govr Royal Shakespeare Theatre 1981–, memb Hodgson Ctee on Profits from Crime and their Recovery 1981–82, pres Old Abingdonian Club 1982–84, chm Cornhill Club 1985–86; Freeman City of London 1973, Liveryman Worshipful Co of Carmen 1978; FCA 1963, FIPA 1985; *Books* Receivership Manual (with C J Hughes, 1987); *Recreations* waiting on my family; *Clubs* Leander, Cornhill, Reading Abbey Rotary; *Style*— Martin Iredale, Esq; ✉ Holybrook Farm House, Burghfield Bridge, Reading RG30 3RA (☎ 0118 957 5108); Coopers & Lybrand, 9 Greyfriars Road, Reading RG1 1JG (☎ 0118 960 7708, fax 0118 960 7703)

IREDALE, Dr Peter; s of Henry Iredale (d 1965), of Brownhills, Staffordshire, and Annie, *née* Kirby (d 1992); *b* 15 March 1932; *Educ* King Edward VI GS, Univ of Bristol (BSc, PhD); *m* 11 April 1957, Judith Margaret, da of John Herod Marshall (d 1976), of Long Eaton, Nottingham; 1 s (John b 1960), 3 da (Susan b 1962, Helen b 1964, Alison b 1966); *Career* AERE Harwell: res on nuclear instrumentation 1955–69, non-destructive testing 1969–70, computer storage 1970–73, head of Nuclear Instrumentation Gp 1975–77, head of Mktg and Sales Dept 1973–74 and 1977–79, head of Marine Technol Support Unit 1979–81, chm UK Wave Energy Steering Ctee 1979–84, dir of engrg 1981–86, dep dir Harwell 1986–87, dir Harwell Laboratory 1987–90, dir Culham and Harwell Sites 1990–92; chm Oxfordshire Health Authy 1992–; pubns and scientific papers on high energy physics and nuclear instrumentation; supernumary fell Wolfson Coll; Hon DSc Oxford Brookes Univ 1993; FInstP, FIEE; *Recreations* family, music, working with wood, gardening, walking; *Style*— Dr Peter Iredale; ✉ Oxfordshire Health Authority, Old Road, Headington, Oxford OX3 7LG (☎ 01865 227160)

IREDALE, Prof Roger Oliver; s of Fred Iredale (d 1978), of Sussex, and Elsie Florence, *née* Hills (d 1990); *b* 13 Aug 1934; *Educ* Harrow Co GS, Univ of Reading (BA, MA, PhD), Peterhouse Cambridge; *m* 1968, Mavis, da of Charles Frederick Bowtell, of York; 1 s (Simon Crispian b 1974), 1 da (Rachel Samia b 1971); *Career* teacher Hele's Sch Exeter 1959–61, lectr (later sr lectr) Bishop Otter Coll Chichester 1962–70, Br Cncl offr and maitre de conferences Univ of Algiers 1970–72, lectr Chichester Coll of Further Educn 1972–73, Br Cncl offr Madras 1973–75, lectr in educn Univ of Leeds 1975–79, chief educn advsr Overseas Devpt Admin FCO 1983–93 (educn advsr 1979–83), prof of int educn Univ of Manchester 1993–96 (dir Sch of Educn 1994–96, prof emeritus 1996–); memb Cwlth Scholarship Cmmn 1984–93, cmmr Sino-Br Friendship Scholarship Scheme 1986–96; govr: SOAS 1983–95, Queen Elizabeth House Oxford 1986–87, The Cwlth of Learning 1988–93; writer of poems for BBC Radio 3 and in anthologies and jls; hon fell Royal Coll of Preceptors 1995; *Publications* Turning Bronzes (poems, 1974), Out Towards the Dark (poems, 1978); articles in Comparative Education and other jls; *Recreations* sailing, poetry, writing, restoring the discarded; *Style*— Prof Roger Iredale; ✉ 57 Whaley Lane, Whaley Bridge, Derbyshire SK12 7BA (☎ and fax 01663 732400, e-mail Roger.Ireland@man.ac.uk)

IRELAND, Adrian William Velleman; *b* 1 March 1945; *Educ* Stowe; *m* 19 July 1975, (Victoria) Jane, da of Maj Myles Harry Cooper (d 1986), of Bideford, Devon; 2 s (Rupert b 1977, Frederic b 1979); *Career* with Akroyd and Smithers stock jobbers until 1986, dir S G Warburg Securities 1986–93, dir Winterflood Gilts Ltd 1994–; memb London

Stock Exchange 1968; *Recreations* travel, cricket, food; *Clubs* City of London, Boodle's, MCC; *Style*— Adrian Ireland, Esq; ✉ 7 Dalebury Rd, London SW17; Winterflood Gilts Ltd, Walbrook House, 23–29 Walbrook, London EC4N 8LA (☎ 0171 621 0004, fax 0171 626 8133)

IRELAND, John; s of Victor Edwin Ireland (d 1986), of Ipswich, Suffolk, and Mina Mary, *née*, Bugler; *b* 14 July 1942; *Educ* Ipswich Sch, Westminster Hosp Med Sch; *m* 24 Sept 1972, Shahla Monireh, da of General A Samsami; 2 s (Michael b 1973, David b 1978), 1 da (Roya b 1974); *Career* formerly: sr registrar Royal Nat Orthopaedic Hosp, conslt surgn Dept of Orthopaedics King George Hosp Ilford Essex; currently conslt orthopaedic surgn: Knee Surgery Unit Holly House Hosp Buckhurst Hill Essex, Royal Nat Orthopaedic Hosp London; memb Int, Euro and Br Assocs for Surgery of the Knee; FRCS 1971; *Publications* author of scientific papers on knee surgery and arthroscopy; *Recreations* golf, music, wine, gardening; *Clubs* RAC; *Style*— John Ireland, Esq; ✉ 17 Kings Avenue, Woodford Green, Essex IG8 0JD (☎ 0181 505 3211, fax 0181 559 1161); Royal National Orthopaedic Hospital, 45 Bolsover Street, London W1P 8AQ (☎ 0171 383 5656)

IRELAND, Richard Henry; s of George Thomas Ireland (d 1970), of Eltham, and Irene Edith, *née* Lunt (d 1993); *b* 30 April 1946; *m* 30 Sept 1967, Joan Florence, da of William Thomas Smith (d 1958), of Lewisham; 1 s (Robert b 1972), 1 da (Suzanne b 1975); *Career* admitted slr 1978; Slaughter and May 1978; ptnr: Eaton & Burley 1982, Rowe & Maw 1984–94, Ireland & Associates 1994–; exec dir Lawyers In Mind Ltd 1994–; Freeman: City of London, Worshipful Co of Slrs; memb: Law Soc 1978, Int Bar Assoc 1987, IOD 1996; *Recreations* fly fishing, golf, music, reading; *Clubs* The Directors; *Style*— Richard Ireland, Esq; ✉ Lawyers In Mind Ltd, 110 Gloucester Avenue, London NW1 8JA (☎ 0171 483 2155, fax 0171 483 2177)

IRELAND, Sheriff Ronald David; QC (Scot 1964); s of William Alexander Ireland (d 1969), and Agnes Victoria Brown (d 1958); *b* 13 March 1925; *Educ* Watson's Coll Edinburgh, Balliol Coll Oxford (MA), Univ of Edinburgh (LLB); *Career* advocate of the Scottish Bar 1952, prof of Scots law Univ of Aberdeen 1958–71 (dean of the Faculty of Law 1964–67); Sheriff of Lothian and Borders 1972–88, dir Scottish Cts Admin 1975–78, Sheriff Princ of Grampian Highland and Islands 1988–93; Hon LLD Aberdeen 1994; *Clubs* New (Edinburgh), Royal Northern and Univ (Aberdeen), Highland (Inverness); *Style*— Sheriff Ronald Ireland, QC; ✉ 6a Greenhill Gardens, Edinburgh

IRETON, Barrie Rowland; s of Philip Thomas Ireton, and Marjorie Ireton; *b* 15 Jan 1944; *Educ* Trinity Coll Cambridge (MA), LSE (MSc); *m* 1965, June; 2 s (Paul b 1969 (decd), Stephen b 1976), 1 da (Helen b 1971); *Career* economic statistician to Zambian Govt Office of National Devpt and Planning 1965–69, economist Industrial Development Corporation Zambia 1968–69, LSE 1969–70, devpt sec Office of the President of The Gambia 1970–73; ODA: econ advsr on British Dependencies 1973–74, sr econ advsr Africa and ME aid progs 1974–77, sr econ advsr Asia, Latin America, Caribbean and Pacific aid progs 1977–80, head Aid Policy Economists Gp 1980–84, head Aid Policy Dept 1984–88, princ fin offr and under sec Aid Policy and Fin Div 1988–93, under sec Africa Div 1993–96, dir gen programmes 1996–; *Style*— Barrie Ireton, Esq; ✉ ODA, 94 Victoria Street, London SW1E 5JL (☎ 0171 917 0480)

IRISH, John George Augustus; CBE (1989); s of Albert Edwin Irish (d 1986), of Hinton St George, Somerset, and Rosa Anna Elizabeth, *née* Norris (d 1963); *b* 1 Aug 1931; *Educ* Crewkerne Sch, LSE (BSc); *m* 1, 1953 (m dis 1967), Joan, *née* Hall; 1 da (Nicola b 1962), 1 s (Timothy b 1964); m 2, 1968, Isabel Josephine, o da of Bernhard Berenzweig (d 1965), and Irma Berenzweig (d 1996), of Harrow-on-the-Hill, Middx; 4 s (Jonathan b 1970, Nicholas b 1972, Hugo b 1979, Charles b 1981); *Career* cmmnd Nat Serv 1952–54; exec Marks and Spencer 1954–65, retail dir David Greig 1965–70; chm: Eight Till Late Ltd 1981–91, Spar (UK) Ltd 1983–93 (md 1981–93), Spar Landmark Ltd 1993–94; chief exec: Spar Landmark Services 1985–94, Landmark Cash and Carry Ltd 1986–91; dir IGD (Amsterdam based trading co of International Spar) 1983–94; non-exec dir NAAFI 1989–; chm: OSTA Ltd 1994–, Numark 1994–; non-exec dir Wessex Quality Meat Ltd 1996–; dep chm Retail Consortium 1981–91, vice pres British Retail Consortium 1991–; hon pres Spar National Guild 1994– (vice chm 1984–94); formerly: chm Voluntary Group Assoc, memb Cncl Inst of Grocery Distribution, memb NEDC Distributive Trades, memb Cncl and Fund Raising Ctee Nat Grocers' Benevolent Fund 1983–90; govr Orley Farm Sch Middx 1980–, tstee One Plus One 1986–; Supermarketing Man of the Year 1986, Independent Grocer Gold Award 1987; FIGD 1985, FRSA 1989, fell Inst of Euro Business Suppliers (FIEBS) 1996; *Recreations* history, conservation, education; *Clubs* IOD; *Style*— John Irish, Esq, CBE; ✉ Burford House, Burford, Nr Shepton Mallet, Somerset BA4 4PA (☎ 01749 890608); 50 Iverna Court, London W8 6TS (☎ 0171 937 9544)

IRONS, Jeremy John; s of Paul Dugan Irons (d 1983), and Barbara Anne Brereton Brymer, *née* Sharpe; *b* 19 Sept 1948; *Educ* Sherborne, Bristol Old Vic Theatre Sch; *m* 23 March 1977, Sinead Cusack, *qv*, da of late Cyril Cusack; 2 s (Samuel b 16 Sept 1978, Maximilian b 17 Oct 1985); *Career* actor; joined Bristol Old Vic Theatre Co 1971; *Theatre* incl: A Winter's Tale, What the Butler Saw, Hayfever, Godspell 1971, Wild Oats (RSC) 1975, Simon Gray's Rear Column (Clarence Derwent Award) 1976; RSC 1986–87 incl: A Winter's Tale, The Rover, Richard II; Broadway: The Real Thing (Tony Award Best Actor, Drama League Distinguished Performance Award) 1984; *Television* incl: Brideshead Revisited (TV Times Best Actor Award) 1982; *Films* incl: French Lieutenant's Woman (Variety Club Best Actor Award), Moonlighting 1982, The Captain's Doll (BBC TV film) 1982, The Wild Duck (Aust film of Ibsen play) 1983, Betrayal 1983, Swann in Love 1983, The Mission 1985, Dead Ringers (Best Actor NY Critics Award, Best Actor Canada Genie Award) 1988, Chorus of Disapproval 1988, Danny Champion of the World 1988, Australia 1989, Reversal of Fortune (Golden Globe Best Actor Award, Academy Best Actor Award) 1990, Kafka 1991, Waterland 1992, Damage 1993, M Butterfly 1994, House of the Spirits 1994, voice of Scar in The Lion King 1994, Die Hard with a Vengeance 1995, Stealing Beauty 1995; *Recreations* sailing, riding, skiing; *Style*— Mr Jeremy Irons; ✉ c/o Hutton Management Ltd, 200 Fulham Road, London SW10 9PN (☎ 0171 352 4825, fax 0171 352 8579)

IRONS, Keith Donald; s of Donald Henry Irons (d 1967), of Winchester, Hants, and Muriel, *née* Ridley-Kitt; *b* 16 Nov 1941; *Educ* Peter Symonds Sch Winchester, Eastleigh Coll, Royal Sch of Mines; *m* 8 June 1968, Diana Elizabeth, da of Stanley Frederick George Ransom (d 1992), of Warwick, and Dorothy, *née* Perceval; 2 s (Nicholas Guy b 6 Oct 1970, Rupert Charles b 24 May 1972); *Career* journalist: Hampshire Chronicle 1961–64, Evening Telegraph Coventry 1964–66, Birmingham Post 1966–69; PRO RST Ltd 1969–73, PR mangr RTZ Group 1973–76, dir of public affairs Blue Circle Industries plc 1976–87, public affairs conslt Charter Consolidated plc 1987–88, vice pres Minorco SA 1988–90; chm and ceo: RMR Group Ltd 1990–91, Bankside Consultants Ltd 1991–; Parly candidate (Cons) Newham NW gen election 1983; FIPR 1993 (MIPR 1974); *Recreations* sailing; *Clubs* Little Ship, Sea View Yacht; *Style*— Keith Irons, Esq; ✉ Bankside Consultants Ltd, Suite 306, 45 Curlew Street, Butlers Wharf, London SE1 2ND (☎ 0171 403 5325, fax 0171 407 7819)

IRONS, Norman MacFarlane; CBE (1995), JP (1983), DL (1984); *b* 4 Jan 1941; *Educ* George Heriot's Sch Edinburgh, Borough Road Coll London, Napier Coll Edinburgh (student of the yr, IMechE prize); *m* 16 July 1966, Anne Wyness, *née* Buckley; 1 s (Kenneth b 2 Sept 1968), 1 da (Elizabeth b 26 Dec 1969); *Career* Lord Provost and Lord Lt of the City of Edinburgh 1992–96; ptnr IFP Consulting Engrs; joined SNP 1973, elected to Edinburgh City Cncl (Drumbrae Ward) 1976, subseq contested elections 1977, 1980, 1984, 1988 and 1992; chm Sec of State for Scotland's Advsy Ctee on Health Serv Appts 1994–; memb Cncl Royal Zoological Soc of Scotland; Hon DLitt Napier Univ 1993; Rotary Int Paul Harris fell; Hon FRSC(Ed) 1994; CEng, MIMechE, MCIBSE; *Recreations* sharing life with wife, rugby football (pres Lismore RFC 1989–); *Style*— Norman Irons, Esq, CBE, JP, DL; ✉ 141 Saughton Hall Drive, Edinburgh EH12 5TS

IRONSIDE, Hon Charles Edmund Grenville; s and h of 2 Baron Ironside; *b* 1 July 1956; *m* 17 Aug 1985, Hon Elizabeth Mary Law, eldest da of 2 Baron Coleraine; 1 s (Frederick Thomas Grenville b 22 April 1991), 2 da (Emily Charlotte Olivia b 23 Oct 1988, Alice Octavia Louise b 12 March 1990); *Career* dir Stace Barr Underwriting Agencies at Lloyd's; Liveryman Worshipful Co of Skinners; *Style*— The Hon Charles Ironside; ✉ 46 Mayford Rd, London SW12 8SN

IRONSIDE, 2 Baron (UK 1941); Edmund Oslac Ironside; s of Field Marshal 1 Baron Ironside, GCB, CMG, DSO (d 1959); *b* 21 Sept 1924; *Educ* Tonbridge; *m* 1950, Audrey Marigold, da of late Col the Hon Thomas George Breadalbane Morgan-Grenville, DSO, OBE, MC (3 s of late Lady Kinloss in her own right); 1 s, 1 da; *Heir* s, Hon Charles Ironside; *Career* Lt RN 1943–52; Marconi Co 1952–59, English Electro Leo Computers 1959–64, Cryosystems Ltd 1964–68, International Research and Development Co Ltd 1968–84, NEI plc 1984–89, def conslt Rolls Royce IPG 1989–95; memb: Organising Ctee Br Library 1972–74, Select Ctee European Communities 1974–90; chm Sci Reference Library Advsy Ctee 1975–85; pres: Electric Vehicle Assoc of Great Britain 1975–83, European Electric Road Vehicle Assoc 1980–82 (vice-pres 1978–80), Sea Cadet Corps Chelmsford 1959–88; vice-pres: Inst of Patentees and Inventors 1976–90, Parly and Scientific Ctee 1977–80 and 1983–86 (dep chm 1974–77); treas All Pty Energy Studies Gp 1979–92, hon sec All-Pty Def Study Gp 1992–94 (chm 1994–); memb: Privy Cncl of Ct City Univ 1975–94 (memb Cncl 1986–88), Ct Univ of Essex 1982– (memb Cncl 1984–87); Hon FCGI 1986; memb Ct of Assts Worshipful Co of Skinners (Master 1981–82); *Books* Highroad to Command (1972); *Clubs* Royal Ocean Racing; *Style*— The Rt Hon the Lord Ironside; ✉ Priory House, Old House Lane, Boxted, Colchester Essex CO4 5RB

IRONSIDE, Graham; s of James Mackie Ironside (d 1981), of Aberdeen, Scotland, and Nan, *née* Thomson; *b* 12 Sept 1942; *Educ* Robert Gordon's Coll Aberdeen; *m* 25 July 1963, Sheena Jane Simpson, da of Catherine Simpson, of Balmedie, Aberdeenshire; 1 da (Gillian); *Career* head of regnl progs Yorkshire TV 1982–92 (news ed 1971, ed Calendar 1974), dir of ops and devpt Yorkshire Programmes plc 1992–95, TV conslt 1995–; *Recreations* golf, gardening, grandsons; *Style*— Graham Ironside; ✉ Television Programme Services, 90 Leeds Road, Bramhope, Leeds, West Yorks (☎ 0113 281 7410, fax 0113 281 7410)

IRONSIDE WOOD, Timothy Swainston; s of Lt-Col F D I Wood, RA (d 1986), and Olga Madeleine, *née* Mills-Browne; *Educ* Wellington, Univ of Manchester (BA); *m* 28 May 1978, Jane Elizabeth Ursula, da of Ian Alexander Ross Peebles (d 1980); 2 s (Robert b 1980, Nicholas b 1982); *Career* theatre and TV actor 1970–72; BBC TV: prodr and dir music and arts 1976–79, assoc prodr drama 1978–82, prodr plays and films 1983–; prodns incl works by: Edward Bond, David Hare, Graham Reid, Christopher Hampton, Barry Hines; series incl: Ties of Blood 1985, The Ginger Tree 1989; memb BAFTA; *Recreations* cricket, snooker, fishing; *Style*— Timothy Ironside Wood, Esq; ✉ BBC Films, Television Centre, Wood Lane, London W12 7RJ (☎ 0181 576 1275, fax 0181 576 4767)

IRVIN, Albert Henry Thomas; s of Albert Henry Jesse Irvin (d 1947), of London, and Nina Lucy, *née* Jackson (d 1944); *b* 21 Aug 1922; *Educ* Holloway Co Sch, Northampton Sch of Art, Goldsmiths' Coll Sch of Art London (NDD); *m* 1947, Beatrice Olive, da of John Wagner Nicolson; 2 da (Priscilla Jane b 24 July 1949, Celia Ann b 26 Feb 1959); *Career* artist; princ lectr in painting Goldsmiths' Coll Sch of Art London 1962–83; memb London Gp 1965–; *Solo Exhibitions* incl: 57 Gallery Edinburgh 1960, New Art Centre London 1963, 1965, 1971 and 1973, Galerie Skulima Berlin 1972 and 1978, Städtische Kunstsammlungen Ludwigshafen 1974, Galerie Lüpke Frankfurt 1972, 1976, 1992 and 1995, Berlin Opera House 1975, Aberdeen Art Gallery 1976, Acme Gallery London 1980, Gimpel Fils Gallery London 1982, 1984, 1986, 1990, 1992, 1994 and 1996, Aberdeen Art Gallery 1983, Ikon Gallery Birmingham 1983, Coventry Gallery Sydney 1985, Kilkenny Castle 1985, Hendriks Gallery Dublin 1986, Campo Gallery Antwerp 1987, 1989 and 1993, Talbot Rice Gallery Edinburgh 1989, Gimpel and Weitzenhoffer New York 1988, Serpentine Gallery London 1990, Spacex Gallery Exeter 1990, Gallery Monochrome Brussels 1990, Welsh Arts Cncl 1990, Playhouse Gallery Harlow 1991, Lancaster Univ Gallery 1991, Galeria Punto Valencia 1992, Chapter Gallery Cardiff 1994, Galerie Wassermann Munich 1994, RHA Gallery Dublin 1995, Oriel Theatr Clwyd 1996; *Group Exhibitions* incl: John Moores Liverpool 1961, 1980, 1982 (prize winner), 1987, 1989, 1991 and 1995, London Group (regularly), British Painting 74 (Hayward Gallery) 1974, British Art Show tour 1979, ROSC 84 Dublin 1984, Home and Abroad (Serpentine Gallery) 1985, Int Print Biennale Bradford (prize winner) 1986, Royal Acad Summer Exhibition 1987– (prize winner 1987 and 1989), Hoyland Beattie Irvin (Sunderland) 1988, Great British Art Show (Glasgow) 1990, Goldsmiths' Centenary Exhibition 1991, Courtauld Inst Loan Collection 1991–93, Design for Diversions Dance Co 1992, Here and Now (Serpentine Gallery) 1994; *Work in collections* of: Tate Gallery, Arts Cncl of GB, Br Cncl, private and public collections in Britain and abroad; *Commissions* incl painting for Maternity Wing Homerton Hosp Hackney 1987, painting for Chelsea and Westminster Hosp 1995; *Awards* Arts Cncl Award (for visit to USA 1968, Major Award 1975, Purchase Award 1980), Gulbenkian Print Award 1983, Giles Bequest Prize from V & A Museum and Br Museum at Int Print Biennale Bradford 1986; *Recreations* music, reading, football; *Clubs* Chelsea Arts; *Style*— Albert Irvin, Esq; ✉ 19 Gorst Rd, London SW11 6JB (☎ 0171 228 2929); 71 Stepney Green, London E1 3LE; c/o Gimpel Fils, 30 Davies St, London W1Y 1LG (☎ 0171 493 2488, fax 0171 629 5732)

IRVIN, Thomas Thoburn; s of Thomas Thoburn Irvin (d 1969), of Aberdeen, Scotland, and Catherine, *née* Argo (d 1985); *b* 14 Sept 1940; *Educ* Aberdeen GS, Univ of Aberdeen (MB ChB, PhD, ChM); *m* 7 Aug 1965, Joan Marr, da of James Reid (d 1980), of Aberdeen, Scotland; 2 s (Thomas b 1970, Simon b 1974), 1 da (Rachel b 1968); *Career* lectr in surgery Univ of Leeds 1970–73 and 1974, res surgn Univ of California San Francisco 1973–74, reader in surgery Univ of Sheffield (sr lectr in surgery 1974–78), conslt surgn Royal Devon and Exeter Hosp 1978–; memb: Br Soc of Gastroenterology, Int Coll of Surgns; chm med staff Exeter Health Authy; memb Assoc of Surgns GB 1974; FRCSEd 1968; *Books* Wound Healing! Principles and Practice (1981); *Recreations* music, squash; *Style*— Thomas Irvin, Esq; ✉ Royal Devon and Exeter Hospital, Barrack Road, Exeter, Devon EX2 5DW (☎ 01392 411611)

IRVINE, Brian Alexander; s of William Irvine, of Airdrie, and Isobel, *née* Garden; *b* 24 May 1965; *Educ* Airdrie Acad, Glasgow Tech Coll; *m* 27 May 1988, Donna Frances, da of Donald Rennie Main; 2 da (Hannah Danielle b 25 Sept 1990, Christina Frances b 12 Sept 1994); *Career* professional footballer; Falkirk 1984–85 (debut v Morton 1984, 44 appearances), Aberdeen 1985– (over 350 appearances); Scotland: 9 full caps (first full cap v Romania 1990), 2 semi-professional caps 1985; Scottish Cup winners' medal 1990 v Celtic (scored winning penalty in penalty decider), Skol Cup winners' medal 1990 v Rangers (losers' medal 1988 and 1989); Clydesdale Bank 1981–84; *Recreations* committed Christian; *Style*— Brian Irvine, Esq; ✉ Aberdeen Football Club, Pittodrie Stadium, Aberdeen AB2 1QH (☎ 01224 632328)

IRVINE, Sir Donald Hamilton; kt (1994), CBE (1987, OBE 1979); s of late Dr Andrew Bell Hamilton Irvine, and Dorothy Mary, *née* Buckley; *b* 2 June 1935; *Educ* King Edward VI GS Morpeth, Med Sch Univ of Newcastle upon Tyne (MB BS, MD); *m* 1, 16 July 1960 (m dis 1985), Margaret Mary, da of late Francis McGuckin of Ponteland, Northumberland; 2 s (Alastair b 1962, Angus b 1968), 1 da (Amanda b 1966); m 2, 28 June 1986, Sally, da of Stanley Arthur Day, of Bellingen, NSW; *Career* princ GP Lintonville Med Gp Northumberland 1960–95, regnl advsr GP Regnl Postgrad Inst for Med and Dentistry Univ of Newcastle upon Tyne 1973–95; pres GMC 1995– (memb 1979–); RCGP: memb Cncl 1968–95, hon sec 1972–78, chm of Cncl 1982–85; memb: Jt Ctee on Postgrad Trg for GP 1976–91 (chm 1988–91), UK Central Cncl for Nursing Midwifery and Health Visiting 1983–93; chm Bd of Govrs MSD Fndn 1983–89, memb The Audit Cmmn 1990–95; fell: BMA, RSM; FRCGP 1972 (MRCGP 1965); *Books* The Future General Practitioner - Learning and Teaching (jtly, 1972), Managing for Quality in General Practice (1990), Making Sense of Audit (1991), The Practice of Quality (1996); *Recreations* gardening, walking, bird watching, theatre; *Style*— Sir Donald Irvine, CBE; ✉ Mole End, Fairmoor, Morpeth, Northumberland NE61 3JL (☎ 01670 517546, fax 01670 510046); General Medical Council, 178–202 Great Portland Street, London W1N 6JE (☎ 0171 580 7642, fax 0171 637 7278)

IRVINE, Edmund (Eddie); s of Edmund Irvine, of Conlig, N Ireland, and Kathleen, *née* McGowan; *b* 10 Nov 1965; *Educ* Regent House GS; *Career* motor racing driver; racing debut Irish Formula Ford 1600 Series 1983; achievements incl: RAC Championship winner 1987, winner ESSO Championship 1987, Formula Ford Festival champion 1987, Br Formula Three Championship winner 1988, third Int Formula 3000 Championship 1990, second Japanese Formula 3000 Championship 1993, second Le Mans 24 Hour Race 1994; Formula One debut 1993, driving for Sasol Jordan team 1993–96, with Ferrari 1996–; Formula One career: 33 races, third Australian Grand Prix 1996; *Recreations* golf, cars; *Style*— Eddie Irvine, Esq; ✉ c/o Ferrari Grand Prix Racing

IRVINE, His Hon James Eccles Malise; yr s of Brig-Gen Alfred Ernest Irvine, CB, CMG, DSO, late DLI (d 1962), of Wotton-under-Edge, Glos, and Katharine Helen (d 1984), eld da of Lt-Gen H M C W Graham, CMG, late RMLI; *b* 10 July 1925; *Educ* Stowe (scholar), Merton Coll Oxford (MA, Postmaster); *m* 24 July 1954, Anne, eld da of Col Geoffrey Egerton-Warburton, DSO, TD, JP, DL (d 1961; ggs of Rev Rowland Egerton-Warburton, bro of 8 and 9 Bts Grey-Egerton), of Grafton Hall, Malpas, Cheshire, and Hon Georgiana Mary Dormer, MBE (d 1955), eld da of 14 Baron Dormer; 1 s (David Peter Gerard b 1963), 1 da (Susan Caroline Jane b 1961); *Career* WWII served Grenadier Gds 1943–46 (France and Germany Star, Hon Capt 1946); called to the Bar Inner Temple 1949 (Poland Prize in Criminal Law), prosecuting counsel for Inland Revenue on Oxford circuit 1965–71, dep chm Glos QS 1967–71, circuit judge (Midland and Oxford Circuit) 1972–96; Lay Judge of Ct of Arches for Province of Canterbury and of Chancery Ct of York for Province of York 1981–; *Books* Parties and Pleasures - The Diaries of Helen Graham 1823–26 (1954); *Style*— His Hon James Irvine; ✉ School House, Caulcott, Bicester OX6 3NE (☎ 01869 343267)

IRVINE, John Ferguson; CB (1983); s of Joseph Ferguson Irvine (d 1980), of Scotland, and Helen Dick, *née* Gardner (d 1985); *b* 13 Nov 1920; *Educ* Ardrossan Acad, Univ of Glasgow (MA); *m* 1, 1945, Doris, da of Thomas Partidge (d 1952), of Birmingham; 1 s (Graham b 1946), 1 da (Gwyneth b 1949); m 2, 1980, Christine Margot, da of Thomas Tudor, of Staffs; 2 s (Thomas b 1982, William b 1983), and 2 step s (Richard b 1970, John b 1977); *Career* Flt Lt flying boat capt Atlantic, North Sea and Indian Ocean; administrative civil servant: Scottish Office 1946, N Ireland Civil Serv 1948, asst sec 1959, under sec 1971, permanent sec 1976, ret 1983 as permanent sec Dept of Environment for N Ireland; seconded chief exec Ulster Transport Authy and N Ireland Transport Hldg Co 1976–78; chief exec Indust Therapy Organisation (Ulster) Ltd 1984–94, conslt in public admin 1994–; *Recreations* distance running, soccer, Mallorca, yoga, swimming; *Style*— John F Irvine, Esq, CB; ✉ Consultant in Public Administration, 7 Bullseye Park, Downpatrick, Co Down BT30 6RX (☎ 01396 614272, fax 01396 614272)

IRVINE, Kate; *see:* Taylor, Bernard Irvin

IRVINE, Prof (John) Maxwell; s of John MacDonald Irvine (d 1977), of Edinburgh, and Joan Paterson, *née* Adamson (d 1982); *b* 28 Feb 1939; *Educ* George Heriot's Sch, Univ of Edinburgh (BSc), Univ of Michigan (MSc), Univ of Manchester (PhD); *m* 14 Sept 1962, Grace Irvine, da of Edward Ritchie, of Edinburgh; 1 s (Ritchie b 26 April 1971); *Career* res assoc Cornell Univ 1966–68, head Nuclear Theory Gp SERC Daresbury Laboratory 1974–76; Univ of Manchester: asst lectr 1964–66, lectr 1968–73, sr lectr 1973–76, reader 1976–82, prof 1983–91, dean of sci 1989–91; princ and vice chllr: Univ of Aberdeen 1991–96, Univ of Birmingham 1996–; vice pres Inst of Physics 1983–87 (memb Cncl 1981–87 and 1988–92); chm: SERC Nuclear Structure Ctee 1984–88, Ctee of Scottish Univ Principals 1994–96, Cncl Assoc of Cwlth Univs 1994–95; memb: Cncl EPS 1989–92, SCDI 1992–96, Scottish Economic Cncl 1993–96, Scottish Ctee Br Cncl 1994–96, Scottish Forum BT 1994–96; dir: Grampian Enterprise Ltd 1992–96, Rowett Res Inst 1992–96, HEQC Ltd 1994–; Hon DSc William and Mary Coll, Hon DEd Robert Gorn Univ 1995; CIMgt 1995; FInstP 1971, FRAS 1986, Hon FRCSEd 1995, FRSA 1993, FRSE 1993; *Books* Basis of Modern Physics (1967), Nuclear Structure Theory (1972), Heavy Nuclei, Super Heavy Nuclei and Neutron Stars (1975), Neutron Stars (1978); *Recreations* tennis, hill walking; *Clubs* Athenaeum, Caledonian, Royal Northern and University (Aberdeen); *Style*— Prof Maxwell Irvine, FRSE; ✉ Meadwocroft, Edgbaston Park Road, Birmingham B15 2RS University of Birmingham, Edgbaston, Birmingham B15 2TT (☎ 0121 414 4535, fax 0121 414 4534)

IRVINE, Michael Fraser; s of Rt Hon Sir Arthur James Irvine, QC, MP (d 1978), of London, and Eleanor, *née* Morris; *b* 21 Oct 1939; *Educ* Rugby, Oriel Coll Oxford (BA); *Career* called to the Bar Inner Temple 1964; Parly candidate (C) Bishop Auckland 1979, MP (C) Ipswich 1987–92, PPS to the Attorney Gen 1990–92; *Recreations* hill walking in Scotland; *Style*— Michael Irvine, Esq; ✉ 1 Crown Office Row, Temple, London EC4Y 7HH (☎ 0171 583 9292, telex 8953152, fax 0171 353 9292)

IRVINE OF LAIRG, Baron (Life Peer UK 1987), of Lairg, District of Sutherland; Alexander Andrew Mackay Irvine; QC (1978); s of Alexander Irvine and Margaret Christina, da of late Alexander Macmillan; *b* 23 June 1940; *Educ* Inverness Royal Acad, Hutchesons' Boys' GS Glasgow, Univ of Glasgow (MA, LLB), Christ's Coll Cambridge (scholar, BA, LLB); *m* 1974, Alison Mary, yst da of Dr James Shaw McNair, MD, and Agnes McNair, MA; 2 s (Hon David b 1974, Hon Alastair b 1976); *Career* lectr LSE 1965–69; called to the Bar Inner Temple 1967, bencher 1985; head of chambers 11 King's Bench Walk 1981–, recorder 1985–88, dep judge High Ct 1987–; shadow Lord Chllr 1992–; hon fell Christ's Coll Cambridge 1996–; *Recreations* collecting paintings, reading, theatre, cinema, travel; *Clubs* Garrick; *Style*— Baron Irvine of Lairg, QC; ✉ 11 King's Bench Walk, Temple, London EC4Y 7EQ (☎ 0171 583 0610, fax 0171 583 9123/3690)

IRVING, Dr Barrie Leslie; s of Herbert Leslie Irving, of Jersey, CI, and Joan Fletcher, *née* Robinson (d 1976); *b* 6 Oct 1942; *Educ* Stowe, Pembroke Coll Cambridge (BA), Graduate Sch of Univ of California at Berkeley (MA), Univ of Cambridge (PhD); *m* 1, 11 July 1964 (m dis 1982), (Pamela) Jane, da of Capt Ronald Leese (ka 1943); 1 s (Dominic Paul b 25 May 1972), 1 da (Samantha Jane b 15 May 1968); m 2 (sep), Susan Margaret, da of Alec John Davey (d 1971); 1 s (Benjamin Alec James b 16 March 1985); *Career* psychologist and criminologist; res staff Inst of Human Devpt Univ at California Berkeley 1965–66, professional staff (later memb Mgmnt Ctee) Tavistock Inst of Human Relations London 1966–79; dir: The Police Fndn 1980–, Forensic Technology Ltd 1995–; vice chm Nat Stepfamily Assoc 1992–96; special assignments incl: conslt to the official slr for Sir Henry Fisher's Inquiry into the Murder of Maxwell Confait 1977, res conslt to the Royal Cmmn on Criminal Procedure 1979, res conslt to the Royal Cmmn on Criminal Justice 1991; *Books* The Psychological Dynamics of Smoking (1968), Tied Cottages in British Agriculture (1975), Police Interrogation (1980), Regulating Custodial Interviews (1988), Police Interrogation (1989), Human Factors in the Quality Control of CID Investigations (1993); *Recreations* tennis, golf, piano; *Clubs* Naval and Military; *Style*— Dr Barrie Irving

IRVING, Dr (John) Bruce; s of Edward James Bruges Irving (d 1976), of Balgownie, Kirkintilloch, and Marjorie Olive, *née* Dumbleton; *b* 19 June 1942; *Educ* Lenzie Acad, Univ of Glasgow (BSc, PhD), Univ of Stirling (MSc); *m* 14 June 1969, Margaret Anne, da of James Elgin McWilliam (d 1976), of Uphall, W Lothian; 2 s (Christopher b 1971, Peter b 1973), 1 da (Anna b 1978); *Career* researcher Nat Engrg Lab E Kilbride 1969–78, info systems mangr (formerly project coordinator) Chloride Tech Ltd Manchester 1978–85, dir info technol Dumfries and Galloway Regnl Cncl 1986–96; Laird of Bonshaw; former pres: Ayrshire Philatelic Soc, Dumfries Philatelic Soc; chm: Dumfries and Galloway Int Family Assoc 1992–94, Data General User Group 1993–96; chm Dumfries and Galloway Family History Soc 1992–95; FIMgt 1988, FSA(Scot) 1989; *Recreations* outdoor pursuits, family history, philately; *Style*— Dr Bruce Irving; ✉ Bonshaw Tower, Kirtlebridge, Lockerbie, Dumfriesshire DG11 3LY (☎ 01461 500256)

IRVING, (Edward) Clifford; CBE (1981); s of William Radcliffe Irving (d 1950), of Peel, IOM, and Mabel Henrietta, *née* Cottier (d 1920); *b* 24 May 1914; *Educ* Douglas HS, Chatham and Oshawa Collegiates Canada; *m* 11 Oct 1941, Norah Constance, da of Harold Page (d 1960), of Luton, Beds; 1 s (Paul Julian b 1949), 1 da (Caroline b 1953); *Career* cmmnd RA 1940, later at War Office responsible for economic matters in ex-Italian colonies under mil govt; dir Irvings Ltd 1950–84; chm: Bank of Wales (IOM) Ltd 1985–87, Etam (IOM) Ltd 1985–, Bank of Scotland (IOM) Ltd 1987–, Refuge (IOM) Ltd 1988–; memb House of Keys 1955–61, 1966–81 and 1984–87 (actg speaker 1971–81); memb IOM Govt Depts: Airports 1955–58, Assessment 1955–56, Social Security 1956, Local Govt 1956–62, Harbours 1985–87, Home Affairs 1985–86, Health 1985–86, Indust Advsy Cncl 1961–62 and 1971–81, Civil Serv Cmmn 1976–81, Indust Dept 1988–94; memb: Exec Cncl IOM Govt 1968–81, Legislative Cncl IOM 1987–95; chm: Exec Cncl 1977–81, IOM Tourist Bd 1971–81, IOM Sports Cncl 1971–81, IOM Harbours Bd 1985–87, IOM Govt TT Race Ctee 1971–81; pres: Douglas Angling Club, IOM Angling Assoc, Manx Parascending Club, Manx Nat Powerboat Club, Wanderers Male Voice Choir, Douglas Branch RNLI, Douglas Bay Yacht Club; *Recreations* powerboating, angling; *Style*— Clifford Irving, Esq, CBE; ✉ Highfield, Belmont Road, Douglas, IOM IM1 4NR (☎ 01624 73652)

IRVING, Dr Henry Charles; s of Dr Gerald Ian Irving, of Leeds, and Sonia Carol, *née* Sinson; *b* 6 Oct 1950; *Educ* Leeds GS, King's Coll and Westminster Med Sch London Univ (MB BS); *m* 8 July 1973, (Alison) Jane, da of Peter Brackup, of Leeds; 2 da (Juliet b 1975, Georgina b 1978); *Career* conslt radiologist and head Ultrasound Dept St James's Univ Hosp Leeds 1979–, sr clinical lectr radiodiagnosis Univ of Leeds 1979–; RCR regional postgrad educn advsr 1996–; pres Br Med Ultrasound Soc 1994–95; memb Editorial Bd: British Jl of Radiology, Radiology Now, Radiography; memb Bd Faculty RCR, memb Examining RCR, FRCR 1978; *Books* chapters in: Ultrasound in Inflammatory Diseases (1983), A Text Book of Radiology, Vol 4, The Alimentary Tract (1988), Practical Ultrasound (1988), Clinical Ultrasound - A Comprehensive Text (1992); *Recreations* golf, tennis; *Clubs* Moor Allerton Golf, Chapel Allerton Lawn Tennis; *Style*— Dr Henry Irving; ✉ Wingfield House, 22 Street Lane, Leeds LS8 2ET (☎ 0113 237 0321, fax 0113 237 0336)

IRVING, Prof Sir Miles Horsfall; kt (1995); s of Frederick William Irving (d 1953), of Southport, Lancs, and Mabel, *née* Horsfall (d 1988); *b* 29 June 1935; *Educ* King George V Sch Southport, Univ of Liverpool (MB ChB, MD, ChM), Univ of Sydney; *m* 13 Nov 1965, Patricia Margaret, da of Dr Richard Alexander Blaiklock, late Capt RAMC, of Alnwick, Northumberland; 2 s (Peter Miles b 1970, Simon Richard b 1974), 2 da (Katherine Susan b 1966, Jane Elizabeth b 1967); *Career* house surgn Broadgreen Hosp Liverpool 1960 (house physician 1959–60), Robert Gee fell in human anatomy Univ of Liverpool Med Sch 1961–62 (anatomy demonstrator 1960–61), registrar in gen surgery Liverpool Royal Infirmary 1963–64 (sr casualty offr 1962–63, sr house offr in orthopaedics 1963), sr house offr in neurosurgery Newcastle Gen Hosp 1965 (sr house offr in plastic surgery 1964–65), Phyllis Anderson surgical res fell Sydney Univ Med Sch 1965–67, registrar in gen surgery Dudley Rd Hosp Birmingham 1967–68, sr registrar in gen surgery N Middx Hosp 1968–69, reader in surgery and asst dir Professorial Surgical Unit Bart's London 1972–74 (sr registrar in gen surgery 1969–71), prof and head Univ Dept of Surgery Hope Hosp Salford 1974–, chm Sch of Surgical Scis Univ of Manchester 1974–92, head Dept of Surgery Manchester Royal Infirmary 1992–95; dir NHS Health Technol Prog 1994–; regnl dir of res and devpt North Western RHA 1992–94, non-exec memb Salford Health Authy 1992–94; hon conslt surgn to the Br Army; numerous guest lecturerships and external examinerships since 1974 in Europe, Scandinavia, Australia, NZ, Canada, USA, Saudi Arabia and the Far East; Royal Coll of Surgeons: former memb Cncl, former chm External Affrs Bd, memb numerous Cncl ctees; Dept of Health: former memb Working Gps on Health Care Workers and HIV Infection and Health Care Workers and Hepatitis Infection, memb Expert Advsy Gp on AIDS, former memb Trauma Centre Evaluation Advsy Gp, chm Standing Gp on Health Technologies 1993–; memb Editorial Bd: Urgentis Chirurgiae Commentaria, Br Jl of Surgery, Current Practice in Surgery; exec memb Editorial Ctee INJURY; advsr to Med Records Mgmnt Devpt Prog Health Servs Mgmnt Unit Univ of Manchester (hon fell 1995), advsr in surgery Cwlth Scholarship Cmmn; past pres: Ileostomy Assoc of GB and I, Int Surgical Gp, Assoc of Surgns of Great Br and Ireland; pres Section of Coloproctology Royal Soc of Med 1997–98, pres elect Assoc of Coloproctology; memb: GMC (and its Overseas and Educn Ctees) 1990–92, Cncl Inst of Accident Surgery; chm Fedn of Surgical Speciality Assocs; Hon DSc Univ of Salford 1996; hon memb Br Orthopaedic Trainees Assoc; hon fell: Br Assoc for Accident and Emergency Med, Faculty of Emergency Med; memb: Liverpool Med Inst, Br Soc of Gastroenterology, Surgical Res Soc, Euro Soc for Surgical Res, Br Columbia Surgical Soc, James IV Assoc of Surgns, Int Surgical Soc, Med Soc of London; FRSM; fell: Assocs of Surgeons of GB and I, Manchester Med Soc (hon fell 1995); *Publications* Gastroenterological Surgery (1983), Intestinal Fistulas (1985), A B C of Colo Rectal Diseases (1993), Minimal Access Surgery (1996); author of over 200 articles in surgical and other med jls; *Recreations* reading the Spectator, mountain climbing, opera; *Style*— Prof Sir Miles Irving; ✉ 18 Albert Road, Heaton, Bolton, Lancs BL1 5HE (☎ 01204 841182); University Department of Surgery, Hope Hospital, Eccles Old Rd, Salford, Greater Manchester M6 8HD (☎ 0161 787 4358, fax 0161 787 7432)

IRVING, (James) Wyllie; TD; s of John Irving, MBE (d 1931), and Jessie Howatson Mitchell Wyllie (d 1925); *b* 21 April 1914; *Educ* Fettes, Univ of Glasgow; *m* 31 March 1937, Henrietta Mary, da of Henry Purcell (d 1940), of Co Dublin; 2 da (Christine b 1946, Pamela b 1948); *Career* Maj Cheshire Regt 1939–45; KOSB (TA) 1948–59; controller SW Scot Civil Def Gp 1960–68; slr; ptnr (and conslt) Primrose and Gordon Dumfries, ret; memb Bd of Mgmnt Dumfries and Galloway Hosps 1965–71 (chm 1968–71); chm: Bd of Mgmnt Dumfries and Galloway and Crichton Royal Hosps 1972–74, Dumfries and Galloway Health Bd 1973–80; sec: County of Dumfries Valuation Appeal Ctee 1956–72, SW Scot Local Employment Ctee 1960–74, Local Bd of Dirs Scot Union & Nat Insur Co 1973–85; dir Dumfries Trading Estate Ltd 1961–89; SSC, Hon Sheriff South Strathclyde Dumfries and Galloway 1963–, Notary Public; *Recreations* reading, gardening; *Style*— J Wyllie Irving, Esq, TD; ✉ The Glebe, Lochrutton, Nr Dumfries DG2 8NH (☎ 01387 73301); Primrose and Gordon, 92 Irish Street, Dumfries (☎ 01387 67316)

IRWIN, Basil William Seymour; MC (1945), TD (1946 2 Clasps), DL (Greater London 1967); s of Maj William James Irwin (d 1960); *b* 27 May 1919; *Educ* Tonbridge; *m* 1949, Eleanor Ruth, da of Edwin Burgess; *Career* Brevet Col, served Europe and ME; TAVR, ADC to HM The Queen 1968–73; former merchant banker, vice chm Ionian Bank Ltd until 1978, dir Archimedes Investment Trust plc; *Clubs* Special Forces; *Style*— Basil Irwin, Esq, MC, TD, DL; ✉ The Thatch, Stansted, Essex (☎ 01279 812207)

IRWIN, Maj-Gen Brian St George; CB (1975); s of Lt-Col Alfred Percy Bulteel Irwin, DSO (d 1976), of Maumfin, Moyard, Co Galway, and Eileen, *née* Holberton (d 1974); *b* 16 Sept 1917; *Educ* Rugby, RMA Woolwich, Trinity Hall Cambridge (MA); *m* 23 Dec 1939, Audrey Lilla (d 1994), da of Lt-Col Hugh Barkley Steen, IMS (d 1951), of Dunboe, Shepperton-on-Thames, Middx; 2 s (Michael St George b 1940, (Brian) Christopher b 1946); *Career* cmmnd 2 Lt RE 1937; WWII served: Western Desert 1941–43 (despatches), Sicily and Italy 1943–44 (despatches), Greece 1944–45; Cyprus 1956–59 (despatches) and 1961–63, dir of mil survey MOD 1965–69, Maj-Gen 1969–74, dir gen Ordnance Survey 1969–77, ret Army 1974; under sec Civil Serv 1974–77; Col Cmdt RE 1977–82; FRICS 1949 (memb Cncl 1969–70 and 1972–76), FRGS 1960 (memb Cncl 1966–70, vice pres 1974–77); *Recreations* golf, fishing, genealogy; *Clubs* Army and Navy; *Style*— Maj-Gen Brian Irwin, CB; ✉ 16 Northerwood House, Swan Green, Lyndhurst, Hampshire SO43 7DT (☎ 01703 283499)

IRWIN, Christopher Conran; s of John Conran Irwin, of Petersfield, Hants, and Helen Hermione, *née* Fletcher; *b* 2 April 1948; *Educ* Bedales Sch, Univ of Sussex; *m* Stephanie Jane, da of Hilary Noble Ball (d 1972); 1 s (John Phineas Hilary b 20 June 1978), 2 da (Bryony b 12 Jan 1972, Tamsin b 25 April 1974); *Career* freelance broadcaster BBC Radio Brighton 1968–69, Fed Tst for Educn and Res 1969–75, sr visiting fell Univ of Sussex 1971–72, Secretariat N Atlantic Assembly Brussels 1973–74, current affrs prodr BBC World Serv 1975–77, sr res assoc IISS 1977–78; various BBC appointments incl: sec of BBC Scot 1978–79, head of radio BBC Scot 1979–82, gen mangr Satellite devpt 1982–84, chief exec Satellite Broadcasting Bd 1984–85; sold concept for Br Satellite Broadcasting to Pearson plc 1985; gen mangr new media devpt Pearson plc 1986–88, controller of resources and admin BBC World Serv 1989–90, chief exec BBC World Service Television Ltd 1990–94, md Guinness Publishing Ltd 1994–, pres Guinness Media Inc, dir Guinness Verlag GmbH, dir Guinness Media SAS; contrib to: International Affairs, Strategic Survey; memb: RTS, Rail Users' Consultative Ctee for W of England; media govr World Economic Forum; *Books* The Security of Western Europe (with Sir Bernard Burrows, 1972), Electing the European Parliament (1973), Towards a Peaceful Europe (1974); *Recreations* gardening, historical topography, timetables; *Style*— Christopher Irwin, Esq; ✉ Bourton House, Bourton, Bishops Cannings, nr Devizes, Wilts SN10 2LQ (☎ 01380 860252, fax 01380 860119)

IRWIN, Prof David George; s of George Archibald Raven Irwin (d 1973), of London, and Doris, *née* Tetlow (d 1988); *b* 24 June 1933; *Educ* Holgate GS Barnsley, Queen's Coll Oxford (MA, open exhibitioner, Laurence Binyon prize), Courtauld Inst of Art Univ of London (PhD); *m* 26 March 1960, Francina Mary, da of Richard Kaikhrusru Sorabji (d 1950), of Oxford; 1 s (Dickon b 1966), 1 da (Saskia b 1963); *Career* Nat Serv 1951–53, Capt RAEC 1952–53; lectr in history of fine art and asst keeper of univ art collections Univ of Glasgow 1959–70, prof of history of art and head of dept Univ of Aberdeen 1970–; memb Editorial Bd British Journal for Eighteenth Century Studies, pres Br Soc for Eighteenth Century Studies; memb Ctee: Aberdeen Art Gallery, Architectural Heritage Soc of Scotland; memb: Art Panel of Scottish Arts Cncl, Cncl of Walpole Soc, Cncl of Europe Exhibition Ctee 1972; FSA 1968, FRSA 1974; *Books* English Neoclassical Art (1966), Paul Klee (1968), Visual Arts, Taste and Criticism (1969), Winckelmann: Writings on Art (1972), Designs and Ornaments of the Empire Style (1974), Scottish Painters: At Home and Abroad 1700 to 1900 (jtly with Francina Irwin, 1975), John Flaxman: Sculptor, Illustrator, Designer (1979), Neoclassicism (1997); *Recreations* travel, gardening; *Style*— Prof David Irwin, FSA; ✉ 43 Don Street, Old Aberdeen, Aberdeen AB24 1UH

IRWIN, Denis; *b* 31 Oct 1965; *Career* professional footballer (defender); clubs: Leeds Utd 1982–86, Oldham Athletic 1986–90, Manchester Utd (transferred for £625,000) 1990–; honours with Manchester Utd: Euro Cup Winners' Cup 1991, League Cup 1992, winners inaugural FA Premier League Championship 1992/93, Charity Shield 1993, winners League and FA Cup double 1994 and 1996 (setting record); over 350 League appearances; Republic of Ireland: over 20 full caps, memb World Cup squad 1994; *Style*— Denis Irwin, Esq; ✉ Manchester United FC, Old Trafford, Manchester M16 0RA (☎ 0161 872 1661)

IRWIN, (Frederick George) Ernest; MBE (1989); s of George Irwin, and Margaret Irwin; *b* 19 Nov 1933; *Educ* Trinity Coll Dublin (BA, BAI), Univ of Iowa State (MSc); *m* 11 Sept 1964, Juliet Faith, da of Antony Alexander Fitzgerald Tatlow; 1 s (George b 14 April 1972), 2 da (Katharine b 19 March 1969, Aisling b 31 May 1966); *Career* area engr DuPont Construction 1958–61; Ove Arup and Ptnrs: design engr London 1961–64, chief engr Ghana 1964–68, regnl assoc 1968–75, dir 1975–96, responsible for engrg design of Int Convention Centre Birmingham, Nat Exhibition Centre extension and land reclamation projects; dir Ove Arup Partnership 1989–96; memb Senate Engrg Cncl; Royal Acad of Engrg visiting prof Univ of Birmingham; hon ed ICE Jl Civil Engineering; tstee Lench's Tst; FICE (Garth Watson medal 1994), FIStructE; *Recreations* golf, drawing; *Clubs* Edgbaston Golf; *Style*— Ernest Irwin, Esq, MBE; ✉ 46 Selly Wick Rd, Selly Park, Birmingham B29 7JA; Ove Arup & Ptnrs, 3 Duchess Place, Edgbaston, Birmingham, B16 8NH (☎ 0121 454 6261, fax 0121 454 8853, telex 339468)

IRWIN, (David) Gwyther Broome; s of Gwyther William Powell (d 1960), and Barbara Ethel, *née* Dallimore; *b* 7 May 1931; *Educ* Bryanston, Central Sch of Art & Design; *m* 10 April 1960, Elizabeth Anne, da of Robert Gowlett; 2 s (Brom Gwyther Giles b 1 Oct 1962, Capel Robert Powell b 10 April 1967), 1 da (Charlotte Alicia Estelle b 26 Dec 1963); *Career* artist; lectr: Bath Acad of Art 1963, Chelsea Sch of Art 1967–69; head of fine art Brighton Poly 1969–84; designed and cut Rectangular Relief for BP House 1965–68, large paintings cmmnd by Glaxo for Stevenage offices 1993; works embrace paper collages, construction, acrylic on canvas and watercolours; Greater London Arts Assoc Award 1978; *Solo Exhibitons* Gallery One 1957, AIA Gallery 1957, ICA 1958, Gimpel Fils (various years 1959–87), New Art Centre 1973, 1975, 1977, Newcastle Poly Gallery 1978, Kettle's Yard Cambridge 1981, John Jones Gallery 1992, The Sixties (Barbican) 1993, Redfern Gallery 1994, major retrospective (Royal Cornish Museum) 1995 and (Royal West of England Academy) 1996; *Group Exhibitions incl* Young Contemporaries 1953, Paris Biennale 1960, Collage (Museum of Modern Art NY) 1961, John Moores Liverpool Exhibitions 1961, 1963, 1978, British Kunst Denmark 1963, XXXII Venice Biennale 1964, Recent British Painting (Tate) 1967, Contemporary British Painting (Albright Knox Art Gallery USA) 1974, Three Decades of Artists (Royal Acad) 1983, Recalling the 50s (Serpentine Gallery) 1985, Print 86 (Barbican) 1986, Summer Show (Royal Acad) 1986–94; *Works in Public Collections incl* Tate, Arts Cncl of GB, DOE, Peggy Guggenheim Venice, Yale; *Recreations* poker, chess, maritime activities; *Clubs* Chelsea Arts; *Style*— Gwyther Irwin, Esq; ✉ winter: 21 Hillbury Rd, London SW17 8JT (☎ 0181 673 7930); summer: 2 The Glyddins, Rock, Wadebridge, Cornwall (☎ 01208 863186)

IRWIN, Ian Sutherland; CBE (1982); s of Andrew Campbell Irwin (d 1967), of Glasgow, and Elizabeth Ritchie, *née* Arnott (d 1994); *b* 20 Feb 1933; *Educ* Whitehill Sr Secdy Sch Glasgow, Univ of Glasgow (BL); *m* 2 May 1959, (Margaret Miller) Maureen, da of John Scoullar Irvine (d 1990), of Edinburgh; 2 s (Graeme Andrew b 1961, Derek John b 1965); *Career* Nat Serv 1 Bn Seaforth Highlanders 1957–59; Hon Col 154 Regt RCT (V) 1986–93; commercial mangr Scottish Omnibuses Ltd 1960–64; Scottish Transport Group: gp accountant 1965–68, gp sec 1969–75, dir and md 1975–86, chm and chief exec 1987–; a non-exec dir Scottish Mortgage & Trust 1986–; hon vice pres Int Union Public Tport, pres Bus and Coach Cncl 1979–80, vice pres Inst of Tport 1984–87; CA, MIPFA, FCIT, CIMgt, FInstD; *Recreations* golf, foreign travel, reading; *Clubs* Caledonian (London), MCC, The Bruntswood Links Golfing Society Ltd; *Style*— Ian Irwin, Esq, CBE; ✉ 10 Moray Place, Edinburgh EH3 6DT (☎ 0131 225 6454); Scottish Transport Group, 57 Castle Street, Edinburgh EH2 3DN (☎ 0131 226 7491)

IRWIN, Lord; James Charles Wood; s and h of 3 Earl of Halifax; *b* 24 Aug 1977; *Educ* Eton; *Style*— Lord Irwin; ✉ Garrowby, York YO4 1QD

IRWIN, Dr Michael Henry Knox; s of William Knox Irwin, FRCS, MD (d 1973), of Watford Heath, Herts, and Edith Isabel Mary, *née* Collins; descendant of John Knox; *b* 5 June 1931; *Educ* Merchant Taylors' Sch, St Bartholomew's Hosp London (MB BS), Columbia Univ NY (MPH); *m* 1, 1958 (m dis 1982), Elizabeth Miriam, *née* Naumann; 3 da (Christina, Pamela, Diana); m 2, 1983 (m dis 1991), Frederica Todd, *née* Harlow; m 3, 1994, Patricia Anne, *née* Tullock, formerly w of Sir Peter Walters; *Career* physician; joined UN 1957, UN medical dir 1969–73, dir of personnel UN Devpt Programme 1973–76, UNICEF rep in Bangladesh 1977–80, sr advsr UNICEF 1980–82, medical dir UN, UNDP and UNICEF 1982–89, dir Health Servs Dept World Bank 1989–90; conslt American Assoc of Blood Banks 1984–90, advsr ActionAid 1990–91, dir Westside Action 1991–93, int health conslt 1993–95; chm: UN Assoc 1996–97 (vice chm 1995), Vol Euthanasia Soc 1996–; Offr Cross Int Fedn of Blood Donor Organisations 1984; *Books* Overweight: a Problem for Millions (1964), What Do We Know About Allergies? (1972), Nuclear Energy: Good or Bad? (1984), The Cocaine Epidemic (1985), Can We Survive Nuclear War? (1985), Talpa (1990), Peace Museums (1991); *Recreations* windmills, writing, politics; *Clubs* Royal Soc of Medicine (London); *Style*— Dr Michael Irwin; ✉ 15 Hovedene, 95 Cromwell Rd, Hove, Sussex BN3 3EH

IRWIN, Prof William James; *b* 9 March 1942; *Educ* Univ of London (BPharm, PhD, DSc); *m* 1968; 2 c; *Career* prof of pharmaceutics and dean Faculty of Life and Health Scis Aston Univ 1995–; CChem, FRSC 1976 (ARIC 1968), FRPharmS 1990 (MPS 1969); *Books* Analytical Pyrolysis: A Comprehensive Guide (Vol 2, 1982), Kinetics of Drug Decomposition (1990), Encyclopedia of Analytical Science (contrib, 1995); numerous papers in academic jls on drug stability, absorption and delivery; *Style*— Prof William Irwin; ✉ Faculty of Life and Health Sciences, Aston University, Aston Triangle, Birmingham B4 7ET (☎ 0121 359 3611, fax 0121 359 0733)

ISAACS, Dr Anthony Donald; s of David Isaacs (d 1995), of London, and Rosa, *née* Hockman; *b* 18 Jan 1931; *Educ* Univ of London, Charing Cross Hosp London Univ (MB BS, DPM); *m* 15 Dec 1963, Elissa, da of Isaac Cedar (d 1977), 1 s (Timothy b 13 Sept 1967), 1 da (Catharine b 28 Oct 1964); *Career* Nat Serv RAMC Lt to Capt 1955–57; conslt psychiatrist Bethlem Royal and Maudsley Hosp 1963–90, conslt psychiatrist and dep exec med dir Charter Nightingale Hosp; sub dean Inst of Psychiatry Univ of London 1982–90; vice chm Grants Ctee King Edward's Hosp Fund for London; Freeman City of London 1962; FRCP, FRCPsych, FRSM; *Books* Studies in Geriatric Psychiatry (1978), Psychiatric Examination in Clinical Practice (1981, 3 edn 1990); *Style*— Dr Anthony Isaacs; ✉ 138 Harley St, London W1M 1AH (☎ 0171 935 1963/0554, fax 0171 724 8294)

ISAACS, Anthony Hyman; s of Eric Hyman Isaacs (d 1985), and Marjorie Josephine, *née* Solomon (d 1983); *b* 9 Aug 1934; *Educ* Cheltenham Coll, Pembroke Coll Cambridge (BA); *m* 31 March 1964, Jennifer Irene Isaacs, JP, da of Sir James Cameron, CBE, TD (d 1991); 3 s (Roderick b 1968, Matthew b 1972, Oliver b 1976), 2 da (Jessica b 1966, Diana b 1970); *Career* RN 1952–54, Sub Lt RNVR; Stephenson Harwood (formerly Stephenson Harwood & Tatham): admitted slr 1960, ptnr 1964, sr ptnr 1987–96, conslt 1996–; dir: Thornton & Co Limited 1987–91, Andrew Weir & Company Limited 1991–; memb: Slrs Disciplinary Tbnl 1988–, chm Peper Harow Trusts, Advsy Ctee The Rehearsal Orchestra, Law Soc, Cncl of Lloyds' (nominated memb) 1993–; *Recreations* music, gardening, reading, theatre; *Clubs* Garrick, City Law; *Style*— Anthony Isaacs, Esq; ✉ Stephenson Harwood, One St Paul's Churchyard, London EC4M 8SH (☎ 0171 329 4422, fax 0171 606 0822, telex 886789 SHSPC G)

ISAACS, Dr Anthony John; s of Benjamin H Isaacs, of Finchley, and Lily, *née* Rogol; *b* 22 Oct 1942; *Educ* Wanstead County HS, Hertford Coll Oxford (BA), Westminster Med Sch (MA, BM BCh); *m* 1, 12 Dec 1971 (m dis), Jill, da of Paul Elek (d 1976), of Highgate; 3 s (Jeremy b 1973, Adrian b 1976, Nicholas (twin) b 1976); m 2, 24 Oct 1986, Edie Lynda, *née* Friedman; 1 da (Anna b 1988); *Career* Dept of Health: SMO Meds Div 1984–85, PMO Meds Div and assessor Ctee on Safety of Meds 1985–86, sr PMO, under sec and head of Med Manpower and Educn Div 1986–91; hon conslt endocrinologist Middx Hosp and UCH 1986–, on secondment to London Sch of Hygiene and tropical Med 1991–93, conslt in clinical audit N Thames Regnl Health Authy 1993–95 and Barnet Health Authy 1995–, conslt endocrinologist Charing Cross Hosp 1993–95 and Chelsea & Westminster Hosp 1993–; first govr Hendon Sch 1992– (parent govr 1987–92); MRCP 1971, MSc 1992; *Books* Anorexia Nervosa (with P Dally and J Gomez, 1979); *Recreations* table tennis, music, cinema; *Clubs* Royal Society of Medicine; *Style*— Dr Anthony Isaacs; ✉ Chelsea & Westminster Hospital, 369 Fulham Road, London SW10 9NH

ISAACS, Geoffrey Lewis; s of Laurence Isaacs (d 1955), of Northwood, Middx, and Gladys Rachel, *née* Jacobs (d 1982); *b* 29 Sept 1935; *Educ* Merchant Taylors', Coll of Law; *m* 23 Sept 1960, (Barbara) Jane, da of Charles Stanley Catlow, of 66 Church Way, Weston Favell, Northampton; 2 s (Mark b 1961, Tom b 1968), 1 da (Caroline b 1964); *Career* admitted slr 1958, ptnr Tarlo Lyons 1960–; dir: SIP Ltd, Whippendell Electrical Ltd, Soil Structures International Ltd, OH1 UK Ltd, Servequip Ltd, Broadoak Flexible Packaging Ltd, Returnreal Ltd, Hireright Ltd, Trade Links (Europe) Ltd, Ralvin Pacific Properties Inc California; Freeman: City of London 1979, Worshipful Co of Painter Stainers 1979; memb Law Soc 1958; *Recreations* golf, skiing, travel, theatre, walking; *Clubs* City Livery, Moor Park Golf, Old Merchant Taylors'; *Style*— Geoffrey Isaacs, Esq; ✉ Benthills, 1 Kings Farm Rd, Chorleywood, Herts WD3 5HF (☎ 01923 283340); Tarlo Lyons, Watchmaker Court, 33 St John's Lane, London EC1M 4DB (☎ 0171 405 2000, fax 0171 814 9421)

ISAACS, Sir Jeremy Israel; kt (1996); s of Isidore Isaacs, and Sara, *née* Jacobs; *b* 28 Sept 1932; *Educ* Glasgow Acad, Merton Coll Oxford (MA, pres Oxford Union); *m* 1, 1958, Tamara (d 1986); 1 s, 1 da; m 2, 1988, Gillian Mary Widdicombe; *Career* TV prodr: Granada TV 1958–63 (progs incl What the Papers Say, All Our Yesterdays), Associated-Rediffusion 1963–65 (This Week), BBC 1965–67 (Panorama); Associated-Rediffusion (renamed Thames Television 1968): controller of features 1967–74, dir of progs 1974–78, prodr The World at War 1974, conslt Hollywood series; ind prodr: A Sense of Freedom (Scottish TV), Ireland - A Television History (13 part series BBC TV), Cold War (Turner Broadcasting) 1995–; chief exec Channel 4 1981–87, gen dir Royal Opera House 1988– (dir 1985–88); awarded: Desmond Davis Award for outstanding contrib to TV 1972, George Polk Meml Award 1973, Cyril Bennett Award for outstanding contrib to TV programming (RTS) 1982; govr BFI 1979, BFI fellowship 1986; memb Bd Open Coll 1986–; Hon DLitt: Univ of Strathclyde 1984, CNAA 1987, Univ of Bristol 1988; fell British Acad of Film and TV 1985; RTS Hall of Fame 1996; Cdr Order of Arts and Letters (France) 1988, L'Ordre National du Mérite (France) 1992; *Recreations* walking, reading; *Style*— Sir Jeremy Isaacs; ✉ Royal Opera House, 45 Floral Street, London WC2E 9DD (☎ 0171 240 1200)

ISAACSON, Laurence Ivor; s of Henry Isaacson (d 1980), of Liverpool, Lancs, and Dorothy Hannah, *née* Levitt (d 1976); *b* 1 July 1943; *Educ* Quarry Bank GS Liverpool, LSE (BSc), Northwestern Univ Chicago (summer business course); *Career* restaurateur; various business traineeships 1962–64 (Commercial Bank of Italy Milan, Shell Italiana Genoa, Manpower Inc Milwaukee), mgmnt trainee rising to account exec Unilever plc 1964–67, account mangr Doyle Dane Bernbach advtg 1967–70, sr int account mangr Foote Cone & Belding advtg 1970–72; The Creative Business Ltd: fndr md 1974–81, dep chm 1981–83, chm 1986–90; dir Amis du Vin Group Ltd and fndr ptnr/dir Café des Amis Ltd 1972–83 (sold to Kennedy Brookes plc 1983), bd dir i/c mktg and gourmet restaurant gp Kennedy Brookes plc 1983–86, fndr ptnr/dep chm Groupe Chez Gérard plc (Chez Gérard, Bertorelli's, Café Fish, Soho Soho, Scotts and Chutney Mary) 1986–; non-exec dir: Cullens Holdings plc 1984–87, Lazard Food & Drink Fund Ltd 1987–90, Katie's Kitchen Ltd 1988–91, Metabolic Services Ltd 1991–94, London Tourist Board Ltd 1994–; Contemporary Dance Trust: tstee 1980–, govr 1982–, chm Fundraising Ctee 1983–88, chm Bd 1989–94; dir Bd Assoc for Business Sponsorship of the Arts 1989– (memb Cncl 1985–), chm Covent Garden Festival 1993– (fndr/dep chm 1990–93); memb Covent Garden Forum of Representatives 1976 (hon treas 1978–80), MIAA (memb UK Branch Ctee 1979–, chm Activities Ctee 1982–83); FHCIMA 1996; *Recreations* the arts, travel; *Clubs* Groucho; *Style*— Laurence Isaacson, Esq; ✉ Groupe Chez Gerard PLC, 8 Upper St Martins Lane, London WC2H 9EN (☎ 0171 240 9240, fax 0171 836 2200)

ISAAMAN, Gerald Michael; OBE (1994); s of Asher Isaaman (d 1975), and Lily Finklestein (d 1993); *b* 22 Dec 1933; *Educ* Dame Alice Owens GS; *m* 1962, Delphine, da of Arnold Bertram Walker, of Whitby, Yorks; 1 s (Daniel); *Career* journalist and editorial conslt; N London Observer Series 1950, gen mangr and ed Hampstead and Highgate Express 1990–94 (joined 1955, ed 1968–94), editorial conslt Home Counties Newspapers plc 1994–, dir Pipistrel Retail Solutions Ltd 1994–, dir Pipistrel Education Systems 1995–; external examiner Dept of Journalism City Univ 1994–; press conslt to China-Britain Trade Gp mission to China 1994; memb Press Complaints Cmmn 1993–95; chm: Mgmnt Bd Camden Arts Tst 1970–82, Exhibitions Ctee Camden Arts Centre 1971–82, Russell Housing Soc 1976–82, Tstees King's Cross Disaster Fund 1987–89; memb: Camden Festival Tst 1982–93, Bd Assoc of Br Eds 1985–; fndr tstee Arkwright Arts Tst 1971; special presentation for distinguished servs to journalism British Press Awards 1994; FRSA; *Recreations* listening to jazz, collecting postcards, pontificating; *Clubs* Garrick; *Style*— Gerald Isaaman, Esq, OBE; ✉ 10 Salmon Mews, West End Lane, London NW6 1RH (☎ 0171 794 3950)

ISDELL-CARPENTER, Peter; s of Richard Isdell-Carpenter, OBE (d 1986), and Rosemary, *née* Ashworth (d 1995); *b* 18 Nov 1940; *Educ* Marlborough, St John's Coll Oxford (BA); *m* 28 Sept 1966, Antoinette, da of Louis Cass (d 1952), and Mary, *née* Whetherly; 1 s (Simon b 1968), 2 da (Katherine b 1968, Nicola b 1970); *Career* Birds Eye Foods Ltd 1964–69, Grey Advertising 1969–70, dir Young and Rubicam Advertising Ltd 1970–78, md Sea Tack Ltd 1978–81, dir Young and Rubicam Europe Ltd 1981–96; *Recreations* sailing, skiing, golf, music; *Clubs* Boodle's, Sloane; *Style*— Peter Isdell-Carpenter, Esq; ✉ Field House, Bentworth, nr Alton, Hants GU34 5RP (☎ 01420 563687)

ISHAM, Sir Ian Vere Gyles; 13 Bt (E 1627), of Lamport, Northamptonshire; s of Lt-Col Vere Arthur Richard Isham, MC (d 1968); suc kinsman Sir Gyles Isham, 12 Bt (d 1976); *b* 17 July 1923; *Educ* Eton, Worcester Coll Oxford; *Heir* bro, Norman Murray Crawford Isham, OBE, *qv*; *Career* marketing analyst and cartographer; *Clubs* Overseas; *Style*— Sir Ian Isham, Bt; ✉ 40 Turnpike Link, Croydon, Surrey (☎ 0181 686 1256)

ISHAM, Norman Murray Crawford; OBE (1988); s of late Lt-Col Vere Arthur Richard Isham, MC; hp of bro, Sir Ian Vere Gyles Isham, 13 Bt, *qv*; *b* 28 Jan 1930; *Educ* Stowe, Univ of Cape Town (B Arch); *m* 1956, Joan, da of late Leonard James Genet, of Umtali, Zimbabwe; 2 s (Richard Leonard Vere b 1958, Vere Murray Gyles b 1960), 1 da (Elizabeth Angela (Mrs Richard N Brayshaw) b 1957); *Career* architect, civil serv; RIBA; *Style*— Norman Isham, Esq, OBE; ✉ 5 Langton Way, Park Hill, Croydon, Surrey CRO 5JS

ISHIGURO, Kazuo; OBE (1995); s of Shizuo Ishiguro, and Shizuko Michida; *b* 8 Nov 1954; *Educ* Woking Co GS, Univ of Kent (BA), Univ of East Anglia (MA); *m* Lorna Anne, da of Nicol Mackechnie MacDougall; 1 da (Naomi b 29 March 1992); *Career* author; work translated into 26 languages; Hon DLitt Univ of Kent 1990, Hon DLitt Univ of E Anglia 1995; memb: Soc of Authors 1989, PEN 1989; hon foreign memb American Acad of Arts and Sciences 1993; FRSL 1989, FRSA 1990; *Books* novels: A Pale View of the Hills (1982, Winifred Holtby award 1983), An Artist of the Floating World (1986, Whitbread Book of the Year 1986), The Remains of the Day (1989, Booker prize 1989, Merchant-Ivory film 1993), The Unconsoled (1995); TV plays: A Profile of Arthur J Mason (broadcast 1984), The Gourmet (broadcast 1987); *Recreations* playing musical instruments; *Style*— Kazuo Ishiguro, Esq, OBE, FRSL; ✉ Rogers, Coleridge and White Ltd, 20 Powis Mews, London W11 1JN (☎ 0171 221 3717, fax 0171 229 9084)

ISLE OF WIGHT, Archdeacon of; *see:* Banting, Ven (Kenneth) Mervyn Lancelot Hadfield

ISLES, Maj-Gen Donald Edward; CB (1978), OBE (1968), DL (Lincs 1990); s of Harold Isles (d 1956), and Kathleen, *née* Trenam (d 1979); *b* 19 July 1924; *Educ* Roundhay Sch Leeds, Univ of Leeds, RMCS, Jt Serv Staff Coll; *m* 1948, Sheila Mary, *née* Thorpe; 3 s, 1 da; *Career* cmmnd Duke of Wellington's Regt 1943; CO 1 DWR 1965–67, Col GS Royal Armaments Res and Devpt Estab 1971–72, dir of Munitions Br Def Staff Washington 1972–75, dir-gen of Weapons MOD 1975–78, Col DWR 1975–82, ret; dir and dep mangr British Manufacturing & Research Co Ltd Grantham 1979–89; county pres Royal Br Legion Lincs and S Humberside 1991–96; *Recreations* shooting; *Clubs* MCC, Army and Navy; *Style*— Maj-Gen Donald Isles, CB, OBE, DL

ISRAEL, Rev Dr Martin Spencer; s of Elie Benjamin Israel (d 1980), of Johannesburg, SA, and Minnie, *née* Israel (d 1957); *b* 30 April 1927; *Educ* Parktown Boys HS Johannesburg SA, Univ of the Witwatersrand SA (MB ChB); *Career* RAMC 1955–57, Capt; registrar in pathology Royal Hosp Wolverhampton 1953–55; RCS: res fell in pathology 1957–60, lectr in microbiology 1961–66, sr lectr in pathology 1967–81, hon lectr 1982; curate St Michael Cornhill London 1974–76, asst priest Holy Trinity with All Saints S Kensington 1977–82 (priest i/c 1983); pres Churches' Fellowship for Psychical and Spiritual Studies; MRCP 1952, FRCPath 1975; *Books* General Pathology (with J B Walter, 1963), Summons to Life (1974), Precarious Living (1976), Smouldering Fire (1978), The Pain that Heals (1981), Living Alone (1982), The Spirit of Counsel (1983), Healing as Sacrament (1984), The Discipline of Love (1985), Coming in Glory (1986), Gethsemane (1987), The Pearl of Great Price (1988), The Dark Face of Reality (1989), The Quest for Wholeness (1989), Creation (1989), Night Thoughts (1990), A Light on the Path (1990), Life Eternal (1993), Dark Victory (1995), Angels (1995); *Style*— The Rev Dr Martin Israel; ✉ Flat 2, 26 Tregunter Rd, London SW10 9LH

ISSA, Moneim; s of Mustapha Issa (d 1987), of Alexandria, Egypt, and Zakeya, *née* Zaky; *b* 21 Aug 1939; *Educ* Alexandria Univ (BChD); *m* 1962, Christa Sylvia, da of Balthasar Sima (d 1973), of Marquartstein, Germany; 1 s (Thomas b 1963), 1 da (Alexandra b 1971); *Career* lectr Univ of Alexandria 1961–62, clinical asst Eastman Dental Hosp 1964–65, sr house surgn Leicester Royal Infirmary 1966, sr registrar Bart's 1969–73 (registrar 1966–68), conslt oral and maxillofacial surgn and postgrad tutor W Middx Univ Hosp 1973–79, conslt oral and maxillofacial surgn to Oxford RHA and NW Thames RHA 1973–, clinical dir Head and Neck Reconstructive Surgery Unit Heatherwood and Wexham Hosps Tst E Berks 1995; conslt to BA in oral and maxillofacial surgery 1986–; former chm BDA Windsor Section, memb Windsor Med Soc; FFD RCSI 1968, FDS RCS 1969, fell Br Assoc of Oral and Maxillofacial Surgns 1973, memb Hosp Conslts and Specialists Assoc 1974; *Books* Oral Surgery section in Hamlyn Medical Encyclopaedia (1978), Maxillo Facial Injuries section in Operative Plastic & Reconstructive Surgery (1980); *Recreations* tennis, skiing, waterskiing, chess; *Style*— Moneim Issa, Esq; ✉ St Bernards, Oak End Way, Gerrards Cross, Bucks SL9 8DB (☎ 01753 888123); Consulting Rooms: Alma Medica, 47 Alma Rd, Windsor; Hospitals: Wexham Park Hospital, Slough, St Mark's Hospital, Maidenhead, Princess Margaret Hospital, Windsor, Mount Vernon Hospital, Northwood, Middlesex (☎ 01753 868754)

ISSERLIS, Steven John; s of George Isserlis, and Cynthia Saville; gs of Julius Isserlis, Russian composer and pianist; *b* 19 Dec 1958; *Educ* City of London Sch, Int Cello Centre (with Jane Cowan), Oberlin Coll Ohio (with Richard Kapuscinski); *m* Pauline Anne Mara; 1 s (Gabriel Mara b 26 April 1990); *Career* cellist; recitals and concerts all over Europe, N America, S America, Far East and Australia with all maj worldwide orchs, played with: English Baroque Soloists, London Classical Players; worked with conductors incl: Sir Georg Solti, Christoph Eschenbach, André Previn, Roger Norrington, Richard Hickox, John Eliot Gardiner, Oliver Knussen, Jiri Behlolavek, Gennadi Rozhdestvensky, Mark Wigglesworth, Vladimir Ashkenazy; has played a leading role in many prestigious chamber music projects incl own festival Schumann and his Circle (Wigmore Hall London), several television films incl Channel 4 films on Saint-Saëns and Schumann 1997; *Recordings* incl: Elgar Cello Concerto Opus 85, Bloch Schelomo (with LSO and Richard Hickox, 1989), Tchaikovsky etc works for cello and orchestra (with Chamber Orchestra of Europe and John Eliot Gardiner, 1990), works by Britten, Bridge, Brahms, Fauré and Martinu (1985–89), Boccherini 2 concertos and 3 sonatas (with Ostrobothnian Chamber Orch and Maggie Cole, 1991), John Tavener The Protecting Veil and Threenos and Britten Suite no 3 (with LSO and Gennadi Rozhdestvensky, 1992, Gramophone Magazine Contemporary Music Award 1992, shortlisted for Mercury Prize and Grammy Award), Strauss Don Quixote (with Minnesota Orchestra under Edo de Waart, 1992), Saint Saëns: Concerto no 1, Sonata no 1, The Swan and others (with LSO under Michael Tilson Thomas, with Dudley Moore, Pascal Devoyon and others, CD and video), works by Tavener and Bloch (with Moscow Virtuosi Spivakov, CD, 1994), Mendelssohn cello works (with Melvyn Tan, 1994), Fauré cello works (with Pascal Devoyon, 1995), Liszt, Grieg and Rubinstein cello works (with Stephen Hough, 1995), Shostakovitch, Prokofiev and Janacek cello works (with Olli Mustonen, 1996), Barber Concerto (with St Louis Symphony Orch under Leonard Slatkin); *Recreations* sleeping, eating, talking, generally wasting time (my own and others'), trying to understand how my son's toys work, picking dried contact-lens solution out of my eyelashes; *Style*— Steven Isserlis, Esq; ✉ c/o Harrison/Parrott Ltd, 12 Penzance Place, London W11 4PA (☎ 0171 229 9166, fax 0171 221 5042)

ISTEAD, Peter Walter Ernest; CB (1988), OBE (1978), GM (1965); s of Walter David Charles Istead (d 1992), and Marie, *née* Flukiger (d 1939); *b* 7 Aug 1935; *Educ* Whitgift Trinity Sch Croydon; *m* 1961, Jennifer Mary, da of Leslie Swinson (d 1974); 1 s (Peter James b 1967), 1 da (Sally Marie b 1964); *Career* enlisted Scots Gds 1952, cmmnd Queen's Royal Regt 1954, King's African Rifles 1954–56, transferred RAOC 1956, last posting DG Logistic Policy MOD (London); chief exec Inst of Brewing 1989–96; Freeman City of London 1985, Liveryman Worshipful Co of Gold and Silver Wyre Drawers 1990 (memb Ct of Assts); *Recreations* angling; *Clubs* Naval and Military; *Style*— Maj-Gen Peter Istead, CB, OBE, GM

ISTED, Barrington James (Barry); s of James William Isted (d 1978), of Croydon, and Gwendolyne Irene, *née* Fleetwood (d 1995); *b* 12 July 1935; *Educ* Wallington County GS Surrey, Univ of Nottingham (BA); *m* 31 May 1963, Glenda Jeanne, da of Thomas Leonard Bunyan (d 1991), of Broxbourne, Herts; 2 s (Jonathan b 1964, Daniel b 1965); *Career* corporate ed: Pyrene Ltd 1957–58, Formica Ltd 1958–59; dir of personnel: Potterton International Ltd 1968–72, De La Rue Group 1977–88 (corp ed 1960–63, pubns mangr 1963–65, trg offr 1965–67, manpower controller 1973–77); co sec De La Rue plc 1985–88, dir Chandler Gooding Ltd 1993–; Br Assoc of Communicators in Business: nat chm 1967–68, chm of Senate 1981–84, vice pres 1984–89 and 1996–, pres 1989–95; govr London Business Sch 1984–87 (chm Business Liaison Ctee); memb: Industl Tribunals for Eng and Wales 1984–, London Bd of Crimestoppers 1987–88; Freeman: City of London 1987, Worshipful Co of Makers of Playing Cards 1987; Fedn of Euro Industl Eds Assoc Dip of Honour 1974; fell Br Assoc of Communicators in Business (FCB) 1968, FIMgt 1980; *Books* British Industry's Editors and Their Views (1981); *Recreations* writing, travel, food and drink; *Clubs* Reform; *Style*— Barry Isted, Esq; ✉ Pinnacles, Hatfield Broad Oak, Bishops Stortford, Hertfordshire CM22 7HS (☎ and fax 01279 718397)

ITO, Kazue; *b* 19 March 1939, Nagoya, Japan; *Educ* Nanzan Univ Nagoya (BA); *m* Masako; 2 s (Katsuya, Kanta); *Career* Honda Motor Company Ltd: instr Honda Sales Trg Sch Tokyo 1966–71, branch mangr Honda Motor Kyoto 1971–72, pres Honda World (retailing subsid) Nagoya 1972–76, planning mangr automobiles Honda Motor Tokyo 1976–78, pres Honda Philippines 1978–84, dep md Asia Sales Div 1984–85, gen mangr Singapore Office 1985–86, pres Honda Italia Rome 1986–89, exec vice pres Honda Motor Europe Reading 1989–94, group main bd dir Honda Motor Tokyo 1992–, pres Honda Motor Europe Ltd and group chief operating offr Europe, Middle E and Africa 1994–; *Style*— Kazue Ito, Esq; ✉ Honda Motor Europe Ltd, Caversham Bridge House, Waterman Place, Reading, Berkshire RG1 8DN (☎ 0118 956 6399, fax 0118 950 2266)

IVANOVIĆ, Ivan Stevan (Vane); s of Dr Ivan R Ivanović (d 1949), of Zagreb, and Milica, *née* Popović (d 1969); *b* 9 June 1913; *Educ* Westminster, Peterhouse Cambridge (BA, MA); *m* 1939, June Veronica, da of Rev John L Fisher, Canon of Colchester (d 1970); 2 s (Ivan Božidar, Andrija), 1 da (Milica); *Career* serv WWII, Middle E & Italy, Maj; chm: Yugoslav Shipping Ctee 1941 (memb 1941–45), Assoc of Free Yugoslavs 1949–76, Ivanovic & Co 1949–67; consul gen Monaco in London 1967–89; Offr Order of Grimaldi (Monaco) 1975, Cdr Order of Grimaldi 1994; *Recreations* diving and spear fishing, track and field athletics, jogging; *Clubs* White's, MCC, Brooks's; *Style*— Vane Ivanović, Esq; ✉ Flat 12, 17 Blvd Albert I, Monte Carlo, Monaco 98000; 4 Cromwell Place, London SW7 2JE (☎ 0171 584 8499, fax 0171 581 8161/589 5995)

IVEAGH, 4 Earl of (UK 1919); Sir Arthur Edward Rory Guinness; 4 Bt (UK 1885); also Baron Iveagh (UK 1891), Viscount Iveagh (UK 1905), and Viscount Elveden (UK 1919); er s of 3 Earl of Iveagh (d 1992), and Miranda Daphne Jane, *née* Smiley; *b* 10 Aug 1969; *Heir* bro, Hon Rory Michael Benjamin Guinness b 12 Dec 1974; *Style*— The Rt Hon the Earl of Iveagh; ✉ 41 Harrington Gardens, London SW7 4JU

IVENS, Michael William; CBE (1983); s of Harry Guest Ivens, and Nina Ailion; *b* 15 March 1924; *Educ* Quinton Sch London; *m* 1, 3 March 1951, Rosalie Joy, da of Bertrand Turnbull (d 1943); 3 s (1 decd), 1 da; m 2, 17 July 1971, Katherine Patricia, da of John Kellock Laurence; 2 s; *Career* mangr Communication Dept ESSO 1955–59, jt ed Twentieth Century 1967–72, dir Standard Telephone 1970–71; dir: Fndn for Business Responsibilities 1968–92, Aims of Industry 1971–; jt fndr & vice pres Freedom Assoc 1976–, jt fndr & tstee Res Fndn for Study of Terrorism 1986–, memb Cncl Poetry Soc 1989 (hon treas 1989); *Books* The Practice of Industrial Communication (1963), Case Studies in Management (1964), The Case for Capitalism (1967), Industry and Values (1970), Prophets of Freedom & Enterprise (1975); Bachman Book of Freedom Quotes (jt ed, 1978); *Poetry* Another Sky (1963), Last Waltz (1964), Private and Public (1968), Born Early (1975), No Woman is an Island (1983), New Divine Comedy (1990); author of columns, articles and booklets as Yorick; *Recreations* dog walking, reading, campaigning; *Style—* Michael Ivens, Esq, CBE; ✉ Aims of Industry, 2 Mulgrave Road, London NW10 1BT (☎ 0181 452 8884, fax 0181 452 8084)

IVERSEN, Dr Leslie Lars; s of Svend Iversen, and Anna Caia Iversen; *b* 31 Oct 1937; *Educ* Heles Sch, Trinity Coll Cambridge (BA, MA, PhD, prize fellowship); *m* 1961, Susan Diana; 1 s, 1 da (and 1 da decd); *Career* Nat Serv Educn Branch RN 1956–58; Harkness fell of the Cwlth Fund Nat Inst of Mental Health Harvard Med Sch 1964–66, res fell Trinity Coll and Dept of Pharmacology Cambridge 1966–71, Locke res fell Royal Soc London 1967–71, dir MRC Neurochemical Pharmacology Unit Cambridge 1971–83, vice pres Neuroscience Research Centre Merck Sharp & Dohme Research Laboratories Harlow 1987–95 (exec dir 1983–87), visiting sr scientist Dept of Pharmacology Univ of Oxford 1995–; assoc of neurosciences Res Prog MIT USA 1975–84, foreign hon memb American Acad of Arts and Sciences 1981, Rennebohm lectr Univ of Wisconsin USA 1984, visiting prof Inst of Psychiatry Univ of London 1985, assoc memb Royal Coll of Psychiatrists UK 1986, foreign assoc memb Nat Acad of Sciences USA 1986, hon prof Beijing Med Univ China 1988; memb: Academia Europaea, American Coll of Neuropsychopharmacology, Bayliss and Starling Soc, Biochemical Soc UK, BBC Science Consultative Gp, Br Pharmacological Soc, Collegium Internationale Neuro-Psychopharmacologicum, Euro Molecular Biology Orgn, Feldberg Fndn 1989, Int Brain Res Orgn, Int Soc for Neurochemistry, Physiological Soc UK, Royal Acad of Med Belgium, Royal Soc of Med London, Save Br Science, Soc for Drug Res UK, Soc for Neuroscience USA; pres Euro Neuroscience Assoc 1980–82 (vice pres 1978–80); FRS 1980; *Books* The Uptake and Storage of Noradrenaline in Sympathetic Nerves (1967), Behavioural Pharmacology (with S D Iversen, 1975), author of numerous articles in learned jls; *Style—* Dr Leslie Iversen, FRS; ✉ University Department of Pharmacology, University of Oxford, Mansfield Road, Oxford OX1 3QT (☎ 01865 271850, fax 01865 271882)

IVERSON, Ann; da of John Earl Van Eenenaam (d 1950), of Michigan, and Dorothy Ann Knight (d 1988); *b* 1944; *Educ* Arizona State Univ; *m* (m dis); 1 s (Steven), 1 da (Leslie); *Career* exec trainee and dept mangr Bullock's Department Stores LA 1960–66, various buying positions in stores in Arizona 1966–80, buying dir Harzfield's (div of Brooks Bros) Kansas City 1980–82, buying dir/stores dir T H Mandy (div of US Shoe) Merrifield Virginia 1982–84, operating vice pres Bloomingdale's stores NY and NJ 1984–89, sr vice pres stores and regnl vice pres Bonwit Teller NY 1989–90; Storehouse plc group: dir of stores British Home Stores (BhS) 1990–92, chief exec Mothercare 1992–94, gp main bd dir 1993–94; pres and chief exec Kay-Bee (toystore div of Melville Inc) USA 1994–95, chief exec Laura Ashley Holdings plc UK 1995–; *Recreations* music and ballet, theatre, swimming, walking; *Style—* Ms Ann Iverson; ✉ Laura Ashley Holdings plc, 27 Bagleys Lane, Fulham, London SW6 2AR (☎ 0171 880 5100, fax 0171 880 5151)

IVES, Prof Eric William; s of Frederick Henry Ives (d 1981), of Trowbridge, and Ethel Lily, *née* Hall; *b* 12 July 1931; *Educ* Brentwood Sch, Queen Mary Coll (BA, PhD); *m* 1 April 1961, Christine Ruth, da of Norman Henry Denham (d 1971), of Dewsbury; 1 s (John b 1967), 1 da (Susan b 1963); *Career* res History of Parliament Tst 1957; Univ of Birmingham: fell Shakespeare Inst 1958–61, sr lectr in modern history 1972–83 (lectr 1968–72), prof of English history 1987– (reader 1983–87), dean Faculty of Arts 1987–89 (dept dean 1982–84), pro vice-chllr 1989–93, head Dept of Modern History 1994–; lectr in modern history Univ of Liverpool 1962–68 (asst lectr 1961–62); memb Cncl Hist Assoc 1968–77; govr: Warwick Schs Fndn 1980– (chm Ctee Govrs Warwick Sch 1985–), Coventry Sch 1985–88, Westhill Coll 1991– (tstee and chm of Govrs); memb: Cncl Regents Park Coll Oxford 1988–, Ct Univ of Warwick 1989–, Cncl Selly Oak Colls 1993–96, Cncl Surgeons Coll 1993– (Academic Bd 1987–); non-exec dir Birmingham Women's Health Care NHS Tst 1993–; tstee Warwick Municipal Charities (charity of Henry VIII) 1996–; chm Stratford-upon-Avon Choral Soc 1985–91; FRHistS 1963, FSA 1984; *Books* Letters & Accounts of William Brereton (1976), God in History (1979), Faction in Tudor England (1979, 2 edn 1986), The Common Lawyers of Pre-Reformation England (1983), Anne Boleyn (1986); *Recreations* choral singing, lay preaching; *Style—* Prof E W Ives, FSA; ✉ School of History, University of Birmingham, Birmingham B15 2TT (☎ 0121 414 5743, fax 0121 414 3656)

IVES, Kenneth Ainsworth; s of Lawrence George Ives (d 1956), and Margaret, *née* Walker (d 1979); *b* 26 March 1934; *Educ* Queen Mary's GS Walsall, Pembroke Coll Oxford (MA), RADA (Leverhulme scholar); *m* 1, Ann Brown; m 2, Imogen Hassall; m 3, 1985, Lynne Shepherd (the comedienne Marti Caine) (d 1995), former w of Malcolm Stringer; *Career* Mil Serv Lt RN; director: over fifty plays for BBC TV, NT and West End, seven plays by Harold Pinter; latest theatre work The Philanthropist (by Christopher Hampton, with Edward Fox in leading role); called to the Bar Middle Temple 1993; *Recreations* cricket, opera, reading, walking; *Clubs* Garrick, MCC; *Style—* Kenneth Ives, Esq

IVES, Prof Kenneth James; CBE (1996); s of Walter Leslie Ives (d 1966), of London, and Grace Amelia, *née* Curson (d 1983); *b* 29 Nov 1926; *Educ* William Ellis GS London, UCL (BSc, PhD, DSc); *m* 29 March 1952, Brenda Grace, da of Rev Frederick Walter Tilley (d 1987), of Leatherhead, Surrey; 1 s (Matthew b 1962), 1 da (Cherrill (Mrs Theobald) b 1953); *Career* asst engr Metropolitan Water Bd London 1948–55; UCL: lectr, reader and prof 1955–84, Chadwick prof of civil engrg 1984–92, emeritus prof 1992; res fell Harvard Univ USA 1958–59, visiting assoc prof Univ of N Carolina USA 1964, visiting prof Univ of Delft Netherlands 1977; expert advsr on environmental health WHO 1966–92, hon exec ed Int Assoc on Water Quality 1984–; memb Badenoch Ctee on Cryptosporidium in Water Supplies 1989–90; JP Kingston upon Thames 1967–72; author of numerous articles in jls; FICE 1952, MASCE 1959, FEng 1986; *Books* The Scientific Basis of Filtration (1975), The Scientific Basis of Flocculation (1978), The Scientific Basis of Flotation (1984); *Recreations* ballroom dancing; *Style—* Prof Kenneth Ives, CBE, FEng; ✉ Department of Civil and Environmental Engineering, University College London, Gower St, London WC1E 6BT (☎ 0171 387 7050, fax 0171 380 0986)

IVORY, (James) Angus; s of Basil Gerritsen Ivory (d 1973), of Jamaica, and Joan Mary, *née* White; *b* 31 July 1932; *Educ* Eton, Toronto Univ Canada (BA); *m* 26 Oct 1956, Nancy Ann, da of William Park, of Toronto, Canada; 2 s (Gavin b 1957, Colin b 1959), 1 da (Gillian b 1964); *Career* dir Clark Dodge & Co Inc 1960–74, chm Wall Street Int Corp 1967–70, currently md Brown Brothers Harriman Ltd; memb Cncl: US Investmt Community 1967–70, Securities Indust 1980–82; chm UK Assoc of New York Stock Exchange; *Recreations* various; *Clubs* White's, Lansdowne, Toronto; *Style—* J Angus Ivory, Esq; ✉ Greenway Farm, Tockenham, Swindon SN4 7PP (☎ 01793 852367); 11F Warwick Square, London SW1 (☎ 0171 834 5968); Brown Brothers Harriman Ltd, Veritas House, 125 Finsbury Pavement, London EC2A 1PN (☎ 0171 588 6166, fax 0171 614 2446)

IVORY, Brian Gammell; s of Eric James Ivory (d 1988), and Alice Margaret Joan, *née* Gammell (d 1984); *b* 10 April 1949; *Educ* Eton, Magdalene Coll Cambridge (MA); *m* 21 Feb 1981, Oona Mairi Macphee, *qv*, da of Archibald Ian Bell-MacDonald (d 1987); 1 s (Euan b 1986), 1 da (Roseanna b 1989); *Career* CA; The Highland Distilleries Co plc: dir 1978–, md 1988–94, gp chief exec 1994–; chm Matthew Gloag & Son Ltd 1994– (dir 1987–), chm and chief exec Macallan-glenlivet PLC 1996–; vice chm Cncl Scottish Arts Cncl 1988–92 (memb Cncl 1983–92); memb Arts Cncl of GB 1988–92; FRSA 1993; *Recreations* the arts, farming, hillwalking; *Clubs* New (Edinburgh), RSAC (Glasgow); *Style—* Brian Ivory, Esq; ✉ Brewlands, Glenisla, by Blairgowrie, Perthshire PH11 8PL; 12 Ann St, Edinburgh EH4 1PJ; The Highland Distilleries Company plc, 106 West Nile St, Glasgow G1 2QY (☎ 0141 332 7511, fax 0141 332 4854)

IVORY, James Francis; s of Capt Edward Patrick Ivory, US Army (d 1967), of Dinuba, California, and Hallie Millicent, *née* De Loney (d 1963); *b* 7 June 1928; *Educ* Univ of Oregon (BA), Univ of Southern California (MA); *Career* fdnr Merchant Ivory Productions (with Ismail Merchant and Ruth Prawer Jhabvala) 1963; Guggenheim fell 1975; memb: Dirs' Guild of America, Writers' Guild of America; *Films* incl: Shakespeare Wallah 1965, Savages 1972, Autobiography of a Princess 1975, Roseland 1977, Hullabaloo Over Georgie and Bonnie's Pictures 1978, The Europeans 1979, Quartet 1981, Heat and Dust 1983, The Bostonians 1984, A Room with a View (Best Dir nomination Acad Awards 1987) 1986, Maurice (Silver Lion Venice Film Festival) 1987, Slaves of New York 1989, Mr and Mrs Bridge 1990, Howards End (Best Dir nomination Acad Awards 1993) 1992, The Remains of the Day (Best Dir nomination Acad Awards 1994) 1993, Jefferson in Paris 1995, Surviving Picasso 1996; *Recreations* looking at pictures; *Style—* James Ivory, Esq; ✉ Patroon St, Claverack, NY 12513, USA (☎ 00 1 518 851 7808); Merchant Ivory Productions, 46 Lexington St, London W1R 3LH (☎ 0171 437 1200/0171 439 4335)

IVORY, Oona Mairi MacPhee; da of Archibald Ian Bell-MacDonald (d 1987), and Mary Rae, *née* Macphee (d 1983); *b* 21 July 1954; *Educ* Royal Scottish Acad of Music & Drama, King's Coll Cambridge (MA), Royal Acad of Music (ARCM); *m* 21 Feb 1981, Brian Gammell Ivory, *qv*; 1 s (Euan b 1986), 1 da (Roseanna b 1989); *Career* dir RSAMD 1989–, chm Scottish Ballet 1995– (dir 1988–), fndr The Piping Centre 1996; FRSA 1996; *Recreations* The Arts, sailing, hillwalking, wild places; *Style—* Mrs Oona Ivory; ✉ Brewlands, Glenisla, Blairgowrie, Perthshire PH11 8PL; 12 Ann Street Edinburgh EH4 1PJ; Scottish Ballet, 261 West Princes Street, Glasgow G4 9EE (☎ 0141 331 2931, fax 0141 331 2629)

IWANIEC, Prof (Stanisława) Dorota; da of Count Kazimierz Czartoryski (d 1944), of Krasiczyn, nr Przemyśl, Poland, and Ewa Elżbieta, *née* Pruszyńska (d 1944); *b* 20 April 1940; *Educ* Gimnażium Oleandry Kraków, Jagielonian Univ Kraków (MA, DipEd), Univ of Leicester (CQSW, PhD); *m* 1, 1960, Zygfryd Iwaniec, s of Aleksander Iwaniec; 2 c (Zygmunt Witold b 16 Oct 1961, Andrzej Jan b 12 July 1966); m 2, 1993, Prof James Stevens Curl, *qv*, s of George Stevens Curl (d 1974); *Career* teacher Liceum Sienkiewicza Kraków 1959–60, generic social worker Leicester Social Servs Dept 1971–75, therapist/researcher Dept of Child Health Leicester Royal Infirmary and Univ of Leicester Med Sch 1977–82, dir Student Trg Unit Leicester 1982–89, team ldr Practice Teaching Resource Centre Univ of Leicester/Social Servs Dept 1989–92; Queen's Univ Belfast: chair of social work and head Dept of Social Work 1992–, dir Centre for Child-Care Research 1994–; memb: Britsh Assoc of Behavioural Psychotherapy, Britsh Assoc of Social Workers; ABPS; *Publications* Working with Children and Their Families (1987), Failure-to-thrive in Children, Emotional Abuse, Prediction of Child Abuse and Neglect (1989), The Emotionally Abused and Neglected Child: Identification, Assessment, and Intervention (1995); *Recreations* walking, opera, theatre, food & wine, travel; *Style—* Prof Dorota Iwaniec; ✉ 15 Torgrange, Holywood, Co Down BT18 0NG (☎ 01232 425141); Social Work Department, School of Social Sciences, Queen's University of Belfast, 7 Lennoxvale, Belfast BT9 5BY (☎ 01232 335426/7, fax 01232 665465)

IZAT, (Alexander) John Rennie; JP; s of Sir James Rennie Izat (d 1962), of Balliliesk, and Lady (Eva Mary Steen) Izat, *née* Cairns (d 1984); *b* 14 July 1932; *Educ* Trinity Coll Glenalmond, Oriel Coll Oxford (MA); *m* 12 April 1958, Frederica Ann, da of Colin Champness McNiel, of Hants; 2 da (Davina b 1959, Rosanna (who m Hon Charles Fane Trefusis, *qv*) b 1963), 1 s (Alexander b 1960); *Career* stockbroker, farmer; ptnr Williams de Broe & Co London 1955–75; John Izat & Partners: Balliliesk and Naemoor 1961–87, High Cocklaw 1987–; chm: Shires Income plc, United Auctions (Scotland) plc, U A Properties Ltd, U A Forestry Ltd, Fraser Tennant (Insurance Brokers) Ltd, Moredun Research Institute; dir: Cromlix Estates, C Champness & Co, Wiston Investment Co, Glasgow Investment Managers Ltd, Pentlands Science Park Ltd, Moredun Foundation Ltd, Moredun Scientific Ltd; past pres Fife-Kinross NFU & Kinross Agric Assoc; dir Royal Highland Agric Soc 1985–97 (hon treas 1992–96); memb Cncl Glenalmond Coll 1975–95 (chm of Ctee 1989–95); *Recreations* shooting, Suffolk sheep; *Clubs* Caledonian; *Style—* John Izat, Esq, JP; ✉ High Cocklaw, Berwick-upon-Tweed TD15 1UZ (☎ 01289 386591, fax 01289 386775)

J

JACK, Ian Grant; s of Henry Jack (d 1981), and Isabella, *née* Gillespie; *b* 7 Feb 1945; *Educ* Dunfermline HS Fife; *m* 1, 1979 (m dis 1992), Aparna Bhagat, da of Ganesh Bagchi; *partner* Rosalind Sharpe; 1 da (Isabella b 16 July 1992), 1 s (Alexander b 9 Oct 1993); *Career* trainee journalist 1965–66 (Glasgow Herald, Cambuslang Advertiser and East Kilbride News), Scottish Daily Express 1966–70; Sunday Times London 1970–86: chief sub-ed, ed Look pages and Atticus column, feature writer/foreign corr (newspaper and magazine) 1979–86; writer under contract Observer London and Vanity Fair NY 1986–89; Independent on Sunday: dep ed 1989–91, exec ed 1991–92, ed 1992–95; ed Granta magazine 1995– (former contrib); also contrib to: New Statesman, Spectator, TLS and London Review of Books; *Awards* Journalist of the Year 1985, Magazine Writer of the Year 1985, Reporter of the Year 1988, Nat Newspaper Ed of the Year 1992; *Books* Before the Oil Ran Out (1987); *Recreations* reading, music, steam navigation, Indian history; *Clubs* India International Centre (New Delhi); *Style*— Ian Jack, Esq; ✉ Editor, Granta, 2–3 Hanover Yard, Noel Road, London N1 8BE (☎ 0171 704 9776, fax 0171 704 0474)

JACK, Janet Marie; da of Albert Frederick Kaye (d 1951), and Ida, *née* Hancock (d 1951); *b* 5 June 1934; *Educ* Architectural Assoc Sch of Architecture (AADipl, GradDiplCons(AA)); *m* 8 Feb 1963, William Jack, s of Col Frank Weaver Jack, TD (d 1984); 1 s (Angus b 1963 d 1990), 1 da (Amy b 1965); *Career* architect; Architects Co-Ptnrship 1957–58, Harry Weesse Assocs Chicago 1958–59, IM PEI NY 1960, Planning and Devpt Ltd 1960–63, Dame Sylvia Crowe 1965–66, own landscape practice 1967–81; Building Design Partnership: joined 1981, ptnr 1986, sr ptnr 1988; own landscape practice 1991–; Landscape Inst: publicity offr 1984–88, memb External Affrs Ctee 1984–; memb Landscape Advsy Ctee on Trunk Roads Dept of Tport 1987–94; RIBA 1961, FRSA 1987, FLI 1994 (ALI 1973); *Books* The Design of Atria (contrib, 1983), The Design of Shopping Centres (contrib, 1989); *Recreations* yoga, opera, art, architecture, the environment; *Style*— Mrs Janet Jack

JACK, Rt Hon (John) Michael; PC (1997), MP (C) Fylde (majority 20,991); s of Ralph Niven, of York, and Florence Edith, *née* Reed; mother's family Hewish of Devon said to have arrived with William the Conqueror; *b* 17 Sept 1946; *Educ* Bradford GS, Bradford Tech Coll, Univ of Leicester (BA, MPhil); *m* 1976, Alison Jane, da of Cncllr Brian Rhodes Musgrave; 2 s (Edmund b 1979, Oliver b 1981); *Career* formerly with Marks & Spencer and Procter & Gamble, sales dir L O Jeffs Ltd 1980–87; Parly candidate Newcastle Central Feb 1974, MP (C) Fylde 1987–, PPS to Rt Hon John Gummer as min of state for local govt then for agric fisheries and food 1988–90, Parly under sec Miny of Social Security 1990–92, min of state Home Office 1992–93, min of state MAFF 1993–95, fin sec to the Treasy 1995–; jt sec Cons Tport Ctee 1987–88, sec Cons NW Membs Gp 1988–90, vice pres Think Green 1989–90; *Recreations* motor sport, dinghy sailing, playing Boules; *Style*— The Rt Hon Michael Jack, MP; ✉ House of Commons, Westminster, London SW1A 0AA

JACK, His Hon Judge Raymond Evan; QC (1982); s of late Evan Stuart Maclean Jack (d 1992), and Charlotte, *née* Fry (d 1993); bro of Roland Maclean Jack; *b* 13 Nov 1942; *Educ* Rugby, Trinity Coll Cambridge (MA); *m* 1 Oct 1976, Elizabeth Alison (Liza), da of Canon James Seymour Denys Mansel, KCVO (d 1995); 1 s (Alexander b 1986), 2 da (Katherine b 1979, Lucy b 1981); *Career* called to the Bar Inner Temple 1966; SE Circuit; recorder Crown Ct 1989–91, circuit judge (Western Circuit) 1991–, liaison judge to Dorset magistrates 1991–94, first mercantile judge Bristol 1994–; *Publications* Documentary Credits (1991, 2 edn 1993); *Style*— His Hon Judge Raymond Jack, QC; ✉ c/o The Law Courts, Small Street, Bristol BS1 1DA

JACK, Prof Robert Barr; CBE (1988); s of Robert Hendry Jack (d 1966), of Largs, Ayrshire, and Christina Alexandra, *née* Barr (d 1961); *b* 18 March 1928; *Educ* Kilsyth Acad, Glasgow HS, Univ of Glasgow (MA, LLB); *m* 1958, Anna Thorburn, da of George Harris Thomson (d 1991), of Glasgow; 2 s (Robert Thomson Barr b 1961, David George b 1963); *Career* slr; former sr ptnr McGrigor Donald Glasgow Edinburgh and London (ret 1993); prof of mercantile law Univ of Glasgow 1978–94; memb: Co Law Ctee Law Soc of Scotland 1971–95 (convener 1978–85), Scot Law Cmmn 1974–77, Advsy Panel Co Law DOT 1980–83, Cncl of the Stock Exchange 1984–86, Securities and Futures Authy (formerly Securities Assoc) 1986–94, The Securities and Investments Bd 1994–, UK Panel of Arbitrators Int Centre for Settlement of Investment Disputes 1989–, Panel on Takeovers and Mergers 1992–; lay memb Cncl for the Securities Indust 1983–85; Scot observer Insolvency Law Review Ctee DOT 1977–82, chm Review Ctee on Banking Servs Law 1987–89, legal advsr Accounting Standards Bd 1991–94; chm Joseph Dunn (Bottlers) Ltd 1983–; dir: Brownlee plc 1974–86 (chm 1984–86), Scottish Metropolitan Property plc 1980– (dep chm 1991–), Clyde Football Club Ltd 1980–, Bank of Scotland 1985–96 (chm W of Scotland Bd 1991–96), Gartmore Scotland Investment Trust plc 1991–; Scottish Mutual Assurance plc (formerly Scottish Mutual Assurance Society): dir 1987–, dep chm 1991–92, chm 1992–; dir Glasgow Devpt Agency 1992–; memb Scottish HE Funding Cncl 1992–96; chm Scottish Nat Cncl of YMCAs 1966–73 (pres 1983–), govr Hutchesons' Educnl Tst Glasgow 1978–87 (chm 1980–87), chm The Turnberry Tst 1983–; memb: Ctee of Mgmnt Malin Housing Assoc Turnberry Ayrshire 1971–, Bd of Govrs Beatson Inst for Cancer Res Glasgow 1989–; FRSA; *Publications* author of papers on various aspects of company law, banking law and practice and the statutory regulation and self regulation of the City; *Recreations* golf, music, football; *Clubs* Caledonian, Western (Glasgow), Pollok Golf, Shiskine Golf and Tennis (Isle of Arran); *Style*— Prof R B Jack, CBE; ✉ 50 Lanton Road, Newlands, Glasgow G43 2SR (☎ 0141 637 7302, fax 0141 637 8115)

JACK, Prof Ronald Dyce Sadler; s of Muirice Jack (d 1982), of Ayr, and Edith Emily Sadler (d 1984); *b* 3 April 1941; *Educ* Ayr Acad, Univ of Glasgow (MA, DLitt), Univ of Edinburgh (PhD); *m* (Christabel) Kirsty Margaret, da of Rev Maj Angus Macdonald Nicolson, TD (d 1975), of Ayr; 2 da (Fiona b 1968, Isla b 1972); *Career* Dept of English Lit Univ of Edinburgh: lectr 1965, reader 1978, assoc dean 1971–73, prof of Scot and medieval lit 1987–; visiting prof Univ of Virginia 1973–74; govr Newbattle Abbey Coll 1984–88, memb Scot Consultative Ctee on the Curriculum 1987–89, dir UCAS (formerly UCCA) 1989–94; Beinecke res fell Yale Univ 1992, visiting prof Univ of Strathclyde 1993; *Books include* The Italian Influence on Scottish Literature (1972), Scottish Prose 1550–1700 (ed, 1978), Choice of Scottish Verse 1560–1660 (ed, 1978), The Art of Robert Burns (co-ed, 1982), Alexander Montgomerie (1985), Scottish Literature's Debt to Italy (1986), Patterns of Divine Comedy (1989), The Road to the Never Land (1991), William Dunbar (1996); *Recreations* golf; *Style*— Prof Ronald Jack; ✉ 54 Buckstone Rd, Edinburgh EH10 6UN (☎ 0131 443 3498); Department of English Literature, University of Edinburgh, David Hume Tower, George Square, Edinburgh EH8 9JX (☎ 0131 650 3617)

JACK, Dr Timothy Michael (Tim); s of Michael Henry Fingland Jack (d 1990), of Teignmouth, S Devon, and Margaret Joyce, *née* Baker (d 1978); *b* 5 July 1947; *Educ* King Edward's Sch Birmingham, Guy's Hosp (MB BS); *m* 20 Oct 1979, (Veronica) Jane, da of Richard Christopher Warde (d 1953), of Orpington, Kent; 2 s (Benjamin b 1983, Jonathan b 1986); *Career* anaesthetist Shanta Bhawan Hosp Kathmandu Nepal 1974–76, sr registrar Nuffield Dept of Anaesthetics Radcliffe Infirmary Oxford 1978–82, conslt anaesthetist Leeds Gen Infirmary and hon lectr Univ of Leeds 1982–90, conslt in pain relief and clinical dir Oxford Regnl Pain Relief Unit Oxford 1990–; memb: Exec Ctee Christian Med Fellowship 1987–95, Personnel Ctee Interserve (UK) 1978–, Cncl The Pain Soc 1993–; FFARCS 1977; *Recreations* sailing, mountain-walking, gardening, bird-watching; *Style*— Dr Tim Jack; ✉ 46 Eaton Road, Appleton, Abingdon, Oxon OX13 5JH (☎ 01865 864900)

JACK, William; s of Col Frank W Jack, TD, JP (d 1984), of Aberdeenshire, Scotland, and Edith Margaret, *née* Forsyth (d 1974); *b* 12 Dec 1933; *Educ* Aberdeen GS, Aberdeen Coll of Architecture, Cornell Univ (MArch); *m* 8 Feb 1963, Janet Marie, da of Albert Frederick Kaye (d 1951); 1 s (Angus b 31 Dec 1963 d 1990), 1 da (Amy Frances b 28 July 1965); *Career* Building Design Ptnrship: joined 1961, ptnr 1966, sr ptnr 1968, chm 1989–92, conslt 1992–94; designer of many projects in UK and overseas memb Bd London Docklands Development Corp 1993– (chm Planning Ctee 1993–); RIBA; *Recreations* opera, theatre, architecture, golf; *Style*— William Jack, Esq

JACKAMAN, Michael Clifford John; s of Air Cdre Clifford Thomas Jackaman, OBE, and Lily Margaret Jackaman; *b* 7 Nov 1935; *Educ* Felsted Sch Essex, Jesus Coll Cambridge (MA); *m* 1960, Valerie Jane, *née* Pankhurst; 1 s, 1 da; *Career* dep md Harveys of Bristol 1976–78, marketing dir Allied Breweries 1978–83; Allied Domecq plc (Allied-Lyons plc until 1994): dir 1978–, vice chm 1988–92, chm 1991–96; dir Kleinwort Benson Group PLC 1994–; chm: Hiram Walker Allied Vintners 1983–91, John Harvey & Sons Ltd 1983–92; memb Cncl of Admin Château Latour 1983–93, dir Fintex of London Ltd 1986–92, non-exec dir Rank Organisation plc 1992–; govr Univ of the West of England Bristol (formerly Bristol Poly) 1988–91; appeal chm Royal Hosp for Sick Children Bristol; memb: Keepers of the Quaich (Scotland), Commanderie des Bontemps du Médoc et des Graves (France); *Recreations* walking, tennis, potting; *Style*— Michael Jackaman, Esq; ✉ Allied-Domecq plc, 24 Portland Place, London W1N 4BB (☎ 0171 323 9000, fax 0171 436 0689)

JACKLIN, Anthony (Tony); CBE (1990, OBE 1970); s of Arthur David Jacklin, of Bottesford, South Humberside, and Doris Lillian Jacklin; *b* 7 July 1944; *Educ* Doncaster Road Secdy Modern Scunthorpe; *m* 1, 1966, Vivian (d 1988); 2 s (Bradley Mark b 12 Nov 1969, Warren b 10 Sept 1972), 1 da (Tina b 27 March 1975); m 2, Dec 1988, Astrid May, da of Tormod Waagen; 1 s (Sean b 1991), 1 step s (Alistair James b 11 Aug 1981), 1 step da (Anna-May b 17 Feb 1979); *Career* professional golfer 1962–; began playing golf 1953, Lincolnshire jr champion 1959–61, Lincolnshire Open champion 1961, memb Br Boys team 1960, turned professional 1962, Br Asst Pro champion 1964, Coombe Hill Assts champion 1964; winner of 24 tournaments worldwide incl: Jacksonville Open 1968 and 1972, Br Open 1969, US Open 1970, Br PGA 1972 and 1982, Italian Open 1973, Dunlop Masters 1973, Scandinavian Open 1975, Eng Nat PGA Championship 1977, German Open 1979; played in 7 Ryder Cup matches 1967–79; capt Euro Ryder Cup team: 1983, 1985 (won), 1987 (won), 1989 (drawn); memb PGA Senior Tour; dir of golf San Roque Club Cadiz Sapin 1988–, currently golf course designer; life vice pres and hon memb PGA 1970 (hon life memb Euro Tournament Players Div), hon memb numerous golf clubs; *Books* Golf With Tony Jacklin (1969), The Price of Success (1979), Jacklin's Golfing Secrets (with Peter Dobereiner, 1983), Tony Jacklin: The First Forty Years (1985), Golf My Way (1990); *Recreations* shooting; *Style*— Tony Jacklin, Esq, CBE; ✉ c/o IMG, 1 Erieview Plaza, Cleveland, Ohio 44114, USA

JACKLIN, Walter William (Bill); s of Harold Jacklin (d 1964), of London, and Alice Mary, *née* Jones (d 1988); *b* 1 Jan 1943; *Educ* Walthamstow Sch of Art, Royal Coll of Art (MA, ARA); *m* 1, 1979 (m dis 1992), Lesley Sarina, da of Monty Berman; m 2, Janet Ann, da of Frank Russo; *Career* artist; teaching at various art colls 1967–75, artist in residence Br Cncl Hong Kong 1993–94; *Solo Exhibitions* Nigel Greenwood Inc London 1970, 1971 and 1975, Hester Van Royen Gallery London 1973 and 1977, Marlborough Fine Art London 1980, 1983, 1988, 1992 and 1997, Marlborough Gallery New York 1985, 1987, 1990 and 1997, Urban Portraits 1985–92 (retrospective, Museum of Modern Art Oxford 1992, touring to Santiago and Compostella Spain 1992–93), Urban Portraits Hong Kong (British Cncl, Hong Kong Arts Centre) 1995, Marlborough Graphics London 1996; included in numerous int gp exhibitions; *Public Collections* Art Gallery of Sydney Aust, Arts Cncl of GB, Br Cncl London, Br Museum, Govt Arts Collection GB, Metropolitan Museum of Art, NY, Tate Gallery, V & A, Yale Centre for Br Art Newhaven Conn; RA 1992; *Books* Monograph on Bill Jacklin (by John Russell-Taylor, 1997); *Recreations* walking, planting trees; *Clubs* Chelsea Arts; *Style*— Bill Jacklin, Esq, RA; ✉ c/o Marlborough Fine Art, 6 Albermarle St, London W1 (☎ 0171 629 5161)

JACKMAN, Frederick Charles; s of Stanley Charles Jackman (d 1978), of Brentwood, Essex, and Lilian May, *née* Brassett (d 1991); *b* 29 Feb 1944; *Educ* Warren Sch Dagenham, Barking Coll of Technol, Borough Poly (HNC); *m* 14 June 1969, Zarene, da of Karim Gulam Husain (d 1973), of London; *Career* Stinton Jones & Ptnrs 1960–64, Costain Construction 1964–66, T P Bennett & Son 1966–69, Arup Assocs 1969–73, Upton Associates bldg servs consulting engrs 1973– (resident Dubai 1976, sr ptnr 1979–, Malaysia 1991); CEng, FCIBSE, FIHEEM; *Recreations* travel, walking, fishing; *Style*— Frederick Jackman, Esq; ✉ New House, Holyport Rd, Maidenhead, Berks; Upton Associates, Pilot House, West Wycombe Rd, High Wycombe, Bucks HP12 3AB (☎ 01494 450931, fax 01494 531464)

JACKOWSKI, Andrzej Aleksander; s of Henryk Soplica Jackowski (d 1978), and Anne Biernaczak; *b* 4 Dec 1947; *Educ* Holland Park Sch, Camberwell Coll of Art, Falmouth Sch of Art (Dip AD), RCA (MA); *m* 1, 1 May 1970 (m dis 1989), Nicolette Tester; 1 da (Laura b 3 Feb 1972); *partner*, Eve Ashley; 1 s (Louis b 5 Oct 1990); *Career* artist; lectr 1977–86 (RCA, Byam Shaw Sch of Art Brighton); *Solo Exhibitions* Univ of Surrey 1978–79, Moira Kelly Fine Art 1982, Bluecoat Gallery Liverpool (touring) 1984, Marlborough Fine Art 1986, 1989 and 1990, Gardner Centre Gallery Brighton 1989, Castlefield Gallery Manchester transferred Nottingham Castle Museum 1989; *Gp Exhibitions* incl: John Moores Exhibitions (Walker Art Gallery Liverpool) 1976, 1980–81 and 1982–83, Narrative Painting (Arnolfini Bristol, travelling) 1979–80, Inner Worlds (Arts Cncl of GB, travelling), Eight in the Eighties (Britain Salutes New York Festival, NY) 1983, Interiors (Anne Berthoud Gallery) 1983–84, New Works on Paper (Br Cncl Travelling Exhibition) 1983–85, House and Abroad (Serpentine) 1984, The Image as Catalyst (Ashmolean Oxford) 1984, Human Interest, Fifty Years of British Art About People (Cornerhouse Manchester) 1985; Introducing with Pleasure: Star Choices from the Arts Cncl Collection (travelling exhibition, Gardner Centre Brighton) 1987; An Anthology: Artists who studied with Peter de Francia (Camden Arts Centre 1987; Cries and Whispers: New Works for the Br Cncl Collection (travelling exhibition Aust and NZ) 1988; 150 Anniversary Exhibition, Exhibition Road Painters at the RCA (RCA) 1988; Object and Image: Aspects of British Art in the 1980s (City Museum and Art Gallery, Stoke on Trent) 1988; The New British Painting (The Contemporary Arts Centre Cincinnati, travelling exhibition) 1988, The Tree of Life (South Bank Centre travelling exhibition Cornerhouse Gallery Manchester) 1989, School of London Words on Paper (Odette Gilbert Gallery) 1989, Now for the Future (South Bank Centre) 1990, Picturing People (Br Cncl travelling exhibition, Nat Art Gallery Kuala Lumpur, Hong Kong Museum of Art, The Empress Palace Singapore) 1990, On View (Marlborough) 1990, Tribute to Peter Fuller (Beaux Arts Bath) 1990; *Public Collections* incl: Arts Cncl of GB, Br Cncl, Contemporary Arts Soc, Euro Parl, RCA, SE Arts, Univ of Liverpool, Univ of Surrey; SE Arts fell Univ of Surrey 1978–79, Tolly Cobbold/Eastern Arts Major prize 1981; *Style*— Andrzej Jackowski, Esq; ✉ c/o Purdy Hicks Gallery, 65 Hopton Street, London SE1 9GZ (☎ 0171 237 6062)

JACKSON, Alan Francis; *b* 25 April 1935; *Educ* Westminster; *m* Jean Elizabeth; 1 da (Kate); *Career* J H Minet & Co Ltd 1955–58, worked in Canada 1958–62, underwriter Robert Bradford Ltd 1962–78, Alan Jackson Underwriting Agencies Ltd 1979–92 (merged with Wren Underwriting Agencies Ltd 1986); chm: Wren Syndicates Management Ltd, Wren Holdings Ltd 1994, Wren Holdings Group Plc 1995; sr dep chm Cncl of Lloyd's 1991; Freeman Worshipful Co of Goldsmiths; FIIC, ACII; *Recreations* golf; *Style*— Alan Jackson, Esq; ✉ Wren Syndicates Management Ltd, 12 Arthur Street, London EC4R 9AB (☎ 0171 623 3050, fax 0171 283 2150)

JACKSON, Andrew Graham; s of Thomas Armitage Geoffrey Jackson (d 1985), and Hilda Marion Jackson; *b* 5 May 1937; *Educ* Denstone Coll, Jesus Coll Cambridge (MA); *m* 1964, Christine Margaret, da of Charles Edward Chapman, of Oundle; 1 s (Matthew b 1971), 2 da (Sarah b 1967, Claire b 1969); *Career* Nat Serv 1955–57, Lt served Suez 1956; Stewarts & Lloyds Corby 1960–67; Denco Holdings Ltd: joined 1967, sales mangr 1967–69, sales dir dep md 1972–77, gp md 1977–85; dir AMEC Projects Ltd 1985–86, chm and md Keg Services Ltd 1996– (md 1986–); Lloyd's underwriter; pres Hereford Dist Scouts Assoc; Liveryman: Worshipful Co of Carmen, Worshipful Co of Engrs (memb Ct of Assts); CEng, FIMechE, FIMgt; *Recreations* squash, water skiing, scuba diving; *Clubs* RAC; *Style*— Andrew Jackson, Esq; ✉ The Orchard, Lyde, Hereford HR4 8AA (☎ 01432 272830, fax 01432 358745); Keg Services Ltd, Twyford Rd, Hereford HR2 6JR (☎ 01432 353300, fax 01432 268141)

JACKSON, Andrew Malcolm; s of Douglas MacGilchrist Jackson, of Milford on Sea, and Mabel Pauline, *née* Brand; *b* 4 May 1945; *Educ* Marlborough Coll, Middx Hosp Med Sch Univ of London (MB BS); *m* Anne Marie, da of Joseph Lucas, of 38 Regency Drive, Silksworth, Sunderland; 2 s (Charles b 1979, Adam Stuart b 1981); *Career* conslt orthopaedic surgn: UCH 1981–91, Hosp for Sick Children Gt Ormond St 1981–91, Queen Mary's Univ Hosp Roehampton 1991–94, St George's Hosp 1994–; hon conslt Royal Nat Orthopaedic Hosp 1983; Freeman City of London 1981, Liveryman Worshipful Soc of Apothecaries; FRCS 1979, memb RSM; *Recreations* sailing, fishing; *Style*— Andrew Jackson, Esq; ✉ 107 Harley St, London W1 (☎ 0171 935 9521)

JACKSON, Andrew Michael; s of Anthony Hargreaves Jackson (d 1990), of Boughton, Northampton, and Evelyn Mary, *née* Anson (d 1987); *b* 27 Feb 1940; *Educ* Sedbergh; *m* 1 April 1967, Jillian Felicity, da of Denys Gordon Parfitt, of Shalford, Guildford, Surrey; 1 s (Capt David Richard Anthony RE b 5 March 1968); *Career* admitted slr 1965; ptnr Hutson Poole 1984–, Notary Public 1986; memb Guildford Rotary Club, past pres Guildford C of C; memb: Law Soc 1965, Notaries Soc 1986; *Recreations* inland cruising, carriage driving; *Style*— Andrew M Jackson, Esq; ✉ Oaklands, Horsham Lane, Ewhurst, Cranleigh, Surrey GU6 7SW (☎ 01483 275085); Hutson Poole Solicitors, 17 & 18 Quarry St, Guildford, Surrey GU1 3XA (☎ 01483 565244, fax 01483 575961)

JACKSON, Ashley Norman; s of Norman Valentine Jackson (POW Malaya, executed 1944/45), and Dulcie Olga, *née* Scott (Mrs Haigh); *b* 22 Oct 1940; *Educ* St Joseph's Singapore, Holyrood Barnsley S Yorks, Barnsley Coll of Art; *m* 22 Dec 1962, (Patricia) Anne, da of Donald Hutchinson, of Barnsley, S Yorks; 2 da (Heather b 11 Nov 1968, Claudia b 15 Sept 1970); *Career* artist; exhibited: RI, RBA, RWS, Britain in Watercolour, UA; one man shows: Upper Grosvenor Gallery, Mall Gallery, Christina Foyle Gallery, Spanish Inst of Culture, London, New York, Chicago, San Francisco, Washington, Dallas, one-man exhibition in Huddersfield opened by HRH The Prince of Wales 1987; works in the collections of: Barnsley Coll (house permanent collection of 26 originals), MOD, RN, NCB, British Gas, NUM, Harold Wilson, Edward Heath and John Major; own TV series on: Yorkshire TV (A Brush with Ashley 1990, 1992, 1993 and 1994), BBC1, Channel 4 and PBS in America; chm Crimestoppers Yorks region, memb Bd Yorkshire Young Achievers Awards; FRSA 1964; *Books* My Own Flesh and Blood (1981), The Artist's Notebook (1985), Ashley Jackson's World of Art 1 and 2 (1988), Painting in the Open Air (1992), A Brush With Ashley (1993), Painting the British Isles - a watercolourist's journey (1994); *Style*— Ashley Jackson, Esq; ✉ Ashley Jackson Galleries, 13–15 Huddersfield Rd, Holmfirth, Huddersfield HD7 1JR (☎ 01484 686460, fax 01484 681766)

JACKSON, Barry Trevor; s of late Arthur Stanley Jackson, of Chingford, and Violet May, *née* Fry; *b* 7 July 1936; *Educ* Sir George Monoux GS, King's Coll London, Westminster Med Sch (entrance scholar, MB MS); *m* 1962, Sheila May, *née* Wood, of Bollington Cheshire; 2 s (Simon, James), 1 da (Sarah); *Career* Serjeant Surgn to HM The Queen 1991– (Surgn to HM's Household 1983–91); conslt surgn: St Thomas' Hosp 1973–, Queen Victoria Hosp East Grinstead 1977–, King Edward VII Hosp for Offrs 1983–; pres Assoc of Surgns of GB and Ireland 1994–95 (hon sec 1986–91, vice pres 1993–94), hon conslt surgn to the Army 1990–; memb: Ct of Examiners RCS England 1983–89, Cncl RSM 1987–92 (pres Section of Coloproctology 1991–92), Cncl Assoc of Coloproctology of GB and Ireland 1990–93, Cncl RCS 1991–; ed Annals RCS England 1992– (asst ed 1984–91); memb Ct of Assts Worshipful Co of Barbers, Liveryman Worshipful Soc of Apothecaries; FRCS; *Recreations* book collecting, reading, opera, the arts generally; *Clubs* Athenaeum; *Style*— Barry Jackson, Esq; ✉ St Thomas' Hosp, London SE1 7EH; The Consulting Rooms, York House, London SE1 7UT

JACKSON, Prof Bernard Stuart; s of Leslie Jackson (d 1989), of Liverpool, and Isabelle, *née* Caplan (d 1944); *b* 16 Nov 1944; *Educ* Liverpool Collegiate Sch, Univ of Liverpool (LLB), Univ of Oxford (DPhil), Univ of Edinburgh (LLD); *m* 1967, Rosalyn, *née* Young; 1 s (Iain Charles b 1970), 1 da (Judith Deborah b 1973); *Career* called to the Bar Gray's Inn 1966; lectr Dept of Civil Law Univ of Edinburgh 1969–76, princ lectr Div of Law Preston Poly 1976, prof of law Liverpool Poly 1980–85 (head Dept of Law 1977–85), prof of law Univ of Kent at Canterbury 1985–89, Queen Victoria prof of law Univ of Liverpool 1989–; sr assoc fell Oxford Centre for Postgrad Hebrew Studies 1984–, pres The Jewish Law Assoc 1984–88 (chm 1980–84), sec-gen and treas Int Assoc for the Semiotics of Law 1987–93, chm BILETA Inquiry into Computer Provision in UK Law Schs 1989–91, pres Br Assoc for Jewish Studies 1993; memb Editorial Bd: Archivos Latinoamericanos de Metodologia y Filosofia, Advsy Bd Center for Semiotic Res in Law Govt and Economics Penn State Univ, Int Jl for the Semiotics of Law, International Jl of the Legal Profession, Semiotic Crossroads; ed: The Jewish Law Annual 1978–, The Liverpool Law Review 1979–85; memb: Conseil d'administration Association Européenne pour la philosophie du droit, Soc for Old Testament Study 1974–, Br Assoc for Jewish Studies 1974–, Société d'Histoire du Droit 1975–, Soc for the Study of Theology 1976–, Mgmnt Ctee Nat Centre for Cued Speech 1985–89, Mgmnt Ctee UK Law Tech Centre 1989–92, Northern Circuit Ctee on Computer Support for Litigation 1991, Lord Chllr's Area Criminal Justice Advsy Ctee 1992–, Liverpool Branch Soc for Computers and Law; visiting appts: visiting asst prof Univ of Georgia Law Sch 1968–69, assoc fell Oxford Centre for Postgrad Hebrew Studies 1974 (Littman fell 1977), Br Cncl lectr Univ of Rotterdam and Univ of Amsterdam 1975, faculty lectr Faculty of Theology Univ Coll of N Wales 1980, Lady Davis visiting prof Dept of Bible Hebrew Univ of Jerusalem 1981, speaker's lectr in Biblical studies Univ of Oxford 1983–86, professeur invité Université de Paris-X Nanterre 1987–88, professore a contratto Università di Bologna 1988, Caroline and Joseph Gruss visiting prof in Talmudic legal studies Harvard Law Sch 1992, Gastprofessor Rechtstheorie Katholieke Universitet Brussels 1992–93 and 1994–95, assoc prof University of Paris I (Panthéon-Sorbonne) 1994; *Books* Theft in Early Jewish Law (1972), Essays in Jewish and Comparative Legal History (1975), Semiotics and Legal Theory (1985), Law, Fact and Narrative Coherence (1988), Making Sense in Law (1995), Making Sense in Jurisprudence (1996), Wisdom Laws (1997); ed of numerous legal books and jls; *Style*— Prof Bernard Jackson; ✉ Faculty of Law, University of Liverpool, PO Box 147, Liverpool L69 3BX (☎ 0151 794 2814, fax 0151 794 2829)

JACKSON, Betty (Mrs David Cohen); MBE (1987); da of Arthur Jackson (d 1977), of Lancs, and Phyllis Gertrude, *née* Rains (d 1983); *b* 24 June 1949; *Educ* Bacup and Rawtenstall GS Lancs, Birmingham Coll Art and Design; *m* 14 Jan 1986, David Cohen, s of Mansour Cohen (d 1977), of Marseille, France; 1 s (Oliver Mansour b 1987), 1 da (Pascale Phyllis b 1986); *Career* chief designer Quorum 1975, fndr Betty Jackson Ltd 1981, launched Betty Jackson for Men 1986; Cotton Designer of the Year 1983, Br Designer of the Year 1985, Fil D'Or award by International Linen 1985 and 1989, Viyella award by Coates Viyella 1987; hon fell: Univ of Birmingham 1988, RCA 1989, Univ of Central Lancashire 1992; RDI 1988; *Clubs* Groucho; *Style*— Miss Betty Jackson, MBE; ✉ 33 Tottenham St, London W1P 9PE (☎ 0171 631 1010, fax 0171 323 0609)

JACKSON, Very Rev Dr Brandon Donald; s of Herbert Jackson (d 1977), and Millicent, *née* Haddock (d 1980); *b* 11 Aug 1934; *Educ* Stockport Sch, Univ of Liverpool, Univ of Oxford (LLB, Dip Theol); *m* 1958, Mary Lindsay, da of John Philip; 2 s (Timothy Philip b 1959, Robert Brandon b 1961), 1 da (Sarah Lindsay b 1964); *Career* curate: Christ Church New Malden Surrey 1958–61, St George Leeds 1961–65; vicar St Peter's Shipley 1965–77, provost Bradford 1977–89, dean of Lincoln 1989–; memb: Gen Synod of the C of E 1970–77 and 1980–89, Gen Synod Marriages Cmmn 1974–78; church cmmr 1971–73; memb: Cncl of Wycliffe Hall Oxford 1971–85, St John's Coll Nottingham 1986–89; govr: Harrogate Coll 1974–84, Bradford GS 1977–89, Bishop Grosseteste Coll Lincoln 1989–, Lincoln Christ's Hosp Sch 1989–; religious advsr to Yorkshire TV 1969–79; scriptwriter conslt: Stars on Sunday, Emmerdale Farm, etc; Hon DLitt Univ of Bradford 1990; *Recreations* sport, cricket, running, fell-walking, fishing, reading; *Style*— The Very Rev Dr Brandon Jackson; ✉ The Deanery, Eastgate, Lincoln LN2 1QG (☎ 01522 523608, fax 01522 538320)

JACKSON, (Barbara Amy) Bridget; da of Walter Dumolo Jackson (d 1979), and Vera Joan, *née* Pepper (d 1990); *b* 10 July 1936; *Educ* Bredenbury Court Herefordshire, Gardenhurst Burnham-on-Sea; *Career* co sec and dir P F Jackson Ltd Birmingham 1975–85; int golfer; Br Girls Champion 1954, Staffs Ladies Champion 1954, 1956–59, 1963–64, 1966–69 and 1976, Midland Ladies Champion 1954, 1956–60 and 1969; toured Aust and NZ with Br Jr Team 1955, Eng Ladies Champion 1956, German Ladies Champion 1956, Canadian Ladies Champion 1967; represented GB and I v USA 1958, 1964 and 1968; represented GB and I v Europe 1959, 1963, 1965 and 1967 (non playing capt 1973 and 1975); represented GB in Cwlth tournament 1959 and 1967; represented Eng in home int 1955–59 and 1963–66 (non playing capt 1973–74); int and nat selector 1983–88; tstee Rhodes Almshouses Birmingham 1983–; pres: Midlands Div Eng Ladies Golf Assoc 1988–91, Staffs Ladies Golf Assoc 1988–89, English Ladies Golf Assoc 1993–95; *Recreations* embroidery, golf, watching other sports; *Clubs* Edgbaston and Royal St David's Golf, Handsworth Hunstanton and Killarney Golf (hon life memb); *Style*— Miss Bridget Jackson

JACKSON, Bryan Alan; s of Michael Jackson, and Mildred, *née* Segal; *b* 26 Feb 1956; *Educ* Hutchesons GS, Glasgow Coll of Technol (Scottish HND in Accountancy); *m* 12 Aug 1980, Frances Lauren, da of Ronnie Freedman; 3 da (Leigh Sarah b 28 Jan 1982, Dawn Michele b 24 March 1985, Kara Nicole b 3 Aug 1987); *Career* articled clerk Ernst and Whinney Glasgow 1977–81; Pannell Kerr Forster: insolvency mangr 1981–85, ptnr (insolvency) 1985–94, managing ptnr 1995–; lectr ICAS, spokesperson in insolvency to media, speaker on insolvency to professionals, govt agencies, Fraud Squad, Consumer Credit Assoc and debt counselling bodies; examiner in Scotland of the personal insolvency paper for the Jt Insolvency Examinations; treas Children's Aid (Scotland) Ltd; MICAS 1981; memb: Inst of Credit Mgmnt 1989, Insolvency Practitioners' Assoc 1989, Soc of Practitioners of Insolvency 1992; *Recreations* squash (rep GB Maccabiah Games Israel 1993, rep Scotland (silver medal) Euro Maccabi Games 1995), karate, skiing, football; *Style*— Bryan Jackson, Esq; ✉ Pannell Kerr Forster, 78 Carlton Place, Glasgow G5 9TH (☎ 0141 429 5900, fax 0141 429 5901, mobile 0802 470478)

JACKSON, Calvin Leigh Raphael; s of Air Cdre John Arthur George Jackson, CBE, DFC, AFC, of Wimbledon Common, London, and Yolanda, *née* de Felice; *b* 13 Aug 1952; *Educ* Douai Sch, King's Coll London (LLB, LLM), CCC Cambridge (MPhil); *m* 14 Aug 1993, Caroline Mary, da of Colin Herbert Clout; *Career* called to the Bar Lincoln's Inn 1975, in practice 1981–83, govt legal serv 1983–85, sr compensation conslt William M Mercer Ltd 1985–87, princ Coopers & Lybrand 1987–92, head of strategic compensation consltg and ptnr Watson Wyatt Partners 1992–; memb Hon Soc of Lincoln's Inn; *Clubs* Utd Oxford and Cambridge; *Style*— Calvin Jackson, Esq; ✉ Watson Wyatt Partners, 21 Tothill Street, London SW1H 9LL (☎ 0171 222 8033)

JACKSON, Dr Caroline Frances; MEP (C) Wiltshire North and Bath (majority 8,787); *b* 5 Nov 1946; *Educ* Sch of St Clare Penzance, St Hugh's Coll Oxford (MA), Nuffield Coll Oxford (DPhil); *m* 1975, Robert Victor Jackson, MP, *qv*; 1 s (decd); *Career* res fell St Hugh's Coll 1972, memb Oxford City Cncl 1970–73, Parly candidate (C) Birmingham Erdington 1974, MEP (C): Wiltshire 1984–94, Wiltshire North and Bath 1994–; EDG: secretariat Luxembourg 1974–76, Brussels 1976–78, head London Office 1979–84; dir: Peugeot Talbot UK Ltd 1987–, Inst Euro Environment Policy; memb: Nat Consumer Cncl 1982–84, UK Nat Ctee for Euro Environment Year 1987; *Books* A Student's Guide to Europe (1985 and 1996), Europe's Environment: A Conservative Approach (1989);

Recreations walking, painting, tennis, golf; *Style*— Dr Caroline Jackson, MEP; ✉ 14 Bath Road, Swindon, Wilts SN1 4BA (☎ 01793 422663, fax 01793 422664)

JACKSON, Charles Vivian; s of Louis Charles Jackson, MC, of E Sussex, and Sylvia, *née* Kerr; *b* 2 July 1953; *Educ* Marlborough, Magdalen Coll Oxford (MA), Stanford (MBA); *m* 12 Feb 1982, Frances Miriam, da of Frederick Schwartzstein (d 1982), of NJ; 1 s (David b 1985), 1 da (Rebecca b 1983); *Career* Harkness fell 1976–78; md Mercury Asset Management Holdings 1987–90, dep chm Warburg Asset Management 1988–95, vice chm Mercury Asset Management plc 1993–; dir: Warburg Investment Management 1985–87, Mercury Bond Fund 1985–, Munich London 1986–90, Warburg Asset Management 1988–95, Mercury Asset Management plc 1990–, Mercury Asset Management Group plc 1993–; *Clubs* Brooks's, Travellers', Seaview Yacht; *Style*— Charles Jackson, Esq; ✉ Mercury Asset Management plc, 33 King William St, London EC4R 9AS (☎ 0171 280 2800)

JACKSON, Christopher Murray; s of Rev Howard Murray Jackson (d 1955), and Doris Bessie Jackson (d 1995); *b* 24 May 1935; *Educ* Kingswood Sch Bath, Magdalen Coll Oxford (MA), Univ of Frankfurt, LSE; *m* 1971, Carlie Elizabeth, da of Bernard Sidney Keeling; 1 s, 1 da; *Career* Nat Serv cmmnd Pilot RAF; former: dir of corp devpt Spillers plc, sr mangr Unilever plc; MEP (C) Kent East 1979–94, Hon MEP 1994–; Cons Pty spokesman on: co-operation with developing countries 1981–86, agric 1987–89, foreign affrs and defence 1991–91, economics and monetary affrs and industrial policy 1992–94; dep chm and dep ldr Cons MEPs 1989–91; dir: Westminster Communications Ltd 1988–95, Politics International Ltd 1995–; nat chm Agriculture and Countryside Forum 1995–; chm CJA Consultants Ltd 1995–; memb Cons Nat Union Exec 1995–; memb Lloyd's 1985–; *Books* Europe and the Third World (1985), Careers in Europe (2 edn 1991), Shaking the Foundations - Britain and the New Europe (1990), Your Watchdogs in Europe (1990), The Maastricht Summit (with B Pattersen, 1992), Whose Job Is It Anyway? - Subsidiarity in the EC (1992); *Recreations* music, gardening, skiing, sailing; *Style*— Christopher Jackson, Esq; ✉ 8 Wellmeade Drive, Sevenoaks, Kent TN13 1QA (☎ 01732 741117, fax 01732 743061)

JACKSON, Colin Ray; MBE; *b* 18 Feb 1967; *Career* athlete (110m hurdles); memb Brecon Athletics Club, UK int 1985– (jr int 1984); honours incl: Silver medal Euro Jr Championships 1985, Gold medal World Jr Championships 1986, Silver medal Cwlth Games 1986, Silver medal Euro Cup 1987, Bronze medal World Championships 1987, Silver medal Olympic Games 1988, Silver medal World Cup 1989, Gold medal Euro Cup 1989, 1991 and 1993, Gold medal Cwlth Games 1990 and 1994, Gold medal World Cup 1992, Gold medal (and new world record) World Championships 1993 (Silver medal 4 x 100m relay); honours at 60m hurdles: Silver medal World Indoor Championships 1989 and 1993, Gold medal Euro Indoor Championships 1989 and 1994 (Silver medal 1987), new world record 1994; numerous Welsh, UK, Euro and Cwlth records; *Style*— Colin Jackson, Esq, MBE; ✉ c/o Susan Barrett, "Nuff" Respect, 107 Sherland Road, Twickenham, Middx; fan club (with Linford Christie MBE): LCJ Club, PO Box 295, Twickenham, Middx TW1 4XJ

JACKSON, Prof David Cooper; s of Rev James Jackson (d 1983), and Mary Emma Jackson; *b* 3 Dec 1931; *Educ* Ashville Coll Harrogate, Brasenose Coll Oxford (BCL, MA); *m* 1967, Roma Lilian, da of late William Pendergast; *Career* called to the Bar Inner Temple 1957, pt/t prof of law Univ of Southampton (prof of law 1971–84, dean 1972–75 and 1978–81, dep vice chllr 1983–84); dir Inst of Maritime Law Southampton 1983–84 and 1987–89, conslt Shipping Legislation UNCTAD 1979–80 and 1983–84; vice pres Immigration Appeal Tbnl 1984–96 (chm pt/t 1996–); visiting prof: QMC London 1969, Arizona State Univ 1976; Sir John Latham prof of law Monash Univ Aust 1966–70; *Books* Principles of Property Law (1967), The Conflicts Process (1975), The Enforcement of Maritime Claims (1985, 2 edn 1996), World Shipping Laws (gen ed, 1979), Civil Jurisdiction and Judgments: Maritime Claims (1987), Immigration Law and Practice (1996); *Recreations* travel; *Style*— Prof David Jackson; ✉ office: 231 Strand, London (☎ 0171 353 8060)

JACKSON, Dr David Edward Pritchett; s of Reginald Robert George Pritchett Jackson, of Newark on Trent, Notts, and Dorothy Elizabeth, *née* Hodgson (d 1989); *b* 9 Dec 1941; *Educ* Rossall Sch, MECAS Shemlan Lebanon, Pembroke Coll Cambridge (BA, MA, PhD, Judo half blue); *m* 9 July 1982 (m dis 1994), Margaret Letitia, da of Melville Brown (d 1993), of St Andrews, Fife; 1 s (Anthony David), 1 da (Carolyn Ellen); *Career* Lt-Cdr RNR 1972–82; res fell Pembroke Coll Cambridge 1967–70; Univ of St Andrews: lectr in Arabic language and lit 1967–68, lectr in Arabic studies 1968–84, sr lectr in Arabic studies 1984–95, chm dept 1979–86, dir Sch of Abbasid Studies 1979–95; ed Occasional Papers Sch of Abbasid Studies 1982–96; memb: Union Européenne d'Arabisants et d'Islamisants (UEAI), ME Studies Assoc of America (MESA), Br Soc for the History of Mathematics; memb RNA St Andrews and NE Fife branch (memb Ctee 1984–86); fell Br Soc for Middle Eastern Studies 1974, RUSI; *Books* Saladin - the Politics of the Holy War (with M C Lyons, 1982), Chambers Dictionary of World History (contrib, 1993), Egypt and Syria in the Fatimid, Ayyubid and Mamluk Eras (contrib, 1995); *Recreations* the river, music, food, golf, Italian language and lit, Venice; *Clubs* Hawks', Leander, Oriental, Royal and Ancient Golf (St Andrews); *Style*— Dr David Jackson; ✉ 4 Woodside Crescent, Elie, Fife KY9 1DY (☎ 01333 330258); c/o Department of Arabic Studies, The University, St Andrews, Scotland KY16 9AL (☎ 01334 476161)

JACKSON, David John; *b* 25 Jan 1953; *Educ* Univ of Bristol (LLB); *Career* articled clerk Grey Lloyd & Co slrs 1975–77, asst slr Barlow Lyde and Gilbert 1977–79, slr The Nestlé Company Ltd 1979–81, asst gp legal advsr Chloride Group plc 1981–87, head of legal Matthew Hall plc 1987–89, co sec and dir of legal servs PowerGen plc 1989–; *Recreations* rugby, tennis, sailing; *Clubs* Royal Ocean Racing, Seaview Yacht, RAC, Harlequins FC; *Style*— David Jackson, Esq; ✉ PowerGen plc, 53 New Broad Street, London EC2M 1JJ (☎ 0171 826 2743, fax 0171 826 2712)

JACKSON, Sir (John) Edward; KCMG (1984, CMG 1977); *b* 24 June 1925; *Educ* Ardingly, Corpus Christi Coll Cambridge; *m* 1952, Eve Stainton, *née* Harris; 2 s, 1 da; *Career* Sub Lt, RNVR 1943–46; Dip Serv FO 1947–49, Br Embassy Paris 1949–52, Br Embassy Bonn 1956–59, Br Embassy Guatemala 1959–62, NATO Def Coll 1969, cnsllr and political advsr Br Mil Govt Berlin 1969–73, head Def Dept FCO 1973–75, ambass to Havana 1975–79, head UK Delgn on Mutual and Balanced Reduction of Forces in Central Europe (ambass) 1980–82, ambass to Brussels 1982–85; chm Spadel Ltd (formerly Brecon Beacons Natural Waters) 1985–; dir Armistice Festival 1985–89, dir Anglo-Belgian Club 1993–; tstee Imperial War Museum 1985–95, chm Anglo-Belgian Soc 1987–, dep chm Belgian-Luxembourg C of C 1987–, vice-pres Int Menuhin Assoc 1991–; *Recreations* tennis, the arts; *Clubs* Anglo-Belgian, Hurlingham; *Style*— Sir Edward Jackson, KCMG; ✉ 17 Paultons Square, London SW3 5AP (☎ 0171 352 8501)

JACKSON, Gordon Ackroyd; s of Neville Ackroyd Jackson, of Ripley, Surrey, and Althea, *née* Landon (d 1993); *b* 25 March 1952; *Educ* Reeds Sch Cobham, Univ of Newcastle upon Tyne (Robinson prize, LLB); *m* 1975, Susan Mary, da of George Harry Pattinson, OBE; 2 s (Christopher Ackroyd b 17 March 1980, Timothy George b 19 Jan 1982), 1 da (Rebecca Mary b 5 Nov 1985); *Career* slr; articled Bartlett & Gluckstein 1976–78, slr Bartlett & Gluckstein, Crawley & de Reya 1978–81, ptnr Bartletts de Reya 1978–88, ptnr and head of commercial dept Taylor Garrett 1988–89; Taylor Joynson Garrett: managing ptnr 1989–93, chm Int 1991–; memb City of London Co of Slrs 1991; tstee Windermere Nautical Tst; *Recreations* steam boats, photography, walking; *Style*— Gordon Jackson, Esq; ✉ Taylor Joynson Garrett, Carmelite, 50 Queen Victoria Embankment, Blackfriars, London EC4Y 0DX (☎ 0171 353 1234, fax 0171 936 2666)

JACKSON, Graeme; s of Lewis Reginald Jackson, and Winifred Ivy Jackson; *b* 13 March 1943; *Educ* Brighton Coll; *m* 1, 22 Nov 1963, Elizabeth (decd); 1 s (Richard Andrew St John b 22 April 1964); m 2, 10 Aug 1972 (m dis 1980), Janet, da of Robert Tyndall; *Career* jr surveyor Ibbet Moseley Card 1959–61, surveyor Donaldson & Co 1961–64, dir Central of Dist Properties plc 1966–71 (surveyor 1964–66), chm London and Manchester Securities plc 1971–83, chm and chief exec Warringtons plc 1986–91, chief exec BSS Ltd 1991–; *Recreations* ocean racing, real tennis, opera; *Clubs* RORC, Island SC, Queens Royal Berkshire; *Style*— Graeme Jackson, Esq; ✉ BSS Ltd, 121 Mount Street, London W1Y 5HB (☎ 0171 499 4994, fax 0171 493 4994)

JACKSON, Helen; MP (Lab) Sheffield Hillsborough (majority 7,068); da of Stanley Price, and late Katherine Price; *b* 19 May 1939; *Educ* Berkhamsted Sch for Girls, St Hilda's Coll Oxford (MA, CertEd); *m* 1960, Keith Jackson, s of Hugh Jackson; 2 s, 1 da; *Career* asst librarian Queen's Coll Oxford 1960–61, asst teacher City of Stoke-on-Trent 1961–62, voluntary playgroup organiser and occasional researcher Liverpool City Cncl Social Servs 1962–70, teacher Lancs 1972–74, teacher Sheffield 1974–80; cncllr Huyton UDC 1973–74; Sheffield City Cncl: cncllr 1980–91, chm Public Works Ctee 1981–83, chm Employment and Econ Devpt Ctee 1983–91, chm Sheffield Econ Regeneration Ctee 1987–91; MP (Lab) Sheffield Hillsborough 1992–; memb House of Commons Select Ctee on the Environment 1992–, co-chair Parly Lab Pty Women's Ctee 1992–, chair All-Pty Parly Water Gp; memb: Sheffield Partnerships Ltd until 1991, Sheffield Science Park until 1991, Sheffield Devpt Corp 1986–91; chm and fndr memb Centre for Local Econ Strategies, occasional tutor Yorks Dist WEA; *Recreations* walking, music; *Style*— Ms Helen Jackson, MP; ✉ 6 Stephen Lane, Grenoside, Sheffield, S Yorks S30 3QZ (☎ 0114 232 2439, fax 0114 285 5808); House of Commons, London SW1A 0AA (☎ 0171 219 4587/2342, fax 0171 2192442)

JACKSON, Hugh Richard; *b* 2 June 1946; *Educ* King's Sch Canterbury, Keble Coll Oxford (BA), Coll of Law; *m*; 3 c; *Career* Norton Rose: articled clerk (admitted 1971), ptnr Property Team Private Client Dept 1977–; memb: Law Soc, City of London Slrs' Co; *Recreations* family, sport, travel; *Style*— Hugh Jackson, Esq; ✉ Norton Rose, Kempson House, Camomile Street, London EC3A 7AN (☎ 0171 283 6000, fax 0171 283 6500)

JACKSON, Jane Therese (Tessa); *b* 5 Nov 1955; *Educ* Univ of E Anglia (BA), Univ of Manchester (dip in museum studies); *Career* museum asst Art Dept Castle Museum Norwich 1977–78, art ed Oxford University Press 1978–80, exhbns organiser Soc for the Protection of Ancient Bldgs London 1981–82, actg curator Eyemouth Museum Berwickshire 1982, curator Collins Gallery Univ of Strathclyde Glasgow 1982–88, seconded as visual arts offr Festivals Office Glasgow City Cncl 1988–91, dir Arnolfini Bristol 1991–; memb: Architectural Heritage Soc of Scotland 1984–90 (variously chair and ctee memb), Eurocreation Steering Ctee England 1990–91, Advsy Bd Tate Gallery St Ives Cornwall 1993–, Bd Bristol Cultural Devpt Partnership 1994–; tstee Forest of Dean Sculpture Tst 1993–; external examiner BA(Hons) Fine Art Bath Coll of Higher Educn 1995, govr Falmouth Coll of Arts Cornwall 1995; *Books* George Washington Wilson and Victorian Glasgow (with John R Hume, 1983), Henry Moore in Scotland (ed, 1990), Dice Works - An Installation by George Lappas (1990), Le Cinq - French Contemporary Art (ed with Nicola White, 1990), Temperamenti - Art from Northern Italy (with Dr Pier Giovanni Castagnoli, 1990); *Style*— Ms Tessa Jackson; ✉ Arnolfini, 16 Narrow Quay, Bristol BS1 4QA (☎ 0117 929 9191, fax 0117 925 3876)

JACKSON, (Henry) John; s of James William Jackson, and Annie Margaret, *née* Best; *b* 10 Sept 1937; *Educ* Hackney Downs GS, Pitman's Coll; *m* 17 Aug 1972, Jill Yvonne, da of Albert Horace Ireson, OBE, of Seaford, E Sussex; *Career* served: 67 Trg Regt RAC 1955, 1 King's Dragoon Gds 1956–58, 28 Cwlth Inf Bde, 17 Gurkha Div Malaya; journalist Press Assoc 1952–54, The Scotsman 1954–55, Press Assoc 1958–62, Daily Telegraph 1962–66, Ilford Pictorial 1966–67, educn and Parly corr London Evening News 1967–75, Parly rep Press Assoc 1975–76, freelance 1976–79, Saudi Press Agency 1979–80, publishing dir Municipal Jl 1989–90 (ed 1980, dir 1986–89), ed Public Money 1990–91, ed Insurance Age 1992– (publisher and ed 1995–); memb: Cromwell Assoc, Br Horse Soc, Redbridge LBC 1968–74; Parly candidate (Cons) Erith Crayford 1970 and Hornchurch 1974; Br Soc of Magazine Editors Business Editor of the Year 1995; Freeman City of London; Liveryman Worshipful Co of Loriners; *Recreations* horseriding, cricket, English Civil War history; *Clubs* MCC; *Style*— John Jackson, Esq; ✉ Wingfield Farm, Wing, Leighton Buzzard LU7 0LD (☎ 01296 688972); Insurance Age, 33–39 Bowling Green Lane, London EC1R 0DA (☎ 0171 505 8181, fax 0171 505 8187)

JACKSON, John David; CBE (1993); s of Cecil Jackson (d 1986), and Gwendoline Jackson (d 1976); *b* 7 Dec 1933; *Educ* Oundle, McGill Univ Montreal (BComm, LA); *m* 11 Dec 1966, Hilary Anne, da of Sir Rudolph Lyons, QC (d 1991), of Leeds; 4 da (Johanna b 1971, Julie b 1974, Jenny b 1976, Janie (twin) b 1976); *Career* dir: William Baird plc, Baird Textile Holdings Ltd, Leeds City Development Co Ltd, Nidd Vale Motors Ltd, British Appaarel and Textile Confedn; vice chm Br Clothing Indust Assoc, chm Leeds Western Health Authy 1988–91; memb Bd: Leeds Health Authy 1991–96, Leeds Development Corporation (UDC) 1988–95; pres Leeds Chamber of Commerce and Indust 1990–92, chm Yorkshire and Humberside Region Br Clothing Indust Assoc 1990–94; memb Inst of Chartered Accountants of Quebec; *Recreations* tennis, sailing, skiing (water & snow); *Style*— John D Jackson, Esq, CBE; ✉ Red Oaks, Manor House Lane, Leeds LS17 9JD; William Baird plc, Leeds Office, New Centaur House, The Granary Building, 1 Canal Wharf, Leeds LS11 5BB

JACKSON, John Edgar; s of Wilfred Jackson JP (d 1965), of Burnley, and Sarah, *née* Duckworth (d 1956); *b* 11 Dec 1939; *Educ* Burnley GS, Kansas City CHS; *m* 1, 1963 (m dis 1987), Marilyn Cooper Jackson; 1 s (Jonathan b 1967), 1 da (Rebekah b 1965); m 2, 30 Sept 1988, Kathryn Lesley, da of Roland H Hughes, BEM, of Manchester; *Career* called to the Bar Middle Temple 1970; chm Burnley FC 1981–84 (dir 1976–84); *Recreations* soccer, sailing; *Style*— John E Jackson, Esq; ✉ Far Laithe, Lower Chapel Lane, Grindleton, Lancs BB7 4RN (☎ 01200 441561); 40 King St, Manchester (☎ 0161 832 9082)

JACKSON, Judith Margaret (Mrs John Horam); da of Ernest Jackson, MBE (d 1970), and Lucy Margaret Jackson (d 1990); *b* 1 May 1936; *Educ* Dartington Hall Sch, Univ of London (BA, LGSM), Univ of Paris (Dip Civ Fr); *m* 1, 6 June 1963 (m dis 1976), Peter Jopp, s of George Jopp (d 1969); 2 s (Fraser b 1965, Lincoln b 1968); m 2, 4 April 1987, John Rhodes Horam, MP, *qv*; *Career* TV presenter: Associated Rediffusion 1961–65, BBC 1965–80; motoring ed: The Sunday Times 1970–84, The Guardian 1987–91; dir: UK 2000 1987–90, Dartington Summer Arts Fndn 1984– (also tstee); chm Women on the Move Against Cancer 1996– (hon treas 1985), govr Orpington Coll 1992–; *Books* Man and the Automobile (1979), With a Little Help from Our Friends (ed, 1991), Every Woman's Guide to the Car (1993); *Recreations* music, cookery; *Style*— Ms Judith Jackson; ✉ 6 Bovingdon Rd, London SW6 2AP (☎ 0171 736 8521, fax 0171 736 7795)

JACKSON, Kenneth A; *Educ* Cannock HS, Birmingham Coll of Commerce, Univ of Birmingham; *Career* asst news ed The Journal Newcastle-on-Tyne 1962–64, business desk Express & Star Wolverhampton 1964–66, dep business ed/property ed Birmingham Post 1966–68, PR mangr Reliant Motor Company 1968–70, industl ed/property ed Birmingham Evening Mail 1970–77; Tarmac plc: divnl mktg advsr Housing Div 1977–80, gp press advsr 1980–83, head of press and public affrs 1983–90 (led Tarmac's successful Channel Tunnel PR and mktg campaign), dir of corp affrs 1990–93; fndr Jackson-Brown & Associates media rels, public rels and corp affrs conslts 1993– (appointed conslt to Govt Inner Cities Initiative, Wolverhampton City Challenge and CISC, DOE Award for best City Challenge community newspaper in GB 1994); non-exec dir First Community Health Tst Mid Staffs; fndr memb: Wolverhampton Business Initiative, Communications Through Conventions; involved in various charity work; FRSA, FIPR; *Clubs* Birmingham Press; *Style*— Kenneth A Jackson, Esq; ✉ Little Orchard, Wolseley Road, Rugeley, Staffs WS15 2EN (☎ 01889 579525)

JACKSON, Kenneth (Ken); s of Joseph Henry Jackson (d 1965), of Dewsbury, and Ada, *née* Smith (d 1981); *b* 23 Sept 1939; *Educ* Dewsbury Wheelwright GS, Batley Tech and Art Coll, Harvard Business Sch; *m* 25 Aug 1962, Elisabeth Joyce, da of David William Wilks (d 1975), of Dewsbury; 1 s ((Stephen) David b 8 Feb 1970); *Career* md Spencer & Halstead Ltd 1971 (personnel dir 1968–); vice pres Bonded Abrasives Europe Carborundum & Co USA 1978, vice pres (sales and mktg) Abrasives Carborundum Div Sohio 1981, gp md Carborundum Abrasives plc (became Carbo plc 1984), chief exec The Hopkinsons Group plc 1993–; *Recreations* travel, gardening; *Style*— Ken Jackson, Esq; ✉ Savile Ings Farm, Holywell Green, Halifax, W Yorks HX4 9BS (☎ 01422 372608); The Hopkinsons Group plc, Lakeside, Trafford Park, Manchester M17 1HP (☎ 0161 872 8291, fax 0161 872 1471, telex 667344 CARBOM G)

JACKSON, Very Rev Lawrence; s of Walter Jackson (d 1947), and Edith, *née* Gray (d 1955); *b* 22 March 1926; *Educ* Alderman Newton's Sch Leicester, King's Coll London (AKC); *m* 1955, Faith Anne, da of Philip Henry Seymour, of Suffolk; 4 da (Charlotte b 1955, Deborah b 1957, Rachel b 1961, Lucy b 1966); *Career* asst curate St Margaret's Leicester 1951–54; vicar of: Wymeswold 1955–59, St James The Greater Leicester 1959–65, Coventry 1965–73; canon of Coventry Cathedral 1967–73, provost of Blackburn 1973–92; memb Gen Synod of the C of E 1974–, church cmmr 1981–, sr chaplain ACF Leics, Rutland and Warwick 1955–70; Liveryman Worshipful Co of Fruiterers; *Recreations* music, architecture, theatre, countryside, after dinner speaking; *Clubs* Lord's Taverners, Forty, Lighthouse; *Style*— The Very Rev Lawrence Jackson; ✉ Northcot, Brook Lane, Newbold-on-Stour, Stratford-upon-Avon, Warwicks CV37 8UA (☎ 01789 450721)

JACKSON, Michael; s of Stanley Jackson, and Maisie Joan Jackson; *b* 12 March 1948; *Educ* St Nicholas GS Northwood, Univ of Salford (BSc); *m* 21 July 1973, Jacqueline Yvonne Doreen, da of Jesse Hudson; 1 s (Robert b 5 May 1976), 1 da (Helen Sara b 17 Oct 1978); *Career* industl engr Hawker Siddeley 1970–73, fin controller Citibank NA 1975–76 (expense controller 1973–75), chief of staff Citifin Finanziaria 1976–82, consumer banking dir Citibank Savings 1985–86 (customer servs dir 1982–85), head of Europe Middle East and Africa operations Bank of America 1988–90 (head of consumer loans 1986–88), chief exec Birmingham Midshires Building Society 1990–; non-exec dir Wolverhampton TEC 1994–; FMS 1989, FRSA 1991, CIMgt 1993, FCIB 1994, FInstD 1995; *Recreations* model making, music, sport; *Style*— Michael Jackson, Esq; ✉ Birmingham Midshires Building Society, Pendeford Business Park, Wobaston Road, Wolverhampton WV9 5HZ (☎ 01902 302000, fax 01902 28849, mobile 0374 428809)

JACKSON, HE (Richard) Michael (Mike); CVO (1983); s of Richard William (Dick) Jackson (d 1979), of Newbiggin-by-the-Sea, Northumberland, and Charlotte, *née* Wrightson (d 1978); *b* 12 July 1940; *Educ* Darlington Queen Elizabeth GS, Paisley GS, Univ of Glasgow (MA); *m* 27 Dec 1961, Mary Elizabeth (Mollie), da of Dr Andrew Symington Kitchin (d 1978), of Colintraive, Strathclyde; 1 s (Andrew b 1968), 1 da (Dorothy b 1963); *Career* Scottish Office 1961–73, seconded to MAFF 1971–72, seconded to FCO and served The Hague 1973–74; HM Dip Serv: Panama 1977–79, Buenos Aires 1981–82, Stockholm 1982–87, dep head of mission Seoul 1987–91; HM ambassador: Bolivia 1991–95, Costa Rica 1995–; Cdr of the Order of the Northern Star (Sweden) 1983; *Recreations* bird watching, conservation, real ale; *Style*— HE Mr Mike Jackson, CVO; ✉ c/o Foreign and Commonwealth Office (San José), King Charles St, London SW1A 2AH

JACKSON, Maj-Gen Michael David (Mike); CB (1996), CBE (1992, MBE 1979); s of Maj George Michael Jackson (d 1982), of Camberley, Surrey, and Ivy, *née* Bower; *b* 21 March 1944; *Educ* Stamford Sch, Univ of Birmingham (BSocSc), RMA Sandhurst; *m* 2, 4 May 1985, Sarah Carolyn, da of Col Brian Jackson Coombe, GM; 2 s (Mark b 1973, Thomas b 1990), 1 da (Amanda b 1971); *Career* Bde Maj Berlin Inf Bde 1977–78, Co Cdr 2 Para 1979–80, directing staff Staff Coll 1981–83, CO 1 Para 1984–86, sr directing staff Jt Serv Def Coll 1986–88, serv fell Wolfson Coll Cambridge 1989, Cdr 39 Inf Bde 1989–92, DG Personal Servs (Army) 1992–93, GOC 3 (UK) Div 1994–96, Cdr Multi-national Div South West (Bosnia) 1996, DG Development and Doctrine 1996–; memb MENSA; Freeman City of London 1988; *Books* Central Region vs Out-of-Area: Future Commitments (Tri-Service Press, contrib, 1990); *Recreations* skiing, tennis, music; *Style*— Maj-Gen M D Jackson, CB, CBE; ✉ c/o RHQ Para Regt, Browning Barracks, Aldershot, Hants GU11 2AU

JACKSON, Michael Edward Wilson; s of Sqdn Ldr Edward Grosvenor Jackson, of The Field House, E Rigton, Yorks, and Yvonne Brenda Jackson, OBE, *née* Wilson; *b* 16 March 1950; *Educ* The Leys Sch, Univ of Cambridge (LLB); *m* 1, 19 April 1980 (m dis), Prudence Elizabeth Robinson, da of Michael John Boardman, of White Howe, Norfolk; m 2, 18 Nov 1989, Harriet Leigh, da of Air Cdre Denis Wilson; *Career* dir The Guidehouse Group plc 1983–90, currently md Elderstreet Investments Ltd (fndr chm 1990); dep chm Sage Group plc; FCA 1976; *Recreations* tennis; *Clubs* The Vanderbilt Tennis, Royal Automobile, Annabel's; *Style*— Michael Jackson, Esq; ✉ Elderstreet Investments Ltd, 32 Bedford Row, London WC1R 4HE (☎ 0171 831 5088)

JACKSON, Prof Michael Peart; JP; s of Herbert Jackson (d 1976), and Norma, *née* Peart; *b* 1 July 1947; *Educ* Univ of Hull (BA, MA); *m* Sylvia; 1 da (Karen b 16 June 1978), 1 s (Callum b 12 Nov 1980); *Career* Univ of Stirling: lectr Dept of Sociology 1970–79, sr lectr 1979–86, head Dept of Sociology 1984–86, prof of human resource mgmnt 1986–, chm Bd of Studies for Mgmnt and Soc Scis 1986–89, head Sch of Mgmnt 1989–91, sr dep princ 1991–; visiting appts: Dept of Sociology Meml Univ of Newfoundland 1979, Indstl Relations Research Unit Univ of Warwick 1981; chm Scottish Univs Staff Devpt Ctee; former chm Social Security Appeal Tribunal; memb: Cncl of Validating Univs, UCAS Scottish HE Ctee, COSHEP (working gp for response to Dearing Ctee); assoc ed Int Jl of Sociology and Social Policy, memb Ed Bd Int Jl of Human Resource Mgmnt, memb Advsy Bd Unemployment Unit; conslt: Highlands and Islands Devpt Bd 1971, Lovable/Pagan Ltd 1973, T&GWU 1975, Open Univ 1979, OECD 1981, EEC/Euro Centre for Work and Society 1983, Cumbernauld Devpt Corp 1988, Robert Taylor Holdings 1990; grad memb Inst of Personnel Devpt, memb Br Univs Industl Relations Assoc, memb Int Industl Relations Assoc; *Books* Labour Relations on the Docks (1973), The Price of Coal (1974), Industrial Relations (1977, 2 edn 1982, 3 edn 1985), Financial Aid Through Social Work (with B M Valencia, 1979), Work Creation: International Experiences (ed with V J B Hanby, 1979), Trade Unions (1982, 2 edn 1988), British Job Creation Programmes (with V J B Hanby, 1982), Youth Unemployment (1985), Strikes (1987), Policy Making in Trade Unions (1991), An Introduction to Industrial Relations (1991), Decentralisation of Collective Bargaining (with J Leopold and K Tuck, 1993); also author of numerous articles in learned jls; *Style*— Prof Michael Jackson, JP; ✉ University of Stirling, Stirling FK9 4LA (☎ 01786 467013, fax 01786 462057, e-mail MPJ1@Stirlan.ac.uk)

JACKSON, Michael Richard; s of Ernest Jackson, and Margaret, *née* Kearsley; *b* 11 Feb 1958; *Educ* King's Sch Macclesfield, Poly of Central London (BA); *Career* organiser Channel Four Gp (pressure gp campaigning for independent access to fourth channel) 1979–81, freelance prodr 1981–82, fndr Beat Productions (progs for C4 incl The Media Show, Open the Box and Whose Town Is It Anyway?) 1983–87; BBC Television: joined 1987, ed The Late Show BBC2 1988–90, ed Late Show Productions (incl Naked Hollywood, Moving Picture, The Lime Grove Story) 1990–91, head of music and arts 1991–93, controller BBC2 1993–96, dir of television and controller BBC1 1996–; *Recreations* reading, walking, cinema; *Style*— Michael Jackson, Esq; ✉ BBC Television, Television Centre, Wood Lane, London W12 7RJ (☎ 0181 743 8000)

JACKSON, Sir Nicholas Fane St George; 3 Bt (UK 1913), of Eagle House, Wimbledon, Surrey; s of Sir Hugh Nicholas Jackson, 2 Bt (d 1979), and Violet Marguerite Loftus, *née* St George; the 1 Bt, Sir Thomas Graham Jackson, was the architect responsible for many buildings in Oxford incl Examination Schools, Brasenose, Hertford and Trinity Colls; *b* 4 Sept 1934; *Educ* Radley Coll, Wadham Coll Oxford, Royal Acad of Music; *m* 1, 1961 (m dis 1968), Jennifer Ann, da of F A Squire, of Marylebone St, London; m 2, 1972, Nadia Françoise Genevieve, da of Georges Michard, of St Etienne, France; 1 s (Thomas Graham St George b 1980); *Heir* s, Thomas Graham St George Jackson b 5 Oct 1980; *Career* organist, harpsichordist and composer; organist: St Anne's Soho 1963–68, St James's Piccadilly 1971–74, St Lawrence Jewry 1974–77; organist and master of the choristers St David's Cathedral 1977–84, musical dir and fndr St David's Cathedral Bach Festival 1979; concert tours: USA, France, Germany, Spain, Belgium; dir Festival Bach at Santes Creus Spain 1987–89; dir Concertante of London 1987–; hon fell Hertford Coll Oxford 1995; memb Ct of Assts Worshipful Co of Drapers (Master 1994–95), Liveryman Worshipful Co of Musicians; LRAM, ARCM; *Recordings* organ and harpsichord recordings for Decca, RCA, Abbey, Oryx and Priory Records; *Compositions* various (incl one opera) published by Boosey & Hawkes, Cardiff University Press, Anglo-American Publishers and Alfred Lengnick; *Recreations* travel, sketching; *Style*— Sir Nicholas Jackson, Bt

JACKSON, (Kevin) Paul; s of late T Leslie Jackson, of Ealing, and Jo, *née* Spoonley, of Caersws, Powys; *b* 2 Oct 1947; *Educ* Gunnersbury GS, Univ of Exeter (BA); *m* 21 Aug 1981, Judith Elizabeth, da of John Charles Cain, DSO, of Cowden, Kent; 2 da (Amy b 1981, Katie b 1984); *Career* formerly stage mangr: Marlowe Theatre Canterbury 1970, Thorndike Theatre Leatherhead 1971; prodr BBC TV 1971–82 (progs incl The Two Ronnies, Three of a Kind, Carrott's Lib, The Young Ones and Happy Families), freelance prodr and dir 1982–84 (progs incl Cannon and Ball and Girls on Top), prodr and chm Paul Jackson Productions 1984–86 (progs incl Red Dwarf, Don't Miss Wax and Saturday Live), md NGTV 1987–91, md Carlton Television Ltd 1993–94 (dir of progs 1991–92), md Carlton UK Productions 1995–96, freelance prodr/dir 1996–97, head of entertainment BBC 1997–; memb ITV Broadcast Bd 1993–94; exec prodr Appointments of Dennis Jennings (winner Oscar for Best Live Action Short 1989), BAFTA awards 1983 and 1984; chm: Comic Relief 1985–, Charity Projects 1993– (vice chm 1990–92), Royal Television Soc 1994–96; Stanford Executive Programme 1993, academic visitor Univ of Exeter 1996; FInstD 1992, FRTS 1993; *Recreations* theatre, rugby, travel, food and wine, friends and family; *Style*— Paul Jackson, Esq; ✉ c/o BBC Television Centre, Wood Lane, London, W12 7RJ (☎ 0181 743 8000)

JACKSON, Paul Edward; s of George Edward Jackson, of Kington St Michael, Wilts, and Joan, *née* Barry; *b* 8 July 1953; *Educ* Taunton Sch, Watford Sch of Art, Canterbury Coll of Art (BA), Univ of Bradford; *m* 8 May 1982, Jane Frances, da of Frank Haseler; 1 s (Nicholas Edward Jackson b 16 Feb 1990); *Career* account exec Saatchi and Saatchi 1978–80, account exec Mathers 1980–81, account supr Fletcher Shelton Delaney 1981–83, account mangr Publicis 1983–85, bd dir BSB Dorland 1985–92, md Kevin Morley Marketing 1992–95, vice chm and exec managing ptnr Ammirati Puris Lintas (following merger) 1995–; MIPA, FRSA; *Recreations* sailing, painting, classical music; *Clubs* Little Ship; *Style*— Paul Jackson, Esq; ✉ Ammirati Puris Lintas, 84 Eccleston Square, London SW1V 1PX (☎ 0171 932 8888, fax 0171 932 8421)

JACKSON, Peter John; *b* 16 Jan 1947; *Educ* Univ of Leeds (BA Econ); *m* Anne; 2 s (David b 1977, Andrew b 1983), 1 da (Rosemary b 1980); *Career* sr dir level appts Perkins Engines Gp 1976–87, dir Associated British Foods plc 1984–, exec dir British Sugar plc 1987–88, chief exec British Sugar Group 1989– (dep md 1988–89), dir C Czarnikow Sugar Ltd 1993–; *Style*— Peter Jackson, Esq; ✉ British Sugar plc, Oundle Road, Peterborough PE2 9QU (☎ 01733 63171, fax 01733 63067)

JACKSON, His Hon Judge Dr Peter John Edward; s of David Charles Jackson (d 1977), of Kent, and Sarah Ann, *née* Manester; *b* 14 May 1944; *Educ* Brockley County GS, Sprachen und Dolmetscher Inst Hamburg, Univ of London (LLB), Tübingen Univ W Germany (Dr Jur); *m* 23 Sept 1967, Ursula Henny, da of Paul Schubert (d 1945), and Henny Schubert (d 1980), of Hamburg; 2 da (Philippa b 1972, Pia b 1984); *Career* called to the Bar Middle Temple 1968, and N Ireland 1982, dep circuit judge 1979–81, asst recorder 1982–83, recorder of Crown Ct 1983–92, on Attorney-Gen's list of prosecuting counsel 1986–92; circuit judge (SE Circuit) 1992–; memb Arbitration Panel Int C of C 1990, co-opted memb Int Practice Sub-ctee Gen Cncl of the Bar 1991–92; govr Newbold Coll Bracknell 1990–95; reg speaker Pump Ct Chambers and other seminars; *Recreations* horse riding, travel, German language, German law; *Style*— His Honour Judge Dr Peter Jackson; ✉ 3 Pump Court, Temple, London EC4Y 7AJ (☎ 0171 353 0711, fax 0171 353 3319); D 7000 Stuttgart 50, Seelbergstrasse 8 (☎ 00 49 954646–0, fax 00 49 95464–46)

JACKSON, Peter Michael; s of Frederick Jackson (d 1984), and Henzey, *née* Hingley (d 1954), of Stourbridge; *b* 2 June 1931; *Educ* King Edward VI Sch Stourbridge, Royal Army Educnl Corps, St Paul's Coll Cheltenham, Inst of Educn Univ of Bristol (CertEd); *m* 1955, Jean, *née* McGregor; 1 da (Elizabeth Anne b 1959), 1 s (James Richard b 1964); *Career* head of geography Royston Secdy Sch 1956–61, dep head Willian Sch Letchworth 1961–65, headmaster Highfield Sch Letchworth 1965–94, field offr (Herts and Beds) Assoc of Teachers and Lecturers 1994–; fndr memb, hon sec and later chm Geography Bd CSE E Anglian Regnl Examination Bd 1964–84, chm Geography Panel London E Anglian Examination Bd GCSE 1984–86 (memb Schs Examination Cncl Geography), UK rep EC Environmental Educn Advsy Gp 1976–86, co-opted memb Herts CC Educn Ctee 1985–94, memb and later pres Herts Co NAHT 1965–94; govr Letchworth Garden City Heritage Fndn 1995–; 25 yrs as fndr headmaster Highfield Sch commemorated by naming of Peter Jackson rose by Harkness Rose Growers 1990; *Recreations* European travel, rose growing, water colours; *Style*— Peter Jackson, Esq; ✉ 32 South View, Letchworth Garden City, Herts SG6 3JJ (☎ 01462 683800, fax 01462 484413)

JACKSON, Dr Peter Warren; s of Dr Robert Edward Jackson (d 1990), and Rosina Kathleen, *née* Warren; *b* 7 Feb 1935; *Educ* St Bees Sch Cumbria, Victoria Univ Manchester (MB ChB); *m* 1, 23 April 1960 (m dis 1980), Ann, da of Sydney James Wrigglesworth (d 1965); 3 s (Nicholas b 1961, David b 1963, Michael b 1964), 1 da (Susan b 1964); m 2, 30 May 1980, Susan Evelyn, da of Peter John Tyndall (d 1987); *Career* conslt anaesthetist Manchester Royal Infirmary 1968–95; hon conslt anaesthetist Central Manchester Healthcare NHS Trust 1995–; fell Manchester Med Soc (pres Section of Anaesthetics 1988–89); memb: BMA, Assoc of Anaesthetists, fell Royal Coll of Anaesthetists; *Books* Practical Anaesthesia for Surgical Emergencies (ed); *Recreations* golf, fishing, shooting, bowls; *Clubs* Aberfeldy Golf, Ollerton Gun; *Style*— Dr Peter Jackson; ✉ Cluain, Tom Na Croich, Fortingall, By Aberfeldy, Perthshire PH15 2LJ

(☎ 01887 830298); Dept of Anaesthetics, Royal Infirmary, Manchester (☎ 0161 276 4551, car 0860 635799)

JACKSON, Raymond Allen (JAK); s of Sgt Maurice Jackson (d 1960), and Mary Ann, *née* Murphy; *b* 11 March 1927; *Educ* Clipstone Road Sch London, Lyulph Stanley Central, Willesden Sch of Art (Nat Cert in Drawing, Dip in Illustration); *m* Claudie Sidonie, da of Henri Grenier (d 1974); 1 s (Patrick b 1 Oct 1959), 2 da (Dominique b 20 Sept 1957, Nathalie b 5 Feb 1965); *Career* Nat Serv Sgt RAOC 1945–48 (attached Educn Corps); Link House Group 1950–51, Keymers Advertising 1951–52, cartoonist Evening Standard 1952–; *Books* JAK Annuals 1971–; *Recreations* judo; *Clubs* Judokan; *Style*— Raymond Jackson, Esq; ✉ The Evening Standard, Northcliffe House, 2 Derry St, London W8 5EE (☎ 0171 938 7556)

JACKSON, Richard Anthony; s of Harold Reginald Jackson (d 1948), of Harrogate, N Yorks, and Irene Dallas, *née* Nelson (d 1968); *b* 31 March 1932; *Educ* Cheltenham; *Career* theatre producer; Nat Serv RE 1950–52; salesman Henry A Lane & Co Ltd 1953–56, merchandising asst Walt Disney Productions Ltd 1956–59, dir Richard Jackson Personal Management Ltd (actors representation); life memb BAFTA; Offr de l'Ordre des Arts et des Lettres (France) 1993; *Theatre* West End and Fringe incl: Madame de Sade (Kings Head) 1975, Charles Trenet in concert (Royal Albert Hall) 1975, The Bitter Tears of Petra Von Kant (New End) 1976, An Evening with Quentin Crisp (Duke of Yorks and Ambassadors) 1978, The Singular Life of Albert Nobbs, Alterations, Tribute to Lili Lamont (New End) 1978, Flashpoint (New End and Mayfair) 1978, A Day in Hollywood, A Night in The Ukraine (New End and Mayfair, Evening Standard Award for Best Musical and Plays and Players Award for Best Comedy) 1979, The Square, La Musica, Portrait of Dora (New End) 1979, Appearances (Mayfair) 1980, A Galway Girl (Lyric Studio) 1980, Bar and Ger (Lyric Studio) 1981, Latin (Lyric Studio) 1983, The Human Voice (with Susannah York, performed world-wide since 1984), Swimming Pools at War (Offstage) 1985, Matthew, Mark, Luke and Charlie (Latchmere) 1986, I Ought to be in Pictures (Offstage) 1986, Pier Paola Pasolini (Offstage) 1987, Creditors, Latin (New End) 1989 Beached (Old Red Lion) 1990, Hamlet (Howarth Festival USA) 1990, Eden Cinema (Offstage, Peter Brook Empty Space Award) 1991, Noonbreak (French Inst) 1991, Beardsley (Offstage) 1992, Don't Play With Love (French Inst and Rudolf Steiner House) 1992, Play With Cocaine (New Grove) 1993, The Eagle has Two Heads (Lilian Baylis) 1994, Happy Days (French Institute) 1994, The Star-Spangled Girl (Grace at the Latchmere) 1994, Suzanna Andler (BAC) 1995, Independent State, The First Years, Beginnings, Last Legs (all Grace Theatre at the Latchmere) 1995; *Recreations* table tennis, crosswords; *Clubs* Green Room; *Style*— Richard Jackson, Esq; ✉ 48 William Mews, London SW1X 9HQ (☎ 0171 235 3759); 59 Knightsbridge, London SW1X 7RA (☎ 0171 235 3671, fax 0171 235 6126)

JACKSON, Richard Peter; s of Richard Charles Jackson (d 1982), of Fowlmere, Cambs, and Allison Mary Clare, *née* Hicks; *b* 21 March 1944; *Educ* Bishop's Stortford Coll Herts, City Univ London (BSc); *m* 1, 30 April 1966 (m dis 1986), Rosemary Phyllis Choat Stickels, da of Samuel Harry Choat Jenkins, of Bury St Edmunds, Suffolk; 2 s (Piers b 1970, Giles b 1972); m 2, 24 July 1987, Annabel Gemma Jane (formerly Mrs Gunn), da of Maj Rodney Charles Hitchcock (d 1969), of Hampstead, London; *Career* indentured engr George Wimpey & Co London 1963–69, structural engr Firth Cleveland Jamaica 1969–71, sec engr Bullen & Ptnrs Croydon 1971–73, assoc John Powlesland & Assoc Colchester 1973–76, sr ptnr Richard Jackson Partnership Ipswich, Cambridge, Norwich and London 1976–; memb Ctee E Anglian AICE; CEng 1969, MICE 1971, MConsE 1983, FIStructE 1983; *Recreations* tennis, sailing, skiing; *Clubs* Lansdowne, Placemakers, Lighthouse; *Style*— Richard Jackson, Esq; ✉ Hill Barn, Hitcham, Ipswich, Suffolk IP7 7PT (☎ 01449 741399); Richard Jackson Partnership, Consulting Civil & Structural Engineers, 26 High St, Hadleigh, Ipswich, Suffolk IP7 5AP (☎ 01473 823939, fax 01473 823226)

JACKSON, Sir Robert; 7 Bt (UK 1815), of Arlsey, Bedfordshire; s of Maj Francis Gorham Jackson (d 1942, 2 s of 4 Bt); suc kinsman, Sir John Montrésor Jackson, 6 Bt, 1980; *b* 16 March 1910; *Educ* St George's Coll; *m* 1943, Maria Esther, da of Leon P Casamayou, of Montevideo, Uruguay; 2 da (Victoria Maria b 1945, d 1993, Bertha Mary b 1949); *Heir* kinsman, Keith Arnold Jackson b 24 April 1921; *Clubs* English (Montevideo); *Style*— Sir Robert Jackson, Bt; ✉ Bulevard Artigas 266, Flat 601, Montevideo, Uruguay (☎ 00 598 2 71 5032)

JACKSON, Robert Kenneth; s of John Kenneth Jackson (d 1977), of Kendal, Cumbria, and Laura Theresa, *née* Rankin (d 1976); *b* 26 Feb 1933; *Educ* Heversham GS, Clare Coll Cambridge (MB BCh, MA), St Thomas's Hosp Med Sch; *m* 21 June 1967, Margaret Elizabeth, da of Norman Dixon, of Aycliffe, Co Durham; 1 s (Robert Andrew b 2 April 1970), 1 da (Emma Jane b 20 Feb 1968); *Career* Surgn Spec RAF 1960–64; chief asst Orthopaedic Dept St Thomas' Hosp London 1966–71, conslt orthopaedic surgn Southampton Gen Hosp 1971–95; pres Br Scoliosis Soc 1993–94, chm Med Advsy Ctee Southampton Health Authy 1991–94; fell: Br Orthopaedic Assoc, Scoliosis Research Soc; FRCS 1964; *Books* More Dilemmas in the Management of the Neurological Patient (1987); *Recreations* fishing, orienteering, mountaineering; *Clubs* RAF; *Style*— Robert Jackson, Esq; ✉ Well Cottage, Pilley, Lymington, Hants SO41 5QR

JACKSON, Robert Victor; MP (C) Wantage (majority 16,473); *b* 24 Sept 1946; *Educ* Falcon Coll S Rhodesia, St Edmund Hall Oxford, All Souls Coll Oxford; *m* 1975, Dr Caroline Frances Jackson, MEP, *qv*, da of G H Harvey; 1 s decd; *Career* memb Oxford City Cncl 1969–71, political advsr to Employment sec 1973–74, Parly candidate (C) Manchester Central Oct 1974, memb Cabinet of Sir Christopher Soames (later Lord Soames), EEC Cmmn 1974–76, chef de cabinet to Pres EEC Econ and Social Ctee Brussels 1976–78, MEP (C) Upper Thames 1979–84, special advsr to Lord Soames as Govr Rhodesia 1979–80, rapporteur European Parl Budget Ctee 1982–; MP (C) Wantage 1983–; Parly under sec of state: DES with responsibility for higher educn and sci 1987–90, Dept of Employment with responsibility for training and the Employment Serv 1990–92; Parly sec Office of Public Serv and Sci 1992–93; former ed The Round Table and Int Affrs (Chatham House); author of several books; *Style*— Robert Jackson, Esq, MP; ✉ House of Commons, London SW1A 0AA

JACKSON, (Michael) Rodney; s of John William Jackson (d 1992), of N Humberside, and Nora, *née* Phipps (d 1984); *b* 16 April 1935; *Educ* Queen Elizabeth GS Wakefield, Queens' Coll Cambridge (MA, LLM); *m* 1968, Anne Margaret, da of Prof Eric William Hawkins, CBE, of N Humberside; 2 s (Nicholas b 1969, Richard b 1972); *Career* admitted slr 1962, NP 1967, recorder of the Crown Ct 1985–, slr advocate (all Higher Cts) 1996–; sr ptnr Andrew M Jackson & Co Slrs 1992–94 (currently conslt); *Recreations* fell walking, steam railway photography; *Style*— Rodney Jackson, Esq; ✉ 11 The Paddock, Swanland, North Ferriby, East Yorkshire HU14 3QW (☎ 01482 633278); Andrew M Jackson & Co, PO Box 47, Essex House, Manor Street, Hull HU1 1XH (☎ 01482 325242, fax 01482 212974)

JACKSON, Dr (William) Roland Cedric; s and h of Sir (William) Thomas Jackson, 8 Bt, *qv*; *b* 9 Jan 1954; *Educ* Wycliffe Coll, St Peter's Coll Oxford (MA), Exeter Coll Oxford (DPhil); *m* 1977, Nicola Mary, yr da of Prof Peter Reginald Davis, of St Mawes, Cornwall; 3 s (Adam William Roland b 1982, James Anthony Foljambe b 1984, Oliver Thomas Peter b 1990); *Career* head of science Backwell Sch 1986–89; educn advsr ICI 1989–93, head of educn Nat Museum of Science and Indust 1993–; FRSA; *Style*— Dr Roland Jackson; ✉ Summer Hill, 14 Glebe Rd, Welwyn, Herts AL6 9PB (☎ 01438 840255)

JACKSON, Rupert Matthew; QC (1987); s of George Henry Jackson (d 1981), and Nancy Barbara, *née* May; *b* 7 March 1948; *Educ* Christ's Hosp, Jesus Coll Cambridge (MA, LLB); *m* 20 Sept 1975, Claire Corinne, da of Harry Potter (d 1979); 3 da (Corinne b 1981, Chloe b 1983, Tamsin b 1985); *Career* called to the Bar Middle Temple 1972, practising SE Circuit, recorder 1990–, head of chambers; chm Professional Negligence Bar Assoc 1993–95; FRSA; *Books* Jackson and Powell on Professional Negligence (jtly, 3 edn 1992); *Clubs* Reform; *Style*— Rupert Jackson, Esq, QC; ✉ 2 Crown Office Row, Temple, London EC4Y 7HJ (☎ 0171 797 8000, fax 0171 797 8001)

JACKSON, (Francis) Sydney; s of Francis David Jackson, of Liverpool, and Edith Isobel Bold, *née* Butler; *b* 16 Sept 1926; *Educ* Liverpool Collegiate Sch, Univ of Sheffield (BSc), Univ of London (Dip); *m* Margaret Gillian, da of Sydney Alfred Hood White; 1 da (Sally Gillian b 1 April 1964), 1 s (Nicholas David b 15 May 1962); *Career* served Fleet Air Arm 1943–47; Esso: various tech and mgmnt positions Fawley Refinery 1951–65, supply mangr London 1965–67, marine ops mangr London 1967–74, transportation advsr Exxon Corp NY 1974–76, refinery mangr Milford Haven Refinery 1976–84, transportation mangr Esso Petroleum 1984–87; refinery mangr Rabigh Saudi Arabia 1990–91; chm: City Homes (UK) Ltd 1987–90, E Dorset Health Authy 1987–90, Royal Bournemouth and Christchurch Hosps NHS Trust 1991–95, ret; MInstD, FInstPet; *Recreations* gardening, walking, running church and village activities; *Clubs* Beaulieu River Sailing; *Style*— Sydney Jackson, Esq; ✉ Puffins, Bucklers Hard, Beaulieu, Hants SO42 7XD (☎ 01590 616304)

JACKSON, Sir (William) Thomas; 8 Bt (UK 1869), of The Manor House, Birkenhead; s of Sir William Jackson, 7 Bt (d 1985), and his 1 w, Lady Ankaret Cecilia Caroline Howard (d 1945), da of 10 Earl of Carlisle; *b* 12 Oct 1927; *Educ* Mill Hill, RAC Cirencester; *m* 1951, Gilian Malise, eld da of Col John William Stobart, MBE (d 1986), formerly of Farlam Ghyll, Brampton, Cumbria; 3 s ((William) Roland Cedric b 1954, Piers Anthony b 1955, Jolyon Thomas b 1957); *Heir* s, (William) Roland Cedric Jackson, *qv*; *Style*— Sir Thomas Jackson, Bt; ✉ Fell End, Mungrisdale, Penrith, Cumbria CA11 OXR

JACKSON, Thomas St Felix; s and h of Sir Michael Roland Jackson, 5 Bt; *b* 27 Sept 1946; *Educ* Stowe, Southampton Univ (BA); *m* 1980, Georgina Victoria, da of George Harold Malcolm Scatliff, of Springlands Farm, Wineham, Sussex; 2 da (Lucy Harriet b 1982, Charlotte Dare b 1986); *Career* md Billington Jackson Advertising Ltd; *Recreations* golf, cricket, photography, reading, topiary; *Clubs* Royal Wimbledon Golf, MCC; *Style*— Thomas Jackson, Esq; ✉ 70 Marryat Road, London SW19 5BN (☎ 0181 947 3045); Billington Jackson Advertising Ltd, 219A King's Road, London SW3 5EJ (☎ 0171 351 0006)

JACKSON, William Clifford Maurice; s of Arthur Newton Jackson (d 1986), and Helen Monica, *née* Maurice; *b* 23 Jan 1943; *Educ* Bedales Sch Petersfield Hampshire, Univ of Perugia; *m* 30 Sept 1967, Carol Janet, da of John Patterson; 1 s (Alexander William Maurice b 12 March 1970), 1 da (Amy Fiona Gibb b 10 Nov 1968); *Career* PA to md J Davey & Son 1963–68; Aitken Dott Ltd the Scottish Gallery (formerly Aitken Dott & Son): PA to sole proprietor William J Macaulay 1968–72, jr ptnr 1971–72, sr ptnr 1975–84, md Edinburgh 1984–88, md Edinburgh and London (Aitken Dott plc) 1988–91; former md William Jackson Gallery; writer lectr and broadcaster on Scot art; pubns: Herdsmans Liverpool (1966), A Patron of Art (managing ed and contrib, 1990–); MInstD; memb: Ctee Scot Crafts Centre 1970–73, Mgmnt Ctee Arts Educn Tst 1983–86, Selection Ctee of Art 1989–, Business Design Centre Islington 1989–; *Recreations* music, opera, cinema, classic cars; *Clubs* The Arts, Citroen Maserati, Lasham Gliding; *Style*— William Jackson, Esq

JACKSON, Gen Sir William Godfrey Fothergill; GBE (1975, OBE 1957), KCB (1971), MC (1940, and bar 1943); s of Col Albert Jackson (d 1956), and Eleanor Mary Fothergill (d 1978), of Ravenstonedale, Cumbria; *b* 28 Aug 1917; *Educ* Shrewsbury, RMA Woolwich (King's medallist), King's Coll Cambridge (MA); *m* 1946, Joan Mary, da of Capt C P Buesden, of Bournemouth; 1 s, 1 da; *Career* cmmnd RE 1937; served WWII: Norway, N Africa, Sicily, Italy, Far East; CO Queen's Gurkha Engrs 1958–60, dep dir Staff Duties WO 1962–64, IDC 1965, dir CDS's Unison Planning Staff 1966–68, asst CGS Op Requirements MOD 1968–70, GOC-in-C Northern Cmd 1970–72, QMG 1973–76, mil historian Cabinet Office 1977–88, govr and C-in-C Gibraltar 1978–82; ADC Gen to HM The Queen 1974–76; Col Cmmdt: RE 1971–81, Gurkha Engrs 1971–76, RAOC 1973–78; Kermit Roosevelt exchange lectr to USA 1975, Hon Col Engr and Rlwy Staff Corps RE TAVR 1977–94, chm Friends of Gibraltar's Heritage 1989–94; KStJ 1978; *Books* Attack in the West (1953), Seven Roads to Moscow (1957), Battle for Italy (1967), Battle for Rome (1969), Alexander of Tunis (1971), The North African Campaigns (1975), Overlord: Normandy 1944 (1978), Vol VI British Official History of the Mediterranean and Middle East Campaigns (Pt 1 1984, Pt 2 1987, Pt 3 1988), Withdrawal from Empire (1986), Rock of the Gibraltarians (1987), Alternative Third World War (1987), Britain's Defence Dilemmas (1990), The Chiefs - A History of the British Chiefs of Staff (1991), The Governor's Cat (1992), Fortress to Democracy: A Political Biography of Sir Joshua Hassan (1995), British Military Campaigns in the Middle East 1798–1992 (Vol I - The Pomp of Yesterday (1995), Vol II - With Nineveh and Tyre (1996)); *Clubs* Army and Navy; *Style*— Gen Sir William Jackson, GBE, KCB, MC; ✉ West Stowell, Oare, Marlborough, Wilts SN8 4JU (☎ and fax 01672 563782)

JACKSON, Dr William Thomas; s of William Thomas Jackson (d 1967), of Bulwell, Nottingham, and Elizabeth, *née* Martin (d 1950); *b* 22 Aug 1926; *Educ* Henry Mellish GS, Glasgow Vet Coll, Univ of Edinburgh (DVSM), Univ of Berne (DrMedVet) Coll of Law; *m* 11 July 1953, Anthea June (d 1994), da of Capt Robert Richard Gillard (d 1950), of Sholing, Southampton; 2 da (Elizabeth Helen Anthea b 1954, Barbara Anne (Mrs Rockwell) b 1956); *Career* asst vet surgn 1948–53; vet offr Miny of Agric 1953; stationed: Worcs 1959, Birkenhead Port 1964, Beverley E Yorks 1971; DVO Lewes E Sussex 1987 (Animal Welfare Section Tolworth 1977); called to the Bar Lincoln's Inn 1975; nat del and local treas IPCS 1964–71; memb Cncl Br Inst of Agric Conslts, Boy Scout Cmmr 1969–71, legal assessor and memb Cncl Soc for Vet Ethology 1986– (sec 1977–86), pres Sussex BVA 1985–87, dir Raystede Animal Welfare Centre 1987–; vice chm Kent and E Sussex Agric Wages Bd, chm E Sussex Agric Dwelling Houses Advsy Ctee; MRCVS, FCIArb, FBIAC; *Recreations* violin, sailing, cycling, walking, cross country skiing, swimming, English literature; *Style*— Dr William Jackson; ✉ 19 Ravens' Croft, Eastbourne, East Sussex BN20 7HX (☎ and fax 01323 733589)

JACKSON, William Unsworth (Bill); CBE (1985), DL (Kent 1992); s of William Jackson (d 1959), and Margaret Esplen, *née* Sunderland (d 1984); *b* 9 Feb 1926; *Educ* Alsop HS Liverpool; *m* 27 Sept 1952, Valerie Annette, da of Robert Henry Llewellyn (d 1966); 1 s (Philip Robert b 1957), 1 da (Deborah Ann b 1954); *Career* slr; dep co clerk Kent CC 1970–73, chief exec Kent CC 1973–86; dir Kent Econ Devpt Bd 1982–86, govr Henley Mgmnt Coll 1983–86, pres Soc of Local Authy Chief Execs 1985–86, memb Tunbridge Wells DHA 1986–, tstee Charity Aid Fndn 1986–, chm UK Steering Ctee on Community Tsts 1988–91, adjudicator on political restrictions in local govt England and Wales 1989–; *Recreations* gardening; *Clubs* Royal Over-Seas League; *Style*— Bill Jackson, Esq, CBE, DL; ✉ 34 Yardley Park Rd, Tonbridge, Kent TN9 1NF (☎ 01732 351078)

JACOB, Sir Isaac Hai (Jack); kt (1979), QC (1976); s of Jacob Isaiah Jacob (d 1936), of Shanghai, China; *b* 5 June 1908; *Educ* Shanghai Public Sch for Boys, LSE, UCL (Joseph Hume scholar, LLB); *m* 1940, Rose Mary Jenkins (d 1995), da of John Samwell (d 1918); 2 s; *Career* Nat Serv WWII RAOC 1940, Lt 1942, Staff Capt WO 1943–45; Cecil Peace prize 1930; called to the Bar Gray's Inn 1930 (Arden scholar) (hon bencher 1978); sr master Supreme Ct Queen's Bench 1975–80 (master 1957–75), Queen's Remembrancer 1975–80; hon lectr in law (principles of civil litigation) UCL 1959–74 (fell 1966, visiting prof of English law 1974–87); visiting prof: Univ of Sydney NSW 1971, Osgoode Hall Law Sch, York Univ Toronto 1971; dir of Inst of Advanced Legal Studies Univ of London 1986–88; memb Lord Chllr's Dept Ctees on: Funds in Ct (Pearson Ctee) 1958–59, Revision of Rules of Supreme Ct 1960–65, Enforcement of Judgement Debts (Payne Ctee) 1965–69, Personal Injuries Litigation (Winn Ctee) 1966–68, Foreign Judgements (Kerr Ctee) 1976–80; chm Working Pty on Form of Writ of Summons and Appearance 1978; advsy ed Court Forms 1962–, ed Annual Practice 1961–66; gen ed: Supreme Court Practice 1967–97 (emeritus ed 1997–), Civil Justice Quarterly 1982–; pres: Univ of London Law Students' Soc 1930, Univ of London Jewish Students Union 1931, Bentham Club UCL 1986 (chm 1965–85), Assoc of Law Teachers 1977–84 (vice pres 1965–76); vice pres: Selden Soc (cncl memb), Inst of Legal Execs, Industl Law Soc; memb Gen Ctee Bar Assoc for Commerce, Fin and Indust; memb Senate of Inns of Ct and the Bar 1975–78; memb: Ct of Govrs Poly of Central London 1970–88, Broderers' Co 1977; Freeman: City of London 1976; hon memb: Cncl of Justice 1987, Soc of Public Teachers of Law, Int Assoc of Procedure Law; hon fell: Univ of Westminster (formerly Poly of Central London) 1988, Acad of Experts; Hon LLD: Univ of Birmingham 1978, Univ of London 1981, Staffordshire Univ 1994; Dr Juris hc Univ of Würzburg 1982; *Books* The Fabric of English Civil Justice: Hamlyn Lectures (1986), Annual Practice (ed 1961–66), Supreme Court Practice (ed, 1967–97, emeritus ed 1997–), Chilty and Jacob Queen's Bench Forms (ed, 19 edn 1965, 20 edn 1969, 21 edn 1986), Practice and Proceedure (Halsbury's Laws, 4 edn Vol 37, 1982), Bullen and Leake and Jacob Precedents of Pleadings (ed, 12 edn 1975, 13 edn 1990), Pleadings Principles and Practice (1990), Malaysian Court Practice (conslt ed, 1995); *Style*— Sir Jack Jacob, QC; ✉ Ellern Mede, 31 Tottridge Common, London N20

JACOB, Nicholas Allen Swinton; s of Cdr John Jacob, and Rosemary Elizabeth Allen, *née* Shuter; *b* 25 June 1954; *Educ* Sherbourne Sch Dorset, Univ of Nottingham (BA, BArch); *m* 1979, Frederike Mathilde Maria Wilhelma, da of Theodorus Doreleijers; 1 s (Ian b 12 March 1983), 1 da (Philippa b 4 June 1985); *Career* Suffolk Co Architects' Dept 1979–81, joined Peter Cleverly (architect in Wetheringsett, Suffolk) 1981–84, ptnr Cleverly & Jacob Architects Stowmarket, ptnr Purcell Miller Tritton & Partners (following merger) 1985–; work incl: repair to Little Hall Lavenham (for Suffolk Building Preservation Tst) 1981–, repairs and alterations Newnham Coll Cambridge 1985–, alterations and repairs to Snape Maltings Concert Hall (Aldeburgh Fndn) 1988–, repairs to Hedingham Castle Essex 1990–, extension and repairs to St John's Church Stratford Broadway 1992–; exec memb Ipswich Building Preservation Tst 1984–, memb Ipswich Conservation Advsy Panel 1986–, dir Suffolk Building Preservation Tst 1990–; RIBA 1980; *Recreations* choir of St Margaret's Church (Ipswich), walking, skiing, golf, sketching, painting; *Clubs* Rotary (Ipswich Wolsey); *Style*— Nicholas Jacob, Esq; ✉ 8 Gainsborough Road, Ipswich, Suffolk IP4 2UR (☎ 01473 250379); Partner, Purcell Miller Tritton & Partners, St Mary's Hall, Rawstorn Road, Colchester, Essex CO3 3JH (☎ 01206 549487, fax 01206 763408, car 0831 404941)

JACOB, Prof (John) Peter; s of William Thomas Jacob (d 1960), and Doris Olwen, *née* Llewellyn (d 1991); *b* 13 May 1942; *Educ* Sir William Borlase's Sch, Univ of Durham (BA), Univ of Newcastle (BArch); *m* 21 July 1982, Lesley Diana, da of Alfred Charles Thomas James, of Maidenhead, Berks; 1 da (Katharine b 1985); *Career* Kingston Univ (formerly Kingston Poly) Sch of Architecture: princ lectr 1972–83, dep head 1983–87, head of sch 1987–, prof 1993–; chm Kingston Chapter RIBA 1980–82, memb Cncl RIBA 1983–89, memb Bd Architectural Educn Architect's Registration Cncl 1987– (memb RIBA/ARCUK Joint Validation Panel 1995–), chm RIBA Publications Ltd 1989–94, dir RIBA Companies Ltd 1990–93; RIBA 1967, FRSA 1988; *Recreations* reading, riding, motoring; *Style*— Prof Peter Jacob; ✉ 8 The Poplars, South Ascot, Berks (☎ 01344 20894); School of Architecture, Kingston University, Knights Park, Kingston upon Thames Surrey (☎ 0181 547 2000, fax 0181 547 7186)

JACOB, Hon Mr Justice; Hon Sir Robert Raphael Hayim (Robin); kt (1993); s of Sir Jack I H Jacob, of London, and Rose Mary, *née* Samwell; *b* 26 April 1941; *Educ* Mountgrace Comp Sch, St Paul's, Trinity Coll Cambridge, (MA), LSE (LLB); *m* 1967, Wendy, da of Leslie Huw Thomas Jones; 3 s (Sam b 1970, Matthew b 1972, Oliver b 1975); *Career* called to the Bar Gray's Inn 1965, bencher 1989; jr counsel to Treasury in patent matters 1976–81, QC 1981, QC (NSW) 1989, judge of the High Court of Justice (Chancery Div) 1993–; dep chm Copyright Tribunal 1989–93, apptd to hear Trade Mark Appeals to Bd of Trade 1989–93; govr LSE 1994–; *Style*— The Hon Mr Justice Jacob; ✉ Royal Courts of Justice, Strand, London WC2A 2LL (☎ 0171 936 6671, fax 0171 936 6624, e-mail rjacob@lix.compulink.co.uk)

JACOB, Ven Dr William Mungo; s of John William Carey Jacob (d 1982), of Ringstead, Norfolk, and Mary Marsters, *née* Dewar (d 1959); *b* 15 Nov 1944; *Educ* King Edward VII Sch King's Lynn, Univ of Hull (LLB), Linacre Coll Oxford (BA, MA), Univ of Edinburgh (Dip), Univ of Exeter (PhD); *Career* asst curate Wymondham Norfolk 1970–73, asst chaplain Univ of Exeter 1973–75, dir of pastoral studies Salisbury and Wells Theol Coll 1975–80 (vice princ 1977–80), sec Ctee for Theol Educn Advsy Cncl for Church's Miny 1980–86, warden Lincoln Theol Coll and prebendary of Gretton in Lincoln Cathedral 1986–96, archdeacon of Charing Cross 1996–; *Style*— The Ven the Archdeacon of Charing Cross; ✉ 4 Cambridge Place, London W8 5PB (☎ 0171 937 2560); The Old Deanery, Dean's Court, London EC4V 5AA (0171 248 6233)

JACOBI, Sir Derek George; kt (1994), CBE (1985); *b* 22 Oct 1938; *Career* actor; artistic dir Chichester Festival Theatre 1995–; narrator of The Iliad (talking book) 1993; *Theatre* RSC: Benedick in Much Ado About Nothing (tour to NY and Washington, Tony Award), title role in Peer Gynt, Prospero in The Tempest, title role in Cyrano De Bergerac (tour to NY and Washington), Macbeth 1993; Old Vic: title role in Hamlet (tour), Thomas in The Lady's Not for Burning, title role in Ivanov; Haymarket Theatre: Breaking The Code 1987, To Know, title role in Becket (UK tour); Octavius in Antony and Cleopatra (Cambridge Theatre Co), Apimantus in Timon of Athens (New Shakespeare Co), Charles Dyer in Staircase (Oxford Playhouse), Byron in The Lunatic, The Lover and The Poet (Lyric Hammersmith), Semyon in The Suicide (Anta Theatre NY), Breaking The Code (Neil Simon Theatre, nominated for Tony Award) 1987–88, Richard II/Richard III (Phoenix Theatre) 1988–89, Narrator in The Wedding Bouquet (Royal Opera House), title role in Kean (Old Vic Toronto), Frederick William Rolfe in Hadrian VII (Chichester Festival Theatre) 1995; *Television* BBC: Man of Straw, The Pallisers, title role in I Claudius, Richard II, Hamlet, The Vision Thing; other credits incl: Skin (Anglia), The Stranger Left No Card (Anglia), Philby, Burgess and MacLean (Granada), Budgie (LWT), The Strauss Family (ATV), My Pye (Channel 4), In My Defence (Oyster TV), Wolves Are Howling (Yorkshire), Cadfael (Central) 1994; *Films* incl: The Day of the Jackal, Blue Blood, The Odessa File, The Medusa Touch, The Human Factor, Charlotte, The Man Who Went Out In Smoke, The Hunchback of Notre Dame, Inside The Third Reich, Little Dorrit (dir Christine Edzard), The Tenth Man, Henry V (dir Kenneth Branagh), The Fool (dir Christine Edzard), Dead Again (dir Kenneth Branagh); *Style*— Sir Derek Jacobi, CBE; ✉ c/o ICM Ltd, Oxford House, 76 Oxford Street, London W1N 0AX (☎ 0171 636 6565, fax 0171 323 0101)

JACOBS, Brian David Lewis; s of John Barry Lewis Jacobs, of Pennypot Cottage, Pennypot Lane, Chobham, Surrey, and Elizabeth, *née* Mendes; *b* 14 Dec 1949; *Educ* Charterhouse; *m* 26 Nov 1983, Rosalind Mary, da of late Leslie Jory; 2 da (Katherine Alice (Katie) b 3 Sept 1985, Emily Rose b 13 Dec 1988); *Career* messenger rising to res asst Horniblow Cox-Freeman 1968–71, media and market res exec Southern TV 1971–74, market res exec Access 1974, media res mangr Davidson Pearce 1974–80; Leo Burnett Advertising: assoc media dir 1980, media dir 1985, exec media dir 1986, international media dir 1990–95; media devpt dir Aegis Group plc 1995–96, md Carat International 1996–; memb CAM, FIPA 1982; *Books* Spending Advertising Money (with Dr Simon Broadbent, 1984); *Recreations* golf, family, reading, the media, travel, watching ads; *Clubs* Sunningdale Golf; *Style*— Brian Jacobs, Esq; ✉ 61 Woodlawn Road, London SW6 6PS (☎ 0171 731 3854); Carat International, 2–6 Broadway, London SW6 1AA (☎ 0171 381 8010)

JACOBS, David Lewis; CBE (1996), DL (Greater London 1983); s of late David Jacobs and late Jeanette Victoria, *née* Goldsmid; *b* 19 May 1926; *Educ* Belmont Coll, Strand Sch; *m* 1, 15 Sept 1949 (m dis 1972), Patricia Bradlaw; m 2, 1975, Caroline Munro (d 1975); m 3, 1979, Mrs Lindsay Stuart Hutcheson; 1 s (Jeremy decd), 3 da (Carol, Joanna, Emma), 1 step s (Guy); *Career* radio and television broadcaster; RN 1944–47; first broadcast Navy Mixture 1944, announcer Forces Broadcasting 1944–45, chief announcer Radio SEAC Ceylon 1945–47 (asst station dir 1947), newsreader BBC Gen Overseas Serv 1947, sometime commentator British Movietone News, freelance 1947–; numerous film appearances; dir: Duke of York's Theatre 1979–85, Man in the Moon UK Ltd 1986–, Video Travel Guides 1988–91; chm: Kingston FM 1995–96, Thames FM 1996; chm Kingston Theatre Tst 1990–, formerly vice chm RSPCA, chm Think Br Campaign 1985 (dep chm 1983–85), pres Kingston Branch Royal Br Legion, Kingston Alcohol Advsy Service, Wimbledon Girls Choir; vice pres: Stars Orgn for Spastics (formerly chm), Royal Star and Garter Home Richmond, Kingston Div St John Ambulance, BA Cabin Staff Entertainment Soc; 6 Royal Command Performances; rep DL Royal Borough of Kingston upon Thames 1984–; Hon Doctorate Kingston Univ 1994; *Radio* incl: Housewives' Choice, Journey into Space, BBC Jazz Club, Pick of the Pops, Any Questions?, Any Answers?, Melodies for You, The David Jacobs Show, Easy Does It, Soundeasy; *Television* incl: Make Up Your Mind, Tell The Truth, Juke Box Jury, Top of the Pops, David Jacobs Words and Music, Sunday Night With David Jacobs, Little Women, Where Are They Now?, What's My Line?, Miss World, Eurovision Song Contest, Come Dancing, Questions, Primetime, Countdown; *Awards* top disc jockey BBC and Radio Luxembourg 1947–53, TV Personality of the Year Variety Club of GB 1960, Personality of the Year BBC Radio 1975, Sony Gold Award 1984 (later admitted to Hall of Fame), Richard Martin Award RSPCA 1978; *Books* Jacobs Ladder (1963), Caroline (1978), Any Questions? (with Michael Bowen, 1981); *Recreations* talking and listening, hotels; *Clubs* Garrick, St James's, Helford River Sailing; *Style*— David Jacobs, Esq, CBE, DL; ✉ 203 Pavilion Rd, London SW1X 0BJ (fax 0171 259 5697)

JACOBS, Godfrey Frederick; s of Frederick George Jacobs (d 1963), of Woodford, Essex, and Louise Lily, *née* Phipps; *Educ* South West Essex Tech Coll, Wansfell Coll Essex; *m* Hazell Thirza, *née* Robertson; 2 da (Lorne Alison b 10 June 1958, Clare Morag b 13 April 1960); *Career* Nat Serv Tport Cmd RAF 1949–51; dir (overseas) English Property Corporation 1968–75, gen property mangr MTRC Hong Kong 1976–79; 1979–86: exec dir US Assets Ltd, dir and pres AMP Property Services Inc of San Francisco, chm Copthorn Holdings Ltd (Toronto); chm Suncrest Developments plc 1986–; memb: World Wildlife Fund of Canada, Community Assoc for Riding for Disabled (Canada), 200 Canadians for Wildlife, Utd Wards Club of London; Freeman City of London 1964, Master Worshipful Co of Painter Stainers 1996–97, former Master Hon Co of Freemen of the City of London in N America; FSVA 1963, AIMgt 1966, FCIArb 1977, FInstD 1961; *Recreations* charity work; *Clubs* Naval, City Livery; *Style*— Godfrey Jacobs, Esq; ✉ Fort Anner, 25 Retreat Road, Friars Lane, Richmond, Surrey TW9 1NN

JACOBS, Prof Howard Saul; s of Flt Lt Joseph Jacobs, of 79 Marlborough Mansions, Cannon Hill, London NW6, and Florence Jacobs (d 1950); *b* 9 June 1938; *Educ* Malvern, Gonville and Caius Coll Cambridge (BA), Middx Hosp Med Sch (MB BChir), Univ of London (MD); *m* 15 July 1962, Sandra Rose, da of Mark Garelick; 3 da (Caroline, Susanna, Amber); *Career* asst prof UCLA 1969–74, sr lectr St Mary's Hosp Med Sch 1974–81, prof Univ Coll London and Middx Sch of Medicine 1983– (reader in gynaecological endocrinology 1981–83), civilian conslt endocrinology RAF 1985–; memb Ctee on Safety of Medicines 1983–; chm: Biologicals Sub-ctee Ctee on Safety of Meds 1993–, Br Fertility Soc 1993–95; pres Endocrine Section RSM 1993–95; FRCP, FRCOG; *Recreations* tennis, music, reading, theatre; *Style*— Prof Howard Jacobs; ✉ 169 Gloucester Ave, London NW1 8LA (☎ 0171 722 5593, fax 0171 722 5243); Middlesex Hosp, Mortimer St, London W1N 8AA (☎ 0171 380 9451, fax 0171 636 9941)

JACOBS, Prof John Arthur; s of Arthur George Jacobs (d 1949), and Elfrida Malvine Beck (d 1952); *b* 13 April 1916; *Educ* Dorking HS, Dorking County Sch, Univ Coll London (BA, MA, PhD, DSc); *m* 1, 1942, Daisy Sarah Ann Montgomerie (d 1974); 2 da (Coral Elizabeth b 1942, Margaret Ann b 1948); m 2, 1974 (m dis 1981), Margaret Jones; m 3, 24 June 1982, Ann Grace Wintle, da of Albert James Wintle (d 1990); *Career* instructor Lt RN 1941–46; lectr in mathematics Royal Holloway Coll Univ of London 1946–51, assoc prof of geophysics Univ of Toronto 1951–57, prof of geophysics Univ of British Columbia 1957–67, dir Inst of Earth Sciences Vancouver 1961–67, Killam Memorial prof of science Univ of Alberta 1967–74, dir Inst of Earth and Planetary Physics Univ of Alberta 1970–74, prof of geophysics Univ of Cambridge 1974–83, emeritus prof of geophysics Univ of Cambridge 1983–, hon prof Inst of Earth Studies Univ of Wales Aberystwyth 1988–; memb many nat and int ctees on geophysics; vice master Darwin Coll Cambridge 1978–83; Hon DSc Univ of British Columbia Vancouver; Centennial Medal of Canada 1967, Gold Medal Canadian Assoc of Physicists 1975, J Tuzo Wilson Medal Canadian Geophysical Union 1982, Price Medal Royal Astrophysical Soc 1994, John Adam Fleming Medal American Geophysical Union 1994; FRSC 1958, FRAS 1951, fell American Geophysical Union 1975; *Books* Physics & Geology (with R D Russell and J T Wilson, 1959 and 1974), The Earth's Core and Geomagnetism (1963), Geomagnetic Micropulsations (1970), A Textbook on Geonomy (1974), The Earth's Core (1975 and 1987), Reversals of the Earth's Magnetic Field (1984 and 1994), Deep Interior of the Earth (1992); *Recreations* walking, music; *Style*— Prof John Jacobs; ✉ 4 Castell Brychan, Aberystwyth SY23 2JD (☎ 01970 623 436); Institute of Earth Studies, University of Wales, Aberystwyth SY23 3DB (☎ 01970 622646, fax 01970 622659)

JACOBS, Rabbi Dr Julian Godfrey; s of Maurice Jacobs (d 1991), and Blooma, *née* Friedenberg (d 1980); *b* 6 March 1934; *Educ* Avigdor HS London, Jews' Coll London, UCL (BA, MA, PhD); *m* 27 Aug 1975, Margaret, da of late Albert Harris; 1 da (Aviva Nechama b 6 Aug 1976); *Career* rabbinic trg 1951–61; rabbi: Richmond Synagogue 1961–69, W Hackney Synagogue 1969–78, Blackpool Synagogue 1978–82, Liverpool Old Hebrew Congregation 1982–89, Ealing Synagogue 1989–; Chief Rabbi's rep for interfaith rels 1990–; *Books* The Ship has a Captain (1987), From Week to Week (1992), Judaism looks at Modern Issues (1993); *Recreations* reading, writing and study; *Style*— Rabbi Dr Julian Jacobs; ✉ 12 Ascott Avenue, Ealing, London W5 5QB (☎ 0181 567 0527)

JACOBS, Hon Sir Kenneth Sydney; KBE (1976); s of Albert Sydney Jacobs; *b* 5 Oct 1917; *Educ* Knox GS NSW, Sydney Univ Aust (BA, LLB); *m* 1952, Eleanor Mary Neal; 1 da; *Career* barr NSW 1947, QC 1958, Supreme Court of NSW Australia: judge 1960, judge of appeal 1966, pres Court of Appeal 1972, justice of High Ct of Aust 1974–79;

Style— The Hon Sir Kenneth Jacobs, KBE; ✉ Crooks Lane Corner, Axford, Marlborough, Wilts SN8 2HA

JACOBS, Rabbi Louis; CBE (1990); s of Harry Jacobs (d 1968), of Manchester, and Lena, *née* Myerstone (d 1956); *b* 17 July 1920; *Educ* Manchester Central HS, UCL (BA, PhD); *m* 28 March 1944, Sophie, da of Israel Lisagorska (d 1945), of London; 2 s (Ivor b 1945, David b 1952), 1 da (Naomi b 1947); *Career* rabbi: Central Synagogue Manchester 1948–1954, New West End Synagogue London 1954–60; tutor Jews' Coll London 1959–62, dir Soc Study of Jewish Theology 1962–64, rabbi New London Synagogue 1964–; visiting prof: Harvard Divinity Sch 1985–86, Univ of Lancaster 1988–; hon fell: UCL 1988, Leo Baeck Coll London 1988; former pres London Soc for Study of Religion, pres Assoc for Jewish Studies; hon citizen: Texas 1961, New Orleans 1963; Hon DHL: Spertus Coll 1987, Hebrew Union Cincinnati 1989, Jewish Theological Seminary New York 1989; Hon DLitt Lancaster 1991; *Books* We Have Reason To Believe (1957), Studies in Talmudic Logic (1961), Principles of the Jewish Faith (1964), A Jewish Theology (1973), Hasidic Prayer (1977), Jewish Mystical Testimonies (1977), The Talmudic Argument (1985), Helping With Inquiries - An Autobiography (1989), Holy Living - Saints and Saintliness in Judaism (1990), God Torah Israel (1990), Structure and Form of the Babylonian Talmud (1991), Religion and the Individual (1991), Turn Aside From Evil (trans, 1995), The Jewish Religion: A Companion (1995); *Recreations* hillwalking, theatre, cinema; *Style*— Rabbi Louis Jacobs, CBE; ✉ 27 Clifton Hill, St John's Wood, London NW8 0QE (☎ 0171 624 1299); The New London Synagogue, 33 Abbey Rd, London NW8 (☎ 0171 328 1026/7)

JACOBS, Michael Edward Hyman; s of Harry Ronald Jacobs, CC (d 1966), of London, and Edmonde, *née* London; *b* 21 May 1948; *Educ* St Paul's, Univ of Birmingham (LLB); *m* 5 March 1973, Ruth; 2 s; *Career* admitted slr 1972; Nicholson Graham & Jones: ptnr 1976–, head of Tax Dept 1981–; legal expert in employee benefits and share schemes; ed Tolley's Trust Law International (formerly Trust Law and Practice) 1989–95 (memb Editorial Bd 1986–89, conslt ed 1995–); author of articles on corporate and personal taxation; fndr memb and vice chm Share Scheme Lawyers Gp 1989–, govr Tax Res Unit KCL 1993–, fndr memb and sec Trust Law Ctee 1994–; memb: Tax Working Pty ProShare 1992–95, Taxation Sub-ctee CISCO 1993–, VAT Practitioners Gp Trafalgar Chapter 1993–, Private Tsts Ctee Assoc of Corp Tstees 1996–; Freeman City of London 1983, Liveryman Worshipful Co of Slrs 1987; memb: Law Soc 1972, Inst for Fiscal Studies 1984, Int Fiscal Assoc 1985, Assoc of Pension Lawyers 1986, City of London Law Soc 1986, Int Bar Assoc 1991, Charity Lawyers Assoc 1992, Soc of Tst and Estate Practitioners 1993, BFI; FIMgt 1983, FRSA 1993; *Books* Tax on Takeovers (1989, 6 edn 1994), Tolley's Tax on Takeovers (1990), Tolley's Tax Planning (contrib 1989, 7 edn 1994–95), Tolley's VAT Planning (contrib, 2 edn 1994–95), The Director's Guide to Employee Benefits (IOD, contrib 1991), Longman's Financial Precedents (contrib 1992); *Clubs* RAC; *Style*— Michael Jacobs, Esq; ✉ Nicholson Graham & Jones, 110 Cannon Street, London EC4N 6AR (☎ 0171 648 9000, fax 0171 648 9001)

JACOBS, Norman Nathaniel; OBE (1994), ERD (1964); s of Abram Gershon Jacobs (d 1953), of London, and Deborah, *née* Nabarro (d 1969); *b* 8 Aug 1930; *Educ* Christ's Hosp Horsham, Exeter Coll Oxford (MA); *m* 11 July 1957, Elizabeth Rose, da of Dr Raphael Shaffer (d 1965), of Cheltenham; 2 s (Simon Anthony b 1962, David Raphael b 1968), 2 da (Ruth Helen b 1960, Susan Naomi b 1965); *Career* 2 Lt Army 1949–51, Capt AER 1955; admitted slr 1958; ptnr Slaughter & May 1973–90; govr Christ's Hosp, steward Br Boxing Bd of Control 1960–93, memb Sports Cncl 1988–93, chm Football Licensing Authy 1990–96, tstee Sports Aid Fndn 1992–; Freeman City of London 1970; FRSA 1989; *Recreations* walking, trekking, Freemasonry, music, spectating; *Clubs* MCC, Naval and Military, Rugby Club of London; *Style*— Norman Jacobs, Esq, OBE, ERD; ✉ 64 Moss Lane, Pinner, Middx HA5 3AU (☎ 0181 866 0840, fax 0181 868 9116)

JACOBS, Prof Patricia Ann; da of Cyril Jacobs, and Sadie, *née* Jones; *b* 8 Oct 1934; *Educ* Univ of St Andrews (BSc, DSc, D'Arcy Thomson medal, Sykes medal); *m* 1972, Newton Ennis Morton; 3 step s, 2 step da; *Career* res asst Mount Holyoke Coll Mass USA 1956–57, scientist MRC 1957–72, prof Dept of Anatomy and Reproductive Biology Univ of Hawaii Sch of Med 1972–85 (Regents medal 1983), prof and chief Div of Human Genetics Dept of Paediatrics Cornell Univ Med Coll NY 1985–87, dir Wessex Regional Genetics Lab 1988–; hon sr lectr Dept of Med Univ of Edinburgh 1966–72, hon prof of human genetics Univ of Southampton Med Sch 1988–; Allan Award American Soc of Human Genetics 1981; fndr memb American Bd of Med Genetics 1979–82; memb Cncl: RCPath 1991–94, Royal Soc 1993–95; author of over 200 articles; FRSE 1977, FRCPath 1987, FRS 1993; *Recreations* botany, gardening, walking; *Style*— Prof Patricia Jacobs, FRS; ✉ Wessex Regional Genetics Laboratory, Salisbury District Hospital, Salisbury SP2 8BJ (☎ 01722 336262 ext 4080, fax 01722 338095)

JACOBS, Paul Granville; s of Thomas Granville Jacobs, of London, and Marjorie Rosina, *née* Walters; *b* 15 Feb 1946; *Educ* The Leys Sch Cambridge, Univ of Exeter (LLB); *Career* admitted slr 1970; commercial property ptnr: Clifford-Turner 1978–87, Clifford Chance 1987–; Freeman City of London; *Recreations* horse racing, the arts; *Clubs* RAC; *Style*— Paul Jacobs, Esq; ✉ Clifford Chance, 200 Aldersgate St, London EC1A 4JJ (☎ 0171 600 1000, fax 0171 600 5555, telex 887847 LEGIS G, mobile 0836 743698)

JACOBS, Paul Martin; s of Colin Alfred James Jacobs, of Ruthin, Clwyd, and Betty Mary, *née* Rowse; *b* 11 Dec 1951; *Educ* Oundle, The Queen's Coll Oxford (MA), Univ of Liverpool (MB ChB); *m* 11 Feb 1989, Deborah Clare Josephine, da of Arthur Ernest Smith, of Haslemere, Surrey; 1 s (Edmund Charles b 22 Nov 1991); *Career* resident surgical offr Moorfields Eye Hosp 1982–85; conslt ophthalmic surgn: Univ Hosp Nottingham 1988–92, Borders Gen Hosp 1992–94, York District Hosp 1995–; FRCS Glasgow 1984, FRCOphth 1988; *Recreations* music, skiing, angling; *Clubs* Royal Soc of Med; *Style*— Paul Jacobs, Esq; ✉ Department of Ophthalmology, York District Hospital, Wigginton Road, York YO3 7HE (☎ 01904 631313)

JACOBS, Peter; s of Bertram Jacobs (d 1982), and Phyllis Jacobs (d 1982); *b* 26 Sept 1938; *Educ* Merchant Taylors', Queen's Coll Cambridge (MA); *m* 21 Dec 1974, Susan Frances, da of Eric Simeon Boyes; 2 da (Sarah b 1977, Helen b 1978); *Career* 2 Lt 1958–59, Royal Hampshire Regt 1957–59; fencing: Br Epée Champion (1962, 1964, 1970), Br Olympic Teams (1964, 1968), Cwlth Team (1962, 1966, 1970), mangr Br Olympic Team (1972, 1976), World Univ Epée Champion 1963; vice pres Amateur Fencing Assoc, memb Exec Ctee Int Fencing Fedn 1985–88 and 1993– (memb Statutes Ctee 1977–); market researcher; Liveryman Worshipful Co of Weavers 1971; *Style*— Peter Jacobs, Esq; ✉ c/o Amateur Fencing Association, 1 Barons Gate, 33–35 Rothschild Road, London W4 5HT (☎ 0181 742 3032, fax 0181 742 3033)

JACOBS, Peter Alan; s of Cyril Jacobs (d 1971), and Sadie, *née* Jones (d 1973); *b* 22 Feb 1943; *Educ* Univ of Glasgow (BSc), Aston Univ (Dip in Mgmnt Studies); *m* 30 May 1966, Eileen Dorothy, da of Dr Leslie Naftalin; 2 s (Andrew, Michael (twins) b 4 Feb 1969), 1 da (Katrina b 14 July 1972); *Career* prodn controller Toy Div Tube Investments Ltd 1968–70 (graduate trainee 1965–67), prodn mangr Pedigree Petfoods Ltd 1970–83 (prodn shift mangr 1970–72, Purchasing Dept 1972–81), sales dir Mars Confectionery 1983–86, chief exec Berisford International plc and chm subsid British Sugar Ltd 1986–91, chief exec BUPA 1991–; *Recreations* reading, music, theatre, tennis, sailing; *Clubs* RAC; *Style*— Peter Jacobs, Esq; ✉ BUPA, Provident House, Essex Street, London WC2R 3AX (☎ 0171 353 5212)

JACOBS, Sir Piers; KBE (1989, OBE 1981); s of Selwyn Jacobs, and Dorothy, *née* Fredman; *b* 27 May 1933; *Educ* St Paul's; *m* 13 April 1964, Josephine Lee; 1 da (Isobel Lee b 9 July 1966); *Career* Army Legal Serv 1955–57; former Hong Kong Govt slr, asst registrar gen 1968–76, registrar gen 1976–82, sec for econ serv 1982–86, fin sec 1986–91; vice chm China Light and Power Co Ltd; hon pres: Hong Kong PHAB Assoc, Soc for Child Health & Devpt; hon vice pres Hong Kong Girl Guides Assoc; memb Law Socs of Eng & Wales and Hong Kong; *Recreations* walking, swimming and reading; *Clubs* Hong Kong, Hong Kong Jockey, Oriental; *Style*— Sir Piers Jacobs, KBE; ✉ c/o Sir Elly Kadoorie & Sons Ltd, St George's Building, Hong Kong (☎ 00 852 2524 9221)

JACOBSON, Prof Dan; s of Hyman Michael (d 1975), and Liebe, *née* Melamed (d 1961); *b* 7 March 1929; *Educ* Kimberley Boys' HS, Univ of the Witwatersrand SA (BA); *m* 1954, Margaret Dunipace, *née* Pye; 2 s (Simon Orde b 1955, Matthew Lindsay b 1958), 1 da (Jessica Liebe b 1966); *Career* writer; fell in creative writing Stanford Univ Calif 1956–57, visiting prof Syracuse Univ NY 1965–66, visiting fell SUNY Buffalo NY 1972; Univ Coll London: lectr 1975–79, reader in English 1980–87, prof of English 1988–94 (emeritus prof 1994–); John Llewelyn Rhys Award 1958, W Somerset Maugham Award 1962, H H Wingate Award 1979, J R Ackerley Prize 1986, Mary Elinore Smith Poetry Prize 1992; FRSL 1974; *Fiction* The Trap (1955), A Dance in the Sun (1956), The Price of Diamonds (1957), The Evidence of Love (1960), The Beginners (1966), The Rape of Tamar (1970), Inklings - Selected Stories (1973), The Wonderworker (1973), The Confessions of Jozef Baisz (1977, H H Wingate Award 1979), Her Story (1987), Hidden in the Heart (1991), The God-Fearer (1992); *Criticism* The Story of the Stories (1982), Adult Pleasures (1988); *Travel* The Electronic Elephant (1994); *Autobiography* Time and Time Again (1985); *Recreations* tennis, reading, walking; *Clubs* Athenaeum, Templars Tennis; *Style*— Prof Dan Jacobson, FRSL; ✉ c/o A M Heath & Co, 79 St Martin's Lane, London WC2N 4AA (☎ 0181 836 4271, fax 0171 497 2561)

JACOBSON, Howard; s of Max Jacobson, of Manchester, and Anita, *née* Black; *b* 25 Aug 1942; *Educ* Stand GS Whitefield, Downing Coll Cambridge (BA, MA, Table Tennis half blue); *m* 1, 1964 (m dis 1972), Barbara, *née* Starr; 1 s (Conrad b 1968); *m* 2, 1978, Rosalin Joy, da of Allan Sadler, of Balnarring, Aust; *Career* lectr in Eng lit Univ of Sydney 1965–67, Eng tutor Selwyn Coll Cambridge 1969–72, sr lectr Wolverhampton Poly 1974–81, novelist and critic 1981–; reg contrib Modern Painters 1988– (currently memb Editorial Bd); *Books* Shakespeare's Magnanimity (with Wilbur Sanders, 1978), Coming From Behind (1983), Peeping Tom (1984), Redback (1986), In The Land of Oz (1987), The Very Model of a Man (1992), Roots Schmoots (1993), Seriously Funny: An Argument for Comedy (1997); *Television Films* Into the Land of Oz (1991), Yo, Mrs Askew (1991), Roots Schmoots (3 parts, 1993), Sorry, Judas (1993), Seriously Funny: An Argument for Comedy (5 parts, 1997); *Recreations* appearing on television; *Style*— Howard Jacobson, Esq; ✉ Peters Fraser & Dunlop, 503–4 The Chambers, Chelsea Harbour, London SW10 0XF (☎ 0171 376 7676, 0171 352 7356, fax 0171 351 1756)

JACOBSON, Ivor Julian; s of Harry Jacobson (d 1980), and Rae, *née* Tatz (d 1950); *b* 6 May 1940; *Educ* King Edward VII Sch Johannesburg, Univ of Witwatersrand S Africa (BComm); *m* 23 Dec 1963, Joan Yocheved, da of Isiah Adelson (d 1974); 1 s (Russell b 1965), 2 da (Lauren b 1968, Amanda b 1970); *Career* chief exec and controlling stockholder Trade and Industry Group (with subsids in many countries incl S Africa, UK, USA and Bermuda) 1968–; chm and pres: Liberty Finance Corporation, Fundex Capital Corporation; md I J Holdings (Pty) Ltd, CA (SA); *Recreations* squash, horse riding; *Style*— Ivor J Jacobson, Esq; ✉ 200 North St, Harrison, New York 10528, USA (☎ 00 1 914 967 7299); Liberty Finance Corporation, 555 Theodore Fremd Avenue, Rye, New York 10580, USA (☎ 00 1 914 967 2227, fax 00 1 914 967 6650)

JACOBSON, Prof Werner Ulrich (Jacob); s of Dr Otto Jacobson (d 1968), of San Francisco, California, and Paula Margaret, *née* Masur; *b* 4 Jan 1906; *Educ* Momsen Gymnasium Berlin, Univ of Heidelberg (MD), University of Cambridge (PhD, ScD); *m* 14 Feb 1934, Gertrude Elena (d 1969), da of Prof Eric Ebler (d 1925); *Career* Home Guard 1940–45; Univ of Cambridge: academic assistance grant 1933–34, Rockefeller grant 1934–35, Sir Halley Stewart prof of med res 1978– (res fell 1935–78); visiting sr res assoc Galveston Univ Texas Med Branch 1948–49, Harvard Med Sch 1949–54, visiting prof Harvard Med Sch 1969–70 and 1972; contrib to various med books and publications; memb: Physiological Soc, Int Soc of Haematology; MNYAS; fell Cambridge Philosophical Soc; FRCP 1986, FRCPath 1986, FRSM, FRSTM; *Recreations* gardening, classical music, Limoges enamels; *Style*— Prof W Jacobson; ✉ Dept of Paediatrics, University of Cambridge, Level 8, Addenbrooke's Hospital, Cambridge CB2 2QQ (☎ 01223 217544)

JACOMB, Sir Martin Wakefield; kt (1985); s of Hilary Jacomb, and Félise Jacomb; *b* 11 Nov 1929; *Educ* Eton, Worcester Coll Oxford (MA); *m* 1960, Evelyn Helen, *née* Heathcoat Amory; 2 s, 1 da; *Career* called to the Bar Inner Temple 1955, practised at bar 1955–68; with Kleinwort Benson 1968–85, Commercial Union Assurance Co plc 1984–93 (dep chm 1987–93), dep chm Barclays Bank plc 1985–93; chm: Barclays de Zoete Wedd 1986–91, Postel Investment Management Ltd 1991–95, The British Cncl 1992–, Delta plc 1993–, Prudential Corporation plc 1995– (non-exec dir 1994–); non-exec dir: Bank of England 1986–95, The Telegraph plc (formerly Daily Telegraph) 1986–95, Rio Tinto Zinc Corporation plc 1988– (non-exec dir CRA Ltd Dec 1995–), Marks and Spencer PLC 1991–; external memb Fin Ctee OUP 1971–95; memb Nolan Ctee 1995–; tstee Nat Heritage Meml Fund 1982–; Liveryman Worshipful Co of Merchant Taylors; *Style*— Sir Martin Jacomb; ✉ Prudential Corporation plc, 142 Holborn Bars, London EC1N 2NH (☎ 0171 548 3900, fax 0171 548 3631)

JACQUES, Dr Martin; s of Dennis Arthur Jacques, of Bury St Edmunds, Suffolk, and Dorothy *née* Preston (d 1989); *b* 1 Oct 1945; *Educ* King Henry VIII Sch Coventry, Univ of Manchester (BA, MA), King's Coll Cambridge (scholar, PhD); *m* 1969 (m dis 1975), Brenda Simson; *partner* 1976–94, Philippa Anne, da of Sqdn Ldr Lloyd Norman Langton, RAF (ret); m 2, 1996, Harinder Kaur Veriah; *Career* lectr in econ and social history Univ of Bristol 1971–77, ed Marxism Today 1977–91; columnist: Sunday Times 1988–94, The Times 1990–91, L' Unità (Rome) 1990–93; dep ed The Independent 1994–96; currently writer Observer and Guardian, also occasional contrib: The Independent, The Financial Times, Daily Mail, Daily Telegraph, The NY Times, Int Herald Tribune, Wall Street Journal, New Republic, Volkskrant, La Stampa, Corrière della Sera, Le Monde Diplomatique; reg broadcaster on TV and radio; Cncl memb European Policy Forum 1992–; chm Advsy Cncl Demos 1992–; memb Exec Ctee Communist Pty 1967–90 (memb Political Ctee 1978–80 and 1982–90); memb Econ History Soc 1971–77; FRSA 1991; *Books* Forward March of Labour Halted (co-ed and contrib, 1981), The Politics of Thatcherism (co-ed and contrib, 1983), New Times (co-ed and contrib, 1989); contrib to various other books and publications; *Recreations* squash, tennis, skiing, running, motor racing, reading, cooking; *Style*— Dr Martin Jacques; ✉ 31 Sussex Way, London N7 6RT (☎ 0171 272 0885, fax 0171 281 2402)

JACQUES, Peter Roy Albert; CBE (1990); s of George Henry Jacques (d 1984), and Ivy Mary, *née* Farr (1988); *b* 12 Aug 1939; *Educ* Archbishop Temple's Sch, Newcastle upon Tyne Poly (BSc), Univ of Leics; *m* 21 Aug 1965, Jacqueline Anne, da of Robert George Sears, of Worthing; 1 s (Jonathan Peter), 1 da (Tamsin Eleanor); *Career* building labourer 1955–58, market porter 1958–62, student 1962–68, sec Social Insur and Industl Welfare Dept TUC 1971–92 (asst 1968–71); sec: BMA/TUC Ctee 1972–, TUC Social Insur and Industl Welfare Ctee 1972–92, TUC Health Servs Ctee 1979–92; special advsr TUC; memb: Health and Safety Cmmn 1974–95, Industl Injuries Advsy Cncl 1972–92, Exec Ctee Royal Assoc for Disability and Rehabilitation 1975, Nat Insur Advsy Ctee 1976–79, EEC Ctee on Health and Safety 1976, NHS London Advsy Ctee 1979, Social Security

Advsy Ctee 1980–91, Health Educn Cncl 1984–87, Civil Justice Review Advsy Ctee 1985, Royal Cmmn on Environmental Pollution 1989–94; non-exec dir Redbridge and Waltham Forest Health Authy 1994–96 (chm); appointed to Employment Appeal Tribunal 1996; *Recreations* yoga, gardening, walking, golf, reading, climbing; *Style*— Peter Jacques, Esq, CBE; ✉ 7 Starling Close, Buckhurst Hill, Essex IG9 5TN (☎ 0181 505 5327)

JAFFA, Robert Harvey (Sam); s of Leslie Jaffa, and Dorothy, *née* Rakusen (d 1994); *b* 4 March 1953; *Educ* Allerton Grange Sch Leeds, Univ of Hull (BSc), Univ of Wales Coll of Cardiff (DipJour), Univ of London (pt/t MA); *m* 28 Aug 1988, Celia, da of Philip Barlow; 1 s (Lewis b 28 Feb 1992), 1 da (Lucy b 27 Jan 1995); *Career* trainee journalist Essex County Newspapers until 1980; BBC: reporter BBC Radio Humberside 1980–82, prodr BBC Radio Stoke 1982 (covered Ballykelly pub bombing while visiting N Ireland 1982), reporter National BBC Radio News 1984–91 (major assignments incl sinking of ferry Herald of Free Enterprise Zeebrugge, Bradford football stadium fire, Piper Alpha oil platform disaster), New York reporter 1991, reporter Business & Economics Unit 1992–95, N American business corr 1995–; *Books* Maxwell Stories (1992); *Style*— Sam Jaffa, Esq; ✉ BBC Business & Economics Unit, Room 3071, Broadcasting House, Portland Place, London W1A 1AA (☎ 0171 765 4991, fax 0171 636 4808)

JAFFÉ, Prof (Andrew) Michael; CBE; s of Arthur Daniel Jaffé, OBE, of London, and Marie Marguerite, *née* Strauss; *b* 3 June 1923; *Educ* Eton (King's scholar), King's Coll Cambridge (Fndn scholar, MA, DLitt), Courtauld Inst of Art, Harvard, NY Inst of Fine Arts; *m* Patricia Anne Milne Henderson, da of Alexander Roy Milne Henderson; 2 s (Daniel, Benjamin), 2 da (Deborah, Dorothea); *Career* served RNVR, Lt Cdr, ret; dir Fitzwilliam Museum Cambridge 1973–90 (prof of history of western art 1973–90), fell King's Coll Cambridge 1952–, fell Cwlth Fund Harvard and NY Univ 1951–53, asst lectr in fine arts Univ of Cambridge 1956 (lectr 1961), prof of renaissance art Washington Univ 1960–61, visiting prof Harvard 1961 and 1968–69, head Dept of History of Art Univ of Cambridge 1969–73 (reader in history of western art 1968), organiser Jordaens Exhibition Ottawa 1968–69; memb Cambridge Festival Bd, memb Bd Eastern Arts Assoc 1987–90; memb Nat Tst: Regnl Ctee (Wessex) 1971–93, Art Panel; govr Br Inst of Florence (representing vice-chllrs and princs of univs in the UK) 1971–91; Nat Art Collections Fund Award for Life Service to the Arts 1989; FRSA 1969; Officier Ordre de Léopold (Belgium), Ordre des Arts et Lettres (France), hon foreign memb American Acad of Arts and Sciences; *Books* Van Dyck's Antwerp Sketchbook (1966), Rubens (1967), Jordaens (1968), Rubens and Italy (1977), Rubens: catalogo completo (1989), The Devonshire Collection of Italian Drawings (4 vols, 1993); author of articles and reviews (art historical) in various Euro and N American jls; *Recreations* viticulture; *Clubs* Brooks's, Beefsteak, Turf; *Style*— Prof Michael Jaffé, CBE; ✉ Clifton Maybank, Yeovil, Somerset BA22 9UZ

JAFFERJEE, Aftab Asger; s of Asger A Jafferjee, of Colombo, Sri Lanka, and Tara H, *née* Kajiji; *b* 25 June 1956; *Educ* St Paul's Sch Darjeeling India, Rugby, Univ Coll Durham (BA); *Career* called to the Bar Inner Temple 1980, specialist in criminal law; memb: Ctee Criminal Bar Assoc 1992–94, Professional Conduct Ctee Bar Cncl 1994–; sec Central London Bar Mess 1994–; *Recreations* theatre, travel; *Style*— Aftab Jafferjee, Esq; ✉ 2 Harcourt Buildings, Temple, London EC4Y 9DB (☎ 0171 353 2112, fax 0171 353 8339)

JAFFRAY, Sir William Otho; 5 Bt (UK 1892), of Skilts, Studley, Warwickshire; s of Col Sir William Edmund Jaffray, 4 Bt, TD, JP, DL (d 1953), and his 2 w, Anne, *née* Paget; *b* 1 Nov 1951; *Educ* Eton; *m* 9 May 1981, Cynthia Ross, *née* Corrington, da of Mrs William M Geering, of Montreal, Quebec, Canada; 3 s (Nicholas Gordon Alexander b 18 Oct 1982, Jack Henry William b 3 Aug 1987, William Lawrence Paget b 5 March 1990), 1 da (Alexandra Marina Ross b 1984); *Heir* s, Nicholas Gordon Alexander Jaffray b 18 Oct 1982; *Career* property conslt; *Style*— Sir William Jaffray, Bt; ✉ The Manor House, Priors Dean, Petersfield, Hants

JAFFREY, Saeed; OBE (1995); s of Dr Hamid Hussain Jaffrey (d 1984), of Lucknow, Uttar Pradesh, India, and Hadia Imam (d 1987); *Educ* Wynberg-Allen Sch and St George's Coll Mussoorie UP India, Univ of Allahabad UP India (MA), RADA, The Catholic Univ of America Washington DC USA (Fulbright scholar, MA); *m* 1, 1958 (m dis 1966), Madhur Jaffrey; 3 da (Zia b 1959, Meera Shameem b 1960, Sakina b 1962); m 2, 1980 Jennifer Irene, da of William Edward Sorrell, of Rustington, W Sussex; *Career* actor; formed own Eng theatre co Delhi, became first Indian actor to tour and perform Shakespeare across the US; joined Actors' Studio NY where played leads in: Lorca's Blood Wedding, Rashomon, Twelfth Night; Broadway debut as Prof Godbolé in A Passage to India, toured US in Brecht on Brecht, produced wrote and narrated the NY radio programme Reflections of India, recorded The Art of Love - A Reworking with Music of the Kama Sutra (new version released 1992); retrospective of work Birmingham Film and TV Festival 1996; *Theatre* West End incl: Brahma in Kindly Monkeys, On a Foggy Day (St Martin's), Captain Brassbound's Conversion (Cambridge), My Giddy Aunt (Churchill Theatre Bromley), A Touch of Brightness (Royal Court), The Mother Country (Riverside Studios), Oberon in A Midsummer Night's Dream (Regent's Park), Ibrahim in White Chameleon (RNT); *Television* incl: Jimmy Sharma in Tandoori Nights (Channel 4), Nawab in Jewel In The Crown (Granada), Frankie Bhoolabhoy in Staying On, Biju Ram in The Far Pavilions, leading role in A View From The Window (BBC2), three maj roles in Partition (Channel 4), Rafiq in Gangsters (BBC), Minder, Tales of the Unexpected, Callan, Destiny (Play for Today), Love Match (BBC2), A Killing on the Exchange (Anglia), Hard Cases (Central), Rumpole of the Bailey (Thames), Little Napoleons (Channel 4), Two Oranges and a Mango (BBC2); *Films* incl: Billy Fish in The Man Who Would Be King, The Guru, Hullabaloo Over Georgie and Bonnie's Pictures, Courtesans of Bombay, Hussain in The Deceivers, The Wilby Conspiracy, Nasser in My Beautiful Laundrette, Patel in Gandhi, Hamidullah in A Passage To India, three lead roles (incl Lord Krishna) in Masala 1992, lead in After Midnight, The Chessplayers (first film in India); *Radio* writer and broadcaster of hundreds of scripts in Hindi, Urdu and English, actor in numerous plays for BBC Radio 4 incl The Pump (played nine roles), other radio work incl the Rajah in In The Native State (BBC Radio 3) and Village By The Sea (BBC Radio, played all 39 characters); *Awards* nominated for BAFTA Best Supporting Actor for My Beautiful Laundrette, winner Filmfare and Film World awards (India) for Best Actor in The Chessplayers, winner numerous awards in India for Best Actor for Ram Teri Ganga Maili, winner other awards for Dil and Henna, nominated for Canadian Academy Award (Genie) for Best Actor for Masala, selected for Norman Beaton Award for multi-cultural achievements; *Recreations* snooker, cricket, languages, cartooning, cooking, building cultural bridges; *Clubs* Union (Stratford-upon-Avon), Gerry's (Soho), Ealing Snooker, The Br Legion; *Style*— Saeed Jaffrey, Esq, OBE; ✉ c/o Magnolia Management, 136 Hicks Avenue, Greenford, Middx UB6 8HB (☎ 0181 578 2899, fax 0181 575 0369)

JAGGARD, Anthony John Thorrold; JP (1976); s of Rev Arthur William Percival Jaggard (d 1967), of Guilsborough Vicarage, Northamptonshire, and Isabel Louise May, *née* Capell (d 1972); *b* 5 June 1936; *Educ* Bedford Sch, Liverpool Sch of Architecture Univ of Liverpool; *m* 29 April 1961, (Elizabeth) Jane, da of Col Sir Joseph William Weld, OBE, TD (d 1992, Ld-Lt Dorset 1964–84), of Lulworth Castle, Dorset; 2 s (Oliver b and d 3 April 1970, Simon b (twin) 3 April 1970), 3 da (Victoria (Mrs Nigel Beer) b 14 Jan 1962, Charlotte (Mrs David Swann) b 27 Jan 1964, Sarah (Mrs Robin Price) b 5 March 1968); *Career* Cheshire (Earl of Chester's) Yeomanry 1958–67 (Capt 1964, Adj 1967), RARO 1967–86; ptnr John Stark and Partners architects 1965–; projects incl consultation on: Callaly Castle Northumberland, Hoddam Castle Dumfries, Ince Castle Cornwall, Lulworth Castle Dorset, Wardour Castle Wiltshire; designed or remodelled new houses at Gaston Grange Bentworth Hants, Longford House Sydling St Nicholas Dorset, Lulworth Castle House Dorset, Oakfield Park Mortimer Berks; contrib Archaeological Journal; memb Exec Cncl S Dorset Cons Assoc 1965–81, pres Dorset Nat Hist and Archaeological Soc 1994– (memb cncl 1969–, tstee 1993–); memb cncl: Dorset Cncl of St John 1978–81, Royal Archaeological Inst 1987–91; dir Dorset Bldgs Preservation Tst 1984–89, Liveryman Worshipful Co of Painter Stainers 1975; FRSA 1986; FSA 1990; *Recreations* old buildings, gardening, shooting; *Clubs* Cavalry and Guards'; *Style*— Anthony Jaggard, Esq, JP, FSA; ✉ Winfrith Court, Winfrith Newburgh, Dorset DT2 8JR (☎ 01305 852 800); John Stark and Partners, 13 and 14 Princes St, Dorchester DT1 1TW (☎ 01305 262636, fax 01305 260960)

JAGGER, Cedric Sargeant; s of Charles Sargeant Jagger, MC, ARA (d 1934), of London, and Violet Constance, *née* Smith (d 1964); *b* 14 June 1920; *Educ* Westminster; *m* 1, 22 March 1952 (m dis 1972), Jane Angela, da of James Hynds (d 1975); 1 s (Christopher b 18 May 1958), 1 da (Lindsay b 19 Sept 1954); m 2, 5 April 1972, Christine, da of James Fergus Brown, of Sevenoaks, Kent; *Career* WWII RA 1940–46, served 8 Army ME 1942, then N Africa, Sicily and Italy, WO at end of war; perm staff ICI 1938–72, pt/t memb and chm of selection bds CS Cmmn 1973–86, pt/t asst curator then first keeper The Clockmakers' Co Collection Guildhall London 1974–88 (conslt 1992–94); horological historian and author 1968–; fndr memb Antiquarian Horological Soc 1953–; memb: The Stables Theatre Tst, Soc of Authors 1987–94, Ctee Friends of St Mary-in-the-Castle 1993–94; life memb Hastings and St Leonards Museums Assoc, friend of The Rye Harbour Nature Reserve, friend of The Royal Acad 1977–; JP Hants 1975–84; Hon Liveryman Worshipful Co of Clockmakers 1980 (Freeman 1975); *Books* Clocks (1973), The World's Great Clocks and Watches (1977), Royal Clocks - The British Monarchy and its Timekeepers 1300–1900 (1983), The Artistry of the English Watch (1988), Macmillan's Dictionary of Art (contrib, 1993); *Recreations* principally work - also photography and music; *Clubs* The Arts; *Style*— Cedric Jagger, Esq

JAGGER, Harriett Alexis (Mrs Simon Gaul); da of Philip Charles Upfill Jagger, of Warwicks, and Claudine, *née* Goodfellow (d 1996); *b* 30 Oct 1959; *Educ* Kings HS for Girls Warwick, Marlborough Coll, London Coll of Fashion (Dip in Journalism); *m* 1984, Simon Gaul; 1 s (Hamilton John Alexander b 12 June 1992), 1 da (India Louisa Savannah b 17 Nov 1995); *Career* fashion asst Observer Newspaper 1982–85, fashion ed Elle Magazine 1985–89, sr fashion ed Vogue Magazine 1989–92, fashion and style dir Harpers & Queen Magazine 1992–94, fashion dir Tatler Magazine 1994–; *Recreations* theatre, cricket, gardening, horse-racing, travel, all aspects of design and photography; *Style*— Miss Harriett Jagger; ✉ Tatler, Vogue House, Hanover Square, London W1R 0AD (☎ 0171 499 9080)

JAGGER, Michael Philip (Mick); s of Joe Jagger, and Eva Jagger; *b* 26 July 1943; *Educ* LSE; *partner* Marsha Hunt; 1 da (Karis b 1971); m 1, 12 May 1971 (m dis 1980), Bianca Rose Perez, *née* Moreno de Macias; 1 da (Jade b 21 Oct 1971); m 2, 21 Nov 1991, Jerry Hall; 1 s (James b 28 Aug 1985), 2 da (Elizabeth Scarlett b 2 March 1984, Georgia May Ayeesha b Jan 1992); *Career* singer and songwriter; Rolling Stones formed London 1962; signed recording contracts with: Impact Records/Decca 1963, London Records/Decca 1965, CBS 1983, Virgin 1992; has worked with David Bowie, Peter Tosh, Michael Jackson, Carly Simon and others; albums with Rolling Stones: The Rolling Stones (1964, reached UK no 1), The Rolling Stones No 2 (1965, UK no 1), Out of Our Heads (1965, UK no 2), Aftermath (1966, UK no 1), Big Hits (High Tide and Green Grass) (compilation, 1966, UK no 4), got LIVE if you want it! (live, 1967), Between The Buttons (1967, UK no 3), Flowers (US compilation, 1967, US no 3), Their Satanic Majesties Request (1967, UK no 3), Beggars Banquet (1968, UK no 3), Through The Past Darkly (Big Hits Volume 2) (compilation, 1969, UK no 2), Let It Bleed (1969, UK no 1), Get Yer Ya-Ya's Out! (live, 1970, UK no 1), Stone Age (compilation, 1971, UK no 4), Sticky Fingers (1971, UK no 1), Hot Rocks 1964–71 (US compilation, 1972, US no 4), Exile On Main Street (1972, UK no 1), More Hot Rocks (US compilation, 1973, US no 9), Goats Head Soup (1973, UK no 1), It's Only Rock'N'Roll (1974, UK no 2), Made In The Shade (compilation, 1975, UK no 14), Rolled Gold - The Very Best of the Rolling Stones (compilation, 1975, UK no 7), Black and Blue (1976, UK no 2), Love You Live (live, 1977, UK no 3), Some Girls (1978, UK no 2), Emotional Rescue (1980, UK no 1), Tattoo You (1981, UK no 2), Still Life (American Concert 1981) (live, 1981, UK no 4), Undercover (1983, UK no 3), Rewind 1971–84 (compilation, 1984, UK no 23), Dirty Work (1986, UK no 4), Steel Wheels (1989, UK no 2), Flashpoint (live, 1991, UK no 6), Voodoo Lounge (1994, UK no 1); solo albums: She's The Boss (1985, UK no 6), Primitive Cool (1987, UK no 26), Wandering Spirit (1993, UK no 13) and charity single Dancing In The Street (with David Bowie, 1985, UK no 1); concert films: Sympathy For The Devil (dir Jean Luc Godard) 1969, Gimme Shelter 1970, Ladies and Gentlemen, The Rolling Stones 1977, Let's Spend The Night Together (dir Hal Ashby) 1983, Imax film of 1991 Steel Wheels Tour, 1991; feature films: Performance 1970, Ned Kelly 1970, Fitzcarraldo (dir Werner Herzog) 1981, FreeJack 1992; *Style*— Mick Jagger, Esq; ✉ c/o Marathon Music, 5 Church Row, Wandsworth Plain, London SW18 1ES

JAGGS, Rev Michael Richard Moore; s of Rev Arthur Ernest Jaggs (d 1975), of Tilford Vicarage, Tilford, Surrey, and Mary Enid, *née* Moore; *b* 7 Nov 1937; *Educ* Wells Cathedral Sch, Pierrepont Sch, City Univ (FBDO, PhD); *m* 1, 15 Sept 1962 (m dis), Gillian, da of (Francis) Allen Eyre, MBE (d 1969); 2 s (Richard, Alexander), 2 da (Sarah, Sophie); m 2, 30 Aug 1980, Janet Elizabeth, *née* Talbot; *Career* qualified dispensing optician 1956, in private practice 1961–; hosp appointment Salisbury District Hosp; in control of: Moore Jaggs Ltd, Crofting Ltd (investmt co); past chm Assoc of Contact Lens Manufacurers; Freeman City of London, Liveryman Worshipful Co of Spectacle Makers; fell: Assoc of Br Dispensing Opticians, Royal Soc of Health, Br Contact Lens Assoc (past pres); ordained deacon 1995, priest 1996; *Books* Scleral lenses - A Clinical Guide (1980); *Recreations* skiing, sailing, swimming; *Style*— The Rev Michael Jaggs; ✉ Turnpike Field, Hartley Wintney, Hampshire RG27 8HY (☎ 01252 842658); 19 Duchess Mews, London W1 (☎ 0171 580 9192)

JAIN, Dr Virendra Kumar (Viren); s of Trilok Chandra Jain (d 1974), and Roop Wati Jain (d 1995); *b* 3 Aug 1935; *Educ* Agra (BSc, MB BS); *m* 23 Nov 1960, Kamlesh, da of Jagdish Prashad Jain (d 1944); 1 s (Sanjiv b 1965), 2 da (Angela b 1964, Meena b 1977); *Career* sr registrar in psychiatry Powick Hosp Worcester 1966–68, lectr in psychiatry and sr registrar Professorial Unit Univ of Liverpool 1968–70, conslt psychiatrist Barnsley District Gen Hosp 1970–, med dir Barnsley Community and Priority Servs NHS Tst 1991–; chm: Barnsley Div Br Med Assoc (memb Yorks Regnl Cncl), Barnsley Div Overseas Doctors' Assoc; cmmr Mental Health Act Cmmn; memb: Bd of Examiners RCPsych 1990–, Standing Conference of Asian Organisation UK Nat Cncl, Br Assoc of Med Mangrs, Assoc of Tst Med Dirs, BMA, Br Soc of Med and Dental Hypnosis, Br Assoc of Psychopharmacology; life memb Wakefield Civic Soc; FRCPsych, DPM RCP and RCS; *Books* A Short Introductory Guide to Clinical Psychiatry (1984); also several articles on depression and psychopharmacology; *Recreations* entertaining, playing tennis and golf, listening to Indian classical music; *Clubs* Sandal Lawn Tennis, Walton Hall Country, Waterton Park Golf; *Style*— Dr Viren Jain; ✉ Shantiniketan, 17 Beechfield, Sandal, Wakefield, West Yorkshire WF2 6AW (☎ 01924 255207); Department of Psychological Medicine, Kendray Hospital, Doncaster Road, Barnsley, South Yorkshire S70 3RD (☎ 01226 730000, fax 01226 296782)

JAINE, Tom William Mahony; s of William Edwin Jaine (d 1970), and Aileen, *née* Mahony (d 1943); *b* 4 June 1943; *Educ* Kingswood Sch Bath, Balliol Coll Oxford (BA); *m* 1983, Sally Caroline, da of Andrew Agnew, of Crowborough, and Hon Joyce Violet, *née* Godber; 4 da (Harriet b 1974, Elizabeth b 1976, Matilda b 1985, Frances b 1987); *Career* restaurateur 1973–84; ed: Good Food Guide 1989–93, Journal of the International Wine and Food Society 1989–91, publisher Prospect Books 1993–; freelance writer (Sunday Telegraph, and others) 1993–; *Recreations* baking; *Style*— Tom Jaine, Esq; ✉ Allaleigh House, Blackawton, Totnes, Devon TQ9 7DL (☎ 01803 712269)

JAK, *see:* Jackson, Raymond Allen

JAKOBOVITS, Baron (Life Peer UK 1988), of Regent's Park in Greater London; Sir Immanuel Jakobovits; kt (1981); s of Rabbi Dr Julius Jakobovits, of Königsberg, Germany; *b* 8 Feb 1921, Konigsberg, Germany; *Educ* Univ of London (PhD), Jews' Coll London, Yeshivah Etz Chaim London (DD), City Univ (DLitt), DD (Lambeth); *m* 1949, Amélie, da of Rabbi Dr Elie Munk; 2 s (Dr Hon Julian b 1950, Rabbi Hon Samuel b 1951), 4 da (Esther (Hon Mrs Pearlman) b 1953, Jeanette (Hon Mrs Turner) b 1956, Aviva (Hon Mrs Adler) b 1958, Elisheva (Hon Mrs Homburger) b 1966); *Career* minister of three London synagogues 1941–49, Chief Rabbi of Ireland 1949–58, rabbi Fifth Ave Synagogue (New York) 1958–67, Chief Rabbi of The United Hebrew Congregations of Br Cwlth of Nations 1967–91 (Chief Rabbi Emeritus 1991–); pres Conf of Euro Rabbis; awarded Templeton Prize for Progress in Religion 1991; Hon DD Univ of Wales 1992; *Books* Jewish Medical Ethics (1959), Jewish Law Faces Modern Problems (1965), Journal of a Rabbi (1966), The Timely and the Timeless (1977), 'If Only My People..' Zionism in My Life (1984), Dear Chief Rabbi (1995); co-author of The Jewish Hospital Compendium (1963) and others; Centenary Edition of The Authorised Daily Prayer Book (ed, 1990); *Style*— The Rt Hon Lord Jakobovits, Emeritus Chief Rabbi; ✉ 44a Albert Rd, London NW4 2SJ (☎ 0181 203 8667, fax 0181 203 8826)

JAMAL, Dr Goran Atallah; s of Atallah Jamal (Al-Talabani), of Iraq, and Nusrat Jamal (d 1987); *b* 19 July 1953; *Educ* Baghdad Univ (MB ChB), Univ of Glasgow (PhD, MD); *m* 15 Dec 1983, Vian, da of Maj-Gen Mohamad Salih Anber (ret), of Iraq; 1 da (Lazia b 23 May 1986), 1 s (Arie b 3 June 1992); *Career* sr registrar in neurology Bart's Med Sch 1986–88, conslt Dept of Neurology and sr clinical lectr Univ of Glasgow 1988– (res fell in neurology 1981–86), sr lectr in neurosciences Dept of Educn Strathclyde Region 1988–; chm Kurdish Relief Assoc UK (a registered charity); memb: Assoc of Br Neurologists, The EEG Soc, Assoc of Br Clinical Neuro-physiologists, Scottish Assoc of Neurosciences, New York Acad of Sci, American Assoc of Electrodiagnostic Med, American EEG Soc; FRCPGlas; *Publications* author of over 105 articles, papers and book chapters; *Clubs* The Pond Leisure (Glasgow); *Style*— Dr Goran Jamal; ✉ 1 Camstradden Drive West, Bearsden, Glasgow G61 4AJ (☎ 0141 942 8687); Glasgow University, Department of Neurology, Institute of Neurological Sciences, Southern General Hospital, Glasgow G51 4TF (☎ 0141 201 2462, fax 0141 201 2148)

JAMAL, Mahmood; s of Maulana Jamal Mian, of Firangi Mahal, and Kaniz Fatima Asar; *Educ* St Joseph's Sch Dacca, SOAS, Univ of London (BA); *Career* poet, film producer and director; poems broadcast on Radio 3 and published in various magazines incl London Magazine; co-fndr Retake Film and Video Collective (winner BFI Independent Film and TV Award 1988), co-ed Black Phoenix Magazine 1979–82; dir Epicflow Films; winner Minority Rights Gp Award for poetry and translation 1985, lit advsr to Gtr London Arts 1986–88, advsr and memb Editorial Bd Third Text Quarterly 1987–92; script-writer first Br Asian serial Family Pride (Central TV Birmingham) 1991–92, co-prodr History of Indian Cinema (Channel 4) 1990–91, ex-prodr/dir Songs and Memories (26 part series, Channel 4), prodr/dir Islamic Conversations (6 part series on contemporary issues in the Muslim World) 1992–93, prodr/dir Quarrels (4 part series, Channel 4) 1994, prodr/writer Turning World (new drama, Channel 4); *Books* Coins for Charon (1976), Silence Inside A Guns Mouth (1984), Penguin Book of Modern Urdu Poetry (ed and translator, 1986); *Recreations* tennis, squash, cricket; *Clubs* South Hampstead Lawn Tennis; *Style*— Mahmood Jamal, Esq; ✉ 69 Dartmouth Rd, London NW2 4EP (☎ 0181 452 8170); 19 Liddell Rd, London NW6 (☎ 0171 328 8768)

JAMAL, Patricia Barbara; da of Lt Cdr John Enda Bernard Healy, RNVR (d 1967), and Barbara Maud, *née* Taylor; *b* 3 Sept 1943; *Educ* St Maur's Convent Weybridge, Ursuline Convent Wimbledon, Brooklands Coll Weybridge; *m* 16 Dec 1971, (Nizar) Ahmed Jamal, s of Abdulmalek Ahmed Jamal, of Vancouver, Canada; 3 da (Jenna b 1977, Sarah b 1980, Isabel b 1982); *Career* business devpt offr Bank of Montreal London 1983–87, chief dealer GTS Corp Servs Barclays Bank 1987–92, dir Barclays Metals Ltd 1992–95, md Global Money Market Sales Barclays Bank plc 1994–96, md Fin Instns BZW 1996–; dir Aston Charities Tst Ltd 1978–; *Recreations* family, reading, music, riding; *Style*— Mrs Patricia Jamal; ✉ Managing Director, Financial Institutions, BZW, First Floor, Seal House, Swan Lane, London EC4R 3UD (☎ 0171 623 2323)

JAMES, Prof Alan Morien; s of Willie James (d 1983), of Newport, Gwent, and Martha, *née* John (d 1990); *b* 20 Jan 1933; *Educ* Newport HS, LSE (BSc); *m* 1, 18 Aug 1956 (m dis 1980), Jean Valerie, da of Ernest Hancox, of Newport, Gwent; 4 s (Morien b 1958, Gwyn b 1962, Gareth b 1964, David b 1965), 3 da (Helen b and d 1959, Nesta b 1961, Ceri b 1969); m 2, 19 March 1981, Lorna, da of Frank Eric Lloyd, of Chester; *Career* LSE: asst lectr, lectr, sr lectr, reader 1957–73; Rockefeller res fell Inst of War and Peace Studies Columbia Univ USA 1968, prof and head of Dept of Int Rels Univ of Keele 1974–91 (res prof 1990–); visiting prof: Dept of Int Rels Univ of Ife Nigeria 1981, Sch of Int Studies Jawaharlal Nehru Univ New Delhi 1983, Nat Inst for Defense Studies Tokyo 1993; chm Br Int Studies Assoc 1979–83, memb Soc Studies Sub Ctee Univ Grants Ctee 1983–89, advsr in politics and int studies Univ Funding Cncl 1989–93, chm Int Law Section Int Studies Assoc (USA) 1992–93; *Books* The Politics of Peacekeeping (1969), The Bases of International Order (ed 1973), Sovereign Statehood - The Basis of International Society (1986), Peacekeeping in International Politics (1990), States in a Changing World - A Contemporary Analysis (co-ed 1993), Britain and the Congo Crisis, 1960–63 (1996); *Recreations* hill and coast walking, golf, supporting Port Vale FC, music, food; *Clubs* Royal Commonwealth Soc; *Style*— Prof Alan James; ✉ 23 Park Lane, Congleton, Cheshire CW12 3DG (☎ and fax 01260 271801); Department of International Relations, University of Keele, Keele, Staffordshire ST5 5BG (☎ 01782 583210, fax 01782 583088, telex 36113 UNKLIB G)

JAMES, Albert (Alby); s of Albert Samuel James (d 1982), of London, and Florence Cassetta Renalda, *née* Thomas (d 1989); *Educ* St David's C of E Sch London, Southgate Technical Coll London, Univ of E Anglia (BA), Univ of London; *m* 5 Jan 1980, Vanessa Mary, da of Capt Christopher Simmonds; 2 s (William Marcus b 17 March 1980, Benjamin Andrew b 16 April 1982), 1 da (Eloise Sarah b 4 Aug 1988); *Career* currently freelance radio and theatre dir/prodr and dramaturg; Arts Cncl trainee asst dir English Stage Company 1979–80, asst dir Royal Shakespeare Company (Barbican) 1982–83, artistic dir and chief exec Temba Theatre Company 1984–93; productions incl: Mr Wilberforce, MP (Westminster Theatre) 1980, Meetings (Hampstead Theatre) 1982, Scrape off the Black (Temba) 1985, Porgy and Bess (assoc dir, Glyndebourne Festival Opera 1986 and 1987, Royal Opera House, BBC TV and Primetime TV 1992), Fences (Liverpool Playhouse and The Garrick London) 1990, Dona Rosita, The Spinster (RADA) 1990, Ghosts (Temba tour) 1991, A Killing Passion (Temba tour) 1992, The Constant Wife (RADA) 1992, King Lear and The Shelter (RADA) 1993, My Children, My Africa (Watermill Theatre) 1993, Mamma Decemba (BBC Radio 4) 1994, The Ramayama (BBC Radio 4) 1994; writer and speaker on theatre and multi-culturalism; specialist advsr for performing arts CNAA 1989–92; memb: BBC Gen Advsy Cncl 1987–91, Dirs' Guild of GB; *Recreations* listening to music, reading, photography, religion and politics, foreign travel; *Style*— Alby James, Esq; ✉ 45 Cranworth Gardens, London SW9 0NR (fax 0171 793 9976); c/o Marmont Mangement (☎ 0171 637 3183)

JAMES, Bill; *see:* Tucker, (Allan) James

JAMES, His Hon Judge Charles Edwin Frederic; s of Frederic Crockett Gwilym James (d 1970), formerly treas of the Great Universal Stores Ltd, and Marjorie Peggy, *née* Peace (d 1976); *b* 17 April 1943; *Educ* Trent Coll Derbyshire, Selwyn Coll Cambridge (MA); *m* 1968, Diana Mary Francis, da of James Francis Thornton (d 1977), formerly chm and md William Thornton & Sons Ltd; 2 s (Daniel b 1971, Philip b 1973); *Career* called to the Bar Inner Temple 1965, junior Northern Circuit 1966, barr-at-law on the Northern Circuit 1965–93, recorder of the Crown Ct 1982–93, circuit judge (Northern Circuit) 1993–; *Recreations* family pursuits; *Clubs* Cambridge Univ Cricket, Royal Liverpool Golf, Royal Mersey Yacht; *Style*— His Hon Judge Charles James

JAMES, Hon Charles Walter Henry; eldest s & h of 5 Baron Northbourne, *qv*; *b* 14 June 1960; *Educ* Eton, Magdalen Coll Oxford (MA), Henley Management Coll, Brunel Univ (MBA); *m* 3 Oct 1987, Catherine Lucy, o da of W Ralph Burrows, of Prescot, Lancs; 2 s (Henry Christopher William b 3 Dec 1988, Alexander Oliver Charles b 27 Feb 1996), 1 da (Anastasia Aliki b 18 Feb 1992); *Career* dir: Betteshanger Investments Ltd, Betteshanger Farms Ltd; *Style*— The Hon Charles James; ✉ Northbourne Court, Northbourne, Kent CT14 0LW (☎ 01304 374617); Home Farm, Betteshanger, Kent CT14 0NT (☎ 01304 611281, fax 01304 614512)

JAMES, Christopher John; s of John Thomas Walters James, MC (d 1978), of Monmouth, and Cicely Hilda, *née* Purton (formerly Motteram) (d 1970); *b* 20 March 1932; *Educ* Clifton, Magdalene Coll Cambridge (MA); *m* 20 Sept 1958, Elizabeth Marion Cicely, da of Thomas Finlayson Thomson (d 1977), of Winchester; 1 s (Timothy b 10 Dec 1959), 1 da (Caroline b 10 Oct 1962); *Career* Nat Serv cmmn RA 1951–52, TA 1952–60; admitted slr 1958, sr ptnr Martineau Johnson 1989–94; chm Birmingham Midshires Building Society 1990–96, ret; dep chm R Griggs Group Ltd 1994– (dir 1993–), dir Police Mutual Assurance Soc Ltd 1996–; pres Birmingham Law Soc 1983–84, chm Cncl Edgbaston HS for Girls 1987–90; FRSA 1991; *Clubs* Little Aston Golf; *Style*— Christopher James, Esq

JAMES, His Honour Judge; Christopher Philip; s of Herbert Edgar James, CBE (d 1977); *b* 27 May 1934; *Educ* Felsted, Magdalene Coll Cambridge (MA); *Career* cmmnd RASC 1953; called to the Bar Gray's Inn 1959, recorder of the Crown Ct 1979, circuit judge (SE Circuit) 1980–; *Clubs* United Oxford and Cambridge Univ; *Style*— His Honour Judge James; ✉ Lambeth County Court, Court House, Cleaver Street, Kennington Road, London SE11 4DZ

JAMES, Clive Vivian Leopold; s of late Albert Arthur James, and Minora May, *née* Darke; *b* 7 Oct 1939; *Educ* Sydney Tech HS, Univ of Sydney, Pembroke Coll Cambridge (pres Footlights); *Career* writer, TV presenter and entertainer; feature writer The Observer 1972– (TV critic 1972–82); fndr Watchmaker Productions 1994; *Television* presenter TV series: Cinema, Up Sunday, So It Goes, A Question of Sex, Saturday Night People, Clive James on Television, The Late Clive James, The Late Show with Clive James, Saturday Night Clive, The Talk Show with Clive James; TV documentaries: Shakespeare in Perspective - Hamlet 1980, The Clive James Paris Fashion Show 1981, Clive James and the Calendar Girls 1981, The Return of the Flash of Lightning 1982, Clive James in Las Vegas 1982, Clive James meets Roman Polanski 1984, The Clive James Great American Beauty Pageant 1984, Clive James in Dallas 1985, Clive James meets Katherine Hepburn 1986, Clive James on Safari 1986, Clive James and the Heroes of San Francisco 1987, Clive James in Japan 1987, Postcard from Rio 1989, Postcard from Chicago 1989, Postcard from Paris 1989, Clive James meets Jane Fonda, Clive James on the 80s 1989, Postcard from Miami 1990, Postcard from Rome 1990, Postcard from Shanghai 1990, Clive James meets Ronald Reagan 1990; *Music* record lyricist for Pete Atkin; albums incl: Beware of Beautiful Strangers, Driving through the Mythical America, A King at Nightfall, The Road of Silk, Secret Drinker, Live Lible, The Master of the Revels; song-book A First Folio (with Pete Atkin); *Non-fiction* incl: The Metropolitan Critic (1974), The Fate of Felicity Fark in the Land of the Media (1975), Peregrine Prykke's Pilgrimage through the London Literary World (1976), Britannia Bright's Bewilderment in the Wilderness of Westminster (1976), Visions Before Midnight (1977), At the Pillars of Hercules (1979), First Reactions (1980), Charles Charming's Challenges on the Pathway to the Throne (1981), Crystal Bucket (1981), From the Land of Shadows (1982), Glued to the Box (1982), Flying Visits (1984), Snakecharmers in Texas (1988); autobiographies: Unreliable Memoirs (1980), Falling Towards England: Unreliable Memoirs II (1985), May Week Was in June: Unreliable Memoirs III (1990); *Fiction* Brilliant Creatures (1983), The Remake (1987), Brrm! Brrm! (1992), The Silver Castle (1996); *Verse* Fan-mail (1977), Poem of the year (1983), Other Passports: poems 1958–85; *Style*— Clive James, Esq; ✉ Watchmaker Productions, The Chrysalis Building, Bramley Road, London W10 6SP (☎ 0171 465 6000, 0171 465 6060)

JAMES, Rt Rev Colin Clement Walter; s of late Canon Charles Clement Hancock James, and Gwenyth Mary James; *b* 20 Sept 1926; *Educ* Aldenham, King's Coll Cambridge (MA), Cuddesdon Theological Coll; *m* 1962, Margaret Joan Henshaw; 1 s, 2 da; *Career* asst curate Stepney Parish Church 1952–55, chaplain Stowe Sch 1955–59, BBC Religious Broadcasting Dept 1959–67, vicar St Peter's Bournemouth 1967–73, bishop suffragan of Basingstoke 1973–77, chm Church Information Ctee 1976–79, bishop of Wakefield 1977–85, bishop of Winchester 1985–95, ret; chm Central Religious Advsy Ctee to BBC and IBA 1979–84, chm C of E Liturgical Cmmn 1986–93, pres Woodward Corporation 1978–93; *Recreations* theatre, travelling, radio and television; *Style*— The Rt Rev Colin James; ✉ 5 Hermitage Road, Lansdown, Bath BA1 5SN (☎ 01225 312720)

JAMES, Darrel; s of Desmond James, of Ystalyfera, Swansea; *b* 10 Dec 1959; *Educ* UCW Aberystwyth (LLB), Sidney Sussex Coll Cambridge (LLM); *Career* contracts offr S4C 1985–86, contracts offr HTV Group 1986–88; S4C: prog acquisition mangr 1988–89, head of business affrs and prog acquisition 1989–93, concurrently head of co-prodns 1991–93, involved with numerous co-prodns incl The Legend of Lochnagar (with BBC), Shakespeare - The Animated Tales (with BBC, Home Box Office USA and Fujisankei Japan), Rules of Engagement (with La Sept France/Germany) and In Times of War (with BFI and ZDF and Frankfurter Filmproduktion Germany); head of business affairs ITV Network 1993–94, dir of business devpt Scottish Television plc 1994–; *Recreations* squash, cinema, literature, music; *Style*— Darrel James, Esq; ✉ Scottish Television plc, 200 Gray's Inn Road, London WC1X 8XZ (☎ 0171 843 8350)

JAMES, Prof David Edward; s of Charles Edward James (d 1982), of Eastleigh, Hants, and Dorothy Hilda, *née* Reeves (d 1984); *b* 31 July 1937; *Educ* Peter Symonds Sch Winchester, Univ of Reading (BSc), Univ of Oxford (DipEd), Univ of London (Dip in Further Educn), Univ of Durham (MEd); *m* 30 March 1963, Penelope Jane, da of Lt Cdr Edward J Murray, of Bradford-on-Avon, Wilts; 2 s (Philip b 1966, Christopher b 1969), 1 da (Lucy b 1964); *Career* lectr in zoology and psychology City of Bath Tech Coll 1961–63, lectr in sci and psychology St Mary's Coll of Educn Newcastle upon Tyne 1963–64; Univ of Surrey: lectr in educnl psychology 1964–68, res lectr in educn 1968–69, dir of adult educn 1969–80, prof of adult educn 1980–81 and 1993–, prof and head of Dept of Educnl Studies 1981–93, dean of Assoc Instns 1996–; md: Interactive Educational Systems International Ltd, IV Epoch Productions Ltd 1989–93; non-exec dir: Transnational Satellite Education Co Ltd 1991–94, ICON Productions Ltd 1993–95;

chm: Cncl of Sci & Technol Regnl Orgn for Surrey 1983–93, Surrey Retirement Assoc 1984–, Br Assoc for Educnl Gerontology 1986–, High Coombe Tst for Midwife Educn 1990–, Moor Park Tst for Christian Adult Educn 1992–, Age Concern Waverley 1993–96, Cmmn for Social Service Users & Carers (Surrey) 1994–; vice chm: Br Assoc for Servs to the Elderly 1991–94, Cncl of Assoc of Business Execs 1994–; pres Preretirement Assoc of GB and NI 1993–; memb: Bd of Educn RCN 1980–92, Educn Ctee Royal Coll of Midwives 1986–91, Governing Body Centre for Int Briefing 1975–, Gen Nursing Cncl 1972–80, UK Central Cncl for Nursing Midwifery and Health Visiting 1980–83, English Nat Bd for Nursing Midwifery and Health Visiting 1983–88, Exec Ctee Guildford Branch English Speaking Union 1985–; CBiol, MIBiol 1963, CPsych, AFBPsS 1966, FRSH 1974, FRSA 1974, FITD 1991; *Books* A Students Guide to Efficient Study (1966), Introduction to Psychology (1968); *Recreations* farming; *Style*— Prof David James; ✉ Department of Educational Studies, University of Surrey, Guildford GU2 5XH (☎ 01483 300800, fax 01483 300803, telex 859331)

JAMES, Derek Claude; OBE (1989); s of Cecil Claude James (d 1987), and Violet, *née* Rudge (d 1974); *b* 9 March 1929; *Educ* King Edward's GS Camphill, Birmingham, Open Univ (BA); *m* 16 Oct 1954, Evelyn, *née* Thomas; 1 s (Stephen b 1955), 1 da (Kathryn (Mrs Dawson) b 1956); *Career* RA 1947–49; local govt 1946–69 (Birmingham, Coventry, Bradford); Leeds City Cncl: princ offr 1969–73, dep dir of social servs 1973–78, dir of social servs 1978–89; pres Nat Assoc of Nursery and Family Care 1988–92, chm Nightstop Leeds (scheme to assist homeless young people) 1989–; memb: St Anne's Shelter & Housing Action Ltd Leeds 1976–89, Yorks RHA 1976–82, Cncl Wm Merritt Disabled Living Centre 1981– (chm 1994–), Nat Advsy Cncl for Employment of Disabled People 1985–89, Panel of Experts Registered Homes Tribunal 1990–95, Health Advsy Serv 1990–92, Assoc of Dirs of Social Servs; vice chair Nat Cncl Family Serv Units 1992– (memb 1991–); Sanctuary Housing Assoc: memb N Region Ctee 1991–92, chm N & W Yorks Area 1992–, memb Nat Cncl 1993–; *Recreations* doing the bidding of my granddaughters, gardening, attempting to work with wood; *Style*— Derek James, Esq, OBE; ✉ Hill House, Woodhall Hills, Calverley, Pudsey, West Yorkshire LS28 5QY (☎ 0113 257 8044)

JAMES, Eirian; da of Dewi William James, of Cardigan, and Martha Ann, *née* Davies; *b* 7 Sept 1952; *Educ* Preseli Secdy Sch Crymych Pembrokeshire, RCM; *m* 29 Dec 1975 (m dis 1993), Alan Rowland Davies; 1 da (Sara Elen b 11 March 1990); *Career* soprano/mezzo-soprano; hosts own TV series on S4C featuring popular folk and operatic arias; *Roles* with Kent Opera incl: Olga in Eugene Onegin, title role in L'Incoronazione di Poppea, Rosina in The Barber of Seville, Nero in Agrippina, Dido in Dido and Aeneas, Cherubino in The Marriage of Figaro, Meg Page in Falstaff, Man Friday in Robinson Crusoe; with other cos incl: title role in La Perichole (Singers Co), Dorabella in Cosi fan Tutte (Singers Co, Aix-en-Provence), title role in Ariodante (Buxton Festival), Medea in Cavalli's Jason (Buxton Festival), Hänsel in Hänsel and Gretel (Geneva), Second Lady in The Magic Flute (Geneva), Cupid in Orpheus in the Underworld (Houston, ENO), Siebel in Faust (Houston), Sextus in Julius Caesar (Houston, Scottish Opera), Annina in Der Rosenkavalier (Covent Garden), Smeaton in Anna Bolena (Covent Garden), Nancy in Albert Hering (Covent Garden), Hermia in A Midsummer Night's Dream (Aix-en-Provence), Isolier in Count Ory (Lyon), Orlofsky in Die Fledermaus (WNO), Olga in Eugene Onegin (Covent Garden), Zerlina in Don Giovanni (Parma, Amsterdam, Ludwigsburg, London), Cherubino in Marriage of Figaro (Bordeaux, Bastille Paris), Despina in Cosi Fan Tutte (Garnier Paris), Diane in Hippolyte et Aricie (Garnier Paris); *Recordings* Reuben in Christmas Rose (conducted by Howard Williams), Second Lady in The Magic Flute (conducted by Roger Norrington) 1990, Despina in Cosi Fan Tutte (conducted by John Eliot Gardiner), Zerlina in Don Giovanni (conducted by John Eliot Gardiner), Sextus in Julius Caesar (conducted by Jean-Claude Malgoire); *Recreations* gardening; *Style*— Ms Eirian James; ✉ c/o Peter Alferink, Apollolaan 181, 1077 Amsterdam, Holland (☎ 31 (0) 20 664 31 51, fax 31 (0) 20 675 24 26)

JAMES, Elizabeth Sheila (Liz); (Mrs C Drummond Challis); da of Edward Leonard James, of Westerham, Kent, and Sheila Florence, *née* Jordan; *b* 24 Aug 1944; *Educ* Micklefield Sch for Girls Sussex, Ravensbourne Coll of Art and Design (BA); *m* 4 Oct 1984, (Christopher) Drummond Cremer Challis, s of Christopher George Joseph Challis; *Career* graphic designer: Crosby Fletcher Forbes 1965–66, Total Design Holland 1966–68, Pentagram 1968–74; freelance graphic designer Holland and London 1974–83, fndr ptnr Lambton Place Design 1983–87, head of design Phaidon Press 1994–95, dir Liz James Design Associates 1987–; clients incl: Michael Samuelson Lighting, RICS, Gardiner and Theobald, Clifford Chance, Sun Life, Barclay's Premier Card; awards: D&AD nomination for work on Colonial Mutual, Br Business Calendar Silver Award for work on Cine-Europe; PPL 1977; memb: D&AD 1983, DBA 1983 (dir 1992–93); FCSD 1986 (memb Cncl 1992–95), FRSA 1992; *Recreations* art, music, ceramics, skiing, sailing, dance and movement; *Style*— Ms Liz James; ✉ Liz James Design Associates, 18 Middle Row, London W10 5AT (☎ 0181 960 3251 or 0181 348 4313, fax 0181 960 6150)

JAMES, Rev Canon Eric Arthur; s of John Morgan James, and Alice Amelia James; *b* 14 April 1925; *Educ* Dagenham County HS, King's Coll London (MA, DD, FKC); *Career* asst curate St Stephen with St John Westminster 1951–55, chaplain Trinity Coll Cambridge 1955–59, select preacher to Univ of Cambridge 1959–60, vicar St George Camberwell and warden Trinity Coll Mission 1959–64, dir Parish and People 1964–69, canon residentiary and precentor Southwark Cathedral 1966–73, proctor in convocation 1964–72, canon residentiary and missioner Diocese of St Albans 1973–83 (canon emeritus 1990–), hon canon 1983–90, preacher to Gray's Inn 1978–; commissary to: Bishop of Kimberley 1965–67, Archbishop of Melanesia 1969–93; examining chaplain to: Bishop of St Albans 1973–83, Bishop of Truro 1983–93; hon dir Christian Action 1979–; chaplain to HM The Queen 1984–94 (extra chaplain 1995–); select preacher to Univ of Oxford 1991–92; DD Lambeth 1993; FRSA 1992; *Books* The Double Cure (1957, 2 edn 1980), Odd Man Out (1962), Spirituality for Today (ed, 1968), Stewards of the Mysteries of God (ed, 1979), A Life of Bishop John A T Robinson, Scholar, Pastor, Prophet (1987), Where Three Ways Meet (ed, 1987), God's Truth (ed, 1988), Judge Not - A Selection of Sermons Preached in Gray's Inn Chapel 1978–88 (1989), Collected Thoughts - Fifty Scripts for BBC's Thought For The Day (1990), A Last Eccentric - A Symposium concerning the Rev Canon F A Simpson, Historian, Preacher and Eccentric (ed, 1991), Word Over All - Forty Sermons 1985–1991 (1992), The Voice Said, Cry Forty Sermons 1990–93 (1994); *Recreations* music; *Clubs* Reform, Royal Cwlth Soc; *Style*— The Rev Canon Eric James; ✉ 11 Denny Crescent, Kennington, London SE11 4UY

JAMES, Dr (David) Geraint; s of David James (d 1928), of Treherbert, Wales, and Sarah, *née* Davies (d 1978); *b* 2 Jan 1922; *Educ* Pontypridd Co Sch, Jesus Coll Cambridge (MA, MD), Middx Hosp Univ of London (MRCS, LRCP, MRCP), Columbia Univ NY; *m* 15 Dec 1951, Prof Dame Sheila Patricia Violet Sherlock, DBE, *qv*; 2 da (Amanda b 15 Sept 1958, Auriole b 7 Dec 1963); *Career* Surgn-Lt RNVR 1946–48; serv: HMS Halcyon, HMS Theseus; conslt physician RN 1972–85; dean of studies Royal Northern Hosp London 1968–88 (conslt physician 1959–), prof of med Univ of London and Miami, conslt ophthalmic physician St Thomas' Hosp London; pres: Harvey Soc London 1963, Osler Club London, Med Soc London 1980; fndr London Med Ophthalmology Soc 1964, organising soc World Congress History of Med 1972; cncl memb: RCP 1983, Hunterian Soc 1984; fndr pres World Assoc of Sarcoidosis 1987, ed International Journal Sarcoidosis, vice pres Postgrad Med Fedn; hon corr Thoracic Soc of: France, Italy, Portugal, French Nat Acad of Med; pres London Glamorganshire Soc 1971–75, white robed memb Bardic Circle of Wales 1984; Freeman: Worshipful Soc of Apothecaries 1960–, City of London; Hon LLD Univ of Wales 1982; FRCP 1964, Hon FACP 1990; *Books* Textbook of Infections (1957), Colour Atlas of Respiratory Diseases (1981), Sarcoidosis (1985), W B Saunders; *Recreations* tennis, rugby, international Welshness; *Clubs* Athenaeum; *Style*— Dr D Geraint James; ✉ 41 York Terrace East, Regent's Park, London NW1 4PT (☎ 0171 486 4560); 149 Harley St, London W1N 1HG (☎ 0171 935 4444)

JAMES, Geraldine; da of Gerald Thomas (d 1987), of Cornwall, and Annabella, *née* Doogan (d 1987); *b* 6 July 1950; *Educ* Downe House Sch Newbury, Drama Centre London; *m* 28 June 1986, Joseph Sebastian Blatchley, s of John Blatchley (d 1994); 1 da (Eleanor b 20 June 1985); *Career* actress; worked in repertory theatre 1972–75: Chester, Exeter, Coventry; numerous venues London Fringe; *Theatre* roles incl: Miss Julie, Desdemona, Raina, Annie Sullivan; other works incl: The White Devil (Oxford Playhouse) 1981, When I was a Girl I Used to Scream and Shout (Whitehall) 1987, Cymbeline (NT) 1988, Portia in The Merchant of Venice (Peter Hall Co, London and Broadway, Tony Award nomination 1990) 1989, Death and the Maiden (Duke of York) 1992, Lysistrata (Old Vic) 1993, Hedda Gabler (Manchester Royal Exchange) 1993; *Television* Dummy 1977 (BAFTA Best Actress nomination, Critics' Assoc Best Actress Award), Love Among The Artists 1978, The History Man 1980, Jewel In The Crown (BAFTA Best Actress nomination), Blott on the Landscape (BBC) 1984, Echoes 1987, Stanley and the Women 1991, The Doll's House 1991, Ex 1991, The Healer 1994, Kavanagh QC 1994, Band of Gold 1994 and 1995 (BAFTA Award nomination for Best Actress), Over Here 1995, Rebecca 1996; *Films* incl: Sweet William 1978, Night Cruiser 1978, Gandhi 1981, Wolves of Willoughby Chase 1988, The Tall Guy 1988, She's Been Away 1989 (Vencie Film Festival Best Actress Award), If Look's Could Kill 1990, The Bridge 1990, Beltenebros 1991, Losing Track 1991, No Worries 1992, Doggin' Around 1994, Moll Flanders, Watch that Man 1996; *Recreations* music; *Style*— Miss Geraldine James; ✉ c/o Julian Belfrage Associates, 46 Albemarle Street, London W1X 4PP (☎ 0171 491 4400, fax 0171 493 5460)

JAMES, Glen William; s of Clifford Vizetelly James, of Long Ashton, Bristol, and Kathleen Mary Flora, *née* Doull; *b* 22 Aug 1952; *Educ* King's Coll Sch Wimbledon, New Coll Oxford (MA); *m* 15 Aug 1987, Amanda Claire, da of Philip Dorrell, of Worcester; *Career* admitted slr 1976, ptnr Slaughter and May 1983–; Freeman Worshipful Co of Solicitors; memb Law Soc; MSI; *Recreations* music, reading, various sports; *Clubs* RAC; *Style*— Glen James, Esq; ✉ Slaughter and May, 35 Basinghall St, London EC2V 5DB (☎ 0171 600 1200, fax 0171 600 0289, telex 883486/888926)

JAMES, Rt Rev Graham Richard; *see:* St Germans, Bishop of

JAMES, Helen; *née* Shaw; da of Peter Shaw, and Joan Mary, *née* Turner; *b* 29 March 1951; *Educ* Cheadle Hulme Sch, Girton Coll Cambridge (MA); *m* 30 August 1976, Allan James, s of Thomas Raymond James; 1 s (Peter Thomas b 26 March 1979), 2 da (Clare Elizabeth b 21 Oct 1980, Sarah Linda b 29 Sept 1985); *Career* actuary; trainee Equity and Law 1972–74; Alexander Clay & Partners: joined 1975, ptnr 1977–94, currently princ actuary; *Style*— Mrs Helen James; ✉ 15 Church Ave, Ruislip, Middx HA4 7HX (☎ 01895 631 758); Alexander Clay, Carnegie House, Peterborough Road, Harrow HA1 2AJ (☎ 0181 970 4619, fax 0181 970 4798)

JAMES, Henry Leonard; CB (1979); s of Leonard Mark James (d 1967), of Birmingham, and Alice Esther, *née* Jones (d 1971); *b* 12 Dec 1919; *Educ* King Edward VI Sch Birmingham; *m* 26 March 1949, Sylvia Mary (d 1989), da of Rupert John George Bickell (d 1952), of Bournemouth; *Career* ed The Window (Miny of Nat Insur) 1947–51, press offr Miny of Pension and Nat Insur 1951 55, head films radio and tv Admty 1955–61, dep chief info offr Miny of Educn 1961–64, dep press sec to PM 1964–69 (press sec 1970–71 and 1979), chief info offr Miny of Housing 1969–70, dir of info DOE 1971–74, dir gen COI 1974–78, PRO Vickers Ltd 1978, dir gen Nat Assoc of Pension Funds 1980–86; assoc dir Godwins Ltd 1987–95, editorial conslt Tolleys Ltd 1987–, dir Pielle Ltd 1989–, vice pres Retirement Tst 1992–; memb: BOTB 1980–84, Cncl RSPCA 1980–83; FIPR (pres 1979), FCAM (vice pres 1984–), FRSA; *Recreations* literary and visual arts; *Style*— Henry James, Esq, CB; ✉ 17 Beaumont Avenue, Richmond, Surrey TW9 2HE (☎ and fax 0181 940 9229)

JAMES, Dr Ian Meurig; s of late Thomas John James, of Norton, Swansea, and Margery, *née* Bennett; *b* 15 Feb 1937; *Educ* Gowerton GS, UCH Med Sch London (MB BS), Gonville and Caius Coll Cambridge (PhD); *m* 1, 16 Nov 1968 (m dis 1986), Margery Lia; 2 da (Alice Margery b 25 Aug 1969, Emily Angela b 19 Jan 1971); m 2, 28 March 1987, Jane Elizabeth, da of Hugh Faulkner, of Bucks; 1 s (Jeremy Rhidian b 24 Aug 1990), 1 da (Henrietta Louise b 6 July 1995); *Career* MacKenzie MacKinnan-Streatfield res fell RCP and RCS held at Univ of Cambridge 1965–68; Royal Free Hosp: conslt physician 1972–, sr lectr Med Sch 1972–94, reader clinical pharmacology 1984–; vice chm Britten Sinfonia; former chm: Br Performing Arts Medicine Tst, Int Soc for Study of Tension in Performance; hon physician to Royal Soc of Musicians 1993–; FRCP 1975, FRSA 1988; *Recreations* music and the arts; *Style*— Dr Ian James; ✉ Victoria House, The Green, Sarratt, Rickmansworth, Herts WD3 6AY (☎ 01923 265066); Division of Clinical Pharmacology, Department of Medicine, Royal Free Hospital, Pond St, Hampstead, London NW3 2QG (☎ 0171 794 0500)

JAMES, Prof Ioan Mackenzie; s of Reginald Douglas James (d 1966), of Heathfield, Sussex, and Jessie Agnes, *née* Surridge (d 1982); *b* 23 May 1928; *Educ* St Paul's, Queen's Coll Oxford; *m* 1 July 1961, Rosemary Gordon, da of William George Stewart (d 1953); *Career* Cwlth fund fell: Princeton, Berkeley, Inst for Advanced Study 1954–55; Tapp res fell Gonville and Caius Coll Cambridge 1956, reader in pure mathematics Oxford 1957–69, sr res fell St John's Coll Oxford 1959–69, Savilian prof of geometry Oxford 1970–95, emeritus prof Univ of Oxford 1995; hon fell St John's Coll Oxford 1987–, professorial fell New Coll Oxford 1987–95, emeritus prof New Coll Oxford 1995, pres London Mathematical Soc 1985–86 (treas 1969–79), govr St Paul's Sch and St Paul's Girls' Sch 1970; hon prof Univ of Wales 1989; Hon DSc Univ of Aberdeen 1993; FRS 1968; *Books* The Topology of Stiefel Manifolds (1976), General Topology and Homotopy Theory (1984), Topological and Uniform Spaces (1987), Fibrewise Topology (1988), Introduction to Uniform Spaces (1990); *Style*— Prof Ioan James, FRS; ✉ Mathematical Institute, 24–29 St Giles, Oxford OX1 3LB (☎ 01865 273541)

JAMES, Prof James Roderick; s of James Henry James (d 1933), and Muriel May, *née* Trueman; *b* 20 June 1933; *Educ* Headlands GS Swindon, Univ of London (external student, BSc, PhD, DSc); *m* 5 March 1955, Pamela Joy, da of William Henry Frederick Stephens; 1 s (Julian Maxwell b 8 May 1962), 1 da (April Louise b 24 Feb 1956); *Career* Nat Serv RAF 1952–54; AERE Harwell 1950–52, radar devpt engr E K Cole Ltd 1954–58, applications engr Semiconductors Ltd 1958–61, demonstrator RMCS 1961–65, sr scientific offr AERE 1966; RMCS: sr lectr 1967, sr princ scientific offr and res prof 1976, dep chief scientific offr 1982, currently prof of electromagnetic systems engrg, dir Wolfson RF Engrg Centre, chm Sch of Electrical Engrg and Science 1989; chm: Inst of Electronic and Radio Engrs Papers Ctee 1973–76, IEE Professional Gp on Antennas and Propagation 1980–83, IEE Int Conf on Antennas and Propagation 1983, Electronics Div IEE 1988–89; memb IEE Electronics Divnl Bd, pres Inst of Electronic and Radio Engrs 1984–85 (rep on Ctees of Engrg Cncl); FIEE, FIMA, FEng 1987; *Style*— Prof J R James, FEng; ✉ Royal Military College of Science (Cranfield University), Shrivenham, Swindon, Wilts SN6 8LA

JAMES, Jeffrey Russell; CMG (1994); *b* 13 Aug 1944; *Educ* Whitgift Sch Croydon, Univ of Keele (BA Int Rels); *m* 5 July 1965, (Carol) Mary, *née* Longden; 2 da (Alison b 7 Dec 1965, Lindsay b 4 April 1969); *Career* HM Dip Serv: joined 1967, Br Embassy Tehran 1969–70, second sec Br Embassy Kabul 1970–73, FCO 1973–78, dep political advsr Br Mil Govt Berlin 1978–82, Cabinet Office and FCO 1982–86, head of chancery Br Embassy Pretoria/Cape Town 1986–88, head Economic and Commercial Dept Br High Cmmn New Delhi 1988–92, head Edinburgh EC Unit 1992–93, chargé d'affaires Br Embassy Tehran 1993–; *Recreations* bird watching, hill walking, golf, tennis; *Clubs* Tandridge Golf (Oxted), Royal Commonwealth Society; *Style*— Jeffrey James, Esq, CMG; ✉ 7 Rockfield Close, Oxted, Surrey RH8 0DN; c/o Foreign and Commonwealth Office (25444), King Charles Street, London SW1A 2AH

JAMES, John Anthony; s of Charles Thomas James (d 1979), of Sutton Coldfield and Tenby, and Gwenith Aylwin, *née* Jones; *b* 15 July 1945; *Educ* King Edward VI GS Lichfield, Univ of Bristol (LLB); *m* 10 Sept 1973, Gwyneth Jane, da of Ambrose Elwyn Evans (d 1975), of Altrincham; 2 da (Harriet Lucy b 24 Sept 1975, Emily Jane b 22 Nov 1977); *Career* admitted slr 1969, ptnr Edge & Ellison 1974–93 (conslt 1993–); sr jt hon sec Birmingham Law Soc 1987–91 (memb Cncl 1986–93), sec W Midlands Assoc of Law Socs 1991–93, memb Editorial Advsy Bd Law Soc Gazette; former chm and dir Birmingham City 2000 (currently chm International Ctee), sec Midlands Branch IOD, tstee Birmingham Repertory Theatre Fndn, chm Birmingham Press Club; govr: Matthew Boulton Coll, Coll of Food Tourism and Creative Studies; memb Law Soc 1970, FInstD 1985; *Recreations* reading, writing, theatre, opera; *Clubs* Solihull Sporting, Belfry Sporting, Moseley Rugby, Birmingham & Solihull Rugby, Avenue Bowling, Warwickshire Co Cricket; *Style*— John James, Esq; ✉ Edge & Ellison, Rutland House, 148 Edmund St, Birmingham B3 2JR (☎ 0121 200 2001, fax 0121 200 1991)

JAMES, John Arthur William; s of Dr Peter Michael James (d 1971), and Eileen Mary, *née* Walters (d 1993); *b* 7 Jan 1942; *Educ* Douai Sch Berks; *m* 5 Aug 1967, Barbara, da of Maj William Nicholls (d 1955); 1 s (John-Leo b 1982), 2 da (Jessica b 1968, Alice b 1970); *Career* admitted slr 1967, sr ptnr Hand Morgan & Owen Stafford 1988; under sheriff Staffs and W Midlands 1983, dep coroner S Staffs 1987, clerk to Cmmrs of Taxes Stafford and Cannock 1987, adjudicator on immigration 1986–91; chm Mid Staffs NSPCC 1976–95; memb Bd Stafford Prison 1975–93 (chm 1983–86); Cdr St John Ambulance Staffordshire 1994–; OStJ 1992; *Recreations* walking, shooting; *Clubs* Stafford County; *Style*— John James, Esq; ✉ Presford House, Butterbank, nr Seighford, Stafford, Staffs; 17 Martin St, Stafford, Staffs (☎ 01785 211411, fax 01785 48573)

JAMES, John Christopher Urmston; s of John Urmston James (d 1964), of Llandeilo, Dyfed, and Ellen Irene, *née* Walker; *b* 22 June 1937; *Educ* Hereford Cathedral Sch; *m* 1 (m dis 1982), Gillian Mary, *née* Davies; m 2, 20 Nov 1982, Patricia Mary, da of Arthur Leslie Walter White (d 1983), of Peckham, London; 2 s (David Henry Urmston b 3 Feb 1960, Christopher Hammond Urmston b 1 Jan 1961); *Career* trainee buyer Harrods 1954; rep: Jaeger 1961, Pringle 1972; sec LTA 1981– (asst sec 1973–81), dir British Olympic Assoc; memb: Nat Tst, Friends of the Earth, Trinity Hospice, Ealing Nat Tst; tstee British Olympic Educn Tst; *Recreations* tennis, rugby union, walking, architecture, topography, the countryside; *Clubs* Queen's, Questors, London Welsh, West Hants, International Lawn Tennis Club of GB, IOD; *Style*— John James, Esq; ✉ c/o Lawn Tennis Association, The Queen's Club, West Kensington, London W14 9EG (☎ 0171 381 7000, fax 0171 381 5965, telex 895 6036)

JAMES, John Denis; s of Kenneth Alfred James, of Alvechurch, Worcestershire, and Pauline Audry, *née* Haymen; *b* 30 Aug 1950; *Educ* Bridley Moor GS Redditch; *m* 3 Sept 1975, Barbara Elizabeth, da of John Thorpe, of Birmingham; 1 s (Christopher John b 1975), 1 da (Emma Louise b 1978); *Career* trainee photographer Redditch Indicator 1965, sr photographer Birmingham Post and Mail 1972–; Midland Photographer of the Year 1981 and 1987, Midland News Photographer of the Year 1987 and 1991, Nat Br Press Award Photographer of 1987, Kodak News Photographer of 1987; memb Inst of Journalists; *Recreations* game fishing; *Style*— John James, Esq; ✉ c/o Birmingham Post and Mail, Colmore Circus, Birmingham B4 6AX (☎ 0121 236 3366)

JAMES, John Douglas; OBE (1996); s of late William James and Agnes James; *b* 28 July 1949; *Educ* Spalding GS, IOD (Dip); *Career* articled pupil William H Brown & Son 1967–68, Geest Industries 1969–71, John Player & Sons 1971–77; The Woodland Trust: joined 1977, first dir 1980, exec dir 1985, chief executive 1992–; ptnr Focus Gallery Nottingham 1995–; memb Inst of Charity Fundraising Mangrs, MInstD; FRSA; *Films* Locked Up 1964, The Story of Springfields 1966, Woodland Rescue (prodr, BBC) 1980; *Style*— John D James, Esq, OBE; ✉ The Woodland Trust, Autumn Park, Dysart Road, Grantham, Lincs NG31 6LL (☎ 01476 581111, fax 01476 590808)

JAMES, Jonathan Elwyn Rayner; QC (1988); s of Basil James, of London, and Moira Houlding, *née* Rayner; *b* 26 July 1950; *Educ* King's Coll Sch Wimbledon, Christ's Coll Cambridge (MA, LLM), Univ of Brussels (Licencié Spécial en Droit Européen); *m* 3 Jan 1981, Anne, da of Henry McRae (d 1984); 1 s (Daniel Charles Rayner b 23 Dec 1981); *Career* called to the Bar Lincoln's Inn 1971 (Hardwicke scholar), Rayner bencher Lincoln's Inn 199, asst recorder of the Crown Court 1994–; memb Editorial Bd Entertainment Law Review; *Books* EEC Anti Trust Law (jt ed, 1975), Encyclopaedia of Forms and Precedents Vol 15 (consulting jt ed, 1989), Copinger and Skone James on Copyright (jt ed 1980 and 1991); *Recreations* DIY, squash, music, travel; *Clubs* RAC; *Style*— Jonathan James, Esq, QC; ✉ 5 New Square, Lincoln's Inn, London WC2A 3RJ (☎ 0171 404 0404, fax 0171 831 6016)

JAMES, Prof Keith; s of George Stanley James (d 1940), of Cumbria, and Alice, *née* Dixon (d 1989); *b* 15 March 1938; *Educ* Whitehaven GS, Univ of Birmingham (State scholar, MRC studentship, BSc, PhD); *m* 30 Sept 1967, Valerie Spencer, *née* Jubb; 3 s (Mark b 21 Nov 1971, Stephen Gordon b 26 Feb 1975, Daniel b 18 April 1978); *Career* res fell Univ of Birmingham 1962–64, res asst Univ of California 1964–65, prof Dept of Surgery Univ of Edinburgh 1991– (sr lectr 1965–77, reader 1977–91); sec-gen Int Union of Immunological Socs 1992; FRSE 1976, FRCPath 1982, FIBiol 1987; *Books* Introducing Immunology (with N Staines and J Brostoff, 1985, 2 edn 1993); author of 230 scientific papers; *Recreations* hill walking, photography, watching rugby; *Style*— Prof Keith James, FRSE; ✉ Department of Surgery, University of Edinburgh Medical School, Teviot Place, Edinburgh EH8 9AG (☎ 0131 650 3557, fax 0131 667 6190)

JAMES, (David) Keith Marlais; s of James Lewis James (d 1993), and Margaret Evelyn James; *b* 16 Aug 1944; *Educ* Cardiff HS, W Monmouth Sch, Queens' Coll Cambridge (BA, MA); *m* 4 Aug 1973, Kathleen Linda, da of Wilfred Lawson Marrs, OBE (d 1981), of Cyncoed, Cardiff; 1 s (Thomas b 1983), 2 da (Alys b 1978, Elizabeth b 1980); *Career* slr; ptnr (currently chm) Eversheds (formerly Eversheds Phillips and Buck) 1969–; dir: various cos in Hamard Group 1977–86, Bank of Wales plc 1988–, AXA Insurance Co Ltd 1992–; chm: Welsh Exec of UN Assoc 1977–80, Welsh Centre for Int Affrs 1979–84; memb: UK Mgmnt Ctee Freedom from Hunger Campaign 1978–87, Welsh Mgmnt Ctee IOD 1985–94, Ct UWIST 1985–88, Cncl UWIST 1985–88, Advsy Panel Cardiff Business Sch 1986–, Cncl Univ of Wales Coll of Cardiff 1988–94, Editorial Bd Welsh Economic Review 1989–92, Representative Body of the Church in Wales 1989–95, Gen Advsy Cncl BBC 1991–92; non-exec dir HTV Gp 1997–; vice pres Cardiff Business Club 1987–, dep chm Inst of Welsh Affrs 1987–, non-exec memb Welsh Health Common Servs Authy 1991–95; memb: Law Soc, IOD; FRSA; *Recreations* golf; *Clubs* Cardiff and County, United Oxford & Cambridge Univ; *Style*— Keith James, Esq; ✉ Trehedyn Cottage, Peterston-Super-Ely, S Glamorgan; Eversheds, Fitzalan House, Fitzalan Court, Cardiff CF2 1XZ (☎ 01222 471147, fax 01222 463447) and Senator House, 85 Queen Victoria Street, London EC4V 4JL (☎ 0171 919 4500, fax 0171 919 4919)

JAMES, Keith Royston; s of William Ewart Gladstone James (d 1990), of Birmingham, and Lilian Elizabeth James (d 1966); *b* 22 Aug 1930; *Educ* King Edward VI Camp Hill Sch Birmingham, Univ of Birmingham; *m* 6 May 1961, Venice Imogen, da of Maj Henry St John Murray Findlay (d 1954); 1 s (William b 1964), 3 da (Rohaise b 1966, Selina b 1968, April b 1971); *Career* admitted slr 1954, sr ptnr Needham & James 1956–94 (ptnr 1994–); dir Technology and Law 1980–; sec The Lace Market Development Co Ltd; author of articles on the application of technology to the law; chm Michael Blanning Tst, tstee Solihull Hosp Fndn; gen cmmr for taxes; chm Soc for Computers and Law 1988–90; *Books* A Guide to the Electronic Office for Practising Solicitors; *Recreations* shooting, walking, golf; *Clubs* Athenaeum, Birmingham, Ingon Manor Golf; *Style*— Keith R James, Esq; ✉ Norton Curlieu, nr Warwick CV35 8JR (☎ 01926 842372); Needham & James, 11 Vyse Street, Birmingham B18 6LT (☎ 0121 237 1130, fax 0121 237 1135)

JAMES, Sir (Cynlais) Kenneth Morgan; KCMG (1985, CMG 1976); s of Thomas and Lydia James; *b* 29 April 1926; *Educ* Trinity Coll Cambridge; *m* 1953, Mary Teresa, da of Richard Désiré Girouard and Lady Blanche Maud de la Poer Beresford (da of 6 Marquess of Waterford, KP, and Lady Beatrix Fitzmaurice, da of 5 Marquess of Lansdowne), also sis of the architectural historian Mark Girouard, *qv*; 2 da; *Career* served RAF 1944–47; FO (now FCO): joined 1951, former 1 sec Moscow, head W Euro Dept FCO and min Paris, ambass to Poland 1981–83, under sec of state FCO 1983, ambass to Mexico 1983–86; DG Canning House 1987–92; dir: Latin American Investment Trust plc, Foreign and Colonial Emerging Markets PLC, Darwin Instruments; assoc of Europrincipals; chm Br Inst Paris, chm Inst of Latin American Studies, memb Franco-Br Cncl; Chevalier de la Légion d'Honneur (France), Order of the Aztec Eagle (First Class, Mexico), Order of Andreas Bello (First Class) Venezuela, Order of Merit (Chile); Dr (hc) Mexican Acad of Int Law; *Clubs* Brooks's, Pratt's, Travellers' (Paris), Beefsteak, MCC; *Style*— Sir Kenneth James, KCMG; ✉ c/o Brooks's, St James's Street, London SW1

JAMES, Lesley; da of Albert Harry Showell (d 1978), of Birmingham, and Esme Kathleen, *née* Robinson; *b* 7 April 1949; *Educ* Lordswood Grammar Technical Sch, Open Univ (BA 1977), Univ of Warwick (MA 1977); *m* John William James; *Career* sec Joseph Lucas Ltd 1965–70, personnel mangr Delta Metal Co Ltd 1973–77 (PA 1970–73), personnel admin mangr Rank Hovis MacDougall Ltd 1977–79, mgmnt devpt mangr Sketchley Ltd 1979–80; Savacentre Ltd (subsid of J Sainsbury plc): personnel mangr 1980–83, checkout ops mangr 1983–85; Tesco Stores Ltd: regnl personnel mangr 1985–87, personnel dir (head office/distribution) 1987–89, personnel dir (retail) 1989–93, personnel and trg dir 1993–95; human resources dir Tesco plc 1995–; MIPD; *Style*— Mrs Lesley James; ✉ Tesco plc, Tesco House, Delamare Road, Cheshunt, Herts EN8 9SL (☎ 01992 644145, fax 01992 644741)

JAMES, Linda; *Educ* Univ of York; *Career* television prodr; prodn asst TV commercials Sid Roberson Productions 1980, prodr Sgrin (82) Ltd (independent prodrs of progs for S4C) 1981–83 (prodr award-winning drama series Joni Jones with dir Stephen Bayly 1982); Red Rooster Films Ltd (now subsid of Chrysalis plc): co-fndr with Stephen Bayly 1983, md until 1995, currently chief exec; govr: Br Film Inst 1991–95, Nat Film and TV Sch 1991–; chair Edinburgh Int TV Festival 1992, memb Br Screen Advsy Cncl 1993–96, memb awards juries for BAFTA, RTS and BFI; *Programmes* Red Rooster prodns incl: And Pigs Might Fly (feature-length film for S4C, prodr) 1983, The Works (feature-length film, English/Welsh versions for S4C and Channel 4, prodr) 1984, Coming Up Roses (feature-length comedy for S4C and cinema release, prodr) 1985–86, Homing (for S4C, exec prodr) 1986, Just Ask for Diamond (feature film for Coverstop, Children's Film Fndn and British Screen, prodr) 1987–88, Travelling Hopefully (documentary for HTV, exec prodr) 1988–89, The Gift (series for BBC, prodr) 1989–90, The Diamond Brothers - South by South East (series for TVS, exec prodr) 1990–91, The Life and Times of Henry Pratt (comedy drama series for Granada, exec prodr) 1992, Body and Soul (drama series for Carlton, exec prodr) 1992–93, Smokescreen (drama series for BBC, exec prodr) 1993, Crocodile Shoes (drama series for BBC, exec prodr) 1994, The Sculptress (drama series for BBC, prodr), wilderness (drama series for ITV, exec prodr); *Awards* numerous incl: Chicago Children's Awards (for Joni Jones and And Pigs Might Fly), official selection Cannes Film Festival 1986 (Coming Up Roses), Golden Pierrot (first prize) for Best First Feature Vevey Int Festival of Comedy Film and Special Jury Prize Golden Plaque Chicago Int Film Festival 1986 (for Coming Up Roses), Best Adventure Film Moscow Film Festival 1988 (for Just Ask for Diamond); *Style*— Ms Linda James; ✉ Red Rooster Film and Television Entertainment Ltd, 29 Floral Street, London WC2E 9DP (☎ 0171 379 7727, fax 0171 379 5756)

JAMES, Mark Hugh; s of Roland Malcolm Dennis James, of Stamford, Lincolnshire, and Doreen Vivien Eugenie Bayard, *née* Wace; *b* 28 Oct 1953; *Educ* Stamford Sch; *m* 18 Oct 1980, Jane Ann; *Career* professional golfer; winner English Amateur Championships 1974, runner up Br Amateur Championships 1975; turned professional 1976, winner numerous maj Euro tournaments and various others worldwide; winner Tenerife Open 1993; int appearances: Ryder Cup 1977, 1979, 1981, 1989 (winners), 1991, 1993, 1995 (winners), Hennessy Cup 1978, 1980, 1982 and 1984, Dunhill Cup 1988, 1989, 1990, 1993 and 1995, World Cup 1978, 1980, 1982, 1984, 1987, 1988, 1990 and 1993; Rookie of the Year 1976; *Recreations* American football, gardening, science; *Style*— Mark James, Esq; ✉ c/o PGA European Tour, Wentworth Club, Virginia Water, Surrey (☎ 0344 842881)

JAMES, Martin Jonathan; s of Kenneth Charles James, of Christchurch, NZ, and Beatrice Rose, *née* Dickson; *b* 22 Sept 1961; *Educ* NZ Sch of Dance; *m* 8 Feb 1985, Adrienne Jane Terehunga, da of Flt Lt James Matheson, DFC, of Christchurch, NZ; 1 da (Rachael Unaiiki b 31 July 1990), 1 s (Marcus Sebastian Tane James b 20 Oct 1992); *Career* ballet dancer; Royal NZ Ballet 1981, awarded Queen Elizabeth II Arts Cncl Grant for study in America 1982, gained int recognition Fourth World Ballet Competition Japan 1984; princ dancer: English Nat Ballet 1987–90 (joined 1985), Deutsche Oper Berlin (at invitation of Peter Schaufuss) 1990–94, Royal Danish Ballet 1994–; first one man graphic arts exhibition Molesworth Gallery NZ 1984; ARAD 1979, Solo Seal 1980; *Performances* incl: Albrecht and Hilarion in Giselle, Franz in Coppelia, Prince in The Nutcracker (with Lynn Seymour), Toreador in Petit's Carmen, Romeo and Paris in Ashton's Romeo and Juliet, Blackamoor in Petrushka, world premiere Christopher Bruce's Symphony in 3 movements, Ben Stevenson's Three Preludes, Kevin Haigen's Meditation (cr role with Natalia Makarova) 1987, Spectre de la Rose 1987, Le Corsaire 1987, cr role of Benno in Makarova's Swan Lake 1987 (also role of Seigfried), title role in Cranko's Onegin 1987 (and with Ekaterina Maximova 1989), Oedipus in Glen Tetley's Sphinx, title role in Balanchine's Apollo 1987 and 1992, Balanchine's Symphony in C 1987, Bournonville's Napoli 1987, Christopher Bruce's Land 1987, Bull in Christopher Bruce and Lyndsey Kemp's Cruel Garden 1987 (and that ballet's German première 1992), leading soldier in Antony Tudor's Echoing Trumpets 1990, Donner and Hagen in Bejart's Ring um den Ring 1990, The Chosen One in Bejart's Sacre du Printemps and Firebird 1991, Tchaikovsky Pas de Deux (Kirov Theatre Leningrad) 1991, Albrecht in Peter Schaufuss' Giselle 1991, lead role in Kenneth Macmillan's Different Drummer 1991, James in Schaufuss' La Sylphide 1991, Prince in Valery Panov's Cinderella 1991 (Badische Zeitung Critics' Award), title role in Tales of Hoffman (Hong Kong Ballet) 1991, Albrecht in Paris Opera version of Giselle (with Inoue Ballet Fndn Japan) 1992, Le Corsaire Pas de Deux (with Sylvie Guillem, Paris Gala) 1992, Albrecht in Giselle (guest artist Kirov Theatre St Petersburg) 1993; roles with Royal Danish Ballet incl:

world premiere of Anna Laekenson's Dromme 1994, Albrecht in Giselle 1994, Romeo, Paris and Benvolio in Ashton's Romeo and Juliet 1994, premiere of Marie Bronlin's Tanis Dance Piece 1994, James and Gurn in La Sylphide 1994, Paul Taylor's Aureole 1994, Flower Festival of Genzano 1994, title role in Crankos' Onegin 1994, Dance Master in Conservatoire 1995, The King in Fleming Flint's Caroline Mathilde 1995, Peter Martin's Ash 1995, King in Peter Schaufuss' Hamlet 1996; guest appearances in: Spain, London, France, Denmark, Russia, NZ, Berlin, Finland; Genée Awards 1988 and 1989; film and TV performances incl: Gillian Lynne's Look of Love (princ role as Eros) 1989, Natalia Makarova's Swan Lake, James in La Sylphide (live, New Zealand) 1990; *Recreations* tennis, painting, swimming; *Style*— Martin James, Esq; ✉ Royal Danish Ballet, Det Kongelige Teater Og Kapel, Postbox 2185, Copenhagen K, DK1017 Denmark

JAMES, Michael Leonard (Michael Hartland); s of late Leonard James, of Portreath, Cornwall; *b* 7 Feb 1941; *Educ* Latymer Upper Sch, Christ's Coll Cambridge (MA); *m* 1975 (m dis 1992), Jill Elizabeth, da of George Tarján, OBE, of Budapest; 2 da (Ruth b 1978, Susanna b 1980); *Career* writer and broadcaster; entered Br Govt Serv (GCHQ) 1963, private sec to Rt Hon Jennie Lee MP as Min for the Arts 1966–68, DES 1968–71, planning unit of Rt Hon Margaret Thatcher MP as Sec of State for Educn & Sci 1971–73, asst sec 1973, DCSO 1974, advsr to OECD Paris and UK govr Int Inst for Mgmnt of Technol (IIMT) Milan 1973–75, int negotiations on non-proliferation of nuclear weapons 1975–78, dir Int Atomic Energy Agency Vienna 1978–83, advsr on int rels Cmmn of the Euro Union Brussels 1983–85; feature writer and book reviewer for: The Times (resident thriller critic 1990–91), Sunday Times, Guardian, Daily Telegraph 1986– (resident thriller critic 1993–); chm Wade Hartland Films Ltd 1991–; govr: E Devon Coll of Further Educn Tiverton 1985–91, Colyton GS 1985–90, Sidmouth Community Coll 1988–; chm: Bd of Govrs Axe Vale Further Educn Centre Seaton 1987–92, Civil Serv Selection Bds 1983–90; memb: Exeter Social Security Appeal Tbnl 1986–, Immigration Appeal Tbnl 1987–, Child Support Appeal Tbnl 1993–, Devon and Cornwall Rent Assessment Panel 1990–; hon fell Univ of Exeter; FRSA; *Books* novels (as Michael Hartland): Down Among the Dead Men (1983), Seven Steps to Treason (1985, SW Arts Literary Award, dramatized for BBC Radio 4 1990), The Third Betrayal (1986), Frontier of Fear (1989), The Year of the Scorpion (1991); other publications (as M L James): Internationalization to Prevent the Spread of Nuclear Weapons (1980), articles on int relations and nuclear energy; *Television and Radio* incl: Sonja's Report (ITV documentary, 1990), Masterspy (interviews with KGB defector Oleg Gordievsky, BBC Radio 4, 1991); *Clubs* Athenaeum, United Oxford and Cambridge University, Int PEN, Devon and Exeter Institution; *Style*— Michael James, Esq; ✉ Cotte Barton, Branscombe, Devon EX12 3BH

JAMES, Dame Naomi Christine; DBE (1979); da of Charles Robert Power, of Rotorua, New Zealand; *b* 2 March 1949; *Educ* Rotorua Girls' HS NZ; *m* 1, 1976, Robert A James (d 1983), of Andover, Hants, s of J S James; 1 da (Lois Anne b 1983); m 2, 4 Sept 1990 (m dis), Eric G Haythorne, o s of G V Haythorne, of Ottawa, Canada; *Career* former language teacher and hairdresser; yachtswoman: winner Binatone Round Br and Ireland Race in Trimaran Colt Cars GB 1982, NZ Yachtsman of the Year 1978, recipient RYS Chichester Trophy 1978, winner Ladies' prize Observer Transatlantic Race 1980 (women's record for solo crossing), circumnavigated world as first woman solo via Cape Horn Sept 1977–June 1978; tstee Nat Maritime Museum 1985–92, memb Cncl Winston Churchill Memorial Tst; writer and presenter BBC Documentary Polynesian Triangle (Great Journeys Series) 1989; *Books* Women Alone (1978), At One With the Sea (1979), At Sea on Land (1981), Courage at Sea (1987); *Recreations* walking, literature; *Clubs* Royal Lymington Yacht, Royal Dart Yacht, Royal Western Yacht; *Style*— Dame Naomi James, DBE

JAMES, Prof the Hon Oliver Francis Wintour; o s of Baron James of Rusholme (Life Peer, d 1992), and Cordelia Mary, *née* Wintour; *b* 23 Sept 1943; *Educ* Winchester, Balliol Coll Oxford (MA, BM BCh); *m* 4 Sept 1965, Rosanna, er da of Maj Gordon Bentley Foster (d 1963), of Sleightholme Dale, Fadmoor, York; 1 s (Patrick Esmond b 4 May 1967), 1 da (Helen b 26 Jan 1970); *Career* landowner (170 acres); Univ of Newcastle upon Tyne: prof of geriatric med 1985–, head Dept of Med 1994–, head Sch of Clinical Med Sciences 1995–; censor RCP, sr vice pres RCP 1997–99; pres Br Assoc for Study of the Liver; tstee Sir James Knott Tst; FRCP 1981; *Books* Ageing Liver and Gastrointestinal Tract (ed 1987); *Recreations* golf, gardening; *Style*— Prof the Hon Oliver James; ✉ Department of Medicine, Floor 4, Clinical Block, Medical School, Framlington Place, Newcastle upon Tyne NE2 4HH; Sleightholmedale Lodge, Kirbymoorside, York YO6 6JG

JAMES, (William) Paul; s of Sir Frederick Seton James, KCMG, KBE (d 1934), and Lady Doris Francis James (d 1956); *b* 22 Aug 1921; *Educ* Haileybury, PCL (DipArch); *m* 4 Jan 1947, (Florence) Peggy, da of Josephy Harvey; 1 s (Julian Paul b 1958), 3 da (Jennifer b 1948, Fenella b 1952, Caroline b 1954); *Career* WWII RAF 1940–45; architect on staff of Lord Holford 1950–60, princ in private practice 1960–67, seconded planning conslt DHSS 1967–68, fndr ptnr and chm Hosp Design Partnership (London, Leeds and Birmingham) 1968–79, int conslt in hosp planning 1979–; author of numerous articles in professional jls 1970–85; FRIBA 1970 (ARIBA 1950); *Books* Hospitals - Design and Development (1986), Hospital Architecture (1992); *Recreations* walking, reading, travel, writing; *Style*— Paul James, Esq; ✉ Lawnside, 3 Hungershall Park, Tunbridge Wells, Kent (☎ 01892 525726)

JAMES, Dr Peter David; s of Thomas Geraint Illtyd James, of Ealing Common, London, and Dorothy Marguerite, *née* John; *b* 20 Aug 1943; *Educ* Mill Hill, Middlesex Hosp Med Sch and Univ of London (MB BS); *m* 14 Sept 1968, Angela Judith, da of William Robert Hearn, of Hovingham, North Yorks; *Career* lectr in pathology: Makerere Univ Kampala Uganda 1970–72, Bland-Sutton Inst Middx Hosp London 1972–73 (asst lectr 1967–70); conslt and hon sr lectr in histopathology Univ Hosp Nottingham 1973–; memb: BMA, Br Soc of Gastroenterology, Br Div Int Acad of Pathology; *Recreations* squash, shooting, horse riding; *Style*— Dr Peter James; ✉ Histopathology Department, University Hospital, Nottingham NG7 2UH (☎ 0115 970 9175)

JAMES, Peter John; s of John Burnett James, and Cornelia, *née* Kates; *b* 22 Aug 1948; *Educ* Charterhouse, Ravensbourne Coll of Art and Design; *m* 21 April 1979, Georgina Valerie James, da of T D Wilkin, of Hove, Sussex; *Career* dir: Quadrant Films Toronto 1972–75, Yellowbill Ltd 1977; currently dir: Cornelia James Ltd, Ministry of Vision plc; film prodr: Dead of Night 1973, Spanish Fly 1976, Biggles 1985 (assoc prodr); Royal Warrant Holder Queen's Warrant for Glove Mfrs; memb: Soc of Authors, Soc for Psychical Res; Freeman City of London 1980, Liveryman Worshipful Co of Glovers; author; *Books* Dead Letter Drop (1981), Atom Bomb Angel (1982), Billionaire (1983), Possession (1988), Dreamer (1989), Sweet Heart (1990), Twilight (1991), Prophecy (1992), Host (1993), Alchemist (1996), Getting Wired (1996), The Truth (1997); *Recreations* golf, tennis, skiing, fast cars, smoking, white burgundy; *Clubs* Tramp; *Style*— Peter James, Esq; ✉ c/o Cornelia James Ltd, 123 Havelock Rd, Brighton BN1 6GS (☎ 01273 508866, fax 01273 541656, telex 877057, e-mail scary@pavilion.co.uk)

JAMES, Prof (William) Philip Trehearne; CBE (1993); s of Jenkin William James (d 1944), and Lilian Mary, *née* Shaw (d 1992); *b* 27 June 1938; *Educ* Ackworth Sch Pontefract Yorks, UCL (BSc), UCH (MB, BSc, MD), Cambridge Univ (MA), London Univ (DSc); *m* 1961, Jean Hamilton, da of James Lingford Moorhouse (d 1977); 1 s (Mark), 1 da (Claire); *Career* asst dir MRC Dunn Nutrition Unit Cambridge 1974–82, dir Rowett Res Inst Aberdeen 1982–, hon res prof Univ of Aberdeen; memb DHSS Ctees on Medical Aspects of Food Policy and Novel Foods, memb EU Scientific Ctee for Food 1992–95, formerly chm Working Pty on Nat Advsy Ctee of Nutrition Educn, vice chm FAO/WHO/UNU Expert Consultation on Energy and Protein Requirement of Man 1981–85; chm: FAO Expert Consultation on Nat Energy Needs 1987, UK Nat Food Alliance 1987–90 (pres 1990–), Coronary Prevention Group 1988–96, WHO Int Task Force on Obesity; memb Nutrition Advsy Ctee WHO Euro Region 1985–, chm Consultation on Nutrition and Health WHO 1989–91, special advsr to WHO DG 1989–; chm Scottish Working Pty on: Diet and Scottish Public Health 1992–93, Obesity Management; lectures: Cuthbertson Meml Lecture 1979, Peter Beckett Lecture Dublin 1983, Ames Meml Lecture 1985, Mehta Oration India 1985, Middleton Meml Lecture 1986, Davidson Meml Lecture 1987, Minshull Meml Lecture 1989, Hallberg Oration 1994, Gopalan Oration 1994; FRCP 1978, FRSE 1986, FIBiol 1987; *Books* incl: The Analysis of Dietary Fibre in Food (1981), Assessing Human Energy Requirements (1990); papers on nutrient absorption, energy and protein metabolism, health policy and food labelling; *Recreations* talking, writing government reports, eating; *Clubs* Athenaeum (London); *Style*— Prof Philip James, CBE, FRSE; ✉ Wardenhill, Bucksburn, Aberdeen, Scotland AB2 9SA (☎ 01224 712623, fax 01224 713292); The Rowett Research Institute, Greenburn Road, Bucksburn, Aberdeen, Scotland AB2 9SB (☎ 01224 712751, fax 01224 715349)

JAMES, Richard Austin; CB, MC (1945); s of Thomas Maurice James (d 1962), of Kent, and Hilda Joan, *née* Castle (d 1987); *b* 26 May 1920; *Educ* Clifton, Emmanuel Coll Cambridge; *m* 1948, Joan Betty, da of Albert Malcolm Boorer (d 1932); 1 da (Sally), 2 s (Thomas, Andrew); *Career* RE 1939–41, Queen's Own Royal West Kent Regt 1941–46, served in ME and Europe (despatches); Home Office 1948, private sec to Chllr of the Duchy of Lancaster (the late Lord Hill and the late Mr Iain Macleod) 1960 (asst sec 1961), the receiver Met Police Dist 1977–80 (dep receiver 1970–73), dep under sec of state Home Office 1980 (asst under sec 1974–76); memb Cncl of Mgmnt of Distressed Gentlefolk Aid Assoc 1982–88 (gen sec 1981–82, vice pres 1990–95), memb Ctee of Mgmnt Sussex Housing Assoc for the Aged 1985–90; pres The Brunswick Boys' Club Tst 1990–95; Freeman City of London; *Recreations* cricket, garden construction; *Clubs* Athenaeum, MCC; *Style*— Richard James, Esq, CB, MC; ✉ 5 Gadge Close, Thame, Oxfordshire OX9 2BD

JAMES, Richard Daniel; *Educ* King's Coll; 3 s, 1 da; *Career* health authority administrator; charge nurse: Harris Hosp Texas 1973–74, Central Middlesex Hosp 1975–77; nursing offr: Harefield Hosp 1975–77, Hammersmith Hosp 1977–79; sr nursing offr Ham Green Hosp and Clevedon Hosp 1979–82, dir Nursing Services Hosp and Community Bristol and Weston Health Authy 1983–85, unit gen mangr (gen) Salisbury Health Authy 1989–92 (unit gen mangr (community) 1986–89), chief exec Severn NHS Tst Gloucester 1992–; SRN 1972, RCNT 1975, NDN 1983; *Style*— Richard James, Esq; ✉ Pidgemore Farm, Nupend, nr Stonehouse, Glos GL10 3SU; Severn NHS Trust, Rikenel, Montpellier, Gloucester GL1 1LY (☎ 01452 529421, fax 01452 383045)

JAMES, Rita; da of Harry James Butcher (d 1993), of Leiston, Suffolk, and May Gladys, *née* Songer; *b* 18 March 1946; *Educ* Leiston GS, Hornsey Coll of Art (BA), RCA (MDesRCA); *m* 16 Dec 1967 (m dis), William David James; *Career* womenswear apparel fabric designer; freelance work for textile mfrs and fashion designers incl Br Wool Mktg Bd, Harris Tweed UK, Promostyl, Sekine, Daniel Hechter, Cacharel, Jean-Charles de Castelbajac France and Echo scarves USA until 1979, fashion co-ordinator (womenswear fabrics) Int Wool Secretariat 1979–84, in own consultancy Design Works (specialising in colour prediction and woven fabric design) 1985–; recent clients incl: Anglo Fabrics USA, Marumasu Company Japan, Yusung Company S Korea, Taiwan Textile Fedn Taiwan; lectr in woven textiles at various colls/instns, external moderator in woven textiles Central Saint Martin's Coll of Art and Design; rep on many indust working ctees; Burton Group Design Award 1974; FRSA 1971, FCSD 1986, Design Cncl registered 1991; *Recreations* opera at Covent Garden, cinema, hill walking; *Style*— Ms Rita James; ✉ Design Works, 16 Westfields Avenue, Barnes, London SW13 0AU (☎ 0181 878 3381 and 0181 878 5327, fax 0181 876 4158)

JAMES, Roger; *m* Johanna; 1 da (Anna); *Career* Central Television: joined Central Independent TV 1982, sometime head of documentaries, controller of factual progs Central Productions Ltd 1990–94, head of documentaries and int co-prodns Carlton UK Productions 1995–; dir: Central Observer Ltd; tstee TV Tst for the Environment; incl on UN Global 500 Roll of Honour for outstanding environmental achievement; FRSA; *Style*— Roger James, Esq; ✉ Head of Documentaries and International Co-Productions, Carlton UK Productions, 35–38 Portman Square, London W1H 9FH (☎ 0171 486 6688)

JAMES, Roy Lewis; s of David John James (d 1981), and Eleanor, *née* Rees (d 1940); *b* 9 Feb 1937; *Educ* Llandysul GS, Univ Coll of Wales Aberystwyth (BSc, DipEd); *m* 1962, Annie Mary, da of Evan David Williams; 1 da (Llinos James b 1968); *Career* asst mathematics master Strodes GS Surrey 1959–60; head Mathematics Dept: Lampeter Comp Sch 1960–62, Cyfarthfa Castle Sch 1962–70; HM inspr of Schs 1970–84, seconded as sec Schools Cncl Ctee for Wales 1975–77, staff inspr 1984–90, chief inspr 1990–92, HM chief inspr of schs (Wales) Office of Her Majesty's Chief Inspector of Schools 1992–; *Recreations* reading, walking, travel, snooker, chess; *Style*— Roy James, Esq; ✉ Office of Her Majesty's Chief Inspector of Schools, 7th Floor, Phase 1, Government Buildings, Ty Glas Road, Llanishen, Cardiff CF4 5FQ (☎ 01222 761456, fax 01222 758182)

JAMES, Russell; *see:* Logan, Russell James Vincent Crickard

JAMES, Simon Robert; s of Alan William James (d 1994), and Dorothy Denise James; *b* 1 April 1952; *Educ* LSE (BSc Econ, MSc), Open Univ (MBA, MA), CDipAF DipM; *Career* res asst LSE 1974–76, reader in economics Univ of Exeter 1996– (lectr 1976–88, sr lectr 1988–96); specialist conslt to New Shorter Oxford English Dictionary 1990–93; FRSA 1990, FTII 1992, ACIM 1996; *Books* incl: Self Assessment for Income Tax (with N A Barr and Prof A R Prest, 1977), The Economics of Taxation (with Prof C W Nobes, 1978, Chinese edn 1988, 5 edn 1996), A Dictionary of Economic Quotations (1981, 2 edn 1984), Pears Guide to Money and Investment (1982), A Dictionary of Sexist Quotations (1984), A Dictionary of Legal Quotations (1987, Indian edn 1994), The Comprehensibility of Taxation (1987), A Dictionary of Business Quotations (jtly, 1990), Chambers Sporting Quotations (1990), Collins Dictionary of Business Quotations (jtly, 1991), Trapped in Poverty? (jtly, 1992), Putting the Family First: Identities, Decisions, Citizenship (jtly, 1994), Self-Assessment and the UK Tax System (1995); *Recreations* distance learning, cooking, St John Ambulance, quotations; *Style*— Simon James, Esq; ✉ Department of Economics, University of Exeter, Amory Building, Rennes Drive, Exeter EX4 4RJ (☎ 01392 263204, fax 01392 263242, telex 42894 EXUNIV G, e-mail S.R.James@exeter.ac.uk)

JAMES, Stephen Lawrence; s of Walter Amyas James (d 1978), of Clifton, Bristol, and Cécile Juliet, *née* Hillman (d 1970); *b* 19 Oct 1930; *Educ* Clifton, St Catharine's Coll Cambridge (BA); *m* 1955 (m dis 1986), Patricia Eleanor Favell, da of Reginald Cave (d 1968), of Bristol; 2 s (Oliver, Benedict), 2 da (Gabrielle, Miranda); *Career* called to the Bar Gray's Inn 1953, admitted slr 1959; Simmons & Simmons: ptnr 1961–80, sr ptnr 1980–92, conslt 1992–; dir: Horace Clarkson plc, Greycoat plc, Kiln Capital plc; memb Worshipful Co of Glaziers 1964; memb Law Soc 1959; *Recreations* yachting (yacht 'Jacobite'), gardening; *Clubs* Royal Yacht Sqdn, Royal Thames Yacht, Royal Lymington Yacht, Royal Ocean Racing; *Style*— Stephen James, Esq; ✉ Widden, Shirley Holms, Lymington, Hants SO41 8NL; Simmons & Simmons, 21 Wilson Street, London EC2M 2RJ (☎ 0171 628 2020, fax 0171 628 2070)

JAMES, Terence (Terry); s of Robert Joseph James (d 1986), of Long Stratton, Norfolk, and Nellie Wallis, *née* Beare; *b* 6 June 1935; *Educ* Paston Sch, Magdalene Coll Cambridge (MA); *m* 12 Aug 1958, Julie Estelle, da of Charles Anderson Robson (d 1953), of Shelford, Cambs; 1 s (Michael b 1962), 1 da (Linda b 1961); *Career* Nat Serv RAF 1953–55; dir Fisons plc 1976–80; chm: FBC Ltd 1980–86, Chlor-Chem 1982–90, Schering Holdings Ltd 1986–90 (non-exec dir 1990–94), Meconic Plc 1990–; non-exec dir Meristem Plc 1992–; chm Anglia Poly Univ 1993–96, conslt Nordic Synthesis; treas Cambridge Fndn 1990–96 (tstee 1989–96); chm AgrEvo Pension Fund 1994–; Univ of Cambridge: memb Investment Ctee 1993–, memb Fin Ctee 1994–, chm Venture Capital Ctee 1995–; FInstD 1984; *Recreations* golf, contemplative indolence; *Clubs* John O'Gaunt Golf; *Style*— Terry James, Esq; ✉ 215 Wimpole Road, Barton, Cambridge CB3 7AE (☎ 01223 262070, fax 01223 263776)

JAMES, Thomas Garnet Henry (Harry); CBE (1984); s of Thomas Garnet James (d 1956), and Edith, *née* Griffiths (d 1958); *b* 8 May 1923; *Educ* Neath GS, Exeter Coll Oxford (BA, MA); *m* 15 Aug 1956, Diana Margaret, da of Harold Lancelot Vavasseur Durell (d 1929); 1 s (Stephen Garnet Vavasseur b 1958); *Career* WWII cmmnd RA served NW Europe 1942–45; keeper of Egyptian antiquities Br Museum 1974–88 (joined 1951, subsequently dep keeper then asst keeper); Laycock student Worcester Coll Oxford 1954–60, Wilbour fell The Brooklyn Museum NY 1964, visiting prof Coll de France Paris 1983; hon chm Bd of Govrs Inst of Egyptian Art & Archaeology Memphis State Univ 1985– (visiting prof 1990); vice pres Egypt Exploration Soc 1990 (chm 1983–89), chm Mgmnt Ctee Freud Museum 1986–; FBA 1976; *Books* The Mastaba of Khentika (1953), Hieroglyphic Texts in the Br Museum (I 1961, IX 1970), The Hekanakhte Papers (1962), Corpus of Hieroglyphic Inscriptions in The Brooklyn Museum (I 1974), Pharaoh's People (1984), Ancient Egypt (1988), Howard Carter, The Path to Tutankhamun (1992), Egypt: The Living Past (1992), A Short History of Ancient Egypt (1995); *Recreations* music, cooking; *Clubs* United Oxford and Cambridge Univ; *Style*— T G H James, Esq, CBE, FBA; ✉ 113 Willifield Way, London NW11 6YE (☎ 0181 455 9221)

JAMES, Tzena; da of Nesho Karaneshev, of Sofia (d 1958), and Anna, *née* Vitanova (d 1991); *b* 22 Feb 1937; *Educ* Sofia HS, Architectural Faculty of Civil Engineering Sofia (Dip in Architecture); *m* 28 Feb 1965 (m dis 1986), Dennis Edward James; 1 da (Anna-Maria b 29 Nov 1972); *Career* architectural asst private practice Vienna 1963–64, project architect Miny of Trade Dept of Architecture Bulgaria 1964–65, architectural asst Dept of Architecture and Civic Design GLC 1965–75, freelance architect Bureau d'Etude Brussels 1976–77; sr architect: Architectural RES Partnership 1979–80, Dept of Architecture Royal Borough of Kingston 1980–83; princ architect Slough Corp Architects Div 1983–87, team ldr Tech Servs Dept London Borough of Ealing 1987; sr project architect: Broadway Malyan Chartered Architects 1987–88, Boyer Design Gp 1988–89; sr professional tech offr PSA Building Mgmnt South East Heritage Dept 1989–94, fndr own architectural practice 1995; RIBA: memb Cncl until 1996, chm SAG Ctee, memb Int Affairs Ctee, Kingston District Branch, Membership Bd, Euro Affairs Ctee; awarded dip in project mgmnt RICS; *Recreations* modern languages (Bulgarian, Russian, German, French), classical music, visual arts, politics, skiing, swimming; *Style*— Mrs Tzena James; ✉ 14 Temple Road, Kew, Richmond, Surrey TW9 2ED (☎ and fax 0181 940 4068)

JAMES, Prof Vivian Hector Thomas; s of William Percy James (d 1970), of London, and Alice May James (d 1936); *b* 29 Dec 1924; *Educ* Latymer's Upper Sch, Univ of London (BSc, PhD, DSc); *m* 20 April 1958, Betty Irene, da of Frederick Pike (d 1941), of London; *Career* joined RAF 1942, served as cmmnd pilot in UK and M East, released Flt Lt 1946; sci staff Nat Inst for Med Res 1952–56, reader in chemical pathology St Mary's Hosp Med Sch 1962–67 (lectr 1956–62), prof of chemical endocrinology Univ of London 1967–73, prof and head of Dept of Chemical Pathology St Mary's Hosp Med Sch Univ of London 1973–90 (emeritus prof of chemical pathology 1991–); chm Div of Pathology St Mary's Hosp 1981; ed Clinical Endocrinology 1972–74; memb Herts AHA 1967–72, sec Clinical Endocrinology Ctee MRC 1976–82, chm Human Pituitary Collection MRC, pres Section of Endocrinology RSM 1976–78, gen sec Soc for Endocrinology 1979–83 (treas 1983–91), dep sec gen Int Soc of Endocrinology 1986–, sec gen Euro Fedn of Endocrine Socs 1987–94; ed-in-chief Endocrine-related Cancer 1993–, editorial advsr Euro Jl of Endocrinology 1994–; Freedom of Haverfordwest; FRCPath, Hon MRCP, Fiorino D'Oro City of Florence 1977, Clinical Endocrinology Tst Medal 1990, Leverhulme Emeritus Fellowship 1991, Soc for Endocrinology Jubilee Medal 1992; *Books* Hormones in Blood (1983), The Adrenal Gland (1979, 2 edn 1992); *Recreations* languages; *Clubs* RSM; *Style*— Prof Vivian James; ✉ Unit of Metabolic Medicine, St Mary's Hospital Medical School, London W2 1PG

JAMES, Prof Walter; CBE (1977); s of George Herbert James, and Mary Kathleen, *née* Crutch; *b* 8 Dec 1924; *Educ* Royal GS Worcester, St Luke's Coll Exeter, Univ of Nottingham (BA); *m* 21 Aug 1948, Joyce Dorothy, da of Frederick George Allan Woollaston (d 1975); 2 s (Alan b 1962, Andrew b 1965); *Career* lectr in adult educn Univ of Nottingham 1948–69, prof of educnl studies Open Univ 1969–84 (dean and dir 1969–77); UK rep Cncl of Europe working parties on: Devpt of Adult Educn 1973–81, Adult Educn for Community Devpt 1982–87, Adult Educn for Change 1988–93 (project dir 1982–87); cncllr Eastbourne BC 1994–; chm: Nat Cncl for Voluntary Youth Servs 1970–76, Review of Trg p/t Youth and Community Workers 1975–77, Religious Advsy Bd, Scout Assoc 1977–82, In Serv Trg and Educn Panel for Youth and Community Work 1978–82, Cncl for Educn and Trg in Youth and Community Work 1982–85, Nat Advsy Cncl for the Youth Serv 1986–88, Diocese of Southwark LNSM Cncl 1992–95; memb: C of E Gen Synod Bd of Educn 1991–, Scout Assoc Community Devpt Ctee 1991–95; tstee: Trident Educnl Tst 1972–86, Young Volunteer Force Fndn 1972–77, Community Projects Fndn 1977–90, Community Devpt Fndn 1990–; pres: Inst of Playleadership 1972–74, Fair Play for Children 1979–82, Regnl Youth Work Unit for London and the SE 1992–94; *Books* The Standard of Living (with F J Bayliss, 1964), Virginia Woolf Selections from her Essays (ed, 1966); contrib: Encyclopaedia of Education (1968), Teaching Techniques in Adult Education (1971), Mass Media and Adult Education (1971); The Development of Adult Education (with H Janne and P Dominice, 1980), The 14 Pilot Experiments Vols 1–3 (1984), Handbook on Co-operative Monitoring (1986), Role of Media in Adult Education and Community Development (1988), An Excellent Enterprise (1994), Youth A Part (jtly, 1996), Tomorrow is Another Country (jtly, 1996); *Recreations* living; *Style*— Prof Walter James, CBE; ✉ 25 Kepplestone, Staveley Rd, Eastbourne, E Sussex BN20 7JZ (☎ 01323 417029)

JAMES, William Stirling; s of Wing Cdr Sir Archibald William Henry James, KBE, MC (d 1980), and Eugenia, *née* Morris (d 1991); *b* 20 Nov 1941; *Educ* St George's Coll Rhodesia, Stonyhurst, Magdalene Coll Cambridge (MA); *Career* Morgan Grenfell & Co Ltd 1964–65; Touche Ross & Co: London 1965–68, NY 1968–69; dir Hill Samuel & Co Ltd 1980– (joined 1969); farmer; external memb Lloyd's; FCA 1978 (ACA 1968); *Recreations* shooting, bridge; *Clubs* Boodle's, Pratt's, Annabel's; *Style*— William James, Esq; ✉ 14 Queensberry Mews West, London SW7 2DU (☎ 0171 584 6750); Champions Farm, Pulborough, Sussex RH20 3EF; Hill Samuel & Co Ltd, 100 Wood St, London EC2P 2AJ (☎ 0171 600 6000)

JAMES DUFF OF HATTON, David Robin Millais; s of Capt Christopher Alexander James, RN (d 1969), and Cynthia Swire (d 1970); *b* 29 May 1945; *Educ* Trinity Coll Glenalmond, RAC Cirencester; *m* 1, 14 March 1970 (m dis 1982), Monica Jean, da of Thomas G Browne; 1 s (Rory b 1978), 3 da (Fiona b 1971, Tania b 1973, Nicola b 1980); m 2, 20 Feb 1988, Jayne Elizabeth, da of James Bryce, of Coupar Angus; 2 s (Gardie William Beauchamp b 1993, Patrick Alexander b 1995); *Career* chm BFSS in Scotland 1990– (former vice chm), coordinator for Operation Raleigh Grampian Region; memb Queen's Bodyguard for Scotland (The Royal Co of Archers); *Recreations* golf, cricket, tennis, field sports; *Clubs* Royal and Ancient, MCC; *Style*— David James Duff of Hatton; ✉ Hatton Castle, Turriff, Aberdeenshire AB5 8ED (☎ 01888 562279); Estate Office, Hatton Estates, Turriff (☎ 01888 563624)

JAMES OF HOLLAND PARK, Baroness (Life Peer UK 1991); Phyllis Dorothy James (P D James); OBE (1983); da of late Sydney Victor James, and late Dorothy May Amelia, *née* Hone; *b* 3 Aug 1920; *Educ* Cambridge HS for Girls; *m* 8 Aug 1941, Connor Bantry White (d 1964), s of Harry Bantry White, MC; 2 da (Hon Clare Bantry (Hon Mrs Flook) b 1942, Hon Jane Bantry (Hon Mrs McLeod) b 1944); *Career* admin NHS 1949–68, princ Serving Police and Criminal Policy Dept Home Office 1968–79; novelist; chm: Soc of Authors 1984–86, Booker Prize Judges 1987; memb Bd Br Cncl 1988–93, chm Lit Advsy Panel and memb Arts Cncl 1988–92, govr BBC 1988–93; assoc fell Downing Coll Cambridge; FRSL, FRSA; Hon DLitt Buckingham Univ 1992; Hon DLit: Univ of London 1993, Univ of Hertfordshire 1994, Univ of Glasgow 1995; Hon Doctor Univ of Essex 1996; *Books* Cover her Face (1962), A Mind to Murder (1963), Unnatural Causes (1967), Shroud for a Nightingale (1971), The Maul and the Pear Tree (with T A Critchley, 1971), An Unsuitable Job for a Woman (1972), The Black Tower (1975), Death of an Expert Witness (1977), Innocent Blood (1980), The Skull Beneath the Skin (1982), A Taste for Death (1986), Devices and Desires (1989), The Children of Men (1992), Original Sin (1994); *Recreations* reading, exploring churches, walking by the sea; *Clubs* The Detection; *Style*— The Rt Hon Baroness James of Holland Park, OBE; ✉ c/o Greene and Heaton Ltd, Literary Agent, 37 Goldhawk Rd, London W12 8QQ (☎ 0181 749 0315)

JAMESON, Derek; s of Mrs E Barrett; *b* 29 Nov 1929; *Educ* elementary schs East London; *m* 1, 1948, Jacqueline Sinclair (decd); 1 s, 1 da; m 2, 1971 (m dis 1977), Pauline Tomlin; 2 s; m 3, 1988, Ellen Petrie; *Career* Reuters 1944–60; ed: London American 1960–61, Daily Express 1961–63, Sunday Mirror 1963–75; northern ed Daily Mirror 1975–76, managing ed Daily Mirror 1976–77; ed: Daily Express 1977–78, Daily Star 1978–80, News of the World 1981–83; TV and Radio commentator; *Style*— Derek Jameson, Esq; ✉ BBC Radio 2, Broadcasting House, Glasgow G12 8DG (☎ 0141 353 0358)

JAMESON, Air Cdre Patrick Geraint (Jamie); CB (1959), DSO (1943), DFC (1940, and bar 1941); s of Robert Delvin Jameson (d 1952), of Delvin Lodge, and Katherine Lenora Jameson, *née* Dick (d 1965); *b* 10 Nov 1912; *Educ* Hutt Central, Hutt Valley HS; *m* 1941, Hilda Nellie Haiselden, da of Bertie Fitzherbert Webster, of NZ; 1 s (John), 1 da (Suzanne); *Career* joined RAF 1936, No 8 FTS Montrose 1936, posted to No 46 Fighter Sqdn Norwegian Campaign 1940, cmd 266 Spitfire Sqdn (Battle of Britain), 12 Gp Wing Leader based at Wittering 1941–42, (Dieppe Operation) Wing Leader North Weald leading Norwegian Spitfire Wing 1942–43, HQ No 11 Gp 1943, planning fighter ops 1943–44, Cdr 122 Mustang Wing in Normandy Beach-head then Tempest Wing, Belgium, Holland, Germany, Denmark 1944–45, Staff Coll Haifa 1946, Air Miny Fighter Operational Trg 1947–49, OC Day Fighter Leaders Sch & Gp Capt Ops Central Fighter Estab 1949–52, OC RAF Station Wunstorf Germany 1952, SASO HQ No 11 Gp 1954–56, Air Cdre 1956–59, apptd SASO of 2nd TAF RAF Germany, Task Force Cdr Operation Grapple (Christmas Island) 1959, ret 1960; mentioned in despatches 5 times; Norwegian War Cross with Swords, Cdr Order of Orange-Nassau Netherlands, American Silver Star; *Recreations* fishing, shooting, golf; *Clubs* RAF, Hutt, Hutt Golf; *Style*— Air Cdre Jamie Jameson, CB, DSO, DFC; ✉ 70 Wai-iti Crescent, Lower Hutt, New Zealand (☎ 00 644 569 7693)

JAMESON, (Arthur) Roy; s of Arthur Jameson (d 1945), and Jessie, *née* Wright (d 1947); *b* 27 Dec 1930; *Educ* Hutton GS, Univ of London (LLB, LMRTPI); *m* 5 Aug 1961, Pauline, da of John Charles Crook (d 1966); 1 s (Andrew Roy b 1965), 2 da (Caroline Judith b 1963, Alison Claire b 1968); *Career* slr and NP; clerk Fulwood UDC 1968–74; hon sec Preston Incorporated Law Soc 1976–80 (pres 1986–87), currently actg sec Assoc of North Western Law Socs (pres 1988–89), local rep Slrs' Benevolent Assoc, memb Cncl Notaries' Soc 1987–; clerk to: Bd of Mgmnt Royal Cross Sch for the Deaf Preston 1969–90, Withnell Parish Cncl 1974–77; govr Hutton GS, chm Gt Manchester and Lancashire Rent Assessment Ctee 1989–; *Recreations* fencing, amateur drama (pres Preston Drama Club 1993–); *Style*— Roy Jameson, Esq; ✉ 11 Regent Drive, Fulwood, Preston, Lancashire PR2 3JA (☎ 01772 719312); 69 Friargate, Preston, Lancashire PR1 2LD (☎ 01772 555616, fax 01772 203569)

JAMIESON, Andrew Thomas; s of Alexander Jamieson (d 1960), and Catherine Elizabeth, *née* MacDonald (d 1977); *b* 16 Feb 1928; *Educ* George Heriot's Sch Edinburgh, Univ of Edinburgh (BSc); *m* 18 March 1953, Evelyn Hall, da of James Andrew Hiddleston (d 1983); 1 da (Elizabeth Helen Hall b 1955), 1 s (Alexander James Andrew b 1958); *Career* Nat Serv 1950–52; dir Panmure Gordon Ltd 1986–96 (ptnr 1964–86), dir FTSE Int 1995–; chm Hemel Hempstead Cons Assoc 1972–74; Freeman City of London, Liveryman Worshipful Co of Actuaries; FFA 1951, AIA, FSS 1956; *Books* Investment Management (with J G Day, 1974); *Recreations* hill walking, cattle rearing; *Clubs* Caledonian, Actuaries; *Style*— Andrew Jamieson, Esq; ✉ Rookwoods, Sible Hedingham, Essex CO9 3QG; Château de la Commanderie, St Siffret, 30700 France

JAMIESON, Crawford William; s of Crawford John Baird Jamieson (d 1978), and Elizabeth, *née* McAulay (d 1991); *b* 28 Sept 1937; *Educ* Dulwich, Guy's Hosp Med Sch Univ of London (MB BS, MS, FRCS); *m* 18 Nov 1961, Gay Jane, da of Brig Albert Gillibrand, DSO, TD (d 1942); 1 s (Crawford Philip b 1966); *Career* res fell Tulane Univ New Orleans 1968, Hunterian prof RCS of England 1970, asst dir Surgical Unit St Mary's Hosp 1970–72, conslt surgn St Thomas' Hosp, dir Surgical Servs Guy's and St Thomas' Hosp Tst; chm Br Jl of Surgery; memb: Surgical Res Soc, Cncl Vascular Surgical Soc (pres); *Books* Surgical Management of Vascular disease (1982 and 1992), Current Operative Surgery: Vascular Surgery (1985), Vascular Surgery: Issues in Current Practice (1987), Limb Salvage & Amputation for Vascular disease (1988); *Recreations* fishing, shooting, gun dog training; *Style*— Crawford Jamieson, Esq; ✉ The Consulting Rooms, York House, 199 Westminster Bridge Rd, London SE1 7UT (☎ 0171 928 3013)

JAMIESON, David; MP (Lab) Plymouth Devonport (majority 7,412); s of late Frank Jamieson, and Eileen Jamieson; *b* 18 May 1947; *Educ* Tudor Grange GS Solihull, St Peter's Coll Birmingham, Open Univ (BA); *m* 11 Dec 1971, Patricia, *née* Hofton; 2 s, 1 da; *Career* asst mathematics teacher Riland-Bedford Sch Sutton Coldfield 1970–76, head of mathematics Crown Hills Community Coll Leicester 1976–81, sr vice princ John Kitto Community Coll Plymouth 1981–92; Parly candidate (Lab): Birmingham Hall Green Feb 1974, Plymouth Drake 1987; MP (Lab) Plymouth Devonport 1992–, memb Commons Select Ctee on Educn 1992–, private members Bill - Activity Centres (Young Persons' Safety) Act 1995; cncllr Solihull CBC 1970–74 (vice chm Housing Ctee 1973–74); *Recreations* music, tennis, gardening; *Style*— David Jamieson, Esq, MP; ✉ House of Commons, London SW1A 0AA (☎ 0171 219 6252, fax 0171 219 2388, constituency office ☎ 01752 704677)

JAMIESON, Prof Ian Miller; s of James Miller Jamieson (d 1959), and Winifred Emma Jamieson (d 1980); *b* 10 Nov 1944; *Educ* Brockley County GS, Hastings GS, Univ of Surrey (BSc, PhD), Univ of Leicester (PGCE); *m* 1975, Anne Emmery, da of Aksel Pederson; 1 s (Erik b 15 June 1976), 1 da (Claire b 27 Oct 1984); *Career* Ealing Coll of

HE (now Thames Valley Univ): variously lectr, sr lectr, head of sociology 1969–77; evaluator then co-dir Schs Cncl industry project Schs Cncl London 1978–84, reader in business and mgmnt Thames Valley Univ 1984–85; Univ of Bath: lectr in educn and industry 1985–89, prof of educn 1989–, head Dept of Educn 1990–93, pro-vice-chllr 1994–; non-exec dir Western Educn and Trg Partnership; ed Br Jl of Educn and Work; memb Steering Ctee Int Partnership Bd; memb: Br Educnl Research Assoc, Br Educnl Mgmnt Assoc; FRSA 1991; *Books* Capitalism and Culture (1980), Schools and Industry (1982), Industry and Education (1985), Mirrors of Work: Work Simulations in Schools (1988), Rethinking Work Experience (1991), School Effectiveness and School Improvement (1996); *Recreations* tennis, theatre, opera, writing; *Clubs* Lansdown Tennis; *Style*— Prof Ian Jamieson; ✉ 35, Richmond Heights, Lansdown, Bath BA1 5QJ; University of Bath, Claverton Down, Bath BA2 7AY (☎ 01225 826013, fax 01225 826113, e-mail I.M.Jamieson@bath.ac.uk)

JANES, (John) Douglas Webster; CB (1975); s of John Arnold Janes (d 1949), and Maud Mackinnon, *née* Webster (d 1938); *b* 17 Aug 1918; *Educ* Trinity Acad Edinburgh, Southgate Co Sch Middx, City and Guilds Coll Univ of London (BSc Eng, ACGI, DIC); *m* 1943, Margaret Isabel, *née* Smith (d 1978); 1 s, 2 da; m 2, 1986, Joan Walker; *Career* princ fin offr Miny of Housing and Local Govt DOE 1968–73 (dep sec 1973), chief exec Maplin Devpt Authy 1973–74, dep sec NI Office 1974–79; various mgmnt orgn reviews 1979–81; memb Home Grown Timber Advsy Ctee 1979–81 (chm 1981–93); sec Bach Choir 1981–89; *Recreations* singing in choirs, using my hands; *Style*— Douglas Janes, Esq, CB

JANNER, Hon Greville Ewan; QC (1971), MP (Lab) Leicester West (majority 3,978); s of Baron Janner (Life Peer, d 1982), and Elsie Sybil, CBE, JP, *née* Cohen (d 1994); *b* 11 July 1928; *Educ* Bishop's Coll Sch Canada, St Paul's Sch, Trinity Hall Cambridge, Harvard Law Sch USA; *m* 1955, Myra Louise, *née* Sheink (d 1996); 1 s (Daniel), 2 da (Marion, Laura); *Career* called to the Bar 1955, author, journalist, broadcaster; Parly candidate (Lab) Wimbledon 1955; MP (Lab): Leicester North West 1970–74, Leicester West 1974–; chm Select Ctee on Employment 1992–96; chm All Pty Safety Gp, co-chm All Pty Employment Gp 1996–, vice chm All Pty Parly Ctee for Release of Soviet Jewry, pres Inter-Parly Cncl Against Anti-Semitism 1990–; pres Retired Exec's Action Clearing House (REACH) 1980–; vice pres World Jewish Congress 1981–; former dir Jewish Chronicle Newspaper Ltd; non-exec dir Ladbroke plc 1986–95; pres Bd of Deputies of British Jews 1979–85, first pres Cwlth Jewish Cncl 1982–; chm Holocaust Educnl Tst 1990–, pres Maimonides Fndn 1993–; FIPD 1976; *Books* 65 books incl: Janner's Complete Speechmaker (Century Business, 5 edn, 1991); *Recreations* Magic Circle, languages, swimming; *Style*— The Hon Greville Janner, QC, MP; ✉ House of Commons, London SW1A 0AA (☎ 0171 219 4469)

JANSEN, N Elly; OBE (1980); da of Jacobus Gerrit Jansen, of Wisch, Holland, and Petronella Suzanna, *née* Vellekoop; *b* 5 Oct 1929; *Educ* Paedologisch Inst Free Univ Amsterdam, Boerhave Kliniek (SRN), Univ of London; *m* 1969, (Alan Brian Stewart) George Whitehouse; 3 da; *Career* fndr and dir Richmond Fellowship for Community Mental Health 1959–91, chief exec offr Richmond Fellowship International 1981–, fndr Fellowship Charitable Fndn 1983–; fndr Richmond Fellowship of: America 1968, Australia 1973, New Zealand 1977, Austria 1978, and subsquently of Barbados, Bangladesh, Bolivia, Canada, Costa Rica, France, Ghana, Grenada, Hong Kong, India, Israel, Jamaica, Malta, Mexico, Nigeria, Peru, Philippines, Trinidad & Tobago, Uruguay and Zimbabwe; dep chm Richmond Fellowship Enquiry 1981–82; conslt to: Pan-American Health Organisation 1987–, Min of Social Affairs Holland 1969–73; advsr to many govts on community care legislation and servs; organiser of Int Confs on Therapeutic Communities 1973, 1975, 1976, 1979, 1984 and 1988; fell German Marshall Meml Fund 1977–78; Templeton award 1985–86; *Books* The Therapeutic Community Outside The Hospital (ed, 1980), Mental Health and the Community (contrib 1983), Towards a Whole Society (contrib, 1985); *Recreations* nature, reading, music, photography; *Style*— Mrs N Elly Whitehouse-Jansen, OBE; ✉ Clyde House, 109 Strawberry Vale, Twickenham TW1 4SJ (☎ 0181 744 9585, fax 0181 891 0500)

JANSON-SMITH, (Peter) Patrick; s of John Peter Janson-Smith, of London, and Diana Mary, *née* Whittaker, of Sérignac-sur-Garonne, France; *b* 28 July 1949; *Educ* Cathedral Sch Salisbury, Cokethorpe Park Sch Witney Oxon; *m* 1, 22 April 1972 (m dis), Lavinia Jane, da of Robert Hugh Priestley, MBE; 1 da (Emma Mary b 12 Dec 1975), 1 s (Mark Robert b 19 July 1978); m 2, 12 June 1987, Pamela Jean, da of Cdr Anthony William Gossage, RN; 2 s (Oscar William Patrick b 9 Jan 1989, Daniel Alexander b 15 Jan 1991); *Career* publisher; asst to export publicity mangr University of London Press Ltd (Hodder & Stoughton) 1967–69; Granada Publishing; asst to publicity mangr Panther Books Ltd 1969–70, ed Mayflower Books 1970–71 and 1973–74, press offr 1971–72; publicity mangr Octopus Books 1972; Transworld Publishers: ed Corgi Books 1974–78, assoc editorial dir Corgi Books 1978–79, editorial dir Nationwide Book Serv 1979–81, publisher Corgi & Black Swan Books 1981–95, publisher Transworld Publishers Adult Trade Div 1995–; memb: Ctee Soc of Young Publishers 1969–71, Whitefriars Soc 1992–, Bd Edinburgh Book Festival 1994–; *Recreations* book collecting, late 19th and early 20th century illustrations, wine and food, serious laughter; *Clubs* Garrick; *Style*— Patrick Janson-Smith, Esq; ✉ Transworld Publishers, 61–63 Uxbridge Road, London W5 5SA (☎ 0181 579 2652, fax 0181 579 5479)

JANSONS, Mariss; s of Arvid Jansons, conductor; *b* 1943; *Educ* Leningrad Conservatory, 2nd Vienna Acad; *Career* conductor; trained with Prof Hans Swarowsky in Vienna and with Herbert von Karajan in Salzburg (winner Herbert von Karajan Competition 1971); Leningrad (now St Petersburg) Philharmonic: assoc princ conductor 1985, conducted orch on numerous tours to Europe, N America and Japan; Oslo Philharmonic: music dir 1979–, conducted orch at numerous international venues incl Salzburg Festival and Edinburgh Festivals, Carnegie Hall NY, Suntory Hall Tokyo, Vienna Musikverein and BBC Proms; princ guest conductor London Philharmonic Orch 1992–, prof of conducting St Petersburg Conservatoire 1993–, music dir Pittsburgh Symphony Orch 1997–; conducted numerous other orchs incl: Boston, Chicago, Baltimore and Pittsburg Symphonies, Cleveland Orch, Philadelphia Orch, Los Angeles Philharmonic, Toronto and Montreal Symphonies, Vienna Symphony and Philharmonic, Berlin Philharmonic, Royal Concertgebouw Amsterdam, NDR Symphony Germany, Israel Philharmonic, LSO, LPO, The Philharmonia; recorded TV series Jansons Conducts for BBC Wales 1991; awarded Anders Jahre Norwegian Culture Prize, Cdr with Star Royal Norwegian Order of Merit 1995, EMI Classics' Artist of the Year 1996; *Recordings* with St Petersburg Philharmonic incl Shostakovich's 7th Symphony 1989 (winner Eddison Award Holland 1989); with Oslo Philharmonic incl: complete Tchaikovsky Symphonies (Chandos), numerous for EMI incl Sibelius and Prokofiev violin concertos (with Frank-Peter Zimmerman), Wagner overtures, Dvorak's Symphonies 5 (winner Penguin Award), 8 and 9, Saint-Saens Sympphony No 3 (winner Spellemannsprisen Norway), other works by Bartok, Mussorgsky, Ravel, Respighi, Shostakovich and Svendsen; *Style*— Mariss Jansons, Esq; ✉ c/o IMG Artists Europe, Media House, 3 Burlington Lane, London W4 2TH (☎ 0181 233 5800, fax 0181 233 5801)

JANTET, Georges Henry; s of Auguste Jantet (d 1955), and Renée, *née* Jacob (d 1978); *b* 5 Oct 1927; *Educ* Lycée Français de Londres, St Benedict's Sch Ealing, St Mary's Hosp Med Sch London (MB BS, Martin John Turner prize); *m* 4 June 1955, Alice, da of Jean-François Moulin, of St Etienne, France; 1 s (Bruno b 16 April 1957), 3 da (Martine (Mrs Cremer) b 4 March 1956, Blandine (Mrs Manière) b 24 March 1959, Nadine (Mrs Pistolesi) b 16 March 1963); *Career* Mil Serv with Serv de Santé des Armées Paris and Lyon 1952–53; house surgeon St Mary's Hosp then The Miller Hosp 1951–52, resident surgical offr Hôpital Français London 1953–54, sr house offr Royal Marsden Hosp 1954–55; St Mary's Hosp: prosector in anatomy and demonstrator Dept of Anatomy Med Sch 1953, resident casualty surgeon 1954, surgical registrar Surgical Professorial Unit 1955–57, sr registrar in surgery 1959–66 (also Regnl Hosp Bd NW Thames), assoc teacher Med Sch 1970–; lectr in surgery and research fell Surgical Professorial Unit St Thomas' Hosp and Med Sch 1957–59, research fell and asst in surgery Dept of Surgery Peter Bent Brigham Hosp Harvard 1961–62, conslt in gen and vascular surgery The Ealing Hosp and Assoc Hosps 1966–92; hon conslt surgeon: Dispensaire Français London 1967–, The Italian Hosp London 1967–, Hammersmith Hosp and Royal Postgrad Med Sch 1974–92 (also sr lectr in surgery); RCS: surgical tutor 1973–77, regnl advsr 1977–88, memb Manpower Advsy Panel 1987–92, memb Euro Gp 1989–, chm Ct of Examiners 1986–87; memb numerous ctees NW Thames Regnl Health Authy (chm Surgeons' Ctee 1989–92); FRCS 1955 (MRCS 1951), FRSM 1966; memb: BMA 1960, Cncl Assoc of Surgeons of GB & Ireland 1987–94 (fell 1966), Vascular Surgical Soc of GB & Ireland, Cncl Hunterian Soc 1975–90 (fell 1966, pres 1986–87), Société Clinique Française 1985– (pres 1987–90), Br Lymphology Interest Gp 1987–92; pres Union Internationale de Phlébologie 1995– (vice pres 1992–95); memb Editorial Bd various learned jls; *Books* New Trends In Basic Lymphology (co-ed, 1967), Phlebology 1985 (co-ed, 1986); author of chapters in various books; *Recreations* family and social life, tennis, sailing, fishing, skiing, travelling, history, current affairs, music; *Clubs* Surgical Specialists Soc, Roehampton; *Style*— Georges Jantet, Esq; ✉ 14 Rue Duroc, 75007 Paris, France (☎ 00 331 47 34 46 28, fax 00 33 1 47 34 26 78)

JANVRIN, Robin Berry; CB (1997), CVO (1994, LVO 1983); s of Vice Adm Sir (Hugh) Richard Benest Janvrin, KCB, DSC (d 1993), and Nancy Edyth, *née* Fielding (d 1994); *b* 20 Sept 1946; *Educ* Marlborough, BNC Oxford; *m* 22 Oct 1977, Isabelle, da of Yann de Boissonneaux de Chevigny; 2 s, 2 da; *Career* RN: RNC Dartmouth 1964, HMS Devonshire 1965, HMS Lynx 1970, HMS Ganges 1973, HMS Royal Arthur 1974; Dip Serv: FCO 1975, 1978 and 1984, first sec UK Delgn NATO 1976, New Delhi 1981, cnsllr and dep head Personnel Dept 1985–87; dep private sec to HM The Queen 1996– (press sec 1987–90, asst private sec 1990–95); *Style*— Robin Janvrin, Esq, CB, CVO; ✉ Buckingham Palace, London SW1 1AA

JAQUES, Geoffrey Wilfred; s of Jack Kearsley Jaques, of Sevenoaks, Kent, and Yvette, *née* Hopkins; *b* 14 Sept 1942; *Educ* Downside, Univ of Manchester (LLB); *m* 18 Sept 1965, Marcia Hemming, da of late Norman Cowan Woodhead; 2 da (Sarah Lucy (Mrs Vavasour) b 17 June 1966, Sophie Victoria b 10 Oct 1970), 2 s (Charles Alexander Kearsley b 4 June 1968, Justin Geoffrey Kearsley b 10 March 1972); *Career* called to the Bar Lincoln's Inn 1963 (Mansfield scholar), admitted to NSW Bar 1990, bencher of Lincoln's Inn 1991, head of chambers, asst Parly cmmr 1992–95, dep registrar in bankruptcy High Ct 1996–97; *Books* Butterworth's Encyclopedia of Forms and Precedents (co-ed, 4th edn, vols 18 & 19 sale of land, 1969); *Recreations* watching cricket; *Clubs* MCC; *Style*— Geoffrey Jaques, Esq; ✉ 17 Old Buildings, Lincoln's Inn, London WC2A 3UP (☎ 0171 405 9653, fax 0171 404 8089)

JAQUES, John Michael; MBE (1988); s of William Edward Jaques (d 1994), of Rochester, Kent, and Gertrude, *née* Scott (d 1980); *b* 29 Sept 1930; *Educ* Cambridge HS, Sch of Architecture The Polytechnic (DipArch); *m* 27 Jan 1962, Caroline, da of Philip Reddie Knapman, of Stanton Drew, Somerset; 2 s (Rupert b 1962, Matthew b 1964); *Career* architect; early design experience with Design Research Unit and Sir William Whitfield; sr ptnr Jaques Muir & Ptnrs chartered architects; practice cmmns incl: buildings for sport and recreation, theatres and museums, restoration of historic buildings; 1989 Civic Tst Commendation for the restoration of the Palace Theatre London; architect for major restoration work to Church of the Holy Sepulchre Jerusalem; visiting tutor Thames and Central London Polys 1972–75, hon sec The Soc of St John Chrysostom; memb Cncl: The Anglo Jordanian Soc 1980–86 and 1991–94, Friends of St John Ophthalmic Hosp Jerusalem 1982–86, Appeal Ctee Royal Soc of Br Sculptors; OStJ 1985, Order of El Istiqlal (Jordan) 1977; RIBA, FRSA; *Recreations* reading, shooting, stalking, fishing, painting, Eastern Mediterranean studies; *Clubs* Arts, Cantabrigian Rowing (pres 1976–77); *Style*— John M Jaques, Esq, MBE; ✉ 14 Macduff Road, London SW11 4DA (☎ 0171 720 1770, fax 0171 357 7650)

JARAY, Tess; da of Francis Ferdinand Jaray (d 1987), and Pauline, *née* Arndt; *b* 31 Dec 1937; *Educ* St Martin's Sch of Art, Slade Sch of Art; *children* 2 da (Anna Vaux b 1964, Georgia Vaux b 1966); *Career* artist; teacher Hornsey Coll of Art 1964–68, teacher Slade Sch of Art 1968–; *Solo Exhibitions* Grabowski Gallery 1963 (with Marc Vaux, *qv*), Hamilton Gallery 1965 and 1967, Demarco Gallery Edinburgh 1967, Axiom Gallery London 1969, Graves Art Gallery Sheffield 1972, City Art Gallery Bristol 1972, Whitechapel Art Gallery 1973 (with Marc Vaux), Flowers Gallery 1976, Adelaide Festival Centre Australia 1980, Whitworth Art Gallery Manchester 1984, Ashmolean Museum (Prints and Drawings) Oxford 1984, Serpentine Gallery 1988; *Gp Exhibitions* Galleria Trastevere Rome 1962, John Moores Exhbn Liverpool 1963–78, Fine Art for Industry (RCA) 1969, 7 From London (Bern) 1973, British Painting 1974 (Hayward Gallery) 1974, Artists of the Sixties (Tate) 1977, 80 Prints by Modern Masters (Flowers Gallery) 1982, Platforms for Artists (BR/Gateshead Borough Cncl) 1987, and others; *Commissions* mural British pavilion Expo 1967 Montreal 1967, terrazzo floor Victoria Stn London 1985, decorative paving Stoke-on-Trent Garden Festival 1986, decorative paving Midlands Art Centre 1987, Centenary Square Birmingham 1988, Cathedral Precinct Wakefield 1989, and others; *Work in Public Collections* Tate Gallery, Arts Cncl, Stadtisches Museum Leverkusen, British Cncl, Peter Stuyvesant Fndn Holland, UCL, Walker Art Gallery Liverpool, DOE, Univ of Warwick, Sundvalls Museum Stockholm, Museum of Modern Art Belgrade, V & A, Graves Art Gallery Sheffield, Museum of Fine Art Budapest, Contemporary Art Soc, and others; *Style*— Ms Tess Jaray

JARDINE, Sir Andrew Colin Douglas; 5 Bt (UK 1916), of Godalming, Surrey; er s of Brig Sir Ian Liddell Jardine, 4 Bt, OBE, MC (d 1982), and Priscilla, *née* Scott-Phillips; *b* 30 Nov 1955; *Educ* Charterhouse, Royal Agric Coll/Univ of Reading 1993–96 (BSc); *Heir* bro, Michael Ian Christopher Jardine b 4 Oct 1958; *Career* served Royal Green Jackets 1975–78; C T Bowring & Co 1979–81, Henderson Administration Group plc 1981–92, Gartmore Investment Management Ltd 1992–93, Strutt & Parker 1996–; memb The Queen's Body Guard for Scotland (Royal Co of Archers); *Style*— Sir Andrew Jardine, Bt; ✉ 99 Addison Rd, London W14 8DD (☎ 0171 603 6434)

JARDINE, Sheriff James Christopher Macnaughton; s of James Jardine (d 1952), of Glasgow, and Jean Paterson, *née* Stuart (d 1966); *b* 18 Jan 1930; *Educ* Glasgow Acad, Gresham House Sch Ayrshire, Univ of Glasgow (BL); *m* 1955, Vena Gordon, da of Daniel Gordon Kight (d 1973), of Renfrewshire; 1 da (Susan); *Career* slr; princ Nelson & Mackay 1955–56, ptnr McClure Naismith Brodie & Co Slrs Glasgow 1956–69; Sheriff: Stirling Dunbarton and Clackmannan (later N Strathclyde) at Dumbarton 1969–79, Glasgow and Strathkelvin 1979–95, ret; *Recreations* boating, music, theatre, ballet, opera; *Style*— Sheriff James Jardine

JARDINE, Michael Ian Christopher; s of Brig Sir Ian Liddell Jardine, 4 Bt, OBE, MC (d 1982), and Priscilla, Lady Jardine; hp of bro, Sir Andrew Jardine, 5 Bt, *qv*; *b* 4 Oct 1958; *Educ* Charterhouse; *m* Jan 1982, (Maria) Milky Pineda; 2 s (Oliver Michael Ian b 20 Feb 1983, Adrian Douglas Francis b 3 Dec 1986); *Style*— Michael Jardine, Esq; ✉ 12 Graham Ave, Ealing, London W13 9TQ

JARDINE, Prof Nicholas; s of Michael James Jardine (d 1988), and Jean Caroline, *née* Crook; *b* 4 Sept 1943; *Educ* Monkton Combe, King's Coll Cambridge (Trevelyan scholar, BA, PhD); *m* 1992, Marina, da of Mario Frasca-Spada; 4 c by previous marriages; *Career* Royal Society research fell 1968–73, sr research fell King's Coll Cambridge 1971–75 (jr research fell 1967–71); Univ of Cambridge: univ lectr in history and philosophy of science 1975–85, reader 1985–91, prof of history and philosophy of the sciences 1991–; fell Darwin Coll Cambridge 1975–; ed Studies in History and Philosophy of Science 1982–; *Books* Mathematical Taxonomy (with R Sibson, 1971), The Birth of History and Philosophy of Science (1984), The Fortunes of Inquiry (1986), The Scenes of Inquiry (1991); *Recreations* fungus hunting; *Style*— Prof Nicholas Jardine; ✉ Department of History and Philosophy of Science, University of Cambridge, Free School Lane, Cambridge CB2 3RH (☎ and fax 01223 334546)

JARDINE OF APPLEGIRTH, Sir Alexander Maule; 12 Bt (NS 1672), of Applegirth, Dumfriesshire; 23 Chief of Clan Jardine; s of Col Sir William Edward Jardine of Applegirth, 11 Bt, OBE, TD, JP, DL (d 1986), and Ann Graham Maitland; *b* 24 Aug 1947; *Educ* Gordonstoun, Scottish Agric Coll Aberdeen (Dip in Farm Business Orgn & Mngt 1988); *m* 9 Oct 1982, Mary Beatrice, posthumous only child of Hon John Michael Inigo Cross (yst s of 2 Viscount Cross), and Sybil Anne, *née* Murray, who m subsequently Lt Cdr James Parker-Jervis, RN; 3 s (William Murray b 1984, John Alexander Cross b 1991, Douglas Edward b 1994), 2 da (Kirsty Sybil b 1986, Jean Maule b 1988); *Heir* s, William Murray Jardine, yr of Applegirth b 4 July 1984; *Career* herb farmer; memb Queen's Body Guard for Scotland (Royal Co of Archers); *Recreations* shooting, fishing, curling; *Style*— Sir Alexander Jardine of Applegirth, Bt; ✉ Ash House, Thwaites, Millom, Cumbria LA18 5HY (☎ 01229 716331)

JARMAN, Prof Brian; OBE (1988); *Educ* MB BS, MA, DIC, PhD; *Career* house physician St Mary's Hosp London 1969, house surgn St Bernard's Hosp Gibraltar 1970, resident in med Beth Israel Hosp Harvard Med Sch 1970, trainee GP London 1971, princ (currently pt/t princ) in GP Lisson Grove Health Centre London 1971–, prof of primary health care and gen practice and head of dept St Mary's Hosp Med Sch 1984– (pt/t sr lectr 1973–83); memb: MRC Health Servs Research Ctee 1987–89, English Nat Bd 1988–90, Kensington Chelsea and Westminster FHSA 1990–, King's Fund Mgmnt Ctee 1994–; author of numerous papers in academic jls and research advsr to various bodies nationally and internationally; FRCGP 1984, FRCP 1988, MFPHM 1994; *Style*— Prof Brian Jarman, OBE; ✉ St Mary's Hospital Medical School, Imperial College of Science Technology and Medicine, Norfolk Place, London W2 1PG (☎ 0171 725 1075, fax 0171 706 8426, e-mail BJarman@sm.ic.ac.uk)

JARMAN, Nicolas Francis Barnaby; QC (1985); s of Archibald Seymour Jarman (d 1982), of Brighton, and Helen Marie Klenk; *b* 19 June 1938; *Educ* Harrow, ChCh Oxford (MA); *m* 1, 1973 (m dis 1977), Jennifer Michelle, da of Michael Lawrence Lawrence-Smith (d 1988), of Suffolk; 1 da (Jemima b 1975); m 2, Julia Elizabeth, da of Leonard Owen John (d 1995), of Swansea; *Career* JUO Mons Offr Trg Sch 1957, cmmnd RA 1957, served Cyprus; called to the Bar Inner Temple 1965, in practice Midland & Oxford circuit, recorder of the Crown Ct 1982–, head of chambers; jt chm Bucks Berks and Oxon Barristers-Slrs Jt Liaison Ctee 1985–96; *Recreations* flyfishing, France; *Style*— Nicolas Jarman, Esq, QC; ✉ 13 Blithfield St, London W8 6RH (☎ 0171 937 0982); 4 King's Bench Walk, Temple, London EC4 (☎ 0171 353 3581); Sous Chateau, Castelnau Valence, 30190 St Chaptes, France

JARMAN, Roger Whitney; s of Reginald Cecil Jarman (d 1989), and Marjorie Dix, *née* Whitney (d 1970); *b* 16 Feb 1935; *Educ* Cathays HS Cardiff, Univ of Birmingham (BSocSc); *m* 1959, Patricia Dorothy, da of Trevor Henry Odwell (d 1977); 1 s (Christopher b 1960); *Career* instr in Lib studies Vauxhall Motors 1960–62, recruitment offr Vauxhall Motors 1962–64, asst sec Appt Bd Univ of Bristol 1964–68, princ Civil Serv Cmmn 1968–72, princ Welsh Office Euro Div 1972–74, asst sec Devolution Div 1974–78, asst sec Perm Sec Div 1978–80, under sec Land Use Planning Gp 1980–83, under sec Tport Highways and Planning Gp Welsh Office 1983–88, under sec Housing Health and Social Servs Policy Gp 1988–94, under sec Local Govt Finance Housing and Social Sevs Gp 1994–95; *Recreations* reading, cooking, walking; *Clubs* Civil Serv; *Style*— Roger Jarman, Esq; ✉ Cooper's Lea, 72 Mill Road, Lisvane, Cardiff CF4 5XJ (☎ 01222 756405)

JARRATT, Sir Alexander Anthony (Alex); kt (1979), CB (1968), DL (Essex 1995); s of Alexander Jarratt (d 1943), and Mary Jarratt (d 1970); *b* 19 Jan 1924; *Educ* Royal Liberty GS Essex, Univ of Birmingham (BCom); *m* 1946, Mary Philomena, da of Louis Keogh (d 1932); 1 s, 2 da; *Career* Petty Offr Fleet Air Arm, served Far East; civil servant: Miny of Power 1949–64, seconded Treasy 1953–54, Cabinet Office 1964–65, sec Prices and Incomes Bd 1964–68, dep under sec Dept of Employment and Productivity 1968–70, dep sec Miny of Agric 1970; chief exec IPC and IPC Newspapers 1970–74, chm and chief exec Reed International 1974–85 (dir 1970–85), chm Smiths Industries plc 1985–91 (now non-exec dir); dep chm: Midland Bank plc 1980–91, Prudential Corporation 1987–91 and 1992–94; non-exec dir ICI plc 1975–91; pres Advertising Assoc 1979–83, former memb NEDC; former chm CBI Econ Policy Ctee and Employment Policy Ctee, former memb President's Ctee CBI; chm: Industl Soc 1975–79, Henley Admin Staff Coll 1976–89, Centre for Dispute Resolution 1990–; chllr Univ of Birmingham 1983–; Liveryman Worshipful Co of Marketors; Hon LLD Birmingham, Hon DSc Cranfield, Hon DUniv Brunel; Hon CGIA; FRSA; *Recreations* the countryside, theatre, reading, music; *Style*— Sir Alex Jarratt, CB, DL; ✉ Smiths Industries plc, 765 Finchley Rd, Childs Hill, London NW11 8DS (☎ 0181 458 3232, telex 928761)

JARRATT, Dr John Anthony; s of Leslie Jarratt (d 1958), and Lily, *née* Tweedie (d 1977); *b* 26 Dec 1939; *Educ* Spalding GS, Univ of Sheffield Med Sch (MB ChB); *m* 21 Feb 1970, Patricia Anne, da of Jack Madin, of Alford, Lincolnshire; 2 s (Mark b 24 Nov 1971, Paul b 5 Aug 1975); *Career* Nat Hosp for Nervous Diseases London: academic registrar 1969–70, MRC res fell 1970–72, registrar in clinical neurophysiology 1972; registrar in neurology Middx Hosp 1972, sr registrar Dept of Clinical Neurophysiology Rigshospitalet Copenhagen 1973, conslt in clinical neurophysiology Sheffield AHA 1976–, hon lectr in neurology Univ of Sheffield 1976–; author of numerous scientific pubns; pres Assoc of Br Clinical Neurophysiologists 1990–93 (sec 1984–88); memb Jt Neurosciences Ctee 1984–88, chm SAC on Higher Med Trg in Clinical Neurophysiology RCP 1988– (memb 1984–88), memb Expert Panel EEC 1989; memb: Assoc of Br Neurologists 1978, EEG Soc 1991; FRCP 1981; *Recreations* golf, photography, music, travel, technical innovation; *Style*— Dr John Jarratt; ✉ Department of Clinical Neurophysiology, Royal Hallamshire Hospital, Sheffield S10 2JF (☎ 0114 271 2399)

JARRATT, Prof Peter; s of Edward Jarratt (d 1988), and Edna Mary Eliza, *née* Pearson (d 1976); *b* 2 Jan 1935; *Educ* Bingley GS, Univ of Manchester (BSc), Univ of Bradford (PhD); *m* 1 June 1971, Jeanette, da of Lucien Adrian Debeir (d 1946); 1 s (Robin Alexander Debeir b 1972), 1 da (Sophie Amanda Debeir b 1978); *Career* sr lectr Univ of Bradford 1963–72, dir of Computing Laboratory Univ of Salford 1972–75; Univ of Birmingham: prof of computer sci 1975–, dir of Computer Centre 1975–90, dean of Faculty of Sci 1985–88, exec chm for info technol 1992–93, devpt advsr to Vice Chllr 1991–; dir: TV and Film Unit 1983–95, Birmingham Res Park 1985–88, Computer Based Learning Centre 1993–; govr Royal Nat Coll for the Blind 1986–96; memb Exec Ctee Lunar Soc of Birmingham 1991–94, tstee Nat Fndn for Conductive Educn 1985–88, patron Henshaw's Soc for the Blind 1993–; author of numerous scientific pubns; FIMA 1968, FBCS 1968, FSS 1972, CEng 1990; *Recreations* gardening, mountain walking, opera, chess, power boating; *Clubs* Athenaeum; *Style*— Prof Peter Jarratt; ✉ 42 Reddings Road, Moseley, Birmingham B13 8LN (☎ 0121 449 7160); The University of Birmingham, Edgbaston, Birmingham B15 2TT (☎ 0121 414 3487, fax 0121 414 4281)

JARRETT, Eur Ing Dr (Boaz) Antony; s of Frank Jarrett (d 1963), of Cox Corner, Ockley, Surrey, and Ethel Mary, *née* Budden (d 1990); *b* 24 July 1923; *Educ* Windsor Co Boys' Sch, Imperial Coll London (BSc, PhD, DIC, ACGI); *m* 2 Oct 1948, Patricia Eveline, da of Arthur White (d 1976), of Forest Row, Sussex; 2 da (Lianne b 6 Sept 1951, Naomi b 11 Sept 1955); *Career* Sub Lt (A) RNVR air engr 1943–46; res contract Imperial Coll 1946–48, gen factory mangr Lucas Cav Ltd 1949–63, md Eaton-Env Ltd 1963–66, tech dir Lucas Cav Ltd 1966–81, gp dir product technol Lucas Industries plc 1981–86; pres Old Centralians (Engrs' Alumnus Assoc of Imperial Coll) 1986–87, memb Tech Ctee RAC 1984–94, former govr Claremont Fan Ct Sch Esher (chm CDT Ctee); Freeman City of London 1984, Liveryman Worshipful Co of Engrs 1984; memb British Assoc for the Club of Rome 1988–; FIMechE 1965, MSAE 1978, FCGI 1981, FEng 1983, FRSA 1984–95 (resigned), Eur Ing 1989; *Clubs* RAC; *Style*— Eur Ing Dr Antony Jarrett, FEng; ✉ c/o Royal Automobile Club, 85 Pall Mall, London SW1Y 5HS

JARRETT, Rt Rev Martyn William; *see:* Burnley, Bishop of

JARRETT, Paul Eugene Marcus; s of Dr Maurice Eugene Decimus Jarrett (d 1987), of Woking, Surrey, and Doris Mabel Lake, of Cobham, Surrey; *b* 18 Feb 1943; *Educ* Queen Elizabeth's GS Blackburn Lancs, Downing Coll Cambridge (MA), St Thomas' Hosp London (MB BChir, DObstRCOG); *m* 1 April 1966, Ann, da of George Wilson (d 1982), of Blackburn, Lancs; 1 s (Michael b 1972); *Career* dir of surgical servs Kingston Hosp 1987– (conslt surgn 1978–); chm Healthcare Holdings plc 1993–94; former tstee Princess Alice Hospice Esher, former chm Br Assoc of Day Surgery, pres-elect Int Assoc of Ambulatory Surgery; FRCS 1972; *Recreations* medical antiques, golf; *Style*— Paul Jarrett, Esq; ✉ Langleys, Queens Drive, Oxshott, Surrey KT22 0PB (☎ 01372 842259, fax 01372 844257); Kingston Hospital, Wolverton Ave, Kingston-upon-Thames, Surrey KT2 7QB (☎ 0181 546 7711)

JARROLD, Kenneth Wesley; CBE (1997); s of William Stanley Jarrold (d 1981), and Martha Hamilton, *née* Cowan; *b* 19 May 1948; *Educ* St Lawrence Coll Ramsgate, Sidney Sussex Coll Cambridge (Whittaker scholar, BA, pres Cambridge Union Soc), Inst of Health Servs Mgmnt (dip); *m* 1973, Patricia, da of William Hadaway; 2 s (Luke b 28 Jan 1977, Paul b 6 April 1979); *Career* nat mgmnt trainee E Anglian Regnl Health Bd 1969–70, Briggs Ctee on Nursing 1970–71, dep supt Royal Hosp Sheffield 1971–74, hosp sec Derbyshire Royal Infirmary 1974–75, sector admin Nottingham Gen and Univ Hosps 1975–79, asst dist admin (planning) S Tees Health Authy 1979–82, dist gen mangr Gloucester Health Authy 1985–89 (dist admin 1982–84), chief exec Wessex RHA 1990–94; NHS Executive: dir of human resourses 1994–95, dir of human and corp resources 1995–; pres Inst of Health Serv Mgmnt 1985–86 (memb Nat Cncl 1977–89), memb NHS Trg Authy and chm Trg Ctee 1984–87, chm MESOL Project Gp 1986–89 and 1991–93; MHSM 1972; *Recreations* being with family, fitness training; *Style*— Kenneth Jarrold, Esq, CBE; ✉ 20 Dunottar Avenue, Eaglescliffe, Stockton on Tees, Cleveland TS16 0AB; NHS Executive, Department of Health, Quarry House, Quarry Hill, Leeds LS2 7UE (☎ 01532 545171, fax 01532 545173)

JARROLD, HE Nicholas Robert; s of A R Jarrold (d 1964), and D V Jarrold, *née* Roberts (d 1977); *b* 2 March 1946; *Educ* Shrewsbury Sch, Western Reserve Acad Ohio (ESU scholar), St Edmund Hall Oxford (exhibitioner, MA); *m* 1972, Anne Catherine, *née* Whitworth; 2 s (Henry b 1976, Peter b 1979); *Career* HM Dip Serv: FCO 1968–69, third sec The Hague 1969–72, second sec Dakar 1972–75, FCO 1975–79, first sec and head of chancery Nairobi 1979–83, FCO 1983–89, cnsllr and dep head of mission Havana 1989–91, visiting fell St Antony's Coll Oxford 1991–92, cnsllr (economic and commercial) Brussels 1992–96, ambass Latvia 1996–; *Recreations* reading history, cricket, the theatre; *Style*— HE Mr Nicholas Jarrold; ✉ c/o Foreign and Commonwealth Office (Riga), King Charles Street, London SW1A 2AH (☎ 00 371 733 8126, fax 00 371 733 8132)

JARROW, Bishop of 1990–; Rt Rev Alan Smithson; *b* 1 Dec 1936; *Educ* Bradford GS, Queen's Coll Oxford (MA), Queen's Theol Coll Birmingham; *m* Margaret Jean, *née* McKenzie; 2 da (Catherine b 1965, Joanna b 1973), 2 s (Timothy b 1967, Jonathan b 1971); *Career* ordained: deacon 1964, priest 1965; curate: Skipton 1964–68, St Mary the Virgin with St Cross and St Peter Oxford 1968–72; chaplain: Queen's Coll Oxford 1969–72, Reading Univ 1972–77; vicar of Bracknell 1977–83, team rector 1983–84, canon residentiary Carlisle Cathedral and dir of Trg Inst 1984–90, diocesan dir of trg 1985–90; *Recreations* watercolour painting, fell walking, camping, cello music; *Style*— The Rt Rev the Bishop of Jarrow; ✉ The Old Vicarage, Hallgarth, Pittington, Durham DH6 1AB (☎ 0191 372 0225, fax 0191 372 2326)

JARVIS, David; s of Harold Jarvis (d 1945), and Phyllis Emma, *née* Hart; *b* 9 March 1941; *Educ* Gillingham GS, Maidstone Coll of Tech; *m* 9 Feb 1963, Williamina Bell, da of William Herbert Colby; 1 s (Julian David b 1966), 2 da (Andrea Claire b 1968, Nicola Emma b 1976); *Career* Anderson Clayton: controller and treas Milne and Cosa 1963–68, fin admin Peru 1968–70, gen mangr Consumer Prods Div Mexico 1970–78; gen mangr Int Business Devpt The Pillsbury Co USA 1978–81, vice chm and chief fin offr Norwest Corp USA 1981–86, md Salomon Bros USA UK 1986– (currently co-head of Euro investmt banking); voyageur Outward Bound Sch Minnesota, ex tstee Fin Accounting Standards Bd USA; ACMA 1960; *Recreations* tennis, golf; *Clubs* Johns Island, Canning, Queens, Annabel's; *Style*— David Jarvis, Esq; ✉ Salomon Bros International, Victoria Plaza, 111 Buckingham Palace Road, London SW1W OSB (☎ 0171 721 3974, fax 0171 627 8464, telex 886441)

JARVIS, David William; s of George Harry Jarvis, and Doris Annie, *née* Mabbitt; *b* 25 April 1947; *Educ* City of London Sch, Univ of Exeter (BA); *m* 1972, Elizabeth Ann Rowena, da of Fergus Ferguson (d 1969); 2 da (Rowena Gillian b 1978, Katherine Elizabeth b 1980), 1 s (John David George b 1982); *Career* joined Allied-Lyons Group 1972; former dir John Harvey & Sons Ltd; fin dir Harveys of Bristol Ltd 1984–88, md Allied Distillers Ltd 1988–90, chm George Ballantine and Son Ltd, chm William Teacher and Sons Ltd, dir Hiram Walker-Allied Vintners Ltd 1990–91, sector chm Far East and Special Markets Hiram Walker-Allied Vintners Ltd 1990–91, chm and chief exec J Lyons & Co (Food Sector Allied-Lyons plc) 1991–92, chief exec Allied Domecq Spirits & Wine Ltd (formerly The Hiram Walker Group Ltd) 1992–95, dir Allied Domecq plc 1991–95, chief exec Hilton International Ltd and main bd dir parent co Ladbroke Group plc 1996–; FCCA; *Recreations* sports, walking, reading, current affairs; *Style*— David Jarvis, Esq; ✉ Hilton International, Maple Court, Central Park, Reeds Crescent, Watford, Herts WD1 1HZ (☎ 01923 434000, fax 01923 434001)

JARVIS, Debra Ann (Debbie); da of Peter Alan Jarvis, of Leicester, and Lucia, *née* Gospodarek; *b* 16 Jan 1964; *Educ* St Paul's RC Secdy Sch, Wyggeston and Queen Elizabeth Sixth Form Coll, North London Poly; *m* 30 April 1993, Mark Darling, s of Michael Darling, of Ramsey, Cambs, and Diana; *Career* yachtswoman (470 class); began sailing aged 5, competed at club level from age 7, memb youth squad 1978, memb women's squad and int debut 1987; achievements incl: winner UK Women's Nat Championships 1987, winner Br Olympic Trials 1988, runner-up Palamos Olympic Regatta Spain 1989, winner Eurolymp Nat Championships 1990 and 1991, third Euro Championships Norway 1991; also competed in Olympic Games Seoul 1988 and Barcelona 1992; sales rep L'Oreal 1985–87, currently nat account exec Coca-Cola & Schweppes Beverages Ltd (joined 1987); *Recreations* sailing, renovating my old house, golf; *Style*— Ms Debbie Jarvis; ✉ c/o Royal Yachting Association, RYA House, Romsey Rd, Eastleigh, Hants SO5 4YA (☎ 01703 629962/629924)

JARVIS, Gerald Joseph; s of Maurice Jarvis (d 1956), and Sarah, *née* Brown (d 1964); *b* 4 Jan 1947; *Educ* Pembroke Coll Oxford (BA), Univ of Oxford Sch of Med (BM, BCh); *m* 1 Oct 1977, Elizabeth Honor, da of Gordon Wilson Izatt, of Earlsferry, Fife; 2 s (Thomas Edward Maurice b 11 Sept 1979, Alexander James Patric b 11 Dec 1984), 1 da (Emma Elizabeth b 25 Feb 1982); *Career* conslt obstetrician and gynaecologist St James Univ Hosp Leeds 1981–, hon lectr in med Univ of Leeds 1981–; author of various publications on obstetrics and gynaecology; examiner RCOG 1989–, convenor of Nat Course on the Treatment of Female Urinary Incontinence; FRCSEd 1975, FRCOG 1989; *Books* Female Urinary Incontinence (1990), Obstetrics and Gynaecology (1994); *Recreations* playing piano, egyptology; *Clubs* United Oxford & Cambridge Univ; *Style*— Gerald Jarvis, Esq; ✉ Beechwood House, Raby Park, Wetherby LS22 6SA (☎ 01937 582218); St James's University Hospital, Beckett Street, Leeds LS9 7TF (☎ 0113 243 3144); BUPA Hospital, Roundhay Hall, Jackson Ave, Leeds LS8 1NT (☎ 0113 269 3939)

JARVIS, John Manners; QC; s of Donald Edward Manners Jarvis, TD, of Rockbourne, Hants, and Theodora Brixie, *née* Bryant (d 1991); *b* 20 Nov 1947; *Educ* King's Coll Sch Wimbledon, Emmanuel Coll Cambridge (MA); *m* 5 May 1972, Janet Rona, da of Eric Cresswell Kitson, OBE (d 1975), of Mersham, Kent; 2 s (Christopher b 1974, Fergus b 1976); *Career* called to the Bar Lincoln's Inn 1970, in practice at Commercial Bar, recorder of the Crown Ct; chm Commercial Bar Assoc; govr King's Coll Sch Wimbledon; *Publications* Lender Liability (jtly, 1994), Banks, Liability and Risk (contrib, 2 edn); int ed Jl of Banking and Finance Law and Practice; *Recreations* tennis, sailing, horse riding, skiing, cycling, music; *Clubs* Hurlingham; *Style*— John Jarvis, Esq, QC; ✉ 3 Gray's Inn Place, Gray's Inn, London WC1R 5EA (☎ 0171 831 8441, fax 0171 831 8479)

JARVIS, Martin; s of Denys Jarvis, and Margot Jarvis; *b* 4 Aug 1941; *Educ* Whitgift Sch, RADA; *m* 1; 2 s; m 2, 23 Nov 1974, Rosalind Ayres, *qv*, da of Sam Johnson (d 1986); *Career* actor; first appearance Nat Youth Theatre 1960–62 (played Henry V Sadler's Wells 1962); dir Children's Film Unit 1993–; pres Croydon Histrionic Soc 1984–; contrib Comic Relief and Children in Need; *Theatre* incl: Manchester Library Theatre 1962–63, Poor Bitos (Duke of York's) 1963, Man and Superman (Vaudeville) 1966, The Bandwagon (Mermaid) 1970, The Rivals (USA) 1973, title role in Hamlet (Festival of Br Theatre) 1973, The Circle (Haymarket) 1976, She Stoops to Conquer (Canada and Hong Kong Arts Festivals) 1977, Caught in the Act (Garrick) 1981; NT incl: Importance of Being Earnest 1982, Victoria Station 1983, The Trojan War Will Not Take Place 1983; later theatre work incl: Woman in Mind (Vaudeville) 1986, The Perfect Party (Greenwich) 1987, Jerome in Henceforward (Vaudeville) 1989, Viktor in Exchange (Vaudeville 1990, LA 1992), Sir Andrew Aguecheek in Sir Peter Hall's revival of Twelfth Night (Playhouse) 1991, title role in Leo in Love (Nuffield Theatre and nat tour) 1992, Dennis in the revival of Ayckbourn's Just Between Ourselves (Greenwich) 1992, starred in Make and Break (LA) 1993, starred in On Approval (Playhouse) 1994, starred in Ayckbourn's Man of the Moment (LA) 1994 and Table Manners (LA Theatre Works) 1995; *Television* incl: The Forsyte Saga 1967, Nicholas Nickleby 1968, David Copperfield 1975, Rings on their Fingers 1978, Breakaway 1980, The Black Tower 1985, Chelworth 1988, Rumpole of the Bailey 1988–89, Countdown 1989–95, all voices in children's animated series Huxley Pig 1989–90, You Say Potato (LA) 1990–, all voices on animation series Fourways Farm (American series, Channel 4) 1993–95, Scarlet and Black (film series) 1993, Touch of Love (BBC) 1994, starred as Brillat Savarin (BBC) 1994; guest star: Inspector Morse (Greeks Bearing Gifts, feature length TV film) 1991, Maurice Howling in Murder Most Horrid (BBC 2) 1991, Woof (Central) 1992, Charles Longmuir in The Good Guys (LWT) 1992, Boon (Central) 1992, Casualty (BBC) 1992, Library of Romance (1993), Countdown (1993), Pebble Mill (1993), House Party 1993, Lovejoy 1994, Murder She Wrote 1995, A Touch of Frost 1995, Fantastic Mr Fox 1995, Space - Above and Beyond (USA) 1996, Walker - Texas Ranger (USA) 1996; commentaries for TV film documentaries and arts programmes; *Radio* numerous radio performances incl: Charles Dickens in The Best of Times, one-man series Jarvis' Frayn, Lord Illingworth in Wilde's A Woman of No Importance (BBC Radio) 1991; adapted and read over 60 of Richmal Crompton's William stories for radio, TV and cassette; prodr and performer Speak After the Beep (Radio 4); *Recordings* cassette recordings incl: Just William vols 1–5 (BBC), David Copperfield 1991, Jarvis's Frayn (CSA Telltapes) 1992, Tales From Shakespeare (LA) 1993, Honor Among Thieves (USA) 1993, narrator/host Concorde Playhouse 1994–95, Oliver Twist 1996, Goodbye Mr Chips 1997; *Films* incl: The Last Escape, Ike, The Bunker, Taste the Blood of Dracula, Buster, Emily's Ghost (CFU/Channel 4) 1993, Calliope 1993, Absence of War 1995, Titanic 1997; *Awards* nominated Best Actor Sony Radio Awards 1991, recipient NY Int Radio Award 1994, winner Peabody Award USA for Fourways Farm, winner Brit Talkies Award 1995; *Publications* Bright Boy (play, 1977), Just William Stories (ed, 1992); short stories for radio, articles in The Listener, Punch, Evening Standard, High Life, Fourth Column, Tatler, BBC Afternoon Shift; *Recreations* Indian food, Beethoven, Mozart, people-watching; *Clubs* BBC; *Style*— Martin Jarvis, Esq; ✉ c/o Sally Long-Innes, ICM Ltd, Oxford House, 76 Oxford Street, London W1N 0AX (☎ 0171 636 6565, fax 0171 323 0101)

JARVIS, Paul William; s of Malcolm Jarvis, of Caldicot, Gwent, and Marjorie, *née* Lofthouse; *b* 29 June 1965; *Educ* Bydales Comp Sch Marske-by-Sea Cleveland; *m* 3 Dec 1988, Wendy Jayne; 1 s (Alexander Michael b 13 June 1989), 1 da (Isabella Grace b 21 March 1993); *Career* professional cricketer; Yorkshire CCC: debut 1981, awarded county cap 1986; joined Sussex CCC 1994; England under 19 v W Indies 1982 and Aust 1983; 9 test matches: v NZ (2) 1988, v W Indies (2) 1988, v Aust (2) 1989, v India (2) 1993, v Sri Lanka 1993; 16 one day Ints: v Aust 1988, v NZ (4) 1988, v India (6) 1993, v Sri Lanka (2) 1993, v Aust (3) 1993; memb unofficial England team touring S Africa 1989/90 (subsequently banned from test cricket until winter 1992), memb England team touring India and Sri Lanka 1992/93; youngest player to represent Yorkshire aged 16; *Recreations* fishing, golf, drinking in the local pub; *Style*— Paul Jarvis, Esq; ✉ c/o Sussex County Cricket Club, County Ground, Eaton Road, Hove, E Sussex BN3 3AN (☎ 01273 732161)

JARVIS, Peter Jack; CBE (1995); *b* 1 July 1941; *Educ* Christ's Coll Cambridge (MA); *Career* various sales and mktg appts with Unilever 1964–76; Whitbread PLC: joined as sales and mktg dir Long John International 1976, gp mktg dir 1978, main bd dir 1979–, int md (responsible for all overseas ops) 1981–83, md Trading Div 1983–85, gp md 1985–90, gp chief exec 1990–97; non-exec dir: Burton Group plc, Rank Organisation plc 1995–, Barclays Bank 1995–; govr Bolton Sch; memb Brewers and Retailers' Assoc, fell Inst of Grocery Distribution; memb Ct of Assts Worshipful Co of Brewers; *Style*— Peter Jarvis, Esq, CBE; ✉ Whitbread PLC, Chiswell Street, London EC1Y 4SD (☎ 0171 606 4455)

JASKEL, Martin Stephen; s of David Jaskel (d 1956), and Fanny Jaskel (d 1981); *b* 3 June 1946; *Educ* St Marylebone GS, Univ of Manchester (BA); *m* 13 May 1976, Antone Sheila; 1 da (Felicity b 1981); *Career* gilt edged salesperson Phillips & Drew 1967–72, gilt edged exec Capel Cure Myers 1972–75, ptnr W Greenwell & Co 1981–86 (gilt edged exec 1976–81), dir Greenwell Montagu Gilt Edged 1986–88, treasy sales dir Midland Montagu 1988–90, dir of global mktg NatWest Treasury 1990–94, md of global trade and banking servs NatWest Markets 1994–; Freeman City of London 1980; memb: Stock Exchange 1972, Co of World Traders 1987; *Recreations* cricket, opera, books, travel; *Clubs* MCC, Carlton, City; *Style*— Martin Jaskel, Esq; ✉ 12 St Ann's Terrace, London NW8 6PJ (☎ 0171 722 1921); NatWest Markets, 135 Bishopsgate, London EC2M 3UR (☎ 0171 375 4906, fax 0171 375 6006, car 0468 728743)

JASON, David; OBE (1993); s of Arthur White, and Olwen, *née* Jones; *b* 2 Feb 1940; *Educ* Northside Secdy Sch; *Career* actor; first professional job with Bromley Repertory 1965; early work incl: 3 months in Crossroads, tour with Ron Moody in Peter Pan, Summer seasons with Bob Monkhouse and Dick Emery; *Theatre* incl: Under Milk Wood (Mayfair), Bob Acres in The Rivals (Sadler's Wells), No Sex Please...We're British! (Strand) 1972, Darling Mr London 1975–76, Fancourt Babberley in Charley's Aunt, Norman in The Norman Conquests (Oxford Playhouse) 1976, Lord Foppington in The Relapse (Cambridge Theatre Co), Buttons in Cinderella, Tom Bryce in The Unvarnished Truth (Middle and Far East) 1983, Look No Hans! (Strand Theatre and tour) 1985–86; *Television* incl: Do Not Adjust Your Set 1967, The Top Secret Life of Edgar Briggs (LWT) 1973–74, Mr Stabbs (Thames) 1974, Blanco in Porridge (BBC) 1975, Lucky Feller (LWT) 1975, A Sharp Intake of Breath (ATV) 1978, Granville in Open All Hours (with Ronnie Barker, several series, BBC), Del Trotter in Only Fools and Horses (several series, BBC), Skullion in Porterhouse Blue (C4) 1986, Ted Simcock in A Bit of a Do (2 series, YTV) 1988–89, Single Voices: The Chemist (monologue by Roy Clarke, BBC) 1989, George in Amongst Barbarians (screenplay, BBC) 1989, Pa Larkin in The Darling Buds of May (YTV) 1990–93, Inspector Jack Frost in A Touch of Frost (YTV) 1992–, The Bullion Boys (1993, Int Emmy for Best Drama 1994); voice of many cartoon characters incl Dangermouse and Count Duckula; *Films* Under Milk Wood, Royal Flash 1974, The Odd Job 1978, Only Fools and Horses (BBC), Toad in The Wind in the Willows; *Awards* Radio Times Funniest Actor, Variety Club Personality of the Year, Sony Radio Award, Water Rats Personality of the Year, TV Times Actor of the Year, TV Times Funniest Actor, BAFTA Award for Best Actor 1988, BAFTA Award for Best Light Entertainment Performer 1990, Nat Television Awards Special Recognition Award for Lifetime Achievement in Television, Favourite Situation Comedy Performer at Aunties (BBC); *Recreations* skin diving, gliding, restoration of old machines, work; *Style*— David Jason, Esq, OBE; ✉ The Richard Stone Partnership, 25 Whitehall, London SW1A 2BS (☎ 0171 839 6421, fax 0171 839 5002)

JASON, Gillian Brett; da of Anthony Romney Francis Bosworth (d 1963), of London, and Joan Lena, *née* Brett; *b* 30 June 1941; *Educ* Dominican Convent Staffs, Ely House Sch for Girls Wolverhampton, Royal Ballet Sch London, London Opera Centre; *m* 21 March 1961, Neville Jason; 1 s (Alexander b 1970), 1 da (Elinor b 1967); *Career* former singer and ballerina, currently gallery director; work incl: Cobweb in A Midsummer Night's Dream (Old Vic) 1957, ENO Ballet 1959, London's Festival Ballet 1959–60, Schubert and Schumann lieder recital (Wigmore Hall) 1962, title role in Cinderella (Richmond Theatre) 1964, Moses and Aaron (Royal Opera House) 1965, Karl Ebert Master Class (BBC TV) 1967, alto solos and arias in St John Passion and St Matthew Passion (Bad) for Southern Opera, Handel Opera Soc and concert in Queen Elizabeth Hall, concert of Mahler Symphony No 2 and three songs 1969; curator Campbell and Franks (Fine Arts) London 1973–79, private dealer 1980–, md Gillian Jason Gallery 1981–; dir: Wolseley Fine Arts plc 1990–, Jason & Rhodes 1994–; *Awards* Br Ballet Orgn award (for Royal Ballet Sch) 1957, Vaughan-Williams Tst bursary (for London Opera Centre) 1966, Countess of Munster Tst award (for further singing studies) 1966, finalist Kathleen Ferrier Meml scholarship (RAM) 1966; *Recreations* music, yoga, theatre, tennis, roadrunning; *Style*— Mrs Gillian Jason; ✉ 42 Inverness St, London NW1 7HB (☎ 0171 267 4835, fax 0171 267 4835)

JASPAN, Andrew; s of Mervyn Aubrey Jaspan (d 1974), and Helen, *née* Wright; *b* 20 April 1953; *Educ* Beverley GS, Marlborough, Univ of Manchester (BA); *Career* founding ed New Manchester Review 1975–77; sub ed: Daily Telegraph 1978–80, Daily Mirror 1981; reporter Journalists in Europe (Paris) 1982, sub ed and reporter The Times 1983–85, asst news ed The Sunday Times 1985–88; ed: The Sunday Times Scotland 1988, Scotland on Sunday 1989–94, The Scotsman 1994–95, The Observer 1995–96; publisher and md The Big Issue 1996–; *Recreations* reading, squash, psephology; *Clubs* Glasgow Art; *Style*— Andrew Jaspan, Esq

JASPER, Robin Leslie Darlow; CMG (1963); s of Thomas Darlow Jasper (d 1969), of Beckenham, Kent, and Clara Ada Maud, *née* Emberley (d 1962); *b* 22 Feb 1914; *Educ* Dulwich, Clare Coll Cambridge (open scholar, BA); *m* 1, 1940 (m dis 1965), Jean, da of late Brig-Gen J K Cochrane, CMG; 1 da; m 2, 1966, Diana Speed, da of Maj G West; 2 step da; *Career* Wing Cdr RAFVR 1940–45; graduate apprentice Hotels Dept LNER 1936–39, bursar Dominion Students Hall Tst (London House) 1939–40; HM Dip Serv: princ India Office (later FCO) 1945, concerned with resettlement of the Sec of State's services in India 1947–48, Br dep high cmmr Lahore Pakistan 1949–52, advsr London Conferences on Central African Fedn 1952–53, cnsllr HM Embassy Lisbon 1953–55, visited Portuguese Africa 1954, Cwlth Rels Office 1955–60 (head of Info Policy Dept 1958–60); attached to UK delgn to the UN 1955 and 1956, Br dep high cmmr Ibadan Nigeria 1960–64, cnsllr Cwlth Office 1965–67, consul-gen Naples 1967–71, ret 1972; *Recreations* real tennis, rugby fives, wind music, 17th century church sculpture, claret, jazz; *Clubs* MCC, Jesters; *Style*— Robin Jasper, CMG; ✉ Ashburnham Lodge, 62 London Road, St Leonards on Sea, East Sussex TN37 6AS (☎ 01424 438575)

JAUNCEY OF TULLICHETTLE, Baron (Life Peer UK 1988), of Comrie in the District of Perth and Kinross; Charles Eliot Jauncey; PC (1988); o s of Capt John Henry Jauncey, of Tullichettle, DSO, RN (d 1958), and Muriel Charlie, eldest da of Adm Sir Charles Dundas of Dundas, KCMG, 28 Chief of Dundas; *b* 8 May 1925; *Educ* Radley, Ch Ch Oxford (MA, hon student 1990), Univ of Glasgow (LLB); *m* 1, 1948 (m dis 1969), Jean, o da of late Adm Sir Angus Edward Malise Bontine Cunninghame Graham, KBE, CB, of Ardoch, Cardross, Dunbartonshire; 2 s (Hon James Malise Dundas b 1949, Hon Simon Helias b 1953), 1 da (Hon Arabella Bridget Rachel b 1965); m 2, 1973 (m dis 1977), Elizabeth, da of Capt R H V Sivewright, DSC, RN, and wid of Maj John Ballingal, MC; m 3, 1977, (Sarah) Camilla, da of late Lt-Col Charles Frederick Cathcart, DSO (ggs of 2 Earl Cathcart); 1 da (Hon Cressida Jane b 1981); *Career* served WWII Sub Lt RNVR; advocate 1949; Kintyre Pursuivant of Arms 1955–71; QC 1963; Sheriff Principal Fife and Kinross 1971–74, judge Cts of Appeal Jersey and Guernsey 1972–79, senator Coll of Justice Scotland 1979–88, Lord of Appeal in Ordinary 1988–96, Hon Master of Bench of Middle Temple 1988; memb Historic Bldgs Cncl for Scotland 1972–92; memb Royal Co Archers (Queen's Bodyguard for Scotland); *Recreations* shooting, fishing, genealogy, bicycling; *Clubs* Royal (Perth); *Style*— The Rt Hon Lord Jauncey of Tullichettle, PC; ✉ Tullichettle, Comrie, Perthshire (☎ 01764 70349); House of Lords, London SW1A 0PW

JAVER, Monique Alicia; da of Gerald Milton Javer, and Anne Heather, *née* Clark; *b* 22 July 1967; *Educ* St Matthew's Episcopal Sch, Crocker Sch Hillsborough Calif, San Diego Univ; *Career* tennis player; professional debut 1988; represented GB: debut Maureen Connolly Brinker Cup under 21 1988, Wightman Cup 1988, Federation Cup Atlanta 1990, Euro Cup (finalist) 1990, Federation Cup Nottingham 1991, European Cup Nantes (finalist) 1991, Barcelona Olympics 1992; achievements incl: winner Jr Orange Bowl under 21 Amateur Championships Calif 1984 and 1985, winner Singapore Open 1988 (semi-finalist 1989), semi-finalist Br Nationals 1989, semi-finalist Virginia-Slims Arizona 1990; competed at various Grand Slam events; number one ranked collegiate player USA 1986 and 1987, number one ranked player GB 1990; *Recreations* ballet, figure skating, theatre, animals; *Style*— Miss Monique Javer; ✉ 60 Knightwood Lane, Hillsborough, Calif 94010, USA (☎ 415 344 7562, fax 415 692 4675)

JAWARA, Hon Sir Dawda Kairaba; kt (1966), Hon GCMG (1974); *b* 16 May 1924; *Educ* Methodist Boys' HS Banjul, Achimota Coll (Vet Sch) Ghana, Univ of Glasgow;

Career princ vet offr for The Gambia Govt 1957–60 (vet offr 1954–57); ldr Proctectorate People's Party (later People's Progressive Party) The Gambia 1960, elected memb House of Representatives 1960, min of Educn 1960–61, premier 1962–63, PM 1963–70, pres The Republic of The Gambia 1970–94; chm: CILSS Heads of State Conf, Authy of Heads of State and Govt of Econ Community of W African States (ECOWAS) 1988–90; Grand Cross Order of Lebanon 1966, Nat Order of Republic of Senegal 1967, Order of Propitious Clouds of China (Taiwan) 1968, Nat Order of Republic of Guinea 1973, Grand Offr Order of Islamic Republic of Mauritania 1967, Grand Cordon of Most Venerable Order of Knighthood Pioneers of Republic of Liberia 1968, Grand Commander Nat Order of Federal Republic of Nigeria 1970, Grand Master Order of the Republic of The Gambia 1972, Commander of Golden Ark (Netherlands) 1979, Pertinger Gold medal Pertinger-Collegium Munich 1979, Agricola medal 1980; Hon LLD Ife Univ Nigeria 1978, Hon Dr Sci and Vet Med Colorado State Univ 1986, Hon LLD Univ of Glasgow 1990; MRCS 1953; FRCVS 1988, fell W African Coll of Physicians 1988; *Books* Sir Dawda Speaks (1971), Sunrise in the Sahel (forthcoming); *Recreations* golf, gardening, sailing; *Style*— Hon Sir Dawda Jawara, GCMG

JAY, Sir Antony Rupert; kt (1988), CVO (1993); s of Ernest Jay (d 1957), of London, and Catherine Mary, *née* Hay (d 1981); *b* 20 April 1930; *Educ* St Paul's (scholar), Magdalene Coll Cambridge (Major scholar, MA); *m* 15 June 1957, Rosemary Jill, da of Leslie Watkins, of Stratford upon Avon; 2 s (Michael b 1959, David b 1972), 2 da (Ros b 1961, Kate b 1964); *Career* Nat Serv Royal Signals 1952–54 (2 Lt 1953), Lt TA 1954; BBC 1955–64: ed Tonight 1962–63, head talks features 1963–64; freelance writer and prodr 1964–; ed A Prime Minister on Prime Ministers 1977; writer: Royal Family (1969), Yes Minister (3 series with Jonathan Lynn, 1980–82), Yes Prime Minister (2 series, 1985 and 1987) Elizabeth R (1992); BAFTA Writers' Award 1988; chm Video Arts Ltd 1972–89; memb Annan Ctee on Future of Broadcasting 1974–77; Hon MA Sheffield 1987, Hon DBA Int Mgmnt Centre Buckingham 1988; FRSA, CIMgt 1991; *Books* Management and Machiavelli (1967), To England with Love (with David Frost, 1967), Effective Presentation (1970), Corporation Man (1972), The Complete Yes Minister (with Jonathan Lynn, 1984), Yes Prime Minister (1986, vol II 1987), Elizabeth R (1992), The Oxford Dictionary of Political Quotations (ed, 1996); *Style*— Sir Antony Jay, CVO; ✉ c/o Video Arts Ltd, Dumbarton House, 68 Oxford St, London W1N 9LA (☎ 0171 637 7288)

JAY, Prof Barrie Samuel; s of Maurice Bernard Jay (d 1959), of London, and Julia, *née* Sterling (d 1965); *b* 7 May 1929; *Educ* Perse Sch Cambridge, Gonville and Caius Coll Cambridge (MB BChir, MA, MD); *m* 19 Jan 1954, Marcelle Ruby, da of Alan Byre (d 1968), of Paris; 2 s (Robert b 1959, Stephen b 1961); *Career* conslt ophthalmic surgn London Hosp 1965–79, conslt surgn Moorfields Eye Hosp 1969–92; dean Inst of Ophthalmology London 1980–85, conslt advsr in ophthalmology DHSS 1982–88, prof of clinical ophthalmology Univ of London 1985–92 (emeritus 1992); pres Faculty of Ophthalmologists 1986–88; vice pres: Coll of Ophthalmologists 1988–92, Royal Philatelic Soc 1996–; Liveryman: Worshipful Soc of Apothecaries (memb Ct 1985–, Master 1995–96), Worshipful Co of Barbers; hon sec: Royal Philatelic Soc 1992–, Acad of Med Royal Colls 1994–, Specialist Trg Authy of Med Royal Colls 1996–; FRCS 1962, FRPSL 1986, FCOphth 1988, Hon FRCOphth 1994, Hon FCPCH 1996; *Books* System of Ophthalmology vol XI (jtly 1969), Postal History of Great Britain and Ireland (jtly 1981), British County Catalogue of Postal History, vols 1–5 (jtly 1978–96); *Recreations* postal history, gardening; *Style*— Prof Barrie Jay; ✉ 10 Beltane Drive, London SW19 5JR (☎ 0181 947 1771, fax 0181 946 0474)

JAY, John Philip Bromberg; s of Alec Jay (d 1993), and (Helena) June Jay; *b* 1 April 1957; *Educ* UCS, Magdalen Coll Oxford (BA); *m* 1, 1987 (m dis 1992), Susy, da of Donald Streeter; m 2, 19 Oct 1992, Judi Bevan; *Career* reporter Western Mail 1979–81; city reporter: Thomson Regional Newspapers 1981–83, Sunday Telegraph 1984–86; city ed Sunday Times 1986 (dep business ed 1988), city & business ed Sunday Telegraph 1989–95, managing ed business news and city Sunday Times 1995–; *Recreations* walking, cinema, theatre; *Style*— John Jay, Esq; ✉ The Sunday Times, 1 Pennington Street, London E1 9XW (☎ 0171 782 5000)

JAY, Marion; *see:* Spalding, Ruth Jeanie Lucile

JAY, Hon Martin; yr s of Baron Jay, PC (Life Peer, d 1996), and his 1 w, Margaret Christian, *née* Garnett; *Educ* Winchester, New Coll Oxford (BA); *m* 1969, Sandra, *née* Williams; 1 s (Adam b 1976), 2 da (Claudia b 1971, Tabitha b 1972); *Career* industrialist; md and chief exec Vosper Thornycroft Holdings PLC 1989–; *Style*— The Hon Martin Jay; ✉ Bishop's Court, Bishop's Sutton, Alresford, Hants; Vosper Thornycroft Holdings PLC, Victoria Road, Woolston, Southampton SO9 5GR (☎ 01703 445144, fax 01703 421539)

JAY, HE Sir Michael Hastings; KCMG (1997, CMG 1993); s of Capt Alan David Hastings Jay, DSO, DSC, RN (d 1978), and Felicity, *née* Vickery; *b* 19 June 1946; *Educ* Winchester Coll, Magdalen Coll Oxford, SOAS Univ of London; *m* 1995, Sylvia, *née* Mylroie; *Career* Miny of Overseas Devpt 1969–73, UK delgn to IMF and World Bank Washington 1973–75, Miny of Overseas Devpt 1975–78, first sec Br High Cmmn New Delhi 1978–81, FCO London 1981–85, cnsllr Cabinet Office 1985–87, cnsllr Br Embassy Paris 1987–90, asst under sec for EC affrs FCO 1990–94, dep under sec for EU and economic affrs 1994–96, Br ambass Paris 1996–; sr assoc memb St Antony's Coll Oxford 1996; *Recreations* cinema, tennis, poetry; *Style*— HE Sir Michael Jay, KCMG; ✉ c/o Foreign & Commonwealth Office (Paris), King Charles Street, London SW1A 2AA

JAY, Hon Peter; er s of Baron Jay, PC (Life Peer, d 1996), and his 1 w, Margaret Christian, *née* Garnett; *b* 7 Feb 1937; *Educ* Winchester, ChCh Oxford (MA); *m* 1, 1961 (m dis 1986), Hon Margaret Ann Callaghan (now Baroness Jay of Paddington, *qv*, Life Peer), er da of Baron Callaghan of Cardiff, KG, PC, *qv*, Life Peer; 1 s (Hon Patrick James Peter b 1971), 2 da (Hon Tamsin Margaret b 1965, Hon Alice Katharine b 1968); m 2, Emma Bettina, da of Peter Kai Thornton; 3 s (Thomas Hastings b 1987, Samuel Arthur Maxwell b 1988, James William Hagen Thornton b 1992); issue by Jane Tustian (Nicholas James Tustian b 1980); *Career* Midshipman and Sub Lt RNVR 1956–57; former pres Oxford Union; HM Treasy: asst princ 1961–64, private sec to Jt Perm Sec 1964, princ 1964–67; economics ed The Times 1967–77, assoc ed Times Business News 1969–77, presenter Weekend World (London Weekend Television) 1972–77, ambass to USA 1977–79, conslt Economist Group 1979–81, dir Economist Intelligence Unit 1979–83, chm and chief exec TV-am plc 1980–83, chm Nat Cncl for Voluntary Orgns 1981–86, presenter A Week in Politics (Channel Four) 1983–86, ed Banking World 1983–86, chief of staff to Robert Maxwell 1986–89, economics ed BBC 1990–; dir New Nat Theatre Washington DC 1979–81; chm United Way (UK) Ltd 1982–83 and various United Way subsids; memb Cncl Cinema and TV Benevolent Fund 1982–83, govr Ditchley Fndn 1982–; holder of various broadcasting honours and TV awards; visiting scholar Brookings Inst 1979–80, Wincott Meml lectr 1975, Copland Meml lectr 1980; *Clubs* Garrick; *Style*— The Hon Peter Jay; ✉ Hensington Farmhouse, Woodstock, Oxon OX20 1LH (☎ 01993 811222, fax 01993 812861)

JAY OF PADDINGTON, Baroness (Life Peer UK 1992), of Paddington in the City of Westminster; Margaret Ann Adler; *née* Callaghan; er da of Baron Callaghan of Cardiff, KG, PC (Life Peer), *qv*; *b* 18 Nov 1939; *Educ* Blackheath HS, Somerville Coll Oxford (BA); *m* 1, 1961 (m dis 1986), as his 1 w, Hon Peter Jay, *qv*; 1 s (Hon Patrick James Peter b 1971), 2 da (Hon Tamsin Margaret (Hon Mrs Raikes) b 1965, Hon Alice Katharine b 1968); m 2, 26 March 1994, Prof Michael William Adler, *qv*; *Career* current and further educn depts BBC TV 1965–67, political res asst Senator John Tunney (Dem, Calif) 1969–70, freelance work for ABC TV and Nat Public Radio Washington DC 1977–82, memb Paddington and N Kensington DHA 1984–, reporter Panorama and This Week BBC TV 1981–88, reporter and prodr Thames TV 1986–88, fndr dir Nat Aids Trust; oppn princ spokesperson on health House of Lords 1994–; non-exec dir: Carlton Television 1996–, Scottish Power 1996–; non-exec memb Kensington Chelsea Westminster Health Authy 1996–; govr South Bank Univ 1995–; memb: Advsy Ctee Meteorological Office 1995–, Cncl Overseas Devpt Inst 1994–; tstee Int Crisis Gp 1995–; chm Nat Assoc of League of Hosp Friends 1994–; patron: Help the Aged, REACTION Tst; *Books* Battered - The Story of Child Abuse (co-author 1986); *Style*— The Rt Hon Lady Jay of Paddington; ✉ 44 Blomfield Road, London W9 2PF; Elm Bank, Glandore, Co Cork, Republic of Ireland

JAYACHANDRA, Dr Chickaballapur Reddiyappa; s of Chickaballapur Reddiyappa (d 1931), and Lakshmamma, *née* Kempaiah (d 1979); *b* 21 Nov 1928; *Educ* in India (MB BS); *m* 6 Sept 1961, Sujaya, da of Nanjunda Gowda (d 1977); *Career* paediatric registrar Walton Hosp and Children's Hosp Liverpool 1961–67, conslt paediatrician NW RHA 1968–93, hon conslt paediatrician for screaming baby servs Royal Oldham Hosp 1993–; memb Oldham Health Authy 1977–87; memb BPA 1969; life memb World Inst of Acheivement (USA) 1990, life fell American Biographical Inst 1991, FRCPE 1986; *Books* Child Management - Five Universal Basic Principles (1988), Screaming Babies - Certainly Curable (1992), author of several articles constant crying and sleep disturbances of infants and toddlers; *Recreations* gardening, tennis, badminton; *Style*— Dr C R Jayachandra; ✉ The Royal Oldham Hospital, Oldham, Lancs (☎ 0161 624 0420)

JAYAWANT, Prof Bhalchandra Vinayak; s of (Rao Saheb) Vinayak Laxman Jayawant (d 1971), of Nagpur, India, and Indira Jayawant (d 1948); *b* 22 April 1930; *Educ* Univ of Bombay (BE), Univ of Bristol (PhD), Univ of Sussex (DSc); *m* 3 Sept 1960, (Elizabeth) Monica, da of George William Bowdler (d 1985); 1 s (Richard Anthony b 4 April 1962), 1 da (Frances Rachael b 12 Aug 1964); *Career* jr engr Metropolitan Vickers Manchester 1956–60, lectr in electrical engrg Queen's Univ Belfast 1960–65; Sch of Engrg Univ of Sussex: reader in electrical engrg 1965–72, prof of electrical engrg 1972–, dean 1985–90; IEE: chm Sussex Centre, chm Computing and Control Div, memb Cncl; Sir Harold Hartley medal 1988; FIEE, FInstMC, FRSA; *Books* Induction Machines (1968), Electromagnetic Suspension and Levitation Techniques; *Recreations* walking on the Downs, French wines; *Style*— Prof Bhalchandra Jayawant; ✉ School of Engineering and Applied Sciences, University of Sussex, Falmer, Brighton BN1 9QT (☎ 01273 606755, fax 01273 678399)

JAYSON, Prof Malcolm I V; *Educ* Middx Hosp Sch, Univ of London (MB BS), Univ of Bristol (MD), London (FRCP); *m* 1 July 1962, Judith; 2 s (Gordon b 1963, Robert b 1966); *Career* lectr and sr lectr in med (rheumatology) Univ of Bristol and Royal Nat Hosp for Rheumatic Diseases Bath 1967–77, prof of rheumatology and dir of Rheumatism Res Laboratories Univ of Manchester 1977–, dir Manchester and Salford Back Pain Centre 1993–; pres: Int Soc for Study of the Lumbar Spine, Section of Rheumatology and Rehabilitation RSM; sec gen Int Back Pain Soc; *Books* Total Hip Replacement (1971), Stills Disease: Juvenile Chronic Polyarthritis (1976), Collagen In Health and Disease (1982), Locomotor Disability In General Practice (1983), Lumbar Spine and Back Pain (1992), Back Pain - The Facts (1992), Rheumatism and Arthritis (1991); *Recreations* antiques, music, trout fishing; *Style*— Prof Malcolm I V Jayson; ✉ The Gate House, 8 Lancaster Road, Didsbury, Manchester M20 2TY (☎ 0161 445 1729, fax 0161 448 8195); Rheumatic Diseases Centre, Hope Hospital, Eccles Old Road, Salford M6 8HD (☎ 0161 787 4369, fax 0161 787 4687)

JAYSTON, Michael (*né* Michael James); s of Vincent Aubrey James (d 1937), of Nottingham, and Edna Myfanwy, *née* Llewelyn (d 1950); *b* 29 Oct 1935; *Educ* Becket GS Nottingham, Guildhall Sch of Music and Drama (scholar, Restoration Prize, Microphone Prize, Comedy Prize, Shakespeare Prize, Poetry Prize); *m* 1, 1965 (m dis 1970), Lynn, *née* Farleigh; m 2, 1971 (m dis 1977), Heather, *née* Sneddon; 2 s (Tom Robert b 1971, Ben Patrick b 1973); m 3, 1978, Elizabeth Ann, *née* Smithson; 1 s (Richard John b 1981), 1 da (Katharine Sarah b 1985); *Career* actor; fell Guildhall Sch of Music and Drama 1981; author of chapter in County Champions (cricket book), articles for The Cricketer and Wisden's Monthly; *Theatre* Salisbury Playhouse: Macduff in Macbeth 1962, Henry II in Becket 1962; Bristol Old Vic: Beyond The Fringe 1963, title role in All In Good Time 1963, title role in Scent of Flowers 1963; RSC: Laertes in Hamlet 1965, Storyteller in Thwarting of Baron Bolligrew 1965, Exeter in Henry V 1965, Lennie in The Homecoming (Broadway) 1966, Oswald in Ghosts (Aldwych) 1967, Reader in Hollow Crown 1967, Bertram in Much Ado About Nothing 1968, Young Fashion in Relapse 1968, Custer in Indians 1969; Old Vic: Appleby in Eden End 1974, Dysart in Equus (also Albery) 1976–77; other credits incl: Elyot in Private Lives (Duchess) 1980–81, Captain von Trappe in The Sound of Music (Apollo) 1981–82, Mirabell in Way of the World (Haymarket) 1984, Rev in Woman In Mind (Vaudeville) 1986, Father Jack in Dancing At Lughnasa (Garrick) 1992, Ratty in Wind in the Willows (RNT) 1995; *Television* Thames: Dowling in The Power Game 1969, title role in Charles Dickens 1970; BBC: Wilfred Owen (solo performance) 1970, Sassoon in Mad Jack 1970, title role in Beethoven 1970, Rochester in Jane Eyre 1972, Royce in Rolls and Royce 1973; YTV: Neville in A Bit of a Do 1989 and 1990, Bristow in Darling Buds of May; other credits incl: Seddon in The Ladykillers (Granada) 1981, Outside Edge (Carlton) 1995; *Radio* BBC: Chekhov Short Stories 1969, Camus Stories 1970, Alpha Beta 1972; *Audio* Winston Churchills History of the 2nd World War (CD, reading); *Films* Ireton in Cromwell 1969, Nicholas in Nicholas and Alexandra 1970, Teddy in The Homecoming 1971, Hardy in Bequest to the Nation 1972; *Recreations* playing cricket, chess, darts; *Clubs* MCC, Lord's Taverners', Gelding Colliery CC (vice pres), Rottingdean CC (pres), Cricketers', Cricket Soc, Sussex CC; *Style*— Michael Jayston, Esq; ✉ c/o Michael Whitehall Ltd, 125 Gloucester Road, London SW7 4TE (☎ 0171 244 8466, fax 0171 244 9060)

JEAN, Vadim; s of Claude Jean, of Sonoma, N California, and Mary, *née* Gadd; *b* 9 Dec 1963; *Educ* Bristol GS, Univ of Warwick (BA); *Career* director, producer and writer; runner on Mike Figgis' film Stormy Monday 1987, fndr prodr Jean-Hicks Assoc (corp and non-bdcast video prodn co) 1988; memb BECTU; *Video* dir Elton John's True Love video 1993; *Commercials* as dir incl: Stone's Bitter, Mercury One-2-One, Blockbuster, The Observer; *Films* Leon the Pig Farmer (co-dir/co-prodr) 1992, Beyond Bedlam (dir) 1993, The Line (screenplay) 1993, Clockwork Mice (dir) 1995; *Awards* for Leon the Pig Farmer incl: Chaplin Award for Best First Feature Film Edinburgh Festival 1992, Int Critics' Prize Venice Film Festival 1992; others incl: David Harlech democracy prize for documentary Isle of Gorf (Channel Four) 1987, Most Promising Newcomer Award Evening Standard Awards 1994, winner Best Film Giffoni Int Children's Film Festival 1995; *Recreations* hockey, movie watching; *Clubs* Tulse Hill Hockey, Thames Barge Sailing, Triumph Motorcycle Owners; *Style*— Vadim Jean, Esq; ✉ c/o Gavin Knight, Peters Fraser & Dunlop Ltd, 503 The Chambers, Chelsea Harbour, Lots Road, London SW10 0XF (☎ 0171 352 4446, fax 0171 352 7356)

JEANS, Michael Henry Vickery; s of Henry Tendron Wilson Jeans, of Walton-on-Thames, Surrey, and Joan Kathleen, *née* Vickery; *b* 14 March 1943; *Educ* St Edward's Sch Oxford, Univ of Bristol (BA); *m* 1, 27 June 1970 (m dis 1981), Iris Carla, da of Franco Dell'Acqua, of Milan, Italy; m 2, 12 Jan 1987, Paula Wendy, da of David Arthur Spraggs, of Thorpe Bay, Essex; 1 s (James b 25 Aug 1987), 1 da (Rebecca (twin) b 25 Aug 1987); *Career* CA; trainee accountant Peat Marwick McLintock (formerly Peat Marwick Mitchell) 1964–67, asst accountant Blue Circle Group 1967–70; KPMG: conslt

1970–81, ptnr 1981–94, special advsr 1994–; non-exec dir Ross Group plc 1995–; independent business advsr The Planning Inspectorate 1992–; chm of govrs Haberdashers' Aske's Sch Elstree, memb St Matthew's Bayswater PCC; Freeman City of London 1965; first Master Guild of Mgmnt Conslts; Liveryman: Worshipful Co of Haberdashers 1965 (memb Ct of Assts 1985), Worshipful Co of CAs 1991; MBA (hc) Univ of Cranfield 1996; FCA 1967, FIMC 1970 (pres 1990–91), FCMA 1971 (memb Cncl 1994–), MMS 1984; *Recreations* tennis, opera, theatre, Italy; *Clubs* RAC, Kingston Rowing, Mensa, Soc of London Ragamuffins; *Style—* M H V Jeans, Esq; ✉ 36 Bark Place, Bayswater, London W2 4AT (☎ 0171 229 7303, fax 0171 221 5346); Via Lanza 56/2, Celle Ligure, 17015 Savona, Italy (☎ 00 39 19 993393); KPMG, 8 Salisbury Square, Blackfriars, London EC4Y 8BB (☎ 0171 311 8799, fax 0171 311 8885, telex 8811541 PMMLON G)

JEANS, Royston (Roy); s of Ronald Henry Jeans, of Bordon, Hants, and Phyllis Margaret, *née* Kent; *b* 22 Sept 1956; *Educ* Heath End Sch, Farnham VI Form Coll, Univ of Sheffield (BA), Univ of Southern Calif (MA); *m* 15 Oct 1983, Amelia, da of Ubaldo Marini (d 1975); 1 da (b 1993), 1 s (b 1996); *Career* teaching asst Univ of Southern Calif 1979–81, classified rep Farnham Herald 1982–83; advtg exec: Regional Newpaper Advertising Bureau (RNAB) 1983–86, Advertising Media Representation Agency (AMRA) 1986–87; Cordiant plc (formerly Saatchi & Saatchi Co plc): regnl media mangr Saatchi & Saatchi Advertising 1987–88, regnl media dir Zenith Media 1988–90, md Zenith Outdoor 1989–90, TV buying dir Zenith Media 1990–91, exec dir of press Zenith Media 1991–94, gen mangr Zenith Media 1994–95; md AMRA 1995–; memb Editorial Bd Headlines magazine 1989–, chm Regnl Press Club 1995–; winner Media Mind (jtly) 1991; MIPA 1991, MInstD 1995; *Books* News from a Square World (with Alan Kamin, Unwin Paperbacks, 1986); *Recreations* travel, cinema, literature, modern art; *Style—* Roy Jeans, Esq

JEAPES, Maj Gen Anthony Showan; CB (1987), OBE (1977), MC (1959); s of Stanley Arthur Bernard (d 1971), and Dorothy Irene, *née* Showan (d 1979); *b* 6 March 1935; *Educ* Raynes Park GS, RMA Sandhurst, Staff Coll Camberley, NDC Latimer; *m* 1959, Jennifer Clare, da of Lt-Col O G W White, DSO, OBE (d 1975); 1 s (Benjamin Patrick b 1965), 1 da (Antonia Clare b 1968); *Career* enlisted 1953, cmmnd Dorset Regt 1955, joined 22 Special Air Serv Regt Malaya 1958; serv: Oman and Trucial States, India, Kenya, USA, Malaysia; DS Army Staff Coll 1972–74, CO 22 SAS Regt 1974–77, BMAT Bangladesh 1977–79, dep cmdt Sch of Inf 1979–81, cmd 5 Airborne Bde 1982–85, cmd LF NI 1985–87, GOC SW Dist 1987–90 (ret); vice chm Romanian Orphanage Tst 1991–, memb Lord Chllr's Panel of Ind Inspectors 1991–; *Books* SAS - Operation Oman (1981), SAS - Secret War (1996); *Recreations* offshore sailing, country pursuits; *Clubs* Army and Navy; *Style—* Maj Gen Anthony Jeapes, CB, OBE, MC; ✉ c/o National Westminster Bank, 80 Market Place, Warminster, Wilts

JEBB, Lionel Richard; s of Richard Lewthwaite Jebb (d 1961), of Ellesmere, and Marjorie Joy, *née* Jacobs; *b* 21 Dec 1934; *Educ* Shrewsbury, Merton Coll Oxford (MA); *m* 28 May 1960, Corinna Margaret, da of late Charles Peter Elmhirst Hawkesworth, of Boroughbridge, N Yorks; 2 s (Richard b 1961, Andrew b 1966), 1 da (Sophie b 1963); *Career* farmer and landowner; cncllr Shropshire CC 1970–81; chm: Shropshire Conservation Devpt Tst 1981–88, Shropshire Ctee of COSIRA 1982–91, Shropshire Branch CLA 1985–88, Shropshire Rural Devpt Forum 1985–96; lay chm Ellesmere Deanery Synod 1970–74 and 1980–85, vice chm Walford Coll of Agric 1981–88, chm Adcote Sch Shrewsbury 1989–; memb: Cncl CLA 1975–88, Rural Voice 1981–88, Shropshire Regnl Bd Prince's Youth Business Tst 1989–92, Shropshire Trg and Enterprise Cncl 1990–96; High Sheriff of Shropshire 1991; *Recreations* conservation, shooting; *Clubs* Royal Overseas League; *Style—* L R Jebb, Esq; ✉ The Lyth, Ellesmere, Shropshire SY12 0HR

JEBB, Dom (Anthony) Philip; s of Reginald Douglas Jebb, MC (d 1977), of King's Land, Shipley, Horsham, Sussex, and Eleanor Philippa (d 1979), da of Hilaire Belloc; *b* 14 Aug 1932; *Educ* Downside, Christ's Coll Cambridge (MA); *Career* clothed as a monk of Downside 1950, ordained priest 1956, curate Midsomer Norton 1960–62, headmaster Downside Sch 1980–91 (teacher 1960–, housemaster 1962–75, dep headmaster 1975–80), prior Monastic Community of Downside 1991–; archivist and annalist English Benedictine Congregation 1972–; tstee Somerset Archaeological and Natural History Soc 1989– (pres 1993–94); memb: Cncl Somerset Records Soc 1975–, Univ of Bath 1983–87, Ctee area 7 Secdy Heads Assoc 1984–87, HMC, SHA 1980–91; Chaplain Magistral Obedience Br Assoc SMOM 1978–; chm: EBC Theol Cmmn 1979–82 (memb 1969–82), SW Div HMC 1988; del to Gen Chapter EBC 1980–; vice pres SW Amateur Fencing Assoc, princ speaker AGM of WI in The Albert Hall 1988; *Books* Missale de Lesnes (ed, 1964), Religious Education (ed, 1968), Widowed (1973), Consider Your Call (contrib, 1978), A Touch of God (contrib, 1982), By Death Parted (ed 1986); *Recreations* fencing, archaeology, cosmology, canoeing; *Clubs* Stratton-on-the-Fosse Cricket (vice pres); *Style—* Dom Philip Jebb; ✉ Downside Abbey, Stratton-on-the-Fosse, Bath BA3 4RH (☎ 01761 232295)

JEENS, Robert Charles Hubert; s of John Rolfe Hinton Jeens (d 1982), and Mary Margaret, *née* Hubert; *b* 16 Dec 1953; *Educ* Marlborough, Pembroke Coll Cambridge (MA); *m* 8 July 1978, Gillian Frances, da of (David) Gurney Arnold Thomas; 3 s (Richard b 6 Oct 1980, Henry b 2 May 1982, Edward b 15 Feb 1985); *Career* with Touche Ross & Co 1975–87 (ptnr 1984–87); Kleinwort Benson: fin dir Kleinwort Benson Securities Ltd 1987–88, fin dir Kleinwort Benson Ltd 1989–94, fin dir Kleinwort Benson Group plc 1992–96; fin dir Woolwich Building Society 1996–; FCA 1978; *Recreations* family life, skiing, wine, bridge, philately; *Style—* Robert Jeens, Esq; ✉ Woolwich Building Society, Corporate Headquarters, Watling Street, Bexleyheath, Kent DA6 7RR (☎ 0181 298 5000)

JEEVES, Prof Malcolm Alexander; CBE (1992); s of Alexander Frederic Thomas Jeeves (d 1977), and Helena May, *née* Hammond (d 1975); *b* 16 Nov 1926; *Educ* Stamford Sch, St John's Coll Cambridge (MA, PhD), Harvard Univ; *m* 7 April 1955, Ruth Elisabeth, da of Oscar Cecil Hartridge (d 1983); 2 da (Sarah b 1958, Joanna b 1961); *Career* Army 1945–48, cmmnd Royal Lincs Regt, served 1 Bn Sherwood Foresters BAOR; lectr Dept of Psychology Univ of Leeds 1956–59, fndn prof and head of Dept of Psychology Univ of Adelaide S Aust 1959–69 (dean Faculty of Arts 1963–64); Univ of St Andrews: fndn prof of psychology 1969–93, vice princ 1981–85, hon research prof 1993–; ed in chief Neuropsychologia 1990–93; pres: Int Neuropsychological Symposium 1985–91, Psychology Section Br Assoc for the Advancement of Sci 1988–89; memb: Cncl Sci and Engrg Res Cncl 1985–89, Neuroscience and Mental Health Bd MRC 1985–89, Manpower Sub-ctee ABRC 1990–93; pres Royal Soc Edinburgh 1996– (vice pres 1990–93, memb Cncl 1986–89); Hon Sheriff E Lothian and Tayside; memb Experimental Psychology Soc; Hon DSc Univ of Edinburgh 1993, Leverhulme emeritus fell 1994; FRSE 1980, FBPsS 1958; *Books* Thinking in Structures (with Z P Dienes, 1965), The Effects of Structural Relations upon Transfer (with Z P Dienes, 1968), The Scientific Enterprise and Christian Faith (1969), Experimental Psychology: an Introduction For Biologists (1974), Psychology and Christianity: the view both ways (1976), Analysis of Structural Learning (with G B Greer, 1983), Free to be Different (with R J Berry and D Atkinson, 1984), Behavioural Sciences: A Christian Perspective (1984), Psychology - Through the Eyes of Faith (with D G Myers, 1987), Mind Fields (1994), Collosal Agensis - A Natural Split Brain? (with M Lassonde, 1994), Human Nature at the Millenium (1997); *Recreations* fly-fishing, music, walking; *Clubs* New (Edinburgh); *Style—* Prof Malcolm Jeeves, CBE, PRSE; ✉ 7 Hepburn Gardens, St Andrews, Fife, Scotland (☎ 01334 473545); School of Psychology, University of St Andrews, St Andrews, Fife, Scotland KY16 9JU (☎ 01334 462072, fax 01334 477441)

JEFFARES, Prof Alexander Norman (Derry); s of Cecil Norman Jeffares (d 1950), and Agnes, *née* Fraser (d 1970); *b* 11 Aug 1920; *Educ* HS Dublin, Trinity Coll Dublin (BA, MA, PhD), Oriel Coll Oxford (MA, DPhil); *m* 29 July 1947, Jeanne Agnes, da of Emil Calembert (d 1932), of Brussels; 1 da (Felicity Anne b 1 Jan 1949); *Career* lectr in classics Trinity Coll Dublin 1943–44, lectr in Eng Groningen Univ 1946–48, lectr Univ of Edinburgh 1949–51, Jury prof of Eng Univ of Adelaide S Aust 1951–56, prof of Eng lit Univ of Leeds 1957–74, prof of Eng studies Univ of Stirling 1974–86; md Academy Advisory Services Ltd 1970–, dir Colin Smythe Ltd 1978–; vice pres Film & TV Cncl S Aust 1951–56; vice chm: Muckhart Community Cncl 1976–86, Scottish Arts Cncl 1978–84 (vice chm 1980–84); pres PEN Scotland 1986–89, chm Book Tst Scotland 1985–88, vice pres The Royal Soc of Edinburgh 1988–90; memb ACGB 1980–84, life fell Assoc for Cwlth Lit and Language Studies (chm 1966–68), hon life pres Int Assoc for the Study of Anglo-Irish Lit 1973–; FAHA 1970, FRSL 1965, FRSE 1981, FRSA 1963, AM 1988; *Books* W B Yeats - Man and Poet (1949, 1966, 1996), A Commentary on the Collected Poems of Yeats (1968), The Circus Animals (1970), A Commentary on the Collected Plays of Yeats (with A S Knowland, 1975), Restoration Drama (4 vols, 1974), A History of Anglo-Irish Literature (1982), Poems of Yeats - A New Selection (1984, 1987), A New Commentary on the Poems of W B Yeats (1984), Brought Up in Dublin (poems, 1987), Brought Up to Leave (poems, 1987), An Irish Childhood - An Anthology (with Antony Kamm, 1987, 1992), W B Yeats - A New Biography (1988), Yeats's Poems (1989, 1996), W B Yeats - A Vision (1990), W B Yeats - The Love Poems (1990), Swift - The Selected Poems (1992), Joycechoyce (with Brendan Kennelly, 1992), Ireland's Women: Writings Past and Present (with Katie Donovan and Brendan Kennelly, 1994), The Collins Dictionary of Quotations (with Martin Gray, 1995), Images of Imagination (essays, 1996), Victorian Love Poetry - An Anthology (1996); *Recreations* drawing, motoring, restoring old houses; *Clubs* Athenaeum, Royal Cwlth Soc; *Style—* Prof Derry Jeffares, FRSE; ✉ Craighead Cottage, Fife Ness, Crail, Fife (☎ and fax 01333 450898)

JEFFCOATE, Dr William James; s of Prof Sir (Thomas) Norman Arthur Jeffcoate (d 1992), and Josephine, *née* Lindsay (d 1981); *b* 31 May 1947; *Educ* Liverpool Coll, St John's Coll Cambridge (MA), Middx Hosp Med Sch (MB BChir); *Career* conslt physician and endocrinologist City Hosp Nottingham 1979–; FRCP; *Publications* Lecture Notes on Endocrinology (5th edn, 1993), The Diabetic Foot: An Illustrated Guide to Management (with R M Macfarlane, 1995); author of papers on diabetes and endocrinology; *Style—* Dr William Jeffcoate; ✉ Nottingham City Hospital, Hucknall Rd, Nottingham NG5 1PB (☎ 0115 969 1169)

JEFFCOCK, David Philip; s of William Philip Jeffcock (d 1963), of Worlingham Grove, Suffolk, and Margaret Renée (d 1976), 2 da of Sir Everard Cayley, 9 Bt, and wid of Cdr E H Rideout, RN (d 1923); *b* 8 July 1933; *Educ* Ampleforth, Trinity Coll Cambridge (BA); *m* 14 Dec 1963, Josephine Anne, da of Maj Harold George Warde-Norbury (d 1974), of Hooton Pagnell Hall, Doncaster; 2 s (Capt John Jeffcock b 1968, George b 1970), 2 da (Venetia b 1964, Cordelia Caroline (Mrs Jason Patrick Barbour) b 1965); *Career* Parly candidate 1964; co-author various pubns on tax and law reform for Sir Alec Douglas-Home 1965; patron Court Jeffcock AOF, chm Euro Movement Hampshire Central 1993–; memb The Stock Exchange 1971–92, MSI 1992–; *Recreations* books, history, music; *Style—* David Jeffcock, Esq; ✉ Wellington House, Captains Row, Lymington, Hampshire SO41 9RR (☎ 01590 672237, fax 01590 673592)

JEFFCOTT, Prof Leo Broof; s of late Edward Ian Broof Jeffcott, and Pamela Mary, *née* Hull; *b* 19 June 1942; *Educ* Caius Sch Shoreham by Sea, Brighton Tech Coll, Royal Vet Coll Univ of London (BVetMed, PhD), Univ of Melbourne (DVSc), Univ of Cambridge (MA); *m* 14 June 1969, Tisza Jacqueline, *née* Hubbard; 2 da (Julie Marie b 9 Feb 1972, Michele Anne b 7 March 1978); *Career* Equine Res Station Animal Health Tst: asst pathologist 1967–71, radiologist and clinician 1972–77, head Clinical Dept 1977–82; prof of clinical radiology Vet Coll Swedish Univ of Agric Sciences 1981–82; Univ of Melbourne: prof of vet clinical sciences 1983–91, head Dept of Vet Clinical Sciences 1985–89, dep dean Faculty of Vet Science 1985, dir Vet Clinic and Hosp 1986–91; Univ of Cambridge: prof of vet clinical studies 1991–, dean Vet Sch 1992–, professorial fell Pembroke Coll 1993; official veterinarian Int Equestrian Fedn at: Seoul Olympics 1988, Stockholm World Equestrian Games 1990, Barcelona Olympics 1992, The Hague World Equestrian Games 1994, Atlanta Olympics 1996; Sir Frederick Hobday Meml Lecture 1977, Peter Hernquist Meml Lecture 1991, Share Jones Lectureship 1993; elected Univ of Kentucky Equine Res Hall of Fame 1991; G Norman Hall medal 1978, Richard Hartley Clinical prize 1980, Tierklinik Hochmoor Int prize 1981, Open award Equine Vet Jl 1982, John Hickman Orthopaedic prize 1991, Animal Health Tst Outstanding Scientific Achievement Award 1994; memb: BVA, Br Equine Vet Assoc, Br Vet Radiological Assoc, Australian Vet Assoc, Australian Equine Vet Assoc; hon memb: Societa Italiana di Ippologie 1977, Equine Section of the Swedish Soc for Veterinary Med 1992; FRCVS 1978; *Publications* Comparative Clinical Haematology (jt ed, 1977), Equine Exercise Physiology 3 (jt ed, 1991), Osteochondrosis in the 90's (jt ed, 1993), On to Atlanta '96 (jt ed, 1994), Thermonegulatory Responses During Competitive Exercise in the Performing Horse (jt ed, Vol 1 1995, Vol 2 1996); author of 259 articles in learned jls; *Recreations* photography, swimming, horse riding; *Style—* Prof Leo Jeffcott; ✉ Department of Clinical Veterinary Medicine, University of Cambridge, Madingley Road, Cambridge CB3 OES (☎ 01223 337664, fax 01223 337671)

JEFFERIES, David George; CBE; s of George Jefferies (d 1981), of Upminster, Essex, and Emma, *née* Braybrook (d 1979); *b* 26 Dec 1933; *m* 12 Dec 1959, Jeanette Ann (Jean); *Career* chief engr Southern Electric 1972–74, dir NW Region CEGB 1974–77, dir of personnel CEGB 1977–81, chm LEB 1981–86, dep chm Electricity Cncl 1986–90; chm: National Grid Company plc 1990–96, National Grid Group plc 1995–, Electricity Pensions Ltd 1986–96, Electricity Pensions Trustees Ltd 1986–, Northern Ireland Electricity 1994–; Freeman City of London 1982, Liveryman Worshipful Co of Wax Chandlers; Hon DTech, Hon LLD; FEng 1989, FIEE (vice pres), CIMgt, FInstE (past pres); *Recreations* golf, gardening, music; *Clubs* Athenaeum, RAC, Foxhills; *Style—* David Jefferies, Esq, CBE, FEng; ✉ The National Grid Group plc, 185 Park Street, London SE1 9DY (☎ 0171 620 8323, fax 0171 620 8229)

JEFFERIES, James (Jim); s of James Jefferies, of Wallyford, Midlothian, and Helen, *née* Johnstone; *b* 22 Nov 1950; *Educ* Musselburgh GS; *m* 24 June 1972, Linda, da of Joseph Sidonio; 1 s (Calum b 10 April 1983), 1 da (Louise b 19 Nov 1980); *Career* professional football manager; player Heart of Midlothian 1967–81: professional 1969, debut v East Fife 1972, latterly capt; mangr: Berwick Rangers 1988–90 (player 1981–84), Falkirk 1990–95, Hearts 1995–; honours with Hearts: runners up Scot Cup 1976, Scot Div 1 Championship 1980 (capt); mangr of the month Dec 1990; insurance sales mangr 1984–90; *Recreations* golf (club champion 9 times); *Style—* Jim Jefferies, Esq; ✉ c/o Heart of Midlothian FC, McLeod Street, Edinburgh EH11 2NL

JEFFERIES, Roger David; s of George Edward Jefferies, of Cirencester, Glos, and Freda Rose, *née* Marshall; *b* 13 Oct 1939; *Educ* Whitgift Sch Croydon, Balliol Coll Oxford (BA, BCL); *m* 1, 1962 (m dis 1974), Jennifer Anne, da of Leslie Ernest Southgate (d 1984), of Rowhedge, Essex; 1 s (William b 1965), 2 da (Sophie b 1967, Polly b 1970); m 2, 1974 (m dis 1984), Margaret Sealy, *née* Pointer; m 3, 1984, Pamela Mary Elsey, da of Benjamin

Arnet Holden (d 1992), of Harpenden, Herts; 1 s (Harry b 1986); *Career* articled clerk to Sir Charles Barratt town clerk Coventry 1961–64, admitted slr 1965, asst slr Coventry City Cncl 1965–68, asst town clerk Southend Co Borough Cncl 1968–70, dir Ops London Borough of Hammersmith 1970–75; chief exec: London Borough of Hounslow 1975–90, London Borough of Croydon 1990–93; Housing Assoc Tenants' ombudsman 1993–; hon sec Cmmn for Local Democracy 1993–95; clerk: Mortlake Crematorium Bd 1973–90, W London Waste Authy 1986–90; under-sec (on secondment) DOE 1983–85; sec Hounslow Arts Tst 1975–90; memb: Cncl RIPA 1982–88, Bd of Public Fin Fndn 1987–93, Regnl Advsy Ctee Arts Cncl 1984–88, Lewisham Theatre Advsy Bd 1994–; tstee South African Advanced Educn Project 1989–; dir: Extemporary Dance Co 1989–91, SOLOTEC 1992–93, Croydon Business Venture 1991–93; pres Soc of Local Authy Chief Execs 1990–91; memb Law Soc 1975; *Books* Tackling the Town Hall (1982); *Recreations* theatre, cooking, growing vegetables; *Style*— Roger Jefferies, Esq

JEFFERIES, Sheelagh; CBE (1987); da of Norman Jefferies (d 1944), and Vera, *née* Bradley (d 1954); *b* 25 Aug 1926; *Educ* Harrogate GS, Girton Coll Cambridge (MA), Smith Coll Northampton Mass USA (MA); *Career* archivist RIIA 1947–50 and 1951–52, info offr Office of the Chllr of the Duchy of Lancaster 1960–61, press offr PM's Office 1961–67, princ info offr Privy Cncl Office 1967–69, chief press offr Miny of Housing of Local Govt 1969–71, head of Parly liaison then head of news Dept of the Environment 1971–74, chief info offr Dept of Prices & Consumer Protection 1974–77; COI: info offr 1953–60, dir of overseas press and radio 1977–78, controller (Home) 1978–83, dep dir gen 1983–86, actg dir gen 1987; media conslt WRVS HQ 1988–92; FIPR 1986, FCAM 1989; *Style*— Miss Sheelagh Jefferies, CBE; ✉ 17 Beaumont Avenue, Richmond, Surrey TW9 2HE (☎ 0181 940 9229)

JEFFERIES, Stephen; s of George Frederick Jefferies, of Birmingham, and Kitty Barbara, *née* Salisbury; *b* 24 June 1951; *Educ* Turves Green Sch Birmingham, Royal Ballet Sch (Upper); *m* 1972, Rashna, da of Homi B Minocher Homji; 1 s (Christopher b 1985), 1 da (Lara b 1982); *Career* ballet dancer; joined Sadler's Wells Royal Ballet 1969, charter princ dancer 1993, sr princ dancer Royal Ballet 1979–93 (princ dancer 1973–76 and 1977–79); all maj roles with the Royal Ballet & Nat Ballet of Canada, over 25 roles created; rehearsal dir Rambert Ballet 1995, artistic dir Hong Kong Ballet 1996; ARAD Hons; *Recreations* golf; *Style*— Stephen Jefferies, Esq; ✉ Royal Opera House, Covent Garden, London WC2 (☎ 0171 240 1200)

JEFFERISS, Christopher David; s of Derek Jefferiss, TD (d 1987), and Vivien Margaret, *née* Hodges (d 1983); *b* 18 Nov 1940; *Educ* Sherborne, Middx Hosp Univ of London (MB BS); *m* 16 April 1966, Madlen Elizabeth Prys, da of William Prys Roberts (d 1992), of Old Abbey Court, Exeter; 1 s (Fredric b 1968), 2 da (Elizabeth b 1970, Emily b 1974); *Career* SHO Middx and Central Hosps 1964–66, surgical registrar W Dorset Hosps 1966–69, registrar and sr registrar Southwest RHA 1970–76, conslt orthopaedic surgn Exeter 1976–; articles in med and legal press on: orthopaedics, hand surgery, med litigation; memb: SICOT, BMA, BSSH, BOFSS, BOA, Medico-legal Soc; FRCS 1970; *Style*— Christopher Jefferiss, Esq; ✉ Lindrick, 405 Topsham Road, Exeter, Devon EX2 7AB (☎ 01392 873292)

JEFFERS, Prof John Norman Richard; s of Lt-Col J H Jeffers, OBE (d 1980), of Woodhall Spa, Lincs, and Emily Matilda Alice, *née* Robinson (d 1974); *b* 10 Sept 1926; *Educ* Portsmouth GS, Benmore Forestry Sch Dunoon; *m* 25 July 1951, Edna May, da of Ernest Reginald Parratt (d 1973), of Farnham, Surrey; 1 da (Ysanne b 11 July 1963); *Career* Forestry Cmmn: res forester 1944–53, princ statistician 1953–68, dir Merlewood Res Station Nature Conservancy 1968–73; Inst of Terrestrial Ecology (NERC): dep dir 1973–75, dir 1976–86; visiting prof: Maths Inst Univ of Kent 1988–, Dept of Chemical and Process Engineering Univ of Newcastle 1990–94, Dept of Mechanical, Materials and Mfrg Engrg Univ of Newcastle 1994–, Sch of Mathematics, Statistics and Computing Univ of Greenwich 1994–; chm Grange and Dist Concert Club; DSc (hc) Univ of Lancaster; memb Biometric Soc; CStat, CBiol, CIFor; *Books* Experimental Design and Analysis in Forestry (1953), An Introduction to Systems Analysis: with ecological examples (1978), Modelling (1982), Practitioner's handbook on the modelling of dynamic change in ecosystems (1988), Microcomputers in Environmental biology (1992); *Recreations* military history; *Clubs* Athenaeum; *Style*— Prof John Jeffers; ✉ Glenside, Oxenholme, Kendal, Cumbria LA9 7RF (☎ 01539 734375, fax 01539 734378, e-mail MEJNRJ@UK.AC.NMW.UA)

JEFFERS, Raymond Jackson; s of George Dennis Jeffers, of Albany, Ipswich, Suffolk, and Jeannine, *née* Jacquier; *b* 5 Aug 1954; *Educ* Stanwell Sch Penarth, Aberystwyth Univ Coll of Wales (LLB), Wadham Coll Oxford (BCL); *m* 4 Sept 1982, Carol Elizabeth, da of John Bernard Awty, of Freshwater, IOW; 3 da (Alice Elizabeth b 19 Aug 1994, Lara Victoria b 27 Jan 1996, Florence May (twin) b 27 Jan 1996); *Career* admitted slr 1980, ptnr Corporate Dept Linklaters & Paines 1986–; memb Employment Law Sub-Ctee City of London Slrs Co 1987 (memb Commercial Law Sub-Ctee 1986); memb Law Soc 1980; *Recreations* ornithology, badminton, golf, tennis; *Style*— Raymond Jeffers, Esq; ✉ Linklaters & Paines, Barrington House, 59–67 Gresham St, London EC2V 7JA (☎ 0171 606 7080, fax 0171 606 5113, telex 884349/888167)

JEFFERSON, (John) Bryan; CB (1989), CBE (1983); s of John Jefferson (d 1940), of Sheffield, Yorks, and Marjorie, *née* Oxley; *b* 26 April 1928; *Educ* Lady Manners Sch Bakewell Derbyshire, Univ of Sheffield (DipArch); *m* 26 July 1954 (m dis 1965), Alison Mary, da of Basil Gray (d 1960); 3 s (Timothy b 1955, David b 1958, Peter b 1960); *Career* Nat Serv RAF 1948–50; asst Morrison and Partners Derby 1956–57, estab practice Sheffield 1957, Jefferson Sheard and Partners (London, Sheffield, Peterborough) 1960–84; DOE: dir-gen of design Property Services Agency 1984–90, chm of PSA Projects 1990–92; chief architectural advsr to Sec of State Dept of Nat Heritage 1993–; visiting prof Sch of Architecture Univ of Sheffield 1992–; pres Sheffield Soc of Architects 1973–74, chm RIBA Yorks Region 1974–75, pres Concrete Soc 1977–78, pres RIBA 1979–81; Freeman City of London 1982; Hon Doctorate in Civil Engrg Univ of Bradford 1987, Hon DLitt Univ of Sheffield 1992; RIBA 1954, RSA 1983, Hon FRAIC 1981, Hon ARICS 1990; *Recreations* sailing, music, skiing; *Clubs* Royal Western Yacht; *Style*— Bryan Jefferson, Esq, CB, CBE; ✉ 6 St Andrews Mansions, Dorset St, London W1H 3FD (☎ and fax 0171 486 6219)

JEFFERSON, David John; s of Edward Hemmings Jefferson (d 1959), of Maidenhead, Berks, and Margaret Agatha, *née* Young (d 1977); *b* 14 June 1932; *Educ* Windsor GS, Coll of Law; *m* 6 Jan 1962, Barbara Anne, da of Richard Bevington Cooper, of Arnside, Cumbria; 1 s (Peter b 1968), 2 da (Sarah b 1963, Lucy b 1970); *Career* 2 Lt Intelligence Corps 1957–58; sr ptnr Maxwell Batley Slrs 1985–91 (ptnr 1963–91); dep taxing master Supreme Ct 1991–, pt/t immigration adjudicator 1993–; hon legal advsr The Victorian Soc; memb Cncl Law Soc 1968–92, chm Incorporated Cncl of Law Reporting for England and Wales 1987–92; memb: Datchet Parish Cncl 1965–83 (chm 1971–73), Eton RDC 1967–74, Royal Borough of Windsor and Maidenhead Cncl 1974–83; chm Church Adoption Soc 1977–88; Freeman City of London 1969, Liveryman Worshipful Co of Slrs 1969; memb Law Soc 1957; *Recreations* conversation, music, ballet, opera, theatre, swimming, skiing, collecting books, drawings and water colours; *Clubs* Special Forces, Royal Thames Yacht, City of London, Leander; *Style*— David Jefferson, Esq; ✉ The Vyne, Deep Field, Datchet, Berks SL3 9JS (☎ 01753 543087)

JEFFERSON, Sir George Rowland; kt (1981), CBE (1969); s of Harold Jefferson, and Eva Elizabeth Ellen; *b* 26 March 1921; *Educ* Dartford GS; *m* 1943, Irene, da of Frederick Watson-Browne; 3 s; *Career* engrg apprentice Royal Ordnance Factory Woolwich 1937–42, cmmnd RAOC 1942, transferred REME 1942, served 1942–45 Anti-Aircraft Cmd on heavy anti-aircraft gun mounting devpt, subsequently memb Miny of Supply staff Fort Halstead until 1952; joined Guided Weapons Div English Electric Co Ltd 1952 (chief res engr 1953, dep chief engr 1958), dir English Electric Aviation (Guided Weapons) Ltd 1963 (dep md 1964, memb Bd 1965–77, md 1966–68, chm and md 1968–77); dir Br Aerospace and chm and md Dynamics Gp 1977–80 (memb Organizing Ctee 1976–77); dir: British Aerospace (Australia) Ltd 1968–80, British Scandinavian Aviation AB 1968–80, Engineering Sciences Data Unit Ltd 1975–80, Hawker Siddeley Dynamics 1977–80, Babcock International 1980–87, Lloyds Bank 1986–89, AMEC plc 1988–92; chm BAC (Anti-Tank) 1968–78, dep chm Post Office 1980; chm: British Telecommunications plc 1981–87 (chief exec 1981–86), Matthew Hall plc 1987–88, City Centre Communications 1988, Videotron Holdings plc 1989–; memb: NEB 1979–80, NICG 1980–84, NEDC 1981–84; Freeman City of London; Hon DSc Univ of Bristol 1984, Hon DUniv Essex 1985; FEng 1978, Hon FIMechE, FIEE, FRAeS, FRSA, CIMgt, FCGI; *Style*— Sir George Jefferson, CBE, FEng; ✉ 449 Kingsway, Landsdale, Perth 6065, Western Australia

JEFFERSON, John Malcolm; s of Arthur Jefferson, of Driffield, N Humberside, and Gladys Evelyn Jefferson; *b* 26 June 1945; *Educ* Bridlington GS; *m* 30 March 1967, Gillian Mary, da of Joseph Healy; 2 s (Nathan b 28 Sept 1974, Daniel b 13 June 1978); *Career* news reporter Bridlington Free Press and Scarborough Evening News, chief reporter Redcar, industl ed and dep news ed Evening Gazette Teesside; news prodr: BBC Radio Durham, BBC Radio Cleveland, BBC Radio Carlisle; prog organiser BBC Radio Humberside, station mangr and fndr BBC Radio York, managing ed BBC Radio Leeds 1988–96, fndr JJ Media Services 1996; former memb: Carlisle Round Table, Holderness Rotary Club Hull, Viking Rotary Club York; former chm York Branch Br Heart Fndn; *Style*— John Jefferson, Esq; ✉ JJ Media Services, Mile End Park, Pocklington, York YO4 2TH (☎ and fax 01759 304875, e-mail j.jefferson@pock.karoo.co.uk)

JEFFERSON, William Hayton; OBE (1986); s of Stanley Jefferson, of Abbeytown, Cumbria, and Josephine, *née* Hayton (d 1986); *b* 29 July 1940; *Educ* Nelson-Thomlinson GS Wigton Cumbria, Wadham Coll Oxford (MA); *m* 1, 1963 (m dis 1986), Marie-Jeanne, *née* Mazenq; 3 s (Jean-Marc b 1963, Jean-Michel b 1964, Vincent b 1970); m 2, 1986, Fadia George, *née* Tarraf; 1 s (William b 1986); *Career* Russian teacher 1963–66; British Council: Tripoli 1967–70, Kuwait 1970–72, Algeria 1972–75, dir Doha Qatar 1975–79, dir Overseas Cooperation London 1979–82, dir United Arab Emirates 1982–85, dir Algeria 1985–90, dir Czechoslovakia and cultural cnsllr British Embassy Prague 1990–96, dir Portugal and cnsllr British Embassy Lisbon 1996–; Czech Scientific Univ Gold Medal 1995, Charles Univ Prague Silver Medal 1996, Olomouc Uni Moravia Medal of Hon 1996, Masaryk Univ Brno Silver Medal 1996; *Recreations* wine, cooking, antiques, horse-racing; *Style*— William Jefferson, Esq, OBE; ✉ 3 Marine Terrace, Silloth, Cumbria CA5 4BZ (☎ 01697 332526); The British Council, Rua de Sao Marcal 174, 1294 Lisbon Codex, Portugal

JEFFERY, David John; s of Stanley John Friend Jeffery (d 1972), and Sylvia May, *née* Mashford; *b* 18 Feb 1936; *Educ* Sutton HS Plymouth, RNC Greenwich, Croydon Coll of Technol, RCDS; *m* 28 March 1959, Margaret, da of George Yates (d 1983); 1 s (Christopher b 6 Aug 1968), 2 da (Karen b 6 Sept 1962, Susan b 22 July 1964); *Career* Nat Serv RAOC 1954–56; Admty and MOD 1956–70 (Devonport, Risley, Singapore, London), princ Treasy Centre for Admin Studies 1970–72, mgmnt sci trg advsr Malaysian Govt Kuala Lumpur 1972–74, princ Civil Serv Dept 1974–76, sr princ MOD 1976–80, asst sec 1980–84, dir Armaments and Mgmnt Servs RN Supply and Tport Serv 1984–86; chief exec and bd memb Port of London Authority 1986–; tstee dir Pilots National Pension Fund 1988–95; dir: British Ports Federation Ltd 1988–92, Estuary Services Ltd 1988– (chm 1988, 1991, 1993, 1995 and 1996), UK Major Ports Group Ltd 1993–, British Ports Industry Training Ltd 1993–; chm: Trade Facilitation Ctee, Int Assoc of Ports and Harbours 1992–96 (conference vice pres 1995–); vice chm European Sea Ports Orgn 1993–; Freeman: City of London 1987, Worshipful Co of Watermen and Lightermen of the River Thames 1987; *Style*— David Jeffery, Esq; ✉ Port of London Authority, Devon House, 58 St Katharine's Way, London E1 9LB (☎ 0171 265 2656, fax 0171 265 2699)

JEFFERY, Jack; CBE (1995); s of Philip Jeffery (d 1973), and Elsie, *née* Carr; *b* 10 March 1930; *Educ* Stanley GS Co Durham, King's Coll Durham (BSc Chemistry and Bacteriology, MSc); *m* 1 (m dis 1983); 3 da (Wyn b 28 March 1951, Carole b 1 Dec 1953, Jill b 26 Feb 1958); m 2, 28 May 1983, Deborah Mary, da of Kenneth Hyde; *Career* scientist NCB 1953–61, chemist and bacteriologist SW Suburban Water Co 1961–73 (asst gen mangr 1968–73); North Surrey Water: water quality controller 1973–77, gen mangr 1977–87, md 1987–95, chm 1990–; also chm: General Utilities Projects Ltd, Tendring Hundred Water Services Ltd; dir: WRC plc, East Surrey Holdings plc, Durham County Waste Management Ltd; chm Water Cos Assoc 1987–90, pres Instn of Water Offrs 1991, dep chm Cncl of RIPHH 1993–, chm Surrey First 1993–96, tstee World Humanity Action Tst 1993–, chm Careers Advsy Bd Univ of Newcastle 1995–; hon memb: Instn of Water Offrs 1992, American Waterworks Assoc 1994; Distinguished Serv Certificate BSI 1995; author of various papers on water quality and treatment and water privatisation (incl regulation); Freeman City of London 1980, Liveryman, memb Ct of Assts and immediate past Master Worshipful Co of Plumbers; FCIWEM 1987, FRIPHH 1987, FRSA 1989, CIMgt 1994; *Recreations* music, watching sport, books, wine; *Clubs* Lansdowne, MCC, Forty, Durham CCC; *Style*— Jack Jeffery, Esq, CBE; ✉ Laleham House, Hedley on the Hill, Stocksfield, Northumberland NE43 7SW (☎ 01661 843729, fax 01661 844058); North Surrey Water Ltd, The Causeway, Staines, Middlesex TW18 3BX (☎ 01784 455464, fax 01784 426336)

JEFFERY, Paul Francis; s of Arthur Felgate Sinclair Jeffery, of Storrington, West Sussex, and Muriel Carmen, *née* Privett (d 1992); *b* 27 Jan 1946; *Educ* Eastbourne Coll; *m* 13 March 1971, Patricia Ann Jeffery, OBE, da of Edward Frederick Emes; 1 s (Edward Paul b 21 Oct 1972); *Career* CA; articled clerk: Harry Price & Co Eastbourne 1964–66, Jones Avens Worley & Piper Chichester 1966–68; Thomas McLintock & Co: London office 1969–77, ptnr Norwich office 1977–87 (managing ptnr 1986–87), memb Quality Review Gp 1981–84, UK dir of quality review 1984–86; ptnr specialising in insolvency and investigations KPMG (following merger of Thomson McLintock and Peat Marwick Mitchell in 1987): London office 1991–94, St Albans office 1994–; pres Norfolk and Norwich Soc of CAs 1982–83, chm Norwich Enterprise Agency Tst 1989–92 (memb Bd 1986–92), treas Mid Norfolk Cons Assoc 1993–96, asst area treas (Norfolk) Cons Pty 1994–, treas Norfolk Cons Euro Constituency Cncl 1994–; govr Eastbourne Coll 1992–; FCA 1979 (ACA 1969), Insolvency Licence (ICAEW) 1987, memb Soc of Practitioners in Insolvency 1990; *Recreations* golf, swimming, travelling, reading; *Style*— Paul Jeffery, Esq; ✉ KPMG, Aquis Court, 31 Fishpool Street, St Albans, Hertfordshire AL3 4RF (☎ 01727 733000)

JEFFERY, Very Rev Canon Robert Martin Colquhoun; s of Norman Clare Jeffery (d 1972), and Gwenedd Isabel, *née* Field; *b* 30 April 1935; *Educ* St Paul's, King's Coll London (BD, AKC); *m* 4 May 1948 (m dis 1995), Ruth Margaret, da of Everard Tinling (d 1978), of Surrey; 3 s (Graham b 1969, Hilary b 1971, Charles b 1975), 1 da (Phillipa b 1975); *Career* asst curate: St Aidan Grangetown 1959–61, St Mary Barnes 1961–63; asst sec Missionary and Ecumenical of Church Assembly 1964–68, sec Dept of Mission and Unity Br Cncl of Churches 1968–71, vicar St Andrew Headington 1971–78, rural dean Cowley 1972–78, Lichfield diocesan missioner 1978–80, memb Gen Synod of C of

E 1982, archdeacon of Salop 1980–87, dean of Worcester 1987–96 (dean emeritus 1996), canon residentiary and sub-dean Christ Church Oxford 1996–; memb Gen Synod Standing Ctee 1990–96; *Books* Unity in Nigeria (1964), Christian Unity and the Anglican Community (with D M Paton, 1965 and 1968), Areas of Ecumenical Experiment (1968), Ecumenical Experiments - A Handbook (1971), Case Studies in Unity (1972), By What Authority (1987), Anima Christi (1994); *Recreations* local history, cooking; *Clubs* RSA; *Style*— The Very Rev Canon Robert Jeffery; ✉ Christ Church, Oxford OX1 1DP (☎ 01865 276278)

JEFFERY, Timothy Arthur Rodney; s of Rodney Albert Jeffery, of Lymington, Hants, and Edith Rosina, *née* Meeks; *b* 13 June 1956; *Educ* Methodist Coll Belfast, Univ of Kent at Canterbury (BA); *m* 14 April 1984, (Margaret) Jennifer, da of Harold Gibson; 1 da (Kate Elizabeth Rosina b 4 Dec 1987); *Career* features ed Yachting World 1978–88, yachting corr The Daily Telegraph 1988–; former chm UKC Sports Fedn, memb Yachting Journalists' Assoc 1977; *Books* Sail of the Century (1983), Practical Sailing (1986), Sailing Year (1987), The Official History of The Champagne Mumm Admiral's Cup (1994); *Recreations* sailing, golf, skiing, tennis; *Clubs* Royal Ocean Racing; *Style*— Timothy Jeffery, Esq; ✉ The Daily Telegraph, 1 Canada Square, Canary Wharf, London E14 5DT (☎ 0171 538 5000, fax 0171 513 2507)

JEFFORD, Barbara Mary; OBE (1965); da of Percival Francis Jefford (d 1961), and Elizabeth Mary Ellen, *née* Laity (d 1979); *b* 26 July 1930; *Educ* Weirfield Sch Taunton, Eileen Hartly-Hodder Studio Bristol (LGSM), RADA London (Bancroft Gold Medal); *m* 1, (m dis 1961), Terence Longdon; m 2, 13 May 1967, John Arnold Turner, s of William John Turner; *Career* actress; extensive radio and tv work throughout career, incl House of Elliot (series, BBC) 1991; *Theatre* Shakespearean debut as Viola in Twelfth Night (Dolphin Theatre Brighton) 1949, worked at Shakespeare Meml Theatre 1950, 1951 and 1954, led co with Anthony Quayle on Australasian Tour 1953, leading lady at Old Vic 1956–62 (incl tours of UK, USA, Europe and USSR), led HM Tennant Co with Ralph Richardson on tour of S America and Europe to mark Shakespeare's Quartercentenary 1964, roles in West End and with regnl cos (incl Oxford Playhouse) 1960s, 70s and 80s, int tours for Br Cncl (The Labours of Love, two-handed show with husband, John Turner), Prospect Prodns and Bristol Old Vic; leading roles with: NT 1976 and 1987, RSC 1967, 1989–90 and 1992–94; recent work 1994–96 incl: A Collier's Friday Night, The School for Scandal, Night Must Fall; *Films* debut as Molly Bloom in Ulysses; subsequent films incl: The Shoes of The Fisherman, And The Ship Sails On, Where Angels Fear to Tread; *Awards* Clarence Derwent Award 1988, Pragnell Shakespeare Prize 1994; *Recreations* music, swimming, gardening; *Style*— Ms Barbara Jefford, OBE; ✉ c/o Peters Fraser & Dunlop Ltd, 503 The Chambers, Chelsea Harbour, Lots Road, London SW10 0XF (☎ 0171 352 4446, fax 0171 352 7356)

JEFFREY, Gordon Boyd Buchanan; s of William Barclay Boyd Jeffrey (d 1982), of Southport, Lancs, and Jean Ross, *née* Macgregor; *b* 12 April 1935; *Educ* Merchant Taylors', Univ of Liverpool (LLB); *m* 11 May 1963, Jill Virginia, da of William Frederick Baker (d 1980), of Southport; 3 s (Andrew b 20 April 1965, Robert b 4 April 1967, Jonathan b 22 Aug 1973), 1 da (Sarah Jane b and d 1970); *Career* Nat Serv cmmnd Royal Artillery 1958–60, served with 2 Field Regt RA and 17 Gurkha Div during terrorist emergency in Malaya; admitted slr 1958, ptnr Laces & Co (now Lace Mawer) 1963–; jt chm World Amateur Golf Cncl 1989–92; memb Law Soc; *Recreations* golf, fishing; *Clubs* Royal & Ancient Golf (chm Gen Ctee 1988–91, capt 1994–95), Royal Birkdale Golf (tstee), Pine Valley Golf (New Jersey); *Style*— Gordon Jeffrey, Esq; ✉ Lace Mawer, Castle Chambers, 43 Castle St, Liverpool L2 9SU (☎ 0151 236 2002, fax 0151 236 2585)

JEFFREY, John; s of James Jeffrey, OBE, DL, and Margaret Lambie, *née* Young; *b* 25 March 1959; *Educ* Merchiston Castle Sch Edinburgh, Univ of Newcastle (BSc); *Career* former rugby union flanker; represented: English Univs, British Univs; clubs: Kelso RFC (capt 1987–93, twice Scottish champions), South of Scotland 1982–91 (capt 1988–91), Barbarians RFC; 3 caps Scotland B; Scotland: debut v Aust 1984, Five Nations debut v Ireland 1985, tour Romania 1984, tour USA 1985, France 1986, memb World Cup Squad 1987 and 1991, tour NZ 1990, Championship and Grand Slam winners 1990, record 11 tries scored by a forward, 40 caps, Scotland int selector; British Lions: IRB celebration team 1986, tour Aust 1989; occasional rugby TV pudit; farmer Kersknowe, Frogden and Deuchrie farms; dir: Moredun Fndn, Kelso Grain Consultants, Scott Country Potato Growers; *Recreations* golf, sailing, water skiing, spoofing; *Clubs* MENSA, Farmers'; *Style*— John Jeffrey, Esq; ✉ Kersknowe, Kelso, Roxburghshire, Scotland TD5 8AA (☎ and fax 01573 440212)

JEFFREY, John Christopher; s of Cyril Henry Jeffrey (d 1985), and Mary Elizabeth, *née* Jones; *b* 21 July 1942; *Educ* Clifton Coll Bristol; *m* 27 Sept 1974, Diana Lisa, da of Cecil Raymond Messiter-Tooze (d 1988); 2 s (Justin b 1971, Nicholas b 1975); *Career* CA; Deloitte Haskins & Sells: ptnr Zambia 1970–75, ptnr i/c Kitwe Zambia 1975–78, managing ptnr Lusaka Zambia 1978–84, ptnr i/c Leeds Bradford 1984–85, ptnr i/c Liverpool until 1995; FCA 1965; *Recreations* golf, rugby, skiing; *Style*— John C Jeffrey, Esq; ✉ Mill House, Mill Lane, Willaston, S Wirral, Cheshire L64 1RP (☎ 0151 327 4423)

JEFFREY, Nicholas; s of Manfred Jeffrey, and Doris MacKay, *née* Spouge; *b* 6 June 1942; *Educ* Ecclesfield GS, Univ of Sheffield (LLB); *m* 1965, Dianne Michelle, da of Cyril Cantor (d 1985); 2 s (Alexander b 1966, David b 1969), 2 da (Danya b 1968, Miranda b 1971); *Career* exec dep chm H & C Furnishings plc and all subsidiary companies 1980– (dir 1967–), chm Hallamshire Investments plc 1990, chm Neepsend Plc 1994–; Liveryman Worshipful Co of Furniture Makers; *Recreations* shooting, sailing; *Style*— Nicholas Jeffrey, Esq; ✉ Riley Croft, Eyam, Derbyshire; H & C Furnishings plc, 164–170 Queens Rd, Sheffield S2 4DY (☎ 0114 276 6461, fax 0114 276 9070, telex 547037)

JEFFREY, Richard Stephen; s of Alexander Arthur Jeffrey, of Hertfordshire, and Heather Eve, *née* Royan; *b* 20 Aug 1957; *Educ* Haileybury and ISC, Univ of Bristol (BSc, MSc(Econ)); *m* 29 Sept 1984, Marion Bernadette, da of John Roach; 3 s (Edward Alexander John b 13 Feb 1988, Harry Richard Matthew and Stephen Michael Murdo (twins) b 2 Sept 1989); *Career* trainee accountant Thompson McLintock 1978–80; Hoare Govett: joined as economist 1981, head of Economics and Strategy Dept 1988–92; Charterhouse plc: joined gp as head of research Charterhouse Tilney 1992, dir Charterhouse Tilney Ltd, currently gp economist Charterhouse plc; FRSA; *Publications* Quarterly Review of the UK Economy (UK Economica); *Style*— Richard Jeffrey, Esq; ✉ Charterhouse plc, 1 Paternoster Row, St Paul's, London EC4M 7DH (☎ 0171 246 2472, fax 0171 522 3785)

JEFFREY, Dr Robin Campbell; s of Robert Stewart Martin Jeffrey (d 1962), and Catherine Campbell McSporran (d 1995); *b* 19 Feb 1939; *Educ* Kelvinside Acad, Royal Coll of Science and Technol Univ of Glasgow (BSc), Pembroke Coll Cambridge (PhD), Templeton Coll Oxford (Harvard Univ mgmnt course); *m* 28 July 1962, Barbara Helen, da of Prof Sir Austin Robinson; 2 s (Alan b 17 Jan 1967, David b 9 Dec 1968), 1 da (Catherine b 19 Nov 1971); *Career* engrg res mangr Babcock & Wilcox 1956–60 and 1964–79; SSEB (now Scottish Power): tech servs mangr 1979–80, mangr Torness Power Station Project 1980–88, chief engr 1988–89, md Engrg Resources 1990–92; chm Scottish Nuclear Ltd 1995– (chief exec 1992–), jt dep chm British Energy plc 1995–; visiting prof Univ of Strathclyde; FEng 1992, FIChemE 1992, FIMechE 1993; *Books* Open Cycle MHD Power Generation (co-author, 1969); *Recreations* squash, tennis, skiing, playing musical instruments; *Clubs* Cambridge Univ Royal Tennis, Glasgow Academical Squash; *Style*— Dr Robin Jeffrey, FEng; ✉ 71D Partickhill Road, Glasgow G11 5AD (☎ 0141 357 3079); Scottish Nuclear Ltd, 3 Redwood Crescent, Peel Park, East Kilbride G74 5PR (☎ 01355 262410, fax 01355 262419)

JEFFREY, William Alexander; s of Alexander Jeffrey (d 1979), and Joyce, *née* McCrindle; *b* 28 Feb 1948; *Educ* Allan Glen's Sch Glasgow, Univ of Glasgow (BSc); *m* 2 June 1979, Joan, da of Duncan MacNaughton; *Career* Home Office: various positions 1971–84 (incl private sec to the Perm Sec 1975–76), asst sec 1984–91, under sec (ops and resources) Immigration and Nationality Dept 1991–94; dep head Economic and Domestic Secretariat Cabinet Office 1994–; *Recreations* reading, hill-walking, watching football; *Style*— William Jeffrey, Esq; ✉ Cabinet Office, 70 Whitehall, London SW1A 2AS

JEFFREY-COOK, John; *b* 5 Jan 1936; *Educ* Whitgift Middle (Trinity) Sch Croydon; *m* 12 May 1962, Gillian Audrey, da of Ronald Albert Kettle (d 1982), of Croydon; 2 s (Richard Daniel b 1964, Malcolm John b 1970 d 1981), 1 da (Fiona Elizabeth b 1966); *Career* managing ed of taxation books Butterworth Law Publishers 1966–77, dir of pubns Deloitte Haskins & Sells 1977–85, ptnr Moores Rowland 1985–; ed Moores Rowland's Yellow and Orange Tax Guides 1987–, conslt ed Encyclopaedia of Forms and Precedents 1993–; memb Editorial Bd: Simons Direct Tax Serv 1977–, Taxation 1989–, Taxation Practitioner 1992–; memb: Ctee London & Dist Soc of CA's 1966–77, Cncl Chartered Inst of Taxation 1977–90 (treas 1981–88), Cncl Assoc of Taxation Technicians 1989–, Addington Soc 1966 (chm 1993–95); Freeman City of London 1980, memb Worshipful Co of CA's 1980, clerk Guild of Tax Advisers 1996–; FCA 1958, FCIS 1959, FTII 1964, ATT 1989; *Books* Simon's Taxes (ed, 1970), de Voil's Value Added Tax (1973), Simon's Tax Intelligence and Cases (1973), Butterworths Orange Tax Handbook (1976), Foster's Capital Taxes Encyclopaedia (1976), Moores Rowland's Taxation of Farmers and Farming (1989); *Recreations* genealogy, cinema, history; *Style*— John Jeffrey-Cook, Esq; ✉ 32 Campion Close, Croydon, Surrey CR0 5SN (☎ 0181 688 3887); Moores Rowland, 6 Bedford Park, Croydon, Surrey CRO 2AP (☎ 0181 686 9281, fax 0181 760 0411)

JEFFREYS, Alan Howard; QC (1996); s of Hugh Jeffreys (d 1988), and Rachel Mary, *née* Evans; *b* 27 Sept 1947; *Educ* Ellesmere Coll, King's Coll London (LLB); *m* 1975, Jane Olivia, da of Richard Duncan Sadler; 1 da (Cerian Olivia Sophia b 7 July 1979), 1 s (Hugo Harri Richard b 8 July 1981); *Career* called to the Bar Gray's Inn 1970, in practice SE Circuit, recorder 1993– (asst recorder 1989); memb: London Common Law and Commercial Bar Assoc, Personal Injuries Bar Assoc; *Recreations* fishing, golf, chess, music; *Clubs* Hurlingham; *Style*— Alan Jeffreys, Esq, QC; ✉ Farrar's Building, Temple, London EC4Y 7BD (☎ 0171 583 9241, fax 0171 583 0090)

JEFFREYS, Prof Sir Alec John; kt (1994); s of Sydney Victor Jeffreys, of Corton, Lowestoft, Suffolk, and Joan, *née* Knight (d 1994); *b* 9 Jan 1950; *Educ* Luton GS, Luton Sixth Form Coll, Merton Coll Oxford (MA, DPhil); *m* 28 Aug 1971, Susan, da of Frederick Charles Robert Miles (d 1975), of Luton, Beds; 2 da (Sarah Catherine b 1979, Elizabeth Jane b 1983); *Career* postdoctoral res fell Euro Molecular Biology Orgn Univ of Amsterdam 1975–77, prof of genetics Univ of Leicester 1987– (lectr 1977–72, Lister Inst res fell 1982–, reader 1984–87), devpt of genetic fingerprinting system 1984–; Wolfson res prof of Royal Soc 1991–; memb: EMBO, HUGO, Genetical Soc, Biochemical Soc; Hon DUniv Open Univ 1991, Hon DSc Univ of St Andrews 1996; hon fell: Merton Coll Oxford, Univ of Luton 1995; fell Forensic Sci Soc of India, fell Linnean Soc 1994, FRCPath 1991, Hon FRCP 1992, FRS; *Recreations* swimming, walking, postal history; *Style*— Prof Sir Alec Jeffreys, FRS; ✉ Dept of Genetics, Adrian Building, University of Leicester, University Rd, Leicester LE1 7RH (☎ 0116 252 3435, fax 0116 252 3378)

JEFFREYS, 3 Baron (UK 1952); Christopher Henry Mark Jeffreys; s of 2 Baron Jeffreys (d 1986), and Mrs Sarah Clarke, of Foxhill House, Hawling, Glos; *b* 22 May 1957; *Educ* Eton; *m* 22 Aug 1985, Anne Elisabeth, da of Antoine Denarie, of Johannesburg, and Mrs Derek Johnson, of Boden Hall, Scholar Green, Cheshire; 1 s (Hon Arthur Mark Henry b 1989), 1 da (Hon Alice Mary b 1986); *Heir* s, Hon Arthur Mark Henry Jeffreys b 18 Feb 1989; *Career* futures broker; Johnson Matthey & Wallace Ltd 1976–85, GNI Ltd 1985–90, stockbroker Raphael Zorn Hemsley 1992–; currently sits as Cons peer in House of Lords with interests in environmental matters, the City and the EC; *Recreations* shooting, fishing, sailing, golf, skiing; *Clubs* White's; *Style*— The Rt Hon the Lord Jeffreys; ✉ Bottom Farm, Eaton, Grantham, Lincolnshire NG32 1ET (☎ 01476 870498); Raphael Zorn Hemsley, 10 Throgmorton Avenue, London Wall, London EC2N 3DP (☎ 0171 628 4000)

JEFFREYS, Martyn Edward; s of William Herbert Jeffreys (d 1961), of Ealing, and Nora Emilie, *née* Crane (d 1995); *b* 20 Jan 1938; *Educ* St Clement Danes, Univ of Bristol (BSc); *m* 29 Oct 1960, Carol, da of Marcel Faustin Boclet (d 1964), of Twickenham; 2 s (Andrew b 1962, Adam b 1968), 1 da (Katy b 1965); *Career* operational res scientist BP 1961–63, sr mathematician and mangr Mathematical Programming Div SD-Scicon (formerly CEIR Ltd) 1964–67, chief mgmnt scis conslt and head professional servs SIA Ltd 1968–70, sr ptnr Wootton Jeffreys & Ptnrs 1971–84, exec chm Wootton Jeffreys Systems Ltd 1985–86, chm Jeffreys Systems plc 1987–; FBCS 1973, CEng 1990; *Style*— Martyn Jeffreys, Esq; ✉ 196 Epsom Road, Merrow, Guildford, Surrey GU1 2RR (☎ 01483 39598); Jeffreys Systems plc, Jeffreys House, 21 Normandy Street, Alton, Hampshire GU34 1DD (☎ 01420 541541, fax 01420 541640)

JEFFRIES, Prof Donald James; s of Edmond Frederick Jeffries (d 1976), and Eileen Elizabeth, *née* Elton (d 1993); *b* 29 Aug 1941; *Educ* William Ellis GS, Royal Free Hosp Sch of Med (BSc, MB BS, MRCPath); *m* 11 Aug 1966, Mary Millicent, da of Eric John Bray; 1 da (Caroline Mary b 31 Jan 1967), 2 s (Paul James b 5 Jan 1969, Richard Anthony b 21 June 1973); *Career* St Mary's Hosp Med Sch: sr registrar in microbiology 1970–72, head Div of Virology 1982–90, dir of clinical studies 1985–90, reader and hon conslt in clinical virology 1987–90 (lectr 1972–74, sr lectr 1974–87); prof and head of virology Bart's 1990–, clinical dir of virology Royal Hosps Tst 1994–; conslt in virology St John Ambulance 1994–, sr examiner Univ of London 1993–, chm Panel of Examiners in Virology RCPath; visiting prof Riyadh 1988, C T Huang lectr Hong Kong 1991, Wellcome visiting prof Med Coll S Africa 1993; memb: Soc for General Microbiology 1970–, Hospital Infection Soc 1980– (memb Cncl 1980–83 and 1990–93), Advsy Ctee on Genetic Modification HSE 1988–, Assoc of Profs of Medical Microbiology 1991–, Expert Advsy Gp on AIDS 1992–, Advsy Ctee on Dangerous Pathogens Dept of Health 1993–, Diagnostics and Imaging Panel Standing Gp on Health Technol, NHS R & D Directorate; FRCPath 1986; *Publications* Lecture Notes on Medical Virology (1987), Current Topics in AIDS Vol I (1987, Vol II 1989), Antiviral Chemotherapy (1995); *Recreations* ornithology, walking, medical history; *Style*— Prof Donald Jeffries; ✉ Department of Virology, St Bartholomew's and the Royal London School of Medicine and Dentistry, 51–53 Bartholomew Close, West Smithfield, London EC1A 7BE (☎ 0171 601 7350, fax 0171 726 4248)

JEFFRIES, Lionel Charles; s of Bernard Jeffries, and Elsie Jackson; *b* 10 June 1926; *Educ* Queen Elizabeth's GS Wimborne Dorset, RADA (Dip, Kendal Award 1947); *m* 30 June 1951, Eileen Mary, da of William Walsh (d 1963); 1 s (Timothy), 2 da (Elizabeth, Martha); *Career* actor 1949–, film producer, director and screen writer; War Serv 1939–45, Capt Oxford and Bucks LI Burma, RWAFF (Burma Star 1945); *Theatre* roles incl: Carrington VC, The Enchanted, Blood Wedding, Brouhaha, Hello Dolly (Prince of Wales) 1984, See How They Run, Two Into One, Rookery Nook (Shaftesbury) 1985–86, Pygmalion (Plymouth) 1987, The Wild Duck (Phoenix) 1990, When we are Married (Savoy) 1996; *Television* incl: Cream In My Coffee 1980, Shillingbury Tales 1981, Father

Charlie, Tom, Dick and Harriet 1983, Bed 1994: *Films* over 100 appearances incl: Colditz Story, Bhowani Junction, Lust for Life, The Baby and The Battleship, Doctor at Large, Law and Disorder, The Nun's Story, Idle on Parade, Two Way Stretch, The Trials of Oscar Wilde, Fanny, The Notorious Landlady, The Wrong Arm of the Law, The First Men in the Moon, The Truth about Spring, Arrivederci Baby, The Spy with a Cold Nose, Camelot, Chitty Chitty Bang Bang, Eyewitness, The Prisoner of Zenda, Ménage à Trois, Chorus of Disapproval, Danny Champion of the World, Ending Up, First and Last, Look at it This Way; as writer and dir: The Railway Children 1972 (St Christopher Gold Medal Hollywood for Best Film), The Amazing Mr Blunden (Cinema Fantastique Paris Gold Medal Award for Best Screen Play) 1972, Wombling Free 1977; co-writer and dir The Water Babies 1979; *Recreations* oil painting, swimming; *Clubs* St James; *Style*— Lionel Jeffries, Esq; ✉ c/o ICM Ltd, Oxford House, 76 Oxford Street, London W1N 0AX (☎ 0171 636 6565, fax 0171 323 0101)

JEFFRIES, Dr Michael Godfrey; *b* 16 April 1943; *Educ* Univ of Birmingham (BSc, MB ChB, DCCH), FRCGP; *m* 28 Aug 1965, Sheila; 2 s (Simon b 12 Dec 1967, Nick b 30 Dec 1975), 1 da (Clare b 28 Jan 1970); *Career* med dir Clwyd Community Care NHS Tst; memb Cncl RCGP; MRCGP 1984; *Style*— Dr Michael Jeffries; ✉ Clwyd Community Care NHS Trust, Catherine Gladstone House, Hawarden Way, Mancot, Flintshire CH5 2EP (☎ 01244 538883, fax 01244 538884)

JEFFRIES, Michael Makepeace Eugene; s of William Eugene Jeffries (d 1975), of Port of Spain, Trinidad, and Margaret, *née* Makepeace; *b* 17 Sept 1944; *Educ* Queens Royal Coll Port of Spain Trinidad, Poly of North London (Dip Arch); *m* 10 Sept 1966, Pamela Mary, da of Sir Gordon Booth, KCMG, CVO, of Kingswood, Surrey; 2 s (Andrew b 1969, Simon b 1973), 2 da (Kathryn b 1971, Victoria b 1975); *Career* John Laing and Sons Ltd 1963–67, Deeks Bousell Ptnrship 1968–73, Bradshaw Gass and Hope 1973–75; ASFA Ltd (WS Atkins Gp) 1975–: dir 1978, chm and md 1979; dir WS Atkins Conslts 1979, chief exec W S Atkins plc 1995– (dir 1992–95); chm Banstead Round Table 1980, memb Cncl London C of C; RIBA 1973, FRSA 1987; *Recreations* golf, sailing, skiing, water colours, antiquarian horology; *Style*— Michael Jeffries, Esq; ✉ Ellerslie House, The Glade, Kingswood, Surrey KT20 6LL (☎ 01737 832081); W S Atkins plc, Woodcote Grove, Ashley Rd, Epsom, Surrey KT18 5BW (☎ 01372 726140, fax 01372 743006, car tel 0860 366251, telex 266701 ATKINS G)

JEFFRIES, Neil; *b* 1959; *Educ* St Martin's Sch of Art, Slade Sch of Fine Art; *Career* artist; artist in residence Kingston Poly 1984–85, artist in Schools Project Whitechapel 1986; pt/t lectr: Slade Coll of Art 1985–, Ruskin Sch 1985–; sculputre cmmn Scott Tallon & Walker; *Solo exhibitions* Arnolfini 1985, Blond Fine Art 1986, Flowers East 1990, Angela Flowers Gall 1992, Galeria Ray Gun 1994, Stadt Tuttlingen Stadtische Galerie Tuttlingen Germany 1995, Flowers East 1996; *Group exhibitions* incl: Stowells Trophy Exhbn (RA) 1982, The New Contemporaries (ICA) 1982, The Best of 1982 (Christies) 1982, New Directions in Sculpture (Blond Fine Art) 1984, Artist of the Day (Angela Flowers Gall) 1984, Home and Abroad (Serpentine Gall) 1984, Summer Show (Blond Fine Art) 1984, Contemporary Art Society Fair (Five Dials Gall) 1984, Monstrous Craws (Actors Inst) 1984, A View From My Window (Angela Flowers Gall) 1984, Ten Painters (St Martin's Sch of Art) 1985, International Contemporary Art Fair (Olympia) 1985, Group Show (Blond Fine Art) 1985, In Their Circumstances (Usher Gall) 1985, Art for Ethiopia (Bonham's) 1985, Newbury Arts Festival 1985, Proud and Prejudiced (Twining Gall NY) 1985, Figures and Figures (Manchester Arts Centre) 1985, Peter Moores Project (Walker Art Gall) 1986, Living Art (Ideal Home Exhbn) 1986, Britain in Vienna (Kunstlerhaus) 1986, Modern Art? It's a Joke! (Cleveland Gall) 1986, State of the Nation (Herbert Art Gall) 1987, Small Is Beautiful (Angela Flowers Gall) 1987, The Big Fight (Vanessa Devereux Gall) 1987, London (Royal Festival Hall) 1987, Contemporary Portraits (Flowers East) 1988, Small Is Beautiful - Part 6 (Flowers East) 1988, A Personal View (Nigel Greenwood Gall) 1988, Big Paintings (Flowers East) 1989, Ingenious Inventions (Harris Art Gall) 1989, 30 Tage (Galerie Siegart) 1990, Academicians Choice (Mall Galls) 1990, Summer Exhbn (RA) 1990 and 1991, Flowers East (Watermans Art Centre) 1991, Artist's Choice Exhbn (Angela Flowers Gall) 1992, Decouvertes (Grand Palais Paris) 1993, But Big is Better (Flowers East) 1993, Inner Visions (Flowers East) 1994, The Twenty Fifth Anniversary Exhibition (Flowers East) London Fields 1995; *Public Collections* Arts Cncl of GB, British Cncl; *Awards* Boise Travelling Scholarship 1984, Wollaston Award Summer Exhibition RA 1991; *Style*— Neil Jeffries, Esq; ✉ c/o Flowers East, 199 Richmond Road, London E8 3NJ (☎ 0181 985 3333)

JEFFS, Julian; QC (1975); s of Alfred Wright Jeffs (d 1974); *b* 5 April 1931; *Educ* Mostyn House Sch, Wrekin Coll, Downing Coll Cambridge (MA, assoc fell); *m* 1966, Deborah, *née* Bevan; 3 s (Daniel b 1968, Alexander b 1970, Benjamin b 1972); *Career* called to the Bar Gray's Inn 1958; recorder 1975, bencher Gray's Inn 1981, ret from practice 1991; chm Patent Bar Assoc 1981–89; memb Ctee of Mgmnt Int Wine and Food Soc 1965–67 and 1971–82, gen cmmr of Income Tax 1983–91; memb: Senate of the Inns of Ct and Bar 1984–85, Bar Cncl 1988–89; pres Circle of Wine Writers 1991– (chm 1970–72); gen ed Faber's Wine Series; *Books* Sherry (1961, 4 edn 1992), Clerk & Lindsell on Torts (co-ed, 13 edn 1969, 16 edn 1989), The Wines of Europe (1971), Little Dictionary of Drink (1973), Encyclopedia of United Kingdom and European Patent Law (jtly, 1977); *Recreations* wine, walking, old cars, Iberian things; *Clubs* Beefsteak, Garrick, Reform, Saintsbury; *Style*— Julian Jeffs, Esq, QC; ✉ Church Farm House, East Ilsley, Newbury, Berks (☎ 01635 281216, fax 01635 281756)

JEFFS, Dr Nicholas Graham; s of John Grahame Jeffs (d 1974), and Evelyn Maude, *née* Cattermole; *b* 20 Nov 1950; *Educ* Lycee Victor Hugo Marrakesh Morocco, Nottingham HS, Middx Hosp Med Sch (MB BS); *m* 18 Jan 1975, Jennifer Mary, da of Robert Herbert Rogers, of 9 Gainsborough Rd, Colchester, Essex; 2 s (Richard b 1978, Thomas b 1983); *Career* anaesthetist; registrar London Hosp 1976–78, lectr Univ of London 1978–79, sr registrar St Mary's Hosp 1981–82, conslt and dir Intensive Care Unit Luton and Dunstable Hosp 1982–; FFARCS 1978, fell Coll of Anaesthetics, memb Intensive Care Soc; *Recreations* model engineering, shooting; *Clubs* N London Rifle; *Style*— Dr Nicholas Jeffs; ✉ 28 Ludlow Ave, Luton, Bedfordshire LU1 3RW (☎ 01582 451504); Luton and Dunstable Hospital, Lewsey Road, Luton, Bedfordshire LU4 0DZ (☎ 01582 497230)

JEGER, Baroness (Life Peer UK 1979), of St Pancras in Greater London; Lena May Jeger; da of Charles Chivers (d 1971), of Yorkley, Glos, and Eugenie Alice James (d 1969); *b* 19 Nov 1915; *Educ* Southgate Co Sch Middx, Birkbeck Coll London Univ (BA); *m* 1948, Dr Santo Wayburn Jeger, MP (d 1953); *Career* sits as Labour peer in House of Lords; Civil Serv: HM Customs & Excise, Miny of Info and FO 1936–49, Br Embassy Moscow 1947 (asst ed British Ally (weekly Br Govt pubn in Russian)); on London staff The Guardian 1951–54 and 1961–; MP (Lab): LCC 1951–54, Holborn and St Pancras South Nov 1953–59 and 1964–74, Camden Holborn and St Pancras South 1974–79; memb Nat Exec Ctee Labour Party 1968–80 (vice chm 1978–79, chm 1979–80); UK rep Status of Women Cmmn UN 1967, memb Consultative Assembly of Cncl of Europe and Western Euro Union 1969–71, memb Chm's Panel House of Commons 1971–79; oppn spokesman (Lords) Social Security 1983–89; hon fell Birkbeck Coll 1994; *Style*— The Rt Hon the Lady Jeger; ✉ 9 Cumberland Terrace, Regent's Park, London NW1

JEHANGIR, Sir Hirji Cowasji; 3 Bt (UK 1908), of Bombay; s of Sir Cowasji Jehangir, 2 Bt, GBE, KCIE (d 1962); *b* 1 Nov 1915; *Educ* St Xavier's Sch Bombay, Magdalene Coll Cambridge; *m* 10 Aug 1952, Jinoo, er da of Kakushroo H Cama; 2 s (Jehangir b 1953, Ardeshir b 1956); *Heir* s, Jehangir Hirji Jehangir, b 23 Nov 1953, m 21 March 1988, Jasmine, da of Beji Billimoria (1 s, Cowasji b 28 March 1990, 1 da Simone b 19 July 1994); *Career* merchant and landlord; chm: Jehangir Art Gallery Bombay, Cowasji Jehangir Charity Tst; pres Parsi Public Sch Soc; *Clubs* Willingdon (Bombay), Royal Over-Seas League; *Style*— Sir Hirji Jehangir, Bt; ✉ Readymoney House, 49 Nepean Sea Rd, Bombay-400 036, India; 24 Kensington Court Gdns, Kensington Court Place, London W8

JEHU, Jeremy Charles Rhys; s of Thomas Colin Jehu, of Pyrford, Surrey, and Betty Burrows, *née* Wilson; *b* 31 Aug 1955; *Educ* Royal GS Guildford, Univ Coll Durham (BA); *Career* journalist; Surrey Daily Advertiser: joined 1976, chief reporter main area office 1978–79, sub ed 1979; The Stage and Television Today: joined 1979, news ed 1986, dep ed 1986–92, ed 1992–94; freelance journalist and conslt 1995–; fndr memb Arts Correspondent Gp 1981 (memb Ctee 1981–90), memb Bdcasting Press Guild 1989 (memb Ctee 1990–92); *Recreations* shooting, classic car ownership, gossip, politics, all the usual cultural pursuits; *Clubs* Savage, Green Room (hon memb), London and Middx Rifle Assoc, Tennessee Squires Assoc, CAA (hon memb); *Style*— Jeremy Jehu, Esq; ✉ 11 Rita Road, London SW8 1JX (☎ 0171 587 0423)

JEJEEBHOY, Sir Jamsetjee; 7 Bt (UK 1857), of Bombay; s of Rustamjee J C Jamsetjee (d 1947), n of 4 Bt; suc kinsman Sir Jamsetjee Jejeebhoy 1968, when he assumed the name of Jamsetjee Jejeebhoy in lieu of Maneckjee Rustamjee Jamsetjee; *b* 19 April 1913; *Educ* Univ of Bombay (BA); *m* 1943, Shirin, da of late Jehangir Hormusjee Cama; 1 s (Rustomjee, *qv*, b 16 Nov 1957), 1 da (Ayesha b 1952); *Heir* s, Rustomjee Jejeebhoy b 16 Nov 1957; *Career* chm: Sir Jamsetjee Jejeebhoy Charity Fund, Sir J J Parsee Benevolent Instn, Zoroastrian Bldg Fund, Seth Rustomjee Jamsetjee Jejeebhoy Gujarat Sch Fund, M F Cama Athornan Instn & M M Cama Educn Fund, Bombay Panjrapole, HB Wadia Atash-Behram Funds, Parsee Dhandha Rojgar Fund, Fasli Atash-Kadeh Tst, Iran League, K R Cama Oriental Inst, Framjee Cowasjee Inst; tstee: A H Wadia Charity Tst, Byramjee Jeejeebhoy Parsi Charitable Instn, Nanabhoy Jejeebhoy Charities, Cowasji Behramji Divecha Charity Tst, Parsee Surat Charity Fund, H D Saher Fire Temple & Charity Tst, Ashburner Fire Temple Tst, Vatcha Fire Temple & Charity Tst, Eranee Charity Funds and Dharamhala; dir: Enjay Estates Pvt Ltd 1972, Beaulieu Investment Pvt Ltd 1975, Palmera Investment Pvt Ltd 1984, Dawn Threads Pvt Ltd 1984; memb Exec Ctee Bomanjee Dinshaw Petit Parsee Gen Hosp; created Special Exec Magistrate 1977; Hon Freeman and Liveryman Worshipful Co of Clockmakers 1995; *Clubs* Willingdon Sports, WIAA, Royal Western India Turf, Ripon; *Style*— Sir Jamsetjee Jejeebhoy, Bt; ✉ Beaulieu, 95 Worli Seaface, Bombay 400 025, India (☎ 00 91 22 493 0955); Maneckjee Wadia Building, 127 Mahatma Gandhi Rd, Fort, Bombay 400 001, India (☎ 00 91 22 2673843)

JEJEEBHOY, Rustomjee; s and h of Sir Jamsetjee Jejeebhoy, 7 Bt, of Bombay, and Shirin Jamsetjee Jejeebhoy; *b* 16 Nov 1957; *Educ* Bombay Univ (BCom, LLM); *m* 1984, Delara Jal Bhaisa, da of Jal Nariman Bhaisa, of Bombay; 1 s (Jehangir b 20 Jan 1986); *Career* tstee: Sir Jamsetjee Jejeebhoy Parsee Benevolent Instn, Sir Jamsetjee Jejeebhoy Charity Fund, Seth Rustomjee Jamsetjee Jejeebhoy Gujarat Sch Fund, Parsee Dhandha Rojgar Fund, Eranee Charity Funds and Dharamshala; dep mangr (legal) TATA Exports Ltd Bombay 1983–; dir: Beaulieu Investment Pvt Ltd 1975, Dawn Threads Pvt Ltd 1984, Palmera Investment Pvt Ltd 1984, Special Paints Ltd 1996; *Clubs* Willingdon Sports, Royal Western India Turf; *Style*— Rustomjee Jejeebhoy, Esq; ✉ Beaulieu, 95 Worli Seaface, Bombay 400 025 (☎ 00 91 22 493 8517); Block A, Shivsagar Estates, Dr Annie Besant Rd, Worli, Bombay 400018 (☎ 00 91 22 494 8573)

JELLICOE, (Patricia) Ann; OBE (1984); da of Maj John Andrea Jellicoe (d 1975), and Frances Jackson Henderson (d 1995); *b* 15 July 1927; *Educ* Polam Hall Sch Darlington, Queen Margaret's Sch Castle Howard York, Central Sch of Speech & Drama; *m* 1962, David Roger Mayne; 1 s (Tom b 1969), 1 da (Katkin b 1966); *Career* theatre director, playwright and actress; fndr Cockpit Theatre Co to experiment with Open Stage 1952–54, taught acting and directed plays Central Sch of Speech and Drama 1954–56, literary mangr Royal Court Theatre 1972–74, set up first community play Lyme Regis 1978, fndr and dir Colway Theatre Tst (to produce and develop community plays); Elsie Fogarty prize 1947, 3rd prize Observer Playwriting Competition 1956; *Books* Some Unconscious Influences in the Theatre (1967), The Shell Guide to Devon (with Roger Mayne, 1975), Community Plays-How to Put Them on (1987); *Plays* The Sport of My Mad Mother (1958), The Knack (1962), Shelley (1965), The Giveaway (1969), Flora and the Bandits (1975), The Bargain (1979); for children: The Rising Generation (1967), You'll Never Guess! (1973), Clever Elsie, Smiling John, Silent Peter (1974), A Good Thing or a Bad Thing (1974); community plays incl: The Reckoning (1978), The Tide (1980), The Western Women (1984), Money & Land (1988), Under the God (1989), Changing Places (1992); translations and adaptations: Rosmersholm (1959), The Lady From the Sea (1961), The Seagull (1964), Der Freischutz (1964); *Recreations* reading theatrical biography; *Style*— Ms Ann Jellicoe, OBE; ✉ Colway Manor, Lyme Regis, Dorset DT7 3HD

JELLICOE, 2 Earl (UK 1925); George Patrick John Rushworth Jellicoe; KBE (1986), DSO (1942), MC (1944), PC (1963); also Viscount Jellicoe of Scapa (UK 1917), and Viscount Brocas of Southampton (UK 1925); s of Adm of the Fleet 1 Earl Jellicoe, GCB, OM, GCVO (d 1935); *b* 4 April 1918; *Educ* Winchester, Trinity Coll Cambridge (exhibitioner); *m* 1, 23 March 1944 (m dis 1966), Patricia Christine, o da of late Jeremiah O'Kane, of Vancouver, Canada; 2 s (Viscount Brocas b 1950, Hon Nicholas Charles b 1953), 2 da (Lady Alexandra Patricia Gwendoline Wilson b 1944, Lady Zara Lison Josephine b 1948); m 2, 1966, Philippa Ann, da of late Philip Dunne, of Gatley Park, Leominster; 1 s (Hon John Philip b 1966), 2 da (Lady Emma Rose b 1967, Lady Daisy b 1970); *Heir* s, Viscount Brocas; *Career* page of honour to HM King George VI; WWII: ME Lt-Col Coldstream Gds, 1 SAS Regt, Special Boat Serv Regt (wounded, despatches thrice, Legion of Honour, French Croix de Guerre, Greek War Cross); Dip Serv 1947–58 (served Washington, Brussels and Baghdad (as dep sec gen Baghdad Pact)); Lord-in-Waiting to HM The Queen Feb-June 1961; Parly under-sec Miny of Housing and Local Govt 1961–62, Min of State Home Office 1962–63, First Lord of the Admty 1963–64, Min of Defence for the RN 1964, Lord Privy Seal, Min i/c Civil Service and Leader of the House of Lords 1970–73; dir Tate & Lyle plc 1973–93 (chm 1978–83); chm: Davy Corporation 1985–90, Booker Tate 1988–91, European Capital Ltd 1991–95, Greece Fund 1987–94; dir: Sotheby's Holdings 1973–93, S G Warburg & Co 1973–88, Morgan Crucible 1974–88, Smiths Industries 1973–86; pres: London C of C 1980–83, Br Heart Fndn 1992–95, Royal Geographical Soc 1993–; chm: Br Overseas Trade Bd 1983–86, E Euro Trade Cncl 1986–90 (pres 1990–95), Parly & Scientific Ctee 1980–83, Prevention of Terrorism Act Review 1982–83, Cncl of King's Coll London 1974–83, MRC 1982–90; chllr Southampton Univ 1984–; Liveryman Worshipful Co of Mercers; Legion of Honour and Croix de Guerre (France), Grand Cdr of the Order of Honour (Greece) 1991; FRS 1990; *Recreations* travel, skiing; *Clubs* Brooks's, Special Forces; *Style*— The Rt Hon the Earl Jellicoe, KBE, DSO, MC, PC, FRS; ✉ Tidcombe Manor, Tidcombe, nr Marlborough, Wilts (☎ 01264 731 225); 97 Onslow Square, London SW7 (☎ 0171 584 1551)

JELLICOE, Dr Jillian Ann; da of George Molyneux Jellicoe (d 1972), of Liverpool, and Ellen, *née* Fitzsimmons (d 1991); *b* 28 June 1947; *Educ* Holly Lodge HS for Girls Liverpool, KCH Med Sch; *m* 29 Sept 1973, Alan Fitzgerald, s of Raymond Charles Fitzgerald, of Brockenhurst, Hants; *Career* house surgn and house physician Hereford Hosps 1970–71; sr house offr in: obstetrics Royal Victoria Hosp Bournemouth 1972, anaesthetics Whiston Hosp Lancs 1972–73; GP Bournemouth 1973–77, registrar Liverpool RHA 1978–80, sr registrar Wessex Region 1981–84, conslt anaesthetist Shackleton Dept of Anaesthetics Southampton Gen Hosp 1985–, clinical sub-dean Sch of Med Univ of Southampton 1989–; memb: BMA, Assoc of Anaesthetists, Assoc of Cardio-Thoracic Anaesthetists; LRCP, MRCS 1970, DObstRCOG 1972, DA 1973, FFARCS 1980; *Recreations* reading, watching cricket, cats, church architecture; *Style*— Dr Jillian Ann Jellicoe; ✉ Shackleton Department of Anaesthetics, Southampton General Hospital, Tremona Road, Southampton (☎ 01703 777222)

JENCKS, Charles Alexander; s of Gardner Platt Jencks (d 1989), and Ruth Dewitt, *née* Pearl; *b* 21 June 1939; *Educ* Brooks Sch, Harvard Univ (BA, MA), Univ of London (Fulbright scholar, PhD); *m* 1, Pamela Balding; 2 s (Ivor Cosimo b 1969, Justin Alexander b 1972); m 2, 1978, Maggie (d 1995), da of Sir John Henry Keswick, KCMG (d 1982); 1 s (John Keswick b 1979), 1 da (Lily Clare b 1980); *Career* writer on architecture 1966–, lectr and prof 1969–, TV writer and sometime participant 1971–, architect and designer 1976–, writer on art 1985–, garden designer 1989–, writer on non architectural subjects 1989–; author of numerous books and articles on the subject of modern architecture and its successors; furniture and drawings exhibited; lectures at over 40 int univs; memb: AA, RSA; Nara Gold Medal for Architecture 1992; *Clubs* Groucho, Athenaeum, Chelsea Arts; *Style*— Charles Jencks, Esq; ✉ Academy Editions, 42 Leinster Gardens, London W2 (☎ 0171 402 2141, fax 0171 723 9540)

JENKALA, Adrian Aleksander; s of Georgius Ihorus Jenkala, and Olena, *née* Karpynec; *b* 21 May 1957; *Educ* Latymer Upper Sch, Univ of London (BSc, LLB); *Career* called to the Bar Middle Temple 1984; practising barr 1984–, lectr in law London Guildhall Univ 1985–92, instr Inns of Ct Sch of Law 1989–; legal sec to Int Cmmn of Inquiry into 1932–33 Famine in Ukraine 1987–90 (report presented to UN in 1990); Sch of Slavonic and East European Studies (SSEES): chm Ukrainian Studies Tst Fund Ctee 1991–, hon res fell 1993–; official international observer at the referendum and presidential elections in Ukraine 1991; chm Assoc of Ukrainian Lawyers 1987–, memb Bd World Congress of Ukrainian Lawyers 1992– (vice pres (Europe) 1994–); sec Br-Ukrainian Law Assoc 1993–; memb: Bd of Foreign Advisers Ukrainian Legal Fndn Kiev, Central and E European Sub-Ctee of the Int Practice Ctee of Bar Cncl, Hon Soc of the Middle Temple; Freeman City of London; ACIArb; *Books* Ukrainian Legal Dictionary (ed, 1994); *Recreations* squash, skiing, ski instructing; *Style*— Adrian Jenkala, Esq; ✉ 11 Bolt Court, London EC4A 3DQ (☎ 0171 353 2300, fax 0171 353 1878)

JENKIN, Hon Bernard Christison; MP (C) Colchester N (majority 16,492); yr son of Baron Jenkin of Roding, PC, *qv*; *b* 9 April 1959; *Educ* Highgate, William Ellis Sch, Corpus Christi Coll Cambridge; *m* 24 Sept 1988, Anne Caroline, da of late Hon Charles Strutt, and sis of 6 Baron Rayleigh, *qv*; 2 s (Robert Patrick Christison b 13 May 1989, Peter Andrew Graham b 29 July 1991); *Career* sales and mktg exec Ford Motor Co Ltd 1983–86, with 3i plc 1986–92, mangr Legal and General Ventures Ltd until 1992, advsr Legal & General Group plc 1992–95; election asst to Sir Hugh Rossi MP 1979 and 1983, res asst to Sir Leon Brittan MP 1986–89, Parly candidate Glasgow Central 1987, MP Colchester N 1992–; memb Social Security Select Ctee 1993–, PPS to Rt Hon Michael Forsyth, MP (Sec of State for Scotland) 1995–; *Recreations* sailing, music (esp opera), fishing, family, DIY; *Style*— The Hon Bernard Jenkin, MP; ✉ House of Commons, London SW1A 0AA (fax 0171 219 5963)

JENKIN, Rear Adm (David) Conrad; CB (1983); s of C O F Jenkin; yr bro of Baron Jenkin of Roding (Life Peer), *qv*; *b* 25 Oct 1928, ; *Educ* RNC Dartmouth; *m* 1958, Jennifer Margaret Nowell; 3 s, 1 da; *Career* RN 1942, Flag Offr First Flotilla 1981–82, Cmdt Jt Servs Def Coll 1982–84; *Style*— Rear Adm Conrad Jenkin, CB; ✉ Knapsyard House, West Meon, Hants GU32 1LF (☎ 01730 829227)

JENKIN, Ian Evers Tregarthen; OBE (1984); s of late Henry Archibald Tregarthen Jenkin, OBE (d 1951), of The Firs, Norton, Worcs, and Dagmar, *née* Leggott (d 1969); *b* 18 June 1920; *Educ* Stowe, Slade Sch of Fine Art, Camberwell Sch of Art and Crafts, Trinity Coll Cambridge (MA); *Career* Mil Serv RA 1940–46; Open Coll of the Arts: co-fndr (with Lord Young of Dartington) 1986, dir 1986–89, pres 1989–91, vice pres 1991–; curator Royal Acad Schs 1985–86, princ Camberwell Sch of Art and Crafts 1975–85, ret; sec and tutor Slade Sch of Fine Art UCL 1949–75; memb: Art Panel Arts Cncl 1979–82 (also vice chm), Crafts Cncl 1981–84 (also chm Educn Ctee), Nat Advsy Body for Public Sector Higher Educn Art and Design Working Gp 1982–85, Nat Conservation Advsy Ctee 1984–86, Arts Ctee RSA 1989–93; chm: Selection Bd for Scholarships and Awards in Painting 1982–91, Gulbenkian Fndn Craft Initiative Working Pty 1985–89; Br Sch at Rome: memb Cncl 1981–90, chm Painting Faculty 1977–86, Fine Arts Faculty 1986–90, memb Fin and Gen Purposes Ctee 1986–90, memb Mgmnt Ctee 1990–95; govr: Hounslow Borough Coll 1976–81, W Surrey Coll of Art and Design 1975–94, Wimbledon Sch of Art 1985–90, Loughborough Coll of Art and Design 1985–94, Norfolk Inst of Art and Design 1988–90, Surrey Inst of Art & Design 1994–95; memb Exec Ctee Arts Servs Grants Ltd 1977–90 (vice chm 1983–90), fndr and tstee Camberwell Residential Academic and Fellowship Tst, pres Dulwich Decorative and Fine Arts Soc 1984–95; memb: Exec Ctee and Restoration Advsy Ctee City and Guilds of London Art Sch 1985–, Fine Art Advsy Bd Amersham Coll of Further Educn 1990–92, Arts Consultative Ctee Langley Coll 1991–93; moderator City and Guilds of London Inst Graduateship Awards 1992–, vice pres The Nine Elms Group of Artists 1991–, art adjudicator Koestler Awards to UK (prisoners and patients in special hosps) 1990–; tstee: Sir Stanley Spencer Meml Tst 1982–, Birgit Skiöld Meml Tst 1988–; memb Advsy Ctee Paintings in Hospitals 1982–; chm: E Vincent Harris Fund for Mural Decoration 1993–, Edwin Austin Abbey Meml Scholarships 1994– (memb Cncl 1985–94); dir Guild of St George 1986– (companion 1984–); Hon Dr Arts CNAA 1987, hon fell W Surrey Coll of Art and Design 1993, hon memb City and Guilds of London Inst 1995; FRSA 1975; *Publications* Disaster Planning and Preparedness, A Survey of Practices and Procedures (British Library R & D Report, 1986), An Outline Disaster Control Plan (British Library Information Guide, 1987), William Johnson, His Contribution to Art Education (1981); contribs to DNB; *Recreations* painting, gardening, farming; *Clubs* Athenaeum, Bucks, Arts; *Style*— Ian Tregarthen Jenkin, Esq, OBE; ✉ Grove Farm, Fifield, Maidenhead, Berks SL6 2PF (☎ 01628 24486)

JENKIN OF RODING, Baron (Life Peer UK 1987), of Wanstead and Woodford in Greater London; (Charles) Patrick Fleeming Jenkin; PC (1973); s of Charles O F Jenkin (d 1939), of Gerrards Cross, Bucks; er bro of Rear Adm David Conrad Jenkin, *qv*; *b* 7 Sept 1926; *Educ* Clifton, Jesus Coll Cambridge; *m* 1952, Alison Monica, eldest da of late Capt Philip Skelton Graham, RN; 2 s (Rev Hon Charles Alexander Graham Jenkin b 1954, Hon Bernard Christison Jenkin MP, *qqv*, b 1959), 2 da (Hon Nicola Mary b 1956, Hon Flora Margaret b 1962); *Career* Queen's Own Cameron Highlanders 1945–48; called to the Bar Middle Temple 1952–57, Distillers Co Ltd 1957–70; memb Hornsey Borough Cncl 1960–63; govr Westfield Coll Univ of London 1964–70; MP (C) Wanstead and Woodford 1964–87, jt vice chm Cons Parly Trade and Power Ctee 1966, oppn front bench spokesman on Treasy, Trade and Econ Affrs 1965–70, fin sec to Treasy 1970–72, chief sec to Treasy 1972–74, min for Energy Jan-March 1974, memb Shadow Cabinet and shadow spokesman on Energy 1974–76 and on Social Servs 1976–79; sec of state for: Social Servs 1979–81, Indust 1981–83, DOE 1983–85; chm Friends' Provident Life Office; memb Supervisory Bd Achmea Holding NV Netherlands, dir Nat Econ Res Assocs Inc (UK office); advsr: Andersen Consulting, Sumitomo Tst and Bank Ltd, Marsh & McLennan Group of Companies Int Advsy Bd (US); dir UK-Japan 2000 Gp (chm 1986–90); chm: Forest Healthcare NHS Tst, Westfield Coll Tst; tstee: Monteverdi Choir and Orch Ltd, Queen Elizabeth's Fndn for the Disabled People Devpt Tst; dep chm Cncl Imperial Cancer Res Fund; vice pres: Foundation for Science and Technology, Nat Assoc of Local Cncls, Nat Federation of Housing Assoc, Assoc of Metropolitan Authorities; tstee Conservative Agents Superannuation Fund; jt pres Assoc of London Govt; pres British Urban Regeneration Assoc; memb Cncl Guide Dogs for The Blind Assoc; chm Visual Handicap Gp; memb advsry bd UK CEED; advsr Thames Estuary Airport Co Ltd; memb Internat Advsry Bd Nijenrode Univ (Netherlands); patron: Stort Tst, St Clair Hospice Tst, Roding Conservation Gp, Redbridge Community Tst, Waltham Forest Alcohol Counselling Servs; *Recreations* gardening, music, bricklaying, sailing, DIY; *Clubs* West Essex Cons; *Style*— The Rt Hon the Lord Jenkin of Roding, PC; ✉ 15 Old Bailey, London EC4M 7AP (☎ 0171 329 4454, fax 0171 248 6332)

JENKINS, Alan Dominique; s of Ian Samuel Jenkins, of Dorset, and Jeannette Juliette Jenkins; *b* 27 May 1952; *Educ* Clifton Coll, New Coll Oxford (BA); *m* 30 June 1979, Caroline, da of Paul Treverton Jones (d 1983), of Gwent; 1 s (Mark b 30 May 1982), 3 da (Claire b 13 April 1984, Alice 17 Oct 1989, Emily b 9 Nov 1991); *Career* admitted slr 1977, ptnr Frere Cholmeley Bischoff 1983–; memb: Law Soc, City of London Slrs' Co, Int Bar Assoc; FRSA; *Recreations* sport; *Clubs* MCC, Roehampton; *Style*— Alan Jenkins, Esq; ✉ Frere Cholmeley Bischoff, 4 John Carpenter Street, London EC4Y 0NH (☎ 0171 615 8000, fax 0171 615 8080, telex 27623 FRERESG)

JENKINS, Alan Niell; s of John Niell Jenkins, of Neston, Wirral, and Elizabeth Alice Griffiths, *née* May; *b* 24 July 1947; *Educ* Wirral GS, Liverpool Art Coll; *Career* motor racing design engr; asst designer McLaren International 1980–84 (engr to world champion Alain Prost 1984), chief designer Penske Racing Indy cars 1985–87 (champions 1985, winners Indianapolis 500 1985 and 1987), chief designer Onyx Grand Prix 1988–90, tech dir Footwork Grand Prix International 1990–; *Recreations* following my wife's passion for show horses; *Style*— Alan Jenkins, Esq; ✉ Footwork Grand Prix International, 39 Barton Rd, Water Eaton Industrial Estate, Bletchley, Milton Keynes MK2 3HW

JENKINS, (Thomas) Alun; QC (1996); s of Seward Thomas Jenkins, of Abergavenny, and Iris Jenkins; *b* 19 Aug 1948; *Educ* Ebbw Vale Tech Sch, Univ of Bristol (LLB); *m* 1971, Glenys Maureen, da of Maj John Constant, of Abergavenny; 2 da (Clare Elizabeth b 19 Sept 1976, Katie Jane b 19 Dec 1982), 1 s (Christopher Alun b 7 Nov 1985); *Career* called to the Bar Lincoln's Inn 1972, in practice in Bristol 1972–, asst recorder of the Crown Ct 1992–; *Recreations* horse riding, horse racing, point to point, rugby, motor cars, reading; *Style*— Alun Jenkins, Esq, QC; ✉ All Saints Chambers, 9/11 Broad Street, Bristol BS1 2HP (☎ 0117 921 1966, fax 0117 927 6493, mobile 0973 135238)

JENKINS, Anne; da of Roy Dudley, of Blackpool, Lancs, and Georgina Ledlie, *née* McKeen (d 1996); *Educ* Elmslie Girls' Sch Blackpool, Univ of Manchester (BA); *m* 24 Sept 1988, Peter Lewis Jenkins, s of David Jenkins (d 1994); 1 da (Victoria Anne b 14 June 1993), 1 s (William Dudley b 23 April 1996); *Career* Neville Russell CAs Stockport 1980–84 (ACA 1983), Peat Marwick CAs London 1984–85, The Financial Training Co 1986–90, ind trg conslt in fin 1990–; ICAEW: memb Cncl 1993–, chm Recruitment and Promotion Ctee 1994–96, memb Educn and Trg Directorate 1994–; memb Ctee Women in Accountancy 1994–, memb Business Law Ctee 1996–; awarded FCA 1994; *Recreations* swimming, running, cycling, skiing, theatre; *Clubs* LA Fitness (Isleworth); *Style*— Mrs Anne Jenkins; ✉ Anne Jenkins Training, 50 Beaconsfield Road, St Margarets, Middx TW1 3HU (☎ 0181 287 4003)

JENKINS, Prof Aubrey Dennis; s of Arthur William Jenkins (d 1982), and Mabel Emily, *née* Street (d 1970); *b* 6 Sept 1927; *Educ* Dartford GS, Sir John Cass Tech Inst, King's Coll London (BSc, PhD, DSc); *m* 29 Dec 1987, Jitka, da of Josef Horský (d 1975); *Career* res chemist Courtaulds Fundamental Res Laboratory 1950–60, res mangr Gillette Fundamental Res Laboratory 1960–64, prof of polymer sci Univ of Sussex 1971– (joined 1964); sec: Macromolecular Div Int Union of Pure and Applied Chemistry 1985–93, Br High Polymer Res Gp 1991–; memb Brighton Health Authy 1983–90; Heyrovský Gold Medal for Chemistry Czechoslovak Acad of Sciences 1990; FRSC 1957; *Books* Kinetics of Vinyl Polymerization (1958), Reactivity Mechanism and Structure in Polymer Chemistry (1974), Polymer Science (1972); *Recreations* music, travel; *Clubs* GB, E Europe Centre; *Style*— Prof Aubrey Jenkins; ✉ Shoe Box Cottage, 115 Keymer Road, Hassocks, W Sussex BN6 8QL (☎ and fax 01273 845410); School of Chemistry and Molecular Sciences, Univ of Sussex, Brighton, Sussex BN1 9QJ (☎ 01273 678419, fax 01273 677196)

JENKINS, Sir Brian Garton; GBE (1991); s of Owen Garton Jenkins (d 1963), and Doris Enid, *née* Webber (d 1986); *b* 3 Dec 1935; *Educ* Tonbridge, Trinity Coll Oxford (MA); *m* 2 Jun 1967, (Elizabeth) Ann, da of John Philip Manning Prentice (d 1981), of Suffolk; 1 da (Julia b 1971), 1 s (Charles b 1973); *Career* 2 Lt RA 1955–57, served Gibraltar; ptnr Coopers & Lybrand 1969–95; chm Woolwich Building Society May 1995– (dir 1994–); pres ICAEW 1985–86; govr Royal Shakespeare Theatre 1981–; memb: Cmmn for New Towns 1990–, Ctee Automobile Assoc 1995–; tstee Charities Aid Fndn 1994–; Alderman City of London 1980– (Sheriff 1987–88); Lord Mayor of London 1991–92; Liveryman: Worshipful Co of CAs 1980– (Master 1990), Worshipful Co of Merchant Taylors 1984– (memb Ct 1989–, Warden 1996), Worshipful Co of Information Technologists 1985– (Master 1994–95); Hon Liveryman Worshipful Co of Cordwainers; hon bencher Inner Temple; hon fell Trinity Coll Oxford; Hon DSc City Univ, Hon DLitt London Guildhall Univ; FCA 1974 (ACA 1963), FRSA 1980; *Books* An Audit Approach to Computers (jtly, 4 edn, 1992); *Recreations* garden construction, old books, large jigsaw puzzles, ephemera; *Clubs* Brooks's, City of London, City Livery; *Style*— Sir Brian Jenkins, GBE; ✉ 12 Devereux Court, Strand, London WC2R 3JJ (☎ 0171 353 6775, fax 0171 353 6778)

JENKINS, Brian Stuart; s of Harold Griffith Jenkins (d 1970), of Christleton, Chester, and Ida Lily, *née* Stuart (d 1986); *b* 26 May 1934; *Educ* Shrewsbury; *m* 5 Sept 1959, Teresa Sheelagh, da of Stephen George Ronan (d 1980), of St Asaph, N Wales; 2 s (Nicolaus Stuart b 13 March 1961, Simon Spencer b 26 March 1962), 1 da (Vanessa Stephanie b 7 July 1965); *Career* RN 1952–54, Midshipman 1953 (served HMS Surprise, fleet despatch vessel Med Fleet), Mersey Div RNR, ret Lt 1960; CA; sr ptnr Haswell Bros 1970–93; chm: Wrexham Water plc 1987– (dir 1969–), Dee Valley Water plc 1994–; dir Mersey RHA 1990–94; former memb Wales Regnl Bd TSB Gp plc; FCA 1966; *Recreations* sailing, shooting, travel; *Clubs* Royal Yacht Sqdn, Royal Ocean Racing; *Style*— Brian Jenkins, Esq; ✉ Beeston House, Tarporley, Cheshire CW6 9ST (☎ 01829 260326)

JENKINS, Catrin Mary; da of Charles Bryan Jenkins, of Southerndown, Mid Glamorgan, and Anne, *née* Davies-Jones; *b* 22 Dec 1958; *Educ* Llanelli Girls GS, Univ Coll Cardiff (LLB); *Career* admitted slr 1983; ptnr: Eversheds Phillips & Buck 1988–95, Francis & Buck 1995–; *Style*— Miss Catrin Jenkins; ✉ 15 Hollybush Rise, Cyncoed, Cardiff, Wales (☎ 01222 562316); Francis & Buck, Celtic House, Cathedral Road, Cardiff, Wales CF1 9LJ (☎ 01222 344995)

JENKINS, Hon Charles Arthur Simon; s of Baron Jenkins of Hillhead (Life Peer), *qv*; *b* 25 March 1949; *Educ* Winchester, Holland Park Sch, New Coll Oxford; *m* 11 Sept 1971, Ivana Alexandra, da of Ing Ivo Vladimir Sertic (d 1986), of Zagreb, Croatia; 2 da (Alexandra Dorothea b 14 March 1986, Helena Harriet b 13 May 1988); *Career* European ed Economist Intelligence Unit 1975–, ed Euro Trends (quarterly magazine on European affairs); memb Exec Ctee Be Section European League for Economic Coperation; memb

Clapham Action on Tport; *Style*— The Hon Charles Jenkins; ✉ Economist Intelligence Unit, 15 Regents Street, London SW1Y 4LR (☎ 0171 830 1036)

JENKINS, (James) Christopher; CB (1987), Hon QC (1994); s of Percival Si Phillips Jenkins (d 1988), and Dela, *née* Griffiths (d 1983); *b* 20 May 1939; *Educ* Lewes Co GS, Magdalen Coll Oxford (Mackinnon scholar, MA); *m* 1962, Margaret Elaine, da of late Rt Hon John Edwards; 2 s, 1 da; *Career* slr Slaughter and May 1962–67; Parliamentary Counsel Office: joined 1967, seconded to Law Cmmn 1970–72 and 1983–86, first parliamentary counsel 1994–; *Style*— Christopher Jenkins, Esq, CB, QC; ✉ Parliamentary Counsel Office, 36 Whitehall, London SW1A 2AY (☎ 0171 210 6640)

JENKINS, Prof David; s of Alfred Thomas Jenkins (d 1960), and Doris Cecilia, *née* Hutchings (d 1994); *b* 1 March 1926; *Educ* Marlborough, Royal Vet Coll (MRCVS), Univ of Cambridge (MA), Univ of Oxford (DPhil, DSc); *m* 8 April 1961, Margaret, da of James Wellwood Johnston (d 1958); 1 da (Fenella b 1967), 1 s (Gavin b 1969); *Career* vertebrate ecologist Nature Conservancy 1956–72; asst dir res Scotland NC 1966–72, Inst of Terrestrial Ecology 1972–86 (head Banchory Res Station), hon prof of zoology Univ of Aberdeen 1986–; memb NE Regnl Bd Nature Conservancy Cncl for Scotland and Scottish Natural Heritage 1992–95; chm Sci Advsy Ctee World Pheasant Assoc 1976–94; FRSE 1986; *Publications include* Population control in protected partridges (1961), Social behaviour in the partridge (1963), Population studies on red grouse in N E Scotland (with A Watson and G R Miller, 1963), Population fluctuations in the red grouse (with A Watson and G R Miller, 1967), Structure and regulation of a shelduck population (with M G Murray and P Hall, 1975), several papers on ecology of otters in Scotland; *Recreations* international wildlife conservation, editing, natural history, gardening; *Style*— Prof David Jenkins, FRSE; ✉ Whitewalls, Aboyne, Aberdeenshire AB34 5JB (☎ 013398 86526)

JENKINS, Dr David Anthony Lawson; s of Phillip Ronald Jenkins (d 1969), of Folkestone, Kent, and Olive Lilian, *née* Lear; *b* 5 Dec 1938; *Educ* Dauntsey's Sch Wilts, Clare Coll Cambridge (BA, DPhil); *m* 13 Feb 1963, Evanthia, da of Spirithonos Nicolopoulou, of Patras, Greece; 2 s (Charles David b 19 June 1969, Anthony Phillip b 8 Aug 1970); *Career* BP: joined 1961, chief geologist Exploration 1979–82, sr vice pres Exploration and Prodn Canada 1983–84, gen mangr Exploration 1985–88, chief exec Technol Exploration 1988–, dir Exploration 1989–, dir Canada 1989–; chm Oil Industry Int Exploration and Prodn Forum 1991–, dir Petroleum Sci and Technol Inst 1990–, memb Advsy Cncl AAPG 1991–; FGS, AAPG; *Recreations* shooting, tennis, opera, gardening, current affairs; *Style*— Dr David Jenkins; ✉ Ardennes, East Road, St George's Hill, Weybridge, Surrey KT13 0LB; BP Exploration Operating Co Ltd, Chertsey Road, Sunbury-on-Thames, Middx TW16 7LN 1BP (☎ 01932 764281, fax 01932 762384, telex 888811 BPLDN)

JENKINS, Rt Rev David Edward; er s of Lionel Charles Jenkins, and Dora Katherine, *née* Page; *b* 26 Jan 1925; *Educ* St Dunstan's Coll Catford London, Queen's Coll Oxford (MA); *m* 1949, Stella Mary, da of Henry Leonard Peet (d 1976); 2 s (Christopher, Timothy), 2 da (Deborah, Rebecca); *Career* temp cmmn RA 1945–47, Capt; priest 1954, succentor Birmingham Cathedral 1953–54, fell chaplain and praelector in theology The Queen's Coll Oxford 1954–69, dir of humanum studies World Cncl of Churches Geneva 1969–73, dir William Temple Fndn Manchester 1974–79 (chm 1987–94), prof of theology Univ of Leeds 1979–84, bishop of Durham 1984–94, hon asst bishop Diocese of Ripon 1994–; chm SCM Press 1989–95; Hon DD: Univ of Durham 1987, Trinity Coll Toronto 1989, Univ of Aberdeen 1990; Hon DLitt Univ of Teeside 1993, Hon DCL Univ of Northumbria 1994, Hon DD Univ of Birmingham 1996, Hon DD Univ of Leeds 1996, Hon DUniv Open Univ 1996; hon fell: St Chad's Durham 1986, Sunderland Poly (now Univ) 1986, Queen's Coll Oxford 1990; *Books* Guide to the Debate about God (1966), The Glory of Man (1967, republished 1984), Living with Questions (1969), Man Fallen and Free (contrib, 1969), What is Man? (1970), The Contradiction of Christianity (1976, republished 1985), God, Miracles and the Church of England (1987), God, Politics and the Future (1988), God, Jesus and Life in the Spirit (1988), Still Living With Questions (1990, revised version of Living With Questions), Free to Believe (with Rebecca Jenkins, 1991); *Recreations* music (opera), walking, travel, books; *Style*— The Rt Rev David Jenkins; ✉ Ashbourne, Cotherstone, Barnard Castle, Co Durham DL12 9PR (☎ 01833 650804, fax 01833 651714)

JENKINS, Derek William; s of William Jenkins (d 1961), of Burnley, Lancs, and Annie, *née* Haydock (d 1993); *b* 12 Sept 1934; *Educ* Burnley GS; *m* 3 June 1961, Hazel, da of late George Watson; 2 da (Fiona Louise (Mrs Fiona Seabrook) b 22 Dec 1962, Alison Helen (Mrs Alison Winter) b 8 Feb 1966); *Career* articled clerk Proctor and Proctor CAs Burnley 1950–58 (Nat Serv 1952–54), various appts Binder Hamlyn & Co 1958–66, asst tax administrator Texaco UK Ltd 1966–68; RMC Group plc: gp taxation mangr 1968–77, gp financial controller 1977–80, fin dir 1981–; Freeman City of London 1982, Liveryman Worshipful Co of Chartered Accountants in England and Wales 1982; FCA 1958, ATII 1962, FCT 1990; *Recreations* cartophily, swimming, golf, Burnley FC (past and present); *Clubs* Wentworth, Camberley Heath Golf, RAC; *Style*— Derek W Jenkins, Esq; ✉ RMC Group plc, RMC House, Coldharbour Lane, Thorpe, Egham, Surrey TW20 8TD (☎ 01932 568833, fax 01932 568422)

JENKINS, Edward Victor; s of Ernest Victor Jenkins (d 1977), of Keynsham, Bristol, and Winifred Agnes, *née* Capron (d 1983); *b* 17 Aug 1932; *Educ* Frays Coll Uxbridge, Ealing GS, Northampton Engrg Coll (BSc), Imperial Coll London (DIC); *m* 5 Sept 1959, Elisabeth, da of Hubert Deacon Harrison, OBE, MC (d 1987), of Victoria, Vancouver, BC, Canada; 1 s (Christopher b 1965), 1 da (Victoria b 1968); *Career* Nat Serv RE 1956–58; engrg pupil 1951–55, Holland and Hannen & Cubitts Ltd 1958–66; G Maunsell & Ptnrs: section and resident engr 1966–72, sr engr 1972–73, assoc 1973–75, project ptnr seconded to Maunsell Consultants Asia Hong Kong 1978–81, md G Maunsell & Partners 1987–93; chm Guy Maunsell International Ltd 1993–96, currently conslt; FEng 1991, FICE, MConsE; *Publications* co-author: M25 North-East Sector: Design of Holmesdale and Bell Common Tunnels (in Proceedings Institution of Civil Engineers, 1978), Hand-dug Caissons or Wells (chapter in Civil Engineering for Underground Rail Transport, 1990); *Recreations* sailing, rugby football, choral singing; *Clubs* Army & Navy, Royal Hong Kong Yacht; *Style*— Edward Jenkins, Esq, FEng; ✉ Maunsell House, 160 Croydon Rd, Beckenham, Kent BR3 4DE (☎ 0181 663 6565, fax 0181 663 6723, telex 946171)

JENKINS, Sir Elgar Spencer; kt (1996), OBE (1988); s of Spencer Jenkins (d 1984), and Mabel, *née* Gower (d 1996); *b* 16 June 1935; *Educ* Monmouth Sch, St Edmund Hall Oxford, St Luke's Coll Exeter (CertEd), Open Univ (BA); *Career* Short Serv Cmmn 1956–59; asst sch master Bath and Bristol 1962–73, dep headmaster St Gregory's Sch Bath 1973–88; chm: Bath and Dist HA 1989–93, Bath Mental Health Care NHS Tst 1993–; memb: Bath City Cncl 1966–72 and 1973–96 (Mayor, ldr of Cncl, chm 5 major ctees), Assoc of Dist Cncls 1985–96 (Cons ldr 1991–96, dep chm then vice chm 1991–96); Parly candidate (Cons) Ebbw Vale 1970, chm Cons Pty Nat Advsy Ctee on Local Govt 1994; memb Nat Advsy Ctee on Libraries 1995–, chm Tourism and Leisure Consortium 1996–; memb Bath Archaeological Tst, chm of Tstees Bath Postal Museum 1985–; FRSA 1993; *Recreations* history and reading; *Style*— Sir Elgar Jenkins, OBE; ✉ 2 Elm Croft, St Saviour's Road, Bath BA1 6SE (☎ 01225 314834); Bath Mental Health Care NHS Trust, St Martin's Hospital, Midford Road, Bath BA2 5RP (☎ 01225 832255)

JENKINS, (John) Emyr; s of Llywelyn Jenkins (d 1957), of Machynlleth, Powys, and Mary Olwen, *née* Jones (d 1967); *b* 3 May 1938; *Educ* Machynlleth Co Sch, Univ Coll of Wales (BSc); *m* 1964, Myra Bonner, da of Brynley Samuel; 2 da (Manon Bonner b 1965, Ffion Llywelyn b 1968); *Career* BBC: trainee studio mangr BBC Radio London 1961–62, asst studio mangr BBC Cardiff 1962–63, staff announcer and compere 1963–71, prog organiser BBC Wales 1971–77; dir Royal National Eisteddfod of Wales 1978–93, dir Welsh Arts Cncl 1993–94, chief exec Arts Cncl of Wales 1994–; Hon MA Univ of Wales 1993; FRSA 1992; *Recreations* music, theatre, sport, walking; *Style*— Emyr Jenkins, Esq; ✉ Arts Council of Wales, Museum Place, Cardiff CF1 3NX (☎ 01222 394711, fax 01222 221447)

JENKINS, Very Rev Frank Graham; s of Edward Jenkins (d 1961), of Glamorgan, and Miriam Martha, *née* Morse (d 1978); *b* 24 Feb 1923; *Educ* Cyfarthfa Castle Sch Merthyr Tydfil, Port Talbot Secdy GS, St David's Coll Lampeter (BA), Jesus Coll Oxford (BA, MA), St Michael's Coll Llandaff; *m* 1 Aug 1950, Ena Doraine, da of Eardley Morgan Parry (d 1970), of Port Talbot; 2 s (Timothy b 1955, Peter b 1958), 1 da (Caroline b 1951); *Career* cmmnd Welsh Regt 1944–46 (Capt), CF (TA) 1956–61; curate of Llangeinor 1950–53, minor canon Llandaff Cathedral 1953–60, vicar of Abertillery 1960–64, vicar of Risca 1964–75, vicar of Caerleon 1975–76, dean of Monmouth 1976–90; *Style*— The Very Rev F G Jenkins; ✉ Rivendell, 209 Christchurch Road, Newport, Gwent NP9 7QL (☎ 01633 255278)

JENKINS, Garin Richard; s of Eirvil Jenkins, of Ynysybwl, Pontypridd, and Anne, *née* Williams; *b* 18 Aug 1967; *m* 20 June 1992, Helen Susan, da of late Michael Voyle; 1 s (Owen Richard b 20 July 1993); *Career* rugby union player (flanker); currently with Swansea RFC; former rep: Pontypridd Schs under 11 and under 15, Rhonnda and E Glamorgan under 11's, Boys Clubs of Wales under 19, Mid-District under 19 and under 21 (v NZ), 10 appearances King Country NZ incl Ranfurly Shield v Auckland 1988; Wales: debut v France 1991, 4 appearances World Cup 1991, memb World Cup squad 1995, pack-leader Five Nations Championship 1992, 30 caps; employment: miner, labourer, timber mill worker NZ, leisure mgmnt, currently schs devpt offr Swansea Cricket and Football Club; *Recreations* football, swimming, boxing, tennis; *Style*— Garin Jenkins, Esq; ✉ Swansea RFC, St Helens, Bryn Rd, Swansea SA2 0AR (☎ 01792 466593, fax 01792 473042)

JENKINS, Prof George Charles; s of John Robinson Jenkins (d 1969), of Stoneygate, Leics, and Mabel Rebecca, *née* Smith (d 1985); *b* 2 Aug 1927; *Educ* Wyggeston GS Leics, St Bartholomew's Hosp Med Coll Univ of London (MB BS, PhD); *m* 28 April 1956, Elizabeth Claire, da of Cecil Joseph Welch (d 1963), of Carlton Rd, Ealing; 1 s (Mark Andrew b 15 Nov 1957), 2 da (Nicola Claire b 11 April 1961, Camilla Anne b 3 Jan 1963); *Career* Sqdn Ldr RAF (Med Branch) 1952–54, civilian conslt haematologist RN 1978–92 (emeritus 1992–); conslt haematologist: N Middx Hosp 1963–65, Royal London Hosp 1965–92, consulting 1992–; reader in haematology Univ of London 1971–74, prof of haematology Univ of London at London Hosp Med Coll 1974–92 (emeritus 1992–); vice pres RCPath 1981–84, pres Br Soc for Haematology 1988–89, pres Br Acad of Forensic Sci 1990–91 (chm Exec Cncl 1985–89), memb Ctee on Dental and Surgical Materials (Ctee of Safety of Meds of Dept of Health) 1990–92; patron Home Farm Tst (govr 1993–); Freeman City of London 1961, memb Worshipful Co of Spectacle Makers 1961; FRCPath 1975, FRSM 1989, FRCPE 1990, FRSA 1991; *Books* Advanced Haematology (jt ed and author), Infection and Haematology (jt ed and author, 1994); *Recreations* fishing, music, theatre going; *Style*— Prof George Jenkins; ✉ 19 Bush Hill, London N21 2DB (☎ and fax 0181 360 1484); London Hosp Medical College, Whitechapel, London E1 2AD (☎ 0171 377 7000)

JENKINS, Graeme James Ewers; s of Kenneth Arthur Jenkins, of London, and Marjorie Joyce, *née* Ewers; *b* 31 Dec 1958; *Educ* Dulwich, Gonville and Caius Coll Cambridge (MA), RCM London; *m* 19 July 1986, Joanna, da of Christopher Charles Cyprian Bridge, ERD, of E Sussex; 2 da (Martha Nancy b 18 May 1989, Isabella Dinah b 20 Dec 1991); *Career* music dir Glyndebourne Touring Opera 1985–91; has conducted at: Glyndebourne Festival Opera, ENO, Scottish Opera, Kent Opera, Opera North, Geneva Opera, Netherlands Opera, Paris Opera, Canadian Opera, Australian Opera, Cologne Opera; music dir Dallas Opera 1993–, princ Br and several Dutch and German orchs; artistic dir Arundel Festival 1992–; Freeman City of London 1989–, Freeman Worshipful Co of Goldsmiths 1989; ARCM; *Recreations* reading, cooking; *Clubs* Savile, Beefsteak; *Style*— Graeme Jenkins, Esq; ✉ Philipston House, Winterborne Clenston, Blandford Forum, Dorset DT11 0NR (☎ 01258 880100, fax 01258 880870)

JENKINS, Prof Harold; s of Henry Jenkins (d 1932), of Shenley Church End, Bucks, and Mildred, *née* Carter (d 1959); *b* 19 July 1909; *Educ* Wolverton GS, UCL (BA, MA, fell 1991); *m* 23 Jan 1939, Gladys Grace (d 1984), da of Albert George Victor Puddifoot (d 1960), of London; *Career* Quain student in English UCL 1930–35, William Noble fell Univ of Liverpool 1935–36; Univ of Witwatersrand SA: jr lectr in English 1936–38, lectr 1938–44 (DLitt 1944), sr lectr 1945; reader in English UCL 1946–54 (lectr 1945–46), prof of English Westfield Coll London 1954–67, visiting prof Duke Univ USA 1957–58, Regius prof of rhetoric and English literature Univ of Edinburgh 1967–71 (emeritus prof 1971–), visiting prof Univ of Oslo 1974; gen ed The Arden Shakespeare 1958–82; memb Editorial Bd: Shakespeare Survey 1964–72, Studies in English Literature 1961–78; contrib: Modern Language Review, Review of English Studies, The Library, Studies in Bibliography, Shakespeare Survey; pres Malone Soc 1989– (cncl memb 1955–89); awarded Shakespeare Prize Stiftung FVS Hamburg 1986; Hon DLitt Iona Coll New Rochelle NY USA 1983; memb: Int Shakespeare Assoc, Int Assoc of Univ Profs of English; FBA 1989; *Publications* The Life and Work of Henry Chettle (1934), Edward Benlowes (1952), The Structural Problem in Shakespeare's Henry IV (1956), The Catastrophe in Shakespearean Tragedy (1969), Hamlet (ed, 1982); *Clubs* Athenaeum; *Style*— Prof Harold Jenkins, FBA; ✉ 22 North Crescent, Finchley, London N3 3LL

JENKINS, Howard Max Lewis; s of Sqdn Ldr Lewis Max Jenkins, MBE (d 1981), of Bournemouth, and Georgina Ann, *née* Beasant (d 1989); *b* 30 July 1947; *Educ* Bournemouth Sch, Univ of London Middx Hosp (MB BS); *m* 20 Nov 1971, Carol Ann, da of Christopher Downs Hankinson (d 1958), of Southampton; 2 da (Catherine b 1976, Sarah b 1979); *Career* house surgn Middx Hosp 1972, registrar Professorial Unit Nottingham 1976–79; clinical teacher Univ of Nottingham 1985– (med res fell 1979–81, clinical lectr in obstetrics and gynaecology 1981–85), med dir Derby City Gen Hosp 1996– (conslt obstetrician and gynaecologist 1985–); author of many papers in professional jls and chapters in books; memb Examination Ctee and examiner RCOG, examiner Univ of Nottingham; memb: Nuffield Visiting Soc, Birmingham and Midland Obstetrics and Gynaecology Soc; DM Univ of Nottingham 1984; DObst RCOG 1973, FRCOG 1990 (MRCOG 1977); *Recreations* family and home, any machinery (mechanical, electrical and electronic); *Style*— Mr Howard Jenkins; ✉ Derby City General Hospital, Uttoxeter Rd, Derby DE22 3NE (☎ 01332 340131); 14 Vernon St, Derby DE1 1FT (☎ 01332 347314)

JENKINS, Hugh Royston; CBE (1996); s of Hubert Graham (d 1977), of Llanelli, S Wales, and Violet, *née* Aston; *b* 9 Nov 1933; *Educ* Llanelli GS; *m* 1988, Mrs Beryl Kirk; *Career* Nat Serv RA 1954–56; valuer London CC 1956–62, md Coal Industry (Nominees) Ltd 1968–72 (asst controller 1962–68), dir gen of superannuation investments NCB 1972–85, chief exec Heron Financial Corporation LA 1985–86, gp investmt dir Allied Dunbar Assurance plc 1986–89, dep chm and chief exec Allied Dunbar Unit Trusts 1986–89, chm Dunbar Bank plc 1988–89, chm and chief exec Allied Dunbar Asset Management 1987–89; dir: Unilever Pensions Ltd 1985–89, IBM Pensions Trust PLC 1985–89; exec dir Prudential Corporation PLC 1989–95, chief exec Prudential Portfolio

Managers Ltd 1989–95; dir: Rank Organisation PLC 1995–, Thorn EMI plc 1995–96; dep chm Thorn plc and dir EMI Group PLC (following demerger of Thorn EMI) 1997–; chm Property Advsy Gp DoE 1990; memb The City Capital Markets Ctee 1982, lay memb The Stock Exchange 1984–85; FRICS, FPMI; *Recreations* theatre, golf; *Clubs* Garrick; *Style*— Hugh Jenkins, Esq, CBE; ✉ 41 Tower Hill, London EC3N 4HA (☎ 0171 480 5000)

JENKINS, Ian David Pearson; s of Norman Marsden Jenkins, of Emsworth, and Beryl Margaret Andrews, *née* Pearson; *b* 24 Aug 1946; *Educ* Denstone Coll, King's Coll London (LLB); *m* 6 Jan 1973, Judy Mary, da of John Ernest Middleton Rogers (d 1971), of Salisbury, Rhodesia; 2 s (Peter b 27 June 1979, David b 22 March 1982); *Career* sr ptnr Barlow Lyde & Gilbert 1989–; dir: Crowe Insurance Group Ltd 1990–, R J Kiln & Co Ltd 1993–; *Recreations* sailing; *Clubs* Royal Thames Yacht, Ocean Cruising; *Style*— Ian Jenkins, Esq; ✉ 39 Sheen Common Drive, Richmond, Surrey TW10 5BW (☎ 0181 876 6905, fax 0181 876 3325); Barlow Lyde & Gilbert, Beaufort House, 15 St Botolph Street, London EC3A 7NJ (☎ 0171 247 2277, fax 0171 782 8500, telex 913281)

JENKINS, Dr Ivor; CBE (1970); s of Thomas Jenkins (d 1955), of Gwynfryn, Kingsbridge, Gorseinon, Swansea, and Mary Emily Ellen, *née* Evans (d 1959); *b* 25 July 1913; *Educ* Gowerton GS, Univ Coll Swansea (BSc, MSc, DSc); *m* 19 April 1941, Caroline Wijnanda, da of William John James (d 1961), of Harrow, Middx; 2 s (Brian James b 3 April 1944, Peter Anthony b 15 Feb 1947); *Career* chief metallurgist GEC Hirst Res Centre 1952–61; dir for res: Manganese Bronze Holdings Ltd 1961–69, Delta Metal Co Ltd 1969–78; Williams prize Iron and Steel Inst 1946, Platinum medal The Metals Soc 1978; fell UC Swansea 1986, pres Onehouse Harleston and Shelland (Suffolk) Community Cncl 1974–80; FEng 1979, FIM 1948 (pres 1965–66 and 1968–69); fell American Soc of Metals; *Books* Controlled Atmospheres for the Heat Treatment of Metals (1946); *Recreations* walking, swimming; *Clubs* Anglo-Belgian; *Style*— Dr Ivor Jenkins, CBE, FEng; ✉ 31 Trotyn Croft, Aldwick Felds, Aldwick, Bognor Regis, W Sussex PO21 3TX (☎ 01243 828749)

JENKINS, John George; CBE; s of George John Jenkins, and Alice Maud, *née* Prickett; *b* 26 Aug 1919; *Educ* Winchester, Univ of Edinburgh; *m* 1948, Chloe Evelyn, da of John Kenward; 1 s (Martin), 3 da (Alison, Penelope, Jocelyn); *Career* farmer (1,750 acres) and landowner (694 acres); dir Agricultural Mortgage Corp 1969–90, chm United Oilseeds Ltd 1983–87; pres NFU of Scotland 1960–61; *Recreations* music, bridge; *Clubs* Farmers'; *Style*— John Jenkins, Esq, CBE

JENKINS, Sir Michael Nicholas Howard; kt (1997), OBE (1991); s of Maj Cyril Norman Jenkins (d 1985), and Maud Evelyn Sophie, *née* Shorter; *b* 13 Oct 1932; *Educ* Tonbridge, Merton Coll Oxford (BA); *m* 28 Sept 1957, Jacqueline Frances, da of Francis Jones (d 1979); 3 s (Howard Michael Charles b 1958, (Edward) Hugo b 1961, Oliver John b 1966); *Career* Nat Serv 2 Lt RA 1951–53; Shell-Mex and BP 1956–61, IBM UK 1961–67, ptnr Robson Morrow Management Consultants 1967–71, tech dir The Stock Exchange 1971–77, md European Options Exchange Amsterdam 1977–80, chief exec London International Financial Futures Exchange (LIFFE) 1981–92, non-exec chm London Commodity Exchange 1992–96, chm The Futures & Options Assoc 1993–; chm The London Clearing House 1996– (dir 1990–), dir Tradepoint Investment Exchange 1995–; *Recreations* games, music, woodworking; *Clubs* Wilderness (Sevenoaks); *Style*— Sir Michael Jenkins, OBE; ✉ The London Clearing House Ltd, Aldgate House, 33 Aldgate High Street, London EC3N 1EA (☎ 0171 426 7000, fax 0171 667 7354)

JENKINS, Sir Michael Romilly Heald; KCMG (1990, CMG 1984); s of Romilly James Heald Jenkins (d 1969), and Celine Juliette, *née* Haeglar; *b* 9 Jan 1936; *Educ* King's Coll Cambridge (BA); *m* 1968, Maxine Louise, da of Dudley Hodson (d 1982); 1 s (Nicholas b 1975), 1 da (Catherine b 1971); *Career* HM Dip Serv (Paris, Moscow, Bonn) 1959–93: dep sec-gen of Euro Cmmn 1981–83, asst under-sec of state FCO 1983–85, min HM Embassy Washington 1985–87, Br ambass to the Netherlands 1988–93 (ret); vice chm Kleinwort Benson Group plc 1993–, dir Aegon NV 1995–; memb Pres's Advsy Gp Atlantic Cncl 1994–, chm Br Gp Trilateral Cmmn 1996–; memb Gen Purposes Ctee MCC 1993–; *Books* Arakcheev, Grand Vizier of the Russian Empire (1969), A House in Flanders (1992); *Clubs* Brooks's, MCC; *Style*— Sir Michael Jenkins, KCMG; ✉ Kleinwort Benson Group plc, 20 Fenchurch St, London EC3M 3LB

JENKINS, Neil Martin James; *b* 9 April 1945; *Educ* Westminster Abbey Choir Sch (chorister), Dean Close Sch Cheltenham (music scholar), King's Coll Cambridge (choral scholar, MA), RCM; *m* 1, 1969, Sandra, *née* Wilkes; *m* 2, 26 April 1982, Penny Maxwell, *née* Underwood; 5 c (Tom, Sam, Nicholas, Benjamin, Rosie); *Career* tenor; recital debut Kirckman Concert Series Purcell Rooms 1967, operatic debut Menotti's The Consul Israel Festival 1968; Geoffrey Tankard Lieder prize 1967, Nat Fedn of Music Socs award 1972; prof of singing RCM 1975–76, teacher various summer schs incl Dartington, Canford and Wellington 1989–, pres Grange Choral Soc Hampshire; vice-pres: Huntingdonshire Philharmonic, Brighton Competitive Music Festival; *Roles incl* Ottavio in Don Giovanni (Kent Opera) 1971, Fenton in Falstaff (BBC) 1972, Ferrando in Cosi fan Tutte (Kent Opera) 1974, Almaviva in The Barber of Seville (WNO) 1974, Quint in Turn of the Screw (Eng Music Theatre 1977, Kent Opera 1979), title role in Return of Ulysses (Kent Opera) 1978 and 1990, Nadir in The Pearl Fishers (Scottish Opera) 1981–82, title roles in Peter Grimes (New Sussex Opera) 1981 and Robinson Crusoe (Kent Opera) 1983, Cat/Milkman in Higglety Pigglety Pop (Glyndebourne Festival Opera), Junger Diener in Elektra (Geneva) 1986 and 1990, Herod in Salome (WNO) 1991 and (Scottish Opera) 1993, Valzacchi in Der Rosenkavalier (WNO) 1994, Sellem in Stravinsky's The Rake's Progress (WNO) 1996, Berg's Lulu (BBC Proms) 1996; *Recordings* incl: Rossini's Elisabetta Regina D'Inghilterra, Mozart's Le Nozze di Figaro, Bernstein's Candide, Purcell's St Cecilia's Day Ode, Bach's St Matthew Passion and Cantata 131, Handel's Wedding Anthem, Schumann's Scenes From Faust, Henze's Kammermusik, Britten's Peter Grimes, Vaughan Williams' Hugh the Drover, Maxwell Davies' Resurrection; *Film Soundtracks incl* Chariots of Fire, Revenge of the Pink Panther, SOS Titanic, Lion of the Desert; *Books* Carol Singer's Handbook, O Praise God, O Holy Night, Sing Solo Sacred; *Recreations* visiting ancient monuments, 18th century music research; *Style*— Neil Jenkins, Esq; ✉ c/o Music International, 13 Ardilaun Road, London N5 2QR (☎ 0171 359 5813)

JENKINS, Neil Roger; s of Roger John Jenkins, of Church Village, Pontypridd, and Eileen Jenkins; *b* 8 July 1971; *Educ* Bryn Celynog Comp Sch; *partner* Catherine Harry; *Career* rugby union player (fly half); over 50 appearances Pontypridd RFC; Wales: rep E Wales under 11 1981, 2 youth caps 1990, B cap v Holland 1990, under 21 caps v NZ 1990 and Scot 1991, full debut v England 1991, memb tour to Aust 1991 (2 appearances), memb World Cup squad 1995, 41 full caps; Pontypridd Player of the Year 1991 and 1992, Supporters Player of the Year 1992; occupation scrapper; *Recreations* baseball, golf, swimming; *Style*— Neil Jenkins, Esq; ✉ Pontypridd RFC, New Clubhouse, Sardis Rd, Pontypridd, Mid Glamorgan

JENKINS, Nicholas Garratt Primrose; s of Edward Adam Primrose (d 1965), and Betty, *née* Warburton; *b* 16 Feb 1939; *Educ* Bradfield, Byam Shaw Sch of Art, St Martin's Sch of Art; *m* 1, 1959, Marie France Aries; 2 da (Nathalie b 1959, Carolyn b 1962); *m* 2, 1983, Jane Hiller; 2 da (Alys b 1985, Lucy b 1987); *Career* display designer Simpson's Piccadilly 1961–62, art dir New English Library 1963–64, sr tutor RCA 1965–75, co-fndr Guyatt/Jenkins (renamed The Jenkins Group) 1975 (currently chm); significant achievements incl: two solo exhibitions of poster designs (RCA and Univ of Marseilles), design of corporate identities for W H Smith, The Nat Gallery, Queen's Silver Jubilee, Mowlem Construction and Macmillan Publishers, awarded first prize Israel Museum Book Design; visiting prof Nottingham Trent Univ 1994; chm Design Week Awards 1990, 1991 and 1992, chm BTEC Advsy Bd on Design, co-fndr Design Business Assoc; fell RCA, FCSD (pres 1996–), FRSA; *Books* Photographics, David Hicks Living With Design, The Monarchy Book, The Business of Image; *Recreations* writing and jazz; *Style*— Nicholas Jenkins, Esq; ✉ The Jenkins Group, 9 Tufton Street, London SW1 (☎ 0171 799 1090, fax 0171 222 6751)

JENKINS, (Graham) Nicholas Vellacott; s of Gwynne Jenkins (d 1988), of Radlett, Herts and Irene Lillan, *née* Vellacott; *b* 15 Dec 1945; *Educ* Radley; *m* 23 April 1977, Margaret Alice, *née* Bailey; 4 s (Nicolas Edward Vellacott b 9 May 1978, Jonathan William Vellacott b 16 July 1980, Edward Henry Vellacott b 20 March 1984, William Alexander Vellacott b 7 April 1987); *Career* CA; Whinney, Smith & Whinney (now Ernst & Young): articled clerk London 1964, Cardiff office 1968, London 1969; ptnr Moores Rowland 1974– (joined 1970); Freeman City of London, Liveryman Worshipful Co of Barbers; FCA (ACA 1969); *Recreations* fishing, golf; *Clubs* Hon Artillery Co, Flyfishers', Ashridge Golf, Royal Porthcawl Golf; *Style*— Nicholas Jenkins, Esq; ✉ Moores Rowland, Clifford's Inn, Fetter Lane, London EC4A 1AS (☎ 0171 831 2345, fax 0171 831 6123)

JENKINS, Peter Sefton; s of John Harry Sefton Jenkins (d 1978), of Brackley, Northants, and Helen Summers, *née* Staveley; *b* 9 Feb 1948; *Educ* King's Sch Canterbury, St Edmund Hall Oxford (MA); *m* 8 June 1972 (m dis 1991), Jacqueline, da of John Mills (d 1976); 2 s (Benjamin b 13 June 1975, Christopher b 7 April 1979); *Career* HM Customs and Excise 1969–86: private sec to chm 1972–74, Cabinet Office 1974–77, involved in EC negotiations on customs duty harmonisations 1977–79, private sec to Chllr of Exchequer 1979, asst sec VAT Admin 1983–86; nat ptnr VAT and Customs Gp Ernst & Young 1990– (Ernst & Whinney 1986–90); memb VAT Practitioners' Gp 1988; *Recreations* squash, music (violin, singing), opera, walking; *Clubs* Reform; *Style*— Peter Jenkins, Esq; ✉ Ernst and Young, Rolls House, 7 Rolls Buildings, Fetter Lane, London EC4A 1NH (direct ☎ 0171 931 2299)

JENKINS, Dr Rachel; da of Peter Osborne McDougall, of Durham, and Beryl, *née* Braddock; *b* 17 April 1949; *Educ* Monmouth Sch for Girls, St Paul's Girls' Sch, Girton Coll Cambridge (BA, MA, MB BChir, MD); *m* 6 July 1974, (David) Keith Jenkins, s of Lt Cdr David Edward Jenkins, of Chesterfield; 1 s (Benjamin b 1983), 1 da (Ruth b 1979); *Career* registrar Maudsley Hosp 1975–77, conslt psychiatrist and sr lectr Bart's 1985–88, hon sr lectr Inst of Psychiatry 1985– (res worker and Wellcome fell 1977–82, sr lectr 1982–85), princ MO Mental Health, Elderly, Disability and Ethics Div Dept of Health 1988–; 90 pubns in res jls; memb: Inst of Psychiatry Ctee of Mgmnt, Int Fedn of Psychiatric Epidemiologists, RCPsych Cncl; FRCPsych, FRIPHH; *Books* Sex Differences in Minor Psychiatric Morbidity (1985), The Classification of Psychosocial Problems in Primary Care (1987), Post Viral Fatigue Syndrome (1991), Indicators of Mental Health in the Population (1991), Preventing Mental Ill Health at Work (1992), The Prevention of Depression and Anxiety - The Role of the Primary Care Team (1992), The Primary Care of Schizophrenia (1992), Promoting Mental Health Policies in the Workplace (1993), Prevention of Suicide (1994); *Recreations* wild orchids, travel, walking, reading; *Style*— Dr Rachel Jenkins; ✉ 4 Roseway, Turney Road, London SE21 7JT; Le Fresse, Palluaud, St Severin, Charente, France; Mental Health, Elderly, Disability and Ethics Division, Department of Health, Wellington House, 133–135 Waterloo Rd, London SE1 8UG (☎ 0171 972 4334, fax 0171 972 4340)

JENKINS, His Hon Judge; Richard Peter Vellacott; s of Gwynne Jenkins (d 1988), of Radlett, Herts, and Irene Lillian, *née* Vellacott; *b* 10 May 1943; *Educ* Edge Grove Sch Aldenham, Radley, Trinity Hall Cambridge (MA); *m* 5 April 1975, (Agnes) Anna Margaret, da of Howard Mullan; 1 s (Daniel Gwynne b 1978), 1 da (Isobel Sarah b 1982); *Career* called to the Bar Inner Temple 1966; memb: Midland Circuit 1968–71, Midland and Oxford Circuit 1972–89 (asst treas and remembrancer 1985–89); recorder 1988–89, circuit judge (Midland and Oxford Circuit) 1989–; jt assigned judge: Lincs County Courts 1995–, Humberside Probation Ctee 1996–; liaison judge Lincs and S Humberside Magistrates 1995–; Freeman City of London, Liveryman Worshipful Co of Barbers 1967; *Clubs* MCC, Glamorgan CCC, London Welsh RFC; *Style*— His Hon Judge Jenkins; ✉ Hall Barn, Far End, Boothby Graffoe, Lincoln LN5 0LG; Lincoln Combined Court Centre, 360 High St, Lincoln (☎ 01522 883000)

JENKINS, Simon David; s of Rev Dr Daniel Jenkins, and Agatha Helen Mary (Nell), *née* Cree (d 1992); *b* 10 June 1943; *Educ* Mill Hill Sch, St John's Coll Oxford (BA); *m* 1978, Gayle Hunnicutt, *qv*, the actress; 1 s (Edward Lloyd b 24 Feb 1982), 1 step s (Nolan); *Career* £ournalist; Country Life 1965, news ed Times Education Supplement 1966–68, columnist Evening Standard 1968–74, Insight ed Sunday Times 1974–75, ed Evening Standard 1976–78 (dep ed 1975–76), political ed The Economist 1979–86, columnist Sunday Times 1986–90 (ed Books Section 1988–89, Journalist of the Yr 1988); The Times: ed 1990–92, columnist 1992– (Br Press Awards Columnist of the Year 1993); memb: Bd BR 1979–90, Millenium Cmmn 1994–; dep chm English Heritage 1989–90, chm Buildings Books Tst 1995–; *Books* A City at Risk (1971), Landlords of London (1974), Insight on Portugal (ed, 1975), Newspapers: The Power and The Money (1979), The Companion Guide to Outer London (1981), The Battle for the Falklands (with Max Hastings, 1983), Images of Hampstead (1983), With Respect Ambassador (with Anne Sloman, 1985), The Market for Glory (1986), The Selling of Mary Davies and Other Writings (1993), Accountable to None (1995); *Style*— Simon Jenkins, Esq; ✉ The Times, 1 Virginia Street, London E1 9BD (☎ 0171 782 5655)

JENKINS, Dr (Bernard) Stephen; s of Bernard Pizzy Terence Jenkins (d 1952), and Jane, *née* Webb; *b* 21 Dec 1939; *Educ* Christ's Coll Cambridge (MA, MB BChir); *m* 1, 4 July 1964 (m dis 1983), Diana, da of Edward Farmer (d 1985), of Henley-on-Thames; m 2, 3 Nov 1995, Elizabeth, da of Eric Winder, of Harrogate; *Career* conslt cardiologist St Thomas' Hosp 1971–, dist gen mangr West Lambeth Health Authy 1985, chief exec St Thomas' Hosp 1991; memb Br Cardiac Soc, FRSA, FRCP; *Recreations* music; *Style*— Dr Stephen Jenkins; ✉ 53 Fontarabia Road, London SW11 5PE (☎ 0171 223 6242, fax 0171 223 8020); St Thomas' Hospital, Lambeth Palace Rd, London SE1 7EH (☎ 0171 928 9292, fax 0171 261 1488)

JENKINS, Thomas Islwyn David (Tom); s of David Jenkins, of Dyfed, and Elizabeth, *née* Davies (d 1976); *b* 17 Oct 1950; *Educ* Ardwyn GS Aberystwyth, Craft Design and Technol Coll London (HND advtg and mktg); *m* 1983, Bridget Anne Sellers, step da of John Saunders; 2 da (Katherine Alice Myfanwy b 19 Aug 1985, Lydia Branwen b 4 Aug 1987); *Career* began advtg career as copywriter J Walter Thompson, later joined Davidson Pearce until 1981 (winner D&AD, Cannes, Br TV and Campaign Silvers for The Observer), Abbott Mead Vickers 1981–85 (award-winning work on Volvo, Olympus Sports stores, Waterstone's Bookshops, Paul Masson Wine and Sainsbury's); subsequently creative dir: Colman's (D&AD and Cannes Silvers for work on Citroën), Horner Collis Kirvan (awards for Peugeot and Majestic Wine Warehouses), Weiden and Kennedy US; currently sr copywriter/bd dir Abbott Mead Vickers BBDO Ltd; memb D&AD (memb Ctee 1991–92); *Recreations* learning to ride, reading, writing, watching rugby; *Clubs* Chelsea Arts; *Style*— Tom Jenkins, Esq; ✉ Abbott Mead Vickers BBDO Ltd, 191 Old Marylebone Road, London NW1 5DW (☎ 0171 402 4100, fax 0171 935 5883)

JENKINS OF HILLHEAD, Baron (Life Peer UK 1987), of Pontypool in the Co of Gwent; Roy Harris Jenkins; OM (1993), PC (1964); o s of Arthur Jenkins (d 1946);

MP (Lab) Pontypool 1935–46, Parly sec Miny Town and Country Planning then Educn 1945 and PPS to Rt Hon Clement Attlee (later 1 Earl Attlee) 1940–45, and Hattie Jenkins; *b* 11 Nov 1920; *Educ* Abersychan GS, Balliol Coll Oxford (hon fell 1969); *m* 1945, Dame (Mary) Jennifer Jenkins, DBE (chm Nat Tst 1986–91; former chm: Historic Bldg Cncl for England 1975–85, Consumers' Assoc; tstee The Wallace Collection), da of Sir Parker Morris (d 1972 expert on housing after whom Parker Morris standards are named); 2 s (Hon Charles Arthur Simon Jenkins, *qv*, b 1949, Hon Edward Nicholas b 1954), 1 da (Hon Cynthia Delanie (Hon Mrs Crosthwait) b 1951); *Career* RA 1942–44, special intelligence 1944–46 (Capt); ICFC 1946–48, contested (Lab) Solihull 1945; MP (Lab): Southwark Central 1948–50, Birmingham Stechford 1950–76; former chm and memb Exec Fabian Soc; PPS to Cwlth Relations Sec 1949–50, memb UK Delgn to Cncl of Europe 1955–57; min of Aviation 1964–65, home sec 1965–67 and 1974–76, chllr of the Exchequer 1967–70, dep ldr Lab Party 1970–72, vice pres Inst Fiscal Studies 1970–; awarded Charlemagne and Robert Schuman prizes for services to Euro unity 1972; pres Br in Europe (EEC membership referendum) 1975, dep chm Common Market Campaign, pres Lab Ctee for Europe, chm Lab Euro Ctee; pres: UK Cncl Euro Movement, UWIST 1975–81, Euro Cmmn 1977–81; tstee Pilgrims Tst 1973–; dir: John Lewis Partnership 1962–64, Morgan Grenfell Holdings 1981–82; fndr memb: Cncl for Social Democracy Jan 1981, SDP March 1981; contested (SDP) Warrington 1981; MP (SDP) Glasgow Hillhead (by-election) 1982–87; elected first SDP ldr 1982, resigned 1983 having led Alliance with Rt Hon David Steel into June 1983 Election; chllr of Oxford Univ 1987–; pres Royal Soc of Literature 1988–; memb Ctee of Mgmnt Soc of Authors, former govr Br Film Inst; Liveryman Worshipful Co of Goldsmiths; Hon FBA 1993; *Publications include* Mr Attlee: An Interim Biography, Pursuit of Progress, Mr Balfour's Poodle, Sir Charles Dilke, Asquith, Afternoon on the Potomac, What Matters Now, Nine Men of Power, Partnership of Principle, Truman, Baldwin, Gallery of Twentieth Century Portraits European Diary 1977–81, A Life at the Centre, Portraits and Miniatures, Gladstone; *Clubs* Brooks's, Athenaeum, Reform, Beefsteak, Pratt's; *Style*— The Rt Hon Lord Jenkins of Hillhead, OM, PC; ✉ St Amand's House, East Hendred, Oxon; 2 Kensington Park Gdns, London W11; House of Lords, London SW1 (0171 219 6661)

JENKINS OF PUTNEY, Baron (UK 1981), of Wandsworth, Greater London; Hugh Gater Jenkins; s of Joseph Walter Jenkins (d 1955), and late Florence, *née* Gater; *b* 27 July 1908; *m* 1, 1936, Marie Ethel (d 1989), da of Sqdn-Ldr Ernest Christopher Crosbie, RAF; m 2, 1991, Helena Maria (d 1994), da of Nicolas Pavlidis (d 1994), of Athens; *Career* sits as Lab Peer in House of Lords; served WWII, Flt-Lt RAF, UK, Burma, Pacific; with Prudential Assurance Co 1930–40; head English Programmes Rangoon Radio 1945, research offr National Union of Bank Employees (editor The Bank Officer) 1946–50; asst gen-sec Actors Equity 1950–64; MP (Lab) Wandsworth (Putney) 1964–79, min of Arts 1974–76; memb: Arts Cncl 1968–71, Drama Panel 1972–74, National Theatre Bd 1976–80; dir Theatres' Trust 1977–86, jt life pres 1995–, writer and broadcaster; vice pres Theatres' Advsy Cncl 1980–95, pres 1995–, pres Battersea Arts Centre 1985–88, vice pres CND 1981– (chm 1979–81, Aldermaston marcher); *Books* The Culture Gap (1979), Rank and File (1980); *Recreations* politics, reading, writing, listening, talking, viewing, theatre and concert-going, avoiding retirement; *Style*— The Rt Hon the Lord Jenkins of Putney; ✉ House of Lords, London SW1A 0PW (☎ 0171 219 6706, 0171 836 8591, fax 0171 219 5979)

JENKINSON, Dermot Julian; s of Julian Charles Lewis Jenkinson, and Diana Catherine, *née* Baird; *b* 2 Dec 1954; *Educ* Eton, Eurocentre (Lausanne and Cologne), Carnegie Mellon Univ Pittsburgh (GSIA); *m* 2 May 1979, Miranda Jane, da of John Maxwell Menzies, *qv*; 1 s (Oliver John Banks b 1984), 1 da (Emily Lavinia b 1981); *Career* dir: John Menzies plc 1985–, Frank Smythson Inc 1985–; currently chm: Smythson of Bond Street, Terry Blood Distribution (TBO), Universal Office Supplies, Early Learning Centre; currently non-exec dir: Regal Hotel Group plc, Verine Ltd; *Clubs* Turf, New (Edinburgh); *Style*— Dermot J Jenkinson, Esq; ✉ Philpstoun House, Linlithgow, West Lothian EH49 7NB (☎ 0150 683 4287); John Menzies plc, 108 Princes Street, Edinburgh EH2 3AA (☎ 0131 225 8555)

JENKINSON, Dr James Lawrence; s of William Sinclair Jenkinson (d 1973), of Haddington, and Eleanora Cree, *née* Lawrie; *b* 9 Jan 1939; *Educ* Edinburgh Acad, Univ of Edinburgh (MB ChB); *m* 7 Aug 1963, (Isabella) Annette Livingstone, da of Rev Alexander Downie Thomson (d 1995), of Gifford; 3 da (Sheila b 1965, Fiona b 1969, Clare b 1972); *Career* conslt anaesthetist 1972, pt/t sr lectr Univ of Edinburgh 1987–94 (hon sr lectr 1994–); examiner: RCSEd 1981–, RCS 1986–92, Univ of Glasgow 1987–90, RCAnaes 1992–; pres: N Br Pain Assoc 1985–88, Neuroanaesthesia Soc 1995–; memb Cncl Intractable Pain Soc of GB & I 1986–89; memb Assoc of Anaesthetists 1965–, Standing Ctee in Scotland Coll of Anaesthetists 1988–94; FFARCS 1969, FRSM 1988; *Recreations* music, hill walking; *Style*— Dr James Jenkinson; ✉ Department of Clinical Neurosciences, Western General Hospital Trust, Crewe Road, Edinburgh EH4 2XU (☎ 0131 537 1000)

JENKINSON, Sir John Banks; 14 Bt (E 1661), of Walcot, Oxfordshire, and Hawkesbury, Gloucestershire; o s of Sir Antony Banks Jenkinson, 13 Bt (d 1989), and Frances, *née* Stremmel (d 1996); *b* 16 Feb 1945; *Educ* Eton, Univ of Miami; *m* 1979, Josephine Mary, da of late Samuel William Marshall-Andrew; 1 s (George Anthony Samuel Banks b 1980), 1 da (Samantha Emma b 1983); *Heir* s, George Anthony Samuel Banks Jenkinson b 8 Nov 1980; *Style*— Sir John Jenkinson, Bt; ✉ Hawkesbury Home Farm, Hawkesbury, Badminton GL9 1AY

JENKS, Sir (Maurice Arthur) Brian; 3 Bt (UK 1932), of Cheape, in the City of London; s of Sir Richard Atherley Jenks, 2 Bt (d 1993), and Marjorie Suzanne Arlette, *née* du Cros; *b* 28 Oct 1933; *Educ* Charterhouse; *m* 1962, Susan Lois, eldest da of (Frank) Leslie Allen, of Glenside, Star Lane, Hooley, Surrey; 1 da ((Marjorie) Emma (Mrs William Wellesley) b 1964), 1 adopted s (Timothy Charles b 1967); *Heir* bro, Richard John Peter Jenks b 1936; *Career* FCA; Past Master Haberdashers' Co; chm sch govrs; *Recreations* wine, racing; *Style*— Sir Brian Jenks, Bt; ✉ Warren House, Savernake, Marlborough, Wilts SN8 3BQ (☎ 01672 870442)

JENKYNS, Richard Henry Austen; s of Henry Leigh Jenkyns (whose mother Winifred was gda of the Rev James Austen-Leigh, himself n of Jane Austen), of Aldeburgh; *b* 18 March 1949; *Educ* Eton, Balliol Coll Oxford; *Career* writer and classicist; fell All Souls Oxford 1972–81, lectr in classics Univ of Bristol 1978–81, fell Lady Margaret Hall Oxford 1981–, reader in classical languages and literature Univ of Oxford 1996–; *Books* The Victorians and Ancient Greece (1980, winner of Arts Cncl Nat Book Award 1981 and Yorkshire Post Book Award 1981), Three Classical Poets (1982), Dignity and Decadence (1991), Classical Epic: Homer and Virgil (1992), The Legacy of Rome (ed, 1992); *Recreations* playing the piano, looking at buildings, walking; *Style*— Richard Jenkyns, Esq; ✉ Lady Margaret Hall, Oxford OX2 6QA (☎ 01865 274300, fax 01865 511069)

JENNER, Michael Eugene; s of Eugene Jenner (d 1945), and Beatrice Jenner (d 1976); *b* 7 Jan 1936; *Educ* St George's Coll Surrey; *m* 9 June 1962, Jane Elizabeth, da of Harold Goodhew Turner, CMG (d 1978); 1 s (Mark Eugene b 1963), 2 da (Clare Elizabeth b 1967, Lucy Jane b 1972); *Career* CT Bowring 1952–80 (latterly chief exec), jt dep chm CT Bowring (Insurance Holdings) Ltd 1976, chief exec CT Bowring Insurance 1979, dir Parent Bd CT Bowring & Co 1979; dir: Bowring Tyson, CTB Offshore Oil UK, Terra Nova Insurance Brokers, Premium Underwriting plc; fndr and chm: Jenner Fenton Slade Group Ltd 1980, JFS Reinsurance Brokers 1981; chm LIBC 1987; ACII; *Recreations* golf; *Clubs* Piltdown Golf, Royal St George's Golf, Annabel's; *Style*— Michael Jenner

JENNER, Prof Peter George; s of George Edwin Jenner, of Gravesend, Kent (d 1948), and Edith, *née* Hallett; *b* 6 July 1946; *Educ* Gravesend GS, Chelsea Coll London (BPharm, PhD, DSc); *m* 1 Dec 1973, Katherine Mary Philomena, da of Hilary David Harrison Snell (d 1958); 1 s (Terence Martin b 19 Oct 1977); *Career* postgrad fell Dept of Pharmacy Chelsea Coll London 1970–72; Univ of London Dept of Neurology Inst of Psychiatry: lectr in biochemistry 1972–78, sr lectr 1978–85, reader in neurochemical pharmacology 1985–89; reader in neurochemical pharmacology King's Coll Hosp 1985–89 (hon sr lectr 1983–85), prof of pharmacology and head of dept King's Coll 1989–, co-dir Neurodegenerative Diseases Research Centre King's Coll 1994–; hon sr lectr Inst of Neurology 1988–, dir Parkinson's Disease Soc Experimental Res Laboratories 1988–; elected memb Cncl of Mgmnt Parkinson's Disease Soc 1993–; memb: Br Pharmacological Soc, Drug Res Soc, Euro Neurochemistry Soc, Brain Res Assoc, Euro Neuroscience Assoc, Int League Against Epilepsy; FRPharmS 1994; *Books* Drug Metabolism - Chemical & Biochemical Aspects (with B Testa, 1976), Concepts in Drug Metabolism (co-ed B Testa, pt A 1980, pt B 1981), Approaches to the Use of Bromocriptine in Parkinson's Disease (co-ed, 1985), Recent Developments in Parkinson's Disease (co-ed, 1986), Neurological Disorders (co-ed, 1987), Neurotoxins and their Pharamcological Implications (ed, 1987), Disorders of Movement (co-ed, 1989); *Recreations* gardening, driving; *Style*— Prof Peter Jenner; ✉ Pharmacology Group, Biomedical Sciences Division, King's College London, Manresa Rd, London SW3 6LX (☎ 0171 333 4716, fax 0171 376 4736)

JENNER, Air Vice-Marshal Timothy Ivo (Tim); CB (1996); s of Harold Ivo Jenner, and Josephine Dorothy Jenner; *b* 31 Dec 1945; *Educ* Maidstone GS, RAF Coll Cranwell; *m* 1968, Susan Lesley, da of Colin Stokes (d 1994); 2 da; *Career* with RAF; helicopter sqdn pilot UK, ME and Germany 1968–75, Puma pilot and instr 1976–78, desk offr Helicopter MOD 1979–80, Army Staff Coll Camberley 1981, OC 33 Sqdn 1982–84; mil asst to: ACDS (Commitments) 1985, DCDS (Programmes & Personnel) 1986; OC RAF Shawbury 1987–88, RCDS 1989, dep dir Air Force Plans 1990–91, dir Def Programmes 1992–93, AO Plans HQ Strike Cmd 1993, ACDS (Costs Review) 1993–95, Asst Chief of Air Staff 1995–; non-exec dir NATS Ltd 1996–; chm RAF Gliding and Soaring Assoc; *Recreations* gliding, old cars, photography, mountain walking; *Clubs* Royal Air Force; *Style*— Air Vice-Marshal Tim Jenner, CB; ✉ Assistant Chief of Air Staff, Ministry of Defence, Main Building, Whitehall, London SW1A 2HB (☎ 0171 218 6565)

JENNETT, Prof (William) Bryan; CBE (1992); s of Robert William Jennett (d 1956), of Twickenham, and Jessie Pate, *née* Loudon (d 1975); *b* 1 March 1926; *Educ* King's Coll Sch Wimbledon, King George V Sch Southport, Univ of Liverpool (MB ChB, MD); *m* 15 Sept 1950, Sheila Mary, da of Herbert Pope (d 1966), of Liverpool; 3 s (Peter Dennis b 1953, Martin Robert b 1954, John Duncan b 1964), 1 da (Hilary Anne b 1957); *Career* Maj RAMC 1951–53; conslt neurosurgeon Glasgow 1963–68, prof of neurosurgery Inst of Neurological Sci 1968–91, memb Court Univ of Glasgow 1986–91 (dean Faculty of Med 1981–86); pres Section of Neurology RSM 1986–87; memb: MRC 1979–83, Chief Scientist Ctee Scotland 1984–94; DSc (hc) Univ of St Andrews 1993; *Books* Epilepsy After Non-Missile Head Injuries (2 edn, 1975), Management of Head Injuries (with G Teasdale, 1981), High Technology Medicine: Benefits and Burdens (1986), Introduction to Neurosurgery (5 edn, 1994); *Recreations* writing, sailing; *Clubs* RSM; *Style*— Prof Bryan Jennett, CBE; ✉ 83 Hughenden Lane, Glasgow G12 9XN (☎ and fax 0141 334 5148); Department of Neurosurgery, Institute of Neurological Sciences, Glasgow G51 4TF (☎ 0141 201 2023, fax 0141 201 2995)

JENNETT, Frederick Stuart; CBE (1985); s of Horace Frederick Jennett (d 1948), of Rhiwbina, Glam, and Jenny Sophia Hall (d 1969); *b* 22 April 1924; *Educ* Whitchurch GS, Welsh Sch of Architecture UWIST (DipArch with Distinction); *m* 9 July 1948, Nada Eusebia, da of George Allan Phillips (d 1968), of Pontypridd, Glam; 2 da (Sara Elizabeth b 9 June 1950, Claire Katy b 21 Feb 1955); *Career* Lt RS 1942–46, served Far East; architect Alwyn Lloyd & Gordon Cardiff 1949–51; architect and planner: Cwmbran Devpt Corp 1951–55, Louis de Soissons & Ptnrs Welwyn Garden City 1955–56; assoc S Colwyn Foulkes & Ptnrs 1956–62, chm and sr ptnr Percy Thomas Partnership Bristol 1971–89 (assoc 1962–64, ptnr 1964–89); conslt architect and town planner Frederick S Jennett 1990–; conslt to: Studio BAAD (architects) West Yorks 1990–94, Mouchel Management Ltd West Byfleet 1990–92, NHS Estates Leeds 1991–92, Carnell Green & Nightingale architects 1993; collaboration with garden designer Nada Jennett at Weston Park Shropshire and Everton Parks Beds; author of papers on: hosp planning, fast-track construction, refurbishment of historic bldgs; memb Cncl for Protection of Rural England; FRIBA 1949, MTPI 1955, FRSA 1985; *Recreations* hill walking, watercolour painting, running; *Clubs* Royal Over-Seas League; *Style*— Frederick S Jennett, Esq, CBE; ✉ Portland Lodge, Lower Almondsbury, Bristol BS12 4EJ (☎ 01454 615175)

JENNINGS, Alex Michael; s of Michael Thomas Jennings, of Shenfield, Essex, and Peggy Patricia, *née* Mahoney; *b* 10 May 1957; *Educ* Abbs Cross Tech HS Hornchurch Essex, Univ of Warwick (BA), Bristol Old Vic Theatre Sch; *ptnr* Lesley Moors; 1 s (Ralph Jennings Moors b 23 March 1990); 1 da (Georgia Jennings Moors b 14 April 1992); *Career* actor; *Theatre* incl: The Scarlet Pimpernel (Her Majesty's) 1985, The Country Wife (Royal Exchange Manchester), Too Clever By Half (Old Vic) 1988, The Liar (Old Vic), The Wild Duck (Peter Hall Co), The Importance of Being Earnest (Aldwych) 1993; work for the RSC: Hyde Park, The Taming of the Shrew, Measure For Measure 1987–88, Richard II 1990–91, Peer Gynt (Young Vic), Oberon in A Midsummer Night's Dream (also US tour and Broadway) Measure for Measure 1995–96, Much Ado About Nothing, Hamlet 1998–97; work for RNT: Ghetto, The Recruiting Officer; *Television* incl: Smiley's People (BBC), The Franchise Affair (BBC), Alfonso Bonzo (BBC), Ashenden (BBC/Kelso Films), Inspector Alleyn - Death at the Bar (BBC), Inspector Morse - Sins of the Fathers (Central), Dread Poet's Soc (BBC), Bye Bye Columbus (Channel 4), Hard Times (BBC); *Films* War Requiem (dir Derek Jarman), A Midsummer Night's Dream, The Wings of the Dove; *Awards* for Too Clever By Half: Drama Magazine Best Actor Award 1988, Plays and Players Actor of the Year Award 1988, Olivier Award for Comedy Performance of the Year 1988; Olivier Award for Best Actor (for Peer Gynt) 1996; *Style*— Alex Jennings, Esq; ✉ c/o Marmont Management Ltd, Langham House, 308 Regent Street, London W1R 5AL (☎ 0171 637 3183, fax 0171 323 4798)

JENNINGS, Prof Barry Randall; s of Albert James Jennings (d 1981), of Worthing, Sussex, and Ethel Victoria Elizabeth, *née* Randall (d 1983); *b* 3 March 1939; *Educ* St Olave's and St Saviour's GS Tower Bridge, Univ of Southampton (BSc, PhD, DSc); *m* 1 Sept 1964, Margaret Penelope (Penny), da of Lionel Wall (d 1977), of Newport, Gwent; 2 da (Carolyn b 1966, Samantha b 1969); *Career* res fell Strasbourg Univ 1964–65, ICI fell Univ of Southampton 1965–66, lectr in physics Queen Elizabeth Coll London 1966–71, visiting prof Univ of San Luis and Santa Rosa Argentina 1979, head of physics Brunel Univ 1982–84 (reader 1971–77, prof of experimental physics 1977–84), estab prof of physics Univ of Reading 1984–89, res dir ECC International Ltd 1990–93, dir of res ECC plc group of companies 1994–; visiting prof of physics Univ of Reading 1990–93, visiting prof of chemistry Univ of Bristol 1992–, visiting prof of optoelectronics South Bank Univ 1994–; author of 200 scientific articles and holder of ten patents; vice pres Minerals Indust Res Orgn 1991–; memb: Ctee Standing Conf of Profs of Physics 1984–90, Scientific Ctee Assoc for Int Cancer Res 1984–90; chm Int Ctee for Molecular Electro-optics 1988–94, pres Br Biophysical Soc 1982–83, chm Polymer Physics Gp Royal Soc of Chem 1981–87; ed: Int Journal of Biological Macromolecules 1979–84, Polymer Journal 1983–, Semiconductor Sci and Technol 1986–87; hon ed Journal of

Physics D (Applied) 1986–90; memb Bd of Govrs Univ of Plymouth 1995–; Cowan-Keedy prize Southampton Univ 1961, Soc of Chemical Indust Polymer prize 1969, Kerr medal Int Electro-Optics Gp 1994, Founders lectr Sci Chem Ind 1994; pres Cornish Fedn of Male Voice Choirs 1991–; FInstP 1970, CPhys 1985, CChem 1994, FRSC 1994; *Books* Atoms in Contact (with V J Morris, 1974), Electro-optics and Dielectric of Macromolecules (1979), Colloid & Molecular Electro-optics (with S P Stoylov, 1992); *Recreations* swimming, long cased clocks, church activities; *Style*— Prof Barry Jennings; ✉ Luney Barton House, Lower Sticker, St Austell, Cornwall PL26 7JH (☎ 01726 882219); ECC plc, John Keay House, St Austell, Cornwall PL25 4DJ (☎ 01726 818011, fax 01726 818029, telex 45526 ECCSAU G)

JENNINGS, Charles James; s of (Douglas) Vivian Jennings, MC, Witley Manor, Witley, Surrey, and Virginia, *née* Turle (d, 1996); *b* 27 Oct 1951; *Educ* Harrow, Univ of Durham (BA); *m* 8 May 1976, Julia Frances, da of Philip Whiffen, of Mole End, Oxshott, Cobham, Essex; 1 s (Simon Charles b 1980), 1 da (Anna Frances b 1978); *Career* slr; Freshfields 1980–82, ptnr Wilde Sapte 1986–95, dir Henderson Crosthwaite Corporate Finance Ltd 1995; memb: Law Soc, City of London Solicitors Co; *Recreations* tennis, gardening; *Clubs* City of London; *Style*— Charles Jennings, Esq

JENNINGS, Prof David Harry; s of Harry Jennings (d 1982), of Cirencester, and Doris, *née* Hewitson (d 1961); *b* 30 March 1932; *Educ* Merchant Taylors' Crosby, Univ of Cambridge (BA), Univ of Oxford (MA, DPhil); *m* Ruth Mary, da of Capt Gerald Hope Sworder (d 1959), of St Teath, Cornwall; 2 da (Alison b 1960, Hilary b 1962); *Career* King George VI meml fell Univ of Rochester 1956–57; Univ of Leeds: ICI fell 1957–60, lectr in botany 1960–66, reader in plant physiology 1966–68; Univ of Liverpool: prof of botany 1969–92 (emeritus 1992), head Dept of Botany 1975–85, dean Faculty of Sci 1977–80 and 1988–91, pro-vice chllr 1981–84; pres Br Mycological Soc 1986; govr Chester Coll 1988–92; memb Cwlth Scholarships Cmmn 1987–94; dir: Liverpool Playhouse 1986–91, Merseyside Innovation Centre 1984–91; FIBiol 1971; *Books* The Absorption of Solutes by Plant Cells (1963), Serpula lacrymans: Fundamental Biology and Control Strategies (with A F Bravery, 1991), Stress Tolerance of Fungi (1993), The Physiology of Fungal Nutrition (1995), Microbial Culture (with S Isaac, 1995), Fungal Biology (with G Lysek, 1996); *Recreations* architecture, painting, walking, exploring cities; *Style*— Prof David Jennings; ✉ 3 St George's Road, Hexham, Northumberland NE46 2HG (☎ 01434 600428); Department of Genetics & Microbiology, The University, PO Box 147, Liverpool L69 3BX (☎ 0151 794 4414, fax 0151 708 4401, tlx 627095 UNILPL G)

JENNINGS, Ven David Willfred Michael; s of Rev Willfred Jennings (d 1970), of Kensington, London, and Nona Janet, *née* de Winton; *b* 13 July 1944; *Educ* Radley, KCL (AKC); *m* 11 Oct 1969, Sarah Catherine, da of Dr Robert Fynn, of Harare, Zimbabwe; 3 s (Andrew Willfred Mark b 1971, Peter Timothy John b 1974, Michael Robert James b 1978); *Career* asst curate: Walton PC Liverpool 1967–69, Christ Church Priory Hampshire 1969–73; vicar: of Hythe Southampton 1973–80, of Romford St Edward 1980–92; rural dean of Havering 1985–92, non-residentiary canon of Chelmsford Cathedral 1987–92, archdeacon of Southend 1992–; *Recreations* exploring the buildings of the British Isles; *Style*— The Ven the Archdeacon of Southend; ✉ 136 Broomfield Road, Chelmsford, Essex CM1 1RN (☎ 01245 258257, fax 01245 250845)

JENNINGS, Elizabeth Joan; CBE (1992); da of Dr Henry Cecil Jennings, of Oxford, and Mary Helen, *née* Turner; *b* 18 July 1926; *Educ* Oxford HS, St Anne's Coll Oxford (BA); *Career* asst Oxford City Library 1950–58, reader for Chatto & Windus Ltd 1958–60; poet; poetry incl: Poems (1953, Arts Cncl prize), A Way of Looking (1955, Somerset Maugham award 1956), A Sense of the World (1958), The Batsford Book of Children's Verse (ed, 1958), Song for a Birth or a Death (1961), Michelangelo's Sonnets (trans, 1961), Recoveries (1964), The Mind Has Mountains (1966, Richard Hillary prize 1966), The Secret Brother (for children, 1966), Collected Poems (1967), The Animals' Arrival (1969, Arts Cncl bursary 1969), A Choice of Christina Rosetti's Verse (ed, 1970), Lucidities (1970), Relationships (1972), Growing Points (1975), Consequently I Rejoice (1977), After The Ark (for children, 1978), Selected Poems (1980), Moments of Grace (1980), The Batsford Book of Religious Verse (1981), Celebrations and Elegies (1982), In Praise of Our Lady (anthology, 1982), Extending the Territory (1985), A Quintet (for children, 1985), Collected Poems 1953–86 (1986, W H Smith award 1987), Tributes (1989), Times and Seasons (1992), In the Meantime (1996), A Spell of Words (for children, 1997); prose incl: Let's Have Some Poetry (1960), Every Changing Shape (1961), Robert Frost (1964), Christianity and Poetry (1965), Seven Men of Vision (1976); poems and articles published in: New Statesman, New Yorker, Botteghe Oscure, Observer, Spectator, Listener, Vogue, The Independent; *Recreations* theatre, cinema, looking at pictures, collecting; *Clubs* Soc of Authors; *Style*— Miss Elizabeth Jennings, CBE; ✉ c/o David Higham Associates Ltd, 5–8 Lower John St, London W1R 4HA

JENNINGS, Geoffrey Arthur (Geoff); OBE (1988); *b* 21 Oct 1931; *Educ* Ilford Co HS; *m* 1953, Jean Georgina; *Career* commercial dir Abbey Goodman Display Ltd 1955–68, chm and md Designwise Ltd 1968–87, chief exec Brentwood Enterprise Agency 1987–92, chm Havering Hosps NHS Tst 1992–; ldr: Brentwood DC 1982–89, Cons Gp Assoc of DCs 1987–89; memb: Rotary Club of Brentwood, Brentwood and Ongar Cons Assoc; memb Inst of Mktg 1964; *Recreations* golf, music, bridge; *Clubs* Thornton Park Golf; *Style*— Geoff Jennings, Esq, OBE; ✉ Havering Hospitals NHS Trust, Harold Wood Hospital, Gubbins Lane, Romford, Essex RM3 0BE (☎ 01708 708128, fax 01708 384730)

JENNINGS, John Southwood; CBE (1985); s of George Southwood Jennings (d 1978), of Crowle, Worcs, and Irene Beatrice, *née* Bartlett; *b* 30 March 1937; *Educ* Oldbury GS, Univ of Birmingham (BSc), Univ of Edinburgh (PhD, Shell res student), London Business Sch (Sloan fell); *m* 1961 (m dis), Gloria Ann, da of Edward Albert Griffiths (d 1985), of Hope Cove, Devon; 1 s (Iain), 1 da (Susan); *Career* chief geologist Shell UK Exploration and Production Ltd London 1968–70, exploration mangr Petroleum Development Oman Ltd 1971–75 (prodn mangr 1975–76), gen mangr and chief rep Shell Group of Companies Turkey 1976–79, md exploration and prodn Shell UK Ltd London 1979–84, exploration and prodn co-ordinator Shell International Petroleum Maatschappij BV The Hague 1984–89, md Royal Dutch Shell Group 1987–, chm Shell Transport and Trading Co plc 1993–; vice pres Liverpool Sch of Tropical Med 1991–; memb Cncl RIIA 1994–; govr: London Business Sch 1992–, NIESR 1995–; Hon DSc Univ of Edinburgh 1991; Commandeur de l'Ordre National du Merite Gabon 1989; FGS, FRSE 1992; *Recreations* flyfishing, travel; *Clubs* Flyfishers', Brooks's; *Style*— John Jennings, Esq, CBE, FRSE; ✉ Shell Transport and Trading Company plc, Shell Centre, London SE1 7NA (☎ 0171 934 5554)

JENNINGS, The Very Rev Kenneth Neal; s of Reginald Tinsley Jennings (d 1976), and Edith Dora, *née* Page (d 1982); *b* 8 Nov 1930; *Educ* Hertford GS, Corpus Christi Coll Cambridge (MA), Cuddesdon Theological Coll; *m* 9 Sept 1972, Wendy Margaret, da of Sir John Arthur Stallworthy (d 1993); 1 s (Mark Nicholas b 1976), 1 da (Katharine Rachel b 1975); *Career* Nat Serv RA 1950–51; asst curate Holy Trinity Ramsgate 1956–59; vice princ: Bishop's Coll Calcutta 1961–66 (lectr 1959–61), Cuddesdon Coll Oxford 1967–73; vicar St Mary's Hitchin 1973–76, team rector Parish of Hitchin 1977–82, dean of Gloucester 1983–Nov 1996, ret; *Recreations* fell walking, music; *Style*— The Very Rev Kenneth Jennings

JENNINGS, Dr Kevin; s of Kevin Jennings, and Bridget, *née* Flynn; *b* 9 March 1947; *Educ* Downside, St Bartholomew's Med Sch (MB BS); *m* 24 June 1978, Heather Joanne, da of Ray Wolfenden; 2 s (Mark b 1979, Thomas b 1981), 1 da (Debra b 1987); *Career* registrar: King's Coll London 1976–78, London Chest Hosp 1978–80; sr registrar Freeman Hosp Newcastle 1980–83, conslt cardiologist Aberdeen Royal Infirmary 1983–; FRCP 1988; *Publications* Acute Cardiac Care (OUP, 1993), author of several articles on ischaemic heart disease and cardiac imaging; *Style*— Dr Kevin Jennings; ✉ Department of Cardiology, Royal Infirmary, Foresterhill, Aberdeen AB9 2ZB (☎ 01224 681818, fax 01224 208402)

JENNINGS, Marie Patricia; da of Harold Robert Jennings, and Phyllis Hortense; *b* 25 Dec 1930; *Educ* Presentation Convent Coll Srinagar Kashmir; *m* 1 (m dis), Michael Keegan; 1 s (Michael Geoffrey b 18 July 1962); m 2, 3 Jan 1976, Eur Ing (Harry) Brian Locke, *qv*, s of Harry Locke; *Career* md The Roy Bernard Co Ltd 1960–65; special advsr: Stanley Tools 1961–89, The Unit Trust Association 1976–90, The Midland Bank Group 1978–; dir: Lexington Ltd (JWT) 1971–75, The PR Consultants' Association 1979–84, Cadogan Management Ltd 1984–90; Woman of the Year 1969; Nat Assoc of Women's Clubs: memb Fin and Gen Purposes Ctee, hon treas 1977–87, pres 1993–; memb: Cncl Fin Int Mangrs and Brokers Regnl Assoc 1986–, Insur Ombudsman Bureau 1988–, Exec Ctee Wider Share Ownership Cncl 1987–91, Consumer Panel Personal Investmt Authy; chm Legislation Ctee Nat Fedn Cons Gps 1991–; memb NUJ, MIPR, FRSA, FInstD; *Books include* The Money Guide (1983), Getting the Message Across (1988), Women and Money (1988), Money Go Round (1977), Moneyspinner (1985), A Guide to Good Corporate Citizenship (1990), Ten Steps to the Top (1992), Better Money Management (1994), Perfect PR (1995), Perfect Personal Finance (1996), Your Family and Money (1996); *Recreations* reading, writing; *Clubs* IOD; *Style*— Ms Marie Jennings; ✉ Cadogan Grange, Bisley, Stroud, Glos GL6 7AT (☎ 01452 770003, fax 01452 770058)

JENNINGS, Patrick Thomas; s of Charles Thomas Jennings (d 1983), of Witham, Essex, and Helen Joan, *née* Scorer; *b* 23 Feb 1948; *Educ* Forest Sch; *m* Jayne, da of Ronald Stanley Green; 1 s (Edward Thomas Patrick b 16 Aug 1990), 3 da (Victoria Anne b 3 June 1977, Joanna Emily b 6 Oct 1979, Charlotte Joy b 16 Oct 1983); *Career* articled clerk H Kennard & Son 1967–72; Slaughter and May: joined 1973, ptnr 1979, currently property group ptnr; chm Building Contracts Ctee of the Construction Law Ctee Int Bar Assoc 1985–89; memb: Law Soc, Anglo-American Real Property Inst, City of London Slrs Co; author of various articles and papers on construction law; *Style*— Patrick Jennings, Esq; ✉ Slaughter and May, 35 Basinghall St, London EC2V 5DB (☎ 0171 600 1200, fax 0171 600 0289)

JENNINGS, Peter Nevile Wake; s of Archibald Eaton de Burgh Jennings (d 1953), and Veronica Jennings, MBE, *née* Gwynne (d 1988); *b* 19 Aug 1934; *Educ* Marlborough, Staff Colls Shrivenham and Camberley (psc(m), grad sr wing staff coll), Armed Forces Staff Coll Norfolk Va USA (osc(US)); *m* Shirley Anne, da of Capt B J Fisher, DSO, RN, Ret; 1 s, 2 da; *Career* cmmnd 2 Lt Royal Marines 1952, ret as Major 1976; appointed to staff House of Commons 1976, Serjeant at Arms 1995–; *Style*— Peter Jennings, Esq; ✉ House of Commons, London SW1A 0AA (☎ 0171 219 3030)

JENNINGS, Prof Sir Robert Yewdall; kt (1981), QC (1969); s of Arthur Jennings, of Idle, Yorks; *b* 19 Oct 1913; *Educ* Belle Vue GS Bradford, Downing Coll Cambridge (LLB), Harvard Univ; *m* 1955, Christine Dorothy, da of late H Bernard Bennett, of Lydd, Kent; 1 s, 2 da; *Career* served WWII Intelligence Corps Maj; asst lectr in law LSE 1938–39; Jesus Coll Cambridge: fell 1939, sr tutor 1949–55, subsequently pres, hon fell 1982; Whewell prof of int law Univ of Cambridge 1955–81, reader in int law Cncl of Legal Educn 1959–70; called to the Bar Lincoln's Inn 1943 (hon bencher 1970), judge Int Ct of Justice The Hague 1982– (pres 1991–94); jt ed: International and Comparative Law Quarterly 1955–61, British Year Book of International Law 1960–; vice pres Inst of Int Law 1979–81 (pres 1981–83, hon memb 1985); Hon LLD: Univ of Hull 1987, Univ of Rome 1990, Univ of Cambridge 1993, Univ of Leicester 1995; Hon Dr Juris Univ of Saarland 1988, hon fell LSE 1993, Hon DCL Oxford 1996; Manley O Hudson medal American Soc of Int Law 1993; *Clubs* Utd Oxford and Cambridge Univ, Haagsche Plaats Royaal (The Hague); *Style*— Prof Sir Robert Jennings, QC; ✉ Jesus College, Cambridge CB5 8BL; Peace Palace, 2517 KJ The Hague, Netherlands

JENSEN, David; *b* 4 July 1950, Victoria, BC, Canada; *m* June 1975, Gudrun; 1 da (Anna Lisa), 2 s (Alexander, Viktor); *Career* radio and television personality; weekly newspaper/magazine columns: FAB 208 1973–75, Record Music 1974–75, Daily Star 1978–80, Daily Mirror 1982–84, The People 1984–92; non-exec dir Fabergé 1982–84; *Radio* local radio presenter Canada 1966–67, presenter/prodr Jensen's Dimensions Radio Luxembourg 1968–75, sr presenter and asst head of music Radio Trent 1975–76, own music and topical features show BBC Radio 1 1976–80, news anchor and documentary presenter Turner Broadcasting System and CNN Atlanta Georgia 1980–82, rejoined BBC Radio 1 1982–84; Capital Radio plc London: presenter national Network Chart Show 1984–94, mid-morning chat show 1984–87, Drive-Time show 1987–; *Television* presenter numerous shows and series incl: 45 (Granada for ITV) 1974–75, Pop Quest (YTV for ITV) 1975–76, Top of the Pops (regular guest presenter, BBC) 1976–80, British Rock and Pop Awards (BBC) 1976–80, Worldwise (TVS for ITV) 1986–87, Razzmatazz (Tyne Tees for ITV) 1986–87, The Roxy (presenter and assoc prodr, Tyne Tees for ITV) 1986–87, Run the Gauntlet (Thames for ITV) 1987, US World Baseball Series (Channel 4) 1988, LWT Telethon 1990, documentary series Jensen's Canadian Crossing (Discovery Channel) 1988, Love Call (Anglia) 1993–, World Series Baseball (Sky Sports) 1993–94, Central Weekend (Central) 1994–; numerous voice-overs and corporate/in-flight video prodns; *Awards* incl: Variety magazine Top UK Presenter 1977, Emmy nomination for CNN/TBS special on US Iranian hostages 1980, Melody Maker Top Br Radio Personality 1983, TV and Radio Industries Club Top UK Radio Show (for Network Chart Show) 1985, Sony Awards Local Radio DJ of the Year 1989; *Style*— David Jensen, Esq; ✉ Capital Radio plc, Euston Tower, London NW1 3DR (☎ 0171 608 6080, fax 0171 387 2345)

JENSEN, Michael Harold; s of Eric Axel Jensen (d 1964); *b* 24 Oct 1942; *Educ* St Lawrence Coll; *m* 1969, Linda, da of Ernest Edwards; 2 da; *Career* md: Eden Ct Property Co Ltd 1968–79, HL Thomson Ltd 1976–81, HL Thomson (E Anglia) Ltd 1977–81, Hogg Robinson Gardner Mountain International Ltd 1977–81; exec dir Willis Faber & Dumas Ltd (insurance brokers) 1981–87; chm: Jensen Dickens Ltd (insurance brokers), Thamesgate Holdings Ltd; Freeman City of London 1978, Liveryman Worshipful Co of Carmen 1978; memb Lloyd's 1980; *Recreations* shooting, sailing (yacht Bulldog I); *Clubs* Little Ship; *Style*— Michael Jensen, Esq; ✉ Oaken, Falconers Park, Sawbridgeworth, Herts CM21 0AU; Jensen Dickens Ltd, Lloyd's Ave House, 6 Lloyd's Ave, London EC3N 3AX (☎ 0171 480 6474, fax 0171 480 7605)

JEPHCOTT, Sir (John) Anthony; 2 Bt (UK 1962), of East Portlemouth, Co Devon; s of Sir Harry Jephcott, 1 Bt (d 1978), and Doris, da of Henry Gregory; *b* 21 May 1924; *Educ* Aldenham, St John's Coll Oxford, LSE (BCom); *m* 1, 1949 (m dis 1978), Sylvia Mary, da of Thorsten F Relling, of Wellington, NZ; 2 da (Helen Mary (Mrs Asbury) b 1953, Caroline Ruth (Mrs Nigel Clark Flower) b 1955); m 2, 1978, Josephine Agnes, da of Philip Sheridan, of Perth, WA; *Heir* bro, Neil Welbourn Jephcott b 3 June 1929; *Career* served WWII with REME, later RAEC; formerly manufacturer of anaesthesia equipment; md: Penlon Ltd 1952–73, Pen Medic Ltd NZ 1973–78; contrib to scientific journals; Hon FFARACS 1990, Hon FANZCA 1992; *Books* A History of Longworth Scientific Instrument Co Ltd (1988); *Style*— Sir Anthony Jephcott, Bt; ✉ 26 Sage Road, Kohimarama, Auckland 5, New Zealand

JEPHCOTT, Neil Welbourn; s of Sir Harry Jephcott, 1 Bt (d 1978), and hp of bro, Sir Anthony Jephcott, 2 Bt; *b* 3 June 1929; *Educ* Aldenham, Emmanuel Coll Cambridge (MA);

m 1, 1951, Mary Denise (d 1977), da of Arthur Muddiman, of Abbots Mead, W Clandon, Surrey; 2 s (David Welbourn b 1952, Mark Lanwer b 1957), 1 da (Penelope Mary b 1955); m 2, 1978, Mary Florence, da of James John Daly (d 1950); *Career* professional engr; *Recreations* sailing; *Clubs* Royal Ocean Racing; *Style—* Neil Jephcott, Esq; ✉ Thalassa, East Portlemouth, Salcombe, S Devon

JEREMIAH, Melvyn Gwynne; CB (1994); s of Bryn Jeremiah (d 1967), of Gwent, and Fanny Evelyn Mary, *née* Rogers (d 1987); *b* 10 March 1939; *Educ* Abertillery County Sch; *m* 1960 (m dis 1970), Clare, da of William Bailey, of Devon; *Career* civil servant; appt HO 1958, Customs and Excise 1963, Cabinet Office 1975, Treasy 1976, Welsh Office 1979, Dept of Health 1987–95; chm Wage and Salary Cmmn Republic of Namibia 1995–; chief exec Disablement Servs Authy 1987–91; dir Ashley Gardens Freeholds Ltd 1986–89, sec Assoc of First Div Civil Servants 1967–70; *Recreations* public service reform (memb Commonwealth Assoc for Public Admin and Mgmnt), genealogy (memb Soc of Genealogists); *Clubs* Reform; *Style—* Melvyn Jeremiah, Esq, CB; ✉ PO Box 24331, Windhock, Namibia

JERRARD, Donald George; s of Harold George Jerrard, of Warsash, Hants, and Margaret Kathleen, *née* Pomeroy; *b* 21 March 1950; *Educ* Winchester (scholar), Emmanuel Coll Cambridge (MA, Rodwell prize for law), Coll of Law; *m* 10 Sept 1977, Susan Christine, da of John Henry Collett; 2 s (Peter George Eveleigh b 2 April 1984, Andrew David Eveleigh b 22 March 1987); *Career* admitted slr 1976; Lovell White & King: articled clerk 1974–76, asst slr 1976–77; Baker McKenzie: joined as asst slr 1977, later ptnr, head Intellectual Property and Technology Law Dept 1983–; bd memb Fedn Against Software Theft 1988–91; editorial bd memb: Computer Law and Practice, Computer Law and Security Report; memb Law Soc; *Books* Protecting Computer Technology (European ed, 1986); *Recreations* gardening, travel, watching sport of all kinds, swimming; *Style—* Donald Jerrard, Esq; ✉ The Coach House, Petersfield Rd, Greatham, nr Liss, Hampshire (☎ 01420 538392); Baker & McKenzie, 100 New Bridge Street, London EC4V 6JA (☎ 0171 919 1808, fax 0171 919 1999)

JERROM, Michael George Lindsay; s of late Maj Michael Francis Jerrom, and Irene Edith, *née* Fry; *b* 14 April 1942; *Educ* Sherborne, Univ of Oxford (MA); *m* 1, 1 June 1968 (m dis), Rosalind Mary, da of late Dr Bernard James Sanger, of Walberswick, Suffolk; 1 s (Charles Lindsay b 11 May 1973), 1 da (Amanda Suzanne b 25 Aug 1970); m 2, 8 Sept 1979, Dorothy Fay Allgood; *Career* audit mangr Thornton Baker & Co London 1968–70 (accountancy articles 1964–67), section leader Overseas Containers Ltd 1971–72, co sec Int Caledonian Assets Ltd and Argyle Securities Ltd 1972–73; dir: Jardine Properties Ltd 1973–75, Norwest Holst International Ltd 1975–77, CCL Financial Services Ltd 1977–, Axis Property Management Ltd; md: Selective Construction Projects plc 1984–91, CCL Developments plc 1986–91; chm The Vector Collection plc 1988–90, dir Look at Languages Communications Experts Ltd 1989–, fin conslt, ptnr Jerrom & Co Chartered Accountants 1993–; memb Pubns Review Panel ICAEW 1990–91; FCA 1968; *Recreations* golf, local affairs, ex chairman conservative branch; *Clubs* East India, Thorpe Hall, Wrotham Heath, Royal Cinque Ports, Rye Golf, Oxford and Cambridge Golfing Soc, Oxford Soc; *Style—* Michael Jerrom, Esq; ✉ 18 Avenue Road, Belmont Sutton, Surrey SM2 6JD (☎ 0181 770 0422, fax 0181 770 3832)

JERSEY, Dean of; *see:* Seaford, Very Rev John Nicholas

JERVIS, Hon Edward Robert James; s and h of 7 Viscount St Vincent, *qv*; *b* 12 May 1951; *Educ* Radley; *m* 1977, Victoria Margaret, da of late Wilton Joseph Oldham, of Jersey; 1 s (James Richard Anthony b 1982), 1 da (Emma Margaret Anne b 1980); *Career* co dir; *Recreations* skiing, water sports, chess; *Style—* The Hon Edward Jervis; ✉ Colinas Verdes 26, Bensafrim, Lagos 8600, Algarve, Portugal

JERVIS, Simon Swynfen; s of Capt John Swynfen Jervis (ka 1944), and Diana Elizabeth, *née* Marriott (now Mrs Christopher Parker); *b* 9 Jan 1943; *Educ* Downside, Corpus Christi Coll Cambridge; *m* 19 April 1969, Fionnuala, da of Dr John MacMahon (d 1961); 1 s (John Swynfen b 25 June 1973), 1 da (Thalia Swynfen b 5 Jan 1971); *Career* student asst, asst keeper of art Leicester Museum and Art Gallery 1964–66; Dept of Furniture V & A: asst keeper 1966–75, deputy keeper 1975–89, acting keeper 1989, curator 1989–90; guest scholar J Paul Getty Museum 1988–89; dir Fitzwilliam Museum Cambridge 1990–95; National Trust: memb Arts Panel 1982–95 (chm 1987–95), memb Properties Ctee 1987–95, historic buildings sec 1995–; ed Furniture History Society 1987–92, dir The Burlington Magazine 1993–; Soc of Antiquaries: memb Cncl 1986–88, memb Exec Cncl 1987–90, pres 1995–; tstee The Royal Collection Tst 1993–; FSA 1983, FRSA 1990; *Books* Victorian Furniture (1968), Printed Furniture Designs Before 1650 (1974), High Victorian Design (1983), Penguin Dictionary of Design and Designers (1984), Furniture from Austria and Hungary in the Victoria and Albert Museum (1986); *Recreations* tennis; *Style—* Simon Jervis, Esq, PSA; ✉ 45 Bedford Gardens, London W8 7EF (☎ 0171 727 8739)

JERVOISE, John Loveys; DL (Hants 1994); s of Capt John Loveys, MC (d 1974), of Chudleigh, Devon, and Barbara Tristram Ellis (d 1992), o da of Arthur Tristram Ellis Jervoise (d 1942); descended maternally from Sir Thomas Jervoise, MP (d 1654) (*see* Burke's Landed Gentry, 18 edn, vol I, 1965); *b* 16 July 1935; *Educ* Hardye's Sch Dorchester, MacDonald Coll McGill Univ, Seale-Hayne Agric Coll; *m* 12 Aug 1961, Jane Elizabeth, eldest da of James Henry Lawrence Newnham (d 1975); 2 s (John Tristram b 3 May 1962, Anthony Richard b 2 Aug 1964), 2 da (Sarah Jane b 18 Nov 1965, Anne Elizabeth (twin) b 18 Nov 1965); *Career* Nat Serv Lt Devonshire Regt 1953–56, Capt 4/5 Bn Royal Hampshire Regt TA 1960–68; farmer and landowner; cncllr: Basingstoke Rural DC 1964–74, Basingstoke and Deane Borough Cncl 1974–78; dir Mid Southern Water Co 1974–91, chm Hampshire Branch Country Landowners' Assoc 1986–88, pres Black Welsh Mountain Sheep Breeders' Assoc 1980–82; High Sheriff of Hampshire 1989–90; *Recreations* hunting, shooting, walking; *Clubs* Naval and Military; *Style—* John Loveys Jervoise, Esq, DL; ✉ Grange Farmhouse, Herriard, Basingstoke, Hampshire RG25 2QB

JESS, Digby Charles; s of Ronald Ernest Jess, of Cornwood, Devon, and Cordelia Brookes, *née* Cundy; *b* 14 Nov 1953; *Educ* Plymouth Coll, Univ of Aston (BSc), Univ of Manchester (LLM); *m* 4 Aug 1980, Bridie Ann, da of Bartholomew Connolly, of Galway, Eire; 1 s (Piers Bartholomew Digby b 1988); *Career* called to the Bar Gray's Inn 1978, in practice 1981–, lectr in law (pt/t) Univ of Manchester 1986–87; memb Ctee: NW Branch CIArb 1984–95 (chm 1992–93), Gtr Manchester and W Pennines Region BIIBA Liability Soc (dep chm 1992–93, chm 1993–); memb: Professional Negligence Bar Assoc, Northern Circuit Commercial Bar Assoc; FCIArb 1992 (ACIArb 1984); *Books* The Insurance of Professional Negligence Risks: Law and Practice (1982, 2 edn 1989), The Insurance of Commercial Risks: Law and Practice (1986, 2 edn 1993), vol on Insurance in The Encyclopaedia of Forms and Precedents (vol 20, 1988), Butterworths Insurance Law Handbook (consulting ed, 3 edn 1992); numerous articles for legal jls; *Recreations* family, walking, theatre; *Style—* Digby C Jess, Esq; ✉ 8 King Street Chambers, Manchester M2 6AQ (☎ 0161 834 9560, fax 0161 834 2733); 26 Carlton Avenue, Wilmslow, Cheshire SK9 4EP (☎ 01625 536191)

JESSEL, Sir Charles John; 3 Bt (UK 1883), of Ladham House, Goudhurst, Kent; s of Sir George Jessel, MC, 2 Bt (d 1977); *b* 29 Dec 1924; *Educ* Eton, Balliol Coll Oxford, Northampton Inst of Agric (dip), Inst of Optimum Nutrition (dip); *m* 1, 1956, Shirley Cornelia (d 1977), da of John Waters, of Northampton; 2 s (George Elphinstone b 1957, Alastair John b 1959), 1 da ((Cornelia) Sarah b 1963); m 2, 1979 (m dis 1983), Gwendoline Mary, da of late Laurence Devereux, OBE, and widow of Charles Langer; *Heir* s, George Elphinstone Jessel b 15 Dec 1957, *qv*; *Career* Lt 15/19 Hussars (despatches) WWII; farmer 1953–85, farmer in ptnrship with son 1985–, nutrition conslt 1987–; JP Kent 1960–78; chm: Ashford NFU 1963–64, Canterbury Farmers' Club 1972; pres: Kent Branch Men of the Trees 1979–83 and 1996–, Br Soc of Dowsers 1987–93; hon fell Psionic Med Soc 1977; memb Inst of Allergy Therapists 1990–, memb Parly Gp for Alternative and Complementary Medicine 1991–, govr Inst of Optimum Nutrition 1994; *Books* An Anthology of Inner Silence (1990); *Recreations* gardening, walking, planting trees, opera; *Clubs* Cavalry and Guards'; *Style—* Sir Charles Jessel, Bt; ✉ South Hill Farm, Hastingleigh, nr Ashford, Kent TN25 5HL (☎ 01233 750325)

JESSEL, David Greenhalgh; s of Robert George Jessel (d 1954), and Penelope, *née* Blackwell (later Dame Penelope Jessel, DBE, d 1996); *b* 8 Nov 1945; *Educ* Dragon Sch Oxford, Eton (scholar), Merton Coll Oxford (exhibitioner, MA); *m* 1974, Samantha Joyce Lynn; 2 s (Benjamin Christian b 11 Jan 1978, Robert Ashton b 16 Dec 1980); *Career* reporter BBC Radio World at One (Paris riots) 1968, reporter/presenter World at One and World This Weekend 1969–72, reporter 24 Hours and Midweek (BBC TV) 1972–76; presenter: Morning Show (LBC) 1976, Newsweek (BBC TV) 1977–79; writer/presenter (for BBC TV): Heart of the Matter 1979–85, Out of Court 1980–86, Rough Justice 1987–88, Taking Liberties 1989; presenter Trial & Error (Channel 4) 1992; fndr dir Just Television Ltd 1992–; winner: Royal Television Soc Int Current Affairs Award, UN Media Peace Prize, Bar Cncl Special Award; *Books* Brainsex (with Anne Moir, 1989), Trial and Error (1994), A Mind to Crime (1995); numerous misc contribs to periodicals; *Recreations* sailing; *Clubs* Chelsea Arts; *Style—* David Jessel, Esq; ✉ Just Television, 11–15 Emerald Street, London WC1 (☎ 0171 404 6744, fax 0171 242 3346)

JESSEL, George Elphinstone; s and h of Sir Charles John Jessel, 3 Bt, *qv*, and Shirley Cornelia, *née* Waters (d 1977); *b* 15 Dec 1957; *Educ* Milton Abbey, RAC Cirencester; *m* 10 Dec 1988 (m dis 1993), Rose Amelia, yr da of James Coutts-Smith, of Wallington, Herts; *Career* cmmnd Lt 15/19 Royal Hussars, Germany, Canada and Cyprus 1978–82; farmer (ptnr with father) 1985–; *Recreations* skiing, Cresta, travelling; *Clubs* Farmers'; *Style—* George Jessel, Esq; ✉ Stoakes Cottage, Hastingleigh, Ashford, Kent TN25 5HG (☎ 01233 750 216); South Hill Farm, Hastingleigh, Ashford, Kent TN25 5HL (☎ 01233 750325)

JESSEL, Oliver Richard; er s of Cdr Richard Frederick Jessel, DSO, OBE, DSC (d 1988), of Marden, Kent; er bro of Toby Jessel, MP, *qv*; *b* 24 Aug 1929; *Educ* Rugby; *m* 1950, Gloria Rosalie Teresa, *née* Holden; 1 s, 5 da; *Career* chm: numerous cos in Jessel Group 1954–89, London Australian & General Exploration Co 1960–75, Charles Clifford Industs (non-ferrous metals gp) 1978–81, Thomas Seager plc 1993–; pioneer of specialised unit tsts, responsible for numerous mergers incl Johnson and Firth Brown and Maple Macowards; fndr: Castle Communications plc, New Issue and Convertible Issue Permanent Investment Trusts, Gold & General Unit Trust, 27 other quoted cos and tsts; *Clubs* Garrick; *Style—* Oliver Jessel, Esq; ✉ Tilts House, Boughton Monchelsea, Maidstone, Kent ME17 4JE

JESSEL, Toby Francis Henry; MP (C) Twickenham (majority 5,711); yr s of Cdr Richard Jessel, DSO, OBE, DSC, RN (d 1988), and Winifred May (d 1977), da of Maj Walter Levy, DSO, and Hon Mrs Levy (later Hon Mrs Ionides), da of 1 Viscount Bearsted; bro of Oliver Jessel, *qv*; *b* 11 July 1934; *Educ* RNC Dartmouth, Balliol Coll Oxford (MA); *m* 1, 1967 (m dis); 1 da (decd); m 2, 1980, Eira Heath; *Career* Sub Lt RNVR 1954; memb GLC for Richmond-upon-Thames 1967–73; Parly candidate (C): Peckham 1964, Hull N 1966; MP (C) Twickenham 1970–; chm: Indo-Br Parly Gp (hon sec 1972–87), Anglo-Belgian Parly Gp 1983, Cons Parly Arts and Heritage Ctee 1983 (vice chm 1979); memb Cncl of Europe 1976–92; Liveryman Worshipful Co of Musicians; Order of Polonia Restituta (Polish Govt in Exile) 1975; Order of Merit (Liechtenstein) Fourth Class 1979; Chevalier de l'Ordre de la Couronne (Belgium) 1980; *Recreations* piano, gardening, skiing, swimming; *Clubs* Garrick, Hurlingham; *Style—* Toby Jessel, Esq, MP; ✉ Old Court House, Hampton Court, E Molesey, Surrey KT8 9BW; House of Commons, London SW1A 0AA (☎ 0171 219 6377)

JESSOP, Sheriff Alexander Smethurst; s of Thomas Alexander Jessop (d 1953), of Montrose, and Ethel Marion, *née* Robertson; *b* 17 May 1943; *Educ* Montrose Acad, Fettes Coll, Univ of Aberdeen (MA, LLB); *m* 16 Sept 1967, Joyce Isobel, *née* Duncan; 2 s (Graeme b 15 Nov 1969, Andrew b 14 Feb 1978), 1 da (Alison b 9 June 1972); *Career* apprentice then ptnr Campbell Middleton Burness & Dickson Montrose; depute procurator fiscal Perth 1976–78, asst slr Crown Office 1978–80, regnl procurator fiscal Aberdeen 1984–87, regnl procurator fiscal Glasgow 1987–90 (sr asst procurator fiscal 1980–84), Sheriff of Grampian Highland & Islands Aberdeen 1990–; memb Scottish Legal Aid Bd; *Recreations* golf; *Clubs* Royal Montrose Golf; *Style—* Sheriff Alexander Jessop; ✉ Sheriff Court House, Castle Street, Aberdeen AB10 1WP (☎ 01224 648316)

JEUNE, Senator Reginald Robert; CBE (1996, OBE 1979); s of Reginald Valpy Jeune (d 1974), and Jessie Maud, *née* Robinson (d 1945); *b* 22 Oct 1920; *Educ* De La Salle Coll Jersey; *m* 1946, Monica Lillian, da of Hedley Charles Valpy, of Jersey; 2 s (Richard Francis Valpy b 1949, Nicholas Charles b 1954), 1 da (Susan Elizabeth b 1958); *Career* slr Royal Ct of Jersey 1945; ret sr ptnr Mourant du Feu & Jeune (now conslt); Senator of States of Jersey (pres Policy and Resources Ctee); chm: Cwlth Parly Assoc (Exec Jersey Branch), Jersey Electricity Co Ltd; dir: S G Warburg & Co (Jersey) Ltd, Mercury Asset Management Channel Islands Ltd; OStJ, Chevalier of the Order of Orange Nassau, Offr of the Ordre de Merite Nationale; *Recreations* golf; *Clubs* RAC, MCC, Victoria (Jersey), United, Royal Jersey Golf, La Moye Golf; *Style—* Senator Reginald R Jeune, CBE; ✉ 22 Grenville St, St Helier, Jersey, CI (☎ 01534 609000, fax 01534 609333, telex 4192064)

JEWELL, David John; s of Wing Cdr John Jewell, OBE (d 1985), of Porthleven, Cornwall, and Rachel, *née* Miners (d 1962); *b* 24 March 1934; *Educ* Blundell's, St John's Coll Oxford (MA, MSc); *m* 23 Aug 1958, Katharine Frida, da of Prof Hans Sigmund Heller (d 1974), of Bristol; 1 s (John Edward), 3 da (Rachel Susannah, Sarah Josephine, Tamsin Mary Katharine); *Career* Nat Serv Pilot Offr RAF 1952–54; head of Sci Dept: Eastbourne Coll 1958–62, Winchester Coll 1962–67; dep head Lawrence Weston Sch Bristol 1967–70; head master: Bristol Cathedral Sch 1970–79, Repton 1979–87; master Haileybury and Imperial Serv Coll 1987–96; nat rep and chm HMC sub-ctees, chm HMC 1990; govr: Blundell's Sch 1994–, Truro Sch 1990– (chm 1996–); memb Engrg Trg Authy; FRSA 1981; *Recreations* music, cricket, Cornwall; *Clubs* East India, MCC, Bristol Savages, British Sportsman's, Lord's Taverners; *Style—* David Jewell, Esq; ✉ Coombe Orchard, Compton Martin, Bristol BS18 6JA (☎ 01761 221264)

JEWELL, Dr Derek Parry; s of Ralph Parry Jewell, of Bishopsteignton, Teignmouth, Devon, and Eileen Rose, *née* Champion; *b* 14 June 1941; *Educ* Bristol GS, Pembroke Coll Oxford (MA, DPhil, BM BCh); *m* 6 July 1974, Barbara Margaret, da of late Leonard Pearson Lockwood; 1 s (Christopher b 1979), 1 da (Carolyn b 1981); *Career* visiting asst prof Stanford Univ Sch of Med 1973–74, sr lectr in med Royal Free Hosp 1974–80, conslt physician and reader in med Univ of Oxford 1980–; memb Res Ctee RCP 1978–87; memb Editorial Bds: Gut, Clinical Science, European Journal of Gastroenterology and Hepatology; ed Topics in Gastroenterology 1973 and 1984–89; FRCP 1979 (MRCP 1970); *Books* Clinical Gastrointestinal Immunology (1979); *Recreations* music, gardening; *Style—* Dr Derek Jewell; ✉ Madison, Brill Road, Horton-cum-Studley, Oxford OX33 1BN (☎ 01865 351315); Radcliffe Infirmary, Oxford (☎ 01865 224829, fax 01865 790792)

JEWELL, Prof Peter Arundel; s of Percy Arundel Jewell (d 1960), of Bude, Cornwall, and Ivy Dorothea, *née* Ennis (d 1962); *b* 16 June 1925; *Educ* Wandsworth Sch, Univ of Reading (major open scholar, BSc), St John's Coll Cambridge (BA, Wright's prizeman,

MA, Gedge prizeman, PhD, ARC postgrad scholar, Wellcome res scholar); *m* 26 June 1958, Juliet, da of Alan Clutton-Brock (d 1970); 3 da (Sarah Abigail b 1959, Vanessa Topsy b 1961, Rebecca Tamsin b 1963); *Career* lectr RVC 1951–61, res fell Zoological Soc 1961–66, prof of biology and dir Div of Biological Sci Univ of Nigeria 1966–67, sr lectr in zoology UCL 1966–72 (dir MSc course in conservation 1968–70), prof of zoology Royal Holloway Coll London 1972–77; Mary Marshall and Arthur Walton prof of physiology of reproduction 1977–92, prof emeritus Univ of Cambridge 1992–; fndr memb and vice pres Rare Breeds Survival Tst; fndr memb Experimental Earthwork Ctee; fell St John's Coll Cambridge; FIBiol 1960, CBiol 1985; *Books* Island Survivors: The Ecology of the Soay Sheep of St Kilda (1974), Problems in Management of Locally Abundant Wild Mammals (1987), Large African Mammals in their Environment (1989); *Recreations* breeding Gloucester cattle (Arundel herd), life drawing, African cultures and conservation of African elephants, pottery, Cornish history, promoting real ale; *Style—* Prof Peter Jewell; ✉ University of Cambridge, Department of Zoology, Downing St, Cambridge CB2 3EJ (☎ 01223 336600, fax 01223 336676)

JEWITT, Anthony John; s of John Jewitt, and Ellen, *née* Tatlock; *b* 7 Oct 1935; *Educ* Chingford GS, Harvard Business Sch; *m* 26 July 1958, Janet Julia, *née* Smith; 3 da (Marie Julia Anne b 28 June 1960, Jennie Anne Louise b 15 July 1962, Catherine Jane b 8 April 1965); *Career* served as Capt in Army 1958–60; gp chm Marcom Group plc; MIMgt, MInstM, MICSA; *Recreations* skiing, tennis, horse racing; *Clubs* St James's; *Style—* Anthony Jewitt, Esq; ✉ Majenca, Pelling Hill, Old Windsor, Berks SL4 2LL (☎ 01753 865289, fax 01753 856751); Marcom Group plc, Marcom House, 1 Heathlands, Heath Gardens, Twickenham, Middlesex TW1 4BP (☎ 0181 891 5061, fax 0181 892 9028)

JEWITT, (Anselm) Crispin; s of Vivian Henry Anselm Jewitt, of Brackley, Northants, and Helen Phyllis, *née* Charles (d 1986); *b* 30 July 1949; *Educ* The Skinners' Sch Tunbridge Wells, Poly of N London; *m* 1 July 1970, Mary *née* Lee; 1 da (Alexandra b 20 June 1977), 2 s (Michael b 23 Nov 1978, Henry b 6 May 1984); *Career* Br Library: joined 1974, curator Map Library 1980–88, dir Nat Sound Archive 1992– (asst dir 1988–92); tstee: Nat Life Stories Collection, Wildlife Sound Tst; govr and treas Hever C of E Primary Sch; memb: Kent Archaeological Soc, The Charles Close Soc; ALA 1974; *Books* Maps for Empire (1992); *Recreations* singing, family holidays, whisky drinking; *Style—* Crispin Jewitt, Esq; ✉ National Sound Archive, 29 Exhibition Road, London SW7 2AS (☎ 0171 412 7424, fax 0171 412 7422, e-mail crispin.jewitt@bl.uk)

JEWITT, Ronald William; s of Cyril George Jewitt (d 1982), of Newport, Gwent, and Hilda Laura Jewitt (d 1972); *b* 25 Jan 1942; *Educ* Newport HS, Newport and Mon Tech Coll, Brunel Coll of Advanced Tech; *m* 30 March 1963, June Rose, da of Reginald Barley (d 1982), of Newport, Gwent; 2 s (Peter Ronald b 1964, David Charles b 1965), 1 da (Penelope Anne b 1967); *Career* asst chemist Monsanto Chemicals Ltd 1958–62, dep analyst Expandite Ltd 1962–64, res and devpt chemist Burt Boulton and Haywood Ltd 1964–66, analytical chemist London Transport 1966–89 (chief chemist 1989–); pres: Caversham and Mapledurham Royal Br Legion, Reading Mid-Week Assoc Cricket League; vice pres: Caversham Cons Club, Royal Berks Sports and Social Club; chm Caversham Cons Assoc; memb: Reading Borough Cncl 1973–91 (housing chm 1979–84, Mayor 1984–85, Dep Mayor 1985–86), Berks CC 1977–93 (ldr 1986–90); *Recreations* walking, swimming; *Style—* Ronald Jewitt, Esq; ✉ 98 Chiltern Road, Caversham, Reading, Berkshire RG4 OJD (☎ 0118 948 1147); 55 Lot's Road, London SW10 (☎ 0171 352 3727 ext 37)

JEWKES, Sir Gordon Wesley; KCMG (1990, CMG 1980); s of Jesse Jewkes (d 1943), and Anne Plumb (d 1983); *b* 18 Nov 1931; *Educ* Barrow in Furness GS, and elswhere; *m* 1954, Joyce, da of John Lyons (d 1975); 2 s (Nigel, Stephen); *Career* Nat Serv and Army Emergency Reserve (AER), cmmnd RAOC 1950–61; Home Civil Serv 1948–68, first sec Cwlth Office later FCO, consul (commercial) Chicago 1969–72, dep high cmmr Port of Spain 1972–75, head of Fin Dept FCO, fin offr Dip Serv 1975–79; consul gen: Cleveland 1979–82, Chicago 1982–85; govr Falkland Islands and high cmmr Br Antarctic Territory 1985–88, consul gen NY and dir gen Trade and Investmt USA 1989–91, ret; non-exec dir: Hogg Group plc 1992–94, Slough Estates 1992–; exec dir The Walpole Ctee 1992–96; memb: Cncl Univ of Buckingham 1996–, Marshall Aid Commemoration Cmmn 1996–, Salvation Army London Advsy Bd 1996–; *Recreations* music, walking, travel; *Clubs* Travellers'; *Style—* Sir Gordon Jewkes, KCMG; ✉ 19 Furzefield Road, Beaconfield, Bucks HP9 1PG (☎ 01494 681830)

JEWKES, Josephine Michaela Ingam; da of Michael Withy Jewkes, and Catherine Maxine, *née* Edwards, of Isleworth; *b* 6 Oct 1964; *Educ* Solihull Sch of Ballet, Royal Ballet Sch White Lodge, Bush Davies Sch; *Career* ballet dancer; princ dancer with English National Ballet (formerly London Festival Ballet) 1982–96, Rambert Dance Company 1996–; trained also with Mme Cleo Nordi and Svetlana Beriosova, currently trains with Mme Maria Fay; choreographed Menotti's The Medium for Opera Shop 1988; winner Noreen Bush Award for Classical Ballet 1978, Dance and Dancers magazine's Most Improved Dancer 1988, Dancer of the Month (Dancing Times) Aug 1993; *Roles* first major role Swanilda in Gable's Coppèlia 1981; roles created for Eng Nat Ballet incl: Youngest Child in Christopher Bruce's Land (Coliseum) 1985, leading roles in Haigen's Nocturne and A'Winged 1987, role in Michael Clarke's Drop Your Pearls... 1987, lead in Bruce's Symphony in Three Movements (Coliseum) 1989, Blue Duet in S Davies' Dancing Ledge 1990, Nastenka in Brandstrup's White Nights 1992; other major Eng Nat Ballet roles incl: Tatiana in Onegin (Coliseum) 1988, Odette in Makarova's Swan Lake 1988, Sugar Plum Fairy and Snow Queen in The Nutcracker (Royal Festival Hall) 1989, Juliet in Sir Frederick Ashton's Romeo and Juliet 1989, Swanilda in Coppèlia 1990, Myrtha in Giselle 1991, title roles in Wainrot's Anne Frank (Coliseum) 1991, Cinderella 1992 and Giselle 1994, guest appearance as Aurora in Sleeping Beauty (tour of Germany) 1994, Juliet in Nureyev's Romeo and Juliet 1995, principal in Balanchine's Square Dance 1995, title role in Michael Corder's Cinderella (new prodn) 1996, Sister With Glasses in MacMillan's My Brother, My Sister; also created non-singing role of Young St Thérèse of Lisieux as a child in John Tavener's opera Thérèse (Royal Opera House Covent Garden) 1979; *Books* The Art of Teaching Classical Ballet (by Woytec Lowski, ed, 1994); author of articles: A Dancer Prepares (Dance Now, March 1992), Carry on Touring with ENB (Dancing Times, Oct 1993); *Recreations* applied arts, DIY, gardening (especially old roses), antiques (especially antique fans), music, Maria Callas; *Style—* Ms Josephine Jewkes; ✉ Rambert Dance Company, 94 Chiswick High Road, London W4 1SH (☎ 0181 995 4246); personal fax 0181 287 2227

JEWSON, Richard Wilson; s of Charles Boardman Jewson (d 1981), of Norfolk, and Joyce Marjorie, *née* Laws; *b* 5 Aug 1944; *Educ* Rugby, Pembroke Coll Cambridge (MA); *m* 1965, Sarah Rosemary, da of Henry Nevill Spencer, of Kenilworth; 1 s (William b 1968), 3 da (Henrietta b 1966, Charlotte b 1971, Camilla b 1977); *Career* md Jewson Ltd 1974–86; Meyer International plc: dir 1984–93, md 1986, chm 1991–93; non-exec chm: Ideal Hardware plc 1994–, Savills plc 1995– (dir 1994–); non-exec dir: Anglian Water plc 1991– (dep chm 1994–), Queens Moat House plc 1994–, Grafton Group plc 1995–; dir Eastern Counties Newspaper Group Ltd 1982–96; memb Cncl Univ of E Anglia 1980–; CIMgt, fell Inst of Wood Sciences; *Recreations* gardening, golf, tennis; *Clubs* Boodle's, Queen's, Royal W Norfolk Golf, RSA; *Style—* Richard Jewson, Esq; ✉ Dades Farm, Barnham Broom, Norfolk NR9 4BT (☎ 01603 759237, fax 01603 759685)

JHABVALA, Ruth Prawer; da of Marcus Prawer (d 1948), and Eleonora, *née* Cohn (d 1983); *b* 7 May 1927; *Educ* Hendon Co Sch London, Univ of London (MA); *m* 16 June 1951, Cyrus Jhabvala, s of Shiavakshah Jhabvala (d 1973); 3 da (Renana b 1952, Ava b 1955, Firoza b 1957); *Career* authoress and screenwriter; collaborations with Ismail Merchant and James Ivory 1963–; Hon DLitt Univ of London, Hon LHD Hebrew Union Coll NY; FRSL; *Films* incl: Shakespeare Wallah 1964, Autobiography of a Princess 1975, The Bostonians 1985, A Room With A View 1986 (Oscar for Best Screenplay Adaptation), Mr and Mrs Bridge 1990, Howards End 1992 (Oscar for Best Screenplay Adaptation); *Books* To Whom She Will (1955), The Nature of Passion (1956), A Stronger Climate (1968), Heat and Dust (1975, winner Booker Prize), Out of India (1986), Three Continents (1987), Poet and Dancer (1993), Shards of Memory (1995); *Style—* Mrs Ruth Jhabvala; ✉ 400 East 52nd St, New York, NY 10022, USA

JIA, Dr Yizhen; da of Zhijie Jia, and Tianquan Dai, of 73 Binhe Rd, Lanzhou City, China; *b* 19 Oct 1963; *Educ* Gansu Univ of Traditional Chinese Med (BA), Tianjing Univ of Traditional Chinese Med (MSc), Univ of Surrey (Med Microbiology); *Career* acupuncturist and herbalist specialising in gynaecological problems (esp infertility, period problems, PMT and menopausal problems), stress-related problems, skin complaints, sports injuries, arthritis and back pain; formerly asst lectr on gen med and gynaecology Ganshu Univ of Traditional Chinese Med and practising doctor of gen in univ hosp; lectr Br Coll of Acupuncture 1991–; memb Br Acupuncture Assoc 1990; *Style—* Dr Yizhen Jia; ✉ British College of Acupuncture, 8 Hunter Street, London WC1N 1BN (☎ 0171 837 6429, and 0171 833 8164)

JIANG, Enzhu; HE Mr Jiang Enzhu; *b* 7 Dec 1938, Jiangsu; *Educ* univ graduate; *m*; 1 s; *Career* diplomat of the People's Republic of China; teacher Beijing Foreign Languages Inst 1964, staff memb then attaché Office of the Chargé d'Affaires London 1964–72, third then second sec London 1972–77, dep dir Dept of W Euro Affrs Miny of Foreign Affrs 1978–81, research fell Center for Int Affrs Harvard Univ and sr visiting scholar Brookings Instn USA 1981–82, successively dir, dep DG then DG Dept of W Euro Affrs Miny of Foreign Affrs 1983–90, asst min Miny of Foreign Affrs 1990–91, vice foreign min 1991–95, ambass to the Ct of St James's 1995–; *Style—* HE Mr Jiang Enzhu; ✉ Embassy of the People's Republic of China, 49–51 Portland Place, London W1N 4JL (☎ 0171 636 9375)

JILLINGS, Godfrey Frank; s of Gerald Frank Jillings (d 1991), of Worcester Park, Surrey, and Dorothy Marjorie, *née* Smith (d 1996); *b* 24 May 1940; *Educ* Tiffin Boys' Sch Kingston; *m* 1967, Moira Elizabeth, *née* McCoy (d 1986); 1 s (Simon Andrew b 1969; *Career* with S G Warburg & Co 1956–58; National Westminster Bank: joined 1958, head Industl Section 1983–85, sr project mangr 1985–86, chief exec NatWest Personal Financial Management Ltd 1986–89, dir County Unit Trust Managers Ltd 1986–87, dir NatWest Stockbrokers Ltd 1986–89, dir NatWest Stockbrokers Financial Services Ltd 1987–89, dir NatWest PEP Nominees Ltd 1988–89, sr exec Gp Chief Exec's Office 1989–90; chief exec FIMBRA 1990–94, dep chief exec Personal Investmt Authy 1992–94, dir Financial Services Initiative Wales 1994–, dir DBS Management plc 1994–, dir Baronsmead VCT plc 1995–; ACIB 1961; *Recreations* travel, chess; *Clubs* Athenaeum; *Style—* Godfrey Jillings, Esq; ✉ 47 Hurlingham Square, London SW6 3DZ (☎ and fax 0171 736 9083); Financial Services Initiative, 10 Charles II Street, London SW1Y 4AA (☎ 0171 925 0453)

JIP, Dr James; s of Joseph Wing Jip (d 1980), of Liverpool, and Lai Jip (d 1977); *b* 10 July 1949; *Educ* Liverpool Collegiate Sch, Liverpool Univ Med Sch (MB ChB); *m* 20 Nov 1972, Margaret Victoria Ann, da of Victor Matthew Boulton (d 1970), of St Helens, Merseyside; 2 s (Edward James b 5 Jan 1976, Paul Francis b 13 Dec 1977), 1 da (Caroline Ann b 20 Aug 1981); *Career* house physician Whiston Hosp Merseyside 1972–73, house surgn St Helen's Hosp Merseyside 1973, registrar pathology Walton Hosp Merseyside 1974–75 (sr house offr pathology 1973–74), sr registrar haematology Mersey RHA 1975–80, conslt haematologist Bolton Gen Hosp 1980–; Br Soc Haematology, Br Blood Transfusion Soc, NW Regnl Haematology Sub-Ctee; FRCPath 1991 (MRCPath 1979); *Recreations* foreign travel, chess, piano; *Clubs* Bolton Chess; *Style—* Dr James Jip; ✉ The Dept of Haematology, Bolton Gen Hosp, Minerva Rd, Bolton, Lancs BL4 0JR (☎ 01204 390390)

JIRICNA, Eva Magdalena; CBE (1994); da of Josef Jiricny (d 1973), and Eva, *née* Svata; *b* 3 March 1939; *Educ* Tech Univ of Prague, Prague Acad of Fine Arts; *Career* architect; GLC's Sch Division 1968–69, Louis de Soissons Partnership 1969–78 (assoc architect), in practice with David Hodges 1978–82, freelance working for Richard Rogers Partnership 1982–84, fndr ptnr own practice with Kathy Kerr 1984–86, reformed co as Eva Jiricna Architects 1986–; interior work for clients incl: Lloyd's Headquarters Buildings, Harrods, Joseph, Legends, Joan & David, Bergdorf Goodman, Vitra International; conslt Sir John Soanes Museum; lectr various venues; RIBA (memb Cncl), memb Cncl AA; hon fell RCA 1990; RDI 1991; *Style—* Ms Eva Jiricna, CBE; ✉ Eva Jiricna Architects Ltd, 7 Dering Street, London W1R 9AB (☎ 0171 629 7077, fax 0171 491 3370)

JO, Sumi; *b* 22 Nov 1962; *Educ* Seoul, Santa Cecilia Rome; *Career* soprano; *Roles* international debut as Gilda in Rigoletto at Teatre Verdi Trieste 1986; others incl: Oscar in Un Ballo in Maschera (Salzburg Festival, under Sir Georg Solti) 1990, Gilda in Rigoletto (Met Opera NY) 1990, Queen of Night in The Magic Flute (Vienna Staatsoper, Chicago Lyric Opera) 1990, Zerbinetta in Ariadne auf Naxos (Rome) 1990, Olympia in Les Contes d'Hoffman (Royal Opera House Covent Garden 1991 and 1992), Constance in Carmelites (Rome) 1991, Adina in L'Elisir D'Amore (Covent Garden) 1992, Elvira in I Puritani (Covent Garden) 1992, Queen of the Night (Covent Garden) 1993; *Recordings incl* Oscar in Un Ballo in Maschera (under von Karajan, Deutsche Grammophon), Queen of Night in The Magic Flute (under Solti on Decca and Jordan on Erato), Countess in Le Comte Ory (under John Eliot Gardiner, Philips), Fiorilla in Il Turco in Italia (under Sir Neville Marriner, Philips), Rossini's Messe Di Gloria (under Marriner, Philips), Falcon in Die Frau Ohne Schatten (under Solti, Decca), Mahler's Symphony No 8 (under Sinopoli, Deutsche Gramophone); *Style—* Ms Sumi Jo; ✉ c/o Diana Mulgan, IMG Artists Europe, Media House, 3 Burlington Lane, Chiswick, London W4 2TH (☎ 0181 747 9977)

JOACHIM, Julian; *b* 20 Sept 1974; *Career* professional footballer; with: Leicester City 1992–96, Aston Villa (for fee of £1.5m) 1996– (winners Coca-Cola Cup 1996); former memb England under 21 team; *Style—* Julian Joachim, Esq; ✉ c/o Aston Villa FC, Villa Park, Trinity Road, Birmingham B6 6HE

JOB, Peter James Denton; s of Frederick Job (d 1944), and Marion Pickard; *b* 13 July 1941; *Educ* Clifton Coll, Exeter Coll Oxford (BA); *m* 1966, Christine, da of Frederick Cobley; 1 da (Laura b 21 May 1971), 1 s (Luke b 5 Sept 1973); *Career* Reuters: joined 1963, served as reporter then mangr in Paris, New Delhi, Kuala Lumpur, Jakarta and Buenos Aires 1963–78, mangr Reuters in Asia (mainly based Hong Kong) 1978–90, full main bd dir 1989–, chm Visnews Ltd 1991–92, chief exec Reuters Holdings plc 1991–; non-exec dir Grand Metropolitan plc 1994–; memb: DTI Multimedia Advsy Gp, DTI Japan Trade Gp 1994–, HM Treasy City Promotion Panel 1995–, High Level Advsy Gp on Info Soc EU 1996–, INSEAD UK Nat Cncl 1993–; memb Advsy Cncl Green Coll and hon fell 1995–; *Recreations* theatre, classical music, boating, golf, shooting, tennis; *Clubs* Hong Kong; *Style—* Peter Job, Esq; ✉ Reuters Holdings plc, 85 Fleet Street, London EC4P 4AJ (☎ 0171 250 1122)

JOBSON, Anne Margaret; OBE (1992); da of Colin Thomas Figgins Bell, of Fareham, Hants, and Margaret, *née* Porter; *b* 12 Jan 1952; *Educ* Purbrook Park Co GS, City of London Poly (BA); *m* 10 July 1976, (Stephen) Andrew Jobson, s of Norman Jobson, of Walkden, Manchester; *Career* called to the Bar Gray's Inn 1975; barr at law (in practice as Anne Bell); memb London Regnl Passenger Ctee; prospective Parly candidate (Cons) Birmingham Yardley; *Recreations* gardening, walking, theatre, watching cricket, keeping fit; *Style*— Mrs Anne Jobson, OBE; ✉ 24 Parkfield Crescent, North Harrow, Middx HA2 6JZ (☎ 0181 428 5868); Holborn Chambers, 6 Gate Street, Holborn, London WC2A 3HP (☎ 0171 242 6060, fax 0171 242 2777, car 0831 424983)

JOBSON, Timothy Akers; s of Maj E O A Jobson (d 1965), and Joan, *née* Webb (d 1991); *b* 16 July 1944; *Educ* Bromsgrove, Keble Coll Oxford (MA); *m* 1, 27 July 1970 (m dis 1980), Lee Bazeley; 1 s (Simon b 1973), 1 da (Annie b 1974); m 2, 7 April 1982, Susan F Jeavons; *Career* admitted slr 1968; ptnr: Lyon Clark & Co W Bromwich 1970–84, Keely Smith & Jobson Lichfield 1985–95, Oldham Rust Jobson Stafford 1995–; co sec Barnt Green Waters Ltd; dep chm W Bromwich & Dist YMCA; *Recreations* sailing, swimming, gardening; *Clubs* Barnt Green Sailing, Oxford Univ Yacht; *Style*— Timothy Jobson, Esq; ✉ 6 Redhouse Road, Tettenhall, Wolverhampton WV6 8ST

JOCELYN, Prof Henry David; s of John Daniel Jocelyn (d 1956), and Phyllis Irene, *née* Burton (d 1977); *b* 22 Aug 1933; *Educ* Canterbury Boys' HS NSW, Univ of Sydney (BA), St John's Coll Cambridge (MA, PhD); *m* 22 Oct 1958, Margaret Jill, da of Bert James Morton (d 1984); 2 s (Luke b 1962, Edmund b 1968); *Career* memb academic staff Univ of Sydney 1960–73, Hulme prof of latin Univ of Manchester 1973–96; FBA 1982; *Style*— Prof Henry D Jocelyn, FBA; ✉ 52 Vicarage Road, Oxford OX1 4RE; Faculty of Arts, University of Manchester, Manchester M13 9PL (☎ 0161 275 3022)

JODRELL, Michael Francis Mostyn Owen; s of Col Herbert Lewis Mostyn-Owen (d 1972), and Susan Dorothy, *née* Ramsden-Jodrell (d 1965); *b* 9 Dec 1935; *Educ* Eton; *m* 25 April 1964, Veronica Mary, da of Lt-Col Oscar Leslie Boord, MC (d 1967); 2 s (Henry b 28 April 1967, William b 8 Oct 1969); *Career* Lt Grenadier Gds; ptnr Rowe & Pitman 1972–86, dir Mercury Mgmnt plc 1989–, vice chm Mercury Asset Mgmnt Private Investors Gp Ltd 1988–; Liveryman Worshipful Co of Fishmongers; *Recreations* photography, gardening, shooting; *Clubs* Pratt's, Boodle's; *Style*— Michael M O Jodrell, Esq; ✉ Leigh Court, Shaftesbury, Dorset SP7 9EJ (☎ 01747 828261); Mercury Asset Management plc, 33 King William St, London EC4 (☎ 0171 280 2800)

JOEL, Victoria Lynne Roberts (Vicky); da of Llywellyn James Roberts Joel (d 1970), of Gravesend, Kent, and Nora, *née* Bagshaw (d 1981); *b* 18 July 1952; *Educ* Ashford Sch for Girls Kent, Univ of Manchester (BA); *m* Stephen Bobasch; *Career* mktg asst Taylor Law & Co Ltd 1973–75, prod mangr Lyons Maid Ltd 1975–77, gp prod mangr Book Club Associates 1977–80; DDM Advertising Ltd: account mangr 1980–85, account dir 1985–87, client servs dir 1987–88; Eng area mangr and vice pres for Euro Time-Life Books 1989–91, Euro mktg dir Marvel Entertainment Group Inc 1992–95, mktg dir Enid Blyton Co 1996–; memb Cncl and dir BDMA 1989–91, memb Mktg Soc 1989–92, memb Inst of Director Mktg 1994; FZS 1996; *Style*— Ms Vicky Joel; ✉ Enid Blyton Company, 40 Shaftesbury Avenue, London W1V 7DD (☎ 0171 434 1880, fax 0171 434 1882)

JOFFE, Joel Goodman; s of Abraham Michael Joffe (d 1984), of Johannesburg, and Dena, *née* Idelson (d 1984); *b* 12 May 1932; *Educ* Univ of Witwatersrand Johannesburg (BCom, LLB); *m* 1 Nov 1962, Vanetta, da of François Pretorius (d 1975), of Port Elizabeth, S Africa; 3 da (Deborah b 11 June 1963, Lisa b 13 Aug 1964, Abigail b 4 Sept 1969); *Career* human rights lawyer SA 1954–65; admin dir Abbey Life Assurance plc 1966–70, dep chm (formerly dir and md) Allied Dunbar Assur plc 1971–91; chm Swindon Cncl of Voluntary Servs 1973–80, Oxfam 1980– (tstee, hon sec and and currently chm), chm Swindon Health Authy and NHS Tst 1988–94; *Recreations* tennis, skiing, cycling; *Style*— Joel Joffe; ✉ c/o Oxfam, 274 Banbury Road, Oxford OX2 7DZ

JOFFRE, Hugues; s of Bernard Joffre, of Paris, and Muriel, *née* Robert; *b* 7 July 1958; *Educ* Lycée Champollion Grenoble, Lycée Edouard Herriot Lyon, Univ of Grenoble; *m* Nazan, da of late Ismail Agar; 1 step da (Lara Stoby b 4 July 1980); *Career* Contemporary Art Dept Sotheby's: expert 1982–86, dep dir 1986–88, dir 1988–91, sr dir 1991–92; sr dir 20th Century Pictures Christies 1993–, dir Christies Paris 1995–, DG Christies France SA 1996– (dep chm 1995–96); *Style*— Hugues Joffre, Esq; ✉ Christies, 6 rue Paul Baudry, F-75008 Paris, France

JOHANSEN-BERG, Rev John; s of John Alfred Johansen-Berg, of Middlesbrough, Cleveland, and Caroline, *née* Gettings; *b* 4 Nov 1935; *Educ* Acklam Hall GS, Univ of Leeds (BA, BD), Univ of Cambridge (MA); *m* 17 July 1971, Joan Scott, da of James Parnham, of Leeds, Yorks; 2 s (Mark b 1973, James (Jake) b 1977), 1 da (Heidi b 1974); *Career* tutor Westminster Coll Cambridge 1961–62, ordained 1962, min St Ninian's Presbyterian Church Luton Beds 1962–70, fndr min St Katherine of Genoa Church Dunstable Beds 1966–70, frontier mission work in Everton Liverpool resulting in the bldg of the Rock Church Centre 1970–77, min St Andrew's United Reformed Church Ealing 1977–86, min Rubery URC 1992–, fndr Community for Reconciliation 1984 (pastoral ldr Birmingham 1986–); moderator: United Reformed Church 1980–81, Free Church Federal Cncl 1987–88; memb: Br Cncl of Churches Assembly 1987–90, SA Advsy Ctee, Namibia Advsy Gp, Forum of Churches Together in England 1990–; sponsor Christian Concern for SA; memb and former chm: Christian Fellowship Tst, Namibia Christian Exchange; former chm: Clergy Against Nuclear Arms, Church and Soc Dept of URC 1972–79, Ecumenical Working Party which produced Non-Violent Action: A Christian Appraisal (SCM 1973) and Violence, Non-Violence and Social Change (BCC 1977), URC Gp which produced Good News the Poor: New Enterprise in Mission (URC 1982); fndr: Ecumenical Order of Miny 1990, Romania Concern 1990; jt ed The Journal of the Presbyterian Historical Soc 1964–70; *Books* Arian or Arminian? Presbyterian Continuity in the Eighteenth Century (1969), Prayers of The Way (1987, revd edn 1992), Prayers of Pilgrimage (1988), Prayers of Prophecy (1990), Prayer for Pilgrims (1993), A Celtic Collection (1996); *Recreations* walking, mountain climbing/walking, badminton, tennis, golf; *Style*— The Rev John Johansen-Berg; ✉ Barnes Close, Chadwich Manor, nr Bromsgrove, Worcs B61 ORA (☎ 01562 710231); Community for Reconciliation, Barnes Close, Chadwich Manor, nr Bromsgrove, Worcs B61 ORA (☎ and fax 01562 710213)

JOHANSON, Capt Philip; s of Stanley Theodore Johanson (d 1991), and Betty Johanson (d 1984); *b* 10 April 1947; *Educ* Alderman Cogan C of E Sch Kingston upon Hull, Wilson Carlile Coll of Evangelism; *Career* Church Army: head of missions 1975–83, dir of evangelism 1983–90, chief sec 1990–; chm African Pastor Fellowship; memb: C of E Bd of Mission in England Ctee, Cncl Evangelical Alliance, Partnership World Mission Ctee; *Recreations* theatre, music, travel, reading; *Clubs* Royal Cwlth; *Style*— Capt Philip Johanson; ✉ Church Army Headquarters, Independents Rd, Blackheath, London SE3 9LF (☎ 0181 318 1226, fax 0181 318 5258)

JOHN, (Richard) Alun; s of Thomas Guy John (d 1969), and Edith, *née* John (d 1979); *b* 7 April 1948; *Educ* Whitchurch GS; *m* 14 June 1980, (Elizabeth) Sara, da of Denis W Kent, of Beaconsfield, Bucks; 1 s (Guy b 7 Oct 1985), 1 da (Lucy b 5 April 1989); *Career* photographer South Wales Echo and Western Mail 1966, photographer The Press Assoc 1977, ed The Associated Press; dep picture ed: Evening Standard 1981, Mail on Sunday 1982; picture ed The Independent 1986, gp picture ed Mirror Group Newspapers 1989–91, exec vice chm Syndication International 1989–91, md Alun John Communications Ltd 1991–; external examiner Univ of Sheffield, selector RPS Exhibitions 1988–89, conslt picture ed Thomson Fndn; Gerald Barry award from What the Papers Say 1987; *Books* Newspaper Photography (1988); *Recreations* travel, writing, shooting; *Style*— Alun John, Esq

JOHN, Daniel Howard; s of Michael Hanlon John, of London, and Patricia Ann, *née* Hawkes; *b* 6 June 1961; *Educ* Archbishop Tenison's GS London; *Career* trainee journalist West London Observer 1979–83, sr reporter West Kent Extra Series 1983–84, industl reporter Kent Evening Post 1984–86, fin reporter Birmingham Post 1986–88, freelance reporter 1988–89 (The Guardian, Mail on Sunday, Daily Star), financial corr, tport corr and dep financial news ed The Guardian 1989, freelance Australian corr Jan-Oct 1993, rejoined The Guardian as home news ed Oct 1993–96, managing ed (News) The Observer 1996–; received Proficiency Test Cert from Nat Cncl for Trg of Journalists; NEC memb NUJ 1986–87; memb: Charter 88, Friends of the Earth; *Recreations* reading, current affairs, music, cooking, entertaining, cricket, golf; *Clubs* Fleet Street Strollers Cricket; *Style*— Daniel John, Esq; ✉ c/o The Observer, 119 Farringdon Road, London EC1R 3ER (☎ 0171 713 4526)

JOHN, David Glyndwr; s of William Glyndwr John (d 1967), of Pontypridd, Mid Glamorgan, and Marjorie, *née* Gaze (d 1985); *b* 20 July 1938; *Educ* Llandovery Coll (Thomas Phillips Fndn scholar, Johnes scholar), Christ's Coll Cambridge (MA), Columbia Univ NY (NATO Research Studentship, MBA), Harvard Business Sch (Int Sr Mgmnt Prog); *m* 22 Aug 1964, Gillian, da of Henry J Edwards; 1 da (Emma Victoria b 7 July 1967), 1 s (Ceri David b 30 July 1968); *Career* graduate trainee then shift mangr United Steel Companies Sheffield 1962–64, mgmnt conslt then mktg dir subsid Hardman and Holden Ltd RTZ Corporation 1966–73; Redland Group plc: gen mangr Land Reclamation Co 1973–77, regnl dir Middle E and Far E Redland Industrial Services 1977–80, md Redland Purle 1980, md Cleanaway Ltd 1980–81; Inchcape plc: chief exec subsid Gray Mackenzie & Co Ltd Bahrain 1986–87 (devpt dir 1981–85), chief exec Inchcape Berhad Singapore 1987–90, main bd dir 1988–95, chm Inchcape Berhad 1990–95, exec chm Inchape Toyota Motors 1994–95; chm The BOC Group plc 1996– (non-exec dir 1993–); govr SOAS Univ of London 1994–; *Recreations* sailing, skiing, reading; *Clubs* United Oxford and Cambridge, Oriental; *Style*— David John, Esq; ✉ BOC Group plc, Chertsey Road, Windlesham, Surrey GU20 6HJ (☎ 01276 477222, fax 01276 471333)

JOHN, Elton Hercules (born Reginald Kenneth Dwight); CBE (1996); s of Stanley Dwight, and Sheila, *née* Sewell; *b* 25 March 1947; *Educ* Pinner GS, RAM; *Career* pop singer and pianist; keyboard player with R & B band Bluesology 1965, first album Empty Sky released 1969, US debut at Troubadour Folk Club 1970, single Your Song first UK and US Top 10 record 1971, renowned during 1970s for outlandish costumes and ludicrous spectacles, albums Goodbye Yellow Brick Road, Captain Fantastic and The Brown Dirt Cowboy and Blue Moves confirmed worldwide stardom, toured Communist Bloc (played eight sell-out dates in Leningrad), album A Single Man 1978 and subsequent tour stripped away razzmatazz of early 1970s shows, album Two Low for Zero 1983 provided four worldwide hits, broadcast of Live in Australia album viewed by record Australian TV audience of six million 1987, stage costumes and memorabilia sold by Sotheby's 1988, 34th album Sleeping with the Past released 1989, No 1 in UK Album Charts July 1990, over 3 million copies sold worldwide, double A-Sided single Sacrifice/Healing Hands No 1 five weeks in UK (first UK No 1, all proceeds donated to AIDS related charities), No 1 double album The Very Best of Elton John released Dec 1990 (over 9.5 million copies sold worldwide), album The One released 1992, album Duets released 1993, wrote music for film The Lion King (lyrics by Sir Tim Rice) 1994, album Made In England released 1995; significant achievements: record seven sell-out shows Madison Square Gardens, first artist to enter Billboard US Album chart at No 1, seven consecutive No 1 US albums, writer of over 600 songs and has released over 30 albums, more weeks spent in UK chart than any other recording artist during 1970s, winner Best Male Artist BRIT Awards 1991, Lifetime Achievement award BRIT Awards 1995, Oscar for Can You Feel The Love Tonight? (from The Lion King) 1995, Polar Music Prize 1995; chm Watford FC 1979–90; fndr Elton John Aids Fndn 1993; involved in many charities incl: Nordoff Robbins Music Therapy, Terence Higgins Tst, Body Positive, London Lighthouse; *Recreations* Watford FC (life pres); *Style*— Elton John, Esq, CBE; ✉ John Reid Enterprises, 32 Galena Rd, London W6 0LT (☎ 0181 741 9933, fax 0181 741 3938)

JOHN, Geraint Morton; s of Frederick William John (d 1977), of Swansea, and Gwladys Mary John (d 1970); *b* 2 April 1938; *Educ* Swansea GS, Bartlett Sch of Architecture UCL (DipArch); *m* Jan 1959, Jane Doreen, da of William Aurelius Williams; 1 s (Dylan William b 1964), 2 da (Catrin Elizabeth b 1959, Betsan Sarah b 1961); *Career* architect; articled to Sir Percy Thomas 1954–58; Maxwell Fry and Jane Drew 1961–63, Denys Lasdun 1963–64, Arup Associates 1964–65, Parkin Associates Toronto Canada 1965–66, Hertfordshire CC 1966–69, Architects and Bldgs Branch DES 1969–72, head Tech Unit for Sport and chief architect to Sports Council 1975–96 (joined 1972), sr lectr in architecture Faculty of Design & Technology Univ of Luton 1996–; memb: Arts Cncl Planning Bd 1988–93, Cncl Int Union of Architects 1990–93, RIBA Overseas Ctee 1985–93; chm RIBA/UIA Co-ordinating Ctee 1987–93, dir Sports Leisure and Tourism Prog Int Union of Architects 1984–, corr on sports bldgs for Architects Jl 1978–82; Companion Inst of Sports & Recreation Management 1993–; sec Sports and Leisure Work Gp Int Union of Architects 1994–; pres: Old Albanians RFC 1983–85, St Albans Welsh Soc 1980–83; memb: Editorial Advsy Bd Crowd Management magazine Int Assoc of Auditorium Managers, ILAM, Tech Ctee Sports Ground Initiative; RIBA (ARIBA 1962), FRSA; *Books* Handbook of Sports and Recreational Building Design (4 vols, jt ed 1981), Handbook of Sports and Recreation Design (revised edn, 3 vols, jt ed, 1994), Stadia Design (jtly, 1994); *Recreations* sketching; *Style*— Geraint John, Esq; ✉ 125 Verulam Rd, St Albans, Herts AL3 4DL (☎ 01727 857682); Faculty of Design & Technology, University of Luton, Park Square, Luton (☎ 01582 34111, fax 01582 489224)

JOHN, Dr Joshy; s of late Prof P V Ulahannan Mapilla, of Changanachery, Kerala, India, and late Mary, *née* Joseph; *b* 9 Oct 1940; *Educ* St Berchmans' HS, Kerala Univ (BSc, MB BS), Univ of Sheffield (MD); *m* 25 Jan 1970, Tresa, da of K J Jacob, of Kerala, India; 2 s (Jason Joseph b 30 June 1974, James George b 7 Nov 1983), 1 da (Mary Anne b 14 March 1979); *Career* conslt physician genito-urinary med St Albans City Hosp Herts; hon conslt HIV and AIDS Unit Chelsea and Westminster Hosp; former conslt physician genito-urinary med: Derby Royal Infirmary, Derby and Chesterfield Royal Hosp, St Mary's Hosp Luton; former hon lectr Med Div Univ of Sheffield; memb: Int Union Against VD and Treponematoses, Med Soc Study of VD, American VD Assoc, Indian Assoc Study of Sexually Transmitted Diseases, Int Soc for AIDS, Herts HIV/AIDS and Sexual Health Working Pty; chm Clinical Sub Gp on AIDS/HIV Infection St Albans and Hemel Hempstead NHS Tst; FRSM; *Books* papers on non-gonococcal urethritis therapy, asymptomatic gonorrhoea in male and abnormal forms of trichomonas vaginalis; *Recreations* tennis, swimming, reading; *Style*— Dr Joshy John; ✉ Department of Genito-urinary Medicine and HIV and AIDS Unit, St Albans City Hospital, Waverley Road, St Albans AL3 5PN (☎ 01727 866122, fax 01727 860261); 104 Harley Street, London W1N 1AF (☎ 0171 935 6554, fax 0171 935 6652); 60 Wimpole Street, London W1M 7DE (☎ 0171 487 4644); The Clementine Churchill Hospital, Sudbury Hill, Harrow HA1 3RX (☎ 0181 422 3464, fax 0181 846 1747)

JOHN, Katherine (real name Karen Watkins); da of Harry Glyn-Dwr Jones, of Pontypridd, and Gerda, *née* Salewski; *b* 30 May 1948; *Educ* Pontypridd Girls' GS, Swansea Coll (dip); *m* 28 Dec 1968, Trevor John Watkins, s of Arthur Watkins; 2 s (Ralf Spencer b 13 Dec 1974, Ross Michael b 12 Feb 1980), 1 da (Sophie Amelia b 11 May 1976); *Career* writer; teaching, youth and social work 1969–74; memb: Soc of Authors 1992–, PEN 1992–, Crime Writers Assoc 1992–; *Books* Without Trace (1990), Six Foot Under (1993), Murder of a Dead Man (1994), By Any Other Name (1995); under pseudonym of Catrin Collier: Hearts of Gold (1992), One Blue Moon (1993), A Silver

Lining (1994), All That Glitters (1995), Such Sweet Sorrow (1996); *Recreations* riding, sailing, swimming; *Style—* Ms Katherine John; ✉ c/o A M Heath & Co, 79 St Martin's Lane, London WC2N 4AA (☎ 0171 836 4271)

JOHN, Maldwyn Noel; s of Thomas Daniel John (d 1944), of Pontypridd, Glamorgan, and Beatrice May, *née* Clare (d 1971); *b* 25 Dec 1929; *Educ* Pontypridd GS, Univ Coll Cardiff (BSc); *m* 27 June 1953, Margaret, *née* Cannell; 2 s (Steven Thomas b 1959, Paul David b 1962); *Career* Metropolitan Vickers Electrical Co Manchester 1950–59, Atomic Energy Estab UKAEA Winfrith 1959–63, chief engr and divnl mangr AEI/GEC Manchester 1963–69; Kennedy & Donkin Consulting Engrs: chief electrical engr 1969–72, ptnr 1972–87, chm 1987–94, conslt Rust Kennedy & Donkin Ltd 1994–; pres Inst of Electrical Engrs 1983–84; memb: Ct UWIST 1984–88, Overseas Projects Bd 1987–90; dir Nat Inspection Cncl for Electrical Installation Contractors (NICEIC) 1988–91; Freeman City of London 1987, CEng 1966, FIEE 1969, MConsE 1973, FEng 1979, FIEEE 1985; *Books* Practical Diakoptics for Electrical Networks (jtly, 1969), Power Circuit Breakers Theory & Design (jtly, 1 edn 1975, 2 edn 1982); *Recreations* golf, bridge; *Clubs* Bramley Golf (Surrey); *Style—* M N John, Esq, FEng; ✉ Rust Kennedy & Donkin Ltd, Westbrook Mills, Godalming, Surrey GU7 2AZ (☎ 01483 425900, fax 01483 425136, telex 859373 KDHO G)

JOHN, Sir Rupert Godfrey; kt (1971); s of Donelley Westmore John (d 1951); *b* 19 May 1916; *Educ* St Vincent GS, London Univ (BA, DipEd), New York Univ; *m* 1937, Hepsy, da of Samuel Norris; 3 s (and 1 s decd), 1 da; *Career* called to the Bar Gray's Inn; first asst master St Kitts and Nevis GS 1943, asst master St Vincent GS 1944–52, private law practice St Vincent 1952–58, magistrate Grenada WI 1958–60, acting attorney gen Grenada 1960–62, human rights offr UN 1962–70, memb int team of observers Nigeria 1969–70, sr human rights offr 1970, govr St Vincent 1970–76; memb: Barclays Bank Int Ltd Policy Advsy Ctee (St Vincent) 1977–85, West India Ctee, special fellow to UN Inst of Trg and Res 1978–85, founded Assoc of Sr Citizens of St Vincent and The Grenadines, pres Caricare, Caribbean Inst for observance and protection human rights and democratic and humanitarian principles 1987–88; Caricare Human Rights Awards 1988; KStJ 1971; *Recreations* reading, walking, swimming; *Clubs* Royal Commonwealth Soc; *Style—* Sir Rupert John; ✉ PO Box 677, Cane Garden, St Vincent, West Indies (☎ 809 4561500)

JOHN, Stewart Morris; OBE (1992); s of Ivor Morgan John (d 1989), of Shepperton, Middx, and Lilian, *née* Morris (d 1989); *b* 28 Nov 1938; *Educ* Porth Co GS, N Staffs Tech Coll, Southall Tech Coll (HNC); *m* 3 July 1961, Susan Anne, da of William Alfred Cody; 1 s (Philip Andrew b 23 May 1964), 1 da (Sarah Margaret b 10 Nov 1967); *Career* BOAC apprentice aeronautical engr 1955–60, seconded as station engr to Kuwait Airways 1961–65, seconded as chief engr Borneo to Malaysia-Singapore Airlines E Malaysia 1965–67 (gen inspr and project engr Singapore 1963–66), engr Avionics Devpt London Airport 1967–70, asst to Gen Manager Maintenance 1970–71, works supt Mechanical Workshops 1972–73, aircraft maintenance supt 1973–74, maintenance mangr American Aircraft 1975–77, engrg dir Cathay Pacific Airways 1980–93 (dep dir engrg and maintenance Hong Kong 1977–80); dep chm Hong Kong Aircraft Engineering 1987–93 (dir 1982–93), chm Assoc Engineers Ltd Hong Kong 1990–93, ret; dir of quality and memb Cncl Aviation Trg Assoc; memb Cncl RAeS: pres elect, Regnl Affairs Bd; memb: Aerospace Bd Rolls-Royce 1993–, Bd British Aerospace Aviation Services 1993–, Bd Taikoo Aircraft Engineering Co Xiamen 1993–, Bd Airlines of Britain Holdings 1995–, Bd of Tstees Brooklands Museum Tst, Bd Hong Kong Aero Engine Service Limited (HAESL) 1996–; pres Int Fedn of Airworthiness 1993–96; Gold medal Br Assoc of Aviation Conslts 1991; FEng 1990, FHKIE, FRAeS, FRSA, FInstD; *Recreations* golf, classic cars, rugger; *Clubs* The Hong Kong, Shek-o Country, Hong Kong Aviation, Burhill Golf, Bentley Drivers; *Style—* Stewart John, Esq, OBE, FEng; ✉ Strawberry Fields, 12A Fairmile Avenue, Cobham, Surrey KT11 2JB (☎ 01932 868298, fax 01932 867477)

JOHNS, Prof Allan Thomas; s of William George Johns (d 1995), of Exeter, Devon, and Ivy Maud, *née* Camble; *b* 14 April 1942; *Educ* St Luke's Sch Exeter, Univ of Bath (BSc, PhD, DSc); *m* 23 Sept 1972, Marion, da of Charles Franklin (d 1952); 2 da (Louisa Anne b 1979, Victoria Helen b 1981); *Career* asst dist engr SW Electricity Bd 1963–68, reader in power systems Univ of Bath 1976–84 (res fell 1968–69, lectr in electrical engrg 1969–76), head of Electrical Electronic and Information Engineering Dept and dir of Power and Energy Systems Research Centre City Univ 1988–91 (prof of electrical and electronic engineering 1984–88), prof of electrical engineering Univ of Bath 1991– (head Sch of Electronic and Elctrical Engrg 1992–), non-exec dir EEM Consulting Engineers Hong Kong 1994–; chm SERC Electricity Research Co-Funding Ctee 1989–94, memb SERC Electromechanical Engrg Ctee (chm Electrical Power Industs Gp 1991–94); conslt: GEC, NGC, British Technol Group; ed: IEE Power Engineering Series 1984–, IEE Power Engineering Journal 1989–; govr Greendown Secdy Sch Swindon (vice chm); author of over 200 res papers, awarded 4 learned soc premiums (1968, 1982, 1988 and 1995); FIEE 1981, FRSA 1988, CEng; *Recreations* ice skating, bowls, walking, piano, singing (professional concert tenor); *Clubs* Swindon NE Bowling (pres 1990–); *Style—* Prof Allan T Johns; ✉ Head of School of Electronic and Electrical Engineering, University of Bath, Claverton Down, Bath BA2 7AY (☎ 01225 826330, fax 01225 826412, e-mail A.T.Johns@bath.ac.uk)

JOHNS, Prof David John; *b* 29 April 1931; *Educ* St Brendan's Coll Bristol, Univ of Bristol (BSc, MSc), Loughborough Univ of Technol (PhD, DSc); *Career* student apprentice (later tech offr section ldr) Br Aeroplane Co Ltd 1949–57, sr tech offr Sir W G Armstrong Whitworth A/C Ltd 1957–58, lectr Cranfield Coll of Aeronautics 1958–63; Loughborough Univ of Technol 1964–83: reader, prof, head of Dept of Tport Technol, dean of Sch of Engrg, sr pro vice chllr; fndn dir City Poly Hong Kong 1983–89; vice chllr and princ Univ of Bradford 1989–; memb: Aeronautical Res Cncl Dynamics Ctee 1970–80 (later chm), Cncl Inst of Acoustics 1979–83 (later vice pres and pres elect), Environmental Pollution Advsy Ctee Hong Kong 1984–88 (later chm), Vocational Trg Cncl (Hong Kong) 1984–89, Hong Kong Productivity Cncl 1984–89, Cncl Hong Kong Inst of Engrs 1984–89, Cncl Royal Acad of Engrg 1993–96; chm Univs Assoc for Continuing Educn 1990–94; CEng 1968, FRAeS 1969, FHKIE 1984, FAeSI 1986, FEng 1990; *Books* Thermal Stress Analyses (1965); *Recreations* theatre, bridge, music; *Clubs* Athenaeum, Hong Kong, Royal Hong Kong Jockey; *Style—* Prof David Johns, FEng; ✉ Vice Chancellor's Office, University of Bradford, W Yorks BD7 1DP (☎ 01274 383012, fax 01274 383003)

JOHNS, Michael Alan; s of John William Johns, of Sevenoaks, Kent, and Kathleen Eva, *née* Hummerston (d 1982); *b* 20 July 1946; *Educ* Judd Sch Tonbridge, Queens' Coll Cambridge (BA, MA); *Career* Inland Revenue 1967–79, Central Policy Review Staff 1979–80, Inland Revenue 1980–84, seconded Orion Royal Bank 1985, Inland Revenue 1986– (dir Business Ops Div 1993–); *Recreations* skiing, teaching (adults), moral philosophy; *Style—* Michael Johns, Esq; ✉ Board of Inland Revenue, South West Wing, Bush House, Strand, London WC2B 4QN (☎ 0171 438 6171, fax 0171 438 6440)

JOHNS, Michael Charles; s of Arthur Charles Johns, of Crediton, Devon, and Margaret Mary Johns (d 1986); *b* 20 Dec 1947; *Educ* Tiffin Sch, St Edmund Hall Oxford (BA, Cross Country blue 1967 and 1968), Law Soc Finals (New Inn prize); *m* Sept 1970, Lucy Mary; 2 da (Kathryn Helen b 23 Oct 1973, Clare Louise b 16 April 1976); *Career* ptnr: Withers 1974–87 (joined 1970), Ashurst Morris Crisp 1987–; dir: London Forfaiting Company PLC 1984–, Exco plc 1985–, Fairway Group Plc 1996–; tstee Leonard Cheshire Fndn 1992–; *Style—* Michael Johns, Esq; ✉ Ashurst Morris Crisp, Broadwalk House, 5 Appold St, London EC2 (☎ 0171 638 1111, fax 0171 972 7990)

JOHNS, Michael Stephen Mackelcan; s of Jack Elliott Mackelcan Johns (d 1968), of Starveacres, Radlett, Herts, and Janet, *née* Price; *b* 18 Oct 1943; *Educ* Marlborough; *m* 1, 20 Sept 1968 (m dis 1975), Joanna Turner, *née* Gilligan; 2 s (Alexander b 16 Sept 1971, Toby b 1 Sept 1973); m 2, 10 March 1979, Gillian, da of Geoffrey Duckett White, of Perth, Western Aust; 1 da (Sophie b 2 Feb 1984); *Career* slr; managing ptnr Nicholson Graham & Jones 1987– (ptnr 1973–); chm Merchant Retail Group plc (dir 1979–); memb: Law Soc, IOD; *Recreations* golf, cricket, gardening; *Clubs* MCC, Hurlingham, St George's Hill Golf; *Style—* Michael Johns, Esq; ✉ 22 Bowerdean St, London SW6 3TW (☎ 0171 731 7607); Nicholson Graham & Jones, 110 Cannon Street, London EC4N 6AR (☎ 0171 648 9000, fax 0171 648 9001)

JOHNS, Milton; né John Robert Milton; s of Arthur Wallace Milton (d 1956), and Olive Grace, *née* Trobridge (d 1968); *b* 13 May 1938; *Educ* Merrywood GS Bristol, Bristol Old Vic Theatre Sch; *m* 1961, Bella, da of Arthur Buckley Horsfield; 1 s (Simeon Robert b 1969), 1 da (Leah b 1964); *Career* actor; newspaper columnist The Stage 1992–95; Br Actors Equity: memb Cncl 1972–, memb Exec 1972–92, hon treas 1975–92; dir Equity Tst Fund 1988– (vice chm 1995–), chm Acting Accreditation Bd of Nat Cncl for Drama Trg 1991–95, memb exec cncl The Actors' Benevolent Fund 1992–; *Theatre* various repertory incl: Sheffield, Coventry, Leicester and Farnham (also dir); various seasons incl: Bristol Old Vic 1961–62, Chichester Festival Theatre and Royal Exchange Manchester; credits incl: She Stoops to Conquer (debut, Theatre Royal Bristol) 1960, Swiss Cheese in Mother Courage 1961, Czar Alexander II in War and Peace (West End debut, Old Vic and Phoenix) 1962, Peter Shirley in Major Barbara (RSC, Aldwych) 1970, The Woman in Black (Fortune) 1991; *Television* Shop at Sly Corner (debut, BBC) 1960; began by playing various unsavoury characters in detective series; roles since incl: Parker in Pickwick Papers (BBC), William Potter in Death of a Ghost (BBC), Kistiacowski in Oppenheimer (BBC), Rev Horsley in Horseman Riding By (BBC), Griffiths in The Florence Bravo Mystery (BBC), Cassidy in Murphy's Mob (Central), Fred Mitchell in South Riding (Yorkshire), Arnold Haithwaite in The Intruder (Granada), Brendan Scott in Coronation Street (Granada), Adolf Eichmann in War and Remembrance (USA); *Recreations* horse racing, reading, music, cricket (full memb of Assoc of Cricket Umpires); *Clubs* Garrick, Club's Taverners; *Style—* Milton Johns, Esq; ✉ c/o Hilda Physick Agency, 78 Temple Sheen Rd, London SW14 7RR (☎ 0181 876 0073)

JOHNS, Peter Andrew; s of Lt John Francis, DSC, RNVR, of Porthcawl, and Megan, *née* Isaac; *b* 31 Dec 1947; *Educ* Bridgend GS, UCL (BSc); *m* 12 Aug 1985, Rosanne Helen Josephine, da of Capt William John Howard Slayter, RA, of Oxted, Surrey; 3 s (Jack b 1987, Robert b 1989, Harry b 1994), 1 da (Megan b 1996); *Career* non-exec dir Merchant Bank of Central Africa 1985–91, dir NM Rothschild & Sons Ltd 1987–, dir New Court Financial Services Ltd, chm New Court Commercial Finance Ltd; ACIB 1975; *Recreations* golf, skiing, tennis, books; *Clubs* RAC, Mottram Hall; *Style—* Peter Johns, Esq; ✉ Withinlee Brow, Withinlee Road, Mottram St Andrew, Cheshire SK10 4QE (☎ 01625 820062); NM Rothschild & Sons Ltd, Trinity Court, 16 John Dalton Street, Manchester M2 6HY (☎ 0161 827 3800, fax 0161 839 2465)

JOHNS, Prof Richard Bell; s of Charles Walter Johns (d 1962), and Cynthia, *née* Gamble (d 1986); *b* 10 Aug 1929; *Educ* St Paul's, Guy's Hosp London (LDSRCS, PhD); *m* 1954, Pamela Marie, da of Charles Henry Thurgood; 3 da (Susan b 1957, Katharine b 1958, Lucy b 1963), 2 s (Nicholas b 1961, Timothy b 1965); *Career* own NHS dental practice 1956–58; Guy's Hosp: lectr 1969–74, sr lectr 1974–79, reader 1979–81; Univ of Sheffield: prof of restorative dentistry 1981–93 (emeritus prof 1993), dean of dental studies Sch of Clinical Dentistry 1984–88; clinical dir Inst for Dental Implants 1991–; memb GDC 1989–94; memb Advsy Bd Denplan 1988–96, tstee Dental Implant Research Tst 1988–; ed Jl of the Br Endodontic Soc 1973–78; external examiner Univs of Surrey, Tulane, Manchester, London, Dundee, Cork, Bristol, Liverpool, Edinburgh, Leeds, Birmingham and Hong Kong; pres Odontological Section RSM 1994–95; memb: Br Endodontic Soc (past pres), Br Soc for Restorative Dentistry (past pres), Int Assoc of Dental Research, Br Soc for Dental Research, Implant Dental Research Gp, Acad of Osseointegration (USA), Euro Assoc of Osseointegration, BDA; *Books* contrib chapters: The Scientific Foundation of Dentistry (1976), General Dental Practice (1986), Dental Care for the Elderly (1986), A Companion to Dental Studies (1986), The Brånemark Osseointegrated Implant (1989); *Style—* Prof Richard Johns; ✉ Institute for Dental Implants, 43 Penninsular Square, Winchester SO22 4QA (☎ 01962 866956, fax 01962 855129, e-mail rbjohns@legend.co.uk)

JOHNS, Air Chief Marshal Sir Richard Edward; KCB (1994, CB 1991), CBE (1985, OBE 1978), LVO (1972); s of Lt-Col Herbert Edward Johns, RM (d 1977), of Emsworth, Hants, and Marjory Harley, *née* Everett; *b* 28 July 1939; *Educ* Portsmouth GS, RAF Coll Cranwell; *m* 23 Oct 1965, Elizabeth Naomi Anne, da of Air Cdre Frederick John Manning (d 1988), of Eynsham, Oxford; 1 s (Douglas b 1972), 2 da (Victoria b 1970, Harriet b 1974); *Career* RAF, No 64 (F) Sqdn 1960–63, No 1417 (FR) Flt Aden 1965–67, flying instr duties 1968–71 (including tuition of HRH The Prince of Wales 1970–71), Staff Coll 1972, PSO/AOC in C NEAF 1973, No 3 (F) Sqdn as CO 1975–77, MOD Air Staff 1978–81, Station Cdr and Harrier Force Cdr RAF Gutersloh 1982–84, ADC to HM the Queen 1983–84, RCDS 1985, SASO HQ RAF Germany 1986–88, SASO HQ Strike Cmd 1989–91 (incl Dir of Operations for Op Granby at JHQ High Wycombe), AOC No 1 Gp 1991–93, COS/Dep C-in-C HQ Strike Cmd 1993–94, AOC-in-C Strike Cmd 1994, C-in-C Allied Forces Northwestern Europe 1994–; Hon Col 73 Engr Regt (V) 1994–; *Recreations* military history, rugby, cricket, equitation; *Clubs* RAF; *Style—* Air Chief Marshal Sir Richard Johns, KCB, CBE, LVO, RAF; ✉ c/o Lloyds Bank, Cox's & Kings Branch, PO Box 1190, 7 Pall Mall, London SW1Y 5MH

JOHNS, Stratford (*né* Alan Edgar Stratford Johns); s of Sidney Johns (d 1927), and Esther Grove Stratford (d 1965); *b* 22 Sept 1925; *Educ* St Charles Coll PMB Natal, NUC PM BTRG; *m* 21 March 1955, Nanette Sybil, da of Morris Parsons; 3 da (Frith Mary, Peta Anne, Lissa Jane), 1 s (Alan Paul); *Career* actor; *Theatre* incl: Annie (Victoria), Run For Your Wife (Comedy and Criterion), An Italian Straw Hat (Comedy and Shaftesbury), Seasons Greetings (Far and Middle East tour), The Shape of the Table (NT), Scrooge (nat tour), The Good Guys (nat tour), Minder (nat tour); *Television* BBC incl: The Jail Diary of Albie Sachs, 1001 Nights, Dear Brutus, Winston Churchill - The Wilderness Years, Doctor Who, Great Expectations, Blakes Seven, Softly, Softly, Z Cars, Barlow At Large, Second Verdict (series), The Beggar's Opera, A Small Mourning, The Secret Agent, Scarlet and Black; other credits incl: Union Castle (series, Granada), Jemima Shore Investigates (Thames), Little Match Girl (HTV), Brond (Channel 4), Boon (Central), Perfect Scoundrels (TVS), Master of the Game (mini-series), SS (mini-series); *Films* incl: The Naked Edge, The Valiant, The Fiendish Plot of Dr Fu Manchu, Wild Geese II, Car Trouble, Foreign Body, The Tragedy of Salome, The Lair of the White Worm, The Fool, A Demon in my View, Splitting Heirs; *Books* Gumphlumph; *Recreations* walking round supermarkets; *Style—* Stratford Johns, Esq; ✉ c/o Michael Whitehall Ltd, 125 Gloucester Road, London SW7 4TE (☎ 0171 244 8466, fax 0171 244 9060)

JOHNSON, *see:* Campbell-Johnson

JOHNSON, Alan Arthur; s of Stephen Arthur Johnson and Lillian May Johnson; *b* 17 May 1950; *Educ* Sloane GS Chelsea; *m* 1, (m dis), Judith Elizabeth, *née* Cox; 1 s, 2 da; m 2, 1991, Laura Jane, *née* Patient; *Career* postman 1968; UCW: branch official 1976, memb Exec Cncl 1981, nat officer 1987–93, gen sec 1993–95; jt gen sec Communication Workers Union (following merger with Nat Communication Union) 1995–; memb: TUC Gen Cncl 1993–95, Nat Exec Lab Pty 1995–, Postal, Telegraph & Telephone Int World Exec; dir Unity Trust Bank plc; govr Ruskin Coll; Duke of Edinburgh Cwlth Study Conf 1992; *Recreations* music, tennis, reading, football, radio; *Style*— Alan Johnson, Esq; ✉ Communication Workers Union, CWU House, Crescent Lane, Clapham, London SW4 9RN (☎ 0171 622 9977, fax 0171 720 6853)

JOHNSON, Prof Alan Godfrey; s of Dr Douglas Johnson (d 1991), of Pulborough, Sussex, and Dorothy Middleton, *née* James (d 1996); *b* 19 Jan 1938; *Educ* Epsom Coll, Trinity Coll Cambridge (MA, MB MChir); *m* 7 July 1962, Esther Caroline, da of James Millner Vellacott (d 1983); 2 s (Paul b 1964, Andrew b 1966), 1 da (Fyona b 1970); *Career* house physician and surgn UCH 1963–64, sr house offr and surgical registrar Redhill Gen Hosp 1965–67, res fell and lectr Charing Cross Hosp (surgical registrar 1967–68), sr lectr then reader in surgery Univ of London 1971–79, prof of surgery Univ of Sheffield 1979–; Hunterian prof RCS 1973–74; pres Assoc of Surgns of GB and Ireland 1993–94, chm Specialist Advsy Ctee in Gen Surgery 1992–95, vice chm Standing Med Advsy Advsy Ctee to Sec of State for Health; chm Christian Med Fellowship Tst, chm Int Christian Med and Dental Assoc; govr Birkdale Sch; memb: Surgical Res Soc, Br Soc of Gastroenterology, Surgical Travellers; FRCS, hon fell American Surgical Assoc, fell Euro Surgical Assoc; *Books* Aims and Motives in Clinical Medicine (1975), Techniques of Vagotomy (1979), Liver Disease and Gallstones - The Facts (2 edn, 1992), Pathways in Medical Ethics (1990), Current Surgical Practice Nos 6 and 7 (ed, 1993); *Recreations* ornithology, hill walking, music (organ), painting (watercolour); *Style*— Prof Alan G Johnson; ✉ University Surgical Unit, Royal Hallamshire Hospital, Glossop Rd, Sheffield S10 2JF (☎ 0114 282 1290, fax 0114 271 3791)

JOHNSON, Alan Michael Borthwick; s of Dennis Daniel Borthwick Johnson, OBE (d 1976), of Calderstones, Liverpool, and Nora, *née* MacLeod (d 1992); *b* 7 June 1944; *Educ* Liverpool Coll 1951–63, CCC Oxford (MA); *Career* called to the Bar Middle Temple (Harmsworth scholar) 1971, ad eundem Gray's Inn 1973; memb Criminal Bar Assoc; *Clubs* Oxford Society; *Style*— Alan Johnson, Esq; ✉ 1 Farm Place, London W8 7SX; 1 Gray's Inn Square, Gray's Inn, London WC1R 5AA (☎ 0171 405 8946/8, fax 0171 405 1617)

JOHNSON, Air Vice Marshal Alan Taylor; s of Percy Johnson (d 1988), and Janet, *née* Taylor (d 1990); *b* 3 March 1931; *Educ* Mexborough GS, Univ of Sheffield (MB ChB, DipAvMed, FFOM, MFCM, Sir Arthur Hall trophy 1956, Richard Fox-Linton prize 1982); *m* 24 Aug 1954, Margaret Ellen, da of Albert Mee (d 1983); 3 s (Simon Rusell b and d 1957, Adrian Robert Alexander b 1959, Matthew William Edward b 1964), 3 da (Deborah Anne b 1955, Bridget Louise b 1958, Lisa Charlotte b 1962); *Career* RAF: cmmnd 1957, MO RAF Gaydon 1957–59, Princess Mary's RAF Hosp Akrotiri Cyprus 1959–61, No 1 Parachute Trg Sch RAF Abingdon 1961–65, RAF Changi Singapore 1965–67, RAF Inst of Aviation Med 1967–71, RAF Bruggen Germany 1971–74, Med S O (Air) HQ RAF Support Cmd 1974–77, RAF Brize Norton 1977–78, chief aerospace med HQ SAC Offutt AFB USA 1978–91, dep dir health and res (aviation med) 1981–84, OC Princess Alexandra Hosp RAF Wroughton 1984–86, asst surgn gen (environmental med and res) MOD 1986, PMO HQ RAF Germany 1986–88, PMO HQ Strike Cmd 1988–91, ret; dir of occupational health Met Police Serv 1991–95; QHS 1986–91; hon med advsr Br Parachute Assoc 1967–71, chm Safety and Trg Ctee BPA 1968–71, head Br Delgn World Parachuting Championships 1970, 1972 and 1974, hon memb Assoc of Mil Surgns (USA) 1980; pres Adastrian Cricket Club 1986–91, vice pres RAF Cricket Assoc 1990–91; OStJ 1976, FRAeS 1983; *Recreations* music, cricket, sport parachuting; *Clubs* Royal Air Force; *Style*— Air Vice-Marshal Alan Johnson; ✉ c/o Lloyds Bank, 99 High St, Huntingdon, Cambs PE18 6DU

JOHNSON, Dr (James) Barry; s of James Johnson, of Myerscough, Lancs, and Dorothea, *née* Tomlinson; *b* 2 June 1945; *Educ* Greaves Secdy Mod, Kirkham GS, Univ of Liverpool (BVSc); *m* 25 July 1976, Carolyn Ann, da of Tony Battersby; 6 s (John Robert James b 11 May 1974, David Barry b 4 Sept 1977, Michael Thomas b 11 Feb 1979, Andrew Peter b 30 July 1980, Paul Robert b 8 Dec 1981, Steven Tony b 16 July 1986); *Career* in vet practice: Kirkham Lancs 1969–71, Gloucester 1971–73, Myerscough then Goosnargh Lancs 1974– (currently sr ptnr); lectr Myerscough Coll 1974–; pres: Lancs Vet Assoc 1983, Royal Coll of Veterinary Surgns 1993–94 (memb Cncl 1985–), Farmers' Club; memb Cncl Animal Health Tst 1994; Freeman: City of Lancaster, City of London 1994; Hon DVSc Univ of Liverpool 1994; memb BVA, MRCVS; *Recreations* children's support at sports; *Clubs* Rotary; *Style*— Dr Barry Johnson; ✉ Brook House, Bilsborrow, nr Preston, Lancs PR3 0RD (☎ 01995 640254); J B Johnson and Partners, Oakhill Veterinary Centre, Langley Lane, Goosnargh, nr Preston, Lancs PR2 2JQ (☎ 01772 861300)

JOHNSON, Prof Barry Edward; s of Edward Johnson (d 1964), of Burgess Hill, Sussex, and Evelyn May, *née* Bailey (d 1980); *b* 1 Aug 1937; *Educ* Epsom Co GS, Hobart State HS, Univ of Tasmania (BSc), Univ of Cambridge (PhD); *m* 1 Nov 1961 (m dis 1979) Jennifer Pat; 2 s (Martin b 1963, Adrian b 1966), 1 da (Susan b 1964); m 2, 15 June 1991, Margaret Blyth; *Career* instr Univ of California Berkeley 1961–62, lectr Univ of Exeter 1963–65; Univ of Newcastle-upon-Tyne: lectr 1965–68, reader 1968–69, prof of pure mathematics 1969–, dean Faculty of Sci 1986–89; visiting prof: Univ of Yale New Haven USA 1970–71 (visiting lectr 1962–63), Univ of California LA 1990–91; auditor Higher Educn Quality Cncl Div Quality Audit 1993–; pres London Mathematical Soc 1980–82 (memb Cncl 1975–78), govr Royal GS Newcastle 1987–; FRS 1978; *Books* Cohomology in Banach Algebras (1970); *Recreations* reading, travel; *Style*— Prof Barry Johnson, FRS; ✉ 63 Montagu Court, Gosforth, Newcastle upon Tyne NE3 4JL (☎ 0191 213 1013); Department of Mathematics and Statistics, The University, Newcastle upon Tyne NE1 7RU (☎ 0191 222 7314, fax 0191 261 1182)

JOHNSON, Prof Brian Frederick Gilbert; *b* 11 Sept 1938; *Educ* Univ of Nottingham (BSc, PhD), Univ of Cambridge (MA); *m*; 2 c; *Career* post-doctoral fell: MIT 1963–64, Univ of Manchester 1964–65; lectr in chemistry Univ of Manchester 1965–67, lectr UCL 1967–70, reader in inorganic chemistry Univ of Cambridge 1978–90 (lectr 1970–78); Fitzwilliam Coll Cambridge: fell 1970–90, steward 1972–77, asst dir of studies in chemistry 1975–90, fndn lectr 1984, dean 1987–90, pres 1989–90, acting master 1989–90; head Dept of Chemistry and Crum Brown chair of inorganic chemistry Univ of Edinburgh 1991–95, prof Dept of Chemistry and head of Inorganic Sector Univ of Cambridge 1995–; visiting prof: Simon Fraser Univ BC 1982, Univ of Wisconsin USA 1985, Texas A&M Univ USA 1986; RSC: Corday-Morgan medal and prize 1976, Chemistry and Electrochemistry of Transition Metals award 1982; memb RSC: Dalton Cncl 1984–87 and 1994–, Working Party 2000, Exempting Qualifications Panel; memb: Cncl of Senate Univ of Cambridge, Senate Univ of Edinburgh; FRS 1991, FRSC 1991, FRSE 1992; *Publications* Transition Metal Clusters (1982), author of over 600 papers and review articles; *Style*— Prof Brian Johnson, FRS, FRSE; ✉ University of Cambridge, Department of Chemistry, Lensfield Road, Cambridge CB2 1EW (☎ 01223 336337)

JOHNSON, Brian Joseph; s of Joseph Johnson, of Billinge, nr Wigan, and Margary, *née* Nichson; *b* 12 Oct 1953; *Educ* Grange Park Tech Sch St Helens, Univ of Manchester Sch of Architecture (BA, BArch); *m* 1 Sept 1979, Marie, da of John O'Brien; 1 da (Emma b 19 Sept 1986); *Career* student architect Gearey Blair Weed Dickenson Partners Liverpool 1976–77, architect Weightman and Bullen Partnership Liverpool 1979–81; Holford Associates 1982–: assoc 1984–88, salaried ptnr 1988–92, equity ptnr (i/c educnl sector) 1992–; Civic Tst Award (for Lincoln House Manchester) 1987; memb ARUCK, RIBA; *Recreations* travel, squash, skiing; *Style*— Brian Johnson, Esq; ✉ Beacon Cottage, 17 Beacon Road, Billinge, nr Wigan, Greater Manchester WN5 7HE (☎ 01744 895991); Holford Associates, 6th Floor, Barnet House, 53 Fountain Street, Manchester M2 2AN (☎ 0161 228 3566, fax 0161 228 3569, mobile 01585 240762)

JOHNSON, Brian Michael; s of Frederick William Johnson, of Woking, and Helen Josephine, *née* Whitmarsh; *b* 1 May 1939; *Educ* Finchley GS, Univ of Sheffield (BEng); *m* 1, 24 Aug 1963 (m dis 1973), Jennifer Ann, da of Thomas Kenneth Derham (d 1989), of Earsham Hall, Norfolk; 3 s (Arawn b 1964, Jess b 1971, James b 1973), 2 da (Fiona b 1965, Emily b 1974); m 2, 31 March 1973, Maureen Patricia, *née* Haines (d 1981); m 3, 10 July 1982, Diana Victoria, *née* Armstrong; *Career* trainee engr Balfour Beatty & Co Ltd 1961–64, site agent Costain Civil Engrg 1964–70, contracts mangr Tilbury Gp 1970–73, chm and md Anglo Dutch Dredging Co Ltd 1973–; papers on engrg subjects and contract law; memb Central Dredging Assoc 1980–, assoc memb Hydraulics Res 1985–, chm Fedn of Dredging Contractors 1989–90 (memb 1973–, chm 1981–82), memb Code of Practice Maritime Structures BSI (chm 1989–90); author papers on engrg subjects and contract law; CEng 1967, FICE 1988 (MICE 1967); *Recreations* music, violin (Windsor & Maidenhead Symphony Orch), art-antiques, classic cars, historic rallying, tennis, cycling; *Clubs* Athenaeum; *Style*— Brian Johnson, Esq; ✉ Old Thatch, Tittle Row, Maidenhead, Berks SL6 4PZ (☎ 01628 23963); Anglo-Dutch Dredging Co Ltd, The Old Rectory, Windsor End, Beaconsfield, Bucks HP9 2JW (☎ 01494 675646, fax 01494 678628, car 0831 835743)

JOHNSON, Carlton (Carl); s of Ronald James Johnson (d 1990), and Margaret Ruth, *née* Vincent; *b* 3 Nov 1958; *Educ* Barton Peveril Coll Eastleigh Hampshire, Keble Coll Oxford (BA); *m* 29 Oct 1990, Linda Suzette; 2 s (Michael James b 16 Jan 1991, Christian Charles b 26 March 1993); *Career* account exec Ogilvy & Mather advtg agency 1981–83, account mangr then dir Publicis 1983–85, account dir Gold Greenlees Trott 1985–88 (assoc bd dir 1987, bd dir 1988), chief exec Simons Palmer Clemmow Johnson 1996– (md 1988–95, gp md 1995–96); *Recreations* music, books, cinema, sport; *Style*— Carl Johnson, Esq; ✉ Simons Palmer Clemmow Johnson Ltd, 19–20 Noel Street, London W1V 3PD (☎ 0171 287 4455, fax 0171 734 2658)

JOHNSON, Prof Charles Edward; s of Charles Montague Johnson (d 1980), of Watford, Herts, and Margaret Joyce, *née* Cordy (d 1982); *b* 21 Oct 1928; *Educ* Watford GS, Balliol Coll Oxford (MA, DPhil); *m* 1, 27 July 1957 (m dis 1980), Anne-Grete, da of Dr Arne Gorm Lauritzen, of Seattle, USA; 3 s (Paul b 1960, Ian b 1962, Michael b 1964); m 2, 29 July 1983, Jacqueline Anne, da of Brian Birch, of Southport; 2 s (William b 1987, Benjamin b 1988), 2 da (Lisa b 1984, Zoë b 1992); *Career* Nat Serv RAF 1947–49; DSIR res fell Clarendon Laboratory Oxford 1955–57, Fulbright fell Univ of California Berkeley 1957–59, res assoc Argonne Nat Laboratory Univ of Chicago 1962–63, princ scientific offr AERE Harwell 1963–70 (sr res fell 1959–62), Royal Soc/NSERC visiting prof Univ of Toronto 1986–87, Lyon Jones prof of physics Univ of Liverpool 1987– (prof of experimental physics 1970–86, dean Faculty of Sci 1991–94), Erskine lectr Univ of Canterbury NZ 1991; contrib to books and scientific jls; served on Ctees SERC, pres of STEM (Sci and Technol Educn on Merseyside); FInstP; *Books* Mössbauer Spectroscopy and its Applications (1985); *Recreations* walking, reading; *Style*— Prof Charles Johnson; ✉ Oliver Lodge Laboratory, Univ of Liverpool, PO Box 147, Liverpool L69 3BX (☎ 0151 794 3359, fax 0151 794 3441, telex 627095 UNILPL G)

JOHNSON, Christopher Louis McIntosh; s of Donald McIntosh Johnson, MP for Carlisle 1955–64 (d 1978); *b* 12 June 1931; *Educ* Winchester, Magdalen Coll Oxford; *m* 1958, Hon Anne, da of Baron Robbins, CH, CB (Life Peer, d 1984); 1 s, 3 da; *Career* Capt RAEC; Financial Times: foreign ed 1965–67, managing ed 1967–70, dir Business Enterprises Div 1971–72 dir 1972–76; econ advsr Lloyds Bank 1976–91, visiting prof of economics Univ of Surrey 1986–89, UK advsr Assoc for the Monetary Union of Europe 1991–, chm British section Franco-British Cncl 1993–; Chevalier de la Légion d'Honneur (1996); *Books* Anatomy of UK Finance, North Sea Energy Wealth, Measuring the Economy, The Economy under Mrs Thatcher 1979–90, In with the Euro, Out with the Pound; *Recreations* music, windsurfing; *Clubs* Royal Soc of Arts; *Style*— Christopher Johnson Esq; ✉ 39 Wood Lane, London N6 (☎ 0181 340 4970)

JOHNSON, Colin Trevor; s of Richard Johnson (d 1986), of Eccles, Manchester, and Annie Evelyn, *née* Breakwell; *b* 11 April 1942; *Educ* Worsley Tech Coll, Salford Sch of Art, Manchester Coll of Art; *Career* artist; artist-in-residence: Manchester Festival 1980, City of London Festival 1984, Wigan Int Jazz Festival 1986 and 1987, Int Nuclear Physics Conf 1986; dir: Swinton & Pendlebury Festival 1973, Bolton Festival 1979, Teignmouth Festival 1996; assoc memb Penwith Soc of Arts, hon friend Manchester Camerata Orchestra; memb Manchester Acad of Fine Arts, memb Exeter and Dist Writers' Club, fndr memb NAG of Teignmouth (new arts gp); *Exhibitions* solo incl: Monks Hall Museum and Art Gallery Eccles 1961, 1963, 1969, 1972 and 1978, Portico Library and Gallery Manchester 1988 and 1995, NW Arts Centre Manchester 1974, Victoria Gallery Harrogate 1975 and 1977, Granada TV 1968, 1969, 1973 and 1976, RNCM 1974, 1978 and 1987, Theatre Royal York 1976, Derby City Art Gallery 1980, Salt House Gallery St Ives Cornwall 1981 and 1984, Liberty's London 1983, Barbican 1984, Guildhall Art Gallery London 1985, Harrogate Gallery 1986, Brewhouse Art Centre Tauton 1987, Falmouth Art Gallery 1987 and 1990, Buxton Art Gallery 1988, Blackburn Art Gallery 1988 and 1995, Bridgewater Art Centre 1989, Swinton Art Gallery 1969, 1972 and 1989, St Giles Cripplegate London 1990, Maclaurin Art Gallery Ayr 1990, Univ of Salford 1990, Bristol Guild 1992, Bury Art Gallery 1992, Winchester Cathedral 1992, Guildhall Gallery Winchester 1993, Tiverton Museum 1993 and 1994, Foyles Bookshop London 1993, 2 year nat tour commencing St Ives May 1995, Torre Abbey Torquay 1995; mixed incl: Park Sq Gallery Leeds 1972–74, Manchester Acad and Manchester City Art Gallery 1976 and 1982–95, Royal Acad Business Galleries 1983–85; *Work in Public Collections* incl: BBC TV, Derby City Art Gallery, Lancs Libraries, Univ of Manchester, Univ of Salford, City of London, City of Manchester; *Commissions* Granada TV 1968, BBC NW 1975, Royal Exchange Theatre Manchester 1978; *Recreations* travelling, jazz, collecting books, tiles, jugs; *Style*— Colin Johnson, Esq; ✉ 43 Higher Brimley, Teignmouth, Devon TQ14 8JU (☎ 01626 776395)

JOHNSON, Colpoys Guy (Matt); s and h of Sir Peter Johnson, 7 Bt; *b* 13 Nov 1965; *Educ* Winchester, King's Coll London (BA); *m* 1990, Marie-Louise, da of John Holroyd, of Guildford, Surrey; 2 s (Colpoys William b 28 Dec 1993, Rufus George b 27 May 1996); *Career* HSBC plc; FRGS; *Recreations* yachting, fly-fishing; *Clubs* Royal Ocean Racing, Royal Lymington Yacht; *Style*— Colpoys Johnson, Esq; ✉ 21 Elthiron Road, London SW6 4BN (☎ 0171 731 7202)

JOHNSON, Daniel Benedict; s of Paul Bede Johnson, of London, and Marigold E G Hunt, MBE; *b* 26 Aug 1957; *Educ* Langley GS, Magdalen Coll Oxford (BA); *m* 1988, Sarah Cynthia Charlotte, da of J W M Thompson, CBE; 2 s (Tycho b 1990, Leo b 1994), 1 da (Edith b 1992); *Career* research student Peterhouse Cambridge 1978–81, Shakespeare scholar Berlin 1979–80, teaching asst in German history Queen Mary Coll 1982–84, dir of pubns Centre for Policy Studies 1983–84; The Daily Telegraph: leader writer 1986–87, Bonn corr 1987–89, Eastern Europe corr 1989–90; The Times leader writer 1990–91, literary ed 1992, currently editorial dept; *Books* German Neo-Liberals and the Social Market Economy (co-ed, 1989), Death In Venice (Thomas Mann, intro

1991); *Recreations* chess; *Style*— Daniel Johnson, Esq; ✉ The Times, 1 Pennington Street, London E1 9XW (☎ 0171 782 5000)

JOHNSON, David Bryan; s of Bernard Johnson, and Audrey, *née* Warrender; *b* 27 Feb 1957; *Educ* John Hunt Comp Sch Telford, Walker Tech Coll, Univ of Sheffield (BA); *m* Gillian; 1 s (Martyn b 4 Aug 1986); *Career* hosp porter Lodge Moor Hosp Sheffield 1978–79, housing offr Manchester City Cncl 1979–80, NHS Mgmnt Trg Scheme 1980–83 (asst hosp admin Birch Hill Hosp Rochdale), asst then dep hosp admin Manchester Royal Infirmary 1983–85, unit gen mangr Acute and Maternity Servs Pontefract Health Authy 1985–90, chief exec St James's Univ Hosp NHS Tst 1992–95 (dir of ops 1990–92, dep chief exec 1991–92), chief exec St James's and Seacroft University Hosps NHS Tst (following name change) 1995–; MHSM; *Recreations* golf, swimming, running, music, theatre, travel; *Style*— David B Johnson, Esq; ✉ St James's and Seacroft University Hospitals NHS Trust, Beckett Street, Leeds LS9 7TF (☎ 0113 283 6925, fax 0113 283 7037, mobile 0831 585323)

JOHNSON, David Gordon; s of Sidney Burnup Johnson, of Newcastle upon Tyne, and Pearl, *née* Jenkinson; *b* 13 Dec 1951; *Educ* Dame Allan's Boys' Sch Newcastle upon Tyne, Univ of Manchester (BSc); *m* 1 (m dis 1986), Lesley Annis Johnson; 2 s (James Scott b 1981, Mark David b 1983); m 2, 17 May 1988, Judith Ann, da of Gerald Arthur Vernon Leaf, of Leeds; 2 s (Edward Matthew b 1989, William Charles b 1992), 1 da (Jessica Aimée b 1991); *Career* ptnr Duncan C Fraser and Co 1977, dir William M Mercer Ltd 1986–; pres Soc of Pension Conslts 1990–92; Freeman: City of London 1989, Worshipful Co of Actuaries 1989, Guild of Air Pilots and Navigators 1991; FIA 1976; *Recreations* private aviation, motor racing; *Clubs* Reform; *Style*— David G Johnson, Esq; ✉ Summerhill, 2 Aldenham Grove, Radlett, Herts; William M Mercer Ltd, Telford House, 14 Tothill St, London SW1H 9NB (☎ 0171 222 9121, fax 0171 222 6140)

JOHNSON, HE David John; CMG (1995), CVO (1994); s of Herbert John Victor Johnson (d 1994), of Folkestone, Kent, and Mildred Frances, *née* Boyd (d 1991); *b* 2 March 1938; *Educ* Harvey GS Folkestone; *m* 10 May 1976, Kathy Johanna, da of Albert Hicks; 3 da (Philippa Jane and Alison Victoria (twins) b 27 Aug 1981, Verity Rose b 13 April 1983); *Career* Nat Serv RAF 1957–59; HM Dip Serv: entered 1959, FO 1959–62, third sec Moscow 1962–64, second sec Dakar 1965–68, second sec Ulan Bator 1969, second sec UK Mission to the UN Geneva 1969–73, first sec UK Delgn to the Negotiations on Mutual and Balanced Force Reductions Vienna 1973–75, first sec Moscow 1975–78, first sec FCO 1978–82, cnsllr NATO Def Coll Rome 1982, seconded to NATO Int Staff Brussels 1982–85, cnsllr and head of Chancery Islamabad 1985–89, cnsllr FCO 1989–92, dep ldr UK Delgn to CSCE Meeting Helsinki 1992, high cmmr to Guyana and ambass to Surinam 1993–; *Recreations* marquetry, music, reading, walking; *Style*— HE Mr David Johnson, CMG, CVO; ✉ c/o Foreign and Commonwealth Office (Georgetown), King Charles Street, London SW1H 2AH

JOHNSON, David John Crump; s of Stanley Charles Johnson (d 1983), of Stourbridge, West Midlands, and Mary, *née* Blunsom; *b* 10 March 1938; *Educ* King Edward VI GS Stourbridge, Univ of Bristol; *m* 25 Aug 1962, Valerie Margaret, JP, da of Arthur Henry Heathcock, of Wollescote, Stourbridge; 3 da (Katherine Jane b 1966, Victoria Louise b 1968, Kirsty Valerie b 1972); *Career* CA 1962; articled clerk Agar Bates Neal & Co (now Coopers & Lybrand Deloitte) Birmingham 1958–62, Stanley C Johnson & Son Stourbridge 1962–; High Sheriff of W Midlands 1989–90; gen cmmr of Income Tax Div of Dudley; pres: Wollaston Lawn Tennis Club 1977–85, Stourbridge Rotary Club 1978–79; tstee and chm of govrs King Edward VI Coll Stourbridge (also collector to tstees); memb Inst of Taxation; FCA; *Recreations* lawn tennis, walking, literature; *Style*— David Johnson, Esq; ✉ Yew Tree House, Shenstone, Kidderminster, Worcs DY10 4BY (☎ 01562 777464); Stanley C Johnson & Son, 22 Worcester St, Stourbridge, West Midlands DY8 1BH (☎ 01384 395380/372008, fax 01384 440468)

JOHNSON, David Leonard; s of Richard Lewis Johnson, of Las Palmas, Canary Islands, and Olive Mary, *née* Bellamy; *b* 2 Feb 1956; *Educ* Wellington Coll, Univ of Durham; *m* 13 Dec 1986, Susan, da of James Fitzjohn, of Carlton in Lindrick, nr Worksop, Notts; 1 s (Edward James b 1988), 2 da (Caroline Francesca b 1990, Sarah Cordelia b 1996); *Career* admitted slr 1981; Rowe & Maw 1979–87, ptnr D J Freeman 1988– (slr 1987–88), gp head Construction and Property Litigation; memb Law Soc 1981; ACIArb 1987; *Style*— David Johnson, Esq; ✉ D J Freeman, 1 Fetter Lane, London EC4A 1BR

JOHNSON, Dr Donald Arthur Wheatley; s of Arthur Edwin Johnson (d 1982), of London, and Ellen Victoria, *née* Wheatley (d 1983); *b* 18 April 1934; *Educ* Nat Univ of Ireland (MD), Univ of Manchester (MSC, DPM), Univ of London (DPM); *m* 3 Aug 1957, Dr Sheila MacDonald Johnson, da of Dr Hector MacDonald Walker (d 1969), of Manchester and Banff Scotland; 2 s (Ian James b 23 Nov 1960, Angus Howard b 9 June 1964); *Career* Capt RAMC 1960–63; lectr Univ of Manchester 1969–, res fell Oxford; conslt psychiatrist: N Manchester Gen Hosp 1971–74, Univ Hosp of S Manchester 1974–; magistrate in Manchester 1977–88, chm NW Div RCPsych 1986–90 (past sec, convener and exec memb), regnl advsr in psychiatry N W Health Authy 1987–, advsr Dept of Health, chm N W Mental Health Advsy Ctee, clinical dir Dept of Psychiatry Univ Hosp of S Manchester, former chm of N Manchester Med Soc, former sec and pres Psychiatry Section Manchester Med Soc, fndr memb Br Assoc for Psychopharmacology; DRCOG 1963, FRCPsych 1977 (MRCPsych 1972); *Books* New Perspectives in Treatment of Schizophrenia (1985), Causes and Management of Depression in Schizophrenia (1985), Maintenance Treatment of Chronic Schizophrenia (1989), Modern Trends in the Treatment of Schizophrenia (1991); *Recreations* walking, shooting, fishing; *Clubs* Lancashire CCC, Mere Golf and Country; *Style*— Dr Donald Johnson; ✉ Lyndhurst, Warrington Road, Mere, Cheshire WA16 0TE (☎ 01565 830 188); Lavina Cottage, Greenhead, Sidbury, Sidmouth, Devon; Department of Psychiatry, University Hospital of South Manchester, West Didsbury, Manchester M20 8LR (☎ 0161 445 8111)

JOHNSON, Emma Louise; MBE (1996); da of Roger George Johnson, of Petts Wood, Kent, and Mary, *née* Froud; *b* 20 May 1966; *Educ* Newstead Wood Sch, Sevenoaks Sch, Pembroke Coll Cambridge; *Career* clarinettist; debuts: London (Barbican Centre) 1985, Austria (Konzerthaus Vienna) 1985, France (Montpellier Festival with the Polish Chamber Orch) 1986, Africa (tour of Zimbabwe) 1988, USA (Newport Festival) 1989, Tokyo 1990, USSR 1990; tours with: Royal Philharmonic Orch, Bournemouth Sinfonietta, Eng Chamber Orch; concerts with Royal Liverpool Philharmonic, City of London Sinfonia, Halle, New Japan Philharmonic; Netherlands Radio Symphony, Warsaw Sinfonia (with Sir Yehudi Menuhin), LSO, London Mozart Players, Schubert Festival Hohenems (with Arleen Auger); various tv appearances; composed Variations on a Hungarian Folk Tune (for solo clarinet) 1988; *Recordings* for ASV: Mozart Clarinet Concerto with the Eng Chamber Orch under Leppard (1985), Crusell Clarinet Concerto number 2, Weber, Baermann, Rossini with the Eng Chamber Orch with Eco/Groves (1986), Weber Clarinet Concerto number 1, Crusell, Tartini, Debussy with the Eng Chamber Orch under Tortelier (1987), La Clarinette Francaise (1988), Weber Concerto no 2, Crusell Concerto no 3, Spohr Concerto no 1 with Eco/Schwartz, A Clarinet Celebration (1990), Emma Johnson plays Weber (1991), Crusell Concerto no 1, Krommer Concerto, Kozeluh Concerto with RPO under Gunther Herbig (1991), Finzi Concerto and Stanford Concerto with Sir Charles Groves (1992), Encores with Piano and Harp (1992), Michael Berkeley Concerto (1993), Pastoral - British Music for Clarinet and Piano (1994), Encores II (1994), Complete Clarinet Works of Sir Malcolm Arnold (1995); *Awards* winner BBC Young Musician of the Year 1984, Eurovision Young Musician of the Year Bronze award 1984, Wavenden award 1986, USA Young Concert Artists award 1991; *Recreations* learning languages, literature, theatre, writing about music; *Style*— Miss Emma Johnson, MBE; ✉ Lies Askonas Ltd, 6 Henrietta Street, London WC2E 8LA (☎ 0171 379 7700, fax 0171 242 1831)

JOHNSON, Frank Robert; s of Ernest Johnson, pastry cook and confectioner, and Doreen, *née* Skinner; *b* 20 Jan 1943; *Educ* Chartesey Secdy Sch Shoreditch, Shoreditch Secdy Sch; *Career* reporter local and regnl press 1960–69, political staff Sun 1969–72, Parly sketch writer and ldr writer Daily Telegraph 1972–79, columnist Now! Magazine 1979–81; The Times: Parly sketch writer 1981–83, Paris diarist 1984, Bonn corr 1985–86, Parly sketch writer 1986–87, assoc ed 1987; dep ed Sunday Telegraph 1988–95, ed The Spectator 1995–; awards: Parly Sketch Writer of the Year Award Granada What the Papers Say 1977, Columnist of the Year British Press Awards 1981; *Books* Out of Order (1982), Frank Johnson's Election Year (1983); *Recreations* opera, ballet; *Clubs* Beefsteak, Garrick; *Style*— Frank Johnson, Esq; ✉ The Spectator, 56 Doughty Street, London WC1N 2LL (☎ 0171 405 1706, fax 0171 242 0603)

JOHNSON, Sir Garry Dene; KCB (1990), OBE (1978, MBE 1971), MC (1965); *b* 20 Sept 1937; *Educ* Christ's Hosp; *m* 20 Aug 1962, Caroline Sarah, *née* Frearson; 2 s (Charles b 1963, Nicholas b 1969); *Career* cmmnd 1956, cmd 1 Bn Royal Green Jackets 1976–79, cmd 11 Armoured Bde 1981–82, Asst Chief of Def Staff 1985–87, cmd Br Forces Hong Kong and memb Exec Cncl Hong Kong Govt 1987–89, Inspr Gen Doctrine and Trg 1989–91, Gen 1992, C-in-C Allied Forces Northern Europe 1992–94; Col 10 Princess Mary's Own Gurkha Rifles 1985–95, Col Cmdt Light Div 1989–; dir Johnson Walker Associates Ltd 1995–; chm: International Defence Advsy Bd to the Baltic States 1995–, TEC National Cncl 1995–; tstee Gurkha Welfare Tst 1985–, memb Cncl RUSI 1986–92, chm Ogilvy Tst 1991–; FRGS, FRSA; *Books* Brightly Shone the Dawn (1980); *Recreations* travel; *Clubs* Army and Navy; *Style*— Sir Garry Johnson, KCB, OBE, MC; ✉ c/o Holts Bank, Lawrie House, Victoria Road, Farnborough, Hants GU14 7NR

JOHNSON, Geoffrey Edwin; s of Leslie Edwin Johnson (d 1982), of Nottingham, and Rosaline Ada, *née* Allsop (d 1980); *b* 12 Oct 1947; *Educ* County HS Nottingham, Univ of Sheffield (BA); *m* Caron Nicole, *née* Reed; 1 s (Gregory b 1983), 1 da (Valentine b 1989); *Career* Price Waterhouse: joined Nottingham Office 1969, transferred to London Office 1973, Washington DC 1974, ptnr 1979–, London staff and planning ptnr 1982–85, dir London Audit and Business Advsy Servs Practice 1988–90, dir UK Ops 1990–93 (memb UK Exec, European Mgmnt Bd and Worldwide General Cncl), currently managing ptnr Price Waterhouse Europe (memb UK Exec, European Mgmnt Bd and World Bd); FCA 1972; *Recreations* sailing, swimming; *Style*— Geoffrey Johnson, Esq; ✉ Price Waterhouse, Southwark Towers, 32 London Bridge Street, London SE1 9SY (☎ 0171 939 3000, fax 0171 939 3698, car 0831 273505)

JOHNSON, Dr Gordon; s of Robert Johnson (d 1960), of South Shields, Durham, and Bessie, *née* Hewson (d 1956); *b* 13 Sept 1943; *Educ* Richmond Sch Yorkshire, Trinity Coll Cambridge (MA, PhD, Thirlwall Prize, Seeley Medal, Royal Cwlth Soc Walter Frewn Lord Prize); *m* 1973, Faith, da of Wilfred Sargent Lewis, of New Haven, Conn, and North Haven, Maine; 3 s (Timothy Foy b 14 May 1975, Nathaniel James b 10 May 1977, Orlando Benedict b 19 Jan 1980); *Career* Univ of Cambridge: fell Trinity Coll 1966–74, fell Selwyn Coll 1974–93 (tutor 1975–93), univ lectr in history of S Asia 1974–, dir Centre of S Asian Studies 1983– (sr proctor 1977–78), pres Wolfson Coll 1994– (pres elect 1993); memb: Library Syndicate 1978–, Press Syndicate 1981– (chm 1993–), Syndicate of the Govt of the Univ (The Wass Syndicate) 1988–89; chm Faculty of Oriental Studies 1984–87 (sec 1971–76); memb: Gen Bd of the Faculties 1979–82 and 1985–90, Cncl of the Senate 1985–92; tstee: Cambridge Cwlth Tst, Cambridge Overseas Tst, The Nehru Tst for Cambridge Univ, The Hinduja Tst for Cambridge Univ; *Books* Provincial Politics and Indian Nationalism (1973), University Politics: F M Cornford's Cambridge and his advice to the Young Academic Politician (1994), Cultural Atlas of India (1995); The New Cambridge History of India (ed); ed Modern Asian Studies (CUP quarterly) 1971–; *Style*— Dr Gordon Johnson; ✉ The President's Lodge, Wolfson College, Cambridge CB3 9BB (☎ 01223 35900)

JOHNSON, Graham Rhodes; OBE (1994); s of John Edward Donald Johnson (d 1986), and Violet May, *née* Johnson; *b* 10 July 1950; *Educ* Hamilton HS Bulawayo Zimbabwe, Royal Acad of Music London; *Career* concert accompanist; accompanied Elisabeth Schwarzkopf, Victoria de Los Angeles, Peter Shreier, Dame Margaret Price, Dame Janet Baker, Dame Felicity Lott, Ann Murray, Sarah Walker, Anthony Rolfe Johnson, Brigitte Fassbaender, Philip Langridge, Elly Ameling, Thomas Hampson, Christine Schäfer, Matthias Görne; appeared as accompanist at numerous festivals incl: Aldeburgh, Bath, Edinburgh, Feldkirch (Hohenems), Munich and Salzburg; has taught various classes worldwide, prof of accompaniment at Guildhall Sch of Music; fndr The Songmakers' Almanac 1976, writer of BBC series for TV and radio, song advsr to the Wigmore Hall London 1992; recordings incl: a complete Schubert Lieder series for Hyperion beginning 1988, Hyperion French Song Edn beginning 1993, Hyperion Schumann Edn beginning 1996; FRAM 1985, FGSM 1988; *Books* The Unashamed Accompanist by Gerald Moore (contrib, 1984), The Britten Companion (contrib, 1984), Song on Record (contrib, 1986), The Spanish Song Companion (contrib, 1992), The Songmakers Almanac 1976–96 (1996); *Recreations* restaurants and fine wine, book collecting; *Style*— Graham Johnson, Esq, OBE; ✉ 83 Fordwych Rd, London NW2 3TL (☎ 0181 452 5193, fax 0181 452 5081)

JOHNSON, Harold Graham; s of Harold Johnson (d 1979), of Chatteris, Cambs, and Irene Hetherington, *née* Clowes (d 1988); *b* 11 Dec 1933; *Educ* March GS, QMC London (BSc), Imperial Coll London (DIC); *m* 5 Nov 1966, Jennifer Mary, da of Leonard Victor Harold Hazelton (d 1959), of St Albans, Herts; 2 s (Adrian b 1970, Philip b 1972); *Career* Nat Serv Lt RE 1956–58; asst engr Miny of Works Aldermaston 1954–56, engr Balfour Beatty (Tanzania and Nigeria) 1961–63, exec engr Govt of Uganda 1964–66, dir Sir William Halcrow and Ptnrs Ltd 1982–94 (asst engr 1958–61, engr 1966–77, assoc 1977); ptnr: Halcrow Int Partnership 1983–94, The Halcrow Partnership 1988–94; dir Christian Engineers in Development (CED) 1994–; memb Mgmnt Bd ICID; churchwarden St Helen Abingdon; former memb: PCC (Holy Trinity Brompton, St Mary Beaconsfield); former sec UNA Beaconsfield; cuidadano honorario San Pedro Sula Honduras 1975; CEng, FICE, FCIWEM, CDipAF, FRSA; *Recreations* sailing, walking, gardening; *Clubs* Royal Over-Seas League; *Style*— H Graham Johnson, Esq; ✉ Caledon, 23 Picklers Hill, Abingdon, Oxon OX14 2BB, (☎ 01235 520907, fax 01235 520067)

JOHNSON, (William) Holly; s of Eric William Francis Johnson, of Wavertree, Liverpool, and Clarissa Patricia, *née* McGloughlin; *b* 9 Feb 1960; *Educ* Liverpool Collegiate GS; *partner* Wolfgang Kuhle; *Career* multimedia artist, singer, songwriter and author; bass player Big in Japan 1977, solo artist 1978–81, lead singer and major songwriter Frankie Goes To Hollywood 1982–87 (toured USA 1984, world 1985 and Europe 1987), solo singer/songwriter 1987–; various platinum, gold and silver UK discs, other discs from Canada and Europe; awards: Best Contemporary Song Ivor Novello Awards 1984, Best Newcomer and Best Single BPI Awards 1984, Diamond awards 1986 and 1990; memb: Performing Rights Soc, Equity, Screen Actors Guild; *Books* A Bone In My Flute (autobiography, 1994); *Recreations* oil painting, silk screen printing, art collector; *Style*— Holly Johnson, Esq; ✉ c/o Wolfgang Kuhle, Pleasuredome Productions, PO Box 425, London SW6 3TX (fax 0171 736 9212)

JOHNSON, Hugh Eric Allan; s of Maj Guy Francis Johnson, CBE (d 1969), of London, and Grace Enid Marian, *née* Kittel; *b* 10 March 1939; *Educ* Rugby, King's Coll Cambridge (BA, MA); *m* 13 March 1965, Judith Eve, da of Col Antony Gibbons Grinling, MBE, MC (d 1982), of Dyrham, Glos; 1 s (Redmond b 1970), 2 da (Lucy b 1967, Kitty-Alice b 1973); *Career* staff writer Vogue and House & Garden 1960–63, ed Wine & Food (sec Wine & Food Soc 1963–65), travel ed Sunday Times 1967 (wine corr 1962–67), ed Queen 1968–70, pres Sunday Times Wine Club 1973–, editorial dir The Garden 1975–90 (conslt 1990–), gardening corr New York Times 1985–86; chm: Winestar Productions Ltd, The Movie Business, The Hugh Johnson Collection Ltd; dir Société Civile de Château Latour; wine conslt: Jardines Wine Tokyo, Riche Monde Hong Kong and Br Airways; churchwarden St James Great Saling 1974–; *Films* How to Handle A Wine (video 1984), Wine - A Users Guide (with KQED San Francisico, 1986), Vintage - A History of Wine (with WGBH Boston and Channel 4, 1989), Return Voyage (for Star TV Hong Kong, 1992); *Books* Wine (1966, revised 1974), The World Atlas of Wine (1971, revised 1977, 1985 and 1994), The International Book of Trees (1973, revised 1984 and 1993), The California Wine Book (with Bob Thompson, 1976), Hugh Johnson's Pocket Wine Book (annually 1977–), The Principles of Gardening (1979, revised 1984, republished as Hugh Johnson's Gardening Companion 1996), Understanding Wine (1980), Hugh Johnson's Wine Companion (1983, revised 1987 and 1991), How to Enjoy Wine (1985), The Atlas of German Wines (1986, revised 1995), The Hugh Johnson Cellar Book (1986), The Wine Atlas of France (with Hubrecht Duijker, 1987), The Story of Wine (1989), The Art & Science of Wine (with James Halliday, 1992), Hugh Johnson on Gardening (1993); many articles on gastronomy, gardening and travel incl Tradescant's Diary in The Garden (monthly for 20 years); *Recreations* gardening, travel, pictures; *Clubs* Garrick, Saintsbury; *Style*— Hugh Johnson, Esq; ✉ Saling Hall, Great Saling, Essex CM7 5DT; 73 St James's St, London SW1; Domaine des Boutons, 03190 Hérisson, Allier, France

JOHNSON, Hugh Nicholas Tysilio; s of Basil Tysilio Johnson, and Stella Gwendolen Johnson (d 1987); *b* 7 June 1957; *Educ* Lancing; *m* 21 Dec 1983, Hazel, da of Ian Francis and Ann Digby; 1 s (Frederick Charles Tysilio b 19 March 1989), 1 da (Camilla Henrietta b 18 March 1985); *Career* photographer; advertising and editorial photographer (specialising in still life, location, people, animals and cars) 1980–; clients incl: BP, Sony, BMW, VW, Volvo, IBM, Texaco, Br Govt, Bundesbank, Benson & Hedges, World of Interiors, Vogue, Silk Cut, ICI, Carling Black Label, Coca Cola, Harrods; numerous pictures in various books; recipient: Grand Prize at NY Festival of Arts and Advertising, Gold Award Internationaler Druckschriften Wettbewerb 1993 and 1994, Bronze Award Art Dirs' Club Germany 1994, Gold Award Art Dirs' Club NY 1994; other awards from: AFAEP, Campaign Posters, Campaign Press, D&AD, Creative Circle; work selected for special mention by George Roger (fndr memb of Magnum photographic agency), only living English photographer selected for Photography Now (V & A exhibition celebrating 150 year anniversary of photography); memb: AFAEP, SCCC, CRCC; *Recreations* travelling, art, wildlife, sports; *Style*— Hugh Johnson, Esq; ✉ Hugh Johnson Studio, 1A Chance St, London E1 6JT (☎ 0171 729 1989, fax 0171 729 1504)

JOHNSON, Hugh Stringer; s of Richard Stringer Johnson, CBE, TD (d 1981), of Medbourne Manor, Market Harborough, Leics, and Isabel Alice, *née* Hezlett; *b* 24 May 1939; *Educ* Sherborne, Gonville and Caius Coll Cambridge (MA, LLB); *m* 4 March 1967, Marie-Odile, da of Comte Antoine Tillette De Clermont-Tonnerre, of Versailles; 2 s (Antony b 1967, Charles b 1971), 1 da (Marie-Caroline b 1969); *Career* admitted slr 1966, sr ptnr Biddle & Co 1992–96 (ptnr 1966–96); Freeman City of London 1970, Liveryman Worshipful Co of Ironmongers 1970 (memb Ct 1988); *Style*— Hugh Johnson, Esq; ✉ 5 Lichfield Rd, Kew, Richmond, Surrey TW9 3JR (☎ 0181 948 4518); Hauranne, 1 Allee Adrienne, Bois De La Chaize, Noirmoutier-En-L'Ile, France

JOHNSON, Ian Frederick; s of Alan Frederick Johnson, of Oswestry, Shropshire, and Betty, *née* Edwards; *b* 10 March 1960; *Educ* Oswestry Boys HS, Univ of Reading (LLB); *m* 18 March 1989, The Hon Elizabeth Anne Cynlais, da of Lord and Lady Evans of Claughton, of Claughton, Birkenhead; 1 da (Lucy Eva b 9 Oct 1995); *Career* called to the Bar Gray's Inn 1982; memb Northern Circuit, barr at law 1983–; memb: Chancery Bar Assoc, Northern Chancery Bar Assoc; *Recreations* golf, sports cars, skiing; *Clubs* Prestatyn Golf; *Style*— Ian Johnson, Esq; ✉ 1 Oaklea Road, Irby, Wirral L61 3US (☎ 0151 648 7645); 20 North John St, Liverpool (☎ 0151 236 6757); 5 Stone Buildings, Lincoln's Inn, London (☎ 0171 242 6201)

JOHNSON, Prof Ian Richard; s of William Henry Johnson, of Eltham; *b* 14 July 1948; *Educ* Christ's Hosp Horsham, London Hosp Med Coll (BSc, MB BS), Univ of Nottingham (DM); *m* 1970, Jane, da of Frank Lewis Lockley (d 1984); *Career* sr house offr obstetrics and gynaecology Nottingham 1975–76 (house offr med and surgery 1974–75), lectr in physiology Univ of Nottingham 1977–78, registrar obstetrics and gynaecology Mansfield and Nottingham 1979–80, lectr in obstetrics and gynaecology Univ of Nottingham 1980–83, sr lectr and conslt North Staffs Med Centre Univ of Keele 1983–87, prof of obstetrics and gynaecology Univ of Nottingham 1987– (head of dept 1992–), hon conslt City Hosp Nottingham 1987–; memb Gynaecological Visiting Soc; FRCOG 1988 (MRCOG 1978); *Books* MCQ's for Undergraduates in Obstetrics and Gynaecology (1985, 2 edn 1994); *Recreations* gardening, antiques; *Style*— Prof Ian Johnson; ✉ Department of Obstetrics and Gynaecology, University of Nottingham, Queen's Medical Centre, Nottingham (☎ 0115 962 7666 and 0115 962 7670)

JOHNSON, Air Vice-Marshal James Edgar; CB (1965), CBE (1960), DSO (and two Bars 1943, 1944), DFC (1941, and Bar 1942), DL (Leicestershire); s of Alfred Edward Johnson (d 1953), and Beatrice May Rossell (d 1978); *b* 9 March 1915; *Educ* Loughborough GS, Univ of Nottingham; *m* 14 Nov 1942 (m dis), Pauline Ingate; 2 s (Michael James Barrie b 1944, Christopher b 1946); *Career* Air Offr cmd Middle East 1963–65 (ret 1966); dir: Aircraft Equipment (International) Ltd, Westminster Scaffolding Ltd; Legion of Merit (USA), DFC (USA), Air Medal (USA), Legion d'Honneur (France), Order of Leopold (Belgium), Croix de Guerre (Belgium); *Recreations* fishing and writing; *Clubs* RAF; *Style*— Air Vice-Marshal James Johnson, CB, CBE, DSO, DFC, DL; ✉ The Stables, Hargate Hall, Buxton, Derbyshire SK17 8TA (☎ 01298 871522)

JOHNSON, Prof James Henry; s of James William Johnson (d 1955), of Belfast, and Martha Moore, *née* Linton (d 1983); *b* 19 Nov 1930; *Educ* Belfast Royal Acad, Queen's Univ Belfast (BA), Univ of Wisconsin (MA), Univ of London (PhD); *m* 31 March 1956, Jean, da of Dr John James McKane (d 1969), of Salford; 2 s (David b 1969, Owen b 1971), 2 da (Ruth b 1957, Kathleen b 1958); *Career* Whitbeck fell Univ of Wisconsin 1953–54; UCL: lectr 1954–65, reader 1965–74; Univ of Lancaster: prof of geography 1974–95 (prof emeritus 1995–), head of geography 1974–84 and 1993–94, princ Lonsdale Coll 1982–87, dean of graduate studies 1985–92, princ Charlotte Manson Coll Ambleside 1994–95; pres Inst of Br Geographers 1989; memb Assoc of American Geographers; govr: Lytham Schs Fndn 1995–, HOST 1996–; FRGS; *Books* Urban Geography (1967), Trends in Geography (co-ed, 1969), Housing and The Migration of Labour in England and Wales (jtly, 1974), An Advanced Geography of The British Isles (jtly, 1974), Urbanisation (1980), Suburban Growth (ed, 1974), The Structure of Nineteenth Century Cities (co-ed, 1982), Geography and Regional Planning (ed, 1983), Geography Applied to Practical Problems (ed, 1985), Labour Migration (co-ed, 1990), Population Migration (jtly, 1992), Human Geography of Ireland (1994); *Style*— Prof James H Johnson; ✉ The Coach-House, Wyreside Hall, Dolphinholme, Lancaster LA2 9DH (☎ 01524 791046); Department of Geography, University of Lancaster, Lancaster LA1 4YB (☎ 01524 65201, fax 01524 847099, e-mail j.johnson@Lancaster.ac.uk)

JOHNSON, Sir John Rodney; KCMG (1988, CMG 1980); s of Edwin Done Johnson, OBE (d 1967), of Kendal, Cumbria, and Florence Mary, *née* Clough (d 1980); *b* 6 Sept 1930; *Educ* Manchester GS, Univ of Oxford (BA, MA); *m* 11 Sept 1956, Jean Mary, da of Ernest Lewis (d 1949), of Manor Farm, Eyton; 3 s (Nicholas b 1957, Charles b 1962, Edward b 1967), 1 da (Julia b 1959); *Career* Nat Serv 2 Lt RA 1949–51; HM Overseas Civil Serv 1955–64, dist offr later dist cmmr Kenya; sr admin asst Ctee of Vice Chllrs and Princs of UK Univs 1964–65; HM Diplomatic Serv 1966–90, 1 sec FCO 1966–69, head of Chancery British Embassy Algiers 1969–72, dep high cmmr Barbados 1972–74, political cnsllr Br High Cmmn Nigeria 1975–78, ambass to Chad and head of W African Dept FCO (concurrently) 1978–80, Br high cmmr to Zambia 1980–84, asst under sec of state Africa 1984–86; Br high cmmr to Kenya 1986–90; dir Univ of Oxford Foreign Serv Prog 1990–95, special elect fell Keble Coll Oxford 1990–95, cmmr Countryside Cmmn for Eng 1995–96 (chm 1991–95); pres Friends of the Lake District 1995–, pres Long Distance Walkers Assoc 1995–; vice pres: Royal African Soc 1994–, Youth Hostels Assoc 1995–, Chiltern Soc 1995–; FRGS; *Recreations* walking, mountains, travel in remote places; *Clubs* Travellers', Alpine, Climbers', Mombasa; *Style*— Sir John Johnson, KCMG

JOHNSON, Kathryn Louise (Kathy); da of Robert Henry Edwards, former professional footballer, of Grimston, King's Lynn, and Benita, *née* Langdon; *b* 21 Jan 1967; *Educ* Springwood HS Kings Lynn; *m* 7 July 1990, Peter George Johnson, s of George Henry Johnson; 1 s (Daniel George b 10 March 1995); *Career* int hockey player; memb: Pelicans Ladies Hockey Club 1980–89, Leicester Ladies Hockey Club 1989–; represented Norfolk and East at under 18, under 21 and sr level; England: under 18, under 21, 67 full caps; 36 GB caps 1991–; int honours: fourth place World Cup Sydney 1990, Gold medal Euro Championship 1991 (top scorer with 9 goals), Bronze medal Olympic Games Barcelona 1992, ninth place World Cup Dublin 1994, fourth place Olympic Games Atlanta 1995; computer operator and clerical asst; *Recreations* all sports; *Style*— Mrs Kathy Johnson; ✉ 8 Loke Road, King's Lynn, Norfolk PE30 2AB (☎ 01553 766686)

JOHNSON, Prof Louise Napier; *b* 26 Sept 1940; *Educ* Wimbledon HS GPDST, UCL (BSc), Royal Inst London (PhD); *m* Aug 1968; 1 s, 1 da; *Career* Univ of Oxford: lectr in molecular biophysics 1973–90, reader in molecular biophysics 1990, David Phillips prof of molecular biophysics 1990–, professorial fell Corpus Christi Coll 1990–, hon fell Somerville Coll 1991– (additional fell 1973–90); Kaj Linderström-Lang prize 1989; memb: Euro Molecular Biology Orgn 1991, Biochemical Soc, Biophysics Soc, Br Crystallographic Assoc; FRS 1990; *Books* Protein Crystallography (with T L Blundell, 1971), Glycogen Phosphorylase (with K R Acharya, D I Stuart and K Varvill, 1991); *Recreations* family, horses; *Style*— Prof Louise Johnson, FRS; ✉ Laboratory of Molecular Biophysics, Rex Richards Building, University of Oxford, South Parks Road, Oxford OX1 3QU (☎ 01865 275365, fax 01865 51054, e-mail LOUISE@BIOP.OX.AC.UK)

JOHNSON, Dr Margaret Anne; da of Dr Frederick William Johnson, of Hinton Charterhouse, and Dr Margaret Rosemary Johnson, *née* Burke; *b* 7 Feb 1952; *Educ* Convent of the Sacred Heart Woldingham Surrey, Royal Free Hosp Med Sch Univ of London (MB BS, MRCP, MD); *m* John William Winston Studd; 1 s (Thomas Joseph Benjamin b 16 Oct 1981), 2 da (Sarah Anne Victoria b 7 Dec 1984, Josephine Clare Francesca b 18 Feb 1992); *Career* house physician Royal Free Hosp 1976–77; SHO: postgrad trg scheme Whittington Hosp 1977–78, in thoracic med London Chest Hosp 1978, Nat Hosp for Nervous Diseases 1978–79; registrar rotation in gen med St Mary's Hosp Paddington 1979–81, research registrar Brompton Hosp 1981–83, sr registrar rotation in gen med and thoracic med Royal Free and Brompton Hosps 1983–89, conslt physician in gen med, HIV, AIDS and thoracic med Royal Free Hosp NHS Tst and hon sr lectr in virology Royal Free Hosp Sch of Med 1989–; chm AIDS Planning Gp and dep chm ID/STD/AIDS Speciality Gp Royal Free Hosp; memb: Expert Advsy Gp on AIDS to the Dept of Health, AIDS Action Gp to Dept of Health, All Pty Parly Gp on AIDS, HIV Infection and AIDS Clinical Trials Working Pty MRC, Med Advsy Ctee to the Home Office on HIV/AIDS in Prisons, Med Advsy Ctee London Lighthouse; tstee, dir and memb Mgmnt Ctee Positively Women; FRCP 1993; *Books* HIV Infection in Women (jt ed with F Johnstone, 1993), An Atlas of HIV and AIDS: a Diagnostic Approach (with M C I Lipman and T A Gluck, 1994); numerous related articles in refereed jls; *Recreations* family, theatre, opera, tennis; *Style*— Dr Margaret Johnson; ✉ Director of Aids Services, Royal Free Hosptital, Pond Street, London NW3 2QG (☎ 0171 794 0500, fax 0171 830 2201)

JOHNSON, Martin; s of Basil Johnson, of Shipston-on-Stour, Warwicks (d 1993), and Bridget Natalie, *née* Wilde, of Stratford on Avon; *b* 23 June 1949; *Educ* St Julian's HS Newport, Monmouth Sch; *m* 1985, Teresa Mary, da of Reginald Victor Wright; 1 s (Andrew Joseph b 25 Nov 1984), 1 da (Charlotte Elizabeth b 25 Dec 1986); *Career* sports writer; trainee RG French Ltd advtg agency Liverpool 1967–68, steelworks labourer 1968–69, trainee journalist South Wales Argus Newport 1969–72; Leicester Mercury: sports writer and sub-ed 1973–86, cricket corr 1974–86, rugby corr 1979–86; cricket corr The Independent 1986–95, Daily Telegraph sports feature writer 1995–; highly commended Br Sports Journalism Awards 1993 and 1994; *Books* The Independent Book of 1987 World Cup India and Pakistan (anthology, 1987), David Gower: the Autobiography (co-author, 1992); *Recreations* golf; *Clubs* Cosby Golf (Leics); *Style*— Martin Johnson; ✉ Sports Feature Writer, The Daily Telegraph, 1 Canada Square, Canary Wharf, London E14 5DT (☎ 0171 538 5000)

JOHNSON, Prof Martin Hume; s of Reginald Hugh Ben Johnson, of Cheltenham, and Joyce Florence, *née* Redsell; *b* 19 Dec 1944; *Educ* Cheltenham GS, Christ's Coll Cambridge (scholar, BA, PhD); *Career* Univ of Cambridge: jr res fell Christ's Coll and MRC 1969–73, Elmore res studentship Physiological Lab 1973, sr res fell 1973–74, lectr Dept of Anatomy 1974–84, reader 1984–91, prof of reproductive sciences 1992–, head Dept of Anatomy 1995–; dir: Reproduction Research Information Service Ltd 1986–88, Company of Biologists Ltd 1986–94; co sec Cambridge Fertility Consultants 1989–91; inspr Human Fertilisation and Embryology Authy 1993– (memb 1994–); Harkness fell Johns Hopkins Univ and Univ of Colorado 1971–73, Br Cncl fell Inst for Res in Reproduction Bombay and Indian Inst of Science 1979, Frank R Lillie fell Marine Biological Lab 1982, MRC res fell 1984–87, lectr CIBA Fndn Public Debate 1990, hon sr lectr United Med & Dental Schs of Guy's and St Thomas's Hosps London 1991–, Hammond lectr Soc for the Study of Fertility 1992, visiting fell La Trobe Univ Melbourne 1993, annual public lectr Australasian Soc for Human Biology 1993; Halliburton lectr 1994; memb: Soc for the Study of Fertility, Br Soc for Cell Biology, Euro Soc for Human Reproduction and Embryology, Soc of Scholars Johns Hopkins Univ 1993, Cambridge Philosophical Soc; chm Br Soc for Developmental Biology 1984–89, hon memb Stoke's Soc, hon sec Professional Advsy Gp for Infertility and Genetic Servs 1989–94; King's Fund prize for Innovation in Med Educn 1993; *Publications* Immunobiology of Trophoblast (ed with R G Edwards and C W S Howe, 1975), Physiological Consequences of Immunity to Reproductive Hormones (ed with R G Edwards, 1976), Development in Mammals (ed, Vol 1 1976, Vol 2 1977, Vol 3 1978, Vol 4 1980, Vol 5 1983), Immunobiology of Gametes (ed with M Edidin, 1977), Essential Reproduction (with B J Everitt, 1 edn 1980, 2 edn 1984, 3 edn 1988, 4 edn 1995); author of over 150 papers; *Recreations* opera, dance, walking; *Style*— Prof Martin Johnson; ✉ Department of Anatomy, University of Cambridge, Downing Street, Cambridge CB2 3DY (☎ 01223 333789, fax 01223 333786)

JOHNSON, Michael Francis George; s of Dr Walter James Johnson (d 1979), of Great Witley, Worcester, and Phyllis Lucy, *née* Hayward (d 1979); *b* 26 March 1942; *Educ* Shrewsbury, INSEAD (MBA); *m* 1, 1971 (m dis 1983), Jose Marie Lucie Simone, da of Dr Alfred Viau (d 1968), of Port Au Prince, Haiti; 1 s (Benjamin b 1974), 1 da (Alix b 1976); m 2, 1 Feb 1984, Jane Elisabeth, da of John Merrick, of Stedham, Midhurst, W

Sussex; 2 s (Jeremy b 1982, Oliver b 1985); *Career* CA 1966; md Synkin SA Brussels 1973–78, ptnr The Needham Partnership, chm W Notting Ltd 1988–; dir: Eurovein plc 1989–, ReActions Publishing Group Ltd 1991–; vice chm Octavia Hill Housing Tst 1988–; *Recreations* tennis, cross country running; *Style*— Michael Johnson, Esq; ✉ 9 Needham Rd, London W11 2RP (☎ 0171 229 5423); Top House, Exton, Nr Oakham, Rutland LE15 8AX (☎ 01572 813444)

JOHNSON, Michael Ross; s of Myron Johnson (d 1972), of Delphi, Indiana, USA, and Eileen Rahilly Johnson (d 1975); *b* 23 Nov 1938; *Educ* San Jose State Coll (BA), Columbia Univ NY; *m* 28 May 1966, Jacqueline, da of Joseph Zimbardo; 3 da (Stephanie, Raphaëlle, Delphine); *Career* editorial staff Hayward Daily Review 1960–61; The Associated Press: corr Charleston W Virginia 1962–63, ed NY 1964–66, corr Moscow 1967–71; bureau chief McGraw-Hill World News Paris 1971–76, dir McGraw-Hill World News NY 1976–82, ed in chief International Management 1982–92; editorial dir CEP Publications Paris 1990–92, dir of media servs Burson-Marsteller UK 1992–; memb: American Soc of Magazine Editors, Paris America Club, Overseas Press Club, Foreign Press Assoc; *Books* Business Buzzwords (1989), French Resistance: The Individual vs The Company in French Corporate Life (1996); *Recreations* piano; *Clubs* Wig and Pen; *Style*— Michael Johnson, Esq; ✉ Burson-Marsteller, 24–28 Bloomsbury Way, London WC1A 2PX

JOHNSON, Michael Sloan; s of Maj Harold Bell Johnson, TD, TA (d 1975), and Jean Louise, *née* Sloan; *b* 3 June 1947; *Educ* Upper Canada Coll Toronto, St Andrews Scots Sch Buenos Aires Argentina, Trinity Coll Cambridge (BA, LLB, MA, LLM); *m* 27 July 1972, Judith Mary, da of Arthur Lawton, of Crewe, Cheshire; 1 s (Matthew Richard b 7 Sept 1979), 1 da (Rosalind Mary b 5 Nov 1980); *Career* called to the Bar Lincoln's Inn 1971, in practice Northern Circuit 1972–, Chancery practitioner Manchester 1972–, chm VAT Tbnls 1994–; asst recorder of the Crown Ct 1994–; reader St Mary's Parish Church Hawkshaw Bury Lancs 1992– (churchwarden 1986–91); pres Cambridge Univ Law Soc 1969, memb Ecclesiastical Law Soc 1988–; *Recreations* music, modern languages, wine; *Clubs* Portico Library Manchester, Lancs CCC; *Style*— Michael Johnson, Esq; ✉ 7 Troutbeck Close, Hawkshaw, Bury, Lancs BL8 4LJ (☎ 0120 488 4088); chambers: 9 St John Street, Manchester M3 4DN (☎ 0161 955 9000, fax 0161 955 9001)

JOHNSON, Col Neil Anthony; OBE (Mil 1989), TD (1986), DL (Greater London 1993); s of Anthony Johnson, of Glamorganshire, and Dilys Mabel Vera, *née* Smith; *b* 13 April 1949; *Educ* Canton Sch Cardiff, RMA Sandhurst; *m* 1, 1971 (m dis 1996); 3 da (Sarah b 1973, Amanda b 1975, Victoria b 1977); m 2, 22 Nov 1996, Mrs Elizabeth J Hunter Johnston, *née* Robinson; *Career* exec dir British Leyland Ltd 1977–82, dir Jaguar Cars Ltd 1982–86, CO 4 Bn The Royal Green Jackets 1986–89, dir Rover Group Plc 1989–92, DG Engrg Employers Fedn 1992–94, chief exec offr Royal Automobile Club 1994–; Hon Col 157 Regt RLC (Pembroke Yeomanry); Freeman City of London, memb Ct Worshipful Co of Coach Makers and Coach Harness Makers; FIMI, FRSA, MInstM, CIMgt; *Recreations* shooting, reading, music; *Clubs* Army and Navy, Beefsteak, Cardiff & County, RAC, Royal Green Jackets, Fadeaways; *Style*— Col Neil Johnson, OBE, TD, DL; ✉ c/o Royal Automobile Club, Pall Mall, London SW1Y 5HS

JOHNSON, Nevil; s of Geoffrey Enoch Johnson (d 1962), of Darlington, and Doris, *née* Thompson, MBE; *b* 6 Feb 1929; *Educ* Queen Elizabeth GS Darlington, Univ Coll Oxford (BA, MA); *m* 29 June 1957, Ulla, da of Dr Peter van Aubel, Distinguished Serv Cross of Fed Repub of Germany (d 1964), of Dusseldorf; 2 s (Peter b 4 June 1961, Christopher b 3 Oct 1964); *Career* Nat Serv Army REME 1947–49; admin class Home Civil Serv 1952–62 (princ Ministries of Supply, Housing, Local Govt); lectr in politics Univ of Nottingham 1962–66, sr lectr in politics Univ of Warwick 1966–69; reader in comparative study of insts and professorial fell Nuffield Coll Univ of Oxford 1969–96 (emeritus fell 1996–), hon ed Public Admin Journal of Royal Inst of Public Admin 1967–81, memb Econ and Social Res Cncl 1981–87, pt/t memb Civil Serv Cmmn 1982–85; chm: Bd Faculty of Social Studies Univ of Oxford 1976–78, Study of Parl Gp 1984–87; town cncllr Abingdon 1976–78; memb Political Studies Assoc; *Books* Parliament & Administration: the Estimates Ctee 1945–65 (1966), Government in the Federal Republic of Germany (1973 and 1983), In Search of the Constitution (1977 and 1980), The Limits of Political Science (1989); *Recreations* walking, gardening; *Style*— Nevil Johnson, Esq; ✉ 2 Race Farm Cottages, Race Farm Lane, Kingston Bagpuize, Oxon (☎ 01865 820777)

JOHNSON, Prof Newell Walter; s of Otto James Johnson, of Melbourne, and Lorna Dorothy Gardner, *née* Guy; *b* 5 Aug 1938; *Educ* Univ HS Melbourne, Univ of Melbourne (MDSc), Univ of Bristol (PhD); *m* 1965 (m dis 1984), Pauline Margaret, *née* Trafford; 2 da (Sarah Kathryn b 1967), Nicola Dale b 1970); *Career* sr demonstrator in pathology and prosthetic dentistry Univ of Melbourne 1960–62, lectr in dental surgery UCL 1963–64, res scientist MRC Dental Res Unit Univ of Bristol 1965–67; London Hosp Med Coll: reader in experimental oral pathology 1968–76, prof of oral pathology 1977–83, hon dir MRC Dental Res Unit 1983–93; King's Coll Sch of Med and Dentistry: prof of oral pathology 1994–, dir Res and Univ Postgrad Educn 1994–95; Nuffield res prof of dental sci RCS 1984–; conslt: WHO, Pan American Health Orgn, Fedn Dentaire Internationale, USPHS, numerous health authys, univs and res cncls; hon conslt dental surgn Royal Hospitals Tst and King's Healthcare Tst; memb: RSM (pres Section of Odontology 1989–90), Br Soc of Peridontology (pres 1992–93), Fedn Dentaire Internationale, BDA, Int Assoc for Dental Res, Int Assoc of Oral Pathology, Pathological Soc; fell Royal Australasian Coll of Dental Surgeons; FDSRCS; FRCPath, FRCPA; *Books* Oral Diseases in the Tropics (1991), Risk Markers for Oral Diseases (1991); author of over 150 scientific papers in jls; *Recreations* music, theatre, film, museums and art galleries; *Style*— Prof Newell Johnson; ✉ RCS Dental Sciences / Department of Oral Medicine and Pathology, King's College School of Medicine and Dentistry, Caldecot Road, London SE5 9RW (☎ 0171 346 3608, fax 0171 346 3624)

JOHNSON, Nigel Derrick Marson; s of Grosvenor Marson Johnson (d 1981), and Diana Margery Joan, *née* Webb (d 1972); *b* 8 Dec 1942; *Educ* Oakmount Sch, Epsom Coll; *m* 26 Sept 1970, Dr Wendy Jane Johnson, da of Frank William Higlett; *Career* articled clerk Woolley and Waldron Southampton 1960–65, qualified chartered accountant 1966; ptnr: Woolley & Waldron 1969–76, Whinney Murray & Co 1976–81, Ernst & Whinney 1981–89, Ernst & Young 1989–96; FCA 1977 (ACA 1966); *Recreations* cricket, golf, skiing; *Clubs* MCC, Hampshire Hogs CC, Rioteers CC, Hockley Golf; *Style*— Nigel Johnson, Esq; ✉ Summerhill, Fairfield Rd, Shawford, nr Winchester, Hampshire SO21 2DA (☎ 01962 713115)

JOHNSON, Dr Norman McIntosh; s of Dr Donald McIntosh Johnson (d 1978), of Sutton, Surrey, and Betty Muriel, *née* Plaisted (d 1979); *b* 1 Feb 1948; *Educ* Westminster, Bart's (MB BS, MD, FRCP); *m* 22 July 1972, Penelope Norah, da of Dr Trevor Alan Morris Johns; 2 s (Daniel b 22 Aug 1975, William b 14 Oct 1978), 2 da (Claire b 23 Dec 1973, Alice b 10 Feb 1981); *Career* conslt physician and clinical dir of med: Whittington Hosp, King Edward VII Hosp for Offrs, St Luke's Hosp for the Clergy; hon sr lectr Univ Coll London Med Sch; formerly sr lectr in med and undergrad sub dean Univ Coll and Middx Hosp Med Sch (formerly postgrad sub dean and clinical tutor); *Books* Pocket Consultant in Respiratory Medicine (1989); *Recreations* family and DIY; *Style*— Dr Norman Johnson; ✉ 146 Burbage Road, London SE21 7AG; 81 Harley Street, London W1N 1DE (☎ 0171 224 2016, fax 0171 274 2086)

JOHNSON, Paul Bede; s of William Aloysius Johnson (d 1943), and Anne, *née* Hynes (d 1982); *b* 2 Nov 1928; *Educ* Stonyhurst, Magdalen Coll Oxford; *m* Marigold Edgerton Gigneac, da of Dr Thomas Hunt, of Upper Harley St, London W1 (d 1983); 3 s (Daniel Benedict b 1957, Cosmo James Theodore b 1958, Luke Oliver b 1961), 1 da (Sophie Jane Louise b 1963); *Career* Nat Serv Capt Army 1949–51; asst exec ed Realities Paris 1952–55, ed New Statesman London 1964–70 (asst ed then dep ed 1955–64), memb Bd New Statesman Publishing Co 1964–76; contrib: London Times, Daily Telegraph, Daily Mail, Wall Street Journal, New York Times, Washington Post, and various other newspapers and periodicals; frequently involved in broadcasting and the prodn of TV documentaries, int lectr to academic govt and business audiences; De Witt Wallace Prof of Communications American Inst for Public Policy Res Washington 1980; memb: Royal Commission on the Press 1974–77, Cable Authority 1984–90; winner numerous literary prizes incl: Yorkshire Post Book of the Year award 1975, Francis Boyer award for servs to public policy 1979, Krug award for excellence (literature) 1982; *Books* A History of Christianity (1976), A History of the Modern World (1983), A History of the Jews (1987), Intellectuals (1988), The Birth of the Modern World - World Society 1815–1830 (1992); *Recreations* hill walking, painting; *Clubs* Beefsteak; *Style*— Paul Johnson, Esq; ✉ The Coach House, Over Stowey, nr Bridgewater, Somerset (☎ 01278 732 393); 29 Newton Rd, London W2 5JR (☎ 0171 229 3859, fax 0171 792 1676)

JOHNSON, Paula Joan; da of Maj Grosvenor Marson Johnson (d 1981), and Diana Margery Joan, *née* Webb (d 1972); *b* 12 Sept 1953; *Educ* Atherley C of E Church Sch Southampton, Univ of Exeter (BA); *m* 20 April 1985, Lance Hamilton, s of John Harold Poynter, of Cowes, IOW; 1 s (Jago b 1994); *Career* asst literary ed: Now! Magazine 1979–81, Mail on Sunday 1982–83; literary ed Mail on Sunday 1983–; *Style*— Ms Paula Johnson; ✉ Donnington, nr Newbury, Berks; Billing Place, London; The Mail on Sunday, Northcliffe House, 2 Derry St, London W8 5TS (☎ 0171 938 6000, fax 0171 937 0081)

JOHNSON, Peter Alec Barwell; s of Oscar Ernest Johnson (d 1968), of Rippington Manor, Gt Gransden, Cambridgeshire, and Marjorie, *née* Barwell (d 1991); *b* 26 July 1936; *Educ* Uppingham; *m* 3 July 1965, Gay Marilyn, da of Douglas Bennington Lindsay; 2 da (Juliet b 1966, Annabel b 1970); *Career* fndr: The Br Sporting Art Tst, Ctee of the World of Watercolours and Drawing Fair, East Anglian Ctee of the Historic Houses Assoc; chm and md Arthur Ackermann & Peter Johnson Ltd; memb Cncl Br Antique Dealers' Assoc 1970–80; chm: Cleaner Royal Borough 1989–91, Hans Town Ward Cons 1969–72; Br delegate Conseil Internationale de la Chasse; govr Kimbolton Sch 1993–; guide Chelsea Physic Garden, memb Cncl Iris Fund 1985–, inventor (with John Barwell) of a weed-gathering hoe (Jo-hoe) 1994; *Books* The Nasmyth Family (with E Money, 1977); *Recreations* gardening, riding, reading; *Clubs* Buck's, Hurlingham; *Style*— Peter Johnson, Esq; ✉ 86 Onslow Gardens, London SW7 3BS (☎ 0171 373 7038); Rippington Manor, Great Gransden, Cambridge; Arthur Ackermann & Peter Johnson Ltd, 27 Lowndes Street, London SW1X 9HY (☎ 0171 235 6464, fax 0171 823 1057)

JOHNSON, Peter Charles; s of Dr William Arthur Johnson (d 1993), of London, and Suzanne Renee, *née* Roubitschek; *b* 12 Nov 1950; *Educ* Merchant Taylors' Sch Crosby, Pembroke Coll Cambridge (MA); *m* 27 July 1974, Judith Anne, da of Vincent Larvan, of Southport; 2 s (Matthew b 1980, Elliot b 1982), 2 da (Charlotte b 1987, Sophie (twin) b 1987); *Career* Herbert Smith and Co 1973–75, admitted slr 1975, sr ptnr Alexan Johnson; Freeman City of London, Liveryman Worshipful Co of Distillers 1978; memb Law Soc; *Recreations* sailing; *Clubs* United Oxford and Cambridge Univ, Wig and Pen; *Style*— Peter Johnson, Esq; ✉ Alexan Johnson, 11 Lanark Square, Glengall Bridge, Isle of Dogs, London E14 (☎ 0171 537 7000, fax 0171 538 2442)

JOHNSON, Sir Peter Colpoys Paley; 7 Bt (GB 1755), of New York, in North America; s of Lt-Col Sir John Paley Johnson, 6 Bt, MBE (d 1975); *b* 26 March 1930; *Educ* Wellington, RMC of Science Shrivenham; *m* 1, 1956 (m dis 1972), Clare, da of Dr Nigel Patrick Bruce; 1 s (Colpoys Guy b 1965), 2 da (Marina Grace b 1960, Alison Fiona b 1961); m 2, 1973, Caroline Elisabeth, da of Wing Cdr Sir (Eric) John Hodsoll, CB (d 1971); 1 s (Nicholas Frederick b 1977); *Heir* s, Colpoys Guy Johnson b 13 Nov 1965; *Career* publisher; RA 1949–61 (Capt); dir Nautical Publishing Co Ltd 1971–81, publisher nautical books Macmillan London Ltd 1981–86, author and consultant editor 1986–; Hon Col King's Royal Regt of New York (Canadian); *Books* Ocean Racing and Offshore Yachts (1970 and 1972), Boating Britain (1973), Guinness Book of Yachting Facts and Feats (1975), Guinness Guide to Sailing (1981), This is Fast Cruising (1986), Encyclopedia of Yachting (1989), Yacht Clubs of the World (1994), and 3 reference works; *Recreations* sailing, DIY; *Clubs* Royal Yacht Squadron, Royal Ocean Racing, Royal Lymington Yacht; *Style*— Sir Peter Johnson, Bt; ✉ Dene End, Buckland Dene, Lymington, Hampshire SO41 9DT (☎ 01590 675921, fax 01590 672885)

JOHNSON, Brig Peter Dunbar; s of Dr P Dunbar Johnson (d 1984), and Barbara Leigh, *née* Hutton (d 1994); *Educ* Sherborne, RMA Sandhurst, Staff Coll (psc), Jt Servs Staff Coll (jssc), Royal Coll of Defence (RCDS); *m* 1961, Marthe Marie Eugenie, da of Yves de Simon de Palmas (d 1975), of Loches, France; 3 s (Mark, Stephen, Paul); *Career* cmmnd Royal Sussex Regt 1951, CO 5 Queens 1971–73; dep dir Manning 1981–84; ADC to HM The Queen 1983–84; gen sec Offr Assoc 1984–; *Recreations* golf, skiing, gardening; *Clubs* Army & Navy, Royal St George's (Sandwich); *Style*— Brig P D Johnson; ✉ The Coach House, Mystole, Chartham, Kent CT4 7DB (☎ 01227 738496); Officers Association, 48 Pall Mall, London SW1Y 5JY

JOHNSON, Prof Peter Malcolm; s of Ronald John Johnson (d 1968), and Beryl Mary, *née* Donaldson; *b* 20 April 1950; *Educ* Dulwich, Jesus Coll Oxford (BA, MA, DSc), Univ of London (PhD); *m* 11 Nov 1972, Wendy Susan, da of James Macer Wright, of London; 2 da (Katherine b 1976, Nicole b 1978); *Career* Royal Soc visiting fell Rikshospitalet Univ Hosp Oslo 1975–76, prof Dept of Immunology Univ of Liverpool 1985– (lectr 1977–80, sr lectr 1980–82, reader 1982–85), dep dean Univ of Liverpool Med Sch 1994–, hon conslt scientist Royal Liverpool Univ Tst 1992–; Cancer Tissue Bank Res Centre Univ of Liverpool: dir 1992–95, dep dir 1995–; co-fndr and chm Br Materno-Fetal Immunology Gp 1978–86, cncllr and sec-gen Int Soc of Immunology of Reproduction 1986–95, vice pres American Soc of Immunology of Reproduction 1991–93; chm: Med Advsy Panel Nat Eczema Soc 1992–96, Cancer Res Ctee Univ of Liverpool 1992–96; memb: Cncl NW Cancer Res Fund 1992–, Academic Ctee Univ of Liverpool 1991–; chief ed Jl of Reproductive Immunology 1996–; author of 200 papers and reviews concerning human immunology, notably the immunology of pregnancy; FRCPath 1993; *Recreations* sailing (memb Int GP14 Class Ctee 1996–), squash, football; *Clubs* West Kirby Sailing, Oxford and Cambridge Sailing; *Style*— Prof Peter Johnson; ✉ Department of Immunology, University of Liverpool, PO Box 147, Liverpool L69 3BX (☎ 0151 706 4354, fax 0151 706 5814, e-mail mq22@liv.ac.uk)

JOHNSON, Peter Michael; s of James Victor Johnson (d 1982), and Nancy Evelyn, *née* Taylorson; *b* 3 July 1947; *Educ* Bromley GS, St Edmund Hall Oxford (Open exhibitioner, MA, BPhil); *m* 1972, Janet Esther, da of William Philip Ashman; 2 s (Simon Christopher b 1976, Timothy Paul b 1979), 1 da (Sarah Elizabeth b 1983); *Career* Unilever plc 1970–73; Redland: joined 1973, gp treas 1978–81, dir of planning 1981–84, md Redland Bricks 1984–89, exec dir Redland plc 1988–96; chief exec The Rugby Group plc 1996–; memb Cncl Building Material Producers 1989–, pres Tuiles et Briques Européennes (TBE) 1994–96; *Recreations* tennis, music, cricket; *Style*— Peter Johnson, Esq; ✉ Rugby Group plc, Crown House, Rugby, Warwickshire CV21 2DT (☎ 01788 542666)

JOHNSON, Philip Robert; s of Robert Johnson, of Stockport, and Cicely, *née* Swalwell; *b* 12 Oct 1946; *Educ* Dialstone Sch Stockport; *m* 27 Aug 1969, Janette Anne, da of Arthur Gowling; 2 da (Clare Louise b 6 May 1976, (Nicola) Kate b 23 Sept 1978); *Career* articled clerk Pitt & Co Manchester 1964–69, qualified chartered accountant 1969, firm merged to become Mann Judd & Co 1970; ptnr: Mann Judd 1977, Touche Ross 1979– (following merger, now Deloitte & Touche); ACA 1970; *Recreations* travel, watching all forms of sport; *Style—* Philip R Johnson, Esq; ✉ Deloitte & Touche, Abbey House, 74 Mosley St, Manchester (☎ 0161 228 3456)

JOHNSON, Rex Sutherland; s of Adam Sutherland Johnson (d 1950), and Grace Elizabeth, *née* Bedwell (d 1988); *b* 24 Aug 1928; *Educ* Royal HS Edinburgh, George Heriot's Sch Edinburgh, Northern Poly Sch of Architecture (DipArch); *m* 24 Aug 1957, Betty Elsie, da of Herbert Charles Manning (d 1974), of Witham, Essex; 2 s (Mark Sutherland b 1958, Michael Charles b 1960); *Career* RN 1947–48; sr architect TP Bennett & Son London 1946–61, jr ptnr Oliver Law & Partners London 1961–63, ptnr Ronald Ward & Partners London 1963–89; dir: Ronald Ward International Ltd 1980–89, Tate Hindle Design Ltd 1991–96; ptnr RWP 1989–; memb Cncl London C of C and Indust 1976–90, former chm Platt Cons Soc Kent 1976–79; past pres: United Wards Club of the City of London, Westminster and Pimlico Rotary Club; govr Royal Wanstead Fndn 1984–; Freeman City of London 1969, Master Guild of Freeman City of London 1991–92; Liveryman: Worshipful Co of Carmen, Worshipful Co of Woolmen (Upper Warden); FRIBA 1968, FCIArb 1971, MBAE 1991; *Recreations* golf, photography, architecture, travel; *Clubs* City Livery, Victory Services; *Style—* Rex Johnson, Esq; ✉ Whitepines, Longmill Lane, Crouch, nr Sevenoaks, Kent TN15 8QB (fax 01732 883027); RWP and Tate Hindle Design, Ramillies Buildings, Hills Place, 215 Oxford Street, London W1R 1AG (☎ 0171 287 2412, fax 0171 437 3148)

JOHNSON, Richard Keith; s of Keith Holcombe Johnson (d 1972), of Essex, and Frances Louisa Olive, *née* Tweed (d 1962); *b* 30 July 1927; *Educ* Parkfield Sch, Felsted, RADA; *m* 1, 9 Feb 1957 (m dis 1964), Sheila, da of Herbert Sweet (d 1988), of London; 1 s (Jervis b 1959), 1 da (Sorel b 1961); m 2, 15 March 1965 (m dis 1966), (Marilyn Pauline) Kim Novak, the actress; m 3, 2 July 1982 (m dis 1989) Marie Louise, *née* Norlund, of London; 1 s (Nicholas b 1979), 1 da (Jennifer b 1984); *Career* actor and producer; served RN (supply asst HM Yacht Victoria and Albert) 1945–48; assoc dir RSC 1962; memb Cncl BAFTA 1976–78, fndr United Br Artists 1982; *Theatre* first stage appearance Hamlet (Opera House Manchester) 1944; major roles incl: Marius Tertius in The First Victoria 1950, Pierre in The Madwoman of Chaillot 1951, Demetrius in A Midsummer Night's Dream 1951, George Phillips in After my Fashion 1952, Beauchamp Earl of Warwick in The Lark 1955, Laertes in Hamlet 1955, Jack Absolute in The Rivals 1956, Lord Plynlimmon in Plaintiff in a Pretty Hat 1956; RSC roles 1957–62 incl: Orlando in As You Like It, Mark Antony in Julius Caesar, Leonatus in Cymbeline, Ferdinand in The Tempest, Romeo in Romeo and Juliet, Sir Andrew Aguecheek in Twelfth Night, title role in Pericles, Don John in Much Ado About Nothing; National Theatre roles 1975–78 incl: Charles in Blithe Spirit, Pinchwife in the Country Wife, Pilate in The Passion, title role in The Guardsman; other work incl: Death Trap (UK tour) 1982, Antony in Antony & Cleopatra, King of France in All's Well that End's Well (RSC) 1992–93, Birling in An Inspector Calls (West End) 1994, Sir Anthony Absolute in The Rivals (West End and tour) 1994–95, Freddie Mays in Gangster No1 (Almeida) 1995, Tyrone in Long Day's Journey into Night (Young Vic) 1996, Serebyakov in Uncle Vanya (West End) 1996; as prodr of London plays incl: The Biko Inquest, Sarjeant Musgrave's Dance, Playboy of the Western World, Old Times; *Television* first TV appearance 1949; leading roles incl: Rembrandt, Antony and Cleopatra, Claudius in Hamlet, The Member for Chelsea, Cymbeline, The Camomile Lawn 1991, Anglo-Saxon Attitudes 1991 (Best Actor 1992 Bdcasting Press Guild), Heavy Weather 1995, Breaking the Code 1996; recent US TV films incl: A Man for All Seasons 1988, Voice of the Heart 1988, Crucifer of Blood 1990; *Films* first film appearance in Captain Horatio Hornblower 1950; roles incl: Never So Few 1959, The Haunting 1963, The Pumpkin Eater 1964, Operation Crossbow 1965, Khartoum 1966, Deadlier than the Male 1966, Hennessy 1975, Turtle Diary 1984, Treasure Island 1989; as prodr of films incl: Turtle Diary, Castaway, The Lonely Passion of Judith Hearne; *Books* Hennessy (original story for film 1974); *Recreations* cooking, gardening, music, travel; *Style—* Richard Johnson, Esq; ✉ c/o Jeremy Conway, 18–21 Jermyn Street, London SW1Y 6HP (☎ 0171 287 0077, fax 0171 287 1940)

JOHNSON, Hon Mr Justice; Hon Sir Robert Lionel; kt (1989); s of Edward Harold Johnson (d 1986), and Ellen Lydiate Johnson (d 1989); *b* 9 Feb 1933; *Educ* Watford GS, LSE (LLB); *m* 1957, Linda Mary, da of Charles William Bennie (d 1975), of Durham; 1 s (Robert b 1968), 2 da (Melanie b 1961, Edwina b 1962); *Career* served 5 Royal Iniskilling Dragoon Gds 1955–57 (Capt), ADC to GOC-in-C Northern Cmd 1956–57, Inns of Court Regt 1957–64; called to the Bar Gray's Inn 1957, recorder of the Crown Ct 1977–89, QC 1978, bencher 1986, judge of the High Court of Justice (Family Div) 1989–; jr counsel to Treasury in probate matters 1975–78, legal assessor GNC 1977–82; chm: Bar Fees and Legal Aid Ctee 1984–86, Family Law Bar Assoc 1984–86, Family Law Ctee of Justice 1990–94; memb: Bar Cncl 1981–88 (vice chm 1987, chm 1988), Supreme Ct Procedure Ctee 1982–87, Law Soc Legal Aid Ctee 1981–87, Judicial Studies Bd 1989–94; memb Nat Exec Ctee and tstee Cystic Fibrosis Res Tst 1964–, hon sec Int Cystic Fibrosis (Mucoviscidosis) Assoc 1984–90; *Recreations* gardening, charitable work; *Style—* The Hon Mr Justice Johnson; ✉ Royal Courts of Justice, Strand, London WC2A 2LL

JOHNSON, Robert William Greenwood; s of Robert William Johnson (d 1960), and Susan, *née* Mills (d 1980); *b* 15 March 1942; *Educ* Licensed Victuallers' Sch Ascot Berks, Univ of Durham (MB BS, MS); *m* 30 July 1966, Dr Carolyn Mary Johnson, da of Dr John Edmund Vooght, of Newbury, Berks; 1 s (Julian Robert Greenwood b 20 Aug 1972), 1 da (Melanie Jane b 16 June 1969); *Career* asst prof of surgery Univ of California 1973–74, conslt surgn Manchester Royal Infirmary 1974–, hon conslt surgn Manchester Children's Hosp; hon reader in surgery Univ of Manchester, Hunterian prof RCS 1980; pres Br Transplant Soc, memb Transplant Advsy Panel Dept of Health, chm Clinical Audit Ctee Central Manchester Health Care Tst; former chm Med Exec Ctee Central Manchester Health Authy; Freeman Worshipful Co of Innholders 1965; FRCS 1970, FRCSEd 1994; *Recreations* golf, tennis, skiing; *Style—* Robert Johnson, Esq; ✉ Evergreen, Chapel Lane, Hale Barns, Cheshire WA15 0AJ (☎ 0161 980 8840); Renal Transplant Unit, Royal Infirmary, Manchester M13 9WL (☎ 0161 276 4413, fax 0161 273 3163)

JOHNSON, Roy Arthur; s of Leonard Arthur Johnson (d 1974), of Hove, Sussex, and Cicely Elsie, *née* Turner (d 1995); *b* 3 March 1937; *Educ* Lancing; *m* 31 July 1965, Heather Campbell, da of Alfred John Heald, of Hove, Sussex; 2 s (Mark b 1967, Paul b 1968); *Career* CA 1960; ptnr: Coopers & Lybrand 1966–92, Cork Gully 1981–92; Inst of CAs of Scotland: moderator of Examination Bd 1975–87, memb Cncl 1984–90, convenor of Fin and Gen Purposes Ctee 1986–90; dir Glasgow C of C 1988–; Univ of Strathclyde: memb Ct 1992–, treas 1994–; dir Strathclyde Graduate Business Sch 1992–; govr Glasgow Acad 1996–; chm Prince's Tst Volunteers Strathclyde Region 1991–; gen cmmr of Income Tax 1993–; Deacon of the Incorporation of Cordiners of Glasgow 1976 (memb 1968), Deacon Convener of the Trades House of Glasgow 1990; Freeman City of London 1992; MIPA 1986; *Recreations* golf, photography, gardening; *Clubs* Western (Glasgow); *Style—* Roy Johnson, Esq; ✉ 8 Hillcrest Drive, Newton Mearns, Glasgow G77 5HH (☎ 0141 639 3800, fax 0141 616 0986)

JOHNSON, Dr Roy Harold; s of Arthur Harold Johnson (d 1985), of Wolverhampton, and Ethel Lancaster, *née* Pratt (d 1973); *b* 18 April 1931; *Educ* Wolverhampton GS, Wednesbury Tech Coll, Univ of Sheffield (BMet, PhD, Brunton Medal); *m* 3 July 1954, Anne Jillian, da of Horace Davies (d 1975); 2 s (Philip William Digby b 22 Oct 1958, Simon Charles Alister b 11 June 1961), 1 da (Rachel Diana Caroline b 25 Oct 1963); *Career* student trainee metallurgist Stewarts & Lloyds Ltd Bilston 1949–54, res offr Central Electricity Generating Bd Berkeley Nuclear Labs 1959–67, Fulbright scholar res associateship Stanford Univ Calif 1966–67; Electricity Cncl Res Centre: res offr 1967–70, section leader, electrometallurgy, head of electrometallurgy, res mangr metals and materials div 1970–91, chm Sr Mangrs Gp 1990–91, dir external relations Electricity Association Technology Ltd 1991–93, dir post grad trg partnership between EAT Ltd and UMIST 1992–93, conslt British Nat Ctee for Electroheat 1994–96; FIM 1973 (memb Cncl IOM 1991–94), FEng 1992; *Recreations* caravanning, gardening, photography; *Style—* Dr Roy Johnson, FEng; ✉ 33 Walmoor Park, Chester CH3 5UT (☎ 01244 329380, fax 01244 347454)

JOHNSON, Stanley Patrick; s of Wilfred Johnson, and Irene Johnson; *b* 18 Aug 1940; *Educ* Sherborne, Exeter Coll Oxford (MA); *m* 1, 1963 (m dis 1979), Charlotte Offlow Fawcett; 3 s (Alexander, Leo, Joseph), 1 da (Rachel (Mrs Ivo Dawnay)); m 2, 1981, Mrs Jennifer Kidd; 1 s (Maximilian), 1 da (Julia); *Career* on staff: World Bank 1966–68, Int Planned Parenthood Fedn London 1971–73; conslt to UN Fund of Population Activities 1971–73, head of Prevention of Pollution and Nuisances Div EEC 1973–77, advsr to head of Environment and Consumer Protection Service EEC 1977–79, MEP (EDG) IOW and E Hants 1979–84, environmental advsr to EEC Cmmn Brussels; special advsr Coopers and Lybrand 1991, dir Environmental Resources Management 1992–94; Newdigate prize for Poetry 1962, RSPCA Richard Martin award, Greenpeace prize 1984; *Books* Life Without Birth (1970), The Green Revolution (1972), The Population Problem (1973), The Politics of the Environment (1973), Antarctica - Last Great Wilderness (1984), World Population and the United Nations (1988), The Environmental Policy of the European Communities (2 edn, 1994); *Novels* Gold Drain (1967), Panther Jones for President (1968), God Bless America (1974), The Doomsday Deposit (1980), The Marburg Virus (1982), Tunnel (1984), The Commissioner (1987), Dragon River (1989); *Recreations* writing, travel; *Style—* Stanley Johnson, Esq; ✉ West Nethercote, Winsford, Minehead, Somerset TA24 7HZ

JOHNSON, Stuart Peter; s of Brian Fredrick Nelson Johnson, of Twyford, Berks, and Yvonne Knowles, *née* Walker; *b* 17 May 1957; *Educ* Willink Sch Reading, Westminster Coll (City and Guilds); *m* Penelope Linda, da of Hugh Anthony Valentine; 1 da (Lucy Victoria b March 1988), 1 s (Edward Rory b Feb 1991); *Career* mgmnt trg scheme Savoy Hotel plc 1974–78, asst banqueting mangr Claridges Hotel 1978–80, mangr The Bishops Table Hotel Farnham 1980–82, personnel and purchasing mangr The Connaught Hotel London 1982–86, res mangr Clivedon 1986–90, hotel mangr The Savoy 1990–94, dir/gen mangr Clivedon (AA Five Red Stars, Egon Ronay 92%) 1994–; Freeman City of London; Master Innholder 1995; FHCIMA 1995; *Recreations* riding, golf, squash, skiing; *Style—* Stuart Johnson, Esq; ✉ Cliveden, Taplow, Berkshire SL6 0JF (☎ 01628 668561, fax 01628 661837)

JOHNSON, Timothy Richard (Tim); s of Michael Johnson, and June Margaret, *née* Murgatroyd; *b* 29 Feb 1964; *Educ* Beckfield Sch York, York Coll of Arts & Technol; *m* 20 May 1989, Sarah Elizabeth; 2 da (Lucy Katherine b 20 May 1989, Rebecca June Olga b 29 June 1992); *Career* art dir: Bernstein Loxton Golding & Klein Advertising SA 1982–85, art dir Saatchi & Saatchi London 1985–90; fndr ptnr and creative dir Cowan Kemsley Taylor 1990–; awards incl: Cannes Silver 1990, Irish Advtg Awards Silver 1990, American One Show Silver 1990; *Style—* Tim Johnson, Esq; ✉ Cowan Kemsley Taylor Ltd, 37 Dean Street, London W1V 5AP (☎ 0171 734 9090, fax 0171 734 9097)

JOHNSON, Trish; *b* 17 Jan 1966; *Career* professional golfer; amateur victories: S W Championships 1983, under 23/21 English Championships 1984, English Matchplay Championships 1985, English Strokeplay Championships 1985, English under 23 champion 1985, Curtis Cup 1986; tournament victories since turning professional 1987: McEwans Wirral Classic 1987, Bloor Homes Eastleigh Classic 1987 and 1990, Woolmark Ladies Matchplay 1987, The Hennessy Cup 1990, Ladies Euro Open 1990, Longines Classic 1990, Skol La Manga Classic 1992, Las Vegas Int 1993, Atlanta Women's Championship 1993; European rep Solheim Cup 1990, 1992 and 1994, English rep Sunrise Cup 1992; finished top Order of Merit European tour 1990, 10th US Order of Merit 1993; *Recreations* tennis, badminton, football; *Style—* Ms Trish Johnson; ✉ 113 Shaftsbury Way, Strawberry Hill, Twickenham, Middlesex TW2 5RW

JOHNSON, Prof William; eld s of James Johnson (d 1968), and Elizabeth, *née* Riley (d 1968); *b* 20 April 1922; *Educ* Manchester Central High GS, Manchester Coll of Technol (now UMIST) (BSc Tech), Univ of London (BSc), Univ of Manchester (DSc); *m* 6 April 1946, Heather Marie, da of John B Thornber; 3 s (Philip James b 5 May 1948, Christopher John b 19 July 1951, Jeremy William b 16 June 1954), 2 da (Helen b 23 April 1953, Sarah b 6 Feb 1959); *Career* HM Forces 1943–47: cmmnd REME 1944, served UK, Italy and Austria; admin grade Civil Serv 1948–50; lectr in mechanical engrg: Northampton Poly (now City Univ) 1950–51, Univ of Sheffield 1952–56; sr lectr Univ of Manchester 1956–60, prof and head of Dept of Mechanical Engrg UMIST 1960–75, prof of mechanics Univ of Cambridge 1975–82 (now prof emeritus); visiting prof Industrial Engrg Dept Purdue Univ USA 1983–85, United Technologies Distinguished Prof of Engrg 1988 and 1989, various visiting professorships overseas; fndr and ed IJMechSci 1960–87 and IJImpactEng 1983–87; IMechE: T Bernard Hall Prize 1965 and 1966, James Clayton Fund Prize 1972 and 1977, best paper for Safety 1980 and 1991, James Clayton Prize (for Educn and Res) 1987, Silver medal Inst of Sheet Metal Engrg, Adv Mats Proc Tech Gold Medal 1995; Hon DTech Univ of Bradford 1976; Hon DEng: Univ of Sheffield 1986, UMIST 1995; fell Univ Coll London 1981; foreign fell: Acad of Athens 1982, Russian Acad of Sciences (Urals Branch) 1993; FIMechE 1960, FRS 1982, FEng 1983; *Books* Mechanics of Metal Extrusion (with H Kudo, 1962), Engineering Plasticity (with P B Mellor, 1967 and 1973), Plane Strain Slip Line Fields (with J B Haddow and R Sowerby, 1968), Impact Strength of Materials (1972), Engineering Plasticity: Metal Forming Processes (Vol II, with A G Mamalis, 1976), A Source Book of Plane Strain Fields for Metal Deformation Processes (with R Sowerby and R D Ventner, 1982); *Recreations* scrambling, travel, heavy gardening; *Style—* Prof William Johnson, FRS, FEng; ✉ Ridge Hall, Chapel-en-le-Frith, via Stockport, Cheshire SK12 6UD (☎ 01298 812441)

JOHNSON-FERGUSON, Sir Ian Edward; 4 Bt (UK 1906), of Springkell, Co Dumfries, Kenyon, Newchurch-in- Culcheth, Co Palatine of Lancaster, and Wiston, Co Lanark; s of Sir Neil Edward Johnson-Ferguson, 3 Bt, TD, JP, DL (d 1992), and Sheila Marian, *née* Jervis (d 1985); *b* 1 Feb 1932; *Educ* Ampleforth, Trinity Coll Cambridge (BA), Imperial Coll London (DIC); *m* 9 April 1964, Rosemary Teresa, yr da of Cecil John Whitehead (d 1989), of Edenbridge, Kent; 3 s (Mark Edward, b 14 Aug 1965, Paul Duncan b 20 Aug 1966, Simon Joseph b 23 July 1967); *Heir* s, Mark Edward Johnson-Ferguson b 14 Aug 1965; *Style—* Sir Ian Johnson-Ferguson, Bt; ✉ Copthall Place, Upper Clatford, Andover, Hants SP11 7LR

JOHNSON-GILBERT, Christopher Ian; s of Thomas Ian Johnson-Gilbert, of London, and Gillian June, *née* Pool; *b* 28 Jan 1955; *Educ* Rugby, Worcester Coll Oxford (BA); *m* 25 July 1981, Emma Davina Mary, da of Hon C M Woodhouse, DSO, OBE; 1 s (Hugh b 22 Oct 1991), 3 da (Cordelia b 14 June 1983, Jemima b 24 July 1985, Imogen b 11 Jan 1990); *Career* admitted slr 1980; ptnr Linklaters & Paines 1986–; memb: City of London Slrs' Co, Int Bar Assoc; *Clubs* MCC, RAC, Vincent's (Oxford), Grannies; *Style—* Christopher Johnson-Gilbert, Esq; ✉ 79 Thurleigh Road, London SW12; Linklaters & Paines, Barrington House, 59–67 Gresham St, London EC2V 7JA (☎ 0171 606 7080, fax 0171 606 5113)

JOHNSON-HILL, Nigel; s of Kenelm Clifton Johnson-Hill, JP (d 1977), and Joyce Wynne, *née* Booth (d 1994); *b* 8 Dec 1946; *Educ* Rugby; *m* 23 Oct 1971, Catherine, da of Edward

Sainsbury, TD; 1 s (Sam b 1978), 2 da (Chloe b 1976, Anna b 1981); *Career* bank offr Hongkong & Shanghai Banking Corp 1965–73, stockbroker W I Carr (Overseas) 1973–78, md Hoare Govett 1978–87; stockbroker and chief exec Hoenig & Co Ltd 1988–; MSI (memb Stock Exchange 1979); *Recreations* wine, skiing, tennis; *Clubs* City of London, Oriental, Hong Kong; *Style—* Nigel Johnson-Hill, Esq; ✉ Park Farm, Milland, Liphook, Hampshire, GU30 7JT; Hoenig & Co Ltd, 5 London Wall Buildings, Finsbury Circus, London EC2M 5NT (☎ 0171 588 6622, fax 0171 588 6497)

JOHNSON-LAIRD, Dr Philip Nicholas; s of Frederick Ryberg Johnson-Laird (d 1962), of Middlesbrough, and Dorothy, *née* Blackett (d 1947); *b* 12 Oct 1936; *Educ* Culford Sch, Univ Coll London (BA, PhD); *m* 1 Aug 1959, Maureen Mary Bridget, da of John Henry Sullivan (d 1948); 1 s (Benjamin b 1966), 1 da (Dorothy b 1971); *Career* asst lectr in psychology Univ Coll London 1966–67 (lectr 1967–73), visiting memb The Inst for Advanced Study Princeton New Jersey 1971–72, reader in experimental pyschology Univ of Sussex 1973–78 (prof 1978–82), visiting fell Cognitive Sci Prog Stanford Univ Spring 1980; visiting prof in psychology: Stanford Univ Spring 1985, Princeton Univ Spring 1986 and 1987; asst dir MRC Applied Psychology Unit Cambridge 1983–89 (fell Darwin Coll Cambridge 1986–89), prof of psychology Princeton Univ 1989– (Stuart prof 1994–); memb: Psychology Ctee SSRC 1975–79, Linguistics Panel SSRC 1980–82, Advsy Cncl Int Assoc for Study of Attention and Performance 1984; memb: Linguistics Assoc 1967, Experimental Psychology Soc 1968, Cognitive Sci Soc 1980, Assoc for Computational Linguistics 1981, Br Psychology Soc; Hon DPhil Göteborg Sweden 1983, FBA 1986, FRS 1991; *Books* Thinking and Reasoning (ed jtly, 1968), Pyschology of Reasoning (with P C Wason, 1972), Language and Perception (with G A Miller, 1976), Thinking (ed jtly, 1977), Mental Models (1983), The Computer and the Mind (1988), Deduction (with R M J Byrne, 1991), Human and Machine Thinking (1993); *Style—* Dr Philip Johnson-Laird, FRS, FBA; ✉ Department of Psychology, Princeton University, Princeton, NJ 08544, USA (☎ 00 1 609 258 4432, fax 00 1 609 258 1113)

JOHNSON SMITH, Rt Hon Sir Geoffrey; PC (1996), kt (1982), DL (E Sussex 1986), MP (C) Wealden (majority 20,931); s of J Johnson Smith; *b* 16 April 1924; *Educ* Charterhouse, Lincoln Coll Oxford; *m* Jeanne Pomeroy, MD; 2 s, 1 da; *Career* WWII Capt RA 1942–47, served UK, Belgium and India; BBC TV 1953–54 and 1955–59; memb LCC 1955–58; MP (C): Holborn and St Pancras South 1959–64, East Grinstead 1965–83, Wealden 1983–; PPS BOT and Miny of Pensions 1960–63, opposition whip 1965, vice chm Cons Party 1965–71, Parly under sec of state for defence 1971–72, Parly sec CSD 1972–74; chm: Select Ctee for Membs Interests 1979–96, Cons Defence Ctee 1988–92, jt Treasure Br-American Parly Gp; memb: Exec 1922 Ctee 1979– (vice chm 1988), Mil Ctee N Atlantic Assembly 1981– (chm 1985, leader of Br Delgn to NAA 1987–, vice pres 1990–92, treas 1996–); former memb IBA Gen Advsy Cncl; govr British Film Inst 1981–87; chm: Thames Salmon Tst 1987, Salmon and Trout Research Tst; *Recreations* fishing, visiting country houses and gardens; *Clubs* Travellers'; *Style—* The Rt Hon Sir Geoffrey Johnson Smith, DL, MP; ✉ House of Commons, London SW1A OAA (☎ 0171 219 4158)

JOHNSTON, Hon Lord; Alan Charles Macpherson; s of Hon Lord Dunpark (d 1991), and Katherine Margaret, *née* Mitchell (d 1982); *b* 13 Jan 1942; *Educ* Loretto, Jesus Coll Cambridge (BA), Univ of Edinburgh (LLB); *m* 30 July 1966, Anthea Jean, da of John Blackburn (d 1985); 3 s (Alexander b 1969, Charles b 1971, Nicholas b 1974); *Career* advocate 1967, standing jr counsel Scottish Home and Health Dept 1972–78, QC 1980, dean Faculty of Advocates 1989–94 (treas 1978–89, advocate depute 1979–82); chm: Industl Tbnl 1982–88, Med Appeal Tbnl 1984–89; senator of the Coll of Justice 1994–; *Recreations* fishing, golf, shooting; *Clubs* New (Edinburgh), Univ Pitt Cambridge; *Style—* The Hon Lord Johnston; ✉ 3 Circus Gardens, Edinburgh EH3 6TN (☎ 0131 225 1862); Parkend, Stichill, Roxburghshire; Advocates' Library, Parliament House, Edinburgh (☎ 0131 226 5071)

JOHNSTON, Alastair John Carmichael; OBE (1990); s of Harry Scott Johnston (d 1973), of Tayport, Fife, and Jean Carmichael (d 1966); *b* 16 Sept 1928; *Educ* Harris Academy Dundee, Univ of St Andrews (BSc); *m* 7 Sept 1953, Morag Elizabeth, da of Robert Campbell (d 1956), of Tayport, Fife; 2 s (Malcolm b 1957, Scott b 1963); *Career* North British Rubber Co Edinburgh 1953–59, plant mangr Armstrong Cork Co Gateshead 1960–70, dir Wm Briggs & Sons Ltd Dundee 1970–74; md: Permanite Ltd Essex 1974–77, Trident Equipment Ltd Herts 1977–81; dir Uniroyal Ltd Dumfries 1982–85, md The Gates Rubber Co Ltd Edinburgh and Dumfries 1980–91, chm Duncan Honeyman Ltd Stirling 1992–95, chm Lyndalware Ltd Auchterarder 1993–; memb Scottish Cncl CBI 1983–91, dep chm Dumfries and Galloway Enterprise Co 1990–92; *Recreations* hill walking; *Style—* Alastair Johnston, Esq, OBE; ✉ Roseburn, 15 West Moulin Road, Pitlochry, Perthshire PH16 5EA (☎ 01796 473900)

JOHNSTON, Alexander David; s of Sir Alexander Johnston, GCB, KBE (d Sept 1994), and Betty Joan, CBE, *née* Harris (d Nov 1994); *b* 3 Sept 1951; *Educ* Westminster, Corpus Christi Coll Cambridge (MA); *m* 1980, Jackie Barbara, da of Ernie Stephenson; 2 s (Mark Edward b 29 June 1987, George Frederick b 1 March 1990); *Career* dir Lazard Bros 1973–; *Recreations* music, reading, skiing; *Style—* Alexander Johnston; ✉ Lazard Brothers, 21 Moorfields, London EC2P 2HT (☎ 0171 588 2721)

JOHNSTON, Andrew Ian; s of Maurice Johnston, of Harrogate, and Pauline Mary, *née* Teasdale; *b* 10 Jan 1956; *Educ* Harrogate GS, St Edmund Hall Oxford (Open exhibitioner, MA); *m* 9 April 1988, Sara Lesley, da of late Geoffrey R T Lewis; 1 da (Harriet Louise b 26 Jan 1990); *Career* Government Actuary's Dept: trainee actuary (public sector pensions) 1978–82, actuary (social security income and expenditure forecasting) 1982–91, chief actuary (public serv pensions) 1991–; FIA; *Clubs* National Liberal; *Style—* Andrew Johnston, Esq; ✉ Government Actuary's Department, 22 Kingsway, London WC2B 6LE (☎ 0171 211 2651, fax 0171 211 2630)

JOHNSTON, Barrie Colin; OBE (1994); s of Alfred John Johnston, OBE (d 1964); *b* 7 Aug 1925; *Educ* Epsom Coll; *m* 1952, Cynthia Anne, *née* Clark; 1 s (Alastair John), 1 da (Nicola Mary); *Career* Lt RM Far East; merchant banker (ret); dir: Charterhouse Japhet Ltd 1973–84, T H White Ltd 1981–87, Mountleigh Group plc 1983–89, Mornington Building Society 1988–91; memb: Mgmnt Ctee The Pension Fund Property Unit Trust 1966–89, Mgmnt Ctee Charities Property Unit Trust 1967–88, Cncl Barnardo's 1980–95, Cncl King George's Fund for Sailors 1982– (hon treas 1985–96), Fin Ctee The Spastics Soc (now Scope) 1984–88, Cncl Hearing Aids for the Deaf 1993–; hon treas Royal Marines Assoc 1972–, tstee Charities Aid Fndn 1989– (chm Investment Ctee 1976–96); memb Ct of Assts Worshipful Co of Turners (Master 1990–91); FPMI, FRSA, AIIMR; *Recreations* sport, travel; *Style—* Barrie C Johnston, Esq, OBE; ✉ Yew Cottage, 8 The Green, Ewell, Surrey (☎ 0181 393 2920)

JOHNSTON, David Lawrence; OBE (1997); s of Herbert David Johnston (d 1983), and Hilda Eleanor, *née* Wood, of Chichester, Sussex; *b* 12 April 1936; *Educ* Lancastrian Sch Chichester, King's Coll Univ of Durham (BSc); *m* 7 July 1959, Beatrice Ann, da of John Turnbull Witten (d 1973); 3 da (Fiona b 1959, Pauline b 1960, Kate b 1970); *Career* Lt RN 1959–62, electrical offr HMS Eastbourne 1960–62; MOD: overseeing Wallsend 1962–63, design Bath 1963–66, prodn and project mgmnt Devonport Dockyard 1966–73, dockyard policy Bath 1973–76, design Bath 1976–79, prodn and planning Portsmouth Dockyard 1979–81, mgmnt systems, planning and prodn Devonport Dockyard 1981–84, asst under sec of state and md Devonport Dockyard 1984–87; chm DDL (mgmnt buy out co) 1985–87, dep chm DML 1987, mgmnt conslt 1988, dir gen Nat Inspection Cncl for Electrical Installation Contracting (NICEIC) 1989–, chm and chief exec National Quality Assurance Ltd (NQA) 1993– (dir 1989–), dir National Quality Assurance, USA Inc 1993–; dir: NSCIA Ltd 1989–90, NACOSS Ltd 1996–; HSE: memb Electrical Equipment Certification Mgmnt Bd 1990–, chm BASEEFA Advsy Cncl 1990–; memb Advsy Ctee for Electrical Electronic and Telecommunications Engrg City & Guilds of London Inst 1996–, memb Open Govt Appeals Panel 1996–; FIEE 1980, FIMgt 1982, RCNC; *Recreations* walking, gardening, modernizing houses; *Style—* David Johnston, Esq, OBE; ✉ The Laurels, Hill Road, Haslemere, Surrey GU27 2NH (☎ 01428 658774); 70 Elm Quay Court, Nine Elms Lane, London SW8 5DF (☎ 0171 498 1824); NICEIC, Vintage House, 37 Albert Embankment, London SE1 7UJ (☎ 0171 582 7746, fax 0171 820 0831)

JOHNSTON, Dr Derek Iain; s of John Johnston, and Anna, *née* Howitt; *b* 31 May 1943; *Educ* Collyers Sch, Queens' Coll Cambridge (MA, MD, BChir); *m* 19 April 1969, Heather Christine, da of Donald Stuart; 3 s (Andrew b 1971, Robert b 1976, James b 1979), 1 da (Emily b 1972); *Career* conslt paediatrician and endocrinologist 1976–; FRCP 1982 (MRCP 1970); *Books* Essential Paediatrics (3 edn 1993); *Recreations* sailing; *Style—* Dr Derek Johnston; ✉ Children's Department, University Hospital, Queens Medical Centre, Nottingham NG7 2UH (☎ 0115 924 9924)

JOHNSTON, Frederick Patrick Mair; CBE (1993); s of Frederick Mair Johnston (d 1973), of Falkirk, and Muriel Kathleen, *née* Macbeth (d 1994); the Johnston family have had a major interest in Johnston Press plc and its predecessor since 1767; *b* 15 Sept 1935; *Educ* Lancing, New Coll Oxford (MA); *m* 1961, Elizabeth Ann, da of Robert Thomas Jones, of Montgomery, Wales; 2 s (Michael b 1962, Robert b 1964); *Career* cmmnd Royal Scots Fusiliers, served East Africa 4 Uganda Bn KAR 1955–56; chm: Johnston Press plc (F Johnston & Co Ltd until 1988) 1973–, Dunn & Wilson Group 1976–; dir Scottish Mortgage & Trust plc 1991–; pres: Young Newspapermen's Assoc 1968–69, Forth Valley C of C 1972–73, Scottish Newspaper Proprietors' Assoc 1976–78; memb Press Cncl 1974–88, chm Central Scot Manpower Ctee 1976–83, chm Edinburgh Book Festival 1996–; treas: Soc of Master Printers of Scotland 1981–86, Cwlth Press Union 1987–91; pres Newspaper Soc 1989–90; FRSA 1992; *Recreations* reading, travelling; *Clubs* New (Edinburgh), Caledonian; *Style—* Frederick P M Johnston, Esq, CBE; ✉ Johnston Press plc, 53 Manor Place, Edinburgh EH3 7EG (☎ 0131 225 3361)

JOHNSTON, Geoffrey Edward Forshaw; s of Ronald Douglas Graham Johnston (d 1985), of Fenwick, Ayrshire, and Nancy Forshaw, *née* Price; *b* 20 June 1940; *Educ* Loretto, Univ of St Andrews (LLB); *m* 21 Dec 1964, Elizabeth Anne, da of Maj William C Lockhart, of Irvine; 2 da (Susannah b 12 May 1968, Victoria b 14 Aug 1969); *Career* apprentice CA then qualified asst with Wilson Stirling & Co 1959–65; Arbuckle Smith Group 1965–: mgmnt trainee 1965–67, md Arbuckle Smith & Co 1972, MBO 1984, gp md 1984–; md Petrasco Services Ltd 1984–; dir: Cambria Investments Ltd 1984–, Lomond School Ltd Helensburgh, Central Coll of Commerce Glasgow, Scottish Friendly Assurance Society Ltd, Glasgow Chamber of Commerce 1980– (pres 1994–95); chm Scottish Chambers of Commerce 1996–; memb Scot Valuation Advsy Cncl 1982–; nat chm BIFA (formerly Inst of Freight Forwarders) 1990–91; memb Merchants' House City of Glasgow; Belgian consul for Glasgow, W of Scot and Northern Isles 1988–94; FIFF, FCIT, FILog; *Recreations* sailing, skiing, hillwalking, gardening, golf, DIY; *Clubs* Royal Northern and Clyde Yacht, Scottish Ski, Buchannan Castle Golf; *Style—* Geoffrey Johnston, Esq; ✉ Arbuckle Smith & Co Ltd, Ferry Road, Yorkhill, Glasgow G3 8QU (☎ 0141 337 8000, fax 0141 337 3888)

JOHNSTON, Gilbert; CBE (1992); s of David Kidd Johnston, of Dundee (d 1953), and Agnes Penman, *née* Neish (d 1957); *b* 11 March 1932; *Educ* Harris Acad Dundee; *m* 24 April 1957, Aileen, da of John Brown (d 1955), of Dundee; 2 s (Scott b 1959, Derek b 1962); *Career* Nat Serv 2 Lt Army 1956–58; chartered accountant 1956; worked ICI and Rolls Royce; J C Bamford Excavators Ltd: mangr dealer development 1964, gp planning dir 1972, gp chief exec 1975–92, dep chm 1992–94, ret; CIMgt; *Recreations* swimming, scuba diving, golf, gardening, music, travel and wildlife; *Style—* Gilbert Johnston, Esq, CBE; ✉ The Gables, 26 Church Road, Rolleston on Dove, Burton on Trent, Staffs DE13 9BE (☎ and fax 01283 813254)

JOHNSTON, HE Gordon MacKenzie; OBE (1996); s of William Johnston (d 1979), of Kelso, and Betty Isabel Lamond, *née* MacKenzie; *b* 24 June 1941; *Educ* Robert Gordon's Coll Aberdeen, Dingwall Acad; *m* 16 Aug 1963, Barbara Glenis, da of Alexander Christie; 1 s (Gavin MacKenzie b 18 Jan 1965), 1 da (Melanie Susan b 22 Sept 1966); *Career* HM Dip Serv: joined FCO 1959, registrar Berne 1963–65, pro-consul Tamsui 1966–67, asst desk offr SE Asia Dept FCO 1967–69, desk offr Office Servs and Tport Dept FCO 1969–71, entry clearance offr Islamabad 1971, desk offr Consular Dept FCO 1972, desk offr Personnel Servs Dept 1972–74, commercial attaché Paris 1974–77, second sec Chancery Georgetown 1978–81, press offr News Dept FCO 1981–84, first sec (commercial) Belgrade 1984–88, first sec (economic) Dublin 1989–90, liaison offr Gulf Emergency Unit FCO 1990–91, head Policy and Planning Unit Overseas Estate Dept FCO 1991–92, ambass to Slovenia 1992–; *Recreations* golf, reading; *Style—* HE Mr Gordon Johnston, OBE; ✉ c/o FCO (Ljubljana 16331), King Charles Street, London SW1A 2AH; British Embassy, TRG Republike 3, 61000 Ljubljana, Slovenia (☎ 00 386 61 1257 191, fax 00 386 61 1250 174)

JOHNSTON, Sheriff (Alexander) Graham; WS (1971); s of Hon Lord Kincraig, *qv*, and Margaret Joan, *née* Graham; *b* 16 July 1944; *Educ* Edinburgh Acad, Strathallan Sch, Univ of Edinburgh (LLB), Univ Coll Oxford (BA, Golf blue); *m* 1, 1972 (m dis 1982), Susan Gay Horne; 2 s (Robin Graham b 30 Nov 1973, Paul Mark b 20 Oct 1975); *m* 2, 6 Feb 1982, Dr Angela Astrid Synnove Anderson, da of Mayer Olsen, of Newport-on-Tay; *Career* ptnr Hagart & Burn-Murdoch WS 1972–82; Sheriff: Grampian Highlands & Islands Aberdeen 1982–85, Glasgow & Strathkelvin at Glasgow 1985–; ed Scottish Civil Law Reports 1987–92; hon fell Inst of Professional Investigators 1979; hon pres: Family Law Assoc, Strathclyde Stepfamily Assoc; memb Incorporation of Barbers (Glasgow); *Recreations* photography, information technology, computers, puzzles, bridge, cooking; *Clubs* Vincent's (Oxford); *Style—* Sheriff Graham Johnston, WS; ✉ 3 North Dean Park Ave, Bothwell, Lanarkshire G71 8HH (☎ 01698 852177); Sheriff Court House, 1 Carlton Place, Glasgow (☎ 0141 429 8888)

JOHNSTON, Dr Ian Alistair; CB (1995); s of Donald Dalrymple Johnston (d 1985), and Muriel Joyce Johnston (d 1994); *b* 2 May 1944; *Educ* Royal GS High Wycombe, Univ of Birmingham (BSc, PhD); *m* 1973, Mary Bridget, da of Francis Patrick Lube (d 1985); 1 s (Donald b 1979), 1 da (Claire b 1981); *Career* Dept of Employment: asst princ 1969, princ 1973, asst sec 1978, under sec 1984, private sec to Sir Denis Barnes 1972–74, first sec Br Embassy Brussels 1975–78, Advsy Conciliation Serv 1978–84, dir Planning and Resources MSC 1984–85 (chief exec VET Gp 1985–87), dep dir gen Dept of Employment Trg 1987–92, dir Resources and Strategy Directorate Dept of Employment 1992, dir gen Dept for Educn and Employment Trg 1992–95; dep to Vice Chllr and Princ Sheffield Hallam Univ 1995– (dep chm 1991–94); study gp expert educn and trg strategy DGXXII Euro Cmmn 1995–; hon treas Industrial Soc 1992–; memb Cncl BTEC 1995–; CIMgt, FIPD, FRSA; *Recreations* bird watching, skiing, tennis; *Style—* Dr Ian Johnston, CB; ✉ Sheffield Hallam University, Pond Street, Sheffield S1 1WB (☎ 0114 253 4486, fax 0114 253 2042, e-mail IJohnston@SHU.AC.UK)

JOHNSTON, Prof Ian Alistair; *b* 13 April 1949; *Educ* Univ of Hull (BSc, PhD); *Career* NERC postdoctoral research fell Univ of Bristol 1973–76, lectr in physiology Univ of St Andrews 1976–78, visiting lectr Univ of Calif Irvine USA 1978–81, visiting sr lectr Univ of Nairobi 1981–84; Univ of St Andrews: reader in physiology 1984–85, prof of comparative physiology (personal chair) 1985–, fndr chm Dept of Biological and Preclinical Med 1987–91, head Sch of Biological and Med Scis 1991–92, chm Research Div of Environmental and Evolutionary Biology 1992–; dir Gatty Marine Lab St Andrews 1985–; visiting prof Univ of Nairobi 1993, visiting scientist to various outside orgns, numerous research visits abroad; memb: Animal Biology Section Ctee Soc of Experimental Biology 1985–87, Exec Ctee Heads of Univ Biological Scis 1989–91, Cncl Marine Biological Assoc UK 1991–94 (chm Research Ctee 1993–94), Bd Scottish Assoc of Marine Scis 1991– (memb Cncl 1994–), Antarctic Research Ctee Royal Soc 1993–96; RSE rep Scottish Marine Biological Assoc Bd 1991–, advsr Assoc of Cwlth Univs Scholarship and Fellowship Plan 1991–94, scientific coordinator NERC InterUnivs Marine Lab and Univs of Dundee, St Andrews and Stirling 1992– (past memb various ctees, bds and panels NERC); memb Editorial Bd: Jl of Fish Physiology and Biochemistry, Physiological Zoology, Marine Behaviour and Physiology, Jl of Comparative Physiology; dir The Company of Biologists (publishers of Present Development, Jl of Cell Science, Jl of Experimental Biology and Bioessays); Royal Soc John Murray travelling studentship in oceanography and limnology 1983, Scientific Medal Zoological Soc of London 1984, Silver Medal 8th Plymouth Marine Sci lectr USA 1994; memb Physiological Soc 1982, scientific fell Zoological Soc of London 1985, FRSE 1987; *Books* Essentials of Physiology (jtly, 3 edn 1991), Phenotypic and Evolutionary Adaptation of Animals to Temperature (jt ed); various book chapters, numerous reviews and original refereed papers; *Style*— Prof Ian Johnston, FRSE; ✉ School of Biological and Medical Sciences, University of St Andrews, St Andrews KY16 8LB

JOHNSTON, Ian David; s of Robert Johnston (d 1964), of Melbourne, and Shirley, *née* Potter (d 1970); *b* 18 June 1947; *Educ* Carey GS Melbourne, Univ of Melbourne (BCom); *m* 1977, Georgina, da of Kelvin Paton; 1 s (Charles Nicholas Paton b 24 March 1980); *Career* Unilever plc: mktg cadet rising to gen mangr of mktg Rosella 1977–78, mktg mangr Thomas J Lipton Canada 1978–80, mktg strategist head office Unilever London 1980 then head office Rotterdam 1981; Cadbury Schweppes plc: sales and mktg dir Cadbury Confectionery Australia 1982–89, md Schweppes Australia 1990–91, md Schweppes Cottees Foods 1991–94, md Cadbury Ltd UK 1994–96, md Confectionery Stream Cadbury Schweppes 1996–; AASA; rep Australia in Olympic Games 1960; *Recreations* golf, skiing, horse racing, jogging; *Style*— Ian Johnston, Esq; ✉ Cadbury Schweppes Plc, 25 Berkeley Square, London W1X 6HT (☎ 0171 409 1313, fax 0171 830 5200)

JOHNSTON, Prof Ivan David Alexander; s of David Johnston, and Mary, *née* Clarke; *b* 4 Oct 1929; *Educ* Royal Belfast Acad, Queen's Univ Belfast (MB Bch, MCH); *m* 1, 3 Sept 1959, Elizabeth (d 1987); 2 s (Stephen Robert David b 29 Nov 1961, Philip Ivan b 11 Dec 1962); m 2, 16 Dec 1989, Annette, *née* Elphinstone; *Career* lectr in surgery Queen's Univ 1954–59, res asst Mayo Clinic USA 1959–61, sr lectr and conslt surgn Royal Post Grad Med Sch London 1963–66, prof and head of Dept of Surgery Univ of Newcastle 1966–, sr surgn Royal Victoria Infirmary 1966–; pres: Int Surgical Gp 1991–92, Travelling Surgical Soc of GB 1992–95, Int Assoc Endocrine Surgns 1993–95; Hon Col 201 NGen Hosp RAMC 1989; memb: Northumberland Health Authy, Cncl RCS; FRSM, FRCS 1959, Hon FACS 1985, FRCSEd 1987; *Books* Metabolic Basis of Surgical Care (1968), Advances in Parenteral Nutrition (1980), Modern Trends in Surgical Endocrinology (1986); *Recreations* gardening, photography; *Clubs* RSM, 1942, Grey Turner Surgical; *Style*— Prof Ivan Johnston; ✉ Department of Surgery, Medical School University of Newcastle, Framlington Place, Newcastle upon Tyne (☎ 0191 222 7067)

JOHNSTON, Maj-Gen James Frederick Junor; CB (1993), CBE (1984); s of William Johnston (d 1972), and Margaret Macrae Ward, *née* Junor (d 1986); *b* 5 Aug 1939; *Educ* George Watson's Coll, Welbeck Coll, RMA Sandhurst, RMCS (BSc), Staff Coll Camberley (psc), RCDS; *Career* cmmnd REME 1959, cmd 7 Field Workshop 1974–76, directing staff Staff Coll 1976–79, Cdr maintenance 3 Armd Div 1979–81, Dep COS 4 Armd Div 1981–84, ACOS HQ BAOR 1986–89, dir of manning (Army) 1989–90, DG army manning and recruiting 1990–93, ret 1993; Col Comdt REME 1993–; chm: Westminster Gardens Ltd 1992–, Broomleigh Housing Association Ltd 1996–; tstee various Service and civilian charities; CEng 1967, FIMechE 1982, FIMgt 1983, Eur Ing 1989, FInstD 1988; *Recreations* travel, photography, postal history, genealogy; *Clubs* Army and Navy, Cavalry & Guards, Fadeaways; *Style*— Maj-Gen James Johnston, CB, CBE; ✉ c/o Royal Bank of Scotland, Lawrie House, Victoria Road, Farnborough GU14 7NR

JOHNSTON, Sir John Baines; GCMG (1978, KCMG 1966, CMG 1962), KCVO (1972); s of Rev Andrew Smith Johnston (d 1966); *b* 13 May 1918; *Educ* Banbury GS, Queen's Coll Oxford (MA); *m* 1969, Elizabeth Mary, da of John Foster Crace (d 1960); 1 s (John b 1970); *Career* served WWII Maj Gordon Highlanders; Colonial Office 1947–57, dep high cmmr S Africa 1959–61; Br high cmmr: Sierra Leone 1961–63, Rhodesia 1963–65, Malaysia 1971–74, Canada 1974–78, ret; chm ARELS Examination Tst 1982–94, govr BBC 1978–85, memb Disasters Emergency Ctee 1985–92; *Style*— Sir John Johnston, GCMG, KCVO; ✉ 5 Victoria Road, Oxford OX2 7QF (☎ 01865 556927)

JOHNSTON, Lt-Col Sir John Frederick Dame; GCVO (1987, KCVO 1981, CVO 1977, MVO 1971), MC (1945); s of Frederick Horace Johnston (d 1935), and Winifred Emily, *née* Dame (d 1983); *b* 24 Aug 1922; *Educ* Ampleforth; *m* 4 Nov 1949, Hon Elizabeth Rosemary (d 1995), da of 2 Baron Hardinge of Penshurst, GCB, GCVO, MC, PC (d 1960); 1 s (Christopher Michael b 1951), 1 da (Joanna Elizabeth b 1953); *Career* Grenadier Gds 1941–64 (cmd 1 Bn 1962–64); comptroller Lord Chamberlain's Office 1981–87 (asst comptroller 1964–81); pres King George's Pension Fund for Actors and Actresses; dir: Theatre Royal Windsor, Claridge's Hotel; pres Hearing Dogs for the Deaf; Freeman City of London 1985; recipient of 32 foreign orders and decorations; *Recreations* gun dogs, golf; *Clubs* Swinley Forest Golf; *Style*— Lt-Col Sir John Johnston, GCVO, MC; ✉ Stone Hill, Newport, Dyfed; Studio Cottage, The Great Park, Windsor, Berks SL4 2HP

JOHNSTON, Mark Steven; s of Ronald Johnston, of Gartmore, by Stirling, Scotland, and Mary Woods, *née* Nicol; *b* 10 Oct 1959; *Educ* McLaren HS Calander Stirlingshire, Univ of Glasgow; *m* 8 June 1985, Deirdre Munro, da of Dr Duncan Ferguson, of Bearsden, Glasgow; *Career* veterinary practice 1983–86; racehorse trainer 1987–; horses trained incl: Marina Park, Quick Ransom, Starstreak, Lifewatch Vision, Mister Baileys, Branston Abby, Double Trigger, Millstream, Jural, Love You Millions, Double Eclipse, Bijon D'Inde; races won incl: Lanson Champagne Stakes, Goodwood 1993, Royal Lodge Stakes Ascot 1993, Princess Margaret Stakes Ascot 1992, Tote Ebor 1992, Portland Handicap 1989, Cock of the North Stakes 1989, White Rose Stakes Ascot 1990, 2000 Guineas 1994, Northumberland Plate 1994, Curragh Stakes 1994, Futurity Stakes 1994, Cornwallis Stakes 1994, Sweet Solera Stakes 1994, Chartwell Stakes 1994, Tattersalls Breeders Stakes 1994, Ascot Gold Cup 1995, Sagaro Stakes 1995, Henry II Stakes 1995, Goodwood Cup 1995, Futurity Stakes 1995, Ballyogan Stakes 1995; MRCVS 1983; *Style*— Mark Johnston, Esq; ✉ Kingsley House, Middleham, Leyburn, N Yorks (☎ 01969 622237, fax 01969 622484, car 0378 654105)

JOHNSTON, Lt-Gen Sir Maurice Robert; KCB (1981), OBE (1971); s of Brig Allen Leigh Johnston, OBE (d 1967); *b* 27 Oct 1929; *Educ* Wellington, RMA Sandhurst; *m* 24 Aug 1960, Belinda Mary, o da of Capt Geoffrey Mainwaring Sladen, DSO, DSC, RN (d 1985); 1 s (Philip William b 18 April 1963), 1 da (Lucinda Helen b 25 Oct 1961); *Career* cmmnd RA 1949, transferred Queen's Bays 1954, Mil Asst to CGS 1968–71, CO 1 Queen's Dragoon Gds 1971–73, Cdr 20 Armd Bde 1973–75, Brig Gen Staff HQ UK Land Forces 1977–78, Sr Directing Staff RCDS 1979–80, Asst CGS 1980, Dep Chief of Defence Staff 1981–83, ret 1984; dir Cargotec (UK) Ltd 1984–; govr Dauntsey's Sch; High Sheriff of Wilts 1993–94; Lord-Lt of Wilts 1996– (DL 1990–96); *Recreations* fishing, shooting, skiing, gardening; *Style*— Lt-Gen Sir Maurice Johnston, KCB, OBE; ✉ Ivy House, Worton, Devizes, Wilts (☎ 01380 723727)

JOHNSTON, Peter William; s of William Johnston (d 1974), and Louisa Alice, *née* Pritchard; *b* 8 Feb 1943; *Educ* Larbert HS, Univ of Glasgow (MA, LLB); *m* 1967, Patricia Sandra, da of late Alexander Yates MacDonald; 1 da (Wendy Ann b 7 May 1969), 1 s (Alasdair Peter b 10 Dec 1970); *Career* ptnr MacArthur & Co Slrs 1971–76 (asst 1968–76), procurator fiscal Procurator Fiscal Service 1978–86 (sr legal asst 1976–78), Crown Office 1986–89 (latterly asst slr), chief exec and sec ICAS 1989–; memb Law Soc of Scotland 1967; FRSA 1990; *Recreations* music, sailing, languages; *Clubs* New (Edinburgh); *Style*— Peter Johnston, Esq; ✉ 34 York Road, Trinity, Edinburgh EH5 3EQ (☎ 0131 479 4809); Institute of Chartered Accountants of Scotland, 27 Queen Street, Edinburgh EH2 1LA (☎ 0131 225 5673, fax 0131 225 3813)

JOHNSTON, Richard Arthur; s of Arthur Robert Court Johnston, of Beaumont, Carlisle, Cumbria, and Sylvia Fay, *née* Lightfoot; *b* 10 April 1955; *Educ* St Bees Sch Cumbria, Ealing Tech Coll; *m* 1 April 1989, Julia Mary, da of Anthony John Harvey, of Birmingham; 2 s (William Richard b 14 March 1990, Max Harvey b 28 March 1995), 1 da (Hannah Lily b 4 Jan 1992); *Career* theatre dir Birmingham Hippodrome Theatre 1980–88, chief exec Contemporary Dance Tst 1988–90; chief exec Stoll Moss Theatres Ltd 1990–; *Recreations* environment, sport, theatre; *Style*— Richard Johnston, Esq; ✉ Fairholme, Hawks Hill, Hedsor, Bourne End, Bucks SL8 5JQ; Stoll Moss Theatres Ltd, 21 Soho Square, London W1V 5ED (☎ 0171 494 5200)

JOHNSTON, Prof Ronald John (Ron); s of Henry Louis Johnston (d 1989), and Phyllis Joyce, *née* Liddard; *b* 30 March 1941; *Educ* Commonweal Co GS Swindon, Univ of Manchester (BA, MA), Monash Univ (PhD); *m* 16 April 1963, Rita, *née* Brennan; 1 s (Christopher Martin b 18 Sept 1964), 1 da (Lucy Carolyn b 30 July 1966); *Career* Monash Univ: teaching fell 1964, sr teaching fell 1965, lectr 1966; Dept of Geography Univ of Canterbury: lectr 1967–69, sr lectr 1969–73, reader 1973–74; Univ of Sheffield: prof Dept of Geography 1974–92, pro-vice chllr for academic affairs 1989–92; vice-chllr Univ of Essex 1992–95, prof of geography Univ of Bristol 1995–; Inst of Br Geographers: sec 1982–85, vice-pres 1988–89, pres 1990; honors award for scholarly distinction Assoc of American Geographers 1991; FRGS (Murchison award 1985, Victoria medal 1990); *Books* author of thirty, ed of over thirty; *Recreations* bell-ringing (pres Yorks Assoc of Change Ringers 1989–92, pres Central Cncl of Church Bellringers 1993–96 (vice-pres 1990–93)); *Style*— Prof Ron Johnston; ✉ Department of Geography, University of Bristol, Bristol BS8 1SS (☎ 0117 928 9116, fax 0117 928 7878, e-mail R.Johnston@uk.ac.bristol)

JOHNSTON, Sir (David) Russell; kt (1985), MP (Lib Dem) Inverness, Nairn and Lochaber (majority 458); s of David Knox Johnston (d 1972); *b* 1932; *Educ* Portree HS Isle of Skye, Univ of Edinburgh (MA); *m* 1967, Joan Graham, da of Donald Menzies; 3 s; *Career* Nat Serv cmmnd Intelligence Corps 1958; history teacher Liberton Secdy Sch Edinburgh 1961–63; memb Exec Scottish Lib Pty 1961–, res asst Scottish Lib Pty 1963–64; MP (Lib until 1988, now Lib Dem): Inverness 1964–83, Inverness, Nairn and Lochaber 1983–; Lib spokesman on: foreign and cwlth affrs 1970–75 and 1979–85, Scotland 1970–73, 1975–83 and 1985–87; Alliance spokesman on Scotland and Euro Community Affrs 1987; Lib Dem spokesman on: foreign and cwlth affrs 1988–89, Europe and East/West rels 1989–; one of first UK Lib membs of Euro Parl 1973–75 and 1976–79 (vice pres Political Ctee 1976–79), stood at first Euro direct election 1979 and 1984; pres Scottish Lib Dems 1988–94 (chm 1970–74, ldr 1974–88); dep ldr Lib Dems 1989–92; memb: Royal Cmmn on Scottish Local Govt 1966–69, Western Euro Union Assembly (rep to Cncl of Europe 1984–86, 1987 and 1988–, pres Lib Gp 1994–, pres Sub-ctee on Youth and Sport 1992–95, pres Ctee on Culture & Educn 1995–); vice pres: Euro Lib Democratic and Reform Parties 1990–92, Liberal International; vice chm Bd of Govrs Westminster Fndn for Democracy; winner of debating trophies: The Scotsman 1956 and 1957, The Observer Mace 1961; *Publications* Highland Development, 'To be a Liberal' and 'Scottish Liberal Party Conference Speeches' 1971–78 and 1979–86; *Clubs* Scottish Liberal; *Style*— Sir Russell Johnston, MP; ✉ House of Commons, London SW1A 0AA (☎ 0171 219 5180)

JOHNSTON, Samuel (Sam); OBE, JP (1974); *b* 28 Feb 1933; *Educ* Methodist Coll Belfast; *m* 1959; 3 c (Stephen b 1960, Laureen b 1963, Valerie b 1965); *Career* gen sec/leader Portadown YMCA, asst gen sec Liverpool YMCA 1960–64, gen sec Swansea YMCA 1964–68, gen sec West Bromwich YMCA 1968–78, regn YMCA sec 1978–82, nat legal sec Nat Cncl of YMCAs (Inc) England 1982–93, assoc nat sec 1993–94, actg nat sec 1994, ret; *Recreations* golf and travel; *Style*— Sam Johnston, Esq, OBE, JP; ✉ 13 Sterndale Close, Girton, Cambridge CB3 0PR (☎ 01223 276391); National Council of YMCAs, 640 Forest Road, London E17 3DZ (☎ 0181 520 5599)

JOHNSTON, Thomas Alan; *Educ* Univ of Glasgow (BSc, DPA); *m*; *Career* civil engr (specialising in reservoir and highway engrg); Babtie Shaw & Morton 1956–61, John Laing Construction Ltd 1961–67, Thyssen (Great Britain) Ltd 1967–68, currently sr conslt Babtie Group Ltd (joined as projects engr 1968, subsequently assoc dir, ptnr then chief exec); recent projects incl major reservoirs, flood prevention works and land reclamation schemes (incl Colliford Dam Roadford and Carsington Reservoirs); memb Reservoirs Ctee Inst of Civil Engrs 1991–94; former memb: Ctee Glasgow and W of Scotland Assoc Inst of Civil Engrs, Cncl Inst of Highways and Transportation; chm British Dam Soc 1995; CEng 1960, FICE 1976, FIWEM 1976, FIHT 1976, FEng 1995; *Publications* author of various papers and pubns incl An Engineering Guide to the Safety of Embankment Dams (jtly, Dept of the Environment, 1990); *Style*— T Alan Johnston, Esq, FEng; ✉ Babtie Group Ltd, 95 Bothwell Street, Glasgow G2 7HX (☎ 0141 204 2511, fax 0141 226 3109)

JOHNSTON, Sir Thomas Alexander; 14 Bt (NS 1626), of Caskieben, Aberdeenshire; only s of Sir Thomas Alexander Johnston, 13 Bt (d 1984), and Helen Torrey, *née* Du Bois; *b* 1 Feb 1956; *Heir* kinsman, William Norville Johnston b 1922; *Style*— Sir Thomas A Johnston, Bt

JOHNSTON, Dr Thomas Lothian (Tom); DL (City of Edinburgh 1987); s of T B Johnston (d 1981), and Janet Bell, *née* Lothian (d 1969); *b* 9 March 1927; *Educ* Hawick HS, Univ of Edinburgh (MA, PhD), Univ of Stockholm; *m* Joan Winifred, da of Ernest Chalmers Fahmy, FRCSE, FRCPE, FRCOG (d 1983), of Edinburgh; 2 s, 3 da; *Career* Sub Lt RNVR 1944–47; lectr in political economy Univ of Edinburgh 1953–65; prof of economics Heriot-Watt Univ 1966–76, chm MSC Scot 1977–80, economic conslt to Sec of State for Scot 1977–81, memb Scottish Economic Cncl 1977–91, princ and vice chllr Heriot-Watt Univ 1981–88 (now princ emeritus); chm Univ Authorities Pay Panel 1985–88; arbitrator and mediator; chm Enquiry into staff representation London Clearing Banks 1978–79, chm Scottish Milk Indust Arbitrations Bd 1983–94, head of Inquiry into Water Dispute 1983; overseas corr Nat Acad of Arbitrators USA; memb: Scottish Milk Marketing Bd 1967–72, Scottish Telecommunications Bd 1977–81, nat Industl Relations Ct 1970–74; dir: First Charlotte Assets Trust 1981–92, Scottish Life Assurance Co 1989–, Hodgson Martin Ltd 1989–, Academic Residences in Scotland 1990–; visiting academic: Univ of Illinois 1962–63, Queen's Univ Canada 1965, Int Inst of Labour Studies Geneva 1973, Western Australia Inst of Technol 1979; chm for Scotland Industry Year 1986 and Industry Matters 1987–89; pres Scottish Economic Soc 1978–81, pres Royal Soc of Edinburgh 1993–96; tstee Nat Galleries of Scotland 1989–95; chm Scottish Ctee Royal Soc of Arts 1991–95; Hon DUniv Edinburgh 1986, DEd, CNAA 1989, FEIS 1989, Hon LLD Univ of Glasgow 1989, Hon DUniv Heriot-Watt 1989; foreign memb Royal Swedish Acad of Engrg Sciences; FRSE 1979, CIMgt 1983, FRSA 1983, FIPM 1985; Cdr Royal Swedish Order of the Polar Star 1985; *Recreations* walking, gardening; *Style*— Dr Tom Johnston, DL, FRSE; ✉ 14 Mansionhouse Rd, Edinburgh EH9 1TZ (☎ and fax 0131 667 1439)

JOHNSTON, Very Rev William Bryce; s of William Bryce Johnston, ISO (d 1963), of Edinburgh, and Isabel Winifred Chester, *née* Highley (d 1953); *b* 16 Sept 1921; *Educ* George Watson's Coll Edinburgh, Edinburgh Univ (MA, BD); *m* 9 Oct 1947, Ruth Margaret, da of Rev James Arthur Cowley (d 1960), of Edinburgh; 1 s (Iain Arthur Bryce b 19 Dec 1950), 2 da (Fiona Margaret b 6 Nov 1952, Rosemary Swan (Mrs McCulloch) b 18 Feb 1958); *Career* Chaplain to the Forces 1945–49; minister: St Andrew's Church Bo'ness 1949–55, St George's Church Greenock 1955–64, Colinton Parish Church 1964–91; Chaplain HM Prison Greenock 1959–64; convenor Gen Assembly Ctees: Church and Nation 1972–76, Inter-Church Relations 1979–81; moderator of the Gen Assembly 1980–81, chaplain-in-ordinary to HM The Queen in Scotland 1981–91, extra chaplain 1991–; chm Judicial Cmmn 1986–93, visiting lectr in social ethics Heriot-Watt Univ 1966–87, tstee Scottish Nat War Memorial 1981–92, memb Bdcasting Cncl for Scotland 1983–87; Hon DD Aberdeen Univ 1980, Hon DLitt Heriot-Watt Univ 1989; *Books* translation: Karl Barth - Dogmatics (1960), John Calvin - Epistle To The Hebrews (1963); Ethics and Defence (ed 1987); *Recreations* organ music, bowls; *Clubs* New (Edinburgh); *Style*— The Very Rev William Johnston; ✉ 15 Elliot Rd, Edinburgh EH14 1DU (☎ 0131 441 3387)

JOHNSTON, William James; s of Thomas Hamilton Johnston (d 1951), of Enniskillen, Co Fermanagh, and Mary Kathleen, *née* Bracken (d 1977); *b* 3 April 1919; *Educ* Portora Royal Sch Enniskillen Co Fermanagh; *m* 6 Dec 1943, Joan Elizabeth Nancye, da of Rev William John Young (d 1927), of Newtownbutler, Co Fermanagh; 2 da (Heather b 1945, Janet (Mrs Moore) b 1948); *Career* qualified CA 1942; dep sec Antrim CC 1944–68, dep town clerk Belfast Corp 1968–73, town clerk and chief exec Belfast City Cncl 1973–79, sec Assoc of Local Authorities NI 1979–82; memb: NI Advsy Bd Abbey Nat Bldg Soc 1982–89, BBC NI Advsy Cncl 1965–69, Bd of Arts Cncl of NI 1974–80, Local Govt Staff Cmmn 1974–84, NI Tourist Bd 1980–85, NI Australian Bicentennial Ctee; chm: Public Serv Trg Cncl 1974–83, Nat House Bldg Cncl (NI) 1989–95; FCA; *Recreations* golf, live theatre, travel; *Clubs* Royal Portrush Golf, Cushendall Golf, Ulster Reform; *Style*— William Johnston, Esq; ✉ 19A Windsor Avenue, Belfast BT9 6EE (☎ 01232 669373); 4 Riverside Close, Cushendall, Ballymena BT44 0NR (☎ 012667 72013)

JOHNSTON OF ROCKPORT, Baron (Life Peer UK 1987), of Caversham, Co Berks; Sir Charles Collier Johnston; TD; s of Capt Charles Moore Johnston (ka Battle of Somme 1916), and Muriel Florence Edmeston, *née* Mellon (d 1963); *b* 4 March 1915; *Educ* Tonbridge; *m* 1, 15 June 1939 (m dis 1979), Audrey Boyes, da of late Edgar Monk; 2 s (Hon Michael Charles b 20 Oct 1942, Hon Timothy Courtenay b 29 May 1945); m 2, 1 Sept 1981, Mrs Yvonne Shearman, da of late Reginald Marley; *Career* chm Standex International Ltd 1951–77 (formerly Roehlen-Martin Ltd, md 1948–76), engravers and engrs, of Cheshire; dir: Thames and Kennet Marina Ltd 1982– (chm 1982–94), James Burn International 1983–, Standex Hldgs Ltd 1986–, Macclesfield Constituency Cons Assoc 1961–65; memb Cons Bd of Finance 1965–71, hon treas NW Area Cons (chm 1971–76), memb Exec Ctee Nat Union of Cons and Unionist Assocs 1965–88 (chm 1976–81), pres Nat Union of Cons and Unionist Assocs 1986–87, nat chm Cons Friends of Israel 1983–86, jt treas Cons Party 1984–88; memb Boyd Cmmn as official observers of elections held in Zimbabwe/Rhodesia April 1980; *Recreations* spectator sports, travelling, gardening; *Style*— The Rt Hon the Lord Johnston of Rockport, TD; ✉ House of Lords, London SW1

JOHNSTONE, Dr Adrian Ivor Clive; *b* 14 Jan 1960; *Educ* St Dunstan's Coll London, Royal Holloway Coll Univ of London (BSc, PhD); *Career* Royal Holloway Coll Univ of London: research fell 1984–86, lectr 1986–, dean Faculty of Science 1994–; visiting lectr in VLSI design: Curtin Univ of Technol Perth Australia June-Oct 1991, King's Coll London 1991–92; tech dir Soroban Ltd 1987–91, visiting industl fell Image Inspection Ltd 1990–93; memb/chm various Coll and Univ Ctees and Bds; assoc memb: Inst of Electrical and Electronic Engrs (USA), Assoc for Computing Machinery (USA); memb: Machine Vision Assoc, Assoc for Science Educn, Euro Assoc of Deans of Science; MBCS, MIEE; *Books* LATEX, concisely (1992, revised edn and trans into Japanese 1994); also author of numerous articles and papers in learned jls; *Style*— Dr Adrian Johnstone; ✉ Faculty of Science, Royal Holloway, University of London, Egham, Surrey TW20 0EX

JOHNSTONE, Air Vice-Marshal Alexander Vallance Riddell; CB (1966), DFC (1940), AE; s of Alexander Lang Johnstone (d 1950), and Daisy, *née* Riddell; *b* 2 June 1916; *Educ* Kelvinside Acad; *m* 1940, Margaret, da of James T Croll, of Glasgow; 1 s, 2 da; *Career* RAF 1935–68; fndr and first CAS Royal Malayan Air Force 1957–58, dir of personnel Air Miny 1962–64, Cdr Air Forces Borneo 1964–65, Air Offr Scotland 1965–68, Cdr Air N Atlantic 1965–68; vice chm Cncl TA and VRA 1969–79, chm Climax Cleaning Co Ltd 1980–90; *Recreations* golf; *Clubs* RAF; *Style*— Air Vice-Marshal Alexander Johnstone, CB, DFC, AE; ✉ 36 Castle Brooks, Framlingham, Woodbridge, Suffolk IP13 (☎ 01728 723770)

JOHNSTONE, Dr Christopher John Maxwell; s of Dr John Maxwell Johnstone (d 1989), and Ashley Margaret, *née* Ord; *b* 10 Feb 1958; *Educ* Oundle, Univ of Dundee (MB ChB, FRCGP), DCH (Glasgow); *m* 1986, Anne Marie Elizabeth, da of John Michael Carey, of Helensburgh, Dumbartonshire; 1 s (Alasdair John Maxwell b 1990), 2 da (Jennifer Catherine Maxwell b 1992, Kirsty Anne Maxwell b 1995); *Career* princ in gen practice Paisley 1987–; audit facilitator 1991–, asst ed Hoolet 1994–; trainer in gen practice 1992–, memb UK Cncl RCGP 1993–95, ARISE assoc 1995–; *Recreations* collecting books and American comics, foreign studies; *Style*— Dr Christopher Johnstone; ✉ 21 Potterhill Avenue, Paisley PA2 8BA (☎ 0141 884 2364, fax 0141 884 4072); Johnstone, Johnson and Hislop, 29 Glasgow Road, Paisley PA1 3PA (☎ 0141 889 3732, fax 0141 889 7502)

JOHNSTONE, David William Robert; s of William Johnstone (d 1948), and Elizabeth Hankin, *née* Hedley (d 1995); *b* 20 Nov 1936; *Educ* St Bees Sch, Clare Coll Cambridge (MA); *m* 1962, Penelope Susan, da of Dr David Robert Sloan, of Bristol; 3 da (Penelope Harriet b 1964, Jessica Lucy b 1966, Bryony Aileen b 1969); *Career* CA; ptnr Thomson McLintock & Co 1969–79; non-exec dir: JT Group Ltd 1979–, Avon Health Authy 1983–; local dir Bain Hogg Ltd 1983–; FCA, ACIArb; *Recreations* gardening, walking, theatre, music; *Style*— David Johnstone, Esq; ✉ 5 West End, Somerset Street, Kingsdown, Bristol BS2 8NE (☎ and fax 0117 924 7276)

JOHNSTONE, Hon Francis Patrick Harcourt (Vanden-Bempde-); s and h of 5 Baron Derwent, LVO, *qv*; *b* 23 Sept 1965; *Educ* Eton, Univ of Edinburgh; *m* 6 Oct 1990, Cressida, o da of Christopher Bourke, of London; *Style*— The Hon Francis Vanden-Bempde-Johnstone; ✉ Hackness Hall, Scarborough, N Yorks

JOHNSTONE, Iain Gilmour; s of Jack Johnstone (d 1990), of Perth, Scotland, and Gillie Gilmour (d 1979); *b* 8 April 1943; *Educ* Campbell Coll Belfast, Univ of Bristol (LLB, slr finals (distinction)); *m* Maureen, da of Robert Watson; 1 s (Oliver b 1 March 1990), 2 da (Sophie b 22 June 1981, Holly b 28 Aug 1983); *Career* film critic; newscaster ITN 1966–67, reporter The Times 1967, prodr BBC TV 1968–74 (devised Ask Aspel, Film '71 and Friday Night Saturday Morning), visiting prof Univ of Boston 1975, presenter Film 83 and Film 84 (BBC), film critic The Sunday Times 1983–93; chm Screenplay BBC Radio 4 1986–95, UK host Academy Awards 1991 and 1992; BAFTA nomination for best documentary (Snowdon on Camera) 1981; *Books* The Arnhem Report (1976), The Man With No Name (1978), Dustin Hoffman (1980), Cannes: The Novel (1990), Wimbledon 2000 (1992); *Film* Fierce Creatures (with John Cleese, 1996); *Recreations* lawn tennis, Egyptology, genetics, sand castles; *Clubs* Garrick, Groucho, Queen's, Campden Hill Lawn Tennis; *Style*— Iain Johnstone, Esq; ✉ Fish Productions, 84 Ladbroke Road, London W11 3NU

JOHNSTONE, Sir (John) Raymond; kt (1993), CBE (1988); o s of Capt Henry James Johnstone, RN, of The Myretoun, Menstrie, Clackmannanshire (d 1947, fourth in descent from John Johnstone, who commanded the artillery at the Battle of Plassey, to which victory he substantially contributed, and who was s of Sir James Johnstone, 3 Bt), and Margaret Alison McIntyre (d 1984); *b* 27 Oct 1929; *Educ* Eton, Trinity Coll Cambridge (BA); *m* 1979, Susan Sara, da of Christopher Gerald Gore (d 1955), widow of Peter Quixano Henriques (d 1974), and of Basil Ziani de Ferranti; 5 step s, 2 step da; *Career* chm: Murray Johnstone Ltd 1984–92 (md 1968–88, hon pres 1992–), Murray Split Capital Trust PLC 1991–, Dominion Insurance Ltd 1978–95, Scottish Amicable Life Assurance Soc 1983–85 (dir 1971–97), Scottish Financial Enterprise 1989–92, Summit Group plc 1989–, Forestry Commission 1989–94, Yamaichi-Murray Johnstone Ltd 1986–, Lomond Underwriting PLC 1993–, The Patrons of the Nat Galleries of Scotland 1995–, The Nuclear Tst 1996–, The Nuclear Generation Decommissioning Fund Limited 1996–; dir: Murray Income Trust plc 1989–, Murray International Trust plc 1989–, Murray Smaller Market Trust plc 1989–, Murray Ventures plc 1984–, Murray Enterprise plc 1989–, R J Kiln & Co Limited 1995–; hon pres: Scottish Opera (chm 1983–86); ACA 1955; *Recreations* fishing, music, farming; *Style*— Sir Raymond Johnstone, CBE; ✉ Wards, Gartocharn, Dunbartonshire G83 8SB (☎ 01389 830471, fax 01389 830493)

JOHNSTONE, Sir (George) Richard Douglas; 11 Bt (NS 1700), of Westerhall, Dumfriesshire; s of Sir Frederic Allan George Johnstone, 10 Bt (d 1994); *b* 21 Aug 1948; *Educ* Magdalen Coll Oxford; *m* 1976, Gwyneth, da of Arthur Bailey, of Hastings; 1 s (Frederic Robert Arthur b 18 Nov 1981), 1 da (Caroline Anne b 1983); *Heir* s, Frederic Robert Arthur Johnstone b 18 Nov 1981; *Career* md DBI Associates Ltd mgmnt conslts; *Style*— Sir Richard Johnstone, Bt

JOHNSTONE, Prof William; s of Rev Thomas Kennedy Johnstone (d 1981), of Ashburn, New Galloway, and Evelyn Hope, *née* Murray (d 1987); *b* 6 May 1936; *Educ* Hamilton Acad, Univ of Glasgow (MA, BD), Univ of Marburg; *m* 25 June 1964, Elizabeth Mary, da of Thomas Ward, of Oswaldtwistle, Lancs; 1 s (Adam Ward b 14 Feb 1969), 1 da (Anna b 15 Nov 1970); *Career* prof of Hebrew and Semitic languages Univ of Aberdeen 1980– (lectr 1962–72, sr lectr 1972–80, dean Faculty of Divinity 1984–87); memb Soc Old Testament Study (pres 1990); *Recreations* gardening, travel; *Style*— Prof William Johnstone; ✉ 37 Rubislaw Den South, Aberdeen AB15 4BD; King's College, University of Aberdeen, Old Aberdeen AB24 3UB (☎ 01224 272378, fax 01224 273750)

JOHNSTONE, William Neill (Bill); s of Harry McCall Johnstone (d 1985), of Forfar, and Ethel Mary Neill; *b* 16 May 1938; *Educ* Forfar Acad, Edinburgh Acad, Univ of Edinburgh, Scottish Coll of Textiles, RCA; *m* (m dis); 2 da (Catriona Mhairi b 14 Dec 1964, Lilian MacDonald b 14 March 1966); m 2, 14 Dec 1991, Mara Lukic; 1 s (James Ilya Neill b 27 Oct 1993), 1 da (Louise Jelena b 20 Aug 1995); *Career* designer then design dir R G Neill & Son 1961–70, md and design dir Neill of Langholm 1970–85, design dir Illingworth Morris Group and co-ordinator trg programme 1982–85; fndr: Neill Johnstone Ltd 1986 (specialises in providing seasonal collections for int apparel fabric markets), Fabric Design Consultants International Ltd 1989–; IWS design conslt 1978–90; memb C B W T Steering Ctee 1981–85 (chm 1982–85); indust on selection panel S D A/S W I Designer Graduate Attachment Scheme; RDI 1989, FRSA 1991; *Recreations* climbing, hill walking, collecting inuit carvings; *Style*— Bill Johnstone, Esq; ✉ Neill Johnstone Ltd, William St, Langholm, Scotland DG13 0BN (☎ 01387 381122, fax 01387 381106)

JOICEY, 5 Baron (UK 1906); Sir James Michael Joicey; 5 Bt (UK 1893); s of 4 Baron Joicey, DL (d 1993), and Elisabeth Marion, *née* Leslie Melville; *b* 28 June 1953; *Educ* Eton, ChCh Oxford; *m* 16 June 1984, (Agnes) Harriet Frances Mary, yr da of Rev William Thompson, of Oxnam Manse, Jedburgh, Roxburghshire; 2 s (Hon William James b 21 May 1990, Hon Richard Michael b 17 Feb 1993), 2 da (Hon Hannah Elisabeth b 25 June 1988, Hon Claire Vida b 1 Dec 1994); *Heir* s, Hon William James Joicey b 21 May 1990; *Style*— The Rt Hon the Lord Joicey; ✉ East Flodden Farmhouse, Milfield, Wooler, Northumberland NE71 6JF

JOICEY-CECIL, James David Edward; s of late Edward Wilfrid George Joicey-Cecil (d 1985), gs of 3 Marquess of Exeter, and Rosemary Lusia, *née* Bowes-Lyon (d 1989), gd of 14 Earl of Strathmore and Kinghorne, and of 5 Earl of Portarlington; *b* 24 Sept 1946; *Educ* Eton; *m* 1975, Jane Susanna Brydon, da of Capt P W B Adeley (d 1968); 2 da (Katherine Mary b 1978, Susanna Maud b 1981); *Career* Whinney Murray & Co 1965–72; James Capel & Co 1972–96, HSBC Investment Bank plc (formerly James Capel & Co) 1996–; dir HSBC Financial Services (Middle East) Ltd; memb London Stock Exchange 1978–92, MSI 1992–; FCA 1979; *Clubs* Annabel's, Boodle's, City; *Style*— James Joicey-Cecil, Esq; ✉ 49 Clapham Common South Side, London SW4 9BX (☎ 0171 622 0576); HSBC Investment Bank plc, 10 Queen Street Place, London EC4R 1BL (☎ 0171 621 0011); Keeper's Cottage, Delcombe, Milton Abbas, Blandford, Dorset DT11 0BT

JOINER, Craig Alexander; s of Michael Roy Joiner, and Helen Forbes, *née* Taylor; *b* 21 April 1974; *Educ* Dunfermline HS, Merchiston Castle Sch (Sch of the Year Whitbread Rugby Awards 1991), Heriot Watt Univ; *partner* since 1993, Hilary Livingstone; *Career* rugby union back; clubs: Melrose RFC 1992 and 1993–96 (64 appearances), Eastern Suburbs Sydney Australia 1993, Leicester RFC 1996–; represented Scottish Schs: U15 v Wales Schs 1989, U18 1990–92; Scotland: U19, first full cap v Argentina (on tour) 1994, played in all Scotland's matches Rugby World Cup S Africa 1995, scorer of 2 tries, 12 full caps; Dunfermline District Cncl Sports Personality of the Year 1995; currently student; *Recreations* skiing, golf; *Style*— Craig Joiner, Esq; ✉ c/o Ian McLaughlan Associates, 35 Chester Street, nr Haymarket, Edinburgh EH3 7EN (☎ 0131 226 2277); c/o Leicester RFC, Aylestone Road, Leicester LE2 7LF

JOLL, Christopher Andrew; s of Sqdn Ldr Ian K S Joll, DFC, AE, RAuxAF (d 1978), and Eileen Mary Sassoon Sykes; *b* 16 Oct 1948; *Educ* Oundle, RMA Sandhurst (Armorers and Braziers Co young offrs prize), Mansfield Coll Oxford (MA); *Career* PR and investor relations exec; served Br Army: joined RMA Sandhurst 1966, cmmnd 2 Lieut Life Gds 1968, served NI 1969, 1970, 1972 and 1974, ret 1975; gen mangr Michael Peters & Partners Ltd 1978 (joined 1977), dir corp affrs United Scientific Holdings 1988 (joined 1978), chief exec Charles Barker City Ltd 1989 (dir 1988), dir Charles Barker Ltd 1989, chief exec Georgeson & Co Ltd 1991–93, dir Kleinwort Benson Securities Ltd 1993–95, dir Focus Communications LTd 1996–; chm: Christopher Joll Consulting Ltd 1995–, The Room Ltd 1995–; memb: Queen's Silver Jubilee Appeal (chm Ideas Ctee) 1976–77, Mansfield Coll Oxford Appeal 1978, Mktg Ctee ENO 1986–89; co prodr José Carreras And Friends concert in aid of José Carreras Int Leukaemia Fndn 1990–91; dir Br Youth Opera 1993–; FRSA 1994; *Recreations* field sports, bridge, charity fund raising and sponsorship; *Clubs* Brooks's; *Style*— Christopher Joll, Esq; ✉ 1A Hyde Park Gate, London SW7 5EW (☎ 0171 584 8102); Focus Communications Ltd (☎ 0171 600 1392)

JOLLES, Bernard Nathan; s of Dr Benjamin Jolles (d 1985), of Northampton, and Miriam, *née* Blake; *b* 23 Aug 1949; *Educ* Bedford Sch, St John's Coll Cambridge (MA), Balliol Coll Oxford (MSc), London Business Sch (MSc); *m* 1 Dec 1986, Pamela, da of Horace Knight (d 1973), of Hastings; 1 da (Antonia Sarah b 21 Jan 1989); *Career* merchant banker; dir: Samuel Montagu & Co Ltd 1982–87, Henry Ansbacher & Co Ltd

1988–94, Campbell Lutyens & Co Ltd 1995–; *Recreations* flying, golf, skiing, tennis; *Style*— Bernard N Jolles, Esq; ✉ 110 Regent's Park Rd, London NW1 8UG (☎ 0171 722 5522)

JOLLIFFE, John Anthony; s of Donald Norman Jolliffe (d 1967), of Dover, Kent, and Edith Constance Mary, *née* Lovegrove (d 1993); *b* 1 Aug 1937; *Educ* Dover Coll; *m* 1, 5 June 1965 (m dis 1983), Jacqueline Mary, *née* Smith, 1 s (Jeffrey b 1968), 1 da (Jenny b 1966); m 2, 3 Aug 1984 (m dis 1986), Irmgard Elizabeth, *née* Melville; 1 s (Andrew b 1985); m 3, 11 Aug 1990 (m dis 1994), Dorothy Jane, *née* Saul; *Career* Nat Serv RAF 1955–57; ptnr R Watson & Sons 1967–91 (joined 1957), princ J A Jolliffe & Co 1991–; examiner in pension funds Inst of Actuaries 1970–75 (tutor 1965–70), memb UK Steering Ctee for Local Govt Superannuation 1975–, chm ACA Local Govt Superannuation Ctee 1975–, treas Assoc of Consulting Actuaries 1980–84; dir: London Aerial Tours Ltd 1983–, Highverse Ltd 1991–; chm Capital Pension Trustees Ltd 1992–; memb Cncl Nat Assoc of Pension Funds 1983–91; chm: NAPF Int Ctee 1986–88, Euro Fedn of Retirement Provision 1988–91; pres Sarl Auvers Berck France 1990–; Freeman City of London, Liveryman Worshipful Co of Actuaries, Liveryman Guild of Air Pilots and Air Navigators; FIA 1964, ASA (USA) 1971, FPMI 1977; *Recreations* flying, tennis, travel; *Clubs* Reform; *Style*— John Jolliffe, Esq; ✉ Hurst House, Clay Lane, Redhill, Surrey RH1 4EG (☎ 01737 779997, fax 01737 778478)

JOLLIFFE, Hon William Henry Martin; s and h of 5 Baron Hylton, DL; *b* 1 April 1967; *Educ* Ampleforth, Univ of York, RAC Cirencester; *Career* voluntary serv in Zimbabwe, Romania and Calcutta 1992–94, Missionaries of Charity London 1995–; *Style*— The Hon William Jolliffe; ✉ 24– Smith Terrace, London SW3 4DL

JOLLY, Michael Gordon; *b* 21 Sept 1952; *Career* The Tussauds Group (incl Alton Towers, Chessington World of Adventures, Warwick Castle, Madame Tussaud's London, The London Planetarium, Rock Circus London, Madame Tussaud Scenerama Amsterdam and Port Aventura Spain): exec dir 1987–92, chief operating offr 1992–94, chm and chief exec 1994–; *Style*— Michael Jolly, Esq; ✉ The Tussauds Group Limited, Maple House, 149 Tottenham Court Road, London W1P 0DX (☎ 0171 312 1131, fax 0171 465 0864)

JOLLY, Nicholas John; s of Michael Harvey Jolly, and Anne Margaret, *née* Saunders; *b* 11 March 1962; *Educ* St Francis Xavier's Coll Liverpool, Worthing Sixth Form Coll, W Sussex Coll of Art, Glos Coll of Art (BA), Royal Acad Schs (post grad dip); *Career* artist; *Solo Exhibitions* Paton Gallery London 1991 and 1993, Beaux Arts London 1996; *Gp Exhibitions* John Player Portrait Awards (Nat Portrait Gallery) 1984, Young Masters - Ten Young Painters (Solomon Gallery London) 1985, Royal Inst of Oil Painters (Mall Galleries London) 1987, Young Masters (Kunsthaus im Welserhof Augsburg) 1988, New Faces II (Paton Gallery) 1989, Royal Over-Seas League Annual Exhbn 1989, 1990 and 1991, On the Threshold of Meaning - Two Man Exhbn (Plymouth City Museum & Art Gallery 1990), The Bridge Show (Lannon Gallery NY) 1994, The Kasen Summer Collection (touring exhbn Glasgow, London) 1994–95, Osaka Triennale (Japan) 1996, Premio Marco (Monterrey, Mexico) 1997; *Public Collections* Metropolitan Museum of Art NYC, Durban Museum of Art SA; awarded Elizabeth Greenshields Fndn Grant 1989, Susan Kasen Travel Scholarship (6 Months in Connecticut) 1993, Pollock-Krasner Fndn Grant 1995; *Recreations* intemperance and torpidity; *Style*— Nicholas Jolly, Esq; ✉ c/o Beaux Arts, 22 Cork Street, London W1X 1HB (☎ 0171 437 5799)

JOLLY, Peter Stanley; s of Stanley Kenyon Jolly, and Gertrude Ethel May, *née* Scott (d 1977); *b* 11 Nov 1941; *Educ* Fairfax HS, Coll of Technol Southend; *m* 9 Sept 1967, Barbara Olive, da of William Arthur Warren (d 1945); 3 s (Martin Peter b 1969, Adrian Stanley b 1978, Christopher William b 1984); *Career* Spicer & Pegler 1966–68; Consolidated Gold Fields Gp: mgmnt accountant 1968, chief accountant 1977, gp internal auditor and admin mangr 1980, operations fin gp exec 1986, fin dir CGF Euro Sales Ltd 1987–89; conslt Hanson Gp 1989–90, chief exec designate Enterprises Devpt & Trg Ltd 1989–90, gp internal review exec Smith & Nephew plc 1990–; memb: Scout Movement 1983–85, Info Technol Ctee Inst CA, Internal Audit Sleeping Ctee of CA 1996–; govr and vice chm Belfairs Community Coll 1993–; FCA 1966, ATII 1966; *Recreations* scouting (Queen Scout), swimming, genealogy; *Clubs* Scout Movement; *Style*— Peter Jolly, Esq; ✉ 167 Hadleigh Rd, Leigh-on-Sea, Essex SS9 2LR (☎ 01702 76912)

JOLLY, (Arthur) Richard; s of late Arthur Jolly, and Flora Doris, *née* Leaver; *b* 30 June 1934; *Educ* Brighton Coll, Magdalene Coll Cambridge (BA, MA), Yale Univ (MA, PhD); *m* 1963, Alison Bishop; 2 s, 2 da; *Career* community devpt offr Baringo Dist Kenya 1957–59, sec Br Alpine Hannibal Expedition 1959, research fell Makerere Coll Uganda 1963–64, research offr Dept of Applied Economics Univ of Cambridge 1964–66, advsr Parly Select Ctee on Overseas Aid and Devpt 1974–75; Univ of Sussex: professorial fell 1971–, dir Inst of Devpt Studies 1972–81; dep exec dir UNICEF 1982–96, special advsr UNDP 1996–; memb: Founding Ctee Euro Assoc of Devpt Insts 1972–75, Editorial Bd World Devpt 1973–, UK Cncl on Int Devpt 1974–78, Triennial Review Gp Cwlth Fund for Tech Co-operation 1975–76, Governing Cncl for Society for Int Devpt 1976–85 (vice pres 1982–85), UN Ctee for Devpt Planning 1978–81; chm North-South Round Table 1988–96 (memb 1976–); Master Worshipful Co of Curriers 1977–78; Hon DLitt: Univ of E Anglia 1988, Univ of Sussex 1992; *Publications* Cuba: The Economic and Social Revolution (jtly, 1964), Planning Education for African Development (1969), Redistribution with Growth (jtly, 1974), The Impact of World Recession on Children (ed jtly, 1984), Adjustment with a Human Face (ed jtly, 1987); author various articles in professional jls; *Recreations* billiards, croquet, nearly missing trains and planes; *Style*— Richard Jolly, Esq; ✉ Institute of Development Studies, University of Sussex, Brighton, Sussex BN1 9RE (☎ 01273 606261); UNDP, 1 United Nations Plaza, NY 10017, USA (☎ 00 1 212 906 5764, fax 00 1 212 906 6661)

JOLOWICZ, Prof John Anthony (Tony); QC (1990); s of Prof Herbert Felix Jolowicz (d 1954), of London and Oxford, and Ruby Victoria, *née* Wagner (d 1963); *b* 11 April 1926; *Educ* Oundle, Trinity Coll Cambridge (MA); *m* 8 Aug 1957, Poppy, da of Norman Stanley; 1 s (Nathaniel Herbert b 20 July 1963), 2 da (Kate (Mrs Little) b 4 May 1959, Sophie b 26 June 1961); *Career* Lt RASC 1944–48; called to the Bar 1952, master of the bench Gray's Inn 1978; Univ of Cambridge: asst lectr 1955, lectr 1959, reader 1972, prof of comparative law 1976–93, chm Faculty of Law 1984–86, fell Trinity Coll 1952–; prof associé Univ de Paris II 1976, Lionel Cohen lectr Univ of Jerusalem 1983; pres SPTL 1986–87, a vice pres Int Acad of Comparative Law 1994–; ed of various law jls and author of various legal works; HonD Universidad Nacional Autónoma de México 1985; memb Academia Europaea; *Recreations* reading, music, travel; *Clubs* Leander, RAC; *Style*— Prof J A Jolowicz, QC; ✉ West Green House, Barrington, Cambridge CB2 5SA (☎ 01223 870495, fax 01223 872852); La Truffière, 47120 St Jean-de-Duras, France; Trinity College, Cambridge CB2 1TQ (☎ 01223 338400, 01223 338461, fax 01223 338564)

JOLY, Simon Michael Bencraft; 2 s of Richard Bencraft Joly (d 1956), and Joan Letitia Brooke, *née* Parnell (d 1993); *b* 14 Oct 1952; *Educ* Christ's Hospital, CCC Cambridge (MA); *Career* conductor; music staff Welsh National Opera 1974–78, asst then assoc chorus master ENO 1978–1980, conductor BBC Singers 1987–95 (asst conductor 1980–87); asst to Pierre Boulez with BBC Singers Paris, Berlin, London; guest conductor BBC Symphony and Concert Orchs FRCO; *Performances* BBC Singers' concerts incl: 70th Anniversary (music by Britten, Messiaen, Ligeti, Poulenc, Xenakis); BBC Proms: Stravinsky Les Noces, Giles Swayne CRY, Steve Reich, The Desert Music; work with BBC Symphony Orch incl: Charles Ives Three Places in New England, Gavin Bryars The War in Heaven, Hindemith Cello Concerto, Martinu Symphony No 6, Debussy La Damoiselle Élue and Le Martyre de St Sebastien, Stravinsky Canticum Sacrum, Messiaen Le Tombeau Resplendissant and L'Ascension, David Bedford First Symphony, Henze The Raft of the Medusa; work with other orchs incl: London Sinfonietta, Bournemouth Sinfonietta, City of London Sinfonia, Ulster Orch, Endymion Ensemble, New London Orch; *Operas* various Wexford Festivals, The Bartered Bride (ENO), Cosi Fan Tutte (Irish National Opera), Peter Grimes (Dublin and Royal Danish Opera), Carmen (with José Carreras), Berio's Co Ro (BBC Singers and London Sinfonietta at La Scala); operas for BBC: Max Brand Maschinist Hopkins, Wagner-Régeny The Burghers of Calais, Weber Peter Schmoll; *Recordings* incl complete choral works Peter Maxwell Davies (CD); *Recreations* theatre, films, reading, food; *Style*— Simon Joly, Esq; ✉ 49b Disraeli Road, Putney, London SW15 2DR (☎ and fax 0181 785 9617)

JOLY DE LOTBINIÈRE, Thomas Henry; s of Lt-Col Sir Edmond Joly de Lotbinière (d 1994), by his 1 w, Hon Elizabeth Jolliffe, da of 3 Baron Hylton (d 1993); *b* 18 July 1929; *Educ* Eton, Trinity Coll Cambridge (MA); *m* 15 Sept 1953, Prudence Mary, da of Thomas Richard Bevan (d 1970), of Hadlow Down; 1 s (Nicholas b 1955), 2 da (Lucy b 1957, Henrietta b 1960); *Career* sr ptnr Grenfell & Colegrave (stockbrokers) 1978–86, vice pres Canadian Imperial Bank of Commerce 1986–91, dep chm Brown Shipley Asset Management 1991–93, dir Fleming Private Asset Management 1993–; MSI (memb Stock Exchange 1959); *Recreations* gardening, shooting; *Clubs* City of London; *Style*— Thomas Joly de Lotbinière, Esq; ✉ Fleming Private Asset Management, 20 Finsbury Street, London EC2Y 9AQ (☎ 0171 814 2730, fax 0171 814 2850)

JONAH, Sam Esson; s of Thomas Jonah (d 1987), of Obuasi, Ghana, and Beatrice, *née* Sampson (d 1978); *b* 19 Nov 1949; *Educ* Adisadell Coll Ghana, Camborne Sch of Mines Imperial Coll of Science and Technol (MSc, DIC); *m* Theodora, da of Winfred Arthur; 2 s (Richard b 17 Nov 1975, Andrew b 30 Aug 1977), 2 da (Tamara b 10 Aug 1982, Samantha b 17 Jan 1988); *Career* Ashanti Goldfields Co Ltd: joined 1969, dep md 1982–86, chief exec 1986–; exec dir Lonrho plc 1992–; dir: Ghana Minerals Cmmn 1985–, Ghana Investment Centre 1986–; chm Ghana Airways 1994–96; winner: Nat Worker of the Year Award TUC of Ghana 1992, Mktg Personality of the Year Award Inst of Mktg Ghana 1993, Chief Exec of the Year Award ING Bank Emerging Markets 1994; Hon DSc Cambrone Sch of Mines; CEng, fell Ghana Inst of Mgmnt, fell Ghana Instn of Engrs; *Recreations* fishing, swimming, squash; *Clubs* Goldfields Sporting (chm); *Style*— Sam Jonah, Esq; ✉ Ashanti Goldfields Co Ltd, Gold House, PO Box 2665, Accra, Ghana (☎ 00 233 21 774913/772190, fax 00 233 21 776750)

JONAS, Christopher William; CBE (1994); s of Philip Griffith Jonas, MC (d 1982), of Oxted, Surrey, and Kathleen Marjory, *née* Ellis; *b* 19 Aug 1941; *Educ* Charterhouse, Coll of Estate Mgmnt, London Business Sch; *m* 30 Nov 1968, (Jennifer Susan) Penny, da of Bernard Leslie Barker (d 1976), of Fulbeck, Grantham; 3 s ((Leslie) Peter b 16 April 1970, Toby Philip b 10 Nov 1971, Max Christopher b 2 Feb 1977), 1 da (Freya Josephine Wendy b 4 Feb 1981); *Career* TA Inns of Ct Regt 1959–66; Jones Lang Wootton 1959–67; Drivers Jonas: ptnr 1967–82, managing ptnr 1982–87, sr ptnr 1987–95; fndr Christopher Jonas/Strategy for Corporate Property 1995–; pres RICS 1992–93; property advsr Staffs CC 1982–, tstee Property Centre City Univ, chm Economics Res Assoc (USA) 1987–93; memb: Port of London Authy 1985–, Bd Securities and Futures Authy 1988–91, Business in the Community 1991–, British Rail Property Bd 1991–94, British Railways Bd 1993–94, Further Educn Funding Cncl 1992–; ind dir: Railtrack Group plc 1994–, Tate Gallery Projects Ltd 1996–; memb: Urban Land Inst USA, American Soc of Real Estate Cnsllrs, Governing Body Charterhouse 1995–; Liveryman: Worshipful Co of Clothworkers 1962 (Warden 1994), Worshipful Co of Chartered Surveyors 1978 (asst 1990); FRICS 1975, FRSA, FInstD; *Recreations* music (especially Wagner), golf, tennis; *Clubs* Toronto (Toronto); *Style*— Christopher William Jonas, Esq, CBE; ✉ Christopher Jonas, 12 Barton Street, London SW1P 3NE (☎ 0171 222 5141, fax 0171 222 5142)

JONAS, George Siegfried; s of George Jonas (d 1942), and Frieda, *née* Glaser (d 1942); *b* 2 Jan 1928; *Educ* Barnton Brunner Sr Sch, LSE (LLB); *m* 23 Dec 1951, Frieda, da of the late Marcus Reinert; 1 s (Steven Michael b 1956), 1 da (Helen Ann b 1959); *Career* slr; conslt (formerly sr ptnr) George Jonas & Co; chm Bd of Mgmnt City of Birmingham Symphony Orch 1974–92 (dep chm 1971–74, memb 1966–), fndr tstee Cannon Hill Tst, pres The Margery Fry Meml Tst 1991– (chm 1970–85), former chm W Midlands Campaign for Abolition of Capital Punishment; memb Birmingham City Cncl 1959–65 and 1966–69 (chm Public Library Ctee 1962–65); Parly candidate (Lab) Hall Green 1966; awarded Gold medal of the Birmingham Civic Soc 1986; cncl memb Birmingham Law Soc 1965– (pres 1979–80, vice pres 1978–79, hon life memb 1985–), chm Litigation and Legal Aid Ctee 1972–79, chm No 6 Regnl Duty Slr Ctee 1984–87; *Recreations* music, cricket, modern transport; *Clubs* The Birmingham; *Style*— George S Jonas, Esq; ✉ 16 Burke Ave, Birmingham B13 9XB (☎ 0121 777 3773); 190 Corporation St, Birmingham B4 6QD (☎ 0121 212 4111, fax 0121 212 1770)

JONAS, Peter; CBE (1993); s of Walter Adolf Jonas (d 1965), of Hamburg and London, and Hilda May, *née* Ziadie; *b* 14 Oct 1946; *Educ* Worth Sch, Univ of Sussex (BA), Royal Northern Coll of Music (LRAM), Royal Coll of Music (CAMS), Eastman Sch of Music, Univ of Rochester USA; *m* 22 Nov 1989, Lucy, da of Christopher Hull, and Cecilia, *née* Pollen; *Career* Chicago Symphony Orch: asst to music dir 1974–76, artistic admin 1976–85; dir of artistic admin Orchestral Assoc of Chicago 1977–85 (Chicago Symphony Orch, Civil Orch of Chicago, Chicago Symphony Chorus, Allied Arts Assoc, Orchestra Hall), gen dir ENO 1985–93, staatsintendant (gen dir) Bavarian State Opera Munich 1993–; memb: Bd of Mgmnt Nat Opera Studio 1985–93, Cncl of Mgmnt London Lighthouse 1990–93, Kuratorium Richard Strauss Gesellschaft 1993–, Beirat (Advsy Bd) Bayerische Vereinsbank Munich 1994–; Hon DMus Univ of Sussex 1994; FRCM 1989 (memb Cncl 1988–95), FRSA 1989; memb: Assoc Internationale de Directeurs de L'Opera 1985, Deutsche Bühnenverein 1993; *Recreations* music, theatre, cinema, cricket, 20th century architecture; *Clubs* Athenaeum, Pegs; *Style*— Peter Jonas, Esq, CBE; ✉ Prinzregentenstrasse 72, D-81675 Munich, Germany (☎ 00 49 89 470 9530, fax 00 49 89 470 9640); Bayerische Staatsoper, Nationaltheater, Max-Joseph-Platz 2, D-80539, Munich, Germany (☎ 00 49 89 2185 1000, fax 00 49 89 2185 1003)

JONES, Adrianne Shirley (Ann); MBE; da of Adrian Arthur Haydon (d 1973), and Doris, *née* Jordan (d 1986); *b* 17 Oct 1938; *Educ* Kings Norton GS; *m* 1962, Philip Frank Jones (d 1993); 2 s (Michael Andrew b 1973, Christopher Haydon b 1978), 1 da (Philippa Ann (Pippa) b 1971); *Career* former international table tennis and lawn tennis player; *table tennis career* 66 England caps 1954–58, memb English Corbillon Cup Team 1954–58, singles finalist World Championships Stockholm 1957, winner 10 Euro Nat Singles Championships; *tennis career* memb Br Wightman Cup Team 1957–67, 1970 and 1975, winner Wimbledon singles and mixed doubles 1969, winner French Open 1961 and 1966; finalist: Wimbledon singles 1967, Forest Hills USA 1961 and 1967, semi-finalist Wimbledon singles 1958, 1960, 1962, 1963, 1966 and 1968; holder Nat Singles Championships 1966: GB (hard courts), France, Italy, Russia; indoor champion: GB, France, Germany; world rankings: No 3 1961, No 5 1962 and 1963, No 8 1964, No 5 1966, No 2 1967, No 1 1968, No 2 1969; capt: Br Fedn Cup Team 1963–66 and 1971, Wightman Cup Team 1971 and 1972; capt for Br Team 1988: Wightman Cup, Fedn Cup, Euro Cup, Maureen Connelly Trophy; chm Women's Int Tennis Cncl 1977–84, Euro dir of ops Women's Tennis Assoc 1978–84, Women's Int team capt, tennis commentator BBC, referee Women's Tennis Tournament circuit; BBC Sports Personality of The Year 1969; *Books* Tackle Table Tennis My Way (1958), A Game to Love (1971);

Recreations most sports, foreign languages and travel, most books, psychology, astronomy; *Clubs* Edgbaston Priory Lawn Tennis, All England Lawn Tennis; *Style—* Mrs Ann Jones, MBE; ✉ 85 Westfield Rd, Edgbaston, Birmingham B15 3JF (☎ and fax 0121 680 5586)

JONES, Alan Wingate; s of Gilbert Victor Jones (d 1971), of Kingswood, Surrey, and Isobel Nairn Wilson; *b* 15 Oct 1939; *Educ* Sutton Valence, King's Coll Cambridge (MA); *m* 6 July 1974, Judith Ann, da of George William Curtis (d 1952); 1 s (Mark b 1975), 1 da (Sophie b 1980); *Career* md Plessey Electronic Systems, former dir Plessey Co plc; chm and chief exec Westland Group plc 1989–95, dir GKN plc 1994–95; chief exec BICC plc 1995–; non-exec dir Fisons plc 1995–96; FEng 1989, FIEE, FRAeS 1992; *Recreations* shooting, opera; *Clubs* RAC; *Style—* Alan W Jones, Esq, FEng; ✉ BICC plc, Devonshire House, Mayfair Place, London W1X 5FH (☎ 0171 629 6622)

JONES, Alec Norman; s of Norman Albert Jones, of Birmingham, and Iris Doreen, *née* Philips; *b* 23 Dec 1951; *Educ* West Bromwich GS, Univ of Nottingham (BA); *m* Mary Cherie; 2 da (Nicola Cherie b 21 July 1982, Sophie Elizabeth b 23 March 1984); *Career* ptnr Price Waterhouse 1981– (joined 1972); ACA 1975; *Recreations* all sports especially golf; *Style—* Alec Jones, Esq; ✉ Price Waterhouse, Cornwall Court, 19 Cornwall Street, Birmingham B3 2DT (☎ 0121 200 3000, fax 0121 200 2464, car 0836 584924)

JONES, (Thomas) Allan; MBE (1982); s of Thomas Jones (d 1963), and Ellen Fawkner, *née* Stevenson; *b* 24 Dec 1940; *Educ* Univ of Wales (BSc(Econ)), McMaster Univ (Rotary fndn fell, MA); *m* 1979, Hilary, *née* Joman; 1 da (Sarah b 5 Aug 1982); *Career* asst lectr Boston Coll of FE 1967–68, lectr Macclesfield Coll of FE 1970; British Council: Nepal 1970–73, Tanzania 1974–76; assoc tutor FE Staff Coll Coombe Lodge 1976–77; British Council 1977–97: educn offr 1977–79, Bangladesh 1979–82, Kenya 1982–86, dir Educn Devpt Unit 1986–90, dir Botswana 1990–96, temp posts 1996–97; *Recreations* reading, photography, wildlife conservation; *Style—* Allan Jones, Esq, MBE

JONES, Allen; s of William Jones, and Madeline, *née* Aveson; *b* 1 Sept 1937; *Educ* Ealing GS for Boys, Hornsey Sch of Art, RCA; *m* 1, 1964 (m dis 1978), Janet, *née* Bowen; 2 da (Thea b 1967, Sarah (twin) b 1967); *m* 2, 1994, Deirdre Morrow; *Career* painter; teacher of lithography Croydon Coll of Art 1961–63, teacher of painting Chelsea Sch of Art 1966–68; RA; first int exhibition Paris Biennale 1961; *Solo Exhibitions* incl: Arthur Tooth & Sons (London), Neuendorf (Hamburg), Zwirner (Cologne), Galeria Milano (Milan), Crispolti (Rome), Bischofberger (Zurich), Ariadne (Vienna), Von Wentzel (Cologne), Springer (Berlin), Thorden Wetterling (Gothenburg), Heland Wetterling (Stockholm), C Cowles (NY), Richard Feigen Gallery (NYC, Chicago and Los Angeles), Marlborough Fine Art (London), Waddington Galleries (London), James Corcoran Gallery (Los Angeles), Galerie Patrice Trigano (Paris), Barbican Art Gallery (London); *Museum Group Exhibitions* incl: ICA Graphic Retrospective 1978, Graphic Retrospective UCLA 1978, Retrospective of Painting Walker Art Gallery (Liverpool, touring England and Germany) 1979, Young Contemporaries Paris Biennale, British Art Today, San Francisco Touring Exhibition, Decade Painting and Sculpture Tate Gallery, Chelsea Harbour Festival 1993; *Commissions* incl: Liverpool Int Garden Festival 1984, sculpture for Cottons Atrium London Bridge City 1987, sculpture for Heathrow Sterling Hotel 1990, St Stephen's Hosp London 1992, sculpture for London Dock Devpt Corp 1994, sculpture and mural for Mezzo restaurant (Sir Terence Conran) 1995; designer of sets for TV and stage in UK and Germany (incl sets and costumes for Rambert Dance Co 1989, Royal Ballet 1996); *Books* Allen Jones Figures (1969), Allen Jones Projects (1971), Waitress (1972), Sheer Magic (1979), Allen Jones (monograph, 1993), Allen Jones Prints (1995); *Recreations* gardening; *Clubs* Chelsea Arts, Garrick; *Style—* Allen Jones, Esq, RA; ✉ 41 Charterhouse Square, London EC1M 6EA (fax 0171 600 1204)

JONES, (Robert) Alun; QC (1989); *Educ* BSc; *Career* called to the Bar Gray's Inn 1972, recorder of the Crown Court; *Style—* Alun Jones, Esq, QC; ✉ 3 Raymond Buildings, Gray's Inn, London WC1R 5BH (☎ 0171 831 3833, fax 0171 242 4221)

JONES, Dr Alun Denry Wynn; s of Thomas D Jones (d 1982), of Penygroes, Dyfed, and Ray, *née* Morgan (d 1994); *b* 13 Nov 1939; *Educ* Amman Valley GS Ammanford, ChCh Oxford (MA, DPhil); *m* 22 Aug 1964, Ann, da of Brinley Edwards (d 1955), of Betws, Dyfed; 2 da (Helen b 1966, Ingrid b 1969); *Career* sr student Cmmn for the Exhibition of 1851 1964–66, sr res fell UKAEA 1966–67, Lockheed Missiles and Space Co Calif 1967–70, tutor Open Univ 1971–82, dep ed Nature (Macmillan Journals) 1972–73 (joined 1971), BSC 1974–77, British Steel Overseas Services 1977–81, asst dir Tech Change Centre 1982–85, dir and sec Wolfson Fndn 1987–90 (dep dir 1986–87), chief exec Inst of Physics 1990–; BAAS: sec Working Pty on Social Concern and Biological Advances 1972–74, memb Section X Ctee 1981–92; Br Library: memb Advsy Cncl 1983–85, Document Supply Centre Advsy Ctee 1986–89; memb Cncl Nat Library of Wales 1987–94 (govr 1986–94), govr UCW Aberystwyth 1990–92, govr City Univ 1991–; memb Cncl for Sci and Technol Inst 1990–, assessor Sci Bd Sci and Engrg Res Cncl 1991–94; memb Cncl Standing Conf on Schools' Science and Technol 1992–96; FInstP 1973, CDipAF 1977, CPhys 1987; *Books* Our Future Inheritance: Choice or Chance (jtly, 1974); *Recreations* Welsh culture, gardening, theatre; *Clubs* Athenaeum; *Style—* Dr Alun Jones; ✉ 4 Wheatsheaf Close, Woking, Surrey GU21 4BP; The Institute of Physics, 76 Portland Place, London W1N 4AA (☎ 0171 470 4800)

JONES, Alun Richard; s of Howell Jones (d 1993), and Olive Kathleen, *née* Williams; *b* 9 March 1948; *Educ* Kingston GS, St Catharine's Coll Cambridge (British Steel scholar, MA); *m* 18 Sept 1971, Gail Felicity; 1 da (Hannah Clare Rhys b 2 June 1979); *Career* Price Waterhouse: joined 1970, transferred to Century City California 1975–77, ptnr 1981–, sr client ptnr 1993, memb Supervisory Ctee; FCA 1973; *Recreations* golf, tennis, opera, concerts, living in France; *Clubs* Effingham Golf; *Style—* Alun Jones, Esq; ✉ Price Waterhouse, Southwark Towers, 32 London Bridge Street, London SE1 9SY (☎ 0171 939 2014, fax 0171 378 0647, mobile 0802 794468)

JONES, Most Rev Alwyn Rice; *see:* Wales, Archbishop of

JONES, Andrew Bryden; s of David Jones, of Stirling, Scotland, and Ellen Milne, *née* Rennie (d 1983); *b* 31 March 1948; *Educ* HS of Stirling; *m* 9 Feb 1974, Rosemary Ann, da of Norman Thomas Clarke, of Buckhurst Hill, Essex; 2 s (Alasdair David b 1975, Douglas Ian b 1976); *Career* CA; apprentice Dickson Middleton & Co Stirling 1965–70, qualified 1970, sr accountant in tax Arthur Andersen Glasgow 1970–71, mangr in tax Edward Moore & Co London 1971–74, supervisor to mangr Whinney Murray London 1974–79; Ernst & Whinney: ptnr 1979, ptnr i/c tax London 1984–88, nat tax ptnr 1988, coordinating ptnr of firms exec 1988; Ernst & Young: ptnr i/c int tax 1989–90, nat tax ptnr 1990–95, memb Firm's Exec 1992–, managing ptnr UK 1995–; MICAS 1970; *Recreations* golf, reading; *Style—* Andrew B Jones, Esq; ✉ Ernst & Young, Becket House, 1 Lambeth Palace Road, London SE1 7EU (☎ 0171 928 2000, fax 0171 928 1345)

JONES, Andrew Robert; s of Barry David Jones, and Yvonne Mary, *née* Grady; *b* 5 April 1961; *Educ* Seaford Coll Petworth, City of London Poly (BA Economics), Inst of Mktg (Dip); *m* 16 Aug 1986, Clare Elizabeth, da of Thomas M G Hanley; 1 da (Olivia Alice Tabitha b 20 April 1990), 1 s (Christopher Robert Jasper b 17 May 1993); *Career* mangr student servs City of London Poly 1982–85, sr mktg and media research exec Bates Dorland 1985–89, brand planner lagers Courage Ltd 1988–89, account planner BMP Business Communications (pt of DDB Needham) 1989–91, planning dir Countrywide Porter Novelli Ltd (formerly Countrywide Communications Ltd) 1991– (bd dir 1994–); speaker at indust confs, misc contribs to trade press; *Books* Public Relations 1996 Kampagnen - Trends and Tips (Baerns & Klewes Germany); *Recreations* road running, gardening, watercolour painting; *Clubs* Royal Anglo-Belgian; *Style—* Andrew Jones, Esq; ✉ Countrywide Porter Novelli Ltd, Bowater House East, 68 Knightsbridge, London SW1X 7LH (☎ 0171 584 0122, fax 0171 584 6655)

JONES, Prof Anne; da of Sydney Joseph Pickard (d 1987), and Hilda Everitt, *née* Bird; *b* 8 April 1935; *Educ* Harrow Weald Co Sch, Westfield Coll London (BA), King's Coll London (PGCE); *m* 9 Aug 1958 (m dis 1988), Cyril Gareth Jones, s of Lyell Jones (d 1936); 1 s (Christopher Lyell b 24 July 1962), 2 da (Catherine Rachel b 8 Aug 1963, Rebecca Madryn b 15 March 1966); *Career* asst mistress: Malvern Girls Coll 1957–58, Godolphin and Latymer Sch 1958–62, Dulwich Coll 1964; sch cnsllr Mayfield London 1965–71, dep head Thomas Calton Sch London 1971–74; head: Vauxhall Manor Sch 1974–81, Cranford Community Coll 1981–87, under sec (dir of educn) Employment Dept 1987–91, visiting prof of educn Univ of Sheffield, educn and training conslt 1991–, prof of continuing educn Brunel Univ 1991–; dir: West London Leadership 1995–, Business Link London NW 1995–; chair: Assoc of Child Psychology and Psychiatry 1979–80, Area Manpower Bd for London South and West 1983–87; former memb: Schools' Bdcasting Cncl, Home Office Advsy Ctees on Drugs and on Sexual Offences; former cncl memb: CRAC, NICEC, Grubb Inst, W London Inst of HE, RSA Examination Bd; hon memb City and Guilds Inst; Hon FCP 1990; fell Queen Mary & Westfield Coll 1992 (memb Cncl), FRSA (former memb Cncl), FIMgt; *Books* Counselling Adolescents: School and After (1986), Leadership for Tomorrow's Schools (1987); *Recreations* walking, dining, swimming, boating; *Style—* Prof Anne Jones; ✉ 23 Queen Street, Henley-on-Thames RG9 1AR (☎ 01491 578672, fax 01491 571853, e-mail 100734.1176@compuserve.com)

JONES, Arfon; *b* 21 April 1943; *Educ* Bristol GS, Clare Coll Cambridge (MA); *m* 27 Sept 1970, Janet Myra Hoskins; 2 s (Rupert b 8 April 1971, Oliver b 18 April 1976), 1 da (Victoria b 28 Nov 1972); *Career* admitted slr 1968; head Corp Fin Dept Cameron Markby Hewitt 1994– (ptnr 1970–); non-exec dir Camford Engineering plc 1976–86; chm of govrs Rokeby Sch 1996–; memb: Law Soc 1968, City of London Slrs' Co; *Recreations* golf, skiing, hockey; *Clubs* Royal Wimbledon Golf; *Style—* Arfon Jones, Esq; ✉ Cameron Markby Hewitt, Sceptre Court, 40 Tower Hill, London EC3N 4BB (☎ 0171 702 2345, fax 0171 702 2303)

JONES, Arthur Edward; CBE (1993); s of Arthur Albert Jones, DCM (d 1963), of Chigwell, Essex, and Mary Alice, *née* Clements (d 1987); *b* 20 Feb 1922; *Educ* Leyton Co HS; *m* 28 June 1947, (Hannah) Elizabeth, da of Albert Storey (d 1933); 1 s (Stephen Arthur b 1950), 1 da (Jill Elizabeth b 1952); *Career* served RN 1941–46; dir A & M Jones & Sons Ltd 1946–85; pres Essex Co Badminton Assoc 1993–94 (vice pres 1973–93), chm Br Badminton Olympic Ctee 1986–90; Badminton Assoc of England: memb Cncl 1956–73, vice pres 1973–86, chm 1975–84, pres 1986–90; Int Badminton Fedn: memb Cncl 1976–84, vice pres 1984–90, pres 1990–93, immediate past pres 1993–; *Recreations* philately (memb Royal Philatelic Soc 1992–), swimming, golf; *Style—* Arthur Jones, Esq, CBE; ✉ 2 Broadstrood, Loughton, Essex IG10 2SE (☎ 0181 508 7218, fax 0181 508 3146)

JONES, Prof Arthur S; s of John Jones (d 1986), of Newcastle upon Tyne, and Anne, *née* Hamilton (d 1938); *b* 17 May 1932; *Educ* Gosforth GS, Kirkley Hall Farm Inst Northumberland, King's Coll Univ of Durham (BSc), Univ of Aberdeen (PhD); *m* 6 January 1962, Mary Margaret, da of George Smith (d 1974), of Aberdeen; 3 s (Graeme Angus b 19 Nov 1962, Roland Philip b 17 May 1964, Nathan Mark b 13 Oct 1966), 1 da (Camilla Anne b 10 March 1970); *Career* cmmnd Army 2 Lt 1955–57, pilot offr RAF Vol Res 1958–62; Rowett Res Inst: scientific offr Applied Biochemistry Dept 1959, sr scientific offr Applied Biochemistry Dept and head of Pig Section Applied Nutrition Dept 1961, princ scientific offr head of Applied Nutrition Dept 1966, sr princ scientific offr head of Applied Nutrition Dept 1971, sr princ scientific offr and chm Applied Sciences Div 1975, dep chief scientific offr and dep dir 1983, govr 1987–; princ North of Scotland Coll of Agric and head Sch of Agric Univ of Aberdeen 1986–90, Strathcona Fordyce prof of agric Univ of Aberdeen 1986–90; chm of Scottish Beef Developments Ltd 1988–, princ Royal Agric Coll Cirencester 1990–; govr Aberdeen Centre for Land Use 1986, govr Henley Coll of Mgmnt 1996–, chm Acad Advsy Cncl 1996–; chm RAC Enterprises Ltd 1992–; Trehane tstee 1993, tstee Geoffrey Claghill Memorial 1993–; memb: Cncl RASE, Cncl Arable Res Centres 1991–96; author of numerous scientific pubns in the field of agric; FIBiol 1968, FIMgt 1978, FRSA 1989, FIAgrM 1992; *Recreations* yachting; *Style—* Prof Arthur Jones; ✉ Bailey Lodge, Stroud Rd, Cirencester, Gloucestershire GL7 6JS (☎ 01285 652531); Royal Agricultural College, Cirencester, Gloucestershire GL7 6JS (☎ 01285 655035, fax 01285 680219)

JONES, Rt Hon Aubrey; PC (1955); s of Evan and Margaret Aubrey Jones; *b* 20 Nov 1911; *Educ* Cyfarthfa Castle Secdy Sch Merthyr Tydfil, LSE; *m* 1948, Joan, da of G Godfrey-Isaacs; 2 s; *Career* editorial and foreign staff memb The Times 1937–39 and 1947–48; Parly candidate: SE Essex 1945, Heywood and Radcliffe 1946; MP (Unionist) Birmingham Hall Green 1950–65; PPS: to Min of State for Econ Affrs 1952, to Min of Materials 1953; min of fuel and power 1955–57, min of supply 1957–59; chm Prices and Incomes Bd 1965–70; pres Oxford Energy Policy Club 1976–88, sr res assoc St Antony's Coll Oxford 1979–82, fell commoner Churchill Coll Cambridge 1972 and 1982–86; dir: Black & Decker 1977–83, Thomas Tilling 1970–82; former dir GKN and Courtaulds; chm Cornhill Insurance 1971–74, former chm Staveley and Laporte Industries; visiting fell Sci Policy Res Unit Univ of Sussex 1986 (hon fell 1993); hon fell LSE 1959 (memb Ct of Govrs 1964), Hon DSc Bath; *Style—* The Rt Hon Aubrey Jones; ✉ Arnen, 120 Limmer Lane, Felpham, Bognor Regis, W Sussex PO22 7LP (☎ 01243 582722)

JONES, Prof (Norman) Barrie; s of Leslie Robert Jones, of Bebington, Merseyside, and Edith, *née* Morris; *b* 3 Jan 1941; *Educ* Liverpool Inst, Univ of Manchester (BSc), McMaster Univ (MEng), Univ of Sussex (DPhil); *m* 13 July 1963, Sandra Mary, da of George Albert Potts (d 1976), of Liverpool; 1 s (Geoffrey Stephen b 7 May 1968), 1 da (Victoria Mary b 21 Oct 1965); *Career* Univ of Sussex: lectr 1968–73, reader 1973–84, dir Centre for Med Res 1982–84; Univ of Leicester: prof of engrg 1985–, head Dept of Engrg 1988–95; memb Biomedical Section Br Assoc; CEng 1978, FIEE 1984; *Style—* Prof N Barrie Jones; ✉ Department of Engineering, The University, Leicester LE1 7RH (☎ 0116 223 1300, telex 347250, fax 0116 252 2619)

JONES, (Stephen) Barry; MP (Lab) Alyn and Deeside (majority 7,851); s of Stephen Jones (d 1988), and Grace Jones (d 1944); *b* 1938; *m* Janet, da of F W Davies; 1 s (Stephen); *Career* head Eng Dept Deeside Secdy Sch, regnl offr NUT, Parly candidate (Lab) Northwich Cheshire 1966; MP (Lab): Flint East 1970–83, Alyn and Deeside 1983–; PPS to the Rt Hon Denis Healey 1972–74, Parly Under Sec of State for Wales 1974–79, Oppn spokesman on employment 1980–83, chief Oppn spokesman on Wales 1983–92, memb Lab Shadow Cabinet 1983–87 and 1988–92; memb Intelligence and Security Ctee (appointed by PM) 1995; formerly memb Welsh Exec Ctee and Cncl of Europe, memb Speaker's Panel of Chairmen; govr: Nat Library of Wales, Nat Museum of Wales; life memb Royal Liverpool Philharmonic Soc, fell Industry and Parliament Tst; *Style—* Barry Jones, Esq, MP; ✉ House of Commons, London SW1A OAA (☎ 0171 219 3556)

JONES, Dr (Richard) Barry; s of Richard Humphrey Jones (d 1973), and Catherine Ann, *née* Herbert; *b* 27 Jan 1935; *Educ* Haberdashers' Aske's, BNC Oxford, Guy's Med Sch (MA, BM BCh); *m* 20 July 1962, Dorothee, da of Bernhard Franz Siebel, of W Germany; 5 s (Llewellyn b 1960, Alexander b 1963, Robert b 1965, Michael b 1968, Peter b 1975), 3 da (Deborah b 1960, Rebecca b 1963, Katherine b 1966); *Career* ed Child Care Health and Development 1974–94; conslt developmental paediatrician: Moorfields Eye Hosp 1975–, Hosp for Sick Children London 1975–94; hon sr lectr in developmental paediatrics Univ of London: Inst of Ophthalmology 1975–, Inst of Child Health 1975–94; dir Donald Winnicott Centre 1975–95; hon paediatrician: RNIB, Sense (chm Children's Interest Gp); FRCP, FRCOphth; *Recreations* philosophy of medicine, walking; *Style*— Dr Barry Jones; ✉ 17 Dartmouth Row, London SE10 8AW (☎ 0181 692 7989); Moorfields Eye Hospital, City Rd, London EC1V 2PD (☎ 0171 253 3411)

JONES, Prof Barry Edward; s of Frederick Edward Jones (d 1994), of Winchcombe, Glos, and Margaret Alice, *née* Redwood (d 1975); *b* 11 March 1940; *Educ* Cheltenham GS, N Gloucestershire Tech Coll, Univ of Manchester (BSc, MSc, PhD, DSc); *m* 7 Dec 1963, Julie, da of William Pritchard (d 1993), of Torquay, Devon; 2 da (Ruth Gillian Sarah b 1966, Jennifer Claire b 1969); *Career* scientific asst Govt Communications Headquarters Cheltenham 1956–60, lectr in electrical engrg Univ of Manchester 1964–81, pt/t tutor Faculty of Technol The Open Univ 1972–84, sr lectr Dept of Instrumentation and Analytical Sci UMIST 1981–86; Brunel Univ: Hewlett Packard prof of mfrg metrology 1986–91, prof of mfrg metrology 1991–, dir The Brunel Centre for Mfrg Metrology 1986–; chm IEE Professional Gp on Fundamental Aspects of Measurement 1980–81, hon ed Jl of Physics E Sci Inst 1983–87, memb CNAA 1983–85; CEng 1970, FInstMC 1979, FInstP 1982, FIEE 1984, CPhys 1986, fell SPIE 1992, EurIng 1992, FRSA 1992; *Books* Instrumentation, Measurement and Feedback (1977), Instrument Science and Technology (ed and contrib vol 1 1982, vol 2 1983, vol 3 1985), Current Advances in Sensors (ed and contrib, 1987); *Recreations* music, gardening, Methodist local preacher; *Style*— Prof Barry Jones; ✉ The Brunel Centre for Manufacturing Metrology, Brunel University, Uxbridge, Middlesex UB8 3PH (☎ 01895 274000 ext 2514, fax 01895 232806, telex 261173 G)

JONES, Barry Malcolm; s of Albert George Jones (d 1980), and Margaret Eileen, *née* Clark; *b* 4 April 1951; *Educ* Battersea GS, Charing Cross Hosp Med Sch Univ of London (MS, FRCS, MB BS, LRCP, MRCS); *m* 12 May 1973, Janine Diane, da of Laurence Henry Gilbey, of London; 1 s (Huw b 1984), 1 da (Georgina b 1986); *Career* sr registrar in plastic surgery Mount Vernon Hosp 1982–85, fell in craniofacial surgery Hôpital des Enfants Malades Paris 1985, currently conslt plastic and cranio-facial surgn The Hosp for Sick Children Gt Ormond St London and Univ Coll Hosp Gower St London; memb: Br Assoc Plastic Surgns, Br Assoc Aesthetic Plastic Surgns, Int Soc of Aesthetic Plastic Surgns, Int Soc of Craniomaxillofacial Surgns, Euro Craniofacial Soc, Euro Assoc Plastic Surgns, Craniofacial Soc of GB, Int Microsurgical Soc, Hand Soc; Freeman: City of London 1982, Worshipful Soc of Apothecaries; *Recreations* exercise, golf, literature, culinary arts, oeneology; *Clubs* RAC, Moor Park Golf; *Style*— Barry M Jones, Esq; ✉ 14A Upper Wimpole St, London W1M 7TB (☎ 0171 935 1938, fax 0171 935 6607, car 0860 449616); The Hospital for Sick Children, Great Ormond St, London WC1; University College Hospital, Gower St, London W1

JONES, Brian Robert; s of Charles Robert Jones (d 1973), and Ellen Elsie Walker (d 1990); *b* 7 Jan 1946; *Educ* Wallington GS; *m* 1968, Sandra Thirlwall, da of William Davies (d 1953); 1 da (Elaine b 1969); *Career* dir Customer Services and actuary Royal London Mutual Insurance Society Ltd 1987– (dir 1985–), chm Royal London General Insurance Company Ltd 1995– (dir 1985–), chm Royal London Homebuy Ltd; FIA; *Recreations* gardening, opera, reading, enjoyment of the countryside; *Style*— Brian Jones, Esq; ✉ Tarkwa, Daisy Green, Groton, Sudbury, Suffolk CO10 5EN (☎ 01787 210814); Royal London Mutual Insurance Society Ltd, Royal London House, Middleborough, Colchester, Essex CO1 1RA (☎ 01206 761761, fax 01206 369649)

JONES, Dr (Robert) Brinley; s of John Elias Jones, and Mary Ann, *née* Williams; *b* 27 Feb 1929; *Educ* Tonypandy GS, Univ Coll Cardiff (BA, DipEd, fell), Jesus Coll Oxford (DPhil), Int Inst for Advanced Studies Clayton Mo (MA); *m* 1971, Stephanie Avril Hall; 1 s; *Career* educn offr RAF Kidlington and Bicester 1955–58 (cmmnd 1955); asst master Penarth GS 1958–60, lectr Univ Coll Swansea 1960–66, asst registrar Univ of Wales 1966–69, dir Univ of Wales Press 1969–76, Warden Llandovery Coll 1976–88, memb Broadcasting Standards Council 1988–91; chm Cathedrals and Churches Cmmn Wales 1994–; memb: Literature Ctee Welsh Arts Cncl 1968–74 and 1981–87, Bd Br Cncl 1987–96 (chm Welsh Ctee 1987–96), Court and Cncl Nat Library of Wales 1974–82, Cncl St David's Univ Coll Lampeter 1977– (hon fell 1987), Governing Body Church in Wales 1981–, Welsh Acad 1981–, Electoral Coll of Church in Wales, Court Univ Coll Swansea 1983–, Cncl Trinity Coll Carmarthen 1984–; chm Dinefwr Tourism Gp 1988–96, managing tstee St Michael's Theol Coll 1982–94, hon memb Druidic Order Gorsedd of Bards 1979–, vice pres Llangollen Int Musical Eisteddfod 1989–; ed The European Teacher 1964–69; Hon DD Faraston Theological Seminary Longview Washington 1992; FSA 1971, FCP 1982, FRCS 1988; *Books* The Old British Tongue (1970), Writers of Wales (ed with M Stephens, 1970–), Anatomy of Wales (contrib and ed, 1972), Astudiaethau ar yr Hengerdd: studies in old Welsh poetry (ed with R Bromwich, 1978), Introducing Wales (1978, 3 edn 1988), Certain Scholars of Wales (1986), Songs of Praises (1991, 2 edn 1995), Prize Days (1992), William Salesbury (1994), 'A Lanterne to their Feete' (1994); *Recreations* walking, farming, music; *Style*— Dr R Brinley Jones, FSA; ✉ Drovers Farm, Porthyrhyd, Llanwrda, Dyfed SA19 8DF (☎ 01558 650649)

JONES, Carey Frederick; s of Clifford William Jones (d 1990), of Bonvilston, S Glam, and Mary Gwendoline, *née* Thomas; *Educ* Llandovery Coll Univ of Wales Aberystwyth (BSc), Selwyn Coll Cambridge (MA); *m* 2 Dec 1979, Bernadette Marie, da of Anthony Fulgoni; 1 s (Alexander Anthony b 10 Feb 1985), 1 da (Mariclare Dominique b 2 July 1981); *Career* graduate surveyor MAFF 1975–79, surveyor Mid Glam CC 1979–80, sr surveyor Cardiff City Cncl 1980–82 (surveyor 1980–81), sole princ Crown & Co Chartered Surveyors 1982; chief exec Royal Life Estates West 1988–92, dir and gen mangr Crown and Company Estate Agents 1993–94, md Knights Chartered Surveyors 1994–; FRICS 1991 (ARICS 1979); *Recreations* skiing, equine pursuits, classic cars; *Clubs* Pitt; *Style*— Carey Jones, Esq; ✉ Knights Chartered Surveyors, 70 Albany Road, Cardiff CF2 3RS (☎ 01222 455550, fax 01222 455551)

JONES, Rev Carmel Emmanuel; MBE (1991); s of Arthur Jones (d 1980); *b* 8 Oct 1937; *Educ* Wandsworth Tech Coll, City and Guilds of London Inst (mech engrg); *m* 2 Nov 1957, Iveline, da of Cordinal Rhule; 2 da (Elaine b 26 Oct 1958, Lorna b 11 June 1963), 1 s (Lionel b 11 June 1963); *Career* mechanical engr until 1980; community devpt dir/min of religion; currently serving three directorates incl exec dir New Assembly of Churches; pt/t prison chaplain; MIMgt; *Recreations* theatre, music, cricket; *Clubs* Diners'; *Style*— The Rev Carmel Jones, MBE; ✉ New Assembly of Churches, 15 Oldbridge Road, London SW12 8PL (☎ 0181 673 0595, fax 0181 675 8768)

JONES, Catherine Zeta; da of David James Jones, of Swansea, S Wales; *Career* actress; *Theatre* incl: The Pyjama Game (Number One Tour), Annie, Bugsy Malone (West End), Peggy Sawyer in 42nd Street (West End), Mae Jones in Street Scene (ENO); *Television* incl: Darling Buds of May (YTV), Out of the Blue (BBC); *Films* incl: lead in Scheherazade, Marie in Coup de Foudre, Splitting Heirs 1993, Blue Juice 1995; *Style*— Ms Catherine Zeta Jones; ✉ c/o ICM Ltd, Oxford House, 76 Oxford Street, London W1N 0AX (☎ 0171 636 6565, fax 0171 323 0101)

JONES, Ceri Jayne; da of David Arnold, of South Petherton, Somerset, and Julie, *née* Raymond; *b* 3 July 1958; *Educ* Ilminster Girls' GS, Wadham Comp, Univ of Keele, Univ of Liverpool; *m* Tom Cuthbert, s of Jack Cuthbert; 2 s (Rory Clark b 11 April 1990, Hadleigh Jack b 25 April 1993); *Career* staff writer Planned Savings; successively ed: Pensions and Employee Benefits, Pensions Management, Financial Adviser, Investors Chronicle; Pensions Journalist of the Year 1987; *Recreations* keen horsewoman; *Clubs* Holmes Place Gym; *Style*— Ms Ceri Jones; ✉ Investors Chronicle, Financial Times Magazines, Greystoke Place, Fetter Lane, London EC4A 1ND (☎ 0171 405 6969, fax 0171 405 5276)

JONES, Prof Charles; s of Charles Jones (d 1962), of Glasgow, and Margaret, *née* Fagan; *b* 24 Dec 1939; *Educ* St Aloysius Coll Glasgow, Univ of Glasgow (MA, BLitt); *m* 12 Aug 1966, Isla, da of Alexander Shennan (d 1989); *Career* lectr Dept of English: Univ of Hull 1964–67, Univ of Edinburgh 1967–78; prof Sch of English Univ of Durham 1978–90, Forbes prof of English language Univ of Edinburgh 1990–; chm: Scots Language Resource Centre 1992–96, Educn Ctee Saltire Soc 1994–, Mgmnt Ctee Scots Language Project Scottish Consultative Cncl on the Curriculum 1994–96; memb Ct Univ of Edinburgh 1993–96, memb Cncl Saltire Soc 1995; FRSE 1995; *Books* Introduction to Middle English (1973), Phonological Structure and The History of English (1974), Grammatical Gender in English (1988), A History of English Phonology (1989), A Treatise on the Provincial Dialect of Scotland (Sylvester Douglas (Lord Glenbervie), ed 1991), Historical Linguistics: Problems and Perspectives (ed, 1993), A Language Suppressed (1995); *Recreations* breeding Soay sheep; *Clubs* Scottish Arts; *Style*— Prof Charles Jones, FRSE; ✉ Laggan Cottage, Faladam, Midlothian EH37 5SU (☎ 01875 833652); Department of English Language, University of Edinburgh, David Hume Tower, George Square, Edinburgh EH8 9JX (☎ 0131 650 3506)

JONES, Christopher Kenneth; Lord's Taverners; s of William Henry Jones (d 1942), and Dorothy Irene, *née* Tonge (d 1990); *b* 22 March 1939; *Educ* Sir Roger Manwood's GS Sandwich, Univ of Southampton Sch of Navigation; *m* 29 June 1963, (Moira) Jane, da of Gp Capt David Fowler McIntyre, AFC (d 1957), of Lochgreen House, Troon, Ayrshire; 2 s (Mark b 1964, Neil b 1965), 1 da (Amanda b 1967); *Career* third offr Union-Castle Mail SS Co Ltd 1957–62, merchandise dir Peter Robinson/Top Shop Ltd 1964–72, dep md Richard Shops Ltd 1972–76, md Bally London Shoe Co Ltd 1976–80, chief exec Lillywhites Ltd 1980–84, md retail activities Seaco Inc 1984–86, sr ptnr Sunningdale Marketing Management; dir: Robert Burns Heritage Collection (Crestock Ltd), Sport Retail Management Ltd 1993–; Freeman City of London; FRSA 1974; *Recreations* skiing, golf; *Style*— Christopher Jones, Esq; ✉ Stack Cottage, Windlesham Road, Chobham, Surrey GU24 8SY (☎ 01276 856132, fax 01276 855441)

JONES, (John) Clement; CBE (1972); only s of Clement Daniel Jones (d 1916), of Haverfordwest; *b* 22 June 1915; *Educ* Ardwyn, Aberystwyth, Open Univ (BA); *m* 1938, Marjorie, da of George Gibson (d 1991), of Llandrindod Wells; 3 s; *Career* journalist and broadcaster; ed and dir Express and Star Wolverhampton 1960–75, media conslt Cwlth and UNESCO 1975–, exec dir Beacon Radio (programming) 1974–78; pres Guild Br Newspaper Editors 1967, govr Br Inst of Human Rights 1971–85; FRSA; *Recreations* gardening, beekeeping, writing, broadcasting; *Clubs* Athenaeum; *Style*— J Clement Jones, Esq, CBE; ✉ The Annex, Summerhaugh Cottage, St Marybourne, Hants SP11 6BJ (☎ 01264 738190)

JONES, Clive Hugh; s of David John Jones, of Harrow, Middx and Marjorie Viola, *née* Hobbs (d 1981); *b* 25 Aug 1958; *Educ* Merchant Taylors', St John's Coll Oxford (BA); *m* 23 July 1988, Judith Helen, da of Gwynfryn George Bond, of Sabden, Lancashire; 1 s (Matthew Alexander b 15 Oct 1991), 1 da (Sophie Victoria b 19 Dec 1993); *Career* called to the Bar Middle Temple 1981; Freeman: City of London 1984, Worshipful Co of Merchant Taylors; ACIArb 1986; *Recreations* golf, the arts and travel; *Clubs* Sudbury Golf; *Style*— Clive H Jones, Esq; ✉ 1 New Square, Lincoln's Inn, London WC2A 3SA (☎ 0171 405 0884, fax 0171 831 6109)

JONES, Clive Lawson; CBE (1997); s of John Lawson Jones (d 1986), and Gladys Irene, *née* Daines; *b* 16 March 1937; *Educ* Cranleigh Sch, Univ of Wales (BSc); *m* 4 April 1961, Susan Brenda, da of late Walter Angus McLeod; 1 s (Robin b 26 Dec 1964), 1 da (Tracy b 28 Dec 1966); *Career* with: BP 1957–61, Texaco Trinidad 1961–68; princ DTI 1968–73, asst sec Dept of Energy 1973–77, energy cnsllr Br Embassy Washington DC 1977–81, under sec Dept of Energy 1981–82, dir energy policy EC 1982–86, dep dir-gen for energy EC Cmmn 1987–94, sec gen European Energy Charter Conf 1991–96; *Style*— Clive Jones, CBE; ✉ Energy Charter Secretariat, c/o EEC - DGXVII, 200 rue de la Loi, 1049 Brussels, Belgium (☎ 00 32 2 295 7096)

JONES, Clive William; s of Kenneth David Llewellyn Jones, of Pontllanfraith, Gwent, S Wales, and Joan Muriel, *née* Withers; *b* 10 Jan 1949; *Educ* Newbridge GS Gwent S Wales, LSE (BSc Econ); *m* 1, 1971 (m dis 1987), Frances Jones; 2 s (Paul Dafydd b 24 Oct 1973, Samuel Alun b 7 Sept 1975), 1 da (Angharad Elizabeth Louisa b 7 May 1979); m 2, 12 Nov 1988, Fern Mary Philomena, da of Tony Britton, the actor, of London; 2 s (Harry b 14 Dec 1993, Jack (twin) b 14 Dec 1993); *Career* journalist Yorkshire Post Group 1970–73, news ed and asst ed Morning Telegraph 1973–78, prodr Yorkshire TV 1978–82, managing ed then ed TV-am 1982–84; Television South: joined 1984, dep md and dir of regnl progs and dir TVS Entertainment Ltd and TVS Television Ltd until 1992; md London News Network 1992–94 (dir LNN Ltd 1992–), md Central Independent Television 1994–95 (dir 1994–), md Carlton UK Broadcasting (following t/o of Central by Carlton) 1995, chief exec Carlton UK Television 1996– (dir 1994–); FRTS 1995; *Recreations* books, films, rugby; *Style*— Clive Jones, Esq; ✉ Carlton UK Television Ltd, 101 St Martin's Lane, London WC2N 4AZ (☎ 0171 240 4000)

JONES, (John) David; s of John Trevor Jones, of Liverpool, and Mair Eluned Jones; *b* 11 Oct 1955; *Educ* Liverpool Coll, Univ of Oxford (MA), Univ of London (PhD); *Career* insur analyst L Messel & Co 1981–83, asst dir and head of French res E B Savory Milln & Co 1983–86, divnl dir and head of French res Warburg Securities 1986–91, dir and head of French res Bacot-Allain, jt head of res and dir CCF Elysées Bourse 1991–92, md CCF Equities 1992, first vice pres and French specialist Merrill Lynch Pierce Ferner & Smith Ltd 1992–93, chm Moonfleet Investments 1993–; registered rep Stock Exchange 1987, memb Société Française des Analystes Financiers 1988; *Recreations* classical music, theatre, cinema, reading; *Clubs* United Oxford and Cambridge University, Travellers, Oxford Soc, Bow Group; *Style*— David Jones, Esq; ✉ Moonfleet Investments, Longcause House, Dartingdon, Nr Totnes, Devon TQ9 6DQ (☎/fax 01803 865941)

JONES, David; *Career* various sr engrg, commercial and mgmnt posts South Western and Midlands Electricity Bds, former gp chief exec South Wales Electricity; chief exec: National Grid Company plc 1994– (chm 1996–), National Grid Group plc 1995–; *Style*— David Jones, Esq; ✉ The National Grid Group plc, National Grid House, Kirby Corner Road, Coventry CV4 8JY (☎ 01203 537777)

JONES, David Alan Freeborn; s of Daniel Edward (d 1966), of King's Norton, Birmingham, and Winnifred Kate, *née* Freeborn (d 1990); *b* 28 March 1943; *Educ* King's Norton GS, Univ of Nottingham (LLB); *m* 15 Feb 1969 (m dis 1995), Mavis, da of John Douglas (d 1961), of Northumbria; 1 s (Nicholas 1971), 2 da (Rachel b 1973, Hannah b 1980); *Career* law lectr Birmingham Coll of Commerce 1965–68, called to the Bar Gray's Inn 1967, in practice Birmingham 1969–, head of chambers 1985, recorder of the Crown Ct 1994– (asst recorder 1990–94); organiser, deliverer and publisher of annual lecture to the Birmingham Bar and Midland and Oxford Circuit on criminal law; memb Criminal Bar Assoc; *Recreations* cricket, golf, ornithology, gardening, tennis; *Clubs* Alvechurch CC, Fulford Heath and Aberdovey Golf, RSPB; *Style*— David Jones, Esq; ✉ 12 Cherry Hill Avenue, Barnt Green, Birmingham B45 8LA (☎ 0121 445 1935); 3 Fountain Court, Steelhouse Lane, Birmingham B4 6DR (☎ 0121 236 5854, fax 0121 236 7008)

JONES, Prof David Alwyn; s of late Trefor Jones, of London, and Marion Edna, *née* Miles; *b* 23 June 1934; *Educ* St John's Sch Leatherhead, Corpus Christi Coll Cambridge (BA), Magdalen Coll Oxford (DPhil); *m* 29 Aug 1959, Hazel Cordelia, da of Dan Lewis,

FRS, of London and Berks; 2 s (Edmund b 6 June 1963, Hugh b 2 Sept 1965), 1 da (Catherine b 26 Dec 1961); *Career* lectr in genetics Univ of Birmingham 1961–73, prof of genetics Univ of Hull 1973–89, prof and chm Dept of Botany Univ of Florida 1989–; Br Assoc for the Advancement of Science: memb Ctees of Sections D and K 1974–89, chm Co-ordinating Ctee for Cytology and Genetics 1974–87; chm Membership Ctee Inst of Biology 1982–87; co-ed Jl of Chemical Ecology 1994–; pres Int Soc of Chemical Ecology 1987–88; FIBiol 1974; *Books* Variation and Adaptation in Plant Service (with D A Wilkins, 1971), Analysis of Populations (with T J Crawford, 1976); *Style*— Prof David Jones; ✉ 7201 SW 97th Lane, Gainesville, Florida 32608–6378, USA (☎ 00 1 352 338 0680); Department of Botany, 220 Bartram Hall, University of Florida, Gainesville, FL 32611, USA (☎ 00 1 352 392 1175, fax 00 1 352 392 3993, e-mail djones@botany.ufl.edu)

JONES, Dr David Arthur; s of Eric Langley Jones (d 1973), of Liverpool, and Loris Edith, *née* Cook (d 1969); *b* 31 May 1927; *Educ* Roundhay Sch Leeds, Univ of Leeds (BSc, PhD); *m* 17 Sept 1955, Heather Ann St Clair, da of Humphrey St Clair Gilby (d 1979), of Perth, Australia; 1 s (Robin b 1959); *Career* British Thompson-Houston Co Ltd 1950–52; Brush Electrical Engineering Co Ltd: joined 1952, PA to tech dir 1953–55, res mangr 1960–64; lectr Univ of Leeds 1955–60, asst dir of engrg The English Electric Co Ltd 1964–69; dir: Ewbank Consulting Ltd 1969–82, Old Ship Hotel Brighton Ltd 1980–87, Ewbank Preece Group Ltd 1982–87; chm Cncl Brighton Poly (now Univ of Brighton) 1983–87 (dep chm Bd of Govrs 1987–94); chm ISIS Medical Technology Ltd 1996–; pres: Inst of Electrical Engrs 1990–91, Fin Ctee Royal Acad of Engrg (pension tstee); judge of Prince of Wales award for Industl Innovation; hon fell Univ of Brighton; FIEE 1968, FRSA 1987, FEng 1987; *Recreations* boating, photography, computers; *Clubs* IEE Council Dining, Dynamicables, 25; *Style*— Dr David Jones, FEng; ✉ Thatchcroft, Clayton Avenue, Hassocks, W Sussex BN6 8HD (☎ and fax 01273 846469)

JONES, David George; s of Fredrick George Jones (d 1987), and Dorothy, *née* Steele; *b* 31 May 1941; *Educ* High Storrs GS Sheffield; *m* 1962, Leonie Usherwood, da of Alfred Smith (d 1962); 3 s (Adrian George b Aug 1965, Robert George b May 1967, Christopher David b Sept 1971); *Career* civil servant; MOD: joined as exec offr 1960, asst private sec to Army Min 1970–71, princ Central Fin Planning Div 1973–77, private sec to Min of State for Defence 1977–80, regnl mktg dir Defence Sales Orgn 1980–84, asst sec air systems Controllerate 1984–85, dep dir gen Al Yamamah Project Office 1985–88, dir gen Aircraft 2 Air Systems Controllerate MOD (PE) 1988–89, civil sec Br Forces Germany 1989–92, dir gen Naval Bases and Supply 1993–96, asst under sec Fin Mgmnt 1996–; FILog 1994; *Recreations* gardening, travel; *Clubs* Civil Service; *Style*— David Jones, Esq; ✉ Ministry of Defence, Assistant Under Secretary (Financial Management), Main Building, Whitehall, London SW1A 2HB (☎ 0171 218 6182)

JONES, Rev David Ian Stewart; s of Rev John Milton Granville Jones (d 1986), and Evelyn Moyes Stewart, *née* Chedburn (d 1965); *b* 3 May 1934; *Educ* St John's Sch Leatherhead, Selwyn Coll Cambridge (MA); *m* 19 Aug 1967, Susan Rosemary, da of Eric Arthur Hardy-Smith (d 1958); 1 s (Benedict b 12 Sept 1970), 1 da (Katherine (twin) b 12 Sept 1970); *Career* RCS 1952–54; ordained priest Manchester Cathedral 1960, curate Oldham Parish Church 1959–62, vicar All Saints Elton Bury Lancs 1962–66, conduct and sr chaplain Eton 1970–74 (asst conduct and chaplain 1966–70), headmaster Bryanston 1974–82, rector Bristol City Parish 1982–85; dir Lambeth Charities 1985–, hon priest vicar of Southwark Cathedral 1985–93, govr Forest Sch 1987–93, chm Inner Cities Young People's Project 1989–; *Recreations* reading, walking, music; *Clubs* East India, Devonshire, Sports and Public Schools; *Style*— The Rev David Jones; ✉ 127 Kennington Road, London SE11 6SF (☎ 0171 735 2531, office 0171 735 1925)

JONES, Dr David Martin; *b* 14 Aug 1944; *Educ* Univ of London (BSc, BVetMed); *Career* The Zoological Soc of London: vet offr Whipsnade Park Zoo 1969–75, sr vet offr and head Dept of Vet Sci 1975–84, asst dir of zoos 1981–84, dir of zoos 1984–91, gen dir 1991–92, dir Conservation & Consultancy 1992–94; dir North Carolina Zoological Park 1994–; overseas conslt, fund-raiser, author of scientific papers and articles; chm Brooke Hosp for Animals, memb Cncl WWF (USA); MRCVS, FIBiol; *Style*— Dr David Jones; ✉ North Carolina Zoological Park, 4401 Zoo Parkway, Asheboro, North Carolina, NC 27203 (☎ 00 910 879 7102, fax 00 910 879 2891)

JONES, David Morris; s of Capt Morris Jones, MN (ka 1941), of Beaumaris, Anglesey, and Menna Lloyd, *née* Evans; *b* 24 March 1940; *Educ* Beaumaris GS, Univ Coll Bangor (BA, DipEd); *m* 3 Dec 1971, Patricia Jones; 2 da (Sian b 24 Nov 1976, Eira b 17 Feb 1980); *Career* journalist Liverpool Daily Post and Echo Ltd 1962–63; BBC News: journalist 1963–64, sr news asst 1964–67, chief news asst 1967–71, TV news prodr 1971–82, managing ed news and current affrs Wales 1982–85, head of news and current affrs BBC Wales 1985–89; controller of news and current affrs TVS Television Ltd 1989–92, head of prog devpt HTV plc 1994–96, currently md Merlin Broadcast Ltd; dir: Merlin TV Ltd, Merlin Media Services Ltd, Splash Post Productions Ltd, Splash Computer Graphics Ltd, McCarthy Communications Ltd, NewsNet UK Ltd, The National Radio Corporation Ltd; memb: RTS, Radio TV News Dirs' Assoc (USA), Inst of Welsh Affrs, BAFTA, ESU; *Recreations* sailing; *Style*— David Morris Jones, Esq; ✉ 21 Uppercliff Close, Penarth, South Glamorgan CF64 1BE (☎ 01222 707018); Merlin Broadcast Ltd, The Wharf, Schooner Way, Cardiff Bay, Cardiff CF1 5EQ

JONES, Della Louise Gething; da of Cyril Vincent Jones (d 1982), and Eileen Gething Jones; *Educ* Neath Girls' GS, Royal Coll of Music (LRAM, ARCM, GRSM); *m* 2 April 1988, Paul Anthony Hooper Vigars, s of Norman Vigars; 1 s (Raphael b 1989); *Career* mezzo-soprano; soloist ENO 1977–82, Sung with all maj Br opera cos and at opera houses and concert halls throughout Europe, USA, USSR and Japan (specializing in Rossini, Handel and Mozart); Dido in Les Troyens (WNO) 1987, Ramiro in Finta Giardinera and Cecilio in Lucio Silla (Mostly Mozart Festival NY), Sorceress in Dido and Aeneas (Buckingham Palace tercentenary celebration of William and Mary 1988), Rosina in Il Barbier di Siviglia (Covent Garden) 1990, Handel's Riccardo Primo (in Cyprus and Covent Garden, to celebrate 800th anniversary of Richard I's arrival in Cyprus) 1991, Sesto in Mozart's La Clemenza de Tito (with Acad of Ancient Music, Japan) 1991; Laurence Olivier Award nomination for Rosina in The Barber of Seville ENO 1988; extensive recordings (incl Recital of Rossini arias 1990, and Spanish and French songs), frequent radio and tv broadcasts incl soloist Last Night of the Proms 1993; hon fell Welsh Coll of Music and Drama 1995; *Recreations* collecting elephants, visiting Venice for Bellini, writing cadenzas, animal welfare; *Style*— Miss Della Jones; ✉ c/o Music International, 13 Ardilaun Road, Highbury, London N5 2QR (☎ 0171 359 5183)

JONES, Denis Raymond; s of Joseph David Jones (d 1981), of Marton, Cleveland, and Gladys Margaret, *née* Lennox; *b* 24 Sept 1950; *Educ* Eston Co Modern Sch; *m* 15 June 1990, Linda, da of Czeslaw Dworowski; 1 s (Samuel Joseph b 6 Feb 1989); *Career* press photographer; trainee marine engr 1966–70, maintenance engr London Zoo 1970–72, photographer Fleet St News Agency 1972–74, freelance photographer (Daily Express, Evening News, Sun) 1974–76; staff photographer: Evening News (mainly fashion assignments) 1976–80, Evening Standard 1985– (freelance 1980–85); *Recreations* video photography, collecting nostalgia, mountain trekking, country walks; *Clubs* Marylebone Rifle and Pistol, London Practical Shooting; *Style*— Denis Jones, Esq; ✉ Evening Standard, Northcliffe House, 2 Derry St, London W8 5EE (☎ 0171 938 7562 mobile 0836 241158)

JONES, Rev Derwyn Morris; s of Alun Jones (d 1949), and Ethel, *née* Morris (d 1955); *b* 6 Sept 1934, Rhos, Wrexham; *Educ* Ruabon GS, UCNW Bangor, (BA, BD), Bala-Bangor Independent Theol Coll; *m* 23 July 1960, Eileen, da of Owen Glyndwr Roberts; 1 da (Bethan Morris (Mrs Batten) b 2 July 1962), 1 s (Alun Morris (b 17 July 1966); *Career* min of the Gospel: Horeb Welsh Congregational Church Penydarren Merthyr Tydfil 1959–66, Christian Temple Welsh Congregational Church Ammanford Dyfed 1966–81 (Mayor's chaplain Co Borough of Merthyr Tydfil during disaster at Aberfan); gen sec Union of Welsh Independents 1981–, pres Cytun (Churches Together in Wales) 1993–94 (first moderator of steering ctee 1990–92); Union of Welsh Independents rep: Cncl of Churches Britain and Ireland, Conf of Euro Churches, World Alliance Reformed Churches, World Cncl of Churches; chm Int Congregational Fellowship 1994–97, sec Welsh Inter-denominational Hymn Book (in preparation); author of religious and literary articles in Welsh periodicals; *Recreations* reading (particularly biographies), walking, listening to music (particularly the organ); *Style*— The Rev Derwyn Morris Jones; ✉ General Secretary, Union of Welsh Independents, Tŷ John Penri, 11 St Helen's Road, Swansea, W Glamorgan SA1 4AL (☎ 01792 467040/652542, fax 01792 650647)

JONES, Diana Wynne; da of Richard Aneurin Jones (d 1953), of Thaxted, Essex (d 1953), and Marjorie, *née* Jackson; *b* 16 Aug 1934; *Educ* Friends' Sch Saffron Walden, St Anne's Coll Oxford (BA); *m* 1956, Prof John Anthony Burrow, s of William Burrow; 3 s (Richard William b 1958, Michael Peter b 1961, Colin John b 1963); *Career* author (mainly of children's books) 1942–, completed first book 1946; books published USA, Japan, Germany, Holland, France, Scandinavia and Italy; winner: Guardian award for Children's Books 1978, Boston Globe/Horn Book (Honours) award 1984 and 1986; judge: Guardian Award Panel 1979–81, Whitbread Award Panel (Children's Section) 1988; memb Soc of Authors; *Books* Changeover (1970), Wilkins' Tooth (1973), The Ogre Downstairs (1974), Eight Days of Luke (1975), Cart and Cwidder (1975), Dogsbody (1975), Power of Three (1976), Drowned Ammet (1977), Charmed Life (1977), Who Got Rid of Angus Flint? (1978), The Spellcoats (1979), The Magicians of Caprona (1980), The Four Grannies (1980), The Homeward Bounders (1981), The Time of the Ghost (1981), Witch Week (1982), Warlock at the Wheel and other stories (1984), The Skivers' Guide (1984), Archers' Goon (1984, televised BBC 1992), Fire and Hemlock (1985), Howl's Moving Castle (1986), A Tale of Time City (1987), The Lives of Christopher Chant (1988), Chair Person (1989), Wild Robert (1989), Hidden Turnings (1989), Castle in the Air (1990), Black Maria (1991, US version Aunt Maria), Yes Dear (1992), A Sudden Wild Magic (1992), The Crown of Dalemark (1993), Hexwood (1993), Fantasy Stories (1994), The Tough Guide to Fantasyland (1996), Minor Arcana (1996); *Style*— Ms Diana Wynne Jones; ✉ 9 The Polygon, Bristol BS8 4PW (☎ 0117 927 7845); c/o Laura Cecil, 17 Alwyne Villas, London N1 2HG (☎ 0171 354 1790)

JONES, Prof Douglas Samuel; MBE (1945); s of Jesse Dewis Jones (d 1932), and Bessie, *née* Streather (d 1992); *b* 10 Jan 1922; *Educ* Wolverhampton GS, CCC Oxford (MA, hon fell 1980), Univ of Manchester (DSc); *m* 23 Sept 1950, Ivy, da of Henry Styles (d 1932); 1 s (Philip b 1960), 1 da (Helen b 1958); *Career* WWII Flt Lt RAFVR 1941–45; fell Cwlth Fund MIT 1947–48; Univ of Manchester (asst lectr, lectr, sr lectr) 1948–57, res prof NY Univ 1955, prof of mathematics Univ of Keele 1957–64, visiting prof Courant Inst 1962–63, Ivory prof of mathematics Univ of Dundee 1964–92 (emeritus 1992); memb: Mathematical Sci Sub Ctee 1971–86 (chm 1976–86), Cncl Royal Soc 1973–74, UGC 1976–86, Computer Bd 1977–82, Visiting Ctee Open Univ 1982–87, Cncl Inst of Mathematics and its Applications 1982– (pres 1988–89); Keith prize Royal Soc of Edinburgh 1974, van der Pol Gold medal of Int Union of Radio Sci 1981, Naylor prize of London Mathematical Soc 1987; Hon DSc Univ of Strathclyde 1975; CMath, CEng, FIMA 1964, FRSE 1967, FRS 1968, FIEE 1989; *Books* Electrical and Mechanical Oscillations (1961), Theory of Electromagnetism (1964), Generalised Functions (1966), Introductory Analysis (Vol 1 1969, Vol 2 1970), Methods in Electromagnetic Wave Propagation (1979, reissued as two volumes 1987, 2 edn (one vol) 1994), Elementary Information Theory (1979), The Theory of Generalised Functions (1982), Differential Equations and Mathematical Biology (1983), Acoustic and Electromagnetic Waves (1986), Assembly Programming and the 8086 Microprocessor (1988), 80x86 Assembly Programming (1991); *Clubs* United Oxford and Cambridge Univ; *Style*— Prof Douglas Jones, MBE, FRSE, FRS; ✉ Department of Mathematics and Computer Science, The University, Dundee DD1 4HN (☎ 01382 223181 and 344486)

JONES, Dr (Hilary) Edgar; s of Edgar George Jones, and Beryl Gertrude, *née* Mathews; *b* 20 July 1953; *Educ* St Clement Danes GS London, Oriel Coll Oxford (MA), Nuffield Coll Oxford (DPhil), United Medical and Dental Schools (Guy's Campus) London (PhD); *m* 1993, Dr Rachel Ann Lyons; 1 da (Imogen b 2 July 1996); *Career* partnership historian Ernst & Whinney 1979–81, historian GKN plc 1982–89, partnership historian Price Waterhouse 1989–; academic visitor Business History Unit LSE 1981–88, pt/t lectr in business history UCL 1985–88, sr res fell LSE 1993–96; hon treas Business Archives Cncl 1984–88; FRHistS 1984; *Books* Accountancy and the British Economy 1840–1980: the Evolution of Ernst & Whinney (1981), Industrial Architecture in Britain 1750–1939 (1985), A History of GKN (2 vols, 1987 and 1990), The Memoirs of Edwin Waterhouse (ed, 1988), True and Fair, A History of Price Waterhouse (1995); *Recreations* cricket, recreations, fell walking; *Clubs* MCC, Wasps FC; *Style*— Dr Edgar Jones

JONES, Edward David Brynmor; s of David Jones, and Margot, *née* Derricourt; *b* 20 Oct 1939; *Educ* Haileybury, AA Sch of Architecture (AA Dipl); *m* 1 (m dis); 1 s, 2 da; m 2, Margot, *née* Griffin; 1 s, 2 da; *Career* architect; princ in private practice 1973–89, in partnership with Jeremy Dixon 1989–; cmmns incl: Royal Opera House 1983–, Henry Moore Fndn Perry Green 1989–, Henry Moore Inst Leeds 1989–93, Darwin Coll Univ of Cambridge 1989–93, Robert Gordon Univ Aberdeen 1991–93, superstores for J Sainsbury plc (Plymouth and Bath), Univ of Portsmouth 1993, luxury housing New Delhi, Nat Portrait Gallery London 1994–, Oxford Sch of Business Univ of Oxford 1996; tutor: AA, Poly of Central London and Univ Coll Dublin 1968–72; sr tutor RCA Sch of Environmental Design 1973–83; adjunct prof Univ of Toronto 1983–89 (visiting prof 1973–82); visiting prof: Univ Coll Dublin 1971–73, Cornell, Rice, Harvard, Yale, Princeton Univs 1973–; RIBA external examiner: Kingston Univ, Portsmouth Univ, Heriott Watt Univ, Univ of Wales, AA 1985; vice pres AA 1995– (memb Cncl 1993–); *Awards* first prize: Northampton County Offices 1973, Mississauga City Hall Canada 1982 (Govr General's Award for Architecture 1988), Bus Station Venice - A Gateway for Venice 1990, Venice Biennale 1991; *Books* A Guide to the Architecture of London (with Christopher Woodward, 1983); contrib to architectural jls; *Clubs* RAC; *Style*— Edward Jones, Esq; ✉ Jeremy Dixon Edward Jones, 41 Shelton Street, London WC2H 9HJ (☎ 0171 240 7044, fax 0171 240 7114)

JONES, Gen Sir (Charles) Edward Webb; KCB (1989), CBE (1985); s of late Gen Sir Charles Jones, GCB, CBE, MC (d 1988), of Amesbury Abbey, Amesbury, Wilts, and Ouida Margaret Jones; *b* 25 Sept 1936; *Educ* Portora Royal Sch Enniskillen NI; *m* 20 Feb 1965, Suzanne Vere, da of G R P Leschallas, of Little Canon, Wateringbury, Kent; 2 s (Hume b 1967, Benjamin b 1978), 1 da (Jemma b 1971); *Career* cmmnd Oxford and Bucks LI 1956, Green Jackets 1958, Royal Green Jackets 1967, Maj DAA and QMG HQ 7 Armd Bde 1968, Lt-Col directing staff Staff Coll 1973, CO 1 Bn Royal Green Jackets 1974, Col MO4 MOD 1976, RCDS 1980, Brig Cdr 6 Armd Bde 1981, Cdr Br Military Advsy and Trg Team Zimbabwe 1983, Maj-Gen Dir Gen TA and Orgn 1985, Col Cmdt Royal Army Educnl Corps 1986–93, Cdr 3 Armd Div 1987, Lt-Gen QMG 1988, Col Cmdt 3 Bn Royal Green Jackets 1988, Gen UK Mil Rep HQ NATO 1992–95; Black Rod House of Lords 1995–; *Recreations* fishing, golf; *Clubs* Army and Navy; *Style*— Gen Sir Edward Jones, KCB, CBE; ✉ House of Lords, London SW1A 0PW

JONES, Emlyn Bartley; MBE (1975); s of Ernest Jones, MM (d 1955), of Buckley, Clywd, and Sarah Jones (d 1982); *b* 9 Dec 1920; *Educ* Alun GS Mold Clywd, Normal Coll Bangor N Wales (CertEd), Loughborough Coll (Dip in PE); *m* 27 March 1944, (Constance) Inez, da of Richard William Jones, of Mold, Clwyd; 1 da (Madeleine Bartley (Mrs Ward) b 11 Oct 1946); *Career* Flt Lt Radar Branch 1941–46, cmmnd Flt Lt 1943, demobbed 1946; teacher history and physical educn Flint Modern Secdy Sch Clwyd 1946, tech rep CCPR N Wales 1947–51, tech advsr CCPR London HQ 1951–62, TV sports commentator ITV 1955–, dir Crystal Palace Nat Sports Centre 1962–78, dir gen The Sports Co 1978–83, self employed conslt (sport and leisure) 1983–; chm The Top 100 Club; pres and hon fell Br Inst of Sports Admins, vice pres Nat Assoc of Boys' Clubs, individual memb CCPR; FIMgt 1984; *Books* Learning Lawn Tennis (1960), Sport in Space (1985); *Recreations* golf, skiing, watching sport, reading, walking; *Clubs* Royal Air Force; *Style*— Emlyn Jones, Esq, MBE; ✉ Chwarae Teg, 1B Allison Grove, Dulwich, London SE21 7ER (☎ 0181 693 7528)

JONES, Prof Emrys; s of Samuel Garfield Jones (d 1969), and Annie, *née* Williams (d 1983); *b* 17 Aug 1920; *Educ* Aberdare Boys' GS, Univ Coll of Wales Aberystwyth (BSc, MSc, PhD); *m* 7 Aug 1948, Iona Vivien, da of Richard Hywel Hughes (d 1972); 2 da (Catrin b 1955, Rhianon b 1958, d 1980); *Career* asst lectr in geography Univ Coll London 1947–50, lectr and sr lectr Queen's Univ Belfast 1950–58, reader and prof LSE 1959–84, emeritus 1984; conslt in planning and urbanisation; Royal Geographical Soc: memb Cncl 1972–78, vice pres 1978–83; Hon Soc of Cymmrodorion: memb Cncl 1978–, chm 1983–89, pres 1989–; memb Govt Ctee of Enquiry into Allotment 1969, chm Regnl Studies Assoc 1968–70; Royal Geographical Soc Victoria Medal 1977; fell: Univ of Wales 1946–47, Rockefeller Fndn NY; FRGS 1947; hon fell Univ Coll of Wales 1991, Hon DSc Queen's Univ Belfast 1978, Hon DUniv Open Univ 1990; *Books* Social Geography of Belfast (1960), Introduction to Human Geography (1964), Towns and Cities (1965), Atlas of London (1970), Cities (with E Van Zandt, 1974), Introduction to Social Geography (with J Eyles, 1977), Metropolis (1990); *Recreations* books, music; *Clubs* Athenaeum; *Style*— Prof Emrys Jones; ✉ 51 Lower King's Road, Berkhamsted, Herts HP4 2AA

JONES, Prof Emrys Lloyd; s of Peter Jones (d 1984), and Elizabeth Jane, *née* Evans; *b* 30 March 1931; *Educ* Neath GS, Magdalen Coll Oxford (BA, Violet Vaughan Morgan scholarship, Charles Oldham Shakespeare prize); *m* 1 Sept 1965, Barbara Maud, da of Leonard Everett; 1 da (Hester b 1967); *Career* Univ of Oxford: fell and tutor Magdalen Coll 1955–77, reader in English 1977–84, Goldsmiths' prof of English lit 1984–, fell New Coll 1984–; FBA 1982; *Books* Scenic Form in Shakespeare (1971), The Origins of Shakespeare (1977), Poems of Henry Howard, Earl of Surrey (ed 1964), Antony and Cleopatra (1977), New Oxford Book of Sixteenth-Century Verse (1991); *Recreations* looking at buildings, opera; *Style*— Prof Emrys Jones, FBA; ✉ New College, Oxford OX1 3BN (☎ 01865 279522)

JONES, Dr Emyr Wyn; s of Evan Walter Jones, of Bodelen, Ffordd Caerdydd, Pwllheli, Gwynedd, and Buddug Morwenna Jones; *b* 23 Feb 1950; *Educ* Pwllheli GS, Univ of Nottingham (DM), Univ of Liverpool (MB ChB); *m* 19 April 1974, Patricia Anne, da of Crowley Hammond (d 1989), of Walton on Naze, Essex; 1 s (Dafydd Benjamin b 28 Nov 1981), 3 da (Anne-Mair b 11 May 1976, Rhiannon Clare b 27 July 1978, Sioned Patricia b 17 March 1980); *Career* registrar in med Royal Liverpool Hosp 1976–78, clinical res fell and hon sr registrar Dept of Med Univ Hosp Queen's Med Centre Nottingham 1979–86, conslt physician specialising in diabetes mellitus and endocrinology 1986–; author of papers on: platelets, thrombosis, diabetes; clinical tutor Doncaster Postgrad Med Fedn, dir of clinical servs Med Directorate Doncaster Royal and Montagu Hosp NHS Tst; memb Med and Scientific Section Br Diabetic Assoc; memb BMA, FRCP 1992 (MRCP 1978); *Recreations* playing guitar in a rock 'n' roll band, all sorts of music, ornithology; *Style*— Dr Emyr Jones; ✉ 16 St Eric's Rd, Bessacarr, South Yorkshire DN4 6NG (☎ 01302 531059); Doncaster Royal Infirmary, Armthorpe Rd, Doncaster, S Yorks DN2 5LT (☎ 01302 366666)

JONES, Dr Eurfron Gwynne; da of William Gwynne Jones (d 1967), and Annie, *née* Harries (d 1975); *b* 24 Sept 1934; *Educ* Aberdare Girls' GS, Univ Coll Cardiff, Univ of Wales (BSc, PhD); *m* 13 Sept 1968, Michael John Coyle; 1 s (David Michael Gwynne b 17 Sept 1975); *Career* joined BBC as gen trainee 1959; prodr educn programmes for sch and adults 1959–75, freelance writer and broadcaster, media conslt for Int Children's Centre and Educn Cmmn of the States 1975–83, asst head of Sch BBC Radio 1983–84, BBC head of Sch TV 1984–87, controller educnl broadcasting 1987–92, dir of educn 1992–94; visiting prof Inst of Educn London 1995–; memb Cncl Royal Inst, vice pres RTS; Hon LLD Exeter 1990, Hon Doctorate Open Univ 1996; fell Univ of Wales Cardiff 1996; FRTS; *Books* Children Growing UP (1973), The First Five Years (1975), Television Magic (1978); *Recreations* photography; *Style*— Dr Eurfron Gwynne Jones

JONES, Sir Ewart Ray Herbert; kt (1963); s of William Jones (d 1924); *b* 16 March 1911; *Educ* Grove Park Sch Wrexham, Univ Coll of N Wales Bangor, Univ of Manchester (MA, DSc, PhD); *m* 1937, Frances Mary Copp; 1 s, 2 da; *Career* Sir Samuel Hall prof of chemistry Manchester Univ 1947–55, Waynflete prof of chemistry Univ of Oxford 1955–78, emeritus prof 1978; hon fell Magdalen Coll Oxford (fell 1955–78); chm Anchor and Guardian Housing Assoc 1979–84; FRS; *Style*— Sir Ewart Jones, FRS; ✉ 6 Sandy Lane, Yarnton, Oxford OX5 1PB (☎ 01865 372581)

JONES, Frederick Charles (Freddie); s of Charles Edward Jones, of Stoke-on-Trent, and Ida Elizabeth, *née* Goodwin; *b* 12 Sept 1927; *Educ* Longton HS, Rose Bruford Coll of Speech & Drama (acting prize, radio prize); *m* Jennifer Elizabeth, da of Reginald Heslewood (d 1990); 3 s (Toby Edward b 7 Sept 1966, Rupert Frederick b 6 July 1968, Caspar Boyd b 16 Nov 1971); *Career* actor; worked in repertory at: Stockton on Tees, Bridlington, Lincoln, Bristol Old Vic, The Flora Robson Playhouse, University Theatre Newcastle upon Tyne, The Royal Exchange Theatre; *Theatre* London incl: season with RSC (Aldwych), Mister (Duchess), Dear Janet Rosenberg (Hampstead), The Cloud (Hampstead), The Dresser (Queen's), Tramway Road (Lyric Hammersmith), One Man Show John Clare (Lyric Hammersmith), Sunset and Glories (The Playhouse Leeds); RSC incl: The Marat Sade, Birthday Party, Afore Night Come, The Lower Depths, Touch of the Poet (toured Venice and Dublin), Death of a Salesman (toured Hong Kong), Malvolio in Twelfth Night 1991–92, title role in Shadwell's The Virtuoso 1991–92; *Television* incl: Secret Orchards, Brensham People, Germinal, Uncle Vanya, Nana, Sword of Honour, Sweeney Todd, The Caesars, Pennies from Heaven, Joe's Ark, Ghosts, John Clare Omnibus, Tiny Revolutions, The Last Evensong, Vanity Fair, Kremlin Fairwell, Mashenka, Shoot the Revolution, Vaclav Havel's The Interview, Inspector Morse; *Radio* numerous incl the solo performances of: Look Here Old Son, John Clare in a Song in the Night, Gogol, Skelton - The Winking Goose, Peter Barnes' People: *Film* incl: The Bliss of Mrs Blossom, Antony and Cleopatra, Far From The Madding Crowd, Accident, Juggernaut, Zulu Dawn, The Elephant Man, Fire Fox, Krull, Dune, Fellini's E la Nave va (and The Ship Sails On), Erik the Viking, Karel Kachyna's The Last Butterfly, The Chronicles of Young Judy, Never Ending Story III, Cold Comfort Farm; *Awards* Monte Carlo Golden Nymph Best Actor for Claudius in The Caesars; *Recreations* gardening, cooking, golf; *Clubs* Garrick; *Style*— Freddie Jones, Esq; ✉ c/o James Sharkey Associates Ltd, 21 Golden Square, London W1R 3PA (☎ 0171 434 3801, fax 0171 494 1547)

JONES, Dr Gareth; s of Lyell Jones (d 1937), and Ceridwen, *née* Jenkins (d 1992); *b* 28 May 1933; *Educ* Nantyglo GS, Christ's Coll Cambridge (MA), Birkbeck Coll London (PhD); *m* 1, 9 Aug 1958 (m dis 1988), Anne, da of Sidney Pickard (d 1987), of Bampton, Oxfordshire; 1 s (Christopher b 24 July 1962), 2 da (Katy b 8 Aug 1963, Becky b 15 March 1966); m 2, 7 April 1989, Helen Patricia Rahming; *Career* RAF 1954–56; Stationers' Company's Sch 1957–59, Dulwich Coll 1959–63, Esso Petroleum Co 1963–69, Booz Allen and Hamilton mgmnt conslts 1969–85 (vice pres 1973, managing ptnr UK 1974), dir Booz Allen & Hamilton Inc 1981–84, managing ptnr Ernst & Whinney mgmnt conslts 1985–89; chm Nevill Hall & District NHS Tst 1994–; non-exec dir: Gwent Health Authy 1990–92, Welsh Nat Opera 1990–94, Powys Health Care NHS Tst 1992–93; chm: Wales 2010, Inst of Welsh Affairs (chm Research Ctee 1994–), Welsh Advsy Ctee Br Cncl 1993–, Mansel Thomas Tst 1995–; dir Shaw Homes 1996–; memb Welsh Health Planning Forum 1989–95, govr Univ of Glamorgan 1992–; FIAM 1987; *Books* Wales 2010: Creating Our Future (jtly, 1993), Welsh Roots and Branches (1994); *Recreations* travel, walking, opera; *Clubs* Cardiff and County, IOD; *Style*— Dr Gareth Jones; ✉ Tre Graig House, Tre Graig Road, Bwlch, Powys LD3 7SJ (☎ 01874 730650, fax 01874 730629)

JONES, Prof (David) Gareth; s of William John Jones (d 1973), of Cray, Powys, and Katie Blodwen, *née* Jones; *b* 7 March 1934; *Educ* Priory GS Shrewsbury, Univ Coll of Wales Aberystwyth (BSc, PhD, DSc); *m* 25 June 1960, Anita Mary, da of Kenneth Joseph John (d 1982), of Neath, W Glamorgan; 3 s (Richard Huw, Philip Alun Rhys, Justin Gareth); *Career* RAF aircrew Coastal Cmd 1952–54; microbiologist Welsh Plant Breeding Station 1959–65; Dept of Agric Scis Univ Coll Wales: lectr 1965–68, sr lectr 1968–81, reader 1981–85, prof 1985–; sec Fedn of Br Plant Pathologists 1971–76, pres Assoc of Applied Biologists 1990 (memb 1973, sec 1976–86, pres elect 1989), memb Cncl Parly and Scientific Ctee 1976–, reviews ed Sci in Parliament 1993–; memb: Soc of Applied Bacteriology 1960, Br Mycological Soc 1966; *Books* Cereal Diseases - Their Pathology and Control (1978), Plant Pathology - Principles and Practices (1987); *Recreations* walking, surfing, fishing, travel; *Style*— Prof Gareth Jones; ✉ Welsh Institute of Rural Studies, University of Wales, Aberystwyth, Dyfed SY23 3DD (☎ 01970 622215)

JONES, Gareth D; *m*; 1 s, 1 da; *Career* Abbey National plc: joined as asst gen mangr and treas 1989, dir of retail ops until 1993, exec dir and treas 1993–, also i/c Europe 1994–95, md Treasy & Wholesale Banking 1996–; FCA, FCT; *Recreations* steam engines, model engineering, politics, opera, reading; *Clubs* RAC; *Style*— Gareth D Jones, Esq; ✉ Abbey National plc, Abbey House, Baker Street, London NW1 6XL (☎ 0171 612 4378, fax 0171 612 4464)

JONES, Prof Gareth Hywel; QC (1986); s of Benjamin Thomas Jones (d 1967), and Mabel Jane Jones (d 1977); *b* 10 Nov 1930; *Educ* Porth Co GS, VCL (LLB), St Catharine's Coll Cambridge (MA, LLD), Harvard Univ (LLM); *m* 21 March 1959, Vivienne Joy, da of Colin Edward Paukridge (d 1983); 2 s (Christopher b 1960, Steven b 1961), 1 da (Alison b 1965); *Career* fell Trinity Coll Cambridge 1961– (vice master 1986–92), Downing prof of the laws of England Cambridge 1975–; chm Fitzwilliam Museum Syndicate 1987–; fell UCL 1988; FBA 1982; foreign memb Royal Netherlands Acad of Arts & Sci 1991; *Clubs* Beafsteak; *Style*— Prof Gareth Jones, QC, FBA; ✉ Trinity Coll, Cambridge CB2 1TQ (☎ 01223 338473)

JONES, His Hon (John) Geoffrey Ramon Owen; s of Wyndham Christopher Jones (d 1948), of Llanelli, and Lilias Rosalind Christina, *née* Johns (d 1992); *b* 14 Sept 1928; *Educ* Brighton and Hove GS, St Michael's Sch Bryn Llanelli Dyfed (head boy), St David's Coll Lampeter, UCL (LLB, LLM 1985); *m* 17 July 1954, Sheila, da of Harry John Gregory (d 1936); 3 s (Geraint Timothy b 13 Nov 1959, Simon David b 30 July 1962, William John b 21 Sept 1965); *Career* cmmnd RASC 1946–48; dir electrical wholesale co 1949–52, called to the Bar Gray's Inn 1956 (Holker Jr scholar), pupilages with late His Hon Geraint Rees, and John Dexter Stocker, Esq (now Rt Hon Sir John D Stocker) 1956–57, in practice on Midland Circuit: from chambers Leicester 1958–70, from chambers London 1970–75; circuit judge (Midland & Oxford Circuit) 1975–96, chm Mental Health Review Tbnl for Wales 1996–; memb Bar Cncl 1970–72, hon sr academic fell De Montfort Univ (formerly Leicester Poly), Hon LLD De Montfort Univ; *Recreations* golf; *Style*— His Hon Geoffrey Jones; ✉ Leicester County Court, Wellington Street, Leicester (☎ 0116 265 3400)

JONES, George Briscoe; CBE (1988); s of Arthur Briscoe Jones (d 1975), and Mary Alexandra, *née* Taylor (d 1982); *b* 1 June 1929; *Educ* Caldy Grange GS, Wallasey GS; *m* 26 March 1955, Audrey Patricia, da of Thomas Arthur Kendrick (d 1976); 2 da (Christine Jennifer (Mrs Hawkins) b 22 May 1958, Deborah Ann (Mrs Campbell) b 4 July 1961); *Career* Army 1947–49; clerk rising to commercial mangr and co sec BEC Ltd 1949–67, planning mangr Agric Div Unilever 1967–71, chm Unitrition International Ltd 1976–82; dir: BOCM Silcock 1974–82 (corp planning mangr 1971–74), Cooperative Development Agency 1982–90, Job Ownership Ltd 1984–95, Partnership in Business Ltd 1988–94; *Recreations* reading, drama, painting, sculpture; *Clubs* Wallaseyans; *Style*— George Jones, Esq, CBE; ✉ 32 Cleveland Drive, Little Sutton, South Wirral L66 4XY (☎ 0151 347 1448)

JONES, George Quentin; s of John Clement Jones, of Walton on Naze, Essex, and Marjorie, *née* Gibson (d 1991); *b* 28 Feb 1945; *Educ* Highfield Sch Wolverhampton; *m* 1, April 1972 (m dis 1989), Diana, *née* Chittenden; 1 s (Timothy Edward b 13 Jan 1979), 1 da (Jennifer Lucy b 2 Jan 1976); m 2, 29 Dec 1990, Teresa Grace, da of John Lancelot Rolleston; *Career* trainee journalist Eastern Daily Press 1963–67, journalist South Wales Argus and Western Mail 1967–69, Reuters London 1969, Parly staff The Times 1969–73, Parly and political corr The Scotsman 1973–82; political corr: The Sunday Telegraph 1982–85, The Sunday Times 1985–86, The Daily Telegraph 1986–88; political ed The Daily Telegraph 1988–, regular bdcaster BBC and independent radio; chm Journalists Parly Lobby 1987–88, chm Parly Press Gallery 1996–97; *Clubs* Athenaeum; *Style*— George Jones, Esq; ✉ The Daily Telegraph, 1 Canada Square, Canary Wharf, London E14 5DT (☎ 0171 538 5000)

JONES, Prof George William; s of George William Jones (d 1973), of Wolverhampton, and Grace Annie, *née* Cowmeadow (d 1982); *b* 4 Feb 1938; *Educ* Wolverhampton GS, Jesus Coll Oxford (BA, MA), Nuffield Coll Oxford (DPhil); *m* 14 Sept 1963, Diana Mary, da of Henry Charles Bedwell (d 1982), of Kidlington; 1 s (Maxwell b 1969), 1 da (Rebecca b 1966); *Career* lectr Univ of Leeds 1965–66 (asst lectr 1963–65); LSE: lectr 1966–71, sr lectr 1971–74, reader 1974–76, prof of govt 1976–, chm LSE Graduate Sch 1990–93, vice chm Appts Ctee 1996–; Layfield Ctee on Local Govt Fin 1974–76, vice chm Political Sci and Int Rels Ctee of Social Sci Res Cncl 1978–81 (memb 1977–81); memb: Nat Consumer Cncl 1991–, DOE Jt Working Pty on the Internal Mgmnt of Local Authorities in England 1992–93; FRHistS 1980, memb RIPA 1963 (memb Cncl 1984–90); *Books* Borough Politics (1969), Herbert Morrison (co-author, 1973), Political Leadership in Local Authorities (jt ed, 1978), New Approaches to the Study of Central-Local Government Relationships (ed, 1980), The Case for Local Government (jt author, 1985), Between Centre and Locality (jt ed, 1985), West European Prime Ministers (ed, 1991), The Government of London (co-author, 1991), The Impact of Population Size on Local Authority Costs and Effectiveness (co-author, 1993), Local Government: The Management Agenda (1993), Joint Working Between Local Authorities (jt author, 1995), The Role of the Local Authority Chief Executive in Local Governance (jtly, 1996); *Recreations* cinema, eating, reading, dancing; *Clubs* National Film; *Style*— Prof G W Jones; ✉ Department of

Government, London School of Economics and Political Science, Houghton St, London WC2A 2AE (☎ 0171 955 7179, fax 0171 831 1707, telex 24655 LSELON G)

JONES, Geraint Martyn; s of Robert Kenneth Jones, of Luton, and Frances Elizabeth, *née* Mayo; *b* 15 July 1948; *Educ* St Albans Sch, Christ's Coll Cambridge (MA, LLM), Inns of Court Sch of Law; *m* 29 July 1978, Caroline Mary Jones, da of Lt Peter Edwin Cecil Eyres, RNVR (d 1975); 1 s (Robert b 1980), 1 da (Louisa b 1982); *Career* called to the Bar Gray's Inn 1972; in practice (principally in commercial, property and planning law): London 1972–74, SE Circuit (mainly in Cambridge) 1974–; memb Chancery Bar Assoc, chm Rent Assessment Ctees 1985–, sr circuit rep Cambridge Bar Mess 1991, memb SE Circuit Ctee 1991–94; asst cmmr Parly Boundary Cmmn 1992–; chm Madingley Sch Tst 1988–91, chm of Govrs Bourn Sch 1993–; Liveryman Worshipful Co of Glaziers 1992; memb: RYA, RNLI, OGA, Cruising Assoc, BASC; *Recreations* sailing, shooting, jazz, carpentry, cooking; *Clubs* Little Ship, Royal Norfolk and Suffolk Yacht, Grafham Water Sailing; *Style*— Geraint Jones, Esq; ✉ Fenners Chambers, 3 Madingley Rd, Cambridge CB3 OEE (☎ 01223 368761, fax 01223 313007); 8–12 Priestgate, Peterborough PE1 1JA

JONES, Geraint Stanley; CBE (1993); s of Rev David Stanley Jones (d 1974); *b* 26 April 1936; *Educ* Pontypridd GS, UCNW Bangor (BA, DipEd, hon fell 1988); *m* 1961, Rhiannon, da of Emrys Williams (d 1971); 2 da (Sioned b 1965, Siwan b 1966); *Career* served RAEC, Sgt; BBC Wales: studio mangr 1960–62, prodn asst Current Affrs (TV) 1962–65, TV prodr Current Affrs 1965–69, prodr Features and Documentaries 1969–73, asst head of progs Wales 1973–74, head of progs Wales 1974–81, controller BBC Wales 1981–85, dir of public affrs 1986–87; md BBC Regnl Bdcasting 1987–89, chief exec S4C (Welsh Fourth Channel Authy) 1989–94; broadcasting conslt 1994–; dir WNO 1985–94; memb: Court and Cncl Univ Coll Wales Aberystwyth 1990–96, Arts Cncl of Wales, Br Cncl Film and TV Advsy Ctee; chm: Welsh Coll of Music and Drama, Euro Bdcasting Union TV Prog Ctee 1990–96, Ryan Davies Tst, Nat Language Centre; vice pres: Hay on Wye Festival of Literature, Llangollen Int Eisteddfod, Cardiff Business Club, Pendyrus Male Choir; memb UK Freedom from Hunger Ctee; FRSA, FRTS; *Recreations* music, painting, horse riding; *Clubs* Cardiff and County; *Style*— Geraint Stanley Jones, Esq, CBE

JONES, (Robert) Gerallt Hamlet; OBE (1996); s of Rev Richard Emrys Jones (d 1969), of Ynys Môn, and Elizabeth Ellen (d 1988); *b* 11 Sept 1934; *Educ* Denstone Coll, UCNW (BA, MA, Dip Ed); *m* 15 Sept 1962, Susan Lloyd, da of Richard Heber Lloyd Griffith (d 1975), of Borth-y-Gest; 2 s (Rhys Gerallt b 1969, Dafydd Gerallt b 1972), 1 da (Ceri Rhiannon b 1964); *Career* lectr in educn Univ of Wales 1960–65, princ Mandeville Teachers' Coll Jamaica 1965–67, warden and headmaster Llandovery Coll 1967–76, sr tutor Extra-Mural Dept Univ of Wales 1979–88, warden and dir Gregynog Hall Univ of Wales 1988–95; author of TV documentaries and series incl Joni Jones; winner: Prose Medal Nat Eisteddfod 1977 and 1979, Hugh McDiarmid Trophy 1987, Welsh Arts Cncl Poetry Award 1990; ed: Taliesin 1986–92, Books From Wales 1992–; memb Broadcasting Cncl Wales 1967–72, chm Welsh Acad 1982–87, dir Aberystwyth Devpt Studies Course 1986–; memb: Welsh Arts Cncl 1987–, Welsh Books Cncl 1992–, S4C Authy 1991–96; chm: Wales Film Cncl 1992–95, Mid Wales Centre for the Arts Tst 1993–; memb Yr Academi Cymreig (the Welsh Acad) 1964–; *Books* author of 35 vols in Welsh and English incl: Ymysg y Drain (1959), Cwlwm (1962), Y Foel Fawr (1962), Poetry of Wales 1930–70 (1972), Jamaican Landscape (1969), Jamaican Interlude (1972), Triptych (1977), Cafflogion (1979), Tair Drama (1988), Seicoleg Cardota (1989), Cerddi 1959–89 (1989); *Recreations* cricket, hill-walking; *Style*— Gerallt Jones, Esq, OBE; ✉ Leri, Dolybont, Borth, Dyfed (☎ 01970 871525)

JONES, (Thomas) Glanville; s of Evan James Jones (d 1981), of London, and Maggie, *née* Evans (d 1972); *b* 10 May 1931; *Educ* Clement Danes GS, Univ Coll London (LLB), Inns of Ct Sch of Law; *m* 29 Aug 1964, Valma Shirley, da of Ivor Jones, of Swansea; 3 s (Aled Prydderch b 1966, Dyfan Rhodri b 1968, Geraint Islwyn b 1971); *Career* called to the Bar 1956, recorder of the Crown Ct; chm The Guild for the Promotion of Welsh Music 1970–; *Recreations* music, rugby, reading; *Clubs* Ffynone (Swansea); *Style*— T Glanville Jones, Esq; ✉ Gelligron, 12 Eastcliff, Southgate, Swansea, West Glamorgan SA3 2AS (☎ 01792 233118); Angel Chambers, 94 Walter Rd, Swansea SA1 5QA (☎ 01792 464623)

JONES, Prof (Walton) Glyn; s of Emrys Jones, and Dorothy Ada, *née* North; *b* 29 Oct 1928; *Educ* Manchester GS, Pembroke Coll Cambridge (BA, MA, PhD); *m* 1, 12 June 1953 (m dis 1981), (Karen) Ruth, da of Vilhelm Olaf Fleischer; 2 s (Stephen b 1 Dec 1956, Olaf b 11 June 1958), 2 da (Monica b 9 June 1962, Anna b 29 June 1965); m 2, 30 Nov 1981, Kirsten, da of Christen Gade; *Career* reader in Danish UCL 1966–73 (Queen Alexandra lectr in Danish 1956–66), visiting prof of Danish Univ of Iceland 1971, prof of Scandinavian studies Newcastle upon Tyne 1973–86, prof of literature Faroese Acad 1979–81, prof of European literature UEA 1986–94 (emeritus prof 1994); memb Cncl Anglo-Danish Soc, hon memb Swedish Literary Soc Finland 1985, fell Royal Norwegian Acad of Sciences 1988; corresponding memb Danish Soc of Authors 1989; Kt Royal Danish Order of the Dannebrog 1994; *Books* Johannes Jørgensens modne Aår (1963), Johannes Jørgensen (1969), Denmark (1970), William Heinesen (1974), Faero og Kosmos (1974), Danish - A Grammar (with Kirsten Gade, 1981), Tove Jansson (1984), Vägen Från Mumindalen (1984), Denmark - A Modern History (1986), Georg Brandes Selected Letters (1990), Blue Guide to Denmark (with Kirsten Gade, 1992), Faroese Literature chapter in A History of Danish Literature (ed S H Rossel, 1992), Colloquial Danish (with Kirsten Gade, 1993), Colloquial Norwegian (with Kirsten Gade and Kari Båtveit, 1994); *Recreations* music, Danish church architecture; *Style*— Prof W Glyn Jones; ✉ c/o School of Modern Languages and European Studies, University of East Anglia, Norwich NR4 7TJ (☎ 01603 56161, fax 01603 250599)

JONES, Rev Canon Glyndwr; s of Bertie Samuel Jones (d 1965), of Birchgrove, Swansea, and Elizabeth Ellen Jones; *b* 25 Nov 1935; *Educ* Dynevor Sch Swansea, St Michael's Theol Coll Llandaff Univ of Wales (DipTheol); *m* 1, 13 Dec 1961, Cynthia Elaine Jenkins (d 1964); m 2, 23 July 1966, (Marion) Anita, da of David Morris (d 1969), of Plasmarl, Swansea; 1 da (Susan b 30 June 1968), 1 s (Robert b 11 Aug 1970); *Career* Nat Serv 1954–56, RAPC attached 19 Field Regt RA, served Korea, Hong Kong, demobbed Sgt AER; ordained Brecon Cathedral: deacon 1962, priest 1963; curate: Clydach 1962–64, Llangyfelach 1964–67, Sketty 1967–70; rector: Bryngwyn with Newchurch and Llanbedr, Painscastle with Llandewi Fach 1970–72; Missions to Seamen: port chaplain Swansea and Port Talbot 1972–76, sr chaplain Port of London 1976–81, sec gen The Missions to Seamen 1990– (aux ministries sec 1981–85, asst gen sec 1985–90); memb Cncl: Marine Soc 1990–, Ptnrship for World Mission 1990–, Int Christian Maritime Assoc 1990–, Merchant Navy Welfare Bd 1990–; hon chaplain Royal Alfred Seafarers Soc 1987–93, hon canon St Michael's Cathedral Kobe Japan 1988; chaplain: Worshipful Co of Information Technologists 1989, Worshipful Co of Innholders 1990, Worshipful Co of Farriers 1990, Worshipful Co of Carmen 1990; Freeman City of London 1990; chaplain to HM The Queen 1990, chaplain to the Lay Sheriff of London 1993–94; Hon Liveryman Worshipful Co of Carmen 1995; *Recreations* sport, music, reading, theatre, travel; *Style*— The Rev Canon Glyndwr Jones; ✉ The Missions to Seamen, St Michael Paternoster Royal, College Hill, London EC4R 2RL (☎ 0171 248 5202, fax 0171 248 4761)

JONES, Sir Gordon Pearce; kt (1990); s of Alun Pearce Jones (d 1979), of Swansea, and Miriam Jones; *b* 17 Feb 1927; *Educ* Swansea GS, Univ of Wales (BSc); *m* 15 Dec 1951, Gloria Stuart, da of Stuart Carr Melville, of Edinburgh; 2 s (Huw b 3 Feb 1960, Hywel (twin) b 3 Feb 1960), 1 da decd; *Career* Lt RN 1947–51; scientist: Br Iron and Steel Res Assoc 1951–56, raw material and energy planning Iron and Steel Indust 1956–64, UK industl sales mangr Esso Petroleum Co Ltd 1961–64, mktg/sales dir English Steel Corp 1964–68, dir and gen mangr Murex 1968–70, md Rotherham Tinsley Steels 1970, md Firth Vickers 1974–79, dir TW Ward plc 1979–82, chm Yorkshire Water plc 1983–96; chm Water Authorities Assoc 1987–89, memb Pres's Ctee CBI 1988–89; hon fell Univ Coll Swansea, hon DSc Univ of Bradford; Hon FIWEM; CIMgt; *Recreations* reading, music, opera, railway history, travel; *Clubs* Naval and Military; *Style*— Sir Gordon Jones

JONES, (David) Graham; *b* 16 June 1951; *Educ* Queen Elizabeth GS Wakefield, Keble Coll Oxford (MA), UCW Cardiff; *m* 23 March 1977, Lynne Francis; *Career* leader writer Glasgow Herald 1973–74; reporter: Sheffield Star 1973, The Sun 1974–79; Now! Magazine 1979–81 (reporter, dep foreign ed), Foreign Desk Daily Mail and Mail On Sunday 1981–83, Daily Telegraph 1983–89 (reporter, political staff, asst news ed, chief asst news ed, dep news ed), news ed Daily Star 1989–94, asst ed (news) Sunday Express 1994–96; *Books* Forked Tongues (1984), Own Goals (1985), The Forked Tongues Annual (1985), Plane Crazy (1986), I Don't Hate Men But.../I Don't Hate Women But... (1986), Boat Crazy (1987), The Official Candidate's Book of Political Insults (1987), I Love Sex/I Hate Sex (with Lynne Jones, 1989), The Book of Total Snobbery (with Lynne Jones, 1989); *Recreations* writing, politics, photography, gardening; *Style*— Graham Jones, Esq; ✉ 32 Kingsmead, Barnet, Herts EN5 5AY (☎ and fax 0181 441 7787)

JONES, Graham Edward; s of Edward Thomas Jones (d 1980), and Dora Rachel, *née* Hughes; *b* 22 Sept 1944; *Educ* Birkenhead Sch, Fitzwilliam Coll Cambridge (MA); *m* 29 Oct 1976, Vanessa Mary Heloïse, *née* Smith; *Career* asst master Charterhouse 1967 (later head of economics and politics and housemaster), awarder in economics Oxford and Cambridge Examination Bd 1979–91, reviser in economics JMB 1981–91, seconded to BP 1981, headmaster Repton 1987–; FRSA; *Recreations* painting, walking, music, cooking, the classics; *Style*— Graham Jones, Esq; ✉ The Hall, Repton, Derby DE6 6FH (☎ 01283 559220)

JONES, His Hon Judge (Anthony) Graham Hume; s of Sir Edward Warburton Jones (d 1993), of Co Down, and Margaret Anne Crosland Smellie (d 1953); *b* 16 Aug 1942; *Educ* Trinity Coll Glenalmond, Trinity Coll Dublin (BA); *m* 5 Nov 1966, Evelyn Ann, da of W Brice Smyth; 2 s (Hume Riverdale b 26 July 1968, Benjamin Brice b 4 March 1972), 1 da (Katharine Ann Crosland b 22 May 1975); *Career* mgmnt trainee Mardon Son & Hall Bristol 1966–71, called to the Bar Gray's Inn 1971, in practice Western Circuit 1971–93, circuit judge (Western Circuit) 1993–; *Recreations* sailing, golf; *Clubs* Royal Co Down Golf, Royal Ocean Racing, Trearddur Bay Sailing; *Style*— His Hon Judge Graham Jones; ✉ c/o Western Circuit Office, Bridge House, Sion Place, Clifton, Bristol BS8 4BN

JONES, His Hon Judge Graham Julian; s of David John Jones, CBE (d 1974), and Edna Lillie Jones, *née* Marshall; *b* 17 July 1936; *Educ* Porth Co GS, Univ of Cambridge (MA, LLM); *m* 30 Aug 1961, Dorothy, da of James Smith Tickle (d 1980), of Abergavenny; 2 s (Nicholas David Julian b 1963, Timothy James Julian b 1968), 1 da (Sarah Elizabeth b 1965); *Career* ptnr Morgan Bruce & Nicholas (slrs Cardiff) 1961–85; dep circuit judge 1975–78, recorder 1978–85; Wales & Chester Circuit: circuit judge 1985–, circuit official referee 1993–, assigned and designated judge Cardiff Co Ct 1994–; pres Assoc Law Soc of Wales 1982–84; memb: Lord Chllr's Legal Aid Advsy Ctee 1980–85, Ct Univ of Wales Coll of Cardiff 1996–, Mgmnt Ctee Centre for Professional Legal Studies Cardiff Law Sch 1996–; *Recreations* golf, boats; *Clubs* Cardiff and County, Radyr Golf (Cardiff), Royal Porthcawl Golf; *Style*— His Hon Judge Graham Jones; ✉ Civil Justice Centre, 2 Park Street, Cardiff (☎ 01222 376400)

JONES, Gwilym Haydn; MP (C) Cardiff North (majority 2,969); s of Evan Haydn Jones, and Mary Elizabeth Gwenhwyfar, *née* Moseley; *m* 1974, Linda Margaret, da of David Mathew John (d 1980), of Cardiff; 1 s (Grant), 1 da (Fay); *Career* insur broker, dir Bowring Wales Ltd 1980–92; memb Cardiff City Cncl 1969–72 and 1973–83, Parly election agent SE Cardiff 1974; MP (C) Cardiff North 1983–, memb Select Ctee on Welsh Affrs 1983–92, sec Welsh Cons Backbenchers 1984–92, PPS to Min of State for Transport 1991–92, Parly under-sec of state Welsh Office 1992–; sec All Party Parly Gp for the Fund for the Replacement of Animals in Med Experiments 1987–92; fell Welsh Livery Guild; *Recreations* golf, model railways; *Clubs* County Conservative, Cardiff & County, Rhiwbina Rugby, United Services Mess, Carlton; *Style*— Gwilym Jones, Esq, MP; ✉ House of Commons, London SW1A 0AA (☎ 0171 219 5084)

JONES, Rev Prof Gwilym Henry; s of John Lloyd Jones (d 1971), and Jennie, *née* Roberts (d 1973); *b* 16 July 1930; *Educ* Pwllheli GS, Univ Coll of N Wales Bangor (BA, PhD, DD), Jesus Coll Oxford (MA); *m* 28 March 1959, Mary Christabel, da of Owen Tudor Williams (d 1972); 2 s (Rhys b 18 May 1966, Huw b 24 Jan 1969), 1 da (Ruth b 13 April 1975); *Career* min Presbyterian Church of Wales 1956–61, prof of Hebrew Theological Coll Aberystwyth 1961–66; Univ Coll of N Wales Bangor: lectr 1966, sr lectr 1979, reader 1984, prof of religious studies 1987–95, emeritus prof 1995–, dean of arts 1988–91; dean Bangor Sch of Theology 1980–83 and 1992–95, dean of divinity Univ of Wales 1987–90; pres Soc for Old Testament Study 1995; *Books* Arweiniad i'r Hen Destament (1966), Gwirionedd y Gair (1974), Cerddi Seion (1975), Gramadeg Hebraeg y Beibl (1976), Diwinyddiaeth yr Hen Destament (1979), Y Gair Ddoe a Heddiw: Eseia o Jerwsalem (1988), 1 and 2 Kings (New Century Bible) (1984), The Nathan Narratives (1990), 1 and 2 Chronicles (Old Testament Guides) (1993), Hen Destament 1988 (1995); *Recreations* walking, gardening, music; *Style*— The Rev Prof Gwilym Jones; ✉ Coed Gadlys, Llansadwrn, Menai Bridge, Unys Môn LL59 5SE (☎ 01248 712226)

JONES, Dame Gwyneth; DBE (1986, CBE 1976); da of late Edward George Jones, and late Violet, *née* Webster; *b* 7 Nov 1936; *Educ* Twmpath Secdy Modern Sch Pontypool, RCM, Accademia Chigiana Siena, Zürich Int Opera Studio; *m* Till Haberfeld; 1 da; *Career* principal dramatic soprano: Royal Opera House Covent Garden 1963–, Vienna Staatsoper 1966–, Bavarian State Opera 1966–, Deutsche Oper Berlin 1966–; guest artiste: Paris, Met Opera NY, La Scala Milan, Zürich, Hamburg, Barcelona, Buenos Aires, Tokyo, San Francisco, Chicago, Rome, Madrid, Oslo, Moscow, Geneva, Bayreuth Festival, Salzburg Festival, Verona Festival, Edinburgh Festival; hon memb Vienna State Opera; Hon DMus: Univ of Wales, Univ of Glamorgan; Kammersängerin Austria and Bavaria, Shakespeare Prize FRG 1987; Bundesverdienstkreuz FRG 1988, commandeur de l'Ordre des Artes et des Lettres France 1992; FRCM; *Roles* incl: Ariadne in Ariadne auf Naxos, Die Feldmarschallin in Der Rosenkavalier, Brünnhilde in Die Walküre, Siegfried and Götterdämmerung, Isolde in Tristan und Isolde, Elisabeth in Tannhäuser, Senta in Der Fliegende Holländer, Leonore in Fidelio, Lady Macbeth in Macbeth, Desdemona in Otello, Kostelnicka in Jenufa, La Voix Humaine, title roles in Elektra, Salome, Helen of Egypt, Aida, Tosca, Madame Butterfly, Turandot and Norma; film, CD recordings and television roles incl: Isolde, Aida, Turandot, Brünnhilde, die Feldmarschallin, Leonore, Poppea in L'Incoronazione di Poppea, La Voix Humaine and Erwartung, title role in The Merry Widow; *Style*— Dame Gwyneth Jones, DBE; ✉ PO Box 556, CH 8037 Zürich, Switzerland

JONES, Gwyneth Ann; da of Desmond James Jones, and Mary Rita, *née* Dugdale; *b* 14 Feb 1952; *Educ* Notre Dame Convent Sch Manchester, Univ of Sussex (BA); *m* 1976, Peter Wilson Gwilliam; 1 s (Gabriel Jimi Jones b 4 Sept 1987); *Career* author; children's books under own name: Water In The Air (1977), The Influence of Ironwood (1978),

The Exchange (1979), Dear Hill (1980), Seven Tales and a Fable (1995); children's books under name of Ann Halam: Ally Ally Aster (1981), The Alder Tree (1982), King Death's Garden (1986), The Daymaker (1987), Transformations (1988), The Skybreaker (1990), Dinosaur Junction (1992), The Haunting Raven (1994), The Fear Man (1995); novels under own name: Divine Endurance (1984), Escape Plans (1986), Kairos (1988), The Hidden Ones (1988), White Queen (1991, winner of James Tiptree Jr award), Flowerdust (1993), North Wind (1994, short listed Arthur C Clarke Award); memb: SE Arts Literature Panel 1988–94, Science Fiction Foundation 1986–; *Recreations* walking, gardening, book reviewing; *Clubs* Shape; *Style*— Ms Gwyneth Jones; ✉ c/o David Higham Associates, 5–8 Lower John Street, Golden Square, London W1R 4HA (☎ 0171 437 7888, fax 0171 437 1072)

JONES, Prof Hamlyn Gordon (Lyn); s of Douglass Gordon Jones (d 1978), and Mary Elsie, *née* Hoadley (d 1966); *b* 7 Dec 1947; *Educ* St Lawrence Coll Ramsgate, St John's Coll Cambridge (MA, Lister entrance scholarship, Wright Prize), Australian National Univ (PhD, ANU scholarship); *m* 1972, Amanda Jane, da of Sir James Perowne Ivo Myles Corry; 2 da (Katherine Myleta Gordon b June 1974, Julia Patricia Gordon b Nov 1976); *Career* res scientist Plant Breeding Inst Cambridge 1972–76, Title A res fellow St John's Coll Cambridge (Henry Humphreys prize) 1973–76, lectr in botany Univ of Glasgow 1977–78, ldr Stress Physiology Gp East Malling Res Station Maidstone 1978–88; International Research Horticulture: dir Crop Science Res 1988–95, dir Res Strategy 1995–; special prof Univ of Nottingham 1992–, hon prof Univ of Birmingham 1995–; visiting prof: Univ of Toronto 1981, Univ of Basilicata 1989–90; memb Cncl Soc of Experimental Biology 1986–90; govr South Warwickshire Coll FE 1988–89, hon lectr Univ of Glasgow 1978–; FIHort 1993; author of over 120 scientific pubns; *Books* Plants and Microclimate (1983, last edn 1992) and joint ed of 4 books; *Recreations* squash, tennis, mountains, lounging; *Style*— Prof Lyn Jones; ✉ 13 Mill Street, Warwick CV34 4HB; Horticulture Reseach International, Wellesbourne, Warwick CV35 9EF (☎ 01789 470382, fax 01789 470552)

JONES, Sir Harry Ernest; kt (1971), CBE (1955); s of Harry Charles Ofield Jones (d 1947); *b* 1 Aug 1911; *Educ* Stamford Sch, St John's Coll Cambridge (BA); *m* 1935, Phyllis Eva, da of Alfred Dixon (d 1963); *Career* entered NI Civil Serv 1934, perm sec Miny of Commerce 1955, agent in GB for NI 1970–76; *Recreations* fly-fishing; *Clubs* Stowe Fly-Fishing; *Style*— Sir Harry Jones, CBE; ✉ Homelea, Nassington, Peterborough (☎ 01780 782675)

JONES, Heather; da of Harold Bentham Gledhill (d 1975), of Coventry, and Bessie, *née* Johnson; *b* 24 April 1941; *Educ* Stoke Park GS for Girls Coventry, Bedford Coll London (BSc, post grad DES scholarship); *m* 8 Aug 1964, Ivan Arthur Francis Jones; 2 s (Alexander Francis b 19 Oct 1966, Matthew Bentham b 21 March 1969); *Career* teacher: biology, botany and zoology Camden Sch for Girls London 1963–66, pt/t science HM Borstal Usk 1967–68, pt/t biology and chemistry Henley Coll of Further Educn Coventry 1969–70, pt/t human biology and English for foreign students Brooklyn Tech Coll Birmingham 1970–73, pt/t biology and chemistry Boldmere HS Sutton Coldfield 1972–74, pt/t biology and gen science Coleshill Secdy Sch 1973–74, pt/t Latin and science Chetwynd House Prep Sch Sutton Coldfield 1974, biology, chemistry and environmental studies then head of science and dir of studies (sr teacher) Handsworth Wood Girls' Sch Birmingham 1974–80, dep head Bournville Sch 1980–87, headteacher Yardleys Sch Birmingham 1987– (commended HM Sch Inspectorate 1992, Independent Parents' Choice selection 1992, winner of numerous regnl and nat environmental awards); fndr sch conservation project - 22 acre abandoned allotments site Acocks Green 1992 (exhibited Green Show 1992); memb Professional Assoc of Teachers 1975–91, memb NAHT 1992–; fndr memb Rotary Club of Birmingham Breakfast; *Recreations* foreign travel, conservation work, horticulture, listening to classical music, reading, tapestry; *Style*— Mrs Heather Jones; ✉ Yardleys School, Warwick Road, Tyseley, Birmingham B11 2LT (☎ 0121 693 6821, fax 0121 693 6824)

JONES, Helen Mary; *b* 28 April 1955; *Educ* chartered secretary 1976; *Career* graduate trainee (Finance) Coventry Climax 1976–77, co secretarial asst Ernst and Whinney 1977–79, asst co sec rising to legal advsr corp fin Guinness PLC 1979–87; asst co sec and gp mangr fin ops Kingfisher plc 1987–91; Woolworths plc (part of Kingfisher) 1991–95: successively mktg mangr Home, head of buying Stationery, logistics mangr Stationery, mangr Range Mgmnt; gp co sec Kingfisher plc 1995–; memb London Regnl Cncl CBI 1996; FCIS 1996; *Style*— Ms Helen Jones; ✉ Kingfisher plc, 119 Marylebone Road, London NW1 5PX (☎ 0171 724 7749, fax 0171 724 0355)

JONES, Dr (John) Howel; s of John Emrys Jones (d 1969), and Mary, *née* Edwards (d 1972); *b* 4 March 1928; *Educ* Ardwyn GS Aberystwyth, Wrekin Coll Wellington Shropshire, Sidney Sussex Coll Cambridge (MA, MD), St George's Hosp Med Sch; *m* 27 June 1953, Sheila Mary, da of Thomas Forster (d 1982); 2 s (Hugh, David), 1 da (Elizabeth); *Career* RAMC Capt in UK and Far East 1954–56; house offr and registrar posts: St George's Hosp London, Brompton Hosp, Queen Elizabeth Hosp Birmingham 1952–61; sr med registrar St George's Hosp and Central Middx Hosp 1961–66, conslt physician W Midlands RHA Coventry and Rugby 1966–91; MO: GB Olympic Team 1976–84, England Cwlth Games Team 1978–82; hon med advsr Cwlth Games Fedn 1982–90; memb Br Soc of Gastroenterology 1964; FRCP 1973; *Recreations* gardening, reading; *Style*— Dr Howel Jones; ✉ 6 Staverton Leys, Rugby, Warwicks CV22 5RD (☎ 01788 812632)

JONES, Sir Hugh; *see:* Hugh-Jones, Sir Wynn Normington

JONES, His Hon Judge Hugh Duncan Hitchings; s of Norman Everard Jones (d 1971), of Mountain Ash, and Ann, *née* Hitchings (d 1991); *b* 25 May 1937; *Educ* Mountain Ash GS (State scholar), UCL (LLB); *m* 1966, Helen Margaret, da of Norman Kingsley Payne; 3 da (Gweno Elizabeth b 19 April 1967, Siriol Ann (twin) b 19 April 1967, Rhian Margaret b 30 May 1970); *Career* admitted slr 1961, registrar Cardiff Co Court 1978–91, circuit judge (Wales and Chester Circuit) 1991– (recorder 1988–91); memb: Law Soc 1961–, Ctee of Registrars' Assoc 1985–91, Co Court Rules Ctee 1994–; *Recreations* gardening, cricket, golf, holidays; *Clubs* Mountain Ash Golf; *Style*— His Hon Judge Hugh Jones; ✉ The Cottage, Cwmpennar, Mountain Ash, Mid Glamorgan CF45 4DB (☎ 01443 472784); c/o Wales & Chester Circuit Office, Churchill House, Churchill Way, Cardiff CF1 4HH

JONES, Hywel; s of William John Russel Jones, of Cardiff, S Wales, and Estelle, *née* Harris; *b* 28 Nov 1965; *Educ* St Teilo's C of E HS, Llanishen High Sixth Form, Plymouth Coll of Art & Design; *m* 9 Feb 1989, Luci, da of Miguel Ximenez; *Career* photographer; awards incl: Assoc of Photographers Annual Award 1993, John Kobal Portrait Award 1993; memb Assoc of Photographers 1992; *Style*— Hywel Jones, Esq; ✉ Bethnal Green, London E2 9PB (☎ 0181 981 9810)

JONES, Hywel Francis; s of Brymmor Jones (d 1957), of Morriston, Swansea, and Maggie Beatrice, *née* Francis (d 1987); *b* 28 Dec 1928; *Educ* Swansea GS, St John's Coll Cambridge (BA, MA); *m* 10 March 1959, Marian Rosser, da of Sidney Craven (d 1951), of Morriston, Swansea; 1 da (Sharon); *Career* Nat Serv RAPC 1953–55; dep county treas Breconshire CC 1956–59, asst county treas Carmarthenshire CC 1959–66, borough treas Port Talbot Borough Cncl 1966–75, Cmmn for Local Admin in Wales 1975–91 (sec 1975–85), local ombudsman 1985–91; memb Public Works Loan Bd 1971–75, fin advsr AMC 1972–74, memb Lord Chllr's Advsy Ctee for W Glamorgan 1990–; treas: Royal Nat Eisteddfod of Wales 1975–95, Gorsedd of Bards 1992– (memb 1977); CIPFA 1953; *Recreations* music, reading, gardening; *Style*— Hywel F Jones, Esq; ✉ Godre'r Rhiw, 1 Lon Heulog, Baglan, Port Talbot SA12 8SY (☎ 01639 813 822)

JONES, Ian; s of Reginald Sampson Jones (d 1977), of Birmingham, and Florence, *née* Lees; *b* 3 July 1947; *Educ* Queensbridge Sch Birmingham, Hall Green Tech Coll Birmingham, Birmingham Poly Sch of Fine Art (BA), RCA (MA); *m* 2 July 1966, Carole Ann, da of Albert Percival Holmes; 2 s (Antony Ian b 27 Dec 1966, Stuart Timothy b 12 Oct 1968); *Career* artist; apprentice toolmaker W H Doherty Co Ltd 1963–69; toolmaker: Aero Coldform Co Ltd 1969–72, Producit Co Ltd 1972–75; teacher of art: Limerick Coll of Art & Design, Birmingham Sch of Fine Art, St Martin's Coll of Art London, Kingston Poly, Canterbury Art Coll, Brighton Poly Sch of Fine Art, Univ of E London; *Major Works* Head (Father) 1982, Drinking & Smoking 1982, The Engineer 1982, The Life Raft 1985, Tightrope Walker 1986, A Quick Trip to Ireland 1987, Hi Heel Sneakers 1987, There'll Be a Bit of a Breeze Tonight 1987, The Wedding 1988, Shoes on a Custard Carpet 1989, Celebrating the Buff Envelope 1989, The Karin B 1989, Brummagem 1989, Sweet Smell of Success 1989, Reflections 1989, Money Talks 1990, Big Legs Tight Skirts 1990, Eight Hour Stay 1991, Yates's 1991, Northfied Girls 1991, Swimmer 1991, Stare 1991, Traffic 1992, Obsession III and IV 1992, Hot Hatch Six Pack 1993, Fast Ford 1993, Move It On Over 1993, Any Road Up 1993, Female Heads I, II, III, IV, V 1995; *Solo Exhibitions* Chapter Art Centre Cardiff 1984, 21 Days Work (Leamington Spa 1985, Stratford upon Avon 1986), Recent Paintings and Drawings (Consort Gallery ICST) 1987, Some New Work (Vortex Gallery London) 1987, Recent Paintings (Camden Arts Centre London) 1988, Anderson O'Day Gallery London 1989–91 and 1995, Big Paintings for the Barbican (Concourse Gallery Barbican) 1993, Cornhill Exhibition 1995 and 1996; *Group Exhibitions* incl: Drawings (Foyle Gallery Birmingham) 1975, 5 Painters (Consort Gallery) 1981, New Contemporaries (ICA Gallery) 1982, New Blood on Paper (MOMA Oxford) 1983, Gallery 24 London 1984, Open Studios (Fish Island Artists London) annually 1985–91, Print Show (The Grannery Limerick) 1986, Mead Gallery Warwick Univ 1987, Athena Awards (Barbican) 1988, The Falklands Factor (Manchester City Art Gallery and tour) 1988, Jumping Ship (Vortex Gallery London) 1989, Images of Paradise (Harewood House, Yorks) 1989, Contemporary London (Transart Cologne) 1989, Salon de la Jeune Peinture Grand Palais Paris 1990, Summer Exhibition (Anderson O'Day Gallery London) 1990 and 1991, Art Frankfurt 1991, The Discerning Eye (Mall Galleries) 1991, Dieppe-Brighton Exchange (Dieppe) 1992, Chelsea Arts Club London 1995, Royal Acad Summer Show 1995, The Motor Show (Herbert Museum and Art Gallery Coventry and tour) 1996, Wheels on Fire (Wolverhampton Art Gallery and tour) 1996; *Work in Public Collections* Unilever, Nordstern Cologne, WEA, Guiness Brewing Worldwide, Pepsi Cola, Br Airports Authy, EMI Worldwide, Glaxo Holding; *Awards* Whitworth Wallis prize 1976, John Minton award 1982, major award Greater London Arts award 1983, short list prize Athena Awards 1988, Unilever prize Portobello Festival 1989; *Recreations* music; *Clubs* Chelsea Arts; *Style*— Ian Jones, Esq; ✉ Anderson O'Day Gallery, 255 Portobello Rd, London W11 1LR

JONES, Ian Geoffrey; s of Geoffrey Frederick Jones, and Ann Elizabeth, *née* Taylor; *b* 18 Aug 1965; *Educ* Bolton Sch, West Glamorgan Inst of Higher Educn (HND), Bournemouth Art Coll (PQE); *Career* chief photographer Skishoot 1987–91, freelance 1991–, Daily Telegraph photographer 1992–; projects incl: maj home and world news assignments and Royal foreign tours; *Awards* highly commended Martini Royal Photographer Awards 1992, winner Canon News Photographer of the Year 1992 and Fuji News Photographer of the Year 1992, Martini Royal Photographer of the Year 1993 and 1994, Martini Royal Photographer of the Decade 1996; memb: Newspaper Publishers' Assoc, Old Boltonians' Assoc; *Recreations* skiing, fishing; *Style*— Ian Jones, Esq; ✉ c/o The Daily Telegraph, Picture Desk, 1 Canada Square, Canary Wharf, London E14 5DT (mobile 0850 329349)

JONES, (Charles) Ian McMillan; s of Wilfred Charles Jones (d 1986), of Wroxham, Norfolk, and Bessie, *née* McMillan; *b* 11 Oct 1934; *Educ* Bishop's Stortford Coll, St John's Coll Cambridge (MA, PGCE, Capt Camb Univ Hockey XI 1958/59); *m* 9 Aug 1962, Jennifer Marie, da of Alec Potter (d 1980), of Hertford; 2 s (William Ian b 18 Jan 1964, Robert Andrew b 28 Jan 1970); *Career* Nat Serv 1953–55, cmmnd RA, Subalt 45 Field Regt in BAOR, regtl motor tport offr, TA 1955–57, Lt Herts Yeomanry; head Geography Dept Bishop's Stortford Coll 1960–70 (asst to Headmaster 1967–70), vice princ King William's Coll IOM 1971–75, headmaster Bedford Sch 1975–86, dir studies Britannia RNC Dartmouth 1986–88, project dir The Centre for Br Teachers Negara Brunei Darussalam 1988–91, Malaysia 1990–91, educnl advsr Kolej Tuanku Ja'afar Malaysia 1988–91, dir CfBT Educn Servs SE Asia 1992–94, grants administrator CfBT Educn Servs 1995–; played for: England Hockey XI 1959–64, GB Hockey XI 1959–64; competed in Rome and Tokyo Olympics, mangr/coach England Hockey XI 1967–69; English Schoolboy Hockey Assoc: chm 1976–86, pres 1980–88; mangr England Schoolboy Hockey XI 1967–77; memb: Ctee of Headmasters' Conf 1981–83, IOM Sports Cncl 1972–75; chm ISIS Central 1981–83; contributed feature articles: on hockey to The Guardian 1969–72, on educn and travel to The Borneo Bulletin 1990–94; govr Bishop's Stortford Coll 1985–, non-exec dir Norwich Community Health Partnership 1995–; FIMgt 1981, FRSA 1981; *Recreations* hockey, cricket, squash, golf; *Clubs* MCC, Hawks' (Cambridge), Pantai Mentiri Golf (Brunei), Royal Norwich Golf; *Style*— Ian Jones, Esq; ✉ Riverain, Staitheway Road, Wroxham, Norwich NR12 8TH (☎ and fax 01603 782307); CfBT Education Services, 1 The Chambers, East Street, Reading RG1 4JD (☎ 0118 952 3900, fax 0118 952 3924)

JONES, Ian Michael; s of Derek Jones, of Newbury, Berks, and Jean, *née* Norton; *b* 5 Sept 1949; *Educ* St Bartholomew's GS Newbury, Fitzwilliam Coll Cambridge (BA); *m* 1976, Vivien, *née* Hepworth; 2 s (Samuel Martin b 16 Aug 1983, William Max 4 Aug 1986); *Career* civil servant; Home Office 1972–83, DTI 1983–85, asst sec Small Firms Div Dept of Employment 1985–89, sec BOTB 1989–90, regnl dir SE Region DTI 1990–94, head Textiles and Retail Div DTI 1994–96, dir Post Office Retail and Textiles Directorate DTI 1996–; leader London City Action Team 1992–94; *Recreations* cricket, birds; *Style*— Ian Jones, Esq; ✉ Post Office, Retail and Textiles Directorate, Department of Trade and Industry, 151 Buckingham Palace Road, London SW1W 9SS (☎ 0171 215 2969, fax 0171 215 1500)

JONES, Ian Quayle; WS; s of Arnold Bates Jones (d 1977), of Poynton, Cheshire, and Lilian Quayle Jones (d 1989); *b* 14 July 1941; *Educ* Strathallan Sch, Univ of Edinburgh (MA, LLB); *m* 24 Feb 1968, Christine Ann, da of Kenneth Macrae, WS (d 1984), of Edinburgh; 2 s (Simon Quayle b 1977, Richard Ian b 1980), 1 da (Stephanie Margaret b 1974); *Career* ptnr Cowan and Stewart WS 1968–72, fund mangr Ivory & Sime 1972–74, dir Br Linen Bank Ltd 1974–83 (mangr, asst dir), chief exec Quayle Munro Holings PLC 1983–; non-exec chm Nevis Range Development Co plc 1989–; govr Strathallan Sch; *Recreations* golf, skiing, fishing; *Clubs* Hon Co of Edinburgh Golfers; *Style*— Ian Jones, Esq, WS; ✉ 24 Ann Street, Edinburgh (☎ 0131 332 7141); Quayle Munro Ltd, 8 Charlotte Square, Edinburgh EH2 4DR (☎ 0131 226 4421, fax 0131 225 3391)

JONES, Ieuan; s of David Edward Humphries Jones, of Mathrafal, Meifod, Powys, Wales, and Beryl Elizabeth Mary, *née* Proudlove; *b* 24 Jan 1963; *Educ* Llanfair Caereinion Sch, RCM (Most Distinguished Student award, Tagore Gold medal, Winner Royal Over-Seas League music competition, runner up Israel Harp contest); *m* 18 June 1992, Penny Gore Browne, *née* Thomson; 1 step s (Edward), 1 step da (Alexandra); *Career* harpist; prof of harp RCM 1996–; appointed harpist to the House of Commons 1984,

London debut Purcell Room 1985, Wigmore Hall debut 1987; recitals incl: Dusseldorf 1986 and 1990, Amsterdam 1987, Ireland 1987, Vienna 1987, Holland 1987, Valencia 1987 and 1988, Mid West tour USA 1989, Wigmore Hall 1990, Paris 1990, St David's Hall Cardiff 1988 and 1990, Madrid 1994; tours with: Bournemouth Sinfonietta 1986, 1987 and 1988, Welsh Chamber Orch 1988, London Festival Orch 1989, 1990 and 1994; TV and radio appearances incl: Wogan 1986, Daytime Live 1988, AVRO TV Holland 1987, Billy Butler Show 1988 and 1990, Derek Jameson 1988, Gloria Hunniford 1988 and 1990; appearances at many festivals in the UK and abroad; private appearance before HRH Queen Elizabeth the Queen Mother at the Royal Lodge Windsor 1986, guest appearance St James' Palace 1988 and Holyrood House 1989, Birthday Honours series with London Festival Orch at London S Bank 1991, Eng Heritage series 1991, World Harp Congress Cardiff 1991, Welsh premier of Rodrigo Concerto 1991, Spanish recitals 1991, soloist with Enrique Batiz and the Mexican State Orchestra, guest appearance Rodrigo Celelbration Concert for EXPO Seville 1992, premiered work by William Mathias at Newbury Festival 1993 and Welsh premiere at Machynlleth Festival 1993, world premiere Concerto for Harp and Marimba World Harp Festival 1994, cmmnd and premiered work by Jean-Michel Damase Wigmore Hall 1994, Concertgebouw debut with Ginastera Concerto 1995, Hong Kong, Phillippines and Australia solo debut tour 1995; recordings: The Uncommon Harp (1987), The Two Sides of Ieuan Jones (1988), ...In The French Style (1990), Mozart in Paris (1990), All Through the Night (1992), French Chamber Music (1994), William Alwyn 1994, Concerto D'Aranjuez/Batiz (1995); ARCM 1981; *Recreations* health & fitness, travel; *Style*— Ieuan Jones, Esq; ✉ 85 Elm Bank Gardens, London SW13 0NX (☎ 0181 876 1013, fax 0181 878 4712)

JONES, Ieuan Wyn; MP (Plaid Cymru) Ynys Mon (majority 1,106); s of Rev John Jones (d 1977), of Gwynedd, and Mair Elizabeth Jones, *née* Pritchard; *b* 22 May 1949; *Educ* Pontardawe GS, Ysgol-Y-Berwyn Y Bala Gwynedd, Liverpool Poly (LLB); *m* 1974, Eirian Llwyd, da of John Nefydd Jones, of Clwyd; 2 s (Gerallt b 1975, Owain b 1978), 1 da (Gwenllian b 1977); *Career* admitted slr 1973, ptnr William Jones & Talog Davies Ruthin Clwyd 1974 (ptnr Llangefni Branch 1985–); MP (Plaid Cymru) Ynys Mon 1987–; memb Select Ctee: on Welsh Affairs 1989–92, on Agriculture 1992–; sponsored Hearing Aid Cncl (Amendment) Act 1989 private members bill; nat chm Plaid Cymru 1980–82 and 1990–92; *Books* Europe: The Challenge for Wales (1996); *Recreations* sport, local history; *Style*— Ieuan Wyn Jones, Esq, MP; ✉ Ty Newydd Rhosmeirch, Llangefni, Gwynedd (☎ 01248 722261, 01248 723599); House of Commons, London SW1A 0AA (☎ 0171 219 5021)

JONES, Jack James Larkin; CH (1978), MBE (1950); s of George Jones (d 1963), of Liverpool, and Ann Devoy (d 1969); *b* 29 March 1913; *Educ* Elementary Sch, Toxteth Tech Sch Liverpool; *m* 1938, Evelyn Mary, da of Joseph Taylor (d 1954), of Knutsford; 2 s (Jack, Michael); *Career* served Spanish Civil War (wounded Ebro Battle 1938); first employed in engrg and docks industs, dep chm Nat Ports Cncl 1967–79, gen sec TGWU 1969–78, vice pres Int Tport Workers Fedn 1972–, memb Bd ACAS 1974–78, chm Int Ctee Nationalised Industs and Tport Ctees of TUC; pres EFTA Trade Union Cncl 1972–74, Royal Cmmn on Criminal Procedure 1978–80, chm of tstees Nat Museum of Labour History 1983–, pres Nat Pensioners' Convention 1992–, vice pres Euro Fedn of Ret and Elderly Persons 1991–; Hon DLitt Univ of Warwick 1978; fell: Liverpool John Moores Univ 1989, Univ of Central Lancashire 1993; FCIT 1970; *Books* The Incompatibles (1967), Industry's Democratic Revolution (1974), A to Z of Trades Unionism and Industrial Relations (with Max Morris, 1982), Union Man (autobiography, 1986); *Recreations* walking; *Clubs* Tom Mann Trades (Coventry); *Style*— Jack Jones, Esq, CH, MBE; ✉ 74 Ruskin Park House, Champion Hill, London SE5 8TH (☎ 0171 274 7067)

JONES, Rt Rev James Stuart; *see:* Hull, Bishop of

JONES, Hon Mr Jeffrey Richard; CBE (1979); s of Rev Thomas Jones (d 1962), and Winifred, *née* Williams (d 1994); *b* 18 Nov 1921; *Educ* Grove Park Wrexham, Denstone Coll Staffs, Keble Coll Oxford (MA); *m* 1955, Ann Rosaleen, da of Michael Carberry (d 1963), of Derbys; 1 s (Thomas), 1 da (Philippa); *Career* Flt Lt (Pilot) RAFVR 1941–46; art master Mountgrace Comp Sch Middx 1953–54, called to the Bar Middle Temple 1954, ed Law Reports Northern Nigeria 1968–75; chief justice: Kano State Nigeria 1975–80, Repub of Kiribati 1980–85; pres Ct of Appeal Kiribati 1981–85; memb Ct of Appeal: Solomon Islands 1983, Vanuatu 1984; pres Rotary Club Kano 1977; *Publications* Some Cases on Criminal Procedure and Evidence (1967 and 1968), Criminal Procedure of the Northern States of Nigeria (1975); *Recreations* duck shooting, sea fishing, golf, art; *Style*— Hon Mr Jeffrey Jones, Esq, CBE; ✉ Bradley Cottage, Bradley Lane, Holt, Wilts (☎ 01225 782004)

JONES, Prof (William) Jeremy; s of Thomas John Jones (d 1975), of Llandeilo, Dyfed, and Margaret Jeremy (d 1958); *b* 15 Aug 1935; *Educ* Llandeilo GS, UCW Aberystwyth (BSc, MSc), Trinity Coll Cambridge (PhD); *m* 29 June 1963, (Margaret) Anne, da of Dr Frederick Greystock Robertson, of Cobourg, Ontario, Canada; 2 s (Jeremy b 18 May 1964, d 1987, Michael b 28 March 1968), 1 da (Suzanne b 19 June 1970); *Career* Univ of Cambridge: external res student Trinity Coll 1958–60, title A res fell Trinity Coll 1960–64, demonstrator in physical chemistry 1965–70, lectr 1970–78, tutor Trinity Coll 1973–78 (fell and dir studies 1964–78); res student Courtaulds 1958–61, fell Nat Res Cncl of Canada 1962–64, prof and head Dept of Chemistry UCW Aberystwyth 1978–88; Univ of Wales Swansea: prof of chemistry 1988–, dean Faculty of Sci 1992–96; memb Optical Soc of America 1978; FRSC 1978; *Recreations* golf, gardening, walking; *Style*— Prof Jeremy Jones; ✉ 2 Knoll Ave, Uplands, Swansea SA2 0JN (☎ 01792 298149); Department of Chemistry, University of Wales Swansea, Singleton Park SA2 8PP (☎ 01792 295507)

JONES, John Elfed; CBE (1987), DL; s of Urien Maelgwyn Jones (d 1978); *b* 19 March 1933; *Educ* Blaenau Ffestiniog GS, Denbighshire Tech Coll, Heriot-Watt Coll; *m* 1957, Mary Sheila, da of David Thomas Rosser; 2 da (Bethan, Delyth); *Career* Flying Offr RAF; chartered electrical engr CEGB 1949–1969, dep md Anglesey Aluminium Metal Ltd 1969–79, under sec (indust) Welsh Office 1979–82; chm: Welsh Water Authy 1982–89, Welsh Water PLC 1989–93, HTV Wales/Cymru 1992–, International Greetings plc 1996–; dep chm HTV (Group) plc 1992–; chm Bwrdd Yr Iaith Gymraeg (Welsh Language Bd) 1988–93, pres Univ Coll of Wales Lampeter (St David's Univ) 1992–; fell Univ of Wales Aberystwyth 1991; CEng, FIEE, FRSA, CIMgt; *Recreations* fishing (salmon and trout), attending Eisteddfodau; *Style*— John Elfed Jones, Esq, CBE, DL; ✉ Ty Mawr, Coety, Penybontarogwr, Morgannwg Ganol CF35 6BN (☎ 01656 653039); HTV Group plc, Culverhouse Cross, Cardiff

JONES, (Henry) John Franklin; s of late Lt-Col James Walker Jones, DSO, and Doris Marjorie, *née* Franklin; *b* 6 May 1924; *Educ* Blundell's, Merton Coll Oxford; *m* 10 Dec 1949, Jean Verity, da of Samuel Robinson, CMG (d 1973), of London; 1 s, 1 da; *Career* WWII serv Ordinary Seaman RN 1943, Intelligence Staff Eastern Fleet 1944; Univ of Oxford: fell and tutor in jurisprudence 1949–56, univ sr lectr 1956–62, fell and tutor in Eng lit 1962–79, prof of poetry 1979–84; Dill Meml Lectr Queen's Univ Belfast 1983; football corr The Observer 1956–59; TV appearances incl The Modern World 1988; *Publications* incl: The Egotistical Sublime (1954, 5 edn 1978), The British Imagination (contrib, 1961), On Aristotle and Greek Tragedy (1965, 5 edn 1980), Dickens and the Twentieth Century (contrib, 1962), John Keats' Dream of Truth (1969, 2 edn 1980), The Morality of Art (1969), The Same God (1971), Dostoevskey (1983, 2 edn 1985), Shakespeare at Work (1995); *Style*— John Jones, Esq; ✉ Garden Flat, 41 Buckland Crescent, London NW3 5DJ (☎ 0171 586 1808); Yellands, Brisworthy, Shaugh Prior, Plympton, Devon (☎ 01752 839310)

JONES, Sir John Lewis; KCB (1983), CMG (1972); *b* 17 Feb 1923; *Educ* Christ's Coll Cambridge (MA); *m* 1948, Daphne Nora, *née* Redman; *Career* RA 1942–46, Sudan Govt 1947–55, MOD 1955–85; *Clubs* United Oxford and Cambridge; *Style*— Sir John Jones, KCB, CMG

JONES, John Maurice; s of Maurice Parry Jones, of Llwynderw, Bala, N Wales, and Armorel Winifred, *née* Adams; *b* 6 March 1943; *Educ* Llandovery Coll, Middx Hosp Univ of London (MB BS); *m* 17 Feb 1968, Valerie Patricia; 1 s (Richard b 1973), 2 da (Katie b 1970, Vanessa b 1971); *Career* surgical registrar Edinburgh 1970–74, orthopaedic registrar St George's Hosp London 1974–76, sr registrar Cardiff 1976–80, orthopaedic conslt Leicester 1980–; fell Presbyterian St Luke's Chicago; memb BSSH, fell BOA, FRCSEd; *Style*— John Jones, Esq; ✉ 8 Knighton Dr, Leics LE2 3HB (☎ 0116 270 6961); BUPA Hospital, Gartree Rd, Leics LE2 2FF (☎ 0116 272 0888, fax 0116 272 0666, car 0860 553135)

JONES, Prof John Richards; s of William Jones (d 1972), of Tregaron, and Mary Ann, *née* Richards (d 1994); *b* 27 Dec 1937; *Educ* Tregaron Co Sch, UCW (BSc, PhD, DSc); *m* 28 Dec 1963, Eirlys Williams, da of Trevor Thomas (d 1966), of Pontlliw; 2 da (Carys b 1964, Siân b 1965); *Career* Battersea Coll of Advanced Technol: asst lectr in physical chemistry 1961–63, lectr in physical chemistry (and Univ of Surrey) 1963–82, reader 1982–88, head of Chemistry Dept 1984–85 and 1991–, personal chair radiochemistry 1988–; FRSC; *Books* The Ionisation of Carbon Acids (1973), Handbook of Tritium NMR Spectroscopy and Applications (with E A Evans, D C Warrell and J A Elvidge 1985); *Recreations* cricket, gardening; *Style*— Prof John R Jones; ✉ Heatherdale, New Park Rd, Cranleigh, Surrey GU6 7HJ (☎ 01483 273483); Chemistry Department, University of Surrey, Guildford, Surrey GU2 5XH (☎ 01483 259313, fax 01483 259514)

JONES, Jon Owen; MP (Lab) Cardiff Central (majority 3,465); s of Gwynfor Owen Jones, and Dorothy Jones; *b* 19 April 1954; *Educ* Ysgol Gyfun Rhydfelin, UEA, UC Cardiff; *m* 11 Feb 1989 Allison Mary, *née* Clement; 2 s; *Career* science and biology teacher 1977–92; MP (Lab) Cardiff Central 1992– (also contested 1987), Lab Welsh whip; Cardiff City Cncl: cncllr 1987–, vice chm Fin Ctee 1987–91, chm Econ Devpt Ctee 1991–; pres: Caerphilly NUT 1983, Mid Glamorgan NUT 1984; sec Cardiff Central Lab Pty 1984–85, chm Campaign for Welsh Assembly 1988–91; *Recreations* walking, cooking, natural history, watching rugby, family, golf; *Style*— Jon Owen Jones, Esq, MP; ✉ House of Commons, London SW1A 0AA

JONES, Very Rev Keith Bynmor; s of John Brynmor Jones (d 1970), of Shrewsbury, Shropshire, and Mary Emily, *née* Evans (d 1980); *b* 27 June 1944; *Educ* Univ of Cambridge (MA); *m* 1973, Viola Mary, da of Henry Leigh Jenkyns; 3 da (Sophia b 27 Dec 1974, Olivia b 6 June 1977, Isabel b 3 July 1980); *Career* curate Limpsey with Titsey Dio of Southwark 1969–72, dean's vicar Cathedral and Abbey Church of St Albans 1972–76, vicar (subsequently team vicar) St Michael's Boreham Wood Team Miny Herts 1976–82, vicar St Mary le Tower Ipswich 1982–96, rural dean of Ipswich 1992–96, hon canon St Edmundsbury Cathedral 1993–96, dean of Exeter 1996–; chm St Matthew Soc (housing project Ipswich) 1990–95, vice pres Exeter Museums and Art Gallery; *Recreations* gardening, music, theatre, vigorous exercise on foot or a bicycle; *Style*— The Very Rev Keith Jones, Dean of Exeter; ✉ The Deanery, Exeter, Devon EX1 1HT (☎ 01392 272697, fax 01392 498769)

JONES, Dr Keith Howard; *b* 14 Oct 1937; *m* Dr Lynne Jones; 3 s; *Career* various positions in clinical med and research at teaching hosps in Cardiff, Edinburgh and Cambridge 1960–67, head Med Dept Agrochemical Div Fisons, head of safety assessment in clinical pharmacology Beecham Pharmaceuticals, exec dir (medical affairs) Merck Sharp & Dohme Research Laboratories, chief exec Medicines Control Agency 1992– (dir 1989–92); former adjunct prof of med Thomas Jefferson Med Sch; UK rep Pharmaceutical Ctee EU, UK rep Standing Ctee EU; author of numerous pubns on clinical and metabolic med, pesticide and drug toxicology and clinical pharmacology and drug devpt; FRCP, FRCPE, FRSM; *Recreations* sailing, tennis; *Style*— Dr Keith Jones; ✉ Medicines Control Agency, Market Towers, 1 Nine Elms Lane, London SW8 5NQ (☎ 0171 273 0100, fax 0171 273 0548)

JONES, Hon Sir Kenneth George Illtyd; kt (1974); s of late Richard Arthur Jones; *b* 26 May 1921; *Educ* Brigg GS, Univ Coll Oxford (MA); *m* 1, 1947, Dulcie Thursfield (d 1977); 1 s, 2 da; *m* 2, 1978, June Patricia, da of late Leslie Arthur Doxey; *Career* served WWII RA; called to the Bar Gray's Inn 1946, bencher 1969, treas 1987; QC 1962; recorder: Shrewsbury 1964–66, Wolverhampton 1966–71; recorder of the Crown Ct 1972, circuit judge 1972, judge of the High Court of Justice (Queen's Bench Div) 1974–88; *Style*— The Hon Sir Kenneth Jones; ✉ c/o Royal Courts of Justice, Strand, London WC2A 2LL

JONES, Laurance Aubrey; s of Aubrey Joseph Goldsmid Jones (d 1990), of Godmanchester, Huntingdon, and Frances Laura, *née* Ward; *b* 7 April 1936; *Educ* King's Sch Rochester; *m* 8 July 1961, Joan, da of Douglas Stanley Sargeant, of Staplehurst, Kent; *Career* Nat Serv RAF 1954–56; Royal Insurance Group 1953–54 and 1956–57, National Employers Mutual General Insurance Association Ltd 1957–58, co sec Marchant & Tubb Ltd 1959–67, jt sec Tollemache & Cobbold Group Cambridge 1967–70, dep sec International Timber Corporation Ltd 1970–77, gp sec Land Securities plc 1977–; Freeman: Maidstone 1957, City of London 1981; Liveryman Worshipful Co of Chartered Secs and Administrators 1981; FCIS 1972 (assoc 1968); *Recreations* tennis, skiing, golf, travel, bridge; *Clubs* City Livery, Broad Street Ward; *Style*— Laurance Jones, Esq; ✉ 242 Cromwell Tower, Barbican, London EC2Y 8DD; 99 Le Panoramic, Thollon Les Memises, 74500 Evian Les Bains, France; Land Securities plc, 5 Strand, London WC2N 5AF (☎ 0171 413 9000)

JONES, Lucy Katharine; da of Anthony Tom Brett-Jones, CBE, and Ann, *née* Fox; *b* 21 Feb 1955; *Educ* Byam Shaw Sch of Art, Camberwell Sch of Art (BA), RCA (MA, Cubitt award for painting, Anstruther award for painting), Br Sch in Rome (Rome scholar in painting); *m* Peter Leach; *Career* self employed artist and painter; formerly visiting tutor at various art colls incl: Ruskin Sch of Art, Byam Shaw Sch of Art, West Surrey Coll of Art and Design, Winchester Sch of Art; currently pt/t tutor Chelsea Coll of Art and Slade Sch of Art; *Solo Exhibitions* Angela Flowers Gallery London 1986, 1987, and 1989, Spitalfields Health Centre in assoc with Whitechapel Art Gallery 1987, Drumcroon Art Educn Centre Wigan 1990, Flowers East London 1991, 1993 and 1995; *Gp Exhibitions* incl: RA Summer Exhibition 1981 and 1990, The Pick of Graduate Art (Christies Inaugural) 1982, 10 Artisti della Accademia Britannica (Palazzo Barberini Rome) 1984, Canvas-New British Painters (John Hansard Gallery and Milton Keynes City Art Gallery) 1986, Artist of the Day (Angela Flowers Gallery) 1986, Young Masters (The Solomon Gallery London) 1986, Whitechapel Open 1987 and 1992, Passage West (Angela Flowers Ireland Co Cork) 1987, The Subjective City (The Small Mansion Arts Centre London) 1988, London Glasgow NY: New Acquisitions (Metropolitan Museum of Art NYC) 1988, Contemporary Portraits (Flowers East) 1988, Big Paintings (Flowers East) 1989, XXI International Festival of Painting Cagnes-sur-Mer-France 1989, Flowers at Moos (Gallery Moos NYC) 1990, The Subjective City (Cleveland Gallery Middlesbrough and tour) 1990, Rome 1980–90 (RCA) 1990, Rome scholars 1980–90 (RCA) 1990, Drumcroon The First Ten Years (Drumcroon Educn Art Centre) 1990, Anglo/Soviet Landscapes (Peterborough and Leningrad) 1991, Foregrounds and Distances (Galleria de Serpenti Rome) 1992, The Discerning Eye (Mall Galleries) 1992,

But Big is Better (Flowers East) 1993, Overcoming Obstacles: Women Artists in NW Collections (Blackburn Museum and Art Gallery) 1993, featured artist Art 24 '93 (Basel) 1993, Two Women Artists (with Eileen Cooper, Collyer Bristow London) 1993, Inner Visions (Flowers East) 1994, Downeen Decade (Angela Flowers Gallery) 1994, Ireland Small is Beautiful Park XII: Night and Day (Flowers East) 1994, The Twenty Fifth Anniversary (Flowers East) 1995, John Moore's Exhbn (Walker Art Gallery) 1995, Small is Beautiful Part XIII: Food and Drink (Flowers East) 1995, In the Looking Glass: Contemporary Self Portraits by Women Artists (Usher Gallery Lincoln and touring) 1996; works in the public collections of: Sheffield City Art Gallery, Univ of Reading, Arts Cncl, Security Pacific, Metropolitan Museum of Art, Rugby Museum, Drumcroon Education Art Centre Wigan, Unilever plc, Contemporary Art Soc, Arthur Andersen, Clifford Chance, Deutsche Bank AG London, Harris Museum and Art Gallery Preston, Proctor & Gamble London, Univ of Hull, Univ of Southampton, Westminster and Chelsea Hosp; awards: Oppenheim-John Downes Meml Tst 1986, Daler-Rowney award (best work in oil) Royal Acad Exhibition 1989, John Moore's Exhbn prize winner Walker Art Gallery Liverpool 1995; *Recreations* swimming, music, opera, cooking, sailing; *Style*— Ms Lucy Jones; ✉ Angela Flowers Gallery plc, Flowers East, 199–205 Richmond Rd, London E8 3NJ (☎ 0181 985 3333, fax 0181 985 0067)

JONES, Dr Lynne Mary; MP (Lab) Birmingham Selly Oak (majority 2,060); da of Stanley Stockton, and Jean Stockton; *b* 26 April 1951; *Educ* Univ of Birmingham (BSc, PhD); *children* 2 s; *Career* res fell Univ of Birmingham 1972–86, housing association mangr 1987–92, MP (Lab) Birmingham Selly Oak 1992–; *Style*— Dr Lynne Jones, MP; ✉ House of Commons, London SW1A 0AA

JONES, Prof Malcolm Vince; s of Reginald Cross Jones (d 1986), and Winifred Ethel, *née* Vince (d 1992); *b* 7 Jan 1940; *Educ* Cotham GS Bristol, Univ of Nottingham (BA, PhD); *m* 27 July 1963, Jennifer Rosemary, da of Frederick Walter Durrant (d 1987); 1 s (Alexander b 30 May 1967), 1 da (Helen b 5 Dec 1968); *Career* asst lectr in Russian Sch of Euro Studies Univ of Sussex 1965–67, prof Dept of Slavonic Studies Univ of Nottingham 1980– (lectr 1967–73, sr lectr 1973–80), dean Faculty of Arts Univ of Nottingham 1982–85 (vice dean 1976–79), pro-vice chllr Univ of Nottingham 1987–91; memb Editorial Bd Birmingham Slavonic Monographs 1976–, gen ed Cambridge Studies In Russian Literature; hon pres: Assoc of Teachers of Russian 1985–86, Br Universities Assoc of Slavists 1986–88 (hon sec 1974–76); hon vice pres Br Assoc For Soviet Slavonic and E Euro Studies 1988–90; hon pres: Coordinating Cncl for Area Studies Assoc 1991–93 (hon vice pres 1988–91), Univ of Nottingham Convocation 1992–; memb Humanities Research Bd British Acad 1994–, pres Int Dostoevsky Soc 1995–; *Books* Dostoyevsky The Novel of Discord (1976), New Essays On Tolstoy (ed, 1978), New Essays On Dostoyevsky (jt ed, 1983), Dostoyevsky after Bakhtin (1990); *Recreations* painting; *Clubs* University (Nottingham); *Style*— Prof Malcolm Jones; ✉ University of Nottingham, Department of Slavonic Studies, University Park, Nottingham NG7 2RD (☎ 0115 951 5825)

JONES, Mark Ellis Powell; s of John Ernest Powell Jones, of Cranleigh, Surrey, and Ann Elizabeth, *née* Murray; *b* 5 Feb 1951; *Educ* Eton, Univ of Oxford, Courtauld Inst of Art; *m* Dr Ann Camilla, da of Stephen Toulmin; 2 da (Sarah b 9 Oct 1974, Agnes b 7 Feb 1987), 2 s (Luke b 27 Aug 1985, William b 31 Dec 1988); *Career* keeper Dept of Coins and Medals British Museum 1990–92 (asst keeper 1974–90), dir National Museums of Scotland 1992–; memb Advsy Ctee Royal Mint 1994–, sec British Art Medal Soc 1982–94, pres Fédération Internationale de la Médaille 1994–; ed The Medal 1983–; Liveryman Worshipful Co of Goldsmiths; *Publications* The Art of the Medal (1977), Impressionist Paintings (1979), Catalogue of French Medals in the British Museum (Vol I 1982, Vol II 1988), Fake: The Art of Deception (ed, 1990), Why Fakes Matter (ed, 1992), Designs on Posterity (ed, 1994); *Clubs* New (Edinburgh); *Style*— Mark Jones, Esq; ✉ 39 Regent Street, Portobello, Edinburgh EH15 2AY (☎ 0131 657 3335); National Museums of Scotland, Chambers Street, Edinburgh (☎ 0131 247 4260, fax 0131 220 4819)

JONES, Prof Martin Kenneth; s of John Francis Jones, and Margaret Olive, *née* Baldwin; *b* 29 June 1951; *Educ* Eltham Coll, Peterhouse Cambridge (Frank Smart prize); *m* 29 June 1985, Lucienne Mary, da of Clive Walker; 1 s (Alexander b 20 Dec 1987), 1 da (Leonie b 6 Aug 1990); *Career* environmental archaeologist Oxford Archaeological Unit 1973–78, res asst Botany Sch Univ of Oxford 1978–81, sr lectr Univ of Durham 1989–90 (lectr 1981–89), George Pitt-Rivers prof of archaeological science Univ of Cambridge 1990–; FSA 1990; *Books* Environment of Man: The Iron Age to the Anglo Saxon Period (1981), Integrating the Substance Economy (1983), England before Domesday (1986), Archaeology and the Flora of the British Isles (1988); *Recreations* walking, sketching, cooking and eating; *Style*— Prof Martin Jones, FSA; ✉ Department of Archaeology, Downing Street, Cambridge CB2 3DZ (☎ 01223 333507, fax 01223 333503)

JONES, Martyn David; MP (Lab) Clwyd South West (majority 4,941); s of Vernon Pritchard Jones, of Wrexham, and Violet Gwendoline Jones, *née* Griffiths; *b* 1 March 1947; *Educ* Grove Park GS Wrexham, Trent Poly; *m* 1974 (m dis 1991), Rhona, da of Roger Bellis, of Wrexham; 1 s (Nicholas b 1984), 1 da (Linzi b 1974); *Career* MP (Lab) Clwyd SW 1987–, an oppn whip 1988–92, memb Agric Select Ctee 1988–94 and 1995–, frontbench spokesperson on food agriculture and rural affairs 1994–95; county cncllr 1981–89; MIBiol; *Recreations* backpacking, target shooting, sailing; *Clubs* Wrexham Lager Sports & Soc; *Style*— Martyn Jones, Esq, MP; ✉ 20 High Street, Johnstown, Wrexham LL14 2SN (☎ 01978 845938); House of Commons, London SW1A 0AA (☎ 0171 219 3417)

JONES, Martyn Eynon; s of Cledwyn Jones, and Megan, *née* Eynon; *b* 22 July 1951; *Educ* Dynevor GS, Denbigh GS, Univ Coll of Swansea (BSc); *m* 15 Sept 1973, Doreen Judith, da of late Russell Long, of Carlisle; *Career* chartered accountant; Robson Rhodes and Deloitte Haskins & Sells 1972–77, Accountancy Tuition Centre 1977–81, under sec then sec Auditing Practices Ctee 1981–84, UK and Ireland advsr to Int Auditing Practices Ctee 1983–84; Touche Ross (Deloitte & Touche): sr mangr 1984–87, nat audit tech ptnr 1987–; memb City Regulatory Panel CBI 1993–; ICAEW: memb Business Law Ctee 1993–, chm Special Reports of Accountants Sub-Ctee 1993–, chm Working Party on Guidance on Audit Ctees, memb Res Bd 1995, vice chm Tech and Practical Auditing Ctee 1995–, sole advsr on Handbook 1995–; memb Audit Procedures Task Force Deloitte Touche Tohmatsu International 1990–, memb DTI Working Party on revision of co law 1993, memb Int Sub-Ctee Auditing Practices Bd 1991– (chm Task Force on future mission of audit and governing principles of auditing 1994–, chm Working Party on reporting on prospective fin info 1996–); FCA 1981; *Books* Safely past the perils - the new investment business accounting requirements (jtly, 1987), The Audit Committee and its Chairman (jtly, 1993), The Finance Director and the Audit Committee (jtly, 1993), Progress Reports on the Financial Aspects of Corporate Governance (jtly, 1993–), Corporate Governance Handbook (conslt ed, 1996), Taking Fraud Seriously (jtly, 1996); *Recreations* gardening; *Style*— Martyn E Jones, Esq; ✉ Deloitte & Touche, 1 Little New Street, London EC4A 3TR (☎ 0171 303 4465, fax 0171 353 9820, e-mail martyn_jones@deloitte.touche.co.uk)

JONES, Maude Elizabeth; CBE (1973); 2 da of Edward William Jones (d 1953), of Dolben, Ruthin, N Wales; *b* 14 Jan 1921; *Educ* Brynhyfryd Sch for Girls Ruthin; *Career* joined Foreign Rels Dept Joint War Orgn BRCS and Order of St John 1940, dir Jr Red Cross 1960 (dep dir 1949), dep dir gen for branch affrs BRCS 1966, memb Jt Ctee Order of St John and BRCS 1966–77, dep dir gen Br Red Cross Soc 1970–77; memb: Nat Cncl of Social Serv 1966–77, FANY 1966–77; govr St David's Sch Ashford Middx; SSStJ 1959; *Recreations* music, gardening, reading; *Clubs* New Cavendish; *Style*— Miss Maude Jones, CBE; ✉ Dolben, Ruthin, N Wales (☎ 01824 702443)

JONES, Medwyn; s of Capt Ieuan Glyn Du Platt Jones, of Llandbedr Duffryn, Clwyd, N Wales, and Margaret, *née* Owen; *b* 13 Sept 1955; *Educ* Scorton Sch, Chester GS, Univ of Sheffield (LLB), The Coll of Law; *m* 1990, Rita, da of Raymond Bailey; 1 s (George Thomas b 1992), 1 da (Harriet Rhys b 1994); *Career* slr Theodore Goddard 1980–81 (articled clerk 1978–80), ptnr Walker Martineau 1983–92 (slr 1981–83), ptnr Cameron Markby Hewitt 1992–94, ptnr Film, TV and Theatre Dept Harbottle & Lewis slrs 1994–; Freeman City of London; memb Law Soc 1980, memb Royal Television Soc 1994; *Recreations* skiing; *Style*— Medwyn Jones, Esq; ✉ Harbottle & Lewis, Hanover House, 14 Hanover Square, London W1R 0BE (☎ 0171 667 5000, fax 0171 667 5100, DX 44617 Mayfair)

JONES, Dr Miah Gwynfor (Gwyn); s of Robert Jones (d 1979), of Porthmadog, Gwynedd, and Jane Irene, *née* Evans (d 1981); *b* 2 Dec 1948; *Educ* Ysgol Eifionydd Porthmadog, Univ of Manchester (BSc), Univ of Essex (PhD); *m* 10 Jan 1976, Maria Linda, da of Kenneth Johnson (d 1984), of Swansea; 2 da (Victoria Rachel Sian b 1980, Holly Alexandra Jane b 1982); *Career* British Steel 1975–77, ICL 1977–81, chm and chief exec Corporate Technology Group plc 1981–87, chm Welsh Devpt Agency 1988–93; non-exec dir: Tesco plc 1992–, ACT Group plc 1989–95, Invesco English and Int Tst 1993–, Welsh Water Enterprises Ltd 1990–93; memb Cncl Univ of Wales 1990–95; BBC: nat govr for Wales 1992–97, memb S4C Authy 1992–97, HBO & Co (UK) Ltd 1995–; hon fell Univ of Glamorgan (formerly Poly of Wales) 1991; FBCS; *Recreations* travel, boating, walking; *Style*— Dr Gwyn Jones; ✉ c/o BBC, Broadcasting House, Cardiff CF5 2YQ (☎ 01222 572070, fax 01222 572280)

JONES, Michael Abbott; s of Ronald Edgar Jones (d 1980), and Irene Gertrude, *née* Abbott; *b* 3 May 1944; *Educ* Felsted, Magdalen Coll Oxford (BA, DipEd); *m* 13 June 1973, Wendy Christine, da of Stanley Saward; 2 da (Cressida b 14 Nov 1976, Miranda (twin) b 14 Nov 1976); *Career* jt sec The Life Offices' Assoc 1982 (joined 1968), chief exec ABI 1987–93 (mangr Legislation Dept 1985–87), head of corp affairs Sun Alliance Group plc 1993–96, head of corp affairs Royal & Sun Alliance Insurance Group plc 1996–; *Style*— Michael Jones, Esq; ✉ 10 Parkhill Road, London E4 7ED; Royal & Sun Alliance Insurance Group plc, 1 Bartholomew Lane, London EC2N 2AB (☎ 0171 826 1812, fax 0171 826 1095)

JONES, Prof Michael Christopher Emlyn; s of late Reginald Luther Jones, and Megan Bevan Jones; *b* 5 Dec 1940; *Educ* Rugeley GS, Univ of Leicester, Trinity Coll Oxford (MA, DPhil, DLitt); *m* 1966, Elizabeth Marjorie, *née* Smith; 1 s; *Career* tutor in medieval history Univ of Exeter 1966–67; Univ of Nottingham: asst lectr 1967–69, lectr 1969–81, sr lectr 1981–84, reader in medieval history 1984–91, prof of medieval French history 1991–; sr scholar Wolfson Fndn 1975, Euro fell Leverhulme Tst 1977, visiting fell All Souls Coll Oxford 1984–85; jt ed Renaissance and Modern Studies 1986–89, ed Nottingham Medieval Studies 1989–; jt literary dir Royal Hist Soc 1990–; FRHistS 1971, FSA 1977; *Books* Ducal Brittany 1364–1399 (1970), Philippe de Commynes - Memoirs, the Reign of Louis XI (trans, 1972), Recueil des actes de Jean IV, duc de Bretagne (2 vols, ed 1980–83), Philippe Contamine - War in the Middle Ages (trans, 1984), John Le Patourel - Feudal Empires Norman and Plantagenet (ed, 1984), Gentry and Lesser Nobility in Later Medieval Europe (ed, 1986), The Family of Dinan in England in the Middle Ages (1987), The Creation of Brittany (collected papers, 1988), England and Her Neighbours 1066–1453 - Essays in Honour of Pierre Chaplais (ed with Malcolm Vale, 1989), The Bretons (with Patrick Galliou, 1991, also French and Italian edns), Aimer les Châteaux de Bretagne (with Prof Gwyn Meirion-Jones, 1991, also English and German edns), Les Châteaux de Bretagne (with Prof Gwyn Meirion-Jones, 1992), Manorial Domestic Buildings in England and Northern France (ed with Prof Gwyn Meirion-Jones, 1993), Recueil des actes de Charles de Blois et Jeanne de Penthievre, duc et ducesse de Bretagne (1341–1364) (1996); numerous papers and reviews in hist jls; *Recreations* browsing in book shops, gardening, philately; *Clubs* MCC, Athenaeum; *Style*— Prof Michael Jones, FSA; ✉ 3 Florence Boot Close, University Park, Nottingham NG7 2QF (☎ 0115 922 1744, e-mail Michael.Jones@Nottingham.ac.uk)

JONES, Michael Frederick; s of Glyn Frederick Jones, of Glos, and Elizabeth, *née* Coopey; *b* 3 July 1937; *Educ* Crypt Sch Glos; *m* 28 Feb 1959, Sheila Joan, da of Charles Dawes, of Chaldon, Surrey; 3 s (Edward b 1966, John b 1968, Richard b 1970); *Career* reporter: Maidenhead Advertiser 1956–59, Northern Echo 1959–61, Manchester Evening News 1961–64; lab reporter: Financial Times 1964–65, The Daily Telegraph 1965–67; news ed then asst ed The Times Business News 1967–70, managing ed The Asian Hong Kong 1971; The Sunday Times: assoc news ed 1972–75, political corr 1975–84, political ed 1984–95, assoc ed (politics) 1995–; chm Parly Press Gallery 1989–91; *Recreations* travel, history; *Style*— Michael Jones, Esq; ✉ The Sunday Times, 1 Pennington St, Wapping, London E1 9XW (☎ 0171 782 5834)

JONES, Michael Lynn Norman; s of Lynn Daniel Jones, of Rhiwbina, Cardiff, and Mary Hannah, *née* Edwards (d 1992); *b* 14 Jan 1943; *Educ* Neath Boys GS, Jesus Coll Oxford (BA, MA), Coll of Law; *m* 16 April 1974, Ethni, da of Gwynfryn Morgan Daniel (d 1960), of Llys-y-Coed, West Orchard Cres, Llandaff, Cardiff; 1 s (Garmon b 1975), 3 da (Mererid b 1976, Gwenfair b 1979, Rhiannon b 1982); *Career* slr; ptnr C Hugh James & Ptnrs Cardiff 1966, sr ptnr Hugh James Jones & Jenkins Cardiff 1970–; memb: Wales and Chester Circuit Advsy Ctee 1971–77, Curriculum Cncl Wales 1988–91; asst sec Cardiff and Dist Law Soc 1969–91 (vice pres 1991–92); govr: Coed-y-Gof Welsh Primary Sch 1985– (chm 1989–92), Glantaf Welsh HS 1988; elder Salem Presbyterian Church of Wales Canton Cardiff 1988; memb: Law Soc 1966, CIArb 1987; *Recreations* gardening, walking; *Clubs* Cardiff & County, Oxford Union; *Style*— Michael Jones, Esq; ✉ Hugh James Jones & Jenkins, Arlbee House, Greyfriars Road, Cardiff CF1 4QB (☎ 01222 224871, fax 01222 388222)

JONES, (Philip) Michael Thyer; s of Philip Emlyn Thyer Jones, DFC (d 1974), of Gorseinon, S Wales, and Elizabeth Vivien Thyer, *née* Fannon; *b* 21 April 1914; *Educ* Roan Sch Blackheath; *m* 21 May 1965, Barbara Mary, da of George Johnstone, of Thornhill, Dumfriesshire, Scotland; 3 da (Fiona b 1968, Alison b 1970, Katey b 1974); *Career* Int Stock Exchange 1959–63; Capel-Cure Myers: various posts 1959–63, head investmts 1969–70, ptnr fin and admin 1970–85; tech servs dir Capel-Cure Myers Capital Management; MInstAM 1970; *Recreations* flying, rock climbing, deep sea fishing, skiing, shooting; *Style*— Michael Jones, Esq; ✉ Capel-Cure Myers Capital Management, The Registry, Royal Mint Court, London EC3N 4EY (☎ 0171 488 4000, fax 0171 481 3798)

JONES, Nicholas Graham; s of Albert William Jones, and Gwendolen Muriel Taylor-Jones, *née* Phillips; *b* 13 Aug 1948; *Educ* Latymer Upper Sch, St Catherine's Coll Oxford (MA); *m* 25 Sept 1976, Shelagh Ann, da of Robert Maitland Farror; 1 s (Benjamin Nicholas Farror b 1986); *Career* film ed and prodr BBC 1969–73; called to the Bar Inner Temple 1975, recorder S Eastern Circuit 1994–; memb Criminal Bar Assoc; *Recreations* sailing, walking, music; *Clubs* Royal London Yacht, Royal Ocean Racing, Bar Yacht (Rear Cdre and hon sec); *Style*— Nicholas Jones, Esq; ✉ 4 Brick Court, Temple, London EC4Y 9AD (☎ 0171 583 8455, fax 0171 353 1699)

JONES, Nicholas Michael Houssemayne; s of Henry J E Jones, of Kitsbury Orchard, nr Moreton-in-Marsh, Glos, and Patricia Rose, *née* Holland; *b* 27 Oct 1946; *Educ* Winchester, London Business Sch (MSc); *m* 25 March 1971, Veronica Anne, da of Brig the Hon R G Hamilton-Russell, DSO, LVO, DL; 1 s (Oliver Mark b 5 April 1977), 1 da

(Rowena Rose b 5 Sept 1975); *Career* Peat Marwick Mitchell 1965–73, dir J Henry Schroder Wagg & Co 1975–87, md Lazard Brothers & Co 1987–; chm The National Stud 1991–; govr: James Allens Girls' Sch 1989–93, Birkbeck Coll 1995–; memb London Business Sch Devpt Bd 1996–; FCA 1969; *Recreations* racing, tennis, stalking, bridge, gardening; *Clubs* Turf; *Style*— Nicholas Jones, Esq; ✉ The Manor, Coln St Dennis, Cheltenham, Gloucestershire GL54 3JU; 12 Paulton's St, London SW3 5DR; Lazard Brothers & Co, Limited, 21 Moorfields, London EC2P 2HT (☎ 0171 588 2721, fax 0171 920 0239)

JONES, Nigel; MP (Lib Dem) Cheltenham (majority 1,668); s of late A J Jones, and Nora Jones; *b* 30 March 1948; *m* 21 May 1981, Katy, *née* Grinnell; 1 s, 2 da (twins); *Career* computer operator Westminster Bank Ltd 1965–67, computer programmer ICL Computers 1967–70, systems analyst Vehicle and General Insurance 1970–71, systems programmer Atkins Computing 1971, systems designer rising to project mangr ICL Computers 1971–92; cncllr (Cheltenham Park) Glos CC 1989–93; MP (Lib Dem) Cheltenham 1992–; Lib Dem spokesman: on England, local govt and housing 1992, on sci and technol 1993 and on consumer affrs 1995–; memb governing body of British Assoc for Central and Eastern Europe; *Recreations* watching Swindon Town FC, cricket, gardening; *Clubs* National Liberal; *Style*— Nigel Jones, Esq, MP; ✉ House of Commons, London SW1A 0AA

JONES, Nigel Michael; s of Ralph Michael Jones, of Wolverhampton, and Patricia May, *née* Phelps; *b* 23 Sept 1960; *Educ* Wolverhampton GS, Keble Coll Oxford (exhibitioner, BA); *m* 27 June 1987, Gillian Hazel, da of Eric Keith Philpot; *Career* advertising exec; currently head of planning BMP DDB (joined as graduate trainee 1984, bd dir 1988); accounts worked on: Quaker Cereals, Schering-Plough, Alliance & Leicester Building Society, Scottish Amicable Life Assurance, Courage, ICI Dulux, AIDS Health Education Authy, Birds Eye; winner of: US TV and Radio Commercials Festival Mobius award 1987, 1st prize IPA Advertising Effectiveness Awards 1988, 1st prize and grand prix IPA Advertising Effectiveness Awards 1990, various chess championships 1971–83; *Recreations* music, bonsai, walking, chess, Wolverhampton Wanderers; *Style*— Nigel Jones, Esq; ✉ BMP DDB, 12 Bishops Bridge Rd, London W2 6AA (☎ 0171 258 3979)

JONES, Rt Rev Noel Debroy; *see:* Sodor and Man, Bishop of

JONES, Prof Norman; s of Edward Valentine Jones, and Mary Alice, *née* Collins; *b* 18 March 1938; *Educ* Liverpool Poly (ordinary Nat Cert), UMIST (BScTech, MScTech, PhD), Univ of Manchester (DSc); *m* 11 July 1964, Jenny, da of Fred Schofield (d 1946); 2 da (Alison Elizabeth b 29 Aug 1967, Catherine Ann b 8 March 1971); *Career* pt/t lectr Dept of Mech Engrg Manchester Coll of Sci and Technol 1961–63, James Clayton fell IMechE 1962–63, asst lectr Faculty of Technol Univ of Manchester 1963–65; asst prof: Dept of Mech Engrg Georgia Inst of Technol USA 1965–66, Dept of Engrg Brown Univ USA 1966–68; Dept of Ocean Engrg MIT USA: asst prof 1968–70, assoc prof 1970–77, prof 1977–79; Univ of Liverpool: prof of mechanical engrg (AA Griffith prof of mechanical engrg since 1993) 1979–, head Dept of Mech Engrg 1982–90; ed in chief Int Jl of Impact Engineering 1988– (ed 1982–87), assoc ed Applied Mechanics Reviews 1995–; memb Editorial Bd: Jl of Ship Research 1972–80, Int Jl of Mechanical Sciences 1975–, Acta Mechanica Sinica 1991–, Dymat Jl 1992–; memb: Safety in Mines Res Advsy Bd 1985–, Ductile Collapse Ctee 3.1 Int Ship Structures Congress 1985–88, Hull and Machinery Ctee Def Scientific Advsy Cncl 1989–95, Man-made Hazards Ctee Inter-Engrg Inst Hazards Forum 1990– (chm 1991–95), Solid Mechanics Conf Ctee Euro Mechanics Cncl 1990– (chm 1995–), Euromech Cncl 1992–; IMechE William Sweet Smith Prize 1989, Ludwig Mond Prize 1992; memb: ASME 1966 (fell 1990), P Eng Massachusetts 1972, FIMechE 1980, FRINA 1980; *Books* Structural Crashworthiness (1983), Structural Failure (1989), Structural Impact (1989), Structural Crashworthiness and Failure (1993); *Recreations* walking, classical music; *Style*— Prof Norman Jones; ✉ Department of Mechanical Engineering, The University of Liverpool, Liverpool L69 3BX (☎ 0151 794 4858, fax 0151 794 4848, telex 627095 UNILPL G, e-mail njones@mechnet.liv.ac.uk)

JONES, Dr Norman Fielding; s of William John Jones (d 1968), of Aberbeeg, Gwent, and Winifred, *née* Evans (d 1974); *b* 3 May 1931; *Educ* Christ Coll Brecon, King's Coll Cambridge (MA, MD), St Thomas' Hosp Med Sch London (MB, BChir), Univ of N Carolina; *m* 15 March 1958, Ann Pye, da of Dr Charles Cecil Howard Chavasse (d 1971), of Alcester, Warwicks; 3 s (Christopher b 1960, Richard b 1963, Michael b 1967); *Career* Nat Serv 1949–50; conslt physician St Thomas' Hosp London 1967–93 (emeritus consulting physician 1993–), physician King Edward VII's Hosp for Offrs 1977–95, chm Dist Mgmnt Team and Staff Ctee St Thomas' Hosp 1977–78, conslt physician to The Met Police 1980–92, hon conslt physician to The Army 1980–93; RCP: chm Ctee on Renal Disease 1980–92, chm Ctee on Legal Aspects of Med 1989–93, sr censor 1989–90, treas 1991–96; chief med offr Equitable Life Assurance Society 1985–96, hon conslt physician Royal Hosp Chelsea 1987–93, vice chm W Lambeth Health Authy 1989–90, special tstee St Thomas' Hosp 1989–94; memb Nat, European and Int Socs of Nephrology; FRCP 1970, FRSA 1992; *Books* Recent Advances in Renal Disease (ed 1975), Renal Disease (ed with Sir Douglas Black, 1979), Recent Advances in Renal Medicine (ed with D K Peters, 1982); *Recreations* iconology, modern English literature; *Style*— Dr Norman Jones; ✉ The Old Coach House, Forest Park Road, Brockenhurst, Hants SO42 7SW

JONES, His Hon Judge Norman Henry; QC (1985); s of Warrant Offr Henry Robert Jones, DFM (d 1992), of Bideford, N Devon, and Charlotte Isabel Scott, *née* Davis; *b* 12 Dec 1941; *Educ* Bideford GS, North Devon Tech Coll, Univ of Leeds (LLB, LLM); *m* 28 March 1970, Trudy Helen, da of Frederick George Chamberlain (d 1974), of Werrington, Peterborough; 2 s (Gareth b 22 Dec 1977, Nicholas b 14 April 1981), 1 da (Helena b 6 April 1983); *Career* called to the Bar Middle Temple 1968, recorder 1987, circuit judge (NE Circuit) 1992–; govr Guiseley Sch; *Recreations* boating, walking; *Style*— His Hon Judge Norman Jones, QC; ✉ The Leeds Courthouse, Oxford Road, Leeds LS1

JONES, Olwen Elizabeth; da of William Jones (d 1991), of Rowhedge, Colchester, and Margaret Olwen Jones (d 1995); *b* 1 March 1945; *Educ* Harrow Sch of Art (NDD), Royal Acad Schs (silver medal in drawing, bronze medal in painting, David Murray travelling scholar); *m* 1970, Charles Bartlett, s of late Charles Henry Bartlett; *Career* artist; pt/t lectr: Putney Sch of Art 1966–71, Harrow Coll of Art 1070–86, City & Guilds of London Art Schs 1993–94; RE 1982 (ARE 1979), RWS 1992 (ARWS 1989); *Exhibitions* solo exhbns incl: Zaydler Gallery London 1971, Oldham Art Gallery 1971, Dudley Museum and Art Gallery 1972, Halesworth Gallery 1973, travelling exhbn (Oldham Art Gallery, Wrexham Library and Art Centre, Lewes Art Centre) 1975, Craftsman Gallery Colchester 1977, Bohun Gallery Henley 1979, 1985 and 1988, travelling exhbn (Minories Colchester, Usher Gallery Lincoln, Univ of Durham, Oriel Theatre Clkwyd, Towner Art Gallery Eastbourne, Anthony Dawson Gallery London) 1984, Coach House Gallery Guernsey 1989, Printworks Colchester 1991 and 1993, Royal Exchange Theatre Manchester 1994, Hayletts Gallery Colchester 1994; gp exhbns incl: RA regularly 1996–, RE regularly 1968–, Barbican Centre London 1985 and 1987, Modern English Graphics Moscow; *Collections* work in numerous private and public collections incl: Dept of the Environment, Beecroft Art Gallery Southend, Bradford City Art Gallery, Graves Art Gallery Sheffield, Norwich Castle Museum, Nat Museum of Wales, Greenwich Library, Dudley Museums and Art Gallery, Reading Museums and Art Gallery, Usher Art Gallery Lincoln, art galleries of Huddersfield, Salford, Plymouth, Bolton, Keighley and Oldham; *Style*— Ms Olwen Jones

JONES, Paul Adrian; né Pond; s of Norman Henry Pond, of Worthing, W Sussex, and Amelia Josephine, *née* Hadfield; *b* 24 Feb 1942; *Educ* Portsmouth GS, Edinburgh Acad, Jesus Coll Oxford; *m* 1, 1963, Sheila MacLeod; 2 s (Matthew b 21 Oct 1963, Jacob b 10 Jan 1965); m 2, Fiona Jayne, da of Hugh Holbein Hendley; *Career* singer, musician, composer, actor, writer and presenter; *Music* gp lead singer Manfred Mann 1962–66 (composer The One in the Middle, 5–4–3–2–1 for TV pop show Ready Steady Go! and others), solo singer 1966–; memb: The Blues Band 1979–, The Manfreds 1994–; songs recorded by numerous artists incl Helen Shapiro and Eric Clapton, has played harmonica for other recording artists, TV and TV advertisements, Royal Ballet Sinfonia featured soloist Street (world premiere) 1993; composer of theme music incl: BBC TV series The Wednesday Play and Fighting Back, films Privilege, The Committee and Intimate Reflections, BBC documentary The Last Vacation; *Theatre* incl: debut as Jack Argue in Muzeeka (Open Space Theatre) 1969, Conduct Unbecoming (Queen's Theatre 1969–70, Ethel Barrymore Theatre NY 1970–71), The Banana Box (Apollo Theatre) 1973, Pippin (Her Majesty's Theatre) 1973–74, Hamlet (Ludlow Festival) 1976, Drake's Dream (Shaftesbury and Westminster Theatres) 1977–78, Cats (New London Theatre) 1982, The Beggar's Opera/Guys and Dolls (Nat Theatre) 1982–83, The Pyjama Game (Leicester Haymarket and tour) 1985–86, Kiss Me Kate (RSC Stratford and tour, Old Vic) 1987, Julius Caesar (Ludlow Festival) 1989; *Films* Privilege 1966, The Committee 1968, Demons of the Mind 1971, The Blues Band 1980; *Television* incl: Top of the Pops, Ready Steady Go! (and other pop shows), A Bit of Discretion (Yorkshire TV) 1968, Square One (LWT) 1971, Z-Cars (BBC) 1972, The Protectors 1973, A Different Kind of Frost, Jackanory, The Sweeney, Space 1999, Great Big Groovy Horse, Twiggy Show (BBC), A Matter of Taste (BBC), The Songwriters (BBC) 1978, The Beggar's Opera (Channel 4) 1983, Weekend (Granada) 1983–84, A Plus 4 (Thames and Channel 4) 1984–85, Beat the Teacher 1985–86, John Lennon - A Journey in the Life 1985, A Royal Celebration 1985, Lyrics by Tim Rice 1985, Live from the Palladium 1988, Uncle Jack series 1990–95; author of play They Put You Where You Are (BBC) 1966; *Radio* Paul Jones on Music (Radio 4) 1983, Counterpoint (BBC World Serv) 1982–92, BBC Radio 2 1985–, GLR 1988–90, Jazz FM 1990–; *Recordings* incl: The Andrew Lloyd Webber Collection (Pickwick Records), The Blues Band: Fat City (RCA Records), Groovin' With The Manfreds (EMI Recrods); *Awards* UK Male Vocalist Br Blues Connection Awards 1990 and 1991, Scroll of Honour (Outstanding Contribution to the Blues) 1993, Gold Badge Award Br Acad of Songwriters, Composers and Authors 1996; memb: Br Actors' Equity, Musicians' Union, Br Acad of Songwriters, Composers and Authors; *Recreations* music, books, walking, food, conversation; *Style*— Paul Jones, Esq; ✉ c/o Chatto and Linnit, Prince of Wales Theatre, Coventry Street, London W1V 7FE (☎ 0171 930 6677, fax 0171 930 0091)

JONES, Brig Peter; CBE (1988, MBE 1975); s of Trevor Jones, of Stoud, and Mona Mary, *née* Bishop (d 1975); *b* 17 Aug 1938; *Educ* Cheshunt GS, UCL (LLB); *Career* RA: 2 Lt TA 1960–63, Lt 42 Med Regt UK and BAOR 1963–66, Capt (adj) 324 HYAD Regt TA UK 1966–67, Capt (adj) 101 Med Regt TA UK 1967–68, Capt (adj) 25 Lt Regt UK and Hong Kong 1968–71, Maj (DAA & QMG) 8 Inf Bde NI 1971–75, Maj (battery cmd) 3RHA UK NI Cyprus Belize 1975–77, Lt Col (GSOI) Staff Coll UK 1977–80, CO 49 FD Regt 1980–82, Col (Chief instr) Royal Sch Artillery UK 1982–84, Col (ACOS) HQ BRIT Forces Falkland Islands 1984–85, Col (ACOS) HQ NI 1984–88, Col (Col ops) HQ AFNORTH Norway 1988–89, mil attaché Br Embassy Moscow 1989–93, ret; chief of technical servs UNPROFOR (Croatia) 1993; *Recreations* hockey, squash, industrial archaeology; *Clubs* Army & Navy; *Style*— Brig Peter Jones, CBE

JONES, Peter Eldon; s of Wilfrid Eldon Jones (d 1985), of Kingston upon Thames, and Jessie Meikle, *née* Buchanan (d 1970); *b* 11 Oct 1927; *Educ* Surbiton GS, Kingston Poly, UCL (DipTP); *m* 1, 1954 (m dis 1984), Gisela Marie, da of Maj Landforstmeister Karl Heinrich von Arnswaldt (d 1985), of Celle, Germany; 2 s (Christopher b 1955, Andrew b 1958), 1 da (Hella b 1962); m 2, 1985, Claudia Ann Mary Milner-Brown, da of John Alan Laurence, of Gt Waltham, Essex; *Career* sr asst architect Powell and Moya 1950–54, joined Architects Dept LCC 1954, dep sch archit LCC 1960–65, town devpt architect and planner GLC 1965–71, tech policy architect GLC 1971–74, acting dir of architecture GLC 1980–82 (educn architect 1974–82), dir of architecture and superintending architect Met Bldgs GLC/ILEA 1982–86, dir Watkins Gray Peter Jones Ltd 1986–92; conslt: Watkins Gray International 1988–, Dept for Educn 1988–92; dir Assoc of Small Historic Towns & Villages of the UK 1992–95; pres Soc Chief Architects of Local Authys 1983–84, memb EC Advsy Ctee on Educn and Trg of Architects 1986–91; Freeman: City of London 1968, Worshipful Co of Chartered Architects 1988; vice pres RIBA 1985–86, FRIBA, FRTPI; *Books* Good House Design (1956); *Recreations* travel, bridge, golf; *Clubs* Woking Golf; *Style*— Peter Jones, Esq; ✉ Dene Cottage, The Green, Pirbright, Surrey GU24 0JE

JONES, Peter George Edward Fitzgerald; CB (1985); s of Dr John Christopher Jones (d 1960), of Warwickshire, and Emily Isabel Howell (d 1954); *b* 7 June 1925; *Educ* Fairfield Sch Birmingham, Dulwich, Croydon Tech, Battersea Poly (BSc); *m* 1, 8 July 1950, Gwendoline Iris (d 1964), da of George Edwin Humphreys (d 1952), of London; 2 s (Graham b 1951, Laurence b 1956 (decd)); m 2, 17 June 1967, Jacqueline Angela, da of Clifford Meyer Gilbert (d 1993), of Newbury; 2 s (Christopher b 1968, Jason b 1971), 1 da (Tracey b 1969); *Career* pilot F/O RAF 1943–47 (India, Malaya, China); sr scientist GEC Res Labs Wembley 1951–54; UKAEA 1954–73 and MOD 1973–87: sr sci offr 1954–58, princ 1958–63, supt electronics res 1964–66, sr supt warhead electronics 1966–68, sr supt special systems 1968–74, chief of warhead devpt 1974–76, dep dir 1976–80, princ dep dir 1980–82, dir AWRE 1982–87 (ret 1987); conslt MOD: on nuclear safety 1987–, on nuclear research 1995–; thermonuclear tests Christmas Island 1957–58, participation with USA under mutual def agreement 1958–87 (with underground tests 1974–87), devpt of Chevaline and Trident 1968–87; FInstP; *Recreations* motoring; *Style*— Peter Jones, Esq, CB; ✉ Rhyd-y-Felin, Upper Llanover, Abergavenny, Gwent NP7 9DD (☎ 01873 880779)

JONES, Peter Henry Francis; s of Eric Roberts Jones, MBE, of Swansea, and Betty Irene, *née* Longhurst (d 1981); *b* 25 Feb 1952; *Educ* Bishop Gore GS Swansea, Newport HS Gwent, Balliol Coll Oxford (MA); *m* 3 June 1978, Anne Elizabeth, da of David Jones, DFC (d 1995), of Cheadle; 2 da (Clare b 14 May 1980, Eleanor b 14 July 1982); *Career* admitted slr 1977; ptnr: Darlington & Parkinson 1979–87, John Howell & Co Sheffield 1987–95; memb Law Soc's Family Law Ctee 1986–92; memb: Lord Chllr's Legal Aid Advsy Ctee 1983–92, Children Act Procedure Advsy Gp 1990, conslt to NAO Review of Legal Aid 1991–92, memb Legal Aid Bd 1992–95; actg provincial stipendiary magistrate 1992, asst recorder 1993, provincial stipendiary magistrate S Yorks Cmmn Area 1995; *Recreations* cricket, tennis, rugby, reading; *Clubs* Dethreau Boat, Scorpions Cricket, Druidstone (Dyfed); *Style*— Peter Jones, Esq; ✉ The Law Courts, PO Box 49, College Road, Doncaster DN1 3HT (☎ 01302 366711)

JONES, Prof Peter Howard; s of Thomas Leslie Jones (d 1963), of London, and Hilda Croesora, *née* Parkinson (d 1982); *b* 18 Dec 1935; *Educ* Highgate Sch, Queens' Coll Cambridge; *m* 8 Oct 1960, (Elizabeth) Jean, da of Robert James Roberton, JP (d 1972), of Morebattle, Roxburghshire; 2 da (Rachel b 1964, Laura b 1969); *Career* Br Cncl 1960–61, res scholar Univ of Cambridge 1961–63, asst lectr in philosophy Univ of Nottingham 1963–64, prof of philosophy Univ of Edinburgh 1984– (lectr then reader 1964–84), dir Inst for Advanced Studies in the Humanities Edinburgh 1986–; visiting prof of philosophy: Rochester Univ NY 1969–70, Dartmouth Coll New Hampshire 1973 and

1983, Carleton Coll Minnesota 1974, Oklahoma Univ 1978, Baylor Univ 1978, Univ of Malta 1993; visiting fell: Humanities Res Centre Australian Nat Univ 1984, Calgary Inst for the Humanities 1992; Lothian lectr 1993, Gifford lectr Univ of Aberdeen 1994–95, Loemker lectr Emory Univ 1995–96; tstee: Nat Museums of Scotland, Univ of Edinburgh Development Tst, Fettes Tst, Morrison's Acad; FRSE 1989, FRSA, FSA Scot; *Books* Philosophy and the Novel (1975), Hume's Sentiments (1982), A Hotbed of Genius (1986), Philosophy and Science in The Scottish Enlightenment (ed, 1988), The Science of Man in the Scottish Enlightenment (ed, 1989), Adam Smith Reviewed (ed, 1992); *Recreations* opera, chamber music, architecture, arts, travel; *Clubs* New (Edinburgh); *Style—* Prof Peter Jones, FRSE; ✉ Institute for Advanced Studies, University of Edinburgh, Hope Park Square, Edinburgh EH8 9NW (☎ 0131 650 4671, fax 0131 668 2252)

JONES, Peter Ivan; s of Glyndwr Jones (d 1995), of Bridport, and Edith Evelyn, *née* Whittaker; *b* 14 Dec 1942; *Educ* Gravesend GS, LSE (BScEcon); *m* 1 (m dis 1969), Judith, *née* Watson; 1 da (Claire Amanda Markham b 1964), 1 s (Nicholas Francis Markham b 1968); m 2, 15 Aug 1970, Elizabeth, da of Raymond Gent; 1 da (Victoria Louise b 1975), 1 s (Matthew Alexander b 1978); *Career* dir Boase Massimi Pollitt Partnership 1968–75, chief exec Boase Massimi Pollitt plc 1989 (non-exec dir 1983–88), chm BBDO Ltd 1989–90, dir Omnicom Inc 1989–94, chief exec Omnicom UK plc 1989–94, pres Diversified Agency Services (DAS) 1994–; pres Racehorse Owners' Assoc 1990–93; memb: Br Horseracing Bd 1992–, Horserace Betting Levy Bd 1993–95, Tote Bd 1995–, Dorset Police Authy 1995–; MIPA 1971; *Publications* Trainers Record (1973–87); *Recreations* horse racing; *Style—* Peter Jones, Esq; ✉ Melplash Farmhouse, Melplash, Bridport, Dorset DT6 3UH (☎ 01308 488383, fax 01308 488650); 38A Rossetti Garden Mansions, Flood St, London SW3 5QX (☎ 0171 352 6510); DAS, 239 Old Marylebone Road, London NW1 5QT (☎ 0171 298 7000, fax 0171 724 8292)

JONES, Sir (Thomas) Philip; kt (1986), CB (1978); *b* 13 July 1931; *Educ* Cowbridge GS, Jesus Coll Oxford (MA); *m* 1955, Mary Phillips; 2 s; *Career* asst princ MOS 1955, princ Miny of Aviation 1959, on loan to HM Treasy 1964–66, PPS to min of Aviation 1966–67, asst sec Miny of Technol subsequently Miny of Aviation Supply 1967–71; under sec: DTI 1971, Dept of Energy 1974; dep sec Dept of Energy 1976–83; chm: Total Oil Marine plc, Total Oil Holdings Ltd 1991–, IVO Energy Ltd; memb Br Nat Oil Corp 1980–82, chm Electricity Cncl 1983–90; Hon Fell Jesus Coll Oxford; *Style—* Sir Philip Jones, CB; ✉ Total Oil Marine plc, 33 Cavendish Square, London W1M 0HX (☎ 0171 416 4339, fax 0171 416 4497)

JONES, Dr Philip Edward; s of Edward Thomas Jones (d 1946), and Stella Mary, *née* Coën (d 1992); *b* 5 Oct 1945; *Educ* Manchester GS, Univ of Birmingham Med Sch (MRCP); *m* 2 Sept 1972, Bernadette Catherine, da of John Terence Cain (d 1978); 3 da (Nina b 1980, Stephanie b 1984, Sarah b 1988); *Career* house physician Dudley Rd Hosp Birmingham 1968–69, registrar Univ Coll Hosp and Whittington Hosp 1972–75, registrar and res fell Hammersmith Hosp 1975–77, sr registrar Manchester Royal Infirmary 1977–82, conslt physician Wythenshawe Hosp 1982–, med dir S Manchester Univ Hosp Tst 1996–; memb: Br Soc of Gastroenterology, N W Gastroenterology Soc, Manchester Med Soc; FRCP 1989; *Recreations* swimming, music; *Style—* Dr Philip Jones; ✉ Wythenshawe Hospital, Department of Gastroenterology, Southmoor Rd, Wythenshawe, Manchester M23 9LT (☎ 0161 291 2394)

JONES, Philip Mark; CBE (1986, OBE 1977); s of John Jones (d 1957), and Mabel, *née* Copestake (d 1980); *b* 12 March 1928; *Educ* RCM (ARCM); *m* 1 Aug 1956, Ursula, da of Walter Strebi (d 1981); *Career* pioneer of brass chamber music; princ trumpet with all maj orchestras London 1949–72, fndr and dir Philip Jones Brass Ensemble 1951–86; dir Wind and Percussion Dept: RNC Manchester 1975–77, Guildhall Sch of Music and Drama City of London 1983–88; princ Trinity Coll of Music London 1988–94; ed Just Brass Series Chester Music London 1975–89; created over fifty gramophone records with Philip Brass Ensemble; vice chm Exec Ctee Musicians' Benevolent Fund 1993–95, chm Musicians' Benevolent Fund 1995–; memb: Arts Cncl GB 1984–88, Royal Soc Musicians 1951–; memb Worshipful Co of Musicians 1987–, Freeman City of London 1988; FRNCM 1977, FRCM 1983, FRSA 1983, FGSM 1984, Hon FTCL 1988; Hon RAM 1991; *Recreations* mountain walking, skiing; *Style—* Philip Jones, Esq, CBE; ✉ 14 Hamilton Terrace, London NW8 9UG (☎ 0171 286 9155)

JONES, Prof Reginald Victor; CH (1994), CB (1946), CBE (1942); s of Harold Victor Jones (d 1953), and Alice Margaret, *née* May (d 1978); *b* 29 Sept 1911; *Educ* Alleyn's Sch Dulwich, Wadham Coll Oxford, Balliol Coll Oxford (MA, DPhil); *m* 21 March 1940, Vera Margaret (d 1992), da of Charles Cain (d 1920); 1 s (Robert Bruce b 11 Feb 1944), 2 da (Susan Primrose (Mrs Addison) b 10 Feb 1941 d 1992, Rosemary Anne (Mrs Forsyth) b 21 July 1950); *Career* dir intelligence res Air Miny 1946 (asst dir 1941–46), prof of natural philosophy Univ of Aberdeen 1946–81, dir scientific intelligence MOD 1952–53, hon memb Electronic Security Cmd USAF 1981–; author of numerous papers on scientific and def topics; chm: Infra-Red Ctee Miny of Supply and Aviation 1950–64, Br Tport Common Res Advsy Cncl 1954–55, Safety in Mines Res Advsy Bd 1956–60 (memb 1950–56); pres Crabtree Fndn 1958, chm Inst of Physics Ctee on Univ Physics 1961–63, memb Carriers Panel 1962–63, chm Paul Fund Ctee Royal Soc 1962–84 (vice pres 1971–72), chm Air Def Working Pty 1963–64, memb Scientific Advsy Cncl War Office 1963–66, chm Electronics Res Cncl Miny of Aviation and Technol 1964–70, govr Dulwich 1965–79, jt ed Notes and Records of the Royal Soc 1969–89, rapporteur Euro Convention on Human Rights 1970, chm Br Nat Ctee for History of Sci Med and Technol 1970–78, pres Section A Br Assoc 1971, life govr Haileybury 1978, hon fell Coll of Preceptors 1978, visiting prof Univ of Colorado 1982, companion Operational Res Soc 1983, visitor RMCS 1983; hon fell: Inst of Measurement and Control 1984, Br Horological Inst 1985, Wadham Coll Oxford, Balliol Coll Oxford; memb other various ctees on electronics, scientific res, measurement, def and educn; Hon Mayor San Antonio Texas 1982, Hon Freeman Clockmaker's Co 1984, hon memb American Soc of Precision Engrg 1990; Hon DSc: Univ of Strathclyde 1969, Univ of Kent 1980, Westminster Coll Missouri 1992; Hon DUniv: Univ of York 1976, Open Univ, Univ of Surrey 1979; Hon LLD Univ of Bristol 1979, Bailie of Benachie 1980; FRSE 1949, FRS 1965, Hon FIEE 1983, CPhys, CEng; BOIMA Prize Inst of Physics 1934, US Medal of Freedom with Silver Palm 1946, US Medal for Merit 1947, Duddell Medal Physical Soc 1960, Parsons Medal 1967, Hartley Medal Inst of Measurement and Control 1972, Mexican Miny of Telecommunications Medal 1973, Rutherford Medal USSR 1 977, RG Mitchell Medal 1979, Old Crows Medal 1980, CIA Medal 1993; *Books* Most Secret War (1978), Instruments and Experiences (1988), Reflections on Intelligence (1989); *Recreations* history, fishing; *Clubs* Athenaeum, Special Forces, Royal Northern and Univ (Aberdeen); *Style—* Prof Reginald Jones, CH, CB, CBE, FRS, FRSE; ✉ 8 Queen's Terrace, Aberdeen AB1 1XL (☎ 01224 648184); The White House, Corgarff, Aberdeenshire (☎ 019756 51406)

JONES, Rhidian Huw Brynmor; s of Rev Preb Ivor Brynmor Jones, RD (d 1982), of Sutton Coldfield, Warwickshire, and Elizabeth Mary, *née* Morris; *b* 13 July 1943; *Educ* Queen Mary's GS Walsall, Keble Coll Oxford (MA); *m* 8 Aug 1970, Monica Marianne, da of Bror Eric Sjunne Sjöholm (d 1957), of Halmstad, Sweden; 1 s (Gavin b 1982), 1 da (Anna b 1978); *Career* trainee sec asst Selection Tst Ltd 1966–68, legal asst Total Oil GB Ltd 1968–69, co sec J E Lesser (Hldgs) Ltd 1969, asst sec Granada Group Ltd 1970–76, articled clerk and asst slr Herbert Smith and Co 1976–80, sr asst slr Kenneth Brown Baker 1980–81, ptnr Turner Kenneth Brown 1981– (merged with Nabarro Nathanson May 1995); non-exec dir: Mornington Building Society 1986–91, Serco Group Plc 1987–94 and 1996–, The Mortgage Agency plc 1988–93, Britannia Building Society 1993–; vice pres Ealing FC (RU), tstee and hon legal advsr Middx Co RFU Youth Tst, former cncl memb Anglo Swedish Soc; Freeman City of London Slrs' Co 1979, Liveryman Turners' Co 1993 (Freeman 1992); FCIS 1976, memb Law Soc 1978, FIMgt 1987, MInstD 1987; *Recreations* rugby, military history, Celtic and Scandinavian studies; *Clubs* Rotary Club of London, Wig and Pen; *Style—* Rhidian Jones, Esq; ✉ Roseleigh, 80 Elers Road, Ealing, London W13 9QD (☎ 0181 579 9785); Nabarro Nathanson, 50 Stratton Street, London W1X 6NX (☎ 0171 493 9933, fax 0171 629 7900, car 0831 175744)

JONES, Dr Richard Arnold Yardley; s of Thomas Richard Jones (d 1989), and Marjorie Yardley Jones (d 1994); *b* 8 April 1936; *Educ* Rydal Sch, Clare Coll Cambridge (scholar, MA), Churchill Coll Cambridge (PhD), Yale Univ (MS); *m* 1959, Barbara Anne, da of Claude Stuart Whiteley; 1 s (Dr Andrew Richard Jones b 1961), 1 da (Gwynneth Anne (Mrs Clay) b 1963); *Career* research fell Churchill Coll Cambridge 1960–61, asst lectr Dept of Chemistry Univ of Sheffield 1961–63; Univ of East Anglia: lectr then sr lectr 1963–95, dean Sch of Chemical Scis 1984–90, pro-vice-chllr 1990–, sr fell 1995–; chm: Ctee of Heads of Univ Chemistry Depts/HE Chemistry Conf 1991–93; sec IUPAC Cmmn on Physical Organic Chemistry 1979–89; corporation memb Univ of Suffolk 1995–; FRSC 1971, CChem 1975, FRSA 1990; *Books* Physical and Mechanistic Organic Chemistry (1979 and 1984), Chemistry: Principles and Applications (1988); *Style—* Dr Richard Jones; ✉ 27 Newfound Drive, Cringleford, Norwich, Norfolk NR4 7RY (☎ 01603 451182); University of East Anglia, Norwich, Norfolk NR4 7TJ (☎ 01603 592735, fax 01603 507753)

JONES, Richard Colwyn; s of late William Meirion Jones, and Doris, *née* Hill; *b* 24 June 1950; *Educ* Penlan Comp Sch, Bournemouth Coll (HND Business Studies); *m* 1973, Angela, da of Hugh Scriven; 1 s (Andrew Stephen b 1974), 1 da (Karen Elizabeth b 1978); *Career* trainee accountant BP 1972–74, Aluminium Co of America 1974–85 (successively devpt accountant, chief mgmnt accountant, fin controller, fin dir & co sec, mangr ops accounting Euro Region, md); with Coopers & Lybrand 1985– (successively sr conslt, managing conslt, assoc dir, currently ptnr i/c World Class Fin Service Gp); former pres Swansea & W Wales Dist ACCA; FCCA, MCIS, MIMC; *Recreations* tennis, badminton, gardening, reading, walking; *Clubs* National Liberal, Congresbury Tennis (chm); *Style—* Richard Jones, Esq; ✉ Beech Hay, Wrington Road, Congresbury, Bristol BS19 5AR (☎ 01934 832413); Coopers and Lybrand, 1 Embankment Place, London WC2N 6NN (☎ 0171 213 3006, fax 0171 213 3103)

JONES, Richard Henry; QC (1996); s of Henry Ingham Jones (d 1993), of Teignmouth, Devon, and Betty Marian, *née* Allison; *b* 6 April 1950; *Educ* Moseley GS Birmingham, St Peter's Coll Oxford (MA Jurisprudence); *m* 1, 1978 (m dis 1983), Gillian Margaret Lang; m 2, Sarah Jane, da of Peter Wildsmith; 1 s (Christopher b 12 March 1991), 1 da (Bryony Alice b 21 July 1994); *Career* called to the Bar Inner Temple 1972, in practice 1972–80 and 1986–; legal advsr: Crown Life Insurance Group 1980–82, Financial Times Group 1982–86; *Recreations* cricket and rugby (as spectator); *Clubs* MCC, RAC, Harlequins RFC; *Style—* Richard Jones, Esq, QC; ✉ 1 Crown Office Row, Temple, London EC4Y 7HH (☎ 0171 583 9292, fax 0171 353 9292)

JONES, Robert; s of Robert Aldwyn Jones, of Sanderstead, Surrey, and Joyce Margaret, *née* Madley; *b* 21 Nov 1956; *Educ* Trinity Sch of John Whitgift Croydon, Royal Coll of Music (jr exhibitioner in piano), Christ Church Oxford (music scholar, MA), Univ of London (Music Teacher's Cert); *m* 23 May 1981, Eleanor Anne, da of Kenneth Michael Harre; 3 s (Edward b 12 Nov 1984, Henry b 4 Feb 1987, Alexander b 16 June 1990); *Career* organist Trinity Sch 1972–75, organist and choirmaster St Mary's Church Addington 1973–75, academical clerk (choral scholar) Christ Church Oxford and conductor Steeple Aston Choral Soc and Nuova Cappella of Oxford 1975–78, asst organis Hampstead Parish Church and St Clement Danes 1978–79, lay clerk St George's Chapel Windsor Castle and organist/choirmaster All Saints Windsor 1979–83, also visiting tutor Eton Coll and pt/t music teacher Tiffin Girls' Sch 1979–83, dir of music Putney Parish Church and conductor Feltham Choral Soc and Thames Voyces 1983–85, lay clerk Westminster Cathedral 1985–88, dir of music St Bride's Fleet St 1988–; fndr memb Tallis Scholars; freelance organ recitalist in venues incl St Paul's Cathedral and Sydney Cathedral, regular oratorio soloist; numerous bdcasts and recordings with choir of St Bride's, Tallis Scholars (Gramophone Record of the Year 1987), Orlando Consort (Gramophone Early Music Award 1996) and Gabrieli Consort; ARCM 1974, FRCO (chm) 1975, ADCM 1979, LRAM 1979; *Recreations* watching cricket, current affairs, good food, real ale; *Style—* Robert Jones, Esq; ✉ 19 Hatch Lane, Windsor, Berks SL4 3QU (☎ and fax 01753 853573); St Bride's Church, Fleet Street, London EC4Y 8AU (☎ 0171 353 1301, fax 0171 583 4867)

JONES, Robert Brannock; MP (C) Hertfordshire West (majority 13,940); s of Ray Elwin and Iris Pamela Jones; *b* 26 Sept 1950; *Educ* Merchant Taylors', Univ of St Andrews (MA); *m* 1989, Jennifer Anne, da of Mrs Iris Sandercock and the late Lewis Sandercock; *Career* memb: St Andrews Burgh Cncl 1972–75, Fife CC 1973–75, Chiltern DC 1979–83; Parly candidate (C): Kirkcaldy Oct 1974, Teesside Stockton 1979; MP (C) Herts W 1983–, PPS to Min of Aviation, Roads and Traffic 1986–87, chm Environment Select Ctee 1992–94 (memb 1983–94), Parly under-sec of state Dept of Environment 1994–95, min of state Dept of Environment 1995–; Liveryman Worshipful Co of Merchant Taylors; *Recreations* squash, tennis, music, shove-halfpenny; *Style—* Robert Jones Esq, MP; ✉ House of Commons, London SW1A 0AA

JONES, Prof Robert Maynard; s of Sydney Jones (d 1956), of Cardiff, and Edith Jones (d 1981); *b* 20 May 1929; *Educ* Univs of Wales and Ireland (MA, PhD, DLitt); *m* 27 Dec 1952, Anne Elizabeth, da of John James (d 1979), of Clunderwen; 1 s (Rhodri Siôn), 1 da (Lowri Dole); *Career* former head of Dept of Welsh Language and Lit Univ of Wales Aberystwyth 1980 (lectr and sr lectr 1955–77, reader 1978, now emeritus prof); memb Editorial Bd Welsh Nat Dictionary; fell Yr Academi Gymreig 1965; hon vice pres UCCF 1986, FBA 1993; *Books include* Nid Yw Dŵr yn Plygu (1958), I'r Arch (1959), Cyflwyno'r Gymraeg (1964), Ci Wrth y Drws (1968), System in Child Language (1970), Traed Prydferth (1973), Tafod y Llenor (1974), Llên Cymru a Chrefydd (1977), Seiliau Beirniadaeth (1984–88), Casgliad o Gerddi (1988), Crio Chwerthin (1990), Dawn Gweddwon (1992), Cyfriniaeth Gymraeg (1994), Canu Arnaf (1995), Epistol Serch a Selsig (1996); *Clubs* Y Bedol (Aberystwyth); *Style—* Prof Emeritus Robert Jones, FBA; ✉ Tandderwen, Heol Llanbadarn, Aberystwyth, Dyfed SY23 1HB (☎ 01970 623603)

JONES, Robert Nicholas; s of Cliff Jones, and Marian Jones; *b* 10 Nov 1965; *m* 8 August 1987, Megan, da of Clive Rowlands, OBE; *Career* rugby union scrum-half; clubs: Swansea RFC (formerly capt) until 1996, transferred to Bristol RFC 1996–, Barbarians RFC; rep Wales B (debut 1985); Wales: debut v England 1986, memb World Cup squad 1987 (5 appearances), memb Triple Crown winning team 1988 (capt 1990), tour NZ 1988 (1 test appearance), partnered Jonathan Davies, *qv*, 22 times, memb World Cup squad 1991 and 1995, 54 caps; memb Br Lions tour Aust 1989 (3 test appearances) and NZ 1993 (no tests); rep Wales in cricket on three age levels; business devpt exec; *Recreations* golf, cricket; *Style—* Robert Jones, Esq; ✉ c/o Bristol RFC, Memorial Ground, Filton Avenue, Horfield, Bristol BS7 0AQ (☎ 0117 951 4448)

JONES, Robert (Rob); *b* 5 Nov 1971; *Career* professional footballer (defender); with Crewe Alexander 1987–91; Liverpool FC: joined for £300,000 1991, FA Cup winners 1992, winners Coca-Cola Cup 1995; England: 8 full caps; *Style—* Rob Jones; ✉ Liverpool FC, Anfield Road, Anfield, Liverpool L4 0TH (☎ 0151 263 2361)

JONES, (James) Roger; s of Albert James Jones, and Hilda Vera, *née* Evans (d 1989); *b* 30 May 1952; *Educ* Shrewsbury, St Catharine's Coll Cambridge (sr scholar, MA); *Career* called to the Bar Middle Temple 1974 (Lloyd Jacob Meml exhibitioner, Astbury scholar), practised Oxford and Midland Circuit 1975–83, Office of the Parliamentary Counsel 1983–91, with Law Commission 1988–91, dep parliamentary counsel 1991–94; head Antique Dept Colefax & Fowler 1994–; *Recreations* walking the dog; *Style*— Roger Jones, Esq; ✉ Colefax & Fowler, 39 Brook Street, London W1Y 2JE

JONES, Ronald Fitzgerald; OBE (1989); s of Henry Fitzgerald Jones (d 1941), of Liverpool, and Margaret Chisholm, *née* Mackenzie (d 1964); *b* 16 Feb 1926; *Educ* Skerry's Coll Liverpool, Wallasey Catering Coll (CGLI Diplomas 150 and 151); *m* 1, 1951, Jeanette Pamela (d 1975), da of Samuel Wood; 2 s (Graham Stuart b 1955, Russell Brent b 1959); m 2, 1978, Eve Helen Hunter Macpherson, da of David Warren; *Career* WWII RN 1944–46; trainee hotel mangr 1946–53, gen mangr Dornoch Hotel Scotland 1956–57, sr asst mangr Midland Hotel Manchester 1957–58; gen mangr: Turnberry Hotel Ayrshire 1958–61, Station Hotel Hull 1961–64, Queen's Hotel Leeds 1964–67, Central Hotel Glasgow 1967–69, Royal Garden Hotel London 1969–72, Athenaeum Hotel London 1972–84; dir and gen mangr Claridge's London 1984–94, dir Dormy House Hotel Broadway 1995–, prtnr Jones and Jones Hotel Management Services 1995–; Master Innholder 1979, Hotelier of the Year 1988; Freeman City of London 1979, Hon Citizen City of New Orleans 1979, Liveryman Worshipful Co of Distillers 1987, Freeman Worshipful Co of Innholders 1990; FHCIMA 1979 (memb 1969); *Books* Grand Hotelier (1997); *Recreations* painting, music, travel, theatre; *Style*— Ronald Jones, Esq, OBE; ✉ 714 Willoughby House, Barbican, London EC2Y 8BN

JONES, Prof Ronald Mervyn; s of Cdr Glyn Owen Jones, MBE, OStJ (d 1987), and Doris, *née* Woodley (d 1983); *b* 24 April 1947; *Educ* Devonport HS Plymouth, Univ of Liverpool (MD); *m* 1, 1970 (m dis 1988), Angela Christine, *née* Parsonage; 1 s (Alex b 1979), 1 da (Emily b 1976); m 2, 22 Sept 1989, Caroline Ann, da of Dr Neill Wordsworth Marshall; 2 da (Catherine Elizabeth b 17 Feb 1992, Lucy Clare b 21 Jan 1995); *Career* memb Faculty: Karolinska Inst Stockholm 1978, Univ of Michigan USA 1979–80; conslt Nottingham Hosps 1981–82, sr lectr and conslt Guy's Hosp 1982–90, prof of anaesthetics Imperial Coll London and conslt anaesthetist St Mary's Hosp 1990–, conslt anaesthetist Northwick Park Hosp 1992; memb Advsy Ctee on NHS Drugs (Dept of Health); academician Euro Acad of Anaesthesiology; hon life memb Aust Soc of Anaesthetists; FFARCS; *Books* Medicine for Anaesthetists (1989), Clinical Anaesthesia (1995); *Recreations* music, history, sailing; *Clubs* Royal Naval Sailing Association; *Style*— Prof Ronald Jones; ✉ Department of Anaesthetics, St Mary's Hospital, London W2 1NY (☎ 0171 725 1681, fax 0171 725 6425, e-mail h.kenna@ic.ac.uk)

JONES, Prof Ronald Samuel; s of Samuel Jones (d 1974), of Chapel House, Old Racecourse, Oswestry, Shropshire, and Gladys Jane, *née* Philips (d 1953); *b* 29 Oct 1937; *Educ* Oswestry Boys' HS, Univ of Liverpool (BVSc); *m* 21 April 1962, Pamela, da of Wilfred Evans, of Rock Cottage, Pant Oswestry, Shropshire; 2 da (Rachel Mary Patricia b 1963, Alison Jane b 1966); *Career* Univ of Glasgow: house surgn 1960–61, univ asst 1961–62; Univ of Liverpool: lectr 1962–77, sr lectr 1977–86, reader 1986–89, prof 1990–; RCVS: memb Cncl 1986–, treas 1993–95, pres 1996–; FRCVS 1981 (MRCVS 1960), FIBiol 1988, DVSc Pretoria 1992; *Recreations* gardening, horse racing, philately, fly-fishing; *Clubs* Farmers'; *Style*— Prof Ronald S Jones; ✉ 7 Birch Road, Oxton, Birkenhead, Merseyside L43 5UF (☎ 0151 653 9008, fax 0151 706 5884); University Department of Anaesthesia, Royal Liverpool Hospital, University of Liverpool, PO Box 147, Liverpool L69 3BX (☎ 0151 706 4006, fax 0151 653 7551)

JONES, Rupert James Livingston; s of Walter Herbert Jones (d 1982), and Dorothy Jocelyn, *née* Dignum (d 1989); *b* 2 Sept 1953; *Educ* King's Coll Sch Wimbledon, Univ of Birmingham (LLB); *m* 24 June 1978, Sheila Carol, da of Andrew Kertesz (d 1993); 3 s (Oliver b 10 June 1984, Stephen b 13 Sept 1989, Michael b 20 Feb 1994), 1 da (Philippa b 31 Jan 1987); *Career* admitted slr 1978, ptnr Allen and Overy 1985– (articled clerk 1976–78, asst slr 1978–85); chm London Young Slrs Gp 1987–88 (Ctee 1984–89); memb Nat Ctee of Young Slrs Gp 1986–89, chm Whittington Ctee of City of London Slrs Co 1992–94 (memb 1988–94); memb Worshipful Co of Slrs 1985–; memb Law Soc 1976; *Recreations* gardening, cinema, motoring; *Style*— Rupert Jones, Esq; ✉ Allen & Overy, One New Change, London EC4M 9QQ (☎ 0171 330 3000, fax 0171 330 9999)

JONES, Russell Alan; *b* 26 May 1960; *Educ* Greenshaw HS Sutton, Univ of Kent at Canterbury (BA); *Career* orch personnel mangr Royal Liverpool Philharmonic Soc 1981–86, concerts mangr Scottish Chamber Orch 1986, chief exec and co sec Nat Fedn of Music Socs 1987– (joined as admin/dir); admin Haydn Orch 1986–, jt fndr/admin/co sec Southwark Music Festival 1988–90; currently chm Nat Music Cncl of GB (memb Exec Ctee 1987–94); memb: Cncl London Symphony Chorus 1987–89 and 1991–94, Cncl Amateur Music Assoc 1987–89, Steering Ctee Nat Music Day, Cncl Nat Fedn of Young Choirs, Panel PRS Awards for Enterprise; memb: Music Ctee Lords Taveners, Musicians' Union, Events Ctee Musicians' Benevolent Fund, Nat Campaign for the Arts, Nat Tst, Friends of the Phil (RLPO); patron Slaithwaite Philharmonic Orch; tenor: London Symphony Chorus, London Choral Soc, New London Collegium (currently hon treas); *Recreations* music, singing, piano, violin, current affairs, Br and American politics, cooking and entertaining, wine (memb Sunday Times Wine Club), badminton, golf; *Style*— Russell Jones, Esq; ✉ National Federation of Music Societies, Francis House, Francis Street, London SW1P 1DE (☎ 0171 828 7320, fax 0171 828 5504, e-mail POSTMASTER@NFMS.DEMON.UK.DOC)

JONES, Samuel; CBE (1996), DL (Leics 1992); s of late Rev Samuel Jones, of Nairn, Scot, and late Sarah Johnston, *née* McCulloch; *b* 27 Dec 1939; *Educ* Morpeth GS, Univ of Manchester (LLB), Univ of Kent (MA); *m* 17 Oct 1964, Jean Ann, da of Frank Broadhurst, of Macclesfield, Cheshire; 2 da (Allison b 1 March 1967, Tracey b 16 Oct 1970); *Career* chief exec Leics CC 1976–91, clerk of Lieutenancy Leics 1976–91, sec Lord Chancellor's Advsy Ctee for Leics 1976–91; town clerk Corp of London 1991–96; chm designate Heathrow Airport Consultative Ctee, chm N Devon Mktg Bureau, memb Cncl on Tbnls; memb Law Soc; Class III Ordem de Merito (Portugal) 1993; *Style*— Samuel Jones, Esq, CBE, DL; ✉ Middleborough House, Baggy Point, Croyde, Devon EX33 1PA (☎ 01271 890210, fax 01271 890879)

JONES, Dr Schuyler; s of Schuyler Jones, of Wichita, Kansas, and Ignace, *née* Mead; *b* 7 Feb 1930; *Educ* Wichita HS, Univ of Edinburgh (MA), Univ of Oxford (MA, DPhil); *m* 20 Dec 1955, Lis Margit Søndergaard, da of Malling Rasmussen, of Karlby, Denmark; 1 s (Peter Rasmussen b 2 Aug 1956), 1 da (Hannah Lis b 3 Oct 1962); *Career* Univ of Oxford; lectr in ethnology 1970–71, dir Pitt Rivers Museum (asst curator 1971–85, curator 1985–), head Dept of Ethnology and Prehistory 1985–91, chm Sch of Anthropology and Museum Ethnography 1993–; anthropological expeditions: N Africa, The Sahara, W Africa 1951, French Equatorial Africa, Belgian Congo, E Africa 1952, S Africa, The Zambezi and Congo Rivers 1953, French W Africa, The Sahara 1954, Eastern Med 1956, Greek Is 1957, Turkey, Iran, Afghanistan, Pakistan, India, Nepal 1958, Pakistan, Kashmir, Afghanistan 1959, Nuristan 1960–70, Central China, Gobi Desert, Chinese Turkestan 1984, E Africa 1985, Central China, Tibet, Gobi Desert 1986, S China, Chinese Turkestan, Hunza, Gilgit 1988, Greenland 1991, E Africa and Greenland 1993; cncl memb RAI 1986–90, tstee Horniman Museum London 1989–94; *Books* Sous le Soleil Africain (1955), Under the African Sun (1956), Annotated Bibliography of Nuristan (Kafiristan) & the Kalash Kafirs of Chitral (1966), The Political Organization of the Kam Kafirs (1967), Men of Influence in Nuristan (1974), Nuristan (with Lennart Edelberg, 1979), Hunting and Trading on the Great Plains 1859–1875 (ed, 1986), Afghanistan (1992), The Arts and Crafts of Tibet: Environment, Pastoral Economy, and Material Culture (1996); *Style*— Dr Schuyler Jones; ✉ Pitt Rivers Museum, Univ of Oxford, South Parks Rd, Oxford OX1 3PP (☎ 01865 270924)

JONES, Sir Simon Warley Frederick Benton; 4 Bt (UK 1919), of Treeton, West Riding of Yorks, JP (Lincs 1971); s of Lt-Col Sir Peter Fawcett Benton Jones, 3 Bt, OBE (d 1972), and Nancy, *née* Pickering; *b* 11 Sept 1941; *Educ* Eton, Trinity Coll Cambridge (MA); *m* 14 April 1966, Margaret Fiona, OBE, eldest da of David Rutherford Dickson, of Bury St Edmunds, Suffolk; 3 s (James Peter Martin b 1973, David William Anthony b 1975, Alastair Frederick Malcolm b 1981), 2 da (Fiona Charlotte b 1967, Fleur Alexandra b 1970); *Heir* s, James Peter Martin Benton Jones b 1 Jan 1973; *Career* farmer; High Sheriff Lincs 1977–78; *Recreations* shooting, fishing; *Style*— Sir Simon Benton Jones, Bt, JP; ✉ Irnham Hall, Grantham, Lincs (☎ 0147 684212); Sopley, Christchurch, Dorset

JONES, (John) Stanley; s of George White Jones (d 1958), of Wigan, Lancs, and Elizabeth Jones; *b* 10 June 1933; *Educ* Wigan GS, Wigan Art Sch (NDD), Slade Sch of Art UCL (Slade Dip in Fine Art), Ecole des Beaux Arts Paris; *m* 18 March 1961, Jennifer Francis, da of Lawrence Frederick Stone; 1 s (Matthew b 4 June 1965), 1 da (Liza b 17 Dec 1962); *Career* lectr in lithography Slade Sch of Fine Art UCL 1958, co fndr Curwen Studio London 1958; dir: Curwen Prints Ltd 1962–92, Curwen Chilford Prints; pres Printmakers' Cncl; *Books* Lithography for Artists (1963); *Recreations* photography, walking, appreciation of music; *Style*— Stanley Jones, Esq; ✉ Curwen Prints Ltd, 4 Windmill St, London W1 (☎ 0171 636 1459); Curwen Chilford Prints, Chilford Hall, nr Linton, Cambridgeshire (☎ 01223 893544, fax 01223 894056)

JONES, Dr (William) Stanley; s of William Cyril Jones (d 1967), and Catherine Ruby, *née* Paton; *b* 20 Nov 1941; *Educ* St Asaph GS, UCNW Bangor (BSc, PhD); *m* 1, 1967, Brenda Mary, *née* Charles; 1 s (Carl William b 27 March 1974), 1 da (Alexandra Elizabeth b 14 Feb 1972); m 2, 24 May 1978, Margaret Ann, da of Leslie Ernest Cyril James; 1 s (David Michael b 16 Feb 1978); *Career* section head Corp Res Labs Texas Instruments Ltd UK and Dallas 1966–71, head of section Scientific Servs Dept CEGB Wythenshawe rising to head of Control and Instrumentation Technol Section CEGB Res Labs 1971–79, project dir Software Sciences Ltd 1979–82, tech mktg dir rising to gp md Hugh Pushman Associates Ltd 1982–85; Rolls Royce Group: dir NEI Electronics Ltd 1988 (joined as gen mangr C&I Systems Business Unit 1985), md R-R Industrial Controls Ltd 1989–96, md Reyrolle Ltd 1992–96, md Rolls-Royce Transmission & Distribution Ltd 1996–; memb Safety Critical Software Advsy Gp IEE; chm: Northern SATRO, Northern Training Awards, S Tyneside Enterprise Partnership; dep chm: Tyneside TEC, Tyneside Careers; dir Newcastle City Challenge; FIEE 1986, FIMgt 1990, FEng 1991; *Books* Micros for Managers (1981); *Recreations* walking, photography, birdwatching; *Style*— Dr Stanley Jones, FEng; ✉ Rolls-Royce T&D Ltd, Hebburn, Tyne & Wear NE31 1UP (☎ 0191 401 5101, fax 0191 401 5577)

JONES, Stephen John Moffat; s of Gordon Jones, of Marlow, Bucks, and Margaret, *née* Moffat; *b* 31 May 1957; *Educ* Liverpool Coll, St Martin's Coll of Art (BA); *Career* model millinery designer 1981–, estab diffusion range Miss Jones/Jones Boy 1989; first British milliner to work for French designer collections (clients since 1984 incl John Paul Gaultier, Thierry Mugler, Comme des Garcons and Claude Montana); designer of hats for film, TV and music business; work in perm collections of: V&A London, Australian Nat Gallery Canberra, Brooklyn Museum NY; references of work included in Status, Style, Glamour (Colin McDowell, Thames and Hudson, 1982); estab: SJ Scarves and Handkerchiefs 1988, SJ Kimonos 1989, SJ Handbags and Gloves 1993; other design projects incl: Shiseido Color Creator (Shiseido Cosmetics Japan) 1987, design conslt to Nissan Cars Ltd; *Recreations* painting, sculpture; *Style*— Stephen Jones, Esq; ✉ Stephen Jones Millinery Ltd, 36 Great Queen Street, Covent Garden, London (☎ 0171 242 0770, fax 0171 242 0796)

JONES, Stephen Roger Curtis; s of Roger Henry Curtis Jones (d 1979), and Kate Alice, *née* Pearson (d 1989); *b* 31 March 1944; *Educ* Brentwood Sch Essex, Univ of Southampton (BA, MA), RSA/UCLES (TEFL 1996); *m* 1973, Janet, *née* Corkett; 2 da (Marianne Isabel b 16 July 1975, Alyson Kate b 26 Aug 1977); *Career* asst princ grade MOD 1968–70, UK Delgn to NATO 1971–73; DES 1973–82: princ grade 1973–76, private sec to Sec of State (Rt Hon Shirley Williams) 1976–78, asst sec 1978–81; asst dir City of London Poly 1982–85; DES (now DFEE) 1986–94: attached to HMI 1986–88, head of Int Rels Div 1988–92, head of Int Rels Youth and Gen Branch 1992–94; educn conslt 1994–96; *Recreations* choral singing, walking; *Style*— Stephen Jones, Esq

JONES, Stewart Elgan; QC (1994); s of Gwilym John Jones (d 1987), of Flecknoe, Warwickshire, and Elizabeth, *née* Davies; *b* 20 Jan 1945; *Educ* Cheltenham, Queen's Coll Oxford (MA); *m* 21 July 1979, Jennifer Anne, da of Maj James Ian Leonard Syddall (d 1963), of Riseley, Berks; 2 da (Eleanor b 1980, Clementine b 1981), 2 step c (Katherine b 1969, James b 1971); *Career* called to the Bar Gray's Inn 1972, memb Western Circuit, recorder of the Crown Ct 1990–; *Recreations* home, hearth, the great outdoors; *Clubs* Athenaeum; *Style*— Stewart E Jones, Esq, QC; ✉ 3 Paper Buildings, Temple, London EC4Y 7EU (☎ 0171 583 8055, fax 0171 353 6271)

JONES, Stuart Kingston; s of Peter Jones (d 1990), and Barbara Ann Jones; *b* 26 May 1951; *Educ* Shrewsbury, Hotchkiss Sch USA (Winston Churchill scholarship, 3 Dips); *Career* sub editor and writer The Field Magazine 1972–74; The Times Newspaper: sub editor 1974–80, asst sports editor 1980–81, football corr 1981–93, sports and tennis corr 1993; *Recreations* sport (especially golf, tennis and cricket), photography, reading; *Style*— Stuart Jones, Esq

JONES, Terence Graham Parry (Terry); s of late Alick George Parry Jones, and Dilys Louise, *née* Newnes (d 1971); *b* 1 Feb 1942; *Educ* Royal GS Guildford, St Edmund Hall Oxford; *m* 20 June 1970, Alison, da of James Veitch Telfer; 1 s (William George Parry b 1976), 1 da (Sally Louise Parry b 1974); *Career* writer and performer Monty Python's Flying Circus BBC TV 1969–74; film dir, actor and co-writer: Monty Python and the Holy Grail 1974, Monty Python's Life of Brian 1978, Monty Python's Meaning of Life 1981; dir Personal Services 1986; dir, writer and actor: Erik the Viking 1989, The Wind in the Willows 1996; TV writer and presenter: So This Is Progress 1991, Crusades 1994/95; TV dir and co-writer: Ripping Yarns 1978, More Ripping Yarns 1980, Dr Fegg's Encyclopeadia (sic) of All World Knowledge 1984; *Books* Chaucer's Knight (1980), Fairy Tales (1981), The Saga of Erik the Viking (1983), Nicobobinus (1986), The Curse of the Vampire's Socks (1988), Attacks of Opinion (1988), Fantastic Stories (1992), Crusades (jtly, 1994), Lady Cottington's Book of Pressed Fairies (jtly, 1994); *Style*— Terry Jones, Esq; ✉ c/o Mayday Management, 68A Delancey Street, London NW1 7RY (☎ 0171 284 0242)

JONES, Thomas Henry (Tom); OBE (1996); s of Cadwaladr Jones (d 1986), and Olwen Ellyw, *née* Humphreys (d 1993); *b* 8 Feb 1950; *Educ* Tywyn Sch Merioneth, Univ Coll of Wales Aberystwyth (BA); *m* 20 Sept 1980, Dr Margaret Elizabeth Jones, da of John Wyn Jones, of Plas Gwyn, Llangyniew, Welshpool, Powys; 2 s (Owain b 1 Sept 1985, Steffan b 24 Nov 1991), 1 da (Siwan b 12 Jan 1988); *Career* farmer; former vice-pres Farmers' Union of Wales, former pres Young Farmers' Clubs of Wales; chm Wales Ctee Nat Lottery Charities Bd; memb: Sec of State's Wales Agric Advsy Panel, Countryside Council for Wales, Agric Trg Bd; formerly: memb S4C Authy, memb National Parks Review Panel, govr Welsh Agricultural Colls; FRAgS; *Books* Brain Yn Y Brwyn (1976),

Dyddiadur Ffarmwr (1985); *Style*— Tom Jones, Esq, OBE; ✉ Plas Coch, Dolanog, Welshpool, Powys (☎ 01938 810553)

JONES, (David) Timothy; s of David Percy Jones (d 1993), and Elvair Jones (d 1990); *b* 21 Aug 1944; *Educ* Queen Elizabeth GS Carmarthen, Univ of Salford, Univ of Leeds (PhD), INSEAD (MBA); *m* 30 March 1968, Jean Margaret; 4 da; *Career* British Petroleum: jr posts Refineries Dept London and Paris and Aden refinery S Yemen 1969–76, mangr liquid petroleum gas and N Sea gas BP Gas London 1979, dep refinery mangr Deutsche BP Hamburg 1979–81, planning mangr BP Oil London 1981–85, gen mangr with Deutsche BP Hamburg 1985–88, dir BP France Paris 1988–89, chief exec oil trading and refining BP Oil London 1990, dir BP Oil Europe Brussels 1990–93; dep chm and chief exec offr Lloyd's Register of Shipping 1993–; MRSC; *Recreations* golf, squash, watching rugby; *Style*— Timothy Jones, Esq; ✉ Lloyd's Register of Shipping, 100 Leadenhall Street, London EC3A 3BP (☎ 0171 709 9166, fax 0171 488 4796)

JONES, Timothy Arthur; s of Canon Idwal Jones, of Leam Cottage, Birdingbury, Warwicks, and Jean Margaret, *née* Shuttleworth; *b* 20 April 1951; *Educ* Christ's Hosp Horsham (Almoners' Nominee Open scholar), Jesus Coll Cambridge, LSE, Coll of Law Chancery Lane; *children* 1 da (Harriet b 1980); *Career* called to the Bar: Inner Temple 1975, King's Inn Dublin 1990; practising Midland and Oxford Circuit (specialising in commercial, landlord and tenant, planning and administrative law); Parly candidate (Lib later Lib Democrat): Warwick and Leamington 1974, Mid Staffordshire 1983, 1987 and 1990; pres Cambridge Univ Liberal Club 1970; memb Standing Ctee Cambridge Union 1971, vice chm League of Friends Rugeley Hosp 1985–89; memb: Lib Democrat Federal Policy Ctee 1990–92, Lib Democrats' Federal Appeals Panel 1990–; pres Rugeley Lib Democrats 1994–; memb: Planning and Environmental Bar Assoc, Admin Law Bar Assoc, Union des Avocats Européens; *Recreations* theatre, walking, ornithology; *Style*— Timothy Jones, Esq; ✉ 7 Fountain Court, Steelhouse Lane, Birmingham B4 6DR (☎ 0121 236 8531, fax 0121 236 4408); Arden Chambers, 59 Fleet Street, London EC4Y 1JU (☎ 0171 353 3132, fax 0171 353 2774)

JONES, Timothy Duncan; s of Robert Walter Jones, and Doreen, *née* Price; *b* 16 Jan 1967; *Educ* Dartmouth HS, Great Barr Birmingham; *Career* memb GB swimming team for: Olympic Games 1988, Euro Championships 1989, Cwlth Games 1986 and 1990; holder Br record 200m butterfly, ranked number 1 in GB 1988, 1989, 1990 and 1991; finalist in Euro Championships 1989; coach to England team at Cwlth Games 1994; coach to GB team: Euro Championships 1995, Olympic Games Atlanta 1996; chief coach Scottish Amateur Swimming Assoc (City of Edinburgh); *Recreations* golf, electronic music, travelling; *Style*— Timothy Jones, Esq; ✉ 43 Gateside Avenue, Haddington, East Lothian EH41 3SE (☎ 01620 826324); Royal Commonwealth Pool, 21 Dalkeith Road, Edinburgh EH16 5BB (☎ 0131 667 7211, fax 0131 662 0265)

JONES, Tom, *né* Thomas Jones Woodward; *b* 7 June 1940; *m*; *Career* singer; formed first band Tommy Scott & The Senators 1963; released first solo single Chills and Fever 1964; hit singles incl: It's Not Unusual (1965, reached UK no 1), Thunderball (from film, 1966), Green Green Grass of Home (1966, UK no 1), Detroit City (1967, UK no 8), I'll Never Fall in Love Again (1967, UK no 2), I'm Coming Home (1967, UK no 2), Delilah (1968, UK no 2), 'Til (1971, UK no 2), A Boy From Nowhere (1987, UK no 2), Kiss (with Art of Noise, 1988, UK no 5); albums incl: Along Came Jones (1965, UK no 11), From The Heart (1966, UK no 23), Green Green Grass of Home (1967, UK no 3), Live At the Talk of the Town (1967, UK no 6), Delilah (1968, UK no 1), Help Yourself (1969, UK no 4), This Is Tom Jones (1969, UK no 2), Tom Jones Live In Las Vegas (1969, UK no 3), Tom (1970, UK no 4), She's A Lady (1971, UK no 9), 20 Greatest Hits (1975, UK no 1), I'm Coming Home (1978, UK no 12), Matador (musical soundtrack, 1987, UK no 26), Under Milk Wood (with George Martin, 1988), Carrying A Torch (with Van Morrison, 1991, UK no 44), The Lead and How to Swing It (1994); TV shows incl: Billy Cotton Band Show 1965, The Ed Sullivan Show 1965, Call In On Tom 1965, Sunday Night At The London Palladium, Spotlight 1967, This Is Tom Jones 1969, Comic Relief 1991, Tom Jones - The Right Time 1992; fell Welsh Coll of Music and Drama 1994; *Style*— Tom Jones, Esq; ✉ Tom Jones Enterprises, 10100 Santa Monica Boulevard, Suite 205 Century City, Los Angeles, Calif 90067, USA (☎ 00 1 310 552 0044, fax 00 1 310 552 0714)

JONES, Sir (Owen) Trevor; kt (1981); s of Owen and Ada Jones, of Dyserth; *b* 1927; *Career* memb: Liverpool City Cncl 1968, Liverpool Metropolitan District Cncl 1973–91 (ldr 1981–83); memb Merseyside Devpt Corpn 1981; pres Liberal Party 1972–73, contested (Lib) Liverpool Toxteth 1974; *Style*— Sir Trevor Jones; ✉ 221 Queen's Drive, Liverpool L15 6YE

JONES, Trevor; s of John Jones (d 1995), of New Penshaw, Tyne and Wear, and Florence Mary, *née* Rogerson (d 1978); *b* 23 Dec 1950; *Educ* New Coll Durham, Washington GS; *m* Hazel, da of Robert Oliver; *Career* served local govt 1969–78, regnl auditor then head of financial policy and planning Northern RHA 1978–83, dep treas S Manchester Health Authy 1983–86, gen mangr Waltham Forest Health Authy 1989–91 (dir of fin and dep gen mangr 1986–89), chief exec Forest Healthcare NHS Tst 1991–95, gen mangr Lothian Health Board 1995–; CIPFA 1973, FCCA 1981, FCIS 1982, MIMgt 1979; *Recreations* golf, squash, Durham CCC, photography, Sunderland AFC; *Clubs* Dunelm Cricket Soc; *Style*— Trevor Jones, Esq; ✉ Lothian Health Board, 148 The Pleasance, Edinburgh EH8 9RS (☎ 0131 536 9001)

JONES, Trevor Courtney; s of William Jones (d 1979), of Hereford, and Edith Frances, *née* Webb (d 1963); *b* 14 Aug 1929; *Educ* Newport HS, Cardiff Univ (MM); *m* 24 Oct 1975, Rosemary Morley, da of Henry Vaughan Lowndes (d 1951), of Cheshire; 1 s (Simon Geoffrey b 30 Oct 1977); *Career* master mariner Union Castle Mail Steamship Co 1952–60, theatre mangr Royal Opera House 1971– (asst theatre mangr 1960–71); memb Hon Co of Master Mariners 1970; *Recreations* sailing, music, opera, ballet, theatre, reading; *Style*— Trevor Jones, Esq; ✉ 132 Tachbrook St, London SW1 (☎ 0171 834 5273); The White Lodge, The Warren, Caversham, Berks; L'Observatoire, Côte de Grace, Honfleur, Calvados, France 14600; Royal Opera House, Covent Garden, London WC2E 9DD (☎ 0171 240 1200, fax 0171 836 1762, telex 27988 COVGAR G)

JONES, Dr Trevor Mervyn; s of Samuel James Jones (d 1992), of Finchampstead, Berks, and Hilda May, *née* Walley (d 1978); *b* 19 Aug 1942; *Educ* Wolverhampton Sch, King's Coll London (BPharm, PhD); *m* 9 April 1966, Verity Ann, da of Richard Bates (d 1963), of Emsworth, Hants; 1 s (Timothy Damian b 1971), 1 da (Amanda Melissa (Mrs Lawrence Richard Kerr) b 1968); *Career* lectr Univ of Nottingham, formerly head of devpt The Boots Co Ltd, dir of R & D and med Wellcome plc, DG The Assoc of the British Pharmaceutical Industry; visiting prof King's Coll London and Univ of Strathclyde, fell King's Coll London 1994–; author various pubns; memb Ed Bd: Jl of Pharmacy and Pharmacology, Drug Development and Industrial Pharmacy, Int Jl of Pharmaceutics, Drugs and the Pharmaceutical Sciences; memb: UK Medicines Cmmn, Cncl King's Coll London, Nuffield Cncl on Bioethics expert gp on the use of human tissue, Bd of Pharmaceutical Scis Fèderation Internationale Pharmaceutique; dir Sci Policy Support Gp, memb Bd of Honorary Advsrs The Glynn Research Fndn, govr Croydon HS; pres Bd of Maurice-Marie Janot Int Ctee; Freeman: Worshipful Soc of Apothecaries 1988, City of London 1994; Hon Doctorate Univ of Athens 1993, Hon DSc Univ of Strathclyde 1994; Harrison Meml Medal 1987, Gold Medal Comenius Univ 1992, Charter Gold Medal Royal Pharmaceutical Soc of GB 1996; hon fell Faculty of Pharmaceutical Med RCP 1995; FPS, CChem, FRCS, MCPP; *Books* Drug Delivery to the Respiratory Tract (1987), Advances in Pharmaceutical Sciences (1992); *Recreations* gardening, opera, golf; *Clubs* Athenaeum; *Style*— Dr Trevor Jones; ✉ The Association of the British Pharmaceutical Industry, 12 Whitehall, London SW1A 2DY (☎ 0171 930 3477)

JONES, Prof Tudor Bowden; s of Idris Jones (d 1961), of Ystradgynlais, S Wales, and Tydvil Ann, *née* Bowden (d 1978); *b* 8 Nov 1934; *Educ* Univ of Wales, Univ Coll Swansea (BSc, PhD, DSc); *m* 16 Aug 1960, Patricia (Pat); 2 s (Owen Bowden b 14 Jan 1968, Hywel Bowden b 11 Sept 1970); *Career* sr res assoc US Nat Acad of Sci 1971–72, conslt on ionospheric radiowave propogation to UK US and Canadian Govt Agencies; Univ of Leicester: former lectr, sr lectr and reader, prof of ionospheric physics 1980, head Dept of Physics and Astronomy 1993–; memb various ctees SERC; awarded: Appleton Prize Royal Soc 1993, Charles Chree Prize Inst of Physics 1994; IEE Appleton Lecture 1996/97; FInstP, FIEE, CEng, FRAS; *Books* Ionospheric Radiowave Propagation (1969); *Recreations* classical music, rugby football; *Style*— Prof Tudor Jones; ✉ Physics and Astronomy Department, University of Leicester, University Road, Leicester LE1 7RH (☎ 0116 252 3561, fax 0116 252 3555)

JONES, Vincent Peter (Vinnie); s of Peter Jones, and Glenda, *née* Harris; *b* 5 Jan 1965; *Educ* Langleybury Sch Herts, Bedmond Sch, Brookmans Park Sch; *children* 1 s (Aaron b 29 May 1991); *Career* professional footballer; formerly amateur player Wealdstone; Wimbledon 1985–89 (debut v Nottm Forest), Leeds Utd 1989–90 (joined for £650,000), Sheffield Utd 1990–91 (joined for £700,000), Chelsea 1991–92 (joined for £575,000), Wimbledon 1992– (rejoined for £700,000); currently memb Welsh Nat squad; honours: FA Cup winners Wimbledon 1988, Div 2 Championship winners Leeds Utd 1990; *Recreations* shooting, fishing, golf, helping handicapped people, children; *Style*— Vinnie Jones, Esq; ✉ Wimbledon FC, Selhurst Park, London SE25 6PU (☎ 0181 653 4462)

JONES, Dr William George (Bill); s of Arthur Constable Jones (d 1987), of Widnes, Cheshire, and Edna May, *née* Rickart (d 1981); *b* 26 Dec 1945; *Educ* Wade Deacon GS Widnes, Univ of Birmingham (MB ChB); *m* 28 June 1969, Anthea Jane, da of Arie Heesterman, of Leeds, W Yorks; 2 da (Penny b 1972, Karen b 1975); *Career* registrar and sr registrar Central Birmingham Hosps 1970–75, conslt radiotherapist and oncologist W Glamorgan Health Authy Swansea 1975–78, lectr then sr lectr in radiotherapy Univ of Leeds 1978–92; currently: conslt in radiotherapy and oncology United Leeds Teaching Hosps NHS Tst and St James's Univ Hosp NHS Tst, hon clinical sr lectr Univ of Leeds; memb: MRC Working Party on Testicular Tumours, Urological Gp Euro Organisation for Res on Treatment of Cancer, Br Inst of Radiology, Trout and Salmon Assoc, Rotary Int (Leeds Elmete); DMRT 1972, FRCR 1974, FRSM 1976, memb Br Inst of Radiology 1978; *Books* Germ Cell Tumours (ed with C K Anderson and A Milford Ward, 1981), Germ Cell Tumours II (ed with C K Anderson and A Milford Ward, 1985), Prostate Cancer and Testicular Cancer (ed with D W W Newling, 1990), Germ Cell Tumours III (ed with P Harnden and I Appleyard, 1994); *Recreations* game fishing, gardening, reading; *Style*— Dr Bill Jones; ✉ 32 Adel Towers Court, Adel, Leeds LS16 8ER (☎ 0113 261 0330); Cookridge Hospital, Leeds LS16 6QB (☎ 0113 292 4276, fax 0113 292 4441)

JONES, William George Tilston; s of Thomas Tilston Jones (d 1976), and Amy Ethel, *née* Millar (d 1991); *b* 7 Jan 1942; *Educ* Portsmouth GS, Portsmouth Poly (BSc); *m* 18 Dec 1965, Fiona Mary; 1 da (Zoë Samantha b 1966); *Career* PO: exec engr 1965–69, head of gp 1969–75, head of section 1975–78, head System X Devpt Div 1978–80; British Telecommunications: dep dir System X 1980–83, dir System Evolution and Standards Div 1983–84, chief exec (technol) 1984–86, dir of technol studies 1988–90; engrg conslt 1990–; exec in residence Int Mgmnt Inst Geneva 1987; hon fellowship Portsmouth Univ (formerly Portsmouth Poly) 1989; FIEE; *Recreations* theatre, debating society, camping; *Style*— William Jones, Esq; ✉ 1a The Drive, Radlett, Herts WD7 7DA (☎ 01923 854448)

JONES, (Ieuan) Wyn; JP (1972); s of Tom Jones (d 1978), of Haverfordwest, and Dilys Vaughan Jones, *née* Williams (d 1959); *b* 8 Dec 1928; *Educ* Ellesmere Coll, Univ of London (BA), Univ of Liverpool (Dip CD); *m* 11 July 1959, Elfrida Mary, da of Michael Ionides (d 1978), of Surrey; 1 s (Gareth b 1962), 1 da (Emma b 1960); *Career* architect; dep architect MOD Iraq 1956–59; ptnr: Hirst & Jones, Moore Simpson & Ptnrs 1959–68, Wyn Jones, Paul Andrews & Associates 1968–92; conslt The Andrews Partnership 1992–; cmmns incl numerous domestic & commercial buildings in West Wales, PCC Admin Building Texaco Refinery; also numerous restorations incl St Mary Haverfordwest, Picton Castle & Pembroke Castle; awarded: 3 Civic Tst Awards 1968, 1970 and 1982, Welsh Office Housing Medal 1968; Burgess of the Guild of Freemen of Haverfordwest 1982; architect to St David's Diocesan Bd of Finance 1985–; High Sheriff of Dyfed 1995–96; FRIBA 1969; *Recreations* hunting, gardening, sketching, historical buildings; *Style*— Wyn Jones, Esq, JP; ✉ Blaencilgoed House, Ludchurch, Narberth, Pembrokeshire SA67 8LA (☎ and fax 01834 831605); 22 High Street, Haverfordwest, Pembrokeshire SA61 2DA (☎ 01437 765156, fax 01437 760885)

JONES, (Graham) Wyn; QPM (1987); s of Thomas James Jones (d 1984), of Talgarreg, Dyfed, and Mary Elizabeth, *née* Almrott; *b* 12 Oct 1943; *Educ* Thornbury GS, Univ of Exeter (LLB, capt Rugby XV, Eng Univs XV); *m* 5 Sept 1970, Joan, da of John Goodbrook (d 1986), of Elberton, Glos; *Career* Glos Constabulary: joined 1963, Inspr 1968–73, Chief Inspr 1973–76, Supt 1976–79; Thames Valley Police: Chief Supt Oxford 1979–82, Asst Chief Constable 1982–84; Met Police: Dep Asst Cmmr (CID) 1984, Asst Cmmr (Personnel and Trg) 1989–93; sec Personnel and Trg Ctee ACPO, govr Police Staf Coll Bramshill, tstee Police Convalescent Home Goring; memb: Police Trg Cncl for England and Wales, Police Negotiating Bd for England and Wales; *Recreations* music, theatre, golf, horse riding; *Style*— Wyn Jones, Esq, QPM; ✉ New Scotland Yard, Broadway, London SW1H 0BG (☎ 0171 230 3228)

JONES, Wynne Melville; s of Rev John Melville Jones (d 1972), and Eirlys, *née* Davies; *b* 7 Aug 1947; *Educ* Co Secondary Sch Tregaron, Swansea Coll of Art, Trinity Coll Carmarthen; *m* 1971, Linda Rees, da of John Verdun Rees; 2 da (Meleri Wyn, Manon Wyn); *Career* head of PR Welsh League of Youth 1975 (co organiser Camarthenshire 1969, publicity offr headquarters 1971), fndr Strata Public Relations & Advertising Aberystwyth 1979, exec dir Strata Matrix 1989– (result of merger between Strata and Cardiff Design & Advertising Co); fndr ptnr Deli Cymru Aberystwyth (delicatessan specialising in fine food from Wales and the rest of the world) 1994–; chm Nat Cncl Welsh League of Youth, memb Bd of Dirs Golwg (Welsh language current affrs magazine); memb Ct Univ Coll of Wales; fell Welsh PR Assoc (fndr memb); *Recreations* art appreciation, swimming, hill walking, rural activities; *Style*— Wynne Melville Jones, Esq; ✉ 23/25 North Parade, Aberystwyth, Dyfed SY23 2JN (☎ 01970 625552, fax 01970 612774); 1 Talbot St, Cardiff CF1 9BW (☎ 01222 231231, fax 01222 372798)

JONES-LEE, Prof Michael Whittaker; s of Lt-Col Walter Whittaker Jones-Lee (d 1977), of Leybourne, Kent, and Christina, *née* Hamilton (d 1985); *b* 3 April 1944; *Educ* Prince Rupert Sch Wilhelmshaven, Bishop Wordsworth's Sch Salisbury, Univ of Sheffield (BEng), Univ of York (DPhil); *m* 20 Dec 1969, Hazel, da of Arthur Stephen Knight; 2 s (Rupert 1974, Ben 1976), 1 da (Sarah b 1979); *Career* sr lectr Dept of Political Econ Univ of St Andrews 1971–72; Univ of York: Esmée Fairbairn lectr in fin 1967–71, sr lectr Dept of Econs 1972–76, reader Dept of Econs 1976–77; Univ of Newcastle upon Tyne: prof Dept of Econs 1977–, head of dept 1984–95, dean Faculty of Social Sci 1984–88; conslt: Dept of Tport, TRL, HSE, London Underground and New Zealand Miny of Tport; *Books* The Value of Life: An Economic Analysis (1976), The Value of Life and Safety (ed, 1982), The Economics of Safety and Physical Risk (1989); *Recreations* shopping and old sports cars; *Style*— Prof Michael Jones-Lee; ✉ Department of

Economics, University of Newcastle upon Tyne, Newcastle upon Tyne NE1 7RU (☎ 0191 222 6549, fax 0191 222 6548, telex 53654)

JONSSON, Ulrika; *b* 16 Aug 1967; *children* 1 s (Cameron); *Career* television presenter; incl: weather slot (TV-am) 1989–92, Gladiators (with John Fashanu, *qv*, LWT) 1992–, Big Breakfast (guest presenter, Channel 4) Sept 1995, Shooting Stars (team capt, BBC2) 1995–, Nat Lottery Live (guest presenter, BBC) July 1996, Des Res (LWT) 1996; Auntie's TV Favourites (comedy nominations, BBC) 1996; *Awards* incl: Gotcha Oscar (Noel's House Party) 1992, Rear of the Year 1992, Spectacle Wearer of the Year 1994; *Style*— Ms Ulrika Jonsson; ✉ c/o Cantor Wise Representation, 109 Crouch Hill, London N8 9RD (☎ 0181 347 7770, fax 0181 347 5550)

JONZEN, Karin; da of Uno Lowenadler, and Gerda Munck, *née* Fulkila; *b* 22 Dec 1914; *Educ* Wimbledon HS, Slade Sch of Art, Royal Acad Stockholm; *m* 1, 26 Feb 1944, Basil Jonzen (d 1969), s of Birger Jonzen; 1 s (Martin b 1948); m 2, 1972, Ake Sucksforff; *Career* Ambulance Serv 1941–45; artist; extra mural lectr in art appreciation 1965–71, lectr Camden Arts Centre 1968–72; Prix de Rome 1939, Theodorn Glelchen Award 1947, Gold Medal Academia della Arte e Lavore Parma, Gold Medal Int Parly for Safety and Peace USA, Silver Medal RBS; memb London Gp; FRBS; *Solo Exhibitions* Heffers Gallery Cambridge 1994, David Messum Gallery Cork St London 1994; *Works in Galleries* incl: The Tate, Glasgow, Liverpool, Brighton, Bradford, Southend, Doncaster, Melbourne Aust, Andrew White Museum Cornell Univ USA, Nat Portrait Gallery; *Portraits* incl: Sir Monty Finniston, Donald Trelford, Lord Constantine of Stanmore, Lord Porter of Luddenham, Sir Hugh Casson, Paul Scofield; *Works in Public Collections* incl: over life size bronze gp Guildhall forecourt, life size bronze London Wall Moorgate, life size youth WHO Bldg New Delhi, life size torso bronze WHO Bldg Geneva, over life size bust of Samuel Pepys Seething Lane, bronze of Dame Ninette de Valois at Sadler's Wells Theatre, young girl Lower Sloan St; *Work in Churches* carving on Guildford Cathedral, Madonna and Child Pieta Swedish Church, Madonna and Child St Mary le Bow, Madonna and Child St Saviour's Church Warwick Ave, Madonna and Child St Mary and St Gabriel S Harting, St Michael St Michael's Church Golders Green, Acension Gp Selwyn Coll Chapel Cambridge, St Ann and St Mary Gp St Ann and St Mary Church Lewes; *Books* Karin Jonzen Sculptor (1976), Karin Jonzen Sculpture (1994); *Style*— Mrs Karin Jonzen; ✉ The Studio, 6A Gunter Grove, London SW10 0UJ (☎ 0171 351 0594)

JOPLING, Rt Hon (Thomas) Michael; PC (1979), DL, MP (C) Westmorland and Lonsdale (majority 16,436); s of late Mark Bellerby Jopling; *b* 10 Dec 1930; *Educ* Cheltenham, King's Coll Newcastle; *m* 1958, Gail, da of late Ernest Dickinson; 2 s; *Career* farmer; Parly candidate (C) Wakefield 1959, memb Nat Cncl NFU 1962–64; MP (C): Westmorland 1964–83, Westmorland and Lonsdale 1983–; PPS to Min of Agric 1970–71, asst Govt whip 1971–73, a Lord Cmmr of the Treasy (Govt whip) 1973–74, oppn whip 1974, oppn spokesman on Agric 1974–79, shadow min for agric 1975–76, Parly sec to Treasy and Govt chief whip 1979–1983, min of agric, fisheries and food 1983–87; pres EEC Cncls of Agric and Fishery Ministers 1986; hon sec Br and American Parly Gp 1987–; ldr UK delegation OSCE Parly Assembly 1991–; memb: Foreign Affrs Select Ctee 1987–, Int Exec Cwlth Parly Assoc 1988–89 (memb UK Exec 1974–79 and 1987, vice chm 1977–79), Select Ctee on Sittings of the House (chm 1991–92); pres Auto Cycle Union 1989–; Liveryman Worshipful Co of Farmers; Hon DCL Newcastle 1992; *Style*— The Rt Hon Michael Jopling, DL, MP; ✉ Ainderby Hall, Thirsk, N Yorks YO7 4HZ

JORDAN, (Leslie) Alan; DL (Essex 1988); s of Dr Leslie Jordan (d 1930), and Ellen Florence, *née* Holmes; *b* 10 Oct 1930; *Educ* King's Sch Ely, RAC; *m* July 1957, Elizabeth (d 1994); 1 da (Rebecca Elizabeth b 13 June 1961); *Career* cmmnd Royal Norfolk Regt 1948–51; currently bd dir and chm: Gent Fairhead Ltd, Tacchi's Nurseries Ltd; High Sheriff of Essex; chm Essex Scout Cncl; Freeman City of London, Liveryman Worshipful Co of Farmers; memb RICS; *Recreations* fishing, shooting, gardening; *Clubs* Farmers', Flyfishers'; *Style*— Alan Jordan, Esq, DL; ✉ The Great Lodge, Great Bardfield, Braintree, Essex CM7 4QD (☎ 01371 810776, fax 01371 811398)

JORDAN, Andrew; s of Andrew Jordan, of Belfast, and Bessie, *née* Gray (d 1977); *b* 12 March 1950; *Educ* Queen's Univ Belfast (BSc), Darwin Coll Cambridge (Dip in Mathematical Statistics), Cranfield Sch of Mgmnt (MBA); *Career* statistician Unilever Research Ltd 1974–77, statistician Overseas Devpt Admin 1977–79, investmt controller 3I 1980–84, ptnr Coopers & Lybrand 1985–; FRSS; *Recreations* skiing, ballet, opera; *Style*— Andrew Jordan, Esq; ✉ 22 Northumberland Place, London W2 5BS (☎ 0171 229 0546); Coopers & Lybrand, 1 Embankment Place, London WC2N 6NN

JORDAN, Andrew Kevin (Andy); s of William John Jordan, and Elsa, *née* Brewer; *b* 10 June 1950; *Educ* Univ of Bristol (BA), St Mary's Coll Southampton (Dip in Drama); *Career* producer and director; fndr Bristol Express Theatre Co 1978, fndr assoc dir Playfair Film and TV Productions Ltd 1980; Scotsman Fringe First Awards: A Respectable Family by Maxim Gorki Edinburgh 1977, Lunatic and Lover by Michael Meyer Edinburgh 1978; radio drama prodr BBC 1988–; Radio Awards incl: Giles Cooper Award 1989 and 1991, Sony Award 1994, EBU Award 1995; memb: CND, Friends of the Earth, Greenpeace, Anti-Apartheid Movement; memb: Directors' Guild GB, 1quity, BECTU; *Recreations* travel, reading, cinema, theatre; *Style*— Andy Jordan, Esq; ✉ Flat 2, 28 Saville Road, Chiswick, London W4 5HG (☎ 0181 742 3952)

JORDAN, Prof Carole; da of Reginald Sidney Jordan, and Ethel May, *née* Waller; *b* 19 July 1941; *Educ* Harrow Co GS for Girls, UCL (BSc, PhD); *Career* res assoc Jt Inst for Laboratory Astrophysics Univ of Colorado USA 1966, post doctoral appt UKAEA Culham Lab 1966–69; SRC's Astrophysics Res Unit Culham Laboratory: post doctoral res asst 1969–71, sr scientific offr 1971–73, princ scientific offr 1973–76; univ lectr Dept of Theoretical Physics Univ of Oxford, reader in physics 1994–96, prof in physics 1996–; fell and tutor in physics Somerville Coll Oxford 1976–; RAS: sec 1981–90, vice pres 1990–91 and 1996–, pres (first female to hold position) 1994–96; memb SERC 1985–90, memb PPARC 1994–; FRAS 1966, memb IAU 1967, FInstP 1973, FRS 1990; *Recreations* gardening; *Style*— Prof Carole Jordan, FRS; ✉ Department of Physics (Theoretical Physics), University of Oxford, 1 Keble Rd, Oxford OX1 3NP (☎ 01865 273980, fax 01865 273947, telex 83245 NUCLOX)

JORDAN, Diane-Louise; da of Harold Jordan, and Norma Jordan; *b* 27 Feb 1960; *Educ* Rose Bruford Coll of Speech and Drama; 1 adopted da (Justine (niece) b 1986); *Career* radio and television presenter; actress 1983–89; fndr writer's club 1990–93; patron The Anne Frank Day (Anne Frank Educnl Tst UK); hon memb Morris Minors Club of GB; NHC Action for Children; *Theatre* as actress incl: Eliza Doolittle in Pygmalion (Harrogate), Helen in To Kill A Mockingbird, Peggy in Playboy of The West Indies (both Contact Theatre Manchester), Hermia in A Midsummer Night's Dream (Nottingham Playhouse), Soloman and the Big Cat (Young Vic), Toffee Jenkins in Pied Piper (RNT); *Television* as actress for BBC incl: Amazing Grace in South of the Border, Difficult People, Handles; other acting credits incl: young Elphida in Elphida (Working Title Films/Channel 4), Coronation Street (Granada); as co/guest/presenter for BBC incl: Corners 1989, Jackanory, Blue Peter 1990–96, Good Morning Summer 1995, Antiques Roadshow - The Next Generation 1995, Fancy That, Summer Holiday 1996, Grandstand (The Great North Run 1996, London Marathon 1997), Songs of Praise 1996–, Bright Sparks 1996, On Christmas Day - in The Morning 1996; for ITV Beyond Belief 1996; appearances incl: Pebblemill, Noel's House Party, GMTV, Hearts of Gold, Live and Kicking, The Disney Channel; *Radio* as actress Ruby in Rent (series, Radio 4); as presenter incl: Time to Move (Radio 5) 1993–, New Presenters (Radio 2) 1996–, Poetry Corner (Radio 3) 1996–, Children in Need (Radio 2) 1996; *Films* High Hopes (dir Mike Leigh, *qv*); *Recreations* playing piano, art galleries, reading, interiors, antiques, music, meeting people, keep fit, computers; *Style*— Ms Diane-Louise Jordan; ✉ c/o Harris Personal Management, 171 Junction Road, London N19 3PZ; (☎ 0171 281 0445, fax 0171 561 0105)

JORDAN, Francis Leo (Frank); CBE (1989), QPM (1982); s of Leo Thomas Jordan (d 1967), of Stone, Staffs, and Mary, *née* Moloney (d 1982); *b* 15 June 1930; *Educ* St Joseph's Coll; *m* 1951, Ruth, da of James Ashmore (d 1970), of Cheshire; 1 s (Francis b 1958), 2 da (Karen b 1957, Diane b 1962); *Career* joined Staffs Police 1950 attaining rank of Chief Superintendent, seconded to Cyprus Police during EOKA emergency 1956–58, staff offr to HO Police Inspectorate 1975, asst chief constable W Midlands 1976, dep chief constable of Kent 1979, chief constable of Kent 1982–89; chm Kent Children's House Soc 1979–81 (hon patron), vice pres Assoc of Kent CCs 1982–89; memb: Kent Co Ctee SSAFA 1986–89, Assoc Men of Kent and Kentish Men, Band of Brothers; appointed to Parole Bd 1990–93; CIMgt 1985, FRSA 1990; OStJ 1988; *Recreations* walking, old buildings, travel; *Clubs* Royal Over-Seas League, Hopper's Tie; *Style*— Frank Jordan, Esq, CBE, QPM; ✉ c/o Police Headquarters, Sutton Rd, Maidstone, Kent ME15 9BZ (☎ 01622 690690, telex 96132)

JORDAN, Graham Harold Ben; s of Harold Jordan (d 1967), and Violet Emily, *née* Wakefield (d 1989); *b* 1 April 1945; *Educ* Chislehurst and Sidcup GS, Downing Coll Cambridge (Whitby scholar, MA), Brunel Univ (MTech); *m* 19 Nov 1977, Jean Anne, da of Thomas Henry Swale; *Career* operational analyst Defence Operational Analysis Estab W Byfleet 1967–77, operational analyst Dept of the Chief Scientist RAF 1977–78, div head Defence Operational Analysis Estab 1978–82, head Defensive Weapons Dept Royal Aircraft Estab Farnborough 1985–87 (div head 1982–85), head Civil Serv Personnel Mgmnt Div HM Treasy 1987–90; MOD: scientific advsr Command Information Systems 1990–91, asst chief scientific advsr Capabilities 1991–95, dep chief scientist Scrutiny and Analysis 1995–; *Books* Learning From Experience: A Report On The Arrangements For Managing Major Projects In The Procurement Executive (1988); *Recreations* riding, small scale farming, music, domestic maintenance; *Style*— Graham Jordan, Esq; ✉ Ministry of Defence, Main Building, Whitehall, London SW1A 2HB (☎ 0171 218 2034)

JORDAN, (Michael) Guy; s of Maj Michael Edward Jordan, of Tavistock, Devon, and Elizabeth Marcia Dermot, *née* Harris; *b* 10 June 1955; *Educ* Downside Sch, Univ of Durham; *m* 12 July 1980, Helena Mary, da of Arthur Lawrence Moore, of Charlton Musgrove, Somerset; 2 s (Adam b 11 Oct 1986, Miles b 20 April 1991), 1 da (Lucy b 13 Dec 1988); *Career* admitted slr 1980; ptnr Masons 1986–; memb Law Soc 1980; *Recreations* fishing, shooting, sheep farming; *Style*— Guy Jordan, Esq; ✉ Masons, 30 Aylesbury St, London EC1R 0ER (☎ 0171 490 4000)

JORDAN, Michael Anthony; s of Charles Thomas Jordan (d 1956), of Duffield, Derbys, and Florence Emily, *née* Golder (d 1977); *b* 20 Aug 1931; *Educ* Haileybury; *m* 1, 9 Dec 1956 (m dis 1989); 1 s (Mark b 1959), 1 da (Fiona b 1961); m 2, Feb 1990, Dorothea Rosine Estelle, *née* Coureau; *Career* ptnr: R H March Son & Co 1959–68 (joined 1958), Saker & Langdon Davis 1963, W H Cork Gully & Co 1968–80, Coopers and Lybrand 1980–93; sr ptnr Cork Gully (Coopers & Lybrand's insolvency practice) 1983–93; High Ct of Justice Isle of Man (jt inspr into affairs of The Savings and Investment Bank Ltd 1983); govr Royal Shakespeare Theatre 1979–; Liveryman Worshipful Co of Bakers; FCA; *Recreations* opera, DIY; *Style*— Michael Jordan, Esq; ✉ Ballinger Farm, Ballinger, nr Great Missenden, Bucks HP16 9LQ (☎ 01494 863298)

JORDAN, Dr Michael John; s of Dr John Jordan (d 1963), of Kidderminster, Worcs, and Margaret Tuer Jordan, MBE, *née* Harper (d 1992); *b* 26 May 1949; *Educ* Malvern, Trinity Hall Cambridge, St Thomas's Hosp Med Sch; *m* 12 May 1984, (Gena) Rosamund, da of Alan Rigby Horler; 3 da (Camilla b 1986, Olivia b 1988, Isobel b 1991); *Career* Anaesthetics Dept St Thomas's Hosp: sr house offr 1976, registrar 1977, sr registrar 1979; visiting asst prof of anaesthesiology Univ of Texas Dallas USA 1981–82; conslt anaesthetist: Bart's 1983–95, St Peter's Hosp Chertsey 1995–; FFARCS 1978; memb: Anaesthetic Res Soc, BMA, Assoc of Anaesthetists; *Recreations* photography, music, cinema, theatre; *Clubs* Hurlingham, RSM; *Style*— Dr Michael Jordan; ✉ 29 Acfold Rd, London SW6 2AJ (☎ 0171 731 4356); Department of Anaesthesia, St Peter's Hospital, Chertsey, Surrey KT16 0PZ (☎ 01932 872000, mobile 0802 312244)

JORDAN, Philip Spencer; s of Frank William Jordan, and Morfydd Enid, *née* Thomas; *b* 24 Feb 1953; *Educ* Swavesey Village Coll, Leicester Poly (DipArch); *m* 28 Oct 1989, Marilyn, da of Fred Longden; 2 s (Paul David b 1980, Keir Richard b 1982), 1 da (Emily Keziah b 1988); *Career* architect: Cound Page Cambridge 1980–82, Covell Matthews Wheatley Architects 1982–85; ptnr Philip Jordan Architects 1985–87, md Forum Architects (London) Ltd 1989– (ptnr 1987–89); dir: Jordan & Bateman Architects Ltd, Domicile Design Ltd, Stadio Ltd; exhibitor International 40 Under 40 exhibition RIBA; vice pres RIBA 1987–89 (memb and memb Cncl), fndr memb Building Experiences Tst; *Recreations* family, sport, gardening and painting; *Style*— Philip Jordan, Esq; ✉ Colon, 113 High St, Trumpington, Cambridge CB2 2JD (☎ 01223 562705, car 0836 690213)

JORDAN, Terence Frank; s of Frank William Jordan, of Papworth Everard, Cambridge, and Morfydd Enid Jordan; *b* 16 Oct 1941; *Educ* Leicester Coll of Art and Design (DipArch); *m* 1, 1963 (m dis 1976), Christine Ann; 1 s (Simon David b 23 April 1972), 1 da (Elizabeth Ann b 25 March 1964); m 2, 7 April 1978, Anita Lesley, da of Douglas Richard Reed, of Cambridge; 1 s (Daniel Thomas b 24 Nov 1981), 1 da (Sarah Louise b 7 Sept 1986); *Career* fndr ptnr Clark and Jordan 1973–76, md Covell Matthews Wheatley 1985–92 (fndr dir 1976), dir CMW Group plc 1990–92, fndr ptnr T Jordan Assoc 1993–; former memb Mgmnt Ctee Cambridge Preservation Soc, former chm Fin and Property Ctee 1978–84; RIBA, FRSA; *Recreations* music, golf, gardening; *Style*— Terence Jordan, Esq; ✉ Grove Cottage, 40 Church St, Haslingfield, Cambridge CB3 7JE (☎ 01223 872346, fax 01223 871432)

JORDAN, William Brian (Bill); CBE (1992); s of Walter Jordan (d 1974), and Alice, *née* Heath; *b* 28 Jan 1936; *Educ* Barford Rd Secdy Modern Birmingham; *m* 8 Nov 1958, Jean Ann, da of Ernest Livesey; 3 da (Pamela, Lisa, Dawn); *Career* former machine tool fitter GKN; pres AEEU 1986–95, gen sec Int Confedn of Free Trade Unions 1995–; formerly: memb NEDC, memb Gen Cncl and major ctees TUC, chair Euro-Strategy Ctee TUC, memb Exec Ctee and chair Engrg Ctee CSEU, pres Euro Metalworkers Fedn, memb Exec Cncl Int Metalworkers Fedn, memb Engrg Trg Authy, memb ACAS, memb UK Skills Cncl, memb Fndn for Mfrg and Indust; currently: memb Cncl Industl Soc, vice pres W Midland Productivity Assoc, govr LSE, BBC, Ashridge Mgmnt Coll and Henley Coll, vice pres Involvement and Participation Assoc (IPA), memb English Partnerships; Hon Doctorate: Univ of Central England, Cranfield Univ; City and Guilds Insignia Award (hc); *Recreations* reading, most sports (particularly football, supporter Birmingham City FC); *Style*— Bill Jordan, Esq, CBE; ✉ International Confederation of Free Trade Unions, Boulevard Emile Jacqmain 155, B-1210 Brussels (☎ 00 32 2 224 02 11, fax 00 32 2 201 58 15)

JORDAN-MOSS, Norman; CB (1972), CMG (1965); s of Arthur Moss, and Ellen, *née* Jordan Round; *b* 5 Feb 1920; *Educ* Manchester GS, St John's Coll Cambridge (MA); *m* 1, 1965, Kathleen, *née* Lusmore (d 1974); 1 s, 1 da; m 2, 1976, Philippa Rands; 1 da; *Career* Miny of Econ Warfare 1940–44; HM Treasy 1944–80: asst rep ME 1945–48 (princ 1948), first sec (econ) Belgrade 1952–55, fin cnsllr Washington 1956–60, asst sec 1956–68, cnsllr UK Perm Delgn to OECD Paris 1963–66, under sec 1968–71, dep sec 1976–80; dep under sec of state DHSS 1971–76; dir 1928 Investment Tst 1980–85, conslt Hambros Bank 1981–83; dir: Crown Life Assurance Co 1980–84, Crown Life Pensions 1980–90, Crown Life Management Services 1980–90, Crown Financial Management 1984–90; *Recreations* music, theatre; *Clubs* Travellers'; *Style*— Norman Jordan-Moss, Esq, CB, CMG; ✉ Milton Way, Westcott, Dorking, Surrey

JOSEPH, Bernard Michael; s of Harry Toby Joseph (d 1989), of London, and Esther, *née* Markson; *b* 27 Sept 1948; *Educ* Bede GS for Boys; *m* 12 Oct 1980, Ruth Lesley-Ann, *née* Trent; 1 s (Darren Paul b 2 Sept 1985), 1 da (Danielle Natasha b 20 May 1983); *Career* CA; trainee Jennings Johnson 1971–75, Peat Marwick & Mitchell 1957–77, Nash Broad & Co 1977–79, sole practitioner 1979–88, ptnr Johnsons 1988–90, sr ptnr Joseph & Co 1990–; treas Voluntary Action Westminster; Freeman: City of London, Worshipful Co of CAs; FICA 1975; *Clubs* 41 (vice chm), Rotary; *Style*— Bernard Joseph, Esq; ✉ 3 Hillersdon Ave, Edgware, Middx, HA8 7SG (☎ 0181 905 3721); Joseph & Co, 40 Bowling Green Lane, London EC1R 0NE (☎ 0171 415 7115, fax 0171 410 0043)

JOSEPH, His Honour Judge; (Thomas John) Cedric; s of Thomas Rhees Joseph (d 1979), of St Dogmaels, Pembrokeshire, and Catherine Ann, *née* Davies; *b* 25 Aug 1938; *Educ* Cardigan GS, LSE (LLB); *m* 12 Oct 1960, Mary, da of Harry Weston; 3 da (Sarah Jane, Catherine Mary, Emma Fiona); *Career* called to the Bar Gray's Inn 1960, crown counsel Malawi 1962–64, recorder 1992–94 (asst recorder 1987–92), circuit judge (SE Circuit) 1994–; *Recreations* music, golf, travel; *Clubs* Royal Wimbledon Golf; *Style*— His Hon Judge Joseph; ✉ Snaresbrook Crown Court, 75 Hollybush Hill, Snaresbrook, London E11 1QW (☎ 0181 982 5500)

JOSEPH, Hon Sir James Samuel Joseph; 3 Bt (UK 1943), of Portsoken, City of London; o s of Baron Joseph, CH, JP (Life Peer and 2 Bt; d 1994), and his 1 w, Hellen Louise, *née* Guggenheimer; *b* 27 Jan 1955; *Educ* Harrow; *Heir* Sam Nathan Joseph; *Style*— James Joseph, Esq

JOSEPH, Jane; da of Leonard Joseph (d 1989), and Hannah Joyce, *née* Stern; *b* 7 June 1942; *Educ* Downe House, Camberwell Sch of Arts and Crafts (NDD, Leverhulme travelling award); *Career* painter and printmaker; teacher principally at Morley Coll London and Wimbledon Sch of Art; Abbey Award in Painting British Sch at Rome 1991; *Solo Exhibitions* Morley Gallery London 1973, The Minories Colchester 1982, Angela Flowers Gallery 1987, Flowers East 1989 and 1992, Edinburgh Printmakers 1994; *Group Exhibitions* S Wales Gp 1971, Air Gallery 1981, Gardner Centre Univ of Sussex 1984, Imperial Coll London 1985, 100 Yrs - Artists and Morley (Morley Coll) 1990, Gardner Centre Univ of Sussex 1992, Artists Market, Cleveland Int Drawings Biennale, Int Print Biennale Bradford, London Gp, RA Summer Exhbns and others; *Public Collections* Br Museum, Castle Museum Norwich, Chelsea and Westminster Hosp, Govt Picture Collection, Imperial Coll London, Univ of Northumbria at Newcastle, Unilever House, Arts Cncl of Wales, Paintings in Hosps; *Clubs* Chelsea Arts; *Style*— Ms Jane Joseph; ✉ 105 Cambridge Gardens, London W10 6JE

JOSEPH, Jenny; da of Louis Joseph (d 1979), and Florence Ethel, *née* Cotton (d 1989); *b* 7 May 1932; *Educ* Badminton Sch, St Hilda's Coll Oxford (scholar, BA); *m* late Charles Anthony Coles; 1 s (Martin Louis b 1961), 2 da (Penelope Clare b 1963, Rebecca Ruth b 1965); *Career* poet, writer, broadcaster and lectr; journalist: Bedfordshire Times, Oxford Mail, Drum Publications (Johannesburg, S Africa); awarded travelling scholarship Soc of Authors 1995; *Books* The Unlooked-for Season (1960, Gregory Award), Rose in the Afternoon and Other Poems (1974, Cholmondeley Award), The Thinking Heart (1978), Beyond Descartes (1983), Persephone: A Story (1986, James Tait Black Meml Prize Award), The Inland Sea (1989), Beached Boats (with photographs by Robert Mitchell, 1991), Selected Poems (1992), Ghosts and Other Company (1995); for children (with Katherine Hoskyns): Boots (1966), Wheels (1966), Wind (1967), Water (1967), Tea (1968), Sunday (1968); *Style*— Miss Jenny Joseph; ✉ 17 Windmill Road, Minchinhampton, Gloucester GL6 9DX; agent: John Johnson Ltd, Clerkenwell House, 45–47 Clerkenwell Green, London EC1R 0HT

JOSEPH, Joe; *b* 20 May 1955; *m* Jane Louise, *née* Winterbotham; 2 s (Thomas Daniel b 20 Nov 1989, Charles Benjamin b 2 Dec 1992), 1 da (Eliza Rose b 6 March 1995); *Career* formerly with Reuters News Agency (London, NY), feature writer and columnist The Times (formerly Tokyo corr); *Books* The Japanese: Strange but not Strangers (Viking Penguin, 1993); *Style*— Joe Joseph, Esq; ✉ The Times, 1 Pennington St, London E1 9XN (☎ 0171 782 5000)

JOSEPH, Julian; *b* 1966; *Educ* Interchange's Weekend Arts Course Kentish Town, Berklee Sch of Music Boston (ILEA scholar); *Career* pianist, composer; fndr: own quartet 1990, Julian Joseph Trio, electric gp KillaJules; int tours of USA, Canada, Bermuda, India, Australia and Caribbean with Branford Marsalis, Wynton Marsalis, Bobby McFerrin, Joe Williams, George Coleman, Gary Bartz, Courtney Pine; festival appearances incl: Montreaux Jazz, North Sea Jazz, Brecon, Glasgow, Aldeburgh, City of London, Cheltenham, Bermuda; projects incl: The Two Sides of Julian Joseph Weekend Barbican 1994 (Classics meets Jazz with Royal Philharmonic Concert Orch, Total Jazz with Julian Joseph Big Band), jazz series Wigmore Hall 1994 with Johnny Griffin, Eddie Daniels, Andy Sheppard and Jason Rebello, Ronnie Scott's Club, Jazz Cafe, BBC Proms 1995, Concertgebouw Amsterdam 1996, Queen Elizabeth Hall (Julian Joseph Trio and first appearance of KillaJules) 1996, concert series with Residence Orkest Hague 1996; *Recordings* The Language of Truth 1991, Reality 1993, Julian Joseph in Concert at the Wigmore Hall 1995, Universal Traveller (Julian Joseph Trio) 1996; *Style*— Julian Joseph, Esq; ✉ c/o James Joseph Music Management, 85 Cicada Road, Wandsworth, London SW18 2PA (☎ 0181 874 8647, fax 0181 877 9783, e-mail 100544, 3473)

JOSEPH, Michael Peter; s of Edward Albert Joseph (d 1959), and Eleonore Cecilie Therese, *née* Seffers; *b* 28 May 1941; *Educ* Michaelhouse Balgowan Natal SA, London Coll of Printing and Graphic Arts London; *m* Julia Lillian, da of George Mallison Hogg (ka 1944); 2 da (Joanna Victoria b 22 Oct 1971, Justine Samantha b 14 Nov 1972), 1 s (Jay Edward Jonathon b 14 June 1974); *Career* advtg and portrait photographer; early career experience as reportage photographer; cmmnd by Town magazine to cover shark fishing in Ireland, the primative painters Chesher, Lloyd and Holzhandler 1963 and to cover the Vietnam War 1964 (photos bought by Paris Match, Sunday Times, The Guardian and The Mirror); subsequent advtg cmmns for clients incl: Aer Lingas, Benson & Hedges, Ford Cars, White Horse Whiskey; other assignments incl Beggars Banquet album cover (Rolling Stones); co-fndr TV prodn co Joseph Dixon Hogg, estab photographic studio Clapham Common 1980; numerous D&AD awards for advtg campaigns; memb Assoc of Photographers (vice chm 1968); *Books* The World of Children (main contrib, 1966), Complete Photography Course (1993), Illustrated Hitchhiker's Guide to the Galaxy (1994); *Recreations* sailing, tennis and primarily photography; *Style*— Michael Joseph, Esq; ✉ 46 Clapham Common North Side, London SW4 0AA (☎ 0171 720 9044/0124, fax 0171 622 6366)

JOSEPH, Richard Lewis; s of Alfred Joseph (d 1967), of London, and Rose Sarah, *née* Melzack; *b* 24 July 1949; *Educ* Algernon Road Sch, Haberdashers' Aske's Sch; *m* March 1974, Linda Carol, da of Frank Hyams; 1 s (Mark Alan b Nov 1981), 1 da (Danielle Frances b July 1978); *Career* articled clerk: Lewis Bloom, Blick Rothenberg & Noble; qualified chartered accountant 1972, Stoy Hayward & Co 1972, Elliott Woolfe & Rose 1977–78, fin controller Unit Tst Gp 1978–82, private practice 1978–; fndr Micro Computer Gp of N London, chm Ctee N London Soc of CAs 1990–91 (joined 1986); London Soc of CAs: memb Main Ctee, memb PR Ctee; chm LSCA Ed Bd 1992–, memb Support Task Force ICAEW 1995–, memb Ctee Edgware & Burnt Oak C of C; FCA (ACA 1972); *Recreations* golf, music, cricket, football, rock and blues guitarist; *Clubs* Elstree Golf; *Style*— Richard Joseph, Esq; ✉ 2nd Floor, 65 Station Rd, Edgware, Middlesex HA8 7HX (☎ 0181 952 5407, fax 0181 951 0779)

JOSEPHS, John Irving; s of David Josephs (d 1972), and Freda, *née* Weiner; *b* 12 March 1944; *Educ* Newcastle Royal GS, Univ of Durham (BA(Econ)); *m* 29 July 1969, Marion Ruth, da of Walter Sharman; 2 s (Daniel Adam b 13 April 1972, David Simon b 18 Feb 1974), 1 da (Kate Louisa b 26 April 1982); *Career* articled clerk Harris Kafton CAs 1965–69, CA Whinney Murray 1969–70, CA Robert Miller Tate 1970–89; Metro Radio plc: non-exec dir 1974–89, fin dir 1989–92, md 1993–95; md The Radio Partnership Ltd 1995–; non-exec dir Ivy Court Leisure Clubs Ltd 1995–; FCA; *Recreations* family, running, Newcastle United FC, bridge, reading; *Clubs* Heaton Harriers; *Style*— John Josephs, Esq; ✉ 22 Osbaldeston Gardens, Gosforth, Newcastle upon Tyne NE3 4JE (☎ 0191 285 1912)

JOSEPHS, Dr Wilfred; s of Philip Isaac Josephs (d 1955), and Rachel, *née* Block; *b* 24 July 1927; *Educ* Rutherford GS Newcastle upon Tyne, Univ of Durham (BDS); *m* 2 Sept 1956, Valerie Gloria (sep); 2 da (Philippa b 1961, Claudia b 1963); *Career* Capt RADC 1952–53 (Lt 1951); composer in residence: Univ of Wisconsin Milwaukee 1970, Roosevelt Univ Chicago 1972; distinguished visiting prof and composer in residence Ohio State Univ Columbus 1992 (Spring and Summer); music conslt London Int Film Sch 1988–, lectr film and TV music Dartington Int Summer Sch of Music; important works: requiem, 12 symphonies, 23 concertos, 11 overtures, 4 string quartets, chamber works, ballets including Equus and Cyrano de Bergerac; operas: Rebecca and Pathelin, Through the Looking Glass, Alice in Wonderland; A Mass for St Cuthbert of Durham; written music for 119 TV prodns incl: The Great War, I Claudius, Horizon, Art of the Western World; 26 feature and 33 documentary films; memb: Performing Rights Soc, Composers' Guild of GB, Royal Philharmonic Soc, BAFTA, Ctee Friends of LIFS; memb: Assoc Professional Composers; Hon DMus Univ of Newcastle upon Tyne 1978; *Recreations* cinema, video, music, swimming; *Style*— Dr Wilfred Josephs; ✉ 6 Grand Union Walk, Kentish Town Road, Camden Town, London NW1 9LP (☎ and fax 0171 485 1634); The Wilfred Josephs Society, Hill House, Corsiehill, Perth PH2 7BN (☎ and fax 01738 442079)

JOSHI, Sanjay; *b* 2 May 1961; *Educ* Univ of Kent at Canterbury (BA(Econ), MA(Econ)); *m*; 1 s, 1 da; *Career* research offr and lectr City Univ Business Sch 1984–86, sr economist CBI 1986–87, sr economist Baring Bros 1987–90, chief economist and head of bond research Daiwa Europe Ltd 1990–; regular pubns: Quarterly Fixed Income Strategy, Yen Comment, Market Comment; regular Gilt Column The Times 1990–, regular portfolio selection The Economist 1990–; also contrib: CBI Economic Situation Report, Euromoney, IFR; *Style*— Sanjay Joshi, Esq

JOSHUA, Rosemary; *Career* soprano; winner: Van Der Beugel Opera Prize, Royal Philharmonic Soc Debut Award 1992, Gold medal RCM; *Performances* incl: Blonde in Die Entführung aus dem Serail (Buxton Festival), Zerlina in Don Giovanni (Scottish Opera), Adele in Die Fledermaus (ENO), Yum Yum in The Mikado (ENO), Norina in Don Pasquale (ENO), title role in Princess Ida (ENO), Pamina in The Magic Flute (Covent Garden Festival and Opera N Ireland), Angelica in Orlando (Aix-en-Provence Festival), Sophie in Der Rosenkavalier (ENO), Poussette in Manon (Royal Opera House), Poppea in Agrippa (Cologne Opera), Susanna in Marriage of Figaro (Cologne Opera), Ilia in Idomeneo (Lisbon), Calisto title role in La Monnaie (Brussel), title role in Semele (BBC Proms 1996); *Style*— Ms Rosemary Joshua; ✉ c/o IMG Artists Europe, Media House, 3 Burlington Lane, Chiswick, London W4 2TH (☎ 0181 747 9977, fax 0181 747 9131)

JOSIPOVICI, Prof Gabriel David; s of Jean Josipovici, of Italy, and Sacha Elena, *née* Rabinovitch; *b* 8 Oct 1940; *Educ* Victoria Coll Cairo Egypt, Cheltenham Coll, St Edmund Hall Oxford; *Career* prof Univ of Sussex 1963– (formerly lectr and reader), Lord Weidenfeld prof of comparative lit Univ of Oxford 1996–97; author; plays for the stage incl: Dreams of Mrs Fraser (Theatre Upstairs) 1972, Flow (Edinburgh Lyceum) 1973, Marathon (ICA) 1978; radio plays incl: Playback (1972), AG (1977), Vergil Dying (1980), Mr Vee (1989); *Books* The Inventory (1968), The World and The Book (1971), Mobius the Stripper (1975), Migrations (1977), Conversations in Another Room (1984), Contre-Jour (1986), In the Fertile Land (1987), The Book of God: A Response to the Bible (1988), Steps: Selected Fiction and Drama (1990), The Big Glass (1991), Text and Voice: Essays 1981–91 (1992), In a Hotel Garden (1993), Moo Pak (1994), Touch (1996); *Style*— Prof Gabriel Josipovici; ✉ Univ of Sussex, Arts Building, Falmer, Brighton, Sussex (☎ 01273 606755)

JOSLIN, Paul; s of Edgar Alfred (d 1958), and Mary Elizabeth Elsie, *née* Buckeridge; *b* 20 Nov 1950; *Educ* City of Portsmouth Tech HS, Royal Coll Music (GRSM, LRAM, ARCM), Univ of Reading (MMus); *m* 2 August 1975, Gwenllian Elfyn, da of Rev Ifor Elfyn Ellis, of St Asaph, North Wales; *Career* organist and dir of music St Paul's Onslow Sq London 1972–77; Holy Trinity Brompton London: associate dir of music 1977–79, organist and dir 1979–92; organist and dir St Luke's Redcliffe Sq SW10 1992–; asst conductor Brompton Choral Soc 1977–81, actg dir of music St Catherine Sch Twickenham 1993; solo and organ accompanist; continuo work with London Bach Orchestra, Thames Chamber Orchestra and English Chorale, concerto soloist with and memb of Eng Chamber Orchestra, choral and orchestral conductor BBC Radio and TV (team organist and dir Daily Service 1989–94, organist Rome Pilgrimage Daily Service Tour 1992), dir of music Let's Celebrate St Paul's Cathedral 1993–96, vice pres London Organist Guild 1994–, visiting lectr Reading Univ 1994–95; memb Br Inst of Organ Studies; *Recreations* architecture, swimming, 35mm photography, collection 78rpm classical records; *Style*— Paul Joslin, Esq; ✉ 109 Hanover Rd, London NW10 3DN (☎ 0181 459 5547); St Luke's, Redcliffe Square, London SW10 (☎ and fax 0171 370 0338)

JOSLIN, Chief Constable Peter David; QPM (1983); s of Frederick William Joslin (d 1992), of Essex, and Emma, *née* Smith (d 1979); *b* 26 Oct 1933; *Educ* King Edward VI GS Chelmsford, Univ of Essex (BA); *m* 5 Oct 1960, Kathleen Josephine, da of Patrick Monaghan, of Eire; 2 s (Russell b 1961, Stephen b 1964), 1 da (Angela b 1972); *Career* police offr; police constable to supt Essex Police 1954–74, asst chief constable (ops) Leics Constabulary 1976 (chief supt 1974), currently chief constable Warwickshire Constabulary (dep chief 1977); *Recreations* cricket, football, golf, gardening, house renovation, after dinner speaking, good wines; *Style*— Chief Constable Peter Joslin, QPM; ✉ Warwickshire Constabulary, PO Box 4, Leek Wootton, Warwick CV35 7QB (☎ 01926 415 000, fax 01926 415188)

JOSLING, Frederick John; s of John Frederick Josling (d 1975), and Emily Esther, *née* Baker (d 1987); *b* 22 Sept 1930; *Educ* St Albans Sch; *m* 1 April 1961, Elisabeth Mary, da of Thomas Reginald Harrison (d 1970); 2 s (Nicholas b 1966, William b 1970), 1 da (Emma b 1963); *Career* dir Lopex plc 1980–83, dep chm Kirkwoods 1981–86, md Interlink 1973–80 (chm 1981); chm: ASL Central 1986–88, Alliance International Ltd 1987–90; dir Social Service Advertising 1990–94; FIPA, FCAM; *Recreations* cricket, gardening; *Clubs* MCC, Lord's Taverners (chm 1976–78), Reform; *Style*— F J Josling, Esq; ✉ Badger's Holt, Caddington, nr Luton, Beds LU1 4AD (☎ 01582 23797)

JOSS, Timothy Hans (Tim); *b* 27 June 1955; *Educ* Harrow, The Queen's Coll Oxford, Univ of Grenoble, RAM; *m* 1983, Elizabeth Morag, *née* Wallace; 1 da (Hannah b 18 May 1987); *Career* Live Music Now! 1980–82, music and dance offr NW Arts 1982–89, concerts dir Bournemouth Sinfonietta rising to sr mangr Bournemouth Orchs 1989–93, artistic dir and chief exec Bath Festivals Tst 1993–; chm Cmmn for Community Music

Int Soc for Music Educn 1992–94; *Books* Directory of Community Music (1993); *Style*— Tim Joss; ✉ Bath Festivals Trust, 2 Midland Bridge Road, Bath BA2 3EQ (☎ 01225 462231, fax 01225 445551)

JOSS, William Hay; s of Lt Col William Taylor Barron Joss, MC, TD, late of RAMC (d 1972), of Nottingham, and Dr Elizabeth Lilly Lindsay Joss, *née* Smith (d 1978); *b* 20 May 1927; *Educ* Worksop Coll, Exeter Coll Oxford (BA); *m* 20 July 1961, Rosemary Sarah (Sally), da of James Dogherty; 2 s (Timothy Simon b 1962, William Anthony b 1966); *Career* 14/20 Kings Hussars (latterly 2 Lt) 1945–48, Capt 307 South Notts Hussars (TA) 1948–53; industl prodn mangr 1950–62; called to the Bar 1957, practising barrister 1962–, recorder of the Crown Court 1982–; *Recreations* golf; *Clubs* Nottingham and Notts United Services; *Style*— William Joss, Esq; ✉ 1 High Pavement, Nottimngham NG1 1HF (☎ 0115 941 8218, fax 0115 941 8240)

JOSSE, Dr (Silvain) Edouard; OBE (1983); s of Albert Josse, of London, and Charlotte, *née* Karolicki; *b* 8 May 1933; *Educ* Highgate Sch, Middx Hosp Med Sch, Univ of London (MB BS, MRCS, LRCP); *m* 1, 15 May 1960 (m dis 1983), Lea, da of Alter Majer Ber (d 1977); 2 s (David b 22 July 1961, Jeremy b 14 July 1968), 1 da (Ann b 19 Sept 1964); m 2, 27 Oct 1991, Yvonne, da of Harry Levine (d 1970); *Career* gen med practitioner 1962, sr forensic med examiner Metropolitan Police 1964, former regnl advsr in gen practice and assoc dean of postgrad med N Thames (E) Region Br Postgrad Med Fedn Univ of London 1976–95, former GP memb NE Thames RHA; memb Standing Ctee on Postgrad Med and Dental Educn, former memb Enfield and Haringey Family Practitioners' Ctee, former chm Enfield and Haringey Local Med Ctee; sec gen UEMO 1982–86; Liveryman Worshipful Soc of Apothecaries; MA London 1989; FRCGP 1977, DMJ 1970, FZS, APS, MLS, BAFS, MAE; memb: BMA 1956, RSM 1978; *Recreations* skiing, gardening, history, good wine tasting; *Clubs* MCC, Middx CC, RAC, Carlton; *Style*— Dr Edouard Josse, OBE; ✉ 2 Shirehall Gardens, London NW4 2QS (☎ 0181 202 7740, fax 0181 903 9891); Brownlow Medical Centre, 140–142 Brownlow Road, London N11 2BD (☎ 0181 888 7775, fax 0181 888 3450)

JOST, Dr H Peter; CBE (1969); s of Leo Jost (d 1941); *b* 25 Jan 1921; *Educ* Liverpool Tech Coll, Manchester Coll of Technol; *m* 1948, Margaret Josephine, da of Michael Kadesh (d 1952); 2 da; *Career* chm: K S Paul Group 1973– (md 1955–89), Associated Technology Group Ltd 1976–, Eley Estate Co Ltd 1989; Lord President's nominee for Ct of Univ of Salford 1970–87, first pres Int Tribology Cncl 1973–, chm Manchester Technol Assoc in London 1976–87; Cncl Engrg Instns: memb Bd 1977–84, memb Exec 1979–83 (chm Home Affrs Ctee 1980–83), memb Parly and Scientific Ctee 1976–, memb Steering Ctee 1983–91, memb Cncl (formerly Steering Ctee) and Gen Purpose Ctee 1991–93, hon sec 1990–93, vice pres 1993–95, vice chm 1995–; pres: Inst of Prodn Engrs 1977–78, Manchester Technol Assoc 1984–85; vice pres Inst of Mech Engrs 1987–92; fell Soc of Mfrg Engrs (USA) 1988, memb Ct Univ of Middlesex 1996; awarded: Derby Medal Liverpool Engrg Soc 1955, Gold Medal Slovak Tech Univ 1984, 1st Nuffield Medal IProdE 1981, Georg Vogelpohl Insignia German Tribology Soc 1979; hon industl prof Liverpool John Moores Univ (formerly Liverpool Poly) 1983–, hon prof of mech engrg Univ of Wales 1986–; tstee Michael John Tst 1986–; Hon DSc Univ of Salford 1970, Hon DTech CNAA 1987, Hon DSc Slovak Univ 1987, Hon DEng Univ of Leeds 1989, Hon DSc Univ of Bath 1990, Hon DSc Tech Univ Budapest 1993; Liveryman Worshipful Co of Engrs, Freeman City of London; State Legislative Commendation of State of California (USA) 1978, Gold Insignia of Order of Merit of Polish People's Republic 1986, Offr Cross of Order of Merit Fed Republic of Germany 1992, Officier de l'Ordre des Palmes Academique (France) 1995; hon foreign memb Russian Acad of Engrs 1991 (first hon foreign memb), hon memb Chinese Mechanical Engrg Soc 1986 (one of first eight foreign membs), hon memb Ukranian Acad of Tport 1994, hon foreign memb Belarus Acad of Engrg and Technology 1996; Hon FIEE 1980; *Recreations* music, gardening; *Clubs* Athenaeum; *Style*— Dr H Peter Jost, CBE; ✉ Hill House, Wills Grove, Mill Hill, London NW7 1QL (☎ 0181 959 3355); K S Paul Products Ltd, Eley Rd, Eley Estate, London N18 3DB (☎ 0181 345 5566, fax 0181 807 2023)

JOURDAN, Martin Henry; s of Henry George Jourdan (d 1990), of Dumfries, Scotland, and Jocelyn Louise, *née* Courtney (d 1962); *b* 7 Oct 1941; *Educ* Bishopshalt GS, Guy's Hosp Med Sch (MB BS, BSc, LRCP, PhD, MS, FRCS); *m* 22 Oct 1966, May, da of John McElwain (d 1960), of Glasgow; 2 s (Iain Campbell b 1967, Adam Ramsay b 1985), 2 da (Anthea b 1969, Gabrielle b 1970); *Career* conslt surgn Guy's Hosp 1978–, external examiner in surgery to Univs of Bristol and W Indies 1978–87, reader in surgery Univ of London 1982, sub-dean Guy's Hosp Med Sch 1984–89, sr examiner in surgery Univ of London 1984–, memb Ct of Examiners RCS 1986–; Freeman City of London, memb Ct of Assts Worshipful Soc of Apothecaries of London; memb BMA, Surgical Res Soc Assoc of Surgns; FRSM; *Recreations* tennis, reading, opera; *Clubs* Athenaeum; *Style*— Martin Jourdan, Esq; ✉ 55 Shirlock Rd, Hampstead, London NW3 (☎ 0171 267 1582); Department of Surgery, Guy's Hospital, London SE1 (☎ 0171 955 4052)

JOWELL, Prof Jeffrey Lionel; Hon QC (1993); s of Jack Jowell, of Cape Town, SA, and Emily, *née* Katzenellenbogen; *b* 4 Nov 1938; *Educ* Univ of Cape Town (BA, LLB), Hertford Coll Oxford (BA, MA), Harvard Law Sch (LLM, SJD); *m* 8 Dec 1963, Frances Barbara, da of Dr Moses Suzman, of Johannesburg, and Helen Suzman, DBE; 1 s (Daniel b 11 June 1969), 1 da (Joanna b 2 Sept 1967); *Career* called to the Bar Middle Temple 1965; res asst Harvard Law Sch 1966–68, fell Jt Centre Urban Studies Harvard and MIT 1967–68, assoc prof of law and admin studies York Univ Toronto 1968–71; LSE: Leverhulme fell in urban legal studies 1972–74, lectr in law 1974–75; Faculty of Law UCL: prof of public law 1975–, dean 1979–89, head of dept 1982–89; vice provost and head Grad Sch UCL 1992–; Lionel Cohen lectr in Hebrew Univ of Jerusalem 1986, visiting prof Univ of Paris 1991; non-exec dir: UCL Press 1994–95, Camden and Islington Community Health Tst 1994–; SSRC: chm Social Sci and Law Ctee 1981–84, vice chm Govt and Law Ctee 1982–84; Bd Inst of Cwlth Studies 1994–; tstee: John Foster Meml Tst 1986–, Int Centre for Public Law 1993–; govr Hull Centre for European Law 1993–, memb Nuffield Ctee Town and Country Planning 1983–86, chm Ctee of Heads Univ Law Schs 1984–86; Br delegate CSCE Conf Oslo 1991; Hon DJur Athens 1987, Hon LLD Ritsumeikan 1988; *Books* Law and Bureaucracy (1975), Lord Denning: The Judge And The Law (jt ed, 1984), The Changing Constitution (jt ed, 1985, 1989 and 1994), Judicial Review of Administrative Action (jt author, 1995); *Recreations* tennis, Exmoor and London; *Style*— Prof Jeffrey Jowell, QC; ✉ UCL, Gower St, London WC1 (☎ 0171 391 1405)

JOWELL, Tessa; MP (Lab) Dulwich (majority 2,056); da of Dr Kenneth Palmer, and Rosemary Palmer; *b* 17 Sept 1947; *Educ* St Margaret's Sch Aberdeen, Univ of Aberdeen, Univ of Edinburgh, Goldsmiths' Coll London; *m* 17 March 1979, David Mills; 1 s, 1 da, 3 step c; *Career* child care offr London Borough of Lambeth 1969–71, social worker The Maudsley Hosp Camberwell 1972–74, asst dir MIND 1974–86, dir Community Care Special Action Project Birmingham 1987–90, dir Joseph Rowntree Fndn Community Care Programme 1990–92; Parly candidate Ilford N 1979, MP (Lab) Dulwich 1992–; cncllr London Borough of Camden 1978–86, vice chm then chm Social Servs Ctee Assoc of Met Authorities 1978–86, govr Nat Inst for Social Work 1985–, tstee Employment Policy Inst, visiting fell Nuffield Coll Oxford; *Style*— Ms Tessa Jowell, MP; ✉ House of Commons, London SW1A 0AA

JOWETT, Richard Lund; s of Harry Jowett (d 1975), of W Yorkshire, and Vera Millicent, *née* Gent; *b* 29 April 1937; *Educ* Bradford GS, Magdalen Coll Oxford, Middlesex Hosp Med Sch (MA); *m* 27 Aug 1966, (Catherine) Louise, da of Maj Robert Pitts Heaton (d 1985); 3 s (Andrew b 1971, James b 1972, Charles b 1978); *Career* conslt orthopaedic surgn Poole Hosp NHS Tst 1974–; memb Int Surgical Soc for the Study of Orthopaedics and Traumatology (SICOT) 1992–; FRCS 1968; *Recreations* golf, cricket; *Clubs* Parkstone Golf, Medical Golfing Soc, MCC, Oxford and Cambridge Golfing Soc, County Cricketers' Golfing Soc; *Style*— Richard Jowett, Esq; ✉ Sandecotes Lodge, 34 Sandecotes Rd, Parkstone, Poole, Dorset BH14 8NZ (☎ 01202 740696)

JOWITT, Hon Mr Justice; Hon Sir Edwin Frank; kt (1988); s of Frank and Winifred Jowitt; *b* 1 Oct 1929; *Educ* Swanwick Hall GS, LSE (LLB); *m* 1959, Anne Barbara, *née* Dyson; 3 s, 2 da; *Career* called to the Bar Middle Temple 1951, memb Midland & Oxford Circuit 1952–80, dep chm QS: Rutland 1967–71, Derbyshire 1970–71; QC 1969, recorder of the Crown Court 1972–80, circuit judge (Midland & Oxford Circuit) 1980–88 (a sr circuit judge 1987–88), judge of the High Court of Justice (Queen's Bench Div) 1988–, presiding judge Midland & Oxford Circuit 1996–; bencher 1977, hon recorder Birmingham 1987–88; *Recreations* fell-walking and cycling; *Style*— The Hon Mr Justice Jowitt; ✉ Royal Courts of Justice, Strand WC2A 2LL

JOWITT, Prof Paul William; s of Stanley Jowitt, of Thurcroft, Yorks, and late Joan Mary, *née* Goundry; *b* 3 Aug 1950; *Educ* Maltby GS, Imperial Coll London (BSc, PhD); *m* 11 Aug 1973, Jane Catriona, da of Lt Ronald George Urquhart, of Romford, Essex; 1 s (Christopher b 17 Feb 1978), 1 da (Hannah b 29 June 1980); *Career* lectr in civil engrg Imperial Coll 1974–86 (warden Falmouth Hall 1980–86), chm Tynemarch Systems Engineering Ltd 1984–86 (dir 1984–91), ed Journal of Civil Engineering Systems 1985–; Heriot-Watt Univ: prof 1987–, head Dept of Civil Engrg 1988–91, head Dept of Civil and Offshore Engrg 1991–; author of various specialist tech pubns and jl articles; memb various nat and local assoc ctees ICE; CEng 1988, FICE 1994 (MICE 1988), FRSA 1996; *Recreations* painting, Morgan 3–wheelers, restoring old houses; *Clubs* Chaps, Links, MTWC; *Style*— Prof Paul Jowitt; ✉ 22 Fountainhall Road, The Grange, Edinburgh EH9 2LW (☎ 0131 667 5696); Department of Civil and Offshore Engineering, Heriot-Watt University, Edinburgh EH14 4AS (☎ 0131 449 5111, fax 0131 451 3170)

JOWITT, Peter John Russell; s of Harold John Duncan Mackintosh Jowitt, of Southwell, Notts, and Kathleen Joyce, *née* Clark; *b* 30 July 1942; *Educ* Bryanston, Univ of Nottingham (BEd); *Career* asst master Cheltenham Coll 1979–82, dep headmaster Cokethorpe Sch 1982–84, head of modern languages Claire's Court Sch 1985–89, dir Monksoft Ltd 1988–91, researcher Language Centre Univ of Buckingham 1989–, head of modern languages St Edmund's Sch Hindhead 1991–96, head of IT Thomas's Prep Battersea 1996–; memb Ctee Nat Sch's Regatta 1973–, selector GB Jr Rowing Team 1974–76, chm Jr Rowing Ctee and memb Exec Ctee Amateur Rowing Assoc 1978–79, memb Jr Cmmn FISA 1979–84 (holder umpire's licence 1971–); chef de mission Moscow 1979, chm Kitchin Soc 1989–91 (sec 1986–89); LRPS 1993; *Recreations* photography, ocean racing, rowing administration, computer assisted language learning; *Clubs* Lloyd's Yacht, Leander; *Style*— Peter Jowitt, Esq; ✉ Burgage Paddock, Southwell, Notts NG25 0ER (☎ and fax 01636 813545)

JOY, (Arthur) Anthony; *b* 3 June 1936; *m* 1 (m dis 1971), Jeanette Strafford; 4 s (b 1957, 1959, 1960 and 1963); m 2, Lena Elsa Warner, *née* Svanberg; 1 s (b 1979) and 1 step s (b 1966); *Career* served HM Forces 1957–59; HM Dip Serv: CRO 1960–61, Delhi 1961–65, Salisbury 1965, Lusaka 1965, CRO 1966, vice-consul Damascus 1966–67, vice-consul Strasbourg 1967–69, second sec Ibadan 1969–70, FCO 1970–72, vice-consul (commercial) Rio de Janeiro 1972–75, first sec (energy) Washington 1976–80, first sec FCO 1980–85, cnsllr Overseas Inspectorate FCO 1985–86, cnsllr (fin and admin) New Delhi 1986–89; consul-gen: Vancouver 1990–93, Rio de Janeiro 1993–96; *Style*— Anthony Joy, Esq; ✉ 7 Giles House, 158 Westbourne Grove, London W11 2RJ

JOY, David; CBE (1983); s of Harold Oliver Joy (d 1995), of West Kirby, Wirral, and Doris Kate, *née* Buxton (d 1950); *b* 9 Dec 1932; *Educ* Hulme GS Oldham, St Catharine's Coll Cambridge (MA); *m* 24 July 1957, Montserrat Morancho Saumench, only da of Angel Morancho Garreta, of Zaragoza; 1 s (Clive Douglas Christopher b 1958), 1 da (Jennifer-Marina Josephine b 1961); *Career* HMOCS N Rhodesia 1956–64; HMOCS Zambia 1964–70: Cabinet Office 1964, under sec (Cabinet) 1968, seconded town clerk Lusaka City Cncl 1969, under sec Miny of Commerce and Industry 1970; Ashridge Management Coll 1970; HM Dip Serv: FCO 1971–73, first sec (Inf) Caracas 1973–75, head Chancery Caracas 1975–77, asst head Mexican and Caribbean Dept FCO 1977–78, cnsllr and head Chancery Warsaw 1978–82, cnsllr and head British Interests Section Buenos Aires 1982–84, head Mexico and Central America Dept FCO 1984–87, ambass to Honduras and El Salvador 1987–89, consul-gen Barcelona 1989–92, ret 1992; company chm and sr conslt 1993–; *Recreations* reading, tennis, golf; *Clubs* United Oxford and Cambridge Univ, Circulo del Liceo (Barcelona), Rotary International; *Style*— David Joy, Esq, CBE; ✉ Maria Agustin 4, Casa 2, 7A, 50004 Zaragoza, Spain (☎ and fax 00 34 76 435218)

JOY, David Anthony Welton; s of Richard Clapham Joy (d 1964), of York, and Annie Doreen, *née* Welton; *b* 14 June 1942; *Educ* St Peter's Sch York; *m* 28 March 1967, Judith Margaret, da of Wilfrid Agar (d 1963), of York; 2 s (Richard b 10 March 1970, Thomas b 1 Aug 1975), 1 da (Fiona b 6 March 1968); *Career* gen reporter Yorkshire Post 1962–65, books ed Dalesman Publishing Co 1970–88 (ed asst 1965–70), ed The Dalesman 1988–93, ed Garden Rail 1993–; sec Craven Branch CPRE, managing ed Atlantic Transport Publishers 1995–; *Books* Settle-Carlisle Railway (with W R Mitchell, 1966), Main Line Over Shap (1967), Cumbrian Coast Railways (1968), Whitby-Pickering Railway (1969), Railways in the North (1970), Traction Engines in the North (1970), George Hudson of York (with A J Peacock, 1971), Steamtown (1972), Railways of the Lake Counties (1973), Regional History of the Railways of Great Britain: South and West Yorkshire (1975, 2 edn 1984), Railways in Lancashire (1975), Settle-Carlisle Centenary (with W R Mitchell, 1975), Railways of Yorkshire: The West Riding (1976), North Yorkshire Moors Railway (with Peter Williams, 1977), Steam on the North York Moors (1978), Yorkshire Railways (with A Haigh, 1979), Steam on the Settle and Carlisle (1981), Yorkshire Dales Railway (1983), Settle-Carlisle in Colour (1983), Regional History of the Railways of Great Britain: The Lake Counties (1983), Portrait of the Settle-Carlisle (1984), The Dalesman: A Celebration of 50 Years (1989), Life in the Yorkshire Coalfield (1989), Settle - Carlisle Celebration (1990), Uphill to Paradise (1991), Yorkshire's Christmas (1992), The Dalesman Bedside Book (1993), Yorkshire's Farm Life (1994), Railways in your Garden (with David Pratt, 1994); *Recreations* photography, walking, modelling; *Style*— David Joy, Esq; ✉ Hole Bottom, Hebden, Skipton, North Yorkshire BD23 5DL (☎ 01756 752369, fax 01756 753370)

JOYCE, Lionel; s of Cornelius Aloysius Frederic Peter Joyce (d 1989), of Kent, and Kathleen Mary, *née* Keane (d 1982); *b* 21 March 1947; *Educ* St Joseph's Coll Beulah Hill, City of London Coll of Laws; *m* Hilary Turner; 1 s (Luke b 8 Nov 1981), 2 da (Joanna b 28 April 1978, Rosalind b 19 Aug 1979); *Career* NHS: joined Personnel Dept Nottingham Dist 1973, princ admin asst S Nottingham Dist 1975–83, sector admin Nottingham Mental Health Sector 1983–85, unit gen mangr Newcastle Mental Health Unit and Newcastle DHA 1985–91, chief exec Newcastle Mental Health (NHS) Tst 1991–94, chief exec Newcastle City Health NHS Tst 1994–; *Style*— Lionel Joyce, Esq; ✉ Newcastle City Health NHS Trust, Newcastle General Hospital, Westgate Road, Newcastle upon Tyne NE4 6BE (☎ 0191 273 8811, fax 0191 273 2340)

JOYCE, Peter Stuart Langford; QC (1991); s of Horace Langford Joyce (d 1984), of Porthmadog, Gwynedd, and Nancy, *née* Dryden; *b* 5 Feb 1946; *Educ* Oundle, Coll of Law; *m* 1971, Helen Christina, da of John Lazenby; 2 s, 2 da; *Career* called to the Bar

Inner Temple 1968, recorder Midland & Oxford Circuit 1986–; *Recreations* golf, sailing, gardening, reading; *Style*— Peter Joyce, Esq, QC; ✉ 1 High Pavement, Nottingham NG1 1HF (☎ 0115 941 8218, fax 0115 941 8240)

JOYCE, Thomas Richard (Tom); s of Thomas Joyce (d 1988), and Margaret, *née* Scanlan (d 1995); *b* 5 Oct 1939; *Educ* St John's Univ Minnesota (BA), Notre Dame Law Sch (LLB, ed Notre Dame Lawyer Vol 38); *m* 1, 1962, Patricia Nepper (d 1993); 2 da; m 2, 1995, Annette Atkins; *Career* corp fin lawyer; Shearman & Sterling: assoc New York Office 1963–72, ptnr 1972–96, New York 1972–78, London Office 1978–81, New York 1981–84, managing ptnr Hong Kong 1985, based New York 1986–89, managing ptnr London 1989–95; ptnr Freshfields London 1996–; regent St John's Univ Minnesota 1980–95, memb Library Advsy Ctee Inst of Advanced Legal Studies, chm Soc of Eng and American Lawyers 1991–94; *Recreations* walking, travel, reading, the arts; *Clubs* RAC, University (NY); *Style*— Tom Joyce, Esq; ✉ Freshfields, 65 Fleet Street, London EC4Y 1HS (☎ 0171 936 4000, fax 0171 832 7001)

JOYNER, Prof Richard William; s of Stanley William Joyner, of Carrickfergus, Co Antrim, and Jenny Kane, *née* Hagan; *b* 20 Dec 1944; *Educ* Belfast HS, Queen's Univ Belfast (BSc, DSc), Univ of Bradford (PhD); *m* 1 Sept 1967, (Ann) Jenepher, da of George Wilson Grange, of Belfast; 2 da (Clare b 24 July 1970, Carol b 9 Dec 1974); *Career* res fell Univ of California Berkeley 1970–71, memb Staff Chemistry Dept Univ of Bradford 1971–80, head Fundamentals of Catalysis Res Gp and Res Assoc BP Res Sunbury-on-Thames 1980–87, dir Leverhulme Centre for Innovative Catalysis and prof of chemistry Univ of Liverpool 1987–94, dir of res Nottingham Trent Univ 1994–; former chm Br Vacuum Cncl; memb: Cncl Int Union Vacuum Sci Technol and its Applications, Editorial Bd Catalysis Letters; chm Ctee Surface Reactivity and Catalysis Gp Royal Soc of Chemistry 1990–94 (sec 1982–86), hon sec Save British Science; FRSC 1989; *Publications* about 130 scientific publications in international journals, 2 books and several book chapters; *Recreations* music, wine, biographies; *Style*— Prof Richard Joyner; ✉ Research Office, The Nottingham Trent University, Newton Building, Burton Street, Nottingham NG7 2JF (☎ 0115 948 6837, fax 0115 948 6838)

JOYNSON, Dr David Huw Malcolm; s of David Cyril Joynson (d 1989), of High Cross, Newport, Gwent, and Rosetta, *née* Gough; *b* 4 Oct 1943; *Educ* Bassaleg GS, Univ of Wales Coll of Med (MB BCh), Univ of London (DipBact); *m* 15 July 1967, Menna Bennett, da of Emrys Bennett Owen (d 1988); 1 s (Owain Bennett), 2 da (Nia Bennett, Heledd Bennett); *Career* conslt med microbiologist W Glamorgan Health Authy 1975–, dir Public Health Laboratory Swansea and head of Toxoplasma Reference Unit; FRCP 1993 (MRCP 1971), FIBiol 1990 (MIBiol 1980), FRCPath 1996; *Recreations* welsh culture, golf, skiing, watching rugby; *Style*— Dr David Joynson; ✉ Public Health Laboratory, Singleton Hospital, Sgeti, Swansea, Wales SA2 8QA (☎ 01792 205666, fax 01792 202320)

JOYNSON, Kenneth Mercer; s of Edgar Hilton Joynson (d 1974), and Nellie, *née* Clansey (d 1943); *b* 8 Oct 1926; *Educ* Lymm GS Cheshire, Wolverhampton Tech Teachers Coll (CertEd); *m* 22 Sept 1951, Ruth Madeleine, da of Cyril Bentley Jackson (d 1931); 1 s (Richard b 25 Jan 1956); *Career* CA; asst accountant Bell & Nicolson Ltd Birmingham 1951–57, accountant Newey Eyre Ltd Birmingham 1957–59, sr audit mangr Impey Cudworth Co Birmingham 1959–62, princ Joynson & Co Sutton Coldfield 1963–66, sr lectr and head accounting studies Peterborough Regnl Coll 1967–80, lectr and examiner Chartered Building Socs' Inst 1972–86, princ Joynson & Co Market Deeping 1981–; disabled through polio 1931, vice chm (later chm) Polio Fellowship Birmingham 1953–65; various offices W Midland Lib Pty, Rutland and Stamford Lib Assoc and Stamford and Spalding Lib Assoc 1958–86, now memb Lib Dems; cncllr: Deeping St James Parish Cncl 1979–83, South Kesteven DC 1983– (vice chm Cncl 1994–96, chm 1996–); ACA 1951, FCA 1961; *Recreations* marathon running, association football; *Clubs* Peterborough Athletic, Stamford Town FC; *Style*— Kenneth M Joynson, Esq; ✉ 39 Manor Way, Deeping St James, Peterborough PE6 8PS (☎ 01778 343 506); Joynson & Co, 89A High Street, Market Deeping, Peterborough PE9 8ED (☎ 01778 346706)

JUBB, Brian Patrick; s of Charles Patrick Jubb (d 1992), and Patricia Elizabeth, *née* Parry (d 1968); *b* 25 Aug 1948; *Educ* The King's Sch Canterbury, Inns of Court Sch of Law; *m* 1, 16 Nov 1974 (m dis 1982), Susan Patricia Taylor; 1 da (Alexandra b 10 June 1978); m 2, 13 Sept 1985, Susan Elizabeth Lunn; 1 da (Lucy b 13 July 1988); *Career* called to the Bar Gray's Inn 1971, head of chambers 1994–; *Recreations* general aviation, scuba diving, reading; *Style*— Brian Jubb, Esq; ✉ Gray's Inn Chambers, Gray's Inn, London WC1R 5JA (☎ 0171 404 1111, fax 0171 430 1522 and 0171 430 1050)

JUDA, Annely; da of Dr Kurt Brauer (d 1951), of London, and Margaret, *née* Goldmann (d 1971); *b* 23 Sept 1914; *Educ* High Sch, Reimann Sch of Art and Design London; *m* 1939, Paul Juda; 1 s (David, *qv* b Feb 1946), 2 da (Carol b April 1942, Susan b May 1951); *Career* admin Eric Estorick's art collection 1956–58, with Kaplan Gallery London 1958–60, dir and fndr Molton Gallery London 1960, Hamilton Galleries London 1963; opened own gallery Annely Juda Fine Art with son David Juda 1968 (merged with Rowan Gallery 1982 to form Juda Rowan Gallery before reverting to former name and status 1987); exhibitions administered incl: Russian Works (Tokyo Gallery Japan) 1983, Dada-Constructivism: The Janus Face of the Twenties Sept-Dec 1984, Dada and Constructivism (The Seibu Museum of Art Tokyo) Oct-Nov 1988, The Seibu Tsukashin Hall Amagaski Nov-Dec 1988, The Museum of Mordern Art Kamakura Jan-Feb 1989, Centro de Arte Sofia Madrid March-May 1989, The Non-Objective World exhibition (at the invitation of the South Bank Centre (Arts Cncl) touring 4 venues in UK) 1992–93; memb Art Dealers' Assoc; winner art prize Cologne 1992; *Style*— Mrs Annely Juda; ✉ Annely Juda Fine Art, 23 Dering St, London W1R 9AA (☎ 0171 629 7578, fax 0171 491 2139)

JUDA, David; s of Paul Juda, and Annely Juda, *qv*; *Educ* Ibstock Place Froebel Sch, John Kelly Secdy Modern, Kilburn Poly; *m* March 1983, Yuko Shiraishi, *qv*, da of Masahiro Shinoda; *Career* ptnr Annely Juda Fine Art 1978 (joined 1967); memb Exec Ctee Fine Art and Antiques Export Ctee 1971–; vice chm Soc of London Art Dealers 1986–90 and 1995– (memb 1970–); *Recreations* skiing; *Clubs* Groucho's; *Style*— David Juda, Esq; ✉ Annely Juda Fine Art, 23 Dering Street, London W1R 9AA (☎ 0171 629 7578, fax 0171 491 2139)

JUDD, Baron (Life Peer UK 1991), of Portsea in the County of Hampshire; Frank Ashcroft Judd; s of Charles W Judd, CBE (d 1974), of Surrey, and Helen Osborn Judd, JP, *née* Ashcroft (d 1982); *b* 28 March 1935; *Educ* City of London Sch, LSE (BSc); *m* 1961, Christine Elizabeth Louise, da of Frederick Ward Willington (d 1966), of Kent; 2 da (Hon Elizabeth b 1967, Hon Philippa b 1969); *Career* F/O RAF 1957–59; sec gen Int Voluntary Serv 1960–66; MP (Lab): Portsmouth W 1966–74, Portsmouth N (following boundary change) 1974–79; memb Public Accounts Ctee 1966–69, chm PLP Overseas Aid and Devpt Gp 1967–70, jt sec All-Pty Parly Gp for UN 1967–72, PPS to Min for Housing and Local Govt 1967–70, memb Commons Select Ctee on Overseas Devpt 1969–74, memb Br Parly Delgn to Cncl of Europe and WEU 1970–73, jt PPS to Rt Hon Harold Wilson as Ldr of Oppn 1970–72, jr oppn def spokesman 1972–74, Parly under sec of state for Def (RN) 1974–76, Parly sec Miny for Overseas Devpt 1976, min for Overseas Devpt 1976–77, min of state FCO 1977–79; assoc dir Int Defence & Aid Fund for Southern Africa 1979–80, dir VSO 1980–85, chm Centre for World Devpt Educn 1980–85, dir Oxfam 1985–91, chm Int Cncl of Voluntary Agencies 1985–90 (memb Exec Ctee 1990–91), memb House of Lords Oppn front bench foreign affrs team 1991–92; House of Lords princ front bench spokesman on: educn 1992–94, overseas devpt cooperation 1992–; memb House of Lords Oppn front bench defence team 1995–; chm Geneva World Economic Forum Conf on future of Southern Africa 1990 and 1991, dir Nat Housing and Tenant Resource Centre 1992–94; chm: Oxford Diocesan Bd for Social Responsibility 1992–95, Selly Oak Colls Birmingham 1994–; advsr on security matters, educn and community rels to World Humanity Action Tst (conslt administrator 1993–), The Forbes Tst, De Montfort Univ; sr fell Saferworld; memb: Int Cmmn on Global Governance 1992–, World Health Orgn Task Force on Health and Devpt 1994–; memb: Labour Pty 1951–, Fabian Soc (former chm), MFI, G&MWU, Governing Body Queen Elizabeth House Univ of Oxford 1989–94; hon vice pres Intermediate Devpt Technol Gp, govr LSE, govr Westminster Coll Oxford, govr Lancaster Univ, chair Cncl of Selly Oak Colls; tstee: International Alert, Portsmouth Cathedral Devpt Tst; freedom of the City of Portsmouth 1995; hon fell Univ of Portsmouth, Hon DLitt Univ of Bradford; FRSA; *Books* Radical Future (jtly, 1967), Fabian International Essays (jtly, 1970), Purpose in Socialism (jtly, 1973); *Recreations* hill walking, family holidays; *Clubs* Cwlth Tst; *Style*— The Rt Hon Lord Judd; ✉ House of Lords, London SW1A 0PW

JUDD, James; s of Eric Judd (d 1986), and Winifred Judd; *b* 30 Oct 1949; *Educ* Hertford GS, Trinity Coll of Music; *m* 1, (m dis) Sue; m 2, 25 Sept 1993, Valerie; *Career* conductor; music dir Florida Philharmonic 1988–, Florida Grand Opera 1993–96; fndr memb Chamber Orch of Europe; has conducted numerous other major orchs incl: English Chamber Orch, Hallé Orch, Royal Philharmonic Orch, LSO, LPO, Royal Scottish National Orch, Vienna Symphony Orch, Prague Symphony Orch, Berlin Philharmonic, Orchestre National de France, Zurich Tonhalle, Orchestre de la Suisse Romande; also conducted numerous operas incl: Il Trovatore, La Traviata, The Barber of Seville, Rigoletto and The Marriage of Figaro (all with ENO), La Cenerentola (Glyndebourne Festival) 1985, Don Giovanni (US operatic debut, Miami) 1988; *Recordings* incl: Mahler Symphony No 1 (with Florida Philharmonic Orch), Elgar Symphony No 1 (with Hallé Orch) 1992, live recordings of Mahler Symphonies No 9 and 10, complete recordings of Meyerbeer and Donizetti operas on Opera Rara, various others with Euro Community Youth Orch, Gustav Mahler Youth Orch, English Chamber Orch, Hallé Orch and Chamber Orch of Europe; *Recreations* almost anything; *Style*— James Judd, Esq; ✉ Tennant Artists, Unit 2, 39 Tadema Road, London SW10 0PY (☎ 0171 376 3758, fax 0171 351 0679)

JUDD, James Hubert; s of Capt Leslie A Judd (d 1967), of Leighton Buzzard, and Enid, *née* Crichton (d 1974); *b* 27 March 1933; *Educ* Eton; *m* 19 March 1982 (m dis 1992), Lady Zinnia Rosemary, *née* Denison, da of 4 Earl of Londesborough (d 1937); *Career* 2 Lt Irish Gds 1952–53; chm and md Walter Judd Ltd 1971–; MIPA; *Recreations* hunting, shooting, skiing, farming; *Clubs* City of London, MCC, White's; *Style*— James Judd, Esq; ✉ Walter Judd Ltd, 64 Queen St, London EC4R 1AJ (☎ 0171 236 4541, fax 0171 248 8139)

JUDD, Lionel Henry; s of John Basil Thomas Judd (d 1983), and Cynthia Margaret Georgina, *née* White-Smith; *b* 24 Oct 1945; *Educ* The Leys Sch Cambridge, Downing Coll Cambridge (MA); *m* 19 Sept 1970, Janet Elizabeth, da of Arthur Boyton Fraser (d 1966), of Stansted, Essex; 1 s (Edward b 1972), 1 da (Alexandra b 1975); *Career* admitted slr 1972; ptnr Darley Cumberland (now Cumberland Ellis Piers) 1975–; memb Exec Ctee Abbeyfield Soc (Bucks) 1980–, tstee Downing Coll Boathouse Centenary Tst 1995–; *Recreations* rowing, country pursuits, travel; *Clubs* Leander, Caledonian; *Style*— Lionel Judd, Esq; ✉ Little Coombe, Wendover, Bucks HP22 6EQ; Columbia House, 69 Aldwych, London WC2B 4RW (☎ 0171 242 0422, fax 0171 831 9081)

JUDD, Vincent Sydney; s of Sydney Arthur Judd, of Wheathampstead, Herts, and Hilda Lillian Judd; *b* 15 April 1944; *Educ* St Albans Sch; *m* 16 Sept 1968, Betty, da of James Humphrey, of Leagrave, Beds; 4 da (Christine b 1971, Eve b 1972 d 1973, Sally b 1976, Fiona b 1978); *Career* insolvency practitioner; ACA 1966, memb SPI; *Recreations* transport, photography, gardening; *Style*— Vincent Judd, Esq; ✉ 69–71 High St, Harpenden, Herts (☎ 01582 762649, fax 01582 460674)

JUDGE, Ian; s of John Judge, of Southport, Merseyside, and Marjorie Judge; *b* 21 July 1946; *Educ* King George V GS, Guildhall Sch of Music & Drama; *Career* opera and theatre director; *Theatre* joined RSC 1975; Stratford: Henry IV Parts 1 and 2, Henry V, The Merry Wives of Windsor and Coriolanus (asst dir); assoc dir Poppy (Barbican, re-worked for the Aldephi), The Wizard of Oz (Stratford and Barbican) 1987 and 1988, The Comedy of Errors 1990, Love's Labour's Lost 1993, Twelfth Night (UK and world tour) 1994, The Relapse 1995, Troilus and Cressida 1996, The Merry Wives of Windsor 1996; other directing credits incl: The Rivals and King Lear (Old Vic), The Orchestra (King's Head Theatre Club), Rookery Nook (Barbican Centre), Musical Chairs (Chichester Festival Theatre Studio), Peg (Yvonne Arnaud Theatre and Phoenix Theatre), Friends of Dorothy and How Lucky Can You Get (Donmar Warehouse), Banana Ridge and Peter Pan (Shaw Festival Canada), Henry the Eighth and Love for Love (Chichester Festival Theatre), A Christmas Carol; *Musicals* incl: Oh Kay! (Chichester Festival Theatre, The Swan-Down Gloves (RSC)), Merrily We Roll Along (Guildhall Theatre Barbican, Arts Theatre Cambridge and Bloomsbury Theatre London), Bitter Sweet (New Sadler's Wells Opera), A Little Night Music (Chichester Festival Theatre and Piccadilly Theatre), Show Boat (RSC, Opera North and London Palladium), West Side Story (Aust); *Opera* Ariodante (Buxton Festival), Faust (ENO and Opera North), The Merry Widow, Cavalleria Rusticana, Pagliacci, Don Quixote and La Belle Vivette (ENO), Macbeth, Tosca, Acis and Galatea, Boris Godunov and Attila (Opera North), Falstaff (Bremer Theatre Germany, Scottish Opera), Lohengrin (Wiesbaden Germany), Tosca and Madama Butterfly (Los Angeles Opera), Faust, The Tales of Hoffmann, Don Quixote (both Victoria State Opera), Macbeth (Cologne Opera), The Flying Dutchman (Royal Opera House), The Tales of Hoffmann (Houston Grand Opera), Norma (Scottish Opera); *Awards* winner Best Musical Revival Olivier Awards (for Show Boat), Green Room Theatre Best Dir Awards Victoria Aust (for Faust, The Tales of Hoffman, West Side Story); *Style*— Ian Judge, Esq; ✉ c/o Simpson Fox Associates Ltd, 52 Shaftesbury Avenue, London W1V 7DE (0171 434 9167, fax 0171 494 2887)

JUDGE, Kenneth Franklin (Ken); *b* 1 Jan 1948; *Educ* Sidney Sussex Coll Cambridge (BA, PhD, Essay prize); *m*; 2 c; *Career* lectr in social policy: Univ of Bristol 1974–79, Civil Service Coll 1979–80; sr res fell and dep dir Personal Servs Res Unit Univ of Kent 1980–85, dir King's Fund Policy Inst 1986–; visiting prof of social policy LSE, external examiner LSHTM, Harkness fell advsr Commonwealth Fund; memb: Research Priorities Bd ESRC, Ed Bd Health Services Management Research; *Books* Rationing Social Services, Changing for Social Care, Tackling Inequalities in Health; author of numerous books and reports in learned pubns; *Style*— Ken Judge, Esq

JUDGE, Sir Paul Rupert; kt (1996); s of Rupert Cyril Judge (d 1985), and Betty Rosa Muriel, *née* Daniels; *b* 25 April 1949; *Educ* Christchurch Sch Forest Hill London, St Dunstan's Coll Catford, Trinity Coll Cambridge (MA), Wharton Business Sch Univ of Pennsylvania (MBA); *m* 25 June 1983, Anne Marie, da of late John James Foff; 2 s (Christopher Paul, Michael James); *Career* Cadbury Schweppes plc: fin analyst then fin planning mangr Overseas Gp 1973–76, internal memb Gp Strategic Planning Project 1976–77, gp dep fin dir 1977–79, planning dir N American Regn 1980, md Cadbury Schweppes Kenya Ltd 1980–82, md Cadbury Typhoo 1982–84, gp planning dir and memb Gp Exec Ctee 1984–85; Premier Brands Ltd: led MBO of food business of Cadbury Schweppes 1986, md 1986–87, chm 1987–89, co sold to Hillsdown Holdings plc 1989; chm Food From Britain 1990–92, DG Conservative Party 1992–95, special advsr to Rt Hon Roger Freeman as Chllr of the Duchy of Lancaster 1995–96; non-exec dir: Grosvenor Development Capital plc 1989–93, Boddington Group plc 1989–93, Strategy Ventures plc 1989–, Isoworth Ltd 1989– (chm), Concourse Communications Ltd 1990– (chm), WPP

Group plc 1991–, Schroder Income Growth Fund plc 1995–; memb: Cncl Food and Drink Fedn 1988–89, Milk Mktg Bd 1989–92, Cncl Royal Agric Soc of England 1991–96, Cncl Assoc of MBAs 1992–; govr Bromsgrove Sch 1990–96, chm Advsy Bd Cambridge Univ Inst of Mgmnt Studies 1991–, tstee Cambridge Fndn 1991–; listed in Business Magazine Top 40 under 40 1986, food industry personality of the year Food Processing Awards 1992; Freeman City of London 1970, Liveryman Worshipful Co of Marketors 1993; Hon LLD Univ of Cambridge 1995; FRSA 1971, FInstD 1988, FIGD 1989, fell Mktg Soc 1991, CIMgt 1994; *Recreations* family, travel; *Clubs* Athenaeum, Carlton, St Stephen's Constitutional, Mombasa (Kenya); *Style*— Sir Paul Judge; ✉ Grange Farm, Elmbridge, Worcs WR9 0DA

JUKES, Rt Rev John; OFMConv; s of Francis Bernard Jukes, and Florence, *née* Stampton (d 1988); *b* 7 Aug 1923; *Educ* St Joseph's Acad Blackheath, Pontifical Faculty of St Bonaventure Rome (STL); *Career* Civil Serv 1940–45, agricultural student 1945–46, entered Franciscan Order (Order of Friars Minor Conventual Liverpool) 1946, ordained priest (St Anthony of Padua Liverpool) 1952, rector Franciscan Order's Seminary Anglesey N Wales 1953–59, parish priest St Clare's High Blackley Manchester 1959–64, vice-provincial 1960–69, parish priest Patrick's Waterloo 1964–69, lectr in canon law and vice-princ Franciscan Study Centre Canterbury 1969–79, vicar episcopal for religious Dio of Southwark 1973–81, min provincial of the English Province 1979, aux bishop of Southwark (RC) and titular bishop of Strathearn 1980–, area bishop for Kent (with special responsiblity for Deaneries of Canterbury, Chatham, Dover, Gravesend, Maidstone, Ramsgate and Tunbridge Wells); VG; memb Exec Ctee and former chm Kent Ecumenical Cncl, chm World of Work Ctee Bishops' Conf of England and Wales, memb Ecumenical Body Churches Cncl on Industl Mission, ecclesiastical advsr to the Catholic Teachers' Fedn, chm Bd of Govrs St Mary's Coll of HE Twickenham; author of numerous articles in theol reviews and Canon Law pubns; *Style*— The Rt Rev John Jukes; ✉ The Hermitage, More Park, West Malling, Kent ME19 6HN (☎ 01732 845486, fax 01732 847888)

JUKES, John Andrew; CB (1968); s of Capt (Andrew) Munro Jukes (d 1918), and Gertrude Elizabeth, *née* King (d 1957); *b* 19 May 1917; *Educ* Shrewsbury, St John's Coll Cambridge (MA), LSE (BSc Econ); *m* 19 June 1943, Muriel, da of Frederick James Child; 2 s (Andrew b 1946, David b 1952), 2 da (Margaret (Mrs Condick) b 1944, Rosemary (Dr Fowler) b 1950); *Career* hon cmmn RAF 1940; econ advsr: Econ Section Cabinet Office and Treasy 1948–54, UKAEA 1954–64; dep DG and dep sec Dept of Econ Affrs 1964–69, dep sec Miny of Tport 1969–71; dep sec DOE: econs and resources 1970–72, environmental protection 1972–74; DG Highways Dept of Tport 1974–77, memb Exec Bd CEGB 1977–80; memb: SDP 1981–87, Merton and Sutton DHA 1986–90; pres Sutton Lib Democrats 1990–93 (memb 1988–); London Borough of Sutton: rep on Cncl for Social Democracy 1982–86, cncllr 1986–90, chm Resources Sub Ctee; *Recreations* gardening, sometime orienteer and Himalayan trekker; *Style*— John Jukes, Esq, CB; ✉ 38 Albion Rd, Sutton, Surrey SM2 5TF (☎ 0181 642 5018)

JULIAN, Prof Desmond Gareth; CBE (1993); s of Dr Frederick Bennett Julian, MC (d 1958), and Jane Frances, *née* Galbraith (d 1956); *b* 24 April 1926; *Educ* Leighton Park Sch, St John's Coll Cambridge (MA, MD), Middx Hosp London; *m* 1, 8 July 1956, Mary Ruth (d 1964), da of John Jessup (d 1968); 1 s (Paul Richard b 1962), 1 da (Claire Frances b 1960); m 2, 10 Dec 1988, Claire, da of Frederick Bolam Marley; *Career* RNVR 1949–51; conslt cardiologist Sydney Hosp Aust 1961–64, conslt cardiologist Royal Infirmary Edinburgh 1964–74, prof of cardiology Univ of Newcastle upon Tyne 1975–86, conslt med dir Br Heart Fndn 1986–93; second vice pres RCP 1990; MD Gothenburg 1986; FRCP: London, Edinburgh, Aust; *Books* Cardiology (1970, 6 edn 1992); *Recreations* gardening, walking; *Clubs* Garrick; *Style*— Prof Desmond Julian, CBE; ✉ Flat 1, 7 Netherhall Gardens, London NW3 5RN (☎ and fax 0171 435 8254)

JULIEN, Michael Frederick; *b* 22 March 1938; *Educ* St Edward's Sch Oxford; *m* Ellen; 1 s (Mark), 2 da (Heidi, Christine); *Career* gp fin dir: BICC plc 1976–83, Midland Bank PLC 1983–86; md (fin and admin) Guinness PLC 1987–88, gp chief exec Storehouse PLC 1988–92, chm First Choice Holidays PLC 1993–; non-exec dir: Guinness PLC 1988– (joined as exec dir 1987), Medeva PLC; Liveryman Worshipful Co of Barbers; FCA, FCT; *Clubs* Athenaeum; *Style*— Michael F Julien, Esq; ✉ First Choice Holidays PLC, First Choice House, London Road, Crawley, West Sussex RH10 2GX (☎ 01293 588013, fax 01293 539039)

JULIUS, Dr DeAnne; da of Marvin G Julius, of Iowa, USA, and Maxine M, *née* Meeske; *b* 14 April 1949; *Educ* Iowa State Univ (BSc), Univ of California (MA, PhD); *m* 21 Nov 1976, Ian Alexander Harvey, s of Dr Alexander Harvey (d 1987), of Cardiff; 1 s (Ross b 9 Dec 1980), 1 da (Megan b 28 March 1979); *Career* lectr Univ of Calif 1972–75, econ advsr World Bank 1975–82, md Logan Associates Inc 1982–86, dir of economics RIIA 1986–89; chief economist: Royal Dutch/Shell 1989–93, British Airways 1993–; chm British Airways Pension Investment Mgmnt Ltd; memb: Cncl Royal Economics Soc, Cncl Inst of Devpt Studies, Editorial Bd Int Affairs; tstee BA Pension Fund; non-exec dir: MAI plc 1995–96, London Health Economic Consortium Ltd 1993–; *Books* Global Companies and Public Policy: The Growing Challenge of Foreign Direct Investment (1990), The Economics of Natural Gas (1990), The Monetary Implications of the 1992 Process (1990); *Clubs* IOD; *Style*— Dr DeAnne Julius; ✉ British Airways, Speedbird House, PO Box 10, Heathrow Airport, Hounslow TW6 2JA (☎ 0181 562 3488, fax 0181 562 3486)

JULIUS, Rosamind; da of Maurice Hille (d 1968), of London, and Ray Hille (d 1986); *Educ* North London Collegiate Sch Canons, Regent St Poly, St Martin's Sch of Art; *m* 20 Feb 1944, Leslie Julius (d 1989), s of late Harold Julius; 1 da (Corinne); *Career* WRNS 1943–45; trainee surveyor George Wimpey & Son; Hille International Ltd: joined 1945, various appts in sales and mktg, fndr Contract Div, dir Design Unit 1950–84; fndr Julius International Design Consultants 1984–; Int Design Conference Aspen USA: advisor to Bd, programme chm 1986, presented Insight and Outlook (views of Br design) with Kenneth Grange; Gold Medal RSA bicentennial 1972; Hon: FRIBA, FCSD, FRSA; *Recreations* tennis, skiing, sailing, art, architecture; *Clubs* Arts; *Style*— Mrs Rosamind Julius; ✉ Julius International Design Consultants, 15 Ulster Terrace, Regents Park, London NW1 4PJ (☎ 0171 487 4832, fax 0171 935 2994)

JUMP, Roger Thomas; s of George William Jump (d 1962), and Alice Redfern, *née* Swann (d 1981); *b* 23 April 1943; *Educ* King George V Sch Southport Lancs (capt of sch), Gonville and Caius Coll Cambridge (MA); *m* Anne Victoria, da of James Henry Westwood (d 1993); 2 s (Simon, Timothy (twins) b 1969), 1 da (Sarah b 1973); *Career* Central Electricity Generating Bd: graduate trainee engr 1964–66, shift engr Meaford Power Stn 1966–68, various technical and managerial appts 1968–81, stn mangr Eggborough Power Stn 1981–82, stn mangr Drax Power Stn 1982–86, dir of generation CEGB SW Region 1986–88, dir of construction CEGB Construction Div 1988–89; exec dir and gen mangr engrg and business servs PowerGen plc (following privatisation) 1989–; non-exec dir: South Yorkshire Supertram, South Yorkshire Light Railway Ltd; special prof Univ of Nottingham; FIMechE, MInstD; *Recreations* golf, swimming; *Style*— Roger Jump, Esq; ✉ PowerGen plc, Westwood Way, Westwood Business Park, Coventry CV4 8LG (☎ 01203 424800, fax 01203 425448)

JUNG, Dr Roland Tadeusz; *b* 8 Feb 1948; *Educ* St Anselm's Coll Birkenhead, Pembroke Coll Cambridge (exhibitioner, fndn scholar, MA, MB BChir, MD), St Thomas' Hosp London (LRCP, MRCS, MRCP); *m* 1974, Felicity Helen, da of Prof J O L King; 1 da (b 1987); *Career* MRC clinical research scientific offr Dunn Nutrition Unit Cambridge 1977–79, sr registrar in endocrinology and diabetes Hammersmith Hosp and Royal Postgrad Med Sch London 1980–82, conslt physician/specialist in endocrinology and diabetes Ninewells Hosp Dundee 1982–, hon reader in med Ninewells Hosp and Med Sch Dundee 1991–, clinical director of med Dundee Teaching Hosps NHS Tst 1991–94; Card Medal Western Gen Hosp Edinburgh 1987; memb: Scottish Soc of Physicians 1984, Assoc of Physicians of UK and I 1987; FRCP(Edinburgh), FRCP(London); *Books* Endocrine Problems in Cancer (jt ed, 1984), Colour Atlas of Obesity (1990); *Recreations* gardening; *Style*— Dr Roland Jung; ✉ Diabetic Centre, Ninewells Hospital and Medical, School, Dundee, Tayside

JUNGELS, Dr Pierre; Hon CBE (1988); s of Henri Jungels, former pres of Labaz; *b* 18 Feb 1944; *Educ* Univ of Liege (Ing Civ), California Inst of Technol (PhD); *m* 2, 1988, Caroline, da of Dr Z Benc, of Worcester; 2 children; *Career* gen mangr and chief exec Petrangol (Angola) 1977–80, md and chief exec Petrofina (UK) 1981–89, chm/dir various Petrofina subsidiaries in UK, Belgium, USA, Italy, Angola, Zaire and Norway, elected to Main Bd of Petrofina SA Brussels, dir Fina Inc USA 1990; pres The Inst of Petroleum 1986–88, md (Exploration-Prodn) Petrofina SA 1989; *Recreations* tennis, skiing, shooting; *Style*— Dr Pierre Jungels, CBE; ✉ Petrofina SA, Rue de L'Industrie, 52, B 1040 Brussels, Belgium

JUNGIUS, Vice Adm Sir James George; KBE (1977), DL (Cornwall 1982); s of Maj E Jungius, MC; *b* 15 Nov 1923; *Educ* RNC Dartmouth; *m* 1949, Rosemary Frances Turquand Matthey; 3 s; *Career* RN: served WWII Atlantic and Med, Commando Ops Adriatic, asst naval attaché Washington 1968–70, asst chief Naval Staff Operational Requirements 1972–74, Rear Adm 1972, Vice-Adm 1974, Dep Supreme Allied Cdr Atlantic 1975–77, Supreme Allied Cdr Atlantic's Rep Europe 1978–80, ret; memb SW War Pensions Ctee; county pres Royal British Legion 1995; Vice Lord-Lt of Cornwall 1994; chm Cncl Order of St John Cornwall 1987–95; CStJ; CIMgt; *Recreations* enjoying myself; *Clubs* Pilgrims, RN Club of 1765 and 1785, Royal Cornwall Yacht, Mylor Yacht; *Style*— Vice Adm Sir James Jungius, KBE, DL; ✉ c/o National Westminster Bank, 26 Molesworth St, Wadebridge, Cornwall PL27 7DL

JUNIPER, Richard Pudan; s of Leonard Alfred Vey Juniper (d 1988), of London, and Edna Amy, *née* Pudan (d 1996); *b* 11 April 1938; *Educ* Highgate Sch London, Guy's Hosp London (MB BS, BDS); *m* 19 Feb 1971, Honor Murray, da of Denis Fargher Glass, of Charing, Kent; 1 s (Matthew b 1973), 1 da (Zoe b 1975); *Career* sr registrar in oral and maxillo facial surgery Queen Victoria Hosp E Grinstead 1970–72; conslt oral and maxillo-facial surgn: Brighton Health Dist 1972–82, Oxford Health Authy 1982–; clinical lectr Oxford Univ Med Sch 1982–; hon sec: Odontological Section RSM 1979, Br Assoc of Oral and Maxillo-Facial Surgns 1983–86; memb Bd of Faculty of Dental Surgery RCS 1989–; Freeman City of London, Master Worshipful Co of Poulters 1994 (memb Ct 1982–); Hon MA Univ of Oxford; FDS RCS 1968, FRSM 1968, fell BAOMS 1982; memb: BMA, BDA, Intractable Pain Soc, Craniofacial Soc 1986; *Books* Emergencies in Dental Practice (with B Parkins, 1990); *Style*— Richard Juniper, Esq; ✉ Dept of Oral and Maxillo-Facial Surgery, John Radcliffe Hospital, Oxford OX3 9DU

JUNKIN, John Francis; s of Detective Inspector John Junkin (d 1972), and Elizabeth, *née* Cavanagh; *b* 29 Jan 1930; *Educ* Aylesbury GS, Holy Cross Acad Edinburgh, West Ham GS, St Mary's Coll Twickenham; *m* 16 Sept 1977 (sep), Jennifer, da of George Henry (Harry) Claybourn (d 1965), of Goole, Yorks; 1 da (Annabel b 1978); *Career* actor; over 1,000 tv appearances, theatre work incl 12 months with Joan Littlewood's Theatre Workshop and five West End appearances; writer and co-writer of approximately 1,500 tv and radio shows; memb: SOS, Variety Club GB; Freeman City of London 1985; *Recreations* crosswords, board games, reading; *Style*— John Junkin, Esq; ✉ c/o Elaine Murphy Associates, 1 Aberdeen Lane, London N5 2EJ (☎ 0171 704 9913)

JUNOR, Brian James Ross; s of Donald Junor, MBE (d 1986), of Dundee, and Ann Russell, *née* Mackie (d 1985); *b* 10 Feb 1946; *Educ* Dundee HS, Univ of St Andrews (MB ChB), Univ of Dundee (MD); *m* 1, 4 Feb 1972, Sheena MacLeod (d 1972), da of Sir Donald Douglas, of White House, Nevay Newtyle; m 2, 19 Jan 1979, Elizabeth Jane, da of John Fotheringham, OBE, of St Helen's, Elie, Fife; 1 s (Malcolm b 1980), 1 da (Katherine b 1982); *Career* sr registrar of medicine Aberdeen Royal Infirmary 1976–78, Aust Kidney Res Fndn fell Univ of Melbourne 1978–79, hon clinical lectr Univ of Glasgow 1979–, conslt nephrologist Gtr Glasgow Health Authy 1979–; currently sec Specialty Section in Nephrology Union of Euro Med Specialists; former memb Jt Ctee for Higher Med Training, former chm Specialist Advsy Ctee in Renal Diseases; memb BMA 1970, FRCPS 1982, FRCPE 1987; *Recreations* skiing, gardening, golf; *Style*— Brian Junor, Esq; ✉ The Barn, Ballagan, Strathblane, Glasgow (☎ 01360 70767); Renal Unit, Western Infirmary, Dunbarton Rd, Glasgow (☎ 0141 211 2000)

JUNOR, Sir John; kt (1980); s of Alexander Junor, of Black Isle; *b* 15 Jan 1919; *Educ* Univ of Glasgow (MA); *m* 1942, Pamela Welsh; 1 s, 1 da; *Career* served WWII RNVR; Parly candidate (Lib): Kincardine and W Aberdeen 1945, Edinburgh E 1948, Dundee W 1951; journalist; dir Express Newspapers (formerly Beaverbrook Newspapers) 1960–86, chm Sunday Express 1968–86 (ed 1954–86); columnist: Sunday Express 1973–89, Mail on Sunday 1990–; dir Fleet Holdings 1982–85; *Books* The Best of JJ (1981), Listening for a Midnight Tram (memoirs, 1990); *Recreations* golf; *Clubs* Royal and Ancient, Walton Heath; *Style*— Sir John Junor; ✉ c/o Bank of Scotland, 16 Cockspur Street, London SW1

JUNOR, Penelope Jane (Penny); da of Sir John Junor, *qv*, and Pamela Mary, *née* Welsh; *b* 6 Oct 1949; *Educ* Benenden, Univ of St Andrews; *m* 8 Sept 1970, James Stewart Leith; 3 s (Sam b 1 Jan 1974, Alexander b 23 July 1976, Jack b 17 Jan 1985), 1 da (Peta b 31 Dec 1987); *Career* trainee IPC Young Magazine Gp 1969–70, feature writer 19 Magazine 1970–71, writer Londoners' Diary Evening Standard 1971–73, freelance journalist 1974–, columnist Private Eye 1974–81, reporter Collecting Now (BBC) 1981, presenter 4 What It's Worth (C4) 1982–89, presenter The Travel Show (BBC) 1988–, co presenter The Afternoon Show 1984–85; gen ed John Lewis Partnership 1994–; *Books* Newspaper (1980), Babyware (1982), Diana, Princess of Wales (1982), Margaret Thatcher, Wife, Mother, Politician (1983), Burton - The Man Behind the Myth (1985), Charles (1987), Charles and Diana - Portrait of a Marriage (1991), Queen Elizabeth - Pictorial Celebration of her Reign (1991), The Major Enigma (1993); *Recreations* walking, tennis; *Style*— Ms Penny Junor; ✉ c/o Curtis Brown, 4th Floor, Haymarket House, 28–29 Haymarket, London SW1Y 4SP (☎ 0171 396 6600)

JUPP, Jeffrey Addison; s of Leonard James Jupp (d 1988), and Elizabeth, *née* Addison (d 1984); *b* 30 Dec 1941; *Educ* Enfield GS, Queens' Coll Cambridge (MA); *m* 1965, Margaret Elizabeth, da of Ronald Peatchey; 1 da (Elizabeth Jane b 1971), 1 s (Richard James b 1974); *Career* Aerodynamics Dept Hawker Siddeley Aviation (subsequently British Aerospace) Hatfield: aerodynamicist 1964–73, head Fluid Motion Section 1973–80, type aerodynamicist Airbus and head Airbus Section 1980–84, asst chief aerodynamicist Devpts 1984; British Aerospace Airbus Ltd Filton: asst chief engr Airbus 1984–87, chief engr A330/A340 (BAe), chief engr Airbus 1988–92, dir Engrg 1992–; chm Tech Dirs Ctee Airbus Industries 3Es Research Prog, chm Indust Advsy Ctee to Supervisory Bd of Euro (Cryogenic) Transonic Windtunnel Cologne; memb: Cncl Aircraft Research Assoc, Tech Bd SBAC, ARB CAA 1995–; author of numerous published lectures and papers; FRAeS 1990, FEng 1996; *Awards* jt winner Esso Energy Award Royal Soc Gold Medal 1987, Br Bronze Medal Royal Aeronautical Soc 1992, Queen's Award for Technol 1994; *Recreations* coastal sailing, listening to classical music, choral singing; *Style*— Jeffrey Jupp, Esq, FEng; ✉ British Aerospace Airbus Ltd, New Filton House, Filton, Bristol BS99 7AR (☎ 0117 936 2272, fax 0117 936 5274)

JUPP, Hon Sir Kenneth Graham Jupp; kt (1975), MC (1943); s of Albert Leonard Jupp, shipbroker; *b* 2 June 1917; *Educ* Perse Sch Cambridge, Univ Coll Oxford (MA); *m* 1947, Kathleen Elizabeth, da of Richard Owen Richards, farmer, of Morton Hall, Morton, Salop; 2 s, 2 da; *Career* Maj, served WWII, Europe and N Africa 1939–43, on WO Selection Bd 1943–46; called to the Bar Lincoln's Inn 1945, dep chm Cambs and Isle of Ely QS 1965–71, QC 1966, rec Crown Ct 1972–75, judge High Ct (Queen's Bench) 1975–90, presiding judge NE Circuit 1977–81; chm Ind Schs Tbnl 1964–67, chm Public Enquiry into Fire at Fairfield Home Nottingham 1975; *Recreations* music, language, reading, occasional writing and lecturing; *Clubs* Garrick; *Style*— The Hon Sir Kenneth Jupp, MC

JURY CRAMP, Felicity; da of Cecil Walter Cramp, of Horsham, and Hilary, *née* Napper (d 1971); *b* 9 July 1961; *Educ* Horsham HS for Girls, W Sussex Coll of Art & Design, Sir John Cass Faculty of Art City of London Poly (dip), Royal Coll of Art (MA); *Career* early design experience with Alain Mikli Paris 1985–86, Optyl Vienna 1987, IDC Paris 1989–90, Betty Jackson 1990–91, Katherine Hamnett 1991–; fndr memb The New RenaisCAnce (multi media co specialising in fashion and accessory design, display, styling and video prodn) 1991–; exhbns incl: Fouts and Fowler Gallery London 1991, The World of The New RenaisCAnce (Royal Festival Hall and Parco Gallery Tokyo) 1992, Court Couture (Kensington Palace) 1992, Vision Gallery London 1992; TV and video work incl title sequences for BBC1, Channel 4 and Carlton, window design for Liberty and Harvey Nichols London; *Style*— Ms Felicity Jury Cramp; ✉ W5 Cockpit Yard Studios, Northington Street, London WC1N 2NP (☎ 0171 916 9858, fax 0171 916 2455)

JUSTE, Adrian; *Educ* Guthlaxton GS Wigston Leics; *Career* comedian/disc jockey; with: BBC Radio 1 until 1993, Fox FM Oxford 1994–95, London News Talk 1995–96; formerly regular guest presenter Top of the Pops (BBC1), numerous other TV appearances; early career as motor mechanic and shoe salesman; *Recreations* speedway, horseracing; *Style*— Adrian Juste, Esq; ✉ c/o John Miles Organisation, Cadbury Camp Lane, Clapton-in-Gordano, Bristol BS20 9SB (☎ 01275 854675, fax 01275 810186)

K

KABERRY, Hon Sir Christopher Donald (Kit); 2 Bt (UK 1960), of Adel cum Eccup, City of Leeds; s of Baron Kaberry of Adel, TD, DL (Life Peer and 1 Bt, d 1991), and Lily Margaret, *née* Scott (d 1992); *b* 14 March 1943; *Educ* Repton; *m* 25 March 1967, Gaenor Elizabeth Vowe, yr da of Cecil Vowe Peake, MBE, of Redbourn, St Albans, Herts; 2 s (James Christopher b 1970, Angus George b 1972), 1 da (Claire Elizabeth b 1974); *Heir* s, James Christopher Kaberry b 1 April 1970; *Career* chartered accountant; FCA 1967; *Style*— The Hon Sir Kit Kaberry, Bt; ✉ Rock View, Chiddingstone Hoath, Kent TN8 7BT (☎ 01892 870539)

KADOORIE, Hon Michael David; o s of Baron Kadoorie, CBE (Life Peer; d 1993), and Muriel, *née* Gubbay; *b* 19 July 1941; *Educ* King George V Sch Hong Kong, Le Rosey Switzerland; *m* 1984, Betty, da of Juan E Tamayo, of Coral Gables, Florida, USA; 1 s (Philip b 1992), 2 da (Natalie b 1986, Bettina b 1987); *Career* chm: The Hongkong & Shanghai Hotels Ltd, Heliservices (HK) Ltd, Rotair Ltd, China Energy & Investment Co; sr vice-chm China Light & Power Co Ltd; dir: Sir Elly Kadoorie & Sons Ltd, Schroders Asia Ltd, Hutchison Whampoa Ltd, and other cos; memb Bd Deportation Tribunal; tstee: Kadoorie Fndn, Incorporated Tstees of the Jewish Community of Hong Kong; fell The Duke of Edinburgh Int Award Fndn; Liveryman Guild of Air Pilots and Air Navigators; Chevalier de la Legion d'Honneur, Commandeur de l'Ordre de Leopold II; *Recreations* world travel, flying, motor cars, skiing, photography; *Clubs* Hong Kong, American (Hong Kong), Eagle Ski (Gstaad), Vintage Sports Car, Hong Kong Aviation, Hong Kong Jockey, and others; *Style*— The Hon Michael Kadoorie; ✉ 24th Floor, St George's Building, No 2 Ice House Street, Central, Hong Kong (☎ 00 852 2524 9221, fax 00 852 2845 9133)

KADRI, Sibghatullah; QC (1989); s of Alhaj Maulana Firasatullah Kadri (d 1990), and Begum Tanwir Fatima, *née* Hamidi (d 1986); *b* 23 April 1937; *Educ* Christian HS Budaun UP India, SM Sci Coll Karachi Univ Pakistan, Inns of Court School of Law London; *m* 1963, Carita Elisabeth da of Ole Idman (d 1973), of Helsinki; 1 s (Sadakat b 1964), 1 da (Maria Fatima b 1965); *Career* BBC External Serv 1965–68, prodr and presenter BBC Home Serv, visiting lectr in Urdu Holborn Coll 1966–68; called to the Bar Inner Temple 1969, head of chambers 1973–, memb Midland and Oxford Circuit; Pakistan Students Fedn in Britain: gen sec 1961–62, vice pres 1962–63; pres Inner Temple Students Assoc 1968–69; Standing Conference of Pakistani Orgn: gen sec 1975–78, pres 1978–84; convener Asian Action Ctee 1976, vice chm Jt Ctee Against Racism, chm Soc of Black Lawyers 1981–83, sec Br Lawyers Ctee for Human Rights and Justice in Pakistan 1984–, chm Asian Lawyers Conference, memb Bar Cncls Race Rels Ctee 1982–85, 1988 and 1989; FRSA 1991; *Clubs* National Liberal; *Style*— Sibghatullah Kadri, Esq, QC; ✉ 6 Kings Bench Walk, Temple, London EC4Y 7DR (☎ 0171 353 4931/2, 0171 583 0695/8, fax 0171 353 1726)

KAFETZ, Dr Kalman Meir; s of Vivian Kafetz, of Regent's Park, London (d 1969), and Rose, *née* Gilbert (d 1982); *b* 3 Dec 1947; *Educ* Eton, St Thomas's Hosp Med Sch (BSc, MB BS); *m* 11 Oct 1972, Marion Linda, da of Gerald Singer, of Mill Hill, London; 2 s (Alexander b 1976, Sebastian b 1980), 1 da (Cordelia b 1983); *Career* conslt physician Dept of Medicine for Elderly People Whipps Cross Univ Hosp London 1982–, hon sr lectr Med Coll St Bartholomew's Hosp 1994– (hon lectr 1987–94), teacher Univ of London 1987–; memb: Br Geriatrics Soc, Old Etonian Med Soc, London Jewish Med Soc; FRCP 1994 (MRCP 1976); *Books* Clinical Tests - Geriatric Medicine (1986); *Style*— Dr Kalman Kafetz; ✉ 22 Offham Slope, London N12 7BZ (☎ 0181 445 5119); Old Court Cottage, Kenegie Manor, Gulval, Penzance, Cornwall TR10 8YW; Connaught Day Hospital, Whipps Cross Hospital, London E11 1NR (☎ 0181 539 5522 ext 5266, fax 0181 535 6970)

KAHN, Paula; da of Cyril Maurice Kahn, and Stella, *née* Roscoe; *b* 15 Nov 1940; *Educ* Chiswick Co HS, Univ of Bristol (BA); *Career* teacher and admin 1962–66; Longman Group: ed then publisher, publishing dir, divnl md 1966–79, md ELT Div, Dictionaries Div and Trade and Reference Div 1980–85, md Int Sector 1986–88, chief exec of publishing 1988–89, chm and chief exec 1990–94; project dir World Learning Network 1995–96, md Phaidon Press 1996–; memb: Bd Inst of Int Visual Arts, Eng Teaching Advsy Ctee Br Cncl, Forum UK; CIMgt, FRSA; *Recreations* cinema, theatre, France, books; *Style*— Ms Paula Kahn; ✉ Phaidon Press Ltd, Regent's Wharf, All Saints Street, London N1 9PA (☎ 0171 843 1000, fax 0171 843 1212)

KAHRMANN, Rainer Thomas Christian; s of Dr Johannes Wilhelm Karl Kahrmann, of W Germany, and Therese, *née* Gillrath; *b* 28 May 1943; *Educ* Neusprachliches Gymnasium Erkelenz W Germany, Univ of Fribourg (LicRerPol, DrRerPol); *m* 8 Dec 1972, Christiane Jeanne Maria, *née* De Muller; 2 da (Louise b 27 Sept 1979, Alice b 19 Nov 1981); *Career* apprenticeship Commerzbank AG W Germany 1963–64, Dow Chemical Co (Dow Banking Corp) 1969–88, md EBC Amro Bank Ltd 1974–89, chm EBC Asset Management Ltd 1989–; *Recreations* work, family, antiquarian horology; *Style*— R C Kahrmann, Esq; ✉ c/o EBC Asset Management Ltd, East India House, 109–117 Middlesex Street, London E1 7JF (☎ 0171 621 0101, fax 0171 626 7915, telex 8811001)

KAIN, Prof Roger James Peter; s of Peter Albert Kain (d 1981), of Harrow, Middx, and Ivy, *née* Sharp; *b* 12 Nov 1944; *Educ* Harrow Weald Middx Co GS, UCL (BA, PhD); *m* 1970, Annmaree, da of Sidney Frank Wallington; 2 s (Simon Peter Wallington b 1986, Matthew James Wallington b 1991); *Career* tutor Bedford Coll London 1971; prof of geography Univ of Exeter 1991– (lectr 1972–91); Gill Meml Award RGS 1990, McColvin Medal Library Assoc 1996; FBA 1990, FSA 1992; *Books* The Tithe Surveys of England and Wales (1985), Atlas and Index of the Tithe Files (1986), Cadastral Maps in the Service of the State (1992), The Tithe Maps of England and Wales (1995); *Recreations* mountain walking, fishing, gardening; *Clubs* Geographical; *Style*— Prof Roger Kain, FBA, FSA; ✉ Department of Geography, University of Exeter, Exeter EX4 4RJ (☎ 01392 263333, fax 01392 263342/01395 223754, e-mail R.J.P.Kain@exeter.ac.uk)

KAKKAD, Sunil Shantilal; s of Shantilal Kalyanji Kakkad, of London, and Usha Shantilal, *née* Kanani; *b* 19 May 1959; *Educ* Alder Sch, Barnet Coll, Univ of Hull (LLB); *m* 23 Aug 1984, Darshna Sunil, da of Kantilal Vithaldas Hindocha, of Harrow, Middx; 1 s (Rajiv Sunil b 1990), 1 da (Radhika Sunil b 1996); *Career* admitted slr 1984; slr Hill Dickinson & Co 1984–89, ptnr Hill Taylor Dickinson 1989–; memb Law Soc; *Recreations* reading, music, cinema, theatre; *Style*— Sunil Kakkad, Esq; ✉ Hill Taylor Dickinson, Irongate House, Duke's Place, London EC3A 7LP (☎ 0171 283 9033, 0171 283 1144, telex 888470)

KALDERON, Dr David; OBE (1987); s of Prof Solomon Kalderon (d 1968), of Belgrade, Yugoslavia, and Diana, and, *née* Konforti (d 1989); *b* 24 Nov 1928; *Educ* Univ of Vienna (Dip Ing), City and Guilds Coll London (DIC), Univ of London (PhD); *m* 12 June 1955, Eva Suzanne, da of Fritz B Hoffmann (d 1983), of London; 2 s (Mark Adam b 1 March 1957, Daniel David b 1 Aug 1959); *Career* dep chief turbine engr GEC 1961–65, turbine plant design engr GEGB 1965–70, asst md GEC Turbine Generators Ltd 1980–89 (engrg dir 1970–89), tech dir and asst md Electromechanical Div GEC Alsthom 1989–91, conslt on power generation engrg 1991–; author of various tech articles; FIMechE 1970, FEng 1979; *Recreations* music, visual arts, theatre; *Style*— Dr David Kalderon, OBE, FEng; ✉ 86 Tiddington Rd, Stratford upon Avon, Warwickshire CV37 7BA (☎ 01789 293804, fax 01789 293804)

KALE, Stuart Guy; s of Ernest Guy Kale (d 1989), of Skewen, Swansea, and Eileen Beryl, *née* Ward (d 1983); *b* 27 Oct 1944; *Educ* Neath GS, Guildhall Sch of Music, London Opera Centre; *m* 4 Sept 1989, Deborah Ann, da of Derek Raymond Wellbrook; 2 s (Adam Nicholas Ward b 23 July 1990, Simon Edward Henry b 12 Oct 1991), 1 da (Sophie Alexandra Rose b 6 April 1996); *Career* tenor; with WNO 1972–73, princ tenor ENO 1975–87, freelance 1987–; *Roles* int debut in Albert Herring (Phoenix Opera) 1972, ENO debut Beppe in I Pagliacci 1972; roles with WNO incl: Don Ottavio in Don Giovanni, Red Whiskers in Billy Budd, The Prince in Lulu; with ENO incl: Don Ottavio, Michel in Julietta, Pierre in War and Peace, Nanki-Poo in The Mikado, title role in Orpheus in the Underworld, Don Basilio in The Marriage of Figaro, Guillot de Morfontaine in Manon, Valzacchi in Der Rosenkavalier, Zinovy in Lady Macbeth of Mtsensk, Vogelgesang in Die Meistersinger, Spoletta in Tosca, Menelaus in La Belle Hélène, Truffaldino in The Love for Three Oranges 1990, Peter Quint in The Turn of the Screw (Coliseum and Russian tour) 1990; others incl: The Captain in Wozzeck (Strasbourg 1987, Parma 1989, Canadian Opera Co 1989, San Francisco 1990, Geneva and Bologna 1995), Mephistopheles, Jacob Glock and Agrippa in The Fiery Angel (Adelaide), Podesta in La Finta Giardiniera (Drottningholm), Guillot de Morfontaine in Manon (Royal Opera House Covent Garden), Drum Major in Wozzeck (Turin) 1989, Lucano in L'Incoronazione di Poppea (Paris) 1989, Bob Boles in Peter Grimes (Covent Garden 1989, Munich 1992), High Priest in Idomeneo (Covent Garden) 1989, Shursky in Boris Godunov (Strasbourg 1990, Bordeaux 1992–93), Zinovy in Lady Macbeth of Mtsensk (Toulouse) 1991, title role in Idomeneo (Drottningholm) 1991, The Prince/Manservant/Marquis in Lulu (Le Châtelet Paris) 1991, Aegisthe in Elektra (Karlsruhe) 1991, Vogelgesang in Die Meistersinger (Trieste) 1992, Schwetzingen in L'Occasione fa il Ladro (Cologne) 1992, Dormont in Scala di Seta (Cologne) 1992, Alfred in Die Fledermaus (Opera Durhin) 1992–93, Captain Vere in Billy Budd (Cologne) 1992–93, Valzacchi in Der Rosenkavalier (Le Châtelet) 1993–94, Albert Gregor in The Makropoulos Case (Opera Durhin, Lisbon) 1993–94, Herod in Salome (Lisbon, Strasbourg) 1994, title role in Peter Grimes (Regersburg) 1996, Prince Shuisky in Boris Godunov (Montpellier) 1996, Prologue/Peter Quint in The Turn of the Screw (Barcelona) 1996, title role in La Clemenza di tito (Nennes) 1996; *Recordings* incl: Rodrigo in Otello (under Mark Elder, EMI), title role in Orpheus in the Underworld (under Mark Elder, TER), Brother II in The Seven Deadly Sins (under Michael Tilson Thomas, Philips), Dr Suda in Osud (under Sir Charles Mackerras), Mr Bumble in Oliver (under John Owen Edwards, TER), Bob Boles in Peter Grimes (under Bernard Haitink, EMI); *Recreations* reading, golf, fine wines; *Style*— Stuart Kale, Esq; ✉ c/o Athole Still International Management, Foresters Hall, 25–27 Westow St, London SE19 3RY (☎ 0181 771 5271, fax 0181 771 8172)

KALETSKY, Anatole; s of Jacob Kaletsky (d 1989), and Esther, *née* Feinsilber; *b* 1 June 1952; *Educ* King's Coll Cambridge (hon sr scholarship, BA, DipEcon), Harvard Univ Graduate Sch (Kennedy memorial scholarship, MA); *m* 5 Dec 1985, Fiona Elizabeth, da of Christopher Murphy; 2 s (Michael b 10 Dec 1988, Jacob Alexander Christopher (Sasha) b 27 Feb 1992), 1 da (Katherine b 2 Nov 1986); *Career* fin writer The Economist 1976–79; The Financial Times: ldr and feature writer 1979–81, Washington corr 1981–84, int economics corr 1984–86, chief New York Bureau 1986–90, Moscow corr 1990, sr features writer April-Sept 1990; The Times: economics ed 1990–, assoc ed 1992–; Specialist Writer of the Year Br Press Awards 1980 and 1992, BBC Press Awards Commentator of the Year 1995; conslt: UN Devpt Ctee, UN Conf on Trade and Devpt, Twentieth Century Fund; memb Advsy Bd UK Govt Know-How Fund for Eastern Europe; numerous television and radio appearances; *Books* The Costs of Default (1985); *Style*— Anatole Kaletsky, Esq; ✉ The Times, 1 Pennington St, London E1 9XN (☎ 0171 782 5000, fax 0171 782 5229)

KALICHSTEIN, Joseph; s of Isaac Kalichstein (d 1959), of Tel Aviv, and Mali, *née* Bendit (d 1995); *b* 15 Jan 1946; *Educ* The Juilliard Sch NY; *m* 1971, Rowain, da of late Edward Schultz; 2 s (Avshalom b 1974, Rafael b 1977); *Career* pianist; recital debut NY 1967, London debut LSO (conductor André Previn) 1969, formed Kalichstein-Laredo-Robinson trio 1976; appearances with major orchestras incl: LSO, LPO, Berlin Philharmonic, Israel Philharmonic, Chicago, Cleveland, Boston, NY, Baltimore, Montreal, San Francisco, LA, St Louis, Dallas, Pittsburgh; conductors worked with: Barenboin, Boulez, Conlon, De Waart, Dohnanyi, Dutoit, Foster, Leinsdorf, Lopez-Cobos, Macal, Mata, Mehta, Previn, Sanderling, Slatkin, Szell, Zinman; solo recordings incl: Bartok and Prokofiev 1968, Chopin 1973, Brahms 1975, Schumann and Schubert 1990; recordings with trio incl: Mendelssohn Trios, Brahms Trios, Beethoven Triple with ECO, two Beethoven Trios; various Mendelssohn recordings incl No 1 with LSO 1971 and No 1 and No 2 with Scot Chamber Orch 1987; first prize Leventritt Int Piano Competition 1969; *Recreations* chess, books, acrostic puzzles; *Style*— Joseph Kalichstein, Esq; ✉ c/o Harrison/Parrott Ltd, 12 Penzance Place, London W11 4PA (☎ 0171 229 9166, fax 0171 221 5042)

KALKHOF, Peter Heinz; s of Heinz Emil Kalkhof (d 1945), and Kate Ottilie, *née* Binder (d 1976); *b* 20 Dec 1933; *Educ* Sch of Arts and Crafts Braunschweig, Acad of Fine Art Stuttgart, Slade Sch of Fine Art London, École des Beaux Arts Paris; *m* 1962, Jeanne The Soen Nio; 1 s (Peter T L b 1964); *Career* artist; Slade Sch travel grant Br Isles 1961; lectr in painting Univ of Reading 1970– (pt/t lectr in lithography and etching 1964–70); artist in residence: Osnabruck Germany 1985, Künstlerhaus Schieder-Schwalenberg Germany 1995 (six months); memb: Br Museum Soc, Soc for Anglo-Chinese Understanding; friend of the Royal Acad; *Solo Exhibitions* Galerie in der Garage Stuttgart 1964, Oxford Gallery 1970, Annely Juda Fine Art London 1970, 1974, 1977,

1979 and 1990, Wellmann Galerie Dusseldorf 1973, Galerie HS Erkelenz 1974, Royal Shakespeare Theatre 1975, Oliver Dowling Gallery Dublin 1976, Kulturgeschichtliches Museum Osnabruck 1977, Hertfordshire Coll of Art and Design St Albans 1978, Kunstverein Marburg 1979, Goethe Inst London 1981, Juda Rowan Gallery London 1983, Galerie Altes Rathaus Worth am Rhein 1987, Landesmuseum Oldenburg 1988, Camden Arts Centre London 1989, Ostpreussisches Landesmuseum Luneburg 1989, Galerie Rösch Neubrunn 1993, Galerie Rösch Karlsruhe 1994, Rathaus Galerie Balingen Germany 1995, Prignitz Museum am Dom Havelberg Germany 1996, Stadt Museums Galerie Schieder-Schwalenberg Germany 1996; *Group Exhibitions* incl: Spectrum 1971 (Alexandra Palace London) 1971, International Biennale of Drawing (Middlesbrough) 1973 and 1979, British Painting 74 (Hayward Gallery London) 1974, Celebrating 8 Artists (Kensington and Chelsea Arts Cncl Exhibition) 1977, Six Painters (Univ of Reading Art Gallery) 1984, Three Decades of Contemporary Art (Juda Rowan Gallery) 1985, From Prism to Paint Box (Welsh Arts Cncl touring exhibition) 1989–90, A Centenary Exhibition (Univ of Reading Art Gallery) 1992; *Recreations* travelling, reading, listening to music, seeing films, visiting museums, exhibitions, art galleries etc; *Style*— Peter Kalkhof, Esq; ✉ c/o Annely Juda Fine Art, 23 Dering St, London W1R 9AA

KALKHOVEN, Ir Paul; *b* 25 May 1955; *Educ* Triniteits Lyceum Haarlem The Netherlands, Dept of Architecture and Town Planning Tech Univ Delft The Netherlands (Ingenieur); *Career* architect; MacCormac Jamieson & Prichard 1980–85, Foster & Partners 1986– (currently dir); ARCUK 1984; *Style*— Ir Paul Kalkhoven; ✉ Foster & Partners, Riverside 3, 22 Hester Road, London SW11 4AN (☎ 0171 738 0455)

KALMS, Sir Stanley; kt (1996); s of Charles Kalms (d 1978), and Cissie, *née* Schlagman (d 1990); *b* 21 Nov 1931; *Educ* Christ's Coll Finchley; *m* 28 Feb 1954, Pamela Audrey, da of Morris Jimack (d 1968), of London; 3 s (Richard b 10 March 1955, Stephen b 3 Dec 1956, Paul b 6 March 1963); *Career* chm Dixons Group plc (joined 1948); non-exec dir British Gas plc 1987–; chm King's Healthcare NHS Tst 1993–96, memb Funding Agency for Schs 1994–; non-exec dir Centre for Policy Studies 1991–, govr Dixons Bradford City Technol Coll; tstee: Industry in Education Ltd 1993–, The Economic Education Trust 1993–; hon fell London Business Sch; Hon DLitt 1991, Hon Dr Univ of North London 1994, Hon FCGI 1988, hon fell London Business Sch 1995; *Recreations* communal educnl activities, sailing, opera; *Clubs* Carlton; *Style*— Sir Stanley Kalms; ✉ Dixons Group plc, 29 Farm Street, London W1X 7RD (☎ 0171 499 3494, fax 0171 499 3436)

KALMUS, Prof George Ernest; s of Hans Kalmus (d 1988), and Anna, *née* Rosenberg; *b* 21 April 1935; *Educ* St Albans Co GS, UCL (BSc, PhD); *m* 15 June 1957, Ann Christine, da of Ernest Henry Harland (d 1984); 3 da (Susan Jane b 1960, Mary Elisabeth b 1962, Diana Christine b 1965); *Career* Lawrence Radiation Laboratory Univ of California Berkeley: res assoc 1962–63 and 1964–67, sr physicist 1967–71; UCL: res assoc 1959–62, lectr Physics Dept 1963–64, visiting prof 1984–; Rutherford Appleton Laboratory: gp ldr Bubble Chamber and Delphi Gps 1971–86, dir Particle Physics 1986–; FRS 1988; *Recreations* skiing, reading, cycling; *Style*— Prof George Kalmus, FRS; ✉ 16 South Avenue, Abingdon, Oxon OX14 1QH (☎ 01235 523340); Rutherford Appleton Laboratory, Chilton, Didcot, Oxon OX11 0QX (☎ 01235 445443, fax 01235 446733, telex 83159 RUTHLB G)

KAMDAR, Batookrai Anopchand; s of Anopchand Keshavlal Kamdar, and Lilavati, *née* Shah; *b* 29 Oct 1939; *Educ* Gujarat Univ (MB BS), FRCS (tutor); *m* 27 May 1964, Dr Beni Kamdar, da of Dr Chandulal Chhotalal Shah, of Baroda, India; 1 s (Neel b 1965), 1 da (Sujata b 1967); *Career* orthopaedic registrar: Hammersmith Hosp 1970–71, Heatherwood Hosp Ascot Berks 1971–72; sr orthopaedic registrar Royal Free Hosp London 1973–75, conslt orthopaedic surgn Dartford and Gravesham Health Dist 1975–; memb: RSM, BMA, Br Orthopaedic Assoc; FRCSEd; *Pubns:* Complications Following Total Knee Replacement (1974), Soft Tissue Calcification Following Total Hip Replacement (1976), Early Soft Tissue Release in CTEV (1977); *Recreations* reading, music, philately, cricket, skiing, golf; *Clubs* MCC, London Golf; *Style*— Batookrai Kamdar, Esq; ✉ 7 Liskeard Close, Chislehurst, Kent BR7 6RT (☎ 0181 467 9851); West Hill Hospital, Dartford, Kent (☎ 01322 223223); Blackheath Hospital, Blackheath, London; Fawkham Manor Hospital, Fawkham, Kent (☎ 01474 879900)

KAMIL, His Hon Judge Geoffrey Harvey; s of Peter Kamil of Leeds, and Sadie, *née* Morris; *b* 17 Aug 1942; *Educ* Leeds GS, Univ of Leeds (LLB); *m* 17 March 1968, Andrea Pauline, da of Gerald Ellis, of Leeds; 2 da (Sharon b 1969, Debra b 1971); *Career* admitted slr of the Supreme Ct 1968, ptnr J Levi Leeds 1974–87; stipendiary magistrate: W Midlands 1987–90 (dep 1985), W Yorkshire 1990–93; recorder of Crown Ct 1991–93 (asst recorder 1986–91), circuit judge (NE Circuit) 1993–; memb: Ctee of Leeds Law Soc 1982–87, Leeds Cts Ctee 1983–87, Leeds Duty Slr Ctee 1985–87, Magisterial Ctee Judicial Studies Bd 1991–93, Center for Criminal Justice Studies Univ of Leeds; sec Stonham's Kirkstall Lodge Hostel Leeds 1974–87; *Recreations* golf, sailing, swimming; *Clubs* Moor Allerton Golf; *Style*— His Hon Judge Kamil; ✉ The Law Courts, Exchange Square, Drake Street, Bradford, W Yorkshire BD1 1JA

KAMINSKY, (Roman) David; s of Orest Kaminsky (d 1963), and Marion, *née* Jones (d 1992); *b* 28 Dec 1950; *Educ* Stockland Green Bi-Lateral Sch, Manchester Coll of Art; *m* 24 May 1975, Elizabeth Louise, da of Albert Edward Walter Morley (d 1975); 1 s (Jonathan David b 27 Oct 1982), 1 da (Lydia Rose Marion b 7 Aug 1981); *Career* prodn mangr Constantine Colour Finishing Ltd 1980–87 (hand printer 1972–80), fndr Kaminski Photographic Labs Ltd 1987–; memb BIPP Fellowship and Associateship Selection Panel (sector 3); BIPP: licentiate 1978, assoc 1985, fell 1986; *Recreations* fly fishing, photography, classic car restoration; *Style*— David Kaminsky, Esq; ✉ Kaminski Professional Photographic Laboratories Ltd, 112–116 Park Hill Rd, Harborne, Birmingham B17 9HD (☎ 0121 427 1160, fax 0121 428 1442)

KAN, Sir Yuet-Keung; GBE (1979, CBE 1967, OBE 1959), kt (1972), JP; s of Kan Tong Po, JP; *b* 26 July 1913; *Educ* Hong Kong Univ, London Univ (BA); *m* 1940, Ida; 2 s, 1 da; *Career* slr; chm Hong Kong Trade Devpt Cncl 1970–75 and 1979–83; pro chllr Chinese Univ of Hong Kong; Hon LLD: Hong Kong Univ, Chinese Univ; *Style*— Sir Yuet-Keung Kan, GBE, JP; ✉ Swire House, 11 Floor, Chater Rd, Hong Kong (☎ 00 852 238181)

KANABUS, Annabel; da of Sir Robert Sainsbury, and Lisa, *née* Van den Bergh; *b* 22 Jan 1948; *Educ* Francis Holland Sch, Univ of East Anglia (BSc); *m* 13 March 1975, Peter John Kanabus, s of Edward Kanabus; 2 s (Jason b 9 June 1976, Adrian b 15 Feb 1978); *Career* fndr and tstee of the charity Avert 1986–; tstee Sainsbury Centre for Visual Arts Univ of East Anglia; *Recreations* farming, watching television; *Style*— Mrs Annabel Kanabus; ✉ Avert, 11 Denne Parade, Horsham, West Sussex RH12 1JD (☎ 01403 210202, fax 01403 211001)

KANAKARATNAM, Dr Gunaseelan; s of Dr Arumugam Kanakaratnam (d 1994), of Canberra, Australia, and Pathmawathy Pichamuttu (d 1985); *b* 20 April 1933; *Educ* Royal Coll Colombo Sri Lanka, Univ of Ceylon (MB BS), RCS (DPM); *Career* registrar Fairfields Hosp Hitchin Herts 1965, conslt psychiatrist Fairfields Hosp 1971–; FRCPsych 1971; *Recreations* cricket, swimming, gardening, travel; *Style*— Dr Gunaseelan Kanakaratnam; ✉ Fairfield Hospital, near Stotfold, Hitchin, Herts SG5 4AA (☎ 01462 730123)

KANCHELSKIS, Andrei; *b* 23 Jan 1969; *Career* professional footballer (midfielder); initially with Dynamo Kiev and Doneztsk; transferred to Manchester Utd (for £650,000) 1991–95, transferred to Everton (for £4m) 1995–; honours: Super Cup 1992, League Cup 1992, winners inaugural FA Premier League Championship 1992/93, Charity Shield 1992, 1993 and 1994, winners League and FA Cup double 1994; *Style*— Andrei Kanchelskis, Esq; ✉ Everton FC, Goodison Park, Liverpool L4 4EL

KANDER, Nadav; *b* 1961; *Career* photographic asst London 1981–85, established own studio in London and worked freelance on numerous major advertising campaigns 1986–; awards incl: AFAEP Gold award for landscape Photography 1989, award from Art Directors Club of NY 1989, Silver award for Best Photography from Creative Circle Honours 1990, 2 Awards of Excellence from Communications Arts 1990, winner Eurobest Photography 1990, 4 finalists' positions in Press Photography Eurobest Competition, AFAEP Silver award for landscape photography, Assoc of Photographers Gold award for portfolio 1993; exhibitions or publications of work incl: Selections of 1987 Image Magazine, Photographers Gallery London 1987, Special Photographers Co London 1987 and 1990, D & AD Annual 1988, 1989 and 1990, Lurt's Archive 1988, V & A 1988, New Tate Gallery, Communication Arts Photography Annual 1989 and 1990, Creative Circle Annual 1990; articles in various pubns incl: British Journal of Photography 1987, Direction Magazine 1988, SLR Magazine 1989, Campaign Press 1989, Graphis Magazine 1989, Conde Nast's Traveler Magazine; memb: AFAEP 1986, D & AD Assoc 1988, Judging Ctee of Photography Assoc of the Netherlands 1991; *Style*— Nadav Kander, Esq; ✉ c/o Nadav Kander Photography, 1/7 Britannia Row, London N1 (☎ 0171 359 5207)

KANE, (David) John; s of Harry Fitchet Kane (d 1987), and Mary, *née* Gordon Philip (d 1988); *b* 27 Oct 1945; *Educ* Brechin HS, Arbroath HS, Glasgow Acad of Music and Drama; *m* 1, 5 Jan 1965 (m dis 1972), Rosemary Rimmer; 1 da (Alice Tiffany b 17 Aug 1965); m 2, 14 Oct 1972, Alison Mary Hope Robine, *née* Warner; 1 s (Simon Leplastrier b 3 Nov 1974), 1 da Susanna Mary Louise b 27 Aug 1976); *Career* actor and writer; visiting dir of theatre studies Lafayette Coll Easton Pennsylvania 1991–92, drama tutor Oxford Overseas Study Course 1993–94; *Theatre* roles incl: Puck in A Midsummer Night's Dream and Prince Myshkin in Subject to Fits 1965–72, Caliban in The Tempest 1988–89, Bob in Outside Edge at Hampstead and The Globe; as writer stage plays incl: The Rise and Fall of Rumplestiltskin, Murder Dear Watson, Plastic Birthday, The Scarlet Blade, Jack and the Beanstalk, Wizard of Oz, The Other Side of Paradise, Jumpin' Jehovah, Blue Murder, Death Reel, Antiphony, The Impressario, Time of Miracles, Tallulah Who?; *Television* writer or creator of series incl: Black Beauty, Dick Turpin, Son of The Bride, The Vamp, Cloppa Castle, The Feathered Serpent, Four Idle Hands, Smuggler, A Little Touch of Wisdom, Happy Ever After, Me and My Girl, Terry and June, Never the Twain, All in Good Faith, The Return of Sherlock Holmes, The Magical Adventures of Mumfie; *Recreations* reading, music, old films; *Style*— John Kane, Esq; ✉ c/o ICM Ltd, Oxford House, 76 Oxford Street, London W1N 0AX (☎ 0171 636 6565, fax 0171 323 0101)

KANE, Martin Christopher; s of Bernard Kane, of Milngavie, Glasgow, and Rosina, *née* Maguire; *b* 3 June 1958; *Educ* St Andrew's HS Clydebank Glasgow, Edinburgh Coll of Art (BA); *Career* artist; *Solo Exhibitions* Artist of the Day (Angela Flowers Gallery) 1988, Memory and Imagination (Jill George Gallery London) 1990, Reflections (Jill George Gallery London) 1992, Beyond the Wall (Jill George Gallery) 1993, New Paintings (Beaux Arts Gallery) 1996; *Group Exhibitions* incl: student annual exhibition (Royal Scottish Acad) 1986 and 1987, New Generation (Compass Gallery Glasgow) 1987, Obsessions (Raab Gallery London) 1987, Two Scottish Artists (Boundary Gallery) 1988, Int Art Fair (LA with Thumb Gallery) 1989, 1990, 1991 and 1992, Art 90, Art 91, Art 92, Art 93, Art 94, Art 95 and Art 96 (Design Centre London), London to Atlanta (Thumb Gallery, Atlanta USA) 1990, Lineart 95 (Gent) 1995, Small Paintings (Beaux Arts); *Public Collections* Glasgow District Cncl, Cleveland Museum Middlesbrough, CBS Collection, Scottish Devpt Agency Glasgow, Unilever PLC Collection London, Gartmore Investments; *Recreations* music, classic cars; *Style*— Martin Kane, Esq; ✉ Beaux Arts Gallery, 22 Cork Street, London W1X 1HB (☎ 0171 437 5799, fax 0171 437 5798)

KANE, Richard George; s of Charles Edward Wright (d 1974), of Lincoln, and Mary Kathleen Wright; *b* 17 Sept 1938; *Educ* City Sch Lincoln, Univ of Leeds, RADA; *m* 1, 1967 (m dis 1972), Jean Hastings; m 2, 1975 (m dis 1993), Jenny Lee; 1 s (Tom b 1977); *Career* actor; *Theatre* repertory work incl: Dundee, Glasgow Citizens, Bristol Old Vic, Oxford Playhouse, Manchester Stables, Chichester Festival Theatre, Edinburgh Lyceum; London Fringe: Royal Court, Hampstead Theatre Club, Greenwich Theatre, Bush Theatre, Open Space Theatre; West End roles incl: Mark Gertler in Bloomsbury (Phoenix) 1974, Nightingale in Vieux Carré (Piccadilly) 1978, Roger Dervish in Outside Edge (Queens) 1979, Leslie Bainbridge in Taking Steps (Lyric) 1980, Sir Benjamin Backbite in The School for Scandal (Duke of Yorks) 1983, Ben Weeks in The Normal Heart (Albany) 1985, William Featherstone in How The Other Half Loves (Duke of Yorks) 1988, Sidney Hopcroft in Absurd Person Singular (Whitehall) 1990, Travels with my Aunt (Wyndhams and Whitehall) 1992; wrote play Sweet Dreams (performed Colchester Mercury Theatre 1982, King's Head Theatre Club 1982, BBC Radio 1984); *Television* incl: two series of Hot Metal (LWT) 1984 and 1986, The Insurance Man, Blind Justice (BBC), Inspector Morse (Zenith); *Radio* incl: Kenrio Watanabe in Sweet Dreams (BBC) 1984, Henry in Henry And The Dogs 1986, Branston in The Event of The Season (BBC) 1987; *Film* incl: Col Weaver in A Bridge Too Far 1976, Gen Jaruselski in Squaring The Circle 1982; *Awards* Scottish Television Theatre Award 1969, nominated Most Promising Newcomer of the Year 1968; *Recreations* football, reading; *Style*— Richard Kane, Esq; ✉ c/o Kerry Gardner Management, 15 High Street Kensington, London W8 5NP (☎ 0171 937 4478, fax 0171 376 2587)

KANIS, Prof John Anthony; s of Max Kanis (d 1957), of London, and Elizabeth Mary, *née* Mees; *b* 2 Sept 1944; *Educ* Univ of Edinburgh (MB ChB); *m* 1, 11 April 1966 (m dis 1984), Patricia Sheila, *née* Mclaren; 4 da (Lisa b 13 Dec 1967, Emma b 24 Sept 1969, Sarah b 4 July 1971, Rebecca b 2 Jan 1975); m 2, 19 June 1989, Monique Nicole Christiane, da of Georges Marie Benéton, of Route du Moulinet, 45290 Varennes-Changy, France; *Career* Wellcome sr res fell Univ of Oxford 1976–79; conslt: Royal Hallamshire Hosp 1979–, Ministry of Health France 1981–; prof of human metabolism Univ of Sheffield 1982–; pres Euro Fndn for Osteoporosis and Bone Disease 1987–, advsr on osteoporosis WHO 1988–90, dir WHO Collaborating Centre for Metabolic Bone Disease Sheffield; ed Bone jl, author of 400 scientific pubns on bone disease; FRCP 1984, FRCPE 1986, MRCPath 1982; *Books* Paget's Disease of the Bone, Osteoporosis; *Recreations* antiques restoration, genealogy; *Style*— Prof John Kanis; ✉ Park Elms, 3 Park Lane, Broomhall Park, Sheffield S10 2DU (☎ 0114 266 1242, fax 0114 268 3995); Department of Human Metabolism & Clinical Biochemistry, University of Sheffield Medical School, Beech Hill Rd, Sheffield S10 2RX (☎ 0114 271 2649, fax 0114 273 9176, telex 547216 UGSHEF G)

KANTOROWICZ-TORO, Donald; s of Rodolph Kantorowicz, and Blanca Livia, *née* Toro; *b* 4 Aug 1945; *Educ* Jesuit Sch Cali Colombia, Hochschule für Welthandel Vienna (MBA), Faculté de Droit et Sciences Economiques Paris (DEconSc); *m* 12 Sept 1973 (m dis 1986), Chantal, *née* Lancrenon; 2 da (Melanie b 1976, Johana b 1978); *Career* Banque de L'Union Européenne Paris 1969–71, vice pres and mangr Bank of America Paris and Madrid 1972–79, md and chief exec Consolidado UK/Vestcor Partners Ltd 1980–94, private banker Merrill Lynch 1994–; memb French Fin Assoc Paris; *Recreations* skiing, sailing, classical music, history; *Clubs* Overseas Bankers, Interallie Paris; *Style*— Donald Kantorowicz-Toro, Esq; ✉ 11 South Terrace, London SW7 2BT (☎ 0171 584 8185); Merrill Lynch, 33 Chester Street, London SW1X 7XD (☎ 0171 867 6043, fax 0171 867 6028);

KAO, Prof Charles Kuen; CBE (1993); s of Chun-Hsian Kao (d 1996), of Hong Kong, and Sin-Fang, *née* King (d 1976); *b* 4 Nov 1933; *Educ* St Joseph's Coll Hong Kong, Univ of London (BSc, PhD); *m* 19 Sept 1959, Gwen May-Wan, da of Ping-Sum Wong (d 1946), of UK; 1 s (Simon b 1961), 1 da (Amanda b 1963); *Career* Standard Telephones and Cables Ltd 1957–60, Standard Telecommunications Laboratories Ltd 1961–70, chm Dept of Electronics The Chinese Univ of Hong Kong 1970–74, chief scientist and dir engrg Electro-Optical Products Div ITT Roanoke Va USA 1974–82, exec scientist and corp dir res ITT Advanced Technology Centre Connecticut USA 1982–87, vice chancellor The Chinese Univ of Hong Kong 1987–96; Hon DSc: The Chinese Univ of Hong Kong 1985, Univ of Sussex 1990, Univ of Durham 1994; Hon DEng Univ of Glasgow 1992, Hon DUniv Griffith Univ Australia 1995; Gold Medal for Engrg Excellence (WFEO) 1995; memb Nat Acad of Engrg USA, fell Academia Sinica Taiwan, foreign memb Royal Swedish Academy of Engrg Sciences Sweden, academician Chinese Acad of Scis; FIEE, FIEEE, FEng, FRSA; *Books* Optical Fibre Systems: Technology, Design and Applications (1982), Optical Fibre (IEE Materials and Devices Series 6, 1988), A Choice Fulfilled: The Business of High Technology (1991); *Recreations* tennis, hiking, gourmet cooking; *Clubs* Hong Kong Jockey, The Hong Kong Country, The American; *Style—* Prof Charles Kao, CBE, FEng; ✉ (e-mail ckao@ie.cihk.edu.hk and chaskao@minerva.cis.yale.edu)

KAPLICKY, Jan; s of Josef Kaplicky (d 1962), and Jirina, *née* Florova (d 1984); *b* 18 April 1937; *Educ* Coll of Applied Arts and Architecture Prague (Dip in Architecture); *m* 1991, Amanda, *née* Levete; 1 s (Josef b 18 April 1995); *Career* architect; private practice Prague 1964–68, Denys Lasdun & Partners 1969–71, Piano & Rogers 1971–73, Spence & Webster 1974–75, Louis de Soissons 1975–77, Foster Assocs 1977–83; fndr: Future Systems 1979, Czechoslovak Architectural Fndn 1990; unit master Architectural Assoc 1982–88; teacher: Hochschule für Kunste Bremen 1990, Sch of Architecture Bordeaux 1992, RMIT Melbourne 1992, Technische Universitat Berlin 1992; *Exhibitions* incl: Jan Kaplicky Projects (Art-Net, 1978), Future Systems (RIBA, 1982, The Graham Fndn Chicago, 1987, Architectural Assoc, 1987), Nouvelles Tendances (Pompidou Centre, 1987), Bibliothèque de France (Insitut Francais d'Architecture, 1989), Royal Acad Summer Show (1990, 1993 and 1995), Future Systems: Architecture (RIBA, 1991), Future Systems: Recent Work (Store-Front New York, 1992), Permanent Collection (Pompidou Centre, 1993), Contemporary British Architecture (Los Angles and Chicago); *TV* incl: Architect's Choice (BBC Late Show) 1990, Art is Dead and Long Live TV? (Scottish TV) 1991, Future Systems: Architecture (BBC Late Show) 1991 *Awards* first prize: Industrial Estates Competition Newcastle 1976, Future House Competition UK 1978, Liverpool Focus on the Centre Competition 1978, Landmark Competition Melbourne 1979, AJ/Bovis Royal Acad 1993, Aluminium Imagination Architectural Award; second prize: Bridge of the Future Competition Tokyo 1987, Int Competition Bibliothèque de France Paris 1989; highly commended: Design Week (Product Design) 1992, British Construction Industry 1992; Graham Fndn Chicago 1986, NASA Certificate of Recognition 1989, finalist Designer of the Year The Prince Philip Prize 1991, Geoffrey Gribble Meml Conservation Award; *Books* Future Systems: The Story of Tomorrow (by Martin Pawley, 1993), For Inspiration Only (1996); *Recreations* history of modern architecture; *Clubs* Architecture, Architectural Assoc; *Style—* Jan Kaplicky, Esq; ✉ Future Systems, 199–205 Old Marylebone Road, London NW1 5QP (☎ 0171 723 4141, fax 0171 723 1131)

KAPLIN, Dayan Rabbi (Cyril) David; s of Noah Kaplin (d 1975), of London, and Rachel Kaplin (d 1966); *b* 1 Oct 1931; *Educ* Letchworth GS, Gateshead Talmudical Coll, Hebron Yeshiva Jersualem, Inst for Higher Rabbinical Studies Gateshead; *Career* formerly: dayan Fedn of Synagogues, rabbi Shomrei Hadath Synagogue Hampstead, vice princ Tree of Life Coll London NW11, princ Bet Hatalmud Golders Green; currently ecclesiastical judge Ct of the Chief Rabbi; co ed Hed Eliyahu, ed SRIDIM (Standing Ctee Conf of Euro Rabbis); FRZS, memb Jewish Historical Soc; *Publications* Keter David, Toldot Noach; *Style—* Dayan Rabbi David Kaplin; ✉ London Beth Din Court of the Chief Rabbi, 735 High Road, London N12 0US (☎ 0181 343 6270)

KAPOOR, Anish; *Educ* Hornsey Coll of Art London, Chelsea Sch of Art; *Career* artist, sculptor; teacher Wolverhampton Poly 1979, artist in residence Walker Art Gallery Liverpool 1982; *Awards* Premio Duemila Venice Biennale 1990, Turner Prize 1991; *Solo Exhibitions* incl: Patrice Alexandre Paris 1980, Lisson Gallery 1983, 1985, 1988, 1989–90 and 1993, Walker Art Gallery Liverpool 1982 and 1983, Barbara Gladstone Gallery NY 1984, 1986, 1989–90 and 1993, Stedelijk Van Abbermuseum Erndhoven 1986, Anish Kapoor: Recent Sculpture and Drawings (Univ Gallery Massachusetts) 1986, Anish Kapoor: Works On Paper 1975–87 (Ray Hughes Gallery) 1987, Kohji Ogura Gallery Japan 1989, Br Pavilion Venice 1990, Anish Kapoor Drawings (Tate Gallery) 1990–91, Centre National d'Art Contemporain Grenoble 1990–91, Palacio de Velazguez Madrid 1991, Kunstverein Hannover 1991, Feuerle Koln 1991, The Sixth Japan Ushimado Int Art Festival Japan 1991, Galeria Soledad Lorenzo Madrid 1992, San Diego Museum of Contemporary Art 1992–93, Designs for a Dance (South Bank Centre London) 1993, Tel Aviv Museum of Art 1993, Mala Galerija Moderna Galerija Ljubljana 1994, Echo (Kohji Ogura Gallery) 1994, Anish Kapoor (Tillburg Nishimura Gallery Tokyo) 1995, Prada Milanoarte Milan and also Lisson Gallery London 1995–96, Anish Kapoor. Sculptures (Aboa Vetus & Ars Nova Finland) 1996, Anish Kapoor. Two Sculptures (Kettle's Yard Cambridge) 1996, Galleria Massimo Minini Brescia 1996, Gourd Project 1993–95 (Freddie Fong Contemporary Art San Francisco) 1996, Kunst-Station Sankt Peter Cologne 1996; *Group Exhibitions* incl: Art Into Landscape 1 (Serpentine Gallery London) 1974, Young Contemporaries (Royal Academy London) 1975, London/New York 1982 (Lisson Gallery London) 1982, Paris Biennale (Paris) 1982, India: Myth and Reality (Museum of Modern Art Oxford) 1982, Finland Biennale (Helsinki) 1983, Sculpture 1983 (Van Krimpen Gallery Amsterdam) 1983, New Art (Tate Gallery) 1983, An International Survey of Recent Painting and Sculpture (Museum of Modern Art NY) 1984, Nouvelle Biennale de Paris (Paris) 1985, Europa oggi/Europe now (Museo d'Arte Contemporanea Italy) 1988, Starlit Waters, British Sculpture: An International Art 1968–88 (Tate Gallery Liverpool) 1988, Heroes of Contemporary Art (Galerie Saqqarah Switzerland) 1990–91, British Art Now (touring) 1990–91, Gallery Shirakawa Kyoto 1991, Feuerle Gallery 1991, Anish Kapoor and Abstract Art in Asia (Fukuoka Art Museum Japan) 1991–92, Whitechapel Open 1992, British Sculpture from the Arts Cncl Collection (Derby Museum and Art Gallery) 1993, Punti Dell'Arti (Italian Pavilion Vanice Biennale) 1993, Art Against Aids (Venice Biennale) 1993, Sculpture (Leo Castelli Gallery NY) 1993, Sculptors' Drawings (Tate Gallery) 1994, Re Rebaudengo Sandretto Collection Turin 1994, Ars 95 Helsinki (Museum of Contemporary Art Helsinki) 1995, Ideal Standard Summertime (Lisson Gallery London) 1995, British Abstract Art Part II: Sculpture (Flowers East Gallery London) 1995, Féininmasculin. Le sexe de l'art (Centre Georges Pompidou Paris) 1996, New Art on Paper 2 (Philadelphia Museum of Art) 1996, Un siècle de sculpture anglaise (Jeu de Paume Paris) 1996, Anish Kapoor, Barry X Ball (Angles Gallery Santa Monica USA) 1996; subject of numerous books, articles and reviews; *Style—* Anish Kapoor, Esq; ✉ Lisson Gallery (London) Ltd, 67 Lisson St, London NW1 5DA (☎ 0171 724 2739, fax 0171 724 7124)

KAPOSI, Prof Agnes Aranka; da of Imre Kristof (d 1962), and Magda Csengeri; *b* 20 Oct 1932; *Educ* Kossuth Zsuzsa Girls' Sch Budapest, Tech Univ of Budapest (Dipl Ing); *m* 1952, Janos Ferenc Kaposi, s of Ernö Kaposi; 2 da (Esther Julia b 1959, Anna Jane b 1963); *Career* sr res engr and head of Digital Systems Gp Ericsson Telephones Beeston 1957–60, princ res engr and head of Storage Electronics ICL Research Laboratories Stevenage 1960–64, lectr Cambridgeshire Coll of Arts and Technol 1964–67, princ lectr and dir of res and postgrad studies Kingston Poly (now Univ of Kingston-upon-Thames) 1967–77, head Dept of Electrical and Electronic Engrg South Bank Poly (now South Bank Univ) 1977–88; formerly: dir Polytechnic Consultants, ptnr ARC Consultants Ltd; ptnr Kaposi Associates 1986–; visiting prof Engrg Design Centre City Univ 1990–95, academic govr Richmond The American Int Univ in London 1992–, memb Nat Bd Academic Accreditation of the Hungarian Govt 1994–97; former memb WSET Ctee Office of Sci and Technol; Instn of Electrical Engrs: former memb Cncl, Public Affrs Bd and Accreditation Ctee, currently memb Pool of Accreditors and Info Engrg Ctee, chair London Branch IEE 1994–95; memb Nominations Ctee Engrg Cncl; EPSRC: memb Electromechanical Engrg Ctee, memb Info Technol Liaison Ctee; memb Cncl Women's Engrg Soc, editorial advsr West Indian Journal of Engrg; FIEE 1977 (MIEE 1958), FEng 1992; *Books* Systems, Models and Measures (with M Myers, 1994); *Recreations* reading, music, walking, debating, bridge; *Style—* Prof Agnes Kaposi, FEng; ✉ Kaposi Associates, 3 St Edwards Close, London NW11 (☎ 0181 458 3626, fax 0181 458 0899)

KAPP, Carlo David; s of Robert Scope Kapp (d 1975), of Hayling Is, Hants, and Paola Luisa, *née* Putoto; *b* 31 July 1947; *Educ* Ladybarn Sch Manchester; *m* 1, 28 March 1970 (m dis 1978), Jean Gillian, da of Aubrey Charles Overington (d 1980), of Richmond, Surrey; 1 da (Kelli Anne b 4 July 1977); m 2, 30 Oct 1979, Basia Evelyn, da of Dr Abraham Seinwel Bardach (d 1988), of London; 1 s (Daniel Joseph Scope b 5 Oct 1980), 1 da (Pippa Luisa b 25 Feb 1983); *Career* creative servs mangr Estee Lauder Group (UK) 1974–81; chm and md: Dawson Kapp Overseas 1981–88, The DKO Group plc 1988–; chm The Best Group Ltd 1988–; govr RNLI; memb: The Little Ship Club, Greenpeace; *Recreations* shooting, golf, skiing, marathon running, sailing; *Clubs* RAC, LSC, Wimbledon Park Golf; *Style—* Carlo Kapp, Esq; ✉ The DKO Group PLC, 145 Kensington Church Street, London W8 7LR (☎ 0171 229 5050, fax 0171 229 6964)

KARAT, David Spencer; s of Lt Rene Karat, and Frances, *née* Levy; *b* 1 Aug 1951; *Educ* Merchant Taylors, Univ of Leicester (LLB); *m* 1 Sept 1976, Shirley Lessels, da of Capt Edward Addison Williams; 2 da (Florence Louisa b 22 Sept 1980, Emma Rachel b 21 May 1985); *Career* slr Slaughter & May 1976, gp counsel Royal Bank of Canada 1980; Merrill Lynch: assoc dir 1984, exec dir 1986, md 1989; md and head of debt capital mkts then UK corp fin Salomon Brothers International Limited 1990–96, md and co-head Fin Instns BZW 1996–; memb Law Soc; *Recreations* tennis, running, theatre, jazz and classical music; *Clubs* RAC; *Style—* David S Karat, Esq; ✉ Barclays de Zoete Wedd Ltd, Seal House 1 Swan Lane, London EC4R 3UD (☎ 0171 956 2860, fax 0171 956 2955)

KARK, Austen Steven; CBE (1987); s of Maj Norman Kark, and Ethel, *née* Goldberg (d 1980); *b* 20 Oct 1926; *Educ* Upper Canada Coll Toronto, Nautical Coll Pangbourne, RNC, Magdalen Coll Oxford (MA); *m* 1, 1949 (m dis 1954), Margaret Solomon, da of S Schmahmann, of S Africa; 2 da (Catherine b 1950, Teresa b 1953); m 2, 1954, Nina Mary (novelist Nina Bawden, *qv*), da of Cdr Charles Mabey (d 1976), of Herne Bay; 1 da (Perdita b 1957), 2 step s (Nicholas Bawden (d 1983), Robert Bawden); *Career* Midshipman RIN 1944–46, E Indies Fleet, HMS Nelson, HMS London; dir first prodn of Sartre's The Flies Oxford 1948; BBC: joined 1954, head S Euro Serv 1964, E Euro and Russian Serv 1972, ed World Serv 1973, controller Eng Servs 1974, advsr to late Lord Soames on election broadcasting Rhodesia, chm Harare Govt Report on Radio and TV Zimbabwe, md external broadcasting 1984–86 (dep md 1981–84), ret 1986; chm: seminar in American Studies UK Alumni Salzburg 1979–85, CPC Guide Books 1987; memb UK Delgn CSCE London Info Forum 1989; tstee Cwlth Journalists Assoc 1993; *Books* Attic in Greece (1994); *Recreations* real tennis, travelling, mosaics; *Clubs* Oriental, MCC, Royal Tennis Ct; *Style—* Austen Kark, Esq, CBE; ✉ 22 Noel Rd, London N1 8HA

KARLWEIS, Georges Joseph Christophe; s of Oskar Karlweis, and Ferdinanda Gabrielle, *née* Coulon; *b* 25 Jan 1928; *Educ* Univ of Paris (LLB); *m* 6 June 1986, Brigitte, da of Robert Camplez; *Career* economics corr AGEFI Paris 1946–52, sec gen Société Industrielle des Huiles au Maroc Casablanca Morocco 1952–55; currently on the bd of various international Groupe Edmond de Rothschild cos, vice chm Banque Privée Edmond de Rothschild SA Geneva, non-exec dir N M Rothschild & Sons Ltd; *Clubs* Golf of Geneva, Golf of Cannes-Mougins, Golf of Mortefontaine (Paris), Maxim's Business (Paris and Geneva); *Style—* Georges Karlweis, Esq; ✉ La Petite Pommeraie, 3 Chemin Palud, 1292 Pregny-Geneva, Switzerland (☎ 00 41 22 758 2479); Le Verger, 281 route de Saint Mathieu, 06130 Grasse, France (☎ 00 33 93 40 87 62); Banque Privée Edmond de Rothschild SA, 18 rue de Hesse, 1204 Geneva, Switzerland (☎ 00 41 22 818 9111, fax 00 41 22 818 9128)

KARMILOFF-SMITH, Prof Annette Dionne; da of late Jack Smith, and Doris Ellen Ruth, *née* Findlay; *b* 18 July 1938; *Educ* Edmonton Co GS, Inst Français de Londres, Univ of Lille (Certificat d'Etudes Bilingues), Holborn Coll of Law and Languages (Dip Int Conf Interpreting), Univ of Geneva (Diplôme Général de Psychologie de l'Enfant, Licence en Psychologie, Diplôme de Spécialisation en Psychologie Génétique, Doctorat en Psychologie Génétique et Expérimentale); *m* 1966 (m dis 1991), Igor Alexander Karmiloff; 2 da; *Career* int conf interpreter UN 1966–70, research conslt UNWRA/UNESCO Inst of Educn Beirut 1970–72, research collaborator Int Centre for Genetic Epistemiology Geneva 1972–76, chargé du cours Faculty of Medicine Univ of Berne 1977–79, dir of studies Univ of Geneva 1979, visiting research assoc Max-Planck Inst Nijmegen 1978–82, special appointment career scientist Cognitive Devpt Unit MRC 1988– (sr scientist 1982–88), hon prof of psychology UCL 1982–; visiting lectr: Free Univ of Brussels 1985, Max-Planck Inst Munich 1986, Univ of Chicago 1987, Univ of Barcelona 1988, Carnegie Mellon Univ 1991–92, Univ of Aix-Marseilles 1995, Univ of Madrid 1995; Sloan fell: Yale Univ 1978, Univ of California at Berkeley 1981; hon professorial fell in cognitive science Univ of Sussex 1979–81; memb and former memb Editorial Bds on numerous learned jls 1982–; memb: Soc for the Study of Behavioural Phenotypes, Br Psychological Soc (memb Cncl 1988–91), US Soc for Philosophy & Psychology, US Cognitive Science Soc; memb Academia Europaea 1991, FBA 1993; *Books* A Functional Approach to Child Language (1979, 2 edn 1981), Child Language Research in ESF Countries (jtly, 1991), Beyond Modularity: A Developmental Perspective on Cognitive Science (1992, British Psychological Society Book Award 1995), Baby It's You: A unique insight into the first three years of the developing baby (1994), Rethinking Nativism: Connectionism in a Developmental Framework (jtly, 1996); also author of numerous book chapters and of articles in learned journals; *Recreations* antique collecting, working out, going on multiple diets, writing/reading poetry; *Style—* Prof Annette Karmiloff-Smith, FBA; ✉ Medical Research Council, Cognitive Development Unit, 4 Taviton Street, London WC1H OBT (☎ 0171 387 4692, fax 0171 383 0398, e-mail annette@cdu.ucl.ac.uk)

KARN, Prof Valerie Ann; da of Arthur Frederick Thomas Karn (d 1968), and Winnifred Alice Whisson; *b* 17 May 1939; *Educ* Newquay Co GS, Lady Margaret Hall Oxford (BA), Univ of the Punjab Lahore Pakistan, Grad Sch of Design Harvard Univ; *children* 1 da (Jacqui Solomonides b 1974); *Career* res fell Inst of Social and Econ Res York Univ 1964–66, sr lectr Centre for Urban and Regnl Studies Univ of Birmingham (formerly res assoc then lectr) 1966–84, res fell Urban Inst and advsr to the Dept of Housing and Urban Development Washington DC USA 1979–80, prof of environmental health and housing Salford Univ and dir Salford Centre for Housing Studies 1984–94, chair Dept of Environmental Health and Housing Univ of Salford 1990–94, prof of housing studies Sch of Social Policy Univ of Manchester 1994–; memb: NW Regnl Ctee

Anchor Housing Assoc 1986–88, Ctee of Inquiry into Glasgow's Housing 1986–88, Advsy Gp Housing Assoc Tenants Ombudsman 1994–, Co-ordinating Ctee Euro Network for Housing Research; chm Supervisory Gp of the Feasibility Study for Hulme Estate Manchester 1986–91, dir Nat Housing and Tenant Resource Centre 1991–93, govr Peabody Tst 1993–, co-opted memb Apna Housing Assoc, former chm Special Projects Ctee Copec Housing Tst Birmingham; res offr to the Central Housing Advsy Ctee 1967–69 (memb Housing Mgmnt Sub Ctee The Cullingworth Ctee 1967–69), memb Housing Servs Advsy Gp DOE 1976–79, memb Duke of Edinburgh's Inquiry into Br Housing 1984–85 and 1990–91, special cmmr Cmmn for Racial Equality (on an inquiry into Liverpool City Cncl's housing allocations), chm Res Steering Gp Nat Fedn Housing Assocs 1988– (memb 1984–93), external advsr Inst of Housing's professional qualification, co-ordinator Joseph Rowntree Fndn Ctee on Housing Standards 1992–94; chm Editorial Bd Roof (Shelter's housing jl) 1979–86; memb Chartered Inst of Housing; *Books* various articles and books incl: Retiring to the Seaside (1977), The Consumers Experience of Housing (ed with C Ungerson, 1980), Home Ownership in the Inner City (with P Williams and J Kemeny, 1985), Race, Class and Public Housing (with J Henderson, 1986), Comparing Housing Systems (with H Wolman, 1992), Neighbour Disputes, Responses by Social Landlords (1993), Housing Quality in the 1990's (with L Sheridan, 1994); *Recreations* gardening, walking; *Style*— Prof Valerie Karn; ✉ 4 Ashcott Close, Bolton, Lancs BL6 4RW; School of Social Policy, University of Manchester, Dover Street, Manchester M13 9PL (☎ 0161 275 4844, fax 0161 275 4724)

KARNEHM, Jack Richard Horace; s of Vaclav Karnehm (d 1940), and Louise, *née* Harler (d 1960); *b* 18 June 1917; *Educ* Hungerford Sch London; *m* 30 Sept 1939, Jean, da of John Saunders-Hastie; 1 s (Richard Vaclav b 30 Dec 1940); *Career* served REME No 1 Coastal Defence and Far East 1939–46; manufacturing optician, apprenticeship Hatton Garden London, originator and world patent holder billiard spectacles; snooker commentator; billiards player: London and Southern England champion 9 times (7 consecutively) 1951–61, English champion 1969, world champion London 1969 (runner-up NZ 1964), UK professional champion 1980; fndr chm Nat Coaching Scheme 1970 (nat coach for 15 years), chm Billiards World Governing Body 1967–70, memb WPBSA 1970–; *Books* Billiards and Snooker (1972), Understanding Billiards and Snooker (1976), World Snooker 1 (1981), World Snooker 2 (1982); *Recreations* more billiards, home life; *Style*— Jack Karnehm, Esq

KARNEY, Andrew Lumsdaine; s of Rev Gilbert Henry Peter Karney (d 1996), and Celia Finch Wigham, *née* Richardson (d 1994); gf Rt Rev Arthur B L Karney, First Bishop of Johannesburg; *b* 24 May 1942; *Educ* Rugby, Trinity Coll Cambridge; *m* 1969, Beryl Fleur Goldwyn, MRAD, prima ballerina of Ballet Rambert 1950–60, da of late Louis Goldwyn, of Australia; 1 s (Peter John b 1972); *Career* staff memb UN Relief and Works Agency Beirut and Gaza 1963–64, devpt engr for STC (now Northern Telecom) London and Paris 1965–68, sr scientist GEC Hirst Res Centre 1968–71, planning engr communications Gas Council (now British Gas) 1972–73; Logica plc 1973–94: chm Logica Space and Communications Ltd 1984–94, fndr dir Logica General Systems Spa (Italy) 1984–94, fndr dir Logica Ltd (Hong Kong) 1986–94, dir Logica Data Architects Inc (USA) 1988–90, dir Logica Aerospace and Defence Ltd 1989–91, fndr dir Speedwing Logica Ltd 1990–94; fndr dir Cable London plc 1984–86; non-exec dir Integrated Micro Products plc 1995–96, non-exec chm Language Line Ltd 1996–; ind conslt to various UK and int companies; memb Ctee Nat Electronics Cncl 1989–; Freeman City of London, Liveryman Worshipful Co of Info Technologists; memb: Royal Photographic Soc, RIIA; CEng, FIEE, FInstD, FRSA; *Recreations* travel, photography; *Style*— Andrew Karney, Esq; ✉ 16 Kemplay Rd, London NW3 1SY (☎ 0171 435 4293, fax 0171 435 9146, e-mail 100277,1343@compuserve.com)

KARSTEN, Ian George Francis; QC (1990); s of Dr Frederick Karsten, and Edith Karsten; *b* 27 July 1944; *Educ* William Ellis Sch Highgate, Magdalen Coll Oxford (MA, BCL); *m* 25 May 1984, Moira Elizabeth Ann, da of Wing Cdr Laurence O'Hara; 1 s (Charles Frederick Laurence b 9 Feb 1993), 2 da (Lucy Caroline Jane b 9 Oct 1985, Emma Catherine Louise b 17 June 1988); *Career* called to the Bar Gray's Inn 1967, in practice Midland and Oxford Circuit 1970–, recorder of the Crown Ct 1994–, head of chambers; lectr in law: Univ of Southampton 1966–70, LSE 1970–88; delegate to Hague Conf on Private Int Law 1973–77 (Convention on the Law Applicable to Agency, appointed rapporteur), ldr UK Delegation to Unidroit Conf (Convention on Agency in the Int Sale of Goods) Bucharest 1979 and Geneva 1983, legal assessor UK Cncl for Nursing Midwifery and Health Visiting 1989–; diplomé Hague Acad of Int Law; *Books* Conflict of Laws - Halsbury's Laws of England (co-author 4 edn, 1974); *Recreations* opera, travel, chess; *Style*— Ian Karsten, Esq, QC; ✉ Queen Elizabeth Building, Temple, London EC4Y 9BS

KARTER, John Francis; s of Bruno Eric Karter (d 1992), of Kingston-upon-Thames, and Margaret Ruth, *née* Kennedy; *b* 26 July 1945; *Educ* Haberdashers' Aske's, Univ of Leeds (LLB); *m* (m dis), Paula; 2 s (Ben John b 14 July 1978, Ryan Paul b 2 Feb 1982); *Career* horse racing journalist; racing ed The Times 1973–86; racing corr: The Independent 1986–90, The Sunday Times 1990–; winner Sporting Life Naps Table 1988–89; *Books* Lester - Return of a Legend (biog of Lester Piggott, 1992), Frankie Dettori - The Pictorial Biography (1995); *Recreations* badminton, cycling; *Style*— John Karter, Esq; ✉ 20 Albany Mews, Albany Park Road, Kingston-upon-Thames, Surrey KT2 5SL (☎ 0181 541 1438); The Sunday Times, 1 Pennington St, London E1 9XW (☎ 0171 782 5714)

KASER, Prof Michael Charles; s of Charles Joseph Kaser (d 1983), of St Albans, Herts, and Mabel Lucina, *née* Blunden (d 1976); *b* 2 May 1926; *Educ* Gunnersbury Catholic GS, Wimbledon Coll, King's Coll Cambridge (MA), Univ of Oxford (MA, DLitt 1993); *m* 13 May 1954, Elizabeth Ann Mary, da of Cyril Gascoigne Piggford (d 1956), of Springs, SA; 4 s (Gregory b 1955, Matthew b 1956, Benet b 1959, Thomas b 1962), 1 da (Lucy b 1968); *Career* economist; chief sci advsr div Miny of Works 1946–47, Economic Intelligence Dept FO 1947–51, second sec HM Embassy Moscow 1949, economic affrs offr UN Economic Cmmn for Europe Geneva 1951–63, visiting prof Graduate Inst of Int Studies Univ of Geneva 1959–63; Univ of Oxford: Leverhulme res fell St Antony's Coll 1960–62, faculty fell St Antony's Coll 1963–72, faculty lectr in Soviet economics 1963–72, professorial fell St Antony's Coll 1972–93 (emeritus fell 1993–), reader in economics 1972–93 (reader emeritus 1993–), assoc fell Templeton Coll 1983–, dir Inst of Russian Soviet and East Euro Studies 1988–93; princ Charlemagne Inst Edinburgh 1993–94; chm Advsy Cncl for Adult Educn Oxford 1972–78, Latin preacher Univ Church of St Mary the Virgin 1982; visiting fell Henley Mgmnt Coll 1986–; sec Cwlth Assoc of Geneva 1956–63; memb: Cncl Royal Economic Soc 1976–86 and 1987–90, Royal Inst of Int Affrs 1979–85 and 1986–92, Exec Ctee Int Economic Assoc 1974–83 and 1986– (gen ed 1986–), Int Social Sciences Cncl (UNESCO) 1980–90, Advsy Bd Inst for East-West Security Studies NY 1989–90; chm: Coordinating Cncl of Area Studies Assocs 1986–88 (memb 1980–93 and 1995), Wilton Park Acad Cncl (FCO) 1986–92 (memb 1985–), Sir Heinz Koeppler Tst 1992– (tstee 1987–); pres: Br Assoc for Soviet Slavic and East Euro Studies 1988–91 (previously first chm and memb Ctee Nat Assoc for Soviet and East Euro Studies 1964–88, vice pres 1991–93), Albania Soc of Britain 1992–95, Keston Inst Oxford 1994–, Br Assoc of Former UN Civil Servants 1994–; sec Br Acad Ctee for SE Euro Studies 1988–93; govr Plater Coll Oxford 1968–95 (emeritus govr 1995–), memb HEFCE Advsy Cncl on Former Soviet and E European Studies 1995–; hon fell Univ of Edinburgh 1993–, hon prof Univ of Birmingham 1994–; Hon DSocSc Univ of Birmingham 1994; KSG 1990; *Books* Comecon - Integration Problems of the Planned Economies (1965 and 1967), Soviet Economics (1970), Planning in Eastern Europe (jtly, 1970), The New Economic Systems of Eastern Europe (jtly, 1975), The Soviet Union since the Fall of Khrushchev (jtly, 1975), Health Care in the Soviet Union and Eastern Europe (1976), Soviet Policy for the 1980s (jtly, 1982), The Cambridge Encyclopaedia of Russia and the Soviet Union (ed, 1982 and 1994), The Economic History of Eastern Europe 1919–75 (ed, 3 vols 1985–86), The Central Asian Economies after Independence (jtly, 1992 and 1996), Privatization in the CIS (1995); *Clubs* Reform; *Style*— Prof Michael Kaser; ✉ 7 Chadlington Rd, Oxford OX2 6SY (☎ and fax 01865 515581)

KASMIN, Aaron Augustus; s of John Kasmin, of London, and Jane, *née* Nicholson; *b* 23 Aug 1963; *Educ* Bousfield London, Ashfold Bucks, Port Regis Dorset, David Game Tutors London, Hogarth Tutors London, Chelsea Sch of Art; *m* 30 Sept 1988, Sarah Elizabeth, da of David Patrick Shane; *Career* artist; solo exhibitions: Gallery 24 1986, Albermarle Gallery 1987 and 1988; gp exhibitions: Artist of The Day (Angela Flowers Gallery) 1985, Albemarle Gallery 1987 and 1991, Contemporary Art Soc Art Market 1988–89; *Recreations* collecting tribal art, carpet croquet, travelling; *Style*— Aaron Kasmin, Esq; ✉ 49 Bishops Mansions, Bishops Park Road, London SW6 6DZ

KASPSZYK, Jacek; *b* 1952; *Career* conductor; debut aged 14, studied in Warsaw, Warsaw Opera debut 1975, international debut Düsseldorf Opera 1976, US debut NY 1978, UK debut Royal Festival Hall 1980; princ conductor Polish Nat Radio Symphony Orch 1977–82 (music dir 1980–82), princ conductor Wren Orch 1983–91, princ conductor and artistic advsr North Netherlands Orch 1991–, princ guest conductor English Sinfonia 1992–; worked with orchs incl: Berlin Philharmonic, French National, Stockholm Philharmonic, Bavarian Radio Symphony, Rotterdam Philharmonic, Czech Philharmonic, Hallé, Bournemouth Symphony, Scottish Nat, Ulster Orch, BBC Scottish and Welsh Symphony Orchs, Northern Sinfonia, Scottish Chamber, Cincinnati Symphony, San Diego Symphony, Calgary Philharmonic, Oslo Philharmonic, Orchestre National de France, Spanish Nat, Danish Radio, New Swiss Philharmonic (incl 1987 Euro tour), Vienna Symphony, Berlin Radio Symphony, Yomiuri Nippon, London Philharmonic, Philharmonia, London Symphony Orch, Royal Philharmonic Orch; appeared at venues incl: La Scala Milan, various London venues, Paris, Linz, Musikverein Vienna, the Netherlands, Australia, Japan, N America, Scandinavia; *Opera* work incl: A Midsummer Night's Dream (Lyons Opera), Eugene Onegin (Bordeaux), The Magic Flute (Opera Comique Paris, Stockholm Opera), The Seven Deadly Sins (Lyons), Die Fledermaus (Scottish Opera), The Flying Dutchman (Opera North), The Barber of Seville (ENO); *Recordings* incl: Il Signor Bruschino (with Warsaw Chamber Opera, first complete recording in Italian), various with London Philharmonic, London Symphony Orch, Royal Philharmonic Orch, Philharmonia; *Style*— Mr Jacek Kaspszyk; ✉ c/o English Sinfonia, 5 Park Mews, Sandy, Beds SG19 1JB (☎ 01767 691006, fax 01767 691012)

KATIN, Peter Roy; s of Jerrold Katin (d 1991), and Gertrude May Katin (d 1975); *b* 14 Nov 1930; *Educ* RAM; *Career* pianist; musical talent evident at age of four, admitted to RAM at age of twelve; debut: Wigmore Hall 1948, Henry Wood Promenade Concert (with Tchaikovsky's second Concerto) 1952; first postwar Br artist to make a solo tour of the USSR 1958; early influences incl: Clifford Curzon, Claudio Arrau, Myra Hess; recordings incl: complete Mozart Sonatas, Chopin Nocturnes and Impromptus, complete Chopin Waltzes and Polonaises, complete Grieg Lyric Pieces, Clementi, Schubert and Chopin (on square piano), works by Schubert, Liszt, Tchaikovsky, Schumann, Rachmaninov, Brahms, Scarlatti and Mendelssohn; composer of various piano pieces and songs, the song cycle Sequence (words by Charlotte Morrow) and various cadenzas to Beethoven and Mozart Concertos; series of subscription recitals and master classes for young artists 1968–78, prof RAM 1956–60, visiting prof Univ of W Ontario 1978–84, prof RCM 1992–; writer of articles on various aspects of music-making and composing, currently writing autobiography; Hon DMus RAM 1994; ARCM 1952, FRAM 1960; *Awards* Eric Brough Meml prize 1942, Chopin Arts Award 1977; *Recreations* theatre, literature, writing, photography, record collections; *Style*— Peter Katin, Esq; ✉ Maureen Lunn Management, Top Farm, Parish Lane, Hedgerley, Bucks SL2 3JH (☎ 01753 645008, fax 01753 647431)

KATZ, Alan Jacob; s of Berl Katz, and Edith Lena, *née* Seidel; *b* 29 Sept 1945; *Educ* Salford GS, LSE (BSc); *m* Susan Ernesta, *née* Rees; 2 da (Nicola b 6 March 1977, Joanna b 8 Dec 1979); *Career* CA; Arthur Andersen: articled clerk 1966–69, mangr 1972–78, ptnr 1978–; memb: ICA 1969, IPA 1989, SPI 1991; *Recreations* walking, swimming, theatre; *Clubs* St James (Manchester); *Style*— Alan Katz, Esq; ✉ Arthur Andersen, St Paul's House, Park Square, Leeds LS1 2PJ (☎ 0113 243 8222, fax 0113 245 9240)

KATZ, Sir Bernard; kt (1969); s of Max Katz (d 1971); *b* 26 March 1911; *Educ* Univ of Leipzig (MD), Univ of London (PhD, DSc); *m* 1945, Marguerite Penly; 2 s; *Career* served WWII Flt Lt RAAF; prof and head of Biophysics Dept UCL 1952–78, emeritus prof 1978–; Nobel prize (jtly) for Physiology and Medicine 1970; FRS 1952; *Style*— Sir Bernard Katz, FRS; ✉ University College, London WC1E 6BT (☎ 0171 387 7050)

KAUFFMANN, Prof C Michael; s of Arthur Kauffmann (d 1983), and Tamara, *née* Karp (d 1977); *b* 5 Feb 1931; *Educ* St Paul's, Merton Coll Oxford (Postmaster), Warburg Inst Univ of London (jr res fell, PhD); *m* 1954, Dorothea, *née* Hill; 2 s (Francis b 1957, Martin b 1962); *Career* asst curator Photographic Collection Warburg Inst 1957 (jr research fell 1953–55), keeper Manchester City Art Gallery 1958–60; V & A Museum: asst keeper 1960–75, asst to the Dir 1963–66, keeper Dept of Prints & Drawings and Paintings 1975–85, prof of history of art and dir Courtauld Inst of Art Univ of London 1985–95, ret; FBA 1987, FMA, FSA; *Books* The Baths of Pozzuoli: Medieval Illuminations of Peter of Eboli's Poem (1959), An Altar-piece of the Apocalypse (1968), Victoria & Albert Museum Catalogue of Foreign Paintings (2 vols, 1973), British Romanesque Manuscripts 1066–1190 (1975), Catalogue of Paintings in the Wellington Museum (1982), John Varley 1778–1884 (1984), Studies in Medieval Art (1992); *Clubs* Ealing-Acton Labour Party; *Style*— Prof C M Kauffmann, FSA, FBA

KAUFMAN, Rt Hon Gerald Bernard; PC (1978), MP (Lab) Manchester Gorton (majority 16,279); s of Louis Kaufman, and Jane Kaufman; *b* 21 June 1930; *Educ* Leeds GS, Queen's Coll Oxford; *Career* political staff Daily Mirror 1955–64, political corr New Statesman 1964–65, Lab Pty press liaison offr 1965–70; MP (Lab): Manchester Ardwick 1970–83, Manchester Gorton 1983–; Parly under sec Environment 1974–75, Parly under sec Indust 1975, min of state Dept of Indust 1975–79; oppn front bench spokesman and memb Shadow Cabinet: Environment 1980–83, Home Affrs 1983–87, Foreign and Cwlth Affairs 1987–92; memb Labour Party Nat Exec Ctee 1991–92, chm House of Commons Nat Heritage Ctee 1992–; *Style*— The Rt Hon Gerald Kaufman, MP; ✉ 87 Charlbert Court, Eamont St, London NW8 (☎ 0171 219 3000)

KAUKAS, Bernard Aloysius; MBE (1984); s of Joseph Kaukas (d 1964), of Stamford Hill, and Ethel Mary, *née* Morgan-Adlam (d 1979); *b* 30 July 1922; *Educ* St Ignatius Coll Stamford Hill, Northern Poly London (DipArch); *m* 23 May 1945, Pamela Dora, da of David Widdowson, MBE (d 1980), of Hampstead Garden Suburb; 1 s (Christopher David b 6 Sept 1946), 1 da (Amanda Mary (Mrs Burroughs) b 18 June 1954); *Career* RN 1941–46; MCC 1952–54, LCC 1954–56, private practice 1956–59, Br Tport Cmmn 1959–64; BR Bd: planning offr 1964–68, chief architect 1968–74, devpt dir Property Bd 1974–77, dir of environment 1977–84; planning conslt to Michael Burroughs Assoc 1984–; memb Int Cncl on Monuments and Sites; fell Science Museum 1984–89; ARIBA

1952, FRSA 1977; *Recreations* painting, writing, collecting; *Clubs* Savage; *Style*— Bernard Kaukas, Esq, MBE; ✉ 13 Lynwood Road, Ealing, London W5 1JQ (☎ 0181 998 1499)

KAVANAGH, Prof Dennis Anthony; s of Patrick Joseph Kavanagh, and Agnes, *née* Campbell; *b* 27 March 1941; *Educ* St Anselm's Coll, Univ of Manchester (BA, MA); *m* 13 Aug 1966, Monica Anne, *née* Taylor; 1 s (David b 20 Nov 1970), 3 da (Jane b 24 July 1968, Catherine b 4 Nov 1972, Helen b 3 Jan 1981); *Career* former prof of politics and head Dept of Politics Univ of Nottingham, currently prof of politics Univ of Liverpool; visiting prof: European Univ Inst Florence 1977, Univ of Stanford California 1985; memb ESRC; *Books include* Constituency Electioneering, The British General Election of February 1974 (with Dr David Butler, *qv*), The British General Election of 1979 (with David Butler), British Politics Today (with W Jones), New Trends in British Politics (ed, with Richard Rose), The Politics of the Labour Party (ed), Political Science and Political Behaviour, The British General Election 1983 (with David Butler), Thatcherism and British Politics, The British General Election of 1987 (with David Butler), Consensus Politics from Attlee to Thatcher (with Peter Morris), The Thatcher Effect (ed, with Anthony Seldon), Comparative Government and Politics, Personalities and Politics, The British General Election of 1992 (with David Butler), The Major Effect (with Anthony Seldon), Electoral Politics, The New Marketing of Politics; *Recreations* running, tennis; *Style*— Prof Dennis Kavanagh; ✉ Politics Department, Liverpool University, Roxby Building, PO Box 147, Liverpool L69 3BX (☎ 0151 794 2889)

KAVANAGH, Patrick Joseph; s of H E (Ted) Kavanagh (d 1958), and Agnes O'Keefe (d 1985); *b* 6 Jan 1931; *Educ* Douai Sch, Lycée Jaccard, Merton Coll Oxford (MA); *m* 1, 1956, Sally (d 1958), da of Hon Mrs R N Philipps (Rosamond Lehmann), and Wogan Philipps (Lord Milford); m 2, 1965, Catherine, da of Sir John Ward, GCMG, of St Margaret's Bay, Kent; 2 s (Cornelius b 1966, Bruno b 1969); *Career* writer; actor 1959–70, columnist The Spectator 1983–96, columnist Times Lit Supplement 1996–; FRSL; *Poetry* One and One (1960), On the Way to the Depot (1977), About Time (1970), Edward Thomas in Heaven (1974), Life Before Death (1979), Selected Poems (1982), Presences (1987), An Enchantment (1991), Collected Poems (1992); *Novels* A Song and Dance (1968, Guardian Fiction Prize), A Happy Man (1972), People and Weather (1979), Only by Mistake (1986), The Perfect Stranger (autobiography, Richard Hillary Prize 1966); *Children's books* Scarf Jack (1978), Rebel for Good (1980); *Anthologies* ed: Collected Poems of Ivor Gurney (1982), The Essential G K Chesterton (1985), Oxford Book of Short Poems (with James Michie), A Book of Consolations (1992), Voices in Ireland - A Literary Companion (1994); *Essays* People and Places (1988); *Travel* Finding Connections (1990); *Style*— P J Kavanagh, FRSL; ✉ Peters Fraser & Dunlop, 5th Floor, The Chambers, Chelsea Harbour, Lots Rd, London SW10 0XT

KAVANAGH, Paul; *b* 14 Dec 1966; *Career* radio presenter 1980–85, head of music Radio Nova 1985–86, prog dir Sunshine 101 Dublin 1986–89, gen mangr and dir Atlantic 252 1994–96 (prog dir 1989–94), gp prog dir EMAP Radio 1996–; *Style*— Paul Kavanagh, Esq; ✉ EMAP Radio, Castle Quay, Castlefield, Manchester M15 4PR (☎ 0161 288 5000)

KAVANAGH, Peter Richard Michael; s of Patrick Bernard Kavanagh, CBE, QPM, of Epsom, and Beryl Annie, *née* Williams (d 1984); *b* 20 Feb 1959; *Educ* Wimbledon Coll, Gonville and Caius Coll Cambridge (BA, MA); *m* 16 Nov 1985, Vivien Mary, da of Gordon Samuel Hart, of Bromham, Bedfordshire; 1 da (Emma b 1988); *Career* admitted slr 1984; ptnr Theodore Goddard 1989– (currently head Corp Gp); memb Law Soc; *Style*— Peter Kavanagh, Esq; ✉ Theodore Goddard, 150 Aldersgate St, London EC1A 4EJ (☎ 0171 606 8855, fax 0171 606 4390)

KAVANAGH, Trevor Michael Thomas; s of Bernard George Kavanagh (d 1978), and Alice Rose, *née* Thompson; *b* 19 Jan 1943; *Educ* Reigate GS; *m* 1967, Jacqueline Gai, da of John Swindells; 2 s (Benjamin b 14 June 1969, Simon John b 20 March 1971); *Career* currently political ed The Sun; chm The Lobby House of Commons Westminster 1990–91; *Recreations* golf, swimming; *Clubs* RAC, Pall Mall; *Style*— Trevor Kavanagh, Esq; ✉ The Sun, 1 Virginia St, London E1 9XP (☎ 0171 782 4000)

KAY, Sir Andrew Watt; kt (1973); s of David Watt Kay; *b* 14 Aug 1916; *Educ* Ayr Acad, Univ of Glasgow (MD, ChM, DSc); *m* 1, 1943, Janetta Main Roxburgh; 2 s, 2 da; m 2, 1992, Phyllis Gillies; *Career* served WWII Maj RAMC; prof of surgery Univ of Sheffield 1958–64, regius prof of surgery Univ of Glasgow 1964–81, pt/t chief scientist Scottish Home and Health Dept 1973–81, chm Scottish Hosp Endowments Res Tst 1982–89; FRCS, FRSE 1971, Hon DSc, FRACS, FACS, FCM (S Africa), FRCSI, FRCS (Canada); *Books* Textbook of Surgical Physiology; *Recreations* gardening; *Style*— Sir Andrew Kay, FRSE; ✉ 5 Loch Road, Milngavie, Glasgow G62 8BB (☎ 0141 956 3378)

KAY, Prof (Anthony) Barrington (Barry); s of Anthony Chambers, and Eva Gertrude, *née* Pearcey (later Mrs Kay, now Mrs Reuben); *b* 23 June 1939; *Educ* King's Sch Peterborough, Univ of Edinburgh (MB ChB, DSc), Jesus Coll Cambridge (MA, PhD), Harvard Med Sch; *m* 1966, Rosemary Margaret, da of Hugh Johnstone; 3 da (Emma Rosalind b 21 Sept 1968, Rebecca b 13 May 1975, Eleanor Elizabeth b 19 Nov 1976); *Career* various posts as house physician and surgn City and Eastern Gen Hosps Edinburgh 1963; student Univ of Cambridge 1964–65; house physician City Hosp Edinburgh 1965–66; post grad student Dept of Pathology Univ of Cambridge and hon registrar Addenbrooke's Hosp Cambridge 1966–69; research fell Harvard Med Sch at Robert B Brigham Hosp Boston 1969–71; Univ of Edinburgh: lectr in respiratory diseases 1971–74, pt/t sr lectr 1974–76, sr lectr in experimental pathology 1977–79, reader Dept of Pathology 1979–80; dep dir and conslt Immunology Div SE Scot Regnl Blood Transfusion Serv Royal Infirmary Edinburgh 1974–76; currently prof of clinical immunology and dir Dept of Allergy and Clinical Immunology Nat Heart and Lung Inst London 1980–; hon conslt physician Royal Brompton and Nat Heart and Lung Hosp 1980–; pres: Euro Acad of Allergology and Clinical Immunology 1989–92, Br Soc of Allergy and Clinical Immunology 1993–; T K Stubbins research fell RCP 1969–71; scientific achievement award Int Assoc of Allergology and Clinical Immunology 1991; hon fell American College of Allergy 1986; hon memb: American Assoc of Physicians 1988, Hungarian Soc of Allergology and Clinical Immunology 1990, Swiss Soc of Allergology and Clinical Immunology 1991; FRCPE 1975, FRCP 1980, FRCPath 1989, FRSE 1993; *Books* Clinical and Experimental Allergy (co-ed, since 1984), Asthma: Clinical Pharmacology and Therapeutic Progress (ed, 1986), Allergy and Inflammation (ed, 1987), Allergic Basis of Asthma (ed, 1988), Allergy and Asthma: New Trends and Approaches to Therapy (ed, 1989), Eosinophils, Allergy and Asthma (ed, 1990), Eosinophils in Allergy and Inflammation (ed, 1993), Allergy and Allergic Diseases (ed, 1997); also numerous scientific articles on asthma and allergy; *Recreations* Baroque and modern bassoon, tennis, country walks; *Clubs* Hurlingham; *Style*— Prof Barry Kay, FRSE; ✉ Stamford Brook House, 12 Stamford Brook Avenue, London W6 0YD (☎ 0181 741 5899, fax 0181 563 0074); National Heart and Lung Institute, Royal Brompton Hospital, Dovehouse Street, London SW3 6NP (☎ 0171 351 8181, fax 0171 376 3138)

KAY, Brian Christopher; s of Noel Bancroft Kay (d 1980), of York, and Gwendoline, *née* Sutton; *b* 12 May 1944; *Educ* Rydal Sch, King's Coll Cambridge (choral scholar), New Coll Oxford; *m* 1, 1970, Sally, *née* Lyne; 1 s (Jonathan b 22 June 1973), 1 da (Charlotte Joanna b 24 Feb 1975); m 2, 1983, Gillian Elizabeth Fisher, *qv*; *Career* conductor, singer, radio and TV presenter; fndr memb and bass The King's Singers 1968–82, chorus master Huddersfield Choral Soc 1984–93, freelance singer various vocal gps incl John Alldis Choir, London Voices and BBC Singers; conductor: Cecilian Singers of Leicester 1987–91, Cheltenham Bach Choir 1989–97, Leith Hill Musical Festival 1996–; presenter various BBC progs incl: Cardiff Singer of the World (BBC TV), Choir of the Year (BBC TV), Mainly for Pleasure (Radio 3) 1983–91, Music in Mind (weekly prog Radio 4) 1989–96, arts prog Radio 2, Record Review (World Serv), Brian Kay's Sunday Morning (Radio 3) 1992–, Classics with Kay (weekly prog Radio 4) 1996–, Comparing Notes (Radio 4) 1996–; Music Presenter of the Year Award Sony Radio Awards 1996; appeared in feature film Amadeus as voice of Schickenaeder; lay vicar Westminster Abbey 1968–71; pres: Harrogate Choral Soc, Market Harborough Singers, Nottingham Choral Tst, Friends of the Llangollen Int Music Festival, Derbyshire Singers, Bristol Bach Choir; vice pres: Stars Orgn for Spastics, Assoc of Br Choral Dirs; vice chm Young Persons' Concert Fndn; *Recreations* reading, gardening, the local pub; *Style*— Brian Kay, Esq

KAY, Dr Clifford Ralph; CBE (1977); s of Maurice Witt Kay (d 1971), of Chester, and Fay Celia Kay (d 1992); *b* 17 Oct 1927; *Educ* King's Sch Chester, Univ of Liverpool (MB ChB, MD), Univ of Manchester (PhD); *m* 1950, Yvette Adele, da of Maurice Hytner; 1 s (Roger Neil b 1952), 1 da (Alison Jane b 1954); *Career* Nat Serv Sqdn Ldr RAF Med Branch 1952–53; fndr of gen practice Didsbury 1955–95 (became Barlow Med Centre 1971), md Bd of Mgmnt Barlow Med Centre 1990–95; travelling lectr in gen practice research Canada 1970; pt/t sr research fell Dept of Gen Practice Univ of Manchester 1971– (hon sr research fell 1992–), conslt NHS Exec for pilot trial of barcoded prescription printing in gen practice 1994–; WHO temp conslt on contraceptive research Indian Cncl for Med Research 1972, (Br Cncl) advsr Danish Med Research Cncl on the initiation of a Gen Practice Research Unit in Denmark 1978, expert advsr to Chief Scientist DHSS 1973–76; memb: UK Health Servs Research Bd 1973–76, Clinical Research Advsy Ctee NW RHA 1972–82, MRC Advsy Ctee on Hormone Replacement Therapy 1977–82, Research Ctee World Orgn of Nat Colls and Academies of Gen Practice 1979–83, MRC Contraceptive Clinical Research Ctee 1983–87, NHS Exec Info Mgmnt and Technol Forum 1985–; non-exec dir Stockport Healthcare NHS Tst 1996–; RCGP: memb NW England Faculty Bd 1953–95 (provost 1991–92), pt/t dir Manchester Research Unit 1968– (conslt 1994–), memb Cncl 1970–95, memb Scientific Fndn Bd 1970–82, chm Research Ctee 1973–82, exec dir Meds Surveillance Orgn 1981–; author of numerous original papers in academic jls; Sir Charles Hastings Research Prize BMA 1961, Mackenzie Medal RCPEd 1975, travelling lectr in gen practice research SA 1975, Fndn Cncl Award RCGP 1978, Mackenzie lectr RCGP 1979, Gregory Pincus Meml Lecture Detroit USA 1982, Jane Berry Meml Lecture Southampton 1984, visiting professorship Univs of Edmonton and Calgary 1987, Hippocrates Medal (Societas Internationalis Medicinae Generalis for outstanding contrib to gen practice in Europe) 1990, George Swift Meml Lecture Portsmouth 1992; pres Manchester Med Soc 1988–89; FRCGP 1971 (MRCGP 1958); hon fell Faculty of Family Planning and Reproductive Health RCOG 1994; *Recreations* photography, gardening, sailing; *Style*— Dr Clifford Kay, CBE; ✉ 12 Dene Park, Didsbury, Manchester M20 2GF (☎ 0161 445 9686, fax 0161 434 2040, e-mail 100530,262@compuserve.com)

KAY, Jason (JK); *b* 1971; *Career* lead singer with Jamiroquai; albums: Emergency On Planet Earth (debut, 1993, UK no 1), Return of the Space Cowboy (1994, UK no 2), Travelling Without Moving (1996, UK no 2); top ten singles: Too Young To Die, Blow Your Mind, Return of the Space Cowboy, Virtual Insanity, Cosmic Girl; *Recreations* classic cars; *Style*— Jason Kay, Esq; ✉ c/o Dave Woolf, 4th Floor, 180–182 Tottenham Court Road, London W1P 9LE (☎ and fax 0171 436 5529)

KAY, (Robert) Jervis; QC (1996); s of Philip Jervis Kay, VRD, of Suffolk, and late Pamela, *née* Carter; *Educ* Wellington, Univ of Nottingham (LLB); *m* 1, 1975 (m dis 1986), Rosemary, da of late Dr Arthur Pollard; m 2, 1988, Henrietta Kathleen, da of Maj Guy Ward, RA; 3 da (Pamela Felicity Iona b 1988, Katherine Elizabeth Skye b 1992, Lucinda Valentine Ailsa b 1995), 1 s (Philip Alexander Guy b 1990); *Career* called to the Bar Lincoln's Inn 1972, called to the Bar of NSW 1984, specialist in admty and commercial shipping; memb Ctee London Common Law & Commercial Bar Assoc; memb: Br Maritime Law Assoc, Commercial Bar Assoc, London Maritime Arbitrators' Assoc (supporting); *Books* Atkins Court Forms (ed Vol 3, Admiralty, 1979, 1990 and 1994); *Recreations* sailing, cricket; *Clubs* Turf, MCC, Royal London Yacht, Royal Ocean Racing, Bar Yacht; *Style*— Jervis Kay, Esq, QC; ✉ 4 Field Court, Gray's Inn, London WC1R 5EA

KAY, Prof John Anderson; s of James Scobie Kay (d 1983), of Edinburgh, and Allison, *née* Anderson; *b* 3 Aug 1948; *Educ* Royal HS Edinburgh, Univ of Edinburgh (MA), Nuffield Coll Oxford (MA); *m* 1986, Deborah, da of Raymond Freeman; *Career* Univ of Oxford: fell St John's Coll Oxford 1970–, univ lectr in economics 1971–79; Inst for Fiscal Studies: research dir 1979–82, dir 1982–86; London Business Sch: prof of economics 1986–96, dir Centre for Business Strategy 1986–91; dir Sch of Mgmnt Studies Univ of Oxford 1997–; chm London Economics 1986–96; dir: Govett Strategic Investment Trust plc 1982–95, Investors' Compensation Scheme 1991–95, Halifax Building Society 1991–, Foreign & Colonial Special Utilities Investment Trust plc 1993–, Undervalued Assets Trust plc 1994–, Value and Income Trust plc 1994–; memb Cncl and Exec Ctee NIESR, bd memb Social Market Fndn 1992–94; *Books* Concentration in Modern Industry (with L Hannah, 1977), The Reform of Social Security (with A W Dilnot and C N Morris, 1984), The Economic Analysis of Accounting Profitability (with J Edwards and C Mayer, 1987), The British Tax System (with M A King, 1989), Foundations of Corporate Success (1993), The Business of Economics (1996); *Recreations* travelling, walking; *Style*— Prof John Kay; ✉ London Economics, 66 Chiltern Street, London W1M 1PR (☎ 0171 446 8400, fax 0171 446 8484/5)

KAY, Hon Mr Justice; Hon Sir John William Kay; kt (1992); s of Christopher Herbert Kay (d 1970), of Blundellsands, nr Liverpool, and Ida Muriel, *née* Harper; *b* 13 Sept 1943; *Educ* Denstone Coll, Christ's Coll Cambridge (MA); *m* 13 Aug 1966, Jeffa, da of Maj Graham Bourke Connell, MBE (d 1968); 1 s (Benedict b 1975), 2 da (Amanda b 1969, Tiffany b 1971); *Career* called to the Bar Gray's Inn 1968, bencher 1992; tutor in law Univ of Liverpool 1968–69, in practice Northern Circuit 1968–92, recorder of the Crown Ct 1982–92, QC 1984, judge of the High Court of Justice (Queen's Bench Div) 1992–, presiding judge Northern Circuit 1994–; memb Gen Cncl of the Bar 1988–92; pres Waterloo RUFC 1995–; *Recreations* gardening, genealogy, horse racing; *Style*— The Hon Mr Justice Kay; ✉ The Royal Courts of Justice, The Strand, London WC2A 2LL

KAY, Hon Mr Justice; Hon Sir Maurice Ralph; kt (1995); s of Ralph Kay (d 1981), of Knutsford, and Hylda Jones; *b* 6 Dec 1942; *Educ* William Hulmes GS Manchester, Univ of Sheffield (LLB, PhD); *m* 24 July 1968, Margaret Angela, da of Joseph Bernard Alcock, of Formby (d 1985); 4 s (Jonathan b 1969, Dominic b 1971, Oliver b 1975, Tristan b 1982); *Career* lectr: Univ of Hull 1967–72, Univ of Manchester 1972–73; prof of law Univ of Keele 1973–83; called to the Bar Gray's Inn 1975, QC 1988, recorder of the Crown Court 1988–95 (asst recorder 1987–88), a judge of the High Court of Justice (Queen's Bench Div) 1995–, a judge of the Employment Appeal Tbnl 1995–, a presiding judge of the Wales & Chester Circuit 1996–; memb Gray's Inn, bencher 1995; ed and contrib legal text books; *Recreations* music, theatre, sport; *Clubs* Reform; *Style*— The Hon Mr Justice Maurice Kay; ✉ c/o Royal Courts of Justice, Strand, London WC2A 2LL

KAY, Neville Rupert Mason; TD; s of Hubert Maurice Kay (d 1990), and Moira Fredricka, *née* Mason (d 1985); *b* 22 June 1934; *Educ* High Pavement GS Nottingham, Univ of Sheffield (LRCMPS); *m* 14 Nov 1958, Josephine, da of late Horace Alcock, of Pocklington; 1 s (Christopher b 1962), 2 da (Suzanne b 1959, Sarah b 1978); *Career* MO

Flt Lt RAF 1980–84, currently Lt-Col RAMC (TA); conslt orthopaedic surgn Claremont Hosp Sheffield and Thornbury Hosp Sheffield (formerly Royal Hallamshire Hosp, King Edward VII Orthopaedic Hosp Rivelin); former hon lectr in orthopaedics Univ of Sheffield, former pres S Yorks Medico-Legal Soc 1984; fell Br Orthopaedic Assoc, FRCS; *Books* Complications of Total Joint Replacement (1985); *Recreations* skiing, hill walking; *Style*— Mr Neville Kay, TD; ✉ Westwood House, 11 Brocco Bank, Sheffield S11 8RQ (☎ 0114 266 2988)

KAY, Susan Elaine; da of Donald Jackson Hodgson, of Manchester, and Joyce, *née* Martyn; *b* 24 June 1952; *Educ* Brookway HS Manchester, Mather Coll of Educn (Cert in Teaching), Univ of Manchester (BEd); *m* 1974, Norman Kay, s of Norman Kay (d 1975); 1 s (Tristan Andrew b 18 Feb 1979), 1 da (Sarah Elizabeth b 23 April 1982); *Career* author; infant sch teacher until 1979; *Books* Legacy (1985, Historical Novel prize in memory of Georgette Heyer 1985, Betty Trask Award for a first novel 1985), Phantom (1990, winner Romantic Novel of the Year Award 1991, ALA Best Book for Young Adults Award 1991); *Recreations* theatre, craft work, writing; *Style*— Mrs Susan Kay; ✉ c/o Heather Jeeves, 9 Dryden Place, Edinburgh EH9 1RP (☎ 0131 668 3859)

KAY, Thomas Anthony (Tony); *Career* admitted barr and slr NZ 1961, in practice until 1968; admitted slr England 1969, in practice London 1969–; Norton Rose: managing ptnr 1987–93, sr ptnr 1994–, chm Norton Rose M5 Gp 1995–; various non-exec positions Nat Autistic Soc (currently chm Supervisory Cncl); *Style*— Tony Kay, Esq; ✉ Norton Rose, Kempson House, Camomile Street, London EC3A 7AN (☎ 0171 283 6000, fax 0171 283 6500)

KAY, William John; s of William Jarvie Kay (d 1988), and Agnes Sutherland Walker; *b* 12 Sept 1946; *Educ* Westminster City Sch, The Queen's Coll Oxford (Open Scholar, MA); *m* 1968 (m dis 1986), Deborah Stacy, *née* Rosen; 2 s (Andrew James b 15 Aug 1972, Benjamin William Matthew b 3 Nov 1973); *Career* fin journalist: London Evening News 1968–72, London Evening Standard 1972–77, Daily Telegraph 1977–79; features ed Financial Weekly 1979, dep business ed Now magazine 1979–81, fin writer The Sunday Times Business News 1981–84, City ed The Times 1984–86, freelance journalist (The Times, The Sunday Times, The Sunday Telegraph, The Independent, Independent on Sunday and Mail on Sunday) 1986–95, fin ed Independent on Sunday 1995, City ed Mail on Sunday 1995–; *Books* A-Z Guide to Money (1983), Tycoons (1985), Big Bang (1986), The Stock Exchange: A Marketplace for Tomorrow (The Stock Exchange, ed, 1986), Battle For the High Street (1987), Nightmare - The Ernest Saunders Story (ghosted, by-line James Saunders, 1989), Modern Merchant Banking (ed, 1990), The City and the Single European Market (ed, 1991), Charity Appeals (ghosted, by-line Marion Allford, 1993), The Bosses (1994); *Recreations* cricket, golf, travel, good food; *Clubs* MCC, Hendon Golf; *Style*— William Kay, Esq; ✉ The Mail on Sunday, Associated Newspapers, Northcliffe House, 2 Derry Street, Kensington, London W8 5TS (☎ 0171 938 6878, fax 0171 795 6437)

KAYE, *see:* Lister-Kaye

KAYE, Alan; s of Wallace Kaye (d 1978), of Horwich, and Nellie Elizabeth, *née* Cookson; *b* 24 June 1936; *Educ* Rivington and Blackrod GS; *m* 21 June 1958, Betty, da of Ernest Rainford (d 1970), of Adlington, Lancs; 1 s (Andrew b 1960), 1 da (Janet b 1961); *Career* dep gen mangr Filter Div Automotive Products plc 1969–70; Dobson Park Industries plc (taken over by Harnischfeger Industries Inc 1995): chief exec Mining Equipment Div 1974–80 (fin dir 1970–74), dep chief exec 1984, chief exec 1985–92, chm 1991–95, ret; non-exec dir M & G Equity Investment Trust PLC 1996–; FCIS, FCIMA; *Recreations* gardening, music, reading, walking; *Style*— Alan Kaye, Esq; ✉ Mill Hill Farm, Mill Lane, Goosnargh, Preston, Lancs PR3 2JX (☎ 01722 865014, fax 01722 863185)

KAYE, David Raymond; s of Michael Kaye (d 1981), and Elizabeth, *née* Wasserman; *b* 29 March 1932; *Educ* Nottingham HS, St Paul's, Univ of Cambridge (MA), Univ of Michigan USA, Univ of Oxford (Dip in Stats); *m* 15 Oct 1966, Sara Frances, da of Edwyn Lyte (d 1979); 2 s (James b 1970, George b 1972), 1 da (Sophie b 1967); *Career* 2 Lt RA 1952; Shell International Petroleum 1958–62, ptnr Andersen Consulting 1967–90 (joined 1962), dean City Univ Business Sch 1992–; FSS, FIMC; *Books* Gamechange: the impact of information technology on corporate strategies and structures: a boardroom agenda (1989); *Recreations* walking, sculpture; *Clubs* Athenaeum; *Style*— David Kaye, Esq; ✉ 37 Wood Lane, London N6 5UD (☎ 0181 340 1624); Middle Howton, Howton, Moretonhampstead, Devon TQ13 8PP (☎ and fax 01647 440147); City University Business School, Frobisher Crescent, Barbican Centre, London EC2Y 8HB (☎ 0171 477 8601, fax 0171 477 8899)

KAYE, Sir Emmanuel; CBE (1967); *b* 29 Nov 1914; *Educ* Richmond Hill Sch, Twickenham Tech; *m* 1946, Elizabeth, *née* Cutler; 1 s, 2 da; *Career* jt fndr chm Lansing Bagnall Ltd 1943–89, fndr chm The Kaye Organisation Ltd 1966–89, Kaye Steel Stockholders Ltd 1978–95, Hart Ventures plc 1989–, pres Lansing Linde Ltd 1989–, fndr chm Kaye Enterprises Ltd 1989–, Elvetham Hall Ltd; memb Econ and Fin Policy Ctee CBI 1985–91; chm Thrombosis Res Tst and fndr chm Thrombosis Res Inst 1990–; Liveryman Worshipful Co of Farriers; FIMgt, FRSA; *Clubs* Brooks's; *Style*— Sir Emmanuel Kaye, CBE

KAYE, Dr Georges Sabry; s of Dr Georges Kaye, of Beirut, The Lebanon, and Claire, *née* De las Case; *b* 21 May 1949; *Educ* Villa St Jean, Fribourg, Ratcliffe, King's Coll London (BSc), Westminster Hosp Med Sch (MB BS); *m* 1992, Dr Stephanie Anne O'Mahony; *Career* physician i/c Occupational Health Dept Cromwell Hosp 1982–; Euro med dir to General Electric Co; currently co physician to: Salomon Bros International, Air France, Hill Samuel Financial Services, Claris International; memb International Commission on Occupational Health; memb BMA and Royal Soc of Med 1974; *Books* La Soif (The Thirst) (1976); *Recreations* French literature, lute playing; *Clubs* The Reform; *Style*— Dr Georges Kaye; ✉ 2 Pennant Mews, London W8 5JN (☎ 0171 460 2000, fax 0171 370 4633); Braco Castle, Perthshire

KAYE, Jeremy Robin; s of Kenneth Brown Kaye (d 1985), of Doncaster, and Hannah Eleanor Christabel, *née* Scott (d 1991); *b* 25 Sept 1937; *Educ* Eastbourne Coll, Worcester Coll Oxford (MA); *Career* Nat Serv Bombardier RA 1956–58; called to the Bar Inner Temple 1962; asst sec Limmer and Trinidad Lake Asphalt Co Ltd 1962–67, chief legal offr and asst sec Limmer Holdings Ltd 1967–72; sec: Arbuthnot Latham Holdings Ltd 1975–81, Dow Scandia Holdings Ltd 1982–86, Secure Trust Group plc 1987–, Arbuthnot Fund Managers Ltd 1987–; dir: Arbuthnot Latham Bank Ltd 1984–91 (sec 1973–91); lay chm East Grinstead Deanery 1977–87 (sec 1967–77, treas 1993–); memb: Chichester Diocesan Synod 1970–73 and 1988–, Chichester Diocesan Bd of Finance 1992–; FCIS; *Recreations* gardening, cricket, golf; *Clubs* MCC, Holtye Golf; *Style*— Jeremy Kaye, Esq; ✉ Mallards, 52 Moat Road, East Grinstead, West Sussex RH19 3LH (☎ 01342 321 294); Royex House, Aldermanbury Square, London EC2V 7HR (☎ 0171 600 3831, fax 0171 626 7041)

KAYE, Laurence Martin; s of Moss Kaye, and Beatrice, *née* Herman; *b* 1 Sept 1949; *Educ* Haberdashers' Aske's, Sydney Sussex Coll Cambridge (Whittaker scholar, MA); *m* 1 July 1976, Lauren Merrill, *née* Shaymow; 1 s (David Benjamin b 22 Sept 1978), 1 da (Debra Ann b 16 Oct 1981); *Career* admitted slr 1975; ptnr: Brecher & Co 1977 (articled clerk 1972–75), Saunders Sobell Leigh & Dobin 1980–94, The Simkins Partnership (head of publishing and multimedia) 1994–; legal advsr to Euro Publishers' Cncl and Directory Publishers' Assoc; former chm Mount Vernon Cleft Lip and Palate Assoc Ltd, former chm Meher Baba Assoc Ltd; memb: Law Soc, Int Bar Assoc, Network 92 (assoc of law firms in Europe); *Recreations* tennis, golf, theatre, music, yoga; *Clubs* Radlett Lawn Tennis; *Style*— Laurence Kaye, Esq; ✉ The Simkins Partnership, 45–51 Whitfield Street, London W1P 6AA (☎ 0171 631 1050, fax 0171 436 2744, e-mail simkins@simkins.com)

KAYE, Mary Margaret (Mollie); da of Sir Cecil Kaye, CSI, CIE, CBE (d 1935), and late Margaret Sarah (Daisy), *née* Bryson; *Educ* The Lawn Sch Clevedon Somerset; *m* Maj-Gen Goff Hamilton, CB, CBE, DSO (d 1985); 2 da; *Career* author; illustrator of other books for children; FRSL 1990; *Books* Six Bars at Seven (1939), Potter Pinner Meadow (1937, one of a series of five Potter Pinner books), Strange Island (1940, reprinted as Death in the Andamans, 1985), Death Walks in Kashmir (1953, reprinted as Death in Kashmir, 1984), Death Walks in Berlin (1955, reprinted at Death in Berlin, 1985), Death Walks in Cyprus (1956, reprinted as Death in Cyprus, 1984), The House of Shade (1959, reprinted as Death in Zanzibar, 1983), Later Than You Think (1958, reprinted as Death in Kenya, 1983), Shadow of the Moon (1957, reprinted 1979), Trade Wind (1963, reprinted 1981), The Far Pavilions (1978), The Golden Calm (ed diary of Emily Metcalf, 1980), The Ordinary Princess (children's Book, 1980), Thistledown (1981), Moon of Other Days (ed selection of Kipling's poems, 1988), The Sun In The Morning (autobiography, vol I, 1990); omnibus edns of 'Death in-' books: Murder Abroad (1992), House of Shade (1993); *Recreations* painting; *Style*— Ms M M Kaye, FRSL; ✉ c/o David Higham Associates Ltd, 5–8 Lower John St, Golden Square, London W1R 4HA (☎ 0171 437 7888, fax 0171 437 1072)

KAYE, Michael; OBE (1991); s of Harry Kaye (d 1973), and Annie, *née* Steinberg (d 1943); *b* 27 Feb 1925; *Educ* West Ham Secdy Sch; *m* 1, 28 March 1950 (m dis 1959), Muriel, da of Barnet Greenberg (d 1973), of London; 1 da (Ann b 9 July 1952); m 2, 6 Sept 1962, Fay, da of Morris Bercovitch (d 1950), of London; *Career* REME 1943–45, Intelligence Corps 1945–47; journalist and PR exec 1947–53, PR and mktg tobacco indust 1953–61, PR mangr Rothmans Ltd 1961–74, PR dir Carreras Rothmans Group 1974–76, dir Peter Stuyvesant Fndn 1963–76, gen admin Rupert Fndn 1972–76, md LSO 1976–80, arts dir GLC 1980–83; gen admin: South Bank Concert Halls 1980–83, Young Concert Artists Tst 1983–92; festival dir City of London Festival 1984–94; chm Fin and Gen Purposes Ctee and tstee Whitechapel Art Gallery 1964–75, tstee Youth & Music 1970–78, tstee A M Purnell Charitable Tst/Bath Mozartfest 1994–; memb: Exec Ctee Carl Flesch Int Violin Competition 1989–94, Cncl Centre for Jewish Studies and Jewish-Christian Relations 1989–94; FRSA 1986; *Recreations* music, photography; *Style*— Michael Kaye, Esq, OBE; ✉ 3 Coppice Way, London E18 2DU (☎ 0181 989 1281)

KAYE, Paul; *b* 1 July 1937; *Educ* Hendon GS; *m* Adrienne; 2 s (Simon b 14 Feb 1962, Julian b 28 Feb 1964), 1 da (Suzy b 11 Feb 1967); *Career* portrait photographer; formerly employed in advtg and printing, freelance 1959–, chm Paul Kaye Studio Ltd London 1968–; photographed various heads of state worldwide, lectr in various countries on portrait photography; dir: The Family Photographers Group Ltd, Cover Shots International Ltd; chm Portrait Qualifying Panel Royal Photographic Soc, formerly chm Portrait Qualifying Panel Br Inst of Professional Photography, hon memb Fellowship Ctee BIPP; Photographic Craftsman (Cr.Photog, USA), FBIPP, FRPS, FMPA; *Publications* The Photographers Bulletin (monthly, 1988–); *Style*— Paul Kaye, Esq; ✉ Paul Kaye Studio Ltd, 20 Park Road, London NW1 4SH (☎ 0171 723 2444, fax 0171 262 5966, e-mail 101735.2726@compuserve.com)

KAYE, Maj Sir Paul Henry Gordon; 5 Bt (UK 1923), of Huddersfield, Co York; s of Sir David Alexander Gordon Kaye, 4 Bt (d 1994), and his 2 w, Adelle Frances, *née* Thomas; *b* 19 Feb 1958; *m* 1984, Sally Ann Louise; *Heir* bro, John Egidio Gordon Kaye b 1967; *Career* cmmnd RAE 1982, currently Maj Aust Intelligence Corps; memb National Party of Qld; *Recreations* rugby union, scuba diving; *Style*— Maj Sir Paul Kaye, Bt; ✉ 15 Muston Court, Carrara, Qld 4211, Australia

KAYE, Roger Godfrey; TD (1980, 1985), QC (1989); s of Anthony Harmsworth Kaye (d 1971), and Heidi Alice, *née* Jordy (d 1984); *b* 21 Sept 1946; *Educ* King's Sch Canterbury, Univ of Birmingham (LLB); *m* 15 April 1974, Melloney Rose, da of Rev H Martin Westall (d 1994); *Career* called to the Bar Lincoln's Inn 1970; jr Treasy counsel in Insolvency Matters 1978–89, dep High Ct bankruptcy registrar 1984–94, dep High Ct judge 1990–, recorder 1995–; chm: Bar Cncl Fees Collection Ctee 1990–93, Bristol and Cardiff Chancery Bar Assoc 1990–95; memb Bar Cncl Professional Conducts Ctee 1995–; dep chllr Dio of St Albans Southwark 1995–; FRSA 1995; *Recreations* going home; *Clubs* RAC, Army and Navy, Special Forces; *Style*— Roger Kaye, Esq, TD, QC; ✉ 24 Old Buildings, Lincoln's Inn, London WC2A 3UJ (☎ 0171 404 0946, fax 0171 405 1360)

KAYE, Simon; s of Isaac Kaye (d 1964), of London, and Dora, *née* Libovitch (d 1964); *b* 22 July 1935; *Educ* Wycombe Sch; *m* 8 Sept 1957, Sylvia Adrienne, da of Michael Kagan (d 1982); 2 s (Jeremy b 22 Oct 1959, Trevor b 6 May 1966), 1 da (Elaine b 24 Sept 1962); *Career* film sound recordist; entered film indust 1953, sound mixer 1962, dir Siren Sound 1967–89, recorded over 100 Br and American films; winner of Oscars (for Platoon and Last of the Mohicans), 2 other Oscar nominations (for Reds and Ghandi), 3 BAFTA Awards (for Oh! What a Lovely War, A Bridge Too Far and Cry Freedom), 10 Br Acad Award nominations (for The Charge of the Light Brigade, The Lion in Winter, Oh! What a Lovely War, Sunday Bloody Sunday, A Bridge Too Far, Reds, Ghandi, Indiana Jones and the Temple of Doom, Cry Freedom and Last of the Mohicans); *Style*— Simon Kaye, Esq; ✉ 39 Bellfield Avenue, Harrow Weald, Middx HA3 6ST (☎ 0181 428 4823)

KAYE, Prof Stanley Bernard; *b* 5 Sept 1948; *Educ* Roundhay Sch Leeds, Charing Cross Hosp Med Sch London (BSc, MB BS, MD); *Career* jr hosp posts in med oncology and gen med 1972–79, acting staff specialist in med oncology Ludwig Institute for Cancer Research Sydney 1980–81, prof of med oncology Univ of Glasgow 1985– (sr lectr 1981–85), head Cancer Research Campaign Beatson Laboratories; MRC/UKCCCR: memb Working Pty on Testicular Cancer 1984, memb Cancer Therapy Ctee 1986–93, memb Gynaecological Cancer Working Pty 1990, memb Working Parties on Lung and Gynaecological Cancer 1986–90; memb: Bd of Clinical Dirs Cancer Research Campaign 1986, Scottish Cancer Coordinating and Advsy Ctee 1992, Scottish Cancer Therapy Network 1993; clinical ed British Jl of Cancer 1993; memb Editorial Bd: Prescribers Jl, European Jl of Cancer, Int Jl of Oncology, Current Drugs, Current Clinical Cancer, Anti Cancer Research; author of various med pubns; FRCP 1989, FRCP (Glas) 1992, FRCR 1993; *Style*— Prof Stanley Kaye; ✉ CRC Department of Medical Oncology, University of Glasgow, Alexander Stone Building, Garscube Estate, Switchback Rd, Bearsden, Glasgow G61 1BD (☎ 0141 330 4171, fax 0141 330 4127)

KAZANTZIS, Prof George; s of Constantine Kazantzis (d 1981), of Ealing, London, and Andromache, *née* Karamanolis (d 1991); *b* 18 Sept 1924; *Educ* Univ of London (MB BS, PhD); *m* 24 June 1973, Virginia Iphegenia, da of George Valassis (d 1977), of Thessaloniki, Greece; 1 s (Alexander b 1976), 1 da (Ariadne b 1974); *Career* appts in med and surgery St Bartholomew's and London Hosps 1950–58, clinical scientific staff MRC 1958–65; London Sch of Hygiene: sr lectr then reader 1979–86, prof of occupational med 1986–89; hon conslt physician The Middx Hosp 1986–89 (lectr then sr lectr Med Professorial Unit 1965–78), emeritus prof Univ of London 1990–, visiting prof Imperial Coll London 1992–; 135 pubns on occupational and environmental med in int jls; memb: Study Gp on pollution control priorities The Royal Soc, Working Gp WHO Air Quality Guidelines for Europe; pres: Section in Occupational Med RSM 1984–85, Hellenic Soc of Professional People and Scientists; FRCS 1957, FRCP 1979, FFCM (RCP) 1979, FFOM (RCP) 1979; *Books* contrib: Handbook On The Toxicology of Metals (1986), Oxford

Textbook of Medicine (1987), The Oxford Medical Companion (1994); *Recreations* music, being with family; *Clubs* The Athenaeum; *Style*— Prof George Kazantzis; ✉ 35 Mount Park Crescent, Ealing, London W5 2RR (☎ 0181 997 3287); Environmental Geochemistry Research, Royal School of Mines, Imperial College, Prince Consort Rd, London SW7 2BP (☎ 0171 594 6386, fax 0171 594 6408, telex 929484), Dept of Medicine, The Middlesex Hospital, London W1N 8AA

KEABLE-ELLIOTT, Dr Robert Anthony (Tony); OBE; s of Robert Keable (d 1927), and Jolie, *née* Buck (d 1924); *b* 14 Nov 1924; *Educ* Sherborne, Guy's Hosp London (MB BS); *m* 9 May 1953, Gilian Mary, da of Brig Colin Ross Marshall Hutchison, DSO, MC (d 1943); 4 s (David b 1954, Ian b 1956, Trevor b 1958, Simon b 1960); *Career* GP 1948–88; BMA: memb 1949–, memb Cncl 1964–94, chm Gen Med Servs Ctee 1964–68, treas 1981–86; memb Fin Corp of Gen Practice 1974–79, dir BMA Services Ltd, chm Jl Ctee BMA 1988–94; fndr memb Chiltern Med Soc 1956 (pres 1964); chm Ibstone Parish Cncl, memb Gen Med Cncl 1989–94; Freeman: City of London 1986, Worshipful Soc of Apothecaries 1986; FRCGP 1964, fell BMA 1987 (Gold medal 1994); *Recreations* golf, sailing, gardening; *Style*— Dr Tony Keable-Elliott, OBE; ✉ Peels, Ibstone, High Wycombe, Bucks

KEAL, Anthony Charles (Tony); s of Maj Kitchener Keal, of Thornton Dale, Yorkshire, and Joan Marjorie, *née* Ayling; *b* 12 July 1951; *Educ* Stowe, New Coll Oxford (BA); *m* 24 Nov 1979, (Janet) Michele, da of late John Charles King, of Javea, Spain; 4 s (Julian Charles b 1982, Jonathan David b 1986, Christopher James b 1987, Alexander Anthony b 1989); *Career* slr Allen & Overy 1976, slr and co sec Libra Bank plc 1976–78, ptnr Allen & Overy 1982– (slr 1978–82); memb Worshipful Co of Slrs; memb Law Soc; *Recreations* sailing, travel, family, opera; *Style*— Tony Keal, Esq; ✉ Allen & Overy, One New Change, London EC4M 9QQ (☎ 0171 330 3000, fax 0171 330 9999)

KEALEY, Gavin Sean James; QC (1994); s of Paul E Kealey, and Evelyn, *née* Fegali; *b* 2 Sept 1953; *Educ* Charterhouse, Univ Coll Oxford (Fletcher scholar, BA Jurisprudence); *m* 28 Feb 1981, Karen Elizabeth, da of Robert Nowak; 3 da (Alexandra Louise b 22 March 1983, Eleanor Victoria b 26 March 1986, Rowena Charlotte Ambrosiana b 19 Feb 1992); *Career* lectr in laws King's Coll London, called to the Bar Inner Temple 1977; *Style*— Gavin Kealey, Esq, QC; ✉ 7 King's Bench Walk, Temple, London EC4Y 7DS (☎ 0171 583 0404, fax 0171 583 0950)

KEANE, Dillie; da of Dr Francis Keane, of Portsmouth, and Miriam, *née* Slattery; *b* 23 May 1952; *Educ* Convent of the Sacred Heart Woldingham, Trinity Coll Dublin, LAMDA; *Career* entertainer, actress, broadcaster and columnist; fndr memb Fascinating Aïda with Marilyn Cutts and Adele Anderson and dir Nica Burns (nominated for Perrier Award 1984, winners City Limits Most Popular Cabaret Act Award 1985, Olivier Award nomination for Best Entertainment 1995); one woman shows: Single Again (nominated for Perrier Award 1990), Citizen Keane 1991; nominated Best Actress Manchester Evening News for Maggie in Dancing at Lughnasa; *Recordings* with Fascinating Aïda: Sweet FA and A Load of Old Sequins, Live at the Lyric; *Books* Fascinating Who? (1987), The Joy of Sequins (1994); *Recreations* working, tapestry, shopping, eight nephews and three nieces; *Clubs* Indian; *Style*— Miss Keane; ✉ c/o Conway van Gelder Robinson Ltd, 18–21 Jermyn Street, London SW1Y 6HP (☎ 0171 287 0077, fax 0171 287 1940)

KEANE, Fergal Patrick; OBE (1997); s of Eamon Brendan Keane (d 1990), and Mary, *née* Hasset; *b* 6 Jan 1961; *Educ* Terenure Coll Dublin, Presentation Coll Cork; *m* 11 July 1986, Anne Frances, da of Frank Coleman Flaherty; *Career* trainee reporter Limerick Leader 1979–82; reporter: Irish Press Group Dublin 1982–84, Radio Telefis Eireann Belfast 1986–89 (Dublin 1984–86); BBC Radio: Northern Ireland corr 1989–91, S Africa corr 1991–94, Asia corr 1994–; *Awards* Reporter of the Year Sony Silver Award 1992 and Sony Gold Award 1993, Amnesty International Press Awards Int Reporter of the Year 1993, RTS Journalist of the Year 1994; *Books* Irish Politics Now (1987), The Bondage of Fear (1994), Season of Blood: A Rwandan Journey (1995); *Recreations* fishing, golf, poetry; *Style*— Fergal Keane, Esq, OBE; ✉ c/o BBC News and Current Affairs, Radio, Broadcasting House, London W1A 1AA

KEANE, Sheriff Francis Joseph; s of Thomas Keane (d 1967), of W Lothian, and Helen Flynn; *b* 5 Jan 1936; *Educ* Blairs Coll Aberdeen, Gregorian Univ Rome (PHL), Univ of Edinburgh (LLB); *m* 19 April 1960, Lucia Corio, da of John Morrison (d 1983), of Glasgow; 2 s (Paul b 1963, Mark b 1965), 1 da (Lucy b 1961); *Career* slr; ptnr McCluskey Keane & Co Edinburgh 1959; depute procurator fiscal: Perth 1961, Edinburgh 1963; sr depute procurator fiscal Edinburgh 1971, sr legal asst Crown Office Edinburgh 1972, procurator fiscal Airdrie 1976, regnl procurator fiscal S Strathclyde, Dumfries and Galloway 1980; pres Procurators' Fiscal Soc 1982–84; Sheriff Glasgow and Strathkelvin 1984–93, Sheriff Lothians and Borders 1993–; *Recreations* music, tennis, painting; *Style*— Sheriff Francis Keane; ✉ Sheriffs' Chambers, Sheriff Court House, 27 Chambers Street, Edinburgh EH1 1LB (☎ 0131 225 2525)

KEANE, (Mary) Georgina; da of Dr Henry Anthony Keane, of Eire and S Wales, and Patricia Josephine, *née* Nolan; *b* 3 Feb 1954; *Educ* Convent of the Sacred Heart Woldingham Surrey; *m* 21 Dec 1978, Dr Saad Al-Damluji, s of Prof Salem Al-Damluji, of Abu Dhabi, United Arab Emirates; 2 s (Salem b 1981, Hassan b 1982); *Career* barr 1975–84 (chambers in London, Colchester Ipswich and Norwich), legal advsr Employment Affrs Directorate CBI 1984–86, conslt barr Titmuss Sainer & Webb 1986–88; admitted slr 1988; ptnr and head employment unit: Titmuss Sainer Dechert (formerly Titmuss Sainer & Webb) 1988–96, Richards Butler 1996–; *Recreations* theatre, avoiding domestic chores; *Style*— Miss Georgina Keane; ✉ Richards Butler, Beaufort House, 15 St Botolph Street, London EC3A 7EE (☎ 0171 247 6555, fax 0171 247 5091)

KEANE, John Charles; s and h of Sir Richard Michael Keane, 6 Bt, *qv*; *b* 16 Sept 1941; *Educ* Eton, Ch Ch Oxford; *m* 1977, Corinne, da of Jean Everard de Harzir, of Waroux, Alleur, Belgium; 2 s (Christopher b 1981, Gregory b 1982), 1 da (Amelia b 1987); *Style*— John Keane Esq; ✉ c/o Cappoquin House, Cappoquin, Co Waterford, Ireland

KEANE, Prof John Charlick; s of Ronald Melville Keane (d 1974), of Adelaide, and Mavis Matilda, *née* Charlick (d 1978); *b* 3 Feb 1949; *Educ* King's Coll Adelaide, Univ of Adelaide (Tinline scholar, BA, Archibald Grenfell Price prize, Charles Fenner prize), Univ of Toronto (Canadian Cwlth scholar and fell, MA, PhD); *m* Kathleen Margaret, *née* O'Neil; 4 c (Rebecca Allison b 1974, Leo Lawson-O'Neil b 1980, George b 1991, Alice b 1992); *Career* Nuffield fell King's Coll Cambridge 1979–80; visiting lectr Inter-Univ Centre of Dubrovnik Yugoslavia (March-April 1982, 1983 and 1985); Social Scis Research Cncl fell Freie Universität Berlin FRG Sept-Dec 1983; DAAD research fell Universität Bielefeld FRG May-June 1984; overseas teaching and research fell Griffith Univ Australia July-Sept 1984; research fell Zentrum für Interdisziplinäre Forschung Universität Bielefeld FRG Jan-July 1987; prof of politics Univ of Westminster 1988– (dir Centre for the Study of Democracy 1989–); visiting sr fell Dept of Politics and Soc Scis Euro Univ Inst Florence April 1990; visiting prof Depts of Political Sci and Communications Univ of California at San Diego Aug-Sept 1990 and 1994; visiting prof Central Euro Univ Prague Nov 1990; Anglo-German Br Cncl Research Award Universität Bremen and Freie Universität Berlin FRG 1991; Andrew Mellon sr fell American Philosophical Soc Philadelphia 1991–92; PCFC Award Europe in the Twenty-First Century 1992–93; Univ of Westminster Euro Awareness Fund 1992; Br Cncl travel grant 1993; DEVR/QR Research Assessment Exercise Award CSD 1993–; Deutsch - Englische Gesellschaft fell 1994; memb: Governing Bd Institutum Studium Humanitatis Ljubljana Slovenia May 1992–, Assoc Thomas Paine (Paris) June 1990–, Editorial Bd The Political Quarterly June 1989–, Jan Hus Educnl Fndn (with frequent contribs to parallel university lectrs and seminars in Brno and Prague) 1984–1989; Superdon Award The Times (London) 1994; FRSA 1992; *Books* Public Life and Late Capitalism: Towards a Socialist Theory of Democracy (1984), Contradictions of the Welfare State (ed and translator, 1984), The Power of the Powerless: Citizens Against the State in Central-Eastern Europe (ed, 1985), Disorganized Capitalism (ed and co-translator, 1985), After Full Employment (co-author with John Owens, 1986), Nomads of the Present: Social Movements and Individual Needs in Contemporary Societies (co-ed with Paul Mier, 1988), Civil Society and the State: New European Perspectives (ed and translator, 1988), Democracy and Civil Society (1988), The Media and Democracy (1991), Tom Paine: A Political Life (1995), Reflections on Violence (1996); *Recreations* walking, running, gardening, film, theatre, cooking; *Style*— Prof John Keane; ✉ Centre for the Study of Democracy, 70 Great Portland Street, London W1N 5AL (☎ 0171 911 5138, fax 0171 911 5164)

KEANE, John Granville Colpoys; s of Granville Keane (d 1990), and Elaine Violet Meredith Doubble; *b* 12 Sept 1954; *Educ* Cheam Sch Newbury Berks, Wellington, Camberwell Sch of Art (BA); *m* June 1996, Rosemary Ann McGowan (television prodr); *Career* artist; official Br war artist Gulf Crisis 1991; work in several public collections incl: Imperial War Museum, The Economist, The Guardian; artist in residence Whitefield Sch London 1985–86; *Exhibitions* solo incl: Peking, Moscow, Milton Keynes (Minsky's Gallery London) 1980, Some of it Works on Paper (Centre 181 London) 1982, War Efforts (Pentonville Gallery London) 1984, Conspiracy Theories (Angela Flowers Gallery London) 1985, Perspective '85 (Basel Art Fair Switzerland) 1985, Work Ethics (Angela Flowers Gallery London) 1986, Bee Keeping in the War Zone (Angela Flowers Gallery) 1988, Against the Wall (Turnpike Gallery Leigh Gtr Manchester) 1988, The Accident (cmmnd painting and screenprint for Greenpeace, Flowers East London) 1988, Divided States (Terry Dintenfass Gallery NY) 1989, Forum (Hamburg Germany) 1989, The Other Cheek? (Flowers East London) 1990, Cloth Caps and Hang-Gliding (cmmnd exhibition about Ollerton Mining Community, Angel Row Gallery Nottingham) 1991, Before the War (Kelvingrove Art Gallery Glasgow) 1991, Gulf (Imperial War Museum London) 1992, Fairytales of London (Lannon Cole Gallery Chicago) 1992, Burden of Paradise, Paintings of Guatemala (Flowers East) 1992, The Struggle for the Control of the Television Station (Terry Dintenfass Gallery, Flowers East) 1993, Gulf (Norton Gallery of Art Florida) 1993, Graham Greene and the Jungle of Human Dilemma (Flowers East) 1995; gp exhibitions incl: Whitechapel Open (Whitechapel Art Gallery London) 1983, 1984 and 1987, Art for Schools (Wells Centre Norfolk) 1983, Artists Against Apartheid (Royal Festival Hall London) 1986, Athena Art Award (Barbican Art Gallery London) 1987, Self Portrait (Artsite Gallery Bath) 1987, State of the Nation (Herbert Art Gallery Coventry) 1987, Art for the City (Lloyd's Building London) 1987, The Print Show (Angela Flowers Gallery London) 1988, Nutidskunst Silkesborg (Kunstmuseum Copenhagen) 1988, 4th International Young Artists Competition (Union of Fine Artists Sofia Bulgaria) 1989, The Thatcher Years - an Artistic Retrospective (Flowers East London) 1989, Flowers at Moos (Gallery Moos NY) 1990, Where There is Discord (Cleveland Gallery Middlesbrough) 1990, Angela Flowers Gallery 1990 (Barbican Concourse Gallery London) 1990, New Figurative Painting (Salander O'Reilly Galleries LA) 1993; cmmnd set design for Salsa Celestina (Palace Theatre Watford) 1993; *Books* Conflicts of Interest (by Mark Lawson, 1995); *Clubs* Groucho's; *Style*— John Keane, Esq; ✉ Flowers East, 199–205 Richmond Road, London E8 3NJ (☎ 0181 985 3333, fax 0181 985 0067)

KEANE, Philip Vincent; s of Bernard Vincent Keane (d 1983), of London, and Brenda Ellen Margaret, *née* Ford; *b* 11 Aug 1940; *Educ* Wimbledon Coll GS, LSE (BSc); *m* 18 Sept 1965, (Kathleen) Winifred, da of William Aloysius Thomson (d 1987), of London; 2 da (Angelina Teresa b 14 Sept 1968, Noelle Francesca b 16 Dec 1969); *Career* sr investmt analyst Esso Pension Tst 1967–71, head of investmt res Mercantile & General Reinsurance 1971–75, equity fund mangr Prudential Pensions 1976–77, investmt mangr Rea Bros Ltd 1977–81; dir: Wardley Investmt Mgmnt Ltd, HK Unit Tst Mangrs Ltd 1981–82, Rea Bros (Investmt Mgmnt) Ltd 1982–89, CS Investmt Mgmnt Ltd 1989–91; assoc dir IBJ International plc (subsid of the Industrial Bank of Japan) 1991–; AIIMR; *Recreations* travel, photography, skiing, literature; *Style*— Philip Keane, Esq; ✉ 70 Pine Grove, off Lake Rd, Wimbledon, London SW19 7HE; IBJ International plc, Bracken House, 1 Friday Street, London EC4M 9JA (☎ 0171 236 1090)

KEANE, Sir Richard Michael; 6 Bt (UK 1801), of Cappoquin, Co Waterford; s of Lt-Col Sir John Keane, 5 Bt, DSO (d 1956), and Lady Eleanor Hicks-Beach (d 1960), da of 1 Earl St Aldwyn; *b* 29 Jan 1909; *Educ* Sherborne, Ch Ch Oxford; *m* 1939, Olivia Dorothy, da of Oliver Hawkshaw, TD, of Chisenbury Priory, Wilts; 2 s (John Charles b 1941, David Richard b 1950), 1 da (Vivien Eleanor (Mrs Simon Pleydell-Bouverie) b 1940); *Heir* s, John Charles Keane, *qv*; *Career* served with Co of London Yeo and 10 Royal Hussars 1939–44, liaison offr (Maj) with HQ Vojvodina Yugoslav partisans 1944, attached British Military Mission Belgrade 1944–45; diplomatic corr: Reuters 1935–37, Sunday Times (also asst to editor) 1937–39; publicity conslt to ICI Ltd 1950–62; farmer; *Recreations* fishing, farming; *Clubs* Kildare Street; *Style*— Sir Richard Keane, Bt; ✉ Cappoquin House, Cappoquin, Co Waterford, Ireland (☎ 0158 54004, fax 0158 54698)

KEARLEY, Chester Dagley Hugh; s of late Hon Mark Hudson Kearley (s of 1 Viscount Devonport); kinsman and hp of 3 Viscount Devonport, *qv*; *b* 29 April 1932; *m* 1974, Josefa Mesquida; *Style*— Chester Kearley, Esq; ✉ S Patos 466, Denia, Alicante, Spain

KEARNEY, Hon Sir William John Francis; kt (1982), CBE (1976); s of W J K Kearney; *b* 8 Jan 1935; *Educ* Wolstanton CGS, Sydney GS, Sydney Univ, Univ Coll London; *m* 1959, Jessie, da of L Yung; 3 da; *Career* dormant cmmn as admin and high cmmr of PNG 1973–75, judge Supreme Ct PNG 1976–82, dep chief justice 1980–82, judge Supreme Ct Northern Territory 1982–; Aboriginal land cmmr 1982–86, chm Law Reform Ctee 1982–90; *Style*— The Hon Sir William Kearney, CBE; ✉ Judges' Chambers, Supreme Court, Darwin, NT 0800, Australia

KEAST, Roger John; s of Horace Keast, of Gwellyets, Truro, Cornwall, and Margaret, *née* Legard; *b* 4 Dec 1942; *Educ* Truro Sch, Univ of Exeter (LLB); *m* 1, 25 March 1970 (m dis 1975), Anne Elizabeth, da of Norman Samuel Cross, of Lanteague, Goonhavern, Truro, Cornwall; m 2, 9 July 1976, (Elizabeth) Ann, da of Albert John Folland (d 1982), of W Forde, Stockleigh Pomeroy, Devon; 1 s (Paul Edward John b 15 Nov 1977), 2 step da (Sarah Annette Radford b 14 July 1966, Carole Suzanne Radford b 20 Nov 1967); *Career* Stephens & Scown St Austell and Exeter: articled clerk 1963–66, slr 1966–70, ptnr 1970–, dep sr ptnr 1986–91, sr ptnr 1991–; memb Exeter City Cncl 1968–81, Mayor City of Exeter 1977–78; hon slr: Devon Young Farmers Club 1968–, Somerset and Dorset Railway Club 1982–, Exeter and District Hoteliers Assoc 1989–; pres Exeter Male Voice Choir 1979–; memb Cncl Exeter Univ 1979–90, Privy Cncl's appointee Ct of Exeter Univ 1980–, fndr memb Exeter Castle Rotary Club 1985–; hon alderman; Hon MA Univ of Exeter 1978; memb Law Soc 1966; *Style*— Roger Keast, Esq; ✉ Stephens & Scown, 25–28 Southernhay East, Exeter EX1 1RS (☎ 01392 210700, fax 01392 74010)

KEAT, Alan Michael; s of Ernest Frank Keat, of Liphook, Surrey, and Joyce Evelyn, *née* Curtis; *b* 12 May 1942; *Educ* Charterhouse, Merton Coll Oxford (MA); *m* 9 July 1966, Lorna Marion, da of Horace Henry Wilson, of Chesterfield, Derbys; 3 da (Anna b 19 Oct 1968, Jane b 18 Sept 1972, Rebecca b 22 June 1975); *Career* admitted slr 1966, ptnr Travers Smith Braithwaite 1970–; non-exec dir Beazer plc 1986–89; *Style*— Alan Keat,

Esq; ✉ Travers Smith Braithwaite, 10 Snow Hill, London EC1A 2AL (☎ 0171 248 9133, fax 0171 236 3728)

KEATES, Jonathan Basil; s of Richard Herbert Basil Keates (d 1949), and Sonia Evangeline, *née* Wilcox; *b* 7 Nov 1946; *Educ* Bryanston Sch (scholar), Magdalen Coll Oxford (Thomas Shepherd exhibitioner, MA), Univ of Exeter (PGCE); *Career* author; asst English master City of London Sch 1974–; regular contrib to: The Observer, The Independent, TLS; judge Booker Prize 1991; Hawthornden Prize 1984, James Tait Black Prize 1984; memb Ctee London Library 1993; FRSL 1993; *Books* The Companion Guide to Shakespeare Country (1979), Allegro Postillions (1983), Handel: the man and his music (1985), The Stranger's Gallery (1986), Tuscany (1988), Umbria (1991), Italian Journeys (1991), Stendhal (1994), Purcell (1995); *Recreations* music, travel, libraries, friendship; *Clubs* Academy; *Style*— Jonathan Keates, Esq, FRSL; ✉ c/o Felicity Bryan, 2A North Parade, Banbury Road, Oxford OX2 6PE (☎ 01865 513816, fax 01865 310055)

KEATING, Caron Louisa; da of Don Keating, and Gloria Hunniford, *qv*; *b* 5 Oct 1962; *Educ* Univ of Bristol (BA); *m* 15 June 1991, Russell Grant Lindsay, *qv*; 1 s (Charlie Jackson b 1994); *Career* presenter religious and youth oriented progs in NI (incl Green Rock and Channel One) until 1986; Blue Peter (BBC 1): co-presenter 1986–92, Special Assignment Russia 1987, Special Assignment USA 1988, filmed in Kampuchea for famine appeal (later fronting the appeal); presenter Wide Angle (ITV), Summer Scene (BBC 1) 1992; reporter Barcelona Olympics for Radio 5 1992, presenter Family Affairs (BBC 1) 1993–94, The Late Lunch (Radio 5), showbusiness corr London Tonight (London News Network); presenter: Schofield's Quest 1994, After 5 (Carlton/London News Network) 1994–96, Routes and Rhythms (BBC 1) 1995; *Recreations* reading, painting, theatre; *Style*— Ms Caron Keating; ✉ James Grant Media Group Ltd, Syon Lodge, London Road, Syon Park, Middlesex TW7 5BH (☎ 0181 232 4100, fax 0181 232 4101)

KEATING, David George Michael; s of George Francis Keating (d 1989), and Una Rosalie, *née* Metters (d 1990); *b* 31 Jan 1943; *Educ* Univ Coll Sch London, King's Coll Durham (LLB), Coll of Law; *m* 1, 18 Dec 1965, Alicia Gay, da of Frederick Johnson (d 1978); 2 da (Ruth b 31 Oct 1967, Rebekah b 21 July 1973), 1 s (Daniel b 30 Dec 1968); m 2, 5 July 1980, Jane, da of Dr Henry Thistlethwaite; *Career* admitted slr: Eng & Wales 1967, Western Pacific High Cmmn 1969 (also barr 1969), Republic of Ireland 1992; advocate Jt Tbnl New Hebrides 1971; articled clerk: Gouldens London 1965–66, London Borough of Bromley 1966–67 (asst slr 1967–68); asst slr County Borough of Hartlepool 1968–89, estab first practice in Solomon Is then practised in Vanuatu (formerly New Hebrides) 1969–72; Smith & Graham Hartlepool: asst slr 1972–74, ptnr 1974–96, conslt 1996–; memb Cncl Law Soc (chm Int Ctee), memb Law Advsy Ctee Br Cncl, former sec and pres Hartlepool Law Soc, legal advsr Hartlepool Victim Support Scheme, dir Hartlepool Enterprise Agency Ltd, memb Cncl Durham & N Yorks Law Soc; chm: Br Albanian Law Assoc, Br Romanian Law Assoc; govr Hartlepool Sixth Form Coll, memb Bd Three Rivers Housing Assoc; former chm: Easington CAB, NE Legal Servs Ctee; NP 1973; *Recreations* walking, postal history, the Balkans; *Clubs* East India, Royal Over-Seas League, West Hartlepool (pres); *Style*— David Keating, Esq; ✉ Hesleden Hall, Monk Hesleden, Hartlepool TS27 4QB

KEATING, Frank; s of Bryan Keating, of Cheltenham, Glos, and Monica, *née* Marsh; *b* 4 Oct 1937; *Educ* Belmont Abbey, Douai; *m* 1987, Jane A Sinclair; 1 s, 1 da; *Career* prodr Independent Television 1963–74; columnist: The Guardian 1975–, Punch 1982–89, The Spectator 1989–95; TV series incl: Maestro (BBC 1), Italy, My Italy (ITV); Sportswriter of the Year 1978, 1980 and 1988; Magazine Writer of the Year 1987; *Books* incl: Bowled Over, Half-Time Whistle (autobiography, 1992), Band of Brothers; *Recreations* Channel 4, Radio 4, gardening; *Clubs* Chelsea Arts; *Style*— Frank Keating, Esq; ✉ Church House, Marden, Hereford; The Guardian, 119 Farringdon Rd, London EC1R 3DA (☎ 0171 278 2332)

KEATING, Henry Reymond Fitzwalter (Harry); s of John Hervey Keating (d 1950), and Muriel Margharita, *née* Clews (d 1986); *Educ* Merchant Taylors' Sch, Trinity Coll Dublin (BA); *m* 3 Oct 1953, Sheila Mary, da of William Ford Mitchell, ISO (d 1968); 3 s (Simon b 1955, Piers b 1960, Hugo b 1964), 1 da (Bryony b 1957); *Career* Army 1945–48; journalist 1952–63; chm: Crime Writers' Assoc 1970–71, Soc of Authors 1982–84; pres The Detection Club 1986–; FRSL 1990; *Books* Death and the Visiting Firemen (1959), The Perfect Murder (1964), The Murder of the Maharajah (1980), The Lucky Alphonse (1982), Under A Monsoon Cloud (1986), Dead on Time (1988), Inspector Ghote - His Life and Crimes (1989), The Iciest Sin (1990), The Rich Detective (1993), Going Wrong (1994), The Good Detective (1995), The Bad Detective (1996), Asking Questions (1996); *Style*— Harry Keating, FRSL; ✉ 35 Northumberland Place, London W2 5AS (☎ and fax 0171 229 1100)

KEATING, John David; s of Peter Steven Keating (d 1944, war casualty), of York, and Muriel Emily Alice Lamport; *b* 18 June 1943; *Educ* King Edward VI Chelmsford, Highbury Coll Portsmouth; *m* 28 Aug 1970, Linda Margaret, da of Sidney Reginald Hall, of Blackheath, London; 1 s (Matthew b 1971), 1 da (Sarah b 1973); *Career* seagoing purser with P & O 1960–70, Lt Reserve Serv RN 2 Submarine Div 1970–71; asst to md CWS 1972–74, UK divnl accountant Borden Chemical Corp 1975–81, fndr dir and proprietor WRA Ltd 1982–; dir: WRA Holdings Ltd 1984–, WRA (Offshore) Ltd (Sub-Sea Devpt) 1985–, Russell Square Management Co Ltd 1991–, Martel-Wessex Composites Ltd 1991–, Euro-Maritime Ltd 1992–; md Wessex Resins & Adhesives Ltd; elected memb for Ringwood South Ward of New Forest Dist Cncl 1987–; FCCA 1977, MHCIMA, ACCA; *Recreations* sailing, skiing; *Clubs* Naval, Royal Naval Sailing Assoc, Ski Club of GB; *Style*— John Keating, Esq; ✉ Greenways, Hightown Hill, Ringwood, Hampshire (☎ 01425 475446); Chalet Florence, Le Villard, Méribel les Allues, France (☎ and fax 00 33 79 00 37 28); Wessex Resins & Adhesives Ltd, Cupernham House, Cupernham Lane, Romsey, Hampshire (☎ 01794 521111, fax 01794 517779)

KEATING, (Kay) Rosamond Blundell; da of Geoffrey Blundell Jones, and Avis Marguerite, *née* Dyer; *b* 3 Oct 1943; *Educ* Maynard Sch Exeter, St Hugh's Coll Oxford (MA); *m* 1, 18 Dec 1965, Edmund Anthony Deighton (d 1974); 1 da (Natasha b 9 June 1966 d 1993); m 2, 2 Dec 1978, Donald Norman Keating, QC (d 1995); 1 s (Oliver Sebastian b 19 June 1981); *Career* called to the Bar Gray's Inn 1966; metropolitan stipendiary magistrate 1987–; *Recreations* tennis, travel, opera, walking; *Style*— Mrs Rosamond Keating; ✉ Horseferry Road Magistrates Court, 70 Horseferry Road, London SW1P 2AY (☎ 0171 233 2000)

KEATINGE, Sir Edgar Mayne; kt (1960), CBE (1954); s of Gerald Francis Keatinge, CIE (d 1965); *b* 3 Feb 1905; *Educ* Rugby, South Africa; *m* 1930, Katharine Lucile (d 1990), da of Reginald John Burrell (d 1948); 1 s (Prof William Richard Keatinge, *qv*), 1 da (Bridget); *Career* joined Suffolk Yeo 1937, Cmdt School of Artillery W Africa 1942–43, Lt-Col RA; MP (C) West Suffolk Bury St Edmunds Div 1944–45; memb Panel Land Tbnl SW Area 1948–74, chm Wessex Area Nat Union of Cons Assocs 1951–54, govr Sherborne Sch 1951–74; memb Cncl Royal African Soc 1970–80; *Clubs* Carlton, Boodle's; *Style*— Sir Edgar Keatinge, CBE; ✉ Teffont, Salisbury, Wilts SP3 5RG (☎ 0172 276 224)

KEATINGE, Richard Arthur Davis; *b* 30 Aug 1947; *Educ* Portora Royal Sch, Trinity Coll Dublin (BA), University Coll Dublin (MBA), Wharton Business Sch (AMP); *m* 1970, Athene; 2 s (Benjamin b 17 Aug 1973, Douglas b 5 May 1976), 1 da (Rebecca b 4 Sept 1979); *Career* fin journalist: Reuters Ltd 1969–71, The Irish Times 1971–78; Bank of Ireland: dir and corp fin exec 1978–83, head of gp strategy 1983–86, chief exec UK 1986–90, exec dir Britain 1990–91; chm NCB Corporate Finance 1991–92, dir NCB Group 1991–92; dir Hardwicke Ltd Dublin 1992–93, chm and md IBI Corporate Finance Ltd; *Recreations* golf, fishing, tennis; *Clubs* Kildare Street and Univ, Royal St George Yacht, Connemara Golf, Carrickmines Golf; *Style*— Richard Keatinge, Esq; ✉ IBI Corporate Finance Ltd, 26 Fitzwilliam Place, Dublin 2 (☎ 00 353 1 661 6633, fax 00 353 1 661 6821)

KEATINGE, Prof William Richard; s of Sir Edgar Keatinge, *qv*, Salisbury, Wilts, and Katherine Lucille; *b* 18 May 1931; *Educ* Upper Canada Coll, Rugby, Univ of Cambridge (MA, MB BChir, PhD); *m* 15 Oct 1955, Margaret Ellen Annette, da of David Hegarty (d 1973); 1 s (Richard), 2 da (Claire, Mary); *Career* RNVR seconded for res at Univ of Cambridge 1956–58; dir of studies in med and jr res fell Pembroke Coll Cambridge 1958–60, fell Cardiovascular Res Inst San Francisco 1960–61, MRC post and fell Pembroke Coll Oxford 1961–68; head of Physiology Dept: London Hosp Med Coll 1981–90 (reader 1968–71, prof 1971–), Queen Mary and Westfield Coll 1990–96; memb: Physiological Soc 1959, RSM; FRCP 1990 (MRCP 1984); *Books* Survival In Cold Water, Local Mechanisms Controlling Blood Vessels; *Recreations* archaeology, sailing; *Style*— Prof William Keatinge; ✉ Department of Physiology, Queen Mary and Westfield Coll, Mile End Rd, London E1 4NS (☎ 0171 982 6365)

KEATLEY, (Robert) Bryan; TD (1961); s of James Walter Stanley Keatley (d 1978), of Royston, and Helen Rankin Thompson; *b* 21 March 1930; *Educ* Aldenham, St Catharine's Coll Cambridge (MA); *m* 14 Sept 1957, Diana, da of Frank Harvey, of Bishops Stortford; 2 da (Georgina b 1960, Rebecca (Mrs Meyrick) b 1962), 2 s (Robert b 1967, Richard (twin) b 1967); *Career* chartered surveyor and land agent; Nat Serv 1949–50; conslt Humberts London 1990–95 (ptnr 1962–90, sr ptnr 1980–85); underwriting memb of Lloyds; TA Cambs Regt (16 Airborne Div), Maj & OC Herts Regt; Nat Tst: Fin Ctee 1983, Estates Panel 1983–96, Enterprise Bd 1984; dir: Landplan Ltd 1974, Glen Rinnes Ltd 1990–; chm Formfield (BES) 1984, dir Rural Assets 1987 (chm 1990); govr Wellington Coll 1992–, cmmr of taxes 1960–95, chm Herts (Hadhams Branch) Royal Br Legion 1984–95; Freeman City of London 1978, Liveryman Worshipful Co of Farmers; FRICS, FRSA; *Recreations* shooting, conservation, gardens, browsing; *Clubs* Boodle's, Farmers'; *Style*— Bryan Keatley, Esq, TD; ✉ Bonjedward Hill, Jedburgh, Roxburghshire TD8 6SF (☎ 01835 863636); Estate Office (☎ and fax 01835 864626)

KEATLEY, John Rankin Macdonald; s of James Walter Stanley Keatley (d 1978), of Royston, and Helen Rankin Thompson; *b* 20 Aug 1933; *Educ* Aldenham, RAC Circencester; *m* 1964 (m dis 1980), Carolyn Margaret, da of Rodney Telford Morell, of Melbourne, Australia; 1 s (James b 1965), 1 da (Arabella b 1967); *Career* 2 Lt Duke of Wellington's Regt, Korea 1952–53, Capt Hertfordshire Regt TA 1953–60; Parly candidate (C) Hemsworth 1964; leader Cambridge CC 1967–69; dir REA Holdings plc 1978–, chm Applied Botanics plc 1984; chm The Keatley Tst 1968–; tstee: Cambridge Museum of Technol 1970–, Decorative Arts Soc 1990–; pres: SW Cambridgeshire Cons Assoc 1987, Arts Cncl of North Hertfordshire 1991–; memb: Ctee Contemporary Art Soc 1989–95 (buyer 1990), Syndicate Fitzwilliam Museum Cambridge 1990–; hon fell Guild of Designer Bookbinders 1989; *Clubs* Lansdowne (chm 1979–); *Style*— J R M Keatley, Esq; ✉ Melbourn Lodge, Royston, Herts SG8 6AL (☎ 01763 260680)

KEATLEY, William Halliday; TD (1970); s of James Walter Stanley Keatley (d 1978), of Royston, and Helen Rankin, *née* Thompson; *b* 22 Sept 1935; *Educ* Aldenham, St Catharine's Coll Cambridge (MA); *m* 3 Sept 1965, (Elizabeth) Jane, da of Capt Thomas Abdy Combe (d 1984); 2 da; *Career* 2 Fd Battery Gold Coast RWAFF 1954–56, Cambs Regt and Suffolk and Cambs Regt 1956–72; ptnr John Prust & Co 1965–71 (joined 1959), ptnr Laurence Prust & Co 1971–85 (dep sr ptnr 1983–85), sr ptnr and chm Laurence Keen Ltd 1986–; non-exec dir Pershing Ltd 1987–, dep chm Rathbone Bros Plc 1995–; *Style*— William Keatley, Esq, TD; ✉ Heddon Hall, Parracombe, N Devon EX31 4QL (☎ 01598 763409); Laurence Keen Ltd, 49–51 Bow Lane, Cheapside, London EC4M 9LX (☎ 0171 489 9493)

KEAY, Dr Ronald William John; CBE (1977, OBE 1966); s of Harold John Keay (d 1962), of Richmond, Surrey, and Marion Lucy, *née* Flick (d 1971); *Educ* King's Coll Sch Wimbledon, St John's Coll Oxford (BSc, MA, DPhil); *m* 18 Aug 1944, Joan Mary, da of Rev Alfred Edward Walden; 1 s (Martin John b 1951), 2 da (Alison Marian (Mrs Eldridge) b 1946, Hilary Ruth (Mrs Kinnell) b 1948); *Career* Colonial Forest Serv 1942–62, dir forest res Nigeria 1960–62; exec sec Royal Soc 1977–85 (dep exec sec 1962–77), visiting prof Univ of Essex 1990–93; numerous papers on: tropical African plant ecology and taxonomy, sci policy; pres: Sci Assoc Nigeria 1961–62, African Studies Assoc 1971–72; vice pres Nigerian Field Soc 1987– (chm UK branch 1985–91), pres Inst of Biology 1988–90 (hon fell), treas Linnean Soc of London 1989–95 (vice pres 1961–65, 1971–73, 1974–76), scientific advsr Earthwatch Europe; church warden St Martin-in-the-Fields 1981–87; hon fell RHS; *Books* Flora of West Tropical Africa Vol 1 (1954–58), Nigerian Trees (1960–64), Trees of Nigeria (1989); *Recreations* gardening; *Clubs* Athenaeum; *Style*— Dr Ronald Keay, CBE; ✉ 38 Birch Grove, Cobham, Surrey KT11 2HR (☎ 01932 865677)

KEBLE-WHITE, (Arthur) James; s of Capt Geoffrey Meredith Keble-White, RN (d 1961), of Hants, and Violet Gertrude Alice, *née* Preston (d 1963); *b* 29 May 1930; *Educ* Winchester, Trinity Coll Cambridge (MA); *m* 7 May 1955, Penelope Mary, da of John Newsam McClean (d 1986), of Cirencester, Glos; 3 da (Caroline b 1957, Julia b 1959, Diana b 1964); *Career* chartered engr; Carrier Engineering Co Ltd 1957 (md 1972), Pell Frischmann & Partners 1974, Ove Arup & Partners 1981 (dir 1988–92); CEng, FIMechE, FCIBSE; *Recreations* horse riding, photography, woodwork; *Style*— James Keble-White, Esq; ✉ Abbots Place, Putley, Ledbury, Herefordshire HR8 2QW (☎ and fax 01531 670929); Ove Arup & Partners, 13 Fitzroy Street, London W1P 6BQ (☎ 0171 636 1531)

KECK, Colleen; *b* 23 Oct 1958; *Educ* Univ of Saskatchewan (BA, LLB), Univ of London (LLM); *Career* lawyer specialising in intellectual property; admitted slr and called to the Bar Alberta Canada 1983, admitted slr England and Wales 1988; articled student Bennet Jones Barristers and Solicitors Canada 1982–83, barr and slr Home Oil Co Ltd 1983–88, ptnr Allen & Overy 1992– (asst 1988–92); frequent lectr on technol, IP, IT and media topics; memb Exec Ctee: Int Trade Marks Assoc, Licensing Execs Soc; memb: Law Soc of England and Wales, Law Soc of Alberta, Canadian Bar Assoc; *Publications* Information as Property (Patent World, 1987), Collaboration Agreements in the Pharmaceutical and Biotechnology Industries (Int Corp Law, 1993), IP and the convergence of technology and media (Managing Intellectual Property, 1995), Banks as Suppliers of IT goods and services (Banking Technology, 1995), Contractual Construction and Interpretation: A comparison of the Canadian, US and English Rules and their ramifications in choosing a governing law (jtly, Canadian Int Lawyer, 1995), Copyright and Related Rights in the Information Society - the EC Green Paper (jtly, IBC Conf, 1995); *Style*— Ms Colleen Keck; ✉ Allen & Overy, One New Change, London EC4M 9QQ (☎ 0171 330 3000, fax 0171 330 9999)

KEE, Prof (Alexander) Alistair; s of Robert Kee (d 1983), and Agnes Stevenson Kee (d 1963); *b* 17 April 1937; *Educ* Clydebank HS, Univ of Glasgow (MA, BD, Dickson prize, DLitt), Union Theological Seminary NY (Scots fell, STM, PhD); *m* 1961, Anne Mary Paterson (d 1992); 2 s (David Graeme b 1967 d 1968, Colin Cameron b 1969), 1 da (Hilary Moira b 1970); *Career* lectr Dept of Theology Univ Coll Rhodesia 1964–67, lectr Dept of Theology Univ of Hull 1967–76, reader Univ of Glasgow 1983–88 (sr lectr 1976–83), prof Dept of Theology and Religious Studies Univ of Edinburgh 1991– (reader 1988–91); Karl Jaspers lectureship Ripon Hall Oxford 1975, Ferguson lectureship Univ of Manchester 1986; memb: Soc for the Study of Theology, Br Assoc for the Study of

Religion; *Books* The Way of Transcendence (1971), Seeds of Liberation (1973), A Reader in Political Theology (1974), The Scope of Political Theology (1978), Constantine Versus Christ (1982), Domination or Liberation (1986), Being and Truth (1986), The Roots of Christian Freedom (1988), Marx and the Failure of Liberation Theology (1990), From Bad Faith to Good News (1991); *Recreations* golf; *Style*— Prof Alistair Kee; ✉ 24 Colinton Road, Edinburgh EH10 5EQ (☎ 0131 447 0209); Department of Theology and Religious Studies, University of Edinburgh, New College, Mound Place, Edinburgh EH1 2LX (☎ 0131 650 8953, e-mail alistair.kee@ed.ac.uk)

KEE, Robert; s of Robert Kee (d 1958), and Dorothy Frances, *née* Monkman (d 1964); *b* 5 Oct 1919; *Educ* Rottingdean Sch Sussex, Stowe, Magdalen Coll Oxford (MA); *m* 1, 1948, Janetta, da of G H J Woolley; 1 da (Georgiana); m 2, 1960, Cynthia Charlotte, da of Edward Judah; 2 s (Alexander, Benjamin (decd)), 1 da (Sarah); m 3, 1990, The Hon Catherine Mary, da of Lord Trevelyan; *Career* served RAF 1940–46, Picture Post 1948–52; author, translator journalist and broadcaster, TV interviewer, presenter and documentary maker 1958–; radio broadcaster 1946–; Richard Dimbleby Award 1976, Jacobs Award (Dublin) for BBC Ireland 1981; memb: BECTU, Equity; *Publications* A Crowd is not Company (1947, republished 1982), The Impossible Shore (1949), A Sign of the Times (1956), Broadstrop in Season (1959), Refugee World (1961), The Green Flag (1972), Ireland: A History (1981, up-dated paperback 1996), The World We Left Behind (1984), The World We Fought For (1985), Trial and Error (1986), Munich: The Eleventh Hour (1988), The Picture Post Album (1989), The Laurel and The Ivy: C S Parnell and Irish Nationalism (1993); *Clubs* Reform; *Style*— Robert Kee, Esq; ✉ Rogers Coleridge and White, 20 Powis Mews, London W11 1JN (☎ 0171 221 3717)

KEEBLE, Sir (Herbert Ben) Curtis; GCMG (1982, KCMG 1978, CMG 1970); s of Herbert Keeble (d 1949), of Walton on the Naze, and Gertrude Keeble, BEM, *née* Hardy (d 1969); *b* 18 Sept 1922; *Educ* Clacton Co HS, Univ of London; *m* 2 April 1947, Margaret Ellen Stephenson Stuart, da of John Fraser, of Edinburgh; 3 da (Dr Suzanne (Richardson) b 1949, Sally b 1951, Jane b 1955); *Career* served HM Forces 1942–47; HM Dip Serv: served Berlin, Washington and Jakarta, former cnsllr and head Euro Econ Orgns Dept FCO, commercial cnsllr Berne 1965–68, min Canberra 1968–71, asst under sec of state FCO 1971–73, ambass GDR 1974–76, dep under sec FCO (chief clerk) 1976–78, ambass USSR 1978–82, ret; conslt to FCO 1984–; advsr House of Commons Foreign Affrs Ctee 1985–86; govr BBC 1985–90; memb Cncl: RIIA 1984–90, Sch of Slavonic and East European Studies 1984–93; chm: GB and USSR Assoc 1985–92, Britain-Russia Centre 1992–, Fndn for Accountancy and Financial Mgmnt 1993–; *Books* The Soviet State (ed, 1985), Britain and the Soviet Union 1917–89 (1990); *Recreations* sailing; *Clubs* Travellers', Cruising Association; *Style*— Sir Curtis Keeble, GCMG; ✉ Dormers, St Leonard's Road, Thames Ditton, Surrey KT7 0RR (☎ 0181 398 7778)

KEEBLE, Giles; s of Thomas Whitfield Keeble (d 1994), and Ursula, *née* Scott-Morris; *b* 12 Nov 1949; *Educ* The King's Sch Canterbury, St John's Coll Cambridge (MA); *m* 1, 1981 (m dis 1988), Gillian, *née* Perry; 2 s (Nicholas, Sam); m 2, 1992, Caroline, *née* de Meric; 1 da (Hannah), 2 step da (Polly, Chloë); *Career* account handler JWT 1971–73, account mangr BMP 1973–75, sr account mangr and account planner FGA 1975–76; copywriter: FGA 1976–77, Abbott Mead Vickers 1978–81, WCRS 1981–88 (dir 1984); creative ptnr Leo Burnett 1994–95 (exec creative dir 1988–94), creative dir McBain Noel-Johnson (Abbott Mead Vickers gp integrated communications subsid) 1996–; winner various advertising indust awards; *Recreations* sport, music, reading, friends; *Clubs* Hawks, Groucho; *Style*— Giles Keeble, Esq; ✉ McBain Noel-Johnson, 7 Fitzroy Square, London W1P 6HJ (☎ 0171 387 7474, fax 0171 887 9798)

KEEBLE, John Francis; s of Frank Edward Keeble (d 1989), and Lilith Louise Keeble (d 1993); *b* 26 April 1933; *Educ* Slough GS, Acton Tech Coll (BSc); *m* 29 March 1958, Vivienne, da of Reginald William Anderson; 1 s (Peter b 1960), 1 da (Elizabeth b 1964); *Career* 2 Lt RCS 1954–56; methods study asst Pharmaceutical Co 1956–60 (res asst 1950–54), sr admin BBC TV 1968–83 (orgn and methods conslt 1960–66, asst to head TV drama 1966–68), sr admin dir business admin and dep chief exec BBC Enterprises Ltd 1983–92; dir: BBC Telecordiale 1988–92, BBC Sub TV Ltd 1990–92, Twin Network Ltd 1990–92, BBC World Service Television Ltd 1991–92; company sec UK Gold Television Ltd and UK Living Ltd 1992–; FRTS (memb 1970–); *Recreations* theatre, ballet, travel; *Style*— John Keeble, Esq; ✉ 4 Turner Rd, Slough, Berks SL3 7AN (☎ 01753 533850, fax 01753 719678)

KEEFE, Prof Terence (Terry); s of Wilfrid Patrick Keefe (d 1979), and Laura Clara, *née* Mitchell; *b* 1 Feb 1940; *Educ* Five Ways GS Birmingham, Univ of Leicester (BA, MA), Univ of London (BA); *m* 30 June 1962, Sheila Roberta, da of John Parkin (d 1975), of Gt Yarmouth; 1 s (Simon Patrick b 24 Dec 1968), 1 da (Rosanna Jancis b 24 April 1971); *Career* asst master Lincoln City GS 1963–65, asst lectr then lectr then sr lectr in French Univ of Leicester 1965–88, prof of French studies Univ of Lancaster 1988–; memb: Exec Ctee French Studies Soc, Assoc of Univ Professors of French; *Books* Simone De Beauvoir: A Study of Her Writings (1983), French Existentialist Fiction (1986), Zola and the Craft of Fiction (co-ed, 1990), Beauvoir: Les Belles Images, La Femme Rompue (1991), Autobiography and the Existential Self (ed, 1994); *Recreations* golf; *Style*— Prof Terry Keefe; ✉ Department of Modern Languages, Lonsdale College, University of Lancaster, Lancaster LA1 4YN (☎ 01524 592667)

KEEFFE, Barrie Colin; s of Edward Thomas Keeffe, and Constance Beatrice, *née* Marsh; *b* 31 Oct 1945; *Educ* East Ham GS; *m* 1, 1969 (m dis 1979), Dee Sarah Truman; m 2, 1981, Verity Eileen Proud, *née* Bargate (d 1981); 2 step s; m 3, 1983 (m dis 1993), Julia Lindsay; *Career* actor Nat Youth Theatre, journalist, writer-in-residence Shaw Theatre, resident playwright Royal Shakespeare Co 1978, assoc writer Theatre Royal Stratford East 1986–91; also theatre and radio plays dir; memb Bd of Dirs: Soho Theatre Co 1978–89, Theatre Royal Stratford 1989–91; UN ambass 1995; *Theatre* Only a Game 1973, A Sight of Glory 1975, Scribes 1975, Here Comes the Sun 1976, Gimme Shelter 1977, A Mad World My Masters 1977, Barbarians 1977, Gotcha 1977, Frozen Assets 1978, Sus 1979, Bastard Angel 1980, She's So Modern 1980, Black Lear 1980, Chorus Girls 1981, Better Times 1985, King of England 1988, My Girl 1989, Not Fade Away 1990, Wild Justice 1990, We Lost Our Library 1993, I Only Want to be With You 1995; *Television* plays: Nipper 1977, Champions 1978, Hanging Around 1978, Waterloo Sunset 1979, King 1984; TV series No Excuses 1983, Paradise 1991; *Films* The Long Good Friday 1981; *Awards* French Critics Prix Revelation 1978, Giles Cooper Best Radio Plays 1980, Mystery Writers of America Edgar Allan Poe Award 1982; *Novels* Gadabout (1969), No Excuses (1983); *Recreations* origami; *Style*— Barrie Keeffe, Esq; ✉ 110 Annandale Rd, Greenwich, London SE10 0JZ

KEEGAN, John Desmond Patrick; OBE (1991); s of Francis Joseph Keegan (d 1975), of London, and Eileen Mary, *née* Bridgman; *b* 15 May 1934; *Educ* King's Coll Taunton, Wimbledon Coll, Balliol Coll Oxford (BA, MA); *m* 10 Dec 1960, Susanne Ingeborg, da of Dr Thomas Everett, of Horsington, Somerset (d 1974); 2 s (Thomas b 1963, Matthew b 1965), 2 da (Lucy Newmark b 1961, Rose Keegan b 1965); *Career* sr lectr in war studies RMA Sandhurst 1960–86, defence ed Daily Telegraph 1986–; Lees Knowles lectr in mil history Cambridge 1986–87; visitor Sexey's Hosp Bruton Somerset, dir East Somerset NHS Tst, tstee Nat Heritage Meml Fund; fell Princeton Univ 1984, Delmas distinguished prof of history Vassar Coll 1997; FRHistS, FRSL; *Books* The Face of Battle (1976), World Armies (1978), Six Armies in Normandy (1982), The Mask of Command (1987), The Price of Admiralty (1988), The Second World War (1989), A History of Warfare (1993, Duff Cooper prize 1993), Warpaths (1995); *Clubs* Garrick, Beefsteak, Pratt's, The Brook (NY); *Style*— John Keegan, Esq, OBE, FRSL; ✉ The Manor House, Kilmington, Warminster, Wilts BA12 6RD (☎ 01985 844574); The Daily Telegraph, 1 Canada Square, Canary Wharf, London E14 5DT (☎ 0171 538 5000)

KEEGAN, (Elizabeth) Mary; da of Michael Keegan (d 1991), of Upminster, Essex, and Elizabeth, *née* Sarginson; *b* 21 Jan 1953; *Educ* Brentwood Co HS for Girls, Somerville Coll Oxford (Caroline Haslett meml scholar, Coombs exhibitioner, MA, rowing blue); *Career* Price Waterhouse CAs: articled London 1974, Paris 1979, Chicago 1982, ptnr 1985–, nat tech ptnr 1991–, dir Professional Standards Europe 1994–; chm Fin Reporting Ctee and memb Cncl ICAEW 1994–; memb Urgent Issues Task Force Accounting Standards Bd 1993–; FCA 1983 (ACA 1977), FRSA; *Recreations* classical music, sailing; *Style*— Miss Mary Keegan; ✉ Price Waterhouse, Southwark Towers, 32 London Bridge Street, London SE1 9SY (☎ 0171 939 3000, fax 0171 378 0647)

KEEGAN, William James Gregory; s of William Patrick Keegan (d 1995), of Durham, and Sheila Julia, *née* Buckley (d 1976); *b* 3 July 1938; *Educ* Wimbledon Coll, Trinity Coll Cambridge (MA); *m* 1, 7 Feb 1967 (m dis 1982), Tessa, *née* Young (wid of John Ashton); 2 s, 2 da; m 2, 24 Oct 1992, Hilary Stonefrost (barr), da of Maurice Stonefrost, CBE, DL, *qv*, and Audrey Stonefrost; 1 da (Caitlin Clare b 5 Sept 1994); *Career* Nat Serv 5 Royal Tank Regt RASC (cmmnd 1958) 1957–59; journalist: Financial Times 1963–64, Daily Mail 1964–67; economics corr Financial Times 1967–76, worked Econ Intelligence Dept Bank of England 1976–77, economics ed The Observer 1977– (assoc ed 1982–); memb: BBC Advsy Ctee on Business and Industl Affrs 1981–88, Cncl Employment Inst 1987–92, Advsy Bd Dept of Applied Economics Univ of Cambridge 1988–92; visiting prof of journalism Univ of Sheffield 1989– (hon res fell 1990–), memb CNAA (memb Ctee for Social Sci 1991–92); Hon DLitt Univ of Sheffield 1995; *Books* fiction: Consulting Father Wintergreen (1974), A Real Killing (1976); non-fiction: Who Runs The Economy (jtly, 1978), Mrs Thatcher's Economic Experiment (1984), Britain Without Oil (1985), Mr Lawson's Gamble (1989), The Spectre of Capitalism (1992); *Clubs* Garrick, MCC; *Style*— William Keegan, Esq; ✉ The Observer, 119 Farringdon Road, London EC1 3ER (☎ 0171 278 2332)

KEELING, Christopher Anthony Gedge; s of Sir Edward Keeling, MC, MP, DL (d 1954), of London SW1, and Martha Ann, *née* Darling; *b* 15 June 1930; *Educ* Eton, RMA Sandhurst; *m* 1, 20 Sept 1955 (m dis 1972), Veronica, da of Alec Waugh, writer (d 1980), of Edrington, Silchester, Berks; 2 s (Simon Alexander Edward d 1982, Julian James), 1 da (Nicola Sara); m 2, 1974, Rachael Macdonald; *Career* Capt Grenadier Gds 1948–56; chm Minories Underwriting Agencies Ltd; Freeman City of London, Liveryman Worshipful Co of Fishmongers 1955; *Recreations* shooting, reading, watching cricket; *Clubs* White's, MCC, Beefsteak; *Style*— Christopher Keeling, Esq; ✉ Leyden House, Thames Bank, London SW14 7QR (☎ 0181 876 7375); Minories Underwriting Agencies Ltd, 18 Mansell St, London E1 8AA (☎ 0171 264 7000, fax 0171 488 2789)

KEELING, Surgn Rear Adm John; CBE (1978); *b* 28 Oct 1921; *Educ* Queen Elizabeth's Sch Hartlebury, Univ of Birmingham; *m* 1948, Olwen Anne, *née* Dix; 2 s (1 decd); *Career* RN 1946; Fleet Air Arm until 1975, dir of environmental med 1975–77, dep med dir-gen (Naval) 1977–80, dir of med policy and plans MOD 1980–83, chm NATO Jt Civil/Mil Med Gp 1981–83; QHP 1977–83; memb Cncl of Mgmnt Herefordshire Nature Tst 1989–; MFOM, memb Soc of Occupational Med; *Recreations* caravanning, microcomputers; *Style*— Surgn Rear Adm John Keeling, CBE; ✉ Merlin Cottage, Brockhampton, Hereford HR1 4TQ (☎ 01989 740649)

KEEMER, Peter John Charles; s of Frederick George Keemer (d 1973), and Queenie Ellen, *née* Gaston (d 1972); *b* 27 Jan 1932; *Educ* Price's Sch Fareham, City of London Coll, Univ of Bath (MPhil); *m* 5 Aug 1954, Yvonne, da of late Henry Griffin; 2 s (Jeremy b and d 1958, Nigel Richard b 1962), 1 da (Caroline Jane b 1959); *Career* Nat Serv Sgt Royal Army Educn Corps 1950–52; Exchequer and Audit Dept: asst auditor then auditor 1952–62, private sec to Comptroller and Auditor Gen 1962–65, seconded to Office of Parly Cmmr for Admin as chief exec offr 1966–70, chief auditor 1970–74, dep dir 1974–77, dir 1978, seconded to Euro Ct of Auditors as dir 1978–86; Nat Audit Office (formerly Exchequer and Audit Dept): dir 1986–89, asst auditor gen 1989–93; hon treas Inst of Cancer Research 1996– (dir 1994–), external auditor European Univ Inst Florence 1994–, chm of tstees Breakthrough Breast Cancer; memb CIPFA 1982; *Clubs* Royal Anglo-Belgian; *Style*— Peter Keemer, Esq; ✉ How Green Cottage, How Lane, Chipstead, Surrey CR5 3LL (☎ and fax 01737 553711, e-mail keemer@premier.co.uk)

KEEN, Alan; MP (Lab) Feltham and Heston (majority 1,995); s of late Jack Keen, and Gladys Keen; *b* 25 Nov 1937; *Educ* Sir William Turner's Sch Redcar; *m* 20 June 1980, Ann Lloyd, *née* Fox; 1 s, 1 da; *Career* various positions 1963–92, pt/t tactical scout Middlesbrough FC 1969–85, sometime fire protection conslt; cncllr London Borough of Hounslow 1986–90, MP (Lab, Co-op Pty) Feltham and Heston 1992–; memb Select Ctees on: Deregulation 1995–, Educn 1995–; *Recreations* music, football, athletics; *Style*— Alan Keen, Esq, MP; ✉ House of Commons, London SW1A 0AA

KEEN, Charles William Lyle; s of Harold Hugh Keen (d 1974), and Catherine Eleanor Lyle, *née* Cummins (d 1991); *b* 4 July 1936; *Educ* Winchester, New Coll Oxford (MA); *m* 21 July 1962, Lady (Priscilla) Mary Rose, da of 6 Earl Howe, CBE (d 1984); 1 s (William b 1970), 3 da (Laura (Hon Mrs Nicholas Beatty) b 1963, Eleanor b 1965, Alice (Mrs Peter Oswald) b 1966); *Career* Lt The Royal Dragoons; local dir Barclays Bank: Reading 1967–71 (sr local dir 1974–81), Nottingham 1971–74; dir: Barclays Unicorn Group Ltd 1978–81, Barclays Merchant Bank 1981–87, Barclays de Zoete Wedd Holdings Ltd 1986–87; regnl dir Barclays Bank 1987–96; tstee Shaw Tst Wells Preservation Tst 1996; AIB 1964; *Books* The Mondragon Experience (jtly, 1977); *Recreations* rural sports and pastimes; *Style*— Charles Keen, Esq; ✉ The Old Rectory, Duntisbourne Rous, Cirencester GL7 7AP (☎ 01285 653569)

KEEN, Maurice Hugh; s of Harold Hugh Keen (d 1974), and Catherine, *née* Cummins; *b* 30 Oct 1933; *Educ* Winchester (scholar), Balliol Coll Oxford (BA); *m* 20 July 1968, Mary Agnes, da of Francis Keegan; 3 da (Catherine b 1969, Harriet b 1971, Clare b 1973); *Career* Nat Serv 2 Lt Royal Ulster Rifles 1952–54; jr res fell The Queen's Coll Oxford 1957–61, fell and tutor in medieval history Balliol Coll Oxford 1961–; govr Blundell's Sch 1970–89, fell Winchester Coll 1989–; FSA 1987, FBA 1990; *Books* The Outlaws of Medieval Legend (1961), The Laws of War in the Later Middle Ages (1965), Pelican History of Medieval Europe (1968), England in the Later Middle Ages (1973), Chivalry (1984), English Society in the Later Middle Ages (1990); *Recreations* fishing, shooting; *Style*— Maurice Keen, Esq, FSA, FBA; ✉ Balliol College, Oxford OX1 3BJ (☎ 01865 277777)

KEEN, Richard Sanderson; QC (Scot 1993); s of Derek Michael Keen, of Wester Balgedie, Kinross-Shire, and Jean, *née* Sanderson; *b* 29 March 1954; *Educ* King's Sch Rochester, Dollar Acad, Univ of Edinburgh (Beckman scholar, LLB Hons); *m* 7 April 1980, Jane Carolyn, da of Dr William Marr Anderson; 1 s (Jamie Marr Sanderson b 29 Sept 1983), 1 da (Sophie Jane b 29 Sept 1985); *Career* Bar apprentice with Messrs Balfour and Manson, admitted Faculty of Advocates 1980, standing jr counsel DTI Scotland 1986–93; *Recreations* opera, golf, shooting, skiing; *Clubs* New (Edinburgh), Bruntsfield Links Golfing Soc, Grange (Edinburgh); *Style*— Richard Keen, Esq, QC; ✉ 18 India Street, Edinburgh EH3 6EZ (☎ 0131 225 8340, fax 0131 225 5801); Advocates Library, Parliament House, Parliament Square, Edinburgh EH1 1RF (☎ 0131 226 5071, clerk 0131 260 5699)

KEENE, Bryan Richard; s of Edward Stanley William Keene (d 1963), of Weybridge, and Sybil White, *née* Holmes (d 1991); *b* 14 Sept 1937; *Educ* St James' Boys Sch

Weybridge; *Career* Securities Agency Ltd and Drayton Corporation Ltd 1963–74, asst dir Samuel Montagu & Co Ltd 1974–84; dir: Elliot Assocs Ltd 1984–, Anglo-Scottish Securities Ltd 1986–, Staple Investment Trust Ltd 1986–, Invesco Trustee Corporation 1986–, Anglo-Scottish Amalgamated Corporation Ltd 1993–, Invesco Pension Trustees Ltd 1994–; ptnr Raleigh Manor Hotel Wheddon Cross Somerset; FCIS 1968, ATII 1977; *Style*— Bryan Keene, Esq; ✉ Woodside, Winterbourne Grove, Weybridge, Surrey (☎ 01932 841708); 11 Devonshire Square, London EC2M 4YR (☎ 0171 626 3434)

KEENE, Hon Mr Justice; Hon Sir David Wolfe; kt (1994); s of Edward Henry Wolfe Keene (d 1987), and Lilian Marjorie, *née* Conway; *b* 15 April 1941; *Educ* Hampton GS, Balliol Coll Oxford (Eldon scholar, BA, BCL, Winter Williams prize), Inner Temple (Public Int Law prize); *m* 1965, Gillian Margaret, da of Geoffrey Lawrance; 1 s (Edward Geoffrey Wolfe b 1970), 1 da (Harriet Margaret b 1968); *Career* called to the Bar Inner Temple 1964, bencher 1987; QC 1980–94, recorder of the Crown Court 1989–94, judge of the High Court of Justice (Queen's Bench Div) 1994– (dep High Ct judge 1993); judge Employment Appeal Tbnl; visitor Brunel Univ 1995–; chm Examination-in-Public Cumbria Structure Plan 1980, inspector County Hall (London) Public Inquiry 1987, chm Local Govt and Planning Bar Assoc 1994, sometime memb Final Selection Bd Planning Inspectorate DOE; memb Exec Ctee Amnesty International (Br section) 1965–68; *Books* The Adult Criminal (co-author 1967); *Clubs* Athenaeum; *Style*— The Hon Mr Justice Keene; ✉ Royal Courts of Justice, Strand, London WC2A 2LL

KEENE, Gareth John; s of Victor Horace Keene, of Kent, and Muriel Olive, *née* Whitehead; *b* 31 March 1944; *Educ* Tonbridge, St John's Coll Cambridge (Choral scholar, MA, LLM); *m* 1, 1969 (m dis 1983), Georgina, da of David Walter Patrick Thomas, of Cambs; 3 s (Timothy b 1973, David b 1975, Jonathan b 1979); m 2, 1983, Charlotte Louise, da of Peter Frank Lester (d 1985), of Devon; *Career* called to the Bar Gray's Inn 1966; sec Allen & Hanburys Ltd 1968–73, admin Dartington Coll of Arts 1973–78 (later govr), sec The Dartington Hall Tst 1978–83; dir: TSW Television South West Holdings plc 1980–82, Gamida for Life BV (formerly Eryphile Group) Netherlands 1989–; chm Ganidor Ltd 1994–; sec Euro Community Chamber Orchestra Tst, chm Beaford Arts Centre; Freeman City of London 1971, Liveryman Worshipful Co of Skinners 1974; *Books* Sacred and Secular (with Adam Fox, 1975); *Recreations* music; *Clubs* RSM; *Style*— Gareth Keene, Esq; ✉ Buttermead, Manaton, Newton Abbot, Devon TQ13 9XG (☎ 01647 221208, fax 01647 221410)

KEENE, Martin Elliott; s of John Keene, and Pamela, *née* Richards; *b* 8 Sept 1957; *Educ* Felsted, Sidney Sussex Coll Cambridge (BA); *Career* photographer: Torquay Herald Express 1978–82, Torbay News Agency 1982–87; The Press Association: joined as staff photographer 1987, special responsibility for royal coverage 1990, chief photographer 1992–95, picture ed 1995–; *Books* Practical Photojournalism - a professional guide (1993); *Style*— Martin Keene, Esq; ✉ c/o The Press Association, 292 Vauxhall Bridge Road, London SW1V 1EA (☎ 0171 963 7155)

KEENE, Raymond Dennis; OBE (1985); s of Dennis Arthur Keene (d 1992), of Worthing, and Doris Anita, *née* Leat (d 1969); *b* 29 Jan 1948; *Educ* Dulwich, Trinity Coll Cambridge (MA); *m* 1974, Annette Sara, da of Walter Goodman; 1 s (Alexander Philip Simon b 21 March 1991); *Career* chess corr: The Spectator 1977–, The Times 1985–, Thames Television 1986–, Channel 4 TV 1993–, Classic FM Radio 1993–; chess contrib to Encyclopaedia Britannica; memb Eng Olympic chess team 1966, 1968, 1970, 1972, 1974, 1976, 1978 and 1980, Br Chess Champion 1971, Olympic Bronze medal 1976, Bronze medal Cwlth Chess Championship Melbourne 1983; winner various int chess tournaments: Johannesburg 1973, Camaguey (Cuba) 1974, Alicante 1977, Sydney 1979, Dortmund 1980, London (Lloyds Masters) 1981, Adelaide 1983, Valletta 1985; chess grandmaster 1976 (life title); chief oraniser: World Chess Championship London 1986, World Memory Championship London 1991, World Draughts Championship London 1992, second World Memory Championship London 1993, World Chess Championship between Kasparov and Short London 1993, World Draughts Championship Human v Computer Boston 1994, third World Memory Championship London 1994; *Books* author of over 90 books on chess (the world record) incl: Duels of the Mind, Kingfisher Pocket Book of Chess, Batsford Chess Openings (with Garry Kasparov), Buzan's Book of Genius (co-author, 1994); *Recreations* attending ballet, theatre, opera, collecting modern British art; *Clubs* Athenaeum, RAC; *Style*— Raymond Keene, Esq, OBE; ✉ 86 Clapham Common North Side, London SW4 9SE (☎ 0171 228 7009, fax 0171 924 6472); Times Newspaper, News International, 1 Virginia St, London E1 (fax 0171 402 6183)

KEENLYSIDE, Brig Richard Headlam (Dick); CBE (1957), DSO (1946); s of Capt Guy Francis Headlam Keenlyside (ka France 1914), and Rose Margaret, *née* Knyvett (d 1969); *b* 13 May 1909; *Educ* Charterhouse, RMA Woolwich; *m* 1, 1937, Aileen Evelyn D'Auvergne (d 1960), da of Capt Nigel Hogg (ka 1916); 2 da (Susan (Mrs Lionel Vale) b 1939, Jane (Mrs John Jacob) b 1940); m 2, 28 April 1962, Ann Christian (d 1988), wid of Maj-Gen F N Mitchell, da of Maj Nigel Livingstone-Learmonth (ka 1915); 3 step da (Dame Mona Mitchell, DCVO, Josephine (Mrs John Robinson), Marion (Mrs Ian Weston)); *Career* cmmnd 2 Lt 1929, served England 1929–34, India (now Pakistan) 1935–39, (Capt) France 1939, (Maj) France, Belgium, Dunkirk, England 1940; Egypt, Sudan, Eritrea, Palestine 1940–42; Lt-Col Tripoli, Algeria, Normandy, Belgium, Holland, Germany 1943–45; Regtl Cdr and WO England 1945–50, SO Germany 1950–53, Regtl Cdr England 1953–54, SO Singapore 1954–57, Cdr RA 56 (London) Div 1958–61, ret 1961; dir CLA Game Fair 1963–74; The Netherlands Bronze Cross 1946; *Recreations* watching shooting and golf, playing the piano; *Clubs* Army and Navy; *Style*— Brig R H Keenlyside, CBE, DSO; ✉ Valley Farm, Blackford, Yeovil, Somerset BA22 7EF (☎ 01963 440304)

KEENS, David Wilson; s of Wilson Leonard Keens (d 1959), and Olive Ivy, *née* Collins; *b* 16 Aug 1953; *m* Shirley Ann, da of Cyril Charles Cardnell; 1 s (Benjamin David b 17 Nov 1983), 1 da (Emma Louise b 15 Oct 1985); *Career* Gale Brown & Co Essex: articled clerk 1970–75, chartered accountant 1975–77; RJR Nabisco Inc 1977–86: successively chief fin offr Tunis, fin controller Liverpool, fin dir Lancashire, planning dir and treas Berks; Next plc: dir of treasy then gp fin dir 1986–; ACA 1975, ACT 1989; *Style*— David Keens, Esq; ✉ Next plc, Desford Rd, Enderby, Leicestershire LE9 5AT (☎ 0116 286 6411, fax 0116 286 7178, mobile 0374 606888)

KEEYS, Geoffrey Foster; s of Richard Kipling Foster Keeys, and Joan, *née* Anderson; *b* 29 Oct 1944; *Educ* Abingdon Sch, Univ of Manchester (LLB); *m* 4 April 1970, Christine Mary (Donna), da of Henry Albert Lavers, of Newbury; 1 s (Henry Foster b 16 April 1976), 1 da (Georgia Ellen b 22 May 1974); *Career* graduate trainee Mobil Oil 1966–68, various personnel positions to dir of personnel and industl relations (Euro and world export) Massey Ferguson 1968–82, dir gp personnel Chubb & Son plc 1982–84, dir of Personnel and Business Servs Prudential Corporation plc 1984–95, md Strategic Thinking Group 1995–; dir IPD Enterprises Ltd; non-exec memb Bd HM Prison Service until 1995 (resigned); memb Advsy Bds: Personnel Management (magazine of Inst of Personnel Mgmnt), Centre for Strategic Mgmnt and Change Univ of Warwick; tstee Pension Fund NABC; FIPM; *Recreations* golf, cricket; *Clubs* RAC, Wisley Golf; *Style*— Geoffrey Keeys, Esq; ✉ Strategic Thinking Group, 211 Piccadilly, London W1V 9LD (☎ 0171 917 2867, fax 0171 917 2868)

KEFFER, John W; s of James Morgan Keffer (d 1935), and Dove, *née* Douglas (d 1934); *b* 5 June 1923; *Educ* Texas Technol Univ (BA), The Univ of Texas (JD), Johns Hopkins Univ (MA); *m* 25 Aug 1954, Natalia, da of Baron Giulio Blanc (d 1978), of Le Château, Tolochenaz, Switzerland; 2 s (Charles b 1955 d 1959, John b 1957); *Career* ensign USNR 1943; served Europe 1944–45: Normandy Invasion 1944, Invasion Southern France 1944, Lt (JG); served Pacific 1945–46: Okinawa, Philippines, occupation of Japan; lawyer 1950–53: Schuster & Davenport NY, Travieso Paul Caracas Venezuela; gen counsel: Esso Standard Oil Havana Cuba 1954–60, Coral Gables Florida 1960–63, Creole Petroleum Corp Caracas Venezuela 1964–73, Esso Europe London 1973–85; counsel Fulbright & Jaworski London 1986–; chm tstees American Museum in Br 1982– (tstee 1979–), memb Advsy Bd Royal Acad 1987–; memb: Int Bar Assoc, American Bar Assoc, Texas Bar; *Recreations* photography, collecting paintings, drawings, watercolours, antiques; *Clubs* Garrick, Brooks's, Univ (NY), Circolo Della Caccia (Rome); *Style*— John Keffer, Esq; ✉ Fulbright & Jaworski, 2 St James's Place, London SW1A 1NP (☎ 0171 629 1207, fax 0171 493 8259, telex 28310)

KEFFORD, Anthony John Roland; s of Harry Roland Kefford, of Basildon, Essex, and Joyce, *née* Reeves; *b* 18 Jan 1954; *Educ* City of London Sch, QMC (BSc), Poly of Central London (Dip Law); *m* 21 Nov 1981, Janet Maureen, da of Douglas Malcolm Grant, of Wickford, Essex; 2 da (Edith b 20 July 1983, Harriet b 11 April 1991); *Career* called to the Bar Middle Temple 1980; in practice Norwich 1981–; *Style*— Anthony Kefford, Esq; ✉ East Anglian Chambers, 57 London St, Norwich NR3 1HR

KEIGHLEY, Dr Brian Douglas; s of Jeffrey Torrance Keighley, of Bishopbriggs, Glasgow, and Alice Winifred, *née* North; *b* 21 May 1948; *Educ* Glasgow Acad, Univ of Glasgow (MB ChB, MRCGP, DFM); *m* 11 Sept 1976, Ruth Patricia, da of James Kevin Maguire; 2 s (Douglas John b 31 Aug 1978, Andrew James b 5 May 1981); *Career* house offr: in gen med Law Hosp Lanarkshire 1972–73, in gen surgery Stobhill Hosp Glasgow 1973; sr house offr: in obstetrics and gynaecology Robroyston Hosp Glasgow 1973–74, in paediatrics Falkirk Royal Infirmary Falkirk 1974; trainee GP 1974–75, princ in gen practice 1975–; police surgn 1975– (dep 1975–83), GP trainer 1978–94, MO Ballikinrain Sch 1983–; memb: Scottish Gen Med Servs Ctee 1978– (chm 1995–), Forth Valley Area Med Ctee (chm 1989–92), Forth Valley Local Med Ctee (chm 1986–89), Scottish Rural Practices Fund Ctee 1986– (chm 1989–95), Scottish Cncl BMA 1990–, Gen Med Servs Ctee UK 1992–, Private Practice and Professional Fees Ctee BMA 1992–94, Jt Ctee on Postgrad Trg for Gen Practice 1990–, Scottish Cncl for Postgrad Med and Dental Educn 1993–, GMC 1994–; memb Assoc of Police Surgns 1975; fell RSM 1988, FRCGP 1990; *Recreations* angling, jogging, squash; *Clubs* RSM, Western Medical (Glasgow); *Style*— Dr Brian Keighley; ✉ Hector Cottage, Bankers Brae, Balfron, Stirlingshire G63 0PY (☎ 01360 440520, fax 01360 440829); The Clinic, Buchanan Street, Balfron, Stirlingshire G63 0TS (☎ 01360 440515, fax 01360 440831, car 0831 174139)

KEIGHLEY, Prof Michael Robert Burch; s of Rev Dr R A S Keighley, TD (d 1988), and Dr J V Keighley, *née* Burch; *b* 12 Oct 1943; *Educ* Monkton Combe Sch nr Bath, Bart's Med Coll London (MB BS, MS); *m* 27 Sept 1969, Dr D Margaret Keighley, da of J H Shepley (d 1985); 1 s (Nicholas John Alexander b 23 Jan 1974), 1 da (Helen Louise b 28 Oct 1971); *Career* Univ of Birmingham: prof of gastrointestinal surgery 1985–88, Barling prof and head Dept of Surgery 1988–; Hunterian prof RCS 1976, Jacksonian prize RCS 1980, Boerhaave prof of surgery Univ of Leiden 1985, Eybers visiting prof Univ of Blomfontein 1988, visiting prof Harvard 1990, Penman visiting prof Univ of Cape Town 1991; treas and memb Cncl Br Jl of Surgery; memb: American Soc of Colorectal Surgns, Br Soc of Gastroenterology (formerly memb Cncl), Coloproctology Section RSM (formerly sec and memb Cncl), Cncl Surgical Res Soc, Assoc of Surgns of GB & I; hon fell Brazilian Coll of Surgns, FRSCEd 1970, FRCS 1971; *Books* Antimicrobial Prophylaxis in Surgery (1980), Inflammatory Bowel Diseases (1983 and 1990), Gastrointestinal Haemorrhage (1985), Textbook of Gastroenterology (1986 and 1993), Surgery of the Anus, Rectum & Colon (1993); *Recreations* painting, music, writing, travel, botony, walking, sailing; *Clubs* RSM, Athenaeum; *Style*— Prof Michael Keighley; ✉ Department of Surgery, Queen Elizabeth Hospital, Edgbaston, Birmingham B15 2TH (☎ 0121 627 2276, fax 0121 472 1230)

KEIGHTLEY, Maj-Gen Richard Charles; CB (1987); s of Gen Sir Charles F Keightley, GCB, GBE, DSO (d 1974), and Joan Lydia, da of Brig-Gen G N T Smyth-Osbourne, CB, CMG, DSO (d 1942); *b* 2 July 1933; *Educ* Marlborough, RMA Sandhurst; *m* 21 Oct 1958, Caroline Rosemary, da of Col Sir Thomas Butler, 12 Bt, DSO, OBE, MVO (d 1994); 3 da (Charlotte (Mrs Jenkinson) b 21 March 1961, Arabella (Mrs O'Connell) b 31 July 1962, Victoria b 3 Dec 1965); *Career* cmmnd 5 Royal Inniskilling Dragoon Gds 1953; served Suez Canal Zone, Far East, Libya, NI, Germany, Cdr 1972–75; Cdr: Task Force E 1978–79, Western Dist 1982–83; Cmdt RMA Sandhurst 1983–87, Col 5 Royal Inniskilling Dragoon Gds 1986–91; chm: Combined Servs Polo Assoc 1982–87, Dorset Health Authy 1988–95, Dorset Healthcare NHS Tst 1995–; pres Dorset Co Royal Br Legion 1992–; *Recreations* equitation, field sports, cricket, farming; *Style*— Maj-Gen Richard Keightley, CB; ✉ Kennels Cottage, Tarrant Gunville, Blandford, Dorset DT11 8JQ (☎ 01258 830418), fax 01258 830651); 11 Shelley Road, Boscombe, Bournemouth, Dorset BH1 4JQ (☎ 01202 443081)

KEIL, Charles George; *b* 7 March 1933; *Educ* St Bartholomew's GS Newbury, QMC London; *m* 23 April 1960, Janette Catherine; 2 s (Duncan b 1963, Ewan b 1964), 1 da (Fiona b 1962); *Career* fighter pilot RAF 1951–55, Flt Lt; served Canada, Germany, France, Cyprus; ed of monthly aviation journal Aircraft Engineering 1959–65, assoc ed (London) Indian Aviation 1963–66, gp ed Thomas Reed Publications Ltd 1965–66, dir John Fowler & Ptnrs Ltd (PR conslts) 1971–73, md Harrison Cowley PR Birmingham Ltd 1974–94; chm: Harrison Cowley PR Gp (Birmingham, Bristol, Cardiff, Edinburgh, Maidenhead, Manchester and Southampton) 1988–, Birmingham Readers' and Writers' Festival 1992–96, Brumhalata Storytelling Co 1995–; mktg dir Birmingham Centre for Drama 1994–95; mktg advsr Business in the Arts 1992–, session leader Understanding Industry 1992–, memb Servs Ctee Birmingham City 2000 1995–; MRAeS, CEng; *Books* Aerodynamics (jt ed and trans with Janette C Loder, textbook); *Recreations* border collies, reading, walking, painting, skiing, activity holidays; *Clubs* RAF; *Style*— Charles Keil, Esq; ✉ Illyria, 536 Streetsbrook Rd, West Midlands B91 1RD (☎ 0121 705 0773); Harrison Cowley Public Relations, 154 Great Charles St, Birmingham B3 3HU (☎ 0121 236 7532)

KEILL, (William Richard) Ian; s of Cdre W J D Keill (d 1980), and Annie Mavis, *née* Dash; *b* 11 May 1937; *Educ* Liverpool Coll, RADA (Dip); *m* 1963 (m dis 1977), Carole Ann, *née* Bishop; 1 s (Jeremy William Richard b 8 Oct 1964); m 2, 1990, Enid Averil, *née* Musson; *Career* actor then dir prodr and writer; BBC TV: prodr and dir Up Sunday 1971–73, 30 documentaries in the One Mans Weeks series 1971–74, The End of the Pier Show 1974; pioneered electronic fantasy on TV with: The Snow Queen 1976, The Light Princess 1978, The Mystery of the Disappearing Schoolgirls 1980, The Ghost Downstairs 1982; prodr strip cartoon Jane, dir and prodr two schoolgirl dramas 1982–83, prodr History of Westerns 1987, dir children's ghost serial 1988, prodr Lucinda Lambton in Desirable Dwellings Forty Minutes 1988, prodr Frederic Raphael in Frontiers 1989; currently freelance; directed 3 progs in Dream Gardens (series for BBC 2) 1991, dir Gardener's World 1992, prodr and dir Quest for the Rose (TV documentary series in Britain, America and China) 1993, currently developing Terry Pratchett's Discworld for television; *Recreations* collecting books and recorded music, photography; *Style*— Ian Keill, Esq; ✉ Dovedale Cottage, Moor End Common, Lane End, Bucks HP14 3EZ (☎ 01494 881541)

KEIR, Prof Hamish Macdonald; s of Esme Charles Robson Keir (d 1967), of Ayr, Scotland, and Mabel Munro, *née* Blackstock (d 1979); *b* 5 Sept 1931; *Educ* Ayr Acad, Univ of Glasgow (BSc, PhD, DSc); *m* 1, Eleanor Louise, da of Ivor Campbell (d 1974), of Oban, Scotland; 2 da (Catriona Louise b 1959, Deirdre Jean b 1961), 1 s (Kenneth

James Macdonald b 1962); m 2, Linda Margaret, da of William A G Gerrie, MC, of Aberdeen, Scotland; 2 da (Lindsay Helen Margaret b 1988, Catherine Elizabeth b 1992); m 3, Evelyn Mary, da of Richard J Cook, of Royston; *Career* Univ of Glasgow: asst lectr in biochemistry 1956–59, lectr 1960–66, sr lectr 1966–68; James Hudson Brown res fell in pharmacology Yale Univ 1959–60, vice princ Univ of Aberdeen 1982–84 (Prof of biochemistry 1968–96); govr Rowett Res Inst 1968–94 (chm 1989–93), pres Fedn of Euro Biochemical Socs 1981–83, memb Br Nation Ctee for Biochemistry Royal Soc 1986–90; chm: Jt Purchasing Consortium Univs of Scotland 1986–96, The Biochemical Soc 1986–89; govr and vice chm Macaulay Land Use Res Inst 1987–, pres Euro Union of Socs for Experimental Biology 1989–96, Euro Sci Fndn, Euroconferences 1989–; govr Longridge Towers Sch 1987–, branch chm Exec Cncl Ross Skye & Inverness W Conservation & Unionist Assoc 1996–; FRSE 1969; *Recreations* piano, travel, golf; *Clubs* Conservative Club, Aberdeen; *Style*— Prof Hamish Keir, FRSE; ✉ Dundalachie, Cathedral Square, Fortrose, The Black Isle, Ross & Cromarty IV10 8TB (☎ 01381 621239)

KEIR, James Dewar; QC; s of Lt-Col David Robert Keir, DSO (d 1947), of Edinburgh, and Elizabeth Lunan, *née* Ross (d 1975); *b* 30 Nov 1921; *Educ* Edinburgh Acad, ChCh Oxford (MA); *m* 7 July 1948, Jean Mary, da of Rev Edward Percival Orr (d 1970), of Diss, Norfolk; 2 s (Robert b 17 Sept 1954, Simon b 29 March 1957), 2 da (Alison b 22 Aug 1950, Caroline b 11 Feb 1952); *Career* Capt Black Watch RHR served: ME, Italy, Austria; called to the Bar Inner Temple 1949, legal advsr United Africa Company Ltd 1954, head of legal servs Unilever Ltd 1973, jt sec Unilever NV and Unilever plc 1976–84; dir Open University Educational Enterprises Ltd 1983–88; pres E Grinstead RFC 1969–88; chm: City and E London Family Practitioner Ctee 1985–89, Pharmacists Review Panel 1986–, E Grinstead Decorative and Fine Arts Soc 1987–92, Professional Ctee Royal Coll of Speech and Language Therapists 1993–; memb Monopolies and Mergers Cmmn 1987–92; lay memb NHS Pharmaceutical Appeals Panel 1992–; *Recreations* watching rugby, opera, reading; *Clubs* Caledonian; *Style*— James Keir, Esq, QC; ✉ The Crossways, 1 High St, Dormansland, Lingfield, Surrey RH7 6PU (☎ 01342 834621)

KEITH, Alan; OBE (1991); *b* 19 Oct 1908; *Educ* Dame Alice Owen's Sch, RADA; *m* 1941, Pearl Rebuck; 1 s (Brian Richard (Hon Mr Justice Keith, *qv*)), 1 da (Linda Margaret b 7 May 1946); *Career* stage work incl: Late Night Final (Phoenix), Dinner At Eight (Palace), Magnolia Street (Adelphi); deviser and presenter of numerous programmes for radio incl Your Hundred Best Tunes 1959–; *Books* Your Hundred Best Tunes (1977); *Recreations* reading any book dealing with the theatre, talking politics; *Style*— Alan Keith, Esq, OBE; ✉ c/o BBC Radio 2, Broadcasting House, London W1A 1AA

KEITH, Hon Mr Justice; Hon Brian Richard; s of Alan Keith, OBE, *qv*, and Pearl, *née* Rebuck; *b* 14 April 1944; *Educ* UCS, Lincoln Coll Oxford (MA), Harvard Law Sch; *m* 16 Nov 1978, Gilly Mary, da of late Air Cdre Ivan James de la Plain, CBE; 1 s (Benjamin b 15 March 1982), 1 da (Joanna b 22 Oct 1980); *Career* called to the Bar Inner Temple 1968, in practice 1969–91, asst recorder 1988, QC 1989, a judge of the High Ct Hong Kong 1991–, recorder of the Crown Ct 1993–, presiding judge Admin Law List High Ct of Hong Kong 1996–; hon lectr Faculty of Law Univ of Hong Kong 1994–; memb Judicial Studies Bd Hong Kong 1994–; *Recreations* playing tennis, stamp collecting; *Clubs* The Hong Kong; *Style*— The Hon Mr Justice Keith; ✉ The Supreme Court, 38 Queensway, Hong Kong (☎ 852 2825 4422)

KEITH, Ian Douglas; s of Leonard Douglas Keith, and Bertha Musker, *née* Strachan; *b* 13 Oct 1929; *Educ* Strathallan Forgandenny Perth; *m* 5 Sept 1959, Rosemary Enriqueta, da of Col William Herbert Treays, RE (d 1960); 3 da (Sophie Henrietta b 1963, Sarah Louise b 1965, Fiona Mary b 1967); *Career* admitted slr 1960, ptnr Whitley Hughes & Luscombe 1963 (amalgamated with Donne Mileham & Haddock 1986); Notary Public 1963; chm Govrs Handcross Park Prep Sch 1976–87, sole clerk to NHSS Tbnl for Eng and Wales; memb Law Soc; *Recreations* sailing, tennis, gardening; *Clubs* Bosham Sailing, United & Cecil; *Style*— Ian Keith, Esq; ✉ East Hookers, Twineham, nr Haywards Heath, W Sussex RH17 5NN (☎ 01444 881345)

KEITH, Penelope Anne Constance; OBE (1989); da of Frederick Arthur William Hatfield, and Constance Mary, *née* Nutting; *b* 2 April 1940; *Educ* Webber Douglas Acad; *m* 1978, Rodney Timson; *Career* actress; worked in repertory Chesterfield, Lincoln, Manchester and Salisbury, seasons with RSC; pres Actors' Benevolent Fund 1989; govr Queen Elizabeth's Fndn for the Disabled People 1990, govr Guildford Sch of Acting; tstee Yvonne Arnaud Theatre Guildford; memb HFEA 1990; *Theatre* roles incl: Maggie Howard in Suddenly at Home (Fortune) 1971, Sarah in The Norman Conquests (Greenwich and Globe) 1974, Lady Driver in Donkey's Years 1976, Orinthia in The Apple Cart (Chichester and Phoenix) 1977, Epifania in the Millionairess (Haymarket) 1982, Sarah in Moving (Queen's) 1981, Maggie in Hobson's Choice (Haymarket) 1982, Lady Cicely Waynflete in Captain Brassbound's Conversion (Haymarket) 1982, Judith Bliss in Hayfever (Queen's) 1983, The Dragon's Tail (Apollo) 1985, Miranda (Chichester) 1987, The Deep Blue Sea (Haymarket) 1988, Dear Charles (Yvonne Arnaud Theatre) 1990, The Merry Wives of Windsor (Chichester) 1990, The Importance of Being Earnest 1992, On Approval Glyn and It (all Yvonne Arnaud Theatre) 1994, Monsieur Amilcar (Chichester); dir: Relatively Speaking 1992, How the Other Half Loves 1994; *Television* Six Shades of Black, Kate, The Pallisters, Jackanory, Saving it for Albie, The Morecambe and Wise Christmas Show, Tickle on the Tum, Woof, The Good Life, To the Manor Born, Law and Disorder, Sweet Sixteen, Executive Stress, No Job for a Lady, Next of Kin (BBC) 1995 and 1996; former presenter: What's My Line, Capability Brown, Growing Places, Behind the Scenes 1994; *Films* The Priest of Love 1980; *Awards* BAFTA 1976 and 1977, SWET 1976, Variety Club of GB 1976 and 1979, Pye Female Comedy Star 1977, Radio Industries 1978 and 1979, Daily Express 1979/80/81/82, BBC TV Swap Shop 1977–78 and 1979–80, TV Times 1976, 1977–78, 1979–80, 1983 and 1988, United States TV and Radio Mobius 1988; *Style*— Miss Penelope Keith, OBE; ✉ c/o London Management, 2–4 Noel Street, London W1V 3RB (☎ 0171 287 9000, fax 0171 287 3036)

KEITH-LUCAS, Prof David; CBE (1973); s of Dr Keith Lucas, FRS (ka 1916), and Alys, *née* Hubbard (d 1955); *b* 25 March 1911; *Educ* Gresham's, Gonville and Caius Coll Cambridge (MA); *m* 1, 25 April 1942, Dorothy De Bauduy (d 1979), da of Leslie S Robertson (d 1916); 2 s (Michael b 1944, Christopher b 1949), 1 da (Mary (now Mrs Benjamin) b 1943); m 2, 11 July 1981, Phyllis Marion Everard, da of Bertram William Whurr (d 1939); *Career* Short Bros & Harland Ltd: chief designer 1949–58, tech dir 1958–65; Cranfield Inst of Technol: prof of aircraft design 1965–72, chm Coll of Aeronautics 1972–76, pro vice chllr 1970–73, prof emeritus 1976; pt/t dir John Brown & Co 1970–77, chm N I Assoc of Boys' Clubs 1952–65; memb: Senate Queen's Univ of Belfast 1955–65, Roskill Cmmn on Third London Airport 1968–70; pres Royal Aeronautical Soc 1968–69 (Gold medal 1975), memb Bd CAA 1972–80, chm Airworthiness Requirements Bd 1973–81; Hon DSc: Queens Univ Belfast 1968, Cranfield 1975; FIMechE 1949, Hon FAIAA 1974, FEng 1978, Hon FRAeS 1979; *Books* The Shape of Wings to Come (1952); *Recreations* vintage car, vintage cabin cruiser; *Style*— Prof David Keith-Lucas, CBE, FEng; ✉ Manor Close, Emberton, Olney, Bucks MK46 5BX (☎ 01234 711552)

KEITH-MURRAY, Maj Peter; s of David Keith-Murray (d 1968), and Nancy Mai, *née* Gautschi; hp of kinsman, Sir Patrick Murray of Ochtertyre, 12 Bt, *qv*; *b* 12 July 1935; *m* 15 June 1960, Judith Anne, da of William Andrew Tinsley (d 1962), of Sarnia, Ontario; 1 s ((David) Andrew b 7 Dec 1965), 1 da (Leslie Anne b 30 Jan 1961); *Career* RCAF 1954–91 (ret); Canadian Forces Decoration with 2 clasps (long service and good conduct); *Style*— Maj Peter Keith-Murray; ✉ 895 Brentwood Heights, Brentwood Bay, BC V8M 1A8, Canada (☎ and fax 00 1 604 652 0574)

KEITH OF CASTLEACRE, Baron (Life Peer UK 1980), of Swaffham in the county of Norfolk; Kenneth Alexander Keith; kt (1969); s of Edward Charles Keith (d 1972), naturalist and writer, of Swanton Morley House, Dereham, Norfolk; *b* 30 Aug 1916; *Educ* Rugby; *m* 1, 25 April 1946 (m dis 1958), Lady Ariel Olivia Winifred Baird, 2 da of 1 Viscount Stonehaven, GCMG, DSO, PC, and (Ethel) Sydney, Countess of Kintore; 1 s, 1 da; m 2, 1962 (m dis 1972), Mrs Nancy (Slim) Hayward, *née* Mary Raye Gross (d 1990), formerly w of (1) Howard Hawks, the film dir, and (2) Leland Hayward, theatre and film agent; m 3, 1973, Marie-Luz, da of Capt Robert Peel Dennistoun-Webster, RN, and formerly wife of (1) Adrian Donald Henderson and (2) James Robert Hanbury; *Career* British banker and industrialist; trained as chartered accountant; 2 Lt Welsh Gds 1939, Lt-Col 1945, served in N Africa, Italy, France and Germany (despatches, Croix de Guerre with Silver Star); asst to Dir-Gen Political Intelligence Dept Foreign Office 1945–46, asst to md Philip Hill & Partners London 1946–48 (dir 1947), dir Philip Hill Investment Tst 1949 (md 1951); md: Philip Hill Higginson & Co Ltd 1951–59, Philip Hill Higginson Erlangers Ltd 1959–62 (chm 1962–65); dep chm and chief exec Hill Samuel & Co 1965–80 (gp chm 1970–80); dir: Bank of Nova Scotia 1958–86, Eagle Star Insurance Co 1955–75, National Provincial Bank 1967–69, British Airways 1971–72, Times Newspapers Ltd 1967–81; vice chm BEA 1964–71, chm and chief exec Rolls-Royce Ltd 1972–80, chm Arlington Securities 1982–90, dir Standard Telephone and Cables Ltd 1977–85 (chm 1985–89), chm Beecham Group Ltd 1985–86 (vice chm 1956–65 and 1974–87); pres: Br Standards Instn 1989–94, Royal Norfolk Agricultural Assoc 1989, RoSPA 1989–92; memb NEDC 1964–71, chm Economic Planning Cncl for E Anglia 1965–70; govr NIESR, vice pres EEF; memb Cncl Manchester Business Sch; hon companion Royal Aeronautical Soc; FRSA, FIMgt; *Recreations* farming, shooting, golf; *Clubs* White's, Links (NY); *Style*— The Rt Hon the Lord Keith of Castleacre; ✉ The Wicken House, Castle Acre, Norfolk PE32 2BP (☎ 01760 755225)

KEITH OF KINKEL, Baron (Life Peer UK 1976), of Strathtummel in District of Perth and Kinross; Hon Sir Henry Shanks Keith; GBE (1997), PC (1976); o s of Baron Keith of Avonholm (Life Peer, d 1964), and Jane Maitland, *née* Bennet; *b* 7 Feb 1922; *Educ* Edinburgh Acad, Magdalen Coll Oxford (hon fell 1977), Univ of Edinburgh; *m* 17 Dec 1955, Alison Hope Alan, JP, yr da of Alan Brown, of Fairways, St Andrews; 1 da (Hon Deborah Jane b 1957), 4 s (Hon James Alan b 1959, Hon Thomas Hamilton b 1961, Hon Hugo George b 1967, Hon Alexander Lindsay (twin) b 1967); *Career* Scots Gds 1941–45 (despatches); advocate Scottish Bar 1950, called to the Bar Gray's Inn 1951, bencher 1976, QC (Scot) 1962, Sheriff of Roxburgh, Berwick and Selkirk 1970–71; dep chm Parly Boundary Cmmn for Scotland 1971; Senator of College of Justice in Scotland with judicial title of Lord Keith 1971–77, Lord of Appeal in Ordinary 1977–96; memb Ctee on Law of Defamation 1970–73, chm Ctee on Powers of the Revenue Depts 1980–83; *Clubs* Flyfishers'; *Style*— The Rt Hon the Lord Keith of Kinkel, GBE, PC; ✉ House of Lords, London SW1A 0PW

KELBIE, Sheriff David; s of Robert Kelbie, of Plymouth, and Monica Eileen Pearn; *b* 28 Feb 1945; *Educ* Inverurie Acad, Univ of Aberdeen (LLB); *m* 1966, Helen Mary, da of William Ross Smith, of Aberdeen; 1 s (Alasdair David b 1975), 1 da (Catriona Helen b 1972); *Career* advocate 1968; Sheriff: North Strathclyde at Dumbarton 1979–86, Grampian, Highland and Islands, Aberdeen, Stonehaven 1986–; ed Scottish Civil Law Reports 1996–; *Recreations* sailing; *Style*— Sheriff David Kelbie; ✉ 38 Earlspark Drive, Bieldside, Aberdeen (☎ 01224 868237); Aberdeen Sheriff Court (☎ 01224 648316)

KELLAS, Arthur Roy Handasyde; CMG (1963); s of Henry Kellas (d 1923), of Aberdeen, and Mary, *née* Brown (d 1956); *b* 6 May 1915; *Educ* Aberdeen GS, Univ of Aberdeen (MA), Balliol Coll Oxford (BA), École des Sciences Politiques Paris; *m* 27 Aug 1952, (Katharine) Bridget, da of Sir John Le Rougetel, KCMG, MC (d 1975), of Alton, Hants; 2 s (Ian b 1955, Roger b 1958), 1 da (Miranda b 1953); *Career* WWII 2 Lt 7 Bn Border Regt 1939–40 (10 Ind Company 1940), Lt 1 Bn Parachute Regt 1941–43, Capt SOE 1943–44; HM Dip Serv: third sec 1939, third sec Tehran Embassy 1944–47, first sec Helsinki Legation 1949–51, first sec Cairo Embassy 1951–52, first sec Baghdad Embassy 1954–58, cnsllr Tehran Embassy 1958–62, cnsllr Tel Aviv Embassy 1964–65, ambass Kathmandu 1966–70, ambass Aden 1970–72, high cmmr Tanzania 1973–75; FRGS 1960; Pahlavi Order (Taj) Iran 1960; *Books* Down to Earth (war memoirs, 1990); *Clubs* United Oxford and Cambridge Univ; *Style*— Arthur Kellas, Esq, CMG; ✉ Inverockle, Achateny, Acharacle, Argyll, Scotland (☎ 01972 510265); 59 Cockburn St, Edinburgh (☎ 0131 2262398)

KELLAWAY, Prof Ian Walter; s of Leslie William Kellaway (d 1975), and Margaret Seaton, *née* Webber; *b* 10 March 1944; *Educ* King Edward VI GS Totnes, Univ of London (BPharm, PhD, DSc); *m* 2 Aug 1969 (m dis 1995), Kay Elizabeth, da of Raymond Cyril Downey, of Ystrad Mynach; 1 s (Robert b 5 July 1972), 1 da (Jane b 21 May 1974); *Career* lectr in pharmaceutics Dept of Pharmacy Univ of Nottingham 1969–79, prof of pharmaceutics Welsh Sch of Pharmacy Univ of Wales Cardiff 1979–; memb Welsh Scheme for the Devpt of Health and Soc Res; fell Royal Pharmaceutical Soc 1969; *Recreations* gardening, travel; *Style*— Prof Ian Kellaway; ✉ 9 Dan-Y-Bryn Ave, Radyr, S Glamorgan, Wales (☎ 01222 842427); Welsh School of Pharmacy, UWC, PO Box 13, Cardiff CF1 3XF (☎ 01222 874159)

KELLEHER, Brig Dame Joan Evelyn; DBE (1965); da of Kenneth George Henderson, barr-at-law; *b* 24 Dec 1915; *m* 1970, Brig M F H Kelleher, OBE, MC, late RAMC; *Career* joined ATS 1941, cmmnd 1941, WRAC 1949, dir WRAC 1964–67; Hon ADC to to HM The Queen 1964–67; *Recreations* golf, gardening; *Style*— Brig Dame Joan Kelleher, DBE

KELLETT, Anthony; s of Albert Kellett (d 1980), and Lilian, *née* Holroyd; *b* 24 Sept 1937; *Educ* Batley GS, Leeds Sch of Architecture (DipArch); *m* 1, 4 Sept 1964 (m dis 1984); 2 s (Anthony John b 1967, Martin James b 1970); m 2, 1992, Enid Mary; *Career* architect; ptnr: Davidson Marsh & Co 1971–79, Kellett & Robinson 1980–; former pres IOM Soc of Architects and Surveyors; FASI, ACIArb, RIBA, FRSA; *Recreations* choral singing, gardening, painting; *Clubs* Ellan Vannin, Rotary of Rushen and Western Mann; *Style*— Anthony Kellett, Esq; ✉ Rish-y-Lheeaney, 9 Bradda View, Ballakillowey, Colby, Castletown, IOM (☎ 01624 836151); Kellett & Robinson, Sydney Mount, Bucks Rd, Douglas, IOM (☎ 01624 628141)

KELLETT, Sir Stanley Charles; 7 Bt (UK 1801), of Lota, Cork; s of Sir Stanley Everard Kellett, 6 Bt (d 1983), and Audrey Margaret, *née* Phillips; *b* 5 March 1940; *m* 1, 1962 (m dis 1968), Lorraine May, da of F Winspear; m 2, 1968 (m dis 1974), Margaret Ann, da of James W Bofinger; m 3, 1982, Catherine Lorna, da of W J C Orr; 1 da (Leah Catherine Elizabeth, b 1983); *Heir* uncle, Charles Rex Kellett b 1916; *Style*— Sir Stanley Kellett, Bt; ✉ 58 Glad Gunson Drive, Eleebana, Newcastle, NSW 2280, Australia

KELLETT-BOWMAN, Edward Thomas; JP (Middx 1966), MEP (EPP) Itchen, Test and Avon (majority 6,903); s of Reginald Edward Bowman (d 1934), and Mabel Bowman; *b* 25 Feb 1931; *Educ* Reed's Sch, Slough Coll of Technol (DMS), Cranfield Univ (MBA); *m* 1, 1960, Margaret Blakemore (d 1970); 3 s, 1 da; m 2, 1971, (Mary) Elaine Kellett (Dame Elaine Kellett-Bowman, MP, *qv*); *Career* MEP (EDG): Lancs E 1979–84, Hampshire Central 1988–94, Itchen, Test and Avon 1994–; Liveryman Worshipful Co of Wheelwrights; FIMgt; *Recreations* shooting, tennis, swimming; *Style*— Edward

Kellett-Bowman, Esq, JP, MEP; ✉ Constituency Office: 18a Bargates, Christchurch, Dorset BH23 1QL (☎ and fax 01202 475548)

KELLETT-BOWMAN, Dame (Mary) Elaine; *née* Kay; DBE (1989), MP (C) Lancaster (majority 2,953); da of late Walter Kay; *b* 8 July 1924; *Educ* Queen Mary's Sch Lytham, The Mount Sch York, St Anne's Coll Oxford; *m* 1, 1945, Charles Norman Kellett (d 1959); 3 s, 1 da; m 2, 1971, Edward Thomas Kellett-Bowman, JP, MEP, *qv*; 3 step s, 1 step da; *Career* farmer; welfare worker London and Liverpool; called to the Bar Middle Temple 1964, in practice 1968–74; cncllr Denbigh BC 1951–55; Parly candidate (C): Nelson and Colne 1955, S W Norfolk 1959 and 1959 by-election, Buckingham 1964 and 1966; MP (C) Lancaster 1970–, MEP (EDG) Cumbria 1979–84 (delegate to the European Parliament 1974–79); memb Press Cncl 1964–68; Alderman London Borough of Camden 1968–74, chm Welfare Ctee 1969; *Style*— Dame Elaine Kellett-Bowman, DBE, MP; ✉ House of Commons, London SW1A 0AA

KELLEY, John Victor; s of William Kelley (d 1988), and Beatrice, *née* Armitage (d 1984); *b* 20 Feb 1947; *Educ* Harold Hill GS; *m* 1974 (sep), Anne; 1 s (John William b 28 Feb 1980), 1 da (Rosemary Anne b 26 June 1982); *Career* jr art dir Brunning Advertising 1963–66; copywriter: Foote Cone & Belding 1966–69, PKL (later BBDO) 1969–75, Collett Dickenson Pearce 1976–81 (rising to gp head); fndr ptnr Lowe Howard Spink 1981–82, copywriter/bd dir Abbott Mead Vickers 1982–83, creative dir Geers Gross 1983–85, vice chm and exec creative dir Abbott Mead Vickers 1985–93, creative dir Publicis 1993–95, vice chm and sr creative TBWA 1996–; D&AD Silver Awards for: best 15 sec TV commercial (Great Northern Bitter) 1973, most outstanding direction of TV campaign (Daily Express) 1977, most outstanding 45 sec TV commercial (Heineken) 1981, most outstanding typography in an advertisement (Long John Whisky) 1981, most outstanding direction of cinema commercial (Benson & Hedges) 1982; other awards incl: Br TV ITV Award for best commercial (EMI Records) 1978, Film & TV Festival of NY Gold Award (Bass Charrington) 1984, Br Cinema Advtg Awards Gold Award (Britvic Corona) 1988, NY One Show Merit Awards (Cow & Gate) 1990 and 1991; memb Exec Ctee D&AD; *Style*— John Kelley, Esq; ✉ TBWA, 8 Crinan Street, Battle Bridge Basin, London N1 9UF (☎ 0171 833 5544)

KELLEY, Malcolm Percy; s of Percy William Alfred Kelley (d 1978), and Gladys Beatrice Kelley (d 1986); *b* 21 July 1931; *Educ* Thames Valley GS; *m* 24 Aug 1957, Pamela, da of John Ernest Conway (d 1968); *Career* sales dir: Penguin Books Ltd 1970–72, Ladybird Books Ltd 1972–73; md Ladybird Books Ltd 1973–91; dir: Longman Group UK 1981–91, Pickwick Group plc 1988–91; chm: Ladybird Books Inc 1985–91, Sunbird Publishing Ltd 1986–91; founding tstee RAINBOWS (East Mids Children's Hospice) 1992–; *Recreations* following rugby football, reading, cooking, gardening, travelling; *Clubs* Rosslyn Park RFC, Leicester RFC; *Style*— Malcolm Kelley, Esq; ✉ 50 Outwoods Rd, Loughborough, Leics LE11 3LY

KELLS, Ronald David (Ronnie); *b* 14 May 1938; *Educ* Bushmills GS, Sullivan Upper Sch Holywood, Queen's Univ Belfast (BSc (Econ)), Babson Coll Boston Mass; *m* 30 July 1964, Elizabeth; 1 da (Louise), 1 s (Jeremy); *Career* formerly with Wm F Coates and Co and Wm Patterson and Co stockbrokers Belfast; Ulster Bank: joined 1964, investmt mangr 1969, dep head of related banking servs 1976–79, head of planning and mktg 1979–82, seconded to National Westminster Bank plc 1982–84, dir and head Branch Banking Div (later Retail Servs Div) 1984–94, chief exec 1994–; hon memb Cncl NSPCC (also memb Fundraising Ctee), dir Bryson Community Enterprise; FCIS; *Recreations* golf, winter sports, gardening, walking; *Style*— Ronnie Kells, Esq; ✉ Ulster Bank Ltd, 47 Donegall Place, Belfast BT1 5AU (☎ 01232 898472, fax 01232 898588)

KELLY, Anthony; CBE (1988), DL (Surrey 1993); *b* 25 Jan 1929; *Educ* Presentation Coll Reading, Univ of Reading (scholar, BSc), Trinity Coll Cambridge (PhD, ScD); *m* Christina Margaret, *née* Dunleavie; 4 c; *Career* scientist and engr; researcher Illinois Univ, ICI res fell Univ of Birmingham, asst prof then assoc prof of metallurgy and materials science Technological Inst of North Western Univ Chicago, lectr in metallurgy Univ of Cambridge 1958, founding fell and dir of studies in natural sciences Churchill Coll Cambridge until 1967, dep dir Materials Gp National Physical Laboratory 1969–74 (supt Div of Inorganic and Metallic Structure 1967–69), seconded to ICI 1974, vice chancellor Univ of Surrey 1975–94 (prof 1988); former visiting prof: Univ of Göttingen, Carnegie-Mellon Univ, Ecole Polytechnique Federale de Lausanne; dir British Non-Ferrous Metals Research Association 1970–72; chm: Engineering Materials Requirements Bd Dept of Indust 1976–80, Standing Ctee on Structural Safety (estab by Inst of Civil and Structural Engrs) 1987–; fndr Euro Assoc for Composite Materials 1984, currently: dir Johnson Wax, dir Quo-Tec Ltd, non-exec dir NPL Management Ltd; extraordinary fell Churchill Coll Cambridge 1985, Medal of Excellence Univ of Delaware USA 1984; foreign assoc Nat Acad of Engrg of USA 1986, FRS 1973, FEng 1979; author of numerous scientific papers and five books; *Style*— Prof Anthony Kelly, CBE, FRS, FEng, DL; ✉ Churchill College, Cambridge CB3 0DS

KELLY, Barbara Mary; CBE (1992), DL (Dumfries and Galloway); da of John Maxwell Prentice, JP, (d 1990), of Dalbeattie, Stewartry of Kirkcudbright, and Barbara Bain, *née* Adam (d 1989); *b* 27 Feb 1940; *Educ* Dalbeattie HS, Kirkcudbright Acad, Moray House Edinburgh; *m* 28 July 1960, Kenneth Archibald Kelly, s of Thomas Archibald Grant Kelly (d 1960); 3 s (Hamish Grant b 1961 d 1961, Neil Grant b 1963, Jonathan Ormiston b 1965, d 1985), 2 da (Joanna Barbara b 1970, Christian Maxwell b 1972); *Career* ptnr in mixed farming enterprise; dir Clydesdale Bank plc; chm Scottish Consumer Cncl 1985–90, memb Nat Consumer Cncl 1985–90, pres Rural Forum Scotland 1992– (chm 1988–92), memb Scottish Enterprise 1990–95, cmmr in Scotland for EOC 1991–95; memb: Scottish Econ Cncl, Scottish Tourist Bd, Scottish Bd BP plc, Priorities Bd MAFF 1990–93, Scottish Nat Heritage 1995–; chm: Training 2000, BBC Scotland Rural Affairs Advsy Ctee; convenor Millenium Forest for Scotland Tst; former chm Dumfries and Galloway Area Manpower Bd, memb UK Advsy Ctee Duke of Edinburgh Award 1981–85 (former chm Scottish Advsy Ctee); tstee Scottish Silver Jubilee Tst; *Recreations* family, music, the pursuit of real food, gardening of necessity; *Style*— Mrs Barbara Kelly, CBE, DL; ✉ Barncleugh, Irongray, Dumfries, Dumfries and Galloway DG2 9SE (☎ 01387 730210)

KELLY, Bernard Noel; s of Sir David Kelly, GCMG, MC (d 1959), of Tara House, Co Wexford, and Comtesse Renée Marie Noële Ghislaine de Vaux (d 1995); *b* 23 April 1930; *Educ* Downside; *m* 11 July 1952, Lady Mirabel Magdalene Fitzalan Howard, sister of 17 Duke of Norfolk, *qv*; 7 s, 1 da; *Career* Capt 8 Queen's Royal Irish Hussars incl reserves 1948–60; admitted slr 1956; ptnr Simmons and Simmons 1958–62; banker; md Compagnie Monegasque de Banque SAM 1976–80; dir: S G Warburg & Co 1963–76, Barnes Gp Inc USA 1975–91, Insilco USA 1978–89, Lazard Bros and Co Ltd 1980–90 (vice-chm and md 1981–85), PXRE USA 1988–, American Phoenix Investment Ltd 1990–, LET Ventures plc 1990–95, Société Générale Investissement (LUX) 1990–, Campbell Lutgens & Co Ltd (chm 1990–92); chm: International Select Fund Ltd 1988–, First Equity Holdings Ltd 1987–, Nexus Structured Finance Ltd 1993–; *Clubs* Athenaeum, Brooks's, Kildare Street and University (Dublin); *Style*— Bernard Kelly, Esq; ✉ 45 Fernshaw Road, London SW10 (☎ 0171 352 8272)

KELLY, Air Vice-Marshal (Herbert) Brian; CB (1983), LVO (1960); s of Surgn Capt James Cecil Kelly, DSC (d 1961), of Clonmore, Charing, Kent, and Meta Matheson, *née* Fraser (d 1971); *b* 12 Aug 1921; *Educ* Epsom Coll, St Thomas's Hosp London Univ (MB BS MD, DCH, FRCP); *Career* registered med practitioner; med offr RNVR 1945–48; registrar and lectr in medicine St Thomas's Hosp 1948–53; conslt in med RAF Hosps: Aden, Ely, Nocton Hall, Singapore, Cyprus, Germany; med branch RAF 1953–83, sr conslt to RAF 1979–83 (formerly conslt advsr in med), ret; conslt med advsr to PPP Medical Centre 1983–91, conslt advsr to CAA 1974–93; QHS 1978–83; Liveryman Worshipful Soc of Apothecaries, Freeman City of London; fell RSM 1948, MFOM 1982; *Recreations* choral singing, DIY; *Clubs* RAF; *Style*— Air Vice-Marshal Brian Kelly, CB, LVO; ✉ 32 Chiswick Quay, Hartington Rd, London W4 3UR (☎ 0181 995 5042)

KELLY, Brian Owen; s of George Alfred Kelly (d 1983), and Delia, *née* Cafferkey (d 1983); *b* 9 Jan 1943; *Educ* Presentation Coll Reading, Farnborough Coll of Technol; *m* 17 Oct 1970, (Anne) Christine, da of Fred Payne (d 1985); *Career* scientific asst Service Electronics Res Laboratory 1959–64, experimental offr Admty Compass Observatory 1964–70, sr engr Bendix Aerospace Michigan USA 1970–73, vice pres United Detector Technology LA 1973–78, gen mangr Centronic Optical Systems Ltd Croydon 1978–85, md Centronic Ltd 1985–95; chm: Centronic Ltd Croydon, Spanoptic Ltd Glenrothes, Centronic Inc USA; dir Laser Diode Inc USA; chm of govrs Addington HS Croydon; MIEEE (USA) 1975, MInstP 1979, FIMgt 1980, CPhys, MINucE 1992; *Recreations* golf, bridge, chess; *Style*— Brian Kelly, Esq; ✉ Green Roofs, Dower House Crescent, Tunbridge Wells, Kent TN4 0TT; Centronic House, King Henry's Drive, Croydon CR9 0BG (☎ 01689 842121, fax 01489 843053, telex 876 474 CENTRO G)

KELLY, Charles Henry; CBE (1986), QPM (1978), DL (Staffs 1979); s of Charles Henry Kelly (d 1984), and Phoebe Jane Kelly (d 1948); *b* 15 July 1930; *Educ* Douglas HS for Boys IOM, London Univ (LLB); *m* 1952, Doris; 1 s (Kevin), 1 da (Lynne); *Career* asst chief constable Essex 1972–76, chief constable Staffordshire 1977–96 (dep chief constable 1976–77), assoc prof Criminal Justice Dept Michigan State Univ 1990–; chm ACPO Communications Ctee 1983–92 (sec 1992), No 3 ACPO Regnl Conf 1985–93; Hon MUniv Keele 1991; KStJ 1991; *Recreations* music, cricket, reading; *Clubs* Special Forces; *Style*— Charles Kelly, Esq, CBE, QPM, DL; ✉ c/o Chief Constable's Office, Staffordshire Police, Cannock Road, Stafford ST17 0QG

KELLY, Christopher Michael; s of Patrick Joseph Kelly, and Una Kelly; *b* 29 Oct 1945; *Educ* Downside; *m* 30 March 1970, Margaret; 1 s (Timothy b 7 June 1979), 1 da (Samantha 27 Sept 1975); *Career* mktg trainee Shell Mex & BP Ltd 1963–65, account dir Cogent Elliott Advertising 1965–75, sales and mktg dir Hertz Europe Ltd 1975–79; md: Hertz UK Ltd 1979–84, Reed Executive plc 1984–; *Style*— Christopher Kelly, Esq; ✉ 33 Dukes Ave, London W4 2AA; Reed Executive plc, Tolworth Tower, Tolworth, Surrey KT6 7EL (☎ 0181 339 4885, fax 0181 339 4851)

KELLY, Christopher William; s of Dr Reginald Edward Kelly (d 1990), and Peggy Kathleen, *née* Stone; *b* 18 Aug 1946; *Educ* Beaumont Coll, Trinity Coll Cambridge (MA), Univ of Manchester (MA); *m* 1970, Alison Mary Collens, da of Dr Henry Durant (d 1982), and Peggy Durant; 2 s (Jake b 1974, Toby b 1976), 1 da (Rachel b 1980); *Career* HM Treasy: asst princ 1970, private sec to Fin Sec 1971–73, sec to Wilson Ctee of Inquiry into Fin Instns 1978–80, asst sec 1981, under sec Pay and Industl Relations Gp in Treasy 1987–90, under sec Social Servs and Territorial Gp 1990–92, under sec Gen Expenditure Policy Gp 1992–94, dir of fiscal and monetary policy 1994–95, dir of budget and public fins 1995, head Policy Gp Dept of Social Security 1995–; *Recreations* narrow boating, walking; *Style*— Christopher Kelly, Esq; ✉ Department of Social Security, The Adelphi, 1–11 John Adam Street, London WC2N 6HT (☎ 0171 712 2498)

KELLY, Dr David Roy; s of Roy Alfred Kelly, and Marie Rose Kelly; *b* 16 April 1955; *Educ* Univ of Salford (BSc, PhD), Univ of Waterloo Canada, Univ of Maryland, Univ of Oxford; *m* 13 Sept 1980, Judith Wendy, da of Eric Hadfield, of Marsden, Yorkshire; 1 da (Lauren Rachael Olivia b 14 July 1990); *Career* post doctoral fell: Univ of Waterloo 1979–80, Univ of Maryland 1980–81, Univ of Oxford 1981–84; New Blood lectr in organic chem Univ Coll Cardiff 1984–, speaker The Chemistry of Sexual Attraction; over 50 pubns in jls; broadcaster (several TV and radio appearances); sec: Euro Symposium on Bioorganic Chemistry 1986–90 (memb Ctee 1986–), Gregynog Symposium for Young Br Chemists 1987–; memb: ACS, SCI; MRSC (C Chem) 1979, ECLAIR 209; *Books* Biotransformations in Preparative Organic Chemistry (with S M Roberts, H G Davies and R H Green, 1989); *Recreations* cabinet making; *Style*— Dr David R Kelly; ✉ School of Chemistry and Applied Chemistry, University of Wales, College of Cardiff, PO Box 912, Cardiff CF1 3TB (☎ 01222 874063, fax 01222 874030, mobile 0831 231465)

KELLY, Dr Desmond Hamilton Wilson; s of Norman Wilson Kelly, OBE (d 1976), and Anne Elizabeth, *née* Megarry (d 1976); *b* 2 June 1934; *Educ* King's Sch Canterbury, St Thomas' Hosp Univ of London (Crawford Exhibitioner, MB BS, MRCP, Plank Prize in psychiatry); *m* 6 Feb 1960, Angela Marjorie, da of Stuart Way Shapland; 2 s (Jonathan Desmond b 6 Jan 1963, Simon James 16 Nov 1965); *Career* St Thomas' Hosp: med casualty offr 1958, house surgn 1959, psychiatric house physician 1959; RAMC 1960–63; St Thomas' Hosp: res registrar 1963–65, sr registrar 1965–67, chief asst psychiatry 1968–69; registrar The Maudsley Hosp 1965, Nuffield Fndn Medical Fellowship Johns Hopkins Hosp USA 1967–68, conslt psychiatrist St George's Hosp 1971–79 (sr lectr and hon conslt 1969–71), med dir The Priory Hosp 1980–; visiting prof of psychiatry Univ Coll London 1991–; lectr in USA & ME; Pavlovian Award and Medal Soc of N America 1971, physician of the year 1981; gp med dir the Priory Hosps Gp 1993 (dir 1981, chm 1988–93); memb: Assoc of Univ Teachers of Psychiatry 1970, Int Ctee for the Prevention and Treatment of Depression UK (chm 1976), Cncl Psychiatric Section of RSM 1977–80; pres UK Branch Int Stress and Tension Control Soc 1985–88, pres Int Stress Mgmnt Assoc 1988–92; FRSM 1963, DPM 1961, MD 1965, MRCPsych 1971, FRCPsych 1975, FRCP 1977; *Books* Anxiety and Emotions: physiological basis and treatment (1980), A Practical Handbook for the Treatment of Depression (co-ed,1987), author of over 50 papers; *Recreations* tennis, skiing, windsurfing, gardening; *Clubs* Roehampton; *Style*— Dr Desmond Kelly; ✉ The Priory Hospital, Priory Lane, London SW15 5JJ (☎ 0181 876 8261, fax 0181 876 4015)

KELLY, Desmond Hugh; s of Fredrick Henry Kelly (d 1973), of Harare, Zimbabwe, and Mary Josephine, *née* Bracken; *b* 13 Jan 1942; *Educ* Christian Brothers Coll Bulawayo Zimbabwe, Elaine Archibald Ballet Sch Bulawayo Zimbabwe, Ruth French Dance Acad London; *m* 4 Jan 1964, Denise Jeanette, da of Henri Charles le Comte; 1 s (Joel Henry b 1 June 1973), 1 da (Emma Louise b 30 Dec 1970); *Career* dancer; princ London Festival Ballet 1964 (joined 1959), Zurich Ballet 1966–67, ballet master teacher and princ dancer New Zealand Ballet 1967–68, Nat Ballet of Washington 1968–70 (most notable role James in La Sylphide with Margot Fonteyn), The Royal Ballet 1970–76 (ballets incl Swan Lake, Giselle and Romeo and Juliet); Sadler's Wells Royal Ballet: princ dancer 1976–78, ballet master 1978–, asst to dir 1988, currently asst dir; recent roles incl: Thomas in La Fille Mal Gardee, Dr Coppelius in Coppelia, Dago in Facade, Mr Hobson in David Bintley's Hobson's Choice; various TV appearances; *Recreations* theatre, gardening, cooking, reading; *Style*— Desmond Kelly, Esq; ✉ Birmingham Royal Ballet, Birmingham Hippodrome, Thorp St, Birmingham B5 (☎ 0121 622 2555, fax 0121 622 5038)

KELLY, (Reay) Diarmaid Anthony; s of Capt Edward Raymond Anthony Kelly (d 1991), of Belgrave Mews North, London, and Bridget Ramsay, *née* Hornby; *b* 8 July 1959; *Educ* Ampleforth; *m* 18 April 1991, Candida, eld da of Peter Meinertzhagen; 2 s (Barnaby b 15 Jan 1993, Augustus b 15 June 1995); *Career* sales exec Henderson Crosthwaite & Co 1981–84, dir Baring Securities Ltd (later ING Baring Securities Ltd) 1984–96, fndr dir CrossBorder Capital 1996–; *Recreations* racing; *Clubs* Boodle's, Pratt's, Turf; *Style*— Diarmaid Kelly, Esq; ✉ 50 Chepstow Villas, London W11; CrossBorder

Capital, 3/4 Royal Exchange Buildings, London EC3V 3LL (☎ 0171 623 9119, fax 0171 623 4006)

KELLY, Prof Donald Francis; s of John Francis Kelly (d 1963) of Chelmsford, Essex, and Blanche Helen, *née* Murphy; *b* 20 July 1933; *Educ* King Edward VI GS Chelmsford Essex, Univ of Bristol (BVSc), Univ of Cambridge (MA, PhD); *m* 13 Oct 1962, Patricia Ann, da of William Septimus Holt (d 1965), of Bolton, Lancs; 3 s (Andrew b 1964, Ian b 1966, David b 1972); *Career* Nat Serv 1951–53, 2 Lt RASC, RAVC (RARO); demonstrator in animal pathology Univ of Cambridge 1965–66 (demonstrator in pathology 1962–64), asst/assoc prof of pathology Sch of Vet Med Univ of Pennsylvania 1966–70, sr lectr in vet pathology Univ of Bristol, 1970–79, prof and head Dept of Vet Pathology Univ of Liverpool 1979–; pres Euro Coll of Veterinary Pathologists 1995–; MRCVS 1957, FRCPath 1980; *Books* Notes on Pathology for Small Animal Clinicians (with V M Lucke and C J Gaskell, 1982), Color Atlas of Veterinary Cardiology (with P G G Darke and J D Bonagura, 1996); *Recreations* photography, reading, walking, house maintenance; *Clubs* Backwell Working Men's; *Style*— Prof Donald Kelly; ✉ Department of Veterinary Pathology, University of Liverpool, PO Box 147, Liverpool L69 3BX (☎ 0151 794 4265, fax 0151 794 4268, telex 627095 UNILPL G, e-mail DKELLY@ .liv.ac.uk)

KELLY, Prof Francis Patrick (Frank); s of Francis Kelly, and Margaret, *née* McFadden; *b* 28 Dec 1950; *Educ* Van Mildert Coll Durham (BSc), Emmanuel Coll Cambridge (PhD); *m* 1972, Jacqueline Pullin; 2 s; *Career* operational res analyst Scicon Ltd 1971–73; Univ of Cambridge: asst lectr in engineering 1976–78, lectr Statistical Laboratory 1978–86, fell Christ's Coll 1976– (variously dir of studies, tutor, memb Coll Cncl, memb Investmts Ctee), Nuffield Fndn sci res fell 1986–87, reader in mathematics of systems 1986–90, prof of the mathematics of systems 1990–, dir Statistical Laboratory 1991–93, Royal Soc Leverhulme Tst sr res fell 1994–95; Rollo Davidson prize 1979, Guy medal in silver (RSS 1989), Lanchester prize (Operation Res Soc of America 1992); chm Lyndewode Research Limited 1987–; assoc ed: Stochastic Models 1983–86, Annals of Probability 1984–90, Jl of the Royal Statistical Soc 1986–90, Probability in the Engineering and Informational Scis 1986–, Combinatorics, Probability and Computing 1991–95; FRS 1989, CStat; *Books* Reversibility and Stochastic Networks 1979, numerous articles in mathematical & statistical jls; *Recreations* skiing, football with children; *Style*— Prof Frank Kelly, FRS; ✉ Statistical Laboratory, 16 Mill Lane, Cambridge CB2 1SB (☎ 01223 337963, fax 01223 337956)

KELLY, (Robert Henry) Graham; s of Thomas John Kelly (d 1960); *b* 23 Dec 1945; *Educ* Baines GS Poulton-Le-Fylde; *m* 18 July 1970, Elizabeth Anne, *née* Wilkinson; 1 s (Stephen b 1974), 1 da (Alison b 1972); *Career* Barclays Bank 1964–68, sec Football League 1979–88, chief exec FA 1989–; tstee: Football Grounds Improvement Tst 1985–88, Football Tst 1989–; memb Nat Olympic Ctee; FCIS 1974; *Style*— Graham Kelly, Esq; ✉ 16 Lancaster Gate, London W2 3LW (☎ 0171 402 7151, fax 0171 402 0486, telex 261110)

KELLY, Jane Maureen; da of Adrian Morgan Kelly (d 1995), of Bristol, and Monica Dallas, *née* Edwards; *b* 20 Sept 1948; *Educ* Notre Dame HS Sheffield, Univ of Birmingham (LLB); *m* 1, 1975, (m dis 1981); *m* 2, 1 July 1994, Michael Randolph Peter Blanckenhagen, s of John Stanley Blanckenhagen (d 1974); *Career* admitted slr 1971; slr in private practice in Eng and Far East 1971–79; AMI Healthcare Group plc 1979–90: legal advsr 1979, co sec 1983, dir of corporate health servs 1988; dir AMI Healthcare Group plc 1987–90; independent mgmnt conslt 1990–; chm W Middx Univ Hosp NHS Tst 1992–; hon visiting fell Dept of Health Sciences Univ of York 1996–; chm Women in Mgmnt 1987–89, lay memb Gen Cncl and Register of Osteopaths 1990–95, chm Jt Cncl of the Lay and Monastic Communities of Worth Abbey 1991–95; memb Cncl English Nature 1992–, tstee Lifecare Charitable Tst 1992–, memb Cncl Nat Tst 1994–; *Clubs* Reform; *Style*— Miss Jane Kelly; ✉ Chairman, West Middlesex University Hospital NHS Trust, Twickenham Road, Isleworth, Middx TW7 6AF

KELLY, John Anthony Brian; RD (1974); s of Lt Cdr Brian John Parmenter Kelly, DSC (d 1994), of Bangor, Co Down, N Ireland, and Ethne Mary, *née* Ryan (d 1977); *b* 21 Aug 1941; *Educ* Bangor GS N Ireland, Fort Augustus Abbey Sch Scotland, Queen's Univ Belfast (LLB); *m* 28 March 1973, Denise Anne, da of Ronald James Circuit, of St Albans; 2 s (Christopher b 1977, Nicholas b 1982), 2 da (Katrina b 1973, Joanna b 1975); *Career* Lt Cdr RNR 1959–84; Price Waterhouse and Co 1963–68 (qualified 1967), exec Old Broad St Securities 1968–70, exec and assoc Laurie Milbank and Co 1971–78, dir Brown Shipley and Co Ltd 1982–92 (mangr 1978); dir: Close Brothers Ltd 1992–96, Close Securities Ltd 1996–; non-exec dir Cosalt plc 1986; Liveryman Worshipful Co of Founders; FCA; *Recreations* walking, reading, poetry, tennis; *Clubs* The Naval, Royal Ulster Yacht; *Style*— John Kelly, Esq, RD; ✉ Cherrytrees, Penn Rd, Beaconsfield, Bucks HP9 2LW; Close Securities Ltd, 12 Appold Street, London EC2A 2AA (☎ 0171 426 4000)

KELLY, HE John Philip; LVO (1994), MBE (1984); s of William Kelly (d 1989), and Norah Kelly (d 1983); *b* 25 June 1941; *Educ* Oatlands Coll Stillorgan Dublin; *m* 2 May 1964, Jennifer Anne, *née* Buckler; 1 s (Oliver b 1969); *Career* HM Dip Serv: entered FO 1959, archivist Leopoldville 1962–65, Cairo 1965–68, Bonn 1968–70, News Dept FCO 1970–73, Canberra 1973–76, vice consul (commercial) Antwerp 1977–78, second sec FCO 1978–80, on loan to DTI 1980–82, resident rep Grenada 1982–86, first sec Middle Eastern Dept FCO 1986–89, dep govr Bermuda 1989–94, dep head W Indian and Atlantic Dept FCO 1994–96, govr Turks and Caicos Islands 1996–; memb Royal Victoria League for Cwlth Friendship; *Recreations* golf, walking, theatre; *Style*— HE Mr John Kelly, LVO, MBE; ✉ Government House, Grand Turk, Turks and Caicos Islands (☎ 00 1 809 946 2308, fax 00 1 809 946 2903)

KELLY, Rt Hon Sir John William (Basil); kt (1984), PC (1984), PC (NI 1969); s of Thomas William Kelly (d 1955), of NI, and Emily Frances, *née* Donaldson (d 1966); *b* 10 May 1920; *Educ* Methodist Coll Belfast, Trinity Coll Dublin (BA, LLB); *m* 1957, Pamela, da of Thomas Colmer Colthurst (d 1960), and Marjorie Colthurst; *Career* called to the Bar: NI 1944, Middle Temple 1970; MP NI 1964–72, attorney gen NI 1968–72, judge of the High Court NI 1973–84, Lord Justice of Appeal Supreme Court of Judicature NI 1984–95; chm: Bar Cncl of NI 1968–70, Cncl of Legal Educn NI 1989–93, Judicial Studies Bd NI 1993–95; memb Legal Advsy Ctee British Cncl 1983–93; UK judicial representative Int Assoc of Judges 1982–94; *Recreations* golf, travel, music; *Style*— The Rt Hon Sir Basil Kelly; ✉ c/o Royal Courts of Justice, Belfast BT1 3JF

KELLY, Judith Pamela (Jude); da of John Kelly, of Hatch End, Middlesex, and Ida Kelly; *b* 24 March 1954; *Educ* Calder HS Liverpool, Univ of Birmingham; *m* Michael Bird (professionally known as Michael Birch); 1 da (Caroline b 21 Oct 1986), 1 s (Robbie b 4 Sept 1989); *Career* director; began career as freelance folk and jazz singer 1970–75; actress with Michael Bogdanov's Co (Leicester Phoenix Theatre) 1975–76; fndr dir Solent People's Theatre Hampshire (over 42 community shows) 1976–80; artistic dir BAC 1980–85 (also co-fndr BAC based General Theatre Co 1983); prodns incl: Fascinating Aida 1983, Second from Last in the Sack Race (also tour) 1983, The Devil Rides Out - A Bit (also Lyric Hammersmith and tour) 1984; freelance dir (Nat Theatre of Brent) 1982–85; prodns incl Harvey and the Wallbangers (3 nat tours, 2 TV shows); other prodns incl: The Pink Briefcase (Lyric Hammersmith and tour) 1985, Lynchville (RSC festival, joined as asst dir) 1986, Sarcophagus 1987 (The Pit, transferring to Mermaid (two nominations Olivier Awards)), Affairs in a Tent 1988, A Garden Fete 1988 (both Bristol Old Vic); artistic dir York Festival and Mystery Plays 1988 (joined pt/t 1985–88); chief exec West Yorkshire Playhouse 1993– (artistic dir 1988–); prodns incl: Wild Oats, Safe in our Hands, Getting Attention, The Pope and the Witch, Second from last in the Sack Race, Pratt of the Argus, The Revenger's Tragedy, Wicked Old Man, Happy Days, The Taming of the Shrew, Comedians, Gypsy, The Merchant of Venice, Mail Order Bride, Call in the Night, King Lear; fndr memb Noroc 1992 (cultural exchange initiative between Br and Romania); awarded Br Jr C of C Outstanding Young Person's Cultural Achievement 1993; memb: Leeds Initiative, Univ of Leeds Court, Univ of Leeds Cncl, Arts Cncl Drama Panel 1995–97; Hon Dr Univ of Leeds 1995, Hon Dr Univ of Bradford 1996; *Recreations* windsurfing; *Style*— Ms Jude Kelly; ✉ West Yorkshire Playhouse, Playhouse Square, Quarry Hill, Leeds LS2 7UP (☎ 0113 244 2141, fax 0113 244 8252)

KELLY, Laurence Charles Kevin; s of Sir David Kelly, GCMG, MC (d 1959), and Comtesse Renée Marie Noële Ghislaine de Vaux (d 1995); *b* 11 April 1933; *Educ* Downside, New Coll Oxford (MA); *m* 1963, Linda, da of Maj R G McNair Scott (d 1995), and Hon Mrs Scott (d 1996), of Huish House, Old Basing, Hants; 1 s, 2 da; *Career* Lt Life Gds 1949–52; served FO (Northern Dept) 1955–56, Guest Keen and Nettlefolds 1956–72; Helical Bar plc: non-exec dir 1972–93, dep chm 1981–84, chm 1984–88, vice chm 1988–93; dir: GKN International Trading 1972, Morganite International Ltd 1984–92, KAE Mintel International Ltd 1985–88; chm Queenborough Steel Co 1980–89; vice chm British Steel Consumers' Cncl 1974 (res 1985); memb: Bd N Ireland Devpt Agency 1972–78, Monopolies and Mergers Cmmn 1982–88; sr assoc memb St Antony's Coll Oxford 1985–92; FRGS; *Books* Lermontov - Tragedy in the Caucasus (1978), Travellers' Companion to St Petersburg (1981), Travellers' Companion to Moscow (1983), Travellers' Companion to Istanbul (1987), Proposals (with A L Kelly); *Recreations* swimming; *Clubs* Brooks's, Turf, Beefsteak, University (Dublin); *Style*— Laurence Kelly, Esq; ✉ 44 Ladbroke Grove, London W11 2PA (☎ 0171 727 4663); Lorton Hall, Low Lorton, nr Cockermouth, Cumbria CA13 7UP (☎ 01900 85252)

KELLY, (Richard) Martin; s of Norman Keith Kelly, of Bishop Burton, and Gwendoline, *née* Fisher; *b* 25 April 1954; *Educ* Beverley GS, Leeds Poly (Dip Landscape Architecture), Oxford Poly (Dip Urban Design, MA); *m* 10 May 1986 (m dis), Anna Acton-Stow; 1 da (Victoria Grace b 1987); *Career* asst planning offr Landscape and Reclamation Section Sheffield Met Dist Cncl until 1979; ptnr Derek Lovejoy Partnership London 1986– (joined 1979); landscape infrastructure work undertaken for public and private sector clients; expert witness at public enquiries; dir Derek Lovejoy Touchstone Ltd; memb SE Chapter Landscape Ctee; author various articles and book reviews for tech press; FLI 1990, FIHT 1990; *Style*— Martin Kelly, Esq; ✉ Derek Lovejoy Partnership, 8–11 Denbigh Mews, Denbigh Street, London SW1V 2HQ (☎ 0171 828 6392, fax 0171 630 6958)

KELLY, Matthew David Alan; s of Ronald Nugent Kelly, and Olive Hilda, *née* Rixon; *b* 9 May 1950; *Educ* Urmston GS, Manchester Poly (DipEd), Open Univ (BA 1996); *m* 1970, Sarah Elizabeth, *née* Gray; 1 s (Matthew David (stage name Matthew Rixon) b 1970), 1 da (Ruth Emma b 1972); *Career* actor and television personality; theatre 1967–, TV 1977–; early leading TV role as Fitz in sitcom Holding the Fort (LWT) 1979–82; presenter: Game for a Laugh (LWT) 1981–83, You Bet! (LWT) 1990–95, Stars in their Eyes (Granada) 1990–; pres Neuromuscular Centre Cheshire 1990–; *Style*— Matthew Kelly, Esq; ✉ c/o Stella Richards Management, 42 Hazlebury Road, London SW6 2ND (☎ 0171 736 7786, fax 0171 731 5082)

KELLY, Matthias John; s of Ambrose Kelly, of Dungannon, Co Tyrone, N Ireland, and Anne, *née* McKiernan (d 1973); *b* 21 April 1954; *Educ* St Patrick's Secdy Sch and St Patrick's Acad Dungannon Co Tyrone, Trinity Coll Dublin (BA, LLB), Cncl of Legal Educn London; *m* 5 May 1979, Helen Ann, da of Peter Joseph Holmes (d 1974), of Longford, Ireland; 1 s (Peter b 1986), 1 da (Anne b 1987); *Career* called to the Bar: Gray's Inn 1979, N Ireland 1983, Republic of Ireland 1983; admitted attorney: New York 1986, USA Federal Bar 1987; hon life memb Br Soc of Criminology 1986, memb Soc of Labour Lawyers 1979, past memb Mgmnt Ctee Gray's Inn; chair: EVA Campaign, Children Act Housing Action Gp, Mgmnt Ctee Alcohol Recovery Project; sec Personal Injuries Bar Assoc, memb Environmental Law Fndn; *Recreations* squash, walking, cycling, reading; *Style*— Matthias Kelly, Esq; ✉ 1 Verulam Buildings, Gray's Inn, London WC1 (☎ 0171 831 0801, fax 0171 405 1387)

KELLY, Dr Michael; CBE (1983), JP (Glasgow 1973), DL (1983); s of David Kelly (d 1972); *b* 1 Nov 1940; *Educ* Univ of Strathclyde (BSc, PhD); *m* 1965, Zita, da of Hugh Harkins; 3 c; *Career* economics lectr Univ of Strathclyde 1967–84, md Michael Kelly Associates 1983–; Lord Provost of Glasgow (and ex officio Lord-Lieut) 1980–84, Lord Rector Univ of Glasgow 1984–87; chm RSSPCC 1987–96, pres Strathclyde Branch Inst of Mktg 1986–89, dir Celtic FC 1990–94; memb: Scottish ABSA 1986–90, Scottish Ctee Nat Art Collections Fund 1990–94; Hon LLB Univ of Glasgow 1983; OStJ 1984; FIM 1989; *Books* Paradise Lost, The Struggle for Celtic's Soul (1994), London Lines: The Capital by Underground (1996); *Recreations* football, photography, philately, phillumeny (collecting match books & boxes); *Style*— Dr Michael Kelly, CBE, JP, DL; ✉ 50 Aytoun Rd, Glasgow G41 5HE

KELLY, Prof Michael Howard; s of Kenneth Howard Kelly, of Hull, and Kathleen Mary, *née* Lucas (d 1994); *b* 19 Nov 1946; *Educ* Hull GS, Univ of Warwick (BA, PhD), Univ of Southampton Mgmnt Sch (MBA); *m* 3 Jan 1975, Josephine Ann, da of Patrick Joseph Doyle, of Dublin; 2 s (Thomas Doyle b 1980, Paul Doyle b 1983); *Career* lectr in French Univ Coll Dublin 1972–86, prof of French Univ of Southampton 1986–; chair Univ Cncl of Modern Languages; assoc ed French Cultural Studies; former pres Assoc of Univ Profs of French, former chm Irish Cncl for Civil Liberties; FRSA; *Books* Pioneer of the Catholic Revival: Emmanuel Mounier (1979), Modern French Marxism (1982), Hegel in France (1992), French Cultural Studies: An Introduction (1995); *Recreations* tennis, golf, cinema; *Style*— Prof Michael Kelly; ✉ School of Modern Languages, The University, Southampton SO17 1BJ (☎ 01703 592191, fax 01703 593288, e-mail mhk@ lang.soton.ac.uk)

KELLY, Prof Michael Joseph; s of Steve Kelly (d 1988), and Mary Constance, *née* Powell (d 1987); *b* 14 May 1949; *Educ* Francis Douglas Meml Coll NZ, Victoria Univ of Wellington (scholar, MSc), Univ of Cambridge (MA, PhD, DSc); *m* 1 June 1991, Ann Elizabeth, da of Dr Daniel Brumhall Cochrane Taylor; 1 da (Constance Frances b 12 Feb 1993); *Career* res fell Trinity Hall Cambridge 1974–77, IBM res fell Univ of California 1975–76, SRC advanced fell Cavendish Laboratory and staff fell Trinity Hall 1977–81, res asst GEC 1981–92; University of Surrey: prof of physics and electronics 1992–96, head Electronic and Electrical Engrg Dept 1996–; conslt GEC Marconi 1992–93, visiting researcher Cavendish Laboratory 1988–92; Paterson medal and prize Inst of Physics 1989, Nelson Gold medal GEC 1991; holder of 13 patents on semiconductor devices; memb American Inst of Physics; CPhys, FInstP 1988, FIEE 1989, FRS 1993; author of 195 papers, review articles and book chapters in refereed jls; *Books* The Physics and Fabrication of Microstructures and Microdevices (ed, 1986), Low Dimensional Semiconductors: Physics, Materials, Technology, Devices (1995); *Recreations* music, literature; *Style*— Prof Michael Kelly, FRS; ✉ Department of Electronic and Electrical Engineering, University of Surrey, Guildford, Surrey GU2 5XH (☎ 01483 259410, fax 01483 34139)

KELLY, Patricia Mary (Pat); MBE (1977); da of Edward James Kelly (d 1941), of Newbury, Berks, and Elizabeth Lilian, *née* Hyde (d 1956); *b* 6 Jan 1938; *Educ* Newbury Girls' GS, UCL (BA); *m* 21 May 1984, William Eduard (Bob) Drysdale, s of Charles Drysdale (d 1963); *Career* joined Govt Serv 1964, Dept of Economic Affrs 1964–66, asst private sec to Sec of State for Foreign Affrs 1966–68, third sec Singapore 1968–71, Hong Kong Dept FCO 1972–74, second later first sec (info) The Hague 1974–78, first sec Personnel Dept FCO 1978–80, consul Rio de Janeiro 1981–82, seconded to private sector London 1982–83, first sec (commercial) Caracas 1984–88, dep head Commercial Mgmnt and Exports Dept FCO 1988–90; consul gen: Rio de Janeiro 1990–93, Naples 1993–97, ret; hon citizen State of Rio de Janeiro Brazil 1993; memb London Business Sch Alumni Assoc; *Style*— Miss Pat Kelly, MBE; ✉ c/o Foreign and Commonwealth Office, King Charles Street, London SW1A 2AH

KELLY, Peter; *b* 1931; *Educ* Loxford Central Sch Ilford, West Ham Sch of Art and Technol (graphic design), Central Sch of Art & Design London; *Career* artist; Nat Serv Royal Signals 1950–52; graphic designer 1952–57, painter and illustrator 1957–; *Exhibitions* solo: Hallam Gallery London, John Adams Fine Art London; two man: Llewelyn Alexander Gallery London, John Adams Fine Art London, Adam Gallery Bath; gp exhbns incl: Waterman Fine Art, Mall Gallery, Westminster Central Hall, Roy Miles Gallery, RA Summer Exhbn, Royal Soc of Portrait Painters; awards: Laing Competition (5 times), Berol Drawing Prize, painting prize Beecroft Gallery Essex, Pro Arte Brush Award, RBA Daler Rowney Award, Higgs & Hill Bursary, Artist Magazine Drawing Prize, Jeffrey Archer Prize; cmmns from numerous British and foreign companies and galleries; RBA 1982 (ARBA 1980); *Style*— Peter Kelly, Esq; ✉ c/o Llewellyn Alexander Ltd, 124–126 The Cut, London SE1 8LN

KELLY, Philip John; s of William Kelly (d 1979), of Crosby, Merseyside, and Mary Winifred, *née* Ellison; *b* 18 Sept 1946; *Educ* St Mary's Coll Crosby, Univ of Leeds (BA); *m* 12 Nov 1988, Dorothy Margaret Jones; 2 s (Matthew b 1980, Robert b 1986); *Career* freelance journalist and PR conslt 1970–87; co-fndr: Leveller 1976, State Research 1977; ed Tribune 1987–91; advsr and press offr to Michael Meacher, MP (Shadow Sec of State for Social Security) 1991; journalist and political conslt 1992–; chm London Freelance Branch NUJ 1983; cncllr (Lab) London Borough of Islington 1984–86 and 1990–; Parly candidate (Lab) Surrey SW 1992; *Recreations* railways, model railways; *Clubs* Red Rose; *Style*— Philip Kelly, Esq; ✉ 56 Windsor Rd, London N7 6JL (☎ 0171 272 9093)

KELLY, Dr William Francis; s of William Francis Kelly (d 1951), of Wolverhampton, and Lilian Rose, *née* Foister (d 1986); *b* 16 June 1942; *Educ* Royal Wolverhampton Sch, Univ of London (BSc), St Mary's Med Sch London (MB BS, MD); *m* 21 Aug 1971, Miranda Jane, da of Leonard Oscar Goddard, of Wonersh, Surrey; 1 s (Adam John William b 1974), 1 da (Juliet Miranda b 1977); *Career* qualified CA 1964 (resigned 1972); conslt physician S Tees Health Authy 1983, hon clinical tutor Charing Cross and Westminster Med Schs 1987, clinical lectr Univ of Newcastle 1988, chm Sr Med Staff Ctee S Tees Acute Hosps 1990–93; author of 34 articles in endocrine and diabetic jls, editorial asst Clinical Endocrinology 1986–93, memb Editorial Bd Cinical Endocrinology 1994–; chm Northern Region Advsy Gp for Diabetes 1993–96; memb: Br Diabetic Assoc 1976 (pres S Tees Branch), Endocrine Section RSM 1978, FRCP 1989 (MRCP 1975); *Recreations* walking, literature, photography; *Style*— Dr William Kelly; ✉ Diabetes Care Centre, Middlesbrough General Hospital, Ayresome Green Lane, Middlesbrough, Cleveland TS5 5AZ (☎ 01642 850850 ext 5722)

KELMAN, Alistair Bruce; s of James Bruce Edward Kelman (d 1983), of London, and Florence Gwendoline, *née* Cutts (d 1987); *b* 11 Aug 1952; *Educ* Haberdasher's Askes', Univ of Birmingham (BSc); *m* 2 Sept 1978, Diana Elizabeth, da of Prof Joseph Tinsley, of Aberdeen; *Career* called to the Bar Middle Temple 1977, specialist in computer law 1979–; litigation: R v Bedworth (computer addiction defence) 1993, McConville v Barclays and others (group action against UK banks over phantom withdrawals from automatic teller machines) 1993, IBCOS v Poole and Barclays (software copyright in the UK) 1994; currently working and advising in London, Brussels and Luxembourg on computer related legal problems; visiting lectr Computer Security Research Centre LSE 1995; reviewer ESPRIT project CITED (copyright in transmitted electronic documents); fndr memb Parly Info Technol Ctee House of Parl; AMBCS 1982, ACIArb 1986; *Books* The Computer in Court (with R Sizer, 1982), Computer Fraud in Small Businesses (1985); *Recreations* writing, piano playing and composing; *Style*— Alistair Kelman, Esq; ✉ 37 Station Road, Hendon, London NW4 4PN (☎ 0181 202 5675, fax 0181 202 8045)

KELNAR, Dr Christopher John Harvey; s of Dr John Kelnar (d 1979), of London, and Rose, *née* Stoller (d 1992); *b* 22 Dec 1947; *Educ* Highgate Sch London, Trinity Coll Cambridge (MA, MB BChir, MD), Bart's Med Coll London (DCH, MRCP); *m* Alison Frances, da of Dr Ernst Adolf Schott (d 1984); 2 da (Clare Deborah Rosemary b 5 April 1976, Rachel Catherine Ruth b 9 May 1978), 1 s (David John Samuel b 12 June 1981); *Career* successively registrar in paediatrics rising to research fell in paediatric endocrinology Middx Hosp London then sr paediatric registrar Hosp for Sick Children Great Ormand St and clinical tutor Inst of Child Health London 1976–83, conslt paediatrician, endocrinologist and diabetologist Royal Hosp for Sick Children Edinburgh and pt/t sr lectr Dept of Child Life and Health Univ of Edinburgh 1983–; memb: Cncl and Symposium Ctee RCPEd, Cncl British Paediatric Assoc, Jt Paediatric Ctee Scottish Royal Colls, Cncl British Paediatric Assoc (rep for SE Scotland), Exec Ctee Br Paediatric Assoc Surveillance Unit; Sydney Watson Smith lectr RCPEd; memb Scientific Ctees: Euro Soc for Paediatric Research Edinburgh 1993, Int Colloquium on Growth and Growth Disorders Pisa 1994, Euro Soc for Paediatric Endocrinology Edinburgh 1995; memb: Br Soc for Paediatric Endocrinology, Euro Soc for Paediatric Endocrinology, Br Paediatric Assoc; FRCPEd 1985; *Books* The Sick Newborn Baby (with D R Harvey, 1981, 3 edn 1995), Childhood and Adolescent Diabetes (ed, 1995); contrib chapters to other med books and author of over 50 reveiws and original scientific papers; *Recreations* music, gardening; *Style*— Dr Christopher Kelnar; ✉ 9 Easter Belmont Road, Edinburgh EH12 6EX (☎ 0131 337 3195); Department of Child Life and Health, University of Edinburgh, 20 Sylvan Place, Edinburgh EH9 1UW (☎ 0131 536 0690, fax 0131 536 0821)

KELSALL, Prof Malcolm Miles; s of Alec James Kelsall, and Hetty May, *née* Miles; *b* 27 Feb 1938; *Educ* William Hulme's GS Manchester, Brasenose Coll Oxford (state scholar, MA, Sr Hulme scholar, BLitt); *m* 5 Aug 1961, Mary Emily, da of George Hurley Ives (d 1978); *Career* staff reporter The Guardian 1961, asst lectr Univ of Exeter 1963–64, lectr Univ of Reading 1964–75, prof English Dept Univ Coll Cardiff 1988– (head 1975–88); visiting prof: Univ of Paris 1978, Univ of Hiroshima 1979, Univ of Madison 1996; advsy ed The Byron Journal, memb Mgmnt Ctee Welsh Nat Drama Co 1976–77; *Books* Sarah Fielding's David Simple (ed, 1969), Thomas Otway's Venice Preserved (ed, 1969), William Congreve's Love for Love (ed, 1969), Joseph Trapp's Lectures on Poetry (ed, 1973), JM Synge's The Playboy of the Western World (ed 1975), Christopher Marlowe (1981), Congreve: The Way of the World (1981), Joseph Trapp's The Preface to the Aeneis (ed 1982), Studying Drama (1985), Byron's Politics (1987, awarded Elma Dangerfield prize, 1991), Encyclopedia of Literature and Criticism (ed, 1990), The Great Good Place: The Country House and English Literature (1992), British Academy Warton Lecture (1992); *Recreations* theatre, long distance running; *Style*— Prof Malcolm Kelsall; ✉ Ashbrook, Cae Rex, Cowbridge, S Glamorgan CF71 7JS (☎ 01446 772627); University of Wales, PO Box 94, Cardiff CF1 3XB (☎ 01222 874244)

KELSEY, Alan Howard Mitchell; s of Emanuel Kelsey (d 1985), of London, and Dorothy Mitchell, *née* Smith; *b* 10 April 1949; *Educ* King's Coll Sch Wimbledon, Oriel Coll Oxford (BA, MA); *m* 12 March 1977, Sarah D'Oyly, da of Robin Carlyle Sayer, of Little Walsingham, Norfolk; 2 s (Guy b 22 Feb 1980, William b 27 July 1981), 1 da (Keziah b 19 Jan 1978); *Career* Kitcat & Aitken: tport investmt analyst 1975–88, head of res 1987–89, head of corp fin 1989–90; dir: RBC Dominion Securities International 1988–91, RBC Dominion Securities Inc 1989–91, Merrill Lynch International (formerly Smith New Court) 1992–96; dir of corp devpt National Express Group PLC 1996–; chm local Cons Assoc 1985–88, memb Cncl Soc of Investmt Analysts 1986–88; assoc IIM, MSI (dip), FCIT; *Recreations* fishing; *Clubs* Brooks's; *Style*— Alan Kelsey, Esq; ✉ The Priory, Little Waldingfield, Suffolk CO10 0SW; Flat 2, 26 Lennox Gardens, London SW1X 0DQ (☎ 0171 584 4238); National Express Group PLC, Worthy Park House, Abbots Worthy, Winchester, Hants SO21 1AN

KELSEY, John; CBE (1968); s of Benjamin Richard Kelsey and Daisy, *née* Powell; *b* 1 Nov 1920; *Educ* Royal Masonic Sch, Emmanuel Coll Cambridge, Royal Mil Coll of Sci (BSc); *m* 1944, Phyllis Margaret (d 1995), da of Henry Smith, of Chingford; 1 s (Peter), 1 da (Diana); *Career* RE 1940 (N Africa and Europe), Mil Survey Units in UK, North Africa, West Indies and Germany; sr instr Geodsy Sch of Mil Survey 1951–53; offr Ordnance Survey 1954–59, dir of field survey 1969–72, dir of mil survey MOD 1972–77, sec Western Euro Sub Cmmn of Int Cmmn for Artificial Satellites 1967–71 (pres 1971–75); chm: Working Party Satellite Geodsy 1975–86, Survey and Mapping Conference Steering Gp 1981–87; non-exec dir Wild Heerburg UK Ltd, consIt to Wild Heerburg Ltd and Ernst Leitz Wetzlar GmbH 1978–91; FRICS; *Style*— John Kelsey, Esq, CBE

KELSEY, Linda; da of Samuel Cohen, and Rhona, *née* Fox, of London; *b* 15 April 1952; *Educ* Woodhouse GS, Univ of Warwick; *m* 1972 (m dis 1980); partner Christian Testorf; 1 s (Thomas Testorf b 1988); *Career* trainee sub ed Good Housekeeping 1970–72, sub ed, asst features ed then features ed Cosmopolitan 1972–78; dep ed Company Magazine 1978–81, dep ed Options Magazine 1981–82, ed Cosmopolitan 1985–89 (dep ed 1982–85), ed SHE Magazine 1989–95, ed-at-large Nat Magazine Co 1996–; chair Br Soc of Magazine Editors 1987 (memb), memb Women's Financial Forum 1993; Editor of the Year award for Cosmopolitan Periodical Publishers Assoc 1989, Women's Magazine Editor of the Year award for SHE Br Soc of Magazine Editors 1990; *Recreations* family, reading, hill-walking, sleeping; *Clubs* Groucho, RAC; *Style*— Ms Linda Kelsey; ✉ c/o National Magazine Co, 72 Broadwick House, London W1V 2BP

KELTON, Michael John St Goar; s of Gerald St Goar Kelton (d 1972), and Beatrice Millicent (d 1993), da of J B Body (md S Pearson & Co, responsible for many engrg devpts in Mexico *ca* 1900 incl: draining of Valley of Mexico, construction of Vera Cruz harbour, founding Mexican Eagle Oil Co); *b* 25 March 1933; *Educ* Stowe, Queens' Coll Cambridge (MA); *m* 19 June 1958, Joanna Elizabeth, da of Sir (William) John Peel, MP (C) Leicester SE 1957–74; 3 s (Jeremy b 1960, Andrew b 1961, Simon b 1966); *Career* stockbroker; Capt 3 Carabiniers (now Royal Scots Dragoon Gds); merchant banker Lazard Bros and Co Ltd 1957–, dir Lazard Securities until 1971; dir Raphael Zorn Hemsley Ltd 1976–; *Recreations* shooting, fishing, golf; *Clubs* Cavalry and Guards', Flyfishers', Hankley Common Golf; *Style*— Michael Kelton, Esq; ✉ Pipers Well, Churt, Farnham, Surrey GU10 2NT (☎ 01428 713194); Raphael Zorn Hemsley Ltd, 10 Throgmorton Ave, London EC2 (☎ 0171 628 4000)

KEMBALL, Christopher Ross Maguire; MBE (Mil 1973); s of John Patrick Gerard Kemball, of Vila Praia De Ancora, Portugal, and Rachel Lucy, *née* Vernon; *b* 29 Dec 1946; *Educ* Ampleforth, Pembroke Coll Cambridge (BA); *m* 3 Feb 1979, Frances Maria, da of Flt Lt Richard Peter Monico, RAF (d 1945); 1 s (Charles b 1983); *Career* Regular Army Capt (actg Maj) Royal Green Jackets 1968–75, Sultan's Armed Forces, Maj Northern Frontier Regt 1972–73; dir Kleinwort Benson Ltd 1975–86, vice chm Kleinwort Benson Hldgs Inc 1984–86, md Dillon Read & Co Inc 1986–91, exec md and co-head Dillon Read Ltd 1987–91, head of corp fin (emerging markets) and dir Baring Brothers & Co Ltd (now ING Barings) 1992–; *Recreations* opera, swimming, skiing, shooting, sailing; *Clubs* Royal Green Jackets, Brooks's, Royal Automobile; *Style*— Christopher Kemball, Esq, MBE; ✉ ING Barings, 60 London Wall, London EC2M 5TQ (☎ 0171 767 1000)

KEMBER, Anthony Joseph; s of Thomas Kingsley Kember (d 1968), and May Lena, *née* Pryor (d 1972); *b* 1 Nov 1931; *Educ* St Edmund Hall Oxford (MA); *m* 3 Aug 1957, Drusilla Mary, da of Geoffrey Lionel Boyce, of Twickenham, Middx; 1 s (Julian James Kingsley b 18 May 1960), 2 da (Selina May b 28 April 1962, Perdita Jane b 15 Jan 1965); *Career* dep house govr and sec to Bd of Govrs Westminster Hosp 1961–69, gp sec Hillingdon Gp Hosp Mgmnt Ctee 1969–73, area admin Kensington and Chelsea and Westminster AHA (teaching) 1973–78, gen mangr SW Thames RHA 1978–89, communications advsr Dept of Health 1989–91; Disabled Living Fndn: tstee 1981–, chm 1993–; memb Lord Chllr's SW London Area Advsy Ctee for the appointment of JPs 1994–; chm: Richmond Art Soc 1995–, Roehampton Art Gp 1995–; MHSM (DipHSM), CIMgt; *Publications* The NHS - a Kaleidoscope of Care = conflicts of service and business values (1994); *Recreations* real tennis, lawn tennis, painting, golf; *Clubs* Roehampton, Exiles, Royal Tennis Court Hampton Court Palace; *Style*— Anthony Kember, Esq; ✉ 16 Orchard Rise, Richmond Upon Thames, Surrey TW10 5BX (☎ 0181 876 5192)

KEMBERY, John Philip; s of Alec George Kembery, of Keynsham, Somerset; *b* 6 Oct 1939; *Educ* Queen Elizabeth's Hosp Bristol, Univ of Surrey; *m* 1964, Marjorie Carolyn, da of Gilbert James Bowler, of Bridge End House, Much Cowarne, Herefordshire; 2 s (Jonathan Alexander b 1967, Nicholas Philip b 1969); *Career* md: Alcan Extrusions 1975–80, Alcan Metal Centres 1980–81; chm: McKechnie Metals non-ferrous metal mfrs (md 1981–87), PSM Int plc; dir and chm Metals and Engrg Divs McKechnie plc 1986–92, business conslt and chm MW Technologies 1992–95; non-exec chm: Wheelpower International 1993–94, Black and Luff Holdings Ltd 1994–, Sunleigh plc 1995–; non-exec dir: Brasway plc 1994–, Trigon Packaging Systems (Europe) Ltd, Trigon Packaging Systems (UK) Ltd, Trigon Cambridge Ltd 1993–95, Crosrol Ltd 1995–, Eadie Holdings PLC 1996–; pres Br Non-Ferrous Metals Fedn 1988–90; fell Inst of Metals, FInstD; *Recreations* golf, shooting, good food; *Style*— John Kembery, Esq; ✉ 12 Parkfields, Arden Drive, Dorridge, W Midlands (☎ 01564 730168, fax 01564 778057, mobile 0421 892685)

KEMP, Alan Scott; s of Alexander Scott Kemp (d 1968), of Edinburgh, and Christina Margaret, *née* Stocks (d 1965); *b* 2 April 1944; *Educ* George Heriots Sch Edinburgh; *m* 9 Dec 1967, June, da of John Christie (d 1986), of Edinburgh; 2 s (Graeme, Martin); *Career* dep mangr The Edinburgh Investment Trust plc 1974–84, dep chief exec Dunedin Fund Managers Ltd 1990–95 (investmt dir 1985–90); memb Murrayfield and Cramond Rotary Club; MICAS; *Recreations* golf; *Style*— Alan Kemp, Esq; ✉ Brae Park House, 5 Brae Park Road, Edinburgh EH4 6DN (☎ 0131 317 7976)

KEMP, Arnold; s of Robert Kemp (d 1968), of Edinburgh, and Meta Elizabeth, *née* Strachan; *b* 15 Feb 1939; *Educ* Edinburgh Acad, Univ of Edinburgh (MA); *Career* sub ed: The Scotsman 1959–62, The Guardian 1962–65; The Scotsman: prodn ed 1965–70, London ed 1970–72, dep ed 1972–81; ed The Herald (formerly Glasgow Herald) 1981–94, conslt ed Caledonian Publicity 1984–; Hon Dr Univ of Edinburgh 1992, Hon DLitt Univ of Strathclyde 1993, Hon DUniv Univ of Paisley 1993; *Publications* The Hollow Drum (1993); *Clubs* Caledonian, Glasgow Arts; *Style*— Arnold Kemp, Esq; ✉ 2 Queen Margaret Drive, Glasgow G12 8DQ (☎ 0141 339 3329, fax 0141 339 0937)

KEMP, Brian William; s of William Kemp (d 1984), of Solihull, and Muriel Beatrice, *née* Taylor; *b* 29 Jan 1939; *Educ* Moseley GS Birmingham; *m* 1, 15 Feb 1964 (m dis 1988), Mary Christine, da of Harry Hughes, of Birmingham; 2 s (Andrew b 1970, Jonathan b 1973), 1 da (Alison b 1967); *m* 2, 20 May 1988, Sheila Margaret, da of Walter Patrick, of Birmingham; *Career* sr ptnr Allenbrooke Kingsley Mills (formerly R Kingsley Mills and Co) 1986– (ptnr 1970–); FCA 1962, ATII 1965; *Recreations* yachting; *Clubs* Salcombe Yacht; *Style*— Brian Kemp, Esq; ✉ Allenbrooke Kingsley Mills, 614 Stratford Rd, Birmingham B11 4BE (☎ 0121 777 6762, fax 0121 777 2319)

KEMP, Charles James Bowring; s of Capt Michael John Barnett Kemp, ERD (d 1982), of Winchcombe, Glos, and Brigid Ann Vernon-Smith, *née* Bowring; *b* 27 April 1951; *Educ* Shrewsbury, UCL (LLB); *m* 21 Dec 1974, Fenella Anne, da of Harry Herring (d 1995), of Cropwell Butler, Nottingham; 1 s (Marcus b 28 Feb 1979), 1 da (Sophie b 11 Feb 1977); *Career* called to the Bar Gray's Inn 1973, recorder 1991– (asst recorder 1987–91); *Recreations* tennis, swimming, cricket, golf, country pursuits, music; *Style*— Charles Kemp, Esq; ✉ Keepers, Cinder Hill, Chailey, nr Lewes, East Sussex BN8 4HP (☎ 01825 723168, fax 01825 724106); 1 King's Bench Walk, Temple, London EC4Y 7DB (☎ 0171 583 6266, fax 0171 583 2068); King's Bench Chambers, 174 High Street, Lewes, E Sussex (☎ 01273 486266, fax 01273 486478)

KEMP, David A M; QC (1973); *Educ* Winchester, Corpus Christi Coll Cambridge (BA); *Career* called to the Bar Inner Temple 1948, bencher of the Inner Temple; memb Bars: Gibraltar, Hong Kong, Kenya, Malaysia; ret from Bar 1996; FCIArb; *Style*— David Kemp, Esq, QC; ✉ c/o 4 Raymond Buildings, Gray's Inn, London WC1R 5BP

KEMP, David Stephen; s of Stephen Nicholas Kemp (d 1967), of Bromley, Kent, and Mary Grace, *née* Gibbs (d 1976); *b* 14 Dec 1928; *Educ* Tonbridge, Brasenose Coll Oxford (MA); *m* 16 April 1966, Marion Elizabeth, da of Dr Maurice Sibley Blower (d 1982), of Rake, Hants; 3 s (Anthony David b 1967, William James Stephen b 1971, Peter John b 1973); *Career* 2 Lt Duke of Wellington's Regt 1948; articled clerk E F Turner & Sons 1952; admitted slr 1955; Tonbridge Sch: asst master 1956, housemaster 1969, second master 1971, actg headmaster 1990; played hockey for Kent; memb Tunbridge Wells Health Authy 1984–89, Mental Health Act mangr Weald of Kent NHS Tst, chm Govrs Marlborough House Sch; govr: Tonbridge Sch, The Judd Sch; chm: Kent CCC 1993– (pres 1992), Swifts Sports Tst 1993–; pres: Old Tonbridgian CC 1988–, Old Tonbridgian Soc 1992–; hon treas The Cricketer Cup; First Warden Worshipful Co of Skinners 1996; *Recreations* cricket, golf, reading; *Clubs* Vincent's (Oxford), MCC, Bude & N Cornwall Golf; *Style*— David Kemp, Esq; ✉ Summerlands, Portman Park, Tonbridge, Kent TN9 1LW (☎ 01732 350023); Rosamond Cottage, Marhamchurch, North Cornwall EX23 0EP

KEMP, Rt Rev Eric Waldram; *see:* Chichester, Bishop of

KEMP, Gene; da of Albert Rushton, of Tamworth, Staffs, and Alice Anne, *née* Sutton; *Educ* Wigginton C of E Sch, Tamworth Girls' HS Staffs, Univ of Exeter (BA); *m* 1 (m dis), Norman Charles Pattison, s of Charles Pattison; m 2, Allan William Kemp, s of late William Kemp; 1 s (Richard William), 2 da (Judith Eve, Chantal Jennifer); *Career* author; teacher: Wychbury HS Hagley Worcs, Drewsteignton CP Sch Devon, St Sidwell's Combined Sch Exeter, Rolle Coll Devon; govr: Central and Middle Schs Exeter 1975–85, Montgomery Sch Exeter 1994–; Hon MA Univ of Exeter 1984; memb: Lab Pty, Soc of Authors; *Awards* The Other Award 1977, Carnegie Medal 1978; shortlisted: Whitbread Award 1985, Smarties Award 1986 and 1990; *Books* incl: Tamworth Pig Stories, Cricklepit Combined School Stories (incl Turbulent Term of Tyke Tiler, Gowie Corby Plays Chicken and Just Ferret), The Well, Dog Days and Cat Naps (short stories), Mr Magus is Waiting for You (TV drama), Ducks and Dragons (poetry, ed), The Mink War (narrative poem), Roundabout, Puffin Book of Ghosts and Ghouls, The Wacky World of Wesley Baker, Zowey Corby's Story (fiction, Faber & Faber Ltd), Goosey Farm (HarperCollins), Rebel, Rebel (anthology, Faber & Faber); *Recreations* gardening, reading, grandchildren; *Style*— Mrs Gene Kemp; ✉ c/o Gerald Pollinger, Laurence Pollinger, 18 Maddox Street, Mayfair, London W1R 0EU (☎ 0171 629 9761); c/o Faber & Faber Ltd, 3 Queen Square, London WC1N 3AU (☎ 0171 465 0045, fax 0171 465 0034); c/o Puffin, 27 Wrights Lane, London W8 5TZ (☎ 0171 416 3000, fax 0171 416 3099)

KEMP, Hubert Bond Stafford (Hugh); s of John Stafford Kemp (d 1966), of Cardiff, and Cecilia Isabel, *née* Bond (d 1964); *b* 25 March 1925; *Educ* Cardiff HS, Univ of South Wales, St Thomas' Hosp Med Sch London (MB BS, MS); *m* 22 June 1967, Moyra Ann Margaret, da of William Arthur Odgers (d 1951), of Johannesburg; 3 da (Siân b 16 Jan 1961, Sarah b 10 Oct 1962, Louise b 4 June 1975); *Career* hon conslt Royal Nat Orthopaedic Hosp London and Stanmore 1965–74, hon sr lectr in orthopaedics 1974–90 (sr lectr 1965–74), conslt Royal Nat Orthopaedic Hosp London and Stanmore 1974–90 (hon conslt 1992–), Hunterian prof RCS 1969; visiting prof VII Congress of Soc Latino America de Orthopedia y Traumatologica 1971; chm London Bone Tumour Unit 1985–91; memb MRC working parties: Tuberculosis of the Spine 1974–, Osteosarcoma 1985–94; MRCS 1947, LRCP 1947, FRCSE 1960, FRCS 1970; *Books* Orthopaedic Diagnosis (jtly 1984), Harris and Birch Postgraduate Textbook of Clinical Orthopaedics (contrib 1985, 2 edn 1995), Bailliere's Clinical Oncology (contrib 1987), Rob and Smith's Operative Surgery (contrib, 1991), Cuschieri Essential Surgical Practice (3 edn 1995); *Recreations* fishing, painting; *Style*— Hugh Kemp, Esq; ✉ 55 Loom Lane, Radlett, Herts WD7 8NX (☎ 01923 854265); Royal National Orthopaedic Hospital Trust Private Consulting Rooms, 45 Bolsover Street, London W1P 5AQ (☎ 0171 383 5656, fax 0171 383 5107)

KEMP, (Edmund) Jeremy James; s of Edmund Reginald Walker (d 1994), of Felixstowe, Suffolk, and Elsa May, *née* Kemp (d 1983); *b* 3 Feb 1935; *Educ* Abbotsholme Sch Staffs, Central School of Speech and Drama (Dip Dramatic Art); *Career* actor; Nat Serv 1953–55, served Duke of Wellington Regt, cmmnd 2 Lt 1 Bn Gordon Highlanders; memb of Br Actors Equity Cncl for last 5 years; *Theatre* Old Vic 1958–60; plays incl: St Joan (Warwick), The Winters Tale (Leontes), Henry VIII (Norfolk); *Television* incl: Z-Cars (Bob Steele original cast), Colditz (Sqdn Ldr Shaw), Peter the Great, Winds of War, War and Remembrance (US TV); *Films* over thirty films incl: Operation Crossbow, The Blue Max, Darling Lili; *Recreations* course games, cricket, golf, skiing, walking, natural history; *Style*— Jeremy Kemp, Esq; ✉ 29 Britannia Road, London SW6 2HJ; 8749 Wonderland Avenue, Los Angeles, California 90046, USA (☎ 00 1 213 654 7920); c/o Marina Martin Associates, 12–13 Poland Street, London W1V 3DE (☎ 0171 734 4818, fax 0171 734 4832)

KEMP, Prof Martin John; s of Frederick Maurice Kemp (d 1990), of Watton, Norfolk, and Violet Anne, *née* Tull; *b* 5 March 1942; *Educ* Windsor GS, Downing Coll Cambridge (BA, MA), Courtauld Inst of Art Univ of London; *m* 27 Aug 1966, Jill, da of Dennis William Lightfoot, of Bisham, Marlow, Bucks; 1 s (Jonathan b 1976), 1 da (Joanna b 1972); *Career* lectr in history of western art Dalhousie Univ Nova Scotia Canada 1965, lectr in fine arts Univ of Glasgow 1966–81; Univ of St Andrews: prof of fine arts 1981–90, memb Ct 1988–91, prof of the history and theory of art 1991–95, provost St Leonard's Coll 1991–94; prof of history of art Univ of Oxford 1995–; memb Inst for Advanced Study Princeton 1984–85, Slade prof Univ of Cambridge 1987–88, Benjamin Sonenberg visiting prof Inst of Fine Arts NY Univ, Wiley prof Univ of North Carolina Chapel Hill 1993, Br Acad Wolfson Res prof 1993–; tstee: Nat Galleries of Scotland 1982–87, Victoria and Albert Museum 1986–89, British Museum 1995; hon prof of history Royal Scottish Acad 1985–, pres Leonardo da Vinci Soc 1987–, chm Assoc of Art Historians 1989–92, memb Exec Scottish Museums Cncl 1990–, dir and chm Graeme Murray Gallery 1990–92; dir: Interalia Bristol 1992–, Museums Training Inst 1993–; memb Cncl Br Soc for the History of Science 1994–; Hon DLitt Heriot-Watt Univ 1995; hon memb American Acad of Arts and Sciences 1996; FRSA 1983, HRSA 1985, HRIAS 1988, FBA 1991, FRSE 1992; *Books* incl: The Science of Art - Optical Themes in Western Art from Brunelleschi to Seurat; *Recreations* sport (especially hockey); *Style*— Prof Martin Kemp, FBA, FRSE; ✉ Trinity College, Oxford OX1 3BH

KEMP, Michael Alfred Lawrence; s of Alfred Lawrence Kemp (d 1968), and Margaret, *née* Smith; *b* 19 March 1941; *Educ* Greenwich Central Sch; *m* 1, 1965, Janet Anne, da of Charles Blogg, OBE; 1 s (Lawrence Michael b 1968); m 2, Patricia Deborah, da of Jack Kitching (d 1986); 1 s (Paul Lawrence Michael b 1971), 1 da (Lindsey b 1974); *Career* md: G & L Ralli Investment & Trustee Co Ltd 1977– (dir 1973–), G & L Ralli Finance Co Ltd 1977– (dir 1972–), Ralli Investment Co Ltd 1979–; chm Frowds Ltd 1992– (dir 1983); dir Ely Fund Managers Ltd 1996–; AIIMR; *Recreations* gardening, rugby union supporter, horseracing; *Clubs* City of London; *Style*— Michael A L Kemp, Esq; ✉ 5 Westott Close, Bickley, Kent BR1 2TU (☎ 0181 468 7347)

KEMP, (Bernard) Peter; s of William Gordon Kemp, of Chorley, Lancashire, and Teresa, *née* Howarth; *b* 16 Oct 1942; *Educ* Thornleigh Coll Bolton, King's Coll Univ of London (BA, MPhil); *Career* lectr in English Middx Poly 1968–88; regular book reviewer: The Listener 1978–91, TLS 1980– (weekly TV and radio column 1982–86); fiction ed Sunday Times 1995– (regular fiction reviewer 1987–95); theatre reviewer The Independent 1986–90; regular broadcaster on: Kaleidoscope, Critics' Forum, Third Opinion, Night Waves, Meridian; *Books* Muriel Spark (1974), H G Wells and The Culminating Ape (1982, 2 edn 1996); *Recreations* travel, art galleries, music, gardening; *Style*— Peter Kemp, Esq; ✉ The Sunday Times, 1 Pennington Street, London E1 9XW (☎ 0171 782 5777, fax 0171 782 5798)

KEMP, (Charles) Richard Foster; s of (Charles) Ian Taggart Kemp, of Beaconsfield, Bucks, and late Jean Maisie, *née* Foster; *b* 5 Jan 1957; *Educ* Bedford Sch, Queens' Coll Cambridge (MA); *Career* mangr Chemical Bank London and NY 1978–84; dir: Charterhouse Development Capital Ltd London 1984–87, Brown Shipley Venture Managers Ltd London 1988–; memb Br Venture Capital Assoc 1987; *Recreations* golf, climbing, skiing; *Style*— Richard Kemp, Esq; ✉ Brown Shipley Venture Managers Ltd, Founders Court, Lothbury, London EC2R 7HE (☎ 0171 606 6555, fax 0171 600 2279)

KEMP, Robert Thayer; s of Robert Kemp (d 1968), and Ada, *née* Thayer (d 1990); *b* 18 June 1928; *Educ* Bromley GS, Univ of London (BA); *m* 1951, Gwendolyn Mabel, da of Rev Charles Stanley Minty (d 1930); *Career* dir Export Credits Guarantee Dept 1985–88 (asst sec 1970–75, under sec 1975–85), export credit conslt and non-exec dir Sedgwick Credit Ltd 1989–95; *Publications* Review of Future Status Options for ECGD (1989); *Recreations* gardening, theatre, music; *Style*— Robert Kemp, Esq; ✉ Aldersgate, 294 Tubbenden Lane South, Farnborough, Orpington, Kent BR6 7DN (☎ 01689 853924)

KEMP, Roger John; s of Ivor Kemp, of York, and Audrey, *née* Hobbs; *b* 18 Dec 1945; *Educ* Hitchin GS, Univ of Sussex (BSc); *m* 3 Aug 1968, Joan Caroline, da of Kenneth and Winifred Walker (both decd); 1 da (Deborah Rachael b 29 Oct 1971), 1 s (Nicholas Ian b 15 Dec 1972); *Career* electrical and mechanical engr; science teacher Malaysia VSO 1964–65, control systems engr Reyrolle Parsons Automation Ltd Edinburgh and Newcastle 1969–71; British Railways Bd Derby: Research Dept 1971–74, head of Advanced Passenger Train (APT) Electrical Design 1974–79; devpt mangr electric vehicles Lucas Batteries Ltd Birmingham 1979–81, GEC Traction Ltd Manchester 1981–85, engrg dir GEC Transportation Projects Ltd Manchester 1985–89, directeur des Etudes d'Ensemble GEC Alsthom SA Paris 1989–91, project dir Eurostar Paris 1991–93, sales and mktg dir GEC Alsthom Traction Ltd Preston 1994–95, dir Systems Devpt GEC Alsthom Tport Div 1996–; memb IEE Professional Gp P2 (Railway Traction and Signalling) 1984–89 (chm 1987–89), chm Railway Engrs' Forum 1988, memb Railway Div Bd IMechE 1987–89, memb TC9X Working Gp CENELEC 1989–90, memb UIC/UNIFE Working Gp on Interoperability of High Speed Trains 1992–95; memb Editorial Bd Proceedings IMechE (part F) 1994–; author of numerous papers in various professional jls; CEng, FIEE, FIMechE, FEng 1995; *Recreations* playing double bass, music, theatre, cycling and hillwalking; *Style*— Roger Kemp, Esq, FEng; ✉ 6 Oakwood Gardens, Lancaster LA1 4PF (☎ 01524 69471); GEC Alsthom Transport Division, PO Box 134, Manchester M60 1AH (☎ 0161 875 4191, fax 0161 875 2131)

KEMP, Prof Terence James; s of Thomas Brynmor Kemp (d 1978), and Emily Maud, *née* Spriggs (d 1982); *b* 26 June 1938; *Educ* Cardiff HS, Watford GS, Jesus Coll Oxford (MA, DPhil, DSc); *m* 8 April 1961, Sheila Therese, da of Henry Francis Turner (d 1972); 1 s (Jeremy b 1964), 2 da (Celia b 1966, Penelope b 1969); *Career* Univ of Warwick: asst lectr 1965, lectr 1966, sr lectr 1970, reader 1974, prof 1980–, pro-vice chllr 1983–89, seconded pt/t to HEQC Quality Assurance Group 1995–; specialist subject assessor HEQC 1993–95; memb Int Evaluation Ctee Univ of Namibia 1993; CChem, FRSC 1969, FRSA 1986; OM Polish Repub 1985; *Books* Introductory Photochemistry (1971), Dictionary of Physical Chemistry (1992); *Recreations* philately, cinema, walking; *Style*— Prof Terence Kemp; ✉ 93 Leamington Rd, Coventry CV3 6GQ (☎ 01203 414735); Department of Chemistry, University of Warwick, Coventry CV4 7AL (☎ 01203 523235, fax 01203 524112, e-mail msrhp@snow.warwick.ac.uk)

KEMP-GEE, Mark Norman; s of Bernard Kemp-Gee (d 1993), and Ann, *née* MacKilligin; *b* 19 Dec 1945; *Educ* Marlborough, Pembroke Coll Oxford (MA); *m* 26 July 1980, The Hon Lucy Lyttelton, 3 da of late Viscount Cobham KG; *Career* chm Greig Middleton & Co Ltd (stockbrokers); *Recreations* tennis, skiing; *Style*— Mark Kemp-Gee, Esq; ✉ Greig Middleton & Co Ltd, 66 Wilson St, London EC2A 2BL (☎ 0171 392 4000, fax 0171 392 4242)

KEMP-WELCH, John; s of Peter Wellesbourne Kemp-Welch, OBE (d 1964), and Peggy Penelope, *née* Hunter; sr rep of the family descended from Martin Kemp-Welch (1772–1837), who assumed, by Royal Licence, 1795, the additional name of Welch, in compliance with the testamentary injunctions of his maternal unc, George Welch, banker and fndr of the banking house of Welch Rogers Olding and Rogers; *b* 31 March 1936; *Educ* Winchester; *m* 1964, Diana Elisabeth, da of Dr A W D Leishman (d 1978); 1 s, 3 da; *Career* memb Stock Exchange 1959, jt sr ptnr Cazenove & Co (stockbrokers) 1980–94; chm: Lowland Investment Co plc, Updown Investment Co plc, The Scottish Eastern Investment Trust plc 1993–, British Invisibles 1994–; chm London Stock Exchange 1994– (dir 1991–); dir: Garrows Farm Ltd 1964, Savoy Hotel plc 1985–, Royal & Sun Alliance Insurance Group plc 1994–, The Financial Reporting Council Limited 1994, The Securities and Futures Authority Limited 1994, Claridge's Hotel Limited 1995, ProShare (UK) Limited 1995; govr Ditchley Fndn; memb Courtauld Inst of Art Tst; tstee: King's Medical Res Tst, Game Conservancy Tst, The Dulverton Tst; CIMgt 1984, FRSA; *Recreations* the hills of Perthshire, country life, cricket, champagne, claret, Impressionist paintings, heather moorland management; *Clubs* White's, City of London, MCC; *Style*— John Kemp-Welch, Esq; ✉ The London Stock Exchange, Old Broad Street, London EC2N 1HP (☎ 0171 797 1000, fax 0171 334 8932)

KEMPSELL, John Douglas (Jake); s of Alfred Kempsell (d 1986), of Dumfries, and Elizabeth Agnes, *née* Ashmore (d 1993); *b* 24 March 1940; *Educ* Dumfries Acad, Edinburgh Coll of Art (Andrew Grant Bequest and post-dip scholarships, DA); *m* 1, 1961 (m dis 1982), Elizabeth Wilma, da of Gavin Gordon Lennox; 1 s (Gavin Lennox Ashmore b Jan 1968), 1 da (Karen Elizabeth b July 1962); m 2, April 1984, Elizabeth Anne, da of Robert Wood; *Career* sculptor; lectr in sculpture Edinburgh Coll of Art 1965–75, dir of sculpture Duncan of Jordanstone Coll Univ of Dundee 1975–; fndr memb Scottish Sculpture Tst; various professional ctees incl: Scottish Arts Cncl Visual Awards Panels, WASPS, CNAA; external assessor: Univ of London Goldsmiths' Coll 1982–84, Edinburgh Coll of Art and Univ of Edinburgh MA courses 1983–87 and 1991–92, RCA 1994; has completed number of sculpture cmmns and has exhibited extensively in sculpture parks at Glenshee and Carrbridge in Scotland, Wakefield in Yorks and Margam in Wales; *Exhibitions* first one person show (Richard Demarco Gallery) 1970; other exhibitions incl: The British Art Show 1979–80, Built in Scotland (travelling exhibition) 1983–84, Art in the Garden (Glasgow Garden Festival) 1988, Nine Sculptors in Scotland (Edinburgh Festival exhibition) 1994, Scandex (touring exhibition of contemporary Scottish sculptures to various Scandinavian venues) 1994–95; *Seminal Works* Eve Figure (1962), Celtic Harpy (1967), Archaic Sunrise (1976), Squaring the Circle (Almost) (1979), Luminous and Cool (1990), Breaking the Plane of Time (1993); *Recreations* building the occasional motor car and golf; *Clubs* Broughty Golf; *Style—* Jake Kempsell, Esq; ✉ Duncan of Jordanstone College, Perth Rd, Dundee DD1 4HT (☎ 01382 223261 ext 5228)

KEMSLEY, Adrian Bruce; s of Norman Patric Bruce Kemsley, of Harlow, Essex, and Margret Elizabeth, *née* Langley; *b* 11 Aug 1958; *Educ* Mark Hall Comp, Ware Coll of Art; *m* 10 Oct 1991, Geraldine Maria, da of Christopher Finnerty; *Career* with Saatchi & Saatchi Advertising 1983–90, fndr creative dir Cowan Kemsley Taylor 1990–93, assoc then creative dir Ammirati Puris Lintas (formerly S P Lintas) 1994–96 (joined as creative gp head 1993), exec creative dir Collett Dickenson Pearce 1996–; winner: D&AD Awards 1984, 1985, 1986 and 1989, 5 Gold and Silver Campaign Awards 1986; memb D&AD; *Recreations* photography, cinema, books; *Style—* Adrian Kemsley, Esq; ✉ Collett Dickenson Pearce & Partners Ltd, 33–34 Soho Square, London W1V 6DP (☎ 0171 292 4000)

KEMSLEY, Arthur Joseph; s of Joseph Alfred Kemsley (d 1966), of Stepney, East London, and Ivy Elizabeth Everet; *b* 21 May 1936; *Educ* Nicholas Gibson Secdy Sch; *m* 1967, Maureen (d 1989); 1 da (Gemma Louise b 29 Sept 1983); *Career* SAC RAF 1953–58; photographer; copy boy Advertising Dept Kemsley Newspapers 1951–52, gen asst Pathe Pictorial 1952–53, TV prodr/dir BAA 1989– (formerly Heathrow Airport Ltd, joined 1958, chief photographer 1965–89); R&D on video-visual imaging system for recording condition and quality of runway approach lights at airports (first of its kind) 1993–95; 2 Gold and 3 Silver medals World Airports Photographers competition 1988, Bronze medallion USAF (for photographing the space shuttle Discovery); memb Professional Photographers of America; MBKS, FRPS, FBIPP; *Recreations* research and development in new visual imaging, bringing up daughter; *Style—* Arthur Kemsley, Esq; ✉ BAA, Building 224, Norwood Crescent, Heathrow Airport, Hounslow, Middlesex (☎ 0181 745 7461, fax 0181 745 7099)

KEMSLEY, 2 Viscount (UK 1945); Sir (Geoffrey) Lionel Berry; 2 Bt (UK 1928), DL (Leics 1972); Baron Kemsley (UK 1936); s of 1 Viscount Kemsley, GBE (d 1968); *b* 29 June 1909; *Educ* Marlborough, Magdalen Coll Oxford; *m* 1933, Lady Helen Candida Hay, da of 11 Marquess of Tweeddale (d 1967); 4 da; *Heir* nephew, Richard Gomer Berry, b 1951, s of late Hon Denis Gomer Berry, TD; *Career* served WW II Grenadier Gds (invalided out 1942); dep chm Kemsley Newspapers Ltd 1938–59, MP (C) Buckingham 1943–45; Master Worshipful Co of Spectacle Makers 1949–51 and 1959–61; CC Northants 1964–70; High Sheriff Leics 1967; chm St Andrew's Hosp Northampton 1973–84, pres Assoc of Independent Hosps 1976–83; FRSA; KStJ; *Clubs* Pratt's, Royal Over-Seas League; *Style—* The Rt Hon the Viscount Kemsley, DL; ✉ Field House, Thorpe Lubenham, Market Harborough, Leics LE16 9TR (☎ 01858 462816)

KENCH, Eric Arthur; s of Joseph Peter Kench, of Oxfordshire, and Ethel Catherine, *née* Younger; *b* 30 Sept 1952; *Educ* Henley GS; *m* 20 July 1974, Kathleen Jennifer, da of Philip Hague (d 1980); 1 s (David b 1979), 2 da (Caroline b 1981, Sarah b 1982); *Career* CA; fndr E A Kench & Co 1982–; former chm Thames Valley Young CAs Gp; memb: ICAEW Smaller Practitioners' Ctee 1984–90, ICAEW Gen Practitioner Bd 1990–; pres Thames Valley Soc of CAs 1987–88; FCA; *Recreations* squash, cycling, flying (private pilot), reading, working; *Style—* Eric Kench, Esq; ✉ E A Kench & Co, 8 Station Rd, Henley-on-Thames RG9 1AY (☎ 01491 578207)

KENDAL, Felicity Anne; CBE (1995); da of Geoffrey Kendal, of Chelsea, London, and Laura May, *née* Liddell (d 1992); *Educ* convents in India; *m* 1, 1969 (m dis 1976), Drewe Henley; 1 s (Charles b 23 Jan 1973); m 2, 1983 (m dis 1991), Michael Edward Rudman, *qv*, s of Duke Rudman, of Dallas, Texas; 1 s (Jacob Henry b 1 Oct 1987); *Career* grew up touring and acting with parents' theatre co in India and Far East, London debut in Minor Murder (Savoy) 1967; *Theatre* Henry V and The Promise (Leicester) 1968, Back to Methuselah (NT) 1969, A Midsummer Night's Dream and Much Ado About Nothing (Regents Park) 1970, Kean (Oxford 1970 and London 1971), Romeo and Juliet,' Tis Pity She's a Whore 1972, The Three Arrows 1972, The Norman Conquests (Globe) 1974, Once Upon a Time (Bristol) 1976, Arms and the Man (Greenwich) 1978, Clouds (Duke of York's) 1978, Amadeus (NT) 1979, Othello (NT) 1980, On the Razzle (NT) 1981, The Second Mrs Tanqueray (NT) 1981, The Real Thing (Strand) 1982, Jumpers (Aldwych) 1985, Made in Bangkok (Aldwych) 1986, Hapgood (Aldwych) 1988, Much Ado About Nothing and Ivanov (Strand) 1989, Hidden Laughter (Vaudeville) 1990, Tartuffe (Playhouse) 1991, Heartbreak House (Yvonne Arnaud Guildford and Haymarket) 1992, Arcadia (RNT) 1993, An Absolute Turkey (Globe) 1994, Indian Ink (Aldwych) 1995, Mind Millie for Me (Haymarket) 1996; *Television* Barbara in The Good Life 1975–77, Twelfth Night 1979, Solo 1980 and 1982, The Mistress 1985, The Camomile Lawn 1992, Honey for Tea (BBC) 1994; *Films* Shakespeare Wallah 1965, Valentino 1976; *Awards* Variety Club Most Promising Newcomer 1974, Best Actress 1979, Clarence Derwent Award 1980, Variety Club Woman of the Year Best Actress Award 1984, Evening Standard Best Actress Award 1989, Actress of the Year Sony Radio Awards 1992; *Style—* Miss Felicity Kendal, CBE; ✉ c/o Chatto & Linnit, Prince of Wales Theatre, Coventry Street, London W1V 7FE (☎ 0171 930 6677, fax 0171 930 0091)

KENDALL, Bridget; MBE (1994); da of David George Kendall, and Diana Louise, *née* Fletcher; *b* 27 April 1956; *Educ* Perse Sch for Girls Cambridge, Lady Margaret Hall Oxford (BA), Harvard Univ (Harkness fell), St Antony's Coll Oxford, Voronezh Univ USSR (Br Cncl scholar), Moscow State Univ (Br Cncl postgrad scholar); *m* July 1989, Nicholas John Whinfrey Worrall; *Career* BBC: prodr and reporter BBC World Service, BBC Radio 4 and Newsnight 1983–89, Moscow corr 1989–93, made series of special reports on Russia for Newsnight and Panorama 1993–94, Washington corr 1994–; James Cameron Meml Award for Journalism 1992, Voice of the Listener and Viewer Award for Excellence in Bdcasting 1993; *Recreations* literature, music, theatre and film; *Style—* Ms Bridget Kendall, MBE; ✉ BBC Washington Bureau, 2030 M Street NW, Washington DC, USA (☎ 00 1 202 223 2050); Foreign Affairs Unit, BBC Radio News and Current Affairs, Broadcasting House, London W1A 1AA

KENDALL, David Richard; s of Frederick Richard Kendall, of Lutterworth, Leics, and Gwendoline Florence, *née* Blackwell; *b* 17 Sept 1955; *Educ* Lutterworth GS, Univ of Birmingham (LLB), City of London Poly (MA), Sprachen und Dolmetsch Institut Munich (Dip); *m* 28 June 1980, Marsha Alexa, da of Allan Rothenberg; 1 da (Sarah Louise b 13 Feb 1982), 2 s (Ralph Alexander b 14 Sept 1984, Ian William b 1 April 1986); *Career* Messrs Hedleys: articled clerk 1979–81, asst slr 1981–85, ptnr 1985–88; head of insurance dept D J Freeman 1991– (ptnr 1988–); panel arbitrator Lloyd's 1993–; memb: Law Soc 1977, Fedn of Insurance and Corp Counsel 1993; ARIAS; *Recreations* tennis, woodwork; *Style—* David Kendall, Esq; ✉ D J Freeman, 43 Fetter Lane, London EC4A 1NA (☎ 0171 583 4055, fax 0171 353 7377)

KENDALL, Rev Frank; s of Norman Kendall (d 1976), of Ripon, Yorkshire, and Violet, *née* Bloor; *b* 15 Dec 1940; *Educ* Bradford GS, Corpus Christi Coll Cambridge (MA), London Univ (Dip in Religious Studies); *m* 20 Feb 1965, Brenda, da of Walter Isaac Pickin (d 1982), of Royston; 1 s (Andrew b 1970), 1 da (Angela b 1969); *Career* asst princ then princ Miny of Public Building and Works 1962–70, princ Dept of Economic Affairs 1967–68, princ and asst sec DOE 1970–84, under sec and NW regnl dir Depts of the Environment and Tport 1984–89; chief exec St Helens Met Borough Cncl 1989–91, dir St Helens and Knowsley Community Health (NHS) Trust 1995–, chm Liverpool Diocesan Bd for Social Responsibility 1996–; inspr of schools 1993–; conslt Solace international 1995–; ordained: deacon 1974, priest 1975; hon curate: Lingfield 1974–75 and 1978–82, Sketty 1975–78 (Diocese of Swansea and Brecon), Limpsfield 1982–84 (Diocese of Southwark); licensed preacher: Diocese of Manchester 1984–89, Diocese of Liverpool 1989–; FRSA 1990; *Recreations* painting, DIY; *Style—* The Rev Frank Kendall; ✉ Cromwell Villa, 260 Prescot Road, St Helens, Merseyside WA10 3HR (☎ 01744 27626)

KENDALL, George Langton; JP (1966 Bucks); s of Gordon Kendall (d 1972), of Leics, and Elsie Winifred, *née* Breese (d 1989); coat of arms 1448 confirmed under seal by Clarenceux King of Arms; John Kendall, sec to Richard III, killed at Bosworth Leics; *b* 19 June 1927; *Educ* Haileybury; *m* 13 June 1959, Elizabeth Jane, da of W G E Shand, FRCS, of NZ; 1 s (Angus b 1960), 1 da (Mary-Anne b 1962); *Career* Sub Lt RNVR, served Far East; chartered surveyor; chm and sr ptnr Raffety Buckland 1980–89 (ret 1989); memb: Bow Gp 1955–65, Cncl RICS 1956–59, Wycombe Borough Cncl 1966–69, Cncl Univ of Buckingham 1986–96 (chm Bldgs and Devpt Ctee 1986–96); memb and chm Personnel Ctee Bucks CC 1970–77; gen cmmr of taxes 1983–93; High Sheriff Bucks 1986–87; chm Bucks St John Ambulance Centenary Appeal (memb Cncl 1987–95); Norwich Diocesan Synod: chm Property Ctee 1994–, memb Exec Bd 1995–; life memb Primrose League; former Liveryman Worshipful Co of Chartered Surveyors; FInstD (ret); OStJ 1993; *Recreations* golf, shooting, fishing, painting, pottery, sailing (crew memb Taiseer IV, first winner Britannia Cup Cowes 1951), PC and internet; *Clubs* Naval, MCC, Blakeney Sailing; *Style—* George Langton Kendall, Esq, JP; ✉ York Cottage, Blakeney, Norfolk NR25 7NU; Meadow Cottage, by Hughenden, Bucks

KENDALL, Howard; s of John James Kendall, and May, *née* Atkinson; *b* 22 May 1946; *Educ* Washington GS; *m* Cynthia Ruth; 1 s (Simon), 2 da (Hayley, Lisa); *Career* professional football manager; player: Preston North End 1961–67, Everton 1967–74, Birmingham City 1974–77; player-coach Stoke City 1977–79, player-mangr Blackburn Rovers 1979–81; mangr: Everton 1981–87 and 1990–93 (resigned), Athletic Bilbao Spain 1987–89, Manchester City 1989–90; coach Xanthi (Greece) 1994; mangr: Notts County FC until April 1995 (winners Anglo Italian Cup 1995), Sheffield Utd FC 1995–; England caps: schoolboy, youth, under 23; achievements as mangr Everton: League Championships 1985 and 1987, FA Cup 1984, Euro Cup-Winners' Cup 1985; *Recreations* golf, cricket; *Style—* Howard Kendall, Esq; ✉ Sheffield United FC, Bramall Lane, Sheffield S2 4SU (☎ 0114 273 8955, fax 0114 272 3030)

KENDALL, (Gilbert) John; s of Arthur Charles Kendall (d 1983), of Crickhowell, Powys, and Hilda Mary, *née* Morgan; *b* 31 May 1950; *Educ* Rugby (scholar), New Coll Oxford (exhibitioner, MA), King's Coll London; *m* 4 Oct 1986, Jennifer Lynne, da of Peter Owen Watton; *Career* slr; articled clerk Stephenson Harwood 1973; Allen & Overy: slr 1977–, ptnr 1985–, specialist in litigation, arbitration and construction law, managing ptnr Litigation Dept 1994–; consulting ed Building Law Monthly; chm Alternative Dispute Resolution Sub-Ctee Int Bar Assoc; chm Friends United Network (children's charity); Freeman City of London; memb City of London Law Soc; FCIArb; *Publications* Expert Determination (2 edn 1996), author numerous articles; *Recreations* walking, opera; *Style—* John Kendall, Esq; ✉ 6 Lanchester Road, Highgate, London N6 4TA (☎ and fax 0181 883 6385); Allen & Overy, One New Change, London EC4M 9QQ (☎ 0171 330 3000, fax 0171 330 9999); Chairman, Friends United Network, 404 Camden Road, London N7 0SJ

KENDALL, John Melville; s of Capt Charles Edward Kendall (d 1978), of Great Nineveh, Benenden, Kent, and Cara Honoria, *née* Pelly (d 1996); *b* 1 Sept 1931; *Educ* Ampleforth; *m* 23 Feb 1971, Anthea Diana, da of Col T D Partridge; 1 s (Mark b 12 Jan 1972), 1 da (Sophia b 4 July 1973); *Career* Lt RN 1952–56; chm Charles Kendall Group of Cos 1978–; Order of Sultan Qaboos Sultanate of Oman; *Recreations* sailing, skiing, hunting; *Clubs* Brooks's; *Style—* John Kendall, Esq; ✉ Coombe Priory, Shaftesbury, Dorset; Charles Kendall Group of Companies, 7 Albert Court, Prince Consort Road, London SW7 2BJ (☎ 0171 589 1256, fax 0171 581 5761, telex 919060)

KENDALL, Nicholas John (Nick); s of Leonard and Barbara Kendall; *b* 29 Sept 1959; *Educ* Manchester GS, Christ Church Oxford (BA); *m* 23 Sept 1989, Patrice Rosanna, da of Roy Charlton Chasteau; *Career* account exec Sharps Advertising 1981–82, account planner Burkitt Weinreich Clients & Co 1982–87; Bartle Bogle Hegarty: account planner 1987–93, bd dir 1989–, head of planning 1993–; Gold (IPA Effectiveness Awards) 1992; memb: Effectiveness Ctee IPA 1993, MRS; *Recreations* work, my wife; *Style—* Nick Kendall, Esq; ✉ Bartle Bogle Hegarty, 60 Kingly Street, London W1R 6DS (☎ 0171 734 1677, fax 0171 437 3666)

KENDALL-TAYLOR, Prof Pat; da of Kendall-Taylor, CBE, of Wimbledon, and Dorothy, *née* Lawton (d 1958); *b* 17 Feb 1937; *Educ* RCM (ARCM), Royal Free Hosp Univ of London (MD); *Career* lectr in med Univ of Sheffield 1968–74, prof of endocrinology Univ of Newcastle upon Tyne 1985– (sr lectr and reader in med 1980–85), conslt physician Royal Victoria Infirmary Newcastle upon Tyne; memb Assoc Physicians 1973, FRCP; *Books* Casebook in Endocrinology (1987), numerous chapters and papers on endocrinology and medicine; *Recreations* fell walking, gardening, bird watching, music; *Style—* Prof Pat Kendall-Taylor; ✉ Royal Victoria Infirmary, Newcastle on Tyne NE1 4LP (☎ 0191 232 5131, fax 0191 222 0723)

KENDELL, Dr Robert Evan; CBE (1992); s of Robert Owen Kendell (d 1954), and Joan, *née* Evans (d 1986); *b* 28 March 1935; *Educ* Mill Hill Sch, Peterhouse Cambridge (BA, MA, MB BChir, MD), King's Coll Hosp Med Sch London; *m* 2 Dec 1961, Dr Ann Whitfield, da of Dr Gerald Whitfield (d 1972), of Lindfield, Sussex; 2 s (Patrick b 1968, Harry b 1970), 2 da (Katherine b 1965, Judith b 1966); *Career* registrar then sr registrar The Maudsley Hosp London 1962–66, assoc prof Univ of Vermont Coll of Med USA 1969–70, reader in psychiatry Inst of Psychiatry London 1970–74 (res worker 1966–70), dean Faculty of Med Univ of Edinburgh 1986–90 (prof of psychiatry 1974–91), chief med offr Scottish Office Home and Health Dept 1991–96, pres RCPsych 1996–; WHO: chm Expert Ctee on Alcohol Consumption 1979, memb Expert Advsy Panel on Mental Health 1979–91; Gaskell Gold medal RCPsych 1967, Paul Hoch medal American Psychopathological Assoc 1988, Marcé Soc medal 1994; memb MRC 1984–88; Hon FRCSEd 1995, Hon FRCPS (Glasgow) 1995; FRCP 1974, FRCPE 1977, FRCPsych 1979, FRSE 1993; *Books* The Classification of Depressive Illnesses (1968), Psychiatric Diagnosis in New York and London (1972), The Role of Diagnosis in Psychiatry (1975), Companion to Psychiatric Studies (ed 3–5 edns, 1983–93); *Recreations* overeating, walking up hills; *Clubs* Climbers'; *Style—* Dr R E Kendell, CBE, FRSE; ✉ 3 West Castle Rd, Edinburgh EH10 5AT (☎ 0131 229 4966); Royal College of Psychiatrists, 17 Belgrave Square London SW1X 8PG (☎ 0171 235 2351)

KENDREW, Sir John Cowdery; kt (1974), CBE (1963); s of Wilfrid Kendrew; *b* 24 March 1917; *Educ* Clifton, Trinity Coll Cambridge (ScD, PhD); *Career* served WWII Miny of Aircraft Prodn, Hon Wing Cdr RAF ME and SE Asia; dep chm MRC Laboratory of Molecular Biology Cambridge 1946–74, dir gen Euro Molecular Biology Laboratory 1975–82; jt winner Nobel Prize for Chemistry 1962, Royal Soc Royal Medal 1965; chm Governing Cncl UN Univ 1983–85 (memb 1980–86); pres: St John's Coll Oxford 1981–87,

Br Assoc for the Advancement of Sci 1974, Int Cncl of Scientific Unions 1983–88; hon fell: Peterhouse and Trinity Coll Cambridge, St John's Coll Oxford; Hon DSc: Reading, Keele, Exeter, Buckingham, Madrid, Siena, Chile, Pécs; Hon DUniv Stirling, hon prof Univ of Heidelberg 1982; FRS; *Clubs* Athenaeum; *Style—* Sir John Kendrew, CBE, FRS; ✉ The Old Guildhall, 4 Church Lane, Linton, Cambridge CB1 6JX (☎ 01223 891545)

KENEALLY, Thomas Michael (Tom); AO (1983); *m*, Judith; 2 da (Margaret, Jane); *Career* author and playwright; contrib to numerous magazines and newspapers incl: New York Times Book Review, Boston Globe, Washington Post, The Times, The Guardian, The Independent, Observer Colour Magazine, Time, Newsweek, The Australian, Sydney Morning Herald, Medical Journal of Australia; work translated into over 15 languages incl: French, German, Spanish, Hebrew, Czechoslovakian, Flemish, Japanese; distinguished prof Dept of English Creative Writing Sch Univ of Calif Irvine 1991–95 (prof 1985–), visiting prof and Berg prof Dept of English Creative Writing Sch New York Univ 1988; inaugural memb Australia-China Cncl 1978–83; pres: Aust Nat Book Cncl 1985–89, Aust Soc of Authors 1990 (cncl memb 1981–, chm 1987–90); dir Australian Republican Movement Movement 1993– (inaugural chairperson 1991–93); memb: Lit Bd Aust Cncl 1985–, Advsy Panel Aust Constitutional Cmmn 1985–88, Aust Writers' Guild, US Screenwriters' Guild; Hon DLit: Queensland Univ 1993, Nat Univ of Ireland 1994, Fairleigh Dickenson Univ USA 1994, Rollins Coll USA 1995; Univ Medal Univ of Calif Irvine 1995; FRSL, FAAAS 1993; *Books* incl: Bring Larks and Heroes (1967, Miles Franklin Award), Three Cheers for the Paraclete (Miles Franklin Award 1968), The Survivor (1969, Captain Cook Bi-Centenary Prize 1970), The Chant of Jimmie Blacksmith (1972, Booker McConnell shortlisted, RSL Prize 1973, later filmed), Gossip from the Forest (1975, The Age Fiction Prize, Booker McConnell shortlisted 1977, filmed 1979), Ned Kelly and the City of Bees (for children, 1978), Confederates (1979, Booker McConnell shortlisted), Schindler's Ark (1982, Booker McConnell Prize, Los Angeles Times Prize for Fiction 1983, titled Schindler's List in US), A Family Madness (1985), The Playmaker (1987), Towards Asmara (1989), Flying Hero Class (1991), Now And In Time To Be (1991), Place where Souls are Born (1992), Woman of the Inner Sea (1992), Jacko (1993), A River Town (1995); *Non-Fiction* The Utility Player (1993), Our Republic (1993), Homebush Boy - A Memoir (1995); *Plays* incl: Childermas (1968), An Awful Rose (1972), Gossip from the Forest (1983), The Playmaker (adapted from novel, 1988); *Film and TV scripts* incl: Too Many People are Disappearing, Silver City (Critics' Circle award for Best Screenplay 1985), Libido, Catalpa - The Australian Break, Corroboree; *Style—* Tom Keneally, Esq, AO, FRSL; ✉ c/o Rogers Colleridge and White, 20 Powis Mews, London W11 1JN (☎ 0171 221 3717)

KENILWORTH, 4 Baron (UK 1937); (John) Randle Siddeley; only s of 3 Baron Kenilworth (d 1981); *b* 16 June 1954; *Educ* Northease Manor, London Coll of Furniture; *m* 1, 1983 (m dis 1990), Kim, only da of Danie Serfontein, of Newcastle upon Tyne; m 2, 15 Aug 1991, Mrs Kiki McDonough, *née* Axford; 2 s (Hon William Randle b 24 Jan 1992, Hon Edward Oscar b 4 Feb 1994); *Heir* s, Hon William Randle Siddeley b 24 Jan 1992; *Career* dir Siddeley Landscapes Ltd; *Style—* The Rt Hon the Lord Kenilworth; ✉ c/o House of Lords, London SW1A 0PW

KENNA, Michael; s of Walter Kenna, and Eva, *née* Sherrington (d 1968); *b* 20 Nov 1953, Widnes, Cheshire; *Educ* Upholland Coll Lancs, Banbury Sch of Art Oxon, London Coll of Printing (HND Photography); *m* 1991, Camille, *née* Solyagua; 1 da from prev m (Olivia Morgan b 1985); *Career* photographer/master printer since 1978 (specialising in the interacton between the natural landscape and urban structures); advertising clients 1990– incl: BR, Chrysler Corporation, Powergen, RAF and Volvo (Britain), DHL, Marubeni and Mazda (Japan), Bank of America, Infiniti, KBA, Simpson Paper Co and Toshiba (USA), Adidas, PSI (Germany), Rolls Royce (Hong Kong); *Exhibitions* over 150 selected one-man exhbns in USA, Europe and Japan incl: Contrasts Gallery London 1982, Equivalents Gallery Seattle Washington 1983, Stephen Wirtz Gallery San Francisco 1984, 1987, 1990 and annually since 1993, Weston Gallery Carmel Calif 1985, 1988, 1991, 1992, 1994 and 1995, Madison Art Center Madison Wisconsin 1985, XVI Rencontres Internationales de la Photographie (Gallery Rue Balze Arles) 1985, Zur Stockeregg Gallery Zurich 1986 and 1994, Gallery MIN Tokyo 1987 and 1990, Michele Chomette Gallery Paris 1987, Fox Talbot Museum Lacock Wilts 1987, Halsted Gallery Birmingham Michigan 1988, 1990, 1992, 1994, 1995 and 1996, National Centre for Photography Bath Avon 1988, Long Beach Museum of Art Long Beach Calif 1988, Tampa Museum of Art Tampa Florida 1988, Germans Van Eck Gallery NY 1989 and 1993, Hamiltons Gallery London 1989 and 1992, Fuerte Gallery Tokyo 1990, Catherine Edelman Gallery Chicago Illinois annually 1990–, G Gibson Gallery Seattle Washington 1991, 1993, 1994, 1995 and 1996, Jackson Fine Art Atlanta Georgia 1991, 1994 and 1996, Robert Klein Gallery Boston Massachusetts 1992, 1993 and 1997, Cleveland Art Museum Cleveland Ohio 1992, University Art Museum Ann Arbor Michigan 1992, Int Center for Photography NY 1993, Photo Picture Space Osaka Japan 1994, Spectrum Gallery Rochester NY 1995, Craig Krull Gallery Los Angeles 1995 and 1996, Il Tempo Gallery Tokyo 1995, Industrial Relations - The Rouge and other sites (Detroit Inst of Arts) 1995, Marly le Roi (Clark Humanities Museum Claremont) 1997, Les Notre's Gardens (Huntingdon Library Pasadena) 1997, Musée Marly-le-Roi (Louveciennes France) 1997, Robert Mann Gallery NY 1997; over 150 selected gp exhbns in USA, Europe and Japan incl: Architecture: Subject, Object or Pretext? (Musee des Beaux-Art Argen) 1983, Lay of the Land (Palo Alto Cultural Center Palo Alto Calif) 1985, Museotrain Les Collections Photographiques des FRAC (France) 1986, Silver Image Exhibition (Gallery MIN Tokyo) 1988, The Landscape at Risk (Houston Center for Photography Texas) 1989, Picturing California (organized by The Oakland Museum Calif) 1990, La Conversation - Recent Acquisitions (Museum of Modern Art Strasbourg) 1990, Galerie Michele Chometta Paris 1991, Le Desert de Retz (Palace of the Legion of Honor San Francisco) 1991, Jane Jackson Fine Arts Atlanta Georgia 1991, Selenographie (Observatoire Astronomique Strasbourg) 1991, Der Europaische Ausbruch/L'Echapee Europeenne (travelling exhbn, Le Departement Culturrel de Bayer Leverkusen Germany), Le Mois de la Photographie 1992 (Pavillon des Arts Paris) 1992, Portraits d'une Capitale (Musee Carnavalet Paris) 1992, Recent Acquisitions (San Francisco Museum of Art) 1993, Sites/Fragile Ecologies (Smithsonian travelling exhbn, Washington DC) 1993, Contemporary Photographs from the Museum Collection (The Art Museum Princeton Univ) 1994, Latent August: The Legacy of Hiroshima and Nagasaki (Fort Mason Center San Francisco) 1995, Water (Robert Klein Gallery Boston) 1995, Trees (Galerie zur Stockeregg Zurich) 1995, Now and Then: The first eight years (Catherine Edelman Gallery Chicago) 1996, La Lune (l'Espace Lezard France) 1996, A Centennial Exposed (Jackson Fine Art Atlanta) 1996; *Selected Collections* work included in the permanent collections of over 60 museums in USA, Europe, Australia and Japan incl: Australian Nat Gallery Canberra, Bibliotheque Nationale Paris, The Museum of Decorative Arts Prague, The San Francisco Museum of Modern Art, Yale Univ Art Gallery New Haven Connecticut, V & A London; *Awards* Imogen Cunningham Award (San Francisco) 1981, Zellerbach Award (San Francisco) 1981, Art in Public Buildings Award (California Arts Cmmn Sacramento) 1987, The Inst for Aesthetic Devpt Award (Pasadena) 1989; *Selected Books and Catalogues* The Hound of the Baskervilles (Arthur Conan Doyle, Arion Press San Francisco, photographic illustrations, 1985), Michael Kenna 1977–1987 (MIN Gallery Tokyo, 1987), Night Walk (The Friends of Photography San Francisco, 1988), Le Desert de Retz (Arion Press San Francisco, 1990), Michael Kenna (MIN Gallery Tokyo, 1990), The Elkhorn Slough and Moss Landing (The Elkhorn Slough Fndn, photographic illustrations, 1991), Michael Kenna - A Twenty Year Retrospective (Treville Tokyo, 1994), The Rouge (Ram Publications Los Angeles, 1995); *Style—* Michael Kenna, Esq; ✉ c/o Hamiltons Photographers Ltd, The Studio, 25 Fentiman Road, London SW8 1LD (☎ 0171 820 9660, fax 0171 820 9669)

KENNAIR, William Brignall; s of Joseph Terry Kennair, of Newcastle upon Tyne, and Nancy, *née* Neasham; *b* 6 June 1956; *Educ* Royal GS Newcastle upon Tyne, UCL (LLB); *m* 2 Aug 1980, Karen Elizabeth, da of Keith John Williams, of Cardiff; *Career* ptnr John Venn & Sons London 1986– (articled clerk 1978–83, assoc 1983–86), Notary Public (John Venn & Sons, Notaries and Translators); Freeman City of London 1983–, Liveryman Worshipful Co of Scriveners 1983–, Freeman Worshipful Co of Information Technologists 1993–; memb Assoc Int De Jeunes Avocats 1985–, assoc memb American Bar Assoc 1994–; co-representative of Soc Public Notaries of London to the Union Internationale du Notariat Latin; *Recreations* computing, cuisine, wine, travel; *Style—* William Kennair, Esq; ✉ John Venn & Sons, 95 Aldwych, London WC2B 4JF (☎ 0171 395 4300, fax 0171 395 4310, modem 0171 395 4312)

KENNARD, Lt Col Sir George Arnold Ford; 3 Bt (UK 1891), of Fernhill, Co Southampton; s of late Sir Coleridge Arthur FitzRoy Kennard, 1 Bt; suc bro, Sir Laurence Ury Charles Kennard, 2 Bt, 1967; *b* 27 April 1915; *Educ* Eton; *m* 1, 1940 (m dis 1958), Cecilia Violet Cokayne, da of Maj Cecil John Cokayne Maunsell, JP (d 1948); 1 da (Zandra (Mrs John Powell) b 1941); m 2, 1958 (m dis 1974), Mrs Molly Jesse Rudd Miskin, da of late Hugh Wyllie, of Fishbourne, Sussex; m 3, 1985, Nicola, da of Capt Peter Gawan Carew (d 1966) and formerly w of Charles Louis Breitmeyer; m 4, 14 Dec 1992, Georgina, da of Sir Harold Augustus Wernher, 3 and last Bt, GCVO, TD (d 1973), and widow of Lt-Col Harold Pedro Joseph Phillips (d 1980); *Heir* none; *Career* WWII 1939–45 (despatches twice, POW), Lt Col (cmdg) late 4 Queen's Own Hussars; Midland rep for Cement Marketing Co; *Books* Loopy (autobiography, 1990); *Clubs* Cavalry and Guards'; *Style—* Lt Col Sir George Kennard, Bt; ✉ 13 Burton Court, Franklins Row, London SW3 4TA

KENNARD, Dr Olga (Lady Burgen); OBE (1988); da of Joir Weisz, and Catherina, *née* Sternberg (d 1988); *b* 23 March 1924; *Educ* Prince Henry VIII GS, Univ of Cambridge (ScD); *m* 1, 1948 (m dis 1961), Dr David William Kennard; 2 da (Susanna Clare b 1955, Julia Sarah b 1958); m 2, 5 Dec 1993, Sir Arnold Stanley Vincent Burgen, *qv*; *Career* res asst Cavendish Laboratory Cambridge 1944–48; MRC: memb Scientific Staff Vision Res Unit 1948–51, Nat Inst for Med Res 1951–61, Chem Laboratory Univ of Cambridge 1961–, special appt 1971–89; scientific dir Cambridge Crystallographic Data Centre 1965–, visiting prof Univ of London 1988–90; author of scientific papers and books on scientific data; memb numerous ctees of scientific socs; FRS 1987; *Recreations* swimming, modern architecture, reading; *Style—* Dr Olga Kennard, OBE, FRS; ✉ Cambridge Crystallographic Data Centre, 12 Union Rd, Cambridge CB2 1EZ (☎ 01223 336408)

KENNARD, Peter; *b* 1949, London; *Educ* Byam Shaw Sch of Art, Slade Sch of Art, RCA; *Career* artist/photographer; photomontages used for varied film and video work incl: Lab Pty election bdcast 1983, State of Emergency - South Africa (Bandung File C4) 1986, Heartfield - The Father of Photomontage (Granada TV) 1991; work published in newspapers and jls incl: The Guardian (regular contrib), The Listener, Time Magazine, Washington Post, New Scientist, Sunday Times; book covers cmmnd by: Penguin, Pluto Press, Paladin, Verso; work in the collections of: Magdalen and St Catherine's Colls Oxford, V & A, Imperial War Museum, Arts Cncl of GB, Saatchi Collection London; *Exhibitions* one man incl: St Catherine's Coll Oxford 1968, Gardner Arts Centre Univ of Sussex (artist in residence) 1971, Photographers Gallery Univ of Southampton 1973, A Document of Chile (Half Moon Gallery London and touring) 1978, Images for Disarmament (ICA London and Arnolfini Gallery Bristol) 1981, Despatches from an Unofficial War Artist (opening GLC Peace Year County Hall London and touring) 1982–83, Images Against War 1965–85 (Barbican Centre London) 1985, Photomontages for Peace (UN Palais des Nations Geneva) 1989, Images for the End of the Century (Gimpel Fils Gallery London and Imperial War Museum London) 1990, Reading Room (Gimpel Fils Gallery) 1996; group incl: Photographer as Printmaker (Arts Cncl touring) 1981, Art of the Comic Strip (Gimpel Fils Gallery London) 1984, Whitechapel Open 1985–88, Invention D'un Art (Pompidou Centre Paris) 1989, Shocks to the System (Festival Hall London and touring) 1991, Photomontage Now (Manchester City Art Gallery) 1991; *Books* No Nuclear Weapons (jtly, 1981), Jobs for a Change (1983), Keep London out of the Killing Ground (jtly, 1983), Target London (1985), About Turn (jtly, 1986), Images for the End of the Century (1990); *Style—* Peter Kennard, Esq; ✉ c/o Gimpel Fils Ltd, 30 Davies Street, London W1Y 1LG (☎ 0171 493 2488)

KENNAWAY, Eur Ing Prof Alexander; s of Dr Noah Barou (d 1955), and Mrs Sophie Barou (d 1956); bro of Liliana Archibald, *qv*; *b* 14 Aug 1923; *Educ* St Paul's, Pembroke Coll Cambridge (MA); *m* 1, 1947 (m dis 1970), Xenia Rebel; 1 s (Igor b 1947), 1 da (Nadia b 1950); m 2, 1973, Jean Simpson, da of Stanley Church (d 1982); *Career* WWII Lt Cdr RN served: Med, East Indies, Pacific; consltg engr 1966–; dir: BTR Industries 1960–66, Lankro Chemicals 1970–77, Thomas Jourdan Group 1976–82; chm Terrafix Ltd 1983–90; visiting prof of chemical (then mechanical) engrg Imperial Coll 1976–96, sr lectr Conflict Studies Res Centre RMA Sandhurst MOD; memb Bd CAA 1979–82, former memb Standing Advsy Ctee on Artificial Limbs DHSS; advsr: to Chilean Univs on design and innovation, to former Soviet orgns on product quality, design and conversion of military factories to civilian use; CEng, FIM; *Books* contrib: Plastics in Surgery (1956), Polythene, Its Technology and Uses (1958), The British Malaise (1982); sole author: Engineers in Industry, A Management Guide to Self Improvement (1981), Working in a market economy (in Russian, 1994); *Recreations* sailing, chess, music, self-education, thinking; *Clubs* Royal Naval Sailing Assoc; *Style—* Eur Ing Prof Alexander Kennaway; ✉ 12 Fairholme Crescent, Ashtead, Surrey KT21 2HN (☎ 01372 277 678); Conflict Studies Research Centre, RMA Sandhurst, Camberley, Surrey GU15 4PQ

KENNAWAY, John-Michael; s and h of Sir John Lawrence Kennaway, 5 Bt, and Christina Veronica, *née* Urszenyi; *b* 17 Feb 1962; *Educ* King Edward's Sch Bath, Hampshire Coll of Agriculture; *m* 22 Oct 1988, Lucy Frances, yr da of Dr Jeremy Houlton Bradshaw-Smith, of Ottery St Mary, Devon; 2 da (Olivia Ursula b 17 Nov 1993, Jessica Imogen b 31 May 1995); *Career* ornamental fish farmer, landowner (1200 acres); *Recreations* shooting, scuba diving; *Style—* John-Michael Kennaway, Esq; ✉ Escot, Ottery St Mary, Devon EX11 1LU (☎ 01404 822188)

KENNEDY, Dr Alexander; s of late Alexander Kennedy, and late Florence Edith, *née* Callin; *b* 20 April 1933; *Educ* Merchant Taylors', Univ of Liverpool (MB ChB, MD); *m* 6 Aug 1960, Marlene Joan Campbell, da of Alfred Beveridge (d 1939), of Edinburgh; 1 s (Alistair b 1969), 1 da (Fiona b 1963); *Career* RAF Med Branch, Flt Lt pathologist RAF Hosp Wroughton 1958–61; lectr in pathology Univ of Liverpool 1961–67, visiting asst prof Dept of Pathology Univ of Chicago 1968, sr lectr Dept of Pathology Univ of Sheffield 1968–77, hon conslt pathologist Sheffield Area Health Authy 1969–77, currently conslt histopathologist Northern Gen Hosp NHS Tst Sheffield, hon clinical lectr Univ of Sheffield; memb: Pathological Soc of GB and Ireland, Int Acad of Pathology, Sheffield Medico-Chirurgical Soc (pres elect), British Thoracic Soc, Trent Regnl Thoracic Soc, Pulmonary Pathology Club; churchwarden St Andrews Sharrow; FRCPath 1985 (MRCPath 1966); *Books* Essentials of Surgical Pathology - A Programmed Instruction Text (with A C Daniels and F Strauss, 1974), Basic Techniques in Diagnostic Histopathology (1977); *Recreations* cycling, walking, music, gardening; *Style—* Dr

Alexander Kennedy; ✉ Department of Histopathology, Northern General Hospital, Herries Road, Sheffield S5 7AU (☎ 0114 243 4343 ext 4849)

KENNEDY, Alison Louise; da of Prof R Alan Kennedy, and Edwardine Mildred, *née* Price; *b* 22 Oct 1965; *Educ* HS of Dundee, Univ of Warwick (BA); *Career* writer; co-ordinator of creative writing for Project Ability 1989–94, writer in residence SAC/Strathclyde Regnl Social Work Dept 1990–92; *Awards* Social Work Today Special Award 1990, Scottish Arts Cncl Book Award 1991, Saltire First Book Award 1991, Mail on Sunday/John Llewellyn Rees Prize 1991, Best of British Young Novelist list Granta 1993, Edinburgh Festival Fringe First 1993, Scottish Arts Cncl Book Award 1994, Somerset Maugham Award 1994, Saltire Best Book Award 1995, Scottish Arts Council Book Award 1995, Encore Award 1996; *Film* Stella Does Tricks (1997); *Books* Night Geometry and the Garscadden Trains (1991), Looking for the Possible Dance (1993), Now That You're Back (1994), So I am Glad (1995), Original Bliss (1997), The Life And Death of Colonel Blimp (1997); *Recreations* cinema, clarinet; *Clubs* Scottish Amateur Fencing Union; *Style—* Miss A L Kennedy; ✉ c/o Antony Harwood, Aitken & Stone, 29 Fernshaw Road, London SW10 0TG (☎ 0171 351 7561, fax 0171 376 3594)

KENNEDY, Andrew David; s of Maj Denis George Kennedy (d 1970), of London, and Catherine Clementina, *née* MacGregor; *b* 20 May 1943; *Educ* Downside, Gonville and Caius Coll Cambridge (MA); *m* 3 Jan 1970, Mary Frances, da of Frank Turnbull (d 1981), of Lancs; 2 s (James Andrew b 21 Sept 1970, Mark Richard b 4 Nov 1972); *Career* admitted slr 1965; sr ptnr Beachcroft Stanleys 1988–96 (ptnr 1970–); former chm E Surrey Water Plc 1995–96 (dir 1979), Sutton District Water Plc 1988–96, Cheam Group Plc 1991–96; chm Slrs' Indemnity Fund 1993–; dir: MMI Companies Inc 1996–, Edward Lumley Holdings Ltd 1996–; govr: Wimbledon Coll, Woldingham Sch; Liveryman Worshipful Co of Slrs 1994, Freeman City of London 1993; memb Law Soc 1965 (memb Cncl 1986); *Recreations* golf, music, cricket; *Clubs* MCC, City Law, Royal Wimbledon Golf; *Style—* Andrew Kennedy, Esq; ✉ Friars Croft, 19 Wool Rd, Wimbledon, London SW20 OHN (☎ 0181 946 3208); Beachcroft Stanleys, 20 Furnival St, London EC4R 1BN (☎ 0171 242 1011, telex 264607, fax 0171 831 6630)

KENNEDY, Dr Cameron Thomas Campbell; s of Thomas Kennedy (d 1981), and Dorian, *née* Talbot; *b* 30 Jan 1947; *Educ* Forest Sch Snaresbrook, Queens' Coll Cambridge and UCH (MA, MB BChir); *m* 19 May 1973, Dr Rosalind Penolope, da of Raymond Whittier Baldwin, of Alderley Edge, Cheshire; 3 s (Nicholas b 5 June 1979, Thomas b 3 March 1981, Stephen b 29 Jan 1984); *Career* registrar in dermatology London Hosp 1973–75, sr registrar St George's Hosp 1975–80; Bristol Royal Infirmary: conslt dermatologist 1981–, postgraduate clinical tutor 1985–89; conslt dermatologist: Southmead Hosp Bristol 1981–, Bristol Children's Hosp 1981–; hon chm Br Soc of Paediatric Dermatology 1994– (hon treas/sec 1991–94); memb Br Assoc of Dermatologists, non-resident fell American Acad of Dermatology; FRCP 1986, FRSM; *Recreations* gardening, reading; *Clubs* Bristol Savages; *Style—* Dr Cameron Kennedy; ✉ 16 Sion Hill, Clifton, Bristol BS8 4AZ (☎ 0117 974 1935); Bristol Royal Infirmary, Department of Dermatology, Marlborough St, Bristol BS2 8HW (☎ 0117 928 2520)

KENNEDY, Charles Peter; MP (Lib Dem) Ross, Cromarty and Skye (majority 7,630); s of Ian Kennedy and Mary MacVarish, *née* MacEachen, of Fort William; *b* 25 Nov 1959; *Educ* Lochaber HS Fort William, Glasgow Univ (MA), Univ of Indiana USA (Fulbright Scholarship); *Career* broadcaster and journalist BBC Highland Inverness 1982, graduate student/lecturer (speech communications and British politics) Univ of Indiana USA 1982–83, MP (SDP until 1987, now Lib Dem) Ross, Cromarty and Skye 1983–; chm SDP Cncl for Scotland 1985–87, Alliance spokesman on social security 1987; SDP spokesman on Scotland, health and social security 1983–87, SLD spokesman on trade and industry 1988–89; Lib Dem spokesman on: health 1989–92, Europe 1992–; pres Lib Dem Party 1990–94; *Recreations* journalism, lecturing, broadcasting, music, reading, writing; *Clubs* National Liberal; *Style—* Charles Kennedy, Esq, MP; ✉ House of Commons, London SW1A 0AA (☎ 0171 219 5090, fax 0171 219 4881)

KENNEDY, Prof Clive Russell; s of Thomas Kennedy (ka 1941), of Paisley, Renfrewshire, and Victoria Alice, *née* Russell; *b* 17 June 1941; *Educ* Liverpool Coll, Univ of Liverpool (BSc, PhD, DSc); *m* 1, 23 Feb 1963, Beryl Pamela (d 1978), da of David Redvers Jones (d 1979), of Portargothi, Nantgaredig, Carmarthen; 1 s (Aidan b 1970), 1 da (Kate b 1971); m 2, 5 May 1979, Margaret Hilary, da of Bernard Wise (d 1973), of Oxford; *Career* asst in zoology Univ Coll Dublin 1963–64, asst lectr in zoology Univ of Birmingham 1964–65; Univ of Exeter: lectr in biological sci 1965–76, reader in zoology 1976–86, prof of parasitology 1986–, dean of sci 1990–93, head of dept 1996–; visiting prof King's Coll London 1986–90; memb: Ctee NERC 1984–88, Regional Fisheries Advsy Ctee Nat Rivers Authy, Br Soc of Parasitology 1968 (vice pres 1992–94, pres 1994–96), Fisheries Soc of the Br Isles 1969; hon memb Russian Parasitology Soc; *Books* Ecological Animal Parasitology (1975), Ecological Aspects of Parasitology (1976), numerous papers in sci jls; *Recreations* walking, churches, glass, rugby; *Style—* Prof Clive Kennedy; ✉ Department of Biological Sciences, The University, Exeter EX4 4PS (☎ 01392 263757, fax 01392 263700, telex 42894 EXUNIVG, e-mail biology@exeter.ac.uk)

KENNEDY, David; s of Lilian Alice Kennedy; *b* 7 Nov 1940; *Educ* Ryhope Robert Richardson GS Co Durham, City Of London Coll; *m* 5 Sept 1964, Peta Jennifer, *née* Hatton; 2 da (Karen Jane b 15 Feb 1972, Sarah Louise b 5 May 1975); *Career* various posts Exchequer and Audit Dept Home Civil Serv 1959–69; Commonwealth War Graves Commission: worked in personnel 1969–74, dir of Mgmnt Servs 1974–79, dir of Outer Area (Far East and Africas) 1979–84, dir of France Area 1984–86, dir of Personnel 1986–87, dep DG 1987–92, attended Royal Coll of Defence Studies 1992, DG 1993–; *Recreations* sport, tennis, skiing, golf, photography, travel; *Style—* David Kennedy, Esq; ✉ Commonwealth War Graves Commission, 2 Marlow Road, Maidenhead, Berks SL6 7DX (☎ 01628 34221, fax 01628 771208)

KENNEDY, Lord David Thomas; s of 7 Marquess of Ailsa, OBE, DL (d 1994); bro and hp of 8 Marquess, *qv*; *b* 3 July 1958; *Educ* Strathallan Sch, Berks Coll of Agric; *m* 19 Dec 1991, Anne, da of Bernard Kelly, of Warwick; 1 s (Archibald David b 7 Sept 1995), 1 da (Katherine Jean b 22 Oct 1993); *Career* farmer; *Recreations* vintage car restoration, travel; *Clubs* New (Edinburgh), Glasgow Art; *Style—* The Lord David Kennedy; ✉ Morriston Farm, Maidens, Maybole, Ayrshire KA19 8LB

KENNEDY, Sir Francis; KCMG (1986), CBE (1977, MBE 1958); s of James Kennedy (d 1961), and Alice, *née* Bentham (d 1978); *b* 9 May 1926; *Educ* Preston Catholic Coll, Univ of Manchester (BA), Univ of London (BA); *m* 4 March 1957, Anne O'Malley; 2 s (Mark b 1960, Jonathan b 1966), 2 da (Sarah b 1958, Ruth b 1965); *Career* RN 1944–46; HM Colonial Serv Nigeria 1953–64, Dip Serv 1964–86: served Kuching, Dar es Salaam, Istanbul, Atlanta, Lagos; ambass to Angola and ambass non-resident to São Tomé and Principe 1981–83, HM consul-gen at NY and DG Br Trade Devpt USA 1983–86; British Airways 1986– (bd memb 1987–96), chm British Airways Regnl 1994–; dir: Global Analysis Systems Ltd 1986–88, Leslie & Godwin 1986–90, Fluor-Daniel 1986– (chm 1989–), Hambourne Development Co Ltd 1987–94, Smith & Nephew plc 1988–96, Fleming Overseas Investment Trust 1988–, Brunner Mond 1992–; memb Bd of Inward 1986–90; memb Bd of Govrs: Br Liver Fndn 1990–93, Univ of Central Lancs 1988–95; chllr Univ of Central Lancashire 1995–; *Recreations* watching cricket, golf, gardening; *Clubs* Brooks's; *Style—* Sir Francis Kennedy, KCMG, CBE; ✉ British Airways, Berkeley Square House, Berkeley Square, London W1X 6BA

KENNEDY, Graham Norbert; CVO (1993); *b* 21 Oct 1936; *Career* dir Ockham plc; chm: Anglo Pacific Resources plc, Dwyer plc; former dir London Stock Exchange (and memb Cncl's Quotations Ctee); MSI 1974; *Recreations* golf, shooting, music; *Clubs* Boodle's, City of London; *Style—* Graham Kennedy, Esq, CVO; ✉ Hatchetts, Church Lane, Worting, Basingstoke, Hants (☎ 01256 21764)

KENNEDY, Iain Manning; s of William Stanley Kennedy (d 1983), and Pamela Ellen, *née* Manning; *b* 15 Sept 1942; *Educ* Glenalmond, Pembroke Coll Cambridge (MA); *m* 18 Aug 1971, Ingrid Annette, da of Andersson Holgar Adolf Herr (d 1986); 2 da (Lucy Gunilla b 1974, Anna Ingrid b 1976); *Career* Church & Co plc: dir 1974–, jt md 1991–; *Recreations* golf, philately; *Style—* Iain Kennedy, Esq; ✉ 3 Townsend Close, Hanging Houghton, Northampton NN6 9HP (☎ 01604 880755, office ☎ 01604 751251)

KENNEDY, Jane; MP (Lab) Liverpool Broad Green (majority 7,027); da of Clifford Hodgson, and Barbara Hodgson; *b* 4 May 1958; *Educ* Haughton Comp Sch, Queen Elizabeth Sixth Form Coll, Univ of Liverpool; *m* 14 Dec 1977, Malcolm Kennedy; 2 s; *Career* residential child care offr Liverpool City Cncl 1979–83, care asst Liverpool Social Servs 1984–88, area organiser NUPE 1988–92 (branch sec 1983–88), MP (Lab) Liverpool Broad Green 1992–; memb: Social Security Select Ctee Oct 1982–July 1984, Environment Select Ctee May 1995 - Oct 1995; opposition whip Oct 1995–; memb Governing Body: Liverpool Poly 1986–88, Oldham Sixth Form Coll 1990–92; memb: Lab Pty 1978–, Ramblers' Assoc, Belgian Shepherd Dog Assoc; *Style—* Jane Kennedy, MP; ✉ Liverpool office: 302/304 Kensington, Liverpool L7 2RS (☎ 0151 261 0007, fax 0151 261 0007); London office: (☎ 0171 219 4523, fax 0171 219 6838); House of Commons, London SW1A 0AA

KENNEDY, Jane; *b* 28 Feb 1953; *Educ* Sch of Architecture Univ of Manchester, Sch of Architecture Manchester Poly (DipArch); *m* John Maddison, artist and writer; 2 s; *Career* asst in Historic Buildings Gp Planning Dept Gtr Manchester Cncl 1974–75, Manchester Poly 1975–78, architect with Br Waterways Bd Rugby 1978–80, asst to David Jeffcoate Architect London 1980–81, pt/t work (due to family) 1981–86, historic buildings architect Planning Dept Norwich City Cncl 1986–88; Purcell Miller Tritton and Partners: joined Norwich Office as asst 1988, assoc 1989, ptnr Ely Office 1992–; memb Norwich Diocesan Advsy Ctee 1993– (representing Eng Heritage for Norwich), conslt inspecting architect Eng Heritage 1994–, surveyor to the Fabric of Ely Cathedral 1994– (asst surveyor 1990), memb Cncl for the Care of Churches 1996–; occasional lectr at Univs of York, Cambridge and Edinburgh; tstee and vice chm Church and Community Tst 1992–; memb: The Victorian Soc (ctee memb Manchester and E Anglia), Soc for the Protection of Ancient Buildings, National Tst; memb ARCUK 1979, RIBA; FRSA 1994; *Recreations* walking and family life; *Style—* Ms Jane Kennedy; ✉ Partner, Purcell Miller Tritton & Partners, 46a St Mary's Street, Ely, Cambridgeshire CB7 4EY (☎ 01353 666367, fax 01353 669191)

KENNEDY, Joanna Alicia Gore; *née* Ormsby; OBE (1995); da of Capt Gerald Anthony Gore Ormsby, DSO, DSC, RN (d 1992), of Oxon, and Nancy Mary (Susan), *née* Williams (d 1974); *b* 22 July 1950; *Educ* Queen Anne's Sch Caversham, Lady Margaret Hall Oxford (MA); *m* 21 July 1979, Richard Paul Kennedy, *qv*; 2 s (Peter b 1985, David b 1988); *Career* Ove Arup & Ptnrs consltg engrs: design engr 1972, asst resident engr (Runnymede Bridge) 1977, sr engr 1979, Arup Associates 1987, Arup Project Management 1990–, associate 1992, assoc dir 1994, project dir redevpt of South Bank Centre 1995–, dir 1996–; memb: Engrg Cncl 1984–86 and 1987–90, Cncl Inst of Civil Engrs 1984–87, Advsy Cncl RNEC Manadon 1988–94, Engrg and Technol Prog Advsy Gp PCFC 1989–91, Engrg Bd SERC 1990–93, Engrg and Technol Bd SERC 1993–94, Tech Opportunities Panel EPSRC 1994–, Cncl Univ of Southampton 1996–; vice pres Friends of Whittington Hosp, govr Channing Sch; tstee Science Museum 1992–; Hon DSc Univ of Salford 1994; CEng, FICE, ACIArb, FRSA; *Style—* Mrs Joanna Kennedy, OBE; ✉ Ove Arup & Partners, 13 Fitzroy St, London W1P 6BQ (☎ 0171 465 2003, fax 0171 465 2143)

KENNEDY, Rt Rev Monsignor John; s of James Kennedy (d 1961), and Alice, *née* Bentham (d 1978); *b* 31 Dec 1930; *Educ* St Joseph's Coll Upholland, English Coll Rome (PhL, STL), Campion Hall Oxford (MPhil); *Career* curate: St John's Wigan 1956–64, St Austin's St Helens 1964–66, St Edmund's Waterloo Liverpool 1966–68; lectr Christ's Coll Liverpool 1968–83 (head Dept of Theology 1975–83), rector English Coll Rome 1984–91, parish priest Southport Merseyside 1991–; *Books* Priest & People (contrib, 1968); *Recreations* golf, cricket; *Clubs* Royal Birkdale Golf (Southport), Royal Over-Seas League; *Style—* The Rt Rev Monsignor Kennedy; ✉ Holy Family, 1 Brompton Rd, Southport, Merseyside PR8 6AS (☎ 01704 532613)

KENNEDY, John Maxwell; s of George Steel Kennedy (d 1979), of Cardiff, and Betty Gertrude, *née* Bennett (d 1983); *b* 9 July 1934; *Educ* Univ Coll London (LLB); *m* 1958, Margaret Joan, da of Dr Trevor Davies; 4 s (Simon b 1959, Alexander b 1960, David b 1965, Hamish b 1964); *Career* slr; Allen & Overy: joined 1954, ptnr 1962–94, sr ptnr 1986–94; chm: The Law Debenture Corporation plc, Angerstein Underwriting Trust plc, Lloyd's Corp Capital Assoc; dir Nuclear Generation Decommissioning Fund Ltd; memb Bd Securities and Investments Board; Freeman City of London; *Recreations* music, reading, sport; *Clubs* City of London, City Law, Bankers, Hurlingham, Royal Wimbledon Golf; *Style—* John Kennedy, Esq; ✉ 16 Kensington Park Road, London W11 3BU (☎ 0171 727 6929, fax 0171 727 3262); The Law Debenture Corporation, Princes House, 95 Gresham Street, London EC2V 7LY (☎ 0171 606 5451, fax 0171 606 0643)

KENNEDY, Louise; da of James Kennedy, of Tipperary, Ireland, and Margaret, *née* McCormack (d 1984); *b* 28 June 1960; *Educ* St Annes Mount Merrion Avenue Dublin, Coll of Mktg & Design Dublin, Grafton Acad of Design Dublin; *Career* fashion designer (under own label) 1984–; designer of inauguration outfit for Mary Robinson (first female pres of Ireland) 1989, selected to join Br Designer Gp and exhibit at London Designer Show 1990, elected Tipperary Person of the Year (for outstanding achievements in Irish fashion 1992); other Irish fashion awards incl: Best Irish Coat Collection 1985, Irish Designer of the Year 1989 and 1990, Best Suit and Best Coat Award 1991, Best Irish Designer Collection (Fashion Oscar Award) 1992, Best Coat and Suit Collection Designer of the Year Awards 1993, first female designer to receive award for Outstanding Achievements in Fashion from Irish Clothing Indust 1994; *Style—* Ms Louise Kennedy; ✉ 22 South William Street, Dublin 2, Ireland (☎ 00 353 1 6719564, fax 00 353 1 6798689)

KENNEDY, Sir Ludovic Henry Coverley; kt (1994); s of Capt Edward Kennedy, RN (ka 1939; ggs of Hon Robert Kennedy, bro of 1 Marquess of Ailsa and 3 s of 11 Earl of Cassillis), and Rosalind, da of Sir Ludovic Grant, 11 Bt of Dalvey; *b* 3 Nov 1919; *Educ* Eton, Ch Ch Oxford; *m* 1950, Moira Shearer (formerly ballerina with Sadler's Wells Ballet, actress (including The Red Shoes), and writer, da of Harold King; 1 s, 3 da; *Career* writer and broadcaster; served WWII, Lt RNVR; private sec and ADC to Govr of Newfoundland 1943–44; librarian Ashridge Coll 1949, lectr British Cncl 1955–56; Parly candidate (Lib) Rochdale: 1958 by-election, 1959 gen election; columnist: Newsweek International 1974–75, Sunday Standard 1981–82; chm Royal Lyceum Theatre Co of Edinburgh 1977–84, Voltaire Meml lectr 1985, dir The Spectator 1988–89; pres Voluntary Euthanasia Soc 1995–; *Television and Radio Work* incl: newscaster Independent Television News 1956–58; introducer: This Week (AR) 1958–59, Time Out (BBC) 1964–65, World at One 1965–66; commentator Panorama (BBC) 1960–63; presenter: Lib Party's Gen Election TV Bdcasts 1966, The Middle Years (ABC) 1967, The Nature of Prejudice (ATV) 1968, Face the Press (Tyne-Tees) 1968–69 and 1970–72, Against the Tide (Yorkshire TV) 1969, Living and Growing (Grampian TV) 1969–70, 24 Hours (BBC) 1969–72, Ad Lib (BBC) 1970–72, Midweek (BBC) 1973–75, Newsday (BBC) 1975–76, Tonight (BBC) 1976–78, A Life with Crime (BBC) 1979, Change of Direction (BBC) 1979, Lord Mountbatten Remembers 1980, Did You See? 1980–88,

Timewatch 1984, Indelible Evidence 1987 and 1990, A Gift of the Gab 1989, Portrait 1989; *TV Films* incl: The Sleeping Ballerina, The Singers and the Songs, Scapa Flow, Battleship Bismarck, Life and Death of the Scharnhorst, U-Boat War, Target Tirpitz, The Rise of the Red Navy, Lord Haw-Haw, Coast to Coast, Who Killed the Lindbergh Baby, Elizabeth - The First Thirty Years, Happy Birthday, dear Ma'am, Consider the End, Murder in Belgravia: The Lucan Affair; *Awards* Rockefeller Fndn Atlantic Award in Literature 1950, winner Open Finals Contest English Festival of Spoken Poetry 1953, Richard Dimbleby BAFTA Award 1988; pres Nat League of Young Liberals 1959–61, memb Lib Party Cncl 1965–67; Hon LLD: Strathclyde 1985, Southampton 1993; Hon DUniv: Edinburgh 1990, Stirling 1991; FRSA 1974–76; West German Cross of Merit First Class 1979; *Books* Sub-Lieutenant (1942), Nelson's Band of Brothers (1951), One Man's Meat (1953), Murder Story (play, 1956), Ten Rillington Place (1961), The Trial of Stephen Ward (1964), Very Lovely People (1969), Pursuit - The Chase and Sinking of the Bismarck (1974), A Presumption of Innocence - The Amazing Case of Patrick Meehan (1975), Menace - The Life and Death of the Tirpitz (1979), The Portland Spy Case (1979), Wicked Beyond Belief (1980), A Book of Railway Journeys (ed, 1980), A Book of Sea Journeys (ed, 1981), A Book of Air Journeys (ed, 1982), The Airman and the Carpenter (1985), On My Way to the Club (autobiography, 1989), Euthanasia - The Good Death (1990), Truth to Tell (collected writings, 1991), In Bed with an Elephant: A Journey Through Scotland (1995); *Clubs* Brooks's, Army and Navy; *Style*— Sir Ludovic Kennedy; ✉ c/o Rogers, Coleridge & White, 22 Powis Mews, London W11 1JN

KENNEDY, Dr Malcolm William; s of William Kennedy (d 1970), of Gosforth; *b* 13 March 1935; *Educ* Univ of Durham (BSc), Univ of Newcastle upon Tyne (DPhil); *m* June 1962, Patricia Ann, da of George Arthur Forster; 1 da (Clare Rachel b 10 Oct 1967); *Career* apprentice to C A Parsons & Co Ltd; Merz and McLellan: joined 1964, ptnr 1981, sr ptnr 1988–91, first chm and md (following incorporation) 1991–94, exec chm 1995–; non-exec dir Port of Tyne Authy 1994–, non-exec chm Parsons Brinckerhoff International 1996–; advsr Dept of Energy on privatisation of electricity indust 1989–90, memb Electricity Panel MMC 1992–, head Northern Engrg Centre 1994–; vice pres IEE 1989 and 1994–; CEng 1967, FIEE 1974, FEng 1986, CIMgt 1992; *Recreations* Methodist local preacher, cricket, railways; *Clubs* National; *Style*— Dr Malcolm Kennedy, FEng; ✉ Merz and McLellan Ltd, Amber Court, William Armstrong Drive, Newcastle Business Park, Newcastle upon Tyne NE4 7YQ (☎ 0191 226 1899, fax 0191 226 1104)

KENNEDY, (William) Michael Clifford; s of Dr Clifford Donald Kennedy (d 1989), and Isobel Sinclair Kennedy (d 1984); *b* 29 Oct 1935; *Educ* Rugby, Merton Coll Oxford (BA); *m* 1962, Judith Victoria, da of Kenneth Fulton Gibb, of Fife; 1 s (Niall b 1964), 1 da (Tessa b 1965); *Career* CA; dep chm The Scottish Life Assurance Co 1976–; dir: Venture Assocs SA 1978–, Martin Currie Pacific Tst 1985–, Adam & Company Group PLC 1996–, Fleming Income & Growth Investment Trust PLC 1996–, Moorgate Investment Trust (non-exec) 1996–; non-exec dir Royal Infirmary of Edinburgh NHS Tst 1993–; *Recreations* shooting, fishing, golf, gardening, music; *Clubs* New (Edinburgh), Hon Co of Edinburgh Golfers; *Style*— Michael Kennedy, Esq; ✉ Oak Lodge, Inveresk, Midlothian EH21 7TE (☎ 0131 665 8822)

KENNEDY, His Hon Judge Michael Denis; QC (1979); s of Denis George Kennedy (d 1970), of London, and Clementina Catherine, *née* MacGregor; *Educ* Downside, Gonville & Caius Coll Cambridge; *m* 1964, Elizabeth June, *née* Curtiss; 2 s (Laurence James Denis b 8 Oct 1965, Benedict Michael b 24 March 1969), 2 da (Rachel Mary Helen b 6 June 1967, Alice Catherine Elizabeth b 12 Feb 1971); *Career* called to the Bar Inner Temple 1961, recorder 1979–84, circuit judge (SE Circuit) 1984–; memb Ct Univ of Sussex 1980–90; Univ of Brighton: chm Students Appeals Ctee 1992, memb Bd of Govrs 1993; *Recreations* music, hedge-laying, flint-walling, fishing; *Clubs* S of England Hedge-Laying Soc, Schola Gregoriana (Cambridge); *Style*— His Hon Judge Kennedy, QC

KENNEDY, Sir Michael Edward; 8 Bt (UK 1836), of Johnstown Kennedy, Co Dublin; s of Lt-Col Sir (George) Ronald Derrick Kennedy, 7 Bt, OBE (d 1988), and Noelle Mona, *née* Green; *b* 12 April 1956; *Educ* Rotherfield Hall Sussex; *m* 1984, Helen Christine, da of Patrick Lancelot Rae, of Nine Acres, Halstead, Kent; 1 s (George Matthew Rae b 9 Dec 1993), 2 da (Constance Andrea Rae b 4 Aug 1984, Josephine Jennifer Rae b 6 Dec 1986); *Heir* s, George Matthew Rae Kennedy b 9 Dec 1993; *Career* memb Standing Cncl of the Baronetage; *Style*— Sir Michael Kennedy, Bt; ✉ 48 Telston Lane, Otford, Kent TN14 5LA

KENNEDY, Neil Richard; s of Walter Kennedy (d 1988), and Vera Nancy Kennedy; *b* 6 March 1946; *Educ* Uppingham; *m* 1, Georgina Theresa, *née* Tolhurst (d 1979); 2 s (Angus b 19 Jan 1973, James b 7 Sept 1978), 2 da (Caroline b 28 Oct 1971, Elizabeth b 8 Oct 1976); m 2, 28 Nov 1980, Johanna, da of Gert Woudstra, of Holland; *Career* Colman Prentis & Varley Ltd 1963–65, dep md Childs-Greene Associates Ltd 1965–76, md Brunnings plc 1976–78, vice chm Bates Dorland Ltd 1978–96, exec vice-pres Bates Europe 1988–96, dir The Countryside Business Group 1996–; non-exec dir: Allders Dept Stores 1995–, Steven Sharp PLC; FIPA; *Books* Retail Handbook (1988); *Recreations* skiing, sailing, shooting; *Clubs* Royal Burnham Yacht (tstee, former cdre), Royal Thames Yacht; *Style*— Neil Kennedy, Esq; ✉ Stokes Hall, Althorne, Essex CM3 6DS

KENNEDY, Nigel Alan; s of Alan Ridsdale Kennedy (d 1980), of Claygate, Surrey, and Joan, *née* Mellows; *b* 2 Feb 1956; *Educ* Ardingly, Trinity Coll Oxford (MA); *m* 11 Sept 1982, Nicola Helen, da of Christopher Maurice Spencer; 2 da (Rachel b 21 Dec 1985, Rosalind b 16 Feb 1988), 1 s (Michael b 4 June 1990); *Career* public affrs offr: Mobil Oil Co Ltd London 1979–81, Total Oil Great Britain Ltd London 1981–84, co-ordinator (Northern Europe) Total Compagnie Française des Pètroles Paris 1984–86, dir The Communication Group plc 1986–93, md The Grayling Group 1993–; *Recreations* soccer, cricket, tennis, squash, travel; *Style*— Nigel Kennedy, Esq; ✉ The Grayling Group, 4 Bedford Square, London WC1B 3RA (☎ 0171 255 1100, fax 0171 631 0602)

KENNEDY, Nigel Paul; s of John Kennedy, and Scylla, *née* Stoner; *b* 28 Dec 1956; *Educ* Yehudi Menuhin Sch, Juillard Sch of Performing Arts; *Career* solo violinist; debut at Festival Hall with Philharmonia Orch 1977, Berlin debut with Berlin Philharmonia 1980, Henry Wood Promenade debut 1981, New York debut with BBC Symphony Orch 1987, tour of Hong Kong and Aust with Hallé Orch 1981, extensive tours USA and Europe; recordings incl: Tchaikovsky, Sibelius, Vivaldi (Double Platinum Disc), Elgar Violin Concerto (Record of the Year 1985, Gold Disc), Bruch and Mendelssohn (Gold Disc), Walton Violin and Viola, and Let Loose, Kafka 1996; *Style*— Nigel Kennedy, Esq; ✉ c/o Russells Solicitors, Regency Hosue, 1/4 Warwick Street, London W1R 6LJ (☎ 0171 439 8692)

KENNEDY, Rt Hon Lord Justice; Rt Hon Sir Paul Joseph Morrow Kennedy; kt (1983), PC (1992); s of late Dr Joseph Morrow Kennedy, of Sheffield, and late Bridget Teresa Kennedy; *b* 12 June 1935; *Educ* Ampleforth, Gonville and Caius Coll Cambridge; *m* 1965, Hon Virginia, da of late Baron Devlin; 2 s, 2 da; *Career* called to the Bar Gray's Inn 1960; recorder of the Crown Ct 1972, QC 1973, bencher 1982, judge of the High Court of Justice 1983–92, presiding judge NE Circuit 1985–89, a Lord Justice of Appeal (Queen's Bench Div) 1992–; chm Criminal Ctee 1993–96, memb main bd Judicial Studies Bd 1993–96; *Style*— The Rt Hon Lord Justice Kennedy; ✉ Royal Courts of Justice, Strand, London WC2A 2LL

KENNEDY, Prof Paul M; *b* 1945; *Educ* Univ of Newcastle (BA), Univ of Oxford (DPhil); *m* Catherine; 3 s; *Career* UEA: lectr 1970–75, reader 1975–82, prof 1982–83; J Richardson Dilworth prof of history Yale Univ 1983– (dir of int security studies); co-dir of the Secretariat to the Int Advsy Gp's Report - The UN in its Second Half Century; res awards from British Acad, Leverhulme Fndn, Alexander von Humboldt Fndn, Beit Fund Oxford, Social Science Res Cncl, German Academic Exchange Serv; Hon MA Yale Univ, Hon DLitt Univ of Newcastle, Hon DHL Long Island Univ, Hon DHL Univ of New Haven, Hon LLD Ohio Univ; supernumary fell St Antony's Coll Oxford; fell: Inst for Advanced Study Princeton 1978–79, American Philosophical Soc, Soc of American Historians, Alexander von Humboldt Fndn; FRHS, FAAAS; *Books* Pacific Onslaught 1941–43 (1972), Conquest: The Pacific War 1943–45 (1973), The Samoan Tangle: A Study in Anglo-German-American Relations 1878–1900 (1974), The Rise and Fall of British Naval Mastery (1976), The Rise of the Anglo-German Antagonism 1860–1914 (1980), The Realities Behind Diplomacy: Background Influences on British External Policy 1865–1980 (1981), Strategy and Diplomacy, 1870–1945: Eight Essays (1983), The Rise and Fall of the Great Powers: Economic Change and Military Conflict from 1500–2000 (1988), Preparing for the Twenty-First Century (1993); reg contrib to numerous jls and publications incl The New York Times, The Los Angeles Times, The Atlantic and others; *Recreations* coaching soccer, helping to run local soup kitchen; *Style*— Prof Paul Kennedy; ✉ Department of History, Yale University, New Haven, Conn, USA (☎ 00 1 203 432 6246, fax 00 1 203 432 6250)

KENNEDY, Peter Francis; s of Maurice Joseph Kennedy (d 1980), of Bradford, and Mary Josephine, *née* Benson; *b* 31 May 1941; *Educ* St Bede's GS Bradford, Univ of Leeds (MB ChB, DPM), Univ of Edinburgh (MD); *m* 1965, Sarah Elizabeth, da of Lawrence Arthur Inman; 2 s (John b 1966, Andrew b 1971), 1 da (Juliette b 1967); *Career* medical houseman York 1965–68, scientist MRC Epidemiology Unit Edinburgh 1968–71, sr lectr in psychiatry and hon conslt psychiatrist Univ of Edinburgh 1973–80 (lectr 1971–73), gen mangr Mental Health Servs York 1985–88, dist gen mangr York Health Authy 1988–92, chief exec York Health Servs NHS Tst 1992–; conslt in mental health WHO: Burma 1975, India 1978, Athens 1982, Qatar 1989 and 1990; FRCPsych 1982; *Books* Trends in Suicide and Attempted Suicide in Europe (WHO) 1982; *Recreations* sailing; *Style*— Dr Peter Kennedy; ✉ 10 St George's Place, York YO2 2DR (☎ 01904 621636); York Health Services NHS Trust, Bootham Park Hospital, York YO3 7BY (☎ 01904 610700, fax 01904 631823)

KENNEDY, Prof Peter Graham Edward; s of Philip Kennedy, of London, and Gertrude Sylvia, *née* Summer; *b* 28 March 1951; *Educ* Univ Coll Sch London, UCL and UCH (MB BS, MPhil, MLitt, MD, PhD, DSc); *m* 6 July 1983, Catherine Ann, da of Christopher King; 1 s (Luke b 1988), 1 da (Vanessa b 1991); *Career* hon res asst MRC Neuroimmunology Project UCL 1978–80, sr registrar (formerly registrar) in neurology Nat Hosp London 1981–84, asst prof of neurology Johns Hopkins Univ Sch of Med USA 1985, Burton prof and head Dept of Neurology Univ of Glasgow 1987– (sr lectr in neurology and virology 1986–87), conslt neurologist Inst of Neurological Sciences Glasgow 1986–; visiting fell in med Jesus Coll Cambridge 1992, Fogarty int scholar-in-residence Nat Insts of Health USA 1993–94; memb Med Res Advsy Ctee Multiple Sclerosis Soc, chm Med Res Advsy Ctee Scot Motor Neurone Disease Assoc; assoc ed Guarantor of Brain; memb Editorial Bds: Neuropathology and Applied Neurobiology 1986–92, Journal of Neuroimmunology, Jl of Neurovirology, Seminars in the Neurosciences, Neurobiology of Disease; BUPA Med Fndn Doctor of the Year Res Award 1990, Fleming Lecture RCPSGlas 1990, Linacre Medal and Lecture RCP 1991, T S Srinivasan Endowment Lecture and Gold Medal 1993; memb: Assoc of Br Neurologists, American Neurological Assoc, Soc for Gen Microbiology, Assoc of Clinical Profs of Med, Br Soc for the Study of Infection, Euro Neurological Soc, Scottish Assoc of Neurological Sciences, Scottish Soc of Physicians, Royal Medico-Chirurgical Soc Glasgow, Assoc of Physicians of GB and I; fell: Fellowship of Postgrad Med, Br Astronomical Assoc; MRCPath 1988, FRCP 1988, FRCPG 1989, FRSM, FRSE 1992; *Books* Infections of the Nervous System (ed with R T Johnson, 1987); author of numerous papers on neurology and neurovirology; *Recreations* astronomy, philosophy, walking in country, tennis, music; *Style*— Prof Peter Kennedy, FRSE; ✉ 23 Hamilton Ave, Pollokshields, Glasgow G41 4JG (☎ 0141 427 4754); Glasgow University Department of Neurology, Institute of Neurological Sciences, Southern General Hospital, Glasgow G51 4TF (☎ 0141 201 2474, fax 0141 201 2993)

KENNEDY, Richard Paul; s of David Clifton Kennedy, of Southampton, and Evelyn Mary Hall, *née* Tindale; *b* 17 Feb 1949; *Educ* Charterhouse (foundation scholar), New Coll Oxford (exhibitioner, BA, MA); *m* 21 July 1979, Joanna Alicia Gore Kennedy, OBE, *qv*, da of late Capt Gerald Anthony Gore Ormsby, DSO, DSC, RN; 2 s (Peter Michael Andrew b 1985, David Anthony James b 1988); *Career* asst master: Shrewsbury Sch 1971–77, Westminster Sch 1977–84; dep headmaster Bishop's Stortford Coll 1984–89, headmaster Highgate Sch 1989–; GB int athlete 1973–76; memb Acad of St Martin-in-the-Fields Chorus 1977–; govr: The Hall Sch Hampstead 1989–, Wycombe Abbey Sch 1992–; HMC: memb Sports Sub-Ctee 1992–95, memb Ctee 1995–, chm London Div 1996; memb Bd Architectural Educn 1992–; *Recreations* choral music; *Clubs* East India, Devonshire, Sports and Public Schs, Vincent's (Oxford); *Style*— Richard Kennedy, Esq; ✉ Highgate School, North Road, London N6 4AY (☎ 0181 340 1524, fax 0181 340 7674)

KENNEDY, Rory Hugh; s of Thomas Kennedy (d 1986), of Fulham, London, and Philomena, *née* McCormack; *b* 3 April 1964; *Educ* Riddlesdown HS Sanderstead Surrey, Croydon Coll of Technol; *m* 8 Oct 1983, Pauline, da of Wallace Joseph Frith-Loney; 1 s (Fraser b 31 March 1988), 2 da (Hayley b 9 June 1989, Abigail b 14 Oct 1994); *Career* second commis de cuisine Mount Royal Hotel London 1978–79, chef de partie (sauce and larder) Naval and Military Club London 1979–80; chef de partie (all sections): Hyatt Carlton Towers London W1 1981–84, Connaught Hotel London 1984–87; second sous chef Britannia Hotel London 1987–88, exec sous chef Le Meridien Hotel London 1988–90, exec chef Hanbury Manor Hotel (from its opening) 1990–96, head chef Rules Restaurant London 1996–; awards for Hanbury Manor Hotel: 5 stars AA 1992, 4 rosettes AA 1992–93, Co Restaurant of the Yr 1992, Best Newcomer Good Food Guide 1992, 4 rosettes AA 1993–94, RAC Merit Award for Hospitality Comfort and Restaurant 1993; memb Academie Culinaire de France Filiale de Grande Bretagne 1994; *Recreations* family, architecture, jazz music, most sports (rugby, football, cricket, cycling); *Style*— Rory Kennedy, Esq; ✉ Rules, 35 Maiden Lane, Covent Garden, London WC2 (☎ 0171 379 0258)

KENNEDY, Tessa Georgina (Mrs Elliott Kastner); da of late Geoffrey Farrer Kennedy, and Daska McLean, *née* Ivanovic; *b* 6 Dec 1938; *Educ* Oak Hall Haslemere Surrey, Ecole de Beaux Arts Paris; *m* 1, 27 Jan 1958 (m dis 1969), Dominick Evelyn Bede Elwes, s of Simon Elwes (d 1975); 3 s (Cassian b 1959, Damian b 1960, Cary b 1962); m 2, 26 June 1971, Elliott Kastner; 1 s (Dillon b 1970), 1 da (Milica b 1972); *Career* interior designer; former clients incl: John Barry, Sam Spiegel, Richard Burton, Stanley Kubrick, Viscount Hambledon, De Beers, BUPA Hosps, HM King of Jordan, Michael Winner, Candice Bergen, Rudolf Nureyev, George Harrison; currently Claridges, Berkeley Hotels, Aspinall Club; dir Euro Region IIDA; Fell IIDA; *Recreations* tennis, movies, watching American football; *Clubs* Vanderbilt, Harbour; *Style*— Miss Tessa Kennedy; ✉ 2 Hyde Park Gdns, London W2 2LT; 1 East 62nd St, New York, NY 10021 (☎ 00 1 212 753 4418); 314 N Foothill, Beverly Hills, Los Angeles, CA 90210 (☎ 00 1 310 273 4097); Studio 5, 91/97 Freston Rd, London W11 4BD (☎ 0171 221 4546, fax 0171 229 2899, car 0836 201 980)

KENNEDY-SANIGAR, Patrick; s of William Adrian George Sanigar, of Aldreth, Cambridgeshire, and Patricia Anne, *née* Kay; *b* 27 Sept 1957; *Educ* Soham GS Cambs,

Soham Village Coll Cambs, Gordonstoun, Canterbury Coll of Art Sch of Architecture (BA, DipArch); *m* 12 Oct 1989, Melena Kay, da of Alan Mark Kennedy; 3 da (Courtney Oneka b 24 July 1991, Ottilie Fabien b 6 April 1993, Sydney Camille b 27 Aug 1995); *Career* head of design Townscape Homes Ltd 1981 (site agent 1979); fndr: Townscape Designs Ltd (dir and head of design) 1982, Townscape Interiors Ltd 1984, Harbour Studios 1986 (having resigned all directorships of the Townscape Group); head of design 691 Promotions Ltd 1991–95, head of design servs Faithdean Interiors Ltd Chatham 1995– (design conslt 1991–95); dir: Domus Estates Ltd 1992–, Honeywood Forestry Ltd 1993; projects incl: The Tube shoe retail chain 1985 (featured Designers Journal 1986), restoration in assoc with Lionel March The How House (LA) 1986, The Cocoon concert bldg 1991, Swedish Knotty Timber project 1991/92 and 1994/95, The Penguin Café Canterbury, The Kent Bio-power Renewable Energy Project 1993/95; memb Visiting Bd Panel RIBA 1987–89; FCSD 1988 (co chm of Interiors Gp and memb Cncl 1990), fell Br Inst of Interior Design 1988; *Recreations* qualified open water scuba diver, qualified gymnasium instructor, swimming, motor racing, earth sheltered housing; *Style*— Patrick Kennedy-Sanigar, Esq; ✉ 7 Little Meadow, Upper Harbledown, Canterbury, Kent CT2 9BD (☎ 01227 767967); Harbour Studios, Harbour Buildings, Sea St, Whitstable, Kent CT5 1AF (☎ 01227 265556, fax 01227 276190)

KENNELLY, Brendan; *b* 1936; *Educ* St Ita's Coll Co Kerry, Trinity Coll Dublin (BA, MA, PhD), Univ of Leeds; *Career* poet, dramatist and lectr; prof modern literature Trinity Coll Dublin 1973– (lectr 1963–71), Guidersleeve prof Barnard Coll NYC 1971, Cornell prof of literature Swarthmore Coll Penn 1971–72; hon doctorate Trinity Coll Conn 1992; *Publications* The Real Ireland (text, photos by Liam Blake, 1984), Ireland Past and Present (ed, 1985), Landmarks of Irish Drama (1988); *Poetry* My Dark Fathers (1964), Collection One - Getting Up Early (1966), Good Souls to Survive (1967), Dream of a Black Fox (1968), A Drinking Cup (1970), Selected Poems (1969), The Penguin Book of Irish Verse (ed, 1970, 2 edn 1981), Selected Poems (1971), Love Cry (1972), The Voices (1973), Shelley in Dublin (1974), A Kind of Trust (1975), New and Selected Poems (1976), Islandman (1977), A Small Light (1979), The Boats Are Home (1980), The House That Jack Didn't Build (1982), Moloney Up and At It, Cromwell (1983 Eire, 1987 UK), Selected Poems (1985), Mary (1987), Love of Ireland - Poems from the Irish (trans, 1989), A Time for Voices - Selected Poems 1960–90 (1990), The Book of Judas (1991, Suday Independent/Irish Life Award for Poetry), Joycechoyce: The poems in verse and prose of James Joyce (ed jtly with A N Jeffares, 1992), Breathing Spaces (1992); *Novels* The Crooked Cross (1963), The Florentines (1967); *Plays* Antigone (1983, Peacock Theatre Dublin), Medea (1988, Dublin Theatre Festival), Cromwell (1986, Damer Hall Dublin), Trojan Women (1993, Peacock Theatre Dublin); *Style*— Brendan Kennelly, Esq; ✉ Department of English, Trinity College, Dublin 2, Ireland (☎ 00 353 1 7021161, fax 00 353 1 6772694)

KENNERLEY, Prof James Anthony Machell (Tony); s of William James Kennerley, of Hale, Cheshire, and Vida May, *née* Machell (d 1984); *b* 24 Oct 1933; *Educ* Altrincham GS, Rhyl GS, Univ of Manchester (BSc), Imperial Coll London (MSc); *m* 12 Jan 1978, Dorothy Mary, da of George Paterson Simpson; 1 s (David James b 20 Nov 1978), 1 da (Elizabeth Lindsay (twin) b 20 Nov 1978); *Career* Univ and RAF Pilot Training 1952–55; aerodynamicist: AV Roe & Co Manchester 1955–58, Pratt & Whitney USA 1958–59; Flying Offr RCAF 1959–62; asst prof of mathematics Univ of New Brunswick Canada 1962–67, dir of graduate studies Manchester Business Sch 1967–69, assoc prof of business mathematics Columbia Univ Business Sch NY 1969–70, sr lectr in mktg and quantitative methods London Business Sch 1970–73, dir and prof Strathclyde Univ Business Sch 1973–83; exec dir Business Graduates' Assoc 1983–86, dir Intermatrix Ltd (Mgmnt Conslts) 1984–89, ind mgmnt conslt 1983–, visiting prof City Univ 1991–95, prof of health mgmnt Univ of Surrey 1993–; memb Advsy Bd Meta Generics 1991–96, chm W Surrey and NE Hants Health Authy 1986–93, chm NW Surrey Health Authy 1993–95, chm W Surrey Health Cmmn 1995–96, chm Cncl for Professions Supplementary to Medicine 1990–96, arbitrator ACAS 1976–; dir First Step Housing Co Waverley BC 1990–93; memb: Legal Aid Advsy Ctee 1991–93, Monopolies and Mergers Ctee 1991–, Cncl Br Inst of Mgmnt 1991–; CEng, AFIMA, MIMechE, AFRAeS, FIMgt; *Books* Guide To Business Schools (1985), Arbitration, Cases in Industrial Relations (1994); *Recreations* flying, travelling; *Clubs* Reform, Caledonian; *Style*— Prof Tony Kennerley; ✉ 5 Old Rectory Gardens, Busbridge, Godalming, Surrey GU7 1XB (☎ 01483 428108); West Surrey Health Commission, The Ridgewood Centre, Old Bisley Road, Camberley, Surrey GU16 5QE (☎ 01276 671718, fax 01276 21760)

KENNERLEY, Peter Dilworth; TD (1989); s of John Dilworth Kennerley, and Margery, *née* Dugard (d 1977); *b* 9 June 1956; *Educ* Collyers Sch, Sidney Sussex Coll Cambridge (MA); *m* 1989, (Anne Marie) Ghislaine du Roy, da of late Hon Sir Thomas Galbraith, KBE, MP; 1 s (Samuel John Maximilian b 21 July 1992), 1 da (Sarah Marie Louise b 30 Jan 1991); *Career* TA Maj Royal Yeo 1986; Simmons & Simmons: joined 1979, admitted slr 1981, ptnr 1986–; sec Panel on Takeovers and Mergers 1986–88; cncllr London Borough of Wandsworth; memb Law Soc; *Clubs* Cavalry and Guards'; *Style*— Peter Kennerley, Esq; ✉ 112 Streathbourne Rd, London SW17 8QY (☎ 0181 672 7305); Simmons & Simmons, 21 Wilson St, London EC2M 2TX (☎ 0171 628 2020, fax 0171 628 2070, telex 888562)

KENNET, 2 Baron (UK 1935); Wayland Hilton Young; s of 1 Baron Kennet, GBE, DSO, DSC, PC (d 1960), and Kathleen, da of Rev Canon Lloyd Stewart Bruce (3 s of Sir James Bruce, 2 Bt) and widow of Capt Robert Falcon Scott, CVO, RN, the Antarctic explorer; Lady Kennet was a sculptor whose works include the statue of her first husband in Waterloo Place, London; *b* 2 Aug 1923; *Educ* Stowe, Trinity Coll Cambridge (MA), Univ of Perugia; *m* 24 Jan 1948, Elizabeth Ann, da of Capt Bryan Fullerton Adams, DSO, RN; 1 s, 5 da; *Heir* s, Hon Thoby Young; *Career* sits as Lab peer in House of Lords; RN 1942–45, FO 1946–47 and 1949–51, del Parly Assemblies WEU and Cncl of Europe 1962–65, Parly sec Miny of Housing and Local Govt 1966–70, Labour oppn spokesman Foreign Affrs and Science Policy 1971–74; chm: Advsy Ctee on Oil Pollution of the Sea 1970–74, CPRE 1971–72, Int Parly Conferences on the Environment 1972–78; MEP 1978–79, SDP whip in House of Lords 1981–83, SDP spokesman on Defence and Foreign Affrs 1981–90; vice chm Parly Office of Sci and Technol 1990–93, vice pres: Parly and Sci Ctee 1988–, The Chartered Inst of Environmental Health 1984–, The Arboricultural Assoc 1977–; pres: The Architecture Club 1984–94, The Avebury Soc; memb Bd of Advsrs to Centre for Medical Law and Ethics, King's Coll London 1990–; author and journalist; Hon FRIBA; *Books* novels: The Deadweight, Now or Never, Still Alive Tomorrow; non-fiction: The Italian Left, Strategy for Survival, The Montesi Scandal, The Profumo Affair, Eros Denied, Thirty Four Articles, The Futures of Europe, Preservation, The Rebirth of Britain; jtly (with wife Elizabeth Young): Old London Churches, London's Churches, Northern Lazio: An Unknown Italy (first prize Euro Fedn of Tourist Press 1990); *Recreations* sailing, music, walking; *Style*— Lord Kennet; ✉ House of Lords, London SW1A 0PW

KENNETT, Ronald John (Ron); s of William John Kennett (d 1980), of Thornhill, Dewsbury, W Yorks, and Phyllis Gertrude, *née* Whipp (d 1972); *b* 25 March 1935; *Educ* Bishopshalt Sch, Bradford Tech Coll (HNC in electrical engrg); *m* 16 March 1957, Sylvia, da of Tom Barstow (d 1976), of Thornhill, Dewsbury, W Yorks; 1 s (Andrew Martyn b 1958), 3 da (Julie Elizabeth b 1959, Stephanie Louise b 1964, Ruth Victoria b 1967); *Career* Lucas Aerospace Ltd: various engrg appts Bradford 1956–78, chief engr Hemel Hempstead 1978–86, quality assur mangr Hemel Hempstead 1986–88; dir Royal Aeronautical Soc 1988–; FRAeS 1981, AFAIAA 1992, FIMgt 1990, FInstD 1990, FCIT 1994, FRSA 1994; *Recreations* reading, music, walking, photography, Persian cats; *Clubs* IOD; *Style*— Ron Kennett, Esq; ✉ Greenbanks, Toms Hill Rd, Aldbury, nr Tring, Herts HP23 5SA (☎ 01442 85268); The Royal Aeronautical Society, 4 Hamilton Place, London W1V 0BQ (☎ 0171 499 3515, fax 0171 499 6230, car 0860 660324)

KENNETT BROWN, David; s of Thomas Kennett-Brown (d 1979), and Vanda, *née* Low; *b* 29 Jan 1938; *Educ* Durston House Ealing, Monkton Combe Sch Bath, Lincoln Coll Oxford (MA), Univ of London (Dip Crim); *m* 1966, Wendy Margaret, da of Frederick Gordon Evans (d 1984); 1 s (Neil b 1969), 2 da (Kathryn b 1967, Alison b 1971); *Career* slr in private practice 1965–82; JP Willesden 1975–82, met stipendiary magistrate 1982–, dep chm Juvenile & Domestic Cts Panel 1979–82, chm London Rent Assessment Panel 1979–82, chm Inner London Family Proceedings Cts 1983–, Crown Ct recorder 1989–; pres Central and S Middx Law Soc 1982; FCIArb; *Recreations* walking, gardening, family life; *Style*— David Kennett Brown, Esq; ✉ Marylebone Magistrates' Court, 181 Marylebone Road, London NW1 5QJ

KENNEY, Anthony; s of Eric Alfred Allen Kenney (d 1992), of West Mersea, Essex, and Doris Winifred, *née* Dollwood (d 1995); *b* 17 Jan 1942; *Educ* Brentwood Sch, Gonville and Caius Coll Cambridge (MA), The London Hosp Med Coll (MB BChir); *m* 1, 1966 (m dis 1973), Elizabeth Dain Fielding; 2 s (Christopher Julian b 1967, Nicholas Charles b 1970); m 2, 17 March 1973, Patricia Clare, da of Maj Rafe Trevor Newbery, MBE (d 1981); 2 s (Alexander William b 1974, Simon Rafe b 1977), 1 da (Louise Clare b 1980); *Career* formerly: sr registrar Westminster and Kingston Hosps, sr house surgn Queen Charlotte's and Chelsea Hosp for Women, res accoucheur The London Hosp; currently conslt obstetrician and gynaecologist St Thomas' Hosp London; examiner: Univ of London, Royal Coll of Obstetricians and Gynaecologists; former examiner Univs of Cambridge and Liverpool; FRCS 1970, FRCOG 1987 (MRCOG 1972); *Recreations* canal cruising, foreign travel; *Clubs* RSM, Med Soc of London; *Style*— Anthony Kenney, Esq; ✉ 17 Wimpole St, London W1M 7AD (☎ 0181 942 0440)

KENNEY, Antony Reginald; LVO (1995); s of Herbert Howard Kenney (d 1976), of Carshalton, and Winifred Charlotte, *née* Wilson (d 1980); *b* 23 Feb 1931; *Educ* John Fisher Sch Purley, Christ's Coll Cambridge (MA), Birkbeck Coll London (BSc); *m* 31 July 1970, Carol Jane, da of Thomas Noel Charles Izod, of Leamington Spa; 2 s (James Benedict Thomas b 11 Feb 1973, Benedict Antony b 15 July 1987), 1 da (Louise Mary b 29 Nov 1971); *Career* St Benedict's Sch Ealing 1956–59, St Mary's Univ Coll Twickenham 1959–96; tstee Prince's Tst 1984–94; govr St Charles' Sch Weybridge; MUniv Surrey 1996; Knight of St Gregory the Great (Papal honour) 1996; *Books* incl a variety of educnl works; *Recreations* woodcarving, DIY; *Style*— Antony Kenney, Esq, LVO; ✉ 28 St Alban's Avenue, Weybridge, Surrey KT13 8EN (☎ 01932 841300)

KENNEY, Edward John; s of George Kenney, and Emmie Carlina Elfrida, *née* Schwenke; *b* 29 Feb 1924; *Educ* Christ's Hospital, Trinity Coll Cambridge (Craven scholar, Craven student, Chancellor's medallist, MA); *m* 18 June 1955, (Gwyneth) Anne, da of late Henry Albert Harris; *Career* served WWII: Royal Signals UK and India 1943–46, cmmnd 1944, Lt 1945; asst lectr Univ of Leeds 1951–52; Univ of Cambridge: res fell Trinity Coll 1952–53, asst lectr 1955–60, lectr 1966–70, reader in Latin lit and textual criticism 1970–74, Kennedy prof of Latin 1974–82; Peterhouse Cambridge: fell 1953–91, dir of studies in classics 1953–74, librarian 1953–82, tutor 1956–82, sr tutor 1962–65, Perne librarian 1987–91, domestic bursar 1987–88; jt ed Classical Quarterly 1959–65, Sather prof of classical lit Berkeley 1968, Carl Newell Jackson lectr Harvard Univ 1980 (James C Loeb fell in classical philology 1967–68); author of articles and reviews in classical jls; pres: Jt Assoc of Classical Teachers 1977–79, Classical Assoc 1982–83; treas and chm Cncl of Almoners Christ's Hospital 1984–86; FBA 1968, foreign memb Royal Netherlands Acad of Arts and Scis 1976; *Books* P Ouidi Nasonis Amores etc (ed, 1961, 2 edn 1994), Ovidiana Graeca (ed with Mrs P E Easterling, 1965), Appendix Vergiliana (ed with W V Clausen, F R D Goodyear, J A Richmond, 1966), Lucretius De Rerum Natura III (ed, 1971), The Classical Text (1974, Italian trans 1995), Cambridge History of Classical Literature II (ed and contrib, 1982), The Ploughman's Lunch (1984), Ovid Metamorphoses (introduction and notes, 1985), Ovid, The Love Poems (introduction and notes, 1990), Apuleius Cupid & Psyche (ed, 1990), Ovid, Sorrows of an Exile (Introduction and Notes, 1992), Ovid, Heroides XVI-XXI (ed, 1996); *Recreations* cats, books; *Style*— Prof E J Kenney, FBA; ✉ Peterhouse, Cambridge CB2 1RD

KENNY, Sir Anthony John Patrick; kt (1992); s of John Kenny, and Margaret, *née* Jones; *b* 16 March 1931; *Educ* St Joseph's Coll Upholland, Gregorian Univ Rome, St Benet's Hall Oxford (DPhil); *m* 2 April 1966, Nancy Caroline, da of Henry T Gayley Jr, of Ithaca, NY, USA; 2 s (Robert b 1968, Charles b 1970); *Career* master Balliol Coll Oxford 1978–89, pro-vice chllr Univ of Oxford 1985–97, warden and sec Rhodes Tst Oxford 1989–; chm Br Library Bd 1993–96; Hon DLitt Bristol 1982, Hon DHumLitt Denison Ohio 1986, Hon DCL: Oxon 1987, Belfast 1994; Hon DLitt: Liverpool 1988, Glasgow 1990, Lafayette Pennsylvania 1990, Trinity Coll Dublin 1992, Hull 1993, Warwick 1995, Sheffield 1995; FBA 1974 (vice pres 1986–88, pres 1989–93); *Books* Descartes (1968), Wittgenstein (1973), Will, Freedom and Power (1975), Freewill and Responsibility (1978), The God of the Philosophers (1979), A Path from Rome (1986), The Road to Hillsborough (1986), The Heritage of Wisdom (1987), Reason and Religion (1987), The Metaphysics of Mind (1989), Aristotle on the Perfect Life (1992), What is Faith? (1992), Aquinas on Mind (1992), The Oxford Illustrated History of Western Philosophy (ed, 1994), Frege (1995); *Clubs* United Oxford and Cambridge Univ, Athenaeum; *Style*— Sir Anthony Kenny, FBA; ✉ Rhodes House, Oxford OX1 3RG

KENNY, His Hon Judge Anthony Marriott; s of Noel Edgar Edward Marriott Kenny, OBE (d 1972), of Zimbabwe and Zambia, and Cynthia Margaret Seton, *née* Melville; *b* 24 May 1939; *Educ* St Andrew's Coll Grahamstown, Christ's Coll Cambridge (MA); *m* 1969, Monica, da of Hector Bennet Grant Mackenzie, of S Africa; 3 s (Julian Hector Marriott b 1972, Christian Edward Mackenzie b 1977, Nicholas William Mackenzie b 1983); *Career* called to the Bar Gray's Inn 1963; rec of the Crown Ct 1980–87, circuit judge (SE Circuit) 1987–, princ judge for civil matters Berkshire and Buckinghamshire 1990, designated family judge Berkshire 1990; hon pres Thames Valley Family Lawyers' Soc 1991; *Recreations* travelling, skiing, music, reading, tennis; *Style*— His Hon Judge Kenny; ✉ Reading County Court, 160–163 Friar Street, Reading RG1 1HE

KENNY, Gen Sir Brian Leslie Graham; GCB (1991, KCB 1985), CBE (1979); s of Brig James Wolfenden Kenny, CBE (d 1978); *b* 18 June 1934; *Educ* Canford; *m* 1958, Diana Catherine Jane, da of Brig Felton Arthur Hamilton Mathew, OBE, MC (d 1977); 2 s; *Career* CO Queen's Royal Irish Hussars 1974–76, Col GS HQ 4 Armd Div 1976–78, Brig 1978, cmd 12 Armd Bde 1978–80, Maj-Gen 1982, GOC 1 Armd Div 1982–83, dir Army Staff Duties MOD 1983–85, cmd 1 (BR) Corps 1985–87, C-in-C BAOR/Cmd NORTHAG 1987–89, D SACEUR 1990–93; govr Royal Hosp Chelsea 1993–; Col Cmdt Royal Army Veterinary Corps 1983–95, Col QRIH 1985–93, Col Cmdt RAC 1989–93; govr Canford Sch 1983–; *Recreations* cricket, tennis, skiing; *Clubs* MCC, I Zingari, Free Foresters; *Style*— Gen Sir Brian Kenny, GCB, CBE; ✉ Governor's Appartment, Royal Hospital, Chelsea, London SW3 4SR

KENNY, Michael James; s of James Kenny, of Blackburn, Lancashire, and Ellen, *née* Gordon; *b* 10 June 1941; *Educ* St Francis Xavier's Coll Liverpool, Liverpool Coll of Art, Slade Sch of Fine Art; *m* 1, July 1962 (m dis), Gillian Wainwright; m 2, June 1968 (m dis), Rosemary Flood; 1 s, 2 da; m 3 (m dis 1992), 20 Dec 1978, Angela Helen; m 4, 1993, Susan Rowland; *Career* sculptor; visiting lectr Slade Sch of Fine Art 1970–82, dir of fine art studies Goldsmiths' Coll London 1983–88, princ City & Guilds of London Art Sch 1995–; treas Royal Acad of Arts 1995–; works in collections of: Tate Gallery, V & A Museum, British Museum; numerous one man exhibitions incl Paris, Milan, Tokyo and Frankfurt; public sculptures in: Scotland (Lumsden), Paris (Parc de la Courneuve), Cambridge (Addenbrooke's Hosp), Japan (Yokohama Business Park, Muraoka-Cho, Hyogo Prefecture 1992), London (Docklands Limehouse Link Eastern Terminal 1992–93), Prittlewell Sch Essex 1993–94; RA 1986 (ARA 1976), FRBS 1992; *Recreations* ornithology; *Clubs* Chelsea Arts, Arts; *Style*— Michael Kenny, RA; ✉ City & Guilds of London Art School, 124 Kennington Park Road, London SE11 4DJ (☎ 0171 790 3409); 71 Stepney Green, London E1 3LE (☎ 0171 790 3409)

KENNY, Prof Phillip Herbert; s of Robert Kenny, of King's Lynn, and Moira, *née* Davies; *b* 9 Aug 1948; *Educ* Univ of Bristol (LLB), Univ of Cambridge (Dip in Criminology), Univ of Columbia (LLM); *m* 7 Aug 1970, Ann Mary, da of Harold Langley (d 1970), of Winchester; 1 s (Stephen b 1982), 3 da (Julia b 1975, Angharad b 1977, Helen b 1979); *Career* slr; head of Law Dept Univ of Northumbria at Newcastle (formerly Newcastle Poly) 1980–, former univ and poly lectr, legal dir Educn Assets Bd; conslt Messrs Dickinson Dees Slrs Newcastle upon Tyne; *Publications* Conveyancing Law, Study of Law, Conveyancing Law and Practice, Licensed Conveyancers the New Law, Sweet and Maxwell's Law Files, Mines and Minerals in Conveyancing, Property Law Statutes, Leasehold Reform Housing and Urban Development Act 1994, Covenants for Title; *Recreations* shooting, walking, sailing, golf; *Clubs* Keswick Golf; *Style*— Prof Phillip Kenny; ✉ 105 Kenton Rd, Gosforth NE3 4NL; University of Northumbria at Newcastle, Ellison Building, Ellison Place, Newcastle Upon Tyne NE1 8ST (☎ 0191 232 6002, fax 0191 235 8017)

KENRICK, Dr (John Edward) Arthur; OBE (1994); s of Kenrick Kenrick (d 1935), and Martha Jane, *née* Roberts (d 1970); *b* 7 July 1935; *Educ* Boys' GS Bala Merioneth, Welsh Nat Sch of Med Univ of Wales (MB BCh); *m* 1959, Gwyneth, da of John Owen Williams; 1 da (Dr Rhian Mair Kenrick b 15 Nov 1960), 1 s (Ioan Gwynne b 16 June 1964); *Career* house surgn United Cardiff Hosps then house physician Professorial Dept of Child Health Cardiff 1958–59, SHO in obstetrics and gynaecology Stanley Hosp St Asaph Clwyd 1959–60, MO RAMC 1960–64, princ in gen med practice Llanrwst Gwynedd 1964–95; med sec Gwynedd Local Med Ctee 1978–88; chm: Gwynedd Family Practitioner Ctee 1988–89, Gwynedd FHSA 1989–96, N Wales HA 1996–; advsr Nat Sick Doctor Scheme 1983–88, Welsh rep Advsy Ctee on Borderline Substances DHSS 1983–88; memb Cncl: Univ of Wales Bangor 1996–, Univ of Wales Coll of Med 1996–; retired memb BMA; *Recreations* music, people and places; *Style*— Dr Arthur Kenrick, OBE; ✉ North Wales Health Authority, Preswylfa, Hendy Road, Mold, Flintshire CH7 1PZ (☎ 01352 700227, fax 01352 754649)

KENRICK, Martin John; s of William Edmund Kenrick (d 1981), of Birmingham, and Elizabeth Dorothy Magdalen, *née* Loveday; family non-conformists who settled with others in Midlands; *b* 5 Feb 1940; *Educ* Newlands, Rugby, Trinity Coll Dublin (MA, BComm), Cranfield Inst of Technol (MSc); *m* 21 Feb 1970, Christine Mary, da of Charles Ronald Wingham (d 1972), of St Albans, Herts; 1 s (Hilgrove b 1977), 2 da (Tanya b 1972, Helen b 1973); *Career* guardian Birmingham Assay Office 1971–, cmmr of taxes 1972–, chm Archibald Kenrick & Sons Ltd 1978–91 (md 1973–78); dir: Birmingham R & D Ltd 1985– (chm 1985–87), Rote Public Relations 1991–92, Jones & Barclay Ltd 1991–93, Martin Kenrick Associates 1991–; managing conslt Directormatch 1993–; Univ of Birmingham: hon life memb Ct of Govrs 1978, memb Cncl 1981–96, memb Fin and Gen Purpose Ctee 1987–88; memb Mgmnt Ctee W Midlands Regnl Mgmnt Centre 1978–82; Birmingham C of C and Indust: memb Cncl 1981–, memb Gen Purposes Ctee 1982–93, chm Educn Ctee 1985–89, memb Working Pty for Indust Year 1985–86, vice pres 1988–90, pres 1990–91; dir: Birmingham Chamber Training Ltd 1986–87, Black Country Museum Tst 1987–; chm: Policy Gp Birmingham Local Employer Network 1987–89, W Midlands Region Indust Matters 1987–90, Birmingham Educn Business Ptnrship 1989–93, Policy Advsy Ctee Birmingham City Centre 1995–; govr Fndn for Schs of King Edward VI Birmingham 1990–93; *Recreations* ornithology, skiing, tennis, gardening; *Style*— Martin J Kenrick, Esq; ✉ The Mount, 37 Richmond Hill Rd, Edgbaston, Birmingham B15 3RR (☎ 0121 454 4720, fax 0121 455 0184, e-mail mkenrick@waverider.co.uk)

KENSINGTON, 8 Baron (I 1776 and UK 1886); Hugh Ivor Edwardes; s of Capt Hon Owen Edwardes (d 1937, 2 s of 6 Baron Kensington, CMG, DSO, TD, JP, DL); suc unc, 7 Baron, 1981; *b* 24 Nov 1933; *Educ* Eton; *m* 1961, Juliet Elizabeth Massy, da of Capt Alexander Massy Anderson (d 1943); 2 s (Hon Owen b 21 July 1964, Hon Rupert b 25 Jan 1967), 1 da (Hon Amanda); *Heir* s, Hon (William) Owen Alexander Edwardes; *Career* farmer and thoroughbred breeder; *Recreations* horse breeding, shooting; *Clubs* Boodle's, Durban; *Style*— The Rt Hon the Lord Kensington; ✉ Friar Tuck, PO Box 549, Mooi River, 3300 Natal, S Africa (☎ 00 27 333 36323)

KENSINGTON, Bishop of 1996–; Rt Rev Michael John Colclough; s of Joseph Colclough, of Stoke-on-Trent, and Beryl, *née* Dale (d 1969); *b* 29 Dec 1944; *Educ* Stanfield Tech HS 1957–65, Univ of Leeds (BA), Cuddesdon Coll Oxford; *m* 24 Sept 1983, Cynthia Flora Mary, da of Joseph Christopher de Sousa, MBE; 2 s (Edward Joseph, Aidan Michael); *Career* curate: St Werburgh Burslem 1971–75, St Mary S Ruislip 1975–79; vicar of St Anselm Hayes 1979–86, area dean of Hillingdon 1985–92; priest-in-charge: St Margaret and St Andrew Uxbridge and St John Uxbridge Moor 1986–88, St Vedast-alias-Foster London 1994–96, St Magnus the Martyr London 1995–96; team rector of Uxbridge 1988–92, archdeacon of Northolt 1992–94, personal asst to the Bishop of London 1994–96; dep priest in Ordinary to HM The Queen 1995–96; *Recreations* English countryside, family, reading; *Style*— The Rt Rev the Bishop of Kensington; ✉ 19 Campden Hill Square, London W8 7JY (☎ 0171 727 9818, fax 0171 229 3651)

KENSIT, Patricia Jude Francis (Patsy); da of James Henry Kensit (d 1986), and Margie, *née* Doohan (d 1993); *b* 4 March 1968; *Educ* St Catherine's Convent Sch Twickenham; *m* 1992 (m dis 1996), Jim Kerr, *qv*; 1 s (James b 4 Sept 1992); *Career* actress; *Theatre* Cinderella 1982, Richard III (RSC) 1983; *Television* For the Love of Ada 1973, King Arthur 1974, Prince Regent 1975, Penmarric 1975, Life of Charles Dickens 1976, The Foundation 1978, Jemima Shore 1978, Luna 1980, Pollyanna 1980, Great Expectations 1982, Frost in May 1982, Diana 1983, The Corsican Brothers 1984, The Prattling Princess 1984, Silas Marner 1984, Arms and the Man 1989, Adam Bede 1991, Tales from the Krypt 1993, Fall From Grace 1994, The Mia Farrow Story 1994; *Films* The Great Gatsby 1972, Hanover Street 1975, The Blue Bird 1976, Absolute Beginners 1985, The Countrymen of God 1987, A Chorus of Disapproval 1988, Lethal Weapon 2 1989, Chicago Joe and the Showgirl 1989, The Atlantic 1989, The Three Tornados 1990, Timebomb 1990, Twenty One 1990, Does This Mean We're Married 1990, Beltenebros 1991, Blame it on the Bellboy 1991, Turn of the Screw 1992, Bitter Harvest 1993, Kleptomania 1993, The Pack 1993, Angels and Insects 1994; *Awards* nominated best actress Independent Spirit Awards 1992; *Recreations* skiing, horse riding; *Style*— Ms Patsy Kensit; ✉ Peters Fraser & Dunlop Ltd, 503 The Chambers, Chelsea Harbour, Lots Road, London SW10 0XF (☎ 0171 352 4446, fax 0171 352 7356)

KENSWOOD, 2 Baron (UK 1951); John Michael Howard Whitfield; s of 1 Baron Kenswood (d 1963); *b* 6 April 1930; *Educ* Trinity Coll Sch Ontario, Harrow, Grenoble Univ, Emmanuel Coll Cambridge; *m* 1951, Deirdre Anna Louise, da of Colin Malcolm Methven, of Errol, Perthshire; 4 s (Hon Michael b 1955, Hon Anthony b 1957, Hon Steven b 1958, Hon Benjamin b 1961), 1 da (Hon Anna Louise b 1964); *Heir* s, Hon Michael Christopher Whitfield b 6 July 1955; *Style*— The Rt Hon the Lord Kenswood; ✉ Domaine de la Foret, 31340 Villemur sur Tarn, France

KENT, Brian Hamilton; s of Clarence Kent (d 1946), of Hyde, Cheshire, and Edyth Kent (d 1963); *b* 29 Sept 1931; *Educ* Hyde GS, Univ of Salford (BSc Eng); *m* 15 May 1954, Margery, da of Laurence Foulds (d 1974), of Bredbury, Cheshire; 1 s (Peter Hamilton b 15 April 1958), 2 da (Wendy Susan (Mrs Martin) b 13 July 1960, Linda Anne (Mrs Lynch) b 10 Oct 1961); *Career* Lt RN(t) 1954–57; mangr Mather and Platt Contracting Ltd 1960, mktg dir Morganite Carbon Ltd 1965, md Alfa Laval UK Ltd 1970; chm: Staveley Industries plc 1987–94 (chief exec and gp md 1980), Wellington Holdings plc 1994–; formerly chm Industry and Parliamentary Tst, past cncl memb CBI, pres IMechE 1994, memb Cncl (now Senate) Engrg Cncl (elected 1995); Hon DSc Univ of Salford 1995; FIMechE, FIEE, FEng 1995; *Recreations* boating, bridge, tennis; *Clubs* RAC, Directors; *Style*— Brian Kent, Esq, FEng; ✉ Collingwood, 16 Woodlands Rd, Surbiton, Surrey KT6 6PS; Wellington Holdings plc, 130 Oldfield Road, Hampton, Middx TW12 2HT (☎ 0181 941 2244, fax 0181 941 0417)

KENT, Sir Harold Simcox; GCB (1963, KCB 1954, CB 1946), QC (1973); s of Percy Horace Braund Kent, OBE, MC (d 1963), of Clavering, Cooden, Sussex, and Anna Mary, *née* Simcox; *b* 11 Nov 1903; *Educ* Rugby, Merton Coll Oxford; *m* 14 April 1930, Zillah (d 1987), da of Henry Rees Lloyd; 1 s, 1 da (decd); *Career* called to the Bar Inner Temple 1928; Parly counsel 1940–53; HM procurator-gen and Treasy slr 1953–63; slr: Bank Rate Tribunal 1957, Vassall Tribunal 1962; standing counsel to Church Assembly and Gen Synod 1964–72; memb Security Cmmn 1967–72; vicar-gen Province of Canterbury 1970–76, dean of Arches Ct of Canterbury and auditor of Chancery Ct of York 1972–76, commissary to Dean and Chapter of St Paul's Cathedral 1976–; *Books* In on the Act (1979); *Clubs* United Oxford and Cambridge Univ; *Style*— Sir Harold Kent, GCB, QC; ✉ Alderley, Calf Lane, Chipping Campden, Glos GL55 6JQ (☎ 01386 840421)

KENT, Dr John Philip Cozens; s of John Cozens Kent, DCM (d 1990), and Lucy Ella, *née* Binns (d 1984); *b* 28 Sept 1928; *Educ* Minchenden Co GS, UCL (BA, PhD); *m* 21 Oct 1961, Patricia Eleanor, da of Lionel Maldwyn Bunford (d 1961); 1 s (Philip b 1962), 1 da (Hilary b 1965); *Career* Nat Serv 1951–53, 2 Lt RASC 1952; Br Museum Dept of Coins and Medals: asst keeper 1953–74, dep keeper 1974–83, keeper 1983–90; hon lectr in numismatics Univ of Birmingham 1993–; pres: Br Assoc of Numismatic Socs 1974–78, Royal Numismatic Soc 1984–89, London and Middx Archaeological Soc 1985–88, Barnet and Dist Local Hist Soc 1980–; memb: International Numismatic Commission 1986–91, Instituto de Sintra 1986; Derek Allen Prize (in numismatics) British Acad 1996; medals: Royal Numismatic Soc 1990, American Numismatic Soc 1994; FRNS 1948, FSA 1961, FBA 1986, FMA 1988; *Books* Late Roman Bronze Coinage (jtly 1960), Wealth of the Roman World (with K S Painter, 1977), Roman Coins (1978), 2000 Years of British Coins and Medals (1978), Roman Imperial Coinage Vol VIII, The Family of Constantine I 337–364 (1981), Vol X: The Divided Empire and Fall of the Western Parts 395–491 (1994), A Selection of Byzantine Coins in the Barber Institute of Fine Arts (1985), British Museum Catalogue of Celtic Coins Vol I: Catalogue of Silver Coins of the East Celts and other Balkan Peoples (with M R Mays, 1987), Vol II: Silver Coins of North Italy, South and Central France, Switzerland and South Germany (1990); *Recreations* local history and archaeology, mediaeval music, railway history; *Style*— Dr John Kent, FBA, FSA; ✉ 16 Newmans Way, Hadley Wood, Barnet, Herts EN4 OLR

KENT, Justin; s of Rodney Derrick Kent (d 1993), of Harrogate, and Edwina, *née* Rakusen; *b* 15 Dec 1964; *Educ* Bootham Sch York, Middx Business Sch & Tübingen Fachhochschule W Germany (BA); *m* 22 Aug 1992, Paula Myra, *née* Tomlin; 1 s (Isaac b 5 July 1993), 1 da (Asha b 4 Oct 1994); *Career* advtg exec; planner Gold Greenlees Trott 1986–90, bd dir and sr planner Still Price Court Twivy d'Souza 1990–95, ptnr and head of planning Mellors Reay & Partners 1995–; winner IPA Gold Award for Advtg Effectiveness (for Peperami campaign "It's a Bit of an Animal") 1994, Account Planning Gp Creative Planning Award (for Peperami campaign) 1994; memb: Market Research Soc, Account Planning Gp; *Recreations* rock climbing, skiing, family; *Style*— Justin Kent, Esq; ✉ Mellors Reay & Partners, 65–66 Frith Street, London W1V 5TA (☎ 0171 439 2686, fax 0171 437 0166)

KENT, Michael Harcourt; QC (1996); s of Capt Barrie Harcourt Kent, RN, of Petersfield, Hants, and Margaret, *née* Wightman; *b* 5 March 1952; *Educ* The Nautical Coll Pangbourne, Univ of Sussex (BA); *m* 1977, Sarah Ann, da of Alan John Ling; 2 s (Rupert Haworth Harcourt b 2 April 1982, Leo Jonathan Harcourt b 2 Feb 1985); *Career* called to the Bar Middle Temple 1975, memb Supplementary Panel of Jr Counsel to the Crown (Common Law) 1988–96; *Recreations* sailing; *Style*— Michael Kent, Esq, QC; ✉ 2 Crown Office Row, Upper Ground Floor, Temple, London EC4Y 7HJ (☎ 0171 797 8100, fax 0171 797 8101)

KENT, Dr Paul Welberry; JP (1972); s of Thomas William Kent (d 1975), of Doncaster, and Marion, *née* Cox (d 1954); *b* 19 April 1923; *Educ* Doncaster GS, Univ of Birmingham (BSc, PhD), Jesus Coll Oxford (MA, DPhil, DSc); *m* 23 Aug 1952, Rosemary Elizabeth Boutflower, da of Maj Charles Herbert Boutflower Shepherd, MC, TD (d 1980), of Oxford; 3 s (Anthony b 1955, Richard b 1961, Peter b 1964), 1 da (Deborah b 1957); *Career* asst lectr subsequently ICI fell Univ of Birmingham 1946–50, visiting fell Princeton Univ NJ 1948–49, demonstrator in biochemistry Univ of Oxford 1950–72, tutor and Dr Lees reader Ch Ch Coll Oxford 1955–72 (emeritus student 1972–), master Van Mildert Coll Univ of Durham 1972–82 (res dir 1972–82); biochemical conslt, visiting prof Windsor Univ Ontario 1971 and 1980; memb: Oxford City Cncl 1964–72, Ctee Biochemical Soc 1963–67, Chemical Cncl 1965–70, Advsy Ctee Cystic Fibrosis Res Cncl 1977–82; govr: Oxford Coll of Technol (subsequently Oxford Poly) 1964–72 and 1983–88 (vice chm 1966–69, chm 1969–71), St Chad's Coll Durham 1976–88, Pusey House Oxford 1983– (registrar 1993–96); memb Oxford Poly Higher Educn Corp (now Oxford Brookes Univ) 1988–; Rolleston Prize 1951, Medal of the Société de Chemie Biologique Paris 1969, hon fell Canterbury Coll Ontario 1974, Hon DLitt Drury Coll USA 1973, Hon DSc CNAA 1991; Order of Merit (Germany) 1970; author of articles in scientific jls and jt author of scientific monographs; FRSC 1950; *Books* Biochemistry of the Amino Sugars (with M W Whitehouse, 1955), International Aspects of the Provision of Medical Care (1976); *Recreations* travel, flute and organ music; *Clubs* Athenaeum; *Style*— Dr Paul Kent, JP; ✉ Briscoe Gate, Baldersdale, Barnard Castle, Co Durham DL12 9UL; 18 Arnolds Way, Cumnor Hill, Oxford OX2 9JB (☎ 01865 862087)

KENT, Roderick David; s of Dr Basil Stanley Kent (d 1991), of Ramsdell, Hants, and Vivien Margaret, *née* Baker; *b* 14 Aug 1947; *Educ* King's Sch Canterbury, CCC Oxford (MA), INSEAD (MBA); *m* 12 Aug 1972, Belinda Jane, da of W H Mitchell (d 1983), of Grouville, Jersey; 3 da (Sophie b 1974, Nicola b 1976, Tiffany b 1978); *Career* with J Henry Schroder Wagg & Co Ltd 1969–71, Banque Blyth (Paris) 1971, MBA 1971–72, Triumph Investment Tst 1972–74; Close Brothers gp: dir Close Brothers 1974–, md Close Brothers 1975–84, md Close Brothers Group plc 1984–; non-exec dir: Wessex Water plc 1989–, English and Scottish Investors plc 1989–, M & G Group plc 1995–; Liveryman of Worshipful Co of Pewterers; *Recreations* sport; *Style*— Roderick Kent, Esq; ✉ Wolverton Cottage, Wolverton, nr Basingstoke, Hants RG26 5SX (☎ 01635 298276); Close Brothers Group plc, 12 Appold Street, London EC2A 2AA (☎ 0171 426 4000, fax 0171 247 1203)

KENT, Sarah Ann; da of Hugh Kent (d 1989), of Cornwall, and Joan Eileen, *née* Mather (d 1972); *b* 19 Nov 1941; *Educ* Haberdashers' Aske's Sch for Girls, Slade Sch of Fine Art (dip in fine art, painting and printmaking), UCL (MA), Univ of London Inst of

Educn (advanced dip in art educn); *m* 1961 (m dis 1965), John Howard Drane; 1 s (Matthew Pendarell); *Career* artist, exhibition curator, lectr, bdcaster, writer and magazine ed; pt/t lectr various art schs 1965–77 (incl Hornsey, London Coll of Printing, Harrow and Byam Shaw); lectr in art history and criticism: City Literary Inst London 1965–76, Extra-mural Dept Univ of London 1967–75; visual arts ed: Time Out magazine 1976–, 20/20 magazine 1989–90; dir of exhibitions ICA London 1977–79; *Exhibitions as curator* since 1979: Br section of Lichtbildnisse (historical survey of portrait photography Bonn) 1982, Serpentine Summer Exhibition 1984, Retrospective of Elisabeth Frink's Sculpture, Drawings and Prints (Royal Acad) 1985, Br section of Sydney Biennale (Art Gallery of NSW) 1986, Peripheral States (Benjamin Rhodes London), Photo 94 (Photographers' Gallery); *Exhibitions as artist* solo: Redmark Gallery London 1968, Design Progression London 1970; mixed: Young Contemporaries 1965, Arts Cncl Touring 1965, Slade/Royal Coll Show 1966, Free Painters and Sculptors 1966, Ben Uri Gallery 1966, Reeves Bicentennial Exhibition 1966, Survey '67 (Camden Arts Centre) 1967, Lancaster Arts Festival 1967, Arts Cncl Touring Exhibition 1969–71, Cleveland Int Drawing Biennale 1973 (prizewinner), Cleveland Int Drawing Biennale Touring Exhibition 1979–80, Aspects of Drawing (House Gallery London) 1981, Fully Exposed - The Male Nude in Photography (Photographers' Gallery London) 1990, Artists in the Arts (John Jones Gallery London) 1992; work in collections incl: Arts Cncl of GB, Camden Arts Cncl, Cleveland BC, numerous private collections; as writer and broadcaster numerous contribs to TV and radio incl: Art and Technology, Arena, The South Bank Show, The Late Show, J'Accuse, Private View, Critics' Forum, Third Ear, Third Opinion, After Eight, Kaleidoscope, Meridian; numerous contribs to art jls and magazines incl: Studio International, Art Monthly, Flash Art, Artscribe, Arte, Tema Celeste, Art in America, Time Out; memb Jury: Turner Prize Tate Gallery 1992, Gulbenkian New Horizons Award 1992, Barclay Young Artists Awards 1993, SE Arts Purchasing Award 1993, British Tport Painting Competition 1993, Arts Fndn Fellowship 1995; external examiner: Chelsea Sch of Art (Sculpture MA) 1986–90, Trent Poly (MA Fine Art) 1982–86, Staffs Poly (Sculpture BA) 1990–93, Univ of Nottingham (Contemporary Art Practice BA) 1993–95, Glasgow Sch of Art (Fine Art MA) 1993–96; *Publications* Berlin a Critical View: Ugly Realism 20's-70's (with Eckhart Gillen, 1978), Elisabeth Frink: Sculpture (1985), Women's Images of Men (with Jacqueline Morreau, 1985 and 1990), Shark Infested Waters (1994), Composition (1995); contrib to: Fotografie als Kunst: Kunst als Fotografie (by Floris M Neususs, 1979), Lichtbildnisse (by Klaus Honeff, 1982), Drawings and Graphics (by Jacqueline Morreau, 1986), Nudes in Budapest (by James Cotier); photographs published in: The Naked and the Nude (by Jorge Lewinski, 1987), Fully Exposed: the Male Nude in Photography (by Emmanuel Cooper, 1990), Running Scared (by Peter Lehman, 1993); *Recreations* walking, travelling, dancing, drumming, reading; *Style*— Ms Sarah Kent; ✉ Time Out Magazine, Universal House, 251 Tottenham Court Road, London W1P 0AB (☎ 0171 813 3000, fax 0171 813 6001)

KENT, Trevor Lincoln; s of Ernest George Kent (d 1987), and Evelyn Gertrude Mary, *née* Fuller, of Gerrards Cross, Bucks; *b* 28 March 1947; *Educ* Denstone Coll, London Coll of Commerce; *m* 7 July 1979, Angela Christine (d 1996), da of Gp Capt John Thornhill Shaw, DSO, DFC, AFC (d 1975), and Doreen Lilian Shaw, of Salisbury; 4 s (Toby d 1980, Lincoln b 1982, Warwick b 1983, Leicester b 1987); *Career* princ Trevor Kent & Co estate agents and auctioneers 1971–; freelance journalist and broadcaster specialising in residential property and related finance; co-presenter: Moving and Improving, Housebuying Explained; dist cncllr South Bucks DC 1978–82; media spokesman Nat Assoc of Estate Agents 1987– (pres 1989–90); memb Inter Professional Working Pty on the Transfer of Residential Property 1989–, licensed asst CoE; FNAEA, hon memb Du Page Assoc of Realtors Chicago USA; *Recreations* playing cricket, watching the garden grow, separating the boys, not dieting; *Clubs* Middlesex and Bucks County Cricket; *Style*— Trevor Kent, Esq; ✉ Trevor Kent & Co, Kent House, Oxford Rd, Gerrards Cross, Bucks SL9 7DP (☎ 01753 885522, fax 01753 887777, message pager 01399 728338)

KENTFIELD, Graham Edward Alfred; s of Edward Leonard Harvey Kentfield (d 1984), and Frances Elfrida May, *née* Tucker; *b* 3 Sept 1940; *Educ* Bancroft's Sch, St Edmund Hall Oxford (BA); *m* 29 April 1965, Ann Dwelley, da of James Préaud Hewetson; 2 da; *Career* Bank of England: joined 1963, Econ Intelligence Dept 1964–66, seconded to Dept of Applied Economics Univ of Cambridge 1966–67, Foreign Exchange Operations 1967–69, Overseas Dept 1969–74 (a mangr 1972–74), mangr Monetary Policy Forecasting 1974–76, Govr's speechwriter 1976–77, ed Bank of England Quarterly Bulletin 1977–80, sr mangr Financial Statistics Div 1980–84, advsr Banking Dept 1984–85, dep chief Banking Dept 1985–91, chief Banking Dept and chief cashier 1991–94, dep dir and chief cashier 1994–; hon treas Soc for the Promotion of Roman Studies 1991–; FCIB; *Recreations* Roman history, genealogy, philately; *Style*— Graham Kentfield, Esq; ✉ Bank of England, Threadneedle St, London EC2R 8AH (☎ 0171 601 4361, fax 0171 601 3092)

KENTRIDGE, Sydney; QC (1984); s of Morris Kentridge (d 1964), of Johannesburg, and May, *née* Shafner (d 1971); *b* 5 Nov 1922; *Educ* King Edward VII Sch Johannesburg, Univ of Witwatersrand (BA), Univ of Oxford (MA); *m* 15 Jan 1952, Felicia, da of Max Geffen, of Johannesburg (d 1977); 2 s (William, Matthew), 2 da (Catherine, Elizabeth); *Career* WWII Lt SA Forces served E Africa, Sicily, Italy; admitted Johannesburg Bar 1949, sr counsel SA 1965, called to the Bar Lincoln's Inn 1977, bencher 1986; hon fell Exeter Coll Oxford, Roberts lectr Univ of Pennsylvania 1979, Granville Clark prize (USA) 1978; sometime judge of the Cts of Appeal of Jersey, Guernsey and Republic of Botswana, actg justice of the Constitutional Ct of SA 1995–96; Hon LLD: Leicester 1985, Cape Town 1987, Seaton Hall, New Jersey 1978, Natal 1989, London 1995; *Recreations* opera-going; *Clubs* Athenaeum; *Style*— Sydney Kentridge, Esq, QC; ✉ Brick Court Chambers, 15–19 Devereux Court, London WC2 (☎ 0171 583 0777, 0171 583 9401)

KENWARD, Elizabeth; MBE (1986); da of Brian Charles Durant Kemp-Welch (d 1950), of Kineton, Warwicks, and Verena, *née* Venour (d 1968); *b* 14 July 1906; *Educ* privately and Les Tourelles Brussels; *m* 22 June 1932 (m dis 1942), late Capt Peter Trayton Kenward, s of late Edward Kenward, of Tenterden, Kent; 1 s (Jim Trayton b 1933); *Career* social ed; the original Jennifer of Jennifer's Diary (Tatler 1944–59, Queen Magazine 1959–70, Harpers & Queen 1970–91); Officer Sister Order of St John 1986; *Books* Jennifer's Memoirs (1992); *Recreations* flat racing, theatre, flying (quickest trip Caracas and back for a dinner party by Air France Concorde); *Clubs* Annabel's, The Jockey Club Rooms Newmarket; *Style*— Mrs Elizabeth Kenward, MBE; ✉ c/o Harpers & Queen, 72 Broadwick Street, London W1V 2BP

KENWORTHY, Joan Margaret; da of Albert Kenworthy (d 1984), and Amy, *née* Cobbold (d 1965); *b* 10 Dec 1933; *Educ* GS for Girls Barrow-in-Furness, St Hilda's Coll Oxford (BLitt, MA); *Career* temp tutorships: St Hugh's Coll Oxford 1958–59, Bedford Coll London 1959–60; sr lectr Univ of Liverpool 1973–77 (asst lectr 1960–63, lectr 1963–73); warden: Salisbury Hall 1966–77, Morton House 1974–77; princ St Mary's Coll Univ of Durham 1977–; contrib to several books on climatology and Africa; memb: Geographical Assoc, African Studies Assoc, Inst of Br Geographers; FRGS, FRMetS; *Clubs* Royal Cwlth Tst, Royal Overseas League; *Style*— Miss Joan M Kenworthy; ✉ 1 Elvet Garth, South Rd, Durham DH1 3TP (☎ 0191 384 3865); St Mary's College, University of Durham, Durham DH1 3LR (☎ 0191 374 7119, fax 0191 374 7473)

KENWORTHY, (Frederick) John; s of Rev Fred Kenworthy, MA, BD (d 1974), and Ethel Kenworthy, *née* Radcliffe; *b* 6 Dec 1943; *Educ* William Hulme's GS Manchester, Univ of Manchester (BA); *m* 1968, Diana, da of Reginald Flintham (d 1948); 1 da (Hannah Frances b 1983); *Career* asst princ MOD (Navy) 1966, Treasy centre for Admin Studies 1968–69, Br Steel Corp Sheffield 1969; princ MOD 1972, asst sec Royal Cmmn on the Press Secretariat 1974, dir Weapons Resources and Progs (Naval) MOD 1979–83; head of RN Size and Shape Policy Div MOD 1983–86; DHSS: dir of ops Disablement Servs Div 1986–87, dir ops Disablement Servs Authy 1987–88; DSS: under sec 1989, chief exec IT Servs Agency 1990–93; mgmnt conslt ICL International 1993–95; independent mgmnt conslt 1995–; *Recreations* music, sport, photography; *Clubs* Lansdown Tennis and Squash, Racquets (Bath), Hendon Golf; *Style*— F John Kenworthy, Esq; (☎ 0181 208 1043)

KENWORTHY-BROWNE, District Judge (Bernard) Peter Francis; s of Bernard Evelyn Kenworthy-Browne (d 1979), and Margaret Sibylla (d 1985), da of late Sir George Hadcock, KBE, FRS; *b* 11 May 1930; *Educ* Ampleforth, Oriel Coll Oxford (MA); *m* 1, 1975 (m dis 1982), Jane Elizabeth, da of late Denis Malcolm Mackie; m 2, 1989, Elizabeth Anne, da of late Dr J A Bowen-Jones; *Career* Nat Serv 2 Lt Irish Guards 1949–50; called to the Bar Lincoln's Inn 1955, Oxford and Midland and Oxford circuits 1957–82, recorder of the Crown Ct 1981–82, registrar of the Family Div of High Ct of Justice 1982–91, district judge of the Principal Registry of the Family Div 1991–; *Recreations* music, field sports, photography; *Clubs* Cavalry and Guards; *Style*— Peter Kenworthy-Browne, Esq; ✉ 30 Dewhurst Road, London W14 0ES (☎ 0171 602 9580)

KENWRIGHT, Bill; s of Albert Kenwright, of Liverpool, and Hope, *née* Jones; *b* 4 Sept 1945; *Educ* Liverpool Inst HS for Boys; *m* (m dis) Anouska Hempel (Lady Weinberg); *Career* stage and film producer; actor 1964–70, theatre prodr 1970–; chm and prodr Olivier Awards Soc of London Theatres; dir Everton FC; Hon Dr John Moores Univ Liverpool 1994; *Theatre* over 500 prodns worldwide incl: Joseph and His Amazing Technicolor Dreamcoat (toured for over 13 years) 1979, The Business of Murder 1981–89, A Streetcar Named Desire 1984, Stepping Out 1984–87, Blood Brothers 1988–, Shirley Valentine 1989–93, Dancing at Lughnasa 1991–93; West End shows in 1993 incl: Medea, An Absolute Turkey, No Man's Land, The Gift of Gorgon, Separate Tables, An Ideal Husband, She Stoops to Conquer, Present Laughter, September Tide, Moonlight, The Deep Blue Sea; recent prodns incl: Piaf, Only the Lonely, On Approval, The Winslow Boy, The Miracle Worker, Hamlet, The Cherry Orchard, Lysistrata, A Streetcar Named Desire, Passion, Shakespeare for My Father; *Films* as exec prodr incl: Stepping Out 1991, The Day After the Fair; *Awards* winner numerous awards incl: Tony Awards, Olivier Awards, Evening Standard Awards, Scouser of the Year 1991, 1992; *Recreations* football; *Style*— Bill Kenwright, Esq; ✉ Bill Kenwright Ltd, 55–59 Shaftesbury Avenue, London W1V 7AA (☎ 0171 439 4466, fax 0171 437 8370)

KENYON, Antony Howard; s of Frank Kenyon (d 1988), and Kathleen, *née* Richards; *b* 1 Oct 1954; *Educ* St Albans GS for Boys, Univ of Manchester (BSc); *m* 6 Sept 1985, Linda, da of John Burke; 1 s (James b 6 Dec 1986), 2 step da (Nicola West b 24 April 1974, Samatha West b 12 May 1975); *Career* trainee Benton & Bowles 1977–78, media buyer Allen Brady & Marsh 1978–80, media mangr McCann-Erickson 1980–83, exec media dir Dorland Advertising 1983–88, md IDK Media Ltd 1988–; *Recreations* flyfishing; *Style*— Antony Kenyon, Esq; ✉ IDK Media Ltd, 15/19 Great Titchfield Street, London W1P 7FB (☎ 0171 580 4441, fax 0171 580 5416)

KENYON, Sir George Henry; kt (1976), JP (Cheshire 1959), DL (Chester 1969), DL (Manchester 1983); s of George Henry Kenyon; *b* 10 July 1912; *Educ* Radley, Manchester Univ (BSc, LLD); *m* 1938, Christine Dorey, *née* Brentnall (d 1996); 2 s (Christopher, John), 1 da (Elisabeth); *Career* chm: William Kenyon & Sons Ltd 1961–82 (dir 1942–92), Williams and Glyn's Bank Ltd 1978–83 (dir 1972–83), S Tameside Bench 1974–82, Cncl Manchester Univ 1972–80; dir: Manchester Ship Canal 1972–87, Royal Bank of Scotland 1979–83; *Style*— Sir George Kenyon, JP, DL; ✉ Limefield House, Hyde, Cheshire (☎ 0161 368 2012)

KENYON, Guy Stuart; s of Horace Stuart Kenyon, of Hunstanton, Norfolk, and Katherine Mary, *née* Chapman; *b* 6 Jan 1948; *Educ* Perse Sch Cambridge, Univ of Edinburgh (BSc, MB ChB, MD), Univ of Surrey (MBA); *m* 30 Sept 1989, Judith Elizabeth, da of Edward Meirion Morgan, of Kettering, Northants; 2 s (James Edward Stuart b 1 Feb 1991, Benjamin Raymond Guy b 20 Dec 1993); *Career* RNR 1979–88, Surgn Lt Cdr; training in gen surgery United Bristol and Royal Northern Hosps 1977–80, registrar and sr registrar in otolaryngology London Hosp, Royal Free Hosp and Royal Surrey County Hosp Guildford 1981–87; conslt surgn in otolaryngology: London Hosp 1987–, Hosps for Sick Children London 1987–92, conslt surgn St Luke's Hosp for the Clergy 1987–; contrib papers on neuro-otology and head and neck cancer; memb: Med Soc of London, The Otorhinolaryngological Res Soc 1983, The Joseph Soc 1987; FRCSEd 1980, FRCS 1982; *Books* Hutchinson's Clinical Examination (1984 and 1994), Textbook of Otolaryngology (contrib, 1988), many articles in medical journals; *Recreations* skiing, swimming, music, reading; *Clubs* RSM, Royal Naval Medical, Blizzard; *Style*— Guy Kenyon, Esq; ✉ Pentlands, East Common, Harpenden, Herts AL5 1DG (☎ 01582 767593, fax 01582 767751)

KENYON, Dr Julian N Jessel-; s of Dr Joseph Bernard Kenyon, of Worsthorne, nr Burnley, Lancs, and Marie Therese, *née* Rudant; *b* 8 March 1947; *Educ* Lancaster Royal GS, Univ of Liverpool Med Sch (scholar, MB ChB, MD); *m* 1, 1970 (m dis 1985), Margaret Angela, *née* O'Connor; 2 s (Benjamin b 21 Nov 1974, Rupert b 18 Jan 1978), 2 da (Rachel b 31 March 1973, Abigail b 28 Feb 1984); m 2, 1987, Rachel Staveley Jessel, da of Dr Thomas Bonsor Staveley Dick; 1 da (Meis Barbara b 9 June 1989); *Career* house surgn Broadgreen Hosp Liverpool 1971 (house physician 1970–71), demonstrator Dept of Anatomy Univ of Liverpool Med Sch 1971–72, lectr in child health Univ of Liverpool 1972–74, princ in gen practice Crosby Liverpool 1974–76, full-time private practice in med alternatives 1976–82; currently: co-dir The Centre for the Study of Complementary Med Southampton, dir The Dove Healing Tst; hon specialist Pain Relief Fndn Clinic Walton Hosp Liverpool 1980–82, visiting prof Calif Inst for Human Sci; pres Int Assoc of Auricular Therapy; fndr Innovated Medical Technologies Ltd; memb: Ctee Br Holistic Med Assoc, Bd of Advsrs Findhorn Holistic Health Centre Forres Scotland, Br Soc for Clinical Ecology, Br Med Acupuncture Soc (fndr chm 1980); pres Int Auricular Med Soc; FRCSEd 1972; contrib to/author or editor of numerous books and booklets on acupuncture and related subjects; *Recreations* playing violin, gardening; *Style*— Dr Julian N Kenyon; ✉ The Centre for the Study of Complementary Medicine, 51 Bedford Place, Southampton, Hampshire SO1 2DG (☎ 01703 334752, fax 01703 231835); 14 Harley House, Upper Harley Street, London NW1 4PR (☎ 0171 935 7848, fax 0171 224 4159)

KENYON, 6 Baron (GB 1788); Sir Lloyd Tyrell-Kenyon; 6 Bt (GB 1784); eldest s of 5 Baron Kenyon, CBE, DL (d 1993), and Leila Mary, *née* Cookson; *b* 13 July 1947; *Educ* Eton, Magdalene Coll Cambridge (BA); *m* 1971, Sally Carolyn, da of Jack Frank Page Matthews, of The Firs, Thurston, Bury St Edmunds; 2 s (Hon Lloyd Nicholas b 9 April 1972, Hon Alexander Simon b 29 Nov 1975); *Heir* s, Hon Lloyd Nicholas Tyrell-Kenyon b 9 April 1972; *Career* High Sheriff of Clwyd 1986; memb: Wrexham Maelor BC 1991–96, Wrexham County Borough Council 1996–, EU Ctee of the Regions 1994–; *Style*— The Rt Hon the Lord Kenyon; ✉ Gredington, Whitchurch, Shropshire SY13 3DH (☎ 01948 830305)

KENYON, Ronald James; s of Fletcher Kenyon (d 1981), of Penrith, Cumbria, and Isabella, *née* Winter; *Educ* Queen Elizabeth's GS Penrith, Trent Poly; *m* 27 April 1985, Anne Christine, da of William Eckersall; 1 s (Michael Fletcher b 14 Oct 1990), 1 da (Catherine Sarah b 31 Oct 1993); *Career* chartered accountant; articled clerk F T Kenyon and Son (founded by grandfather), ptnr Saint and Company (formerly F T Kenyon and Son then Kyle Saint and Co) 1980–; dir Penrith Building Society 1993–; chm: Cumberland Dist Soc of CAs 1991, Penrith Civic Soc 1989–91, Eden Climbing Wall Appeal 1992–96 (now opened), Eden Sports Cncl 1996–; treas: Penrith Amateur Savoyards 1981–84, Eden Valley Visitors Assoc 1983–95, Penrith Agric Soc 1986–, Penrith Lions 1988–90, Greenpeace Eden Valley Support Gp 1991–93, Juniper Tst 1996–; pres Penrith Mountain Rescue Team 1992–; memb: Greenpeace, Amnesty Int, Tibet Support Group; winner Penrith Sports Superstar 1976; FCA (ACA 1975); *Books* Rock Climbers' Guide - North of England (1978), Rock Climbers' Guide - Borrowdale (1986 and 1990), Recent Developments of Rock Climbs in the Lake District (1984, 1986, 1988 and 1990); *Recreations* rock climbing, fell running; *Clubs* Eden Valley Mountaineering, Fell and Rock Climbing (vice pres 1992–94), Borderliners Orienteering, Penrith Lions, TVR; *Style*— Ronald Kenyon, Esq; ✉ 30 Wordsworth Street, Penrith, Cumbria CA11 7QY (☎ 01768 864728); Saint and Company, Poets Walk, Penrith, Cumbria CA11 7HJ (☎ 01768 865189, fax 01768 891003, car 0831 887982, e-mail ron@saintacc u-net com)

KEOGH, Andrew John; s of George Augustine Keogh (d 1961), of Bolton, Lancs, and Flora Theresa Furt Keogh, JP, *née* Angler (d 1981); *b* 9 Jan 1938; *Educ* Salesian Coll Bolton, Univ of Glasgow (MB ChB); *m* 19 Jan 1967, Mary Ruth, da of Frederic Newman, of Sidcup, Kent; 2 s (Edward John b 25 Feb 1972, George b 25 May 1977), 2 da (Emma Louise b 25 Feb 1969, Amy Victoria b 28 Jan 1970); *Career* serv TA; SHO and registrar in orthopaedics Bromley Gp Hosps 1964–65; registrar: in surgery Lewisham 1967–69, in neurosurgery Woolwich 1969–72; sr registrar and lectr in neurosurgery Univ of Sheffield 1972–78; conslt neurosurgn NW Regn 1978–, head of Dept of Neurosurgery Preston 1987–, clinical dir neurosciences Preston 1991–; FRCS 1969; memb: Soc of Br Neurological Surgns 1972, BMA 1980; *Style*— Andrew Keogh, Esq; ✉ Grantham House, 21 Beech Grove, Ashton, Preston PR2 1DX (☎ 01772 726475); Royal Preston Hospital, Sharoe Green Lane, Preston (☎ 01772 716565)

KEOGH, Colin Denis; s of John Denis Keogh, and Hillary Joan, *née* Campbell; *b* 27 July 1953; *Educ* St John's Coll SA, Eton, Univ Coll Oxford (MA), INSEAD (MBA); *m* 26 Aug 1978, Joanna Mary Martyn, da of John Frederick Leapman; 2 s (Thomas b 27 March 1983, William b 6 May 1987), 2 da (Kate b 6 Nov 1984, Georgina b 10 Aug 1990); *Career* Arthur Andersen & Co 1978–82, INSEAD 1982–83, Saudi Int Bank 1983–85, chief exec Close Brothers Ltd 1986–96; currently: chm Close Brothers Corporate Finance Ltd, dir Close Brothers Group plc; memb Inst of Taxation; *Recreations* sport, theatre; *Style*— Colin Keogh, Esq; ✉ Manor Farm, North Oakley, nr Basingstoke, Hants RG26 5TT (☎ 01256 780686); Close Brothers Corporate Finance Ltd, 12 Appold Street, London EC2A 2AA (☎ 0171 426 4000, fax 0171 247 1214)

KEOGH, Eddie Patrick; s of Edward Keogh, of London, and Elizabeth, *née* Kelly; *b* 6 Nov 1962; *Educ* St Benedict's Sch Ealing, Paddington Coll, Richmond Coll (NCTJ course in photography); *m* 8 Sept 1990, Cathy, da of James Stimpson; *Career* sports photographer; Mercury Press Agency Liverpool 1983–84, Fleet St News Agency 1984–85, freelance photographer 1985–86 (Mail on Sunday, Daily Mirror, Today), sports photographer Today newspaper 1986–95, sports photographer The Sun 1995–; *Style*— Eddie Keogh, Esq; ✉ The Sun, 1 Virginia Street, London E1 9BS (☎ 0171 782 4111)

KEOGH, Malcolm Christopher; s of late Ronald Keogh, of Bowdon, Cheshire, and Dorothy, *née* Bulley; *b* 13 April 1944; *Educ* Stonyhurst, Coll of Law London, Liverpool Poly; *m* 30 Aug 1969, Marie-Catherine, da of Henri Pouplard, of Angers, France; *Career* admitted slr 1969; sr ptnr Ronald Keogh & Co Altrincham 1974–87, consular agent of France for Manchester 1985–94, ptnr Pritchard Englefield London 1987–, dir Pannone Law Group EEIG (int grouping of lawyers) 1988–; chm: Northern Chamber Orch 1984–89, Franco Br Business Club Manchester 1988–91; pres Franco Br Cultural Assoc Manchester 1990–; memb: Law Soc 1969– (Int Promotion Ctee 1989–), Manchester Law Soc 1969–94; Officier de l'Ordre Nationale du Merite France; *Books* (part author) Daily Telegraph Guide to Buying Property in France (1990); *Recreations* flying, languages, international affairs, wine, electronics, DIY; *Clubs* Franco-British Business; *Style*— Malcolm Keogh, Esq; ✉ Pritchard Englefield, 14 New Street, London EC2M 4TR (☎ 0171 972 9720, fax 0171 972 9723)

KEOGH, (Anthony) Patrick; s of Arthur Wilfrid Keogh (d 1947), of Enfield, Middlesex, and Vere Alberta, *née* Stock (d 1981); *b* 10 Aug 1929; *Educ* St Ignatius Coll London, Univ of London (MA, LLB, LLM); *m* 3 May 1952, Eileen, da of Michael Lynch (d 1964), of Farran, County Cork; 3 s (Kevin b 8 Feb 1953, Dominic b 5 July 1955, Benedict (twin) b 5 July 1955), 2 da (Angela b 16 March 1959, Fiona b 2 May 1962); *Career* Flying Offr RAF 1949–51; admitted slr 1959, pres N Middlesex Law Soc 1972–73, admin Highgate Duty Slr Scheme 1985–90; Grand Knight (Edmonton) Knights of St Columba May 1964; chm: Edmonton Freedom from Hunger Campaign 1964, Hornsey Round Table 1969–70; pres: Southgate Catenian Assoc 1974–75 and 1984–85, Province 14 1993–94; Freeman City of London 1963, Liveryman Worshipful Co of Slrs 1963; memb Law Soc, memb Br Legal Assoc (treas 1992–); Knight Commander of St John of Jerusalem 1978, Knight of the Holy Sepulchre 1991; *Recreations* my family, walking, skiing, swimming; *Style*— Patrick Keogh, Esq; ✉ St Thomas More's, 28 Methuen Park Road, Muswell Hill, London N10 2JT (☎ 0181 444 6900), Attorneys' Bench, 335 Muswell Hill Broadway, Muswell Hill, London N10 1BW (☎ 0181 883 4412, fax 0181 883 6278)

KEOUGH, Linda; da of Michael John Keough, of Basingstoke, and Barbara Anne, *née* Sullivan; *b* 26 Dec 1963; *Educ* The Vyne Sch Basingstoke, Queen Mary's Coll Basingstoke; *m* 11 Nov 1995, Gary Staines (athlete); *Career* athlete; English Schs Intermediate 400m champion 1979 and 1980, full UK int 1980– (over 30 appearances); Gold medal 200m UK Championships 1991; achievements at 400m: Gold medal UK Championships 1985, 1988 and 1989 (Silver 1987), Gold medal WAAA Championships 1987, 1988 and 1989 (Silver 1984, 1985 and 1990), fifth European Championships 1990, Silver medal Cwlth Games 1990; achievements at 4 x 400m relay: Bronze medal European Championships 1990, Gold medal Cwlth Games 1990 and 1994 (Silver 1986), Bronze medal World Championships 1993 (fourth 1991), Gold medal World Cup 1994; achievements at 800m: Silver medal WAAA Championships 1993, Silver medal UK Championships 1993; *Style*— Ms Linda Keough

KER, David Peter James; s of Capt David John Richard Ker, MC, DL, JP, of Aldworth, Reading, Berks, and Virginia Mary Eloise, *née* Howard, of Berkshire and Suffolk; *see* Burke's Landed Gentry and Irish Family records Ker of Portavo; *b* 23 July 1951; *Educ* Eton; *m* 27 June 1974, Alexandra Mary, da of Vice Adm Sir Dymock Watson, KCB, CBE, DL (d 1987), of Trebinshwyn, nr Brecon, Powys; 1 da (Claire Rose b 23 Nov 1977), 2 s (David Edward Richard b 18 Dec 1979, d 17 March 1980, David Humphry Rivers b 11 Oct 1982); *Career* fndr and sole proprietor David Ker Fine Art 1980–; dir: Parc St Roman SA 1977–79, Oceanic Development Co (Bahamas) Ltd 1979–80, Ker Management Ltd 1980–, Belgrave Frames Ltd 1986–92, John Paravicini Ltd 1988–92, James Ronndell Ltd 1995–; md Simon Dickinson Ltd, dir Simon Dickinson Inc; memb Soc of London Art Dealers 1986; *Recreations* shooting, fishing, collecting fine art, racing; *Clubs* White's, Turf, Beefsteak, Pratt's, The Brook (NY); *Style*— David Ker, Esq; ✉ 58 Jermyn Street, London SW1Y 6LX (☎ 0171 493 0340, fax 0171 493 0796, mobile 0385 777105)

KERBY, John Vyvyan; s of Dr Theo Rosser Fred Kerby (d 1947), and Constance Mary, *née* Newell (d 1954); *b* 14 Dec 1942; *Educ* Eton, ChCh Oxford (MA); *m* 23 June 1978, Shirley Elizabeth, da of Sydney John Pope (d 1970); 1 step s, 1 step da; *Career* temp asst princ Colonial Office 1965–67, asst princ Miny of Overseas Devpt 1967–70, private sec to Parly Under Sec FCO 1970–71; princ: ODA 1971–74, Civil Serv Selection Bd 1974–75; ODA 1975–: princ 1975–77, asst sec 1977–83, head Br Devpt Div SA 1983–86, under sec and princ estabs offr 1986–93, dir Asia 1993–; govr Centre for International Briefing Farnham Castle 1986–; *Recreations* gardening, entomology, cricket; *Style*—John Kerby, Esq; ✉ Overseas Development Administration, 94 Victoria Street, London SW1 (☎ 0171 917 0352)

KEREVAN, Austin James (Jim); s of James Kerevan (d 1983), of Lincoln, and Olive, *née* Stroud; *b* 18 May 1935; *Educ* City Sch Lincoln; *m* 14 May 1966, Yvonne, da of John Burns (d 1985); 2 s (Mark James b 22 July 1968, Thomas James b 19 Sept 1984), 1 da (Emily Jane b 4 Nov 1971); *Career* RAF 1959–61; qualified CA 1959; KPMG Peat Marwick: joined Peat Marwick Mitchell 1961, London office 1961–75, Reading 1975–92; currently chm W Berks Priority Care Serv NHS Trust; non-exec dir Marbaix (Holdings) Ltd; dep chm Berkshire Enterprise Agency; tstee Rhos-y-Gwalian Outdoor Educn Centre; govr: Abbey Sch Reading, St Andrews Sch Pangbourne; FCA (ACA 1959); *Recreations* family, golf, reading (all sorts), bridge, studying railways; *Clubs* West Hill Golf, Huntercombe Golf, Trevose Golf; *Style*— Jim Kerevan, Esq; ✉ Springfield, The Street, Mortimer, Berkshire RG7 3PE (☎ and fax 0118 933 1008)

KERLY, Sean Robin; MBE (1993); *b* 29 Jan 1960; *m* Jacqueline; 3 da; *m*; 2 c; *Career* hockey player (centre forward); former memb: Southgate Hockey Club, Bournemouth Hockey Club; currently playing for Richmond (2nd Div) 1996–; scored 110 goals in 190 appearances for Eng and GB 1981–92; int honours incl: Bronze medal Olympic Games LA 1984 (scored 8 goals), Silver medal World Cup London 1986, Silver medal Euro Cup Moscow 1987, Gold medal Olympic Games Seoul 1988 (scored 7 goals); UK agent Glasgkoch 1996–, conslt Amey Sport-Tec 1996–; *Style*— Sean Kerly, Esq, MBE; ✉ c/o The Hockey Association, The Stadium, Silbury Boulevard, Milton Keynes MK9 1NR

KERMODE, Prof Sir (John) Frank; Kt (1991); s of John Pritchard Kermode (d 1966), and Doris Pearl, *née* Kennedy (d 1967); *b* 29 Nov 1919; *Educ* Douglas HS, Univ of Liverpool; *Career* lectr: Univ of Durham 1947–49, Univ of Reading 1950–58; prof: Univ of Manchester 1955–65, Univ of Bristol 1965–67, UCL 1967–74, Univ of Cambridge 1974–82, Harvard Univ 1977–78, Columbia Univ 1983 and 1985; memb Arts Cncl of GB 1969–71; Hon Dr: Chicago Univ, Univ of Amsterdam, Yale Univ, Univ of Newcastle, Univ of Liverpool; FRSL 1957, FBA 1973; *Books* author of numerous works incl: Romantic Image (1957), The Sense of an Ending (1967), The Genesis of Secrecy (1979), Forms of Attention (1985), The Uses of Error (1990), Not Entitled (memoirs, 1996); *Recreations* squash; *Clubs* Savile; *Style*— Sir Frank Kermode, FBA, FRSL; ✉ 9 The Oast House, Grange Road, Cambridge CB3 9AP (☎ 01223 357931)

KERN, Jan; *Educ* St Joseph's Convent Redhill Surrey, Purley Co GS; *m* (m dis 1988), Cyril Kern; 1 s (Joshua b 12 Dec 1980), 1 da (Tamara b 15 May 1974); *Career* trainee buyer Selfridges Ltd 1959–63, mktg exec Braemar Knitwear 1963–66, fashion dir Clothing Export Cncl 1966–70, design dir Reldan Ltd 1970–86, merchandise dir Conran Design Gp 1986–90, buying dir Littlewoods Chain Store 1990–92, dir Littlewoods International 1992–96; vice pres Cottage Homes Charity 1983– (pres of appeal 1989); *Style*— Mrs Jan Kern

KERNICK, Robert Charles (Robin); CVO (1992); s of John Wilson Kernick, OBE (d 1974), and Myrth Gwendoline, *née* Whittall (d 1989); *b* 11 May 1927; *Educ* Blundell's, Sidney Sussex Coll Cambridge (MA); *m* 1, 1951, Gillian, da of late Brig John Burne; 1 s (Mark Robert John b 1957), 1 da (Georgina Mary b 1954); m 2, Elizabeth, da of Surgn Rear Adm Sir Henry White, KCVO, CBE (d 1976); *Career* Capt Queen's (late King's) Dragoon Gds (served Palestine and N Africa); dir Grand Metropolitan Ltd 1972–75, md IDV Ltd 1972–75, chm Corney and Barrow Ltd 1981–88; Clerk of The Royal Cellars 1979–92, Clerk of the Prince of Wales' Cellar 1992–; *Recreations* golf, shooting; *Clubs* Cavalry & Guards, MCC, Huntercombe Golf, Swinley Forest Golf; *Style*— Robin Kernick, Esq, CVO; ✉ 79 Canfield Gardens, London NW6 3EA (☎ and fax 0171 328 5758)

KERR, Alan Grainger; s of Joseph William Kerr (d 1974), and Eileen, *née* Allen (d 1989); *b* 15 April 1935; *Educ* Methodist Coll Belfast, Queen's Univ Belfast (MB BCh, BAO, DRCOG); *m* 14 April 1962, Patricia Margaret, da of Edward Stewart McNeill; 2 s (Jonathan Richard b 5 June 1963, Anthony Michael b 16 Oct 1965), 1 da (Rosalind Patricia b 18 Dec 1966); *Career* basic med trg Belfast Hosps, otolaryngology trg Belfast Hosps and Harvard Med Sch, conslt otolaryngologist Royal Victoria Hosp and Belfast City Hosp 1968–; prof of otorhinolaryngology Queen's Univ Belfast 1979–81; Harrison prize RSM, Jobson Horne prize BMA, Howells prize Univ of London; past pres: Section of Otology RSM, Otorhinolaryngological Res Soc, Int Otopathology Soc; pres Br Assoc of Otorhinolaryngologists 1993–; FRCS 1964, FRSCEd 1987; *Books* Scott-Brown's Otolaryngology (ed, 5 edn 1987, 6 edn 1996); *Recreations* squash, tennis, skiing; *Clubs* RSM; *Style*— Alan Kerr, Esq; ✉ 6 Cranmore Gardens, Belfast BT9 6JL (☎ 01232 669181, fax 01232 663731); Eye and Ear Clinic, Royal Victoria Hospital, Belfast (☎ 01232 240503 ext 4102)

KERR, Eur Ing Allan Marshall; s of Dr Hugh Findlay Kerr (d 1967), of Greenock, Scotland, and Dorothy Mary Allan, *née* Martin (d 1978); *b* 25 Nov 1934; *Educ* Greenock Acad, HS of Glasgow, Paisley Tech Coll Combined (S&M Dept of T Cert); *m* 1, 2 Aug 1961, Joan Sorbie (d 1988), da of Thomas Millar (d 1961), of Glasgow; 2 s (Allan Thomas b 1963, David Marshall b 1966); m 2, 31 Dec 1988, Barbara Judith, *née* Nairn, widow of Richard Crosthwaite; 1 step s (Adam Johnathan Crosthwaite b 1967), 2 step da (Philippa Jill (Mrs MacLean) b 1963, Belinda Kate (Mrs Hazell) b 1964); *Career* apprentice Scotts S&E Co Ltd Greenock 1953–58; engr offr Merchant Navy: Furness Withy Ltd 1958–62, Union Castle Line 1963–64; engr mangr Ardossan Dockyard 1962–63, superintendent engr Clyde Shipping Co Ltd Glasgow 1964–75, dir and gen mangr Forth Tugs Ltd Grangemouth 1975–86, md Tees Towing Co Ltd 1986–90, md Cory Towage (Tees) Ltd 1990–93, ret; chm: Firth of Forth Shipowners Assoc 1982–84, Br Tug Owners Assoc 1984–86, Tees Wharf Operators Assoc 1990–93; fell Inst of Marine Engrs 1961; *Recreations* golf, DIY, rough gardening; *Clubs* Middlesbrough Golf; *Style*— Eur Ing Allan M Kerr; ✉ Rook House, Skutterskelfe, Yarm, North Yorkshire TS15 0JP (☎ 01642 700855, fax 01642 700855)

KERR, Andrew Mark; s of William Mark Kerr, WS (d 1985), of Edinburgh, and Katharine Marjorie Anne, *née* Stevenson (d 1989); *b* 17 Jan 1940; *Educ* Edinburgh Acad, Univ of Cambridge (BA), Univ of Edinburgh (LLB); *m* 23 Sept 1967 (Jane) Susanna, da of James Cumming Robertson, CBE, of Cockburnspath, Berwickshire; 1 da (Elizabeth Louise b 1971); *Career* slr; British Petroleum 1961–62, apprentice Davidson & Syme WS (now Dundas & Wilson CS) 1964–67; Bell & Scott Bruce & Kerr WS (now Bell & Scott WS): joined 1967, ptnr 1969, sr ptnr 1987–96; clerk Soc of Writers to HM Signet 1983–; RNR 1961–76; sec Edinburgh Festival Fringe Society Ltd 1969–, vice chm Edinburgh New Town Conservation Ctee 1972–76; chm: Edinburgh Solicitors' Property Centre 1976–81, The Arts Trust of Scotland 1996–, The Dunedin Concerts Trust 1996–; memb: Cncl Edinburgh Int Festival 1978–82, Cncl St George's Sch for Girls Edinburgh 1985–93, Scottish Arts Cncl 1988–94 (chm Drama Ctee 1988–91 and 1993–94), Bd of Govrs The New Sch Butterstone 1995–; *Recreations* architecture, hill walking, music, ships, skiing, theatre; *Clubs* New (Edinburgh); *Style*— Andrew Kerr, Esq; ✉ 16 Ann Street, Edinburgh EH4 1PJ (☎ 0131 332 9857)

KERR, Hon Mr Justice; Hon Sir Brian Francis; kt (1993); s of James William Kerr (d 1959), of Lurgan, Co Armagh, and Kathleen Rose, *née* Murray (d 1996); *b* 22 Feb 1948; *Educ* St Colman's Coll Newry, Queen's Univ Belfast (LLB); *m* 31 Oct 1970, Rosemary Gillian Owen, da of John Owen Widdowson; 2 s (John James b 6 May 1977, Patrick Brian b 11 Jan 1980); *Career* called to the Bar NI 1970 (Eng and Wales 1974), QC (NI) 1983, sr crown counsel NI 1988–93 (jr crown counsel 1978–83), bencher of Inn of Ct NI 1990–, judge of the Supreme Ct of NI 1993–; chm Mental Health Cmmn NI 1988–; *Style*— The Hon Sir Brian Kerr; ✉ The Royal Courts of Justice, Chichester Street, Belfast BT1 3JF

KERR, Caroline; da of John Joseph Kerr, of Surbiton, Surrey, and Maureen, *née* McNulty; *b* 27 May 1962; *Educ* St Catherine's Sr Sch Strawberry Hill Middx, Newnham Coll Cambridge (BA); *m* 5 Feb 1994, Gerard Harvey, s of Patrick Harvey; *Career* ITN: trainee 1984–86, prodr 1986–89, reporter Channel 4 Daily 1989–92 (assignments incl fall of Berlin Wall and subseq end of communist rule in Eastern Europe, Gulf War from Jordan, Israel and liberated Kuwait), gen reporter ITN 1992–94 (assignments incl Bangkok riots 1992, Bombay bombings 1993), Asia corr 1994–; *Recreations* reading, swimming, cooking, watching movies; *Clubs* Foreign Correspondents' (Hong Kong); *Style*— Ms Caroline Kerr; ✉ Independent Television News, 200 Gray's Inn Road, London WC1X 8XZ (☎ 0171 833 3000)

KERR, Prof David James; s of Robert James Andrew Kerr, and Sarah, *née* Hogg; *b* 14 June 1956; *Educ* Eastwood HS Glasgow, Univ of Glasgow (BSc, MB ChB, MSc, MD, PhD, FRCPG); *m* 12 July 1980, Anne Miller, da of William Young, of Glasgow; 1 s (Stewart b 26 Oct 1981), 2 da (Sarah b 6 Dec 1982, Fiona b 9 Dec 1985); *Career* sr lectr in med oncology and hon conslt physician Beatson Oncology Centre Western Infirmary Glasgow 1989–92, prof of med oncology Univ of Birmingham 1992–; visiting prof Univ of Strathclyde Glasgow 1990–; memb: Cancer Res Campaign, Br Assoc for Cancer Res, Assoc of Cancer Physicians, Euro Orgn for Cancer Treatment and Res; *Books* Advances in Oncology (1990), Oxford Textbooks of Oncology (1991), plus six others; *Recreations* football, busking; *Clubs* Partick Thistle Supporter's; *Style*— Prof David Kerr; ✉ The CRC Institute for Cancer Studies, CRC Trials Unit, Clinical Research Block, The Medical School, Edgbaston, Birmingham B15 2TT (☎ 0121 414 3788)

KERR, Prof David Nicol Sharp; CBE (1992); s of William Sharp Kerr (d 1972), and Elsie May Ransted (d 1989); *b* 27 Dec 1927; *Educ* George Watson's Boys Sch Edinburgh, Univ of Edinburgh (MB ChB), Univ of Wisconsin (MSc); *m* 2 July 1960, Mary Eleanor Jones, da of Capt John Roberts, of Holyhead, Gwynedd; 1 da (Jane b 1961), 2 s (Gordon b 1963, Ian b 1965); *Career* RNVR Surgn Lt 1953–55, RNR Surgn Lt Cdr 1963; prof of med Univ of Newcastle upon Tyne 1968–83, dean Royal Postgraduate Med Sch 1984–91, prof of renal med Univ of London 1986–93 (prof emeritus 1993–); postgraduate med advsr NW Thames RHA 1991–96, med awards admin Cwlth Scholarships Cmmn 1993–; Br Heart Fndn: memb Cncl 1991–, chm Fellowships Ctee 1992–; RCP: Goulstonian lectr 1968, Lumleian lectr 1983, censor 1982–84, sr censor 1990–91, ed 1994–; non-exec dir Ealing Hosp NHS Tst 1991–95; formerly: pres Renal Assoc UK, conf pres Euro Renal Assoc, memb Cncl Int Soc of Nephrology; memb MRC Systems Bd; FRCP 1968 (MRCP 1955), FRCPE 1967 (MRCPE 1955); *Books* Short Textbook of Renal Disease (1968), Oxford Textbook of Clinical Nephrology (ed, 1992), sections in med textbooks; *Recreations* fell walking; *Clubs* Athenaeum; *Style*— Prof David Kerr, CBE; ✉ 22 Carbery Ave, London W3 9AL (☎ and fax 0181 992 3231); 12 Brundholme Gardens, Keswick, Cumbria CA12 4NZ (☎ 017687 74382); Royal College of Physicians, 11 St Andrew's Place, London NW1 4LE (☎ 017 935 1174, ext 288); Commonwealth Scholarships Commission, 36 Gordon Square, London WC1H 0PF (☎ 0171 387 8572 ext 224)

KERR, Dr Finlay; s of Robert Cunningham Kerr (d 1979), and Mary MacKay, *née* Macaskill; *b* 8 Aug 1941; *Educ* Keil Sch, Univ of Glasgow (MB ChB); *m* 1968, Margaret Ann Carnegie, da of Samuel Allan; 1 s (Finlay b 3 Oct 1970), 3 da (Fiona Mary Allan b 4 Oct 1964 d 1983, Joanna Margaret b 1 Nov 1973, Marsaili Barbara Carnegie b 8 May 1979); *Career* jr house offr: Western Infirmary Glasgow 1965–66, Ruchill Hosp Glasgow 1966–67, Queen Mother's Hosp Glasgow 1967; SHO Western Infirmary Glasgow 1967–68, fell Univ of Southern California 1968–70, lectr Dept of Med Univ of Edinburgh 1970–73, sr registrar Edinburgh Hosps 1973–75, conslt physician/cardiologist Raigmore Hosp Inverness 1976–; RCPEd: regional advsr 1992–, memb Cncl 1994–95; memb: Exec Ctee Scottish Soc of Physicians 1989–94, Cncl Scottish Cardiac Soc 1993–96; chm: Bd of Dirs Highland Hospice 1986–87, Highlands and Western Isles Hosp Med Servs Ctee 1979–82, Hosp Sub-ctee Area Med Ctee 1987–88, Hosp Med Staff Assoc 1987–88, Highland Area Med Ctee 1993–96; FRCPGlas, FRCPEd; *Recreations* piping, skiing, sailing, windsurfing, golf; *Style*— Dr F Kerr; ✉ The Birks, 2 Drummond Place, Inverness IV2 4JT (☎ 01463 234779); Raigmore Hospital NHS Trust, Inverness IV2 3UJ (☎ 01463 704000)

KERR, Dr Graeme Douglas; s of Douglas Kirkland Kerr (d 1963), and Louie Ellen, *née* Stevens; *b* 1 Jan 1933; *Educ* Waitaki Public Sch, University of Otago (MB ChB); *m* 1960, Annette, da of George Denney; 1 s (Iain b 1966), 1 da (Jane b 1963); *Career* res fell Morrow Dept of Gastroenterology Royal Prince Alfred Hosp Sydney, Australia 1966; conslt gastroenterologist: Waikato Hosp 1967–71, Dept of Gastroenterology Royal Shrewsbury Hosp 1972–; memb: Br Soc of Gastroenterology, Med Equestrian Soc, Aust Gastroenterological Soc, NZ Gastroenterological Soc; FRACP 1973, FRCP 1978; *Recreations* horse trials, scuba diving; *Clubs* BHS Horse Trials Gp, British Sub-aqua Gp; *Style*— Dr Graeme Kerr; ✉ Chaney Plough, Exfordsgreen, Longden, Shrewsbury SY5 8HH (☎ 01743 718651); Royal Shrewsbury Hospital, Mytton Oak Rd, Shrewsbury, Shropshire SY3 8XF (☎ 01743 261065, fax 01743 261066)

KERR, Hugh; MEP (Lab) Essex West and Hertfordshire East (majority 3,067); s of John Kerr and late Mary Kerr; *b* 9 July 1944; *Educ* Kilmarnock Acad, Newbattle Abbey Adult Coll, LSE, Univ of Essex; *m* 9 July 1988, Devam Hendry; 1 s; *Career* lectr then sr lectr specialising in European social policy Univ of North London 1968–94, MEP (Lab) Essex West and Hertfordshire East 1994–, chm Euro Parly Australian Delegation, rapporteur on the revision of the Acquired Rights Directive; memb: Social Affrs & Employment Ctee, and also Culture, Youth, Education and Media Ctee; Socialist Gp spokesman on drug abuse prevention and public health issues; memb Harlow DC 1991–95; visiting prof Univ of Iowa USA 1983–84, visiting sr lectr Univ of South Australia 1986–87; chm of tstees Gibberd Garden Tst; memb Bd Landscape Fndn; former memb: Harlow Playhouse Bd, West Essex Community Health Cncl; *Recreations* opera (pres Parly Friends of Music Gp), the Edinburgh Festival, motor-cycling, collecting Scottish art; *Style*— Hugh Kerr, Esq, MEP; ✉ 14 Home Close, Harlow, Essex CM20 3PD

KERR, Jill; da of Eric David Kerr, MC, of Barn Cottage, Cryers Hill Lane, Widmer End, High Wycombe, Bucks, and Betty, *née* Knight; *b* 2 July 1949; *Educ* Univ of York (BA, MA); *Career* Dept of MSS and Early Printed Books Trinity Coll Dublin 1971–72, Photo-Archives Courtauld Inst Univ of London 1973–75, dean and chapter Canterbury Cathedral (estab system for recording the restoration of the stained glass) 1975, Radcliffe Tst Scheme for the Crafts 1974–75, sec Corpus Vitrearum Medii Aevi GB (Br Acad) 1975–84, inspr Historic Bldgs and Monuments Cmmn for England (English Heritage) 1984–88, head Western Region Historic Bldgs Div English Heritage 1988–91, head SW Region (Cons) English Heritage 1991–; author of various contribs to specialist lit; memb: Br Soc of Master Glass Painters 1969–86 (memb Cncl and hon jt ed of jl 1983–86), Br Archaeological Assoc 1972–85 (memb Cncl 1981–85), Assoc for Studies in the Conservation of Historic Bldgs 1984– (visits sec 1988–, memb Cncl 1990–), Stained Glass Advsy Ctee Cncl for the Care of Churches of the C of E 1984–91; hon sec to the Tstees Ely Stained Glass Museum 1978–84; Freeman City of London 1984, Liveryman Worshipful Co of Glaziers Painters and Stainers of Glass; *Recreations* talking, travelling; *Style*— Miss Jill Kerr; ✉ English Heritage, 23 Savile Row, London W1X 2HE (☎ 0171 973 3021, fax 0171 973 3001)

KERR, Jim; *b* 9 July 1959; *m* 1, 5 May 1984, Chrissie Hynde; 1 da (Yasmin Paris b 1985); m 2, 1992 (m dis 1996), Patsy Kensit, *qv*; 1 s (James b 4 Sept 1992); *Career* singer; memb Johnny & the Self Abusers 1977, co fndr Simple Minds 1977; albums with Simple Minds: Life In A Day (1979, reached UK no 30), Real To Real Cacophony (1980), Empires And Dance (1980, UK no 41), Sons And Fascinations/Sister Feelings Call (two albums released as one double, 1981, UK no 11), Celebration (1982, UK no 45), New Gold Dream (81, 82, 83, 84) (1982, UK no 3), Sparkle In The Rain (1984, UK no 1), Once Upon A Time (1985, UK no 1), Live In The City of Light (live, 1987, UK no 1), Street Fighting Years (1989, UK no 1), Themes - Vol 1–4 (compilation discs, 1990), Real Life (1991, UK no 1), Glittering Prize (Best of) 1992, Good News from the Nexworld (1995, UK no 2); performances incl: Live Aid (Philadelphia) 1985, Amnesty Conspiracy of Hope 1985, Nelson Mandela 70th Birthday 1988; *Style*— Jim Kerr, Esq; ✉ c/o Simple Minds Ltd, 26a Alva Street, Edinburgh EH2 4PY (☎ 0131 225 1707)

KERR, Lord John Andrew Christopher; s of late Capt Andrew William Kerr, RN (gs of 7 Marquess of Lothian) and bro of 12 Marquess of Lothian; raised to the rank of a Marquess's son 1941; *b* 1927; *Educ* Ampleforth, Christ Church Oxford; *m* 1949, Isabel Marion, da of Sir Hugh Gurney, KCMG, MVO, and Mariota, da of Rt Hon Sir Lancelot Carnegie, GCVO, KCMG (d 1933); 3 s (William b 1950, David b 1952, Andrew b 1955), 2 da (Marion b 1960, Catherine b 1965); *Career* late Capt Scots Guards; chm Bloomsbury Book Auctions 1983– (formerly dir book dept of Sotheby's); *Style*— The Lord John Kerr; ✉ Holly Bank, Wootton, Woodstock, Oxford

KERR, Sir John Olav; KCMG (1991, CMG 1987); s of Dr and Mrs J D O Kerr; *b* 22 Feb 1942; *Educ* Glasgow Acad, Pembroke Coll Oxford; *m* 1965, Elizabeth Mary, da of Wilfrid George Kalaugher, of Newcastle; 2 s, 3 da; *Career* HM Dip Serv: joined 1966, served FO Moscow Rawalpindi and FCO, private sec to Permanent Under Sec FCO 1974–79, head DM1 Div HM Treasury 1979–81, princ private sec to Chancellor of the Exchequer 1981–84, head of Chancery Washington 1984–87, asst under sec of state FCO 1987–90, ambass and UK perm rep to EC 1990–95, ambass Washington 1995–; *Style*— Sir John Kerr, KCMG; ✉ c/o Foreign & Commonwealth Office (Washington), King Charles St, London SW1A

KERR, Rt Hon Sir Michael Robert Emanuel; kt (1972), PC (1981); s of Alfred Kerr; *b* 1 March 1921; *Educ* Germany, Switzerland, France, Aldenham, Clare Coll Cambridge; *m* 1, 1952 (m dis 1982), Julia (actress, played Mrs Dale's da-in-law in Mrs Dale's Diary on BBC radio), da of Joseph Braddock; 2 s, 1 da; m 2, 1983, Diana Sneezum, yr da of late H Neville Sneezum, of Gothic House, E Bergholt, Suffolk; 1 s, 1 da; *Career* served WWII Flt Lt RAF; barr 1948, QC 1961, dep chm Hants QS 1961–71, High Ct Judge (Queen's Bench Div) 1972–81, chm Law Commission 1978–81, Lord Justice of Appeal 1981–89, first chm Supreme Ct Procedure Ctee 1982–86; pres: Chartered Inst of Arbitrators 1983–86, London Ct of Int Arbitration 1984–94 (hon pres 1994–), Br German Jurists Assoc 1985–91; memb Cncl of Mgmnt Br Inst for Int and Comparative Law 1973–, chm Lord Chllr's Inter-Departmental Ctee on EEC Judgements Convention 1974–81, vice pres Br Maritime Law Assoc 1977–, memb Inst for Advanced Legal Studies 1979–85, chm Ctee of Mgmnt Centre for Commercial Law Studies QMC 1980–89, chm Appeal Ctee Panel on Takeovers and Mergers; hon fell: Clare Coll Cambridge, Queen Mary and Westfield Coll London; hon life memb: American Bar Assoc, Canadian Bar Assoc, American Law Inst; Int Arbitrator; German Order of Merit 1991; *Clubs* Garrick, Pilgrims; *Style*— The Rt Hon Sir Michael Kerr; ✉ Essex Court Chambers, 24 Lincoln's Inn Fields, London WC2A 3ED (☎ 0171 813 8000, fax 0171 813 8080)

KERR, Lord Ralph William Francis Joseph; s of 12 Marquess of Lothian, KCVO; *b* 7 Nov 1957; *Educ* Ampleforth; *m* 1, 1980 (m dis 1987), Lady Virginia Mary Elizabeth, da of 11 Duke of Grafton, KG; m 2, 5 March 1988, Marie-Claire Gordon, yr da of (Michael) Donald Gordon Black, MC, of Edenwood, Cupar, Fife; 3 s (John Walter Donald Peter b 8 Aug 1988, Frederic James Michael Ralph b 23 Oct 1989, Francis Andrew William George b 5 Sept 1991), 1 da (b Amabel Mary Antonella 5 Jan 1995); *Career* political researcher, currently estate mangr, songwriter, Sotheby's rep; dir Grange Estates (Newbattle) Ltd, pres of tstees Treetops Hospice 1988–, Co pres St John Ambulance 1994–, memb Queen's Body Guard for Scotland (Royal Company of Archers); *Recreations* playing the piano; *Style*— The Lord Ralph Kerr; ✉ 20 Upper Cheyne Row, London SW3 5JN (☎ 0171 352 7017); Melbourne Hall, Melbourne, Derby DE7 1EN (☎ 01332 862163)

KERR, Rose; da of William Antony Kerr, of Almeley, Herefordshire, and Elizabeth, *née* Rendell; *b* 23 Feb 1953; *Educ* Convent of Sacred Heart Hammersmith, Belmont Abbey Hereford, SOAS Univ of London (BA), Languages Inst of Beijing; *m* Stephen Charles Lord; *Career* fell Percival David Fndn of Chinese Art 1976–78; V&A Far Eastern Dept: res asst 1978, asst keeper 1979, keeper 1987; memb: Exec Cncl GB-China Assoc 1989, Cncl Oriental Ceramic Soc, Br Assoc for Chinese Studies, GB-China Educational Tst 1995; *Books* Kiln Sherds of Ancient China (with P Hughes-Stanton, 1980), Guanyin - A Masterpiece Revealed (with John Larson, 1985), Chinese Ceramics - Porcelain of the Qing Dynasty (1986), Later Chinese Bronzes (1990), Chinese Art and Design (The T T Tsui Gallery of Chinese Art) (ed and contrib, 1991), Ceramic Evolution in the Middle Ming Period (with Rosemary E Scott, 1994); *Recreations* walking, reading, gardening; *Style*— Ms Rose Kerr; ✉ Far Eastern Dept, Victoria & Albert Museum, London SW7 2RL (☎ 0171 938 8263, fax 0171 938 8667, e-mail far.east@vam.ac.uk)

KERR, Thomas Henry; CB (1983); s of Albert Edward Kerr, of Westborough, Newark (d 1963); *b* 18 June 1924; *Educ* Magnus GS Newark, Univ Coll Durham (BSc); *m* 1946, Myrnie Evelyn Martin, da of Edward Hughes, of Newark, Notts (d 1965); *Career* Flt Lt, served Europe and Africa, pilot RAFVR 1942–53, Aero Flight RAE 1949–55, head Supersonic Flt Gp 1955–59, sci advsr to C-in-C Bomber Cmd High Wycombe 1960–64, head Assessment Div Weapons Dept RAE 1964–66, dep dir and dir Def Operational Analysis Estab 1966–70, head Weapons Res Gp Weapons Dept RAE 1970–74; dir: Nat Gas Turbine Establishment 1974–80, Royal Aircraft Establishment 1980–84, Hunting Engineering 1985–94 (tech dir 1986–88); R & D dir Royal Ordnance plc 1984–85; pres RAeS 1985–86; Freeman City of London, Liveryman Guild of Air Pilots and Air Navigators; *Recreations* bridge, water-skiing, tennis, badminton; *Style*— Thomas Kerr, Esq, CB; ✉ Bundu, 13 Kingsley Ave, Camberley, Surrey GU15 2NA (☎ 01276 25961)

KERR-DINEEN, Michael Norman Colin; s of Frederick George Kerr-Dineen (d 1988), and Hermione Iris, *née* Macdonald; *b* 14 July 1952; *Educ* Marlborough, Univ of Edinburgh (MA); *m* 1, 1976 (m dis 1981), Catharine, da of Alexander McCrindle; 1 s (Robert Crockford b 4 Oct 1979); m 2, 1988 (m dis 1995), Sally, da of Raymond Leonard; 1 s (Luke Giles b 26 Feb 1989), 1 da (Iris Sophie b 20 May 1992); *Career* Economic Intelligence Dept Bank of England 1975–79, PA to chm and chief exec British National Oil Corporation 1979–81, exec Alastair Morton & Co 1981–82; md: Guinness Peat Group 1982–88, Cambridge International Partners NY 1988–89; chief-exec: Laing & Cruickshank Investment Management 1989, Credit Lyonnais Laing 1990; *Recreations* horse racing, golf, skiing, opera; *Clubs* Athenaeum, Turf, MCC, St Mellion; *Style*— Michael Kerr-Dineen, Esq; ✉ Credit Lyonnais Securities, Broadwalk House, 5 Appold Street, London EC2A 2DA (☎ 0171 588 4000, fax 0171 588 0290)

KERR-MUIR, James; *Educ* Univ of Oxford (BA), Harvard Business Sch (MBA); *Career* formerly vice pres finance Redpath Industries Toronto, md UK Div Tate & Lyle 1988–92 (gp fin dir 1984–88), fin dir Kingfisher plc 1992–95; chm Millet's Limited 1996–; non-exec dir: Graseby plc, The Boddington Group plc 1993–95, Gartmore Micro Index Tst, The Senior Engineering Group plc 1996–; *Style*— James Kerr-Muir, Esq; ✉ 8/71 Elm Park Gardens, London SW10 9QE (☎ 0171 795 0339, fax 0171 352 1286)

KERRIGAN, Greer Sandra; da of Wilfred McDonald Robinson, of Trinidad, and Rosina, *née* Ali (d 1964); *b* 7 Aug 1948; *Educ* Bishop Anstey HS Trinidad, Coll of Law Cncl of Legal Education; *m* 11 May 1974, Donal Brian Matthew Kerrigan, s of Daniel Patrick Kerrigan, QC; 1 s (Dylan Brian Rum b 25 April 1976), 1 da (Lanra Lee Gin b 24 Jan 1979); *Career* legal advsr to Public Utilities Cmmn Trinidad 1972–74, various positions DSS 1974–96, currently legal dir Dept of Health; *Recreations* bridge, reading, squash; *Style*— Mrs Greer Kerrigan; ✉ New Court, 48 Carey Street, London WC2A 2LS (☎ 0171 412 1341, fax 0171 412 1583)

KERRUISH, Sir (Henry) Charles; kt (1979), OBE (1964); *b* 23 July 1917; *Educ* Ramsey GS; *m* 1, 1944, Margaret Gell; 1 s, 3 da; m 2, 1975, Kay Warriner; *Career* farmer; speaker House of Keys 1962–90 (memb 1946–90), regnl cncllr Br Isles & Med Cwlth Parly Assoc 1975–77, pres Cwlth Parly Assoc (vice pres 1983), pres of Tynwald (and Legislative Cncl) 1990–; memb Ct Univ of Liverpool 1974–90; Hon LLD Univ of Lancaster 1990; *Style*— Sir Charles Kerruish, OBE; ✉ Ballafayle, Maughold, IOM (☎ 01624 812293)

KERRY, Knight of; *b* 27 Feb 1917; *see:* Fitzgerald, Sir George Peter Maurice

KERRY, Sir Michael James; KCB (1982, CB 1976), QC (1984); s of Russell Kerry (d 1948), and Marjorie, *née* Kensington (d 1967); *b* 5 July 1923; *Educ* Rugby, St John's Coll Oxford (MA); *m* 1952, Sidney Rosetta Elizabeth, *née* Foster; 1 s (Patrick b 1965), 2 da (Lucy, Frances); *Career* called to the Bar Lincoln's Inn 1949, joined BOT as legal asst 1951, slr DTI 1973–80 (princ asst slr 1972), HM procurator gen and treasy slr 1980–84, bencher Lincoln's Inn 1984, dep chm Lautro Ltd 1987–90; hon fell St John's Coll Oxford 1986; *Recreations* golf; *Style*— Sir Michael Kerry, KCB, QC; ✉ S Bedales, Lewes Rd, Haywards Heath, W Sussex (☎ 0144 4831 303)

KERSHAW, Sir (John) Anthony; kt (1981), MC (1943), DL; s of Judge John Felix Kershaw (d 1927); *b* 14 Dec 1915; *Educ* Eton, Balliol Coll Oxford (BA); *m* 1939, Barbara, da of Harry Mitton Crookenden (d 1953); 2 s, 2 da; *Career* WWII: 16/5 Lancers, Reserve Forces 1946–56, CO Royal Gloucs Hussars 1953–56, (C) psc; barr 1939; City of Westminster cncllr 1946–49, cncllr LCC 1948–51, MP (C) Stroud 1955–87, Parly sec Miny of Public Building and Works 1970, Parly under sec of state FCO 1970–73, Parly under sec of State for Def (RAF) 1973–74, chm House of Commons Select Ctee on Foreign Affrs 1979–87, vice chm British Cncl 1975–87; Vice Lord-Lt Glos 1991–92; *Recreations* field sports; *Clubs* White's; *Style*— Sir Anthony Kershaw, MC, DL; ✉ West Barn, Didmarton, Badminton, Glos GL9 1DT (☎ 01454 238630)

KERSHAW, David Andrew; s of Lawrence Morris Kershaw (d 1991), of Malaga, Spain, and Rona, *née* Levy; *b* 26 Feb 1954; *Educ* Bedales Sch, Univ of Durham (BA), London Business Sch (MBA); *m* 1993, Clare Elizabeth, *née* Whitley; *Career* advtg exec; account exec Wasey Campbell Ewald 1977–80, London Business Sch 1980–82; Saatchi & Saatchi Advertising: account dir 1982–86, gp account dir 1986–90, md 1990–94, chm and chief exec offr 1994–95, resigned; ptnr M&C Saatchi 1995–; memb Mktg Soc, MIPA; *Recreations* music (playing clarinet), opera, golf, tennis; *Clubs* RAC, Groucho; *Style*— David Kershaw, Esq; ✉ M&C Saatchi Ltd, 34–36 Golden Square, London W1R 4EE (☎ 0171 543 4500, fax 0171 543 4501)

KERSHAW, David Robert; s of Noel Ernest Kershaw, TD, and Dorothy Anne, *née* Cheyne, b 1953; *Educ* Urmston GS, Trinity Coll Cambridge (MA); *m* 1978, Christine Anne, da of John Spear Sexton (d 1986); 3 s (Oliver James b 1979, Toby Thomas b 1984, Charles Henry Alexander b 1986), 1 da (Isabelle Alice Katharine b 1989); *Career* admitted slr 1978; specialist in corporate fin, mergers and acquisitions, insolvency and banking; ptnr Ashurst Morris Crisp 1986–; *Recreations* classical guitar, violin, windsurfing, tennis, literature; *Style*— David Kershaw, Esq; ✉ Ashurst Morris Crisp, Broadwalk House, 5 Appold St, London EC2A 2HA (☎ 0171 638 1111, fax 0171 972 7990)

KERSHAW, Jane; *b* 16 Feb 1959; *Educ* St Paul's Girls' Sch, Univ of Bristol (BA); *Career* initially teaching (Egypt) and computing; mgmnt conslt KPMG Peat Marwick (formerly Peat Marwick McLintock) 1986–87, prog dir Business in the Community 1987–93, head of European and Canadian Ops VSO 1993–95, head of Secretariat Cmmn on the Future of the Voluntary Sector NCVO 1995–96; FRSA; *Recreations* all forms of music, travel; *Style*— Ms Jane Kershaw; ✉ NCVO, Regent's Wharf, 8 All Saints Street, London N1 9RL (☎ 0171 713 6161)

KERSHAW, His Hon Judge (Philip) Michael; QC (1980); s of His Honour Philip Charles Stones Kershaw (d 1986), and Michaela, *née* Raffael (d 1993); *b* 23 April 1941; *Educ* Ampleforth, St John's Coll Oxford (MA); *m* 30 Dec 1980, Anne; 1 s (Francis Edward b 23 Aug 1984); *Career* called to the Bar Gray's Inn 1963, recorder 1980–90, commercial circuit judge Northern Circuit 1990–92, mercantile circuit judge Northern Circuit 1992–; FCIArb 1991; *Style*— His Hon Judge Kershaw, QC; ✉ The Crown Court, Crown Square, Manchester M60 9DJ

KERSHAW, Hon Peter John; s of 1 Baron Kershaw, OBE (d 1961); *b* 19 July 1924; *Educ* Queen Elizabeth's GS Barnet, King's Coll London (BSc); *m* 1948, Brenda Margaret, da of James Austin Smith (d 1966), of Brighton; 1 s (Michael b 1951); *Career* Sub Lt RNVR 1945–46; chartered civil engr; dir and chief engr Sir Robert McAlpine & Sons Ltd 1977–87; FEng 1981, FICE; *Style*— The Hon Peter Kershaw, FEng; ✉ 22 Orchard Rise, Richmond, Surrey TW10 5BX (☎ 0181 876 2660)

KERSHAW, Richard Ruegg; s of Raymond Newton Kershaw, CMG, MC (d 1981), of Warren Row, Berks, and Hilda Mary, *née* Ruegg (d 1989); *b* 16 April 1934; *Educ* Cheltenham, Clare Coll Cambridge, Univ of Virginia Grad Sch; *m* 1, 22 April 1962 (m dis 1967), Venetia, da of Basil Murray (d 1938); 1 da (Sophy Charlotte b 1963), 1 step s (Rupert Birch b 1959); m 2, 15 April 1994, Jann Parry, *qv*; *Career* Nat Serv 2 Lt RA 1952–54, served BAOR; asst princ Cwlth Rels Office 1958–59, features writer Financial Times 1959–60, dip corr The Scotsman 1960–63, ed Africa Confidential 1963–68, memb BBC Panorama reporting team 1965–75; presenter: Newsday then Newsweek (BBC TV) 1975–80, Nationwide (BBC1) 1980–83, The World Tonight (BBC Radio 4) 1983–94, The Business Programme (Channel Four) 1988–89; pres Dip and Cwlth Writers' Assoc 1965–67; memb Cncl: Overseas Devpt Inst 1975–, Minority Rights Gp 1975–94, Cheltenham Coll 1977–, RGS 1979–82, Lord's Taverners 1992–; first Eisenhower fell from UK to USA 1963; FRGS 1978; *Recreations* cricket, skiing; *Clubs* Brooks's, Beefsteak, MCC, Hurlingham; *Style*— Richard Kershaw, Esq; ✉ 82 Prince of Wales Mansions, Prince of Wales Drive, London SW11 4BL (☎ 0171 622 3453)

KERSHAW, (John) Stephen; s of Raymond Newton Kershaw, CMG, MC (d 1981), and Hilda Mary, *née* Ruegg (d 1989); *b* 21 Dec 1931; *Educ* Cheltenham, New Coll Oxford; *Career* investmt mgmnt (including in developing countries of Br Cwlth); former dir: Bandanga Tea Plantations Ltd, Henckell du Buisson & Co Ltd, Plantation Tst Co plc; author of various articles in investment and economic jls and newspapers; fndr memb Stock Exchange Sailing Assoc 1961; Bow Group: memb Corp Taxation Res Gp 1967–69, memb Overseas Devpt Res Gp 1974–76, memb Trade and Industry Ctee 1993–; memb: Cons Cwlth and Overseas Cncl 1972–76, Economic Res Cncl 1993–; *Publications* Referendum (jtly, 1975), Loan Trusts for Small and Medium Sized Enterprises in the UK (1996); *Recreations* travel, reading, old cars; *Clubs* Oriental; *Style*— Stephen Kershaw, Esq; ✉ 5 Valonia Gardens, West Hill, London SW18 1PY

KERSHAW, Stephen; s of John Bertram Kershaw, of Ashington, Egley Road, Mayford, Woking, Surrey, and Joyce Mary, *née* Robson; *b* 24 April 1955; *Educ* Dr Challoner's GS Amersham Bucks; *m* 1978, Alison Deborah, da of Thomas Charles Garrett, of 10 Brushwood Drive, Chorleywood; 1 s (Carl Thomas b 15 Sept 1985), 1 da (Deborah Stephanie b 12 Dec 1982); *Career* salesman Cavenham Foods 1973–75; Wilkinson Sword Ltd: salesman 1975–76, mktg asst 1977–78, product mangr 1978; Cadbury Ltd: product mangr 1978–79, sr product mangr 1980–82, product gp mangr 1983–84; head of mktg Britvic Ltd 1984–86, currently bd dir/team ldr Bartle Bogle Hegarty advtg (joined as account dir 1986, subsequently business devpt dir/mgmnt rep); memb Mktg Soc; *Style*— Stephen Kershaw, Esq; ✉ Bartle Bogle Hegarty, 60 Kingly Street, London W1R 6DS (☎ 0171 734 1677, fax 0171 437 3666)

KERSHAW, Walter; s of Walter Kershaw, of Ashford, Middx, and Florence, *née* Ward; *b* 7 Dec 1940; *Educ* De La Salle Coll Salford, Univ of Durham (BA); *Career* war artist King's Regt NI 1976; artist and pioneer of large external mural painting; UK work: Manchester Trafford Park 1993, Science Museum, Manchester United FC, CEGB, Univ of Salford 1979–89, Br Aerospace and Granada TV 1984–88, Wensum Lodge Norwich 1985, Italian Consulate Manchester 1991, P&O Manchester Arndale 1996; work abroad: Brazil, São Paulo and Recife 1983–95, Sarajevo Int Arts Festival 1996; works exhibited: V&A, Tate Gallery, Nat Portrait Gallery, Gulbenkian Fndn, Arts Cncl and Br Cncl Berlin, Brazil and Edinburgh; in conversation BBC Radio Four with Sue MacGregor 1984; *Recreations* travel, cricket, photography; *Clubs* Littleborough Cricket; *Style*— Walter Kershaw, Esq; ✉ Studio, Todmorden Rd, Littleborough, Lancashire OL15 9EG (☎ 01706 379653)

KERSLAKE, Dennis David; s of Denis Henry Kerslake, and Doreen Mary, *née* Carl; *b* 30 June 1957; *Educ* Whitgift Sch S Croydon, Univ of Exeter (BA, Hockey blue); *m* 13 Aug 1983, Jacqueline Ann, da of Brian Anthony Murphy; 1 s (Benjamin Thomas b 17 June 1989), 1 da (Hannah May b 7 May 1991); *Career* asst product mangr Beecham Group 1980 (graduate mktg trainee 1979), account mangr International Marketing and Promotions 1982 (account exec 1981), brand mangr Courage Ltd 1984, dir Purchasepoint Group 1986 (account dir 1985); md: LGM Marketing Services 1989–96 (dir 1987), Carlson Marketing Group 1996–; memb Ctee Sales Promotion Conslts Assoc 1992–93; memb Mktg Soc; hockey player Full Surrey Hockey XI, formerly rep Eng Univs Cricket and Surrey Young Cricketers, winner Annual Int Sledge Race Bormio 2000 Italy 1989; *Recreations* music, theatre, wine, travel; *Clubs* Purley Hockey, Poisoned Dwarfs, Soho Strollers; *Style*— Dennis Kerslake, Esq; ✉ Carlson Marketing Group, 116 Putney Bridge Road, London SW15 (☎ 0181 875 0060)

KERSLEY, Dr Jonathan Bernard; s of Edward Kersley (d 1976), of London, and Hilda, *née* Stone; *b* 4 March 1942; *Educ* Christ's Coll Finchley London, St Bartholomew's Hosp Med Coll Univ of London (MB BS), FRCSEng; *m* 13 April 1969, Susan Esther, da of Prof William W Mushin, CBE, of Cardiff; 1 s (Benjamin Alexander b 8 Aug 1973), 2 da (Deborah Anne b 26 March 1971, Sarah Rebecca b 16 Dec 1976); *Career* sr house offr Luton and Dunstable Hosp 1971–72, registrar in surgery St Bartholomew's Hosp 1973 (house surgn to Professorial Surgical Unit 1967 and Thoracic Unit 1968), registrar in surgery Portsmouth Hosp 1972–74 (house physician 1967), sr orthopaedic registrar Addenbrooke's Hosp Cambridge 1974–78; conslt orthopaedic surgn: Birmingham Heartlands Hosp 1978–95, Birmingham Orthopaedic Service 1995–; memb: Int Soc of Arthroscopy Knee Surgery and Orthopaedic Sports Med, Euro Soc of Knee Surgery and Arthroscopy, Br Assoc for Surgery of the Knee, BMA; MB BSLRCP, DObstRCOG, Fell Br Orthopaedic Assoc, FRCS; *Recreations* gardening, ornithology, aviculture; *Style*— Dr Jonathan B Kersley; ✉ Treverven, 41 Moor Green Lane, Moseley, Birmingham B13 8NE (☎ 0121 449 1707, fax 0121 442 4987); Birmingham Nuffield Hospital (☎ 0121 456 2000 or 0121 456 1709)

KESSELER, Dr Michael Edward; s of Sydney Joseph Kesseler (d 1989), and Edith Maud, *née* Smith (d 1978); *b* 18 Dec 1946; *Educ* King Edward's Sch Five Ways Birmingham, Univ of Birmingham (MB ChB); *m* 15 April 1978, Gale, da of Clifford Narbett, of Snitterfield, Warwickshire; *Career* sr registrar in dermatology Royal S Hants Hosp 1978–83, conslt dermatologist and clinical dir Rotherham Dist Gen Hosp and hon lectr in dermatology Univ of Sheffield 1983–; past chm Rotherham BMA; MRCP 1978, FRSM, FRCP 1989; *Recreations* wine, theatre; *Style*— Dr Michael Kesseler; ✉ The Beeches, Doncaster Rd, Thrybergh, Rotherham S65 4NU (☎ 01709 850307); Rotherham District General Hospital, Moorgate Rd, Oakwood, Rotherham, S Yorks S60 2UD (☎ 01709 820000)

KESSLER, George Bernard; s of William Kessler, of London, and Joanna, *née* Rubner; *b* 17 Aug 1953; *Educ* City of London Sch, Univ of Nottingham (BSc); *m* 25 Oct 1986, Deborah Susan, da of Beni Baltfried Jaffe, of London; 2 da (Madeleine b 1987, Flora b 1988); *Career* conslt Logica 1976–77, prodn dir Kesslers International 1984–87, ops dir Kesslers Group 1987–, md Kesslers Manufacturing 1989–; dir of 9 companies; chm: Newham Compact Steering Ctee (jtly) 1990–93, Newham Community Coll 1992–93, London E TEC Educn Advsy Gp 1991–95, London Regnl Competitiveness Gp 1995–; dep chm London E TEC 1994–; memb: London Regnl Ctee FE Funding Cncl 1993–, RSA Learning Soc Exchange 1993–95, Educn Ctee RSA 1994–, Bd E London Strategic Forum 1993–95, CBI Educn Advsy Gp 1994–, Steering Ctee Campaign for Learning 1994–, Fndn for Sci and Technol 1994–, Futures 1994–95, Jt CBI/LCCI Gp on Mfrg in London 1995–, London Bd Business Link 1996–; MRI 1975, FRSA 1994; *Recreations* contemporary art, reading, theatre; *Clubs* Savile; *Style*— George Kessler, Esq; ✉ 22 Tanza Road, London NW3 2UB; Kesslers International Ltd, 1 Warton Road, London E15 2NF (☎ 0181 522 3000, fax 0181 522 3129)

KESTER, Prof Ralph Charles; s of John David Kester, of Peterborough, Canada, and Christine Petronella, *née* Miller; *b* 16 Feb 1938; *Educ* Univ of Cape Town (MB ChB, MD, ChM); *m* 19 Sept 1964, Ilse Helga, da of John Phillip Meyer (d 1969), of Knysna, Cape Province, SA; 1 s (Bruce b 1967), 1 da (Anthea b 1966); *Career* sr surgical registrar Dundee Teaching Hosps 1970–74, sr Fulbright travel scholar and res fell Univ of California San Diego 1971–72, sr surgical lectr Univ of Leeds, hon surgn St James's Univ Hosp Leeds 1974–80, Hunter prof of surgery 1982, Arris and Gale lectr RCS 1974, currently conslt gen and vascular surgn St James's Univ Hosp Leeds, prof of vascular surgery Univ of Leeds 1995–; hon surgn to Yorkshire Rugby Union; pres elect Vascular Surgical Soc of GB and I; memb: Surgical Res Soc, Assoc of Surgns of GB and I; FRCS 1965; *Books* A Practice of Vascular Surgery (1981); *Recreations* rugby union football; *Style*— Prof Ralph Kester; ✉ Department of Vascular Surgery, St James's University Hospital, Beckett Street, Leeds, West Yorks LS9 7TF (☎ 0113 243 3144)

KESWICK, Hon Mrs (Annabel Térèse (Tessa)); *née* Fraser; yr da of 15 Lord Lovat, DSO, MC, TD (d 1995); *b* 15 Oct 1942; *Educ* Woldingham, French Baccalaureat Course (Paris); *m* 1, 1964 (m dis 1978), 14 Lord Reay; 2 s, 1 da; m 2, 1985, Henry Neville Lindley Keswick, eld s of Sir William Johnston Keswick (d 1990); *Career* early career with J Walter Thompson and journalist on Telegraph and Spectator, London ed Business and Energy International 1974–78, dir Cluff Investments and Trading 1981–95 (also fndr memb Cluff PLC 1973); special advsr to Rt Hon Kenneth Clarke QC, MP (as Sec of State for Health then Educn and Sci, Home Sec and Chllr of the Exchequer) 1989–95, exec dir Centre for Policy Studies 1995–; Parly candidate (Cons and Unionist) Inverness, Nairn and Lochaber 1987; cncllr Queensgate Ward RBKC 1982–86; memb City of

London and Westminster Assoc (ctee memb St James's Ward), memb Cons Women's Parly Sub-Ctee and Foreign Affrs Forum; fndr memb and tstee Aids Crisis Tst; memb: Inst of Strategic Studies, RIIA; *Recreations* collecting antiques, gardening and travel; *Style*— The Hon Mrs Keswick; ✉ 6 Smith Square, London SW1; The Centre for Policy Studies, Rochester Row, London SW1 (☎ 0171 828 1176)

KESWICK, Sir (John) Chippendale Lindley (Chips); kt (1993); s of Sir William Johnston Keswick (d 1990), and Mary, *née* Lindley; *b* 2 Feb 1940; *Educ* Eton, Univ of Aix Marseilles; *m* 1966, Lady Sarah Ramsay, da of 16 Earl of Dalhousie, KT, GCVO, GBE, MC, *qv*; 3 s (David b 1967, Tobias b 1968, Adam b 1973); *Career* Hambros Bank Ltd: chief exec 1985–96, chm and chief exec 1986–95, non-exec chm 1995–; chief exec Hambros PLC 1995– (jt dep chm 1990–95); non-exec dir: Persimmon plc 1984–, Hunters & Frankau Group Ltd 1986–, The Edinburgh Investment Trust plc 1992–, De Beers Consolidated Mines Ltd 1993–, Bank of England 1993–, IMI plc 1994–, Anglo American Corporation of South Africa Ltd 1995–; vice cnsllr Cancer Res Campaign 1978–, hon treas Children's Co Holidays Fund; memb Royal Co of Archers (Queen's Body Guard for Scotland); *Recreations* bridge, country pursuits; *Clubs* White's, Portland; *Style*— Sir Chips Keswick; ✉ Hambros PLC, 41 Tower Hill, London EC3N 4HA (☎ 0171 480 5000, telex 883851, fax 0171 702 9262)

KESWICK, Henry Neville Lindley; s of Sir William Johnston Keswick (d 1990), and Mary, *née* Lindley; *b* 29 Sept 1938; *Educ* Eton, Trinity Coll Cambridge (MA); *m* 1985, Annabel Thérèse (Tessa), da of 15 Lord Lovat; *Career* Nat Serv cmmnd Scots Guards 1956–58; dir: Jardine Matheson & Co Ltd 1967 (chm 1972–75), Sun Alliance & London Insurance 1975–, Royal & Sun Alliance Insurance Group plc 1989– (dep chm 1993–), Robert Fleming Holdings, Mandarin Oriental Ltd, Dairy Farm Int Ltd, The Telegraph plc; chm: Matheson & Co Ltd 1975–, Jardine Matheson Holdings Ltd, Jardine Strategic Holdings Ltd, Hong Kong Assoc; *Recreations* country pursuits; *Clubs* White's, Turf, Third Guards'; *Style*— Henry Keswick, Esq; ✉ Matheson & Co Ltd, 3 Lombard St, London EC3V 9AQ (☎ 0171 528 4000, fax 0171 623 5024)

KESWICK, Simon; s of Sir William Johnston Keswick (d 1990), and Mary, *née* Lindley; the firm of Jardine Matheson was founded in 1832 by William Jardine and James Matheson; the Keswicks of Dumfries married into the Jardine family in the mid-nineteenth century; *Educ* Eton, Trinity Coll Cambridge; *Career* chm: Trafalgar House plc until 1996, Kwik Save Group plc 1990–; dir: Matheson Holdings Ltd 1988– (chm 1983–89), Hanson plc 1991–; *Style*— Simon Keswick, Esq; ✉ Matheson & Co, 3 Lombard St, London EC3

KETT, George Anthony; s of George Robert Kett, and Lilian Hester, *née* Groves (d 1987); *b* 15 Feb 1943; *Educ* Christ's Coll Blackheath; *m* 23 May 1970, Margaret Anne; 1 s (Nicholas George b 1 June 1973), 1 da (Georgina Anne b 14 Sept 1978); *Career* subst underwriter of Red Star Policies Lloyd's 1960–65, underwriter of Corinthian Motor Policies Lloyd's 1977 (dep underwriter 1965–77); dir Marchant and Kett Underwriting Ltd 1992; chm Lloyd's Motor Underwriters' Assoc 1994; govr Christ's Coll Blackheath; *Recreations* golf, gardening, reading; *Style*— George Kett, Esq

KETTELEY, John Henry Beevor; s of John Joseph Beevor Ketteley (d 1975), and Violet, *née* Robinson (d 1995); *b* 9 Aug 1939; *Educ* Brentwood Sch Essex, Hackley Sch Tarrytown NY USA; *m* 15 April 1967, Susan Elizabeth, da of Robert Charles Jay Gordon, of Great Wakering, Essex; 2 s (Stephen b 13 Nov 1973, Thomas b 20 Aug 1985), 2 da (Sara b 11 July 1969, Alexandra b 15 Nov 1970); *Career* exec dir S G Warburg & Co Ltd 1972–81, md Rea Bros plc 1981–83, exec dir Barclays De Zoete Wedd Ltd 1983–87; non-exec dep chm Sutcliffe Speakman plc 1991–95; non-exec dir: Boosey & Hawkes plc 1987–, Throgmorton Preferred Income Trust plc 1993–95, Calorex Heat Pumps plc 1995–; non-exec chm: BTP plc 1978–, Prolific Income Trust plc 1994–; Freeman City of London 1978, Liveryman Worshipful Co of CAs 1978; FCA 1970; *Recreations* sailing, golf, tennis; *Clubs* Royal Burnham Yacht, Royal Corinthian Yacht; *Style*— John Ketteley, Esq; ✉ Keeway, Ferry Rd, Creeksea, Burnham on Crouch, Essex CM0 8PL (☎ 01621 783748, fax 01621 784966, car 0860 252941)

KETTLE, Martin James; *b* 7 Sept 1949; *Educ* Leeds Modern Sch, Balliol Coll Oxford; *m* Alison Hannah; 2 s; *Career* journalist and writer; asst ed and columnist The Guardian; *Books* Policing the Police (with Peter Hain 1980), Uprising (with Lucy Hodges 1982); *Style*— Martin Kettle, Esq; ✉ 3 Avenue Road, St Albans, Herts AL1 3QG; The Guardian, 119 Farringdon Rd, London EC1R 3ER (☎ 0171 278 2332)

KETTLEWELL, Cmdt Dame Marion Mildred; DBE (1970, CBE 1964); da of George Wildman Kettlewell, and Mildred Frances, *née* Atkinson; *b* 20 Feb 1914; *Educ* Godolphin Sch Salisbury, St Christopher's Coll Blackheath; *Career* worked for Fellowship of Maple Leaf Alta Canada 1935–38, worked for local cncl 1939–41; joined WRNS 1941, cmmnd as Third Offr 1942, Supt WRNS on staff of Flag Offr Air 1961–64, Supt Trg and Drafting 1964–67, dir WRNS 1967–70, gen sec GFS 1971–78, pres Assoc of Wrens 1981–92; *Recreations* needlework, walking, ornithology; *Style*— Cmdt Dame Marion Kettlewell, DBE; ✉ Flat 2, 9 John Islip St, London SW1P 4PU

KETTLEY, John Graham; s of Harold Kettley, of Littleborough, Lancs, and Marian, *née* Greenwood; *b* 11 July 1952; *Educ* Todmorden GS, Lanchester Poly Coventry (BSc); *m* 12 Sept 1990, Lynn Nicola; 2 s (Charles William b 19 Sept 1992, George Kit b 26 Sept 1994); *Career* Meteorological Office 1970– (Meteorological Res Flight Farnborough then Fluid Dynamics Dept Bracknell 1970–80), television weatherman for BBC and ITV Nottingham Weather Centre 1980–85, forecaster BBC Television and Radio 1985–, resident weather expert The Travel Show BBC 2 1988–91; guest appearances on Blankety Blank (BBC), Telly Addicts (BBC), Through the Keyhole (ITV); subject of song John Kettley is a Weatherman (Tribe of Toffs) 1988; memb Inst Broadcast Meteorology; *Recreations* cricket, horse racing, photography, fell-walking, gardening, cycling, brewing; *Clubs* Lords' Taverners; *Style*— John Kettley, Esq; ✉ BBC Weather Centre, Room 2027, BBC TV, London W12 7RJ (☎ 0181 225 7769)

KEVILL-DAVIES, Christopher Evelyn (Kit); CBE (1973); s of William A S H Kevill-Davies, JP (ka 1915), of Croft Castle, Hereford, and Dorothy Mortlock, *née* Lacon (d 1965); *b* 12 July 1913; *Educ* Radley; *m* 23 June 1938, Virginia Louisa, da of Adm Ronald Arthur Hopwood, CB (d 1949), of Sloane Gardens, London; 1 s (Rev Christopher Charles Kevill-Davies b 1944), 1 da (Anna Margaret (Mrs Bartholomew) b 1939); *Career* served WWII Suffolk Yeo 1939–43 and Grenadier Gds 1943–45 in France, Belgium and Germany, Capt; memb Gt Yarmouth Borough Cncl 1946–53; chm Norfolk Mental Deficiency HMC 1950–69, vice chm E Anglian Regnl Health Authy 1974–82, chm E Lacon & Co (brewers) Gt Yarmouth 1963–75 (dir 1936, vice chm 1946), memb Gen Cncl King Edward Hosp Fund for London 1972–91; JP 1954–82, High Sheriff of Norfolk 1965, DL Norfolk 1974–82; Liveryman Worshipful Co of Fishmongers 1967; *Clubs* Cavalry and Guards', RAC, Norfolk; *Style*— Christopher Kevill-Davies, Esq, CBE; ✉ 11 Hale House, 34 de Vere Gardens, London W8 5AQ (☎ 0171 937 5066)

KEY, Anthony Henry Lawrence (Tony); s of Harry Joseph Lawrence Key (d 1987), of Worthing, Sussex, and Lillian Coke (d 1982); *b* 22 June 1936; *Educ* Stanley Tech Coll, Croydon Poly; *m* 1958, Josephine Ann, da of Edward J Becket; 3 da (Joanne b 1963, Bridget b 1965, Belinda b 1973); *Career* qualified as mechanical engr, designer in precision engrg of teleprinters and fax machines, designer of domestic appliances Morphy Richards, designer and engr Seiscom geophysical exploration, industl offr Design Council until 1984, design mangr British Airports 1984–87; corp head of design: British Telecommunications plc 1987–95, BBC 1995–; award for design mgmnt 1990, Engr of the Year Inst of Engrg Designers 1976; Freeman City of London 1984, Liveryman Worshipful Co of Gardeners 1996; FRCA, MIED, FCSD (memb Cncl 1996–); *Recreations* game fishing, golf; *Style*— Tony Key, Esq; ✉ Head of Corporate and Brand Design, BBC, Room 104, Henry Wood House, 3 and 6 Langham Place, London W1A 1AA (☎ 0171 765 5808, fax 0171 765 3192)

KEY, Geoffrey George Bamford; s of George Key (Sgt RA, d 1967), of Manchester, and Marion, *née* Bamford; *b* 13 May 1941; *Educ* Manchester High Sch of Art, Manchester Regnl Coll of Art (NDD, Dip of Associateship of Manchester, Postgrad in Sculpture); *Career* sculptor; major exhibitions: Salford Art Gallery 1966, Univ of Manchester 1969, Erica Bourne Gallery London 1974, Salon d'Automne Clermont Ferrand France 1974, Nancy France 1974, Gallery Tendenz Germany 1977, Lausanne Switzerland 1980, Madison Avenue NY 1980, Solomon Gallery Dublin 1983, Solomon Gallery London 1985, Damme Belgium 1990, Moret-sur-Loing France 1991, Hong Kong 1992 and 1993; work incl in the collections of: Salford Art Gallery, Manchester City Art Gallery, Bolton Art Gallery, NW Arts Assoc, Univ of Manchester, Wigan Corp, Granada TV, Chateau de St Oven France, Jockey Club Hong Kong; cncl memb: Friends of Salford Art Gallery, Manchester Acad of Fine Art (memb 1970); *Books* G Key A Book of Drawings and Interview (1975), Daydreams (1981); *Recreations* collecting 16th & 17th century works of art; *Style*— Geoffrey Key, Esq; ✉ 59 Acresfield Rd, Pendleton, Salford 6, Lancashire (☎ 0161 736 6014)

KEY, (Simon) Robert; MP (C) Salisbury (majority 8,973); s of Rt Rev John Maurice Key (d 1984), and (Agnes) Joan Dence (d 1995); Rt Rev Maurice Key (d 1984) was Bishop of Sherborne (1946–60) and Bishop of Truro (1960–73); *b* 22 April 1945; *Educ* Salisbury Cathedral Sch, Sherborne, Clare Coll Cambridge (MA), Cert Ed; *m* 1968, Susan Prisilla Bright, da of Very Rev Thomas Thurstan Irvine, former Dean of St Andrews; 2 s (James (decd), Adam b 1974), 2 da (Sophy b 1977, Helen b 1979); *Career* asst master: Loretto Sch Edinburgh 1967–69, Harrow Sch 1969–83; MP (C) Salisbury 1983–, memb Commons Select Ctee on Educn Sci and the Arts 1983–86; PPS to: Rt Hon Edward Heath 1984–85, Min of State for Energy 1985–87, Rt Hon Chris Patten at Miny of Overseas Devpt and Dept of the Environment 1987–90; Parly under sec of state: DOE 1990–92, Nat Heritage 1992–93, Transport 1993–94; memb Defence Select Ctee 1995–; chm Cncl for Educn in the Cwlth 1984–87; memb: UK Nat Cmmn for UNESCO 1985–86, MRC 1989–90; *Style*— Robert Key, Esq, MP; ✉ House of Commons, London SW1A 0AA (☎ 0171 219 3000)

KEYES, Hon Charles William Packe; s and h of 2 Baron Keyes, *qv*; *b* 8 Dec 1951; *m* 1, 1978 (m dis), Sadiye Yasmin, da of Mahir Coskun, of Istanbul; m 2, 1984, Sally, da of Thomas Jackson; 1 da (Anna Merula b 1985); *Career* paper conservator; *Recreations* botany, aviation history, drawing; *Style*— The Hon Charles Keyes; ✉ 2 Long Bessels, Hadleigh, Ipswich, Suffolk IP7 5DB

KEYES, 2 Baron (UK 1943); Sir Roger George Bowlby Keyes; 2 Bt (UK 1919); s of Adm of the Fleet 1 Baron Keyes, GCB, KCVO, CMG, DSO (d 1945), and Eva Mary Salvin, *née* Bowlby (d 1973); *b* 14 March 1919; *Educ* King's Mead Sch Seaford, RNC Dartmouth; *m* 6 Dec 1947, Grizelda Mary, da of late Lt-Col William Packe, DSO (d 1993); 3 s (Hon Charles, *qv*, Hon John, Hon Adrian), 2 da (Hon Mrs Crompton 1950, Hon Mrs Young b 1958); *Heir* s, Hon Charles Keyes (b 1951); *Career* WWII serv RN, N Sea and Med 1939–45, ret 1949; co dir, author; Liveryman Worshipful Co of Pattenmakers; *Books* Outrageous Fortune, King Leopold III of the Belgians (1984, winner S E Arts Literary prize 1984), Un Règne Brisé (1985), Echec au Roi (1986), Een Beproeft Koning (1986), Complot Tegen de Koning (1988); *Clubs* Anglo-Belgian, House of Lords Yacht; *Style*— The Rt Hon the Lord Keyes; ✉ East Farleigh House, Lower Road, East Farleigh, nr Maidstone, Kent ME15 0JW (☎ 01622 726295, fax 01622 721471)

KEYNES, Stephen John; OBE (1993); s of Sir Geoffrey Langdon Keynes, FRCS, FRCP, FRCOG, MD (d 1982), and Margaret Elizabeth, *née* Darwin (d 1974); *b* 19 Oct 1927; *Educ* Oundle, King's Coll Cambridge (sr scholar, MA); *m* 10 April 1955, Mary, da of Senator the Hon Adrian Knatchbull-Hugessen, QC (Canada) (d 1972); 3 s (Gregory Robert Edward b 1956, Toby William b 1959, Zachary Edmund b 1962), 2 da (Elizabeth Harriet b 1957, Martha Paganel b 1961); *Career* ind documentary film prodr; RA 1949–51; formerly merchant banker, ptnr J F Thomasson & Co private bankers 1961–65; dir: Charterhouse Japhet Ltd and Charterhouse Finance Corporation 1965–72, Sun Life Assurance Society plc 1965–89, Arbuthnot Latham Holdings Ltd 1973–80, Premier Consolidated Oilfields plc 1975–, English Trust Company plc 1980–90, Hawkshead Ltd 1987–91; memb: Ctee Islington Family Serv Unit 1956–68 (also treas), Advsy Ctee Geffrye Museum 1964–87, IBA (formerly ITA) 1969–74; chm: Whitechapel Art Gallery 1978–, William Blake Tst 1981–, English Chamber Theatre 1986–92; tstee: Centerprise Community Project 1971–75, Needham Res Inst (E Asian History of Sci Tst) 1984–; *Recreations* medieval manuscripts, painting, gardening, travelling; *Clubs* Roxburghe; *Style*— Stephen Keynes, Esq, OBE; ✉ 14 Canonbury Park South, Islington, London N1 2JJ (☎ and fax 0171 226 8170); Lammas House, Brinkley, Newmarket, Suffolk CB8 0SB (☎ 01638 507 268); 24 Baltic Street West, London EC1Y 0UL (☎ 0171 251 9111, fax 0171 251 2609, telex 94011991)

KEYS, David Chaloner; s of John Henry Keys (d 1982), of Sussex, and Jean Winifred, *née* Glover (d 1970); *b* 12 Feb 1934; *Educ* Merchant Taylors', St John's Coll Oxford (MA); *m* 20 June 1959, Pamela Helen, da of Philip Henry Megson (d 1984), of Cheshire; 3 da (Charlotte b 1962, Harriet b 1965, Rebecca b 1973); *Career* Nat Serv RAF 1953–55; private sec to Dep Govr Bank of England 1963 (joined 1958), seconded to UK Treasy Delgn Washington 1964–66, seconded as md Bank of Mauritius 1968–70, with Morgan Grenfell 1971–88; dir: Morgan Grenfell and Co Ltd 1973–88, Morgan Grenfell Group plc 1987–88, A De Gruchy and Co Ltd 1982– (chm 1988–), Norwich Union Insurance Group 1988–, Robert M Douglas Holdings plc 1989–91, Tilbury Douglas plc 1991– (dep chm 1996–); chm HFC Bank plc 1989– (dir 1982–); dir: Maples Holdings Ltd (later chm) 1975–80, Thomas Borthwick and Sons plc 1981–84, Target Group plc 1986–87; chm E Surrey Health Authy 1988–90; *Recreations* reading, travelling, ornithology; *Clubs* United Oxford & Cambridge, Norfolk; *Style*— David Keys, Esq; ✉ HFC Bank plc, North Street, Winkfield, Windsor, Berks SL4 4TD (☎ 01344 890000)

KEYS, Richard John; s of Henry John Keys, of Rustington, Sussex, and Bessie, *née* Taylor; *b* 10 April 1951; *Educ* Lewes Co GS for Boys; *m* 5 Oct 1974, Helen Kathryn, da of Alan Herbert Jackson; 2 da (Emily Sarah b 19 Feb 1986, Letitia Mary b 2 March 1990); *Career* articled clerk Singleton Fabian Derbyshire 1969–73; Coopers & Lybrand: joined Cooper Bros & Co 1973, ptnr Coopers & Lybrand 1984–, seconded to Dept of Environment (water finance) 1983–84, memb Energy Water and Tport Mkt Bd 1989– (chm 1989–96), memb Audit Bd 1993–96; memb Tech Ctee ICAEW 1988–90; FCA (ACA 1973); *Recreations* shooting, opera, gardening; *Style*— Richard Keys, Esq; ✉ Coopers & Lybrand, 1 Embankment Place, London WC2N 6NN (☎ 0171 583 5000, fax 0171 213 2112)

KEYTE, Malcolm William; s of William Keyte (d 1977), of Sandsgate, Chagford, Devon, and Grace Mary, *née* Bocking (d 1983); *b* 23 Feb 1944; *Educ* Tonbridge (1st VIII cross country); *m* May 1983, Nicola Anne, da of Arthur Leonard Spiller; 3 da (Sophie Victoria b 30 March 1985, Charlotte Mary b 10 Jan 1987, Alice Joanna b 18 Dec 1990), 1 s (Thomas William b 25 March 1993); *Career* princ Keyte & Co CAs 1973– (articled clerk 1961–67); Croydon and Dist Soc of CAs: memb 1968–, pres 1991–92, chm Gen Practitioner Bd 1994–; memb: Gen Practitioner Bd ICAEW 1994–, Cncl Small Firms Lead Body 1995–; capt Purley Squash Club 1981–84; fell World Wildlife Fund 1985–; FCA 1979 (ACA 1968); *Recreations* gardening, tennis, walking; *Style*— Malcolm W

Keyte, Esq; ✉ Keyte & Co, Coombe Avenue, Croydon CR0 5SD (☎ 0181 688 6551, fax 0181 760 1951)

KHABRA, Piara Singh; JP (1987), MP (Lab) Ealing Southall (majority 6,866); *b* 20 Nov 1924; *Educ* Punjab Univ (BA, BEd); *Career* cncllr (Lab) London Borough of Ealing 1978–82, MP (Lab) Ealing Southall 1992–; *Recreations* reading; *Style*— Piara Khabra, Esq, MP, JP; ✉ House of Commons, London SW1A 0AA

KHALSA, Guru Dharam Singh; s of Richard Hinchcliffe Ainley (d 1966), of London, and Dr Rowena Woolf (d 1967); *b* 7 Jan 1956; *Educ* UCS London, Diss GS Norfolk, Park Lane Coll of FE Leeds, London Sch of Acupuncture and Traditional Chinese Med (Dip), London Coll of Chinese Herbal Med (Dip); *m* 1983, Satnam Kaur Khalsa, da of William Dumphy; *Career* teacher of Kundalini yoga and meditation 1982–, vice princ London Acad of Oriental Med 1988–, fndr practitioner Lotus Healing Centre 1990–, tutor in Chinese med London Acad of Chinese Herbal Med 1991–; memb Kundalini Yoga Fedn of GB 1987–; min of Sikh Dharma; *Recreations* nature, music; *Style*— Guru Dharam Khalsa, Esq; ✉ Lotus Healing Centre Ltd, 7 Newcourt Street, London NW8 7AA (☎ 0171 722 5797, fax 0171 722 5751)

KHAMBATA, Ardeshir Shiavax; s of Shiavax Sorabjee Khambata (d 1969), of Bombay, India, and Coomi, *née* Lam; *b* 13 Oct 1935; *Educ* Cathedral Sch Bomba, Univ of Bombay (MB BS), FRCS; *Career* conslt ENT surgn and conslt laryngologist 1973–; conslt laryngologist: Royal Coll of Music, Royal Opera House Covent Garden, ENO; memb: RSM, The Harveian Soc, Med Soc London; *Books* contrib: Music And the Brain (1977), Diseases of the Ear, Nose and Throat (1979), Voice (1983); *Recreations* music, singing, opera; *Style*— Ardeshir Khambata, Esq; ✉ 152 Harley Street, London W1 (☎ 0171 935 8868)

KHAN, (Mohammed) Ilyas; s of Mahammed Yasin Khan (d 1970), of Gillingham, Kent, and Hafiza Begum; *b* 14 Oct 1945; *Educ* Duke of Gloucester Sch Nairobi Kenya; *m* 14 April 1972, Amtul Naseer, da of Abdul Rehman Qureshi (d 1965); 1 da (Maham Hina b 1988), 1 s (Shamail Ahmed Nadeem b 1992); *Career* Cncl of Legal Educn 1965–68, called to the Bar Lincoln's Inn 1969, res magistrate Kenya 1977–80, immigration adjudicator 1992– (pt/t 1983–92), special asylum adjudicator 1993–; recorder of the Crown Ct 1996– (asst recorder 1991); *Recreations* cricket, squash; *Style*— Ilyas Khan, Esq; ✉ 12 Halfway Close, Great Barr, Birmingham B44 8JL

KHAN, Dr Kamaluddin; s of Fida Husain Khan (d 1945), and Jameelunisa Begum; *b* 5 July 1937; *Educ* Univ of Liverpool (PhD); *m* 1963, Ghazala Parveen, da of Hamid Husain Khan, of Gorakhpur, India; 3 s (Dr Salahuddin Khan b 17 June 1965, Asif Kamal b 27 March 1972, Yousuf Kamal b 22 Sept 1982); *Career* conslt psychiatrist Clatterbridge and Arrowe Park Hosp 1977–96 (emeritus conslt psychiatrist), hon clinical lectr in psychiatry Univ of Liverpool 1979–96, med advsr to Br Memb Cncl of World Veterans Fedn 1984–, Lord Chllr's pt/t med visitor 1989–; med memb Mental Health Review Tbnl, med advsr Ex-Services Mental Welfare Soc; memb: Post Grad Advsy Panel in Psychiatry, World Fedn of Mental Health; FRCPsych; *Recreations* travelling, chess, reading; *Style*— Dr Kamaluddin Khan

KHAN, Rosemarie; *b* 29 July 1947; *Educ* GDC (Dip in Dental Hygiene), Univ of Manchester (BEd, MEd); *m* Mohammad Aslam; 1 s (Alexander b 24 Nov 1965), 1 da (Sophia b 5 June 1973); *Career* formerly dental hygienist Dental Dept St Mary's Hosp Whitworth Park Manchester, dental hygienist in gen dental practice 1971–, tutor dental hygienist Univ of Manchester Dental Hosp 1971–; nat pres Br Dental Hygienists Assoc 1984–86 (memb Cncl 1981–84), UK dir Int Dental Hygienists Fedn 1986–89; memb: Central Examining Bd for Dental Hygienists 1976–, Panel of Examiners Central Examining Bd for Dental Hygienists 1982–; elected as Dental Auxiliary memb GDC 1991– (memb Dental Auxiliaries Ctee 1985–); *Recreations* family, reading, travel; *Style*— Mrs Rosemarie Khan; ✉ School of Dental Hygiene, University Dental Hospital of Manchester, Higher Cambridge Street, Manchester M15 6FH

KHAN, Dr Saeed Ahmad; s of Muhammed Khawas Khan (d 1976), of Peshwar, NW Frontier, Pakistan, and Khudija, *née* Ahmad (d 1965); *b* 1 Nov 1936; *Educ* Islamia Coll, Peshawar Univ, Karachi Univ (MB BS), Univ of London (DTM & H); *m* 25 Oct 1965, Selma Mubaraka, da of Wilfred Benjamin Reynolds (d 1971), of Ackworth, W Yorks; 3 s (Khalid b 1969, Karim b 1970, Imran b 1973), 1 da (Tahira b 1966); *Career* resident house physician Dow Med Coll Civil Hosp Karachi 1960–61; sr house offr: Manchester and Salford Skin Hosp 1962–63, St John's Hosp for the Diseases of the Skin 1963–64, gen med Middleton Hosp Ilkley 1964, gen med and dermatology Pinderfields Hosp Wakefield 1964–65; locum conslt dermatologist The Royal Infirmary Edinburgh 1968 (registrar Dept of Dermatology 1965–67, hon lectr and sr registrar Dept of Dermatology 1967–71); conslt dermatologist: Wakefield and Dewsbury Dist Hosps 1971–87, Wakefield Dist Hosps 1987–; contrib to pubns incl: Scottish Medical Journal (1968), British Medical Journal (1970), British Journal of Dermatology (1971), Archives of Dermatology (1972), Practitioner (1978 and 1981); pres Ahmaddiya Muslim Assoc Spen Valley; memb: Br Assoc of Dermatologists, N of England Dermatological Soc; memb BMA, MRCP 1965, FRCP 1985; *Recreations* walking, bee keeping, charity work; *Style*— Dr Saeed Khan; ✉ Firdene, Fusden Lane, Off Spen Lane, Gomersal, West Yorkshire (☎ 01274 873907); Pinderfields General Hospital, Aberford Rd, Wakefield, W Yorkshire WF1 4DG (☎ 01924 814803)

KHARITÒNOV, Dimitri; s of Anatolij Ivanovich Kharitònov, and Valentina Nikolaievna, *née* Loboda; *b* 18 Oct 1958; *Educ* Rimsky-Korsakov Coll of Music Leningrad State Conservatoire, Odessa State Conservatoire; *m* Nicoletta; 2 s (Vadim b 9 April 1987, Georgij b 13 Oct 1994); *Career* baritone; princ baritone Odesa State Filpharmonie Sociaty 1982–84, princ baritone Odessa State Opera 1983–85, leading baritone Bolshoi Theatre 1985–89, leading baritone Bolshoi Theatre Moscow, corso di perfezionaniento La Scala Milan, based in UK/Italy 1989–; winner: Zolotaja Osen all-Ukrainian Competition for Concert Interpretation Kiev 1983, all-Ukrainian Lysenko Competition for Opera Singers Odessa 1984, all-USSR Michail Ivanovich Glinka Competition 1984 (with special prize for best interpretation of Rimsky-Korsakov works), Grand Prix Verviers Int Opera Competition Belgium 1987, gold medal Bastianini Int Competition Siena Italy 1988, Voci Verdiane Competition Busseto Italy 1988, Carlo Alberto Cappelli Competition Arena di Verona for winners of international competitions; *Performances* regular roles with Bolshoi incl: title role in Eugene Onegin, Prince Yeletsky in Queen of Spades, Duke Robert in Iolanta, Silvio in I Pagliacci, Ferdinando in Duenna, Giorgio Germont in La Traviata, Figaro in Il Barbiere di Siviglia; with Odessa State Opera: most of the above, also Seaman Zarev in Semion Kotko, Matveev in Po to storonu 1980/81; others incl: Bill in Mahagonny (Maggio Musicale Fiorentino) 1990, Shchelkalov in Boris Godunov (Maggio Musicale Fiorentino) 1991, Jokanaan in Salome (UK debut role at Edinburgh Festival 1989, ENO 1991), Giorgio Germont in La Traviata (Liège, Dublin Grand Opera), Orbazzano in Tancredi (Buxton Festival), Sonora in La Fanciulla del West (Chicago Lyric Opera 1990–91), Prince Andrei Bolkonsky in War and Peace and Escamillo in Carmen (San Francisco War Meml Opera House 1991), Prince Yeletsky in The Queen of Spades (Barcelona Liceum Opera 1992, Glyndebourne Festival 1992 recorded on BBC Video), Enrico in Lucia di Lammermoor and Renato in Un Ballo in Maschera (both at LA Music Center), title role in Nabucco (Teatro Communale Carlo Felice Genoa) 1994, Renato in Un Ballo in Maschera (Dresden Semperoper and Sächische Staatsoper) 1994, Sharpless in Madama Butterfly (Teatro Colon Buenos Aires) 1994; gala concert at Palais des Beaux Arts Brussels 1992, recitals (with pianist Leif Ove Andsens) Olympic Games Cultural Prog Oslo, Lillehammer and Hamer 1994, recitals at Royal Opera House, Hamburg Symphony Hall, Ceseria Teatro Alessandro Bonei, Buxton Festival and Bergamo; *Style*— Dimitri Kharitònov, Esq; ✉ c/o IMG Artists Management, Media House, 3 Burlington Lane, Chiswick, London W4 2TH (☎ 0181 747 9977, fax 0181 742 8758)

KHASRU, (Mohammed) Ameer; s of Abdur Rahman Khasru, of Bangladesh, and Saleha Khasru; *b* 28 Jan 1942; *Educ* Collegiate Sch Chittagong, Univ of Dhaka (BCom); *m* 4 March 1965, Chantal Berthe, da of Andre Faucher (d 1979), of France; 1 s (Stephane Reza b 1966), 1 da (Ambreen Joy b 1970); *Career* sr ptnr Khasru & Co London; chm Thai Pavilion Restaurants; chief accountant: Burmah Eastern Ltd, Chittagong Bangladesh 1968–71; sr lectr Business Studies SW London Coll 1971–74, trg mangr 1974–78; FCA; *Recreations* swimming, tennis, theatre, reading, good food; *Style*— Ameer Khasru, Esq; ✉ Khasru & Co, 121 Kennington Rd, London SE11 6SF

KHAW, Prof Kay-Tee; da of Kai-Boh Khaw (d 1972), of Kuala Lumpur, and Chweegeok, *née* Tan; *b* 14 Oct 1950; *Educ* Victoria Inst Kuala Lumpur, Univ of Cambridge (MA, MB BChir), LSHTM (MSc), FRCP, MFPHM; *m* 1980, Dr James William Fawcett; 1 da (Nicola b 21 Dec 1981), 1 s (Andrew b 14 Feb 1984); *Career* house physician and surgn St Mary's Hosp 1975–76, sr house offr Whittington Hosp 1977–78, registrar KCH 1978–79; Wellcome Tst res fell: St Mary's Hosp and LSHTM 1980–82, Univ of California 1982–84; asst prof Univ of California 1985–89; Univ of Cambridge: sr registrar (community med) 1986–89, prof of clinical gerontology 1989–; FRCP; *Style*— Prof Kay-Tee Khaw; ✉ Clinical Gerontology Unit, University of Cambridge, Addenbrooke's Hospital, Cambridge CB2 2QQ (☎ 01223 217292, fax 01223 336928)

KHAYAT, Georges Mario; QC (1992); s of Fred Khayat (d 1973), of Israel and the USA, and Julie, *née* Germain (d 1990); *b* 15 Aug 1941; *Educ* Terra Sancta Coll Nazareth, Prior Park Coll Bath; *Career* called to the Bar Lincoln's Inn 1967, pupillage with K Zucker (now His Hon Judge Zucker, QC), mixed practice later specialising in prosecution and defence in criminal cases, recorder 1987–; *Recreations* music, reading, boating, riding and travelling; *Style*— Georges M Khayat, Esq, QC; ✉ 10 King's Bench Walk, Temple, London EC4Y 7EB (☎ 0171 353 2501, fax 0171 353 0658)

KHODOR, HE Mohammad; *b* 1932; *Educ* Military Coll Syria, Lenin Acad Moscow; *m*; 1 s; *Career* Syrian diplomat; Lt rising to Lt-Col Syrian Army 1953–63; counsellor Miny of Foreign Affairs 1963–64, counsellor Embassy Buenos Aires 1964–66, gen consul Consulate Saõ Paulo Brazil 1966–68, dir Trg and Coordination Dept Miny of Foreign Affairs 1968–71, minister plenipotentiary charge d'affaires Embassy Cyprus 1971–77, dir Arab Nation Dept Miny of Foreign Affairs 1977–81, ambassador to India 1982–89, non-res ambassador to Sri Lanka, Nepal, Bangladesh, Afghanistan and Burma 1983–89, dir Dept of Western Europe Miny of Foreign Affairs, ambassador to Ct of St James 1991–; participant in many Arab summit, Euro-Arab and non-aligned confs; del: to the Arab Israeli Peace Conf Madrid, to the Peace Talks Washington; *Recreations* playing football, music, reading, horse riding; *Style*— HE Mr Mohammad Khodor; ✉ Syrian Embassy, 8 Belgrave Square, London SW1X 8PH

KHOO, Francis Kah Siang; s of late Teng Eng, and Swee Neo, *née* Chew; *b* 23 Oct 1947; *Educ* Univ of Singapore (LLB), Univ of London (MA); *m* 29 Jan 1977, Dr Swee Chai Ang, da of Peng Liat Ang; *Career* advocate and slr Singapore 1971–77, business and political journalist London 1980–87, gen sec War on Want London (Br Devpt Aid Agency) 1988–89, asst slr Law Soc of England and Wales; vice chm and fndr memb Medical Aid for Palestinians 1984–; memb: NUJ 1979–, Singapore Law Soc 1971–; *Books* Bungaraya Blooms All Day (1978), The Rebel and The Revolutionary (1994); *Recreations* hill walking, swimming, camera designing; *Style*— Francis Khoo, Esq; ✉ 17 Knollys House, 39 Tavistock Place, London WC1H 9SA (☎ 0171 380 0648)

KHOURY, Dr Ghassan George; s of George Sammaan Khoury, of Amman, Jordan, and Margaret, *née* Rizik; *b* 14 July 1954; *Educ* Bryanston, UCL, UCH; *m* 7 Aug 1984, Sonia, da of Jubran Khoury, of Jifna, Ramallah, Israel; 2 s (George Ghassan b 1986, Timothy b 1993), 1 da (Genevieve b 1996); *Career* lectr in radiotherapy and oncology Univ of Leeds 1986–89, conslt in radiotherapy and oncology Portsmouth 1989–; memb radiotherapy co-op gp EORTC; MRCP 1981, FRCR 1985; memb: BMA 1978, British Oncological Assoc 1987; *Recreations* swimming, squash; *Style*— Dr Ghassan Khoury; ✉ St Mary's Hospital, Milton Rd, Portsmouth PO3 6AD (☎ 01705 822331, fax 01705 866313)

KIBAZO, Joel Serunkuma; s of Godfrey Serunkuma Lule, and Margaret Mary, *née* Namusisi; *b* 24 June 1961; *Educ* HS for Boys Swindon, Kingsbury HS London, Sunderland Poly (BA), Univ of Reading (MA), Univ of Bradford (MBA); *Career* trainee reporter New Life 1986–87, political corr The Voice 1987–88; Financial Times: gen reporter 1988–89, stockmarkets reporter 1989–90, researcher/reporter FT TV 1990–91, markets reporter 1992–; co fndr: Black Journalists' Assoc 1989, Br Uganda Soc (former chm); *Recreations* swimming, African history, Third World development issues; *Style*— Joel Kibazo, Esq; ✉ Financial Times, 1 Southwark Bridge, London SE1 9HL (☎ 0171 873 3227, fax 0171 873 4348)

KIDBY, Robert James; s of James Clarence Kidby, of Vixenlaw, Warninglid, Sussex, and Myrtle Eileen, *née* Wright; *b* 27 Feb 1951; *Educ* Steyning GS, Univ of London (LLB); *m* 3 Dec 1977, Stephanie Elizabeth Mary, da of Morris Shipley, of Hook, Basingstoke, Hants; 1 s (Samuel Robert b 4 Aug 1985), 1 da (Harriet Elizabeth Cynthia b 6 Nov 1988); *Career* admitted slr 1977; ptnr: Durrant Piesse 1985–88, Lovell White Durrant 1988– (currently head of Property Dept); Freeman Worshipful Co of Slrs 1984; memb Law Soc 1978; *Recreations* electric guitar, Antarctic memorabilia; *Style*— Robert Kidby, Esq; ✉ Lovell White Durrant, 65 Holborn Viaduct, London EC1A 2DY (☎ 0171 236 0066)

KIDD, John Edward Aitken; s of Maj Edward Daltrey Kidd (d 1979), and Hon Janet Gladys, *née* Aitken (d 1988), da of 1 Baron Beaverbrook; *b* 12 Dec 1944; *Educ* Harrow; *m* 2 April 1973, Wendy Madeleine, da of Sir John Rowland Hodge, MBE (d 1995); 1 s (Jack Edward b 1973), 2 da (Jemma Madeleine b 1974, Jodie Elizabeth b 1978); *Career* Jr Euro Individual Showjumping Champion 1962, represented GB in Europe, USA and Africa 1964–72, represented England 11 v The Commonwealth (Polo) on Int Day at Windsor 1972; dir: London United Investments plc 1977–81, Aitken Home plc 1982–86, Careplus Inc USA 1987–, All England Jumping Course Hickstead 1989–; chm Columbia Laboratories Inc USA 1987–; *Books* Reins In Our Hands (1966), Take Off (1974), Biographies On Showjumping Career; *Recreations* polo; *Clubs* Buck's; *Style*— John Kidd, Esq; ✉ Holders House, St James, Barbados; Suite 1809, 745 Fifth Ave, New York City, NY, USA

KIDD, Richard; *Educ* Univ of Newcastle, British Sch Rome; *Career* artist; teacher: Trent Poly and Univ of Reading 1975–76, Univ of Newcastle 1976–80; Harkness fell San Francisco 1980, moved to NY 1981, returned to UK 1987; *Solo Exhibitions* incl: Sunderland Arts Centre 1976, Rowan Gallery 1977, 1979 and 1980, Turnpike Gallery Leigh 1978, Armand Bartos NY 1983, Alexander Milliken Gallery NY 1983, Juda Rowan Gallery 1983, Mayor Rowan Gallery 1990; *Gp Exhibitions* incl: Northern Painters and Sculptors (Peter Stuyvesant Fndn Sunderland Arts Centre) 1974, John Moores Liverpool Exhibition 9 and 10 1974 and 1976, Mostra 75 (Rome) 1975, Growing up with Art (Leics Collection Whitechapel Gallery) 1980, Br Artists in NY (Newhouse Gallery NY) 1983, New Works on Paper (Br Cncl tour) 1984–86; *Collections* incl: Arts Cncl of GB, Kunsthaus Zurich, Museum of Modern Art Rio de Janeiro, Sainsbury Centre Norwich, Ulster Museum Belfast, Clare Coll Cambridge; equal first prize Peter Stuyvesant Fndn

1974, prize John Moores Liverpool Exhibition 9 1974, Abbey major scholar Rome 1974, Arts Cncl award 1976, N Arts fell 1976; *Style*— Richard Kidd, Esq

KIDD, Sir Robert Hill; KBE (1979), CB (1975); s of Andrew Kidd (d 1947), and Florence, *née* Hill (d 1963); *b* 3 Feb 1918; *Educ* Royal Belfast Academical Inst, Univ of Dublin (BA, BLitt); *m* 1942, Harriet Moore, da of Rev E H Williamson, PhD, of Ballina and Tralee, Eire; (3 s, 2 da); *Career* Actg Maj SEAC, cmmnd 1942, RUR, later attached to Intelligence Corps; NI Civil Serv 1947–79 (head of NICS 1976–79); dir Allied Irish Banks Ltd 1979–85, chm Belfast Car Ferries Ltd 1983–88, NI chm of Cooperaton North 1982–86; pro chancellor and chm of Cncl New Univ of Ulster 1980–84, tstee Scot Irish Tst 1980–96, chm Ulster Historical Fndn 1988–93; dir Irish American Partnership 1988–91; Hon DLitt Univ of Ulster 1985; *Recreations* gardening, photography; *Clubs* Civil Service; *Style*— Sir Robert Kidd, KBE, CB; ✉ 24 Massey Court, Belfast BT4 3GJ (☎ 01232 768694)

KIDGELL, John Earle; s of Maj Gilbert James Kidgell, TD, RA and TA (d 1989), and Cicely Alice Whitfield, *née* Earle (d 1982); *b* 18 Nov 1943; *Educ* Eton House Sch Southend, Univ of St Andrews (MA), LSE (MSc); *m* 30 March 1968, Penelope Jane, da of Kenneth Tarry (d 1970); 1 s (James Kenneth b 1974), 2 da (Clare Louise b 1972, Alexandra Frances b 1981); *Career* NIESR 1967–70, Gallup Poll 1970–72, statistician Central Statistical Office and Treasury 1972–79, chief statistician DOE and PSA 1979–88, under sec (grade 3) Office of National statistics (formerly Central Statistical Office) 1988– (dir Macro-Economic Statistics and Analysis Gp 1994–); FRSS; *Recreations* tennis, hill walking, reading; *Style*— John Kidgell, Esq; ✉ Office for National Statistics, Room 57A/2, Great George Street, London SW1P 3AQ (☎ 0171 270 6040, fax 0171 270 6085)

KIDNER, Michael James; s of Norman William Kidner (d 1931), of Kettering, and Kathleen Kidner (d 1976); *b* 11 Sept 1917; *Educ* Bedales Sch, Univ of Cambridge (MA); *m* 24 Feb 1951, Marion, da of Morton Frederick (d 1975), of NY, USA; 1 s (Simon Morton b 15 Sept 1962, d 10 March 1982); *Career* Nat Serv Royal Canadian Signal Corps 1942–46; artist and sculptor; one man shows incl: ACGB Expo Serpentine Gallery London 1984, Museum of Contemporary Art Lodz Poland 1985, Joszefvarosi Kaillito Teerem Gallery Budapest Hungary 1986, Amos Anderson Museum Helsinki Finland 1987, The Wave: Concepts in Construction (Galerie Hubert Winter Vienna Austria) 1990 and 1992, At-tension to the Wave (CICA NYC) 1990, Galerie Bismarck Bremen 1992, Galerie Schlege Zurich 1991, Critics' Choice (Cowling Gallery) 1992, Michael Kidner 1958–93 (Galerie Hoffmann Friedberg Germany) 1993–94, Michael Kidner (Gallery Emilia Slacia Ettlingham Germany) 1995; numerous gp expos worldwide; public collections incl: Tate Gallery, Museum of Mod Art NY, Nat Gallery of Aust Canberra, Amos Anderson Museum Helsinki, Manchester City Art Gallery, Victoria and Albert Museum, Sainsbury Collection; recent cmmns: sculpture for the Museo Internazionale di Scultura all'Aperto Citta di Portofino Italy 1988, sculpture in Vissingen Holland 1989, sculpture in Dresdener Bank Merseburg Germany 1995; *Books* Elastic Membrane (1980); *Style*— Michael Kidner, Esq; ✉ 18 Hampstead Hill Gardens, London NW3 2PL (☎ 0171 435 9630)

KIDWELL, Raymond Incledon; QC (1968); s of Montague Ernest Kidwell (d 1988), and Dorothy, *née* Incledon (d 1980); *b* 8 Aug 1926; *Educ* Whitgift Sch, Magdalen Coll Oxford (BCL, MA); *m* 1, 1951 (m dis) Enid, *née* Rowe; 2 s (Barry Gerard b 1956, Nicholas Justin b 1958); m 2, 26 June 1976, Dr Carol Kidwell, da of Warren Garnet Hopkins (d 1962), of Ottawa, Canada; *Career* Nat Serv RAFVR 1944–48; called to the Bar Gray's Inn 1951 (bencher 1978), recorder 1972, dep High Ct judge 1976, head of chambers until 1996; *Recreations* travel, photography; *Clubs* United Oxford and Cambridge Univ; *Style*— Raymond Kidwell, QC; ✉ Sanderstead House, Rectory Park, Sanderstead, Surrey CR2 9JR (☎ 0181 657 4161); 2 Crown Office Row, Temple, London EC4Y 7HJ (☎ 0171 797 8100, fax 0171 583 8101)

KIELY, Dr David George; s of George Thomas Kiely (d 1964), of Ballynahinch, Co Down, and Susan, *née* Wolfenden (d 1972); *b* 23 July 1925; *Educ* Down HS Downpatrick, Queen's Univ Belfast (BSc, MSc), Sorbonne (DSci), Royal Naval Staff Coll (psc); *m* 17 Aug 1956, Dr Ann Wilhelmina, da of John William Kilpatrick (d 1961), of Hillsborough, Co Down; 1 s (Patrick b 1964), 1 da (Fiona b 1961); *Career* Civil Serv (MOD); RNS Serv: joined 1944, head of Electronic Warfare Div ASWE 1965–68, head of Communications and Sensor Dept ASWE 1968–72, under sec 1972, dir gen Telecommunications PE MOD 1972–74, dir gen Strategic Electronic Systems PE MOD 1974–76, dir gen Electronics Res 1976–78, dir Naval Surface Weapons ASWE 1978–83, The Chief Naval Weapon Systems Engr 1983–84; chm R&D Policy Ctee of the Gen Lighthouse Authys of the UK and Eire 1974–89; gp chief exec Chemring plc 1984–85; conslt engr; govr: Portsmouth Coll of Technol 1965–69, Springfield Sch Portsmouth 1993–; chm Cncl Chichester Cathedral 1985–89 (memb 1982–89); CEng, FIEE, CPhys, FInstP; *Books* Dielectric Aerials (1953), Marine Navigational Aids for Coastal Waters of the British Isles (1987), Naval Electronic Warfare (1988), Naval Surface Weapons (1988), Naval Command and Control (1989), Defence Procurement (1990), The Future for the Defence Industry (1991); *Recreations* fly fishing, gardening, aviculture; *Clubs* Naval and Military; *Style*— Dr D G Kiely; ✉ Cranleigh, 107 Havant Rd, Emsworth, Hampshire PO10 7LF (☎ 01243 372250)

KIELY, John Andrew; s of Nicholas Joseph Kiely (d 1989), and Maureen, *née* O'Neill; *b* 12 Dec 1961; *Educ* Stonyhurst, UCL (BA); *m* 1 June 1991, Sarah, da of Maj Peter Challen; 1 s (Alexander Fergus b 11 June 1993), 1 da (Georgia Francesca b 14 Oct 1994); *Career* Broad Street Associates PR 1986–88, fndr dir Square Mile Communications 1988–95, dir Lowe Bell Financial 1995–; *Recreations* sports, good food and drink; *Clubs* Queen's, Rye Golf, Royal Worlington and Newmarket Golf; *Style*— John Kiely, Esq; ✉ Lowe Bell Financial Ltd, 20 Red Lion Court, London EC4A 3HE (☎ 0171 353 9203, fax 0171 353 7980, mobile 0385 275665)

KIER, Michael Hector; s of Mogens Kier, and Birthe, *née* Andreasen; *b* 22 Oct 1946; *Educ* Repton, King's Coll London; *m* 15 May 1971, Jane Elizabeth, da of J R Childs; *Career* jt md: Fielding Juggins Money & Stewart 1981–86, Heath Fielding Insurance Broking Ltd 1986–89; chm C E Heath Latin America Ltd 1986–91; C E Heath plc: insur broker 1968–77, dir 1986–, md 1989–92, chm 1992–; *Style*— Michael H Kier, Esq; ✉ C E Heath plc, 133 Houndsditch, London EC3A 7AH (☎ 0171 234 4000, fax 0171 234 4184, telex 8813001)

KIERAN, Patrick Oliver; *b* 17 June 1938; *Career* Argyll Group plc: joined 1957, dir 1989–95, dep chm Safeway plc 1995 (md 1993–95), ret; *Style*— Patrick Kieran, Esq

KIERNAN, Patrick Justin; s of Bernard Kiernan (d 1987), of Cavan, Ireland, and Elizabeth, *née* Johnson (d 1994); *b* 28 April 1944; *Educ* Salesian Coll Battersea, LSE (BSc(Econ)), Univ of Manchester (Dip in Business); *m* 1982, Jillian, *née* Sheppard; 2 s (Michael b 1983, Matthew b 1985); *Career* salesman ICL 1968–69 (graduate trainee 1967); Price Waterhouse: mgmnt conslt 1969–74, mangr 1974–79, ptnr 1979–, various mgmnt roles in UK 1979–89, vice chm UK Firm Supervisory Ctee 1992– (memb 1988–), dir International Client Services Network 1992, sr client ptnr 1993, memb Euro Firm Supervisory Bd 1993–; *Recreations* sport; *Clubs* Riverside, Racquet Centre; *Style*— Patrick Kiernan, Esq; ✉ Price Waterhouse, No 1 London Bridge, London SE1 9QL (☎ 0171 939 6067, fax 0171 939 6222)

KIFF, Ken; *b* 29 May 1935; *Educ* Hornsey Sch of Art; *m*; 1 s (Sam), 1 da (Anna); *Career* artist; pt/t teacher various schs incl Chelsea Sch of Art and RCA; *Solo Exhibitions* Gardener Centre Gall Univ of Sussex 1980, Nicola Jacobs Gall 1980, 1983 and 1985, Talbot Rice Art Centre 1987, Edward Thorp Gall NY 1981, 1982 and 1986, Serpentine Gall (and tour) 1986, Fischer Fine Art 1988, Pamela Auchincloss Gall NY (monotypes) 1990, Marlborough Fine Art 1991, Marlborough Graphics 1991, National Gall 1993–94, Marlborough Fine Art 1996; *Group Exhibitions* incl: Critic's Choice 1970, Magic and Strong Medicine (Walker Art Gall) 1973, Narrative Painting (Arnolfini and tour) 1979, New Work on Paper 1 (Museum of Modern Art, NY and tour USA) 1981, New Art (Tate Gall) 1983, Tenth Anniversary Exhibition: Content - A Contemporary Focus 1974–84 (Hirshhorn Museum Smithsonian Inst, Washington DC) 1984, The Proper Study: Contemporary Figurative Art From Britain (Lalit Kala Academy, New Delhi) 1984, Metaphor and/or Symbol (National Museum of Modern Art, Tokyo) 1984, Eros in Albion: Six English Painters (Arezzo) 1989, Sammlung Sandven: Zur Kunst der Zweiten Hälfte des 20 Jahrhunderts (Staatliche Kunstsammlung, Liechtenstein) 1992–93, Acchrochage (Marlborough Fine Art) 1994, Here and Now (Serpentine Gall) 1994; *Work in Public Collections* Arts Cncl, Br Cncl, Göteborgs Konstmuseum, Metropolitan Museum of Art NY, Museum of Modern Art NY, Rugby Museum and Art Gall, Tate Gall; assoc artist National Gall 1991–93; RA; *Clubs* Chelsea Arts; *Style*— Ken Kiff, Esq; ✉ c/o Marlborough Fine Art (London) Ltd, 6 Albemarle Street, London W1X 4BY (☎ 0171 629 5161, fax 0171 629 6338)

KILBANE, Dr (Mary) Paula Jane; da of Dr Mathew Clement Kelly (d 1971), of Warrenpoint, and Dr Margot Kelly, *née* King; *b* 17 May 1950; *Educ* Trinity Coll Dublin, Queen's Univ Belfast (MB BCh), London Sch of Hygiene and Tropical Med (MSc), RCP (MFCM); *m* 3 Nov 1979, James Kilbane, s of James Kilbane; 1 da (Caroline b 23 Feb 1981), 1 s (James Patrick b 24 March 1983); *Career* jr doctor posts Royal Victoria Hosp Belfast 1973–76, registrar then sr registrar LSHTM and City and East London Area Health Authy 1976–80, conslt in public health med NE Thames RHA 1980–84, jt conslt and lectr LSHTM Islington 1982–86, conslt Eastern Health and Social Servs Bd Belfast 1986–90, chief exec Southern Health and Social Servs Bd 1993–95 (dir of public health 1990–93), chief exec Eastern Health and Social Servs Bd 1995–; memb: Health Economics Gp, Soc of Social Med, NI Higher Educn Cncl 1993–; FFPHM (memb Bd 1991–93); *Books* AIDS Responding to the Challenge - A Comparative Study of Local AIDS Programmes in the UK (jtly, 1989), Oxford Textbook of Public Health (contrib, 1991); author of numerous published papers in learned periodicals; *Recreations* France, food and wine; *Style*— Dr Paula Kilbane; ✉ Eastern Health and Social Services Board, Champion House, 12/22 Linenhall Street, Belfast, Co Antrim BT2 8BS (☎ 01232 321313, fax 01232 321520)

KILBORN, Dr John Robert; s of Charles James Kilborn (d 1995), of Desborough, Northants, and Winifred Jane, *née* Fenton; *b* 22 April 1939; *Educ* Kettering GS, Univ of Durham, Univ of Newcastle upon Tyne (BSc, PhD, MB BS); *m* 3 July 1965, Jean Margaret (Jan), da of Stewart Allen (d 1966), of Newcastle upon Tyne; 3 s (David John b 1970, Andrew James b 1973, Christopher Richard b 1975); *Career* physician Royal Victoria Infirmary Newcastle 1969–71, clinical res physician Hoffman la Roche 1971–73, SMO Glaxo Group 1973–77, cardiovascular clinical res leader then med dir UK Laboratories d'Etudes et de Recherche Synthélabo Paris and London 1977–83; md: Lorex Pharmaceuticals Ltd 1983–88, Eurocetus UK Ltd 1988–93; med dir Worldwide Clinical Trials Ltd 1995–; chief exec offr Morphosys GmbH 1994; author of various publications on clinical pharmacology and therapeutics; FFPM, FInstD; *Style*— Dr John Kilborn; ✉ 2 Moreton End Lane, Harpenden, Herts AL5 2EX (☎ 01582 712500, fax 01582 760072); Worldwide Clinical Trials Ltd, 27 Harley Street, London W1N 1DA

KILBRACKEN, 3 Baron (UK 1909); John Raymond Godley; DSC (1945); s of 2 Baron Kilbracken, CB, KC (d 1950), and his 1 w, Elizabeth, *née* Hamilton; gs of 1 Baron who was Gladstone's private sec and perm under sec for India, and bro of Prof Hon Wynne Godley, *qv*; *b* 17 Oct 1920; *Educ* Eton, Balliol Coll Oxford (MA); *m* 1, 1943 (m dis 1949), Penelope, da of Rear Adm Sir Cecil Reyne, KBE (d 1958); 1 s (Hon Christopher b 1945, and 1 s decd Simon b and d 1947); m 2, 1981 (m dis 1989), Susan, da of Norman Heazlewood; 1 s (Hon Seán b 1981); *Heir* s, Hon Christopher Godley; *Career* sits as Lab peer in House of Lords; serv WWII RNVR Fleet Air Arm (pilot) 1940–46, Lt Cdr (A) 1945; journalist and author; life memb NUJ; *Books* Tell Me The Next One (1950), The Master Forger (1951), Living Like A Lord (1954), A Peer Behind The Curtain (1959), Shamrocks & Unicorns (1962), Van Meegeren (1967), Bring Back My Stringbag (1979), The Easy Way to Bird Recognition (1982, TES Information Book Award for children aged 10–16 1982), The Easy Way to Tree Recognition (1983), The Easy Way to Wild Flower Recognition (1984); the Easy Way books were republished as The Easy Way Guides (1995); *Recreations* chess, birdwatching; *Style*— The Rt Hon Lord Kilbracken, DSC; ✉ Killegar, Co Leitrim, Ireland (☎ and fax 00 353 49 34309)

KILBURN, Alan Edward; OBE (1990); s of Edward Kilburn (d 1979), and Ethel, *née* Doidge; *b* 15 April 1936; *Educ* Wellfield A J Dawson GS Wingate Co Durham; *m* 27 July 1963, Doreen, da of Richard Edward Gratton; 1 s (Matthew Charles b 24 Nov 1970), 1 da (Jessica b 9 Jan 1974); *Career* Peterlee Devpt Corp 1952–63; housing mangr: Ashington Urban DC 1963–65, Knottingley Urban DC 1965–66, Felling Urban DC 1966–69; asst dir of housing Newcastle upon Tyne City Cncl 1969–73, regnl dir N Br Housing Assoc Ltd 1973–74, dep dir of housing Nottingham City Cncl 1974–76, chief exec Home Housing Assoc 1976–; memb Inquiry into Br Housing; pres Inst of Housing 1982–83 (fell 1972); *Recreations* sport: assoc football, rugby football, cricket, golf; theatre and music; *Clubs* Lansdowne; *Style*— Alan Kilburn, Esq, OBE; ✉ Home Housing Association, Ridley House, Regent Centre, Gosforth, Newcastle-upon-Tyne NE3 3JE (☎ 0191 285 0311, fax 0191 284 0634)

KILBY, Michael Leopold; s of Guy Kilby (d 1972), and Grace Kilby; *b* 3 Sept 1924; *Educ* Coll of Technol; *m* 21 March 1952, Mary, da of Eric Sanders (d 1981); 3 s (Guy, Marcus, Robert); *Career* General Motors Corporation: head of Euro planning, govt and trade relations 1972–79, mktg and serv mangr Euro sales, plant mangr 1966–71; MEP (C) Nottingham 1984–89; author; *Novels incl* Man at the Sharp End, Mammon's Ladder; *Recreations* cricket; *Clubs* Beds CC, Dunstable Town CC, Luton CC; *Style*— Michael Kilby, Esq; ✉ Grange Barn, Haversham Village, Milton Keynes, Bucks MK19 7DX (☎ 01908 313613)

KILDARE, Marquess of; Maurice FitzGerald; s and h of 8 Duke of Leinster by his 2 w, Anne, *née* Smith; *b* 7 April 1948; *Educ* Millfield; *m* 1972, Fiona Mary Francesca, da of late Harry Hollick, of Sutton Courtenay, Abingdon; 1 s, 2 da (Lady Francesca b 6 July 1976, Lady Pollyanna b 9 May 1982); *Heir* s, Earl of Offaly b 12 Jan 1974; *Career* landscape gardener and designer Maxwell Communication Corporation plc Headington Oxon 1984–92; pres Oxfordshire Dyslexia Assoc 1978–; *Recreations* shooting, fishing, riding, squash, sailing; *Style*— Marquess of Kildare; ✉ Courtyard House, Oakley Park, Frilford Heath, Oxon OX13 6QW

KILFOYLE, Peter; MP (Lab) Liverpool Walton (majority 28,299); s of Edward Kilfoyle, and Ellen Kilfoyle; *b* 9 June 1946; *Educ* St Edward's Coll Liverpool, Univ of Durham, Christ's Coll Liverpool; *m* 27 July 1968, Bernadette, *née* Slater; 2 s, 3 da; *Career* building labourer 1965–70 and 1973–75, student 1970–73, teacher 1975–85, Lab Pty organiser 1985–91, MP (Lab) Liverpool Walton July 1991–; *Recreations* reading, music, spectator sports; *Style*— Peter Kilfoyle, Esq, MP; ✉ House of Commons, London SW1A 0AA

KILGOUR, Dr John Lowell; CB (1987); s of Ormonde John Lowell Kilgour (d 1946), of Aberdeen, Scot, and Catherine, *née* MacInnes (d 1925); *b* 26 July 1924; *Educ* St Christopher's Hove Sussex, Aberdeen GS, Univ of Aberdeen (MB ChB); *m* 24 Oct 1955, Daphne, da of Walter Tully (d 1958), of Otterburn, Northumberland; 2 s (Alastair Hugh

Lowell, Simon Walter Lowell); *Career* Lt RAMC 1947–48, Capt RAMC 1948–50; Maj: 26 Field Ambulance Korea 1950–52, Depot and Trg Estab RAMC 1953–54; Lt-Col CO 23 Parachute Field Ambulance 1954–57 (served Suez, Cyprus), registrar Queen Alexandra Mil Hosp 1957–59, Gen Staff Coll Camberley 1959–60, DADG WO 1960–61, ADMS GHQ FARELF (Singapore, Brunei) 1961–64, JSSC 1964–65, Cmdt RAMC Field Trg Sch 1965–66; gen mangr WF Schlesinger 1966–68; joined Med Civil Serv 1968, med offr in med manpower postgrad med educn implementation of Todd Report, sr med offr 1970–71, princ med offr head of Int Health Div DHSS 1971–73, chief med advsr and under sec Miny of Overseas Devpt 1973–78, seconded dir of coordination (D2) WHO Geneva until 1983, dir and under sec Prison Med Serv Home Office 1983–89, chm science Recruitment Advsy Service 1989–91 and Industrial Accident Med Bds, assessor for Dept of Social Servs and various commercial consultancies 1989–94, private conslt and occupational health assessor 1994–; ldr of UK delgns to WHO and Cncl of Euro Public Health Ctees 1971–78 (chm 1976); chm: Ctee for Surveillance of Communicable Diseases WHO 1976, EPHC 1976; govr London Sch of Tropical Med and Hygiene 1973–89 (visiting lectr 1973–89); memb: UN Advsy Ctee on Coordination 1978–83, Exec Ctee Royal Cwlth Soc of the Blind 1983–89, Cncl Liverpool Sch of Tropical Med 1973–87; Cons Speaking Prize (London and SE) 1967, Cantacuzino Medal for servs to int health (Bucharest) 1981; MRCGP 1961, FFCM 1974, FFPHM 1989; *Books* Medical Migration (1971), Global Impact of AIDS (1988), plus numerous contributions to med and general publications; *Clubs* Athenaeum, Hurlingham, Royal Windsor Racing; *Style*— Dr John L Kilgour, CB; ✉ Stoke House, 22 Amersham Road, Chesham Bois, Bucks HP6 5PE (☎ and fax 01494 726100)

KILKENNY, Bernard Crook; s of William Kilkenny (d 1985), of Branksome Park, Poole, Dorset, and Lilian, *née* Crook; *b* 6 Sept 1928; *Educ* Beaumont Coll, New Coll Oxford (BA, BSc, DPhil, MA); *m* 1 Feb 1958 (m dis 1985; re-m 27 April 1991), Victoria Patricia Ann, da of Thomas William Howard, of Northwood, Middx; 2 s (Charles b 1965, Neville b 1966), 2 da (Elizabeth b 1959, Caroline b 1961); *Career* RHA 1952–54, HAC 1954–62; dir: Allied Breweries 1969–78 (jt md (UK) Ltd 1973–88, dep chm (UK) Ltd, chm (UK) Ltd & subsid Cos 1975–78); dir Scottish & Newcastle Breweries plc 1978–88, ret; former chm: Thistle Hotels, William Younger & Co, Home Brewery, Waverley Vintners Ltd; dir Invergordon Distillers Group plc 1989–93; chm: Innsite International Ltd 1990–92, National Leisure Catering Ltd 1993–94; Hon Asst Worshipful Co of Brewers (former Master); *Recreations* golf, sailing, skiing, shooting, bridge; *Clubs* Royal Thames Yacht, Moor Park Golf, Hon Co of Edinburgh Golfers, New (Edinburgh); *Style*— Bernard Kilkenny, Esq; ✉ Cleeve House, Mill Road, Goring-on-Thames, Oxon RG8 9DD (☎ 01491 875842)

KILL, Michael John; s of Edwin Charles Kill, and Margaret Jean, *née* Biddlecombe; *b* 12 March 1953; *Educ* Price's Sch Fareham, Pembroke Coll Oxford (MA PPE); *m* (m dis); *Career* Barclays Bank plc: Mgmnt Devpt Prog 1974–79, instructor Training Sch 1980, mangr 54 Lombard Street branch 1980–84, mangr Cost Control Unit 1984–86, asst to Gen Mangr 1986–87, head of planning 1987–88, head of UK planning 1988–89, sr mangr UK ops review 1989–90, head of network planning 1990–91, business sector mktg dir 1991–; ACIB 1977; *Recreations* golf, opera; *Style*— Michael Kill, Esq; ✉ Barclays Bank plc, PO Box 120, Longwood Close, Westwood Business Park, Coventry CV4 8JN (☎ 01203 532440)

KILLALA, Neal John Patrick; s of Ernest Killala (d 1978), and Joan Lambert, *née* Evans; *b* 20 Jan 1945; *Educ* Dulwich, St John's Coll Cambridge (MA, MB BChir); *m* 3 Feb 1973, Jennifer Ann, da of Norman Francis Lee (d 1986); 2 s (Stewart b 18 March 1975, James b 13 Aug 1986), 5 da (Anne b 1 June 1978, Helen b 3 Feb 1980, Lucy b 17 Nov 1981, Janet b 26 June 1984, Fiona b 13 Aug 1986); *Career* psychiatric registrar: Belmont Hosp Surrey 1974–76, Maudsley Hosp London 1978–80; sr registrar N Middlesex Hosp 1981–, conslt psychiatrist Runwell Hosp Essex 1981–, conslt Anorexia and Bulimia Care; hon conslt psychiatrist St Luke's Hosp for the Clergy; med dir Southend Drug and Alcohol Advsy and Treatment Serv; memb: BMA, N Thames Regnl Conslts and Hosp Specialists Ctee, N Thames Regnl Psychiatric Advsy Ctee, Mgmnt Ctee Fair Havens Christian Hospice Southend-on-Sea, Mgmnt Ctee Greenwoods Therapeutic Community Stock, West Ham Central Mission, Mgmnt Ctee Alcohol & Drugs Advsy Service Harlow (also tstee), Soc for Study of Addiction, Med Cncl on Alcoholism, New Directions in the Study of Alcohol Gp, Mgmnt Ctee Essex Christian Healing Tst, Acorn Apostolate, Assoc of Christian Psychiatrists; DCH 1973, DObstRCOG 1973, DPM 1975, MRCPsych 1978; *Recreations* reading, music, walking, swimming; *Style*— Neal J P Killala, Esq; ✉ 16 Drake Rd, Westcliff-on-Sea, Essex SS0 8LP (☎ 01702 354819); Roche Unit, Union Lane, Rochford, Essex SS4 1RB (☎ 01702 541100, fax 01702 541931)

KILLANIN, 3 Baron (UK 1900); Sir Michael Morris; 3 Bt (UK 1885); MBE (Mil, 1944), TD (1945); s of Lt-Col Hon George Morris, Irish Gds (ka 1914, yr bro of 2 Baron) by his w Dora Wesley Hall; gs of 1 Baron, formerly Lord Chief Justice of Ireland and later Lord of Appeal in Ordinary; suc unc 1927; *b* 30 July 1914; *Educ* Eton, Sorbonne, Magdalene Coll Cambridge (MA, pres Cambridge Univ Footlights Dramatic Club and literary ed Varsity Weekly); *m* 1945, Mary Sheila, MBE, da of late Rev Canon Douglas Dunlop, of Co Galway; 3 s, 1 da; *Heir* s, Hon Redmond Morris; *Career* journalist Daily Express then Daily Mail 1935–38 (reported on Chinese/Japanese War 1937, latterly asst political and diplomatic corr Daily Mail and political columnist Sunday Dispatch); served WWII KRRC, Bde Maj 30 Armd Bde (Normandy Landing 1944); former dir: Irish Shell Ltd, Beamish & Crawford Ltd, Ulster Bank Ltd, Aspro Nicholas of Ireland Ltd; former chm: Northern Telecom (Ireland) Ltd, Gallaher (Dublin) Ltd, Chubb Ireland Ltd, Hibernian Life Assoc Ltd, Ulster Investmt Bank Ltd, Lombard & Ulster Banking Ireland Ltd, Northern Telecom (Ireland) Ltd, Bovril (Ireland) Ltd, Fitzwilton Ltd, Four Provinces Films Ltd; pres: Galway C of C 1952–53, Incorporated Sales Managers Assoc Ireland (now Mktg Inst of Ireland) 1955–56; memb: Cultural Relations Ctee 1947–72, Nat Monuments Advsy Cncl 1947–80 (chm 1961–65), Irish Sailors and Soldiers Land Tst 1947–, Cncl Irish Red Cross Soc 1947–72 (hon sec 1952–68 and 1973), Ctee of Mgmnt RNLI 1959–89 (memb Exec Ctee 1970–84, vice pres 1972, life vice pres 1989); fndr memb An Taisce (Nat Tst for Ireland) 1950, chm Nat Heritage Cncl 1988–; pres Olympic Cncl of Ireland 1950–73 (hon life pres 1981); Int Olympic Ctee: memb 1952, memb Exec Bd 1967, vice pres 1968, pres 1972–80, hon life pres 1980; memb: Galway Race Ctee 1947 (chm 1969–85), Irish Nat Hunt Steeplechase Ctee 1966, Irish Sports Cncl 1970–72, Irish Turf Club 1971– (steward 1973–75 and 1981–83); chm Irish Govt Cmmn on Thoroughbred Breeding and Racing 1982–85; hon consul gen for the Principality of Monaco in Ireland 1961–84; chm Dublin Theatre Festival 1958–70 (patron 1971); associated with prodn of film The Quiet Man (with John Ford) 1952, subsequently produced various films incl The Rising of the Moon, The Playboy of the Western World and Gideon's Day, associated with prodn of Young Cassiday and Alfred the Great; memb: Irish Govt Cmmn on Film Indust 1957, John Huston's Cmmn on the Film Indust 1968; Hon LLD Nat Univ of Ireland 1975, Hon DLitt New Univ of Ulster 1977; Chubb fell Yale 1981; decorations include: Knight of Honour and Devotion SMOM 1943, Medal Miroslav Tyrs (Czech) 1970, Cdr Grand Cross (FDR) 1972, Star of Sacred Treasure (2 class, Japan) 1972, Grand Offr Order of Merit (Italy) 1973, Knight Grand Cross Order of Civil Merit (Spain) 1976, Grand Offr Order of Republic (Tunisia) 1976, Grand Offr Order of Phoenix (Greece) 1976, Order of Madara Rider (Bulgaria), Cdr Legion of Honour (France) 1980, Order of Merit with Flag (Yugoslavia) 1984; Olympic Order of Merit (Gold) 1980; memb: Royal Irish Academy 1952, French Acad of Sports 1974; hon life memb: Royal Dublin Soc 1981, NUJ, ACTT, Chambers of Commerce of Ireland, Mktg Inst of Ireland; fell Irish Mgmnt Inst, FRSA, FSA Ireland; *Books* Four Days (ed and contrib, 1938), Sir Godfrey Kneller (1947), The Shell Guide to Ireland (with Prof Michael Duignan, 1962), The Olympic Games (with John Rodda, 1975), The Olympic Games - Moscow - Lake Placid (with John Rodda, 1979), The Olympic Games 1984 (with John Rodda, 1983), My Olympic Years (autobiography, 1983), Lord Killanin - Olympic Speeches 1970–1981 (1984), My Ireland (1987); *Clubs* Garrick, County (Galway), Stephen's Green (Dublin); *Style*— The Rt Hon the Lord Killanin, MBE, TD; ✉ 9 Lower Mount Pleasant Ave, Dublin 6; St Annins, Spiddal, Co Galway

KILLEARN, 3 Baron (UK 1943); Sir Victor Miles George Aldous Lampson; 4 Bt (UK 1866); s of 1 Baron Killearn, GCMG, CB, MVO, PC (d 1964), by his 2 w Jacqueline Aldine Leslie, da of late Marchese Senator Aldo Castellani, KCMG; suc half-bro, 2 Baron Killearn (d 1996); *b* 9 Sept 1941; *Educ* Eton; *m* 1971, Melita Amaryllis Pamela Astrid, da of Rear Adm Sir Morgan Charles Morgan-Giles, DSO, OBE, GM, DL, lately MP Winchester; 2 s (Hon Miles Henry Morgan b 1977, Hon Alexander Victor William b 1984), 2 da (Hon Pamela Camilla Roxana b 1973, Hon Miranda Penelope Amber b 1975); *Heir* s, Hon Miles Henry Morgan Lampson b 10 Dec 1977; *Career* late Capt Scots Gds; ptnr Cazenove & Co 1979–; *Clubs* White's, Pratt's, City of London; *Style*— The Rt Hon Lord Killearn

KILLICK, Elizabeth Audrey; da of George Wellstead Killick (d 1976), of Rhodes Minnis, Kent, and Winifred Rose, *née* Baines (d 1941); *b* 10 Sept 1924; *Educ* Streatham Hill HS, Altrincham Co HS, Univ of St Andrews (BSc, DSc); *Career* radar mechanic LACW WAAF 1943–46, lab asst RAF Inst of Aviation Med 1947, res and devpt Admiralty Signal and Radar Estab 1951–69, Admty Underwater Weapons Estab 1969–84 (head Submarine Sonar Systems Div 1969–75, head Weapons Dept 1975–84); memb Bd Marine Technology Directorate Ltd 1986–92; FIEE 1980, FEng 1982; *Recreations* gardening, skiing, local history; *Style*— Miss Elizabeth Killick, FEng

KILLICK, Sir John Edward; GCMG (1979, KCMG 1971, CMG 1966); s of Edward William James Killick (d 1972); *b* 18 Nov 1919; *Educ* Latymer Upper Sch, UCL (fell), Univ of Bonn; *m* 1, 1949, Lynette du Preez, da of William Oxenham Leach (d 1984); m 2, 1985, Irene Monica Harries, OBE (d 1995), da of Malcolm Henry Easton; *Career* WWII Capt (Army) W Africa and W Europe; Dip Serv 1946–; asst under sec of state 1968–71, ambass USSR 1971–73, dep under sec of state 1973–75, ambass and perm UK rep to NATO 1975–79, ret; dir Dunlop SA 1980–85; pres Br Atlantic Ctee 1985–92, vice pres Atlantic Treaty Assoc 1992–94; chm Southborough Soc 1990–94; *Recreations* golf; *Clubs* Garrick, East India Devonshire, Sports and Public Schs; *Style*— Sir John Killick, GCMG; ✉ Challoner's Cottage, 2 Birchwood Ave, Southborough, Kent TN4 0UE

KILLICK, Dr Stephen Robert; s of Herbert Percy Killick, of Poulton-le-Fylde, Lancs, and Lois Margaret, *née* Richardson (d 1985); *b* 30 Dec 1952; *Educ* Univ of London Guy's Hosp Med Sch (BSc, MB BS, MD); *m* 25 May 1985, Diane, da of George Hall Billings (d 1980); 2 da (Georgina b 15 Oct 1987, Harriet b 10 Nov 1990); *Career* SE England jr hosp doctor 1976–79, surgical registrar Soweto SA 1979–80, SE England jr hosp doctor qualifying in gynaecology 1980–82, res fell Univ of Manchester 1982–87, conslt obstetrician and gynaecologist and sr lectr Univ of Manchester 1987–92, currently prof of reproductive med and surgery Univ of Hull; numerous articles in med pubns; pres Withington Hosp Obstetric Fund; FRCOG; *Recreations* rugby, badminton, gardening; *Style*— Prof Stephen Killick; ✉ Department of Obstetrics and Gynaecology, University of Hull, Hull HU6 7RX (☎ 01482 676647, fax 01482 676646)

KILMAINE, 7 Baron (I 1789); Sir John David Henry Browne; 13 Bt (NS 1636); s of 6 Baron Kilmaine, CBE (d 1978); *b* 2 April 1948; *Educ* Eton; *m* 1982, Linda, yr da of Dennis Robinson; 1 s, 1 da (Alice b 1985); *Heir* s, Hon John Francis Sandford Browne b 4 April 1983; *Career* dir: Fusion (Bickenhill) Ltd 1969–, Whale Tankers Ltd 1974–; *Style*— The Rt Hon the Lord Kilmaine

KILMARNOCK, 7 Baron (UK 1831); Alastair Ivor Gilbert Boyd; s of 6 Baron Kilmarnock, MBE, TD (d 1975), and Hon Rosemary Guest (d 1971), da of 1 Viscount Wimborne. Lord Kilmarnock's f (6 Baron) changed his family name from Hay to Boyd 1941, having succeeded his bro, the 22 Earl of Erroll (in the UK Barony only) the same year; 5 in descent from the 18 Earl of Erroll cr 1 Baron Kilmarnock who m (1820) Elizabeth FitzClarence, a natural da of William IV by the actress Mrs Jordan; *b* 11 May 1927; *Educ* Bradfield, King's Coll Cambridge; *m* 1, 1954 (m dis 1969), Diana Mary (d 1975), da of D Grant Gibson; m 2, 1977, Hilary Ann, da of Leonard Sidney Bardwell; 1 s (James Charles Edward Boyd b 27 Jan 1972); *Heir* bro, Hon Robin Jordan Boyd; *Career* Lt Irish Gds, serv Palestine 1947–48; joined SDP 1981, chief SDP whip in House of Lords 1983–86, dep ldr SDP peers 1986–87, chm All-Pty Parly Gp on AIDS 1986–96, tstee AIDS Awareness Tst 1991–, gen sec Euro Public Health Fndn 1994–; co sec and ed conslt Social Market Fndn; chief of Clan Boyd, page to Lord High Constable of Scotland at Coronation of HM King George VI; *Books* Sabbatical Year (1958), The Road from Ronda (1969), The Companion Guide to Madrid and Central Spain (1974), The Essence of Catalonia (1988), The Sierras of the South (1992); *Clubs* Pratt's; *Style*— The Lord Kilmarnock; ✉ House of Lords, London SW1 0PW

KILMISTER, (Claude Alaric) Anthony; s of Dr Claude Emile Kilmister (d 1951), of Swansea, and Margaret E Mogford, *née* Gee; *b* 22 July 1931; *Educ* Shrewsbury; *m* 24 May 1958, Sheila, da of Lawrence Harwood (d 1984), of Hyde, Cheshire; *Career* Nat Serv 1950–52, cmmnd Army; with NCB 1952–54, Cons Pty Orgn 1954–60; gen sec Cinema and TV Benevolent Fund 1962–72 (asst sec 1960–61), exec dir Parkinson's Disease Soc 1972–91, fndr memb Ctee Action for Neurological Diseases 1987–91, fndr Prostate Research Campaign UK 1994–; memb: Exec Ctee Anglican Assoc 1976–, Int Cncl for the Apostolic Faith 1987–93; chm of Prayer Book Soc 1989– (fndr memb and dep chm incl BCP Action Gp (its forerunner) 1972–89), memb Standing Ctee Assoc for the Apostolic Ministry 1989–96; *Books* The Good Church Guide (1982), When Will Ye be Wise? (1983), My Favourite Betjeman (1985); *Recreations* writing, walking; *Clubs* Athenaeum; *Style*— Anthony Kilmister, Esq; ✉ 36 The Drive, Northwood, Middx HA6 1HP (☎ 01923 824278)

KILMORE, Bishop of (RC) 1972–; Most Rev Francis Joseph MacKiernan; s of Joseph MacKiernan (d 1970), of Stradrinan, Ballinamore, Co Leitrim, and Ellen, *née* MacTague (d 1949); *b* 3 Feb 1926; *Educ* St Patrick's Coll Cavan, St Patrick's Coll Maynooth, UC Dublin (BA, BD, Higher Dip in Educn); *Career* St Malachy's Coll Belfast 1951–52, St Patrick's Coll Cavan 1952–62, pres St Felim's Coll Ballinamore 1962–72; *Books* Diocese of Kilmore Bishops and Priests 1136–1988 (1989); *Recreations* local history; *Style*— The Most Rev the Bishop of Kilmore; ✉ Bishop's House, Cullies, Cavan, Republic of Ireland (☎ 00 353 49 31496)

KILMORE, ELPHIN AND ARDAGH, Bishop of 1993–; Rt Rev Michael Hugh Gunton Mayes; s of Thomas David Dougan Mayes (d 1983), and Hilary, *née* Gunton (d 1986); *b* 31 Aug 1941; *Educ* The Royal Sch Armagh, Trinity Coll Dublin (BA), Univ of London (BD); *m* 1966, Elizabeth Annie Eleanor, da of James Irwin; 1 s (Patrick Dougan James b 18 Nov 1967), 2 da (Soren Elizabeth Hilary b 15 June 1969, Natalya Vivienne Ann b 6 April 1974); *Career* ordained: deacon 1964, priest 1965; asst curate: St Mark's Portadown 1964–67, St Columba's Portadown 1967–68; USPG Missionary Japan 1968–74, USPG area sec Ireland 1974–75, incumbent St Michael's Union Cork 1975–86, archdeacon of Cork Cloyne and Ross 1986–93; incumbent: Moviddy Union Cork 1986–88, Rathcooney Union Cork 1988–93; warden of lay readers Cork Cloyne and Ross 1986–93, co-ordinator aux miny trg Church of Ireland 1989–; *Recreations* music, photography, reading, golf, walking; *Style*— The Rt Rev the Bishop of Kilmore, Elphin and Ardagh; ✉ The See House, Kilmore, Co Cavan, Ireland (☎ 00 353 49 31336, fax 00 353 49 62829)

KILNER, John Stephen; s of Stephen Roy Kilner, and Sheila Mary, *née* West; *b* 4 Feb 1952; *Educ* Rugby, Gonville & Caius Coll Cambridge (MA); *m* 13 Oct 1979, Mary Josephine, *née* Crowley; 1 s (James b 1984), 5 da (Eleanor b 1982, Sarah b 1987, Olivia b 1989, Diana b 1991, Isabelle b 1993); *Career* slr; articled clerk Stephenson Harwood & Tatham 1974–76, ptnr Linklaters & Paines 1985– (slr 1976–85); *Style*— John Kilner, Esq; ✉ Linklaters & Paines, Barrington House, 59–67 Gresham Street, London EC2V 7JA (☎ 0171 606 7080, fax 0171 606 5113)

KILPATRICK OF KINCRAIG, Baron (Life Peer UK 1996), of Dysart in the District of Kirkcaldy; Sir Robert Kilpatrick; kt (1986), CBE (1979); s of Robert Kilpatrick (d 1974), of Coaltown of Wemyss, Fife, and Catherine Sharp, *née* Glover (d 1944); *b* 29 July 1926; *Educ* Buckhaven HS, Univ of Edinburgh (MB ChB, MD); *m* 28 Oct 1950, Elizabeth Gibson Page, da of Alexander Sharp Forbes, of Smeeton Westerby, Leics; 2 s (Hon Neil b 25 March 1956, Hon John b 28 May 1959), 1 da (Hon Katherine b 9 Aug 1951); *Career* Univ of Sheffield: lectr 1955–56, prof of clinical pharmacology and therapeutics 1966–75, dean Faculty of Med 1970–73; Univ of Leicester: dean Faculty of Med 1975–89, prof and head Dept of Clinical Pharmacology and Therapeutics 1975–83, prof of med 1984–89; pres GMC 1989–95; Hon DUniv Edinburgh 1987, Hon LLD Dundee 1992, Hon DSc Univ of Hull 1994, Hon DSc Univ of Leicester 1994, Hon LLD Univ of Sheffield 1995; Hon FRCS 1995, Hon FRCP(Dublin) 1995, Hon FRCSEd 1996; FRCPE 1963, FRCP 1975, FRCP(Glas) 1991; memb Physiological Soc 1960; *Recreations* idling; *Clubs* Reform, Royal and Ancient; *Style*— The Rt Hon Lord Kilpatrick of Kincraig, CBE; ✉ 12 Wester Coates Gardens, Edinburgh EH12 5LT (☎ 0131 337 7304)

KILROY, Thomas; s of Thomas Kilroy, of Callan, Co Kilkenny, Ireland, and Mary, *née* Devine; *b* 23 Sept 1934; *Educ* St Kieran's Coll Kilkenny, Univ Coll Dublin; *m* 1, 1963 (m dis 1980), Patricia, *née* Cobey; 3 s; m 2, 1981, Julia Lowell, *née* Carlson; 1 da; *Career* writer; lectr in Eng Univ Coll Dublin 1965–73, prof of modern Eng Univ Coll Galway 1979–89; Guardian Fiction Prize 1971, short listed for Booker Prize 1971, Heinneman Award for Literature 1972, AIB Literary Prize 1972, American-Irish Fndn Award 1975; memb: AOSDANA, Irish Acad of Letters; FRSL; *Novels* The Big Chapel 1971; *Plays* The Death and Resurrection of Mr Roche 1968, Tea and Sex and Shakespeare 1976, Talbot's Box 1977, Double Cross 1986, The Madame MacAdam Travelling Theatre 1991, Gold in the Streets 1993, The Secret Fall of Constance Wilde 1997; *Adaptations* The Seagull 1981, Ghosts 1989, Six Characters in Search of An Author; *Style*— Thomas Kilroy, Esq, FRSL; ✉ Kilmaine, County Mayo, Ireland (☎ 00 353 93 33361); Casarotto Ramsay Ltd, 60–66 Wardour Street, London W1V 3HP (☎ 0171 287 4450, fax 0171 287 9128)

KILROY-SILK, Robert; s of William Silk (d 1943); *b* 19 May 1942; *Educ* Secdy Modern Sch, Sparkhill Commercial Sch, Saltley GS, LSE; *m* 1963, Jan, da of William Beech; 1 s, 1 da; *Career* lectr Univ of Liverpool 1966–74, govr Nat Heart and Chest Hosp 1974–77; MP (Lab): Ormskirk Feb 1974–83, Knowsley North 1983–86; PPS to Min of Arts 1975–76, memb Select Ctee on Race Relations and on Wealth Tax 1974–75, vice chm PLP Home Affrs Gp 1976–79, chm PLP Civil Liberties Gp 1979–84, chm Parly Penal Affrs Gp 1979–86, memb Select Ctee Home Affrs 1979–84, chm PLP Home Affrs Gp 1983–84, frontbench spokesman Home Affrs 1984–86; TV presenter Kilroy! 1986–; columnist: The Times 1987–90, The Daily Express 1990–96; chm The Kilroy Television Co 1989–; *Publications* Socialism since Marx (1973), The Ceremony of Innocence (novel, 1984), Hard Labour: The Political Diary of Robert Kilroy-Silk (1986); *Recreations* gardening; *Style*— Robert Kilroy-Silk, Esq; ✉ Kilroy Television Company, Teddington Studios, Teddington Lock, Middx TW11 9NT (☎ 0181 614 2866)

KILSHAW, David Andrew George; s of George Arthur Kilshaw (d 1963), and Margaret Annie, *née* Bridgwater (d 1991); *b* 18 March 1953; *Educ* Keil Sch Dumbarton; *m* 17 June 1976, Judith Margaret, da of John Sydney Milner; 3 s (Ross David b 26 May 1980, Craig John b 18 Feb 1982, Iain George b 21 Oct 1985); *Career* qualified asst Messrs Brunton Miller, Alexander & Martin Slrs Glasgow 1979–80 (legal apprenticeship 1974–79), slr Borders Regnl Cncl 1980–82, NP 1982, ptnr Messrs Cullen Kilshaw Slrs Galashiels and Melrose 1982–; chm Borders Health Bd 1993– (non-exec memb 1991–93); children's panel safeguarder Borders Regnl Cncl 1987–; memb: Law Soc of Scotland 1979; *Recreations* dir of rugby Peebles Rugby FC, golf, fishing, listening to music; *Style*— David Kilshaw, Esq; ✉ Cullen Kilshaw, Solicitors and Estate Agents, 27 Market Street, Galashiels TD1 3AF (☎ 01896 758311, fax 01896 758112)

KIMBALL, Baron (Life Peer UK 1985), of Easton, Co Leics; Marcus Richard Kimball; kt (1981), DL (Leics 1984); s of late Maj Lawrence Kimball, JP, DL, sometime MP Loughborough, by his 1 w, Kathleen Joan, only surviving da of Richard Ratcliff, of Stanford Hall, Loughborough, by his w Christine, 3 da of Vaughan Hanning Vaughan-Lee, JP, DL, sometime MP W Somerset; *b* 18 Oct 1928; *Educ* Eton, Trinity Coll Cambridge; *m* 1956, June Mary, only da of Montagu John Fenwick (whose mother Millicent was da of Rt Hon Lord Robert Montagu, 2 s of 6 Duke of Manchester), of Great Stukeley Hall, Huntingdon; 2 da (Hon Mrs Gibbs, Hon Mrs Straker); *Career* Lt Leics Yeo (TA) 1947, Capt 1952, Maj 1955; MP (C) Gainsborough Div of Lincs 1956–83, CC Rutland 1955–63, PC rep Cncl of RCVS 1969–82 (Hon ARCVS 1982); external memb Cncl Lloyd's 1982–91; chm: South East Assured Tenancies 1988–96, Fire Arms Consultative Ctee 1989–94, Univ of Cambridge Vet Sch Tst 1989–, British Greyhound Racing Fund Ltd 1993–96; pres: Hunters Improvement Soc 1989, Olympia Int Show Jumping Championships 1991–, British Inst of Innkeeping 1992–, Br Field Sports Soc 1995– (chm 1966–82); *Recreations* fox hunting, past jt master of FitzWilliam and Cottesmore; *Clubs* White's, Pratt's; *Style*— The Rt Hon the Lord Kimball, DL; ✉ Great Easton Manor, Great Easton, Market Harborough, Leics LE16 8TB (☎ 01536 770333)

KIMBER, Sir Charles Dixon; 3 Bt (UK 1904), of Lansdowne Lodge, Wandsworth, Co London; s of Sir Henry Dixon Kimber, 2 Bt (d 1950); *b* 7 Jan 1912; *Educ* Eton, Balliol Coll Oxford (BA 1933); *m* 1, 1933 (m dis 1950), Ursula (d 1981), da of late Ernest Roy Bird, MP; 3 s (Timothy Roy Henry b 1936, Nicholas John b 1937, Robert b 1941); m 2, 1950 (m dis 1965), Margaret, o da of late Francis John Bonham, of Wimbledon; 1 da (Rhys Catherine (Mrs Michael Fox) b 1951); *Heir* s, Timothy Roy Henry Kimber, *qv*; *Style*— Sir Charles Kimber, Bt; ✉ No 2 Duxford, Hinton Waldrist, nr Faringdon, Oxon SN7 8SQ (☎ 01865 820004)

KIMBER, Timothy Roy Henry; s and h of Sir Charles Dixon Kimber, 3 Bt, *qv*; *b* 3 June 1936; *Educ* Eton; *m* 1, 1960 (m dis 1974), Antonia Kathleen Brenda, da of late Sir Francis John Watkin Williams, 8 Bt, QC; 2 s (Rupert Edward Watkin b 1962, Hugo Charles b 1964); m 2, 1979, Susan Hare, da of late J K Brooks, and widow of Richard Coulthurst North, of Newton Hall, Lancs; *Career* Nat Serv Midshipman/Sub Lt 2 Submarine Sqdn 1955–57; banker; dir Lazard Bros & Co Ltd, ret 1990; currently dir: Adam & Co Investment Management, Noble Group, Invesco Japan Discovery Trust plc, Border Asset Management, Cumberland Building Society, Jardine Fleming India Asset Management Ltd, Jardine Fleming India Fund Inc; currently chm: Martin Currie Pacific Trust plc, Exeter Preferred Capital Investment Trust plc, Dartmoor Investment Trust plc, Taiwan Opportunites Fund Ltd; currently dep chm NZ Investment Tst plc; dep treas Univ of Lancaster 1995–96; High Sheriff of Lancashire 1996–97; *Clubs* Boodle's, Royal Lytham St Anne's Golf; *Style*— Timothy Kimber, Esq; ✉ Newton Hall, via Carnforth, Lancashire LA6 2NZ (☎ 015242 71232, fax 015242 71552, work 015242 72146 or 72941)

KIMBERLEY, 4 Earl of (UK 1866); Sir John Wodehouse; 11 Bt (estab 1611); also 6 Baron Wodehouse (GB 1797); s of 3 Earl of Kimberley, CBE, MC (d 1941), and Frances Margaret Irby, niece of Lord Boston; *b* 12 May 1924; *Educ* Eton, Magdalene Coll Cambridge; *m* 1, 1945 (m dis 1948), Diana Evelyn, da of late Lt-Col the Hon Sir Piers Walter Legh, GCVO, KCB, CMG, CIE, OBE (yr s of 2 Baron Newton); m 2, 1949 (m dis 1952), Carmel June (Dunnett) (d 1992), da of late Michael Maguire, of Melbourne, Aust; 1 s; m 3, 1953 (m dis 1960), Mrs Cynthia Abdy Westendarp, da of E Abdy Collins, FRCS, MRCP, of Saxmundham, Suffolk; 2 s; m 4, 1961 (m dis 1965), Margaret, da of Alby Simons; 1 s; m 5, 1970 (m dis 1982), Gillian, da of Col Norman Ireland-Smith, and formerly w of John Raw; m 6, 1982, Jane, da of Lt-Col Christopher d'A P Consett, DSO, MC, of N Riding, Yorks; *Heir* Lord Wodehouse b 1951, *qv*; *Career* served as Lt Gren Gds in Gds Armd Div 1943–45; Br Bobsleigh Team 1950–58, Cresta rider 1948–58; former Lib spokesman on aviation & aerospace, defence and voluntary community servs; expelled from Lib Pty May 1979, has since sat as Cons Peer in House of Lords; delegate to N Atlantic Assembly 1981–93, pres House of Lords All Pty Defence Study Gp 1992– (hon sec 1978–92); memb: Air League Cncl 1981–95, Assoc of Cons Peers, Br Maritime League Cncl, Royal Utd Services Inst, Int Inst for Strategic Studies, Br Atlantic Ctee; vice pres World Cncl on Alcoholism, chm National Cncl on Alcoholism 1982–85; chm J & P Security Services Ltd 1993–; ARAeS; *Recreations* fishing, shooting, racing, gardening, bridge; *Clubs* White's, MCC, Naval and Military, House of Lords Yacht, House of Lords Fly Fishing, Falmouth Shark Angling (pres); *Style*— The Rt Hon the Earl of Kimberley; ✉ Hailstone House, Cricklade, Wilts SN6 6JP (☎ 01793 750344, fax 01793 752078)

KIMMINS, Malcolm Brian Johnston; s of Lt-Gen Sir Brian Charles Hannam Kimmins, KBE, CB, DL (d 1979), and Marjory, *née* Johnston (d 1992); *b* 12 Feb 1937; *Educ* Harrow, Grenoble Univ; *m* 1968, Jane, da of Thomas Douglas Pilkington; 1 s, 2 da; *Career* chm Corney & Barrow Group plc; tstee The Ascot Authy; Liveryman Worshipful Co of Distillers; *Recreations* horse racing, golf, shooting; *Clubs* White's, Jockey; *Style*— Malcolm Kimmins, Esq; ✉ Corney & Barrow Group plc, 12 Helmet Row, London EC1V 3QJ (☎ 0171 251 4051, fax 0171 608 1373)

KINAHAN, Sir (Robert George Caldwell) Robin; kt (1961), ERD (1946), JP (1950); s of Henry Kinahan (d 1958); *b* 24 Sept 1916; *Educ* Stowe; *m* 1950, Coralie Isabel, da of Capt Charles de Burgh, DSO, RN (d 1968); 2 s, 3 da; *Career* Capt RA 1939–45, served France and Far East; cncllr and alderman Belfast Corpn 1949–64; High Sheriff: Belfast 1955, Co Antrim 1969; MP (NI) Clifton 1958–59, Lord Mayor of Belfast 1959–61; dir: Gallaher Ltd 1967–81, National Westminster Bank 1973–83, Eagle Star Insurance Co (local) until 1981, STC (NI) Ltd, Abbey Life (Ireland) Ltd 1981–87; chm: Bass Ireland Ltd 1958–78, Inglis & Co Ltd 1962–82, E T Green Ltd 1964–82, Ulster Bank Ltd 1970–82 (dep chm 1964–70), Abbeyfield Belfast Soc 1983–, Cheshire House (NI) 1983–91; Lord Lt Co Borough of Belfast 1985–91 (DL 1962); Liveryman Worshipful Co of Vintners; Hon LLD Queen's Univ Belfast 1961; *Recreations* family, politics; *Style*— Sir Robin Kinahan, ERD, JP; ✉ Castle Upton, Templepatrick, Co Antrim, N Ireland (☎ 018494 32466)

KINCADE, Dr James; CBE (1988); s of George Kincade (d 1965), and Rebecca Jane, *née* Lyons (d 1983); *b* 4 Jan 1925; *Educ* Foyle Coll Londonderry, Trinity Coll Dublin (MA), Oriel Coll Oxford (MA, BLitt), Univ of Edinburgh (PhD); *m* 26 Aug 1952, (Elizabeth) Fay, da of James Anderson Piggot, OBE, JP, DL (d 1961); 1 s (James Anderson b 26 Aug 1953), 1 da (Ruth b 20 Feb 1956); *Career* RAF 1943–47 (cmmnd 1944); head of English Merchiston Castle Sch 1955–61 (teacher 1952–61), visiting prof of philosophy Indiana Univ 1959; headmaster: Dungannon Royal Sch 1961–74, Methodist Coll Belfast 1974–88; Queen's Univ Belfast: memb Senate, chm External Relations Ctee, memb Standing Ctee; nat govr for NI BBC 1985–91, dir Design Cncl NI 1990–93 (chm 1993–94); tstee: Housing the Homeless Fund, Pantridge Fndn NI; chm Broadcasting Cncl NI 1985–91; memb: Educn Ctee UTV 1979–85, SHA 1961–88, HMC 1974–88, Design Cncl 1993–94; *Recreations* gardening, walking; *Style*— Dr James Kincade, CBE; ✉ Harry's Rd, Culcavy, Co Down BT26 6HJ (☎ 01846 683865)

KINCAID, Brig John William Martin (Bill); s of Maj John Brian Shortt Kincaid (d 1944), and Stella May, *née* Martin (d 1980); *b* 1 July 1940; *Educ* Cheltenham Coll, RMA Sandhurst, Fitzwilliam Coll Cambridge (BA, MA); *m* 17 June 1965, Hilary Jane, da of Elmore Cooper (d 1989); 2 s (John b 2 April 1966, Charles b 27 Aug 1968), 1 da (Rebecca b 28 Dec 1972); *Career* regtl duty RA 1961–72, army staff course Shrivenham and Camberley 1973–74, MOD 1977–79, Battery Cdr 50 Missile Regt 1977–79, Maj MGO Secretariat MOD 1979–81, NDC 1981, Lt-Col MOD LSOR 6 1981–84, Lt-Col MOD MLRS 1984–87, Col MOD LSOR 6 1987–91, Brig MOD DOR (Land) 1991–95, ret; dir TheSAURAS Ltd 1995–; *Recreations* cricket, choral singing, gardening; *Clubs* Royal Artillery Cricket, Stragglers of Asia Cricket, Sunbury Cricket (capt); *Style*— Brig Bill Kincaid; ✉ c/o National Westminster Bank, 12 High Street, Shepperton, Middx TW17 9AN

KINCRAIG, Hon Lord; Robert Smith Johnston; s of William Turner Johnston, of Glasgow; *b* 10 Oct 1918; *Educ* Strathallan, St John's Coll Cambridge, Univ of Glasgow; *m* 1943, Margaret Joan (decd), da of Col A Graham, of Glasgow; 1 s, 1 da; *Career* advocate 1942, QC 1955, Sheriff princ Roxburgh & Berwick 1964–70, senator Coll of Justice and Lord of Session 1972–87 (with title of Lord Kincraig); dean Faculty of Advocates 1970–72; *Recreations* gardening, golf; *Clubs* Hon Co Edinburgh Golfers, RSAC (Glasgow); *Style*— The Hon Lord Kincraig; ✉ Westwood Cottage, Longniddry, E Lothian EH32 0PL (☎ and fax 01875 853583)

KINDER, Eric; s of William Kinder (d 1979), of Ashton-under-Lyne, nr Manchester, and Amy, *née* Grimshaw (d 1967); *b* 26 Dec 1927; *Educ* Ashton-under-Lyne GS, Accrington GS; *m* 1953, Isobel Margaret, da of Joseph Clarence Barnes; 1 s (Christopher William b 8 Jan 1956), 1 da (Katie b 18 Jan 1960); *Career* served RAF 1946–48; industl liaison offr Br Cotton Indust Res Assoc 1949–53, tech mangr Lostock Hall Spinning Co 1953–57; Smith & Nephew plc: joined 1957, gp main bd dir 1972–97, chief exec 1982–90, dep chm 1986–90, chm 1990–97; chm Brunner Mond Holdings Ltd 1992–; non-exec dir: Christie Hosp NHS Tst Manchester 1993–, Intermediate Capital Group PLC 1994–; ATI; *Recreations* tennis, game fishing, golf; *Clubs* Queen's, Lord's Taverners; *Style*— Eric Kinder, Esq; ✉ c/o Smith & Nephew plc, 2 Temple Place, Victoria Embankment, London WC2R 3BP (☎ 0171 836 7922, fax 0171 240 1343)

KINDER, John Russell; s of Herbert Kinder, of Leicester, and Kathleen Margaret, *née* Sarson; *b* 10 Nov 1937; *Educ* Wyggeston GS Leicester, Corpus Christi Coll Oxford (MA in PPE); *m* 1964, Diana Christine, da of Frederick Gordan Evans (d 1984); 4 s (Mark Russell b 1966, Andrew John b 1967, Stephen James b 1970, Jonathan Charles b 1974); *Career* RAF 1956–58; dir William Brandts Sons & Co Ltd 1975–77; jt md Warwick Engineering Investmts Ltd 1978–80; md CH Industrials plc 1980–90; dir: Aston Martin Lagonda 1980–83, Aston Martin Tickford 1981–90; sr industl ptnr Merton Associates 1991–92, chief exec Kinder Consultants mgmnt and exec search conslts 1992–; FCA; *Recreations* tennis, sailing, christian youth work; *Style*— John Kinder, Esq; ✉ 23 Woodville Gardens, Ealing, London W5 2LL (☎ 0181 997 1207); Kinder Consultants, 23 Woodville Gardens, Ealing, London W5 2LL (☎ 0181 932 3744, fax 0181 723 3672)

KINDERSLEY, Christian Philip; s of Hon Philip Leyland Kindersley, of Aldbourne, Wilts, and Violet Valerie Gwendolen, *née* French; *b* 19 March 1950; *Educ* Eton; *m* 1,

1973 (m dis 1991), Hilary Luise, da of David Radcliffe Guard (d 1979); 1 s (Alexander b 1982), 2 da (Vanessa b 1980, Davina b 1986); m 2, 1992, Lara Hepburn, da of Frederick George Pohl, of Constantia, Cape Town, S Africa; 1 da (Rosanna b 1995); *Career* ptnr Cazenove & Co 1982– (joined 1970); Freeman City of London 1983, Liveryman Worshipful Co of Fishmongers 1983; *Recreations* shooting, tennis, scuba; *Clubs* White's, City of London, MCC; *Style*— Christian Kindersley, Esq; ✉ Cazenove & Co, 12 Tokenhouse Yard, London EC2R 7AN (☎ 0171 588 2828, fax 0171 606 9205, telex 886758)

KINDERSLEY, Gay; s of Hon Philip Leyland Kindersley (d 1995; 4 s of 1 Baron Kindersley, GBE), by his 1 w, Oonagh (d 1995), yst da of Hon (Arthur) Ernest Guinness (2 s of 1 Earl of Iveagh), who m 2, 4 Baron Oranmore and Browne and 3, Miguel Ferreras; *b* 2 June 1930; *Educ* Eton; *m* 1, 1956 (m dis 1976), Margaret, da of Hugh Wakefield, of Mount St, Mayfair; 2 s, 2 da; m 2, 1976, Philippa Harper; 2 s; *Career* gentleman rider (amateur jockey) and trainer; *Clubs* Turf; *Style*— Gay Kindersley, Esq; ✉ Laines, Aldbourne, Marlborough, Wiltshire SN8 2NW (☎ 01672 841369); office (☎ 01672 841356, car 0836 507319)

KINDERSLEY, 3 Baron (UK 1941); Robert Hugh Molesworth Kindersley; s of 2 Baron Kindersley, CBE, MC (d 1976), and Nancy Farnsworth (d 1977); *b* 18 Aug 1929; *Educ* Eton, Trinity Coll Oxford, Harvard Business Sch; *m* 1, 4 Sept 1954 (m dis 1989), Venice Marigold (Rosie), da of late Capt Lord (Arthur) Francis Henry Hill (yr s of 6 Marquess of Downshire); 3 s (Rupert John Molesworth b 11 March 1955, Hugh Francis b 22 June 1956 (d 6 March 1991), Dickon Michael b 9 March 1962), 1 da (Anna Lucy b 19 June 1965); m 2, 1989, Patricia Margaret (Tita), o da of late Brig Hugh Ronald Norman, DSO, MC, of St Clere, Kemsing, Kent, and former w of Henry Colum Crichton-Stuart; *Career* Lt Scots Gds served Malaya 1949; dir: London Assurance 1957–, Witan Investment Co Ltd 1958–85, Steel Co of Wales 1959–67, Lazard Bros and Co Ltd 1960–91, Marconi Co Ltd 1963–68, Sun Alliance & London Insurance Group 1965–96, English Electric Co Ltd 1966–68, GEC Ltd 1968–70, British Match Corporation Ltd 1969–73, Swedish Match Co 1973–85, Maersk Co Ltd 1986–, Maersk India 1990–; chm: Cwlth Devpt Corpn 1980–89, Siam Selective Growth Trust 1990–, Brent Walker Group plc 1991–92; dep chm Advsy Cncl ECGD 1975–80; fin advsr Export Gp for the Constructional Industs 1961–85; chm BBA 1976–78, pres Anglo-Taiwan Trade Ctee 1976–86; memb Inst Int d'Etudes Bancaires 1971–85; chm Smith's Charity 1990–; memb Ct Worshipful Co of Fishmongers 1973– (Prime Warden 1989–90); *Recreations* all sports, deer, gardening; *Clubs* All England Lawn Tennis and Croquet (memb Ctee), Queen's, MCC, Vincent's, Pratt's; *Style*— The Rt Hon The Lord Kindersley; ✉ West Green Farm, Shipbourne, Kent TN11 9PU (☎ 01732 810293, fax 01732 810799); 5A Crescent Grove, London SW4 7AF (☎ and fax 0171 622 1198)

KINDERSLEY, Hon Rupert John Molesworth; s and h of 3 Baron Kindersley; *b* 11 March 1955; *Educ* Eton; *m* 2 Aug 1975, Sarah Anne, da of late John D Warde; 1 s (Frederick b 1987), 1 da (Rebecca b 1985); *Career* Freeman City of London, Liveryman Worshipful Co of Fishmongers 1990; FIMBRA 1987; *Style*— The Hon Rupert Kindersley

KINDERSLEY, Tania; da of Gay Kindersley, of Aldbourne, Wilts, and Margaret Fisher, *née* Wakefield; *b* 30 Jan 1967; *Educ* Marlborough, Christ Church Coll Oxford (MA); *Career* writer; *Books* Out To Lunch (1991), Here for the Season (1992), Goodbye Johnny Thunders (1996), Don't Ask Me Why (1997); *Recreations* reading, cinema, travelling, eating, theatre, talking on the telephone; *Clubs* Groucho, Green Street; *Style*— Miss Tania Kindersley; ✉ c/o Dinah Wiener Ltd, 27 Arlington Road, London NW1 7ER

KING, Sir Albert; kt (1975), OBE (1958), JP; s of George King (d 1915); *b* 20 Aug 1905; *Educ* Primrose Hill Leeds; *m* 1928, Pauline Riley; 1 da; *Career* full-time offr AUEW 1942–70: sec Leeds Div 1942–52, div organiser 1952–70, TUC regnl sec 1958–70, ret; ldr Labour Gp Leeds Met DC 1959–78; *Recreations* walking, reading; *Clubs* Beeston WMC; *Style*— Sir Albert King, OBE, JP; ✉ 25 Brookhill Ave, Leeds LS17 8QA (☎ 0113 268 4684)

KING, Prof Anthony Stephen; s of Harold Stark King (d 1949), and Marjorie Mary, *née* James (d 1982); *b* 17 Nov 1934; *Educ* Queen's Univ Kingston Ontario Canada (BA), Univ of Oxford (BA, DPhil); *m* 1, 1965, Vera Korte (d 1972); m 2, Janet Frances Mary, da of Adm of the Fleet Sir Michael Pollock, KGCB, DSO, *qv*, of The Ivy House, Churchstoke, Montgomery, Powys; *Career* fell Magdalen Coll Oxford 1961–65; Univ of Essex 1966–: sr lectr in govt 1966–67, reader 1967–69, prof 1969–, academic pro vice chllr 1986–89; fell Center for Advanced Study in the Behavioral Scis Stanford California 1977–78, visiting prof of public int affrs Princeton Univ 1984, hon foreign memb American Acad of Arts and Sciences 1993–; memb Nolan Ctee 1994–; *Books* Westminster and Beyond (with Anne Sloman, 1973), British Members of Parliament (1974), Why is Britain Becoming Harder to Govern? (ed, 1976), Britain Says Yes: The 1975 Referendum on the Common Market (1977), The British Prime Minister (ed, 2 edn 1985), The New American Political System (ed, 2 edn 1990), Britain at the Polls (ed, 1992), SDP: The Birth, Life and Death of the Social Democratic Party (with Ivor Crewe, 1995), Running Scared: Why America's Politicians Campaign Too Much and Govern Too Little (1997); *Recreations* music, holidays, walking; *Clubs* Royal Cwlth Soc; *Style*— Prof Anthony King; ✉ Department of Government, University of Essex, Wivenhoe Park, Colchester, Essex CO4 3SQ (☎ 01206 873393, fax 01206 873598)

KING, Barbara Sarah; da of John Henry Otty (d 1978), of Yorks, and Florence Harriet, *née* Robinson (d 1985); *b* 14 June 1946; *Educ* Secdy Modern Otley, privately; *m* 21 July 1962, James King; 1 s (James Martin b 1964, d 1964), 1 da (Sarah Jane b 1972); *Career* md Slimming Magazine Clubs Ltd 1988– (exec dir 1985–); dir: Argus Consumer Magazine Division 1988, Argus Press Group, Argus Business Publications 1990–; contrib to health and diet pubns; MInstD MInstM; *Recreations* reading, writing, wine making, DIY enthusiast(!); *Style*— Mrs Barbara King

KING, Col Bryan Arthur George; TD (1972); s of late George Henry King, of Wallasey; *b* 29 April 1930; *Educ* Birkenhead Sch; *m* 21 May 1960, Elizabeth, da of late Jack Oddy, of Chester; 2 da (Jane b 1962, Julia b 1967); *Career* conslt (formerly sr ptnr) Wayman-Hales Slrs Chester, hon slr Cheshire Regt; memb Cncl Law Soc 1982–94; govr The Queen's Sch Chester, pres Deeside Ramblers Hockey Club 1986–93; TA 1959–79, 4 Bn Cheshire Regt, Mercian Vols and Cheshire ACF, Col 1978, memb Regtl Cncl Cheshire Regt, vice chm NW Eng TAVR; *Recreations* travel, gardening; *Clubs* Army and Navy, Chester City; *Style*— Col Bryan King, TD; ✉ Taluca, Church Lane, Upton By Chester, Cheshire (☎ 01244 381 436); Wayman-Hales Solicitors, 12 White Friars, Chester (☎ 01244 321122, fax 01244 343642)

KING, Christopher John; s of Kavan John King, of New Malden, Surrey and Gwendoline June, *née* Kent (d 1985); *b* 15 Oct 1959; *Educ* King's Coll Sch Wimbledon, Univ of Edinburgh; *m* 1989, Gayle Shiona, da of John Thomson, of Dollar, Clackmannanshire; 1 s (James Alexander b 4 Oct 1990), 1 da (Georgie Louisa b 10 Feb 1992); *Career* cmmnd Royal Regt of Fus 1978–; brand mangr Proctor and Gamble Limited 1982–84, account supervisor Ted Bates Advertising 1984, account dir Grey Advertising Limited 1985–87; bd dir: Jenner Keating Becker Reay 1989–91 (account dir 1987–88), Reay Keating Hamer 1991–94, Mellors Reay and Partners 1994–; MIPA; *Style*— Christopher King, Esq; ✉ Mellors Reay and Partners, 65–66 Frith St, London W1V 5TA (☎ 0171 439 2686)

KING, David; s of Charles King (d 1942), and Maria, *née* Ward (d 1942); *Educ* Sir Roger Manwood's Sch Sandwich Kent, RAF Radio/Radar Sch Cranwell, RAF Flying Coll, RAF and RCAF Navigation Sch; *m* 1, 1958 (m dis 1987), Siv Mail, da of late Sam Owen Jansson, of Stockholm; 2 s (Ian David b 1960, Robin Timothy Owen b 1964); m 2, Sept 1991, Kerstin Birgitta Walters, da of late Rev Johan Domeij; 2 step s (Nicholas, Alexander), 1 step da (Ingrid); *Career* served as aircrew offr and navigator 224 Sqdn Gibraltar and 203 Sqdn Topcliffe, acceptance trials for Victor and Vulcan bombers Experimental Test Centre Boscombe Down, project navigator TSR2 trials for Vickers 1962–63; Procter & Gamble 1963–74: joined as salesman, subsequently area mangr, dist mangr, nat account and sales promotion mangr, sales dir Sweden 1972–74; sales dir Bovril Ltd 1974–82; SmithKline Beecham plc (formerly Beecham plc) 1982–93: gen mangr sales and mktg Beecham Foods 1982–83, md Food and Drinks Div 1984–86, chm Food and Drinks Div 1986–88, chm UK Consumer Brands 1988–93, ret; non-exec dir: Baxters Speyside, Parsons of Hull; non-exec chm Catalina; chm London Telethon Ball, memb Exec Ctee Africa 95, chm Br Dyslexia Assoc Ball, pres Nat Advertisers' Benevolent Soc (NABS) 1992; Freeman City of London, Liveryman Worshipful Co of Tinplate alias Wire Workers 1990; FInstD 1988, fell Inst of Grocers 1991; *Recreations* golf, theatre, opera; *Clubs* Wentworth, City Livery, IOD; *Style*— David King; ✉ Fieldmoor, Gorse Hill Road, Virginia Water, Surrey GU25 4AS (☎ 01344 842344, fax 01344 842883)

KING, Prof David Anthony; s of Arnold Tom Wallis King, of Johannesburg, SA, and Patricia Mary Bede, *née* Vardy; *b* 12 Aug 1939; *Educ* St John's Coll Johannesburg, Univ of Witwatersrand SA (BSc, PhD), UEA (ScD); *m* 5 Nov 1983, Jane Margaret Lichtenstein (uses maiden name), da of Hans Lichtenstein, of Llandrindod Wells, Wales; 3 s (Benjamin Tom b 11 Nov 1973, Tobias Alexander b 15 Sept 1975, Zachary Adam b 17 Sept 1986), 1 da (Emily Sarah b 20 Feb 1984); *Career* Shell scholar Imperial Coll London 1963–66, lectr in chemical physics UEA Norwich 1966–74, Brunner prof of physical chemistry Univ of Liverpool 1974–88; Univ of Cambridge: 1920 prof of physical chemistry 1988–, fell St John's Coll 1988–95, head Dept of Chemistry 1993–, Master Downing Coll 1995–; pres AUT 1976–77; chm Leverhulme Tst Res Awards Advsy Ctee 1995–, memb Direction Ctee Fritz Haber Inst Berlin 1981–93; ed Chemical Physics Letters 1989–, chm Kettle's Yard (House and Art Gallery) Cambridge 1989–; FInstP 1977 (MInstP 1967), FRSC 1974 (medal and award for surface chem 1978, Tilden lectr 1988–89, Liversidge lecture and medal 1997); Br Vac Cncl medal and award for research 1991; FRS 1991; *Publications* numerous scientific pubns on the chemical physics of solid surfaces and gas/surface interactions; *Recreations* art, photography; *Style*— Prof David King, FRS; ✉ Department of Chemistry, University of Cambridge, Lensfield Rd, Cambridge CB2 1EW (☎ 01223 336300); The Master's Lodge, Downing College, Cambridge CB2 1DQ (☎ 01223 336338, fax 01223 336332)

KING, David E; *b* 18 Aug 1945; *Educ* MBA; *m*; 4 c; *Career* various financial positions overseas until 1982, returned UK 1982; London Metal Exchange: joined as first dir of fin and admin 1987, chief exec 1989–; dir London Clearing House Ltd, dir Futures and Options Assoc; author of various articles and business papers; FCCA 1976; *Style*— David King, Esq; ✉ The London Metal Exchange, 56 Leadenhall Street, London EC4A 2BJ (☎ 0171 264 5555, fax 0171 680 0505)

KING, Diana Mary; da of Robin Garnett Milton Bull (d 1990), of Nesscliffe, Shropshire, and Phyllis Rosemary, *née* Hill; *b* 22 June 1953; *Educ* Sutton Coldfield Girls GS, Univ of Sheffield (BA); *m* 23 May 1981, Philip Adrian King, s of Harry King, OBE (d 1984); *Career* Univ of Sheffield OTC 1972–75, 3 Bn Yorks Vol 1975–80, ret with rank of Capt; admitted slr 1979, private practice as litigation slr 1979–85, chief exec Eng Ski Cncl 1985–; Exec Ctee Central Cncl for Physical Recreation, City of Birmingham Symphony Chorus; *Recreations* gliding, music, gardening; *Clubs* Midland Gliding, Herefordshire Gliding, Stratford-upon-Avon Gliding; *Style*— Mrs Diana King; ✉ English Ski Council, Area Library Building, Queensway Mall, The Cornbow, Halesowen, W Midlands B63 4AJ (☎ 0121 501 2314)

KING, Francis Henry; CBE (1985); s of Eustace Arthur Cecil King (d 1937), and Faith Mina, *née* Read (d 1992); *b* 4 March 1923; *Educ* Shrewsbury, Balliol Coll Oxford (MA); *Career* author; Br Cncl offr 1960–63; lectr: Florence Italy 1950–51, Salonica and Athens Greece 1951–57; asst rep Finland 1957–58, regnl dir Kyoto Japan 1958–63; drama critic Sunday Telegraph 1976–88; int vice-pres PEN 1989– (int pres 1986–89); FRSL 1958; *Books* The Dividing Stream (1951, Somerset Maugham Award), The Man on the Rock (1957), The Custom House (1961), The Needle (1975), Act of Darkness (1983), Voices in an Empty Room (1984), The Woman Who Was God (1988), The Ant Colony (1991), Secret Lives (1991), Yesterday Come Suddenly (autobiography, 1993), The One and Only (1994), Ash on an Old Man's Sleeve (1996), A Hand at the Shutter (1996); *Recreations* mountaineering and pot-holing; *Style*— Francis King, Esq, CBE; ✉ 19 Gordon Place, London W8 4JE (☎ 0171 937 5715)

KING, Gen Sir Frank Douglas; GCB (1976, KCB 1972, CB 1971), MBE (1953); s of Arthur King; *b* 9 March 1919; *Educ* Wallingford GS; *m* 1946, Joy Emily; 1 s, 2 da; *Career* joined Army 1939, serv WWII, cmd Parachute Bn Gp Cyprus 1960–62, cmd Inf Bde Gp Germany 1962–64, Brig 1962, Maj-Gen 1966, dir Land/Air Warfare MOD (Army) 1966–68, Cmdt RMCS 1969–71, Lt-Gen 1971, GOC-in-C Strategic Cmd 1971, dep C-in-C UKLF 1972–73, GOC NI 1973–75, Gen 1976, Cdr Northern Army Gp and C-in-C BAOR 1976–78, ADC Gen to HM The Queen 1977–78, ret; chm: John Taylor Tst 1978–88, Assets Protection International Ltd 1981–86; mil advsr Short Bros Ltd Belfast 1979–84; dir: Control Risks Ltd 1979–86, Kilton Properties, Springthorpe Property Co, PLAZA Fish Ltd, Airborne Forces Charitable Devpt Tst 1988; tstee Airborne Forces Security Tst 1981–, memb Cncl Air League 1982–89; *Style*— Gen Sir Frank King, GCB, MBE; ✉ c/o Royal Bank of Scotland, 1 Fleet Street, London EC4 1BD

KING, Harold Samuel; s of Manuel King (d 1971), of Durban, SA, and Hettie, *née* Lichtenstein (d 1966); *b* 13 May 1949; *Educ* Univ Ballet Sch Cape Town; *Career* formerly ballet dancer: CAPAB Ballet Co Cape Town SA 1968–70, Scottish Ballet (formerly Western Theatre Ballet), Opera Ballet Royal Opera House Covent Garden, Nat Ballet of Zimbabwe, ret as dancer 1978; artistic co-ordinator: Victor Hochhauser Gala Ballet Season Royal Festival Hall 1978, two Rudolf Nureyev seasons London Coliseum; artistic dir London City Ballet 1978–96; fndr and artistic dir City Ballet of London 1996–; prodns for London City Ballet incl: Dances from Napoli, Prince Igor, The Nutcracker Suite, Carmen (choreographer); series of Strauss Galas (choreographer, Victor Hochhauser); most recently choreographer for A Little Princess and The Lion, The Witch and the Wardrobe 1995; prodr La Sylphide (Phillipine Dance Theatre) 1990; *Recreations* painting and designing, travel, all music except country & Western, people; *Style*— Harold King, Esq; ✉ City Ballet of London, International Buildings, 71 Kingsway, London WC2B 6SX (☎ 0171 405 0044, fax 0171 405 2050)

KING, Henry Edward St Leger; s of Robert James King, and Dorothy Louisa Marie, *née* Wickert; *b* 11 Oct 1936; *Educ* Whitgift Middle Sch, Fitzwilliam Coll Cambridge (MA, LLB); *m* 10 April 1964 (m dis 1989), Kathleen Bridget, da of William Wilcock (d 1971); 1 s (Simon b 1969, d 1984), 1 da (Alexandra b 1966); 2 March 1996, Margaret Evelyn, da of Ronald Charles Empson (d 1982); *Career* Nat Serv 2 Lt 1955–57; admitted slr 1964, ptnr Denton Hall 1967–96 (chm 1993–96), conslt 1996–; dir: City Centre Restaurants plc (chm 1996–), Rentokil Group plc (chm 1994–), GKR Group (chm 1995–), Brambles Securities plc, Brambles Investments plc; memb Bucks Co Cncl 1977–81; *Recreations* travel, theatre, music; *Style*— Henry King, Esq; ✉ Denton Hall, 5 Chancery Lane, Clifford's Inn, London EC4A 1BU (☎ 0171 242 1212)

KING, Ian Ayliffe; s of Jack Edward King (d 1990), of Henley on Thames, and Hilda Bessie King; *b* 25 April 1939; *Educ* Bromsgrove Sch; *m* 1963, Rosemary Frances, da of

Sir Gordon Wolstenholme, OBE; 4 c (Joanna Susan b 24 Aug 1965, Giles Edward Ayliffe b 12 Nov 1966, Oliver Charles Ayliffe b 2 Jan 1972, Philippa Rosemary b 1 Sept 1977); *Career* chartered accountant; nat chm Kidsons Impey 1992– (ptnr 1968); dir: E Walters (Ludlow) Ltd 1968–85, Baker & Sons (Margate) Ltd 1975–, The All England Lawn Tennis Ground Ltd 1991–, LTA Trust Ltd 1991–94, The Queens Club Ltd 1993–, The South Birmingham Mental Health NHS Trust Ltd 1994–; tstee: Sir Barry Jackson Tst, The Jack Kendall Tennis Tst; govr Whitford Hall Sch 1973–90; Lawn Tennis Assoc: memb Cncl 1981–87 (representing Hereford & Worcester County Lawn Tennis Assoc), memb Bd of Mgmnt 1984– (chm 1991–93), dep pres 1988–90, pres 1991–93, int rep 1995–; Wimbledon: memb Ctee of Mgmnt of the Championships 1987–, memb Ticket Ctee 1987–90 and 1994, memb Media Ctee 1990, memb Royal Box Ctee 1991–93, memb Tport Ctee 1995–; chm Hereford & Worcester County Lawn Tennis Assoc 1980– (memb Ctee 1969–), memb Ctee of Mgmnt Int Tennis Fedn 1995– (memb Fin Ctee, chm Women's Circuit Ctee); Liveryman Worshipful Co of CAs in England and Wales 1991; FCA 1962; *Recreations* tennis, cricket, theatre, travel; *Clubs* The All England Lawn Tennis and Croquet, Birmingham, Buckland, Barnt Green Tennis, Chartered Accountants Dining, Edgbaston Priory Tennis, The International Lawn Tennis Clubs of GB and Aust, West Hants Tennis; *Style—* Ian King, Esq; ✉ The Mount, Stoke Prior, Bromsgrove, Worcestershire B60 4JU (☎ 01527 831281, fax 01527 579592); Kidsons Impey, Bank House, 8 Cherry Street, Birmingham B2 5AD (☎ 0121 631 2631, fax 0121 631 2633)

KING, Ian Charles; *b* 28 Dec 1934; *Educ* Univ Coll Sch Hampstead, Bartlett Sch of Achitecture Univ of London (Dip Arch); *m* 1 (m dis); m 2, 5 Feb 1980, Nathalie Wareham, *née* Singh; *Career* architect in private practice 1964–, Ian C King Associates Architects; Freeman City of London 1981; Liveryman: Worshipful Co of Glass Sellers 1982, Worshipful Co of Chartered Architects 1988; MRIBA 1960; *Recreations* lawn tennis, theatre, veteran cars; *Clubs* All England Lawn Tennis and Croquet, Hurlingham (past chm), Athenaeum; *Style—* Ian C King, Esq; ✉ Flat 28, Sherwood Court, Riverside Plaza, Chatfield Road, London SW11; Berkeley House, 73 Upper Richmond Road, London SW15 2SZ (☎ 0181 785 3408, fax 0181 780 1949)

KING, Jack Naisbitt; s of John George King (d 1944), and Grace, *née* Naisbitt (d 1989); *b* 19 Sept 1928; *Educ* Emmanuel Coll Cambridge (BA, MA), Univ of Adelaide (MA); *m*; 4 s, 3 da; *Career* Wolfson Coll Cambridge: founding fell 1965–, bursar and sec of tstees (fundraising and college building) 1968–79, dir Wolfson Course and Programme 1979–94 (vice pres 1984–88), sr fell 1984–95, hon fell 1995–, ed College Magazine 1979–; sr proctor Univ of Cambridge 1991–92; memb Ctee of Mgmnt Inst of Criminology 1991–95; memb: Cambridge Police Authy 1980–89 and 1991–92, Ctee Drinking Fountain Assoc 1990–; chm Fairleigh Dickinson Fndn New Jersey 1981–95 (hon tstee 1996); memb: Royal Opera House Tst 1985–89, Royal Opera House Endowment Tst 1985–, Cluff Fndn, St Mary-at-Hill Restoration Tst, London Cncl Anglo Hong Kong Tst 1995–; patron Churchill Archives Centre; Freeman City of London, Freeman and hon memb Ct of Assts Co of Watermen and Lightermen of the River Thames; Liveryman: Worshipful Co of Blacksmiths, Worshipful Co of Broderers; hon memb Sr Common Room Oriel Coll Oxford 1996–; Yates Medallion 1980, Hon DHL William Jewell Coll Missouri; Chev de l'Ordre des Coteaux de Champagne 1992; FRSA; *Clubs* Leander, RAF, Travellers, Beefsteak, Hawks' (dir 1996–); *Style—* Jack N King, Esq; ✉ Wolfson College, Cambridge, Cambs CB3 9BB (☎ 01223 335900)

KING, James Archibald; s of John Howard King (d 1973), of Ballater, and Margaret Whyte Smail, *née* Bannatyne; *b* 25 May 1951; *Educ* Melville Coll Edinburgh, Univ of Strathclyde (BA); *m* 1, 8 Oct 1977 (m dis 1982), Amanda Jane, da of Alan Lea Ferrand, of Woodside, Minshull Vernon, Cheshire; m 2, 29 Jan 1983, Katharine Stein, da of Henry Stein McCall, of High Auchengare, Rhu, Dunbartonshire; *Career* account exec Grey Advertising 1972–74; account dir: French Gold Abbott 1974–79, Abbott Mead Vickers 1979–81; dir Ogilvy & Mather (Scotland) 1981–87, client servs dir Hall Advertising 1987–89, dir James King Consultancy 1989–, head of mktg Oasis Group Ltd 1990–93, int mktg dir Sybase Inc 1994–96; chm Central New Town Assoc of Edinburgh 1990–94; Freeman Citizen of Glasgow Incorporation of Gardeners, Incorporation of Coopers; MIPA 1982; *Recreations* sailing, shooting, skiing, photography; *Clubs* RORC (memb Ctee 1980–81), Royal Northern & Clyde Yacht (memb Ctee 1981–83), Annabel's; *Style—* James King, Esq; ✉ Rosebank, St Margaret's Road, North Berwick, East Lothian EH39 4QH

KING, Jennifer Hilary Laura; da of Rev Thomas Symmons Magson, of Highworth, Wilts, and Rita, *née* Carter; *b* 7 Nov 1947; *Educ* Commonweal Sch Swindon, Queenswood, Univ of Bristol (LLB); *m* 11 July 1977 (m dis 1985); 2 s (Alan b 17 Sept 1977, John b 20 June 1980); *Career* admitted slr 1973, currently ptnr Townsends (specialist in family law); accredited family mediator and memb Family Mediators' Assoc; memb Law Soc Children Panel; legal advsr: RELATE, The Samaritans; soroptomist; *Style—* Mrs Jennifer King; ✉ Townsends, 42 Cricklade Street, Swindon, Wilts SN1 3HD (☎ 01793 410800, fax 01793 616294)

KING, John Arthur Charles; *b* 7 April 1933; *Educ* Sir Joseph Williamson's Mathematical Sch Rochester Kent, Univ of Bristol (BSc); *m*; 2 s; *Career* IBM 1956–70, UK md Telex Computer Products 1971–73, dir UK Data Processing Div Metra Consulting 1974–75, UK dir of Mktg rising to Euro dir of Business and Market Devpt ITT Business Systems and Communications Group 1976–81, commercial dir Philips International Business Communications Systems 1981–83, md Overseas Div and main bd dir BT plc 1983–88; chm: Quotron International Citicorp Information Business 1988–91, Analysys Ltd 1991–, Olivetti UK Ltd (non exec dir 1991–); vice chm Leeds Permanent Building Society 1995–96 (non-exec dir 1991–); dir Science Research Associates Ltd 1992–93; sec gen European Fndn for Quality Management 1993–94; memb Restrictive Practices Court 1995, non-exec memb Bd Child Support Agency 1996; Liveryman Worshipful Co of Info Technologists 1992; CIMgt, FBCS, FInstD, FRSA; *Recreations* sport (tennis), bridge, music; *Style—* J A C King, Esq; ✉ 1 Washington Close, Beech Road, Reigate, Surrey RH2 9LT; Analysys Ltd, St Giles Court, Castle Street, Cambridge CB3 0AJ (☎ 01223 460600, fax 01223 460866)

KING, John B; *Educ* MB BS, LRCP; *Career* sr lectr in orthopaedic and trauma surgery London Hosp Med Coll and hon conslt in orthopaedic and trauma surgery Royal London Hosp, dir Academic Dept of Sports Med The London Hosp Med Coll; former chm Br Assoc of Sports Med, sr examiner in sports med Worshipful Soc of Apothecaries, external advsr to Bath Distance Learning Course for Doctors in Sports Med, surgical conslt i/c Sports Clinic The London Hosp, orthopaedic conslt to Nat Sports Centre Crystal Palace London; memb Bd: Int Soc of the Knee, Nat Sports Med Inst; academic assoc The Univ of London Interdisciplinary Research Centre in Biomedical Materials, memb Editorial Bd Int Jl of Orthopaedic Trauma; Robert Milne prize in orthopaedic and related subjects 1977, Br Orthopaedic Assoc Euro travelling fell 1977; memb: Biological Engrg Soc, Biological Repair and Growth Soc (fndr memb), Br Assoc for Surgery of the Knee (fndr memb), Acad of Surgical Research, BMA, RSM, Br Orthopaedic Assoc, Int Knee Soc, Euro Soc of Sports Traumatology, Knee Surgery and Arthroscopy; *Publications* author of 73 pubns in learned jls and books; *Clubs* Athenaeum; *Style—* John B King, Esq; ✉ Royal London Hospital, Whitechapel, London E1 1BB

KING, Sir John Christopher; 4 Bt (UK 1888), of Campsie, Stirlingshire; s of Sir James Granville Le Neve King, 3 Bt, TD (d 1989), and Penelope Charlotte, *née* Cooper-Key (d 1994); *b* 31 March 1933; *Educ* Eton; *m* 1, 3 Oct 1958 (m dis 1972), Patricia Monica, o da of late Lt-Col Kingsley Osbern Nugent Foster, DSO, OBE; 1 s, 1 da; m 2, 1984, Mrs (Aline) Jane Holley, er da of Col Douglas Alexander Brett, GC, OBE, MC; *Heir* s, James Rupert King b 24 May 1961; *Career* Sub Lt RNVR, 1 Lt Berkshire Yeo TA; memb Stock Exchange 1958–73; *Recreations* sailing, shooting; *Clubs* Brooks's; *Style—* Sir John King, Bt; ✉ Stillwater, Box 218 Mathews Courthouse, Virginia 23109, USA (☎ 001 804 725 9873)

KING, John Keeley; s of George Frederick John King (d 1965), and Winifred Florence, *née* Hayes; *b* 24 June 1938; *Educ* Hove Coll; *m* 23 March 1968, Susan Ann, da of Lt-Col Harry Loe, OBE, RASC (d 1968), of Hampshire; 2 da (Alison Jane b 8 May 1972, Joanna Emily, b 11 March 1977); *Career* dir G J King Group Co 1975–; ACIOB 1980, FInstD 1987; *Recreations* motor sport, classic car collector, boating, golf; *Clubs* Dyke Golf, AMOC, Rotary (Brighton), Brighton & Hove MC (pres); *Style—* John King, Esq; ✉ 110 Woodland Drive, Hove, East Sussex BN3 6DE (☎ 01273 508486); G J King Business Centre, Reeds Lane, Sayers Common, Hassocks, Sussex BN6 9LS (☎ 01273 832314, fax 01273 832892, car 0402 596248)

KING, (Kenneth George) Jonathan; s of George Farquhar Janes King, and Ailsa King; *b* 6 Dec 1945; *Educ* Trinity Coll Cambridge (BA); *Career* entertainer; entered TV indust 1964, recording artist Everyone's Gone To The Moon 1965; TV presenter and creator Entertainment USA and No Limits (BBC 2), columnist Sun and other newspapers, show host Talk Radio 1995–; *Books* The Polish Boy and the Pope, Bible II, Adventures of Tim; publishes record industry Tip Sheet magazine; *Style—* Jonathan King, Esq; ✉ 1 Wyndham Yard, Wyndham Place, London W1H 1AR (☎ 0171 402 7433, fax 0171 402 2866)

KING, Julian Rex; s of Sqdn Ldr Arthur Herbert Edward King (d 1977), of Esher, Surrey, and Ada Marion, *née* Algar (d 1986); *b* 31 March 1944; *Educ* St John's Sch Leatherhead, Kingston Poly; *m* 1 (m dis 1994), Gillian Mary; 2 s (Matthew b 1976, Thomas b 1981), 1 da (Sarah b 1973); m 2, 25 June 1994, Diana Mary; *Career* mangr Regency Bookshop Surbiton Surrey 1964–66, mangr and fndr College Bookshop Kingston Surrey 1966–69, co proprietor and co fndr Centre Bookshop Croydon Surrey 1969–73, co proprietor, co fndr (with Colin Spooner) and md Prism Press Book Publishers Ltd Dorset, New York and Sydney 1974–; *Recreations* reading; *Style—* Julian King, Esq; ✉ Prism Press Book Publishers Ltd, The Thatched Cottage, Partway Lane, Hazelbury Bryan, Sturminster Newton, Dorset DT10 2DP (☎ 01248 817164, fax 01258 817635)

KING, Justin Matthew; s of Alan Sydney King, of Alton, Hants, and Elaine, *née* Adams; *b* 17 May 1961; *Educ* Tudor Grange Sch Solihull, Solihull Sixth Form Coll, Univ of Bath (BSc); *m* 12 May 1990, Claire Andrea, da of Neville Simmons; 1 da (Briony Justine b 25 April 1991), 1 s (Jordan Wesley b 26 Feb 1994); *Career* univ sponsorship to Lucas Electrical Birmingham 1979–83; various positions Mars Confectionery incl: mfrg mangr 1983–84, servs buyer 1984–85, nat account mangr 1986–89; various positions Pepsi Cola International incl: sales devpt mangr Cyprus 1989–90, sales and mktg dir Egypt 1990; md Haagen-Dazs UK Ltd 1990–93, mktg dir Allied Maples (Div of Asda plc) 1993–94, dir of drinks and kiosks Asda 1994–; *Recreations* sailing; *Clubs* Hayling Island Sailing; *Style—* Justin King, Esq

KING, Laurence Richard; s of (Cecil) Francis Harmsworth King, of London, and Jenifer Mary, *née* Beckett; *b* 28 July 1955; *Educ* Winchester, Jesus Coll Cambridge (BA); *m* Caroline Monica Elizabeth Ann, *née* Schofield; *Career* Calmann & King Ltd (formerly Calmann & Cooper Ltd until 1983): asst ed 1976–80, sales dir 1980, md 1983–; fndr Laurence King Publishing 1991; *Style—* Laurence King, Esq; ✉ 6 St Martin's Road, London SW9 0SW (☎ 0171 733 5120); Laurence King Publishing, 71 Great Russell Street, London WC1B 3BN (☎ 0171 831 6351, fax 0171 831 8356)

KING, Malcolm James Geoffrey; s of late Douglas James Edward King; of Hadley Wood, Herts, and Betty Alice, *née* Martin; *b* 10 April 1945; *Educ* Harrow, Coll of Estate Mgmnt, Univ of Western Ontario (MBA); *m* 6 June 1970, Jennifer Kate, da of Arthur Charles Rose; 1 s (Oliver James b 25 March 1975), 1 da (Annabel Kate b 11 Jan 1973); *Career* chartered surveyor Gerald Eve 1963–68; King & Co: joined 1968, head Investment Dept 1970, assoc 1972–75, ptnr 1975–88, jt sr ptnr 1988–94, sr ptnr 1994–; Freeman City of London; memb: Worshipful Co of Wheelwrights, Worshipful Co of Chartered Surveyors, Worshipful Co of Chartered Surveyors; FRICS; *Recreations* fly fishing, golf, shooting, stalking, helicopter flying, gardening; *Clubs* Flyfishers', Wentworth, Mortons; *Style—* Malcolm King, Esq; ✉ King Sturge & Co, 7 Stratford Place, London W1N 9AE (☎ 0171 493 4933, fax 409 0676)

KING, Martina; *née* Doyle; *b* 7 March 1961; *Educ* Bonus Pastor RC Sch Bromley Kent; *m* 1996, Simon King; *Career* personnel exec GLC 1980–82, telephone sales canvasser The Observer 1982–84; The Guardian 1984–93: classified sales exec 1984–86, display sales exec 1986–88, gp head (Display Sales) 1988–89, display sales mangr 1989–93; Capital Radio 1993–: client sales dir Jan-Aug 1993, sales dir Aug 1993–94, station dir 1994–; *Recreations* watersports, music, family life and friends; *Style—* Mrs Martina King; ✉ Capital Radio, Euston Tower, Euston Road, London NW1 3DR (☎ 0171 608 6276, fax 0171 962 6044)

KING, Mary Elizabeth; da of Lt Cdr Micheal Dillon Harding Thomson, RN (ret), and Patricia Gillian, *née* Hole; *b* 8 June 1961; *Educ* King's GS Ottery St Mary Devon, Evendine Court (cordon bleu coll) Malvern Worcs; *m* 1995, (Alan) David Henry King; 1 da (Emily Maria b Jan 1996); *Career* three day eventer; began with Axe Vale Pony Club, trained with Sheila Wilcox 1977–80, fndr own yard 1981–; achievements incl: winner Windsor Horse Trials 1988, 1989 and 1992, Br Open champion 1990 and 1991, team Gold medal Euro Championships Ireland 1991, winner Badminton Horse Trials 1992 (runner-up 1989), winner Althorp Maverick Championships 1993, team Gold individual 4th World Equestrian Games 1994, winner Punchestown and Compiegne Int Events 1995, team Gold individual Bronze Euro Championships 1995, Br Open Champion 1996; GB rep Olympic Games: Barcelona 1992 (team sixth, individual ninth), Atlanta 1996 (individual twelfth); ranked no 1 British event rider 1993 and 1994, holds world record for consecutive 3–day event wins (5 in 1991–92); watch leader on the Sir Winston Churchill tall ship 1980, chalet girl Zermatt 1980–81; Sun Systems Outstanding Rider of the Year 1990, Animal Health Tsts Equestrian Personality of the Year 1991, The Times/Minet Supreme Award 1992; *Video* Mary Thomson - Rider of the World (1995); *Books* Mary Thomson's Eventing Year (1993); *Recreations* tennis, snow and water skiing, deep sea diving; *Style—* Mrs Alan King; ✉ Matford Park Farm, Exminster, Exeter, Devon (☎ 01392 73880)

KING, Prof Mervyn Allister; s of Eric Frank King, and Kathleen Alice, *née* Passingham; *b* 30 March 1948; *Educ* Wolverhampton GS, King's Coll Cambridge (BA, MA); *Career* jr res offr Dept of Applied Economics (memb Cambridge Growth Project) 1969–73, Kennedy Scholarship Harvard Univ 1971–72; Univ of Cambridge: fell and dir studies St John's Coll 1972–77, res offr Dept of Applied Economics 1972–76, lectr Faculty of Economics 1976–77; Esmée Fairbairn prof of investmt Univ of Birmingham 1977–84, prof of economics LSE 1984–95; chief economist and exec dir Bank of England 1991–; visiting prof of economics: Harvard Univ 1982 and 1990, MIT 1983–84; pres Euro Econ Assoc 1993; memb: Meade Ctee on Taxation (sec) 1975–78, Prog Ctee Econometric Soc Congress 1974, 1979, 1985, Economics Ctee ESRC 1980–82, Res Ctee ENSAE Paris 1985, Exec Ctee IFS 1985, Econ Policy Panel 1985–86, CLARE Gp 1976–85, Ed Bd Jl of Industl Economics 1977–83, Cncl and Exec Ctee Royal Econ Soc 1981–86, Bd The Securities Assoc 1987–89, City Capital Markets Ctee 1988–90; res assoc NBER 1978–91, co-dir

ESRC Res Prog on Taxation Incentives and Distribution of Income LSE 1979–90 fell Centre for Econ Policy Res 1984–91, co-dir (with C Goodhart) Financial Markets Gp LSE 1987–91; asst ed Economic Journal 1974–75, assoc ed Journal of Public Economics 1982–, managing ed Review of Economic Studies 1978–83, memb Editorial Bd American Economic Review 1985–88, chm Soc of Econ Analysis; Walras-Bowley lectr Econ Soc, Review of Economics lectr Cambridge, assoc memb Inst of Fiscal and Monetary Policy Miny of Fin Japan; conslt: NZ treasy 1979, OECD 1982, Royal Cmmn on Distribution of Income and Wealth; res fell INSEE Paris 1977, hon res fell UCL; Helsinki Univ medal 1982; sr vice pres Aston Villa FC 1995–98 (former vice pres); FBA 1992; *Books* Public Policy and the Corporation (1977), The British Tax System (with J A Kay, 1978, 5 edn 1990), Indexing for Inflation (ed with T Liesner, 1975), The Taxation of Income from Capital: A Comparative Study of the US, UK, Sweden and West Germany (with D Fullerton et al, 1984), author of numerous articles; *Style*— Prof Mervyn King, FBA; ✉ Bank of England, Threadneedle St, London EC2R 8AH (☎ 0171 601 4963, fax 0171 601 3047)

KING, Michael Bruce; s of Bruce Eugene King, of Napier, NZ, and Patricia Alfredith, *née* Maxwell; *b* 10 Feb 1950; *Educ* Canterbury Univ Christchurch NZ (sr scholar in zoology, BSc), Sch of Med Auckland Univ (sr scholar in med, Sims travelling Cwlth scholar, BSc, MB ChB, MD, sr prize for med, MRCP, MRCGP, MRCPsych), Dip in Health Economics (Aberdeen), Univ of London (PhD); *Career* pre-registration/physicians trg Auckland 1976–77, GP trg Hammersmith Hosp 1978–81, trg in psychiatry Royal Bethlem and Maudsley Hosps 1981–84; Inst of Psychiatry: res worker/hon sr registrar 1984–86, clinical lectr/hon sr registrar 1986–88, sr lectr/hon conslt 1988–89, hon sr lectr 1989–; Dept of Psychiatry Royal Free Hosp Sch of Med: sr lectr and hon conslt 1989–94, reader, hon conslt and head of dept 1994–96, prof and head of dept 1996–; memb: Dept of Health's Expert Advsy Gp on AIDS, Cncl Section of Psychiatry RSM (pres elect), AIDS Working Pty RCGP; memb: Educn Ctee RCPysch (1992–95), Standing Ctee Assoc of Univ Teachers of Psychiatry, Steering Gp for the Mental Health Fndn/Dept of Health Sr Educnl Fellowship in Mental Health and Gen Practice, Primary Care Working Pty Mental Health Fndn, Nat Panel of Referees for the Nat Mental Health R&D Prog (NHS Mgmnt Exec); asst ed Jl of Psychosomatic Research 1990–93; memb Editorial Bd: British Jl of General Practice, Br Jl of Psychiatry; memb Int Editorial Bd AIDS Care; Dennis Hill Prize Maudsley Hosp/Inst of Psychiatry 1983; FRCGP 1991, FRCP 1996; *Books* Male Victims of Sexual Assault (ed and jt author, 1992), AIDS, HIV and Mental Health (1993); contrib: Eating Disorders and Disordered Eating (1988), The Scope of Epidemiological Psychiatry (1989), Epidemiology and the Prevention of Psychiatric Disorder (1989), The Public Health Impact of Mental Disorder (1990), Principles of Social Psychiatry (1993), Recent Advances in Clinical Psychiatry (1993), The Medical Annual 1993/94 (1993), Psychiatry and General Practice (1994), Research Foundations for Psychotherapy Research (1995), Assessment of Parenting (1995); author of numerous original papers in learned jls; *Recreations* swimming, languages; *Style*— Michael King, Esq; ✉ Head University Department of Psychiatry, The Royal Free Hospital School of Medicine, Rowland Hill Street, London NW3 2PF (☎ 0171 830 2397, fax 0171 830 2808, e-mail mike@RFHSM.ac.uk); Institute of Psychiatry, De Crespigny Park, London SE5 8AF (☎ 0171 919 3136)

KING, Eur Ing Prof Michael Stuart; s of Edward Roy King (d 1963), of Thornham, Norfolk, and Jessie Margaret, *née* Davis; *b* 2 June 1931; *Educ* St Edward's Sch Oxford, Univ of Glasgow (BSc), Univ of California (MS, PhD); *m* 1, 9 June 1962 (m dis 1983), Margaret Helen Hoeschen, da of Theodore de Vassily Bujila (d 1979), of Montreal, Canada; 2 s (Bernard John Edward b 1967, David Matthew Stuart b 1971), 1 da (Sarah Bernadine Margaret b 1966); m 2, 21 Oct 1989, (Shirley) Georgina King, OBE, da of Dr the Hon Walter Symington Maclay (d 1963), of Newbury, Berks; *Career* prof of geological engrg Univ of Saskatchewan Canada 1966–81, prof of mechanical engrg Univ of California Berkeley USA 1981–86, Phoebe Apperson Hearst distinguished prof 1986, oil indust prof of petroleum engrg Imperial Coll 1986–96 (prof emeritus 1996); FIMechE 1985, FGS 1985, FRSA 1990, Eur Ing 1991; *Recreations* foxhunting, shooting, music; *Style*— Eur Ing Prof Michael King; ✉ Cedar House, Hellidon, nr Daventry, Northamptonshire NN11 6LG (☎ 01327 261919); Royal School of Mines, Imperial College of Science, Technology and Medicine, London SW7 2BP (☎ 0171 594 7330 fax 0171 594 7444, telex 929484)

KING, Mike; *b* 22 Sept 1962; *Educ* St Benedict's Ealing; *Career* photographer, progressively: jr in small sports photographic agency, with Allsport agency, chief sports photographer The Observer; currently chief sports photographer The Sunday Telegraph; Sports Cncl Black and White Photographer of the Year 1989, Nikon Sports Photographer of the Year 1989 and 1990, IAF Athletics Photographer of the Year; *Recreations* cycling; *Style*— Mike King, Esq; ✉ 28 Beauval Road, London SE22 8UQ (☎ 0181 299 0484)

KING, Vice Adm Sir Norman Ross Dutton; KBE (1989); s of Sir Norman King, KCMG (d 1963), and Mona, *née* Dutton (d 1982); *b* 19 March 1933; *Educ* Fonthill Sch, RNC Dartmouth; *m* 1967, Patricia Rosemary, da of Dr Lionel Brian Furber (d 1981); 2 da (Annabelle b 1970, Melissa b 1978); *Career* CO HMS Leopard 1967–68, Exec Offr HMS Intrepid 1972–73, NA to Second Sea Lord 1975–77, RCDS 1978, CO HMS Newcastle 1979–80, Dir of Naval Offr Appts (Seaman Offrs) 1983–84, Cmdr Br Navy Staff Washington, Br Naval Attaché Washington, UKNLR to SACLANT 1985–86, Naval Sec 1987, COS to Cdr Allied Naval Forces S Europe 1988–91, ret 1991; chm: Bucks Health Authy, Safety Centre Milton Keynes 1991–96; *Recreations* tennis, golf, music, chess; *Clubs* Royal Navy of 1765 and 1785; *Style*— Vice Adm Sir Norman King, KBE; ✉ c/o Lloyds Bank, Faversham, Kent

KING, Air Vice-Marshal Peter Francis; CB (1987), OBE (1964); s of William George King, MBE (d 1968), of Huntingdon, and Florence Margaret, *née* Sell (d 1955); *b* 17 Sept 1922; *Educ* Framlingham Coll, King's Coll London, Charing Cross Hosp London, Univ of Edinburgh (DLO); *m* 1945, Doreen Maxwell, da of Jorgen Hansen-Aaröe (d 1960), of Northwood; 1 s (Nigel), 1 da (Suzanne); *Career* cmmnd RAF 1945, serving offr and conslt in otolaryngology, specialist in otorhinolaryngology, employed in Cosford, Ely, Fayid, Halton and CME, conslt in otorhinolaryngology 1955, Hunterian prof RCS 1964, conslt advsr in otorhinolaryngology 1966–83, Air Cdre 1976, reader in aviation med Inst of Aviation Med 1977–79, Whittingham prof in aviation med IAM and RCP 1979–83, Air Vice-Marshal 1983, dean RAF Med 1983–85, sr conslt RAF 1985–87; conslt: Herts Health Authy 1963–94, CAA 1973–95, King Edward VII Hosp Midhurst 1987; hon surgn to HM The Queen 1979–87, examiner for Dip in Aviation Med RCP 1980–87, pres section of otology RSM 1977–78, chm Br Soc of Audiology 1979–81, vice chm RNID 1980–88 (vice pres 1990–); memb Cncl Br Assoc of Otolaryngologists 1960–89; memb Editorial Bd Br Jl of Audiology 1980–89; CStJ (1987); FRCSE; *Recreations* sculpture, looking at prints; *Clubs* RAF; *Style*— Air Vice-Marshal Peter King, CB, OBE; ✉ 5 Churchill Gate, Woodstock, Oxon OX20 1QW (☎ 01993 813115)

KING, Prof Phillip; CBE (1974); s of Thomas John King (d 1973), of UK, France and N Africa, and Gabrielle Laurence, *née* Liautard (d 1975); *Educ* Mill Hill Sch, Univ of Cambridge (MA); *m* 1 (m dis); 1 s (Anthony Thomas b 1965 d 1984); m 2, 1991, Judith Corbalis; *Career* prof of sculpture: RCA 1981–90 (emeritus prof 1990–), RA Schs 1990–; memb Visual Arts Ctee Arts Cncl, tstee Tate Gallery 1967–69; RA 1987 (ARA 1977); *Recreations* travelling, swimming, music, windsurfing; *Style*— Prof Phillip King, CBE, RA

KING, Prof Preston Theodore; s of Clennon King (d 1975), of Albany, GA, USA, and Margaret, *née* Slater (d 1990); *b* 3 March 1936; *Educ* Fisk Univ (BA), Oberlin Coll, Univ of Atlanta, Univ of Vienna, Univ of Strasbourg, Univ of Paris, LSE (MSc, PhD); *m*; 1 s (Slater b 1969), 1 da (Oona b 1967); *Career* tutor: LSE 1958–60, Univ of Maryland 1961; lectr: Univ of Keele 1961–62, Univ of Ghana 1963–66, Univ of Sheffield 1966–68; reader Univ of E Africa Nairobi 1968–70, sr res assoc Acton Soc Tst 1970–72; Univ of Nairobi: prof 1972–76, chm of dept 1972–74, founded Diplomacy Training Prog for Anglophone Africa 1972–73, dir DTP 1973–74; prof of political sci Univ of NSW 1976– (head of sch 1978–80), prof of politics Univ of Lancaster 1986– (head of dept 1986–87); visiting prof: Univ of Dar es Salaam 1973, Institut des Relations Internationales Univ of Cameroun 1976, McGill Univ 1981, Philosophy Dept LSE 1983 (Politics Dept 1979), Univ of Auckland 1995; external examiner: Makerere Univ 1973, Univ of Khartoum 1974–75, Univ of the S Pacific Fiji 1977–83, Univ of Liverpool 1988–91; gen ed: Aust Nat Univ Monograph Series in Social and Political Thought 1977–80, Int Series in Social and Political Thought 1980–; author of numerous articles and reviews on socio-political related topics published in nat and int jls; broadcaster; memb: Exec Ctee Conference for the Study of Political Thought, Exec Ctee Research Ctee for Political Philosophy (IPSA), Advsy Ctee Centre for Res in Ethnic Relations Univ of Warwick; involvement in various int political orgns and conferences; *Books* incl: Fear of Power (1967), The History of Ideas (1983), The Ideology of Order (1974), Toleration (1976), Federalism and Federation (1982), An African Winter (1986), Thomas Hobbes: Critical Assesments (4 vols, 1993), Socialism and The Common Good: New Fabian Essays (1996); *Style*— Prof Preston King; ✉ Department of Politics, University of Lancaster, Lancaster LA1 4YL (☎ 01524 594282, fax 01524 594238, telex 65111 LANCUL G)

KING, Sir Richard Brian Meredith; KCB (1975, CB 1970), MC (1944); s of Bernard King (d 1968), of Claygate, Surrey, and Dorothy, *née* Scrivener (d 1974); *b* 2 Aug 1920; *Educ* King's Coll Sch Wimbledon; *m* 24 Dec 1944, (Blanche) Phyllis, da of Edward Owen Roberts (d 1975), of Shalbourne, Wilts; 2 s (Hilary b 1949, Julian b 1956), 1 da (Pauline b 1946); *Career* cmmnd N Irish Horse 1941, Capt 1944, Maj 1945, served N Africa and Italy; Civil Serv: Air Miny 1939–41, Miny of Works 1946, seconded to HM Treasy 1953–55, PPS to Min of Works 1956–57, seconded to Cabinet Secretariat 1958–61, sec gen of independence constitutional conferences for Malta 1959 (Kenya 1960, W Indies Fedn 1960, Fedn for Rhodesia, N Rhodesia and Nyasaland 1961), asst sec Dept of Tech Cooperation 1961, perm sec Miny of Overseas Devpt 1973 (under sec 1964, dep sec 1968), exec sec World Bank/IMF Jt Devpt Ctee 1976–80, sr advsr to S G Warburg & Co Ltd 1980–85, devpt fin conslt 1985–; *Books* Planning the British Aid Programme (1971), Criteria for Europe's Development Policy to the Third World (1974); *Recreations* music, lawn tennis, gardening; *Clubs* All-England Lawn Tennis; *Style*— Sir Richard King, KCB, MC; ✉ Woodlands Farm House, Woodlands Lane, Cobham, Surrey KT11 3PY (☎ 01372 843 491)

KING, Robert John Stephen; s of Stephen King, of Wolverhampton, and Margaret Digby; *b* 27 June 1960; *Educ* Radley, St John's Coll Cambridge (MA); *Career* conductor and harpsichordist; dir The King's Consort (Baroque orch) 1980–; conductor and dir on over sixty records on Hyperion (exclusive contract); guest dir: Orquesta de Cadaques, Choir of New Coll Oxford, Uppsale Chamber Orchestra, Orquesta Sinfonica Euskadi, Orebro Chamber Orchestra, RTL Symphony Orchestra, Netherlands Chamber Orchestra and Chamber Choir, Koninklijk Filharmonisch Orkest van Vlaanderen; concert tours: France, Holland, Belgium, Spain, Finland, Italy, Japan, Hong Kong, Taiwan, Turkey, S America, USA; TV and radio appearances all over Europe and the UK, ed of much 1600–1750 music (publisher Faber Music); *Recreations* skiing, cricket, graphic design; *Style*— Robert King, Esq; ✉ 34 St Mary's Grove, London W4 3LN (☎ 0181 995 9994, fax 0181 995 2115)

KING, Prof Roger Patrick; *b* 31 May 1945; *Educ* St Anselm's GS Birkenhead, St George's GS Hong Kong and Singapore, Wimbledon Coll, Univ of London (external BSc), Univ of Birmingham (MSc); *m*; *Career* exec offr Miny of Housing & Local Govt London 1963–64, sales mangr United Glass Ltd 1964–65, sales mangr Marley Tiles Ltd 1965–66; lectr then sr lectr in social science Manchester Poly 1970–75; princ lectr Dept of Behavioural Sciences Huddersfield Poly 1976–82 (head of dept 1982–85); Univ of Lincs and Humberside (Humberside Poly until 1992): dep dir (resources) 1985–89, dir and chief exec 1989–92, vice chllr 1992–, personal professorship 1992–; Br Cncl: Ctee for Int Co-operation in Higher Educn 1991–, Ctee for Asia and the Oceans 1991–95; memb Funding Gp PCFC 1988–89, memb Libraries and Learning Resources Review Gp and chm Managing Libraries Sub-Gp Higher Educn Funding Cncl 1993–94; Ctee of Dirs of Polys: memb Funding of Teaching Gp 1991–, memb Student Issues Gp 1992–; CVCP: memb Fin Ctee 1992–, memb European Ctee 1992–, memb Student Affairs Ctee 1992–; memb Exec Bd Poly and Colls Employers Forum 1992–, memb Cncl Humberside TEC 1991–; chm Int Centre for Mgmnt Educn Singapore 1992–; CNAA: memb Combined Studies (Social Sciences) Sub-Ctee 1985–88, memb Sociological Studies Bd 1984–88; memb: Political Studies Assoc, Soc for Res into Higher Educn; author of numerous res papers and pubns; *Style*— Prof Roger King; ✉ The University of Lincolnshire and Humberside, Cottingham Road, Hull HU6 7RT (☎ 01482 440550, fax 01482 440846)

KING, Ronald Gordon; s of Basil King (d 1991), and Jacqueline Marie Catherine, *née* Timmermans (d 1994); *b* 31 Dec 1946; *Educ* Jesuit Coll Antwerp; *Career* ed: Viewpoint 1965–, Warfare 1972–, The Keys of Peter 1969–; sec: Christian Centre Pty, Napoleon Soc, Pugin Guild; *Books* Catholicism and European Unity (1980), Zionism and the Vatican (1981), Napoleon and Freemasonry (1985); *Clubs* Hon Librarian, Army and Navy; *Style*— Ronald King, Esq; ✉ 157 Vicarage Rd, London E10 5DU (☎ 0181 539 3876)

KING, (Derek) Ross; s of David Johnstone King, of Glasgow, and Isabel Moore McLeod, *née* Ross; *b* 21 Feb 1964; *Educ* Victoria Drive Secdy Sch Glasgow; *Career* radio and TV presenter; *Theatre* world premiere of Butterfly Children (musical, King's Theatre Glasgow), Charley's Aunt; pantomime: Cinderella, Aladdin, Mother Goose, Dick Whittington, Snow White, Babes in the Wood; *Television* for BBC: Children In Need, The 8.15 From Manchester, Holiday, The Wetter the Better, The Ross King Show (Pebble Mill), Hot Chefs, Pop Goes Summer, King of the Road, Newshound, Pebble Mill, Summer in The City, CTV 1 (BBC Scot); for Yorkshire: Pick of the Week, The Calendar Fashion Show, Who's Into, Living It Up); for Granada: Young Krypton, Quiz Night, My Secret Desire; other credits inc: Auto TX (LWT), Bros In 2 Summer (Sky), Telethon (ITV), Run the Gauntlet (Thames); *Radio* Radio Clyde Glasgow, Capital Radio (Eurochart Show for ILR Network), BBC Radio 5; *Awards* Local Radio DJ of the Year Sony Radio Awards 1988, Sony Radio Award 1993 (for outstanding sports presentation of Barcelona Olympics); *Recreations* sport, theatre, cinema; *Clubs* Ham Polo; *Style*— Ross King, Esq; ✉ BBC Midlands & East, Broadcasting Centre, Pebble Mill, Pebble Mill Road, Birmingham B5 7QQ (☎ 0121 414 8888, fax 0121 414 8634)

KING, Dame Ruth; *see:* Railton, Dame Ruth

KING, Stephen Harris Morley; *b* 25 Feb 1931; *Educ* Harrow, CCC Oxford (capt squash team); *Career* J Walter Thompson: joined 1957, worked on agency's maj accounts, set up UK's first account planning dept 1968, responsible for specialist units for advtg res and new product devpt, chm MRB Group 1979–86; non-exec dir: WPP Group 1989–93, The Henley Centre; *Books* Developing New Brands (1973, 2 edn 1984); *Style*— Stephen King, Esq; ✉ The Henley Centre, 9 Bridewell Place, London EC4V 6AY (☎ 0171 353 9961, fax 0171 353 2899)

KING, Stephen James (Steve); s of Joseph Henry King, of Leicester, and Jean, *née* Bond; *b* 11 Sept 1956; *Educ* Bosworth Upper Sch Leics, Charles Keene Coll Leicester (OND); *m* 14 July 1984, Philippa Jane, da of George Walter Lay; 1 s (James b 21 May 1992); *Career* presenter and prodr: Loughborough Hosp Broadcasting 1978–81, University Radio Loughborough 1978–81, Centre Radio Leicester 1981–83; Viking Radio Hull: joined as presenter 1984, head of music Viking Radio 1985–88, presentation controller 1988–89, prog controller 1989–91, also gen mangr Viking FM 1990–91; prog controller Hallam FM Sheffield, Yorks regnl prog controller Metro Radio Group plc (parent co of Viking Radio and Radio Hallam, and others) 1993–, prog dir Radio Hallam Ltd 1993–96, md West Yorkshire Broadcasting plc (parent co of The New 96.3 Aire FM and magic 828, pt of Emap Radio Ltd) 1996–; *Recreations* national economics, football, badminton; *Style*— Steve King, Esq; ✉ West Yorkshire Broadcasting plc, 51 Burley Road, Leeds LS3 1LR (☎ 0113 245 2299, fax 0113 244 0445)

KING, Stephen William Pearce; s of William Raymond Pearce King, CBE (d 1980), and Edna Gertrude, *née* Swannock (d 1971); *b* 21 Jan 1947; *Educ* King Edward's Sch Birmingham; *m* 22 Sept 1973, Angela Denise, da of Dennis George Gammon, of Worcester; 2 s (Alexander b 1976, Jeremy b 1978); *Career* admitted slr 1973; princ Stephen King & Co slrs (specialists in child care, criminal and matrimonial law); *Recreations* sport, music, charity work, writing, theatre, travelling, meeting interesting people, art, conservation; *Style*— Stephen W P King, Esq; ✉ Stephen King & Co, 258 High Street, Erdington, Birmingham B23 6SN (☎ 0121 382 8222)

KING, Thea; OBE (1985); da of Henry Walter Mayer King, MBE, and Dorothea Louise King; *b* 26 Dec 1925; *Educ* Bedford HS, RCM; *m* Jan 1953, Frederick Thurston, CBE (d Dec 1953); *Career* clarinettist; Sadler's Wells Orch 1950–52, Portia Wind Ensemble 1955–68, London Mozart Players 1956–84, Vesuvius Ensemble 1965–76, Melos Ensemble of London 1974–93; currently memb: English Chamber Orch, Robles Ensemble; frequent soloist broadcaster and recitalist; prof: RCM 1962–87, Guildhall Sch of Music 1988–; recordings: music by Mozart and Brahms, lesser-known 19th-century works and 20th-century works by Lutoslawski, Finzi, Ireland, Maconchy, Britten and other British composers; pubns: Clarinet Solos (Chester Woodwind series, 1977), arrangement of J S Bach Duets for Two Clarinets (1979), Schumann For The Clarinet (1991), Mendelssohn for the Clarinet (1993), The Romantic Clarinet - A Mendelssohn Collection (1994), Tchaikovsky (1995); FRCM, ARCM, FGSM; *Recreations* skiing, cows, pillow-lace; *Style*— Ms Thea King, OBE; ✉ 16 Milverton Rd, London NW6 7AS (☎ 0181 459 3453)

KING, Thomas George (Tom); s of Thomas Herbert King (d 1974), of Cambridge, and Cecilia Edith, *née* Tromp (d 1986); *b* 21 May 1938; *Educ* Royal Sch of Mines Imperial Coll London (BSc, ARSM, Inst of Petroleum Prize 1958); *m* Jan 1960, Judith Mary Clarke; 2 s (Aivars Thomas b Feb 1961, Warwick Ralph b July 1962), 1 da (Tania Ann b Nov 1963); *Career* Shell Group of Cos 1960–66; Gulf Oil Corp 1966–82: Kuwait Oil Co 1966–74, gen mangr Zaïre 1974–78, mangr planning 1978–79, vice pres and gen mangr Cabinda Gulf Oil 1979–82; dir of ops Burmah Oil 1984–86 (gen mangr UK 1982–84), pres and chief exec Trafalgar House Oil and Gas Inc 1986–87; LASMO plc: dir Prodn 1988–89, dir Exploration & Prodn 1990–93, dir New Business 1993–; Ordre National du Zaïre; memb Soc of Petroleum Engrs, FGS, FInstPet, FInstD; *Recreations* rugby, cricket, boating; *Style*— Tom King, Esq; ✉ LASMO plc, 100 Liverpool Street, London EC2M 2BB (☎ 0171 945 4558, fax 0171 638 6954, mobile 0378 538634, e-mail tom.king@lasmo.com)

KING, Rt Hon Thomas Jeremy (Tom); CH (1992), PC (1979), MP (C) Bridgwater (majority 9,716); s of John H King, JP, of Langford, Somerset; *b* 13 June 1933; *Educ* Rugby, Emmanuel Coll Cambridge; *m* 1960, (Elizabeth) Jane, 3 and yst da of late Brig Robert Tilney, CBE, DSO, TD, DL, Lord of the Manor of Sutton Bonington (maternal gs of Sir Ernest Paget, 1 Bt); 1 s, 1 da; *Career* Nat Serv Somerset LI and King's African Rifles (Tanganyika and Kenya), formerly with E S & A Robinson Ltd Bristol (rising to div gen mangr), chm Sale Tilney & Co 1971–79 (dir 1965–79); MP (C) Bridgwater 1970–; PPS: to Min of Posts and Telecommunications 1970–72, to Min for Industl Devpt 1972–74; vice chm Cons Parly Indust Ctee 1974; oppn front bench spokesman on: indust 1975–76, energy 76–79; min of state for Local govt and environmental servs DOE 1979–83; sec of state for: enviroment Jan-June 1983, transport June-Oct 1983, employment Oct 1983–85, Northern Ireland 1985–July 1989, defence July 1989–1992; chm Intelligence and Security Ctee; memb Nolan Ctee 1995; *Style*— The Rt Hon Tom King, CH, MP; ✉ House of Commons, London SW1A 0AA

KING, Timothy Roger Alan; QC (1991); s of Harold Bonsal King (d 1992), of Liverpool, and Dorothy, *née* Watts; *b* 5 April 1949; *Educ* Liverpool Inst (Margaret Bryce scholar), Lincoln Coll Oxford (MA, BCL); *m* 7 June 1986, Bernadette Tracy, *née* Goodman; *Career* called to the Bar Lincoln's Inn 1973, practising barr Chambers of Henry Lachs 1974–91, currently barr on Northern Circuit, recorder 1991–; memb Hon Soc of Lincoln's Inn 1969–; *Recreations* travel; *Clubs* Liverpool Athenaeum; *Style*— Timothy King, Esq, QC; ✉ Byrom Chambers, 25 Byrom Street, Manchester M3 4PF (☎ 0161 829 2100, fax 0161 829 2101); Byrom Chambers, 61 Fleet Street, London EC4Y 1JU

KING, His Hon Judge Timothy Russell; s of Charles Albert King (d 1988), and Elizabeth Lily, *née* Alexander (d 1996); *b* 4 June 1946; *Educ* St Mary's Coll Southampton, Inns of Court Sch of Law; *m* 1, 1973 (m dis 1979); 2 s (Anthony Laurence b 25 Nov 1973, Gregory James b 14 Oct 1974); m 2, 1989, Rotraud (Jane) Webster-King, da of Wilhelm Karl Oppermann (d 1994), of Hannover, Germany; *Career* HM Dip Service (Colonial Office) 1966–67, called to the Bar Gray's Inn 1970, in practice 1971–86, dep judge advocate 1986–90, asst judge advocate gen 1990–95, asst recorder 1989–93, recorder of the Crown Ct 1993–95, circuit judge (SE Circuit) 1995–; *Recreations* sailing, skiing, classical music, reading, walking, cooking and (occasional) golf; *Clubs* Royal London Yacht (Cowes), Naval and Military; *Style*— His Hon Judge Timothy King; ✉ The Crown Court at Snaresbrook, Hollybush Hill, London E11 1QW (☎ 0181 982 5500)

KING, Sir Wayne Alexander; 8 Bt (UK 1815), of Charlestown, Roscommon; s of Sir Peter Alexander King, 7 Bt (d 1973), and Jean Margaret, *née* Cavell; *b* 2 Feb 1962; *Educ* Sir Roger Mawood's Sch Sandwich Kent, Algonquin Coll Ontario Canada; *m* 1984, Laura Ellen, da of Donald James Lea, of Almonte, Ontario; 1 s (Peter Richard Donald b 1988); *Heir* s, Peter Richard Donald King b 4 May 1988; *Style*— Sir Wayne King, Bt; ✉ 146 High St, Almonte, Ontario, Canada KOA 1AO

KING, William Lawrence; s of Ian Lawrence King (d 1974), and Maisie, *née* Cooke (d 1988); *b* 29 Dec 1947; *Educ* Oundle, Trinity Hall Cambridge (MA); *m* 24 May 1975, Jane, da of Philip George Wrixon, of Norton Canon, Hereford; 2 s (Edward b 1979, Tom b 1981); *Career* slr Macfarlanes: joined 1970, ptnr 1979–, Master Worshipful Co of Slrs; *Recreations* beagling; *Style*— William King, Esq; ✉ Macfarlanes, 10 Norwich St, London EC4A 1BD (☎ 0171 831 9222, fax 0171 831 9607)

KING-FARLOW, Charles Roderick; s of Roderick Sydney King-Farlow, of Birmingham, and Alice Frances Joan, *née* Ashley; *b* 16 Feb 1940; *Educ* Eton, Trinity Coll Oxford (MA); *m* 1965, Tessa, da of Robert Lawrence Raikes, of Llanvethrine, nr Abergavenny; 1 s (Joshua Michael b 1971), 1 da (Alice Caroline 1968); *Career* admitted slr 1965; ptnr Pinsent Curtis (formerly Pinsent & Co) 1969–; dir ISS Europe Ltd 1969–; pres Birmingham Law Soc 1991–92, vice pres Fedn of European Bars 1992–93; chm Midlands Arts Centre 1985–89; memb: CBSO Cncl of Mgmnt 1972–80, Friends of Birmingham Museums and Art Gallery Ctee 1972–78 and 1983–88, Bd City of Birmingham Touring Opera 1987–92, Public Art Cmmns Agency 1990–, Taxation Ctee of Historic Houses Assoc 1980–; contrib to Taxation and International Journal of Museum Management; *Recreations* gardening, fishing, skiing; *Clubs* Oriental; *Style*— Charles King-Farlow, Esq; ✉ 8 Vicarage Rd, Edgbaston, Birmingham B15 3ES (☎ 0121 455 0902); Pinsent Curtis, 3 Colmore Circus, Birmingham B4 6BH (☎ 0121 200 1050)

KING-HAMILTON, His Hon (Myer) Alan Barry; QC (1954); s of Alfred King-Hamilton (d 1959), of Oxshott, Surrey, and Constance Clyde Druiffe (d 1962); *b* 9 Dec 1904; *Educ* Bishop's Stortford GS, Trinity Hall Cambridge (MA, pres Union Soc); *m* 1935, Rosalind Irene (d 1991), da of Dr Abraham Ellis; 2 da (Mary, Jane); *Career* serv WWII Sqdn Ldr RAF; recorder: Hereford 1954, Gloucester 1956, Wolverhampton 1961; bencher Middle Temple 1961; dep chm Oxford County Quarter Sessions 1955, ldr Oxford Circuit 1961, cmmr of Assizes 1961 and 1963, legal memb Med Practices Ctee Miny of Health 1961; additional judge Central Criminal Ct 1964, ret 1979; dep circuit judge 1980–84; legal memb ABTA Appeal Bd 1980–95; pres: W London Synagogue 1965–72 and 1975–83 (hon life pres 1995), Westlon Housing Assoc 1977 (hon life pres 1995), Birnbeck Housing Assoc 1995 (memb Ctee 1982); tstee Barnet Community Tst 1985–88, memb Arts and Library Ctee MCC 1985–89, chm Pornography and Violence Res Tst (formerly Mary Whitehouse Res and Educn Tst) 1986–96; Freeman City of London 1965, Master Worshipful Co of Needlemakers 1969; memb Bar Cncl 1956–60; *Books* And Nothing But the Truth (autobiography 1982); *Recreations* cricket, gardening, theatre, reading; *Style*— His Hon Alan King-Hamilton, QC; ✉ c/o RAF Club, 128 Piccadilly, London W1V 0PY

KING OF WARTNABY, Baron (Life Peer, UK 1983), of Wartnaby in Co of Leicestershire; John Leonard King; kt (1979); yr s of Albert John King, and Kathleen King; *b* 1918; *m* 1, 1941, Lorna Kathleen Sykes (d 1969); 3 s (Richard, Philip and Rupert (twins)), 1 da (Rachel); m 2, 1970, Hon Isabel Monckton, 3 and yst da of 8 Viscount Galway; *Career* fndr Whitehouse Industries Ltd and Ferrybridge Industries Ltd 1945; chm: Pollard Ball & Roller Bearing Co Ltd 1961–69 (md 1945), FKI Babcock plc (formerly Babcock & Wilcox Ltd, subsequently Babcock International plc) 1970–94 (currently pres), Dennis Motor Holdings Ltd 1970–72, SKF (UK) Ltd 1976–89, British Nuclear Associates Ltd 1978–89, British Airways PLC 1981–93 (pres 1993–), R J Dick Inc USA and Dick Corporation USA until 1992, Aerostructures Hamble 1992–95; chm: National Nuclear Corporation 1981–89, Royal Ordnance plc 1985–88; dir: First Union Corporation USA until 1989, Short Brothers plc 1989–, Norman Broadbent International Ltd 1990–, Sabena World Airlines 1990, Daily Telegraph plc 1990–, York Trust 1990–92, Wide Range Engineering Services Ltd 1992–, The Spectator (1828) Ltd 1993–; chm NEB 1980–81 (dep chm 1979–80); chm: City and Industl Liaison Cncl 1973–85, Review Bd for Govt Contracts 1975–78, Br Olympic Appeals Ctee 1975–78, Macmillan Appeal for Continuing Care (cancer relief) 1977–78, Alexandra Rose Day Fndn 1980–85; memb: Engrg Industs Cncl 1975, NEDC Ctee on Fin for Investmt 1976–78, Grand Cncl and Fin Policy Ctee CBI 1976–78, Ctee Ranfurly Library Serv, Advsy Ctee Optima Fund Management LP USA, Advsy Cncl Westinghouse Electric Europe, Advsy Cncl Prince's Youth Business Tst, Advsy Ctee on Foreign Investments to the Venezuelan President; vice pres Cancer Relief Macmillan Fund (formerly Nat Soc for Cancer Relief) 1988; tstee: Royal Opera House Tst, Liver Res Unit Tst 1988–, Blenheim Fndn; Freeman City of London 1984, Companion Royal Aeronautical Soc 1985–87 (pres Heathrow Branch); MFH: Badsworth Foxhounds 1949–58, Duke of Rutland's Foxhounds Belvoir 1958–72; chm Belvoir Hunt 1972–; currently farmer own estate in Leicestershire; winner Nat Free Enterprise Award 1987; Hon DUniv Gardner-Webb Coll USA 1980, Hon DSc Cranfield Inst of Technol 1989, Hon City and Guilds Insignia award in Technol; Cdr of Royal Order of the Polar Star (Sweden) 1983; ARAeS 1982, FCIT 1982, FIMgt 1978; *Recreations* hunting, field sports, painting; *Clubs* White's, Pratt's, Brook (New York); *Style*— The Rt Hon the Lord King of Wartnaby; ✉ Wartnaby, Melton Mowbray, Leics LE14 3HY; British Airways PLC, Berkeley Square House, Berkeley Square, London W1X 6BA (☎ 0171 930 4915)

KING-SMITH, Ronald Gordon (Dick); s of Capt Ronald King-Smith, DSO, MC (d 1980), of Bitton, Glos, and Gay, *née* Boucher (d 1980); *b* 27 March 1922; *Educ* Marlborough, Univ of Bristol (BEd); *m* 6 Feb 1943, Myrle, da of Gp Capt Tom Harry England, DSC, AFC (d 1975), of Malta; 1 s (Giles b 1953), 2 da (Juliet b 1945, Elizabeth (Mrs Rose) b 1948); *Career* WWII serv Lt Grenadier Gds 1941–46 (wounded Italy 1944, despatches); farmer 1947–67, teacher 1976–82, writer of children's books 1978–; *Books* incl: The Fox Busters (1978), Daggie Dogfoot (1980), The Mouse Butcher (1981), Magnus Powermouse (1982), The Queen's Nose (1983), The Sheep-Pig (1983), Harry's Mad (1984), Saddlebottom (1985), Noah's Brother (1986), Tumbleweed (1987), The Toby Man (1988), Martin's Mice (1988), George Speaks (1988), Dodos are For Ever (1989), Paddy's Pot of Gold (1990), The Water Horse (1990), Alphabeasts (1990), Jungle Jingles (1990), and a great many more; *Recreations* writing children's books; *Style*— Dick King-Smith, Esq; ✉ Diamond's Cottage, Queen Charlton, Keynsham, Bristol BS18 2SJ (☎ 0117 986 4655)

KINGDOM, Leonard Grantley; s of Thomas Kingdom (d 1957), of Leics, and Amy Kingdom (d 1968); *b* 24 June 1919; *Educ* Wyggeston Sch Leicester, King's Coll Cambridge (MA, MB BChir), St Bartholomew's Hosp (FRCS); *m* 1, 4 Dec 1943 (m dis 1969), Joyce Elizabeth Mary, da of Sqdn Ldr William Catchpole, AFC (d 1935); 1 s (Richard b 31 March 1946 d 1971), 1 da (Susan b 6 June 1948); m 2, 3 Dec 1969, Susan Elizabeth, da of William King (d 1971), of Bexley; 1 s (William b 8 Dec 1971), 1 da (Sarah b 21 Feb 1976); *Career* Capt RAMC 1943–47, graded surgical specialist BLA 1944; served: Mobile Neurosurgical Unit, Field Surgical Unit (O/C); jr hosp appts at Bart's and Royal Free Hosp, demonstrator of anatomy Univ of Cambridge 1942, chief asst Bart's 1948–52, conslt otologist LCC 1950–64; conslt ENT surgn: UCH 1952–78, Queen Mary's Hosp for Children 1950–64, St Luke's Hosp for the Clergy 1964–80, Hosp of St John and St Elizabeth 1978–80; memb of Ct City Univ 1980–85, memb Br Assoc of Otolaryngologists 1952; Freeman City of London, Liveryman Worshipful Co of Fan Makers (memb of Ct 1967–, Master 1979–80), pres City of London Past Masters Assoc 1980–81; FRSM 1948; *Recreations* large dogs and travelling; *Style*— Leonard Kingdom, Esq; ✉ Stoneygate, Top Park, Gerrards Cross, Bucks SL9 7PW (☎ 01753 883615)

KINGHAN, Neil; s of Derek Kinghan (d 1991), and Esmé, *née* Webb; *b* 20 Aug 1951; *Educ* Brentwood Sch, Hertford Coll Oxford (MA, MPhil); *m* 1994, Dr Lilian Pusavat; *Career* DOE: private sec to Parly Under Sec 1978–80, princ 1980–87, private sec to Mins of Housing Ian Gow then John Patten 1984–87, head Sport and Recreation Div 1987–90, head Homelessness Policy Div 1990–92, head Housing Private Fin Div Jan - June 1992, dir Housing Policy and Private Sector 1992–94, dir Departmental Task Force 1994–96, dir Local Govt Fin Policy 1996–; *Recreations* walking my dog, cricket, skiing; *Clubs* Surrey CC; *Style*— Neil Kinghan, Esq; ✉ 39 Magdalen Road, London SW18 3ND; Department of the Environment, 2 Marsham Street, London SW1P 3EB (☎ 0171 276 3159, fax 0171 276 4466)

KINGHORN, Dr George Robert; s of Alan Douglas Kinghorn, of Allendale, Northumberland, and Lilian Isobel, *née* Henderson; *b* 17 Aug 1949; *Educ* Royal GS Newcastle upon Tyne, Univ of Sheffield (MB ChB, MD); *m* 14 July 1973, Sheila Anne, da of Haydn Wilkinson Littlewood, of Sheffield; 1 s (Robert b 1978), 1 da (Joanne b 1982); *Career* trg in gen med Royal Hosp and Royal Infirmary Sheffield 1972–76, sr registrar in genito-urinary med Royal Infirmary Sheffield 1976–78, conslt in genito-urinary med General Infirmary Leeds 1979; Univ of Sheffield: conslt in genito-urinary med and clinical lectr i/c Sub-Dept of Genito-Urinary Med 1979, clinical dir of communicable diseases 1991–; WHO conslt: Sri Lanka 1985, Tunisia 1987; EEC conslt Kenya 1988; chm Advsy Sub-Ctee on Genito-urinary Med Trent Region 1989–93 (memb 1978–, vice chm 1985–89), memb Trent Regnl Med Ctee 1989–93, chm Special Advsy Ctee Ctee in GU Med 1986–87 (memb 1981–84, sec 1984–86), chm Regnl Educn Ctee GUM 1993–; hon sec Br Co-operative Clinical Gp 1983–93 (chm 1996–), chm Ctee on Genito-urinary Med RCP 1991–95 (memb 1983–86, hon sec 1986–90); memb: UK Working Pty MRC and INSERM Concorde Study 1988–, Clinical Medicine Bd RCP 1994–95; memb: Med Soc for Study of Venereal Diseases 1976–, E Midlands Soc of Physicians 1979–, Assoc of Genitourinary Medicine; MRCP 1986, FRCP 1988; *Recreations* travel, home computers, sport; *Style—* Dr George Kinghorn; ✉ Dept of Genitourinary Medicine, Royal Hallamshire Hospital, Glossop Rd, Sheffield S10 2JF (☎ 0114 271 3524, fax 0114 271 3408)

KINGMAN, Sir John Frank Charles; kt (1985); s of Dr Frank Edwin Thomas Kingman (d 1983), and Maud Elsie, *née* Harley (d 1951); *b* 28 Aug 1939; *Educ* Christ's Coll Finchley, Pembroke Coll Cambridge (MA, ScD); *m* 16 Dec 1964, Valerie, da of Frank Cromwell, OBE, ISO (d 1978); 1 s (John b 1969), 1 da (Charlotte b 1972); *Career* mathematician; prof of maths and statistics Univ of Sussex 1966–69, prof of maths Univ of Oxford 1969–85, vice chllr Univ of Bristol 1985–; chm Sci and Engrg Res Cncl 1981–85; non-exec dir IBM UK Holdings Ltd; vice pres Parly and Scientific Ctee 1986–89 (vice chm 1983–86); pres: Royal Statistical Soc 1987–89, London Mathematical Soc 1990–92; memb Brighton Co Borough Cncl 1968–71; Freeman City of London, Liveryman Worshipful Co of Goldsmiths 1987; Hon DSc: Univ of Sussex 1983, Univ of Southampton 1985; Hon LLD Univ of Bristol 1989; Officier des Palmes Académiques (France) 1989; FRS 1971; *Books* Introduction to Measure and Probability (with S J Taylor, 1966), The Algebra of Queues (1966), Regenerative Phenomena (1972), Mathematics of Genetic Diversity (1980), Poisson Processes (1993); *Clubs* Lansdowne, United Oxford and Cambridge Univ; *Style—* Sir John Kingman, FRS; ✉ Senate House, University of Bristol, Tyndall Avenue, Bristol BS8 1TH (☎ 0117 928 9000, fax 0117 930 4263)

KINGS NORTON, Baron (Life Peer UK 1965), of Wotton Underwood, Co Buckingham; Harold Roxbee Cox; kt (1953); s of William John Roxbee Cox (d 1931), of Birmingham, and Amelia, *née* Stern (d 1949); *b* 6 June 1902; *Educ* Kings Norton GS, Imperial Coll London (FIC, PhD); *m* 1, 12 July 1927, Doris Marjorie (d 1980), da of Ernest Edward Withers (d 1939), of Northwood; 2 s (Christopher, Jeremy); m 2, 1982, Joan Ruth Pascoe, da of late W G Pack, of Torquay; *Career* chm: Landspeed Ltd 1975–, Cotswold Research Ltd 1979–, Berger Jenson & Nicholson Ltd 1967–75, Metal Box Co 1961–67; dir: Dowty Rotol 1968–75, Ricardo & Co (Engrs) 1927 Ltd 1965–77, Br Printing Corp 1968–77, Hoechst UK 1970–75; pres: Royal Aeronautical Soc 1947–49, Royal Instn 1969–76; chm: Cncl for Scientific and Industl Res 1961–65, Cncl for Nat Academic Awards 1964–71; chllr Cranfield Univ 1969–; Freeman City of London 1987, Liveryman Guild of Air Pilots and Air Navigators 1987; Hon DSc: Univ of Birmingham 1954, Cranfield Inst of Technol 1970, Univ of Warwick 1986; Hon DTech Brunel Univ 1966, Hon LLD CNAA 1969; Bronze Medal Univ of Louvain 1946, Medal of Freedom with Silver Palm (USA) 1947; FIMechE, Hon FRAeS, FEng 1976 (fndr fell); *Recreations* collecting aeronautical antiquities; *Clubs* Athenaeum; *Style—* The Rt Hon Lord Kings Norton; ✉ Westcote House, Chipping Campden, Glos GL55 6AG (☎ 01386 840440)

KINGSALE, 30 Baron (I c 1340, precedence 1397); John de Courcy; Premier Baron of Ireland; s of Lt-Cdr Hon Michael de Courcy, RN (d 1940; s of 29 Baron Kingsale who was fifth in descent from the Lord Kingsale who successfully claimed from George III the hereditary privilege of keeping his hat on in front of the king; his cous and predecessor had also successfully claimed this privilege under William III, though the legend that King John granted the permission first is probably apocryphal), and Joan Reid (d 1967); *b* 27 Jan 1941; *Educ* Stowe, Sorbonne, Salzburg Univ; *Heir* 3 cous twice removed, Nevinson Russell de Courcy; *Career* 2 Lt Irish Guards 1962–65; formerly: bingo caller, film extra, safari park driver, barman in local pub; occasional broadcaster, plumber, builder and carpenter; chm Strand Publications 1970; dir: D'Olier Grantmesnil & Courcy Acquisitions 1970, Banaid International Brisbane 1987, De Courcy-Daunt Brisbane 1987, Kinsale Development Corporation; pres Impex Consultants 1987; chm Nat Assoc of Serv to Realm 1979, patron L'Orchestre de Monde 1987; columnist Ukonline 1995; *Recreations* shooting, venery, palaeontology; *Clubs* Cavalry and Guards'; *Style—* The Rt Hon Lord Kingsale; ✉ 15 Dallimore Mead, Nunney, Frome, Somerset BA11 4NB

KINGSBURY, Derek John; CBE (1988); s of Maj A Kingsbury, BEM, of Virginia Water, Surrey; *b* 10 July 1926; *Educ* Strodes Secdy Sch Egham, City and Guilds Coll London (BSc); *m* 1; 1 c (and 1 c decd); m 2, 1980, Sarah; 1 c; *Career* chm: Fairey Group plc 1987–96 (gp chief exec 1982–91), David Brown Group plc 1992–96, Goode Durrant plc 1992–96; non-exec dir: Vickers 1981–91, Acal plc 1991–94; dep chief exec Dowty Group until 1982; memb Cncl CBI 1980–86 (chm Overseas Ctee 1980–84), memb Review Bd for Govt Contracts 1986–94; vice pres Def Manufacturers' Assoc 1993– (memb Cncl 1985–92, chm Fin and Gen Purposes Ctee 1990–92, chm 1987–90), chm CET Pilot Scheme Steering Ctee 1987–90; memb Engrg Cncl 1990–93, pres Br Heart Fndn Horse Show 1977–; Liveryman Worshipful Co of Scientific Instrument Makers, Freeman City of London; FEng 1991, FIEE, FCGI, FRSA, CIMgt; *Recreations* golf (pres Aircraft Golfing Soc 1995–); *Clubs* MCC, Lord's Taverners', RAC, Beaconsfield Golf, St Enodoc Golf; *Style—* Derek Kingsbury, Esq, CBE, FEng; ✉ Trecaven, Rock, Cornwall PL27 6LB

KINGSDOWN, Baron (Life Peer UK 1993), of Pemberton in the County of Lancashire; Sir Robert (Robin) Leigh-Pemberton; KG (1994), PC (1987); s of Capt Robert Douglas Leigh Pemberton, MBE, MC, JP (d 1964), of Torry Hill, Sittingbourne, Kent, and Helen Isabel, *née* Payne-Gallwey (d 1985); *b* 5 Jan 1927; *Educ* Eton, Trinity Coll Oxford; *m* 8 July 1953, Rosemary Davina, OBE (1995), da of Lt-Col David Walter Arthur William Forbes, MC (ka 1943), of Callander, Falkirk, and Diana (d 1982; who m 2, 1946, 6 Marquess of Exeter who d 1981, gda of 1 Baron Faringdon); 5 s (Hon John b 16 March 1955, Hon James b 10 Dec 1956, Hon Edward b 10 Jan 1959, Thomas b 22 Sept 1961, d 13 March 1993, Hon William b 20 March 1964); *Career* Lt Grenadier Gds, served Palestine 1946–48; Hon Col: Kent and Sharpshooters Yeo Sqdn 1979–92, 265 (KCLY) Signal Sqdn (V) 1979–92, 5 (Vol) Bn The Queen's Regt 1987–93; pres: SE TA&VR Assoc 1986–95, Kent SSAFA; hon pres: Kent Wing Air Trg Corps; called to the Bar Inner Temple 1954, practised London and SE Circuit 1954–60, hon bencher 1983; dir: Birmid Qualcast 1966–83 (dep chm 1970, chm 1975–77), University Life Assurance Society 1967–78, Redland Ltd 1972–83, Equitable Life Assurance Society 1979–83 (vice pres 1982–83); chm: National Westminster Bank 1977–83 (dir 1972–83, dep chm 1974), Ctee of London Clearing Bankers 1982–83; govr Bank of England 1983–93; non-exec dir: Hambros PLC 1993–, Redland PLC 1993–, Foreign and Colonial Investment Trust PLC 1993–; Lord-Lieut of Kent 1982– (DL 1970, vice Lord-Lieut 1972–82), JP 1961–75, co cncllr Kent 1961–77 (chm Cncl 1972–75); memb NEDC 1982–92; tstee: Royal Acad of Arts Tst 1982–87 (now tstee emeritus), Kent CCC, Kent Co Playing Fields Assoc, Kent Co Agric Soc, Rochester Cathedral Tst, The Kent Fndn; chm Canterbury Cathedral Tst; pres: Kent Co Agric Soc 1984–85, E of England Agric Soc 1986–87, City Disputes Panel 1994–; tstee RASE 1993– (pres 1989–90); pres: Kent Rural Community Cncl, St John Cncl for Kent; patron Red Cross for Kent; hon fell Trinity Coll Oxford 1984, pro chllr Univ of Kent 1977–83, seneschal of Canterbury Cathedral 1983–; Liveryman Worshipful Co of Mercers; Hon DCL Univ of Kent 1983; Hon DLitt: City of London 1988, Loughborough 1989, City Poly 1990; memb RSA, Hon FCIB, KStJ 1983; *Recreations* country pursuits, the arts; *Clubs* Brooks's, Cavalry & Guards'; *Style—* The Rt Hon Lord Kingsdown, KG, PC; ✉ Torry Hill, Sittingbourne, Kent ME9 OSP

KINGSHOTT, (Albert) Leonard; s of Albert Leonard Kingshott, of Ingatestone, Essex, and Katherine Bridget, *née* Connelley; *b* 16 Sept 1930; *Educ* LSE (BSc); *m* 10 Aug 1957, Valerie, da of Ronald Simpson (d 1964); 2 s (Adrian b 1960, Brendan b 1962), 1 da (Nicola b 1958); *Career* RAF (FO) 1952–55; fin analyst BP Corporation 1955–59, economist British Nylon Spinners 1960–62, fin mangr Iraq Petroleum Co 1963–65; treas 1965–70: Ford of Europe, Ford Motor Co, Ford of Britain; fin dir Whitbread Group 1970–72, md (fin) British Steel Corporation 1972–77; Lloyds Bank plc: dir Merchant Banking Div 1977, dir Int Banking Div 1977–89, exec dir Europe 1980, exec dir Marketing & Planning 1983, dep chief exec Marketing & Planning 1985 and dir several assoc cos; exec dir (banking) The Private Bank and Tst Co Ltd 1989–91, exec dir Rosehaugh PLC 1991 (chm 1992–93); appointed Crown Agent 1989–91, memb Monopolies and Mergers Cmmn 1990–96; dir Mutual Management Services 1993–96, md MicroTruce Ltd 1996–; non-exec dir: Shandwick PLC 1993–, New Markets Foods Ltd 1994–; chm Oakbridge Counselling Gp 1990–; govr and assoc memb Faculty Ashbridge Mgmnt Coll; FCIS; *Books* Investment Appraisal (1967); *Recreations* reading, chess, golf; *Style—* Leonard Kingshott, Esq; ✉ 4 Delamas, Beggar Hill, Fryerning, Ingatestone, Essex

KINGSLAND, Charles Richard; s of Richard Alan Kingsland, of Nottingham, and Noreen Monica, *née* Hayes; *b* 29 Oct 1957; *Educ* Mundella GS Nottingham, Univ of Liverpool (MB ChB, MD, DRCOG, MRCOG); *m* Catharine Anne, da of Peter O'Neill; 1 s (Joseph Edward), 2 da (Charlotte Alexandra, Lucy Elizabeth); *Career* house offr Royal Liverpool Hosp 1982–83, registrar Liverpool Hosps 1983–87, res fell Middx Hosp 1987–89, sr lectr in obstetrics and gynaecology Univ of Liverpool 1992–93 (lectr 1989–92), conslt 1993–; memb: BMA 1982, American Fertility Soc 1992, Br Fertility Soc (memb Ctee 1992–); *Recreations* soccer, hiking; *Style—* Charles Kingsland, Esq; ✉ The Women's Hospital, Crown Street, Liverpool L8 7SS (☎ 0151 708 9988, fax 0151 702 4137)

KINGSLAND, Baron (Life Peer UK 1994), of Shrewsbury in the County of Shropshire; Sir Christopher James Prout; kt (1990), PC (1994), TD (1987), QC (1988); s of Frank Yabsley Prout, MC and bar (d 1980), and Doris Lucy, *née* Osborne (d 1983); *b* 1 Jan 1942; *Educ* Sevenoaks Sch, Univ of Manchester (BA), Queen's Coll Oxford (BPhil, DPhil); *Career* TA Offr (Maj) OU OTC 1966–74, 16/5 The Queen's Royal Lancers 1974–82, 3 Armd Div 1982–88, RARO 1988–; called to the Bar Middle Temple 1972, bencher 1996; ESU fell Columbia Univ NYC 1963–64, staff memb Int Bank for Reconstruction and Devpt (UN) Washington DC 1966–69, Leverhulme fell and lectr in law Univ of Sussex 1969–79; MEP (C) Shropshire and Stafford) 1979–94; dep whip Euro Democratic Gp (EDG) 1979–82, chief whip of the EDG 1983–87, chm Parly Ctee on Legal Affrs 1987, ldr of Cons MEPs Euro Parl 1987–94, chm and ldr of the EDG 1987–92, vice chm EPP Parly Gp 1992–94; pres Shrops and W Midlands Agric Show 1993; Master Shrewsbury Drapers Co 1995; La Grande Médaille de la Ville de Paris 1988; Schuman Medal 1995; *Books* Market Socialism in Yugoslavia (1985), Halsbury's Laws of England (contrib Vols 8, 51 and 52, 4 edn); author of misc lectures, pamphlets, chapters and articles; *Recreations* riding, sailing, gardening; *Clubs* Pratt's, Beefsteak, Royal Ocean Racing, Royal Yacht Squadron; *Style—* The Rt Hon Lord Kingsland, PC, TD, QC; ✉ 4 Breams Buildings, Temple, London EC4 (☎ 0171 353 5835)

KINGSLEY, Ben; s of Rahimtulla Harji Bhanji, and Anna Lyna Mary, *née* Goodman; *b* 31 Dec 1943; *Educ* Manchester GS; *Career* actor; associate artist RSC; patron and affiliated memb of many charitable organisations; Hon MA Univ of Salford 1984; memb: BAFTA 1983, American Acad of Motion Picture Arts and Sciences; Padma Sri (India) 1985; *Theatre* incl: RSC 1967–86 (title roles incl Hamlet and Othello), Nat Theatre 1977–78 (leading roles incl Mosca in Volpone); *Films* incl: Gandhi, Betrayal, Turtle Diary, Harem, Silas Marner, Maurice, Slipstream, Testimony, Pascali's Island, Without a Clue, Murderers Amongst Us, Fifth Monkey, The Children, Bugsy, Sneakers, Searching for Bobby Fischer, Dave, Schindler's List, Death and the Maiden, Species, Twelfth Night; *Awards* incl: Oscar, BAFTA (twice), Golden Globe (twice), NY Critics', LA Critics', Evening Standard (Best Actor for Schindler's List) 1995, Grammy, Simon Wiesenthal Humanitarian, Berlin Golden Camera; *Style—* Ben Kingsley, Esq; ✉ c/o ICM Ltd, Oxford House, 76 Oxford Street, London W1N 0AX (☎ 0171 636 6565, fax 0171 323 0101)

KINGSLEY, David John; s of Walter John Kingsley, and Margery, *née* Walden; *b* 10 July 1929; *Educ* Southend HS for Boys, LSE (BSc(Econ)); *m* 1, July 1965 (m dis), Enid Sophia, da of Thomas Jones, MBE (d 1985), of Llandeilo; 2 da (Nichola Sophia b 1962, Nadia b 1964); m 2, May 1968 (m dis), Gillian, da of George Leech (d 1978); 2 s (Andrew John b 1966, Paul David b 1967); m 3, Oct 1988, Gisela Irene, *née* Reichardt; *Career* dir Benton and Bowles Advertising Agency 1961–64, fndr and ptnr Kingsley Manton & Palmer Advertising Agency 1964–78, dir and chm Kimpher Group Communications Group 1969–78, ptnr and chm Kingsley & Kingsley Business Consultancy 1974–; dir Francis Kyle Gallery 1978–, dir Eventability Group 1996–; pres Worldaware - The centre for world devpt educn, chm Cartoon Arts Tst 1994–; govr LSE (memb Standing Ctee) 1966–, memb Devpt Ctee RCM, tstee The Ireland Fund (UK) 1986–; tstee Royal Philharmonic Orch; Lab Parly candidate E Grinstead 1952–54; advsr to: Lab Pty and Govt on Communications 1962–70, Govt of Zambia 1974–82, Govt of Mauritius 1977–81, SDP 1981–87; organiser and creator: The Greatest Children's Party in the World for the Int Year of the Child 1980, HM The Queen's 60th Birthday Celebration; hon doctorate Soka Univ Tokyo; hon fell LSE; hon memb RCM; FRSA, FIPA, MCSD; *Books* Albion in China (1979); *Recreations* music, books, creating happy public events, travel, art; *Clubs* Reform; *Style—* David J Kingsley, Esq; ✉ Kingsley & Kingsley, 81 Mortimer Road, London N1 5AR (☎ and fax 0171 254 4310)

KINGSLEY, Sir Patrick Graham Toler; KCVO (1962, CVO 1950); s of Gerald Kingsley; *b* 1908; *Educ* Winchester, New Coll Oxford; *m* 1947, Priscilla Rosemary, da of Capt A Lovett Cameron; 3 s, 1 da; *Career* serv WWII Queen's Royal Regt; sec and Keeper of the Records Duchy of Cornwall 1954–72 (asst sec 1930–54); *Style—* Sir Patrick Kingsley, KCVO; ✉ West Hill Farm, West Knoyle, Warminster, Wilts

KINGSLEY, Stephen Michael; s of Ernest Robert Kingsley, of Cheadle, Cheshire, and Ursula Renate, *née* Bochenek (d 1972); *b* 1 June 1952; *Educ* Cheadle Hulme Sch, Univ of Bristol (BSc); *m* 18 March 1982, Michelle, da of Oscar Solovici (d 1983), of Paris; 1 da (Natalie b 1984); *Career* Arthur Andersen 1973–: mangr 1979–86, ptnr 1986–, head London Capital Markets Gp 1987–92, dir Euro regnl capital mkts 1988–93, dir Euro regnl banking and capital mkts 1993–; memb Tech Panel Securities and Investmts Bd 1985–87; visiting lectr Coll of Petroleum Studies Oxford; FCA; *Books* Managing A Foreign Exchange Department (contrib, 1985), Currency Options (contrib, 1985), European Banking and Capital Markets - a strategic survey; *Recreations* travel, ballet, classical music, current affairs; *Style—* Stephen Kingsley, Esq; ✉ 23 Gloucester Walk, London W8 4HZ (☎ 0171 937 4525); Arthur Andersen, 1 Surrey Street, London WC2R 2PS (☎ 0171 438 3000, 0171 438 3855, fax 0171 831 1133, telex 8812711)

KINGSNORTH, Andrew Norman; s of John Norman Kingsnorth, of Eynsford, Dartford, Kent, and Kathleen Dorothy, *née* Bassett; *b* 20 Nov 1948; *Educ* Sevenoaks Sch Kent, Royal Free Hosp Sch of Med (BSc, MB BS, MS, FRCS 1984); *m* 1 June 1974, Jane

Mary, da of Mervyn Bryant Poulter; 2 s (Edward Anthony b 1 July 1977, Peter John b 27 March 1982), 1 da (Bryony Jane b 30 June 1980); *Career* house surgn Addenbrooke's Hosp Cambridge 1974–75, sr house offr Norwich Hosps 1976–77, registrar John Radcliffe Hosp Oxford 1977–80, res fell Harvard Univ Boston 1980–81, lectr in surgery Univ of Edinburgh 1982–86, jr conslt Groote Schuur Hosp Cape Town SA 1986–87, sr lectr and reader in surgery Univ of Liverpool 1987–96, prof of surgery Plymouth Postgrad Med Sch 1996–; RCS: Arris and Gale lectr 1984, memb Ct of Examiners 1994; Rodney Smith prize Pancreatic Soc 1993; *Recreations* duplicate bridge, fell walking; *Clubs* Formby Bridge; *Style—* Andrew Kingsnorth, Esq; ✉ Somerville, 43 Thorn Park, Mannamead, Plymouth PL3 4TF; Plymouth Postgraduate Medical School, Department of Surgery, Level 7, Derriford Hospital, Plymouth PL6 8DH (☎ 01752 763017, fax 01752 769724)

KINGSTON, 11 Earl of (I 1768); Sir Barclay Robert Edwin King-Tenison; 15 Bt (I 1682); also Baron Kingston of Rockingham (I 1764), Viscount Kingston of Kingsborough (I 1766), Baron Erris (I 1800), Viscount Lorton (I 1806); s of 10 Earl of Kingston (d 1948); *b* 23 Sept 1943; *Educ* Winchester, RMA Sandhurst; *m* 1, 1965 (m dis 1974), Patricia Mary, da of E C Killip, of Beoley Lodge, Uttoxeter, Staffs; 1 s, 1 da (Lady Maria Lisette b 1970); m 2, 1974 (m dis 1979), Victoria, da of D C Edmonds, of Northwood, Middx; m 3, 9 Feb 1990, Corleen Jennifer Rathbone; *Heir* s, Robert Charles Henry, Viscount Kingsborough b 20 March 1969; *Career* late Lt Royal Scots Greys; *Style—* The Rt Hon the Earl of Kingston; ✉ c/o House of Lords, London SW1A

KINGSTON, Beryl Alma; da of Herbert Edwards, and Ella, *née* Parodi; *b* 28 Jan 1931; *Educ* Streatham Secdy Sch, LCC GS, King's Coll London (BA, AKC); *m* 29 July 1950, Roy Darren Kingston; 1 s (Lawrence b 1 June 1954), 2 da (Mary b 14 July 1956, Caroline b 10 March 1959); *Career* author; teacher in various ILEA schs 1952–54 and 1964–75, head of English Felpham Comp 1975–85; memb: Nat Childbirth Tst 1956, CND 1960, Ctee of 100, Soc of Authors 1980–; *Books* incl: Kisses and Ha'pennies (1986), A Time to Love (1987), The Easter Empire Trilogy (1988–90), London Pride (1990), War Baby (1991), Two Silver Crosses (1993), Maggie's Boy (1994), Alive and Kicking (1995), Laura's Way (1996); *Recreations* swimming, walking, theatre, reading, making music; *Style—* Mrs Beryl Kingston; ✉ c/o Darley Anderson Books, 11 Eustace Road, Fulham, London SW6 1JB (☎ 0171 385 6652)

KINGSTON, (Thomas) David; s of Rev John Howard Kingston (d 1978), of Limavady, Co Derry, and Gertrude Elizabeth Hare (d 1977); *b* 3 March 1943; *Educ* Portora Royal Sch Enniskillen, Wadham Coll Oxford (MA); *m* 24 June 1967, Georgina, da of William George Ashmore; 2 da (Tara Catherine b 4 June 1970, Candia Louise b 22 Sept 1971); *Career* jt asst actuary Scottish Widows Fund Edinburgh 1967–68 (actuarial student 1964–67); Irish Life Assurance plc: sr investmt analyst and dep fund mangr 1968–73, pensions actuary 1973–74, fund mangr 1974–75, pensions mangr 1975–80, mktg ops mangr 1980–83, md 1983–; Lord Mayor's Millenium award 1988; FFA 1967, FPMI 1979, ASIA 1972; *Books* Measuring Investment Performance (1975), Pension Funds & Inflation (1978); *Recreations* tennis, windsurfing, skiing, gardening; *Style—* David Kingston, Esq; ✉ Irish Life Assurance plc, Lower Abbey St, Dublin 1, Ireland (☎ 00 353 1 704 2000, fax 00 353 1 704 1908)

KINGSTON, Jeremy Henry Spencer; s of William Henry Kingston (d 1989), of Brighton, Sussex, and Elsie, *née* Cooper (d 1980); *b* 5 Aug 1931; *Educ* Reigate GS Surrey; *m* 1967, Meg, da of James Ritchie, of Dumbarton; 2 s (Benjamin James b 1968, Rufus William b 1970); *Career* Nat Serv 2 Lt Royal Signals; casually employed Chelsea 1951–55 (coffee houses, sculpture model, barr's clerk's clerk), sec to John Lehmann 1955–57; playwright: No Concern of Mine (Westminster) 1958, Signs of the Times (Vaudeville) 1973, Oedipus at the Crossroads (King's Head) 1977; theatre critic: Punch 1964–75, The Times 1985–; *Books* Love Among The Unicorns (1968), and three children's books; *Recreations* long conversations over meals; *Style—* Jeremy Kingston, Esq; ✉ 65 Romulus Court, Brentford Dock, Middx TW8 8QL (☎ 0181 568 4714); The Times, Pennington St, London E1 9XN

KINGSTON, (William) Martin; QC (1992); s of William Robin Kingston, of Bishops Frome, Worcs, and Iris Edith, *née* Grocott; *b* 9 July 1949; *Educ* Middlewich Secdy Modern Sch, Hartford Coll of Further Educn, Univ of Liverpool (LLB); *m* 9 Sept 1972, Jill Mary, da of Robert Philip Siney Bache; 2 da (Joanna Jessie b 3 Feb 1976, Emma Rachel b 9 Dec 1980), 1 s (Thomas Henry Robin b 22 June 1978); *Career* called to the Bar Middle Temple 1972, recorder 1991– (asst recorder 1987–91); dep chm Agricultural Lands Tbnl 1985–, asst cmmr Parly Boundary Cmmn for England 1992–; *Recreations* fly fishing, skiing, reading, holidays, sheep; *Style—* Martin Kingston, Esq, QC; ✉ 5 Fountain Court, Steelhouse Lane, Birmingham B4 6DR (☎ 0121 606 0500, fax 0121 606 1501)

KINGSTON, Bishop of 1992–; Rt Rev (John) Martin Wharton; s of John Wharton, of Newton-in-Furness, Cumbria, and Marjorie Elizabeth, *née* Skinner (d 1962); *b* 6 Aug 1944; *Educ* Ulverston GS, Univ of Durham (BA), Univ of Oxford (MA); *m* 29 Aug 1970, Marlene Olive; 1 da (Joanna Helen b 17 Nov 1972), 2 s (Andrew Benjamin b 1 March 1974, Mark Richard b 6 March 1978); *Career* Martins Bank Ltd 1960–64; ordained: deacon 1972, priest 1973; curate: St Peter Spring Hill Birmingham 1972–75, St John the Baptist Croydon 1975–77; dir of pastoral studies Ripon Coll Cuddesdon Oxford 1977–83, curate All Saints Cuddesdon 1979–83, sec Bd of Min and Trg Dio of Bradford 1983–92, residentiary canon Bradford Cathedral 1992; *Books* Knowing Me, Knowing You (with Malcolm Goldsmith, 1993); *Recreations* sport; *Clubs* Lancs CCC; *Style—* The Rt Rev the Bishop of Kingston; ✉ 24 Albert Drive, London SW19 6LS (☎ 0181 789 3218); Kingston Episcopal Area Office, Whitelands College, West Hill, London SW15 3SN (☎ 0181 780 2308, fax 0181 789 3985)

KINGSTON, Thomas Archer; s of Leonard James Kingston (d 1982), and Patricia Elisabeth, *née* Clay; *b* 4 Feb 1952; *Educ* Lady Eden's Sch, Highgate Sch, Keble Coll Oxford (MA); *m* 19 April 1980, Margaret, da of Thomas Donnellan (d 1989); 3 da (Joanna b 1983, Philippa b 1985, Helen b 1988); *Career* fin dir Mayfair Catering Co Ltd 1978–83 (co sec 1975), conslt BTR Management Services 1980–83, sr conslt Interactive Incorp 1983–; hon treas Chipperfield Choral Soc; Freeman City of London 1974, Liveryman Worshipful Co of Vintners 1983; MIMgt; *Recreations* music, children's entertainer; *Style—* Thomas Kingston, Esq; ✉ Briarwood, Langley Rd, Chipperfield Herts WD4 9JP (☎ 01923 263 486); Interactive (UK) Ltd, 9 Marlin House, Marlins Meadow, Croxley Centre, Watford WD1 8LW (☎ 01923 227 777)

KINGTON, Miles Beresford; s of William Beresford Nairn Kington, of Vrondeg Hall, nr Wrexham, and Jean Ann, *née* Sanders; *b* 13 May 1941; *Educ* Glenalmond, Trinity Coll Oxford (BA); *m* 1, 29 Feb 1964 (m dis), Sarah, da of Robert Paine, of Canterbury; 1 s (Thomas b 1968), 1 da (Sophie b 1966); m 2, 6 June 1987, Caroline, da of Nick Carter, of Knysna, S Africa; 1 s (Adam b 1987); *Career* freelance writer; former asst gardener in Ladbroke Square, former jazz corr The Times, double bass player with Instant Sunshine, literary ed Punch (cr Let's Parler Franglais column) 1973–80; journeyed through Andes for BBC's Great Train Journeys of The World Series (Three Miles High) 1980; humorous columnist for: The Times (cr Moreover) 1981–87, The Independent 1987–; translator of Alphonse Allais (French humorist); *Plays* Waiting for Stoppard (Bristol New Vic) 1995, The Death of Tchaikovsky - a Sherlock Holmes Mystery (Edinburgh Festival) 1996; *Books* incl: Miles and Miles, Moreover, Moreover Two, Nature Made Ridiculously Simple, The Franglais Lieutenant's Woman, Steaming Through Britain, The Jazz Anthology; *Recreations* bicycling, drinking, trying to remember if I have signed the Official Secrets Act; *Clubs* Ronnie Scott's; *Style—* Miles Kington, Esq; ✉ 40 Lower Stoke, Limpley Stoke, Bath BA3 6HR (☎ 01225 722262, fax 01225 723894)

KININMONTH, James Wyatt; s of Peter Wyatt Kininmonth, of Ashmore, Dorset, and Priscilla Margaret, *née* Sturge; *b* 26 Sept 1952; *Educ* Harrow, RMA Sandhurst; *m* 19 March 1977, Susie, da of Richard William Griffin, of Albermarle, N Carolina, USA; 1 s (Charles b 1985), 2 da (Annabel b 1980, Harriet b 1983); *Career* cmmnd 5 Royal Inniskilling Dragoon Gds 1974, Capt 1977, trans to Reserve 1978; dir Kininmonth Holdings 1982–85; md Kininmonth Lambert North America 1987–91 (dir 1985–); dir: Lowndes Lambert North America Ltd 1990–92, Cooper Gay & Co Ltd 1992–, Cooper Gay Steele & Co Ltd New York 1992–; memb Lloyd's since 1983; Freeman City of London; Liveryman: Worshipful Co of Haberdashers 1982, Worshipful Co of Insurers 1985; *Recreations* shooting, skiing, tennis, golf; *Clubs* City of London, Royal and Ancient, Piltdown; *Style—* J W Kininmonth, Esq; ✉ Lampool, Fairwarp, Sussex TN22 3DS (☎ 01825 712447, fax 01825 712636); Cooper Gay & Co Ltd, International House, 26 Creechurch Lane, London EC3A 5EH (☎ 0171 480 7322, fax 0171 481 4695)

KINKEAD-WEEKES, Prof Mark; s of Lt-Col Alfred Bernard (Bill) Kinkead-Weekes, MC (d 1960), and Vida May, *née* Kinkead (d 1946); *b* 26 April 1931; *Educ* Potchefstroom Boys HS, Univ of Cape Town (Rhodes scholar), Brasenose Coll Oxford; *m* March 1959, (Margaret) Joan, da of Benjamin Irvine (d 1966); 2 s (Paul b 1962, Timothy Guy b 1963); *Career* lectr Univ of Edinburgh 1958–65 (asst lectr 1956–58); Univ of Kent at Canterbury: lectr 1965–66, sr lectr 1966–74, prof of English and American lit 1974–84, pro vice chllr 1974–77, emeritus prof 1984–; FBA 1992; *Books* William Golding: A Critical Study (with I Gregor, 1967, 2 edn 1984), Samuel Richardson: Dramatic Novelist (1973), D H Lawrence: The Rainbow (ed, 1989), D H Lawrence: Triumph to Exile (1996); *Recreations* walking, music; *Style—* Prof Mark Kinkead-Weekes; ✉ 5 Albion Place, Ramsgate, Kent CT11 8HQ (☎ 01843 593168); Rutherford College, The University, Canterbury CT2 7NX (☎ 01227 764000 ext 3437)

KINLOCH, Sir David; 13 Bt (NS 1686), of Gilmerton, East Lothian; s of Maj Sir Alexander Davenport Kinloch, 12 Bt (d 1982), and his 2 w, Hilda Anna (d 1986), da of Thomas Walker, of Edinburgh; *b* 5 Aug 1951; *Educ* Gordonstoun; *m* 1, 1976 (m dis 1986), Susan, da of Arthur Middlewood, of North Side Farm, Kilham; 1 s (Alexander b 1978), 1 da (Alice b 1976); m 2, 1987, Maureen, da of Robert Carswell; 2 s (Christopher Robert b 1988, Matthew Carswell b 20 July 1990); *Heir* s, Alexander Kinloch b 31 May 1978; *Career* civil engr; *Style—* Sir David Kinloch, Bt; ✉ Gilmerton House, Athelstaneford, North Berwick, East Lothian (☎ 01620 880207)

KINLOCH, Sir David Oliphant; 5 Bt (UK 1873), of Kinloch, Co Perth; s of Sir John Kinloch, 4 Bt (d 1992), and Doris Ellaline, *née* Head; *b* 15 Jan 1942; *Educ* Charterhouse; *m* 1, 1968 (m dis 1979), Susan Minette, da of Maj-Gen Robert Elliott Urquhart, CB, DSO; 3 da (Katherine Cecilia b 1972, Emily Nicole b 1974, Nicola Marjorie b 1976); m 2, 1983, Sabine, da of Philippe de Loës, of Geneva, Switzerland; 1 s (Alexander Peter b 30 June 1986), 1 da (Sophie b 28 April 1994); *Heir* s, Alexander Peter Kinloch b 30 June 1986; *Career* CA; dep chief exec Caledonia Investments PLC; dir: British Empire Securities and General Trust plc, Sterling Industries PLC; chm: Ivory & Sime plc, Fleming Chinese Investment Trust plc; *Style—* Sir David Kinloch, Bt; ✉ House of Aldie, Fossoway, Kinross-shire KY13 7QH; 29 Walpole St, London SW3 4QS

KINLOSS, Lady (S Lordship 1602); Beatrice Mary Grenville; *née* Morgan-Grenville; da of Rev the Master of Kinloss (2 s of Lady Kinloss, 11 holder of title, but he suc er bro in courtesy title); suc grandmother as 12 holder of title 1944; *b* 18 Aug 1922; *Educ* Ravenscroft Sch Eastbourne; *m* 1950, Dr Greville Stewart Parker Freeman-Grenville, *qv*, s of Rev Ernest Freeman (changed name with husb to Freeman-Grenville, recognised by Lord Lyon King of Arms 1950); 1 s, 2 da; *Heir* s, Master of Kinloss; *Career* sits as Independent peer in House of Lords; memb House of Lords Ctee on European Communities (Sub Ctee C) 1990–92, has sat on numerous Select Ctees; special interests: disabled persons (especially deaf-blind), water transport, local govt; *Recreations* music, gradening; *Clubs* Civil Service; *Style—* The Rt Hon Lady Kinloss; ✉ North View House, Sheriff Hutton, York YO6 1PT

KINLOSS, Master of; Hon Bevil David Stewart Chandos Freeman-Grenville; s and h of Lady Kinloss, *qv*; *b* 20 June 1953; *Style—* The Master of Kinloss

KINNAIRD, 13 Lord (S 1682); Graham Charles Kinnaird; Baron Kinnaird of Rossie (UK 1860); s of 12 Lord Kinnaird, KT, KBE (d 1972); *b* 15 Sept 1912; *Educ* Eton; *m* 1, 1938 (m dis 1940), Nadia, da of Harold Augustus Fortington, OBE; m 2, 1940, Diana Margaret Elizabeth, da of late Robert Shuckburgh Copeman, of Roydon Hall, Diss, Norfolk; 1 s decd, 4 da (Caroline (Hon Mrs Best), Anna (Hon Mrs Liddell), Susan (Hon Mrs Lea), Mary (Hon Mrs Staib); *Heir* none; *Career* Flying Offr RAFVR, late Lt 4/5 Bn Black Watch (TA); sits as Cons in House of Lords; Liveryman Worshipful Co of Goldsmiths; *Clubs* Brooks's, Boodles; *Style—* The Rt Hon the Lord Kinnaird; ✉ The Garden House, Rossie Priory, Inchture, Perthshire (☎ 01828 686246)

KINNAIRD, Ross Andrew; s of Neil Edgar Henry Kinnaird, of Rugby, Warks, and Mary, *née* Murphy; *b* 1 Sept 1957; *Educ* Abington HS Wigston Leics; *m* Suzanne Marie, da of Francis O'Connor; *Career* news photographer; trained with Loughborough Echo, later joined Trader Group of Newspapers, Empics Photo Agency 1985–95, Allsport UK 1995–; assignments incl: Cwlth Games Auckland 1990, Hockey World Cup Lahore 1990, Soccer World Cup Italy 1990, US Open Tennis NYC, Rugby World Cup UK 1991 and S Africa 1995, Barcelona Olympics 1992, Euro Soccer Championships Sweden 1992, Wimbledon Championships 1992, Br Lions tour of NZ 1993, The Grand National 1988– and other maj domestic events; winner Fuji Sports Photographer of the Year Award 1992, Sports Photographer of the Year (Sports Cncl) 1993; memb: Professional Sports Photographers' Assoc, Association Internationale de la Presse Sportive; *Recreations* tennis; *Clubs* Carisbrooke Lawn Tennis; *Style—* Ross Kinnaird, Esq; ✉ Allsport UK, 3 Greenlea Park, Prince George's Road, London SW19 2JD (☎ 0181 685 1010, fax 0181 648 5240)

KINNEAR, Joseph Patrick Daniel (Joe); s of late Joe Patrick Reddy, of Dublin, and Greta Margaret, *née* O'Reilly (who m 2 Gerald Leo Kinnear (decd)); *b* 26 Dec 1947; *Educ* Leggatts Way Boys' Sch Watford; *m* 1971, Bonita; 1 s (Elliot b 1972), 1 da (Russelle b 1970); *Career* professional football manager; youth player: Watford Boys, Herts under 15 (capt), St Albans City; Tottenham Hotspur: joined 1963, turned professional 1964, league debut v West Ham Utd 1966, 197 league appearances, 105 other appearances, 6 goals; Brighton & Hove Albion 1975–76 (ret due to injury 1976); honours with Tottenham Hotspur: FA Cup winners 1967 (youngest player in final), FA Charity Shield winners 1968, League Cup winners 1971 and 1973, UEFA Cup winners 1972; 26 Republic of Ireland caps 1967–75 (debut v Turkey 1967); asst mangr Doncaster Rovers 1987–89, mangr Wimbledon 1991– (coach 1989–91); Mangr of the Month Award Sept 1993; *Recreations* horse racing; *Style—* Joe Kinnear, Esq; ✉ Timbers, Highwood Hill, Mill Hill, London NW7 4ET (☎ 0181 959 6544); Wimbledon FC, Selhurst Park Stadium, London SE25 6PY (☎ 0181 771 2233, fax 0181 768 0640)

KINNELL, Ian; QC (1987); s of Brian Kinnell (d 1960), and Grace Madeline, *née* Borer (d 1983); *b* 23 May 1943; *Educ* Sevenoaks Sch Kent; *m* 17 March 1970, Elizabeth Jane, da of David Farries Ritchie, of Hereford; 1 s (Alexander Murray b 1978), 1 da (Fiona b 1981); *Career* barr Gray's Inn 1967–89, recorder 1987–89; professional arbitrator; memb London Maritime Arbitrators' Assoc, pt/t chm Immigration Appeal Tbnl; *Style—* Ian Kinnell, Esq, QC; ✉ Woodside House, The Maypole, Monmouth, Gwent NP5 3QH (☎ 01600 713077 and 0171 388 4363, fax 01600 772880)

KINNIMENT, Prof David John; s of Herbert John Kinniment (d 1974), and Iris Henrietta, *née* Vivaudou (d 1987); *b* 10 July 1940; *Educ* Haberdashers' Aske's, Univ of Manchester (BSc, MSc, PhD); *m* 11 Aug 1962, Anne, da of James Lupton, of Burnley, Lancs; 2 da (Michelle Jane b 19 Aug 1964, Sarah Lynne b 15 Sept 1966); *Career* sr lectr in computer sci Univ of Manchester 1971–79 (lectr in electrical engrg 1964, lectr in computer sci 1964–71), head of Dept of Electrical and Electronic Engrg Univ of Newcastle upon Tyne 1982–90 and 1995– (prof of electronics 1979–); SERC: memb Sub Ctee Solid State Devices 1979–83 and Microelectronics Facilities 1982–86, memb Ctee Alvey Industl and Academic Liaison Ctee 1984–87 and Devices Ctee EPSRC 1988–91; memb Cncl Microelectronics Application Res Inst 1983–90, Peer Review Coll for IT (electronics and photonics tech) 1995–; MIEE 1966, MIEEE 1970; *Books* CAD for VLSI (1985); *Recreations* walking, history; *Style*— Prof David Kinniment; ✉ Electrical and Electronic Engineering Department, The University, Newcastle upon Tyne NE1 7RU (☎ 0191 222 7338, fax 0191 222 8180)

KINNOCK, Glenys; MEP (Lab) South Wales East (majority 120,247); *Career* MEP (Lab) South Wales East 1994–; *Style*— Mrs Glenys Kinnock, MEP; ✉ c/o European Parliament, 93–113 Rue Belliard, 1040, Brussels, Belgium

KINNOCK, Rt Hon Neil Gordon; PC (1983); s of late Gordon H Kinnock, steelworker and former coalminer, and Mary, *née* Howells; *b* 28 March 1942; *Educ* Lewis Sch Pengam, Univ Coll Cardiff (BA, DipEd); *m* 25 March 1967, Glenys Elizabeth, da of Cyril Parry; 1 s (Stephen), 1 da (Rachel); *Career* Univ Coll Cardiff: pres Socialist Soc 1963–66, pres Union 1965–66; tutor organiser WEA 1966–70, memb Welsh Hosp Bd 1969–71, former memb BBC Gen Advsy Cncl; MP (Lab): Bedwellty 1970–83, Islwyn 1983–95; PPS to Sec of State for Employment 1974–75, memb Nat Exec Lab Party 1978–94, princ oppn front bench spokesman on educn 1979–83 (memb Shadow Cabinet 1980–92), leader Lab Party and HM Oppn 1983–92, chm Lab Party 1987–88; EU tport cmmr 1995–; memb TGWU; pres Assoc of Lib Educn 1980–82; hon fell Univ Coll Cardiff; Hon LLD: Univ of Wales 1992, Univ of Glamorgan 1996; *Publications* Wales and the Common Market (1971), Making Our Way - Investing in Britain's Future (1986), Thorns and Roses (1992); *Recreations* music (esp male voice choral work and opera), the theatre, rugby football, being with family; *Style*— The Rt Hon Neil Kinnock; ✉ European Commission, rue de la Loi 200, B-1049 Brussels, Belgium

KINNOULL, 15 Earl of (S 1633); Arthur William George Patrick Hay; also Viscount Dupplin and Lord Hay (S 1627, 1633, 1697), Baron Hay (GB 1711); s of 14 Earl of Kinnoull (d 1938); *b* 26 March 1935; *Educ* Eton; *m* 1961, Gay Ann, da of Sir Denys Colquhoun Flowerdew Lowson, 1 Bt (d 1975); 1 s, 3 da; *Heir* s, Viscount Dupplin, *qv*; *Career* sits as Conservative in House of Lords, jr Cons whip House of Lords 1966–68; FRICS; sr ptnr Langley Taylor Scotland; memb Agricultural Valuers' Assoc; pres: National Cncl on Inland Tport 1964–76, Scottish Clans Assoc 1970; vice-pres Nat Assoc of Parish Cncls 1971; chm Property Owners' Building Society, non-exec dir Woolwich Buiding Society; cncl memb Royal Nat Mission to Deep Sea Fishermen 1978–; Cons del Cncl of Europe 1983–92; memb Royal Co of Archers (Queen's Body Guard for Scotland) 1965–; *Clubs* Turf, Pratt's, White's, MCC; *Style*— The Rt Hon the Earl of Kinnoull; ✉ 15 Carlyle Square, London SW3; 12 Little College Street, London SW1P 3SH (☎ 0171 222 1265); Pier House, Seaview, IOW

KINROSS, 5 Baron (UK 1902); Christopher Patrick Balfour; WS; s of 4 Baron Kinross, OBE, TD, DL, and his 2 w, Helen (d 1969), da of Alan Hog and formerly w of Lt-Col Patrick Perfect; *b* 1 Oct 1949; *Educ* Eton, Univ of Edinburgh (LLB); *m* 1974, Susan Jane, da of Ian Robert Pitman; 2 s (Hon Alan, Hon Derek Andrew b 1981); *Heir* s, Hon Alan Ian Balfour b 4 April 1978; *Career* slr and writer to HM's Signet; ptnr Shepherd & Wedderburn WS Edinburgh; memb Royal Co of Archers (Queen's Body Guard for Scotland); hon memb James IV Assoc of Surgns; *Recreations* pistol and rifle shooting, military vehicle restoration, off road Land Rover competition; *Clubs* New (Edinburgh); *Style*— The Rt Hon the Lord Kinross, WS; ✉ 11 Belford Place, Edinburgh EH4 3DH

KINSELLA, Paul; *b* 11 Aug 1947; *Educ* Beaumont Coll Berks, Trinity Hall Cambridge (BA); *m* Karin, *née* Riechers; *Career* Lawrence Graham: articled clerk (qualified 1974), ptnr and head of Commercial Property (Mgmnt Gp) 1978, head Commercial Property Dept 1985–, also head of Int Property; fndr memb: Steering Ctee for NY Assocs Rosenman & Colin, Jt Ctee of ABLE (Associated Business Lawyers in Europe); memb: Bd Br Cncl of Shopping Centres (chm Legislation and Govt Liaison Ctee), Int Real Estate Inst, German British C of C; *Recreations* travel, gardening, reading, conversation, retired cricketer; *Style*— Paul Kinsella, Esq; ✉ Lawrence Graham, 190 Strand, London WC2R 1JN (☎ 0171 379 0000, fax 0171 379 6854)

KINSELLA-BEVAN, Col Richard Dennis; s of late Lt Col Richard Bevan, of Bowelk House, Co Monaghan, and Margot, *née* Kinsella; *b* 5 Jan 1943; *Educ* Brighton Coll, King's Coll Cambridge (MA); *m* 1971, Kitty, da of late Capt A B B J Goor, KRRC, and Judith Bloomfield; 1 s (Desmond b 1 Oct 1975), 2 da (Emma-Louise b 16 March 1977, Edwina b 6 Sept 1979); *Career* cmmnd 5th Royal Inniskilling Dragoon Gds 1965; served: N Africa, Cyprus, Oman, Dhofar War (Sultan's Commendation), BAOR, and Iraq; psc, Cmd Sultan's Armoured Regt (Sultan's Commendation Medal and Order of the Special Emblem) 1984–87; Head Secretariat National Employers' Liaison Ctee for the Reserve Forces until 1995; sr Br loan serv offr (army) SOLF 1996–; author of articles in mil jls; Freeman City of London; FRGS 1985 (Baram-Rejang Expdn 1961, Kinabalu 1962); *Recreations* field sports (MH Shrivenham Beagles 1987–88); *Clubs* Cavalry and Guards, Kildare Street and University (Dublin); *Style*— Col R D Kinsella-Bevan; ✉ Command and Staff College, Sultan's Armed Forces, PO Box 113, Muscat, Sultanate of Oman

KINSEY, Oliver John Raymond; s of Raymond John Kinsey, of Mayfield, East Sussex, and Winifred, *née* Brown (d 1962); *b* 17 July 1945; *Educ* Radley, Queens' Coll Cambridge (MA); *m* 30 June 1973, Sarah Elizabeth Lyon, da of William Robertson Lyon Warnock; 1 s (Robin John Lyon b 19 Oct 1978); *Career* Church Adams Tatham: articled clerk 1968, admitted slr 1970, ptnr 1971–73; Simmons & Simmons: joined 1973, ptnr in jt charge Brussels Office 1975–76, ptnr Litigation Dept London 1977–, head of Insur Litigation Gp and memb Fin and Risk Mgmnt Ctees 1984, managing ptnr Litigation Dept and memb Ops Ctee 1994–; Freeman City of London 1974, Liveryman Worshipful Co of Scriveners 1974 (Ct asst 1993); memb: Law Soc of England and Wales, Int Bar Assoc, American Bar Assoc; *Recreations* golf, tennis, sailing, opera; *Clubs* Royal Ashdown Forest Golf, Nizels Golf, Law Society Yacht, Chipstead Sailing; *Style*— Oliver Kinsey, Esq; ✉ Simmons & Simmons, 21 Wilson Street, London EC2M 2TX (☎ 0171 628 2020, fax 0171 628 2070)

KINSEY, Thomas Richard Moseley; s of late Richard Moseley Kinsey and Dorothy Elizabeth Kinsey; *b* 13 Oct 1929; *Educ* Newtown Sch, Trinity Hall Cambridge (MA); *m* 1953, Ruth, *née* Owen-Jones; 2 s; *Career* ICI Ltd 1952–57, Tube Investments 1957–65; Delta plc: joined 1965, dir 1973–87, jt md 1977–82, dep chief exec 1982–87; dep chief exec Mitchell Cotts plc 1980–87; chm Birmingham Battery and Metal Co 1984–89; dir: Gower International 1984–89, Telcon 1984–89, Unistrut Europe 1989–92; chm Delcan International (formerly Deltacam Systems) 1989; FIMechE, CIMgt, FEng 1982; *Recreations* golf, travel; *Clubs* Athenaeum, Edgbaston Golf; *Style*— Thomas Kinsey, Esq, FEng; ✉ 6 Sutton Lodge, Blossomfield Road, Solihull, West Midlands B91 1NB (☎ 0121 704 2592)

KINSMAN, Rodney; *b* 1943; *Educ* Central Sch of Art; *m* Lisa Sau-Yuk, *née* Ngai; 1 s (Brandon Lee b 19 June 1968), 2 da (Charlie Sam b 24 Nov 1973, Chloe Jessica b 4 Jan 1975); *Career* furniture designer; md OMK Design (fndr 1966); visiting prof RCA 1985–86 (external examiner 1987–88), memb BA Advsy Cncl St Martin's and Central Sch of Art 1989–90, visiting prof The London Inst 1996; work in exhibitions incl: The Way We Live Now (V & A Museum) 1979, Sit (RIBA) 1980, The Modern Chair (ICA) 1989, The Review (Design Museum London) 1989, Evolution of the Modern Chair (Business Design Centre London) 1989, BBC Design Awards (Design Centre London) 1990, In Focus OMK The Designs of Rodney Kinsman (Design Museum) 1992; also chosen to represent Britain in numerous foreign exhibitions; designs featured in: various Museum permanent collection UK and abroad incl V & A, numerous publications, TV and radio broadcasts; awards incl: Observer Design award UK 1969, Design Council award 1984, Resources Cncl Inc 1987, Product Design award USA 1987, Industrial Design Designers Choice USA 1988, D & AD Silver award for most outstanding Br product design for the home UK 1989, The British Design award 1991; Hon FRCA 1988; FCSD 1983, FRSA 1991, RDI 1990; *Publications* Rodney Kinsman - The Logical Art of Furniture (monograph, 1992); *Clubs* Reform, Chelsea Arts, Groucho; *Style*— Rodney Kinsman, Esq; ✉ OMK Design Ltd, 30 Stephen Building, Stephen St, London W1P 1PN (☎ 0171 631 1335, fax 0171 631 3227)

KINTORE, 13 Earl of (S 1677); Sir Michael Canning William John Keith; 4 Bt (UK 1897); also Lord Keith of Inverurie and Keith Hall (S 1677), Baron Stonehaven (UK 1925), and Viscount Stonehaven (UK 1938); er s of 12 Earl of Kintore (d 1989), and Delia, Countess of Kintore; *b* 22 Feb 1939; *Educ* Eton, RMA Sandhurst; *m* 1972, Mary, o da of late Sqdn Ldr Elisha Gaddis Plum, of Rumson, New Jersey, USA; 1 s (Lord Inverurie), 1 da (Lady Iona Delia Mary Gaddis b 1978); *Heir* s, Lord Inverurie, *qv*; *Career* late Lt Coldstream Guards; *Clubs* Caledonian; *Style*— The Rt Hon the Earl of Kintore; ✉ The Stables, Keith Hall, Inverurie, Aberdeenshire AB51 0LD (☎ 01467 620495)

KIPPING, (Stanley Arnold) Brian; s of Dr Frederic Barry Kipping (d 1965), and Margaret Gertrude, *née* Wilkins (d 1955); *b* 5 April 1928; *Educ* The Leys Sch Cambridge, St John's Coll Cambridge (MA); *m* 1951, (Joyce) Evelyn, *née* Tudor; 2 da (Jennifer Anne (Mrs Groves) b 18 Nov 1952, Sally Margaret (Mrs Downs) b 30 Nov 1960), 1 s (John Brian b 14 Feb 1957); *Career* The Boots Co PLC Nottingham 1951–88: research admin 1954–64, admin and prodn planning 1964–69, factory mangr in Airdrie 1969–70, sec to Works Planning Ctee 1970, dep works mangr pharmaceutical prodn 1970–72, quality controller 1972–73, dir Boots Pure Drug Co 1973–78, dir of prodn and memb Bd Dirs Pharmaceutical Div 1978–88; vice chm Nottingham Health Authy 1991–94 (memb 1987–91), chm Nottinghamshire Family Health Servs Authy 1994–96, vice chm N Nottinghamshire Health Cmmn 1994–96; pro-chllr Univ of Nottingham 1994– (memb Cncl 1985–); *Recreations* gardening, home and village life, my family including grandchildren, trout fishing, genealogy and family history; *Style*— S A B Kipping, Esq; ✉ Fallowfields, 119a Main Street, Willoughby-on-the-Wolds, Loughborough, Leicestershire LE12 6SY (☎ and fax 01509 880884)

KIRBY, (Bernard William) Alexander (Alex); s of Frederic William Kirby (d 1953), and Vera Beryl, *née* Crawshaw (d 1989); *b* 11 July 1939; *Educ* King's Coll Taunton, Keble Coll Oxford; *m* 8 April 1972, Belinda Anne, da of Hugh Alfred Andrews (d 1991); 2 s (Edmund b 29 Dec 1978, Thomas b 14 April 1982); *Career* asst curate Isle of Dogs 1965–66, community relations offr London Borough of Newham 1967–70, ed Race Today magazine 1970–73, co-ordinator Br Volunteer Prog Burkina Faso and Niger 1974–75, researcher Prog to Combat Racism World Cncl of Churches 1976–78; BBC: journalist World Service News 1978–83, stringer N Africa 1983–84, actg bureau chief and Cairo corr 1986, reporter BBC Radio News 1986–87, agric and environment corr 1987–96, religious affairs corr 1996–; *Recreations* walking, drinking beer; *Style*— Alex Kirby, Esq; ✉ 28 Prince Edward's Road, Lewes, E Sussex BN7 1BE (☎ 01273 474935); Room 7083, BBC Television Centre, Wood Lane, London W12 7RJ (☎ 0181 576 7870, fax 0181 749 9016)

KIRBY, Prof Anthony John; s of Samuel Arthur Kirby, and Gladys Rosina, *née* Welch; *b* 18 Aug 1935; *Educ* Eton, Gonville and Caius Coll Cambridge (BA, MA, PhD); *m* 1962, Sara Sophia Benjamina Nieweg; 1 s, 2 da; *Career* Nat Serv RCS 1954–55; NATO Postdoctoral fell: Univ of Cambridge 1962–63, Brandeis Univ USA 1963–64; Univ of Cambridge: univ demonstrator 1964–68, lectr and reader in organic chemistry 1985–95 (lectr 1968–85), prof of bioorganic chemistry 1995–, coll lectr Gonville and Caius Coll 1965– (tutor 1966–74, fell 1962–), dir of studies in natural sciences 1968–96; visiting prof: Univ of Paris Orsay 1970, Université Pierre et Marie Curie Paris 1987, The Technion Haifa 1991; res fellowship Japan Soc for the Promotion of Res 1986, visiting scholar Univ of Cape Town 1987, invited lectr in numerous countries; memb: Perkin Editorial Bd RSC 1983–87, Mgmnt Ctee Organic Reaction Mechanisms Gp RSC 1983–86 (chm 1986–90), Sci and Engrg Res Cncl Organic Chemistry Sub-Ctee 1986–89, Chemistry Ctee SERC 1988–, Hooke Ctee Royal Soc 1988–91, Advsy Ctee Salters Advanced Chemistry Project 1989–, Panel of Experts Univ of London 1989–; elector to 1702 Chair of Chemistry at Cambridge 1987; RSC Ingold lectr 1996–97; RSC Award in Organic Reaction Mechanisms 1983, FRS 1987; *Books* The Organic Chemistry of Phosphorus (with S G Warren, 1967), The Anomeric Effect and Related Stereoelectronic Effects at Oxygen (1983), Stereoelectronic Effects (1996), numerous papers and review articles; *Recreations* chamber music, walking; *Style*— Prof Anthony J Kirby, FRS; ✉ University Chemical Laboratory, Cambridge CB2 1EW (☎ 01223 336370, fax 01223 336362)

KIRBY, Dr Brian John; s of George Kirby, of London, and Lily Ann, *née* Deighton; *b* 25 Aug 1936; *Educ* West Ham GS, Univ of Leeds (MB ChB); *m* 23 July 1959, Rachel Mary, da of James Stoddart Pawson, of Halifax; *Career* house appts Leeds 1960–63, registrar Central Middx Hosp London 1963–65, res fell supported by MRC 1965–67, instr in med Med Coll Virginia 1967–68, registrar Royal Postgrad Med Sch 1968–69, lectr in med Univ of Edinburgh 1969–74, dep dir and sr lectr in med Univ of Exeter Postgrad Med Sch 1974–, conslt physician to Royal Devon and Exeter Hosp and W of England Eye Infirmary 1974–; vice chm Dept of Health Review of Medicines Ctee 1987–92 (memb 1984); chm Dept of Health Advsy Bd on the registration of homoeopathic products; memb: Dept of Health Ctee on the Safety of Meds and Safety Efficacy and Adverse Reactions Ctee 1987–; chm Coronary Prevention Gp; chm SW Action on Smoking and Health Ctee; FRCP, FRCPEdin, FRSM; *Recreations* walking, sailing, skiing, reading and music; *Style*— Dr Brian Kirby; ✉ Postgraduate Medical School, Barack Rd, Exeter EX25 5DW (☎ 01392 403015)

KIRBY, Prof Gordon William; s of William Admiral Kirby (d 1950), of Liverpool, and Frances Teresa, *née* Townson (d 1973); *b* 20 June 1934; *Educ* Liverpool Inst HS, Liverpool Tech Coll, Gonville and Caius Coll Cambridge (MA, PhD, SCD, Schuldham Plate); *m* 4 April 1964 (m dis 1983), Audrey Jean, da of Col C E Rusbridge, of Halse, Somerset; 2 s (Giles Peter b 1968, Simon Michael b 1970); *Career* Imperial Coll London: 1851 Exhibition sr studentship 1958–67, asst lectr 1960–61, lectr 1961–67; prof of organic chemistry Loughborough Univ of Technol 1967–72, Regius prof of chemistry Univ of Glasgow 1972–96, prof of organic chemistry (pt/t) Univ of Glasgow 1997–; Corday Morgan medal and prize 1969, Tilden lectureship and medal 1974–75; memb Chemistry Ctee SERC 1971–75; Royal Soc of Chemistry: chm Journals Ctee 1981–84; memb ACS, memb Royal Philosophical Soc of Glasgow; FRSC 1970, FRSE 1975; *Books* Progress in the Chemistry of Organic Natural Products (ed), Comprehensive Organic Functional Group Transformations (ed, vol 4), plus many res papers in journals of the Chemical Soc; *Recreations* hill walking, amateur astronomy; *Style*— Prof Gordon Kirby, FRSE; ✉ Dept of Chemistry, Univ of Glasgow, Glasgow G12 8QQ (☎ 0141 339 8855, ext 4416/4417, fax 0141 330 4888, telex 777070 UNIGLA)

KIRBY, John Edward Weston; s of Lt-Col Robert Fry (John) Kirby, DSO, MBE (d 1996), of The Oak, Beaumont, Clacton-on-Sea, Essex, and Pamela Mary, *née* Weston; *b* 4 Feb 1936; *Educ* Ampleforth, CCC Oxford (MA); *m* 1, 4 Oct 1963, Teruko Frances (d 1974), da of Rear Adm Yoshio Takahashi, of Tokyo, Japan; 2 s (Patrick b 21 Nov 1966, Peter b 30 June 1974); m 2, 11 Feb 1978, Michiko, da of Junichi Wada, of Tokyo Japan; 1 da (Alicia b 21 May 1981); *Career* Bank of England 1959–: fin attaché Br Embassy Tokyo 1974–76, advsr Far East and Australasia 1977–83 (W Europe 1983–85), alternate memb EC Monetary Ctee 1983–85, head Int Div (N America, W Europe and Japan) 1985–88, alternate exec dir Bank for Int Settlements 1985–88, head Int Div (developing countries and int fin insts) 1988–90, min (fin) Br Embassy Tokyo 1990–; memb UK/Japan 2000 Group; *Books* Business in Japan (contrib, 1980); *Recreations* reading, the arts, cricket, photography; *Clubs* Vincent's (Oxford); *Style*— John Kirby, Esq; ✉ The British Embassy, 1 Ichibancho, Chiyoda-ku, Tokyo, Japan (☎ 00 81 3 3265 5511)

KIRBY, John Patrick; s of Robert Kirby, of Liverpool, and Matilda, *née* Carroll (d 1976); *b* 2 Feb 1949; *Educ* Cardinal Godfrey Tech Sch Liverpool, St Martin's Sch of Art (BA), Royal Coll of Art (MA); *Career* artist; *Solo Exhibitions* incl: Other People's Lives (Angela Flowers Gallery Ireland) 1988, Still Lives (Flowers East) 1989, New York and Related Works (Flowers East) 1991; *Gp Exhibitions* incl: John Player Portrait Exhibition (Nat Portrait Gallery) 1984 and 1986, 85 Degrees Show (Serpentine Gallery) 1985, New Acquaintance (Fabian Carlsson Gallery) 1986, Three Artists Show (Underground Gallery, Bath) 1987, Chicago International Art Exposition (Chicago) 1988 and 1989, The London Influence (Slaughterhouse Gallery) 1988, Sex and Sexuality Festival (Diorama Gallery) 1989, Art LA '89 (Los Angeles) 1989, The Thatcher Years: An Artistic Retrospective (Flowers East) 1989, Flowers at Moos (Gallery Moos, NY) 1990, The Soul and Madonnas (Diorama Gallery) 1990; works included in collection of UCW Aberystwyth; shipping clerk American Express Company Liverpool 1965–67, book salesman Burns & Oates 1967–69, voluntary social worker Boy's Town of Calcutta India 1969–71, asst warden Sydney House Hostel 1971–72, probation offr London and Plymouth 1972–77, asst stage doorman Royal Opera House 1977–78, market stall holder Kensington High St 1978–79, probation offr Brixton 1979–82, mothers' help London 1985, hosp porter London 1986; *Recreations* watching TV, contemplating suicide; *Clubs* Copacabana; *Style*— John Kirby, Esq; ✉ c/o Flowers East, 199–205 Richmond Rd, London E8 3NJ (☎ 0181 985 3333, fax 0181 985 0067)

KIRBY, Maj-Gen Norman George; OBE; s of George William Kirby (d 1978), and Laura Kirby (d 1980); *Educ* King Henry VIII Sch Coventry, Univ of Birmingham (MB ChB); *m* 1 Oct 1949, Cynthia Maire, da of Thomas Ian Bradley (d 1954); 1 s (Robert b 22 June 1954), 1 da (Jill b 11 Nov 1958); *Career* regtl MO 10 Parachute Regt TA 1950–51, offr i/c 5 Parachute Surgical Team 1956–59 (served Suez landing 1956), offr i/c Surgical Div BMH Rinteln 1959–60, OC and surgical specialist BMH Tripoli 1960–62, OC and conslt surgn BMH Dhekelia 1967–70, chief conslt surgn Cambridge Mil Hosp 1970–72, conslt surgn HQ BAOR 1973–78; 1978–82: dir of Army surgery, conslt surgn to the Army, hon surgn to the Queen; Hon Col: 308 Gen Hosp RAMC TA 1982–87, 144 Field Ambulance RAMC TA 1985–; Col Cmdt RAMC 1987–92; surgical registrar: Plastic Surgery Unit Stoke Mandeville Hosp 1950–51, Birmingham Accident Hosp 1953–55, Postgrad Med Sch Hammersmith 1964; hon conslt surgn Westminster Hosp 1979–, dir Clinical Servs, Accidents, Emergencies and Admissions Guy's Hosp 1985–93 (conslt accident and emergency surgn 1982–93); chm: Accidents and Emergencies Ctee SE Thames RHA 1983–88, Army Med Dept Working Pty Surgical Support for BAOR 1978–80; memb Med Ctee Defence Scientific Advsy Cncl 1979–82, examiner in anatomy RCS Edinburgh 1982–90, memb Ct of Examiners RCS 1988–94; pres: Br Assoc for Accident and Emergency Med 1990–93, Mil Surgical Assoc 1991–92; vice pres: Br Assoc of Trauma in Sport 1982–88, Faculty of A/E Med 1993–94; hon librarian RSM 1993–; memb Cncl: ICS 1980, Royal Coll of Surgns 1989–94; McCombe lectr RCS Edinburgh 1979, Mitchener medal RCS 1982, memb Editorial Bd Br Jl of Surgery and Injury 1979–82, librarian Med Soc of London 1988–92 (pres 1992–93); Freeman City of London 1980, Liveryman Worshipful Soc of Apothecaries of London; memb HAC; OStJ; Hon FACEP, FRCS, FICS, FRCSEd, FFAEM; *Books* Field Surgery Pocket Book (1981), Baillieres First Aid (1985), Pocket Reference, Accidents and Emergencies (1991); *Recreations* travel, reading, word processing, archaeology; *Clubs* Surgical Travellers'; *Style*— Maj-Gen Norman Kirby, OBE; ✉ Nuffield House, Guy's Hospital, London SE1 1YR (☎ 0171 955 4752, fax 0171 955 4754)

KIRBY, Paul Michael; s of William Raistrick Kirby (d 1968), and Laura, *née* Topham (d 1995); *b* 19 Feb 1948; *Educ* Hanson GS Bradford Yorks; *m* 16 Sept 1967, Vivien, da of Jack Longstaff, of Bradford, W Yorks; 1 s (Anthony b 1980), 2 da (Deborah b 1976, Michelle b 1978); *Career* Provident Finance Group plc: trainee programmer 1966, project mangr (customer accounting systems) 1972; systems devpt mangr ICL 1900 systems 1975, dep md HT Greenwood Ltd 1980; md: Practical Credit Services Ltd 1983, Car Care Plan Ltd 1985–; *Recreations* cricket, rugby, football, squash; *Clubs* Naval and Military; *Style*— Paul Kirby, Esq; ✉ 8 Glenview Close, Nab Wood, Shipley, West Yorks BD18 4AZ (☎ 01274 599877); Car Care Plan Ltd, Bramley District Centre, Bramley, Leeds, West Yorks LS13 2EJ (☎ 0113 256 2133, fax 0113 255 1601, car 0385 324031)

KIRBY, Richard Charles; s of Charles Neil Vernon Kirby (d 1970), and Nora Helena, *née* Corner; *b* 18 Sept 1946; *Educ* Sevenoaks Sch, Jesus Coll Oxford (MA); *m* 18 May 1985, Jill Christine, da of Kenneth Fernie, of Rugby, Warwicks; 3 s (Thomas Charles b 1986, James Edward b 1988, Robert Alexander b 1992); *Career* admitted slr 1971; ptnr Speechly Bircham 1973– (managing ptnr 1989–91); memb Ctee London Young Slrs 1973–74; cncllr Tonbridge and Malling Borough 1971–84 (ldr 1979–82); memb: Exec Tonbridge and Malling Cons Assoc 1978–84 (vice chm 1979–84), Exec SE region Nat Housing and Town Planning Cncl 1980–83, Cncl Mental After Care Assoc 1982– (hon treas 1987–); dir Hortons' Estate Ltd 1996–; slr Worshipful Co of Pewterers 1981– (Freeman 1991), Freeman City of London 1992; *Recreations* reading, theatre, cycling, swimming; *Clubs* Carlton; *Style*— Richard C Kirby, Esq; ✉ 48 Alleyn Rd, Dulwich, London SE21 8AL (☎ 0181 670 2525); Speechly Bircham, Bouverie House, 154 Fleet St, London EC4A 2HX (☎ 0171 353 3290, fax 0171 353 4825/4992)

KIRBY, Ronald Peter; OBE (1996); s of William John Kirby (d 1952), of Liverpool, and Anne Winifred, *née* Murphy (d 1975); *b* 9 July 1934; *Educ* Coalbrookdale HS Shropshire; *m* Carole; *Career* successively: reporter Shrewsbury Chronicle, ed Warrington Examiner, sub-ed Daily Mail, sub-ed then asst ed Lancashire Evening Telegraph, dep ed Evening Echo Hemel Hempstead, dep md Echo and Post Ltd Hemel Hempstead, Euro PR mangr Sime Darby; dir of public affrs The Engineering Council (since its inception) 1983–96, public affairs conslt 1996–; Cwlth Press Union travelling scholar 1965; FIPR, FRSA; *Books* European Engineering Yearbook; *Recreations* managing activities on behalf of Friends of Tyburn Shrine; *Style*— Ronald Kirby, Esq, OBE; ✉ 23 Lisburne Road, Hampstead, London NW3 2NS (☎ 0171 482 2863, fax 0171 485 6789)

KIRDAR, Nemir Amin; s of Amin Jamil Kirdar (d 1958), and Nuzhet Mohammed Ali Kirdar (d 1982); *b* 28 Oct 1936; *Educ* Baghdad Coll, Coll of the Pacific California (BA), Fordham Univ (MBA), Harvard Univ; *m* 1 Feb 1967, Nada, da of Dr Adnan Shakir; 2 da (Rena b 1968, Serra b 1975); *Career* fndr and proprietor Nemir A Kirdar Business Enterprises Iraq 1963–69, trainee then asst treas rising to head SE Asian region and asst vice pres Allied Bank International NY 1969–73, vice pres Nat Bank of N America NY 1973–74, vice pres and head Gulf Div Chase Manhattan Bank NY 1974–81, fndr pres and chief exec offr Investcorp Bank EC Bahrain 1982–; memb: Overseers' Ctee on Univ Resources Harvard Univ, Visiting Ctee John F Kennedy Sch of Govt Harvard Univ, Advsy Bd World Econ Forum Geneva, Washington DC, Bd Int Cncllrs and Advsy Bd of Govrs Global Forum - Leadership 2000 Center for Strategic and Int Studies Washington DC, Visiting Ctee Fordham Univ NY, Bd of Visitors Edmund A Walsh Sch of Foreign Serv Georgetown Univ Washington DC, Advsy Bd Sch of Int and Public Affairs Columbia Univ in City of NY, Bd of Tstees Eisenhower Exchange Fellowship Philadelphia, Bd of Govrs Bahrain Univ; chm Advsy Cncl Center for Contemporary Arab Studies Georgetown Univ Washington DC; tstee Meridian Int Center Washington DC; author of several articles in leading business and fin magazines; *Recreations* reading, skiing, windsurfing, tennis, collecting antiques; *Clubs* Metropolitan (Washington DC), Knickerbocker (NY); *Style*— Nemir Kirdar, Esq; ✉ Investcorp, 48 Grosvenor Street, London W1Y 6DH (☎ 0171 629 6600, fax 0171 887 3333)

KIRK, Prof David; s of Herbert Arthur Kirk (d 1969), of Sutton Coldfield, Warwickshire, and Constance Florence, *née* Mortimer; *b* 26 May 1943; *Educ* King Edward's Sch Birmingham, Balliol Coll Oxford, Clinical Med Sch Oxford (MA, BM BCh, DM); *m* 7 Aug 1965, Gillian Mary, da of Maj Wilson Bell Wroot, of Sutton Coldfield, Warwickshire; 1 s (Robert b 1971), 2 da (Tonya b 1969, Lucy b 1975); *Career* res med appts Radcliffe Infirmary Oxford 1968–69, univ demonstrator Univ of Oxford 1969–70; sr house offr appts 1970–72: Radcliffe Infirmary, Churchill Hosp Oxford, Bristol Royal Infirmary; surgical registrar 1973–75: Royal Infirmary Sheffield, Children's Hosp; res asst in surgery Univ of Sheffield 1975–76; sr surgical registrar 1976–78: Bristol Royal Infirmary, Royal Devon and Exeter Hosp; sr urological registrar 1978–82: Bristol Royal Infirmary, Southmead Hosp; conslt urological surgn Gtr Glasgow Health Bd (W Glasgow Hosps Univ NHS Tst since 1993) 1982–, hon prof Univ of Glasgow 1995– (hon clinical lectr/sr lectr 1982–94), currently urological advsr Nat Med Advsy Ctee Scottish Office; Arris and Gale lectr RCS 1980–81; memb Cncl: Section of Urology RSM 1984–87, Br Assoc of Urological Surgns 1988–91; chm: Scot Urological Oncology Gp 1985–88 (sec 1983–85), Prostate Forum 1991–94 (memb Steering Ctee 1995–), Intercollegiate Bd in Urology; memb/study coordinator Prostate Cancer Working Pty MRC; contrib to multi-author books on mgmnt of urological cancer, memb Editorial Ctee Br Jl of Urology 1990–93; memb Urological Club of GB; FRCS 1973, FRSM 1981, FRCPSGlas 1989; *Recreations* skiing, hill walking, classical music, woodwork; *Style*— Prof David Kirk; ✉ Woodend, Prospect Road, Dullatur, Glasgow G68 0AN (☎ 01236 720778); Urology Department, Gartnavel General Hospital, 1053 Great Western Road, Glasgow G12 0YN (☎ 0141 211 0047, fax 0141 357 1679)

KIRK, (Alistair) Graham; s of Alexander Charles Tansley Kirk, of Longfield, Stokeholy Cross, Norwich, Norfolk, and Dulce Marjory, *née* Ewins; *b* 10 May 1935; *Educ* Windsor GS, Berks Coll of Art and Design (NDD); *m* July 1986, Gillian Ruth, da of Mark Cresswell Bostock; 2 da (Catherine Elizabeth b 26 Oct 1987, Alexandra Claire b 30 May 1989); *Career* art dir various London advertising agencies until 1967, set up own photographic studio London 1968, visiting lectr in photography London Coll of Printing 1969; portfolio incl: location, lifestyle, still life and food photography for advertising and editorial publications, stamp edn series of photographs for PO (Food and Farming Year) 1989 (D&AD award 1989), photography for various internationally renowned chefs; contrib to Sunday Times and Observer magazines, numerous books (esp on French, Italian and Oriental cuisine); fndr memb AFAEP, FCSD 1986; *Recreations* music and gardening; *Style*— Graham Kirk, Esq; ✉ Graham Kirk Photography, 122 Brad St, London SE1 8TD (☎ 0171 928 7051)

KIRK, Col Pierre le Mercier du Quesnay; s of Joseph Leo Delaney Kirk (Rear Adm USNR, d 1990), and (Marie Louise) Valerie le Mercier du Quesnay; *b* 24 March 1945; *Educ* Jesuit HS New Orleans, Tulane Univ New Orleans and Loyola Univ (BA); *m* Rosalind Celeste Olschner; 1 da (Jennifer Anne b 1969), 2 s (John David b 1976, Pierre Edmond b 1977); *Career* military: Armd Cavalry and Transportation (variously Co Cdr, Bn Cdr, Task Force Cdr, various sr staff appts), served Vietnam, Germany, Caribbean and USA; former asst gen mangr New Orleans Public Service Inc (gas, electricity and public transportation), vice pres Terra Firma Tst New Orleans, combat devpt offr transportation US Army Transportation Centre Fort Eustis Va, currently dir of transportation on staff of C in C US Naval Forces Europe; US Decorations incl: Bronze Star Medal with V and Oak Leaf Cluster, Legion of Merit, Purple Heart, Meritorious Service Medal, Jt Servs Commendation Medal, Army Commendation Medal with V and Oak Leaf Cluster, Army Achievement Medal, Navy Achievement Medal with Star; Repub of Vietnam Decorations: Cross of Gallantry, Medal of Honour (1st Class), Civic Actions Medal; memb: Assoc of US Army 1965, Nat Def Transportation Assoc 1968, Propellor Club of the USA 1972, Lime Street Ward Club London; Freeman City of New Orleans; *Recreations* history, reading, shooting, fly fishing, conversation; *Clubs* Naval and Military (London), Royal Soc of St George (London), British American Forces Dining (London), Movement Control Officers (London), Bienville, Pendennis, Sons of the Revolution, Society of the War of 1812 (all New Orleans), Saint Andrew's Soc (Williamsburg Va); *Style*— Col Pierre du Quesnay Kirk; ✉ Haddon Cottage, 3 Haddon Road, Chorley Wood, Herts WD3 5AW (☎ 01923 283326); 2336 Esplanade Ave, New Orleans, Louisiana 70119 (☎ 00 1 504 821 5134); office: 7 North Audley Street, London W1Y 2AL (☎ 0171 514 4404, fax 0171 514 4451)

KIRK, Raymond Maurice; *b* 31 Oct 1923; *Educ* County Secdy Sch W Bridgford Nottingham, Univ of London (MB BS, MS); *m* 2 Dec 1952, Margaret; 1 s (Jeremy), 2 da (Valentine, Louise); *Career* Lt RN 1942–46; hon consulting surgn Royal Free Hosp (conslt surgn 1964–89), currently pt/t lectr in anatomy Royal Free Hosp Sch of Med; RCS: ed Annals 1985–92, memb Cncl 1983–91, memb Ct of Examiners 1975–81, currently dir Overseas Doctors Trg Scheme; examiner Univ of London; former examiner: Univ of Liverpool, Univ of Bristol, Univ of Khartoum, Univ of Colombo, RCPSG; former pres Surgical Section RSM; past pres: Med Soc London, Hunterian Soc; memb: Surgical Res Soc, British Soc of Gastroenterology, Assoc of Surgns of GB and Ireland, Soc of Authors (memb Cncl Med Section); FRCS, FRSM; *Books* General Surgical Operations (4 edn, 1994), Complications of Surgery of the Upper Gastrointestinal Tract (jtly, 1987), Clinical Surgery in General (jt ed 1993, 2 edn 1996), Basic Surgical Techniques (4 edn, 1995); *Recreations* squash, cycling, opera, travel; *Style*— Raymond Kirk, Esq; ✉ 10 Southwood Lane, Highgate Village, London N6 5EE (☎ 0181 340 8575); Royal College of Surgeons of England, 35–43 Lincoln's Inn Fields, London WC2A 3PN (☎ 0171 405 3474 ext 4040), Royal Free Hospital School of Medicine, London NW3 2QG (☎ 0171 794 0500 ext 4355)

KIRKBY, Maurice Anthony (Tony); s of George Sydney Kirkby (d 1972), of Southwell, Notts, and Rose, *née* Marson (d 1958); *b* 12 April 1929; *Educ* Trent Coll, King's Coll Cambridge (Mech Sci Tripos (1st class)); *m* 2 Aug 1954, Muriel Beatrice, da of Robert Longmire; 1 s (Peter Michael b 13 Dec 1955), 1 da (Susan Margaret b 5 June 1958); *Career* Bruntons (Musselburgh) Ltd 1952–54 (chief engr 1954); Anglo-Iranian Oil Co (later British Petroleum): trainee petroleum engr 1954–56, service in Iraq, Kuwait, Tanganyika, Iran, dist supt Iran 1964–67, regnl petroleum engr London 1967–69, chief petroleum engr London 1969–74, gen mangr BP Petroleum Devpt Aberdeen 1974–76, gen mangr Exploration & Prodn London 1976–80, sr vice pres Oil & Gas Standard Oil Co Ohio 1980–82, pres and chief exec BP Canada Inc 1983–88, chm and chief exec Hope Brook Gold Inc 1986–88, ret from BP 1988; dep chm North American Gas Investment Trust 1989–95; dir: Ensign Oil & Gas Inc Denver 1989–, Intera Information Technology Corporation Calgary 1992–96, Atlantis Resources Ltd Calgary 1992–94; also currently ind mgmnt conslt; vice chm: UK Offshore Operators' Assoc 1974–76, IX World

Petroleum Congress (PD 16); chm X World Petroleum Congress (PD 8), memb Business Cncl on Nat Issues Ottawa 1983–88; memb Soc of Petroleum Engrs (dir 1980 and 1981–83); MIMechE 1955, FIMM (memb Cncl 1990), FEng 1980; *Recreations* skiing, golf, gardening; *Clubs* Farnham Golf, Ranchmen's (Calgary, 1983–88); *Style*— Tony Kirkby, Esq, FEng; (fax 01276 855384)

KIRKBY, Prof Michael John (Mike); s of John Lawrence Kirkby (d 1989), of London, and Hilda Margaret, *née* Potts (d 1974); *b* 6 May 1937; *Educ* Radley, Univ of Cambridge (BA, PhD); *m* 1, 24 July 1963 (m dis 1975), Anne Veronica Tennant, da of Philip Whyte (d 1983), of Bedford; 1 s (David b 1967), 1 da (Clare b 1970); m 2, 15 May 1976, Fiona Elizabeth, da of Donald Weston Burley; 2 s (John b 1978, Nicholas b 1982); *Career* Nat Serv 2 Lt REME 1955–57; lectr in geography Univ of Bristol 1967–72, prof of physical geography Univ of Leeds 1973–; author of numerous scientific pubns; FRGS 1963; memb: IBG 1963, BGRG 1966; *Books* Hillslope Form and Process (with MA Carson, 1972), Hillslope Hydrology (ed, 1978), Soil Erosion (ed with RPC Morgan, 1980), Computer Simulation in Physical Geography (jtly, 1987 and 1993), Channel Network Hydrology (ed with K J Beven, 1993), Process models & theoretical geomorphology (ed, 1994); managing ed Earth Surface Processes and Landforms 1976–; *Recreations* hill walking, photography; *Style*— Prof Mike Kirkby; ✉ School of Geography, University of Leeds, Leeds LS2 9JT (☎ 0113 233 3310, fax 0113 233 6758, e-mail mike@geog.leeds.ac.uk)

KIRKE, Rear Adm David Walter; CB (1967), CBE (1962, OBE 1945); s of Percy St George Kirke (d 1966), and Alice Gertrude (d 1959), da of Sir James Gibson-Craig, 3 Bt; *b* 13 March 1915; *Educ* RNC Dartmouth; *m* 1, 1936 (m dis 1950), Tessa, da of Capt Patrick O'Connor; 1 s; m 2, 1956, Marion Margaret, da of late Dr James Gibb; 1 s, 1 da; *Career* Chief of Naval Aviation Indian Navy New Delhi 1959–62, Flag Offr Naval Flying Trg 1965–68; *Recreations* golf; *Clubs* Army and Navy; *Style*— Rear Adm David Kirke, CB, CBE; ✉ Lismore House, Pluckley, Kent (☎ 01233 840439)

KIRKHAM, Donald Herbert; CBE (1996); s of Herbert Kirkham (d 1987), and Hettie, *née* Trueblood; *m* 17 Sept 1960, Kathleen Mary, da of Christopher Lond; 1 s (Richard b 1963), 1 da (Sarah b 1966); *Career* Nat Serv Army 1954–56; The Woolwich Building Society: joined Lincoln Branch 1959, branch mangr Worcester 1963, gen mangr's asst 1967, business prodn mangr 1970, asst gen mangr of ops 1972, gen mangr 1976, appointed to Local Bd for Scotland and NI 1979–84, dep chief gen mangr 1981, memb Main Bd 1982, chief exec 1986–95; vice pres Chartered Bldg Socs Inst 1986 (pres 1981–82), pres Cncl of Inst of Chartered Secs and Admins 1991; chm: Met Assoc of Bldg Socs 1988–89, Building Societies Assoc 1994–95 (dep chm 1993–94), Banque Woolwich SA 1995–, Banca Woolwich SpA 1995–, Woolwich Insurance Services Ltd 1995–96; memb Bd: Horniman Museum 1989–, Building Societies Investor Protection Bd 1995–, Gresham Insurance Co Ltd 1995–96, Bexley and Greenwich Health Authy 1996–; Freeman City of London, memb Ct of Assts Worshipful Co of Chartered Secretaries and Adminstrators (Liveryman); Hon DBA 1991; FCIS 1973, CIMgt 1986, FCIB 1993; *Recreations* boating; *Clubs* IOD; *Style*— Donald Kirkham, Esq, CBE; ✉ 2 Chaundrye Close, The Court Yard, Eltham SE9 5QB (☎ 0181 859 4295, fax 0181 850 7283)

KIRKHAM, Rt Rev John Dudley Galtrey; *see:* Sherborne, Bishop of

KIRKHAM, John Squire; s of Squire Wilfred Kirkham (d 1989), and Una Mary, *née* Baker; *b* 20 Sept 1936; *Educ* Gonville and Caius Coll Cambridge (MA, MB BChir, MChir), Westminster Hosp; *m* 19 Sept 1969, Charlotte, da of Paul Giersing (d 1981), of Aalborg, Denmark; 1 s (Alexander), 1 da (Sophie); *Career* ships surgn Union Castle Line MN 1962–63; house surgeon Westminster Hosp; sr house offr: Birmingham Accident Hosp, The Hosp for Sick Children Gt Ormond St; surgn registrar Aberdeen Royal Infirmary, sr surgical registrar St James's Hosp SW12 and Charing Cross Hosp; conslt surgn St George's Hosp London and St James's Hosp London 1971–90, hon sr lectr St George's Hosp Med Sch, Queen Mary's Univ Hosp Roehampton 1991 (conslt in gen surgery, surgical gastroenterology and digestive endoscopy); examiner: Univ of London, Khartoum, Basra; visiting prof: Khartoum, Basra, Cairo, Melbourne, Alexandria; author papers on: surgical aspects of gastroenterology, gastro-intestinal bleeding, endoscopy, various surgical topics, chapters in surgical textbooks; memb: Save Br Sci, Int Dendrology Soc, Pancreatic Soc of GB and Ireland, Br Soc of Gastroenterology, Assoc of Surgns of GB and Ireland, Int Gastro-Surgical Club, Surgical Specialists Soc; FRSM, FRCS, FRCSEd; *Books* contrib to Maingot's Adbominal Operations (1984), Surgery of Obesity (1984), British Surgical Progress (1990); *Recreations* reading, dendrology, sailing, travelling, fishing; *Clubs* Athenaeum, Naval and Military; *Style*— John Squire Kirkham, Esq; ✉ 149 Harley St, London W1N 2DH (☎ 0171 935 4444, fax 0171 935 3690)

KIRKHAM, Dr Keith Edwin; OBE (1987); s of Thomas Kirkham (d 1977), of Garstang, Lancs, and Clara Prestwich, *née* Willacy (d 1987); *b* 20 Oct 1929; *Educ* Kirkham GS Lancs 1939–46, Univ of Birmingham (BSc), Fitzwilliam Coll Cambridge (dip in agric sci, MA, PhD); *m* 29 July 1953, Dorothea Mary (Mollie), da of Arthur Fisher (d 1949), of Blackpool, Lancs; 2 s (Jonathan Andrew b 2 Nov 1957, Christopher Michael b 28 Sept 1961); *Career* Nat Serv 2 Lt RA 1955–57; demonstrator Sch of Agric Univ of Cambridge 1954–60 (asst in res 1951–53); MRC: scientist Clinical Endocrinology Res Unit Edinburgh 1960–73, asst dir Clinical Res Centre Harrow 1973–88, admin dir Clinical Res Centre Harrow 1988–94; govr Harrow Coll of HE 1983–90 (chm Govrs 1986–90), memb Ct of Govrs Univ of Westminster (formerly Poly of Central London) 1990–; memb Soc for Endocrinology 1969 (memb Ctee and offr 1971–79), Scientific FZS; *Recreations* watching sport, river cruising; *Style*— Dr Keith Kirkham, OBE

KIRKHAM, Hon Rupert William Tyrwhitt; elder son and heir of Pamela Vivien, Baroness Berners (*qv*). and Michael Joseph Sperry Kirkham; *b* 18 Feb 1953; *Educ* New Coll Choir Sch Oxford, Lord Williams Sch Thame; *m* 1994, Lisa Carol (Judy), da of Col Edward Gibson Lipsey, USAF (ret), of Phoenix, Arizona, USA; 1 s (Edward Michael Tyrwhitt b 7 July 1994); *Style*— The Hon Rupert Kirkham; ✉ c/o Lady Berners, Ashwellthorpe, Charlton Lane, Cheltenham, Glos GL53 9EE

KIRKHILL, Baron (Life Peer UK 1975), in District of City of Aberdeen; John Farquharson Smith; s of Alexander Findlay Smith; *b* 7 May 1930; *Educ* Robert Gordon's Colls Aberdeen; *m* 1965, Frances Mary Walker Reid; 1 step da; *Career* Lord Provost of the City and Royal Burgh of Aberdeen 1971–75, min of state Scottish Office 1975–78, chm North of Scotland Hydro-Electric Bd 1979–82; del to Parly Assembly Cncl of Europe 1987–, chm Ctee on Legal Affrs and Human Rights 1991–95; Hon LLD Univ of Aberdeen 1974; *Style*— The Rt Hon the Lord Kirkhill; ✉ 3 Rubislaw Den North, Aberdeen (☎ 01224 314167)

KIRKHOPE, Timothy John Robert; MP (C) Leeds North East (majority 4,244); s of John Thomas Kirkhope (d 1991), of Newcastle upon Tyne, and Dorothy Buemann Kirkhope, *née* Bolt (d 1973); *b* 29 April 1945; *Educ* Royal GS Newcastle upon Tyne, Coll of Law Guildford; *m* 1969, Caroline, da of Christopher Thompson Maling (d 1975), of Newcastle upon Tyne; 4 s (Justin b 1970, Rupert b 1972, Dominic b 1976, Alexander 1979); *Career* slr; ptnr with Wilkinson Maughan Newcastle upon Tyne (formerly Wilkinson Marshall Clayton & Gibson) 1977–87, conslt 1987–90; MP (C) Leeds NE 1987–, PPS to David (now Sir David) Trippier as Min of State for the Environment and Countryside 1989–90, asst govt whip 1990–92, Lord Cmmr to the Treasy (Govt whip) 1993–95, under sec of state Home Office 1995–; vice-chamberlain HM's Household 1995; conslt to Clereys (Solicitors) Aldershot 1992–95; cncllr Northumberland CC 1981–85, memb: Newcastle Airport Controlling Bd 1981–85, Cons Nat Exec Ctee, Northern Region Health Authy 1982–86, Mental Health Act Cmmn 1983–86; *Recreations* swimming, tennis, flying; *Clubs* Northern Counties (Newcastle upon Tyne), Dunstanburgh Castle Golf (Northumberland); *Style*— Timothy Kirkhope, Esq, MP; ✉ c/o House of Commons, London SW1A 0AA

KIRKLAND, Colin James; OBE (1992); s of James Brown Kirkland (d 1984), of Epsom, Surrey, and Marjorie May, *née* Starling (d 1979); *b* 21 April 1936; *Educ* Epsom GS, Westminster Tech Coll (HNC Civil Engrg); *m* 6 June 1959, Sheila Ann, da of Frederick Harry Jordan; 1 s (Graeme Antony James b 21 March 1969), 2 da (Alison Julie b 19 June 1962, Linsay Anne b 31 July 1965); *Career* Nat Serv Survey Section RE 1954–56; Sir William Halcrow & Partners Ltd: draughtsman and engrg student 1952–54, engrg asst Head Office 1956–62, resident engr 1962–68; sub-agent Victoria Line Extension Contract A Waddington and Son tunnelling contractors 1968–72; Sir William Halcrow & Partners Ltd: resident engr London Tport Jubilee Line Contract 1972–75, sr engr Head Office 1975–77, princ engr Head Office 1977–80, assoc 1980–82, dir 1983–, gp devpt dir 1991–; ptnr Halcrow International Partnership 1983–; dir: Halcrow Geotechnics Tranportation & Tunnelling 1983–85, Halcrow Scotland 1983–85; tech dir Eurotunnel (Channel Tunnel) 1985–91, chm Br Tunnelling Soc 1988–90 (James Clark medal 1991), pres Int Tunnelling Assoc 1990–92 (vice pres 1987–90); lectr at various confs and instns at home and abroad, advsr on both construction and contractual procedures for tunnel works, expert witness in tunnelling litigation; past pres Guildford Lions Club, chief steward Guildford Cathedral; FICE 1985, FEng 1991; *Publications* contrib chapter Tunnels and Underground Chambers for Ground Engineers' Handbook (with Sir Alan Muir Wood, 1987), Engineering the Channel Tunnel (ed, 1995); *Recreations* bird watching, music appreciation, theatre; *Style*— Colin J Kirkland, Esq, OBE, FEng; ✉ Sir William Halcrow & Partners Ltd, Vineyard House, 44 Brook Green, London W6 7BY (☎ 0171 602 7282, fax 0171 603 0095)

KIRKMAN, William Patrick (Bill); MBE (1993); s of Geoffrey Charles Aylward Kirkman (d 1976), of New Milton, Hampshire and Bertha Winifred, *née* Hudson (d 1989); *b* 23 Oct 1932; *Educ* Churcher's Coll Petersfield Hampshire, Oriel Coll Oxford (Heath Harrison travelling scholar, MA, MA by incorporation (Cambridge)); *m* 5 March 1959, Anne Teasdale, da of Frank Fawcett (d 1975), of Minster Lovell, Oxon; 2 s (George William Fawcett b 1961, Edward Thomas Fawcett b 1964), 1 da (Eleanor Mary Fawcett b 1968); *Career* Nat Serv RASC 1950–52, Lt Intelligence Corps (TA) 1955–61; memb editorial staff Express & Star Wolverhampton 1955–57; The Times: joined editorial staff 1957, Cwlth staff corr 1960–64, Africa corr 1962–64; asst sec Oxford Univ Appts Ctee 1964–68; fell Wolfson Coll Cambridge (formerly Univ Coll) 1968– (vice pres 1980–84), sec Cambridge Univ Careers Service 1968–92, sec The Cambridge Soc 1992–, advsr on public relations Univ of Cambridge 1992–96; dir Wolfson Coll Press Fellowship Prog 1982–96; chm: Standing Conf Univ Appointments Servs 1971–73, Cambridgeshire Cwlth Gp 1988–96; tstee Sir Halley Stewart Tst 1969–; memb: Mgmnt Ctee Central Services Unit for Careers Servs 1972–76 and 1986–88, Univ of Cambridge Public Relations Ctee, Univ of Cambridge Bd of Continuing Educn 1987–, Training Bd Econ & Social Res Cncl 1990–93, Midlands & East Regnl Advsy Cncl BBC 1992–93, East Regnl Advsy Cncl BBC 1993–96; chm BBC Radio Cambridgeshire Advsy Cncl 1992–96; memb Home Office Panel of Non-Serv Membs of Extended Interview Bd 1993–; memb Ely Diocesan Communications Ctee 1978–88; churchwarden: St Andrew's Headington Oxford 1967–68, St Mary and All Saints Willingham Cambridge 1977–84 and 1996–; FRSA 1990; *Recreations* church activities, travel; *Clubs* Royal Commonwealth Society; *Style*— W P Kirkman, Esq, MBE; ✉ 19 High Street, Willingham, Cambridge CB4 5ES (☎ 01954 260393, e-mail wpk1000@cam.ac.uk); Wolfson College, Cambridge CB3 9BB (☎ 01223 335900, fax 01223 510228)

KIRKPATRICK, Gavin Alexander Yvone; s of Yvone Eustace Sutton Kirkpatrick, OBE, TD (d 1975), and Margaret Hill, *née* Sclanders (d 1990); *b* 8 July 1938; *Educ* Pilgrims Sch Winchester, Cheltenham Coll (Marcon music prize); *m* 1961, Susan Ann Frances, da of Thomas Alford Boyd Parselle, CBE (d 1979); 1 da (Lucy Margaret b 26 April 1964), 2 s (Thomas Sutton b 24 Oct 1966, Alexander John b 29 June 1969); *Career* Nat Serv RN 1957–59; John Trundell & Partners 1959–61; International Computers (& Tabulators) Ltd: worked in tech support and sales 1961–64, various posts in personnel mgmnt 1964–67, int personnel mangr 1967–70; Sperry Rand Corporation (Univac Div): personnel dir (Europe) 1970–76, dir worldwide personnel planning and devpt (Pennsylvania) 1976–78; International Computers plc: gp personnel mangr (Worldwide Mktg Gp) 1978–81, ops personnel mangr (Gp HQ) 1981–89, seconded as chief exec to British Computer Society 1991–92 (prog dir (Europe) 1989–91); chief exec Br Computer Soc 1992–95, ret; vice chm Outer London Gp European Movement 1994–95, hon sec Central & W Dorset Branch European Movement 1996, memb Anglo-German Assoc, friend London Bach Soc; Liveryman Worshipful Co of Information Technologists 1994; MInstD 1970, FIDM 1991, FBCS 1992, FRSA 1992; *Recreations* music, sailing, photography, travel, contemporary European developments; *Style*— Gavin Kirkpatrick, Esq; ✉ West Walks House, Dorchester, Dorset DT1 1RE (☎ 01305 269946, fax 01305 269986, e-mail gkirkpatrick@bcs.org.uk)

KIRKPATRICK, Sir Ivone Elliott; 11 Bt (NS 1685), of Closeburn, Dumfriesshire; s of Sir James Alexander Kirkpatrick, 10 Bt (d 1954), and Ellen Gertrude, *née* Elliott; *b* 1 Oct 1942; *Educ* Wellington, St Mark's Coll Adelaide Univ; *Heir* bro, Robin Alexander Kirkpatrick b 19 March 1944; *Style*— Sir Ivone Kirkpatrick, Bt; ✉ 82 Stanenborough Street, Adelaide, S Australia 5066, Australia

KIRKPATRICK, Jennifer Augustine (Jenny); da of Richard Arthur Seckerson (d 1973), of Wallasey, Merseyside, and Olive Frances Maude, *née* O'Connor; *b* 7 Aug 1946; *Educ* Oldershaw GS Wallasey, Cheshire Coll of Educn, Univ of Keele (BEd); *Career* teacher 1968–79; writer and broadcaster; gen sec Nat Assoc of Probation Offrs 1979–85; dir: Electricity Consumers' Cncl 1985–88, The Paul Hamlyn Fndn 1988–89, Burson-Marsteller 1989–92, Venture Link Investors 1991–93, Lifespan Environmental Affairs Ltd 1992–, LS Research Ltd 1994–, The Strategic Partnership (London) Ltd 1996–; chm: Oxfordshire Community Health NHS Trust 1993–, Gas Consumers' Cncl 1995–; memb MOD Advsy Ctee on Conscientious Objectors 1991–; tstee: Res Inst for Consumer Affrs, Ambache Orchestra, Fndn for Mfrg Indust 1993–; MIPR, FRSA; *Recreations* written and spoken word, public policy, anything obsessional - crosswords, bridge, puzzles, horses; *Style*— Jenny Kirkpatrick; ✉ Mavis Bank, Church Road, Greatworth, Banbury OX17 2DU (☎ 01295 711983)

KIRKUP, Prof James Falconer; s of James Harold Kirkup (d 1958), and Mary Johnson (d 1973); descendant of Seymour Stocker Kirkup (DNB), Thomas Kirkup (DNB), William Falconer (DNB); *b* 23 April 1918; *Educ* S Shields Secdy Sch, King's Coll Univ of Durham (BA); *Career* lectr and prof at various univs in Britain, Europe, USA and Far East, prof of comparative lit Kyoto Univ of Foreign Studies 1976–88, composer An Actor's Revenge (opera); sponsor Inst of Psychophysical Res Oxford 1970; named Ollave Order of Bards, Ovates and Druids 1974; pres Br Haiku Soc 1990–; British Centre for Literary Translation 1995; FRSL; *Books* 20 volumes of poetry incl: The Sense of the Visit (1985), Throwback: Poems towards an Autobiography (1992), Shooting Stars: Haiku (1992), Words for Contemplation: Poems (1993), Look at it This Way: Poems for Young People (1993), Short Takes: One-Line Senryu and Haiku (1993), Blue Bamboo (1994), The Genius of Haiku (1994), Formulas for Chaos (1994), Strange Attractors (1995), An Extended Breath: Collected Longer Poems (1995), Selected Shorter Poems: Omens of Disaster Vol 1 (1995), A Certain State of Mind (1995), How to Cook Women: Selected Poems and Stories of Takagi Kyozo (1996), Burning Giraffes: An Anthology of Modern and

Contemporary Japanese Poets (1996), A Book of Tanka (1996), Utsusemi, tanka (1996), Broad Daylight: Poems East and West (1996), Child of the Tyne (reprint of The Only Child and Sorrows, Passions and Alarms in 1 vol, 1996), Measures of Time: Collected Longer Poems Vol II (1996), Once and for All Vol II (1996), The Patient Obituarist: New Poems (1996); translator of Kawabata, Simone de Beauvoir, Kleist and Pasolini, winner Scott-Moncrieff Prize for Translation 1993 for Painted Shadows by Jean-Baptiste Niel, Blindsight (trans Hervé Guibert, 1995), Paradise (trans Hervé Guibert, 1996); A Poet Could Not But Be Gay (autobiography), I of All People (autobiography), Gaijin On The Ginza (novel), Me All Over: Memoirs of a Misfit (autobiography, 1993), Queens have Died Young and Fair (novel, 1993); *Recreations* reading, music (jazz and classical), cinema, travel; *Style—* Prof James Kirkup, FRSL; ✉ BM-Box 2780, British Monomarks, London WC1N 3XX

KIRKWOOD, Hon Mr Justice; Hon Sir Andrew Tristram Hammett; kt (1993); s of Maj Tristram Guy Hammett Kirkwood, RE (ka 1944), and Margaret Elizabeth Montague Brown (who m 2, Rt Rev Arthur Groom Parham, MC, Bishop of Reading, and 3, Sir Neville Major Ginner Faulks, MBE, TD) (d 1982); *b* 5 June 1944; *Educ* Radley, Christ Church Oxford (MA); *m* 13 July 1968, Penelope Jane, *née* Eaton; 2 s (Tristram b 2 Jan 1972, Edward b 19 June 1977), 1 da (Sophie b 25 Oct 1969); *Career* called to the Bar Inner Temple 1966, recorder of the Crown Court 1987–93, QC 1989, bencher Inner Temple 1993, judge of the High Court of Justice (Family Div) 1993–; chm Leicestershire Inquiry 1992, memb Judicial Studies Bd (co-chm Civil and Family Ctee) 1994–, judge Employment Appeal Tbnl 1996–; *Recreations* the countryside; *Clubs* MCC; *Style—* The Hon Mr Justice Kirkwood; ✉ Royal Courts of Justice, Strand, London WC2R 2LL

KIRKWOOD, (Joan) Antoinette Lindsay; da of Maj Charles Home Kingston Kirkwood (d 1966), of Chelsea, and Ivy Muriel, *née* Burlton (d 1983); *b* 26 Feb 1930; *m* 14 July 1961, Richard Owen Neil Phibbs (d 1987), s of Basil Phibbs (d 1938), of Lisheen, Sligo; 1 s (Harry b 1966), 2 da (Rebekah b 1962, Jessica b 1964); *Career* composer; works as composer: Suite for Strings, Symphony No 1, Sonata for Cello and Piano, Six Intermezzi for Piano Solo; memb: Performing Right Soc, ISM; *Style—* Miss Antoinette Kirkwood; ✉ 56 Sutherland St, London SW1V 4JZ (☎ 0171 828 1683, fax 0171 828 7907)

KIRKWOOD, Archibald Johnston (Archy); MP (Lib Dem) Roxburgh and Berwickshire (majority 4,257); s of David Kirkwood, of Glasgow, and Jessie Barclay (d 1980); *b* 22 April 1946; *Educ* Heriot-Watt Univ (BSc); *m* 1972, Rosemary Jane, da of Edward John Chester; 1 s, 1 da; *Career* slr, NP; MP (Lib until 1988, now Lib Dem) Roxburgh and Berwickshire 1983–, Lib spokesman on health and social security 1985–87, Alliance spokesman on overseas devpt 1987, Lib spokesman on Scotland 1987–88, SLD spokesman on welfare, health and educn 1988–89, Lib Dem chief whip 1992– (dep 1989–92), Lib Dem convenor and spokesman on welfare and social security 1989–94, Lib Dem spokesman on community care 1994–; sponsored Private Member's Bills leading to Access to Personal Files Act 1987 and Access to Medical Reports Act 1988; chm Lib Dem Campaigns Ctee 1989–92; tstee Rowntree Reform Tst 1985–; *Recreations* music, skiing; *Style—* Archy Kirkwood, Esq, MP; ✉ House of Commons, London SW1A 0AA

KIRKWOOD, Colin Bennie; s of Matthew Chrystal Kirkwood (d 1991), of Killearn, Stirlingshire, and Charlotte Margaret, *née* Bennie (d 1993); *b* 6 Dec 1951; *Educ* Glasgow Acad, Napier Coll of Sci and Technol Edinburgh (Dip in Book and Periodical Publishing); *m* 4 April 1987, Isabel Mary, da of David Gordon Johnstone (d 1976); 1 s (Matthew David b 1989), 1 da (Rosanna Mary b 1991); *Career* prodn and editorial asst NFER publishing co 1972–74, gen ed Blackie & Son Ltd 1974–77; John Bartholomew & Son Ltd: editorial mangr Pictorial Div 1977–79, Book Div mangr 1979–81, publishing mangr 1981–83, assoc dir (publishing) 1984–86, publishing dir 1986–89; md The Aberdeen University Press Ltd 1990–92, publishing conslt 1992–93, publishing dir Times Books/Bartholomew Div HarperCollins Publishers Ltd 1993–94, publishing and marketing conslt 1994–95, marketing dir Colin Baxter Photography Ltd 1995–; chm Scot Young Publishers Soc 1979, chm Scot Publishers Assoc 1984–86, dir Tuckwell Press 1994–95, memb Bd Edinburgh Book Festival 1984–89, ed Charles Rennie Mackintosh Soc Newsletter 1976–84; *Books* The National Book League (1972); *Recreations* sailing, tennis, cooking, architecture; *Style—* Colin B Kirkwood, Esq; ✉ Coulnakyle, Nethy Bridge, Inverness-shire PH25 3EA (☎ 01479 821393)

KIRKWOOD, 3 Baron (UK 1951); David Harvie Kirkwood; s of 2 Baron Kirkwood (d 1970, s of 1 Baron, PC, JP, MP Dumbarton Burghs 1922–50, who as David Kirkwood was deported for being the ringleader in a protest against rent increases); *b* 21 Nov 1931; *Educ* Rugby, Trinity Hall Cambridge (MA, PhD); *m* 1965, Judith, da of John Hunt, of Leeds; 3 da (Hon Ruth b 17 Sept 1966, Hon Anne b 24 April 1969, Hon Lucy b 28 July 1972); *Heir* bro, Hon James Stuart Kirkwood, *qv*; *Career* warden Stephenson Hall 1974–79, sr lectr Sheffield Univ 1976–87, hon sr lectr 1987–; CEng; *Style—* The Rt Hon the Lord Kirkwood; ✉ 56 Endcliffe Hall Ave, Sheffield S10 3EL (☎ 0114 266 3107)

KIRKWOOD, The Hon Lord; Ian Candlish Kirkwood; QC (1970); s of John Brown Kirkwood OBE (d 1964), and Constance Kirkwood (d 1987); *b* 8 June 1932; *Educ* George Watson's Boys' Coll Edinburgh, Univ of Edinburgh (MA, LLB), Univ of Michigan (LLM); *m* 1970, Jill, da of Lt-Cdr Trevor P Scott, RN (ret), of Torquay; 2 s (Jonathan b 1973, Richard b 1975); *Career* chm Medical Appeal Tribunal (until 1987); memb Parole Bd for Scotland 1994–; senator Coll of Justice Scotland 1987; *Recreations* tennis, golf, chess; *Style—* The Hon Lord Kirkwood; ✉ 58 Murrayfield Ave, Edinburgh, EH12 6AY (☎ 0131 477 1994); Knockbrex House, nr Borgue, Kirkcudbrightshire (☎ 01557 870269)

KIRKWOOD, Hon James Stuart; s of 2 Baron Kirkwood (d 1970), and hp of bro, 3 Baron Kirkwood, *qv*; *b* 19 June 1937; *Educ* Rugby, Trinity Hall Cambridge; FRICS; *m* 1965, Alexandra Mary, da of late Alec Dyson, of Holt, Norfolk; 2 da; *Style—* The Hon James Kirkwood; ✉ The Cearne, Kent Hatch, Crockham Hill, Edenbridge, Kent

KIRSTEIN, Prof Peter Thomas; s of Walter Kirstein (d 1983), of London; *b* 20 June 1933; *Educ* Highgate Sch London, Gonville & Caius Coll Cambridge (BA), Stanford Univ (MSc, PhD), Univ of London (DSc); *m* 5 July 1958, Gwen Margaret Oldham; 2 da (Sarah Lynn b 1964, Claire Fiona b 1971); *Career* res assoc and lectr W W Hansen Laboratory of Physics Stanford Univ 1957–58, accelerator physicist Centre of European Nuclear Research Geneva Switzerland 1959–63, scientific rep Europe General Electric Company of USA 1963–67, prof of computer systems Univ of London 1970–73 (reader in information processing 1967–70); UCL: prof 1973–, head Dept of Computer Science 1980–95, dir of research 1995–; FBCS 1964, FIEE 1965, FInstP 1965, SMIEEE 1975, FEng 1985; *Books* Space Charge Flow (1967); *Recreations* skiing, tennis, squash; *Clubs* Alpine Ski; *Style—* Prof Peter Kirstein, FEng; ✉ 31 Bancroft Ave, London N2 0AR (☎ 0171 380 7286); Department of Computer Science, University College London, Gower St, London WC1E 6BT (☎ 0171 380 7286, fax 0171 387 1397)

KIRTON, Muriel Elizabeth; da of William Waddell Kirton, of Parkhall, nr Glasgow, and Belle Jean Kirton; *b* 4 July 1950; *Educ* Clydebank HS, Univ of Glasgow (MA, Pitoy prize), Univ of Edinburgh (DipEd), Univ of Kent (MA); *Career* teacher in English and French Cornwall Coll Jamaica 1975–77, French teacher Dane Court Tech HS 1977–78; Univ of Kent 1979–82: lectr, dir Norwegian Study Centre, teacher trainer and dir of EFL studies; Xian Foreign Language Univ lectr and co-ordinator language trg project British Council/ODA China 1982–84; British Council: sr teacher trainer then project dir expatriate English teachers' scheme Hong Kong 1985–89, conslt in educn and teacher trg Turkey 1990, educn offr Cairo 1990–93, country dir Vietnam 1993–96, dir Commonwealth Relations London 1996–; *Recreations* scuba diving, exploration of countries lived in, travel, films and theatre, photography, reading, alternative healing therapies; *Style—* Ms Muriel Kirton; ✉ Policy Directorates, SG401, The British Council, 10 Spring Gardens, London SW1A 2BN (☎ 0171 389 4441, fax 0171 389 4758, e-mail muriel.kirton@britcoun.org)

KIRWAN, Sir (Archibald) Laurence Patrick; KCMG (1972, CMG 1958), TD (1949); s of Patrick Kirwan; *b* 13 May 1907; *Educ* Wimbledon Sch, Merton Coll Oxford; *m* 1, 1933 (m dis 1945), Victoria Edith Joan (d 1989), da of Capt Hon Louis Wentworth Pakington Chetwynd, RN (bro of 8 Viscount Chetwynd, d 1914); 1 da; m 2, 1949, Stella Mary Monck, da of R Buchanan Cock; *Career* served WWII Intelligence Corps, TARO 1939–57, Hon Lt-Col; dir and sec RGS 1945–75 (hon vice pres 1981–); ed Geographical Journal 1945–78; memb: Ct of Arbitration Argentine-Chile Frontier Case 1965–68, Sec of State for Tport's Advsy Ctee on Landscape Treatment of Trunk Rds 1968–81, UN Register of Fact-Finding Experts 1968–75; memb Ct Univ of Exeter 1969–80; *Style—* Sir Laurence Kirwan, KCMG, TD; ✉ c/o Royal Geographical Society, 1 Kensington Gore, London SW7 2AR

KIRYA, HE Prof George Barnabas; *b* 9 Feb 1939; *Educ* Cambridge HS (sch cert, HSC), Univ of E Africa (MB ChB), Univ of Birmingham (MSc), Univ of Manchester (DipBact), Immunology Course in Infectious Diseases Lausanne Switzerland, Int ICRO/UNESCO Trg Course Bratislava Czechoslovakia, Interregional Workshop Taiyuan China; *m*; 5 s, 1 da; *Career* Ugandan high cmmr to Ct of St James's 1990–, concurrently ambass to Ireland 1995–; med house offr Mulago Hosp 1966–67, SHO Dept of Paediatrics and Child Health Makerere Faculty of Med 1967; E African Virus Res Inst Entebbe Uganda: virologist 1967, sr med res offr 1968, princ med res offr and head Dept of Arbovirology 1969; WHO conslt on yellow fever epidemics 1970; Dept of Med Microbiology Faculty of Med Makerere Univ: hon lectr 1970, sr lectr 1973–75, assoc prof and head of dept 1975–78, prof and head of dept 1978–86; memb Senate Makerere Univ 1977–90 (memb Cncl 1981–90, vice chllr 1986–90); dir Central Public Health Labs Uganda, pres Uganda Med Assoc 1982–86 (treas 1978–82), chm weekly Uganda TV medical magazine prog 1984–86; memb Editorial Bds: E African Jl for Med Res, Uganda Med Jl; memb: Confedn of African Med Assocs and Socs, E and Central African Physicians Assoc; *Recreations* games: cricket, football, tennis, athletics; *Clubs* Africa Cricket (Kampala); *Style—* HE Prof George Kirya; ✉ High Commission for Uganda, 58/59 Trafalgar Square, London WC2N 5DX (☎ 0171 839 5783, fax 0171 839 8925)

KISSACK, Nigel Euan Jackson; s of Maj Henry Jackson Kissack, RE (ret), of Sydney, Aust, and formerly Isle of Man, and Ethel Valerie, *née* Kneen; *b* 8 April 1955; *Educ* King William's Coll IOM, Univ of Sheffield (LLB); *m* 11 Oct 1980, Kathryn Margaret, da of Thomas Lloyd-Jones, of Hale, Cheshire; 1 s (Richard Lloyd b 2 Aug 1984), 1 da (Annabel Laura Jayne b 4 Aug 1982); *Career* admitted slr 1979; articled clerk Foysters Manchester, managing ptnr Manchester Office Alsop Wilkinson until 1996, ptnr Dibb Lupton Alsop Manchester (following merger) 1996–; author of various professional articles; *Recreations* rugby, cricket, cycling, reading, golf, skiing; *Clubs* St James's, Bowdon Lawn Tennis, Hale Golf; *Style—* Nigel Kissack, Esq; ✉ Dibb Lupton Alsop, Carlton House, 18 Albert Square, Manchester M2 5PE

KISSIN, Baron (Life Peer UK 1974), of Camden in Greater London; Harry Kissin; s of Israel Kissin, and Reusi, *née* Model; *b* 23 Aug 1912; *Educ* Basle Univ (LLD); *m* 1935, Ruth Deborah, da of Siegmund Samuel; 1 s (Hon Robert David b 1947), 1 da (Hon Evelyn Anne (Hon Mrs Singer) b 1944); *Career* chm: Lewis & Peat Ltd 1961–73, Experanza International Services plc 1970–83, Guinness Peat Group plc 1973–79, Linfood Holdings 1974–81, Lewis & Peat Holdings 1982–87 (pres 1987–); life pres Guinness Peat Gp plc 1979; dir: Tycon Spa Venice 1974–93, Transcontinental Servs Gp NV 1982–86; chm Cncl Inst of Contemporary Arts 1968–75, dir Royal Opera House Covent Garden 1973–84, tstee Royal Opera House Tst 1974–87 (chm 1974–80); govr: Bezadel Acad of Arts & Design 1975–87, Hebrew Univ of Jerusalem 1980–; Commandatore Ordem Nacional do Cruzeiro do Sul (Brazil) 1977, Chevalier Légion d'Honneur 1981; 1300 Years Bulgaria medal 1982; FRSA; *Clubs* Reform, E India, Devonshire Sports, Public Schs; *Style—* The Rt Hon the Lord Kissin; ✉ office: 79 Knightsbridge, London SW1X 7RB; House of Lords, London SW1A 0PW

KISSMANN, Edna; da of Karl Kissmann (d 1983), of Jerusalem, and Frieda Mosser Kissmann, of Tel Aviv; *b* 20 Dec 1949; *Educ* Hebrew Univ HS, Hebrew Univ (BA), Univ of Boston Sch of Public Communications (MSc); *Career* asst press sec PM's Office Govt of Israel 1975, md Ruder and Finn PR Ltd Israel 1976–77 (assoc dir 1973–75); Burson-Marsteller Inc NY: account exec 1978–79, account supervisor 1979–80, client servs mangr 1980–82, gp mangr 1982–85, vice pres then sr vice pres, exec vice pres and unit mangr i/c healthcare communications practice 1985–88; Burson-Marsteller London: EUP/unit mangr of healthcare and mktg 1988–89, jt md 1989–, currently global chair in healthcare practice; winner of several internal Burson-Marsteller awards; vice chm Europe 1993; memb Bd: Business in the Community, London First Centre; fndr memb Israel PR Assoc 1974 (memb London 1990); *Recreations* music, theatre, travel, people, good food and wine; *Clubs* The Reform; *Style—* Miss Edna Kissmann; ✉ 15 Melton Court, Old Brompton Road, London SW7; Burson-Marsteller Ltd, 24–28 Bloomsbury Way, London WC1 2PX (☎ 0171 831 6262, 0171 430 1033)

KITAJ, R B (Ronald); s of Dr Walter Kitaj (d 1982), and Jeanne Brooks Kitaj; *b* 29 Oct 1932; *Educ* Royal Coll of Art; *m* 15 Dec 1983, Sandra Fisher; 2 s (Lem b 1958, Max b 1984), 1 da (Dominie b 1964); *Career* artist; US Army 1955–57; pt/t teacher: Camberwell Sch of Art 1961–63, Slade Sch 1963–67; visiting prof: Univ of California Berkeley 1968, UCLA 1970; Hon DLitt London 1982; Hon Dr: RCA 1991, California Coll of Art & Craft 1995, Durham 1996; memb US Inst of Arts and Letters NY 1982, Nat Acad of Design NY 1987; chevalier des Arts et des Lettres 1996; RA 1991 (ARA 1984); *Solo Exhibitions* Marlborough New London Gallery 1963 and 1970, Marlborough Gallery NY 1975 and 1974, LA Co Museum of Art 1965, Stedelijk Museum Amsterdam 1967, Museum of Art Cleveland 1967, Univ of California Berkeley 1967, Galerie Mikro Berlin 1969, Kestner Gesellschaft Hanover 1970, Boymans-van-Beuningen Museum Rotterdam 1970, Cincinnati Art Museum Ohio (with Jim Dine) 1973, Marlborough Fine Art 1977, 1980 and 1985; *Retrospective Exhibitions* Hirshhorn Museum Washington 1981, Cleveland Museum of Art Ohio 1981, Kunsthalle Düsseldorf 1982, Tate Gallery 1994 and 1996, Los Angeles County Museum 1995, Metropolitan Museum NY 1995, Golden Lion (painting) Venice Biennale 1995; *Style—* R B Kitaj, Esq, RA; ✉ c/o Marlborough Fine Art Ltd, 6 Albemarle St, London W1

KITCHEN, Prof Kenneth Anderson; s of Leslie Dufton Kitchen (d 1994), and Hannah, *née* Sheen (d 1981); *b* 8 June 1932; *Educ* Hawick HS, Kettering GS, Newark Magnus GS, Univ of Liverpool (BA, PhD); *Career* Univ of Liverpool: lectr in Egyptology 1957–74, reader in Egyptology 1974–87, prof of Egyptology (personal chair and Brunner chair) 1987–96; author numerous papers and articles; visiting prof Regent Coll Vancouver Canada 1970, visiting fell Rundle Fndn for Egyptian Archaeology Macquarie Univ Sydney Aust 1985 and 1989; TE Peet Travelling Prize 1962, Sir Ernest Cassell Tst Award 1970, Br Acad Award 1987; *Books* Suppiluliuma and the Amarna Pharaohs (1962), Ancient Orient and Old Testament (1966), Ramesside Inscriptions, Historical and Biographical Vols I-VIII (1968–1990, Trans Vols I-II 1994–95, Notes and Comments Vols I-II 1994–96), The Third Intermediate Period in Egypt (1100–650 BC) (1972, 1986 and 1996), The Bible in its World (1977), Pharaoh Triumphant, Life and Times of Ramesses

II, King of Egypt (1983), Catalogue of the Egyptian Collection in the National Museum Rio de Janeiro (1990), Documentation for Ancient Arabia Vols I-IV (1994–); *Recreations* walking, gardening; *Style*— Prof Kenneth Kitchen; ✉ Oriental Studies, University of Liverpool, 14 Abercromby Square, Liverpool L69 3BX (☎ 0151 794 2468, fax 0151 794 2226)

KITCHEN, Linda Jayne; da of Capt Robert Barry Kitchen, of Heysham, Lancs, and Elaine, *née* Dunstan (d 1988); *b* 20 March 1960; *Educ* Morecambe GS, RNCM Manchester, National Opera Studio; *m* 21 July 1990, Aidan Patrick Lang, s of Bernard Lang; *Career* soprano; princ artist: Royal Opera Co 1986–89, Opera North 1989–; has given concert and recital performances with orchs and ensembles incl: BBC Symphony Orch, BBC Philharmonic Orch, Scottish Chamber Orch, London Mozart Players, Bournemouth Symphony Orch, CBSO, BBC Chamber Orch, Nash Ensemble, Corydon Singers, Huddersfield Choral, Royal Ballet; awarded Heinz Bursary; *Roles* with Royal Opera Co incl: Oscar in Un Ballo in Maschera, Sophie in Werther, Flora in The Knot Garden, Echo in Ariadne auf Naxos, Jano in Jenufa, Papagena in The Magic Flute, Jemmy in Guillaume Tell, Xenia in Boris Godunov; with Opera North incl: Zerlina in Don Giovanni 1985, Cherubino in The Marriage of Figaro 1989, Magnolia in Showboat (Opera North/Royal Shakespeare Co) 1989, Serpetta in La Finta Giardiniera 1989, Polly in The Threepenny Opera 1991, Eurydice in Orpheus in the Underworld 1992, Susanna in The Marriage of Figaro 1992; others incl: Sophie in Der Rosenkavalier (Hong Kong Festival), Tytania in A Midsummer Night's Dream (Netherlands Opera), Blonde in Die Entführung aus dem Serail (Glyndebourne Festival 1983 and Istanbul Int Festival 1995), Jemmy in Guillaume Tell (Geneva Opera) 1991, Zerbinetta in Ariadne Auf Naxos (Garsington Festival and Opera Zuid Holland), Susanna in Le Nozze di Figaro (Bordeaux and Grand Theatre Belfast 1996), Euridice in Orfeo ed Euridice (Lisbon); *Recordings* incl: Haydn's Little Organ Mass (under Denis McCauldin) 1988, Il Crociato in Egitto (under David Parry, Opera Rara) 1990, Serenade to Music (under Matthew Best) 1990; *Recreations* squash, golf, reading, bridge; *Style*— Ms Linda Kitchen; ✉ c/o Julia Maynard, Harrison/Parrott Ltd, 12 Penzance Place, London W11 4PA (☎ 0171 229 9166, fax 0171 221 5042)

KITCHEN, Mervyn John; s of Hubert John Kitchen, and Phyllis Elizabeth, *née* Webber; *b* 1 Aug 1940; *Educ* Backwell Comp Sch Bristol; *m* Anne, *née* Mathias; 1 s (Jody b 6 March 1977), 1 da (Faye b 30 Sept 1975); *Career* cricket umpire; laboratory asst Long Ashton Res Centre 1955–56; professional cricketer Somerset CCC: joined 1957, debut v Middx at Lord's, awarded county cap 1966, testimonial 1973, ret 1979; first class cricket umpire: appointed 1982, test debut Eng v NZ Lord's 1990, one day int debut v India Trent Bridge 1990; honours as player: John Player League winners 1979, runners-up Gillette Cup (Man of the Match award), awarded best batting performance BBC TV Sunday Cricket 1966; jobs during off-seasons whilst player incl: orchard technician, DIY asst, lorry driver, photographic printer, bookmaker's clerk; *Style*— Mervyn Kitchen, Esq; ✉ c/o Test & County Cricket Board, Lord's Cricket Ground, London NW8 8QN (☎ 0171 286 4405)

KITCHEN, Michael; s of Arthur Kitchen, and Betty, *née* Allen; *b* 31 Oct 1948; *Educ* City of Leicester Boys GS, RADA; *children* 2 s (Jack b 7 Oct 1988, James b 25 Nov 1995); *Career* actor; writer of two screenplays and short stories; *Theatre* work incl: Nat Theatre 1974–84, RSC 1987 (roles incl Hogarth, Mercutio, Bolingbroke), Lenny in The Homecoming (West End); *Television* numerous appearances incl: Caught on a Train, Brimstone and Treacle, Home Run, Benefactors, The Brontës, Freud, No Man's Land, Savages, Chancer, The Justice Game, Bedroom Farce, King Lear, A Comedy of Errors, School Play, Love Song, Ball Trap at the Côte Sauvage, To Play the King, Dandelion Dead, Buccaneers, The Hanging Gale (BBC) 1995, Reckless, Wilderness; *Films* incl: Out of Africa, The Russia House, Fools of Fortune, The Dive, Pied Piper, Unman Wittering and Zigo, The Bunker, The Enchanted April, Hostage, The Guilty, The Trial, Mrs Dalloway, Goldeneye; *Recreations* music, guitar, piano, composition, pilot's licence, riding, tennis, skiing, swimming; *Style*— Michael Kitchen, Esq; ✉ c/o ICM Ltd, Oxford House, 76 Oxford Street, London W1N 0AX (☎ 0171 636 6565, fax 0171 323 0101)

KITCHENER, Prof Henry Charles; s of Gershon Kitchener, and Muriel, *née* Jacobs; *b* 1 July 1951; *Educ* Eastwood HS, Univ of Glasgow (MB ChB, MD); *m* 12 June 1977, Valerie Anne, da of Walter Hayes, of Glasgow; 1 da (Sophie); *Career* Florence and William Blair-Bell res fell 1980–82, lectr in obstetrics and gynaecology Univ of Singapore 1983–84, William Blair-Bell memorial lectr RCOG 1985, conslt obstetrician and gynaecologist specialising in gynaecological oncology Aberdeen Royal NHS Tst 1988–96, prof of gynaecological oncology Univ of Manchester 1996–; sec Exec Ctee Br Soc for Colposcopy and Cervical Pathology 1994–; memb Gynaecological Visiting Soc of GB and Ireland; FRCS Glasgow 1989, FRCOG 1994 (MRCOG 1980); *Recreations* golf, hillwalking; *Clubs* Royal Aberdeen Golf, Royal Dornoch Golf; *Style*— Prof Henry Kitchener; ✉ Southlands, Bridge End Drive, Prestbury, Cheshire SK10 4DL; Department of Obstetrics and Gynaecology, St Mary's Hospital, Whitworth Park, Manchester M13 (☎ 0161 276 6461, fax 0161 273 3958)

KITCHENER OF KHARTOUM AND OF BROOME, 3 Earl (UK 1914); Henry Herbert Kitchener; TD, DL (Cheshire 1972); s of Viscount Broome (d 1928, s of 2 Earl and n of the general who won his reputation at the recapture of Khartoum); suc gf 1937; *b* 24 Feb 1919; *Educ* Winchester, Trinity Coll Cambridge; *Career* Maj RCS (TA), ret; pres Lord Kitchener Nat Meml Fund, pres Henry Doubleday Res Assoc; *Clubs* Brooks's; *Style*— The Rt Hon the Earl Kitchener of Khartoum, TD, DL; ✉ Westergate Wood, Eastergate, Chichester, W Sussex PO20 6SB (☎ 01243 543061)

KITCHIN, Alan William Norman; s of Norman Tyson Kitchin (d 1995), and Shirley Boyd, *née* Simpson; *Educ* Oundle, Univ of Cambridge (Squire Univ Scholar, BA, Tapp Postgraduate Scholar, MA); *Career* admitted slr 1978; Ashurst Morris Crisp 1986–: ptnr 1986–, ptnr in charge Tokyo office 1991–; chm Construction Ctee Law Asia; *Books* International Trade for the Nonspecialist (co-author); *Recreations* golf, tennis; *Clubs* Walton Heath Golf; *Style*— Alan Kitchin, Esq; ✉ Ashurst Morris Crisp, Broadwalk House, 5 Appold Street, London EC2A 2HA (☎ 0171 638 1111, fax 0171 972 7990)

KITCHIN, David James Tyson; QC (1994); s of Norman Tyson Kitchin (d 1995), and Shirley Boyd, *née* Simpson; *b* 30 April 1955; *Educ* Oundle, Fitzwilliam Coll Cambridge (MA); *m* 28 Oct 1989, Charlotte, da of Cdr David Jones; 1 da (Lara b 16 June 1991), 1 s (James b 2 July 1993); *Career* called to the Bar Gray's Inn 1977; *Recreations* golf, tennis; *Clubs* Walton Heath, Leander, Hawks (Cambridge); *Style*— David Kitchin, Esq, QC; ✉ 22 Perrymead St, London SW6 (☎ 0171 736 2161); 8 New Square, Lincoln's Inn, London WC2A 3QP (☎ 0171 405 4321)

KITCHING, (Henry) Alan; s of Noel Kitching, JP (d 1975), and Gladys Nichols (d 1961); *b* 9 Feb 1936; *Educ* Leighton Park Reading, Peddie Inst Hightstown NJ USA; *m* 1988, Ann Margaret, *née* Britton; 2 s; *Career* serv RN Sub-Lt; stockbroker; chm Middlesbrough Warehousing Ltd; dir Greig Middleton Ltd; *Recreations* tennis, shooting, fishing, bridge; *Clubs* Cleveland; *Style*— Alan Kitching, Esq; ✉ 9 Victoria Road, Harrogate, N Yorkshire HG2 0HQ

KITCHING, Alan; *b* 29 Dec 1940; *m* 1962, Rita, *née* Haylett (d 1984); 2 s; *Career* compositor to J W Brown & Son Darlington 1956–61, fndr (with Anthony Froshaug) Experimental Printing Workshop Sch of Art Watford Coll of Technol 1964 (first yr work exhibited ICA 1965), freelance design practice working in magazine and book design 1971–78, fndr (with Derek Birdsall) Omnific Studios Partnership Covent Garden 1978, subsequently estab letterpress studio Islington 1986, fndr/designer The Typography Workshop Clerkenwell 1989–; pt/t teacher of typography Central Sch of Art & Design London 1968–72, visiting lectr in typography RCA 1988–, estab letterpress workshops RCA 1993, subsequent workshops at Univs of Brighton and Middx and Glasgow Sch of Art; memb AGI 1994, RDI 1994; *Exhibitions* Pentagram Gallery London (first exhbn of letterpress work) 1992, RCA (retrospective exhbn of typography and printing) 1993; *Books and Publications* Typography Manual (Watford Sch of Art, 1970), Broadside (occasional pubn devoted to the typographic arts, 1 edn 1988); *Clubs* Chelsea Arts; *Style*— Alan Kitching, RDI; ✉ The Typography Workshop, 31 Clerkenwell Close, London EC1R 0AT (☎ 0171 490 4386, fax 0171 490 0063)

KITCHING, John Richard Howard; s of Dr Edwin Howard Kitching (d 1968), and Gwendoline Mary, *née* King; *b* 30 July 1946; *Educ* Rugby, Gonville and Caius Coll Cambridge (BA, MA); *m* 7 Oct 1972, Toril, da of Finn Ness; 1 s (Nicholas Howard b 3 Sept 1973), 1 da (Penelope Ann b 8 Set 1976); *Career* admitted slr 1971; Lovell White Durrant (formerly Lovell White & King): articled clerk 1969–71, asst slr 1971–76, ptnr 1976–; memb: City of London Slrs 1974–, Law Soc 1974–; *Recreations* golf, choral singing; *Clubs* The City Law Club, Mid Herts Golf, Quinta Do Lago Golf; *Style*— John Kitching, Esq; ✉ Lovell White Durrant, 65 Holborn Viaduct, London EC1A 2DY (☎ 0171 236 0066, fax 0171 248 4212)

KITSON, Clare; da of Harry Frederick Kitson (d 1963), of London, and Florence Blanche Maud, *née* Crook; *b* 19 March 1947; *Educ* Sydenham HS for Girls, Putney HS for Girls, St Anne's Coll Oxford (BA); *m* Jan 1981, John Edward Jordan, s of John Clarence Jordan; 1 da (Harriet Elizabeth Kitson Jordan b 16 Sept 1981); *Career* mgmnt trainee Marplan Market Research 1968–69, animation programming County Museum of Art LA 1969–71, freelance writer and involved in film programming London 1971–72, overseas sales of Kung Fu films for Golden Harvest 1972–78, prog offr National Film Theatre 1978–89, commissioning ed animation Channel Four Television 1989–; AIL 1992; *Awards* Channel 4 awarded EU Media Prog Golden Cartoon Award for outstanding contrib to European animation 1993, various awards to Channel 4 cmmnd films incl Academy Award for Best Animated Short 1995; *Recreations* languages, swimming; *Style*— Ms Clare Kitson; ✉ Channel Four Television Corporation, 124 Horseferry Road, London SW1P 2TX (☎ 0171 306 8474, fax 0171 306 8360)

KITSON, Gen Sir Frank Edward; GBE (1985, CBE for gallantry 1972, OBE 1968, MBE 1959), KCB (1980) MC (1955, Bar 1958), DL; s of Vice Adm Sir Henry Kitson, KBE, CB, by his w Marjorie, *née* de Pass; *b* 15 Dec 1926; *Educ* Stowe; *m* 1962, Elizabeth Janet, da of late Col Charles Richard Spencer, OBE, DL; 3 da; *Career* cmmnd 2 Lt Rifle Bde 1946, BAOR 1946–53, served Kenya, Malaya, Cyprus; CO 1 Bn Royal Green Jackets 1967–69, def fellow Univ Coll Oxford 1969–70, Cmd 39 Inf Bde NI 1970–72, Cmdt Sch of Infantry 1972–74, RCDS 1975, GOC 2 Div (subsequently Armoured Div) 1976–78, Cmdt Staff Coll 1978–80, Col Cmdt 2 Bn Royal Green Jackets 1979–87, dep C in C UKLF and inspr gen TA 1980–82, C in C UKLF 1982–85, Rep Col Cmdt RGJ 1982–85, Hon Col Univ of Oxford OTC (V) 1982–87, Gen 1982; ADC Gen to HM The Queen 1983–85; *Books* author of books on war incl: Gangs and Countergangs (1960), Low Intensity Operations (1971), Bunch of Five (1977), Warfare as a Whole (1987), Directing Operations (1989), Prince Rupert: Portrait of a Soldier (1994); *Style*— Gen Sir Frank Kitson, GBE, KCB, MC, DL; ✉ c/o Lloyds Bank, Farnham, Surrey

KITSON, Sir Timothy Peter Geoffrey; kt (1974); s of Geoffrey Kitson; *b* 28 Jan 1931; *Educ* Charterhouse, RAC Cirencester; *m* 1959, Diana Mary Fattorini; 1 s, 2 da; *Career* former memb Thirsk RDC & N Riding Yorks CC; formerly farmed in Australia; MP (C) Richmond (Yorks) 1959–83, PPS to Parly Sec Miny of Agriculture 1960–64, oppn whip 1967–70, PPS to Edward Heath as PM 1970–74, to same as Ldr of oppn 1974–75; chm: Provident Financial 1983–95, Ryeland Properties Ltd 1983, Leeds Overseas Ltd, Fishers Group Ltd, Homecare Insurance Ltd; dir: Leeds Permanent Building Society 1983–, Bradstock Hamilton, London Clubs International 1994; *Style*— Sir Timothy Kitson; ✉ Ulshaw Farm, Middleham, Leyburn, N Yorks DL8 4PU (☎ 01969 624455)

KITTEL, Gerald Anthony (Gerry); s of Francis William Berthold Kittel of Pinner Hill, Middx, and Eileen Winifred, *née* Maybanks (d 1973); *b* 24 Feb 1947; *Educ* Merchant Taylors', Univ of Poitiers (Dip), Ealing Poly; *m* 26 April 1975, Jean Samantha, *née* Beveridge; 2 s (Christian b 1969, Ashley b 1976), 1 da (Natalie b 1979); *Career* mktg dir C E Heath (Insurance Broking) Ltd; memb Int Advertising Assoc, MIPA, MCIM, MInstD; *Recreations* riding, squash, tennis; *Clubs* St James's, Park Place, Old Merchant Taylors' Soc; *Style*— Gerry A Kittel, Esq; ✉ Valence End, Hosey Hill, French Street, Westerham, Kent TN16 1PN (☎ 01959 564009); C E Heath (Insurance Broking) Ltd, 133 Houndsditch, London EC3A 7AH (☎ 0171 234 4000)

KITZINGER, Sheila Helena Elizabeth; MBE (1982); da of Alec Webster, and Clare, *née* Bond; *b* 29 March 1929; *Educ* Bishop Fox GS Taunton, Ruskin Coll Oxford, St Hugh's Coll Oxford (MLitt); *m* 1952, Uwe Kitzinger, *qv*; 5 da (Celia b 1956, Nell b 1958, Tessa (twin) b 1958, Polly b 1961, Jenny b 1963); *Career* writer, lectr; course team ldr Open Univ 1981–83; Writers' Fellowship Award from the Rockefeller Fndn 1988; involved with: Midwives' Info and Resource Serv, Nat Childbirth Tst; memb planning team, module ldr and lectr and examiner in midwifery Queen Charlotte's Coll of Health and Thames Valley Univ, hon prof Thames Valley Univ 1993–; *Books include* The Experience of Childbirth (1962), Pregnancy and Childbirth (1980, revised 1989), Woman's Experience of Sex (1983), Birth Over Thirty (1985, American Health Book Award), Freedom and Choice in Childbirth (1987), The Experience of Breastfeeding (1987), Being Born (1987, American Hornbook Award and Times Educnl Supplement Award), Breastfeeding Your Baby (1989), The Crying Baby (1989), Talking With Children About Things That Matter (with Celia Kitzinger, 1989), Pregnancy Day by Day (with Vicky Bailey, 1990), Homebirth and Other Alternatives to Hospital (1991), Ourselves as Mothers (1992), The Year After Childbirth (1994), Birth Over Thirty-five (1994), The New Pregnancy and Childbirth (1997), Becoming a Grandmother (1997); *Recreations* painting; *Clubs* RSM; *Style*— Ms Sheila Kitzinger; ✉ The Manor, Standlake, nr Witney, Oxford OX8 7RH (☎ 01865 300266, fax 01865 300438)

KITZINGER, Uwe; CBE (1980); *b* 12 April 1928; *Educ* Watford GS, Balliol Coll and New Coll Oxford; *m* 1952, Sheila Helena Elizabeth, *née* Webster, *qv*; 5 da; *Career* Cncl of Europe 1951–56, fell Nuffield Coll 1956–76 (emeritus fell 1976–), fndr ed Journal of Common Market Studies 1961–; visiting prof: Harvard 1969–70, Paris Univ 1970–73; advsr to vice pres of EEC Cmmn i/c external rels Brussels 1973–75, dean Euro Inst of Business Admin INSEAD Fontainebleau 1976–80, dir Oxford Centre for Mgmnt Studies 1980–84, fndr pres Templeton Coll Oxford 1984–91, visiting scholar Harvard 1993–, sr res fell Atlantic Cncl 1993–; fndr chm: Ctee on Atlantic Studies 1967–70, Major Projects Assoc 1981–86; fndr pres Int Assoc of Macro-Engr Socs 1987–92; chm Oxfordshire Radio Ltd 1988, co-fndr Lentils for Dubrovnik 1991; memb Cncl: European Movement 1974–76, RIIA 1976–85, Oxfam 1981–85, Fondation Jean Monnet 1990–, Hon LLD 1986; *Books* German Electoral Politics (1960), The Challenge of the Common Market (1961), Commitment and Identity (1968), Diplomacy and Persuasion (1973), The 1975 Referendum (with D Butler, 1976); *Recreations* sailing (ketch 'Anne of Cleves'); *Clubs* Royal Thames Yacht, Utd Oxford and Cambridge Univ; *Style*— Uwe Kitzinger, Esq, CBE; ✉ Standlake Manor, nr Witney, Oxon (☎ 01865 300266, fax 01865 300438); La Rivière, 11100 Bages, France (☎ and fax 00 33 68 41 70 13); Lowell House, Harvard University, Cambridge, MA 02138, USA (☎ and fax 00 617 495 3495)

KLASSNIK, Robin; s of Dr Benjamin Klassnik, and Leila Fabian, *née* Hammerschalg; *b* 28 Jan 1947; *Educ* Haverstock Comprehensive Sch, Hornsey Coll of Art, Leicester Coll of Art (BA); *m* 1 Dec 1979, Kathryn, da of Henry Halton; 1 s (Tomas b 2 Jan 1981), 1 da (Zoë b 9 Oct 1983); *Career* artist, lectr, gallery owner; gp ldr Fndn Course London Coll of Printing 1979–82, head Complementary Studies Byam Shaw Sch of Art 1982– (visiting lectr 1977–82), res asst (sculpture theory) Statens Kunstakademie Oslo Norway 1990–91; guest lectr: Poznan Acad of Fine Art, Maidstone Sch of Art, Camberwell Sch of Art, Brighton Poly, Slade Sch of Fine Art, Statens Kunstakademie Oslo, Goldsmiths Coll London, RCA London, Valands Konsthogskola Goteborg Sweden, Bath Coll of HE, Chelsea Coll of Art & Design (external examiner sculpture MA); dir New Contemporaries; *Solo Exhibitions* incl: Walk Through Painting (Pavilions in the Park Croydon) 1969, Nine Till Four (Acland Burghley Sch) 1969, Postal Sculpture (Boyd Inst and James Carters Bookshop) 1970, 34'3" x 57' x 11'6" (New Gallery) 1970, Galeria Dois Porto Portugal 1974, Open Studio Martello St 1974, Galeria Akumulatory 2 Poznan Poland 1975, Space Open Studios 1976, Nearly a Sculpture (Galeria Akumulatory 2, Galeria Pawilon Krakow, Whitechapel Art Gallery) 1978–79, Five Pheromones The Incomplete Documentation (Matts Gallery) 1980, Three Works (Spectro Art Gallery Newcastle upon Tyne) 1981, To Be Or Not To Be Original That is The Question (Galeria Akumulatory 2, Piwna 20/26 Warsaw Poland) 1983; fndr owner and dir Matts Gallery 1979; over fifty solo exhibitions to date; publisher artists books and bookworks; *Recreations* cricket; *Clubs* Burger King; *Style*— Robin Klassnik, Esq; ✉ Matt's Gallery, 42–44 Copperfield Road, London E3 4RR (☎ 0181 983 1771)

KLEEMAN, David George; s of Jack Kleeman (d 1984), and Ruth, *née* Stephany (d 1981); *b* 20 Aug 1942; *Educ* St Paul's, Trinity Hall Cambridge (MA); *m* 1968, Manuela Rachel, da of Edouard Cori, of Ave de Wagram, Paris; 4 da (Susanna b 1970, Nicole b 1973, Julie b 1974, Jenny b 1978); *Career* dir: Daman Financial Services Ltd, The Housing Corporation, and other public and private cos; slr; chm New River Health Authy; non-exec dir NHS Supplies Authy; *Recreations* fly-fishing, reading, opera; *Clubs* MCC; *Style*— David Kleeman, Esq; ✉ 141 Hamilton Terrace, London NW8 9QS (☎ 0171 624 2335); Daman Financial Services Ltd, 4th Floor, 74 Chancery Lane, London WC2A 1AA (☎ 0171 430 9329)

KLEEMAN, Harry; CBE (1984); s of Max Kleeman (d 1947); *b* 2 March 1928; *Educ* Westminster, Trinity Coll Cambridge; *m* 1955, Avril, da of Dr Maurice Lees (d 1974); 2 s (John, Daniel), 2 da (Jacqueline, Amanda); *Career* chm Kleeman Plastics Group 1968–94, ret; pres British Plastics Fedn 1979–80 (memb Cncl 1977–85), chm CBI Small Firms Cncl 1988–90 (also memb Cncl); formerly chm: Mgmnt Ctee Polymer Engrg Directorate, Plastic Processing EDC of NEDO; chm: Advsy Ctee on Telecommunications for Small Businesses 1986–88, Plastics and Rubber Inst 1985–87 (memb Cncl 1984–87), Central British Fund for World Jewish Relief 1991–96, Advsy Ctee London Sch of Polymer Technol 1990–94; memb: CBI Cncl 1984–94, Cons Trade and Indust Forum; tstee The Ort Tst; Freeman City of London, Liveryman Worshipful Co of Horners (memb Ct and past Master); FIM; *Recreations* amateur radio, riding, tennis; *Clubs* RSA; *Style*— Harry Kleeman, Esq, CBE; ✉ 41 Frognal, London NW3 6YD (☎ 0171 794 3366, e-mail 100417.1715@compuserve.com); High Trees, Friday St, Dorking, Surrey (☎ 01306 730678)

KLEIN, Gillian; da of Harry Falkow (d 1980), of Johannesburg, and Enid, *née* Ash (d 1985); *b* 13 May 1939; *Educ* Univ of the Witwatersrand (BA, postgrad dip in library and info sci); *children* 1 s (Graeme b 31 Dec 1961), 1 da (Leanne b 20 March 1964); *Career* info offr private indust 1960–61, sch librarian 1967–74, librarian ILEA Centre for Urban Educnl Studies 1974–81, teacher fell Inst of Educn London 1981–82, resources librarian ILEA 1982–90; visiting lectr: Brighton Poly 1986–89, Poly of N London 1987–90, Univ of Warwick 1989–; fndr and ed Multicultural Teaching Jl 1982–, editorial dir Trentham Books Ltd 1984–; rapporteur Cncl of Europe Multicultural Studies in Higher Educn 1983–86; conslt: Children's Book Project of Thailand 1991–, ANC Centre for Educnl Policy and Devpt Kwa-Zulu and Transvaal 1994–; tstee Anne Frank Educational Tst 1995–; FRSA 1993; *publications include* Fancy Dress Party (1981), Resources for Multicultural Education: An Introduction (1982), Scrapbooks (1983), School Libraries for Cultural Awareness (1985), Reading into Racism (1985), Agenda for Multicultural Teaching (with Alma Craft, 1986), Education towards Race Equality (1993), Achieving Publication in Education (with John Eggleston, 1996); *Recreations* family and friends, travel, theatre, art and architecture, swimming, reading, food; *Style*— Gillian Klein; ✉ Trentham Books, Westview House, 734 London Road, Stoke on Trent ST4 5NP

KLEIN, Roland; s of Fernand Klein (d 1982), and Marguerite, *née* Meyer (d 1987); *b* 3 July 1938; *Educ* CEC, BEPC and Beaux Arts Rouen France, Ecole de la Chambre Syndicale de la Haute Couture Parisienne and CAP Paris France; *Career* designer; Nat Serv France 1959–60; asst tailor Jean Patou Paris 1958–59, asst designer Christian Dior Paris 1960–61, asst designer Jean Patou and Karl Lagerfeld 1961–63, designer Nettie Vogue London 1963–66, design dir Marcel Fenez London 1970–88 (designer 1966–70), designer Roland Klein Ltd London and Tokyo 1988–; major projects incl: conslt designer British Airways corporate image clothing 1986, Max Mara and Marina Rinaldi Italy 1988–, British Telecom corporate image clothing 1991, Halifax Building Society 1992, Midland Bank PLC 1993, Russell & Bromley 1993; *Awards* Fil D'or 1987; *Style*— Roland Klein, Esq; ✉ Roland Klein Ltd, 7/9 Tryon St, London SW3 3LG (☎ 0171 823 9179, fax 0171 823 9717)

KLEIN, Prof Rudolf Ewald; s of Dr Robert Klein (d 1958), of Dumfries, and Dr Martha Klein, *née* Szidon; *b* 26 Aug 1930; *Educ* Bristol GS, Merton Coll Oxford (MA, Gibbs prize in modern history); *m* 24 May 1957, Josephine (d 1996), da of Leonard Thomas Parfitt (d 1980), of Guildford; 1 da (Leonora Jane b 1963); *Career* leader writer Evening Standard London 1951–61, leader writer and leader page editor The Observer 1961–71, res assoc London Sch of Hygiene 1971–73, sr fell Centre for Studies in Social Policy 1973–78, prof of social policy Univ of Bath 1978– (dir Centre for the Analysis of Social Policy); memb: Wiltshire Area Health Authy, Bath District Health Authy, various ctees of Social Sci Res Cncl, Econ and Social Res Cncl; specialist advsr to House of Commons Social Servs Ctee; *Books* Complaints Against Doctors (1973), Inflation and Priorities (ed, 1975), The Politics of Consumer Representation (with Janet Lewis, 1976), The Politics of the NHS (1983), The Future of Welfare (co-ed with Michael O'Higgins, 1985), Accountabilities (with Patricia Day, 1987), Inspecting the Inspectorates (with Patricia Day, 1990), How Organisations Measure Success (with Neil Carter and Patricia Day, 1991), The New Politics of the NHS (1995), Managing Scarcity (with Patricia Day and Sharon Redmayne, 1996); *Style*— Prof Rudolf Klein; ✉ 48 Springcroft Avenue, London N2 9JE (☎ 0181 442 1581); School of Social Sciences, University of Bath, Bath BA2 7AY (☎ 01225 826826)

KLEINPOPPEN, Prof Hans Johann Willi; s of Gerhard Kleinpoppen (d 1985), and Emmi, *née* Maass; *b* 30 Sept 1928; *Educ* HS Germany, Univ of Giessen Germany, Univ of Heidelberg Germany, Univ of Tübingen Germany; *Career* Privat-Dozent Univ of Tübingen 1967, visiting fell and prof Univs of Colorado Boulder and Columbia NY 1967–68; Univ of Stirling: prof of experimental physics 1968–, head of Physics Dept 1972–74, dir Inst of Atomic Physics 1974–81, head of Atomic and Molecular Physics Res Unit 1981–; fell Center for Theoretical Studies Univ of Miami 1973, visiting prof Univ of Bielefeld 1978–79; guest research scientist Fritz-Haber Inst of the Max-Planck Soc Berlin 1992–; chm and co-dir various nat and int confs and summer schs on atomic, molecular and optical physics; CPhys, FInstP 1969, FAmPhysSoc 1970, FRAS 1974, FRSE 1987, FRSA 1990; *Publications* Monograph Series on Physics of Atoms and Molecules (ed jtly with P G Burke), ed of 13 books on atomic and molecular physics, author of over 200 scientific research papers in int jls of physics and a comprehensive article on physics of atoms in advanced German textbook; Festschrift for the occasion of 60th birthday: Coherence in Atomic Collision Physics (eds H J Beyer, K Blum and R Hippler, 1988); *Recreations* music, fine art; *Style*— Prof Hans Kleinpoppen, FRSE; ✉ 27 Kenningknowes Rd, Stirling, Scotland; Unit of Atomic and Molecular Physics, University of Stirling, Stirling FK7 9JF, Scotland (☎ 01786 467800/467802)

KLEINWORT, Sir Richard Drake; 4 Bt (UK 1909), of Bolnore, Cuckfield, Sussex; s of Sir Kenneth Drake Kleinwort, 3 Bt (d 1994), and his 1 w, Lady Davina Rose Pepys (d 1973), da of 7 Earl of Cottenham; *b* 4 Nov 1960; *Educ* Stowe, Univ of Exeter (BA); *m* 29 Nov 1989, Lucinda, da of William Shand Kydd, of Buckinghamshire; 1 s (Rufus Drake b 16 Aug 1994), 1 da (Heloise b 28 Feb 1996); *Heir* s, Rufus Drake Kleinwort b 16 Aug 1994; *Career* Kleinwort Benson Geneva 1979, Banco General de Negocios Buenos Aires 1983, banker corp fin Deutschebank AG Hamburg and Frankfurt 1985–88, Biss Lancaster plc 1988–89, Grandfield Rork Collins Financial 1989–91, dir Cardew & Co 1994– (ptnr 1991–94); patron The Cuckfield Soc; pres The Little Black Bag Housing Assoc; fell World Scout Fndn Geneva; memb: The Sussex Club, Royal Horticultural Soc, S of England Agric Soc, British Field Sports Soc (BFSS), Inst King Edward VII Hosp Midhurst, Compagnie Internationale de la Chasse (CIC); *Recreations* photography, travel, sports (in general); *Clubs* Turf, RAC, WWF (1001); *Style*— Sir Richard Kleinwort, Bt; ✉ Heaselands, Haywards Heath, West Sussex RH16 4SA

KLEMPERER, Prof Paul David; s of late Hugh G Klemperer, and Ruth, *née* Jordan; *b* 15 Aug 1956; *Educ* King Edward's Sch Birmingham, Peterhouse Cambridge (BA), Stanford Univ (MBA, PhD); *m* 1989, Margaret, *née* Meyer; 1 s (David b 1995); *Career* conslt Arthur Andersen & Co 1978–80, Harkness fell of the Cwlth Fund 1980–82; Univ of Oxford: lectr in operations research and mathematical economics 1985–90, reader in economics 1990–95, Edgeworth prof of economics 1995–, John Thomson fell and tutor St Catherine's Coll 1985–95, fell Nuffield Coll 1995–; visiting positions: MIT 1987, Univ of California at Berkeley 1991 and 1993, Stanford Univ 1991 and 1993, Yale Univ 1994; ed RAND Jl of Economics 1993–; assoc ed or memb Ed Bd: Oxford Economic Papers 1986–, Review of Economic Studies 1989–, Jl of Industrial Economics 1989–, International Jl of Industrial Organization 1993–; fell Econometric Soc 1994; *Publications* author of articles in economics jls on industrial organization and economic theory; *Style*— Prof Paul Klemperer; ✉ Nuffield College, Oxford OX1 1NF (☎ 01865 278588)

KLETZ, Dr Trevor Asher; s of William Kletz (d 1974), of Manchester, and Frances, *née* Amshewitz (d 1991); *b* 23 Oct 1922; *Educ* King's Sch Chester, Univ of Liverpool (BSc), Loughborough Univ of Technol (DSc); *m* 28 Oct 1958, Denise Valerie (d 1980), da of Stanley Winroope; 2 s (Anthony Michael b 13 May 1961, Nigel Howard b 10 July 1963); *Career* ICI Ltd: Res Dept Billingham 1944–51, various appts in prodn rising to asst mangr Oil Works Billingham 1952–67, safety advsr Heavy Organic Chemicals (later Petrochemicals) Div 1968–82; Dept of Chemical Engrg Loughborough Univ of Technol: visiting industl prof 1978, full-time prof 1982, visiting fell 1986–; visiting prof Univ of Bradford 1991–94; IChemE Cncl Medal 1986, Loss Prevention Symposium Ctee American IChemE Bill Doyle Award 1985, IChemE Ned Franklin Medal 1992, IChemE Brennan Medal 1996; FIChemE 1978 (memb 1976), FRSC 1984 (assoc 1944), FEng 1984, fell American IChemE 1994 (memb 1982); *Books* Hazop and Hazan - Identifying and Assessing Process Industry Hazards (1983, 3 edn 1992), Cheaper, Safer Plants (1984, 3 edn retitled Plant Design for Safety - A User-Friendly Approach, 1991), Myths of the Chemical Industry (1984, 3 edn retitled Dispelling Chemical Engineering Myths, 1996), What Went Wrong? - Case Histories of Process Plant Disasters (1985, 3 edn 1994), An Engineer's View of Human Error (1985, 2 edn 1991), Learning From Accidents (1988, 2 edn 1994), Critical Aspects of Safety and Loss Prevention (1990), Learning From Disaster - How Organisations Have No Memory and Accidents Recur (1993), Computer Control and Human Error (ed, 1995); *Recreations* reading, walking, railways; *Style*— Dr Trevor Kletz, FEng; ✉ 64 Twining Brook Rd, Cheadle Hulme, Cheadle, Cheshire SK8 5RJ (☎ and fax 0161 485 3875, e-mail T.Kletz@lboro.ac.uk.)

KLEVAN, Rodney Conrad; QC (1984); *Educ* Univ of Birmingham (LLB); *Career* called to the Bar Gray's Inn 1966, recorder, head of chambers 18 St John St, ldr Northern Circuit 1992–96, bencher Gray's Inn 1992; *Style*— Rodney C Klevan, Esq, QC; ✉ 18 St John Street, Manchester M3 4EA (☎ 0161 834 9843, fax 0161 835 2051)

KLIMENTOVA, Daria; da of Zdenek Kliment, of Prague, and Ludmila Klimentová; *b* 23 June 1971; *Educ* Sch of Music and Dance Prague State Conservatory; *Career* ballet dancer; studied with Prof Dr Olga Paskova and Prof Jaroslav Slavicky; soloist Nat Theatre Ballet Prague 1989–92, princ Capab/Kruik Ballet Cape Town S Africa 1992–93, princ Scottish Ballet 1993–96, princ English Nat Ballet 1996–; also appeared with: Prague Festival Ballet Portugal and USA, Nat Theatre Ballet of Brno Germany tour; *Roles* with Nat Theatre Ballet of Prague incl: Aurora in Sleeping Beauty, Margarita in Lady with Camillias, Kitri in Don Quixote, title role in Sylvia, solo in Paguita, solo in Return to a Strange Land, Princess in From Tale to Tale; with Capab/Kruik Ballet incl: solo in Walpurgisnacht, solo in Four Last Songs, Titania in A Midsummer Night's Dream, Sugar Plum Fairy/Snow Queen in The Nutcracker, title role in Raymonda, Ophelia in Hamlet; with The Scottish Ballet incl: Swanilda in Coppelia, Solo Navy in Bruch Violin Concerto No 1, Wendy in Peter Pan, title role in Anna Karenina, Odette/Odile in Swan Lake, title role in La Sylphide, A Fond Kiss, Haydn Pieces; *Awards* second prize nat ballet competition Brno Czech Republic 1987, Prize of Paris Dance Fndn 1989, Prix de Lausanne Tokyo 1989, winner int ballet competition Pretoria 1991; *Recreations* reading psychology books, nature and animals, art; *Style*— Miss Daria Klimentova; ✉ English National Ballet, Markova House, 39 Jay Mews, London SW7 2ES (☎ 0171 581 1245, fax 0171 225 0827)

KLINE, Prof Paul; s of Maurice Victor Kline, and Ivy, *née* Simmons; *b* 8 March 1937; *Educ* Trinity Sch Croydon, Univ of Reading (BA), Univ of Aberdeen (MEd), Univ of Manchester (PhD, DSc); *m* 1, 8 Aug 1960 (m dis 1987); 1 s (Merlyn b 1963), 3 da (Anna b 1965, Naomi b 1966, Harriet b 1971); m 2, 28 Nov 1987, Penelope Mary Bennett; *Career* Univ of Exeter: lectr in educn 1966–69, lectr in psychology 1969–73, reader in psychometrics 1973–86, prof of psychometrics 1986–95, ret; *Books* Fact and Fantasy in Freudian Theory (1972), The Psychology of Vocational Guidance (1975), Psychological Testing (1976), Personality Theories and Dimensions (1976), Psychometrics and Psychology (1979), Fact and Fantasy in Freudian Theory (1981), Personality Measurement and Theory (1983), Psychology and Freudian Theory (1984), Handbook of Test Construction (1986), Psychology Exposed, The Emperor's New Clothes (1988), Psychology and Freudian Theory (1988), Intelligence - The Psychometric View (1990), The Handbook of Psychological Testing (1992), Personality - The Psychometric View (1992), An Easy Guide to Factor Analysis (1994); *Style*— Prof Paul Kline; ✉ Department of Psychology, University of Exeter, Exeter, Devon EX4 4QG (☎ 01392 264621)

KLUG, Sir Aaron; kt (1988), OM (1995); s of Lazar Klug, of Durban (d 1971), and Bella Silin (d 1932); *b* 11 Aug 1926; *Educ* Durban HS, Univ of the Witwatersrand (BSc), Univ of Cape Town (MSc), Univ of Cambridge (PhD, ScD); *m* 8 July 1948, Liebe, da of Alexander Bobrow (d 1983), and Annie Bobrow, of Cape Town; 2 s (Adam Brian Joseph b 1954, David Rupert b 1963); *Career* Nuffield res fell Birbeck Coll London 1954–57, ldr virus res project 1958–61; Univ of Cambridge: fell Peterhouse 1962–93, dir of natural sci studies Peterhouse 1962–85, memb staff Med Res Cncl Laboratory of Molecular Biology 1962–, jt head structural studies 1978–86, dir of laboratory 1986–96, hon prof 1989–96; awards: Heineken prize Royal Netherlands Acad 1979, Louisa Gross Horwitz prize Columbia Univ 1981, Nobel prize for chemistry 1982; Hon DSc: Chicago 1978, Witwatersrand 1984, Hull 1985, St Andrews 1987, Western Ontario 1991, Warwick 1994; Hon Dr Columbia 1978, Dr hc Strasbourg 1978, Hon Dr Stockholm 1980, Hon PhD Jerusalem 1984; hon fell: Trinity Coll Cambridge 1983, Peterhouse Cambridge 1993; hon memb Worshipful Co of Salters 1995; Hon FRCP 1986 (Baly medal 1987), Hon FRCPath 1991, memb Biochem Soc (Harden medal 1985), FRS 1969 (Copley medal 1985, pres 1995–); foreign assoc: American Acad of Arts and Sciences 1969, Nat Acad of Sciences of USA 1984, Max-Planck-Gesellschaft FRG, Académie des Sciences Paris 1989; *Recreations* reading, gardening; *Style*— Sir Aaron Klug, OM, PRS; ✉ MRC Laboratory of Molecular Biology, Hills Rd, Cambridge CB2 2QH (☎ 01223 248011)

KLYBERG, Rt Rev (Charles) John; s of Charles Augustine Klyberg (Capt MN, d 1975), and Ivy Lilian, *née* Waddington (d 1978); *b* 29 July 1931; *Educ* Eastbourne Coll, Lincoln Theol Coll; *Career* 2 Lt 1 Bn The Buffs 1952–53; asst estates mangr Cluttons 1953–57; curate St John's E Dulwich 1960–63, rector Fort Jameson Zambia 1963–67, vicar Christ Church and St Stephen Battersea 1967–77, dean Lusaka Cathedral Zambia and rector of parish 1977–85 (vicar gen 1978–85, dean emeritus 1985), bishop of Fulham 1985–96; chm Church Property Devpt Gp 1978–85, UK commissary for Anglican Church in Zambia 1985–89, pres Guild of All Souls 1988–95, archdeacon of Charing Cross 1989–96, guardian Shrine at Walsingham 1991–96; warden Quainton Hall Sch Harrow 1992–96; ret; ARICS; *Recreations* reading, music, travel; *Clubs* Athenaeum; *Style*— The Rt Rev John Klyberg; ✉ 44 Naildown Road, Hythe, Kent CT21 5TB

KNAPMAN, Paul Anthony; s of Frederick Ethelbert Knapman, of Torquay, Devon, and Myra, *née* Smith; *b* 5 Nov 1944; *Educ* Epsom Coll, King's Coll London, St George's Hospital Medical Sch (MB BS, DMJ, MRCS, LRCP), Inns of Court Sch of Law (barrister, Gray's Inn); *m* 1970, Penelope Jane, da of Lt Cdr Michael Cox, of Torquay, Devon; 1 s, 3 da; *Career* medical practitioner and barrister; Surgn Lt RNR 1970; HM coroner Inner West London at Westminster Coroner's Ct 1980–; hon lectr in medical jurisprudence: St George's, St Mary's, Charing Cross and Westminster, Middx and Univ Coll Hosp; memb: Clinical Forensic Med Section RSM (pres-elect 1993), Br Acad of Forensic Scis (memb Cncl 1982–86), Medicolegal Soc, Soc of Doctors of Law, Coroners Soc (memb Cncl 1985–), SE England Coroners Soc (pres 1980); Liveryman Worshipful Soc of Apothecaries (memb Ct 1993–); memb Lloyd's; *Books* The Law and Practice on Coroners (jtly, 3 edn 1985), Medicine and the Law (1989), Casebook on Coroners (1989); *Recreations* beagling, boats and shooting; *Clubs* Athenaeum, Garrick, Royal Torbay Yacht; *Style*— Paul Knapman, Esq; ✉ c/o Westminster Coroner's Court, Horseferry Road, London SW1P 2ED (☎ 0171 834 6515)

KNAPMAN, Roger Maurice; MP (C) Stroud (majority 13,405); s of Harry Arthur Blackmore Knapman (d 1996), of North Tawton, Devon and Joan Margot, *née* Densham (d 1970); *b* 20 Feb 1944; *Educ* St Aubyn's Sch Tiverton, All Hallows Sch Lyme Regis, RAC Circencester; *m* 25 March 1967, Carolyn Trebell, da of Sidney George Eastman (d 1993), of Appledore, near Bideford, N Devon; 1 s (William b 1970), 1 da (Rebecca b 1971); *Career* chartered surveyor; MP (C) Stroud 1987–, PPS to Rt Hon Archie Hamilton as Min of State for the Armed Forces 1990–92 (resigned), asst govt whip 1995–96, a Lord Cmmr HM Treasy (Govt whip) 1996–; vice chm Cons Euro Affrs Ctee 1989–90; memb Agric and Food Research Cncl 1991–94, memb Select Ctee on Agric 1994–95; FRICS 1967; *Recreations* fishing, snooker; *Style*— Roger Knapman, Esq, MP; ✉ 38 Tufton Court, Tufton St, London SW1; c/o Stroud Conservative Association, Carlton Gardens, London Road, Stroud, Glos

KNAPP, Edward Ronald (Ron); CBE (1979); s of Percy Charles Knapp (d 1979), and Elsie Maria, *née* Edwards (d 1978); *b* 10 May 1919; *Educ* Cardiff HS, St Catharine's Coll Cambridge (MA), Harvard Business Sch (AMP); *m* 16 April 1942, Vera Mary, da of Capt William Stephenson, of Cardiff; 2 s (Ian b 1946, William b 1951), 2 da (Vanessa b 1956, Lucille b 1959); *Career* RNVR Lt Cdr 1940–46, HMS Aurora 1941–44, US Naval Res Estab Washington DC 1944–46, Admty 1946; md: Br Timken 1969–79 (joined 1946), Timken Europe 1979–84; dir Timken Co USA 1976; rugby capt: Univ of Cambridge 1940–41, Northampton RFC 1948; played for Wales 1940; govr Nene Coll 1948–89, pres Northants RFC 1986–88; *Recreations* gardening, golf, world travel; *Clubs* East India, Northants and County, Hawk's (Cambridge); *Style*— Ron Knapp, Esq, CBE; ✉ The Elms, 1 Millway, Duston, Northampton (☎ 01604 584737)

KNARESBOROUGH, Bishop of, 1986–; Rt Rev Malcolm James Menin; s of Rev James Nicholas Menin (d 1970), Vicar of Shiplake, Oxon, and Doreen, *née* Dolamore (d 1967); *b* 26 Sept 1932; *Educ* Dragon Sch, St Edward's, Univ Coll Oxford (MA), Cuddesdon Theol Coll; *m* 11 Oct 1958, Jennifer Mary, da of Andrew Patrick Cullen (d 1966); 1 s (Andrew b 1961), 3 da (Catherine b 1959, Brigid b 1963, Sarah b 1965); *Career* ordained (Portsmouth) deacon 1957, priest 1958; asst curate Holy Spirit Southsea 1957–59, asst curate Fareham Hants 1959–62, vicar St Mary Magdalene with St James Norwich 1962–86, rural dean Norwich East 1981–86; hon canon Norwich Cathedral 1982; *Recreations* carpentry, walking, gardening, photography; *Style*— The Rt Rev the Bishop of Knaresborough; ✉ 16 Shaftesbury Avenue, Leeds LS8 1DT (☎ 0113 266 4800)

KNEALE, Prof (Robert) Bryan Charles; s of William Thomas Kneale (d 1963), of Douglas, IOM, and late Lilian, *née* Kewley; *b* 19 June 1930; *Educ* Douglas HS IOM, Douglas Sch of Art IOM, Royal Acad Schs (Rome scholar); *m* 1956, Doreen, da of Clifford Lister; 1 s (Simon Benedict b 1960, d 1996), 1 da (Katherine b 1957); *Career* painter until 1959; first exhibition of paintings Redfern Gallery 1954, recipient Daily Express Young Painters prize 1955; sculptor (mainly in bronze) 1960–, regular exhibitor Redfern Gallery until 1986; head of sculpture Hornsey Coll of Art and Design 1968, prof of sculpture Royal Acad 1980–87; RCA: tutor 1963–80, sr tutor 1980–85, head of sculpture 1985–90, prof of drawing 1990–95; Leverhulme prize 1952, Arts Cncl purchase award 1969; RA 1974 (ARA 1971), fell RCA; *Exhibitions* incl: John Moores 1961, Sixth Congress of Architects Union (Southbank) 1961, Art d'Aujourd'hui Paris 1963, Battersea Park Sculpture Int 1963–66, Profil 2 Bochom 1964, Retrospective (Whitechapel Gallery) 1966, English Eye 1965, British Sculpture of the 60's (Tate Gallery) 1966, City of London Open Air Sculpture 1968, British Sculptors Winter Exhibition (Royal Acad) 1972 (also curator), Holland Park 1973, New Art (Hayward Gallery) 1975, Silver Jubilee Exhibition of British Sculpture (Battersea Park) 1977 (also curator), Monumental Sculpture (Manx Millenium) 1979, Serpentine Gallery 1979, Royal Acad 1985, Retrospective (Henry Moore Gallery) 1986, Fitzwilliam Museum 1987, Sal Uno Rome 1988, Drawing Retrospective (Natural History Museum) 1991, Sculpture and Drawing (bone drawings and sculpture retrospective Manx Museum and National Tst) 1992, Chelsea Harbour sculpture 1993, Retrospective (Royal West of England Acad) 1995; *Clubs* Chelsea Arts; *Style*— Prof Bryan Kneale, RA; ✉ 10a Muswell Rd, London N10 2BG (☎ 0181 444 7617)

KNEALE, David Arthur; *b* 20 Aug 1954; *Educ* Douglas HS IOM, Univ of Nottingham (BA); *m* 13 May 1996, Jacqueline Sylvia, da of Sylvia Agnes Paterson; *Career* treas Student Union Univ of Nottingham 1975–76; The Boots Company 1976–: asst expense controller 1976–77, pet food buyer 1978–80, leisure gp mangr 1980–82, cosmetics gp mangr 1982–83, asst merchandise controller (med merchandise) 1983–85, asst mktg controller (food and own brand meds) 1985–86, buying controller (personal care business centre) 1986–89, gen mangr (personal care) 1989–92, gen mangr (beauty and personal care) 1992–95, dir of merchandise and mktg 1995–; *Recreations* reading, cinema, badminton; *Style*— David Kneale, Esq; ✉ Boots The Chemist, 1 Thane Road West, Nottingham, Notts NG2 3AA (☎ 0115 959 2583, fax 0115 959 2648)

KNECHT, Prof Robert Jean; s of Jean Joseph Camille Knecht (d 1970), and Odette Jeanne Eugenie Juliette, *née* Mioux (d 1983); *b* 20 Sept 1926; *Educ* Lycée Français London, Salesian Coll Farnborough, King's Coll London (BA, MA), Univ of Birmingham (DLitt); *m* 1, 8 Aug 1956, Sonia Mary Fitzpatrick (d 1984), da of Dr Hubert Hodge; m 2, 28 Aug 1986, Maureen Joan, *née* White; *Career* Univ of Birmingham: asst lectr in mod history 1956–59, lectr 1959–68, sr lectr 1968–78, reader 1978–85, prof of French history 1985–92, emeritus prof and hon sr res fell in modern history 1992–; chm: Soc for Renaissance Studies 1989–92, Bd of Govrs Wroxall Abbey Sch Warwick 1985–92; co fndr Soc for Study of French History (chm 1995–); memb Société de l'Histoire de France; FRHistS; *Books* The Voyage of Sir Nicholas Carewe (1959), Francis I (1982), French Renaissance Monarchy (1984), The French Wars of Religion (1989), Richelieu (1990), Renaissance Warrior and Patron (1994), The Rise and Fall of Renaissance France (1996); *Recreations* travel, music, photography; *Clubs* New Cavendish; *Style*— Prof Robert Knecht; ✉ 79 Reddings Rd, Moseley, Birmingham B13 8LP (☎ and fax 0121 449 1916)

KNELLER, Sir Alister Arthur; kt (1996); s of Arthur Harry Kneller, OBE (d 1972), of Chichester, and Hester Muriel, *née* Farr (d 1975), of Mombasa, Kenya; *b* 11 Nov 1927; *Educ* The King's Sch Canterbury, Corpus Christi Coll Cambridge (MA, LLM); *Career* called to the Bar Gray's Inn 1994 (hon bencher 1995); Kenya: resident magistrate 1955, sr state counsel 1962, registrar of the High Ct 1965, puisne judge 1969, judge of the Ct of Appeal 1982–86; Chief Justice of Gibraltar 1986–95, ret; *Recreations* theatre, classical concerts; *Clubs* United Oxford and Cambridge University; *Style*— Sir Alister Kneller

KNIBB, Prof Michael Anthony; s of Leslie Charles Knibb (d 1987), and Christian Vera, *née* Hoggar (d 1978); *b* 14 Dec 1938; *Educ* Wyggeston Sch Leicester, King's Coll London (BD, PhD), Union Theological Seminary NY (STM), Corpus Christi Coll Oxford; *m* 30 Dec 1972, Christine Mary, da of John Henry Thomas and Patricia Mary Burrell, of Leicester; *Career* Old Testament Studies King's Coll London: lectr 1964–82, reader 1982–86, prof 1986–; head of Theology and Religious Studies Dept King's Coll London 1989–93, dep head Sch of Humanities King's Coll London 1992–; memb SOTS 1965–, ed SOTS Book List 1980–86, hon sec Palestine Exploration Fund 1969–76, memb Studiorum Novi Testamenti Societas 1980– (joint convener of seminar on early Jewish writings and the New Testament 1986–91), memb Humanities Research Bd 1995– (chm Postgraduate Ctee 1996–); FBA 1989, FKC 1991; *Books* The Ethiopic Book of Enoch (1978), Het Boek Henoch (1983), Commentary on 2 Esdras (1979), The Qumran Community (1987); *Recreations* hill walking; *Clubs* Athenaeum; *Style*— Prof Michael A Knibb, FBA; ✉ 6 Shootersway Park, Berkhamsted, Herts HP4 3NX (☎ 01442 871459); Department of Theology and Religious Studies, King's College London, Strand, London WC2R 2LS (☎ 0171 873 2455/2341, fax 0171 873 2255)

KNIGHT, A J; da of Marvin Kitman, of NYC, and Carol Kitman; *b* 3 June 1964; *Educ* Leonia HS, Parsons Sch of Design NYC, St Martin's Sch of Art (BA); *m* 10 Feb 1990, David Richard Knight; *Career* asst fashion ed Village Voice 1986–87; fashion ed: Details Magazine 1987–88, In Fashion Magazine 1988–89, Model Magazine 1989–90, Mademoiselle Magazine 1989–91, Company Magazine 1991–95, Brides Magazine 1995–; *Clubs* Groucho; *Style*— Mrs A J Knight; ✉ Brides Magazine, Vogue House, Hanover Square, London W1 (☎ 0171 499 9080)

KNIGHT, Prof Alan Sydney; s of William Henry Knight, of Buckingham, and Eva Maud, *née* Crandon (d 1979); *b* 6 Nov 1946; *Educ* Christ's Hosp Horsham, Balliol Coll Oxford (BA), Nuffield Coll Oxford (DPhil); *m* 1, 1969 (m dis), Carole, da of Gordon Jones; 1 da (Katharine b 1974); m 2, 1985, Lidia, da of Juan Lozano Martin; 2 s (Alexander b 1980, Henry b 1982); *Career* res fell Nuffield Coll and lectr in politics Balliol Coll Univ of Oxford 1971–73, lectr in modern history Univ of Essex 1973–85, visiting prof Centre for US-Mexican Studies Univ of California San Diego 1986; Univ of Texas: Worsham Centennial prof of history 1986–90, C B Smith sr prof of history 1990–92; Univ of Oxford: prof of Latin America history and dir Latin American Centre 1992–, fell St Antony's Coll 1992–; memb: Soc for Latin American Studies 1982–, Latin American Studies Assoc 1986–; Bolton prize Conf on Latin American History 1987, Beveridge prize American Historical Soc 1987, Guggenheim fell 1990–91; *Books* The Mexican Revolution (1986), US-Mexican Relations 1910–40: An Overview (1987), The Mexican Petroleum Industry in the Twentieth Century (ed, 1992); *Recreations* kayaking; *Style*— Prof Alan Knight; ✉ St Antony's College, Oxford OX2 6JF (☎ 01865 274490, fax 01865 58680)

KNIGHT, Ven Alexander Francis; s of Benjamin Edward Knight, of Bridport, and Dorothy Mary, *née* Sherwood; *b* 24 July 1939; *Educ* Taunton Sh, St Catharine's Coll Cambridge (MA), Wells Theol Coll; *m* 23 June 1962, Sheelagh Elizabeth, *née* Desmond Faris; 3 da (Catharine Mary b 2 April 1964, Susannah Elizabeth b 8 June 1966, Helen Clare b 31 Dec 1968), 1 s (William Benjamin James b 22 Jan 1971); *Career* asst curate Hemel Hempstead 1963–68, chaplain Taunton Sch 1968–74, dir The Bloxham Project 1975–81, dir of studies Aston Trg Scheme 1981–83, priest-in-charge Easton and Martyr Worthy 1983–91, archdeacon of Basingstoke 1990–, canon residentiary of Winchester Cathedral 1991–; *Recreations* gardening, theatre, walking; *Style*— The Ven the Archdeacon of Basingstoke; ✉ 1 The Close, Winchester, Hants SO23 9LS (☎ 01962 869374)

KNIGHT, Andrew Stephen Bower; s of M W B Knight, and S E F Knight; *b* 1 Nov 1939; *m* 1, 1966 (m dis), Victoria Catherine Brittain; 1 s (Casimir); m 2, 1975 (m dis 1991), Begum Sabiha Rumani Malik, formerly w of M Aertsens, of Belgium; 2 da (Amaryllis, Afsaneh); *Career* ed The Economist 1974–86; Daily Telegraph plc: chief exec 1986–89, ed-in-chief 1987–89; exec chm News International plc 1990–93 (non-exec chm 1993–95), dir News Corporation 1991–; Stanford Univ: memb Advsy Bd Centre for Econ Policy Res 1981–, memb Advsy Cncl Inst of Int Studies; govr Ditchley Fndn 1981– (memb Mgmnt Cncl 1982–); *Clubs* Brooks's, Royal Automobile; *Style*— Andrew Knight, Esq; ✉ c/o News International plc, Virginia St, London E1 9XY (☎ 0171 782 6000)

KNIGHT, Angela; MP (C) Erewash (majority 5,703); da of Andrew McTurk Cook, and late Barbara Cook; *b* 31 Oct 1950; *Educ* Sheffield Girls HS, Univ of Bristol (BSc); *m* 7 Feb 1981 (m dis), David George Knight; 2 s; *Career* devpt engr Air Products Ltd 1972–77, fndr and md engrg co specialising in heat treatment of metals 1977–92; cnclr Sheffield City Cncl 1987–92 (spokesman on educn, planning and indust), MP (C) Erewash 1992–; memb Educn Select Ctee 1992–93, sec Backbench Environment Ctee 1992–93, PPS DTI 1993–94, PPS to Chllr of the Exchequer 1994–95, economic sec to the Treasy 1995–; *Clubs* Long Eaton, Sandiacre and Draycott Cons Clubs; *Style*— Mrs Angela Knight, MP; ✉ House of Commons, London SW1A 0AA

KNIGHT, Dr Anthony Harrington; s of Dr Bryant William Knight (d 1982), and Gladys Irene, *née* Eldridge; *b* 29 April 1940; *Educ* Univ Coll Sch, St Bartholomew's Hosp Med Sch Univ of London (MB BS); *m* 24 Aug 1963, Sheila Mary, da of Alfred Stanley Brewer (d 1989); 2 s (Jonathan Clive b 1965, Christopher Harrington b 1968); *Career* conslt physician Stoke Mandeville and Royal Bucks Hosps 1974–, fndr and physician in charge Aylesbury Diabetes Educn Treatment Centre 1978–, dist clinical tutor Univ of Oxford 1979–86, vice chm Aylesbury Vale Health Authy 1982–89; memb Br Diabetic Assoc Med Scientific and Educn Sections (sec Educn Section 1986–89, chm 1991–94), pres Aylesbury Dist Br Diabetic Assoc, chm Stoke Mandeville Hosp Post Grad Med Soc, fndr and leader Ridgeway and Vale Diabetes Club; MRCS 1963, FRCP 1980 (MRCP 1968); *Recreations* hill and mountain walking, oil painting; *Style*— Dr Anthony Knight; ✉ The Old Vicarage, 101 Aylesbury Rd, Bierton, Bucks HP22 5BT; 4 Temple Square,

Aylesbury, Bucks; The Diabetes Centre, Stoke Mandeville Hospital, Aylesbury, Bucks (☎ 01296 315533)

KNIGHT, Sir Arthur William; kt (1975); s of Arthur Frederick Knight; *b* 29 March 1917; *Educ* Tottenham Co Sch, LSE; *m* 1, 1945, Beatrice, *née* Oppenheim (d 1968); 1 s, 3 da; m 2, 1972, Sheila Whiteman; *Career* chm: Courtaulds 1975–79, Nat Enterprise Bd 1979–80; non-exec dir Dunlop Holdings 1981–84 (resigned); vice chm Cncl RIIA until 1986; *Style—* Sir Arthur Knight; ✉ Charlton End, Singleton, W Sussex PO18 0HX

KNIGHT, Prof Bernard Henry; CBE (1993), GSM (Malaya) 1956; s of Harold Ivor Knight (d 1984), of Cardiff, and Doris, *née* Lawes; *b* 3 May 1931; *Educ* St Illtyd's Coll Cardiff, Welsh Nat Sch of Med (MD BCh), MRCP, FRCPath, DMJ (Path); *m* 11 June 1955, Jean Gwenllian, da of Charles Ogborne (d 1947), of Swansea; 1 s (Huw David Charles b 1964); *Career* Short Serv Cmmn Capt RAMC specialist in pathology Malaya 1956–59; called to the Bar Gray's Inn; lectr in forensic med Univ of London 1959–62, sr lectr Univ of Newcastle 1965–68, prof of forensic pathology and lectr Univ of Wales 1980– (sr lectr 1968–76, reader 1976–80), Home Office pathologist, conslt pathologist Cardiff Royal Infirmary, dir Wales Inst of Forensic Med 1989–, pathology ed Forensic Sci Int; memb GMC 1979–, vice pres Int Acad of Legal Med 1982–, pres Forensic Sci Soc 1987–89, memb Cncl RCPath, memb Home Office Policy Advsy Bd on forensic pathology, pres Br Assoc of Forensic Med 1991–93 (former sec), hon memb Finnish, Hungarian and German Socs of Forensic Med; *Books* crime novels: The Lately Deceased (1963), The Thread of Evidence (1965), Russian Roulette (1968), Policeman's Progress (1969), Tiger at Bay (1970), Deg Y Dragwyddoldeb (1972), The Expert (1976); historical novels: Lion Rampant (1974), Madoc Prince of America (1977); biography: Autopsy - The Memoirs of Milton Helpern (1977); popular non-fiction: Murder Suicide or Accident (1971), Discovering the Human Body (1980); textbooks: Legal Aspects of Medicine (5 edn, 1992), Sudden Death In Infancy (1982), Coroner's Autopsy (1983), Lawyer's Guide to Forensic Medicine (1983), Forensic Medicine (1986), Essentials of Forensic Medicine (with Polson & Gee, 1985), Simpson's Forensic Medicine (11 edn, 1996), Forensic Pathology (1991, 2 edn 1996); *Recreations* writing: crime and history novels, biography, radio and TV drama; *Style—* Prof Bernard Knight, CBE, GSM; ✉ 26 Millwood, Lisvane, Cardiff CF4 5TL (☎ 01222 752798); Wales Institute of Forensic Medicine, University of Wales College of Med, Royal Infirmary, Cardiff CF2 1SZ (☎ and fax 01222 484258)

KNIGHT, Brien Walter; s of Edward Alfred Knight (d 1993), of Sussex, and Winifred, *née* Stolworthy (d 1976); *b* 27 June 1929; *Educ* Woodhouse GS, Sir John Cass Coll London; *m* 1, 1955, Annette, da of Alfred Scotten (d 1964), of Barnet; 1 s (Darrell b 1963), 4 da (Carolyn b 1961, Judith b 1964, Emma b 1966, Sophie b 1966); m 2, Maria Antoinette (Rita), da of Abraham Van Der Meer (d 1958), of Holland; *Career* dir: Knight Strip Metals Ltd 1951 (chm 1970–), Sterling Springs Ltd 1952–, Knight Precision Wire Ltd 1979– (chm 1979–); Precision Metals NV (Belgium) 1973–; chm Knuway Investmts Ltd 1973–, FInstD; *Recreations* DIY, sailing; *Style—* Brien Knight, Esq; ✉ Millview, 3 Hawthorn Grove, Barnet Rd, Arkley, Herts EN5 3EN; Knuway House, Cranborne Rd, Potters Bar, Herts EN6 3JL

KNIGHT, Charles F; *Career* chm Emerson Electric Co; non-exec dir: British Petroleum Co plc 1987–, Anheuser-Busch, SBC Communications Inc, IBM; *Style—* Charles Knight, Esq; ✉ Emerson Electric Co, 8000 West Florissant, PO Box 4100, St Louis, Missouri 63136, USA; c/o British Petroleum plc, Britannic House, 1 Finsbury Circus, London EC2M 7BA (☎ 0171 496 4000)

KNIGHT, Dominic John Gerard; s of Kenneth Alexander Knight, of Broadstairs, Kent, and Irene Elaine Clements, *née* Robey (d 1992); *b* 15 Nov 1954; *Educ* Chatham House Sch Ramsgate Kent, Exeter Coll Oxford (open scholar, MA); *m* Jane Nina, *née* Askew; 2 s (Sebastian Alexander John b 3 April 1990, Rupert Charles Guy b 19 May 1993); *Career* vice-pres Stockton Press New York 1984–88; Macmillan Press Ltd: gp marketing dir 1989–91, publishing dir 1992–94, md 1994–; *Recreations* playing the violin and the piano, a little golf and walking in the local hills; *Style—* Dominic Knight, Esq; ✉ Macmillan Press Ltd, Brunel Road, Houndmills, Basingstoke RG21 6XS (☎ 01256 29242)

KNIGHT, Francis William (Frank); s of Thomas Francis Knight (d 1959), and Louisa Doreen, *née* Berridge; *Educ* The Roan Sch Blackheath, St John's Coll Cambridge (MA); *m* 1 Aug 1959, Diane Beverley, *née* Knight; 1 s (Timothy Francis b 30 Oct 1973), 2 da (Susan Pernille b 26 Aug 1965, Jennifer Louise b 27 Sept 1969); *Career* Colgate-Palmolive: mktg mgmnt UK 1960–63, mktg mgmnt Denmark 1964–65, md E Africa 1966–68; mgmnt conslt Booz Allen & Hamilton International 1969–70, gp md Bristol-Myers Co 1971–77, chm and chief exec Campbells Soups 1977–81, md United Biscuits 1984–85 (dep md 1981–83), chief exec UB Foods Europe 1986–87; dep gp chief exec United Biscuits (Holdings) plc 1988–91; chm: Field Group PLC 1992–, More O'Ferrall PLC 1996–; dep chm: ASDA Group plc 1992–, Berisford International plc 1991–; non-exec dir: Ocean Group plc 1988–, London International Group plc; *Recreations* golf, chess, opera, Dickensiana; *Style—* Frank Knight, Esq; ✉ More O'Ferrall PLC, 33 Golden Square, London W1R 3PA

KNIGHT, Geoffrey Egerton; CBE (1970); s of Arthur Egerton Knight, and Florence Gladys, *née* Clarke; *b* 25 Feb 1921; *Educ* Stubbington House, Brighton Coll Sussex; *m* 1947, Evelyn Bugle; 2 da; *Career* Royal Marines 1939–46; joined Bristol Aeroplane Co Ltd 1953; dir: Bristol Aircraft Ltd 1956, BAC Ltd 1964–77 (vice-chm 1972–76), Fenchurch Insurance Group Ltd 1975 (chm 1980–92), GPA Group Ltd 1976–93, GPG plc 1975–89 (jt dep chm 1987–89, chm 1989), Trafalgar House plc 1980–91; *Books* Concorde - The Inside Story (1976); *Clubs* Boodle's, White's; *Style—* Geoffrey Knight, Esq, CBE; ✉ 33 Smith Terrace, London SW3 (☎ 0171 352 5391)

KNIGHT, Rt Hon Gregory (Greg); PC (1995), MP (C) Derby North (majority 4,453); s of Albert George Knight, of Leicester, and late Isabella, *née* Bell; *b* 4 April 1949; *Educ* Alderman Newton's GS Leicester, Coll of Law Guildford; *Career* admitted slr 1973, practising until 1983; MP (C) Derby N 1983–; PPS to David Mellor as Min of State at FO 1987–88 and as Min of Health 1988–89, asst Govt whip 1989, a Lord Cmmr of the Treasury (Govt whip) 1990–93, Treasurer HM Household (dep chief whip) 1993–96, min of state DTI 1996–; Leicester City cncllr 1976–79, Leicestershire co cncllr 1977–83, former chm Public Protection Ctee, former dir Leicester Theatre Tst Ltd (former chm of Fin Ctee); *Books* Westminster Words (1988), Honourable Insults (1990), Parliamentary Sauce (1993); *Recreations* arts (especially music), classic cars; *Style—* The Rt Hon Greg Knight, MP; ✉ House of Commons, London SW1

KNIGHT, Heather Ann; da of Jack Knight, of Diss, Norfolk, and Doris Amelia, *née* Foster; *b* 29 April 1944; *Educ* Grays Convent HS, South East Essex Tech Coll; *Career* sec to head of market res Charles Hobson & Grey 1963–65, PA to publicity offr Thames Board Mills 1965–67; PA to head PR: Benton & Bowles 1967–68, Save the Children Fund 1968–71; asst to artistic dir London Festival Ballet 1971–78, office mangr Greenhalgh & Hanson 1978–81, major examinations mangr Royal Acad of Dancing 1981, administrative dir London City Ballet 1981–84, artistic mangr London Festival Ballet 1984–85, administrative dir London City Ballet 1985–93, dir Heather Knight Associates organising int dance touring 1993–; co-opted exec memb Dance UK 1993–; *Recreations* all the arts particularly classical ballet, opera, classical music, travel, people; *Style—* Ms Heather Knight; ✉ Heather Knight Associates, 23 Wolftencroft Close, London SW11 2LB (☎ 0171 223 4034, ☎ and fax 0171 223 8636)

KNIGHT, (William) Jeremy Jonathan; s of Richard Beatty MacBean Knight, of Brighton, and Yvonne Stephanie, *née* Searles; *b* 27 May 1951; *Educ* Brighton Coll; *m* 15 March 1975, Marian Margaret, da of Albert Edward Hoare; 2 s (Richard Andrew b 6 Feb 1978, Simon Peter Edward b 7 July 1979); *Career* CA/insolvency practitioner; articled clerk Graves Goddard & Horton-Stephens 1969–73, National Trading Co Johannesburg 1973–74, Peat Marwick Mitchell 1974–76; ptnr: Chater Spain Brothers 1978–88 (joined 1976), Moores Rowland (following merger) 1988–89; sole practitioner specialising in insolvency Jeremy Knight & Co Brighton and Croydon 1989–; pres SE Soc of CAs 1991–92, memb Cncl ICAEW; FCA 1975, MIPA 1987; *Recreations* flying, target shooting; *Style—* W J J Knight, Esq; ✉ 41 Cornwall Gardens, Brighton, E Sussex BN1 6RH (☎ 01273 558045); Jeremy Knight & Co, 68 Ship St, Brighton, E Sussex BN1 1AE (☎ 01273 203654 or 0181 680 4274, fax 01273 206056, car 0850 994775)

KNIGHT, Dame (Joan Christabel) Jill; DBE (1985, MBE 1964), MP (C) Birmingham Edgbaston (majority 4,307); da of A E Christie (d 1933); *b* 1927; *Educ* Fairfield Sch, King Edward GS for Girls Birmingham; *m* 1947, Montague Knight (decd), s of Leslie Knight of Harpole Hall, Northampton; 2 s; *Career* Parly candidate (C) Northampton 1959 and 1964, MP (C) Birmingham Edgbaston 1966–; memb Select Ctee on: Race Relations and Immigration 1969–72, Home Affrs 1980–84 and 1992–; chm Cons Backbench Ctee Health and Social Services 1981–, memb Cncl Europe 1977–88, chm Lords and Commons All-Pty Child Protection Gp 1983–, pres W Midlands Cons Political Centre 1980–83, vice chm 1922 Ctee 1992–, chm Inter-Parliamentary Union 1994– (memb Exec Ctee 1992–), vice pres Br Fluoridation Soc 1994–; dir Computeach International Ltd 1990–; lectr and broadcaster; memb Northampton Borough Cncl 1956–66; *Style—* Dame Jill Knight, DBE, MP; ✉ House of Commons, London SW1A 0AA

KNIGHT, Michael James; s of Charles Knight (d 1988), of London, and Ellen, *née* Murphy; *b* 29 Aug 1939; *Educ* St Bonaventures Sch London, King's Coll London, St George's Hosp London (MB BS, MS); *m* 1981, Phyllis Mary, da of William Ansel Purcell; 1 s (William Robert Charles b 1981), 1 da (Ellen Harrison b 1983); *Career* surgical registrar: Royal Hampshire County Hosp Winchester 1965–69, St George's Hosp 1969–71 (surgical res fell 1971–72); surgical res fell Washington Univ St Louis Missouri USA 1972–73, sr surgical registrar St George's Hosp London 1973–78, Hunterian prof RCS 1975, hon sr lectr St George's Hosp Med Sch; conslt surgn: St James's Hosp London 1978–88, St George's Hosp London 1978–, Royal Masonic Hosp London 1979–; memb: Pancreatic Soc of GB and Ireland (pres 1987), RSM, Euro Soc of Surgical Res, Ct of Examiners RCS 1988–94; examiner in surgery Univ of London, external examiner RCS in Ireland, Edinburgh and Univ of Colombo; author of numerous publications on gastroenterology, hepatic, pancreatic and biliary tract diseases; FRCS 1967 (MRCS 1963), LRCP; *Recreations* music; *Clubs* Players Theatre (London), St Anthony's (Forest Gate, London); *Style—* Michael Knight, Esq; ✉ 135 Harley Street, London W1N 1DJ (☎ 0171 487 3501)

KNIGHT, Sir Michael William Patrick; KCB (1983, CB 1980), AFC (1964); s of William and Dorothy Knight; *b* 23 Nov 1932; *Educ* BA; *m* 1967, Patricia Ann, *née* Davies; 1 s, 2 da; *Career* Sqdn pilot/Flt Cdr Nos 30, 53, 216, 139 and 249 Sqdns 1955–61, OC 32 Sqdn (RAF Akrotiri) 1961–63, RAF Staff Coll 1964, Miny of Aviation 1965–66, OC Far East Strike Wing (RAF Tengah) 1966–68, OC Flying Tengah 1968–69, RAF Strike Cmd 1969–70, princ mil asst to Chm NATO Mil Ctee 1970–73, OC RAF Laarbruch 1973–74, RCDS 1975, dir of ops Air Force Dept MOD 1976–77, SASO RAF Strike Cmd 1977–80, AOC No 1 Gp RAF Strike Cmd 1980–82, Air Memb for Supply and Orgn 1983–86, UK Mil Rep NATO 1986–89, Air ADC to HM The Queen 1986–89, ret as Air Chief Marshal 1989; Flying Offr RAFVR(T) 1989–; chm Cobham plc 1995– (dep chm 1994–95); dir: Craigwell Research 1989–, FR Group plc 1990–94, Page Group Ltd 1991–, Smiths Industries Aerospace & Defence Systems Group 1992–95, SBAC (Farnborough) Ltd 1996–; chm Air League 1993– (memb Cncl 1989–), pres Cncl NAAFI 1984–86, vice pres Atlantic Cncl of UK 1993–; vice pres: RAF Club 1983–, The Youth Trust 1994–; dir RAF Club Co Ltd 1993–; adj prof Carnegie Mellon Univ Pittsburgh 1989–; chm: Northern Devon Healthcare NHS Tst 1990–94, N Devon Cheshire Fndn FSS 1989–91; Air Force pres Offrs' Assoc 1990–; pres: Aircrew Assoc 1991–, Buccaneer Aircrew Assoc 1994–; pres: RAF Lawn Tennis Assoc 1984–86, RAF Rugby Union 1986–90 (chm 1975–78), Combined Servs RFC 1986–88 (chm 1976–78); memb Ctee RFU 1977–92; memb: Cncl RUSI 1984–87, Cncl Taunton Sch 1987–, Cncl RGS 1995–, Cncl SBAC 1995–; tstee RAF Museum 1983–86; Liveryman Guild of Air Pilots and Air Navigators 1993 (Upper Freeman 1989), Freeman City of London 1989; Hon DLitt; FRAeS, FRGS, FRSA; *Recreations* flying, rugby, other sports, music, writing, lecturing; *Clubs* RAF, East India, Saunton Golf, Colonels (fndr memb); *Style—* Sir Michael Knight, KCB, AFC; ✉ c/o Nat West Bank plc, 24 Derby Steet, Leek, Staffs ST13 5AF; Cobham plc, Brook Road, Wimborne, Dorset BH21 2BJ (☎ 01202 882020)

KNIGHT, Nicholas David Gordon (Nick); s of Michael Anthony Gordon Knight, and Beryl Rose Knight; *b* 24 Nov 1958; *Educ* Hinchingbrooke Sch Huntingdon, Huntingdon Tech Coll, Chelsea Coll Univ of London, Bournemouth and Poole Colle of Art (PQE Dip in Art & Design); *m* 1995, Charlotte Esme, *née* Wheeler; 2 da (Emily Ruby b 1993, Ella May b 1994); *Career* photographer; commissioning picture ed i-D Magazine 1990, contracted photographer for Vogue 1995–; also freelance photographer for: Vanity Fair, The Face, Arena, Interview, Sunday Times, George; lectr: V & A, RCA, Manchester Coll of Art, BFF Germany, Institute Francais de la Mode; fashion and advtg campaigns incl: Yves Saint Laurent, Lancôme, Guerlain, Christian Dior, Levis, Reebok, Yohji Yamamoto, Jil Sander, Martine Sitbon, Jean Paul Gaultier, Paloma Picasso, Alexander McQueen, Mercedes, Audi, Royal Mail, Citroen, Royal Ballet, Royal Opera House; record covers for: Seal, Boy George, David Bowie, Paul Weller, Bryan Ferry, George Michael, Suede; *Exhbns* Photographers Gallery 1982, 20 For Today (Nat Portrait Gallery) 1986, 14–21 Youth Culture Exhbn (V & A) 1986, Out of Fashion (Photographers Gallery) 1989, Ils Annoncent la Colour (Les Rencontres d'Arles) 1989, Festival de la Photo de Mode exhbn (Barcelona 1991, Monaco 1992), Vanités (Paris) 1993, Plant Power (permanent exhbn cmmnd by Nat History Museum) 1993, Biennale di Firenze - Art/Fashion (with Alexander McQueen) 1996, JAM (Barbican Art Gallery) 1996; *Awards* Kodak UK Photographer of the Year Award 1985 and 1987, D & AD Award for Best Book Cover (Skinheads) 1985, Magazine Publishing Award (for i-D Back to School fashion story) 1986, Club des Directors Artistique Award for best luxury goods campaign (for Christoffe Silverware) 1988, Expansion Magazine Awards for most successful banking campaign (Barclays) 1988, Halina Award for best young Br fashion photographer 1989, Gold Award USA for best magazine fashion story (for Arena Magazine fashion story Faith) 1989, Int Festival de la Photo de Mode Best Cataglogue Award (Jil Sander catalogues) 1991 and 1992, XYZ Design Award for best poster (Nat History Museum's Plant Power) 1993, Int Festival de la Photo de Mode Best Studio Photographer Award 1994, voted most influential fashion photographer in the world Face Magazine 1995; *Books* Skinheads (1982), NICKNIGHT (retrospective by Schirmer Mosel, 1994); *Recreations* architecture, natural history; *Style—* Nick Knight, Esq; ✉ 16 Arlington Road, Petersham, Richmond, Surrey TW10 7BY (☎ 0181 940 1086, fax 0181 948 8761)

KNIGHT, Paul; s of William Charles Knight, of Trealaw, Rhondda, and Norma Joan, *née* Jones; *b* 30 April 1961; *Educ* Porth Co GS Mid Glamorgan; *m* 17 July 1982, Jennifer, da of late Arthur John England; 1 da (Nadia Kylie); *Career* rugby union player; clubs: Treorci 1979–80 (youth team 1977–79), 220 appearances Aberavon 1980–88, over 100 appearances Pontypridd 1988–93, Treorchy (Rhondda) RFC (capt 1993–94) 1993–; Wales: debut v Namibia 1990, five nations debut v England 1991, 5 caps as prop; represented Barbarians v Argentina 1990; Player of the Year awards: Treorci Youth and 1st XV, Aberavon, Pontypridd; formerly wages clerk, currently prodn controller; *Recreations* fishing, gardening, DIY; *Style*— Paul Knight, Esq; ✉ Treorchy (Rhondda) RFC, The Club House, Lower Regent Street, Treorchy (☎ 01443 434671)

KNIGHT, Dr Peter Clayton; CBE (1995); s of Norman Knight, and Vera, *née* Jordan; *b* 8 July 1947; *Educ* Bishop Vesey GS, Univ of York (BA, DPhil); *m* 2 April 1978, Catherine Mary, da of Raymond Ward; 1 s (Andrew b 5 March 1979), 1 da (Gail b 29 Aug 1981); *Career* asst dir Plymouth Poly 1979–82, dep dir Lancashire Poly 1982–85, vice chllr Univ of Central England Birmingham 1992– (dir Birmingham Poly 1985–92); memb: Burnham Further Educn Ctee 1976–81, Ctee on Mgmnt Public Sector Higher Educn 1977, Nat Advsy Body for Local Authy Higher Educn 1981–84, Polys and Colls Funding Cncl 1988–; chm: Polys and Colls Employers Forum 1992–, Teacher Training Agency 1995–; nat pres NATFHE 1978–79, chm Soc for Res into Higher Educn; Hon DUniv York; FRAS, CPhys, MInstP; *Style*— Dr Peter Knight, CBE; ✉ Vice Chancellor, University of Central England, Perry Barr, Birmingham B42 2SU (☎ 0121 331 5555, fax 0121 356 5436)

KNIGHT, Peter John; s of William Knight (d 1974), of Ware, Herts; *b* 16 April 1950; *Educ* Trinity Hall Cambridge (MA); *m* Aug 1975, Jennifer Joan, da of late Wilfred Walter Townsend; 4 s (Jonathan William b May 1979, Robert Peter b Dec 1980, Oliver James b July 1984, Christopher Richard b Feb 1987); *Career* admitted slr England and Wales, Hong Kong and NSW Aust; Baker & McKenzie: slr London 1975–76 and 1979–82, slr Sydney 1976–79, managing ptnr Singapore 1987–90 (slr 1982–83, ptnr 1983–87), ptnr London 1990–; govr Tanglin Tst Schs 1987–90, chm Br Assoc of Singapore 1989–90; memb Ctee: Asia Pacific Advsy Gp (DTI) 1992–, London C of C 1993–; memb Bd of Advsrs Japanese and SE Asian Studies, chm Cambridge in the Capital 1995–; memb: Law Soc of England and Wales, Law Soc of Singapore; *Recreations* tennis, sailing, early music, theatre; *Style*— Peter J Knight, Esq; ✉ Baker & McKenzie, 100 New Bridge Street, London EC4V 6JA (☎ 0171 919 1000, fax 0171 919 1999)

KNIGHT, (Warburton) Richard; CBE (1987); s of Warburton Henry Johnston Knight (d 1987), and Alice Gweneth Knight; *b* 2 July 1932; *Educ* Trinity Coll Cambridge (MA); *m* 26 Aug 1961, Pamela, da of Leonard Charles Hearmon; 2 s (James, Matthew), 1 da (Sarah); *Career* Nat Serv 2 Lt RAEC 1950–52; teacher in Middx and Huddersfield 1956–62, asst dir for secdy schs Leicester 1967, asst educn offr for secdy schs and for special and social educn in W Riding 1970, dir Educn Servs Bradford Met DC 1974–91; Hon DLitt Univ of Bradford 1992; *Recreations* cycling, fell walking, music, sport and travelling; *Clubs* Royal Over-Seas League; *Style*— Richard Knight, Esq, CBE; ✉ Thorner Grange, Sandhills, Thorner, Leeds LS14 3DE (☎ and fax 0113 289 2356)

KNIGHT, (John) Roger; s of Tom Knight (d 1966), of Aberystwyth, and Friswyth, *née* Raymond Jones (d 1972); *b* 16 Aug 1946; *Educ* Littleover Derby; *m* 25 Oct 1980, Wendy Laurena, da of Roy Francis May, of Chalfont-St-Peter, Gerrards Cross, Bucks; 1 s (Thomas Roger b 1983), 1 da (Lucy Jane b 1985); *Career* computer systems devpt & troubleshooting Cinema Int Corp Amsterdam 1970–72, computer conslt 1972–77, chm and md J Computer Logic Ltd (designers of software) 1977–96; MBCS 1981; *Recreations* church, cycling, walking, food, restoration of ancient buildings; *Style*— Roger Knight, Esq; ✉ New Mill, Eaton Bishop, Hereford HR2 9QS; J Computer Logic Ltd, Golden Valley Software Factory, PO Box 26, Hereford HR2 9YU (☎ 01981 251 359)

KNIGHT, Dr Roger John Beckett; s of Lt Cdr John Beckett Knight (d 1983), of Bromley, Kent, and Alyson Yvonne Saunders, *née* Nunn; *b* 11 April 1944; *Educ* Tonbridge, Trinity Coll Dublin (MA), Univ of Sussex (PGCE), UCL (PhD); *m* 3 Aug 1968 (m dis 1980), Helen Elizabeth, da of Dr William Magowan (d 1980), of Hawkhurst, Kent; 2 s (William b 1973, Richard b 1976); *Career* National Maritime Museum: custodian Manuscripts 1977–81 (dep 1974–77) dep head Books and Manuscripts 1981–84, head Info Project Gp 1984–86, head Documentation Div 1986–88, head Collections Div and chief curator 1988–93, dep dir and head Display Div 1993–95, dep dir and head Information Div 1995–; memb: Ctee Greenwich Soc 1988–90, Cncl Soc for Nautical Res 1975–79 (vice pres 1992–), Cncl Navy Records Soc 1975–; FRHistS; *Books* Guide to the Manuscripts in the National Maritime Museum (1977, 1980), The Journal of Daniel Paine, 1794–1797 (with Alan Frost, 1983), Portsmouth Dockyard in the American War of Independence, 1774–1783 (1986), British Naval Documents 1204–1960 (jt ed, 1993); *Recreations* sailing, cricket, music; *Style*— Dr Roger Knight; ✉ National Maritime Museum, Greenwich, London SE10 (☎ 0181 312 6617, fax 0181 312 6632)

KNIGHT, Dr Ronald Kelvin; s of Walter Leonard Knight, and Kathleen Elizabeth, *née* Langran; *b* 12 Oct 1945; *Educ* Latymer Upper Sch, Gonville and Caius Coll Cambridge (BA, MA), St Barts Med Coll London (MB BChir, MRCP); *m* 31 March 1984, Clare Louise, da of Donald Scott, of Wrexham; 3 da (Olivia b 26 Feb 1985, Georgia b 18 Feb 1988, Imogen b 9 Sept 1989); *Career* currently conslt physician in gen and respiratory med at Frimley Park, Farnham and Royal Brompton and Nat Heart Hosps; has researched into and contributed several chapters to reference books on respiratory diseases and runs a clinic for patients with cystic fibrosis referred on a nat level; chm Dept of Med Frimley Park Hosp, med advsr Camberley and Dist Asthma Soc, memb Thoracic Assoc; *Books* contrib Chapters to a number of reference books on Respiratory Disease; *Recreations* children, running, association football; *Style*— Dr Ronald Knight; ✉ Brambley Wood, Snowdenham, Links Rd, Bramley, Guildford GU5 0BX (☎ 01483 894392); Frimley Park Hospital, Portsmouth Rd, Frimley, Camberley, Surrey (☎ 01276 692777); Royal and National Heart Hospitals, Fulham Rd, Chelsea, London SW3 (☎ 0171 352 8121)

KNIGHT, Stephen Charles; s of Reginald Frank Knight, of Street, Somerset, and Sheila Ethel Clarice, *née* Jones; *b* 25 Nov 1954; *Educ* Colfe's Sch, Bromley Coll; *m* 30 July 1977, Lesley Joan, da of Harold Leonard Davison, of Petts Wood, Kent; 2 s (Timothy David Stephen b 1988, Joshua James Stephen b 1990); *Career* gen mangr mktg and devpt Newcross Building Society 1983–84, vice pres Citibank 1984–87, chm Private Label Mortgage Services Ltd 1987–; FCIB 1977, MIMgt 1978, MCIM 1979; *Recreations* squash, cricket, freelance writing; *Clubs* IOD; *Style*— Stephen Knight, Esq; ✉ Little Grange, Orpington Rd, Chislehurst, Kent BR7 6RA (☎ 01689 833667); Private Label Mortgage Services Ltd, 14 Great Queen Street, London WC2B 5DW (☎ 0171 404 6966, fax 0171 404 6884)

KNIGHT, Tina Patricia; da of Jack Leonard King (d 1983), of London, and Nellie Irene, *née* Baxter; *b* 28 May 1942; *Educ* Walthamstow Co HS for Girl, SW Essex Tech Coll; *Career* mgmnt conslt and trouble-shooter until 1978, md GSC (UK) Ltd 1978–84, mgmnt conslt Scientific Staff Consultants 1984–85, proprietor and md Nighthawk Electronics Ltd 1985–, md Nighthawk Traders Ltd 1986; non-exec dir: Essex TEC 1990, Nimue (UK) Ltd 1996–; numerous TV and radio appearances incl: Woman's Hour (BBC Radio 4), The Moral Maze (Radio 4), Newsbeat (BBC Radio 1), After Hours (BBC Radio 5), The Six O'Clock News (BBC 1), Breaking Glass (BBC 1), Election Special (Channel 4), Question Time (BBC 1) and various regnl broadcasting appearances; also professional after-dinner and conf speaker incl: Nat Conf Small Business Bureau, Women in Business Int Conf; memb: Bd Prince's Youth Business Tst 1990, Ctee China-Britain Trade Gp 1990, Ctee Advsy Unit Small Business Bureau 1991, Bd TAVRA 1992; chm Fair Play Consortium (Eastern Region) 1994, chm Women Into Business 1995 (dep chm 1992–95), vice chm London Businessmen's Network 1994, vice pres Small Business Bureau, chm Addenbrookes Hosp Food Chain Appeal; runner-up TSB/Options Magazine Women Mean Business 1988, TOBIE Award 1989, runner-up Veuve Clicquot Business Woman of the Year 1989; FInstD 1987, FRSA 1992; *Recreations* bridge, theatre, opera, bookbinding, fishing, art galleries, car rallies, needlepoint; *Clubs* Wig & Pen, Mosimann's, Motcombs; *Style*— Ms Tina Knight; ✉ Nighthawk Electronics Ltd, PO Box 44, Saffron Walden, Essex CB11 3ND (☎ 01799 540881, fax 01799 541713)

KNIGHT, (Christopher) William; s of Claude Thorburn Knight (d 1993), and Hon Priscilla, *née* Dodson (d 1995), da of 2 Baron Monk Bretton, CB; *b* 10 April 1943; *Educ* Eton; *m* 6 Sept 1969, Jonkvrouwe Sylvia Caroline, da of Jonkheer Emile van Lennep, of The Hague, Netherlands; 1 s (Christopher b 20 Oct 1973), 2 da (Alexa b 9 Nov 1971, Louisa b 15 Oct 1977); *Career* princ mangr Portugal The Bank of London and S America 1982–84; dir Lloyds Merchant Bank 1985–91, dir Lloyds Investmt Mangrs 1987–91, md Lloyds Bank Fund Mgmnt 1988–91, fndr William Knight and Associates 1991; dir: Thai Euro Fund, Vietnam Fund, Portugal Property Fund, Portugal Fund (chm), Sonae International (chm), Mauritius Fund Ltd, Korea China Super Fund, L G India Fund; *Recreations* watching cricket, opera, travel writing, wine, East Asian affairs; *Clubs* Boodle's, Shek-O; *Style*— William Knight, Esq; ✉ 82 Lansdowne Rd, London W11 2LS (☎ 0171 221 3911, fax 0171 221 2178)

KNIGHT, William John Langford; s of William Knight, and Gertrude Alice, *née* Wallage; *b* 11 Sept 1945; *Educ* Sir Roger Manwood's Sch Sandwich Kent, Univ of Bristol (LLB); *m* 21 April 1973, Stephanie Irina, da of Lt-Col Edward Jeffery Williams; 1 s (Sam b 1980), 1 da (Sarah b 1977); *Career* admitted slr 1969; Simmons & Simmons Slrs: joined 1967–, ptnr 1973–, i/c Hong Kong office 1979–82, head Corp Dept 1994–96, sr ptnr 1996–; memb Cncl Haydn Mozart Soc; former chm Standing Ctee on Co Law for Law Soc; memb: City of London Slrs Co, Law Soc, Co Law Ctee CCBE; FRSA; *Books* The Acquisition of Private Companies (1975, 6 edn 1992); *Recreations* riding, photography, skiing; *Clubs* Travellers, Hong Kong; *Style*— W J L Knight, Esq; ✉ Simmons & Simmons, 21 Wilson Street, London EC2M 2TX (☎ 0171 628 2020, fax 0171 628 2070, telex 888562)

KNIGHTON, Robert (Bob); *Educ* BA(Econ); *Career* Abbey National plc: joined Abbey National Building Society 1969, various systems devpt appts, gen mangr IT and computer systems 1988–92 (asst gen mangr 1984–88), IT dir 1992–93, md ops and main bd dir 1993–97; *Style*— Bob Knighton, Esq

KNIGHTON, Vicky; da of Robert Gibbs, of France, and Theodora (Theo) Campbell, of Spain; *b* 16 Nov 1950; *Educ* Holy Trinity Convent Bromley, Bedgebury Park Kent; *children* 1 da (Hannah Theodora Edith b 18 Jan 1987); *Career* Independent Television News Ltd: sec 1971–72, editorial asst House of Commons 1972–73, news desk asst 1973–77, asst news ed 1977–82, news ed 1982–90, foreign ed 1990–92; sr news ed London News Network 1992–93; ITN: rejoined as sr foreign ed 1994, head of foreign news 1996–; *Style*— Ms Vicky Knighton; ✉ ITN Ltd, 200 Gray's Inn Road, London WC1X 8XZ (☎ 0171 430 4411)

KNIGHTS, Baron (Life Peer UK 1987), of Edgbaston, Co West Midlands; Philip Douglas Knights; kt (1980), CBE (1976, OBE 1971), QPM (1964), DL (1985); s of Thomas James Knights (d 1978), of Ottershaw, Surrey, and Ethel Ginn (d 1963); *b* 3 Oct 1920; *Educ* E Grinstead Co Sch, King's Sch Grantham, Police Staff Coll; *m* 1945, Jean, da of James Henry Burman (d 1971); *Career* served WWII with RAF; police cadet Lincolnshire Constabulary 1937, all ranks to Chief Supt 1937–57, Dep Cmdt Police Staff Coll 1963–66, Dep Chief Constable Birmingham City Police 1970–72 (Asst Chief Constable 1959–70); Chief Constable: Sheffield and Rotherham 1972–74, S Yorks 1974–75, West Midlands Police 1975–85; memb: Cncl Aston Univ 1985–, Ctee Warwicks CCC 1985–89; tstee Police Fndn 1979–, memb Advsy Cncl Cambridge Inst of Criminology 1986–; Hon DSc Aston 1996; CIMgt 1977; *Recreations* sport, travel, reading; *Clubs* Royal Overseas League; *Style*— The Rt Hon the Lord Knights, CBE, QPM, DL; ✉ House of Lords, London SW1A 0PW

KNIGHTS, Rosemary Margaret; da of Donald James Robson (d 1989), and Margaret, *née* Laverick; *b* 2 Nov 1945; *Educ* Houghton-le-Spring GS, Sunderland Sch of Nursing, Marygate Coll York (SRN, Ophthalmic Nursing Dip, Dip of Nursing); *m* 1, 1966 (m dis 1980), Warren Richardson; m 2, 1983, Michael Atmore Knights, s of Horace Atmore Knights (d 1987); *Career* staff nurse Dryburn Hosp Durham 1967–69, theatre sister Sunderland Eye Infirmary 1969–71, ward sister (Med/Coronary Care Unit) Harrogate Hosps 1971–75, nursing offr Harrogate 1975–78, sr nursing offr North Tees Hosp 1978–81, dir of nursing Central Manchester HA 1981–85, unit gen mangr Manchester Royal Eye Hosp 1985–88, chief nursing offr Central Manchester HA 1987–88, regnl nursing offr Mersey RHA 1988–91 (concurrently exec dir and dep regnl gen mangr 1989–91), exec dir Mgmnt Exec NW Outpost 1991–93, chief exec Warrington Hosp NHS Tst 1993–; hon lectr Univ of Liverpool Dept of Nursing 1989–; hon sec Ophthalmic Nursing Bd 1982–88; memb Gene Therapy Cncl (Ministerial appt) 1994, memb Editorial Bd Clinician in Management; dir N and Mid Cheshire TEC 1995–; memb Royal Coll of Nursing, Tempus associate; *Recreations* music, 'Hallé friend', Greekophile, the NHS!; *Clubs* Soroptimist Int (Manchester); *Style*— Mrs Rosemary Knights; ✉ 21 Crossfield Drive, Worsley, Manchester M28 1GP (☎ 0161 790 1915); Warrington Hospital NHS Trust, Lovely Lane, Warrington WA5 1QG (☎ 01925 662299, mobile 0831 395466)

KNILL, Sir John Kenelm Stuart; 4 Bt (UK 1893), of The Grove, Blackheath, Kent; s of Sir John Stuart Knill, 3 Bt (d 1973); *b* 8 April 1913; *Educ* Downside; *m* 1951, Violette Maud Florence Martin (d 1983), da of Leonard Martin Barnes, of Durban, S Africa; 2 s (Thomas John Pugin Bartholomew b 1952, Jenkyn Martin Benedict Stuart b 1954); *Heir* s, Thomas John Pugin Bartholomew Knill b 23 Aug 1952; *Career* WWII Lt RNVR 1940–45; canal carrier 1948–54, farmer 1956–63, MOD 1963–77; pres: Avon Tport 2000, Association of Canal Enterprises, Commercial Narrowboat Operators' Assoc; vice pres: Cotswold Canals Tst, Hereford and Gloucester Canal Tst; hon life memb Inland Waterways Assoc; *Clubs* Victory Services; *Style*— Sir John Knill, Bt; ✉ 11 St Nicholas Court, Bathampton, Bath BA2 6UZ

KNILL, Sir John Lawrence; kt (1994); s of William Cuthbert Knill (d 1983), of S Croydon, and Mary, *née* Dempsey; *b* 22 Nov 1934; *Educ* Whitgift Sch Croydon, Imperial Coll London (BSc, ARCS, PhD, DIC, DSc); *m* 16 July 1957, Diane Constance, da of John Corr Judge (d 1956), of Hagerstown, USA; 1 s (Patrick b 1966), 1 da (Fiona b 1962); *Career* geologist Sir Alexander Gibb & Ptnrs 1957; Univ of London: asst lectr 1957–59, lectr 1959–65, reader 1965–73, prof of engrg geology 1973–93, head Dept of Geology 1979–88, dean Royal Sch of Mines 1980–83, sr res fell Imperial Coll and prof emeritus 1993–, visiting prof of energy hydrogeology Royal Holloway 1996–; chm: Radioactive Waste Mgmnt Advsy Ctee 1987–95, Natural Environment Cncl 1988–93, UK Coordination Ctee for UN Int Decade of Natural Disaster Reduction 1992–95; dir Donaldson Associates; Hon FCGI 1988, Hon DSc 1992 and 1995, Hon DTech 1996; FICE 1981, FHKIE 1982, FIGeol 1986, FEng 1991; *Books* Industrial Geology (1978); *Recreations* viticulture; *Clubs* Athenaeum; *Style*— Sir John Knill, FEng; ✉ Highwood Farm, Long Lane, Shaw-cum-Dunnington, Newbury, Berks RG14 2TB (☎ 01635 552300)

KNILL, Thomas John Pugin Bartholomew; s and h of Sir John Kenelm Stuart Knill, 4 Bt, *qv*; *b* 23 Aug 1952; *m* 1977, Kathleen Muszynski; *Style*— Thomas Knill, Esq

KNOBEL, Lance; s of Lawrence Roy Knobel (d 1990), and Gladys, *née* Smith; *b* 6 Nov 1956; *Educ* New Trier East HS Winnetka Illinois, Princeton Univ (BA), Worcester Coll Oxford (MA); *Career* asst ed The Architectural Review 1980–82; ed: Designer's Journal 1983–87, Management Today 1987–89; md New International Media Milan Italy 1989–90; editorial dir Haymarket Marketing Publications 1990– (and publishing devpt dir 1991–92), managing ed World Link Publishing 1992–; *Books* Faber Guide to Twentieth Century Architecture (1985), Office Furniture (1987), International Interiors

(1989); *Recreations* scuba diving, trumpet playing, tennis, skiing; *Style—* Lance Knobel, Esq; ✉ World Link Publishing Ltd, Nestor House, Playhouse Yard, London EC4V 5EX (☎ 0171 779 8721, fax 0171 779 8727)

KNOLLYS, 3 Viscount (UK 1911); David Francis Dudley Knollys; also Baron Knollys (UK 1902); s of 2 Viscount Knollys, GCMG, MBE, DFC (d 1966), and Margaret (d 1987), da of Sir Stuart Coats, 2 Bt; *b* 12 June 1931; *Educ* Eton; *m* 1959, Hon Sheelin Virginia, DL (Norfolk 1996), da of Lt-Col the Hon Somerset Arthur Maxwell, MP (d 1942), and sis of 12 Baron Farnham; 3 s, 1 da; *Heir* s, Hon Patrick Knollys; *Career* late 2 Lt Scots Gds; *Style—* The Rt Hon the Viscount Knollys; ✉ The Bailiff's House, Bramerton Hall Farm, Norwich, Norfolk NR14 7DN

KNOPF, District Judge Elliot Michael; s of Harry Knopf (d 1976), and Clara Renée, *née* Weingard; *b* 23 Dec 1950; *Educ* Bury GS, Univ Coll London (LLB); *m* 8 Feb 1976, Elizabeth Carol, da of Eugene Lieberman; 1 s (Anthony Martin b 17 Dec 1979), 1 da (Marcelle Rebecca b 4 Feb 1983); *Career* articled clerk Conn Goldberg Slrs Manchester 1974–76; Pannone March Pearson Slrs Manchester: admitted slr 1976, asst slr 1976–79, equity ptnr 1979–91; dep district registrar of the High Ct and dep registrar of Co Ct (Northern Circuit) 1987–91, district judge of the High Ct and Co Ct 1991–, asst recorder of Crown Ct (Northern Circuit) 1996–; memb Law Soc 1976–; *Recreations* reading, swimming, walking, theatre, foreign travel, the family; *Style—* District Judge Knopf; ✉ The Queen Elizabeth II Law Courts, Derby Square, Liverpool L2 1XA (☎ 0151 473 7373)

KNOPFLER, Mark; s of Erwin Knopfler (d 1993), and Louisa Knopfler; *b* 12 Aug 1949; *Career* musician; former journalist Yorkshire Evening Post and teacher; fndr Dire Straits 1977; has produced: Bob Dylan, Randy Newman and others; albums with Dire Straits: Dire Straits (1978, reached UK no 5), Communique (1979, UK no 5), Making Movies (1980, UK no 4), Love Over Gold (1982, UK no 1), Alchemy - Dire Straits Live (live, 1984, UK no 3), Brothers In Arms (1985, UK no 1, formerly best ever selling UK album), Money For Nothing (compilation, 1988, UK no 1), On Every Street (1991, UK no 1); solo soundtrack albums: Local Hero (1982, UK no 14), Cal (1984, UK no 65), Comfort and Joy (1984), The Princess Bride (1987), Last Exit to Brooklyn (1989); other albums: Stay Tuned (with Chet Atkins, 1986), Missing...Presumed Having A Good Time (as Notting Hillbillies, 1990, UK no 2), Neck And Neck (with Chet Atkins, 1990, UK no 41), Golden Heart (1996); has won Ivor Novello, BRIT, MTV and Grammy awards; *Style—* Mark Knopfler, Esq; ✉ c/o Damage Management, 16 Lambton Place, London W11 2SH (☎ 0171 229 2992, fax 0171 229 2213)

KNOPS, Prof Robin John; s of Joseph Nicholas Jean Toussaint Knops (d 1978), of Weymouth, Dorset, and Rita Josephine, *née* Colombo; *b* 30 Dec 1932; *Educ* Thames Valley GS Twickenham, Univ of Nottingham (BSc, PhD); *m* 2 Sept 1965, Margaret Mary, da of Michael McDonald (d 1977), of Newcastle upon Tyne; 4 s (Andrew b 10 June 1966, Peter b 4 May 1968, Joseph b 12 April 1970, Robert b 22 Oct 1971), 2 da (Geraldine b 9 Aug 1974, Catherine b 9 Jan 1980); *Career* lectr in mathematics Univ of Nottingham 1959–62 (asst lectr 1956–59), reader in continuum mechanics Univ of Newcastle upon Tyne 1968–71 (lectr in applied mathematics 1962–68); Heriot-Watt Univ: prof of mathematics 1971–, head of Dept 1971–83, dean of science 1984–87, vice princ 1988–95, special advsr to princ 1995–; memb Bd of Govrs Scottish Coll of Textiles 1992–; pres: Edinburgh Mathematical Soc 1974–75, Int Soc for the Interaction of Mechanics and Mathematics 1991–; FRSE 1975 (memb Cncl 1982–87, curator 1987–92), FRSA 1989; *Books* Uniqueness Theorems in Linear Elasticity (with L E Payne, 1971); *Recreations* walking, travel, reading; *Style—* Prof R J Knops, FRSE; ✉ Heriot-Watt University, Edinburgh EH14 4AS (☎ 0131 451 3363, fax 0131 449 5153)

KNORPEL, Henry; CB (1982), QC (1988); s of Hyman Knorpel (d 1958), of Guildford, Surrey, and Dora, *née* Lukes (d 1995); *b* 18 Aug 1924; *Educ* City of London Sch, Magdalen Coll Oxford (BCL, MA); *m* 1953, Brenda, da of Harry Sterling (d 1982), of Wembley, Middx; 2 da (Melanie, Helen); *Career* called to the Bar Inner Temple 1947, practised 1947–52, bencher 1990; Govt Legal Serv: Miny of Nat Insur later Miny of Pensions and Nat Insur 1952–65, Law Cmmn 1965–67, Miny of Social Security 1967–68, asst slr DHSS 1968–71, princ asst slr DHSS 1971–78, slr DHSS 1978–85; lectr in law 1950–; counsel to the Speaker House of Commons 1985–95; *Style—* Henry Knorpel, Esq, CB, QC; ✉ Conway, 32 Sunnybank, Epsom, Surrey KT18 7DX (☎ 01372 721394)

KNOTT, Herbert Espenett (Herbie); s of Lt-Col Roger Birbeck Knott, OBE, MC (d 1960), of Wilmslow, Cheshire, and Eva, *née* Conroy (d 1995); *b* 11 March 1949; *Educ* Rugby, Univ Coll Oxford (BA, MA); *Career* mgmnt trainee Atlas Express Ltd 1972–73; photojournalist: London Evening Standard 1977–80, Now! magazine 1980–81, The Sunday Times 1981–86, The Independent 1986–; contrib exhibitions: World Press Photo Exhibitions 1987 and 1989, Telegraph Magazine 25th Anniversary Exhibition, Br Press Photographers Assoc Exhibitions 1986–89, Witness Exhibition (NT) 1990, Politicians (Impressions Gallery York 1992, Stills Gallery Edinburgh 1993 and Battersea Arts Centre London 1994), Fashion Exposures (The Worx London 1993, 1994, 1995 and 1996), London Exhibition (Zwemmer Gallery London 1994); record sleeves Miss Chatelaine (k d lang, 1993); *Awards* Nikon Photographer of the Month June 1983 and Dec 1990, Nikon Photographer of the Election 1987; *Books* Carol Thatcher's Diary of an Election (illustrated, 1983), How They Made Piece of Cake (with Robert Eagle, 1988), Black and White (1990), Glasmoth - Moscow and Back by Tiger Moth (with Jonathan Elwes, 1990); *Recreations* skiing, tennis, gardening, running, aerobics, supporting Wimbledon FC; *Style—* Herbie Knott, Esq; ✉ c/o Rex Features Ltd, Vine Hill, London EC1 (☎ 0171 278 7294)

KNOTT, Prof John Frederick; s of Fred Knott, of Bristol, and Margaret, *née* Chesney; *b* 9 Dec 1938; *Educ* Univ of Sheffield (BMet), Univ of Cambridge (PhD); *m* 1, 16 April 1963 (m dis 1986), Christine Mary, da of William Roberts; 2 s (William Frederick b 28 April 1965, Andrew John b 10 May 1966); m 2, 15 Sept 1990, Susan Marilyn (formerly Mrs Cooke), da of William Jones; 2 step s (Paul Antony b 6 Dec 1966, James Daniel b 21 April 1981); *Career* res offr Central Electricity Res Laboratories Leatherhead 1962–66; Univ of Cambridge: lectr Dept of Materials Sci and Metallurgy 1967–81, univ reader in mechanical metallurgy 1981–90; Churchill Coll Cambridge: Goldsmiths' fell 1967–91, vice master 1988–90, extra-ordinary fell 1991–; Univ of Birmingham: prof and head of Sch of Metallurgy and Materials 1990–, Feeney prof 1994–; hon prof Beijing Univ of Aeronautics and Astronautics 1992–; pres Int Congress on Fracture 1993; pres Int Congress on Fracture 1994– (hon fell 1984); memb: Materials and Processing Advsy Bd Rolls-Royce 1987–, Tech Assessment Gp on Structural Integrity UKAEA 1988–, Res Bd of the Welding Inst 1989–, SERC/DTI LINK Ctee (EEM) 1992–, Advsy Ctee for the Safety of Nuclear Installations 1992–; foreign memb Acad of Sciences of the Ukraine 1992; visiting fell Japan Soc for the Promotion of Sci 1980, Sheffield Soc of Engrs and Metallurgists prize 1958, Mappin medal 1959, Nesthill medal 1959, L B Pfeil prize for Physical Metallurgy 1973, Rosenhain medal for Physical Metallurgy 1978, Leslie Holliday prize (Materials Sci Club) 1978; ScD (Cantab) 1991; FIM 1974 (AIM 1963), CEng 1978, FWeldI 1985, FRSA 1985, FEng 1988, FRS 1990, FIMechE 1994; *Books* Fundamentals of Fracture Mechanics (1973), Worked Examples in Fracture Mechanics (with Dr D Elliott, 1979), Fracture Mechanics - Worked Examples (with Dr Paul Withey, 1993); *Recreations* bridge, cryptic crosswords, listening to traditional jazz, playing the tenor recorder rather badly; *Style—* Prof John Knott, FRS, FEng; ✉ 54 Evesham Road, Stratford upon Avon CV37 9BA (☎ 01789 261977); The University of Birmingham, School of Metallurgy and Materials, Edgbaston, Birmingham B15 2TT (☎ 0121 414 6729, direct line 0121 414 6730, fax 0121 414 7080)

KNOTT, Malcolm Stephen; s of Eric Stephen Knott, of Framlingham, Suffolk, and Grace Lilley, *née* Smith; *b* 22 Aug 1940; *Educ* Mercers' Sch Holborn; *m* 15 Sept 1962, Eileen Margaret (Meg), da of Ernest William Smith-Lane (d 1969), of Potters Bar, Middx; 1 s (Mungo b 1964), 1 da (Nancy b 1967); *Career* slr 1962–67, called to the Bar 1968; head of Chambers Lincoln's Inn 1980–85, Bar Cncl 1985–89, in practice Queen's Bench and Chancery Divs London, recorder Crown and Co Ct; legal assessor RICS; memb Campaign for Bar; Freeman City of London 1959; *Recreations* archery, family history, toy soldiers; *Clubs* The Players Theatre, Society of Genealogists, Crimean War Res Soc; *Style—* Malcolm Knott, Esq; ✉ 48 Oakfield Rd, Southgate, London N14 6LX (☎ 0181 882 3676)

KNOTT, Air Vice Marshal Ronald George; CB (1967), DSO (1945), DFC (1944), AFC (1956); s of Capt George Knott (d 1952), and Edith Rose, *née* Anderson (d 1981); *b* 19 Dec 1917; *Educ* Borden GS; *m* 1941, Hermione Violet, da of Col Robert Bernard Phayre (d 1964); 3 s (Terence, Nicholas (decd), Andrew), 1 da (Alexandra); *Career* RAF Dir of Operational Requirements MOD 1963–67, Sr Air Staff Offr ME Air Force 1967–70, Air Offr Admin Air Support Cmd 1970–72, ret; *Recreations* wine growing, environmentalist; *Style—* Air Vice Marshal Ronald Knott, CB, DSO, DFC, AFC; ✉ Pilgrims Cottage, Charing, Ashford, Kent TN27 0DR

KNOWLAND, Raymond Reginald (Ray); CBE (1992); s of Reginald George Knowland (d 1945), and Marjorie Doris, *née* Alvis; *b* 18 Aug 1930; *Educ* Bristol GS, Sir John Cass Coll; *m* 1 Sept 1956, Valerie Mary, da of Norman Wintour Higgs (d 1969); 3 s (Paul b 1961, Peter b 1963, Jeremy b 1967); *Career* Nat Serv RAF 1955–57; BP Chemicals: works gen mangr Barry Works S Wales 1969–75 (various appts 1957–69), works gen mangr Baglan Bay Works S Wales 1975–78, md BP Chemicals Belgium Antwerp 1978–80, chief exec offr BP Chemicals London 1983–89 (dir 1980–83); md BP Co plc until 1992; currently non-exec dir: Laporte plc, Br Standards Inst, British Nuclear Fuels plc; pres: Br Plastics Fedn 1985–86, Assoc of Petrochemical Prodrs Europe 1985–88, Chemical Industs Assoc 1990–92; vice-pres Soc of Chemical Industry 1992–96; chm of Bd Chemical Indust Ecology and Toxicology Centre 1986–90; Freeman City of London, memb Ct of Assts Worshipful Co of Horners; FRSC 1958, CIMgt 1987 (MIMgt 1958); *Recreations* sailing, photography, rugby football; *Style—* Ray Knowland, Esq, CBE; ✉ Herons Wake, Flowers Hill, Pangbourne, Reading, Berks RG8 7BD (☎ 01734 844576, fax 01734 841741)

KNOWLAND, Viv; *b* 19 Oct 1948; *Career* milliner; early career experience with IPC Young Magazine Div, Joan Chaumeton PR and Browns South Molton Street; subsequently co-fndr Buckle Under Enterprises (accessories design); freelance hat designer and ptnr in design consultancy 1978–80, estab Viv Knowland Hats 1980; stockists in England, Europe, USA and Japan; other design projects incl: work for Ready to Wear labels (Betty Jackson, Laura Ashley, Next, Jaeger), private cmmns for clients including HRH The Princess of Wales; course tutor (MA Millinery) RCA 1989–92, other associations with Ravensbourne, Trent and Central Saint Martin's colls of design; *Style—* Ms Viv Knowland; ✉ Viv Knowland Hats, 1st Floor, 32 Dryburgh Road, London SW15 1BL (☎ 0181 788 8788, fax 0181 789 1100)

KNOWLES, Sir Charles Francis; 7 Bt (GB 1765), of Lovell Hill, Berkshire; s of Sir Francis Gerald William Knowles, 6 Bt, FRS (d 1974), and Ruth, *née* Brooke-Smith; *b* 20 Dec 1951; *Educ* Marlborough, Oxford Sch of Architecture (DipArch); *m* 1979, Amanda Louise Margaret, da of Lance Lee Bromley, of Molyneux St, London W1; 2 s ((Charles) William Frederick Lance b 1985, Edward Francis Annandale Bromley b 7 April 1989); *Heir* s, (Charles) William Frederick Lance Knowles b 27 Aug 1985; *Career* ptnr Charles Knowles Design (architects); RIBA 1978, FRSA 1984; *Recreations* flying, shooting; *Style—* Sir Charles Knowles, Bt; ✉ Wyndham Croft, Turners Hill, West Sussex

KNOWLES, Prof Christopher John; s of Frank Knowles, of Knott End, Lancashire, and Alice Clayton, *née* Sims; *b* 2 March 1943; *Educ* Univ of Leicester (BSc, PhD); *m* 14 July 1968, Denise Henriette, da of Paul Georges Fouquet (d 1976); 1 s (Peter b 1969); *Career* post-doctoral fell: Dartmouth Coll USA 1967–69, Univ of Warwick 1969–70; Univ of Kent at Canterbury: lectr 1970–77, sr lectr 1977–80, reader 1980–84, prof of microbial biochemistry 1984–; sec Euro Environmental Res Orgn; CChem, FRSC 1986, FRSA 1987; *Recreations* walking, skiing, cooking; *Style—* Prof Christopher Knowles; ✉ Biological Laboratory, University of Kent, Canterbury, Kent CT2 7NJ (☎ 01227 764000)

KNOWLES, Dr Colin George; s of George William Knowles (d 1977), and Isabelle, *née* Houghton (d 1980); *b* 11 April 1939; *Educ* King George V GS Southport, CEDEP Fontainebleau France, Trinity Coll (MA, PhD); *m* 1981 (m dis 1994), Mrs Lesley Carolyn Angela (Carla) Johannes; 1 da (Marguerite Isabella (Daisy) b 1984); by earlier m, 2 da (Emma, Samantha); *Career* co sec and head of public affrs Imperial Tobacco Ltd 1960–80, chm Griffin Associates Ltd UK 1980–83, dir TWS Public Relations (Pty) Ltd Johannesburg 1984, chm Concept Communications (Pty) Ltd Johannesburg 1983–84; dir of devpt and public affrs Univ of Bophuthatswana 1985–95, chm Bophuthatswana Region PR Inst of S Africa 1988–91, chm St John Ambulance Fndn Bophuthatswana 1989–94, memb Chapter (Governing Body) Priory of St John for South Africa 1992–; dir The Consumer Cncl of Bophuthatswana 1991–94; dir: Assoc for Business Sponsorship of the Arts 1975–84 (chm 1975–80), The Bristol Hippodrome Tst Ltd 1977–81, The Bath Archaeological Tst Ltd 1978–81, The Palladian Tst Ltd 1979–81; memb Chllr of Duchy of Lancaster's Ctee of Honour on Business and the Arts 1980–81; Freeman City of London 1974, Liveryman Worshipful Co of Tobacco Pipe Makers and Tobacco Blenders London 1973; MInstM, MIPR, FIMgt, FRSA, FPRISA, APR, assoc memb Assoc of Arbitrators of South Africa (AAArb); KStJ 1995 (CStJ 1991, OStJ 1977); *Recreations* game watching, reading, fishing, shooting, travel; *Clubs* Carlton, MCC; *Style—* Dr C G Knowles

KNOWLES, Evelyn; *Educ* Coborn GS for Girls, Ealing Coll of HE (BA); *m* (m dis); 1 s (William), 2 da (Louise, Gillian); *Career* administrator and fundraiser SOS Childrens Villages International 1981–86, trg co-ordinator Cambridge Training and Development 1988–90, trg conslt Women Returning to Work and Women Undergraduates 1987–, dir Victoria Road Community Centre Cambridge 1990–; 300 Group: memb 1983–, memb Nat Exec for several years, chm 1991–92; former rep for: National Alliance of Women's Organisations, Opportunity 2000; memb Fawcett Soc, regular speaker on radio and to groups; cncllr (Lib Dem) City of Cambridge 1987–; memb Cambridge City Cncl Ctee: City Bd, Cambs Crime Reduction Partnership, Environmental Health and Protection; City Cncl rep for: Riverside (chm), Cambridge Community Health Cncl (chm 1994–96), Cambridge City Police Local Consultation Gp; dep gp leader Local Party, prospective Parly candidate, vice chm Exec Ctee Women Liberal Democrats; memb Bd Kelsey Kerridge Sports Hall Tst; FRSA; *Recreations* family, movies, travel, music, books, dining out; *Style—* Ms Evelyn Knowles; ✉ 21 Primary Court, Chesterton, Cambridge CB4 1NB (☎ and fax 01223 316177, business ☎ 01223 311136, e-mail EvelynCK@Cambridge.Gov.UK)

KNOWLES, Ven Graeme Paul; s of Stanley Knowles, and Grace Edith Ellen, *née* Pratt; *b* 25 Sept 1951; *Educ* KCL (AKC), St Augustine's Coll Canterbury (Bishop Hanson prize); *m* 1973, Susan Gail, *née* Marsden; *Career* ordained: deacon 1974, priest 1975; curate St Peter in Thanet 1974–79, sr curate and precentor Leeds Parish Church 1979–81, chaplain precentor Portsmouth Cathedral 1981–87, vicar of Leigh Park 1987–93, rural dean of Havant 1990–93, archdeacon of Portsmouth 1993–; memb: Cncl for the Care of Churches, Ecclesiastical Law Soc; *Recreations* music (Victorian and Edwardian ballads), novels of E F Benson; *Clubs* Naval and Military; *Style—* The Ven the Archdeacon of Portsmouth; ✉ Victoria Lodge, 36 Osborn Road, Fareham, Hampshire PO16 7DS (☎ 01329 280101, fax 01329 281603)

KNOWLES, Peter Francis Arnold; CB (1996); s of Sidney Francis Knowles, and Patricia Anette, *née* New; *b* 10 July 1949; *Educ* Whitgift Sch S Croydon, Univ Coll Oxford (Open scholar, MA); *m* 2 Sept 1972, Patricia Katharine, da of W H M Clifford; 2 s (Henry b 14 July 1977, Toby b 12 March 1980); *Career* called to the Bar Gray's Inn 1971, practised as barr Lincoln's Inn 1973–75, Parliamentary Counsel Office 1975–93 and 1996– (appointed Parliamentary Counsel (grade 2) 1991), seconded as draftsman in charge Law Commission 1993–96; *Style—* Peter Knowles, Esq, CB; ✉ Office of the Parliamentary Counsel, 36 Whitehall, London SW1A 2AY

KNOWLES, Timothy (Tim); s of Cyril William Knowles (d 1966), of Worcester, and Winifred Alice, *née* Hood (d 1965); *b* 17 May 1938; *Educ* Bishop Gore GS Swansea; *m* 30 Sept 1967, Gaynor, da of Edgar Ernest Hallett, of Llandaff, Cardiff; 1 da (Tracy b 1969); *Career* co sec and accountant Louis Marx & Co Ltd 1960–68, controller Modco Valenite 1968–69, asst md HTV Ltd 1981–86 (co sec 1969–78, fin dir 1975–81), gp md HTV Gp plc 1986–88 (fin dir 1976–86); dir: Hyder plc 1989–, Univ Hosp of Wales Healthcare NHS Trust 1995–; fin dir Export Credits Guarantee Dept Insurance Servs Gp 1990–91; Parly candidate (Cons) Swansea E 1966; memb: S Wales Electricity Bd 1981–82, Welsh Water Authy 1982–89; FCA 1960; *Recreations* travel, walking, golf, watching cricket; *Clubs* Cardiff and County, Glamorgan CC, CG90 (chm 1994–); *Style—* Tim Knowles, Esq; ✉ Cae Ffynnon, 12 Ger-y-Llan, St Nicholas, Cardiff CF5 6SY (☎ 01446 760726, fax 01446 760864)

KNOWLES, Trevor; s of Gordon Gray Knowles (d 1972), of Hull, and Leonora Mary Knowles (d 1979); *b* 23 July 1938; *m* 25 June 1966, Elaine, da of William George Day (d 1991); 2 s (Philip b 8 June 1969, Stephen b 8 June 1972); *Career* gen mangr Lincolnshire Publishing Co Ltd Lincoln 1972–81, md Grimsby and Scunthorpe Newspapers Ltd Grimsby 1981–; memb Cncl Newspaper Soc, memb Cleethorpes Rotary Club; FCA 1961; *Recreations* golf; *Clubs* Cleethorpes Golf; *Style—* Trevor Knowles, Esq; ✉ 45 Cromwell Rd, Cleethorpes, Humberside DN35 0AU (☎ 01472 696703); Grimsby Evening Telegraph, 80 Cleethorpe Rd, Grimsby DN31 3EH (☎ 01472 360360, fax 01472 352272)

KNOWLSON, Prof James Rex; s of Francis Frederick Knowlson (d 1972), of Ripley, Derbyshire, and Elizabeth Mary, *née* Platt; *b* 6 Aug 1933; *Educ* Swanwick Hall GS Derbyshire, Univ of Reading (BA, DipEd, PhD); *m* Elizabeth Selby, da of Thomas Albert Coxon (d 1985); 2 s (Gregory Michael b 1960, Richard Paul b 1963), 1 da (Laura Elizabeth b 1968); *Career* asst master Ashville Coll Harrogate 1959–60, lectr in French Univ of Glasgow 1963–69 (asst lectr 1960–63), prof of French Univ of Reading 1981– (lectr 1969–75, Leverhulme res fell 1975–76, sr lectr 1975–78, reader 1978–81); memb: Soc of Authors 1987–, Assoc of Univ Teachers; *Books* Samuel Beckett: An Exhibition (1971), Light and Darkness in the Theatre of Samuel Beckett (1972), Universal Language Schemes in England and France 1600–1800 (1975), Happy Days/Oh les beaux jours (ed, 1978), Frescoes of the Skull: The Later Prose and Drama of Samuel Beckett (with John Pilling, 1979), Samuel Beckett's Krapp's Last Tape (ed, 1980), Happy Days (ed, 1985), The Theatrical Notebooks of Samuel Beckett Vol III - Krapp's Last Tape (ed, 1992), Waiting for Godot Vol I (ed, 1993), Damned to Fame: The Life of Samuel Beckett (1996); *Recreations* badminton, cricket, theatre; *Style—* Prof James Knowlson; ✉ Rivendell, 259 Shinfield Rd, Reading, Berks RG2 8HF (☎ 0118 986 6387); Department of French, The Faculty of Letters and Social Sciences, The University of Reading, Whiteknights, Reading, Berks RG2 (☎ 0118 931 8776, fax 01734 318122)

KNOX, Anthony Douglas (Tony); s of William Trevor Knox, of Bournemouth, and Jean, *née* Calder; *b* 23 March 1945; *Educ* St Dunstan's Coll, ChCh Oxford (MA); *m* 3 Feb 1990, Adele Josephine, *née* Penny; 1 da (Camilla Rose b 26 June 1990), 1 s (Alexander George Douglas b 26 Nov 1992); *Career* PR conslt; chm Financial Dynamics Ltd 1987–; *Recreations* tennis, skiing; *Clubs* Hurlingham, Utd Oxford & Cambridge Univ, City Univ; *Style—* Tony Knox, Esq; ✉ Financial Dynamics Ltd, 30 Furnival Street, London EC2A 1JE (☎ 0171 831 3113, fax 0171 831 7961)

KNOX, Anthony James (Tony); s of Harry Cooke Knox (d 1979), of Belfast, and Lila Mary Knox; *b* 9 Oct 1949; *Educ* Royal Belfast Academical Inst, Wadham Coll Oxford (BA, MA), Queen's Univ Belfast (MA); *m* 30 March 1972 (m dis), Marie-Hélène Clotilde; 2 da (Jessica b 1975, Chloë b 1980); *Career* radio prodr BBC NI 1975–82, prodr South Bank Show LWT 1982–; *Recreations* fishing; *Style—* Tony Knox, Esq; ✉ 109 Marlborough Park South, Belfast BT9 6HW

KNOX, Bernadette Marie; da of Joseph Chapman Knox (d 1979), and Theresa, *née* Birney; *b* 22 Oct 1954; *Educ* Sacred Heart GS Newcastle upon Tyne, St Anne's Coll Oxford (MA); *Career* J Walter Thompson Co Ltd: Media Dept 1976, Planning Dept 1978, bd dir 1989–; *Recreations* books, cinema, listening to music; *Style—* Ms Bernadette Knox; ✉ J Walter Thompson, 40 Berkeley Square, London W1 (☎ 0171 499 4040)

KNOX, (Alexander) David; CMG (1988); s of James Knox (d 1953), and Elizabeth Maxwell, *née* Robertson (d 1961); *b* 15 Jan 1925; *Educ* The Queen's Royal Coll Trinidad W Indies, Univ of Toronto Canada (BA), LSE; *m* 15 July 1950, Beatrice Lily, da of William Benjamin Dunell (d 1963); 1 s (Andrew b 1953), 2 da (Helen b 1954, Julia b 1963); *Career* reader in economics LSE 1955–63 (joined 1949), vice pres Int Bank for Reconstruction and Devpt 1980–87 (joined 1963); *Recreations* walking, opera; *Style—* David Knox, Esq, CMG; ✉ Knights Barn, Manor Farm Lane, East Hagbourne, Oxfordshire OX11 9ND (☎ and fax 01235 817792)

KNOX, Sir David Laidlaw; kt (1993), MP (C) Staffordshire Moorlands (majority 7,410); s of John McGlasson Knox (d 1951), of Lockerbie, and Catherine Helen Campbell, *née* Laidlaw; *b* 30 May 1933; *Educ* Lockerbie and Dumfries Acads, Univ of London; *m* 1980, Margaret E Maxwell, *née* McKenzie; *Career* economist and mgmnt conslt; Parly candidate (C): Birmingham Stechford 1964 and 1966, Nuneaton (by-election) 1967; MP (C): Leek 1970–83, Staffordshire Moorlands 1983–; jt-sec Cons Fin Ctee 1972–73, PPS to Sec of State for Def 1973–74, sec Cons Trade Ctee 1974; vice chm: Cons Pty 1974–75, Cons Employment Ctee 1979–80 (sec 1976–79), Cons Gp for Europe 1984–87; memb: Select Ctee on Euro Legislation 1976–, Chm's Panel of the House of Commons 1983–; *Style—* Sir David Knox, MP; ✉ House of Commons, London SW1A 0AA

KNOX, (William) Graeme; s of William Francis Knox (d 1970), of Glasgow, and Marjorie Evelyn, *née* Milroy (d 1990); *b* 18 Feb 1945; *Educ* Glasgow Acad, Christ Coll Cambridge (MA); *m* 20 June 1969, Jennifer Marion, da of Dr Thomas Russell; 1 s (Mark Tarimo b 3 Feb 1975), 1 da (Karen Ann Hazel b 31 Dec 1976); *Career* Scottish Amicable Life Assurance Society: actuarial student 1966, analyst Investmt Dept 1969, responsible for Investmt Dept and clients 1976, md Scottish Amicable Investment Managers Limited 1984–96; chm Union plc 1996–; FFA 1969; *Recreations* golf, hillwalking, singing; *Style—* Graeme Knox, Esq; ✉ Union plc, 39 Cornhill, London EC3V 3NU (☎ 0171 623 1020, fax 0171 626 9069)

KNOX, Ian Campbell; s of Eric Campbell Knox, and Mary Fyfe, *née* Beattie; *b* 18 Jan 1954; *Educ* Royal HS Edinburgh, Waid Acad Anstruther, Edinburgh Coll of Art, Br Cncl scholarship to Budapest, Nat Film Sch; *m* 19 Jan 1984, Emily Broome Green; *Career* freelance writer and director 1980–; credits incl: The Stronger 1980, The Privilege 1982, Workhorses (BBC) 1983, Shoot for The Sun (BBC) 1986, Down Where The Buffalo Go (BBC) 1987, The Police (BBC) 1990, Spender (BBC) 1991, 99–1 (Carlton) 1993, Between The Lines (BBC) 1994, Hamish Macbeth (BBC) 1994, Call Red (Thames) 1995; *Awards* Scottish Radio and TV awards for Best Play (for Workhorses) 1984, BAFTA award for Best Short film (for The Privilege) 1983, Bilbao Film Festival award for Best Short Fiction (The Privilege) 1983; memb Dirs' Guild 1987; *Recreations* music (bass player), motor cycling, walking; *Style—* Ian Knox, Esq; ✉ 24c Durham Terrace, London W2 5PB (☎ 0171 792 0101)

KNOX, Jack; s of Alexander Knox (d 1986), of Kirkintilloch, and Jean Alexander Gray, *née* Graham (d 1988); *b* 16 Dec 1936; *Educ* Lenzie Acad, Glasgow Sch of Art; *m* 5 July 1960, Margaret Kyle, da of Walter Duncan Sutherland (d 1963), of Linlithgow; 1 s (Kyle Alexander b 1964), 1 da (Emily Barbara b 1967); *Career* artist; lectr Duncan of Jordanstone Coll of Art 1965–81, head Painting Studios Glasgow Sch of Art 1981–92; work in public collections incl: Scottish Nat Gallery of Modern Art, Glasgow Art Galleries, Scottish Nat Portrait Gallery, Aberdeen Art Gallery, Arts Cncl of GB, Contemporary Art Soc, Edinburgh City Arts Centre, Glasgow Univ, Hunterian Museum Glasgow, City Art Gallery Manchester, Royal Scottish Academy Collection, Scottish Arts Cncl, Scottish Television; memb: Scottish Arts Cncl 1974–79, Tstees Ctee Scottish Nat Gallery of Modern Art 1975–81, Bd of Tstees Nat Gallery of Scotland 1982–87; sec Royal Scot Academy 1990–91; external examiner Univ of Dundee 1990; RSA 1979, RGI 1981, RSW 1987; *Exhibitions* solo incl: 57 Gallery Edinburgh 1961, The Scottish Gallery Edinburgh 1966, Richard Demarco Gallery Edinburgh 1969, Serpentine Gallery London 1971, Buckingham Gallery London 1972, Civic Arts Centre Aberdeen 1972, Retrospective (Edinburgh, Fruit Market Glasgow, Third Eye and touring) 1983, The Scottish Gallery Edinburgh 1989, Kelvingrove Art Gallery and Museum Glasgow 1990, Open Eye Gallery Edinburgh 1991, Festival Exhbn Open Eye Gallery Edinburgh 1993 and 1995; group incl: Scottish Art Now (Fruitmarket Gallery Edinburgh) 1982, Six Scottish Painters (Graham Gallery NY) 1983, Arte Escozia Contemporea (Nat Gallery of Brazil) 1985, Moorehead State Univ Minnesota 1987, The Compass Contribution (Tramway Glasgow) 1990, Scottish Art since 1900 (The Barbican London) 1990; *Style—* Jack Knox; ✉ 31 North Erskine Park, Bearsden, Glasgow G61 4LY (☎ 0141 942 6629)

KNOX, Sir John Leonard; kt (1985); s of Leonard Needham Knox (d 1956), and Berthe Helene, *née* Brel (d 1981); *b* 6 April 1925; *Educ* Radley, Worcester Coll Oxford (MA); *m* 1, 1953, Anne Jacqueline (d 1991), da of Herbert Mackintosh; 1 s (Thomas), 3 da (Diana, Catherine, Margaret); *m* 2, 1993, Benedicta Eugenie, da of late Léon Jean Goossens, CBE, FRCM, and widow of Robin Philip Cooksey; *Career* Lt RA 1944–47; barr Lincoln's Inn 1953–85, bencher Lincoln's Inn 1977, QC 1979, attorney-gen Duchy of Lancaster 1984–85, judge of the High Court of Justice (Chancery Div) 1985–96, judge of Employment Appeal Tribunal 1989; dep chm Boundary Cmmn for England 1986–95; *Style—* Sir John Knox

KNOX, Lesley Mary; *née* Samuel; da of Prof Eric Samuel, CBE, of SA, and Vera Eileen; *b* 19 Sept 1953; *Educ* Cheltenham Ladies' Coll, Univ of Cambridge (MA); *m* 1, 1983 (m dis); *m* 2, 1991, Brian Knox; 1 da (Fenella Megan b 27 June 1994); *Career* slr; gp dir Kleinwort Benson; non-exec dir: Strong & Fisher plc, Bank of Scotland, Scottish Provident, Royal Hosps Tst, Dawson International, Fulcrum Investment Tst; *Recreations* fly-fishing, piano, collector of contemporary art; *Style—* Mrs Lesley Knox; ✉ Kleinwort Benson Ltd, 20 Fenchurch Street, London EC3P 3DB (☎ 0171 956 5794, fax 0171 956 6263)

KNOX, (John) Robert; s of John Arthur Knox, and Rosalind, *née* Kingscote; *b* 4 June 1946; *Educ* Univ of Victoria Canada (BA), Univ of Cambridge (MA); *m* 1 Aug 1981, Helen Elizabeth Irène, da of Arnold Zarb; 3 da (Alexandra, Catherine, Antonia); *Career* keeper Dept of Oriental Antiquities British Museum 1994– (asst keeper 1978–92, dep keeper 1992–94); sec Soc for S Asian Studies 1985, vice pres Soc of Antiquaries 1994; *Books* India, Past into Present (with B Durrans, 1982), Explorations and Excavations in Bannu District (jtly, 1991), Amaravati, Buddhist Sculpture from the Great Stupa (1992); *Recreations* walking, music, 78's; *Style—* Robert Knox, Esq; ✉ Department of Oriental Antiquities, The British Museum, Great Russell Street, London WC1B 3DG (☎ 0171 323 8359, fax 0171 323 8999)

KNOX, Robert William (Bob); s of Jack Dallas Knox (d 1983), of Claygate, Surrey, and Margaret Meikle, *née* Elder; *b* 15 Dec 1943; *Educ* Cranleigh; *m* 10 Feb 1968, Susan Mary, da of Cyril Joseph O'Bryen (d 1991), of Weybridge, Surrey; 2 da (Julie b 1970, Katharine b 1972); *Career* Kidsons Impey CAs: ptnr 1972–, managing ptnr London office 1993–; memb London (W End) Dist Trg Bd ICAEW 1984–94, practising memb Acad of Experts 1995–; FCA 1966; *Books* Statements of Source and Application of Funds (1977); *Recreations* occasional golf, bridge, philately; *Style—* Robert W Knox, Esq; ✉ Kidsons Impey, Spectrum House, 20–26 Cursitor St, London EC4A 1HY (☎ 0171 405 2088, fax 0171 831 2206)

KNOX, Hon Sir William Edward; kt (1979); s of late Edward Knox (Air Cdr), and late Dr Alice Knox, *née* Thomas; *b* 14 Dec 1927; *Educ* Melbourne HS; *m* 1956, Doris Alexia Ross; 2 s, 2 da; *Career* MLA Queensland (Lib) for Nundah 1957–89, sec Parly Lib Party 1960–64, sec Jt Govt Parties 1965, min for Transport 1965–72, chm Queensland Road Safety Cncl and memb Aust Transport Advsy Cncl 1965–72, min for Justice and attorney-gen 1971–76, dep ldr Parly Lib Party 1971–76, state treas 1976–78, dep premier and ldr Parly Lib Party 1976–78, min for Health 1978–80, min for Employment and Lab Rels 1980–83, ldr Parly Lib Pty 1983–88; chm St John's Cncl Queensland; CStJ 1990; *Style—* The Hon Sir William Knox; ✉ 1621 Sandgate Rd, Nundah, Queensland 4012, Australia (☎ 00 617 266 9893)

KNOX-JOHNSTON, Sir William Robert Patrick (Robin); kt (1995), CBE (1969), RD (1978, and Bar); s of David Robert Knox-Johnston (d 1970), and Elizabeth Mary, *née* Cree; *b* 17 March 1939; *Educ* Berkhamsted Sch; *m* 1962, Suzanne, da of Denis Ronald Singer; 1 da (Sara b 1963); *Career* yachtsman; first person to circumnavigate the world non-stop & single handed 14 June 1968–22 April 1969, holder Br Sailing Trans Atlantic Record (10 days, 14 hours, 9 mins) 1986, World Champion Class II multihulls 1985, co-skipper Enza NZ (world's fastest circumnavigation under sail, 74 days, 22 hours, 17 mins, 22 secs) 1994; tstee Greenwich Maritime Museum 1992; pres Sail Trg Assoc 1993–, chm Friends of the Nat Maritime Museum 1993–; Hon DSc Maine Maritime Acad, Hon DTech Southampton Inst of Technol 1993; RIN Gold medal 1992; FRGS 1965, FRIN 1994; *Books* World of my Own (1969), Sailing (1975), Twilight of Sail (1978), Last but not Least (1978), Bunkside Companion (1982), Seamanship (1986), The BOC Challenge (1986–87), The Cape of Good Hope (1989), The History of Yachting (1990), The Columbus Venture (1991, Book of the Sea Award), Sea, Ice and Rock (with Chris Bonington, *qv*, 1992), Cape Horn (1994), Beyond Jules Verne (1995); *Recreations* sailing; *Clubs* Royal Yacht Squadron, Little Ship (hon pres), RNSA (Hon Rear Cdre); *Style—* Sir Robin Knox-Johnston, CBE, RD; ✉ St Francis Cottage, Torbryan, Newton Abbot, Devon TQ12 5UR

KNOX-LECKY, Maj-Gen Samuel; CB (1979), OBE (1967); s of John Daniel Lecky (d 1929), of Coleraine, and Mary Thompson, *née* Knox (d 1968); *b* 10 Feb 1926; *Educ* Coleraine Acad, Queen's Univ Belfast (BSc, CEng); *m* 18 Oct 1947, Sheila Constance, da of Hugh Jones (d 1952), of Liverpool; 1 s (Paul b 1955), 2 da (Karla b 1949, Jennifer b 1952); *Career* Army 1946–79, cmmnd REME 1946, DEME BAOR and Cmdt SEME as Brig; DMAO (MOD) and Min (DS) Br Embassy Tehran as Maj-Gen, Hon Col QUB OTC 1978–83, Col Cmdt REME 1980–86; dir-gen Agric Engrs Assoc 1980–88; FIMechE; *Recreations* fishing, sailing; *Clubs* Army and Navy; *Style—* Maj-Gen Samuel Knox-Lecky, CB, OBE

KNOX-PEEBLES, Brian Philip; s of Lt-Col George Edward Knox-Peebles, RTR, DSO (d 1969), and Patricia, *née* Curtis-Raleigh; *b* 19 June 1936; *Educ* Wellington, Göttingen

Univ W Germany, BNC Oxford (MA); *m* 20 Aug 1960, Rose Mary, da of Capt Cyril Telford Latch; 1 s (Brendan b 21 Sept 1965), 3 da (Nina b 16 Nov 1962, Fleur b 3 Feb 1964, Bryonie b 16 Nov 1967); *Career* Daily Mail 1963–64, Evening Standard 1964–65, The Times 1965–67, United Newspapers plc 1967–89; dir: Bradbury Agnew Ltd 1979–82, United Provincial Newspapers 1981–89, gp mktg dir United Newspapers plc 1974–89; dir Webster & Horsfall 1987–; fndr and chm Consultants in Media; fndr memb and first pres Int Newspaper Mktg Assoc (Europe); former Euro dir Int Circulation Managers' Assoc; memb: Mktg Soc, Newspaper Assoc of America, Cwlth Press Union, Int Fedn of Newspaper Publishers; FInstD; *Books* The Fleet Street Revolution; *Recreations* cinema, walking, swimming, reading, writing; *Clubs* Hurlingham; *Style*— Brian Knox-Peebles, Esq; ✉ Consultants in Media, 2 Campden House Terrace, Kensington Church St, London W8 4BQ (☎ 0171 792 0748, fax 0171 792 0398)

KNUTSFORD, 6 Viscount (UK 1895); Michael Holland-Hibbert; DL (1977 Devon); also Baron Knutsford, of Knutsford, Co Chester (UK 1888), and 7 Bt (UK 1853); o s of Hon Wilfrid Holland-Hibbert (d 1961; 2 s of 3 Viscount), and Isabel Audrey, *née* Fenwick; s cousin 5 Viscount 1986; *b* 27 Dec 1926; *Educ* Eton, Trinity Coll Cambridge (BA); *m* 8 May 1951, Hon Sheila Constance Portman, er da of 5 Viscount Portman (d 1942); 2 s (Hon Henry Thurstan, Hon James Edward b 19 May 1967), 1 da (Hon Lucy Katherine b 27 June 1956); *Heir* s, Hon Henry Thurstan Holland-Hibbert b 6 April 1959; *Career* SW regnl dir Barclays Bank 1956–86; memb various ctees Nat Tst 1965–86 (memb Finance Ctee 1986); High Sheriff of Devon 1977–78; *Clubs* Brooks's; *Style*— The Rt Hon the Viscount Knutsford, DL; ✉ Broadclyst House, Exeter, Devon EX5 3EW (☎ 01392 461244)

KOCEN, Dr Roman Stefan; TD (1973); s of late Dr Mieczyslaw and Mrs Lisa Kocen; *b* 20 March 1932; *Educ* Roundhay Sch Leeds, Leeds Sch of Med (MB ChB, MRCP, various prizes); *m* 1, 1963 (m dis 1971), Anna Louise, *née* Derer; 2 da; m 2, 1974, Elisabeth Ann, *née* Glover; 2 s; *Career* house physician then house surgn in neurosurgery Gen Infirmary Leeds 1956–57; Nat Serv Actg Maj/Offr i/c Med Div Br Mil Hosp Kamunting Malaya RAMC 1958–60, neurologist Mobile Neurosurgical Team RAMC AER 1960–75; registrar then sr registrar Nat Hosp Queen Square 1963–68; conslt neurologist: Brook Gen Hosp 1968–70, Nat Hosp Queen Square 1970–; civil conslt neurologist to RAF, hon conslt neurologist British Airways and St Luke's Hosp for the Clergy; sub-dean Inst of Neurology Univ of London 1976–81, chm Med Ctee Nat Hosp 1991–93; formerly sec: Neurology Section RSM, Ctee on Neurology RCP; Freeman City of London; memb: Assoc of Br Neurologists, Br Neuropathological Soc; FRCP 1974; *Recreations* reading, music, walking, skiing, cooking; *Clubs* Garrick; *Style*— Dr Roman Kocen, TD; ✉ National Hospital for Neurology and Neurosurgery, Queen Square, London WC1N 3BG (☎ 0171 837 3611, fax 0171 833 8658)

KOENIGSBERGER, Prof Otto Heinrich Gustav; s of Georg F Koenigsberger (d 1932), of Berlin, and Katharine Mathilde, *née* Born (d 1953); *b* 13 Oct 1908; *Educ* Tech Univ Berlin (Dr-Ing); *m* 20 Dec 1957, Dr Renate Ursula Born, da of Dr Wolfgang Born (d 1949), of Vienna; *Career* memb Swiss Inst for the History of Ancient Egyptian Architecture 1933–35, chief architect and planner Mysore State India 1939–48, dir of housing Miny of Health Govt of India and planning advsr Basildon New Town Essex 1948–51, UN planning and housing advsr to govts of Ghana, Nigeria, Pakistan, Philippines, Ceylon and Singapore 1956–63, planning conslt to govts of Zambia, Brazil and Costa Rica 1956–63, housing advsr to UN Econ Cmmn for Africa 1966–70, Mellon prof of planning Columbia Univ NY 1968, head Dept of Devpt and Tropical Studies Architectural Assoc London 1957–72; UCL: prof of devpt planning and head Devpt Planning Unit 1973–78, emeritus prof and hon res fell 1979–; ed Habitat Int 1976–93; UN Centre for Human Settlements Award Habitat Scroll of Honour 1989; Hon Dr-Ing Univ of Stuttgart 1979; memb A E V Berlin 1932, fndr memb Inst of Town Planners (India) 1948, MRTPI 1952, ARIBA 1968; author of numerous pubns since 1932 on architectural and applied climatology, planning and housing practice and consultancy reports and theory and education; *Clubs* Architectural Assoc; *Style*— Prof Otto Koenigsberger; ✉ 300 West End Lane, (Ground Floor), London NW6 1LN (☎ 0171 794 3475); Development Planning Unit, University College London, 9–11 Endsleigh Gardens, London WC1H 0ED (☎ 0171 388 7581)

KOFFMANN, Pierre; *b* 21 Aug 1948; *Educ* École Jean Jacques Rousseau Tarbes France, Cap de Cuisine et de Salle Tarbes; *m* 16 Sept 1972, Annie; 1 da (Camille b 26 Oct 1983); *Career* Military Service 1967–69; commis Restaurant L'Aubette Strasbourg 1966, commis Grand Hôtel Palais Juan Les Pins 1967, Restaurant Le Provencal La Ciotat 1969–70, Restaurant La Voile d'Or Lausanne 1970, Gavroche Restaurant 1970–71, chef Brasserie Benoist 1971, Waterside Inn Restaurant Bray on Thames Berks 1971–77, chef and proprietor La Tante Claire Restaurant 1977– (awarded 3 Michelin Stars 1993); Restaurant Assoc Best Restaurant of the Year, The Caterer Best Chef of the Year, Egon Ronay Restaurant of the Year; Top Mark: AA Guide, Egon Ronay, Gault et Millau; 5 out of 5 Good Food Guide 1996; memb Relais et Chateaux et Academie Culinaire de France; *Books* Memories of Gascony (1990), La Tante Claire (1992); *Style*— Pierre Koffmann, Esq; ✉ Tante Claire Restaurant Ltd, 68 Royal Hospital Rd, Chelsea, London SW3 4HP (☎ 0171 352 6045, 0171 351 0227, fax 0171 352 3257)

KOHNER, Prof Eva Maria; OBE (1994); da of Baron George Nicholas Kohner, of Szaszberek (d 1945), of Hungary, and Andrea Kathleen, *née* Boszormenyi (d 1985); *b* 23 Feb 1929; *Educ* Baar-Madas Presbyterian Boarding Sch for Girls, Royal Free Hosp Sch of Med London Univ (BSc, MB BS, MD); *m* 26 April 1961 (m dis 1979), Steven Ivan Warman; *Career* med registrar med ophthalmogy Lambeth Hosp 1963–64, res fell Royal Postgraduate Med Sch Hammersmith Hosp London 1965–68, MRC Alexander Wernher Piggott Meml fell NY 1968–69; Moorfields Eye Hosp and Hammersmith Hosp: sr registrar and lectr 1970–77, conslt med ophthalmologist 1977–88, prof med ophthalmology (first full-time prof in Britain) 1988–; worked in field of treatment of diabetic eye disease by laser (in part instrumental in this treatment now being available to all patients in Britain) and pathogenic mechanisms in diabetic eye disease; FRCP 1977 (MRCP 1963), FRCOPath 1991; *Books* over three hundred publications in field of retinal vascular disease; *Recreations* art, travel; *Style*— Prof Eva Kohner, OBE; ✉ 32 Monckton Ct, Strangways Terrace, London W14 8NF

KOK, Nicholas Willem; s of Felix Kok, and Ann, *née* Steei; *b* 30 Dec 1962; *Educ* King's Sch Worcester, New Coll Oxford (organ scholar, BA, ARCO, FRCO), RCM (Lofthouse Memorial Prize, Countess of Munster Award); *m* 19 Sept 1992, Sarah, *née* Hickson; *Career* conductor; music dir Janet Smith and Dancers 1985–87, music dir Epsom Choral Soc 1988–90, asst conductor/repetiteur ENO and music advsr Contemporary Opera Studio 1989–93, princ conductor East of England Orch 1996–; involved in setting up Almeida Opera; conductor: English Touring Opera, Opera Factory, Dublin Grand Opera, The Opera Co, Chelmsford Opera Gp, The Philharmonia, Royal Scottish Nat Orch, London Sinfonietta, Scottish Chamber Orch, Bournemouth Sinfonietta, Endymion Ensemble, Premiere Ensemble, Trinity Coll of Music Sinfonia, London Pro Arte Orch, Philippines Philharmonic, Alvin Ailey Dance Theater London Coliseum 1992; television and radio incl: The Return of Ulysses, The Fairy Queen, Arion and the Dolphin, The Soldier's Tale, The Carnival of the Animals, Reginald Smith Brindle's Journey Towards Infinity, Erollyn Wallen's Mondrial, A Man For All Seasons; interviewer/commentator: Cardiff Singer of the World, Sainsbury's Choir of the Year, BBC Proms; *Style*— Nicholas Kok, Esq; ✉ c/o Andrew Rosner, Allied Artists, 42 Montpelier Square, London SW7 1JZ (☎ 0171 589 6243)

KOLBERT, His Hon Colin Francis; s of Arthur Richard Alexander Kolbert (d 1992), of Barnet and Barnstaple, and Dorothy Elizabeth, *née* Fletcher (d 1996); *b* 3 June 1936; *Educ* Queen Elizabeth's Barnet, St Catharine's Coll Cambridge (MA, PhD), St Peter's Coll Oxford (MA, DPhil); *m* 12 Sept 1959, Jean Fairgrieve, da of Stanley Hutton Abson (d 1964), of Friern Barnet; 2 da (Julia Catharine b 1963, Jennifer Sally b 1965); *Career* RA 1954–56, Cambridge Univ OTC (TAVR) 1969–74; called to the Bar Lincoln's Inn 1961; fell and tutor in jurisprudence St Peter's Coll Oxford 1964–68, fell Magdalene Coll Cambridge 1968– (tutor 1969–88), lectr in law Dept of Land Economy Cambridge 1968–88; recorder SE Circuit 1985–88; circuit judge: SE Circuit 1988–90, NE Circuit 1990–95; independent bd memb and tbnl chm Securities and Futures Authy 1995–; *Clubs* Hawks' (Cambridge), MCC, Farmers', Cambridge Univ Rugby (tstee 1988–), Leeds; *Style*— His Hon Colin Kolbert; ✉ Magdalene Coll, Cambridge CB3 0AG (☎ 01223 322697); 35 Essex Street, London WC2R 3AR (☎ 0171 353 6381, fax 0171 583 178)

KOLTAI, Ralph; CBE (1983); s of Dr Alfred Koltai (d 1970), and Charlotte, *née* Weinstein (d 1987); *b* 31 July 1924; *Educ* Berlin, Central Sch of Arts and Crafts London (DipAD); *m* 29 Dec 1954 (m dis 1976), Mary Annena, da of late George Stubbs, of Liverpool; *Career* stage designer and director; RASC attached Intelligence Corps, served Nuremberg War Crimes Trial and War Crimes Interrogation Unit 1944–47; assoc designer RSC 1963–66 and 1976–; first prodn Angelique for London Opera Club 1950; designs for: Royal Opera House, Sadler's Wells, Scottish Opera, Nat Welsh Opera, Ballet Rambert; RDI 1984, fell Acad of Performing Arts Hong Kong 1994, hon fell The London Inst 1996; *Theatre* RSC prodns incl: The Caucasian Chalk Circle 1962, The Representative 1963, The Birthday Party 1964, The Jew of Malta 1964, Timon of Athens 1965, Little Murders 1967, Major Barbara 1970, Old World 1976, Wild Oats 1977, The Tempest 1978, Hamlet 1980, The Love Girl and The Innocent 1981, Molière 1982, Much Ado About Nothing 1982, Cyrano de Bergerac (SWET Award) 1984, Troilus and Cressida 1985, Othello 1986; NT prodns incl: As You Like It 1967, Back To Methuselah 1969, State of Revolution 1977, Brand (SWET Award) 1978, Richard III 1979, Man and Superman 1981; other prodns incl: Wagner's complete Ring Circle (ENO) 1973, Tannhauser (Sydney) 1973 and Geneva 1986, Fidelio (Munich) 1974, Bugsy Malone 1983, Pack of Lies 1983, Metropolis 1989, dir and designer of The Flying Dutchman 1987 and La Traviata (Hong Kong Arts Festival) 1990, The Planets (Royal Ballet) 1990, The Makropulos Affair (Norwegian Opera) 1992, Hair (Old Vic) 1993, La Traviata (Swedish Opera) 1993, Otello (Essen Opera) 1994, Madam Butterfly (Tokyo) 1995; has worked throughout Europe and in Argentina, USA, Canada, Australia; *Awards* incl: co-winner Individual Gold Medal Prague Quadrienal 1975, Golden Triga 1979 and 1991, Individual Silver Medal 1987; *Recreations* wildlife photography; *Style*— Ralph Koltai, Esq, CBE; ✉ c/o London Management, 2–4 Noel Street, London W1V 3RB (☎ 0171 287 9000, fax 0171 287 3236)

KOLVIN, Prof Israel; s of Philip Kolvin (d 1936), and Rachel, *née* Peimer (d 1974), of Johannesburg; *b* 5 May 1929; *Educ* Univ of S Africa (BA), Univ of Witwatersrand (MB BCh, MD), Univ of Edinburgh (DPsych), FRCPsych 1972, MFPHM 1993; *m* 27 June 1954, Rona, da of Joseph Samuel Idelson (d 1975), of Johannesburg; 1 s (Philip Alan b 4 Aug 1961), 1 da (Jennifer Lee (Mrs Jacobs) b 2 Nov 1957); *Career* registrar Royal Hosp for Sick Children Edinburgh, sr registrar Warneford and Park Hosp Oxford 1961–63, conslt Dept of Psychiatry Univ of Newcastle 1964–90, prof of child psychiatry Univ of Newcastle 1977–90 (former reader, dir of Human Devpt Unit 1974–90), John Bowlby prof of child and family mental health The Royal Free Hosp and Tavistock Centre 1990–94 (now emeritus); visiting prof Cincinatti, McMaster, Utrecht, Brisbane, Brown and Pittsburgh Univs, Wellcome prof South Africa; former memb Ctee of Advsrs to Chief Scientist, memb Mental Health Res Fndn 1986–92; chm: Assoc of Child Psychology and Psychiatry 1993–96, Child Psychiatry Res Assoc 1993–; RCPsych: sometime memb Educn, Manpower, Examinations, Exec and Fin Ctees, sometime memb Cncl and Ct of Electors, chm Exec Ctee Child and Adolescent Section 1985–89, vice pres 1991–92, currently treas; pres Psychiatric Section RSM 1982–83; has carried out research into: low birth weight, deaf children, infantile autism, hyperactive children, evaluation of psychotherapy, depression in childhood, family disadvantage and deprivation, resilience in the face of adversity (jtly) and child sexual abuse (jtly); memb: British Paediatric Assoc, RSM; *Books* Bladder Control and Enuresis (jtly, 1973), Born Too Soon, Born Too Small (jtly, 1976), Speech Retarded & Deaf Children (jtly, 1979), Help Starts Here (jtly, 1981), Cycle of Deprivation (jtly, 1990); *Recreations* travel, theatre, bridge, poetry, watching cricket and rugby; *Style*— Prof Israel Kolvin; ✉ The Tavistock Centre, 120 Belsize Lane, London NW3 5BA (☎ 0171 435 7111, fax 0171 431 7057); The Royal Free Hospital, School of Medicine, Pond St, Hampstead, London NW3 2QG

KOMISSARENKO, HE Prof Sergui; s of Vassiliy Komissarenko (d 1993), and Lubov, *née* Drosovska (d 1994); *b* 9 July 1943; *Educ* Kiev Secdy Sch, Kiev Med Inst (MD), Dept of Mech and Mathematics Kiev Univ, Inst of Biochemistry Kiev (PhD, DSc); *m* 1970, Natalia, da of Boris Ignatiuk (d 1968); 1 da (Anna b 1 Dec 1971); *Career* Ukrainian diplomat, scientist and statesman; Inst of Biochemistry Ukrainian Acad of Scis: scientific researcher 1969–72, scientific sec 1972–74, head Laboratory of Immunochemistry 1975–82, head Dept of Molecular Immunology 1982–89, dir and prof of biochemistry 1989–92; scholar: Pasteur Inst Paris 1974–75, Sloan-Kettering Cancer Inst NY 1981; dep PM Ukraine (responsible for humanitarian sector) 1990–92, Ukrainian ambass to Ct of St James's 1992–; ed-in-chief Ukrainian Biochemical Jl 1989–92, memb Editorial Bd Int Jl of Immunology and Immunopharmacology Italy; Ukrainian State Award 1979; memb Cncl Int Soc for Immunopharmacology USA 1990; full memb: Ukrainian Acad of Sci 1991 (corresponding memb 1990), Ukrainian Acad of Med Sci 1993; *Publications* author of over 200 scientific articles in the field of biochemistry and immunology, and articles on Ukrainian culture and policy; *Recreations* music, skiing, lawn tennis, windsurfing, clay pigeon shooting; *Style*— HE Prof Sergui Komissarenko; ✉ Embassy of Ukraine, 78 Kensington Park Road, London W11 2PL (☎ 0171 727 6312, fax 0171 792 1708)

KONDRACKI, Henry Andrew; s of Pawel Kondracki (d 1986), of 12 Union St, Edinburgh, and Boyce Matilda, *née* Hills (d 1988); *b* 13 Feb 1953; *Educ* Bellevue Secdy Sch Edinburgh, Byam Shaw Sch of Art London, Slade Sch UCL (BA, Sir William Coldstream prize for best figurative work, Slade prize for Fine Art); *m* 2 Oct 1985, Sara, da of Dr Mohamed Gawad Elsarrag; 2 s (Patrick Samuel, Miles); *Career* artist; *Solo Exhibitions* Traverse Theatre Club Edinburgh 1979, The Artist's Collective Gallery Edinburgh 1984 and 1992, Vanessa Devereux Gallery London 1987 and 1989, Michael Wardell Gallery Melbourne Aust 1988, William Jackson Gallery London 1991; *Gp Exhibitions* Off the Wall 1988, Contemporary Drawings (Vanessa Devereux Gallery London) 1989, Royal Acad Summer Show 1989; *Public Collections* Granada Fndn Manchester 1983, Br Arts Cncl 1986, Br Cncl 1989, UCL 1986, Manchester City Art Gallery 1991; awards: materials and cost award Scot Art Cncl 1978 (minor bursary 1979), South Bank Bd prize 1987; selected to participate in The Peter Moores Exhibition (Walker Gallery Liverpool) 1986; memb Cncl Edinburgh Printmakers Workshop; *Style*— Henry Kondracki, Esq

KONIG, Martyn; s of Peter Hans Konig, of Guildford, Surrey, and Dorothy, *née* Vernon; *b* 21 Sept 1957; *Educ* Godalming GS, Univ of Liverpool (LLB); *Career* called to the Bar Gray's Inn 1979; N M Rothschild and Sons: bullion dealing in Treasy Dept 1980–87, asst dir Bullion Trading (USA, Africa, Asia, Aust) 1987–90, dir of trading Treasy Div 1990–96, subsequently with Goldman Sachs Ltd; memb Chartered Inst of Bankers; *Recreations* motor racing, classic cars, boating; *Style*— Martyn Konig, Esq

KONSTANT, Rt Rev David; *see:* Leeds, Bishop of (RC)

KOOLMAN, Alex C; *Educ* Wimbledon Sch of Art, Allan Frazer Coll of Art; *Career* portraitist; sr master Newport Coll of Art, sr lectr Maidstone Coll of Art; pt/t teacher: London Sch of Printing, Harrow Sch of Art, Beckenham Centre for the Arts; RBA de Laszlo Silver Medal 1983–84; hon memb Pastel Soc; RBA, RP; *Style—* Alex Koolman, Esq, RP

KOOPS, Eric Jan Leendert; s of Leendert Koops (d 1990), of Hellingly, Sussex, and Daphne Vera, *née* Myhill; *b* 16 March 1945; *Educ* Eastbourne Coll, Univ of Lancaster (BA); *m* 1, 1968 (m dis 1985); 1 s (Mark Alexander b 20 Feb 1975), 1 da (Amanda Charlotte b 25 Sept 1972); m 2, 11 Sept 1987, Hon Mrs Justice Hogg, *qv*, da of Baron Hailsham of St Marylebone, KG, CH, *qv*; 1 s (William Quintin Eric b 21 Dec 1991), 1 da (Katharine Mary b 17 March 1989); *Career* TA 2 Lt 4/5 KORR 1964–67; investmt banker and dir of several public and private cos in UK and the Benelux; hon chm: The Duke of Edinburgh's Award, World Fellowship; tstee: The Duke of Edinburgh's Award Int Fndn, Inst for Policy Res, Winnicott Clinic of Psychotherapy Charitable Tst; Parly candidate (Cons) Wakefield 1974, chm Political Ctee Carlton Club 1984–88; FCA 1971; *Publications* Money for our Masters (1970), Airports for the Eighties (1980); *Recreations* travel, cricket, biographies; *Clubs* Buck's, Carlton, MCC; *Style—* Eric Koops, Esq; ✉ 16 Moreton Place, London SW1V 2NP (☎ 0171 834 5615, fax 0171 834 1715)

KOPEL, Ellis; *b* 9 May 1924; *Career* served WWII RAF India; former journalist with local weekly newspaper, journalist with The Press Assoc (Parly press gallery/Fleet St HQ) 1954–59, PR Dept ICL 1959–65, own consultancy (public affrs/fin, corp and product PR, later sold to Paragon Communications) 1965–88; clients incl: Gestetner, Low & Bonar Dundee, Metalrax Group Birmingham, Embassy of the FRG, Business Equipment Trade Assoc, Fedn of Bakers; ind PR conslt 1988–; clients incl: Metalrax Group plc, Nat Assoc of Master Bakers, Annuity & Pensions Network Seymour Cooke; fndr Info Serv for Investment Advsrs (ISIA) 1965–88, fndr exec dir PR Organisation International Ltd 1970–94, fndr admin International PR Network 1995–; former memb Int Ctee IPR; memb: NUJ (one-time memb Nat Exec Cncl and chair Press and PR Industl Cncl), IPRA, PRCA (chm Registered Ind Conslts Gp); *Recreations* theatre, bridge, dining out; *Clubs* London Press; *Style—* Ellis Kopel, Esq; ✉ 16 Duncan Terrace, London N1 8BZ (☎ 0171 278 3633, fax 0171 278 3699, e-mail E.KOPEL@mcrl.poptel.org.uk)

KOPELOWITZ, Dr Lionel; JP (Northumberland 1964); s of Dr Maurice Kopelowitz (d 1971), and Mabel, *née* Garston (d 1949); *b* 9 Dec 1926; *Educ* Clifton, Trinity Coll Cambridge (BA), Univ Coll Hosp London (MA); *m* 29 July 1980, Mrs Sylvia Waksman, *née* Galler; *Career* Flt Lt RAF Med Branch 1952–53; princ in gen practice in Newcastle upon Tyne 1953–87; chm: BMA Newcastle Div 1969–70, Newcastle Family Practitioner Ctee 1979–85, Newcastle Local Med Ctee 1980–86; pres: Soc of Family Practitioner Ctees 1978–79, BMA Northern Regnl Cncl 1984–88, Bd of Deps of Br Jews 1985–91, Nat Cncl for Soviet Jewry 1985–91, Euro Jewish Congress 1988–91; memb: Gen Optical Cncl 1979–93, BMA Cncl 1982–94, GMC 1984–94; hon sec BMA Northern Regnl Cncl 1975–84; Liveryman Worshipful Soc of Apothecaries 1966; memb Assur Med Soc 1987; life vice pres Tyneside Cncl of Christians and Jews; vice pres: Trades Advsy Cncl, Br Cncl of Sha'are Zedek Med Centre Jerusalem; pres Old Cliftonian Soc 1991–93; chm St Marylebone Div BMA 1992–; memb Bd of Govrs Haifa Technion 1977–89; *Books* Medical Annual (contrib 1985); *Recreations* contract bridge, continental travel; *Clubs* Athenaeum, Cambridge Union Soc; *Style—* Dr Lionel Kopelowitz, JP; ✉ 10 Cumberland House, Clifton Gardens, London W9 1DX (☎ 0171 289 6375); 7 Sea Lane, Middleton-on-Sea, W Sussex PO22 7RU (☎ 01243 582167)

KOPPEL, Jessica Esther (Jess); da of Heinz Koppel (d 1980), of Cwmerfyn, Aberystwyth, and Renate Hanni, *née* Fischl; *b* 4 April 1963; *Educ* Penglais Aberystwyth, Cardiff Coll of Art (Higher Nat Dip Photography); *Career* photographer; asst to Bryce Attwell 1984–85, freelance photographer 1985– (specialising in food and still life); numerous exhibitions incl: Stages Photographers Gallery 1988, Assoc of Photographers Gallery, F45 Womens Exhibition every year; winner: Silver award Assoc of Photographers, Clio Gold award Int Food Packaging 1988, award of Excellence Mead Show 1989; memb Assoc of Photographers 1985; *Books* incl: Sophie Grigson's Ingredients Book, 10 Minute Cuisine, Henrietta Green's Country Kitchen, Sophie Grigson's Eat Your Greens, Sophie Grigson's Meat Course, Sophie Grigson's Taste of the Times; *Style—* Ms Jess Koppel; ✉ Jess Koppel Studio, 71 White Lion Street, London N1 9PP (☎ 0171 837 8374)

KOPS, Bernard; *b* 28 Nov 1926; *m* 1956, Erica, *née* Gordon; 4 c; *Career* writer; lectr in drama: The Spiro Inst 1985–86, Surrey Educn Authy, Ealing Educn Authy, ILEA, Arts Educnl Schs 1989–90, City Literary Inst 1990–94, The Paines Plough Co 1992–94; recipient Arts Cncl bursary 1957, 1979, 1985 and 1990, C S Lewis fellowship 1981, 1982, 1983 and 1992; *Novels* incl: Awake for Mourning (1958), The Dissent of Dominick Shapiro (1966), The Passionate Past of Gloria Gaye (1972), Partners (1975), On Margate Sands (1978); *Non-Fiction* Neither Your Honey Nor Your Sting - An Offbeat History of the Jews (1985), The World is a Wedding (autobiog, 1963, 1975); *Poetry* Poems (1955), Poems and Songs (1958), Anemone for Antigone (1959), Erica, I Want You to Read Something (1967), For the Record (1971), Barricades in West Hampstead (1988); *Stage Plays* incl: The Hamlet of Stepney Green (1956), The Dream of Peter Mann (1959), Enter Solly Gold (1961, televised 1968), Stray Cats and Empty Bottles (1967, televised 1967), Ezra (1981, on radio 1980), Simon at Midnight (1985, on radio 1982), More Out Than In (1980, on radio 1985), Kafe Kropotkin (1988, also on radio), Sophie! the Last of the Red Hot Mamas (1990), Moss (1991, on radio 1983, televised 1976), Playing Sinatra (1992), Dreams of Anne Frank (1992, winner London Fringe Awards 1993), Who Shall I Be Tomorrow (1992), Call in the Night (1995), Golem (1996), Jacob and the Green Rabbi (1997); *Radio Plays* incl: Return to Stepney Green (1957), Home Sweet Honeycomb (1962), Israel Pt 1 (1963), Israel Pt 2 (1964), I Grow Old, I Grow Old (1979), Over the Rainbow (1981), Trotsky was My Father (1984), Congress in Manchester (1990), Soho Nights (serial, 1993), Sailing With Homer (1994, winner Writer's Guild Award 1994/95), The Jericho Players (1996); *TV Drama/Documentary* incl: I Want to Go Home (1963), The Lost Years of Brian Hooper (1965), It's A Lovely Day Tomorrow (1975), The Geese that Shrieked and The Boy Philosopher (adaptions from Isaac Bashevis Singer 1975), Rocky Marciano is Dead (1977), Nightkids (1983); *Style—* Bernard Kops, Esq; ✉ Sheil Land Associates, 43 Doughty Street, London WC1N 2LF

KORALEK, Paul George; CBE (1984); s of Mr Ernest Koralek (d 1983), and Alice, *née* Muller (d 1989); *b* 7 April 1933; *Educ* Aldenham, Architectural Assoc Sch of Arch (AADipl); *m* 13 Dec 1958, (Audrey) Jennifer, da of Capt Arthur Vivian Chadwick (d 1980); 1 s (Benjamin b 14 July 1967), 2 da (Catherine b 16 March 1961, Lucy b 19 Dec 1962); *Career* ptnr and dir Ahrends Burton & Koralek Architects 1961–; princ works incl: Trinity Coll Dublin (Berkeley Library 1972, Arts Faculty bldg 1979), residential bldg Keble Coll Oxford 1976, Templeton Coll Oxford 1969–88, Nebenzahl House Jerusalem 1972, warehouse and showroom for Habitat Wallingford, factory for Cummins Engines Shotts, J Sainsbury supermarket Canterbury 1984, WH Smith retail HQ Swindon 1985, John Lewis dept store Kingston 1990, St Mary's Hosp Newport IOW 1991, Heritage Centre Dover 1991, stations for extension Docklands Light Railway 1992, new Br Embassy Moscow 1993, Techniquest Science Centre Cardiff 1995, currently Dublin Dental Hosp and Sch; RIBA 1957, RA 1986; *Style—* Paul Koralek, Esq, CBE, RA; ✉ 3 Rochester Rd, London NW1 9JH (☎ 0171 485 9143); Ahrends Burton & Koralek, Unit 1, 7 Chalcot Rd, London NW1 8LH (☎ 0171 586 3311)

KORANY, Stephen; *b* Budapest, Hungary; *Educ* Ecole Hôtelière Nice France; *Career* hotelier; trained Hotel Ruhl Nice, Imperial Palace Annecy and Hotel Chateau Frontenac Paris, receptionist rising to asst mangr Selsdon Park Hotel Sanderstead Surrey 1948–52, gen mangr Society Restaurant and adjoining Pigalle Restaurant Jermyn Street London 1952–53, managing ptnr Basil Street Hotel London until 1995 (mangr 1953, subsequently managing dir until co became a partnership), ret; Freeman City of London; FHCIMA, Master Innholder; memb: Chaîne des Rotisseurs, Réunion des Gastronomes; former memb Restaurateurs Assoc; *Style—* Stephen Korany, Esq; ✉ Flat 63, Swan Court, Chelsea Manor Street, London SW3 5RX (☎ 0171 351 2107)

KORLIPARA, Dr Krishna Rao; s of Laxminarayana Korlipara, of Denduluru, India, and Krishnaveni, *née* Kodali; *b* 14 Sept 1938; *Educ* Kasturba Med Coll Karnatak Univ Mangalore S India (MB BS); *m* 2 May 1963, Uma Devi Korlipara, da of Rajendra Vara Prasad Veeramachaneni; 3 da (b 1964, 1965 and 1968), 1 s (b 1970); *Career* sr house offr in gen med: Manor Park Hosp Bristol 1965–66, Huddersfield 1967, Mansfield Hosp Notts 1967–68; registrar in gen med Bolton Gen Hosp 1969–72, princ in gen practice Horwich 1972–; pt/t clinical asst in cardiology Wythenshawe Hosp Regional Cardiac Centre Univ of S Manchester 1977–, trainer in gen practice 1984–94; fndr chm Bolton District Medical Services Ltd (first GP co-operative) 1977–, chm Nat Assoc of GP Co-operatives; memb: GMC 1984– (memb Professional Conduct Ctee and Oversees Ctee), Bolton Local Med Ctee 1993–; gen sec Overseas Doctors Assoc UK 1979–84; memb: Med Protection Soc 1965, Bolton Med Soc 1972 (pres 1992–93), BMA 1978; FInstD 1994; *Recreations* badminton; *Style—* Dr Krishna Korlipara; ✉ Pike View Medical Centre, Albert Street, Horwich, Bolton BL6 7AN (☎ 01204 699311, fax 01204 668387, car 0385 394450); Rivington View Ltd, Albert Street, Horwich, Bolton BL6 7AW; Bolton District Medical Services Ltd, 506 Chorley Old Road, Bolton BL1 6AB

KORN, Jacqueline; da of Harry Korn (d 1989), of London, and Essie, *née* Simmons; *b* 15 April 1938; *Educ* Harrow Weald Co GS; *m* 14 March 1965, Ralph Glasser; 1 s (Roland b 5 Feb 1973), 1 da (Miranda b 29 Sept 1975); *Career* authors' agent; became jt owner David Higham Associates 1972 (joined 1958); *Recreations* music, theatre, reading, walking; *Clubs* Groucho, RAC; *Style—* Miss Jacqueline Korn; ✉ David Higham Assocs Ltd, 5–8 Lower John St, Golden Square, London W1R 4HA (☎ 0171 437 7888, fax 0171 437 1072)

KORNBERG, Prof Sir Hans Leo; s of Max Kornberg; *b* 14 Jan 1928; *Educ* Queen Elizabeth GS Wakefield, Univ of Sheffield; *m* 1, 1956, Monica King (d 1989); 2 s (Jonathan, (twin) Simon), 2 da (Julia, Rachel); m 2, 28 July 1991, Donna, da of William B Haber, of Los Angeles; *Career* prof of biochemistry Univ of Leicester 1960–75, Sir William Dunn prof of biochemistry Univ of Cambridge 1975–95, fell Christ's Coll Cambridge 1975– (master 1982–95), univ prof and prof of biology Boston Univ 1995–; a managing tstee Nuffield Fndn 1973–93, chm Royal Cmmn on Environmental Pollution 1976–81, chm Sci Advsy Ctee and chm Kuratorium Max-Planck Inst Dortmund 1979–89, memb AFRC 1981–85, memb Advsy Cncl for Applied Res & Devpt 1982–85, chm Advsy Ctee for Genetic Modification 1986–95, memb Priorities Bd for Res in Agric and Food 1985–90, dir UK Nirex 1987–95, memb Advsy Ctee Harkness Fellowships 1989–94, govr Wellcome Tst 1990–95; pres: Br Assoc 1984–85, Biochemical Soc 1990–95, Int Union of Biochemistry and Molecular Biology 1991–94, Assoc Sci Educn 1991–92; memb various int acads; Hon DSc: Cincinnati, Warwick, Leicester, Sheffield, Bath, Strathclyde, South Bank, Leeds; Hon DUniv Essex, Hon MD Leipzig; FIBiol, FRSA, Hon FRCP 1989, FRS 1965; *Style—* Prof Sir Hans Kornberg, FRS; ✉ The University Professors, Boston University, 745 Commonwealth Avenue, Boston, MA 02215, USA (☎ 00 1 617 353 4020, fax 00 1 617 353 5084)

KORNER, Joanna Christian Mary; QC (1993); da of John Hugh George Korner, of House of Elrig, Portwilliam, and Martha Maria Emma, *née* Tupay von Isertingen; *b* 1 July 1951; *Educ* Queensgate Sch London, Inns of Ct Sch of Law; *Career* called to the Bar Inner Temple 1974, tenant in chambers 1975, recorder of the Crown Court 1995– (asst recorder 1992–95), bencher Inner Temple 1996; memb: SE Circuit, Criminal Bar Assoc, Crown Ct Rules Ctee 1994; co-opted memb Gen Cncl of the Bar 1994; *Recreations* collecting books and porcelain, tennis, cinema; *Style—* Miss Joanna Korner, QC; ✉ 6 King's Bench Walk, Temple, London EC4Y 7DR (☎ 0171 583 0410, fax 0171 353 8791)

KOUMI, Margaret (Maggie); da of Yiasoumis Koumi (d 1982), and Melexidia Paraskeva; *b* 15 July 1942; *Educ* Buckingham Gate London; *m* 8 Aug 1980, Ramon Sola; *Career* sec Thomas Cook 1957–60; sub-ed and feature/fiction writer Visual Features Ltd (incl Boyfriend, Top Boys, Big Beat and Boyfriend Annual) 1960–66; sub-ed TV World 1966–67; ed 19 Magazine 1969–86 (prodn ed 1967–69), concurrently ed Hair Magazine (bi-annual then quarterly); managing ed Practical Parenting, Practical Health and Practical Hair & Beauty 1986–87; sole ed Hello! 1993– (jt ed 1988–93); awards for Hello!: Consumer Magazine of the Year PPA and Media Week 1990, Magazine of the Year Br Press Circulation Awards 1991, Editors of the Year for gen interest magazine Br Soc of Magazine Editors 1991, Consumer Magazine of the Year Media Week 1992; *Books* Beauty Care (1981); *Recreations* work; *Style—* Ms Maggie Koumi; ✉ Hello!, Wellington House, 69–71 Upper Ground, London SE1 9PQ (☎ 0171 334 7404, fax 0171 334 7412)

KOVACEVICH, Stephen; s of Nicholas Kovacevich, and Loretta, *née* Zuban; *b* 17 Oct 1940; *Educ* Berkeley HS California; *Career* concert pianist and conductor; studied with Dame Myra Hess, worldwide concert tours, Kimber Award California 1959, Hertz Scholar 1959–61, Mozart Prize London 1962, Edison Award for Bartok Piano Concerto no 2, Gramophone Award and Stereo Review Record of the Year for Brahms Piano Concerto no 1 (with London Philharmonic/Wolfgang Sawallisch) 1993; int chair piano studies RAM; exclusive recording contract with EMI 1991–; *Books* Schubert Anthology; *Recreations* tennis, films, chess, Indian food; *Style—* Stephen Kovacevich, Esq; ✉ c/o Van Walsum Management, 26 Wadham Road, London SW15 2LR (☎ 0181 874 6344, fax 0181 877 0077)

KOVAR, Dr Ilya Zdenek; s of Victor Kovar (d 1971), and Nina, *née* Klein; *b* 17 March 1947; *Educ* Sydney Boys' HS Aust, Univ of Sydney (MB BS); *m* 29 Dec 1974, Cynthia Rose, da of Norbert Sencier; 3 s (Simon b 10 Oct 1976, Benjamin b 23 March 1979, David b 31 May 1984), 1 da (Sarah b 5 Aug 1981); *Career* formerly sr lectr in child health at Charing Cross and Westminster Schs and conslt paediatrician Charing Cross Hosp London, currently conslt in paediatrics and perinatal med Chelsea and Westminster Hosp and Charing Cross Hosp London; author of med, scientific, clinical articles and med texts; MCPCH, FRCP, FRCPC, FAAP, DRCOG; *Books* Textbook for DCH (1984, 1991), Make it Better (1982); *Recreations* riding, reading, music; *Style—* Dr Ilya Kovar; ✉ Neonatal Unit, Chelsea and Westminster Hospital, London SW10 9NH (☎ 0181 846 7195, fax 0181 846 7998)

KOWALSKI, Gregor; s of Mieczeslaw Kowalski (d 1986), and Jeannie Hutcheson, *née* MacDonald; *b* 7 Oct 1949; *Educ* Airdrie Acad, Univ of Strathclyde (LLB); *m* 4 July 1974, Janet McFarlane, da of Andrew McWilliam Pillatt (d 1976); 2 s (Gavin Gregor b 1978, Giles McFarlane b 1980); *Career* asst slr Levy and McRae Glasgow 1973–74 (legal apprentice 1971–73), depute procurator fiscal Glasgow 1974–78; Lord Advocate's Dept London: asst then dep Parly draftsman for Scotland 1978–87, seconded legal draftsman Govt of Seychelles 1982–83, Scottish Parly Counsel 1987–; memb Law Soc of Scotland 1973, fndr sec Soc of Scottish Lawyers in London 1987 (pres 1991–92); *Recreations* music, singing; *Style—* Gregor Kowalski, Esq; ✉ Lord Advocate's Chambers, 2 Carlton Gardens, London SW1Y 5AA (☎ 0171 210 1010)

KRAEMER, (Thomas Wilhelm) Nicholas; s of Dr William Paul Kraemer (d 1982), of London, and Helen, *née* Bartrum; *b* 7 March 1945; *Educ* Lancing, Dartington Coll of Arts, Univ of Nottingham (BMus, ARCM), Guildhall Sch of Music; *m* 22 April 1984, Elizabeth Mary, da of John Anderson; 3 s (Dominic b 1988, Matthew b and d 1990, Daniel b 1991), 2 da (Emma b 1986, Chlöe b 1993); *Career* harpsichordist: Monteverdi Orchestra and English Baroque Soloists 1970–80, Acad of St Martin in the Fields 1972–80; musical dir: Unicorn Opera Abingdon 1971–75, West Eleven Children's Opera 1971–88; fndr and dir Raglan Baroque Players 1978–, musical dir Opera 80 1980–83, princ conductor Divertimenti 1980–, assoc conductor BBC Scottish Symphony Orchestra 1983–85, princ conductor Manchester Camerata 1992–95 (princ guest conductor 1995–); artistic dir: London Bach Orchestra 1985–93, Irish Chamber Orch 1985–90, prog dir Bath Festival 1994; memb Royal Soc of Musicians; *Recreations* swimming, active fatherhood; *Style*— Nicholas Kraemer, Esq; ✉ c/o Ron Gonsalves, 7 Old Town, Clapham SW4 0JT (☎ 0171 622 2244, fax 0171 622 2288)

KRAMER, Louis Deyong; s of Hyman J Kramer (d 1988), of London, and Priscilla Sarah, *née* Deyong (d 1960); *b* 13 July 1926; *Educ* King George V GS Southport, Univ of Liverpool (BDS, MGDS, LDS RCS, Basketball blue); *m* 9 Jan 1951, Anita, *née* Ross; 1 da (Judith b 15 Jan 1954), 1 s (David Ross b 21 April 1957); *Career* house offr Liverpool Dental Hosp 1950–51; Nat Serv Capt RADC 1951–53; in gen dental practice 1953–; pt/t community dental serv Liverpool 1953–58, sr hosp dental offr Liverpool Dental Hosp 1958–64, pt/t lectr Dept of Restorative Dentistry Univ of Liverpool Sch of Dentistry 1964–88, dean of postgraduate dental educn Univ of Liverpool 1985–92, pt/t advsr to Mersey RHA 1985–92; memb GDC 1984–; chm Southport and Dist Local Dental Ctee (vice chm Liaison Ctee of Local Dental Ctees), memb Nuffield Ctee (An Enquiry into Dental Educn) 1980; memb: BDA 1950 (pres W Lancs, W Cheshire and N Wales Branch 1973–74, life memb by election 1992), Liverpool and Dist Odontological Soc 1951 (pres 1980–81), Br Soc of Restorative Dentistry 1975 (pres 1991–92); *Recreations* skiing, walking; *Clubs* RSM; *Style*— Louis D Kramer, Esq; ✉ 21 Albert Road, Southport, Merseyside PR9 0LF (☎ and fax 01704 533603 and 01704 549927, mobile 0860 905454)

KRAMER, Stephen Ernest; QC (1995); s of Frederic Kramer, of Peterborough, and Lotte Karoline, *née* Wertheimer; *b* 12 Sept 1947; *Educ* Hampton GS, Keble Coll Oxford (Open exhibitioner, MA), Coll of Law, Université de Nancy; *m* 12 March 1978, Miriam, da of Siegfried Leopold (d 1992), and Charlotte Leopold; 1 da (Joanna Louise b 13 Sept 1981), 1 s (Robert Paul b 13 Oct 1982); *Career* called to the Bar Gray's Inn 1970, standing counsel (Crime) Customs and Excise SE Circuit 1989–95, recorder of the Crown Court 1991– (asst recorder 1987–91); memb: Bar Cncl 1993–95, Ctee Criminal Bar Assoc 1993–; Parly candidate (Lib) Twickenham 1974 (both elections); *Recreations* theatre, music, swimming, walking; *Style*— Stephen Kramer, Esq, QC; ✉ 1 Hare Court, Ground Floor, Temple, London EC4Y 7BE (☎ 0171 353 5324, fax 0171 353 0667)

KREBS, Prof John Richard; s of Sir Hans Krebs (d 1981), of Oxford, and Margaret Cicely, *née* Fieldhouse (d 1993); *b* 11 April 1945; *Educ* City of Oxford HS, Pembroke Coll Oxford (MA, DPhil); *m* 3 Aug 1968, Katharine Anne, da of John Fullerton (d 1973), of Newport, Gwent; 2 da (Emma Helen b 1977, Georgina Clare b 1980); *Career* asst prof Inst of Animal Resource Ecology Univ of BC 1970–73, lectr in zoology Univ Coll N Wales Bangor 1973–75, fell Wolfson Coll Oxford 1975–81, lectr in zoology Edward Grey Inst Oxford 1975–88 (demonstrator in ornithology 1970), Royal Soc res prof and fell Pembroke Coll 1988– (EP Abraham fell 1981–88), chief exec Natural Environment Research Cncl 1994–; sr scientific conslt AFRC 1991–94; memb: Max Planck Soc 1985–, AFRC 1988–94, Cncl Zoological Soc of London 1991–92, Acadamea Europaea 1995; Hon DSc Sheffield 1993, Hon DSc Wales 1997; Zoological Soc of London Scientific Medal 1981, Linnaean Soc Bicentenary Medal 1983; FRS 1984; *Books* Behavioural Ecology (with N B Davies, 1978, 1984, 1991 and 1997), Introduction to Behavioural Ecology (with N B Davies, 1981, 1987 and 1993), Foraging Theory (with D W Stephens, 1986); *Recreations* running, violin, gardening, travel; *Style*— Prof John R Krebs, FRS; ✉ 11 Brookside, Oxford OX3 7PJ; NERC, Polaris House, Swindon SN2 1EU (☎ 01793 411599, fax 01793 411780)

KREINCZES, Gerald Michael; s of Maurice Kreinczes (d 1985), of London, and Alice, *née* Baker; *b* 28 Oct 1951; *Educ* Kingston GS, Univ of Lancaster (BA); *m* 1976, Catherine, da of Francis J Cronin (d 1993); 1 da (Nicola Catherine b 17 Aug 1985), 1 s (Christopher Gerald b 22 April 1988); *Career* graduate trainee AGB Market Research 1974–75, Findus Ltd 1975–79, dir/head of mktg Allen Brady & Marsh Ltd 1979–84, dir Mgmnt and Mktg Servs Publicis Ltd 1984–86, planning dir Dorlands 1986–89, exec planning dir Allen Brady & Marsh 1989–90, ptnr The Kreinczes Partnership 1990–92, exec planning dir Kevin Morley Marketing 1992–96, planning dir Lintas i 1996, strategic planning dir Ammirati Puris Lintas 1996–; memb Mktg Soc, MCIM; *Recreations* sailing, music, reading; *Style*— Gerald Kreinczes, Esq; ✉ Ammirati Puris Lintas, 84 Eccleston Square, Victoria, London SW1V 1PX (☎ 0171 932 8888)

KRIEGER, Ian Stephen; s of Sid Krieger, and Raie, *née* Dight; *b* 2 Feb 1952; *Educ* Christ's Coll Finchley, Univ of Kent (BA); *m* Caron Meryl, *née* Gluckstein; 3 s (James Michael b 1990, Elliott Charles b 1992, Ben Scott b 1995); *Career* Arthur Andersen: articled clerk 1973–76, CA 1976, ptnr 1985–; FCA 1981; *Books* Management Buy-Outs (1990); *Style*— Ian Krieger, Esq; ✉ Arthur Andersen, 1 Surrey Street, London WC2R 2PS (☎ 0171 438 3000, fax 0171 438 2100)

KRIKLER, Dennis Michael; s of Barnet Krikler (d 1992), and Eva Krikler (d 1986); *b* 10 Dec 1928; *Educ* Muizenberg HS, Univ of Cape Town SA (MB ChB); *m* 3 July 1955, Anne, da of August Winterstein; 1 da (Shirley Jean b 1957), 1 s (Paul Alan b 1961); *Career* fell Lahey Clinic Boston 1956, C J Adams Meml Travelling Fell 1956, sr registrar Groote Schuur Hosp 1957–58 (house physician and registrar 1952–55); conslt physician: Salisbury Central Hosp Rhodesia 1958–66, Prince of Wales Hosp London 1966–73; conslt cardiologist Hammersmith and Ealing Hosps 1973–94, sr lectr in cardiology Royal Postgrad Med Sch 1973–94, ed expert clinicien en cardiologie Ministère des Affaires Sociales Santé France 1983, int lectr American Heart Assoc 1984 (Paul Dudley White Citation for int achievement); visiting prof: Baylor Univ, Indiana Univ and Univ of Birmingham 1985, Boston, Kentucky, and UCLA 1988; Joseph Welker lectr Univ of Kansas, George Burch lectr Association of Univ Cardiologists USA 1989, Henri Denolin lectr Euro Soc of Cardiology, Hideo Ueda lectr Japan Soc of Electrocardiology 1990, visiting prof Univ of Minnesota and H B Burchell lectr 1991; author of papers on cardiology in nat and int jls; ed British Heart Journal 1981–91; memb Editorial Ctee: Cardiovascular Res 1975–91, Archives des Maladies du Coeur et des Vaisseaux 1980–; hon memb: Soc di Cultura Medica Vercellese Italy, Soc de Cardiologia de Levante Spain, Soc Francaise de Cardiologie 1981–; memb Scientific Cncl Revista Portuguese de Cardiologia 1982–, hon fell Cncl on Clinical Cardiology American Heart Assoc 1984; McCullough prize 1949, Sir William Osler Award Miami Univ 1981, medal of honour Euro Soc of Cardiology; Freeman: Worshipful Soc of Apothecaries 1989, City of London 1990; memb Br Cardiac Soc 1971 (Silver medal 1991), FACC 1971, MD 1973, FRCPE 1970, FRCP 1973; *Books* Cardiac Arrhythmias (with J F Goodwin, 1975), Calcium Antagonism in Cardiovascular Therapy (with A Zanchetti, 1981), Amiodarone and Arrhythmias (with D A Chamberlain and W J McKenna, 1983), Workshop on Calcium Antagonists (with P G Hugenholtz, 1984); *Recreations* photography, history; *Style*— Dennis Krikler, Esq; ✉ 55 Wimpole St, London W1M 7DF (☎ 0171 935 2098, fax 0171 486 1542)

KRIKLER, His Hon Judge; Leonard Gideon; s of Maj J H Krikler, OBE, ED (d 1971), of St Brelade Jersey CI, and Tilly Krikler (d 1974); *b* 23 May 1929; *Educ* Milton Sch Bulawayo S Rhodesia; *m* 1955, Thilla (d 1973); m 2, 1975, Lily; 6 s, 2 da; *Career* Crown counsel Cts Martial Appeals Ct 1968, dep circuit judge 1974–80, head of chambers London and Cambridge 1974–84, recorder of the Crown Ct 1980–84, circuit judge (SE Circuit) 1984–; *Recreations* drawing, painting; *Style*— His Hon Judge Krikler; ✉ Lamb Building, Temple, London EC4Y 7AS (☎ 0171 797 7788)

KRIWACZEK, Paul; Oscar Kriwaczek (d 1960), and Alice Lunzer (d 1990); *b* 30 Nov 1937; *Educ* Kilburn GS, London Hospital Med Coll (BDS, LDS); *m* 29 Jan 1966, Jeannette Ann, da of Leslie Donald Parsons, of Timbarra, Neals Lane, Chetnole, Dorset; 2 s (Rohan b 1968, Tamor b 1972), 1 da (Nandi b 1974); *Career* prodr/dir BBC TV: Ancestral Voices (David Munrow) 1975, BBC Computer Literacy Project (RTS prize) 1980, Bellamy's Backyard Safari (BAAS prize) 1982, Orchestra with Jane Glover 1984, Mozart with Jane Glover 1986, Where on Earth Are We Going (with Jonathon Porritt, Shell-Cawston award) 1989; writer/prodr: Imagina (Chicago Film Festival award) 1989, The Well 1989, The Last Exodus (New York Festival gold award) 1990, Living Islam 1993; exec prodr BBC TV 1987–93; AIEE 1988, FRSA 1993; *Style*— Paul Kriwaczek, Esq; ✉ 12 Wessex Gardens, London NW11 9RT (☎ 0181 201 8810)

KROLL, Natasha; da of Dr Hermann Kroll, and Sophie, *née* Rabinovich; *b* 20 May 1914, Moscow; *Educ* Berlin HS; *Career* TV and film designer; teacher of window display Reimann Sch of Art London 1936–40; display mangr: Rowntrees of York 1940–42, Simpsons of Piccadilly 1942–55; sr designer BBC TV 1955–66, freelance 1966–; RDI, FSIAD; *Recreations* painting, entertaining; *Style*— Ms Natasha Kroll, RDI; ✉ 5 Ruvigny Gardens, London SW15 1JR

KROLL, Dr Una Margaret Patricia (Sister Una CJC); da of Brig George Arthur Hill, CB, DSO, MC (d 1970), and Hilda Evelyn Hill, *née* Pediani (d 1965); *b* 15 Dec 1925; *Educ* Malvern Girls' Coll, Univ of Cambridge (MA, MB BChir); *m* 1957, Leopold Kroll, s of Bishop Leopold Kroll (d 1949), of New York; 1 s (Leopold), 3 da (Florence, Elisabeth, Una); *Career* medical practitioner Missionary Serv in Liberia and Namibia 1953–61, GP (England) 1961–81, community health doctor 1981–88; deaconess (C of E) 1970–88; memb: Christian Medical Cmmn 1978–85, CRAC (Churches Religious Advsy Cncl to BBC) 1980–85, Gen Synod of C of E (diocese of Chichester) 1980–87; deacon Church in Wales Dec 1988; *Books* A Signpost to the World (1975), Flesh of my Flesh (1976), Lament for a Lost Enemy (1978), Sexual Counselling (1980), A Spiritual Exercise Book (1985), Growing Older (1988), In Touch with Healing (1991), Vocation to Resistance (1995); *Style*— Sister Una Kroll, CJC; ✉ St Mary's Lodge, Priory Street, Monmouth, Gwent NP5 3BR

KROMBERG, Peter Heinz; s of Heinz Kromberg (d 1941), and Hilde, *née* Fuerst; *b* 29 Dec 1940; *m* 25 March 1972, Nicole, da of Simone Baldini; 2 s (Olivier, Jean-Pierre); *Career* chef's apprenticeship Hotel Duisburger Hof Germany 1955–58, seasonal jobs in leading hotels in Switzerland and Bavaria 1958–63, chef de partie gardemanger Athens Hilton 1963–66; exec chef: Siam Inter-Continental Hotel Bangkok 1966–70, Portman Inter-Continental London 1971–75; Hotel Inter-Continental London: exec chef 1975–, chef patron Le Soufflé Restaurant 1994– (Restaurant of the Year (Egon Ronay Guides) 1994); *Awards* Apprentice of the Year 1958, Gold Medal with Distinction Cookery Olympics Germany 1972 and 1976, Chef of the Year Award (CATEY) 1987, Banqueting Menu of the Year Award (CATEY) 1992, Hotel and Restaurant Chef of the Year (Craft Guild of Chefs) 1994; selected as guest chef on TV series Take Six Chefs; memb: Académie Culinaire of GB, Assoc Internationale Des Maîtres Conseils on Gastronome Francaise, Guild Des Fromagers; hon memb Restaurateurs Assoc of GB, hon int pres Toques Blanches; *Recreations* gardening, skiing, cycling and swimming; *Clubs* Club 9; *Style*— Peter Kromberg, Esq; ✉ Hotel Inter-Continental London, One Hamilton Place, London W1V 0QY (☎ 0171 409 3131 ext 79256 or 0171 493 9502, fax 0171 493 3476)

KROTO, Prof Sir Harold Walter (Harry); kt (1996); *b* 7 Oct 1939; *Educ* Bolton Sch, Univ of Sheffield (BSc, PhD); *Career* post doctoral fell NRC Ottawa 1964–66, memb tech staff Bell Telephone Laboratories 1966–67; Univ of Sussex: tutorial fell 1967–68, lectr 1968–78, reader 1978–85, prof 1985–91, Royal Soc research prof 1991–; Tilden lectr 1981–82; visiting prof: USC 1981, UCLA 1988–93; visiting scientist NRC Ottawa 1976 and 1978; memb Ed Bd: Chemical Soc Reviews 1986–, Zeitschrift für Physik D 1992–, Carbon 1992–; memb Academia Europaea 1992; chm Vega Science Tst; author of 250 research papers in scientific jls and numerous pubns; FRS 1990; *Awards* Int Prize for New Materials American Physical Soc 1992, Italgas Prize for Innovation in Chemistry 1992, Longstaff Medal RSC 1993, Hewlett Packard Europhysics Prize 1994, Moet Hennessy/Louis Vuitton Prize 1994, jt winner Nobel Prize for Chemistry 1996; *Style*— Prof Sir Harry Kroto, FRS; ✉ School of Chemistry, Physics and Environmental Science, University of Sussex, Brighton BN1 9QJ (☎ 01273 678329, fax 01273 677196)

KRUSIN, Sir Stanley Marks; kt (1973), CB (1963); *b* 8 June 1908; *Educ* St Paul's Sch, Balliol Coll Oxford; *m* 1, 1937 (w d 1972); 1 s, 1 da; m 2, 1976 (w d 1988); *Career* served WWII RAFVR; called to the Bar Middle Temple 1932, Parly counsel 1953–69, second Parly counsel 1970–73; Liveryman Worshipful Co of Musicians; *Style*— Sir Stanley Krusin, CB; ✉ 5 Coleridge Walk, London NW11 6AT (☎ 0181 458 1340)

KRUT, Ansel Jonathan; s of Dr Louis Harold Krut, and Rhoda, *née* Robinson; *b* 19 March 1959; *Educ* Witwatersrand Univ SA (BA), RCA (MA); *Career* artist; Cité International des Arts Paris 1982–83, Rome prize Br Sch Rome 1986–87, subsequently lived and worked in Rome 1987–90, returned London 1990; *Exhibitions* Fischer Fine Art London (one man) 1989 and 1990, Gillian Jason Gallery London (one man) 1994, Royal Acad Summer Show 1985, John Moores 14 Liverpool 1985, 12 British Artists (Kunstlerhaus Vienna) 1986, The Human Touch (Fischer Fine Art London) 1986, Artists at the Br Sch at Rome (Rome) 1987, The Self Portrait (Bath and touring) 1988, 3 Ways (Budapest and touring Eastern Europe) 1989, 10 Years of the Br Sch at Rome (RCA London) 1990, The Discerning Eye (Mall Galleries London) 1991, A View of the New (Royal Over-Seas League London) 1991, 20th Century British Art Fair (London) 1992, Contemporary Portraits, Real and Imagined (Gillian Jason Gallery) 1993, Jason and Rhodes Gallery (one man) 1996; work in public collections: Arts Cncl of GB, Br Cncl London, Contemporary Art Soc London, Johannesburg Art Gallery, Govt Art Collection London; *Style*— Ansel Krut, Esq; ✉ The Harris Museum and Art Gallery, Preston, Lancs; Mercer Art Gallery, Harrogate; Jason and Rhodes Gallery, 4 New Burlington Place, London W1X 1FB (☎ 0171 434 1768)

KUDIAN, Mischa; *Career* writer, ed, poet, lectr, painter, specialist trans of Armenian literature, and children's fiction writer; *Publications* trans: Scenes from an Armenian Childhood by Vahan Totovents (1962, 2 ed 1980), Selected Works by Avetik Issahakian (1976), Komitas, the Shepherd of Songs by Levon Miridjanian (1983) The Tailor's Visitors by Shahan Shahnour (1984), Jesus the Son by Nerses Shnorhali (1986), Anoush and Gikor by Hovannes Toumanian (1994); ed and trans: The Bard of Loree by Hovannes Toumanian (1970), Tell Me, Bella by Vahan Totovents (1972), Soviet Armenian Poetry (1974), The Muse of Sheerak by Avetik Issahakian (1975), Lamentations of Narek by Grigor Narekatsi (1977, 2nd edn 1992), Honourable Beggars by Hagop Baronian (1978), Retreat Without Song by Shahan Shahnour (1982), Jonathan Son of Jeremiah by Vahan Totovents (1985), Balthazar by Hagop Baronian (1992), The Pigeon Fancier by Vahan Totovents (1992), The Apricot Tree by Vahan Totovents (1994); ed and reteller: The Saga of Sassoun by Mischa Kudian (1970), The Epic of Sassoun by Mischa Kudian (1995); poetry: Candy Floss (1980), Flutterby (1984), This

Day and Age (1984), Tenpence a Laugh (1984), Witricks Galore! (1984); books: Three Apples Fell from Heaven (1969, 2 edn 1994), More Apples Fell from Heaven (1982), The Last Laugh (1993), Such Sweet Revenge (1995); *Style—* Mischa Kudian, Esq; ✉ c/o Barclays Bank, 15 Langham Place, London W1A 4NX

KUENSSBERG, Nicholas (Nick); s of Dr Ekkehard Von Kuenssberg, CBE, and Constance, *née* Hardy; *b* 28 Oct 1942; *Educ* Edinburgh Acad, Wadham Coll Oxford (BA); *m* 27 Nov 1965, Sally, da of Hon Lord Robertson (Lord of Session); 1 s (David b 1971), 2 da (Joanna b 1973, Laura b 1976); *Career* worked in Europe and Latin America 1965–78, chm Dynacast International Ltd 1978–91; dir: J & P Coats Ltd 1978–91, West of Scotland Bd Bank of Scotland 1984–88, Scottish Power Plc (formerly South of Scotland Electricity Bd) 1984–, Coats Patons Plc 1985–91, Coats Viyella Plc 1986–91, Standard Life Assurance Co 1988–; md: Dawson International Plc 1994–95 (dir 1991–), Baxi Partnership Ltd 1996–, Stoddard Seckers Int plc 1996–; chm: David A Hall Ltd 1996–, Assoc of Mgmnt Educn & Trg in Scotland 1996–; memb: Scottish Legal Aid Bd 1996–, Advsy Gp to sec of State on Sustainable Devpt 1996–; visiting prof Strathclyde Business Sch 1988–91 (visiting fell 1986–87), govr Queen's Coll Glasgow 1989–91; FCIS 1977, CIMgt 1989, FRSA 1993; *Recreations* travel, languages, opera, sport; *Clubs* New (Edinburgh); *Style—* Nick Kuenssberg, Esq; ✉ 6 Cleveden Drive, Glasgow G12 0SE (☎ 0141 339 8345, fax 0141 334 9730)

KUHLMANN, Kathleen; *b* San Franciso; *Educ* Lyric Opera Sch Chicago; *Career* mezzo soprano, specialises in coloratura repertoire; *Performances* Rossini operatic roles: Arsace in Semiramide (Parma 1985, subsequently Bilbao, Naples, Vienna, Bonn, Toulouse, Munich Opera Festival 1990), Angelina in La Cenerentola (Glyndebourne, Cologne, Stuttgart, Semperoper Dresden debut 1992, Teatro Liceu Barcelona debut 1992), Rosina in Il Barbiere di Siviglia (San Francisco, Chicago, Covent Garden, Vienna, Hamburg, Düsseldorf, Cologne, Parma, Bilbao, Miami), Isabella in L'Italiana in Algeri (Pisa, Cologne, Berlin), Falliero in Bianca e Falliero (Miami), Andromaca in Ermione (Naples, San Francisco), title role in Tancredi (Wexford Festival, Berlin), Malcolm in La Donna del Lago (Parma 1989, Concertgebouw Amsterdam debut 1992); Handel operatic roles: Bradamante in Alcina (Covent Garden, Geneva, Paris), Ino/Juno in Semele (Covent Garden, Festival d'Aix-en-Provence), Cornelia in Giulio Cesare (Bavarian State Opera 1994), Amastris in Xerxes (Chicago Lyric Opera, Bavarian State Opera, Cologne Opera); other operatic roles incl: title role in Carmen (Chicago, Sydney, Montreal, Tel Aviv, Cologne, Hamburg, Naples, Vienna, Covent Garden, San Francisco), Charlotte in Werther (Met Opera NY debut 1989, Hamburg State Opera, Cologne Opera), Penelope in Il Ritorno d'Ulisse in Patria (world premiere of Hans Werner Henze's orchestration at Salzburg Festival, Cologne Opera), Orfeo in Orfeo ed Eurydice (Scottish Opera, Cologne, Parma for which won Italian Critics Award 1988), Messagero/Ninfa/Proserpina in Orfeo (Holland Festival debut 1993), Ottavia in L'Incoronazione di Poppea (Schwetzingen Festival 1993, Cologne 1994); concert and recital work incl: appeared at Rossini Gala (on bicentenary of his birth) Avery Fisher Hall NY 1992, Malcolm aria from Rossini La Donna del Lago at Concert of Nations Red Square Moscow 1992, other Rossini works at Seville, BBC Proms and Purcell Room London 1992, Mozart Requiem (with Eng Chamber Orch) and Coronation Mass (with The Philharmonia), Romeo et Juliette (Radio France), Le Nozze di Teti e di Peleo (Rossini Opera Festival), The Dream of Gerontius (Dublin, London), Beethoven 9th Symphony (Zurich Tonhalle and BBC Proms under Tennstedt), Beethoven Missa Solemnis (Essen), Bach B minor Mass (ECO London), Bach St Matthew Passion (Zurich) and St John Passion (Holland); *Recordings* numerous audio for EMI, BMG and Decca; video recordings incl: La Cenerentola (Glyndebourne), Il Ritorno d'Ulisse in Patria (Salzburg Festival), Vivaldi Orlando Furioso (San Francisco Opera), Il Coronazione di Poppea (Schwetzingen Festival); *Style—* Ms Kathleen Kuhlmann; ✉ c/o Haydn Rawstron (UK) Ltd, 36 Station Road, London SE20 7BQ (☎ 0181 659 2659, fax 0181 676 9119), e-mail haydn@dial.pipex.com)

KÜHNL, HE Dr Karel; *b* 12 Sept 1954; *Educ* Charles Univ Prague (LLD), Vienna Univ; *m* 1983, Daniela Magdalena, *née* Kusin; 1 da (Caroline Daniela b 1984), 1 s (Thomas Gabriel b 1988); *Career* Czech diplomat; freelance journalist and analyst E European affairs Vienna Univ 1980–86, ed and analyst E European affairs Radio Free Europe Munich 1986–93 (incl unpaid leave as chief advsr to the PM of the Czech Republic Prague 1991–92 and as advsr to the Czech Min for Economy Prague 1992), ambass of the Czech Republic to the Ct of St James's 1993–; lectr Law Faculty Charles Univ Prague 1991–, memb Bd Czech TV 1992–93; author of various pubns on Czechoslovak and E European affairs; *Style—* HE Dr Karel Kühnl; ✉ Embassy of the Czech Republic, 26 Kensington Palace Gardens, London W8 4QY (☎ 0171 234 1115, fax 0171 727 9654)

KUHRT, Ven Gordon Wilfred; s of Wilfred Nicholas Henry Kuhrt, and Doris Adeline, *née* Goddard; *b* 15 Feb 1941; *Educ* Colfe's GS, Univ of London (BD), Oakhill Theol Coll; *m* 31 Aug 1963, Olive Margaret, da of Raymond Frank Alexander Powell; 3 s (Martin b 1966, Stephen b 1969, Jonathan b 1972); *Career* religious educn teacher 1963–65, vicar Shenstone Dio of Lichfield 1973–79, vicar Emmanuel Croydon Dio of Southwark 1979–89, rural dean Croydon Central 1981–86, hon canon Southwark Cathedral 1987–89, biblical studies lectr Univ of London 1984–89, memb Gen Synod C of E 1986–96, archdeacon Lewisham Dio of Southwark 1989–96, chief sec Advsy Bd for Ministry 1996–; *Books* Handbook for Council and Committee Members (1985), Believing in Baptism (1987), The Church and its Unity (contrib, 1992), Doctrine Matters (ed, 1993), Growing in Newness of Life - Christian Initiation in Anglicanism Today (contrib, 1993), To Proclaim Afresh (ed, 1995); *Style—* The Ven Gordon Kuhrt; ✉ Church House, Great Smith Street, London SW1P 3NZ (☎ 0171 222 9011, fax 0171 799 2714)

KULUKUNDIS, Sir Eddie; OBE; s of George Elias Kulukundis (d 1978), and Eugenia, *née* Diacakis (d 1993); 5th generation shipping family; *b* 20 April 1932; *Educ* Collegiate Sch NYC NY, Salisbury Sch Salisbury Connecticut, Yale Univ; *m* 4 April 1981, Susan Hampshire, OBE (the actress), *qv*, da of George Kenneth Hampshire (d 1964); *Career* chm: Knightsbridge Theatrical Productions Ltd 1970–, Theatre Museum Association 1990–, London Coaching Fndn 1990–, Sport Aid Fndn 1988–93; vice chm Royal Shakespeare Theatre Tst 1984– (dir 1968); vice pres: Traverse Theatre Club, Greenwich Theatre Ltd 1988–; trustee: Salisbury Sch Connecticut 1983–, Sports Aid Fndn Trust 1987–, Theatre Trust 1976–April 1995; govr: Royal Shakespeare Theatre 1976–, The Raymond Mander & Joe Mitchenson Theatre Collection Ltd 1981–, Sports Aid Fndn 1977–; dir: Rethymnis & Kulukundis Ltd 1964–, Rethymnis & Kulukundis (Chartering) Ltd 1969–, London & Overseas Freighters plc 1980–85 and 1989–, Soc of London Theatre, Hampstead Theatre Ltd 1969–, Hampstead Theatre Trust 1969–; memb: Baltic Exchange 1959–, Lloyd's 1964–95 (memb Cncl 1983–89); FRSA; kt 1993; *Productions* London prodns incl (some jtly): Enemy 1969, The Happy Apple 1970, Poor Horace 1970, The Friends 1970, How the Other Half Loves 1970, Tea Party and the Basement (double bill) 1970, The Wild Duck 1970, After Haggerty 1971, Hamlet 1971, Charley's Aunt 1971, Straight Up 1971, London Assurance 1972, Journey's End 1972, Small Craft Warnings 1973, A Private Matter 1973, Dandy Dick 1973, The Waltz of the Toreadors 1974, Life Class 1974, Pygmalion 1974, Play Mas 1974, The Gentle Hook 1974, A Little Night Music 1975, Entertaining Mr Sloane 1975, The Gay Lord Quax 1975, What the Butler Saw 1975, Travesties 1975, Lies 1975, The Seagull 1975, A Month in the Country 1975, A Room with a View 1975, Too True to be Good 1975, The Bed Before Yesterday 1975, Dimetos 1976, Banana Ridge 1976, Wild Oats 1976, Candida 1977, Man and Superman 1977, Once a Catholic 1977, Privates on Parade 1978, Gloo Joo 1978, Bent 1979, Outside Edge 1979, Last of the Red Hot Lovers 1979, Beecham 1980, Born in the Gardens 1980, Tonight at 8.30 1981, Steaming 1981, Arms and the Man 1981, Steafel's Variations 1982, Messiah 1983, Pack of Lies 1983, Of Mice and Men 1984, The Secret Diary of Adrian Mole Aged 13–3/4 1984, Camille 1985, The Cocktail Party 1986, Curtains 1987, Separation 1989, South Pacific 1989, Married Love 1989, Over My Dead Body 1989, Never the Sinner 1990, King and I 1991, Carmen Jones 1991, Noel & Gertie 1992, Slip of the Tongue 1992, Shades 1992, Annie Get Your Gun 1992, Making it Better 1992, The Prime of Miss Jean Brodie 1994, The Killing of Sister George 1995; NY prodns (jtly): How the Other Half Loves, Sherlock Holmes, London Assurance, Travesties, The Merchant, Players, Once a Catholic; *Recreations* theatre, athletics; *Clubs* Garrick; *Style—* Sir Eddie Kulukundis, OBE; ✉ 21 New Fetter Lane, London EC4A 1JJ (☎ 0171 583 2266, fax 0171 583 1040)

KUMAR, Prof (Jagdish) Krishan; *b* 11 Aug 1942; *Educ* William Ellis Sch London, St John's Coll Cambridge (BA, MA), LSE (MSc); *Career* prodr Talks Dept BBC 1972–74, prof of social thought Univ of Kent 1987–96 (lectr in sociology 1967–77, reader in sociology 1977–87), prof Dept of Sociology Univ of Virgina USA 1996–; tstee Action Soc Tst; *Books* Prophecy and Progress (1978), Utopia and Anti-Utopia in Modern Times (1987), Rise of Modern Society (1988), Utopianism (1991), From Post-Industrial to Post-Modern Society (1995); *Style—* Prof Krishan Kumar; ✉ Department of Sociology, University of Virginia, 539 Cabell Hall, Charlottesville, VA 22903, USA

KUMAR, Dr Parveen June; da of Cyril Proshuno Fazal Kumar (d 1982), and Grace Nazira, *née* Faiz; *b* 1 June 1942; *Educ* Lawrence Sch Sanawar N India, Maida Vale HS, Bart's Med Coll (BSc, MD, FRCP, FRCPE); *m* Dr David G Leaver, s of Frances Joseph Leaver; 2 da (Rachel Nira b 28 March 1972, Susannah Kiran b 22 July 1974); *Career* house physician Bart's 1966–67, house surgn Royal Berks Hosp Reading 1968, res registrar in bacteriology Bart's 1968–69, house physician Royal Postgrad Med Sch 1969–70, registrar, sr registrar then lectr Bart's 1970–85, conslt physician St Leonard's and Hackney Hosps 1983, sr lectr in gastroenterology and hon conslt physician Bart's and Homerton Hosps (City and Hackney Health Authy) 1985–94; coll tutor RCP 1988–93, clinical tutor BPMF 1988–96, dir of postgraduate med educn Royal Hosps Tst 1993–96; currently: reader in gastroenterology and hon conslt physician Royal Hosps Tst, conslt physician Homerton Hosp, examiner MB BS, MRCP, MD and PhD, undergraduate sub-dean St Bart's & the Royal London Sch of Med and Dentistry, pro-censor RCP; author of published papers and lectr at home and abroad; memb: Br Soc of Gastroenterology, Br Soc of Immunology, Medicine's Cmmn; *Books* Gastrointestinal Radiology (jtly, 1981), Clincal Medicine (jtly 1987, 3 edn 1994); *Recreations* opera, skiing; *Style—* Dr Parveen Kumar; ✉ St Bartholomew's Hospital, West Smithfield, London EC1A 7BE (☎ 0171 982 6123)

KUNKLER, Dr Ian Hubert; s of Dr Peter Bertrand Kunkler, of Las Fuentes, Spain, and Pamela, *née* Hailey (d 1988); *b* 22 July 1951; *Educ* Clifton, Univ of Cambridge (BA, MA, MB BChir), St Bartholomew's Hosp London; *m* 18 July 1981, Dr (Alison) Jane Kunkler, da of late Ronald George Pearson, of Kenya; *Career* house offr Univ of Leicester Med Sch 1978–79, sr house offr in gen med Nottingham City Hosp 1979–81, sr registrar Western Gen Hosp Edinburgh 1984–88 (registrar 1981–83), EEC and French Govt clinical res fell Inst Gustave Roussy Paris 1986–87; conslt in radiotherapy and oncology: Sheffield 1988–92, Edinburgh 1992–; author of papers on bone scanning in breast cancer, radiotherapy in breast and laryngeal cancer and the value of clinic follow-up in cervical cancer; pres London Med Gp 1977, convener annual conference Pain - A Necessity? Charing Cross Med Sch; hon sec British Oncological Assoc 1993–95; memb BMA 1978, DMRTEd 1983, FRCR 1985, FRSM 1989, FRCPE 1994; *Books* Cambridge University Medical Journal (ed 1974), Walter and Miller's Textbook of Radiotherapy (jt author 5 edn, 1993); *Recreations* fly fishing; *Style—* Dr Ian Kunkler; ✉ Western General Hospital, Crewe Road, Edinburgh EH4 2XU (☎ 0131 537 2214, fax 0131 537 1029)

KUNZELMANN, C Dixon; s of Fabian W Kunzelmann, of Old Bennington, Vermont, USA, and Helen Dixon; *b* 19 Dec 1941; *Educ* St Paul's Sch Concord NH USA, Univ of Freiburg W Germany, Hobart Coll Geneva NY USA, Amos Tuck Hanover NH USA; *m* 3 Feb 1968, Joan, da of Rawson Atwood, of Rumson, NJ, USA; 1 s (Christopher Ely b 1970), 1 da (Laura Rawson b 1973); *Career* JP Morgan: joined 1965, sr vice pres Personnel London 1982–89, sr vice pres Securities Gp NYC 1989–90, sr vice pres Central Personnel NYC 1990–91, md Private Banking NYC 1991–93, md Global Asset Management London 1993–; tstee Hobart Coll NY 1990–, former pres American Friends of Georgian Gp 1989–94, vice chm America Rugby 2000 Appeal, non-exec dir Roxtons Sporting Agency Hungerford, chm Bowdoin Coll Parents' Ctee 1993–95; *Recreations* shooting, fishing, driving; *Clubs* Piscatorial Soc, Flyfishers', Annabel's, Queen's, Pilgrims, Guards' Polo, Links (NY), Union (NY), Adirondack League (NY); *Style—* C Dixon Kunzelmann, Esq; ✉ The Old School House, Fisherton de la Mere, Warminster, Wilts BA12 0PZ (☎ 01985 248264); 1220 Park Ave, New York City, NY 10128, USA (☎ 00 1 212 722 8409); Flat 4, 12 Chelsea Embankment, London SW3 4LE (☎ 0171 352 6333); J P Morgan Investment Management, 28 King Street, London SW1Y 6XA (☎ 0171 451 8630)

KUPER, Prof Adam Jonathan; s of Simon Meyer (d 1963), of Johannesburg, and Gertrude, *née* Hesselson (d 1987); *b* 29 Dec 1941; *Educ* Parktown Boys HS Johannesburg, Univ of the Witwatersrand Johannesburg (BA), King's Coll Cambridge (PhD); *m* 16 Dec 1966, Jessica Sue, da of Sidney Cohen (d 1986), of Johannesburg; 2 s (Simon b 1969, Jeremy b 1971), 1 da (Hannah b 1974); *Career* lectr in social anthropology Makerere Univ of Kampala Uganda 1967–70, lectr in anthropology UCL 1970–76, prof of African anthropology and sociology Univ of Leiden 1976–85, prof of social anthropology Brunel Univ 1985–; visiting appts: asst prof Univ of California 1969, planner Nat Planning Agency Office of PM Jamaica 1972, prof Univ of Gothenburg Sweden 1975; fell Centre for Advanced Study in the Behavioural Sci California 1980–81, memb Inst for Advanced Study Princeton 1994–95; chm Euro Assoc of Social Anthropologists 1989–90; hon doctorate Univ of Gothenburg 1978; memb Academia Europaea; *Books* Kalahari Village Politics (1970), Wives for Cattle: Bridewealth and Marriage in Southern Africa (1982), Anthropology and Anthropologists: The Modern British School (1983), South Africa and the Anthropologist (1987), The Invention of Primitive Society: Transformations of an Illusion (1988); Councils in Action (ed, 1971), The Social Anthropology of Radcliffe-Brown (ed, 1977), The Social Science Encyclopaedia (ed, 1985), Conceptualizing Society (ed, 1992), The Chosen Primate (1994); *Recreations* cricket; *Style—* Prof Adam Kuper; ✉ 16 Muswell Rd, Muswell Hill, London N10 2BG (☎ 0181 883 0400); Brunel University, Dept of Human Sciences, Uxbridge, Middx UB8 3PH (☎ 01895 56461, fax 01895 32806, telex 261173 Brunel G)

KUPFERMANN, Jeannette Anne; da of Nathaniel Weitz (d 1988), and Eva Tarnofsky; *b* 28 March 1941; *Educ* Hendon Co GS, LSE (BA), Univ Coll London (MPhil); *m* 25 June 1964, Jacques H Kupfermann (d 1988), s of Elias Kupfermann (k ca 1940); 1 s (Elias Jonathan b 16 April 1965), 1 da (Mina Alexandra b 10 May 1967); *Career* res librarian Wenner-Gren Fndn Anthropological Res NY 1963–65, actress Woodstock Playhouse NY 1964–67, res asst Univ of London 1976–77; bdcasting 1972–; writer: Man and Myth (Radio 3, award for best radio documentary series 1976), An Introduction to Social Anthropology (1980); presenter and contrib LWT and Thames TV 1970–, panelist on Tomorrow's Child; tech advsr to film dirs: Fred Zinnemann (The Dybbuk) 1972, Barbra Streisand (Yentl) 1982; journalist: Woodstock Times 1965–67, Sunday Times 1984–88, Daily Telegraph 1987; TV critic and feature writer: Daily Mail 1984–, Sunday Times Magazine, You, She, New Woman, The Mail on Sunday; memb Br Bdcasting Press

Guild 1988; *Books* The Mistaken Body (1978), When The Crying's Done - A Journey Through Widowhood (1992); *Recreations* dancing (flamenco), gardening, walking, painting (water colours), studying cosmology; *Clubs* Chelsea Arts; *Style*— Ms Jeannette Kupfermann; ✉ Television Dept, Daily Mail, Northcliffe House, 2 Derry Street, London W8 5EE (☎ 0171 583 8000)

KURLAND, Dr Philip; s of Peter Kurland (d 1975), and Esther Kurland (d 1983); *b* 6 May 1935; *Educ* Strodes Fndn, Univ of London, Guy's Hospital; *m* Michele, da of William Dillon; 5 c (Nicola b 1963, Paul b 1965, Matthew b 1986, Edward b 1988, Thomas b 1988); *Career* dental surgn; private practice 1959–, contribs to learned jls; memb: Br Standards Inst, LDS Club; GDPA 1959, EUD 1970, LDSRCS, FInstD; *Books* Intravenous Techniques in Dentistry (1967); *Recreations* tennis; *Style*— Dr Philip Kurland; ✉ 79 Harley Street, London W1N 1DE (☎ 0171 631 4552)

KURLANSKY, Mervyn Henry; s of Joseph Kurlansky, of Johannesburg, SA, and Jean, *née* Isaacs; *b* 3 March 1936; *Educ* Highlands North HS Johannesburg, Central Sch of Arts London; *children* 2 da (Karen b 6 April 1962, Dana b 2 July 1965); m, Sept 1992, Karen Sofie Blincoe; *Career* graphic designer; freelance practice 1961–62, Planning Unit Knoll International 1962–67, freelance practice 1967–69, Crosby Fletcher Forbes 1969–72, fndr ptnr Pentagram Design Limited 1972–93, in practice Copenhagen 1994–; clients incl: Penguin Books 1967–80, Reuters 1972–90, Rank Xerox 1972, British Telecom (Prestel) 1977, Shiseido 1977 and 1988, Johnnie Walker 1980, ICI 1982, Barclaycard 1983, Faber & Faber 1983, Eureka! The Children's Museum 1987, Museum of Modern Art Oxford 1988, British Library 1988, Edinburgh Park 1991, The Image Bank Inc 1994, Golden Days in Copenhagen 1994; various int exhibitions; memb: Alliance Graphique Internationale; FCSD, FSTD, FRSAMD; *Awards* D&AD Silver 1972 and 1973, Brno Bronze 1978, New York Art Directors' Club Silver 1988, Japanese Package Design Cncl Gold 1988, first prize Anti-Violence worldwide poster campaign 1994, Danish IG Prize 1996; *Books* Ideas on Design (1968), Pentagram (1972), Watching My Name Go By (1974), Living By Design (1978), Pentagram: The Compendium (1994); *Recreations* horse riding, running, swimming, skiing, windsurfing, music; *Clubs* RAC; *Style*— Mervyn Kurlansky, Esq; ✉ Mervyn Kurlansky Design, Pilestraede 8, 1112 København K, Denmark (☎ 00 45 33 15 06 02, fax 00 45 33 93 54 45)

KUSHNER, Lindsey Joy; QC (1992); da of Harry Kushner, of Manchester, and Rita, *née* Alexander; *b* 16 April 1952; *Educ* Manchester HS for Girls, Univ of Liverpool (LLB); *m* 15 Aug 1976, David Norman Kaye; 1 s (Alexander Lewis b 8 Sept 1979), 1 da (Tamara Ruth b 21 July 1981); *Career* called to the Bar 1974, pupilled to Charles Bloom, QC, recorder 1993– (asst recorder 1989–93); legal chm: Medical Appeal Tbnl 1989–, Disablement Appeal Tbnl 1992–; memb Ethnic Minorities Advsy Ctee Judicial Studies Bd; *Recreations* cooking, cinema; *Style*— Miss Lindsey Kushner, QC; ✉ 28 St John Street, Manchester M3 4DJ (☎ 0161 834 8418)

KUT, David; s of Jakob Kut (d 1962), of London, and Frieda Sachs (d 1979); *b* 5 May 1922; *Educ* Adass Real Gymnasium of Berlin Germany, ORT Tech Sch Berlin, Northampton Poly London, Univ of London (BSc); *m* 2 Nov 1952, Seena, da of Itzak Assuschkewitz (d 1950), of London; 1 s (Steven Humphrey b 1959), 1 da (Deborah Helen b 1962); *Career* WWII Aux War Serv; draughtsman Benham and Sons (Engrs) Ltd 1943–46, jr engr Oscar Faber & Ptnrs Consulting Engrs 1946–49, sr engr Powell Duffryn Tech Servs Ltd 1949–54; David Kut and Ptnrs: fndr 1954, sr ptnr 1954–87, conslt 1988–; past chm Professional Affairs Sub Ctee Engrg Cncl Regnl Orgn Ctee London Central, former memb Guide Ctee Inst of Heating and Ventilating Engrs, past memb Engineering Assembly, hon sec Beli Uri Art Soc; CEng, MInstE, MConsE, FIMechE, FCIBS, FCIArb; Eur Ing; *Books* Heating and Hot Water Services in Buildings (1968), Warm Air Heating (1970), Applied Waste Recycling for Energy Conservation (with G Hare, 1981), District Heating and Cooling for Energy Conservation (with R E Diamant, 1981), Dictionary of Applied Energy Conservation (1982), Applied Solar Energy (with G Hare, 1983), Efficient Waste Management (with G Hare, 1989), Illustrated Encyclopaedia of Building Services (1992); *Recreations* graphology, chess, yoga, tropical fish, swimming; *Style*— Eur Ing David Kut; ✉ 5 Thornton Way, London NW11 6RY (☎ 0181 455 7018, fax 0181 731 6044); David Kut & Ptnrs, Rosebery House, Tottenham Lane, London N8 9BY (☎ 0181 348 5171/6, fax 0181 340 8926, telex 291347)

KUTAPAN, Nicola Annette; da of Peter Kutapan (d 1964), and Molly Grace, *née* Hawkins; *b* 21 April 1958; *Educ* Greycoat Hosp Sch; *children* 1 s (b 1995); *Career* 300 Group (all-pty campaign for more women in Parliament and public life): chair 1992–94, treas 1994–95; head of admin CPSA 1992–95, chair Opportunity 2000 Women's Advsy Panel 1993; Lab Pty: Parly candidate Solihull 1992, vice chair Holborn and St Pancras CLP, sec London Central Euroconstituency; London Borough of Camden: cncllr 1986–90, vice chair Planning Ctee and chair Planning Sub-Ctee, vice chair Employment Ctee, chair Public Control Sub-Ctee; dir Seven Dials Monument Co 1986–; dir Fitzrovia Trust 1989–92, govr St Joseph's Sch 1989–91; MInstD; *Style*— Miss Nicola Kutapan; ✉ 23 St George's Court, Garden Row, London SE1 6HD (☎ and fax 0171 401 8485)

KUYPERS, (Andreas) Neville; s of Andreas Kuypers (d 1982), of Liverpool, and Ellen Margaret, *née* Rodgers (d 1987); *b* 18 April 1934; *Educ* Quarry Bank GS Liverpool; *m* Isobel Jean, da of John Clark; 2 s (Timothy John b 3 Nov 1967, Matthew Yacine b 10 March 1971), 2 da (Andrea Jane b 10 March 1964, Nina Sophia b 3 Nov 1972); *Career* photographer; Nat Serv jr technician photographer RAF 1954–56; Elsam Mann and Cooper Ltd 1949–73 (apprentice rising to studio mangr and co dir), formed partnership C J Studios 1973–86, chm Neville Kuypers Photography Ltd 1990– (estab co 1986); memb Admissions and Qualifications Bd BIPP 1990–; awards from BIPP (NW region) incl: Industl award, Commercial award, Scientific award, numerous Merit awards; non-stipendiary minister United Reformed Church; FBIPP; *Style*— A Neville Kuypers; ✉ Neville Kuypers Photography Ltd, 93 New Chester Rd, New Ferry, Wirral, Merseyside L62 1AB (☎ 0151 645 0544, fax 0151 645 8531)

KVERNDAL, Simon Richard; s of Ole Sigvard Kverndal, of Colgates, Halstead, Kent, and Brenda, *née* Skinner; *b* 22 April 1958; *Educ* Haileybury, Sidney Sussex Coll Cambridge (MA); *Career* called to the Bar Middle Temple 1982, practising barr in commercial and maritime law 1983–; Liveryman Worshipful Co of Shipwrights 1983; *Recreations* real tennis, rackets, squash, wine tasting, opera, the Church of England; *Clubs* Hawks', Queen's, MCC; *Style*— Simon Kverndal, Esq; ✉ 48 Ebury St, London SW1W 0LU (☎ 0171 730 4274); Chambers of David Steel, QC, 4 Essex Court, Temple, London EC4Y 9AJ (☎ 0171 797 7970, fax 0171 353 0998, telex 8812528)

KYLE, Andy; *Career* picture ed: The Daily Mail until 1995, Mail on Sunday 1996–; *Style*— Andy Kyle, Esq; ✉ The Mail on Sunday, Northcliffe House, 2 Derry St, London W8 5TT (☎ 0171 938 7017, fax 0171 937 5560)

KYLE, James; CBE (1989); s of John Kyle (d 1978), of Brocklamont, Ballymena, N Ireland, and Dorothy Frances, *née* Skillen (d 1967); *b* 26 March 1925; *Educ* Ballymena Acad, Queen's Univ Belfast (MB BCh, MCh, DSc); *m* 31 July 1950, Dorothy Elizabeth, da of Alexander Galbraith (d 1945); 2 da (Frances b 1952, Maureen b 1956); *Career* lectr in surgery Univ of Liverpool 1957, sr lectr Univ of Aberdeen 1959, sr surgn Aberdeen Royal Infirmary; chm: Grampian Health Bd 1989–93, Raigmore Hosp NHS Tst Inverness 1993–; chm: BMA Rep Body 1984–87, Scot Ctee for Hosp Med Servs 1977–81, Scot Jt Conslts Ctee 1984–89; memb: Exec Int Soc of Surgery 1971–88, Surgical Research Soc 1972–74, Gen Med Cncl 1979–94, Cons Med Soc 1988–92; Burgess of Guild of the City of Aberdeen FRCS 1954, FRCSI 1954, FRCSEd 1964; *Books* Pye's Surgical Handicraft (1962), Peptic Ulceration (1960), Crohn's Disease (1972), Scientific Foundations of Surgery (1967); *Recreations* opera, amateur radio (callsign GM4CHX), philately; *Clubs* Royal Northern, University; *Style*— James Kyle, Esq, CBE; ✉ Grianan, 7 Fasaich, Gairloch, Ross and Cromarty IV21 2BD (☎ and fax 01445 712398); 25 Gordondale Court, Aberdeen, AB15 5GB (☎ 01224 636067); Raigmore Hospital NHS Trust, Old Perth Road, Inverness IV2 3UJ (☎ 01463 704000, fax 01463 711322)

KYLE, Dr Peter McLeod; s of late Andrew Brown Kyle, of Ravens Court, Thorntonhall, and late Janet, *née* McLeod; *b* 19 Aug 1951; *Educ* Glasgow HS, Univ of Glasgow (MB ChB); *m* 25 March 1982, Valerie Anne, da of late James Steele, of Mairi Lodge, Hamilton; 1 s (Alasdair McLeod b 23 Jan 1983), 2 da (Catriona Jane b 20 Dec 1984, Gillian Fiona b 16 Feb 1989); *Career* clinical dir of ophthalmology Southern Gen Hosp Glasgow 1993– (conslt 1982), memb Med Appeal Tbnl 1985–, hon clinical sr lectr Univ of Glasgow 1985 (lectr in ophthalmology 1980–84), ophthalmology convenor Royal Coll of Physicians and Surgns Glasgow; FRCS (Glasgow and Edinburgh), FRCOphth; *Books* Current Ophthalmic Surgery (1990); *Clubs* Glasgow Art, Golf House (Elie); *Style*— Dr Peter Kyle; ✉ 36 Sutherland Ave, Glasgow G41 4ES; The Stables, Earlsferry, Fife

KYLE, (James) Terence; s of James Kyle (d 1976), of Belfast, and Elizabeth, *née* Cinnamond; *b* 9 May 1946; *Educ* The Royal Belfast Acad Inst, Christ's Coll Cambridge (MA); *m* 17 May 1975, Diana, da of Duncan Sager Jackson, of Buxton; 1 s (Robin b 1984), 2 da (Susan b 1979, Alison b 1981); *Career* Linklaters & Paines: asst slr 1972–79, ptnr 1979–95, managing ptnr 1995–; memb City of London Slrs' Co 1979; memb Law Soc 1972; *Recreations* cricket, squash; *Style*— Terence Kyle, Esq; ✉ Linklaters & Paines, Barrington House, 59–67 Gresham St, London EC2Y 7JA (☎ 0171 606 7080, fax 0171 606 5113, telex 884349)

KYNOCH, George Alexander Bryson; MP (C) Kincardine and Deeside (majority 4,495); s of Gordon Kynoch, and late Nesta Kynoch; *b* 7 Oct 1946; *Educ* Glenalmond Coll, Univ of Bristol (BSc(MechEng)); *m* 2 Sept 1971, Dr Rosslyn Margaret McDevitt; 1 s, 1 da; *Career* plant engr ICI Silicones 1968–71; G & G Kynoch plc: joined 1971, fin dir 1975–77, jt md 1977–81, chief exec 1981–90, dir of restructured gp 1990–95; MP (C) Kincardine and Deeside 1992–; PPS to: Alastair Goodlad as Min of State at FO 1992–94, Gillian Shephard as Sec of State for Educn 1994–95; Parly under-sec of state Scottish Office 1995–; memb Scottish Affairs Select Ctee 1992–95; chm Scottish Woollen Publicity Cncl 1983–90, pres Scottish Woollen Indust 1990–91; memb Aberdeen and Dist Milk Mktg Bd 1988–92, chm Laurence J Smith Ltd 1989, dir Moray Badenoch and Strathspey Local Enterprise Co 1991–92; chm Moray Cons and Unionist Assoc 1990 (various offices 1980–92), vice chm Northern Area Scottish Cons and Unionist Assoc 1991; *Recreations* golf, skiing; *Style*— George Kynoch, Esq, MP; ✉ House of Commons, London SW1A 0AA

KYRIAKIDES, John; s of Vassos Kyriakides (d 1976), and Panayiota, *née* Varnava; *b* 13 June 1944; *Educ* Gymnasium Secdy Famagusta Cyprus, Norwood Tech Coll London (City & Guilds Radio Cert (Full Tech), Bd of Trade Radio Offr's Cert, 1st Marconi Marine Prize); *m* 1984, Helen, *née* Matheou; 2 da (Pamela b 1984, Liza b 1988), 1 s (Alexander b 1992); *Career* worked for BFBS Cyprus 1963, emigrated to UK 1964, served Br Merchant Navy 1968, served Greek Merchant Navy 1969–73, property developer 1974, applied for Greek community radio licence for London 1965 and 1974, chm Spectrum Radio Ltd 1985–, London Greek Radio and Spectrum International (London multi-ethnic radio station) granted licences 1989; *Style*— John Kyriakides, Esq; ✉ c/o Navarino, 102 Queensway, London W2 3RR (☎ 0171 229 2244, fax 0171 229 1909)

KYRLE POPE, Rear Adm Michael Donald; CB (1969), MBE (1945), DL (Hertfordshire 1983); s of Cdr Rowland Kyrle Cecil Pope, DSO, OBE, DL, RN (d 1976), of Ledbury, Herefordshire, and Agnes Jessie, *née* Macdonald (d 1968); bro of Sir Ernle Pope, KCB, *qv*; *b* 1 Oct 1916; *Educ* Wellington; *m* Angela Suzanne, da of Adm Sir Geoffrey Layton, GBE, KCMG, DSO (d 1964), of Rowland's Castle, Hants; 1 s (James), 1 da (Emma (*see* Jonathan Leigh)); *Career* joined RN 1934–70, Submarine Serv, HMS Vanguard 1946–47, Sr Naval Offr Persian Gulf 1962–64, Cdre Intelligence Def Intelligence Staff MOD 1965–67, Rear Adm COS to C-in-C Far East Singapore 1967–69; gen mangr Middle East Navigation Aids Serv (Bahrain) 1971–77, dir Jerusalem and East Mission Tst 1978–92; dean's administrator St Albans Cathedral 1977–80; *Recreations* country interests, sailing; *Clubs* Army & Navy; *Style*— Rear Adm Michael Kyrle Pope, CB, MBE, DL; ✉ Hopfields, Westmill, Buntingford, Herts SG9 9LB

KYTE, Peter Eric; QC (1996); s of Eric Frank Kyte (d 1980), and Cicely Evelyn Leslie, *née* Watts; *b* 8 May 1945; *Educ* Dragon Sch Oxford, Wellington, Trinity Hall Cambridge (MA Law); *m* 7 Oct 1969, Virginia Cameron, da of Athelstan Claud Muir Cornish-Bowden; 1 da (Atlanta Rose b 17 July 1975), 1 s (William Simon b 19 March 1980); *Career* mangr Charter Consolidated Ltd 1968–73, account exec Merrill Lynch New York 1973–74, called to the Bar Lincoln's Inn 1975, recorder 1991– (asst recorder 1988); memb Criminal Bar Assoc 1976; *Recreations* tennis, motorcycling, scuba diving, watching son and England perform on the sports field; *Clubs* Aura (Cambridge); *Style*— Peter Kyte, Esq, QC; ✉ Hollis/Whitemar Chambers, Queen Elizabeth Building, Temple, London EC4Y 9BS (☎ 0171 583 5766, fax 0171 353 0339)

KYTE, Thomas Peter (Tom); *b* 4 June 1947; *m* 1970, Lynn Dora Harding; 2 da, 1 s; *Career* HM Inland Revenue 1963–65, investment commentator Financial Times 1970–77 (statistician 1966–70), writer Questor column Daily Telegraph 1977–86, City ed The Independent 1987–88 (dep City ed 1986–87), dir Brunswick Public Relations 1988–; *Recreations* sports, literature, cooking; *Style*— Tom Kyte, Esq; ✉ Brunswick Public Relations, 15–17 Lincoln's Inn Fields, London WC2A 3ED (☎ 0171 404 5959, fax 0171 831 2823)

L

LA ROCHE, Anthony Philip; TD (1978); s of Philip La Roche (d 1988), and Ruby, *née* Peach; *b* 10 July 1944; *Educ* St George's Coll Weybridge Surrey; *m* 18 Sept 1965, Jane Elizabeth, da of Herbert Custerson; 2 da (Amy Jane b 1972, Sophie Elizabeth b 1979); *Career* TA 1962–82; md: Allen Harvey Ross Ltd 1976–81, Cater Allen Futures Ltd 1981–96; dir: Cater Allen Hldgs plc 1982–96, London Int Fin Futures Exchange 1984–; *Recreations* swimming, cycling, field sports; *Clubs* City of London; *Style*— Anthony La Roche, Esq, TD

LA TROBE-BATEMAN, Richard George Saumarez; s of John Saumarez La Trobe-Bateman (d 1996), of Sark, CI, and Margaret Jane, *née* Schmid; *b* 17 Oct 1938; *Educ* Westminster, St Martin's Sch of Art, RCA (MDesRCA); *m* 26 April 1969, Mary Elizabeth, da of Arthur Jolly, JP (d 1984), of Hove; 1 s (Will b 1973), 2 da (Emily b 1971, Alice b 1976); *Career* studied sculpture under Anthony Caro at St Martin's Sch of Art 1958–61, studied furniture under David Pye at RCA 1965–68; exhbns at UK Design Centre, Crafts Cncl, V & A, Br Craft Centre and Contemporary Applied Art and in Belgium, Holland, Denmark, Austria, France, USA and Japan; works in public collections incl: V & A, Crafts Cncl, Leeds City Art Collection, Tyne and Wear Art Collection (Shipley Art Gallery), Portsmouth Museum and Art Gallery, Craft Study Centre Bath, Contemporary Arts Soc; public footbridges in Britain (Cumbria & Essex) and Australia (SA); memb Crafts Cncl 1982–86 (work presented to HRH Prince of Wales by Craft Cncl 1984); prof of furniture San Diego State Univ USA 1986–87; *Clubs* Contemporary Applied Arts; *Style*— Richard La Trobe-Bateman, Esq; ✉ Elm House, Batcombe, Shepton Mallet, Somerset BA4 6AB (☎ 01749 850442)

LABOUCHERE, Sir George Peter; GBE (1965), KCMG (1955); s of Lt-Col Frank Anthony Labouchere (d 1948), of London; *b* 2 Dec 1905; *Educ* Charterhouse, La Sorbonne; *m* 1943, Rachel Katharine (d 1996), da of Hon Eustace Hamilton-Russell (d 1962, 6 s of 8 Viscount Boyne); *Career* FO 1929, cnsllr Nanking 1946, Buenos Aires 1948; min: Vienna 1950–53, Hungary 1953–55; ambass to: Belgium 1955–60, Spain 1960–66 (ret); former pres Shropshire branch CPRE; FRSA; *Recreations* shooting, fishing, oriental ceramics, modern art; *Clubs* Brooks's, Dilettante Soc; *Style*— Sir George Labouchere, GBE, KCMG; ✉ Dudmaston, Bridgnorth, Shropshire WV15 6QN (☎ 01746 780 351)

LABOVITCH, Carey Elizabeth (Mrs S Tesler); da of Neville Labovitch, LVO, MBE, and Sonia Deborah, *née* Barney; *b* 20 April 1960; *Educ* Lycée Français De Londres, St Paul's Girls' Sch London, St Hilda's Coll Oxford (MA); *m* 1990, S Tesler; *Career* magazine publisher 1980–; md The Cadogan Press Group Ltd 1980–91, with The Magazine Business Ltd; fndr publisher: Blitz Magazine 1980, The MDB Magazine Directory 1984, The HMV Christmas Magazine, The Guardian Impact Magazine, The International Press Directory 1992, The Magazine Business Weekly Report 1992, What Magazine and Newspaper Directory 1992; fndr IPD Int Press Awards 1993–; awards for publishing: Guardian Best Graphics Award 1981, Magazine Publishing Entrepreneur of the Year Award (highly commended) 1984, BBC Enterprise Award for Small Businesses 1985, Businesswoman of the Year Award 1986, Blitz Best Feature in a Consumer Magazine 1989, Impact Colour Supplement of the Year Award 1990; yst ever finalist in Veuve Clicquot/IOD Business Woman of the Year Award; judge: Guardian/NUS Student Media Awards annually 1987–, BBC Enterprise Awards 1987; patron of the Virgin Charitable Fndn; *Recreations* cartooning, cinema, photography, reading; *Style*— Ms Carey Labovitch; ✉ The Magazine Business, 8 Tottenham Mews, London W1P 9PJ (☎ 0171 436 5211, fax 0171 436 5290)

LACEY, Christopher John; s of Derrick Roy Lacey (d 1971), of Luton, and Monica Mary, *née* Tofield; *b* 20 March 1953; *Educ* Moorlands Sch Luton, Bedford Sch; *m* Sept 1980, Maria, da of Martin McDermott, of Manchester; 1 da (Emma-Jane b 3 Sept 1983), 1 s (Anthony James b 22 Dec 1986); *Career* Vauxhall Motors: 3 year commercial apprenticeship, subsquently various positions within sales and mktg becoming exec dir 1984, operational in Scotland (Edinburgh) 1985–87, gen sales and mktg mangr (aftersales) 1988–92, mktg dir 1992–95; dir of mktg and sales Opel Hungary (subsid of General Motors) 1995–; dir Motor Indust Trg Standards Cncl (formerly SMMT Educn Affrs and Trg Bd); *Recreations* motorsport; *Style*— Christopher Lacey, Esq

LACEY, Prof (John) Hubert; s of Percy Hubert Lacey, of Leics, and Sheila Margaret, *née* Neal; *b* 4 Nov 1944; *Educ* Loughborough GS, Univ of St Andrews (MB ChB), Univ of London (MPhil), Univ of Dundee (MD), RCOG (DipObst); *m* 7 Feb 1976, Susan Millicent, da of late Richard England Liddiard, CBE, of Wimbledon; 2 s (Ben William Hubert b 1979, Jonathan Rupert Neal b 1982), 1 da (Emma Louise Susan b 1978); *Career* jr hosp appts Dundee, St Thomas's and St George's Hosps 1969–78; hon conslt psychiatrist: Middx Hosp 1978–80, St George's Hosp 1980–; conslt i/c Bulimia Clinic 1980–, prof Univ of London 1991– (sr lectr 1978–86, reader 1987–91), head of adult psychiatry St George's Hosp Med Sch 1987– (chm Dept of Gen Psychiatry 1991–); clinical dir Pathfinder Hosp Tst 1993–, non-exec dir Merton Sutton and Wandsworth Health Authy 1994–96; med advsr BUPA; author of several res papers on anorexia, bulimia, psychosomatic med and psychopharmacology; patron Eating Disorders Assoc; chm gen psychiatry RCPsych, pres Int Coll of Psychosomatic Med; Freeman: City of London 1986, Worshipful Co of Plaisterers 1986; memb RSM, MRCPsych 1974, FRCPsych 1985; *Books* Psychological Management of the Physically Ill (1989); *Recreations* reading, interior decoration, hill walking; *Clubs* Athenaeum, Richmond RFC; *Style*— Prof J Hubert Lacey; ✉ 5 Atherton Drive, Wimbledon, London SW19 5LB (☎ and fax 0181 947 5976); Rock Cottage, Church St, Amberley, W Sussex (☎ 01798 831209); Professor and Chairman, Department of General Psychiatry, Jenner Wing, St George's Hospital Medical School, Tooting, London SW17 0RE (☎ 0181 725 5528/5529, fax 0181 725 3350, telex 945291 SAGEMS G)

LACEY, Nicholas Stephen; s of John Stephen Lacey, of Highgate, London, and Norma, *née* Hayward (d 1995); *b* 20 Dec 1943; *Educ* Univ Coll Sch, Emmanuel Coll Cambridge (MA), Architectural Assoc London (AADip); *m* 1, 1965 (m dis 1976), Nicola, da of Dr F A Mann (d 1991); 2 s (Joshua b 1968, William b 1973), 1 da (Olivia b 1970); m 2, 1981, Juliet, da of Dr Wallace Aykroyd, CBE (d 1979); 2 da (Laetitia b 1978, Theodora b 1980); *Career* ptnr: Nicholas Lacey & Assoc Architects 1971–83, Nicholas Lacey & Ptnrs Architects 1983–; winner: Wallingford Competition 1972, Crown Reach 1977; jt winner Arunbridge 1977, prize winner Paris Opera House Competition 1983; *Recreations* music, theatre, sailing; *Clubs* Athenaeum, Royal Dorset Yacht; *Style*— Nicholas Lacey, Esq; ✉ Nicholas Lacey & Partners, Reeds Wharf, Mill St, London SE1 2BA (☎ 0171 231 5154, fax 0171 231 5633); home (☎ 0171 237 6281)

LACEY, Peter William; s of Maj Eric Oliver Lacey (d 1947), of Moseley, Birmingham, and Edna Joyce Annie (Joy), *née* Bennett (d 1986); *b* 13 Nov 1945; *Educ* The Old Hall Wellington Salop, Solihull; *m* 22 Nov 1969, Pamela Muriel, da of Neville Nicholl (d 1981), of Musbury, Devon; 3 s (David b 1972, Guy b 1975, Benjamin b 1980); *Career* CA; articled clerk Chas Richards & Co Birmingham 1964–68, Goodland Bull & Co Taunton, Robson Rhodes Taunton, Apsleys Wellington 1969–90; dir Community Cncl for Somerset 1990–, co sec Somerset Assoc of Local Cncls 1990–; memb Somerset Co Jt Ctee, memb County Ctee Rural Devpt Cmmn, former chm Somerset Customer Consultative Ctee Wessex Water, chm Somerset Assoc of Local Cncls 1986–89, memb Regnl Bd Wessex and chm Regnl Rivers Advsy Ctee NRA 1989–, memb Regnl Environmental Protection Advsy Ctee 1996–, chm N Wessex Area Environment Gp Environment Agency 1996–; former chm W Buckland Parish Cncl; FCA 1979 (ACA 1969); *Recreations* gardening; *Clubs* Old Silhillians; *Style*— Peter Lacey, Esq; ✉ The Old Forge, West Buckland, Wellington, Somerset TA21 9JS (☎ 01823 662376); Community Council for Somerset, Victoria House, Victoria St, Taunton, Somerset (☎ 01823 331222, fax 01823 323652)

LACEY, Prof Richard Westgarth; s of Jack Lacey, and Sybil Lacey; *b* 11 Oct 1940; *Educ* Felsted, Jesus Coll Cambridge (BA, MB BChir, MD), The London Hosp (DCH); *m* Fionna; 2 da (Miranda, Gemma); *Career* The London Hosp 1964–66, Bristol Royal Infirmary 1966–68, reader Univ of Bristol 1973–74 (lectr 1968–73), conslt in infectious diseases King's Lynn E Anglia RHA 1974–83, conslt in chemical pathology King's Lynn Queen Elizabeth Hosp 1975–83, prof of clinical microbiology Univ of Leeds 1983–; numerous pubns in jls; memb Pathological Soc of GB, conslt to WHO; FRCPath; *Books* Unfit for Human Consumption (1991), Hard to Swallow (1994), Mad Cow Disease (1994); *Recreations* gardening, antique restoration (intermittently); *Style*— Prof Richard Lacey; ✉ Department of Microbiology, University of Leeds, Leeds LS2 9JT (☎ 0113 233 5596, fax 0113 233 5649)

LACEY, Timothy John Twyford; s of William Joseph Lacey (d 1996), of Sunbury on Thames, and Phyllis Edith, *née* Thomas; *b* 17 May 1935; *Educ* Downside; *m* 24 March 1962, Anne Patricia, da of Maj Reginald William Henly-Stuart (d 1987), of Hereford; 2 s (Michael b 1963, Christopher b 1965); *Career* chief exec William Lacey Group plc and of all subsid cos; *Recreations* golf, farming; *Style*— Timothy Lacey, Esq; ✉ Little Wildwood Farm, Wildwood Lane, Cranleigh, Surrey GU6 8JR; Elmbridge House, Elmbridge Lane, Woking, Surrey GU22 9AF (☎ 01483 740700, fax 01483 740675, car tel 0585 291945)

LACHELIN, Dr Gillian Claire Liborel; da of Pierre Joseph Augustin Lachelin (d 1977), and Joan Kathleen Moncaster, *née* Hilbery (d 1963); *b* 5 Feb 1940; *Educ* Princess Helena Coll Sch for Girls, Girton Coll Cambridge (MA, MB BChir), Univ of London (MD); *Career* registrar in obstetrics and gynaecology UCH London 1969–72, lectr and hon sr registrar Univ Coll Med Sch and UCH 1972–77, reader and hon conslt in obstetrics and gynaecology UCL and Middx Sch of Med 1977–; memb Ctee on Safety of Meds Jan 1993–Dec 1995; memb: Blair Bell Res Soc 1975, Soc for Endocrinology 1979, Br Fertility Soc 1981, Soc for Gynecologic Investigation USA 1982; FRCOG 1982 (MRCOG 1969); *Books* Miscarriage: The Facts (1985, 2 edn 1996), Practical Gynaecology (with D T Y Liu, 1989), Clinical Reproductive Endocrinology (1991); *Recreations* travel, photography, gardening; *Style*— Dr Gillian C L Lachelin; ✉ Obstetric Unit, 88–96 Chenies Mews, London WC1E 6HX (☎ 0171 209 6054)

LACHMANN, Prof Peter Julius; s of Heinz Ulrich Lachmann (d 1971), of London, and Thea Emilie, *née* Heller (d 1978); *b* 23 Dec 1931; *Educ* Christ's Coll Finchley (State scholar, HSC), Trinity Coll Cambridge (scholar), UCH (Goldsmid scholar, MA, MB BChir, PhD, ScD (Cantab), Fellowes Silver medal, Tuke Silver medal, Liston Gold medal), FRCP (1973), FRCPath (1981); *m* 7 July 1962, Sylvia Mary, da of Alan Stephenson; 2 s (Robin b 20 June 1965, Michael b 20 Aug 1970), 1 da (Helen b 16 Sept 1967); *Career* house surgn Newmarket General Hosp 1956–57, house physician Med Unit UCH and Rheumatism Unit Canadian Red Cross Meml Hosp 1957–58, John Lucas Walker student, res scholar and BMA science res scholar Trinity Coll Cambridge 1958–60, visiting investigator and asst physician Rockefeller Univ 1960–61; Dept of Pathology Univ of Cambridge: Arthritis and Rheumatism Cncl fell 1962–64, asst dir of res Immunology Div 1964–71; dir of med studies Christ's Coll Cambridge 1969–70 (fell 1962–71), prof of immunology RPMS Univ of London 1971–75; Univ of Cambridge: fell Christ's Coll 1976–, Sheila Joan Smith prof of immunology 1977–, hon dir MRC Molecular Immunopathology Unit 1980–; conslt WHO 1968, hon conslt pathologist Hammersmith Hosp 1971–75, hon conslt clinical immunologist Cambridge HA 1976–; visiting investigator: Basel Inst for Immunology 1971, Scripps Clinic and Res Fndn 1975, 1980, 1986 and 1989; SmithKline and French visiting prof Aust 1984, Mayerhoff visiting prof Dept of Chemical Immunology Weitzmann Inst 1989; visiting prof: Dept of Med RPMS 1986–90, College de France 1993; memb: Medical Advsy Ctee British Council 1983–, Gene Therapy Advsy Ctee Dept of Health 1993–, Int Bioethics Ctee UNESCO 1993–, Scientific Advsy Bd SmithKline Beecham 1995–; RCPath: memb Cncl 1982–85 and 1989–93, pres 1990–93; biological sec and vice pres Royal Soc 1993–; vice pres Br Lung Fndn 1990–, tstee Darwin Tst 1991–; assoc ed Clinical and Experimental Immunology 1990–, pres Cncl and memb Bd of Dirs Int Jl of Experimental Pathology 1991–; memb Ed Bd: Scandinavian Jl of Immunology, Springer Seminars in Immunopathology, Immunological Communications, British Medical Bulletin; memb: Br Soc for Immunology 1959– (Ctee 1966–69), American Assoc of Immunologists 1966–, Norwegian Acad of Science and Letters 1991–, Academia Europaea 1992–; hon memb Societé Française D'Immunologie 1986–, hon fell Faculty of Pathology RCPI 1993; FRSM, FRS 1982, FRPMS 1995; *Publications* Clinical Aspects of Immunology (co-ed, 5 edn 1993); author of numerous papers in professional jls on complement and immunopathology; *Clubs* Athenaeum; *Style*— Prof Peter Lachmann, FRS; ✉ Conduit Head, 36 Conduit Head Road, Cambridge CB3 0EY (☎ 01223 354433); MRC Centre, Hills Road, Cambridge CB2 2QH (☎ 01223 402302, fax 01223 243237)

LACHS, His Hon Judge; Henry Lazarus; s of Samuel Lachs (d 1960); *b* 31 Dec 1927; *Educ* Liverpool Inst HS, Pembroke Coll Cambridge; *m* 1959, Dr Edith Lachs, JP, da of Ludwig Bergel; 4 da; *Career* recorder of the Crown Ct 1972–79, circuit judge (Northern

Circuit) 1979–; regnl chm Mental Health Review Tbnl 1968–79; *Style*— His Hon Judge Lachs; ✉ 41 Menlove Gardens West, Liverpool L18 (☎ 0151 722 5936)

LACK, Dr (John) Alastair; s of Prof Charles Hansard Lack (d 1991), of Salisbury, Wilts, and Janet Doreen, *née* Steele; *b* 1 Sept 1942; *Educ* Westminster, UCH (MB BS), FRCA, Imperial Coll London (DIC); *m* 2 July 1966, (Patricia) Margaret, da of Alec Reynolds; 1 s (Christopher b 7 Jan 1975), 2 da (Juliette b 14 March 1970, Katherine b 18 May 1973); *Career* asst prof of anaesthesia Stanford Med Center San Francisco USA 1971–73, conslt anaesthetist Salisbury Hospitals 1974–, dir resource mgmnt Salisbury Health Authy 1990–95; chm: Soc Computing and Technol in Anaesthesia Soc 1987–92, European Soc Computing and Technology in Anaesthesia and Intensive Care 1992–; memb: Quality of Practice Ctee Royal Coll of Anaesthetists, IT Ctee Conf of Royal Med Colleges Information Gp 1990–93; pres Soc for Computing and Technol in Anaesthesia 1995–; author of books and articles on computing and technology in anaesthesia and intensive care, resource mgmnt; FRCA 1987; *Recreations* music, wine, writing letters to The Times, computing science, classic cars, gardening; *Style*— Dr Alastair Lack; ✉ The River House, Coombe Bissett, Salisbury, Wilts SP5 4LX (☎ 01722 718303); Anaesthetic Department, Salisbury Hospital, Salisbury, Wilts SP2 8BJ (☎ 01722 425050, fax 01722 414143, e-mail 100012.2245@compuserve.com)

LACK, Alastair Iliffe; s of Gordon Iliffe Lack (d 1985), and Joan Hardwick, *née* Riddell; *b* 25 Dec 1944; *Educ* Whitgift Sch, Univ Coll Oxford (BA); *m* 9 Jan 1971, Catherine Noel, da of John Conran Smerdon (d 1984); 1 da (Sarah Charlotte b 10 Dec 1975); *Career* prodn asst further educn BBC TV 1975, prodr evening sequences BBC radio 1977; World Service: talks writer 1971, prodr 1971–77, sr prodr 1977–84, exec prodr 1984–87, asst head current affrs 1987–88, dep head 1988–90, head of prodns in English 1990–94, head of English Progs 1994–; *Recreations* travel, sport, literature; *Clubs* MCC; *Style*— Alastair Lack, Esq; ✉ 77 Whitmore Rd, Harrow, Middlesex HA1 4AE (☎ 0181 423 2755); BBC World Service, Bush House, Aldwych, London WC2 (☎ 0171 257 2374)

LACON, Edmund Richard Vere; s and h of Sir Edmund Vere Lacon, 8 Bt, *qv*; *b* 2 Oct 1967; *Educ* Woodbridge Sch Suffolk; *Career* gen mangr wine bars London; *Recreations* rugby, running, golf; *Style*— Edmund Lacon, Esq

LACON, Sir Edmund Vere; 8 Bt (UK 1818), of Great Yarmouth, Norfolk; s of Sir George Vere Francis Lacon, 7 Bt (d 1980), by his 1 w Hilary; *b* 3 May 1936; *Educ* Woodbridge Sch Suffolk; *m* 1963, Gillian, o da of Jack Henry Middleditch, of Wrentham, Suffolk; 1 s (Edmund Richard Vere b 1967), 1 da (Anna Kathryn b 1965); *Heir* s, Edmund Richard Vere Lacon b 2 Oct 1967; *Career* co sec SAK Venture Ltd; *Clubs* Naval and Military; *Style*— Sir Edmund Lacon, Bt

LACY, Sir John Trend; kt (1992), CBE (1982); s of Rev Hubert Lacy (d 1982), and Gertrude Markham (d 1983); *b* 15 March 1928; *Educ* King's Sch Ely Cambs; *m* 16 June 1956, Pamela, da of John Guerin; 1 s (Nicholas b 23 Dec 1957); *Career* RN 1945–48; Cons Pty agent London and Bucks 1950–60, CCO agent W Mids, Northern and S Eastern Areas 1960–85, gen dir campaigning Cons Pty 1985–93 (ret); memb Nat Soc Cons and Unionist Agents; *Recreations* politics, family, racing; *Clubs* St Stephen's, Carlton; *Style*— Sir John Lacy, CBE; ✉ 18 Windmill Close, Milford-on-Sea, Hants SO41 0SX (☎ 01590 643984)

LACY, Patrick Bryan Finucane; s of Sir Maurice John Pierce Lacy, 2 Bt (d 1965); and hp to Btcy of bro, Sir Hugh Maurice Pierce Lacy, 3 Bt; *b* 18 April 1948; *Educ* Downside; *m* 1971, Phyllis Victoria, da of Edgar P H James; 1 s, 1 da; *Style*— Patrick Lacy, Esq; ✉ 11 Tudor Gdns, Barnes, SW13

LADEJO, Du'aine; s of Paula Enwezoh (Mrs Thorne), and step-s of I D P Thorne, *qv*; *b* 14 Feb 1971; *Educ* Forest Grange Sch Horsham, King Edward's Sch Witley, Medina HS Ohio (scholar), Univ of Texas (capt Univ Athletics team); *Career* athlete; achievements at 400m: UK Outdoor champion 1993, semi-finalist World Championships 1993, UK Indoor champion 1994, Euro Indoor and Outdoor champion 1994, Gold medal Budapest Championships 1994, Silver medal AAA Championships 1994, Silver medal Goodwill Games 1994, Silver medal Commonwealth Games 1994, Euro Indoor champion 1996; achievements in 4 x 400m relay: Bronze medal Olympic Games Barcelona 1992, Gold medal Europa Cup 1993 and 1994, Gold medal Euro Championships 1994, Gold medal World Cup 1994, Gold medal Cwlth Games 1994, Silver medal Olympic Games Atlanta 1996; hon citizen Austin Texas 1993; memb Belgrave Harriers; dir Quiet Storm Associates; presenter Du'aine's World (LWT) 1995–; *Style*— Du'aine Ladejo; ✉ c/o Paula N Thorne, Quiet Storm Associates, PO Box 11, Newark, Notts NG22 0BD (☎ and fax 01623 862771)

LADENBURG, Michael John Carlisle; s of John Arthur George Ladenburg (d 1990), of W Sussex, and Yvonne Rachel Bankier, *née* Carlisle (d 1968); *b* 2 Feb 1945; *Educ* Charterhouse, Christ Church Oxford (MA); *m* 1971, Susan Elizabeth, da of Dr George Denys Laing, of Surrey; 1 s (William b 1980), 2 da (Harriet b 1975, Olivia b 1977); *Career* merchant banker; dir: J Henry Schroder Wagg & Co Ltd 1979–88, Robert Fleming & Co Ltd 1988–91; head of corporate fin Saudi International Bank 1992–; *Recreations* music, sailing, golf, skiing, reading, tennis; *Clubs* Hurlingham, Tandridge Golf; *Style*— Michael Ladenburg, Esq; ✉ 62 Cloncurry St, London SW6 6DU (☎ 0171 736 5605); Saudi International Bank, 1 Knightsbridge, London SW1X 7XS (☎ 0171 259 3456)

LADENIS, Nicholas Peter (Nico); s of Peter Ladenis (d 1960), of Kenya, and Constance, *née* Antoniadis (d 1976); *b* 22 April 1934; *Educ* Prince of Wales Sch Nairobi, Regent St Poly, LSE, Univ of Hull (BSc(Econ)); *m* 29 June 1963, Dinah-Jane, da of Theodore Zissu (d 1942); 2 da (Natasha Nicole b 29 April 1964, Isabella Therese b 28 June 1966); *Career* restaurateur; various appointments incl: Caltex Kenya, Ford Motor Company, Sunday Times; first entered catering 1971; fndr chef and patron: Chez Nico (with wife Dinah-Jane as ptnr) 1973–, Simply Nico 1989–, Nico Central 1992, Chez Nico at Ninety Park Lane 1992–; first distinction Good Food Guide 1976, Chef of the Year 1988, third Michelin Star 1995 (first 1981, second 1984), 5 out of 5 Good Food Guide 1996; *Books* My Gastronomy (1987), Nico (1996); *Recreations* food, travelling, family; *Style*— Nico Ladenis, Esq; ✉ Chez Nico Restaurants, 90 Park Lane, London W1A 3AA (☎ 0171 409 1290, fax 0171 355 4877)

LADER, Prof Malcolm Harold; OBE (1996); s of Abe Lader (d 1979), of Liverpool, and Minnie, *née* Sholl; *b* 27 Feb 1936; *Educ* Liverpool Inst HS, Univ of Liverpool (BSc, MB ChB, MD), Univ of London (PhD, DPM, DSc); *m* 16 April 1961, Susan Ruth, da of Louis Packer (d 1990), of Hendon, Middx; 3 da (Deborah b 1966, Vicki b 1969, Charlotte b 1972); *Career* memb external scientific staff MRC 1966–, conslt Bethlem Royal and Maudsley Hosp 1970–, prof of clinical psychopharmacology Univ of London 1978–; tstee Mental Health Fndn; memb Advsy Cncl Misuse of Drugs; hon fell American Coll of Psychiatrists 1994; FRCPsych 1971; *Books* Psychiatry on Trial (1977), Dependence on Tranquillizers (1984), Biological Treatments in Psychiatry (1996); *Recreations* antiques, English watercolours; *Clubs* RSM; *Style*— Prof Malcolm Lader, OBE; ✉ 11 Kelsey Way, Beckenham, Kent BR3 3LP (☎ 0181 650 0366); 10 Dedham Mill, Dedham, Essex CO7 6DH; Addiction Sciences Building, Inst of Psychiatry, Decrespigny Park, London SE5 8AF (☎ 0171 703 0770, fax 0171 252 5437)

LAFLIN, John Spencer; s of Arthur Spencer Laflin (d 1990), of Tatworth, Somerset, and Gertrude, *née* Norton; *b* 13 Jan 1941; *Educ* Hastings GS, Central Sch of Art Holborn, Hammersmith Coll of Art (NDD); *m* 1964 (m dis 1971), Felicia, da of Donald Sproule; 2 da (Anna b 1965, Natasha b 1967); *partner* Nicola Freud; 3 s (Jack Freud-Laflin b 1980, Harry Freud-Laflin b 1986, Max Freud-Laflin (twin) b 1986), 1 da (Martha Freud-Laflin b 1983); *Career* apprentice working on prodns for Covent Garden and Glyndebourne Harkers Scenic Studios 1958–61, organiser pre-dip 3 dimensional design course E Ham Art Sch 1964–69, freelance textile designer and pt/t lectr Royal Acad Sch of Art and Kingston Sch of Art 1969–74, dir Liberty of London Prints 1981– (joined as design mangr 1974), design dir Liberty plc 1991–; *Recreations* sailing, the Arts (high and low); *Clubs* Chelsea Arts, Brancaster Staithe Sailing; *Style*— John Laflin, Esq; ✉ Liberty Furnishings, Chelsea Harbour Design Centre, London SW10 (☎ and fax 0171 351 2334)

LAFLIN, Eur Ing Reginald Ernest; s of Sydney Ernest Laflin (d 1975), of Rustington, West Sussex, and Rose, *née* Nichols (d 1988); *b* 21 March 1926; *Educ* Sir Walter St John's Public Sch, Battersea Poly (HNC), Borough Poly (HNC); *m* 28 Sept 1952, (Ruby) Elsie, da of George Francis Brown; 1 s (Michael John), 1 da (Susan); *Career* WWII pilot/navigator in trg RAFVR 1943–45; md APV Paralec Ltd (chief engr APV Paramount Ltd) 1952–75, assoc ptnr Revell Hayward & Ptnrs 1975–78, ptnr EG Phillips Son & Ptnrs 1978–88, ptnr Nordale Design Partnership 1988–96, conslt engr to St George's Hosp Med Sch 1989–, electrical conslt John Hall Assocs 1990–92; Eur Ing, CEng, FIEE, MConsE, FIMechE, FICBSE, FIMechIE, MIM, FInstD; *Style*— Eur Ing R E Laflin; ✉ 9 Gorham Avenue, Rottingdean, Brighton, E Sussex BN2 7DP (☎ 01273 390636, fax 01273 275360); Noredale Design Partnership, 51–53 Burney Road, Greenwich, London SE10 8EX (☎ 0181 858 4482, fax 0181 858 5876, telex 8951039)

LAGDEN, Ronald Gordon; s of Reginald Bousfield Lagden, OBE, MC (d 1944), and late Christine, *née* Haig; *b* 4 Sept 1927; *Educ* Marlborough, RMC Sandhurst (Sword of Honour), Harvard, AMP Univ; *m* 1951, Elizabeth Veronica, da of John Kenneth Mathews (d 1972); 2 s, 1 da; *Career* Lt Queen's Own Cameron Highlanders serv Italy; Maconochie Foods 1947–53, Bowater Scott Corporation 1953–63, md Findus Ltd 1963–68, chm and md Quaker Oats Ltd 1968–71 (chm and pres (Europe) Quaker Oats Co 1971–85, non-exec dir 1985–93); dir Pagepine Ltd; non-exec dir: WA Baxter & Sons Ltd, SFS Group Ltd, Just Group plc; non-exec chm Garma Gourmet (UK) Ltd; chm Golf Development International (Brussels); *Books* Principles and Practices of Management (jtly); *Recreations* golf, gardening, reading, bridge, family; *Clubs* Royal and Ancient Golf, Sunningdale Golf, Royal Golf de Belique, West Sussex Golf; *Style*— Ronald Lagden, Esq; ✉ Spear Hill Cottage, Ashington, W Sussex RH20 3BA

LAIDLAW, Charles David Gray; s of George Gray Laidlaw, and Margaret Orr, *née* Crombie; *b* 23 Jan 1954; *Educ* Strathallan Sch, Univ of Edinburgh (LLB); *m* 27 June 1986, Lucy Elizabeth, *née* Brooks; 2 s (Robert Gray b 27 June 1989, Douglas John b 8 May 1991); *Career* political writer D C Thompson Group 1977–79 (reporter 1975–77), reporter Sunday Express 1980, def intelligence analyst MOD 1980–83, exec Good Relations 1983–85, mangr PA Consulting Group 1985–87, gp mangr Reginald Watts Associates 1987–88; dir: Burson-Marsteller and Burson-Marsteller Financial 1988–90, TMA Group 1990, Citigate Scotland 1991–96; chief exec Scottish and Westminster Communications 1992–96, head media and public relations Scottish Rugby Union 1996–; Freeman City of Glasgow (hereditary); MIPR 1986, memb Grand Antiquary Soc; *Recreations* rugby, running, writing; *Clubs* London Scottish; *Style*— Charles Laidlaw, Esq; ✉ SRU, Murrayfield, Edinburgh EH12 5PJ (☎ 0131 346 5000)

LAIDLAW, Sir Christophor Charles Fraser; kt (1982); s of late Hugh Alexander Lyon Laidlaw; *b* 9 Aug 1922; *Educ* Rugby, St John's Coll Cambridge; *m* 1952, Nina Mary Prichard; 1 s, 3 da; *Career* BP Co Ltd: dir of ops 1971–72, md 1972–81, dep chm 1980–81; chm BP Oil 1977–81; exec chm ICL plc 1981–84; dir: Commercial Union Assurance 1978–83, Barclays Bank Int 1980–87, Barclays Bank plc 1981–88, Amerada Hess Corporation 1983–94, Dalgety plc 1984–92, Redland plc 1984–92, Mercedes Benz (UK) 1985–93, Daimler-Benz 1994–; chm Bridon plc 1985–90; pres German Chamber of Indust and Commerce in UK 1983–84, dir INSEAD 1987–94 (chm UK Advsy Bd 1987–93); memb Ct of Assts Worshipful Co of Tallow Chandlers (Master 1988–89); hon fell St John's Coll Cambridge 1996; *Style*— Sir Christophor Laidlaw; ✉ 22 Hill St, Mayfair, London W1X 7FU

LAIDLAW, James Robertson; s of James Laidlaw (d 1969), of Edinburgh, and Margaret, *née* Craig (d 1991); *b* 23 July 1935; *Educ* George Watson's Coll, Sch of Architecture Edinburgh Coll of Art (Andrew Grant travelling scholar, DA); *m* 17 June 1961, Pauline, da of Walter Peckham, of Bury St Edmunds; 1 s (Quentin James b 29 July 1963), 1 da (Julia Margaret b 12 Nov 1966); *Career* architect; with A H Mottram Architects 1958–60; Bamber Gray Partnership (previously Fairbrother Hall & Hedges): joined 1960, ptnr 1965, sr ptnr 1975–93, conslt 1993–; specialist in high-tech industrial, scientific and educnl buildings in UK, Saudi Arabia and Africa; chm Caledon House Investments (Scotland) Ltd; memb Cncl: RIAS 1979–86 (pres 1993–95), RIBA 1982–87 and 1993–; author Laidlaw Report on Commissioning Architects 1989; memb: ARCUK 1987–94, Bd of Architectural Educn 1987–94; govr Edinburgh Coll of Art 1987– (also memb Scholarships and Awards Ctee 1989–, memb Audit Ctee 1995–); High Constable City of Edinburgh 1986; ARIBA 1958, FRIAS 1970 (ARIAS 1958), FRSA 1988; *Recreations* books, boats, booze; *Clubs* New (Edinburgh), Drumseugh (Edinburgh); *Style*— James R Laidlaw, Chartered Architect; ✉ 6 Gillespie Road, Colinton, Edinburgh EH13 0LL; Caledon House Investments (Scotland) Ltd, 73 Kirk Brae, Liberton, Edinburgh EH16 6JN (☎ 0131 664 4671, fax 0131 666 2466)

LAIDLAW, (Henry) Renton; s of Henry Renton Laidlaw (d 1989), of Broughty Ferry, Dundee, and Margaret McBeath, *née* Raiker; *b* 6 July 1939; *Educ* James Gillespie's Edinburgh, Daniel Stewart's Coll Edinburgh; *Career* golf corr Evening News Edinburgh 1957–68, news presenter Grampian TV Aberdeen 1968–70, news presenter and reporter BBC Scotland Edinburgh 1970–73, golf corr Evening Standard London 1973–; golf presenter 1973–: ITV, TWI, Eurosport, Screensport, PGA European Tour Productions; presenter BBC Sport on 2 1985–88; Freeman Worshipful Co of Scriveners; *Books* Play Golf (with Peter Alliss), Tony Jacklin - The First 40 Years (with Tony Jacklin), Play Better Golf, Golfing Heroes, Ryder Cup 1985, 1987 and 1989, Captain of Kiawah (with Bernard Gallacher), Wentworth - 70 Years; *Recreations* theatre-going, playing golf, travelling; *Clubs* Caledonian, Sunningdale Golf, Wentworth Golf, Royal Burgess Golf, Ballybunion Golf (hon), Royal and Ancient Golf (St Andrews); *Style*— Renton Laidlaw, Esq; ✉ Evening Standard, Northcliffe House, Derry Street, London W8 5EE (☎ 0171 938 6000)

LAIGHT, Eur Ing Barry Pemberton; OBE (1970); s of Donald Norman Laight (d 1935), of Astwood Bank, and Norah, *née* Pemberton (d 1946); *Educ* Johnston Sch Durham, Birmingham Central Tech Coll, Merchant Venturers' Tech Coll Bristol, Univ of Bristol (MSc); *m* 17 Feb 1951, Ruth, da of Alfred Sutro Murton, DCM, MM (d 1975), of Warsash, Hants; 1 s (Timothy b 1952), 1 da (Deborah b 1954); *Career* chief aerodynamicist Bristol Aeroplane Co 1947–52, tech dir Blackburn and General Aircraft 1952–61, dir mil projects Hawker Siddeley Aviation 1961–77, engrg dir Short Bros 1977–82, sec RAeS 1982–85 (pres 1974–75); conslt: ETSU 1985–89, Vertical Axis Wind Turbines 1983–93, Renewable Energy Systems 1987–94; memb at various times: NATO Advsy Gp on Aerospace R & D, Aircraft Res Assoc, Int Cncl Aeronautical Scis, ARC, SERC, CEI, CBI, AERO, Mensa; govr Kingston Univ (formerly Kingston Poly); memb Ct: Univ of Surrey, Coll of Aeronautics; FRAeS 1955, FInstD 1975, MAIAA 1982, FEng 1981, FIMechE 1983, Eur Ing 1989; *Recreations* music, mathematics, walking; *Style*— Eur Ing Barry Laight, OBE, FEng; ✉ Dunelm, 5 Littlemead, Esher, Surrey, KT10 9PE (☎ 01372 463216)

LAINE, Clementine Dinah (Cleo); (Mrs John Dankworth); OBE (1979); da of Alexander Campbell, and Minnie, *née* Bullock; *b* 28 Oct 1927; *m* 1, 1947 (m dis 1958), George Langridge; 1 s; m 2, 1958, John Philip William Dankworth, *qv*; 1 s, 1 da; *Career*

vocalist; with The Dankworth Orchestra 1953–58; has appeared on television numerous times and made guest appearances with symphony orchestras in England and abroad; Hon MA Open Univ 1975; Hon DMus: Berklee Coll of Music, York Univ; *Theatre* incl: lead in Seven Deadly Sins (Edinburgh Festival and Sadler's Wells) 1961, A Time to Laugh, Hedda Gabler 1966, The Women of Troy 1967 (both Edinburgh Festival), lead in Showboat 1972; Collette 1980, The Mystery of Edwin Drood 1986 (winner of Theatre World Award, nominated for a Tony Award and Drama Desk Award), Into The Woods 1989 (US nat tour); *Recordings* most recent albums incl: Cleo Laine Jazz 1991, Nothing Without You 1992, Blue and Sentimental 1994, Solitude 1995; Gold records incl: Feel the Warm, I'm a Song, Live at Melbourne; Platinum records incl: Best Friends, Sometimes When We Touch; *Awards* incl: Golden Feather Award LA Times 1973, Edison Award 1974, Variety Club 1977, Singer of the Year (TV Times) 1978, Grammy Award (best female jazz vocalist) 1985, Theatre World Award 1986; *Books* Cleo (autobiog, 1994); *Style*— Miss Cleo Laine, OBE; ✉ The Old Rectory, Wavendon, Milton Keynes, Bucks MK17 8LT (☎ 01908 583151, fax 01908 584414)

LAING, Christopher Maurice; s of Sir Kirby Laing, *qv*, and Joan Dorothy, *née* Bratt (d 1981); *b* 1 May 1948; *Educ* St Lawrence Coll Ramsgate, Herts Coll of Building St Albans; *m* 15 May 1971, Diana Christina, *née* Bartlett; 2 s, 2 da; *Career* with John Laing Services Ltd 1971–, dir John Laing Construction Ltd 1986–, md Grosvenor Laing Urban Enterprise Ltd; dir: Crofton Country Centre Ltd 1989–, Crofton Trust Ltd 1989–, Br Sch of Osteopathy 1992–, Tyringham Foundation Ltd 1993–, Chartered Inst of Building Benevolent Fund Ltd 1994–, Construction Industry Relief and Assistance for the Single Homeless Ltd 1996–; non-exec dir: NPFA Playground Services Ltd 1987–, Eskmuir Properties Plc 1990–, Englemere Services Ltd 1992–; pres Chartered Inst of Building 1992–93 (vice-pres 1989–92), chm Nat Playing Fields Assoc 1993– (memb Cncl 1985–); memb Cncl: Tidy Britain Gp 1993–, Euro Cncl for Building Professionals 1993–; chm: N London Leadership Team 1993–95, Upper Lee Valley Partnership SRB Gp 1995–; memb Ct of Assts Worshipful Co of Paviors 1993– (Liveryman 1971); *Recreations* golf, shooting, tennis, swimming; *Clubs* RAC; *Style*— Christopher Laing, Esq; ✉ John Laing plc, Studio House, Elstree Way, Borehamwood, Herts WD6 1SD (☎ 0181 236 2949, fax 0181 207 3328)

LAING, Gerald; *see:* Ogilvie-Laing, Gerald

LAING, Maj Hugh Charles Desmond; s of Capt Hugh Desmond Bertram Laing (d 1953), and Dorothy Linton, *née* Harvey (d 1986); *b* 24 Dec 1931; *Educ* King's Coll Sch Canada, Millfield, RMA Sandhurst; *m* 2 May 1959 (m dis 1993), Hon Rosemary Laing, *née* Cornwall-Legh, da of 5 Baron Grey of Codnor, CBE, AE, DL (d 1996); 1 adopted da (Camilla Catherine Harvey b 29 June 1964); *Career* cmmnd 2 Lt Scots Guards 1952, Adj Gds Trg Bn Pirbright, GSO3 16 Ind Parachute Bde Gp, Staff Coll Camberley, GSO2 Int Coord Jt Int Staff Hong Kong, Coy Cmd Scots Guards, Sqdn Ldr 22 SAS Regt, GSO2 Br Def Liaison Staff Washington; ret 1973; Sqdn Ldr Duke of Lancaster's Own Yeo 1984–88; called to the Bar Inner Temple 1976, practising Northern Circuit Manchester 1976–91, currently in ind practice; pres: Manchester Branch Scots Guards' Assoc 1973–93, Great Yeldham and Dist Branch Royal British Legion 1995–; chm Millfield Soc 1980–86; *Recreations* golf, walking, photography; *Clubs* Special Forces; *Style*— Maj Hugh Laing; ✉ The Rectory, Toppesfield, Essex CO9 4DQ (☎ 01787 237924)

LAING, Dr Ian Geoffrey; s of George Edward Laing, and Frances May, *née* Hutton; *b* 15 May 1933; *Educ* Leeds GS, Univ of Leeds (BSc, PhD); *m* 5 April 1958, Una, da of Albert Hannam (d 1982); 2 s (Andrew Nicholas b 1962, Jonathan Richard b 1964), 2 da (Deborah Claire b 1960, Rebecca Sarah b 1967); *Career* tech dir Clayton Aniline Co Ltd 1978–85 (prodn dir 1971–77, prodn mangr 1966–71, memb Bd 1971–87), dir of health safety and environment protection Ciba-Geigy plc 1986–93, ret; memb Health and Safety Cmmn's Advsy Ctee on Toxic Substances 1978–85; CIA: memb Carcinogenic Substances Ctee 1963 (chm 1974–86), memb Cncl for Industl Safety Health and Environmental Control 1985–93, chm Task Force for Carcinogens Mutagens and Teratagens 1985–93, chm Dyes Sector Health Safety Ctee 1986–92, chm Dyes Sector Gp Ctee 1992–93; memb Cncl Br Industl Biological Res Assoc 1989–93; FRSC, FSDC; *Recreations* photography, oil and watercolour painting, skiing, walking, cycling; *Style*— Dr Ian Laing; ✉ Shieldaig, Calrofold Lane, Rainow, nr Macclesfield, Cheshire SK11 0AA (☎ 01625 420552)

LAING, Jennifer Charlina Ellsworth; da of James Ellsworth Laing, FRCS (d 1983), of Salisbury, Wiltshire, and Mary McKane, *née* Taylor; *Educ* Godolphin, North Western Poly; *m* (m dis); *Career* bd dir: Saatchi & Saatchi Garland Compton 1977, Leo Burnett 1978; Saatchi & Saatchi Advertising: dep chm 1981–87, jt chm 1987–88; chm and chief exec Aspect Hill Holliday 1988, mgmnt buyout to form Laing Henry Limited 1990–95 (merged with Saatchi & Saatchi Advertising 1995), chairman Saatchi & Saatchi Advertising (London) 1995–96, memb Exec Bd Saatchi & Saatchi Advertising Worldwide 1996–, chief exec N American ops Saatchi & Saatchi (New York) 1996–; non-exec dir Great Ormond Street Hosp for Children NHS Trust, dir London First; fell Mktg Soc, FIPA; *Recreations* racing, ballet, opera; *Style*— Miss Jennifer Laing; ✉ Chief Executive, Saatchi & Saatchi, 375 Hudson Street, New York, NY 10014–3660, USA (☎ 00 1 212 463 2000)

LAING, Sir (William) Kirby; kt (1968), JP (Middx 1965), DL (1978); s of Sir John Laing, CBE (d 1978), and Beatrice, *née* Harland (d 1972); *b* 21 July 1916; *Educ* St Lawrence Coll Ramsgate, Emmanuel Coll Cambridge (MA); *m* 1, 1939, Joan Dorothy (d 1981), da of Capt E C Bratt (d 1965); 3 s; m 2, 1986, Mary Isobel Lewis, da of late Edward Wray; *Career* chm Laing Properties plc 1978–87, dir John Laing plc 1939–80; pres: Nat Fedn of Bldg Trades Employers 1965 and 1967, Inst of Civil Engrs 1974, Royal Albert Hall 1979–92; hon fell: Emmanuel Coll Cambridge 1983, Univ Coll of North Wales 1988; Master Worshipful Co of Paviors 1987–88; Hon DTech PCL 1990, Hon DUniv Edinburgh 1991; FEng 1977; *Clubs* Naval & Military, Royal Fowey Yacht; *Style*— Sir Kirby Laing, JP, DL, FEng; ✉ John Laing plc, Page Street, London NW7 2ER (☎ 0181 959 3636)

LAING, Sir (John) Martin Kirby; kt (1997), CBE (1991), DL (Herts 1987); s of Sir (William) Kirby Laing, *qv*, and Joan Dorothy, *née* Bratt (d 1981); *b* 18 Jan 1942; *Educ* St Lawrence Coll Ramsgate, Emmanuel Coll Cambridge (MA); *m* 6 Oct 1965, Stephanie Stearn, da of Leslie Worsdell; 1 s, 1 da; *Career* John Laing plc: joined gp 1966, dir 1980–, chm 1985–; chm: Nat Contractors Gp of Building Employers' Fedn 1987, Br Urban Devpt 1988–90, CBI Overseas Ctee 1989–96, chm Worldwide Fund for Nature (WWF) UK 1990– (tstee 1988–, tstee WWF International 1991–), Br Overseas Trade Bd 1995–, Construction Indust Employers Cncl 1995–; memb: Ctee for Middle E Trade 1982–86, UK Advsy Ctee Br American C of C 1985–, Cncl CBI 1986–, Cncl World Economic Forum 1986–, Business in the Community 1986– (dir 1995–), Archbishops' Cncl Church Urban Fund 1987–94, Ct Univ of London 1987–95, Home Office Parole Review Ctee 1987–88, UK-Japan 2000 Group 1988–, World Business Cncl for Sustainable Devpt 1991–; dir: Herts Groundwork Tst 1986–91, City of London Sinfonia 1988–95; tstee National Energy Fndn 1988–, govr St Lawrence Coll Ramsgate 1988–95; hon DSc City Univ 1996; Master Worshipful Co of Paviors 1995–96 (Freeman 1964, Upper Warden 1994), Liveryman Worshipful Co of Chartered Surveyors; FRICS 1984, CIMgt 1985, CCIM 1987, FIEx 1987, FRSA 1988, FICE 1993, FCIOB 1995; *Recreations* gardening, music, travel, the environment; *Style*— Sir Martin Laing, CBE, DL; ✉ John Laing plc, Page Street, London NW7 2ER (☎ 0181 959 3636, fax 0181 906 5297)

LAING, Sir (John) Maurice; kt (1965); s of Sir John William Laing, CBE (d 1978), of Mill Hill, London, and Beatrice, *née* Harland (d 1972); *b* 1 Feb 1918; *Educ* St Lawrence Coll Ramsgate; *m* 20 March 1940, Hilda Violet, da of William Tom Steeper Richards (d 1946), of Ramsgate; 1 s (John Hedley b 1959); *Career* WWII RAFVR 1941–45 (seconded Glider Pilot Regt for Rhine crossing 1945); dir: John Laing plc 1939–87 (jt md 1947–54, md 1954–76, dep chm 1966, chm 1976–82), Bank of England 1963–80; pres: Br Employers' Confedn 1964–65, CBI 1965–66, Export Gp for the Constructional Industs 1976–80, Fedn of Civil Engrg Contractors 1977–80, RYA 1983–87; memb: Export Guarantees Advsy Cncl 1959–63, Econ Planning Bd 1961, NEDC 1962–66, NIESR 1964–82, Admin Staff Coll 1965–70; pres London Bible College 1993–; Insignia Award CGLI 1978; Hon LLD Strathclyde 1967, Hon FGLI 1991, Hon DSc Univ of Exeter 1996; Freeman Municipality of Surrey BC Canada 1978; MCIOB 1981; *Recreations* sailing, swimming; *Clubs* Royal Yacht Sqdn, Royal Ocean Racing; *Style*— Sir Maurice Laing; ✉ John Laing plc, Page St, Mill Hill, London NW7 2ER (☎ 0181 959 3636)

LAING, (John) Stuart; s of late Dr Denys Laing, of Limpsfield, Surrey, and Dr Judy Laing, *née* Dods (d 1995); *b* 22 July 1948; *Educ* Rugby, Corpus Christi Coll Cambridge; *m* 12 Aug 1972, Sibella, da of Sir Maurice Dorman, GCMG, GCVO, of West Overton, Wiltshire; 1 s (James b 1974), 2 da (Catriona b 1979, Hannah b 1985); *Career* Dip Serv 1971–: FCO 1971–72, Mecas Lebanon 1972–73, HM Embassy Jeddah 1973–75, UK Perm Representation to EC 1975–78, FCO 1978–83, HM Embassy Cairo 1983–87, FCO 1987–89, HM Embassy Prague 1989–92, HM Embassy Riyadh 1992–95, dir Know How Fund (Central Europe) 1995–; *Recreations* music, hill walking; *Clubs* Athenaeum; *Style*— Stuart Laing, Esq; ✉ JAD (CE), FCO, King Charles Street, London SW1A 2AH (☎ 0171 210 0001)

LAING OF DUNPHAIL, Baron (Life Peer UK 1991), of Dunphail in the District of Moray; Sir Hector Laing; kt (1978); s of Hector Laing, of Edinburgh; *b* 12 May 1923; *Educ* Loretto, Jesus Coll Cambridge; *m* 1950, Marian Clare, da of Maj-Gen Sir John Emilius Laurie, 6 Bt, CBE, DSO (d 1983); 3 s (Hon Mark Hector b 1951, Hon Robert John b 1953, Hon Anthony Rupert b 1955); *Career* WWII served Scots Gds 1942–47 (despatches 1944), demobbed Capt; joined McVitie & Price 1947 (chm 1963), dir United Biscuits 1953 (md 1964, chm United Biscuits (Holdings) plc 1972–90); chm: Food and Drink Industs Cncl 1977–79, Scottish Business in the Community 1982–90, City and Industl Liaison Cncl 1985–90, Business in the Community 1987–91; dir: Bank of England 1973–91, Exxon Corp Inc 1984–94; pres: Goodwill 1983–92, The Weston Spirit 1989–93; treas Cons Pty 1988–93, jt chm The Per Cent Club 1986–90, chm the tstees The Lambeth Fund 1983, govr Wycombe Abbey Sch 1981–94, pres Trident 1992–94; Hon DUniv: Univ of Stirling, Heriot-Watt Univ, FRSE 1989; *Recreations* gardening, walking; *Clubs* White's; *Style*— The Lord Laing of Dunphail, FRSE; ✉ High Meadows, Windsor Road, Gerrards Cross, Bucks SL9 8ST

LAIRD, Sir Gavin Harry; kt (1995), CBE (1988); s of James Laird, and Frances Luxton Laird; *b* 14 March 1933; *Educ* Clydebank HS; *m* 4 Oct 1956, Catherine Gillies (Reena), *née* Campbell; 1 da (Fiona Campbell b 14 April 1961); *Career* AEU: elected regnl offr Scotland 1972, memb Exec Cncl 1975–82, gen sec 1982–95; non-exec dir: Highlands and Islands Development Board 1973–75, Scottish TV 1986–, Court of The Bank of England 1986–94, FS Assurance 1988– (became Britannia Life 1990); chm Greater Manchester Buses North 1994–96; pt/t memb: British National Oil Corporation 1976–86, Scottish Development Agency 1986–91, GSL Scotland 1990–, Scottish Enterprise 1991–92; memb: Gen Cncl of Scottish TUC 1972–75, Arts Cncl of GB 1983–86, Ed Bd European Business Journal, Armed Forces Pay Review Body 1995–, Employment Appeal Tbnl 1996–; govr Atlantic Coll 1988–96; pt/t forestry cmmr 1991–94; hon fell Paisley Tech Coll, Hon DLitt Univ of Keele 1994, Hon DLitt Heriot-Watt Univ 1994; *Recreations* hill walking, music, reading, avoiding work; *Clubs* North Kent Ramblers' Assoc; *Style*— Sir Gavin Laird, CBE; ✉ 35 Southlands Grove, Bromley, Kent BR1 2DA

LAIRD, John Dunn; s of Dr Norman Davidson Laird, OBE, JP, MP (d 1970), of Belfast, and Margaret, *née* Dunn (d 1983); *b* 23 April 1944; *Educ* Royal Belfast Academical Instn; *m* 24 April 1971, Caroline Ethel, da of William John Ferguson, of Dromore, Derrygonnelly, Co Fermanagh; 1 da (Alison Jane b 24 March 1976), 1 s ((John) David b 18 Oct 1977); *Career* Belfast Saving Bank: bank official 1963–67, bank inspr 1967–68, computer programmer 1968–73; memb (UU): St Anne's Div Belfast NI House of Commons 1970–73, W Belfast NI Assembly 1973–75, NI Convention 1975–76; hon treas Ulster Unionist Pty 1974–76; chm John Laird Public Relations 1976–; chm NI Branch Inst of PR 1989–92, visiting prof of PR Univ of Ulster 1993–; memb: Bd of Govrs Royal Belfast Academical Instn 1994–, Cncl Ulster Soc, Bd Ulster Orchestra 1995–, Cncl NI Chest Heart and Stroke Assoc; FIPR 1991; *Videos* Trolleybus Days in Belfast (1992), Swansong of Steam in Ulster (1993), Waterloo Sunset (1994), Rails on the Isle of Wight (1994), The Twilight of Steam in Ulster (1994); *Recreations* transport, travel, cricket and rugby; *Clubs* Queen's Univ Common Room; *Style*— John Laird, Esq; ✉ 43 Earlswood Road, Belfast BT4 3EA, Northern Ireland (☎ 01232 651554); John Laird Public Relations Ltd, 104 Holywood Road, Belfast BT4 1NU, Northern Ireland (☎ 01232 471282, fax 01232 656022, mobile 0836 234369)

LAIRD, Margaret Heather; da of William Henry Polmear (d 1966), and Edith, *née* Tippett (d 1993); *b* 29 Jan 1933; *Educ* The HS Truro, Westfield Coll Univ of London (BA), King's Coll (Cert in Religious Knowledge); *m* 14 Jan 1961, The Rev Canon John Charles Laird; 2 s (Dr Andrew John William Laird b 1963, Rev Stephen Charles Edward Laird b 1966); *Career* divinity mistress: Grey Coat Hosp 1955–59, St Albans HS 1960–62; head of Religious Studies Dept The Dame Alice Harpur Sch 1970–88, Third Church Estates cmmr 1988–; memb Gen Synod 1980–; tstee Lambeth Palace Library 1993–, govr Pusey House Oxford 1993–, memb Allchurches Trust Ltd 1994–, Advsy Bd of Miny selector for the Dioc of St Albans 1994–, vice pres Soc for the Maintenance of the Faith 1995–, memb Exec The Open Churches Tst 1995–; *Recreations* medieval art, architecture, pilgrims' routes; *Clubs* Utd Oxford and Cambridge; *Style*— Mrs Margaret Laird; ✉ Church Commissioners, 1 Millbank, London SW1P 3JZ (☎ 0171 222 7010, fax 0171 233 0171)

LAIRD, Michael Donald; OBE (1983); s of George Donald Struthers Laird (d 1980), and Catherine Brown Dibley, *née* Tennent; *b* 22 March 1928; *Educ* Loretto, Edinburgh Coll of Art (DipArch); *m* 23 March 1957, Hon Caroline (Kirsty) Noel-Paton, da of Baron Ferrier (Life Peer, d 1992); 2 s (Simon b 1958, Magnus b 1962), 1 da (Nicola b 1958); *Career* lectr Dept of Architecture Edinburgh Univ and Coll of Art 1954–57; architect and industl designer: Michael Laird Architect 1954–67, Michael Laird & Partners 1967–92, The Michael Laird Partnership 1992–; MacLaren fellowship 1956–58; works incl: Edinburgh Univ Central Facilities Bldg, head office Standard Life Assurance Co, computer HQ Royal Bank of Scotland; sundry awards: Saltire Soc, Br Steel, Civic Tst, Royal Scottish Acad gold medallist 1968; ARIBA, FRSA, FSIA, FRIAS; *Recreations* sailing, skiing, hill walking; *Clubs* New (Edinburgh); *Style*— Michael Laird, Esq; ✉ 22 Moray Place, Edinburgh EH3 6DB (☎ 0131 225 5859); The Michael Laird Partnership, 5 Forres St, Edinburgh EH3 6DE (☎ 0131 226 6991, fax 0131 226 2771)

LAIRD, Robert Edward; s of Robert Laird (d 1975), of Seaford, Sussex, and Esther Margaret, *née* Stoney (d 1976); *b* 25 Dec 1940; *Educ* Aldenham, Harvard Univ; *m* 8 Aug 1964, Mary Theresa, da of Martin Cooke (d 1969), of Galway, Ireland; 2 s (Robert Richard Martin b 1964, Julian Alexander b 1968), 1 da (Caroline b 1971); *Career* various appts Unilever Ltd 1959–76, dir Carnation Foods 1977–80, md Vandemoortele 1980–86, chm Polar Entertainment Group 1986–88, dir Keith Butters Ltd 1988–89, head of mktg Tate & Lyle Sugars 1989–96; behavioural conslt 1996–; memb Sugar Bureau Ctee 1991–96; Advtg Assoc: memb Int Working Pty 1992–95, chm Food Advtg Ctee 1992–96 (memb

1991), chm Public Affrs Prog Gp 1993–95, memb Exec Ctee 1995–96; memb Cncl Coronary Prevention Gp; Freeman: City of London 1984, Worshipful Co of Upholders 1984; MInstM 1978, FIMgt 1980, MInstD 1982; *Recreations* golf, squash, jogging, reading, genealogy, horse racing; *Clubs* Carlton, Old Aldenhamians, Harvard Business Sch Club of London, The Sportsman; *Style—* R E Laird, Esq; ✉ 42 Elsham Rd, London W14 8HB (☎ 0171 602 2843); 14 Milton Gardens, Wokingham, Berkshire RG40 1DA (☎ 0118 978 4939)

LAISTER, Peter; s of late Horace Laister; *b* 24 Jan 1929; *Educ* King Edward's Sch Birmingham, UMIST (BScTech); *m* 1, 1951, Barbara Cooke; 1 s, 1 da; m 2, 1958, Eileen Alice Goodchild, *née* Town; 1 da; *Career* served RAF 1949–51; Esso Petroleum Co 1951–66, gp md British Oxygen Co Ltd 1969–75; chm: BOC Finance Corporation USA 1974–75, London and Hull Insurance Co Ltd 1976–79, Tollemache and Cobbold Breweries 1978–79, Thorn EMI 1984–85 (chief exec 1983), Park Hotels plc 1985–91, Tower Group plc 1985–90, Oceonics plc 1986–88, Nimbus Records Ltd 1987–93, Nimbus USA Inc 1992–94, MTV Europe 1987–91, Maxwell Communication Corporation plc 1991–92 (dir 1985–, dep chm 1991), Base Ltd 1996–; vice chm Farmsworth 1996–; chief exec Ellerman Lines Ltd 1976–79, md Thorn Electrical Industries 1979–83; dir: Inchcape plc 1982–93, Fluor Daniel Ltd 1985–90, Mirror Group Newspapers plc 1986–90, SelecTV 1987–94, Nimbus CD International 1994–95; memb: Industl Devpt Advsy Bd 1981–83, Cncl Industl Soc 1971–86, Cncl UCL 1978–88, BIM Bd Companions 1985–91; chm: Br Fndn for Res into Ageing 1982–85, Confedn of Info Communication Industs 1989–94; govr BUPA 1982–93; hon fell UMIST; FInstPet, FIChemE, FIInfSc (pres 1990–91), CEng, CIMgt; *Recreations* private flying, photography, fishing, gardening; *Clubs* Athenaeum; *Style—* Peter Laister, Esq; ✉ Thatches, 92 Staines Rd, Wraysbury, Middx TW19 5AA

LAIT, Jacqui; MP (C) Hastings and Rye (majority 6,634); da of late Graham Lait, and Margaret Lait; *b* 16 Dec 1947; *Educ* Paisley GS, Univ of Strathclyde; *m* 1 June 1974, Peter Jones; *Career* PR exec Jute Industries Ltd 1968–70, with Visnews Ltd 1970–74, Govt Info Serv 1974–79, Parly advsr Chemical Industs Assoc 1980–84, independent Parly conslt 1984–92, MP (C) Hastings and Rye 1992–; former PPS to Sec of State for Wales, asst govt whip (first female Tory whip) 1996–; chm: City and E London Family Health Servs Authy 1987–91, Br Section Euro Union of Women 1990–92; *Style—* Mrs Jacqui Lait, MP; ✉ House of Commons, London SW1A 0AA

LAITHWAITE, Prof Eric Roberts; s of Herbert Laithwaite (d 1954), of Kirkham, Lancs, and Florence, *née* Roberts (d 1966); *b* 14 June 1921; *Educ* Kirkham GS, Manchester Univ (BSc, MSc, PhD, DSc); *m* 8 Sept 1951, Sheila Margaret, da of Arthur Haighton Gooddie (d 1981), of Hawkinge, Kent; 2 s (Martin b 1954, Dennis b 1965), 2 da (Helen (Mrs Boam) b 1956, Louise b 1962); *Career* RAF 1941–46, RAE Farnborough 1943–46, lectr Manchester Univ 1951–64, prof of heavy electrical engrg Imperial Coll London 1964–86 (emeritus prof 1986), visiting prof Univ of Sussex 1990–; pres: Assoc for Science Educn 1970, Soc of Environmental Engrs 1991–; dir: Linear Motors Ltd 1971–86, Landspeed Ltd 1975–86, Cotswold Research Ltd; conslt Brian Colquhoun & Partners 1975–91; former conslt: British Rail, Tracked Hovercraft Ltd, GEC, Pilkington Bros; RS SG Brown Award and Medal 1966, Nikola Telsa Award 1986, IEE Achievement Award 1992, Electrical Review Special Award 1995; fell Univ of Hong Kong 1986, fell Imperial Coll 1990; appearances on various TV and radio progs incl: Tomorrow's World, Horizon, The World Around Us, Science Now, Dial a Scientist; CEng, FIEEE, Hon FIEE 1993, FRCA; *Books* incl: Induction Machines for Special Purposes (1966), Propulsion Without Wheels (1966), The Engineer in Wonderland (1967), How to Invent (1970), Engineer Through the Looking Glass (1974), Dictionary of Butterflies and Moths (1981), Invitation to Engineering (1984), Shape is Important (1986), History of Linear Electric Motors (1988), An Inventor in the Garden of Eden (1994); *Recreations* entomology, gardening; *Clubs* Athenaeum; *Style—* Prof Eric Laithwaite; ✉ Department of Electrical Engineering, Imperial College, London SW7 2BT (☎ 0171 589 5111, ext 46176)

LAITY, Mark Franklyn; s of Frank Laity, of Cornwall, and Pamela, *née* Dunn; *b* 18 Dec 1955; *Educ* Redruth County GS, Univ of York (MA); *m* 6 Oct 1990, Sarah Lisa, da of Edward Thomas Parker-Gomm; *Career* trainee and reporter Western Mail 1978–81, news prodr BBC Radio Wales 1981–83; prodr BBC Radio 4: Today 1983–86, Analysis 1986–88; dep ed The World This Weekend Radio 4 1988–89, defence correspondent BBC 1989–; *Recreations* sailing, reading military and maritime history literature; *Clubs* RAF, Thames Sailing; *Style—* Mark Laity, Esq; ✉ Foreign Affairs Unit, BBC News and Current Affairs, Broadcasting House, London W1A 1AA (☎ 0171 765 5305, fax 0171 636 4295, home ☎ and fax 0181 390 1044)

LAKE, David John; *b* 14 J[illegible] 1950; *Educ* Holloway Sch, St Peter's Coll Oxford (MA, Sutton prize for economi[illegible] Janice; 3 da (Elizabeth Megan b 11 Feb 1982, Emily Bronwen b 5 Feb 1985, F[illegible] Dilys b 4 Aug 1989); *Career* formerly industl journalist on various newspapers [illegible]ines, currently md Countrywide Porter Novelli Ltd Oxon (co-fndr as Country[illegible]nications Ltd); *Recreations* sailing, fishing; *Style—* David Lake, Esq; ✉ Coun[illegible]er Novelli Ltd, Communications House, 51 The Green, South Bar, Banbury, Oxon [illegible] 9AB (☎ 01295 272288, fax 01295 270659, car 0374 753020)

LAKE, Sir (Atwell) Graham; 10 Bt (GB 1711), of Edmonton, Middx; s of Capt Sir Atwell Henry Lake, 9 Bt, CB, OBE, RN (d 1972); *b* 6 Oct 1923; *Educ* Eton; *m* 1983, Mrs Katharine Margaret Lister, da of late D W Last; *Heir* bro, Edward Geoffrey Lake b 17 July 1928; *Career* serv in Gilbert & Ellice Mil Forces 1944–45, Col Admin Serv 1945–55, sec to Govt of Tonga 1950–53, Br High Cmmn New Delhi 1966–68, FCO 1969–72; sr tech advsr MOD to 1983, ret; hon sec Abbeyfield Epping Soc 1987–96, chm 1996–; *Recreations* bridge, chess, tennis, landscape gardening; *Clubs* Lansdowne; *Style—* Sir Graham Lake, Bt; ✉ Magdalen Laver Hall, Chipping Ongar, Essex CM5 0EG

LAKE, Dr Lionel Malcolm; s of Colin Frank Lake (d 1962), of Brockworth, Glos, and Marie Moss, *née* Gay, of Harrow, Middx; *b* 5 July 1934; *Educ* Acton Tech Sch, Acton Tech Coll, Chelsea Poly, Birkbeck Coll London (BSc Geology (pt/t)), Imperial Coll London (MSc(Eng), DIC), Univ of Surrey (PhD (pt/t)); *m* 2, 1986, Pamela Margaret, *née* Howe; 2 s (Nicholas Lionel b 1988, Alexander Henry b 1990); 2 da by previous m (Kathryn Maria b 1958, Heather Jane b 1963); *Career* Nat Serv cmmnd 60 HAA Regt RA 1953–55; soil mechanics and foundations technician/engr Ground Explorations Ltd 1955–63, dep chief civil engr Le Grand Sutcliffe & Gell Ltd 1967–71 (geotechnical engr 1963–66), chief engr Soil Mechanics Ltd (John Mowlem & Co) 1971–73; Mott MacDonald (formerly Mott, Hay & Anderson): divnl head 1973–75, assoc dir 1975–77, md Fndn & Geotechnical Div 1977–87, md MOTT YARD Ltd 1987–94, Main Bd dir 1992–94, conslt 1994–; major projects with Mott MacDonald: Tyne & Wear Metro, Channel Tunnel 1973–76, 1978–79 and 1986–94, Lantau Suspension Bridge and New Airport Hong Kong; conslt Environmental Servs Gp John Mowlem & Co 1995–; visiting prof in geotechnical engrg Univ of Newcastle upon Tyne 1987–90, external examiner (postgrad) Dept of Engrg, Geology & Geotechnics Imperial Coll London 1987–91, Royal Acad of Engrg visiting prof in civil engrg design Univ of Brighton 1993–; memb Senate Engrg Cncl, memb Cncl Fndn for Sci and Technol; former memb Environmental and Civil Engrg Ctee SERC, fndr memb and former Ctee memb Assoc of Geotechnical Specialists, former memb Advsy Panel Geotechnique and CIRIA Advsy Ctee on Earthworks and Foundations; author of 29 published papers in public domain and numerous papers and reports with restricted access, numerous lectures to univs, colls, instns and socs; memb: Société des Engenieurs et Scientifiques de France, British Geotechnical Soc, Int Soc of Rock Mechanics, Br Ground Freezing Soc; MACE, MIMM 1966, fell Geological Soc 1966, CEng 1971, FICE 1991 (MICE 1971); *Recreations* sailing, modelling, music, walking, badminton, rugby spectator; *Clubs* Cruising Association, Royal Yachting Association; *Style—* Dr Lionel Lake; ✉ Arden, Snows Ride, Windlesham, Surrey GU20 6PE (☎ 01276 471672, fax 01276 471672)

LAKE, Richard Lawrence Geoffrey; s of Albert Lake (d 1968), and Elsie Lake (d 1995); *b* 11 Nov 1939; *m* 17 Oct 1964, Sheila June, da of Charles Douglas Marsh; 2 da (Amanda b 18 April 1967, Katharina b 1 May 1980); *Career* chartist Laurie Milbank 1969–72; ptnr: Zorn and Leigh-Hunt 1972–76, Grieveson Grant 1976–84, Raphael Zorn 1984–86; dir Swiss Bank Corp 1986–89, chm World Stockmarket Analysis 1989–90, dir Hoare Govett Securities 1991–92, head of technical analysis SBC Warburg 1992–; deacon Duke St Baptist Church Richmond; memb: Securities Inst, Inst of Investment Mgmnt and Research; fell Soc of Technical Analysts; *Recreations* family, running and cycling; *Style—* Richard Lake, Esq; ✉ 285 Petersham Rd, Petersham, Richmond, Surrey TW10 7DA (☎ 0181 940 3795); SBC Warburg, 1 Finsbury Avenue, London EC2M 2PA (☎ 0171 382 4941)

LAKER, Sir Frederick Alfred (Freddie); kt (1978); *b* 6 Aug 1922; *Educ* Simon Langton Sch Canterbury; *m* 1, 1942 (m dis 1968), Joan; 1 s (decd), 1 da (Elaine); m 2, 1968 (m dis 1975), Rosemary Black; m 3, 1975 (m dis 1982), Patricia Gates, of Oklahoma; 1 s (Freddie Jr b 1978); m 4, 1985, Jacqueline Ann Harvey; *Career* with Short Bros Rochester 1938–40, Gen Aircraft 1940–41, ATA 1941–46, md Aviation Traders Gp 1946–65, md Br Utd Airways 1960–65, chm and md Laker Airways (Int) Ltd 1966–82, established Skytrain Holidays 1983, aviation and travel conslt 1982–, chm and md Laker Airways (Bahamas) Ltd 1992–; memb Airworthiness Requirements Bd until 1982, chm benevolent fund Guild of Air Pilots and Air Navigators; memb Lloyd's 1954–; hon fell UMIST; Hon DSc City Univ, Hon DSc Cranfield Inst of Technol, Hon LLD Manchester; *Clubs* Jockey, Eccentric, Little Ship; *Style—* Sir Freddie Laker; ✉ Furzegrove Farm, Chailey, nr Newick, Lewes E Sussex (☎ 01825 722648)

LAKER, Dr Michael Francis; s of Sqdn Ldr Walter John Laker, of Ledbury, and Joyce, *née* Ashill; *b* 9 June 1945; *Educ* Newport HS, Univ of London (MD, BS, Dip BioChem); *m* 13 Dec 1969, Alison Jean, da of Thomas Borland (d 1986), of Tunbridge Wells; 2 s (Christopher b 1981, Jonathan b 1983), 2 da (Hannah b 1974, Bethan b 1977); *Career* lectr in chemical pathology and metabolic disorders St Thomas's Hosp Med Sch 1973–80, res fell Dept of Med Univ of California San Diego 1979–80, sr lectr in clinical biochemistry and metabolic med Univ of Newcastle and conslt chemical pathologist Newcastle Health Authy 1980–89, reader in clinical biochemistry and metabolic med Univ of Newcastle upon Tyne 1989– (sub dean for Admissions The Med Sch 1990–), conslt in clinical biochemistry Royal Victoria Infirmary and Associated Hosps NHS Tst 1989–; memb Ctee Br Hyperlipidaemia Assoc; FRCPath 1988; *Books* Short Cases in Clinical Biochemistry (1984), Cholesterol Lowering Trials - Advice for the British Physicians (1993), Clinical Biochemistry for Medical Students (1995), Multiple Choice Questions in Clinical Pathology (1995); *Recreations* music, computing, gardening; *Style—* Dr Michael Laker; ✉ 9 Campus Martius, Heddon On The Wall, Northumberland NE15 0BP; Department of Clinical Biochemistry and Metabolic Medicine, University of Newcastle upon Tyne, Medical School, Framlington, Newcastle upon Tyne NE2 4HH (☎ 0191 222 6000 ext 8786, fax 0191 222 6227)

LAKES, Gordon Harry; CB (1987), MC (1951); s of Harry Lakes (d 1980), and Annie, *née* Butcher (d 1970); *b* 27 Aug 1928; *Educ* Army Tech Sch Arborfield, RMA Sandhurst; *m* 2 Oct 1950, Nancy (d 1992), da of Joseph Watters Smith (d 1952); 1 da (Alison b 1953); *Career* cmmnd RA 1948, 39 Medium Regt 1949–50, Lt 1950, 170 Ind Mortar Batty 1950–52, pilot 657 Air Op Sqdn RAF 1952–54, Capt 1953, Adj 383 Light Regt RA (DCRH) TA 1954–56, 2 Ind Field Batty RA 1956–58, promoted Maj to cmd Ghana Recce Sqdn Ghana Army 1958–60, ret 1960; asst govr HM Prison Serv 1961, HM Borstal Feltham 1962–65, asst princ Offrs Trg Sch Leyhill 1965–68, govr HM Remand Centre Thorp Arch 1968–70, Prison Serv HQ 1970, govr class 3 1971, HM Prison Pentonville 1974, govr class 2 1975, HM Prison Gartree 1975, Prison Serv HQ 1977, govr class 1 1979, asst controller and HM dep chief inspr of prisons 1982, AUSS and dep dir gen of Prison Serv 1985, memb Cncl of Europe Ctee for Cooperation in Prison Affrs 1986–91; memb Parole Bd 1989–92, conslt to 8th UN Congress on Prevention of Crime and the Treatment of Offenders 1990, chm National AIDS and Prisons Forum 1990–, assessor to Lord Justice Woolf's Inquiry into Prison Disturbances 1990–91, commissioner Mental Health Act 1991–; *Recreations* golf, photography; *Style—* Gordon H Lakes, Esq, CB, MC

LAKEY, Prof John Richard Angwin; s of late William Richard Lakey, and late Edith; *b* 28 June 1929; *Educ* Morley GS, Univ of Sheffield (BSc, PhD); *m* 22 Dec 1955, Dr Pamela Janet Lakey, JP, da of late Eric Clifford Lancey; 3 da (Joanna Margaret, Philippa Mary (Mrs Lewry), Nicola Janet (Dr King)); *Career* res posts Simon Carves Ltd, secondment to AERE Harwell and GEC 1953–60; RNC Greenwich: asst prof 1960–80, prof 1980–89, dean 1984–86 and 1988–89; reactor shielding conslt DG Ships 1967–89, radiation conslt WHO 1973–74, hon visiting lectr Harvard Univ 1984–, hon visiting prof Univ of Surrey 1988–95, radiation protection conslt John Lakey Assocs 1989–; memb CNAA Physics Bd 1973–82, pubns dir Int Radiation Protection Assoc 1979–88, external examiner Univ of Surrey 1980–86, memb Editorial Bd Physics in Med and Biology 1980–83, news ed Health Physics 1980–88, memb Medway Health Authy 1981–90, regnl scientific advsr No 5 Region 1984–93, chm UK Liaison Ctee for Scis Allied to Med and Biology 1984–87, pres Inst of Nuclear Engrs 1988–90 (vice pres 1983–87), vice pres London Int Youth Sci Forum 1988–, pres Int Radiation Protection Assoc 1988–92, vice pres Euro Nuclear Soc 1989–95; Freeman City of London 1988, Liveryman Worshipful Co of Engineers 1988, hon fell Soc for Radiological Protection 1992; Eur Ing, CEng, FINucE, FInstE, CPhys, FInstP, Hon FSRP; memb: Soc for Radiological Protection, US Health Physics Soc, American Nuclear Soc; *Books* Protection Against Radiation (1961), Radiation Protection Measurement: philosophy and implementation (1975), ALARA principles and practices (1987), IRPA Guidelines on Protection Against Non-Ionizing Radiation (1991), Off-site Emergency Response to Nuclear Accidents (1993), Radiation and Radiation Protection (1994), papers on nuclear safety, radiological protection and management of emergencies; *Recreations* yachting, photography, conversation; *Clubs* Athenaeum, Medway Yacht, RNSA; *Style—* Prof John Lakey; ✉ John Lakey Associates, 5 Pine Rise, Meopham, Gravesend, Kent DA13 0JA (☎ and fax 01474 812551)

LAKIN, Sir Michael; 4 Bt (UK 1909), of The Cliff, Borough of Warwick; s of Sir Henry Lakin, 3 Bt (d 1979); *b* 28 Oct 1934; *Educ* Stowe; *m* 1, 1956 (m dis 1963), Margaret, da of Robert Wallace, of Mount Norris, Co Armagh; m 2, 1965, Felicity, da of Anthony Denis Murphy, of Londiani, Kenya; 1 s (Richard Anthony b 1968), 1 da (Mary Jane b 1966); *Heir* s, Richard Anthony Lakin b 26 Nov 1968; *Style—* Sir Michael Lakin, Bt; ✉ Little Sherwood Hill, Tunley, nr Cirencester, Glos

LAKIN, His Hon Judge Peter Maurice; s of Ronald Maurice Lakin (d 1985), of Coventry, and Dorothy Kathleen, *née* Cowlishaw; *b* 21 Oct 1949; *Educ* King Henry VIII GS Coventry, Univ of Manchester (LLB); *m* 11 Dec 1971, Jacqueline, da of John Alexander Jubb; 1 s (Michael John b 25 May 1975), 1 da (Emma Jane b 14 May 1977); *Career* asst slr Conn Goldberg Solicitors 1974–76 (articled clerk 1971–74), ptnr (i/c Forensic and Criminal Litigation) Pannone and Partners Solicitors 1976–95; recorder of the Crown Court 1993–95, circuit judge (Northern Circuit) 1995–; memb Law Soc 1974; *Recreations* fell walking, gardening, opera; *Style—* His Hon Judge Lakin; ✉ Manchester Crown Court, Crown Square, Manchester M3 3FL (☎ 0161 954 1757)

LAL, Prof Deepak Kumar; s of Nand Lal (d 1984), of New Delhi, and Shanti, *née* Devi; *b* 3 Jan 1940; *Educ* Doon Sch Dehra Dun, Stephen's Coll Delhi (BA), Jesus Coll Oxford (MA, BPhil); *m* 11 Dec 1971, Barbara, da of Jack Ballis (d 1987), of New York; 1 s (Akshay b 18 Aug 1981), 1 da (Deepika b 17 March 1980); *Career* Indian Foreign Serv 1963–65, lectr Christchurch Coll Oxford 1966–68, res fell Nuffield Coll Oxford 1968–70, reader political econ UCL 1979–84 (lectr 1970–79), prof of political econ Univ of London 1984–93 (emeritus 1993), James S Coleman prof of devpt studies Univ of Calif at Los Angeles (UCLA) 1990–; conslt Indian Planning Cmmn 1973–74, res admin World Bank Washington DC 1983–87; conslt 1970–: ILO, UNCTAD, OECD, UNIDO, World Bank, Miny of Planning S Korea and Sri Lanka; co-dir Trade Policy Unit Centre for Policy Studies London 1993–; Ohlin Meml lectr 1995, Shenoy Meml lectr 1996; *Books* Wells and Welfare (1972), Methods of Project Analysis (1974), Appraising Foreign Investment in Developing Countries (1975), Unemployment and Wage Inflation in Industrial Economies (1977), Men or Machines (1978), Prices for Planning (1980), The Poverty of Development Economics (1983), Labour and Poverty in Kenya (with P Collier, 1986), Stagflation, Savings and the State (ed with M Wolf, 1986), The Hindu Equilibrium (1988 and 1989), Public Policy and Economic Development (ed with M Scott, 1990), Development Economics, 4 vols (ed 1992), The Repressed Economy (1993), Against Dirigisme (1994), The Political Economy of Poverty, Equity and Growth (with H Myint, 1996); *Recreations* opera, theatre, tennis; *Clubs* Reform; *Style—* Prof Deepak Lal; ✉ 2 Erskine Hill, London NW11 6HB (☎ and fax 0181 458 3713); A 30 Nizamuddin West, New Delhi 110013, India (☎ and fax 00 9111 4629465); 213 Park Wilshire, 10724 Wilshire Boulevard, Los Angeles, CA 90024, USA (☎ and fax 00 1 310 474 7721); Department of Economics, 8369 Bunche Hall, UCLA, 405 Hilgard Avenue, Los Angeles, CA 90024 (☎ 00 1 310 825 4521, fax 00 1 310 206 2382)

LALANDI-EMERY, Lina Madeleine; OBE (1975); da of late Nikolas Kaloyeropoulos, and the late Toula, *née* Gelekis; *Educ* Athens Conservatoire (prizewinner), privately in England; *m* Ralph Emery, *qv*; *Career* first appeared as harpsichord soloist Royal Festival Hall 1954, int career in concert radio and TV, dir Eng Bach Festival Trust 1963– (fndr 1962, specialising in baroque opera and dance); appearances incl Covent Gdn, Versailles and numerous festivals of music (Granada, Athens, Monte Carlo, Madrid); Offr dans l'Ordre des Arts et des Lettres France 1978; *Recreations* cooking, reading, astrophysics, knitting; *Style—* Mrs Lina Lalandi-Emery, OBE; ✉ 15 South Eaton Place, London SW1W 9ER (☎ 0171 730 5925); English Bach Festival Trust, 15 South Eaton Place, London SW1W 9ER (☎ 0171 730 5295, fax 0171 730 1456)

LALIĆ, Susan Kathryn; da of Peter James Walker, of Cheam, Surrey, and Sylvia Dorothy, *née* Bacon; *b* 28 Oct 1965; *Educ* Nonsuch HS for Girls; *m* 1, 1986 (m dis), Keith Charles Arkell, s of Charles Arkell; m 2, April 1994, Bogdan Lalić, s of Dragan Lalić, of Zagreb; 1 s (Peter); *Career* professional chess player; joined Banstead Chess Club aged 13, first represented England aged 14 in girls under 18 team, former rep Surrey, current rep Derbyshire; achievements incl: nat girls under 18 champion 1983, Surrey under 18 mixed champion 1983, third place world girls under 20's Yugoslavia 1985 (fourth Mexico City 1984), winner Br Ladies Championships 1986, 1990, 1991 and 1992, winner Br Womens Prixette annually 1987–91, winner Cwlth Ladies Championships annually 1988–92; rep England in Womens Chess Olympiads: Bd 4 Thessoloniki 1984, Bd 3 Dubai 1986, Bd 1 Thessoloniki 1988, Bd 1 Novi Sad 1990, Bd 1 Manila 1992, Bd 1 Moscow 1994; woman int master title 1985, woman grandmaster title 1988; highest ever rated Br woman chess player, only Br born woman grandmaster; *Books* The Super Clash (co-author, 1987), Trends in the Caro-Kann: Panov-Botvinnik (1993), Trends in the Blumenfeld Gambit (1993), Trends in the French Tarrasch (1994); *Recreations* tennis, table tennis, walking; *Style—* Mrs Susan Lalić; ✉ c/o British Chess Federation, 9a Grand Parade, St Leonards on Sea, E Sussex TN38 0DD (☎ 01424 442500)

LAMB, Adrian Frank; s of Frank Lamb (d 1981), and Mary Elizabeth Graham, *née* Chambers (d 1977); *Educ* Gateshead GS; *m* 4 May 1974, Jane, da of William Moore, of Blyth, Notts; 1 s (Richard b 1982), 3 da (Katharine b 1976, Amy b 1978, Jennifer b 1982); *Career* CA; Richard Ormond Son & Dunn 1960–65, ptnr Coopers & Lybrand 1975–, seconded to Civil Serv Dept 1970; hon treas Int Fedn of Multiple Sclerosis Socs; FCA 1966; *Books* Analysed Reporting (1977), Internal Audit in the Civil Service (jtly, 1971); *Recreations* tennis, bridge, music, gardening; *Style—* Adrian Lamb, Esq; ✉ Lynbury House, Burtons Way, Chalfont St Giles, Bucks HP8 4BP (☎ 01494 764810); Coopers & Lybrand, Embankment Place, London WC2N 6NN (☎ 0171 583 5000, fax 0171 822 4652, telex 887470)

LAMB, Sir Albert Thomas (Archie); KBE (1979, MBE 1953), CMG (1974), DFC (1945); s of Reginald Selwyn Lamb (d 1970), and Violet, *née* Haynes (d 1980); *b* 23 Oct 1921; *Educ* Swansea GS; *m* 8 April 1944, Christina Betty, da of Albert Henry Wilkinson (d 1960); 1 s (Robin b 1948), 2 da (Elizabeth b 1945, Kathryn b 1959); *Career* RAF 1941–46; FO 1938–41, Rome Embassy 1947–50, Genoa Consulate 1950, Bucharest Legation 1950–53, FO 1953–55, MECAS 1955–57, Bahrain (political residency) 1957–61, FO oil desk 1961–65, Kuwait Embassy 1965, political agent Abu Dhabi 1965–68, chief inspr Dip Serv 1968–74; ambass: Kuwait 1974–77, Norway 1978–80; memb Bd BNOC 1981–82, dir Britoil plc 1982–88, memb Bd Samuel Montagu & Co Ltd 1981–85 (advsr 1985–88), sr assoc Conant & Associates Ltd Washington DC 1985–94; clerk of Parish Cncl of Zeals 1991–, memb Bd National Bank of Kuwait (International) plc 1994–; *Recreations* gardening; *Clubs* RAF; *Style—* Sir Archie Lamb, KBE, CMG, DFC; ✉ White Cross Lodge, Zeals, Wilts BA12 6PF (☎ 01747 840321)

LAMB, Allan Joseph; s of Michael Lamb, and Joan Lamb; *b* 20 June 1954, Langebaanweg, SA; *Educ* Wynberg Boys' HS, Abbotts Coll; *m* 8 Dec 1979, Lindsay; 1 s (Richard Edward Thomas), 1 da (Katie-Ann); *Career* professional cricketer; Northamptonshire CCC: debut and county cap 1978, benefit 1988, capt 1989–95, NatWest Trophy winners 1992; overseas teams: Western Province SA 1972–82, Orange Free State SA 1987–88, Western Province SA 1992–93; England: 79 test matches 1982–, 3 tests as capt (made century in first v W Indies Bridgetown 1990), scored 14 test centuries (incl 3 in consecutive tests v W Indies 1984), 122 one day ints; tours: Aust and NZ 1982–83, NZ and Pakistan 1983–84, India and Aust 1984–85, W Indies 1985–86, Aust 1986–87, India and Pakistan (incl World Cup) 1987–88, India and W Indies 1989–90, Aust 1990–91, NZ and Aust (incl World Cup) 1991–92; *Recreations* fly-fishing; *Style—* Allan Lamb, Esq; ✉ Northamptonshire CCC, County Ground, Wantage Rd, Northampton NN1 4TJ (☎ 01604 32917)

LAMB, Andrew Martin; s of Harry Lamb, of Abergele, Clwyd, and Winifred, *née* Emmott; *b* 23 Sept 1942; *Educ* Werneth Sch Oldham, Manchester GS, CCC Oxford (MA); *m* 1 April 1970, Wendy Ann, da of Frank Edward Davies, of Shirley, Solihull, Warwickshire; 1 s (Richard Andrew b 1976), 2 da (Helen Margaret b 1972, Susan Elizabeth b 1973); *Career* investmt mangr then asst gen mangr MGM Assurance 1985–88, chief investmt mangr Friends Provident Life Office 1988–; musicologist; FIA 1972, AIIMR; *Books* Jerome Kern in Edwardian London (1985), Gänzl's Book of the Musical Theatre (with Kurt Gänzl, 1988), Light Music from Austria (1992), Skaters' Waltz: The Story of the Waldteufels (1995); contrib to: Gramophone, Opera, The New Grove Dictionary of Music & Musicians; *Recreations* cricket, music, family; *Clubs* Lancashire CCC; *Style—* Andrew Lamb, Esq; ✉ 12 Fullers Wood, Croydon, CR0 8HZ; Friends Provident Life Office, 15 Old Bailey, London EC4M 7AP (☎ 0171 329 1427)

LAMB, Colin Anthony; s of Wilfred Samuel Lamb (d 1978), of London, and Evelyn Mabel, *née* Straker (d 1982); *b* 17 Nov 1928; *Educ* Dulwich; *m* 7 May 1960, José Dorothy, da of Harold Punt (d 1973), of Hartoft, N Yorkshire; 1 s (Rupert b 22 Oct 1967), 2 da (Henrietta b 26 March 1962, Isabella b 11 Sept 1963); *Career* Nat Serv 2 Lt RASC 1947–49, Capt Middx Regt TA 1954; insurance broker Lloyd's 1950–56, Dist Police, Special Branch and Game Dept Tanganyika HM Overseas Civil Serv 1956–64; called to the Bar Middle Temple 1966, examiner under Ecclesiastical Jurisdiction Measure 1978–, recorder Crown Ct 1989–; *Recreations* cricket, music; *Clubs* The Norfolk; *Style—* Colin Lamb, Esq; ✉ Bure Hse, Millgate, Aylsham, Norfolk (☎ 01263 732555)

LAMB, Hon David Charles; s and h of 2 Baron Rochester, *qv*; *b* 8 Sept 1944; *Educ* Shrewsbury Sch, Univ of Sussex; *m* 9 April 1969, Jacqueline Agnes, yr da of John Alfred Stamp, of Torquay, Devon; 2 s (Daniel b 1971, Joe b 1972); *Career* journalist; *Style—* The Hon D C Lamb; ✉ The Anchorage, 1 Beresford Avenue, Twickenham, Middlesex TW1 2PY (☎ 0181 892 0226)

LAMB, Air Vice-Marshal George Colin; CB (1977), CBE (1966), AFC (1947); s of George Lamb, of Wryville, Hornby, Lancs (d 1953), and Bessie Lamb; *b* 23 July 1923; *Educ* Lancaster Royal GS; *m* 1, 1945, Nancy Mary, da of Ronald Godsmark, of Norwich; 2 s; m 2, 1981, Mrs Maureen Margaret Mepham, da of Thomas Bamford (d 1967), of Hounslow, Middx; *Career* asst cmdt RAF Coll Cranwell 1964–65, dep cdr Air Forces Borneo 1965–66, Air Cdre 1968, OC RAF Lyneham 1969–71, RCDS 1971–72, dir of control (ops) Nat Air Traffic Serv 1972–74, Cdre Southern Maritime Air Region 1974–75, COS No 18 Gp 1975–78, RAF vice pres Combined Cadet Forces Assoc 1978–94; chm Yonex UK Ltd 1995– (md 1990–95); int rugby football referee 1967–72, chief exec Badminton Assoc of England 1978–89, memb Sports Cncl 1983–90; chm: Lilleshall Nat Sports Centre 1983–, Sports Ctee Princes Tst 1985–, Br Int Sports Devpt Aid Tst 1995–; privilege memb RFU 1985 (memb Ctee 1973–85), gen sec London Sports Med Inst 1989–90, Br Int Sports Ctee 1989–, memb Sports Cncl Drug Abuse Advsy Gp 1984–92; pres St Georges Day Club 1994–; FIMgt; *Recreations* rugby union football, gardening; *Clubs* RAF; *Style—* Air Vice-Marshal George Lamb, CB, CBE, AFC; ✉ Hambledon, 17 Meadway, Berkhamsted, Herts HP4 2PN (☎ and fax 01442 862583; office ☎ 0181 742 9777, fax 0181 742 9612)

LAMB, Prof Hubert Horace; s of Prof Ernest Horace Lamb (d 1946), of London, and Lilian, *née* Brierley (d 1969); *b* 22 Sept 1913; *Educ* Oundle, Trinity Coll Cambridge (BA, MA, ScD); *m* 7 Feb 1948, (Beatrice) Moira Milligan, da of Rev Oswald Milligan, DD (d 1940), of Corstorphine, Edinburgh; 1 s (Norman Peter b 1957), 2 da (Catherine Ann (Mrs Gilbride) b 1948, Kirsten Mary (Mrs Reilly) b 1954); *Career* entered Meteorological Office 1936, seconded Irish Meteorological Serv 1939 (later transfd), head forecaster Transatlantic Civil Passenger Air Route 1941–44, researcher UK Meteorological Office 1945–71, forecaster whaling in Antarctic 1946–47, fndr and first dir Climatic Res Unit UEA 1972–78 (now prof emeritus); memb Nat Antarctic Res Ctee 1960–78, former vice pres RMS (Symons Medallist 1987), pres N Norfolk Lib Democrats; contribs incl: Encyclopaedia Britannica, Oxford Dictionary of Natural History; Hon DSc UEA 1981, Hon LLD Univ of Dundee 1981, Hon DSc Univ of Kent 1996; Vega medal Royal Swedish Geographical Soc 1984; hon corresponding memb: Danish Natural History Soc 1978–, Royal Acad of Arts and Sciences Barcelona 1985–; FRMetS 1938, FRGS 1947; *Books* Climate: Present, Past and Future (vol 1 1972, vol 2 1977), Climate, History and the Modern World (1982, 2 edn 1995), Weather, Climate and Human Affairs (1988), Historic Storms of the North Sea, British Isles and Northwest Europe (1991); *Recreations* travel, hill walking; *Style—* Prof Hubert Lamb; ✉ Climatic Research Unit, University of East Anglia, Norwich NR4 7TJ (☎ 01603 456161)

LAMB, John Tregea; s of late Roger Craven Lamb, of Scaynes Hill, W Sussex, and Katherine Honor Lamb; *b* 1 Aug 1952; *Educ* Felsted Sch Essex, Poly of N London (BA); *partner* Dee Robinson; 2 s (Jamie b 25 Nov 1974, Max b 4 April 1984), 2 da (Mary Jane b 14 March 1973, Naomi b 26 Oct 1987); *Career* trainee exec Richmond Towers PR 1970–71, trainee reporter Camberley News Surrey 1971–73, sub ed National Newsagent 1976–77, reporter Computing magazine 1977–78, news ed Computer Talk 1978–80, freelance journalist covering computer and electronics field 1980–88, ed Computer Weekly 1988–96, ed Computer Age supplement Sunday Business 1996; Freeman Worshipful Co of Info Technologists; MBCS; *Recreations* gardening; *Style—* John Lamb, Esq; ✉ 2 Dairy Cottages, Wolterton, Norwich, Norfolk NR11 7LX (☎ 01263 768944)

LAMB, Prof Joseph Fairweather; s of Joseph Lamb (d 1972), of Balnacake, Brechin, Angus, and late Agnes May, *née* Fairweather; *b* 18 July 1928; *Educ* Auldbar Public Sch, Brechin HS, Univ of Edinburgh (MB ChB, BSc, PhD); *m* 1, 10 Sept 1955 (m dis 1989), Olivia Jane, da of Robert Horne (d 1960), of Uganda; 5 s (Joseph William b 1958, John Robert b 1962, Andrew Noel b 1964, James Gerald b 1985, William Finlay b 1987), 1 da (Angela Gail b 1956); m 2, 21 April 1989, Bridget Cecilia, da of John Kingsley Cook (d 1994), of London; *Career* Nat Serv RAF 1947–49, house offr appts 1955–56, lectr Royal (Dick) Vet Coll Univ of Edinburgh 1958–61, lectr then sr lectr in physiology Univ of Glasgow 1961–69, Chandos prof of physiology Univ of St Andrews 1969–93 (emeritus 1993); sec Physiological Soc 1982–85, chm and fndr memb Save Br Sci 1986–; chm and organiser Gas Greed campaign 1994–95; memb RSM, FRCPE 1984, FRSE 1986, FRSA 1987; *Books* Essentials of Physiology (1980); *Recreations* sailing; *Clubs* Sceptre Sailing, RSM, Clyde Cruising; *Style—* Prof Joseph Lamb, FRSE; ✉ Kenbrae, 23 Millbank, Cupar, Fife KY15 5DP (☎ 01334 652791); School of Biological & Medical Sciences, Bute Medical Buildings, Univ of St Andrews, Fife KY16 9TS (☎ 01334 463542, fax 01334 463600)

LAMB, Sir Larry; kt (1980); *b* 15 July 1929; *Educ* Rastrick GS; *m* Joan Mary Denise, *née* Grogan; 2 s, 1 da; *Career* ed: Daily Mail (Manchester) 1968–69, The Sun 1969–72 and 1975–81 (ed dir 1971–81, dep chm News Gp 1979–81), dep chm and ed-in-chief Western Mail Ltd W Aust 1981–82; ed: The Australian 1982, Daily Express 1983–86; chm Larry Lamb Associates 1986–; *Recreations* cricket, fell-walking, fishing; *Style—* Sir Larry Lamb; ✉ 42 Malvern Court, Onslow Square, London SW7 3HY

LAMB, Hon Timothy Michael (Tim); s of 2 Baron Rochester; *b* 24 March 1953; *Educ* Shrewsbury, The Queen's Coll Oxford (MA); *m* 23 Sept 1978, Denise Ann, da of John Buckley, Frinton-on-Sea, Essex; 1 s (Nicholas b 9 Nov 1985), 1 da (Sophie b 15 Sept 1983); *Career* professional cricketer with Middlesex CCC 1974–77, Northants County Cricket Club 1978–83; sec/gen mangr Middlesex CCC 1984–88; chief exec Test and County Cricket Bd 1996– (cricket sec 1988–96); *Recreations* cricket, golf, travel; *Clubs* MCC, Lord's Taverners; *Style—* The Hon Tim Lamb; ✉ c/o Test and County Cricket Board, Lord's Ground, London NW8 8QZ (☎ 0171 286 4405, fax 0171 289 5619)

LAMB, Dr Trevor Arthur John; s of Arthur Bradshaw Lamb, and Ruth Ellen, *née* Eales; *b* 7 Dec 1929; *Educ* Wanstead GS Essex, QMC London (BSc, PhD); *m* 1952, Shirley Isabel, da of Sidney Charles Hubbard (d 1971); 2 s (John b 1957, Martin b 1960), 2 da (Susan b 1960, Karen b 1964); *Career* pt/t lectr Univ of London 1950–52, section ldr Bristol Aeroplane Co Engine Div 1952–56, section head (engrg res) Imperial Chemical Industs 1956–58, factory mangr then gen mangr Leeds Plant Marston Excelsior Ltd (subsid of ICI Metals Div, became Imperial Metal Industs Ltd, styled IMI Ltd) 1958–62, md then exec chm Radiator Gp IMI Ltd 1962–74; IMI plc: main bd dir of overseas and mktg 1974–87, exec chm Australasian, Refinery and Fabrication Gps 1974–77, exec chm Valve Gp 1977–89, exec chm Fluid Power Gp 1981–91, conslt 1992–94; non-exec dir: W Canning plc 1980–96, Richard Burbidge Ltd 1992–96; business conslt 1992–; govr The City Technol Coll Kingshurst 1989–93; Eur Ing, CEng, FIMechE, fell Inst of Refrigeration (FIR); *Recreations* music, golf, tennis, swimming; *Style—* Dr Trevor Lamb; ✉ Mead End, Bushwood Drive, Dorridge, Solihull, W Mids B93 8JL (☎ 01564 773877, fax 01564 779428)

LAMBERT, Dr Andrew David; s of David George Lambert, of Beetley, Norfolk, and Nola, *née* Burton; *b* 31 Dec 1956; *Educ* Hamond's Sch Swaffham, City of London Poly (BA), King's Coll London (MA, PhD); *m* 27 Nov 1987, Zohra, da of Mokhtar Bouznat, of Casablanca, Morocco; 1 da (Tama-Sophie b 29 May 1990); *Career* lectr modern int history Bristol Poly 1983–87, conslt Dept of History and Int Affrs RNC Greenwich 1987–89, sr lectr in war studies RMA Sandhurst 1989–91, sr lectr in war studies King's Coll London 1996– (lectr 1991–96); memb Cncl SS Great Britain Project 1989–, sec Soc Navy Records 1996 (cncllr 1985); FRHistS 1990; *Books* Battleships in Transition: The Creation of the Steam Battlefleet 1815–1960 (1984 and 1985), Warrior: Restoring The World's First Ironclad (1987), The Crimean War: British Grand Strategy Against Russia 1853–56 (1990), The Last Sailing Battlefleet: Maintaining Naval Mastery 1815–1850 (1991), Steam, Steel and Shellfire (1992); *Recreations* running, motorcycling; *Clubs* Vintage Motorcycle; *Style*— Dr Andrew Lambert; ✉ Department of War Studies, King's College London, Strand, London WC2R 2LS (☎ 0171 873 2179, fax 0171 873 2026)

LAMBERT, Angela Maria; da of late John Donald Helps, of Sherborne, Dorset, and Ditha, *née* Schroeder; *b* 14 April 1940; *Educ* Wispers Sch nr Midhurst Sussex, St Hilda's Coll Oxford (BA); *m* 1962 (m dis 1966), Martin John Lambert; 1 s (Jonathan Martin Andrew b 1964), 1 da (Carolyn Ruth (Mrs Butler) b 1963); *partner* 1986–, Tony Price; 1 da from previous ptnr (Marianne Jane Colette b 1971); *Career* author and journalist; PPS to Lord Longford House of Lords 1965–68, freelance journalist 1968–72, TV reporter for News at Ten, LWT and Thames TV 1972–88; feature writer: The Independent 1988–96, The Daily Mail 1996–; memb Ctee English PEN; *Books* Unquiet Souls (1984), 1939: The Last Season of Peace (1989), Love Among The Single Classes (novel, 1989), No Talking After Lights (novel, 1990), A Rather English Marriage (novel, 1992), The Constant Mistress (novel, 1994), The Woman Who Rode on a Lion (novel, 1997); *Recreations* reading, writing, talking, eating, travelling, five grandchildren; *Style*— Ms Angela Lambert; ✉ Flat 4, 15 Collingham Rd, London SW5 ONU (☎ 0171 244 9762, fax 0171 244 8297); c/o The Daily Mail, Northcliffe House, 2 Derry Street, Kensington, London W8 5TT (☎ 0171 938 6000, fax 0171 937 2471)

LAMBERT, Sir Anthony Edward; KCMG (1964, CMG 1955); s of Reginald Everitt Lambert (d 1968), of Pensbury House, Shaftesbury, Dorset, and Evelyn Lambert (d 1968); *b* 7 March 1911; *Educ* Harrow, Balliol Coll Oxford; *m* 28 April 1948, Ruth Mary, da of Sir Arthur Percy Morris Fleming, CBE (d 1960); 3 da (Jane b 1949, Katherine b 1950, Julia b 1953 d 1958); *Career* entered Foreign Serv 1934; cnsllr: Stockholm 1949 and Athens 1951; min to Bulgaria 1958; ambass: Tunisia 1960, Finland 1963, Portugal 1966–70; *Style*— Sir Anthony Lambert, KCMG

LAMBERT, David George; *b* 7 Aug 1940; *Educ* Barry GS, Univ Coll of Wales at Aberystwyth (LLB); *m* 1966, Diana Mary, *née* Ware; 1 s (Nicholas David b 1976), 1 da (Julia Mary b 1978); *Career* called to the Bar 1964; slr and legal advsr (grade 3) Welsh Office 1991– (joined 1966); tutor Law Faculty Univ Coll Cardiff; registrar Diocese of Llandaff, dep chapter clerk Llandaff Cathedral; NP, memb Law Soc; *Recreations* ecclesiastical law, baroque music; *Style*— David Lambert, Esq; ✉ 9 The Chantry, Llandaff, Cardiff CF5 2NN (☎ 01222 568154); Welsh Office, Cathays Park, Cardiff CF1 3NQ (☎ 01222 823510)

LAMBERT, Eva Margaret; da of Frank Holroyd (d 1978), and Elsie Irene, *née* Fearnley; *b* 17 Sept 1946; *Educ* Elland GS; *m* 1; 1 s (Terry Graham Lambert b 16 Dec 1966), 1 da (Justine Louise Lambert b 30 July 1968); m 2, 17 April 1982, Robert Stephen Lambert, s of Robert Lambert; 1 da (Jemma Louise Lambert b 13 April 1983); *Career* health service administrator 1973–83, financial accountant 1983–85, mgmnt accountant 1985–86, dep fin mangr 1986–90, dep unit gen mangr 1990–91, divnl gen mangr 1991–92, chief exec Huddersfield NHS Tst 1992–; AAT 1982, FCCA 1993 (ACCA 1987); *Recreations* tennis, squash, handicrafts; *Style*— Mrs Eva Lambert; ✉ Huddersfield NHS Trust, Trust Headquarters, The Royal Infirmary, Lindley, Huddersfield, W Yorks HD3 3EA (☎ 01484 422191, fax 01484 456275)

LAMBERT, Dr Hannah Eva; *Educ* St Mary's Hosp Med Sch Univ of London (MB BS, DObstRCOG, DMRT); *Career* various house posts in surgery, med, paediatrics, obstetrics and gynaecology 1957–60, registrar obstetrics and gynaecology Edgware Gen Hosp and W Middx Hosp 1961–63, instr of obstetrics and gynaecology Univ of Pittsburgh 1963–65, res asst Dept of Obstetrics and Gynaecology Hammersmith Hosp 1965–69, med offr MRC 1969–70, registrar then sr registrar in radiotherapy and oncology Middx Hosp 1971–75, sr registrar in oncology Mount Vernon Hosp 1975–79, conslt clinical oncologist Hammersmith Hosp 1979–; hon conslt St Mary's Hosp Paddington 1983–; hon sr lectr: Royal Postgradute Med Sch Hammersmith Hosp 1979–, Inst of Obstetrics and Gynaecology 1983–; memb: N Thames Ovary Gp (fndr), MRC Gynaecological Cancer Working Pty, Breast Cancer Diagnostic and Screening Services Gp, PMB Gp, Portland Gynaecological Oncology Gp, Int Gynaecological Cancer Soc, British Gynaecological Cancer Soc, British Oncological Assoc, Rad Soc; FRCR 1976, FRCOG 1981 (MRCOG 1962); *Books* Gynaecological Oncology (with Dr P Blake, 1992); author of numerous pubns, book chapters and papers in med jls; *Style*— Dr Hannah Lambert; ✉ Hammersmith Hospital, 150 Du Cane Road, London W12 0HS (☎ 0181 743 2030)

LAMBERT, Harry Paul; s of James Lambert (d 1979), of Manchester, and Irene, *née* Kennedy; *b* 20 Feb 1944; *Educ* Chorlton Tech High, Stockport Coll; *m* 1974, Shan Elizabeth Rose, da of Trevor Watkins, of Kent; 1 s (Mark James Trevor b 1981), 1 da (Katie Elizabeth b 1982); *Career* chm and chief exec The Adscene Group plc (newspaper and magazine publishers and printers); *Style*— Harry Lambert, Esq; ✉ The Adscene Group plc, Newspaper House, Wincheap Industrial Estate, Canterbury, Kent CT1 3YR (☎ 01227 767321)

LAMBERT, Henry Uvedale Antrobus; s of Roger Uvedale Lambert, MBE (d 1985), of Blechingley, Surrey, and Muriel Froude (d 1982), da of Sir Reginald Antrobus, KCMG, CB; *b* 9 Oct 1925; *Educ* Winchester, New Coll Oxford (MA); *m* 19 Jan 1951, Diana Elsworth, da of Capt Henry Eric Dumbell, Royal Fus (d 1957), of Bridge Vere, Farnham, Surrey; 2 s (Michael Uvedale b 1952, Roger Mark Uvedale b 1959), 1 da (Jennifer (Hon Mrs Andrew Hope-Morley) b 1955); *Career* RN 1939–45, Sub Lt RNVR, later RNR Lt Cdr (ret); chm Barclays Bank Int Ltd 1979–83 (joined Barclays 1948, dir 1966–91, vice chm 1973, dep chm Barclays Bank plc 1979–85); chm: Barclays Bank UK Ltd 1983–85, Sun Alliance & London Insurance Group 1985–93 (vice chm 1978–83, dep chm 1983–85), Agricultural Mortgage Corporation plc 1985–93 (dep chm 1977–85); dir BA 1985–89; tstee: Imperial War Graves Endowment Fund 1987–94, Nat Maritime Museum 1990–95; fell Winchester Coll 1979–91; FCIB 1967; *Recreations* fishing, gardening, naval history; *Clubs* Brooks's, MCC; *Style*— Henry Lambert, Esq; ✉ c/o Barclays Bank plc, Jewry Street, Winchester, Hampshire

LAMBERT, Sir John Henry; KCVO (1980), CMG (1975); s of Col R S Lambert, MC (d 1976), and Mrs H J F Mills (d 1995); *b* 8 Jan 1921; *Educ* Eton, Sorbonne, Trinity Coll Cambridge; *m* 1950, Jennifer Ann, da of Sir Robert Urquhart, KBE, CMG; 1 s, 2 da; *Career* served Grenadier Gds 1940–45; entered Foreign Serv 1945, cnsllr Stockholm 1964, commercial cnsllr and consul-gen Vienna 1971–74, min and dep cmdt Br Mil Govt Berlin 1974–77, ambass to Tunisia 1977–81; dir Heritage of London Tst 1981–96 (vice pres 1996–); chm Channel Tunnel Investments plc 1986–92; Grand Offr Order of Tunisian Republic 1980; *Clubs* Hurlingham, MCC, Royal St George's Golf, Sandwich; *Style*— Sir John Lambert, KCVO, CMG; ✉ 103 Rivermead Court, London SW6 3SB (☎ 0171 731 5007; office: 0171 973 3809)

LAMBERT, 3 Viscount (UK 1945); Michael John Lambert; yr s of 1 Viscount Lambert, PC (d 1958); suc bro, 2 Viscount 1989; *b* 29 Sept 1912; *Educ* Harrow, New Coll Oxford; *m* 5 Sept 1939, Florence Dolores, da of Nicholas Lechmere Cunningham Macaskie, QC; 3 da (Hon Sophia Jane b 1943, Hon Caelia Anne Georgiana (Hon Mrs Pereira) b 1946, Hon Flavia Mary b 1949); *Heir* none; *Style*— The Rt Hon the Viscount Lambert; ✉ Casanuova di Barontoli, 53010 San Rocco a Pilli, Siena, Italy

LAMBERT, Patricia (Pat); OBE (1980); da of Frederick Burrows (d 1961), and Elsie, *née* Mummery (d 1971); *b* 16 March 1926; *Educ* Malet Lambert HS Hull, West Bridgford GS Nottingham; *m* 1949, (m dis 1982), George Richard, s of Richard Palin Lambert (d 1982); 1 s (Warwick b 1954), 1 da (Margaret b 1952); *Career* memb Nat Consumer Cncl 1978–82; Br Standards Inst 1972–91: chm Consumer Standards Advsy Ctee (now Consumer Policy Ctee) 1972–91, memb Bd 1980–86, chm Consumer Standards Advsy Cncl 1980–86, memb Quality Assur Bd 1986 (govr 1986–91), memb various other BSI ctees; memb: Advsy Ctee on Safety of Electrical Appliances Br Tech Approval Bd 1980–86, Direct Mail Servs Standards Bd 1983– (dir 1986–95); dir and vice chm Think Br Campaign 1983–94 (now Invest in Britain); memb: Advsy Panel UTA 1981–91, Nat House Building Cncl 1980–91; public interest dir Life Assur & Unit Tst Regulatory Orgn 1986–95; memb: Gas Consumers Cncl (E Mids Panel) 1988–94, Consumer Panel Personal Investment Authy 1994–; *Style*— Pat Lambert, OBE; ✉ 100 Wolds Drive, Keyworth, Nottingham NG12 5FS (☎ and fax 0115 937 6885)

LAMBERT, Sir Peter John Biddulph; 10 Bt (GB 1711), of London; o s of John Hugh Lambert (d 1977), and Edith, *née* Bance (d 1988); suc kinsman Sir Greville Foley Lambert, 9 Bt (d 1988); *b* 5 April 1952; *Educ* Upper Canada Coll, Trent Univ Peterborough (BSc), Univ of Manitoba Winnipeg (MA), Univ of Toronto (BEd); *m* 2 Sept 1989, Leslie Anne, da of Richard Welkos Lyne; 1 da (Maeve Edith Jean b 7 Oct 1992); *Heir* uncle, Robert William Lambert b 6 June 1911; *Style*— Sir Peter Lambert, Bt; ✉ 483 Spadina Rd, Toronto, Ontario, Canada M5P 2W6

LAMBERT, Sophia Jane; *Career* HM Dip Serv: third sec FCO 1966–68, second sec Br Embassy Bonn 1968–72, first sec FCO 1972, first sec Br Embassy Pretoria 1976–80, first sec FCO 1980–82; asst sec Cabinet Office 1982–85; Dept of Tport: head Int Div 1985–87, head Public Tport Met Div 1987–91, head Int Railways Div 1991–92, dir Road and Vehicle Safety 1992–; *Style*— Miss S J Lambert; ✉ Department of Transport, 2 2/15, 76 Marsham Street, London SW1P 4DR (☎ 0171 271 5000, fax 0171 271 4728, e-mail RVS2.DOT@gtnet.gov.uk)

LAMBERT, Stephen; s of Roger Lambert, of London, and Monika, *née* Wagner; *b* 22 March 1959; *Educ* Thames Valley GS, UEA, Univ of Oxford; *m* 8 April 1988, Jenni, da of Martin Russell, of S Africa; 1 da (Jessica b 1988), 1 s (Harry b 1992); *Career* BBC TV 1983–: Documentary Dept prodr/dir 40 Minutes 1987–90 and Inside Story 1991–92, series prodr/dir True Brits 1994, series ed Modern Times (BBC 2) 1994–; memb BAFTA; *Books* Channel Four (1982); *Recreations* sailing; *Style*— Stephen Lambert, Esq; ✉ BBC TV, White City, 201 Wood Lane, London W12 7TS (☎ 0181 752 6400)

LAMBERT, (Barry) Unwin; s of Henry Benjamin Lambert (d 1981), and Elsie, *née* Organ (d 1977); *b* 28 Jan 1934; *Educ* The John Lyon Sch, Harrow GS, Br Sch of Osteopathy (DO, MRO); *m* 3 Oct 1959, Penelope Frances, da of Harold David Frearson (d 1982); 3 s (Simon b 1960, Jonathan b 1962, Christopher b 1967); *Career* registered osteopath; Gen Cncl and Register of Osteopaths: chm 1971–76 and 1983–92, vice pres 1992–; memb Nat Tst and RSPB; govr Royal Alexandra & Albert Sch Gatton Park Reigate; *Recreations* country pursuits, working with wood; *Clubs* RSM, Rotary (pres 1996–97); *Style*— B Unwin Lambert, Esq; ✉ Fairlead, Chart Lane, Reigate, Surrey RH2 7EG (☎ 01737 245500, 01737 245041, fax 01737 224984)

LAMBERT, Verity Ann; da of Stanley Joseph Lambert, and Ella Corona Goldburg; *b* 27 Nov 1935; *Educ* Roedean, Sorbonne; *Career* prodr BBC TV 1963–74, controller Drama Dept Thames TV 1974–76, chief exec Euston Films 1976–82, dir of prodn and exec prodr Thorn EMI Screen Entertainment 1982–85, ind film prodr 1985– (co name Cinema Verity Ltd), prodr A Cry in the Dark; exec prodr TV films and series incl: Sleepers (BBC), GBH (Channel 4), Boys from the Bush (BBC), Coasting (Granada), Sam Saturday (LWT), Eldorado (BBC) 1992–93, Class Act (Carlton) 1993, Comics (Channel 4), She's Out (Carlton), Capital Lives (Carlton), Heavy Weather (BBC); *Recreations* good books, good food; *Style*— Ms Verity Lambert; ✉ Cinema Verity Productions Ltd, The Mill House, Millers Way, 1A Shepherds Bush Rd, London W6 7NA (☎ 0181 749 8485)

LAMBERTY, Mark Julian Harker; s of Dr G B Lamberty (d 1982), of Rossendale, Lancs, and Dr D S Lamberty; *b* 17 Aug 1947; *Educ* Rugby, Keble Coll Oxford (MA), Univ of Oxford (postgrad BCL); *m* 17 Aug 1991, Pamela Jean Wilson; *Career* called to the Bar Gray's Inn 1970, head of chambers 1994–; *Recreations* cricket; *Clubs* Norden Cricket (tstee); *Style*— Mark Lamberty, Esq; ✉ 5 John Dalton Street, Manchester M2 6ET (☎ 0161 834 6875, fax 0161 834 8557)

LAMBIE-NAIRN, Martin John; *Career* asst graphic designer BBC 1965, graphic designer Rediffusion 1966, freelance graphic designer 1967, art dir Conran Associates 1968, dep sr designer ITN 1968, graphic designer LWT 1970–76; chm and creative dir Lambie-Nairn & Company (brand identity for TV and commercials prodns) 1990– (founded as Robinson Lambie-Nairn 1976); work incl: Channel 4 TV corp identity 1982, creative conslt to Presentation Dept Channel 4 1987, Anglia TV corp identity 1988, review of on-screen presentation for BBC 1 and BBC 2 1989, TFI corp identity 1989, BBC 1 and BBC 2 channel identities 1991, RTSI corp identity 1992, Carlton TV corp identity 1992–93, Showtime (USA) 1994, ARTE (France & Germany) 1995, ITN 1995, The Disney Channel (UK) 1996; Lambie-Nairn & Co recipient of Queen's Award for Export Achievement 1995; devisor of Spitting Image (ITV), designer and dir of numerous TV commercials; chm Graphics Jury BBC Design Awards 1987; subject of BBC Radio 4 profile 1988, winner (with Daniel Barber) BAFTA Award for BBC 2 identity 1992, recipient RTS Judges' Award for 30 yrs of creativity 1995; pres D&AD 1990 (memb Exec Ctee 1985); hon fell Kent Institute of Art and Design 1994; FCSD 1982, RDI 1987; *Style*— Martin Lambie-Nairn, Esq; ✉ Lambie-Nairn & Co, 48 Beak Street, London W1R 3DA (☎ 0171 734 1622, fax 0171 434 1098, e-mail lambie.n@dial.pipex.com)

LAMBIRTH, Andrew Gordon; s of Gordon Frank Trevallion Lambirth, of Ottery St Mary, Devon, and Adelaide Harriet, *née* Betteridge; *b* 2 Jan 1959; *Educ* St John's Sch Leatherhead, Univ of Nottingham (BA); *Career* porter Sotheby's London 1981–82, freelance researcher and writer 1983–, ed and collaborator on Eileen Agar's autobiography A Look At My Life (1988) 1985–88, cataloguer and conslt on papers of Malcolm Muggeridge 1987–88, contrib ed Royal Academy Magazine 1990–; currently contrib: The Sunday Times, World of Interiors, London Magazine, Modern Painters and others; memb Int Assoc of Art Critics 1991–; *Recreations* reading, walking and looking; *Style*— Andrew Lambirth, Esq

LAMBIRTH, Mark Nicholas; s of Peter Mabson Lambirth, of St Albans, and Jean Margaret, *née* Barber; *b* 30 May 1953; *Educ* St Albans Sch, Queens' Coll Cambridge (BA); *m* 7 June 1986, Anne Catherine, da of George Wood; *Career* civil servant; Price Cmmn 1975–77; Civil Service 1977–: princ 1982, Shipping Policy 1982–85, Ports Div 1985–88, sr princ 1988, ministerial speech writer and dep head Info Div 1988–89, asst sec 1989, head Public Tport London Div 1989–92, head Central Fin Div 1992–95, under sec 1995, dir Planning and Tport Directorate Govt Office for London 1995–; *Recreations* poetry, cooking, wine; *Style*— Mark Lambirth, Esq; ✉ 10th Floor, Riverwalk House, 157–161 Millbank, London SW1P 4RR (☎ 0171 217 3151, fax 0171 217 3470)

LAMBLE, Lloyd Nelson; s of William Henry Sylvester Lamble (d 1956), of Melbourne, Australia, and (Francis) Alma Spencer, *née* Potter (d 1971); *b* 8 Feb 1914; *Educ* Wesley Coll Melbourne, Melbourne Univ Conservatorium of Music; *m* 1, Marjorie Ellerton, *née* Barrett; m 2, (Doris) Barbara, da of Dr S A Smith; 1 s (Lloyd William Addison (Tim) b 5 Sept 1941), 1 da (Elizabeth (Mrs Ken White) b 22 Sept 1944); m 3, (Joyce) Lesley Wallis, *née* Jackson; 1 adopted s (Lloyd Wallis Addison b 21 Dec 1962), 1 adopted da (Helene Caroline (b 28 March 1963); *Career* commenced piano studies at age 4, joined travelling circus, became world's youngest radio announcer at age of 17, freelance radio acting, first theatre appearance in Novello's Fresh Fields (Comedy Theatre Melbourne), first starring role as Danny in Night Must Fall (Comedy Theatre Melbourne) 1936, lead in first musical comedy Wild Violets (His Majesty's Melbourne) 1937, founded own drama sch Radio Theatre Guild 1938, toured NZ and starred in Claudia, Arsenic and Old Lace, Kiss and Tell, The Man Who Came to Dinner, Susan And God, The Two Mrs Carrols 1944, formed own company to tour NSW and Queensland 1945, 1 year on fair grounds 1946, toured Australia and NZ in Under the Counter, Born Yesterday (Comedy Theatre Melbourne), Edward My Son, first London play The Martin's Nest (Westminster Theatre) 1952, first tv appearance The Passing Parade (BBC) 1952; 66 years in showbusiness June 1996; *Theatre* most recently incl: The Picture of Dorian Gray (Greenwich), Having a Ball (Liverpool, Salisbury, Hornchurch), On Golden Pond (Dundee), A Month of Sundays (Chester), Habeas Corpus, School for Scandal, The Best Years of Your Life, The Crucible (Pitlochry), Gigi (Welsh tour), Charles in Me and My Girl (Adelphi); *Television* incl: Corridors of Power, Z Cars, Softly Softly, Armchair Theatre, Lady Killers, The Naked Civil Servant, Howard's Way; *Films* over 100 credits incl: Where no Vultures Fly 1952, The Story of Gilbert and Sullivan 1953, The Straw Man 1954, The Dambusters 1954, The Bells of St Trinians (as Inspr Sammie Kemp-Bird) 1954, The Man Who Knew Too Much 1956, The Good Companions, Quatermass II 1957, Blue Murder at St Trinians 1957, Our Man in Havana 1959, The Pure Hell of St Trinians 1960, No Sex Please We're British 1973, Eskimo Nell 1974; *Recreations* classical music, swimming, tennis, golf, writing, philosophy, house building; *Style—* Lloyd Lamble, Esq; ✉ 55 Greencroft Gardens, London NW6 3LL (☎ 0171 624 4320); Janet Mills, PBR Management, 138 Putney Bridge Road, London SW15 2NQ (☎ 0181 871 4139)

LAMBTON, Anne; *Career* actress; *Theatre* Glasgow Citizen's Theatre incl: Women Beware Women, Hedda Gabler, An Ideal Husband, Friends and Lovers, The Spanish Bawd, Blithe Spirit, Judith, She Stoops to Conquer, French Knickers, A Woman of No Importance, The Vortex, Joan of Arc; RSC incl: Country Wife, Elgar's Rondo, Transit of Venus; other roles incl: School for Scandal (Royal Exchange Manchester), Hangover Square (Lyric), Margaret Thatcher in Ronnie's Doing Well, Mainland (tour, Watermans Art Centre), Miss Julie (Westcliff); *Television* incl: Calling the Shots (BBC), Unnatural Causes (ATV), Ghosts of Oxford Street (Middlemarsh Films), The House of Eliott (BBC), Hedgehog Wedding (BBC), Oscar (BBC); *Films* incl: Crimetime (dir George Sluizer), Gulliver's Travels (dir Charles Sturridge), Where the Wolves Howl (dir Laurent Bontonnat), Howards End (dir James Ivory), The Witches (dir Nick Roeg), Sid and Nancy (dir Alex Cox), Half Moon Street (dir Bob Swain); *Style—* Anne Lambton; ✉ c/o Conway van Gelder Robinson Ltd, 18–21 Jermyn Street, London SW1Y 6HP (☎ 0171 287 0077, fax 0171 287 1940)

LAMBTON, Antony Claud Frederick; (Viscount Lambton, by which courtesy title he was known in House of Commons); s of 5 Earl of Durham (d 1970); disclaimed peerages (Earldom of Durham, Barony of Durham and Viscountcy of Lambton) for life 1970; *b* 10 July 1922; *m* 1942, Belinda Bridget, da of Maj Douglas Holden Blew-Jones, of Westward Ho, N Devon; 1 s, 5 da; *Heir* to renounced Earldom of Durham, s, Lord (courtesy title of Baron) Durham; *Career* MP (C) Northumberland (Berwick-on-Tweed) 1951–73; PPS to Min of Supply 1954, parly under-sec of state for Def (RAF) 1970–73; *Books* Snow and Other Stories (1983); *Style—* Antony Lambton, Esq; ✉ Biddick Hall, Lambton Park, Chester-le-Street, Durham; Lambton Castle, Fence Houses, Durham

LAMBTON, (Lady) Lucinda; *née* Lambton; eld da of Antony Lambton (6 Earl of Durham who disclaimed peerage 1970); does not use courtesy title of Lady; *b* 10 May 1943; *m* 1, 16 Jan 1965, Henry Mark Harrod, s of Sir (Henry) Roy Forbes Harrod; 2 s (Barnaby, Huckleberry); m 2, 11 Jan 1986 (m dis), Sir Edmund Fairfax-Lucy, 6 Bt, of Charlecote Park, Warwick; m 3, 11 May 1991, as his 2 w, Sir Peregrine Gerard Worsthorne, *qv*; *Career* photographer, writer and bdcaster; TV programmes: On The Throne, Animal Crackers, Cabinet of Curiosities, The Great North Road, Desirable Dwellings, Hurray for Today (on modern architecture, six part series), Hurray for Today USA (six part series), The Alphabet of Britain (24 part series), One Foot in the Past (nine contribs), The Other House of Windsor, Travels with Pevsner; *Books* Vanishing Victoriana, Temples of Convenience (1978 and 1995), Chambers of Delight, Beastly Buildings, Album of Curious Houses, Magnificent Menagerie, Lucinda Lambton's A-Z of Britain; *Style—* Lucinda Lambton; ✉ The Old Rectory, Hedgerley, Buckinghamshire SL2 3UY (☎ 01753 646167, fax 01753 646914)

LAMBTON, Viscount Viscount; *see:* Durham, Baron

LAMING, Sir (William) Herbert; kt (1996), CBE (1985); s of William Angus Laming, and Lillian, *née* Robson; *b* 19 July 1936; *Educ* Univ of Durham (DSocSci); *m* 1962, Aileen Margaret, *née* Pollard; *Career* probation offr then sr probation offr Nottingham Probation Serv 1961–68, asst chief probation offr Nottingham City and Co Probation Serv 1968–71, deputy dir then dir Hertfordshire CC Social Servs 1971–91, chief inspr Social Servs Inspectorate DHSS 1991–; pres Assoc of Dirs of Social Servs 1982–83; *Style—* Sir Herbert Laming, CBE; ✉ Social Services Inspectorate, Department of Health, Richmond House, 79 Whitehall, London SW1A 2NS (☎ 0171 210 5569, fax 0171 210 4982)

LAMMIMAN, Surgn Rear Adm David Askey; CB (1993), LVO (1978); s of Herbert Askey Lammiman (d 1983), and Lilian Elsie, *née* Park (d 1967); *b* 30 June 1932; *Educ* Wyggeston Sch Leicester, St Bartholomew's Hosp (MB BS, DA, DObstRCOG); *m* 1, 7 Sept (m dis 1984), Sheila Mary, da of Frederick Graham (d 1963); 3 s (Christopher b June 1958, Robert b April 1960, Michael b March 1969), 1 da (Susie b Feb 1967); m 2, 30 Oct 1984, Caroline Dale, da of Francis John Brooks (Lt Cdr RN, ret); *Career* res house offr Redhill County Hosp and St Bartholomew's Hosp 1957–58; joined RN 1959; clinical asst 1966–69: Southampton Gp of Hosps, Alder Hey Children's Hosp, Liverpool/Radcliffe Infirmary Oxford; conslt anaesthetist: RN Hosp Malta 1969–71, RN Hosp Haslar 1971–73 and 1978–82, RN Hosp Gibraltar 1973–75, RN Hosp Plymouth 1975–76; served in ships: HMS Chaplet 1959, HMS Eagle 1967–68, HMY Britannia 1976–78; dir of med personnel MOD 1982–84; med offr i/c: RN Hosp Plymouth 1984–86, RN Hosp Haslar 1986–88; Surgn Rear Adm (Support Med Servs) 1989–90, Med Dir Gen (Naval) Oct 1990–93; QHS 1987–93; memb Assoc of Anaesthetists 1962, FFARCS 1969, FRSM 1989; *Recreations* fly fishing, golf, tennis; *Clubs* Flyfishers'; *Style—* Surgn Rear Adm David Lammiman, CB, LVO; ✉ Magdella Cottage, 75 St Michael's Road, St Helens, Isle of Wight PO33 1JY

LAMONT, Rt Hon Norman Stewart Hughson; PC (1986), MP (C) Kingston upon Thames (majority 10,153); s of Daniel Lamont and Irene Lamont; *b* 8 May 1942; *Educ* Loretto, Fitzwilliam Coll Cambridge; *m* 1971, Alice Rosemary, da of Lt-Col Peter White; 1 s, 1 da; *Career* PA to Duncan Sandys 1965, CRD 1966–68, asset mgmnt N M Rothschild & Sons 1968–79; Parly candidate (C) Hull E 1970, MP (C) Kingston-upon-Thames 1972–; chm: Coningsby Club 1970–71, Bow Gp 1971–72; PPS to Arts Min 1974; oppn spokesman: on consumer affairs 1975–76, on industry 1976–79; under-sec of state Dept of Energy 1979–81; min of state: DTI 1981–85, for defence procurement 1985–86; financial sec to Treasy May 1986–July 1989, chief sec to the Treasy July 1989–Nov 1990, Chancellor of the Exchequer Nov 1990– May 1993; non-exec dir: N M Rothschild & Sons Ltd 1993–95; dir various cos; *Style—* The Rt Hon Norman Lamont, MP; ✉ c/o House of Commons, London SW1A 0AA

LAMONT, Prof William Montgomerie; s of Hector Lamont (d 1985), of Harrow, London, and Hughina Carmichael, *née* MacFadyen (d 1982); *b* 2 Feb 1934; *Educ* Harrow Weald County GS, Univ of London (BA, PGCE, PhD); *m* 5 April 1961, Linda Mary, da of Lionel Stanley Cuthbert Murphy; 3 da (Catriona b 1 Jan 1962, Ailsa b 10 May 1963, Tara b 26 June 1965); *Career* schoolmaster Hackney Downs Secdy Sch 1959–63, lectr Aberdeen Coll of Educn 1963–66, prof of history Univ of Sussex 1966– (lectr 1966, reader 1970), dean Sch of Cultural and Community Studies Univ of Sussex 1981–86, dir Centre for the History of Br Political Thought Folger Library Washington 1985; FRHistS 1969; *Books* Marginal Prynne (1963), Godly Rule (1969), The Realities of Teaching History (ed, 1972), Politics Religion and Literature in the 17th century (jtly, 1975), Richard Baxter and the Millennium (1979), The World of the Muggletonians (jtly, 1983), Richard Baxter A Holy Commonwealth (ed, 1994), Puritanism and Historical Controversy (1996); *Recreations* watching Arsenal; *Style—* Prof William Lamont; ✉ Essex House, University of Sussex, Falmer, Brighton BN1 9QN (☎ 01273 606755)

LAMPARD, Clive; s of Roy Lampard (d 1978), of Maidstone, and Renee Lampard; *b* 25 May 1959; *Educ* Oakwood Park GS Maidstone, Westfield Coll London (BA, MA); *m* 1984, Julia Catherine, da of James Bernard Carr; 1 da (Sarah b 13 Jan 1987), 2 s (Daniel b 22 March 1989, Luke b 12 June 1992); *Career* articled clerk Slaughter and May 1983–85; ptnr Macfarlanes 1991– (joined 1989); author of various articles; govr The Hall Sch Hampstead; memb Law Soc; *Recreations* family, wine, sport, church; *Style—* Clive Lampard, Esq; ✉ Macfarlanes, 10 Norwich Street, London EC4A 1BD (☎ 0171 831 9222, fax 0171 831 9607)

LAMPERT, Catherine Emily; da of Lt Cdr Chester Graham Lampert (d 1981), of Washington DC, USA, and Emily Schubach Lampert; *b* 15 Oct 1946; *Educ* Brown Univ (BA), Temple Univ (MA); *m* 22 Dec 1971 (m dis 1994), Robert Keith Mason; 1 da (Susana b 1990); *Career* sr exhibition organiser Arts Cncl of GB 1973–88, dir Whitechapel Art Gallery 1988–; organiser of several exhibitions incl retrospectives of: Frank Auerbach, Lucian Freud, Michael Andrews, Anthony Caro, Henri Matisse, Drawings and Sculputure, Auguste Rodin, In the Image of Man, Arshile Gorky, Euan Uglow, Richard Diebenkorn, Juan Gris; memb: Slade Ctee Univ of London, Bd Courtauld Inst; memb ICOM, CIMAM; *Books* The Drawings and Sculpture of Auguste Rodin (1987), Lucian Freud: Recent Work (1993); *Style—* Mrs Catherine Lampert; ✉ Whitechapel Art Gallery, 80–82 Whitechapel High Street, London E1 7QX (☎ 0171 522 7888)

LAMPERT, Steven Lee; s of Sam Lampert (d 1977), of New York, and Estelle, *née* Elkin (d 1990); *b* 26 Aug 1949; *Educ* Fairleigh Dickenson Univ, Hunter Coll New York (BA); *m* 7 March 1971, Andrea, *née* Diamond; 1 s (Dylan Lee b 10 Nov 1980), 1 da (Jessica Leigh b 21 Nov 1975); *Career* head of telecommunications: Metpath Laboratories 1976–82, NBC 1985; pres: Communications Technologies Inc 1985–91 (vice pres 1982–85), Long Distance Direct Inc 1991–, Long Distance Direct (UK) Ltd 1993–; *Recreations* long distance running, karate; *Clubs* Dellwood Country; *Style—* Steven Lampert, Esq; ✉ 9 Lansdale Road, New City, New York 10956, USA (☎ 00 1 914 638 1479); Long Distance Direct Inc, 1 Blue Hill Plaza, Pearl River, New York 10965, USA (☎ 00 1 914 620 0765, fax 00 1 914 620 1889, auto 00 1 914 523 9345)

LAMPL, Sir Frank William; kt (1990); s of Dr Otto Lampl (d 1934), and Olga, *née* Jellinek (d Auschwitz 1944); *b* 6 April 1926; *Educ* Faculty of Architecture and Engrg Tech Univ Brno Czechoslovakia; *m* 1948, Blanka, da of Jaroslav Kratochvil (d 1981); 1 s (Thomas b 1950); *Career* various contruction industry appts rising to md in Czechoslovakia before emigrating to UK 1968; Bovis Construction Group: project mangr then construction dir Bovis Ltd 1971, md Bovis Construction Southern Ltd and exec dir Bovis Construction Ltd 1974, chief exec and md Bovis International Ltd 1978, dir Bovis Ltd 1979, chm Bovis Construction Ltd and Bovis International Ltd 1985–89, exec dir Peninsular and Oriental Steam Navigation Co (P&O, parent co of Bovis) 1985–, chm Bovis Construction Group 1986–, dir Lehrer McGovern Bovis Inc New York 1986–, chm Bovis (Far East) Ltd 1987–, chm P&O Developments Ltd 1987–89; chllr Univ of Kingston 1994–; hon doctorates: Brno Tech Univ 1993, Univ of Kingston 1994, Univ of Reading 1995; Pres's Medal Chartered Inst of Bldg 1993; CIMgt, FCIOB; *Clubs* RAC, Carlton; *Style—* Sir Frank Lampl; ✉ Bovis Ltd, Liscartan House, 127 Sloane Street, London SW1X 9BA (☎ 0181 422 3488, fax 0171 730 4722, telex 919435)

LAMPLUGH, Diana Elizabeth; OBE (1992); da of David Gwynydd Howell (d 1971), of Cheltenham, and Eileen Mary, *née* Weddell; *b* 30 July 1936; *Educ* Westonbirt Sch, West London Inst of Higher Education; *m* 18 Oct 1958, Paul Crosby Lamplugh, s of Eric Crosby Lamplugh; 1 s (Richard b 21 Jan 1960), 3 da (Susannah Jane (Suzy) b 3 May 1961, disappeared 28 July 1986 presumed murdered, Tamsin Rose b 13 July 1962, Elizabeth Madge b 16 June 1970); *Career* sec to: Wycliffe Coll 1955–57, Carl Rosa Opera Co 1957–58, controller of programmes BBC TV 1958–60; teacher of swimming (specialist in elderly and disabled), fndr BR Slimnastics Assoc 1973–89, teacher and tutor/assessor of slimnastics relaxation and tension control 1973–89 (created concept of Whole Person Approach to Fitness), res project Disabled Living Fndn 1985 (Sports and Exercise for the Visually Handicapped, published 1989), fndr memb Exec Ctee of Int Stress & Tension Control Soc UK 1980–85, fndr and dir The Suzy Lamplugh Trust (the Nat Charity for Personal Safety) 1986–; writer, speaker, teacher and specialist in personal safety; campaigner for: action to enable people to live safer lives, missing persons helpline and nat missing persons bureau, licensing of minicabs, safer car parks, treatment of sex offenders (so as not to re-offend), an agency for victims of serious crime and personal safety for children; chm Home Office Ctee for Personal Safety for Disabled People 1994–; memb: Ctee on Violence Health & Safety Exec 1987–, Working Pty for Safety of Users of Cabs Dept of Tport 1991–93, Br Transport Police Ctee 1993–, Penal Affairs Consortium 1996; Hon Doctorate Sheffield Hallam Univ; *Books* Slimnastics (1970), Stress and Overstress (1974), A Guide to Good Living (1980), The Whole Person Approach to Fitness (1984) (all with Pamela Nottidge), Beating Aggression (1988), Survive the 9–5 (1989), Physical Activities for Visually Handicapped People (1989), Without Fear (1991), Personal Safety for Schools (with Barbara Pagan); creator core concept of personal safety for educn and trg manuals, videos and courses; *Recreations* opera, sailing, riding, swimming, enjoying my children, being alone with my husband; *Style—* Mrs Diana Lamplugh, OBE; ✉ 14 East Sheen Ave, London SW14 8AS (☎ home 0181 876 1838; business 0181 392 1839, fax 0181 392 1830)

LAMPRELL-JARRETT, Peter Neville; s of Reginald Arthur Lamprell-Jarrett (d 1966), of Margate, Kent, and Phyllis Inez, *née* Heath-Fox; *b* 23 June 1919; *Educ* Cliftonville Coll; *m* 1944, Kathleen, da of Percival Francis Furner (d 1973); 1 s (Peter Jonathan b 1950), 1 da (Sarah Fiona b 1952); *Career* architect and surveyor 1954–93; pres Incorporated Assoc of Architects and Surveyors 1967–68; life vice pres London Caledonian Catholic Assoc; Freeman City of London 1978, Liveryman Worshipful Co of Wheelwrights; FFB, FRSA, FSA (Scot); KCSG 1975, KCHS 1974, Cdr Cross Polonia Restituta (Poland) 1982; *Recreations* fishing, walking, classical music; *Clubs* Royal Cwlth Soc; *Style—* Peter Lamprell-Jarrett, Esq; ✉ 42 Mall Chambers, Kensington Mall, London W8 4DZ (☎ 0171 229 8247); Carrick House, Carrick Castle, by Lochgoil, Argyll PA24 8AF (☎ 01301 703394)

LANCASTER, Christopher; s of George Lancaster (d 1959), of Headingley, Leeds, and Grace Evelyn, *née* Foster (d 1974); *b* 10 Aug 1932; *Educ* Queen Elizabeth GS Wakefield, Trinity Hall Cambridge (MA, LLM); *m* 12 Sep 1959, Aase,da of Kristoffer Böe (d 1965), of Bergen, Norway; 2 s (Stephen b 1960, Richard b 1962), 1 da (Anne-Lise b 1964); *Career* articled clerk Booth and Co 1956–59, asst slr William Henry and Co 1959–60 (ptnr 1960–72), ptnr Wansbroughs Willey Hargrave 1972–88 (conslt 1988–), pres Leeds Law Soc 1979–80 (press offr 1972–79); memb: Headingley Rotary 1974–84, Leeds Skyrack Lions Club 1965–69, tstee Grassington Angling Club 1972–85, Law Soc 1959; *Recreations* fly-fishing, English history, jazz piano; *Style*— Christopher Lancaster, Esq

LANCASTER, Graham; s of Eric Lancaster, of Salford, Gtr Manchester, and Edna, *née* Butterworth; *b* 24 Feb 1948; *Educ* Salford GS, Mid Cheshire Coll (HND), Open Univ (BA); *m* 10 Oct 1971, Lorna Mary, da of William Thomas White (d 1979); *Career* Hawker Siddeley Aviation 1968–69, asst to Dir of Information and Educn The Textile Cncl 1969–70, trg devpt offr Corah Ltd 1971, policy coordinator to Pres CBI 1972–77, head of public affrs ABTA 1977, chm Biss Lancaster plc 1978–, chm Corporate Graphics International (UK) Ltd 1993–, chm Euro RSCG International Communications 1994–; MCIM, MIPR; *Books* The Nuclear Letters (1979), Seward's Folly (1980), The 20 Percent Factor (1987 and 1989), Gravesong (1996); *Recreations* writing; *Clubs* Groucho's, Travellers'; *Style*— Graham Lancaster, Esq; ✉ Biss Lancaster plc, 69 Monmouth Street, London WC2H 9DG (☎ 0171 497 3001, fax 0171 497 8915, telex 894767 BISSPR G)

LANCASTER, Bishop of (RC) 1985–; Rt Rev John Brewer; s of Eric Winston Brewer (d 1977), of Manchester, and Laura Helena Webster (d 1987); *b* 24 Nov 1929; *Educ* Ushaw Coll Durham, Venerable English Coll Rome, Gregorian Univ Rome (STL, JCL, PhL); *Career* vice rector Ven English Coll Rome 1964–71, auxiliary bishop of Shrewsbury 1971–83, co-adjutor to Bishop of Lancaster 1983–85; *Style*— The Rt Rev the Bishop of Lancaster; ✉ Bishop's House, Cannon Hill, Lancaster LA1 5NG (☎ 01524 32231)

LANCASTER, Bishop of 1990–; Rt Rev John (Jack) Nicholls; s of James William Nicholls, of Rossendale, Lancs, and Nellie, *née* Bann (d 1986); *b* 16 July 1943; *Educ* Bacup & Rawtenstall GS, King's Coll London (AKC, Jelf Prize for Theol); *m* 1969, Judith, da of William Ernest Dagnall; 2 s (Antony Paul b 15 May 1971, Michael Patrick David b 11 Nov 1973), 2 da (Rachel Elizabeth b 4 Dec 1977, Clare Frances b 18 April 1979); *Career* curate St Clement with St Cyprian Ordsall Salford 1967–69, vicar All Saints and Martyrs Langley 1972–78 (curate 1969–72), dir of pastoral studies Coll of the Resurrection Mirfield 1978–83, residentiary canon of Manchester Cathedral 1983–90, warden of the community of St Mary the Virgin Wantage 1987–; *Books* A Faith Worth Sharing? A Church Worth Joining? (jtly, 1995); *Recreations* music, reading, listening to and telling stories; *Style*— The Rt Rev the Bishop of Lancaster; ✉ Wheatfield, 7 Dallas Road, Lancaster LA1 1TN (☎ 01524 32897, fax 01524 66095)

LANCASTER, Reg; s of Tim Lancaster, of Leasingham, Lincs, and Elizabeth, *née* McLean; *b* 6 April 1935; *Educ* Bearsden Acad Dumbartonshire, Ballyclare HS Co Antrim; *m* 25 March 1957, Annabelle McLaren, da of John M Allan; 1 s (Raymond b 6 July 1958), 1 da (Heather b 16 June 1960); *Career* photographer; joined Daily Express Scotland 1951–62, Daily Express London 1962– (seconded to Paris office 1965–73); Sports Picture of 1960 Encyclopedia Britannica Award, News Picture of 1978 and 1987 Br Press Awards, Royal Picture 1987 Kodak Awards, winner of many awards at regnl nat and int film-making competitions; fell Inst of Amateur Cinematographers; *Recreations* film-making; *Style*— Reg Lancaster, Esq; ✉ Daily Express, Ludgate House, 245 Blackfriars Rd, London EC1P 1DQ (☎ 0171 928 8000)

LANCASTER, Roger; *b* 4 Feb 1951; *Educ* Univ of Leicester (LLB); *m* Margaret; 2 s, 1 da; *Career* admitted slr 1975; currently sr ptnr Halliwell Landau; *Recreations* cricket, squash; *Style*— Roger Lancaster, Esq; ✉ Halliwell Landau, St James' Court, Brown St, Manchester M2 2JF (☎ 0161 835 3003, fax 0161 835 2994)

LANCASTER-GAYE, Linda Mary; da of Ronald Ernest Treves, of Kenilworth, Warwickshire, and Barbara Gertrude, *née* Shute; *b* 15 Sept 1959; *Educ* Kenilworth GS, St Martin's Sch of Art, Univ of Exeter (BA), Northwestern Univ Evanston Ill (exec devpt prog 1991); *m* Sept 1985 (m dis 1995), Robert Graham Richard Lancaster-Gaye, s of Derek Lancaster-Gaye; *Career* IPC Magazines: grad trg scheme 1983, advtg sales Country Life 1984–86, corp business planning mangr 1986–87, publisher Woman's Own and Woman's Weekly 1987–89 (asst publisher 1987), publishing dir TV Weeklies (TV Times, What's On TV, TV & Satellite Week) 1989–, main bd dir 1994–, md IPC Specialist Gp 1995–; Publisher of the Year PPA Awards 1993, Adwoman Advertising Woman of the Year 1995; *Recreations* opera, theatre, music, tennis, modern art; *Style*— Mrs Linda Lancaster-Gaye; ✉ IPC Magazines Ltd, King's Reach Tower, Stamford Street, London SE1 9LS (☎ 0171 261 5293, fax 0171 261 5157)

LANCASTER SMITH, Dr Michael John; s of Ronald Lancaster Smith, of Hastings, Sussex, and Marie, *née* Wright; *b* 4 Sept 1941; *Educ* Hastings GS, London Hosp Med Sch Univ of London (BSc, MB BS, MD); *m* 11 April 1964, Susan Frances Bayes, da of Lt Arthur Bannister (d 1946); 1 s (Daniel b 1969), 2 da (Catherine b 1966, Naomi b 1971); *Career* registrar and sr registrar The London Hosp 1969–73 (house physician and surgn 1966–68), sr lectr St Bartholomew's Hosp 1973–74, conslt physician Queen Mary's Hosp Sidcup Kent 1974–; memb Br Soc of Gastroenterology (memb Cncl 1993–95), vice chm Bexley Health Authy 1986–89, currently chm South Thames Regnl Gastroenterology Trg Ctee, South Thames Regnl Gastroenterology advsr RCP; memb BMA; FRCP; *Books* Problems in Practice - Gastroenterology (1982), Problems in Management - Gastroenterology (1985), Ulcer and Non Ulcer Dyspepsia (1987); *Recreations* cricket, music, theatre; *Style*— Dr Michael Lancaster Smith; ✉ Stableside House, 36 Southborough Rd, Bickley, Bromley, Kent BR1 2EB (☎ 0181 464 4184); Queen Mary's Hospital, Sidcup, Kent (☎ 0181 302 2678 ext 4231); Blackheath Hospital, London SE3; The Sloane Hospital, Beckenham, Kent

LANCE, Prof (Edward) Christopher; s of F Nevill Lance (d 1987), and Elizabeth, *née* Bagnall (d 1989); *b* 17 Jan 1941; *Educ* Dulwich, Trinity Coll Cambridge (MA, PhD); *m* 9 April 1966, Mary Margaret, *née* Hall; 1 s (Stephen b 1969), 1 da (Elizabeth b 1971); *Career* lectr in pure maths Univ of Newcastle 1965–73, reader Univ of Manchester 1973–78, prof of mathematics Univ of Leeds 1980–; visiting prof Univ of Pennsylvania USA 1971–72, 1978–80 and 1992–93; vice pres London Mathematical Soc 1988–90, sec Euro Mathematical Soc 1990–94; *Recreations* hill walking, music; *Style*— Prof Christopher Lance; ✉ School of Mathematics, The University of Leeds, Leeds LS2 9JT (☎ 0113 233 5142, fax 0113 233 5145)

LANCE, Sean; *b* 1947; *Educ* Christian Brothers Coll Pretoria; *Career* Mil Serv S African Special Forces, qualified as chartered sec and administrator; various positions rising to commercial dir Noristan Group of Companies Ltd (pharmaceuticals) 1967–82, exec chm The Boots Company (South Africa) Pty Ltd 1982–85; Glaxo: md Glaxo South Africa Pty Ltd 1985–87, regnl dir i/c Australia, S Africa, NZ, the Orient and the Far East 1987–89, md Glaxo Pharmaceuticals UK Ltd 1989–93, exec dir i/c Middle E, Africa and S Africa Glaxo Holdings plc 1993, also i/c N Europe, Greece and Latin America 1994, exec dir i/c Europe, Africa, ME and Asia Pacific and gp tech ops Glaxo Wellcome plc 1994–; dir British Pharma Group; Assoc of Br Pharmaceutical Industry: former vice pres, memb International Policy Ctee, memb Strategic Working Party on Health Matters; past pres: Pharmaceutical Mfrs' Assoc of S Africa, Proprietary Assoc of S Africa; *Style*— Sean Lance, Esq; ✉ Glaxo Wellcome plc, Lansdowne House, Berkeley Square, London W1X 6BP (☎ 0171 493 4060, fax 0171 408 0228)

LANCELEY, Ian Kenneth; s of Thomas Peter Kenneth Lanceley, of Paignton, Devon, and Barbara Doreen, *née* Allen; *b* 12 Feb 1946; *Educ* Blundell's, Coll of Law; *m* 12 Dec 1980, Valerie, da of Frederick William Kay (d 1987), of Richmond, North Yorks; 2 s (Adam b 1981, Charles b 1983); *Career* admitted slr 1971; ptnr Freeborough Slack & Co 1977–85, jt sr ptnr Freeboroughs 1985–; dep magistrate Metropolitan Stipendiary 1985–90; memb Law Soc; *Recreations* family, squash, golf, tennis; *Clubs* Roehampton, Royal Wimbledon Golf; *Style*— Ian K Lanceley, Esq; ✉ Freeborough House, 4 Addison Bridge Place, W Kensington, London W14 (☎ 0171 602 3474, fax 0171 603 7004)

LANCELOT, James Bennett; s of Rev Roland Lancelot (d 1983), and Margaret, *née* Tye; *b* 2 Dec 1952; *Educ* St Paul's Cathedral Choir Sch, Ardingly, RCM, King's Coll Cambridge (Organ scholar, MA, MusB); *m* 31 July 1982, Sylvia Jane, da of Raymond Hoare, of Cheltenham; 2 da (Rebecca b 1987, Eleanor b 1989); *Career* asst organist Hampstead Parish Church and St Clement Danes Church 1974–75, sub-organist Winchester Cathedral 1975–85, master of the choristers and organist Durham Cathedral 1985–, conductor Univ of Durham Choral Soc 1987, numerous recordings; memb: Cncl RCO, Cathedrals Liturgical Gp; FRCO (chm 1969), ARCM 1970; *Books* Durham Cathedral Organs (co-author with Richard Hird, 1991), The Sense of the Sacramental (contrib, 1995); *Recreations* railways; *Style*— James Lancelot, Esq; ✉ 6 The College, Durham DH1 3EQ (☎ 0191 386 4766)

LANCHBERY, John; OBE (1990); *Educ* RAM (Henry Smart scholar); *Career* served WWII RAC 1942–45; conductor; musical dir Metropolitan Ballet 1947–49, freelance 1949–51, conductor Sadler's Wells Theatre Ballet 1951–60, princ conductor Royal Ballet (arranged ballet scores incl La Fille Mal Gardee, The House of Birds, The Dream) 1960–72, musical dir Australian Ballet (arranged ballet scores incl Don Quixote, Mayerling, The Merry Widow) 1972–76, guest conductor The Royal Ballet 1976–, music dir American Ballet Theatre 1978–80, guest ballet conductor numerous leading opera houses; composer of music for film and TV incl: The Tales of Beatrix Potter, The Turning Point, Evil Under the Sun, Nijinsky, The Iron Horse, Birth of a Nation; awards: Bolshoi medal, Queen Elizabeth II Coronation award (From Royal Acad of Dance), Carina Ari medal; *Style*— John Lanchbery, Esq, OBE

LANCHIN, Gerald; s of Samuel Lanchin (d 1969), of London, and Sara, *née* Bernstein (d 1967); *b* 17 Oct 1922; *Educ* St Marylebone GS, LSE (BCom); *m* 1951, Valerie Sonia, da of Charles Lyons (d 1970), of London; 1 s (Michael), 2 da (Wendy, Judith); *Career* HM Forces 1942–46; under sec Dept of Trade 1971–82; chm Direct Mail Servs Standards Bd 1983–89, conslt on trade practices; memb: Cncl Consumers' Assoc 1983–88, Data Protection Tbnl 1985–, Consumer Panel Personal Investment Authy 1994–; vice pres Nat Fedn of Consumer Gps 1984–; *Books* Government and the Consumer (1985); *Recreations* photography, music, walking; *Style*— Gerald Lanchin, Esq; ✉ 28 Priory Gardens, Berkhamsted, Herts HP4 2DS (☎ 01442 875283)

LAND, (John) Anthony; *b* 21 Sept 1939; *Educ* Westminster (Queen's scholar), Trinity Coll Cambridge (minor scholar, BA); *m* Deborah Lucy Irene; 2 c; *Career* asst mangr (special pubns) The Times 1962–65; Readers' Digest London: asst, then dep ed (magazines) 1965–71, managing ed (magazines) 1971–74, exec dir (books) 1975–77; Consumers' Assoc: head of publishing 1977–91, asst dir 1987–91; freelance conslt (Thames and Hudson, Joseph Rowntree Fndn, The Planning Exchange, Asia Inc) 1991–93; Design Cncl: dir of publishing 1991–94, resources dir and sec to the Cncl 1994–; non-exec dir Book Tst London 1989–96, memb Parly and Legal Ctee PPA 1989–94; Hon DLitt; FRSA; *Recreations* swimming, walking, opera; *Style*— Anthony Land, Esq; ✉ 32 Holland Avenue, London W11 3QU (☎ 0171 221 9005); Design Council, Haymarket House, 1 Oxendon Street, London SW1Y 4EE (☎ 0171 208 2103, fax 0171 839 6033)

LAND, (Harold) Brook; s of David Land, of London, and Zara, *née* Levinson; *b* 12 March 1949; *Educ* St Paul's; *m* 7 Dec 1975, Anita Penny, da of Leslie Grade; 1 s (Daniel Edward b 30 April 1983), 1 da (Lesley Olivia b 19 Jan 1981); *Career* Nabarro Nathanson Solicitors: articled clerk 1967–72, asst slr 1972–74, ptnr 1974–96, conlst 1996–; memb Law Soc 1972; non-exec dir JLI Group plc 1989, Signet Group plc 1995; *Recreations* reading, TV; *Style*— Brook Land, Esq; ✉ Nabarro Nathanson, 50 Stratton St, London W1X 6NX (☎ 0171 493 9933, fax 0171 629 7900)

LAND, James Gordon Murray; OBE (1979); s of Gordon William Land (d 1964), Marion Lina, *née* King (d 1978); *b* 10 Sept 1932; *Educ* Marlborough; *m* 1, 18 Aug 1956 (m dis 1992), Betty Winifred; 1 s (Tristram b 1957), 1 da (Teresa b 1959); m 2, 19 Feb 1993, Maria del Carmen de Haro Martin; *Career* ptnr Price Waterhouse 1968–93 (joined 1955, served Spain, Italy and Libya); pres Br C of C Spain 1977–79 (vice pres 1992–93), vice pres Cncl Br C of C Continental Europe; memb ICAEW (cncl memb rep EEC 1987–90); dir MYROSE SL; *Recreations* cooking, painting, photography; *Style*— James Land, Esq, OBE; ✉ Rosa de Lima 44, 28290 Las Matas, Madrid, Spain (☎ and fax 00 34 1 630 46 49)

LAND, Prof Michael Francis; s of Prof Frank William Land (d 1990), and Nora Beatrice, *née* Channon (d 1985); *b* 12 April 1942; *Educ* Birkenhead Sch Cheshire, Jesus Coll Cambridge (BA, Frank Smart prize in zoology), UCL (PhD); *m* 1 (m dis 1980), Judith Drinkwater; 1 s (Adam Michael b 1969); m 2, 10 Dec 1980, Rosemary, da of James Clarke; 2 da (Katherine Rosemary b 1981, Penelope Frances b 1983); *Career* asst prof Univ of Calif Berkeley 1969–71 (Miller fell 1967–69); Sch of Biological Sciences Univ of Sussex: lectr 1972–78, reader 1978–84, prof 1984–; sr visiting fell Aust Nat Univ Canberra 1982–84; memb Cncl of the Marine Biological Assoc 1995–; memb Editorial Bd: Proceedings of Royal Soc, Jl of Comparative Physiology; Frink Medal Zoological Soc of London 1994; FRS 1982; *Publications* author of 100 publications on aspects of animal and human vision in learned jls and popular sci jls; *Recreations* gardening, music; *Style*— Prof Michael Land, FRS; ✉ White House, Cuilfail, Lewes, East Sussex BN7 2BE (☎ 01273 476780); School of Biological Sciences, University of Sussex, Brighton BN1 9QG (☎ 01273 678505, fax 01273 678535)

LAND, Peter Anthony; s of Anthony Land (d 1973), and Barbara Williamson, *née* Markland (d 1980); *b* 14 April 1927; *Educ* Bemrose Sch Derby; *m* 1, 15 April 1952, Dorothy Jessica (d 1994), da of Samuel Robert Pritchard (d 1989); 1 s (Patrick b 1956), 2 da (Jane b 1955, Sally b 1961); m 2, Jean Tighe Wagar, da of Cuthbert Hugh Tighe Leeson (d 1985); *Career* cmmnd Sherwood Foresters 1945–48; qualified CA 1950; chief accountant: BTR Industries 1958–63, BR Western Region 1963–67; md: National Carriers 1967–77, md British Transport Hotels 1978–83; chm: J N Dobbin (Hldgs) Ltd 1980–85, Bisham Abbey Nat Sport Centre 1980–84, Wycombe Health Authy 1986–93, S Bucks NHS Tst 1993–; tstee HRH Princess Christian's Hosp 1984–94; Freeman: City of London, Worshipful Co of Cooks; FCA (ACA 1950), CIMgt 1975; *Recreations* golf, travel, formerly cricket, hockey (former Capt Derbys); *Clubs* MCC; *Style*— Peter Land, Esq; ✉ South Riding, Bisham Rd, Marlow, Bucks SL7 1RL (☎ 01628 482898); 3 Vicarage St, Colyton, Devon EX13 6JR (☎ 01297 552092)

LANDALE, Sir David William Neil; KCVO (1993), DL (Nithsdale and Annandale (Dumfriesshire) 1984); s of David Fortune Landale (d 1970), and Louisa Mary Dorothy Charlotte, *née* Forbes, (d 1956), yst da of Charles Forbes of Callander House, Falkirk, Stirlingshire; *b* 27 May 1934; *Educ* Eton, Balliol Coll Oxford (MA); *m* 1961, Norah Melanie, da of Sir Harold Roper, CBE, MC, MP (C) for N Cornwall 1949–59 (d 1971); 3 s (Peter b 1963, William b 1965, Jamie b 1969); *Career* Black Watch Royal Highland Regt 1952–54; Jardine Matheson & Co Ltd: joined 1958, dir 1967–75, worked in Hong Kong, Thailand, Taiwan and Japan; dir: Matheson & Co Ltd 1975–, Pinneys Holdings Ltd 1982–87; chm: T C Farries & Co Ltd 1982–, Timber Growers UK Ltd 1985–87;

appointed sec and keeper of records of The Duchy of Cornwall 1987–93, dir Dumfries & Galloway Enterprise Co 1993–95; pres Royal Highland Agric Soc of Scotland 1994–95; chm: Royal Highland Agric Soc Ingliston Devpt Tst 1995–, Royal Scottish Forrestry Society Trust Co Ltd 1996–, Malcolm Sargent Cancer Fund for Children Ctee for Scotland 1996–; *Recreations* all countryside pursuits, theatre, reading (history); *Clubs* Boodle's, Pratt's, New (Edinburgh); *Style*— Sir David W N Landale, KCVO, DL; ✉ Dalswinton, Dumfries, Scotland DG2 0XZ

LANDAU, Dr David; s of Aharon Landau, of NY, and Evelyne, *née* Conti, of Italy; *b* 22 April 1950, Tel Aviv, Israel; *Educ* Liceo Berchet Milan (Maturitá Classica), Pavia Univ (MD), Wolfson Coll Oxford (MA); *Career* curator Mantegna exhbn Oxford 1979, print curator The Genius of Venice 1500–1600 exhbn Royal Acad 1983, chm Steering Ctee Andrea Mantegna exhbn Royal Acad and Metropolitan Museum NYC 1986–92; co-fndr Italian ice cream business 1983–86; Loot (classified listings paper): fndr and jt md 1985–95, chm 1995–; fndr of other jls: Print Quarterly 1984, Via Via (Holland) 1986, Modern Painters 1988; fndr treas and chm Free Ad Paper Int Assoc 1986–91 (ctee offr 1991–93), jt fndr and treas Young British Friends of the Art Museums of Israel charity 1988–95 (ctee offr 1995–), tstee The Nat Gallery Tst 1995–, dir Nat Gallery Pubns 1995–, memb Ctee Nat Art Collections Fund 1996–; fell Worcester Coll Oxford 1980; FRSA; *Books* Il Catalogo Completo dell'Opera Grafica di Georg Pencz (catalogue of the prints of Georg Pencz, 1978), Federica Galli - Catalogo Completo delle Acqueforti (1982), The Renaissance Print (with Prof Peter Parshall, 1994); numerous articles in jls incl: The Burlington Magazine, Master Drawings, Print Collector, Print Quarterly, Art International, Oxford Art Jl; *Recreations* looking at and collecting art, opera; *Style*— Dr David Landau; ✉ Loot Ltd, Lynwood House, 24/32 Kilburn High Road, London NW6 5TF (☎ 0171 625 0266, fax 0171 625 7921)

LANDAU, Sir Dennis Marcus; kt (1987); s of late Michael Landau, metallurgist; *b* 18 June 1927; *Educ* Haberdashers' Aske's; *m* 2 Dec 1992, Mrs Pamela Garlick; *Career* chief exec Co-operative Wholesale Society Ltd 1980–92, dep chm Co-operative Bank plc 1989–92; vice chm Lancashire Enterprises plc 1989–; chm: Unity Trust Bank plc 1992–, Social Economy Forum; CIMgt, FRSA; *Style*— Sir Dennis Landau; ✉ Unity Trust Bank plc, 130 Minories, London EC3 1NT (☎ 0171 481 3110)

LANDER, Geoffrey Ian; s of Victor Lander; *b* 11 Jan 1951; *m* Lynn; *Career* Nabarro Nathanson: joined as trainee slr 1973, ptnr Property Dept 1980–, head Property Dept 1995–; featured in Euromoney Guide to World's Leading Real Estate Lawyers; memb Bd UK Branch American C of C; chm Dolphin Sq Tenants' Assoc; memb Law Soc 1976; *Recreations* watching Manchester Utd, bridge, golf; *Style*— Geoffrey Lander, Esq; ✉ Nabarro Nathanson, 50 Stratton Street, London W1X 6NX (☎ 0171 518 3254, fax 0171 518 3140, mobile 0585 095912)

LANDER, John Hugh Russell; s of Hugh Russell Lander, of IOW, and Maude Louise, *née* Ellis; *b* 25 Feb 1944; *Educ* Sandown GS, Univ of Sheffield (BSc), Imperial Coll London (MSC, DIC); *m* 1,1972 (m dis); 2 s (Robert b 1976, Edward b 1983), 2 da (Melody b 1975, Annabel b 1982); m 2, 1995, Alexandra Margaret, *née* Waldron; *Career* exploration dir RTZ Oil & Gas Ltd 1983–89, vice pres Exploration Platt Energy Corp 1983–86, md PICT Petroleum plc 1989–95, dir British Borneo Petroleum PLC 1996–; *Recreations* sailing, squash, tennis; *Clubs* RAC, Lensbury, Lagos Yacht; *Style*— John Lander, Esq; ✉ Camelot, 26 The Island, Thames Ditton, Surrey; British Borneo Petroleum Syndicate PLC, Bowater House, Knightsbridge, London SW1X 7JX (☎ 0171 581 8822)

LANDER, Maxwell; s of Gustave Lander (d 1948); *b* 10 May 1914; *Educ* King Edward's Sch Birmingham; *m* 1939, Helena Margaret (d 1996), da of Wolf Halon; 1 da (Pamela Marjorie (Mrs Lander Brinkley)); *Career* former Col GHQ India Cmd; asst sec Admty 1947–50; conslt actuary, jt sr ptnr Duncan C Fraser & Co 1950–84 (ptnr 1984–86), conslt William M Mercer Ltd 1986–; pres: Nat Assoc of Pension Funds 1981–85, Int Employee Benefits Assoc 1994–; memb Ct of Assts Worshipful Co of Actuaries (Master 1986–87), Queen's Silver Jubilee medal 1977; *Recreations* fast cars, reading, theatre, music, food and wine; *Clubs* RAC; *Style*— Maxwell Lander, Esq; ✉ 83 Waterloo Rd, Hillside, Southport, Merseyside PR8 2NW (☎ 01704 67408); c/o William M Mercer Ltd, 30 Exchange Street East, Liverpool L2 3QB (☎ 0151 236 9771)

LANDER, Richard Simon; s of Israel Lennard Lander (d 1991), and Pauline, *née* Shalyt; *b* 18 Oct 1957; *Educ* Manchester GS, Jesus Coll Cambridge (BA), City Univ (MBA 1993–94); *m* 16 June 1988, Sarah Frances, da of Michael Barclay; 1 da (Rebecca Florence b 1993), 1 s (Benjamin Michael Lennard b 1996); *Career* journalist; Reuters Ltd: trainee journalist 1979, corr Hong Kong 1980, corr Aust 1981, corr S Africa 1982–84, London 1984–86; City reporter: The Times 1986, London Daily News 1987; freelance 1987–89, prodr Hard News 1989, news ed Business on Sunday (Channel 4) 1990, asst news ed business The Independent 1991–93, mangr Multimedia Services Dow Jones Telerate Ltd 1994–96, md Lime Media 1996–; Team RTS Award for Hard News feature on Russell Harty; *Books* The Director's Guide to Corporate Finance (ed, 1990); *Recreations* watching sport, walking, swimming, philosophy; *Clubs* RAC; *Style*— Richard Lander; ✉ Lime Media, 36 Westbere Rd, London NW2 3SR (☎ 0171 435 7581, fax 0171 916 4918)

LANDER, Stephen James; CB (1995); *b* 1947; *Educ* Bishop's Stortford Coll, Queens' Coll Cambridge (Open exhibitioner, BA, MA, PhD); *m* Felicity Mary, *née* Brayley; 1 s, 1 da; *Career* Inst of Historical Research 1972–75, DG Security Service 1996– (joined 1975); *Style*— Dr Stephen Lander, CB; ✉ Security Service, PO Box 3255, London SW1P 1AE

LANDERS, Brian James; *b* 21 April 1949; *Educ* Hele's Sch Exeter, St Charles HS Illinois, Univ of Exeter (BA, sabbatical pres Guild of Students and regnl chm NUS 1971–72), London Business Sch (MBA); *Career* Commercial Union 1973–79 (variously mgmnt Argentina, audit), mgmnt auditor Int Planned Parenthood Fedn 1979–82, sr internal auditor then asst to Exec Vice Pres (Europe) Tenneco Automotive Europe 1982–83, MBA London Business Sch 1983–85, chief internal auditor then fin controller Retail Div J Sainsbury Plc 1985–88, Habitat 1990–93 (positions included commercial dir, gp fin dir, gp fin and planning dir, md Habitat Spain), dir of fin HM Prison Service 1993–; memb Exec Euro Movement during EEC Referendum Campaign 1973, govr Walworth Sch London 1987–89; author of articles in Africa Guide and Jl of Inst of Internal Auditors; *Style*— Brian Landers, Esq; ✉ HM Prison Service, Cleland House, Page Street, London SW1P 4LN (☎ 0171 217 6275, fax 0171 217 6746)

LANDES, Emil; s of Wilhelm Landes (d 1983), of London, and Toni, *née* Held; *b* 13 July 1932; *Educ* Parmiter's Sch, King's Coll Hosp London (BDS); *m* 7 Feb 1960, Suzanne Dorrit, da of Paul Fraenkel, of Stockholm, Sweden; 2 s (Anthony b 1963, Jeremy b 1966), 1 da (Viveca b 1961); *Career* Flt Lt dental branch RAF 1958–59 (Flying Offr 1957–58); dental surgn St Thomas' Hosp, St Mary's Hosp, currently in private practice Harley St; int tstee Alpha Omega Dental Fraternity; Freeman City of London 1971; GDC 1956, BDA 1956, SAAD 1971, RSM 1974, EDS 1983; *Recreations* golf, tennis, skiing, chess, reading, biographies; *Clubs* RAC, RAF; *Style*— Emil Landes, Esq; ✉ Penthouse West, Thornbury Sq, London N6 5YW (☎ 0171 281 1843); 22 Harley St, London W1N 1AP (☎ 0171 637 0491, car 0836 248529)

LANDON, Prof John; s of Charles Landon, and Ellen, *née* Hutton; *b* 2 Dec 1931; *Educ* King William's Coll Isle of Man, St Mary's Hosp Med Sch (MD); *m* Mary Ursula; 2 s (Ewan, Mark), 1 da (Bridget); *Career* prof of chemical pathology Bart's Med Coll 1968–95; chm and res dir Therapeutic Antibodies 1984–; FRCP; *Style*— Prof John Landon; ✉ Therapeutic Antibodies Inc, Medical College of St Bartholomew's Hospital, Charterhouse Square, London EC1M 6BQ (☎ 0171 982 6058)

LANDON, Prof (Howard Chandler) Robbins; s of William Grinell Landon (d 1979), and Dorothea, *née* Le B Robbins (d 1982); *b* 6 March 1926; *Educ* Asheville Sch, Lenox Sch, Swarthmore Coll, Boston Univ (MBus); *m* 1, (m dis 1957), Christa; m 2, Else Radant, da of Fritz Schmidt (d 1975); *Career* author and music historian; guest Queen's Coll NY 1969; Univ Coll Cardiff: visiting professional fell 1971–77, John Bird prof of music history 1978–95, ret; guest prof Univ of California 1970, 1975 and 1979; Hon DMus: Boston Univ 1969, Queen's Univ Belfast 1971, Univ of Bristol 1975, New England Conservatory of Music 1988, Univ of Toulouse 1991; Verdientskreuz fur Kunst und Wissenschaft Austria first class (second class) 1975, Golden Cross City of Vienna 1986; *Books* Haydn-Chronicle and Works (5 vols 1978–80), 1791 Mozarts Last Year (1988), Mozart-The Golden Years 1781–91 (1989), The Mozart Compendium (ed, 1990), Mozart and Vienna (1991), Five Centuries of Music in Venice (with J J Norwich, 1991), Une Journée Particulière de Mozart (France, 1992), Vivaldi (1993), The Mozart Essays (1995); *Recreations* swimming, walking, cooking; *Style*— Prof Robbins Landon; ✉ Château de Foncoussières, 81800 Rabastens, (Tarn) France (☎ 00 33 63 40 61 45, fax 00 33 63 33 76 36); Anton Frankgasse 3, Vienna 1180, Austria

LANDON, Theodore Luke Giffard; s of Rev Sylvanus Luke Landon (d 1979; his mother was Jane Mary Giffard, *see* Halsbury, 3 Earl of), formerly vicar of Marldon, Devon, and Florence Faith Loetitia Trelawny, *née* Lowe (d 1972; her mother was Eleanor Salusbury-Trelawny, *see* Sir John Salusbury-Trelawny 13 Bt), Mr Landon is the head of the French Huguenot family of Landon, founded in England by Samuel Landon in 1683; *b* 10 Oct 1926; *Educ* Blundell's, Univ of London; *m* 1956, Joan, da of Frederic Archibald Parker (d 1977), of Alresford, Hants (s of Rev Hon Archibald Parker, sometime rural dean of Wem, Salop, and Hon Maud Bateman-Hanbury, da of 2 Baron Bateman; the dean was 9 s of 6 Earl of Macclesfield); 3 s (Mark b 1958, Philip b 1962, Benjamin b 1967), 2 da (Felicity b 1960, Rohais b 1964); *Career* dep chm and md Terra Nova Insurance Co Ltd 1970–79, dep chm C T Bowring Underwriting Holdings Ltd 1979–83; dir: English and American Insurance Co Ltd 1982–89, La Providence (The French Hosp) 1992–; chm English and American Pension Tst 1994– (dir 1984–94); memb Lloyd's 1961–; govr Kelly Coll Tavistock 1969–; tstee Huguenot Soc 1973– (pres 1989–92); *Recreations* history, music, genealogical research; *Clubs* East India; *Style*— Theodore Landon, Esq; ✉ Great Bromley House, Great Bromley, Colchester, Essex CO7 7TP (☎ 01206 230385)

LANDSHOFF, Prof Peter Vincent; *b* 22 March 1937; *Educ* Univ of Cambridge (mathematical tripos, wrangler, Smith's prize, PhD); *m*; 3 c; *Career* Univ of Cambridge: research fell St John's Coll 1961–63, fell Christ's Coll 1963–, asst lectr 1964–65, lectr 1965–74, reader in mathematical physics 1974–94, prof of mathematical physics 1994–; instructor Princeton Univ 1961–62, visiting assoc prof Univ of California at Berkeley 1966, scientific assoc CERN 1970, 1975–76, 1984–85 and 1991–92; SERC: chm Nuclear Theory Sub-Ctee 1979–82 (memb 1978–82), memb Particle Physics Experiments Selection Panel 1978–79, memb Nuclear Physics Bd 1979–82, memb Postgraduate Trg Ctee 1981–82; memb: Rutherford Lab Experiments Selection Panel 1975, European Ctee for Future Accelerators 1979–82, Ctee Isaac Newton Inst for Mathematical Scis Management (chm 1990–94); currently ed Physics Letters B; *Books* The Analytic S-Matrix (jtly, 1966), Simple Quantum Physics (with A J F Metherell, 1979); *Style*— Prof Peter Landshoff; ✉ Department of Applied Mathematics and Theoretical Physics, University of Cambridge, Silver Street, Cambridge CB3 9EW (☎ 01223 337880, fax 01223 337918, e-mail pvl@damtp.cam.ac.uk)

LANE, Anthony John; CB (1990); s of Eric Marshal Lane, and Phyllis Mary, *née* Hardwick; *b* 30 May 1939; *Educ* Caterham Sch, Balliol Coll Oxford; *m* 1967, Judith Sheila, da of William Herbert Dodson (d 1968); 2 s (Barnaby b 1969, Robin b 1972), 1 da (Lucinda b 1976); *Career* investment analyst Joseph Sebag & Co 1964–65; asst princ Miny of Technology 1965, private sec to Parly Sec 1968–69, princ 1969; private sec: to Min for Aerospace and Shipping 1973–74, to Sec of State for Prices and Consumer Protection 1974–75; asst sec: Dept of Prices 1975, Dept of Trade 1979; under sec Dept of Trade then Dept of Transport 1980–84, under sec DTI 1984–87, dep dir gen OFT 1987–90, dep sec DTI 1990–94, dep sec DOE 1994–; *Recreations* music; *Style*— Anthony Lane, Esq, CB; ✉ Department of Environment, 2 Marsham Street, London SW1

LANE, Barry Douglas; s of Douglas Lane, of Berks, and Dorothy, *née* Chalmers; *b* 21 June 1960; *Educ* Brakenhale Sch Bracknell; *Children* 1 s (Benjamin b 15 Jan 1990), 1 da (Emma b 12 Jan 1992); *Career* professional golfer 1976–; tournaments won: Jamaica Open 1983, Equity and Law Challenge 1987, Bell's Scottish Open 1988, Mercedes German Masters 1992, Canon European Masters 1993, Open de Baleares 1994, Andersen Consulting World Championship 1995; memb team: World Cup 1988 and 1994 (finalists), Dunhill Cup 1988 and 1994 (finalists), Ryder Cup 1993; *Recreations* cars, chess; *Style*— Barry Lane, Esq; ✉ IMG, Pier House, Strand on the Green, Chiswick, London W4 3NN (☎ 0181 233 5000, fax 0181 233 5001)

LANE, Maj-Gen Barry Michael; CB (1984), OBE (1974, MBE 1965); *b* 10 Aug 1932; *Educ* Dover Coll, RMA Sandhurst; *m* 1, 1956, Eveline Jean (d 1986), da of Vice Adm Sir Harry Koelle, KCB; 1 s (Anthony b 1962), 1 da (Juliet b 1959); m 2, 1987, Shirley Ann, da of E V Hawtin; *Career* cmmnd Somerset LI 1954; cmd: 1 LI 1972–75, II Armd Bde 1977–78; RCDS 1979, DAQ 1981–82, vice QMG 1982–83, GOC S W Dist 1984–87, Col LI 1982–87, Hon Col 6 LI (V) and Bristol Univ OTC 1987–; chief exec Cardiff Bay Devpt Corp 1987–92; *Recreations* cricket, gardening, architecture, wines; *Clubs* Army and Navy; *Style*— Maj-Gen Barry Lane, CB, OBE; ✉ c/o Army and Navy Club, London SW1Y 5JN

LANE, David Goodwin; QC (1991); s of James Cooper Lane (d 1981), of Gloucester, and Joyce Lilian, *née* Goodwin; *b* 8 Oct 1945; *Educ* Crypt Sch Gloucester, King's Coll London (LLB, AKC); *m* 31 Aug 1991, Jacqueline Elizabeth, da of Kenneth Frank Cocks (d 1989); *Career* called to the Bar Gray's Inn 1968, recorder of the Crown Court; Freeman City of London; *Style*— David Lane, Esq, QC; ✉ 2 All Saints' Chambers, 9/11 Broad St, Bristol BS1 2HP (☎ 0117 921 1966, fax 0117 927 6493); 11 Bolt Court, Fleet Street, London EC4Y 7DQ (☎ 0171 353 2300, fax 0171 353 1878)

LANE, Rev David John; *b* 12 June 1935; *Educ* Magdalen Coll Oxford (BA, Pusey and Ellerton Hebrew scholar, Hall Houghton Syriac Prize, MA, Kennicott Hebrew fell, BD), Coll of the Resurrection Mirfield; *Career* ordained deacon and priest (Barbados) 1962; lectr then sr tutor Codrington Coll Barbados (affiliated to Univ of Durham) 1961–65, asst curate St Peter's Wolvercote Oxford 1965–66, assoc chaplain and lectr in theol Pembroke Coll Oxford and lectr and tutor in Old Testament studies St Stephen's House Oxford 1966–68, tenured assoc prof Dept of Near Eastern Studies Univ of Toronto 1975–83 (asst prof 1971–75); sec Coll Cncl UC Toronto 1972–74, sr fell Trinity Coll Toronto 1976–82, visiting prof Peshitta Inst Leiden 1977, hon lectr Dept of Theol and Religious Studies Univ of Leeds 1983–; Coll of the Resurrection Mirfield: lectr and tutor in biblical studies 1983–84, dir of studies 1984–90, vice princ 1987–90, princ 1991–; memb: Soc for Old Testament Study 1966, British New Testament Soc 1985; *Publications* numerous Old Testament translations, text editions and papers published; *Style*— The Rev D J Lane; ✉ Principal, College of the Resurrection, Mirfield, W Yorks WF14 0BW

LANE, David Neil; CMG (1983); s of A C Lane (d 1974), of Bath, and H M Lane, *née* Tonner (d 1980); *b* 16 April 1928; *Educ* Abbotsholme Sch, Merton Coll Oxford (MA); *m* 1968, Sara, da of C J Nurcombe, MC (d 1988), of Timberscombe, Somerset; 2 da;

Career HM Foreign (later Diplomatic) Serv 1951–88, Br high cmmr Trinidad and Tobago 1980–85, ambass to the Holy See 1985–88; chm Anglo-Turkish Soc 1995–; Order of St John: asst sec-gen 1989–92, sec 1990–92; *Recreations* music; *Style—* David Lane, Esq, CMG; ✉ 6 Montagu Sq, London W1H 1RA (☎ 0171 486 1673)

LANE, Prof David Philip; *b* 1 July 1952; *Educ* John Fisher Sch, UCL (BSc, PhD); *Career* post doctoral res fell 1976–77, lectr Zoology Dept Imperial Coll of Science and Technol 1977–81, Robertson res fell and CRI fell Cold Spring Harbor Laboratories USA 1978–80, lectr Biochemistry Dept Imperial Coll 1981–85, princ scientist Imperial Cancer Research Fund 1988–90 (sr head scientist 1985–88), dir Cell Transformation Res Gp Cancer Research Campaign 1990–; Gibb fell CRC 1990; memb: Euro Molecular Biology Orgn 1990, CRC Grants Ctee 1991–, MRC Cell and Molecular Biology Bd 1994–, Cncl Royal Soc of Edinburgh 1995–, Scientific Advsy Bd Scotgen Ltd; author of over 160 papers; Charles Rodolphe Brupbacher Fndn Prize 1993, Howard Hughes Int Scholar Award 1993–98, Joseph Steiner Prize 1993, Jan Waldenström Lecture 1994, Yvette Mayent Prize 1995, Lennox Black Prize 1995; FRSE 1992, FRS 1996; *Style—* Prof David Lane, FRS, FRSE; ✉ Cancer Research Campaign Laboratories, Department of Biochemistry, University of Dundee, Dundee DD1 4HN

LANE, David Stuart; *Educ* King Edward's GS Birmingham, Univ of Birmingham (BSocSc), Nuffield Coll Oxford (DPhil), Univ of Cambridge (PhD, by incorporation); *m* Christel, *née* Noritzsch; 1 s (Christopher), 1 da (Julie); *Career* Univ of Birmingham: lectr Faculty of Commerce and Social Sci 1962–64, lectr Centre for Russian and E Euro Studies 1964–67, prof of sociology 1981–90; Univ of Essex: lectr 1967–71, reader 1971–73, chm Sociology Dept 1972–73; Emmanuel Coll Cambridge: univ lectr 1974–80 and 1990–92, reader 1992–, fell 1974–80 and 1990–; visiting scholar Woodrow Wilson Centre Washington DC 1982, 1986 and 1995; visiting prof: Cornell Univ USA 1987, Univ of Graz Austria 1991 and 1996, Harvard Univ 1993; chm W Midlands Branch Campaign for Mentally Handicapped People 1982–83, sec W Midlands Cncl for Disabled People 1983–86, exec ed Disability, Handicap and Society jl 1985–89, vice chm Birmingham Elfrida Rathbone Assoc 1986–90, memb Exec Br Sociological Assoc 1987–92; *Books* incl: The Roots of Communism (1969), Politics and Society in the USSR (1970), The Socialist Industrial State - Towards a Political Sociology of State Socialism (1976), Current Approaches to Down's Syndrome (jt ed, 1985), Soviet Economy and Society (1985), Soviet Labour and the Ethic of Communism - Employment and the Labour Process in the USSR (1987), Soviet Society under Perestroika (1991), Russia in Flux (ed, 1992), Russia in Transition (ed, 1995), The Rise and Fall of State Socialism (1996); *Recreations* playing squash, cinema, theatre, supporting Arsenal FC; *Style—* David Lane; ✉ Emmanuel College, Cambridge CB2 3AP (☎ 01223 334202, fax 01223 334426)

LANE, Sir David William Stennis Stuart; kt (1983); s of Hubert Samuel Lane, MC; *b* 24 Sept 1922; *Educ* Eton, Trinity Coll Cambridge, Yale; *m* 1955, Lesley Anne Mary, da of Sir Gerard Clauson, KCMG, OBE (d 1974); 2 s; *Career* serv WWII RNVR; called to the Bar Middle Temple 1955, Br Iron and Steel Fedn 1948–59 (sec 1956), with Shell International 1959–67; MP (C) Cambridge 1967–76 (had contested Lambeth (Vauxhall) 1964, Cambridge 1966), PPS to Employment Sec 1970–72, Parly under sec Home Office 1972–74; chm: N Kensington Cons Assoc 1961–62, Cmmn for Racial Equality 1977–82, Nat Assoc of Youth Clubs 1982–87; *Recreations* travel, walking, golf; *Clubs* MCC; *Style—* Sir David Lane; ✉ 5 Spinney Drive, Great Shelford, Cambridge CB2 5LY (☎ 01223 843437)

LANE, (Sara) Elizabeth; da of Rt Hon Sir Lionel Heald, QC, MP (d 1981), of Chilworth Manor, Surrey, and Daphne Constance Heald, CBE; *b* 30 April 1938; *Educ* Heathfield and Paris; *m* 15 May 1963, George Henry Lane, MC, s of Ernest Lanyi, of Budapest, Hungary; *Career* dir Seek & Find Ltd 1963–68, advsr on works of art and assoc Baron Martin von Koblitz 1968–78, dir Christie Manson & Woods Ltd 1978–; *Recreations* country pursuits; *Style—* Mrs George Lane; ✉ 12 Petersham Place, London, SW7 5PX (☎ 0171 584 7840); Christie Mansion & Woods Ltd, 8 King St, St James, London SW1Y 6QT (☎ 0171 839 9060, fax 0171 839 1611)

LANE, Baron (Life Peer UK 1979), of St Ippollitts, Co Hertfordshire; Geoffrey Dawson Lane; kt (1966), AFC (1943), PC (1974); s of late Percy Albert Lane, of Lincoln; *b* 17 July 1918; *Educ* Shrewsbury, Trinity Coll Cambridge; *m* 1944, Jan, da of Donald Macdonald; 1 s (Hon Richard b 1948); *Career* served RAF 1939–45, Sqdn Ldr 1942; barr 1946, QC 1962, bencher 1966, dep chm Beds QS 1960–66, recorder Bedford 1963–66, judge High Ct of Justice (Queen's Bench Div) 1966–74, Lord Justice of Appeal 1974–79, Lord of Appeal in Ordinary 1979–80, Lord Chief Justice 1980–92, hon master of the bench Inner Temple 1980–; Hon DCL Cambridge 1984; *Style—* The Rt Hon the Lord Lane, AFC; ✉ Royal Courts of Justice, Strand, London WC2; House of Lords, London SW1

LANE, John Armstrong; s of Dr Sidney William Lane (d 1952), of Leicester, and Freda Lydia, *née* Robinson (d 1980); *b* 7 April 1935; *Educ* Ashby-de-la-Zouch GS, Leicester Sch of Architecture (DipArch); *m* 23 June 1962, Patricia Anne, da of Rowland Fletcher, of Derby; 2 da (Dawn b 9 July 1967, Sonia b 2 Nov 1971); *Career* Nat Serv RAF; fndr Lane, Bremner & Garnett Architects 1961; former govr Glasgow Sch of Art; former pres: RIAS, Glasgow Art Club; FRIBA; *Recreations* family, country house, travel, competitions; *Clubs* Art (Glasgow); *Style—* John Lane, Esq; ✉ 18 Whittinghame Drive, Glasgow G12 0XX (☎ 0141 339 7101); Planetree, Planetree Park, Gatehouse of Fleet, Castle Douglas, Kirkcudbrightshire; 87 Cumberland Mills Square, Saunders Ness Road, London E14 3BJ; Lane, Bremner and Garnett, Chartered Architects, New Bridgegate Church, 69 Dixon Road, Glasgow G42 8AT (☎ 0141 423 1100, fax 0141 424 3113)

LANE, Jonathan William Miles (Jon); *b* 24 July 1958; *Educ* Eton, Clare Coll Cambridge (MA); *Career* civil engr Ove Arup Partnership 1979–86, country rep Nepal WaterAid 1987–91, dir Registered Engineers for Disaster Relief 1991–94, dir WaterAid 1994–; MICE 1985; *Style—* Mr Jon Lane; ✉ Director, WaterAid, Prince Consort House, 27–29 Albert Embankment, London SE1 7UB (☎ 0171 793 4513, fax 0171 793 4545)

LANE, Hon Mrs (Miriam Louisa); *née* Rothschild; CBE (1982); eld da of Hon Nathaniel Charles Rothschild (d 1923); sis of 3 Baron Rothschild; granted the rank and precedence of a Baron's da 1938; *b* 5 Aug 1908; *Educ* privately; *m* 14 Aug 1943 (m dis 1957), Capt George Henry Lane, MC; 1 s living, 3 da living (1 s and 1 da decd); *Career* serv WWII FO (Def Medal); farmer and biologist; tstee Br Museum 1967–75; visiting prof of biology Royal Free Hosp 1970–74, Romanes lectr 1985; author of over 300 scientific pubns; memb: Zoological and Entomological Res Cncl, Marine Biological Assoc, Royal Entomological Soc (pres 1992–93), Systematics Assoc, Soc for Promotion of Nature Reserves, Pubns Ctee Zoological Soc; Wigglesworth Medal Royal Entomological Soc, Silver Medal Int Assoc of Chemical Ecology 1989, Victoria Medal RHS 1991, Bloomer Award Linnean Soc, Gregor Mendel Gold Medal Czech Republic; hon fell St Hugh's Oxford; Hon DSC: Oxford, Gothenberg, Hull, North Western (Chicago), Leicester, Open Univ; FRS; *Books* Fleas Flukes and Cuckoos (5 edn), Dear Lord Rothschild (1983), Catalogue of the Rothschild Collection of Fleas (6 vols) (1953–82), The Butterfly Gardener (1983), Atlas of Insect Tissue (1985), Animals and Man (1986), Butterfly Cooing Like a Dove (1991), The Rothschild Gardens (1996); *Recreations* natural history, conservation; *Clubs* Queens; *Style—* The Hon Mrs Lane, CBE, FRS; ✉ Ashton Wold, Peterborough PE8 5LZ

LANE, Dr Nancy Jane; OBE (1994); da of Temple Haviland Lane (d 1994), of Nova Scotia, and Frances de Forest, *née* Gilbert (d 1967); *Educ* Dalhousie Univ Canada (Allan Pollock scholar, Khaki Univ scholar, Ross Stewart Smith scholar, B'nai B'rith prize, Eugene Harris prize in zoology, BSc, Univ Gold medal, MSc), Univ of Oxford (DPhil), Univ of Cambridge (PhD, DSc); *m* 22 Dec 1969, Prof R N Perham, FRS, *qv*; 1 da (Temple Helen Gilbert b 8 Oct 1970), 1 s (Quentin Richard Haviland b 14 Oct 1973); *Career* res asst prof Dept of Pathology Albert Einstein Coll of Med NY 1964–65, res staff biologist Dept of Biology Yale Univ 1965–68; Univ of Cambridge: research fell Girton Coll 1968–70, official fell and lectr in cell biology Girton Coll 1970–, tutor Girton Coll 1975–, sr princ scientific offr ARC Unit of Invertebrate Chemistry and Physiology (later AFRC Unit) Zoology Dept 1982–90 (sr scientific offr 1968–73, princ scientific offr 1973–82), sr res assoc Zoology Dept 1990–; visiting prof: Siena Univ 1990–93, Padua Univ 1991–94; memb: PM's Advsy Panel for the Citizen's Charter 1991–93, Forum UK 1994–; chair: BTEC's Advsy Bd for Science and Caring 1991–94, Working Pty for Women in Science and Engrg (OST) Cabinet Office 1993–94; non-exec dir: Smith and Nephew plc 1991–, Peptide Therapeutics plc 1995–; Hon LLD Dalhousie Univ 1985, Hon DSc Univ of Salford 1994; memb: Soc for Experimental Biology 1962, American Soc for Cell Biology 1965, Histochemical Soc 1965, American Assoc for the Advancement of Science 1965, Br Soc for Cell Biology 1980 (sec 1982–90), Br Soc for Developmental Biology 1980, fell Royal Microscopical Soc 1965; memb Forum UK 1994; MRI 1987, MInstD 1991, FZS 1986, FIBiol 1991, FRSA 1992; *Publications* author of 180 scientific papers, assoc ed 5 learned jls, and ed-in-chief Cell Biology International; *Recreations* theatre, dance and opera, 20th Century art, travelling; *Clubs* IOD, United Oxford and Cambridge University; *Style—* Dr Nancy J Lane, OBE; ✉ Girton College, Cambridge CB3 0JG (☎ and fax 01223 363752); Department of Zoology, Downing Street, Cambridge CB2 3EJ (☎ 01223 330116/336600, fax 01223 336676/330116)

LANE, (Alan) Piers; s of Peter Alan Lane, of Brisbane, Aust, and Enid Muriel, *née* Hitchcock; *b* 8 Jan 1958; *Educ* Kelvin Grove HS Brisbane, Queensland Conservatorium of Music, RCM London; *Career* concert pianist; prof at Royal Acad of Music; appeared with orchs incl: Royal Philharmonic, London Philharmonic, the Philharmonia, Hallé Orch, BBC Welsh, BBC Scottish, BBC Concert, BBC Symphony, BBC Philharmonic, Scottish Chamber Orch, Australian Chamber Orch, New Zealnad Symphony Orch, Bombay Chamber Orch, Adelaide Symphony Orch, Ensemble Kanazawa, Capetown Symphony, Transvaal Philharmonic, Natal Philharmonic, Royal Liverpool Philharmonic, RTE Orch, Queensland Symphony, W Aust Symphony, Tasmanian Symphony, Melbourne Symphony, Queensland Philharmonic, Auckland Philarmonic, Montpellier Orch, Royal Oman Symphony, Brabants Orkester, Noorhollands Philharmonisch Orkest, Gothenburg Philharmonic; toured extensively in UK, Ireland, Aust, NZ, S America, Western and Eastern Europe, USA, Africa, Japan, India; special prize Bartok-Liszt Int Competition Budapest 1976, best Australian pianist Sydney Int Piano Competition 1977, winner Royal Over-Seas League Competition 1982; Churchill fell 1979; Hon RAM 1994; *Recordings* Moszowski and Paderewski Concertos (with BBC Scottish Symphony Orch and Jerzy Maxymiuk, 1991), Complete Etudes of Scriabin 1992, works by Mussorgsky, Balakirev and Stravinsky 1992, Piano Quintet by Brahms (New Budapest Quartet) 1992, Violin Virtuoso (with Tasmin Little) 1992, Sonatas by Shostakovich, Prokofiev, Schnittke and Rachmaninoff (with cellist Alexander Baillie), Franz Waxman Rhapsody (with Queensland Symphony Orch and Richard Mills), d'Albert Concertos (with BBC Scottish Orch and Alun Francis) 1994, Busch Concerto (with Royal Philharmonic and Vernon Handley) 1994, Vaughan-Williams and Delius Concertos plus Finzi Eclogue (with RLPO and Vernon Handley) 1994, Piano pieces by Alan Bush 1994, Elgar Piano Quintet (with Vellinger String Quartet) 1994, Virtuoso Strauss Transcriptions 1995, Concertos by Parry and Stanford 1995, French Violin Sonatas by Ravel, Debussy and Poulenc (with Tasmin Little) 1995; *Style—* Piers Lane, Esq; ✉ agent for concerts worldwide: c/o Patrick Garvey Management, Top Floor, 59 Lansdowne Place, Hove, E Sussex BN3 1FL (☎ 01273 206623, fax 01273 208484); recitals: Georgina Ivor Associates, 28 Old Devonshire Road, London SW12 9RB (☎ 0181 673 7179, fax 0181 675 8058); Australian agent: Arts Management, 180 Goulburn Street, Darlinghurst NSW 2010, Australia (☎ 02 283 2066, fax 02 264 8201)

LANE, Stevens (Steve); s of William Stevens Moore Lane (d 1960), and Marguerite, *née* Willson; *b* 7 Nov 1921; *Educ* Latymer Upper Sch London, Univ of Edinburgh; *Career* jazz guitarist, cornettist, bandleader and composer; electrical laboratory devpt worker CAV Ltd 1939–42, Meteorological Office 1942, radar mechanic then with Bomber Command RAF 1942–46, various laboratory positions CAV Ltd and Goodmans Loudspeakers 1946–60, instant printer 1960–86; editor: Jazz Music 1950, Jazz Guide until 1986; amateur guitarist 1939–50, fndr The Southern Stompers 1950 (renamed The Red Hot Peppers 1985); *Recreations* medieval churches, Shropshire, politics, anthropology, music; *Style—* Steve Lane, Esq; ✉ c/o Azure Records, Zhdanov Music, 32 Kenton Lane, Harrow, Middx HA3 8TX (☎ 0181 907 5583)

LANE, Terence Maurice; s of Alexander Uriah Lane (d 1927), of Fleet, Hants, and Hilda Rachel, *née* Smith (d 1976); *b* 5 Oct 1918; *Educ* London Univ (BA), Indiana Univ (AB), Coll of Law; *m* 15 Aug 1944, (Bruce) Jacqueline, da of Bruce Alexander Johnston Dunlop, MC; 3 s (Jeremy, Piers, Crispin), 4 da (Litan, Rafael (Mrs Hall), Halcyon (Mrs Heaslop), Meredith (Mrs Sanders)); *Career* RA 1940, cmmnd 2 Lt 1941, seconded 2 Indian Anti-Tank Regt and 28 Mountain Regt RIA 1941, Capt 1944, Maj 1944 (despatches); Colonial Admin Serv Tanganyika Territory (now Tanzania) 1946, dist cmmr Chunya Dist 1948, invalided from serv 1949; slr 1953, fndr ptnr Baker & McKenzie 1961, sr ptnr Lane & Ptnrs 1974, ptnr Marks & Murase NYC 1974; Freeman City of London 1987, Liveryman Worshipful Co of Arbitrators 1987; memb Law Soc 1954, FCIArb 1977; *Books* International Licensing Agreements (1973); *Recreations* riding, hunting, racing; *Clubs* Hampshire Hunt; *Style—* Terence Lane, Esq; ✉ Peregrine House, Rake, Liss, Hampshire (☎ 01730 893138); Lane & Partners, 46–47 Bloomsbury Square, London WC1A 2RU (☎ 0171 242 2626, fax 0171 242 0387, telex 8812495)

LANE FOX, Robin James; s of James Henry Lane Fox, of Middleton Cheney, Oxon, and Anne, *née* Loyd; *b* 5 Oct 1946; *Educ* Eton, Magdalen Coll Oxford (MA); *m* 26 June 1970 (m dis 1993), Louisa Caroline Mary, da of Maj Charles Farrell, MC, of Cutmill House, Watlington, Oxon; 1 s (Henry b 19 Oct 1974), 1 da (Martha b 10 Feb 1973); *Career* fell Magdalen Coll Oxford 1970–73, lectr in classics Worcester Coll Oxford 1974–76, res fell classical and Islamic history Worcester Coll 1976–77, fell and tutor New Coll Oxford 1977–, univ reader in ancient history 1990–; gardening columnist Finanical Times 1970–, Br Press Award Leisure Journalist of Year 1988; garden master New Coll 1979–; FRSL 1974; *Books* Alexander The Great (1973), Variations On A Garden (1974), Search for Alexander (1980), Better Gardening (1982), Pagan and Christians (1986), The Unauthorised Version (1990); *Recreations* gardening, hunting, travelling; *Clubs* Beefsteak; *Style—* Robin Lane Fox, Esq, FRSL; ✉ c/o New College, Oxford OX1 3BN (☎ 01865 279 555)

LANE OF HORSELL, Baron (Life Peer UK 1990), of Woking in the County of Surrey; Sir Peter Stewart Lane; kt (1984), JP (Surrey 1976); s of Leonard George Lane (d 1950); *b* 29 Jan 1925; *Educ* Sherborne; *m* Doris Florence (d 1969), da of Robert Simpson Botsford (d 1955); 2 da (Hon Rosalie (Baroness Trefgarne) b 1946, Hon Alexandra (Hon Mrs (Jeremy) Cresswell b 1956); *Career* Sub Lt RNVR 1943–46; sr ptnr BDO Binder Hamlyn 1979–92; chm: Brent International plc 1985–95, Attwoods plc 1994, Automated Security (Holdings) plc 1994–96; dep chm More O'Ferrall plc 1985–; dir: Christie Group plc 1994–, Reliance Security Group plc 1994–; chm: Air Travel Tst Ctee 1989–, Nuffield Hospitals 1993–96; pres Bd of Gen Purposes United Grand Lodge of England 1991–95; Nat Union of Cons and Unionist Assocs: chm 1983, chm Exec Ctee

1986–91, hon vice pres 1984–; FCA; *Clubs* Boodle's, MCC; *Style*— The Rt Hon Lord Lane of Horsell, JP; ✉ House of Lords, London SW1A 0PW

LANE-SMITH, Roger; s of Harry Lane-Smith (d 1979), of Cheshire, and Dorothy, *née* Shuttleworth; *b* 19 Oct 1945; *Educ* Stockport GS, Guildford Coll of Law (Robert Ellis Memorial prizeman); *m* 1969, Pamela Mary, da of Leonard Leigh; 1 s (Jonathan Roger b 10 Nov 1973), 1 da (Zoe Victoria b 21 June 1971); *Career* admitted slr 1969; ptnr David Blank & Co Manchester 1973–77; Alsop Wilkinson: managing ptnr Manchester Office 1977–88, managing ptnr London Office 1988–92, chm 1992–96; dep sr ptnr Dibb Lupton Alsop 1996–; winner Robert Ellis Meml prize; memb Law Soc; *Recreations* golf, tennis, shooting, deep-sea fishing; *Clubs* Mark's, St James'; *Style*— Roger Lane-Smith, Esq; ✉ Dibb Lupton Alsop, Carlton House, 18 Albert Square, Manchester M2 5PE

LANESBOROUGH, 9 Earl of (1756); Denis Anthony Brian Butler; TD, JP (Leics 1967), DL (Leics 1962); also Baron of Newtown-Butler (I 1715, but eldest s & h usually styled Lord Newtown-Butler), and Viscount Lanesborough (I 1728); s of 8 Earl of Lanesborough (d 1950), by his 2 w Grace, da of Sir Anthony Abdy, 3 Bt; *b* 28 Oct 1918; *Educ* Stowe; *m* 1, 1939 (m dis 1950), Bettyne Ione (d 1989), da of Sir Lindsay Everard, JP, DL, MP (d 1949); 2 da (1 decd); m 2, 3 Nov 1995, Patricia Julia, da of late Frederick William Meston, MC, and Norah Elizabeth Meston; *Heir* none; *Career* Lt Leics Yeo 1939, Maj RA (TA) 1945; memb Nat Gas Consumers' Cncl 1973–78, vice chm Trent RHA 1974–85, chm Loughborough & Dist Housing Assoc 1978–88; pres Guide Dogs for the Blind Assoc 1964–86 (chm 1953–64); *Style*— The Rt Hon Earl of Lanesborough, TD, JP, DL; ✉ Allerly, Gattonside, Melrose, Roxburghshire TD6 9LT (☎ 01896 823482); Bridgeview, Strathdon, Aberdeenshire AB36 8UR

LANG, Prof Andrew Richard; s of late Ernest Lang; *b* 9 Sept 1924; *Career* asst prof Harvard Univ 1954–59; Univ of Bristol: physics lectr 1960–66, reader 1966–79, prof of physics 1979–87, prof emeritus 1987–; FRS 1975; *Style*— Prof Andrew Lang, FRS; ✉ 1B Elton Rd, Bristol BS8 1SJ

LANG, Belinda Lucy; da of Jeremy Hawk, of London, and Joan, *née* Heal; *b* 23 Dec 1953; *Educ* Lycee Français de Londres, Central Sch of Speech and Drama; *m* 15 Oct 1988, Hugh Munro, s of John Hugh Munro Fraser (d 1987); 1 da (Lily Irene b 1990); *Career* actress; *Theatre* incl: Present Laughter (Vaudeville) 1981, Hobsons Choice (Haymarket) 1982, Antigone and Tales from Hollywood (NT) 1983–84, Clandestine Marriage (Albery) 1984, Mrs Klein (Apollo) 1989, Thark (Lyric Hammersmith) 1989, Dark River (Orange Tree) 1992, On Approval (Leatherhead and tour) 1994, Dead Funny (Savoy and tour) 1996; *Television* incl: To Serve Them All My Days (BBC) 1980, Dear John (BBC) 1985, The Bretts (Central) 1986, Bust (LWT) 1988, Alleyn Mysteries (BBC) 1990 and 1993–94, Second Thoughts (LWT) 1991–94, 2 Point 4 Children (BBC) 1991–96; *Recreations* walking, cycling, reading; *Style*— Miss Belinda Lang; ✉ c/o Ken McReddie Ltd, 91 Regent Street, London W1 7TB (☎ 0171 439 1456, fax 0171 734 6530)

LANG, Dr Brian Andrew; *b* 2 Dec 1945; *Educ* Royal High Sch Edinburgh, Univ of Edinburgh (MA, PhD); *m* 1, 1975 (m dis 1982); 1 s; m 2, 1983, Susan, *née* Purnell; 1 s, 1 da; *Career* postgrad res Kenya 1968–71, lectr then sr lectr in social anthropology Aarhus Univ Denmark 1971–75, princ scientific offr Social Science Res Cncl 1977–79 (sr scientific offr 1976–77), head Historic Bldgs Branch Scottish Devpt Dept Edinburgh 1979–80, sec Nat Heritage Meml Fund 1980–87, dir of public affairs National Trust 1987–91, chief exec and dep chm The British Library 1991–; pres Inst of Info Scientists 1993–94 (hon fell 1994), cmmr Library and Information Cmmn 1995–, chm EC Euro Nat Libraries Forum (COBRA) 1993–; tstee Education 2000 1995–; *Style*— Dr Brian Lang; ✉ The British Library, 96 Euston Road, St Pancras, London NW1 2DB (☎ 0171 412 7273, fax 0171 412 7268)

LANG, Lt-Gen Sir Derek Boileau; KCB (1967, CB 1964), DSO (1944), MC (1941), DL (Edinburgh 1978); s of Lt-Col C F G Lang (d 1961), of Whytegates, Church Crookham, Hants; *b* 7 Oct 1913; *Educ* Wellington, RMC Sandhurst; *m* 1, 1942, Morna Helena Casey (d 1953), da of Charles Massy-Dawson, of Sussex; 1 s, 1 da; m 2, 1953 (m dis 1969), Anita Lewis Shields; m 3, 1969, Elizabeth H Balfour (d 1982); m 4, 1983, Maartje McQueen, wid of Charles N McQueen; *Career* 2 Lt Cameron Highlanders 1933, Brig 1958, COS Scot Cmd 1960–61, GOC 51 Highland Div 1962–64, dir Army Trg MOD 1964–66, GOC-in-C Scot Cmd and govr of Edinburgh Castle 1966–69, Lt-Gen 1966, ret 1969; sec Univ of Stirling 1970–74, assoc conslt PA Mgmnt Conslts Ltd 1975–83; OStJ; *Recreations* golf, shooting, fishing, music; *Clubs* Hon Co of Edinburgh Golfers, New (Edinburgh), Sr Golfers'; *Style*— Lt-Gen Sir Derek Lang, KCB, DSO, MC, DL; ✉ Templeland, Kirknewton, Midlothian EH27 8DJ (☎ 01506 883211)

LANG, Rear Adm (William) Duncan; CB (1981); s of James Hardie Lang (d 1936), of Edinburgh, and Elizabeth Foggo Paterson, *née* Storie (d 1965); *b* 1 April 1925; *Educ* Edinburgh Acad; *m* 1947, Joyce Rose, da of Alfred Henry Weeks (d 1936), of Catford; 1 s (James), 1 da (Celia); *Career* serv WWII RN 1943; pilot in 800, 816 and 825 Sqdns, flying instr and test pilot, CO 802 Sqdn 1958–59, CO RNAS Lossiemouth 1970–72, COS to Flag Offr Naval Air Cmd 1975–76, Naval ADC to HM The Queen 1978, Mil Dep to Head of Def Sales 1978–81; dir Naval Security 1981–86; *Recreations* golf (pres RNGS 1979–85); *Clubs* Army & Navy; *Style*— Rear Adm Duncan Lang, CB; ✉ c/o Midland Bank, 19 High Street, Haslemere, Surrey GU27 2HQ

LANG, Hugh; ERD (1967); s of Hugh Lang (d 1981), of Holmwood, Surrey, and Lilian Maydee, *née* Mackay; *b* 22 Dec 1934; *Educ* St Edmunds Sch, Harrow Sch; *m* 11 March 1961, Rosanne Auber, da of Lt-Col Richard Quentin Charles Mainwaring (d 1983), of Cortown, Kells, Co Meath Ireland; 2 s (Alistair Hugh b 15 July 1963, James Richard b 13 March 1966); *Career* 2 Lt 5 Royal Inniskilling Dragoon Gds cmmnd 1954, RARO (AER) 1955–67; ptnr: John Prust & Co 1963–70, Laurence Prust & Co 1970–80; conslt Wallace Smith Trust Co Ltd 1985–92; MSI (memb Stock Exchange 1962), chief exec and sec The Stock Exchange Benevolent Fund 1980–94; govr Crossways Trust Ltd 1980–94, tstee Poyle Charity 1968–94; Offrs' Assoc: memb Exec and Fin Ctee 1985–94, memb Cncl 1995; govr and hon fin advsr Royal National Coll for the Blind, dir RNC Enterprises plc, memb Investmt and Fin Ctee DGAA 1991–92; govr: Bridewell Royal Hosp and King Edward's Sch Witley 1992, St Edmund's Sch Tst Ltd 1992; chm Friends King Edward VII Hosp Midhurst 1996 (memb Ctee 1994); Freeman City of London 1956, Liveryman Worshipful Co of Skinners 1956; *Recreations* shooting, gardening, wine; *Clubs* Sloane, The City of London, MCC; *Style*— Hugh Lang, Esq, ERD; ✉ Durfold Hatch Cottage, Fisher Lane, Chiddingfold, Surrey GU8 4TF (☎ 01428 684286)

LANG, Hugh Montgomerie; CBE (1978); s of John Montgomerie Lang; *b* 7 Nov 1932; *Educ* Univ of Glasgow (BSc); *m* 1, 1959 (m dis 1981), Marjorie Armour; 1 s, 1 da; m 2, 1981, Susan Lynn Hartley; *Career* REME 1953–55; chm: P-E International 1980–92 (dir 1972–92, chief exec 1977–92), Redman Heenan Int 1982–86 (dir 1981–86), Brammer 1990– (dir 1990–), Manganese Bronze Holdings 1992–; chm Technol Transfer Servs Advsy Ctee 1982–85 (memb 1978–85); non-exec dir: Fairey Holdings 1978–82, UKO International 1985–86, B Elliott plc 1986–88, Renaissance Holdings plc 1987–91, Siebe plc 1987–91, Strong & Fisher (Holdings) plc 1988–90, Co-ordinated Land and Estates plc 1988–93, OGC International plc 1993–94, Ericsson Ltd 1993–; memb: Business Educn Cncl 1980–81, CBI Industl Policy Ctee 1980–83, Design Cncl 1983–90 (dep chm 1987–90), Engrg Cncl 1984–86; CEng, FIEE; *Recreations* fishing, gardening, golf, reading; *Clubs* Denham Golf, Brooks's; *Style*— Hugh Lang, Esq, CBE; ✉ Welders Wood, Chalfont St Peter, Bucks SL9 8TT

LANG, Rt Hon Ian Bruce; PC (1990), MP (C) Galloway and Upper Nithsdale (majority 2,468); s of late James Fulton Lang, DSC; *b* 27 June 1940; *Educ* Lathallan Sch Kincardineshire, Rugby, Sidney Sussex Coll Cambridge (BA); *m* 1971, Sandra Caroline, da of John Alastair Montgomerie, DSC; 2 da; *Career* Parly candidate (C): Central Ayrshire 1970, Glasgow Pollok 1974; MP (C): Galloway 1979–83, Galloway and Upper Nithsdale 1983–; asst govt whip 1981–83, a Lord Cmmr of the Treasy 1983–86; Parly under sec of state: Dept of Employment 1986, Scottish Office 1986–87; min of state Scottish Office 1987–90, sec of state for Scotland 1990–95, pres Bd of Trade (sec of state for Trade and Industry) 1995–; vice-chm Scottish Cons Pty 1983–86; tstee W of Scotland Tstee Savings Bank 1974–81; dir: Hutchison and Craft Ltd 1975–81, Hutchison and Craft (Underwriting Agents) Ltd 1976–81; dir Glasgow C of C 1978–81; memb Royal Co of Archers (Queen's Body Guard for Scotland) 1974; OStJ 1974; *Clubs* Western (Glasgow), Prestwick Golf, Pratt's; *Style*— Rt Hon Ian Lang, MP; ✉ House of Commons, London SW1A 0AA

LANG, The Very Rev John Harley; s of Frederick Henry Lang (d 1973), of Rickmansworth, Herts, and Eileen Annie Harley (d 1966); *b* 27 Oct 1927; *Educ* Merchant Taylors', King's Coll London, Emmanuel Coll Cambridge (MA, BD); *m* 1972, Frances Rosemary, da of Reginald Widdowson, of Southwell, Notts; 3 da (Henrietta b 1973, Victoria b 1975, Charlotte b 1977); *Career* curate St Mary's Portsea 1952–54, priest vicar Southwark Cathedral 1957–60, chaplain Emmanuel Coll Cambridge 1960–64, head of religious broadcasting BBC 1971–80 (asst head 1964–71), chaplain to HM The Queen 1976–80, dean of Lichfield 1980–93, dean emeritus 1994; memb: Broadcasting Standards Cncl 1994–, Cathedrals and Churches Advsy Ctee English Heritage 1994–; tstee Historic Churches Preservation Tst 1994–; Freeman Worshipful Company Goldsmiths; Hon DLitt Univ of Keele 1988; *Recreations* music and English history; *Style*— The Very Rev John Lang; ✉ South Barn, Stanton, Broadway, Worcestershire WR12 7NQ (☎ 01386 584251)

LANGAN, Colette Elaine; da of Alfred Langan, of Croydon, and Cynthia, *née* Greinig; *b* 6 June 1960; *Educ* Ashburton HS, Carshalton Coll of FE (City & Guilds); *Career* receptionist rising to front office mangr Holiday Inn Heathrow 1977–85, front office mangr Royal Lancaster Hotel London 1985–87, rooms div mangr The Chelsea Hotel 1987–88, ops exec Sunset View Holiday Village Kusadasi Turkey and Olive Tree Catalkoy N Cyprus 1989–92, gen mangr Marble Arch Appartments 1992–93, gen mangr Ascott Mayfair 1993–; *Recreations* horse riding, tennis, skiing, water skiing; *Style*— Miss Colette Langan; ✉ The Ascott Mayfair, 49 Hill Street, London W1X 7FQ (☎ 0171 499 6868, fax 0171 499 0705)

LANGDALE, Simon John Bartholomew; s of Geoffrey Ronald Langdale (d 1977), of Tunbridge Wells, and Hilda Joan, *née* Bartholomew (d 1991); *b* 26 Jan 1937; *Educ* Tonbridge, St Catharine's Coll Cambridge (MA); *m* 30 July 1962, Diana Marjory, da of Roger Wilby Hall, MVO, JP (d 1973), of West Grinstead, Sussex; 2 s (Andrew Rupert b 1964, Mark Simon b 1970), 1 da (Philippa Kate b 1967); *Career* housemaster Radley Coll 1968–73 (master 1959–73); headmaster: Eastbourne Coll 1973–80, Shrewsbury 1981–88; dir of appeals and special projects The Rank Fndn 1988–; *Recreations* books, gardening, golf; *Clubs* East India, Hawks; *Style*— Simon Langdale, Esq; ✉ Park House, Culworth, Banbury, Oxon OX17 2AP (☎ 01295 760222); The Rank Foundation, 12 Warwick Square, London SW1V 2AA (☎ 0171 834 7731)

LANGDON, (Richard) Benedict (Ben); s of David Langdon, OBE, of Prestwood, Bucks, and April Yvonne Margaret, *née* Sadler-Phillips; *b* 28 Aug 1963; *Educ* Royal GS High Wycombe Bucks, Jesus Coll Oxford (BA); *m* 21 Oct 1989, Vicky, da of George Henderson; 1 s (Max David b 25 Sept 1992), 1 da (Ruby Louise b 25 April 1994); *Career* account mangr: Allen Brady & Marsh advtg agency 1985–87, Lowe Howard Spink 1987–88; Still Price Court Twivy D'Souza Lintas: account dir 1989–90, bd/gp account dir 1990, new business dir 1991–93; md Addition Marketing Jan-June 1993, client servs dir McCann-Erickson Advertising Aug-Oct 1993, chief exec Collett Dickenson Pearce 1995–96 (md 1993–95), chief exec and md McCann-Erickson Advertising 1996–; *Recreations* golf, soccer; *Clubs* Harewood Downs Golf (Little Chalfont), Wentworth, The Oxfordshire; *Style*— Ben Langdon, Esq; ✉ McCann-Erickson Advertising Ltd, McCann-Erickson House, 36 Howland Street, London W1A 1AT (☎ 0171 580 6690)

LANGDON, David; OBE; s of Bennett Langdon, and Bess Langdon; *b* 24 Feb 1914; *Educ* Davenant GS; *m* 1955, April Yvonne Margaret, *née* Sadler-Phillips; 2 s (Ben, Miles), 1 da (Beth); *Career* Sqdn Ldr RAFVR 1945; cartoonist & illustrator; memb of Punch Table, contrib Punch, New Yorker, and others; official artist to: Centre Internationale Audio-Visuel, D'Etudes et de Recherches; *Books* various cartoon collections and book illustrations; *Recreations* golf; *Clubs* RAF; *Style*— David Langdon, Esq, OBE; ✉ Greenlands, Honor End Lane, Prestwood, Great Missenden, Bucks HP16 9QY (☎ 01494 862475)

LANGDON, Prof John Dudley; s of Jack Langdon (d 1984), of London, and Daphne Irene Heloise, *née* Liebsch (d 1988); *b* 24 March 1942; *Educ* Highgate Sch, London Hosp Med Coll (BDS, MB BS, MDS, Med, Surgery and Pathology prize, London prize, Annual Award of Merit American Soc of Dentistry for Children, Harold Fink prize, Charrington prize, James Anderson prize), RCS (LDS, FDS, FRCS); *Career* house surgn Royal London Hosp 1965, sr house surgn Dept of Oral Surgery Royal Dental and St George's Hosp 1965–66, SHO Dept of Oral Surgery Eastman Hosp 1966; registrar: Dept of Oral Surgery Royal London Hosp 1967 (Oral Surgery and Conservative Dentistry 1966–67), Oral Surgery and Maxillofacial Unit Honey Lane Hosp 1967–68; pt/t demonstrator Dept of Dental Anatomy London Hosp Med Coll 1968–69, locum registrar Dept of Oral Surgery St Thomas' Hosp 1969, pt/t lectr London Hosp Med Coll 1970–73, house physician Harold Wood Hosp 1974 (house surgn 1973), locum consIt oral surgn Oldchurch Hosp 1974; sr registrar Dept of Oral and Maxillofacial Surgery: Royal London Hosp 1974–76, KCH 1976–77; tutor RCS 1977, consIt oral and maxillofacial surgn Queen Mary's Hosp 1977–83 (hon consIt 1983–90), sr lectr/consIt Dept of Oral and Maxillofacial Surgery King's Coll Sch of Med and Dentistry 1983–92, special lectr in oral surgery Dental Sch Univ of Bristol 1987–93, prof of oral and maxillofacial surgery King's Coll Sch of Med and Dentistry 1992– (vice dean Faculty of Clinical Dentistry 1987–90), exec dir of patient servs King's Dental Inst 1994–; hon consIt: St George's Healthcare NHS Tst 1984–, Royal Surrey and St Luke's NHS Tst 1993–, Epsom Healthcare NHS Tst 1994–; memb: Cncl Assoc of Head and Neck Oncologists of Great Br 1981–84, Academic Advsy Ctee Oral and Maxillofacial Surgery 1989–, SAC in oral surgery and oral med 1989–94, Speciality Advsy Bd in oral and maxillofacial surgery RCS(Ed) 1990– (chm), Bd Faculty of Dental Surgery RCSE 1994–, BDA, BMA, Br Soc of Dental Res, Craniofacial Soc of Great Britain, Euro Assoc for Cranio-Maxillo-Facial Surgery; hon treas Br Assoc of Oral and Maxillofacial Surgns 1992–; fndr memb Maxillofacial Study Gp, hon sec (Odontology) RSM 1993–95; fndn fell Asian Assoc of Oral and Maxillofacial Surgns; fell: Br Assoc of Oral and Maxillofacial Surgns, Int Assoc of Oral and Maxillofacial Surgns; FRCS 1985; *Books* Malignant Tumours of the Oral Cavity (with J M Henk, 1985), Cancer of the Mouth, Jaws and Salivary Glands (with J M Henk, 1994), Surgical Pathology of the Mouth and Jaws (with R A Canson and J Eveson, 1995); ed (Oncology Section) Int Jl of Oral and Maxillofacial Surgery 1988–, consIt ed (Oral Oncology) Euro Jl of Cancer 1991–; *Recreations* gardening, opera, antiques, cooking; *Style*— Prof John Langdon; ✉ Old School House, 14 North Hill, Highgate Village, London N6 4QA (☎ 0181 340 5169); Department of Oral and Maxillofacial Surgery, King's College School of Medicine and Dentistry, Caldecot Road, London SE5 9RW (☎ 0171 346 3474, fax 0171 346 3185)

LANGDON, His Hon Judge Jonathan Bertram Robert Louis; s of Capt John Edward Langdon, RN, of Hayling Is, and Nancy Langdon; *b* 1 Nov 1939; *Educ*

Hurstpierpoint Coll; *m* 31 March 1962, Hilary Jean, da of John William Fox Taylor, OBE (d 1988), of Spain; 2 s (Andrew William, Stephen John (twin) b 1964), 1 da (Claire Fiona b 1967); *Career* RNC Dartmouth 1958, HM Ships Bermuda, Lincoln, London, Daring 1960–68; called to the Bar Gray's Inn 1970; Far East legal advsr Hong Kong 1973–75, RN Supply Sch 1975–77, Cdr 1977, HMS Norfolk 1977–79, MOD 1979–81, staff of C-in-C Naval Home Cmd 1981–83, asst recorder SE Circuit 1983, sec to Naval Sec MOD 1983–86, Capt 1986, postgrad trg int law 1987–88, Chief Naval Judge Advocate 1988–90, recorder SE Circuit 1989, sec to C-in-C Naval Home Cmd 1990–91, circuit judge (SE Circuit) 1991–; *Recreations* sailing, gardening, history; *Style*— His Hon Judge Langdon; ✉ c/o The Law Courts, Chaucer Road, Canterbury, Kent CT1 1ZA

LANGDON, Richard Norman Darbey; s of Norman Langdon (d 1959), of Shrewsbury, and Dorothy Hewitt, *née* Darbey; *b* 19 June 1919; *Educ* Shrewsbury; *m* 1 Nov 1944, June Phyllis, da of Alexander Ernest Dixon (d 1954), of Kingston, Surrey; 2 s (John Richard Darbey b 1946, Michael Robert Finch b 1948); *Career* offr RA 1939–46; ptnr Spicer and Pegler 1951–84 (managing ptnr 1971–84, sr ptnr 1978–84); chm: Hammond & Champoness Ltd 1966–89, Aspinall Holdings PLC 1983–89, Finlay Packaging plc 1984–92, First National Financial Corporation plc 1984–92, Time Products plc 1984–92; dir Chemring Group 1984–95, dir Rockware Group plc 1985–92; chm Beeson Gregory Ltd 1989–95; treas CGLI 1982–90; memb Cncl Univ of Surrey 1988–90; *Recreations* gardening, bricklaying; *Clubs* City of London, Old Salopian; *Style*— Richard Langdon, Esq; ✉ Whitedale House, Hambledon, Hants PO7 4RZ (☎ 01705 632457)

LANGDON, Sarla Mehta; da of Rama Iyer (d 1957), of Bombay, and Kuppa Iyer; *b* 30 Sept 1944; *Educ* Sophia Coll Bombay (BA); *m* 1, 1964 (m dis 1982), Dr Bogilal Mehta; 1 s (Jayant b 1 July 1966); m 2, 7 Dec 1984, Keith James Langdon, FICE (d 1991); *Career* currently: dir Markmaid Ltd, sr ptnr Langdon Partnership PR; dir W Glamorgan Enterprise Tst 1991–; memb: Ct of Govrs Nat Library of Wales, CBI Cncl Wales 1990–93, CBI Area Ctee W Wales; Sec of State appointee as community health cncllr, business advsr Prince's Youth Business Tst; MIPR 1990; *Books* Pwyll Lord of Dyfed (1989), Brown Waters (co-author, 1989); *Recreations* reading, swimming; *Clubs* New Business (chm), Marriott Leisure; *Style*— Mrs Sarla Langdon; ✉ Markmaid Ltd, 6A Queens Road, Sketty, Swansea SA2 0SD (☎ and fax 01792 280610)

LANGER, Air Cdre John Francis; CBE (1973), AFC, (1958) DL (Gtr London 1983); s of Cecil Edward Langer (d 1966), and Emma Elizabeth Maud, *née* Tucker (d 1988); *b* 24 June 1925; *Educ* Wimbledon Coll; *m* 1951, Doreen Jane, da of Wilfrid Newland-Hodges; 2 s, 1 da; *Career* RAF Serv WWII in SE Asia Cmd, Flt Cdr No 33 Sqdn 1948–50, QFI Cambridge Univ Air Sqdn 1951–53, Cdr Singapore Sqdn MAAF 1953–56, Cdr No 43 (Fighting Cocks) Sqdn 1957–59, chief instr Central Flying Sch 1962–64, Station Cdr RAF Valley 1970–71, dep dir Air Plans MOD 1972, Cdr Singapore Air Force 1973–75, dir Flying Trg MOD 1975–79, ret; UK govt advsr on aviation security 1979–1987; vice chm (Air) TAVR Assoc for Gtr London 1980–1988; aviation security conslt 1987–94; rep DL for Hillingdon 1987–93; FIMgt 1971, MRAeS 1980; *Recreations* cat watching; *Clubs* RAF; *Style*— Air Cdre John Langer, CBE, AFC, DL; ✉ The Walled Garden, Filkins, Lechlade, Glos GL7 3JJ (☎ 01367 860700)

LANGFORD, Bonita (Bonnie); *b* 22 July 1964; *Educ* Arts Educational Sch London, Italia Conti Stage Sch London; *Career* actress, singer, dancer; debut single Just One Kiss 1984; *Theatre* incl: West End debut (aged seven) Bonnie Butler in Gone With The Wind (Theatre Royal Drury Lane), Baby June in Gypsy (Piccadilly), Rumpleteazer in Cats (New London) 1981 and 1983, Kate in Pirates of Penzance (Theatre Royal Drury Lane) 1982, title role Peter Pan - The Musical (Aldwych) 1985, Sally Smith in Me And My Girl (Adelphi) 1988–89, Mabel in Pirates of Penzance (London Palladium) 1990; maj provincial seasons and nat tours with: Peter Pan - The Musical 1985, Pirates of Penzance 1985, 1989 and 1993, Charlie Girl 1987, 42nd Street (playing Peggy Sawyer) 1991–92, The Greatest Shows In Town 1993, Hollywood and Broadway 1993 and 1994, Oklahoma! 1994 (playing Adoannie); numerous pantomime appearances; Broadway debut in Gypsy 1974 (and US tour); *Television* incl: debut (aged 6) on Opportunity Knocks, co-host Junior Showtime (Yorkshire TV), Violet Elizabeth in Just William (LWT) 1976, Lena and Bonnie (Thames TV) 1978, The Hot Shoe Show (BBC) 1983 and 1984, Rub-a-dub-tub (TV-am) 1984, co-host Saturday Starship (Central) 1984, Melanie in Doctor Who (BBC) 1986, This Is Your Life 1986, A Royal Birthday Gala (for HM Queen Elizabeth the Queen Mother's 90th birthday) 1989, Tonight at 8.30 (BBC) 1991, numerous guest appearances; *Radio* debut playing May Belford in Posters of Montmartre (BBC Radio 4) 1991, host two series BBC Radio 5 1993; *Film* work incl: Bugsy Malone, Wombling Free 1980; *Style*— Miss Bonnie Langford; ✉ c/o Lake-Smith Griffin Associates, 15 Maiden Lane, London WC2E 7NA (☎ 0171 836 1020, fax 0171 836 1040)

LANGFORD, 9 Baron (I 1800); Col Geoffrey Alexander Rowley-Conwy; OBE (mil 1943), DL (Clwyd 1977); s of Maj Geoffrey Seymour Rowley-Conwy (ka 1915, himself ggs of 1 Baron, who in his turn was 4 s of 1 Earl of Bective, the Earldom of the same now forming one of the subsidiary dignities of the Marquesses of Headfort), of Bodrhyddan, Rhuddlan, Flintshire; suc 2 cous once removed, 8 Baron Langford, 1953; *b* 8 March 1912; *Educ* Marlborough, RMA Woolwich, Staff Coll Quetta; *m* 1, 1939 (m dis 1956), Ruth St John (d 1991), da of late Albert St John Murphy; m 2, 1957, Grete (d 1973), da of late Col E T von Freiesleben, Danish Army; 3 s; m 3, 1975, Susan, da of C Denham; 1 s (Hon Christopher b 1978), 1 da (Hon Charlotte b 1980); *Heir* s, Hon Owain Grenville Rowley-Conwy b 1958; *Career* cmmnd RA 1932, Lt 1935, Capt 1939, Maj 1941, Lt-Col 1945, serv 1939–45, with RA in Singapore (POW escaped), with Indian Mountain Artillery in Burma (Arakan, Kohima), CO 25 Mountain Regt 1945, DAQMG Berlin Airlift, FASSBERG 1948–49, GSO1 42 Inf Div TA 1949–52, CO 31 Regt RA 1954–57, ret 1957, Hon Col 1967; various appts and ctee memberships with CLA, NRA 1957–, and former Welsh Water Authy; constable of Rhuddlan Castle, lord of the manor of Rhuddlan; Freeman City of London; *Clubs* Army and Navy; *Style*— Col The Rt Hon the Lord Langford, OBE, DL; ✉ Bodrhyddan, Rhuddlan, Clwyd LL18 5SB (☎ 01745 590414)

LANGFORD, Martin Peter Neil; s of Charles William Langford (d 1972), and Barbara Mary Langford (d 1990); *Educ* Dulwich Coll; *m* 1 Sept 1979, Kathleen Langford, da of Hugh Peter Lim; 2 da (Kirstyn Jane b 25 Feb 1985, Katharine Mary b 23 Nov 1986); *Career* PR conslt; Peter West & Associates 1969–70, Russell Greer & Associates 1970–71; Burson-Marsteller: London 1971–73, Hong Kong 1973–79, mangr creative servs London 1979–86, dep chm 1988–89, chief exec London 1989–94, vice chm (Asia) 1994–; PR Professional of the Year award (PR Week Indust) 1987; chm PRCA 1992–94; MIPR 1984; *Recreations* game fishing, cooking; *Clubs* Mosimann's, American (Singapore); *Style*— Martin Langford, Esq; ✉ Burson-Marsteller, 331 North Bridge Road, 16–02/03 Odeon Towers, Singapore 0718

LANGFORD, Prof Paul; s of Frederick Wade Langford, of Cinderford, Glos, and Olive Myrtle, *née* Walters; *b* 20 Nov 1945; *Educ* Monmouth Sch, Hertford Coll Oxford (MA, DPhil); *m* 1970, Margaret Veronica, *née* Edwards; 1 s (Hugh b 1984); *Career* Univ of Oxford: tutorial fell in history Lincoln Coll 1970 (jr res fell 1969), lectr in history 1971–94, reader in modern history 1994–96, prof of modern history 1996–; visiting fell: Huntington Library 1973, American Antiquarian Soc 1974; Ford's lectr in English history Univ of Oxford 1990, Ralegh lectr British Academy 1996; memb Humanities Research Bd 1995–; FRHistS 1979, FBA 1993; *Books* A Polite and Commercial People 1727–83: New Oxford History of England (1989), Public Life and the Propertied Englishman 1689–1798 (1991); *Recreations* gardening; *Style*— Prof Paul Langford, FBA; ✉ Valpys, Noakes Hill, Ashampstead, Berks RG8 8RY (☎ 01635 578181); Lincoln College, Oxford OX1 3DR (☎ 01865 279795, fax 01865 279802)

LANGFORD, Philip Baber; s of Percy Norman Langford (d 1968), and Elizabeth Ellen, *née* Jones (d 1987); *b* 23 March 1934; *Educ* Bromsgrove, BNC Oxford (MA), Univ of London (LLB); *m* 10 March 1987, Catherine Judith, da of late William Arthur Gibbon, of Bowdon, Cheshire and Salisbury, Wiltshire; 2 step s (Edward b 1977, Richard b 1979); *Career* Nat Serv 2 Lt RAEC attached to 2 Bn Coldstream Guards 1959–61; admitted slr 1959; asst slr Kent CC 1961–63, ptnr Thomson Snell & Passmore 1965–92 (joined 1963), dep district judge 1992–; chm: SE Area Legal Aid Ctee 1985, SE Rent Assessment Panel 1992–; pres Tunbridge Wells Tonbridge and Dist Law Soc 1986; memb Law Soc; *Recreations* tennis, reading, travel; *Style*— Philip Langford, Esq; ✉ Baber House, Ticehurst, Wadhurst, East Sussex TN5 7HT (☎ 01580 200978); Thomson Snell & Passmore, 3 Lonsdale Gardens, Tunbridge Wells, Kent TN1 1NX (☎ 01892 510000, fax 01892 549884)

LANGHAM, Sir James Michael; 15 Bt (E 1660), of Cottesbrooke, Northampton, TD; s of Sir John Charles Patrick Langham, 14 Bt (d 1972), and Rosamond Christabel, *née* Rashleigh (d 1992); *b* 24 May 1932; *Educ* Rossall; *m* 1959, Marion Audrey Eleanor, da of Oswald Barratt, of Tanzania; 2 s (John Stephen b 1960, Rupert William b 1963), 1 da (Lucinda Jane b 1966); *Heir* s, John Stephen Langham, *qv*, b 14 Dec 1960; *Style*— Sir James Langham, Bt, TD; ✉ Claranagh, Tempo, Enniskillen, Co Fermanagh, N Ireland

LANGHAM, John Michael; CBE (1976); s of George Langham (d 1951); *b* 12 Jan 1924; *Educ* Bedford Sch, Queens' Coll Cambridge (MA), Admin Staff Coll; *m* 1949, Irene Elizabeth, *née* Morley; 2 s, 1 da; *Career* served RN 1944–46; joined J Stone & Co 1947, divnl chm Stone-Platt Industries PLC 1967–81, exec chm Stone Manganese Marine Ltd 1967–; dir: BPB Industries PLC 1976–92, Barclay Curle Ltd 1985–; chm: Bruntons Propellers Ltd 1960–89, Stone Marine Canada Ltd 1967–, Stone Marine Singapore Pte Ltd 1969–, Vacu-Lug Traction Tyres Ltd 1973–95, Winters Marine Ltd 1975–89, Stone Marine SA Pty Ltd 1977–, Langham Industries Ltd 1981–, Langham Overseas Ltd 1981–, Stone Marine Overseas Ltd 1981–, Stone Fasteners Ltd 1982–89, Stone Foundries Ltd 1982–89, Weardale Steel (Wolsingham) Ltd 1983–, Tridan Engineering Ltd 1988–89, Appledore Shipbuilders Ltd 1989–, Langham Farms Ltd 1990–, Stone Marine Hong Kong Ltd 1993–, Portland Port Ltd 1995–, Portland Harbour Ltd 1996–; memb: Cncl CBI 1967–79 (chm Prodn Ctee 1970–79), Exec Bd BSI 1969–76 (dep chm Quality Assur Cncl 1971–79), Gen Cncl Engrg Employers' Fedn 1974–82 (memb Mgmnt Bd 1979–82); Liveryman Worshipful Co of Shipwrights; Br Foundry Medal and Prize 1954, Award of the American Foundrymen's Soc 1962; CIMgt, FIMechE, FIMarE, FIBF; *Recreations* skiing, sailing, farming; *Clubs* Brooks's, Leander, RMYC, Hawks; *Style*— John Langham, Esq, CBE; ✉ Bingham's Melcombe, Dorchester, Dorset DT2 7PZ

LANGHAM, John Stephen; s and h of Sir James Michael Langham, 15 Bt, *qv*; *b* 14 Dec 1960; *m* 1991, Sarah Jane, da of late John Denis Verschoyle-Greene, of Dromagh, Johnstown, Co Kildare; 1 s (Tyrone Denis James b 13 Aug 1994); *Style*— John Langham, Esq; ✉ Tempo Manor, Tempo, Enniskillen, Co Fermanagh

LANGHAM, Tony; s of Trevor Langham, and Margaret, *née* Harris; *b* 4 June 1961; *Educ* Holgate Comp Notts, Univ of Birmingham (BA); *m* 1993, Clare, da of Anthony Parsons (d 1964); 1 s ((Charles) Alexander b 10 Jan 1994); *Career* sr researcher MORI 1982–84, jt head of retail fin PR Dewe Rogerson 1984–89, co-fndr and jt md (with w, Clare Parsons) Lansons Communications 1989–; assoc memb MRS 1986, MIPR 1989; *Recreations* playing and watching sport, contemporary music, fringe theatre, comedy; *Style*— Tony Langham, Esq; ✉ Lansons Communications, 42 St John Street, London EC1M 4DT (☎ 0171 490 8828, fax 0171 490 5460)

LANGHORNE, Richard Tristan Bailey; s of Eadward John Bailey Langhorne, MBE (d 1995), of Chichester, and Rosemary, *née* Scott-Foster; *b* 6 May 1940; *Educ* St Edward's Sch Oxford, St John's Coll Cambridge (BA, MA); *m* 18 Sept 1971, Helen Logue, da of William Donaldson, CB (d 1988); 1 s (Daniel b 22 Nov 1972), 1 da (Isabella b 29 Aug 1975); *Career* lectr in history Univ of Kent 1966–75 (master Rutherford Coll 1971–74), fell St John's Coll Cambridge 1975– (steward 1975–79, bursar 1975–87), dir Centre of Int Studies Univ of Cambridge 1987–93, dir and chief exec Wilton Park FCO 1993–96, prof of political science and dir Center for Global Change and Governance Rutgers Univ Newark USA 1996–; visiting prof Sch of Int Rels Univ of S California 1986, hon prof of international relations Univ of Kent at Canterbury 1994; chm Br Int History Assoc 1988–93; FRHistS 1985; *Books* The Collapse of the Concert of Europe 1890–1914 (1982), Diplomacy and Intelligence during the Second World War (ed, 1985), The Practice of Diplomacy (with K A Hamilton, 1994); *Recreations* cooking, music, railways; *Clubs* Athenaeum; *Style*— Richard Langhorne, Esq; ✉ 14 Love Lane, Canterbury, Kent CT1 1TZ (☎ 01227 760664); 6 Carleton Court, Maplewood, NJ 07040, USA (☎ 00 1 201 761 1223)

LANGLEY, Bob; *b* 28 Aug 1937; *Career* writer and broadcaster; scriptwriter then studio anchorman evening news/magazine Tyne Tees Television 1969–70; BBC News and Current Affrs: newsreader BBC 1 1970–71, presenter 24–Hours 1971–72, presenter Nationwide 1972–74, numerous reporting assignments incl Falkland Islands 1981; also BBC presenter: Pebble Mill at One, Saturday Night at the Mill, Six Fifty-Five Special, Take Me Back to New Orleans, Nature Trail, Osprey Summer, Northern Country, Making Waves, Bodycare, Langley South, The Pennine Way, Lakeland Summer, Big Day Out, A Week in the Country; *Books* Traverse of the Gods, War of the Running Fox, Lobo, Walking the Scottish Border, Death Stalk, Autumn Tiger, Hour of the Gaucho, Conquistadores, Warlords, The Churchill Diamonds, East of Everest, Avenge the Belgrano, Blood River, Precipice, Message From Baghdad, Prime Force, The Fell Runner; *Style*— Bob Langley, Esq; ✉ c/o Curtis Brown Group Ltd, 28–29 Haymarket, London SW1Y 4SP (☎ 0171 396 6600, fax 0171 396 0110)

LANGLEY, Maj-Gen Sir (Henry) Desmond Allen; KCVO (1983), MBE (1967); s of Col Henry Langley, OBE; *b* 16 May 1930; *Educ* Eton, RMA Sandhurst; *m* 1950, Felicity, da of Lt-Col K J P Oliphant, MC; 1 s, 1 da; *Career* cmmnd Life Gds 1949, cmd Life Gds 1969–71, Lt-Col cmdg Household Cavalry and Silver Stick-in-Waiting 1972–75, Cdr 4 Gds Armd Bde 1976–77, RCDS 1978, Brig Gen Staff HQ UK Land Forces 1979, GOC London Dist and Maj-Gen cmdg Household Div 1979–83, Cdr British Forces Cyprus and Admin Sovereign Base Areas 1983–85, govr and C in C Bermuda 1988–92; govr Church Lads' and Church Girls' Bde 1986–; Freeman City of London 1983, KStJ 1989; *Style*— Maj-Gen Sir Desmond Langley, KCVO, MBE

LANGLEY, Hon Mr Justice; Hon Sir (Julian Hugh) Gordon; kt (1995); s of Gordon Thompson Langley (d 1943), and Marjorie, *née* Burgoyne; *b* 11 May 1943; *Educ* Westminster, Balliol Coll Oxford (MA, BCL); *m* 20 Sept 1968, Beatrice Jayanthi, da of Simon Tennakoon (d 1986), of Colombo, Sri Lanka; 2 da (Ramani Elizabeth b 1969, Sharmani Louise b 1972); *Career* called to the Bar Inner Temple 1966, QC 1983–95, recorder 1986–95, a judge of the High Court of Justice (Queen's Bench Div) 1995–, bencher Inner Temple 1996; *Recreations* music, sport; *Clubs* Travellers; *Style*— The Hon Mr Justice Langley; ✉ Royal Courts of Justice, Strand, London WC2A 2LL

LANGLEY, John William Frederick; s of Reginald John William Langley (d 1973), of Torquay, Devon, and Veronica Mary, *née* King; *b* 17 Feb 1932; *Educ* Hornchurch GS; *m* 23 Sept 1961, Margaret Tait, da of Thomas Ormiston Gow; 1 s (Michael John b 25 Nov 1965), 1 da (Clare Caroline b 28 Nov 1963); *Career* journalist; contrib to local weekly newspapers whilst at sch, reporter The Romford Times 1949, subsequently industl corr Western Morning News and Evening Herald Plymouth, joined News Chronicle

(Manchester office) 1954, motoring corr Daily Sketch 1956–57, subsequently re-joined News Chronicle, gen reporter and motoring writer Daily Telegraph 1961– (motoring corr 1965–); fndr memb and first chm Fleet St Motoring Gp; hon ed Waterfowl (magazine of Br Waterfowl Assoc) 1975–85; *Awards* Motoring Writer of the Year award (twice); memb: Guild of Motoring Writers, Wildfowl Tst, Br Waterfowl Assoc, Kent Tst for Nature Conservation; *Recreations* breeding and watching wildfowl, secondhand books, looking at trees, wildlife, music, real ale, motoring, fishing; *Style—* John Langley, Esq; ✉ Hunters End, Chiddingstone Hoath, Edenbridge, Kent (☎ 01892 870291); The Daily Telegraph, 1 Canada Square, Canary Wharf, London E14 5DT (☎ 0171 538 5000, fax 0171 538 7842)

LANGLEY, Kenneth William; s of William Thomas Charles Langley (d 1984), of Wanstead, London, and Ada Winifred, *née* Looke (d 1979); *b* 13 Jan 1932; *Educ* East Ham Tech HS, East Ham Tech Coll; *m* 16 March 1957, Daisy Rosina, da of Frederick Charles Parsons (d 1956), of Essex; 3 da (Gillian b 1959, Susan b 1961, Elizabeth b 1964); *Career* Nat Serv Sgt RE Egypt and Jordan; chief exec Bryen & Langley Ltd (building contractors); memb: Cncl S London TEC, Cncl CBI, Divnl Cncl RICS, Construction Indust Res and Info Assoc; past chm Kent Branch Jt Consultative Ctee for Bldg Indust; chm of govrs Lewisham Coll, memb Rotary Club Gravesend; Freeman City of London 1972, Liveryman Worshipful Co of Basketmakers 1977; FCIOB 1957, FRICS 1960, ACIArb 1966; *Recreations* music, reading, golf; *Clubs* City Livery; *Style—* Kenneth Langley, Esq; ✉ Bryen & Langley Ltd, 58 Footscray Rd, London SE9 2SU (☎ 0181 850 7775, fax 0181 850 6772)

LANGLEY, Peter James; *b* 18 Feb 1942; *Educ* Brighton Hove and Sussex GS; *children* 1 s (James William b 1973), 1 da (Catherine Jane b 1975); *Career* articled clerk Mileham Scatliff and Allen Brighton 1960–65, admitted slr 1965; ptnr: C F Snow & Co Littlehampton 1966–70 (asst slr 1965–66), Slaughter and May London 1975– (asst slr 1970–75); memb Law Soc; *Recreations* reading, collecting fine bindings, golf; *Clubs* MCC, RAC, Wisley Golf; *Style—* Peter Langley, Esq; ✉ Slaughter and May, 35 Basinghall Street, London EC2V 5DB (☎ 0171 600 1200, fax 0171 726 0038)

LANGMAN, Prof Michael John Stratton; *b* 30 Jan 1935; *Educ* St Pauls, Guys Hosp Med Sch (BSc, MB, MD); *m* Rosemary Ann Langman, JP; 2 s (Nicholas, Benjamin), 2 da (Suzannah, Victoria); *Career* conslt physician, sr lectr, then reader in med Nottingham Teaching Hosps 1968–73, Boots prof of therapeutics med Univ of Nottingham Med Sch 1974–87, William Withering prof of med Univ of Birmingham Med Sch 1987– (dean 1992–); pres elect Br Soc of Gastroenterology 1997; memb: Ctee on Review of Medicines 1980–86, Ctee on Safety of Medicines 1987–; MRCP 1960, FRCP 1974, FFPM 1990; *Recreations* tennis, cricket, opera-going; *Clubs* MCC, Athenaeum; *Style—* Prof Michael Langman; ✉ Queen Elizabeth Hospital, Birmingham B15 2TH (☎ 0121 414 4044)

LANGMEAD, Jeremy John; s of John Sambrook, and Juliet Langmead, *née* Popplewell; *b* 3 Nov 1965; *Educ* St Joseph's Coll Ipswich, Central St Martin's Sch of Art London (BA); *m* 1992, India Knight, da of Michael Lacroix-Aertsens; 2 s (Oscar Augustus b 8 Dec 1992, Archie Jack b 8 Nov 1995); *Career* journalist; previous appts with Tatler, Elle Decoration and Mirabella magazines and freelance contrib to various newspapers incl Sunday Times, Evening Standard and The Guardian; Style ed The Sunday Times 1995– (dep Style ed 1994–95); *Recreations* shopping, television and eating; *Style—* Jeremy Langmead, Esq; ✉ The Sunday Times, 1 Pennington Street, London E1 9XW (☎ 0171 782 5000, fax 0171 782 5120)

LANGRIDGE, Edward James; s of Edward Victor Langridge (d 1977), of Eastbourne, Sussex, and Edith Mabel, *née* Blair; *b* 7 Aug 1946; *Educ* Eastbourne GS; *m* 1, 1967 (m dis 1983), Margaret Dally, *née* Scott; 1 s (Stuart Edward b 12 Oct 1973), 1 da (Nicola Ann b 7 March 1972); m 2, 1982, Judith Anne, da of Stanley Frederick Hammersley; 1 s (Alexander James b 2 July 1988), 1 da (Sophie Clare Henrietta b 9 Feb 1990); *Career* prodn mangr Gordon Scott & Barton Ltd 1966–72 (prodn trainee 1963–66); Smedley McAlpine Ltd: prodn mangr 1972, assoc dir 1975, dir 1980, dep md 1983, md 1987–91; jt md Bastable Hazlitt Partnership (formerly Bastable Advertising and Marketing) 1991–95, exec mktg dir McCarthy & Stone (Developments) Ltd 1996–; FInstM; *Recreations* classic cars, golf; *Clubs* Jaguar Drivers', Villa Golf; *Style—* Edward Langridge, Esq; ✉ Byeways, Gipps Cross Lane, Langton Green, Tunbridge Wells, Kent TN3 01DH (☎ 0189 286 2006); McCarthy & Stone (Developments) Ltd, Homelife House, 26–32 Oxford Road, Bournemouth, Dorset BH8 8EZ (☎ 01202 292480, fax 01202 298616, car 0421 862302)

LANGRIDGE, Philip Gordon; CBE (1994); s of Arthur Gordon, and Elsie Kate, *née* Underhill; *b* 16 Dec 1939; *Educ* Maidstone GS, Royal Acad of Music; *m* 1, 2 Aug 1962, (Margaret) Hilary, da of Rev George Davidson; 1 s (Stephen Maitland b 28 May 1962), 2 da (Anita Jane (Mrs Keith McNicoll) b 11 June 1966, Jennifer Mary (Mrs Richard Strivens) b 19 Dec 1970); m 2, 6 June 1981, Ann Murray, the mezzo soprano, da of Joseph Eugene Murray, of Dublin; 1 s (Jonathan Philip b 20 Oct 1986); *Career* concert and opera singer (tenor); Glyndebourne Festival debut 1964, BBC Proms debut 1970, Edinburgh Festival debut 1970; served on Music Panel for Arts Cncl of GB; LRAM, GRSM, FRAM, ARAM; *Performances* Glyndebourne incl: Idomeneo, Don Giovanni, Titus, King Kong 1977–96; Royal Opera House: Boris Godunov, Jenufa, Idomeneo, Death in Venice, Semele, Das Rheingold, Peter Grimes 1983–96; The Met New York: Cosi Fan Tutte, Das Rheingold, Boris 1985–96; ENO: Mask of Orpheus (world première) 1986, new prodn of Billy Budd 1988, Peter Grimes 1991; Salzburg Festival: Idomeneo 1990, Poppea, Boris, House of the Dead; other prodns incl: Idomeneo Angers 1975, Boris Godunov (with Claudio Abbado) La Scala 1979, Rake's Progress La Scala, Aron 1987 and 1988; *Awards* Grammy Award for Moses und Aron (Schonberg) under Solti 1986, Olivier Award for Osud (Janacek) 1984, winner of RPS Charles Heidsieck Singer of the Year 1988–89; *Recordings* over 50 recordings of early, baroque, classical, romantic and modern music; *Recreations* collecting watercolours; *Style—* Philip Langridge, Esq, CBE; ✉ c/o Allied Artists, 42 Montpelier Square, London SW7 1JZ (☎ 0171 589 6243)

LANGRISH, Rt Rev Michael Laurence; *see:* Birkenhead, Bishop of

LANGRISHE, Sir Hercules Ralph Hume; 7 Bt (I 1777), of Knocktopher Abbey, Kilkenny; s of Capt Sir Terence Hume Langrishe, 6 Bt (d 1973), of Knocktopher Abbey, Co Kilkenny; *b* 17 May 1927; *Educ* Summer Fields (St Leonards), Eton; *m* 1955, Hon Grania Sybil Enid Wingfield, o da of 9 Viscount Powerscourt; 1 s (James Hercules b 1957), 3 da (Miranda Grania (Mrs Christopher J Markes) b 1959, Georgina Emma (Mrs S Ross Wallace) b 1961, Atalanta Sue (Mrs Arthur Pollock) b 1963); *Heir* s, James Hercules Langrishe b 3 March 1957; *Career* 2 Lt 9 Lancers 1947, Lt 1948, ret 1953; *Clubs* Kildare Street and Univ (Dublin); *Style—* Sir Hercules Langrishe, Bt; ✉ Arlonstown, Dunsany, Co Meath, Ireland (☎ 00 353 46 25243)

LANGRISHE, James Hercules; s and h of Sir Hercules Ralph Hume Langrishe, 7 Bt, *qv*; *b* 3 March 1957; *m* 1985, Gemma Mary Philomena, eldest da of Patrick O'Daly, and Rita, *née* Hickey, of Kiltale, Co Meath; 1 s (Richard James Hercules b 8 April 1988), 1 da (Victoria Anna Jean b 1986); *Style—* James Langrishe, Esq; ✉ Derrypatrick, Drumree, Co Meath, Republic of Ireland

LANGSLOW, Dr Derek Robert; s of Alex Langslow (d 1993), and Beatrice, *née* Wright (d 1992); *b* 7 Feb 1945; *Educ* Ashville Coll Harrogate, Queens' Coll Cambridge (MA, PhD); *m* 1969, Helen Katherine Langslow; 1 s (Ian b 1975), 1 da (Sarah b 1980); *Career* res fell Univ of Cambridge 1969–72, lectr in biochemistry Univ of Edinburgh 1972–78; Nature Conservancy Cncl: sr ornithologist 1978–84, asst chief scientist 1984–87, dir policy planning and servs 1987–90; chief exec English Nature 1990–; author of more than 50 scientific pubns; *Style—* Dr Derek Langslow; ✉ English Nature, Northminster House, Peterborough PE1 1UA (☎ 01733 318364, fax 01733 898290)

LANGSTAFF, Brian Frederick James; QC (1994); s of Frederick Sydney Langstaff, of 2 Parsonage Farm, Church St, Boxted, Essex, and Muriel Amy Maude, *née* Griffin; *b* 30 April 1948; *Educ* George Heriot's Sch Edinburgh, St Catharine's Coll Cambridge (BA); *m* 19 July 1975, Deborah Elizabeth, da of Samuel James Weatherup (d 1953), of NI; 1 s (Nicholas b 1980), 1 da (Kerry b 1978); *Career* called to the Bar Middle Temple 1971, sr lectr in law Chelmer Coll 1971–75 (formerly lectr), Harmsworth scholar 1975, in practice 1975–; recorder of the Crown Ct 1995– (asst recorder 1991–95); memb Exec Ctee Personal Injury Bar Assoc 1995–; chm Bd of Govrs Stoke-by-Nayland VCP Sch; parochial church cncllr; *Books* Concise College Casenotes Series: Equity & Trusts (1975); contrib Health and Safety at Work (Halsbury's Laws, 4 edn); *Recreations* tennis, swimming, walking, travel, watching TV, mowing the lawn; *Style—* Brian Langstaff, Esq, QC; ✉ Cloisters, 1 Pump Court, Temple, London EC4Y 7AA (☎ 0171 583 0303, fax 0171 583 2254)

LANGTON, Bryan David; CBE (1988); s of Thomas Langton (d 1974), and Doris, *née* Brown (d 1987); *b* 6 Dec 1936; *Educ* Accrington GS, Westminster Tech Coll (Dip Hotel Operation), Ecole Hotelière de la SSA Lausanne (Operations Dip); *m* 23 Sept 1960, Sylva, da of Herman Heinrich Leo Degenhardt, of Richterstrasse 11, Braunschweig, W Germany; 2 da (Suzanne (Mrs Boyette) b 1962, Michele (Mrs Wijegoonaratna) b 1964); *Career* chm and chief exec offr Holiday Inn Worldwide 1990–; dir Bass plc 1985–; chm: Crest Hotels Ltd 1985–90 (md 1982–88), Bass Horizon Hotels 1985–89, Holiday Inns Int 1988–90, Toby Restaurants Ltd 1988–90; non-exec: Bd memb Wachovia Bank of Georgia 1992, Bd memb National Service Industries 1993, dir Fairfield Communities, dir Caribiner International Inc; vice pres Int Hotel Assoc 1990–; memb President Carter's Atlanta Project 1992; memb Bd of Tstees: Woodruff Arts Center Atlanta 1991–, Northside Hospital Fndn Bd 1991–; hon fell Manchester Poly 1986; FHCIMA; *Recreations* golf, reading, cricket, theatre; *Style—* Bryan D Langton, Esq, CBE; ✉ Holiday Inn Worldwide, Corporate Headquarters, Three Ravinia Drive, Atlanta, Georgia 30346–2149, USA

LANGTON, Edward Langton; s of Lewis Langton, and Louisa Kate, *née* Levy; *b* 30 Oct 1921; *Educ* City of London Sch; *m* 1 Sept 1949, Joye Amelia, da of Jack Isaacs (d 1962); 1 s (Timothy John b 25 July 1953), 1 da (Louise (Mrs P J Rawlins) b 26 June 1950); *Career* WWII serv: Flt Lt and Sqdn Navigation Offr RAF 1941–46; sr ptnr Stoy Hayward CAs 1968–85 (ptnr 1951–86); memb Exec Cncl Horwath and Horwath International 1975–86; dir Conrad Ritblat Sinclair Goldsmith plc; past pres John Carpenter Club, memb Exec Bd Variety Club of GB, memb Bd of Jewish Care, chm Family Welfare Assoc; Liveryman Worshipful Co of Chartered Accountants; FCA; *Recreations* golf, cricket; *Clubs* Hurlingham, MCC; *Style—* Edward Langton Langton, Esq; ✉ Flat 8, 40 Chester Square, London SW1W 9HT (☎ 0171 730 1847)

LANGTON, Lord; James Grenville Temple-Gore-Langton; s and h of 8 Earl Temple of Stowe, *qv*; *b* 11 Sept 1955; *Educ* Winchester; *Style—* Lord Langton; ✉ c/o The Rt Hon the Earl Temple of Stowe, The Cottage, Easton, Winchester, Hants

LANGTON, John Leslie; s of Arthur Laurence Langton (d 1976), and Sarah Jane, *née* Baker; *b* 23 Nov 1948; *Educ* Roan GS Greenwich; *m* 10 Aug 1979, Raymonde, da of Raymond Glinne, of Gembloux, Belgium 5030; 1 da (Jennifer Marie-Anne b 8 Dec 1983); *Career* Strauss Turnbull & Co 1965–69, Scandinavian Bank Ltd 1969–73, Williams & Glyns Bank 1973–74, Bondtrade in Brussels 1974–77, Morgan Stanley International 1977–78, dir Amex Bank Ltd 1979–80, sr exec dir Orion Royal Bank Ltd 1980–85, exec dir Security Pacific Hoare Govett Ltd 1986–87, md Gintel & Co Ltd 1987–89; chief exec and sec gen International Securities Market Association (ISMA); memb Bd ISMA Zurich 1981–, chm International Securities Market Association Ltd 1990–; memb Bd European Capital Markets Inst (ECMI) Copenhagen; MSI; *Recreations* wine, books, travel; *Style—* John L Langton, Esq; ✉ Lerchenbergstrasse 115, CH 8703, Erlenbach - Zürich, Switzerland (☎ and fax 00 411 910 7143); International Securities Market Association (ISMA), Rigistrasse 60, PO Box, CH-8033, Zürich, Switzerland (☎ 00 411 363 4222, fax 00 411 363 7772, telex 815812); International Securities Market Association Ltd, 7 Limeharbour, Docklands, London E14 9NQ (☎ 0171 538 5656, fax 0171 538 4902, telex 8813069)

LANGTON, John Raymond; *b* 28 May 1929; *Educ* Stationers' Co Sch; *m* 4 April 1953, Brenda Olive, *née* Eady; 1 s (Toby b 1970), 2 da (Fiona b 1962, Charlotte b 1966); *Career* fndr and md Sun Life Unit Services Ltd 1980–88, chm Valens Associates Ltd 1988–, chm The Langton Partnership Ltd 1992–; Freeman City of London; ACII 1953; *Style—* John Langton, Esq; ✉ Minden Cottage, Firs Walk, Tewin Wood, Welwyn, Herts AL6 0NZ (☎ 01438 798437)

LANGTON, Simon Guy Charles; s of David Langton (d 1994), of Stratford-upon-Avon, and Mona Rosemary, *née* Copeman (d 1972); *b* 5 Nov 1941; *Educ* Bloxham; *m* 1, 1971 (m dis 1973), Victoria Master; *partner* since 1985, Jan Child; *Career* director; asst stage mangr Folkestone Repertory Theatre 1959, stage mangr Theatre Royal Windsor 1960–62, BBC TV 1963–71, freelance dir 1971–; memb: Directors' Guild of GB 1980, Directors' Guild of America 1983; *Television and Film* credits incl: Microbes & Men (BBC) 1972, Love For Lydia (LWT) 1973, Upstairs Downstairs (LWT) 1974, Duchess of Duke Street (BBC) 1976, Gate of Eden (YTV) 1977, Danger UXB (Euston Films) 1978, Rebecca (BBC) 1979, Therese Raquin (BBC) 1980, Nelson (ATV) 1980, Smiley's People (BBC) 1981, Lost Honour of Katherine Beck (CBS) 1982, Casanova (ABC) 1984, Anna Karenina (CBS) 1985, Laguna Heat (HBO) 1986, Dos Destinos (corporate film for BA) 1986, Whistle Blower (feature) 1987, Out of Darkness (ABC/Robert Halmi) 1987, Mother Love (BBC) 1988, Jeeves & Wooster II (Carnival Films) 1990, Good Guys (Hava Hall Pictures) 1991, Headhunters (BBC) 1992, The Cinder Path (YTV) 1993, Pride and Prejudice (BBC) 1994; *Awards* winner: Peabody Award (for Smiley's People), Tric Award (for Mother Love); for Pride and Prejudice 1996: Tric Award for Best Drama, Broadcasting Press Guild Award for Best Drama Serial, Banff Television Festival Award for Best Mini Series and Grand Prize for Best Programme; nominations incl: BAFTA 1972 (for Microbes & Men), BAFTA 1979 (for Therese Raquin), BAFTA (Mother Love), BAFTA for Best Serial 1996 (for Pride and Prejudice); for Smiley's People: BAFTA, Emmy, Peoples Award; *Recreations* natural history; *Style—* Simon Langton, Esq; ✉ Newnham Hill Farmhouse, Newnham Hill, Henley-on-Thames, Oxon RG9 5TL; c/o agent, Peter Murphy, Curtis Brown Group Ltd, 28–29 Haymarket, London SW1Y 4SP (☎ 0171 396 6600, fax 0171 396 0110)

LANGTRY, (James) Ian; s of Rev Herbert James Langtry (d 1942), and Irene Margaret, *née* Eagleson (d 1995); *b* 2 Jan 1939; *Educ* Coleraine Academical Instn, Queen's Univ Belfast (BSc); *m* 1959, (Eileen Roberta) Beatrice, da of James Burnside Nesbitt (d 1957); 1 s (James Paul Eagleson b 1960), 1 da (Anna Beatrice b 1965); *Career* asst master Bangor GS 1960–61, lectr Belfast Coll of Technol 1961–66, asst dir Civil Serv Cmmn 1966–70; Dept of Educn and Sci: princ 1970–76, asst sec 1976–82, under sec 1982–87; under sec Dept of Health and Social Security 1987–88; educn offr Assoc of CCs 1988–96; *Recreations* golf, sailing; *Clubs* Royal Portrush Golf, West Kent Golf; *Style—* Ian Langtry, Esq; ✉ 11 Allard Close, Orpington, Kent BR5 4EB (☎ 01689 834840)

LANIGAN, Denis George; CBE (1994); s of George Lanigan (d 1961), and Ada Lanigan (d 1988); *b* 26 Jan 1926; *Educ* Drayton Manor Sch, King's Coll Cambridge (MA); *m* 5 Oct 1959, Jean Anne, *née* Sanderson (d 1992); 1 s (Mark b 1960), 1 da (Kate b 1962); *Career* J Walter Thompson Company: chief exec JWT Germany 1959–64, md UK 1966–74, chm

UK 1974–76, pres JWT Europe 1976–80, vice chm Worldwide 1980–82, chief operating offr Worldwide 1982–86; non-exec dir: Marks and Spencer plc 1987–97, TSB Bank 1987–90; chm MM and K Ltd 1988–91; memb: Cambridge Univ Appt Bd 1974–78, East Sussex Area Health Authy 1972–74, Overseas Trade Bd N American Advsy Ctee 1986– (chm 1991), Overseas Trade Bd 1991–; dir Money Mgmnt Cncl 1986–91; *Recreations* music, theatre, gardening; *Clubs* Arts, University (NY); *Style—* Denis Lanigan, Esq, CBE; ✉ 21 Queens Gate Gardens, London SW7 5LZ; Annes, Hadlow Down, East Sussex TN22 4HU

LANKESTER, Sir Timothy Patrick (Tim); KCB (1994); s of Robin Prior Archibald Lankester, and Jean Dorothy, *née* Gilliat; *Educ* Monkton Combe Sch, St John's Coll Cambridge (BA), Jonathan Edwards Coll Yale (Henry fell, MA); *m* 1968, Patricia, *née* Cockcroft; 3 da (Alexandra Kim b 30 April 1970, Olivia Mary b 28 Sept 1971, Laura Camilla b 9 Oct 1981); *Career* economist World Bank 1966–73 (Washington until 1969 and New Delhi until 1973); HM Treasy: princ 1973–77, asst sec 1977, private sec to Rt Hon James Callaghan 1978–79, private sec to Rt Hon Margaret Thatcher 1979–81, seconded to S G Warburg and Co Ltd 1981–83, under sec 1983–85, econ minister Washington (and exec dir World Bank and IMF) 1985–88, dep sec (and dir European Investment Bank) 1988–89; perm sec: ODA 1989–94, Dept for Educn and Employment 1994–95; dir SOAS Univ of London 1996–; non-exec dir: Commercial Union plc, Smith and Nephew plc, Simba Fund; tstee Actionaid; govr Ashridge Coll; *Style—* Sir Tim Lankester, KCB; ✉ School of Oriental and African Studies, Thornhaugh Street, Russell Square, London WC1H 0XG (☎ 0171 323 6025, fax 0171 580 6769)

LANSBURY, Angela Brigid; CBE (1994); da of Edgar Lansbury, and late Moyna Macgill; *b* 16 Oct 1925; *Educ* South Hampstead HS for Girls, Webber Douglas Sch of Singing and Dramatic Art Kensington, Feagin Sch of Drama and Radio NY; *m* 1 (m dis), Richard Cromwell; m 2, 1949, Peter Shaw; 1 s, 1 da, 1 step s; *Career* actress; with Metro-Goldwyn-Mayer 1943–50, freelance 1950–; *Theatre* incl: Hotel Paradiso (Broadway debut) 1957, Helen in A Taste of Honey (Lyceum NY) 1960, Anyone Can Whistle (Broadway musical) 1964, title role in Mame (Winter Garden NY) 1966–68, Dear World (Broadway) 1969, Pretty Belle 1971, All Over 1973, Sondheim - A Musical Tribute 1973, Gypsy (Piccadilly NY and tour) 1973–74, Gertrude in Hamlet (NT) 1975, Counting The Ways and Listening, Anna in The King and I (Broadway) 1978, Mrs Lovett in Sweeney Todd (Broadway) 1979; *Television* incl: Robert Montgomery Presents The Citadel, The Wonderful Night, Lux, Stone's Throw, Robert Montgomery Presents Cakes and Ale, Dreams Never Lie, The Ming Lama, Schilitz Playhouse of Stars, The Crime of Daphne Rutledge, The Indiscreet Mrs Jarvis, Madeira! Madeira!, The Treasure, The Rarest Stamp, The Force of Circumstance, Little Gloria...Happy at Last (mini-series), A Talent for Murder, The Gift of Love - A Christmas Story, Shootdown, Lace (mini-series), Rage of Angels II, The Shell Seekers, The Love She Sought (TV film) 1991, Mrs Arris Goes to Paris (TV film) 1992, Jessica Fletcher in Murder She Wrote (CBS) 1984–96, Mrs Santa Claus (TV musical film) 1996; *Films* Gaslight 1944 (Oscar nomination Best Supporting Actress), National Velvet 1944, The Picture of Dorian Gray 1945 (Oscar nomination best Supporting Actress), Harvey Girls 1946, The Hoodlum Saint 1946, Till the Clouds Roll By 1946, The Private Affairs of Bel-Ami 1947, If Winter Comes 1948, Tenth Avenue Angel 1948, State of the Union 1948, The Three Musketeers 1948, The Red Danube 1949, Samson and Delilah 1949, Kind Lady 1951, Mutiny 1952, Remains to be Seen 1953, A Life at Stake 1955, The Purple Mask 1956, The Court Jester 1956, A Lawless Street 1956, Please Murder Me 1956, The Long Hot Summer 1958, The Reluctant Debutante 1958, Summer of the 17th Doll 1959, Season of Passion 1961, Breath of Scandal 1960, The Dark at the Top of the Stairs 1960, Blue Hawaii 1961, All Fall Down 1962, The Manchurian Candidate 1962 (Oscar nomination for Best Supporting Actress), In the Cool of the Day 1963, The World of Henry Orient 1964, Out of Towners 1964, Dear Heart 1964, The Greatest Story Ever Told 1965, Harlow 1965, The Amorous Adventures of Moll Flanders 1965, Mister Buddwing 1966, Something for Everyone 1970, Bedknobs and Broomsticks 1971, Death on the Nile 1978, The Lady Vanishes 1980, The Mirror Crack'd 1980, The Pirates of Penzance 1982, The Company of Wolves 1983, voice of Mrs Potts in Disney animation Beauty and the Beast 1991; *Awards* incl 16 Emmy Award nominations (12 for Murder She Wrote) and 6 Golden Globe Awards, Woman of the Year Harvard Husty Pudding Theatre Theatricals 1968, Sarah Siddons Award 1974 and 1980, Antoinette Perry Awards: Mame 1968, Dear World 1969, Gypsy 1975, Sweeney Todd 1979; inducted into Theatre Hall of Fame 1982, BAFTA Silver Mask for lifetime achievement 1992, inducted into Television Hall of Fame 1996; *Style—* Ms Angela Lansbury, CBE; ✉ c/o MCA Universal, 100 Universal City Plaza, Universal City, CA 91608, USA (☎ 00 1 818 777 1181, fax 00 1 818 733 1573)

LANSDOWNE, 8 Marquess of (GB 1784); Maj George John Charles Mercer Nairne Petty-Fitzmaurice; PC (1964), JP (Perthshire 1950); also Baron Kerry and Lixnaw (I 1295), Earl of Kerry, Viscount Clanmaurice (both I 1723), Viscount FitzMaurice, Baron Dunkeron (both I 1751), Earl of Shelburne (I 1753), Lord Wycombe, Baron of Chipping Wycombe (GB 1760), Earl Wycombe, and Viscount Calne and Calston (both GB 1784); assumption of additional surnames of Petty-Fitzmaurice recognised by decree of Lord Lyon 1947; s of Maj Lord Charles Mercer-Nairne, MVO (ka 1914, himself 2 s of 5 Marquess, sometime Viceroy of India and Foreign Sec), and Lady Violet Mary Elliot Murray-Kynynmound, da of 4 Earl of Minto; suc 7 Marquess (first cousin, who was ka 1944); *b* 27 Nov 1912; *Educ* Eton, Ch Ch Oxford; *m* 1, 1938, Barbara (d 1965), da of Harold Stuart Chase, of Santa Barbara, California; 2 s, 1 da (and 1 decd); m 2, 1969 (m dis 1978), Hon Selina Polly Dawson, da of 1 Viscount Eccles, KCVO, PC; m 3, 1978, Gillian Anna (d 1982), da of Alured Morgan; m 4, 12 July 1995, Penelope Eve, widow of Hon John Astor, formerly wife of late David Rolt, and da of late Cdr George Francis Norton Bradford, RN; *Heir* s, Earl of Shelburne, *qv*; *Career* served WWII Capt Scots Greys & Maj Free French; private sec to Duff Cooper (1 Visc Norwich) when ambass in Paris 1944; 2 Lt Scottish Horse (TA), a lord in waiting to HM The Queen 1957–58, jt parly under-sec state FO 1958–62, min of state Colonial Affairs 1962–64, DL Wilts 1952–73, sec Junior Unionist League for E Scotland 1939; memb Royal Company of Archers (Queen's Body Guard for Scotland); chm Franco-British Soc 1972–83 (pres 1983–), active pres Franco-Scottish Soc 1973–83 (hon pres 1983–); patron Invalids-at-Home 1989–, pres Royal Surgical Aid Soc 1985–; patron of two livings; memb Ct of Assts Worshipful Co of Fishmongers; *Clubs* Turf, New (Edinburgh); *Style—* The Most Hon the Marquess of Lansdowne; ✉ Meikleour House, Perthshire (☎ 01250 883210)

LANSLEY, Andrew David; CBE (1996); s of Thomas Stewart Lansley, OBE, of Hornchurch, Essex, and Irene, *née* Sharp; *b* 11 Dec 1956; *Educ* Brentwood Sch Essex, Univ of Exeter (BA, pres Guild of Students); *m* 30 Nov 1985, Marilyn Jane, da of Clive Biggs, of Bishops Stortford, Herts; 3 da (Katherine Elizabeth Jane b 1987, Sarah Isabel Anne b 1989, Eleanor Rose Amy b 1993); *Career* private sec to Sec of State for Trade and Indust 1984–85 (joined DOI 1979), princ private sec to Chancellor of the Duchy of Lancaster Cabinet Office 1985–87, dep DG Assoc of British Chambers of Commerce 1989–90 (dir policy and programmes 1987–89), dir Conservative Research Dept 1990–95, dir Public Policy Unit 1995–; prospective Parly candidate for S Cambridgeshire; memb Exec Ctee Nat Union of Cons and Unionist Assocs 1990–95; *Recreations* political biographies, travel, cricket; *Style—* Andrew Lansley, Esq, CBE; ✉ Public Policy Unit, 50 Rochester Row, London SW1P 2JU (☎ 0171 828 6088)

LANTOS, Prof Peter Laszlo; s of Sandor Leipniker (d 1945), and Ilona, *née* Somlo (d 1968); *b* 22 Oct 1939; *Educ* Med Sch Szeged Univ Hungary (MD), Univ of London (PhD, DSc); *Career* Wellcome res fell 1968–69, sr lectr and hon conslt in neuropathology Middx Sch of Med 1976–79 (res asst 1969–73, lectr in neuropathology 1974–75), prof of neuropathology Inst of Psychiatry 1979–; hon conslt in neuropathology: Bethlem Royal and Maudsley Hosps 1979–, KCH 1985–, St Thomas's Hosp 1992–; academic co-ordinator King's Neuroscience Centre 1995–; chm: Scientific Advsy Panel Brain Res Tst 1985–91, Neuropathology Sub-Ctee RCPath 1986–89 (chm Panel of Examiners in Neuropathology 1983–89), Academic Bd Inst of Psychiatry 1988–91; memb: Pathologic Soc of GB and I 1971, Br Neuropathological Soc 1972 (pres 1995–); FRCPath 1987 (MRCPath 1975); *Books* ed Greenfield's Neuropathology; contrib: Brain Tumours: Scientific Basis, Clinical Investigation and Current Therapy (1980), Histochemistry in Pathology (1983), Scientific Basis of Clinical Neurology (1985), Schizophrenia: The Major Issues (1988), Systemic Pathology (3 edn, 1990), Oxford Textbook of Pathology (1992); *Recreations* travel, theatre, fine arts; *Clubs* Athenaeum; *Style—* Prof Peter Lantos; ✉ Institute of Psychiatry, London SE5 8AF (☎ 0171 703 5411)

LANYON, Prof Lance Edward; s of Harry Lanyon (d 1947), of London, and Heather Gordon, *née* Tyrell; *b* 4 Jan 1944; *Educ* Christ's Hosp, Univ of Bristol (BVSc, PhD, DSc, MRCVS); *m* 15 April 1972, Mary, da of Harold Kear (d 1966), of Sevenoaks, Kent; 1 s (Richard b 1975), 1 da (Alice b 1977); *Career* reader in veterinary anatomy Univ of Bristol 1980–83 (lectr 1967–79), prof Tufts Sch of Veterinary Med Boston Mass USA 1983–84 (assoc prof 1980–83); The Royal Veterinary Coll London: prof of veterinary anatomy 1984–89, head Dept of Veterinary Basic Sci 1987–88, princ 1989–; FBOA; memb: Euro Soc for Biomechanics, Orthopaedic Res Soc (US), Anatomical Soc, Bone and Tooth Soc, American Soc for Bone and Mineral Res; author of numerous chapters in books on orthopaedics, osteoporosis and athletic training, and various scientific articles in orthopaedic and bone related jls; *Recreations* building, home improvements, sailing; *Clubs* Christ's Hosp; *Style—* Prof Lance Lanyon; ✉ The Royal Veterinary College, Royal College St, London NW1 0TU (☎ 0171 468 5000, fax 0171 387 7386)

LANYON, (Harry) Mark; s of Henry Lanyon (d 1948), and Heather Gordon, *née* Tyrrell (d 1994); *b* 15 July 1939; *Educ* Ardingly Coll, Univ of St Andrews (BSc); *m* 1970, Elizabeth Mary, da of John Mowbray Morton; 1 da (Eleanor Lucy b 1975), 1 s (Edward James b 1977); *Career* apprentice AWRE Aldermaston 1957–58 and 1962–63, engr cadet Miny of Aviation 1963–65, Aeronautical Inspectorate Rolls Royce 1965–68, Concorde Div Mintech 1968–75; DTI: Shipbuilding Policy Div 1975–77, dep dir SW Regnl Office 1977–82, regnl dir W Midlands Regnl Office 1982–85, Mechanical Electrical Engrg Div 1985–90; asst dir consumer affairs Office of Fair Trading 1990–93, regnl dir Yorks and Humberside Regnl Office DTI 1993–94, regnl dir Government Office for the East Midlands 1994–; CEng, MIMechE; *Style—* Mark Lanyon, Esq; ✉ Government Office for the East Midlands, The Belgrave Centre, Stanley Place, Talbot Street, Nottingham NG1 5GG

LAPOTAIRE, Jane Elizabeth Marie; da of Louise Elise Burgess Lapotaire; *b* 26 Dec 1944; *Educ* Northgate GS Ipswich, Bristol Old Vic Theatre Sch; *m* 1, 1965 (m dis 1967), Oliver Wood; m 2, 1974 (m dis 1982), Roland Joffé; 1 s (Rowan b 1973); *Career* actress; pres Bristol Old Vic Theatre Club 1985–, memb Marie Curie Meml Fndn Appeals Ctee 1986–88, hon pres Shakespeare's Globe Friends 1986–, hon assoc artist RSC 1993–, visiting fell Univ of Sussex 1986–; *Theatre* RSC various periods 1974–94 incl: Viola in Twelfth Night, Sonya in Uncle Vanya, Rosaline in Love's Labours Lost 1978–79, Misalliance 1986, Archbishop's Ceiling 1986, Gertrude in Kenneth Branagh's Hamlet 1993, Mrs Alving in Ghosts 1993 & 1994; NT various periods 1967–84 incl: Measure for Measure, Flea in Her Ear, Dance of Death, Way of the World, Merchant of Venice, Oedipus, The Taming of the Shrew, Eileen in Kick for Touch 1983, Belvidera in Venice Preserv'd, Antigone 1984; other credits incl: Bristol Old Vic Co 1965–67, Vera in A Month in the Country, Lucy Honeychurch in A Room with a View (both Prospect Theatre Co West End) 1975–76, Rosalind in As You Like It (Edinburgh Festival) 1977, title role in Piaf (The Other Place, RSC, Aldwych, Wyndhams and Broadway) 1978–81, title role in St Joan (Compass Co) 1985, Double Double (Fortune) 1986, Greenland (Royal Court) 1988, Joy Davidman in Shadowlands (Queen's) 1990; *Television* freelance 1971–74 & 1976–78; credits incl: Marie Curie (Emmy and BAFTA nomination) 1977, Antony and Cleopatra 1981, Macbeth 1983, Seal Morning 1985, Napoleon and Josephine 1987, Blind Justice (BAFTA nomination) 1988, The Dark Angel 1989, Love Hurts (series 1 & II, BBC) 1991–92, Big Battalions (Channel Four) 1992; *Films* freelance for Paramount, MGM, United Artists 1971–74 & 1976–78; other credits incl: Eureka 1983, Lady Jane 1986, Surviving Picasso (Merchant Ivory) 1996; *Awards* incl: Emmy and BAFTA nominations 1976; awards for performance in Piaf: SWET Award 1979, London Critics' Award 1980, Variety Club Award 1980, Broadway Tony Award 1981; for Blind Justice: Br Press Guild Best Actress Award 1988, Variety Club Award 1989; *Books* Grace and Favour (autobiog, 1989); *Recreations* walking, water colours, cooking; *Style—* Ms Jane Lapotaire; ✉ c/o William Morris Agency (UK) Ltd, 31/32 Soho Square, London W1V 6DG (☎ 0171 434 2191, fax 0171 437 0238)

LAPPERT, Prof Michael Franz; s of the late Julius Lappert, of Brno, Czechoslovakia, and the late Kornelie, *née* Beran; *b* 31 Dec 1928; *Educ* Wilson's GS London, Northern Poly London (BSc, PhD, DSc); *m* 14 Feb 1980, Lorna, da of David McKenzie (d 1974), of Seaton, Workington; *Career* sr lectr N London Poly 1955–59 (asst lectr 1952–53, lectr 1953–55), sr lectr Univ of Manchester Inst of Sci and Technol 1961–64 (lectr 1959–61), prof Univ of Sussex 1969– (reader 1964–69); sr SERC fell Univ of Sussex 1980–85; author of approx 600 papers on organometallic and inorganic chemistry; pres Dalton Div RSC 1989–91; RSC Awards: Main Gp Element 1970, Organometallic Chemistry 1978, Tilden lectr 1972, Nyholm lectr 1994; Kipping Award ACS 1976; Hon Doctorate München 1989; FRS 1979, FRCS, MACS; *Books* Metal and Metalloid Amides: Syntheses, Structures and Physical and Chemical Properties (with P P Power, A R Sanger, R C Srivastava, 1980), Chemistry of Organo-Zirconium and Hafnium Compounds (with D J Cardin, C L Raston, 1986); *Recreations* theatre, opera, art, tennis, walking; *Style—* Prof Michael Lappert, FRS; ✉ 4 Varndean Gardens, Brighton BN1 6WL (☎ 01273 503661); School of Chemistry, Physics and Environmental and Molecular Science, Univ of Sussex, Brighton BN1 9QJ (☎ 01273 678316)

LAPPING, Anne Shirley Lucas; da of Frederick Stone, and Dr Freda Lucas Stone; *b* 10 June 1941; *Educ* City of London Sch for Girls, LSE; *m* 1963, Brian Michael Lapping; 3 da (Harriet, Claudia, Melissa); *Career* journalist: New Society 1964–68, London Weekend Television 1970–73, The Economist 1974–82; dir: Brook Associates 1982–, Scott Tst 1995–; non-exec dir: Channel 4 TV 1989–95, North West London Mental Health Tst 1993–; govr LSE 1995–; memb Bdcasting Res Unit Nat Gas Consumers Cncl 1978–79, memb Social Sci Res Cncl 1978–79; *Recreations* literature, housework; *Style—* Anne Lapping; ✉ 61 Eton Avenue, London NW3 3ET (☎ 0171 586 1047); Brook Associates, 21–24 Bruges Place, Randolph St, London NW1 0TF (☎ 0171 482 6111, fax 0171 284 0626)

LAPPING, Brian; *Career* early career as journalist on Daily Mirror, Guardian, Financial Times and New Society until 1970; Granada Television 1970–88: exec prodr World in Action 1976–79, creator Hypotheticals current affrs format (30 progs produced for Granada); fndr Brian Lapping Associates (independent prodn co) 1988–; Brian Lapping Associates progs incl: six further Hypotheticals series (BBC), Countdown to War (ITV) 1989, The Second Russian Revolution (BBC2, Discovery US, NHK Japan, etc) 1991,

Question Time (BBC1) 1991–94, The Washington Version (BBC2 and Discovery US) 1992, Woolly Al Walks the Kitty Back (BBC2 and Discovery US) 1992, Off the Back of a Lorry (BBC1) 1993, Watergate (BBC2 and Discovery US) 1994, Fall of the Wall (BBC2, Spiegel TV and Discovery US) 1994, The Death of Yugoslavia (BBC2, ORF Austria, Discovery US, Canal Plus France, etc) 1995; *Awards* incl: various for World in Action, RTS Best Documentary Series for The State of the Nation 1979, Silver Medal Int Film and TV Festival NY for Hypotheticals prog Kidnapped 1984, Bdcasting Press Guild Best Documentary Series for Apartheid 1984, Gold Medal Int Film and TV Festival NY for Breakthrough at Reykjavik 1988 (also finalist Prix Italia) and for Countdown to War 1989, RTS and Bdcasting Press Guild Best Documentary Series Awards and Silver Medal Int Film and TV Festival NY for The Second Russian Revolution 1992; for The Death of Yugoslavia: RTS Judges' Award 1996, Best Independent Prodn and Best News & Current Affrs Prodn Indie Awards 1996, Broadcasting Press Guild Best Documentary Series 1996, George Foster Peabody Award Univ of Georgia 1996, BAFTA Best Documentary 1996; *Style—* Brian Lapping, Esq; ✉ Brian Lapping Associates Ltd, 21–24 Bruges Place, Randolph Street, London NW1 0TF (☎ 0171 482 5855, fax 0171 284 0626)

LAPPING, Peter Herbert; s of Dr Douglas James Lapping, MBE (d 1989), of Swaziland, and Dorothy, *née* Horrocks (d 1971); *b* 8 Aug 1941; *Educ* St John's Coll Johannesburg, Univ of Natal (BA), Lincoln Coll Oxford (MA, played cricket for OU Authentics); *m* 1 April 1967, Diana Dillworth, da of Lt Col Eric S G Howard, MC (d 1977), of Stroud, Glos; 1 s (Mark Edward b 1969), 1 da (Joanna Venka b 1970); *Career* asst master Reed's Sch 1966–67, head of hist Loretto Sch 1967–79 (house master Pinkie House 1972–79); headmaster: Shiplake Coll 1979–88, Sherborne 1988–; memb: HMC, SHA; *Recreations* walking, gardening, cooking, travel; *Clubs* Vincent's (Oxford), MCC, East India, Devonshire Sports and Public Schools; *Style—* Peter Lapping, Esq; ✉ Sherborne School, Dorset DT9 3AP (☎ 01935 812249, fax 01935 816628)

LAPSLEY, (Alastair Gourlay) Howard; s of Rev Claude William Lapsley (d 1976), and Florence Lapsley; *b* 20 May 1940; *Educ* Dulwich, Coll of Law; *m* 5 June 1965, Susan Elizabeth, da of Charles Henry Bassingthwaighte (d 1988), of Diss, Norfolk; 1 s (Angus b 1970), 1 da (Catriona b 1972); *Career* admitted slr 1964; dir: JA Gadd Ltd 1975–, RAC Motor Sports Assoc Ltd 1986–; memb Br Motor Sports Cncl 1984–; Br Rally Champion (1300 cc) 1983; memb Law Soc; *Recreations* motor sport, music, travel; *Clubs* RAC; *Style—* Howard Lapsley, Esq; ✉ Farrant & Sinden, 8 Horsefair, Chipping Norton, Oxon (☎ 01608 642063, fax 01608 644429)

LAPTHORNE, Richard Douglas; *b* 25 April 1943; *Educ* Calday Grange GS, Univ of Liverpool (BCom); *m* 1967, Valerie, *née* Waring; 2 s, 2 da; *Career* trainee Unilever Audit UCMDS 1965–67, fin accountant Lever Brothers (Zambia) Ltd 1967–69, accountant Unilever Pensions 1969–71, chief accountant Food Industries Ltd 1971–74, commercial offr Urachem Div Unilever Holland 1974–75; commercial dir: Synthetic Resins Ltd 1975–77, Sheby SA Paris 1977–80, Urachem Div 1980–81, Crosfields Chemicals Ltd 1981–83; Courtaulds plc: gp fin controller 1983–86, gp fin dir 1986–92, pres Courtaulds United States Inc 1986–92; fin dir British Aerospace plc 1992–; non-exec dir Amersham International 1988–; non-exec dir Fndn and Friends of the Royal Botanic Gardens Kew 1991–; FCCA, FCMA, FCTA, CIMgt; *Recreations* gardening, tennis; *Style—* Richard Lapthorne; ✉ British Aerospace plc, Warwick House, PO Box 87, Farnborough Aerospace Centre, Farnborough, Hants GU14 6YU (☎ 01252 373232, fax 01252 383000)

LARCOM, Sir (Charles) Christopher Royde; 5 Bt (UK 1868); s of Sir Philip Larcom, 4 Bt (d 1967), and Aileen Monica Royde, *née* Colbeck; *b* 11 Sept 1926; *Educ* Radley, Clare Coll Cambridge (MA); *m* 1956, Barbara Elizabeth, da of Balfour Bowen; 4 da (Mary Elizabeth (Mrs Joseph W Arnold) b 1957, Jane Catherine (Mrs Andrew J Edyvean) b 1958, Julia Dorothea (Mrs John Dyer) b 1961, Anna Balfour b 1962); *Heir* none; *Career* memb The Stock Exchange London 1959–1987 (memb Cncl 1970–1980), ptnr Grieveson Grant and Co stockbrokers 1960–1986, fin dir Kleinwort Grieveson 1986; *Recreations* sailing, music; *Clubs* Naval and Military, Cruising Assoc, Ocean Cruising, Itchenor Sailing, Island Sailing, Blackwater Sailing; *Style—* Sir Christopher Larcom, Bt; ✉ 4 Village Cay Marina, PO Box 145, Road Town, Tortola, British Virgin Islands

LARCOMBE, Brian; *Career* 3i Group plc: joined 1974, local dir 1982, regnl dir 1988, fin dir 1992–; chm Br Venture Capital Assoc 1994–95; *Style—* Brian Larcombe, Esq; ✉ 3i Group plc, 91 Waterloo Road, London SE1 8XP (☎ 0171 928 3131, fax 0171 620 2805)

LAREDO, Jaime; *b* 1940; *Career* violinist; pupil of: Antonio de Grassi, Frank Houser, Josef Gingold, Ivan Galamian; debut recital 1948, orchestral debut 1951, youngest winner ever Queen Elizabeth competition Brussels 1959; festival appearances with major orchestras worldwide incl: Spoleto, Tanglewood, Hollywood Bowl, Mostly Mozart, Ravinia, Blossom, Marlboro, Edinburgh, Harrogate, The Proms; dir Chamber Music at the 92nd Street Y series NY, memb Kalichstein/Laredo/Robinson Trio, memb Ax, Stern, Laredo Ma Quartet, teacher Artist Faculty Curtis Inst, chamber musician, dir and soloist with int chamber orchestras incl: Scottish Chamber, English Chamber Orchestra, Orchestra of St Luke's; holds post as Distinguished Artist with St Paul Chamber Orchestra; numerous tours worldwide, numerous recordings made; awarded Handel medallion NY; *Style—* Jaime Laredo; ✉ Harold Holt Ltd, 31 Sinclair Road, London W14 ONS (☎ 0171 603 4300, fax 0171 603 0019, telex 22339 HUNTER)

LARGE, Sir Andrew McLeod Brooks; kt (1996); s of Maj-Gen Stanley Eyre Large, MBE (d 1991), of Drumcrannog, Dalbeattie, Kirkcudbrightshire, and Janet Mary, *née* Brooks; *b* 7 Aug 1942; *Educ* Winchester, Univ of Cambridge (MA), INSEAD Fontainebleau (MBA); *m* 17 June 1967, Susan Mary, da of Sir Ronald Melville, KCB, *qv*; 2 s (Alexander b 1970, James b 1972), 1 da (Georgina b 1976); *Career* British Petroleum Ltd 1964–71, md Orion Bank Ltd 1971–79; Swiss Bank Corporation International 1980–87: md 1980–83, chief exec and dep chm 1983–86, gp chief exec and dep chm 1986–87; memb Exec Bd Swiss Bank Corporation 1988–89; chm: Large Smith & Walter Limited 1990–92, Securities and Investments Bd (SIB) 1992–; non-exec dir: Nuclear Electric PLC 1990–94, Ranks Hovis McDougall PLC 1990–92, Phoenix Securities Ltd 1990–92, Dowty Group Plc 1991–92, ECC Group Plc 1991–96; non-exec chm Luthy Baillie Dowsett Pethick & Co Limited 1990–92; dep chm International Securities Regulation Organisation (ISRO) 1985–86, memb Cncl Stock Exchange 1986–87; non-exec chm: The Securities Assoc 1986–87, London Futures and Options Exchange Ltd (London FOX) 1991–92; memb UK Cncl INSEAD 1992–; *Recreations* skiing, walking, photography, music, weather, sailing, gardening; *Clubs* Brooks's; *Style—* Sir Andrew Large; ✉ Securities and Investments Board, Gavrelle House, 2–14 Bunhill Row, London EC1Y 8RA (☎ 0171 638 1240, fax 0171 382 5909); Cui Parc, Talybont-on-Usk, Brecon, Powys LD3 7YW

LARGE, Prof John Barry; s of Tom Large (d 1975), and Ada Large; *b* 10 Oct 1930; *Educ* QMC, Purdue Univ Indiana, Cornell Univ NY, Harvard Univ; *m* 18 Oct 1958, Barbara Alicia, da of William A Nelson (d 1965), of New Westminster, BC, Canada; 2 s (Jonathan William b 13 March 1968, Jeremy Thomas (twin)); *Career* chief of acoustics The Boeing Co Seattle USA 1958–70, prof of applied acoustics Univ of Southampton 1970– (dir Inst of Sound and Vibration Res, dean Faculty of Engrg, chief exec Univ of Southampton Hldgs Ltd); industl affrs conslt: US Dept of Transportation, UK Civil Aviation Authy, BAA plc (formerly Br Airports Authy), BR Bd, Euro Community Environmental Serv; non-exec dir: Hampshire TEC, Hampshire Business Link Co; memb CBI: Regional Cncl, SME Cncl; fell Acoustical Soc; memb Acoustical Soc of America, MSAE (USA), corresponding memb Inst of Noise Control Engrg USA; FInstD, FRAeS; *Recreations* flying, skiing; *Style—* Prof John Large; ✉ Chinook, Southdown Rd, Shawford, Hants SO21 2BY (☎ 01962 712307); University of Southampton, Southampton, Hants SO9 5NH

LARGE, Sir Peter; kt (1993), CBE (1987, MBE 1974); s of Rosslyn Victor Large (d 1955), and Ethel May, *née* Walters (d 1981); *b* 16 Oct 1931; *Educ* Enfield GS, UCL (BSc); *m* 1, 27 April 1962, Susy (d 1982), da of Dr Bernard Fisher (d 1960); 2 step da (Julia b 1947, Anne b 1953), 1 step s (George b 1957); m 2, 16 Oct 1992, Sheenah, da of Joseph James McCaffrey (d 1993); *Career* Nat Serv Sub Lt (E) HM Submarines 1953–55; Shell Int: joined 1956, Nigeria 1957, Ghana 1957–60, SE Arabia 1960–61, Indonesia 1961–62; paralysed by Poliomyelitis; Civil Serv 1966–91; chm: Jt Ctee on Mobility for Disabled People 1971–, Assoc Disabled Professionals 1971–93 (Parly advsr 1993–), Silver Jubilee Ctee on Access for Disabled People 1977–79, Ctee on Restrictions Against Disabled People 1979–82; vice chm Royal Assoc for Disability and Rehabilitation 1995– (memb Exec Ctee 1977–); memb: Access Ctee for England 1984–94, Nat Advsy Cncl on Employment of Disabled People 1987–, Disability Living Allowance Advsy Bd 1991–; govr Motability 1978–, vice chm Disablement Income Gp 1985–93 (Parly advsr 1973–93), dep chm Disabled Persons Tport Advsy Ctee 1986–; tstee Motability 10th Anniversary Tst 1989–; FRSA 1993; *Recreations* living with siamese cats; *Style—* Sir Peter Large, CBE; ✉ 14 Birch Way, Warlingham, Surrey CR6 9DA (☎ 01883 623801)

LARKEN, Anthea; CBE (1991); da of Frederick William Savill (d 1993), of Winchester, and Nance, *née* Williams (d 1993); *b* 23 Aug 1938; *Educ* Stafford Girls' HS; *m* 19 Dec 1987, Rear Adm (Edmund Shackleton) Jeremy Larken, DSO; *Career* range assessor WRNS 1956, cmmnd 1960, qualified photographic interpreter 1961, qualified WRNS Sec Offr 1967, i/c WRNS offrs trg BRNC Dartmouth 1977–79, RN Staff Coll 1978–79, NATO Mil Agency for Standardisation Brussels 1981–84, Chief Staff Offr (admin) to Flag Offr Plymouth 1985–86, Royal Coll of Def Studies 1987, Dir WRNS and ADC to HM The Queen 1988–91, ret Cmdt; dir and co sec Operational Command Training Organisation Ltd 1991–96; *Recreations* theatre, music, reading, home, family and friends; *Clubs* Army and Navy; *Style—* Mrs Anthea Larken, CBE; ✉ c/o Midland Bank plc, 8 Market Square, Stafford, Staffs ST16 2JP

LARKEN, Jasper Wyatt Royds; s of Capt Francis Wyatt Rawson Larken (d 1985), of Rushall Manor, Pewsey, Wilts, and Florence Meriel, *née* Royds, (see Burke's Landed Gentry, 18th Edn Vol 1 1965); *b* 12 Sept 1939; *Educ* Winchester; *m* 20 April 1968, Caroline Lucia Marie, da of Stuart West Little, of NY, USA; 1 s (Jonathan b 1973), 1 da (Melissa b 1970); *Career* Grenadier Gds 1958–61; formerly md Financial Intelligence UK Ltd, currently chm CLD Stationery Ltd; *Recreations* bridge, hunting, tennis, golf; *Clubs* White's, MCC, Berkshire; *Style—* Jasper Larken, Esq; ✉ 6 Cheyne Gardens, London SW3 5QU

LARKEN, Rear Adm (Edmund Shackleton) Jeremy; DSO (1982); s of Rear Adm Edmund Thomas Larken, CB, OBE (d 1965), and Eileen Margaret, *née* Shackleton; *b* 14 Jan 1939; *Educ* Bryanston, Britannia RNC Dartmouth; *m* 1, 1963 (m dis 1987), Wendy Nigella, *née* Hallett; 2 da (Juliet b 1963, Henrietta b 1968); m 2, 1987, Cmdt Anthea Larken, CBE, WRNS, da of Frederick William Savill (d 1993), of Winchester; *Career* joined RN 1957; specialised in submarines 1961; navigator 1964; exchange with USN Submarine Force 1971–73; cmd: HMS Osiris 1969–70, Glamorgan 1975, Valiant 1976–77, Third Submarine Sqdn 1979–81, HMS Fearless 1981–83 (incl Falklands Campaign); Naval Plans 1983–84, Dir Naval Staff Duties 1985, Cdre Amphibious Warfare and Cmd UK/NL Amphib Force 1985–87; Rear Adm 1988, Asst Chief of Def Staff (Overseas) 1988–90; md Operational Command Training Organisation Ltd (OCTO) 1991–; govr Bryanston Sch 1988–; memb Royal Utd Servs Inst for Def Studies; MInstPet, MInstD; *Recreations* maritime and aviation interests, history and strategy, theatre, reading, home, family and friends; *Clubs* Royal Cwlth Soc; *Style—* Rear Adm Jeremy Larken, DSO; ✉ c/o Lloyds Bank plc, 5 The Square, Petersfield, Hants GU32 3HL

LARKIN, Judith Mary; da of Patrick John Larkin, and Sylvia May, *née* Silverthorne; *b* 22 May 1952; *Educ* The North London Coll Sch, City of London Poly; *Career* trainee Unilever plc 1971, corporate PR specialist in IT, telecommunications and electronics industries, head of corporate PR Logica plc 1979–84; dir: Traverse-Healy & Regester 1984–87, Charles Barker 1987; md Fleishman-Hillard UK Ltd 1990–94, fndr ptnr Regester & Larkin Ltd 1994–; chm Br Gp Int PR Assoc; MIPR 1985; *Style—* Ms Judith Larkin; ✉ Regester & Larkin Ltd, 505 Coppergate House, 16 Brune Street, London E1 7NJ (☎ 0171 721 7395, fax 0171 721 7810)

LARKIN, Prof Maurice John Milner; s of Terence John Larkin (d 1964), of Birmingham, and Winifred, *née* Richards (d 1992); *b* 12 Aug 1932; *Educ* St Philip's GS Birmingham, Trinity Coll Cambridge (BA, MA, PhD); *m* 17 Dec 1958, Enid Thelma, da of Clifford Enoch Lowe (d 1988), of Haddington; 1 s (John b 1962), 1 da (Katie b 1965); *Career* Nat Serv 2 Lt RAEC 1950–51, TA Serv Lt RA 1951–55; lectr in history Univ of Glasgow 1961–65 (asst lectr 1958–61), reader in history Univ of Kent 1976 (lectr 1965–68, sr lectr 1968–76), Richard Pares prof of history Univ of Edinburgh 1976–; FRHistS 1986; *Books* Gathering Pace: Continental Europe 1870–1945 (1969), Church and State after the Dreyfus Affair (1974), Man and Society in Nineteenth Century Realism: Determinism and Literature (1977), France Since the Popular Front: Government and People 1936–86 (1988), Religion, Politics and Preferment in France since 1890 (1995); *Recreations* bird-watching, music, cinema; *Style—* Prof Maurice Larkin; ✉ 5 St Baldred's Crescent, N Berwick, E Lothian, Scotland EH39 4PZ (☎ 01620 892777); Department of History, University of Edinburgh, William Robertson Building, George Square, Edinburgh EH8 9JY (☎ 0131 650 3754, fax 0131 668 4565, telex 727442 UNIVED G)

LARKINS, Derrick Alfred; CBE (1987); s of Walter Arthur Larkins (d 1950), and Ada Amelia Larkins (d 1966); *b* 5 July 1926; *Educ* Royal Liberty Sch Romford; *m* 1960, Noël Sarah, da of William White, of Co Meath, Ireland; 1 s (Barry b 1966), 1 da (Trudi b 1968); *Career* served RN Patrol Serv 1943–46; Apex Oilfields Trinidad 1951–54, Ford Motor Co and Chrysler Motors 1954–61, dep chm (formerly chief accountant and jt md) Lansing Bagnall 1961–89; FCMA; *Recreations* gardening, watching sport, music, reading; *Clubs* MCC; *Style—* Derrick Larkins, Esq, CBE; ✉ Kneledore, Barn Close, Church Rd, Tadley, Hants RG26 6AU (☎ 0118 981 4730)

LARLHAM, Christopher; s of Maj Percival Edward Larlham (d 1968), of London, and Cecelia Louise, *née* Farrell; *b* 8 Nov 1949; *Educ* Dulwich; *m* 1, 3 May 1973 (m dis 1984), Caroline Jane, da of Stanley Godfrey, of Ruislip; 3 s (Edward b 1976, Guy b 1978, George b 1980); m 2, 1 Oct 1994, Cecily, da of Robin Hazell, of Bodmin, Cornwall; 1 s Sam Robert b 30 June 1996); *Career* admitted slr 1975; ptnr Cameron Markby Hewitt and its predecessor firms 1976– (managing ptnr 1990–94); capt Cambs and Hunts CBA and Saffron Walden Bridge Club; Liveryman Worshipful Co of Slrs; memb Law Soc; *Recreations* cricket, golf, bridge, wine; *Clubs* MCC, Hanbury Manor Golf, Saffron Walden Golf; *Style—* Christopher Larlham, Esq; ✉ Cameron Markby Hewitt, Sceptre Court, 40 Tower Hill, London EC3N 4BB (☎ 0171 702 2345, fax 0171 702 2303, telex 925779 CAMLAW G)

LARMOUR, Sir Edward Noel; KCMG (1977, CMG 1966); s of Edward Larmour; *b* 25 Dec 1916; *Educ* Royal Belfast Academical Inst, Trinity Coll Dublin, Univ of Sydney; *m* Agnes Margaret, da of Thomas Bill; 1 s, 2 da; *Career* served Royal Inniskilling Fus and 15 Indian Corps in Burma 1940–46, joined CRO 1948, joined HM Diplomatic Serv 1968, Br high cmmr in Jamaica and ambassador (non res) to Haiti 1970–73, Br high cmmr for New Hebrides (res in London) 1973, dep under sec of state FCO 1975–76, ret

1977; *Style*— Sir Edward Larmour, KCMG; ✉ 68 Wood Vale, London N10 3DN (☎ 0181 444 9744)

LARMOUTH, Prof John; TD (1974); s of Herbert Larmouth (d 1963), of Thornaby, Teesside, Cleveland, and Elsie, *née* Grimwood (d 1989); *b* 17 Sept 1941; *Educ* The GS Yarm, Emmanuel Coll Cambridge; *m* 14 April 1973, Carol Anne, da of Albert George Grover (d 1987), of Cambridge; 1 s (James b 1984), 1 da (Sarah-Jayne b 1984); *Career* cmmnd TA 1964, transferred RARO Maj 1983; computing laboratory Univ of Cambridge 1967–76; Univ of Salford: dir of computing serv 1976–82, dir of computing systems res and devpt 1982–86, dir Info Technol Inst 1986–95, dir of telematics applications 1995–; FBCS 1974, CEng 1988; *Books* Standards for Open Systems Interconnection (1987), Understanding Open Systems Interconnection (1995); *Clubs* Bowdon Croquet, Bowdon Squash, Bowdon Tennis; *Style*— Prof John Larmouth, TD; ✉ 1 Blueberry Rd, Bowdon, Altrincham, Cheshire WA14 3LS (☎ 0161 928 1605); Information Technology Institute, University of Salford, Salford M5 4WT (☎ 0161 745 5657, fax 0161 745 8169, telex 668680 SULIB, e-mail j.Larmouth@iti.salford.ac.uk)

LARNER, Gerald; s of Clifford Larner (d 1968), of Leeds, and Minnie, *née* Barraclough (d 1985), of Leeds; *b* 9 March 1936; *Educ* Leeds Modern Sch, New Coll Oxford (sr scholarship, BA); *m* 1, 1959 (m dis 1988), Celia Ruth Mary, da of late Harry Gordon Norman White; 2 da (Alice Elizabeth b 1960, Melissa Ruth b 1962); m 2, 1989, Lynne Catherine Telfer, da of late Stuart George Cameron Walker; *Career* asst lectr German Dept Univ of Manchester 1960–62; The Guardian: music critic and features sub ed 1962–64, dep features ed 1964–65, regnl music and opera critic 1965–93, freelance music critic associated mainly with The Times 1993; specialist writer of prog and sleeve/liner notes, occasional lectr on music and opera; tv and radio broadcaster; memb: NW Arts Music Panel 1975–80, Hallé Orch Advsy Ctee 1990–92; artistic dir Bowden Festival 1980–84; memb The Critics' Circle 1966; *Books* Wolf's Der Corregidor (trans, 1966), McCabe's The Lion The Witch and the Wardrobe (librettist, 1971), The Glasgow Style (1979), The New Grove (contrib, 1980), Opera Grove (1992), Maurice Ravel (1996); *Stage productions* Peter and the Women (Royal Exchange Theatre Manchester and Buxton Festival, 1993), A Chabrier Cabaret (Edinburgh Int Festival, 1994); *Recreations* visual arts incl decorative arts and design, theatre, literature, tennis; *Style*— Gerald Larner, Esq; ✉ 38 Heyes Lane, Alderley Edge, Cheshire SK9 7JY (☎ 01625 585378, fax 01625 590175)

LARRAIN, Prof Jorge; s of Alberto Larrain, of Santiago, Chile, and Rosa, *née* Ibáñez; *b* 7 May 1942; *Educ* Catholic Univ of Chile (BTheol, Licenciate of Sociology), Univ of Sussex (MA DPhil); *m* 26 Dec 1969, Mercedes, da of Alberto Pulido, of Santiago, Chile; 1 da (Caroline); *Career* Univ of Birmingham: lectr in sociology 1977, sr lectr 1984, reader 1987, head Dept of Cultural Studies 1988–92, prof of social theory 1990; *Books* The Concept of Ideology (1979), Marxism Ideology (1983), A Reconstruction of Historical Materialism (1986), Theories of Development (1989), Ideology and Cultural Identity (1994); *Recreations* tennis; *Style*— Prof Jorge Larrain; ✉ University of Birmingham, Department of Cultural Studies, PO Box 363, Birmingham B15 2TT (☎ 0121 414 6216)

LARRECHE, Prof Jean-Claude; s of Pierre Albert Alexis Larreche, of Pau, France, and Odette Jeanne Madeleine, *née* Hau-Sans; *b* 3 July 1947; *Educ* Lyon France (INSA), Univ of London (MSc), INSEAD Fontainebleau France (MBA), Stanford Univ USA (PhD); *m* 10 Sept 1971, Denyse Michèle Joséphine, da of Michel Francis Henri Gros, of Besancon, France; 1 s (Philippe b 1978), 1 da (Sylvie b 1975); *Career* INSEAD: prof of mktg 1974–, dir Euro Strategic Mktg Inst 1985–89, Alfred H Heineken chair 1993–; non-exec dir Reckitt and Colman plc (London) 1983–, chm Strat X Paris France 1985–, memb Bd The Mac Group Boston 1986–89; memb: America Mktg Assoc 1973, Inst of Mgmnt Sci 1975; FInstD; *Recreations* tennis, golf; *Style*— Prof Jean-Claude Larreche; ✉ 85 Rue Murger, 77780, Bourron Marlotte, France (☎ 00 33 1 64 45 62 00, fax 00 33 1 64 45 98 76); INSEAD, 77305, Fontainebleau, France (☎ 00 33 1 60 72 40 00, fax 00 33 1 60 74 55 00, telex 690389 F)

LARSSON, Cmmr John Alfred; s of Sture William Larsson (d 1974), and Flora, *née* Benwell; *b* 2 April 1938; *Educ* Univ of London (BD); *m* 5 July 1969, Freda, *née* Turner; 2 s (Karl b 17 Dec 1971, Kevin b 15 May 1973); *Career* The Salvation Army: cmmnd offr 1957, corps offr and various youth and trg work 1957–80, 2 i/c Chile, Peru and Bolivia 1980–84, princ William Booth Meml Trg Coll London 1984–88, asst to Chief of Staff Int HQ 1988–90; territorial cdr: UK and Republic of Ireland 1990–93, NZ and Fiji 1993–96, Sweden and Latvia 1996–; composer of brass and vocal music incl 10 full length Christian stage musicals; *Books* Doctrine Without Tears (1974), Spiritual Breakthrough (1982), The Man Perfectly Filled with the Spirit (1985), How Your Corps Can Grow (1988); *Recreations* music, walking; *Style*— Cmmr John Larsson; ✉ The Salvation Army Territorial HQ, Östermalmsgatan 71, 11450 Stockholm, Sweden

LASCELLES, Angela Marion; da of James Anthony Greig (d 1967), of Mersham, Kent, and Juliet Felicia, *née* Colvile; *Educ* Ashford Sch Kent, Univ of London (BA); *m* 8 June 1974, Richard Lascelles, s of Dr William Lascelles; 2 s (Edward b 1975, Simon b 1978), 1 da (Rosalind b 1981); *Career* private clients Phillips & Drew Stockbrokers 1968–70, investmt analyst Spencer Thornton Stockbrokers 1970–72, investmt mangr Dawnay Day (Merchant Bank) 1972–74, Associated British Foods Pension Fund 1975–79, Courtaulds Pension Fund 1979–86, exec dir OLIM Ltd 1986–; jt investmt dir: OLIM Convertible Trust plc 1989, Value & Income Trust plc 1986–; govr The London Inst 1989–92; ASIA; *Recreations* tennis, music; *Style*— Mrs Angela Lascelles; ✉ OLIM Ltd, Pollen House, 10–12 Cork St, London W1X 1PD (☎ 0171 439 4400, fax 0171 734 1445)

LASCELLES, Maj-Gen (Henry) Anthony; CB (1967), CBE (1962), DSO (1944); s of Edward Charles Ponsonby Lascelles, OBE (d 1951), of Midhurst, Sussex, and Leila Winifred Leonora, *née* Kennett-Barrington (d 1979); *b* 10 Jan 1912; *Educ* Winchester, Oriel Coll Oxford (MA); *m* 5 March 1941, Ethne Hyde Ussher, *née* Charles; *Career* WWII served Egypt, N Africa, Sicily, Italy; instr Nato Defence Coll 1955–56, Brig RAC 1956–57, NDC Canada 1958, BGS MO War Office 1959–62, COS NI 1962–63, MGGS Far East 1963–66; tstee Winston Churchill Meml Tst 1980– (dir gen 1966–80), pres Br Water Ski Fedn 1979–; *Recreations* squash, tennis, music; *Clubs* Naval and Military; *Style*— Maj-Gen Anthony Lascelles, CB, CBE, DSO; ✉ Manor Farm Cottage, Hedgerley Green, Bucks SL2 3XG (☎ 01753 883582)

LASCELLES, Viscount; David Henry George Lascelles; s of 7 Earl of Harewood; *b* 21 Oct 1950; *Educ* The Hall Sch, Westminster; *m* 1, 12 Feb 1979 (m dis 1989), Margaret Rosalind, da of Edgar Frank Messenger; 3 s (Hon Benjamin George b 19 Sept 1978, Hon Alexander Edgar b 13 May 1980, Hon Edward David b 19 Nov 1982), 1 da (Hon Emily Tsering b 23 Nov 1975); m 2, 11 March 1990, Diane Jane, da of John Prince Howse; *Career* independent film and television producer, chm Harewood House Tst; *Style*— Viscount Lascelles; ✉ Harewood House Trust, Moor House, Harewood, Leeds LS17 9LQ (☎ 0113 288 6331, fax 0113 288 6467)

LASDUN, Sir Denys Louis; CH (1995), kt (1976), CBE (1965); s of Norman Lasdun; *b* 8 Sept 1914; *Educ* Rugby, Architectural Assoc; *m* 1954, Susan Bendit; 2 s, 1 da; *Career* served WWII RE; architect; in practice with Peter Softley 1960–; works incl: Royal Coll of Physicians London, Flats 26 St James's Place, Keeling House Bethnal Green, Univ of London (SOAS, Inst of Educn, Law Inst, project for Courtauld Inst), Nat Theatre and IBM Central Marketing Centre, South Bank London, office bldgs Fenchurch St EC4 and Milton Gate EC2, EEC HQ for Euro Investmt Bank Luxembourg, Univ of East Anglia, Christ's Coll extensions Cambridge, Cannock Community Hosp, design for new Hurva Synagogue Old City Jerusalem, Genoa Opera House competition; tstee British Museum 1975–85, memb Slade Ctee 1976–92; RIBA Gold Medal 1977 and Trustees' Medal 1992, jt winner Wolf Prize in the Arts Israeli Wolf Fndn 1992, Hon Diploma Architectural Assoc 1994, Architects' Jl Centenary Medal 1995; Hon DLitt: E Anglia 1974, Sheffield 1978; hon fell: American Inst of Architects 1966, RIAS 1994; memb: Accademia Nazionale di San Luca 1984, Academie d'Architecture 1984, Int Acad of Architecture Bulgaria 1986; FRIBA, RA 1991; *Books* Architects' Approach to Architecture (1965), A Language and a Theme (1976), Architecture in the Age of Scepticism (1984); suject of the book Denys Lasdun: Architecture, City, Landscape (by William Curtis, 1994); *Style*— Sir Denys Lasdun, CH, CBE, RA; ✉ 146 Grosvenor Rd, London SW1V 3JY (☎ 0171 630 8211, fax 0171 821 6191)

LASK, Dr Bryan; s of Dr Aaron Lask, and Rita, *née* Flax (d 1989); *b* 18 Feb 1941; *m* 15 Sept 1973, Judith, da of Norman Stubbs (d 1981); 2 s (Gideon, Adam); *Career* conslt psychiatrist Gt Ormond St Hosp for Children London, sr lectr Inst of Child Health London, former ed Jl of Family Therapy; ed Clinical Child Psychology and Psychiatry; memb BPA; fell Int Coll of Psychosomatic Medicine, FRCPsych; *Books* Child Psychiatry & Social Work (1981), Children's Problems (1985), Childhood Illness - The Psychosomatic Approach (1989), Childhood - Onset Anorexia Nervosa and Related Eating Disorders (1993); *Recreations* sports, theatre, music; *Style*— Dr Bryan Lask; ✉ Great Ormond Street Hospital for Children, London WC1N 3JH (☎ 0171 827 8679, fax 0171 829 8657)

LASOK, Prof Dominik; QC (1982); s of Alojzy Lasok, of Turza, Poland (d 1956); *b* 4 Jan 1921; *Educ* elementary educn in Poland and Switzerland, Univ of Fribourg (Licence en Droit), Univ of Durham (LLM), Univ of London (PhD, LLD), Polish Univ Abroad (Dr Juris); *m* 7 Aug 1952, Sheila May, da of James Corrigan; 2 s ((Karol) Paul Edward, *qv*, b 1953, (Dominik) Marc Alexander b 1960 d 1993), 3 da (Pia b 1962, Teresa b 1962, Carmen b 1965); *Career* WWII in Polish Army (cmmnd 1944), served Poland, France and Italy 1939–46 (holds Polish, French and British decorations); employed in indust 1948–51; called to the Bar 1954; legal advsr 1954–58, prof of Euro law Univ of Exeter 1968–86, emeritus prof; visiting prof: Williamsburg (1966–67 and 1977), McGill Univ 1976–77, Rennes Univ 1980–81 and 1986, College d'Europe Bruges 1984–86, Aix-Marseille Univ 1986 and 1989, Marmara Univ Istanbul 1987–94, Chukyo Univ Nagoya 1991, Poznan Univ 1994–97, Cracov Univ 1996–97; Hon LLD: Aix-Marseille 1987, Marmara Univ 1996; Officier dans L'Ordre des Palmes Academiques France 1983; *Books* Polish Family Law (1968), Law and Institutions of the European Communities (1972, 6 edn 1994), Polish Civil Law (1975), The Law of the Economy of the European Communities (1980), The Customs Law of the European Community (1983, 2 edn 1991), Professions and Services in the EEC (1986), Conflict of Laws in the European Community (1987), Halsbury's Laws of England (contrib, Vol 51, 3 edn 1996), The Society of England and European Community Problems (trans into Japanese, 1991); *Style*— Prof Dominik Lasok, QC; ✉ Reed, Barley Lane, Exeter (☎ 01392 272582); Ground Floor, Lamb Building, Temple, London EC4Y 7AS

LASOK, Dr (Karol) Paul Edward; QC (1994); s of Prof Dominik Lasok, QC, *qv*, and Sheila May, *née* Corrigan; *b* 16 July 1953; *Educ* Jesus Coll Cambridge (MA), Univ of Exeter (LLM, PhD); *m* 23 Feb 1991, Karen Bridget Morgan, da of Rev Dr Hugh Griffith, HCF (d 1991); 1 da (Frances Katharine Marina b 10 June 1993); *Career* called to the Bar Middle Temple 1977, legal sec Ct of Justice of Euro Communities 1980–84 (locum tenens March-May 1985); private practice: Brussels 1985–87, London 1987–; memb Cons Pty; memb Editorial Bd: European Competition Law Review, Law and Justice; *Books* The European Court of Justice Practice and Procedure (2 edn, 1994), Lasok & Bridge's Law & Institutions of the European Union (6 edn, 1994); contrib to: Halsbury's Laws of England 4 edn vols 51 and 52 (1986), Stair Memorial Encyclopaedia of the Laws of Scotland, Weinberg & Blank on Take-overs and Mergers (1989); *Recreations* walking, music; *Style*— Dr Paul Lasok, QC; ✉ 57 Ellington Street, London N7 8PN (☎ 0171 607 5874); 4 Raymond Buildings, Gray's Inn, London WC1R 5BP (☎ 0171 405 7211, fax 0171 405 2084)

LASS, Jonathan Daniel; s of Jacob Lass, of London, and Regina, *née* Weinfeld; *b* 22 Feb 1946; *Educ* Univ Coll Sch, Downing Coll Cambridge (MA); *m* 24 March 1985, Andria Mina, da of Mervyn Thal; 2 s (Saul Alexander Yentis, Gregory Michael), 1 da (Eliza Gina Thal); *Career* Herbert Oppenheimer Nathan & Vandyk 1970–75; admitted slr 1972, slr Crawley & De Reya 1975–77, vice pres and legal advsr Citibank NA 1977–86, ptnr Lovell White Durrant (formerly Lovell White & King) 1986–89, ptnr Lass Salt Garvin Slrs 1990–; chm Financial Servs Ctee American C of C; memb: Law Soc, Int Bar Assoc, American Bar Assoc; *Recreations* history, opera, theatre, art, antiques, gardening, swimming, tennis; *Clubs* RAC, Annabel's; *Style*— Jonathan D Lass, Esq; ✉ 4 North Square, London NW11 7AA; Lass Salt Garvin, 35 Piccadilly, London W1V 9PB (☎ 0171 434 4433, fax 0171 434 4464)

LASSEN-DIESEN, David Peter; s of Sigurd Lassen-Diesen (d 1986), and Mary Margaret, *née* Wright; *b* 30 Jan 1938; *m* 7 Sept 1968, Valerie Jane, da of Joseph John Ive (d 1964); 2 s (David b 1974, Piers b 1977), 1 da (Karen b 1971); *Career* fndr Finance Centre (first money shop business in UK) 1967, fndr ptnr Diesen Property Co 1967; dir: Frost Holdings 1972–74, Konrad Roberts Ltd 1978, Konrad Roberts plc 1985–, Delter Ltd 1995–, Brandford Ltd 1995–; memb Inst of Dir; *Recreations* yachting; *Style*— David P Lassen-Diesen, Esq; ✉ Roundwood Hall, Norwood Hill, Horley, Surrey RH6 0HS (☎ 01293 862798, fax 01293 862846)

LAST, Maj-Gen Christopher Neville; CB (1990), OBE (1976); s of Jack Neville Last, and Lorna Kathleen Mary, *née* Goodman; *b* 2 Sept 1935; *Educ* Culford Sch, Brighton Tech Coll; *m* 11 Feb 1961, Pauline Mary, da of Henry Percy Lawton (d 1981); 2 da (Caroline Victoria Neville b 3 Aug 1964, Alexandra Louise Neville b 10 June 1969); *Career* Regular Army, Royal Corps of Signals Troop Cdr 1955, Cdr 8 Signal Regt 1980, Brig and Cdr 1 Signal Bde HQ 1 (Br) Corps Germany 1981–83; dir of Mil Cmd and Control Projects (Army) UK 1984, dir of Procurement Policy (special studies) 1985, Maj-Gen and Vice Master Gen of the Ordnance 1986, mil dep to Head of Def Export Servs 1988, Col Cmdt RCS 1990–96; business dir N Wales and Oswestry Tissue Bank 1996; chief exec Clwyd FHSA 1990–96, vice pres N Wales Br Red Cross 1992–, chm Bd of Tstees Royal Signals Inst 1994–; memb: TA & VR Assoc for Wales, CLA, Br Field Sports Soc, Nat Tst, Nat Museum of Army Communications Blandford 1996; Liveryman Worshipful Co of Info Technologists 1992, Freeman City of London 1988; *Recreations* shooting, sailing, skiing; *Clubs* Special Forces, Fadeaways; *Style*— Maj-Gen Christopher Last, CB, OBE; ✉ c/o Nat West Bank plc, 34 North Rd, Lancing, Sussex BN15 9AB

LAST, Prof Joan Mary; OBE (1988); da of Dr Cecil Edward Last (d 1971), of Bletsoe, Littlehampton, Sussex, and Grace Bevington, *née* Jarvis (d 1913); *b* 12 Jan 1908; *Educ* Godolphin Sch Salisbury, piano student Mathilde Verne; *Career* brief career as pianist ended with injury to hand; prof of piano RAM 1959–83; teaching seminars and master classes in UK, USA, Canada, Aust, NZ, Africa, Bermuda, Hong Kong, Scandinavia, Ireland, the Netherlands; compiled over 100 albums of educnl music and 3 textbooks for piano teachers, adjudicator at over 50 competitive festivals in UK and Canada; examiner Associated Examining Bd 1960–85; voluntary work as music presenter The Voice of Progress cassette magazine for the blind; memb: Inc Soc of Musicians 1940, EPTA, Composers' Guild, Performing Rights Soc; Hon ARAM 1965, Hon RAM 1975; *Recreations* photography (memb Littlehampton Camera Club), croquet; *Clubs* RAM, Arun Decorative and Fine Arts Soc, National Tst; *Style*— Prof Joan Last, OBE; ✉ Surya, 11 St Mary's Close, Littlehampton, Sussex BN17 5PZ (☎ 01903 713522)

LAST, Prof John William; CBE (1989); s of late Jack Last (d 1986), and Freda Edith, *née* Evans (d 1976); *b* 22 Jan 1940; *Educ* Sutton GS Surrey, Trinity Coll Oxford (MA); *m* 1967, Susan Josephine, da of late John Holloway Farmer, of Knaresborough; 3 s (Andrew John b 2 Jan 1969, Philip James b 12 June 1971, Peter Charles b 7 June 1973); *Career* corp affrs advsr Littlewoods Orgn (joined 1969), dir of public affrs United Utilities plc (North West Water plc) 1993–; fndr Merseyside Maritime Museum; chm: Walker Art Gallery Liverpool 1977–81, Royal Liverpool Philharmonic Orch 1977–92; memb: Arts Cncl 1980–84, Press Cncl 1980–86, Museums Cmmn 1983–95; tstee: Theatre Museum 1983–86, V&A 1983–86 (memb Advsy Cncl); vice pres Museums Assoc 1983–84; visiting prof in arts admin City Univ 1985–, hon fell Liverpool John Moores Univ 1989, Christie lectr 1990, vice chm Northern Ballet Theatre, chm Museums Trg Inst 1990–, govr Nat Museum of Wales 1994–; Merseyside Gold Medal for Achievement 1991; Hon DLitt City Univ 1995; Freeman City of London 1985, Liveryman Worshipful Co of Barber Surgns 1986; *Recreations* Victoriana, music, swimming; *Clubs* RAC; *Style*— Prof John Last, CBE; ✉ Llannerch Hall, St Asaph, Denbighshire LL17 6BD; United Utilities plc, Dawson House, Great Sankey, Warrington, Cheshire WA5 3LW (☎ 01925 234000, fax 01925 236836)

LASZLO, *see:* de Laszlo

LATCHMAN, Prof David Seymour; *b* 22 Jan 1956; *Educ* Haberdashers' Aske's Elstree Herts, Queens' Coll Cambridge (entrance scholar, fndn scholar, BA, coll prizes 1976, 1977 and 1978), Univ of Cambridge (bachelor scholar, MA, PhD), Univ of London (DSc 1994); *Career* post-doctoral res fell Eukaryotic Molecular Genetics Gp Cancer Res Campaign Dept of Biochemistry Imperial Coll London 1981–84, lectr in molecular genetics Dept of Biology (formerly Zoology) UCL 1984–88, dir Medical Biology Unit Dept of Biochemistry and Molecular Biology UCL and Middlesex Sch of Med 1988–91 (reader 1990), prof of molecular pathology (established chair) and head Dept of Molecular Pathology UCL Med Sch 1991–; chm: Div of Pathology UCL Med Sch 1995–, Science Expert Advsy Ctee Univ of London; memb Univ of London: Central Equipment and Scholarships Fund, Examinations and Assessment Cncl Advsy Bd, Examinations Bd and Biological Subjects Advsy Panel; memb: Med Advsy Panel Parkinson's Disease Soc, Biochemical Soc, Soc for General Microbiology, AAAS, American Soc for Microbiology, NY Acad of Scis; MRCPath; *Books* Gene Regulation - a eukaryotic perspective (1990, 2 edn 1995), Eukaryotic Transcription Factors (1991, 2 edn 1995), Transcription Factors: a practical approach (ed, 1993), From Genetics to Gene Therapy (ed, 1994), PCR Applications in Pathology (ed, 1994), Genetic Manipulation of the Nervous System (ed, 1996); *Style*— Prof David Latchman; ✉ Department of Molecular Pathology, University College London Medical School, The Windeyer Building, 46 Cleveland Street, London W1P 6DB (☎ 0171 380 9343, fax 0171 387 3310)

LATCHMORE, Andrew Windsor; s of Arthur John Craig Latchmore, MBE, FRCS, of Windrush Coll Farm Lane, Linton, Nr Wetherby, W Yorks, and Joyce Mary Latchmore, JP, *née* Raper (d 1993); *b* 9 Feb 1950; *Educ* Oundle, Univ of Leeds (LLB); *m* 1, 20 June 1976 (m dis 1989), Jillian Amanda, da of Victor Hugo Watson, of Moatfield, E Keswick, nr Leeds; 1 s (Jolyon Guy 1981), 1 da (Lucy Emma 1979); *m* 2, Clarissa Mary, da of Maj Peter J Orde; 1 s (Max Andrew b 1993), 1 da (Chloe Roseanna b 1991); *Career* admitted slr 1975; Eversheds: (formerly Hepworth and Chadwick): ptnr 1978–, chm of commercial property 1991–; govr Gateways Sch 1992–94 (sec to govrs 1977–92); hon sec Leeds Law Soc 1982–91; memb The Law Soc; FRSA; *Recreations* music, opera, golf, tennis, skiing, walking, travel; *Clubs* Alwoodley Golf, Collingham Squash; *Style*— Andrew Latchmore, Esq; ✉ Eversheds, Cloth Hall Court, Infirmary Street, Leeds LS1 2JB (☎ 0113 243 0391, fax 0113 245 6188, telex 557917)

LATEY, Rt Hon Sir John Brinsmead; kt (1965), MBE (Mil, 1943), PC (1986); s of William Latey, CBE, QC (d 1976), and Annie (d 1983); *b* 7 March 1914; *Educ* Westminster Sch, ChCh Oxford; *m* 1938, Betty Margaret, da of Dr Edwyn Henry Beresford of London; 1 s, 1 da; *Career* served WWII MEF and WO (Lt-Col); called to the Bar Middle Temple 1936, QC 1957; bencher Middle Temple 1964–; a judge of High Court of Justice (Probate, Divorce and Admty Div, now Family Div) 1965–89; chm Lord Chllr's Ctee on Age of Majority 1965–67, dep chm Oxfordshire Quarter Sessions 1966; *Recreations* golf, fishing, chess, bridge; *Clubs* United Oxford and Cambridge Univ; *Style*— The Rt Hon Sir John Latey, MBE; ✉ 1 Adderbury Park, Adderbury, nr Banbury, Oxon OX17 3EN (☎ 01295 810208)

LATHAM, Cecil Thomas; OBE (1976); s of Cecil Frederick James Latham (d 1942), and Elsie Winifred, *née* Lewis (d 1959); *b* 11 March 1924; *Educ* Rochester Cathedral Choir Sch, King's Sch Rochester; *m* 8 Aug 1945, Ivy Frances, da of Thomas William Fowle (d 1935); 1 s (Martin John b 1954), 1 da (Helen Susan b 1952); *Career* war serv 1942–45; asst clerk Magistrates' Courts: Chatham 1939–42, Maidstone 1945, Leicester 1948–54, Bromley 1954–63; dep clerk to the Justices: Liverpool 1963–65, Manchester 1965–76 (clerk); stipendiary magistrate Greater Manchester (Salford) 1976–94; memb: Royal Cmmn on Criminal Procedure 1978–81, Criminal Law Revision Ctee 1981–; Hon MA Univ of Manchester 1984; *Books* Stone's Justices' Manual (editions 101–109); fndr ed: Family Law Reports 1980–86, Family Court Reporter 1987–; specialist ed J P Reports 1986–; *Style*— Cecil Latham, Esq, OBE; ✉ 12 Oakside Way, Oakwood, Derby DE21 2UH (☎ 01332 544338)

LATHAM, Hon Mr Justice; Hon Sir David Nicholas Ramsay; kt (1992); s of Robert Clifford Latham, CBE (d 1995), of Cambridge, and Eileen Frances, *née* Ramsay (d 1969); *b* 18 Sept 1942; *Educ* Bryanston, Queens' Coll Cambridge (MA); *m* 6 May 1967, Margaret Elizabeth, *née* Forrest; 3 da (Clare Frances (Mrs Jonathan Speight) b 2 Aug 1969, Angela Josephine b 23 Jan 1972, (Rosemary) Harriet b 10 Dec 1974); *Career* called to the Bar Middle Temple 1964, bencher 1989; jr counsel to the Crown Common Law 1979–85, jr counsel to Dept of Trade in export credit guarantee matters 1982–85, QC 1985, recorder of the Crown Court 1983–92, judge of the High Court of Justice (Queen's Bench Div) 1992–, presiding judge Midland and Oxford Circuit 1995–; memb: Gen Cncl of the Bar 1986–92, Judicial Studies Bd 1988–91, Cncl Legal Education 1988–96; vice-chm Cncl for Legal Educn 1992–96; *Recreations* reading, music, food, drink; *Clubs* Leander; *Style*— The Hon Mr Justice Latham; ✉ Royal Courts of Justice, Strand, London WC2A 2LL

LATHAM, David Russell; s of Russell Latham CBE, MC, JP (d 1964), and Elsa Mary, *née* Andrews (d 1980); *b* 9 Nov 1937; *Educ* Rugby; *m* 1963, Susan Elisabeth, da of Charles Alfred Bryant (d 1984); 2 s (Jonathan b 1966, Nicholas b 1968), 1 da (Katherine b 1970); *Career* chm James Latham plc; *Recreations* tennis, golf, skiing; *Style*— D R Latham; ✉ James Latham plc, Leeside Wharf, Clapton, London E5 9NG (☎ 0181 806 3333)

LATHAM, Derek James; s of James Horace Latham, DFC, of Newark-on-Trent, and Mary Pauline, *née* Turner (d 1974); *b* 12 July 1946; *Educ* King Edward VI GS Retford, Leicester Sch of Architecture, Trent Poly Nottingham (DipArch, DipTP, DipLD, ALI); *m* 14 Sept 1968, Pauline Elizabeth, OBE, da of Philip George Tuxworth, of Lincs; 1 da (Sarah Jane b 1972), 2 s (Benjamin James b 1974, Oliver James b 1981); *Career* Clifford Wearden & Assocs (architects and planners) London 1968–70, housing architect and planner Derby CC 1970–73, design and conservation offr Derbyshire CC 1974–78, tech advsr Derbyshire Historic Bldgs Tst 1978–, princ Derek Latham and Assocs 1980–89, chm Derek Latham and Company 1989–; md Michael Saint Developments Ltd 1984; dir: Acanthus Associated Architectural Practices Ltd 1984– (chm 1987–89), Acanthus Europe 1993–; memb Exec Ctee Cncl for Care of Churches 1985–91, govr Nottingham Sch of Interior Design 1986–90, architectural advsr Peak Park Tst 1986–, concept co-ordinator Sheffield Devpt Corp 1987–89; external examiner: Leicester Sch of Architectural Conservation Studies 1983–86, Leicester Sch of Architecture 1988–92, Sch of Architecture Univ of Nottingham 1996–; dir Omega Two Ltd (artworks advsrs) 1990–, master planner Derby City Challenge 1992–94; memb RIBA 1971, MRTPI 1974; memb: Landscape Inst 1978, Soc for the Protection of Ancient Buildings 1974 (memb Ctee 1993–), Ancient Monument Soc 1975, Soc for the Interpretation of Britains Heritage 1976, EASA 1991, Urban Design Gp 1991, RSA 1989 (chm RSA Dean Clough 1995–); *Recreations* squash, sailing, rambling; *Clubs* Duffield Squash and Lawn Tennis, Little Eaton Law Tennis (pres 1991); *Style*— Derek J Latham, Esq; ✉ Hieron's Wood, Vicarage Lane, Little Eaton, Derby DE21 5EA (☎ 01332 832371); Derek Latham and Company, St Michaels, Derby DE1 3SU (☎ 01332 365777)

LATHAM, 2 Baron (UK 1942); Dominic Charles Latham; er (twin) s of Hon Francis Charles Allman Latham (d 1959), and his 3 w Gabrielle Monica, *née* O'Riordan (d 1987), and gs of 1 Baron Latham (d 1970); *b* 20 Sept 1954; *Educ* NSW Univ (BEng 1977, MEngSc 1981); *Heir* bro, Anthony Latham; *Career* civil engr with Electricity Cmmn of New South Wales 1979–88; structural engr with Rankine & Hill consulting engrs 1988–91; sr structural engr with Gerard Barry Assocs 1992; social dancing teacher 1993–; *Recreations* tennis, squash, snooker, electronics, sailboarding; *Style*— The Rt Hon the Lord Latham; ✉ PO Box 355, Kensington, NSW 2033, Australia

LATHAM, James Miles; s of Maj James Francis Latham, TD, JP (d 1966); *b* 24 Jan 1940; *Educ* Haileybury; *m* 1968, Margaret Eleanor, da of Donald Maclenan Gray (d 1946); 2 s (James Alexander b 1969, Piers Francis b 1971); *Career* wood merchant; dir: James Latham plc, Singer Plywood Ltd 1975–, Leeside Services (Guernsey) Ltd 1993–; memb Cncl: Timber Trade Fedn of UK 1974–, Timber Res and Devpt Assoc 1975–; dir Epping Forest Centenary Trust (registered charity) 1985–; gen cmmr of income tax 1986; Freeman Worshipful Co of Blacksmiths (memb 1962, warden 1996); memb Inst of Wood Sci; *Recreations* golf, gardening, field sports; *Clubs* Royal Worlington, Newmarket Golf; *Style*— James Latham, Esq; ✉ Gills Farm, Epping Upland, Essex CM16 6PL; James Latham plc, Leeside Wharf, Clapton, London E5 9NG (☎ 0181 806 3333, fax 0181 442 4396)

LATHAM, John Aubrey Clarendon; s of Geoffrey Chitty Latham (d 1980), of Farnham, Surrey, and Kathleen Anne, *née* Godfrey (d 1970); *b* 23 Feb 1921; *Educ* Winchester, various art colls; *m* 1951, Barbara Mary Leslie, da of Leo Steveni; 2 s (Peter Noa b 1952, John-Paul b 1954), 1 da (Xenia b 1963); *Career* artist; RNVR 1940–46; hon fndr Inst for Study of Mental Images 1954, co-fndr Artist Placement Gp 1965, lectr St Martin's Sch of Art 1965–67; memb Orgn and Imagination; *Work in Public Collections* Museum of Modern Art NY (Shem, Art and Culture), Tate Gallery, Newark Museum New Jersey, Modern Art Museum Caracas, Belfast National Gallery of Modern Art, Washington Gallery of Modern Art, Musee de Calais France, Staatsgalerie Stuttgart, Washington Art Centre Minneapolis USA; *Solo Exhibitions* Kingly Gallery London 1948, Bear Lane Gallery Oxford 1963, Kasmin Gallery London 1963, Alan Gallery NY 1964, Lisson Gallery London 1970, 1987, 1989 and 1992, Gallery House London 1972–73, Kunsthalle Dusseldorf 1975, Stedelijk Van Abbemuseum Eindhoven 1983, Josh Baer Gallery NY 1987 and 1989, Art after Physics (Staatsgalerie Stuttgart and MOMA Oxford) 1991, Tate Gallery (summary exhibit) 1995; several films, videos, tapes, performances and demonstrations; *Publications incl* Report and Offer For Sale (1971), Time-Base & Determination in Events (1975), Event-Structure, Sub Quantum (with Andrew Dipper, 1983), Report of a Surveyor (1984), Dimension: Framework of event discovered via art (with Munro, 1989); *Style*— John Latham; ✉ 210 Bellenden Rd, London SE15 4BW (☎ and fax 0171 639 3597)

LATHAM, (John) Martin; s of William John Lawrence Latham, of Leatherhead, Surrey, and late Kathleen Louise, *née* Ward; *b* 28 July 1942; *Educ* Bradfield Coll Berks, Fitzwilliam Coll Cambridge (MA); *Career* articled clerk to asst mangr Peat Marwick Mitchell & Co London 1965–74; James Capel & Co: corp fin exec 1974–76, co sec 1976–87, head of secretariat 1987–92, compliance dir 1992–96; gp compliance dir HSBC Investment Bank plc 1996–; MSI (memb Stock Exchange 1978), FCA 1979; *Recreations* tennis, golf, yachting; *Clubs* MCC, Roehampton; *Style*— Martin Latham, Esq; ✉ 53 Abbotsbury Close, Holland Park, London W14 8EQ (☎ 0171 603 2591); Thames Exchange, 10 Queen Street Place, London EC4R 1BL (☎ 0171 621 0011, fax 0171 621 0845, telex 888866)

LATHAM, Sir Michael Anthony; kt (1993), DL (Leics 1994); s of Wing Cdr S H Latham (d 1993); *b* 20 Nov 1942; *Educ* Marlborough, King's Coll Cambridge, Dept of Educn Univ of Oxford; *m* 1969, Caroline Susan, da of Maj T A Terry, RE (d 1971); 2 s; *Career* housing and local govt offr CRD 1965–67, co-opted memb GLC Housing Ctee 1967–73, memb Westminster City Cncl 1968–71, dir and chief exec House Builders Fedn 1971–73; MP (C): Melton 1974–83, Rutland and Melton 1983–92; memb: Select Ctee on Energy 1979–82, Public Accounts Ctee 1983–92; advsr on economic and political issues 1993–95, chm Construction Indust Bd 1995–96, pres Br Flat Roofing Cncl 1995–; visiting prof Univ of Northumbria 1995–; reviewer Jt Govt/Indust Review on Procurement/Contractual Problems in the Construction Indust 1993–94; hon vice pres Anglo-Israel Assoc 1994– (pres 1990–94); tstee Oakham Sch 1987–; Anglican lay reader 1988–; hon memb RICS 1996; hon fell: Chartered Inst of Purchasing and Supply 1994, Instn of Civil Engrs 1995, Inst of Bldg Control 1995, Chartered Inst of Bldg 1995, Architects' and Surveyors' Inst 1995; Hon LLD Nottingham Trent Univ 1995; FRSA 1992; *Recreations* cricket, fencing, gardening, listening to classical music; *Clubs* Carlton; *Style*— Sir Michael Latham, DL; ✉ 508 Hood House, Dolphin Square, London SW1V 3LX

LATHAM, (Edward) Michael Locks; DL (Cornwall 1995); s of Edward Bryan Latham, CBE (d 1980); *b* 7 Jan 1930; *Educ* Stowe, Clare Coll Cambridge; *m* 1955, Joan Doris, da of Charles Ellis Merriam Coubrough (d 1967); 1 s, 2 da; *Career* chm: Trebartha Estates Ltd, The Lanlivery Tst 1989–; dir: James Latham plc 1957–91 (chm 1973–87), Bloomsbury Properties Ltd 1991–; pres: Sandringham Assoc of Royal Warrant Holders 1982–83, Timber Trade Fedn 1984–85; memb Exec Ctee Nat Cncl of Bldg Material Prodrs 1985–91; govr St Dunstan's Abbey Sch 1988–93, non-exec dir Royal Cornwall Hosp Tst, pres Royal Cornwall Agric Assoc 1992; High Sheriff of Cornwall 1992, Co Cdr St John Ambulance Cornwall 1993–; *Recreations* tennis, the countryside, classic cars, books; *Clubs* Launceston Golf, Devon Vintage Car, Club Talbot; *Style*— E Michael Latham, Esq, DL; ✉ Trebartha Lodge, Launceston PL15 7PD

LATHAM, Air Vice-Marshal Peter Anthony; CB (1980), AFC (1960); s of Oscar Frederick Latham (d 1945), of Birmingham, and Rhoda, *née* Archer (d 1969); *b* 18 June 1925; *Educ* St Phillip's GS Birmingham, St Catharine's Coll Cambridge; *m* 19 Sept 1953, Barbara Mary, da of Reginald des Landes Caswell (d 1984), of Birmingham; 2 s (Mark b 1958, Phillip b 1960), 6 da (Jane (Mrs Foskett) b 1954, Sarah (Mrs Street) b 1955, Anne (Mrs Lewis) b 1956, Katharine (Mrs Hampden-Smith) b 1959, Margaret (Mrs Lindsell) b 1962, Josephine (Mrs Saville) b 1965); *Career* joined RAF 1944, served in 26, 263, 614, 247 sqdns 1946–54, cmd III Sqdn (ldr Black Arrows Aerobatic Team) 1958–60, MOD jt planning staff 1962–64, cmd NEAF strike and PR wing 1964–66, Gp Capt Ops 38 Gp 1967–69, cmd RAF Tengah Singapore 1969–71, MOD central staff 1971–73, AOC Offr and Aircrew Selection Centre Biggin Hill 1973–74, SASO 38 Gp 1974–76, dir def ops MOD 1976–77, AOC II Gp 1977–81, Cdre RAF Sailing Assoc 1974–80, pres Assoc of Service Yacht Clubs 1978–81, ret RAF 1981; princ Oxford Air Trg Sch and dir CSE Aviation 1981–85, sr air advsr Short Bros plc 1985–90, ptnr Peter Latham Clocks; memb Ctee East Wessex TAVR, tstee RAF Heraldry Tst; pres Br Horological Inst 1996–97;

Freeman City of London 1988, Master Worshipful Co of Clockmakers 1996–97; *Recreations* sailing, horology; *Clubs* RAF; *Style*— Air Vice-Marshal P A Latham, CB, AFC; ✉ c/o Lloyd's Bank, 193 High St, Deritend, Birmingham B12 OLJX

LATHAM, Richard Brunton; QC (1991); s of Frederick Latham, and Joan Catherine, *née* Glover; *b* 16 March 1947; *Educ* Farnborough GS, Univ of Birmingham (LLB); *m* 1 Jan 1972, Alison Mary, da of John Llewellyn Goodall; 3 s (Thomas Richard b 6 Jan 1977, Nicholas John b 30 Aug 1979, Peter James b 5 Feb 1981); *Career* called to the Bar Gray's Inn 1971, recorder Midland & Oxford Circuit 1987–, standing counsel Inland Revenue 1987–91, treas Midland & Oxford Circuit 1992–; *Recreations* sailing, opera, photography; *Style*— Richard Latham, Esq, QC; ✉ 9 Bedford Row, London WC1R 4AZ (☎ 0171 242 3555, fax 0171 242 2511, car 0831 630600)

LATHAM, Sir Richard Thomas Paul; 3 Bt (UK 1919), of Crow Clump, Walton-upon-Thames, Co Surrey; s of Sir (Herbert) Paul Latham, 2 Bt (d 1955); *b* 15 April 1934; *Educ* Eton, Trinity Coll Cambridge (MA); *m* 1958, (Marie-Louise) Patricia, da of late Frederick Hooper Russell, of Vancouver, BC, Canada; 2 da (Nicola Patricia (Mrs Colin D Jones) b 1959, Alison Kathleen (Mrs Gary W Schilds) b 1965); *Heir* none; *Style*— Sir Richard Latham, Bt; ✉ 2125 Birnam Wood Drive, Santa Barbara, Calif 93108, USA

LATHWELL, Mark Nicholas; *b* 26 Dec 1971; *Career* professional cricketer; Somerset CCC: debut 1991, awarded county cap 1992; England: rep U19 v Aust 1991, memb A Team touring Aust 1992/93 and S Africa 1993/94, full debut v Aust 1993; Somerset Player of the Year 1992, Young Player of the Year 1992; *Style*— Mark Lathwell, Esq; ✉ c/o Somerset CCC, The County Ground, Taunton, Somerset TA1 1JT (☎ 01823 272946)

LATIMER, Dr Raymond Douglas (Ray); s of Kenneth Eric Latimer, MBE (d 1975), of London, and Doris Evelyn, *née* Friend; *b* 15 Aug 1941; *Educ* City of London Sch, Univ of Cambridge (MA), Middlesex Hosp Med Sch (LRCP, MRCS, MB BS); *m* 15 May 1965, Patricia Mary, da of Frank Theodore Page; 3 s (Paul b 1968, Mark b 1970, Andrew b 1978), 1 da (Sarah b 1971); *Career* cardiothoracic anaesthetist Papworth Hosp, assoc lectr Univ of Cambridge, ed Jl of Cardiothoracic Anaesthesia; guest lectr: China 1987, Iran 1989, India and China 1991, Romania 1994; fndr Assoc of Cardiothoracic Anaesthetists of GB and I, sec and treas Euro Assoc of Cardiothoracic Anesthesiologists, cncl memb World Assoc of Cardiothoracic and Vascular Anaesthesia; memb Queens' Coll Cambridge; tstee St Stephens Hosp Delhi; FRCA; *Books* author of chapters in pubns on endotoxaemia in cardiac surgery, anaesthesia for heart and lung transplantation, selective phosphodieterase inhibitors in treatment of heart failure and inhaled nitric oxide in pulmonary hypertension; *Recreations* sailing, Christian Youth Leader (Pathfinders); *Clubs* Christian Med Fellowship; *Style*— Dr Ray Latimer; ✉ Oaksway, 15 Braggs Lane, Hemingford Grey, Huntingdon, Cambs PE18 9BW (☎ 01480 463582); Papworth Hospital, Papworth Everard, Cambridge CB3 8RE (☎ 01480 830 541, fax 01480 831143)

LATIMER, Sir (Courtenay) Robert; kt (1966), CBE (1958, OBE 1948); s of Sir Courtenay Latimer, KCIE, CSI (d 1944), and Isabel Primrose, *née* Aikman (d 1981); *b* 13 July 1911; *Educ* Rugby, ChCh Oxford (MA); *m* 1, 3 Oct 1944, Elizabeth Jane Gordon (d 1989), da of William Mitchell Smail (d 1971); 1 s (Colin b 1947), 1 da (Penelope b 1953); m 2, 4 Jan 1990, Frederieka Jacoba Blankert, da of Hermanus Witteveen (d 1959); *Career* ICS and IPS 1935–47, HM Overseas Serv 1948–64 (dep high cmmr for Basutoland, Bechuanaland Protectorate and Swaziland 1960–64), min (Territories) Br Embassy Pretoria 1964–66; registrar Kingston Poly 1967–76; *Recreations* golf; *Style*— Sir Robert Latimer, CBE; ✉ Benedicts, Old Avenue, Weybridge, Surrey KT13 0PS (☎ 01932 842381)

LATOUR-ADRIEN, Hon Sir (Jean Francois) Maurice; kt (1971); s of Louis Constant Emile Adrien (decd), and Maria Ella *née* Latour (decd); *b* 4 March 1915; *Educ* Royal Coll Mauritius, UCL (LLB); *Career* called to the Bar Middle Temple 1940; Mauritius: dist magistrate 1947, crown counsel 1948, additional subst procureur and adv-gen 1954, sr crown counsel 1958, asst attorney-gen 1960, slr-gen 1961–64, DPP 1964–66, puisne judge 1966–70, chief justice 1970–77, actg govr-gen intermittently 1973–76; chm Mauritius Union Assurance Co 1982– (dir 1978–); pres Mauritius Mental Health Assoc 1986– (vice pres 1978–85); Mauritius Commercial Bank Ltd: dir 1980–83, 1984–87, 1988–91 and 1992–95, pres 1993–94 (vice-pres 1992–93); legal conslt: Mauritius Commercial Bank Ltd 1983–, Promotion and Development Co Ltd 1985–, Mauritius Commercial Bank Finance Corp 1991–94, Mauritius Commercial Bank Registry and Securities Ltd 1991–, Promotion and Development Co Ltd 1991–, Caudan Development Co Ltd 1991–, Fincorp Investment Ltd 1994–; pres: Mauritius Red Cross 1978–, War Meml Bd of Tstees 1978–84 (vice pres 1985–), Mauritius Mental Health Assoc 1986– (vice pres 1978–85); vice pres Institut de Droit d'Expression Française, jt ed Mauritius Law Reports 1970–77; *Style*— The Hon Sir Maurice Latour-Adrien; ✉ Vacoas, Mauritius

LATTER, (Henry) James Edward; s of Henry Edward Latter, of Horley, Surrey, and Hilda Bessie, *née* Gyford; *b* 19 April 1950; *Educ* Reigate GS, Trinity Hall Cambridge (BA, MA); *m* 27 May 1978, Penelope Jane, da of Douglas Arthur Morris, of Pto del Duquesa, Spain; 1 s (Christopher b 1983), 1 da (Sarah b 1985); *Career* called to the Bar Middle Temple 1972; chm: Disciplinary Ctee Potato Mktg Bd 1988–94, Milk Mktg Bd 1990–94; pt/t immigration adjudicator 1993, special adjudicator 1994, full-time immigration adjudicator 1995–; churchwarden Parish of Horley 1982–86, reader C of E 1990; *Style*— H J E Latter, Esq; ✉ Immigration Appellate Authority, York House, Feltham, Middx (☎ 0181 893 1000, fax 0181 893 7772)

LATTO, Dr Douglas; s of David Latto (d 1946), of Dundee, and Christina, *née* Gordon (d 1960); *b* 13 Dec 1913; *Educ* St Andrews Univ (MB ChB, DObst); *m* 11 Oct 1945, Dr Edith Monica Latto, da of Capt Arthur Edward Druitt; 1 s (Conrad b 1948), 3 da (Christina b 1947, Elizabeth b 1952, Veronica b 1957); *Career* house surgn Dundee Royal Infirmary 1939, house physician Cornelia and E Dorset Hosp Poole 1940, res obstetrician and gynaecologist Derbys Hosp for Women Derby 1940, res surgical offr Birmingham Accident Hosp 1944, casualty offr Paddington Gen Hosp London 1944, asst in obstetrics and gynaecology Mayday Hosp Croydon 1945, res obstectrician and gynaecologist Southlands Hosp Shoreham-by-Sea Sussex 1946–49, Nuffield Dept of Obstetrics and Gynaecology Radcliffe Infirmary Oxford 1949–51; chm Br Safety Cncl 1971– (Sword of Honour 1985); Freeman City of London 1988, Liveryman Worshipful Soc of Apothecaries 1988; memb BMA; FRPSL 1975, FRCOG 1989; *Recreations* squash, travelling, gardening, philately; *Clubs* RAC, Rolls-Royce Enthusiasts; *Style*— Dr Douglas Latto; ✉ Lethnot Lodge, 4 Derby Road, Caversham, Reading, Berks RG4 0EZ (☎ 0118 947 2282)

LATYMER, 8 Baron (E 1431–32); Hugo Nevill Money-Coutts; s of 7 Baron Latymer (d 1987); *b* 1 March 1926; *Educ* Eton; *m* 1, 1951 (m dis 1965), Hon (Penelope) Ann Clare, da of Thomas Addis Emmet (d 1934), and Lady Emmet of Amberley (Life Peeress, d 1980); 2 s (Hon Crispin James Alan Nevill b 1955, Hon Giles Thomas Nevill b 1957), 1 da (Hon Clare Louise (Hon Mrs Edmunds) b 1952); m 2, 1965, Jinty Ann, da of Peter Calvert (d 1970); 1 s (Hon Henry Eugene b 1967), 2 da (Hon Vera Dulcie Harriet b 1972, Hon Fanny Clara Maria b 1973); *Heir* s, Hon Crispin Money-Coutts; *Career* gardener; *Style*— The Rt Hon the Lord Latymer; ✉ Vivero Hortus, Santa Maria, Mallorca

LAUD, Derek George Henry; s of Alexander Laud; *Career* special advsr to Govt Mins and Cons MPs and professional speechwriter; memb Political Staff House of Commons, political sec to Parly Delgns visiting Washington, S Africa, Hong Kong and Taiwan, campaign mangr gen election 1987, asst Campaign Team for Rt Hon John Major, MP 1990, actively involved gen election campaign 1992; md Ludgate Laud Government Relations Co 1992–; advsr House of Lords Rural Economy Group, govt advsr to FIMBRA, special advsr to the Ed of the Sunday Express, policy advsr to Cncllr Robert Michaels (Chm Westminster City Cncl), conslt Alexander Associates (mgmnt conslts), ptnr Competition Analysis, conslt The Earl of Smith Galleries; alternate memb Economic and Social Ctee of EC; occasional journalist and broadcaster; local govt candidate Hampshire 1990; memb Cons Pty: Westminster and Chelsea Assoc, Romsey and Waterside Assoc; *Recreations* reading poetry, fox hunting, music, staying with the Welby's; *Style*— Derek Laud, Esq; ✉ Ludgate Laud Government Relations Co, 21 Deans Yard, Westminster, London SW1P 3PA (☎ 0171 227 8200)

LAUDERDALE, 17 Earl of (S 1624); Sir Patrick Francis Maitland; 13 Bt (NS 1680); also Lord Maitland of Thirlestane (S 1590), Viscount of Lauderdale (S 1616), Viscount Maitland, and Lord Thirlestane and Boltoun (both S 1624); Hereditary Bearer of National Flag of Scotland by Decrees of Lord Lyon King of Arms (1790 and 1952); s of Rev Hon Sydney George William Maitland (d 1946; 2 s of 13 Earl), and gggggg nephew of 2 Earl and 1 Duke of Lauderdale (the 'L' of Charles II's acronymic CABAL); suc bro, 16 Earl, 1968; f of Lady Olga Maitland, MP; *b* 17 March 1911; *Educ* Lancing, Brasenose Coll Oxford; *m* 1936, Stanka, da of Prof Milivoje Lozanitch, of Belgrade Univ; 2 s, 2 da; *Heir* s, Master of Lauderdale, Viscount Maitland; *Career* sits as Cons in House of Lords; journalist 1933–59, fndr and sometime ed Fleet Street Letter Service, sometime ed The Whitehall Letter; war corr: The Times (Central Europe) 1939–41, News Chronicle (Pacific) 1941–43; MP (C) Lanarkshire (Lanark Div) 1951–59 (resigned whip 1956–58 in protest at withdrawal from Suez); fndr and chm Expanding Cwlth Gp at House of Commons 1955–59 (re-elected chm 1959), chm House of Lords Sub-ctee on Energy Tport and Res 1974–79; dir Elf Petroleum (UK) plc 1980–; pres The Church Union 1956–61, memb (emeritus) Coll of Guardians Nat Shrine of Our Lady of Walsingham 1955–; FRGS; *Books* European Dateline (1945), Task for Giants (1957); *Clubs* New (Edinburgh); *Style*— The Rt Hon the Earl of Lauderdale; ✉ 12 St Vincent St, Edinburgh (☎ 0131 556 5692); 10 Ovington Square, London SW3 1LH (☎ 0171 589 7451 and 0171 219 5452)

LAUGHLAND, His Hon (Graham Franklyn) Bruce; QC (1977); s of Andrew Percy Laughland, of Birmingham (d 1962); *b* 18 Aug 1931; *Educ* King Edward's Sch Birmingham, ChCh Oxford (MA); *m* 1969, Victoria Nicola Christina (fndr Who Cares? Tst, d 1994), da of Archibald Seymour Jarman (d 1982), of Brighton; 1 s; *Career* called to the Bar Inner Temple 1958, standing counsel to the Queen's Proctor 1968–77, recorder of Crown Ct 1972–89, prosecuting counsel to Inland Revenue (Midland & Oxford circuit) 1973–77, bencher of the Inner Temple 1985, acting judge Supreme Ct of the Falkland Islands 1985–, memb Gen Cncl of the Bar 1970, treas Midland & Oxford Circuit 1986–89, circuit judge (SE Circuit) 1989–96, a regular judge of the Central Criminal Ct 1989–96; chm Westminster Assoc for Youth 1984–89; Liveryman Worshipful Co of Curriers; *Clubs* Garrick; *Style*— His Hon Bruce Laughland, QC; ✉ 30 Monmouth Road, London W2 4UT

LAUGHLAND, Hugh William; s of William Laughland (d 1949), and Eleanor Anne Gordon, *née* Wilson (d 1993); *b* 20 Dec 1931; *Educ* Ayr Acad, Merchiston Castle Sch; *m* 24 Aug 1961, Louise Osborne; 1 s (Brian b 1963), 1 da (Tracy b 1966); *Career* Fleet Air Arm 1954–56; dir Scottish Aviation Ltd 1970–75 (joined 1957), chief exec Scottish Universal Investment 1976–79; dir: Thomas Tilling plc 1981–83 (joined 1980), BTR plc 1984–96 (joined following takeover of Thomas Tilling 1983); chm: Low and Bonar plc, Stoddard Sekers International plc; CA, ATII; *Recreations* golf, gardening; *Clubs* Caledonian; *Style*— Hugh Laughland, Esq; ✉ Higher Stratton, Stratton Chase Drive, Chalfont St Giles, Bucks HP8 4NS

LAUGHTON, Prof Michael Arthur; s of William Arthur Laughton (d 1986), of Barrie, Ontario, Canada, and Laura, *née* Heap (d 1987); *b* 18 Dec 1934; *Educ* King Edward Five Ways Birmingham, Etobicoke Collegiate Inst Toronto Canada, Univ of Toronto (BASc), Univ of London (PhD, DSc(Eng)); *m* 1960 (m dis 1994), Margaret Mary, yr da of Brig George Vincent Leigh Coleman, OBE (QVOCG Indian Army, d 1970); 2 s (Mark Michael b 30 July 1968, Thomas George b 16 May 1971), 2 da (Joanna Margaret (Mrs Brogan-Higgins) b 28 June 1963, Katherine Alice (Dr Gardner) b 22 Nov 1965); *Career* graduate apprentice GEC Witton Birmingham 1957–59, project engr GEC Engineering Computer Services 1959–61; Queen Mary Coll (now Queen Mary and Westfield Coll) Univ of London: DSIR res student 1961–64, lectr Dept of Electrical Engrg 1964–72, reader in electrical engrg 1972–77 (prof 1977–), dean Faculty of Engrg 1983–85, pro-princ QMC 1985–89; dean of engrg Univ of London 1990–94; visiting prof: Univ of Purdue USA 1966, Univ of Tokyo Japan 1977; external examiner numerous univs UK and abroad 1970–; co-ed and fndr Int Journal of Electrical Power and Energy Systems 1978–; chm: Tower Shakespeare Company Ltd 1985–93, Queen Mary College Industrial Research Ltd 1988–91 (dir 1979); organising sec Power Systems Computation Confs 1963–81 (chm Exec Ctee 1981–); chm: IEE Working Gp on Applications of New Electronic Techniques in Publishing 1983–87, Working Gp on Renewable Energy 1986–90 (Watt Ctee Exec 1986–); memb: Info Ctee Royal Society 1988–, British Scholars Selection Ctee Fulbright Cmmn 1991–, House of Lords Select Ctee on the Euro Communities 1988– (specialist advsr to Sub Ctee B (Energy, Tport and Technol) on Inquiries into Renewable Resources 1988 and Efficiency of Electricity Use 1989), Cncl IEE 1990–, House of Commons Welsh Ctee (specialist advsr on Inquiry on Wind Energy) 1994; memb Ct Cranfield Inst of Technol 1991–; Freeman City of London 1990, Liveryman Worshipful Co of Barbers 1995; MRI 1973, FIEE 1977 (MIEE 1968), FEng 1989; *Publications* Electrical Engineers Reference Book (with M G Say and G R Jones, 1985, 1993), Expert System Applications in Power Systems (ed with T S Dillon, 1990), Renewable Energy Sources (ed 1990); author of numerous papers on electrical power and energy systems, control and computation; *Recreations* music, following rugby and cricket; *Clubs* Athenaeum; *Style*— Prof M A Laughton, FEng; ✉ 28 Langford Green, Champion Hill, London SE5 8BX (☎ 0171 326 0081); Department of Electronic Engineering, Queen Mary & Westfield College, University of London, Mile End Rd, London E1 4NS (☎ 0171 975 5331, fax 0181 981 0259)

LAUNDER, Prof Brian Edward; s of Harry Edward Launder, of Manchester, and Elizabeth Ann, *née* Ayers; *b* 20 July 1939; *Educ* Enfield GS, Imperial Coll London (BSc(Eng), Bramwell Medal, Unwin Premium, ACGI), MIT (SM, ScD), Univ of London (DSc(Eng), Univ of Manchester (DSc), UMIST (DEng); *m* 20 Sept 1967, Dagny, da of Svend Simonsen; 1 da (Katya Jane b 18 July 1970), 1 s (Jesper David b 12 May 1973); *Career* res asst MIT 1961–64, reader in fluid mechanics Imperial Coll London 1972–76 (lectr in mech engrg 1964–72), prof of mech engrg Univ of California Davis 1976–80; UMIST: prof of mech engrg 1980–, head of Thermodynamics & Fluid Mechanics Div 1980–90, head of Mech Engrg Dept 1983–85 and 1993–95; adjunct prof Pennsylvania State Univ 1984–88; assoc ed ASME Fluids Engrg Jl 1978–81, ed-in-chief Int Jl of Heat & Fluid Flow 1987–; hon prof Nanjing Univ of Aeronautics and Astronautics PRC 1993; FIMechE 1981, FASME 1983, FRS, FEng 1994; *Books* Mathematical Models of Turbulence (with D B Spalding, 1972), Turbulence Models and their Application (with W C Reynolds and W Rodi, 1985); also author of over 200 scientific articles on turbulence and turbulent flow; *Recreations* photography, country walking, cycling; French life, literature, culture, food and wine; *Style*— Prof Brian Launder, FRS, FEng;

✉ Department of Mechanical Engineering, UMIST, PO Box 88, Manchester M60 1QD (☎ 0161 200 3700, fax 0161 200 3723)

LAUNER, Dr Michael Andrew; s of Ellis Launer (d 1978), of Manchester, and Sylvia Launer, *née* Cohen (d 1985); *b* 29 May 1947; *Educ* Manchester GS, Univ of Leeds (DPM), Open Univ (BA); *m* Nov 1972, Hilary Elizabeth, da of Herbert Frederick Coates (d 1955), of Milford Haven, Wales; 1 s (Jack Simon b 1974); *Career* conslt psychiatrist Burnley Healthcare Tst 1977–, fndr Psychonutritional Unit for the Treatment of Eating Disorders Burnley 1984, clinical dir Mental Health Burnley 1995; pioneer in use of Clozapine for schizophrenia; freelance contrib: Hospital Doctor, local radio, TV and newspapers; ed Mespeak (magazine for eating disorder sufferers); hon consIt: NW, Samaritans, Relate; hon conslt advsr: Nat Schizophrenic Fellowship (NSF), SANE, MIND; listed by Anorexic Aid, second opinion doctor Mental Health Cmmn, Law Society approved expert witness, memb Nat Ctee for Sick Doctors, memb Special Professional Panel for Sick Doctors, assessor for conslt appts RCPsych, opinion ldr on schizophrenia; LRCP, MRCS 1970, MRCPsych 1975, memb BMA; FRSA 1996; *Recreations* writing, sport as a spectator, aspiring novelist and communicator, memb med team Manchester Utd FC; *Style*— Dr Michael Launer; ✉ Burnley Health Care Trust, Lamont Clinic, Burnley General Hosp, Casterton Ave, Burnley, Lancs BB10 2PQ (☎ 01282 474736, 01282 420906, fax 01282 474743)

LAURANCE, Anthony John (Tony); s of Dr Bernard Laurance (d 1994), and Audrey, *née* Kidner (d 1968); *Educ* Bryanston, Clare Coll Cambridge (exhibitioner, MA Philosophy and Economics); *m* 1981, Judith, *née* Allen; 2 da (Rachel b 13 March 1982, Miriam b 23 May 1986); *Career* trainee BBC News 1975, various policy jobs DHSS 1975–85, princ private sec to Sec of State for Social Servs 1985–87, Newcastle Central Office DSS 1987–90, territorial dir Benefits Agency 1990–95, regnl dir S&W NHS Exec 1995–; *Recreations* tennis, poker, fiction, family; *Style*— Tony Laurance, Esq; ✉ NHS Executive South and West, Westward House, Lime Kiln Close, Stoke Gifford, Bristol BS12 6SR (☎ 0117 984 1851, fax 0117 984 1852)

LAURANCE, Ben James; s of David Laurance (d 1970), and Helen, *née* Young; *b* 27 May 1956; *Educ* Oakham Sch Rutland, Trinity Coll Cambridge (BA); *Career* Eastern Counties Newspapers 1977–82, business corr then energy ed Lloyd's List 1982–86, dep City ed Daily Express 1986–88, fin reporter then dep fin ed The Guardian 1988–94, investment analyst Smith New Court/Merrill Lynch 1994–96, business ed The Observer 1996–; *Recreations* sailing, cycling, beachcombing; *Style*— Ben Laurance, Esq; ✉ The Observer, 119 Farringdon Road, London EC1R 3ER (☎ 0171 278 2332)

LAURENCE, Andrew David; s of Kenneth Gordon Laurence, of Northants, and Vera, *née* Gilbert; *b* 1 Oct 1957; *Educ* Wellingborough Sch Northants, Univ of Reading (LLB), Inns of Court Sch of Law, Webber Douglas Acad of Dramatic Art (Postgrad Cert); *m* 1982, Priscilla, da of Donald C Bergus; 2 da (Elizabeth Emma b 1991, Katherine Louisa b 1993); *Career* called to the Bar Inner Temple 1981; actor, writer and prodr 1982–84, freelance press and PR rep for West End and touring theatre 1984–85, head of mktg The Orchard entertainment complex Dartford BC 1985–86, PR mangr LDDC 1986–89; main bd dir and md Corp Communications Div Hill & Knowlton (UK) Ltd 1993– (joined 1989); memb: NUJ, Br Actors' Equity; MInstD, MIPR; *Recreations* theatre, film, music, swimming, sub aqua, rugby; *Clubs* British Sub Aqua; *Style*— Andrew Laurence, Esq; ✉ Hill & Knowlton (UK) Ltd, 5–11 Theobalds Road, London WC1X 8SH (☎ 0171 413 3005, fax 0171 413 3131, mobile 0385 380643, e-mail alaurence@hillandknowlton.com)

LAURENCE, Ven (John Harvard) Christopher; s of Hugh Peter Laurence (d 1987), and Enid, *née* Wheeler (d 1978); *b* 15 April 1929; *Educ* Christ's Hosp Horsham, Trinity Hall Cambridge (MA), Westcott House Cambridge; *m* 1952, Evelyn Margaret Elizabeth, da of Herbert William Chappell; 1 s (Peter Jonathan b 1953), 1 da (Margaret Ruth b 1954); *Career* ordained (Lincoln) 1955; asst curate St Nicholas Lincoln 1955–59; vicar: Crosby St George Scunthorpe 1959–74, St Hugh's Missioner (Lincoln Dio) 1974–80; bishop's dir of clergy trg (London Dio) 1980–85, archdeacon of Lindsey 1985–94; *Recreations* sculpture; *Style*— The Ven Christopher Laurence; ✉ 5 Haffenden Road, Lincoln LN2 1PP (☎ 01522 531444)

LAURENCE, George Frederick; QC (1991); s of Dr George Bester Laurence (d 1993), of S Africa, and Anna Margaretha, *née* Niemeyer; *b* 15 Jan 1947; *Educ* Pretoria Boys HS, Univ of Cape Town (Smuts Meml scholar, BA), Univ Coll Oxford (Rhodes scholar, BA); *m* 27 Aug 1976, (Ann) Jessica, da of John Gordon Chenevix Trench; 1 step s (Thomas James Yardley b 14 Sept 1974), 1 da (Catherine Ann b 28 Aug 1978), 1 s (Benjamin George b 24 Oct 1981); *Career* called to the Bar Middle Temple 1972 (Harmsworth scholar); asst recorder 1993–; memb Ed Bd Rights of Way Law Review; tstee: Statute Law Tst, Pretorian Tst; memb: Administrative Law Bar Assoc, Parly Bar Mess, Planning & Local Govt Bar Assoc, Chancery Bar Assoc; *Recreations* cricket, tennis, theatre; *Clubs* Grannies Cricket, Pretoria Country; *Style*— George Laurence, Esq, QC; ✉ 12 New Square, Lincoln's Inn, London WC2A 3SW (☎ 0171 405 3808, fax 0171 831 7376)

LAURENCE, Michael; s of Jack Laurence, MBE (d 1960), of London N2, and Eveleen, *née* Lewis (d 1988); *b* 18 June 1930; *Educ* Stonyhurst, St Mary's Hosp Med Sch, Univ of London (MB BS); *m* 12 Sept 1967, Parvin, da of Jamshid Faruhar (d 1969), of Iran; 1 s (Arian b 1968), 2 da (Nicola b 1970, Hotessa b 1972); *Career* RAMC Capt specialist aneasthetics MELF 1955–57; orthopaedic surgn and conslt: Guy's Hosp, St Olave's Hosp, New Cross Hosp and Lewisham Hosp 1970–94, Hosp of St John and St Elizabeth and Royal London Hosp 1995–; conslt orthopaedic surgn: Hammersmith Hosp 1968–70, Royal Nat Orthopaedic Hosp Stanmore 1968–70; sr lectr Inst of Orthopaedics London Univ 1968–70, lectr Dept of Surgery Royal Post Grad Med Sch 1968–70; chm Med Staff Ctee Hosp of St John & St Elizabeth 1982–88; assoc ed Jl of Bone and Joint Surgery, author of many articles, papers and chapters in books on the subject of Reconstructive Joint Surgery in Chronic Arthritis; pres Rheumatical Arthritis Surgical Soc 1978–79 and 1988–89, chm Bd of Affiliated Socs Cncl Br Orthopaedic Assoc 1989–94, hon treas NHS Support Fedn 1990–92, pres Hampstead Med Soc 1991–93, hon sec Hunterian Soc 1993–; Royal Soc of Med: hon sec Sports Med Section 1993–, pres Orthopaedic Section 1993–94; FRCS; *Recreations* sailing, golf, skiing; *Clubs* Island Sailing (Cowes); *Style*— Michael Laurence, Esq; ✉ 2 Lyndhurst Terrace, Hampstead NW3 5QA; Billingham Manor, nr Newport IOW PO30 3HE; 106 Harley St, London W1N 1AF (☎ 0171 486 3131)

LAURENCE, Prof (Kurt) Michael; s of Gustav Leobenstein (d 1927), of Berlin, and Grete, *née* Heymann (d 1990); *b* 7 Aug 1924; *Educ* Newcastle under Lyme HS, Trinity Hall Cambridge (BA, MA), Univ of Liverpool (MB BCh), Univ of Wales (DSc); *m* 9 July 1949, (Ethel) Rose, da of Thomas James Settle (d 1976), of Coventry; 1 s (Anthony Stephen b 1950), 2 da (Amanda Rose b 1959, Elizabeth Clare b 1961); *Career* registrar in pathology Portsmouth 1953–55, res fell in hydrocephalus and spina bifida Hosp for Sick Children Gt Ormond St London 1955–58, reader in applied genetics Welsh Nat Sch for Med 1969–76 (sr lectr in paediatric pathology 1959–69), prof of paediatric res Univ of Wales Coll of Med 1976–89, hon conslt clinical geneticist S Glam Health Authy 1976–89, co-dir Inst of Med Genetics 1976–89, emeritus prof Univ of Wales 1989–; project ldr Euro Registration of Congenital Malformations for Wales 1985–; memb Vale of Glamorgan Community Health Cncl 1994–; over 300 sci papers on congenital malformations, clinical genetics, paediatric pathology, hydrocephalus and spina bifida, prenatal diagnosis, prevention of malformations; FRCPEd, FRCPath; memb: Clinical Genetics Soc (past sec and pres), Br Paediatric Assoc, Soc for Res into Hydrocephalus and Spina Bifida (past sec and pres), Paediatric Pathology Soc (past pres); *Books incl* Fetoscopy (jtly, 1981), Fetal and Neonatal Pathology (contrib, 1987), Principles and Practice of Medical Genetics (contrib, 1990), Modern Antenatal Care of the Foetus (contrib, 1990), Hydrocephalus (contrib, 1992); *Recreations* music, painting, current affairs, skiing, walking; *Style*— Prof Michael Laurence; ✉ Springside, Pen-y-Turnpike, Dinas Powys, South Glamorgan CF64 4HG (☎ and fax 01222 513248)

LAURENCE, Sir Peter Harold; KCMG (1981, CMG 1976), MC (1944), DL (Devon 1989); s of Ven George Laurence (d 1953); *b* 18 Feb 1923; *Educ* Radley, Ch Ch Oxford; *m* 1948, Elizabeth Aïda, da of H C B Way; 2 s, 1 da; *Career* diplomat; political advsr Berlin 1967–69, visiting fell All Souls Coll Oxford 1969–70, cnsllr (commercial) Paris 1970–74, chief inspr Dip Serv 1974–78, SOAS London 1979, ambass Ankara 1980–83, ret; chm: Br Inst of Archaeology at Ankara 1984–95, Community Cncl of Devon 1986–92; fell Woodard Corp, chm of govrs Grenville Coll Bideford 1988–95, memb Cncl Univ of Exeter 1989–; *Clubs* Army and Navy; *Style*— Sir Peter Laurence, KCMG, MC, DL; ✉ Trevilla, Beaford, Winkleigh, N Devon EX19 8NS

LAURENCE, Capt Timothy James Hamilton; MVO (1989); yr s of Cdr Guy Stewart Laurence, RN (d 1982), and Barbara Alison, *née* Symons; *b* 1 March 1955; *Educ* Sevenoaks, RNC Dartmouth, Univ Coll Durham; *m* 12 Dec 1992, HRH The Princess Royal (*see* Royal Family); *Career* cmmnd RN 1979, Cdr 1988, Capt 1995; asst navigating offr HM Yacht Britannia 1979, cmd HMS Cygnet 1981–82 (despatches), equerry to HM The Queen 1986–89, cmd HMS Boxer 1990–91, MOD 1992–95, cmd HMS Cumberland 1995–96, cmd HMS Montrose and Capt Sixth Frigate Sqdn 1996–; memb: RUSI, IISS; Liveryman Worshipful Co of Coachmakers & Coach Harness Makers; *Style*— Capt Timothy Laurence, MVO, RN; ✉ c/o Buckingham Palace, London SW1

LAURENSON, James Tait; s of James Tait Laurenson (d 1986), of Seal, Kent, and Vera Dorothy, *née* Kidd (d 1968); *b* 15 March 1941; *Educ* Eton, Magdalene Coll Cambridge (MA); *m* 13 Sept 1969, Hilary Josephine, da of Alfred Howard Thompson, DFC (d 1991), of Chatton, Northumberland; 3 da (Emily b 1972, Marianne b 1974, Camilla b 1978), 1 s (Fergus b 1976); *Career* Ivory & Sime Investment Managers 1968–83, dep chm and md Adam & Company Group plc 1984–93, chm Nippon Assets Investments SA 1984–; dir: I & S UK Smaller Companies Trust plc 1983–, Hiscox Harrison Ltd 1992–, NSM plc 1994–, Fidelity Special Values plc 1994–; chm Governing Cncl Erskine Stewarts Melville; FCA 1967; *Recreations* tennis, gardening; *Clubs* New (Edinburgh), Hon Co of Edinburgh Golfers; *Style*— James Laurenson, Esq; ✉ Hill House, Kirknewton, Midlothian EH27 8DR (☎ 01506 881990)

LAURIE, Sir (Robert) Bayley Emilius; 7 Bt (UK 1834), of Bedford Sq, Middlesex; s of Maj-Gen Sir John Emilius Laurie, 6 Bt, CBE, DSO (d 1983), and Evelyn, *née* Richardson-Gardener (d 1987); *b* 8 March 1931; *Educ* Eton; *m* 1968, Laurelie Meriol Winifreda, da of Sir Reginald Lawrence William Williams, 7 Bt, MBE, ED (d 1971); 2 da (Clare Meriol b 1974, Serena Catherine b 1976); *Heir* kinsman, Andrew Ronald Emilius Laurie b 1944; *Career* Capt 11 Bn Seaforth Highlanders (TA) 1951–67; Samson Menzies Ltd 1951–58, CT Bowring & Co Ltd 1958–88, dir CT Bowring (Underwriting Agencies) Ltd 1967–83, chm Bowring Membs Agency Ltd 1983–88, dir Murray Lawrence Membs Agency Ltd 1988–92; memb Lloyd's 1955–; *Style*— Sir Bayley Laurie, Bt; ✉ The Old Rectory, Little Tey, Colchester, Essex (☎ 01206 210410)

LAURIE, Richard Thomas; s of Thomas Werner Laurie (d 1944), of Putney, London SW15, and Elizabeth Mary Beatrice, *née* Blackshaw (d 1967); *b* 4 Oct 1935; *Educ* Bradfield Coll; *m* 29 June 1959 (m dis), Susan, da of John Dring, OBE (d 1991), of Fakenham, Norfolk; 2 s (Daniel b 1959, Thomas b 1963), 1 da (Sophie b 1961); *Career* Nat Serv RASC 1954–56, 2 Lt; creative dir Brockie Haslam Advertising 1970–81, dir The Medicine Men 1993–; ed: Hot News International 1987–, Docklands Business News 1994–; freelance journalist and copywriter; professional jazz musician; memb Exec Ctee Soho Soc 1977–, ed Soho Clarion 1977–; *Recreations* book collecting, magazine editing; *Style*— Richard T Laurie, Esq; ✉ 27 Clarendon Drive, Putney, London, SW15 1AW (☎ 0171 780 1939, fax 0171 780 2137)

LAURIE, Capt Robert Peter; OBE (1994), JP (1974), DL (1979); s of Col Vernon Stewart Laurie, CBE, TD, DL (d 1981), of Brentwood, Essex (*see* Burke's Landed Gentry 18th Edn, vol III), and Mary (d 1989), 2 da of late Selwyn Robert Pryor, of Plaw Hatch, Bishop's Stortford, Essex; *b* 20 Aug 1925; *Educ* Eton; *m* 26 Nov 1952, Oonagh Margaret Faber, 3 da of late William Preston Wild, of Warcop Hall, Westmorland; 3 s (Ranald Martin b 1956, Benjamin William b 1959, Andrew Robert b 1963), 1 da (Marian Doone b 1955); *Career* Coldstream Gds 1943–47 (hon Capt); farmer (ret); memb Stock Exchange 1953–87; ptnr Heseltine Powell & Co (then Heseltine Moss & Co) 1953–80 (conslt 1980–85), dir British Empire Securities & General Trust plc 1954–95 (chm 1973–84); pres Coldstream Gds Assoc Essex Branch 1959–; memb Ct Essex Univ 1979–; govr: Brentwood Sch 1974–95, Alleyn's Sch 1984–95; chm Essex Assoc of Boys Clubs 1977–86 (pres 1986–), a vice-pres Nat Assoc of Boys' Clubs 1986–; pres: Essex Agric Soc 1986–87, Essex Home Workers 1986–, Essex Shire Horse Assoc 1987–, Chelmsford and Mid Essex Samaritans 1986–93, The Essex Club 1984; High Sheriff of Essex 1978–79, Vice Lord-Lieut of Essex 1985–92; chm Essex Co Ctee TAVRA 1987–91, memb Cncl CGLI 1984–; Hon Col Essex Army Cadet Force 1994–; memb Ct of Assts Worshipful Co of Saddlers (Master 1981–82); *Recreations* foxhunting, gardening, reading, agriculture, attempting to behave; *Clubs* City Livery; *Style*— Capt Robert P Laurie, OBE, JP, DL; ✉ Heatley's, Ingrave, Brentwood, Essex CM13 3QW (☎ 01277 810224)

LAURISTON, His Hon (Alexander) Clifford; QC (1972); s of Alexander Lauriston, MBE (d 1960), and Nellie, *née* Ainsworth; *b* 2 Oct 1927; *Educ* Coatham Sch Redcar, Trinity Coll Cambridge (MA); *m* 1954, Inga Louise Cameron, da of E Gregor (d 1987), of Tunbridge Wells; 2 da; *Career* called to the Bar Inner Temple 1952, recorder Crown Ct 1972–76, circuit judge 1976–93; chm Registered Homes Appeals Tbnl 1994–; Freeman City of London 1969, Liveryman Worshipful Co of Loriners 1969; *Clubs* Berkshire Golf, Utd Oxford and Cambridge; *Style*— His Hon Clifford Lauriston, QC; ✉ 199 Strand, London WC2R 1DR

LAUTERPACHT, Prof Elihu; CBE (1989), QC (1970); s of Sir Hersch Lauterpacht, QC (d 1960), and Rachel, *née* Steinberg (d 1989); *b* 13 July 1928; *Educ* Harrow, Trinity Coll Cambridge (MA, LLM); *m* 1, 1955, Judith Maria (d 1970), er da of Harold Hettinger; 1 s (Michael), 2 da (Deborah, Gabriel); m 2, 1973, Catherine Josephine, da of Francis Daly (d 1960); 1 s (Conan b 1980); *Career* international lawyer; called to the Bar Gray's Inn 1950, bencher 1983; Univ of Cambridge: dir Res Centre for Int Law 1983–95, hon prof of int law 1994; pres World Bank Admin Tbnl 1996 (vice pres 1992), chm Asian Devpt Bank Admin Tbnl 1993–95; judge *ad hoc* Int Ct of Justice 1993; chm Dispute Settlement Panel N American Free Trade Agreement 1996; hon memb American Soc of Int Law; govr Westminster Sch, pres Eastern Regn UN Assoc; *Clubs* Garrick; *Style*— Prof Elihu Lauterpacht, CBE, QC; ✉ Res Centre for Int Law, 5 Cranmer Rd, Cambridge CB3 9BL (☎ 01223 335358, fax 01223 300406)

LAVELLE, John Bryan; s of Alexander Joseph Lavelle (d 1970), of Shrewsbury, and Suzanne Mai, *née* Townley (d 1996); *b* 11 June 1937; *Educ* Shrewsbury Sch, Imede Business Sch; *m* 11 Oct 1969, Anna Georgina, da of Walter Harold Bamfield; 2 da (Joanna Katherine b 9 July 1971, Polly Susanna b 30 July 1983), 1 s (William Timothy John b 19 Dec 1973); *Career* Nat Serv 1956–58; prodn mangr J Lyons & Co 1961–67 (trainee mangr 1958–61), dir Findus Ltd 1974–83 (mktg mangr 1967–73), exec dir The Institute of Public Relations 1984–; fell Communication Advtg and Mktg Educn Fndn (CAM); *Recreations* tennis, golf, bridge, horse racing; *Clubs* Hurlingham; *Style*— John Lavelle, Esq; ✉ Grove Crescent, 181 Camberwell Grove, London SE5 8JS (☎ 0171 274

1400); The Institute of Public Relations, The Old Trading House, 15 Northburgh Street, London EC1V 0PR (☎ 0171 253 5151, fax 0171 490 0588)

LAVELLE, Richard John; s of Alexander Joseph Lavelle (d 1970), of Shrewsbury, and Suzanne Mai, *née* Townley (d 1996); *b* 25 Feb 1936; *Educ* Shrewsbury, St Mary's Hosp Med Sch London (scholar, MB BS, MRCS, LRCP); *m* 22 July 1961, Anne Christine, da of late Tom Sims, of Sonning, Berks; 3 s (Jonathan Richard b 5 May 1962, Edward Charles b 5 Aug 1964, Alexander James b 8 May 1971), 1 da (Emma Charlotte b 16 April 1973); *Career* formerly house surgn Royal Nat Throat Nose and Ear Hosp London, sr registrar St Mary's Hosp London (casualty offr 1964) and Royal Marsden Hosp London 1969–71, conslt ENT surgn London Chest Hosp 1973–78, currently conslt i/c ENT Dept and clinical dir in surgical specialities Bart's London and ENT surgn King Edward VII Hosp for Offrs; memb Ct of Examiners RCS, past pres Chelsea Clinical Soc; author of numerous articles on diseases of the ears, nose and throat; FRCS 1967, FRSM; *Clubs* Berkshire Golf (Ascot, capt 1973, pres 1994–), Royal & Ancient Golf (St Andrews), Swinley Forest Golf, Ascot Race, Royal Windsor Race; *Style*— Richard Lavelle, Esq; ✉ Kingsmead, Hatchet Lane, Windsor Forest, Berks SL4 4RJ (☎ 01344 882669); 86 Harley St, London W1N 1AE (☎ 0171 580 3625)

LAVELLE, Roger Garnett; CBE (1987); s of Dr Henry Allman Lavelle (d 1955), and Dr Evelyn Alice Garnett (d 1986); *b* 23 Aug 1932; *Educ* Leighton Park Reading, Trinity Hall Cambridge (BA, LLB); *m* 7 Dec 1956, Gunilla Elsa, da of Prof Hugo Odeberg (d 1973); 3 s (Barnaby b 22 March 1962, Richard b 10 March 1967, Edward b 4 May 1972); 1 da (Katharine b 18 July 1959); *Career* special asst (Common Market) Lord Privy Seal 1961–63, private sec to Chllr of Exchequer 1965–68; HM Treasy: under sec 1975, dep sec 1985–87; head Euro Secretariat Cabinet Office 1987–89, vice pres Euro Investment Bank 1989–93, dir European Bank for Reconstruction and Development 1993–; *Recreations* music, gardening; *Style*— Roger Lavelle, Esq, CBE; ✉ European Bank for Reconstruction and Development, 1 Exchange Square, London EC2A 2EH

LAVENDER, Rt Rev Mgr Gerard; s of Joseph Edward Lavender, and Mary, *née* Sullivan; *b* 20 Sept 1943; *Educ* Ushaw Coll Durham; *Career* ordained 1969, asst priest St Mary's Newcastle upon Tyne 1969–75; chaplain: HMS Heron RNAS 1975–77, RM 1977–79, sea going 1979–80 and 1987–89, RN Hosp Portsmouth 1980–81, exchange with USN San Diego Calif 1981–83, HMS Cochrane Rosyth 1983–85, HMS Nelson Portsmouth 1985–87, HMS Drake Plymouth 1989–90; princ RC chaplain (Navy) 1990–93, ret; parish priest Holy Family Darlington Dio of Hexham & Newcastle 1993–; involved with int military and handicapped children's RN pilgrimages to Lourdes until 1993; *Recreations* golf, tennis, walking; *Style*— The Rt Rev Mgr Gerard Lavender; ✉ Holy Family Presbytery, 60 Cockerton Green, Darlington, Co Durham DL3 9EU (☎ 01325 464848)

LAVENDER, (Christopher) Justin; s of late Alexander Desmond Lavender, of Christchurch, Dorset, and Hilary May, *née* Coleman; *b* 4 June 1951; *Educ* Bedford Modern Sch, QMC London, Guildhall Sch of Music and Drama; *m* 1; 1 s (William b 4 May 1982), 1 da (Catherine b 21 Jan 1984); m 2, Louise, da of Derek William Crane; *Career* tenor; has performed with all major Br orchs; regular contrib The Examiner, The Singer and Opera Now jls; *Performances* professional debut as Nadir in The Pearl Fishers (Sydney Opera House) 1980; other operatic roles incl: Male Chorus in Rape of Lucretia and Belmonte in Die Entführung aus dem Serail (Palermo 1983, regularly Vienna and Berlin State Opera 1992–), cr leading tenor role of Lorenzi in Arrigo's Il Ritorno di Casonova (Geneva 1984, Paris 1985), Don Ottavio in Don Giovanni (Rome 1985, Prague 1990, Venice 1996), cr role of Montezuma in Prodromidès' La Noche Triste (Nancy and Paris) 1989, Arnold in Rossini's Guillaume Tell (Royal Opera House Covent Garden) 1990, Almaviva in The Barber of Seville (Covent Garden) 1990, Tamino in Die Zauberflöte (Vienna State Opera) 1990, title role in Le Comte Ory (La Scala Milan debut) 1991, Fernand in Donizetti's La Favorite (Vichy and Paris 1991, The Hague 1992, Tours 1994), Néocles in Rossini's Siege of Corinth (Madrid 1992 and Corinth 1993), Demodokos in Dallapiccola's Ulisse (Salzburg Festival debut) 1993, Edgardo in Donizetti's Lucia (Auckland) 1996; concert performances incl: Schubert's Mass in E flat with Giulini and Berlin Philharmonic 1988, Bartok's Cantata Profana (with Solti and London Philharmonic) 1989, Rossini's Stabat Mater (with Accardo and the Academia di Santa Cecilia Rome) 1990, Schnittke's Faust Cantata (with Vienna Symphony) 1991, Gerontius (with Philharmonia) 1996; *Recordings* incl: videos of Oedipus Rex 1983 and Mitridate 1993, audio of La Noche Triste 1989, La Favorite 1991, Messiah 1993, I Puritani 1993, The Wreckers 1994, Rossini and Donizetti arias 1994, Britten Song Cycles 1996, Bomtempo Mattutina dei Morti 1996; *Recreations* horse riding, railway modelling; *Style*— Justin Lavender, Esq; ✉ 29 Newlands Avenue, Thames Ditton, Surrey KT7 0HD; c/o Athole Still International Management, Forresters Hall, 25–27 Westow Street, London SE19 3RY (☎ 0181 771 5271, fax 0181 771 8172)

LAVER, Prof John David Michael Henry; s of Harry Frank Laver (d 1985), and Mary, *née* Brearley (d 1994); *b* 20 Jan 1938; *Educ* Churcher's Coll, Univ of Edinburgh (MA, DipPhon, PhD, DLitt); *m* 1, 29 July 1962 (m dis 1974), Avril Morna Anel Macqueen, *née* Gibson; 2 s (Nicholas b 1963, Michael b 1965), 1 da (Claire b 1968); m 2, 1 Aug 1974, Sandra, da of Alexander Traill, of Bonnyrigg, Midlothian; 1 s (Matthew b 1972); *Career* lectr in phonetics Univ of Ibadan 1964–66 (asst lectr 1963–64); Univ of Edinburgh: lectr in phonetics 1966–76, sr lectr 1976–80, reader 1980–85, personal chair in phonetics 1985–, chm Centre for Speech Technol Res 1989–94 (dir 1984–89), res prof in the Faculty of Arts 1994–, vice-princ 1994–97; pres Int Phonetic Assoc 1991–95 (memb Cncl), memb Bd Euro Speech Communication Assoc 1988–93, chm Humanities Res Bd of the British Acad 1994–98, vice pres Royal Soc of Edinburgh 1996–99; FIOA 1988, FBA 1990, memb NY Acad of Sciences 1992, FRSE 1994, FRSA 1995; *Books* The Phonetic Description of Voice Quality (1980), The Gift of Speech (1991), Principles of Phonetics (1994); *Recreations* travel; *Clubs* Athenaeum; *Style*— Prof John Laver, FBA, FRSE; ✉ Humanities Research Board, Playfair Library, University of Edinburgh, Old College, South Bridge, Edinburgh EH8 9YL (☎ 0131 650 8238/2088, fax 0131 650 2088, telex UNIVEDG 727 442)

LAVERICK, Peter Michael; s of Lt Peter Laverick, and Joyce Margaret Carpenter; *b* 7 June 1942; *Educ* Canford Sch, Sch of Law; *m* 25 Feb 1972, Elaine Ruth, da of Leopold Steckler; 2 da (Helen Tanya b 1973, Elise Mary b 1975); *Career* Capt GS (attached Coldstream Guards) 1968–71; slr 1966, Notary Public 1985, sr ptnr Bennett Griffin & Partners Worthing, pres Worthing Law Soc 1995; *Recreations* playing the tuba, sailing and skiing, rowing, punting and skiffing; *Clubs* Leander, Thames Rowing, Royal Ocean Racing, Thames Punting, Kingston Boat, Thames Valley Skiff; *Style*— Peter M Laverick, Esq; ✉ North Barn, Poling, W Sussex (☎ 01903 883205); Bennett Griffin & Partners, 23 Warwick Street, Worthing, W Sussex (☎ 01903 210781, fax 01903 237625)

LAVIN, Deborah Margaret; da of George E Lavin (d 1987), of Johannesburg, SA, and Laura Kathleen Lavin (d 1987); *b* 22 Sept 1939; *Educ* Roedean Sch Johannesburg SA, Rhodes Univ Grahamstown SA, Lady Margaret Hall Oxford (BA, DipEd, MA); *Career* lectr Dept of History Univ of Witwatersrand SA 1962–64, lectr then sr lectr Dept of History Queen's Univ Belfast 1965–80; Univ of Durham: princ Trevelyan Coll 1980–95, dep dean of colleges 1990–93, pres Howlands Trust Univ of Durham 1993–, princ-elect the new coll 1995–, co-dir Research Inst for Study of Change 1995–; FRSA 1996; *Clubs* Reform; *Style*— Miss Deborah Lavin; ✉ Hickmans Cottages, Cat St, East Hendred, Wantage, Oxon OX12 8JT; Howlands Trust, University of Durham, Old Shire Hall, Durham DH1 3HP (☎ 0191 374 4690, fax 0191 374 2928)

LAVIN, John Jeffrey; s of Cynthia, *née* Gledhill; *b* 11 Sept 1953; *Educ* Scarborough HS for Boys, Tal Handaq Services Sch Malta, King Richard's Services Sch Cyprus; *m* 20 March 1982, Janet Audrey, da of late William George Connor; *Career* Dept of Energy: joined as exec offr 1973, various policy posts until 1983, private sec to Under Sec of State for Energy 1983–85, head trg and devpt 1985–88, head indust section Energy Efficiency Office 1988–89; dir of operations Royal Botanic Gardens Kew 1991– (head of admin 1989–91); bd dir: RBG Enterprises 1993–, Assoc of Leading Visitor Attractions (ALVA) 1992–, Chelsea Physic Garden Trading Co 1995–; *Recreations* golf, tennis, squash, football, gardening, cycling, eating out, writing poetry; *Style*— John Lavin, Esq; ✉ Royal Botanic Gardens, 47 Kew Green, Kew, Richmond, Surrey TW9 3AB (☎ 0181 332 5113, fax 0181 948 4237)

LAVINGTON, Prof Simon Hugh; s of Edgar Lavington (d 1982), of Wembley Park, London, and Jane, *née* Nicklen; *b* 1 Dec 1939; *Educ* Haileybury & ISC, Univ of Manchester (MSc, PhD); *m* 6 Aug 1966, Rosalind Margaret, da of Rev George Charles William Twyman, ISO (d 1991), of Herstmonceux, Sussex; 2 s (Damian b 25 Aug 1968, Dominic b 9 April 1970), 2 da (Hannah b 7 Sept 1971, Tamsin b 19 May 1973); *Career* sr lectr Univ of Manchester 1974–86 (lectr 1965–74); prof: Univ of Ife Nigeria 1976–77, Univ of Essex 1986–; memb: various BCS and IEE ctees, EPSRC AIKMS, HEFC JISC/TAP; UN tech expert 1975; CEng, FBCS 1978, FIEE 1985, FRSA 1988; *Books* Logical Design of Computers (1969), History of Manchester Computers (1975), Processor Architecture (1976), Early British Computers (1980), Information Processing 80 (1980), Emerging Trends in Database and Knowledge - Base Machines (1995); *Recreations* sailing, walking; *Clubs* Thames Barge Sailing; *Style*— Prof Simon Lavington; ✉ Lemon Tree Cottage, High Street, Sproughton, Suffolk IP8 3AH (☎ 01473 748478); Department of Computer Science, University of Essex, Colchester CO4 3SQ (☎ 01206 872677, fax 01206 872788, telex 98440 unilib g)

LAW, Andrew Jonathan Parker (Andy); s of Peter Leslie Law, and Audrey Iris, *née* Potter; *b* 25 May 1956; *Educ* Portsmouth GS, Univ of Bristol (BA Jt Hons Classics); *m* 12 April 1986, Amanda Mary, da of Ronald Ernest Southey; 1 s (Thomas Andrew Peter (Tom) b 27 Dec 1988), 1 da (Olivia Rosie Jean b 31 Jan 1993); *Career* account supervisor Wasey Campbell-Ewald advtg 1980 (trainee 1978, asst account exec 1979), account dir Foote Cone & Belding 1981–83 (account supervisor 1980), account dir Collett Dickenson Pearce & Partners 1983–90 (London bd dir 1985, int bd dir 1988); Chiat/Day: business devpt dir 1990–92, client servs dir 1992–93, md London 1993–95, managing ptnr Chiat/Day Inc 1994–95; chm St Luke's Holdings Ltd (after MBO of Chiat/Day London) 1995–; *Recreations* family, reading and translating the classics; *Clubs* RAC; *Style*— Andy Law, Esq; ✉ Robinswood, Park Road, Haslemere, Surrey GU27 2NL; St Luke's Holdings Ltd, 22 Duke's Road, London WC1H 9AB (☎ 0171 380 8888, fax 0171 380 8899)

LAW, Anthony John; s of Victor Frank Law (d 1992), of London, and Hilda Ellen, *née* Whitaker (d 1996); *b* 19 April 1940; *Educ* Christ's Coll Blackheath; *m* 18 July 1970, Pamela Ann, da of late Nelson Stuart Middleton; 2 da (Alexandra Michelle Jane b 7 Feb 1978, Nicola Anne-Marie b 28 May 1980); *Career* publisher Apollo Magazine, The International Magazine of Art and Antiques; memb Inst of Journalists; *Clubs* Rugby; *Style*— Anthony Law, Esq; ✉ 10 Strathmore Close, Caterham, Surrey CR3 5EQ (☎ 01883 348082); Apollo Magazine Ltd, 1 Castle Lane, London SW1E 6DR (☎ 0171 233 8906, fax 0171 233 7159)

LAW, Hon Cecil Towry Henry; s of 7 Baron Ellenborough, MC (d 1945); *b* 17 Oct 1931; *Educ* Eton; *m* 22 Feb 1957, (Daphne Mary) Jean, da of Hon Laurence Paul Methuen (d 1970); 1 s, 3 da; *Career* Lt 1 King's Dragoon Gds 1950–52; Lloyd's insur broker 1952; chm Towry Law plc 1958– (and all assoc cos in Towry Law Group); Liveryman Worshipful Co of Gardeners; *Style*— The Hon Cecil Law; ✉ 6 Sussex Square, London W2 2SJ; Towry Law plc, Towry Law House, High St, Windsor, Berks SL4 1LX

LAW, Charles Ewan; s of Robert Charles Ewan Law, DSO, DFC (ret Gp Capt), of Constantine Bay, Cornwall, and Norah, *née* Eaden; *b* 12 Aug 1946; *Educ* Wrekin Coll, Univ of Nottingham (BSc), Manchester Business Sch (MBA); *m* 5 Sept 1970, Clodagh Susan Margaret, da of Col Eric Steele-Baume, CBE (d 1968); 2 s (Huw b 1974, Henry b 1980), 1 da (Angharad b 1972); *Career* metallurgist British Steel Corp 1969–71, mangr United International Bank 1973–79, vice pres Merrill Lynch International Bank 1979–81, exec dir First Interstate Ltd 1984–87, non-exec dir Continental Illinois Ltd 1987–94 (exec dir 1981–84), md Continental Bank 1988–94, md Bank of America NT & SA 1994–; FRSA; *Recreations* sailing, theatre; *Style*— Charles Law, Esq; ✉ Bank of America NT & SA, 1 Alie Street, London E1 8DE (☎ 0171 634 4368, fax 0171 634 4690)

LAW, Adm Sir Horace Rochfort; GCB (1972, KCB 1967, CB 1963), OBE (1951), DSC (1941); s of Dr Samuel Horace Law, MD (d 1940), of Dublin, and Sybil Mary, *née* Clay; *b* 23 June 1911; *Educ* Sherborne; *m* 13 Dec 1941, Heather Valerie (d 1996), da of Rev Henry Haworth Coryton (d 1956); 2 s (Robert b 1946, Edward b 1952), 2 da (Philippa b 1942, Deborah b 1948); *Career* joined RN 1929; CO: HMS Duchess 1952, HMS Centaur 1958; Capt Britannia RNC Dartmouth 1960; Rear Adm, Flag Offr Sea Trg 1962, Submarines 1963; Vice Adm Controller of the Navy 1965–70; Adm, C-in-C Naval Home Cmd and First and Princ Naval ADC to HM The Queen 1970–72; ret 1972; chm Hawthorn Leslie 1973–81; pres RINA 1979–81; chm Church Army Bd 1979–86; pres offr Christian Union 1970–86; chm Agnes Weston's Royal Sailors Rest 1958–85; Liveryman Worshipful Co of Coachmakers & Coach Harness Makers; Order of William of Orange 1 Class (Netherlands) 1972; *Style*— Adm Sir Horace Law, GCB, OBE, DSC; ✉ Cowpers, West Harting, Petersfield, Hants GU31 5NT (☎ 01730 825511)

LAW, James; QC (Scotland 1970); s of George Law (d 1961), and Isabella Rebecca, *née* Lamb (d 1985); *b* 7 June 1926; *Educ* Kilmarnock Acad, Girvan HS, Univ of Glasgow (MA, LLB); *m* 1956, Kathleen Margaret, da of Alexander Gibson (d 1984); 2 s (George, Bruce), 1 da (Catriona); *Career* called to the Scottish Bar 1950, advocate depute 1957–64, memb Criminal Injuries Compensation Bd 1970–96, temp sheriff 1971–96; chm Temp Sheriffs' Assoc 1975–93; *Clubs* New (Edinburgh), Caledonian (Edinburgh); *Style*— James Law, Esq, QC; ✉ 9/3 Silvermills, Edinburgh EH3 5BF (☎ 0131 558 9376)

LAW, Richard Alastair; *b* 29 April 1953; *Educ* Rendcomb Coll, Exeter Coll Oxford (MA); *m* Monique Ratcliffe; *Career* CA; ptnr Ernst & Young; FCA, ATII; *Recreations* National Hunt racing; *Style*— Richard A Law, Esq; ✉ Ernst & Young, Becket House, 1 Lambeth Palace Road, London SE1 7EU (☎ 0171 928 2000, fax 0171 928 1345)

LAW, Richard Arthur; *b* 1943; *Educ* RAC Cirencester; *m*; 2 c; *Career* chief exec Bruton Knowles Chartered Surveyors Gloucester and branches 1986–, chm Gloucester Market Auctioneers Ltd; memb Lord Chllr's Panel of Arbitrators; Royal Inst of Chartered Surveyors: memb Rural Practice Divnl Cncl 1983–91 (divnl pres 1989–90), memb Gen Cncl 1987–92, memb Agric Land Mgmnt Ctee (chm 1983–86), memb Practice Ctee (chm 1986–87) former memb Educn and Membership Ctees, former memb Pres's Advsy Gp on Arbitrations, memb Avon, Glos, Somerset and N Wilts Branch Ctee (chm 1979), memb Agric Hldgs Policy and other working parties; chm Cncl and Fin Ctee Three Counties Agric Show Soc (vice pres Glos 1993), memb Panel of Agricultural Mortgage Corporation PLC Valuers, sr receiver Crown Estate Cmmrs Wales & W of Severn Estates and Taunton Dunster and N Wyke Estates, vice chm Bd of Govrs Royal Agric Coll (and chm Fin and Gen Purposes Ctee) 1992–; FRICS 1976; *Recreations* travel, rural pursuits, farming, the countryside, sailing, good food, wine; *Clubs* Oriental; *Style*— Richard Law, Esq; ✉ Albion Chambers, 111 Eastgate Street, Gloucester GL1 1PZ (☎ 01452 521267, fax 01452 300184)

LAW, Richard William Evan; MBE (1996); s of George Edward Law (d 1974), of Court-up-Hill, Maplehurst, Sussex, and Margaret Dorothy, *née* Evans, OBE (d 1980); *b* 17 May 1926; *Educ* Westminster, ChCh Oxford (BA, MA); *m* 11 Feb 1955, Joy Patricia, da of Dr Jean-Jacques Spira (d 1972), of London; 1 s (Nicholas b 1957), 2 da (Jennifer b 1957, Katie b 1959); *Career* mgmnt trainee Seligman Brothers 1951–53, Gillett Bros Discount Co 1953–83 (md 1968), chm Int CD Market Assoc 1972–73, dir Kirkland Whittaker Ltd 1974–81, chm Kirkland Whittaker (Italia) Spa Milan 1974–78, cmmr Public Works Loans Bd 1977–89, London advsr to Banca Commerciale Italiana Milan 1983–86, dept chm BCI Ltd 1983–86, chm Euromed Group of Cos 1986–; numerous pubns in jls; annual lectr on banking and money markets to Br Cncl 1968–84, chm Council for Music in Hospitals 1982–96, govr Br Inst of Florence 1984–, memb Cncl of St John's Smith Square 1983–94; *Books* Banking (as Evan Hughes, 1974); *Recreations* music, travel, cooking; *Clubs* Brooks's, Garrick; *Style—* Richard Law, Esq, MBE; ✉ Euromed Investments PLC, 7 Bury Place, London WC1A 2LA (☎ 0171 831 7430, fax 0171 430 1637)

LAW, Hon Rupert Edward Henry; s and h of 8 Baron Ellenborough, *qv*; *b* 28 March 1955; *Educ* Eton; *m* 1981, Hon Grania Janet Grey Boardman, only da of Baron Boardman (Life Peer); 2 s (James Rupert Thomas b 8 March 1983, Frederick George Towry Gray b 9 Sept 1990), 1 da (Georgina Poppy b 16 Dec 1984); *Career* Coldstream Gds until 1988, Maj; Coutts and Co 1988–; *Style—* The Hon Rupert Law; ✉ Bridge House, Clipston, Market Harborough, Leicestershire LE16 9RX

LAWDEN, James Anthony Henry; s of Maj Henry Tipping Lawden, MC (d 1981), of Roehampton, and Claire Phyllis, *née* Berthoud (d 1962); *b* 10 Aug 1955; *Educ* Winchester, New Coll Oxford (MA); *Career* admitted slr 1981; Freshfields: joined 1979, seconded with Aoki, Christensen & Nomoto Tokyo 1984–95, ptnr 1988, resident ptnr Tokyo Office 1992–95, currently resident ptnr Bangkok Office; memb Law Soc; *Recreations* tennis, golf, squash, travelling; *Clubs* Naval and Military, Roehampton, Tokyo American, Bangkok British; *Style—* James Lawden, Esq; ✉ Freshfields, Whitefriars, 65 Fleet Street, London EC4Y 1HS (☎ 0171 936 4000, fax 0171 832 7001, telex 889292)

LAWLER, Geoffrey John; s of Maj Ernest Lawler, and Enid Florence Lawler, of Richmond, N Yorks; *b* 30 Oct 1954; *Educ* Colchester Royal GS, Richmond Sch, Univ of Hull (BSc); *m* 1989, Christine Roth, da of C Roth, of Wyoming, USA; *Career* Cons Res Dept 1980–82, PR exec 1982–83, md The Public Affairs Company 1987–, dir Democracy International Limited 1995–, vice pres International Access Inc 1987–; FCO observer Russian elections 1993, 1995 and 1996, UN observer S African elections 1994; MP (C) Bradford North 1983–87; vice pres Bradford N Cons Assoc 1987–; pres: Univ of Hull Students' Union 1976–77, Br Youth Cncl 1984–87, W Yorks Youth Assoc 1995– (vice pres 1986–95); memb cncl UKIAS 1987–93; Freeman City of London; *Recreations* cricket, travel; *Style—* Geoffrey Lawler, Esq; ✉ The Public Affairs Company, Matthew Murray House, 97 Water Lane, Leeds LS11 5QN (☎ 0113 245 5139, fax 0113 242 9477, e-mail 106072.1221@compuserve.com)

LAWLER, Ivan; s of Roland James Lawler, and Diana Mary, *née* Rabjohns; *b* 19 Nov 1966; *Educ* Hampton Sch; *Career* canoeist; Nat Marathon champion 1986, 1987, 1988 and 1992; memb Br Olympic team 1988, 1992 and 1996; World Cup Marathon winner: with Graham Burns 1989 and 1991, individual 1993, with Steve Harris 1995; World Marathon Championships: second with Graham Burns 1988 and 1990, winner individual 1992, winner with Steve Harris 1994 and 1996; World Sprint Championships: winner with Grayson Bourne 10,000m pairs 1990 (second 1989); winner UNESCO Pierre de Coubertin Fair Play Award; holder of 5 nat sprint titles 1996, ranked no 1 nationally in marathon and sprint; *Style—* Ivan Lawler, Esq

LAWLEY, Susan (Sue); da of Thomas Clifford Lawley (d 1972), and Margaret Jane Lawley; *b* 14 July 1946; *Educ* Dudley Girls' HS, Univ of Bristol (BA); *m* 1, David Arnold Ashby; 1 s (Thomas David Harvey b 1976), 1 da (Harriet Jane b 1980); m 2, Roger Hugh Williams; *Career* trainee reporter and sub ed Western Mail and South Wales Echo 1967–70, BBC Plymouth 1970–72 (freelance reporter, sub ed, TV presenter); TV presenter BBC: Nationwide 1972–75 and 1977–81, Tonight 1976, Budget and gen election progs Nine O'Clock News 1981–82, Six O'Clock News 1982–86, chat shows and other special series incl News '45, Hospital Watch and most recently Here and Now; presenter Desert Island Discs BBC Radio Four 1988–; govr Nat Film & TV Sch 1990–95; Hon LLD: Univ of Bristol 1989, Univ of Wolverhampton 1995; Hon MA Univ of Birmingham 1989; *Recreations* family life, eating, biographies, guarding my own privacy; *Style—* Ms Sue Lawley; ✉ c/o Noel Gay TV Ltd, 1 Albion Court, Albion Place, Galena Road, London W6 0QT (☎ 0181 600 5200)

LAWLOR, Prof John James; s of Albert John Lawlor (d 1938), and Teresa Anne Clare, *née* Knight (d 1954); *b* 5 Jan 1918; *Educ* Ryders Sch, Magdalen Coll Oxford (BA, MA, DLitt); *m* 1, 26 April 1941 (m dis 1979), Thelma Joan, da of Charles Edward Parkes Weeks (d 1964); 1 s (John b 1954), 3 da (Teresa Anne (Mrs Rigby) b 1945, Judith Mary (Mrs Griffiths) b 1947, Penelope Jane (Mrs Jeffrey) b 1949); m 2, 7 Nov 1984, Prof Kimie Imura, *née* Fukuda; *Career* WWII Devonshire Regt 1940–45, cmmnd 1941, Capt 1942–45; asst chief instr Artists' Rifles OCTU 1943–44, serv in Italy with Royal West Kent and Hampshire Regts 1944–45, mil govt Austria 1945; lectr in English BNC and Trinity Coll Oxford 1947–50, univ lectr in English lit 1949–50, prof of English language and lit Univ of Keele 1950–80; fell Folger Shakespeare Library Washington DC 1962, Ziskind visiting prof Brandeis Univ USA 1966, visiting prof Univ of Hawaii 1972; sec gen and treas Int Assoc of Univ Profs of English 1971–95; pres N Staffs Drama Assoc 1955–72, jt sec Advsy Ctee for Adult Educn N Staffs 1957–60; FSA 1966; *Books incl* The Tragic Sense in Shakespeare (1960), Piers Plowman: An Essay in Criticism (1962), Patterns of Love and Courtesy (1966), To Nevill Coghill From Friends (with W H Auden, 1966); *Recreations* any sort of seafaring; *Clubs* Athenaeum; *Style—* Prof John Lawlor, FSA; ✉ Penwithian, Higher Fore St, Marazion, Cornwall TR17 0BQ (☎ 01736 711180); 2–45–13 Misawa, Hinoshi, Tokyo 191 (☎ 00 81 425 944177)

LAWRENCE, Christopher Nigel; s of Rev William Wallace Lawrence (d 1979), and Millicent, *née* Atkinson (d 1983); *b* 23 Dec 1936; *Educ* Westborough HS Westcliff on Sea, Central Sch of Arts and Crafts London (NDD); *m* 1958, Valerie Betty; 2 s (Adrian, Robin), 2 da (Fay, Verity); *Career* goldsmith, silversmith and industl designer 1968–; solo exhbns incl: Galerie Jean Renet London 1970–71, Hamburg 1972, Goldsmiths' Hall 1973, Ghent 1975, Hasselt 1977; maj cmmns: Br & Foreign Govts, Royalty, City Livery cos, banks, mfrg cos; judge and external assessor for art colls, specialist in symbolic presentation pieces and limited edns of decorative pieces, industl designer to leading mfrs of cutlery and hollow ware; TV and radio bdcaster; chm Goldsmiths' Craft Cncl 1976–77; Jacques Cartier Meml Award for Craftsman of the Year 1960, 1963 and 1967 (unique achievement); Liveryman Worshipful Co of Goldsmiths 1978–; FTC, FIPG; *Recreations* badminton, tennis, bowls, carpentry, painting; *Style—* Christopher Lawrence, Esq; ✉ 20 St Vincent's Rd, Westcliff-on-Sea, Essex SS0 7PR (☎ 01702 338443, studio ☎ 01702 344897, fax 01702 436187)

LAWRENCE, Dr Clifford Maitland; s of Ronald Douglas Lawrence, and Irene Rose Emma, *née* Abell; *b* 29 Nov 1950; *Educ* East Ham GS, Univ of Sheffield Med Sch (MB ChB, MD); *m* 2 April 1977, (Patricia) Anne; 3 s (Thomas b 12 Sept 1981, Christopher b 22 June 1986, James b 29 Jan 1991), 1 da (Joanna b 23 Feb 1984); *Career* dermatologist N Staffs Hosp Centre and Royal Victoria Infirmary Newcastle; chm British Soc for Dermatological Surgery; author of papers on: skin surgery, psoriasis, dithranol inflammation; FRCP 1993 (MRCP 1978), MD 1988; *Books* Physical Signs in Dermatology - A Color Atlas and Text (with N H Cox, 1993), Diagnostic Picture Tests in Dermatology (with N H Cox, 1995), An Introduction to Dermetological Surgery (1996); *Recreations* gardening; *Style—* Dr Clifford Lawrence; ✉ Department of Dermatology, Royal Victoria Infirmary, Newcastle NE1 4LP (☎ 0191 227 5088)

LAWRENCE, Clive Wyndham; s of Lt-Col Sir (Percy) Roland Bradford Lawrence, MC, and hp to Btcy of bro, Sir David Roland Walter Lawrence; *b* 6 Oct 1939; *Educ* Gordonstoun; *m* 1966, Sophia Annabel Stuart, da of Ian Hervey Stuart Black, of Bridge of Earn, Perthshire; 3 s (James Wyndham Stuart b 1970, Simon Roland Stuart b 1973, Hugo Hervey Stuart b 1975); *Career* late Lt Coldstream Gds; *Style—* Clive Lawrence, Esq; ✉ Woodside, Frant, nr Tunbridge Wells, Kent TN3 9HW

LAWRENCE, 5 Baron (UK 1869); Sir David John Downer Lawrence; 5 Bt (UK 1858); s of 4 Baron Lawrence (d 1968) by his 1 w, Margaret Jean, *née* Downer (d 1977); *b* 4 Sept 1937; *Educ* Bradfield; *Style—* The Rt Hon the Lord Lawrence; ✉ c/o Bird & Bird, 2 Gray's Inn Sq, London WC1

LAWRENCE, Sir David Roland Walter; 3 Bt (UK 1906), of Sloane Gardens, Chelsea; s of Lt-Col Sir (Percy) Roland Bradford Lawrence, 2 Bt, MC (d 1950); *b* 8 May 1929; *Educ* Radley, RMC; *m* 1955, Audrey, da of Brig Desmond Young, CIE, OBE, MC, and formerly w of 11 Duke of Leeds; *Heir* bro, Clive Wyndham Lawrence b 6 Oct 1939; *Career* late Capt Coldstream Gds; *Style—* Sir David Lawrence, Bt; ✉ 28 High Town Rd, Maidenhead, Berks SL6 1PB

LAWRENCE, Edward George; s of Capt Edward Sear Lawrence (d 1964), of Southgate, London, and Ethel May, *née* Lambert; *b* 26 Feb 1927; *Educ* Edmonton Co GS; *Career* dir Lawrence Bros (Transport) Ltd 1949–77, ret; memb Heraldry Soc 1952–, life govr Royal Soc of St George 1953 (memb Exec Cncl for eight years), silver staff usher Jubilee HM Queen Elizabeth II 1977, wandsman St Paul's Cathedral London 1977–88, usher at wedding of TRH The Prince and Princess of Wales 1981; memb Ctee Middx Fedn of Old Grammarian Socs 1955–64, dep dir of ceremonies of Most Venerable Order of St John 1994– (asst dir 1980); CStJ 1979, KStJ 1989; Freeman City of London 1959; Liveryman: Worshipful Co of Carmen 1960, Worshipful Co of Scriveners 1983; AMInstTA 1947, FFCS 1954, FInstD 1955, FRSA 1963; *Recreations* heraldry, deipnosophism, ceremonial, official and academic dress; *Clubs* City Livery, Wig and Pen, IOD; *Style—* Edward Lawrence, Esq; ✉ 33 Woodmere Court, Avenue Road, Southgate, London N14 4BW

LAWRENCE, Eileen Ellen Mary; *b* 15 Aug 1946; *Educ* Edinburgh Coll of Art (DA Edin); *Career* artist; memb: Scottish Arts Cncl Award Panel 1980–82, Ctee Scottish Arts Cncl 1980–82, Ctee New 57 Gallery Edinburgh 1980–83; winner Scottish Arts Cncl Major Bursary; *Solo Exhibitions* 57 Gallery 1969, Richard Demarco Gallery Edinburgh 1975, New 57 Gallery 1976, Arnolfini Gallery Bristol 1978, Chapter Cardiff 1978, ICA London 1978, Fischer Fine Art London 1980 and 1985, Artsite Bath 1986, The Barn Lincolnshire 1987, Beaux Arts Bath 1988, Paintings 1977–92 Usher Gallery Lincoln and Lincoln Cathedral 1992, Fruitmarket Gallery Edinburgh 1992; *Group Exhibitions* incl: 20 x 57 Univ of Edinburgh 1970, Inscape 1976–77, Fruitmarket Gallery Edinburgh 1976–77, Warehouse Gallery 1976–77, London Ulster Museum Belfast 1976–77, Paris Biennale Musee d'Art Moderne Paris 1977, AIR Gallery London 1977, New Acquisitions (Tate Gallery) 1980, British Drawing 1982, Hayward Annual (Hayward Gallery) 1982, Overland Ikon Gallery Birmingham 1986, Athena Awards (Barbican London) 1987 (prizewinner) and 1988, Artists in National Parks (V & A) 1988, Scottish Art Since 1900 (Scottish Nat Gallery of Modern Art) 1989–90, The Journey (Usher Gallery, Lincoln Cathedral Bishop's Palace Lincoln) 1990, New North (Tate Liverpool) 1990–91; *Public Collections* Tate Gallery, Scottish Nat Gallery of Modern Art, Ulster Museum Belfast, Br Cncl, Arts Cncl of GB, DOE, Contemporary Arts Soc, Nat Gallery of Modern Art Canberra, Scottish Arts Cncl, European Parliament, Univ of Liverpool, Gulbenkian Fndn, Ferens Gallery Hull; *Style—* Ms Eileen Lawrence

LAWRENCE, Francine; *Educ* Twickenham Art Sch; *Career* won Thames TV Design bursary and travelled Caribbean, exhibition of photographs on return New English Library; subsequently: worked with several design gps, asst art dir Fontana and freelance work for Virago Books and Woman's Journal, art dir and assoc ed Living, ed Country Living 1989–95 (art dir 1985); freelance 1995–; Designer of The Year Award Periodical Pubns Assoc 1988, Marc Boxer Award for Art Editors 1989; chair Br Soc of Magazine Eds 1991; *Recreations* photography, cats, gardening, watercolour painting, The Archers; *Style—* Ms Francine Lawrence; ✉ 126 Mortimer Road, London NW10 5SN (☎ and fax 0181 968 7152)

LAWRENCE, Gordon Charles; s of Alfred Charles Lawrence, and Gertrude Emily, *née* Frost; *b* 2 March 1931; *Educ* Isleworth GS; *m* 17 July 1954, Barbara Mary Rees, da of Francis Charles Rees Deacon, MBE (d 1983); 2 s (Simon b 1957, Jonathan b 1963), 1 da (Catriona b 1959); *Career* financial consultant; dir: Schreiber Industs Ltd 1967–70, Helena Rubinstein Ltd 1970–74; National Trust: dir of fin 1977–88, memb Wessex Regnl Ctee 1988–; dir Heritage Educn Trust 1992–; FCA, FCMA, JDipMA; *Recreations* music, sailing; *Style—* Gordon Lawrence, Esq; ✉ Walnut Tree House, Bromham, Wilts (☎ 01380 850294)

LAWRENCE, Sir Guy Kempton; kt (1976), DSO (1943), OBE (1945), DFC (1941); s of Albert Edward Lawrence (d 1951); *b* 5 Nov 1914; *Educ* Marlborough; *m* 1947, Marcia Virginia, da of Prof Harold Clark Powell; 2 s, 1 da; *Career* memb Stock Exchange London 1937–45, chm Findus (UK) Ltd 1967–75; dep chm: Spillers French Holdings Ltd 1972–75, J Lyons & Co Ltd 1950–75; dir Eagle Aircraft Services Ltd 1977; chm Food and Drink Industs Cncl 1973–77, chm Eggs Authy 1978–81; *Recreations* Br ski team 1937–38, farming, squash, carpentry; *Clubs* RAF; *Style—* Sir Guy Lawrence, DSO, OBE, DFC; ✉ Courtlands, Kier Park, Ascot, Berks (☎ 01344 21074)

LAWRENCE, Prof (Clifford) Hugh; s of Ernest William Lawrence, (d 1956), of London, and Dorothy Estelle, *née* Mundy; *b* 28 Dec 1921; *Educ* Stationers' Co Sch, Lincoln Coll Oxford (BA, MA, D Phil); *m* 11 July 1953, Helen Maud, da of Felix Curran, of Dublin and Yorks; 1 s (Peter), 5 da (Clare, Margaret, Felicity, Katherine, Julia); *Career* 2 Lt RA 1943, Lt 1944, Capt Beds and Herts 1945, Maj 1945–46; Bedford Coll Univ of London: lectr in history 1951–62, reader in medieval history 1962–70, dean Faculty of Arts 1975–77, head Dept of History 1980–85; prof of medieval history Univ of London 1970–87, prof emeritus 1987; memb: Press Cncl 1976–80, Governing Body Westfield Coll 1982–86; vice chm of govrs Heythrop Coll 1988–91 (memb Governing Body 1980–91); FRHistS 1960, FSA 1985; *Books* St Edmund of Abingdon, a study in Hagiography and History (1960), The English Church and the Papacy in the Middle Ages (1965), Medieval Monasticism, Forms of Religious Life in Western Europe in the Middle Ages (1984, 2 edn 1989), The Friars: The Impact of the Mendicants on Medieval Society (1994), The University in Church and State (in History of University of Oxford vol 1, ed J Catto), The Life of St Edmund (trans with a biography, 1996); *Recreations* reading, painting, sightseeing; *Clubs* Reform; *Style—* Prof Hugh Lawrence, FSA; ✉ 11 Durham Road, London, SW20 0QH (☎ 0181 946 3820)

LAWRENCE, Sir Ivan John; kt (1992), QC (1981), MP (C) Burton (majority 5,996); s of Leslie Lawrence; *b* 24 Dec 1936; *Educ* Brighton Hove and Sussex GS, Ch Ch Oxford (MA); *m* 1966, Gloria Helene; 1 da; *Career* called to the Bar Inner Temple 1962, in practice S Eastern Circuit, recorder of the Crown Ct 1987, bencher Inner Temple 1990–; MP (C) Burton 1974–; memb Foreign Affrs Select Ctee 1983–92; chm Home Affrs Select Ctee 1992–; chm: Cons Parly Legal Ctee 1987–, All-Pty Jt Parly Barristers Gp 1987–, Cons Parly Home Affrs Ctee 1988–, Exec Ctee UK Branch Cwlth Parly Assoc 1994–;

vice chm Cons Friends of Israel 1994–; memb: Cncl of Justice 1989–95, Exec Ctee Soc of Cons Lawyers 1989–, Exec 1922 Ctee 1988–89 and 1992–; chm Burton Breweries Charitable Tst 1982–; *Recreations* piano, squash, travel; *Style*— Sir Ivan Lawrence, QC, MP; ✉ House of Commons, London SW1A 0AA

LAWRENCE, Jeffrey; s of Alfred Silver (d 1957), and Sylvia, *née* Fishgold; *b* 28 March 1946; *Educ* Carmel Coll, London Business Sch; *m* 8 April 1971, Vivienne Lesley, da of Clifford Arch (d 1987); 2 da (Faith b 1973, Sarah b 1975); *Career* Merrill Lynch: office mangr 1980–84, md corporate fin servs 1984–87, regnl mangr Scandinavia and Netherlands 1987–89, md Merrill Lynch Asset Management 1989–94; dir of sales and mktg American Express Bank Ltd 1994–96, md Lawrence Oliver Ltd (corp fin and asset mgmnt consltss) 1996–; *Recreations* golf, race horse owner; *Clubs* RAC; *Style*— Jeffrey Lawrence, Esq; ✉ Moor Lane House, Moor Lane, Sarratt, Rickmansworth, Herts WD3 6BU; Lawrence Oliver Ltd, Prince Frederick House, Mill Street, London W1

LAWRENCE, Jill; *b* 17 April 1947; *Educ* Loughborough Univ (BA); *m*; *Career* designer and consIt; industrial consIt for product design devpt and mktg to numerous int corporations; course consIt and external examiner at numerous univs and colls incl RCA; memb Steering Ctee YDI (Young Designers into Industry) 1985–89; FRSA 1982; *Style*— Ms Jill Lawrence; ✉ Jill Lawrence Design International, 236a Cricklewood Lane, London NW2 2PU (☎ 0181 452 5190, fax 0181 208 4558)

LAWRENCE, Air Vice-Marshal John Thornett; CB (1975), CBE (1967, OBE 1961), AFC (1945), AE; s of Tom Lewis Lawrence, JP (d 1970), and Beatrice Mary Sollars (d 1977); *b* 16 April 1920; *Educ* Crypt Sch Gloucester; *m* 2 June 1951, Hilary Jean, da of Lewis Davis Owen (d 1968); 3 s (Patrick b 1952, Christopher b 1955, Andrew b 1959), 1 da (Tessa b 1964); *Career* RAFVR 1938, WWII Coastal Cmd 235, 202 and 86 Sqdns, dir staff RAF Flying Coll 1949–53, Co No 14 Sqdn 1953–55, SO 2 ATAF Turkey 1956–58, OC Flying RRFU 1958–61, Gp Capt Ops AFME Aden 1962–64, Co RAF Wittering 1964–66, AOC No 3 Gp Bomber Cmd 1967, Student IDC 1968, dir Orgn and Admin Plans RAF 1969–71, dir Gen Personnel Mgmnt RAF 1971–73, Air Offr Scot and NI 1973–75, ret April 1975; Rolls Royce Ltd 1975–81; vice pres SSAFA Glos 1990–; Order of Leopold II Belgium 1945, Croix De Guerre Belgium 1945; *Recreations* golf, bridge; *Clubs* RAF; *Style*— Air Vice-Marshal John Lawrence, CB, CBE, AFC, AE

LAWRENCE, Sir John Waldemar; 6 Bt (UK 1858), of Lucknow, OBE (1945); s of Sir Alexander Waldemar Lawrence, 4 Bt (d 1939), and Anne Elizabeth Le Poer, *née* Wynne (d 1948); suc bro, Sir Henry Eustace Waldemar Lawrence, 5 Bt (d 1967); *b* 27 May 1907; *Educ* Eton, New Coll Oxford (MA); *m* 1, 1948, Mrs Jacynth Mary Donaldson-Hudson (d 1987), da of Rev Francis George Ellerton; m 2, 1988, Audrey Viola, widow of John Woodiwiss; *Heir* bro, George Alexander Waldemar Lawrence b 22 Sept 1910; *Career* with BBC 1940–42 (Euro intelligence offr and subsequently Euro services organiser), press attaché Moscow 1942–45, chm Centre for Study of Religion and Communism (now Keston Research) 1969–83, pres Keston Inst 1983–; chm GB-USSR Assoc 1970–85; ed Frontier 1958–75; offr of the Order of Orange Nassau; *Books* A History of Russia (1960, 7 edn 1993), Russians Observed (1969), The Journals of Honoria Lawrence (with Audrey Woodiwiss, 1980), The Hammer & The Cross (1986), Lawrence of Lucknow (1990); *Recreations* walking, arguing and reading in ten languages; *Clubs* Athenaeum, Sloane; *Style*— Sir John Lawrence, Bt, OBE; ✉ 59 Iffley Road, Oxford OX4 1EB (☎ 01865 723 812); 1 Naishe's Cottage, Northstoke, Bath BA1 9AT (☎ 0117 932 6076)

LAWRENCE, John Wilfred; s of Wilfred James Lawrence, and Audrey Constance, *née* Thomas; *b* 15 Sept 1933; *Educ* Salesian Coll Cowley Oxford, Hastings Sch of Art, The Central Sch of Art and Design; *m* 14 Dec 1957, Myra Gillian, da of Dr George Douglas Hutton Bell, CBE, FRS; 2 da (Emma b 26 July 1958, Kate b 6 Feb 1960); *Career* book illustrator; lectr in illustration: Brighton Poly 1960–68, Camberwell Sch of Art 1960–92; external assessor of illustration: Bristol Poly 1978–82, Brighton Poly 1982–85, Exeter Coll of Art 1986–89, Duncan of Jordanstone Coll of Art 1986–89, Kingston Poly 1990–93, Edinburgh Coll of Art 1991–94; work represented in: Ashmolean Museum, V & A, Nat Museum of Wales, collections abroad; memb Art Workers' Guild 1972 (Master 1990), RE 1987, Soc of Wood Engravers; *Books* The Giant of Grabbist (1968), Pope Leo's Elephant (1969), Rabbit and Pork Rhyming Talk (1975), Tongue Twisters (1976), George His Elephant and Castle (1983), Good Babies Bad Babies (1987); illustrator of more than 100 books; *Clubs* Double Crown; *Style*— John Lawrence, Esq; ✉ 6 Worts Causeway, Cambridge CB1 4RL (☎ 01223 247449)

LAWRENCE, Michael John; s of Geoffrey Frederick Lawrence, of London, and Kathleen, *née* Bridge (d 1981); *b* 25 Oct 1943; *Educ* Wembley County GS, Univ of Exeter (BSc), Univ of Bristol (PhD); *m* 1967, Maureen, da of Terence Henry Blennerhassett; 3 c; *Career* postgrad research in solid state physics Univ of Nottingham 1965–66, research fell Univ of Bristol 1966–69; Price Waterhouse: joined 1969, qualified CA 1972, ptnr 1978–88; gp fin dir Prudential Corporation plc 1988–93, chief exec London Stock Exchange 1994–Jan 1996; non-exec dir: Port of London Authy 1983–89, London Transport Bd 1994–; external memb Cncl Defence Research Agency 1990–, chm Hundred Gp of Fin Dirs 1992–93; memb Bow Gp 1970–74, cncllr London Borough of Hillingdon 1974–79 (chm Fin Ctee 1978–79); Freeman City of London 1974, memb Ct of Assts Worshipful Co of Tin Plate Workers; FCA; *Recreations* flying, sailing, bridge, tennis; *Style*— Michael Lawrence, Esq; ✉ c/o London Regional Transport, 55 Broadway, London SW1H 0BD (☎ 0171 222 5600, fax 0171 222 5719)

LAWRENCE, Sir (John) Patrick (Grosvenor); kt (1988), CBE (1983), DL (W Midlands 1993); s of Ernest Victor Lawrence, and Norah Grosvenor, *née* Hill; *b* 29 March 1928; *Educ* Denstone Coll Staffs; *m* 1954, Anne Patricia, da of Dr Charles Auld; 1 s (decd), 1 da; *Career* RNVR 1945–48; admitted slr 1954; sr ptnr Wragge & Co Birmingham 1982–93 (ptnr 1959–82); chm Nat Union of Cons and Unionist Assocs 1986–87 (vice pres 1986–), chm Br Shooting Sports Cncl 1996– (vice chm 1985–96), pres W Midlands Cons Cncl 1988–89, chm Birmingham Cathedral in Need Appeal 1990–92; memb Bromsgrove RDC 1967–74, chm W Midlands Rent Assessment Panels 1971–; memb Cncl: Denstone Coll 1989–, Aston Univ 1990–; chm Kidderminster Healthcare NHS Tst 1993–96; Hon DSc Aston Univ 1996; Freeman City of London; *Clubs* Carlton, Law Soc Yacht, Bean (Birmingham), Royal Overseas League; *Style*— Sir Patrick Lawrence, CBE, DL; ✉ c/o Wragge & Co, 55 Colmore Row, Birmingham B3 2AS

LAWRENCE, Dr Peter Anthony; s of Instr Lt Ivor Douglas Lawrence (d 1990), of Swanage, Dorset, and Joy Frances, *née* Liebert; *b* 23 June 1941; *Educ* Wennington Sch Wetherby Yorks, Univ of Cambridge (MA, PhD); *m* 9 July 1971, (Ruth) Birgitta, da of Prof Ake Haraldson (d 1985), of Uppsala, Sweden; *Career* Cwlth (Harkness) fell 1965–67, Genetics Dept Univ of Cambridge 1967–69, MRC Lab of Molecular Biology Cambridge 1969–; parish cnllr; FRS 1983; *Books* Insect Development (ed, 1976), The Making of a Fly (1992); *Recreations* Ascalaphidae, fungi, gardening, golf, theatre, trees; *Style*— Dr Peter Lawrence, FRS; ✉ 9 Temple End, Gt Wilbraham, Cambridge CB1 5JF (☎ 01223 880505); MRC Laboratory Molecular Biology, Hills Rd, Cambridge CB2 2QH (☎ 01223 402282, fax 01223 412142, telex 81532)

LAWRENCE, Richard Foreshew; *b* 1930; *Career* farmer since 1950s; chm of poultry export business, dir of petrol retail business; formerly: vice chm Crewe HA, chm Mid Cheshire Hosps NHS Tst; fell Woodard Corp, chm of local sch govrs; active in both local and agricultural politics; *Recreations* music, particularly opera; *Style*— Richard F Lawrence, Esq; ✉ Sandlow Green Farm, Holmes Chapel, Cheshire CW4 8AS

LAWRENCE, Ruth Isabel; da of Frederick Lawrence, of London, and Clare, *née* Rosenblatt; *b* 13 May 1957; *Educ* East Barnet GS, Clare Coll Univ of Cambridge (MA); *Career* managing ed Sweet and Maxwell Ltd 1980–85, head of publishing and multimedia Law Soc of Eng and Wales 1986– (press offr 1985–86); memb Hon Soc of Middle Temple; Hon MA Univ of Cambridge; *Recreations* flying trapeze, flying light aircraft, classical guitar, walking; *Style*— Ms Ruth Lawrence; ✉ Teddington, Middx; The Law Society, 113 Chancery Lane, London WC2A 1PL (☎ 0171 242 1222)

LAWRENCE, Sandra Elizabeth; da of Brig Roderick Gwynne Lawrence, OBE (d 1976), and Gillian Winifred, *née* Bishop; *Educ* St Mary's Sch Wantage, St Martin's Sch of Art London; *Career* painter (chiefly wild life, still life and portraits); exhibited Royal Acad, Francis Kyle, Fischer Fine Art, Pastel Soc, Tryon Gallery, Grosvenor Gallery, Royal Inst of Oil Painters, Inst of Fine Arts Glasgow, New York, Caracas, Palm Beach; designed: Overlord Embroidery D-Day Museum Portsmouth 1968–72, 275ft of cartoons which hang in the Pentagon Washington DC; ROI 1980; *Recreations* travel, music, reading; *Clubs* Chelsea Arts; *Style*— Sandra Lawrence; ✉ 12 Paultons House, Paultons Square, London SW3 5DU (☎ 0171 352 3866)

LAWRENCE, Stephen Richard; s of Richard Lawrence, of Thrussington, Leicestershire, and Joyce, *née* Howarth; *b* 6 Sept 1951; *Educ* Longslade Coll Leics; *m* 9 April 1983, Linda Corina, *née* Hillier; 1 s (Alexander Guy b 16 Jan 1993); *Career* pilot offr cadet RAF 1971; Civil Service 1969–71, advtg mangr Loughborough Monitor 1971–72, reporter and features writer Leicester Mercury 1972–76, ed Leicester Shopwindow 1976–78, chief sub ed Gulf Mirror Bahrain 1978–79, sr ed Daily Nation Nairobi Kenya 1979–82, fndr Media Management Kenya 1983–86 and London 1986–87, ptnr Raitt Orr & Associates Public Relations 1988–90, press and PR mangr BP Chemicals 1990–; MIPR 1986; *Books* The Complete Guide To Amboseli National Park (1983), The Total Guide To Nairobi National Park (1986), The Total Guide To Amboseli National Park (1986); *Recreations* sailing, sub aqua, natural history; *Clubs* Royal Yachting Assoc (yachtmaster), Little Ship, Cruising Assoc, Pemba Channel Fishing (Kenya), British Sub Aqua, Kenya Soc; *Style*— Stephen Lawrence, Esq; ✉ BP Chemicals, Britannic House, 1 Finsbury Circus, London EC2M 7BA (☎ 0171 496 4827, fax 0171 496 4985)

LAWRENCE, Susanne; da of Julian Lawrence, of Thorpe Bay, Essex, and Irene Leah Esme, *née* Conn (d 1980); *b* 15 Dec 1944; *Educ* Brondesbury & Kilburn HS for Girls, City of London Coll (dip), Inst of Public Relations City of London Coll (cert), Coll for the Distributive Trades; *Career* PR consultancy with Wilcox Press & PR, International News Service and Good Relations 1963–68, editorial asst, asst ed then dep ed Personnel Management 1968–74, ed Personnel Management monthly jl of IPM 1974–94, co-fndr, editorial dir and dep md Personnel Publications Ltd 1981–93, dep chm Personnel Publications Ltd 1993–, chief exec Indigo Publishing Ltd 1996–; launched: Transition magazine for Br Assoc for Commercial & Industrial Educn 1985, Personnel Management Plus mid-monthly magazine for IPM 1990, Human Resource Management Journal as jt publisher 1990, Newsline for Nat Fedn of Retail Newsagents 1994, People Management for Inst of Personnel and Devpt 1995, Supply Management for Chartered Inst of Purchasing and Supply 1996, newsletters for Employers Forum on Age and Employers Forum on Disability 1996; pub charity magazine for Charities Aid Fndn 1996; awards: Specialist Journalist of the Yr Blue Circle Awards for Industrial Journalism 1980, Best Specialist Columnist Magazine Publishing Awards 1983, highly commended Ed of the Yr Award Periodical Publishers Assoc 1993; fndr and hon sec: Equal Pay and Opportunity Campaign 1974–87, David Wainwright Equal Opportunity Devpt Tst 1987– (chair); has served as judge in advtg awards, Personnel Mangr of Year Awards, Parents at Work Employer Awards and in trade union jl awards; MIPR 1968, FIPD 1992; *Recreations* cinema, theatre, travel; *Style*— Ms Susanne Lawrence; ✉ Personnel Publications Ltd, 17 Britton Street, London EC1M 5NQ (☎ 0171 880 6200, fax 0171 336 7635)

LAWRENCE, His Hon Judge; Timothy; s of Alfred Whiteman Lawrence, MBE, and Phyllis Gertrude, *née* Lloyd-Jones; *b* 29 April 1942; *Educ* Bedford Sch; *Career* Slrs' Dept New Scotland Yard 1967–70, ptnr Claude Hornby and Cox 1970–86 (sr ptnr 1976), recorder 1983, circuit judge (SE Circuit) 1986–; memb: Criminal Law Ctee Law Soc 1978–86, No 13 Area Legal Aid Ctee 1983–86, Judicial Studies Bd 1984–87 (Criminal Ctee until 1988), Tribunals Ctee 1991–96; chm: No 14 Area Duty Slr Ctee 1984–86, Exec Ctee of Br Acad of Forensic Sciences 1991– (pres 1992–93); legal memb Mental Health Review Tbnls 1989–; pres: London Criminal Cts Slrs' Assoc 1984–86 (sec 1974–84), Industrial Tribunals for England and Wales 1991–; FRSA; *Clubs* Hurlingham; *Style*— His Hon Judge Lawrence; ✉ 8 Slaidburn Street, London SW10 0JP

LAWRENCE, Timothy Gordon Roland (Tim); s of Lionel Arthur Lawrence (d 1975), and Patricia Mary Young (d 1992); *b* 22 Aug 1936; *Educ* Wimbledon Coll, St George's Coll Weybridge; *m* 19 Sept 1964, (Mabyn) Ann, da of Robert Hugh Shuttleworth Petherbridge; 1 s (Stephen Robert Anthony b 3 April 1966), 2 da (Katherine Ann b 15 July 1967, Joanna Frances b 22 Feb 1972); *Career* Nat Serv 1958–60 (cmmnd Royal Irish Fusiliers); articled clerk Wilson de Zouche & Mackenzie (later Wilson Davis & Co) 1953–58, CA 1958 (won Gold medal of ICAEW for first place in final examination); Cooper Brothers & Co (now Coopers & Lybrand): joined 1960, ptnr 1967–, memb Governing Bd 1975–90, vice chm 1988–90; chm Professional Asset Indemnity Ltd 1993–; chm London Soc of Chartered Accountants 1984–85; FCA; *Recreations* bridge, golf; *Clubs* MCC, Naval and Military, Stoke Poges Golf, Austenwood Bridge; *Style*— Tim Lawrence, Esq; ✉ Whitethorn, Collinswood Rd, Farnham Common, Slough, Berkshire SL2 3LH (☎ 01753 645377, fax 01753 647445); Coopers & Lybrand, 1 Embankment Place, London WC2N 6NN (☎ 0171 583 5000, fax 0171 213 2767)

LAWRENCE, Vernon John; s of Arthur Douglas Lawrence (d 1996), of Berlin, and Lilian Cecily, *née* Collings (d 1956); *b* 30 April 1940; *Educ* Ingleside Coll, Dulwich Coll, Kelham Coll; *m* 10 Sept 1960, Jennifer Mary, da of Maj Michael Henry Cecil Drewe, MBE, JP (d 1986), of Sidmouth, Devon; 2 s (James William b 1964, Jeremy Robert b 1966), 1 da (Sarah Katherine b 1961); *Career* prodr BBC Radio 1963 (studio mangr 1958); BBC TV: dir 1964, prodr 1967–74 (progs incl Top of the Pops, Omnibus, Full House); Yorkshire Television: asst head of entertainment 1974–85, controller of entertainment 1985–92 (progs incl The Darling Buds of May, Let's Face the Music, Rising Damp, Song by Song, Only When I Laugh, Duty Free, The New Statesman, A Bit of a Do, A Touch of Frost, Beecham, James Galway); controller of drama and entertainment ITV Network Centre 1992–95, md United Film and Television Productions (formerly MAI Productions Ltd) 1995–, md Anglia Television Entertainment 1995; memb Cncl BAFTA 1985, FRTS; *Recreations* walking, fishing, gardening, art; *Style*— Vernon Lawrence, Esq; ✉ United Film and Television Productions Ltd, 48 Leicester Square, WC2H 7FB (☎ 0171 389 8555)

LAWRENCE, Sir William Fettiplace; 5 Bt (UK 1867), of Ealing Park, Middx; s of Maj Sir William Lawrence, 4 Bt (d 1986), and Pamela Mary, *née* Gordon; *b* 23 Aug 1954; *Educ* King Edward VI Sch Stratford-upon-Avon; *Heir* cousin, Peter Stafford Hayden Lawrence b 1913; *Career* asst fin accountant: W B Bumpers Ltd, Rockwell International 1980–81; gen mangr Newdawn & Sun Ltd 1981–; proprietor William Lawrence Wines; dir: Unicorn Tourism Ltd 1994–, South Warwickshire Business Partnership 1995–, Stratford-upon-Avon & District Marketing Ltd 1995–, Stratford-upon-Avon Crossroads Care Attendant Scheme Ltd; cncllr Stratford-on-Avon DC 1982– (chm 1990–91); memb S Warwickshire Health Authy 1984–92, non-exec/assoc dir S Warwickshire General Hospitals NHS Tst 1993–; memb W Midlands Arts 1984–91, chm Heart of England Tourist Bd 1991– (non-exec dir 1989–); exec memb Stratford District Cncl for Voluntary

Serv 1986–91; pres: Stratford and Dist MENCAP, Stratford-upon-Avon Chamber Music Soc, Action Unlimited Tst; dir English Music Festivals; memb: Coventry & Warwicks Ctee for Employment of People with Disabilities, Warwicks Branch Rural Devpt Cmmn 1995–; patron Stratford-upon-Avon Age Concern; conslt to The Insite Consultancy on Disability Awareness Training 1995–; memb Ct Univ of Birmingham 1990–, memb Corporation Stratford-upon-Avon Coll; govr: King Edward VI Sch Stratford-upon-Avon, Royal Shakespeare Theatre; *Recreations* horse racing, wine; *Style*— Sir William Lawrence, Bt; ✉ The Knoll, Walcote, nr Alcester, Warwickshire B49 6LZ (☎ 01789 488303)

LAWRENCE-JONES, Sir Christopher; 6 Bt (UK 1831), of Cranmer Hall, Norfolk; s of Cdr Bertram Edward Jones, RN (d 1958), and Margaret Louise, *née* Cookson (d 1980); suc uncle, Sir Lawrence Evelyn Jones, 5 Bt, MC, TD (d 1969); *b* 19 Jan 1940; *Educ* Sherborne, Gonville and Caius Coll Cambridge, St Thomas's Hosp (MA, MB BChir, DIH, FRCP, FFOM); *m* 1967, Gail, da of Cecil Arthur Pittar, FRACS (d 1976), of Auckland, NZ, and Helen Miller, *née* Finlay (d 1973); 2 s (Mark Christopher b 1968, John Alexander b 1971); *Heir* s, Mark Christopher Lawrence-Jones b 28 Dec 1968; *Career* med advsr to various organisations 1967–; ICI Dyestuffs Div 1967–70, BP Co Ltd 1970–73, Health and Safety Exec 1973–75, ICI Paints Div 1975–79, central med advsr ICI 1979–85, gp chief med offr ICI Group HQ 9 Millbank London SW1P 3JF 1985–93, chm Medichem 1986–92; memb Bd Faculty of Occupational Med RCP 1988–91, pres Section of Occupational Med Royal Soc of Med 1990–91, memb Mgmnt Ctee Br Occupational Health Res Fndn 1991–94; *Recreations* cruising under sail (yacht 'Mermerus'); *Clubs* Royal Cruising; *Style*— Sir Christopher Lawrence-Jones, Bt

LAWRENCE-MILLS, Rowena Margaret; da of Edward Charles Leader (d 1982), and Blanche Linda, *née* Calcott (d 1979); *b* 14 July 1931; *Educ* North London Collegiate Sch for Girls, UCL (BSc); *m* John, s of Herbert Harold (d 1964); 1 s (Charles Sebastian b 1966), 1 da (Alexandra Louise b 1968); *Career* former economist Metal Box Co Ltd, chm and chief exec Rowena Mills Associates Ltd, chm packaging working pty NEDO 1988–90; memb: Ctee of Investigation MAFF 1988–, Financial Reporting Cncl 1990–95, NEDO Food Sector Gp 1991–93; cncllr CBI South Western Region 1991–; Freeman City of London, Liveryman Worshipful Co of Plumbers; fellow Inst of Packaging; *Recreations* work, riding, music, theatre, reading, writing; *Clubs* Naval and Military; *Style*— Mrs Rowena Lawrence-Mills; ✉ Manor Farm, Stogumber, Taunton, Somerset TA5 3TQ (☎ 01984 656614)

LAWRENSON, Prof Peter John; s of John Lawrenson (d 1949), of Prescot, and Emily, *née* Houghton (d 1979); *b* 12 March 1933; *Educ* Prescot GS, Univ of Manchester (BSc, MSc, DSc); *m* 5 April 1958, Shirley Hannah, da of Albert Edward Foster, of Macclesfield; 1 s (Mark b 1958), 3 da (Ruth b 1960, Rachel b 1963, Isobel b 1965); *Career* res engr GEC 1956–61; Univ of Leeds: lectr 1961, reader 1965, prof 1966–91, head Dept of Electrical and Electronic Engrg 1974–84, chm Faculty of Sci and Applied Sci 1978–80, chm Faculty of Engrg 1980–81; chm Switched Reluctance Drives Ltd 1980–; author of over 120 papers for various sci jls; awards: Inst Premium IEE 1981, Alfred Ewing Gold Medal Royal Soc and Inst of Civil Engrs 1983, Esso Energy Gold Medal Royal Soc 1985, Faraday Medal IEE 1990; pres IEE 1992–93; memb Cncl Univ of Buckingham 1987–93; FIEE 1974, FIEEE 1975, FEng 1980, FRS 1982; *Books* Analysis and Computation of Electric & Magnetic Fields (with K J Binns, 1963 and 1973), Per Unit Systems (with M R Harris & J M Stephenson, 1970), The Analytical and Numerical Solution of Electric and Magnetic Fields (with K J Binns and C W Trowbridge) 1992; *Recreations* chess, bridge, squash, walking; *Style*— Prof Peter Lawrenson, FEng, FRS; ✉ Switched Reluctance Drives Ltd, East Park House, Otley Road, Harrogate HG3 1PR (☎ 01423 845200, fax 01423 845201)

LAWREY, Keith; JP (Inner London); s of Capt George William Bishop Lawrey, of Bognor Regis, W Sussex, and Edna Muriel, *née* Gass; *b* 21 Aug 1940; *Educ* Colfe's Sch, Heythrop Coll and Birkbeck Coll London (LLB, MA, MScEcon); *m* 20 Dec 1969, (Helen) Jane, da of James Edward Marriott, MBE, and Betty Evelyn, *née* Church; 2 s (David Keith b 1972, Andrew Charles Keith b 1976), 2 da (Sarah Jane b 1970, Katherine Jane b 1979); *Career* called to the Bar Gray's Inn 1972; educn offr Plastics and Rubber Inst 1960–68, lectr and sr lectr Bucks Coll of Higher Educn 1968–74, head Dept of Business Studies Mid-Kent Coll of Higher and Further Educn 1974–78, sec gen The Library Assoc 1978–84, dean Faculty of Business and Mgmnt Harrow Coll of Higher Educn 1984–90, sec and registrar Royal Coll of Veterinary Surgeons 1991, headmaster Cannock Sch 1992–95; hon treas Coll of Preceptors 1987– (also examiner), memb Social Security Appeal Tbnls Panel, lay preacher Methodist church; Freeman City of London, Liveryman Worshipful Co of Chartered Secretaries and Administrators; Rotarian; FCIS 1967, FCollP 1980; *Recreations* preaching, sailing, swimming, theatre, gardening; *Clubs* Dell Quay Sailing, Old Colfeians' Assoc, Orpington Rotary; *Style*— Keith Lawrey, Esq, JP

LAWS, Iain McOlvin; TD (1981); s of Capt Edmund Francis Laws (d 1976), of Banchory, Scotland, and Marion, *née* Cruickshank; *b* 23 Feb 1938; *Educ* Robert Gordon's Coll Aberdeen, Univ of St Andrews (BDS), Univ of Aberdeen (MB ChB); *m* 21 Sept 1963, (Mary) Bridget, da of Thomas Hugh Maguire (d 1952), of Manor Hamilton, Eire; 2 s (Stephen b 3 April 1969, Gavin b 16 May 1973), 2 da (Siobhan b 3 Aug 1964, Diane b 14 Feb 1967); *Career* TA 1969–; sr house offr Nottingham Gen Hosp 1962–63, registrar Mount Vernon Hosp 1963–65, lectr and sr registrar Kings Coll Hosp 1970–73; conslt in oral and maxillo-facial surgery: Royal Free Hosps 1973–86, Hampstead Health Authy 1986–; FDSRCS(Eng); *Recreations* fishing; *Style*— Iain Laws, Esq, TD; ✉ 53 Wimpole St, London W1M 7DF (☎ 0171 935 8239)

LAWS, Hon Mr Justice; Hon Sir John Grant McKenzie; kt (1992); s of Dr Frederic Laws (d 1961), and Dr Margaret Ross Laws, *née* McKenzie; *b* 10 May 1945; *Educ* Durham Sch (King's scholar), Exeter Coll Oxford (Sr open classical scholar, MA 1st class honours); *m* 1973, Sophie Susan Sydenham Cole, *née* Marshall; 1 da (Margaret Grace McKenzie b 1980); *Career* called to the Bar Inner Temple 1970 (Marshall Hall scholar), recorder 1985–92 (asst recorder 1983–85), first jr counsel to the Treasy in Common Law 1984–92, bencher Inner Temple 1985, judge of the High Court of Justice (Queen's Bench Div) 1992–; called to the Bar: New South Wales 1987, Gibraltar 1988; pres Bar Euro Gp 1994–; hon fell Robinson Coll Cambridge; *Recreations* Greece, living in London, philosophy; *Clubs* Garrick; *Style*— The Hon Mr Justice Laws; ✉ c/o Royal Courts of Justice, Strand, London WC2A 2LL

LAWS, Dr Richard Maitland; CBE (1983); s of Percy Malcolm Laws (d 1962), and Florence May Laws, MBE, *née* Heslop (d 1983); *b* 23 April 1926; *Educ* Dame Allan's Sch Newcastle upon Tyne, St Catharine's Coll Cambridge (open scholarship, res scholarship, MA, PhD, ScD); *m* Maureen Isobel Winifred, da of late George Leonard Holmes; 3 s (Richard Anthony, Christopher Peter, Andrew David); *Career* biologist Falkland Is Dependencies Survey 1947–53, biologist and whaling inspr on factory ship Balaena in Antarctic 1953–54, PSO Nat Inst of Oceanography 1954–61; dir: Nuffield Unit of Tropical Animal Ecology Uganda and Univ of Cambridge 1961–67, Tsavo Res Project Kenya 1967–68; Smuts Meml fellowship Univ of Cambridge 1968–69, Leverhulme fellowship 1969, head Life Sciences Div Br Antarctic Survey 1969–73; dir: Br Antarctic Survey 1973–87, NERC Sea Mammal Res Unit 1977–87; Univ of Cambridge: master St Edmund's Coll 1985–96, memb Financial Bd 1988–91, memb Cncl of Senate 1989–92, chm Local Examinations Syndicate 1990–94; hon lectr Makerere Univ Uganda 1962–66; Bruce Meml medal for Antarctic work RSE 1954, scientific medal Zoological Soc of London 1966, polar medal 1976, hon fell St Catharine's Coll Cambridge 1982, hon fell St Edmund's Coll Cambridge 1996; SCAR: UK memb working Gp on Biology 1972–90, memb Gp of Specialists on Seals 1972– (convenor 1972–88), chm Working Gp on Biology 1980–86, memb BIOMASS Exec 1976–91, pres SCAR 1990–94, hon memb 1996; hon memb Soc for Marine Mammalogy 1994, hon warden Uganda Nat Parks 1996; Hon DSc Univ of Bath 1991; FZS 1960 memb Cnl 1982–84, vice pres 1983, sec 1984–88; FIBiol 1973 (vice pres 1983), FRS 1980 (chm Interdisiciplinary Scientific Ctee on Antarctic Res 1988–93); author of numerous res pubns in scientific journals, books and reviews; *Books* Elephants and their Habitats (with I S C Parker and R C B Johnstone, 1975), Scientific Research in Antarctica (jt ed with V E Fuchs, 1977), Antarctic Ecology (ed 1984), Antarctic Nutrient Cycles and Food Webs (jt ed with W R Siegfried and P R Condy, 1985), Antarctica - The Last Frontier (1989), Life at Low Temperatures (jt ed with F Franks, 1990), Antarctica and Environmental Change (jt ed with D J Drewry and J A Pyle, 1992), Antarctic Seals: Research Methods and Techniques (ed, 1993), Elephant Seals: Population Ecology, Behaviour, and Physiology (jt ed with B J Le Boeuf, 1994); *Style*— Dr Richard Laws, CBE, FRS; ✉ 3 The Footpath, Coton, Cambridge CB3 7PX (☎ 01954 210567); The Master, St Edmund's College, Cambridge CB3 0BN (☎ 01223 336250, fax 01223 336111)

LAWS, Stephen Charles; CB (1996); s of late Dennis Arthur Laws, and Beryl Elizabeth, *née* Roe; *b* 28 Jan 1950; *Educ* St Dunstan's Coll Catford, Univ of Bristol (LLB); *m* 1972, Angela Mary, da of John William Deardon; 3 da (Clare Theresa b 10 Aug 1976, Mary Veronica b 20 May 1980, Philippa Jane b 24 Nov 1982), 2 s (Michael Benedict b 11 Feb 1978, Patrick Joseph b 30 July 1985); *Career* asst lectr Univ of Bristol 1972–73, called to the Bar Middle Temple 1973, pupil of Michael Hutchison then Andrew Longmore 1973–74, legal asst Home Office 1975–76; Parly Counsel: asst 1976–82, seconded to Law Cmmn 1980–82 and 1989–91, sr asst 1982–85, parly counsel 1991– (dep parly counsel 1985–91); *Books* Halsbury's Laws: Statutes Title (1983); *Recreations* theatre, cinema, family life; *Style*— Stephen Laws, Esq, CB; ✉ Office of the Parliamentary Counsel, 36 Whitehall, London SW1A 2AY (☎ 0171 210 6639, fax 0171 210 6632)

LAWSON, Anthony Raymond; s of Alexander Lawson (d 1965), of Redcroft, Whitefield, Manchester, and Jeanne Alexandra Lawson (d 1968); *b* 26 Aug 1931; *Educ* Repton; *m* 1, 1955, Anne, da of Dr Walter Martin, MC, of Bury, Lancs; 1 s, 1 da; *m* 2, 1980, Patricia Jane, da of Dr F Lascelles, MC, of Formby, Lancs; *Career* chm and chief exec Hollas Group plc 1970–94 (currently non-exec dir); memb Lloyd's; FRSA, FIMgt; *Recreations* tennis; *Style*— Anthony Lawson, Esq; ✉ Churn Cottage, Budworth Road, Aston-By-Budworth, Cheshire CW9 6LT (☎ 01565 777530); Hollas Group plc, Ocean House, Caspian Road, Altrincham, Cheshire WA14 5HH (☎ 0161 929 2000, fax 0161 929 4121)

LAWSON, Charles John Patrick; s and h of Sir John Charles Arthur Digby Lawson, 3 Bt, DSO, MC, *qv*; *b* 19 May 1959; *Educ* Harrow, Univ of Leeds, RAC Cirencester; *m* 18 Sept 1987, Lady Caroline Lowther, da of 7 Earl of Lonsdale, *qv*; 3 s (Jack William Tremayne b 6 Dec 1989, Thomas Charles Lancelot b 5 May 1992, Ralph Hugh Arthur b 7 Sept 1995), 1 da (Tess b 30 Aug 1988); *Career* princ Jackson-Stops and Staff; ARICS; *Recreations* children, kite flying, shooting, gardening, fell walking (and sometimes running); *Style*— Charles Lawson, Esq; ✉ Heckwood, Sampford Spiney, Yelverton, Devon PL20 6LG (☎ 01822 852269, work ☎ 01392 214222)

LAWSON, Sir Christopher Donald; *b* 1922; *Educ* Magdalen Coll Sch Oxford; *m* 1945, Marjorie Patricia, *née* Bristow; 2 s, 1 da; *Career* serv RAF 1941–50 Sqdn Ldr; joined Thomas Hedley Ltd (sales mangr, mktg, personnel), retail sales mangr Cooper McDougal & Co, md Mars Foods, dir Mars Ltd, pres Mars Snack Master; chm Goodblue Ltd; dir Cons Central Office 1981–; dir: Grant Maintained Schools Ltd, Choice in Educations Ltd; Liveryman Worshipful Co of Broderers; *Clubs* RAF, MCC, Gloucester RFC, Lillybrook, Doublegate (USA), Thurlstone Golf; *Style*— Sir Christopher Lawson; ✉ Church Cottage, Great Witcombe, Glos GL3 4TT (☎ 01452 862591)

LAWSON, Prof David Hamilton; CBE (1993); s of David Lawson (d 1956), of East Kilbride, and Margaret Harvey, *née* White (d 1982); *b* 27 May 1939; *Educ* HS of Glasgow, Univ of Glasgow (MB ChB, MD); *m* 7 Sept 1963, Alison (d 1996), da of William Diamond (d 1974), of Sale; 3 s (Derek b 1965, Iain b 1967, Keith b 1970); *Career* visiting conslt Univ Med Center Boston Mass 1972–90; conslt physician: Royal Infirmary Glasgow 1973–, Dental Hosp Glasgow 1984–; visiting prof Sch of Pharmacy Univ of Strathclyde 1976–, hon prof of med Univ of Glasgow 1993–; advsr on adverse drug reactions WHO Geneva 1984–89, external assessor Scientific Branch Civil Serv Cmmn 1986–; Dept of Health London: chm Ctee on Review of Med 1987–91 (memb 1979–91), memb Ctee on Safety of Med 1987–93, chm Medicines Cmmn 1994–; memb: Br Pharmacological Soc 1976, Assoc of Physicians GB & Ireland 1979, Scottish Soc of Physicians 1975; FRCPEd, FRCPGlas, FFPM, fell American Coll of Clinical Pharmacology; *Books* Clinical Pharmacy & Hospital Drug Management (with R M E Richards, 1982), Current Medicine - 2 (1990), Current Medicine - 3 (1991), Current Medicine - 4 (1994); *Recreations* hill-walking, photography, bird-watching; *Clubs* Royal Commonwealth Soc, London; *Style*— Prof David Lawson, CBE; ✉ 25 Kirkland Avenue, Blanefield, Glasgow G63 9BY; Wards 10 and 11, Royal Infirmary, Glasgow G4 0SF (☎ 0141 211 4000 ext 4291, fax 0141 552 8933)

LAWSON, Denis Stamper; s of Lawrence Lawson (d 1981), of Crieff, Perthshire, Scotland and Phyllis Lawson; *b* 27 Sept 1947; *Educ* Crieff Secdy Sch, Morrisons Acad Crieff, RSAMD; *m* 1 s (Jamie Fletcher b 3 June 1979); *Career* actor; *Theatre* incl: Pal Joey (Albery) 1980–81, Mr Cinders (Fortune) 1983, Lend Me A Tenor (Globe) 1987, Mosca in Volpone (Almeida) 1990, Lust (Hornchurch and Haymarket) 1993, Oleanna (Duke of York's) 1994; *Television* work incl: Dead Head (by Howard Brenton, BBC), That Uncertain Feeling (by Kingsley Amis, BBC), Love After Lunch (BBC), One Way Out (BBC), Born Kicking (BBC), The Justice Game (parts I & II, BBC); *Films* incl: Providence 1977, Local Hero 1983; *Awards* Drama Magazine Award for Most Promising Actor (for Pal Joey) 1981, SWET Award for Best Actor in a Musical (Mr Cinders) 1983; *Recreations* Sheila Gish, music; *Style*— Denis Lawson, Esq; ✉ ICM Ltd, Oxford House, 76 Oxford Street, London W1N 0AX (☎ 0171 636 6565, fax 0171 323 0101)

LAWSON, Hon Dominic Ralph Campden; s of Baron Lawson of Blaby (Life Peer), *qv*, and his 1 w, Vanessa Mary Addison, *née* Salmon (d 1985); bro of Nigella Lucy Lawson, *qv*; *b* 17 Dec 1956; *Educ* Westminster, ChCh Oxford; *m* 1, 11 Sept 1982, Jane Fiona, da of David Christopher Wastell Whytehead, of W Dulwich, London SE21; *m* 2, 30 Dec 1991, Hon Rosamond Mary Lawson, *qv*, *née* Monckton, only da of 2 Viscount Monckton of Brenchley, CB, OBE, MC, *qv*; 3 da (Savannah Vanessa Lucia b 23 Dec 1992, Natalia b and d March 1994, Domenica b 1 June 1995); *Career* res The World Tonight Radio 4 1979–81; The Financial Times: joined staff 1981, energy corr 1983–86, columnist Lex 1986–87, columnist 1991; ed The Spectator 1990–95 (dep ed 1987–90), ed The Sunday Telegraph 1995–; columnist for The Sunday Correspondent 1990; Harold Wincott Prize for financial journalism 1987; *Books* Korchnoi - Kasparov: The London Contest (with Raymond Keene, 1983), Britain in the Eighties (contrib, 1989), The Inner Game (1994, published in US as Endgame); *Recreations* chess, cricket; *Clubs* Academy, MCC, Beefsteak; *Style*— The Hon Dominic Lawson; ✉ Sunday Telegraph, 1 Canada Square, Canary Wharf, London E14 5DT (☎ 0171 538 5000, fax 0171 513 2504)

LAWSON, Edmund James; QC (1988); s of Donald Edmund Lawson, of Norwich, and Veronica, *née* Clancy; *b* 17 April 1948; *Educ* City of Norwich Sch, Trinity Hall Cambridge (BA); *m* 24 Feb 1973, Jennifer Mary, da of James J Cleary (d 1984), of Sheffield; 3 s

(Matthew b 1973, Joseph b 1975, Benjamin b 1980); *Career* called to the Bar Gray's Inn 1971, head of chambers 1989–; *Recreations* music; *Style*— Edmund Lawson, Esq, QC; ✉ 9–12 Bell Yard, London WC2A 2LF (☎ 0171 400 1800, fax 0171 404 1405)

LAWSON, Elizabeth Ann; QC (1989); da of Alexander Edward Lawson (d 1995), of Croydon, Surrey, and Helen Jane, *née* Currie (d 1989); *b* 29 April 1947; *Educ* Croydon HS for Girls, Univ of Nottingham (LLB); *Career* called to The Bar Gray's Inn 1969; chaired inquiries into child abuse London Borough of Lewisham 1985; memb Islington Area Child Protection Ctee 1989, chm Family Law Bar Assoc 1995–; sec St Paul's Bayswater United Reformed Church; *Recreations* knitting, cake decoration; *Style*— Miss Elizabeth Lawson, QC; ✉ Cloisters, 1 Pump Court, Temple, London EC4Y 7AA (☎ 0171 583 0303, fax 0171 583 2254)

LAWSON, Dr Graham Bernard; s of Wilfred Lawson, of Salford, and Bertha, *née* Henshaw (d 1974); *b* 18 May 1942; *Educ* Salford GS, Univ of Manchester (MSc, PhD); *m*, Jacqueline Constance, *née* Clarke; 2 s (Carlton Michael b 1968, Simon John b 1972); *Career* res fell Univ of Aston 1965–67, devpt engr E I Dupont de Nemours Inc Texas 1967–70, project engr Unilever Research Sharnbrook 1970–72, project engr and prodn mangr Mars Ltd Slough 1972–74, section mangr and div mangr Unilever Research Sharnbrook 1974–81, tech dir Crosfield Chemicals Warrington 1981–83, md Crosfield Catalysts Warrington 1983–85, head Med Products Gp Unilever plc London 1985–87, tech dir RTZ Borax 1987–95, chief exec Watts Blake Bearne and Co PLC 1995–; FIChemE 1980, FEng 1993; *Recreations* family, travel, golf, food, wine; *Clubs* RAC; *Style*— Dr Graham Lawson, FEng; ✉ Watts Blake Bearne and Co PLC, Park House, Courtenay Park, Newton Abbot, Devon TQ12 4PS (☎ 01626 332345, fax 01626 332342, car 0836 536514)

LAWSON, Col Sir John Charles Arthur Digby; 3 Bt (UK 1900), of Weetwood Grange, Headingley-cum-Burley, W Riding of Yorks, DSO (1943), MC (1940); s of Maj Sir Digby Lawson, 2 Bt, TD, JP (d 1959), and Iris Mary Fitzgerald (d 1941); *b* 24 Oct 1912; *Educ* Stowe, RMC, Staff Coll Camberley; *m* 1, 17 March 1945 (m dis 1950), Rose (d 1972), da of David Cecil Bingham (d 1914), widow of William M L Fiske, previously w of 7 Earl of Warwick; m 2, 22 Dec 1954, Tresilla Anne Eleanor (d 1985), da of late Maj Eric Buller Leyborne Popham, MC, of Downes, Crediton, and formerly w of John Garland de Pret Roose; 1 s (Charles John Patrick b 1959); *Heir* s, Charles John Patrick Lawson, *qv*; *Career* 2 Lt 11 Hussars (PAO) 1933, served Palestine 1936 (despatches), seconded Trans-Jordan Frontier Force 1939–40, Western Desert 1940–43 (wounded, despatches thrice), Temp Lt-Col 1943 as Gen Montgomery's apptd advsr on armoured reconnaissance to Gen Patton N Africa 1943 (wounded), US Marine Staff Course Quantico Virginia 1944, Personal Liaison Offr to Gen Montgomery at 21 Army GP N France 1944, cmdg Inns of Court Regt 1944–46, ret 1947, Col 11 Hussars (PAO) 1965–69, Col R Hussars 1969–72; chm Fairbairn Lawson Ltd and subsidiary cos 1968–79, memb Cncl Univ of Leeds 1972–79; US Legion of Merit 1943; *Recreations* golf, gardening, country pursuits; *Clubs* Cavalry and Guards', MCC; *Style*— Col Sir John Lawson, Bt, DSO, MC; ✉ Hillmore Cottage, Bishops Hull Rd, Taunton, Somerset TA1 5ER (☎ 01823 325555)

LAWSON, Lesley (Twiggy); da of William Norman Hornby, and Nell Helen, *née* Reeman; *b* 19 Sept 1949; *m* 1, 1977, Michael Whitney Armstrong (d 1983); 1 da (Carly); m 2, 1988, Leigh Lawson, the actor; *Career* actress and singer; came to prominence in modelling career 1966–71; has been the recipient of many awards and honours; *Theatre* incl: Cinderella 1976, Captain Beaky 1982, My One And Only 1983–84; *Television* incl: Twiggy Series 1978, Twiggy And Friends 1980, Pygmalion 1981, Captain Beaky 1982, Little Match Girl 1986, Sun Child 1988, The Young Charlie Chaplin 1989, Princesses (US pilot) 1991; more recently Something Borrowed Something Blue (CBS); *Films* incl: The Boy Friend 1971, W 1975, There Goes The Bride 1979, Blues Brothers 1981, The Doctor And The Devils 1985, Club Paradise 1986, Madame Sousatzka 1988, Harem Hotel Istanbul 1988; *Recordings* incl: Here I Go Again, Please Get The Name Right, London Pride (Songs from the Brit Musicals); *Books* Twiggy (autobiography, 1975), An Open Look (1985); *Recreations* music, design; *Style*— Ms Twiggy Lawson; ✉ c/o ICM Ltd, Oxford House, 76 Oxford Street, London W1N 0AX (☎ 0171 636 6565, fax 0171 323 0101)

LAWSON, Mark Gerard; s of Francis Lawson, of Harpenden, Herts, and Teresa, *née* Kane; *b* 11 April 1962; *Educ* St Columba's Coll St Albans Herts, UCL (BA); *m* 1990, Sarah Gillian Jane, da of Alan John Gilbert Bull; 1 s (William Mark b 25 July 1992), 1 da (Anna Sarah b 15 March 1995); *Career* journalist; jr reporter and TV critic The Universe 1984–85, TV previewer The Sunday Times 1985–86, asst arts ed and TV critic The Independent 1986–89 (Parly sketchwriter 1987–88), chief feature writer The Independent Magazine 1988–95, TV critic The Independent on Sunday 1990–91; columnist and feature writer: The Independent 1993–95, The Guardian 1995–; freelance contrib to numerous pubns since 1984 incl: The Times, Time Out, The Listener, Mirabella, Vogue, New Statesman; writer and presenter of TV documentaries: Byline: Vote For Ron (BBC) 1990, J'Accuse: Coronation Street (Channel 4) 1991; writer and presenter TV and radio progs: The Late Show (BBC 2) 1993–95, Late Review (BBC 2) 1994–, The Big Question (BBC 1) 1996–, Vice or Virtue (Radio 4) 1996–, Burning for Atlanta (Radio 4) 1996; script-writer The Vision Thing (BBC TV) 1993; *Awards* British Press award 1987, BP Arts Journalism awards 1989, 1990 and 1991, TV-am Critic of the Year 1989, TV-am Broadcast Journalist of the Year 1990; *Books* Bloody Margaret: Three Political Fantasies (1991), The Battle for Room Service (1993), Idlewild (1995), Conflicts of Interest: The Art of John Keane (1995); contrib: House of Cards: A Selection of Modern Political Humour (1988), Fine Glances: an anthology of cricket writing (1990); *Recreations* theatre, watching cricket, red wine, reading; *Style*— Mark Lawson, Esq; ✉ The Guardian, 119 Farringdon Road, London EC1R 3ER (☎ 0171 278 2332)

LAWSON, Michael Henry; QC (1991); s of Dr Richard Pike Lawson, MC, of Calne, Wiltshire, and Margaret Haines, *née* Knight (d 1990); *b* 3 Feb 1946; *Educ* Monkton Combe Sch Bath, Univ of London (LLB); *m* Ann Pleasance Symons, da of late John Guy Brisker, CBE, RD, RN; 2 da (Kate Alexandra b 13 Oct 1971, (Antonia) Sophia Louise b 27 Feb 1974); *Career* called to the Bar Inner Temple 1969, primarily in criminal advocacy practice, recorder of the Crown Court 1987– (asst recorder 1983–87); Master of the Bench Inner Temple 1993; Liveryman Worshipful Co of Curriers 1982; *Style*— Michael Lawson, Esq, QC; ✉ 36 Essex Street, London WC2R 3AS (☎ 0171 413 0353)

LAWSON, Nigella Lucy; da of Lord Lawson of Blaby, PC, *qv*, and Lady Ayer, Vanessa Mary Addison, *née* Salmon (d 1985); sis of Hon Dominic Ralph Campden Lawson, *qv*; *b* 6 Jan 1960; *Educ* The Godolphin & Latymer Sch, Lady Margaret Hall Oxford (BA Hons); *m* Sept 1992, John Diamond; 1 da (Cosima Thomasina b 15 Dec 1993), 1 s (Bruno Paul Nigel b 28 June 1996); *Career* journalist and broadcaster; ed Quartet Books 1982–84; Sunday Times: asst on Arts & Review section 1984–86, dep literary ed 1986–88, arts writer 1988–89; restaurant columnist The Spectator 1985–96; columnist: Evening Standard 1989–94, The Times 1995–; food writer Vogue 1996–; *Style*— Nigella Lawson; ✉ c/o Jacquie Drewe, London Management, 2–4 Noel Street, London W1 (☎ 0171 287 9000, fax 0171 287 3036)

LAWSON, Gen Sir Richard George; KCB (1980), kt (1979), DSO (1962), OBE (1968); s of John Lawson, and Florence Rebecca Lawson; *b* 24 Nov 1927; *Educ* St Alban's Sch, Univ of Birmingham; *m* 1956, Ingrid, da of Dr Sture Nikolaus Montelin, of Sweden (d 1979); 1 s; *Career* served with UN peacekeeping force Zaire 1962 when he rescued a Belgian priest from 800 rebels armed only with a swagger-stick (DSO); CO Ind Sqdn Royal Tank Regt Berlin 1963–64, GSO 2 MOD 1965–66, COS S Arabian Army 1967, CO 5 Royal Tank Regt 1968–69, Cdr 20 Armoured Bde 1972–73, Asst Mil Dep to Head of Def Sales 1975–77, GOC 1 Armd Div 1977–79, GOC NI 1979–82, Gen 1982, C-in-C Allied Forces N Europe 1982–84; Col Cmdt Royal Tank Regt 1980–82; Order of Leopold (Belgium) 1962, Kt Cdr Order of St Sylvester (Vatican) 1962; *Books* Strange Soldiering (1963), All The Queen's Men (1967), Strictly Personal (1972); *Recreations* sailing, writing; *Clubs* Army and Navy; *Style*— Gen Sir Richard Lawson, KCB, DSO, OBE

LAWSON, Richard Henry; CBE (1994); s of Sir Henry Brailsford Lawson, MC (d 1980), of Churchmead, Pirbright, Surrey, and Mona, *née* Thorne (d 1990); *b* 16 Feb 1932; *Educ* Lancing; *m* 1958, Janet Elizabeth, da of Hugh Govier, of Shere, nr Guildford, Surrey; 3 s (Anthony b 1966, Charles b 1969, Philip b 1972), 1 da (Sally d 1975); *Career* jt sr ptnr W Greenwell & Co 1980–86, chm Greenwell Montagu Stockbrokers Ltd 1987; Stock Exchange: memb 1959, memb Cncl, dep chm Cncl 1985–86; dep chm Securities Assoc 1986–91, chm Securities and Futures Authy 1991; chm The Investors Compensation Scheme 1992– (dir 1987–); *Recreations* golf, tennis, walking, birdwatching, skiing; *Clubs* Naval and Military; *Style*— Richard Lawson, Esq, CBE; ✉ Cherry Hill, Burrows Lane, Gomshall, Surrey GU5 9QE

LAWSON, Robert Alexander Murdoch; s of Robert McKenzie Lawson (d 1944), and Margaret Perrins Murdoch (d 1985); *b* 11 Feb 1938; *Educ* George Watsons Boys Coll Edinburgh, Univ of Edinburgh (MB ChB); *m* 13 Nov 1965, Elizabeth Ettie, da of Tom Clark (d 1971); 1 s (Tom b 1973), 4 da (Rebecca b 1966, Catherine b 1969, Elizabeth b 1970, Hannah b 1981); *Career* registrar in surgery Bangour Gen Hosp W Lothian 1966–69, registrar then sr registrar Shotley Bridge cardio-Thoracic Unit Co Durham 1969–72, res fell St Vincents Hosp Univ of Oregon Med Sch USA 1973–75, sr registrar Nat Heart and London Chest Hosp Brompton 1975–77, currently conslt cardio-thoracic surgn Wythenshawe Hosp Manchester; memb: Br Cardiac Soc, Soc of Thoracic and Cardiovascular Surgns of UK and Ireland, Euro Assoc for Cardio-Thoracic Surgery; FRCSEd 1966, FRCS 1971; *Recreations* walking; *Style*— Robert Lawson, Esq; ✉ The Hollies, 8 Harboro Road, Sale, Cheshire M33 5AB (☎ 0161 973 3295); Cardio-Thoracic Unit, Wythenshawe Hospital, South Manchester (☎ 0161 998 7070)

LAWSON, Roger Hardman; *b* 3 Sept 1945; *m* Jeni; 3 da (Sarahjane, Annabel, Louise); *Career* special dir Resource (handling substantial investments) 3i plc 1993– (head Int Dept until 1993); dir 3i plc and various UK unlisted trading companies; memb Cncl ICAEW (pres 1994–95), memb Ct City Univ, former chm Bd for Chartered Accountants in Business; Liveryman Worshipful Co of Chartered Accountants; FCA; *Recreations* golf; *Clubs* Royal Wimbledon Golf; *Style*— Roger Lawson, Esq; ✉ 3i plc, 91 Waterloo Rd, London SE1 8XP (☎ 0171 928 3131, fax 0171 928 0058)

LAWSON, Hon Mrs (Rosamond Mary); *née* Monckton; only da of 2 Viscount Monckton of Brenchley, CB, OBE, MC; *b* 26 Oct 1953; *Educ* Ursuline Convent Tildonk Belgium; *m* 30 Dec 1991, as his 2 w, Dominic Ralph Campden Lawson, *qv*, s of Rt Hon Lord Lawson of Blaby, PC, *qv*; 3 da; *Career* asst md Cartier London 1979, sales and exhibition mangr Tabbah Jewellers (Monte Carlo) 1980, promotions mangr Asprey 1982–85, md Tiffany London 1986–; Freeman Worshipful Co of Goldsmiths 1982; *Recreations* books, dogs, voyages; *Style*— The Hon Mrs Lawson; ✉ Tiffany & Co, 25 Old Bond Street, London W1X 3AA (☎ 0171 409 2790)

LAWSON, Sarah; *see:* Maher, Hon Mrs (Sarah Jane)

LAWSON, Sonia; da of Frederick Lawson (d 1968), of Castle Bolton, North Yorks, and Muriel Mary, *née* Metcalfe (both artists); *b* 2 June 1934; *Educ* RCA (MA, postgrad travelling scholarship); *m* 14 Jan 1969, Charles William Congo; 1 da (b 29 May 1970); *Career* artist; currently visiting lectr Royal Acad Schs; Rowney Drawing Prize 1984, Lorne Award 1987, Eastern Arts drawing prize (first prize 1984 and 1989); RWS 1987 (Assoc 1984), RA 1982; *Solo Exhibitions* incl: Zwemmer Gallery London 1960, New Arts Centre London 1963, Queens Square Gallery Leeds 1964, Trafford Gallery London 1967, Billingham/Middlesbrough 1973, Harrogate Art Gallery 1979, retrospective Shrines of Life touring exhbn 1982–83, Central Art Gallery Milton Keynes 1982, Mappin Gallery Sheffield 1982, Cartwright Bradford 1982, Leicester Kimberlin and Hull Ferens 1983, Midnight Muse (City Art Gallery Manchester) 1987, Wakefield City Art Gallery 1988, Bradford Cartwright 1989, Boundry Gallery London 1989 and 1995, Univ of Birmingham 1994, retrospective Dean Clough Halifax 1996; *Group Exhibitions* incl: London Gp, Royal Acad, RWS, 25 Years of British Art (Royal Acad Jubilee) 1977, Fragments Against Ruin (Arts Cncl tour) 1981–82, Moira Kelly Fine Art (London 1982 and NY 1983), Tolly Cobbold Tour 1982–83 and 1985–86, Leeds Poly 'New Art' 1987, Manchester City Art Gallery 1988, London RCA Centenary 1988, Olympia, Islington and Bath Festivals 1989–97, China Br Cncl Touring Exhbn 1989–90, Royal Inst of Fine Art Glasgow 1990, The Infernal Method etchings, Royal Acad London 1990, John Moores Liverpool 1991, Nielson & Wuethrich Inter Fine Art Thun Switzerland 1992, Mercury Gallery Duncan Campbell London 1992, Lamont, Connaught Brown 1994–97; *Work in Collections* incl: Imperial War Museum London (BAOR cmmnd 1984), Arts Cncl GB, Sheffield Graves, Belfast Art Gallery, Leeds Univ, Middlesbrough Art Gallery, Miny Works, RA and RCA Collections, Wakefield, Carlisle, Bolton and Rochdale Galleries, Univ Centre Birmingham (cmmnd 1994), St Peter's Oxford, various educn authys, Vatican Rome (cmmnd 1989), Lambeth Palace (cmmnd 1989), Chatsworth House collection, private collections in Europe, USA, Canada and Aust; *Publications* illustrator for: book of poems by James Kirkup (1993), short story by Fay Weldon (1995); *Clubs* Royal Over-Seas League; *Style*— Sonia Lawson, RA; ✉ Royal Academy of Arts, Piccadilly, London W1 (☎ 0171 494 5680, fax 0171 434 0837, 21812, studio ☎ 01525 850687)

LAWSON, Thomas Vincent; s of John Boyd Lawson, MBE (d 1952), and Mary Alexandra, *née* Chambers (d 1945); *b* 22 Jan 1925; *Educ* Denstone Coll, Univ of Leeds (BSc), Imperial Coll London (DIC); *m* 6 Aug 1948, Pauline Elizabeth, da of William Arthur Gaunt (d 1984); 2 s (Theodore Thomas b 23 Oct 1953, Oscar Charles b 18 May 1958), 4 da (Alexandra Barbara b 14 Oct 1952, Charity Jenny b 5 Sept 1956, Pandora Pauline b 20 July 1964, Darcie Tabitha b 11 Jan 1966); *Career* Univ of Bristol: lectr in aeronautical engrg 1949–62, sr lectr in aeronautical engrg 1962–72, reader in industrial aerodynamics 1972–83, hon sr res fell in aerospace engrg 1983–; conslt in industl aerodynamics and wind engrg 1983–; chm ESDU Wind Engrg Ctee; memb: ESDU Structural Vibration Ctee, BSI BS 6399 Wind Loading Ctee; memb Editorial Bd Journal of Atmospheric Environment; FEng 1987; *Books* Wind Effects on Buildings (2 vols, Design Applications, Statistics and Meteorology, 1980), Wind Loading Handbook (1995); *Recreations* gardening, drawing; *Style*— Thomas Lawson, Esq, FEng; ✉ Hamel Green House, Ham Green, Pill, Bristol BS20 0HF (☎ 01275 372263); Department of Aerospace Engineering, University of Bristol, Bristol BS8 1TR (☎ 0117 928 7700, fax 0117 925 1154)

LAWSON OF BLABY, Baron (Life Peer UK 1992), of Newnham in the County of Northamptonshire; Nigel Lawson; PC (1981); s of late Ralph Lawson, and Joan Elisabeth, *née* Davis; *b* 11 March 1932; *Educ* Westminster, ChCh Oxford; *m* 1, 1955 (m dis 1980), Vanessa Mary Addison (d 1985), 2 da of late Felix Addison Salmon, of Ham Common, Surrey; 1 s (Hon Dominic Ralph Campden b 1956, *qv*), 3 da ((Hon) Nigella Lucy b 1960, *qv*, Hon Thomasina Posy (Hon Mrs Hill) b 1961,d 1993, Hon Horatia Holly b 1966); m 2, 1980, Thérèse Mary Maclear, da of late Henry Charles Maclear Bate, of Putney; 1 s (Hon Thomas Nigel Maclear b 1976), 1 da (Hon Emily Hero b 1981); *Career* Sub-Lt RNVR 1954–56; memb editorial staff Financial Times 1956–60, city ed Sunday Telegraph 1961–63, ed The Spectator 1966–70; Parly candidate (C) Eton and Slough

1970, MP (C) Blaby 1974–92; oppn whip 1976–77, oppn spokesman on Treasy and Economic Affrs 1977–79, fin sec to the Treasy 1979–81, Energy sec 1981–83, Chancellor of the Exchequer 1983–Oct 1989 (resigned); dir Barclays Bank 1990–, chm Central Europe Trust 1990–; pres Br Inst of Energy Economics 1994–; special advsr Cons HQ 1973–74, vice chm Cons Political Centre Nat Advsy Ctee 1972–75; *Books* The View From No 11 (memoirs, 1992); *Style*— The Rt Hon the Lord Lawson of Blaby, PC; ✉ House of Lords, London SW1A 0PW

LAWSON ROGERS, (George) Stuart; QC (1994); s of George Henry Roland Rogers, CBE (d 1983), of Bournemouth, and Mary Lawson (d 1983); *b* 23 March 1946; *Educ* Buckingham Coll Harrow Middx, LSE (LLB); *m* 19 July 1969, Rosalind Denise, da of Lt Dennis Ivor Leach, of Bournemouth; 1 s (Dominic b 1971), 1 da (Lucy b 1972); *Career* called to the Bar Gray's Inn 1969; recorder of the Crown Ct 1990– (asst recorder 1986–89); asst boundary cmmr Boundary Cmmn (Parly) for England and Wales 1981, ad hoc appt asst boundary cmmr Local Govt Boundary Cmmn for England and Wales 1983, appt to Panel of Chairmen of Structure Plan Examinations in Public Dept of Environment 1984, asst recorder 1986–89, appt to Panels of Legal Assessors to GMC and Gen Dental Cncl 1988, inspector Dept of Transport (Merchant Shipping Act 1988 investigations) 1989, inspector DTI (insider dealing investigation) 1989, Standing Counsel to H M Customs and Excise (Criminal S E Circuit) 1989–94; dir Watford AFC 1990–96; memb Hon Soc of Gray's Inn; *Recreations* theatre, music, gardening, reading; *Clubs* Athenaeum; *Style*— Stuart Lawson Rogers, Esq, QC; ✉ 36 Essex St, London WC2R 3AS (☎ 0171 413 0353, 0171 353 3533, fax 0171 413 0374)

LAWSON-TANCRED, Andrew Peter; s and h of Sir Henry Lawson-Tancred, 10 Bt, of Boroughbridge, Yorkshire and Jean Veronica, *née* Foster (d 1970); *b* 18 Feb 1952; *Educ* Eton, Univ of Leeds; *Career* barr at law; memb Hon Soc of the Middle Temple; *Recreations* flying; *Style*— Andrew Lawson-Tancred, Esq; ✉ 13 Musgrave Crescent, London SW6 4PT; The Television Corporation PLC, 30 Sackville Street, London W1X 1DB (☎ 0171 287 5700, fax 0171 287 6524)

LAWSON-TANCRED, Sir Henry; 10 Bt (E 1662), JP (West Riding 1967); s of Maj Sir Thomas Selby Lawson-Tancred, 9 Bt (d 1945); *b* 1924; *Educ* Stowe, Jesus Coll Cambridge; *m* 1, 1950, Jean Veronica (d 1970), da of Gerald Robert Foster (d 1962); 5 s, 1 da; m 2, 1978, Susan Dorothy Marie-Gabrielle, da of late Sir Kenelm Cayley, 10 Bt, and formerly w of Maldwin Drummond; *Heir* s, Andrew Peter Lawson-Tancred; *Career* served with RAFVR 1942–46; *Style*— Sir Henry Lawson-Tancred, Bt, JP; ✉ Aldborough Manor, Boroughbridge, Yorks (☎ 01423 322716)

LAWTON, Commodore Alan Frederick; s of Frederick Lawton (d 1974), of Berkhamsted, and Ivy, *née* Parker (d 1989); *b* 14 Feb 1939; *Educ* Berkhamsted Sch, Britannia RNC Dartmouth, Royal Naval Engrg Coll, Univ of London (BSc), RCDS; *m* 21 Jan 1967, Susan Russell, da of John Torrie Johnston (d 1978), of Glasgow; 2 da (Tina b 1967, Jennifer b 1970); *Career* RNC Dartmouth 1957, Cdr 1975, Trg Cdr HMS Caledonia 1976–78, Dir Marine Engrg RNZN 1978–79, Chief Tech Servs RNZN 1979–80, Marine Engr Offr HMS Bristol 1980–82, Offr i/c Machinery Trials Units 1982–83, Capt 1984, Offr i/c Fleet Maintenance Falklands Is 1984, Asst Dir Naval Plans and Progs 1985–87, memb Royal Coll of Def Studies 1988, Dir Naval Logistic Planning 1989–92, Dir Naval Logistic Staff 1992–93; head of Logistics Engrg Systems and Servs Div British Aerospace Defence 1993–; FIMechE 1993, FIMgt 1991, FInstD 1992; *Recreations* golf, tennis, watching cricket and rugby; *Style*— Alan Lawton; ✉ Head of Logistics Engineering, IJVC Horizon, Kemble House, Kemble Street, London WC2B 4AJ (☎ 0171 489 4110, fax 0171 489 4113)

LAWTON, Charles Henry Huntly; s of Philip Charles Fenner Lawton, CBE, DFC (d 1993), and Emma Letitia Gertrude, *née* Stephenson; *b* 17 April 1946; *Educ* Westminster Sch; *m* 21 April 1979, Sarah Margaret, da of Rev Christopher Lambert; 1 s (Timothy b 1982), 1 da (Hermione b 1984); *Career* admitted slr 1970; legal advsr and head Legal Dept RTZ Corp plc 1985–; *Recreations* walking, reading, fishing; *Clubs* RAC; *Style*— Charles Lawton, Esq; ✉ The RTZ Corporation Plc, 6 St James's Square, London SW1 (☎ 0171 930 2399, fax 0171 930 3249)

LAWTON, Rt Hon Sir Frederick Horace; kt (1961), PC (1972); s of William John Lawton, OBE; *b* 21 Dec 1911; *Educ* Battersea GS, CCC Cambridge; *m* 1937, Doreen, da of Richard John Maker Wilton (d 1979), of Bodmin, Cornwall; 2 s; *Career* London Irish Rifles 1939–41; QC 1957, judge of the High Ct 1961–72, lord justice of appeal 1972–86; chm: Standing Ctee for Criminal Law Revision 1977–86, Advsy Ctee on Legal Educn 1977–86, pres British Acad of Forensic Scis 1964; *Style*— The Rt Hon Sir Frederick Lawton; ✉ 1 The Village, Skelton, York YO3 6XX (☎ 01904 470441)

LAWTON, Jeffrey; s of Harold Lawton (d 1975), of Oldham, and Edna, *née* Penney (d 1978); *b* 11 Dec 1938; *Educ* Greenhill GS, Royal Manchester Coll of Music; *m* 26 Sept 1959, Ann Barbara, da of Alan Whitehead; 2 s (Andrew David b 19 Sept 1966, Robert Jeffrey b 7 May 1969), 1 da (Sara Jane b 17 Oct 1971); *Career* tenor; princ WNO 1982–87 (chorus 1981), freelance 1987–, artistic dir Civit Hills Opera Theatre 1995–, dir Manannan Opera Isle of Man 1995, dir of vocal studies and opera La Tour de France Festival 1995, prof Vocal Studies Dept RSAMD 1995; has sung with various major Br orchs and conductors; appeared at various major festivals incl: Salzburg, Edinburgh, Llangollen, Salisbury, York, BBC Proms; *Performances* with WNO incl: Ringmaster in The Bartered Bride 1982, Tichon in Katya Kabanova 1982, Judge in Un Ballo in Maschera 1982, Large Prisoner in House of the Dead 1982, Laca in Jenufa 1984, Manolious in The Greek Passion 1984, title role in Siegfried 1985 and 1986, Siegfried in Götterdämmerung 1985, title role in Otello (in Brussels, Nancy and Paris) 1987 and 1990, Don Jose in Carmen 1987, Emperor in Die Frau ohne Schatten 1989, Luka in House of the Dead 1991, Aegisthus in Elektra 1992 and 1995, Tristan in Tristan und Isolde 1993; other operatic roles incl: Florestan in Fidelio (Opera North) 1988, Siegmund in Die Walküre (Cologne) 1988, Siegfried in Götterdämmerung (Cologne) 1989, Erik in Der Fliegende Holländer (Opera North) 1989, title role in Otello (Lisbon) 1989 and (Covent Garden) 1990, Radames in Aida (Den Bosch Holland) 1991, Prince Shuisky in Boris Godunov (Opera North) 1992, Laca in Jenufa (New Israeli Opera) 1993, Captain in Wozzeck (Opera North) 1993, Aegisthus in Elektra (Covent Garden) 1994, Tristan in Tristan und Isolde (Scottish Opera, Lisbon and Mainz) 1994, Wird in Der Rosenkavalier (Covent Garden), Apollo in Daphne (Garsington) 1995, Aegisthus in Elektra (Canadian Opera Co) 1996, Laca in Jenufa (New Israeli Opera) 1996, Pedro in Indes de Castro (world premiere, Scottish Opera) 1996; concert performances incl: Das Lied von der Erde (Paris, under Janovski, also bdcast on radio, BBC Proms 1995), Mahler Symphony No 8 (Turin, also televised); *Recordings* incl: The Greek Passion (under Sir Charles Mackerras) 1982, Panait and Adonis, Supraphon (with Brno State Philharmonic Orch); *Clubs* Oldham Athletic FC; *Style*— Jeffrey Lawton, Esq; ✉ c/o Music International, 13 Ardilaun Road, London N5 2QR (☎ 0171 359 5183, fax 0171 226 9792)

LAWTON, Prof John Hartley; s of Frank Hartley Lawton (d 1982), of Leyland, Lancashire, and Mary, *née* Cuerden; *b* 24 Sept 1943; *Educ* Balshaw's GS Leyland, Univ Coll Durham (BSc, PhD); *m* 22 Oct 1966, Dorothy, da of Harold Grimshaw (d 1960), of Leyland Lancs; 1 s (Graham John b 1969), 1 da (Anna Louise b 1968); *Career* Univ of Oxford: departmental demonstrator in zoology 1968–71, lectr in zoology Lincoln Coll 1970–71, lectr in zoology St Anne's Coll 1970–71; Dept of Biology Univ of York: lectr 1971–78, sr lectr 1978–82, reader 1982–85, prof 1985–89; prof of community ecology and dir Centre for Population Biology Imperial Coll of Sci Technol and Med Univ of London 1989–, adjunct scientist Inst of Ecosystem Studies Millbrook NY 1992–; chm: Royal Cmmn on Environmental Pollution, Terrestrial and Freshwater Sci and Technology Bd Nat Environmental Research Cncl; memb: Natural Environment Research Cncl, Br Ecological Soc, American Soc of Naturalists; chm Cncl RSPB; formerly cncl memb Freshwater Biological Assoc; Hon DSc Univ of Lancaster 1993; fell Royal Entomological Soc, fell Br Tst for Ornithology; FRS; *Books* Insects on Plants: Community Patterns and Mechanisms (1984), Blackwell Scientific Oxford (with T R E Southwood and D R Strong), The Evolutionary Interactions of Animals and Plants (ed with W G Chaloner and J L Harper, 1991), Linking Species and Ecosystems (ed with C G Jones, 1994), Extinction Rates (ed with R M May, 1995); *Recreations* bird watching, gardening, photography, running, hill walking, travel; *Style*— Prof John Lawton, FRS; ✉ 17 Course Road, Ascot, Berks SL5 7HQ (☎ 01344 26819); 21 Lime Avenue, York YO3 0BT (☎ 01904 424873); Centre for Population Biology, Imperial College, Silwood Park, Ascot, Berks SL5 7PY (☎ 01344 294354, fax 01344 873173)

LAWTON, District Judge Peter Edward; s of Frank Edward Lawton, of Nottingham, and Ida Hook, *née* Rayner (d 1986); *b* 4 June 1946; *Educ* Henry Mellish GS Nottingham, Univ of Leeds (LLB); *m* 22 May 1976, Joy Ann, da of David John Reavill; 1 s (Mark Edward b 15 June 1977); *Career* admitted slr 1971, ptnr J H Milner & Son Solicitors Leeds 1972–91 (articled clerk 1968–70), dep registrar 1986, district judge 1991–; chief examiner part I slrs' qualifying exam torts 1977–82; attorney at law State of Texas 1980; *Recreations* amateur radio, walking, gardening; *Style*— District Judge Lawton; ✉ Bradford County Court, The Law Courts, Exchange Square, Drake Street, Bradford, West Yorks BD1 1JA (☎ 01274 840274, fax 01274 840275)

LAX, Peter Andrew; s of Carl Werner Lax, BEM, and Lilly Lax; *b* 27 March 1958; *Educ* Barnard Castle Sch, Hatfield Coll Univ of Durham (BA); *m* 27 July 1985, Angela Clare, da of Kenneth Sidney Ansell Davis, of Gayton, Wirral; 1 s (Adam Peter Simon b 14 Aug 1992); *Career* admitted slr 1982; articled clerk John Buckingham Duggan Lea & Co 1980–82, ptnr Pinsent & Co Slrs 1988, jt fndr Bell Lax Litigation Slrs 1995–; memb: Birmingham Canal Navigation Soc, Stourbridge Inst, Warwickshire Industl Locomotive Tst; organiser legal advice session Birmingham CAB; memb Law Soc 1982; *Recreations* rabbit watching, bridge (Birmingham Business Houses pairs champion); *Style*— Peter Lax, Esq; ✉ Wissage Hill House, Covey Close, Lichfield, Staffs WS13 6BS (☎ 01543 250390); Bell Lax Litigation, 2 High Street, Sutton Coldfield, West Midlands (☎ 0121 355 0011, fax 0121 355 0099)

LAY, David John; s of Walter Charles Frederick Lay (d 1984), and June Barbara, *née* Cadman; *b* 15 Aug 1948; *Educ* Magdalen Coll Sch Oxford, CCC Oxford (MA); *m* 1 Sept 1973, Tamara Said, da of Said Pasha Mufti (d 1989), former PM of Jordan; 1 s (Taimour b 1982), 3 da (Sima b 1977, Maya b 1980, Lana b 1982); *Career* BBC radio news reporter 1974–79, presenter Twenty-four Hours BBC World Serv 1979–91, managing ed Oxford Analytica 1988–; *Recreations* tennis, foreign travel, Middle East politics; *Clubs* David Lloyd (Raynes Park); *Style*— David Lay, Esq; ✉ 90 Coombe Lane West, Kingston upon Thames, Surrey KT2 7DB (☎ 0181 336 1325)

LAY, Richard Neville; s of late Edward John Lay, of Banstead, Surrey, and Nellie, *née* Gould; *b* 18 Oct 1938; *Educ* Whitgift Sch; *m* 1, 1964; 1 s (Martin Richard Forbes b 1969), 1 da (Melanie St Clair b 1965); m 2, 19 Dec 1991, Pauline Alison Marguerita Pringle, *née* Howard Dorchy; *Career* chartered surveyor; ptnr Debenham Tewson & Chinnocks 1965–87, chm Debenham Tewson & Chinnocks Holdings plc and subsid cos 1987–, vice chm Central London Bd Sun Alliance and London Insurance Group; tstee Tate Gallery Fndn 1988–94; chm: Market Requirements Ctee RICS (The Lay Report, 1991), Commercial Market Panel RICS 1992–; vice pres Gen Cncl RICS 1995– (memb 1994–); memb: Cncl Br Property Federation 1992–, Bank of England Property Forum 1994–, Advsy Panel on Standards in the Planning Inspectorate 1996–; Liveryman and surveyor to the Worshipful Co of Armourers & Brasiers 1983–; FRICS; *Recreations* gardening, family life; *Clubs* RAC; *Style*— Richard Lay, Esq; ✉ 15 Clareville Grove, London SW7 5AU; 44 Brook St, London W1 (☎ 0171 408 2650, fax 0171 493 8161)

LAYARD, Adm Sir Michael Henry Gordon; KCB (1993), CBE (1983); s of Edwin Henry Frederick Layard (d 1972), of Colombo, Sri Lanka, and Doris Christian Gordon, *née* Spence (d 1965); *b* 3 Jan 1936; *Educ* Pangbourne Coll, BRNC Dartmouth; *m* 17 Dec 1966, Elspeth Horsley Fisher, da of late Rev L C Fisher; 2 s (James Henry Gordon b 1967, Andrew Charles Gordon b 1969); *Career* RN: Seaman Offr 1954–58, flying trg 1958–60, fighter pilot 1960–70, air warfare instr 1964; Cmd: 899 Naval Air Sqdn (Sea Vixens) 1970–71, HMS Lincoln 1971–72; NDC 1974, Directorate Naval Air Warfare MOD 1975–77, Cdr (Air) HMS Ark Royal 1977–78, CSO (Air) to Flag Offr Naval Air Cmd 1979–82, SNO SS Atlantic Conveyor Falklands conflict 1982; Cmd: RNAS Culdrose 1982–84, HMS Cardiff 1984–85 (leader Task Force to Persian Gulf); Dir Naval Warfare (Air) MOD 1985–88, Flag Offr Naval Air Command 1988–90 (latterly Flag Offr Naval Aviation), Dir Gen Naval Manpower Trg 1990–92, head RN Offr Study Gp 1992–93, Second Sea Lord, Chief of Naval Personnel and Adm Pres RNC Greenwich 1993–94, Second Sea Lord and Cdr in Chief Naval Home Command and Flag ADC to HM The Queen 1994–95; chm White Ensign Assoc; pres RN Golfing Soc 1988–94, govr Pangbourne Coll 1995–; tstee Fleet Air Arm Museum 1988–; memb: RN Sailing Assoc, Fleet Air Arm Offrs' Assoc, RUSI, Cncl Royal Patriotic Fund; Ordre de Chevalier Bretvin; *Recreations* music, history, painting, sailing, collecting experiences; *Clubs* Royal Navy Club of 1765 & 1785; *Style*— Adm Sir Michael Layard, KCB, CBE; ✉ c/o Lloyds Bank plc, Cheapside, Langport, Somerset

LAYARD, Prof (Peter) Richard Grenville; s of John Willoughby Layard (d 1974), and Doris, *née* Dunn (d 1973); *b* 15 March 1934; *Educ* Eton, Univ of Cambridge (BA), LSE (MSc); *m* 1991 Molly, *née* Reid; *Career* 2 Lt 4 RHA 1953–54, RA 1952–54; sch teacher LCC 1959–61, sr res offr Robbins Ctee of Higher Educn 1961–64; LSE: dep dir Higher Educn Res Unit 1964–74, lectr 1968–75, head Centre for Lab Economics 1974–90, reader 1975–80, prof of economics 1980–, dir Centre of Econ Performance 1990–; advsr Working Centre for Economic Reform Govt of Russian Fedn 1991–; memb Univ Grants Ctee 1985–89, chm Exec Ctee Employment Inst until 1986 and chm 1987–91; fell Econometric Soc; *Books* More Jobs, Less Inflation (1982), How to Beat Unemployment (1986), Restoring Europe's Prosperity (with O Blanchard and R Dornbusch, 1986), Microeconomic Theory (with A Walters, 1978, reissued 1987), Unemployment, Macroeconomic Performance and the Labour Market (with S Nickell and R Jackman, 1991); *Recreations* walking, tennis; *Style*— Prof Richard Layard; ✉ 45 Cholmeley Park, London N6 5EL (☎ 0181 341 7771); London School of Economics, Houghton Street, London WC2A 2AE (☎ 0171 955 7281, fax 0171 955 6848)

LAYE, Michael George (Mike); s of George Edward Laye, of North Lancing, W Sussex, and Audrey, *née* Ford; *b* 16 May 1948; *Educ* Henley GS Henley-on-Thames, Univ of Manchester (BA); *m* 1, 1968 (m dis 1972), Helen, *née* Capewell; m 2, 1982 (sep) Emily Louise, *née* Goodrum; 2 da (Maybelle Evelyn b 22 Aug 1983, Agnes Annie Webb b 23 May 1986), 1 step da (Selena Cleo b 8 Aug 1978); partner Sandra Ross; 1 s (Sam George Thomas Ross-Laye b 5 Sept 1994); *Career* actor/dir 1972–75, dir ICA Theatre 1975–77, freelance photographer 1977–; AFAEP: Merit Award 1987, Gold, Silver and Merit Awards 1988; chm Assoc of Photographers 1990 (memb Cncl 1987–90); *Recreations* walking, jazz, technology; *Style*— Mike Laye, Esq; ✉ Priory Studios, 252 Belsize Road, London NW6 4BT (mobile 0956 701208)

LAYFIELD, Sir Frank Henry Burland Willoughby; kt (1976), QC (1967); s of Henry Layfield (d 1960); *b* 9 Aug 1921; *Educ* Sevenoaks; *m* 1965, Irene Patricia, da of Capt J D Harvey, RN; 1 s, 1 da; *Career* called to the Bar Gray's Inn 1954; chm: Inquiry into

Greater London Plan 1970–72, Ctee of Inquiry into Local Govt Fin 1974–76, NEDO Working Pty on Constructional Steel Work 1977–82; counsel to Univ of Oxford 1972, bencher Gray's Inn 1974, memb Sec of State's Housing Fin Policy Review 1975–77, general cmmr of taxes 1977–, recorder of the Crown Ct 1979–85, govt inspr on inquiry into Sizewell B Nuclear Power Station 1982–85; pres Assoc of CCs; chm: Tribunal for the Protection of St Paul's Cathedral 1971–, Inst of Environmental Assessment 1992–; hon fell: Coll of Estate Mgmnt 1981, Inst of Landscape Architects 1989, Inc Soc of Valuers and Auctioneers 1978; Hon LLD Univ of Reading 1996; memb Ct of Assts Worshipful Co of Pewterers (Master 1993); Lincoln Land Inst Gold Medal 1983, Property Award Charter Soc 1991; ARICS 1977; *Style*— Sir Frank Layfield, QC

LAYMAN, Rear Adm Christopher Hope; CB (1990), DSO (1982), LVO (1977); s of Capt Herbert F H Layman, DSO, RN (d 1989), and Elizabeth, *née* Hughes (d 1990); *b* 9 March 1938; *Educ* Winchester; *m* 15 Aug 1964, Katharine Romer, da of Capt Stephen Romer Ascherson, RN (d 1955); 1 s (James b 1965), 1 da (Alexandra b 1969); *Career* joined RN 1956, specialised communications and electronic warfare 1966; cmd: HMS Hubberston 1968–70, HMS Lynx 1972–74; exec offr HM Yacht Britannia 1976–78, Capt 7 Frigate Sqdn 1981–83; cmd: HMS Argonaut 1981–82, HMS Cleopatra 1982–83, HMS Invincible 1984–86; Cdr Br Forces Falkland Islands 1986–87, asst dir (CIS) Int Mil Staff NATO HQ 1988–91; ret 1991; conslt in CIS and maritime affairs 1991–; *Publications* Man of Letters (1990), The Falklands and the Dwarf (1995); *Recreations* fishing, archaeology; *Clubs* New (Edinburgh); *Style*— Rear Adm C H Layman, CB, DSO, LVO

LAYTON, Alexander William; QC (1995); s of Paul Henry Layton (d 1989), of London, and Frances Evelyn, *née* Weekes; *b* 23 Feb 1952; *Educ* Marlborough, Univ of Oxford (MA), Ludwig-Maximillian Univ Munich; *m* 1988, Sandy Forshaw, da of late Gordon Alexander Keith Matheson; 2 da (Catherine Emma b 30 June 1989, Lydia Frances b 27 Sept 1991); *Career* called to the Bar Middle Temple 1976; memb Br German Jurists' Assoc (chm 1988–93); *Books* The Bar on Trial (contrib, 1977), European Civil Practice (co-author, 1989); *Style*— Alexander Layton, Esq, QC; ✉ 2 Temple Gardens, Temple, London EC4Y 9AY (☎ 0171 583 6041, fax 0171 583 2094)

LAYTON, Hon Christopher Walter; s of 1 Baron Layton, CH, CBE (d 1966); *b* 31 Dec 1929; *Educ* Oundle, King's Coll Cambridge; *m* 1, 1952 (m dis 1957), Anneliese Margarethe, da of Joachim von Thadden, of Hanover; 1 s, 1 da; m 2, 1961 (m dis), Margaret Ann, da of Leslie Moon; 3 da; m 3, 1995, Wendy Daniels, da of Kenneth Bartlett; 1 da; *Career* Intelligence Corps 1948–49; ICI Ltd 1952, The Economist Intelligence Unit 1953–54, editorial writer Euro affairs The Economist 1954–62; contested (Lib) Chippenham Parly election 1962, 1964 and 1966; econ advsr to Liberal Party 1962–69; dir Centre for European Industrial Studies Bath Univ 1968–71; Cmmn of Euro Communities: Chef de Cabinet to Cmmr Spinelli 1971–73, dir Computer Electronics, Telecommunications and Air Transport Equipment Manufacturing, Directorate-General of Internal Market and Industrial Affairs 1973–81, hon dir-gen EEC 1981–; dir World Order Project Federal Tst 1987–90; ed Alliance 1982–83, assoc ed New Democrat 1983–85; contested (SDP) London W Euro Parly Election 1984; fndng memb Grimstone Community 1990–; *Publications* Transatlantic Investment (1966), European Advanced Technology (1968), Cross-frontier Mergers Europe (1970), Industry and Europe (jtly, 1971), Ten Innovations - International Study on Development Technology and the Use of Qualified Scientists and Engineers in Ten Industries (jtly, 1972), Europe and the Global Crisis (1987), A Step Beyond Fear (1989), The Healing of Europe (1990); *Recreations* painting, sculpture, healing; *Style*— The Hon Christopher Layton

LAYTON, Dr Clive Allan; s of Peter Eric Layton (d 1979), and Joan, *née* Sims; *b* 17 April 1944; *Educ* City of London Sch, King's Coll London, St George's Hosp Med Sch London (MB BS); *m* 2 April 1971, Helen MacLean, da of William Paxton (d 1953); 2 da (Charlotte b 1972, Sarah b 1974); *Career* sr registrar in cardiology The London Hosp 1972–77; consIt cardiologist: Royal Brompton Nat Heart and Chest Hosps The London Chest Hosp (now Royal Hosps Tst The London Chest Hosp) 1977–, NE Thames Regnl Health Authy 1977–; clinical dir in cardiology London Chest Hosp 1991–94; memb Cardiology Ctee RCP; contrib to pubns on cardiology and intensive care; former memb English Fencing Team (Br Schs, Public Schs and Br Junior Fencing Champion); FRCP 1992 (MRCP 1969); *Recreations* equestrian activities and computer programming; *Style*— Dr Clive Layton; ✉ 22 Upper Wimpole St, London W1M 7TA (☎ 0171 486 8961, fax 0171 486 7918, mobile 0385 228166, telex 23621 CARDIO G)

LAYTON, Lt-Col the Hon David; MBE (1946); s of 1 Baron Layton, CH, CBE (d 1966), and Eleanor Dorothea (d 1959), da of Francis Beresford Plumptre Osmaston; uncle and hp of 3 Baron Layton, *qv*; *b* 5 July 1914; *Educ* Gresham's Sch Holt, Trinity Coll Cambridge; *m* 1, 1939 (m dis 1972), Elizabeth, da of Rev Robert Millar Gray, of Hampstead; 2 s, 1 da; m 2, 1972, Joy Parkinson; *Career* 2 Lt RE 1939; md Incomes Data Services 1966–91; chm and fndr Environmental Data Services 1976–; *Clubs* Reform; *Style*— Lt-Col the Hon David Layton, MBE; ✉ 18 Grove Terrace, Highgate Rd, London NW5 1PH (☎ 0171 267 4280)

LAYTON, 3 Baron (UK 1947); Geoffrey Michael Layton; o s of 2 Baron Layton (d 1989), and Dorothy Rose, *née* Cross (d 1994); *b* 18 July 1947; *Educ* St Paul's, Stanford Univ Calif, Univ of Southern Calif; *m* 1, 1969 (m dis 1970), Viviane, da of François P Cracco, of Louvain, Belgium; m 2, 1989, Caroline Jane, da of William Thomas Mason, of Fairford, Glos, and formerly w of Adm Spyros Soulis, of Athens; *Heir* uncle, Lt-Col the Hon David Layton, MBE, *qv*; *Style*— The Rt Hon the Lord Layton; ✉ c/o House of Lords, London SW1

LAZAREV, Alexander; *Educ* Leningrad Conservatory, Moscow Conservatory; *Career* conductor; fndr Ensemble of Soloists Bolshoi Theatre 1978, chief conductor and artistic dir Bolshoi Theatre 1987–95; princ guest conductor: BBC Symphony Orchestra 1992–95, Royal Scottish National Orchestra 1994–; Bolshoi debut 1973, UK debut with Royal Liverpool Philharmonic Orch 1987; worked with orchs incl: St Petersburg Philharmonic, USSR State Symphony, Berlin Philharmonic, Bavarian Radio Symphony, Philharmonic, Munich Philharmonic, Netherlands Radio Philharmonic, Rotterdam Philharmonic, Orchestre National de France, Orchestra Sinfonica del Teatro alla Scala Milan, Orchestra Sinfonica dell'Accademia Nazionale di Santa Cecilia Rome, City of Birmingham Symphony, Royal Scottish National, The Philharmonia, NHK Symphony Orch, Cleveland Orch, Montreal Symphony, Orchestre de la Suisse Romande, New Zealand Symphony Orch; venues incl: Barbican Hall, Royal Festival Hall, Royal Albert Hall (BBC Proms annually 1991–), La Scala Milan, Edinburgh Festival, Metropolitan Opera NY, Theatre Royal de la Monnaie Brussels, Arena di Verona, Bavarian State Opera; various recordings on Melodiya, Virgin Classics, Sony Classical and Erato record labels; first prize USSR nat competition for conductors 1971, first prize and Gold medal Karajan Competition 1972; *Style*— Alexander Lazarev, Esq; ✉ c/o Tennant Artists, Unit 2, 39 Tadema Road, London SW10 0PY (☎ 0171 376 3758, fax 0171 351 0679)

LAZENBY, David William; s of George William Lazenby, of Walton-on-Thames, Surrey, and Jane, *née* Foster; *b* 13 Oct 1937; *Educ* Canford, Battersea Coll of Technol, Imperial Coll London (DIC), City Univ London (Dip, CU); *m* 2 Sept 1961, Valerie Ann, da of Lewis Edward Kent, OBE (d 1972); 1 s (Jonathan b 22 Jan 1965), 1 da (Andrea b 23 Feb 1968); *Career* chm Andrews Kent & Stone consulting engrs 1983– (joined 1962, ptnr 1972); civil and structural engrg work includes: Nat Library of Wales, Merchant Navy Coll, E Sussex County Hall; past pres IStructE, chm European Ctee for Structural Eurocodes; Eur Ing, FCGI, FICE, FIStructE, MConsE; *Books* Cutting for Construction (1978), Structural Mechanics for Students (1984), 1936/85 Structural Steelwork for Students (jtly, 1985); *Recreations* travel, tennis, opera, good food and wine; *Style*— Eur Ing David Lazenby; ✉ Pond Cottage, 28 Sanger Drive, Send, Woking, Surrey GU23 7EB (☎ 01483 223 104); Andrews Kent & Stone Ltd, 69 High Street, Croydon CR9 1PQ (☎ 0181 686 9271, fax 0181 680 2305)

LAZENBY, Terence Michael; s of Ernest Lazenby (d 1990), and Joyce, *née* Spice (d 1987); *b* 29 Nov 1942; *Educ* King's Sch Macclesfield, Univ of Swansea (BSc), Stanford Univ (MSc), Cert Dip of Fin and Accounting; *m* 1971, Eleanor Jane, da of James Livingston Ritchie; 1 s (Simon James b 1975), 1 da (Sarah Jane b 1977); *Career* British Petroluem (BP): univ apprentice 1961–64, technologist 1964–71, process engr 1971–77, engrg mangr Sullom Voe Project 1979–81, tech div mangr BP Developments Aust 1981–84, works gen mangr BP Chemicals Grangemouth 1984–88, dir of mfrg and supply BP Oil UK Ltd 1988–90, gen mangr BP Engineering 1990–92, mangr BP Research and Engrg Site 1993, chief engr BP International 1994–; chm Br Pipeline Agency 1988–; memb Senate Engrg Cncl 1996–; Maj (TA); FInstPet 1991, FIChemE 1992, FEng 1995; *Recreations* golf, swimming, gardening, tennis; *Style*— Terence Lazenby, Esq, FEng; ✉ Seamab, Woodland Drive, East Horsley, Surrey KT24 5AN (☎ 01483 284232); BP International Ltd, Chertsey Road, Sunbury-on-Thames, Middlesex TW16 7LN (☎ 01932 762389)

LE BAILLY, Vice Adm Sir Louis Edward Stewart Holland; KBE (1972, OBE 1952), CB (1969), DL (Cornwall 1982); s of Robert Francis Le Bailly; *b* 18 July 1915; *Educ* RNC Dartmouth, RN Engrg Coll Devonport; *m* 1946, Pamela Ruth, da of Rear Adm Charles Pierre Berthon; 3 da; *Career* joined RN 1929, served WWII, Cdr British Navy Staff and naval attaché Washington DC 1967–69, dir Serv Intelligence MOD 1970, ret 1972; DG of Intelligence MOD 1972–75; memb The Pilgrims; Hon DSc Plymouth; CEng, FIMechE, FIMarE, FInstPet; *Books* The Man around the Engine: From Fisher to the Falklands, Old Loves Return; *Clubs* Naval; *Style*— Vice Adm Sir Louis Le Bailly, KBE, CB, DL; ✉ Garlands House, St Tudy, Bodmin, Cornwall

LE BRUN, Christopher Mark; s of John Le Brun, BEM, QSM, RM (d 1970), of Portsmouth, and Eileen Betty, *née* Miles; *b* 20 Dec 1951; *Educ* Southern GS Portsmouth, Slade Sch of Fine Art (DFA), Chelsea Sch of Art (MA); *m* 31 March 1979, Charlotte Eleanor, da of Gp Capt Hugh Beresford Verity, DSO, DFC, of Richmond, Surrey; 2 s (Luke b 1984, Edmund b 1990), 1 da (Lily b 1986); *Career* artist; awards and cmmns: prizewinner John Moores Liverpool Exhibitions 1978 and 1980, Calouste Gulbenkian Fndn Printmakers Commission Award 1983, designer Ballet Imperial Royal Opera House Covent Garden 1985; DAAD Fellowship Berlin 1987–88; tstee: Tate Gallery 1990–95, Nat Gallery 1996–; *Solo Exhibitions* incl: Nigel Greenwood Gallery London 1980, 1982, 1985 and 1989, Gillespie-Laage-Salomon Paris 1981, Sperone Westwater NY 1983, 1986 and 1988, Fruitmarket Gallery Edinburgh 1985, Arnolfini Gallery Bristol 1985, Kunsthalle Basel 1986, DAAD Galerie Berlin 1988, Galerie Rudolf Zwirner Cologne 1988, Art Center Pasadena 1992, LA Louver Los Angeles 1992, Marlborough Fine Art London 1994, Astrup Fearnley Museum of Modern Art Oslo 1995, Fitzwilliam Museum Cambridge 1995; *Group Exhibitions* incl: Nuova Imagine Milan Triennale 1980, Sydney Biennale 1982, New Art (Tate Gallery London) 1983, An Int Survey of Recent Painting and Sculpture (Museum of Modern Art NY) 1984, The British Show (toured Australia and NZ) 1985, Paris Biennale 1985, San Francisco Biennale 1986, Venice Biennale 1982 and 1984, Falls the Shadow (Recent Br and Euro Art Hayward Gallery London) 1986, British Art of the 1980's (Museum of Modern Art: Oxford, Budapest, Warsaw, Prague) 1987, Avant Garde in the Eighties (LA County Museum) 1987, Br Art of the 1980's (Liljevalchs Museum Stockholm) 1987, The Br Picture (Louver Gallery LA) 1988, New Br Painting (Cincinnati Museum and American tour) 1988–89, Br Art Now (Setagaya Art Museum and Japanese tour) 1990–91, Contemporary Br Art in Print (Scottish Nat Gallery of Modern Art and American tour) 1995–96; *Style*— Christopher Le Brun, Esq; ✉ c/o Marlborough Fine Art (London) Ltd, 6 Albemarle Street, London W1X 4BY (☎ 0171 629 5161)

LE CARPENTIER, Francis Stewart; s of Frank Henry Le Carpentier, of Worthing, W Sussex, and Elizabeth, *née* Stafford (d 1961); *b* 26 Feb 1949; *Educ* Royal Wolverhampton Sch; *m* 2 July 1976 (m dis 1991), Nicole Madeleine Fischer Corderior, da of Willey Fischer, of Brussels; 1 s (Phillipe Alexandre), 1 da (Mercedes Elizabeth); *Career* offr US Armed Forces 1969–71, served Europe and Far East; retail mangr until 1969, gp sales dir Int Property Developers 1971–74, chm and chief exec Paramount Gp 1974–91, jt chief exec Trading Force Ltd (UN Procurement Agency) 1991–; FInstD 1989 (MInstD 1988); *Recreations* skiing, shooting (not animals), motorsports and powercraft racing; *Clubs* Annabel's (London), various in rest of world; *Style*— Francis Le Carpentier, Esq; ✉ El Morapio, Calle 15D, Casa 6D, Las Brisas, Nueva Andalucia, Marbella, Malaga, Spain; Trading Force Ltd, 4 Talina Centre, Bagley's Lane, Fulham, London SW6 2BW (☎ 0171 384 1000, fax 0171 384 3060)

LE CARRÉ, John (pen name of David John Moore Cornwell); s of Ronald Thomas Archibald Cornwell, and Olive, *née* Glassy; *b* 19 Oct 1931; *Educ* Sherborne, Univ of Berne, Lincoln Coll Oxford (BA); *m* 1, 1954 (m dis 1971), Alison Ann Veronica Sharp; 3 s; m 2, 1972, Valerie Jane Eustace; 1 s; *Career* novelist; schoolmaster Eton 1956–58, British Foreign Serv 1959–64 (serv as second sec Bonn then political consul Hamburg); Grand Master Award Mystery Writers of America, Malaparte Prize Italy, Crime Writers' Assoc Diamond Dagger Award 1987; subject of Time and Newsweek cover stories and work subject of many books; hon fell Lincoln Coll Oxford 1984, Hon DLitt Univ of Exeter 1990; *Books* Call for the Dead (1961, filmed as the Deadly Affair 1967), A Murder of Quality (1962, TV film prize winner at Venice Prix Italia 1991), The Spy Who Came in From the Cold (1963, film, Somerset Maugham Award, Crime Writers' Assoc Golden Dagger Award, Best Mystery of the Year Mystery Writers of America Inc), The Looking Glass War (1965, film), A Small Town in Germany (1968), The Naïve and Sentimental Lover (1971), Tinker, Tailor, Soldier, Spy (1974, BBC TV series), The Honourable Schoolboy (1977, James Tait Black Meml Prize, Crime Writers' Assoc Golden Dagger Award), Smiley's People (1980, BBC TV series), The Little Drummer Girl (1983, Warner Bros film), A Perfect Spy (1986, BBC TV series), The Russia House (1989, film, Nikos Kasanzakis Prize 1991), The Secret Pilgrim (1990), The Night Manager (1993), Our Game (1995), The Tailor of Panama (1996); The Karla Trilogy (Smiley's People, Tinker, Tailor, Soldier, Spy and The Honourable Schoolboy) published in one volume as The Quest for Karla,; *Style*— John Le Carré, Esq; ✉ c/o David Higham Associates, 5–8 Lower John Street, Golden Square, London W1R 4HA (☎ 0171 437 7888, fax 0171 437 1072)

LE CHEMINANT, Air Chief Marshal Sir Peter de Lacey; GBE (1978), KCB (1972, CB 1968), DFC (1943, and bar 1951); s of Lt-Col Keith Le Cheminant, TD, of Guernsey, CI, and Blanche Etheldred Wake Clark; *b* 17 June 1920; *Educ* Elizabeth Coll Guernsey, RAF Coll Cranwell; *m* 1940, Sylvia, da of J van Bodegom (d 1963); 1 s, 2 da; *Career* joined RAF 1939, Cmdt Joint Warfare Establishment 1968–70, asst chief of Air Staff (Policy) 1972, memb Permanent Mil Deputies Gp Cen Treaty Orgn 1972–74, vice chief of Defence Staff 1974–76, dep C-in-C Allied Forces Central Europe 1976–79, Lt-Govr and C-in-C Guernsey 1980–85; KStJ 1980; *Recreations* golf, sailing; *Clubs* RAF; *Style*— Air Chief Marshal Sir Peter Le Cheminant, GBE, KCB, DFC; ✉ La Madeleine de Bas, Ruette de La Madeleine, St Pierre du Bois, Guernsey, Channel Islands

LE FANU, Mark; OBE (1994); s of Adm of the Fleet Sir Michael Le Fanu (d 1970), and Prudence, *née* Morgan (d 1980); *b* 14 Nov 1946; *Educ* Winchester, Univ of Sussex (BA), Coll of Law; *m* 1976, Lucy Rhoda, da of John Cowen (d 1982), of Bisley, Stroud, Glos; 3 s (Thomas b 1980, Matthew b 1982, Caspar b 1986), 1 da (Celia b 1985); *Career* Lt RN

1964–73; slr McKenna & Co 1973–78; Soc of Authors 1979– (gen sec 1982–); *Recreations* canals, sailing, golf; *Style*— Mark Le Fanu, Esq, OBE; ✉ 25 St James's Gardens, London W11 4RE (☎ 0171 603 4119); Society of Authors, 84 Drayton Gardens, London SW10 9SB (☎ 0171 373 6642)

le FLEMING, Morris John; DL (1991); s of Maj Morris Ralph le Fleming (d 1969), of Durham, and Mabel, *née* Darling (d 1980); *b* 19 Aug 1932; *Educ* Tonbridge Sch, Magdalene Coll Cambridge (BA); *m* 27 Aug 1960, Jenny Rose, da of Reginald McColvin Weeks, and Eileen Weeks, of Bristol; 1 s (Daniel b 1963), 3 da (Emma b 1961, Bridget b 1965, Alice b 1969); *Career* Nat Serv 2 Lt RA 1951–52, Capt TA 1952–61; admitted slr 1958; asst slr: Worcestershire CC 1958–59, Middx CC 1959, Nottinghamshire CC 1959–63; asst clerk Lincolnshire CC 1963–69; Hertfordshire CC: dep clerk 1969–73, county sec 1973–79, chief exec 1979–90, clerk to the Lieutenancy 1979–90, clerk to Magistrates Cts Ctee 1979–90, sec to Probation Ctee 1979–90; Prince's Youth Business Tst Reg Bd 1987–90, dir Herts TEC 1989–90; chm: Stansted Airport Consultative Ctee 1991–, Herts Scouts 1991–; pres Herts Assoc of Local Cncls 1991–, patron Herts Gardens Tst, dir Herts Groundwork Tst, tstee Herts Community Tst; Hon LLD (Univ of Hertfordshire); *Recreations* theatre, family history, gardening, architecture; *Style*— Morris le Fleming, Esq, DL; ✉ Swangleys Lane, Knebworth, Herts SG3 6AA (☎ 01438 813 152)

LE FLEMING, Sir Quentin John; 12 Bt (E 1705), of Rydal, Westmorland; s of Sir William Kelland Le Fleming, 11 Bt (d 1988), and Noveen Avis, *née* Sharpe; *b* 27 June 1949; *m* 26 June 1971, Judith Ann, da of C J Peck, JP, of Ashhurst, Manawatu, NZ; 2 s (David Kelland b 12 Jan 1976, Andrew John b 4 Oct 1979), 1 da (Josephine Kay b 31 July 1973); *Heir* s, David Kelland Le Fleming; *Style*— Sir Quentin Le Fleming, Bt; ✉ 147 Stanford St, Ashhurst, Manawatu, New Zealand

LE GOY, Raymond Edgar Michel; s of Jean Andre Stanhope Nemorin Michel Le Goy (d 1966), of Mauritius, and May, *née* Callan (d 1976); *b* 20 April 1919; *Educ* William Ellis Sch, Gonville and Caius Coll Cambridge (sec Cambridge Union, MA); *m* 27 Aug 1960, (Silvia) Ernestine, da of Philip Luther Burnett (d 1947), of Trelawny, Jamaica; 2 s (Keith b 1962, Mark b 1964); *Career* Br Army: joined 1940, cmmnd 1941, Staff Capt HQ E Africa 1943–45, Maj 1945; London Passenger Transport Bd 1947, UK civil servant 1947–, princ 1948, asst sec 1958, under sec 1968; dir-gen for Transport EEC 1973–81, a dir-gen Cmmn of the EU 1982–; chm Union of Univ Liberal Soc 1939–40; FCIT; *Books* The Victorian Burletta (1953); *Recreations* theatre, music, race relations; *Clubs* United Oxford and Cambridge University, National Liberal; *Style*— Raymond Le Goy, Esq; ✉ Société Générale De Banque, Agence Européenne, Rond Point Schuman, Brussels B 1040, Belgium

Le GRAND, Julian Ernest Michael; s of Roland John Le Grand (d 1976), of Taunton, Somerset, and Eileen Joan, *née* Baker; *b* 29 May 1945; *Educ* Eton, Univ of Sussex (BA), Univ of Pennsylvania (PhD); *m* 19 June 1971, Damaris May, da of Rev Nigel Robertson-Glasgow, of Fakenham, Norfolk; 2 da (Polly b 1978, Zoe b 1981); *Career* lectr in economics: Univ of Sussex 1971–78, LSE 1978–85; sr res fell Suntory-Toyota Int Centre for Econs and Related Disciplines LSE 1985–87, prof of public policy and dir Sch for Advanced Urban Studies Univ of Bristol 1987–92, Richard Titmuss prof of health policy LSE and professorial fell King's Fund 1993–; conslt: OECD, Euro Cmmn, World Bank, NAO; ESRC: memb Social Affrs Ctee 1982–86, memb Res Grants Bd 1988–92; *Books* The Economics of Social Problems (with R Robinson, 1976, 3 edn 1992), The Strategy of Equality (1982), Privatisation and the Welfare State (ed with R Robinson, 1984), Not Only the Poor (with R Goodin, 1987), Market Socialism (ed with S Estrin, 1989), Equity and Choice (1991), Quasi-Markets and Social Policy (ed with W Bartlett, 1993), Evaluating the NHS Reforms (ed with R Robinson, 1994); *Recreations* drawing, reading; *Style*— Julian Le Grand, Esq; ✉ 31 Sydenham Hill, Cotham, Bristol BS6 5SL (☎ 0117 942 5253, fax 0117 944 2476); London School of Economics, Houghton Street, London WC2A 2AE (☎ 0171 955 7353, fax 0171 955 7415); King's Fund, 11–13 Cavendish Square, London W1M 0AN (☎ 0171 307 2519, fax 0171 307 2581)

LE GRICE, (Andrew) Valentine; s of Charles Le Grice (d 1982), of Penzance, and Wilmay, *née* Ward; *b* 26 June 1953; *Educ* Shrewsbury, Collingwood Coll Univ of Durham (BA); *m* 17 Dec 1977, Anne Elizabeth, da of Philip Moss, of Gt Bookham; 2 s (Charles b 8 Oct 1984, Philip b 16 Aug 1986), 1 da (Alexandra b 24 Nov 1989); *Career* called to the Bar Middle Temple 1977; *Recreations* reading, sailing, watching sport, throwing things away; *Clubs* Travellers', Royal Yacht Sqdn; *Style*— Valentine Le Grice, Esq; ✉ 1 Mitre Court Buildings, Temple, London EC4Y 7BS

LE MARCHAND, Capt Thomas Maitland; s of Col L P Le Marchand, OBE (d 1977), and Sibyl, *née* Rouse; *b* 14 May 1941; *Educ* Tonbridge Sch, Britannia RNC Dartmouth; *m* 29 June 1963, Valerie, da of L Reynolds (d 1963); 1 s (Philip b 4 July 1973), 3 da (Zoë b 15 April 1964, Helen b 26 Sept 1966, Anna b 19 Dec 1968); *Career* joined RN 1959, cmmnd 1962, submarine serv 1963; cmd: HMS Narwhal 1972–74, HMS Valiant 1977 and 1981–83 (Falklands War (despatches 1982)), HMS Cleopatra and 7th Frigate Sqdn 1987–89, 3rd Submarine Sqdn 1989–91, dir Naval Offr Appointing MOD 1991–93 (ret 1994); dir Branch Devpt SSAFA 1994; MRIN, MIPD; *Recreations* squash (Suffolk county veterans 1988), home handyman; *Clubs* IOD, Royal Navy Club of 1765 and 1785, The Naval; *Style*— Capt Thomas Le Marchand, RN; ✉ Lowood, Hasketon, Woodbridge, Suffolk IP13 6JL (☎ 01473 735486)

LE MARCHANT, Sir Francis Arthur; 6 Bt (UK 1841), of Chobham Place, Surrey; s of Sir Denis Le Marchant, 5 Bt (d 1987), and Elizabeth Rowena, *née* Worth; *b* 6 Oct 1939; *Educ* Gordonstoun, Royal Acad Schs; *Heir* kinsman, Michael Le Marchant b 28 July 1937; *Career* painter; solo exhibitions include Agnews, Sally Hunter Fine Art, Roy Miles 1996; mixed exhibitions include Royal Academy Summer Exhibitions, Leicester Galleries, Bilan de l'Art Contomerain Paris, Spink & So "Ten at Spink"; *Style*— Sir Francis Le Marchant, Bt; ✉ c/o Midland Bank, 88 Westgate, Grantham, Lincs

LE MARECHAL, Robert Norford; CB (1994); s of Reginald Le Marechal (d 1976), of Southampton, and Margaret, *née* Cokely; *b* 29 May 1939; *Educ* Taunton's Sch Southampton; *m* 21 Dec 1963, Linda Mary, da of Noel Stanley Williams (d 1983), of Ludlow; 2 da (Kate b 1969, Rebecca b 1971); *Career* Sgt RAEC 1958–60; sr auditor MOD 1971–76 (joined Exchequer and Audit Dept 1957), chief auditor DOE 1976–80, dep dir of audit 1980–83, dir of policy and planning NAO 1984–86, asst auditor gen 1986–89, dep comptroller and auditor gen 1989–; *Recreations* reading, gardening; *Style*— Robert Le Marechal, Esq, CB; ✉ 62 Woodcote Hurst, Epsom, Surrey (☎ 013727 21291); National Audit Office, Buckingham Palace Road, Victoria, London (☎ 0171 798 7381)

LE MÉTAIS, Dr Joanna Petra Fransisca Maria; da of Peter Joseph Bevers, of St Agnes, S Aust, and Geertruda Petronella, *née* van der Zanden; *b* 2 Jan 1949; *Educ* Loreto Abbey Victoria Aust, Croydon Tech Coll, Gipsy Hill Coll Kingston-upon-Thames (Cert in Educn, BEd), Université de Caen (Diplôme d'Études Françaises), Inst of Linguists (final level French), Brunel Univ (MA, PhD); *m* 2 Sept 1972 (m dis 1980), Michel Philippe Alfred Le Métais, s of Alfred Le Métais, of Vimoutiers France; *Career* dep head Modern Languages Dept Redstone Sch Surrey 1974–76 (French teacher 1973–76), head Languages Dept Raynes Park HS 1976–82, pt/t adult educn teacher 1978–79, professional asst Educn Dept London Borough of Hounslow 1982–84; Nat Fndn for Educnl Research: dep head Info Dept, dir EPIC Europe (Educn Policy Info Centre for Europe), head Nat Unit EURYDICE (educn policy info network in the European Community) 1984–; external examiner: Univ of London 1977–81, SE Regnl Examination Bd 1977 and 1978; pres Merton Branch Nat Assoc of Schoolmasters Union of Women Teachers 1980 (vice pres 1979), tstee Inst of Linguists Educnl Tst 1988–90, memb Int Ctee Soc of Educn Offrs 1991–, memb Exec Ctee UK Forum for Int Educn and Trg 1994–, quality assessor HE Funding Cncl for England 1995–; overseas expert Visiting Cmmn Netherlands 1992, attended UNESCO Int Forum for solidarity against intolerance Tbilisi Georgia 1995; life memb Sail Trg Assoc 1990–; MIMgt 1985–89, MInstD 1989–95, FRSA 1979, FIL 1986 (MIL 1978, memb Cncl 1987–90, chm Cncl 1988–90); *Books* Communication and Culture: Foreign Languages in and out of the Curriculum (ed, 1988), The Impact on the Education Service of Teacher Mobility (1990), Quality in Education: standards in Europe (in The Search for Standards, 1992), Teachers' Salaries (in Performance-related Pay in Education, 1992), Making the most of European teachers (in The Supply and Recruitment of Teachers, 1993), Teachers' Salaries in France, Germany and Scotland (1994), A Response from Across the Channel (in Effective Governors for Effective Schools, 1995), Legislating for Change: School Reforms in England and Wales 1979–1994 (1995); *Recreations* people, travel, pottery, sailing; *Style*— Dr Joanna Le Métais; ✉ National Foundation for Educational Research in England and Wales, The Mere, Upton Park, Slough, Berks SL1 2DQ (☎ 01753 574123, fax 01753 691632)

LE PARD, Geoffrey; s of Desmond Allen Le Pard, of Sway, Lymington, and Barbara Grace, *née* Francis; *b* 30 Nov 1956; *Educ* Purley GS, Brockenhurst GS, Univ of Bristol (LLB); *m* 19 May 1984, Linda Ellen, da of Leslie Jones, of Costessey, Norwich; 1 s (Samuel William b 23 April 1990), 1 da (Jennifer Grace b 8 Feb 1993); *Career* articled clerk Corbould Rigby & Co 1979–81, ptnr Freshfields 1987– (asst slr 1981–87); memb: City of London Slrs Co, Anglo American Real Property Inst; *Recreations* cycling, walking long distance footpaths, watching any sport, theatre, good food, gardening, being a dad; *Style*— Geoffrey Le Pard, Esq; ✉ Freshfields, 65 Fleet Street, London EC4Y 1HS (☎ 0171 936 4000)

LE QUESNE, Sir (John) Godfray; kt (1980), QC (1962); 3 s of Charles Thomas Le Quesne, QC (d 1954), of London and Jersey, and Florence Elizabeth Eileen, *née* Pearce Gould (d 1977); bro of Sir Martin Le Quesne, *qv* and Prof Leslie Le Quesne, *qv*; *b* 18 Jan 1924; *Educ* Shrewsbury, Exeter Coll Oxford (MA); *m* 6 April 1963, Susan Mary, da of Rev Thomas Woodman Gill; 2 s, 1 da; *Career* called to the Bar Inner Temple 1947, admitted to Bar of St Helena 1959; dep chm Kesteven Lincs QS 1963–71, judge Ct of Appeal of Jersey 1964–97, judge Ct of Appeal of Guernsey 1964–95, recorder of the Crown Ct 1972–; chm: Cncl Regent's Park Coll Oxford 1958–87, Monopolies and Mergers Cmmn 1975–87; resumed practice 1988; Dato Order of the Crown of Brunei 1978; *Recreations* music, railways, walking; *Style*— Sir Godfray Le Quesne, QC; ✉ 1 Crown Office Row, Temple, London EC4 7HH (☎ 0171 583 9292, telex 8953152)

LE QUESNE, Prof Leslie Philip; CBE (1984); 2 s of Charles Thomas Le Quesne, QC (d 1954), and (Florence Elizabeth) Eileen (d 1977), 3 da of Sir Alfred Pearce Gould, KCVO, FRCS; bro of Sir Martin Le Quesne, *qv* and Sir Godfray Le Quesne, *qv*; *b* 24 Aug 1919; *Educ* Rugby, Exeter Coll Oxford (DM, MCh); *m* 1969, Pamela Margaret, da of Dr Archibald Fullerton, MC (d 1972), of Batley, Yorks; 2 s (Thomas b 1973, William b 1975); *Career* prof of surgery Middx Hosp and dir Surgical Studies Dept 1963–84, dep vice chllr and dean Faculty of Med Univ of London 1980–84; medical awards administrator Commonwealth Scholarship Cmmn 1984–91; FRCS; *Recreations* fishing, sailing; *Style*— Prof Leslie Le Quesne, CBE; ✉ 8 Eton Villas, London NW3 4SX (☎ 0171 722 0778)

LE QUESNE, Sir (Charles) Martin; KCMG (1974); s of Charles Thomas Le Quesne, QC (d 1954); bro of Prof Leslie Le Quesne, *qv* and Sir Godfray Le Quesne, *qv*; *b* 10 June 1917; *Educ* Shrewsbury, Exeter Coll Oxford; *m* 1948, Deirdre Noel Fisher; 3 s; *Career* entered Foreign Office 1946; ambass to: Republic of Mali 1961–64, Algeria 1968–71; dep under sec FCO 1971–74, high cmmr Nigeria 1974–76; memb of the States of Jersey 1978–90; hon fell Exeter Coll Oxford 1990; *Clubs* Reform (chm 1973–74), MCC, United (Jersey), Royal Channel Islands Yacht; *Style*— Sir Martin Le Quesne, KCMG; ✉ Beau Désert, St Saviour, Jersey, CI (☎ 01534 22076)

LE ROUX, François; s of Pierre Le Roux, and Claudie, *née* Blanchard; *b* 30 Oct 1955; *Educ* Madagascar, Univ of Tours; *Career* baritone; studied with François Loup then Opera Studio Paris with Vera Rosza and Elizabeth Grümmer, winner Maria Canals competition Barcelona 1978 and Rio de Janeiro 1979; memb Lyon Opera Co 1980–85, given numerous recitals at various international venues; given masterclasses at: Atelier de l'Opera and Conservatoire Superieur Lyon, Cleveland Inst of Music Ohio 1992, Helsinki Sibelius Acad Finland 1994, 1995 and 1996; *Performances* with Lyons Opera incl: Papageno in The Magic Flute, Figaro in The Barber of Seville, Lescaut in Manon, Pelléas in Pelléas et Mélisande; at Royal Opera House Covent Garden incl: Lescaut 1987, Papageno 1988, Dandini in La Cenerentola 1989 and 1994, Figaro in The Barber of Seville 1991, world premiere of Birtwistle's Gawain 1991 (also in 1994), Dr Malatesta in Don Pasquale 1992, Pelléas 1993, Mercutio in Gounod Romeo and Juliet 1994; others incl: Pelléas (Paris 1985, La Scala Milan 1986, Edinburgh 1986, Vienna Staatsoper 1988, LA 1995, Venice 1995), Ramiro in L'Heure Espagnole (Glyndebourne debut) 1987, title role in Don Giovanni (Paris 1987 for which awarded Critics' Union Prize, Zurich 1989), Count Almaviva in Le Nozze di Figaro (Trieste) 1986, Marcello in La Bohème (Hamburg) 1987, Oreste in Iphigenie en Tauride (Frankfurt) 1987 and (Athens) 1993, Der Prinz von Homburg (Munich 1992 and 1993, Antwerp and Ghent 1995), John Ruskin in world premiere of David Lang's Modern Painters (Santa Fe Opera) 1995; *Recordings* incl: Debussy Pelléas et Mélisande (under Claudio Abbado, DGG), Chabrier L'Etoile (under John Eliot Gardiner, EMI), Poulenc Dialogues of the Carmelites (under Kent Nagano, Virgin), Cimarosa Il Matrimonio Segreto (under Jesus Lopez-Cobos, Cascavelle), Duparc complete songs (REM), Fauré complete songs (REM), La Fontaine Fables in Music (EMI, winner French Academy Award), L'Invitation au Voyage (French songs with orch under John Nelson, EMI), Poulenc songs with ensemble (under Charles Dutoit, DECCA); *Style*— M François Le Roux; ✉ c/o Susana Meyer, IMG Artists Management, 420 West 45th Street, New York, NY 10036, USA (☎ 00 1 212 541 5640, fax 00 1 212 265 5483)

LE SAUX, Graeme Pierre; s of Pierre Le Saux, of Jersey, CI, and late Daphne, *née* Brown; *b* 17 Oct 1968; *Educ* D'Hautree Sch Jersey, Hautlieu, Kingston Poly; *Career* professional footballer; Chelsea 1987–92 (90 appearances); Blackburn Rovers FC: joined 1992–, winners FA Premier League 1994/95; England: 4 under 21 caps, over 12 full caps (first v Denmark 1994); *Recreations* tennis, jazz music, antiques, art, literature, media; *Style*— Graeme Le Saux, Esq; ✉ Blackburn Rovers FC, Ewood Park, Blackburn BB2 4JF (☎ 01254 55432)

LE TISSIER, Matthew Paul; s of Marcus Le Tissier, of Guernsey, and Ruth Elizabeth, *née* Blondel; *b* 14 Oct 1968; *Educ* La Mare De Carteret Secdy Sch CI; *m* 23 June 1990, Catherine Claire, *née* Loveridge; 1 s (Mitchell Paul b 5 Nov 1991); *Career* professional footballer; Southampton 1986–: apprentice then professional, debut 1986, over 200 appearances; England: 5 B caps (debut v Republic of Ireland 1990), first full cap (v Denmark) 1994, 7 full caps (as at Jan 1997); Zenith Data Systems Cup runners-up medal Southampton 1992; Young Player of the Year Professional Footballers' Assoc 1990, Barclays Young Eagle of the Year 1990; *Recreations* snooker, golf, TV; *Style*— Matthew Le Tissier, Esq; ✉ c/o Southampton Football Club, The Dell, Milton Road, Southampton, Hants S09 4XX (☎ 01703 220505)

LEA, The Rev His Hon Christopher Gerald; MC; s of late George Percy Lea, and Jocelyn Clare, *née* Lea, of Franche, Kidderminster, Worcs; *b* 27 Nov 1917; *Educ* Charterhouse, RMC Sandhurst; *m* 1952, Susan Elizabeth, da of Maj Edward Pendarves Dorrien Smith; 2 s, 2 da (1 decd); *Career* called to the Bar Inner Temple 1948; memb:

Assistance Bd Appeal Tribunal Oxford Area 1961–63, Mental Health Review Tbnl 1962–68 and 1983–92; met magistrate 1968–72, dep chm Berks QS 1968–71, circuit judge 1972–90; ordained deacon 1992, asst curate Non-Stipendiary Miny, ordained priest 1993; *Style*— The Rev His Hon Christopher Lea, MC; ✉ Simms Farm House, Mortimer, Reading, Berks (☎ 0118 933 2360)

LEA, Vice Adm Sir John Stuart Crosbie; KBE (1979); s of Lt-Col Edward Heath Lea (d 1947), and Aileen Beatrice Hawthorne, *née* Morris (d 1973); *b* 4 June 1923; *Educ* Boxgrove Sch Guildford, Shrewsbury, RNEC Keyham; *m* 1947, Patricia Anne, da of William Martin Thoseby (d 1955); 1 s, 2 da; *Career* joined RN 1941, Capt 1966, Dep Supt Clyde Submarine Base 1966–68, Imperial Defence Coll 1969, dir of Naval Admin Planning 1970–71, Cdre HMS Nelson 1972–75, Rear Adm 1975, asst chief of Fleet Support 1976–77, dir gen Naval Manpower and Trg 1977–80, Vice Adm 1978, ret; chm GEC Marine and Industrial Gears Ltd 1980–87; chm: Portsmouth Naval Heritage Tst 1983–87, Regular Forces Employment Assoc 1987–89, RN, RMSD & Warrant Officers Benevolent Fund 1993; pres: Hampshire Autistic Assoc 1988–95, Hayling Island Horticultural Soc 1994 (chm 1980–93); vice pres RFEA 1990–93, tstee Hayling Island Community Centre 1982; memb Ct of Assts Worshipful Co of Plumbers (Master 1988–89); *Recreations* walking, woodwork, gardening; *Style*— Vice Adm Sir John Lea, KBE; ✉ Springfield, 27 Bright Lane, Hayling Island, Hants (☎ 0170 5 463801)

LEA, Prof Peter John; s of Dr Alan Joseph Lea (d 1983), of Tamworth, and Jessie, *née* Farrall; *b* 1 Dec 1944; *Educ* Arnold Sch Blackpool, Univ of Liverpool (BSc, PhD, DSc); *m* 30 July 1965, Christine, *née* Shaw; 1 da (Julia b 5 Dec 1966); *Career* res fell Royal Soc 1972–75, princ scientific offr Rothamsted Experimental Station Harpenden Herts 1978–84 (sr scientific offr 1975–78); Univ of Lancaster: prof of biology 1985–, head Div of Biological Scis 1988–91, dean 1994–96; chm Phytochemical Soc Europe (sec 1982–87); FIBiol; *Books* incl: The Genetic Manipulation of Plants and its Application to Agriculture (with G R Stewart, 1984), The Biochemistry of Plant Phenolics (with C F van Sumere, 1986), Biologically Active Natural Products (with K Hostettmann, 1987), Methods in Plant Biochemistry (1989, 1993), The Biochemistry of plants (with B J Miflin, 1990), Plant Biochemistry and Molecular Biology (with R C Leegood, 1993); *Recreations* cricket, collecting wedgwood pottery; *Style*— Prof Peter Lea; ✉ The Old School, Chapel Lane, Ellel, Lancaster LA2 0PW (☎ 01524 751156); University of Lancaster, Division of Biological Sciences, Bailrigg, Lancaster LA1 4YQ (☎ 01524 65201 ext 3510, fax 01524 382212)

LEA, Ruth Jane; da of Thomas Lea, of Warburton, Lymm, Cheshire, and Jane, *née* Brown; *b* 22 Sept 1947; *Educ* Lymm GS, Univ of York (BA), Univ of Bristol (MSc); *Career* HM Treasy 1970–73, lectr in economics Thames Poly (now Univ of Greenwich) 1973–74, Civil Serv Coll 1974–77, HM Treasy 1977–78, CSO 1978–84, DTI 1984–87, Invest in Britain Bureau DTI 1987–88, Mitsubishi Bank 1988–93 (rising to chief economist), chief UK economist Lehman Brothers 1993–94, economics ed ITN 1994–95, head of Policy Unit Inst of Directors 1995–; memb: RPI Advsy Ctee 1992–94, Nat Consumer Cncl 1993–96, Rowntree Fndn Income and Wealth Inquiry Gp 1993–94, Nurses' Pay Review Body 1994–, Research Centres Bd ESRC 1996, Research Priorities Bd 1996–, Statistics Advsy Ctee Office of Nat Statistics 1996–; judge DTI/BBP Innovation Writer of the Year Awards 1995 and 1996; memb: Soc of Business Economists 1988, Royal Economic Soc 1994 (memb Cncl 1995–); FRSA 1993, FSS 1996; *Recreations* music, cats, philately; *Clubs* Oxford and Cambridge Musical, Reform; *Style*— Miss Ruth Lea; ✉ 25 Redbourne Avenue, Finchley, London N3 2BP (☎ 0181 346 3482); Policy Unit, The Institute of Directors, 116 Pall Mall, London SW1Y 5ED (☎ 0171 451 3291, fax 0171 839 2337)

LEA, Sir Thomas William; 5 Bt (UK 1892), of The Larches, Kidderminster, Worcestershire, and Sea Grove, Dawlish, Devon; eldest s of Sir (Thomas) Julian Lea, 4 Bt (d 1990), and Gerry Valerie, o da of late Capt Gibson Clarence Fahnestock, USAF; *b* 6 Sept 1973; *Educ* Uppingham; *Heir* bro, Alexander Julian Lea b 1978; *Style*— Sir Thomas Lea, Bt

LEACH, Allan William; s of Frank Leach (d 1938), of Rotherwick Hants, and Margaret Ann, *née* Bennett (d 1973); *b* 9 May 1931; *Educ* Watford GS, Loughborough Coll, Open Univ (BA, DPA); *m* 1962, Betty, da of William George Gadsby (d 1992), of Bramcote, Notts; 1 s (William b 1967), 1 da (Sarah b 1969); *Career* county librarian Bute 1965–71, burgh librarian Ayr 1971–74, dir of Library Servs Kyle and Carrick 1974–82, dir gen and librarian Nat Library for the Blind 1982–95, ret; memb Standing Ctee IFLA Section of Libraries for the Blind 1983–95 (chm 1985–87, special advsr 1991–93), chm UK Assoc of Braille Prodrs 1991–94; tstee Ulverscroft Fndn 1993–; FLA; *Recreations* people, music, the countryside; *Style*— Allan Leach; ✉ 4 Windsor Rd, Hazel Grove, Stockport, Cheshire SK7 4SW (☎ 0161 285 1287)

LEACH, Clive William; s of Stanely Aubrey Leach, of Kessingland, Suffolk, and Laura Anne, *née* Robinson; *b* 4 Dec 1934; *Educ* Sir John Leman Sch Beccles Suffolk, Univ of Birmingham; *m* 1, 25 Oct 1958; 3 s (Christopher b 1959, Stuart b 1961, Adrian b 1964); m 2, 25 Sept 1980, Stephanie Miriam, da of Patrick McGinn, of Newlands Rd, Sidmouth, Devon; 1 s (Damian b 1981); *Career* gen sales mangr Tyne Tees Television 1968–74, dir of sales and mktg Trident Television 1979–82 (sales dir 1974–79), md Link Television 1982–85; Yorkshire Television Ltd: dir of sales and mktg 1985–88, md 1988–93, chm Yorkshire Television Enterprises Ltd 1988–94 (md 1985–88), chm Yorkshire Television International Ltd 1988–94; Yorkshire-Tyne Tees Television Holdings: gp chief exec 1992–94, also gp chm Oct 1993–94; dir: ITN 1988–93, New Era Television 1988–; chm Butler Advertising 1994–; played first class cricket for Warwicks 1955–57, also for Durham and Bucks counties; *Recreations* golf, travel, entertaining; *Clubs* Harewood Downs Golf, Warwickshire County Cricket, Bucks County Cricket, Clermont, MCC; *Style*— C W Leach, Esq; ✉ The White House, Barkston Ash, Tadcaster, North Yorkshire LS24 9PJ

LEACH, David Andrew; OBE (1987); s of Bernard Howell Leach, CH, CBE (d 1979), of Cornwall, and Edith Muriel, *née* Hoyle (d 1955); *b* 7 May 1911; *Educ* Dauntsey's Sch; *m* 23 April 1938, (Mary) Elizabeth, da of Surgn Cdr Samuel Henry Facey (d 1942), of The Firs, Nyewood, Petersfield, Hants; 3 s (John Henry b 1939, (Paul) Jeremy David b 1941, Simon Andrew b 1956); *Career* WWII DCLI 1941–45; potter; student to Bernard Leach (father), in practice 1930–; former chm Craftsman Potters' Assoc GB, chm Devon Guild of Craftsmen 1985–88; gold medalist Int Acad of Ceramists; memb: Craftsmen Potters' Assoc, Crafts Cncl, Devon Guild of Craftsmen; *Recreations* hockey and tennis; *Style*— David Leach, Esq, OBE; ✉ Lowerdown Pottery, Lowerdown Cross, Bovey Tracey, Devon TQ13 9LE (☎ and fax 01626 833408)

LEACH, Frank; s of George Manley Leach (d 1954), and Ethel Leach (d 1968); *b* 1 May 1935; *Educ* Wirral GS, Univ of London (BA); *m* 1959, Marion, da of Reginald Edwards (d 1975); 2 s; *Career* chartered sec; gp sec The Cunard S/S Co Ltd 1968–74; dir: Br Lion Films Ltd 1974–76, Thorn EMI Screen Entertainment 1977–86, Weintraub Entertainment 1987–91, Lumiere Pictures Ltd 1992–95, ret; *Recreations* painting, gardening; *Clubs* Rotary; *Style*— Frank Leach, Esq; ✉ 11 Upton Quarry, Langton Green, Tunbridge Wells, Kent (☎ 01892 862733)

LEACH, Graham John; s of Vernon Richard Henry Leach, and Doris Elsie Margaret, *née* Richardson; *b* 1 Oct 1948; *Educ* Battersea GS London, Univ of Liverpool (BA); *m* 14 Dec 1974, Ruth, da of Noel Barsby; 3 s (Thomas b 1980, William b 1983, Oliver b 1985); *Career* BBC journalist; news trainee 1971–72, regnl news corr Belfast 1972–74, radio reporter London 1974–77, Bonn corr 1977–81, ME corr 1981–83, SA radio corr 1983–89, Europe corr 1989–95, freelance 1995–; Sony Radio Reporter of the Year 1987; *Books* South Africa No Easy Path to Peace (1985), The Afrikaners Their Last Great Trek (1989); *Recreations* theatre, sailing, skiing, cycling; *Style*— Graham Leach, Esq

LEACH, Adm of the Fleet Sir Henry Conyers; GCB (1978, KCB 1977), DL (Hampshire, 1992); s of Capt John Caterall Leach, MVO, DSO, RN (ka 1941), and Evelyn Burrell, *née* Lee (d 1969); *b* 18 Nov 1923; *Educ* RNC Dartmouth and Greenwich; *m* 15 Feb 1958, Mary Jean (d 1991), da of Adm Sir Henry William Urquhart McCall, KCVO, KBE, CB, DSO (d 1980); 2 da (Henrietta b 1959, Philippa b 1964); *Career* joined RN 1937, Capt 1961, dir Naval Plans 1968–70, Rear Adm 1971, asst chief Naval Staff (Policy) 1971–73, Vice Adm 1974, Flag Offr First Flotilla 1974–75, Vice Chief of Def Staff 1976–77, Adm 1977, C-in-C Fleet and Allied C-in-C Channel and Eastern Atlantic 1977–79, chief of Naval Staff and First Sea Lord 1979–82, Adm of the Fleet 1982; first and princ Naval ADC to the Queen 1979; govr Cranleigh Sch 1983–93; pres: Royal Naval Benevolent Soc 1983–95, Sea Cadet Assoc 1984–93, Royal Bath and West of England Soc 1993 (vice pres 1994–); chm: St Dunstan's 1983–, Cncl King Edward VII Hospital 1987–, Annual Servs for Seafarers 1993–95; patron: Meridian Tst Assoc 1993–, Hants Royal British Legion 1994–; Freeman: City of London 1982, Worshipful Co of Shipwrights, Worshipful Co of Merchant Taylors; *Recreations* fishing, shooting, gardening, repairing antique furniture; *Clubs* Farmers'; *Style*— Adm of the Fleet Sir Henry Leach, GCB, DL; ✉ Wonston Lea, Wonston, Winchester, Hants SO21 3LS (☎ 01962 760344)

LEACH, Robin Anthony Langley; s of Col Anthony Pearce Leach, TD, DL (d 1984), of Clifford, Wetherby, Yorks, and Jeanette Helen Leach; *b* 20 March 1955; *Educ* Sherborne, Univ of St Andrews (MA); *m* 19 Sept 1987, Fiona Susan, da of Hamish Tait Easdale, of Polkerris, Camp Rd, Gerrards Cross, Bucks; 1 s (Charles Anthony Langley b 13 March 1993); *Career* called to the Bar Lincolns Inn 1979; *Recreations* golf, cricket, squash, fishing, shooting, horseracing, photography, travel; *Clubs* MCC, RAC; *Style*— Robin Leach, Esq; ✉ 2 Harcourt Buildings, Temple, London EC4 (☎ 0171 353 2112)

LEACH, Dr Rodney; s of Edward Leach (d 1951), of Thornton Cleveleys, Lancs, and Alice Matthews, *née* Marcroft (d 1988); descendant of one of the Rochdale Pioneers who founded the Worldwide Co-operative movement; *b* 3 March 1932; *Educ* Baines GS Poulton le Fylde Lancs, Univ of Birmingham (BSc, PhD); *m* 1958, Eira Mary, da of David Arthur Tuck (d 1975), of Caterham, Surrey; 3 s (Michael, Stephen, Alan), 1 da (Alison); *Career* ptnr McKinsey & Co Inc 1970–74, exec dir P & O Steam Navigation Co 1974–85; chm: P & O Euro Transport Services Ltd 1974–85, P & O Cruises Ltd 1980–85; fndr chief exec and md VSEL Consortium plc 1985–88, chm and chief exec Vickers Shipbuilding and Engineering Ltd 1986–88, chm Cammell Laird Shipbuilders Ltd 1985–88; dir: United Utilities plc (formerly North West Water Group plc) 1989–, Jasmin plc 1989–, Rennaissance Arts Theatre Tst Ltd 1989–93 (vice chm 1991–93); vice chm S Cumbria Community & Mental Health NHS Tst 1993–; conseiller spécial Chambre de Commerce et d'Industrie de Boulogne sur Mer 1989–93, memb Gen Cncl Cumbria Tourist Bd 1987–92; govr St Anne's Sch Windermere 1991–; Freeman City of London, Liveryman Worshipful Co of Shipwrights; CEng, FRINA, FCIM, FIMgt, FRSA; *Recreations* sailing, reading, gardening, fell walking; *Clubs* RAC, Royal Yachting Assoc; *Style*— Dr Rodney Leach; ✉ Dockwray Cottage, Grasmere, Cumbria LA22 9QD (☎ and fax 015394 35288)

LEADBETTER, Prof Alan James; CBE (1994); s of Robert Pickavant Leadbetter (d 1989), and Edna, *née* Garlick; *b* 28 March 1934; *Educ* Univ of Liverpool (BSc, PhD), Univ of Bristol (DSc); *m* 23 Oct 1957, (Jean) Brenda, da of Percy Williams (d 1966); 1 s (Andrew Robert b 1 Aug 1964), 1 da (Jane b 22 Dec 1966); *Career* postdoctoral res fell Nat Res Cncl Canada Ottawa 1957–59; Univ of Bristol Sch of Chemistry: res asst 1959–62, lectr 1962–72, reader in physical chemistry 1972–74; prof of physical chemistry Univ of Exeter 1975–82; SERC: assoc dir Sci Bd and head Neutron Div 1982–87, assoc dir and head Science Dept (Rutherford Appleton Laboratory) 1987–88, dir Daresbury Laboratory 1988–94; dir adjoint Institut Laue-Langevin 1994–; FRSC, FInstP; *Publications* author of numerous articles in scientific jls; *Recreations* cooking, walking; *Style*— Prof Alan Leadbetter, CBE; ✉ Institut Laue-Langevin, Avenue des Martyrs, BP 156, 38042 Grenoble Cedex 9, France (☎ 00 33 76 20 71 00, fax 00 33 76 96 11 95)

LEAF, Robert Stephen; s of Nathan Leaf, and Anne, *née* Feinman; *b* 9 Aug 1931; *Educ* Univ of Missouri (Bachelor of Journalism, MA); *m* 8 June 1958, Adele Renee; 1 s (Stuart b 4 June 1961); *Career* Burson-Marsteller International: joined 1957, vice pres 1961, exec vice pres 1965, pres 1968, chm 1985; writer in various trade and business pubns for USA, Europe and Asia; speaker on PR marketing and communications in W and E Europe (incl Russia), Asia (incl China), Australia, N and S America; memb: PR consltg (former bd memb), Int Advertising, Foreign Press, PR Soc of America; FIPR 1984 (MIPR 1973); *Recreations* tennis, travel, theatre; *Clubs* Hurlingham; *Style*— Robert Leaf, Esq; ✉ 3 Fursecroft, George St, London W1H 5LF (☎ 0171 262 4846); Burson-Marsteller, 24–28 Bloomsbury Way, London WC1A 2PX (☎ 0171 831 6262, fax 0171 430 1033, telex 267531)

LEAHY, Sir John Henry Gladstone; KCMG (1981, CMG 1973); s of William Henry Gladstone Leahy (d 1941), and Ethel, *née* Sudlow (d 1967); *b* 7 Feb 1928; *Educ* Tonbridge, Clare Coll Cambridge (BA), Yale Univ (MA); *m* 1954, Elizabeth Anne, da of John Hereward Pitchford, CBE; 2 s, 2 da; *Career* served RAF 1950–52; entered FO 1952, head of chancery Tehran 1965–68, FCO 1968, head of personnel servs FCO 1969, head News Dept FCO 1971–73, cnsllr and head of chancery Paris 1973–75, asst under sec state on loan to NI Office 1975–77, asst under sec state FCO 1977–79, ambass SA 1979–82, dep under sec state (Africa and ME) FCO 1982–84, high cmmr Aust 1984–88; dir The Observer 1989–93, chm (non-exec) Lonrho plc 1994–; chm Britain-Australia Soc; govr ctee Tonbridge Sch; pro chllr City Univ; memb Franco-Br Cncl (chm 1989–93); Ct of Worshipful Co of Skinners (master 1993–94); Officier Légion d'Honneur 1996; *Recreations* tennis, golf; *Clubs* United Oxford and Cambridge; *Style*— Sir John Leahy, KCMG; ✉ Manor Stables, Bishopstone, Seaford, E Sussex BN25 2UD (☎ 01323 898898, fax 01323 896037)

LEAKE, Prof Bernard Elgey; s of Norman Sidney Leake (d 1963), and Clare Evelyn, *née* Walgate (d 1970); *b* 29 July 1932; *Educ* Wirral GS Bebington, Univ of Liverpool (BSc, PhD), Univ of Bristol (DSc); *m* 23 Aug 1955, Gillian Dorothy, da of Prof Charles Henry Dobinson, CMG; 5 s (Christopher b 1958, Roger b 1959, Alastair b 1961, Jonathan b 1964, Nicholas b 1966); *Career* Leverhulme res fell Univ of Liverpool 1955–57, res assoc Berkeley California 1966, reader in geology Univ of Bristol 1968–74 (lectr 1957–68); Univ of Glasgow: prof 1974–, head Dept of Geology and Applied Geology 1974–92, hon keeper of geological collections Hunterian Museum 1974–97; author of over 100 res papers and maps, especially of Connemara Western Ireland; treas: Geological Soc London 1980–85 and 1989–96 (pres 1986–88), Geologists' Assoc 1997–; FGS 1956, FRSE 1976; *Books* Catalogue of Analysed Calciferous Amphiboles (1968), The Geology of the Dalradian and associated rocks of Connemara, Western Ireland (1994); *Clubs* Geological Soc; *Style*— Prof Bernard Leake, FRSE; ✉ Dept of Geology & Applied Geology, University of Glasgow, Glasgow G12 8QQ (☎ 0141 339 8855, fax 0141 330 4808)

LEAKE, Christopher Jonathan Piers; s of Kenneth Piers Leake (d 1988), of Frodsham, Cheshire, and Sheila Mary, *née* Salt; *b* 17 May 1951; *Educ* St Olave's Sch York, St Peter's Sch York; *m* 1976, Carol Joan, da of Lawrence Miveld, of Hartford, Cheshire; 1 s (Gerard William b 13 Dec 1982), 1 da (Claire Louise b 21 Oct 1978); *Career* journalist; reporter W Cheshire Newspapers 1970–74, Express and Star Wolverhampton

1974–79 (reporter, industl corr), The Daily Telegraph 1979–82 (Scottish corr, memb industl staff), industl and consumer affrs ed The Mail on Sunday 1982–; *Recreations* squash, running, people, films; *Style*— Christopher Leake, Esq; ✉ The Mail on Sunday, Associated Newspapers plc, Northcliffe House, 2 Derry St, Kensington, London W8 5TS (☎ 0171 938 7034, fax 0171 937 3829)

LEAKER, Dudley Roberts; s of Charles Henry Leaker (d 1941), and Mabel Gwendoline Leaker (d 1967); *b* 22 Dec 1920; *Educ* Dynevor Sch Swansea, Welsh and RWA Schs of Architecture UCL, Strathclyde Univ; *m* 12 June 1945, Mary Venn (Molly) (d 1996), da of Sydney James (d 1958); 1 s (David Charles b 1949), 3 da (Margaret (Mrs Halstead) b 1947, Jane (Mrs Smith) b 1953, Patricia (Mrs Eynon) b 1956); *Career* Civil Def; architect on bomb-damaged cities: Bristol, Plymouth, Coventry 1945–52; sr architect Stevenage New Town 1952–56; chief architect and planner: Cumbernauld New Town 1962–70, Warrington New Town 1970–75; architectural advsr and exec dir Milton Keynes New City 1975–78, hon res fell Open Univ 1979–84, exchange prof of architecture Pennsylvania State Univ 1981–82; chm Int Study Gp invited to Tokyo by Japanese Govt 1985, sr ind inspr at major public inquiries 1978–91, head of team winning Reynolds Award for Community Architecture, and various other architectural awards; chm: Int Working Party on New Towns 1976–87, Bd of Tstees Inter Action (Milton Keynes) 1976–78; external examiner Strathclyde and Sheffield Univs; memb Bd: Oxford Citizen's HSG Assoc 1978–85, S Shrops Rural HSG Assoc 1988–; hon life memb Int Fedn of HSG & Planning, fndr memb Cottage Theatre Cumbernauld; JP Dunbartonshire 1968–75; FRIBA 1952, FRIAS 1958, memb ISOCARP 1962; *Books* New Towns in National Development (1980), New Towns Worldwide (1985); *Recreations* painting, music, travel; *Style*— Dudley Leaker, Esq; ✉ 27 Churchill Road, Church Stretton, Shropshire SY6 6AE

LEAKEY, Dr David Martin; s of Reginald Edward Leakey (d 1969), of Redhill, Surrey, and Edith Doris, *née* Gaze (d 1974); *b* 23 July 1932; *Educ* Imperial Coll London (BSc, PhD, DIC); *m* 31 Aug 1957, Shirley May, da of George Clifford Webster (d 1968), of Bridlington, Yorks; 1 s (Graham Peter b 1967), 1 da (Pamela Susan b 1961); *Career* tech dir GEC Telecoms Ltd 1969–84; dir: Fulcrum Telecommunications Ltd 1985–92, Mitel Inc Canada 1986–92; British Telecom (BT): dep engr-in-chief 1984–86, chief scientist 1986–91, gp technical advsr 1991–92, ret 1992; conslt telecommunications services, systems and networks 1992–; dir: BABT (Br Approvals Bd Telecommunications) 1990–, Wireless Systems International Ltd 1995–; chm BSI/DISC 1996–; visiting prof Univ of Bristol 1985–; Liveryman Worshipful Co of Engrs, Freeman City of London; Hon DEng Univ of Bristol 1995; FEng 1979, FIEE, FCGI; *Recreations* horticulture; *Style*— Dr David Leakey, FEng; ✉ Rocheberie, Grassy Lane, Sevenoaks, Kent TN13 1PW (☎ and fax 01732 453950)

LEAMAN, Adrian John; s of Robert Edgar Leaman, and Rita, *née* Fricker; *b* 20 Oct 1946; *Educ* Tiffin Sch Kingston-upon-Thames, Univ of Sussex (BA); *m* Rita Harland, *née* Russell; 2 step c (Joseph Harland, Katie Harland (now Mrs Kelly); *Career* researcher Science Policy Res Unit Univ of Sussex 1969–71, with RIBA 1971–78 (worked in Res Unit and ed Journal of Architectural Research), sometime teacher and researcher Bartlett Sch of Architecture and Unit for Architectural Studies UCL (co-fndr Space Syntax research programme), lectr computing and statistics Poly of N London 1978–86, md Building Use Studies Ltd (studying human behaviour in buildings) 1987– (joined 1986), dir of research Inst of Advanced Architectural Studies Univ of York 1993–; FRGS 1983, FRSA 1994; *Style*— Adrian Leaman, Esq; ✉ Institute of Advanced Architectural Studies, University of York, The King's Manor, York YO1 2EP (☎ 01904 671280, fax 01904 611338, e-mail al18@york.ac.uk); Building Use Studies Ltd, 42–44 Newman Street, London W1P 3PA

LEAN, (George) Alastair; OBE (1971); s of Daniel Lean (d 1960), of Glasgow, and Edith Janet, *née* Maclellan (d 1966); *b* 19 June 1921; *Educ* Loretto, Royal Technical Coll Glasgow (now Univ of Strathclyde); *m* 1, June 1946 (m dis 1966), Iona Edith Hope, da of Charles Hope Murray (d 1938), of Beith; 1 s ((Daniel) Graham), 2 da (Ferelith Iona, Bryony Edith); m 2, Mrs (Margaret) Anne Little (d 1996), da of Sir Rennie Izat, CIE (d 1966), of Balliliesk, Muckhart; *Career* studied med 1938–40, served RAF Coastal Cmd, Sqdn Ldr 1940–46 (despatches); entered textile indust 1946, dir of various textile mfrg cos 1950–66; md: Carse of Allan Ltd 1966–81, Pauline Hyde & Associates Ltd (outplacement consltS) Scotland 1982, ret 1988; freelance contrib to radio and jls; memb Glasgow Valuation Appeals Ct 1955–67, chm Savings Bank of Glasgow 1964–66 (tstee 1955–83), vice chm Scot Woollen Mfrs Assoc 1965, gen cmmr of Income Tax 1970–96, consul for Finland Glasgow 1973–94, doyen Finnish Consuls in UK 1989–94, chm Personnel Gp Tstee Savings Bank Central Bd 1977–82 (Employers Cncl 1966–76), dir Merchants House of Glasgow 1985–, tstee TSB Fndn (Scotland) 1988–92; Dean Glasgow Consular Corps 1987–89; Freeman City of Glasgow 1985, memb Incorporation of Weavers Glasgow 1985; Commander Order of the Lion of Finland 1994; Knight (Class 1) Order of the White Rose (Finland) 1985; FInstD 1960–88; *Recreations* shooting, countryside, Finnish matters; *Clubs* Western (Glasgow), Clyde Corinthian Yacht (Rhu); *Style*— G Alastair Lean, Esq, OBE; ✉ Birkhill, Muckhart, By Dollar, Scotland FK14 7JW (☎ 01259 781392)

LEAN, Prof Michael Ernest John; s of Maj John Holman Lean, of Suffolk and Cornwall, and Estelle Flower, *née* Oulton; *b* 16 March 1952; *Educ* Trinity Coll Glenalmond, Downing Coll Cambridge (MA), St Bart's Hosp Med Sch (MB BChir, MD); *m* Prof Annie Scott Anderson, da of James Coutts Anderson; 5 c; *Career* currently prof of human nutrition Univ of Glasgow and hon conslt physician Glasgow Royal Infirmary; memb: Br Diabetic Assoc, Nutrition Soc, Bd Health Education for Scotland; André Mayer prize 1986; FRCP (Edin), FRCPS (Glasgow); *Recreations* violin, Scottish music, cross-country and hill running (winner Barmekin Hill race 1991, 1992 and 1993), fishing and mountaineering; *Style*— Prof Michael Lean; ✉ Hatton Castle, Newtyle, Blairgowrie PH12 8UN (☎ 01828 650404); Department of Human Nutrition, University of Glasgow, Glasgow Royal Infirmary, Glasgow (☎ 0141 211 4686, fax 0141 211 4844, e-mail mejlean@clinmed.gla.ac.uk)

LEAPER, David John; s of David Thomas Leaper, of Leeds, and Gwendoline, *née* Robertson; *b* 23 July 1947; *Educ* Leeds Modern GS, Univ of Leeds (MB ChB, MD, ChM); *children* 1 s (Charles David Edward), 1 da (Alice Jane Sophia); *Career* Univ of Leeds: house offr 1970–71, MRC res fell 1971–73, registrar in surgery 1973–76; Univ of London: CRC res fell, sr registrar in surgery 1976–81; conslt sr lectr in surgery Univ of Bristol 1981–96, prof of surgery at North Tees General Hospital 1996–; Hunterian prof of surgery RCS 1981–82, prof of surgery Hong Kong Univ 1988–90; memb Cncl and vice pres RSM (surgery) 1982–88, fndr memb Surgical Infection Soc of Europe, memb Ctee Surgical Res Soc (UK) 1987–88; FRCS 1975, FRCSEd 1974, FICA 1984; *Clubs* RSM London; *Style*— Prof David Leaper; ✉ Professorial Unit of Surgery, North Tees General Hospital, Stockton on Tees, Cleveland TS19 8PE

LEAPMAN, Edwina; da of Charles Morris Leapman (d 1962), of London, and Hannah, *née* Schonfield (d 1988); *b* 21 Oct 1931; *Educ* Farnham Sch of Art, Slade Sch of Fine Art, The Central Sch of Art; *m* Dec 1957 (m dis 1969), John Saul Weiss; *Career* artist; *Solo Exhibitions* The New Art Centre London 1974, Annely Juda Fine Art London 1976, 1980 and 1993, Gallerie Loyse Oppenheim Nyon Switzerland 1979, Gallery Artline The Hague Holland 1979, Juda Rowan Gallery London 1987, Galerie Konstrucktiv Tendens Stockholm Sweden 1990, The Serpentine Gallery London 1991, ACP Viviane Ehrli Galerie Zurich Switzerland 1996; *Group Exhibitions* incl: Signals Gallery London 1956, Four Abstract Painters (ICA, London) 1967, Survey '67 (Camden Art Centre, London) 1967, Silence (Camden Art Centre) 1971, John Moores Exhibition Liverpool 1972, 1974 and 1976, Post Minimal Painting (Scottish Arts Cncl, Edinburgh) 1974, Rini Dippel: A Selection of Six Painters (Air Gallery, London) 1976, Gallerie Loyse Oppenheim Nyon Switzerland 1977, Hayward Annual '78 (Hayward Gallery, London) 1978, A Free Hand (Arts Cncl Touring Exhibition) 1978, The Arts Cncl Collection (Hayward Gallery) 1980, Masters of the Avant-Garde & Three Decades of Contemporary Art (Annely Juda/Juda Rowan) 1986, A Disquieting suggestion (John Hansard Gallery Southampton) 1988, The Presence of Painting: Aspects of British Abstraction (South Bank Touring Exhibition) 1989, The Experience of Painting: Eight Modern Artists (Laing Art Gallery Newcastle, S Bank Touring Exhibition) 1989, From Picasso to Abstraction (Annely Juda Fine Art) 1989, The Arts Cncl Collection (Festival Hall) 1993, Lead and Follow: the continuity of abstraction (Atlantis Gallery) 1994, British Abstract Art: Painting (Flowers East) 1994; *Style*— Ms Edwina Leapman; ✉ Annely Juda Fine Art, 23 Dering St, London W1R 9AA (☎ 0171 722 5311)

LEARMONT, Gen Sir John Hartley; KCB (1989), CBE (1980, OBE 1975); s of Capt Percy Hewitt Learmont, CIE (d 1983), of Curry Rivel, Somerset, and Doris Orynthia, *née* Hartley (d 1982); *b* 10 March 1934; *Educ* Fettes, RMA Sandhurst; *m* 2 March 1957, Susan, da of Thomas Jefferson Thornborrow, (d 1971), of Penrith; 3 s (Mark b 7 Jan 1958, Richard John b 8 June 1960, James Jefferson b 9 Feb 1967); *Career* cmmnd RA 1954, Instr RMA 1960–63, student Staff Coll 1964, served 14 Fld Regt, Staff Coll and 3 RHA 1965–70, MA to C-in-C BAOR 1971–73, CO 1 RHA 1974–75 (despatches 1974), HQ BAOR 1976–78, Cdr 8 Field Force 1979–81, Dep Cdr Cwlth Monitoring Force Rhodesia 1979–80, student RCDS 1981, Chief of Mission Br C-in-C Mission to Soviet Forces in Germany 1982–84, Cdr Artillery 1 (Br) Corps 1985–87, Chief of Staff UKLF 1987–88, Cmdt Staff Coll Camberley 1988–89 Mil Sec MOD 1989–91, QMG MOD 1991–94, Col Cmdt Army Air Corps 1988–94, Col Cmdt RA 1989–, Col Cmdt RHA 1990–, Hon Col 2 Bn The Wessex Regt 1990–95, Hon Col 2 (Vol) Bn The Royal Gloucester, Berkshire and Wiltshire Regt 1995–; pres Army Athletic Assoc 1988–94; FIMgt; *Recreations* fell walking, all sport, theatre; *Clubs* Naval and Military; *Style*— Gen Sir John Learmont, KCB, CBE

LEARY, Brian Leonard; QC (1978); s of late A T Leary, and late M C Leary, *née* Bond; *b* 1 Jan 1929; *Educ* Kings Sch Canterbury, Wadham Coll Oxford (MA); *m* 14 April 1965, Myriam Ann, da of late Kenneth Bannister, CBE, of Mexico City; *Career* called to the Bar Middle Temple 1953; sr prosecuting counsel to Crown 1971–78 (jr 1964–71), master of the bench 1986; chm Br Mexican Soc 1989–92; *Recreations* travel, sailing, growing herbs; *Style*— Brian Leary, Esq, QC; ✉ c/o 5 Paper Buildings, Temple, London EC4Y 9AR

LEASK, Annie Carol; da of Kenneth Roy Leask, of Hatfield, South Yorkshire, and Marion Gladys, *née* Dixey; *b* 23 July 1965; *Educ* Thorne GS, Univ of Kent Canterbury (BA), Nat Cncl for Training Journalists Proficiency Cert; *Career* trainee Croydon Advertiser Newspaper Group 1986–89, presenter and reseacher daily news bulletins Croydon Cable TV 1987–88, freelance journalist 1989 (Thames TV, Sunday Mirror, Evening Standard); Daily Express: showbusiness reporter and music critic 1989–91, dep showbusiness ed 1991–, special projects ed 1992–; memb NUJ 1986; *Recreations* horse riding, squash, skiing, reading; *Style*— Ms Annie Leask; ✉ Daily Express, Ludgate House, 245 Blackfriars Rd, London SE1 9UX (☎ 0171 922 7099, fax 0171 922 7970/7974, car 0836 516079)

LEASK, Lt-Gen Sir Henry Lowther Ewart Clark; KCB (1970, CB 1967), DSO (1945), OBE (1957, MBE 1945); s of Rev James Leask, Rector of Scruton, Yorks, and Margaret Ewart Leask; *b* 30 June 1913; *m* 1940, Zoë de Camborne, da of Col William Patterson Paynter, DSO (d 1958), of Dogmersfield Lodge, Odiham, Hants; 1 s, 2 da; *Career* 2 Lt Royal Scots Fus 1936, served WWII (India, Med and Italy), GSO 1942, Bde Maj Inf Bde 1943, 2 i/c (later CO) 8 Bn Argyll and Sutherland Highlanders 1944–45, CO 1 Bn London Scottish 1946–47, Gen Staff Mil Ops WO 1947–49, Instr Staff Coll 1949–51, CO 1 Bn Parachute Regt 1952–54, Asst Mil Sec to Sec of State for War 1954–57, Cmdt Tactical Wing Sch of Inf 1957–58, Comd Inf Bde 1958–61, Brig 1961, idc 1961, Dep Mil Sec to Sec of State for War 1962–64, Col Royal Highland Fus 1964–69, Col Cmdt Scottish Inf 1968, GOC 52 Lowland Div 1964–66, Maj-Gen 1964, Dir Army Trg MOD 1966–69, Lt-Gen 1969, GOC Scotland 1969–72; Govr of Edinburgh Castle 1969–72; ret; *Recreations* shooting, fishing; *Clubs* Carlton; *Style*— Lt-Gen Sir Henry Leask, KCB, DSO, OBE; ✉ 9 Glenalmond House, Manor Fields, London SW15 (☎ 0181 788 6949)

LEASK OF LEASK AND OF THAT ILK, Madam; Anne Meredith Gordon Fleming; Baroness of Leask and 22 Chief of Clan Leask; da of Alexander Leask Curr, univ lectr, and Anne Marie Stuart Leask; suc Alexander Graham Leask of that Ilk 1968; *b* 1915; *Educ* Lonsdale Sch for Girls Norwich, Blyth GS Norwich, Univ of London (BA), Sorbonne (Diplôme), Univ of Colorado (MA, PhD); *m* Sydney Helgesen; 1 s; *Career* instr Univ of Colorado, asst and assoc prof Univ of Toledo (Ohio) and Kalamazoo Coll (Michigan), prof Cedar Crest Coll (Pa), lectr Inst of Adult Educn Norwich; personally involved with Clan Leask Soc and membs worldwide also church work and with charitable orgns; Chev de l'Ordre des Palmes Académiques 1956; *Books* incl: La Littérature Françaises Contemporaine (1970), French Grammar, Spanish Grammar, The Leasks (1980); *Recreations* theatre, music, swimming; *Clubs* Royal Over-Seas League; *Style*— Madam Leask of Leask and of that Ilk; ✉ 1 Vincent Rd, Sheringham, Norfolk NR26 8BP; Leask, Aberdeenshire

LEASOR, (Thomas) James; s of Richard Leasor, (d 1959), of Erith, Kent, and Christine, *née* Hall (d 1949); *b* 20 Dec 1923; *Educ* City of London Sch, Oriel Coll Oxford (MA); *m* 1 Dec 1951, Joan Margaret (barr-at-law), da of Capt Roland S Bevan (d 1968), of Crowcombe, Somerset; 3 s (Jeremy b 1953, Andrew b 1956, Stuart b 1958); *Career* WWII vol Royal E Kent Regt 1942, cmmnd 2 Lt Royal Berks Regt 1944; serv 1 Lincolns: Burma, India, Malaya, ret Capt 1946; editorial staff London Daily Express 1948–55, magazine conslt Geo Newnes Ltd (later IPC) 1955–59, co fndr and dir Elm Tree Books; FRSA; OStJ; *Books* author of 30 novels incl: the Dr Jason Love series of suspense novels, The Red Fort (1954), War at the Top (1959), Hess, The Uninvited Envoy (1962), Singapore, The Battle that Changed the World (1968), Green Beach (1975), Open Secret (1983), Ship of Gold (1984), Tank of Serpents (1986); *Recreations* walking dogs, swimming, vintage sports cars; *Clubs* Garrick; *Style*— James Leasor, Esq; ✉ Swallowcliffe Manor, Salisbury, Wilts SP3 5PB; Casa Do Zimbro, Praia da Luz, Lagos, Algarve, Portugal

LEATES, Margaret; da of Henry Arthur Sargent Rayner, and Alice, *née* Baker; *b* 30 March 1951; *Educ* Lilley and Stone Girls' HS Newark, King's Coll London (LLB, LLM, AKC); *m* 26 May 1973, Timothy Philip Leates; 1 s (Benjamin b 15 April 1982), 1 da (Lydia b 14 July 1983); *Career* admitted slr 1975; Parliamentary Counsel Office 1976–90, parly conslt 1990–; memb Law Soc; *Recreations* other people's gardens, hermeneutics; *Clubs* Whitstable Yacht; *Style*— Mrs Margaret Leates; ✉ Crofton Farm, 161 Crofton Lane, Orpington, Kent BR6 0BP (☎ 01689 820192, fax 01689 878441); Nyanza, 87 Bennells Avenue, Whitstable, Kent (☎ 01227 272335)

LEATHAM, Simon Patrick; eldest s of Maj Patrick Magor Leatham (d 1951), and Hon Cecily Eveline, *née* Berry (d 1976), da of 1 and last Baron Buckland (d 1928); *b* 9 Nov 1944; *Educ* Eton, Trinity Coll Cambridge; *m* 25 April 1967, Lady Victoria Diana, *née* Cecil, da of 6 Marquess of Exeter (d 1982); 1 s (Richard b 1971), 1 da (Miranda b 1969); *Career* chartered accountant; md Tufton Oceanic Ltd (formerly Oceanic Finance Corp)

1982–; *Recreations* country pursuits, the Arts; *Clubs* Boodle's (chm 1992–95); *Style*— Simon P Leatham, Esq; ✉ Burghley House, Stamford, Lincolnshire PE9 3JY (☎ 01780 63 131, fax 01780 56057); Flat 18, Chelsea House, 24 Lowndes Street, London SW1X 9JE (☎ 0171 245 6366); Tufton House, 3 Dean Trench Street, London SW1P 3HB (☎ 0171 340 2850, fax 0171 976 0772)

LEATHAM, Lady Victoria Diana; *née* Cecil; DL (1993 Cambs); da of 6 Marquess of Exeter, KCMG, and 2 w, Diana, da of Hon Arnold Henderson, OBE (d 1933, 5 s of 1 Baron Faringdon, CH); *b* 1947; *m* 1967, Simon Patrick Leatham, *qv*; 1 s, 1 da; *Career* dir: Preservation Tst, Burghley House; Sotheby's; presenter of tv progs on stately homes; lectr on antiques UK and overseas; tstee Samuel Courtauld Tst; Hon Dr of Arts De Montfort Univ Leicester 1994; Hon Col 158 (Royal Anglian) Regt 1996; The Royal Logistics Corps (Volunteer); *Books* Burghley - The Life of a Great House (1992); *Style*— The Lady Victoria Leatham, DL; ✉ Burghley House, Stamford, Lincs (☎ 01780 63131); Flat 18, 24 Lowndes St, London SW1 (☎ 0171 245 6366)

LEATHARD, Dr John Frederick; s of Herbert Richard Leathard (d 1975), of Scarborough, Yorks, and Gladys Adeline, *née* Carr (d 1977); *b* 15 May 1927; *Educ* Haberdashers' Aske's, Royal GS Guildford, Kingston Tech Coll (Inter BSc), King's Coll Durham Univ (BSc, PhD); *m* 1960, Audrey Mary, da of Sidney Frank Baker; 1 da (Nicola Jane b 1965); *Career* post grad scholarship in naval architecture King's Coll Durham Univ, early training with Swan Hunter and Wigham Richardson Walker Shipyard, temp scientific offr Ship Div Nat Physical Lab 1949–51, ship draughtsman John I Thornycroft Woolston Shipyard 1951–52; naval architect: Devpt Dept Alcan Banbury Oxon 1952–55, Burness Corlett & Partners Basingstoke 1955–61; Richard Dunston (Hessle) Shipbuilders 1961–71 (naval architect, gen mangr, md); dir various subsid cos A & P Appledore Group (servs to marine industry worldwide) 1972–91 (ret 1991); FEng 1987, FRSA 1988, FRINA; *Recreations* piano, theatre, walking, swimming, water-skiing; *Clubs* David Lloyd (Raynes Park), Princes Water-Skiing; *Style*— Dr John Leathard, FEng

LEATHER, Sir Edwin Hartley Cameron; KCMG (1974), KCVO (1975), kt (1962); s of Harold H Leather, MBE; *b* 1919; *Educ* Trinity Coll Sch Ontario, RMC Kingston Ontario; *m* 1940, Sheila Alexie (d 1994), da of A H Greenlees; 2 da (Hope, Sarah); *Career* dir Hogg Robinson and Capel-Cure Ltd and subsid cos 1946–64; MP (C) Somerset N 1950–64; pres Inst of Mktg 1963–67, dir William Baird and Co Ltd 1966–73, chm Nat Union of Cons Assocs 1969–70, govr and C-in-C Bermuda 1973–77, dir N M Rothschild (Bermuda) 1978–90, and others; broadcaster and author; nat govr The Shaw Festival Canada, memb Hon Ctee of the Canadian Meml Fndn, fndr (with Lord Menuhin) Bermuda Festival, tstee Menuhin Fndn of Bermuda, chm Bermuda Ctee Utd World Coll 1975–91; Hon LLD Univ of Bath 1975; Hon FRSA, hon citizen Kansas City, medal of merit Royal Canadian Legion, Gold medal Nat Inst of Social Sciences NY; KStJ 1973; Batchelor of Mil Sci RMC of Canada 1994; *Books* The Vienna Elephant, The Mozart Score, The Duveen Letter; *Recreations* travel, reading, music; *Clubs* Royal Bermuda Yacht, York (Toronto), Hamilton (Ontario); *Style*— Sir Edwin Leather, KCMG, KCVO; ✉ Chelsea, Inwood Close, Paget, Bermuda (☎ 00 1 809 236 0240, fax 00 1 809 236 5534); 130 St Joseph's Drive, Hamilton, Canada L8N 2E8 (☎ 00 1 905 527 1917, fax 00 1 905 523 6383)

LEATHERDALE, Dr Brian Anthony; s of Dennis Hector Leatherdale, and Mary Ann, *née* Sheilds (d 1984); *b* 30 Nov 1942; *Educ* St Joseph's Coll Birkfield, London Hosp Med Coll (BSc, MD, DiplObst); *m* 27 April 1968, Salliebelle, da of Joseph Gilley Dathan (d 1987); 2 s (Anthony Stephen b 15 May 1971, Daniel Brian b 23 March 1973); *Career* sr med registrar King's Coll Hosp 1972–75, conslt physician Dudley Rd Hosp Birmingham 1975–81, conslt physician Royal S Hants Hosp Southampton 1981– (post grad tutor 1983–88); regnl advsr Wessex RCP 1988–94; memb BMA, memb RSM, FRCP 1985; *Recreations* cricket, golf, assoc football; *Clubs* Brockenhurst Manor Golf; *Style*— Dr Brian Leatherdale; ✉ Hewers Orchard, Newtown, Minstead, nr Lyndhurst, Hants SO43 7GD (☎ 01703 812789); Royal South Hants Hospital, Graham Rd, Southampton SO9 4XY (☎ 01703 634288)

LEATHERS, 3 Viscount (UK 1954); Christopher Graeme Leathers; JP; also Baron Leathers (UK 1941); s 2 Viscount Leathers (d 1996), and his 1 w, Elspeth Graeme, *née* Stewart (d 1985); *b* 31 Aug 1941; *Educ* Rugby, Open Univ (BA); *m* 1964, Maria Philomena, da of Michael Merriman, of Charlestown, Co Mayo; 1 s (Hon James Frederick b 27 May 1969), 1 da (Hon Melissa Maria (Hon Mrs Wesley) b 22 April 1966); *Heir* s, Hon James Frederick Leathers b 1969; *Career* with Wm Cory & Son Ltd 1961–83, Mostyn Docks Ltd 1084–86; currently civil servant; Dept of Tport 1988–; memb Inst of Chartered Shipborkers, MIMgt; Liveryman Worshipful Co of Shipwrights; *Style*— The Rt Hon the Viscount Leathers; ✉ Lime Cottage, High Street, Burwash, Etchingham, East Sussex TN19 7HL

LEATHERS, Hon Jeremy Baxter; s of 2 Viscount Leathers (d 1996); *b* 11 April 1946; *Educ* Rugby, Trinity Coll Dublin (BBS); *m* 1969, Fiona Lesley, eldest da of late George Stanhope Pitt, of Rowbarns Manor, Horsley, Surrey; 1 s (Luke Alexander b 1974), 2 da (Tara Charlotte b 1972, Fern Griselda b 1979); *Career* md Stocksigns 1989–; dir: Applied Environmental Research Co (AERC) 1989–, British & Foreign Wharf 1977–; *Recreations* sailing, tennis, reading ski brochures; *Style*— The Hon Jeremy Leathers; ✉ Stocksigns Ltd, Ormside Way, Redhill, Surrey RH1 2LG (☎ 01737 764764, fax 01737 763763)

LEATHWOOD, Barry; *b* 11 April 1941; *m* 15 Aug 1963, (Veronica) Ann; 1 da (Sarah Ann); *Career* sec SW Regnl Trade Gp 1983–87 (dist offr 1973–83), nat sec Rural Agric and Allied Workers Trade Gp TGWU 1987–; ldr Worker Side Agric Wages Bd, co-ordinator for the environment TGWU, vice pres Euro Fedn of Agric Workers Union, formerly cncllr Doncaster Co BC; trade union sec: Home Grown Timber Nat Jt Industl Cncl, Forestry Indust Jt Industl and Trades Cncl; memb: HSE Agric Indust Advsy Ctee, Euro Ctee Int Fedn of Plantation Agric and Allied Workers, Euro Liaison Gp for Agric, Br Socialist Agric Soc; EEC: memb Jt Ctee on Problems Facing Agric Workers, memb Milk and Milk Products Ctee, memb Agric Health and Safety Ctee, memb Agric Statistics Gp; FRSA 1995; *Style*— Barry Leathwood, Esq; ✉ TGWU, Transport House, 16 Palace Street, Victoria, London SW1E 5JD (☎ 0171 828 7788, fax 0171 630 5861)

LEAVER, Sir Christopher; GBE (1981), JP (Inner London); s of Dr Robert Leaver, and Audrey, *née* Kerpen; *b* 3 Nov 1937; *Educ* Eastbourne Coll; *m* 1975, Helen Mireille Molyneux Benton; 1 s (Benedict), 2 da (Tara, Anna); *Career* cmmnd RAOC 1956–58, Hon Col 151 (Gtr London) Tport Regt RCT (V) 1983–88, Hon Col Cmdt RCT 1988–91; chm: Thames Line plc 1987–89, Thames Water plc 1993– (dep chm 1983–93); dir: Bath & Portland Group plc 1983–85, Thermal Scientific plc 1985–88, Unionamerica Holdings Plc 1994–; cncllr Royal Borough of Kensington and Chelsea 1971–74, Alderman Ward of Dowgate City of London 1974– (memb Ct of Common Cncl 1973), Sheriff City of London 1979–80, Lord Mayor of London 1981–82; memb: Bd Brixton Prison 1975–78, Cmmn of Lt for City of London 1982–, Fin Ctee London Diocesan Fund 1983–86, Cncl Mission to Seamen 1983–93, Advsy Gp Royal Parks 1993–96; govr: Christs' Hosp Sch 1975–, City of London Girls' Sch 1975–78, City Univ 1978– (chllr 1981–82), City of London Freemen's Sch 1980–81, Music Therapy Tst 1981–89; chm: Young Musicians' Symphony Orchestra Tst 1979–81, London Tourist Bd 1983–89, Eastbourne Coll 1988–; tstee: London Symphony Orchestra 1983–90, Chichester Festival Theatre; vice pres: Nat Playing Fields Assoc 1983–, Bridewell Royal Hosp 1983–89; church warden St Olave's Hart St 1975–89, church cmmr 1982–93 and 1996–; hon memb GSM 1982; Hon DMus City Univ 1982; Freeman Co of Watermen and Lightermen, Hon Freeman Co of Water Conservators; Hon Liveryman: Worshipful Co of Farmers, Worshipful Co of Environmental Cleaners; Master Worshipful Co of Carmen 1987–88; KStJ 1982; FRSA, FCIT; *Style*— Sir Christopher Leaver, GBE, JP; ✉ 52 Old Church Street, London SW3 5DB (☎ and fax 0171 352 2273)

LEAVER, Prof Christopher John; s of Douglas Percival Leaver (d 1978), and Elizabeth Constance, *née* Hancock; *b* 31 May 1942; *Educ* Lyme Regis GS, Imperial Coll London (BSc, ARCS, DIC, PhD), Univ of Oxford (MA); *m* 8 Oct 1971, Anne, da of Prof Hastings Dudley Huggins (d 1970); 1 s (Tristan), 1 da (Anya); *Career* Fulbright scholar Purdue Univ USA 1966–68, sci offr ARC Plant Physiology Unit Imperial Coll 1968–69, prof of plant molecular biology Univ of Edinburgh 1986–89 (SERC sr res fell 1985–89, reader 1980–86, lectr 1969–80), Sibthorpian prof of plant sciences and head of dept Oxford 1990–; fell St John's Coll Oxford; tstee and memb Cncl John Innes Inst 1987–; memb: Cncl AFRC 1990–94, Priorities Bd MAFF 1990–94; memb: Cncl Euro Molecular Biology Orgn 1992–, ACOST 1992–93, Cncl Royal Soc 1992–94, Advsy Panel CIBA Fellowship Tst 1993–; T H Huxley Gold medal Imperial Coll 1970, Tate and Lyle Award Phytochem Soc of Europe 1984, Academia Europaea 1988; EMBO 1982, FRS 1986, FRSE 1987; *Recreations* walking and talking in Upper Coquetdale; *Style*— Prof Christopher Leaver, FRS, FRSE; ✉ Department of Plant Sciences, South Parks Road, Oxford OX1 3RB (☎ 01865 275143, fax 01865 275144, e-mail chris.leaver@plants.ox.ac.uk)

LEAVER, Colin Edward; s of Edward Roy Leaver, of West Wittering, West Sussex, and Freda Eleanor, *née* Toogood; *b* 25 May 1958; *Educ* Haywards Heath GS, Lincoln Coll Oxford (MA); *m* 10 May 1986, Maria Victoria, da of John Hutton Simpkins, of Alicante, Spain; 2 da (Chirstina b 1987, Mónica b 1991), 1 s (James b 1989); *Career* Simmons & Simmons: articled clerk 1980–82, asst slr 1982–86, ptnr 1986–, based Hong Kong 1989–96, based London 1996–; *Recreations* sailing, philately, aviation; *Clubs* Royal Hong Kong Yacht; *Style*— Colin Leaver, Esq; ✉ Simmons & Simmons, 21 Wilson Street, London EC2M 2TQ (☎ 0171 628 2020, fax 0171 628 2070)

LEAVER, (Mary) Elaine; *b* 16 Nov 1948; *Educ* Lancashire Poly (BA); *Career* Queen Alexandra's Royal Army Nursing Corps 1966–70 (RGN 1970), health visitor student and qualified health worker Blackburn BC 1970–74, health visitor and fieldwork teacher Blackburn Hyndburn and Ribble Valley Health Authy 1974–79 (cert in health educn 1979), community nursing offr Burnley Pendle and Rossendale Health Authy 1979–83; N Manchester Health Authy: dir of nursing servs (community and mental handicap) 1983–86, unit gen mangr Mental Health and Community Unit 1986–88, unit gen mangr Acute Servs Unit 1988–90, chief exec 1990–94; chief exec N Manchester Healthcare NHS Tst 1994–; memb Royal Coll of Nursing, MIHSM; *Style*— Mrs Elaine Leaver; ✉ North Manchester Health Authority, Central Drive, Crumpsall, Manchester M8 6RL (☎ 0161 720 2836, fax 0161 720 2834, mobile 0860 457830)

LEAVER, Peter Lawrence Oppenheim; QC (1987); s of Marcus Isaac Leaver (d 1966), of London, and Lena, *née* Oppenheim (d 1984); *b* 28 Nov 1944; *Educ* Aldenham Sch, Univ of Dublin; *m* 2 June 1969, Jane Rachel, o da of Leonard Pearl (d 1983), of London; 3 s (Marcus, James, Benjamin) 1 da (Rebecca); *Career* called to the Bar Lincoln's Inn 1967, recorder 1994–; memb Gen Cncl Bar 1987–90; chm: Bar Ctee 1989 (vice chm 1988–89), Int Practice Ctee 1990; memb: Ctee on Future of Legal Profession 1986–88, Cncl Legal Educn 1986–90; dir Investment Management Regulatory Organisation Limited 1994–; tstee The Free Representation Unit; *Recreations* refereeing football matches, sport, wine, theatre, opera; *Clubs* Garrick, Groucho, MCC; *Style*— Peter Leaver, Esq, QC; ✉ 5 Hamilton Terrace, London NW8 9RE (☎ 0171 286 0208); 1 Essex Ct, Temple, London EC4Y 9AR (☎ 0171 583 2000, fax 0171 583 0118, telex 889109 ESSEX G)

LEBUS, (Hon) Christina; da of 2 Baron Strathalmond, CMG, OBE, TD (d 1976); *b* 1954; *m* 1974, Timothy Andrew Lebus; 1 s (David b 1983); *Career* business devpt dir Dewe Rogerson Ltd (PR) until 1997, dir WellBeing (The Health Research Charity for Women and Babies) 1997–; *Style*— Mrs Christina Lebus; ✉ Director, WellBeing, 27 Sussex Place, Regent's Park, London NW1 4SP (☎ 0171 262 5337, fax 0171 724 7725)

LECHLER, Prof Robert Ian; s of Dr Ian Sewell Lechler (d 1972), and Audrey Florence, *née* Wilson (d 1979); *b* 24 Dec 1951; *Educ* Monkton Combe Sch, Univ of Manchester (MB ChB), Univ of London (PhD); *m* Valerie Susan, da of Harold Ord Johnston (d 1988); 2 s (Alastair Robert b 4 Feb 1980, Toby Ian b 23 Dec 1982), 1 da (Suzannah Jane b 24 Feb 1988); *Career* sr renal registrar Professorial Med Unit Hammersmith Hosp 1983–84 (renal registrar 1982–83), Wellcome Tst travelling fellowship Laboratory of Immunology Bethesda Maryland USA 1984–86; Royal Postgrad Med Sch: sr lectr in immunology 1986–89, hon conslt in med 1989–, prof and dir of immunology 1994–; chief of immunology serv Hammersmith Hosps Tst 1995–; memb Editorial Bd Transplantation Jl; memb: Renal Assoc 1980, Int Transplantation Soc 1987, Med Res Club 1987, Assoc of Physicians 1988; FRCP 1990 (MRCP 1978), FRCPath 1996; *Recreations* classical music, theatre, family; *Style*— Prof Robert Lechler; ✉ Department of Immunology, Royal Postgraduate Medical School, Hammersmith Hospital, Du Cane Rd, London W12 0NN (☎ 0181 740 3225)

LECHMERE, Sir Berwick Hungerford; 6 Bt (UK 1818), of The Rhydd, Worcestershire, JP (Worcs 1966); s of Capt Sir Ronald Berwick Hungerford Lechmere, 5 Bt (d 1965), and Constance, *née* Long; the estate of Severn End at Hanley Castle, formerly known as Lechmere's Place has been in the family since 11th century; Nicholas Lechmere, chancellor of Duchy of Lancaster for life 1717 cr Baron Lechmere 1721, *dsp* 1727; *b* 21 Sept 1917; *Educ* Charterhouse, Magdalene Coll Cambridge; *m* 1, 24 May 1952 (m annulled 1954), Susan Adele Mary, o child of late Cdr George Henry Maunsell-Smyth, RN; m 2, 17 Nov 1954, Norah Garrett, eldest da of late Lt-Col Christopher Garrett Elkington, DSO, DL, of The Moat House, Cutnall Green, Worcs; *Heir* kinsman, Reginald Anthony Hungerford Lechmere, *qv*; *Career* High Sheriff Worcs 1962, Vice Lord-Lt Hereford and Worcester 1977–92 (DL 1972); FICS; CStJ (1980); *Style*— Sir Berwick Lechmere, Bt, JP; ✉ Church End House, Hanley Castle, Worcester (☎ 01684 592130)

LECHMERE, Reginald Anthony Hungerford; s of Anthony Hungerford Lechmere (d 1954, 3 s of 3 Bt), and Cicely Mary, *née* Bridges (d 1964); hp of kinsman, Sir Berwick Hungerford Lechmere, 6 Bt, *qv*; *b* 24 Dec 1920; *Educ* Charterhouse, Trinity Hall Cambridge; *m* 1956, Anne Jennifer, da of late A C Dind, of Orbe, Switzerland; 3 s (Nicholas Anthony Hungerford b 1960, Adam Francis b 1962, Mark Edmund Dind b 1966), 1 da (Jennifer Sarah b 1959); *Career* formerly Capt 5 Royal Inniskilling Dragoon Gds; antiquarian bookseller; *Style*— Reginald Lechmere, Esq; ✉ Primeswell, Evendine lane, Colwall, Malvern Worcs WR13 6DT (☎ 01684 540340)

LECK, Ann Patricia; MBE (1995); da of Arnold Wilfred Sarson (d 1973), and Annie Elizabeth, *née* Wright (d 1989); *b* 29 Sept 1937; *Educ* Sutton HS for Girls GPDST, Leicester Domestic Sci Trg Coll, Univ of Leicester (CertEd), Manchester Educn Ctee Cert in Counselling and Guidance; *m* 25 July 1959, Prof Ian Maxwell Leck, *qv*; 2 s (Christopher James b 1962, Jonathan Peter b 1967), 2 da (Susan Margaret b 1960, Patricia Mary b 1965); *Career* teacher: Hurlingham Comp Sch 1958–59, Lordswood Tech GS Birmingham 1959–60, Sutton HS for Girls GPDST 1968–71, Shawgrove Sch Manchester 1975–81; Relate marriage guidance: remedial and sex therapy cnsllr 1972–90, memb Nat Exec Ctee 1982–94, vice chm Nat Exec Ctee 1988–90, chm Nat Exec Ctee 1990–94; *Recreations* badminton, sewing, reading, walking; *Style*— Mrs Ann Leck, MBE; ✉ Pembury, 18 Cadogan Park, Woodstock, Oxford OX20 1UW (☎ 01993 811528)

LECK, Prof Ian Maxwell; s of Rev Arthur Simpson Leck (d 1952), and Margaret Mortimer, *née* Jagger (d 1983); *b* 14 Feb 1931; *Educ* Kingswood Sch Bath, Univ of Birmingham (MB ChB, PhD, DSc); *m* 25 July 1959, Ann Patricia Leck, *qv*; 2 s

(Christopher James b 1962, Jonathan Peter b 1967), 2 da (Susan Margaret b 1960, Patricia Mary b 1965); *Career* Lt 1955–56 and Capt 1956–57 RAMC; house offr Walsall Gen Hosp 1954–55, lectr in social med Univ of Birmingham 1959–66 (res fell 1957–59), sr lectr in community med Univ Coll Hosp Med Sch London 1966–71; Univ of Manchester: reader in social and preventive med later community med 1971–78, prof of community med then prof of epidemiology 1979–91, prof emeritus 1991; author of papers and chapters on epidemiology of malformations and cancer; assoc ed Teratology: the Journal of Abnormal Development 1972–80; memb: Ctee Soc for Social Med 1974–77, Editorial Bd Journal of Epidemiology and Community Health 1978–92; hon sec and treas Heads of Academic Depts Gp (social and community med) 1985–87, hon sec Soc for Social Medicine 1993–95, Milroy lectr RCP 1993; MSc (ex officio) Manchester 1982; FFCM 1972, FRCP 1985, FFPHM 1989; *Books* Childhood Cancer in Britain: Incidence, Survival and Mortality (with G J Draper, 1982), God of Science, God of Faith (with D Bridge, 1988); *Recreations* cycling, walking; *Style*— Prof Ian Leck; ✉ Pembury, 18 Cadogan Park, Woodstock, Oxford OX20 1UW (☎ 01993 811528)

LECOMBER, Brian Kenneth; *b* 12 July 1945; *Educ* Dr Challoner's GS Amersham Bucks; *m* 15 Dec 1978, Barbara Joyce, da of Frank Moore; 1 da (Amy b 1987); *Career* journalist 1962–70, wing walker Roaring 20s Flying Circus 1970, chief flying instr Antigua Aero Club W1 1971–73, novelist 1973–78, display aerobatic pilot 1978; memb Rothmans Aerobatic Team touring: UK, Europe, Middle and Far E 1979–80; fndr Firebird Aerobatics 1981, operator and lead pilot Rover Group Aerobatic Team and Microlease Aerobatic Team; has flown a record-breaking 2000 public aerobatic displays, Br freestyle aerobatic champion 1984 and 1988; has flown at air shows incl: Farnborough, Paris, Royal Show, Grand Nat; chm Br Air Display Cncl; memb: Historic Aircraft Assoc, Br Aerobatic Assoc, Aircraft Operators and Pilots Assoc; display evaluator CAA; Liveryman Guild of Air Pilots and Air Navigators; *Books* Turn Killer (1974), Dead Weight (1976), Talk Down (1978); *Recreations* gardening; *Style*— Brian Lecomber, Esq; ✉ Elmers, 94 Ellesborough Road, Wendover, Bucks HP22 6EW (☎ 01296 622739); Firebird Aerobatics Ltd, Old Buckland Wharf, Buckland, Aylesbury, HP22 5LJ (☎ 01296 631102, fax 01296 625883)

LEDDINGTON WRIGHT, Paul; s of Peter Alfred Wright, CVO, of Maidenhead, Berks, and Iris Anne, *née* Carter; *Educ* Desborough Sch Maidenhead, St Catharine's Coll Cambridge (organ scholar, MA); *m* 1977, Sheila Emms; 2 da (Emma Jane b 1979, Lucy Fiona b 1981); *Career* organist; sub-organist Coventry Cathedral 1977–81, asst music master King Henry VIII Sch Coventry, dir of music Coventry Methodist Central Hall until 1981, dir of music Methodist Assoc of Youth Clubs 1982–84, dir of music Coventry Cathedral 1984–95, organist and asst dir of music Coventry Cathedral 1995–; artistic dir Int Church Music Festival 1990–, dir of music Huddersfield Choral Soc 1996–; conductor Songs of Praise (BBC Television); composer various choral works; memb Performing Right Soc 1991; ARCM, FRCO (chm), FTCL; *Recreations* cinema, walking, Indian food; *Style*— Paul Leddington Wright, Esq; ✉ 11 Styvechale Avenue, Earlsdon, Coventry CV5 6DW (☎ 01203 673633, fax 01203 673633); Coventry Cathedral, 7 Priory Row, Coventry CV1 5ES (☎ 01203 227597, fax 01203 631448)

LEDEN, Judy; MBE (1989); da of Thomas Leden, of Wraysbury, Berks, and Nina Mary, *née* Nowell; *b* 23 Dec 1959; *Educ* St Bernard's Convent Slough, WNSM; *Career* hang gliding and paragliding champion; holder of women's world open distance record 1983, Br Women's Open champion 1983, Euro Women's champion 1986, World Women's champion hang gliding 1987 and 1991 and paragliding 1995, Br Women's champion 1988, 1989, 1990, 1991, 1992 and 1993, holder of two women's world records 1990, first female capt Br mixed team 1990, holder world triangle distance record 1991, holder of women's world paragliding open distance record 1992, world altitude balloon drop hang gliding record (39,000 feet) 1994; memb: Br Hang Gliding & Paragliding Assoc, Br Women's Pilots' Assoc, Women's Sports' Fndn; Diplome de Performance French Aeroclub 1988, Pilot of the Year award Fédération des Pilotes Europénne 1992; *Recreations* microlight flying, paragliding, swimming, reading, travel, theatre; *Style*— Ms Judy Leden, MBE

LEDERER, Helen; da of Peter Lederer, and Jeanne Lederer; *b* 24 Sept 1954; *Educ* Blackheath HS, Hatfield Poly (now Hatfield Univ), Central Sch of Speech & Drama; *children* 1 da (Hannah Louise b 28 April 1990); *Career* comedienne and actress; early work at the Comedy Store and similar venues; *Theatre* incl: Bunny in House of Blue Leaves (with Dennis Quilley, Lilian Bayliss Theatre), Educating Rita (with Julian Glover), Doreen in Having A Ball (Comedy Theatre); *Television* appearances incl: The Young Ones, Girls on Top, The French and Saunders Show, Flossie in Happy Families (BBC 2), 5 series of Naked Video (writing and performing own material in between sketches, BBC 2), Wogan, Hysteria, The New Statesman, Bottom, Absolutely Fabulous (BBC), One Foot in the Grave (BBC); *Radio* female actress in BBC Radio 4's In One Ear (Sony Award for Best Comedy); other radio work incl: writer and performer two series of Life With Lederer (Radio 4), short story readings (Radio 3 and 4), Comic Cuts (Radio 5); *Publications* Coping With Lederer, Single Minding (1995); author of numerous articles for New Woman, Options and She magazines, The Guardian; *Recreations* cinema, reading, friends; *Style*— Ms Helen Lederer; ✉ c/o Spotlight, 7 Leicester Place, London WC2H 7BP

LEDERER, Peter J; OBE (1994); s of Thomas Francis Lederer, and Phoebe, *née* Blackman; *b* 30 Nov 1950; *m* 10 Oct 1981, Marilyn Ruth MacPhail; *Career* Four Seasons Hotels Canada 1972–79, vice pres Wood Wilkings Ltd Toronto Canada 1979–81; gen mangr: Plaza Group of Hotels Toronto Canada 1981–83, The Gleneagles Hotel 1983–; dir Guinness Enterprises 1987, md Gleneagles Hotels PLC 1987–; dir Scottish Tourist Board; chm: Tourism Training Scotland, Hospitality Indust Tst Scotland; memb Sec of State's Advsy Scottish Cncl for Educn and Training Targets; prof Univ of Dundee, govr Ardvreck Sch Crieff; Master Innholder (Worshipful Co of Innholders), Freeman City of London; MInstD, MIMgt, FHCIMA; *Recreations* Matthew and Mark; *Style*— Peter J Lederer, Esq, OBE; ✉ The Gleneagles Hotel, Auchterarder, Perthshire, Scotland PH3 1NF (☎ 01764 62231, fax 01764 62134, telex 76105)

LEDERMAN, David; QC (1991); s of Dr E K Lederman, of London, and Marjorie, *née* Smith; *b* 8 Feb 1942; *Educ* Clayesmore Public Sch, Gonville and Caius Coll Cambridge (MA); *m* 10 June 1974, Georgina Anne; 2 da (Samantha b 7 Sept 1970, Chloe b 28 April 1973), 1 s (Ben b 16 Oct 1977); *Career* called to the Bar Inner Temple 1966, recorder of the Crown Court 1990–; *Recreations* horses, skiing; *Style*— David Lederman, Esq, QC; ✉ 5 King's Bench Walk, Temple, London EC4Y 7DN (☎ 0171 797 7600)

LEDERMAN, Geoffrey Lewis Harry; s of David Lederman (d 1945), and Sylvia Doris, *née* Langbart; *b* 9 July 1929; *Educ* Whittinghame Coll; *m* 29 April 1963, Olivia, da of Frederick Russell (d 1978); 2 da (Amanda (Mrs Bishop) b 1965, Caroline (Mrs Kingham) b 1968); *Career* ptnr Smith Bros 1960–73 (joined 1951), dep chm Smith Bros 1976–87, jt chief exec Smith New Court plc 1987–89 (dir 1973–87); memb Stock Exchange; *Recreations* cricket, squash, tennis, golf; *Clubs* MCC, RAC, Incogniti, Annabel's; *Style*— Geoffrey Lederman, Esq; ✉ 145 Hamilton Terrace, London NW8 9QS (☎ 0171 624 4986, car 0836 286339)

LEDGER, Christopher John Walton; JP (1993); s of Peter Walton Ledger, of St Mawes, Cornwall, and Barbara Nancy, *née* Eve; *b* 5 Feb 1943; *Educ* The Nautical Coll Pangbourne; *m* 1, 21 April 1971 (m dis 1973); m 2, 19 Sept 1977, Gillian Penelope, da of Col Paul Heberden Rogers (d 1972); 1 s (James Walton Herberden b 17 July 1981), 1 da (Nicola Kate b 10 Aug 1978); *Career* cmmnd 2 Lt RM 1962, offr 43 Commando 1964, OC Recce Tp 45 Commando 1965–66, ATURM Poole 1966–67, OC HMS Bulwark 1967–69, Adj RM Poole 1969–72, ATT HQ CO Forces 1972–74; Shell UK Ltd: joined 1974, PA mangr Expro 1976–77, mangr Small Business Initiative Films and Educnl Serv 1978–81, dir of PA 1981–84, chief exec World Energy Business 1984–86; chief exec The Phoenix Initiative 1986–91; md: AML 1991–94, Fieldway Ltd 1994–; dir: Elysium Projects, Westgate Water, Ledger Montgomery; chm Preditor II Business Expansion Scheme; Liveryman Worshipful Co of Grocers 1972; FRSA, FInstPet; *Recreations* sailing, shooting; *Clubs* Royal Cornwall Yacht, IOD, Special Forces, Tamesis, RNSA; *Style*— Christopher Ledger, Esq, JP; ✉ The Willows, 29 Broom Water, Teddington, Middx TW11 9QJ (☎ 0181 977 3451, fax 0181 943 9116); Elysium Projects Ltd, 3 Elysium Gate, 126 New King's Road, London SW6 4LZ (☎ 0171 371 9617, fax 0171 371 9521)

LEDGER, Frank; CBE (1992, OBE 1985); s of Harry and Doris Ledger; *b* 16 June 1929; *Educ* Univ of London (BSc); *m* 1953, Alma, *née* Moverley; 2 s; *Career* student apprentice Leeds Corp Electricity Dept 1947, station mangr Cottam 1965, gp mangr Midlands Region 1968, dir computing CEGB 1980, dir operations CEGB 1981, memb Bd for Prodn CEGB 1986–89, dep chm Nuclear Electric plc 1989–92; FIEE 1980, FIMechE 1989, FEng 1990; *Books* Crisis Management in the Power Industry: an Inside Story (jtly, 1994); *Style*— Frank Ledger, Esq, CBE, FEng; ✉ 3 Barns Dene, Harpenden, Hertfordshire AL5 2HH (☎ 01582 762188)

LEDGER, Dr Philip Stevens; CBE (1985); s of Walter Stephen Ledger (d 1986), of Bexhill-on-Sea, and Winifred Kathleen, *née* Stevens; *b* 12 Dec 1937; *Educ* Bexhill GS, King's Coll Cambridge (MA, MusB); *m* 15 April 1963, Mary Erryl, *née* Wells; 1 s (Timothy b 1964), 1 da (Katharine b 1966); *Career* master of music Chelmsford Cathedral 1962–65, dir of music UEA 1965–73 (dean Sch of Fine Arts and Music 1968–71), conductor Univ of Cambridge Musical Soc 1973–82, dir of music and organist King's Coll Cambridge 1974–82, princ RSAMD 1982–; pres: Royal Coll of Organists 1992–94, Incorporated Soc of Musicians 1994–95; Hon LLD Univ of Strathclyde 1987; FRCM 1983, HonRAM 1984, FRNCM 1989, HonGSM 1989, FRSE 1990, FRCO; *Recreations* swimming, theatre-going; *Style*— Dr Philip Ledger, CBE; ✉ Royal Scottish Academy of Music and Drama, 100 Renfrew St, Glasgow G2 3DB (☎ 0141 332 4101, fax 0141 332 8901)

LEDINGHAM, Prof John Gerard Garvin; s of Dr John Ledingham (d 1970), of Ladbroke Square, London, and Dr Una Christina Ledingham, *née* Garvin (d 1965); *b* 19 Oct 1929; *Educ* Rugby, New Coll Oxford (MA, DM), Middx Hosp Med Sch Univ of London (BM BCh); *m* 3 March 1962, Elaine Mary, da of Richard Glyn Maliphant (d 1977), of Cardiff; 4 da (Joanna b 22 March 1963, Catherine b 19 May 1964, Clare b 10 Oct 1968, Sarah b 20 Nov 1971); *Career* Nat Serv 2 Lt RA 1949–50; registrar in med Middx Hosp London 1960–62 (house offr 1957–58), sr registrar Westminster Hosp London 1963–65, visiting fell Univ of Columbia NY 1965–66, conslt physician United Oxford Hosps 1966–74; Univ of Oxford: May reader in med Univ of Oxford 1974–95, prof 1989–95, dir of clinical studies 1977–81 and 1991–95; contrib various med and science jls; tstee: Nuffield Prov Hosps Tst, Beit Tst, Oxford Hosp Devpt and Improvement Fund, Oxford Hosps Servs and Devpt Tst, Commonwealth Scholarships Cmmn 1992–98; examiner in med: Univs of Cambridge, Glasgow, Oxford, London, Southampton, Sheffield, Sultan Qaboos Univ, Royal Coll of Physicians, Royal Coll of Surgns of Ireland; memb GMC; chm Med Research Soc 1988–91, memb Animal Procedures Ctee of Home Sec 1985–92, memb Supra-Regnl Servs Ctee Dept of Health 1983–86, censor RCP 1984–85, former hon sec and hon treas Assoc of Physicians of GB and Ireland, former pres Br Hypertension Soc; fell New Coll Oxford 1974; FRCP 1971; *Books* Oxford Textbook of Medicine (ed with D J Weatherall and D A Warrell, 1983, 1987 and 1995); *Recreations* music, golf; *Clubs* Vincent's (Oxford); *Style*— Prof John Ledingham; ✉ 22 Hid's Copse Rd, Cumnor Hill, Oxford OX2 9JJ (☎ 01865 862023)

LEDLIE, John Kenneth; CB (1994), OBE (1977); s of Reginald Cyril Bell Ledlie (d 1966), and Elspeth Mary, *née* Kaye (d 1982); *b* 19 March 1942; *Educ* Westminster, Brasenose Coll Oxford (MA); *m* 27 Nov 1965, Rosemary Julia Allan, da of Francis Glen Allan (d 1974); 3 da (Rebecca b 1969, Kate b 1971, Joanna b 1973); *Career* admitted slr 1967, private sec to Sec of State for Defence 1969–70, UK delgn to NATO Brussels 1973–76, dep chief of PR MOD 1977–79, seconded to NI Office and Cabinet Office 1979–81, Procurement Exec MOD 1981–83, head Def Secretariat 19 MOD 1983, regnl mktg dir in defence sales 1983–85, chief PR MOD 1985–87, under sec MOD 1987, dep sec NI Office 1990, MOD 1993, partnership sec Linklaters & Paines 1995–; fell Centre for Int Affrs Harvard Univ 1987–88; *Recreations* cricket, tennis, golf, ornithology, hill walking, opera; *Clubs* Oxford and Cambridge; *Style*— John Ledlie, Esq, CB, OBE; ✉ Linklaters & Paines, Barrington House, 59/67 Gresham Street, London EC2V 7JA (☎ 0171 606 7080, fax 0171 606 5113)

LEDWARD, Rodney Spencer; s of Arthur Ledward (d 1984), of Stone, Staffs, and Beatrice Maud, *née* Pritchard (d 1986); *b* 30 June 1938; *Educ* Alleynes GS, Univ of Manchester (BSc, MPS), Univ of Liverpool (MB ChB), Univ of Virginia Charlottesville, Brown Univ RI, Univ of Nottingham (DM); *m* 26 Aug 1983, Lady Jane Annabelle, *née* Howard, sister of 13 Earl of Carlisle, and former w of John David Vaughan Seth-Smith; 1 s (Bertie Arthur Ruthven b 7 Nov 1985); *Career* conslt in obstetrics and gynaecology SE Kent Health Dist 1980–; in private gynaecological practice Kent and London; md Tutorial Systems International; hon sr teaching fell Dept of Obstetrics and Gynaecology The Royal London Hosp, dean Ross Univ Med Sch Ross Univ NY; FRCS 1974, FRSM 1974, FRCOG 1986; *Books* Drug Treatment in Obstetrics (1982, 2 edn 1990), Drug Treatment in Gynaecology (1984, 2 edn 1994), Handbook of Obstetrics and Gynaecology (1986); *Recreations* swimming, riding; *Clubs* RSM, Mosiman's; *Style*— Rodney Ledward, Esq; ✉ Consulting Rooms, St Saviours Hospital, Hythe (☎ 01303 265 581); Chaucer Hospital, Canterbury (☎ 01227 455 466); 144 Harley St, London (☎ 0171 935 0023); Cromwell Hospital, London (☎ 0171 370 4233)

LEDWIDGE, Sir (William) Bernard John; KCMG (1974, CMG 1964); s of Charles Bernard Arthur Ledwidge (d 1945); *b* 9 Nov 1915; *Educ* Cardinal Vaughan Sch, King's Coll Cambridge, Princeton Univ USA; *m* 1, 1948 (m dis 1970), Anne, da of George Henry Kingsley (d 1959); 1 s, 1 da; m 2, Flora, da of André Groult (d 1967); *Career* entered India Office 1939, Indian Army 1941–46, NW Frontier; FO 1948, first sec Kabul 1952–56, political advsr Br Mil Govt Berlin 1956–61, cnsllr FO 1961, head of Western Dept FO 1963–65, min Paris 1965–69; ambass: Finland 1969–72, Israel 1972–75; chm UK Ctee for UNICEF 1976–89, memb Police Complaints Bd 1977–82; *Books* Frontiers (1980), Des Nouvelles de la Famille (1981), De Gaulle (1982), De Gaulle et les Americains (1984), Sappho: la Première Voix de Femme (1987); *Clubs* Travellers' (London), MCC; *Style*— Sir Bernard Ledwidge, KCMG; ✉ 19 Queen's Gate Terrace, London SW7 5PR (☎ 0171 584 4132); 54 Rue de Bourgogne, 75007 Paris, France (☎ 00 33 1 47 05 80 26)

LEE, (Edward) Adam Michael; s of His Hon Judge Michael Lee, DSC, DL (d 1983), of Winchester, Hampshire, and Valerie Burnett Georges, *née* Drake-Brockman (d 1995); *b* 29 June 1942; *Educ* Winchester, ChCh Oxford (MA); *m* 5 July 1975, Carola Jean, da of Capt Frederick Le Hunte Anderson (d 1989), of Hungerford, Berks; 2 s (Frederick Edward Maconchy b 1977, (James) Michael Maconchy b 1981); *Career* called to the Bar Middle Temple 1964; cadet Glyn, Mills & Co 1964; William & Glyn's Bank: sr planner 1969, dep dir City Div 1974; local dir: Child & Co 1977–87, Holts Branches 1978–87, Drummonds 1985–87; asst gen mangr Royal Bank of Scotland 1985–87, gp devpt dir Adam & Co 1988–90; dir: Duncan Lawrie Tst Corp 1990–92, Trustee Resources 1993–, Minmet plc 1993–96, Crediton Minerals plc 1996–; chm Unison International plc

1992–94; conslt to various cos; sec and treas: Inverforth Charitable Tst, Matthews Wrightson Charity Tst; tstee: Chelsea Opera Gp, Southern Pro Arte Orchestra; published articles in: Three Banks Review, Royal Bank of Scotland Review, Humberts Commentary; Freeman City of London, Liveryman Worshipful Co of Dyers 1984; FCIB 1981; *Recreations* opera, tennis, golf, fly fishing, food and wine, travel; *Clubs* Travellers', Rye Golf, Chatham Dining (memb Ctee); *Style*— Adam Lee, Esq; ✉ The Farm, Northington, Alresford, Hants SO24 9TH (☎ and fax 01962 732205)

LEE, Alan Peter; s of Peter Alexander Lee, of Sidmouth, Devon, and Christina, *née* Carmichael; *b* 13 June 1954; *Educ* Cavendish GS Hemel Hempstead; *m* 18 Oct 1980, Patricia Rosemary Drury, da of James Chesshire; 1 s (James Patrick b 19 Feb 1987), 1 da (Victoria Helen b 22 Oct 1984); *Career* sports writer; Watford Observer 1970–74, Hayter's Agency 1974–78; cricket corr: Mail on Sunday 1982–87, The Times 1988–; covered England home test matches 1977–; covered England tours: India and Aust 1976–77, Aust 1978–79, 1982–83, 1986–87, 1990–91 and 1994–95, W Indies 1981, 1986, 1990 and 1994, Pakistan 1983, India 1984–85, NZ 1988 and 1992; covered World Cups 1979, 1983, 1987, 1992 and 1996; highly commended Sports Magazine Writer of the Year 1987; *Books* over 20 on cricket, racing and golf incl: A Pitch in Both Camps (1979), Jump Jockeys (1980), Lambourn (1982), Fred (biography of Fred Winter, 1991), To be a Champion (1992), Lord Ted (1995), Raising the Stakes (1996); *Recreations* national hunt racing, tennis; *Clubs* Cricketers' Club of London, Cricket Writers'; *Style*— Alan Lee, Esq; ✉ 8 The Courtyard, Montpellier St, Cheltenham, Glos GL50 1SR (☎ and fax 01242 572637); The Times, 1 Virginia St, London E1 9XN (☎ 0171 782 5944, fax 0171 782 5211, mobile 0860 299041)

LEE, Dr Christine Ann; *b* 5 March 1943, Hampton, Middx; *Educ* Tiffin Girls' Sch Kingston Surrey, Somerville Coll Oxford (MA, Kirkaldy prize in natural scis), Univ of Oxford Med Sch (clinical entrance scholar, Nuffield travelling scholar, BM BCh, MD, Radcliffe prize in pathology, MRCP, MRCPath); *Career* laboratory technician Dept of Haematology Royal Postgrad Med Sch London 1962, student Somerville Coll Oxford 1962–66, res asst Inst for Haematology Univ Clinic Freiburg W Germany 1966, student Univ of Oxford Med Sch 1966–69, house physician Radcliffe Infirmary Oxford 1970 (house surgn 1969–70); SHO: in renal med Hammersmith Hosp London 1970–71, in neurology United Oxford Hosps 1971, admitting doctor Govt Gen Hosp Zaria Nigeria Aug 1971; SHO: in chest med Brompton Hosp London 1971–72, Renal Med and Dialysis Unit Royal Free Hosp London 1972; research registrar (renal immunology) Royal Postgrad Med Sch Hammersmith Hosp London 1972–73, trainee in GP Chalkhill Health Centre Wembley 1973–74, registrar (haematology) St Mary's Hosp Harrow 1974–76, sr registrar Dept of Haematology St George's Hosp Med Sch London 1976–82, res sr registrar Royal Free Hosp and hon lectr Royal Free Hosp Sch of Med 1983–84, sr lectr in haematology Charing Cross and Westminster Med Sch and hon conslt haematologist Queen Mary's Univ Hosp Roehampton 1984–87, AIDS cnsllr Richmond, Twickenham and Roehampton Health Dist 1985–87, conslt haematologist Haemophilia Centre and Haemostasis Unit Royal Free Hosp 1987– (pt/t hon conslt 1986–87), hon sr lectr Academic Dept of Haematology Royal Free Hosp Sch of Med 1987–, dir Haemophilia Centre and Haemostasis Unit Royal Free Hampstead NHS Tst 1992– (actg dir 1991–92); memb: User Ctee Res Mgmnt Initiative and Audit Ctee Royal Free Hampstead NHS Tst, Educn Ctee and Sch Cncl Royal Free Hosp Sch of Med, MRC HIV Infection and AIDS Clinical Trials Working Pty, Jt Parly Gp on AIDS, UK Haemophilia Dirs Pty (chm HIV Working Pty), Med Advsy Panel Haemophilia Soc of UK, Haemophilia and AIDS Trg Workshop (WHO) New Delhi 1994; sec Int Haemophilia Trg Centres Ctee World Fedn of Haemophilia; memb Editorial Bd AIDS CARE, fndr ed Haemophilia (WFH) 1994; Henri Chagneau prize French Haemophilia Soc 1992; memb: Br Soc of Haematology, World Fedn of Haemophilia, Int Soc of Thrombosis and Haemostasis; FRCP 1990, FRCPath 1994; *Publications* author of numerous published papers, articles and reviews in learned jls, author/ed of various text-books; *Style*— Dr Christine A Lee; ✉ Haemophilia Centre and Haemostasis Unit, Royal Free Hospital School of Medicine, University of London, Rowland Hill Street, London NW3 2QG (☎ 0171 830 2238, fax 0171 830 2178)

LEE, Christopher Frank Carandini; s of Lt-Col Geoffrey Trollope Lee (d 1941), and Contessa Estelle Marie Carandini (d 1981); m descends from one of the six oldest Italian families, created Count 1184 and granted Arms Emperor Charlemagne by Emperor Frederick Barbarossa; *b* 27 May 1922; *Educ* Wellington Coll; *m* 1961, Birgit, da of Richard Emil Kroencke (d 1982); 1 da (Christina b 1963); *Career* actor (entered film indust 1947), author, singer; served WWII RAF 1941–46, Flt Lt, Intelligence and Special Forces, W Desert, Malta, Sicily, Italy and Central Europe (despatches 1944); Offr Arts Sciences et Lettres France 1974, OStJ 1986; *Films* over 200 feature film appearances worldwide incl: Moulin Rouge, Tale of Two Cities, Dracula, Rasputin, The Devil Rides Out, Private Life of Sherlock Homes, The Wicker Man, The Three Musketeers, The Four Musketeers, Man with a Golden Gun, To the Devil a Daughter, Airport 77, The Far Pavilions, 1941, The Return of Captain Invincible, The Disputation (TV), Round the World in 80 Days (TV), The Return of Musketeers, Gremlins II, The French Revolution (TV), Sherlock Holmes and the Leading Lady (TV), Sherlock Holmes and the Incident at Victoria Falls (TV), Death Train, A Feast at Midnight; also theatre, opera and TV; *Books* Christopher Lee's X Certificate (1975), Archives of Evil (1975), Tall, Dark and Gruesome (1977); *Recreations* golf, travel, languages, opera; *Clubs* Buck's, MCC, Hon Co of Edinburgh Golfers, Travellers' (Paris); *Style*— Christopher Lee, Esq; ✉ London Management, 2–4 Noel Street, London W1V 3RB (☎ 0171 287 9000, fax 0171 287 3036)

LEE, Capt (John) Colin Leonard Thornton; OBE (1995), JP (1980), DL (Merseyside 1995); s of John Lee (d 1946), of Birkenhead, and Ann Rebecca, *née* Thornton (d 1979); *b* 14 Jan 1933; *Educ* Birkenhead Sch, Liverpool Poly, RNC Greenwich, Univ of Wales Cardiff; *m* 7 Oct 1961, Jean Pauline, da of Norman Drummond Wilson (d 1977); 1 s (Mark b 8 Feb 1967), 2 da (Alison b 3 March 1963, Catherine b 31 July 1964); *Career* cadet rising to Master Ellerman Lines 1950–67, assoc dir AE Smith Coggins Stevedores and Master Porters Liverpool 1967–72, sr commercial mangr Mersey Docks and Harbour Co 1979–82 (operations mangr 1972–75, customer servs mangr 1975–78), md Delphic Ltd 1982–85, int mgmnt and mktg conslt 1985–; The Seneschal Hon Soc of Knights of the Round Table, Cdr St John Ambulance Co of Merseyside, fndr memb and past pres Rotary Club of Liverpool Exchange, NW area chm Sea Cadet Corps, tstee Sea Cadet Assoc, dep chm Merseyside Advsy Bd Salvation Army, memb Tower Ward Club; Freeman City of London 1985, Warden Hon Co of Master Mariners 1994 (memb 1984, chm and sec NW Area 1987); OStJ 1994; FIMgt 1983; *Recreations* travel, gardening, naval and maritime history; *Clubs* Athenaeum (Liverpool), Royal Over-Seas League; *Style*— Capt Colin Lee, OBE, JP, DL; ✉ Three Oaks, Grove Rd, Mollington, Chester CH1 6LG (☎ 01244 851 253); The Owen Ellis Partnership Ltd, 1 Temple Court, Victoria St, Liverpool L2 6PY (☎ 0151 236 0424, fax 0151 236 3762)

LEE, David; *b* 12 Aug 1929; *Educ* Reay Central Sch, Royal GS Newcastle upon Tyne, Johannesburg Conservatoire of Music; *m* Leila Sklair; 2 da (Laura (Mrs Spicer), Dr Abigail Lee Six); *Career* fndr Jazz FM Radio (first UK jazz radio station) 1990; formerly: pianist and mangr Dankworth Orchestra, musical dir TV progs (incl Here Today, That Was The Week That Was and Not So Much A Programme), musical dir and advsr to Ms Judy Garland, composer and conductor of various film scores and TV signature tunes, music composer various advtg campaigns (incl British Airways, Kelloggs and Persil), composer hits songs incl Goodness Gracious Me (Ivor Novello award 1960); BBC Jazz Musician of the Year 1983, Media Personality of the Year 1990; *Recreations* cricket, swimming, crossword puzzles; *Style*— David Lee, Esq; (☎ 0181 549 2105, fax 0181 549 4601)

LEE, David George; s of George Edward Lee (d 1970), of Manchester, and Elsie, *née* Wathey; *b* 27 July 1952; *Educ* Horsley's Green Sch, St John's Coll of Further Educn, Univ of Nottingham (BA), UCL (MA, Guido Farina scholarship); *m* 1987, Emma Irene Maude, da of Sir Anthony Parsons, GCMG, LVO, MC (d 1996); *Career* freelance writer and art critic 1977–, tutor Photography Dept RCA 1984–89, ed Art Review 1992–; *Recreations* none; *Clubs* Manchester City; *Style*— David Lee, Esq; ✉ Art Review, Hereford House, 23–24 Smithfield Street, London EC1A 9LB (☎ 0171 236 4880, fax 0171 236 4881)

LEE, Prof David John; CBE (1989); s of Douglas Lee (d 1987), and Mildred Amy, *née* Checkley (d 1955); *b* 28 Aug 1930; *Educ* Chislehurst & Sidcup Co GS, Univ of Manchester (BSc Tech), Imperial Coll London (DIC); *m* 6 Dec 1957, Helga; 1 s (Graham b 1961), 1 da (Caroline b 1960); *Career* Nat Serv RE 1950–52, OC (Col) Engr and Tport Staff Corps RE (TA) 1990–95 (Maj 1978, Lt-Col 1982); G Maunsell & Partners: joined 1955, ptnr 1966, managing ptnr 1978–84, chm 1984–93, currently conslt (also conslt to Maunsell Structural Plastics); visiting prof Imperial Coll London; chm Construction Indust Research and Info Assoc (CIRIA) 1989–92; hon pres Fédération Internationale de la Précontrainte (FIP) 1996; FIP Medal 1974, George Stephenson Medal; author of many papers published in learned jnls; Freeman City of London, Liveryman Worshipful Co of Engrs; FIP Medal 1974; FICE 1966, FIStructE 1968 (pres 1985–86), FEng 1980, FCGI 1995; *Books* Civil Engineering Reference Book (contrib), Bridge Bearings and Expansion Joints (1994); *Clubs* East India, Maserati; *Style*— David Lee, CBE, FEng; ✉ 26 Paget Gardens, Chislehurst, Kent BR7 5RX (☎ 0181 325 0942)

LEE, Air Chief Marshal Sir David John Pryer; GBE (1969, KBE 1965, CBE 1947, OBE 1943), CB (1953); s of John Lee (d 1955), and Gertrude Ethel Lee (d 1964), of Bedford; *b* 4 Sept 1912; *Educ* Bedford Sch, RAF Coll Cranwell; *m* 1938, Denise, da of Louis Hartoch (d 1934), of Bedford; 1 s, 1 da; *Career* joined RAF 1930, served WWII, Cmdt RAF Staff Coll Bracknell 1962–64, air memb for personnel 1965–68, UK mil rep NATO 1968–71, ret 1972; chm Grants Ctee RAF Benevolent Fund 1971–88, dir United Services (tstee 1972–88), chm Exec Ctee Nuffield Tst for the Forces of the Crown 1975–96, pres Corps of Commissionaires 1984–88; *Books* Flight From The Middle East (1980), Eastward (1983), Never Stop The Engine When It's Hot (1983), Wings In The Sun (1989), And We Thought The War Was Over (1991); *Recreations* golf; *Clubs* RAF; *Style*— Air Chief Marshal Sir David Lee, GBE, CB; ✉ The Garden House, 12a Catherine Close, Shrivenham, Swindon, Wilts SN6 8ER (☎ 01793 784264)

LEE, David Stanley Wilton; DL (1984); s of Col Kenneth C Lee, TD (d 1964); *b* 17 Sept 1933; *Educ* Uppingham, Queens' Coll Cambridge; *m* June 1957, Jennifer Ann, da of Col John P Hunt, TD (d 1971); 3 s, 2 da; *Career* dir Arthur Lee & Sons plc 1965–93; non-exec dir: Halifax Building Society 1977–94, Iron Trades Insurance Group 1978–, Wire Div Carclo Engineering Group PLC 1993–95; chm SSAFA Sheffield; Liveryman Worshipful Co of Tin Plate Workers; *Recreations* shooting, fishing, farming; *Clubs* The Club (Sheffield), Farmers'; *Style*— D S W Lee, Esq, DL; ✉ 4 Ranmoor Crescent, Sheffield S10 3GU (☎ 0114 230 1633, fax 0114 230 8254)

LEE, Edward David; s of Walter George Lee (d 1974), and Annie Rosina, *née* Wriggle; *b* 23 Dec 1947; *Educ* Southend HS for Boys, Coll of Law (dip in local govt); *m* 9 May 1971 (m dis 1986), Janet Laurie Mitchell; 1 s (Matthew b 13 May 1978), 1 da (Michelle Alexandria b 10 June 1976 d 1993); *Career* slr; Rochford DC: princ legal asst 1980–84, slr to Cncl 1984–85, asst slr 1990–91; ptnr: Wiseman Lee Marshall Essex 1985–89, Kloosmans 1991–; sec Abbeyfield Rochford and Dist Soc Ltd; memb Law Soc 1977; FInstLEx 1967; *Recreations* musician; *Style*— Edward Lee, Esq; ✉ 4 Newhall, Ashingdon, Essex (☎ 01702 548821)

LEE, Francis Henry; s of Colin Lee (d 1968), of Westhoughton, Lancs, and Millie, *née* Tonge; *b* 29 April 1944; *Educ* Horwich Tech Coll; *m* 1, Jean; 1 s (Gary), 1 da (Charlotte); m 2, Gill; 2 s (Jonathan, Nicholas); *Career* flat racehorse trainer; former professional footballer: with Bolton Wanderers, Manchester City and Derby County 1959–76, over 500 appearances and 240 goals, 27 England caps scoring 10 goals (played in World Cup Mexico 1970) 1969–72; chm Manchester City FC 1994–; fndr, owner and chm: FH Lee Ltd Bolton, Highway Safety Systems Ltd; bd dir Hazlewood Foods plc Derby; *Recreations* golf, horse racing, food, wines, keep fit; *Style*— Francis Lee, Esq; ✉ Manchester City Football Club, Maine Road, Moss Side, Manchester M14 7WN (☎ 0161 226 1191/2, fax 0161 227 9418)

LEE, Geoffrey; OBE (1980); s of Clifford Lee (d 1993), of Bolton, Lancs, and Florence Lee (d 1988); *b* 7 Jan 1931; *Educ* Sunning Hill Sch, Lords Commercial Coll Bolton; *m* 1955 (m dis 1986), Shirley, *née* Massey; 2 da (Janet b 1958 d 1981, Caroline b 1956); *Career* insur and investmt broker; underwriting memb Lloyd's; memb Appeals Tbnl for Miny of Pensions and Nat Insur 1961–64, pres Altrincham Dist C of C, Trade and Indust 1965 (treas 1963, chm 1964, memb Exec Ctee 1960–81), chm Assoc of Insur Brokers NW Area 1968–70 (memb Nat Exec Ctee), dir NW Industl Cncl 1993– (memb Ctee 1968–, vice chm 1973–87); Altrincham & Sale Cons Assoc: treas 1969–75, vice pres 1975–83, patron 1983–94, vice pres 1994–; memb: Exec Ctee Knutsford Constituency Cons Assoc 1975–77, Northern Exec Ctee French C of C 1982–87; Cons Central Office: treas's rep NW Area 1993–95, dir of fundraising NW Area 1995–; memb Fundraising Ctee Historic Cheshire Churches Preservation Tst 1992–; Chevalier de St Vincent; ABIBA, IBRC; *Recreations* weight training, keeping fit; *Clubs* St James's (Manchester); *Style*— Geoffrey Lee, Esq, OBE; ✉ Mode Cottage, Church Lane, Mobberley, Cheshire WA16 7RA (☎ 01565 873485, fax 01565 873485)

LEE, Dr Gloria Lulu; da of Alexander John Burton Edlin (d 1989), of Highcliffe-on-Sea, Dorset, and Louise Violet, *née* Theobald (d 1991); *b* 22 Oct 1931; *Educ* St Paul's Girls' Sch London, Univ of London (BSc(Econ)), Univ of Birmingham (MSocSc, PhD); *m* 2 June 1951, Norman Lee, s of Enoch Lee; 3 da (Amanda Lulu b 8 Feb 1953, Roberta Lulu b 1 Feb 1955, Fiona Lulu b 6 May 1958); *Career* Aston Univ: lectr Dept of Industl Admin 1968–86, sr lectr 1986–, dir postgraduate studies Aston Business Sch then dean Faculty of Management, Languages and European Studies 1993–; memb: Acad of Mgmnt, Western Acad of Mgmnt, Br Acad of Mgmnt, Euro Operations Mgmnt Assoc; *Books* Who Gets to the Top? (1981), The Manufacture of Disadvantage (jtly, 1987), Engineers and Management (jtly, 1992); *Recreations* swimming, sailing, windsurfing, canoeing, cruising inland waterways, mountain biking; *Style*— Dr Gloria Lee; ✉ Bridge House, 17 Noddington Lane, Whittington, Lichfield, Staffordshire (☎ 01543 432030, fax 01543 432137); Aston Business School, Aston University, Aston Triangle, Birmingham B4 7ET (☎ 0121 359 3011, fax 0121 333 5774)

LEE, Brig Sir (Leonard) Henry; kt (1983), CBE (1964, OBE 1960); s of Henry Robert Lee (d 1969), of Southsea, Hants, and Nellie, *née* Randall; *b* 21 April 1914; *Educ* Portsmouth GS, Univ of Southampton; *m* 1949, Peggy Metham; *Career* serv WWII BEF, Maj Royal Scots Greys (despatches 1945), Lt-Col 1954, Chief of Intelligence to Dir of Ops of Malaya 1957–60, Col Naval and Mil Attaché Saigon 1961–64, Chief of Personnel and Admin Allied Land Forces Central Europe (France) 1964–66, Brig Chief of Intelligence Allied Forces Central Europe (Netherlands) 1966–69, ret 1969; dep dir Cons Party Bd of Fin 1970–92; *Recreations* gardening, charity work, golf; *Clubs* Kingswood Golf; *Style*— Brig Sir Henry Lee, CBE; ✉ Fairways, Sandy Lane, Kingswood, Surrey (☎ 01737 832577)

LEE, Prof Hermione; da of Dr Benjamin Lee, and Josephine Lee; *b* 29 Feb 1948; *Educ* Lycée de Londres, City of London Sch, Queen's Coll and St Hilda's Coll Oxford (BA, BPhil); *m* 1991, John M Barnard; *Career* instr William and Mary Coll Williamsburg USA 1970–71, lectr Univ of Liverpool 1971–77, prof of English Univ of York 1993– (lectr 1977–88, sr lectr 1988–90, reader 1990–93); judge: Faber Prize 1981, Booker Prize 1981, W H Smith Prize 1987–92, Cheltenham Prize 1987; presenter: Book Four (C4) 1982–86, Booker Prize (LWT) 1984–87; memb: Mgmnt Ctee Lumb Bank Arvon Fndn 1988–92, Advsy Ctee Centre for the Book Br Library, Arts Cncl Literature Panel; FRSL; *Books* The Novels of Virginia Woolf (1977), Elizabeth Bowen (1981), Philip Roth (1982), Willa Cather: A Life Saved Up (1989), Virginia Woolf (1996); editions and anthologies of: Kipling, Trollope, Woolf, Bowen, Cather; The Secret Self (short stories by women writers); *Clubs* Academy; *Style*— Prof Hermione Lee, FRSL; ✉ Dept of English, University of York, Heslington, York YO1 5DD (☎ 01904 433361)

LEE, Howard Andrew Gabriel; s of Jack Lee, of Sydney, Aust, and Nora, *née* Blackburne; *b* 26 Feb 1953; *Educ* St Edward's Sch Oxford, Jesus Coll Cambridge (BA, MA); *m* 16 Dec 1983, Jessica Lena, da of Robert Benton Bottomley; 2 s (James Jonathan b 2 June 1987, Jack b 17 Oct 1995), 2 da (Harriet Aimee b 29 January 1986, Rebecca Elizabeth b 9 March 1989); *Career* with Charles Barker 1974–78, dep dir of info Nat Enterprise Bd 1978–80, public affairs exec British Telecom 1980–82; Valin Pollen: joined 1982, assoc dir 1983, dir 1984, int dir 1985, dir Investor Rels Div 1988, md Carter Valin Pollen Ltd 1988 (chief exec 1989), dir Valin International PLC, dir Valin Pollen PLC 1989 (chief exec 1990); chief exec Gavin Anderson & Company Ltd 1991–; memb City & Financial Group IPR 1985, assoc memb Investor Rels Soc 1989; *Recreations* shooting, wine; *Clubs* Savile; *Style*— Howard Lee, Esq; ✉ Gavin Anderson & Co Ltd, New Liverpool House, 15–17 Eldon Street, London EC2M 7LA (☎ 0171 457 2345, fax 0171 457 2330)

LEE, James Giles; s of John Lee, CBE, and Muriel, *née* Giles; *b* 23 Dec 1942; *Educ* Trinity Coll Glenalmond, Univ of Glasgow, Harvard Univ; *m* 1966, Linn, *née* MacDonald; 1 s (John b 1974), 2 da (Maggie b 1968, Katie b 1971); *Career* conslt McKinsey & Co 1969–80; chm: Penguin Publishing Co 1980–84, Longman Group 1980–84; dir S Pearson & Son 1981–84, dep chm Yorkshire TV 1982–85, chief exec Goldcrest Films and TV 1983–85 (chm 1981–85), chm Direct Bdcasting by Satellite Consortium 1986–87, dir Boston Consulting Group Ltd 1987–92, md Lee & Co 1992–; non-exec dir: Pearson Television Holdings 1993–, Phoenix Pictures Inc 1995–; chm Performing Arts Labs Tst 1990–; *Books* Planning for the Social Services (1978), The Investment Challenge (1979); *Recreations* photography, travelling, sailing; *Clubs* Reform, Harvard (NY); *Style*— J G Lee, Esq; ✉ Meadow Wood, Penshurst, Kent TN11 8AD (☎ 01892 870309)

LEE, Jennifer Elizabeth; da of Ernest M B Lee, and Mary, *née* Fowlie; *b* 21 Aug 1956; *Educ* St Margaret's Sch for Girls Aberdeen, Edinburgh Coll of Art (DipAD), RCA (MA); *m* 29 March 1990, Jake Tilson, *qv*, s of Joe Tilson; 1 da (Hannah Lee Tilson b 26 May 1995); *Career* potter; *Solo Exhibitions* The Scottish Gallery Edinburgh 1981, Anatol Orient London 1984, Crafts Cncl Sideshow ICA London 1985, Rosenthal Studio-Haus London 1985, Craft Centre Royal Exchange Theatre Manchester 1986, Crafts Cncl Shop V & A 1987, Craft Centre and Design Gallery City Art Gallery Leeds 1987, Galerie Besson London 1990, 1992 and 1995, Graham Gallery NY 1991, Galleri Lejonet Stockholm 1993, Röhsska Museum of Arts and Crafts Göteborg 1993, Aberdeen Art Gallery 1994, Osiris Brussels 1994, Galerie Besson London 1995, James Graham and Sons NY 1996; *Group Exhibitions* incl: Three Generations British Ceramics (Maya Behn Zurich) 1984, Jugend Gestaltet (Exempla Munich) 1985, Jugend Formt Keramik (Mathildenhöhe Darmstadt Germany) 1985, British Ceramic Art (Transform NY) 1985, Zeitgenössiche Keramik Aus Grossbritannien (Keramik Studio Vienna) 1986, New British Design (Osaka and Tokyo) 1987, On a Plate (The Serpentine Gallery) 1987, British Ceramics (Marianne Heller Galerie Sandhausen Germany) 1987, The New Spirit (Crafts Cncl Gallery London and tour) 1987, Craft and Folk Museum (Los Angeles) 1988, Ton in Ton (Landesmuseum Germany) 1988, Christmas Exhibition (Galerie Besson London) 1988, Sotheby's Decorative Award Exhibition (Yorakucho Seibu Japan) 1988, Galleri Lejonet (Stockholm) 1989, L'Europe des Ceramistes (Auxerre France touring Spain, Austria, Hungary) 1989, The Royal Scottish Museum (Edinburgh) 1989, Lucie Rie, Hans Coper and their Pupils (Sainsbury Centre Norwich) 1990, Int Art Fair (Chicago) 1990, The Fitzwilliam Museum (Cambridge) 1991, British Ceramics (Int Art Fair Bologna Italy) 1991, British Ceramics (Graham Gallery NY) 1991, Contemporary British Ceramics (Graham Gallery NY) 1992, Int Ceramic Art (Nat Museum of History Taipei Taiwan) 1992, Keramik aus Grossbritannien und Japan (Galerie Hinteregger Austria) 1992, Handbuilt Ceramics (Scottish Gallery Edinburgh) 1993, Towards the Future (Marianne Heller Germany) 1993, Visions of Craft (Crafts Cncl London) 1993, 20th Century European Ceramics (Los Angeles) 1993, Gallery Koyanagi Tokyo 1994, Sculpture, Objects and Functional Art (Chicago) 1994), The David Collection NY 1994, Wim Vromans Amsterdam 1995, James Graham & Sons NY 1995, Design im Wandel (Übersee Museum Bremen Germany) 1996, European Ceramics (Yufuku Gallery Tokyo) 1996; *Collections* work in numerous public collections incl: V & A London, Royal Scottish Museum, Glasgow Museums and Art Galleries, The Scottish Collection SDA Edinburgh, Los Angeles Co Museum of Art, Leeds City Art Gallery, Contemporary Art Society, Crafts Cncl Collection, The Sainsbury Centre (Norwich), Hawkes Bay Art Gallery New Zealand, Peters Fndn London, Buckinghamshire Co Museum, Cleveland Collection Middlesbrough, Thamesdown Collection Swindon, Hove Museum and Art Gallery, Norwich Castle Museum, Aberdeen Art Gallery, Nat Museum of Sweden Stockholm, Trustees Savings Bank Collection, Europa Kunst Handwerk Landesgerwerbeamt Stuttgart, Röhsska Konstslöjdmuseet Göteborg, Norwich Castle Museum, Hove Museum and Art Gallery, Bellerive Museum Zurich, Tochigi Prefectural Museum of Fine Arts Japan; *Awards* David Gordon Meml Tst Prize 1979, Andrew Grant Travelling Scholarship 1979, Allen Lane Penguin Book Award 1983, Mathildenhöhe Award Rosenthal Germany 1984, Jugend Gestaltet Prize Munich 1985, Crafts Cncl Grant 1987, Br Cncl Exhibitions Grant 1991; *Style*— Ms Jennifer Lee; ✉ c/o Galerie Besson, 15 Royal Arcade, 28 Old Bond St, London W1X 3HD (☎ 0171 491 1706)

LEE, Jeremy Charles Roger Barnett; s of Lt Cdr Charles Alexander Barnett Lee, RNR (d 1982), of Phyllis Kathleen Mary, *née* Gunnell (d 1986); *b* 10 July 1944; *Educ* Bristol Cathedral Sch; *m* 4 April 1972 (m dis 1983), Patricia Margaret, *née* Coleridge; 3 da (Veryan Georgina Coleridge b 1974, Isobel Mary b 1977, Caroline Sybella b 1978); *Career* RM: 2 Lt 1962, Troop Cdr 40 Commando serving in Malaya and Sabah 1964–65, Lt 1965, Co Cdr Sultan's Armed Forces Muscat and Oman 1967–69, Adj (later Co Cdr) 40 Commando 1972–74, serving in NI and Cyprus (during Turkish invasion), Capt 1973, invalided 1976; admitted slr 1978; sr ptnr Symes Robinson and Lee (Exeter, Crediton and Budleigh Salterton) 1983–; Cons Pty: area treas Crediton 1980, chm Coldridge Brushford and Nymet Rowland Branch 1981–; Br Red Cross: chm 125 Ctee 1995, chm Invitation Events Ctee 1996–; rugby: Capt RM 1971, RN 1971, Exeter FC 1965–67 and 1969–72; memb: Anglo Omani Soc, Law Soc; ASBAH's Conversationalist of the Year 1990; Sultan's Bravery Medal 1968, Br Red Cross Cert of Commendation; *Recreations* tennis, fox-hunting, walking, gardening, conversation; *Clubs* Army and Navy, LTA; *Style*— Jeremy Lee, Esq; ✉ Frogbury, Coldridge, nr Crediton, Devon EX17 (☎ 01363 83484); Symes Robinson and Lee, Manor Office, North Street, Crediton, Devon (☎ 01363 775566)

LEE, Prof John Anthony; s of Cecil John Lee (d 1977), of Southsea, Hants, and Phyllis Gwendoline, *née* Fry; *b* 18 March 1942; *Educ* The Portsmouth GS, Univ of Sheffield (BSc, PhD); *m* 17 April 1965, Barbara Lee, da of Thomas Harold Wright, of Burton-in-Kendal, Cumbria; 2 s (Richard b 1968, Peter b 1971); *Career* Univ of Manchester: asst lectr in botany 1967, lectr 1970, sr lectr 1979, prof of environmental biology 1988–94, head Dept of Environmental Biology 1986–93; Univ of Sheffield: prof of environmental biology 1994–, chm Dept of Animal and Plant Scis 1995–; ed The Journal of Ecology 1983–90, author of many scientific papers; vice pres Int Ecology Soc 1989–95, pres Br Ecological Soc 1996–97; memb Soc for Experimental Biology; *Recreations* theatre, Portsmouth FC, hill walking; *Style*— Prof John Lee; ✉ Department of Animal and Plant Sciences, PO Box 601, The University of Sheffield S10 2UQ (☎ 0114 282 4371)

LEE, John Desmond (Des); s of Ernest Wilson Lee (d 1988), of Doncaster, and Sarah, *née* Murphy (d 1958); *b* 18 Jan 1942; *Educ* Belmont Abbey Hereford, Doncaster Tech Coll; *m* 30 April 1964, Susan, da of Eric Bott (d 1974), of Doncaster; 1 s (Ryan b 18 March 1970), 1 da (Sadie b 25 April 1967); *Career* computer supervisor NCB 1960–65, computer servs mangr Centre File 1965–67, sr mangr GMS Rowntree Ltd 1967–81, mgmnt servs controller Brooke Bond Oxo Ltd 1981–86, gp head of systems and communications Lloyd's of London 1986–90, info technol dir B&Q PLC (part of Kingfisher Group) 1990–93, conslt The Rank Organisation PLC 1993–94, dir IT Mgmnt Programme PE International 1994–; fndr London Insur Market Network (LIMNET), chm IBM Computer Users' Assoc 1979–81 (hon life pres); int conf speaker on info technol; former memb York 65 Round Table; Liveryman Worshipful Co of Info Technologists 1987, Freeman City of London 1987; FBCS 1981, FIDPM 1978; *Recreations* tennis, golf, motor racing; *Style*— Des Lee, Esq; ✉ PE International, Park House, Wick Road, Egham, Surrey (☎ 01784 476371, fax 01784 476530)

LEE, John Michael Hubert; s of Victor Lee (d 1978), of Wentworth, Surrey, and Renée Annette, *née* Harburn (d 1960); *b* 13 Aug 1927; *Educ* Reading Sch, Christ Coll Cambridge (MA), SOAS Univ of London; *m* 16 July 1960, Margaret Ann, da of James McConnell Russell, ICS; 1 s (Julian b 1968), 1 da (Joanna b 1963); *Career* HM Colonial Serv Gold Coast (Ghana) 1951–58; cadet dist cmmr Transvolta Togoland 1951–52, asst sec Accra 1952–53, asst govt agent (asst dist cmmr) Koforidua 1953, sec to regnl officer (Prov Cmmr) 1953–54, asst govt agent (asst dist cmmr) Kibi 1954–55, govt agent (dist cmmr) Oda Koforidua 1955–56 and Akuse 1957–58, princ asst sec Accra 1958; on staff BBC 1959–65, legal advsr BBC Television Enterprises Dept 1963–65; called to the Bar Middle Temple 1960, in practice Midland circuit 1965–; MP (Lab): Reading 1966–70, Handsworth 1974–79; Parly candidate (Lab) Reading 1964, chm W Midland Gp of Lab MPs 1974–75, memb Parly Ctee on Obsolete Legislation; *Recreations* gardening, watching cricket and tennis, reading, listening to classical music, studying philosophy, trying to promote tactical voting to get rid of Conservatives; *Clubs* Royal Over-Seas League; *Style*— J M H Lee, Esq; ✉ 9 Gough Square, Temple, London EC4A 3DE (☎ 0171 353 5371, fax 0171 353 1344)

LEE, His Hon John Thomas Cyril Lee; s of Cyril Lee (d 1974), and Dorothy Lee (d 1985), of Leadon Bank, Ledbury; *b* 14 Jan 1927; *Educ* Holly Lodge GS, Emmanuel Coll Cambridge (MA, LLB); *m* 1956, Beryl, da of John T Haden (d 1959); 1 s, 3 da; *Career* served HM Forces 1945–48, Royal W African Frontier Force; called to the Bar Gray's Inn 1952; chm various tbnls, circuit judge Midland and Oxford 1972–93; *Recreations* golf; *Clubs* Union & County, Worcester Golf & Country; *Style*— His Hon John Lee; ✉ The Red House, Upper Colwall, Malvern, Worcs WR13 6PX

LEE, Laurie; MBE; s of Reg Lee; *b* 1914; *m* 1950, Catherine Francesca Polge; 1 da (Jessy); *Career* poet and writer; Hon DLitt; FRSL; *Poetry* incl: The Sun My Monument, The Bloom of Candles, My Many-Coated Man, Selected Poems; *Prose* incl: Cider with Rosie (1959), As I Walked Out One Midsummer Morning (1969), A Moment of War (1991, all three published together as Red Sky at Sunrise), A Rose for Winter, The Firstborn, I Can't Stay Long, Two Women; *Drama* The Voyage of Magellan; *Clubs* Chelsea Arts, Garrick; *Style*— Laurie Lee, Esq, MBE, FRSL

LEE, His Hon Judge Malcolm Kenneth; QC (1983); s of Thomas Marston Lee (d 1972), of Birmingham, and Fiona Margaret, *née* Mackenzie; *b* 2 Jan 1943; *Educ* King Edward's Sch Birmingham, Worcester Coll Oxford (MA); *m* 16 May 1970, (Phyllis) Anne Brunton, da of Andrew Watson Speed, of Bromsgrove, Worcs; 3 s (Oliver b 1973, Dominic b 1974, Adrian b 1977), 4 da (Phyllis b and d 1972, Lydia b 1976, Flora b 1979, Georgina b 1981); *Career* Lt 268 Regt (RA) TA 1966–69; called to the Bar Inner Temple 1967; practised Midland Circuit 1967–71, Midland and Oxford Circuit 1972–93, jr counsel to DHSS 1979–83, recorder of the Crown Ct 1980–93, circuit mercantile judge Birmingham 1993–; chm Agric Land Tribunal Midland Area 1994– (dep chm E Midland then Midland Area 1978–93); *Recreations* squash, tennis, walking, reading; *Clubs* Edgbaston Priory; *Style*— His Hon Judge Malcolm Lee, QC; ✉ The Priory Courts, 33 Bull Street, Birmingham B4 6DW (☎ 0121 681 3000)

LEE, Mark; s of Tan Sri Lee Siew Yee, and Puan Sri Lee Siew Lee, of Malaysia; *b* 12 Dec 1956; *Educ* Leys Sch Cambridge, Balliol Coll Oxford (MA), London Business Sch (MSc); *Career* asst dir County Bank Ltd (merchant bankers) 1981–85, princ Watermark & Co (mgmnt consultancy) 1986–, ptnr Priestman Associates (product design) 1990–93, strategy ptnr The Partners (design consltS) 1992–95; FRSA; *Recreations* squash, real tennis, theatre; *Clubs* RAC, Queen's, Royal Selangor Golf, Singapore CC; *Style*— Mark Lee, Esq

LEE, Eur Ing Prof Mark Howard; s of Clifford Howard Lee, of Derby, and Peggy Alice, *née* Osborne; *b* 9 April 1944; *Educ* Univ of Wales (BSc, MSc), Univ of Nottingham (PhD); *m* 24 July 1971, Elizabeth Anne, da of Rev Frank Andrew Willmot (d 1976), of London, 2 s (Matthew Peter Howard b 13 Oct 1976, Joseph Jonathan b 28 March 1979), 1 da (Bethan Louisa b 3 Jan 1984); *Career* lectr City of Leicester Poly 1969–74, prof Univ of Wales Aberystwyth 1987– (lectr 1974–85, sr lectr 1985–87), visiting prof Univ of Auckland NZ 1988; FRSA, FIEE, CEng; *Books* Intelligent Robotics (1989), Intelligent Assembly Systems (ed with J J Rowland, 1995); *Recreations* mountaineering; *Style*— Eur Ing Prof Mark Lee; ✉ Department of Computer Science, University of Wales, Penglais, Aberystwyth, Dyfed SY23 3BD (☎ 01970 622421, telex 35181, fax 01970 622455)

LEE, Prof (John) Michael; s of John Ewart Lee (d 1975), of Castle Donington, and May, *née* Humber (d 1992); *b* 29 March 1932; *Educ* Henry Mellish GS Nottingham, ChCh Oxford (MA, BLitt); *m* 23 June 1962, Mary Joy, da of James Philip Sorby Bowman (d 1962), of Barnack; 1 s (Matthew b 1964), 1 da (Helen b 1966); *Career* lectr and sr lectr in govt Univ of Manchester 1958–67, princ (academic secondment) HM Treasy 1967–69, sr lectr Inst of Cwlth Studies 1969–72, reader in politics Birkbeck Coll 1972–81, dean of Faculty of Social Sciences Univ of Bristol 1987–90 (prof of politics 1981–92, emeritus prof 1992); visiting fell Centre for Int Studies LSE 1993–95; jt ed Jl of RIPA 1974–86, prog sec Romney Street Gp 1994–; FRHistS 1971; *Books* Social Leaders and Public Persons (1963), Colonial Development and Good Government (1967), African Armies and Civil Order (1969), The Churchill Coalition (1980); *Style*— Prof Michael Lee; ✉ 29 Castlebar Rd, Ealing, London W5 2DL (☎ 0181 997 9006)

LEE, Michael James Arthur; s of Brian Arthur Frederick Lee (d 1983), of Newton Abbot, Devon, and Rachel Dorothy Strange, *née* Wickham (d 1992); *b* 22 June 1942; *Educ* Blundell's Sch, Univ of Durham (LLB); *m* 1, 4 March 1974 (m dis 1984), Judith Mary, da of Humphrey David Oliver of Alresford Hants; 1 da (Henrietta Victoria b 4 Oct 1976);

m 2, 18 March 1993, Caroline Mary, da of Duncan Hamilton (d 1994), of Marston Magna, Somerset; 1 da (Olivia Grace b 28 Feb 1994); *Career* admitted slr 1966; articled clerk Lovell White and King 1963–66 (asst slr 1966–67); legal asst New Scotland Yard 1967–69; Norton Rose: asst slr 1970–73, ptnr 1973–, sr litigation ptnr 1993–; memb Worshipful Co of City of London Slrs; memb: Law Soc, Int Bar Assoc; ACIArb; *Recreations* sailing, skiing; *Clubs* RAC, Lttle Ship; *Style*— Michael Lee, Esq; ✉ Norton Rose, Kempson House, Camomile St, London EC3A 7AN (☎ 0171 283 6000, fax 0171 283 6500, telex 883652)

LEE, Prof Michael Radcliffe; s of Harry Lee (d 1982), of Manchester, and Jean Adelaide, *née* Radcliffe (d 1976); *b* 21 Nov 1934; *Educ* Manchester GS, Univ of Oxford (MA, DM, DPhil); *m* 27 Aug 1960, Judith Ann, da of Reginald Horrocks, of Leyland Lancashire; 1 s (Stephen Michael b 21 Dec 1962), 1 da (Karen Elizabeth b 11 March 1965); *Career* lectr in med: Univ of Oxford 1965–69, St Thomas' Hosp 1969–71; med dir then md Weddell Pharmaceuticals 1971–73, sr lectr in clinical pharmacology Univ of Leeds 1973–84, prof Univ of Edinburgh 1984–95; memb: Assoc of Physicians of GB and I, Br Hypertension Soc; FRCP 1976, FRCPE 1985, FRSE 1990; *Books* Renin and Hypertension (1969), Clinical Toxicology (jtly, 1982); *Recreations* gardening, collecting cricket and naval books; *Style*— Prof Michael Lee, FRSE; ✉ 112 Polwarth Terrace, Edinburgh EH11 1NN (☎ 0131 337 7386)

LEE, Brig Michael Richard; OBE (1974); s of Maj Thomas Lee (ka 1941), and Laura Myfanwy, *née* Bushman (d 1987); *b* 1 Nov 1934; *Educ* Eton, RMA Sandhurst; *m* 5 July 1969, Jane Patricia, da of Augustus George Harris; 1 s (William b 1970), 1 adopted da (Prue b 1966); *Career* cmmnd Welsh Gds 1955, psc 1965, DAA and QMG HQ 99 Gurkha Inf Bde 1966, Bde Maj 4 Gds Armd Bde 1969, US Cmd and Gen Staff Coll 1971, CO 1 Bn Welsh Gds 1972, Regtl Lt-Col Welsh Gds 1976; Col Gen Staff: SHAPE 1978, HQ BAOR 1981, HQ UKLF 1983; Cdr 2 Inf Bde and Dep Constable Dover Castle 1984, pres RCB 1988, Dep Dir of Army Security 1990–94, Dir of Army Security 1994–95, ret; *Recreations* game shooting, bird watching, military history; *Clubs* Pratt's; *Style*— Brigadier Michael Lee, OBE

LEE, Maj-Gen Patrick Herbert; CB (1982), MBE (1964); s of Percy Herbert Lee, and Mary Dorothea Lee; *b* 15 March 1929; *Educ* King's Sch Canterbury, Univ of London (BSc Gen, BSc Physics); *m* 1952, Peggy Eveline, *née* Chapman; 1 s, 1 da; *Career* cmmnd RMA Sandhurst 1948, Staff Coll 1960, WO Staff duties 1961–63, CO Parachute Workshop 1964–65, JSSC 1966, mil asst to Master Gen of Ordnance 1966–67, directing staff Staff Coll 1968–69, Cdr REME 2 Div 1970–71, Col AQ Br Corps 1972–75, Dep Cmdt Sch of Electrical Mech Engrg (Army) 1976–77, Cmdt REME Trg Centre 1978–79, DG REME 1980–83, Col Cmdt REME 1983–89; dir Wincanton Logistics (formerly Wincanton Transport then Wincanton Distribution Services Ltd) 1983–; Road Haulage Assoc: dir 1988–, vice chm 1990–94, chm 1994–96; memb Wessex Water Authy 1983–88; CBI: memb Cncl 1991–, chm Somerset County Gp 1992–94, vice chm SW Region Cncl 1992–94, chm SW Region Cncl 1994–96; govr Wellington Sch Somerset 1992–; CEng, FIMechE, FIMgt, FInstD, memb Inst of Environmental Mgmnt; *Recreations* gardening, railways, Roman history, industrial archeology; *Clubs* Army and Navy; *Style*— Maj-Gen Patrick Lee, CB, MBE; ✉ Wincanton Logistics, Cale House, Station Road, Wincanton, Somerset BA9 9AD (☎ 01963 33800)

LEE, Paul Anthony; s of Wilfred Lee (d 1970), of Manchester, and Anne, *née* Molyneux; *b* 26 Jan 1946; *Educ* Central GS Manchester, Clare Coll Cambridge (MA, LLB); *m* 16 Sept 1977, Elisabeth Lindsay, da of Maj Geoffrey Robert Taylor, of Manchester; 2 s (Jonathan b 1980, William b 1985), 1 da (Antonia b 1983); *Career* admitted slr 1970; managing ptnr Addleshaw Sons & Latham Manchester 1991–; dir: Pugh Davies & Co Ltd 1976–, Robert H Lowe plc 1985–, Davies & Metcalfe plc 1986–, NRM5 Group Ltd 1994–; chm: Leaf Properties Ltd 1986–, Bon Marché Ltd (formerly Wiltex by Wilson Ltd) 1994–; chm: Royal Exchange Theatre Co 1986–, Royal Northern Coll of Music 1992–; dir Hallé Concerts Soc 1991–; feoffee Chethams Hosp and Library, chm of Govrs Cethams Sch of Music, chm of Patrons and Associates Manchester City Art Gallery; FRSA 1993; *Recreations* the arts, travel, tennis, wine; *Clubs* St James's (Manchester), Real Tennis and Racquets (Manchester); *Style*— Paul A Lee, Esq; ✉ Riverbank Cottage, Stanton Avenue, W Didsbury, Manchester M20 2PG; Addleshaw Sons & Latham, Dennis House, Marsden Street, Manchester M2 1JD (☎ 0161 832 5994, fax 0161 832 8215)

LEE, Peter Gavin; DL (Essex 1991); s of Lt Cdr John Gavin Lee, RNVR, of Burygate, Felsted, Essex, and late Helena Frances, *née* Whitehead; *b* 4 July 1934; *Educ* Midhurst GS, Wye Coll; *m* 27 April 1963, Caroline Mary, da of Cdr E N Green, RN (d 1976); 2 s (William Gavin b 1964, Jonathan Campbell b 1966), 1 da (Olivia Alice b 1969); *Career* RA Nat Serv 1953–55; chartered surveyor Strutt & Parker 1957– (sr ptnr 1979–96); former chm Anglo American Liaison Ctee Wethersfield USAF; High Sheriff of Essex 1990–91; govr Felsted Sch; Freeman City of London 1977, Liveryman Worshipful Co of Chartered Surveyors 1977; FRICS; *Recreations* flying, country pursuits, vintage cars and aircraft; *Clubs* Boodle's; *Style*— P G Lee, Esq, DL; ✉ Fanners, Great Waltham, Essex CM3 1EA (☎ 01245 360470); Coral Hall, Chelmsford, Essex CM1 2QF (☎ 01245 258201, fax 01245 348897)

LEE, Richard Alan; *b* 31 Aug 1943; *Educ* Univ of Cambridge (MA, Dip in Architecture); *Career* architect; currently: dir of private practice Bristol, dir of Alec French Partnership, external examiner Dept of Architecture Univ of Bath; previous positions incl: chm Avon Branch RIBA, pres Bristol Soc of Architects, chm Wessex Assoc of Conslt Architects, visiting tutor Sch of Architecture Univ of Bristol; RIBA; *Style*— Richard Lee, Esq; ✉ Alec French Partnership, 27 Trenchard Street, Bristol BS1 5AN (☎ 0117 929 3011)

LEE, Robert; *b* 1 Feb 1966; *Career* professional footballer; 293 appearances and 69 goals Charlton Athletic FC 1983–92, transferred to Newcastle Utd FC (for a fee of £700,000) 1992; England: 7 full caps (first full cap v Romania 1994); *Style*— Robert Lee, Esq; ✉ c/o Newcastle Utd FC, St James Park, Newcastle upon Tyne NE1 4ST (☎ 0191 232 8361)

LEE, Robin John; s of John Johnson Lee, of Dublin, and Adelaide Elizabeth, *née* Hayes; *b* 23 Oct 1952; *Educ* Wesley Coll Dublin, Trinity Coll Dublin (BA, MB BCh, MA, MD); *m* 23 Sept 1978, (Sylvia) Jane Lucette, da of Ernest Herbert Bodell, of Dublin; 2 s (Charles b 25 Dec 1982, Christopher (twin) b 25 Dec 1982), 2 da (Sarah b 31 Jan 1981, Victoria b 10 Feb 1992); *Career* sr registrar in otolaryngology: Royal Victoria Eye and Ear Hosp Dublin 1985, Federated Dublin Vol Hops 1986, Beaumont Hosp Dublin 1988; res fell Dept of Otolaryngology Head and Neck Surgery Univ of Iowa 1987, conslt ENT surgn Kettering Gen Hosp 1988–; memb Ctee Young Consultants in Otolaryngology Head and Neck Survery 1989–94; memb: BMA 1988, RSM 1988, Br Assoc of Otolaryngologists 1988, Irish Otolaryngological Soc 1983; FRCSI 1984; *Style*— Robin Lee, Esq; ✉ Kettering General Hospital, Rothwell Rd, Kettering, Northants NN16 8UZ (☎ 01536 492000 ext 2274)

LEE, Rosa; da of William W Y Lee, and Joyce Ying Lee (d 1987); *b* 1 Feb 1957; *Educ* Univ of Sussex (BA), Brighton Poly Faculty of Art and Design, St Martin's Sch of Art (BA), RCA (MA); *m* 7 May 1993, Mark A S Graham; 1 s (Nathan Graham b 1993); *Career* artist; pt/t fine art lectr; work in public collections; *Solo Exhibitions* Artist of the Day (Flowers East Gallery) 1989, Ellipsis (Winchester Gallery) 1989 (touring 1990), Interface (Todd Gallery London) 1990, New Work 1990–1992 (Todd Gallery) 1992, Conceits (La Centrale Galerie Powerhouse Montreal) 1995, New Work 1994–1996 (Todd Gallery) 1996 and 1997; *Group Exhibitions* incl: Whitechapel Open (Whitechapel Gallery) 1989, John Moores 16 (Walker Art Gallery Liverpool) 1989–90, Opening Gp Exhibition (Todd Soho Gallery) 1989, 3 Ways (RCA/Br Cncl touring exhibition) 1990, Works on Paper (Todd Gallery) 1990, Broadgate Art Week 1990, Group Show (Todd Gallery) 1991, (dis)parities (Mappin Art Gallery Sheffield) 1992 and (Herbert Art Gallery & Museum Coventry) 1993, The Discerning Eye (Mall Galleries) 1992, John Moores 18 (Walker Art Gallery Liverpool) 1993–94, Lead and Follow, The Continuity of Abstraction (Bede Gallery Jarrow and Atlantis) 1994, British Abstract Art (Flowers East) 1994, Export-Import (Galerie Rähnitzgasse Dresden) 1994, Contemporary Art Society - Recent Purchases (Butler Gallery Kilkenny Ireland) 1995, A Question of Scale (Winchester Gallery) 1995, Pretext: Heteronyms, Rear Window (Clink Street Studios Soho Wharf) 1995, Permission to Speak (Worcs City Museum and Gallery and tour to Derby and Peterborough) 1996, Shelf Life (Eagle Gallery) 1996, Br Abstract Art Part 3 - Works on Paper (Flowers East) 1996; *Awards* ABTA Award 1986, Cwlth Festival prizewinner 1986, Mario Dubsky Travel Award 1988, visiting fell in painting Winchester Sch of Art 1988–89, John Moores 16 prizewinner 1989, Gtr London Arts Award 1989, Br Cncl Award 1995; *Style*— Ms Rosa Lee; ✉ c/o Todd Gallery, 1–5 Needham Rd, London W11 2RP (☎ 0171 792 1404)

LEE, Samuel George; s of George Alles Lee (d 1966), and Nancy, *née* Moore; *b* 16 Oct 1939; *Educ* Rossall; *m* 12 May 1965, Jennifer Anne, *née* Nye (d 1995); 2 s (Matthew Everett b 1968, Joseph James b 1970); *Career* admitted slr 1963; coroner Blackpool and the Fylde Dist 1989–; chm: Fylde Arts Assoc 1977–81, Blackpool District Scout Cncl 1986–, Blackpool Grand Theatre Tst 1993–, Radiowave Ltd (Fylde coast local radio); vice pres Blackpool Civic Tst; govr: Rossall Sch 1981, Blackpool & the Fylde Coll 1990–; *Recreations* squash, reading, watching rugby; *Style*— Samuel G Lee, Esq; ✉ The Croft, 7 St Clements Avenue, Blackpool FY3 8LT (☎ 01253 391990); John Budd & Co, 283 Church Street, Blackpool FY1 3PG (☎ 01253 26557, fax 01253 751055)

LEE, Maj-Gen (James) Stuart; MBE (1970), CB (1990); s of George Lee (d 1974), and Elizabeth, *née* Hawkins (d 1952); *b* 26 Dec 1934; *Educ* Normanton GS, Univ of Leeds (BA), King's Coll London (MA); *m* 21 March 1960, Lorna Alice, da of James Leonard Powell (d 1983); 1 s (James Alastair Spencer b 29 Dec 1964); *Career* educn offr UK Trg Units 1959–64, mil trg offr Beaconsfield 1964, RMCS and Staff Coll 1964–65; DAQMG HQ: Cyprus Dist 1966, NEARELF 1967; SO2 MOD 1968–70, DAA & QMG HQ FARELF 1970, GSO2 HQ FARELF 1970–71, OC offr trg wing Beaconsfield 1971–74, gp educn offr Rheindahlen 1974–75, chief educn offr NE Dist 1976–78, head offr Educn Branch 1978–79, SO1 trg HQ UKLF 1979, Col chief inspr res 1980–82, Cdr educn HQ BAOR 1983–87, dir army educn 1987–90; res assoc Int Inst of Strategic Studies 1982–83, non-exec dir Exhibition Consultants Ltd 1990–; dep co cmmr Br Scouts Western Europe 1983–87, tstee and sec Gallipoli Meml Lecture 1987–90, pres Army Canoe Union 1987–90, pres Army Chess 1987–90; Dep Col Cmdt AGC 1993–, pres RAEC Assoc 1993–; memb: Bd of Mgmnt Nat Fndn for Educnl Res 1987–90, Nat Advsy Ctee Duke of Edinburgh's award 1987–90, Cncl Scout Assoc 1988–, Governing Body Imperial Coll London 1991–, Ct Univ of Leeds 1994–; City and Guilds of London Inst: memb Cncl 1990–, chm Sr Awards Ctee 1990–, jt hon sec 1993–; FRSA 1987, FITD 1991 (FIPD 1994), Hon FICG 1995; *Recreations* theatre, boats; *Style*— Maj-Gen Stuart Lee, CB, MBE

LEE, Prof Thomas Alexander (Tom); s of Thomas Henderson Lee (d 1970), of Edinburgh, and Dorothy Jane Paton, *née* Norman (d 1990); *b* 18 May 1941; *Educ* Melville Coll Edinburgh, ICAS, Univ of Edinburgh, Inst of Taxation, Univ of Strathclyde (MSc, D Litt); *m* 14 Sept 1963, Ann Margaret, da of John Brown (d 1971), of Edinburgh; 1 s (Richard Thomas b 19 July 1968), 1 da (Sarah Ann (Mrs Birchall) b 17 August 1965); *Career* auditor J Douglas Henderson & Co and Peat Marwick Mitchell 1959–66, lectr Univ of Strathclyde 1966–69; prof: Univ of Liverpool 1973–76, Univ of Edinburgh 1976–90 (lectr 1969–73), Culverhouse endowed chair of accountancy Univ of Alabama 1991–; dir accounting and auditing res ICAS 1983–84, memb Exec Ctee AUTA (BAA) 1971–84, ed AUTA News Review 1971–75; ICAS: memb and convener Scottish Accounting History Ctee 1971–, memb Educn Ctee 1982–88, memb Advsy Ctee on Accounting Educn 1985–87, memb Company Law Strategy Unit 1986–88, memb Res Ctee 1988–, memb Cncl 1989–90; memb Cncl Br Fin and Accounting Assoc 1973–77; memb Editorial Bd: Journal of Business Fin and Accounting 1976–82, Accounting Review 1977–80, Accounting and Business Research 1981–, Accounting, Auditing and Accountability Journal; assoc ed Br Accounting Review 1993–, ed Int Jl of Auditing 1995–; tstee Acad of Accounting Historians 1993– (vice pres 1996–); elder: Church of Scotland 1984–, Presbyterian Church USA 1992–; memb Academic Advsy Ctee ASC 1987–90; memb: ICAS 1964, IT 1966, AAA 1969, AAH 1974, EAA 1978, IIA 1992; FRSA 1983; *Books* incl: Company Auditing (1972), Income and Value (1974), Company Financial Reporting (1976), Cash Flow Accounting (1984), Towards a Theory and Practice of Cash Flow Accounting (1986), The Closure of the Accounting Profession (1989), Corporate Audit Theory (1992), Shaping the Accountancy Profession (1995); *Recreations* road running, cricket, history; *Style*— Prof Tom Lee; ✉ 2013 Foxridge Road, Tuscaloosa, Alabama 35406, USA; Culverhouse School of Accountancy, University of Alabama, 332 Alston Hall, Box 870220, Tuscaloosa, Alabama, AL 35487-0220, USA (☎ 00 1 205 348 7915)

LEE-BROWNE, Col Martin Shaun Lee; CBE (1989, OBE, 1974), TD, DL (Glos); s of Denis William Lee-Browne (d 1960), of Cirencester, and Freda Rosamund Austin (d 1974); *b* 17 Oct 1931; *Educ* Leighton Park Sch Reading, Emmanuel Coll Cambridge (MA); *m* 14 Sept 1957, Diana Frances, da of Dr Geoffrey Richard Ford of Dartford, Kent; 3 s (Jeremy b 1960, Patrick b 1964, Rupert b 1966), 1 da (Alison b 1962); *Career* slr; sr ptnr Wilmot & Co; Col TA (ret 1981), Dep Col The Glos Regt 1985–94, Hon Col 1 Bn The Wessex Regt 1989–95, Hon Col Glos Cadet Bn, The Royal Glos Berks and Wilts Regt (ACF); chm Western Wessex TAVR Assoc 1982–90, vice chm Cncl of TAVR Assocs 1987–90; chm: Cncl of TAVR Assocs Pension Fund, Glos Three Choirs Festival; *Recreations* music, sailing, bookbinding; *Clubs* Army and Navy; *Style*— Col M S Lee-Browne, CBE, TD, DL; ✉ Chester House, Fairford, Glos GL7 4AD (☎ 01285 712102)

LEE-POTTER, Dr Jeremy Patrick; s of Air Marshal Sir Patrick Lee Potter, KBE, MD (d 1983), of Wittersham, Kent, and Audrey Mary, *née* Pollock; *b* 30 Aug 1934; *Educ* Epsom Coll, Guy's Hosp Univ of London (MB BS), DTM&H, DCP; *m* 26 Oct 1957, Lynda, da of Norman Higginson, of Culcheth, Lancs; 1 s (Adam Brunton b 1968), 2 da (Emma Clare b 1958, Charlotte Brodie b 1960); *Career* Sqdn Ldr Med Branch RAF 1960–68, sr specialist in pathology RAF Inst of Pathology and Tropical Med; lectr in haematology St George's Hosp Med Sch Univ of London 1968–69, conslt haematologist Poole Hosp NHS Tst 1969–95; BMA: dep chm Central Conslts and Specialists Ctee 1988–90, chm Cncl 1990–93; memb Standing Med Advsy Ctee 1990–93; memb GMC 1994– (dep chm Professional Conduct Ctee 1996–); FRCPath 1979; *Recreations* printing, print-making, visual arts; *Clubs* Athenaeum, Parkstone Golf; *Style*— Dr Jeremy Lee-Potter; ✉ Icen House, Stoborough, Wareham, Dorset BH20 5AN (☎ 01929 556307, fax 01929 554363)

LEECH, Prof Geoffrey Neil; s of Charles Richard Leech (d 1973), of Overstone, Bredon, Worcs, and Dorothy Eileen Leech (d 1967); *b* 16 Jan 1936; *Educ* Tewkesbury GS, UCL (BA, MA, PhD); *m* 29 July 1961, Frances Anne, da of George Berman, MBE (d 1985), of Lancaster; 1 s (Thomas b 1964), 1 da (Camilla b 1967); *Career* Nat Serv SAC RAF 1954–56; Harkness fell Mass Inst of Technol 1964–65, lectr English UCL 1965–69 (asst lectr 1962–64), visiting prof Brown Univ USA 1972, prof of linguistics and modern Eng language Univ of Lancaster 1974– (reader in Eng language 1969–74), chair Unit for Computer Res on the English Language; memb: Cncl The Philological Soc 1979–83, Eng Teaching Advsy Ctee The Br Cncl 1983–91, Academia Europaea 1990–, Norwegian

Acad of Science and Letters 1993–; hon prof Beijing Univ of Foreign Studies China; Fil Dr Lund Univ Sweden 1987; FBA 1987; *Books* English in Advertising (1966), A Linguistic Guide to English Poetry (1969), A Grammar of Contemporary English (with Randolph Quirk Sidney Greenbaum and Jan Svartvik, 1972), Semantics (1974), Studies in English Linguistics: For Randolph Quirk (ed with Sidney Greenbaum and Jan Svartvik, 1980), Style in Fiction: A Linguistic Introduction to English Fictional Prose (with Michael H Short, 1981), A Comprehensive Grammar of the English Language (with Randolph Quirk Sidney Greenbaum and Jan Svartvik, 1985), An A-Z of English Grammar and Usage (1989), Spoken English on Computer (ed with Greg Myers and Jenny Thomas, 1995); *Recreations* chamber music, playing the piano; *Style*— Prof Geoffrey Leech, FBA; ✉ Department of Linguistics and Modern English Language, University of Lancaster, Bailrigg, Lancaster LA1 4YT (☎ 01524 593036, fax 01524 843085)

LEECH, Maj John Cooper; MVO (1991); s of Raymond Alan Leech (d 1979), of Ipswich, Suffolk, and May Daisy Gertrude, *née* Pledger (d 1971); *b* 25 Feb 1928; *Educ* Northgate GS Ipswich, Inst of Educn Univ of London; *m* 25 April 1964, Pauline Mary, da of Russell James Forth (d 1963), and Kathleen Mary (d 1981), of Cheltenham, Gloucestershire; *Career* cmmnd RASC 1947, RAEC 1953 (served Aust, Malaya, Borneo, Malta, N Africa, BAOR), ret 1978; Chamberlain Lincoln Cathedral 1978–79, State Invitations Asst Lord Chamberlain's Office Buckingham Palace 1979–91; lay steward of St George's Chapel Windsor 1991–, steward Christ Church Cathedral Oxford 1993–; Chevalier du Wissam Alouite (Morocco) 1987, Cavaliere Ordine Al Merito della Repubblica Italiana 1990; *Recreations* video, travel, restoration of old furniture, history, swimming; *Clubs* Army and Navy, Victory Services; *Style*— Maj John Leech, MVO; ✉ 1 Hartley Russell Close, Church Way, Iffley, Oxford OX4 4EA (☎ 01865 711358)

LEECH, Rev Kenneth; s of John Leech, and Annie Leech; *b* 15 June 1939; *Educ* Hyde GS Tameside, King's Coll London (Sambrooke scholar, BA, Barry prize in divinity, AKC), Trinity Coll Oxford (BA), St Stephen's House Oxford; *m* 1970, Rheta; *Career* ordained: deacon 1964, priest 1965; asst priest: Holy Trinity Hoxton London 1964–67, St Annes Soho 1967–71; fndr and dir: Soho Drugs Gp 1967–71, Centrepoint Soho Emergency Night Shelter 1969–71; chaplain and tutor St Augustine's Coll Canterbury 1971–74, relief chaplain HM Prison Canterbury 1971–74, rector St Matthew's Bethnal Green 1974–80, i/c post-ordination training Stepney Episcopal Area 1975–80, advsr on exorcism and the occult to the London Bishops 1976–79; visiting theologian: St Stephen's House Chicago 1978–89, Bishop Brent House Chicago 1990–; race rels field offr General Synod Board of Social Responsibility 1980–87, hon asst priest St Clements Notting Dale 1982–88, dir Runnymede Trust 1987–90, chm Maze Drug Prevention Project 1989–, memb Drug Policy Review Gp 1988–; Christendom fell St Botolph's Church Aldgate 1991; former memb Ctee: Soho Project, Avenues Unlimited Youth Project, Br and Foreign Schs Soc, Inst for Study of Drug Dependence; has given numerous lectures at Univs and Colls in Britain and America; *Books* Drugs for Young People: Their Use and Misuse (with Brenda Jordan, 1967), Keep the Faith Baby (1973), Brick Lane 1978: The Events and their Significance (1980), The Social God (1981), Care and Conflict: Leaves from a Pastoral Notebook (1990), The Eye of the Storm (1992); contrib to numerous learned jls; *Recreations* cartoon drawing, Lancashire dialect poetry, pubs; *Style*— Rev Kenneth Leech; ✉ St Botolph's Church, Aldgate, London EC3N 1AB (☎ 0171 377 0721)

LEECH, His Hon Robert Radcliffe; s of Edwin Radcliffe Leech (d 1947); *b* 5 Dec 1919; *Educ* Monmouth Sch, Worcester Coll Oxford; *m* 1951, Vivienne Ruth, da of A J Rickerby; 2 da; *Career* served Border Regt (despatches twice) 1940–44; called to the Bar Middle Temple 1949, dep chm Cumberland QS 1966, judge County Ct 1970, circuit judge 1971–86, hon recorder City of Carlisle 1985–86; *Recreations* sailing, golf; *Clubs* Oriental; *Style*— His Hon Robert Leech; ✉ Scaur House, Cavendish Terrace, Stanwix, Carlisle CA3 9ND (☎ 01228 21946)

LEEDALE, Prof Gordon Frank; s of William Henry Leedale, and Ivy Victoria Alexandra, *née* Hampton; *b* 10 Oct 1932; *Educ* E Ham GS, QMC (BSc, PhD, DSc); *m* 24 July 1954 (m dis 1981), Hazel Doris, da of Harry Dudley Leeson (d 1984); 1 s (Jonathan Paul b 7 Dec 1967), 2 da (Wanda Siriol Jane b 8 Feb 1960, Siân Vanessa b 13 March 1964); *Career* res fell in pure sci Univ of Durham 1957–59, res fell Devpt Cmmn 1959–60; Univ of Leeds: lectr in botany 1960–65, reader in botany Dept of Plant Sciences 1965–79, prof of botany 1980–91, head Dept of Plant Sciences 1986–87, head Dept of Pure and Applied Biology 1987–90, emeritus prof 1991–, chm Sr Common Room 1995–; Darwin lectr Br Assoc 1965, sec Br Phycological Soc 1965–67, hon ed British Phycological Journal 1967–75, pres Soc of Evolutionary Protistology 1977–79; FIBiol 1981, FLS 1981; *Books* Euglenoid Flagellates (1967); *Recreations* classical music, biological photography; *Style*— Prof Gordon Leedale; ✉ The Cottage, Rigton Hill, N Rigton, Leeds LS17 0DJ (☎ 01423 734348); Dept of Biology, University of Leeds, Leeds LS2 9JT (☎ 0113 233 2870, fax 0113 233 2835); Senior Common Room (☎ 0113 233 2870, fax 0113 233 4161)

LEEDHAM, Dr Peter William; s of William Marshall Leedham, and Winifred, *née* Doswell; *b* 17 March 1941; *Educ* Collyer's Sch Horsham Sussex, King's Coll Hosp Med Sch London (MB BS); *m* 12 June 1965, (Dorothy) Elaine, da of Walter John Witcombe, of Magor, Newport, Gwent; 2 s (Richard b 1966, David b 1971), 1 da (Ruth b 1968); *Career* lectr in morbid anatomy King's Coll Hosp Med Sch 1967 (demonstrator in pathology 1966), lectr in morbid anatomy The London Hosp Med Coll 1969, conslt histopathologist Shropshire Health Dist 1972–; past memb: Shropshire local Med Ctee, Shropshire Health Authy 1979–87; past memb Regnl Scientific Ctee and past chm Combined Laboratory Servs Ctee W Midlands RHA; W Midlands regnl rep RCPath 1989–92; memb Shrewsbury Rotary Club; memb: ACP, BMA, Pathological Soc of GB and Ireland, Int Acad of Pathology (former cncl memb); LRCP, MRCS, FRCPath; *Recreations* golf, gardening; *Style*— Dr Peter Leedham

LEEDS, Archdeacon of; *see:* Oliver, Ven John Michael

LEEDS, Sir Christopher Anthony; 8 Bt (UK 1812), of Croxton Park, Cambridgeshire; s of Maj Geoffrey Hugh Anthony Leeds (d 1962, yr bro of 6 Bt) by his w Yolande Therese Barre, *née* Mitchell (d 1944); suc cous, Sir Graham Mortimer Leeds, 7 Bt, 1983; *b* 31 Aug 1935; *Educ* King's Sch Bruton, LSE (BSc(Econ)), Univ of S California (MA); *m* 1974 (m dis 1980), Elaine Joyce, da of late Sqdn Ldr Cornelius Harold Albert Mullins; *Heir* cous, Anthony Leeds; *Career* author; asst master: Merchant Taylors' Sch 1966–68, Christ's Hosp 1972–75, Stowe 1978–81; sr lectr Univ of Nancy II, visiting lectr Univ of Strasbourg I 1983–87; conslt Business Etiquette; memb RIIA; *Books* incl: Political Studies (1968, 3 edn 1981), European History 1789–1914 (1971, 2 edn 1980), Italy under Mussolini (1972), Management and Business Studies (with R S Stainton and C Jones, 1974, 3 edn 1983), World History-1900 to the present day (1987), Peace and War (1987), English Humour (1989); *Recreations* tennis, modern art, travel; *Clubs* Lansdowne; *Style*— Sir Christopher Leeds, Bt; ✉ 6 Hurlingham, 14 Manor Road, Bournemouth, Dorset BH1 2EE; 7 Rue de Turique, 54000 Nancy, France (☎ 00 33 83 96 43 83)

LEEDS, Bishop of (RC) 1985–; Rt Rev David Every Konstant; s of Antoine Konstant (d 1985), and Dulcie Marion Beresford Leggatt (d 1930); *b* 16 June 1930; *Educ* St Edmund's Coll Ware, Christ's Coll Cambridge (MA), Univ of London Inst of Education (PGCE); *Career* priest Diocese of Westminster 1954, Cardinal Vaughan Sch Kensington 1959, diocesan advsr on religious educn 1966, St Michael's Sch Stevenage 1968, dir Westminster Religious Educn Centre 1970, auxiliary bishop of Westminster (bishop in Central London) 1977–85; chm Nat Bd of Religious Inspectors and Advisers 1970–75; episcopal advsr: Catholic Teachers' Fedn 1980–88, Catholic Inst for Int Relations 1982–; chm: Oxford and Cambridge Catholic Education Bd 1984–86, Dept of Catechetics Bishops Conf 1978–84, Dept of Catholic Educn 1984–, W Yorks Ecumenical Cncl 1986–87; Freeman City of London 1984; FRSA 1996; author of various books on religious educn and liturgy; *Recreations* music, sport of most kinds; *Style*— The Rt Rev the Bishop of Leeds; ✉ Bishop's House, 13 North Grange Road, Headingley, Leeds LS6 2BR (☎ 0113 230 4533, fax 0113 278 9890)

LEEK, Anthony Thomas (Tony); s of Thomas Henry Howard Leek (d 1988), and Mary, *née* Curtis; *b* 15 Feb 1947; *Educ* Forest Sch Snaresbrook, Univ of Southampton (LLB); *Career* admitted slr 1975; ptnr: Austin Ryder & Co 1977–86, Alsop Wilkinson (now Dibb Lupton Alsop) 1987–; memb Law Soc; *Recreations* cricket, theatre, music; *Style*— Tony Leek, Esq; ✉ Dibb Lupton Alsop, 6 Dowgate Hill, London EC4R 2SS (☎ 0171 248 4141, fax 0171 623 8286, telex 995593)

LEEMING, Charles Gerard James; s of Gerard Paschal de Pfyffer Leeming, of Field Dalling Hall, Holt, Norfolk, and Joan Helen Mary (d 1954), da of Edmund Trappes-Lomax (d 1927, *see* Burke's Landed Gentry 1952); *b* 4 May 1936; *Educ* Ampleforth; *Career* admitted slr 1959, sr ptnr Wilde Sapte London 1987–96 (ptnr 1963–96), ret 1996; memb Lloyd's; memb Worshipful Co of Watermen and Lightermen of the River Thames, Liveryman Worshipful Co of Slrs; *Recreations* sailing, music, art, books, bee-keeping, collecting electronic gadgets; *Clubs* Little Ship, Cruising Assoc; *Style*— Charles Leeming, Esq; ✉ Picton House, 45 Strand-on-the-Green, Chiswick, London W4 3PB (☎ 0181 994 0450)

LEEMING, Ian; QC (1988); s of Flt Lt Thomas Leeming (d 1981), of Preston, Lancs, and Lilian, *née* Male (d 1993); *b* 10 April 1948; *Educ* Catholic Coll Preston, Univ of Manchester (LLB); *m* 26 May 1973, Linda Barbara, da of Harold Cook, of Walton-le-Dale, Preston, Lancs; 1 s (Charles b 1985), 2 da (Lucinda b 1976, Angela b 1981); *Career* called to the Bar Gray's Inn 1970, Lincoln's Inn (ad eundem); in practice at the Chancery and Commercial Bars Northern Circuit 1971–, recorder 1989– (asst recorder 1986–89); fndr memb Northern Soc of Cons Lawyers (vice chm 1985–89), chm Heaton Cons Assoc 1986–88, formerly pt/t lectr in law Univ of Manchester; co dir; *Recreations* squash, real tennis; *Clubs* Athenaeum; *Style*— Ian Leeming, Esq, QC; ✉ Lamb Chambers, Lamb Building, Temple, London EC4 7AS (☎ 0171 797 8300); 9 St John Street, Manchester (☎ 0161 955 9000)

LEEMING, Jan; da of Ivan Terrence Atkins, MBE, of Nailsworth, Glos, and Hazel Louise Wyatt, *née* Haysey; *b* 5 Jan 1942; *Educ* St Joseph's Convent GS, Abbey Wood Kent; *m* 1, 10 April 1980 (m dis July 1986), Patrick Geoffrey Lunt, s of Rev Canon Ronald Lunt (d 1994), of Ledbury, Herefordshire; 1 s (Jonathan Patrick Geoffrey b 18 May 1981); m 2; *Career* TV announcer NZ 1962, first woman TV newsreader Sydney Aust 1963, theatre actress 1963–66, presenter Women Only and Report West HTV West 1970–76, Pebble Mill at One and various outside broadcast specials 1976–80, announcer Radio 2, newsreader BBC 1980–87, compère Eurovision Song Contest 1982, presenter The Garden Party (BBC TV) 1989, Makers (ITV This Morning) 1989, 1990 and 1991, Whatever Happened To ......? (BBC 1) 1993, Right or Wrong (series, Central TV) 1994; narrator Peter and the Wolf (with Birmingham Symphony Orch) 1993; contrib holiday articles to Travelling Magazine; winner: Newsreader of the Year 1981 and 1982, TV Personality of the Year 1982; charities: Fight for Sight (patron), BACUP, David Shepherd Conservation Fndn (life memb), Born Free Fndn (life memb), Vale Wildlife Rescue; involved in corporate videos, presentations and conferences; memb: Guild of Freemen City of London 1988, Soc of Amateur Artists; *Books* Working in Television (1980), Simply Looking Good (1984); *Recreations* theatre, reading, painting and embroidery; *Style*— Miss Jan Leeming; ✉ c/o Anne Sweetbaum, Arlington Enterprises, 1–3 Charlotte Street, London W1P 1HD (☎ 0171 580 0702, fax 0171 580 4994)

LEEPER, (Thomas William) Brian; s of Richard Leeper (d 1987), of W Byfleet; bro of Desmond Leeper; *b* 16 June 1927; *Educ* Downside, Magdalene Coll Cambridge; *m* 1951, Edreen Diana, da of Capt Edric Lyte; 4 s (Patrick b 1953, Michael b 1955, James b 1957, Timothy b 1965), 2 da (Mrs Andrew Bruce b 1952, Mrs Johnathon Gidley b 1959); *Career* Mil Serv Irish Gds 1945–48; dir LEP Group Ltd 1970–86; homeopath 1989; *Recreations* aviculture, horticulture, herbalism, photography; *Clubs* Cavalry and Guards'; *Style*— Brian Leeper, Esq; ✉ Bonners, Hambledon, Godalming, Surrey

LEES, Dr Andrew John; s of late Lewis Lees, of Harrogate, and Muriel, *née* Wadsworth; *b* 27 Sept 1947; *Educ* Roundhay Sch, London Hosp Med Coll (MD); *m* 21 July 1973, Juana Luisa Pulin Perez-Lopez, da of Juan Luis Pulin, of Geneva; 1 s (George Luis b 9 April 1975), 1 da (Nathalie Jasmine b 23 June 1976); *Career* conslt neurologist to the Nat Hosp for Neurology and Neurosurgery UCL and Middx Hosps; cncl memb and med advsr Parkinson's Disease Soc, chm Med Advsy Panel Gilles de la Tourette Assoc UK; FRSM, FRCP; *Books* Parkinson's Disease - The Facts (1982), Tics and Related Disorders (1985), Ray of Hope - The Ray Kennedy Story (1993); *Recreations* Hispanic and Latin American studies, memb and hon medical advsr to Liverpool FC; *Clubs* Taurino De Londres; *Style*— Dr Andrew Lees; ✉ The National Hospital for Neurology and Neurosurgery, Queen Square, London WC1N 3BG (☎ 0171 837 3611)

LEES, Sir (William) Antony Clare; 3 Bt (UK 1937), of Longdendale, Co Chester; s of Sir William Hereward Clare Lees, 2 Bt (d 1976), and Dorothy Gertrude, *née* Lauder; *b* 14 June 1935; *Educ* Eton, Magdalene Coll Cambridge (MA); *m* 1986, Joanna Olive Crane; *Heir* none; *Style*— Sir Antony Lees, Bt

LEES, Col Brian Musson; LVO (1979), OBE (1978); s of John Lees (d 1978), and Margaret, *née* Musson (d 1942), of Tamworth; *b* 9 Oct 1931; *Educ* Queen Elizabeth GS Tamworth, Univ of Leeds (BA); *m* 1963, Diana Caroline, da of John Harold Everall; 2 da (Diana (Mrs Richard Howarth) b 1964, Alexia (Mrs Guy Fetherstonhaugh) b 1966); *Career* cmmnd KOYLI 1954; served: Kenya (Mau Mau campaign), Cyprus (EOKA campaign), Arabian Peninsula (S Yemen emergency); CO 5 Bn LI 1971–73, Def Attaché Jedda 1975–79, Def Intelligence Staff MOD 1979–82, Head Br Def Intelligence Liaison Staff Washington 1982–84, Def Attaché Muscat 1984–1986, ret 1987; ME conslt; sr advsr Carlyle International Washington DC; cdr St John Ambulance Shropshire 1994–; FRGS (1989); *Books* The Al Sa'ud, Ruling Family of Saudi Arabia (1980); *Recreations* music, gardening, reading; *Clubs* MCC, Royal Soc for Asian Affrs; *Style*— Col B M Lees, LVO, OBE; ✉ The Old Rectory, Kenley, Shropshire SY5 6NH (☎ 01694 731281, fax 01694 731301)

LEES, His Honour Charles Norman; s of Charles Lees; b 4 Oct 1929; *Educ* Stockport Sch, Univ of Leeds; *m* 1961, Stella (d 1987), da of Hubert Swann; 1 da (Rosemary); *Career* called to the Bar Lincoln's Inn 1951, a dep chm Cumberland QS 1969–72, recorder of Crown Ct 1972–80, circuit judge (Northern Circuit) 1980–96 (designated family judge 1991–96); legal chm Disciplinary Ctee of the Potato Mktg Bd 1965–80, chm Mental Health Review Tbnls (restricted patients) 1983–; *Style*— His Hon C N Lees; ✉ c/o Northern Circuit Office, 15 Quay Street, Manchester M60 9FD

LEES, Christopher James; TD; s and h of Sir Thomas Edward Lees, 4 Bt, *qv*; *b* 4 Nov 1952; *Educ* Eton, Univ of Edinburgh (BSc 1976); *m* 1, 1977 (m dis 1988); m 2, 1989, Clare, da of Austen Young, of Sheffield; 1 s (John b 1992), 3 da (Gabriel b 1990, Rosamund b 1994, Mary b 1995); *Career* farmer; Royal Wessex Yeo; *Style*— Christopher Lees, Esq, TD; ✉ Post Green Farm, Lytchett Minster, Poole, Dorset

LEES, Sir David Bryan; kt (1991); s of Rear Adm Dennis Marescaux Lees, CB, DSO (d 1973), and Daphne May, *née* Burnett (d 1990); *b* 23 Nov 1936; *Educ* Charterhouse; *m* 1961, Edith Mary, da of Brig Ronald Playfair St Vincent Bernard, MC, DSO (d 1943); 2 s, 1 da; *Career* Nat Serv 2 Lt RA 1955–57; articled clerk with Binder Hamlyn & Co (chartered accountants) 1957–62, sr audit clerk 1962–63, chief accountant Handley Page Ltd 1964–68, fin dir Handley Page Aircraft Ltd 1969; GKN Sankey Ltd: chief accountant 1970–72, dep controller 1972–73, dir sec and controller 1973–76; GKN plc: gp fin exec 1976–77, gen mangr (fin) 1977–82, main bd dir 1982–, fin dir 1982–87, gp md 1987–88, chm 1988–; chm Courtaulds plc July 1996– (dir 1991–), non-exec dir Bank of England 1991–; cmmr Audit Cmmn 1983–90; Engrg Employers' Fedn: memb Commercial and Economic Ctee 1985–87, ex-officio memb Mgmnt Bd and Gen Cncl 1987–, memb Policy Ctee 1988–94, vice pres 1988, sr dep pres 1989, pres 1990–92; CBI: memb Cncl 1988–, chm Econ and Financial Policy Ctee (now Economic Affrs Ctee) 1988–94, memb President's Ctee 1988–96; memb: Listed Companies Advsy Ctee 1990–, Midlands Industl Cncl 1988–, Nat Campaign Ctee of Cncl for Charitable Support 1990–, Euro Round Table 1995–, Nat Defence Industries Cncl 1995–; tstee Ironbridge Gorge Museum Devpt Tst 1989–; govr Shrewsbury Sch, hon fell Univ of Wolverhampton (formerly Wolverhampton Poly) 1990; FCA, FRSA 1988; *Recreations* golf, music; *Clubs* MCC; *Style*— Sir David Lees; ✉ GKN plc, 7 Cleveland Row, London SW1A 1DB; Courtaulds plc, 50 George Street, London W1A 2BB (☎ 0171 612 1000, fax 0171 612 1521)

LEES, Prof Peter; CBE (1994); s of Harold Edward Lees (d 1943), of Farnworth, Lancs, and Gladys, *née* Millar; *b* 15 July 1940; *Educ* Canon Slade GS, Chelsea Coll of Sci and Technol (BPharm), RVC London (PhD); *m* 3 Aug 1968, Mary Hogg, da of John Moffat; 1 s (Matthew Peter b 9 June 1975), 1 da (Katherine Mary b 30 March 1978); *Career* Royal Veterinary Coll: asst lectr in pharmacology Dept of Physiology 1964–66, lectr in vet pharmacology Dept of Physiology 1966–76, reader in vet pharmacology 1976–88, prof of vet pharmacology 1988–, head Dept of Vet Basic Scis 1991–; Ciba-Geigy Prize for res in animal health 1985, Open Award Equine Vet Jl 1985, Victory Medal Central Vet Soc 1987, George Fleming Prize Br Vet Jl 1987, Amoroso Award Br Small Animal Vet Assoc 1988; ed Jl of Vet Pharmacology and Therapeutics 1983–93; Peter Wilson bequest lecture Univ of Edinburgh 1989, Bogan Meml lecture Univ of Cambridge 1990, Sir Frederick Smith Meml lecture Br Equine Vet Assoc 1993; memb: Vet Products Ctee 1978–96, Mgmnt Ctee Home of Rest for Horses 1988–96; hon memb Euro Assoc for Vet Pharmacology and Toxicology 1991, hon assoc RCVS 1987; Dr (hc) Univ of Gent 1992; memb: Br Pharmacological Soc 1965–96, Assoc for Vet Clinical Pharmacology and Therapeutics 1976–96, Euro Assoc of Vet Pharmacology and Toxicology 1978–96; FIBiol 1989; *Books* Pharmacological Basis of Large Animal Medicine (jtly, 1983), Veterinary Pharmacology, Toxicology and Therapy in Food Producing Species (jtly, 1988), Proceedings of the 6th International Congress of the European Association for Veterinary Pharmacology and Toxicology (co-ed, 1994); *Style*— Prof Peter Lees, CBE; ✉ Department of Veterinary Basic Sciences, The Royal Veterinary College, Royal College Street, London NW1 0TU (☎ 0171 468 5200)

LEES, Robert Ferguson; s of William Cameron Lees, and Martha, *née* McAlpine; *b* 15 Sept 1938; *Educ* Bellshill Acad, Univ of Strathclyde (LLB); *m* 23 Feb 1966, Elizabeth, da of Robert Loughridge; *Career* Procurator Fiscal Service: legal asst Paisley 1972–75, sr depute procurator fiscal Glasgow 1975–81 (legal asst then sr legal asst), asst procurator fiscal Dundee 1982–88, regnl procurator fiscal N Strathclyde 1989–91, regnl procurator fiscal Lothian and Borders 1991–; memb Cncl Law Soc of Scotland 1990–93, pres Forensic Sci Soc 1995–; *Recreations* music, travel, foreign languages; *Style*— Robert F Lees, Esq; ✉ Procurator Fiscal's Office, 29 Chambers Street, Edinburgh EH1 1LD (☎ 0131 226 4962)

LEES, Air Vice-Marshal Robin Lowther; CB (1985), MBE (1962); s of Air Marshal Sir Alan Lees, KCB, CBE, DSO, AFC (d 1973), of Newbury, Berks, and Norah Elizabeth, *née* Thompson (d 1974); *b* 27 Feb 1931; *Educ* Wellington, RAF Cranwell; *m* 1966, Alison, da of Lt-Col Cuthbert Benson Carrick, MC, TD, JP (d 1966), of Newcastle upon Tyne; 3 s (Timothy, Anthony, Edward); *Career* RAF 1949–86, Air Offr Admin RAF Support Cmd and Head of RAF Admin Branch 1982–86 (AVM); chief exec Br Hospitality Assoc 1986–96; memb Cncl CBI 1990–93, govr Wellington Coll 1990–; rep: Hants, Combined Servs and RAF at squash, RAF at tennis and Cambs at hockey; *Recreations* lawn tennis, real tennis, squash, rackets, golf; *Clubs* All England Lawn Tennis, Jesters, RAF; *Style*— Air Vice-Marshal Robin Lees, CB, MBE; ✉ c/o Barclays Bank Ltd, 6 Market Place, Newbury, Berks

LEES, Ronald; ISO (1992); s of Arthur Lees (d 1946), of Stockport, Cheshire, and Eva, *née* Smith (d 1983); *b* 28 Sept 1933; *Educ* Stockport Coll; *m* 1 June 1957, Arline Margot, da of Albert Williamson (d 1978), of Stockport, Cheshire; *Career* works chemist CWS Ltd until 1959, res chemist Food Industs Res Assoc 1960–65, Info Servs for Industl Miny of Technol 1965, princ Small Firms Info Serv Dept of Indust 1971, divnl head Laboratory of the Govt Chemist 1978–93, ret; sr ptnr Rolton Technical Scientific and symposium Services 1994–; author of over 300 articles on food topics; former pres: Kingston Philatelic Soc, Weybridge Philatelic Soc; FRSC, FRSH, MIFST, CChem; *Books* Sugar Confectionery and Chocolate Manufacture (1973), Food Analysis (1975), Faults, Causes and Remedies in the Sweet and Chocolate Industry (1981), Chemical Nomenclature Usage (ed vol 1 1983, ed vol 2 1993), Design Construction and Refurbishment of Laboratories (ed vol 1 1984, ed vol 2 1993), A History of Sweet and Chocolate Making (1988), An Introduction and Basic Guide to the Manufacture of Sweets and Chocolate (1996); *Recreations* walking, postal history, travel, lecturing on food science, history of sweets and chocolates; *Style*— Ronald Lees, Esq, ISO; ✉ 38 St Vincent Road, Walton on Thames, Surrey KT12 1PB

LEES, Dr (David Arthur) Russell; s of Dr David Lees, CBE (d 1986), of Larch Rd, Glasgow, and Olive Willington; *b* 16 Jan 1948; *Educ* Hamilton Acad, Univ of Glasgow; *m* 21 June 1971, Marie; 4 s (Russell b 1972, Andrew b 1975, Alister b 1982, Peter b 1984); *Career* registrar Dept of Obstetrics and Gynaecology: Robroyston Hosp Glasgow 1974–76, Stobhill Hosp Glasgow 1978–80; sr registrar Queen Mother's Hosp Glasgow 1980–81, conslt obstetrician and gynaecologist Raigmore Hosp Inverness 1981–; area advsr for special needs Inverness, Medal of Merit (and Bar) for servs to Scout Assoc; memb Highland Med Soc; FRCOG; *Style*— Dr Russell Lees; ✉ Crofthill, Daviot (West), Inverness IV1 2XQ (☎ 01463 722230); Dept of Obstetrics, Raigmore Hospital, Inverness IV2 3UJ (☎ 01463 704000)

LEES, Sir Thomas Edward; 4 Bt (UK 1897), of South Lytchett Manor, Lytchett Minster, Dorset, JP (Dorset 1951); s of Col Sir John Victor Elliott Lees, 3 Bt, DSO, MC (d 1955); *b* 1925; *Educ* Eton, Magdalene Coll Cambridge; *m* 1949, Faith Justin, JP (1963) (d 1996), o da of George Gaston Jessiman, OBE, of Great Durnford, Wilts; 1 s (Christopher James b 1952), 3 da (Sarah Margaret (Mrs John M Omond) b 1951, Bridget Selina (Mrs Martin C Green) b 1954, Elizabeth Jane (Mrs Colin Bierton) b 1957); *Heir* s, Christopher James Lees b 4 Nov 1952; *Career* serv RAF 1943–45; High Sheriff of Dorset 1960; memb: Dorset CC 1951–70, General Synod 1970–90; *Recreations* sailing; *Clubs* Royal Cruising; *Style*— Sir Thomas Lees, Bt; ✉ Post Green, Lytchett Minster, Dorset BH16 6AP (☎ 01202 622048, fax 01202 632632)

LEES, Sir Thomas Harcourt Ivor; 8 Bt (UK 1804), of Blackrock, Dublin; s of Sir Charles Archibald Edward Ivor Lees, 7 Bt (d 1963); *b* 6 Nov 1941; *Heir* kinsman, John Cathcart D'Olier-Lees, *qv*; *Style*— Sir Thomas Lees, Bt; ✉ c/o Fosseys, The Street, Slinfold, Horsham, Sussex RH13 7RS

LEES, Dr William; CBE (1971), TD (1962 bar 1968); s of Maj William Lees (d 1986), and Elizabeth, *née* Massey (d 1962); *b* 18 May 1924; *Educ* Queen Elizabeth Sch Blackburn, Victorian Univ Manchester (MB ChB, DPH); *m* 4 Oct 1947, (Winifred) Elizabeth, da of Robert Archibald Hanford (d 1964), of Cheshire; 3 s (William b 1948, John b 1953, Christopher b 1959); *Career* RAMC 1948–50; TA 1950–71: Col Cmdg 257 Gen Hosp TA 1966–71, Col Cmdt NW sector ACF 1971–77; lectr and gynaecologist St Mary Hosp Manchester 1950–59, sr princ med offr Miny of Health DHSS 1959–81 (under sec 1977–81), conslt advsr on med manpower and post graduate educn SW Thames RHA 1981–87; chm Dacorum Cancer Relief and McMillan Fund; Hon Physician to HM The Queen 1970–72; Liveryman Worshipful Co of Apothecaries; OStJ 1968; FROCG 1964, MFCM 1973; *Recreations* golf, music, travel; *Clubs* Athenaeum, St John's; *Style*— Dr William Lees, CBE, TD; ✉ 13 Hill Park Hill, Berkhamsted, Herts HP4 2NH (☎ 01442 863010)

LEES-MILNE, James; s of George Crompton Lees-Milne (d 1949), of Crompton Hall, Lancashire, and Wickhamford Manor, Evesham, Worcs, and Helen Christina (d 1962), da of Henry Bailey, DL, and gda of Sir Joseph Bailey, 1 Bt, of Glanusk Park, Crickhowell, Powys; *b* 6 Aug 1908; *Educ* Eton, Magdalen Coll Oxford, Grenoble Univ; *m* 19 Nov 1951, Alvilde (d 1994), da of late Lt-Gen Sir Tom Molesworth Bridges, KCB, KCMG, DSO, former wife of 3 Viscount Chaplin; *Career* 2 Lt Irish Gds 1940–41 (invalided); private sec to 1 Baron Lloyd 1931–34, on staff Reuters 1935–36, on staff Nat Tst 1936–66, advsr on historic bldgs Nat Tst 1951–66; FRSL 1957, FSA 1974; *Books* The National Trust (ed, 1945), The Age of Adam (1947), National Trust Guide - Buildings (1948), Tudor Renaissance (1951), The Age of Inigo Jones (1953), Roman Mornings (Heinemann Award, 1956), Baroque in Italy (1959), Baroque in Spain and Portugal (1960), Earls of Creation (1962), Worcestershire - A Shell Guide (1964), St Peter's (1967), English Country Houses: Baroque 1685–1714 (1970), Another Self (1970), Heretics in love (1973), Ancestral Voices (1975), William Beckford (1976), Prophesying Peace (1977), Round the Clock (1978), Harold Nicolson (vol 1 1980, vol II 1981, Heineman Award 1982), Images of Bath (with David Ford, 1982), The Country House (1982), Caves of Ice (1983), The Last Stuarts (1983), Midway on the Waves (1985), The Enigmatic Edwardian (1986), Some Cotswold Country Houses (1987), Venetian Evenings (1988), The Fool of Love (1990), The Bachelor Duke (1991), People and Places (1992), A Mingled Measure (1994), Fourteen Friends (1996); *Recreations* visiting the haunts of the illustrious dead; *Clubs* Brooks's; *Style*— James Lees-Milne, Esq, FSA, FRSL; ✉ Essex House, Badminton GL9 1DD (☎ 01454 218288)

LEES-SPALDING, Rear Adm Ian Jaffery; CB (1973); s of Frank Souter Lees-Spalding (d 1970); *b* 16 June 1920; *Educ* Blundells; *m* 1946, June Sandys Lyster, da of Maj Warren Lyster Sparkes, of Devon; 2 da; *Career* joined RN 1938, awarded commendation 1940, joined submarines 1945, CSO (tech) to C-in-C Fleet and inspr gen Fleet Maintenance 1971, ret 1974, ADC 1971; admin London Int Film Sch 1975–79; *Books* Macmillan and Silk Cut Yachtsman's Handbook (ed); *Recreations* music, travel, gardening; *Clubs* Army and Navy; *Style*— Rear Adm I J Lees-Spalding, CB; ✉ St Olaf's, Wonston, Winchester, Hants SO21 3LP (☎ 01962 760249)

LEESON, Ian Arthur; s of Alister Curtis Leeson (d 1991), and Nancy Avis Louise, *née* Cayzer (d 1996); *b* 13 March 1937; *Educ* Rugby, Univ Coll Oxford (MA); *m* 7 Aug 1965, (Eileen) Margaret, da of Col Anderson Kirkwood Tennent, OBE (d 1971); 2 da (Sally b 1968, Patricia b 1971); *Career* CA; ptnr Ernst & Young 1970–96; FCA 1964; *Recreations* golf; *Clubs* Hurlingham, Woking Golf; *Style*— Ian Leeson, Esq; ✉ Eaton House, Eaton Park, Cobham, Surrey KT11 2JF (☎ 01932 868389)

LEFANU, Prof Nicola Frances; da of William Richard LeFanu (d 1995), and Elizabeth Violet Maconchy, DBE (d 1994); *b* 28 April 1947; *Educ* St Mary's Sch Calne Wilts, St Hilda's Coll Oxford (MA), Harkness fellowship, Univ of London (DMus); *m* 16 March 1979, David Newton Lumsdaine; 1 s (Peter LeFanu b 13 Nov 1982); *Career* composer (fifty musical compositions); prof of music Univ of York 1994–; memb: Music Panel ACGB, Cncl SPNM; fndr memb WIM; Hon DMus Univ of Durham; FRCM; *Recreations* conservation, natural history, feminism; *Style*— Prof Nicola LeFanu; ✉ 5 Holly Terrace, York YO1 4DS (fax 01904 610467)

LEFEBVRE, Prof Arthur Henry; s of Henri Lefebvre (d 1975), and May, *née* Brown (d 1972); *b* 14 March 1923; *Educ* Long Eaton GS, Univ of Nottingham (BSc Eng), Imperial Coll London (PhD, Unwin Prize), Univ of London (DSc Eng); *m* Dec 1952, Elizabeth Marcella, *née* Betts; 2 s (David Ivan b 1953, Paul Henry b 1956), 1 da (Anne Marie (Mrs Moore) b 1962); *Career* engrg apprentice Ericsson Telephones 1938–41, combustion engr Rolls Royce Derby 1952–61, prof and head of Sch of Mech Engrg Cranfield Univ 1971–76 (prof of aircraft propulsion 1961–71); Purdue Univ USA: prof and head of Sch of Mech Engrg 1976–80, Reilly prof of combustion engrg 1980–93, Reilly prof emeritus 1993–; visiting prof Cranfield Univ 1993–; Hon DSc Cranfield Univ 1989; memb: ASME, American Inst of Aeronautics and Astronautics; FIMechE, FRAeS, FRSA, FEng 1994; *Awards* Gas Turbine Award ASME 1982, R Tom Sawyer Award 1984, inaugral recipient Propellants and Combustion Award American Inst of Aeronautics and Astronautics 1990, Marshall Award American Inst for Liquid Atomization and Spray Systems 1993, Scholar Award Int Gas Turbine Inst 1995, Aircraft Engine Technology Award Int Gas Turbine Inst 1996; *Books* Gas Turbine Combustion (1983), Atomization and Sprays (1989); *Recreations* music, reading; *Clubs* Athenaeum; *Style*— Prof Arthur Lefebvre, FEng; ✉ Low Furrow, Pebworth, Stratford upon Avon CV37 8XW (☎ and fax 01789 721429)

LEFÈVRE, Robin Charles; s of Jack Lefèvre, and Jean, *née* Syme; *b* 5 May 1947; *Educ* Irvine Royal Acad, The Royal Scottish Acad of Music and Dramatic Art; *m* 2 Oct 1970, Maureen, da of George Webster; 1 da (Laura b 15 Aug 1971); *Career* director; assoc dir Hampstead Theatre, prodns incl: Then and Now, Threads, Writer's Cramp, On the Edge, Fall, Bodies (transfd Ambassadors), Aristocrats (Evening Standard Best Play Award 1988, NY Drama Critics' Award for Best Foreign Play), Valued Friends (Long Wharf Connectictut, Evening Standard Award); for Abbey Theatre Dublin incl: Someone Who'll Watch Over Me (also Hampstead, Vaudeville, and Broadway), The Cavalcaders (also Royal Court), The Bird Sanctuary, Translations; other credits incl: Outside Edge (Queens), Rocket to the Moon (Apollo), Are You Lonesome Tonight? (Evening Standard Best Musical Award), Rowan Atkinson's New Review (Shaftesbury), The Entertainer (Shaftesbury), The Country Girls (Apollo), When We Are Married (NT), The Wexford Trilogy (Bush); *Style*— Robin Lefèvre, Esq

LEFF, Prof Julian Paul; s of Dr Samuel Leff (d 1962), of London, and Vera Miriam, *née* Levy (d 1980); *b* 4 July 1938; *Educ* Haberdashers' Aske's, UCL (BSc, MD); *m* 31 Jan 1975, Prof Joan Lillian Leff, da of Jacob Raphael (d 1970), of Tel Aviv, Israel; 4 s (Michael b 1964, Alex b 1967, Jonty b 1976, Adriel b 1980), 1 da (Jessica b 1975); *Career* career scientist MRC 1972–, hon consit physician Maudsley Hosp 1973–, hon sr lectr London Sch of Hygiene 1974–89, asst dir MRC Social Psychiatry Unit 1974–89, clinical sub-dean Inst of Psychiatry 1974–79, dir Team For Assessment of Psychiatric Servs 1985–, dir MRC Social and Community Psychiatric Unit 1989–95, prof of social and cultural psychiatry Inst of Psychiatry 1987–; memb: Prof Advsy Ctee Nat Schizophrenia Fellowship, Cncl Richmond Fellowship; FRCPsych, MRCP, MFPHM; *Books* Psychiatric Examination in Clinical Practice (1978), Expressed Emotion in Families (1985), Psychiatry Around the Globe (1988), Family Work for Schizophrenia (1992), Principles of Social Psychiatry (1993); *Recreations* squash, swimming, croquet, chess, piano; *Clubs* The 52; *Style*— Prof Julian Leff; ✉ Institute of Psychiatry, De Crespigny Park, London SE5 8AF (☎ and fax 0171 708 3235)

LEGARD, Christopher John Charles; s and h of Sir Charles Thomas Legard, 15 Bt, and his 1 w, Elizabeth (who m 2, 1988, Patrick M L Hibbert-Foy), da of John M Guthrie; *b* 19 April 1964; *Educ* Eton; *m* 1986, Miranda M, da of Maj Fane Travers Gaffney, of

Crossbank Hill, Hurworth, Co Durham; 1 s (Benjamin Fane John b 12 May 1995); *Career* chartered accountant; *Style*— Christopher Legard, Esq; ✉ Grizzlefield House, Felixkirk Road, Thirsk, North Yorkshire YO7 2ED

LEGARD, Jonathan Antony; s of Peter Herbert Legard, of Chester, and Brenda Valerie, *née* Kidd; *b* 17 July 1961; *Educ* Shrewsbury, Univ of Leeds (BA), Peterhouse Cambridge (Postgrad Cert in Educn); *Career* Cambridge Tutors Hong Kong 1984–85, Viper TV Chester 1986, BBC Radio Merseyside 1986–90 (reporter rising to prodr and presenter), BBC Radio Sport 1990–, reporter, football commentator and sports news correspondent Radio 5 Live; *Recreations* golf, cricket, Chester City FC; *Clubs* Delamere Forest Golf; *Style*— Jonathan Legard, Esq; ✉ BBC Radio Sport, Broadcasting House, London W1A 1AA (☎ 0171 765 5050)

LEGG, Barry Charles; MP (C) Milton Keynes SW (majority 4,687); s of Henry Wellman Legg, of Hucclecote, Glos, and Elfreda, *née* Thorp; *b* 30 May 1949; *Educ* Sir Thomas Rich's GS Gloucester, Univ of Manchester; *m* 16 March 1974, Margaret Rose, da of Roy Stewartson, of Roath Park, Cardiff; 1 s (George Alexander b 27 Nov 1987), 2 da (Victoria Rose b 21 Jan 1981, Elizabeth Fiona b 12 Sept 1984); *Career* CA, Courtaulds Ltd 1971–76, Coopers & Lybrand 1976–78, exec dir Hillsdown Holdings plc 1978–92; Parly candidate (C) Bishop Auckland 1983, MP (C) Milton Keynes SW 1992–, memb Treasy and Civil Serv Select Ctee 1992–; FCCA 1975, ATII 1976; *Recreations* cricket; *Clubs* Glos Co Cricket, Glos Exiles; *Style*— Barry Legg, Esq, MP; ✉ House of Commons, London SW1A 0AA (☎ 0171 219 3000)

LEGG, Prof Brian James; s of Walter Legg, of Sheffield, and Mary, *née* Bunting; *b* 20 July 1945; *Educ* Wellingborough GS, Balliol Coll Oxford (BA), Imperial Coll London (PhD); *m* 1972, Philippa, da of John Kenneth Whitehead; 1 s, 1 da; *Career* voluntary work The Gambia VSO 1966–67, res scientist Rothamsted Experimental Station 1967–83; Silsoe Research Inst: head Res Div 1983–90, dir 1990–; visiting scientist Environmental Mechanics Div CSIRO 1980–82, visiting prof Silsoe Coll Univ of Cranfield 1990–, contrib to numerous jls; FEng 1994, CPhys, FInstP, FIAgrE; *Recreations* sailing, skiing, music; *Style*— Prof Brian Legg, FEng; ✉ Silsoe Research Institute, Wrest Park, Silsoe, Bedford MK45 4HS (☎ 01525 860000, fax 01525 860156)

LEGG, (Cyrus) Julian Edmund; s of Cyrus Daniel Jasper Edmund Legg, of Pevensey Bay, E Sussex, and Eileen Doris, *née* Hopkins; *b* 5 Sept 1946; *Educ* Tiffin Sch Kingston-on-Thames; *m* 21 Jan 1967, Maureen Jean, da of James Grahame Lodge (d 1966); 2 s (Cyrus James Grahame b 1968, Julian Clive Edmund b 1969); *Career* Civil Serv Dept 1970–74, ARC 1974–83 (and 1966–70), HM Treasy 1983–87, museum sec The Natural History Museum 1987–; *Recreations* sailing, gardening; *Style*— Julian Legg, Esq; ✉ Museum Secretary, The Natural History Museum, Cromwell Rd, London SW7 5BD (☎ 0171 938 8733, fax 0171 938 9139)

LEGG, Dr Nigel John; s of John Burrow Legg, MBE (d 1957), of Harrow, and Constance Violet, *née* Boatwright (d 1984); *b* 5 Feb 1936; *Educ* Univ Coll Sch, St Mary's Med Sch Univ of London (MB BS); *m* 10 Sept 1960, Margaret Lilian, da of Frank Donald Charles (d 1958), of Harrow; 1 s (Benedick b 1967), 2 da (Kina b 1964, Fiona b 1962); *Career* conslt neurologist Hammersmith Hosp and Royal Masonic Hosp, sr lectr in neurology Royal Postgrad Med Sch and Inst of Neurology 1975–; author of pubns on Parkinson's disease, multiple sclerosis and other neurological diseases, specialises in migraine and medico-legal matters; dir Soc for the Relief of Widows and Orphans of Med Men; memb: Assoc Br Neurologists, Brain Res Assoc; Liveryman Worshipful Soc of Apothecaries, Freeman City of London 1981; *Books* Neurotransmitter Systems and their Clinical Disorders (ed, 1978); *Recreations* Dr Johnson, Bentleys, chamber music; *Clubs* Athenaeum, RSM; *Style*— Dr Nigel Legg; ✉ 12 Rosemont Rd, London NW3 6NE (☎ 0171 794 2630); 152 Harley St, London W1N 1DE (☎ 0171 935 8868, fax 0171 224 2574)

LEGG, Sir Thomas Stuart; KCB (1993, CB 1985), QC (1990); s of Francis Stuart Legg (d 1988), and Margaret Bonté Sheldon, *née* Amos; *b* 13 Aug 1935; *Educ* Horace-Mann Lincoln Sch NY, Frensham Heights Sch Surrey, St John's Coll Cambridge (MA, LLM); *m* 1, Aug 1961 (m dis 1983), Patricia Irene, da of late David Lincoln Dowie; 2 da (Lucy b 1969, Isobel b 1972); m 2, July 1983, Marie-Louise Clarke, da of late Humphrey Jennings; *Career* Royal Marines 1953–55; called to the Bar Inner Temple 1960, Master of Bench 1984; Lord Chllr's Dept: joined 1962, private sec to Lord Chllr 1965–68, asst slr 1975, under sec 1977–82, SE circuit admin 1980–82, dep sec 1982–89, dep clerk of crown 1986, sec cmmns 1988, perm sec to Lord Chllr and clerk of crown in Chancery 1989; chm Civil Service Benevolent Fund 1993–; memb: Bd Inst of Advanced Legal Studies 1989–, Cncl Brunel Univ 1993–, Chllr's Advsy Cncl Univ of Exeter 1995–; hon memb Soc of Professional Teachers of Law 1991–; *Clubs* Garrick; *Style*— Sir Thomas Legg, KCB, QC; ✉ Lord Chancellor's Dept, House of Lords, London SW1 (☎ 0171 219 3246)

LEGGAT, (John) Brian; s of James Leggat (d 1985), and Margaret Robertson Matthew, of Edinburgh; *b* 29 July 1948; *Educ* Edinburgh Acad, Univ of Edinburgh (LLB); *m* 29 April 1972, Iona Laird, da of Wallace Aitken; 1 s ((James) Douglas b 11 April 1982), 1 da (Joanna Rachel b 20 Nov 1983); *Career* apprentice Lindsay Duncan & Black WS 1969–71; Dundas & Wilson: asst slr 1971–73, ptnr 1973–, head of Commercial Property Dept 1984–94, chm 1994–96; memb: Law Soc of Scotland 1971, Soc of Writers to HM Signet 1972; *Recreations* rugby, golf, sailing, curling, horseriding, music; *Clubs* New (Edinburgh), Hon Co of Edinburgh Golfers, Golf House (Elie); *Style*— Brian Leggat, Esq; ✉ Dundas & Wilson, Saltire Court, 20 Castle Terrace, Edinburgh EH1 2EN (☎ 0131 228 8000, fax 0131 228 8888)

LEGGATT, Rt Hon Lord Justice; Rt Hon Sir Andrew Peter; kt (1982), PC (1990); s of Capt W R C (Peter) Leggatt, DSO, RN (d 1983), of Odiham, Hants, and (Dorothea) Joy, *née* Dreyer (d 1992); *b* 8 Nov 1930; *Educ* Eton, King's Coll Cambridge (MA); *m* 17 July 1953, Gillian Barbara (Jill), da of Cdr C P Newton, RN (d 1970), of Petersfield, Hants; 1 s (George b 1957), 1 da (Alice (Mrs Alistair McLuskie) b 1960); *Career* served Rifle Bde 1949–50 and TA 1950–59; called to the Bar Inner Temple 1954, QC 1972, recorder of the Crown Court 1974–82, bencher 1976, judge of the High Court of Justice (Queen's Bench Div) 1982–90; a Lord Justice of Appeal 1990–; memb: Bar Cncl 1971–82 (chm 1981–82), Top Salaries Review Body 1979–82; pres Cncl of the Inns of Ct 1995–; hon fell American Coll of Trial Lawyers 1996; *Recreations* listening to music, personal computers; *Clubs* MCC; *Style*— The Rt Hon Lord Justice Leggatt; ✉ Royal Courts of Justice, Strand, London WC2A 2LL (☎ 0171 936 6635, fax 0171 936 7637)

LEGGATT, Sir Hugh Frank John; kt (1988); s of Henry Alan Leggatt (d 1951), of London, and Beatrice Grace, *née* Burton (d 1934); *b* 27 Feb 1925; *Educ* Eton, New College Oxford; *m* 1, 1953 (m dis 1990), Jennifer, da of Paul Hepworth (d 1964); 2 s (Charles b 1954, Martin b 1955); m 2, 2 Jan 1991, Gaynor, yr da of William Leonard Tregoning, CBE, of Landue, Cornwall, and D M E Tregoning; *Career* Leggatt Bros: joined 1946, ptnr 1952, sr ptnr 1962–92; pres Fine Art Provident Inst 1960–63, chm Soc of London Art Dealers 1966–70, memb Museums & Galleries Cmmn 1983–92; hon sec Heritage in Danger 1974; *Recreations* the Arts; *Style*— Sir Hugh Leggatt; ✉ Rue du Lac 21, CH-1800 Vevey, Switzerland (☎ and fax 00 41 21 923 6810)

LEGGE, (John) Michael; CMG (1994); s of late Dr Alfred John Legge, of Guildford, Surrey, and Marion Frances, *née* James; *b* 14 March 1944; *Educ* Royal GS Guildford, ChCh Oxford (BA, MA); *m* 24 July 1971, Linda, da of John Wallace Bagley, of Haywards Heath, Sussex; 2 s (Christopher b 18 March 1975, Richard b 12 Nov 1978); *Career* MOD 1966–: asst private sec to Def Sec 1970, princ 1971, first sec UK Delgn to NATO 1974, asst sec 1978; Rand Corpn Santa Monica California 1982, asst under sec of state for policy 1987, asst sec-gen for def planning and policy NATO 1988–93; dep under sec of state: NI Office 1993–96, MOD 1996–; *Books* Theatre Nuclear Weapons and the Nato Strategy of Flexible Response (1983); *Recreations* golf, gardening; *Style*— Michael Legge, Esq, CMG; ✉ Deputy Under Secretary, Ministry of Defence, Whitehall, London SW1A 2HB

LEGGE-BOURKE, Hon Mrs (Elizabeth Shân Josephine); *née* Bailey; LVO; o child of 3 Baron Glanusk, DSO (d 1948), and Margaret (who later m 1 Viscount De L'Isle); *b* 10 Sept 1943; *m* 2 June 1964, William Nigel Henry Legge-Bourke, *qv*; 1 s, 2 da; *Career* lady-in-waiting to HRH The Princess Royal 1978–; pres Welsh Cncl of Save the Children Fund; chief pres for Wales St John Ambulance Bde 1990–94, pres Royal Welsh Agricultural Soc 1997; memb Brecon Beacons Nat Park Authority 1989–; High Sheriff of Powys 1991–92; *Style*— The Hon Mrs Legge-Bourke, LVO; ✉ Penmyarth, Glanusk Park, Crickhowell, Powys NP8 1LP (☎ 01873 810230)

LEGGE-BOURKE, Victoria Lindsay; LVO (1986); da of Maj Sir Harry Legge-Bourke, KBE, DL, MP (d 1973), and Lady Legge-Bourke; *b* 12 Feb 1950; *Educ* Benenden, St Hilda's Coll Oxford; *Career* social attaché British Embassy Washington DC 1971–73, dir Junior Tourism Ltd 1974–81, lady-in-waiting to HRH The Princess Royal 1974–86, extra lady-in-waiting to HRH The Princess Royal 1986–; special asst American Embassy London 1983–89, Price Investments Kansas City Mo USA 1989–91, head of protocol American Embassy London 1991–94, exec dir Goldman Sachs International 1995–; memb Cncl The American Museum in Britain 1995–, govr English Speaking Union; *Recreations* cooking, crosswords, music, reading; *Clubs* The Pilgrims; *Style*— Miss Victoria Legge-Bourke, LVO; ✉ 21 Eccleston Square, London SW1V 1NS (☎ 0171 834 0978); Goldman Sachs International, Peterborough Court, 133 Fleet Street, London EC4A 2BB (☎ 0171 774 3360, fax 0171 774 3366)

LEGGE-BOURKE, William Nigel Henry; er s of Sir Harry Legge-Bourke, KBE, DL, MP (d 1973), and (Catherine) Jean, *née* Grant of Monymusk (*see* Lady Legge-Bourke); *b* 12 July 1939; *Educ* Eton, Magdalene Coll Cambridge (MA); *m* 2 June 1964, Hon (Elizabeth) Shân (Josephine) Bailey, LVO, da of 3 Baron Glanusk, DSO (d 1948) (*see* Hon Mrs Legge-Bourke); 1 s (Harry Russell b 1972), 2 da (Alexandra Shân b 1965, Zara Victoria b 1966, m 1985, Capt R Plunkett-Ernle-Erle-Drax); *Career* cmmnd Royal Horse Guards (The Blues) 1958, Capt and Adj, ret 1968; ptnr Grieveson, Grant & Co 1973–86; dir: Kleinwort Benson Securities Ltd 1986–, Kleinwort Benson Ltd 1993–; memb: Cncl and Bd Stock Exchange 1988–92 (chm Domestic Equities Rules Ctee 1991–), Representative Body of the Church in Wales, pres Welsh Scout Cncl 1992–; chm Fin Ctee The Scout Assoc 1985–93; FSA, MSI(Dip); *Recreations* country sports; *Clubs* White's; *Style*— William Legge-Bourke, Esq; ✉ Penmyarth, Glanusk Park, Crickhowell, Powys NP8 1LP (☎ 01873 810230); 8 Kensington Mansions, Trebovir Road, London SW5 9TF; Kleinwort Benson Ltd, 20 Fenchurch Street, London EC3P 2DB (☎ 0171 623 8000)

LEGGETT, Dr Jeremy Kendal; s of Dennis Leslie Kendal Leggett, and Audrey Pamela, *née* Holton; *b* 16 March 1954; *Educ* Hastings GS, Univ of Wales Aberystwyth (BSc), Univ of Oxford (DPhil); *m* 1971 (m dis 1976); 1 da (Jessie b 26 April 1972); m 2, 1990, Abigail Charlot Rebecca Munson; *Career* reader in stratigraphy Imperial Coll of Sci and Techol 1987–89 (lectr in geology Royal Sch of Mines 1978–87), dir of sci Greenpeace UK 1989–92, dir of sci for atmosphere and energy Greenpeace International 1992–; represented UK on Thematic Advsy Panel to Int Ocean Drilling Prog; author of over 50 research papers and numerous articles on environmental issues and policy: The Guardian, The Independent, The Times, The Sunday Times, The Observer, New Scientist, New Statesman; winner of: President's Prize of Geological Soc 1980, Lyell Fund of Geological Soc 1987; treas Save British Sci Soc 1985–86, dir Verification Technol Info Centre 1986–89; FGS 1975; *Books* Trench Fore-arc Geology (1982), Marine Clastic Sedimentology: Models and Case Histories (with G G Zuffa, 1988), Global Warming: the Greenpeace Report (1990), Operation Earth (1991); *Recreations* non-violent direct actions in defence of the natural environment; *Clubs* Oxford and Cambridge Golfing Soc; *Style*— Dr Jeremy Leggett

LEGGETT, Keith Arnold; s of Jack Eric Leggett, of Kirkham, Preston, Lancashire, and Marian Lois, *née* Perkins; *b* 18 March 1940; *Educ* Monkton Combe Sch Bath, Cloverley Hall Whitchurch; *m* 4 Sept 1964, Sonja Ruth, da of Marco Fortune Gareh; 3 s (Stephen b 1966, Oliver b 1968, Robert b 1972); *Career* estate agent, valuer, surveyor and auctioneer; princ N Routledge & Co Sale Cheshire 1964–87, residential sales dir Nationwide Estate Agents 1987–89, md Messenger Leisure Ltd 1993–95, Keith Leggett Consultancy 1995–; former chm: Sale and Dist Round Table, Manchester Branch of Inc Soc of Valuers and Auctioneers, North Cheshire and Sale 41 Club, Sale Festival of Sport and Drama; FSVA, FCIArb; *Recreations* golf, gardening; *Clubs* Hale Golf, N Cheshire 41; *Style*— Keith Leggett, Esq; ✉ Keith Leggett Consultancy, The Ridge, York Drive, Bowdon, Altrincham, Cheshire WA14 3HF (☎ 0161 941 2997, fax 0161 928 7683)

LEGGETTER, Barry H; *m* Patricia; 2 da (Laura, Suzanne); *Career* trainee journalist Home Counties Newspapers Luton 1961–64 (Journalist of the Year NCTJ Trg Scheme 1964); sr journalist: Blackpool Gazette 1964–65, The Sun 1965–68; ptnr Blackpool News Agency 1968–72, PR mangr (Hotels) and dep gp PRO (Edinburgh) Scottish & Newcastle Breweries 1972–74, PR mangr Taylor Woodrow 1974–76, account dir/dir Welbeck Public Relations London 1976–84, jt md Countrywide Communications (London) until 1994 (joined as dir/dep md 1984), md Fleishman-Hillard (UK) Ltd and exec vice pres and sr ptnr Fleishman-Hillard Inc 1994–; awards: HRH The Queen Mother's Award for the Environment, numerous indust awards for creativity incl Int PR Assoc Golden World Award (for Hoffman La Roche Prog); FIPR; *Recreations* travelling, watching sport, reading, popular music; *Style*— Barry H Leggetter, Esq; ✉ 2 Ross Way, Langdon Hills, Essex SS16 6LX (☎ 01268 542489); Fleishman-Hillard (UK) Ltd, 25 Wellington Street, Covent Garden, London WC2E 7DA (☎ 0171 306 9000, fax 0171 497 0096)

LEGH, Hon David Piers Carlis; yr s of 4 Baron Newton (d 1992); *b* 21 Nov 1951; *Educ* Eton, RAC Cirencester; *m* 1974, Jane Mary, da of John Roy Wynter Bee, of West End, Surrey; 2 s (Hugo Peter David b 1979, Thomas John Rowland b 1984), 2 da (Charlotte Mary b 1976, Katherine Anna b 1991); *Career* chartered surveyor; John German chartered surveyors: ptnr 1984–, managing ptnr 1991–95, sr ptnr 1995–; CLA: memb Cncl 1989–, chm Derbyshire Branch 1992–94, chm Taxation Ctee 1993–; Royal Agric Soc of England: memb Cncl, rep Derbyshire 1986–91, nominated memb 1991–94; FRICS, MRAC; *Clubs* Farmers'; *Style*— The Hon David Legh; ✉ Cubley Lodge, Ashbourne, Derbys DE6 2FB (☎ 01335 330297, fax 01335 330159); 1 Lichfield Street, Burton-on-Trent DE6 3QZ (☎ 01283 512244, fax 01283 517896)

LEGON, Prof Anthony Charles; s of George Charles Legon, and Emily Louisa Florence, *née* Conner (d 1993); *b* 28 Sept 1941; *Educ* Coopers' Company Sch, UCL (BSc, PhD, DSc); *m* 20 July 1963, Deirdre Anne, da of Edgar Albert Rivers (d 1944); 2 s (Anthony Daniel Charles b 14 Nov 1979, Edward James b 14 July 1989), 1 da (Victoria May b 11 March 1977); *Career* Turner and Newall fell Univ of London 1968–70, lectr in chemistry UCL 1970–83 (reader 1983–84), prof of physical chemistry Univ of Exeter 1984–89, Thomas Graham prof of chemistry UCL 1989–90, prof of physical chemistry Univ of Exeter 1990–; Tilden lectr and medallist Royal Soc of Chemistry 1989–90; in excess of 260 papers published; memb Physical Chemistry Sub-ctee Chemistry Ctee SERC 1984–87; FRSC 1977; *Recreations* cricket; *Style*— Prof Anthony Legon;

✉ Department of Chemistry, University of Exeter, Stocker Rd, Exeter EX4 4QD (☎ 01392 263488, fax 01392 263434, e-mail ACLegon@exeter.ac.uk)

LEGRAIN, Gérard Marie Francois; s of Jean Legrain (d 1985), and Marie Hélène, *née* Merica (d 1962); *b* 16 April 1937; *Educ* Ecole St Louis de Gonzague, Sorbonne, Faculté de Droit, Inst d' Etudes Politiques, Ecole Nationale d'Administration Paris; *m* 1969, Katrin Ines, da of Harald Tombach, of Altadena, California, USA; 2 s (Philippe b 1973, Pierre b 1980), 1 da (Milli b 1976); *Career* Sub Lt 27 and 15 Bataillons de Chasseurs Alpins 1962; Citibank: Paris 1965, NY 1967, Mexico City 1969; vice pres Citicorp International Bank Ltd London 1972–74; md Int Mexican Bank Ltd London 1974–93; dir: Foreign Banks & Securities Houses Assoc 1991–93, Govett High Income Investment Trust 1993, Govett Emerging Markets Investment Tst 1993; hon treas: The French Clinic 1992, The French Benevolent Soc 1992; *Recreations* skiing, swimming, tennis; *Clubs* Hurlingham; *Style*— Gérard Legrain, Esq; ✉ Hamilton House, 1 Temple Avenue, London EC4Y 0HA (☎ 0171 353 4212, fax 0171 353 3325)

LEHANE, Maureen Theresa (Mrs Peter Wishart); da of Christopher Lehane (d 1970), of London, and Honor, *née* Millar (d 1996); *Educ* Queen Elizabeth's Girls' GS Barnet, Guildhall Sch of Music and Drama; *m* 26 May 1966, Peter Wishart (d 1984); *Career* concert and opera singer; studied under: Hermann Weissenborn, John and Aida Dickens; debut Glyndebourne 1967; speciality Handel, numerous leading roles with Handel opera socs in: England, America, Poland, Sweden, Germany; numerous master classes on the interpretation of Handel's vocal music; title roles in: Handel's Ariodante Sadlers Wells 1974, Peter Wishart's Clytemnestra London 1974, Purcell's Dido and Aeneas Netherlands Opera 1976, castrato lead JC Bach's Adriano London 1982; female lead Hugo Cole's The Falcon Somerset 1983, Peter Wishart's The Lady of the Inn Reading Univ 1983; festival appearances incl: Stravinsky Festival Cologne, City of London, Aldeburgh, Cheltenham, Three Choirs, Bath, Oxford Bach, Göttingen Handel Festival; tours incl: N America, Australia, Far East, Middle East; visits incl: Holland, Belgium, Germany, Lisbon, Poland, Rome, Warsaw; recordings incl: Bach, Haydn, Mozart, Handel (Cyrus in first complete recording Belshazzar); TV appearances incl: BBC, ABC Australia, Belgian TV; regular appearances promenade concerts; memb Jury: Int Singing Comp Hertogenbosch Festival Holland 1982–, Llangollen Int Eisteddfod; fndr: Great Elm Music Festival, Jackdaws Educnl Tst; *Books* Songs of Purcell (co ed Peter Wishart); *Recreations* cooking, gardening, reading; *Style*— Miss Maureen Lehane; ✉ Bridge House, Great Elm, Frome, Somerset BA11 3NY

LEHMAN, Prof Meir M (Manny); s of Benno Lehman (d 1935), and Theresa, *née* Wallerstein (d 1988); *b* 24 Jan 1925; *Educ* Letchworth GS, Imperial Coll (BSc, ARCS, PhD, DIC, DSc); *m* 26 Aug 1953, Chava, da of Moses Robinson (d 1948); 3 s (Benjamin Moses, Jonathan David, Raphael Dan), 2 da (Machla Lea, Esther Dvora); *Career* apprentice Murphy Radio Ltd 1942–50, jr logic designer Ferranti Ltd 1956–57, head digital computers Sci Dept Israel Miny of Defense 1957–64, res staff memb and mangr Project IMP IBM Res Div 1964–72; Imperial Coll of Sci and Technol: prof of computing sci 1972–84, head of section 1972–79, head Dept of Computing 1979–84, emeritus prof Dept of Computing 1984–, sr res fell 1989–; fndr dir IST Ltd 1984–88 (chm 1982–84), fndr and md Lehman Software Technology Associates Ltd 1984–, dir Eureka ESF ICST Profect 1991–94, princ investigator Project FEAST 1996–; author of numerous papers; FEng 1989, FIEE, FBCS, FIEEE, FACM; *Books* Program Evolution - Processes of Software Change (1985); *Recreations* Talmudic studies, DIY, fund raising for charity; *Style*— Prof Manny Lehman, FEng; ✉ Department of Computing, Imperial College of Science, Technology & Medicine, 180 Queen's Gate, London SW7 2BZ (☎ 0171 594 8214, fax 0171 594 8215)

LEICESTER, Archdeacon of; *see:* Edson, Ven Michael

LEICESTER, 7 Earl of (UK 1837); Edward Douglas Coke; also Viscount Coke (UK 1837); s of 6 Earl of Leicester (d 1994), and his 1 w, Moyra, *née* Crossley (d 1987); *b* 6 May 1936; *Educ* St Andrew's Coll Grahamstown S Africa; *m* 1, 28 April 1962 (m dis 1985), Valeria Phyllis, eld da of Leonard A Potter, of Berkhamsted, Herts; 2 s (Viscount Coke, Hon Rupert Henry John b 1975), 1 da (Lady Laura-Jane Elizabeth b 1968); m 2, 1986, Mrs Sarah de Chair, da of Noel Henry Boys Forde, of Wells-next-the-Sea, Norfolk, and formerly wife of Colin Graham Ramsey de Chair; *Heir* s, Thomas Edward, Viscount Coke, *qv* b 6 July 1965; *Style*— The Rt Hon the Earl of Leicester; ✉ Holkham Hall, Wells, Norfolk NR23 1AB (☎ 01328 710227)

LEIFERKUS, Sergei; *b* 4 April 1946; *Career* baritone; appeared at many international venues incl: Royal Opera House Covent Garden, Opera Bastille and Theatre Musical Paris, San Francisco Opera, Metropolitan Opera NY, Chicago Lyric Opera, Dallas Opera, Opera de Montreal, Liceu Barcelona, La Scala Milan, Royal Danish Opera Copenhagen, Netherlands Opera Amsterdam, Cologne Opera, Berlin State Opera, Vienna Staatsoper, Bolshoi Theatre Moscow, Mariinsky Theatre St Petersburg, Teatro Colon Buenos Aires, Concertgebouw Amsterdam, Salzburg Easter Festival, Glyndebourne Festival, Bregenz Festival, Edinburgh Festival, Wexford Festival; performed with numerous major orchs incl: London Symphony, Royal Philharmonic, BBC Symphony Orch, Berlin Philharmonic, Boston Symphony, New York Philharmonic, Philadelphia Orch, San Francisco Symphony, Royal Concertgebouw Orch, Montreal Symphony Orch, Chamber Orch of Europe, Bavarian Radio Symphony Orch; worked with leading conductors incl: Claudio Abbado, Riccardo Chailly, Sir Colin Davis, Bernard Haitink, Nikolaus Harnoncourt, James Levine, Kurt Masur, Zubin Mehta, Riccardo Muti, Seiji Ozawa, Mstislav Rostropovich, Gennadi Rozhdestvensky, Sir Georg Solti; operatic roles incl: Pizarro in Fidelio, Mephistopheles in La Damnation de Faust, Escamillo in Carmen, Zurga in The Pearl Fishers, title role in Prince Igor, Iago in Otello, Enrico in Lucia di Lammermoor, Gerard in Andrea Chenier, Scarpia in Tosca, title role in Eugene Onegin, Nabucco and Don Giovanni, Albert in Werther, Count Almaviva in The Marriage of Figaro, Rangoni in Boris Godunov, Prince Andrei Bolkonsky in War and Peace, Ruprecht in The Fiery Angel, Marcello in La Bohème, Sharpless in Madama Butterfly, Veglasnyi in Mlada, Gryaznoi in The Tsar's Bride, title role in Aleko, Figaro in The Barber of Seville, title role in Mazeppa, Tomsky and Eletsky in The Queen of Spades, Robert and Ibn Hakir in Iolanta, Amonasro in Aida, Renato in Un Ballo in Maschera, Rodrigo in Don Carlos, Don Carlo in La Forza del Destino, title role in Macbeth, Giacomo in Giovanna d'Arco, Iago in Otello, Giorgio Germont in La Traviata, Conte di Luna in Il Trovatore, Telramund in Lohengrin; concert repertoire incl: Bach St Matthew Passion and various cantatas, Beethoven 9th Symphony, Mahler 8th Symphony and Lieder eines fahrenden Gesellen, Mozart Requiem, Brahms Requiem, Mussorgsky Song and Dances of Death, Orff Carmina Burana, Prokofiev Ivan the Terrible, Rachmaninov The Bells and Spring Cantata, Puccini Messa di Gloria, Shostakovich 13th and 14th Symphonies; numerous recitals incl: Royal Opera House Covent Garden, Wigmore Hall, Queen Elizabeth Hall, Purcell Room and St John's Smith Square London, Minterne Abbey Dorset, Theatre Royal Glasgow, Theatre Royal Wexford, Musikverein Vienna, Philharmonie Cologne, Frick Collection and Alice Tully Hall NY, William Jewell Coll Kansas, Sunset Center Carmel, Radio France Paris, Concertgebouw Amsterdam, Hessischer Rundfunk Frankfurt; recordings: various for BMG/RCA, Decca, Philips, Sony, Deutsche Grammophon, Chandos and Teldec, currently recording complete songs of Mussorgsky and Tchaikovsky for BMG/Conifer; *Style*— Sergei Leiferkus, Esq; ✉ c/o Allied Artists Agency, 42 Montpelier Square, London SW7 1JZ (☎ 0171 589 6243, fax 0171 581 5269)

LEIGH, Andrew; s of Walter Leigh (ka 1942), of London, and Marion, *née* Blandford; *b* 17 Feb 1941; *Educ* Bryanston, Christ's Coll Cambridge (MA, Henley Ladies' Plate 1960); *m* 1966, Margaret Anne, da of Robert Lyons; 2 s (Jacob b 1967, Benjamin b 1970), 1 da (Rebecca b 1969); *Career* mangr Palace Theatre Morecambe 1963, gen mangr Citizens' Theatre Glasgow 1965–68 (house mangr 1963–65), prodr Arturo Ui (Edinburgh Festival) and A Day in the Death of Joe Egg (WE and Euro tour) 1968–69, admin The Traverse Theatre Edinburgh 1969–70, gen mangr The Duke's Playhouse Lancaster 1970–73, admin dir The Haymarket and Phoenix Theatres Leciester 1973–79, dir and gen mangr The Old Vic 1979–, exec prodr Into The Woods (Phoenix) 1990–91; dir: Paines Plough Theatre Co, Edinburgh Festival Fringe, Theater Impresariaat Internationaal BV; memb Arts Cncl Drama Panel and Touring Ctees until 1981, co-ordinator Theatre Def Fund 1982–, pres Theatrical Mgmnt Assoc 1985–91, vice chm Theatres' Nat Ctee 1991–; *Books* The Future of the Old Vic (1982), See the Actors Well Bestowed (Hong Kong, 1982); 6 theatre feasibility studies 1977–92; *Recreations* books, photography, food, travel; *Clubs* Garrick; *Style*— Andrew Leigh, Esq; ✉ The Old Vic, Waterloo Road, London SE1 8NB (☎ 0171 928 2651, fax 0171 261 9161)

LEIGH, Bernard Malcolm; s of Lionel Leigh, of London, and Cecilia, *née* Ruderman; *b* 7 Feb 1950; *Educ* William Ellis GS, London Hosp Dental Inst Univ of London (BDS), Eastman Hosp Inst of Dental Surgery; *m* 25 Nov 1973, Yvonne Pamela, da of Leslie Wolfe; 4 s (Daniel b 6 Nov 1976, Jeremy b 24 March 1979, Joshua b 25 July 1984, Avram b 27 July 1989), 2 da (Sara b 20 Nov 1974, Talia b 18 Oct 1980); *Career* house offr London Hosp 1973; practised: City of London 1974–75, Hemel Hempstead 1976–82, London NW11 1976–84, Harley St 1982–; hon clinical asst Dept of Cons Dentistry Inst of Dental Surgery Eastman Dental Hosp 1979–; memb: Alpha Omega (Ctee 1984–88), Br Endodontic Soc (Ctee 1981–82), Gen Dental Practitioners' Assoc, Br Dental Assoc; *Recreations* music, computers, photography, writing; *Style*— Bernard Leigh, Esq; ✉ 137 Harley St, London W1N 1DJ (☎ 0171 935 3394, 0171 935 0187 and 0171 487 4369)

LEIGH, Hon Christopher Dudley Piers; er s (but only one by 1 w) and h of 5 Baron Leigh; *b* 20 Oct 1960; *Educ* Eton, RAC Cirencester; *m* 15 Aug 1990, Sophy-Ann, da of Richard Burrows, MBE, of The Old Hall, Groby, Leics; 1 s (Rupert Dudley b 21 Feb 1994), 1 da (Lucy Alexandra b 2 Nov 1995); *Career* memb: British Field Sports Soc, Royal Agric Soc of England; *Recreations* racing, tennis; *Clubs* Turf; *Style*— The Hon Christopher Leigh; ✉ Fern Farm, Adlestrop, Moreton-in-Marsh, Gloucs GL56 OYL (☎ 01608 658203, fax 01608 658323)

LEIGH, Christopher Humphrey de Verd; QC (1989); s of Wing Cdr Humphrey de Verd Leigh, OBE, DFC, AFC (d 1981), and Johanna Emily, *née* Whitfield Hayes; *b* 12 July 1943; *Educ* Harrow; *m* 18 July 1970, Frances Raymonde, da of Col Raymond Henry Albert Powell, OBE, MC; *Career* called to the Bar Lincoln's Inn 1967, recorder of the Crown Ct 1985; *Recreations* travel; *Style*— Christopher Leigh, Esq, QC; ✉ 1 Paper Buildings, Temple, London EC4Y 7EP (☎ 0171 353 3728)

LEIGH, David Irvine; s of Frederick Leigh (d 1980), of Glasgow, and Mary, *née* David; *b* 16 April 1944; *Educ* Glasgow Sch of Art, Edinburgh Coll of Art Heriot-Watt Univ (DA); *m* 30 Aug 1975, Lynda, da of Frank Thomas Taylor (d 1970), of Hawkhurst, Kent; 1 s (Elliot b 1983), 1 da (Claire Francesca b 1971); *Career* architect; ptnr R J Wood Chapman and Hanson 1974, chm and md Chapman and Hanson 1989–91 (dir 1981–91), chm and md Leigh Blundell Thompson chartered architects and interior designers 1991–94, princ architect E Sussex County Cncl 1995– (sr architect 1994–95); designed HQ bldgs for: Charrington & Co London 1978, R S Components Corby 1984, Electrocomponents Knightsbridge 1987, W M Lighting Northampton 1989; chm Fairlight Tennis Club; RIBA 1969; *Recreations* tennis, swimming, petanque, computing; *Clubs* Inigo Jones; *Style*— David Leigh, Esq; ✉ East Sussex County Council, County Hall, St Anne's Crescent, Lewes, E Sussex BN7 1SG (☎ 01273 841000, fax 01273 423929)

LEIGH, Edward Julian Egerton; MP (C) Gainsborough and Horncastle (majority 16,245); s of Sir Neville Egerton Leigh, KCVO (d 1994), and Denise Yvonne, *née* Branch; *b* 20 July 1950; *Educ* The Oratory, Lycée Francais de Londres, Univ of Durham; *m* 25 Sept 1984, Mary, eldest da of Philip Henry Russell Goodman, of London, and Sophie (Sonia), o da of late Count Vladimir Petrovitch Kleinmichel, CVO; 2 s, 3 da; *Career* barr; memb Inner Temple; former: pres Durham Union Soc, chm Durham Univ Cons Assoc; Parly candidate (C) Middlesbrough 1974, MP (C) Gainsborough and Horncastle 1983–; hon dir Coalition for Peace through Security, chm Nat Cncl for Civil Defence 1980–83, memb House of Commons Select Ctee for Defence 1983–87, vice chm and sec for Backbench Ctees on Agric Employment and Defence 1983–90, Parly private sec to Min of State Home Office 1990–92, under sec of state for Industry and Consumer Affairs DTI 1990–93, memb House of Commons Agric and Social Security Select Ctees; memb: Richmond Borough Cncl 1977–81, GLC 1977–81; Knight of Honour and Devotion SMO Malta 1994–; *Publications* Right Thinking (1976); *Style*— Edward Leigh, Esq, MP; ✉ House of Commons, London SW1A 0AA

LEIGH, Elisabeth Sarah; da of Joshua Levi (d 1955), and Miriam Leigh (d 1980); *b* 14 July 1939; *Educ* Cambs HS for Girls, N London Collegiate Sch, Somerville Coll Oxford (BA), Piccolo Teatro Sch of Mime Milan, Central Sch of Speech & Drama; *m* 1, 1963 (m dis 1966), Michael David Kustow; m 2, 1976 (m dis 1989), Barry George Reynolds; *Career* researcher then dir-prodr Educn, Music and Light Entertainment Depts BBC TV 1963–68, documentary dir (under Tony Essex) Yorkshire Television 1969, freelance film and radio prodr/dir (work incl This Week (Thames TV), Yorks TV documentaries, Capital Radio series etc) 1969–81, food writer Sunday Times 1984–91; articles for Elle, Epicure, Taste, Healthy Living and others; film awards: BISFA Award for Call for Help, British Assoc for the Advancement of Science award for Experiment in Time (Yorks TV); Argos Award for Consumer Journalism 1987; memb Soc of Authors; *Books* The Sunday Times Guide to Enlightened Eating (1986), Greed (novel, 1991), Envy (1993), The Perfect Marriage (1996); *Recreations* cooking for friends, making music; *Style*— Ms Elisabeth Leigh; ✉ David Higham Associates, 5–8 Lower John Street, London W1R 4HA (☎ 0171 437 7888, fax 0171 437 1072)

LEIGH, Sir Geoffrey Norman; kt (1990); s of Morris Leigh, and late Rose Leigh; *b* 23 March 1933; *Educ* Haberdashers' Aske's Hampstead Sch, Univ of Michigan; *m* 1, 1955 (m dis 1975), Valerie Lennard (d 1976); 1 s, 2 da; m 2, 1976, Sylvia Pell; 1 s, 1 da; *Career* chm: Sterling Homes 1980– (md 1965), Allied London Properties 1987– (md 1970–87); fndr and first pres Westminster Jr C of C 1959–63; underwriting memb Lloyd's 1973–; special advsr for the New Towns 1994–; memb: Ctee Good Design in Housing 1978–79, Br ORT Cncl 1979–80, Int Advsy Bd American Univ Washington 1983–, Advsy Cncl Prince's Youth Business Tst 1985–, Main Fin Bd NSPCC 1985–, Appeal Ctee Royal Veterinary Coll 1985–88, London Historic House Museums Tst 1987–, Governing Cncl Business in the Community 1987–, Somerville Coll Appeal 1987–, Art and Architecture Educn Tst Royal Fine Art Cmmn 1988–, Per Cent Club 1988–, Cncl City Technol Colls Tst, City Appeal Ctee Royal Marsden Hosp 1990–, Review Body on Doctors' and Dentists' Remuneration 1990–93, Chllr's Ct of Benefactors Univ of Oxford 1991–, Wellbeing Cncl 1994–, Emmanuel Coll Cambridge Devpt Campaign 1994–; Fulbright Cmmn: cmmr and tstee 1991–, chm Int Advsy Bd 1995–; sponsor The Leigh City Technology Coll Dartford (chm Bd of Govrs 1988–), fndr/sponsor Friends of Br Library 1987–, fndr Margaret Thatcher Centre Somerville Coll Oxford 1991; treas: Cwlth Jewish Cncl 1983–89, Cwlth Jewish Tst 1983–89; treas and tstee Action on Addiction 1991–; tstee: Margaret Thatcher Fndn 1991–, Philharmonia 1992–, Industry in Educn 1993–; patron Hampstead and Highgate Cons Assoc 1991–, a treas Cons Pty 1995–; govr Royal

Sch Hampstead 1991–, chm St Mary's Hosp 150th Anniversary Appeal 1995–; hon memb Emmanuel Coll Cambridge 1994, hon cncl memb NSPCC 1995–; Presidential Citation The American Univ 1987; Freeman City of London 1976, Liveryman Worshipful Co of Furniture Makers (memb Ct of Assts 1992); FRSA; *Recreations* photography, reading, golf; *Clubs* Carlton, United and Cecil, Pilgrims, Royal Automobile, Savile; *Style—* Sir Geoffrey Leigh; ✉ Allied London Properties, 26 Manchester Square, London W1A 2HU (☎ 0171 486 6080, fax 0171 486 5428)

LEIGH, Guy Ian Frederick; s of Arthur Benjamin Leigh, and Amelia, *née* Berger; b 22 Nov 1944; *Educ* Univ of Pennsylvania (BA), Law Sch Univ of Pennsylvania (JD), Trinity Hall Cambridge (DipIntLaw); *m* 9 Aug 1968, Mary Eleanor, da of Maj Ralph Siggins Merkle, of Emporium, Pennsylvania; 1 s (Alexander b 2 May 1976), 1 da (Sarah b 5 May 1980); *Career* admitted slr 1974; articled to Clifford Turner 1972–74; Theodore Goddard: joined 1974, ptnr 1978–, ptnr responsible for competition/anti-trust and regulatory practice Mgmnt Ctee 1988–90; memb Jt Competition Working Pty of the Bars and Law Socs of UK, former int and gen rapporteur Int League of Competition Law; memb: Ctee Competition Law Assoc, Law Soc of England and Wales, European Competition Lawyers Forum, Ctee of Mgmnt Inst of Neurology; *Books* The EEC and Intellectual Property (with Diana Guy, 1981), various articles on EEC competition law; *Recreations* languages (German, Italian, Spanish and French), boating, travel, photography; *Style—* Guy I F Leigh, Esq; ✉ Theodore Goddard, 150 Aldersgate Street, London EC1A 4EJ (☎ 0171 606 8855, fax 0171 606 4390, telex 884678)

LEIGH, Prof Irene May; da of Archibald Allen, of Liverpool, and May Lilian, *née* Whalley; *b* 25 April 1947; *Educ* Merchant Taylors', London Hosp Med Coll (BSc, MB BS); *m* 21 June 1969, Prof (Peter) Nigel Leigh, s of Dr (Archibald) Denis Leigh, of Otford, Kent; 1 s (Piers Daniel b 24 June 1973), 3 da (Andrea Yseult b 11 Oct 1975, Miranda Chloe b 17 June 1982, Rosalino Clio b 12 Jan 1988); *Career* conslt dermatologist London Hosp 1983, hon dir ICRF Skin Tumour Unit 1986, prof of dermatology Royal London Med Coll 1992– (sr lectr 1987–92); FRCP 1989; *Books* Coping with Skin Diseases (1984); *Style—* Prof Irene Leigh; ✉ Department of Dermatology, Royal Hospitals NHS Trust, Whitechapel, London E1 1BB (☎ 0171 377 7000, fax 0171 377 7677)

LEIGH, 5 Baron (UK 1839); John Piers Leigh; s of 4 Baron Leigh (d 1979), and Anne, da of Ellis Hicks Beach (nephew of 1 Earl St Aldwyn); *b* 11 Sept 1935; *Educ* Eton, Oriel Coll Oxford, Univ of London; *m* 1, 1957 (m dis 1974), Cecilia Poppy, da of late Robert Cecil Jackson; 1 s (Hon Christopher, *qv* b 1960), 1 da (Hon Camilla b 1962) (and 1 da decd); m 2, 1976 (m dis 1982), Susan, da of John Cleave, of Whitnash, Leamington Spa; 1 s (Hon Piers b 1979); m 3, 1982, Lea, o da of Col Harry Noel Havelock Wild; *Heir* s, Hon Christopher Dudley Piers Leigh; *Style—* The Rt Hon the Lord Leigh; ✉ House of Lords, Westminster, London SW1A 0PW

LEIGH, John Roland; s of Adam Dale Leigh (d 1978), and Cecilia Winifred Leigh (d 1991); *b* 11 March 1933; *Educ* Winchester, King's Coll Cambridge; *m* 1957, Rosemary Renée, da of late Capt Gordon Furze, MC; 1 s, 3 da; *Career* merchant banker; ptnr Rathbone Bros & Co 1963–88; dir: Greenbank Trust Ltd 1969–81, Albany Investment Trust plc 1979–95, Rathbone Brothers plc 1988–93; chm Blackburn Diocesan Bd of Fin Ltd 1976–; memb: Gen Synod 1995–, Central Bd of Fin Church of England 1995–; ATII; *Clubs* Flyfishers', Athenaeum (Liverpool); *Style—* John Leigh, Esq; ✉ Robin Hood Cottage, Blue Stone Lane, Mawdesley, Ormskirk, Lancs L40 2RG (☎ 01704 822641, fax 01704 822691)

LEIGH, Jonathan; s of Robert Montague Leigh, and Isabel Alexdrina, *née* Villiers; *b* 17 June 1952; *Educ* St George's Sch Windsor (choirister), Eton, Corpus Christi Coll Cambridge (choral exhbn, MA, cert of educn); *m* Emma Mary, da of Rear Adm Michael Kyrle Pope, CB, MBE, DL, *qv*; 1 da (Isabel b 13 Jan 1985), 1 s (Charles b 4 May 1986); *Career* Cranleigh Sch: asst master 1976–83, housemaster 2+3 South House 1983–88, head of history 1988, second master 1988–92; headmaster Blundell's Sch 1992–; memb Ctee ISIS South West 1995; govr St Petroc's Sch Bude 1992–; chm Advsy Cncl Devon Social Service Dept 1994; memb: Admiralty Interview Bd 1993, Interviewing Panel ESU 1996; tstee Inner Cities Young Peoples Project 1996; FRSA 1994; *Recreations* singing, racing, 19th c Africa, painting, labradors; *Clubs* East India; *Style—* Jonathan Leigh, Esq; ✉ Blundell House, Blundell's Avenue, Tiverton, Devon EX16 4DN; Blundell's School, Tiverton, Devon EX16 4DN (☎ 01884 252543, fax 01884 243232)

LEIGH, Prof Leonard Herschel; s of Leonard William Leigh (d 1976), of Edmonton, Canada, and Lillian Mavis, *née* Hayman (d 1965); *b* 19 Sept 1935; *Educ* Strathcona HS Edmonton Canada, Univ of Alberta (BA, LLB), Univ of London (PhD); *m* 17 Dec 1960, Jill Diane, da of George Gale (d 1986); 1 s (Matthew b 1967), 1 da (Alison Jane b 1965); *Career* cmmnd Royal Canadian Artillery 1955, transferred King's Own Calgary Regt 1959–62; called to the Bar: Alberta 1958, NW Territories 1960, Inner Temple 1993; in private practice Alberta 1958–60, advsy counsel Dept of Justice Canada 1960–62, in private practice England and Wales 1994–; LSE: asst lectr 1964–65, lectr in law 1965–71, reader 1971–82, prof of criminal law 1982–, convenor Law Dept 1987–91; visiting prof Queen's Univ Kingston Ontario 1973–74; memb Ed Ctee European Jl of Crime and Criminal Justice 1992–; UK corr: La Revue de Science Criminelle (Paris), La Revue de Droit Penal et de Criminologie (Belgium), La Revue de Droit Africaine (Cameroun), La Revue Trimestrielle des Droits de l'Homme (Belgium); UK chm: Int Assoc of Penal Law 1986–, Université de l'Europe 1986–90; memb Cncl Int Penal and Penitentiary Fndn 1994–; pt/t conslt to govts of Canada, Quebec and Alberta; *Books* The Criminal Liability of Corporations in English Law (1969), Northey & Leigh, Introduction to Company Law (4 edn 1987), Police Powers in England and Wales (2 edn 1985), Strict and Vicarious Liability (1982), Leigh and Edey, Companies Act 1981 (1982), A Guide to the Financial Services Act 1986 (jtly 1986), Blackstone's Criminal Practice 1991– (contrib, 1996); *Recreations* music, walking; *Style—* Prof Leonard Leigh; ✉ 30 Eccles Road, London SW11 1LZ (☎ 0272 978 5529); Law Department, London School of Economics and Political Science, Houghton St, Aldwych, London WC2 2AE (☎ 0171 955 7254); chambers: 2 Pump Court, Temple, London EC4Y 7AH (☎ 0171 353 5597)

LEIGH, Mike; OBE (1993); s of Alfred Abraham Leigh (d 1985), and Phyllis Pauline, *née* Cousin; *b* 20 Feb 1943; *Educ* Salford GS, RADA, Camberwell Sch of Arts and Crafts, Central Sch of Art and Design (Theatre Design Dept), London Film Sch; *m* 15 Aug 1973, Alison Steadman, the actress, da of George Percival Steadman; 2 s (Toby b 1978, Leo b 1981); *Career* dramatist, theatre/television and film director; assoc dir Midlands Arts Centre for Young People 1965–66, asst dir RSC 1967–68, lectr in drama Sedgley Park and De La Salle Colls Manchester 1968–69, lectr London Film Sch 1970–73; memb: Drama Panel Arts Cncl GB 1975–77, Dir's Working Pty and Specialist Allocations Bd 1976–84, Accreditation Panel Nat Cncl for Drama Trg 1978–91, Gen Advsy Cncl IBA 1980–82; Hon MA Univ of Salford 1991; writer-dir: Nat Film Theatre Retrospectives 1979 and 1993, BBC TV Retrospective (incl Arena: Mike Leigh Making Plays) 1982, various US retrospectives incl Museum of Modern Art NY 1992; writer-dir stage plays: The Box Play, My Parents Have Gone To Carlisle, The Last Crusade of the Five Little Nuns (Midlands Arts Centre) 1965–66, Nenaa (RSC Studio Stratford-upon-Avon) 1967, Individual Fruit Pies (E15 Acting Sch) 1968, Down Here And Up There (Royal Ct Theatre Upstairs) 1968, Big Basil 1968, Glum Victoria And The Lad With Specs (Manchester Youth Theatre) 1969, Epilogue (Manchester) 1969, Bleak Moments (Open Space) 1970, A Rancid Pong (Basement) 1971, Wholesome Glory, Dick Whittington and his Cat (Royal Ct Theatre Upstairs) 1973, The Jaws of Death (Traverse, Edinburgh Festival) 1973, Babies Grow Old (Other Place) 1974 (ICA) 1975, The Silent Majority (Bush) 1974, Abigail's Party (Hampstead) 1977, Ecstasy (Hampstead) 1979, Goose-Pimples (Hampstead, Garrick) 1981 (Standard Best Comedy Award), Smelling a Rat (Hampstead) 1988, Greek Tragedy (Belvoir St Theatre Sydney 1989, Edinburgh Festival and Theatre Royal Stratford East) 1990, It's A Great Big Shame! (Theatre Royal Stratford East) 1993; writer-dir BBC Radio play Too Much of A Good Thing 1979; writer-dir BBC TV plays and films: A Mug's Game 1972, Hard Labour 1973, The Permissive Society, Afternoon, A Light Snack, Probation, Old Chums, The Birth Of The 2001 FA Cup Final Goalie 1975, Nuts in May, Knock For Knock 1976, The Kiss of Death, Abigail's Party 1977, Who's Who 1978, Grown-Ups 1980, Home Sweet Home 1982, Four Days In July 1984; writer-dir Channel Four films: Meantime 1983, The Short And Curlies 1987; writer-dir feature films: Bleak Moments 1971 (Golden Hugo, Chicago Film Festival 1972, Golden Leopard Locarno Film Festival 1972), High Hopes 1988 (Critics' Prize Venice Film Festival 1988, Evening Standard Peter Sellers Best Comedy Award 1990), Life Is Sweet 1990 (winner American Nat Soc of Film Critics' Award, Cariddi D'Oro & Maschera di Polifemo Taormina Film Festival 1991), Naked 1993 (winner Best Direction Cannes Film Festival, 1993), Secrets and Lies (winner Palme D'Or, Inter Critics' Prize, Ecumenical Prize Cannes Film Festival, 1996); *Books* Abigail's Party (Penguin, 1983), Goose-Pimples (Penguin, 1983), Smelling A Rat (Nick Hern Books, 1989), Ecstasy (Nick Hern Books, 1989), Naked and Other Screenplays (Faber & Faber, 1995); *Style—* Mike Leigh, Esq, OBE; ✉ c/o Peters Fraser & Dunlop Ltd, 503 The Chambers, Chelsea Harbour, Lots Road, London SW10 0XF (☎ 0171 352 4446, fax 0171 352 7356);

LEIGH, Peter William John; s of John Charles Leigh, JP (d 1961), of Harrow, and Dorothy Grace Jepps Leigh (d 1962); *b* 29 June 1929; *Educ* Harrow Weald Co GS, Coll of Estate Mgmnt; *m* 9 June 1956, Mary Frances, *née* Smith; 2 s (Simon b 1960, Howard b 1965), 1 da (Alison b 1961); *Career* Nat Serv RCS 1947–49; in private surveying practice 1949–53, valuation asst Middx CC 1953–60, commercial estates offr Bracknell Development Corporation 1960–66; dir of valuation and estates GLC 1981–84 (previous sr appts 1966–81), dir of property servs Royal Co of Berks 1984–88, surveying and property conslt 1988–; memb: Exec Local Authy Valuers' Assoc 1981–88, Gen Cncl RICS 1984–86, GP Div Cncl RICS 1993–, Govt Property Advsy Gp 1984–88; visiting lectr Reading Coll of Technol 1990–94; FRICS 1954; *Recreations* editing Old Wealden Assoc newsletter 1978–, drawing and painting, exploring Cornwall, gardening; *Style—* Peter Leigh, Esq; ✉ 41 Sandy Lane, Wokingham, Berks RG41 4SS (☎ 0118 978 2732); Quinley, Bodinnick-by-Fowey, Cornwall PL23 1LX

LEIGH, Ray Hugh; s of Dennis Leigh, OBE (d 1989), of Mickleton, Glos, and Amy Dorothy, *née* Symes; *b* 6 June 1928; *Educ* Morecambe GS Lancs, AA Sch of Architecture London (AADipl); *m* 1952, Jean, da of Col J Wykes, OBE; 1 da (Sarah Jane b 1953), 2 s (Simon Christopher b 1955, David William b 1962); *Career* chartered architect and designer; architectural practice 1952–67; Gordon Russell Ltd (furniture makers): exec dir i/c design 1967–71, md 1971–82, chm 1982–86, re-appointed dir following takeover 1991–94; independent furniture designer and design mgmnt conslt 1986–, chm Luke Hughes & Co (furniture makers) 1990–94; dir: Lygon Arms Hotel Broadway Worcs 1970–86, British Furniture Manufacturers Exports Ltd 1970–93 (past chm), British Furniture Manufacturers Ltd 1994–; memb Crafts Cncl 1977–83, fndr chm Contract Design Assoc 1978–82; chm: Furniture Indust Research Assoc 1980–86, Edward Barnsley Educnl Tst Furniture Workshops 1980–90; pres Glos Guild of Craftsmen 1980–90, memb Furniture Economic Devpt Ctee NEDC 1987–88; memb Ct of Assts Worshipful Co of Furniture Makers (Master 1994–95), chm British Furniture Cncl 1995, dir Design Tst, patron New Designers in Business; RIBA, FCSD, FRSA, Hon FRCA; *Recreations* gardens, fell walking, photography, antiquarian books; *Style—* Ray Leigh, Esq; ✉ Field House, High Street, Broadway, Worcestershire WR12 7AJ (☎ 01386 853654, fax 01386 854825)

LEIGH, Sir Richard Henry; 3 Bt (UK 1918), of Altrincham, Cheshire; s of Eric Leigh (d 1982), and his 1 w, Joan Fitzgerald Lane (d 1973), eldest da of Maurice Charles Lane Freer, of Kiambu, Kenya; suc unc Sir John Leigh, 2 Bt (d 1992); *b* 11 Nov 1936; *Educ* England and Switzerland; *m* 1, 1962 (m dis 1977), Barbro Anna Elizabeth, eldest da of late Stig Carl Sebastian Tham, of Sweden; m 2, 1977, Chérie Rosalind, eldest da of late Douglas Donald Dale, of La Blanchie, Cherval, France, and widow of Alan Reece, RMS; *Heir* half-bro, Christopher John Leigh b 1941; *Style—* Sir Richard Leigh, Bt; ✉ Trythall Vean, Madron, nr Penzance, Cornwall TR20 8SY

LEIGH, (Richard) Rowley; s of Robert Arthur Leigh, of Chulmleigh, and Shelagh Elizabeth, *née* Ruddin; *b* 23 April 1950; *Educ* Clifton Coll Bristol, Tiffin Boys' Sch, Christ's Coll Cambridge (exhibitioner); *m* 1982, Sara Patricia, da of Peter George, the author; 2 da (Ruth Bronwen b 22 Aug 1985, Daisy Dorothy b 2 Oct 1988); *Career* chef tournant Joe Allen Restaurant 1978–79, commis chef Le Gavroche 1979–81, various posts in Roux Restaurants including patisserie, butchery, buying, etc 1981–83, head chef Le Poulbot 1984–87 (sous chef 1983–84), head chef/ptnr Kensington Place 1987–; memb Academie Culinaire 1987; *Recreations* reading, chess, backgammon, poker, golf; *Clubs* Groucho, Green Street; *Style—* Rowley Leigh, Esq; ✉ 21 Frithville Gardens, London W12 7JG (☎ 0181 248 9391); Kensington Place, 201 Kensington Church Street, London W8 7LX (☎ 0171 727 3184, fax 0171 229 2025)

LEIGH FERMOR, Patrick Michael; DSO (1944), OBE (mil 1943); s of Sir Lewis Leigh Fermor, OBE, FRS (d 1954), and Muriel Eileen, da of Charles Taaffe Ambler (d 1972); *b* 11 Feb 1915; *Educ* King's Sch Canterbury; *m* 1968, Hon Joan Elizabeth, da of 1 Viscount Monsell, GBE, PC; *Career* author; WWII: enlisted Irish Guards 1939, 2 Lt I Corps 1940, Lt Br mil mission to Greece, liaison offr Greek forces in Albania, campaigns of Greece and Crete, Maj SOE German occupied Crete 1942–44, team Cdr Allied Airborne Reconnaissance Force N Germany; dep dir Br Inst Athens until 1946; hon citizen: Herakleion Crete 1947, Gytheion Laconia 1966, Kardamyli Messenia 1967; Gold Medal of Honour of the Municipality of Athens, Gold Medal City of Herakleion 1994; Hon DLitt: Univ of Kent 1991, Univ of Warwick 1996, American Coll of Greece; CLit 1991; visiting memb Acad of Athens; Chevalier dans l'Ordre des ArtCs et des Lettres Paris 1994; *Books* The Travellers Tree (Heineman Fndn prize for literature 1950, Kemsley prize 1951), A Time to Keep Silence (1953), The Violins of St Jacques (1953), Mani (1958, Duff Cooper Meml prize, Book Soc's choice), Roumeli (1966), A Time of Gifts (1977, WH Smith & Son literary award 1978), Between the Woods and the Water (1986, Thomas Cook travel book award 1986, int PEN/Time Life Silver Pen award 1986), Three Letters From The Andes (1991); translated: Collete's Chance Acquaintances (1952), George Psychoundakis' The Cretan Runner (1955), Grand Prix Litteraire Jacques Audibertidi de la Ville d'Antibes (1992); *Recreations* travel, reading; *Clubs* Travellers', White's, Pratt's, Beefsteak, Special Forces, Puffins (Edinburgh); *Style—* Patrick Leigh Fermor, Esq, DSO, OBE; ✉ c/o Messrs John Murray Ltd, 50 Albermarle St, London W1

LEIGH-HUNT, Barbara; da of Chandos Austin Leigh-Hunt (d 1970), of Bath, Somerset, and Elizabeth Jones (d 1993), latterly of Stratford-upon-Avon; *b* 14 Dec 1935; *Educ* Bath and Bristol Old Vic Theatre Sch (Bristol Evening Post Award for Most Promising Student 1953); *m* 1967, Richard Edward Pasco, *qv*, s of Cecil Pasco; 1 step s (William b 6 Nov 1961); *Career* actress; frequent bdcaster 1947–, has made many recordings incl a selection from the Psalms with Sir John Gielgud, Richard Pasco and Peter Orr, concert work incl performances with the Medici Quartet and at the Proms and numerous recitals at major UK arts festivals; assoc actor and govr RSC, patron Friends of the RSC; memb

Ctee: Theatrical Ladies' Guild; vice pres Royal Theatrical Fund; pres Friends of the Other Places 1994–96; *Theatre* RSC incl: Winter's Tale, King Lear, Travesties, The Merry Wives of Windsor, That Good Between Us, Hamlet, Richard III; RNT incl: Cat on a Hot Tin Roof, Bartholomew Fair, The Voysey Inheritance, Racing Demon, An Inspector Calls, Absence of War; other roles incl: A Severed Head, Mouse, Are You Within? (all Bristol Old Vic and West End), Sherlock Holmes (Aldwych/Broadway), Every Good Boy Deserves Favour (Festival Hall), The Seagull (Old Vic/Bristol), Getting Married (tour), Pack of Lies (Lyric Theatre and West End), One Thing More or Caedmon Construed (Chelmsford Cathedral), Barnaby and The Old Boys (Theatr Clwyd), A Woman of No Importance (Haymarket Theatre and nat tour), The Importance of Being Earnest (Birmingham Repertory and Old Vic); *Television* BBC incl: The Siegeried Idyll, Search for the Nile, Love Lies Bleeding, Games, Office Story, The Chief Mourner, The Voysey Inheritance, Mary's Wife, Paying Guests, Tumbledown, Pride and Prejudice; LWT incl: One Chance in Four, Cold Feet, A Perfect Hero (with Havahall Pictures), Anna Lee; other prodn incl: Wagner (Channel 4), All for Love (Granada), Inspector Morse (Zenith Prodns), The Best Man to Die (TVS); *Films* Frenzy (dir Alfred Hitchcock), Henry VIII and His Six Wives (dirs Waris Hussein/Mark Shivas), A Bequest to the Nation (dirs James Cellan-Jones and Hal B Wallis), Oh Heavenly Dog (dir Jo Camp), Paper Mask (dir Christopher Morahan); *Awards* Clarence Derwent Award for Best Supporting Actress (as Gertrude) in Hamlet with Michael Pennington (dir John Barton) 1982, Laurence Olivier Award for Best Supporting Actress (as Mrs Birling) in An Inspector Calls (RNT, dir Stephen Daldry) 1993; *Style*— Ms Barbara Leigh-Hunt; ✉ c/o Michael Whitehall Ltd, 125 Gloucester Road, London SW7 4TE (☎ 0171 244 8466, fax 0171 244 9060)

LEIGH PEMBERTON, Jeremy; CBE (1992); s of Capt Robert Douglas Leigh Pemberton, MBE, MC, JP (d 1964), and Helen Isobel, *née* Payne-Gallwey (d 1985); bro of Lord Kingsdown, *qv*; *b* 25 Nov 1933; *Educ* Eton, Magdalen Coll Oxford (MA), INSEAD Fontainebleau (MBA); *m* 1, 30 May 1968 (m dis 1980), Mary, da of John Ames, of Boston, Mass; 1 s (Richard b 13 Dec 1971); m 2, 3 June 1982, Virginia Marion, da of Sir John Curle, KCVO, CMG, *qv*; *Career* Nat Serv Grenadier Gds 1952–54, cmmnd 2 Lt 1953; Brooke Bond Liebig 1957–69 (rising to gp mktg controller), md W & R Balston Group 1973–74 (gp mktg controller and corporate planner 1970–73), dep chm Whatman plc (formerly Whatman Reeve Angel plc) 1990–94 (md 1974–89); chm: Mid Kent Holdings plc, Kent Co Crematorium plc, Fleming Fledgeling Investment Trust plc, Morgan Grenfell Equity Income Trust PLC; dir: London & Manchester Group plc, Bailey Products Ltd, Kent TEC Ltd until 1994, Understanding Industry Trust Ltd, Savoy Hotel plc; chm: Tatem Ltd, Kent Economic Development Board, Business Link Kent Ltd; CBI: former memb Nat Cncl, former memb Econ and Fin Policy Ctee, former memb Fin and Gen Purposes Ctee, fndr chm Kent Area Ctee (later chm SE Regnl Cncl); visiting prof in mktg at INSEAD 1965–70; pres: INSEAD Int Alumni Assoc 1962–66, Kent branch Chartered Inst of Mktg 1988–92, Kent branch Inst of Mgmnt 1992–; chm Fin Ctee Kent Branch Red Cross; tstee Lord Cornwallis Meml Fund; FCIM, FInstD, FRSA; *Recreations* opera, fishing; *Style*— Jeremy Leigh Pemberton, Esq, CBE; ✉ Hill House, Wormshill, Sittingbourne, Kent ME9 OTS (☎ 01622 884472, fax 01622 884784)

LEIGH-PEMBERTON, Robin (Robert); *see:* Kingsdown, The Rt Hon Lord

LEIGH-SMITH, (Alfred) Nicholas Hardstaff; s of Lt-Col Alfred Leigh Hardstaff Leigh-Smith, TD, DL (d 1978), of Stanwell Moor, Middx, and Marguerite Calvert, *née* Calvert-Harrison (d 1983); *b* 21 Dec 1953; *Educ* Epsom Coll, Univ of Leeds (LLB); *Career* called to the Bar Lincoln's Inn 1976; dep clerk: Bromley Justices 1985, Brent Justices 1989; clerk to the justices Cambridge and E Cambridgeshire Justices 1995–; *Recreations* rugby union football, clay pigeon shooting, reading, walking; *Style*— Nicholas Leigh-Smith, Esq; ✉ The Hermitage, 23 Earning Street, Godmanchester, Huntingdon, Cambs PE18 8JD (☎ 01480 433467); 3 & 4 John Street, Penhalhno, N Wales; The Court House, Lion Yard, Cambridge CB2 3NA (☎ 01223 314311, fax 01223 355237)

LEIGHTON, Allan; *b* 12 April 1953; *Educ* Magdalen Coll Sch Oxford, North Oxon Poly; *m*; 1 da, 2 s; *Career* Mars Confectionery 1974–91: direct salesman, area sales mangr, personnel mangr, nat account mangr, regnl sales mangr, nat accounts controller, inter co business mangr, divnl dir Mars Ireland, gen sales mangr UK Grocery Div, business sector mangr; inmarket sales dir Pedigree Petfoods 1991–92; Asda Group plc: gp mktg dir 1992–94, gp retail dir 1994–95, chief exec 1996– (dep chief exec 1995–96); *Recreations* morris dancing, football, cricket, running; *Style*— Allan Leighton, Esq; ✉ Asda Group plc, Asda House, Southbank, Great Wilson Street, Leeds LS11 5AD (☎ 0113 243 5435)

LEIGHTON, (Henry) Gerard Mather; s of Wilfrid Leighton (d 1967), of Burnett, Somerset, and Margaret, *née* Mather; *b* 15 Aug 1932; *Educ* Winchester, Corpus Christi Coll Oxford (MA); *m* 5 June 1982, Amanda Juliet, da of Brig Cedric George Buttenshaw, CBE, DSO, of Worton, nr Devizes, Wiltshire; 1 s (Henry b 1984), 1 da (Alice b 1985); *Career* CA; ptnr Grace Darbyshire & Todd Bristol 1959–68; dir: Tyndall Group Ltd and subsids 1962–86, Gateway Securities Ltd 1965–77; chm Jordan Group Ltd 1985–93 (dir 1968–93), dep chm West of England Trust Ltd 1982– (dir 1972–); hon treas Bristol and Glos Archaeological Soc 1971–; chm: Bristol Diocesan Advsy Ctee for Care of Churches 1974–93, Somerset Record Soc 1977–, Wells Cathedral Fabric Ctee 1991– (dep chm 1987–91); memb Fabric Ctee: Bristol Cathedral 1989–, St Woolo's Cathedral Newport 1995–; FSA; *Recreations* gardening, hunting, archaeology; *Clubs* Travellers'; *Style*— Gerard Leighton, Esq, FSA; ✉ Hassage Manor, Faulkland, nr Bath, Somerset BA3 5XG (☎ 01373 834449); 21 St Thomas St, Bristol (☎ 0117 929 9292)

LEIGHTON, Sir Michael John Bryan; 11 Bt (E 1693), of Wattlesborough, Shropshire; s of Col Sir Richard Tihel Leighton, 10 Bt, TD (d 1957), and Kathleen Irene Linda, *née* Lees (d 1993); *b* 8 March 1935; *Educ* Stowe, RAC Cirencester, Tabley House Agric Sch; *m* 1, 1974 (m dis 1980), Mrs Amber Mary Ritchie; m 2, 1991, Mrs Diana Mary Gamble; 1 da (Eleanor Angharad Diana b 20 Jan 1992); *Heir* none; *Career* photographer of wildlife; ornithologist; *Recreations* panel 'A' gun dog judge, cricket, tennis, golf, writing poetry, cooking; *Clubs* MCC; *Style*— Sir Michael Leighton, Bt; ✉ Loton Park, nr Shrewsbury, Shropshire (☎ 01743 884232)

LEIGHTON, Tom James; s of Thomas James Leighton (d 1974), and Winifred Barclay, *née* Mearns; *b* 2 Oct 1944; *Educ* Cardinal Newman Coll Buenos Aires Argentina, Austin Friars Sch Carlisle, Derby Coll of Art (Dip in Photography); *m* 1, 1964 (m dis 1969), Margaret Louise Lockhart Mure; 1 s (Lee Lockhart-Mure b 20 April 1967); m 2, 1970, Susan Gillian, da of Albert George Hollingsworth; *Career* fashion photographer for many magazines, advertising agencies and catalogues 1975–81, interiors photographer 1981–; assignments incl: American Vogue, World of Interiors, Sunday Times Magazine, Telegraph Magazine, Casa Vogue (Spain), La Casa de Marie Claire (Spain), Domino (Canada), Casa Vogue (Italy), Homes and Gardens, House and Garden, Laura Ashley, Elle Decoration, Architecktur and Wohnen (Germany); Merit award Art Dirs' Club of Toronto 1989 (for work published in Domino magazine); *Photography Books*: Grand Illusions (1988), The Painted House (1988); *Clubs* Pinnacle (Richmond); *Style*— Tom Leighton, Esq; ✉ 17 Cedar Court, Sheen Lane, London SW14 8LY (☎ 0181 876 8497)

LEIGHTON OF ST MELLONS, 2 Baron (UK 1962); Sir John Leighton Seager; 2 Bt (UK 1952); s of 1 Baron, CBE (d 1963), and Marjorie, *née* Gimson (d 1992); *b* 11 Jan 1922; *Educ* Caldicott Sch, Leys Sch Cambridge; *m* 1, 31 Oct 1953, Elizabeth Rosita (d 1979), o da of late Henry Hopgood, of Cardiff; 2 s (Hon Robert b 1955, Hon Simon b 1957), 1 da (Hon Carole b 1958) and 1 da decd; m 2, 1982 (m dis 1994); *Heir* s, Hon Robert William Henry Leighton Seager; *Career* former chm Cardiff & Bristol Channel Shipowners' Assoc, former dir W H Seager & Co Ltd; *Recreations* gardening, photography; *Style*— The Rt Hon the Lord Leighton of St Mellons; ✉ Monkstone House, Penarth Head Lane, Penarth, Cardiff CF64 1BB

LEIMAN, Russell Michael; s of Dr Norman Cecil Leiman (d 1983), and Edith Helen, *née* Rosenberg; *b* 26 Oct 1947; *Educ* King Edward VII Sch Johannesburg S Africa; *m* 15 April 1973, Ashley Elizabeth Chesler, *née* Beer; 2 step da (Samantha Jane b 31 March 1969, Vanessa Claire b 13 April 1971); *Career* clerk I Jacobs (memb Johannesburg Stock Exchange 1968–71); Vickers Da Costa: arbitrage trader London 1971–74, Hong Kong 1974–77, assoc gen mangr Tokyo Branch 1977–85, pres Vickers Da Costa Securities Inc (NY) 1985–88; chief exec Citicorp Scrimgeour Vickers International Ltd (London) 1988–89 (formerly Vickers Da Costa Ltd), chief exec Credit Lyonnais Securities and Laing & Cruickshank Institutional Equities Ops UK 1989–90, dir Int Equity Div Credit Lyonnais 1990–92, chief exec Peregrine Derivatives Ltd 1992–; memb: Int Stock Exchange, Int Ctee NASD Washington 1988; *Recreations* classic cars, music, photography; *Style*— Russell Leiman, Esq; ✉ 7 Kent Terrace, London NW1 4RP (☎ 0171 724 2234); Peregrine Derivatives Ltd, New World Tower, 22nd Floor, 16–18 Queens Road, Central, Hong Kong (☎ 825 1968, fax 845 9411)

LEINSTER, 8 Duke of (I 1766); Gerald FitzGerald; Premier Duke, Marquess and Earl in the Peerage of Ireland, also Baron of Offaly (I *ante* 1203 restored 1554), Earl of Kildare (I 1316), Viscount Leinster of Taplow (GB 1747), Marquess of Kildare, Earl of Offaly (both I 1761), and Baron Kildare (UK 1870); s of 7 Duke of Leinster (d 1976, descended from common ancestors of (1) The Earls of Plymouth, (2) Giraldus Cambrensis the medieval historian, (3) the Earls of Desmond (now extinct), (4) the hereditary Knights of Glin and Kerry and the (extinct) White Knight, (5) the Marquesses of Lansdowne), and his 1 w May, *née* Etheridge (d 1935); *b* 27 May 1914; *Educ* Eton, Sandhurst; *m* 1, 17 Oct 1936 (m dis 1946), Joane, eldest da of late Maj Arthur McMorrough Kavanagh, MC; 2 da (Lady Rosemary Wait b 1939, Lady Nesta Tirard b 1942), and 1 decd; m 2, 12 June 1946, Anne, yr da of Lt-Col Philip Eustace Smith, MC, TD; 2 s (Marquess of Kildare, *qv*, Lord John b 1952); *Heir* s, Marquess of Kildare, *qv*; *Career* served WWII with 5 Royal Inniskilling Dragoon Gds (wounded in Normandy); master: N Kilkenny foxhounds 1937–40, W Percy foxhounds 1945–46, Portman foxhounds 1946–47; *Recreations* shooting, fishing; *Style*— His Grace the Duke of Leinster; ✉ Kilkea House, Wilcote Lane, Ramsden, Chipping Norton, Oxon OX7 3BA

LEINSTER, Prof Samuel John; s of Victor Leinster, of Birmingham, and Jemina Eileen Eva, *née* McGeown; *b* 29 Oct 1946; *Educ* Boroughmuir Sr Secdy Sch Edinburgh, Univ of Edinburgh (BSc, MB ChB), Univ of Liverpool (MD), FRCSEd; *m* 17 July 1971, Jennifer, da of James Woodward, of Wirral; 3 s (Alistair b 1975, David b 1979, Benjamin b 1988), 1 da (Angela b 1972); *Career* RAF Med Branch: PO 1969, Flying Offr 1971, Flt Lt 1972, MO 1972–77, Sqdn Ldr 1977, surgical specialist, ret 1977; lectr in surgery Welsh Nat Sch of Med 1978–81, sr lectr in surgery Univ of Liverpool and hon conslt surgn Liverpool Health Authy 1982–90; Univ of Liverpool: reader in surgery 1990–93, prof of surgery 1993–, dir of med studies 1995–; memb: BMA, Surgical Res Soc, Assoc of Surgns of GB and I, Assoc for the Study of Med Educn, Br Assoc of Surgical Oncology, Christian Med Fellowship; *Books* Systemic Diseases for Dental Students (with T J Bailey, 1983); *Recreations* local preacher, DIY enthusiast, reading, swimming, dinghy sailing; *Style*— Prof Samuel Leinster; ✉ 7 Roman Rd, Meols, Wirral, Merseyside L47 6AG (☎ 0151 632 4468); Department of Surgery, University of Liverpool, PO Box 147, Liverpool L69 3BX (☎ 0151 706 4175, fax 0151 706 5826)

LEISHMAN, Hon Mrs (Marista Muriel); da of 1 Baron Reith, KT, GCVO, GBE, CB, TD (d 1971); *b* 10 April 1932; *Educ* St George's Ascot, Univ of St Andrews (MA); *m* 1960, Murray Leishman (psychotherapist); 1 s (Mark b 1962), 3 da (Iona b 1963, Martha b 1965, Kirsty b 1969); *Career* head of education Nat Tst for Scotland 1978–86, sr conslt The Insite Consultancy, management and trg conslt in Heritage Presentation 1987–; Nat Trg award winner 1989 and 1993; FRSA 1988; *Recreations* music, writing, painting, walking; *Style*— Mrs M Leishman; ✉ 9/23 St Leonards Crag, Edinburgh EH8 9SP (☎ 0131 667 1246)

LEITCH, Alexander Park (Sandy); s of Donald Leitch (d 1949), of Blairhall, Fife, and Agnes Smith, *née* Park; *b* 20 Oct 1947; *Educ* Dunfermline HS; *children* 3 da (Fiona b 1971, Joanne b 1973, Jacqueline b 1975); *Career* chief systems designer National Mutual Life 1969, Hambro Life 1971 (bd dir 1981); Allied Dunbar plc: md 1988, dep chm 1990, chief exec 1993–96, chm Allied Dunbar Assurance PLC 1996–; chief exec Br American Financial Services (UK and Int) Ltd 1996–; chm: Dunbar Bank 1994–, Eagle Star Holdings PLC 1996–, Threadneedle Asset Management 1996–; memb Business in the Community - Employees in the Community Leadership, memb Bd ABI 1996–; MBCS 1966; *Recreations* tennis, football, antiquarian books; *Style*— Sandy Leitch, Esq; ✉ British American Financial Services (UK and Int'l) Ltd, 22 Arlington Street, London SW1A 1RW (☎ 0171 495 5563)

LEITCH, Sir George; KCB (1975, CB 1963), OBE (Mil 1945); s of late James Simpson Leitch, and Margaret Leitch; *b* 5 June 1915; *Educ* Wallsend GS, King's Coll Durham Univ; *m* 1942, Edith Marjorie, da of late Thomas Dawson Maughan; 1 da; *Career* served WWII Army (despatches), Brig 1946; entered Civil Service 1947, dep under sec of state MOD 1965–72, sec (procurement exec) 1972–74, chief exec (perm sec) 1974–75, ret; chm Short Brothers Ltd 1976–83; chm Standing Advsy Ctee on Trunk Rd Assessment 1977–80; *Style*— Sir George Leitch, KCB, OBE; ✉ 10 Elmfield Rd, Gosforth, Newcastle upon Tyne (☎ 0191 284 6559); Black Brae, Port Charlotte, Islay, Argyll (☎ 01496 850430)

LEITCH, Maurice Henry; s of Andrew Leitch (d 1983), of Templepatrick, Co Antrim, NI, and Jean, *née* Coid (d 1973); *b* 5 July 1933; *Educ* Methodist Coll Belfast, Stranmills Trg Coll Belfast (teaching dip); *m* 1, 23 July 1956, Isobel, da of James Scott; 1 s (Paul b 17 Feb 1967), 1 da (Bronagh b 17 Sept 1965); m 2, 18 Nov 1972, Sandra, da of Alfred Hill; 1 s (Daniel b 29 April 1974); *Career* teacher Antrim NI 1954–60; BBC Radio: features prodr Belfast 1960–70, drama prodr London 1970–77, prodr Book at Bedtime 1977–89; author of several novels, TV screenplays, radio dramas, features and short stories; Guardian Fiction Prize 1969, Whitbread Fiction Prize 1981, Pye award for Most Promising Writer New to TV 1980–1981; memb Soc of Authors 1989; *Style*— Maurice Leitch, Esq; ✉ Deborah Rogers, 20 Powis Mews, London W2 (☎ 0171 221 3717)

LEITH, Annie; *see:* Burgh, Anita, Lady; Anita Lorna

LEITH, Hon (Alexander) Gregory Disney; s and h of 7 Baron Burgh, *qv*; *b* 16 March 1958; *m* 1984, Catharine Mary, da of David Parkes; 2 s (Alexander James Strachan b 1986, Benjamin David Willoughby b 1988); *Style*— The Hon Gregory Leith

LEITH, Jake Quintin; s of Jack Leith, of Hove, Sussex, and Louisa Teresa, *née* Quinn; *b* 18 Nov 1958; *Educ* Bushey Meads Sch Bushey Herts, Herts Coll of Art & Design, Loughborough Coll of Art & Design (BA), Birmingham Inst of Art & Design (MA); *Career* chartered designer; export designer Textile Dept Everest Fabrics Ghaziabad India 1983–84, interior designer/textile advsr Europa Shop Equipment Ltd 1984–85, self-employed interior designer Fantasy Finishes 1985–86, ptnr The Jake Leith Partnership interior designers specialising in furnishing fabrics and wall-coverings 1986–; private and commercial cmmns; CSD: memb Textile Bd 1993–, memb: Continual Professional Devpt Ctee 1995–, Professional Standards Ctee 1995–; course conslt/assessor (Printed Textiles/Surface Decoration) Univ of E London 1995–; FCSD 1995 (MCSD 1983), FRSA 1996; *Recreations* classical guitar, printmaking, photography, songwriting, good food; *Clubs* Sopwell House Country; *Style*— Jake Leith, Esq; ✉ The

Jake Leith Partnership, 12 Midland Road, Hemel Hempstead, Herts HP2 5BH (☎ 01442 247010, fax 01442 245495)

LEITH, Prudence Margaret (Prue); OBE (1989); da of Stewart Leith (d 1961), of Johannesburg, SA, and Margaret, *née* Inglis; *b* 18 Feb 1940; *Educ* St Mary's Sch Johannesburg, Univ of Cape Town, Sorbonne Paris (Cours de la Civilisation Francaise); *m* 1974, (Charles) Rayne Kruger (author); 1 s (Daniel b 1974), 1 da (Li-Da b 1974); *Career* restaurateur, caterer, author, journalist; fndr: Leith's Good Food 1961, Leith's Restaurant 1969, Prudence Leith Ltd 1972, Leith's Sch of Food and Wine 1975, Leith's Farm 1976; dir: Br Transport Hotels Ltd 1977–83, BR Bd 1980–85 (pt/t), Prudence Leith Ltd 1972–94 (md), Leith's Ltd 1994–96 (chm), Leith's Restaurant Ltd 1969–95, Safeway plc 1989–96 (formerly Argyll Group plc, joined gp as conslt to Safeway stores 1988), Halifax Building Society (formerly Leeds Permanent Building Society) 1992–, Whitbread plc 1995–; memb Cncl Food From Britain 1983–87, chm Restaurateurs' Assoc of GB 1990–94, govr Ashridge Mgmnt Coll 1992–; appeared in: 26–part TV cookery series on Tyne-Tees TV, Best of Br BBC TV, The Good Food Show, Take 6 Cooks, Tricks of the Trade; memb: Econ Devpt Ctee for the Leisure & Tourism Industs 1986–90, Nat Trg Task Force Dept of Employment 1989–91; FRSA (chm RSA 1995–); *Books* written 12 cookery books between 1972 and 1991, incl Prue Leith's Dinner Parties (Papermac, 1991); *Recreations* riding, tennis, old cookbooks; *Style—* Miss Prue Leith, OBE; ✉ 94 Kensington Park Rd, London W11 2PN (☎ 0171 221 5282)

LEITH-BUCHANAN, Sir Charles Alexander James; 7 Bt (GB 1775), of Burgh St Peter, Norfolk; o s of John Wellesley MacDonald Leith-Buchanan (d 1956); suc kinsman Sir George Hector MacDonald Leith-Buchanan, 6 Bt (d 1973); *b* 1 Sept 1939; *m* 1, 1962 (m dis 1987), Marianne, da of Col Earle Wellington Kelly; 1 s (Gordon Kelly McNicol b 1974), 1 da (Mary Elizabeth b 1964); m 2, 1988, Janice J Jenkins; *Heir* s, Gordon Kelly McNicol Leith-Buchanan b 18 Oct 1974; *Career* pres United Business Machines Inc 1978–; *Style—* Sir Charles Leith-Buchanan, Bt; ✉ 9527 Possum Hollow Drive, Delaplane, Virginia 22025, USA

LEMAN, Adrianne; da of Frank George Jarratt (d 1978), and Frances Hannah, *née* King (d 1975); *b* 19 Feb 1938; *Educ* Edgehill Coll Bideford N Devon, Camberwell Sch of Arts and Crafts (NDD), Royal Coll of Art (ARCA); *m* 1, 1960 (m dis 1969), Martin LeMan, s of Arthur LeMan; m 2, 1977 (m dis 1991), Ian Stirling, s of Col William Stirling; *Career* art dir The Illustrated London News 1970–80, dir Addison Design Company Ltd 1982–87, md Holmes & Marchant Corporate Design 1987–92, fndr md C&FD 1992–; dir DBA 1992–95, pres-elect CSD 1996– (hon treas 1994–96); memb Lab Pty; FRSA; *Recreations* opera, cinema, books, art (seeing and collecting), spending time with friends; *Style—* Ms Adrianne LeMan; ✉ C&FD, 26–27 Great Sutton Street, London EC1V 0DS (☎ 0171 608 3899, fax 0171 608 1190, mobile 0836 610577)

LEMAN, Richard Alexander; s of Dennis Alexander George Leman, and Joyce Mabyn, *née* Pickering; *b* 13 July 1959; *Educ* Gresham's Sch Holt; *Career* hockey player; Bronze medal Olympic Games LA 1984, Silver medal World Cup London 1986, Silver medal Euro Cup Moscow 1987, Gold medal Olympic Games Seoul 1988; dir Olympian Counsultants; *Recreations* golf, flying; *Clubs* East Grinstead Hockey; *Style—* Richard Leman, Esq

LEMKIN, James Anthony; CBE (1986); s of William Lemkin, CBE (d 1991), of Wherwell, Hants, and Rachel Irene, *née* Faith (d 1958); *b* 21 Dec 1926; *Educ* Charterhouse, Merton Coll Oxford (MA); *m* 23 Nov 1960, Joan Dorothy Anne, da of Thomas Casserley (d 1945), of Wellington, NZ; 2 s (Robert b 1961, David b 1968), 2 da (Judith b 1966, Alix b 1968); *Career* served RN 1945–48; admitted slr 1953; ptnr Field Fisher Waterhouse (and predecessors) 1959–90, ret; memb GLC (for Uxbridge) 1973–86: chm Legal and Parly Ctee 1977–78, chm Scrutiny Ctee 1978–81, Cons spokesman on Police 1981–82, oppn chief whip 1982–86; chm Bow Gp 1952, 1956 and 1957–; vice chm Soc of Cons Lawyers 1990–92; govr: Westfield Coll London 1970–83, Royal Marsden Hosp 1984–90, Cwlth Inst 1985–92; parly candidate: (Cons and NL) Chesterfield 1959, (L) Cheltenham 1964; memb Law Soc; High Sheriff of Greater London 1992–93; *Books* Race and Power (ed, 1956); *Recreations* cricket umpiring; *Clubs* Athenaeum, Carlton; *Style—* James A Lemkin, Esq, CBE; ✉ c/o Field Fisher Waterhouse, 41 Vine Street, London EC3 (☎ 0171 481 4841)

LEMMON, David Hector; s of Frederick Robert Lemmon (d 1963), and Sophie Elizabeth, *née* Beadle (d 1934); *b* 4 April 1931; *Educ* Southgate Co GS, Coll of St Mark and St John London (Teacher's Cert, Soccer and Tennis half-colours), Univ of London (BA); *m* 16 Aug 1958, (Jean) Valerie, da of Cornelius Douglas Westneat Fletcher (d 1963); 2 s ((David) Keith b 12 May 1960, Barry Robert b 3 Dec 1964); *Career* writer; Publicity Dept Shell-Mex & BP Co Ltd 1947–49, Nat Serv RAF 1949–51, English and games master Bounds Green Secdy Modern Sch 1953–57, English master Ankara Coll Turkey 1957–60; head of English: Kingsbury HS Warwicks 1960–63, Torells Girls' Sch Thurrock 1963–68; dir of studies Nicholas Comps Sch Basildon 1973–83 (head of English 1968–73), full-time writer 1983–; examiner A-Level Theatre Studies 1980–92, memb TMA/Martini Regnl Theatre award Panel 1993–95, memb Editorial Bd Cricket World 1991–92, compiler Test Match and Texaco Trophy programmes 1984–89, ed TCCB's Tour Guide 1984–89, contrib The Cricketer 1993–94; pres Old Commoners CC, vice pres Southend CC; memb: English Speaking Bd, Cricket Writers Club; assoc Coll of Preceptors 1967; *Books* incl: Benson & Hedges Cricket Year (formerly Pelham Cricket Year, annually 1979–), Summer of Success (1980), Johnny Won't Hit Today (1983), A Walk to the Wicket (with Ted Dexter, 1984), The Great Wicket-Keepers (1984), Percy Chapman (1985), Ken McEwan (1985), The Great All-Rounders (1987), The Crisis of Captaincy (1988), Know Your Sport - Cricket (with Chris Cowdrey, 1989), British Theatre Yearbook (1989 and 1990), Benson & Hedges Theatre Year (1992), Len Hutton: A Pictorial Biography (1990), Cricket's Champion Counties (1991), The Cricketing Greigs (1991), The Guinness Book of Test Cricket Captains (1992), For The Love of The Game (1993), The Book of Essex Cricketers (1994); *Recreations* theatre, music, sport, Arsenal FC, entertaining; *Clubs* MCC, Essex CCC; *Style—* David Lemmon, Esq; ✉ 26 Leigh Rd, Leigh-on-Sea, Essex SS9 1LD (☎ 01702 79640)

LEMMON, Mark Benjamin; s of Edmund Lemmon (d 1984), of Gt Bookham, and Mary Patricia, *née* Bryan; *b* 15 April 1952; *Educ* Wimbledon Coll, Univ Coll London (BA), LSE (MSc); *m* 8 Aug 1980, Anna, da of Prof Tamas Szekely, of Budapest; 3 da (Esther b 1981, Patricia b 1985, Bernadette b 1990); *Career* formerly with: Touche Ross, Grindlays Bank, Guinness Mahon, Hongkong and Shanghai Banking Corporation (sr corp mangr); currently on secondment from HSBC Group as dir of mktg and devpt ECGD; Freeman City of London, memb Billingsgate Ward Club; FCA 1978, ATII 1979, ACIB 1982; *Recreations* squash, opera; *Clubs* Wimbledon Squash and Badminton, LSE; *Style—* Mark Lemmon, Esq; ✉ Director of Marketing and Business Development, ECGD, 2 Exchange Tower, Harbour Exchange Square, London E14 9GS

LEMON, Sir (Richard) Dawnay; kt (1970), CBE (1958), QPM; s of Lt-Col Frederick Joseph Lemon, CBE, DSO (d 1952); *b* 1912; *Educ* Uppingham, RMC; *m* 1939, Sylvia Marie, da of Lt-Col L W Kentish, of Burnham, Bucks; 1 s, 2 da (1 decd); *Career* joined W Yorks Regt 1932; Met Police 1934–37, Leics Constabulary 1937–39; chief constable: E Riding Yorks 1939–42, Hampshire and IOW 1942–62, Kent 1962–74; *Recreations* golf; *Clubs* Band of Brothers Cricket, Free Foresters Cricket, Royal St George's Golf (Sandwich); *Style—* Sir Dawnay Lemon, CBE, QPM; ✉ 9 Milchester House, Staveley Road, Eastbourne, Sussex BN20 7JX

LEMOS-SIMMONDS, HE Dr Carlos; *b* 26 Nov 1933; *Educ* Del Cauca Univ Law Sch (qualified as lawyer); *m* Martha Blanco de Lemos-Simmonds; *Career* Colombian diplomat; cncllr Bogotá 1972–74 and 1986–88, memb House of Reps 1974–78, govr Departamento del Cauca 1976–77, sec gen Office of the Pres of the Republic 1978–79, senator of the Republic 1978–81, min for foreign affrs 1981–82, Colombian ambass to the OAS 1987–89, communications min (actg justice min and devpt min) Feb-Oct 1989, interior min Oct 1989–March 1990, del Nat Constitution Assembly Dec 1990–July 1991, cncllr Santafé de Bogotá 1992 (chm of Cncl Aug-Nov 1992), presidential candidate Aug 1992; Colombian ambass: to the Republic of Austria Feb-Nov 1995, to the Ct of St James's Nov 1995–; Great Cross: Order of Boyacá, Nat Merit Order of Colombia, Civilian Merit of Spain, Merit Order of the Republic of Italy; Knight Cdr Order of Isabel la Católica; prof in the chair of Colombian political history and seminar on parliament Javeriana Univ High Political Studies Sch, prof of Colombian economic history Free Univ and Higher History Inst; dir Consigna magazine 1982–87, perm contrib El Tiempo newspaper, dir of TV progs The Force of History and Caracol Debates; *Publications* Fransico de Paula Santander - an Iconography, Memoirs of an Anti-Government, A Line of Conduct, The Pre-Colombian Economy, The Thieving State, Lemos and the Rescue of Morality in Colombia; *Recreations* music, reading; *Clubs* Canning, Jockey (Bogotá), Metropolitan (Bogotá); *Style—* HE Dr Carlos Lemos-Simmonds; ✉ Colombian Embassy, Flat 3a, 3 Hans Crescent, London SW1X 0LN (☎ 0171 589 9177, fax 0171 581 1829)

LEMPRIERE-ROBIN, Brig Raoul Charles; OBE (1956); s of Capt Charles Harold Robin (ka 1917), and Yvonne, da and heiress of Jurat Reginald Raoul Lempriere, CBE, of Rosel Manor, Jersey (she m 2, 1931, Lt-Col Christopher J M Riley, MC, and d 1948) (*see* Burke's Landed Gentry, 18 edn, vol iii); *b* 6 Sept 1914; *Educ* Eton, Univ Coll Oxford (MA); *m* 6 Jan 1955, Sheelagh, da of Lt-Col Charles Edgar Maturin-Baird, of Langham, Colchester; 1 da (Emma b 1965); *Career* cmmnd Coldstream Gds 1935, served in BEF 1939, Madagascar, India, Italy, Malaya, M East and Jordan (ret as Brig 1966); memb States of Jersey 1969–78; Seigneur de Rosel Jersey; Hereditary Butler to HM The Queen in Jersey; *Recreations* gardening; *Clubs* White's, Pratt's; *Style—* Brig Raoul Lempriere-Robin, OBE; ✉ Rosel Manor, Jersey (☎ 01534 852611)

LENG, Gen Sir Peter John Hall; KCB (1978, CB 1975), MBE (1962), MC (1945); s of J Leng; *b* 9 May 1925; *Educ* Bradfield; *m* 1 (m dis), Virginia Rosemary Pearson; 3 s, 2 da; m 2, 1981, Mrs Flavia Tower, da of Lt-Gen Sir Frederick Browning, KCVO, DSO (d 1965), and Dame Daphne du Maurier, DBE (d 1989); *Career* cmmnd 1944, served WWII, Cdr Land Forces NI 1973–75, Dir Mil Operations MOD 1975–78, Cdr 1 (Br) Corps 1978–80, Master-Gen of the Ordnance 1981–83, ret; Col Cmdt RAVC and RMP 1976–89; chm Racecourse Assoc 1985–89, patron Natural Therapeutic and Osteopathic Soc 1987–93; Liveryman Worshipful Co of Grocers; *Style—* Gen Sir Peter Leng, KCB, MBE, MC; ✉ c/o Naval & Military Club, 94 Piccadilly, London W1

LENHAM, Neil John; s of Leslie John Lenham, and Valerie Ann, *née* Corney; *b* 17 Dec 1965; *Educ* Brighton Coll; *Career* professional cricketer; debut Sussex CCC 1984, awarded county cap 1990; capt Young England tour W Indies 1984; public schs record for runs scored in a season (1534 in 1984); Sussex player of the year 1990; *Recreations* fishing, music, golf, squash; *Style—* Neil Lenham, Esq; ✉ Sussex CCC, County Cricket Ground, Hove, Sussex (☎ 01273 732161)

LENMAN, Prof Bruce Philip; s of Jacob Philip Lenman (d 1986), of Aberdeen, and May, *née* Wishart (d 1976); *b* 9 April 1938; *Educ* Aberdeen GS, Univ of Aberdeen (MA, Forbes Gold medal), St John's Coll Cambridge (MLitt, LittD); *Career* asst prof of history Victoria Univ 1963, lectr in Imperial and Commonwealth history Univ of St Andrews 1963–67, lectr Dept of Modern History Univ of Dundee 1967–72, reader in modern history Univ of St Andrews 1983–88 (lectr 1972–78, sr lectr 1978–83), James Pinckney Harrison prof Coll of William and Mary Virginia 1988–89, prof of modern history Univ of St Andrews 1992– (reader 1989–92); Br Acad fell Newberry Library Chicago 1982, John Carter Brown Library fell Rhode Island 1984, Cncl of Europe res fell 1984, Folger fell Folger Library Washington DC 1988–89, Weddell lectr Virginia Historical Soc 1991 (Mellon fell 1990); past pres Abertay Historical Soc; Scottish Arts Cncl Literary Award 1977 and 1980; FRHistS 1977; *Books* Dundee and its Textile Industry (1969), From Esk to Tweed (1975), An Economic History of Modern Scotland (1977), The Jacobite Risings in Britain (1980), Crime and the Law (ed, 1980), Integration and Enlightenment: Scotland 1746–1832 (1981), Jacobite Clans of the Great Glen (1984), The Jacobite Cause (1986), The Jacobite Threat: A Source Book (with John S Gibson, 1990), The Eclipse of Parliament (1992), Chambers Dictionary of World History (ed, 1993); *Recreations* golf, hill walking, tennis, swimming, Scottish country dancing; *Clubs* Royal Commonwealth, New Golf; *Style—* Prof Bruce P Lenman; ✉ Department of Modern History, University of St Andrews, St Andrews, Fife KY16 9AL (☎ 01334 462923, fax 01334 462927)

LENNARD, Thomas William Jay; s of Thomas Jay Lennard, MBE, of Falkirk, and Elizabeth Jemima Mary Patricia, *née* Poole; *b* 25 Oct 1953; *Educ* Clifton, Univ of Newcastle Upon Tyne (MB BS, MD); *m* 8 July 1978, Anne Lesley, da of Cyril Barber, of Ossett, W Yorks; 3 s (James Matthew Thomas b 1984, Jonathan Alexander Thomas b 1987, Oliver Thames Jay b 1993); *Career* lectr in surgery Univ of Newcastle Upon Tyne 1982–88, sr lectr and conslt surgn Univ of Newcastle Upon Tyne and Royal Victoria Infirmary Newcastle 1988–; memb N of England Surgical Soc; FRCS 1980; *Books* Going into Hospital (1988); *Recreations* fly fishing, gardening; *Style—* Thomas Lennard, Esq; ✉ Ward 46, Royal Victoria Infirmary, Queen Victoria Rd, Newcastle Upon Tyne NE1 4LP (☎ 0191 232 5131)

LENNARD-JONES, Prof John Edward; s of Sir John Lennard-Jones, KBE (d 1954), of Keele, Staffs, and Kathleen Mary, *née* Lennard; *b* 29 Jan 1927; *Educ* King's Coll Choir Sch Cambridge, Gresham's, CCC Cambridge (MA, MD), UCH Med Sch London; *m* 19 Feb 1955, Verna Margaret, da of Ebenezer Albert Down (d 1960); 4 s (David b 1956, Peter b 1958, Andrew b 1960, Timothy b 1964); *Career* med trg posts: UCH, Manchester Royal Infirmary, Central Middx Hosp 1953–65; memb MRC Gastroenterology Res Unit Central Middx Hosp 1963–65, conslt gastroenterologist St Mark's Hosp London 1965–92, conslt physician UCH 1965–74, prof of gastroentology London Hosp Med Coll 1974–87 (emeritus prof 1987–); currently: hon consulting gastroenterologist Royal London Hosp, emeritus conslt gastroenterologist St Mark's Hosp London; author of scientific papers on gen med, gastroenterology and nutrition; Sir Arthur Hurst lecture Br Soc of Gastroenterology 1973, Humphrey Davy Rolleston lecture RCP 1977, Schorstein lecture London Hosp Med Coll 1987, Bryan Brooke lecture and medal Ileostomy Assoc 1991, Robert Annetts lecture Nat Assoc for Colitis and Crohn's Disease 1992, Louis Mirvish meml lectr SA Gastroenterological Assoc 1995; chm Med Ctee St Mark's Hosp 1985–90; Br Soc of Gastroenterology: hon sec 1965–70, pres 1983; memb Cncl RCP 1986–89 (chm Gastroenterology Ctee 1985–89), vice chm Nat Assoc for Colitis and Crohn's Disease 1987–89 (chm Med Advsy Ctee 1979–90, hon life pres 1992), chm British Assoc for Parenteral and Enteral Nutrition 1991–95, pres Br Digestive Fndn 1992–; hon fell RSM; hon memb: Br Soc of Gastroenterology, Swedish Soc of Gastroenterology, Netherlands Soc of Gastroenterology, Ileostomy Assoc, S African Gastroenterology Soc; membre d'honneur: Swiss Soc of Gastroenterology, French Soc of Coloproctology; corresponding memb: Polish Soc of Internal Med, Italian Soc of Gastroenterology; FRCP 1968, FRCS 1992, Fell UCL 1995; *Books* Clinical Gastroentology (jtly, 1968), Intestinal Transit (ed, 1991), Inflammatory Bowel Disease (jtly, 1992), Constipation (jtly, 1994); *Recreations* ornithology, golf, gardening; *Clubs* Athenaeum;

Style— Prof John Lennard-Jones; ✉ 72 Cumberland Street, Woodbridge, Suffolk IP12 4AD (☎ 01394 387717, fax 01394 387742)

LENNOX, *see:* Gordon Lennox

LENNOX, Annie; da of Thomas A Lennox (d 1986), and Dorothy, *née* Ferguson; *b* 25 Dec 1954; *Educ* Aberdeen HS for Girls, RAM (ARAM); *m* 1988, Uri Fruchtmann, s of Benjamin Fruchtmann; 2 da (Lola Lennox Fruchtmann b 10 Dec 1990, Tali Fruchtmann b 9 Feb 1993); *Career* singer; fndr memb (with Dave Stewart): The Tourists 1978–80, Eurythmics 1982–90; solo albums: Diva 1992, Medusa 1995; Eurythmics tours: Folie a Deux (UK Feb-March 1983, Europe March 1983), Kiss Me Quick (UK June 1983, USA (first tour) Aug-Sept 1983), Only Fools and Horses (UK Oct-Dec 1983), Touch (Europe Feb-May 1984, USA May and Aug-Oct 1984), Revenge (World tour Aug 1986–March 1987), Revival (World tour Sept 1989–Jan 1990); singles sales awards: Sweet Dreams (Silver UK, Gold Canada), Who's That Girl (Silver UK), Here Comes The Rain Again (Gold Canada); album sales awards: Sweet Dreams (Platinum UK and Canada), Touch (Double Platinum Canada, Platinum RIAA and UK), Sweet Dreams (Double Platinum Canada), Be Yourself Tonight (Triple Platinum Aust, Double Platinum Canada), Revenge (Triple Platinum Aust, Platinum UK), We Two Are One (Platinum UK and Canada), Savage (Gold Sweden), Diva (Platinum UK and USA); other awards incl: Best UK Video (for Love Is A Stranger) 1982, Best Video Album (for Sweet Dreams) Grammy Awards, Best Female Performance (for Sweet Dreams), Ivor Novello Award for Best Pop Song (Sweet Dreams) Br Acad of Songwriters, winner American Soc of Composers Award, BPI Award for Best Female vocalist 1982/83, 1987/88, 1989/90 and 1992/93, BPI Award for Best Album (Diva) 1992/93, Best Female Video (for Why), Ivor Novello award for Best Song (Why), BRIT Award for Best Female Vocalist 1996, Best Female Pop Vocals (for No More I Love You's) Grammy Awards 1996; other album awards: Replity Effect (with The Tourists, Silver UK, winner Silver UK for single I Only Wanna Be With You), Who's Zoomin Who! (Aretha Franklin, Silver UK); *Style—* Ms Annie Lennox; ✉ c/o 19 Management, Unit 32, Ransomes Dock, 35–37 Parkgate Rd, London SW11 4NP (☎ 0171 228 4000, fax 0171 924 1608)

LENNOX, Michael James Madill; s of Rev James Lennox, of 30 Hazel Beck, Bingley, Yorks; *b* 11 Sept 1943; *Educ* St John's Sch Leatherhead; *m* 4 May 1968, Ingrid Susan Elizabeth, da of Ronald Ewart Binns; 1 s (Timothy b 6 Dec 1974), 1 da (Rebecca b 6 Oct 1972); *Career* CA; Armitage & Norton Bradford 1961–68, Price Waterhouse (Montreal) 1968–70, asst controller Honeywell Ltd Toronto 1970–73, Euro business planning controller Honeywell Europe Brussels 1973–78, fin dir Cutler Hammer Europa Ltd (Bedford) 1978–85; gp fin dir: C P Roberts & Co Ltd 1985–88, Central Trailer Rentco Ltd 1988–90; fin dir Charterhouse Development Capital Ltd 1990–92, gp fin dir Weatherall Green & Smith 1992–; FCA; *Recreations* tennis, squash, skiing; *Style—* Michael Lennox, Esq; ✉ Old Cottage Farm, Top End, Renhold, Bedford MK41 OLS (☎ 01234 870370)

LENNOX-BOYD, Hon Benjamin Alan; s and h of 2 Viscount Boyd of Merton, *qv*; *b* 21 Oct 1964; *Educ* Millfield; *m* 28 Jan 1993, Mrs Sheila Mary Margaret Carroll, da of Harold Emmanuel George Williams, of 343 North Road, West Plymouth; 1 s (Alan George Simon b 11 March 1993), 1 da (Mary Alice b 14 Feb 1994); *Style—* The Hon Benjamin Lennox-Boyd; ✉ South Broadmoor, Saltash, Cornwall

LENNOX-BOYD, Hon Sir Mark Alexander; kt (1994), MP (C) Morecambe and Lunesdale (majority 11,509); s of 1 Viscount Boyd of Merton, CH, PC, DL (d 1983), and Patricia, Viscountess Boyd of Merton; bro of 2 Viscount Boyd of Merton, *qv*; *b* 4 May 1943; *Educ* Eton, ChCh Oxford; *m* 1974, Mrs Arabella Lacloche, o da of Piero Parisi, of Rome; 1 da (Patricia Irene b 1980); *Career* called to the Bar Inner Temple 1968; MP (C): Morecambe and Lonsdale 1979–83, Morecambe and Lunesdale 1983–; PPS to Rt Hon Nigel Lawson as Chllr of the Exchequer 1983–84, govt whip 1984–88, PPS to the Prime Minister 1988–90, Parly under sec of state FCO 1990–94; memb Ct of Assts Worshipful Co of Fishmongers, Liveryman Worshipful Co of Clockmakers; *Style—* The Hon Sir Mark Lennox-Boyd, MP; ✉ c/o The House of Commons, London SW1A 0AA

LENON, Andrew Ralph Fitzmaurice; s of Rev Philip John Fitzmaurice, of Dinton, Wilts, and Jane Alethia, *née* Brooke; *b* 7 April 1957; *Educ* St John's Sch Leatherhead, Lincoln Coll Oxford (BA); *m* 5 Sept 1987, Sheila, da of Donald Cook (d 1977); 1 s (George b 1989), 2 da (Olivia b 1991, Susannah Elizabeth Fitzmaurice b 1995); *Career* called to the Bar Lincoln's Inn 1982; *Style—* Andrew Lenon, Esq; ✉ 1 Essex Court, Temple, London EC4Y 9AR (☎ 0171 583 2000)

LENON, Barnaby John; s of Rev Philip John Fitzmaurice Lenon, of Dinton, Wiltshire, and Jane Alethea, *née* Brooke; *b* 10 May 1954; *Educ* Eltham Coll, Keble Coll Oxford (scholar, MA), St John's Coll Cambridge (Univ Prize for Educn, Coll Prize, PGCE); *m* 27 August 1983, Penelope Anne, da of James Desmond Thain; 2 da (India Elizabeth Jane b 9 Nov 1989, Flora Catherine Dyne b 4 June 1992); *Career* teacher: Eton Coll 1976–77, Sherborne Sch Dorset 1978–79, Eton Coll 1979–90 (latterly head of Geography Dept); dep headmaster Highgate Sch 1990–94, headmaster Trinity Sch of John Whitgift 1995–; FRGS 1987 (memb Cncl 1987–90); *Books* Techniques and Fieldwork in Geography (1982), London (1988), London in the 1990's (1993), Fieldwork Techniques and Projects in Geography (1994), Directory of University Geography Courses 1995 (jt ed, 1995, 2 edn 1996), The United Kingdom: Geographical Case Studies (1995); *Recreations* writing, oil painting, travel, opera; *Clubs* East India; *Style—* Barnaby J Lenon, Esq; ✉ 29 The Ridge Way, Sanderstead, Surrey CR2 0LJ; Trinity School, Shirley Park, Croydon, Surrey CR9 7AT (☎ 0181 656 9541, fax 0181 655 0522)

LENOX-CONYNGHAM, Charles Denis; s of Capt Alwyn Douglas Lenox-Conyngham, RN (d 1990), of Benenden, Kent, and Margaret Cecilia, *née* Clear; *b* 24 Jan 1935; *Educ* Winchester, Magdalen Coll Oxford (MA), Wharton Sch of Business Admin Univ of Pennsylvania; *m* 15 April 1972, Helga Gerrit, da of Lt-Gen Hans von Liebach (d 1966), of Berlin; 1 s (Patrick b 1972), 1 da (Laura b 1974); *Career* cmmnd 2 Lt 13/18 Royal Hussars, served Germany 1954–56; md: Blue Funnel Line 1970, Price and Pierce 1985; exec dir Ocean Transport & Trading 1972–85, chm and chief exec Sealink (UK) Ltd 1985–90, chm Sims Food Group plc 1991–92 (non-exec dir 1992–); chm: Power Group International 1992–94, Atkins Group plc 1992–95, Hartons Group plc 1993–; *Recreations* family, gardening, tennis, walking, skiing; *Clubs* RAC; *Style—* Charles Lenox-Conyngham; ✉ Yew Tree House, Walkhurst Road, Benenden, Kent TN17 4DR (☎ 01580 240630, fax 01580 241996)

LENSKA, Rula (aka Rozamaria Laura Leopoldyna Lubienska); da of Count Ludwig Lubienski, and Elizabeth Carroll, *née* Tyszkiewicz; *b* 30 Sept 1947; *Educ* Jesus & Mary Covent Willesden Green, Ursuline Convent Westgate-on-Sea, Pitmans Secretarial Coll Holborn, Webber Douglas Acad of Dramatic Art; *m* 1 (m dis), Brian Deacon; 1 da (Lara b 17 Aug 1979); m 2, Dennis Waterman, *qv*; *Career* actress; fluent in Polish, French, Italian and German; hot air balloon pilot; fndr memb Elefriends, hon vice pres Operation Raleigh; tstee: CIC, Paul O'Gorman Leukemia Fndn; *Theatre* Suddenly At Home (Durbridge, Windsor and Fortune) 1970–72, Secretary Bird, Lady Capulet in Romeo and Juliet, Titania in Midsummer Night's Dream (Regents Park), Regina in Ghosts (Swan), Doris in Same Time Next Year (Old Vic, Aust, NZ), Double Double, The Real Thing (Guildford, Aust), Elvira in Blithe Spirit (Lyric Hammersmith), Temptation (Palace Theatre London), The Physicists, Annie Wilkes in Misery (no 1 tour), Dangerous Corner (Whitehall and no 1 tour), principal boy in pantomine annually 1988–; *Television* incl: Dixon of Dock Green, Rock Follies, Amazing Stories, Take a Letter Mr Jones, Robin of Sherwood, Return of the Native, Design for Living, Minder, Boon, Conversations with a Stranger, Aubrey Beardsley, Jackanory, The Saint, The Godmother, Cluedo, Kappatoo, The Mixer, Stay Lucky, The Detectives; co-presenter women's prog Sky TV; veteran of voiceovers and TV wildlife documentaries; *Books* Mammoth Hunt (with Col John Blashford-Snell, OBE, 1996); *Recreations* music, reading, snooker, photography, conservation, golf, travel, expeditions, embroidery, making jewellery, alternative medicine and healing; *Clubs* Tramp, Groucho's, Polish Hearth; *Style—* Ms Rula Lenska; ✉ c/o Vernon Conway Ltd, 5 Spring St, Paddington, London W2 (☎ 0171 262 5506/7, fax 0171 402 4834); voice over agent Rhubard (☎ 0171 437 1600)

LENT, Penelope Ann (Penny); da of David Wilson (d 1984), of Stanmore, Middx, and Zipporah, *née* Jacobs; *b* 24 July 1947; *Educ* Whitegate Sch Harrow Weald, Middx Coll Wembley; *m* Nov 1968, Jeffrey Alan Lent; 1 da (Tiffany Dawn); *Career* secretary with advtg and music recording cos 1965–68; London Weekend Television: joined 1968, various location mgmnt positions, headed new business responsible for mktg The London Studios studio and prodn facilities 1988, dir London Studios for sales and mktg, currently dir of sales, mktg and devpt Granada International Resources; *Clubs* Groucho; *Style—* Ms Penny Lent; ✉ The London Studios, The London Television Centre, Upper Ground, London SE1 9LT (☎ 0171 261 3683)

LENTON, John Robert; s of Rev Robert Vincent Lenton, vicar of Lacock, Wilts (ret); *b* 13 May 1946; *Educ* Prince of Wales Sch Nairobi, Exeter Coll Oxford, Harvard Business Sch; *m* 1967, Ann Cathrine; 1 s, 1 da; *Career* specialist in fin mktg; International Factors Ltd: dir sales and mktg 1976, dir ops 1977, dir sales and mktg 1979; sr vice pres int technologies American Express 1994– (vice pres fin and planning 1982–86, vice pres and gen mangr N Europe 1986–88, sr vice pres Euro operating centre 1988–90, sr vice pres and gen mangr S Europe Middle East and Africa 1990–91, sr vice pres customer serv UK 1991–94); chm Agape Ministries Ltd; *Recreations* skiing, choral singing, treble recorder, walking the South Downs; *Style—* John Lenton, Esq; ✉ 11 Wilbury Gardens, Hove, Sussex (☎ office 01273 525455, fax 01273 670802)

LENYGON, Bryan Norman; s of the late Maj Frank Norman Lenygon, of Highfield, Bells Yew Green, E Sussex, and Marjorie Winifred, *née* Healey; *b* 6 May 1932; *Educ* Univ of London (MA, LLB); *m* 27 Oct 1967, Diana Jane, da of Betty Patricia Baxter, of Hingham, Norfolk; 2 da (Fiona b 1957, Sally b 1961); *Career* called to the Bar Gray's Inn 1976; chm: Gartmore Enterprise Trust plc, The Turkey Trust plc, Abtrust Latin American Trust plc, Geared Income Trust plc, Finsbury Technology Trust plc; dir various other investmt tst cos; gen cmmr City of London; Freeman City of London, Liveryman Worshipful Co of Lorimers; FCA, FCIS, ATII; *Recreations* tennis; *Clubs* City of London, City Livery; *Style—* Bryan Lenygon, Esq; ✉ Highfield, Bells Yew Green, E Sussex TN3 9AP (☎ 01892 750343, fax 01892 750609)

LEON, Alexander John; s and h of Sir John Ronald Leon, 4 Bt; *b* 3 May 1965; *Educ* Bryanston; *Career* music prodn musician; *Recreations* skiing, watersports, tennis, cricket; *Style—* Alexander Leon, Esq; ✉ 14 Cliveden Place, London SW1 (0171 730 0803)

LEONARD, Chief Constable (David) Anthony (Tony); QPM (1990); s of Richard Leonard (d 1987), of Stocksmoor, W Yorks, and Elsie Violet, *née* Edwards (d 1991); *b* 10 March 1939; *Educ* Royds Hall GS Huddersfield, LSE (BSc Econ), Univ of Hull (research student (PhD) 1995–); *m* 1962, Kathleen, *née* Rumsey; 1 da (Debra Lynn b 8 July 1963), 1 s (Stuart b 10 March 1966); *Career* Nat Serv RAF Police 1958–60, constable rising to chief inspr Lancs Constabulary 1962–77, Special Course V Police Staff Coll Bramshill 1966–67, supt rising to asst chief constable Derbyshire Constabulary 1977–84 (i/c police response to NUM/NCB dispute 1984), Intermediate Cmd Course Bramshill 1978 (Sr Cmd Course 1981), dep chief constable Sussex Police 1984–91, chief constable Humberside Police 1991–; sr UK police advsr to Czech and Slovak govts (sponsored by FCO Know How Fund) 1990–; external examiner Dept of Applied Social Scis Univ of Hull; various offices Methodist Church; pres: Humberside Inst of Mgmnt 1994–96, Humber Strategic Bd Young Enterprise 1996; memb: Soc for Reform of Criminal Law, Nat Tst; CIMgt 1994; *Recreations* music, theatre, walking, travel; *Style—* Chief Constable Tony Leonard, QPM; ✉ Humberside Police HQ, Queens Gardens, Kingston upon Hull, North Humberside HU1 3DJ (☎ 01482 220113, fax 01482 220561)

LEONARD, Brian Henry; s of William Henry Leonard (d 1986), Bertha Florence, *née* Thomas (d 1977); *b* 6 Jan 1948; *Educ* Dr Challoner's GS, LSE; *m* 1975, Maggy, da of Charles Martin Meade-King; 2 s (Will Martin b 1 Jan 1977, James Henry b 20 July 1979); *Career* Heal & Son Ltd 1969–73, The Price Commission 1973–74; DOE: admin trainee 1974–77, HEO 1977–79, princ 1979–88, seconded to Circle 33 Housing Trust 1982–83, asst sec 1988–93, under sec and regnl dir of Northern Region 1993–94, regnl dir Govt Office for the South West 1994–; fell Hubert Humphrey Inst Minneapolis 1987–88; *Recreations* friends, games; *Clubs* Marylebone Cricket; *Style—* Brian Leonard, Esq; ✉ Government Office for the South West, The Pithay, Bristol BS1 2PB and Phoenix House, Notte Street, Plymouth PL1 2HF

LEONARD, Rev and Rt Hon Dr Graham Douglas; KCVO (1991), PC (1981); s of Rev Douglas Leonard; *b* 8 May 1921; *Educ* Monkton Combe Sch, Balliol Coll Oxford, Westcott House Cambridge; *m* 1943, (Vivien) Priscilla, da of late Dr Swann; 2 s; *Career* served WWII Oxford & Bucks LI as Capt; ordained Church of England 1947, archdeacon Hampstead 1962–64, bishop suffragan of Willesden 1964–73, bishop of Truro 1973–81, 130th Bishop of London 1981–91, received into RC Church and ordained priest *sub conditione* by HE Cardinal Basil Hume OSB 1994; dean of HM's Chapels Royal 1981–91, prelate Order of the British Empire 1981–91; memb House of Lords 1977–91; delegate to fifth Assembly WCC Nairobi 1975, chm Gen Synod Bd for Social Responsibility 1976–83; Green lectr Westminster Coll Fulton Missouri 1987, Hensley Henson lectr Oxford Univ 1991–92; chm: Churches Main Ctee 1981–91, Jerusalem and Middle East Church Assoc 1981–91, Bd of Educn and National Soc 1983–89; church cmmr 1973–91, episcopal canon St George's Cathedral Jerusalem 1981–91, prelate of the Imperial Soc of Knights Bachelor 1986–91; memb Polys and Colls Funding Cncl 1989–93, govr Pusey House Oxford 1990–95; superior gen Soc of Mary 1973–94 (vice pres 1994–), hon guardian Shrine of Our Lady of Walsingham 1970–; hon master of Bench of Middle Temple 1981–, hon fell Balliol Coll Oxford; Hon DD: Episcopal Theological Seminary Kentucky 1974, Westminster Coll Fulton Missouri 1987; Hon DCnL Nashota House USA 1983, STD Siena Coll USA 1984, Hon LLD Simon Greenleaf Sch of Law USA 1987, Hon DLitt CNAA 1989; *Clubs* Garrick; *Style—* The Rev and Rt Hon Dr Graham Leonard, KCVO; ✉ 25 Woodlands Rd, Witney, Oxon OX8 6DR

LEONARD, Jason; *b* 14 Aug 1968; *Career* rugby union player (loose-head prop); former clubs: Barking, Saracens; current club Harlequins; England: B debut 1989 (2 caps v Fiji and France), full debut 1990, memb Grand Slam winning squad 1991 and 1992, memb World Cup runners-up squad 1991, 4th place World Cup S Africa 1995, over 49 caps; memb British Lions' team touring NZ 1993 (2 tests), tour to S Africa 1994; honours incl: Essex Colts Cup winners with Barking, England Colts Under 19s, Essex Cup winners with Barking Seniors, Under 21 County Championship title with Eastern Cos, English Div 2 title with Saracens 1989, England Under 21s Romania; Gorst Clayton Demolition; *Style—* Jason Leonard, Esq; ✉ Harlequins FC, Stoop Memorial Ground, Craneford Way, Twickenham, Middx TW2 7SQ (☎ 0181 892 0822)

LEONARD, Hon Sir (Hamilton) John Leonard; kt (1981); s of Arthur Leonard; *b* 28 April 1926; *Educ* Dean Close Sch Cheltenham, BNC Oxford; *m* 1948, Doreen (d 1996), yr da of late Lt-Col Sidney Parker, OBE; 1 s (Anthony), 1 da (Susan); *Career* served

Coldstream Gds (Capt) 1944–47; called to the Bar Inner Temple 1951, cmmr Central Criminal Ct 1969–71, dep chm Surrey QS 1969–71, QC 1969, recorder Crown Court 1972–78, circuit judge 1978–81, high court judge Queen's Bench 1981–93, presiding judge Wales and Chester Circuit 1982–86; Common Serjeant City of London 1979–81; memb: Gen Cncl of Bar 1970–74, Judicial Studies Bd 1979–82, Cncl Hurstpierpoint Coll 1975–82; govr Dean Close Sch 1986–, former chm Criminal Bar Assoc; Liveryman Worshipful Co of Plaisterers; HM Lt City London 1980–81; *Clubs* Garrick; *Style*— The Hon Sir John Leonard; ✉ Royal Courts of Justice, Strand, London WC2A 2LL

LEONARD, John Patrick; CBE (1994); s of Rt Rev M P G Leonard, DSO (d 1963), and Kathleen Mary, *née* Knights-Smith (d 1994); *b* 3 Sept 1935; *Educ* Glasgow Acad, Trinity Coll Glenalmond, Selwyn Coll Cambridge (BA), Sch of Mil Survey Hermitage (Dip land surveying), Univ Coll Cambridge (Dip Devpt Studies); *m* 6 Aug 1960, Christine Joan, da of Eric Mayer; 1 s (Adam Patrick b 1965 d 1984), 2 da (Catherine b 1963 d 1965, Rachel Anne b 1967); *Career* Midshipman and Sub Lt RN 1954–56; maths teacher Town Close Prep Sch 1957; Directorate of Overseas Surveys (i/c Survey Parties Jamaica, Br Honduras, Nigera, Sierra Leone, Mauritius and Sarawak) 1961–71; Ordnance Survey: regnl mangr W Midlands 1972–78, asst dir surveys 1978–82, head of prodn 1982–84, dir mktg planning and devpt 1984–93, dep DG 1993–95, ret; pres Land Surveyors Div RICS 1990–91, sec gen CERCO (Comitée Européen des Responsables de la Cartographie Officielle) 1996; FRICS 1985 (ARICS 1964); *Recreations* mountaineering, golf, photography; *Style*— John Leonard, Esq, CBE; ✉ Dellbrook, Hubert Road, St Cross, Winchester, Hants S023 9RG (☎ 01962 865093, fax 01962 866273, e-mail 101472.1456@compuserve.com)

LEONARD, (Douglas) Michael; s of Maj Douglas Goodwin Russell Leonard, IXth Jat Regt India (d 1942), and Kathleen Mary Leonard, *née* Murphy; *b* 25 June 1933, Bangalore, India; *Educ* Hallet War Sch Nainital India, Stonyhurst Coll (sch cert), St Martin's Sch of Art (NDD); *Career* artist; freelance illustrator 1957–69, painter 1969–; cmmnd by Reader's Digest to paint portrait of HM the Queen to celebrate her 60th birthday 1984 (presented to Nat Portrait Gall 1986); *Solo Exhibitions* Fischer Fine Art 1974, 1977, 1980, 1983 and 1988, drawings Harriet Griffin NYC 1977, Stiebel Modern NYC 1992, Thomas Gibson 1993; *Retrospectives* Gemeentemuseum Arnhem 1977, Artsite Gallery Bath 1989; *Group Exhibitions* Fischer Fine Art 1972, 1973, 1975, 1976, 1978, 1979, and 1981, Realismus und Realität (Darmstadt) 1975, John Moores Exbhns 10 and 11 Liverpool 1976 and 1978, Nudes (Angela Flowers Gallery London) 1980–81, Contemporary British Painters (Museo Municipal Madrid) 1983, The Self Portrait - A Modern View (touring) 1987–88, In Human Terms (Stiebel Modern NYC 1991); *Public Collections* Museum Boymans-van Beuningen Rotterdam, V & A, Nat Portrait Gallery London, Ferens Art Gallery Hull, New Orleans Museum of Art, Fitzwilliam Museum Cambridge; *Books* Changing - 50 Drawings (intro by Edward Lucie-Smith, 1983), Michael Leonard - Paintings (foreward by Lincoln Kirstein, interviewed by Edward Lucie-Smith, 1985); *Style*— Michael Leonard, Esq; ✉ c/o Thomas Gibson Fine Art, 44 Old Bond Street, London W1X 4HQ

LEONARD, Michael Francis; s of Michael Gerard Leonard (d 1976), and Frances Irene, *née* Kay (d 1994); *b* 25 June 1937; *Educ* Magdalen Coll Sch Oxford, Salesian Coll Oxford (capt of football and cricket, head boy), Oriel Coll Oxford (BA); *m* 19 May 1973, Pamela Georgina, da of Ernest Young, of Weeford, Staffs; 1 s (Paul Francis b 28 Sept 1977); *Career* articled clerk Cocke Vellacott & Hill London 1959, qualified CA 1963; Mann Judd & Co: joined London 1965, ptnr 1970, opened office Newcastle upon Tyne 1977, merged with Touche Ross & Co 1979; sr audit and professional ptnr Touche Ross & Co 1990–94 (ptnr i/c 1979–90); Northern Soc of CAs: sec 1988–90, vice pres 1990–91, dep pres 1991–92, pres 1992–93; memb: NE Industl Devpt Bd 1994–, Ctee Norcare 1995–; FCA 1974 (ACA 1964); *Recreations* golf, gardening, sports and social outdoor pursuits; *Clubs* The Northumberland Golf (treas 1988–93, chm 1993–), Bamburgh Castle Golf, Northern Counties; *Style*— Michael Leonard, Esq; ✉ 237 Darras Road, Ponteland, Newcastle upon Tyne NE20 9AJ (☎ 01661 871150)

LEONARD, Paul Michael; *b* 14 Jan 1942; *Educ* Finchley GS, Univ of Sheffield (LLB); *m* 1970, Diana Clare, *née* Bryce-Curtis; 2 s (Nick, Guy), 1 da (Emily); *Career* admitted slr 1966; Freshfields: articled clerk 1964–66, asst slr 1966–72, litigation ptnr 1972–, managing ptnr Litigation Dept 1988–90, jtly responsible for recruitment of trainee slrs; memb Cncl Trinity Hospice (chm House Ctee); *Recreations* cricket, skiing, Aston Martins, paintings of Paul Marny; *Clubs* MCC; *Style*— Paul Leonard, Esq; ✉ Freshfields, 65 Fleet St, London EC4Y 1HS (☎ 0171 936 4000, fax 0171 832 7246)

LEONARD, Dr Robert Charles Frederick; s of André Lucien Maxime Leonard (d 1977), of Merthyr Tydfil, Wales, and Rosa Mary, *née* Taylor; *b* 11 May 1947; *Educ* Merthyr Tydfil Co GS, Charing Cross Hosp Med Sch (BSc, MB BS, MD); *m* 2 June 1973, Tania, da of Roland Charles Smith, and Keysoe, *née* North, of Louth, Lincs; 3 da (Victoria b 26 Sept 1974, Louisa b 26 Feb 1978, Emily b 18 Sept 1980); *Career* sr house offr: Charing Cross Hosp 1972, Hammersmith Hosp 1973; registrar Oxford Hosps 1974–76, res fell Leukaemia Res Fund 1976–79, lectr and sr registrar Newcastle Hosps 1979–82, fell Cancer Res Campaign 1981–82, res fell Dana Farber Cancer Inst Harvard Med Sch Boston 1982–82, conslt physician and hon sr lectr in clinical oncology Edinburgh 1983–; chm: Lothian Health Bd Ethical Ctee on Med and Oncology, Educnl Ctee Assoc of Cancer Physicians; memb Editorial Bd British Journal of Cancer; FRCPEd 1984, FRCP 1993, American Soc of Clinical Oncology; *Books* Understanding Cancer (1985), Sociological Tumour Marks (1993); author of over 200 scientific papers on cancer and related research; *Recreations* music, piano, soccer; *Style*— Dr Robert Leonard; ✉ Department of Clinical Oncology, Western General Hospital, Crewe Road, Edinburgh EH4 2XU (☎ 0131 537 1000)

LEOPARD, Peter James; s of Charles Henry Leopard (d 1974), of Dinas Powys, Glamorgan, and Dorothy Bertha, *née* Cole; *b* 1 Sept 1938; *Educ* Penarth GS, Guy's Hosp Dental and Med Schs London (MB BS, BDS), FDSRCS, MRCS LRCP, FRCSEd; *m* (m dis), Catherine Mary; 1 da (Claire Angela (Mrs Sams) b 28 Sept 1953), 2 s (Daniel Charles b 12 Aug 1985, Oliver Joseph b 17 June 1987); *Career* conslt maxillofacial surgn N Staffs 1972–; Royal Coll of Surgns: memb Bd Faculty of Dental Surgery 1992–, memb Cncl 1995–, chm Intercollegiate Bd in Oral and Maxillofacial Surgery 1992–95, vice chm Euro Bd of Oral and Maxillofacial Surgery 1994–, chm Faculty Manpower Advsy Panel 1995–, memb Senate of Surgery 1996–; Royal Coll of Surgns of Edinburgh: chm Speciality Advsy Bd 1991–95, chm Hosp Recognition Ctee Faculty of Dental Surgery 1992–95; memb Specialist Workforce Advsy Gp (SWAG) Dept of Health 1995–, chm N Staffs Med Inst 1996–, pres Br Assoc of Oral and Maxillofacial Surgns 1997; divnl surgn St John's Ambulance 1986–92; Down Surgical Prize Br Assoc of Oral and Maxillofacial Surgns 1994/95; memb: N Staffs Med Club, Oral Surgery Club of GB; FRCS (without examination) 1987; *Recreations* skiing, gardening, music, formerly boxing (boxed for Univ of London) and rugby (schoolboy trialist for Wales); *Style*— Peter Leopard, Esq; ✉ Stone House, Basnetts Wood, Endon, Stoke-on-Trent ST9 9DQ (☎ and fax 01782 504095); Department of Maxillofacial Surgery, North Staffordshire Hospital, Stoke-on-Trent ST4 7PA (☎ 01782 716222, fax 01782 714706, mobile 0973 549705)

LEPLEY, Stephen Keith (Steve); s of Ernest Joseph Lepley (d 1989), and Joyce Elsie, *née* Walker; *b* 20 Aug 1954; *Educ* Stratford GS; *m* 11 Dec 1982, Tracey Ann, da of Terry Richardson; 1 s (Samuel b 17 July 1985), 2 da (Ann-Marie b 24 Sept 1979, Lauren b 28 July 1983); *Career* Cartwright Brice Ltd 1970–75 (trainee accountant, asst co accountant), co accountant Owlcliff Ltd 1975–78, asst gp accountant Victoria Sporting Group of Companies (take over by Playboy 1980) 1978–81, chief accountant McCormick Publicis Ltd 1983–84 (regnl accountant 1981–83), fin controller (assoc dir) Gold Greenlees Trott Advertising 1986–88 (accountant 1984–86), fin dir Simons Palmer Denton Clemmow & Johnson Ltd 1988–; *Recreations* most sports particularly rugby and soccer; *Style*— Steve Lepley, Esq; ✉ Simons Palmer Clemmow Johnson Ltd, 19–20 Noel Street, London W1V 3PD (☎ 0171 287 4455)

LEPPARD, Raymond John; CBE (1983); s of Albert Victor Leppard, and Bertha May, *née* Beck; *b* 11 Aug 1927; *Educ* Trinity Coll Cambridge; *Career* fell and lectr in music Trinity Coll Cambridge 1958–68, princ conductor BBC Northern Symphony Orch 1972–80, princ guest conductor St Louis Symphony Orch 1984–90, music dir Indianapolis Symphony Orch 1987–; Hon DUniv Bath 1972; Hon DMus: Indiana Univ 1991, Perdue Univ 1992; hon memb: RAM 1972, GSM 1984; Hon FRCM 1984; Commendatore al Merito Della Republica Italiana 1974; *Books* Monteverdi: Il Ballo Delle Ingrate (1958), L'Incoronazione Di Poppea (1962), L'Orfeo (1965), Cavalli: Messa Concertata (1966), L'Ormindo (1967), La Calisto (1969), Il Ritorno D'Ulisse (1972), L'Eqisto (1974), L'Orione (1983), Authenticity in Music (1988), Raymond Leppard on Music: An Anthology of Critical and Autobiographical Writings (1993); *Recreations* theatre, books, friends, music; *Style*— Raymond Leppard, Esq, CBE; ✉ Colbert Artists Management, 111 West 57th St, New York, NY 10019, USA (☎ 00 1 212 757 0782, fax 00 1 212 541 5179)

LEPRÊTRE-GRANET, Thierry Gerard; s of Georges Leprêtre-Granet, and Michelle, *née* Mairet; *b* 11 June 1962; *Educ* Coll Jean Yole Vendee France, Ecole Hoteliere Ste Anne Saint Nazaire; *m* 6 Feb 1987, Anna, da of Kenneth Wilkinson; 2 da (Céline b 19 June 1989, Claudine b 18 July 1991); *Career* 1 commis chef Hotel Alpina Chamonix 1983, 2 chef Duncow Hotel Dunchurch Warwicks 1984, chef de partie Mallory Court Hotel Leamington Spa 1985–86, chef de partie Hostellerie du Prieure Saumur France 1987, head chef Whitechapel Manor S Molton 1987–93, head chef The Box Tree Restaurant Ilkley 1993–; *Awards* for Whitechapel Manor: 3 AA Rosettes 1988, Egon Ronay Star 1988, Michelin Star 1989; for The Box Tree Restaurant: Egon Ronay Star 1995, 3 AA Rosettes 1995, Michelin Star 1996, Yorkshire Life Magazine Best Yorkshire Restaurant 1996–97; *Recreations* reading, spending time with my wife and children; *Style*— Thierry Lepretre-Granet; ✉ Box Tree Restaurant, 35–37 Church Street, Ilkley, West Yorkshire LS29 9DR (☎ 01943 608484, fax 01943 607186)

LEPSCHY, Prof Giulio Ciro; s of Emilio Lepschy, and Sara, *née* Castelfranchi (d 1984); *b* 14 Jan 1935; *Educ* Liceo Marco Polo Venice, Univ of Pisa (Dott Lett), Scuola Normale Superiore (Dip & Perf Sc Norm Sup); *m* 20 Dec 1962, Prof (Anna) Laura Lepschy, *qv*, da of Arnaldo Momigliano, Hon KBE (d 1987); *Career* Univ of Reading: lectr 1964–67, reader 1967–75, prof 1975–; FBA 1987, corresponding fell Accademia della Crusca 1991; *Publications* A Survey of Structural Linguistics (1970), The Italian Language Today (with A L Lepschy, 1977), Saggi di Linguistica Italiana (1978), Intorno a Saussure (1979), Mutamenti di Prospettiva nella Linguistica (1981), Nuovi Saggi di Linguistica Italiana (1989), Sulla Linguistica Moderna (1989), Storia della Linguistica (1990), La Linguistica del Novecento (1992), A History of Linguistics (1994); *Style*— Prof Giulio Lepschy, FBA; ✉ Department of Italian Studies, The University, Whiteknights, Reading RG6 6AA (☎ 01734 316501)

LEPSCHY, Prof (Anna) Laura; da of Arnaldo Dante Momigliano, Hon KBE (d 1987), of London, and Gemma Celestina, *née* Segre; *b* 30 Nov 1933; *Educ* Headington Sch Oxford, Somerville Coll Oxford; *m* 20 Dec 1962, Prof Giulio Ciro Lepschy, FBA, *qv*, s of Emilio Lepschy, of Venice; *Career* jr fell Univ of Bristol 1957–59, lectr in Italian Univ of Reading 1962–68 (asst lectr 1959–62); UCL: lectr in Italian 1968–79, sr lectr 1979–84, reader 1984–87, prof 1987–; memb: Soc for Italian Studies, Assoc for Study of Modern Italy, Pirandello Soc, Comparative Lit Assoc, Modern Humanities Res Assoc, Associazione Internazionale Studi Lingua and Letteratura Italiana; *Books* Santo Brasca, Viaggio in Terrasanta 1480 (ed, 1967), Tintoretto Observed (1983), Narrativa e Teatro fra Due Secoli (1984), Varietà linguistiche e pluralità di codici nel Rinascimento (1996); *Recreations* swimming; *Style*— Prof Laura Lepschy; ✉ Department of Italian, University College, Gower St, London WC1E 6BT (☎ 0171 380 7784, fax 0171 209 0638)

LEREGO, Michael John; QC (1995); s of Leslie Ivor Lerego, and Gwendolen Frances, *née* Limbert (d 1990); *b* 6 May 1949; *Educ* Manchester GS, Haberdashers' Aske's, Keble Coll Oxford (open scholar, BA jurisprudence, BCL, MA, distinction Law Moderations, Gibbs Prize in Law); *m* 24 June 1972, Susan, da of George Henry Northover (d 1969); 1 s (Colin Andrew b 8 Oct 1976, d 1977); 3 da (Louise Jane b 15 Feb 1979, Caroline Ruth, Victoria Ann (twins) b 26 Aug 1981); *Career* called to the Bar Inner Temple 1972, in practice 1972–; weekender The Queen's Coll Oxford 1972–78; memb: Jt Working Party of Law Soc & Bar on Banking Law 1987–91, Sub-Ctee on Banking Law Law Soc 1991–; arbitrator: Modified Arbitration Scheme Lloyd's 1988–92, Arbitration Scheme Lloyd's 1993–; co-opted govr Wroxham J M I Sch Potters Bar 1995–; *Recreations* watching sport; *Style*— Michael Lerego, Esq, QC; ✉ Fountain Court, Temple, London EC4Y 9DH (☎ 0171 583 3335)

LERNER, Neil Joseph; *b* 31 May 1947; *Educ* Tiffin Sch, St John's Coll Cambridge (MA); *m* 27 June 1972, Susan Elizabeth, *née* Kempner; 2 s (Nicholas b 16 May 1979, Jonathan b 18 July 1981); *Career* KPMG: joined 1968, ptnr 1984–, head Corp Fin UK 1993–; FCA 1971, MSI; *Clubs* Little Ship; *Style*— Neil Lerner, Esq; ✉ KPMG, 8 Salisbury Square, London EC4Y 8BB (☎ 0171 311 8620 (direct), fax 0171 311 8276)

LERWILL, Robert Earl; s of Colin Roy F Lerwill, and Patricia (Luck) Lerwill; *b* 21 Jan 1952; *Educ* Barnstaple GS, Gosport GS, Univ of Nottingham (BA); *m* 1980 (m dis 1994), Carol H G Ruddock 1 s (Henry Robert b 1985), 1 da (Elizabeth Alice b 1991); *m* 2, 1994, Nicola Keddie; 1 da (Anna b 1995); *Career* Arthur Andersen & Co: joined as articled clerk 1973, mangr 1978, sr mangr 1981–86; gp fin dir WPP Group plc 1986–96, fin dir Cable and Wireless plc 1997–; FCA (ACA 1977), MInstD 1987; *Recreations* travel; *Style*— Robert Lerwill, Esq; ✉ Cable & Wireless plc, 124 Theobalds Road, London WC1X 8RX

LESCHLY, Jan; *b* 1940, Denmark; *Career* entered pharmaceutical industry 1972; pres Pharmaceutical Div Novo-Nordisk Corporation until 1979; Squibb Corporation USA: joined B R Squibb and Sons Inc as vice pres commercial devpt 1979, pres US 1981, gp vice pres and bd dir Squibb Corp with responsibility for Worldwide Pharmaceutical Products Group 1984, exec vice pres with responsibility for Squibb Operating Group 1986, pres and chief operating offr 1988–90; SmithKline Beecham plc: joined as chm SKB Pharmaceuticals 1990, bd dir 1990–, chief exec SmithKline Beecham plc April 1994–; memb British Pharma Group; memb: Bd of Dirs Pharmaceutical Research and Mfrs' of America (PhRMA), Bd of Tstees Nat Fndn for Infectious Diseases, Dean's Advsy Cncl Emory Business Sch; *Style*— Jan Leschly, Esq; ✉ SmithKline Beecham plc, One New Horizons Court, Great West Road, Brentford, Middx TW8 9EP (☎ 0181 975 2601)

LESEBERG, Michael; s of Lt Walter Leseberg (ka 1944), of Hamburg, and Karla, *née* Menge (d 1977); *b* 16 Feb 1940; *Educ* Germany Business Studies; *m* 27 Sept 1962, Traute, da of Johannes Plueschau, of Hamburg; 3 da (Birte b 1964, Petra b 1966, Katja b 1968); *Career* md Gilbert J McCaul (Overseas) Ltd 1961–91 (dir 1977–91), mgmnt conslt 1991–; dir: Orimex Handelsgesellschaft GmbH Hamburg 1969–93, London Potato Futures Assoc 1983 (formerly chm), London Commodity Exchange Ltd 1984–87, Baltic Int Freight Futures Exchange 1985, MLC Consultants Ltd 1992–; memb Cncl AFBD 1984–86; memb Baltic Exchange; *Recreations* music, tennis; *Style*— Michael Leseberg,

Esq; ✉ Old Mill House, Gandish Road, East Bergholt, via Colchester, Essex CO7 6UR (☎ and fax 01206 298 301)

LESLIE, Sir (Colin) Alan Bettridge; kt (1986); s of Rupert Colin Leslie, and Gladys Hannah, *née* Bettridge; *b* 10 April 1922; *Educ* King Edward VII Sch Lytham, Merton Coll Oxford (MA); *m* 1, 1953, Anne Barbara, *née* Coates (d 1982); 2 da; m 2, 1983, Jean Margaret (Sally), wid of Dr Alan Cheatle; *Career* cmmnd RSF 1941–46; slr Stafford Clark & Co 1948–60, head of Legal Dept and co sec BOC Group (formerly BOC International) 1960–83; Foreign Compensation Cmmn 1986–90, adjudicator Immigration Appeals 1990–94; pres Law Soc 1985–86 (vice pres 1984–85); *Recreations* fishing; *Clubs* United Oxford and Cambridge Univ; *Style*— Sir Alan Leslie; ✉ Tye Cottage, Alfriston, East Sussex BN26 5TD (☎ 01323 870518); 36 Abingdon Road, London W8 6AS (☎ 0171 937 2874)

LESLIE, Capt Alastair Pinckard; TD; s of Hon John Wayland Leslie (d 1991, s of 19 Earl of Rothes); *b* 29 Dec 1934; *Educ* Eton; *m* 1963, Rosemary, da of Cdr Hubert Wyndham Barry, RN; 1 s (David b 1967, d 1989), 2 da (Fiona (Mrs Richard de Klee) b 1965, Ann b 1973); *Career* Capt Royal Scots Fusiliers (TA); md Willis Faber & Dumas (Agencies) Ltd 1976–85; dir: A P Leslie Underwriting Agency Ltd 1976–90, Wellington Members Agency Ltd and other Lloyds underwriting agencies 1990–95, United Goldfields NL until 1988, Hardy Underwriting Group plc 1996–; memb Queen's Body Guard for Scotland (The Royal Co of Archers); Liveryman and memb Ct of Assts Worshipful Co of Clothworkers; *Recreations* fishing, stalking, shooting; *Clubs* Pratt's, New (Edinburgh); *Style*— Capt Alastair Leslie, TD; ✉ Seasyde House, by Errol, Perthshire PH2 7TA (☎ 01821 642500, fax 01821 642883)

LESLIE, Ann Elizabeth Mary; da of Norman Alexander Leslie (d 1979), of Bourne End, Bucks, and Theodora, *née* McDonald; *Educ* Convent of the Holy Child Mayfield Sussex, Lady Margaret Hall Oxford (BA); *m* 15 Feb 1969, Michael Fletcher, s of Arthur George Fletcher; 1 da (Katharine Cordelia b 8 Sept 1978); *Career* broadcaster and journalist; staff Daily Express 1966–67, freelance journalist 1967–; awards: commendation Br Press Awards 1980, 1983, 1985, 1987, 1991 and 1995, Women of the Yr Award for Journalism and Bdcasting Variety Club 1981, Feature Writer of the Yr Award Br Press Awards 1981 and 1989, Feature Writer of the Yr What the Papers Say (BBC2/Granada TV) 1991; memb NUJ; *Recreations* family life; *Style*— Ms Ann Leslie; ✉ Daily Mail, Northcliffe House, 2 Derry Street, London W8 5TT (☎ 0171 938 6000, fax 0171 938 6039)

LESLIE, David Carnegie; Baron of Leslie; o s of David Brown Leslie (d 1985), of Aberdeen, and Ethel Watson, *née* Kenn; *b* 1 Feb 1943; *Educ* Aberdeen GS, Scott Sutherland Sch of Architecture (DipArch); *m* 7 June 1967, Leslie Margaret, da of Roderick Allen Stuart (d 1970), of Aberdeen; 2 da (Angela Elizabeth b 1970, Yvonne Margaret b 1972); *Career* chartered architect; ptnr Leslie Castle by Insch; restorer of ruined Leslie Castle, ancestral home of the Leslies; Freeman of City of London 1987, Burgess of Trade Aberdeen 1979, Burgess of Guild Aberdeen 1984; RIBA 1974, ARIAS 1979, FSA (Scot) 1981, memb Assoc of Planning Supervisors 1995; KASG 1984; *Recreations* gardening, genealogy; *Style*— The Much Honoured Baron of Leslie; ✉ Leslie Castle, Leslie, by Insch, Aberdeenshire (☎ 01464 820869, fax 01464 821076)

LESLIE, Desmond Peter Arthur; s of Sir (John Randolph) Shane Leslie, 3 Bt (d 1971), and hp of bro Sir John Norman Ide Leslie, 4 Bt, *qv*; *b* 29 June 1921; *Educ* Ampleforth, Trinity Coll Dublin; *m* 1, 1945, Agnes, o da of Rudolph Bernauer, of Budapest, Hungary; 2 s (Shaun Rudolph Christopher b 1947, Christopher Mark b 1952), 1 da (Antonia Kelvey b 1963); m 2, 1970, Helen Jennifer, da of late Lt-Col E I E Strong, of Wiveliscombe, Som; 2 da (Samantha Helen b 1966, Camilla Patricia b 1968); *Career* WWII Flt Sgt Pilot 313 and 131 Squadrons 1942–44; author, composer, film producer, discologist; musical compositions: The Living Shakespeare (an album of 12 LPs of electronic music for Old Vic Cast, Macbeth, Hamlet, Othello, Midsummer Night's Dream, The Tempest, Julius Caesar, Antony and Cleopatra, Measure for Measure, King Lear, Richard III, Henry V); film music: The Day the Sky Fell In, Dr Strangelove, Yellow Submarine, Death of Satan, also numerous library music pieces for Joseph Weinberger; produced and dir films: The Missing Princess, Stranger at My Door; *Books* novels: Careless Lives, Pardon My Return, Angels Weep, Hold Back the Night, The Amazing Mr Lutterworth, The Jesus File, The Daughters of Pan; humour: How Britain Won the Space Race (with Patrick Moore); children's books: Susie Saucer and Ronnie Rocket; non-fiction: Flying Saucers Have Landed (trans in 21 languages, over 1 million copies sold); *Recreations* building cross country courses, falling off horses, teasing evil minded officials, investigating spiritualist and psychic phenomena; *Style*— Desmond Leslie, Esq; ✉ Castle Leslie, Gaslough, co Monaghan, Ireland

LESLIE, Prof Frank Matthews; JP (1984); s of William Ogilvy Leslie (d 1946), of Dundee, and Catherine Pitkethly, *née* Matthews (d 1969); *b* 8 March 1935; *Educ* Harris Acad Dundee, Queen's Coll Dundee, Univ of St Andrews (BSc), Univ of Manchester (PhD), Univ of St Andrews (DSc); *m* 19 Aug 1965, Ellen Leitch, da of William Reoch (d 1945), of Lochee, Dundee; 1 s (Calum William b 6 June 1974), 1 da (Sheena Reoch b 13 June 1969); *Career* asst lectr in mathematics Univ of Manchester 1959–61, res assoc in mathematics MIT USA 1961–62, lectr in mathematics Univ of Newcastle upon Tyne 1962–68, visiting asst prof of mechanics Johns Hopkins Univ USA 1966–67, visiting prof of engrg Tulane Univ USA 1978, prof of mathematics Univ of Strathclyde 1982– (sr lectr 1968–71, reader 1971–79, personal prof 1979–82); visiting prof of engrg: Hokkaido Univ Japan 1985, Pisa Univ Italy 1992; memb Editorial Bds of Jls: Non-Newtonian Fluid Mechanics 1980–, Liquid Crystals 1985–90, Continuum Mechanics and Thermodynamics 1988–, Proceedings of Royal Society (Series A) 1996–; memb Ctee Br Liquid Crystal Soc (chm 1987–91, vice chm 1991–94); Br Soc of Rheology annual award 1982, Sykes Gold Medal Univ of St Andrews 1996; FIMA 1969, FInstPhys 1978, FRSE 1980, FRS 1995; *Recreations* golf, hill-walking, gardening; *Style*— Prof Frank Leslie, JP, FRS, FRSE; ✉ Mathematics Department, University of Strathclyde, Livingstone Tower, Richmond St, Glasgow G1 1XH (☎ 0141 552 4400 ext 3655, fax 0141 552 8657, telex 77472 UNSLIB G)

LESLIE, Ian James; s of James Beattie Leslie (d 1973), of Brisbane, Aust, and Margaret Jean, *née* Ryan; *b* 23 Jan 1945; *Educ* Brisbane Boys' Coll, Univ of Queensland (MB BS), Univ of Liverpool (MChOrth), FRCSEd 1974, FRCS (Eng, ad eundem) 1995; *m* 1 Sept 1975, Jane Ann, da of Col (Allan) Rex Waller, MBE, MC (d 1985), of Waddesdon Manor, Bucks; 1 s (James Henry Rex b 1982), 1 da (Charlotte Ann b 1978); *Career* RAAF 1968–72 (flying offr 1968, Flt Lt 1969, Sqdn Ldr 1971); resident MO Royal Brisbane Hosp Aust 1969, MO RAAF 1970–72 (sr MO Vietnam 1971), teaching surgical registrar Princess Alexandra Hosp Brisbane 1973, registrar then sr registrar Nuffield Orthopaedic Centre Oxford 1974–77, lectr then sr lectr Univ of Liverpool 1978–81, conslt orthopaedic surgn Bristol Royal Infirmary and Avon Orthopaedic Centre, clinical sr lectr Univ of Bristol 1982–; treas Br Orthopaedic Res Soc 1988–90, memb Cncl Br Soc Hand Surgery 1986–88, editorial sec Br Orthopaedic Assoc 1990–92 (hon sec 1994–95), UK rep SICOT 1996–; chm Bd of Mgmnt Jl of Hand Surgery (Br and Euro vol); memb Editorial Bd: Journal of Bone and Joint Surgery, British Journal of Hand Surgery, Current Orthopaedics; examiner MChOrth Liverpool; memb Bd of Govrs Badminton Sch Bristol; memb Aust Orthopaedic Assoc; *Books* Watson-Jones Fractures (contrib), Arthroscopy in Operative Orthopaedics (1979), Operative Treatment of Fractures in Children and Surgery of Wrist in Operative Othopaedics (1989); *Clubs* Army & Navy (London); *Style*— Ian Leslie, Esq; ✉ Collingwood, Easter Compton, Bristol BS12 3RE (☎ 01454 632255, fax 01454 633602); Bristol Royal Infirmary, Marlborough St, Bristol BS2 8HW (☎ 0117 928 3899); 2 Clifton Park, Clifton Bristol BS8 3BS (☎ 0117 973 7113)

LESLIE, James Francis; TD (1974), JP (Co Antrim 1967), DL (Co Antrim 1973); s of Seymour Argent Sandford Leslie, CMG, DL (d 1953), and Eleanor Mary, *née* Stuart (d 1990); *b* 19 March 1933; *Educ* Eton, Queens' Coll Cambridge (MA); *m* 16 June 1956, (Patricia) Elizabeth Jane, da of Col William Anderson Swales, OBE, MC, TD (d 1955); 2 s (James b 1958, John b 1960), 1 da (RoseJane b 1964); *Career* cmmnd N Irish Horse (TA) 1963, Maj Royal Yeo (V) 1968, Hon Col D (N Irish Horse) Sqdn Royal Yeo 1991–93, Hon Col The N Irish Horse and 69 (N Irish Horse) Sqdn R Sigs 1993–; colonial serv (dist offr) Tanganyika 1956–59; farmer 1960–; Maj UDR 1974–85; pres Local Branch Royal Br Legion, chm TA & VRA (NI) 1986–92; High Sheriff of Co Antrim 1967, Vice Lt 1983–; *Recreations* shooting, walking; *Style*— James Leslie, Esq, TD, JP, DL; ✉ Leslie Hill, Ballymoney, Co Antrim BT53 6QL

LESLIE, Lord; James Malcolm David Leslie; s and h of 21 Earl of Rothes, *qv*; *b* 4 June 1958; *Educ* Eton; *Style*— Lord Leslie

LESLIE, Capt Sir John Norman Ide; 4 Bt (UK 1876), of Glaslough, Co Monaghan; s of Sir (John Randolph) Shane Leslie, 3 Bt (d 1971), and Marjory Mary Ide (d 1951); *b* 6 Dec 1916; *Educ* Downside, Magdalene Coll Cambridge (BA); *Heir* bro, Desmond Peter Arthur Leslie, *qv*, b 29 June 1921; *Career* cmmnd 2 Lt Irish Guards 1938, served WWII (POW 1940–45); artist, ecologist, restorer of old buildings; Knight of Honour and Devotion SMO Malta, Knight Cdr Order of St Gregory the Great; landowner (900 acres), previous to Irish Land Act 1910 forty nine thousand acres; *Recreations* ornithology, forestry; *Clubs* Travellers', Circolo della Caccia (Rome); *Style*— Capt Sir John Leslie, Bt; ✉ Glasglough, Co Monaghan, Ireland

LESLIE, Sir Peter Evelyn; kt (1991); s of Dr Patrick Holt Leslie (d 1972), of Oxford, and Evelyn de Berry; *b* 27 March 1931; *Educ* Dragon Sch Oxford, Stowe, New Coll Oxford; *m* 1975, Charlotte, da of Sir Edwin Arthur Chapman-Andrews, KCMG, OBE (d 1979); 2 step s (Francis, Mathew), 2 step da (Alice, Jessica); *Career* cmmnd Argyll and Sutherland Highlanders 1951, served 7 Bn (TA) 1952–56; dep chm Barclays Bank 1987–91 (gen mangr 1973–76, dir 1980, chief gen mangr and md 1985–88), dep chm Midland Bank 1991–92; chm NCM Credit Insurance Ltd; chm: Exec Ctee Br Bankers' Assoc 1978–79, Exports Guarantee Advsy Cncl 1987–92 (memb 1978–81, dep chm 1986–87), Overseas Devpt Inst 1988–95, Cwlth Devpt Corp 1989–95, Queen's Coll 1989–94, Audit Ctee Univ of Oxford 1992–, Stowe Sch 1994– (govr 1983–); govr Nat Inst of Social Work 1973–83; memb Cncl RIIA 1991–; *Recreations* natural history, historical research; *Style*— Sir Peter Leslie; ✉ 153 Sutherland Avenue, London W9 1ES

LESLIE, Stephen Windsor; QC (1993); s of Leslie Leonard Leslie (d 1984), of Hove, Sussex, and Celia, *née* Schulsinger (d 1991); *b* 21 April 1947; *Educ* Brighton Coll, KCL (LLB); *m* 1, 31 May 1974 (m dis May 1989), Bridget Caroline, da of late Edwin George Oldham; 2 da (Lara Elizabeth b 27 Jan 1976, Ophelia Caroline b 19 Nov 1981); m 2, 29 July 1989, Amrit Kumari, da of George Ganesh Mangra; 1 s (Theodore Windsor b 18 July 1992); *Career* called to the Bar Lincoln's Inn 1971 (Sir Thomas More Bursary); *Recreations* travelling, gardening, the telephone and haggling for a bargain; *Clubs* Carlton, The Thunderers; *Style*— Stephen Leslie, Esq, QC; ✉ 1 Crown Office Row, Temple, London EC4Y 7HH (☎ 0171 797 7111, fax 0171 797 7120, mobile 0850 654637)

LESLIE, Thomas Gerard; s of Thomas Leslie, JP (d 1985), formerly of Manuel, Muiravonside, Stirlingshire, and Ellen Slaven (d 1976), da of Hugh Francis McAllister; *b* 1 Aug 1938; *Educ* St Joseph's Coll Dumfries, MOCS Aldershot; *m* 12 June 1982, Sonya Anne, da of Leslie John Silburn (d 1980); 1 s (Thomas John Silburn b 1985); *Career* Nat Serv Scots Gds 1958, cmmnd Argyll and Sutherland Highlanders 1959, Lt HAC RARO; various exec posts: Canada Dry (UK) Ltd, Booker McConnell Ltd, Thos de la Rue; mangr The Corps of Commissionaires 1985–; chm London Caledonian Catholic Assoc 1983–87; memb The Company of Pikemen and Musketeers HAC; Freeman City of London 1974; FSA (Scot) 1980, MECI 1994; *Recreations* shooting, heraldry, genealogy; *Clubs* British American Forces Dining; *Style*— Thomas Leslie, Esq, FSA; ✉ Market House, 85 Cowcross St, London EC1M 6BP (☎ 0171 490 1125, fax 0171 250 1287)

LESLIE MELVILLE, Hon Archibald Ronald; yr s of 14 Earl of Leven and (13 of) Melville; hp to er bro, Lord Balgonie; *b* 15 Sept 1957; *Educ* Gordonstoun; *m* 4 April 1987, Julia Mary Greville, yr da of Basil Fox, of 32 Pembroke Gardens, London; 3 da (Alice Catherine b 12 Nov 1990, Camilla Jane b 29 Aug 1992, Joanne b 6 July 1994); *Career* 2 Lt Queen's Own Highlanders to 1981, Lt 1981, Lt RARO 1982; *Style*— The Hon Archibald Leslie Melville; ✉ Orwell House, Manse Road, Milnathort, Kinross-shire KY13 7LN

LESLIE MELVILLE, (Ian) Hamish; o s of Maj Michael Leslie Melville, TD, DL, s of Lt-Col Hon Ian Leslie Melville (4 s of 11 Earl of Leven and 10 Earl of Melville), and Cynthia, da of Sir Charles Hambro, KBE, MC; *b* 22 Aug 1944; *Educ* Eton, Ch Ch Oxford (BA, MA); *m* 1968, Lady Elizabeth Compton, yr da of 6 Marquess of Northampton; 2 s (James b 1969, Henry b 1975); *Career* dir Hambros Bank Ltd 1975–82, fndr and chief exec Enskilda Securities Ltd 1982–87, chm and chief exec Jamestown Investments Ltd 1987–92; chm: Capel-Cure Myers Capital Management Ltd 1988–91, Dunedin Fund Managers Ltd 1992–95, Scottish Woodlands Ltd, Nat Tst for Scotland; dir: Persimmon PLC, Mithras Investment Tst PLC, Old Mutual South Africa Tst PLC; *Style*— Hamish Leslie Melville, Esq; ✉ Lochluichart Lodge, by Garve, Ross-shire (☎ 01997 414242)

LESNIAK, Alicja Barbara; da of Jozef Lesniak, and Maria, *née* Stachy; *b* 4 Dec 1951; *Educ* Imperial Coll London (BSc), ARCS; *Career* tax sr Arthur Andersen & Co 1974–76 (audit asst 1973–74), project accountant WEA Records Ltd 1976–77, chief accountant Crest 1977–79, mangr Mgmnt Info Systems Lummus & Co 1979–80; Arthur Andersen & Co: asst controller 1980–82, fin controller 1982–86, UK dir of fin 1986–87; Euro gp controller WPP Group plc 1987–89; J Walter Thompson Co Limited: UK gp fin dir 1989–92, md 1989–93; chief fin offr Ogilvy & Mather Worldwide NY 1993–94, fin dir BBDO Europe 1994–; FCA; *Style*— Ms Alicja Lesniak; ✉ BBDO Europe, 2 Allee des Moulineaux, 92441 Issy les Moulineaux, Cedex, France

LESSELS, Norman; CBE (1993); s of John Clark Lessels (d 1981), of Edinburgh, and Gertrude Margaret Ellen, *née* Jack; *b* 2 Sept 1938; *Educ* Melville Coll, Edinburgh Acad; *m* 1, 31 Dec 1960, Gillian Durward, *née* Clark (d 1979); 2 s (Alasdair b 1963, James b 1967, d 1979), 1 da (Sarah b 1965, d 1979); m 2, 27 Jan 1981, Christine, da of George Stevenson Hitchman (d 1971), of Gullane, E Lothian; *Career* qualified chartered accountant 1961; ptnr: Ernst & Whinney (and predecessor firms) 1962–80, Chiene & Tait CAs Edinburgh 1980– (currently sr ptnr); chm: Cairn Energy plc 1988–, Standard Life Assurance Company 1988–, Havelock Europa plc 1989–; non-exec dir: Scottish Eastern Investment Trust plc 1980–, Bank of Scotland 1988–, Robert Wiseman Dairies plc, Scottish Homes 1988–93, Securities and Investments Bd 1989–94; pres Inst of CAs of Scotland 1987–88; *Recreations* golf, music, bridge; *Clubs* New (Edinburgh), Hon Co of Golfers (Edinburgh), Royal & Ancient (St Andrews); *Style*— Norman Lessels, Esq, CBE; ✉ 11 Forres St, Edinburgh EH3 6BJ (☎ 0131 225 5596); Chiene & Tait, 3 Albyn Place, Edinburgh EH2 4NQ (☎ 0131 225 7515, fax 0131 220 1083)

LESSER, Anton; s of late David Lesser, of Birmingham, and late Amelia Mavis, *née* Cohen; *b* 14 Feb 1952; *Educ* Mosely GS Birmingham, Univ of Liverpool (BA), RADA (Bancroft gold medal); *m* Madeleine Adams; *Career* actor; assoc artist RSC, vice pres Friends of Br Theatre; *Theatre* for RSC incl: Richard in Henry VI, Dance of Death, Michael in Sons of Light, Romeo in Romeo and Juliet, Darkie in The Fool, Troilus in Troilus and Cressida (Stratford), Carlos Montezuma in Melons (The Pit), Bill Howell in

Principia Scriptoriae (The Pit), Gloucester in Henry VI (Stratford and Barbican), title role in Richard III (Stratford and Barbican), Joe in Some Americans Abroad (Barbican), Bolingbroke in Richard II (Stratford), Forest in Two Shakespearian Actors (Stratford), Petruchio in The Taming of the Shrew, Ford in The Merry Wives of Windsor; other roles incl: Mark Antony in Julius Caesar (Tyne and Wear), Betty/Edward in Cloud Nine (Liverpool Everyman), Constantin in The Seagull (Royal Court), Hamlet in Hamlet (Warehouse), Kissing God (Hampstead Theatre Club), Family Voices (Lyric Hammersmith), Feste in Twelth Night (Riverside Studios), Stanley in The Birthday Party (RNT), Jack Rover Wild Oats (RNT); *Television* BBC incl: Orestes in The Oresteia, Philip in The Mill on the Floss, Abesey Ivanovitch in The Gambler, Troilus in Troilus and Cressida, Trofimov in The Cherry Orchard, Edgar in King Lear, Wilheim Fliess in Freud, Willy Price in Anna of The Five Towns, Stanley in Stanley Spencer, Vincenzo Rocca in Airbase, Feste in Twelth Night, Mungo Dawson in Downtown Lagos; Channel 4 incl: Cox in Good and Bad At Games, Valerie Chaldize in Sakharov, Mark Hollister in the Politician's Wife, Robert Schumann in Schumann; other prodns incl: Ken in The Daughters of Albion (YTV), London Embassy (Thames), Wiesenthal (TVS/HBO), The Strauss Dynasty (mini-series), David Gaulee in Sharman, Vladic Mesic in Bodyguards, Ezra Jennings in The Moonstone; *Films* incl: The Missionary, Monseigneur Quixote, Moses, One Golden Afternoon; *Style*— Anton Lesser, Esq; ✉ c/o Conway van Gelder Robinson Ltd, 18–21 Jermyn Street, London SW1Y 6HP (☎ 0171 287 0077, fax 0171 287 1940)

LESSING, Charlotte; da of George Fainstone, and Helene Peretz; *b* 14 May 1924; *Educ* Henrietta Barnet Sch, Univ of London (Extension Course Dip in Eng Lit); *m* 25 May 1948, Walter Lessing; 3 da (Diana b 1953, Judith b 1954, Nicola b 1957); *Career* writer of short stories, travel articles and features and occasional broadcaster; ed-in-chief: Good Housekeeping (ed 1973–87, dep ed 1964–73), Country Living 1985–86; editorial conslt and freelance writer 1988–; wine columnist for The Lady; Ed of the Year PPA 1983, Wine Writer of the Year (nat press) Wine Guild 1995; Chevalier de l'Ordre du Mérite Agricole France 1996; *Recreations* travel, wine; *Clubs* Groucho; *Style*— Mrs Charlotte Lessing; ✉ 2 Roseneath Rd, London SW11 6AH (☎ and fax 0171 228 0708)

LESSIR, Mohamed; *b* 1 May 1946; *Educ* Lycée de Sfax, Faculté des Lettres et des Sciences Humaines Tunis (MA), St John's Univ NY; *m* Sept 1979, Samira, *née* Lamari; 3 da (Sana b 23 Dec 1982, Nadia b 19 Oct 1986, Maroua b 9 Oct 1990); *Career* Tunisian diplomat; first sec Int Economic and Financial Cooperation Dept Miny of Foreign Affairs 1970, commercial attaché Tunisian Embassy Belgrade 1973, trg and study courses jtly organised by UNCTAD and ITC in various European capitals 1975, promotion to rank of cnsllr 1978, Foreign Serv Prog Univ of Oxford 1978–79, head Asia Section African and Asian Political Affairs Dept 1979, dep dir for Asian Political Affairs Miny of Foreign Affairs 1981, cnsllr Perm Mission to the UN in NYC (memb Tunisian delegation to Gen Assembly, delegate to Special Political Ctee) 1982, min plenipotentiary of the Republic of Tunisia to UN NYC 1985, ambassador extraordinary and plenipotentiary of Republic of Tunisia to Oman 1987–90, dir Assessment and Follow-up Special Unit Embassies Economic and Commercial Activities 1990, rep of Miny of Foreign Affairs to Higher Cncl for Human Rights and Fundamental Liberties 1991, dir attached to office of Min for Foreign Affairs 1991, DG Tunisian External Communication Agency 1991, ambass extraordinary and plenipotentiary of the Republic of Tunisia to the Ct of St James's 1992–96 (and to Dublin 1993–96); co-patron British Tunisian Soc 1992, patron Tunisians in Britain Soc; delegate to numerous Islamic confs incl Islamic Conf Orgn in Islamabad 1980, and Third Islamic Summit Taief Saudia Arabia 1981; Offr of the Order of the Republic (Tunisia), Offr of the Order of the Nooman (Oman); *Recreations* tennis, jogging, reading; *Clubs* Queen's; *Style*— Mr Mohamed Lessir

LESSORE, John Viviand; s of Frederick Lessore (d 1951), of London, and Helen Lessore, OBE, RA *née* Brook (d 1994); *b* 16 June 1939; *Educ* Merchant Taylors', Slade Sch of Fine Art; *m* 1962, Paule Marie, da of Jean Achille Reveille (Officier de la Légion d'honneur, d 1967), of Paris; 4 s (Remi b 1962, Vincent b 1967, Timothy b 1973, Samuel b 1977); *Career* artist; Korn/Ferry Int Public Award 1991, shortlisted for Jerwood Painting Prize 1994; *Princ Exhibitions* incl: Beaux Arts Gallery 1965, New Art Centre 1971, Theo Waddington 1981, Stoppenbach & Delestre 1983 and 1985, Nigel Greenwood 1990, Theo Waddington and Robert Stoppenbach 1994, Theo Waddington Fine Art Ltd 1996; *Works in Public Collections* incl: Leicester Educn Ctee, Arts Cncl Collection, Royal Acad of Arts, Westminster Hosp, Tate Gallery, Swindon Museum and Art Gallery, CAS, Norwich Castle Museum, Br Cncl; *Style*— John Lessore, Esq; ✉ c/o Theo Waddington, 5a Cork Street, London W1X 1PB (☎ 0171 494 1584, fax 0171 287 0926)

LESTER, Adrian (Anthony); *b* 14 Aug 1968; *Educ* RADA; *Career* actor; memb: Amnesty Int, Green Peace; *Theatre* incl: Hanging the President (Traverse Studio), The Winter's Tale (Manchester Royal Exchange), Kiss of the Spider Woman (Belgrade Coventry), Cory in Fences (Garrick), Paul Poitier in Six Degrees of Separation (Royal Court and Comedy Theatre), Anthony Hope in Sweeney Todd (RNT), As You Like It (Albery and Bouffes du Nord), Company (Albery and Donmar); *Television* incl: For the Greater Good, In the Dark; *Film* incl: Five Years, Touch to Die, Up on the Roof (for Granada); *Awards* winner Time Out Award for Six Degrees of Separation and As You Like It, Olivier Award for Company; *Recreations* dancing, martial arts (orange belt - tae kwon do), music; *Style*— Adrian Lester, Esq; ✉ c/o Kate Feast Management, 10 Primrose Hill Studios, Fitzroy Road, London NW1 8TR (☎ 0171 586 5502, fax 0171 586 9817)

LESTER, Alexander Norman Charles Phillips (Alex); s of John Phillips Lester, of Walsall, W Midlands, and Rosemary Anne, *née* Edgely; *b* 11 May 1956; *Educ* Denstone Coll, Birmingham Poly (Dip in Communication Studies); *Career* presenter/prodr: BBC local radio 1978–81, Independent Radio 1981–86; prodr/announcer Radio 2 1987; freelance presenter, announcer, reporter, voice over and writer Radios 2 and 4 and independent TV and radio 1988–; TV announcer/reporter BSkyB 1990, voice over artist UK Gold, GMTV and The Family Channel, presenter Early Show Nightride and Alex Lester Show (Radio 2), presenter/reporter/announcer Freewheeling, Going Places, Breakaway and It's Your Round (Radio 4); deputises to Ken Bruce, Ed Stewart and Sarah Kennedy; voice trainer and lectr in radio skills BBC Radio Trg; *Style*— Alex Lester, Esq; ✉ BBC Radio 2, G7 Western House, Portland Place, London W1A 4WW (☎ 0171 580 4468 ext 3436)

LESTER, Anthony John; s of Donald James Lester, of Wallingford, Oxon, and Edith Helen Hemmings (d 1982); *b* 15 Sept 1945; *Educ* Gaveston Hall Nuthurst Sussex, St John's Coll Co Tipperary Eire; *Career* ind fine art conslt, art critic, book reviewer and lectr; ed Watercolours, Drawings and Prints 1992–94; publisher and editorial dir Art Prices Review; contribs to numerous magazines incl: Woman, Antique Collecting, Artists' and Illustrators' Magazine, Antique Dealer and Collectors' Guide, Limited Edition, The World of Antiques, The Speculator, Antiques and Decoration, The Collector, The Big Issue, Galleries, Miller's Magazine, Art and Artefact; featured in Farmers' Weekly, Radio Times, Sunday Express Magazine, British Midland Voyager Magazine; regular broadcaster BBC TV Antiques Roadshow 1986–89; memb: Int Assoc of Art Critics, Glass Circle, Glass Assoc; Companion of the Pastel Soc; CRSBA, FRSA; *Books* The Exhibited Works of Helen Allingham (1979), The Stannards of Bedfordshire (1984), BBC Antiques Roadshow-Experts on Objects (contrib, 1987); *Recreations* travel, entertaining friends, charity work; *Style*— Anthony J Lester, Esq; ✉ The Dower House, Hithercroft, Wallingford, Oxfordshire OX10 9ES (☎ 01491 836683); Old Hithercroft House, Hithercroft, Wallingford, Oxfordshire OX10 9ES (☎ 01491 837552)

LESTER, Charles Martin; s of Charles William Lester, of Banbury, Oxon, and Marjory Winnifred, *née* Pursail; *b* 20 March 1942; *Educ* N Oxfordshire Tech Sch, Oxford Coll of Technol, Gwent Coll of HE; *m* 16 March 1963, Patricia Caroline Lester, *qv*, da of Arthur Frederick Wake; 1 da (Georgina Caroline b 28 Oct 1964); *Career* research scientist ICI Fibres 1977–81, teacher of design craft and technol King Henry VIII Sch 1977–81, head Design Craft and Technol Dept Haberdashers' Monmouth Sch 1981–86, dir Charles & Patricia Lester Ltd (textile and fashion design co) 1986–; developed unique method for finely hand pleated silk and hand painted velvets screen printed with metallic/toned designs and using burn-out techniques; work featured in numerous pubns worldwide, major stockists incl Liberty and Lucienne Phillips in London, Bergdorf Goodman, Forgotten Woman and Neiman Marcus in USA, other stockists in Paris, Germany, Italy, Kuwait, Hong Kong and Japan; clients incl HRH Princess Michael of Kent, Shakira Caine, Bette Midler, Sarah Brightman and Barbra Streisand; product range recently extended to incl cushions, bedspreads and silk tapestries and a collection of accessories incl scarves, shawls, throws and waistcoats; *Recreations* Folly Fellowship, Steam Boat Association, rebuilding and restoring vintage boat, photography; *Style*— Charles Lester, Esq; ✉ Charles & Patricia Lester Ltd, Llanfoist House, Llanfoist, Abergavenny, Gwent (☎ 01873 853559, fax 01873 858666)

LESTER, Sir James Theodore (Jim); kt (1996), MP (C) Broxtowe (majority 9,891); s of Arthur Ernest and Marjorie Lester; *b* 23 May 1932; *Educ* Nottingham HS; *m* 1, 1953 (m dis 1989), Iris; 2 s; m 2, Jan 1989, Merry Macey; *Career* MP (C): Beeston Feb 1974–83, Broxtowe 1983–; oppn whip 1975–79, parly under sec state for employment 1979–81, memb Foreign Affrs Select Ctee 1982–, fndr memb CARE (Cons Action to Revive Employment); chm All-Party Gp on: Overseas Devpt, Mgmnt; *Style*— Sir Jim Lester, MP; ✉ House of Commons, London SW1A 0AA (☎ 0171 219 3000)

LESTER, Michael; s of Jack Lester (d 1959), and Mary, *née* Sax (d 1987); *b* 10 March 1940; *Educ* Coopers' Company's Sch, New Coll Oxford (MA); *m* 17 Dec 1967, Pamela Frances Lester, da of Leopold Henry Gillis (d 1988); 1 s (James b 1976), 1 da (Antonia b 1973); *Career* Bigelow teaching fell Univ of Chicago Law Sch 1962–64, articled clerk and slr in private practice 1964–80; GEC plc: dir of legal affrs 1980–, main bd dir 1983–, vice chm 1994–; memb Law Soc, CIMgt; *Style*— Michael Lester, Esq; ✉ 46 Sheldon Ave, London N6 4JR (☎ 0181 340 7868); General Electric Company plc, 1 Stanhope Gate, London W1A 1EH (☎ 0171 493 8484, fax 0171 491 0863)

LESTER, Nigel Martin; s of Geoffrey Charles Lester (d 1992), and Pamela Anne, *née* Goddard (d 1981); *b* 26 March 1953; *Educ* Banbury GS, Univ of Sussex (BSc); *m* 1982, Rosemarie Anne, da of Eric George Skoll (d 1988); 1 s (Jonathan Robert Anthony b 1987), 1 da (Charlotte Nicole Pamela b 1984); *Career* int equity fund mangr Legal and General Assurance Society Ltd London 1974–81, asst dir Schroders and Chartered Hong Kong 1981–84, md Aetna Investment Management (FE) Hong Kong 1984–88, chief invesmt offr and sr vice pres Aetna International Inc Hartford Connecticut USA 1989–90, chief exec County Nat West Investment Management 1990–93, global head of res UBS Ltd 1993–; FIA 1980; *Recreations* real tennis, squash, theatre; *Clubs* MCC, RAC, Queen's, Hong Kong; *Style*— Nigel Lester, Esq; ✉ Squirrel Cottage, 25 Ernle Road, London SW20 0HH (☎ 0181 946 8432); UBS Ltd, 100 Liverpool Street, London EC2M 2RH (☎ 0171 901 1684, fax 0171 901 1571)

LESTER, Patricia Caroline; MBE (1988); da of Arthur Frederick Wake, of NZ, and Dorothy Phyllis, *née* Flew; *b* 11 Feb 1943; *Educ* Thornton Coll; *m* 16 March 1963, Charles Martin Lester, *qv*, s of Charles William Lester; 1 da (Georgina Caroline b 28 Oct 1964); *Career* textile and fashion designer; formerly employed as secretary, subsequently estab small business designing and making children's clothes, fndr and currently dir Charles & Patricia Lester Ltd; developed unique method for finely hand pleated silk and hand painted velvets screen printed with metallic/toned designs and using burn-out techniques; work featured in numerous pubns worldwide, major stockists incl Liberty and Lucienne Phillips in London, Bergdorf Goodman, Forgotten Woman and Neiman Marcus in USA, other stockists in Paris, Germany, Italy, Kuwait, Hong Kong and Japan; clients incl HRH Princess Michael of Kent, Shakira Caine, Bette Midler, Sarah Brightman and Barbra Streisand; product range recently extended to incl cushions, bedspreads and silk tapestries and a collection of accessories incl scarves, shawls, throws and waistcoats; Fit for Work Award (in recognition of commitment to the employment of disabled staff) 1985, Welsh Business Woman of the Yr 1986 and 1987; *Recreations* gardening, painting, Folly Fellowship, Steam Boat Association; *Style*— Mrs Patricia Lester, MBE; ✉ Charles & Patricia Lester Ltd, Llanfoist House, Llanfoist, Abergavenny, Gwent (☎ 01873 853559, fax 01873 858666)

LESTER, Richard; s of Elliott Lester (d 1951), of Pennsylvania, USA, and Ella Young Lester (d 1969); *b* 19 Jan 1932; *Educ* William Penn Charter Sch, Univ of Pennsylvania (BA); *m* 1956, Deirdre Vivian, da of Sqdn Ldr Frederick James Smith (d 1970); 1 s (Dominic), 1 da (Claudia); *Career* director: CBS USA 1951–54, AR (dir TV Goon shows 1956); directed The Running, Jumping and Standing Still Film (Academy Award nomination, 1st prize San Francisco Festival 1960); feature films dir incl: It's Trad, Dad (1962), Mouse on the Moon (1963), A Hard Day's Night (1964), The Knack (1964, Grand Prix Cannes Film Festival), Help! (1965, Best Film Award and Best Dir Award Rio de Janeiro Festival), A Funny Thing Happened on the Way to the Forum (1966), How I Won the War (1967), Petulia (1968), The Bed Sitting Room (1969, Gandhi Peace Prize Berlin Film Festival, Grand Prize Avoriaz Festival 1977), The Three Musketeers (1973), Juggernaut (1974, Best Dir Award Teheran Film Festival), The Four Musketeers (1974), Royal Flash (1975), Robin and Marian (1976), The Ritz (1976), Butch and Sundance: The Early Days (1979), Cuba (1979), Superman II (1981), Superman III (1983), Finders Keepers (1984), Return of the Musketeers (1989), Get Back (1990); Order of Academy of Arts and Letters (France) 1973; *Style*— Richard Lester, Esq; ✉ Courtyards, River Lane, Petersham, Surrey; Courtyard Films Ltd, Twickenham Studios, St Margarets, Middx TW1 2AW (☎ 0181 892 4477)

LESTER OF HERNE HILL, Baron (Life Peer UK 1993), of Herne Hill in the London Borough of Southwark; Anthony Paul Lester; QC (1975); s of Harry Lester (d 1984), of London, and Kate, *née* Cooper-Smith; *b* 3 July 1936; *Educ* City of London Sch, Trinity Coll Cambridge (BA), Harvard Law Sch (LLM); *m* 29 July 1971, Catherine Elizabeth Debora, da of Michael Morris Wassey (d 1969), of London; 1 s (Hon Gideon b 1972), 1 da (Hon Maya b 1974); *Career* 2 Lt RA 1956; called to the Bar Lincoln's Inn 1963 (bencher 1985), memb Northern Ireland Bar and Irish Bar; recorder S Eastern circuit 1987; special advsr to: Home Sec 1974–76, Standing Cmmn on Human Rights in NI 1975–77; former chm and memb Bd of Govrs James Allen's Girls' Sch, pres Interights (Int Centre for Legal Protection of Human Rights), memb Ed Bd Public Law, ed-in-chief Butterworths Human Rights Cases, former chm and treas Fabian Soc, pres Lib Dem Lawyers' Assoc, tstee Runnymede Tst; hon visiting prof of law UCL; *Books* Justice in the American South (1964), Shawcross and Beaumont on Air Law (ed jtly, 3 edn 1964), Race and Law (jtly 1972); conslt ed and contrib Constitutional Law and Human Rights in Halsbury's Laws of England (4 edn, 1973, re-issued 1996); contrib: British Nationality, Immigration and Race Relations in Halsbury's Laws of England (4 edn, 1973, re-issued 1992), The Changing Constitution (ed Jowell and Oliver, 1985); *Recreations* walking, sailing, golf, water colours; *Style*— The Lord Lester of Herne Hill, QC; ✉ 2 Hare Court,

Temple, London EC4Y 7BH (☎ 0171 583 1770, sec 0171 353 4612, fax 0171 583 9269, telex 27139 LINLAW)

LESTOR, Joan; MP (Lab) Eccles (majority 13,226); *b* 1931, Vancouver; *Educ* Blaenavon Secdy Sch (Monmouth), William Morris Secdy Sch Walthamstow, Univ of London; *m*; 1 s, 1 da (both adopted); *Career* nursery sch teacher 1959–66, memb LCC 1962–64; MP (Lab): Eton and Slough 1966–83, Eccles 1987–; Parly under-sec of state: Dept of Education and Science 1969–70 and 1975–76, FCO 1974–75; memb Labour Party NEC 1967–82 (chm 1977–78), co-chm Jt Ctee Against Racism 1978–, chm Int Ctee Labour Party 1978–; memb Shadow Cabinet; oppn front bench spokesperson on: women's rights and welfare 1981, aid and devpt 1987–89, children, juvenile offenders and race 1989–93, children and family 1993–94, overseas devpt 1994–96; *Style*— Joan Lestor, MP; ✉ House of Commons, London SW1A 0AA

LETHBRIDGE, Sir Thomas Periam Hector Noel; 7 Bt (UK 1804), of Westaway House, and Winkley Court, Somerset; s of Sir Hector Wroth Lethbridge, 6 Bt (d 1978), and Evelyn Diana, *née* Noel (d 1996); *b* 17 July 1950; *Educ* Milton Abbey, RAC Cirencester; *m* 1976, Susan Elizabeth, eldest da of Lyle Rocke, of Maryland, USA; 4 s (John Francis Buckler Noel b 1977, Edward Christopher Wroth b 1978, Alexander Ralph Periam b 1982, Henry Charles Hesketh b 1984), 2 da (Georgina Rose Alianore b 1980, Rachael Elizabeth Mary b 1986); *Heir* s, John Francis Buckler Noel Lethbridge b 10 March 1977; *Career* art dealer in sporting subjects of 1700 to date, int agent for distinguished retail names; *Clubs* Farmers', Turf; *Style*— Sir Thomas Lethbridge, Bt; ✉ c/o Drummonds, 49 Charing Cross, SW1

LETLEY, Peter Anthony; s of Sidney Charles Letley (d 1978), of Woodbridge, Suffolk, and Ruby, *née* Berry; *b* 11 Nov 1945; *Educ* Woodbridge Sch Suffolk, St John's Coll Oxford (BA); *m* 21 March 1970, (Alice) Emma Campbell, da of Lt-Col Campbell K Finlay, of W Ardhu, Isle of Mull, Argyll; 1 s (Alfred Thomas b 4 Sept 1988); *Career* joined HSBC Group 1974; Wardley Ltd: head of Lending Dept 1974–78, dir overseas ops and dir 1978–82, jt md Aust 1982–83, chief exec Hong Kong International Trade Finance Ltd (London) 1983–86; fin dir: James Capel Bankers Ltd 1986–87 (md 1987–88), HSBC James Capel & Co 1988–93 (dep chm 1993–); dep chm HSBC Investment Banking Group Ltd 1993–; *Recreations* theatre, opera, reading; *Clubs* Hong Kong Jockey; *Style*— Peter Letley, Esq; ✉ 24 Princedale Rd, London W11 4NJ (☎ 0171 229 1398); James Capel and Co, Thames Exchange, 10 Queen Street Place, London EC4R 1BH (☎ 0171 621 0011, fax 0171 621 0309)

LETTIN, Alan William Frederick; s of Frederick Lettin (d 1959), and Louisa Marion, *née* Tabberer (d 1960); *b* 6 Jan 1931; *Educ* Leyton Co HS for Boys, UCL (MRC scholar, BSc), UCH London (state scholar, MB BS, MRCS, LRCP, MS, Sir Thomas Lewis prize for clinical research); *m* 19 Sept 1953, Patricia Jean, da of Frederick Plumb; 1 da (Jennifer Ann b 1955 d 1967), 3 s (Nicholas Alan b 8 April 1958, Jonathan Frederick b 7 April 1962, Timothy William b 22 Aug 1969); *Career* house physician then house surgn UCH London 1955–56; Nat Serv Flt Lt RAF Med Branch 1957–58; UCH London: casualty surgical offr 1958–59, surgical registrar 1959–61; Royal Nat Orthopaedic Hosp: SHO 1961–62, registrar 1862–64, sr registrar 1964; lectr in orthopaedic surgery Inst of Orthopaedics Univ of London 1964–66; conslt orthopaedic surgn: Bart's 1967–95, Royal Nat Orthopaedic Hosp 1969–93, UCH and Middx Hosps 1993–94; hon conslt orthopaedic surgn: Doctor Barnardo's Homes 1967–71, St Luke's Hosp for the Clergy 1973–90; introduced Stanmore knee, elbow and shoulder artificial joints into clinical practice; variously examiner for RCS and Univs of London, Cambridge and Liverpool; memb Cncl Orthopaedic Section RSM 1971–73, pres Br Orthopaedic Assoc 1993–94, vice pres RCS 1994–96 (memb Cncl 1984–96); Freeman City of London 1973, memb Ct of Assts Worshipful Co of Barbers 1983– (Liveryman 1975, Master 1990); Sir Robert Jones Prize and Gold Medal Br Orthopaedic Assoc 1967; hon fell Inst of Br Surgical Technicians; memb various professional bodies incl: Br Orthopaedic Assoc, Br Orthopaedic Research Soc, Société Internationale de Chirurgie Orthopédique et de Traumatologie, Gen Osteopathic Cncl 1996–, RSM; FRCS; *Books* Fundamental Anatomy for Operative Orthopaedic Surgery (1991), contrib to numerous orthopaedic text-books and author and co-author of many published papers; *Recreations* gardening, photography, DIY; *Style*— Alan Lettin, Esq; ✉ Moat Farm, Swan Lane, Cretingham, Woodbridge, Suffolk IP37 7AZ (☎ 01728 685186); The Royal College of Surgeons, Lincoln's Inn Fields, London WC2A 3PN (☎ 0171 405 3474, fax 0171 973 2183)

LETTS, Anthony Ashworth; s of Leslie Charles Letts, of Old Swaylands, Penshurst, Kent (d 1984), and Elizabeth Mary, *née* Gibson (d 1971); gggf John Letts founded diary publishing business in 1796 as stationer, first diary 1812; *b* 3 July 1935; *Educ* Marlborough, Magdalene Coll Cambridge (MA); *m* 15 Sept 1962, Rosa Maria, da of Avvocato Aminta Ciarrapico, of Rome, Italy (d 1985); 1 s (Philip Leslie b 1966), 1 da (Adalgisa b 1965); *Career* Nat Serv 1954–56 Lt; md Charles Letts & Co Ltd 1965, chm Charles Letts (Holdings) Ltd 1977–94, pres Charles Letts Group Ltd 1994–96; dir: Charles Letts & Co Ltd 1963–63, Letts of London (USA) 1978–96, Letts of London Pty (Australia) 1986–96, Cambridge Market Intelligence 1994–, Accademia Club Ltd 1996–; *Recreations* tennis, sailing, hill walking, theatre; *Clubs* Hurlingham; *Style*— A A Letts, Esq; ✉ 2 The Towers, Soberton, Southampton SO32 3PS (☎ 01489 877684); Accademia Club Ltd, 8/9 Grosvenor Place, London SW1X 7SH (☎ 0171 235 0303)

LETTS, John Campbell Bonner; OBE (1980); s of (Christian) Francis Campbell Letts, of Oakley Hall, Cirencester, Glos (d 1963), and Eveleen Frances Calthrop, *née* Bonner (d 1969); *b* 18 Nov 1929; *Educ* Haileybury, Jesus Coll Cambridge (BA); *m* 21 Sep 1957, Sarah Helen, da of E Brian O Rorke, RA; 3 s (Robert b 1959, Matthew b 1961, Daniel b 1963) 1 da (Vanessa b 1966); *Career* Penguin Books 1959, J Walter Thompson 1960–63, Sunday Times Publications 1964–66, gen mangr Book Club Assoc 1966–69, mktg dir Hutchinson 1969, jt chm (ed and mktg dir) Folio Soc 1971–87; fndr and chm Nat Heritage 1972, tstee and memb ctee Euro Museums Tst, tstee Museum of Empire and Cwlth Tst, fndr and chm The Trollope Soc 1987–; FRSA; *Poetry* A Little Treasury of Limericks (1973); *Recreations* walking in Scotland, reading visiting museums, gardening; *Clubs* Reform; *Style*— John Letts, Esq, OBE; ✉ 83 West Side, Clapham Common, London SW4 (☎ 0171 228 9448); The Trollope Society, 9a North St, London SW4 0HN (☎ 0171 720 6789/071 924 1146)

LETTS, Melinda Jane Frances; da of Richard Francis Bonner Letts, of Cirencester, Glos, and Jocelyn Elizabeth, *née* Adami; *b* 6 April 1956; *Educ* Wycombe Abbey, Cheltenham Coll, St Anne's Coll Oxford (exhibitioner, BA); *m* 13 April 1991, Neil Scott Wishart McIntosh, s of William Henderson McIntosh; 1 s (Fergus George Christian b 15 Oct 1990), 1 da (Isobel Freya Johnstone b 15 Sept 1992); *Career* press and publicity offr Bubble Theatre Co 1980–81, res asst Sociology Dept Brunel Univ 1981–82, head orgn and admin CND 1982–84; VSO: head of admin 1985–86, prog funding mangr 1986–87, regnl mangr S Asia 1987–89; staffing mangr McKinsey & Co Inc 1989–91, chief exec Nat Asthma Campaign 1992– (dep dir 1991–92); tstee Long Term Med Conditions Alliance 1996; MIMgt 1992, FRSA 1993; *Recreations* reading, swimming, photography; *Style*— Ms Melinda Letts; ✉ National Asthma Campaign, Providence House, Providence Place, London N1 0NT (☎ 0171 226 2260, fax 0171 226 4120)

LETTS, Quentin Richard Stephen; s of R F B Letts, of Cirencester, Glos, and Jocelyn, *née* Adami; *b* 6 Feb 1963; *Educ* Haileybury, Bellarmine Coll Kentucky, Trinity Coll Dublin, Jesus Coll Cambridge; *Career* dustman and waiter 1981–84; ed: Oxon Magazine Oxford 1984–85, Mayday Magazine Dublin 1985–86, Filibuster Magazine Dublin 1986–87; journalist The Daily Telegraph 1988–95 (ed Peterborough Column), NY Bureau chief The Times 1995–; *Recreations* restaurants, gossip; *Clubs* Frogs Cricket, Savile; *Style*— Quentin Letts, Esq; ✉ Scrubs' Bottom, Bisley, Glos GL6 7BU (☎ 01452 813899)

LETTS CIARRAPICO, Dr Rosa Maria; *Educ* Univ of Rome (law degree), Brandeis Univ Massachussetts (MA, Fulbright scholar), Courtauld Inst London (BA), Warburg Inst London (MPhil); *Career* history of art and architecture teacher Extra Mural Dept Univ of London 1966–80, lectr on Italian European art (Renaissance and Baroque) and exhbns conslt Educn Dept V&A 1975–82, lectr in Renaissance and Baroque art, Italian modern art design and architecture 1978–85, teacher Italian contemporary design, architecture and fashion Phillip's courses on Contemporary Art 1985–86; fndr dir: Accademia Italiana delle Arti e delle Arti Applicate London 1988–, Euro Acad of the Arts 1994; memb Editorial Advsy Bd Apollo Magazine 1991, cultural cnsllr Italian Embassy London 1992; juror Euro Design Award RSA 1992–93, memb Panel of Judges Swiss Bank Competition for Euro Contemporary Art 1993–95; *Exhibitions* co curator The Splendours of the Gonzaga V&A 1981, curator Letts Keep a Diary The Mall Galleries 1987, co curator Manzu exhbn Museum of Modern Art Rome, Scottish Nat Gallery of Modern Art, Walker Art Gallery Liverpool, Museum of Modern Art Oxford 1987–88, curator Italy by Moonlight Museo de las Belas Artes, Rio De Janiero, Ashmolean Oxford 1990, Accademia Italiana London 1991; Cavaliere Ufficiale della Repubblica Italiana 1990; *Publications* La Pittura Fiorentina (1970, Eng trans 1982), Art Treasures of London (1972, English Art Guides series), Paola Malatesta Gonzaga 1392–1447 (1981, MPhil), The Renaissance (1981, 3rd edn 1991), Italy by Moonlight 1550–1850 (exhbn catalogue, 1990); numerous catalogue essays and articles; *Style*— Dr Rosa Maria Letts Ciarrapico; ✉ European Academy for Arts - Accademia Italiana, 8 Grosvenor Place, London SW1X 7SH (☎ 0171 235 0303, fax 0171 235 0404)

LEUCHARS, Maj-Gen Peter Raymond; CBE (1966); s of Raymond Leuchars (d 1927), and Helen Inez, *née* Copland-Griffiths (d 1979); *b* 29 Oct 1921; *Educ* Bradfield; *m* 1953, Hon Gillian Wightman Nivison, da of 2 Baron Glendyne (d 1967), of E Grinstead, Sussex; 1 s (Christopher); *Career* cmmnd in Welsh Guards 1941, served NW Europe and Italy 1944–45, Adj 1 Bn Welsh Guards Palestine 1945–48, Bde Maj 4 Gds Bde Germany 1952–54, GSO 1 (Instr) Staff Coll Camberley 1956–59, GSO1 HQ 4 Div BAOR 1960–63, cmd 1 Bn Welsh Guards 1963–65, Princ SO to Dir of Ops Borneo 1965–66, cmd 11 Armd Bde BAOR 1966–68, cmd Jt Operational Computer Projects Team 1969–71, Dep Cmdt Staff Coll Camberley 1972–73, GOC Wales 1973–76, Col The Royal Welsh Fus 1974–84; pres Gds Golfing Soc 1977–; St John Ambulance: cmmr-in-chief 1978–80 and 1985–86, chief cdr 1981–89; chm: St John Fellowship 1989–95, Lady Grover's Fund for Officers' Families 1991–; Fell RSPB; Order of Istiqlal (Jordan) 1946; FRGS; KStJ 1978, GCStJ 1989; *Recreations* golf, shooting, travel, photography; *Clubs* Royal and Ancient Golf, Sunningdale Golf (capt 1975), Royal Wimbledon Golf; *Style*— Maj-Gen Peter Leuchars, CBE; ✉ 5 Chelsea Sq, London SW3 6LF (☎ 0171 352 6187)

LEUNG, Prof Clement H C; s of Hon Ming Leung, MBE, of Melbourne, and Suk Wan Leung (d 1954); *b* 10 May 1949; *Educ* McGill Univ Canada (BSc), Univ of Oxford (MSc), UCL (PhD); *m* 24 March 1979, Qui Hoon, da of Suat Eng Choo, of Singapore; 2 s (Timothy b 1986, Philip b 1990); *Career* conslt in mgmnt scis British Oxygen Ltd 1978; lectr in computer sci: Univ of Reading 1979–82, UCL 1982–86; prof of computer sci Birkbeck Coll London 1986–; CEng, FBCS, FRSA; *Books* Quantitative Analysis of Computer Systems (1988); *Recreations* jazz piano, philosophy of religion; *Style*— Prof Clement Leung; ✉ Birkbeck College, University of London, Malet St, London WC1E 7HX (☎ 0171 631 6711, fax 0171 636 4971)

LEUTHOLD, Rudolph; s of Eugen Albert Leuthold (d 1981), of Zurich, and Anna, *née* Wild; *b* 10 May 1949; *Educ* Gymnasium Zurich, Univ of Geneva (MA), McGill Univ Montreal (MBA); *Career* vice pres Morgan Guaranty Trust NY 1981–, md J P Morgan Investment Inc 1984–; AIIMR (memb Soc of Investmt Analysts 1978); *Recreations* music, theatre, literature, skiing; *Clubs* Royal Automobile; *Style*— Rudolph Leuthold, Esq; ✉ J P Morgan Investment Management Inc, 28 King Street, London SW1Y 6XA (☎ 0171 451 8522, fax 0171 451 8080, telex 8954543)

LEVEAUX, David Vyvyan; s of Dr Michael Leveaux, of Derby, and Eve, *née* Powell; *b* 13 Dec 1957; *Educ* Rugby, Univ of Manchester (BA); *Career* director; *Theatre* Almeida: Betrayal, No Man's Land, Moonlight; A Moon for the Misbegotten (Riverside Studios), Easter (Leicester Haymarket), Therese Raquin (Chichester), 'Tis Pity She's A Whore (RSC), The Father (RNT); Berlin: The Dance of Death, Krapp's Last Tape; New York Broadway: A Moon for the Misbegotten (nominee Best Dir Tony Awards 1983/84), Anna Christie (nominee Best Dir and recipient Best Revival Tony Awards 1992/93); New York Off-Broadway: Messiah, Virginia; Tokyo: Les Liaisons Dangereuses, Madame de Sade, Two Headed Eagle, Lady from the Sea; artistic dir Theatre Project Tokyo; *Style*— David Leveaux, Esq; ✉ c/o Simpson Fox Associates Ltd, 52 Shaftesbury Avenue, London W1V 7DE (☎ 0171 434 9167, fax 0171 494 2887)

LEVEN AND MELVILLE, 14 Earl of Leven and 13 of Melville (S 1641); Alexander Robert Leslie Melville; also Lord Melville of Monymaill (S 1616), Lord Balgonie (S 1641), Viscount Kirkaldie, and Lord Raith, Monymaill and Balwearie (both S 1690); DL (Co of Nairn 1961); s of 13 Earl of Leven and (12 of) Melville, KT (d 1947), and Lady Rosamond Foljambe (da of 1 Earl of Liverpool); *b* 13 May 1924; *Educ* Eton; *m* 1953, Susan, da of late Lt-Col Ronald Steuart-Menzies of Culdares; 2 s, 1 da; *Heir* s, Lord Balgonie; *Career* vice pres Highland Dist TA, 2 Lt Coldstream Gds 1943, Capt 1947; ADC to Govr-Gen NZ 1951–52; pres Br Ski Fedn 1981–85; Lord Lieut for Nairn 1969–; convener Nairn Co Cncl 1970–74, chm Bd of Govs Gordonstoun Sch 1971–89; *Recreations* shooting, skiing, fishing; *Clubs* New (Edinburgh); *Style*— The Rt Hon the Earl of Leven and Melville; ✉ Glenferness House, Nairn, Scotland (☎ 01309 651 202)

LEVENE, Ben; s of Mark Levene (d 1987), of London, and Charlotte, *née* Leapman (d 1987); *b* 23 Dec 1938; *Educ* St Clement Danes GS, Slade Sch of Fine Art (DFA); *m* 1; 2 da (Rachael Clare b 19 April 1959, Sophie Rebecca b 22 Sept 1962); m 2, 14 Feb 1978, Susan Margaret; 1 s (Jacob Daniel b 23 April 1979); *Career* artist; former pt/t lectr Camberwell Sch of Art, pt/t lectr RA Schs 1980–, curator RA Schs 1995–; works in various private collections in England and America RA 1986 (ARA 1975); *Solo exhibitons* Thackeray Gallery London 1973, 1975, 1978 and 1981, Browse and Darby London 1988 and 1993 (gallery artist); *Group exhibitions* incl regular exhibitor at RA Summer Exhbn, works shown in Jasper Galleries (Houston and NY); work featured in Oils Master Class (by Sally Bulgin) 1996; *Recreations* gardening under the supervision of my wife; *Style*— Ben Levene, Esq, RA; ✉ c/o Royal Academy of Arts, Piccadilly, London W1V 0DS (☎ 0171 439 7438)

LEVENE, Prof Malcolm Irvin; s of Maurice Mordechai Levene, of Brighton, and Helen, *née* Kutner (d 1983); *b* 2 Jan 1951; *Educ* Guy's Hosp Med Sch (LRCP, MRCS, MB BS, FRCP, MD); *m* 1, 1972, Miriam Ann, *née* Bentley (d 1989); 3 da (Alysa b 20 Aug 1976, Katherine b 10 Jan 1979, Ilana b 13 Feb 1983); m 2, Susan Anne, da of Robert Cave; 1 da (Hannah Sophie b 2 Nov 1992), 1 s (David Jack b 18 May 1994); *Career* house surgn Royal Sussex Co Hosp Brighton March-Oct 1974, house physician Northampton Gen Hosp 1974, locum GP NSW Australia 1975–76, paediatric SHO Charing Cross Hosp 1976–77, registrar Derby Children's Hosp 1977–78, paediatric registrar Charing Cross Hosp 1978–79, hon sr registrar Hammersmith Hosp and Queen Charlotte's Hosp London 1979–82, res lectr in neonatal med Royal Postgrad Med Sch London 1979–82, hon conslt paediatrician Leicester Royal Infirmary and reader in child health Univ of Leicester Med Sch 1988 (sr lectr 1982–88), prof of paediatrics and child health and hon conslt paediatrician Univ of Leeds Med Sch 1989–; Scope (formerly The Spastics Soc): memb

Med Advsy Ctee 1985–91, memb Combined Res Ctee 1986–91; memb Leicestershire Maternity Liaison Ctee 1984–88, chm Res Ctee Action Research 1993– (memb 1992–), chm Centre for Reproduction, Growth and Devpt Research Sch of Med 1995–; ed-in-chief Seminars in Neonatology; memb Editorial Bd: Developmental Med and Child Neurology 1985–93, Jl of Perinatal Med 1987–, Neuropaediatrics 1992–; hon sec Div of Child Health Leicestershire DHA; Handcock prize RCS 1974, British Cncl travelling fellowship 1980, Michael Blecklow Meml prize BPA 1982, Ronnie MacKeith prize BPNA 1984, Guthrie medal BPA 1986, BUPA Nat Res award 1988; memb: BPA, Neonatal Soc, RSM, Paediatric Res Soc, BPNA, British Assoc of Perinatal Med; *Books* A Handbook for Examinations in Paediatrics (jtly, 1981), Ultrasound of the Infant Brain (jtly, 1985), Diseases of Children (jtly, 5 edn 1985), Current Reviews in Paediatrics (1987), Essentials of Neonatal Medicine (jtly, 1987, 2 edn 1993), Fetal and Neonatal Neurology and Neurosurgery (ed jtly, 1988, 2 edn 1994), Jolly's Diseases of Children (ed, 6 edn 1991); author of numerous chapters in books and articles in learned jls; *Recreations* golf, gardening, music; *Style*— Prof Malcolm Levene; ✉ Acacia House, Acacia Park Drive, Apperley Bridge, W Yorks BD10 0PH (☎ 0113 250 9959); Academic Unit of Paediatrics, University of Leeds, D Floor, Clarendon Wing, Leeds General Infirmary, Leeds LS2 9NS (☎ 0113 292 3905, fax 0113 292 3902)

LEVENE, Sir Peter Keith; KBE (1989), JP (City of London 1984); s of Maurice Pierre Levene (d 1970), and Rose Levene (d 1991); *b* 8 Dec 1941; *Educ* City of London Sch, Univ of Manchester (BA (Econ)); *m* 1966, Wendy Ann, da of Frederick Fraiman; 2 s, 1 da; *Career* chm United Scientific Holdings plc 1982–85 (md 1968–85), chm Defence Mfrs Assoc 1984–85, personal advsr to Sec of State for Defence 1984, chief of defence procurement MOD 1985–91, dir UK Nat Armaments 1988–91, chm IEPG (Euro) Nat Armaments Dirs 1989–90, special advsr to Sec of State for the Environment 1991–92, special advsr to Pres of the Bd of Trade 1992–95, efficiency advsr to the Prime Minister 1992–; dep chm Wasserstein Perella & Co Ltd 1991–95, chm Docklands Light Railway 1991–94, chm and chief exec Canary Wharf Ltd 1993–96; govr: City of London Sch for Girls 1984–85, City of London Sch 1985–, Sir John Cass Primary Sch 1985–93 (dep chm); vice pres City of London Red Cross, memb Ct HAC, chm London Homes for the Elderly 1990–93, Hon Col Commandant RLC 1993– (RCT 1991–93); common cncllr Ward of Candlewick 1983–84, Alderman Ward of Portsoken 1984–; Sheriff City of London Sept 1995–96; Master Worshipful Co of Carmen 1992–93; *Recreations* skiing, swimming, watching association football, travel; *Clubs* Guildhall, City Livery, RAC; *Style*— Sir Peter Levene, KBE, JP; ✉ c/o The Cabinet Office, 70 Whitehall, London SW1A 2AS (☎ 0171 270 0275)

LEVENTHAL, Colin David; *b* 2 Nov 1946; *Educ* Univ of London (BA); *Career* slr 1971; head of copyright BBC until 1981, head of programme acquisition Channel Four TV 1981–86, dir of prog acquisition Channel Four TV 1987–, md Channel Four International 1993–; *Recreations* film, television, theatre; *Style*— Colin Leventhal, Esq; ✉ Channel Four TV Corp, 124 Horseferry Road, London SW1P 2TX (☎ 0171 396 4444, fax 0171 306 8353)

LEVER, Hon Bernard Lewis; s of Baron Lever (Life Peer, d 1977), by his w Ray, *see* Baroness Lever; n of Baron Lever of Manchester (Life Peer); *b* 1 Feb 1951; *Educ* Clifton, Queen's Coll Oxford (Neale Exhibitioner, MA); *m* 1985, Anne Helen, da of Patrick Chandler Gordon Ballingall, MBE, of Seaford, E Sussex; 2 da (Helen Jane b 28 Sept 1986, Isabel Elizabeth Rose b 2 March 1991); *Career* called to the Bar Middle Temple 1975, in practice Northern Circuit, recorder of the Crown Court 1995–; co-fndr of SDP in NW 1981, Parly candidate (SDP) Manchester Withington 1983; *Recreations* walking, music; *Clubs* Vincent's; *Style*— The Hon Bernard Lever; ✉ Peel Court Chambers, 45 Hardman St, Manchester M3 3HA (☎ 0161 832 3791, fax 0161 835 3054)

LEVER, Sir (Tresham) Christopher Arthur Lindsay; 3 Bt (UK 1911), of Hans Crescent, Chelsea; s of Sir Tresham Joseph Philip Lever, 2 Bt, FRSL (d 1975), and Frances Yowart Parker, *née* Goodwin (d 1959); step s of Pamela, Lady Lever, da of Lt-Col The Hon Malcolm Bowes-Lyon, former w of Lord Malcolm Avondale Douglas-Hamilton; *b* 9 Jan 1932; *Educ* Eton, Trinity Coll Cambridge (MA); *m* 1, 1970 (m dis 1974), Susan Mary, da of late John Armytage Nicholson, of Crossmolina, Co Mayo, and Dunboyne, Co Meath; m 2, 1975, Linda Weightman McDowell, da of late James Jepson Goulden, of Tennessee, USA; *Heir* none; *Career* author; Lt 17/21 Lancers 1950; Peat Marwick Mitchell & Co 1954–55, Kitcat & Aitken 1955–56, dir: John Barran & Sons Ltd (later plc) 1956–64; conslt: Zoo Check Tst 1984–91, Born Free Fndn 1991–; patron: Rhino Rescue Tst 1985– (tstee 1986–91), Tusk Tst 1990– (chm 1990–), Lynx Educnl Tst for Animal Welfare 1991–, Respect for Animals 1995–, Earth 2000 1996–; memb: Cncl Soc for the Protection of Animals in N Africa 1986–88, Cncl Br Tst for Ornithology 1988–91, SOS Sahel Int (UK) 1995–; chm: African Fund for Endangered Wildlife (UK) 1987–90, Br Tst for Ornithology Nat Centre Appeal 1987–92, Ruaha Tst 1990–95, UK Elephant Gp 1991–92; Int Tst for Nature Conservation: tstee 1980–92, vice pres 1986–91, pres 1991–92; IUCN (World Conservation Union): cmmn memb UK Ctee 1986–, memb Resources Species Survival Cmmn 1988–; hon life memb Brontë Soc 1988; FLS; *Books* Goldsmiths and Silversmiths of England (1975), The Naturalized Animals of the British Isles (1977, paperback edn 1979), Wildlife' 80 - The World Conservation Yearbook (contrib 1980), Evolution of Domesticated Animals (contrib 1984), Naturalized Mammals of the World (1985), Beyond the Bars - The Zoo Dilemma (contrib 1987), Naturalized Birds of the World (1987), For the Love of Animals (contrib 1989), The Mandarin Duck (1990), They Dined on Eland - The Story of the Acclimatisation Societies (1992), The New Atlas of Breeding Birds in Britain and Ireland: 1988–91 (contrib, 1993), Naturalized Animals: The Ecology of Successfully Introduced Species (1994), The Introduction and Naturalisation of Birds (contrib, 1996), Naturalized Fishes of the World (1996), Stocking and Introductions of Fish (1997), European Ornithological Atlas (contrib, 1997); *Recreations* watching and photographing wildlife, fishing, golf; *Clubs* Boodle's, Swinley Forest Golf; *Style*— Sir Christopher Lever, Bt; ✉ Newell House, Winkfield, Berks SL4 4SE (☎ 01344 882604)

LEVER, Colin David; s of Michael Lever (d 1991), of London, and Susan, *née* Cohen (d 1987); *b* 4 Sept 1938; *Educ* Hendon GS, Balliol Coll Oxford (MA); *m* 2 Sept 1962, Ruth, da of Rev Harry Bornstein (d 1943); 1 s (Alexander b 1968), 3 da (Claire b 1966, Joy b 1970, Naomi b 1973); *Career* ptnr Bacon & Woodrow 1966– (actuarial trainee 1960, sr ptnr 1982–93); chm Nat Assoc Pension Funds 1985–87 (memb Cncl 1981–83, vice-chm 1983–85); FIA 1965; *Books* Pension Fund Investment (with D P Hager, 1989); *Recreations* gardening, flying, narrow boating; *Style*— Colin Lever, Esq; ✉ 38 Oakleigh Park South, London N20 9JN (☎ 0181 445 7880); Bacon & Woodrow, St Olaf House, London Bridge City, London SE1 2PE (☎ 0171 357 7171, fax 0171 716 7399, telex 895 3206 BWLON G)

LEVER, Dr Eric G; s of Sam Lever (d 1978), and Freda, *née* Mann; *b* 5 April 1947; *Educ* Quintin Sch, Trinity Coll Cambridge (MA, MB BChir), Univ Coll Med Sch, Univ of Chicago (Endocrinology Diabetes fell), MRCP 1978; *m* 26 Aug 1985, Nicola, da of Bernard Langdon; 4 s (Elliott b 21 Jan 1988, Michael b 2 May 1989, Charles b 27 June 1994, Simon b 22 March 1996); *Career* jr hosp dr appts 1975–88: Univ Coll Hosp, Edgware Gen Hosp, Univ Hosp Nottingham, Royal Marsden Hosp, Hammersmith Hosp, King's Coll Hosp London, Billings Hosp Chicago; full-time private conslt in endocrinology diabetes and gen med 1988–: London Clinic, Humana Hosp Wellington, Lister Hosp; FRSM 1988; author of many papers on endocrinology and diabetes; *Recreations* art, music and the philosophy of ideas; *Style*— Dr Eric G Lever; ✉ 136 Harley St, London W1N 1AH (☎ 0171 935 3386, fax 0171 935 3298)

LEVER, Jeremy Frederick; QC (England and Wales 1972, N Ireland 1988); s of Arnold Lever (d 1980), and Elizabeth Cramer, *née* Nathan (d 1993); *b* 23 June 1933; *Educ* Bradfield, Univ Coll Oxford, Nuffield Coll Oxford, All Souls Coll Oxford (MA); *Career* 2 Lt RA (E African Artillery) 1952–53; called to the Bar Gray's Inn 1957, bencher 1985, head of chambers 1989–96; pres Oxford Union Soc 1957 (tstee 1972–77 and 1988–); non-exec dir: Dunlop Holdings Ltd 1973–80, Wellcome Foundation Ltd 1983–94; memb: Arbitral Tbnl US/UK Arbitration concerning Heathrow Airport User Charges 1988–94, Independent Inquiry Univ of Portsmouth 1995, Cncl and Ctee of Mgmnt Br Inst of Int and Comparative Law; sr dean All Souls Coll Oxford 1988– (fell 1957–, sub warden 1982–84), govr Berkhamsted Schs 1985–95; FRSA; *Books* The Law of Restrictive Trading Agreements (1964), Chitty on Contracts (ed 1961, 1968, 1972, 1977); *Recreations* music; *Clubs* Garrick; *Style*— Jeremy Lever, Esq, QC; ✉ 26 John St, London WC1N 2BL (☎ 0171 831 0351, fax 0171 405 1675); All Souls College, Oxford OX1 4AL (☎ 01865 279379, fax 01865 279 299)

LEVER, John Darcy; s of Prof Jeffery Darcy Lever, of Ystrad Mynach, Mid-Glamorgan, and Margaret Emily, *née* Eastwood; *b* 14 Jan 1952; *Educ* Westminster, Trinity Coll Cambridge (MA, rowing blue), Christ Church Oxford (PGCE); *m* 30 Dec 1981, Alisoun Margaret, da of Dr Alastair Pratt Yule; 2 da (Emily Clare b 10 Aug 1983, Rebecca Mary b 24 May 1988), 1 s (James Edward Darcy 21 Feb 1985); *Career* asst master St Edward's Oxford 1974–76; Winchester Coll: asst master 1976–84, housemaster 1984–92; headmaster Canford Sch 1992–; *Recreations* rowing, walking, solitude; *Style*— John Lever, Esq; ✉ Headmaster's House, Canford School, Wimborne, Dorset BH21 3AD (☎ 01202 882411)

LEVER, His Hon Judge; (John) Michael; QC (1976); s of John Lever (d 1967), and Ida, *née* Donaldson (d 1989); *b* 12 Aug 1928; *Educ* Bolton Sch, Gonville and Caius Coll Cambridge (Blackstone scholar, Tapp scholar, BA); *m* 1964, Elizabeth, *née* Marr; 2 s (Giles b 1968, James b 1970); *Career* Flying Offr RAF 1950–52; called to the Bar Middle Temple; in practice Northern Circuit 1952–81, recorder of the Crown Court 1972–81 (asst recorder Salford 1969–72), circuit judge (Northern Circuit) 1981–, sr res judge Bolton Combined Court Centre 1992–; *Recreations* theatre, fell walking, all sport especially Bolton Wanderers FC; *Style*— His Hon Judge Lever, QC; ✉ Lakelands, Rivington, Bolton, Greater Manchester BL6 7RT

LEVER, Paul Ronald Scott; s of Thomas Denis Lever, of Conningsby House, Sandygate, Sheffield, and Mary Barclay, *née* Scott; *b* 9 Dec 1940; *m* 23 Sept 1964, Elisabeth Barbra, da of Sir Richard Hughes, Bt (d 1970), of Rivelin Cottage, Hollow Meadows, Sheffield; 1 s (Christopher Mark b 17 July 1965), 2 da (Alison Clare b 25 Feb 1967, Catherine Elisabeth b 17 June 1969); *Career* md Tower Housewares (subsidiaries of TI Gp) 1979–83, chm Darius Industrial Investments 1983–86, md Crown Paints Div (subsidiary of Reed International) 1986–88, md Crown Berger Europe Ltd 1988–89 (chm Ireland 1988–89); chm: Cuprinol Ltd 1988–89, Williams European Consumer Productions Division (subsidiaries of Williams Holdings plc) 1989; exec chm Lionheart plc 1989–96; chm: Alexander Drew & Sons Ltd 1990–92, BSM Group plc 1992–, Dan Holdings Ltd 1994–, Ashworth Hosp Authy 1996–; Int Mgmnt Centre Europe: industl fell mktg and business policy 1984, industl prof of strategic mgmnt 1986, elected master teacher 1987, elected memb Cncl 1988, elected chm Cncl 1992; memb Editorial Bd Management Digest 1987; FRSA; *Recreations* cooking, listening to classical music, watching cricket, fishing, shooting; *Clubs* Reform, MCC; *Style*— Paul Lever, Esq

LEVERETT, David; s of George Edgar Leverett, of Nottingham, and Doris, *née* Tebbit; *b* 12 Jan 1938; *Educ* John Player Sch Nottingham, Nottingham Sch of Art (NDD), Royal Acad Schs London (post grad dip, travelling scholar); *m* Sonia Loretta Wilhmena Holme; 2 s (Jason David b 2 June 1967, Simeon b 19 Jan 1970); *Career* artist; variously art teacher at instns incl: RCA, Dublin Coll of Art, Cooper Union NY; currently reg visiting lectr Slade Sch UCL; Sargant fell Br Sch at Rome 1990–91; *Solo Exhibitions* incl: Redfern Gall London 1965, 1968, 1970, 1972, 1987 and 1990, Editions Alecto NY 1970, Studio La Citta Verona 1971, Galleria del Cavallino Venice 1972, Galerie Britta Herberle Frankfurt 1972, Ikon Gall Birmingham 1973, ICA London 1974, Galleria G7 Bologna 1975, Gall Desmos Athens 1975, Galerie Skulima Berlin 1975, Galleria Vinciana Milan 1976, Oliver Dowling Gall Dublin 1977, Janus Suite Riverside Studios London 1979, Studio Gall Palace of Culture Warsaw 1980, Gall III Lisbon 1983, Bildornan Gall Umea Sweden 1984, Curwen Gall London 1985, Jersey Arts Centre St Helier Jersey 1986, Thumb Gall London 1990 and 1992, Jill George Gall London 1995, Gall In Collaboration Santa Monica USA 1996; *Group Exhibitions* incl: British Painting Monte Carlo 1966, British Painting and Sculpture Whitechapel Gall 1968, Play Orbit ICA 1969, British Drawing Angela Flowers Gall London 1972, 6 Artists Inglesi Galleria lo Spazio Berscia and Gall Godel Rome 1974, British Painting 1974 Hayward Gall 1974, Empirica Rimini City Mus 1975, British Painting RA 1952–77 British Drawing from 1945 Whitworth Art Gall Manchester 1979, Cralylus XV Sao Paulo Brazil 1979, Contemporary Choice 1979–81 Contemporary Arts Soc and Serpentine Gall 1982, One of a Kind Maryland Inst Baltimore 1983, Bradford Print Biennale Selection V & A 1986, Decade Exhbn Dublin 1986, Mediterranean Bienal graphic art, Athens 1988, Ogle Fine Art 1989 and 1990, Thumb Gall 1989, Int Art Fair Olympia 1990, Cabinet Paintings Gillian Jason Gall 1991, Special Presentation Merrill Chase Gall Chicago 1991, 1992 and 1995, Contraprint Br Sch at Rome 1991, Omphalos Series Galleria Gianfranco Rosini Riccione Italy 1991, Cyril Gerber Gall 1992, Cabinet Paintings Hove Mus and Art Gall and Glynn Vivian Art Gall and Mus 1992, Drawings 3 Jill George Gall 1995, Drawings V & A 1996; *Public Collections* incl: Arts Cncl of GB, Br Cncl, V & A, Contemporary Arts Soc, Tate Gall, Mus of Peace Hiroshima, Miny of Culture Athens, The State Collection Palace of Culture Warsaw, Mus of Modern Art Sao Paulo Brazil, Mus of Modern Art Campione Switzerland, State Art Gall NSW Aust, Inst of Contemporary Graphics, Mus of Modern Art Zagreb Yugoslavia, Modern Art Gall Koszalim Poland, Umea Kommun Sweden, DOE, Reading Mus of Art, Nottingham City Mus, Univ of Liverpool, Univ of Warwick, British Rail Collection, London Press Exchange; *Publications* incl: A Possible Future - New Painting (1973), Colour in Painting - a European situation (1976), The Citadel (1994), The David Leverett Portfolio (1995); *Style*— David Leverett, Esq; ✉ 132 Leighton Rd, London NW5 2RG (☎ 0171 485 3317)

LEVERHULME, 3 Viscount (UK 1922); Sir Philip William Bryce Lever; 3 Bt (1911), KG (1988), TD, JP; also Baron Leverhulme (UK 1917); s of 2 Viscount (d 1949), by his 1 w, Marion; *b* 1 July 1915; *Educ* Eton, Trinity Coll Cambridge; *m* 1937, Margaret Ann (d 1973), da of John Moon, of Tiverton, Devon; 3 da (Hon Mrs Susan Pakenham, Hon Mrs Peter Tower, Hon Mrs Heber-Percy); *Heir* none; *Career* hon advsy dir Unilever Ltd; Lord-Lt for City and County of Chester 1949–90; Hon Col: Queen's Own Yeo 1979–, RAC TAVR 1972–; memb Nat Hunt Ctee 1961 (steward 1965–68), dep sr steward Jockey Club 1970–73 (sr steward 1973–76); chllr Univ of Liverpool 1980–93; pres NW Tourist Bd 1982–; memb Ct of Assts Worshipful Co of Fishmongers, Liveryman Worshipful Co of Stationers & Newspaper Makers; Hon FRCS; KStJ; *Clubs* Boodle's, Jockey; *Style*— The Rt Hon the Viscount Leverhulme, KG, TD, JP; ✉ Thornton Manor, Thornton Hough, Wirral, Merseyside L63 1JB (☎ 0151 336 4834); Flat 6, Kingston House East, Princes Gate, Kensington, London SW7 1LJ (☎ 0171 589 9322); Badanloch, Kinbrace, Sutherland KW11 6UE (☎ 01431 831269)

LEVESON, Brian Henry; QC 1986; s of Dr Ivan Leveson (d 1980), of Liverpool, and Elaine, *née* Rivlin (d 1983); *b* 22 June 1949; *Educ* Liverpool Coll, Merton Coll Oxford (MA); *m* 20 Dec 1981, Lynne Rose, da of Aubrey Fishel (d 1987), of Wallasey; 2 s (Andrew b 1983, James b 1989), 1 da (Claire b 1984); *Career* called to the Bar Middle Temple 1970; lectr in Law Univ of Liverpool 1971–81, recorder of the Crown Court 1988–, bencher Middle Temple 1995; memb: Cncl Univ of Liverpool 1983–92, Parole Bd 1992–95; *Style*— Brian Leveson, Esq, QC; ✉ 61 Fleet Street, Temple, London EC4Y 1JU (☎ 0171 353 4363, fax 0171 583 1491); 25 Byrom St, Manchester M3 4PF (☎ 0161 829 2100, fax 0161 829 2101)

LEVEY, Sir Michael Vincent; kt (1980), LVO (1965); s of O L H Levey and Gladys Mary Milestone; *b* 8 June 1927; *Educ* The Oratory, Exeter Coll Oxford; *m* 1954, Brigid Antonia (the author Brigid Brophy; d 1995), o da of John Brophy (d 1965); 1 da; *Career* served Army 1945–48; Slade prof of fine art Cambridge 1963–64, dir Nat Gallery 1973–86 (asst keeper 1951–66); Slade prof of fine art Oxford 1994–95; hon fellow Exeter Coll Oxford 1973; Hon DLitt Univ of Manchester; FBA, FRSL; *Books* 14 vols non fiction, 3 vols fiction; *Style*— Sir Michael Levey, LVO, FBA, FRSL; ✉ 36 Little Lane, Louth, Lincolnshire LN11 9DU

LEVI, Peter (Chad Tigar); s of Herbert Simon Levi (d 1956), of Ruislip, Middx, and Edith Mary Tigar (d 1973); *b* 16 May 1931; *Educ* Beaumont and Oxford (MA); *m* 31 March 1977, Deirdre, da of Hon Dennis Craig, MBE (d 1971), of Bath; *Career* former Jesuit priest; tutor and lectr Campion Hall Oxford 1965–76, lectr in classics Christ Church Oxford 1979–82, prof of poetry Univ of Oxford 1984–89; fell St Catherine's Coll 1977–91 (emeritus 1993); author numerous volumes of poetry and some prose; FSA, FRSL; *Poetry* The Gravel Ponds (1960), Water Rock and Sand (1962), The Shearwaters (1985), Fresh Water Sea Water (1966), Ruined Abbeys (1968), Life is a Platform (1971), Death is a Pulpit (1971), Collected Poems (1976), Five Ages (1978), Private Ground (1981), The Echoing Green (1983), Shakespeare's Birthday (1985), Shadow and Bone (1989), Goodbye to the Art of Poetry (1989), The Rags of Time (1994); *Prose* Beaumont (1961), The Lightgarden of the Angel King (1973), In Memory of David Jones (1975), The Noise Made By Poems (1976), The Hill of Kronos (1980), The Flutes of Autumn (1983), A History of Greek Literature (1985), The Frontiers of Paradise (1987), To The Goat (1988), Life and Times of William Shakespeare (1988), Boris Pasternak (1989), The Art of Poetry (1991), Tennyson (1993), Edward Lear (1995), Milton (1996), A Bottle in the Shade (1996); *Thrillers* The Head in the Soup (1979), Grave Witness (1985), Knit One Drop One (1987), Shade those Laurels (with Cyril Connolly, 1990); *Translations* Yevtushenko (1963), The Psalms (1976), Marko the Prince (1983), The Murderess (Papadiamantis, 1983), The Holy Gospel of St John (1985), Revelation (1992); *Recreations* natural wonders and Greek and Roman antiquities; *Style*— Peter Levi, Esq; ✉ Prospect Cottage, The Green, Frampton on Severn, Glos

LEVI, Renato (Sonny); s of Mario Levi (d 1972), and Eleonora, *née* Ciravegna; *b* 3 Sept 1926; *Educ* College de Cannes France, St Paul's Sch Darjeeling India, Bishop Cotton Sch Simla India, Coll of Aeronautical Engrg London; *m* 12 June 1954, Ann Joan, da of John Douglas Watson (d 1969); 2 s (Martin b 1958, Christopher b 1962), 1 da (Gina b 1955); *Career* RAF: joined 1945, cmmnd 1946, demobbed 1948; designer high speed watercraft AFCO Ltd Bombay India 1951–60, chief designer Navaltecnica Anzio Italy 1960–65, freelance designer 1965–; work incl: Cowes-Torquay powerboat race winners, A Speranziella 1963, Surfury 1967, Virgin Atlantic Challenger II (1986 Blue Riband holder); originator of delta hull form and Levi surface propulsion; RDI 1987, FCSD 1989; *Books* Dhows to Deltas (1971), Milestones in My Designs (1992); *Recreations* power boating and travelling; *Clubs* Royal London Yacht; *Style*— Sonny Levi, Esq; ✉ Sandhills, Porchfield, nr Newport, Isle of Wight PO30 4LH (☎ 01983 524713, fax 01983 527238)

LEVIEN, Robin Hugh; s of John Blomeield Levien, of Norwich, Norfolk, and Louis Beryl, *née* Squire; *b* 5 May 1952; *Educ* Bearwood Coll Wokingham Berks, Central Sch of Art and Design (BA), Royal Coll of Art (MA); *m* 21 Aug 1978, Patricia Anne, da of Alan Newby Stainton; *Career* ceramics and glass designer; ptnr: Queensberry Hunt 1982–95 (joined 1977), Queensberry Hunt Levien (following name change) 1995–; mass market products for mfrs and retailers incl: Thomas China, Wedgwood, Ideal Standard, American Standard, Habitat, Dartington Crystal; major products incl: Trend dinnerware shape for Thomas China 1981 (Die Gute Industrieform Award Hanover 1982, Golden Flame Award Valencia 1983), Studio bathroom range for Ideal Standard 1986 (BT Prize BBC Design Awards 1987, runner-up DBA Design Effectiveness Awards 1989), Domi bathroom taps for Ideal Standard 1989 (runner-up Design Week Awards 1990), Symphony range of bathtubs for American Standard 1990 (Interior Design Product Award American Soc of Interior Designers 1991), Kyomi bathroom range for Ideal Standard 1996; lectr RCA, Central St Martins Sch of Art and N Staffordshire Univ; memb Industl Design Course Advsy Panel Central St Martins Sch of Art, external advsr Faculty of Design The Robert Gordon Univ Aberdeen; Design Cncl: memb Design Selection Panel, memb Design Awards Panel 1990, memb Designer Selection Serv Advsy Gp; memb: Task Gp DBA Design Effectiveness Awards, Student Bursary Judging Panel RSA 1991, 1992, 1993 and 1994, Advsy Bd for Design BTEC, Friends of the Earth; fndr memb Brewcombe Woodland Tst; MCSD, FRSA, RDI 1995; *Recreations* 'Fulham Farmer' on 1952 Ferguson tractor, tennis, softball, films, cooking; *Style*— Robin Levien, Esq; ✉ Queensberry Hunt Levien, 24 Brook Mews North, London W2 3BW (☎ 0171 724 3701, fax 0171 723 0508)

LEVIN, (Henry) Bernard; CBE (1990); s of late Phillip Levin, and Rose, *née* Racklin; *b* 19 Aug 1928; *Educ* Christ's Hosp, LSE (BSc); *Career* journalist and author; writer and broadcaster for radio and TV 1952–; regular contributor to many publications 1953–; Sir Dorab Tata Tst lectr India 1990; hon fell LSE 1977; pres English Assoc 1984–85 (vice pres 1985–88); memb Order of Polonia Restituta (by Polish Govt in Exile) 1976; *Publications* The Pendulum Years (1971), Taking Sides (1979), Conducted Tour (1981), Speaking Up (1982), Enthusiasms (1983), The Way We Live Now (1984), A Shakespeare Mystery (English Assoc presidential address, 1985), Hannibal's Footsteps (1985), In These Times (1986), To the End of the Rhine (1987), All Things Considered (1988), A Walk Up Fifth Avenue (1989), Now Read On (1990), If You Want My Opinion (1992), A World Elsewhere (1994), I Should Say So (1995); *Style*— Bernard Levin, Esq, CBE; ✉ c/o The Times, 1 Pennington Street, London E1 9XN (☎ 0171 782 5000)

LEVIN, Eddy; s of Moses Levin, of London, and Sarah, *née* Greenberg (d 1983); *b* 20 March 1932; *Educ* Benoni HS SA, Univ of Pretoria (BChD); *m* Osnath, *née* Bregman; 2 s (Daniel, Phillip); *Career* dentist; in gen practice 1955–56, teacher Hadassa Dental Hosp Jerusalem 1956, Health Serv 1957–65, Harley St practice 1965–, pt/t teacher London Dental Hosp 1965–69; int lectr and author of specialist papers; memb: BDA, RSM, Alpha Omega, Myofunctional Inst USA; FDS; *Recreations* sailing, walking, gardening, study of religion, mysticism, psychology; *Style*— Eddy Levin, Esq; ✉ 42 Harley St, London W1N 1AB (☎ 0171 935 6202)

LEVIN, Richard; OBE (1952); s of late Dr Henry Levin, and late Margaret, *née* Sanders; *b* 31 Dec 1910; *Educ* Clayesmore, Slade Sch, UCL; *m* 1, 1932 (m dis 1958), Evelyn Alexander; 2 da (Leora b 1932, Gillian b 1935); m 2, 4 March 1960, Patricia, da of Dr William Henry Foy; *Career* asst art dir Gaumont Br; exhibition graphics and industl designer in private practice working for BBC Wakefield Ltd, Bakelite Ltd and LEB 1930–39; camouflage offr Bomber 4 Gp Air Miny 1940, exhibition div designer Miny of Info; chief designer Festival of Britain Land Travelling Exhibition 1946, head of design BBC TV Serv 1953–71, exec prodr Crown Int Prodns 1971–73, photographer in private practise 1975–; photographic exhibitions The TV Scene at Hampton Court Palace and Kodak Gallery 1978; RTS: Silver Medal 1972, Award for Lifetimes Contrib to TV 1993; FSIAD 1955, RDI 1975; *Books* Television by Design (1960); *Recreations* fishing; *Style*— Richard Levin, Esq, OBE, RDI; ✉ Sandells House, West Amesbury, Wiltshire SP4 7BH (☎ 01980 623857)

LEVINE, Gemma Jennifer Ann; da of Ellis Josephs (d 1991), and Mae, *née* Phillips; *b* 10 Jan 1939; *Educ* Hasmonean GS; *m* 5 March 1961 (m dis 1986), Eric A Levine, s of Jack D Levine; 2 s (James Andrew b 20 Nov 1963, Adam Edward b 17 June 1965); *Career* antique prints dealer 1961–, interior designer 1970–75, professional photographer 1976–, author 1978–; FRSA 1990; *Exhibitions* Four Seasons (photographs and watercolours, Casson Gallery London) 1977, With Henry Moore (photographs, Serpentine Gallery London (Arts Cncl of GB) and The Arts Club London) 1978, My Jerusalem (photographs and poetry, Jerusalem Theatre Gallery 1982 and The Royal Festival Hall 1983), Henry Moore (photographs, Tel-Aviv Univ) 1982, Henry Moore - Wood Sculpture (The Barbican London 1983, Leeds City Art Gallery 1984 and House of Commons 1985), Jerusalem (photographs, House of Commons) 1983, Tel-Aviv - Faces & Places (Tel-Aviv) 1984, Ethiopian Jews (Manor House London) 1985, Faces of the 80's (The Barbican London, opened by The Rt Hon Margaret Thatcher) 1987, Faces of British Theatre (The Royal Nat Theatre London, opened by HRH Prince Edward) 1990, Gemma Levine 20 Years of Photography - Retrospective (Tom Blau Gallery for Camera Press) 1995, People of the 90's (Catto Gallery Hampstead, Cafe Royal, Barbican, Virgin Airways Terminal 3, Grosvenor House Gallery) 1995; *Publications* 'Israel' Faces and Places (photographs, 1978), Living with The Bible (photographs and watercolours, 1978), With Henry Moore (photographs and taped text, 1978, 4 edn 1984), We live in Israel (photographs and text, 1981), Living in Jerusalem (1982), The Young Inheritors (photographs, 1982), Henry Moore (illustrated biography, 1985), Faces of the 80's (text by Jeffrey Archer, foreword by The Rt Hon Margaret Thatcher, 1987), Faces of British Theatre (text by Jonathan Miller, foreword by John Gielgud, 1990), People of the 90's (caption text by Sheridan Morley, foreward by HRH The Princess of Wales, 1995); *Recreations* art, classical music; *Style*— Mrs Gemma Levine; ✉ The Studio, Flat 2, 65 Wimpole St, London W1M 7DE (home ☎ 0171 486 4040, fax 0171 487 2744)

LEVINE, Sir Montague Bernard; kt (1979); s of late Philip Levine; *b* 15 May 1922; *Educ* RCS in Ireland, RCP in Ireland; *m* 1959, Dr Rose Gold; 1 s, 1 da; *Career* gen practitioner 1956–87, clinical tutor in gen practice St Thomas' Hosp 1972–87, HM coroner for London SE Inner 1988–; currently hon lectr in coronery law: St Thomas' Hosp, King's Coll Hosp, Guy's Hosp; former pres SE England Coroners' Soc; fell Hunterian Soc; *Books* Interparental Violence and its Effect on Children; *Style*— Sir Montague Levine; ✉ Gainsborough House, 120 Ferndene Rd, Herne Hill, London SE24 0AA (☎ 0171 274 9196)

LEVINE, Sydney; s of Rev Isaac Levine (d 1957), of Bradford, and Miriam, *née* Altman (d 1967); *b* 4 Sept 1923; *Educ* Bradford GS, Univ of Leeds (LLB); *m* 29 March 1959, Cécile Rona, da of Joseph Rubinstein (d 1987), of Dublin; 3 s (Iain David b 1960, Simon Mark b 1962, Colin Philip b 1964), 1 da (Emma Rachel b 1969); *Career* called to the Bar Inner Temple 1952, recorder of the Crown Ct 1975–95, head of chambers; *Recreations* acting and directing in amateur theatre, gardening, marathon running; *Style*— Sydney Levine, Esq; ✉ 2A Primley Park Road, Alwoodley, Leeds LS17 7HS (☎ 0113 268 3769); Broadway House, 9 Bank St, Bradford BD1 1TW (☎ 01274 722560, fax 01274 370708)

LEVINGE, Sir Richard George Robin; 12 Bt (I 1704), of High Park, Westmeath; s of Maj Sir Richard Vere Henry Levinge, 11 Bt, MBE (d 1984), and his 1 w, Barbara Mary, da of George Jardine Kidston, CMG (d 1954); *b* 18 Dec 1946; *m* 1, 1969 (m dis 1978), Hilary Jane, da of Dr Derek Mark, of Wingfield, Bray, Co Wicklow; 1 s (Richard Mark b 1970); m 2, 1978, Donna Maria Isabella d'Ardia Caracciolo, yr da of Don Ferdinando d'Ardia Caracciolo dei Principi di Cursi, of Haddington Road, Dublin 4; 1 s (Robin Edward b 1978), 1 da (Melissa Louise b 1980); *Heir* s, Richard Mark Levinge b 1970; *Style*— Sir Richard Levinge, Bt; ✉ Clohamon House, Bunclody, Co Wexford

LEVINSON, Prof Stephen Curtis; *b* 6 Dec 1947; *Educ* King's Coll Cambridge (BA, sr scholar), Univ of Calif Berkeley (MA, Fulbright scholar, special career fell, PhD); *m* 18 Sept 1976, Penelope, *née* Brown; 1 s (b Oct 1980); *Career* teaching asst in linguistic anthropology Univ of Calif Berkeley 1972–73; Univ of Cambridge: asst lctr 1975–78, lectr in linguistics 1978–90, dir of studies archaeology and anthropology Emmanuel Coo 1978–80, Faculty Bd Archaeology and Anthropology Emmanuel Coll 1982–87, reader in linguistics 1991–94; prof Catholic Univ Nijmegen Netherlands 1995–, ldr Cognitive Anthropology Res Gp and dir Max-Planck-Inst for Psycholinguistics Nijmegen; Stanford Univ Calif: visiting prof Linguistic Soc of America Linguistics Inst 1987, visiting assoc prof Dept of Linguistics 1987–88, convenor Res Seminar on Implicature Center for the Study of Language and Information 1987–88; memb Editorial Bd of numerous linguistics jls; memb High Table King's Coll Cambridge 1975–, Nijmegen lectr 1988, Stirling Prize American Anthropology Assoc 1992; memb: Scientific Ctee Fyssen Fndn Paris, Assoc of British Social Anthropologists, Linguistics Assoc of GB, American Anthropological Assoc, Linguistic Soc of America, European Assoc of Social Anthropologists; FBA; *Style*— Prof Stephen Levinson, FBA; ✉ Cognitive Anthropology Research Group, Max Planck Institute, PB 310, NL 6500 AH Nijmegen, Netherlands (☎ 00 31 24 352 1911, fax 00 31 24 352 1300)

LEVINSON, Stephen Michael (Steve); s of Alfred Levinson (d 1976), of London, and Golda, *née* Posner (d 1992); *b* 19 Jan 1949; *Educ* Kilburn GS, Univ of Newcastle upon Tyne (BA); *m* 23 Dec 1973, Vivien Elaine, da of Col James Grant; 1 da (Jemma Debra b 3 Nov 1976), 1 s (Thomas Alex b 13 July 1979); *Career* grad trainee Westminster Press Ltd 1970–71, industl corr South Shields Gazette 1972–73 (educn corr 1971–72); economics corr: Press Association Ltd 1976–86 (sub-ed/copy taster 1973–76), The Independent 1986–88, BBC TV 1988–92, Channel Four News ITN 1993–; Industl Soc Bdcasting Award 1995–96; *Style*— Steve Levinson, Esq; ✉ ITN Ltd, Channel 4 News, 200 Gray's Inn Road, London WC1X 8XZ (☎ 0171 430 4619, fax 0171 430 4608)

LEVISON, Victor Bernard; *Educ* Univ of London (MB BS); *Career* house surgn Radiotherapy Dept Westminster Hosp, sr registrar Radiotherapy Centre Addenbrooke's Hosp Cambridge, consIt radiotherapist Dudley Road Hosp Birmingham and Coventry; currently consIt radiotherapist: N Middx Hosp & Annexes, St Margaret's Hosp Epping, Highlands Hosp London; memb Medico-Legal Soc; MRCS, LRCP 1945, DMRT 1949, FFR 1954, FRCR 1975; *Publications* Pre-operation Radiotherapy and Surgery in the Treatment of Oat Cell Carcinoma of the Bronchus (Clinical Radiology, 1980), What is the Best Treatment of Early Operable Small Cell Carcinoma of the Bronchus? (Thorax, 1980), Effect on Fertility, Libido, Sexual Function of Post-operative Radiotherapy and Chemotherapy for Cancer of Testicle (Clinic Radiology, 1986); *Style*— Victor Levison, Esq; ✉ 20 Priory Close, Totteridge, London N20 8BB (☎ 0181 445 1481); North London Nuffield Hospital, Cavell Drive, Uplands Park Ed, Enfield, Middx EN2 7PR (☎ 0181 366 2122)

LEVVY, George; *b* 30 Nov 1953; *Educ* Robert Gordon's Coll Aberdeen, Univ of Edinburgh (MB ChB); *m*; 1 da, 1 s; *Career* jr hosp doctor Edinburgh and London 1977–83, med dir Excerpta Medica Tokyo 1984–88, commercial mangr Countrywide Communications Group Ltd 1988–91, head mktg and communications British Red Cross 1991–94, chief exec Motor Neurone Disease Assoc 1994–; MICFM, FRSA; *Recreations* sailing, cricket, reading; *Style*— George Levvy, Esq; ✉ Motor Neurone Disease Association, PO Box 246, Northampton NN1 2PR (☎ 01604 250505, fax 01604 24726)

LEVY, Allan Edward; QC (1989); s of Sidney Levy, and Mabel, *née* Lewis; *b* 17 Aug 1942; *Educ* Bury GS, Univ of Hull (LLB), Inns of Ct Law; *Career* called to the Bar Inner Temple 1969, bencher 1993, recorder South Eastern Circuit 1993– (asst recorder 1990–93); chm: Staffordshire Pindown Child Care Inquiry 1990, chm Intercountry Adoption Lawyers' Assoc 1991–95; memb: Cncl of Justice, Cncl Medico-Legal Soc, Editorial Bd Expert Evidence 1992–, Gulbenkian Fndn Cmmn on Children and Violence 1994–95, Howard League Cmmn of Inquiry into Violence in Penal Instns for Young People 1994–95, Bar Cncl 1995–; hon legal advsr Nat Children's Bureau 1990–; fell Int Acad of Matrimonial Lawyers 1992–95; speaker at Seventh Int Congress on Child Abuse Rio de Janeiro 1988, observer (Int Bar Assoc) Hague Conf on Private Int Law on intercountry adoption 1992; FRSM 1993; *Books* Wardship Proceedings (1982, 2 edn 1987), Custody and Access (1983), Adoption of Children (with J F Josling, 10 edn 1985), Focus on Child Abuse (ed and contrib 1989), The Pindown Experience and the Protection of Children (with B Kahan, 1991), One Scandal Too Many: the case for comprehensive protection for children in all settings (contrib, 1993), Re-Focus on Child Abuse (ed and contrib, 1994), Medico-Legal Perspectives in Health Care (contrib, 1996), Children Who Kill (contrib, 1996); *Recreations* travel, reading; *Clubs* Reform; *Style*— Allan Levy, Esq, QC; ✉ 17 Bedford Row, London WC1R 4EB (☎ 0171 831 7314, fax 0171 831 0061)

LEVY, Andrew Paul; s of Isaac Oscar Levy (d 1976), and Ruby, *née* Ottolangui; *b* 17 June 1955; *Educ* Univ of Manchester (BA), Hertford Coll Oxford; *Career* grad trainee Ted Bates advtg, account mangr then planner Colman RSCG 1983–86, fndr ptnr and head of planning Madell Wilmot Pringle 1986–90, planner Lowe Howard-Spink 1990–92, planning dir Lowe Group 1992–93, fndr planning ptnr Mustoe Merriman Herring Levy 1993–; *Style*— Andrew Levy, Esq; ✉ Mustoe Merriman Herring Levy, 133 Long Acre, Covent Garden, London WC2E 9AG (☎ 0171 379 9999, fax 0171 379 8487)

LEVY, Benjamin Keith; s of Col Charles Akiba Levy, RAMC (d 1988), of Brighton, and Florence, *née* Kahn (d 1985); *b* 2 Jan 1934; *Educ* Clifton Coll, King's Coll Cambridge (scholar, MA, LLB); *m* 21 Dec 1962, Ruth, eld da of Dr John Shackleton Bailey; 2 da (Sarah Beatrice b 23 June 1964, Alison Rebecca b 27 Sept 1966); *Career* called to the Bar Lincoln's Inn 1956 (bencher 1989); Staff Sgt RASC 1957–58; in practice at 11 New Sq and then 9 Old Sq Lincoln's Inn 1960–, head of chambers 9 Old Sq 1986–; ed various legal pubns; *Recreations* reading, theatre, sedate travel; *Style*— Benjamin Levy, Esq; ✉ Kara Lodge Studio, 14 Newton Grove, Bedford Park, London W4 1LB (☎ 0181 994 5121); Enterprise Chambers, 9 Old Square, Lincoln's Inn, London WC2A 3SR (☎ 0171 405 9471, fax 0171 242 1447)

LEVY, Prof John Court (Jack); OBE (1984); s of Alfred Levy (d 1978), and Lily, *née* Court (d 1976); *b* 16 Feb 1926; *Educ* Owens Sch, Univ of London, Univ of Illinois; *m* 6 April 1952, Sheila Frances, da of Noah Krisman; 2 s (Richard b 1960, Robert b 1967), 1 da (Ruth b 1957); *Career* The City Univ London: head Dept of Mech Engrg 1966–83, pro vice chllr 1976–82; dir engrg profession The Engrg Cncl London 1983–90; conslt to Institution of Electrical Engrs 1990–; FEng 1988, FIMechE, FRAes, FCGI; *Recreations* theatre, chess; *Clubs* Island Sailing (IOW); *Style*— Prof Jack Levy, OBE, FEng; ✉ 18 Woodberry Way, Finchley, London N12 0HG (☎ and fax 0181 445 1353); 137 Gurnard Pines, Cockleton Lane, Gurnard, IOW (☎ 01983 280939)

LEVY, Prof John Francis; s of Donald Myer Levy (d 1967), and Hilda Rose, *née* Stephens (d 1977); *b* 30 June 1921; *Educ* Ewell Castle Sch Ewell Surrey, Imperial Coll of Sci Technol and Med (BSc, DSc); *m* 3 April 1954, Hazel, da of Bernard Shilton (d 1975); 2 s (Martin John, Timothy James), 2 da (Jain Heather (Mrs Morrissey), Wendy Susan (Mrs Tough)); *Career* Imperial Coll of Sci Technol and Med Univ of London: joined teaching staff Dept of Botany and Plant Technol 1945, lectr 1949, sr lectr in timber technol Dept of Botany 1963, asst dir Dept of Botany 1967–74, reader in wood sci 1974, prof of wood sci 1981, head of plant technol section Dept of Pure and Applied Biology 1983, emeritus prof of wood sci 1986, sr res fell 1986; visiting prof Dept of Botany Kuwait Univ 1970, guest res worker CSIRO Div of Bldg Res Highett Victoria Aust 1977; warden Weeks Hall Imperial Coll 1959–69; hon fell: Portsmouth Univ, Imperial Coll; Inst of Wood Scis: cncl memb 1957–90, pres 1971–73; Br Wood Preserving Assoc: cncl memb 1957–90, hon treas 1960–69, vice pres 1968–76, dep pres 1976–78, pres 1978–80; BSI: memb Chemical Div Cncl 1982–90, chm Wood Preservation Standards Policy Ctee 1982–90; memb: Euro Homologation Ctee 1965–73, Wood Protection Sub Gp Int Union of Forestry Res Orgns 1966–94, Advsy Ctee for Forest Res Forestry Cmmn 1968–80, Int Res Gp on Wood Preservation 1968–, Cncl Timber Res and Devpt Assoc 1980–90, Hull Advsy Panel Mary Rose Tst 1982–, Panel for Evaluation of Efficacy of Wood Preservative Food and Environment Protection Act 1987 91; chm Review Gp on Wood Sci and Processing Forestry Res Co-ordinating Ctee 1983, dir Guarantee Protection Tst 1985–91; memb governing body: Ewell Castle Sch Surrey, Old Palace Sch Surrey; hon memb Royal Sch of Mines Assoc 1989, ARCS, FLS, fell Int Acad of Wood Sci, CBiol, FIBiol, FIWSc; *Recreations* rowing, cricket watching, reading, music; *Clubs* Leander, Thames Rowing (vice pres), Imperial Coll Boat (pres); *Style*— Prof John Levy; ✉ 5 Washington Rd, Barnes, London SW13 9BG (☎ 0181 748 0020); Department of Biology, Imperial College of Science, Technology and Medicine, London SW7 2AZ (☎ 0171 594 5413)

LEVY, Paul; s of Hyman Solomon Levy (d 1980), of Kentucky, USA, and Mrs Shirley Singer Meyers (d 1991); *b* 26 Feb 1941; *Educ* Univ of Chicago (BA, MA), Univ Coll London, Harvard Univ (PhD), Nuffield Coll Oxford; *m* 1977, Penelope, da of Clifford Marcus (d 1952); 2 da (Tatyana b 1981, Georgia b 1983); *Career* journalist and lapsed academic; food and wine ed The Observer 1980–92, wine ed and food columnist You magazine The Mail on Sunday 1992–, sr contributor Europe, Arts and Leisure page Wall Street Journal 1993–, contributing ed Travel and Leisure (USA) 1994–; frequent broadcaster on radio and TV; writer and presenter The Feast of Christmas (C4) 1992 and 1993; national press specialist Writers' Commendations 1985 and 1987; tstee: Strachey Tst, Jane Grigson Tst; FRSL; *Books* G E Moore and the Cambridge Apostles (1977, 3 edn 1989), The Shorter Strachey (ed with Michael Holroyd, 1980, 2 edn 1989), The Official Foodie Handbook (with Ann Barr, 1984), Out to Lunch (1986), Finger-lickin' Good (1990), The Feast of Christmas (1992), The Penguin Book of Food and Drink (ed, 1996); *Recreations* being cooked for, drinking better wine; *Clubs* Groucho, Wednesday; *Style*— Paul Levy, Esq; ✉ PO Box 35, Witney, Oxon OX8 8BF (☎ and fax 01993 883477 and 0171 431 9557)

LEVY, Peter Lawrence; OBE (1991); s of Joseph Levy, CBE, BEM (d 1990), and (Frances) Ninot, *née* Henwood; *b* 10 Nov 1939; *Educ* Charterhouse, Univ of London (BSc); *m* 29 June 1961, Colette, da of Harry Lynford; 1 s (Jonathan David b 8 Aug 1967), 2 da (Claudia Simone b 15 Nov 1962, Melanie Tamsin b 29 June 1965); *Career* ptnr DE & J Levy (surveyors) 1966–87, dir Stock Conversion plc 1985–86, chm Shaftesbury PLC 1986–; chm Inst for Jewish Policy Research, vice pres London Fedn of Clubs for Young People; Freeman City of London; FRICS; *Recreations* tennis, golf, cricket, walking, collecting old books and maps on London; *Clubs* RAC, Reform; *Style*— Peter Levy, Esq, OBE; ✉ Shaftesbury PLC, Pegasus House, 37–43 Sackville Stret, London W1X 2DL (☎ 0171 333 8118, fax 0171 333 0660)

LEVY, Prof Philip Marcus; s of Rupert Hyam Levy (d 1951), and Sarah Beatrice, *née* Naylor; *b* 4 Feb 1934; *Educ* Leeds Mode Sch, Univ of Leeds (BA), Univ of Birmingham (PhD); *m* 8 March 1958, Gillian Mary Levy, da of Ronald Edward Harker, of Grassington, Yorks; 2 da (Lucy b 11 Aug 1965, Mary b 3 Sept 1967); *Career* Nat Serv RAF Flying Offr and psychologist 1959–62; sr res fell then lectr in psychology Inst of Educn Univ of Birmingham 1962–65 (res fell 1956–59), sr lectr in psychology Univ of Birmingham 1969–72 (lectr Dept of Psychology 1965–69); Univ of Lancaster: prof of psychology 1972–94, ret, emeritus prof and pt/t lectr 1994–; ed The British Journal of Mathematical and Statistical Psychology 1975–80; pres Br Psychological Soc 1978–79; ESRC: memb Psychology Ctee 1976–79, chm Psychology Ctee 1979–82, chm Educn and Human Devpt Ctee 1982–87, memb Cncl ESRC 1983–86 and 1987–89, chm Human Behaviour and Devpt Res Devpt Gp 1987–89; FBPsS 1970 (memb 1960); *Books* Tests in Education (with H Goldstein, 1984), Cognition in Action (with M Smyth, 1987, 2 edn, 1994); *Style*— Prof Philip Levy; ✉ Department of Psychology, University of Lancaster, Lancaster LA1 4YF (☎ 01524 65201, fax 01524 843087, telex 65111 Lancul G)

LEVY, Victor Raphael; s of Moise Edward Joseph Levy, and Thelma, *née* Goide; *b* 14 April 1951; *Educ* UCS, Univ of Manchester (BSc); *Career* tax ptnr Arthur Andersen; FCA, FTII; *Style*— Victor Levy, Esq; ✉ Arthur Andersen, 1 Surrey Street, London WC2R 2PS (direct ☎ 0171 438 3473, fax 0171 831 1133, telex 8812711)

LEW, Dr Julian David Mathew; s of Rabbi Maurice Abram Lew (d 1989), of London, and Rachel Lew, JP, *née* Segalov; *b* 3 Feb 1948; *Educ* Univ of London (LLB), Catholic Univ of Louvain (Doctorate Int Law); *m* 11 July 1978, Margot Gillian, da of Dr David Isaac Perk (d 1994), of Johannesburg, SA; 2 da (Ariella b 1981, Lauren b 1983); *Career* called to the Bar Middle Temple 1970, admitted slr 1981, attorney at law state of NY 1985; former ptnr Coudert Brothers, currently ptnr Herbert Smith; head Sch of Int Arbitration Queen Mary and Westfield Coll Univ of London, dir London Ct of Int Arbitration; Freeman City of London 1985; FCIArb 1976; *Books* Selected Bibliography on East West Trade Law (1976), Applicable in International Commercial Arbitration (1978), Selected Bibliography on International Commercial Arbitration (1979), Contemporary Problems in International Commercial Arbitration (ed, 1986), International Trade: Law and Practice (ed jtly, 1985, 2 edn 1990), The Immunity of Arbitrators (ed, 1990), Enforcement of Foreign Judgements (ed jtly, 1994); *Recreations* tennis, reading, religion; *Style*— Dr Julian D M Lew; ✉ Herbert Smith, Exchange House, Primrose Street, London EC2A 2HS (☎ 0171 374 8000, fax 0171 496 0043)

LEWANDO, Sir Jan Alfred; kt (1974), CBE (1968); s of Maurice Lewando, of Manchester, and Eugenie, *née* Goldsmid; *b* 31 May 1909; *Educ* Manchester GS, Univ of Manchester; *m* 1948, Nora, da of William Slavouski; 3 da; *Career* served Br Army WWII in Europe, ME and Far East 1939–45, Br Army Staff Washington DC and Br Miny of Supply Mission 1941–45, Lt-Col 1943; joined Marks & Spencer Ltd 1929 (dir 1954–70), chm Carrington Viyella Ltd 1970–75; pres Br Textile Confedn 1972–73; dir: Heal and Son Holdings Ltd 1975–82, Bunzl Group 1976–86, W A Baxter & Sons Ltd 1975–, Johnston Industs Inc (USA) 1976–84, Royal Worcester Spode Ltd 1978–79, Edgars Stores Ltd SA 1976–82; memb: Br Overseas Trade Bd 1972–77, European Trade Ctee 1973–83, Br Nat Export Cncl 1969–71; chm Appeal Ctee Br Inst of Radiology 1979–84, vice pres Tport Tst 1973– (PRS 1989–91), vice chm Clothing Export Cncl 1966–70; CIMgt, FRSA; Companion Textile Inst 1972, Legion of Merit (USA) 1946; *Style*— Sir Jan Lewando, CBE; ✉ Langham House, Drews Park, Knotty Green, Beaconsfield, Bucks HP9 2TT (☎ 01494 674987)

LEWER, Michael Edward; QC (1983); s of Lt-Col Stanley Gordon Lewer (d 1985), of Ashtead, Surrey, and Jeanie Mary, *née* Hay (d 1980); *b* 1 Dec 1933; *Educ* Tonbridge, Oriel Coll Oxford (MA); *m* 1965, Bridget Mary, da of Harry Anderson Clifford Gill (d 1980), of Buckland, Surrey; 2 s (William b 1966, Simon b 1969), 2 da (Natasha b 1967, Louise b 1977); *Career* called to the Bar Gray's Inn 1958, bencher 1992; recorder of the Crown Court 1983–; memb Criminal Injuries Compensation Bd 1986, chm Criminal Injuries Compensation Appeals Panel 1994; *Clubs* Western (Glasgow); *Style*— Michael Lewer, Esq, QC; ✉ 99 Queens Drive, London N4; Whitehouse Cottage, Horham, Suffolk; Farrars Building, Temple, London EC4Y 7BD (☎ 0171 583 9241, fax 0171 583 0090)

LEWERS, Very Rev Benjamin Hugh; s of Dr Hugh B Lewers, DSO, OBE (d 1950), of Ilfracombe, Devon, and Coral Helen Lewers (d 1995); *b* 25 March 1932; *Educ* Sherborne, Selwyn Coll Cambridge (MA); *m* 1957, Sara, da of Cyprian Claud Blagden; 3 s (Timothy, Michael, Thomas); *Career* Nat Serv 2 Lt The Devon Regt; ordained: deacon 1962, priest 1963; curate St Mary Northampton 1962–65, priest i/c Church of The Good Shepherd Hounslow 1965–68, industl chaplain Heathrow Airport 1968–75, vicar Newark 1975–80, rector 1980–81, provost Derby 1981–, church cmmr; *Recreations* cricket, gardening, music, wine, rug-making; *Style*— The Very Rev the Provost of Derby; ✉ The Provost's House, 9 Highfield Rd, Derby DE22 1GX (☎ 01332 342971); Cathedral Office, St Michael's House, Queen St, Derby DE1 3DT (☎ 01332 341201)

LEWES AND HASTINGS, Archdeacon of; *see:* Glaisyer, Ven Hugh

LEWIN, Christopher George; s of George Farley Lewin, of Ascot, Berks, and Hilda Mary Emily, *née* Reynolds; *b* 15 Dec 1940; *Educ* Coopers' Cos Sch Bow London; *m* 1 Nov 1985, Robin Lynn, da of Robert Harry Stringham; 2 s (Andrew Christopher Philip b 3 July 1987, Peter Edward James b 19 Oct 1990); *Career* actuarial asst: Equity & Law Life Assurance Society 1956–63, London Transport Bd 1963–67; Br Railways Bd: actuarial asst 1967–70, controller corp pensions 1970–80, seconded memb Fin Insts Gp DOE 1981–82, co-ordinator private capital 1980–88; pensions dir Associated Newspapers Holdings Ltd 1989–92, head of gp pensions Guinness plc 1992–; winner: Joseph Burn Prize Inst of Actuaries 1962, Messenger and Brown Prize Inst of Actuaries 1968, Inst of Actuaries Prize for paper Capital Projects (jt author) 1995; chm: Nat Fedn of Consumer Gps 1984–86, Jt Ctee on Capital Projects Inst and Faculty of Actuaries 1993–; memb Cncl Occupational Pensions Advsy Service, memb Cncl Nat Assoc of Pension Funds 1983–87 and 1995–; FIA 1964, FSS, FPMI; author of numerous articles in various actuarial jls 1970–; *Recreations* family life, old books and manuscripts relating to English social history, old board games; *Clubs* Argonauts, Gallio, Scottish Actuaries; *Style*— Christopher Lewin, Esq; ✉ Guinness plc, 33 Pinkhill, Edinburgh EH12 7BA (☎ 0131 346 4373, fax 0131 337 9872)

LEWIN, Prof John; s of Bernard Sidney Lewin (d 1987), of Newport, Dyfed, and Ruth French, *née* Smith (d 1972); *b* 7 May 1940; *Educ* King Edward's Sch Bath, Univ of Southampton (BA, PhD); *m* 9 July 1966, Jane Elizabeth Sarah, da of Capt Cecil Joy (d 1979), of Newport, Dyfed; 2 da (Jenny b 1967, Marianna b 1971); *Career* asst lectr Univ of Hull 1965–68, Univ of Wales Aberystwyth: prof of physical geography 1986–, dean Faculty of Science 1989–91, vice princ 1993–; FRGS 1963; *Books* Timescales in Geomorphology (ed, 1980), British Rivers (ed, 1981), Modern and Ancient Fluvial Systems (ed, 1983), Palaeohydrology in Practice (ed, 1987), Mediterranean Quarternary River Environments (ed, 1995); *Recreations* walking, reading; *Style*— Prof John Lewin; ✉ Institute of Earth Studies, University of Wales, Aberystwyth, Dyfed SY23 3DB (☎ 01970 623111)

LEWIN, Lucille Patricia; da of Michael Witz (d 1969), of SA, and Elaine, *née* Hoffenberg (now Mrs Samuelson); *b* 27 July 1948; *Educ* Redhill Sch for Girls, Univ of Witwatersrand; *m* 1969, Richard Lewin, *qv*; 2 s (Joseph Michel b 1983, Jonathan Toby b 1988); *Career* fashion designer; design res Boston USA 1969–71, buyer Harvey Nichols 1973–76, fndr Whistles 1976– (Br Design-led Retailer award Br Fashion Awards 1993); *Style*— Ms Lucille Lewin; ✉ Whistles, 12 St Christopher's Place, London W1 (☎ 0171 487 4484)

LEWIN, Richard David; s of Max Meyer Lewin (d 1987), of SA, and Evelyn Lilian Lewin (d 1964); *b* 17 Feb 1944; *Educ* Parktown Boys' HS Johannesburg SA, Univ of Witwatersrand SA (BCom, Cert in Theory of Accountancy), Harvard (MBA); *m* 27 July 1969, Lucille Patricia, *qv*, da of Dr Michael Witz; 2 s (Joseph Michael b 23 July 1983,

Jonathan Toby b 29 March 1988); *Career* Schwartz Fine Kane accountants 1966–68, Truworth Group retailers 1968–69, Burton Group fashion retailers 1972–74, Arthur Young consultancy 1975–78, md Whistles Ltd fashion retailers 1978–; CA (SA); *Recreations* skiing, squash; *Clubs* RAC, Harvard Club of London; *Style*— Richard Lewin, Esq; ✉ Whistles, 12–14 St Christopher's Place, London W1 (☎ 0171 487 4484, fax 0171 486 2043)

LEWIN, Adm of the Fleet Baron (Life Peer UK 1982), of Greenwich, in Greater London; Terence Thornton Lewin; KG (1983), GCB (1976, KCB 1973), LVO (1959), DSC (1942); s of E H Lewin (d 1963); *b* 19 Nov 1920; *Educ* Judd Sch Tonbridge; *m* 1944, Jane, da of Rev Charles James Branch Evans (d 1956); 2 s (Hon Timothy Charles Thornton b 1947, Hon Jonathan James b 1959), 1 da (Hon Susan (Hon Mrs Roe) b 1949); *Career* RN 1939, served WWII Home and Med Fleets (despatches), cmd HMS Corunna 1955–56, HMY Britannia 1957–58, Capt 1958, cmd HMS Urchin 1962, HMS Tenby 1963, Dartmouth Trg Sqdn 1962–63, HMS Hermes 1966–67, Rear Adm 1968, Asst Chief of Naval Staff (Policy) MOD 1968–69, Flag Offr second in cmd Far E Fleet 1969–70, Vice Adm 1970, Vice Chief of Naval Staff 1971–73, Adm 1973, C-in-C Fleet, Allied C-in-C Channel and C-in-C Eastern Atlantic Area 1973–75, C-in-C Naval Home Cmd 1975–77, Chief of Naval Staff and First Sea Lord 1977–79, Adm of the Fleet 1979, Chief of Def Staff 1979–82; Naval ADC to HM The Queen 1967–68, Flag ADC to HM The Queen 1975–77 (First and Princ ADC 1977–79); life Col Cmdt Royal Marines 1995; tstee Nat Maritime Museum 1981– (chm 1987–95), elder brother Trinity House 1975; pres: Br Schs Exploring Soc, Shipwrecked Mariners Soc, Soc for Nautical Res, George Cross Island Assoc; Hon Freeman Skinners' Co and Shipwrights' Co, Hon Freeman and Liveryman Stationers' and Newspaper Makers' Co; Hon DSc City Univ, Hon DLitt Greenwich Univ; *Style*— Adm of the Fleet the Rt Hon the Lord Lewin, KG, GCB, LVO,DSC; ✉ House of Lords, London SW1

LEWINSKI, Jorge; s of Stefan Lewinski (d 1946), and Irena, *née* Maliszewska (d 1937); *b* 25 March 1921; *Educ* Gizycki Gimnazium Warsaw, Univ of London (BSc); *m* 1, 1952 (m dis 1973); 2 s (Ian b 1955, Andrew b 1958); m 2, 1974, Mayotte Magnus, *née* Trelaün; *Career* md P D Constable Ltd textile co 1950–66, professional photographer 1967–; sr lectr in photography London Coll of Printing 1968–74, freelance (mainly writing and illustrating books/magazine work) 1974–; memb RPS 1956; *Solo Exhibitions* incl: RPS 1964, Reed House Piccadilly London 1965, San Francisco Museum of Modern Art 1967, Nat Portrait Gallery 1972, Univ of Sussex Brighton 1974, Univ of Wales Cardiff 1977, Photographers' Gallery London 1979, Camden Art Centre London 1980, Galerie et Fils Brussels 1980, Royal Festival London 1987; *Prints in Collections* V & A, Nat Portrait Gallery, Museum of the Univ of California, Bibliotheque National Paris, several private collections; *Books* written: Photography - A Dictionary of Photography (1977), Camera at War (1978), The Naked and the Nude (1987); written and illustrated: Colour in Focus (1976), Shell Guide to Photography of Britain (1982), Book of Photographic Portraiture (with Mayotte Magnus, 1983), Portrait of the Artist (1987); illustrated: Byron's Greece (with Lady Longford, 1975), Writer's Britain (with Margaret Drabble, 1979), One is my Lucky Number (with Daley Thompson, 1981), James Joyce's Odyssey (with Frank Delaney, 1981), Wilderness Britain (with Anthony Burton, 1985), Shell Guide to Archaeology of Britain (with Jacquetta Hawkes, 1986), Smiley's Circus (with David Monaghan, 1986), The Racing World (with Julian Wilson, 1991); illustrated with Mayotte Magnus: Architecture of Southern England (with John Julius Norwich, 1985), Architecture of Northern England (with J M Robinson, 1986), Venice Preserved (with Peter Lauritzen, 1986), English Heritage (with Lord Montague, 1987), By Appointment (with Tim Heald, 1989), The Monument Guide (with Jo Darke, 1991); *Recreations* golf; *Style*— Jorge Lewinski, Esq; ✉ 78 Trinity Road, London SW17 7RJ (☎ 0181 672 2664); c/o Jennifer Kavanagh, 39 Camden Park Rd, London NW1 9AX (☎ 0171 482 3676)

LEWINSOHN, Max Robert; *b* 12 Oct 1946; *m* Dr Jo Krystyna Lewinsohn; 3 c; *Career* chm Industrial Trade and Finance Ltd, sr ptnr Maxwell Allen; former chm: Dominion International Group plc, Southwest Resources plc; FCA; *Recreations* tennis, skiing, windsurfing; *Style*— Max Lewinsohn, Esq; ✉ Tanyard Manor, Sharpthorne, Sussex RH19 4HY (☎ 01342 810246, fax 01342 810797)

LEWINTON, Sir Christopher; kt (1993); s of Joseph Lewinton, and Elizabeth Lewinton; *b* 6 Jan 1932; *Educ* Acton Tech Coll, Univ of London; *Career* Lt REME; pres Wilkinson Sword USA 1960–70, chief exec Wilkinson Sword Group (acquired by Allegheny International 1978) 1970–85, chm Int Ops Allegheny International 1978–85; TI Group plc: chief exec 1986–, chm and chief exec 1989–; non-exec dir: Reed International plc 1990–, Reed Elsevier plc 1993–; memb Supervisory Bd Mannesmann 1996–; FEng 1994, FIMechE, FRAeS; *Recreations* golf, tennis, reading; *Clubs* Buck's, Sunningdale Golf, Metropolitan (NY); *Style*— Sir Christopher Lewinton, FEng; ✉ TI Group plc, 50 Curzon St, London W1Y 7PN (☎ 0171 499 9131, fax 0171 491 2471)

LEWIS, Alan Frederick; s of Frederick Lewis, of Belfast, and Veronica Selina, *née* McCleery; *b* 3 Feb 1950; *Educ* Boys' Model Sch Belfast, Queen's Univ Belfast; *Career* Pacemaker Press (picture agency) Belfast: joined 1971, photographer 1971, chief photographer 1973–76; with Daily Mail 1976–93, fndr Photo Press Picture Agency Belfast 1993–; fndr memb Belfast Press Photographers' Assoc 1979, chm NI Press Photographers' Assoc 1990; *Awards* NI Press Photographer of the Year 1975, NI Press Photographer of the Year 1977, Rothmans NI Photographer of the Year 1980, Carrolls Press Photographers' Assoc of Ireland News Picture of the Year 1980 and 1984, Nikon UK Photographer of the Year 1984, Kodak UK Photographer of the Year 1984, Northern Bank News Picture of the Year 1984, Northern Bank People Picture of the Year 1987, NI Sports Cncl Colour Picture of the Year 1991, Guinness Sports Picture of the Year 1994; *Books* A Day in the Life of Ireland (jtly, 1991); *Recreations* fly fishing for trout and salmon; *Style*— Alan Lewis, Esq; ✉ Photo Press Picture Agency, Belfast (☎ and fax 01232 868682, ☎ 01232 865200, car 0850 988920)

LEWIS, Anthony Meredith; s of Lt-Col G V L Lewis (d 1985), and G Lewis, *née* Fraser; *b* 15 Nov 1940; *Educ* Rugby, St Edmund Hall Oxford (MA); *m* 26 July 1970, Ewa Maria Anna, da of Stanislaw Strawinski (d 1980); 1 s (Alexander Edward Meredith (Beetle) b 1 Oct 1976), 1 da (Antonina Kathryn (Nina) b 18 Sept 1981); *Career* articled clerk then asst slr Freshfields 1964–70 (admitted slr 1966), sr ptnr Joynson-Hicks 1986–89 (ptnr 1971–89), ptnr Taylor Joynson Garret 1989– (sometime jt sr ptnr); chm Birkby plc, chief exec South Thames Properties Ltd and other cos; memb Law Soc; *Recreations* shooting, skiing, tennis, opera, cricket; *Style*— Anthony Lewis, Esq; ✉ Taylor Joynson Garret, Carmelite, 50 Victoria Embankment, Blackfriars, London EC4Y 0DX (☎ 0171 353 1234, fax 0171 936 2666)

LEWIS, Anthony Robert (Tony); DL (Mid-Glamorgan); s of Wilfrid Llewellyn (d 1981), of Swansea, and Florence Majorie, *née* Flower; *b* 6 July 1938; *Educ* Neath GS, Christ's Coll Cambridge (MA, rugby blue, cricket blue and capt); *m* 22 Aug 1962, Joan, da of Owen Pritchard, of Neath; 2 da (Joanna Clare b 29 Nov 1967, Anabel Sophia b 28 July 1969); *Career* former cricketer; Glamorgan 1955–74: capt 1967–72, Eng capt tour to India, Ceylon and Pakistan 1972–73; sports presenter and commentator: HTV Wales 1971–82, BBC Radio and TV cricket progs 1974–, Sport on Four (Radio 4) 1977–84; cricket corr The Sunday Telegraph 1974–92; memb: Sports Cncl for Wales 1972–75, Bd Br Tourist Authy 1992–, Tourism Action Gp CBI 1995–; chm: Glamorgan CCC 1987–93 (tstee 1993–), Wales Tourist Bd 1992–; hon life memb MCC (memb Ctee 1992–94 and 1995–); Wales chm ABSA (Assoc of Business Sponsorship of the Arts) 1988–91; hon fell: St David's Univ Coll Lampeter 1993, Univ of Glamorgan, Univ Coll of Wales Swansea; *Books* Summer of Cricket (1975), Playing Days (1985), Double Century (1987), Cricket in Many Lands (1991), MCC Masterclass (1994); *Recreations* golf, classical music; *Clubs* MCC, Royal and Ancient Golf, Royal Porthcawl Golf; *Style*— A R Lewis, Esq, DL; ✉ Castellau, nr Llantrisant, Mid Glamorgan CF72 8LP (☎ 01443 224228, fax 01443 225627)

LEWIS, Hon Antony Thomas; JP (1979); s of 3 Baron Merthyr, KBE, PC (d 1977), and Violet, *née* Meyrick; *b* 4 June 1947; *Educ* Eton, Univ of Wales (LLM); *m* 1974, Mary Carola Melton, da of Rev Humphrey John Paine; *Career* called to the Bar Inner Temple 1971; lectr in law Univ Coll Cardiff 1976–89; chm: Powys Family Health Servs Authy 1990–96, Powys Health Care NHS Tst 1996–; *Style*— The Hon Antony Lewis, JP; ✉ The Skreen, Erwood, Builth Wells, Powys LD2 3SJ

LEWIS, Dr Barry Winston; s of Alfred Lewis (d 1967), of Essex, and Winifred Alice, *née* Doggett (d 1984); *b* 31 March 1941; *Educ* Hornchurch GS, UCH Med Sch (MB BS, FRCP, DCH); *m* 1, 17 April 1962 (m dis 1982), Rosemary Agnes, da of James Bryant Petter (d 1988); 1 s (Timothy John Barry b 1962), 1 da (Catherine Rosemary b 1964); m 2, 24 June 1982, Josephine Caroline, da of Robert William Cunningham (d 1987), of Swansea; 2 s (Hugo Frederick b 1987 d 1988, Edgar William b 1989); *Career* conslt paediatrician London 1973–, chm London Children's and Women's Hosp 1987–93 (dir 1981–93); fell Hunterian Soc (1983); memb Worshipful Soc of Apothecaries; memb: BPA 1973 (memb Cncl 1979–82), BMA; FRSM; *Recreations* shooting, horses (racing and breeding), cricket; *Clubs* RSM; *Style*— Dr Barry Lewis; ✉ Bungeons Farm, Barking, Suffolk IP6 8HN (☎ 01449 721992); 17 Wimpole St, London W1M 7AD (☎ 0171 486 0044, car tel 0836 271020)

LEWIS, Bernard Walter; CBE (1973), JP (Essex 1970); s of Walter Watson Lewis (d 1949), of Lincoln, and Florence Teresa, *née* Greenbury (d 1979); *b* 24 July 1917; *Educ* Lincoln Sch, Univ of Manchester; *m* 12 May 1943, Joyce Ilston, da of James Issac Storey (d 1932), of Rothbury, Northumberland; 1 s (John Michael b 6 Aug 1947), 1 da (Susan Joan Ilston b 29 June 1945); *Career* joined King's Own Regt 1940, RASC 1941, Capt 1942, Maj 1943, served Middle E 1940–46; chm and md Green's Flour Mills Ltd 1955–90; chm Edward Baker Holdings Ltd 1983–89, ret; chm Flour Advsy Bureau 1979–88, pres Nat Assoc of Br and Irish Millers 1985–86; chm: Dengie and Maldon Essex Bench 1970–88, Maldon Harbour Cmmrs 1978–; Gen Tax Cmmr 1957–93; memb Fin Bd Cons Pty 1966–75, chm Bd of Govrs Plume Sch 1968–83; Liveryman Worshipful Co of Bakers 1973; *Recreations* travel, gardening; *Clubs* RAC, United and Cecil, Essex; *Style*—Bernard Lewis, Esq, CBE, JP; ✉ Roughlees, 68 Highlands Drive, Maldon, Essex (☎ 01621 852981)

LEWIS, Charles William; s of Judge Peter Edwin Lewis (d 1976), of Seaford, and Mary Ruth, *née* Massey; *b* 25 June 1954; *Educ* Eastbourne Coll, Univ Coll Oxford (MA); *m* 20 Sept 1986, Grace Julia Patricia, da of Alphonsus McKenna, of Dublin; 2 da (Cliona Natasha b 14 July 1992, Helena Mary b 17 Feb 1994); *Career* called to the Bar Inner Temple 1977; *Recreations* skiing, bridge, golf, shooting; *Clubs* MCC, East India, Northampton and County; *Style*— Charles Lewis, Esq; ✉ The Dower House, Church Walk, Great Billing, Northampton NN3 9ED (☎ 01604 407189); 36 Bedford Row, London WC1R 4JH (☎ 0171 421 8000, fax 0171 421 8080); 24 Albion Place, Northampton NN1 1UD (☎ 01604 602333, fax 01604 601600)

LEWIS, Very Rev Christopher Andrew; *b* 4 Feb 1944; *Educ* Marlborough, Univ of Bristol (BA), Corpus Christi Coll Cambridge (PhD), Westcott House Theol Coll; *m* 1970, Rhona Jane, *née* Martindale; 1 da (Andrea b 20 Aug 1973), 2 s (Aidan b 5 Feb 1979, Hugh b 27 Sept 1986); *Career* served RN 1961–66; curate Barnard Castle 1973–76, tutor Ripon Coll Cuddesdon 1976–81, priest-in-charge Aston Rowant and Crowell 1978–81, vice princ Ripon Coll 1981–82, vicar of Spalding 1982–87, canon residentiary Canterbury Cathedral 1987–94, dir of Ministerial Trg Dio of Canterbury 1989–94, dean of St Albans 1994–; *Style*— The Very Rev Christopher Lewis; ✉ The Deanery, St Albans, Herts AL1 1BY (☎ 01727 852120, fax 01727 850944, e-mail cathedra@alban.v-net.com)

LEWIS, Clive Hewitt; s of Sqdn Ldr Thomas Jonathen Lewis, OBE, AE (d 1990), of Sway, Hants, and Marguerita Eileen, *née* De Brule (d 1987); *b* 29 March 1936; *Educ* St Peter's Sch York; *m* 7 July 1961, Jane Penelope (Penny), da of Rowland Bolland White (d 1970), of Wakefield, Yorks; 2 s (Simon Nicholas Hewitt b 1962, Mark Hewitt b 1966), 1 da (Victoria Jane b 1968); *Career* Pilot Officer RAF 1956–58, Lt 40/41 Royal Tank Regt (TA) 1958–62; sr ptnr Clive Lewis and Ptnrs 1963–93, jt chm Colliers Erdman Lewis Chartered Surveyors (formerly Edward Erdman) 1993–; dir: St Modwen Properties plc 1985–, Town Centre Securities plc 1994–; chm RICS Journals Ltd 1987–92, dir RICS Business Services Ltd 1987–92, pres gp div RICS 1989–90, pres RICS 1993–94 (vice pres 1991–92, sr vice pres 1992–93); dep chm Merseyside Devpt Corp 1989– (bd memb 1986), pres Euro Cncl of Real Estate Professionals 1990–92; chm Propery Forum (Bank of England) 1994–; pres: Land Aid Charitable Tst, Worldwide FIABCI 1983–84; Hon DLit South Bank Univ; Freeman: City of London 1983, Worshipful Co of Chartered Surveyors; FRICS 1961, FSVA 1980; *Sporting Achievements* Northern Counties sprint champion 1957, Cheshire Co athlete; *Recreations* golf, tennis; *Clubs* Totteridge CC, MCC, Forty, Elstree Golf; *Style*— Clive Lewis, Esq; ✉ Oakhurst, 7 Totteridge Common, London N20 8AP (☎ 0181 445 5109); Colliers Erdman Lewis Chartered Surveyors, 6 Grosvenor Street, London W1X 9FB (☎ 0171 629 8191)

LEWIS, (Peter) Daniel Nicolas David; s of Maj Robert Cholmeley Lewis, TD (d 1993), of Shere, Surrey, and (Miriam) Lorraine, *née* Birnage; *b* 14 Oct 1957; *Educ* Westminster; *Career* day centre dep warden Age Concern Westminster 1976–79, mangr London Business Sch Bookshop 1979–82, ptnr London Town Staff Bureau 1982–88 (taken over by Burns Anderson Recruitment plc 1988), subsequently divnl md Burns Anderson Recruitment plc London Town Div, currently professional legal recruiter Laurence Simons International; dir, vice pres and fell Inst of Employment Consultants 1990–95, treas and govr Abinger Hammer Village Sch Tst 1995; *Recreations* driving, bridge, exploring Africa, flying; *Style*— Daniel Lewis, Esq; ✉ Old Cottage, Shere, Surrey GU5 9JF (☎ 01483 202922); Laurence Simons International, 121 Kingsway, London WC2B 6PA (☎ 0171 831 3270, fax 0171 831 4429)

LEWIS, David Edward; s of Edward Arthur Lewis, of Pontypridd, and Nancy, *née* Williams (d 1992); *b* 26 March 1952; *Educ* Pontypridd Boys' GS, Univ of Exeter (LLB); *m* Susan Enid, da of James Eccleston; 2 s (Gareth Edward b 28 Feb 1986, Anthony David b 15 Jan 1990), 1 da (Alice Rebecca b 23 Nov 1987); *Career* Allen & Overy: articled clerk 1974–76, asst slr 1976–84, ptnr Tax Dept 1984–; memb Law Soc 1976; *Recreations* tennis, skiing; *Clubs* RAC; *Style*— David Lewis, Esq; ✉ Allen & Overy, 9 Cheapside, London EC2V 6AD (☎ 0171 248 9898, fax 0171 236 2192)

LEWIS, Very Rev David Gareth; s of Mordecai Lewis (d 1969), and Bronwen May, *née* Evans (d 1985); *b* 13 Aug 1931; *Educ* Cyfarthfa GS Merthyr Tydfil, Univ of Wales Bangor (BA, DipEd, swimming colours), Oriel Coll Oxford (MA), St Michael's Coll Llandaf; *Career* ordained (Llandaf Cathedral): deacon 1960, priest 1961; curate of Neath 1961–63, vice princ Salisbury Theol Coll 1963–69, dean of Belize 1969–78, lectr Univ of Wales and St Michael's Coll Llandaf 1978–81, vicar of St Mark Newport 1978–82, canon residentiary of Monmouth 1982–90, dean of Monmouth 1990–96; clerical sec Governing Body The Church in Wales 1985–96; chm: Provincial Stewardship 1986–88, Provincial Evangelism and Adult Educn 1988–95; ed Monmouth Diocesan Leaflet 1988–96; pres Rotary Club of Newport 1987; *Books* History of St John's Cathedral Belize, Central America (1976); *Recreations* swimming, travelling; *Style*— The Very Rev David Gareth Lewis; ✉ 7 The Cathedral Green, Llandaf, Cardiff

LEWIS, David Gwyn; s of Rev Gwyn Lewis (d 1984), of Bridport, Dorset, and Annie Millicent (Nancy), *née* Thomas; *b* 5 Aug 1941; *Educ* Ellesmere Coll Salop, Coll of Law London; *m* 8 April 1972, Veronica Mary Viola, da of Alban Edward Courtney Wylde, of RAX House, Bridport, Dorset; 1 da (Angharad b 1976); *Career* 2 Lt 5 Bn The Welch Regt (TA) 1960–63; admitted slr 1966; prosecuting slr: Merthyr CBC 1966–68, Dorset and Bournemouth Police Authy 1968–70, Birmingham City 1970–71; dep chief prosecuting slr Sussex Police Authy 1976–84 (prosecuting sr princ slr 1971–76); chief prosecuting slr: Warwicks 1984–86, Lincs 1986; chief crown prosecutor Cambs and Lincs 1986–93, asst chief crown prosecutor CPS Anglia (Cambs, Norfolk, Suffolk, Essex, Herts and Beds) 1993–96, ret; memb local branch Br Legion; Freeman City of London 1986; memb: Law Soc, Cambridge and Dist Law Soc, Peterborough and Dist Law Soc; *Recreations* cricket, tennis, horse racing (spectator), motoring; *Clubs* MCC, Cambridge Univ CC, Glamorgan CCC; *Style*— David Lewis, Esq

LEWIS, David Gwynder; s of Gwynder Eudaf Lewis (d 1963), of Sketty, Swansea, and Gwyneth, *née* Jones (d 1979); *b* 31 Aug 1942; *Educ* Rugby; *m* 2 July 1966, Susan Joyce, da of Andrew Agnew, of Crowborough; 1 s (George b 1972), 1 da (Alexandra b 1969); *Career* Warrant Offr TA C Battery Hon Artillery Co; Hambros Bank Ltd: banker 1961–, dir 1979–, exec dir 1991–94, vice chm 1994–; currently chm Hambro Pacific Holdings Ltd Hong Kong (md 1974–82), pres Hambro America New York 1982–85, dep chm Hambros Australia Ltd Sydney 1994–; dir: Hunters and Frankau Group Ltd, Hambro Countrywide plc, Pelican Shipping Ltd; ACIB 1967; *Recreations* fishing, music, shooting; *Clubs* Turf, RAC, Madison Square Garden (NY), Hong Kong, Royal Hong Kong Jockey, Shek O Country; *Style*— D G Lewis, Esq; ✉ Hambro Pacific Holdings Ltd, 2110 Jardine House, 1 Connaught Place, Central, Hong Kong; Hambros Bank Ltd, 41 Tower Hill, London EC3N 4HA (☎ 0171 480 5000, fax 0171 702 9827, telex 883851)

LEWIS, David John; s of Eric John Lewis (d 1993), of Nuneaton, Warks, and Vera May, *née* Heath (d 1981); *b* 18 Oct 1942; *Educ* King Edward VI GS Nuneaton; *m* 5 Aug 1967, Vyvian Christine Dawn, da of Eric Hutton Stewart (d 1981), of Coventry; 2 da (Sophie b 1972, Anna b 1975); *Career* qualified CA 1966; Pannell Kerr Forster: Belize 1967–70, Barbados 1970–75 (ptnr 1972–75), Leeds Office 1975–, ptnr 1976–86, sr ptnr 1986–; memb: Leeds Jr C of C 1978–83, Ctee W Yorks Soc of CAs 1982–95 (treas 1982–85, sec 1985–89, vice pres 1989–90, dep pres 1990–91, pres 1991–92); pres CAs Student Soc of Leeds 1984–85; govr Prince Henry's GS Otley 1988–92; memb: Leeds Family Health Serv Authy 1990–92, Otley Round Table 1980–83 (pres 1988), Rotary Club of Otley Chevin 1989– (fndr pres 1989–90); FICA 1966; *Clubs* Leeds, Headingley Taverners; *Style*— David J Lewis, Esq; ✉ 1 Craven Park, Menston, Ilkley, W Yorks LS29 6EQ; Pannell Kerr Forster, Pannell House, 6 Queen St, Leeds LS1 2TW (☎ 0113 244 3541, fax 0113 244 5560)

LEWIS, David John; *b* 17 May 1939; *Educ* Grocers' Sch, Univ of London (BSc); *m* 1961; 4 c; *Career* chartered surveyor; Town & City Properties 1959–62, Maybrook Properties 1962–64, sr ptnr David Lewis & Partners 1964–93; dir Cavendish Land Co 1972–73, dir Hampton Trust 1983–87, dir Mount Martin Gold Mines 1985–92, chm Molyneux Estates plc 1989–95, dir TBI plc 1995–; chm Jewish Blind Soc 1979–89, chm Jewish Care 1991, sr vice pres Jewish Care 1992–, pres European Cncl Jewish Community Services 1992–; FRICS 1969 (ARICS 1961); *Recreations* art, music; *Style*— D J Lewis, Esq; ✉ Catherine House, 76 Gloucester Place, London W1H 4DQ, (☎ 0171 487 3401, fax 0171 487 4211)

LEWIS, Prof David Malcolm; s of Kenneth Stanley Lewis, and Kathleen Elsie, *née* Mann; *b* 24 May 1941; *Educ* Marling Sch Stroud Glos, Univ of Leeds (BSc, PhD); *m* 14 Aug 1965, Barbara, da of Alfred Taylor (d 1965); 2 s (Stephen b 7 March 1967, Matthew b 15 April 1971), 1 da (Catherine b 5 May 1969); *Career* princ devpt offr Int Wool Secretariat 1965–78, sr res scientist CSIRO Geelong Aust 1978–79, princ devpt scientist IWS 1979–87, prof and head of dept Univ of Leeds 1987–; hon visiting prof Xian Textile Inst Xian People's Repub of China 1988; memb Br Nat Ctee for Chemistry, memb and former chm WR Region Soc of Dyers and Colourists; pres Soc of Dyers and Colourists 1993–94; memb American Assoc of Textile Chemists and Colorists; fell Royal Soc of Chemistry 1984, FRSA 1989; *Recreations* tennis, badminton, golf, walking; *Style*— Prof David Lewis; ✉ Department of Colour Chemistry and Dyeing, University of Leeds, Leeds LS2 9JT (☎ 0113 233 2931, fax 0113 233 2947, telex 556473 UNILDS G)

LEWIS, David Thomas Rowell; s of Thomas Price Merfyn Lewis (d 1989); *b* 1 Nov 1947; *Educ* Dragon Sch Oxford, St Edward's Sch, Jesus Coll Oxford (MA); *m* 25 July 1970, Theresa Susan, *née* Poole; 1 s (Tom b 1976), 1 da (Suzannah b 1974); *Career* admitted slr 1972 (Hong Kong 1977); Norton Rose: articles 1969, ptnr 1977, Hong Kong Office 1979–82, head of corp fin 1989–94, head of professional resources 1994–97, sr ptnr 1997–; memb Legal Practice Course Bd Law Soc and Co Law Ctee City Law Soc; govr: Dragon Sch Oxford, Oxford Brookes Univ; pres St Edward's Sch Soc 1995–96; memb: Law Soc, Int Bar Assoc; *Recreations* keeping fit, collecting maps, travel; *Clubs* OUAC, Achilles, Hong Kong; *Style*— David Lewis, Esq; ✉ Norton Rose, Kempson House, Camomile Street, London EC3A 7AN (☎ 0171 283 6000, fax 0171 283 6500)

LEWIS, David Whitfield; *b* 19 Feb 1939; *Educ* Central Sch of Art and Design London (BA), RSA bursary 1960; *Career* industl designer; with Danish design consultancy 1960–68: radio and TV equipment design work for various Danish cos, concurrently worked on product devpt for General Electric USA and on Beolap 5000 series (advanced Hi-Fi music system) for Bang & Olufsen; freelance design conslt 1967–: initial work incl TV equipment for Bang & Olufsen and industl processing machinery and marine products, new design strategies and product renewal progs for Bang & Olufsen since 1980; ID Prize Denmark Design Awards 1982, 1986, 1990 and 1994, EC Design Prize 1988, G-Mark Grand Prix MITI Awards Japan 1991, Int Design Prize State of Badenwurttemberg 1993; design work included in design collection of Museum of Modern Art NY; RDI 1995; *Style*— David Lewis, Esq; ✉ David Lewis Industrial Design APS, St Kongensgade 110C, DK 1264 Kobenhavn, Denmark (☎ and fax 00 45 33 13 69 35)

LEWIS, David Wyn; s of Albert Brinley Lewis, of Newcastle-under-Lyme, Staffs, and Eiluned Gwynedd, *née* Hughes; *b* 1 Nov 1944; *Educ* High Storrs GS, Univ of Sheffield (BArch); *m* 10 July 1971, Meirlys; 1 s (Steffan Gwynedd b 1972), 1 da (Bethan Rhiannon b 1975); *Career* architect and interior designer; sr ptnr David Lewis Assoc 1978– (specialising in large industl buildings, commercial devpt, housing devpt, public houses and listed buildings); pres Sheffield and S Yorks Soc of Architecture 1982–84; ARIBA 1971; *Recreations* gardening; *Style*— David Lewis, Esq

LEWIS, Derek Compton; s of Kenneth Compton Lewis (d 1982), of Zeal Monachorum, Devon, and Marjorie, *née* Buick; *b* 9 July 1946; *Educ* Wrekin Coll, Queens' Coll Cambridge (MA), London Business Sch (MSc); *m* 26 April 1969, Louise, da of Dr D O Wharton (d 1986), of Colwyn Bay, North Wales; 2 da (Annabel b 1983, Julia b 1984); *Career* various appts with Ford Motor Co in Europe and USA 1968–82, chief exec Granada Group plc 1988–91 (joined 1984), chief exec UK Gold Television Ltd 1992–93 (responsible for launch of channel, non-exec chm 1993–), dir gen HM Prison Service in England and Wales 1993–95; non-exec dir Courtaulds Textiles plc 1990–93; *Clubs* Caledonian; *Style*— Derek Lewis, Esq; ✉ c/o UK Gold Television, The Quadrangle, 180 Wardour Street, London W1V 4AE (☎ 0171 306 6100, fax 0171 306 6101)

LEWIS, Derek William; s of Arthur George Lewis (d 1991), of Manor Barn, Snowshill, nr Broadway, Worcs, and Hilda, *née* Rushton; *b* 23 Oct 1944; *Educ* Dean Close Sch Cheltenham; *m* 21 Oct 1972, Bridget Jennifer, da of Maj Bowes Bindon Stoney, of Frant, Sussex; 2 s (Christopher b 4 Feb 1977, James b 14 Feb 1980), 1 da (Sarah-Jane b 30 May 1974); *Career* admitted slr 1967; ptnr Theodore Goddard 1977– (joined 1970); memb: City of London Slrs' Co, Law Soc, Soc of Cons Lawyers; *Recreations* horse racing, golf, tennis; *Clubs* Royal Wimbledon Golf, Roehampton and Cheltenham Steeplechase; *Style*— Derek Lewis, Esq; ✉ Theodore Goddard, 150 Aldersgate St, London EC1A 4EJ (☎ 0171 606 8855, fax 0171 606 4390, telex 884678)

LEWIS, Derek William Richard; s of Percy William Lewis, of Worcs, and Edith, *née* Wisdom (d 1941); *b* 6 July 1936; *Educ* King's Sch Worcester; *m* 16 April 1963, Hedwig Albertine, da of Karl Kamps, of St Arnold, Rheine, W Germany; 2 s (Thomas b 1964, Ron b 1968), 1 da (Stephanie b 1967); *Career* RAEC 1957–59; The Hereford Times 1953–61, The Press Assoc 1961–62; BBC: seconded head of news Radio Zambia Lusaka 1966–68, TV news 1968, dep ed 1970–74 of The World at One, PM, The World This Weekend, ed 1974–76 of The World Tonight, Newsdesk and The Financial World Tonight, ed 1976–88 of The World at One (Radio Programme of the year 1976 and 1979), PM and The World this Weekend (Best Current Affrs Programme 1983); media relations conslt Royal Botanic Gardens Kew, md Diplomatic News Services 1988–; cncllr London Borough of Ealing 1989–94 (chm Planning and Regulatory Ctee 1990–94), cncl memb The Royal Albert Hall; assoc memb Foreign Press Assoc in London; *Recreations* music, association football, exploring US National Parks; *Clubs* Castaways, Ritz; *Style*— Derek Lewis, Esq; ✉ 4 Campbell Rd, London W7 3EA (☎ 0181 567 2478); High View, Jubilee Drive, British Camp, Upper Colwall, Hereford and Worcester WR13 6DW (☎ 01684 540382)

LEWIS, Edward Trevor Gwyn; s of Rev Gwyn Lewis (d 1984), and Annie Millicent, *née* Thomas; *b* 16 March 1948; *Educ* Ellesmere Coll, King's Coll London; *m* 6 April 1974, (Pamela) Gay, da of Lt-Col Jimmy Wilson, DL, of Dorchester, Dorset; 3 da (Leone b 28 Feb 1975, Kim b 23 Jan 1979, Tamsin (twin) b 23 Jan 1979); *Career* called to the Bar Gray's Inn 1972, dep legal mangr Mirror Group Newspapers 1980–83, JP S Westminster Div 1981–84, prosecuting counsel Western Circuit DHSS 1985–, actg stipendiary magistrate 1988–; *Recreations* riding, opera, jogging, skiing, family, motor cars; *Clubs* Garrick; *Style*— Edward Lewis, Esq; ✉ 77 Lexham Gardens, London W8 6JN (☎ 0171 370 3045); Francis Taylor Building, Temple, London EC4 (☎ 0171 353 7768)

LEWIS, Emyr Wyn; s of Thomas Kenneth Lewis, of Carmarthen, and Eleanor Shan, *née* Walters; *b* 29 Aug 1968; *Educ* Ysgol Gyfun Bro Myrddin Secdy Sch Carmarthen; *Career* currently professional rugby union player (no 8, flanker); clubs: Carmarthen Athletic Youth 1985, over 150 appearances Llanelli RFC 1988–94, Cardiff RFC 1994–; Wales: former under 20, under 21 and B rep, full debut v Ireland 1991, memb World Cup squad 1991 and 1995, 41 Welsh caps; other sports: co under 18 shot putt vest, co under 15 football cap; former police offr Carmarthen; *Recreations* fishing, weight training, golf, clay pigeon shooting; *Style*— Emyr Lewis, Esq; ✉ Cardiff RFC, Cardiff Athletic Club, Cardiff, Wales

LEWIS, His Hon Judge Esyr Gwilym; QC (1971); s of Rev Thomas William Lewis (d 1946), of Stamford Hill, London, and Mary Jane May, *née* Selway (d 1974); *b* 11 Jan 1926; *Educ* Mill Hill, Trinity Hall Cambridge (MA, LLM); *m* 1957, Elizabeth Anne Vidler, da of William Origen Hoffmann, of Bassett, Southampton; 4 da (Emma, Clare, Alice, Charlotte); *Career* Intelligence Corps 1944–47; called to the Bar Gray's Inn 1951, bencher 1978, vice treas 1996, treas 1996; ldr Wales & Chester Circuit 1978–80; official referee and circuit judge (SE Circuit) 1984– (sr official referee 1994–); memb Criminal Injuries Compensation Bd 1977–84; Liveryman Worshipful Co of Needlemakers; *Recreations* watching rugby football; *Clubs* Garrick; *Style*— His Hon Judge Esyr Lewis, QC; ✉ 2 South Square, Gray's Inn, London WC1R 5HP (☎ 0171 405 5918); Official Referees' Courts, St Dunstan's House, 133–137 Fetter Lane, London EC4A 1HD (☎ 0171 936 7429)

LEWIS, Geoff; s of late Francis Lewis, and late Dorothy, *née* Rees; *b* 21 Dec 1935; *Educ* Hammersmith Secdy Sch, Lime Grove Tech Coll; *m* 1959, Noelene, da of James Munro; 1 s (Gary James Winter b 1960 (decd)), 1 da (Marianne b 1963); *Career* flat race jockey 1953–79, trainer 1980–; major races won: Derby, Oaks (twice), 2000 Guineas, 1000 Guineas, Prix de L'Arc de Triomphe, Coronation Cup, Eclipse; rode 146 winners in 1969 season, only jockey to win Derby, Coronation Cup and Oaks in same year; *Recreations* golf, fishing, squash; *Style*— Geoff Lewis, Esq; ✉ Thirty Acre Barn, Shepherds Walk, Headley, Epsom, Surrey KT18 6BX (☎ 01372 277662, fax 01372 277366)

LEWIS, Prof Geoffrey; s of Ashley Lewis (d 1971), of London, and Jeanne Muriel, *née* Sintrop (d 1960); *b* 19 June 1920; *Educ* Univ Coll Sch Hampstead, St John's Coll Oxford (BA, MA, DPhil); *m* 26 July 1941, Raphaela Rhoda, da of Reuben Bale Seideman; 1 s (Jonathan b 1949), 1 da (Lalage b 1947, d 1976); *Career* WWII RAF pilot 1940–41, radar 1941–45; Univ of Oxford: lectr in Turkish 1950–54, sr lectr in Islamic studies 1954–64, sr lectr in Turkish 1964–86, prof of Turkish 1986–87, emeritus prof 1987–; visiting prof: Robert Coll Istanbul 1959–68, Princeton Univ 1970–71 and 1974, UCLA 1975, Br Acad Leverhulme Turkey 1984; St Antony's Coll Oxford: fell 1961–87, sub warden 1984–85, sr tutor 1985–87, emeritus fell 1987–; memb Br Turkish Mixed Cmmn 1975–95; Dr (Honoris Causa): Univ of the Bosphorus Istanbul 1986, Univ of Istanbul 1992; corresponding memb Turkish Language Soc 1953–, vice pres Anglo-Turkish Soc 1972–; Turkish Govt Cert of Merit 1973, Turkish Foreign Miny Exceptional Service Plaque 1991; FBA 1979; *Books* Plotiniana Arabica (1959), Albucasis on Surgery and Instruments (1973), The Book of Dede Korkut (1974), Turkish Grammar (1988), Thickhead and other Turkish Stories (1988); *Recreations* bodging, etymology; *Style*— Prof Geoffrey Lewis, FBA; ✉ 25 Warnborough Road, Oxford OX2 6JA

LEWIS, Geoffrey David; s of David Lewis (d 1973), of Brighton, E Sussex, and Esther Grace, *née* Chatfield (d 1978); *b* 13 April 1933; *Educ* Varndean Sch Brighton, Univ of Liverpool (MA); *m* 7 July 1956, Frances May, da of Frederick John Wilderspin (d 1959), of Hove, E Sussex; 3 da (Jennifer b 1958, Heather b 1959, Esther b 1971); *Career* asst curator Worthing Museum and Art Gallery 1950–60, dep dir and keeper of antiquities Sheffield City Museums 1960–65; dir: Sheffield City Museums 1966–72, Liverpool City Museums 1972–74, Merseyside County Museums 1974–77, museum studies Univ of Leicester 1977–89; assoc teacher 1989–92; memb Bd of Tstees of the Royal Armouries 1990–; chm Printing Matters (Bude) Ltd 1991–96, dep chm The Genesis Agendum 1996–; govr Wolvey Sch Warwickshire 1993–; pres: Yorks and Humberside Fedn of Museums and Art Galleries 1969–70, NW Fedn of Museums and Art Galleries 1976–77, Museums Assoc 1980–81, Int Cncl of Museums 1983–89; advsr at various times to: UNESCO, Egyptian Antiquities Orgn, Assoc of Met Authorities, Audit Cmmn for Local Authorities in England and Wales; FMA 1966, FSA 1969, Hon FMA 1989; *Books* Manual of Curatorship (co-ed with J M A Thompson et al, 1984, second edn 1992), For Instruction and Recreation: a Centenary History of the Museums Association (1989); author of various articles on museums and archaeology, also contrib to Encyclopaedia Britannica; *Recreations* reading, writing, walking, computing; *Style*— Geoffrey Lewis, Esq, FSA; ✉ 4 Orchard Close, Wolvey, Hinckley, Leics LE10 3LR (☎ and fax 01455 220708)

LEWIS, Geraint; s of Melvyn Lewis (d 1992), and Mair Eluned, *née* Griffiths (d 1985); *b* 18 Oct 1954; *Educ* Bedwelty GS, Univ of Newcastle upon Tyne (BDS); *Career* photographer; graduated dental surgn Newcastle 1980, subsequently Dept of Oral Surgery London Hosp, in private practice until 1987; full time freelance photographer 1987–; worked with: Independent and Independent on Sunday, Royal Shakespeare Co, Sunday and Daily Telegraph, Evening Standard; dir photo gallery St Leonard's-on-Sea, occasional lectr photojournalism course London Coll of Printing; exhbn of photographs: of Edinburgh Int Festival (Hampstead Theatre) 1993, of Israel (Lyric Theatre Hammersmith) 1993, of Poland (Polish Cultural Inst London) 1995 and (Ty Llyen Gallery

Swansea) 1996, Polish Theatre (Moray House Edinburgh) 1996; highly commended Photography Award Br Arts Journalism Awards 1991 (nominated 1989); *Recreations* cricket, football, cinema, photography; *Clubs* Archery Cricket, BFI, Photographers Gallery, Assoc of Photograhers; *Style—* Geraint Lewis, Esq; (fax 0181 699 9610, mobile 0831 413452)

LEWIS, Gillian Margaret (Gill); da of Gwilym Thomas Lewis (d 1974), and Valerie, *née* Williams (d 1969); *b* 15 Feb 1944; *Educ* Howells Sch Llandaff (head girl), St Hilda's Coll Oxford (BA); *m* 1973, Anthony Joseph Lister, s of late Walter Lister; 2 s (Timothy David b 1 Sept 1979, Adam Anthony b 30 Jan 1981); *Career* worked as advtg exec J Walter Thompson & Co and various sales and mktg appts in food industry 1967–74, gen mangr Europe Green Giant Co 1974–78, mgmnt conslt McKinsey & Co 1979–81, exec search conslt Fisher Dillistone & Associates 1981–86, dir of human resources and memb Gp Exec Ctee Courtaulds plc 1987–91, sr vice pres human resources and corp affrs Nestlé SA Switzerland 1992–94, managing ptnr consumer practice Heidrick & Struggles exec search conslts London 1995–; non-exec dir: Pearson plc 1992–, Zeneca Group plc 1993–; Veuve Clicquot UK Businesswoman of the Year 1977; FIPD 1988, FRSA 1988; *Recreations* theatre, classical music, travel, good food; *Style—* Ms Gill Lewis; ✉ Woodlands, Upper Anstey Lane, Alton, Hants GU34 4BP (☎ 01420 88398); Heidrick & Struggles, 100 Piccadilly, London W1V 9FN (☎ 0171 491 3124, fax 0171 734 9581, mobile 0370 476351)

LEWIS, Henry Nathan; *b* 20 Jan 1926; *Educ* Univ of Manchester (BA(Com)), LSE; *m* 18 Oct 1953, Jenny; 1 s (Jonathan Morris b 1956), 2 da (Deborah Freda (Mrs Goulden) b 1958, Julia Rose (Mrs Alberga) b 1968); *Career* Flt-Lt RAF 1948; formerly: jt md Marks & Spencer plc, chm J & J Fashions, dep chm Berisford International plc; chm Primrose Care Ltd; currently dir: Porter Chadburn plc, Delta Galil, Oasis plc, Value Retail plc, UNO plc, Electronics Boutique plc; former dir: Hunter Saphir plc, Cupid plc, Gabicci plc, Dixons Group plc; *Style—* Henry Lewis, Esq; ✉ 28 Eton Avenue, London NW3 3HL

LEWIS, Hugh Wilson; s of Cdr Hubert Thomas Lewis, OBE, RN (d 1989), and Gwyneth, *née* Ridgway, of Ebford, Exeter, Devon; *b* 21 Dec 1946; *Educ* Clifton, Univ of Birmingham (LLB); *m* 2 Dec 1972, Philippa Jane, da of Lt-Col John Rose Terry (d 1988); 3 s (Edward b 1973, Thomas b 1975, Christopher b 1984), 1 da (Katharine b 1979); *Career* called to the Bar Middle Temple 1970; memb: Western Circuit, Family Law Bar Assoc; *Recreations* walking Dartmoor, archaeology, fly-fishing, skiing; *Clubs* Naval & Military, Devon and Exeter Inst; *Style—* Hugh Lewis, Esq; ✉ 33 Southernhay East, Exeter (☎ 01392 55777, fax 01392 412007); Creaber Cottage, Gidleigh, Chagford, Devon (☎ and fax 01647 433110)

LEWIS, Jack; s of William Lewis (d 1967), of Failsworth, Manchester, and Nora, *née* Taylor; *b* 24 May 1937; *Educ* Chadderton GS; *m* 21 July 1962, Sylvia Ann, da of John William Jordan (d 1978); 2 da (Sarah Jane (Mrs Turner) b 18 July 1965, Gillian Diana (Mrs Richardson) b 5 Feb 1968); *Career* articled clerk J N O Brierley & Son Oldham 1953–60; Nat Serv RAF 1960–62; chartered accountant 1961, ptnr J N O Brierley & Son 1962–70, sr mangr Binder Hamlyn 1970–71, ptnr Josolyne Layton-Bennett & Co 1971–81, ptnr Ernst & Young (formerly Arthur Young) 1981–; FCA 1972, ATII 1962, MSPI 1987; *Recreations* golf, rugby, reading, soccer; *Style—* Jack Lewis, Esq; ✉ Ernst & Young, Southgate House, Wood Street, Cardiff CF1 1EW (☎ 01222 645444, fax 01222 645488)

LEWIS, Jeremy Morley; s of late George Morley Lewis, FRCS, of Seaford, Sussex, and Janet, *née* Iles; *b* 15 March 1942; *Educ* Malvern Coll, Trinity Coll Dublin (BA), Univ of Sussex (MA); *m* 1968, Jane Petra, da of Thomas Anthony Freston; 2 da (Jemima b 5 June 1971, Hattie b 23 Sept 1975); *Career* author; advtg trainee Foote Cone & Belding 1960–61, publicity asst William Collins 1967–69, ed André Deutsch Ltd 1969–70, literary agent A P Watt 1970–76, ed Oxford University Press 1977–79, dir Chatto & Windus Ltd 1979–89, freelance writer and ed 1989–, dep ed London Magazine 1991–94, ed conslt Peters, Fraser & Dunlop 1994; memb Ctee and sec R S Surtees Soc 1990; FRSL 1992; *Books* Playing For Time (1987), The Chatto Book of Office Life, or Love Among the Filing Cabinets (ed, 1992), Kindred Spirits (1995); *Recreations* walking round Richmond Park, carousing with friends; *Style—* Jeremy Lewis, Esq; ✉ 3 Percival Road, London SW14 7QE (☎ 0181 876 2807); c/o Gillon Aitken, Aitken Stone and Wylie Ltd, 29 Fernshaw Road, London SW10 0TG

LEWIS, Ven John Arthur; s of Lt-Col Harry Arthur Lewis (d 1963), and Evaline Helen Ross, *née* Davidson (d 1976); *b* 4 Oct 1934; *Educ* Parkend, Bell's GS Coleford, Univ of Oxford (MA); *m* 6 June 1959, Hazel Helen Jane, da of Albert Morris (d 1942); 1 s (b 1964), 1 da (b 1962); *Career* Nat Serv 1956–58; asst curate: Prestbury Glos 1960–63, Wimborne Minster 1963–66; rector Eastington and Frocester 1966–70; vicar of: Nailsworth 1970–78, Cirencester 1978–88; chaplain Memorial Hosp and Querns Hosp Cirencester 1978–88, archdeacon of Cheltenham 1988–; chm: Diocesan Bd of Educn, Diocesan Redundant Church Uses Ctee, Diocesan Stewardship Ctee 1983–95, Bd of Govrs Nailsworth (CE Controlled) Sch 1970–78, Bd of Govrs Powell's (CE Aided) Sch Cirencester 1978–88, Bd of Govrs Watermoor (CE Controlled) Sch Cirencester 1978–88; cncllr Gloucester RDC 1968–70; govr: Highwood Sch Nailsworth 1970–78, Kingshill Sch Cirencester 1978–88, Deer Park Sch Cirencester 1978–88; hon pres Shortwood AFC 1970–78; memb Cncl Cheltenham Ladies' Coll; hon chaplain Gloucestershire Constabulary; *Recreations* gardening, travel, walking, music; *Style—* The Ven the Archdeacon of Cheltenham; ✉ Westbourne, 283 Gloucester Rd, Cheltenham, Glos GL51 7AD (☎ 01242 522923, fax 01242 235925); Church House, College Green, Gloucester GL1 2LY (☎ 01452 410022, fax 01452 308324)

LEWIS, John Elliott; s of John Derek Lewis, of Whakatane, NZ, and Margaret Helen, *née* Shaw (d 1948); *b* 23 Feb 1942; *Educ* King's Coll Auckland NZ, CCC Cambridge (MA Classical Tripos); *m* 1968, Vibeke, *née* Johansson; *Career* asst master King's Coll Auckland 1964 and 1966–70, jr lectr Classics Dept Univ of Auckland 1965; Eton College: asst classics master 1971–80, master in college 1975–80; head master: Geelong GS Victoria Aust 1980–94, Eton College 1994–; *Style—* John Lewis, Esq; ✉ Eton College, Windsor, Berks SL4 6DW (☎ 01753 671231, fax 01753 671134)

LEWIS, John Henry James; s of late Leonard Lewis, QC, of East Park House, Newchapel, nr Lingfield, Surrey, and Rita Jeanette, *née* Stone (d 1994); *b* 12 July 1940; *Educ* Shrewsbury, UCL (LLB); *m* 30 Nov 1984, Susan Mary Frances, da of Maj Robert Ralph Merton, of The Old Rectory, Burghfield, Berks; 2 s (Barnaby Ralph James b 29 June 1989, Alfred Ralph James b 24 June 1992), 2 da (Daisy Leonora Frances b 1 Jan 1985, Lily Charlotte Frances b 23 Feb 1986); *Career* admitted slr 1966; ptnr Lewis Lewis & Co 1966–82; conslt: Jaques & Lewis 1982–95, Eversheds 1995–; chm: Cliveden Plc, Principal Hotels Plc, Blakeney Holdings Ltd; vice chm John D Wood & Co plc; dir: GR (Holdings) plc, Grayshott Hall Ltd; Br Tourist Authy: memb Bd 1990–96, interim chm 1993; chm: Br Heritage Ctee, The Attingham Tst; memb Cncl Historic Houses Assoc; tstee: The Wallace Collection, The Watts Gallery; Freeman City of London, memb Worshipful Co of Gunmakers; memb Law Soc; *Recreations* sculpture, architecture, tennis, shooting; *Clubs* Brooks's, Garrick; *Style—* John Lewis, Esq; ✉ Shute House, Donhead St Mary, Shaftesbury, Dorset SP7 9DT (☎ 01747 828866); 24 Cadogan Gardens, London SW3 2RP (☎ 0171 730 6466, fax 0171 730 9236); Cliveden Plc, 27A Sloane Square, London SW1W 8AB (☎ 0171 730 5420, fax 0171 730 6608)

LEWIS, Maj John Henry Peter Sebastian Beale; s of Maj Peter Beale Lewis, MC (d 1961), and Mary Evelyn Louise Piers, *née* Dumas (d 1970); *b* 7 July 1936; *Educ* Eton; *m* 21 Dec 1971, Mary Virginia, da of Charles Barstow Hutchinson (d 1978); 2 s (Rupert Henry Alexander b 1974, Antony Rhydian b 1977); *Career* Maj 11 Hussars (PAO) 1955–69; dir: British Bloodstock Agency plc 1976– (vice chm 1992), Lower Burytown Farm 1983–, Nawara Stud Co 1985–; rode over 25 winners under Jockey club rules; represented GB in Bobsleigh; *Clubs* Cavalry and Guards', MCC; *Style—* Maj J P Lewis; ✉ Queensberry House, Newmarket, Suffolk (☎ 01638 665021, fax 01638 660283, telex 817157)

LEWIS, Jonathan; s of Henry Lewis, of London, and Jenny, *née* Cohen; *b* 2 Nov 1955; *Educ* St Paul's, Univ of Manchester (BA Econ); *m* 22 June 1980, Veronique; 2 da (Sara Giselle b 2 July 1983, Tanya Esther 4 May 1987), 1 s (Joshua Prosper b 14 June 1985); *Career* D J Freeman: joined as trainee 1978, admitted slr 1980, ptnr 1982, memb Fin Ctee 1987–90, chief exec 1993–; govr Immanuel Coll; memb City of London Slrs' Co; Br Under 20 Sabre fencing champion 1973; memb Law Soc 1980; *Recreations* fundraising for charity, art, travel; *Style—* Jonathan Lewis, Esq; ✉ D J Freeman, 1 Fetter Lane, London EC4A 1BR (☎ 0171 556 4210, fax 0171 353 1600, mobile 0976 439949, e-mail JML@djfreeman.co.uk)

LEWIS, Jonathan Malcolm; s of Harold Lewis, of London, and Rene, *née* Goldser; *b* 27 March 1946; *Educ* Harrow County Sch, Downing Coll Cambridge (BA, MA); *m* 4 July 1971, Rosemary, da of Lewis Mays (d 1971); 2 s; *Career* admitted slr 1971, ptnr and jt head of Co/Commercial Dept D J Freeman & Co 1974–92, ptnr and head of Insolvency Services Gp Theodore Goddard 1992–; (asst slr 1971–74), columnist (City Comment) Law Soc Gazette 1983–90, insolvency practitioner 1986–; lectr and author on various legal topics; involved in the Scout movement; memb: Law Soc 1971, Int Bar Assoc 1981, Insolvency Lawyers Assoc 1987, Soc of Practitioners of Insolvency 1987; Freeman Worshipful Company of Basketmakers; Freeman Worshipful Co of Solicitors; Freeman of the City of London 1993; *Recreations* walking, theatre, family; *Style—* Jonathan M Lewis, Esq; ✉ Theodore Goddard, 150 Aldergate Street, London EC1A 4EJ (☎ 0171 606 8855, fax 0171 606 4390, telex 884678)

LEWIS, Keith Allan; s of John William Lewis (d 1979), of London, and Violet, *née* Hill; *b* 17 March 1946; *Educ* Henry Thornton GS; *m* 30 March 1968, Sandra Elaine, da of William Slade; 4 s (Clive Matthew b 20 March 1970, David Spencer b 29 Feb 1972, Andrew Christian b 29 June 1973, Jonathan Stuart b 10 June 1976); *Career* Financial Times 1962–78 (journalist, stock market reporter, co commentator, Lex contributor, head City Desk), dir fin pub rels Universal McCann 1978–81; dir: City & Commercial Communications 1981–82, Grandfield Rork Collins Financial 1982–85, Financial Strategy 1985 (merged with Streets); former md Streets Financial Marketing, chief exec Streets Communications 1987–92; chm: The Paternoster Partnership 1992–, Luke-Collins 1993–, The Albemarle Connection 1995–; *Recreations* walking, photography, films; *Clubs* Wig and Pen; *Style—* Keith Lewis, Esq; ✉ The Paternoster Partnership, 99 Charterhouse Street, London EC1M 6HR (☎ 0171 336 7776, fax 0171 336 7736)

LEWIS, Sir Kenneth; DL (Rutland 1973); s of William Lewis (d 1977), and Agnes, *née* Bradley (d 1980); *b* 1 July 1916; *Educ* Jarrow Central Sch, Univ of Edinburgh; *m* 1948, Jane (d 1991), da of Samuel Pearson, of Adderstone Mains, Belford, Northumberland; 1 s (Christopher), 1 da (Katharine); *Career* serv WWII; memb Lloyd's; contested (C): Newton 1945 and 1950, Ashton-under-Lyne 1951, MP (C) Rutland and Stamford 1959–83 and Stamford and Spalding 1983–87; chm Cons Back Bench Labour Ctee 1963–64; former chm Business and Holiday Travel Ltd; *Clubs* Carlton, RAF, Pathfinders; *Style—* Sir Kenneth Lewis, DL; ✉ Redlands, Preston, Uppingham, Rutland (☎ 01572 737320)

LEWIS, Lennox Claudius; *b* 2 Sept 1965; *Career* professional boxer (heavyweight); moved to Canada aged 12; amateur career: first bout 1978, Canadian Super Heavyweight champion 1984–88, winner Gold Medal Cwlth Games 1986, winner Gold Medal Olympic Games (vs Riddick Bowe) 1988, undefeated in 109 contests; turned professional 1989; professional career: winner Euro Heavyweight title 1990, British and Euro Heavyweight champion 1991, WBC champion 1993–94, defended vs Tony Tucker 1993, defended vs Frank Bruno 1993, defended vs Phil Jackson 1994, undefeated in 25 contests, lost title to Oliver McCall 1994, defeated Ray Mercer 1996; Br Boxer of the Year Br Boxing Board of Control Awards 1993; *Style—* Lennox Lewis; ✉ c/o Frank Maloney, Panix Promotions, 99 Middlesex Street, London E1 7DA (☎ 0171 247 1999, fax 0171 247 9855)

LEWIS, Linda Clare; da of Stephen Hood Lewis, of Woodford Green, Essex, and Mary Monica, *née* Wood; *b* 3 Oct 1954; *Educ* Ursuline HS Ilford, Woodford County HS, Univ of Lancaster (BA); *m* 14 Sept 1991, Peter Sergio Allegretti; 2 s (Aubrey Edward Lewis Allegretti b 24 March 1993, Elliott Fraser Lewis Allegretti b 24 Nov 1995); *Career* trainee Mirror Group Newspapers Plymouth 1975–77, news prodr BBC Radio Manchester 1977–79, BBC Parly journalist 1979–80, reporter Today prog BBC Radio 4 1980–83, reporter BBC TV News and Current Affrs 1983–88, corr European Business Channel TV Zürich 1989–90, presenter Financial Times TV London and NHK TV 1990–91, presenter BBC World Service News 1991–92, presenter/reporter business and magazine progs BBC Radio 4 1992–93, presenter PM BBC Radio 4 1993–96; *Recreations* family, classical music, tennis, skiing; *Style—* Ms Linda Lewis; ✉ Knight Ayton Management, 10 Argyll Street, London W1V 1AB (☎ 0171 287 4405)

LEWIS, Lynn Alexander Mackay; s of Victor Lewis (d 1982), journalist; *b* 23 Aug 1937; *Educ* Elizabeth Coll Guernsey, Trinity Kandy Sri Lanka; *m* 1959, Valerie Elaine, da of Harry Procter, journalist, of London; 1 s (Lindon b 1961), 1 da (Carol b 1959); *Career* fndr Corby News 1961, Rome bureau chief Sunday Mirror 1966–68, reporter and presenter Nationwide (BBC TV) 1969–74, fndr and md Nauticalia Ltd 1974 (chm 1988–), fndr chm Lynn Lewis Group Ltd 1984–; chm Marine Trades Assoc 1986–89, dir National Boat Shows Ltd 1988–94; *Recreations* cricket; *Clubs* Shepperton Cricket (chm 1992–94); *Style—* Lynn Lewis, Esq; ✉ Riverdell, Thames Meadow, Shepperton-on-Thames, Middx TW17 8TL (☎ 01932 220794); Nauticalia Ltd, Ferry Works, Shepperton-on-Thames, Middx (☎ 01932 244396, fax 01932 241679, mobile 0831 113501)

LEWIS, Malcolm Neal; s of Neal Stanley Lewis, of Jersey, and Barbara Ann Lewis, *née* Able; *b* 20 Aug 1958; *Educ* Lancing, École Hoteliere de Lausanne (dip); *m* 1, (m dis), Ragnhild Kjaernet; 1 s (David b 18 Aug 1984); m 2, Aug 1996, Florence Patricia Orr; *Career* hotelier; receptionist Hotel Totem Flaine France 1977–78, École Hotelier de Lausanne 1978–81, chef Conaught Hotel London 1981–82, mangr and md Longueville Manor Hotel Jersey 1992–; pres Jersey Hotel and Guest House Assoc; *Recreations* tennis, boating, golf, reading; *Style—* Malcolm Lewis, Esq; ✉ No 2 La Pommeraie Close, St Saviour, Jersey, JE2 7NF; (☎ 01534 619448); Longueville Manor, Longueville Road, St Saviour, Jersey JE2 7WF (☎ 01534 25501)

LEWIS, Mark Robin Llewelyn; s of Gp Capt Howard Llewelyn Lewis, and Joan Blodwen, *née* Williams; *b* 6 Nov 1953; *Educ* Millfield, Exeter Coll Oxford (BA); *m* 29 June 1974, Fay Catherine, da of Patrick Alfred Tester; *Career* Allen & Overy: articles 1976–78, admitted slr 1978, asst slr 1978–81 and 1982–85, ptnr 1985–90; asst slr Cunningham John & Co 1981–82; ptnr: Bevan Ashford 1990–92, Bird & Bird 1992–95, Foot & Bowden 1995–; memb Law Soc; *Recreations* golf, cricket, walking, reading; *Style—* Mark Lewis, Esq; ✉ Foot & Bowden, The Foot & Bowden Building, 21 Derry's Cross, Plymouth PL1 2SW (☎ 01752 675000)

LEWIS, Martyn John Dudley; CBE (1997); s of Thomas John Dudley Lewis (d 1979), of Coleraine, NI, and Doris, *née* Jones; *b* 7 April 1945; *Educ* Dalriada GS Ballymoney NI, Trinity Coll Dublin (BA); *m* 20 May 1970, Elizabeth Anne, da of Duncan Carse, of Fittleworth, Sussex; 2 da (Sylvie b 11 May 1975, Kate b 24 July 1978); *Career* TV journalist, presenter and newsreader; presenter BBC Belfast 1967–68, journalist and broadcaster HTV Wales 1968–70, joined ITN 1970, set up and ran ITN's Northern Bureau Manchester 1971–78; newsreader and foreign corr ITN: News at Ten, News at 5.45 1978–86; ITN reports 1970–86 incl: Cyprus War, Seychelles Independence, Fall of Shah of Iran, Soviet Invasion of Afghanistan, Vietnamese Boat People; co-presenter: ITV gen election programmes 1979 and 1983, ITV Budget programmes 1981–84, wrote and produced Battle for the Falklands video, wrote and presented The Secret Hunters documentary (TVS); joined BBC as presenter One O'Clock News 1986, presenter Nine O'Clock News 1987–94, presenter Six O'Clock News 1994–; presenter Crimebeat (series, BBC 1) 1996 and 1997; host Today's the Day series, BBC 2) 1993–97; BBC documentaries: MacGregor's Verdict, Royal Tournament, Royal Mission Great Ormond Street - A Fighting Chance, Princess Anne - Save The Children, Help is There, Indian Summer, Fight Cancer, Living with Dying, The Giving Business, Health UK; chm and fndr YouthNet UK, chm Drive for Youth, pres United Response; vice pres: Help the Hospices, Marie Curie Cancer Care, Macmillan Cancer Relief; dir: Inst for Citizenship Studies, Friends of Nelson Mandela Children's Fund; patron: Cities in Schools, Youth For Britain, Cambridge Children's Hospice, Hope House Children's Hospice, South West Children's Hospice, Quidenham Children's Hospice, Int Sch for Cancer Care, London Lighthouse, The Dementia Trust; memb: Tidy Britain Gp Policy Advsy Ctee, DNH Volunteering Partnership Forum for England; Freeman City of London 1989; Liveryman Worshipful Co of Pattenmakers; Hon DLitt Univ of Ulster 1994; FRSA 1990; *Books* And Finally (1984), Tears and Smiles - The Hospice Handbook (1989), Cats in the News (1991), Dogs in the News (1992), Go For It (annual, 1993–), Today's the Day (1995), Reflections on Success (1997); *Recreations* photography, tennis, good food; *Clubs* Annabel's, Vanderbilt; *Style*— Martyn Lewis, Esq, CBE; ✉ c/o Anita Land, Simpson Fox Associates Ltd, 52 Shaftesbury Avenue, London W1V 7DE (☎ 0171 434 9167, fax 0171 494 2887)

LEWIS, (Patricia) Mary; da of late Donald Leslie Cornes, of Bayston Hill, nr Shrewsbury, and Eleanor Lillian, *née* Roberts; *Educ* Stonehurst Sch Shrewsbury, St Margaret's Yeaton Peverey Shropshire, Shrewsbury Sch of Art, Camberwell Sch of Arts and Crafts (BA), Central Sch of Art Middx Poly (postgrad); *m* 2, 7 Jan 1992, Robert Moberly, *qv*, s of Sir Walter Moberly, GBE, KCB, DSO (d 1973); 1 da (Scarlett Rose b 28 May 1992); *Career* graphic designer; creative dir and founding ptnr Lewis Moberly Design Consultants 1984–; awards incl: British Design and Art Direction Gold Award for Outstanding Design and 3 Silver Awards for packaging, Design Business Assoc Grand Prix for Design Effectiveness 1993; juror: BBC Design Awards, D&AD Awards, Communication Arts Awards USA; work exhibited: London, Los Angeles, Japan, NYC; pres D&AD 1995, chm BBC Graphic Design Awards 1996; memb Royal Mail Stamps Advsy Ctee 1996; contrib to programme Education (Channel 4); FRSA; *Books* Understanding Brands (co-ed); *Recreations* daughter; *Style*— Ms Mary Lewis; ✉ Lewis Moberly Design Consultants, 33 Gresse Street, London W1P 2LP (☎ 0171 580 9252, fax 0171 255 1671)

LEWIS, Prof Mervyn Keith; s of Norman Malcolm Lewis (d 1982), of Adelaide, and Gladys May Valerie, *née* Way; *b* 20 June 1941; *Educ* Unley HS, Univ of Adelaide (BSc, PhD); *m* 24 Nov 1962, Kay Judith, da of Lt Royce Melvin Wiesner (d 1977), of Adelaide; 4 da (Stephanie b 1966, Miranda b 1967, Alexandra b 1969, Antonia b 1972); *Career* Elder Smith & Co Ltd 1957–58, Cwlth Bank of Aust 1959–64, assoc dean Univ of Adelaide 1981–83 (tutor and lectr 1965–84, sr lectr 1973–79, reader 1979–84), visiting scholar Bank of England 1979–80, conslt Aust Fin System Inquiry 1980–81, Midland Bank prof of money and banking Univ of Nottingham 1984–, visiting prof: of econs Flinders Univ of S Aust 1987, Wirtschaftsuniversität Wien 1987 and 1990–, Int Teachers' Programme Bocconi Univ Milan 1988, Victoria Univ of Wellington 1991; res assoc Center for Pacific Basin Monetary and Economic Studies Federal Reserve Bank of San Francisco 1991–; pres of Cncl Kingston Coll of Advanced Educn 1978–79; elected fell of the Acad of the Social Sciences in Aust 1986; *Books* Monetary Policy in Australia (1980), Australian Monetary Economics (1981), Monetary Control in the United Kingdom (1981), Australia's Financial Institutions and Markets (1985), Personal Financial Markets (1986), Domestic and International Banking (1987), Money in Britain: Monetary Policy, Innovation and Europe (1991), Current Issues in Financial and Monetary Economics (1992), The Australian Financial System (1993), Financial Intermediaries (1995, 2 edn 1996), Monetary Economics (1997); *Recreations* rambling, tennis, music; *Clubs* East India; *Style*— Prof Mervyn Lewis; ✉ 4 Wortley Hall Close, University Park, Nottingham NG7 2QB (☎ 0115 978 7495); The University of Nottingham, Department of Economics, University Park, Nottingham NG7 2RD (☎ 0115 951 5480, fax 0115 951 4159, telex 37346 UNINOT G)

LEWIS, Michael ap Gwilym; QC (1975); s of Rev Thomas William Lewis (d 1946), of London, and Mary Jane May, *née* Selway (d 1975); *Educ* Mill Hill Sch, Jesus Coll Oxford (MA); *m*; 3 s (Meyric b 1962, Gareth b 1964, Evan b 1966), 3 da (Bronwen b 1960, Jennet b 1989, Harriet b 1992); *Career* cmmnd RTR 1952–53; called to the Bar Gray's Inn 1956, bencher 1986; recorder of the Crown Court 1976–, memb Senate 1976–79, memb Criminal Injuries Compensation Bd 1993–; *Style*— Michael Lewis, Esq, QC; ✉ 3 Hare Court, Temple, London EC4Y 7BJ

LEWIS, Dr Mitchell; s of Coleman James Lewis (d 1966), and Fanny, *née* Zweiback (d 1959); *b* 3 April 1924; *Educ* Christian Brothers Coll Kimberley SA, Univ of Capetown (BSc, MB ChB, MD); *m* 23 Oct 1959, Ethel Norma, da of Rachmiel Nochumowitz (d 1958); 1 s (Raymond b 1962); *Career* conslt haematologist Hammersmith Hosp 1961–93, sr res fell Royal Postgrad Med Sch 1989–, emeritus reader Univ of London 1989– (reader in haematology 1970–89); dir WHO Collaborative Centre for Haematology 1987–; past chm Int Cncl for Standardization in Haematology, cnsllr-at-large Int Soc of Haematology, past pres Br Soc for Haematology; FRCPath, FIMLS; *Books* Modern Concepts in Haematology (1972), Dyserythropoiesis (1977), The Spleen (1983), Thromboplastin Calibration (1984), Myelofibrosis (1985), Biopsy Pathology and Bone and Marrow (1985), Quality Assurance in Haematology (1988), Postgraduate Haematology (1989), Practical Haematology (1995), Haematology Laboratory Management and Practice (1995); *Recreations* photography, reading, music, golf; *Style*— Dr Mitchell Lewis; ✉ 6 Salisbury House, Somerset Rd, Wimbledon, London SW19 5HY (☎ 0181 946 2727, fax 0181 946 9146); Royal Postgraduate Medical School, London W12 0NN (☎ 0181 740 3961, fax 0181 946 9146)

LEWIS, Neville Julian Spencer; s of Raymond Malcom Lewis (d 1980), of Llanishen, Cardiff, and Constance Margaret, *née* Jones; *b* 17 March 1945; *Educ* Radley, Pembroke Coll Oxford (MA); *m* 1, 14 July 1967 (m dis 1981), Caroline Joy, da of Robin Homes (d 1987), of Oare, Wiltshire; 1 s (David b 1978), 1 da (Miranda b 1974); m 2, 1994, Anna-Liisa, da of Aake Jarvinen, of Hyvinkää, Finland; 1 s (Kasperi b 1995); *Career* called to the Bar Inner Temple 1970, practises SE Circuit; Parly candidate (Lib) Paddington Feb and Oct 1974; *Books* Guide to Greece (1977), Delphi and the Sacred Way (1987); *Clubs* Nat Lib; *Style*— Neville Spencer Lewis, Esq; ✉ 8 Manor Mansions, Belsize Park Gardens, London NW3 4ND; 12 King's Bench Walk, Temple, London EC4Y 7EL (☎ 0171 583 0811)

LEWIS, Nigel Wickham; s of Henry Wickham Lewis, and Marjorie, *née* Greene; *b* 3 Jan 1936; *Educ* Gayhurst Sch Gerrards Cross Bucks, Greshams' Sch Holt Norfolk, Clare Coll Cambridge (MA); *m* 21 Oct 1961, Chloe Elizabeth, da of John Hershell Skinner; 1 s (Tristram b 1967), 2 da (Derryn b 1964, Venetia b 1969); *Career* graduate apprentice and design engr Vickers-Armstrongs (Aircraft) Ltd 1958–62, sr engr Glacier Metal Co Ltd 1962–68, mgmnt conslt McKinsey & Co Inc 1968–72, md Security Control Engineering Ltd 1972–76, dir 3i plc 1977–91, dir Independent Direction Ltd 1991–; Liveryman Worshipful Co of Cordwainers; CEng, MIMechE, MBCS; *Recreations* lawn tennis, real tennis, garden supression, ceramic restoration, music; *Clubs* Utd Oxford and Cambridge Univs; *Style*— Nigel Lewis, Esq; ✉ Cadsden House, Cadsden Road, Princes Risborough, Bucks HP27 0NB (☎ 01844 274575, fax 01844 274577)

LEWIS, Paul Scott; s of David Harold Lewis (d 1956), of Porthcawl, Mid-Glamorgan, and Margaret Elizabeth, *née* Thomas (d 1991); *b* 29 Nov 1936; *Educ* Monkton Combe Sch Bath (entrance scholar); *m* 31 Aug 1963, Patricia, da of late Kenneth Jospeh Grant; 3 da (Anna b 20 Dec 1966, Erika b 26 April 1969, Suzy b 30 Sept 1971); *Career* articled clerk R H March 1954–59, audit sr mangr Paris and supervising sr Stamford Conn Price Waterhouse 1959–65, int cost mangr Remington Rand Div Sperry Rand Bridgeport Conn 1965, int controller Bridgeport Conn and md Warners UK Ltd Warnaco Inc 1966–71, sr fin analyst Int Div, fin dir Spain, int controller and dir of fin Int Div British Leyland 1971–78, gp fin dir Bestobell plc 1978–82, fin dir Racal Communications and sr vice pres fin Racal Milgo Inc Racal Electronics plc 1982–88; Tate & Lyle plc: gp fin dir 1988–95, dep chm 1993–, dir Bd of Pension Tstees and dir various subsid cos 1988–; non-exec dir: Dairy Crest Group plc 1993–, T & N plc 1995–; memb Listing Policy Ctee London Stock Exchange; FCA 1969 (ACA 1959); *Recreations* sailing, walking, music, reading; *Clubs* Island Sailing; *Style*— Paul Lewis, Esq; ✉ Tate & Lyle PLC, Sugar Quay, Lower Thames St, London EC3R 6DQ (☎ 0171 626 6525, fax 0171 623 5213)

LEWIS, Peter Tyndale; s of Oswald Lewis (d 1966), of Beechwood, Highgate, MP for Colchester 1929–45, and Frances Merriman Cooper; gf founded John Lewis Oxford St in 1864, uncle John Spedan Lewis founded John Lewis Partnership 1929; *b* 26 Sept 1929; *Educ* Eton, ChCh Oxford (MA); *m* 22 July 1961, Deborah Anne, da of Sir William Collins, CBE (d 1976), of St James's Place, London; 1 s (Patrick b 1965), 1 da (Katharine b 1962); *Career* Nat Serv Coldstream Gds 1948–49; called to the Bar Middle Temple 1956; joined John Lewis Partnership 1959; chm: John Lewis Partnership 1972–93, Retail Distributors Assoc 1972; memb: Cncl Industl Soc 1968–79, Design Cncl 1971–74, Cncl Queen's Coll London 1994–; govr: Windlesham House Sch 1979–95, NIESR 1983–; tstee: Jt Educnl Tst 1985–87, Bell Educnl Tst 1987–, Univ of Southampton Devpt Tst 1994–; CIMgt, FRSA; *Recreations* golf; *Clubs* MCC; *Style*— Peter Lewis, Esq; ✉ 34 Victoria Road, London W8 5RG (☎ 0171 937 2662)

LEWIS, Dr Philip Stuart; s of Harold Charles Lewis, of Whitbourne, Herts, and Olwyn, *née* Witcombe; *b* 2 March 1947; *Educ* Buckhurst Hill County HS Chigwell Essex, St Thomas's Hosp Med Sch (BSc, MB BS); *m* 4 April 1970, (Eunice) Brenda, da of Kenneth Herbert Harold Johnson, of E Wittering, W Sussex; 2 s (John b 1985, Charles b 1987), 6 da (Sophia b 1972, Stephanie b 1974, Justine b 1975, Timothea b 1977, Davita b 1978, Octavia b 1990); *Career* house physician St Thomas's Hosp 1972, med registrar W Middx Hosp 1974–76, res fell Dept of Clinical Pharmacology St Mary's Hosp London 1976–78, sr med registrar St Mary's Hospital and Edgware 1978–83, lectr in med Central Middx Hosp 1983–84, conslt cardiovascular physician Stepping Hill Hosp Stockport and Alexandra Hosp Cheadle 1984–; hon lectr in medicine Univ of Manchester Medical Sch; memb: Br Hypertension Soc, British Cardiac Soc, Burnage Family Church; MRCP 1984, FRCP 1992; *Recreations* walking, painting; *Style*— Dr Philip Lewis; ✉ Stepping Hill Hospital, Poplar Grove, Stockport, Cheshire SK2 7JE (☎ 0161 419 5478, fax 0161 419 5478)

LEWIS, (Arthur) Raymond; s of Harold Arthur Lewis (d 1981), of Chislehurst, Kent, and Gladys Nellie, *née* Thompson; *b* 13 Oct 1933; *Educ* Tonbridge; *m* 13 Sept 1957, Anne Margaret Elizabeth, da of John Christie Wishart, MBE (d 1977), of Bromley, Kent; 1 s (Andrew b 1961), 1 da (Katharine b 1962); *Career* PO RAF 1952–54; chm and chief exec Frazer-Nash Group Ltd 1988–90 (md 1974–88), chm Leadership Strategies Ltd 1992–93; chm Surrey Trg and Enterprise Cncl 1990–92, govr Brooklands Coll Weybridge 1993–94; currently chm: Salamander Property Group Ltd and subsids, CIT Holdings Ltd and subsids, RSF Contracting Ltd; currently treas Cranfield Univ; FCA; *Recreations* swimming, music, gardening, reading, gourmet eating, fine wines; *Style*— Raymond Lewis, Esq; ✉ Hilltop, Ruxley Crescent, Claygate, Esher, Surrey KT10 0TX (☎ 01372 462543)

LEWIS, Very Rev Richard; s of Rev Henry Lewis (d 1953), and Amy, *née* Poyner (d 1972); *b* 24 Dec 1935; *Educ* Royal Masonic Sch, Fitzwilliam House Cambridge (MA), Ripon Hall Oxford; *m* 1959, Jill Diane, da of Joseph Alfred Wilford; 2 s (Simon Wilford b 1966, Andrew Richard b 1969); *Career* curate: Hinckley 1960–63, Sanderstead (in charge of St Edmunds) 1963–66; vicar: All Saints S Merstham 1967–72, Holy Trinity and St Peter Wimbledon 1972–79, St Barnabas Dulwich 1979–90; fndn chaplain of Christ's Chapel Alleyn's Coll of God's Gift Dulwich 1979–90, dean of Wells 1990–; tutor in clinical theol 1964–68, gp psychotherapist St George's Hosp Tooting 1972–82, chaplain Worshipful Co of Barber Surgns 1987, occasional speaker's chaplain House of Commons 1988; currently: chm Bd of Govrs Wells Cathedral Sch, memb Bishop's Staff, warden of readers Dio of Bath and Wells, memb Gen Synod, memb Archbishops' Cmmn on Cathedrals, chm Conf of Deans and Provosts of England 1994, memb Crown Appointments Cmmn; *Style*— The Very Rev Richard Lewis; ✉ The Dean's Lodging, 25 The Liberty, Wells, Somerset BA5 2SZ (☎ 01749 670278); The Cathedral Office, West Cloisters Office, Wells, Somerset BA5 2PA (☎ 01749 674483, fax 01749 679184)

LEWIS, Rt Rev (John Hubert) Richard; *see:* St Edmundsbury and Ipswich, Bishop of

LEWIS, Dr Richard Alexander; s of Harold Charles Lewis, of Buckhurst Hill, Essex, and Olwyn, *née* Witcombe; *b* 4 Nov 1949; *Educ* Buckhurst Hill County HS Chigwell Essex, St Thomas's Hosp Med Sch Univ of London (DM, BSc, MB BS); *m* 26 May 1973, Dr Anne Margaret Lewis, da of Cdr Donald Maclennan, of Tong, Stornoway, Isle of Lewis; 2 s (Christopher b 1977, Peter b 1986), 1 da (Elizabeth b 1982); *Career* house physician St Thomas's Hosp London 1975, rotational sr house offr in med Southampton Gen Hosp and Dist Hosp 1976–77, rotational registrar in gen med St Richard's Hosp Chichester and St Thomas's Hosp London 1977–79, res fell Dept of Respiratory Med Unit One Univ of Southampton 1979–82, sr registrar in gen and thoracic med Southampton and Portsmouth Dist Hosp 1982–86; conslt physician specialising in diseases of the chest: Worcester and Dist Health Authy Worcester Royal Infirmary 1986–, Worcester Royal Infirmary NHS Tst 1993–; govr St Richard's Hospice Worcester; pres: Vale of Evesham Asthma Soc, Malvern Asthma Soc; memb: Br Thoracic Soc, Med Res Soc, Christian Med Fellowship; MRCS, MRCP, LRCP, FRCP 1992; *Books* contrib: Pharmacology of Asthma (1983), Drugs and the Lung (1984), Current Treatment of Ambulatory Asthma (1986); *Recreations* running, cycling, mountain walking, gardening, music; *Style*— Dr Richard Lewis; ✉ Crews Court, Suckley, Worcester WR6 5DW (☎ 01886 884552); Worcester Royal Infirmary, Castle St Branch, Worcester WR1 3AS (☎ 01905 763333, fax 01905 26965)

LEWIS, Richard Simon Kirk; s of K J Lewis, of Norfolk, and Josephine, *née* Breadmore; *Educ* Lancing, Andrew Cairn's GS Sussex; *m* 1, (m dis); 2 s (Joshua b 17 Sept 1973, Joel b 31 July 1978); m 2, Alison Brand; *Career* advertising exec; account exec: Lonsdale Hands Advertising (Lonsdale Crowther) London 1967–68 (trainee 1965–67), Alexander Butterfield and Ayer 1968–71; account mangr Rupert Chetwynd & Partners (Chetwynd Haddons) London 1971–75 (accounts handled incl: Lloyds Bank, Carlsberg Lager, Eggs Authority), md Chetwynd Streets Midlands Ltd Leicester 1976–82 (account dir and Bd dir 1975–76), dir Chetwynd Streets (Holdings) Ltd London 1978–82, md Wells O'Brien London and Regions 1982–83, md and fndr ptnr Singer Lewis & Associates 1983–85 (accounts handled incl: Valor Heating, Valor Home Products, Courtaulds Hosiery, Acamas Toys, Greenhall Whitley, Robinsons of Chesterfield, TVR Cars), md Poulter PLC Leeds 1985–; FIPA, memb Mktg Soc; *Style*— Richard Lewis, Esq; ✉ Poulter PLC, 2 Burley Road, Leeds, West Yorkshire LS3 1N3 (☎ 0113 246 9611, fax 0113 244 8796)

LEWIS, Rev Canon Robert Hugh Cecil; s of Herbert Cecil Lewis, OBE (Capt Welsh Regt, d 1967), and Olive Francis, *née* Marsden (d 1980); *b* 23 Feb 1925; *Educ* Swansea GS, Manchester GS, New Coll Oxford (BA, MA), Westcolt House; *m* 15 July 1948, Joan Dorothy, da of Ernest Gordon Hickman (Maj Cheshire Regt, d 1970), and Dorothy Cottier Hickman, *née* Richardson; 1 s (David b 15 June 1949), 1 da (Ruth b 17 Nov 1952); *Career* Mil Serv 1942–47, PO RAFVR 1945, Flying Offr 1946, Flt Lt 1947; ordained: deacon 1952, priest 1953; curate: St Mary Crumpsall 1952–54, St James New Bury 1954–56; incumbent: St Peter Bury 1956–63, St George Poynton 1963–91; rural dean: Stockport 1972–84, Cheadle 1984–86; hon canon Chester Cathedral 1973–91 (now canon emeritus), chaplain to HM the Queen 1987–95; county ecumenical offr for Cheshire 1986–91; *Style*— The Rev Canon Robert Lewis; ✉ 78 Dean Drive, Wilmslow, Cheshire SK9 2EY (☎ 01625 524761)

LEWIS, Hon Robin William; OBE (1988); 4 s of 3 Baron Merthyr, KBE, PC (d 1977), and Violet, *née* Meyrick; *b* 7 Feb 1941; *Educ* Eton, Magdalen Coll Oxford (BA, MA); *m* 28 April 1967, Judith Ann, o da of (Vincent Charles) Arthur Giardelli, MBE, of Pembroke; 1 s (Christopher b 1970), 1 da (Katharine b 1972); *Career* Cwlth Devpt Corp 1964–66, Alcan Aluminium 1967–68, National Westminster Bank Ltd 1968–72, Devpt Corp for Wales 1972–82, md Novametrix Medical Systems Ltd 1982–90 (chm 1989–90), chm and md The Magstim Co Ltd 1990–; High Sheriff of Dyfed 1987–88; chm: Gen Advsy Cncl of Ind Bdcasting Authy 1989–90 (memb 1985–90), National Tst Ctee for Wales 1994– (memb 1983–); dep chm Welsh Devpt Agency 1995– (memb Bd 1994–); *Recreations* sailing; *Clubs* Leander; *Style*— The Hon Robin Lewis, OBE; ✉ The Magstim Co Ltd, Whitland, Carmarthenshire SA34 OHR (☎ 01994 240798, fax 01994 240061)

LEWIS, Roger Charles; s of late Griffith Charles John Lewis, and Dorothy, *née* Russ; *b* 24 Aug 1954; *Educ* Cynffig Sch, Univ of Nottingham (BMus); *m* 5 July 1980, Dr Christine Lewis, da of Leslie Trollope; 2 s (Owen Rhys b 29 March 1985, Thomas Griffith b 16 Feb 1988); *Career* freelance musician 1976–80, music offr Darlington Arts Centre 1980–82, presenter Radio Tees 1982–84, prodr Capital Radio 1984–85, head of music BBC Radio 1 1987–90 (prodr 1985–87), md Classical Div EMI Records 1995 (dir 1990–95), md EMI Premier 1995–; awards incl: Sony Award 1987, 1988 and 1989, NY Grand Award Winner and gold medal 1987 (finalist 1989); Monaco Radio Festival Finalist 1989; chm Music Conf of the Radio Acad 1990; *Style*— Roger Lewis, Esq; ✉ EMI Premier, EMI Records UK, EMI House, 43 Brook Green, London W6 7EP

LEWIS, Prof Roland Wynne; s of David Lewis (d 1958), of Ammanford, Dyfed, and Mary Gladys, *née* Davies (d 1981); *b* 20 Jan 1940; *Educ* Amman Valley GS, Univ College Swansea (BSc, PhD, DSc); *m* 17 April 1965, Celia Elizabeth, da of Haydn Elgar Morris, of Ammanford, Dyfed; 1 s ((David) Andrew b 4 March 1971), 2 da (Caroline b 16 June 1969, Angharad b 11 Feb 1973); *Career* res engr ESSO Canada 1965–69, prof Univ Coll Swansea 1984– (lectr 1969–79, sr lectr 1979–82, reader 1982–84); chm Thermofluids Gp Nat Agency for Finite Element Methods and Standards; FICE 1991 (MICE 1973); *Books* Civil Engineering Systems-Analysis and Design, Finite Elements in the Flow and Deformation of Porous Media, The Finite Element Method in Heat Transfer Analysis; *Recreations* golf, photography, gardening; *Clubs* La Quinta (Spain), Clyne Golf (Swansea); *Style*— Prof Roland Lewis; ✉ Oakridge, 331 Gower Road, Killay, Swansea SA2 7AE (☎ 01792 203166); Civil Engineering Department, University College of Swansea, Swansea SA2 8PP (☎ 01792 295253, fax 01792 295705)

LEWIS, Dr Sean Michael; s of Leonard Leon Lewis (d 1973), of London, and Margaret, *née* Moore (d 1966); *b* 23 Oct 1943; *Educ* St Bonaventure's Sch London, Univ of Liverpool (BSc, PhD); *m* 1971, Jennifer Myra, da of Eric Williams (d 1987); 1 s (Nicholas Eliot Alexander b 21 Oct 1981); *Career* British Cncl: trg in Madrid 1970, trg in London 1970–71, asst rep Enugu Nigeria 1971–73, science advsr London 1973–75, asst rep Colombo Sri Lanka 1975–78, science advsr 1978–79, dep dir Serv Conditions Dept London 1979–84, human resource planner London 1984–88, dir Overseas Educnl Appts London 1988–89, dir Sweden 1989–92, head Film, TV & Video Dept 1992–96, dir Canada 1997–; memb Br Phycological Soc 1967–92, first foreign fell Swedish Soc for Developmental Biology 1992; *Recreations* landscape design, classical/jazz trombonist, cinema, downhill skiing, good beer, country pubs, pyrotechnics; *Style*— Dr Sean Lewis; ✉ The British Council, 80 Elgin Street, Ottawa, Ontario K1P 5K7, Canada (☎ 00 1 613 237 1530, fax 00 1 613 569 1478, e-mail af572@freenet.carleton.ca)

LEWIS, (David) Simon; s of David Lewis, and Sally Elizabeth, *née* Valentine; *b* 8 May 1959; *Educ* Whitefield Sch, Brasenose Coll Oxford (PPE), Univ of California at Berkeley (Fulbright scholar, MA); *m* 1985, Claire Elizabeth, da of Eric Pendry, and late Jean Pendry; 1 s (Thomas Paul b 1989), 1 da (Olivia Rose b 1991); *Career* financial PR exec Shandwick Consultants 1983–86, seconded to S.G. Warburg in run-up to Big Bang 1986, political advsr SDP gen election 1987, head of public relations S G Warburg Group 1987–92 (estab PR dept); dir of corporate affrs: NatWest Group 1992–96, British Gas 1996–; pres IPR 1997– (former chm City and Financial Group); dir and tstee Crime Concern; memb Advsy Bd Cardiff Sch of Journalism; FRSA; *Style*— Simon Lewis, Esq; ✉ Corporate Affairs Department, British Gas, Charter Court, 50 Windsor Road, Slough, Berks SL1 2HA

LEWIS, Stephen John; s of late Douglas John Lewis, of Codsall, Staffs, and late Dorothy Pauline, *née* Shaw; *b* 8 March 1948; *Educ* Wolverhampton GS, Balliol Coll Oxford (BA); *Career* ptnr Phillips & Drew 1980–85, dir Securities Ltd 1985–88, md Fifth Horseman Publications Ltd 1988–92, dir The London Bond Broking Co Ltd 1992– (also chief economist); *Recreations* antiquities; *Clubs* Reform; *Style*— Stephen Lewis, Esq; ✉ The London Bond Broking Co Ltd, 11 Old Jewry, London E2R 8DU (☎ 0171 338 0173)

LEWIS, Stephen Michael; s of Harry Lewis, of Stanmore, Middlesex, and Celia, *née* Softness; *b* 23 Aug 1949; *Educ* Orange Hill Co GS for Boys, St Catherine's Coll Oxford (open exhibition, BA), Univ of London (LLB); *m* 3 March 1974, Erica, da of Jacob Pesate; 1 s (Adrian William b 9 April 1979), 2 da (Ann Marie b 25 April 1976, Francesca Rose b 2 Sept 1986); *Career* mgmnt trainee Reed International 1970–71, articled clerk Clintons slrs 1971–74, legal asst Law Cmmn 1975–80, ptnr Clifford Turner (now Clifford Chance) 1985– (asst slr 1980–85); memb: Law Soc, Sub Ctee on Insurance Law City of London Law Soc; *Recreations* music, reading, swimming, politics; *Style*— Stephen Lewis, Esq; ✉ Clifford Chance, 200 Aldersgate Street, London EC1A 4JJ (☎ 0171 600 1000, fax 0171 600 5555)

LEWIS, Stephen Richard; *b* 11 Jan 1959; *Educ* Deyes HS Maghull Merseyside, Southport Coll of Art, Manchester Poly (BA), Jan Van Eyck Academie Maastricht Netherlands; *Career* artist; visiting artist: Cyprus Sch of Art, Voss Sch Norway, Triangle Artists Workshop NY, Emma Lake Workshop Canada, Hardingham Sculpture Workshop UK; lectr at various art colls and polys; work in various int collections; *Solo Exhibitions* Francis Graham-Dixon Gallery 1988, 1990 and 1993, Holden Gallery Manchester 1990, Stephen Lewis New Sculpture (Christchurch Mansion Ipswich) 1992; *Group Exhibitions* New Contemporaries (ICA), Northern Young Contemporaries (Whitworth Gallery Manchester), The First Picture Show (Norwich), Art in Europe 1991 (Freiberg Germany), Lancashire Contemporaries (Harris Museum Preston) 1992; *Style*— Stephen Lewis, Esq; ✉ Francis Graham-Dixon Gallery, 17–18 Great Sutton Street, London EC1V 0DN (☎ 0171 250 1962, fax 0171 490 1069)

LEWIS, (John) Stuart; s of John Charles Lewis, OBE, JP, and Kathleen Gertrude Clara, *née* Pennick (d 1973); *b* 9 March 1944; *Educ* Downer GS; *m* 19 July 1969, Bridget Margaret, da of Eric Billingham Nash (d 1987); 2 s (James b 1971, Edward b 1983), 1 da (Anna b 1973); *Career* ptnr Fielding Newson-Smith & Co 1975, first vice pres Drexel Burnam Lambert Inc 1986, md Private Fund Managers Ltd 1988–95, md Citiway consultants Ltd; chm Musicale plc; dir WIB (Publications) Ltd; fell Royal Soc for encouragement of Arts Manufacturers and Commerce; chm Beechwood Park Sch Markyate; Freeman City of London; FCIS 1974, MSI 1993; *Recreations* shooting, opera, reading, travel; *Clubs* City of London; *Style*— J Stuart Lewis, Esq; ✉ Greenaway House, Rose Lane, Wheathampstead, Herts AL4 8RA (☎ and fax 01582 834582)

LEWIS, (Christopher) Terence; s of Dr C B Lewis (d 1980), and Rachel, *née* O'Connor (d 1956); *b* 24 May 1944; *Educ* UCL, Westminster Hosp Med Sch (MB BS, LRCP MRCS, FRCS); *m* 1975, Jill, da of Walan Weller; 2 da (Victoria b 1979, Abigail b 1981), 1 s (Freddie b 1985); *Career* conslt then sr conslt cardiothoracic surgn Royal London Hosp 1979–95, conslt cardiothoracic surgn St Bartholomew's Hosp London 1995–Nov 1997, sr conslt cardiothoracic surgn Plymouth Hosps NHS Tst and hon conslt cardiothoracic surgn S Western Region and Derriford Hosp Plymouth Nov 1997–; conslt advsr in cardiothoracic surgery to the RN; memb: Biomaterial and Sensors Ctee SERC, Euro Ctee for the Devpt of Artificial Hearts; *Recreations* fishing, sailing, shooting; *Clubs* Royal Fowey Yach, Fowey Gallants Sailing; *Style*— Terence Lewis, Esq; ✉ until Nov 1997: Department of Cardiothoracic Surgery, St Bartholomew's Hospital, West Smithfield, London EC1A 7BE (☎ 0171 601 7118, fax 0171 601 7117) and 149 Harley Street, London W1N 2DE; from Nov 1997: Plymouth Hospitals NHS Trust, Derriford Hospital, Derriford Road, Plymouth PL6 8DH (☎ 01752 777111)

LEWIS, Terence (Terry); MP (Lab) Worsley (majority 10,012); s of Andrew Lewis; *b* 29 Dec 1935; *Educ* Our Lady of Mount Carmel Sch Salford; *m* 1958, Audrey, da of William Clarke; 2 s (1 decd); *Career* served RAMC 1954–56; formerly personnel offr in food industry, dep ldr Bolton BC (chm Educ Ctee); MP (Lab) Worsley 1983–; memb Select Ctee on: the Environment 1991–93, Members Interests 1993–95; jt vice chm All Pty Parly Gp for Animal Welfare; *Style*— Terry Lewis, Esq, MP; ✉ House of Commons, London SW1A 0AA (☎ 0171 219 3000)

LEWIS, Prof Trevor; CBE (1992); s of Harold Lewis (d 1982), and Maggie, *née* Bakewell; *b* 8 July 1933; *Educ* Imperial Coll London (PhD, DIC), Univ of Cambridge (MA), Univ of Nottingham (BSc, DSc); *m* 21 March 1959, Margaret Edith, da of Frederick George Wells (d 1977); 1 s (Roger b 1 Oct 1963), 1 da (Heather b 15 April 1961); *Career* univ demonstrator in agric zoology Sch of Agric Cambridge 1958–61; Rothamsted Experimental Station: joined 1961, seconded ODA 1970, head Entomology Dept 1976–83, head Crop Protection Div and dep dir 1983–87, head Crop and Environment Protection Div 1987–89, head and dir Inst for Arable Crops Res 1989–93; Lawes Tst sr fell Rothamsted Experimental Station 1994–; sr res fell Univ of West Indies 1970–73, visiting prof of invertebrate zoology Univ of Nottingham 1977– (special lectr 1968–69 and 1973–75); AFRC assessor; memb: MAFF Advsy Ctee on Pesticides 1984–89, Cncl Br Crop Protection Cncl 1985–93, R & D Ctee Potato Mktg Bd 1985–89; dir British Crop Protection Enterprises Ltd 1994–; memb Royal Entomological Soc London 1956 (pres 1985–87), FIBiol; *Books* Introduction to Experimental Ecology (with L R Taylor, 1967), Thrips - Their Biology, Ecology and Economic Importance (1973), Insect Communication (ed 1984); numerous contribs to scientific jls on entomological and agricultural topics; *Recreations* gardening, music; *Style*— Prof Trevor Lewis, CBE; ✉ Institute of Arable Crops Research, Rothamsted Experimental Station, West Common, Harpenden, Hertfordshire AL5 2JQ (☎ 01582 763133, fax 01582 760981, telex 825726)

LEWIS, Trevor Oswin; CBE (1983), DL (Dyfed 1994); suc as 4 Baron Merthyr (UK 1911) in 1977, but disclaimed Peerage for life, and does not use his title of Bt (UK 1896); s of 3 Baron Merthyr, KBE, TD, PC (d 1977); *b* 29 Nov 1935; *Educ* Eton, Magdalen Coll Oxford; *m* 18 April 1964, Susan Jane, da of A J Birt-Llewellin; 1 s, 3 da (Lucy (Mrs Harvey Bradnam) b 1967, Anne b 1970, Jessamy (Mrs Marcus Elmhirst) b 1972); *Heir* to Btcy and disclaimed Barony, s, David Trevor Lewis b 21 Feb 1977; *Career* memb: Dept of Transport Landscape Advsy Ctee 1968–92 (chm 1991–92), Countryside Cmmn 1973–83; JP Dyfed 1969–94; *Style*— Trevor Lewis, Esq, CBE, DL; ✉ Hean Castle, Saundersfoot, Pembrokeshire SA69 9AL (☎ 01834 812222)

LEWIS-BOWEN, His Hon Judge; Thomas Edward Ifor; s of Lt-Col J W Lewis-Bowen (d 1990), and Kathleen, *née* Rice (d 1981); *b* 20 June 1933; *Educ* Ampleforth, St Edmund Hall Oxford; *m* 1965, Gillian, da of the late Reginald Brett, of Puckington, Somerset; 1 s, 2 da; *Career* called to the Bar Middle Temple 1958, recorder of Crown Ct 1974–80, circuit judge (Wales and Chester Circuit) 1980–; *Style*— His Hon Judge Lewis-Bowen; ✉ Clynfyw, Boncath, Pembrokeshire (☎ 01239 841236); 4 Asquith Court, Swansea, W Glamorgan SA1 4QL (☎ 01792 473736)

LEWIS-JONES, Dr (Margaret) Susan (Sue); da of Ian Robert Munro Campbell, of 25 Reform St, Tayport, Fife, Scotland, and Jean Douglas, *née* Ramsay; *b* 12 April 1948; *Educ* Tudor Grange Girls' GS Solihull, Univ of Liverpool Med Sch (MB ChB), FRCP 1994 (MRCP 1982); *m* 7 Aug 1971, David Iwan Lewis-Jones, s of Capt Robert Gwilym Lewis-Jones, CBE, RN, of Man Siriol, Cae Deintur, Dolgellau, Gwynedd, N Wales; 1 s (Sion b 20 Jan 1976), 1 da (Alŷs b 19 May 1978); *Career* medical and surgical house offr 1972–73, demonstrator in anatomy Univ of Liverpool 1973–74, GP 1974–77, medical registrar 1982, conslt dermatologist 1987– (registrar 1982–85, sr registrar 1985–87), currently hon lectr in dermatology Univ of Liverpool and Univ of Wales; memb: BMA, Br Assoc of Dermatologists, American Acad of Dermatology, North of England Dermatological Soc, Liverpool Med Inst; *Recreations* golf, skiing, horse-riding, music; *Clubs* Eaton Golf, Dolgellau Golf (capt 1992); *Style*— Dr Sue Lewis-Jones; ✉ Maelor General Hospital, Croes/Newydd Rd, Wrexham, Clywd, N Wales LL13 7TD (☎ 01978 291100); Grosvenor Nuffield Hospital, Wrexham Rd, Chester, Cheshire CH4 7QP (☎ 01244 680444)

LEWIS OF NEWNHAM, Baron (Life Peer UK 1989), of Newnham in the Co of Cambridgeshire; Sir Jack Lewis; kt (1982); *b* 13 Feb 1928; *Educ* Barrow GS, Univ of London (BSc, DSc), Univ of Nottingham (PhD), Univ of Manchester (MSc), Univ of Cambridge (MA, ScD); *m* 1951, Elfreida Mabel, *née* Lamb; 1 s, 1 da; *Career* sits as an Independent in the House of Lords; lectr Univ of Sheffield 1954–56, lectr Imperial Coll London 1956–57, lectr/reader Univ Coll London 1957–61; prof of chemistry: Univ of Manchester 1961–67, Univ Coll London 1967–70, Univ of Cambridge 1970–95; warden Robinson Coll Cambridge 1975–; visiting prof UCL 1996–; memb: SRC Poly Ctee 1973–79, SRC Sci Ctee 1975–80, Univ Grants Ctee for Physical Scis 1973–80, Jt Ctee SERC/SSRC 1979–84, SERC Cncl 1979–84, Cncl Royal Soc 1982–84, NATO sci Ctee 1986–; chm: DES Visiting Ctee to Cranfield Inst 1982–92, Royal Cmmn on Environmental Pollution 1986–92; pres: Royal Soc of Chemistry 1986–88, Nat Soc for Clean Air and Environmental Protection 1993–95; Chevalier dans l'Ordre des Palmes Académiques, Cdr Cross of the Order of Merit of the Republic of Poland; Hon DUniv: Rennes Univ 1980, Open Univ 1982, Kingston Univ 1993; Hon DSc: UEA 1983, Univ of Nottingham 1983, Univ of Keele 1984, Univ of Birmingham 1988, Univ of Leicester 1988, Univ of Waterloo (Canada) 1988, Univ of Manchester 1990, Univ of Wales 1990, Univ of Sheffield 1992, Cranfield Univ 1993, Univ of Edinburgh 1994, Univ of Bath 1995, Univ of Dundee 1996; hon fell: UCL 1990, UMIST 1990, Univ of Central Lancashire 1993; FRS, FRIC, FRSA; *Style*— The Rt Hon Lord Lewis of Newnham, FRS; ✉ Warden's Lodge, 4 Sylvester Rd, Cambridge (☎ 01223 360222); Robinson College, Cambridge (☎ 01223 339120)

LEWISHAM, Archdeacon of; *see:* Atkinson, Ven Dr David John

LEWISHAM, Viscount; William Legge; s and h of 9 Earl of Dartmouth, *qv*, and his 1 w (now Comtesse Raine de Chambrun); *b* 23 Sept 1949; *Educ* Eton, Christ Church Oxford, Harvard Business Sch; *Career* chm and fndr Kirklees Cable; contested (Cons): Leigh Lancs 1974, Stockport South 1974; FCA; *Style*— Viscount Lewisham

LEWISOHN, His Hon Anthony Clive Leopold Lewisohn; s of John Lewisohn (d 1939); *b* 1 Aug 1925; *Educ* Stowe, Trinity Coll Oxford; *m* 1957, Lone Ruthwen Jurgensen; 2 s; *Career* served Royal Marines and Oxfordshire & Bucks LI 1944–47, Lt; called to the Bar Middle Temple 1951, circuit judge 1974–90, ret; *Style*— His Hon Anthony Lewisohn; ✉ Brackenhurst, Fairoak Lane, Oxshott, Leatherhead, Surrey KT22 0TN

LEWISOHN, Oscar Max; s of Max Lewisohn (d 1973), of Copenhagen, Denmark, and Jenny Lewisohn (d 1984); *b* 6 May 1938; *Educ* Sortedam Gymnasium Copenhagen Denmark; *m* 1, 4 Aug 1962, Louisa Madeleine (d 1985), da of Henry Grunfeld, of London; 3 s (Mark b 1963, Richard b 1965, James b 1970), 1 da (Anita b 1967); m 2, 24 Oct 1987, Margaret Ann, da of Don Paterson, of Wellington, NZ; 2 da (Jenny b 1989, Sophie b 1990); *Career* SG Warburg and Co Ltd 1962–95: exec dir 1969, dep chm 1987–94; dir SG Warburg Group plc 1985–95, dep chm Mercury Bank AG Zurich Switzerland 1990–, dir Private Investors Div Mercury Asset Management plc 1994–; memb: Cncl Imperial Cancer Res Fund, President's Ctee Sloan Kettering Meml Hosp NY 1992; tstee Waitangi Fndn 1990; Knight Order of the Dannebrog (Denmark); FRSA 1992; *Recreations* music; *Style*— Oscar Lewisohn, Esq; ✉ Mercury Asset Management plc, 33 King William Street, London EC4R 9AS (☎ 0171 280 2985, fax 0171 280 2108)

LEWISON, Kim Martin Jordan; QC (1991); s of Anthony Frederick Lewison (d 1993), and Dinora, *née* Pines; *b* 1 May 1952; *Educ* St Paul's, Downing Coll Cambridge (MA, Betha Wolferstan Rylands Prize); *m* 29 Sept 1979, Helen Mary, da of Josef Janecek (d 1980); 1 s (Joshua George b 1982), 1 da (Lydia Miriam b 1984); *Career* called to the Bar Lincoln's Inn 1975, asst recorder 1993–; memb Cncl: Lib Jewish Synagogue 1990–96, Leo Baeck Coll 1996–; *Books* Development Land Tax (1977), The Interpretation of Contracts (1989), Woodfall on Landlord and Tenant (gen ed), Drafting Business Leases (1996); *Recreations* visiting France; *Style*— Kim Lewison, Esq, QC; ✉ Falcon Chambers, Falcon Court, London EC4Y 1AA (☎ 0171 353 2484, fax 0171 353 1261)

LEWITH, Dr George Thomas; s of Frank Lewith (d 1965), and Alice, *née* Schallinger; *b* 12 Jan 1950; *Educ* Queen's Coll Taunton, Trinity Coll Cambridge (MA), Westminster Hosp London (MB BChir), MD (1995); *m* 7 May 1977, Nicola Rosemary, da of Lt Bonham Ley Bazeley, DSC, of Gatehouse Standish, Stonehouse, Gloucestershire; 2 s (Thomas b 1981, Henry b 1986), 1 da (Emily b 1983); *Career* paediatric intern McMaster Univ Ontario 1974, jr positions Westminster Hosp and UCH 1974–78, GP Queensland Australia 1978, WHO studentship in acupuncture Nanjing Coll of Traditional Chinese Med 1978, lectr in general practice (initially trainee) Dept of Gen Practice Univ of Southampton 1979–82, co-dir Centre for the Study of Complementary Med 1982–, hon sr lectr Dept of Med Univ of Southampton; author of numerous learned books and articles, ed Complementary Therapies in Med; formerly vice chm Br Med Acupuncture Soc, memb numerous med orgns and ctees; MRCP 1977, MRCGP 1980; *Recreations* swimming, skiing, sailing, antique collecting, bee keeping, theatre; *Clubs* Royal Lymington Yacht, RSM; *Style*— Dr George Lewith; ✉ Swaywood House, Mead End Road, Sway, Lymington, Hampshire SO41 6EE (☎ 01590 682129); Centre for the Study of Complementary Medicine, 51 Bedford Place, Southampton, Hampshire SO1 2DG (☎ 01703 334752, fax 01703 702459)

LEWTHWAITE, Brig Sir Rainald Gilfrid; 4 Bt (UK 1927), of Broadgate, Parish of Thwaites, Co Cumberland; CVO (1975), OBE (1974), MC (1943); s of Sir William Lewthwaite, 2 Bt, JP (d 1933); suc bro, Sir William Anthony Lewthwaite, 3 Bt (d 1993); *b* 21 July 1913; *Educ* Rugby, Trinity Coll Cambridge; *m* 1936, Margaret Elizabeth, MBE (d 1990), da of Harry Edmonds (d 1982), of NY; 1 s (1 s decd), 2 da (both decd); *Heir* s, David Rainald Lewthwaite b 1940; *Career* cmmnd Scot Gds 1934, 1939–45 served ME and NW Europe, Brig mil attaché 1964 and def attaché Br Embassy Paris 1964–68, Cabinet Office 1952–55, NATO HQ Paris 1961–64, ret 1968; dir Protocol Hong Kong 1969–76; *Recreations* country life; *Style*— Brig Sir Rainald Lewthwaite, Bt, CVO, OBE, MC; ✉ Broadgate, Millom, Cumbria LA18 5JY

LEWTY, (David) Ian; s of Harry Lewty, of Garland, Texas, and late Ruby, *née* Buck; *b* 27 July 1943; *Educ* Lancing, Magdalen Coll Oxford (MA); *m* 25 Feb 1968, Mary, da of late George James Crombie Law; 2 da (Emma Mary Raffan b 7 June 1969, Claire Louise b 24 Dec 1970); *Career* HM Dip Serv: third sec FO 1965–66, MECAS Lebanon 1966–67, third then second sec Ottawa 1967–71, second sec and head of British Interests Section Royal Swedish Embassy Baghdad 1971–72, first sec FCO 1972–76, Jedda 1976–79, L'Ecole Nationale D'Administration Paris 1979–80, UK Delgn OECD Paris 1980–83, FCO 1984–87, cnsllr and consul-gen Khartoum 1987–89, inspr Diplomatic Serv 1989–92, head of Migration and Visa Dept FCO 1992–95, ambass Bahrain 1996–; *Style*— Ian Lewty, Esq; ✉ c/o Foreign and Commonwealth Office (Bahrain), King Charles Street, London SW1A 2AH

LEY, Philip Edward Francis; s of Francis James Ley, of Abingdon, Oxon, and Alexandrina, *née* Moonie (d 1993); *b* 16 July 1960; *Educ* Ampleforth Coll, Univ of Oxford (MA); *m* Feb 1994, Anna Elizabeth, da of David Tate; *Career* Unilever 1982–86: UCMDS trainee Lipton Export Ltd, brand mangr Lipton Yellow Label Tea ME and Scandinavia; Marketing Solutions 1986–87, Trowbridge Ley Partnership specialising in interior design in USA and men's clothing shops in UK 1987–89; Virgin Mastertronic/Sega Europe 1989–94: mktg mangr Sega Products until 1991, mktg dir UK (when Sega bought Virgin Mastertronic) 1991–93, Euro mktg dir 1993–94; mktg dir BSkyB 1994–96, fndr Branded communications agency 1996; Mktg Soc Marketeer of the Yr 1993; memb Mktg Soc 1994; *Recreations* swimming, football, drumming, Manchester Utd supporter; *Clubs* The House (Soho); *Style*— Philip Ley, Esq

LEY, Prof Steven Victor; *b* 10 Dec 1945; *Educ* Univ of Loughborough (BSc, DIS, PhD), Univ of London (DSc); *m*; 1 c; *Career* post doctoral fell Ohio State Univ 1972–74; Imperial Coll London: post doctoral fell 1974–75, probationary lectr 1975–76, lectr 1976–83, prof of organic chemistry 1983–92, head of Dept 1989–92; BP (1702) prof of organic chemistry Univ of Cambridge 1992–, fell Trinity Coll Cambridge 1993–; chm Exec Ctee Ciba Fndn 1993– (memb 1990–); memb: Standing Panel of Experts in Chemistry Univ of London 1993–96, Newly Appointed Lectrs Grant Ctee Nuffield Fndn 1986–; author of over 290 res papers and articles; Royal Soc of Chemistry: Corday Morgan medal and prize for 1980 1982, Tilden lectr and medal 1988, 1989 award for organic synthesis 1990, Pedler lectr, medal and prize 1992, Simonsen lectr and medal 1993–94, 1992 natural products award 1994, pres Perkin Div Royal Soc of Chemistry 1993–96 (memb 1989–96), Flintoff medal 1996; Pfizer academic award 1983, Dr Paul George Kenner prize and lectr Univ of Liverpool 1996, Janssen prize for creativity in organic synthesis Belgium 1996; Hon DSc Loughborough; memb: American Chemical Soc, Chemical Soc of Japan, Soc of Chemical Industry (London), Swiss Chemical Soc, Royal Inst London, American Assoc for the Advancement of Science, Int Soc of Heterocyclic Chemistry; CChem 1980, FRSC 1980, FRS 1990, fell Japanese Soc for the Promotion of Science 1993; *Style*— Prof Steven Ley, FRS; ✉ University Chemical Laboratory, Lensfield Road, Cambridge CB2 1EW (☎ 01223 336398, fax 01223 336442, e-mail svl1000@cam.ac.uk)

LEYSHON, Robert Lloyd; s of Sqdn Ldr Mervyn Leyshon, of Pencoed, Bridgend, Mid Glamorgan, and Joan Hilton, *née* Lloyd (d 1950); *b* 12 Feb 1948; *Educ* Ogmore Vale GS, St Mary's Hosp (BSc, MB BS); *m* 16 July 1977, Catherine (Kay), da of Luther Edwards (d 1984); 1 s (Aled Lloyd b 18 Nov 1978), 1 da ((Catherine) Nia b 23 Feb 1980); *Career* house surgn and casualty offr St Mary's Hosp 1972–74, rotating surgical registrar Cardiff Hosp 1974–77, sr orthopaedic registrar Cardiff and Swansea Hosp 1979–83, sr lectr in orthopaedic surgery Welsh Sch of Med 1983–84, conslt orthopaedic surgn Morriston Hosp Swansea 1984–; author of papers on the use of carbon fibre as ligament replacement, research into post menopausal osteoporosis and reviews of hip prostheses in fractures of femoral neck; hon orthopaedic surgn Llanelli RFC and Welsh National rugby squad; FRCS 1977, fell Br Orthopaedic Assoc 1983; *Recreations* skiing, cricket, tennis, golf; *Clubs* Clyne Golf; *Style*— Robert Leyshon, Esq; ✉ 19 Westport Ave, Mayals, Swansea SA3 5EA (☎ 01792 403003); St David's House, 1 Uplands Terrace, Swansea SA2 0GU (☎ 01792 472922, fax 01792 466803); Orthopaedic Department, Morriston Hospital, Swansea SA6 6NL (☎ 01792 703450)

LIANG, Prof (Wei) Yao; s of Tien Fu Liang, of Hong Kong, and Po Seng Nio, *née* Lie; *b* 23 Sept 1940; *Educ* Pah Chung Chinese HS Jakarta Indonesia, Portsmouth Coll of Technol, Imperial Coll London (BSc, ARCS), Univ of Cambridge (PhD); *m* 17 Aug 1968, Lian Choo, da of Choong Sam; 3 da (Yifan b 12 Feb 1973, Chiafan b 7 July 1977, Hweifan b 10 April 1979); *Career* Univ of Cambridge: demonstrator in physics 1971–75, lectr in physics 1975–92, reader in high temperature superconductivity 1992–93, prof of superconductivity 1994–, dir Interdisciplinary Research Centre 1989– (co-dir 1988–89); Gonville and Caius Coll Cambridge: research fell 1968–71, official fell and lectr 1971–, dir of studies in natural sciences 1975–89, professorial fell 1994–; visiting scientist Xerox Palo Alto Research Centre California (1975 and 1976); visiting prof: EPF Lausanne 1978, Acad Sinica Inst of Semiconductors Beijing 1983; *Books* Polarons and Bipolarons in High Temperature Superconductors and Related Compounds (ed with A S Alexandrov and E K H Salje, 1995); *Recreations* music, conversation, photography; *Style*— Prof Yao Liang; ✉ Interdisciplinary Research Centre in Superconductivity, Madingley Road, Cambridge, Cambridgeshire CB3 0HE (☎ 01223 337077, fax 01223 337074)

LIAO, Donald Poon-Huai; CBE; *Career* architect; former chm Hong Kong Housing Authy, former Hong Kong Govt sec for District Admin and for Home Affrs; non-exec dir: HSBC Holdings plc and HongkongBank Ltd 1990–95, The Morgan Crucible Co plc; memb Cncl Stock Exchange of Hong Kong Ltd; *Style*— D P H Liao, Esq, CBE; ✉ The Morgan Crucible Co plc, Morgan House, Medeira Walk, Windsor SL4 1EP (☎ 01753 837000, fax 01753 850872)

LIBBY, Dr Donald Gerald; s of Herbert Lionel Libby (d 1958), and Minnie, *née* Green (d 1986); *b* 2 July 1934; *Educ* RMA Sandhurst, Univ of London (BSc, PhD); *m* 1, 13 May 1961, Margaret Elizabeth Dunlop (d 1979), da of John Kennedy Dunlop McLatchie; 1 da (Fiona b 1966); m 2, 26 March 1982, June, da of Collin George Belcher, of Newmarket, Suffolk; *Career* Dept of Educn and Science: princ scientific offr 1967–72, princ 1972–74, asst sec 1974–80, asst under sec of state Planning and Int Rels Branch 1980–82, Architects Bldg and Schs Branch 1982–86, Further and Higher Educn Branch 1986–91; Cabinet Office 1991–94: asst under sec of state Office of Sci and Technol, sec Advsy Bd for the Research Cncls; advsr Logica UK Ltd 1995–; memb New York Acad of Sciences; CEng, FIEE, FRSA; *Recreations* music, rowing, golf; *Style*— Dr Donald Libby; ✉ Lygon Cottage, 26 Wayneflete Tower Ave, Esher, Surrey KT10 8QG

LIBOCK MBEI, HE Samuel; *b* 4 Oct 1940; *Educ* BA (Political Sci and Economics) USA; *m* Hermine Libock; 4 c; *Career* Cameroon diplomat; advsr Presidency of Cameroon 1970–80, gen mangr nat oil co and chm Bd of Dirs nat refinery Cameroon 1980–84, min and chief of cabinet of the Pres of Cameroon 1986–89, Cameroon ambass Nigeria 1989–94, Cameroon high cmmr to the Ct of St James's Nov 1995– (ambass April-Nov 1995); many nat and foreign decorations; memb Rotary Int London; *Recreations* golf, theatre, cinema; *Clubs* Highgate Golf, Yaoundé Golf (Cameroon); *Style*— HE Mr Samuel Libock Mbei; ✉ High Commission for the Republic of Cameroon, 84 Holland Park, London W11 3SB (☎ 0171 727 0771, fax 0171 792 9353)

LICHFIELD, Archdeacon of; *see:* Ninis, Ven Richard Betts

LICHFIELD, Dean of; *see:* Wright, Very Rev Dr (Nicholas) Thomas (Tom)

LICHFIELD, 97 Bishop of, 1984–; Rt Rev Keith Norman Sutton; the see of Lichfield was founded by Oswy, King of Mercia in 656; in 1075 it was removed to Chester, in 1102 to Coventry, and finally to its original foundation at Lichfield; patron of one hundred and thirty-four livings, the canonries and prebends in his cathedral and the archdeaconries of Lichfield, Salop and Stoke-upon-Trent; s of Norman and Irene Sutton; *b* 23 June 1934; *m* 1963, Edith Mary Jean Geldard; 3 s, 1 da; *Career* curate St Andrew's Plymouth 1959–62, chaplain St John's Coll Cambridge 1962–67, tutor and chaplain Bishop Tucker Coll Mukono Uganda 1968–73, princ Ridley Hall Cambridge 1973–78, bishop of Kingston-upon-Thames 1978–83, select preacher Univ of Cambridge 1987; admitted House of Lords 1989; chm: Bd of Govrs Queen's Coll Birmingham 1987–94, Bd of Mission and Unity of the Gen Synod 1989–91, Bd of Mission of the Gen Synod 1991–94; memb governing body Derby Univ; Bishop's visitor Uganda RC Bishops Conf; Episcopal visitor Simon of Cyrene Theological Inst 1991–; Hon DUniv Univ of Keele 1992, Hon DLitt Univ of Wolverhampton 1994; *Books* The People of God (1982); author of various articles in The Times, The Guardian and the church press; *Recreations* Russian literature, baroque music, walking, travel in France and Africa; *Style*— The Rt Rev the Bishop of Lichfield; ✉ Bishop's House, The Close, Lichfield, Staffs WS13 7LG (☎ 01543 262251, fax 01543 415801)

LICHFIELD, 5 Earl of (UK 1831); (Thomas) Patrick John Anson; DL (Staffs 1996); also Viscount Anson and Baron Soberton (both UK 1806); s of Lt-Col Viscount Anson (d 1958, s and h of 4 Earl, whom he predeceased) by his 1 w Anne Ferelith Fenella (d 1980, having m 1950 HH Prince Georg of Denmark, CVO, who d 1986), da of Hon John Bowes-Lyon (s of 14 Earl of Strathmore and bro of HM Queen Elizabeth The Queen Mother); suc gf 1960; *b* 25 April 1939; *Educ* Harrow, RMA Sandhurst; *m* 1975 (m dis 1986), Lady Leonora Mary Grosvenor, LVO (1997), da of 5 Duke of Westminster, TD, and sis of former Duchess of Roxburghe; 1 s, 2 da (Lady Rose Meriel Margaret b 1976, Lady Eloise Anne Elizabeth b 1981); *Heir* s, Viscount Anson, *qv*; *Career* served in Grenadier Gds 1959–62 (Lt); photographer; FRPS, FBIPP; *Books* The Most Beautiful Women (1981), Lichfield on Photography (1981), A Royal Album (1986), Lichfield on Travel Photography (1986), Not The Whole Truth (autobiography, 1986), Unipart Calendar Books (1985), Creating the Unipart Calendar (1983), Hotfoot to Zabriskie Point (1985), Lichfield in Retrospect (1988), Courvoisier Book of the Best (ed); *Recreations* arboriculture; *Clubs* White's; *Style*— The Rt Hon the Earl of Lichfield, DL; ✉ Shugborough Hall, Stafford (☎ 01889 881454); studio: 133 Oxford Gardens, London W10 6NE (☎ 0181 969 6161, fax 0181 960 6494)

LICHT, Leonard Samuel; s of Bernhard Licht (d 1982), and Hilde Licht; *b* 15 March 1945; *Educ* Christ's Coll Finchley; *m* 1973, Judith, da of Albert Grossman (d 1980); 1 s (Rupert b 27 July 1974), 1 da (Marina b 19 April 1976); *Career* investmt banker; dir S G Warburg & Co Ltd 1982–85, vice chm and dir Mercury Asset Management Group plc 1985–92, chm Channel Islands and International Investment Trust Ltd 1988–92, chm Beneficial Arts UK Ltd 1989–, dep chief exec and chief investment offr Jupiter International Group PLC 1992–96, dep chm Jupiter Asset Management Ltd 1992–96;

non-exec Royal Free Hosp NHS Trust 1991–, special tstee Royal Free Hosp; *Recreations* tennis, English eighteenth century pottery, restaurants; *Clubs* Brooks's, MCC; *Style*— Leonard Licht, Esq; ✉ c/o St George's Securities Ltd, 25 Queen Anne Street, London W1M 9FB

LICKISS, Sir Michael Gillam; kt (1993); s of Frank Gillam, and Elaine Rheta, *née* Lefeuvre; *b* 18 Feb 1934; *Educ* Bournemouth GS, LSE, Univ of London (BSc); *m* 1, 1959 (m dis 1979), Anita; 2 s, 2 da; m 2, 1987, Anne; 1 s; *Career* articled clerk Bournemouth 1955–58, cmmnd Army 1959–62, CA in practice Bournemouth 1962–68; Grant Thornton (formerly Thornton Baker): Bournemouth office 1968–73, London office 1973–94, exec ptnr 1975–85, nat managing ptnr 1985–89, sr ptnr 1989–94; chm Accountancy Television Ltd 1992–94; non-exec dir United News and Media plc 1996–, chm/dir various smaller companies; DTI inspr (jtly with Hugh Carlisle, QC) 1986–88; lectr UK and overseas, author of numerous articles in learned jls; fndr pres Assoc of Accounting Technicians 1980–82; ICAEW: memb Cncl 1971–81 and 1983–94, pres 1990–91; chm: Somerset Economic Partnership 1993, BTEC 1994–, W of England Devpt Agency 1994–; memb: Cncl FEFC 1992–, Ct of Govrs LSE 1993–, Senate Engrg Cncl; Liveryman Worshipful Co of Chartered Accountants; FCA; *Recreations* walking in Lake District, gardening in Somerset; *Clubs* RAC; *Style*— Sir Michael Lickiss; ✉ 4B Devonshire Mews North, London W1N 1FR

LICKLEY, Sir Robert Lang; kt (1984), CBE (1973); *b* 19 Jan 1912; *Educ* Dundee HS, Univ of Edinburgh, Imperial Coll London (fell 1973); *Career* chief project engr Hawker Aircraft Design Office 1940–46 (joined 1933), prof of aircraft design Coll of Aeronautics Cranfield 1946–51, md Fairey Aviation Ltd 1959–60, dir Hawker Siddeley Aviation Ltd 1960–76 (asst md 1965–76), head of Rolls Royce support staff NEB 1976–79, non-exec dir Fairey Co 1979–85; Hon: MSME, FIMechE; pres: IMechE 1971, IProdE 1981; Hon DSc: Univ of Edinburgh 1973, Univ of Strathclyde 1986; FRSE 1977, FEng 1977, FRAeS, FIEE; *Style*— Sir Robert Lickley, CBE, FRSE, FEng; ✉ Moorfields, Midway, Walton-on-Thames, Surrey KT12 3HY

LICKORISH, Adrian Derick; s of Leonard John Lickorish, CBE, *qv*, and Maris, *née* Wright; *b* 29 Oct 1948; *Educ* Highgate Sch, Univ of London (LLB, LLM); *m* 16 May 1987, Vivien Mary, da of John Bernard Gould, of Wirswall Hall, Whitchurch, Shrops; *Career* slr 1974; ptnr: Durrant Piesse 1981, Lovell White Durrant 1988–; memb Law Soc, Liveryman City of London Solicitors' Co; *Recreations* farming, shooting, fishing, military history; *Clubs* Royal Over-Seas League; *Style*— Adrian Lickorish, Esq; ✉ Woodhouse Farm, Avening, Gloucestershire GL8 8NH; Lovell White Durrant, 65 Holborn Viaduct, London (☎ 0171 236 0066)

LICKORISH, Leonard John; CBE (1975); s of Adrian Joseph Lickorish (d 1957), and Josephine, *née* Rose (d 1953); *b* 10 Aug 1921; *Educ* St George's Coll Weybridge, UCL (BA); *m* 1945, Eileen Maris (d 1983); 1 s (Adrian Lickorish, *qv*); *Career* serv WWII RAF Flt Lt 1941–46; gen mangr Br Travel Assoc 1963–69, dir gen Br Tourist Authy 1970–86; chm Euro Travel Cmmn 1984–86, hon vice chm Euro Travel Cmmn and sec Euro Tourism Action Gp 1987, visiting prof Univ of Strathclyde 1989, vice pres Exhibition Indust Fedn 1989; Liveryman Worshipful Co of Marketors; Order of the Crown of Belgium 1967; *Books* The Travel Trade (1958), Reviews of UK Statistical Sources Tourism (1975), Marketing Tourism (1989), Developing Tourism Destinations (1991); numerous int pubns; *Recreations* gardening, sailing, walking; *Clubs* Royal Overseas League; *Style*— Leonard Lickorish, Esq, CBE; ✉ 46 Hillway, London N6 6EP (☎ 0181 340 8920)

LIDDELL, Alasdair Donald MacDuff; s of Ian Donald Macduff Liddell, WS (d 1976), and Barbara Macduff; *b* 15 Jan 1949; *Educ* Fettes Coll Edinburgh, Balliol Coll Oxford (BA), Thames Poly (DMS); *m* 20 Feb 1976, Jenny Abramsky, *qv*; 1 s (Rob b 22 Feb 1977), 1 da (Maia b 11 Dec 1979); *Career* admin (Planning and Policies) Tower Hamlets Dist 1977–79, area gen admin Kensington and Chelsea and Westminister AHA 1979–82, dist admin Hammersmith and Fulham Health Authy 1984–85, dist gen mangr Bloomsbury Health Authy 1985–88, regnl gen mangr E Anglian RHA 1988–94, dir of planning NHS Executive 1994–; *Recreations* skiing, personal computers, buying wine; *Clubs* Royal Soc of Medicine; *Style*— Alasdair Liddell, Esq; ✉ Room 4W34, Quarry House, Quarry Hill, Leeds LS2 7UE (☎ 0113 254 5807)

LIDDELL, (Andrew) Colin MacDuff; WS (1980); s of Ian Donald MacDuff Liddell, WS (d 1976), and Barbara, *née* Dixon; descendent of MacDuffs of Strathbraan, Perthshire; *b* 21 June 1954; *Educ* Cargilfield Sch Edinburgh, Fettes, Balliol Coll Oxford (BA), Univ of Edinburgh (LLB); *m* 11 Aug 1979, Katrina Louise, da of Dr Kenneth Terence Gruer, MC, of Edinburgh; 2 da (Iona Michelle b 1983, Bryony Marsali b 1985); *Career* slr; ptnr Messrs J & H Mitchell WS Pitlochry and Aberfeldy 1981–; sr pres Speculative Soc of Edinburgh 1983–84, sec Highland Perthshire Development Co Ltd 1985–; govr Cargifield Sch Edinburgh 1985–93 (vice chm 1987–93), tstee Clan Donnachaidh Museum 1992–, chm Pitlochry and District Tourism Mgmnt Prog 1994–; *Publications* Pitlochry - Heritage of a Highland District (1993, 2 edn 1994); *Recreations* skiing, windsurfing, writing, hill walking, curling; *Style*— Colin Liddell, Esq, WS; ✉ Messrs J & H Mitchell WS, 51 Atholl Rd, Pitlochry PH16 5BU (☎ 01796 472606, fax 01796 473198)

LIDDELL, Helen Lawrie; MP (Lab) Monklands East (majority 1,640); da of Hugh Reilly, of Coatbridge, Lanarkshire, and Bridget, *née* Lawrie (decd); *b* 6 Dec 1950; *Educ* Univ of Strathclyde (BA); *m* 22 July 1972, Dr Alistair Henderson, s of Robert Liddell, of Airdrie, Lanarkshire; 1 s (Paul b 1979), 1 da (Clare b 1985); *Career* head Econ Dept Scot TUC 1971–75 (asst sec 1975–76), economics corr BBC Scotland 1976–77, Scottish sec Lab Pty 1977–88, dir of public and corp affrs Scottish Daily Record and Sunday Mail Ltd 1988–92, chief exec Business Venture Prog 1993–94; Parly candidate (Lab) E Fife 1974, MP (Lab) Monklands E 1994–; non-exec dir: Scottish Prison Bd 1992–94, Central Scotland Bdcasting Ltd 1993–94; memb Nat Jt Cncl for Academic Salaries and Awards 1974–76, Cabinet rep Int Women's Year Ctee 1975, chair UN 50th Anniversary Ctee Scotland 1994–95; *Books* Elite (1990); *Recreations* writing, walking; *Style*— Mrs Helen Liddell, MP; ✉ House of Commons, London SW1A 0AA

LIDDELL, Mark Charles; s of Peter John Liddell, DSC (d 1979), of Moorhouse Hall, Carlisle, Cumbria, and Priscilla, *née* Downes; *b* 19 Sept 1954; *Educ* Ampleforth; *m* 21 July 1979, Hon Lucy Katherine, da of 6 Viscount Knutsford, *qv*; 1 s (James b 23 Jan 1987), 2 da (Katherine b 4 June 1983, Sophie b 24 June 1990); *Career* Lloyd's broker 1974–81; dir: Lycetts (Cumbria) Ltd 1981–87, Lycetts (Insurance Brokers) Ltd 1987–, Lycetts (Financial Services) Ltd 1987–; *Recreations* shooting, cricket, classic cars; *Clubs* White's, Northern Counties; *Style*— Mark Liddell, Esq; ✉ Cumrew House, Cumrew, Carlisle, Cumbria CA4 9DD (☎ 01768 896619, fax 01768 896472); Lycetts, Milburn House, Dean St, Newcastle upon Tyne NE1 1PP (☎ 0191 232 1151, fax 0191 232 1873)

LIDDELL, Hon Thomas Arthur Hamish; s and h of 8 Baron Ravensworth, *qv*; *b* 27 Oct 1954; *Educ* Gordonstoun, RAC Cirencester; *m* 18 June 1983, Linda, da of Henry Thompson (d 1986), of Hawthorn Farm, Gosforth, Newcastle-upon-Tyne; 1 s (Henry Arthur Thomas b 27 Nov 1987), 1 da (Alice Lorina b 24 April 1986); *Career* branch chm local NFU and other ctees Northumberland NFU 1989–90; memb ctee Northumberland CLA 1990–; *Recreations* shooting; *Style*— The Hon Thomas Liddell; ✉ Mountain, Whittingham, Alnwick, Northumberland NE66 4UR (☎ 01665 74239, car 0836 359861)

LIDDELL-GRAINGER, David Ian; Baron of Ayton (territorial); s of Capt Henry H Liddell-Grainger, JP, DL (d 1935), of Ayton Castle, Berwickshire, and Lady Muriel Felicia Vere, *née* Bertie (d 1981), da of 12 Earl of Lindsey; *b* 26 Jan 1930; *Educ* St Peter's Coll Adelaide SA, Eton, Univ of London; *m* 14 Dec 1957 (m dis 1982), Anne Mary Sibylla, er da of Col Sir Henry Abel Smith, KCMG, KCVO, DSO, DL (d 1993), of Barton Lodge, Windsor, Berks, and Lady May Cambridge, da of 1 Earl of Athlone and HRH Princess Alice, gda of Queen Victoria through the Queen's 4 s, the Duke of Albany; 4 s (Ian Richard Peregrine b 1959, Charles Montague b 1960, Simon Rupert b 1962, Malcolm Henry b 1967), 1 da (Alice Mary b 1964); issue by Christine, Lady de la Rue; 2 s (David Henry b 1983, Maximilian b 1985); *Career* Scots Gds 1948–50; farmer; Co cncllr 1958–73; has served on Scottish Gas Cncl and cncls of: RNLI, Scot Scout Assoc, Nat Tst for Scot, Royal Agric Soc of England, Scot Landowners Fedn; dep chm Timber Growers UK 1985–88, memb Regnl Advsy Ctee Forestry Cmmn, area cmmr for Scouts in Borders, tstee Shackleton Preservation Tst, pres Berwick-on-Tweed Wildlife Tst; DL (1962–85); Hospitaller Order of St John (Scot) 1977–82, KStJ 1974; Grand Master Mason of Scot 1969–74, memb Queen's Body Guard for Scotland (Royal Co of Archers) 1955–83; FSA (Scot); *Recreations* flying, model engineering, history; *Clubs* New (Edinburgh), MCC; *Style*— David Liddell-Grainger of Ayton; ✉ Ayton Castle, Berwickshire TD14 5RD (☎ 018907 81212, fax 018907 81550)

LIDDERDALE, Sir David William Shuckburgh; KCB (1975, CB 1963), TD; s of late Edward Wadsworth Lidderdale; *b* 30 Sept 1910; *Educ* Winchester, King's Coll Cambridge; *m* 1943, Lola, da of late Rev Thomas Alexander Beckett; 1 s; *Career* served WWII The Rifle Bde (TA), active serv N Africa, Italy; asst clerk House of Commons 1934, Clerk of the House 1974–76; hon vice pres Assoc of Secs-Gen of Parl (Inter-Parly Union); *Publications* The Parliament of France (1951); *Clubs* Travellers', MCC, Pilgrim Soc; *Style*— Sir David Lidderdale, KCB, TD; ✉ 46 Cheyne Walk, London SW3 5LP

LIDDIARD, Michael Richard; s of Richard England Liddiard, CBE (d 1993), of Oxford Lodge, Wimbledon, and Constance Lily, *née* Rook; *b* 15 Nov 1946; *Educ* Oundle, Univ of Exeter (BA), London Business Sch; *m* 14 March 1970, Judith Elizabeth Best, da of Wing Cdr Frederick John Edward Ison, DFC, RAF (d 1978); 1 s (James Stratton b 1973), 1 da (Amanda Brooke b 1975); *Career* C Czarnikow Ltd 1969–92: dir 1981, vice chm 1983; dir C Czarnikow Sugar Ltd 1991–95, exec vice pres C Czarnikow Sugar Inc NY 1995–; dir Lion Mark Holdings 1983–90; memb: Cncl Assoc of Futures Brokers and Dealers 1986–90, London Clearing House Bd 1987–91; govr Haberdashers' Hatcham Coll; Freeman City of London 1970, memb Ct of Assts Worshipful Co Haberdashers 1987 (Liveryman 1971); *Recreations* tennis, shooting; *Clubs* Carlton, Hurlingham, RAC; *Style*— Michael Liddiard, Esq; ✉ C Czarnikow Sugar Inc, Wall Street Plaza, 88 Pine Street, New York, NY 10005, USA (☎ 00 1 212 269 4600, fax 00 1 212 269 9344)

LIDINGTON, Dr David; MP (C) Aylesbury (majority 18,860); s of Roy Lidington, and Rosa Lidington; *b* 30 June 1956; *Educ* Haberdashers' Aske's, Sidney Sussex Coll Cambridge (MA, PhD); *m* 5 Aug 1989, Helen, da of Lt-Col T F Parry; 2 s (Christopher David Parry b 4 June 1993, Thomas Stephen Anders b 21 March 1995); *Career* with BP 1983–86, with RTZ Corporation 1986–87; Parly candidate (C) Vauxhall 1987, special adviser to Rt Hon Douglas Hurd as Home Sec 1987–89 and as Foreign Sec 1989–90, sr conslt Public Policy Unit 1991–92, MP (C) Aylesbury 1992–, PPS to Home Sec 1994–; *Recreations* history, choral singing, reading; *Style*— David Lidington, Esq, MP; ✉ House of Commons, London SW1A 0AA

LIDSTONE, John Barrie Joseph; s of Arthur Richard Francis Lidstone (d 1930), and Lilian May, *née* Teppett (d 1973); *b* 21 July 1929; *Educ* Presentation Coll Reading, Univ of Manchester, RAF Educn Officers' Course; *m* 1957, Primrose Vivien, da of Vincent Russell (d 1947), of Derby; 1 da (b 1960); *Career* Nat Serv RAF 1947–48; English master Repton 1949–52; Shell-Mex and BP and Assoc cos 1952–62, dep md Vicon Agricultural Machinery Ltd 1962–63, dir and gen mangr Marketing Selections Ltd 1969–72; Marketing Improvements Group Plc: joined 1965, dir 1968–, dir and gen mangr 1972–74, dep md 1974–88, dep chm 1988–89, non-exec dir 1989–93; non-exec dir: Kalamazoo Plc 1986–91, North Hampshire Trust Co Ltd 1986–93, St Nicholas' School Fleet Educational Trust Ltd 1982–90 and 1995–96; memb UK Mgmnt Consultancies Assoc 1978–88 (chm 1986–87); sr visiting lectr Univ of Surrey 1990–96; memb: Chemical & Allied Products Indust Trg Bd 1975–79, Nat Inter-Active Video Centre 1988–90; ed Lidstorian 1985–88, marketing ed Pharmaceutical Times 1994–; voted top speaker on mktg in Europe 1974, Dartnell lecture tours USA 1978–82; memb Nat Exec Ctee Chartered Inst of Mktg 1985–90; Freeman City of London, Liveryman Worshipful Co of Marketors, memb Ct of Assts Guild of Mgmnt Consultants 1993; memb BAFTA, FIMC, FIMgt, FInstD, FCIM; *Films and Video* tech advsr and script writer: The Persuaders (EMI 1975), Negotiating Profitable Sales (1979), Training Salesmen on the Job (1981, won highest award for creative excellence at US Industl Film Festival 1982), Marketing for Managers (1985), Marketing Today (1985), Reaching Agreement and Interviewing (1987, 1988); *Books* Training Salesmen on the Job (1975, 2 edn 1986), Recruiting and Selecting Successful Salesmen (1976, 2 edn 1983), Negotiating Profitable Sales (1977, made into two part film by Video Arts 1979), Motivating your Sales Force (1978, 2 edn 1995), Making Effective Presentations (1985), The Sales Presentation (jtly, 1985), Profitable Selling (1986), Marketing Planning for the Pharmaceutical Industry (1987), Manual of Sales Negotiation (1991), Manual of Marketing (for Univ of Surrey, 1991), Beyond the Pay-Packet (1992), Face the Press (1992); contrib chapters to: The Best of Dilemma & Decision (1985), Marketing in the Service Industries (1985), Marketing Handbook (3 edn 1989), Gower Book of Management Skills (2 edn 1992), The Director's Manual (1992 and 1995), The Marketing Book (3 edn 1994), Ivanhoe Guide to Management Consultants (1994), International Encyclopedia of Business and Management (1996); also author of articles contributed to: The Times and Sunday Times, Daily and Sunday Telegraph, Financial Times, Observer, Long Range Planning, International Management, Management Today, Marketing, Marketing Week; *Recreations* writing, cricket, golf (capt N Hants Golf Club 1992–93); *Style*— John B J Lidstone, Esq; ✉ c/o Reform Club, Pall Mall, London SW1Y 5EW

LIEBERMAN, Prof (Alexander) Robert; *b* 7 July 1942; *Educ* UCL (BSc, PhD, DSc); *m* 1 (m dis 1975); 2 s (Gerald b 1963, Nicholas b 1967); m 2, 7 July 1976, Dr Margaret Mary Bird; 2 da (Elizabeth b 1977, Georgina b 1979); *Career* UCL: asst lectr Dept of Anatomy 1965–68, lectr 1968–74, sr lectr 1974–76, reader 1976–87, prof of anatomy Univ of London 1987–, dean Faculty of Life Sciences (biological and medical) 1990–, vice dean University College London Med Sch 1990–; prof of anatomy (neurobiology) Univ of Aarhus Denmark 1983–85; ed-in-chief Jl of Neurocytology 1972–, Euro exec ed Jl of Electron Microscopy 1996–; memb: Scientific Advsy Panel The Brain Res Tst 1991–, Scientific Advsy Bd CNRS/INSERM Unité de Recherches Neurobiologique Marseille 1990–, Sr Advsy Bd Int Jl of Diabetes 1992–, Scientific Ctee R & D Directorate UCL Hosps Tst 1996–; memb Ctee of Mgmnt: Eastman Dental Inst 1995–; memb: BRA, IBRO, ENA, RDA, Soc for Neuroscience, Physio Soc, Anatomical Soc; *Books* contrib: International Review of Neurobiology (1971), Essays On The Nervous System (1974), The Peripheral Nerve (1976), Neuron Concept Today (1976), Local Circuit Neurons (1976), Thalamic Networks for Relay and Modulation (1993), Progress in Neurobiology (1995); *Recreations* cards, backgammon; *Style*— Prof Robert Lieberman; ✉ Department of Anatomy and Developmental Biology, University College London, Gower St, London WC1E 6BT (☎ 0171 387 7050 ext 3357, fax 0171 380 7349)

LIEBERMAN, Dr Stuart; s of Jerome Leon Lieberman, of Miami, Florida, USA, and Libby, *née* Mizus; *b* 4 Oct 1942; *m* 1, 1965 (m dis 1981), Susan Joan Lieberman; 3 s (Samuel, Steven, Simon); m 2, 30 Oct 1986, Sybil Margaret Battersby, da of Joseph Heath, of Wallheath, Wolverhampton; 3 da (Abigail, Gemma, Mel); *Career* Capt USAF 1965–70; hon sr lectr and conslt psychiatrist St George's Hosp Med Sch 1975–92, conslt psychiatrist specialising in psychotherapy Heathlands Mental Health Trust 1992–, conslt-in-charge Eating Disorders Serv Lynbrook Priory Hosp 1995–; fndr memb and treas Inst of Family Therapy London 1976–79, fndr memb and sec Assoc of Family Therapy 1975–78; FRCPsych 1983; *Books* Transgenerational Family Therapy (1 edn 1979, 2 edn 1980); *Style—* Dr Stuart Lieberman; ✉ Lynbrook Priory Hospital, Chobham Road, Knaphill, Woking, Surrey GU21 2QF (☎ 01483 489211)

LIEBERMANN, Frank Alec; s of Alfred H Liebermann, of Iverna Gardens, London, and Ilse, *née* Weisz (d 1991); *b* 13 July 1939, Durban, SA; *Educ* Christian Brothers Coll Cape Town SA, The Neighborhood Playhouse NYC (BA); *m* 1, Jan 1961 (m dis 1965); m 2, 8 Sept 1973, Linda Janice, da of Ian McDougall Marshall; 2 da (Alexis Claire b 15 Dec 1976, Danielle Laura b 11 Sept 1978); *Career* asst stage mangr/actor Hoffmeyer Theatre Cape Town SA 1956, student NYC 1958–60, emigrated to Toronto Canada with various engagements in TV, cinema and theatre 1960–62, emigrated to UK 1962, various employments in TV (starred in own TV series 1965), theatre and cinema, drama teacher The Arts Educnl Tst until 1972; prodr: James Garrett & Partners 1972–75, Brooks Fulford Cramer 1975–77; fndr Thorpe Lieberman Ltd prodn co 1977, prodr BSB Dorland Advertising 1987, dir and head of TV Abbott Mead Vickers BBDO Ltd 1987–; recipient: Gold, Silver and Bronze Awards Cannes Film Festival, Clio Awards (NY), D&AD Awards, Br TV Awards, etc; memb: Equity 1962, ACTT 1974, IPA 1987, D&AD 1988; *Recreations* theatre, cinema, music, reading, travel, food, cooking; *Style—* Frank Liebermann, Esq; ✉ Abbott Mead Vickers BBDO Ltd, 191 Old Marylebone Road, London NW1 5DW (☎ 0171 402 4100, fax 0171 935 5883, car 0850 719557)

LIEBMANN, Dr Stephen James; s of Dr Gehard Liebmann (d 1955), of Aldermaston, and Dora, *née* Badt (d 1989); *b* 4 Sept 1945; *Educ* Reading Sch, Univ of Sheffield (BEng, PhD); *m* 1972, Felicity Anne, da of Geoffrey A E Hodgkinson; 1 s (Nicholas b 11 Jan 1976), 1 da (Charlotte b 22 July 1979); *Career* BBC Radio Sheffield 1966–69 (freelance radio news and feature reporter, prog prodr and editor), journalist Electronics Weekly IPC Business Press 1969–72, Investors Chronicle Throgmorton Pubns 1972–77 (fin journalist, sr memb Editorial and Prodn Team); investmt researcher: J M Finn & Co (stockbrokers) 1977–81, Seymour Pierce & Co (stockbrokers) 1981–83; ptnr i/c private catering business 1983–86, fin conslt 1983–86, gp chief press offr TSB Group plc 1986–87, dir Buchanan Communications Ltd 1987–; *Recreations* sailing; *Style—* Dr Stephen Liebmann; ✉ Buchanan Communications Ltd, 36 St Andrews Hill, London EC4V 5DE (☎ 0171 489 1441, fax 0171 489 1437)

LIESNER, Hans Hubertus; CB (1980); s of Curt Liesner, and Edith, *née* Neumann; *b* 30 March 1929; *Educ* German Schs, Univ of Bristol (BA), Nuffield Coll Oxford (MA); *m* 1968, Thelma; 1 s (Jeremy), 1 da (Raina); *Career* teaching appts 1955–70: LSE, Emmanuel Coll, Univ of Cambridge; under sec HM Treasy 1970–76, chief econ advsr and dep sec DTI 1976–89, dep chm Monopolies and Mergers Cmmn 1989–95 (memb 1995–97); *Recreations* gardening, walking, skiing, cine photography; *Style—* Hans Liesner, Esq, CB; ✉ Monopolies and Mergers Commission, New Court, 48 Carey Street, London WC2A 2JT (☎ 0171 324 1429, fax 0171 324 1400)

LIFFORD, 9 Viscount (I 1781); (Edward) James Wingfield; also Baron Lifford (I 1768); s of 8 Viscount Lifford (d 1987), and (Alison) Mary Patricia, *née* Ashton; *b* 27 Jan 1949; *Educ* Aiglon Coll Switzerland; *m* 1976, Alison, da of Robert Law, of Turnpike House, Withersfield, Suffolk; 1 s (James Thomas Wingfield b 1979), 2 da (Annabel Louise b 1978, Alice Mary b 1990); *Heir* s, James Thomas b 26 Sept 1979; *Career* stockbroker; dir: Rathbone Bros PLC, Winchester Cottage Improvement Society PLC; chm City of Winchester Investments plc; memb Securities Investment Inst; Liveryman Worshipful Co of Armourers and Brasiers; *Recreations* country sports; *Clubs* Boodle's, Pratt's; *Style—* The Rt Hon Viscount Lifford; ✉ Field House, Hursley, nr Winchester, Hants SO21 2LE

LIFFORD, William Lewis (Will); s of George Edward Lifford (d 1993), and Madge Elizabeth, *née* Lewis, of Tunbridge Wells, Kent; *b* 14 Jan 1951; *Educ* Sevenoaks Sch Kent, Univ of Bristol (BSc); *m* 20 Aug 1977, Susanne, da of Stanley Woof; 2 s (David b 18 May 1984, Michael b 24 March 1986); *Career* Deloitte & Co London 1972–79 (qualified CA 1975), Thornton Baker (now Grant Thornton) London 1979–82; Grant Thornton Leeds: ptnr 1982–, head of audit and investigation servs 1991–; memb Urgent Issues Task Force (Accounting Standards) 1994–; FCA 1975; *Recreations* hill walking, photography; *Style—* Will Lifford, Esq; ✉ Grant Thornton, St John's Centre, 110 Albion Street, Leeds LS2 8LA (☎ 0113 245 5514, fax 0113 246 5055, mobile 0585 444114)

LIGENZA-MILDENHALL, Gabriela Maria; da of Tadeusz Ligenza, of Gdynia, Poland, and Gertruda, *née* Szydlowska; *b* 14 May 1959; *Educ* Acad of Fine Arts in Warsaw (MA, UNESCO award); *m* 1, 1978 (m dis), Count Andrzej Borkowski; 1 da (Alicja b 13 Oct 1980); m 2, 1988, Richard Mildenhall; 1 s (Oscar b 8 Nov 1988); *Career* collaboration with Akademia Ruchu visual avant garde theatre in Warsaw and participation in many Euro theatre festivals 1976–83; fndr Gabriela Ligenza (high fashion hat design) 1985–; designed own collections and collaborated with others incl: Missoni, Jasper Conran, Paul Smith, Roland Klein, Laura Ashley, Myrene de Premonville; *Clubs* Chelsea Arts; *Style—* Mrs Gabriela Ligenza-Mildenhall; ✉ c/o Gabriela Ligenza Hats, 291 Brompton Road, London SW3 (☎ 0171 225 1617)

LIGHT, John Vernon; s of Charles Vernon Light (d 1990), and Eva, *née* Blackburn (d 1994); *b* 25 April 1948; *Educ* Sedbergh, Clare Coll Cambridge (MA), Manchester Business Sch (Dip in Business Admin); *m* 1974, Katy, *née* Donald; 1 s (Simon b 1974), 3 da (Jenny b 1975, Anna b 1978, Nicola b 1980); *Career* worked in industry 1969–75, teacher 1975–92, headmaster Oswestry Sch 1992–95, rector Edinburgh Acad 1995–; *Recreations* cricket, squash, golf, mountaineering, acting, choral singing; *Clubs* East India; *Style—* John Light, Esq; ✉ Edinburgh Academy, 42 Henderson Row, Edinburgh EH3 5BL (☎ 0131 556 4603, fax 0131 556 9353)

LIGHTFOOT, Elizabeth (Liz); da of John Richard Lightfoot, of Healing, nr Grimsby, NE Lincolnshire, and Ethne, *née* Stanton; *b* 27 Sept 1950; *Educ* Cleethorpes Girls' GS, Univ of Newcastle (BA), Univ of Durham (MA); *children* 2 s (John Julian, James Stanton (twins) b 6 Dec 1992); *Career* journalist; Hendon Times 1978–81, freelance 1981–83, Parly corr Press Association 1984–86, educn corr Mail on Sunday 1986–92, legal affairs corr Sunday Times 1992–96, educn corr The Daily Telegraph 1996–; *Style—* Ms Liz Lightfoot; ✉ The Daily Telegraph, 1 Canada Square, London E14 5DT (☎ 0171 538 6113)

LIGHTFOOT, James Cecil Emerson; s of George Cecil Lightfoot, of Woodbridge, Suffolk, and Ghetal Angelita, *née* Herschell; *b* 16 Nov 1949; *Educ* Charterhouse, Univ of Oxford; *m* 7 Jan 1977, Hilary Pleydell, da of Robert Cecil Crowhurst, of Newmarket, Suffolk; 2 s (George William b 1980, Harry Robert b 1988), 1 da (Rosalie Pleydell b 1983); *Career* admitted slr, started own practice 1973, currently sr ptnr Lightfoot and O'Brien; memb Cncl The Oxford Soc; *Recreations* sports; *Clubs* United Oxford and Cambridge University, Aldeburgh Golf; *Style—* James Lightfoot, Esq; ✉ Pound Farm, Great Glenham, Saxmundham, Suffolk IP17 2DQ; Lightfoot and O'Brien, 69 The Thoroughfare, Woodbridge, Suffolk IP12 1AH (☎ 013943 6336, fax 01394 380098)

LIGHTFOOT, His Hon Judge; (George) Michael; s of Charles Herbert Lightfoot (d 1941), of Leeds, and Mary, *née* Potter (d 1974); *b* 9 March 1936; *Educ* St Michael's RC Coll Leeds, Exeter Coll Oxford (MA); *m* 20 July 1963, Dorothy, da of Thomas Miller (d 1977), of Rosecroft Farm, Loftus, Cleveland; 2 s (John b 1970, David b 1977), 2 da (Catherine b 1968, Anne b 1973); *Career* Nat Serv 1955–57, York and Lancaster Regt, Intelligence Corps; Exeter Coll Oxford 1957–60, schoolmaster 1962–66; called to Bar Inner Temple 1966, practised NE circuit 1967–86, recorder of the Crown Ct 1985–86, appointed a circuit judge (NE Circuit) 1986–; pres: MENCAP Leeds, Leeds Friends of the Home Farm Tst; *Recreations* cricket and sport in general, reading; *Clubs* Catenian Assoc, City of Leeds Circle; *Style—* His Hon Judge Lightfoot; ✉ Leeds Combined Court Centre, Leeds 1, West Yorkshire LS1 (☎ 0113 283 0040)

LIGHTHILL, Sir (Michael) James; kt (1971); s of Ernest Balzar Lighthill; *b* 23 Jan 1924; *Educ* Winchester, Trinity Coll Cambridge; *m* 1945, Nancy Alice Dumaresq; 1 s, 4 da; *Career* Beyer prof of applied mathematics Univ of Manchester 1950–59, dir RAE 1959–64, res prof Royal Soc 1964–69, Lucasian prof of mathematics Univ of Cambridge 1969–79, provost of UCL 1979–89 (hon res fell 1989–); Gold Medal Inst of Mathematics and Its Applications 1982; *Style—* Sir James Lighthill; ✉ Department of Mathematics, University College London, Gower St, London WC1 (☎ 0181 387 7050, fax 0181 383 5519)

LIGHTMAN, The Hon Mr Justice; Hon Sir Gavin Anthony; kt (1994); *Educ* Univ of London (LLB), Univ of Michigan (LLM); *m* Dr Naomi Lightman; 1 s (Daniel), 2 da (Esther, Sarah); *Career* called to the Bar Lincoln's Inn 1963, QC 1980, bencher Lincoln's Inn 1987, judge of the High Court of Justice (Chancery Div) 1994–; *Style—* The Hon Mr Justice Lightman; ✉ Royal Courts of Justice, The Strand, London WC2A 2LL (☎ 0171 936 6671)

LIGHTMAN, Ivor Harry; CB (1984); s of late Abraham Lightman, OBE, of London, and late Mary Lightman; *b* 23 Aug 1928; *Educ* Abergele Co Sch; *m* 1950, Stella Doris; 1 s (Brian Peter Leon b 1955); *Career* HM Civil Serv: offr Customs & Excise 1949–56, Miny of Works 1957–64, princ HM Treasy 1964–67, asst sec MPBW 1967–70, Civil Serv Dept 1971–73, under sec Price Cmmn 1973–76, Prices and Consumer Protection 1976–78, Dept of Indust 1978–81, dep sec Welsh Office 1981–88, ret; public affairs advsr Touche Ross Management Consultants 1989–91; hon lectr Cardiff Business Sch 1989–95, memb Parole Bd 1990–94; chm: First Choice Housing Assoc 1989–94, All-Wales Advsy Panel on Servs for Mentally Handicapped People 1990–96, Conslt Gp to Contribution Unit on Assembly for Wales 1995–96; *Style—* Ivor Lightman, Esq, CB; ✉ 6 Clos Coed y Dafarn, Lisvane, Cardiff CF4 5ER (☎ 01222 750348)

LIGHTMAN, Prof Stafford Louis; s of Harold Lightman, QC, of Lincoln's Inn, London, and Gwendoline Joan, *née* Ostrer; *b* 7 Sept 1948; *m* 1 May 1977, Susan Louise, da of John Stubbs, of London; 3 s (Sarne Louis b 1978, Joel David b 1979, Leon Alexander b 1982), 1 da (Elewys Gemma b 1987); *Career* prof of clinical neuroendocrinology Charing Cross Hosp London 1988–92, prof of medicine Univ of Bristol 1993–; ed Journal of Neuroendocrinology 1988–96; FRCP; *Books* Neuroendocrinology (ed with B J Everitt, 1986), The Functional Anatomy of the Neuroendocrine Hypothalamus (1992), The Management of Pituitary Tumours: A Handbook (ed with M Powell, 1996), Horizons in Medicine: Vol 7 (ed, 1996); *Style—* Prof Stafford Lightman; ✉ Department of Medicine, University of Bristol, Bristol Royal Infirmary, Bristol BS2 8HW (☎ 0117 928 2871, fax 0117 928 3264)

LIGHTON, Sir Thomas Hamilton; 9 Bt (I 1791), of Merville, Dublin; o s of Sir Christopher Robert Lighton, 8 Bt, MBE (d 1993), and his 2 w, Horatia Edith, *née* Powlett (d 1981); *b* 4 Nov 1954; *Educ* Eton; *m* 1990, Belinda Jean, elder da of John Fergusson, of Castle Douglas, Kirkcudbrightshire; 3 s (James Christopher Hamilton b 20 Oct 1992, Harry John Hamilton b (twin) 20 Oct 1992, Christopher Nicholas Hamilton b 30 Aug 1994, d 25 Nov 1994), 1 da (Celina Hamilton b 26 May 1991); *Heir* s, James Christopher Hamilton Lighton b 20 Oct 1992; *Career* dir Waddington Galleries Ltd, chm Soc of London Art Dealers 1993–95; *Style—* Sir Thomas Lighton, Bt; ✉ c/o Waddington Galleries Ltd, 11 Cork Street, London W1X 1PD

LIJN, Liliane; da of Herman Segall (d 1971), of Geneva, and Helena, *née* Kustanowitz; *b* 22 Dec 1939, NYC; *Educ* Sorbonne Paris, École du Louvre Paris; *m* 1961 (m dis 1970), Takis Vassilakis, s of Athanasios Vassilakis; 1 s (Thanos Vassilakis b 17 April 1962); *partner* Stephen Weiss, s of late Sir Eric Weiss; 1 s (Mischa Weiss-Lijn b 31 May 1975), 1 da (Sheba Weiss-Lijn b 24 Oct 1977); *Career* sculptor, poet and kinetic artist; experimented with fire and acids 1961–62, made and showed first kinetic poems Paris 1963–64, worked using natural forces Athens 1964–66, settled London 1966, numerous cmmns for large public sculptures 1971–; memb Cncl of Mgmnt Byam Shaw Art Sch 1983–90; *Awards* Arts Cncl Award 1976, Alecto Award (Bradford Print Biennale) 1976, Arts Cncl Publishing Award for Crossing Map 1981, Arts Cncl Bursary for holography 1982; *Solo Exhbns* incl: La Librairie Anglaise Paris 1963, Indica Gall London 1967, Germain Gall Paris 1972, Beyond Light Serpentine Gall London 1976, toured Durham LI Museum Durham, Mappin Gall Sheffield and Walker Art Gall Liverpool 1977, Biting Through Alecto Gall London 1977, Circle of Light Eagle Walk Gall Milton Keynes 1980, Roundhouse Gall London 1980, Aberdeen Art Gall Aberdeen 1983, Paton Gall London 1983, Heads Galerie Peter Ludwig Cologne 1985, Imagine the Goddess Fischer Fine Art London 1987, Poem Machines 1962–68 1993 (Nat Arts Library, V & A), Her Mother's Voice (Eagle Gallery London) 1996; *Group Exhbns* incl: Light & Movement Musée d'Art Modern Paris 1967, Kinetic Art Kunstnishus Oslo, Helsinki and Gottenburg 1969 and Hayward Gall London 1970, Agam-Bury-Lijn-Soto-Takis Delson-Richter Galleries Tel Aviv 1973, Art of the Sixties Tate Gall 1976, British Sculpture in the 20th Century Whitechapel Art Gall 1981, Licht-Blicke German Film Mus Frankfurt 1984, 20th Century Drawings & Watercolours V&A 1984, Tecnologia e Informatica Venice Biennale Venice 1986, The Artist's Notebook Galerie Bernard Jordan Paris, Galerie Akiyama Tokyo, Atelier Nishinomiya Nishinomya and Art Works LA Calif 1987, Licht und Transparenz Mus Bellerive Zurich 1988, New Sculpture Gillian Jason Gall London 1990, Chagall to Kitaj - Jewish Experience in 20th Century Art Barbican Art Gall London 1990–, Le Livre Illustre Biblioteque Municipale Besancon 1991, Les Artistes et La Lumiere Le Manege Reims 1991, The Sixties Art Scene in London (Barbican Art Gall) 1993, Art Unlimited (South Bank Centre touring exhibition) 1994, British Abstract Art - Sculpture (Amgela Flowers Gall) 1995, Cabinet Art (Jason and Rhodes) 1995, Livres d'Artistes (Galerie Lara Vincy Paris) 1996, Chimériques Polymères (Musée d'Art Moderne et d'Art Contemporain Nice) 1996; *Public Collections* incl: Tate Gall, Arts Cncl of GB, V&A, Unilever plc, Arthur Andersen & Co, Br Cncl, Contemporary Art Soc London, Glasgow Mus Kelvingrove, Cleveland Educn Ctee, Castle Mus Nottingham, Musée de la Ville de Paris, Robert Mclaughlin Gall Oshawa Ontario, Mus of Modern Art NYC, Chicago Inst, Mus of NSW Sidney Aust, Kunstmuseum Bern; *Publications* incl: Six Throws of the Oracular Keys Paris (poems and drawings, 1982), Crossing Map (autobiographical sci fiction prose poem, 1983), Monument to the French Revolution (with Herman Lelie and Frank Newby, 1987), A Symbolic Structure for the Turn of the Century (1988), Her Mother's Voice (artists' book/oral history, 1996); author of numerous articles for magazines and jls; *Recreations* swimming and gardening; *Style—* Ms Liliane Lijn; ✉ 99 Camden Mews, London NW1 9BU (☎ and fax 0171 485 8524)

LIKIERMAN, Prof (John) Andrew; s of Adolf Likierman (d 1988), and Olga, *née* Heldenbusch (d 1978); *b* 30 Dec 1943; *m* 1987, Meira, da of Joshua Gruenspan; 1 step s (James Thompson b 1979), 1 step da (Ruth Thompson b 1976); *Career* divnl mgmnt accountant Tootal Ltd 1965–68, lectr Dept of Mgmnt Studies Univ of Leeds 1972–74 (asst lectr 1968–69), Qualitex Ltd 1969–72 (md Overseas Div 1971–72), visiting fell Oxford Centre for Mgmnt Studies 1972–74, non-exec chm Ex Libris Ltd 1973–74, non-exec chm Economist's Bookshop Ltd 1987–91 (non-exec dir 1981–91); London

Business Sch 1974–76 and 1979–93: dir Pt/t Masters Prog 1981–85, dir Inst of Public Sector Mgmnt 1983–88, chm Faculty Bd 1986–89, prof of accounting and fin control 1987–93, dean of external affairs 1989–92, ex-officio govr 1990–93 (elected govr 1986–89), dep princ 1990–93; asst sec Cabinet Office and memb Central Policy Review Staff 1976–79 (advsr 1979–82); HM Treasy (on secondment from London Business Sch): head of Govt Accounting Serv and chief accountancy advsr 1993–, dir of fin mgmnt, reporting and audit (princ fin offr) 1994–; advsr House of Commons Select Ctees on: Treasy and Civil Serv 1981–91, Employment 1985–90, Tport 1981 and 1987–90, Social Servs 1988, Social Security 1991; memb Govt Inquiries on: N Sea Cost Escalation 1975, Future of Power Plant Mfrg Indust 1976, Int Comparisons with PO and British Telecom 1981, Monitoring and Control of Nat Industs 1981, Accounting for Econ Costs and Changing Prices 1986, Professional Liability (chm) 1989; memb Editorial Bd Public Money and Management 1988– (chm 1988–93); memb: Fin Ctee Oxfam 1974–84, Ctee on Med Costs Univ of London 1980–81, Current Affairs Advsy Gp Channel 4 1986–87, Academic Advsy Panel Accounting Standards Cte 1987–90 (memb Public Sector Liaison Gp 1984–86), Audit Cmmn 1988–91, Exec Ctee Br Acad of Mgmnt 1988–90, Consultative Ctee of Accountancy Bodies 1989–92, Ctee on Financial Aspects of Corp Governance 1991–95, Auditing Practices Bd 1991–92; memb Cncl: RIPA 1982–88, Consumers' Assoc 1982–85, CIMA 1985–94 (pres 1991–92), Civil Serv Coll 1989–94, Defence Operational Analysis Centre 1992–93; memb Scientific Cncl Euro Inst of Public Admin 1989–92; observer: Accounting Standards Bd 1993–, Fin Reporting Cncl 1994– (memb 1991–94); FCMA, FCCA; *Books* The Reports and Accounts of Nationalised Industries (1979), Cash Limits and External Financing Limits (1981), Public Sector Accounting and Financial Control (jtly, 1983, 4 edn 1992), Structure and Form of Government Expenditure Reports (jtly, 1984, 1985, 1990, 1991 and 1992), Public Expenditure (1988), Accounting for Brands (jtly, 1989), Ethics and Accountants in Industry and Commerce (1990); *Recreations* cycling, tennis, swimming, choral singing, architecture, wine; *Clubs* Reform; *Style*— Prof Andrew Likierman; ✉ 5 Downshire Hill, London NW3 1NR (☎ 0171 435 9888); HM Treasury, Parliament Street, London SW1P 3AG

LILEY, John Garin; s of Warren Stuart Liley, of Wakefield, and Barbara Mary, *née* Gloyne; *b* 21 Aug 1967; *Educ* Eastmoor HS, Wakefield Dist Coll; *m* 26 May 1991, Melanie Jane, *née* Brown; *Career* rugby union full back; clubs: Sandal RUFC 1985–87, Wakefield RFC 1987–88, Leicester FC 1988– (200 appearances, winners Pilkington Cup 1993, winners Courage League Championship 1995, Middx Sevens 1995); rep: Yorks Colts 1985–86, Yorks under 21 1986–88, North of Eng under 21 1988, Yorks 1990–91, Midlands 1991–92 (Dìvnl champions), England B (debut v Namibia 1990); England: debut v Banco Nacion 1990, toured Argentina (replacement in 2 tests) 1990; holder record number of points (447) for Leicester in a season 1995/96; sports attendant 1985–89, trainee accountant Power Thompson CAs 1990–93, accountant Pole Arnold CAs 1993–; MAAT; *Recreations* outdoor activities (sports), photography, travelling; *Style*— John Liley, Esq; ✉ 23 Brook Street, Wymeswold, Leicestershire LE12 6TT (☎ 0116 271 7551, 01509 881175); Leicester FC, Welford Rd, Aylestone Rd, Leicester LE2 7LF (☎ 0116 254 1607)

LILFORD, 7 Baron (GB 1797); George Vernon Powys; s of Robert Horace Powys (d 1940, gggs of 2 Baron Lilford), by his w Vera Grace (d 1989); suc 6 Baron (2 cous twice removed) 1949; *b* 8 Jan 1931; *Educ* St Aidan's Coll Grahamstown SA, Stonyhurst; *m* 1, 1954 (m dis), Mrs Eveline Bird; m 2, 1957 (m dis 1958), Anuta, o da of L F Merritt, of Johannesburg; m 3, 1958 (m dis 1961), Norma Yvonne, o da of V Shell, of Johannesburg; m 4, 1961 (m dis 1969), Mrs Muriel Spottiswoode, *née* Cooke; 2 da (Hon Clare Lynette b 1962, Hon Emma-Jane b 1964); m 5, 1969 (m dis 1991), Margaret, da of Archibald Penman (d 1983), of Roslin, Midlothian; 1 s (Hon Mark Vernon b 1975), 2 da (Hon Sarah Margaret b 1971, Hon Hannah Victoria b 1974); m 6, 1995, Mrs Pamela St Helier Adams; *Heir* s, Hon Mark Vernon Powys b 16 Nov 1975; *Recreations* golf, cricket; *Style*— The Rt Hon the Lord Lilford; ✉ Le Grand Câtelet, St John, Jersey JE3 4EA, CI (☎ and fax 01534 863871)

LILFORD, Prof Richard James; s of Maj Victor Lilford, and Eileen, *née* Gifford; *b* 22 April 1950; *Educ* St John's Coll Johannesburg, PhD, MRCP, MFPHM; *m* 23 May 1981, Victoria Alice Lilford; 1 s (Peter), 2 da (Nicola, Philippa); *Career* formerly conslt obstetrician and gynaecologist Queen Charlottes Hosp London, prof of obstetrics & gynaecology and chm Epidemiology Res Inst Univ of Leeds until 1995, dir of R&D NHS Exec W Midlands 1995–, prof of health servs research Univ of Birmingham 1995–; NHS clinical trials advsr; *Books* Basic Science for Obstetrics and Gynaecology (1984, 3 edn 1989), Prenatal Diagnosis and Prognosis (1990), Computing and Decision Suport in Obstetrics and Gynaecology (1991); *Recreations* flying, tennis; *Style*— Prof Richard Lilford; ✉ Director of R & D, NHS Executive, St Bartholomew House, 142 Hagley Road, Birmingham B16 9PA (☎ 0121 224 4600, fax 0121 220 4601)

LILL, John Richard; OBE (1978); s of G R Lill; *b* 17 March 1944; *Educ* Leyton County HS, Royal Coll of Music; *Career* concert pianist; gave first recital aged nine, London debut playing Beethoven's Emperor (5th) Piano Concerto Royal Festival Hall 1962, first Br pianist to perform complete Beethoven Sonata Cycle (at the Queen Elizabeth Hall 1982, also at the Barbican Hall 1986 and Casals Hall Tokyo 1987); performed with orchs incl: LSO, LPO, CBSO, Royal Liverpool Philharmonic, BBC Welsh and Scottish Symphony Orchs, BBC Symphony, Hallé, Royal Philharmonic, Royal Scottish, Baltimore Symphony, Philadelphia, Cleveland, San Diego Symphony, Boston Symphony, NY Philharmonic, Leipzig Gewandhaus Orch, St Petersburg Philharmonic; worked with conductors incl: Sir Adrian Boult, Sir John Barbirolli, Seiji Ozawa, David Atherton, Eduardo Mata, Simon Rattle, Tadaaki Otaka, Rafael Frühbeck de Burgos, Andrew Davis, Walter Weller, Libor Pesek, Yuri Temirkanov, Kurt Masur; appeared at venues incl: Royal Festival Hall, Queen Elizabeth Hall, Konzerthaus Vienna, Hollywood Bowl, Le Châtalet Paris, Tanglewood, BBC Proms, Cardiff Festival, Swansea Festival; winner Moscow Int Tchaikovsky Competition 1970, adjudicator Van Cliburn Int Piano Competition 1989; *Recordings* incl: Beethoven Piano Concerto Cycle (with Scottish Nat Orch and Sir Alexander Gibson, and with CBSO and Walter Weller), Beethoven Sonata Cycle, Brahms Piano Concertos (with Hallé Orch and James Loughran), Tchaikovsky Piano Concerto No 1 (with LSO and James Judd), Prokofiev Sonatas, Rachmaninov complete works for piano (with BBC Nat Orch of Wales and Tadaaki Otaka); *Recreations* amateur radio, chess, computing; *Style*— John Lill, Esq, OBE; ✉ c/o Harold Holt Ltd, 31 Sinclair Road, London W14 0NS (☎ 0171 603 4600, fax 0171 603 0019, telex 22339 HUNTER)

LILLEY, Prof David Malcolm James; s of Gerald Albert Thomas Lilley, of Colchester, Essex, and Betty Pamela, *née* Dickerson; *b* 28 May 1948; *Educ* Gilberd Sch Colchester, Univ of Durham (BSc, PhD), Univ of London (MSc, E Stickings prize); *m* 1981, Patricia Mary, da of Ronald Biddle; 2 da (Katherine Suzannah b 1982, Sarah Anne b 1985); *Career* res fell Univ of Warwick 1973–75, ICI res fell Univ of Oxford 1975–76, sr res investigator Searle Res Laboratories 1976–81; Univ of Dundee: lectr in biochemistry 1981–84, reader 1984–89, prof of molecular biology 1989–, SERC sr res fell 1991–, dir CRC Nucleic Acid Structure Res Gp 1993–; res fell Royal Soc 1983–90; memb: Biochemical Soc 1974–, Euro Molecular Biology Orgn 1984–; memb Ctee: Br Soc for Cell Biology 1981–83, Tenovus Symposium 1981–83, Nucleic Acids and Molecular Biology Gp 1983–89, Biophysical Soc 1983–86; sec Nucleic Acid Gp 1985–88; Colworth Medal 1982, G J Mendel Gold Medal Czech Acad of Sciences 1994, Prelog Medal for Stereochemistry ETH Zürich 1996; FRSE 1988; *Books* Nucleic Acids and Molecular Biology (jt ed); author of 170 scientific papers; *Recreations* foreign languages; *Style*— Prof David Lilley, FRSE; ✉ CRC Nucleic Acid Structure Research Group, Department of Biochemistry, University of Dundee, Dundee DD1 4HN (☎ 01382 344243, fax 01382 201063)

LILLEY, Prof Geoffrey Michael; OBE (1981); s of Morland Michol Dessau (d 1946), of Ealing, and Emily Lilley (d 1977); *b* 16 Nov 1919; *Educ* Isleworth GS, Imperial Coll London; *m* 18 Dec 1948, Leslie Marion (d 1996), da of Leonard Frank Wheeler (d 1955), of Cranfield, Beds; 1 s (Michael Moreland b 1957), 2 da (Grete Dorothea b 1950, Elisabeth Meta b 1953); *Career* served RAF 1935–36; engrg apprentice 1936–40, asst to chief engr Kodak Ltd 1939–40, Drawing Office, Design, Wind Tunnel and Aerodynamics Dept Vickers Armstrongs Weybridge and Vickers Armstrongs Supermarine Hursley Park 1940–46; lectr then prof of experimental fluid mechanics Coll of Aeronautics 1946–63; prof of aeronautics and astronautics Univ of Southampton 1963–83 (prof emeritus 1983–); visiting prof: Stanford Univ 1977–78, Middle East Tech Univ 1983–89; visiting scientist: ICASE NASA Langley Res Center 1992–93, CTR Stanford Univ 1995; memb: Aeronautical Res Cncl 1957–81, Noise Advsy Cncl (chm Noise from Air Traffic) 1969–81; dir Hampshire Technol Centre 1987–; MIMechE, FRAeS, FIMA; *Books* Complex Turbulent Flows (with S J Kline and B J Cantwell, 1982); *Recreations* hiking, chess, opera; *Clubs* Athenaeum; *Style*— Prof Geoffrey Lilley, OBE; ✉ Highbury, Pine Walk, Chilworth, Southampton SO16 7HQ (☎ 01703 769109); Dept of Aeronautics and Astronautics, University of Southampton, Southampton SO17 1BJ (☎ 01703 594893)

LILLEY, Rt Hon Peter Bruce; PC (1990), MP (C) St Albans (majority 16,404); s of Arnold Francis Lilley, and Lillian, *née* Elliott; *b* 23 Aug 1943; *Educ* Dulwich, Clare Coll Cambridge; *m* 1979, Gail Ansell; *Career* energy industs investmt advsr; Parly candidate (C) Haringey Tottenham Oct 1974, MP (C) St Albans 1983–; chm Bow Group 1973–75, sec Cons Backbench Energy Ctee 1983–84, memb Treasy Select Ctee 1983–84, PPS to Min of State for Local Govt 1984, PPS to Rt Hon Nigel Lawson as Chllr of Exchequer 1985–87, econ sec to the Treasy 1987–89, fin sec to the Treasy 1989–90; sec of state: for Trade and Industry July 1990–92, for Social Security 1992–; FInstPet 1978; *Books* Delusions of Incomes Policy (with Samuel Brittan), Do You Sincerely Want to Win - Defeating Terrorism in Ulster (1972), The End of the Keynesian Era (contrib, ed R Skidelsky, 1980), Thatcherism: The Next Generation (1989), Winning the Welfare Debate (1995); *Style*— The Rt Hon Peter Lilley, MP; ✉ House of Commons, London SW1A 0AA

LILLEYMAN, Prof John Stuart; s of Ernest Lilleyman (d 1992), of Sheffield, and Frances, *née* Johnson; *b* 9 July 1945; *Educ* Oundle, Bart's Med Coll (MB BS, MRCS); *Career* jr med posts Hemel Hempstead and Bart's 1968–70, registrar in haematology Sheffield 1970–72, research fell Cardiff 1972–74, sr registrar Sheffield 1974–75, conslt in haematology Children's Hosp Sheffield 1975–95, Mark Ridgwell chair of paediatric oncology Bart's/ Royal London Med Sch 1995–; first Distinguished Serv Medal RCPath (for establishing UK system of pathology lab accreditation) 1991, personal chair in paediatric haematology Univ of Sheffield (in recognition of research work on childhood leukaemia) 1993; DSc (med) Univ of London 1996; vice pres RCPath 1993–; memb: Br Soc for Haematology 1974, Br Paediatric Assoc 1977; FRCP 1986; *Books* Childhood Leukaemia - the Facts (1994); *Style*— Prof John Lilleyman; ✉ Department of Paediatric Oncology, St Bartholomew's Hospital, West Smithfield, London EC1A 7BE (☎ 0171 601 8381, fax 0171 601 7856)

LILLISTONE, Simon Austin; s of Michael Austin Lillistone, and Jane Elisabeth, *née* Cook, of Grinshill, Shropshire; *b* 13 Feb 1969; *Educ* Meole Brace Secdy Sch, Shrewsbury Sixth Form Coll, Crewe & Alsager Coll of Higher Educn; *Career* cyclist; disciplines: points racing, team pursuit, team time trials; clubs: Mid Shropshire Wheelers 1982–86, Team Haverhill 1987–92, N Wirral Velo 1993–; achievements incl: winner nat jr 30km points race and nat jr 3km pursuit 1987, GB rep Jr World Championships 1987, winner Leon Meredith points race series 1988 and 1989, GB rep Olympic Games Seoul 1988, winner nat amateur 50km points race 1989, 1990, 1991, 1992 and 1993 (setting championship record), GB rep World Championships annually 1989–, winner nat 4km individual pursuit 1990, winner nat club team pursuit (setting championship record) 1990, winner RTTC 100km team time trial 1990, Bronze medal team pursuit Cwlth Games Auckland 1990, winner Welwyn Hatfield Star Trophy 1991, winner nat 4km club team pursuit 1992 (setting championship record), winner 80km Madison Open 1992, winner Girvan 3–day stage race 1992, GB rep Olympic Games Barcelona 1992, winner BCF 100km team time trial 1993, winner RTTC 100km team time trial 1993 (setting championship record), winner nat 4km club team pursuit 1993 (setting championship record), Silver medal team time trial Cwlth Games 1994, 4th 10 mile scratch race Cwlth Games 1994, winner points race and team pursuit Br Nat Championships 1994, team pursuit (setting new Br record) World Championships Bogota Columbia 1995, nat team pursuit champions (new championship record) 1995, team pursuit (setting new Br record) World Championships Manchester 1996; cycling rep on Br Olympic Assoc Competitors Cncl 1991–, rep of BCF Coaching Ctee 1992–94, memb BASS (Br Assoc of Sports Science); mktg trainee Silver Spoon Co; *Recreations* travel, scuba diving, most sports, listening to music; *Style*— Simon Lillistone; ✉ c/o British Cycling Federation, National Cycling Centre, 1 Stuart Street, Manchester M11 4DQ (☎ 0161 230 2301)

LILLY, Prof Malcolm Douglas; s of Charles Victor Lilly (d 1977), and Amy, *née* Gardner (d 1993); *b* 9 Aug 1936; *Educ* St Olave's GS, UCL (BSc, PhD), Univ of London (DSc); *m* 19 Sept 1959, Sheila Elizabeth, da of George Frederick Andrew Stuart (d 1973); 2 s (Andrew Stuart b 14 Nov 1966, Duncan Stuart b 12 May 1968); *Career* RNVR 1953–54, Nat Serv RN 1954–56; dir Whatman Biochemicals 1968–71; UCL: lectr 1963–72, reader 1972–79, prof of biochemical engrg 1979–, fell 1988–, chm Advanced Centre for Biochemical Engrg 1991–; visiting prof Univ of Pennsylvania USA 1969, chm Int Orgn for Biotechnology and Bioengineering 1972–80, memb Cncl Soc of Gen Microbiology 1979–83, memb Br Gas Res Ctee 1982–94, dir Inst of Biotechnology Studies 1983–89, visiting res fell Merck Sharp and Dohme USA 1987, dir Int Inst of Biotechnology 1989–95, memb Biotechnology Jt Advsy Bd 1992–, memb Res Ctee Public Health Lab Serv 1993– (bd memb 1988–94), memb Steering Gp COBIOTECH 1994–; govr St Olave's GS Orpington, observer SE Gp Inst of Advanced Motorists; FIChemE 1980, FEng 1982, FRS 1991; *Books* Fermentation and Enzyme Technology (jtly, 1979); *Recreations* advanced motoring, sailing; *Style*— Prof Malcolm Lilly, FRS, FEng; ✉ Collingwood, 8 Tower Rd, Orpington, Kent BR6 0SQ (☎ 01689 821762); Department of Chemical and Biochemical Engineering, University College London, Torrington Place, London WC1E 7JE (☎ 0171 380 7368, fax 0171 388 0808)

LILLY, Michael Hugh; s of Archibald Hugh Rendall Lilly, of Mount Agar, Carnon Downs, Truro, Cornwall, and Beryl Calenda, *née* Pryor (d 1986); *b* 11 March 1951; *Educ* Hardyes Sch Dorset, Oxford Sch of Architecture (DipArch); *m* 20 Sept 1980, Penelope Sarah Jane, da of Ronald Horace Cranton (d 1993), of Steeple Leaze Farm, Steeple, Dorset; 2 s (James b 1983, Alexander b 1985); *Career* architect; Worshipful Co of Carpenters scholar Philadelphia USA 1978, pt/t design tutor Plymouth Sch of Architecture 1980–83; ptnr: John Crowther & Associates Truro 1983–92, Lilly Lewarne Partnership 1992–; chm Cornwall branch Assoc of Conslt Architects; Freeman City of London, Liveryman Worshipful Co of Carpenters 1982; RIBA 1978; *Recreations* golf, shooting, walking, art; *Style*— Michael Lilly, Esq; ✉ Clifden, Carnon Downs, Truro, Cornwall TR3 6LE

(☎ 01872 863942); Lilly Lewarne Partnership, No 1 Poltisco Wharf, Malpas Road, Truro, Cornwall TR1 1QH (☎ 01872 261000, fax 01872 261001)

LILLYCROP, David Peter; *b* 16 June 1956; *Educ* Univ of Exeter (LLB), Coll of Law London; *m* 1983, Dr Kaye Smith; 2 s (Jonathan b Oct 1985, Christopher b Aug 1988), 1 da (Catherine b Jan 1994); *Career* called to the Bar Middle Temple 1978, legal advsr Mabey & Johnson Ltd 1978–82, gp co sec and legal advsr Mabey Holdings Ltd 1982–85, co sec and legal dir Quaker Oats Ltd 1985–89, gp co sec TI Group plc 1991– (joined 1989); dist cncllr 1979–83; memb Cncl and Mgmnt Ctee Indust and Parliament Tst; memb Int Bar Assoc, FIMgt; *Clubs* Halton Village Lawn Tennis; *Style*— David Lillycrop, Esq; ✉ TI Group plc, Lambourn Court, Abingdon, Oxon OX14 1UH (☎ 01235 540133, fax 01235 554216, mobile 0850 602946)

LIM, Dr Frederick Thomas Keng Sim; s of late Khye Seng Lim, OBE, of Penang, Malaysia, and late Lian Hioh, *née* Goh; *b* 19 April 1947; *Educ* Radley, Middx Hosp London (MB BS); *m* July 1971, Catherine Mary; *Career* Middx Hosp: house surgn 1971, registrar 1974, sr registrar 1977–78; house physician QEII Hosp Welwyn Garden City 1972, sr house offr Lister Hosp 1973, sr registrar Charing Cross Hosp 1975; conslt physician in: genito-urinary med King's Coll Hosp 1979–86, med advsr Elite Premier Model Agency, private practice 1986–; memb: Hampstead Med Soc, Independent Doctors' Forum, MSSVD; MRCP 1974; *Books* Textbook of Genito-Urinary Surgery (jtly, 1985); *Recreations* tennis, music, antiques, travel; *Style*— Dr Frederick Lim; ✉ 26 Devonshire Place, London W1N 1PD (☎ 0171 487 3529, fax 0171 224 1784)

LIM, Kim; *b* 16 Feb 1936; *Educ* St Martins Sch of Art, Slade Sch of Art, Univ Coll London (Dip Fine Art); *m* William Turnbull; 2 s (Alexander b 26 July 1962, Jonathan 29 July 1963); *Career* artist; *Exhibitions* solo: Axiom Gallery 1966 and 1968, Waddington Galleries 1973 and 1990, Alpha Gallery Singapore 1974, Museum of Modern Art Oxford 1975, Experimental Series (Felicity Samuel Gallery) 1975, Temporary Print Exhibition (Tate) 1977, Roundhouse Gallery 1979, Southampton Museum & Art Gallery 1981, Nicola Jacobs Gallery 1982, Arcade Gallery Harrogate 1983, Prints & Drawings 1972–80 (Nicola Jacobs Gallery) London 1984, Nat Museum of Art Singapore 1984, Nicola Jacobs Gallery 1985, Waddington Galleries London 1990, Flowers Graphics London 1993, The Orangery Roche Ct Wilts 1993, Bothy Gallery Yorkshire Sculpture Park 1995; selected group: 26 Young Sculptors (ICA) 1961 Deuxieme Biennale de Paris 1961, Sculpture Today & Tomorrow (Bear Lane Gallery Oxford) 1962, 3rd Int Biennale of Prints (Tokyo) 1962, Sculpture (Battersea Park) 1966, Chromatic Sculpture (Arts Cncl Cambridge) 1966, Expo '67 (Br Pavillion Montreal) 1967, Nagaoka Prize Exhibition (Nagaoka Museum Japan) 1967, Summer Exhibition (Museum of Modern Art Oxford) 1968, Prospect 68 (Düsseldorf) 1968, Open Air Sculpture (Middleheim Antwerp) 1969, Br Sculpture out of the Sixties (ICA) 1970, Print Biennale (Ljubliana Yugoslavia) 1975 and 1981, Inaugural Exhibition (Nat Museum of Art Singapore) 1976, Hayward Annual (Hayward Gallery) 1977, Int Biennale of Prints Tokyo 1979, Biennale of Euro Graphic Art Heidelberg Germany 1979, The First Exhibition (Nicola Jacobs Gallery) 1979, Sculpture for the Blind (Tate) 1981, Women's Art Show 1550–1950 (Notts Castle Museum) 1982, British Sculpture 1951–80 (Whitechapel) 1982, Group Show (Yorks Sculpture Park) 1984, Contemporary Carving (Plymouth Arts Centre, touring) 1984–85, Beyond Appearance Castle Museum (Notts, touring) 1986, Bradford Print Biennale 1986, Premio Internazionale Biella Per L'Incisione 1987 (Turin) 1987, Stoneworks (Powys Castle Welshpool) 1988, Waddington Galleries 1990, New Displays (Tate Gallery) 1992, Tressors (Singapore Art Fair) 1994, British Abstract Art - Sculpture (Flowers East) 1995; *Work in Collections* Arts Cncl of GB, Contemporary Arts Soc, IBM NY, Leics Educn Cncl, Middelheim Museum, Nagaoka Museum of Modern Art, Tate Gallery, Govt Art Collection Wakefield Art Gallery, Southampton Art Gallery, Atkinson Art Gallery Southport, Nat Museum of Art Singapore; *Style*— Ms Kim Lim; ✉ Waddington Galleries Ltd, 11 Cork St, London W1 (☎ 0171 437 8611)

LIMB, Michael James; OBE (1994); s of late Jack Holmes Limb, and late Ada, *née* Farrow; *b* 6 March 1933; *Educ* Woolverston Hall; *m* 1; 1 s (Michael David); m 2, Capt Florence Sylvia McCormack, QARANC, da of late John McCormack, farmer, and Alice, *née* Cowley; *Career* Regular Offr RAF 1951–68; dir RAC (vice chm RAC Br Motor Sports Cncl); dir of various cos; Freeman and Liveryman Worshipful Co of Coachmakers and Coach-Harness Makers; FIMI, FIMgt; *Recreations* sailing, motor sport; *Clubs* RAC, Royal Thames Yacht, Special Forces; *Style*— Michael Limb, Esq, OBE; ✉ 2 Magnolia Close, Kingston Hill, Kingston, Surrey KT2 7JF

LIMB, Sue; da of Lewis Wilfred Limb, of South Woodchester, Glos, and Margaret Winifred, *née* Andrew; *b* 12 Sept 1946; *Educ* Pate's GS for Girls Cheltenham, Newnham Coll Cambridge (scholarship, BA); *m* 1, 1970 (m dis 1979), Roy Sydney Porter; m 2, 1984 (m dis 1991), Jan Vriend; 1 da (Elisabeth Susanna b 18 Feb 1985); *Career* researcher Cambridge 1968–70, clerk Halifax Building Soc 1970, kitchen asst Corpus Christi Cambridge 1971, teacher of English and drama 1971–75; writer and broadcaster 1976–; columnist: Good Housekeeping 1986–91, The Guardian (under name of Dulcie Domum) 1988–; author of numerous articles, children's books, etc; memb Green Party, Euro Parly candidate (Green) Cotswolds 1989; *Books* Captain Oates - Soldier and Explorer (biography, with Patrick Cordingley, 1982, reprinted 1995), Up the Garden Path (novel and radio and TV series, 1984), Love Forty (novel, 1986), The Wordsmiths at Gorsemere (book and radio series, 1987), Love's Labours (novel, 1989), Me Jane (teenage novel, 1989), Big Trouble (teenage novel, 1990), Bad Housekeeping (1990), Sheep's Eyes and Hogwash (1992), Come Back Grandma (1993), Dulcie Dishes the Dirt (1994), Passion Fruit (1995); *Recreations* muck-raking, mostly literal; *Style*— Ms Sue Limb; ✉ c/o Peters Fraser & Dunlop, 5th Floor, The Chambers, Chelsea Harbour, Lots Rd, London SW10 0XF (☎ 0171 352 4233, fax 0171 352 7356)

LIMBU, Capt Rambahadur; VC (1965), MVO (1984); s of Tekbir Limbu (d 1949), and Tunimaya Limbu (d 1952); *b* 1939; *m* 1, Tikamaya (d 1966); 2 s; m 2, 1967, Punimaya, da of Lachuman Rai, of Nepal; 3 s (and 1 s decd); *Career* VC for gallantry against Indonesians in Borneo; 10 Princess Mary's Own Gurkha Rifles 1957, Capt Dipakbahadur Gurung (Gurkha Tport Regt), HM The Queen's Gurkha Orderly Offr 1983–85; employed in Sultanate of Negara Brunei Darussalam 1985–; *Books* My Life Story (1978); *Recreations* football, volleyball, basketball, badminton; *Clubs* VC and GC Assoc; *Style*— Capt Rambahadur Limbu, VC, MVO; ✉ Damak 13 Bikash Marga, Post Office Damak, Jhapa Mechi Zone, East Nepal

LIMERICK, 6 Earl of (I 1803); Patrick Edmund Pery; KBE (1983), DL (W Sussex 1988); also Baron Glentworth (I 1790; from 1834 the gs and h of 1 Earl was designated 'Viscount' Glentworth, now the style of the eldest s and h), Viscount Limerick (I 1800), and sits as Baron Foxford (UK 1815); s of 5 Earl of Limerick, GBE, CH, KCB, DSO, TD (d 1967), by his w Angela, GBE, CH, DStJ (da of Lt-Col Sir Henry Trotter, KCMG, CB, d 1981); *b* 12 April 1930; *Educ* Eton, New Coll Oxford; *m* 1961, Sylvia Rosalind, *qv*; 2 s (Viscount Glentworth b 1963, Hon Adrian b 1967), 1 da (Lady Alison b 1964); *Heir* s, Viscount Glentworth, *qv*; *Career* Kleinwort Benson Ltd: dir 1967–87 vice chm 1983–85, dep chm 1985–87; dir Kleinwort Benson Group plc 1982–90; chm: Mallinson-Denny Ltd 1979–81, Polymeters Response International Ltd 1988–93, Pirelli UK plc 1989–, AMP Asset Management plc 1992–, De La Rue plc 1993– (dir 1983–); dir: Tanks Consolidated Investments plc 1976–83, Union Miniere SA 1976–81, Brooke Bond Group plc 1981–84, Kleinwort Benson Australian Income Fund Inc 1986–, TR Pacific Investment Trust plc 1987–92; sits as Cons peer in House of Lords; Parly under-sec of state for trade 1972–74; chm: Ctee for ME Trade 1975–79 (vice chm 1968–75), Br Overseas Trade Bd 1979–83 (bd memb 1975–91), Br Invisibles 1984–91 (bd memb 1983–91); vice pres Assoc of Br Cs of C 1977– (pres 1974–77), pres Inst of Export 1983–; chm: Ct of Govrs London Guildhall Univ (formerly City of London Poly) 1984–, Ctee of Univ Chairmen 1995–, Tstees City Parochial Fndn 1992– (tstee 1971–); tstee Educn 2000 1986–95; pres: Anglo-Swiss Soc 1984–, S of England Agric Soc 1993–94; Hon Col 71 (Yeo) Signal Regt (Vols) 1993–; pres: Ski Club of GB 1974–81, Alpine Ski Club 1985–87 (vice pres 1975–77), Canning House 1994–; vice pres Alpine Club 1989–91; Master Guild of World Traders 1991–92; MICAS 1957, FCIB 1990; *Recreations* skiing, mountaineering; *Style*— The Rt Hon the Earl of Limerick, KBE, DL; ✉ Chiddinglye, W Hoathly, E Grinstead, W Sussex RH19 4QT (☎ 01342 810214); 30 Victoria Rd, London W8 5RG (☎ 0171 937 0573)

LIMERICK, Countess of; Sylvia Rosalind Pery; CBE (1991); er da of Brig Maurice Stanley Lush, CB, CBE, MC, and Diana Ruth, *née* Hill; *b* 7 Dec 1935; *Educ* St Swithun's Sch Winchester, Lady Margaret Hall Oxford (MA); *m* 22 April 1961, 6 Earl of Limerick, *qv*; 2 s, 1 da; *Career* research asst FO 1959–62, memb Bd of Govrs St Bartholomew's Hosp 1970–74, vice chm Fndn for the Study of Infant Deaths 1971–; pres: UK Ctee for UN Children's Fund 1972–79, Nat Assoc for Maternal and Child Welfare 1973–84; vice-chm Community Health Cncl 1974–77; memb: Ctee of Mgmnt Inst of Child Health 1976–96, Cncl King Edward's Hosp Fund 1977– (memb Ctee of Mgmnt 1977–81 and 1985–89), Kensington Chelsea and Westminster Area Health Authy 1977–82, Eastman Dental Hospital SHA 1990–96, Eastman Dental Inst 1994– (chm 1996–); pres Health Visitors Assoc 1984–, chm Br Red Cross 1985–95 (chm emeritus 1995–), vice pres Int Fedn of Red Cross and Red Crescent Socs 1993–97; chm Chief Medical Offr's Expert Gp to Investigate Cot Death Theories 1994–, non-exec dir University Coll London Hospitals NHS Trust 1996–; Hon DLitt CNAA 1990, Hon FRCP 1994 (Hon MRCP 1990), hon fell Royal Coll of Paediatrics and Child Health (formerly British Paediatric Assoc) 1996 (hon memb BPA 1986), hon fell Inst of Child Health 1996; Hon Freeman Worshipful Co of Salters 1992; FRSocMed 1977; *Books* Sudden Infant Death: Patterns, Puzzles and Problems (jtly, 1985); *Recreations* skiing, music; *Style*— The Rt Hon the Countess of Limerick, CBE; ✉ 30 Victoria Rd, London W8 5RG (☎ 0171 937 0573); Chiddinglye, W Hoathly, E Grinstead, W Sussex RH19 4QT (☎ 01342 810214)

LIMERICK AND KILLALOE, Bishop of 1985–; Rt Rev Edward Flewett Darling; s of Ven Vivian W Darling, BD (Archdeacon of Cloyne, d 1965), and Honor Frances Garde, *née* Flewett (d 1984); *b* 24 July 1933; *Educ* Cork GS, Midleton Coll, St John's Sch Leatherhead, Trinity Coll Dublin (BA, MA); *m* 2 Aug 1958, Edith Elizabeth Patricia, da of Very Rev A W M Stanley Mann (Dean of Down, d 1968); 3 s (David b 1960, Colin b 1961, Philip b 1963), 2 da (Alison b 1966, Linda b 1968); *Career* curate: St Luke's Belfast 1956–59, St John's Orangefield Belfast 1959–62; incumbent St Gall's Carnalea Bangor Co Down 1962–72, rector St John's Malone Belfast 1972–85; *Books* A Child is Born (1966), Choosing the Hymns (1984), Irish Church Praise (ed, 1990); *Recreations* music, gardening; *Style*— The Rt Rev the Bishop of Limerick and Killaloe; ✉ Bishop's House, N Circular Rd, Limerick, Ireland (☎ and fax 0161 451532)

LIMON, Donald William; CB (1993); s of Arthur Limon (d 1986), and Dora Alice, *née* Spice (d 1965); *b* 29 Oct 1932; *Educ* Durham Sch, Lincoln Coll Oxford; *m* 1987, Joyce Beatrice, da of James Butters; *Career* House of Commons: clerk 1956–, sec to House of Commons Cmmn 1979–81, clerk of Fin Ctees 1981–84, princ clerk Table Office 1985–89, clerk of ctees 1989–90, clerk asst 1990–94, clerk of the House 1994–; *Recreations* cricket, golf, singing; *Style*— Donald Limon, Esq, CB; ✉ West Barn, Frog Lane, Kingsdon, Somerton, Somerset TA11 7LL; The House of Commons, London SW1A 0AA (☎ 0171 219 3300)

LINACRE, Sir (John) Gordon Seymour; kt (1986), CBE (1979), AFC (1943), DFM (1941); s of John James Linacre (d 1957), of Norton Woodseats, Sheffield; *b* 23 Sept 1920; *Educ* Firth Park GS Sheffield; *m* 1943, Irene Amy, da of Alexander Gordon (d 1946); 2 da; *Career* WWII RAF; Yorkshire Post Newspapers Ltd: md 1965–83, chm 1983–90, pres 1990–; dep chm United Newspapers Ltd 1983–91 (chief exec 1981–88), dir Yorkshire TV 1968–90, chm Chameleon Television Ltd 1991–; pres Fédération Internationale des Editeurs de Journaux et Publications 1984–88, former chm and dir Press Assoc, chm Leeds TEC 1989–92, former pres Newspaper Soc; chm: Opera North, Univ of Leeds Fndn 1989–; Hon LLD Univ of Leeds 1991; CIMgt, FRSA; *Recreations* golf, fishing, country walking; *Clubs* Alwoodley Golf; *Style*— Sir Gordon Linacre, CBE, AFC, DFM

LINACRE, Nigel Guy Thornton; s of Vivian Thornton Linacre, of Edinburgh, and Joan Linacre; *b* 21 Aug 1957; *Educ* George Heriot's Sch, Imberhorne Sch, Univ of Reading (BA); *m* 1979, Sue, da of Ronald Farish; 2 s (Thomas Edward Benedict b 30 Sept 1986, George Henry Michael b 20 Feb 1989), 2 da (Charlotte Lucy b 28 Nov 1982, Cordelia Mary b 4 Dec 1992); *Career* account exec Charles Barker 1979–82, account mangr Collett Dickenson Pearce Financial 1982–85, advertising dir Boase Massimi Pollit Business 1985–87, exec dir Collett Dickenson Pearce Financial 1987–89, dir Charles Barker 1989–92, md Charles Barker Advertising 1989–92, dir Interactive Telephone Services 1992–96; dir ITS Group plc 1993–96; Parly candidate (C) Ealing Southall 1983, prospective Parly candidate (C) N Cornwall 1993–; Freeman of Chippenham; MIPA 1990; *Books* Advertising For Account Handlers (1987); *Style*— Nigel Linacre, Esq; ✉ 51 St Mary Street, Chippenham, Wiltshire SN15 3JW (☎ and fax 01249 654615)

LINAKER, Dr Barry David; s of Allan Lawrence Linaker (d 1973), and Gwendoline, *née* Higgs; *b* 7 April 1947; *Educ* Wigan GS, KCH Med Sch Univ of London (MB BS, MD); *m* 14 April 1973, Carol Yvonne, da of Lt Cdr John Michael Ogden, of Sunningdale, nr Ascot; 2 da (Emma b 1975, Amanda b 1979); *Career* MRC res fell and sr registrar in gastroenterology Univ Dept of Med Hope Hosp Manchester 1978–80, sr registrar in med Liverpool 1980–81, conslt physician and gastroenterologist Warrington Dist Gen Hosp 1981–; author of papers in various jls especially on mechanisms of histamine stimulated secretion in rabbit ileal mucosa in gut; memb: Br Soc of Gastroenterology, Liverpool Med Inst, N Eng Gastro Soc, Merseyside and N Wales Physicians; memb BMA, FRCP 1989; *Recreations* sailing, clay pigeon shooting, golf, reading, travel; *Clubs* Port Dinorwic Sailing; *Style*— Dr Barry Linaker; ✉ Warrington National Health Trust Hospital, Lovely Lane, Warrington, Cheshire WA5 1QG (☎ 01925 635911 ext 2411)

LINAKER, Lawrence Edward (Paddy); s of late Lawrence Wignall Linaker, and Rose, *née* Harris; *b* 22 July 1934; *Educ* Malvern; *m* 1963, (Elizabeth) Susan, *née* Elam; 1 s (Sam), 1 da (decd); *Career* with Esso Petroleum 1957–63; M & G Group plc: joined 1963, dep chm and chief exec 1987–94, chm M & G Investment Management Ltd 1987–94; non-exec chm: Fisons plc 1994–95, Marling Industries plc 1996–; non-exec dir: Securities Inst 1992–94, Lloyds TSB Group plc 1994–, Fleming Mercantile Investment Trust plc 1994–, SAUL Trustee Company 1994–, Wolverhampton and Dudley Breweries plc 1996–; chm: IFMA 1992–94, YMCA Nat Coll 1992–; dir Childline 1992– (treas 1994–); memb Cncl RPMS 1977–89; memb Governing Body: SPCK 1976–94, Malvern Coll 1989–, Canterbury Christchurch Coll 1992–, FCA; *Recreations* music and gardening; *Clubs* Athenaeum; *Style*— Paddy Linaker, Esq; ✉ Swyre Farm, Aldsworth, Cheltenham, Gloucestershire

LINCOLN, Archdeacon of; *see:* Hawes, Ven Arthur John

LINCOLN, (Fredman) Ashe; QC (1947); s of Reuben Lincoln (d 1954), of London, and Fanny, *née* Fredman (d 1977); *b* 30 Oct 1907; *Educ* Hoe GS Plymouth, Paterson HS USA, Haberdashers Aske's Sch, Exeter Coll Oxford (MA, BCL); *m* 5 Sept 1933, (Eileen) Sybil, da of Samuel Cohen, of London; 1 s (David Hamilton b 1937), 1 da (Roda b 1935); *Career* RNVR: Lt Mine Investigation 1939–42 (Lt Cdr 1941), Marine Commandos 1943 (Cdr 1944, Capt 1952, despatches twice); called to the Bar Inner Temple 1929, master of the

Bench Inner Temple 1955, memb Bar Cncl (memb Exec Ctee and chm Ct Bldgs Ctee) 1957–61, recorder Gravesend 1967, recorder and dep judge Crown Ct 1971–79, head of chambers; pres: RNR Offrs Club, London Devonian Assoc, Royal Masonic Hosp 1993–; nat chm Maritime Volunteer Service; tstee: BMCF, Desmond Wettern Memorial Tst; patron Philip Gren Memorial Tst; Liveryman City of London 1935, Liveryman Worshipful Co of Plaisterers 1935 (Master 1949–50); Knight Grand Cross Order of St John of Jerusalem; *Books* The Starra (1939), Secret Naval Investigator (1952), Odyssey of a Jewish Sailor (1995); *Recreations* yachting; *Clubs* Athenaeum, Navy, MCC, RAC, Royal Corinthian Yacht, Bar Yacht; *Style—* Ashe Lincoln, Esq, QC; ✉ 9 King's Bench Walk, Temple, London EC4Y 7DX (☎ 0171 353 7202 or 0171 353 3909, fax 0171 583 2030)

LINCOLN, Prof Dennis William; s of Ernest Edward Lincoln (d 1951), and Gertrude Emma, *née* Holmes (d 1987); *b* 21 July 1939; *Educ* Bracondale Sch, Essex Inst of Agric, Univ of Nottingham (BSc), Univ of Cambridge (MA, PhD); *m* 1962, Rosemary Alice, *née* Barrell; 1 da (Karen Anne b 4 Oct 1965), 1 s (John Roderick b 13 Sept 1967); *Career* res fell CCC Cambridge 1966–67, lectr, reader and subsequently prof Dept of Human Anatomy Univ of Bristol 1967–82, dir MRC Reproductive Biology Unit Centre for Reproductive Biology 1982–96, dep vice-chllr Griffith Univ Aust 1996–; hon prof Univ of Edinburgh; Hon DSc Univ of Bristol; FRSE; *Recreations* ornithology, travel, wildlife photography; *Style—* Prof Dennis Lincoln, FRSE; ✉ Griffith University, Nathan, Queensland 4111, Australia

LINCOLN, 18 Earl of (E 1572); Edward Horace Fiennes-Clinton; er s of Edward Henry Fiennes-Clinton (ka 1916), and Edith Annie, *née* Guest (d 1965); suc his kinsman 10 and last Duke of Newcastle and 17 Earl of Lincoln (d 1988); *b* 23 Feb 1913; *m* 1, 1940, Leila Ruth, *née* Millen (d 1947); 1 s (Hon Edward Gordon), 1 da (Lady Patricia Elrick); m 2, 3 Dec 1953, Linda Alice, *née* O'Brien; *Heir* s, Edward Gordon Fiennes-Clinton, *qv*; *Style—* The Rt Hon the Earl of Lincoln; ✉ Flat 45, Elanora Villas, 37 Hastie Street, Bunbury, WA 6230, Australia

LINCOLN, 70 Bishop of (1072), 1986–; Rt Rev Robert Maynard Hardy; see founded from two more ancient ones (Lindisfarn at Sidnacester and Middle Angles at Leicester, united in one diocese under see of Leicester; the new entity was firstly removed to Dorchester and secondly, after the conquest, to Lincoln); patron of 154 livings and 21 alternately and by turns or jointly, the Canonries, Precentorship, Chancellor-ship, Sub-Deanery, and the Archdeaconries of Stow, Lincoln and Lindsey, also Prebendal stalls in the Cathedral; s of Harold Hardy, and Monica Mavie Hardy; *b* 5 Oct 1936; *Educ* Queen Elizabeth GS Wakefield, Clare Coll Cambridge (MA); *m* 1970, Isobel Mary, da of Charles Burch; 2 s, 1 da; *Career* deacon 1962, priest 1963, asst curate All Saints and Martyrs Langley Manchester 1962, fell and chaplain Selwyn Coll Cambridge 1965, vicar All Saints Borehamwood 1972, priest-in-charge Aspley Guise 1975, course dir St Albans Diocese ministerial trg scheme 1975, incumbent of United Benefice of Aspley Guise with Husborne Crawley and Ridgmont 1980, bishop suffragan of Maidstone 1980–86, bishop to HM Prisons 1985–; hon fell Selwyn Coll Cambridge 1986, Hon DD Univ of Hull 1992; *Recreations* walking, gardening, reading; *Style—* The Rt Rev the Bishop of Lincoln; ✉ Bishop's House, Eastgate, Lincoln LN2 1QQ (☎ 01522 534701, fax 01522 511095)

LINDISFARNE, Archdeacon of; *see:* Bowering, Ven Michael Ernest

LINDLEY, Dr Bryan Charles; CBE (1982); s of Wing Cdr Alfred Webb Lindley (d 1988), of Lichfield, and Florence, *née* Pratten (d 1975); *b* 30 Aug 1932; *Educ* Reading Sch, UCL (BSc(Eng), PhD); *m* 2 May 1987, Dr Judith Anne Heyworth, da of Robert Heyworth, of Bramhall; 1 s ((John) Julian b 1960); *Career* Nat Gas Turbine Estab 1954–57, Hawker Siddeley Nuclear Power Co Ltd 1957–59, International Research and Development Company Ltd and CA Parsons Nuclear Res Centre 1959–65, mangr R&D Div CA Parsons & Co Ltd 1965–68, chief exec and md ERA Technology Ltd (chm: ERA Patents Ltd, ERA Autotrack Systems Ltd) 1968–1979; dir: of technol Dunlop Holdings plc, Dunlop Ltd; chm: Thermal Conversions (UK) Ltd, Soilless Cultivation Systems Ltd, Dunlop Solaronics Div, Dunlop Bioprocesses Ltd 1979–85; dir technol and planning BICC Cables Ltd, chm: Optical Fibres, Lord Lindley Assocs 1990–, Skand Systems Ltd 1995–; dir: Thomas Bolton & Johnson Ltd 1985–88, RAPRA Technol Ltd 1985–; chief exec Nat Advanced Robotics Res Centre 1989–90; dir Settle-Carlisle Railway Development Co 1991–93; chm N Lakeland Healthcare NHS Tst 1993–; visiting prof Univ of Liverpool 1989–; memb: ACARD 1980–86, Materials Advsy Gp DTI 1984; fell UCL 1979; FIMechE 1968, FIEE 1968, FInstP 1969, FPRI 1980; *Recreations* music, photography, walking, skiing, sailing; *Style—* Dr Bryan Lindley, CBE; ✉ Lindenthwaite, Beacon Edge, Penrith, Cumbria CA11 8BN (☎ 01768 890652)

LINDLEY, Dr David; s of William Lindley (d 1980), and Millicent, *née* Caine; *b* 26 June 1939; *Educ* Manchester Central GS, Univ of Salford (Gen Sir William Platt prize, BSc), Univ of Wales (PhD), Univ of Cambridge (Certificate of Advanced Engrg Design); *m* 14 July 1962, Dorothy, da of John Turnock; 3 s (Simon David b 11 April 1963 d 1993, Nicolas Rhys b 17 Nov 1964, Jonathan Peter b 3 Oct 1969), 1 da (Sarah Jane Kirsty b 31 Dec 1974); *Career* mangr Pump Experimental Dept Mather & Platt Ltd Manchester 1962–63 (apprentice 1955–62), head Turbo Machinery Aero-thermodynamics Dept CEGB 1967–70, sr lectr in mech engrg Univ of Canterbury New Zealand 1970–75, res fell UKAEA 1975–, mangr Energy Systems Group Jet Propulsion Laboratory California Inst of Technol 1975–76, sr lectr Univ of Canterbury New Zealand 1976–78; Taylor Woodrow plc: joined 1978, md Wind Energy Group Ltd 1979–91, dir of Taywood Engineering Ltd 1984–90, vice pres US WEG Inc 1986–91, divnl dir of Taylor Woodrow Construction Ltd 1987–91, memb Severn Tidal Power Gp Mgmnt and Supervisory Bd 1987–91, dir Taylor Woodrow Management and Engineering Ltd 1988–91; md National Wind Power Ltd 1991–96; dir: Euro Wind Energy Assoc 1980– (pres 1986–89), British Wind Energy Assoc 1980–96 (chm 1982 and 1994); memb: Advsy Cncl for Res and Devpt for Fuel and Power 1986–92, Renewable Energy Advsy Gp 1991–92, Electrical Engrg Coll of Peers EPSRC 1993–, Professional Bodies Advsy Gp Design Cncl 1995–; visiting prof Loughborough Univ of Technol and De Montfort Univ 1994–; academician Russian Int Higher Educn Acad of Scis; MASME, memb Inst of Aeronautics and Astronautics, FIMechE, FRMetS, FEng 1993, *Awards* incl: James Watt medal ICE 1987, Stephenson medal Univ of Newcastle 1989, Melchett medal Inst of Energy 1990, Industry Award BWEA 1995, President's Award BWEA 1996; *Recreations* walking, skiing, collecting, sailing, photography, reading, music; *Style—* Dr David Lindley, FEng; ✉ Lindley and Associates, Woodfield, Farm Lane, Jordans, Beaconsfield, Bucks HP9 2UP (☎ 01494 676570, fax 01494 678917)

LINDLEY, Richard Howard Charles; s of Lt-Col (Herbert) Guy Lindley (d 1976), of Winchester, Hants, and Dorothea Helen Penelope Hatchell (d 1996); *b* 25 April 1936; *Educ* Bedford Sch, Queens' Coll Cambridge (exhibitioner, BA, chm Film Soc); *m* 1976 (m dis 1986), Clare Fehrsen; 2 c (Thomas Paul Guy b 29 Dec 1977, Joanna Frances Eleanor b 12 April 1979); *Career* Nat Serv: 2 Lt Royal Hampshire Regt, served Malaya Emergency; prodr TV commercials Foote Cone and Belding 1960–62, reporter presenter and newscaster Southern TV Southampton 1963–64, reporter ITN (in Vietnam, Nigeria, Zimbabwe, Egypt, Israel) 1964–72, reporter and presenter Panorama and Saturday Briefing BBC Current Affairs Gp 1972–88, sr prog offr IBA 1988, reporter and presenter This Week Thames TV 1989–92; presenter: ITN World News 1992–94, Special Reports ITN News at Ten 1995–; dir Lindley Stone Ltd; *Recreations* friends, food, familiar films; *Clubs* Royal Television Soc; *Style—* Richard Lindley; ✉ 46 Oak Village, London NW5 4QL (☎ and fax 0171 267 5870)

LINDOP, Dr George Black McMeekin; s of George Lindop (d 1988); *b* 28 March 1945; *Educ* Hillhead HS Glasgow, Univ of Glasgow (BSc, MB ChB); *m* 22 Jan 1968, Sharon Ann, *née* Cornell; 2 s (Graeme Euan b 1975, Gavin Neil b 1978), 1 da (Amy Elizabeth b 1981); *Career* conslt in histopathology Ayrshire and Arran Health Bd 1976, sr lectr and hon conslt in histopathology Univ of Glasgow and Gtr Glasgow Health Bd; memb: Assoc of Clinical Pathologists 1979, American Soc for Hypertension 1984; FRCPath 1987 (MRCPath 1975), FRCP 1996 (MRCP 1994); *Recreations* sport, music, cinema; *Clubs* Glasgow Golf; *Style—* Dr George Lindop; ✉ 8 Fifth Ave, Glasgow G12 0AT (☎ 0141 211 2390); Dept of Pathology Western Infirmary, Glasgow G11 6NT

LINDOP, Dr Michael John; s of Donald Frederick Lindop, of Birmingham, and Phyllis Alice, *née* Burrows; *b* 29 July 1942; *Educ* King Edward Sch Birmingham, Gonville and Caius Coll Cambridge (MA), Guy's Hosp (MB, BChir); *m* 16 Aug 1968, Kari, da of Per Brachel (d 1955), of Oslo, Norway; 1 s (Tom b 1969), 3 da (Tanya b 1971, Michelle b 1973, Anne-Lise b 1978); *Career* sr registrar Westminster Hosp 1969–74, instr Univ of Washington Seattle USA 1973, conslt in anaesthesia and intensive care 1974–, currently dir anaesthesia servs Addenbrooke's Hosp; examiner Royal Coll of Anaesthetists, MO Howard Mallett Club Cambridge; memb: Intensive Care Soc, Anaesthetic Res Soc; fell Coll Anaesthetists 1971; *Books* contrib: Liver Transplantation (1987), Transplant Surgery (1988); *Recreations* racquet control, weed control; *Style—* Dr Michael Lindop; ✉ Department of Anaesthesia, PO Box 93, Addenbrooke's Hospital, Cambridge CB2 2QQ (☎ 01223 217433, fax 01223 217223)

LINDOP, Sir Norman; kt (1973), DL (Hertford 1989); s of Thomas Cox Lindop, of Stockport, Cheshire, and May Lindop; *b* 9 March 1921; *Educ* Northgate Sch Ipswich, Queen Mary Coll London (MSc); *m* 1974, Jenny Caroline Quass; 1 s; *Career* industl chemist 1942, chemistry lectr Queen Mary Coll 1946, asst dir examinations Civil Serv Cmmn 1951, sr lectr chemistry Kingston Coll of Technol 1953–57 (head of Chem and Geology Dept 1957–63); princ: SW Essex Tech Coll and Sch of Art 1963–66, Hatfield Coll of Technol 1966–69; dir Hatfield Poly 1969–82, princ Br Sch of Osteopathy 1982–90; chm: Hatfield Philharmonic Soc 1970–82, Ctee of Dirs of Polys 1972–74, Cncl for Professions Supplementary to Medicine 1973–81, Cncl of Westfield Coll London 1983–89, Home Office Data Protection Ctee 1976–78, DES Public Sector Validation Enquiry 1984–85, Br Library Advsy Cncl 1986–94; chm Res Cncl for Complementary Med 1989–90; memb: US and UK Educnl Fulbright Cmmn 1971–81, SRC 1974–78, GMC 1979–84, Hertfordshire CC 1993; fell: Queen Mary and Westfield Coll (formerly Queen Mary Coll) London 1976, Univ of Hertfordshire (formerly Hatfield Poly) 1983, Univ of Brighton (formerly Brighton Poly) 1990, Coll of Preceptors; Hon DEd Cncl for Nat Academic Awards 1982, Hon DSc Univ of Ulster 1994; FRSA, FRSC, CChem; *Clubs* Athenaeum; *Style—* Sir Norman Lindop, DL; ✉ 36 Queen's Road, Hertford, Herts SG13 8AZ

LINDOP, Prof Patricia Joyce; da of Elliot David Lindop (d 1973), of Burgess Hill, Sussex, and Dorothy, *née* Jones; *b* 21 June 1930; *Educ* Malvern, St Bartholomew's Hosp Med Coll and Univ of London (BSc, MB BS, PhD, DSc, FRCP); *m* 6 May 1957, Gerald P R Esdale (d 1992), s of Charles August Esdale (d 1949), of Sutton, Surrey; 1 s (Mark Elliott b 11 Aug 1958), 1 da (Patricia Michele b 11 Aug 1963); *Career* registered GP 1954, res and teaching posts in physiology and med radiobiology St Bartholomew's Hosp Med Coll 1955–84, prof of radiation biology Univ of London 1970–84 (currently emeritus prof); author of pubns in field of radiation effects; UK memb Continuing Ctee of Pugwash Confs on Sci and World Affrs (asst sec gen 1961–71), memb Royal Cmmn on Environment 1973–79; Hon MRCR 1972, Hon ARR 1984; *Clubs* Royal Society of Medicine; *Style—* Prof Patricia Lindop; ✉ 58 Wildwood Road, Hampstead, London NW11 6UP (☎ 0181 455 5860)

LINDQVIST, Andrew Nils Gunnar; s of Kjell Gunnar Lindqvist, of Nether Langleys, Tharston, Norwich, and Joan Bernice Kathleen, *née* Skingley; *b* 7 May 1943; *Educ* Gresham's, Trinity Hall Cambridge (MA); *m* 1, 4 Sept 1971 (m dis), Sonia Frances, da of Sqdn Ldr Alfred Basil Charles, MBE (d 1984); 2 da (Hanna b 1980, Annika b 1982); m 2, 29 Oct 1993, Evelyn Jane; *Career* called to the Bar 1968, memb area Legal Aid Ctee 1983; pt/t chm Child Support Appeal Tbnl 1994; *Recreations* sailing, tennis, hockey, languages; *Clubs* Norfolk (Norwich); *Style—* Andrew Lindqvist, Esq; ✉ Home Farm, Rumburgh, Halesworth, Suffolk IP19 0NS (☎ 01986 785467); Octagon House, 19 Colegate, Norwich NR3 1AT (☎ 01603 623186, fax 01603 760519)

LINDSAY, Crawford Callum Douglas; QC (1987); s of Douglas Marshall Lindsay, and Eileen Mary Lindsay; *b* 5 Feb 1939; *Educ* Whitgift Sch Croydon, St John's Coll Oxford (BA); *m* 1963, Rosemary Gough; 1 s, 1 da; *Career* called to the Bar 1961, recorder SE Circuit 1982–, head of chambers; *Style—* Crawford Lindsay, Esq, QC; ✉ 1 Sergeants' Inn, Fleet Street, London EC4Y 1LL (☎ 0171 353 9901)

LINDSAY, Sir James Harvey Kincaid Stewart; kt (1966); s of Arthur Harvey Lindsay (d 1970), and Doris Kincaid Lindsay (d 1944); *b* 31 May 1915; *Educ* Highgate Sch; *m* Marguerite Phyllis Boudville; 1 s, 1 da by previous m; *Career* int mgmnt conslt; formerly: chm and md The Metal Box Co of India Ltd, pres Assoc C of C and Indust of India, dir Int Progs Admin Staff Coll Henly 1969–80; tstee Inst of Family and Environmental Res 1971–91, dir Inst of Cultural Affrs Int Brussels (pres 1981–89), convenor Int Exposition of Rural Devpt 1981–85, dir Int Centre for Organisational Mgmnt 1988–; chm Kambay Resources International (UK) Ltd 1994–; life memb All India Mgmnt Assoc (pres 1967–69); CIMgt, FCInstM; *Recreations* music; *Clubs* East India, IOD; *Style—* Sir James Lindsay; ✉ Christmas Cottage, Lower Shiplake, Oxfordshire RG9 3JT (☎ 0118 940 2859)

LINDSAY, James Martin Evelyn; s and h of Sir Ronald Lindsay of Dowhill, 2 Bt; *b* 11 Oct 1968; *Educ* Shiplake Coll, RMA Sandhurst; *Career* Lt Grenadier Guards 1988–93; *Recreations* tennis, squash; *Clubs* Cavalry and Guards'; *Style—* James Lindsay, Esq; ✉ 104 Edith Road, London W14 9AP (☎ 0171 603 0278)

LINDSAY, 16 Earl of (S 1633); James Randolph Lindesay-Bethune; also Lord Lindsay of the Byres (S 1445), Lord Parbroath (S 1633), Viscount Garnock, and Lord Kilbirnie, Kingsburn and Drumry (both S 1703); s of 15 Earl of Lindsay (d 1989), by his 1 w, Mary, *née* Douglas-Scott-Montagu; *b* 19 Nov 1955; *Educ* Eton, Univ of Edinburgh (MA), Univ of California Davis; *m* 2 March 1982, Diana Mary, er da of Nigel Chamberlayne-Macdonald, LVO, OBE, of Cranbury Park, Winchester; 2 s (Viscount Garnock b 30 Dec 1990, Hon David Nigel b 12 May 1993), 3 da (Lady Frances Mary b 1986, Lady Alexandra Penelope b 1988, Lady Charlotte Diana (twin) b 1993); *Heir* s, William James, Viscount Garnock b 30 Dec 1990; *Career* environmental conslt and landscape architect; dir Tayforth Marketing Group Ltd 1990–; vice chm Inter-Parly Union Ctee on Environment 1994–95 (memb 1993), Parly under-sec of state Scottish Office 1995–; tstee: Gardens for the Disabled, London Gardens Soc; pres: Brighter Kensington and Chelsea Scheme, Int Tree Fndn 1995– (vice pres 1993–95); chm Landscape Fndn 1992–95; memb: Advsy Panel Railway Heritage Tst, World Resource Fndn 1994–, Select Ctee on Sustainable Devpt 1994–95; *Books* Garden Ornament (jtly), Trellis (1991); *Clubs* New (Edinburgh); *Style—* The Rt Hon the Earl of Lindsay; ✉ Lahill, Upper Largo, Fife KY8 6JE

LINDSAY, Hon Mr Justice; Hon Sir John Edmund Fredric; kt (1992); s of George Fredric Lindsay (ka 1944), and Constance Mary, *née* Wright; *b* 16 Oct 1935; *Educ* Ellesmere Coll, Sidney Sussex Coll Cambridge (MA); *m* Patricia Anne, da of late William

Bolton, of Capetown; 3 da; *Career* called to the Bar Middle Temple (Astley Pupillage prizeman and Harmsworth scholar) 1961, jr treasy counsel in bona vacantia, QC 1981, judge of the High Court of Justice (Chancery Div) 1992–; judge Employment Appeal Tbnl 1996–; *Style*— The Hon Mr Justice Lindsay; ✉ c/o Royal Courts of Justice, Strand, London WC2A 2LL

LINDSAY, Prof (John) Kennedy; s of William Gray Lindsay (d 1966), of Ballycraigy, Newtownabbey, and Mary, *née* Kennedy (d 1992); *b* 8 Sept 1924; *Educ* Trinity Coll Dublin (BA), Inst of Historical Res Univ of London, Univ of Edinburgh (PhD); *Career* lectr Univ of S Carolina 1957–59, acting head History Dept Memorial Univ Newfoundland Canada 1959–60, academic staff Royal Military Coll of Canada 1960–61, i/c state papers room Historical Div Canadian Dept of External Affrs Ottawa 1961–62, memb int team which estabd Univ of Nigeria Nsukka 1962–64, Canadian tech cooperation visiting prof Univ of W Indies 1964–69, memb Editorial Bd Third World London 1970–71, MLA S Antrim NI Legislative Assembly 1973–74, ed Ulsterman newspaper 1975–76; legal conslt various cases Euro Cmmn on Human Rights Strasbourg incl: Black v UK, Orchin v UK, Br Ulster Pty v UK 1976–84, memb S Antrim constitutional convention 1976; owner: Dunrod Press UK 1979–, United Book Suppliers Wholesale 1981–96, Ulster Motorway Servs 1994–; *Books* The British Intelligence Services in Action (1980); *Recreations* hiking; *Style*— Prof Kennedy Lindsay; ✉ c/o 8 Brown's Road, Newtownabbey, Co Antrim BT36 8RN (☎ 01232 832362, fax 01232 848780)

LINDSAY, Dr (John) Maurice; CBE (1979), TD (1946); s of Matthew Lindsay (d 1969), of Glasgow, and Eileen Frances, *née* Brock (1954); *b* 21 July 1918; *Educ* Glasgow Acad, Scottish Nat Acad of Music; *m* 3 Aug 1946, Aileen Joyce, da of Evan Ramsay Macintosh Gordon (d 1973); 1 s (Niall Gordon Brock b 1957), 3 da (Seona Morag Joyce b 1949, Kirsteen Ann b 1951, Morven Morag Joyce b 1959); *Career* poet, author, broadcaster, music critic and environmentalist; drama critic Scottish Daily Mail 1946–47, music critic The Bulletin 1946–60, ed Scots Review 1949–50; Border TV: programme controller 1961–62, prodn controller 1962–64, features exec and chief interviewer 1964–67; dir The Scottish Civic Tst 1967–83 (conslt 1983–), hon sec gen Europa Nostra 1982–90 (memb Mgmnt Ctee 1990–), pres Assoc of Scottish Literary Studies 1988–90, hon vice pres Scottish Environmental Educn Ctee 1990–; Hon DLitt Glasgow 1982; Hon FRIAS; *Poetry* The Advancing Day (1940), Perhaps Tomorrow (1941), Predicament (1942), No Crown for Laughter (1943), The Enemies of Love - Poems 1941–45 (1946), Selected Poems (1947), Hurlygush - Poems in Scots (1948), At the Wood's Edge (1950), Ode for St Andrew's Night and Other Poems (1951), The Exiled Heart - Poems 1941–56 (1957), Snow Warning and Other Poems (1962), One Later Day and Other Poems (1964), This Business of Living (1969), Comings and Goings (1971), Selected Poems 1942–72 (1973), The Run from Life (1975), Walking Without an Overcoat - Poems 1972–76 (1977), Collected Poems (1979), A Net to Catch the Winds and Other Poems (1981), The French Mosquitoes' Woman and Other Diversions and Poems (1985), Requiem For a Sexual Athlete (1988), Collected Poems 1940–90 (1990), On The Face of It - Collected Poems Vol 2 (1993), News of the World: Last Poems (1995); *Prose* A Pocket Guide to Scottish Culture (1947), The Scottish Renaissance (1949), The Lowlands of Scotland - Glasgow and the North (3rd edn 1979), Robert Burns, The Man, His Work, The Legend (third edn 1980), Dunoon - The Gem of the Clyde Coast (1954), The Lowlands of Scotland - Edinburgh and the South (3rd edn 1979), Clyde Waters - Variations and Diversions on a Theme of Pleasure (1958), The Burns Encyclopedia (4th paperback edn 1995), Killochan Castle (1960), By Yon Bonnie Banks - A Gallimaufry (1961), Environment - A Basic Human Right (1968), Portrait of Glasgow (second edn 1981), Robin Philipson (1977), History of Scottish Literature (1977, revd edn 1992), Lowland Scottish Villages (1980), Francis George Scott and the Scottish Renaissance (1980), The Buildings of Edinburgh (jt-author, 1980, 2nd edn 1987), Thank You for Having Me - A Personal Memoir, Unknown Scotland (jt-author, 1984), The Castles of Scotland (1986), Count All Men Mortal - A History of Scottish Provident 1837–1987 (1987), An Illustrated Guide to Glasgow 1837 (1989), Victorian and Edwardian Glasgow, Edinburgh Past and Present (1990), Glasgow (1989), The Scottish Dog Book (jtly, 1990); other work incl: A Pleasure of Gardens (jtly, 1990), The Scottish Quotation Book (jtly, 1991), The Music Quotation Book (jtly, 1992), The Theatre and Opera Lover's Quotation Book (jtly, 1993), The Burns Quotation Book (jtly, 1994), A Mini-Guide to Scottish Gardens (jtly, 1994), The Chambers Book of Good Scottish Gardens (jtly, 1995); *Recreations* enjoying compact disc collection, walking, sailing on paddle-steamers; *Style*— Dr Maurice Lindsay, CBE, TD; ✉ 7 Milton Hill, Milton, Dumbarton, Scotland G82 2TS (☎ 01389 62655)

LINDSAY, Col Oliver John Martin; CBE; yr s of Sir Martin Alexander Lindsay of Dowhill, 1 Bt, CBE, DSO (d 1981), and his 1 w, Joyce Emily, *née* Lindsay; *b* 30 Aug 1938; *Educ* Eton, RMA Sandhurst, Staff Coll Camberley, Nat Def Coll Latimer; *m* 27 Oct 1964, Lady Clare Rohais Antonia Elizabeth Giffard, da of 3 Earl of Halsbury; 1 s (Mark Oliver Giffard b 1968), 2 da (Victoria Louise Elizabeth Clare (Mrs Gregory Wheatley) b 1967, Fiona Emily Margaret b 1972); *Career* cmmnd Grenadier Gds 1958, served in W Africa, Cyprus, Hong Kong and Europe, and on staff in Rhodesia, Ottawa and London until 1993; dir Treloar Tst for disabled young people 1993–, memb Royal Co of Archers (Queen's Body Guard for Scotland); lectr (in particular on Far Eastern events 1940–45), historian and author; memb Bd of Govrs: Victoria League for Cwlth Friendship 1986–91, Cwlth Tst 1988–90; ed The Guards Magazine 1993–; Freeman City of London 1994; MICFM 1993, FRHistS 1984; *Books* The Lasting Honour - The Fall of Hong Kong 1941 (1978), At the Going Down of the Sun - Hong Kong and South East Asia 1941–45 (1981), A Guard's General - the Memoirs of Sir Allan Adair (ed, 1986), Once a Grenadier.....The Grenadier Guards 1945–95 (1996); *Recreations* tennis, writing; *Clubs* Boodle's; *Style*— Col Oliver Lindsay, CBE; ✉ c/o Child and Co, 1 Fleet Street, London EC4

LINDSAY, Russell Grant (Russ); s of David Alexander Lindsay, of Catisfield, Hants, and Evelyn, *née* Birrell; *b* 12 July 1961; *Educ* Hardys GS Dorchester, Prices GS Fareham, Southampton Coll of HE; *m* 15 June 1991, Caron Louisa Keating, *qv*; 1 s (Charlie b 1994); *Career* began career as DJ/Radio/TV broadcaster, created Tenball (cue game with Steve Davies), co-prodr of TV progs and radio shows; currently md The James Grant Media Group Ltd; dir: James Grant Management Ltd (fndr with Peter Powell, *qv*, 1984–), James Grant Productions Ltd, James Grant Music Publishing Ltd, James Grant Sports Ltd, James Grant Investments Ltd; also dir: Real Television Ltd, Musical Expectations Ltd, The Licensing Company, Cue 200 (Tenball) Ltd, Showbiz Productions Ltd, Attractions Ltd; owner TV Formats; *Recreations* sport, art, leisure; *Clubs* Wasps RFC, Dukes Dean Golf; *Style*— Russ Lindsay, Esq; ✉ James Grant Media Group Ltd, Syon Lodge, London Road, Syon Park, Middlesex TW7 5BH (☎ 0181 232 4100, fax 0181 232 4101, mobile 083 286103, e-mail jgrant.ftech.co.uk)

LINDSAY-FYNN, Nigel; s of Sir Basil Lindsay-Fynn (d 1988), and (Marion) Audrey Ellen, *née* Chapman (d 1991); *b* 4 May 1942; *Educ* Charterhouse, Oriel Coll Oxford (MA); *m* 12 May 1971, Heleen Vanda Mary, da of Bill Willson-Pemberton, of London; 2 s (Piers b 1975, Charles b 1989), 2 da (Miranda b 1978, Eleanor b 1981); *Career* fin dir Independent Registrars Group Ltd and various private family cos (portfolio mgmnt and trusteeship); memb IMRO; tstee Exeter Cathedral Preservation Tst; treas: Oriel Soc, Devon Co Agric Assoc; vice chm: Bicton Coll of Agric, Friends of Exeter Festival and of numerous other charities; *Clubs* Buck's, Garrick, Kildare St and Univ Dublin, Royal Irish Yacht; *Style*— Nigel Lindsay-Fynn, Esq; ✉ Lee Ford, Budleigh Salterton, Devon EX9 7AJ (☎ 01395 445894, fax 01395 446219); 74 Bedford Gardens, London W8 7EH (☎ 0171 229 1684, fax 0171 792 0024)

LINDSAY-HOGG, Sir Edward William; 4 Bt (UK 1905), of Rotherfield Hall, Rotherfield, Sussex; s of Sir Lindsay Lindsay-Hogg, 1 Bt (d 1923), suc n, Sir William Lindsay-Hogg, 3 Bt, 1987; *b* 23 May 1910; *Educ* Eton; *m* 1, 18 Nov 1936 (m dis 1946), Geraldine Mary, da of Edward Martin Fitzgerald, of Greystones, Co Wicklow; 1 s (Michael Edward b 1940); m 2, 30 Oct 1957, Kathleen Mary, da of James Cooney, of Carrick-on-Suir, Co Tipperary, and wid of Capt Maurice Cadell, MC; *Heir* s, Michael Edward Lindsay-Hogg b 5 May 1940; *Clubs* Kildare Street and University (Dublin); *Style*— Sir Edward Lindsay-Hogg, Bt

LINDSAY-MacDOUGALL OF LUNGA, Colin John Francis; s of John Stewart Lindsay-MacDougall of Lunga, DSO, MC (ka 1943), and Shiela Marion, *née* Sprot; *b* 21 July 1939; *Educ* Radley; *m* 11 Feb 1961 (m dis 1979), Hon Frances Phoebe, da of Capt Hon Anthony Phillimore (ka 1943), of Cappid Hall, nr Henley on Thames, Oxfordshire; 3 s (James, Lucian, Aidan), 2 da (Antonia, Johanna); *Career* Nat Serv 2 Lt Queen's Own Hussars; landowner; *Recreations* sailing, riding, skiing, arts; *Clubs* Glasgow Art; *Style*— Colin Lindsay-MacDougall of Lunga; ✉ Lunga, Ardfern, Argyll (☎ 01852 500237); Lunga Estate, Argyll PA31 8QR (☎ 01852 500237, fax 01852 500639)

LINDSAY OF BIRKER, 3 Baron (UK 1945); James Francis Lindsay; s of 2 Baron Lindsay of Birker (d 1994), and Hsiao Li, da of Col Li Wen Chi, Chinese Army; *b* 29 Jan 1945; *Educ* Canberra HS, Geelong GS Victoria, Bethesda-Chevy Chase HS, Univ of Keele, Univ of Liverpool; *m* 1966 (m dis 1985), Mary Rose, da of W G Thomas, of Cwmbran, Mon; *Heir* cousin, Alexander Sebastian Lindsay b 1940; *Career* formerly lectr Dept of Physics Tunghai Univ Taichung Taiwan Repub of China; second sec Australian Embassy Santiago Chile 1973–76; first sec: Vientiane Laos 1979–80, Dhaka Bangladesh 1982–83, Caracas Venezuela 1986–90, Dept of Foreign Affrs and Trade Canberra 1991–93, dep high cmmr and cnsllr Australian High Cmmn: Islamabad Pakistan 1993–96, Nairobi Kenya 1996–; *Recreations* hiking, mountaineering, tennis; *Style*— The Rt Hon the Lord Lindsay of Birker; ✉ PO Box 39341, Nairobi, Kenya (☎ 254 2 445034, fax 254 2 444617, e-mail mukinduri@tt.sasa.unon.org)

LINDSAY OF DOWHILL, Sir Ronald Alexander; 2 Bt (UK 1962), of Dowhill, Co Kinross; er s of Sir Martin Alexander Lindsay of Dowhill, 1 Bt, CBE, DSO (d 1981), and his 1 w, Joyce, da of Maj the Hon Robert Hamilton Lindsay, 3 s of 26 Earl of Crawford; *b* 6 Dec 1933; *Educ* Eton, Worcester Coll Oxford (MA); *m* 1968, Nicoletta, yr da of Capt Edgar Storich (d 1985), Royal Italian Navy; 3 s (James b 1968, Hugo b 1970, Robin b 1972), 1 da (Lucia b 1974); *Heir* s, James Martin Evelyn Lindsay, *qv*; *Career* Lt Grenadier Gds 1952–54; insur broker (chiefly with Hogg Robinson and with Minet) 1958–80; gen mangr UK branch Ocaso SA of Madrid 1980–84; Lloyd's members' agent 1984–93; dir: AHJ members' agency 1984–88, Sturge Holdings' members' agencies 1989–93, ret; memb Standing Cncl of the Baronetage (chm 1987–89), tstee Baronets' Tst 1986–95 (chm 1990–92); vice pres Anglo-Spanish Soc 1994– (vice chm 1985–93); memb Queen's Body Gd for Scotland (Royal Co of Archers); FCII; Encomienda Orden de Isabel la Católica (Spain) 1988; *Style*— Sir Ronald Lindsay of Dowhill, Bt; ✉ 104 Edith Road, London W14 9AP (☎ 0171 603 0278)

LINDSAY-SMITH, Iain-Mór; s of Edward Duncanson Lindsay-Smith (d 1951); *b* 18 Sept 1934; *Educ* High Sch of Glasgow, Univ of London Extension Dip Course; *m* 1960, Carol Sara, da of Edward Philip Paxman (d 1948); 1 s (Sholto); *Career* cmmnd 1 Bn Cameronians (Scottish Rifles) W Germany 1953–55, 6/7 Bn 1955–63; journalist; Scottish Daily Record 1951–57, Daily Mirror 1957–60, features ed Daily Mail 1968–71 (foreign corr, foreign ed 1960–70), dep ed Yorkshire Post 1971–74, ed Glasgow Herald 1974–77, exec ed The Observer 1977–84; chief exec and md LLP Ltd (Lloyd's of London Press), chm and publisher Lloyd's List; chm: LLP Inc USA 1992– (dir 1984–), Lloyd's Maritime Info Servs Inc (USA), Lloyd's Maritime Info Servs Ltd, LLP Asia Ltd, LLP GmbH (Germany); chm and chief exec LLP Info Servs, chm LLP Business Publishing; dir: Lutine Publications Ltd, DYP Group Ltd, IBJ Associates Ltd, Int Art and Antique Loss Register Ltd, Periodical Publishers' Assoc; memb: Ct Univ of Essex 1985–95, Little Horkesley PCC 1987–91; FRSA; *Recreations* shooting (game and clays), highland bagpipes, gardening; *Clubs* Travellers'; *Style*— Iain-Mór Lindsay-Smith, Esq; ✉ LLP Limited, 69–77 Paul Street, London EC2A 4LQ (☎ 0171 553 1000, fax 0171 553 1117, telex 987321 LLOYDS G)

LINDSELL, Charles Nicholas; s of Brig Robert Anthony Lindsell, MC, and Pamela Rosemary, *née* Cronk; *b* 31 Dec 1953; *Educ* Monkton Combe Sch; *m* 29 March 1980, Jill Penelope, da of Raymond Arthur Gransbury (d 1989); 3 s (David James b 1984, Philip Robert b 1993, Christopher Adam b 1995), 1 da (Nicola Jane b 1986); *Career* fund mangr Phillips & Drew 1972–82, dir Henderson Administration Ltd 1987–88 (joined 1982), dep md then md Midland Montagu Asset Management and chief investmt offr James Capel Asset Management 1988–93, dir int equities Prudential Portfolio Managers Ltd 1993–96, chief investment offr Smith & Williamson Securities 1996–; *Recreations* shooting, fishing, tennis, wine soc; *Style*— Charles Lindsell, Esq; ✉ Smith & Williamson Securities, 1 Riding House Street, London W1 (☎ 0171 637 5377)

LINDSEY, Alan Michael; s of Philip Stanley Lindsey, of Stanmore, Middx, and Doris Frederica Lindsey; *b* 7 Aug 1938; *Educ* Harrow HS, Orange Hill Co GS, LSE (BScEcon); *m* 3 Dec 1967, Dr Caroline Rachel Lindsey, da of Eli Gustav Weinberg; 1 da (Rebecca Adina b 2 Aug 1975); *Career* chartered accountant; articled clerk Baker Sutton & Co (now part of Ernst & Young) 1960–63, exec Corp Fin Dept Hill Samuel and N M Rothschild & Sons 1963–66, mgmnt conslt and fin exec International Timber plc 1966–72, sr investigation mangr Thornton Baker 1972–79, in own practice Alan Lindsey & Co 1979–; author of numerous articles in professional accounting magazines 1967–; memb: Ctee London Dist Soc of CA's 1979–88 (fndr, memb Ctee and past chm North London Branch), Cncl ICAEW 1988–; memb Glyndebourne Festival Soc; FCA 1963; *Recreations* music (especially opera), theatre, cross country skiing, mountain walking, swimming; *Clubs* LSE; *Style*— Alan M Lindsey, Esq; ✉ Alan Lindsey & Co, 23 Gresham Gardens, London NW11 8NX (☎ 0181 455 2882, fax 0181 455 1214)

LINDSEY, Wing Cdr Ian Walter; OBE (1989); s of Walter Richard Lindsey (d 1966), of Bromley, and Christine, *née* Godsman (d 1981); *b* 7 May 1946; *Educ* Univ of Nottingham (BA, MPhil); *m* 1971, Janet, da of Sydney Hewitt; 2 s (Gordon b 1973, Robert b 1979), 1 da (Alison b 1972); *Career* cmmnd RAFVR(T) 1967, Flying Offr 1969, Flt Lt 1973, Sqdn Ldr 1983, Wing Cdr 1984, ret 1988, OC Herts/Bucks Wing ATC, Sqdn Ldr RAFVR 7644 Res Flt 1988–94; mktg exec Williams and Glyn's Bank 1971–75, sr lectr Harrow Coll 1975–77, conslt to Price Cmmn 1977–78, asst gen mangr TSB Trustcard Ltd 1978–83; dir: Save and Prosper Group Ltd 1983–96, Robert Fleming 1988–96, Visa International 1992–96; chm United Communications Ltd 1996–; dir NAAFI 1994–; hon treas Chartered Inst of Bankers; special prof Sch of Finance and Mgmnt Univ of Nottingham; Freeman: City of London 1992, Worshipful Co of Marketors 1995; FCIB 1980; *Publications* Credit Cards (1994); *Recreations* flying; *Clubs* Bankers', HAC; *Style*— Wing Cdr Ian Lindsey, OBE; ✉ 3 Citadel Court, 12 City Road, London EC1Y 2AA (☎ 0171 638 9521)

LINDSEY AND ABINGDON, 14 and 9 Earl of (E 1626 & 1682); Richard Henry Rupert Bertie; also Baron Norreys of Rycote (E 1572); s of Lt-Col Hon Arthur Michael Bertie, DSO, MC (d 1957), and Aline Rose, *née* Arbuthnot-Leslie (d 1948); suc cousin 13 Earl of Lindsey and (8 of) Abingdon 1963; *b* 28 June 1931; *Educ* Ampleforth; *m* 1957, Norah Elizabeth Farquhar-Oliver, 2 da of late Mark Oliver, OBE, and Norah (d 1980), da of Maj Francis Farquhar, DSO, 2 s of Sir Henry Farquhar, 4 Bt, JP, DL; 2 s (Lord Norreys, Hon Alexander Michael Richard b 8 April 1970), 1 da (Lady Annabel Frances Rose b 11 March 1969); *Heir* s, Lord Norreys, *qv*; *Career* sits as Cons Peer in House of Lords; served with Scots Gds 1950 and Royal Norfolk Regt 1951–52, Lt; underwriting memb Lloyd's 1958–; company dir 1965–92, chm Dawes & Henderson (Agencies) Ltd 1988–92; High Steward of Abingdon 1963–, pres Friends of Abingdon 1982–; chm Anglo-Ivorian Soc 1974–77; *Recreations* country pursuits; *Clubs* Pratt's, Turf, White's; *Style*— The Rt Hon the Earl of Lindsey and Abingdon; ✉ Gilmilnscroft, Sorn, Mauchline, Ayrshire KA5 6ND (☎ 01290 551246, fax 01290 552906)

LINDSLEY, David Middleton; s of Richard Middleton Lindsley (d 1960), of Sunderland, Co Durham, and Ethel Muriel, *née* Greig (d 1993); *b* 8 March 1936; *Educ* The Leys Sch Cambridge; *m* 20 Aug 1960, Elizabeth Anne Dickinson, da of Dr William Athelstane Dickinson Oliver (d 1964), of Belgrave, Coxhoe, Co Durham; 1 s ((David) James Middleton b 1971), 2 da ((Elizabeth) Suzanne Middleton b 1963, (Alice) Elspeth Middleton b 1967); *Career* slr, pres Sunderland Law Soc 1986–87; dir: United and Gen Trust Ltd 1977–, Bright and Galbraith Ltd 1977–, Vale Trust Ltd 1977–; cdr Order of Merit SMO of Malta 1988; *Recreations* shooting; *Clubs* The Club (Sunderland); *Style*— David Lindsley, Esq; ✉ Springfield House, Fremington, Richmond, North Yorkshire (☎ 01748 884432); 52 John St, Sunderland, Tyne and Wear (☎ 0191 565 2421, fax 0191 514 5819)

LINE, Frances Mary (Mrs James Lloyd); OBE (1996); da of Charles Edward Line, and Leoni Lucy, *née* Hendriks; *b* 22 Feb 1940; *Educ* James Allen's Girls' Sch; *m* 28 Nov 1972, James Richard Beilby Lloyd, s of James Beilby Lloyd; *Career* BBC: clerk typist 1957, sec in TV and radio 1959–67, prodr Radio 2 1967–73, sr prodr 1973–79, chief asst Radio 2 1979–83, chief asst Radio 4 1983–85, head of Music Dept Radio 2 1985–89, controller Radio 2 1990–96 (UK Station of the Year Sony Radio Awards 1995); fell Radio Acad; FRSA; *Recreations* theatre, Sussex, happy snaps; *Style*— Miss Frances Line, OBE; ✉ 13 Naomi Close, Eastbourne, East Sussex BN20 7UU

LINE, Prof Maurice Bernard; s of Bernard Cyril Line (d 1978), of Bedford, and Ruth Florence, *née* Crane (d 1936); *b* 21 June 1928; *Educ* Bedford Sch, Exeter Coll Oxford (BA, MA); *m* 12 April 1954, Joyce, da of Walter Gilchrist (d 1953), of Paisley; 1 s (Philip b 1955), 1 da (Jill b 1957); *Career* sub librarian Univ of Southampton 1954–65, dep librarian Univ of Newcastle upon Tyne 1965–68; librarian: Univ of Bath 1968–71, Nat Central Library 1971–73; British Library: dir gen Lending Div 1974–85, dir gen Science, Technol and Indust 1985–88, memb Bd 1974–88, conslt 1988–; prof assoc Univ of Sheffield 1980–, visiting prof Loughborough Univ 1987–92; pres Library Assoc 1990; author of: 14 books and 330 articles in learned jls and 40 res reports; hon fell Birmingham Poly (now Univ of Central England in Birmingham) 1992; Hon DLitt Heriot-Watt Univ 1980, Hon DSc Univ of Southampton 1988; FLA 1954, FIInfSci 1975, Hon FLA 1987, CIMgt 1990, FRSA; *Recreations* tennis, walking, music listening, theatre; *Style*— Prof Maurice Line; ✉ 10 Blackthorn Lane, Burn Bridge, Harrogate, N Yorks HG3 1NZ (☎ 01423 872984, fax 01423 879849, e-mail mbl@hgte.demon.co.uk)

LINEEN, Sean Raymond Patrick; s of Terry Raymond Lineen (former All Black), of NZ, and Jeanette, *née* McDonald; *b* 25 Dec 1961, Auckland, NZ; *Educ* Edgewater Coll; *m* Lynne; 1 s (Cameron Jack b 23 July 1996); *Career* rugby union player (centre); former clubs: Pakuranga, Papakura, Counties (NZ), Bombay, Pontypool (championship winners 1985–86); current club Boroughmuir (Player of the Year 1990, Championship winners 1990/91); Scotland: debut v Wales 1989, memb Grand Slam winning team 1990, 29 full caps, holds world record centre partnership (27 matches) with Scott Hastings, *qv*; md Scottish Rugby Edinburgh; feature journalist The Scotsman; *Recreations* racquet sports, golf, athletics; *Style*— Sean Lineen, Esq; ✉ c/o Scottish Rugby, 11 Dock Place, Leith, Edinburgh EH6 6LU (☎ 0131 554 0540, fax 0131 554 0482)

LINEHAN, Stephen John; QC (1993); s of Maurice Gerald Linehan (d 1963), and Mary Joyce, *née* Norrish; *b* 12 March 1947; *Educ* Mt St Mary's Coll, King's Coll London; *m* 1976, Victoria Maria, da of Heiner Rössler; 1 s (Christopher b 1 Aug 1983); *Career* called to the Bar Lincoln's Inn, recorder 1989–; *Style*— Stephen Linehan, Esq, QC; ✉ 5 Fountain Court, Steelhouse Lane, Birmingham B4 6DR (☎ 0121 606 0500)

LINEKER, Gary Winston; OBE (1992); s of Barry Lineker, of 9 Coverdale Rd, The Meadows, Wigston, Leicester, and Margaret Patricia Morris, *née* Abbs; *b* 30 Nov 1960; *Educ* City of Leicester Boys' GS; *m* 5 July 1986, Michelle Denise, da of Roger Edwin Cockayne, of 1 Brickman Close, Forest Farm, Forest East, Leicester; 3 s (George b 2 Oct 1991, Harry b 25 July 1993, Toby b 3 Feb 1996); *Career* former professional footballer, currently journalist and broadcaster; 215 appearances Leicester City 1978–85 (100 goals), 57 appearances Everton 1985–86 (40 goals), 140 appearances FC Barcelona 1986–89 (54 goals), 139 appearances Tottenham Hotspur 1989–92 (80 goals), joined Grampus 8 (Nagoya, Japan) 1993–94, ret 1994; England: debut 1984, played in World Cup Mexico 1986 (leading goal scorer) and Italy 1990, played in Euro Championships W Germany 1988 and Sweden 1992, capt 1990–92, 80 caps, 48 goals, ret 1992; FA Cup winner's medal Tottenham Hotspur 1991; PFA Player of the Year 1986, Football Writers' Assoc Player of the Year 1986 and 1992; host Gary Lineker's Football Night (BBC Radio 5) 1992; regular appearer (occasionally anchor) Football Focus and Match of the Day (both BBC) 1995–, columnist The Observer 1995–, team capt They Think It's All Over (BBC1) 1995–; memb Sports Cncl 1995–; Hon MA: Univ of Leicester 1992, Loughborough Univ 1992; *Recreations* cricket, golf; *Clubs* MCC, Groucho; *Style*— Gary Lineker, Esq, OBE

LING, *see:* de Courcy Ling

LING, Philip Henry; s of Dr Thomas M Ling, and Sylvia Margaret, *née* Burne; *b* 2 April 1946; *Educ* Downside, New Coll Oxford (MA), London Business Sch (MSc); *m* 9 Sept 1969, Mary, da of W Hawley; 2 s (Sebastian b 1977, Alexander b 1983), 1 da (Harriet b 1974); *Career* dir Johnson & Firth Brown plc 1973–82, md London & Midland Industrials plc 1982–84, md Haden plc 1984–86; chm: Haden MacLellan Holdings plc 1987–92, Invesco MIM Development Capital 1992–93; non-exec dir: Ibstock plc 1984–, Fitch plc 1987–, Emess plc 1991–, Channel Holdings plc 1992– (chm), Neepsend plc 1994–, Norman Hay plc; *Recreations* riding, skiing, reading; *Clubs* Lansdowne, Annabel's; *Style*— Philip Ling, Esq; ✉ Channel Holdings plc, Royex House, Aldermanbury Square, London EC2V 7HR (☎ 0171 606 8744, fax 0171 600 4039)

LING, Richard; s of Edwin Arthur Ling (d 1988), of Amersham, and Mary, *née* Green (d 1983); *b* 7 Oct 1939; *Educ* Fettes; *m* 1972, Sandra Margaret, da of John Gaskain; 1 da (Victoria Tamsin b 1978), 1 s (Robert John b 1980); *Career* dir Armour Trust 1971–75, fin dir Croda Polymers Group 1975–79, fin dir Ladbroke Racing and chief exec Ladbroke Racecourse Management 1979–83, chief fin offr Citicorp Diners' Club Europe, ME and Africa 1983–86, md The Corporate Partnership 1986–94, chm March Group plc 1994–, md Austin Friars M & A Ltd 1996–; Master Worshipful Co of Saddlers 1995–96; FCA 1963, FCMA 1971; *Publications* Statistics in Management Information (1966), Return on Capital Employed (1970); *Recreations* sailing, mountaineering, gardening; *Clubs* Fell & Rock Climbing, Tricouni, Hayling Island Sailing; *Style*— Richard Ling, Esq; ✉ 28 White Lion Road, Amersham, Bucks HP7 9JD (☎ and fax 01494 762313, fax 01494 762313); Austin Friars M & A Ltd, Austin Friars House, 2–6 Austin Friars, London EC2N 2HE (☎ 0171 628 5323, fax 0171 628 5324)

LING, Prof Robin Sydney Mackwood; OBE (1992); s of William Harold Godfrey Mackwood Ling (d 1973), of Keighley, W Yorks, and Margaret Mona, *née* Price (d 1979); *b* 7 Sept 1927; *Educ* Shawnigan Lake Sch Vancouver Island Br Columbia, Univ of Oxford (MA, BM BCh), St Mary's Hosp London; *m* 18 Sept 1956, Mary, da of Capt W F Steedman, MC (d 1959); 2 da (Jennifer b 1959, Katherine b 1962); *Career* former conslt orthopaedic surgn: Royal Infirmary Edinburgh, Princess Margaret Orthopaedic Hosp Edinburgh; emeritus conslt orthopaedic surgn Princess Elizabeth Orthopaedic Hosp Exeter (formerly sr conslt); hon prof of bio-engrg Univ of Exeter, past pres Br Orthopaedic Assoc; pres: Br Orthopaedic Res Soc 1979–80, Int Hip Soc 1996–99; visiting prof: Louisiana State Univ 1983, Univ of Arizona 1985, Chinese Univ of Hong Kong 1985, Univ of California 1986, Baylor Univ Texas 1986, Mayo Clinic 1992; memb SICOT; Lt Sir John Charnley Meml lectr Univ of Liverpool 1986, Pridie Meml lectr Univ of Bristol 1987, Robert Jones lectr RCS 1991, W S Baer lectr Johns Hopkins Hospital Baltimore USA 1991, Arthur Steindler lectr Orthopaedic Res Soc and American Acad of Orthopaedic Surgns 1992, Donald Julius Groen Prize IMechE 1993; leading med and scientific jls on hip surgery, implant fixation and properties of biomaterials; FRCS, Hon FRCSEd; *Recreations* sailing; *Clubs* Royal Ocean Racing, Royal Dartmouth Yacht, Royal Soc of Med; *Style*— Prof Robin Ling, OBE; ✉ Lod Cottage, The Lane, Dittisham, nr Dartmouth, Devon TQ6 0HB (☎ 0180 422 451); 2 The Quadrant, Wonford Rd, Exeter EX2 4LE (☎ 01392 37070)

LING, Timothy Andrew; s of Edward Andrew Ling (d 1973), of Maidstone, Kent, and Muriel Garnett, *née* Harford (d 1994); *b* 17 Sept 1948; *Educ* King's Sch Canterbury, Queen's Coll Oxford (MA); *m* 9 May 1981, Sarah Elizabeth, da of David James; 2 s (Edward David b 30 July 1983, Richard James b 19 Jan 1985), 2 da (Emma Sarah b 8 May 1987, Sarah Rebecca b 7 March 1990); *Career* Freshfields: articled clerk 1971–73, asst slr 1973–77, ptnr 1977–, head Corp Tax Dept 1985–91, head Corp Fin Tax Gp 1991–; memb Law Soc (Revenue Law Ctee 1984–91); contrib various taxation pubns 1975–; *Recreations* music, sailing; *Clubs* Royal Harwich Yacht, Orford Sailing, St Mawes Sailing; *Style*— Timothy Ling, Esq; ✉ Freshfields, Whitefriars, 65 Fleet St, London EC4Y 1HS (☎ 0171 936 4000, fax 0171 832 7222)

LINGAM, Dr Sundara; s of Thambu Sabaratnam, of Sri Lanka, and Vijayalaxsmi; *b* 3 April 1946; *Educ* St John's Coll Jaffna Sri Lanka, People's Friendship Univ Moscow (MD(Hons)); *m* 12 June 1985, Susan Heather, da of Alex Reid, of Loughton, Essex; 1 s (Stephen Robert Surajah b 1991), 1 da (Claire Anusha Laura b 1988); *Career* registrar neurology Hosp for Sick Children Gt Ormond St 1980–83, hon sr registrar developmental paediatrics Wolfson Centre Inst of Child Health 1985–88, conslt paediatrician 1988–; hon sr lectr in community paediatrics 1991–, assoc ed World Paediatrics and Child Care; exec med dir Assoc for the Prevention of Disabilities; hon sec and treas Int Coll of Paediatrics and Child Care (ICPCC), hon asst sec/hon asst ed Royal Coll of Paediatrics and Child Health (formerly Br Paediatric Assoc) 1994–, memb and tstee Autism London; FRCP, DCH, DRCOG, LMSSA; *Books* Manual on Child Development (1988), It's Your Life (1982), Case Studies in Paediatric Radiology (1985), A - Z of Child Health (1995), Schedule of Growing Skills (SOGII) (1996); *Recreations* sports, writing, creating models; *Style*— Dr Sundara Lingam; ✉ 42 Westland Drive, Brookmans Park, Herts AL9 2UQ (☎ and fax 01707 662352); St Ann's Hospital, London N15 3TH (☎ and fax 0181 442 6335)

LINGARD, Brian Hallwood; s of Capt Abel Keenan Lingard, MC (d 1955), of Wanstead, London, and Elsie May Lingard, BEM; *b* 2 Nov 1926; *Educ* Stockport GS, Manchester Coll of Art, Sch of Architecture (DA); *m* 20 July 1949, Dorothy Gladys Lingard, da of Capt Herbert Clay (d 1978), of Bramhall, Cheshire; 2 s (Christopher b 1951, Timothy b 1953), 1 da (Rebecca b 1960); *Career* RN 1944–46; served: HMS Wolverine, Gibraltar 1944–45; architect; commenced private practice 1950; ptnr: Brian Lingard & Ptnrs 1972–93, Lingard & Styles Ptnrship (landscape architects) 1975–93, Gallery Lingard (architectural historians) 1982–93; professional awards incl: RIBA Regnl award (Wales), DOE and RIBA Housing medal (7 awards), Civic Tst (21 awards), The Times/RICS Conservation award (2 awards), Prince of Wales Conservation award (3 awards); chm Architects Benevolent Soc 1988–92; ARIBA 1949, FRIBA 1957; *Books* The Opportunities for the Conservation and Enhancement of our Historic Resorts (1983), The State We Were In (1996); *Recreations* swimming, riding, tennis, old buildings; *Clubs* Carlton, RAC; *Style*— Brian Lingard; ✉ Le Bouillon House, St George's Esplanade, St Peter Port, Guernsey CI (☎ 01481 700244); Brian Lingard & Partners, 35 Walpole Street, London SW3 (☎ 0171 730 9233)

LINGARD, Joan Amelia; da of Henry James Lingard (d 1963), and Elizabeth Cunningham Beattie (d 1948); *Educ* Bloomfield Collegiate Sch Belfast, Moray House Coll of Educn Edinburgh; *m*; 3 da; *Career* author; cncl memb Scottish Arts Cncl 1980–85 (memb Lit Ctee 1980–85); memb: PEN, Soc of Authors (chm Scotland 1982–86), Bd Edinburgh Book Festival 1994–; *Adult Novels* Liam's Daughter, The Prevailing Wind, The Tide Comes In, The Headmaster, A Sort of Freedom, The Lord on Our Side, The Second Flowering of Emily Mountjoy, Greenyards, Sisters By Rite, Reasonable Doubts, The Women's House, After Colette, Dreams of Love, Modest Glory; *Children's Novels* The Twelfth Day of July, Across The Barricades, Into Exile, A Proper Place, Hostages to Fortune, The Clearance, The Resettling, The Pilgrimage, The Reunion, Snake Among the Sunflowers, Frying As Usual, The Gooseberry, The File on Fraulein Berg, Strangers in the House, The Winter Visitor, The Freedom Machine, The Guilty Party, Rags and Riches, Tug of War, Glad Rags, Between Two Worlds, Hands Off Our School!, Night Fires, Lizzie's Leaving; *Awards* Scottish Arts Cncl bursary 1967–68, Buxtehuder Bülle Award for children's lit Germany 1986, Scottish Arts Cncl Award 1994; *Style*— Ms Joan Lingard; ✉ c/o David Higham Associates Ltd, 5–8 Lower John Street, Golden Square, London W1R 4HA (☎ 0171 437 7888, fax 0171 437 1072)

LINGENS, Michael Robert; s of Dr Friedrich Otto Lingens, of Stuttgart, W Germany, and Karin Weber; *b* 15 May 1957; *Educ* St Edmund's Sch Canterbury, Trinity Coll Oxford (MA); *m* 9 May 1992, Rachel, da of Charles Fay, *qv*, and Patricia Fay, OBE; 1 s (Matthew b 20 Sept 1995); *Career* admitted slr 1982, ptnr Speechly Bircham, chm Bow Group 1984–85; cncllr London Borough of Hammersmith and Fulham; Parly candidate (C) Bolsover 1987; *Books* The SDP - A Critical Analysis, Beveridge and The Bow Group Generation, Winning on Welfare; *Recreations* real tennis, rackets; *Clubs* Coningsby, The Queen's; *Style*— Michael Lingens, Esq; ✉ 61 Blandford Road, London W4 1EA (☎ home 0181 747 3105, business 0171 353 3290, fax 0171 353 4825)

LINGWOOD, David Frederick; s of Frederick Joseph Lingwood, of Bedford, and Grace Anne, *née* Clark (d 1986); *b* 5 May 1946; *Educ* Royal GS Newcastle upon Tyne, Univ of Newcastle; *Career* PA to md Theatres Consolidated, house mangr for Sadler's Wells Opera London Coliseum, gen mangr Watford Civic Theatre Tst, admin dir Unicorn Theatre, admin Actors Co, asst exec prodr Robert Stigwood Orgn; gen mangr: Mermaid Theatre London, Shaftesbury Theatre London; asst gen mangr Royal Albert Hall; theatre mangr: Duchess Theatre 1987, Queen's Theatre 1987, London Palladium 1988–94; ops mangr Stoll Moss Theatres 1994–; *Recreations* music, theatre, swimming, gardening; *Style*— David Lingwood, Esq; ✉ 17 Elgin Mansions, Elgin Avenue, London W9 1JG

LININGTON, Richard; s of Reginald Friend Linington (d 1981), of Birchington, Kent, and Gwendoline Florence Irene, *née* Amos (d 1986); *b* 31 March 1945; *Educ* Tonbridge, Birmingham Coll of Arts and Crafts (Dip Int Design); *m* 27 Sept 1969 (m dis 1994), (Hilary) Jane, da of Maj Ronald Jasper Lucas, of Westington, Chipping Campden, Glos; 2 s (Noel b 1971, Ben b 1975); *Career* designer; interior designer R Seifert and Ptnrs 1967–69, designer for architect Stephen Garrett 1969–72, assoc with Austin Smith Lord Architects 1972–79, princ Hurley Linington McGirr Design Ptnrshp 1979–87, ptnr

Bloomer Tweedale Architects 1988–91, interior design mangr Austin-Smith Lord 1991–92, princ Linington - Architectural and Interior Design 1992–94, design dir The Chadwick Group London 1994–; pres Int Fedn of Int Designers and Architects 1987–89 and 1991–93; FCSD 1987; *Recreations* music, gardening; *Clubs* East India; *Style*— Richard Linington, Esq; ✉ 3 New Cottages, Potten Street, St Nicholas At Wade, Kent CT7 0QR (☎ 01843 842855)

LINKLATER, Magnus Duncan; s of Eric Robert Linklater, CBE, TD, and Marjorie MacIntyre; *b* 21 Feb 1942; *Educ* Eton, Univ of Freiburg, Sorbonne, Trinity Hall Cambridge (BA); *m* 1967, Veronica Linklater, *qv*, da of Lt-Col Michael Lyle, OBE, JP, DL, of Riemore Lodge, Dunkeld; 2 s (Alexander b 1968, Saul b 1970), 1 da (Freya b 1975); *Career* journalist: Daily Express Manchester 1964–65, Evening Standard (ed Londoner's Diary) 1965–69, The Sunday Times (ed Spectrum pages, ed Colour Magazine, asst ed News, exec ed Features) 1969–83; managing ed The Observer 1983–86; ed: The London Daily News 1986–87, The Scotsman 1988–94; columnist The Times 1994–; presenter BBC Radio Scotland 1994–; chm: Scottish Daily Newspaper Soc 1991–93, Edinburgh Book Festival 1995–96, Scottish Arts Cncl 1996–; Hon Dr of Arts Napier Univ; *Books* Hoax - The Howard Hughes Clifford Irving Affair (with Stephen Fay and Lewis Chester), Jeremy Thorpe - A Secret Life (with Lewis Chester and David May), The Falklands War (with the Sunday Times Insight team), Massacre - the story of Glencoe, The Fourth Reich - Klaus Barbie and the Neo-Fascist Connection (with Isabel Hilton and Neal Ascherson), Not with Honour - the inside story of the Westland Affair (with David Leigh), For King and Conscience - John Graham of Claverhouse, Viscount Dundee (with Christian Hesketh), Anatomy of Scotland (co-ed), Highland Wilderness (photographs by Colin Prior); *Recreations* fishing, book collecting; *Clubs* MCC, Press; *Style*— Magnus Linklater, Esq; ✉ 5 Drummond Place, Edinburgh EH3 6PH (☎ 0131 557 5705, fax 0131 557 9757)

LINKLATER, Veronica; da of Lt-Col Michael Lyle, OBE, JP, DL, of Riemore Lodge, Dunkeld, Perthshire, and Hon Elizabeth Sinclair; *b* 15 April 1943; *Educ* Cranbourne Chase Sch, Univ of Sussex, Univ of London (DipSoc); *m* 1967, Magnus Duncan Linklater, *qv*, s of late Eric Robert Linklater; 2 s (Alexander b 1968, Saul b 1970), 1 da (Freya b 1975); *Career* child care offr London Borough of Tower Hamlets 1967–68, co-fndr Visitors' Centre Pentonville Prison 1971–77, govr three Islington schs 1970–85, Prison Reform Tst project Winchester Prison 1981–82; The Butler Tst Prison Serv Annual Award Scheme: fndr, admin then conslt 1983–87, tstee 1987–; JP Inner London 1985–88, co-ordinator then tstee and vice chm The Pushkin Prizes (Scotland) 1989–, memb Children's Panel Edinburgh South 1989–, pres Soc of Friends of Dunkeld Cathedral 1989–, memb Ctee The Gulliver Award for the Performing Arts in Scotland 1990–, fndr and chm The New Sch Butterstone 1991–, tstee Esmee Fairbairn Charitable Tst 1991–, patron The Sutherland Tst 1993–, tstee The Young Musicians Tst 1993–; Parly candidate (Lib Dem) Perth and Kinross (by-election) 1995; *Recreations* music, theatre, gardening; *Style*— Mrs Veronica Linklater; ✉ 5 Drummond Place, Edinburgh EH3 6PH (☎ 0131 557 5705, fax 0131 557 9757)

LINLEY, Viscount; *see:* Royal Family section

LINLITHGOW, 4 Marquess of (UK 1902); Sir Adrian John Charles Hope; 12 Bt (NS 1698); also Earl of Hopetoun, Viscount Aithrie, Lord Hope (all S 1703), Baron Hopetoun (UK 1809), and Baron Niddry (UK 1814); o son of 3 Marquess of Linlithgow, MC (d 1987), and his 1 w Vivien, *née* Kenyon-Slaney (d 1963); *b* 1 July 1946; *Educ* Eton; *m* 1, 9 Jan 1968 (m dis 1978), Anne Pamela, eld da of Arthur Edmund Leveson, of Hall Place, Ropley, Hants; 2 s (Earl of Hopetoun, *qv*, b 22 May 1969, Lord Alexander b 3 Feb 1971); m 2, 1980, Peta Carol, da of Charles Victor Ormonde Binding, of Congresbury, Somerset; 1 s (Lord Robert b 17 Jan 1984), 1 da (Lady Louisa b 16 April 1981); *Heir* s, Earl of Hopetoun, *qv*; *Style*— The Most Hon the Marquess of Linlithgow; ✉ Hopetoun House, South Queensferry, West Lothian EH30 9SL; 123 Beaufort St, London SW3

LINNELL, David George Thomas; CBE (1987); s of George Linnell, and Marguerite, *née* Gardner; *b* 28 May 1930; *Educ* Leighton Park Sch Reading; *m* 11 March 1953, Margaret Mary, da of Robert John Paterson; 1 s (Mark David b 1955), 1 da (Claire Elizabeth b 1958); *Career* md Thomas Linnell and Sons Ltd 1964–75, chief exec Linfood Holdings Ltd 1975–81, chm Spar Food Holdings 1975–79, pres Inst of Grocery Distribution 1980–82; chm: Eggs Authy 1981–86, Neighbourhood Stores PLC 1983–87, Birkdale Group plc (formerly Brunning Group plc) 1987–95; FIGD 1977, CIMgt 1978; *Clubs* Carlton; *Style*— David Linnell, Esq, CBE; ✉ The Old Rectory, Titchmarsh, Kettering, Northants

LINNELL, Stuart Swain Goodman; s of Capt Eric Henry Goodman Linnell (d 1975), of Birmingham, and Dorothy Mary, *née* Swain (d 1974); *b* 22 Jan 1947, Birmingham; *Educ* King's Norton GS Birmingham; *m* 1981, Susan Marie, da of Desmond Reginald Cleobury, of Coventry; 2 s (Nicholas Charles Goodman b 15 Feb 1983, Matthew Stuart b 4 July 1985); *Career* pt/t freelance bdcaster BBC Radio Birmingham (now BBC Radio WM) 1970–74, sports ed Radio Hallam Sheffield 1974–80, sports ed and afternoon presenter Mercia Sound Coventry 1980–86 (prog controller 1983–86), md Mercia Sound Ltd (formerly Midlands Community Radio plc) and prog controller Mercia FM (formerly Mercia Sound) 1986–94, dep md and gp ops dir Midlands Radio Holdings plc 1988–89, md Leicester Sound Ltd and prog controller Leicester Sound FM 1991–94, station dir Mercia Sound Ltd 1994–95, actg station dir RAM FM Ltd Derby 1994, exec dir Sports Radio UK 1995–; freelance presenter: breakfast show BBC Radio WM 1995–, BBC TV 1995–, BBC Radio 5 Live 1995– (also sports reporter); dir: Cable Advertising Sales (Coventry) Ltd 1986–87, Birmingham Broadcasting Ltd 1988–89, Leicester Communications Ltd (Leicester cable TV) 1992–; memb Labour Rels Ctee AIRC 1987, AIRC rep Sony Radio Awards Ctee 1988–94, memb Programming Ctee AIRC 1992–93; memb Mercia FM Birthday Appeal Ctee 1987–95 (chm 1987–90), tstee Mercia FM/Evening Telegraph Snowball Tst 1988–95, chm Mercia FM Walkathon Ctee 1989–95, chm Coventry Advsy Bd Mercia TAP Agency 1989–90, tstee Midlands Radio Action Community Tst 1990–94, chm Coventry Relate Centre Appeal Ctee 1991–92; vice pres: Baby Lifeline 1991–, Tandem Express Appeal 1992; memb NSPCC Centenary Appeal Coventry Ctee 1994–; Int Radio Festival of NY: Gold Medal for Mercia FM prog format 1990, 2 category Silver Medals and Finalist's Cert of Recognition for prog format 1991, Bronze Medals for jtly-placed prog formats for Mercia FM and Leicester Sound FM 1993; memb Radio Acad; *Recreations* the family, caravanning, watching Coventry City FC, playing golf (badly!); *Clubs* Windmill Village Golf (Coventry), Camping and Caravan Club of GB; *Style*— Stuart Linnell, Esq, MBE; ✉ c/o Terry Smith, Cads Management, 48 Lightwoods Hill, Bearwood, Warley, W Midlands B67 5EB (☎ 0121 420 1996, fax 0121 434 4909)

LINNETT, Simon John Lawrence; s of Prof John Wilfrid Linnett (d 1975), and Rae Ellen Fanny, *née* Libgott; *b* 14 Feb 1954; *Educ* The Leys Cambridge, Balliol Coll Oxford; *m* 28 Nov 1987, Penelope Jane, da of Sir Charles William Willink, Bt, of Highgate, London; 2 s (John Lawrence Humfrey b 1991, Henry Simon Albert b 1993); *Career* NM Rothschild & Sons Ltd: joined 1975, mangr 1982, asst dir 1984, dir 1987, dir Exec Ctee 1989; *Recreations* environmental issues, walking; *Style*— Simon Linnett, Esq; ✉ c/o N M Rothschild & Sons Limited, New Court, St Swithin's Lane, London EC4P 4DU (☎ 0171 280 5062)

LINSCOTT, Gillian; da of Thomas Snow Linscott (d 1988), of Maidenhead, Berks, and Muriel Rosaline, *née* Fountain (d 1978); *b* 27 Sept 1944; *Educ* Maidenhead HS, Somerville Coll Oxford (MA); *m* 1988, Tony Geraghty; *Career* journalist: Liverpool Daily Post 1967–70, Birmingham Post 1970–72, The Guardian 1972–79, BBC 1979–90 (mainly as Parly journalist); freelance writer 1990–; author; memb Crime Writers' Assoc 1984; *Books* A Healthy Body (1984), Murder Makes Tracks (1985), Knightfall (1986), A Whiff of Sulphur (1987), Unknown Hand (1988), Murder, I Presume (1990), Sister Beneath the Sheet (1991), Hanging on the Wire (1992), Stage Fright (1993), Widow's Peak (1994), Crown Witness (1995), Dead Man's Music (1996); *Recreations* horse-riding, gardening, hill walking; *Style*— Ms Gillian Linscott; ✉ c/o David Higham Associates Ltd, 5–8 Lower John Street, Golden Square, London W1R 4HA (☎ 0171 437 7888, fax 0171 437 1072)

LINSELL, Richard Duncan; s of Dr William Duncan Linsell, of Ipswich, and Margaret Sybil, *née* Burns; *b* 21 June 1947; *Educ* Mill Hill Sch, Jesus Coll Cambridge (MA); *m* 25 Oct 1986, Briony Margaret, da of Dr James Wright Anderton Crabtree, OBE, TD (Col and former QHP), of Devon; 1 da (Katherine Jemima Cory b 14 Oct 1987); *Career* admitted slr 1973, ptnr Rowe & Maw 1976–; non-exec dir DHL International (UK) Ltd 1977–, non-exec chm Jas Bowman & Sons Ltd 1991–; memb: Law Soc, Int Bar Assoc; *Recreations* music, golf, walking; *Style*— Richard Linsell, Esq; ✉ 20 Black Friars Lane, London EC4V 6HD (☎ 0171 248 4282, fax 0171 248 2009, telex 262787)

LINSTEAD, Stephen Guy; s of George Frederick Linstead, of Sheffield (d 1974), and May Dorothy, *née* Griffiths; *b* 23 June 1941; *Educ* King Edward VII Sch Sheffield, Corpus Christi Coll Oxford (MA, dip in public and social admin), Univ of Carleton Ottowa (MA); *m* 1, 1971; 2 s (Benjamin, Henry); m 2, 1982, Rachael Marian, *née* Feldman; 2 da (Catherine Eloise, Sheena Mary Gwyneth); *Career* Bd of Trade: joined 1964, asst princ 1964–69, private sec to the Min of State 1967–69, princ 1969–76; asst sec Dept of Prices and Consumer Protection 1976–79, Dept of Trade (now DTI) 1979, Office of Fair Trading 1982–90, under sec and regnl dir West Midlands DTI 1990–94; vice chm Association of First Div Civil Servs 1982–84, memb Steering Gp Industry 96 (West Midlands Festival of Indust and Enterprise) 1994–96, memb Exec Ctee Solihull C of C and Indust 1995–; reader Diocese of Birmingham; *Books* The Law of Crown Privilege in Canada and Elsewhere (1968); *Recreations* biblical criticism, swimming, travel, entertainment; *Clubs* Royal Over-Seas League; *Style*— Stephen G Linstead, Esq; ✉ 20 Silhill Hall Road, Solihull, West Midlands B91 1JU (☎/fax 0121 705 1376, e-mail 100743.326@compuserve.com)

LINTHWAITE, Peter John Nicholas; s of John Linthwaite, ISO, of Johannesburg, SA, and June Margaret Fiennes, *née* Nicoll; *b* 3 Dec 1956; *Educ* Bedford Modern Sch, New Coll Oxford (BA); *m* 18 Sept 1982, Gillian Deborah, da of Rei Oblitas, OBE, ED; 2 da (Sarah Louise Margaret b 1 Jan 1989, Emma Victoria Anne b 6 April 1992); *Career* vice pres Bank of America NT (SA, London and Hong Kong) 1978–86, Standard Chartered Bank Hong Kong 1986–87, dir Tranwood Earl and Co Ltd 1987–90, dir Murray Johnstone Private Equity Ltd 1990–95, md Murray Johnstone (Asia) Pte Ltd 1995–; *Recreations* cricket, skiing, bridge, ballet; *Clubs* MCC, RAC; *Style*— Peter Linthwaite, Esq; ✉ Murray Johnstone Ltd, 30 Coleman St, London EC2R 5AN (☎ 0171 606 6969)

LINTOTT, Lesley Joan; da of John Desmond Hutson (d 1979), of Durham, and Marion Hush, *née* Mallabar (d 1977); *b* 28 June 1950; *Educ* Washington Grammar Tech Sch, St Hilda's Coll Oxford (MA); *m* 19 Aug 1972, Christopher John Lintott, s of John William Lintott (d 1972); *Career* Penningtons: articled clerk 1972–75, ptnr 1978, London admin ptnr 1990–96, head Private Client Dept 1995–, London managing ptnr 1996–; Freeman City of London Slrs' Co 1992, Freeman City of London 1995; memb: City of London Law Soc, Soc of Tsts & Estates Practitioners (STEP); *Books* Butterworths Wills, Probate & Administration Service (revision ed, Wills Div); *Recreations* wine, music, cricket; *Clubs* Wine Soc Dining, Surrey CCC; *Style*— Ms Lesley Lintott; ✉ Penningtons, Bucklersbury House, 83 Cannon Street, London EC4N 8PE (☎ 0171 236 1366)

LINTOTT, Robert Edward; s of Charles Edward Lintott (d 1981), and Doris Mary Lintott (d 1989); *b* 14 Jan 1932; *Educ* Cambridgeshire HS, Trinity Coll Cambridge (MA); *m* 26 July 1958, Mary Alice, da of Canon Frank Hope Scott (d 1971), of Hull; 3 s (Mark b 1959, John b 1961, Benedict b 1965); *Career* Nat Serv PO RAF 1951–52; Esso Petroleum Co/Esso UK 1955–86: dir logistics 1979–81, dir mktg 1981–83, md 1983–86; chief exec The Coverdale Organisation plc 1987–91; chm Materials and Chemical Sector Bd BSI 1991–; conslt Sanders and Sidney plc 1992–; memb Cncl Royal Borough Windsor and Maidenhead 1987–91 (chm Leisure Servs Ctee 1988–91); chm: Exec Ctee Fndn for Mgmnt Educn, Queen's Coll Taunton; FInstPet; *Recreations* vintage motoring, cricket; *Clubs* RAF, MCC; *Style*— Robert Lintott, Esq; ✉ Huish Barton, Watchet, Somerset TA23 0LU (☎ 01984 640208, fax 01984 641147)

LIPKIN, Dr Malcolm Leyland; s of Dr Reuben Lipkin (d 1944), of Liverpool, and Evelyne, *née* Urding (d 1982); *b* 2 May 1932; *Educ* Liverpool Coll, RCM London, Univ of London (BMus, DMus); *m* 5 Aug 1968, Judith Eda, da of Jacob Frankel (d 1968), of Port Elizabeth, S Africa; 1 s (Jonathan b 21 Sept 1970); *Career* lectr in music Dept of External Studies Univ of Oxford 1967–75, lectr Sch of Continuing Educn Univ of Kent at Canterbury 1975–96; composer; premieres incl: Piano Sonata no 3 (Gaudeamus Fndn Int Music Week Holland) 1951, Piano Sonata no 4 (Cheltenham Festival) 1955, Piano Concerto (Cheltenham Festival) 1959, Violin Concerto no 2 (Bournemouth Symphony Orch) 1963, Sinfonia di Roma Symphony no 1 (Royal Liverpool Philharmonic) 1966, Psalm 96 for Chorus and Orch (John Lewis Partnership cmmn) 1969, Clifford's Tower (Cheltenham Festival) 1980, Five Songs (BBC London) 1981, Harp Trio (Rye Festival) 1982, Naboth's Vineyard (Law Soc concerts) 1983, The Pursuit Symphony no 2 (BBC Philharmonic Manchester) 1983, Wind Quintet (BBC cmmn) 1986, Prelude and Dance in Memory of Jacqueline du Pré (City of London Festival) 1988, Piano Sonata no 5 (Gt Comp Festival) 1989, Piano Trio (Purcell Room London) 1989, Oboe Concerto (BBC cmmn) 1990, Variations on a Theme of Bartok for String Quartet (Newbury Spring Festival) 1992, Dance Fantasy for Solo Violin (Carl Flesch Int Violin Competition London) 1992, Sun Symphony No 3 (BBC Philharmonic Manchester) 1993, Five Bagatelles (Wigmore Hall London) 1994; made numerous recordings, broadcasts and performances worldwide; memb Exec Ctee Composers' Guild of GB 1972–76; ARCM, LRAM; *Books* illustrated incl: Handel at Work (1963), A History of Western Music (1974), Casals and the Art of Interpretation (1976), The Nine Symphonies of Beethoven (1981), Tortelier - A Self-Portrait (1984), A Companion to the Concerto (1988); *Recreations* long country walks, travelling; *Style*— Dr Malcolm Lipkin; ✉ Penlan, Crowborough Hill, Crowborough, Sussex TN6 2EA (☎ 01892 652454)

LIPMAN, Dr Harald Martin; s of Dr Isaac Lipman (d 1955), and Dr Rachel Lipman, *née* Caplan (d 1964); *b* 10 Dec 1931; *Educ* City of London Sch, UCH (MB BS, DCH); *m* 19 April 1959, Nahid, da of Jacoub Sahim, of USA; 1 s (Marc b 1963), 1 da (Amanda b 1961); *Career* med advsr Transcare Int 1977–87, conslt physician Repub of the Sudan 1980–87, regnl med advsr Br Embassy Moscow 1987–90; chm Moscow Med Assoc 1987–90, sr med advsr FCO 1992–; dir: Eastern European Travellers Medical Advisory Service Ltd 1991–94, Anglo-Sovmed Ltd 1991–94; vice chm Assoc for Promotion of Healthcare in The Former Soviet Union 1991–93, tstee Tushinskaya Children's Hosp Charitable Tst 1991–; memb: Britain-Russia Centre, Iran Soc, Tibet Soc, Med Soc for Study of Venereal Diseases; Liveryman Worshipful Soc of Apothecaries, Freeman City of London; MRCGP, FRSM; *Books* Encyclopaedia of Russia and the USSR (contrib 2 edn, 1992); *Recreations* skiing, tennis; *Style*— Dr Harald M Lipman; ✉ 43 Wimpole Street, London W1M 7AF (☎ and fax 0171 486 4588)

LIPMAN, Maureen Diane; da of late Maurice Julius Lipman, of Hull, and Zelma Lipman; *b* 10 May 1946; *Educ* LAMDA; *m* 18 Feb 1973, Jack Rosenthal, *qv*, s of Samuel Rosenthal (d 1964); 1 s (Adam b 3 Oct 1976), 1 da (Amy b 7 June 1974); *Career* actress; columnist She Magazine (PPA Columnist of the Year Award 1991), Good Housekeeping 1991–96; Hon DLitt Hull 1994, Hon MA Salford 1995; *Theatre* 3 yrs NT incl Kathleen in A Long Day's Journey into Night (NT); other credits incl: incl: The Knack (Palace Theatre, Watford), Molly in The Front Page (Old Vic), Miss Richland in The Good Natured Man, Celia in As You Like It (RSC); West End incl: Outside Edge, Messiah (both SWET Award nomination for Best Actress), Chapter Two (Lyric Hammersmith), The Meg and Mog Show (Arts Theatre), Kitty McShane On Your Way Riley (Theatre Royal), lead role in Night and Day (Greenwich), See How They Run (Olivier Award for Best Comedy Performance and Variety Club Award), musical debut Ruth in Wonderful Town (Queen's Theatre, Variety Club Award and Olivier Award nomination), devised and appeared in one-woman show Re: Joyce (life of Joyce Grenfell, three seasons, West End and Long Wharf Theatre Connecticut) 1988–91, The Cabinet Minister (Albery) 1991, Lost in Yonkers (Strand Theatre) 1992, The Sisters Rosensweig (Old Vic) 1994; most recently Mrs Malapop in The Rivals (Manchester Royal Exchange), Live and Kidding (solo performance, Chichester, Leeds, also on video); *Television* incl: The Evacuees, Jane Lucas in Agony (BAFTA Award nomination for Best Comedy Performance), Smiley's People, The Evacuees, The Knowledge, Rolling Home, Maggie in Outside Edge (both BAFTA Award nomination for Best Actress), The Princess of France in Love's Labours Lost, Absent Friends, Shift Work, lead in All At No 20 (Thames, TV Times Best Comedy Actress Award), Miss Minchin in The Little Princess (2 series, LWT), About Face (2 series, Central TV) 1989 and 1990, Enid Blyton in Sunny Stories (BBC2, Bookmark), Agony Again 1995, Shani in Eskimo Day 1996; appearances incl Have I Got News for You (BBC) 1994; *Film* incl: Up the Junction (debut), Gumshoe, Educating Rita (BAFTA Award nomination for Best Supporting Actress), Water (with Michael Caine), Carry On Columbus 1992; *Radio* incl: When Housewives Had The Choice (2 series), The Lipman Test 1994; *Books* How Was it for You? (1985), Something to Fall Back On (1987), You Got an 'Ology? (with Richard Phillips, 1989), Thank You For Having Me (1990), When's It Coming Out? (1992), You Can Read Me Like a Book (1995); *Style—* Ms Maureen Lipman; ✉ c/o Hutton Management Ltd, 200 Fulham Road, London SW10 9PN (☎ 0171 352 4825, fax 0171 351 4560)

LIPPIATT, Stuart Ralph; s of Ernest Frank Lippiatt, of Bristol, and Lillian Genevieve, *née* Sage; *b* 26 Oct 1947; *Educ* Bristol GS, Univ Coll Oxford (MA); *Career* graduate computer trainee Rolls-Royce Aero Engines 1969–71, computer programmer, systems analyst and systems mangr Hambro Life Assurance 1972–80; asst slr Norton Rose Solicitors 1982–88 (articled clerk 1980–82); ptnr: D J Freeman & Co Solicitors 1988–91, Norton Rose 1993– (rejoined as asst slr 1991); memb: City of London Solicitors' Co, Law Soc, Assoc of Pension Lawyers; *Books* Taxation of Pension Schemes (co-author, 1996); *Style—* Stuart Lippiatt, Esq; ✉ Norton Rose, Kempson House, PO Box 570, Camomile Street, London EC3A 7AN (☎ 0171 283 6000, fax 0171 283 6500)

LIPSCOMB, (Edwin) Paul; s of Dr A George J Lipscomb (d 1975), and Kathleen A Lipscomb (d 1993); *b* 9 Sept 1933; *Educ* Blackfriars Sch Laxton Northants; *m* 17 June 1961, Pauline Ann, da of Capt Henry John Farrell Palliser (d 1937); 1 s (Christopher John Farrell b 1962), 1 da (Catherine Ann Farrell (Mrs Tony Payton) b 1965); *Career* Nat Serv The Green Howards 1952–54, TA The Green Howards 1955–61, ret as Capt; CA Touche Ross & Co 1955–62; fin dir: Biscuits Belin France (subsid of Nabisco) 1962–64, Levitt & Sons France 1964–65; Euro controller France Mead Corporation 1965–68, mangr fin controls Belgium HQ ITT Europe 1968–72, divnl dir London IHQ Rank Xerox 1972–75, exec vice pres Amsterdam and London Cinema International Corporation 1975–82, fin controller British Airways 1982–85, dir Borthwicks plc 1985–89, gp fin and prodn dir J W Spear & Sons plc 1989–96, chm Corgi Classics Ltd 1995–96; tstee: Fortune Centre for Riding Therapy 1984–, Life Opportunities Tst 1991–; FCA, FIMgt, AFST, FRSA; *Recreations* travel, food & wine; *Clubs* Naval & Military, Savage; *Style—* Paul Lipscomb, Esq; ✉ c/o Naval and Military Club, 94 Piccadilly, London SW1

LIPSCOMBE, Eric Richard; s of Eric Wilfred Lipscombe (d 1965), and Frances Selina Emma, *née* Cowdrey (d 1985); *b* 23 June 1938; *Educ* Churchers Coll Hants; *m* 5 March 1966, Rosemary Christine Frances, da of Maj Harold Ernest White (d 1978); 1 s (Guy b 1968), 2 da (Sophie b 1970, Emily b 1975); *Career* Nat Serv 1960–62, Asst Adj to Sch of Mil Engrg; dep chm White Cross Systems Group Ltd, vice pres Teradata Corp (USA), md Teradata Europe Ltd, chm Teradata UK Ltd; dir: Teradata Deutschland GmbH, Teradata France SA, Teradata Italia 1986–92; non-exec chm European Marketing Consultants; fndr chm and md Computer Peripherals Ltd and subsidiaries 1979–84, dir Micro Business Systems plc 1984–86; Hants rugby player, memb Richmond FC 1962–66; CEng, MICE; *Recreations* sport, music; *Clubs* East India; *Style—* Eric R Lipscombe, Esq; ✉ Bridge End House, Ockham, nr Ripley, Surrey (☎ 01483 222007); White Cross Systems Ltd, 3a Waterside Park, Cookham Road, Bracknell, Berkshire RG12 1RB (☎ 01344 300770)

LIPSEY, David Lawrence; s of Lawrence Lipsey, and Penelope Lipsey; *b* 21 April 1948; *Educ* Bryanston Sch, Magdalen Coll Oxford (BA); *m* 1982, Margaret Robson; 1 da; *Career* journalist; res asst GMWU 1970–72, special advsr to Anthony Crosland MP 1972–77 (DOE 1974–76, FCO 1976–77), PM's Staff 10 Downing St 1977–79, journalist New Society 1979–80, economic ed Sunday Times 1982–86 (political staff 1980–82), ed New Society 1986–88, fndr and jt dep ed Sunday Correspondent 1988–90, assoc ed The Times 1990–92, political ed The Economist 1994– (joined 1992); visiting prof of public admin Univ of Ulster 1993–, non-exec dir Personal Investment Authy 1994–; sec Streatham Lab Pty 1970–72, chm Fabian Soc 1981–82, memb Exec Ctee Charter for Jobs 1984–86; *Books* Labour and Land (1974), The Socialist Agenda: Crosland's Legacy (co-ed Dick Leonard, 1981), Making Government Work (1982), The Name of the Rose (1992); *Recreations* family life; *Style—* David Lipsey, Esq; ✉ 44 Drakefield Rd, London SW17 8RP (☎ 0181 767 3268); The Economist, 25 St James's St, London SW1A 1HG (☎ 0171 830 7000)

LIPTON, Prof Michael; s of Leslie Lipton (d 1977), and Helen, *née* Janssen; *b* 13 Feb 1937; *Educ* Haberdashers' Aske's, Balliol Coll Oxford (BA, MA), Mass Inst of Technol; *m* 9 Dec 1966, Merle, da of Charles Babrow (d 1979); 1 s (Emanuel b 1 March 1974); *Career* res offr with G Myrdal on Asian Drama 1960–61, fell All Souls Coll Oxford 1961–68 and 1982–84; Univ of Sussex: asst lectr 1961–62, lectr 1962–66, reader 1966–71, fell Inst of Devpt Studies and professorial fell 1971–77, 1979–87 and 1990–, prof of devpt economics and dir Poverty Research Unit 1994–; employment devpt advsr Govt of Botswana 1977–78, sr policy advsr World Bank 1981–82, prog dir consumption and nutrition prog Int Food Policy Res Inst Washington DC 1988–89; ed Jl of Devpt Studies 1968–80, chm Br Assoc for South Asian Studies 1985–87; extensive research and consultancy on agric research and technol, rural employment, poverty reduction and land distribution especially in India, Bangladesh, Sri Lanka, Botswana, Sierra Leone and recently SA and Romania; numerous papers and pubns in jls; Hon DLitt Univ of Sussex 1982; memb: Devpt Studies Assoc, Int Assoc of Agric Economists; *Publications* Chess Problems: Introduction to an Art (with R Matthews and J Rice, 1962), Assessing Economic Performance (1968), The Crisis of Indian Planning (with P Streeten, 1968), The Erosion of a Relationship: India and Britain since 1960 (with J Firn, 1975), Migration from Rural Areas: The Evidence from Village Studies (with J Connell, 1976), Why Poor People Stay Poor: Urban Bias and World Development (1977), Botswana: Employment and Labour Use (1979), New Seeds and Poor People (1989), Does Aid Work in India? (with J Toye, 1990), Including the Poor (with J van der Gaag, 1993), How Third World Households Adapt to Dietary Energy Stress (with P Payne, 1994), Successes in Anti-poverty (1995); *Recreations* chess problems, play-going, poetry; *Style—* Prof Michael Lipton; ✉ School of African and Asian Studies, University of Sussex, Brighton BN1 9QN (direct ☎ 01273 678739, fax 01273 623572)

LIPTON, Stuart Anthony; s of Bertram Green, of London, and Jeanette Lipton; *b* 9 Nov 1942; *Educ* Berkhamsted Sch; *m* 16 June 1966, Ruth Kathryn, da of Harry Marks (d 1986), of London; 2 s (Elliot Stephen b 17 March 1969, Grant Alexander b 20 Jan 1975), 1 da (Sarah Joanna b 15 June 1971); *Career* dir: Sterling Land Co 1971–73, First Palace Securities Ltd 1973–; jt md Greycoat plc 1976–83, chief exec Stanhope Properties PLC 1983–95, chief exec Stanhope PLC 1995–; advsr to: Hampton Site Co for Sainsbury Wing Nat Gallery 1985–91, The Sackler Galleries Royal Acad 1988–91, Glyndebourne Productions Ltd for new opera house; memb: Property Advsy Gp DOE 1986–, Mil Bldgs Ctee MOD 1987–, Cncl Br Property Fedn 1986–; tstee Whitechapel Art Gallery 1987–94, cmmr Royal Fine Art Cmmn; memb: Bd Nat Theatre 1988–, Advsy Bd Royal Acad 1987–, Governing Bd Imperial Coll 1987–; dep chm Architecture Fndn; Hon FRIBA; *Recreations* architecture, crafts, art and technology, wine; *Style—* Stuart Lipton, Esq; ✉ Stanhope PLC, 11 Bruton Street, London W1X 7AG (☎ 0171 495 7575, fax 0171 409 7209)

LIPWORTH, Sir (Maurice) Sydney; kt (1991), Hon QC (1993); s of Isidore Lipworth (d 1966), of Johannesburg, SA, and Rae, *née* Sindler (d 1983); *b* 13 May 1931; *Educ* King Edward VII Sch Johannesburg, Univ of Witwatersrand Johannesburg (BCom, LLB); *m* 1957, Rosa, da of Bernard Liwarek (d 1943); 2 s (Bertrand, Frank); *Career* dep chm Allied Dunbar Assurance plc (formerly Hambro Life Assurance plc) 1984–88 (dir 1971–88, jt md 1980–84); chm: Allied Dunbar & Co plc, Allied Dunbar Unit Tsts plc 1985–88 (md 1983–85); dir: J Rothschild Holdings plc 1984–87, BAT Industries plc 1985–88; chm Monopolies and Mergers Cmmn 1988–93 (memb 1981–93), dir and dep chm National Westminster Bank plc 1993–, dir Carlton Communications plc 1993–, dir and chm Zeneca Group PLC 1995–; chm Financial Reporting Cncl 1994–, memb Senior Salaries Review Body 1994; hon bencher Inner Temple 1989 (memb 1991–), chm Bar Assoc for Commerce, Fin and Indust 1991, memb Gen Cncl of the Bar 1991–94; chm NatWest Group Charitable Trust 1994–; tstee: Allied Dunbar Charitable Tst 1971–94, Philharmonia Orchestra 1982– (chm of tstees 1993–), Royal Acad 1988–, Breakthrough (Breast Cancer Res Tst) (memb Advsy Panel) 1991–; memb Bd of Tstees South Bank Foundation Ltd 1996–; govr Sadler's Wells Fndn 1987–90; *Recreations* tennis, music, theatre; *Clubs* Queens, Reform; *Style—* Sir Sydney Lipworth, QC; ✉ National Westminster Bank plc, 41 Lothbury, London EC2 (☎ 0171 726 1000)

LISBURNE, 8 Earl of (I 1776); Capt John David Malet Vaughan; also Viscount Lisburne and Baron Fethard (I 1695); the eld s & h appears to have been styled Lord Vaughan since 1776; s of 7 Earl of Lisburne (d 1965); *b* 1 Sept 1918; *Educ* Eton, Magdalen Coll Oxford; *m* 1943, Shelagh, da of late T A Macauley, of Montreal, Canada; 3 s; *Heir* s, Viscount Vaughan; *Career* 2 Lt Welsh Gds 1939, Capt 1943, served 1939–45; barr Inner Temple 1947–69; dir: British Home Stores plc 1961–87, S Wales Regnl Bd Lloyds Bank Ltd 1978–88, Nationwide Anglia Building Society (Welsh Bd); ret 1990; govr UCW; pres Wales Cncl for Voluntary Action; memb Exec Ctee AA 1981–88; *Clubs* Turf; *Style—* The Rt Hon the Earl of Lisburne; ✉ The Manor House, Hopton Wafers, Kidderminster, Worcs DY14 2NA (☎ 01299 271550)

LISHMAN, Prof (William) Alwyn; s of George Hackworth Lishman (d 1984), and Madge Scott, *née* Young (d 1980); *b* 16 May 1931; *Educ* Houghton Le Spring GS, Univ of Birmingham (BSc, MB ChB, MD, DPM, DSc, MRCP, Gaskell Gold medal Medico Psychological Assoc 1965); *m* 4 June 1966, Marjorie, da of Cecil Victor Loud (d 1987); 1 s (James William Michael b 1973), 1 da (Victoria Alison b 1971); *Career* RAMC Wheatley Mil Hosp Oxfordshire 1957–59; registrar in neurology United Oxford Hosps 1959–60, registrar then sr registrar in psychiatry Maudsley Hosp London 1960–66, conslt psychiatrist Nat Hosp Queen Square London 1966–67, sr lectr in psychological med Royal Postgrad Med Sch Hammersmith 1967–69, conslt psychiatrist Bethlem Royal Hosp and Maudsley Hosp 1967–74, prof of neuropsychiatry Inst of Psychiatry London 1979–93 (reader 1974–79, prof emeritus 1993–), ret 1993; visiting fell Green Coll Oxford 1983; dep chm Neurosciences Bd MRC 1976–77 (memb 1974–78); scientific advsr: DHSS 1979–82, Brain Res Tst 1986–93; chm Br Neuropsychiatry Assoc 1987–93 (hon life pres 1993–), civilian conslt RAF 1987–93, examiner and memb Bd of Examiners Univ of Oxford 1975–79; memb: editorial bds of numerous scientific journals, Experimental Psychology Soc 1975–, Assoc of Br Neurologists 1979–; guarantor of BRAIN 1984–; FRCP 1972, FRCPsych 1972; *Books* Organic Psychiatry: The Psychological Consequences of Cerebral Disorder (1978, 2 edn 1987); *Recreations* organ, piano, harpsichord, travelling; *Style—* Prof Alwyn Lishman; ✉ 9 Elwill Way, Beckenham, Kent BR3 3AB; Institute of Psychiatry, De Crespigny Park, London SE5 8AF (☎ 0171 703 5411)

LISLE, 7 Baron (I 1758); John Nicholas Horace Lysaght; s of Horace George Lysaght (d 1918), and Alice, da of Sir John Wrixon-Becher, 3 Bt; gs of 6 Baron (d 1919); *b* 10 Aug 1903; *m* 1, 1928 (m dis 1939), Vivienne (d 1948), da of Rev M Brew; m 2, 1939, Marie Helen, da of A D Purgold, of Parkgate, Cheshire; *Heir* n, Patrick Lysaght; *Style—* The Rt Hon the Lord Lisle; ✉ The Chestnuts, Barge Farm, Taplow, Bucks SL6 0EA

LISNEY, Cedric Courtenay Dymoke; MBE (1993); s of Dr Arthur Adrian Lisney (d 1963), and Dorothy Ella, *née* Gibbs (d 1973); *b* 7 June 1940; *Educ* Hardye's Sch Dorchester, Birmingham Sch of Architecture (Dip in Architecture), Univ of Edinburgh (post grad Dip in Landscape Architecture), Royal Town Planning Inst (Thomas Adams prize); *m* 1960, Christine, da of Roy Webb (d 1994); 3 s (Andrew Simon b 9 Sept 1962, Christopher Richard b 4 Feb 1964, Thomas Scott b 22 June 1966); *Career* trainee architect F Magnus Austin 1956–57, Farmer and Dark Architects Poole 1962–63, Derek Lovejoy & Assocs 1963–65, dep area planning offr SE Dorset 1965–67, princ planning offr (Landscape) Wilts CC 1967–71, princ Lisney Assocs 1971–; landscape advsr: Scottish Office 1990–, Cardiff Bay Devpt Corp 1990–; chm Joint Cncl for Landscape Industs 1990–92, pres Landscape Inst 1987–89; ARIBA 1963, PPLI 1989 (FLI 1976, ALI 1966); *Awards* Good Design in Housing DOE 1979, USA Award of Excellence (Graphic Design) 1980, Civic Tst Award 1982, twice silver medalist IGF Liverpool 1984, Winchester Preservation Tst 1985 and 1986, Sand and Gravel Assoc Award 1986, Concrete Soc Award 1989 and 1990, Greenleaf Housing Award 1990, Horsham District Design Award 1990, ALCA Grand Award 1991, Award for Environmental Design City of Bath 1993; *Recreations* golf, sailing; *Clubs* Kingsdown Golf; *Style—* Cedric Lisney, Esq, MBE; ✉ Lisney Associates, Landscape Architects, The Green House, 50 St Margarets Street, Bradford on Avon, Wilts BA15 1DE (☎ 01225 868611, fax 01225 868811)

LISNEY, Dr Stephen John William; s of Raymond Laurence Lisney, and Jean Avril, *née* Ladell; *b* 30 April 1951; *Educ* Queen Elizabeth's GS Barnet, Univ of Bristol (BSc, BDS, PhD, Bristol Teaching Hosp's Gold medal, Colgate prize for dental research); *m* 4 Jan 1975, Sandra Jane, da of Bertram Henry Mears; 2 s (Thomas James b 27 May 1977, Robert William b 22 Aug 1981); *Career* MRC travelling fell 1978–79; Univ of Bristol: lectr in physiology 1980–89, sr lectr 1989–, head Dept of Physiology 1995–; author/co-author of articles in scientific jls and books; memb Physiological Soc 1980;

Recreations gardening, outdoor pursuits, antique collecting; *Style*— Dr Stephen Lisney; ✉ Department of Physiology, School of Medical Sciences, University Walk, Bristol BS8 1TD (☎ 0117 928 7802, fax 0117 928 8923, e-mail S.J.W.Lisney@bris.ac.uk)

LISSACK, Richard Anthony; QC (1994); s of Victor Jack Lissack (d 1981), of London, and Antoinette Rosalind Lissack; *b* 7 June 1956; *Educ* Univ Coll Sch Hampstead; *m* 31 May 1986, Carolyn Dare Arscott, da of Gp Capt R H Arscott, CBE; 2 da (Holly Victoria Dare, Lucy Barbara Dare (twins) b 25 July 1994); *Career* called to the Bar Inner Temple 1978, asst recorder 1993–; chm S & W Wilts Hunt 1996–; *Recreations* breeding, competing and falling off thoroughbred horses, farming; *Style*— Richard Lissack, Esq, QC; ✉ 35 Essex Street, Temple, London WC2R 3AR (☎ 0171 353 6381, fax 0171 583 1786, car 0836 727162)

LISTER, Anthony Charles Bramham; s of David Bramham Lister (d 1980), and Monica Joan, *née* Russell (d 1991); *b* 31 Aug 1939; *Educ* Sutton Valence, Coll of Estate Mgmnt St Albans Grove London; *m* 1 June 1963, Susan Kitty, da of (Harold) Norman Funnell (d 1995), of Challock, Ashford; 3 s (Giles Anthony Bramham b 12 Jan 1966, Timothy Norman Bramham (twin) b 12 Jan 1966, Guy Bramham b 16 Oct 1968); *Career* equity ptnr Geering and Colyer Chartered Surveyors 1972–82, Black Horse Agencies 1982–90, dir Lister & Associates (commercial surveyors) 1991–; Freeman City of London 1961, Liveryman Worshipful Co of Leathersellers 1964 (Freeman 1961, 3 Warden 1988–89, memb Ct of Assts 1993); FRICS 1970; *Recreations* sheep farming, golf, sailing; *Clubs* Rye Golf, Whitstable Sailing; *Style*— Anthony Lister, Esq; ✉ Dean Court, Westwell, Ashford, Kent TN25 4NH (☎ 01233 712924); Lister & Associates, 27 Watling Street, Canterbury, Kent CT1 2UD (☎ 01227 763663)

LISTER, John Thomas; s of Albert William Lister (d 1978), of Cardiff, and Joan Trenear, *née* Tarr; *b* 26 Nov 1941; *Educ* Cardiff HS; *m* 1988, Mary; 2 s (Stephen b 29 July 1967, Andrew b 17 Sept 1975), 1 da (Victoria b 13 Nov 1979); *Career* athletics administrator; former athlete Wales 1959–70 and Cardiff Amateur Athletic Club; events competed at: 110m hurdles, decathlon, long jump, high jump (former Welsh record holder); hon treas: Cardiff Amateur Athletic Club 1968– (former pres and chm), AAA 1986–91, British Athletic Fedn 1991–; qualified CA 1964, dir and shareholder Euro Investments Ltd; *Recreations* athletics; *Style*— John Lister, Esq; ✉ 1 The Paddock, Lisvane, Cardiff CF4 5AY (☎ 01222 747734)

LISTER, Moira (Vicomtesse d'Orthez); da of Maj J M Lister (d 1971), of SA, and Margaret Winifred, *née* Hogan (d 1951); *b* 6 Aug 1923; *Educ* Parktown Convent Johannesburg SA; *m* 23 Dec 1951, Jacques Gachassin-Lafite Vicomte d'Orthez, s of Vicomte André d'Orthez (d 1924); 2 da (Chantal (Mrs d'Orthez-Burke) b 1954, Christobel b 1962); *Career* actress; early theatrical appearances as Juliet, Desdemona, Olivia and Kate Hardcastle at the Shakespeare Memorial Theatre (toured Europe with the co when it was led by Sir John Gielgud), played Regan to Gielgud's Lear, world tour of People In Love (one woman show) 1958–59; various radio work; *Theatre* West End credits incl: Present Laughter (with Sir Noel Coward), Love of Four Colonels (with Peter Ustinov), The Gazebo (with Ian Carmichael), Devil May Care (with Ian Carmichael), Birthday Honours, Any Wednesday (with Dennis Price), Getting Married (with Ian Carmichael and Googie Withers); other English prodns incl: Murder Among Friends (Comedy), Lady Windermere's Fan (nat tour), A Friend Indeed (Shaftesbury, with Geoffrey Palmer and Derek Nimmo), No No Nanette (nat tour), The Apple Cart (Haymarket, with Peter O'Toole), Move over Mrs Markham, A Woman Named Anne, Twigs, Deadlock (nat tour with Jack Hedley), Hay Fever (with Derek Nimmo), The Reluctant Debutante, Lloyd George Knew My Father, Aspern Papers (Wyndhams); S African prodns incl: The Sleeping Prince (with Joss Ackland), Bedtime Story (with Derek Nimmo), Lettice and Lovage, The Fan; as dir Present Laughter, Deadly Embrace; *Television* numerous appearances incl: The Very Merry Widow (own comedy series written by Alan Melville), Dramatised Sories (own series reading classic short stories), The Concert (nominated Best TV Actress of the Year), The Whitehall Worrier (own starring series written by Alan Melville), World of One Man Shows (with Robert Morley, Sir John Gielgud, Joyce Grenfell and Dame Peggy Ashcroft), The Guests (solo performance in play by Ronald Harwood); subject of This is Your Life; Have Map will Travel (own documentary, co-prodr with BBC); *Film* incl: The Yellow Rolls Royce (with Rex Harrison), Seven Waves Away (with Tyrone Power), The Deep Blue Sea (with Vivien Leigh), The Double Man (with Yul Brynner), The Choice (with Deborah Shelton); *Awards* The Variety Club of GB's Silver Heart Award for the Best Stage Actress; *Books* The Very Merry Moira; *Recreations* windsurfing, golf, swimming, writing, travel; *Style*— Miss Moira Lister; ✉ c/o Chatto & Linnit, Prince of Wales Theatre, Coventry Street, London W1V 7FE (☎ 0171 930 6677, fax 0171 930 0091)

LISTER, Paul Kenneth; s of Eric Lister, of Yeovil, Somerset, and Molly Ada Patience; *b* 7 Aug 1952; *Educ* Birmingham Sch of Architecture (DipArch), Univ of Aston (BSc); *Career* ptnr Associated Architects Birmingham 1984– (joined 1976), dir Associated Architects Ltd London; fndr memb Birmingham Young Architects' Gp, memb Ctee Birmingham Architectural Assoc 1985–87 and 1988–; RIBA 1979; *Style*— Paul Lister, Esq; ✉ Associated Architects, 35 St Paul's Square, Birmingham B3 1QX (☎ 0121 233 2526, fax 0121 200 1564)

LISTER, Dr Raymond George; s of Horace Lister (d 1971), and Ellen Maud Mary, *née* Arnold; *b* 28 March 1919; *Educ* Cambridge and County HS for Boys, St John's Coll Sch Cambridge, MA, LittD Cantab; *m* 1947, Pamela Helen, da of Frank Bishop Brutnell; 1 s, 1 da; *Career* author, artist, co dir; dir: The Golden Head Press Ltd 1953–70, George Lister & Sons Ltd 1941–94, John P Gray & Sons Ltd 1978–83; emeritus fell Wolfson Coll Cambridge; pres: Royal Soc of Miniature Painters Sculptors and Gravers 1970–80, Architectural Metalwork Assoc 1975–77; chm Bd of Govrs Fedn of British Artists 1976–80, a syndic Fitzwilliam Museum Cambridge 1981–89; Worshipful Co of Blacksmiths: Liveryman 1957–, memb Ct of Assts 1980–95 (now emeritus), Prime Warden 1989–90; *Publications* The Letters of Samuel Palmer (1974), Prints and Printmaking (1984), Samuel Palmer and 'The Ancients' (1984), The Paintings of Samuel Palmer (1985), The Paintings of William Blake (1986), Samuel Palmer: His Life and Art (1987), Catalogue Raisonné of the Works of Samuel Palmer (1988), British Romantic Painting (1989), A M Saint-Léon's Stenochoreography (translation) (1992), With My Own Wings (memoirs, 1994); *Recreations* old-fashioned roses, Ballets Russes; *Clubs* Sette of Odd Volumes; *Style*— Dr Raymond Lister; ✉ 9 Sylvester Road, Cambridge CB3 9AF (☎ 01223 324443)

LISTER, Prof (Margot) Ruth Aline; da of late Dr Werner Bernard Lister, of Manchester, and Daphne, *née* Carter; *b* 3 May 1949; *Educ* Moreton Hall School, Univ of Essex (BA), Univ of Sussex (MA); *Career* dir Child Poverty Action Gp 1979–87 (legal res offr 1971–75, asst dir 1975–77, dep dir 1977–79), prof and head of Dept of Applied Social Studies Univ of Bradford 1987–93, prof of social policy Loughborough Univ 1994–; tstee Friends of Citizens Advice Bureaux 1991–95, vice chm Nat Cncl of Vol Orgns 1991–93, memb Opsahl Cmmn NI 1992–93 (Cmmn on Social Justice 1992–94), chm Jt Univ Cncl Social Policy Ctee 1994–96; Hon LLD Univ of Manchester 1987; *Books* Supplementary Benefit Rights (1974), Welfare Benefits (1981), The Exclusive Society (1990), Women's Economic Dependency and Social Security (1992); numerous articles, pamphlets and chapters in books; *Recreations* walking, tai chi, reading, music, films; *Style*— Prof Ruth Lister; ✉ Department of Social Sciences, Loughborough University, Loughborough, Leicestershire LE11 3TU (☎ 01509 223350)

LISTER, Sandra (Sandie); *b* 16 Aug 1961; *Educ* Whitcliffe Mount Sch, Chelsea Coll of Physical Educn; *Career* int hockey player; memb Ipswich Ladies Hockey Club, England Indoor 1987– (capt 1988–90), 43 GB caps 1989–, 151 Eng caps (over 100 as capt); memb Eng squads: World Cup 1983, 1986, 1990 and 1994, Euro Cup 1984, 1987 (Silver medal), 1991 and 1994 (Gold medal, capt); most capped England player ever; memb GB squad Olympic Games Barcelona 1992 (Bronze medal); PE teacher King Edward VI Sch Bury; *Recreations* all sports; *Style*— Miss Sandie Lister

LISTER, Dame Unity Viola; DBE (1972, OBE 1959); da of Dr Arthur Sydney Webley (d 1931), and Viola, *née* Hockley (d 1938); *b* 19 June 1913; *Educ* St Helen's Blackheath, The Sorbonne; *m* 1940, Samuel William Lister, CEng (d 1995), s of Victor Edward Lister (d 1954); *Career* memb: London CC 1949–65 (dep chm 1963–64), Exec Euro Union of Women 1965– (in vice chm 1963–69); formerly memb Inner London Advsy Ctee on Appointment of Magistrates; govr Royal Marsden Hosp 1957–83; chm: Horniman Museum 1967–95, Women's Nat Advsy Ctee Cons Pty 1966–69, Nat Union of Cons and Unionist Assocs 1970–71; memb Exec: Euro Movement 1970–83, Cons Gp for Europe 1970–83; *Recreations* music, languages, walking, gardening, history; *Clubs* St Stephen's Constitutional; *Style*— Dame Unity Lister, DBE; ✉ 32 The Court Yard, Eltham, London SE9 5QE (☎ 0181 850 7038)

LISTER-KAYE, Sir John Philip Lister; 8 Bt (UK 1812), of Grange, Yorkshire; s of Sir John Christopher Lister Lister-Kaye, 7 Bt (d 1982), and his 1 w, Audrey Helen (d 1979), da of Edwin James Carter, of Westbury-on-Trym, Glos; descended from Sir John Kaye, of Woodsome, Almondbury, Yorkshire, Col of Horse, created Baronet in 1641 by Charles I, also Lord Mayor of York; this Baronetcy became extinct on the death of the 6 Bt in 1809, but Sir John Lister-Kaye, natural s of the 5 Bt, was cr a Bt 1812 for services to George III; Sir John Lister-Kaye, 3 Bt, was groom-in-waiting to Edward VII; *b* 8 May 1946; *Educ* Allhallows Sch; *m* 1, 1972 (m dis 1988), Lady Sorrel Deirdre Bentinck, da of 11 Earl of Portland; 1 s, 2 da (Amelia Helen b 1976, Melanie Jenifer b (twin) 1976); m 2, 17 Feb 1989, Lucinda Anne, eld da of Robin Law, of Withersfield, Suffolk, and formerly w of Hon Evan Baillie; 1 da (Hermione Anne Lucinda Lorne b 27 Sept 1990); *Heir* s, John Warwick Noel Lister Lister-Kaye b 10 Dec 1974; *Career* naturalist, author, lectr, farmer; dir of Aigas Field Centre Ltd 1977–; fndr dir Scottish Conservation Charity The Aigas Tst 1980–; chm Scottish Advsy Ctee RSPB 1986–92; memb: Int Ctee The World Wilderness Fndn 1983, Scottish Ctee of Nature Conservancy Cncl 1990–91; chm: NW Region Nature Conservancy Cncl for Scotland 1991–92, NW Region Scottish Natural Heritage 1992–96, Home Grown Timber Advsy Ctee Forestry Cmmn 1994–96; tstee Environmental Training Organisation 1995–; memb Advsy Cncl of Millenium Forest for Scotland 1996–; recipient of Wilderness Soc Gold Award for Conservation 1984; Hon DUniv Stirling 1995; *Books* The White Island (1972), Seal Cull (1979), The Seeing Eye (1980), Ill Fares the Land (1994), One for Sorrow (1994); *Recreations* breeding horses and Highland cattle; *Clubs* Farmers', Caledonian; *Style*— Sir John Lister-Kaye, Bt; ✉ House of Aigas, Beauly, Inverness IV4 7AD (☎ 01463 782729); Grange Estate Co Office 01463 782443, fax 01463 782097, e-mail GRANGE.est@aigas.ofl.bex400,co.uk)

LISTON, (Edward) Robin; s of David Joel Liston, OBE (d 1990), and Eva Carole, *née* Kauffmann (d 1987); *b* 30 Oct 1947; *Educ* Bryanston, Mercersburg Acad PA USA, Univ of Kent (BA); *m* 6 July 1969 (m dis 1987), Judith Margaret, da of Frederick Tye, CBE; 2 da (Rebecca b 1970, Victoria b 1974); *Career* dist ed Kent Messenger 1969–70, asst ed Benn Bros 1970–72; assoc dir: Forman House PR Ltd 1972–79, Welbeck PR Ltd 1981–84; dir: Carl Byoir Ltd 1984–86, Hill & Knowlton Ltd 1986–88; jt md Buckmans PR 1988–93, freelance conslt 1993–; *Recreations* music, films, railways, suburban architecture; *Style*— Robin Liston, Esq; ✉ Robin Communications, 26 Southern Road, London N2 9JG (☎ 0181 883 7314, fax 0181 444 8834)

LISTOWEL, 5 Earl of (I 1822); William Francis Hare; GCMG (1957), PC (1946); also Baron Ennismore (I 1800), Viscount Ennismore and Listowel (I 1816, usually shortened to Viscount Ennismore when used as courtesy title for eldest s and h), and Baron Hare of Convamore (UK 1869, which sits as); s of 4 Earl (d 1931), by his w Hon Freda Vanden-Bempde-Johnstone (da of 2 Baron Derwent); er bro of Lord (1 Viscount) Blakenham and unc of Lord (3 Earl of) Iveagh; *b* 28 Sept 1906; *Educ* Magdalene Coll Cambridge; *m* 1, 1933 (m dis 1945), Judith, da of Raoul de Marffy-Mantuano, of Budapest; 1 da (Lady Grantley); m 2, 1958 (m dis 1963), Stephanie Sandra Yvonne, da of Sam Wise, of Toronto, and formerly w of Hugh Currie; 1 da; m 3, 1963, Pamela, da of Francis Day, of Croydon, and formerly w of John Read; 2 s, 1 da; *Heir* s, Viscount Ennismore, *qv*; *Career* formerly Lt Intelligence Corps; memb LCC 1937–58; Parly under-sec of state India Office 1944–45, also dep ldr House of Lords 1944–45 (Lab whip 1941–44); sec of state: India 1947, Burma 1947–48; min of state colonial affrs 1948–50, jt Parly sec Miny of Agric & MAFF 1950–51; govr-gen Ghana 1957–60; chm Ctees House of Lords 1965–76, dep chm and dep speaker 1977–; *Style*— The Rt Hon the Earl of Listowel; ✉ 10 Downshire Hill, London NW3 (☎ 0171 431 3327)

LIT, Avtar; *b* Punjab, India; *Educ* RNC Chatham; *Career* presenter Asian World on cable TV 1977, Sina Radio Southall Middx, estab Sina Radio International California, estab Sunrise Radio Asian radio network 1989 (chief exec 1989–) bdcasting on Astra satellite and on cable throughout UK and Europe; chm and chief exec Bradford City Radio, dir Asian Broadcasting Corporation Ltd, dir W London TEC; chm Nat Assoc of Radio Devpt, memb Radio Acad UK; initiated Bangladesh Cyclone Relief Appeal, dir Sunrise Tst; Mother India Int Award for enhancing prestige of India NRI World Convention New Delhi; *Style*— Avtar Lit, Esq; ✉ Sunrise Radio, Sunrise House, Sunrise Road, Southall, Middx UB2 4AU (☎ 0181 574 6666)

LITHERLAND, Robert Kenneth; MP (Lab) Manchester Central (majority 18,037); s of Robert Litherland and Mary, *née* Parry; *b* 1930; *Educ* N Manchester HS for Boys; *m* 1953, Edna; 1 s, 1 da; *Career* MP (Lab) Manchester Central 1979– (GPMU sponsored); cncllr Manchester City Cncl 1971– (dep chm Housing Ctee 1979–), dep chm Public Works Ctee Assoc of Met Authorities 1977–78; memb: Cncl of Europe, Western Euro Union; *Style*— Robert Litherland, Esq, MP; ✉ House of Commons, London SW1A 0AA (☎ 0171 219 3000)

LITHGOW, Sir William James; 2 Bt (UK 1925), of Ormsary, Co Argyll, DL (Renfrewshire 1970); s of Sir James Lithgow, 1 Bt, GBE, CB, MC, TD, JP, DL (d 1952); *b* 10 May 1934; *Educ* Winchester; *m* 1, 1964, Valerie Helen (d 1964), da of Denis Herbert Scott, CBE (d 1958); m 2, 1967, Mary Claire, da of Col Frank Moutray Hill, CBE, of East Knoyle, Wilts; 2 s (James Frank b 13 June 1970, John Alexander b 8 Dec 1974), 1 da (Katrina Margaret b 5 Oct 1968); *Heir* s, James Frank Lithgow b 13 June 1970; *Career* industrialist and farmer; chm: Lithgows Ltd 1959–84 and 1988–, Hunterston Devpt Co Ltd 1987–, Scott-Lithgow Drydocks Ltd 1967–78, Western Ferries (Argyll) Ltd 1972–85; vice-chm Scott Lithgow Ltd 1968–78; dir: Bank of Scotland 1962–86, Landcatch Ltd 1981–, Lithgows Pty Ltd 1972–; memb: Br Ctee Det Norske Veritas 1966–92, Exec Ctee Scottish Cncl Devpt and Indust 1969–85, Scottish Regnl Cncl of CBI 1969–76, Clyde Port Authy 1969–71, Bd Nat Ports Cncl 1971–78, W Central Scotland Plan Steering Ctee 1971–74, Gen Bd Nat Physical Labour 1963–66, Greenock Dist Hosp Bd 1961–66, Scottish Milk Mktg Bd 1979–83; chm Iona Cathedral Tstees Mgmnt Bd 1979–83, memb Cncl Winston Churchill Meml Tst 1979–83, hon pres Students' Assoc, memb Ct Univ of Strathclyde 1964–69; Hon LLD Strathclyde 1979, memb Queen's Body Guard for Scotland (Royal Co of Archers); *Recreations* rural life, invention, photography; *Clubs* Oriental, Western, Royal Scottish Automobile (Glasgow); *Style*— Sir William Lithgow,

Bt, DL; ✉ Ormsary House, by Lochgilphead, Argyllshire (☎ 01880 770252); Drums, Langbank, Renfrewshire (☎ 01475 540606)

LITMAN, Dr Gloria Klein; da of Emil Klein (d 1963), and Sadie Epstein (d 1982); *b* 10 April 1936; *Educ* Hunter Coll New York City (BA), North Texas State Univ (MSc), Univ of London (PhD); *m* 1, 4 Dec 1954 (m dis), Armand Charles Litman (d 1991), s of Charles Louis Litman (d 1987); 2 s (David b 1957, Jonathan b 1960); m 2, 1 May 1993, Dr David Christopher Wallbridge; *Career* sr lectr Inst of Psychiatry 1987, hon conslt psychologist Maudsley Hosp, clinical res psychologist Addiction Res Unit, currently in private practice London; *Recreations* bridge, yoga; *Style*— Dr Gloria Litman; ✉ 14 Phillimore Gardens, London W8 7BH (☎ 0171 937 9267)

LITTLE, (Robert) Alastair; s of Robert Geoffrey Little, of Colne, Lancs, and Marion, *née* Irving; *b* 25 June 1950; *Educ* Kirkham GS Kirkham Lancs, Downing Coll Cambridge (MA); *Career* self-taught chef; head chef Old Compton Wine Bar London 1974–76; chef/proprietor: Le Routier Wrentham Suffolk 1976–79, Simpsons Putney London 1979–81; chef: L'Escargot London 1981–82, 192 Kensington Park Road 1982–85; chef/proprietor Alastair Little: Frith Street 1985–, Lancaster Road 1996–; Times Restaurant of Year 1993; memb Académie Culinaire; *Books* Keep It Simple (1993); *Recreations* reading, mycology, watching sport; *Style*— Alastair Little, Esq; ✉ Alastair Little, 49 Frith Street, London W1V 5TE (☎ 0171 437 6733); Alastair Little, 136a Lancaster Road, London W11 (☎ 0171 243 2220)

LITTLE, Amanda Penelope Wyndham; da of Capt Alec Haines Little, CBE, of Hampshire, and Pamela, *née* Bolt; *b* 19 Jan 1948; *Educ* Winchester; *m* 7 Sept 1979, Kenneth William Elliott, s of John Attewell Elliott, of Notts; *Career* asst PR offr Milk Mktg Bd 1972–79; literary agent Bolt & Watson Ltd 1981–83, dir, pt owner and literary agent Watson Little Ltd 1983–; memb Assoc of Authors' Agents; *Recreations* singing, music, books; *Style*— Ms Amanda Little

LITTLE, Dr (Thomas William) Anthony (Tony); s of Thomas Lowden Little, and Marjorie Annie Little; *b* 27 June 1940; *Educ* Dame Allan's Sch Newcastle upon Tyne, Univ of Edinburgh (BVMS), Univ of London (DipBact, PhD); *m* 1, 1963 (m dis); 1 s, 1 da; m 2, 1985, Sally Anne Headlam; 2 s; *Career* gen vet practice March Cambs 1963–66; MAFF: Cental Vet Lab Weybridge 1966–82, sr res offr Tolworth 1973–82, dep regnl vet offr Tolworth 1982–85, vet head of section Tolworth 1985–86, dep dir CVL 1986–90, chief exec Central Vet Lab 1990–95, chief exec Vet Labs Agency 1995–; MRCVS, FIBiol; *Recreations* travel, food, wine, outdoor activities; *Style*— Dr Tony Little; ✉ Veterinary Laboratories Agency, Woodham Lane, New Haw, Addlestone, Surrey KT15 3NB (☎ 01932 341111, fax 01932 347046)

LITTLE, John Noel; s of Ronald Little (d 1974), and Margaret Elizabeth, *née* Thompson (d 1992); *b* 25 Dec 1935; *Educ* Stockton-on-Tees GS; *m* 1961, Mavis, da of James Sydney Ord (d 1960); 1 s (Mark), 1 da (Elaine); *Career* Lloyds and Scottish plc 1957–84 (exec dir 1973–84), md Lloyds and Scottish Finance Ltd 1969–84; chm: Finance Houses Association 1980–82, London Fiduciary Tst plc 1988–92, J W Galloway Ltd 1985–91, Randsworth Trust plc 1986–87, Tamaris plc 1987–89, Stortext Holdings Ltd 1987–96, Nelson Group Ltd 1994–96; dir Caledonian Trust plc; FInstD; *Recreations* golf, swimming, dog walking, watching sport, bridge; *Clubs* RAC, Royal Burgess Golfing Soc, The Grange; *Style*— John N Little, Esq; ✉ Dunosdale, 22 Cammo Crescent, Edinburgh EH4 8DZ (☎ 0131 339 6948, fax 0131 339 6756)

LITTLE, Michael Robert; s of Robert William Little (d 1973), and Joan, *née* Brown; *b* 10 Sept 1949; *Educ* Blundells; *m* 1, 16 June 1973 (m dis 1977), Susan Elizabeth, da of Desmond Richard Bowden (d 1972), of Ranby Hall, Lincoln; m 2, 18 July 1985 (m dis 1990), Ellen Louise, da of Winston Walker, of Welford upon Avon, Warwickshire; 1 s (Henry Robert William b 7 April 1986); m 3, 9 Aug 1991, Caroline Xania Garnham, *qv*; 1 s (Edward Charles Frank b 21 Nov 1992), 1 da (Georgia Elizabeth Medina b 10 Nov 1995); *Career* St Quintin Son and Stanley 1972–76; ptnr Molyneux Rose 1977–, chm Molyneux Rose Ltd 1987–; Master North Cotswold Hunt 1985–88; FRICS 1981, ACIArb 1980; *Recreations* hunting, shooting, squash; *Clubs* Royal Automobile, IOD; *Style*— Michael Little, Esq; ✉ The Lydes, Toddington, Gloucestershire; (☎ 01242621 419); 51 Connaught Street, London W2 (☎ 0171 706 4320); Molyneux Rose, 143 New Bond Street, London W1Y 9FD (☎ 0171 409 0130, fax 0171 499 7636)

LITTLE, Nigel Stuart; s of Edward Little (d 1963), and Josephine Little; *b* 11 March 1954; *Educ* Queen Elizabeth I Sch (1563), Univ of London (BSc); *m* 17 May 1986, Fiona Mary, da of Henry Arthur Lee, of Foxes' Dale, Blackheath, London SE3; 2 s (Edward Oliver Henry b 11 Nov 1987, Oliver Nigel James b 10 Aug 1990); *Career* sales exec Kitkat & Aitken stockbrokers 1976–78, sr exec and head of Scottish and Irish sales James Capel & Co stockbrokers 1978–88, dir and head of sales (princ of global firm) Morgan Stanley investmt bankers 1988–89; Panmure Gordon & Co stockbrokers: sr dir 1989–, Exec Bd dir, head of sales (globally); Freeman City of London 1982; memb AIP 1979, memb Int Stock Exchange 1982; MSI, FIMgt 1988, MInstD 1994; *Recreations* rugby union, motor sport, golf; *Style*— Nigel Little, Esq; ✉ Panmure Gordon & Co, New Broad Street House, 35 New Broad Street, London EC2M 1NH (☎ 0171 638 4010)

LITTLE, Dr Peter; s of Herbert Edwin Samuel Little, of Durham, and Emily Jewel, *née* Barr; *b* 9 July 1949; *Educ* Rendcomb Coll, Univ of Bristol (BSc, PhD, Rose Bracher Meml prize); *m* 1973, Helen Sheldon, da of Herbert Bruce Cowmeadow; 2 da (Anna Elizabeth b 30 Oct 1981, Abigail Claira b 6 March 1983), 2 s (Angus Stafford b 21 Nov 1984, Andrew Samuel Barnabas b 9 May 1986); *Career* UKAEA Harwell: industl res fell 1974–76, environmental res scientist 1976–79, commercial mangr 1980–87, head of nuclear mktg 1987–; UKAEA Risley: head of mktg and sales 1987–90, commercial mangr AEA Reactor Services 1990–91; commercial and mktg dir Horticulture Research International 1991–; memb Bd of Dirs: Nimtech Northwest 1988–90, Inqual Inc 1990–91, Ornamentals Advice Centre 1993–; memb: Br Ecological Soc 1976–85, Licensing Executives Soc 1988–92, Nuclear Engrg Soc 1989–91, Nat Tst, Woodland Tst, YHA; author of 16 scientific papers; CBiol, MIBiol 1974; *Recreations* family, fell walking, music, travel; *Style*— Dr Peter Little; ✉ Horticulture Research International, Wellesbourne, Warwick CV35 9EF (☎ 01789 470382, fax 01789 470552)

LITTLE, Tasmin Elizabeth; da of George Villiers Little, the actor, of London, and Gillian, *née* Morris; *b* 13 May 1965; *Educ* Yehudi Menuhin Sch, Guildhall Sch of Music (Gold medal); *m* July 1993, Michael Hatch; *Career* violinist; debut Hallé Orchestra 1988; performed as soloist with orchs incl: LSO, Philharmonia, Royal Philharmonic, Royal Liverpool Philharmonic, Hallé, BBC Symphony, Bournemouth Symphony, City of London Sinfonia, Gewandhaus, Berlin Symphony, Stavanger Symphony, Royal Danish; worked with conductors incl: Kurt Masur, Vladimir Ashkenazy, Sir Charles Groves, Sir Charles Mackerras, Vernon Handley, James Loughran, Sir Edward Downes, Richard Hickox, Sian Edwards, Jan Pascal Tortelier, Jerzy Maksymiuk, Sir Yehudi Menuhin, Andrew Davis, Sir Peter Maxwell Davies; author of paper on Delius Violin Concerto for Delius Soc 1991; voted Woman of Tomorrow in the Arts Cosmopolitan Magazine 1990; plays a 1757 Guadagnini; *Performances* in UK incl: world premieres of concertos by Robert Saxton, David Earl and Dominic Muldownie, Vivaldi Four Seasons (Royal Festival Hall and Barbican) 1990, Janacek Violin Concerto with Welsh Nat Opera Orch (BBC Proms debut) 1990, Dvorak Violin Concerto (BBC Proms) 1991, Delius Double Concerto (BBC Proms) 1992, Walton Concerto (BBC Proms) 1993, Elgar Concerto (BBC Proms) 1994, soloist Last Night of the Proms 1995, Sibelius Violin Concerto (BBC Proms) 1996; charity performances incl: Sutton Place for Dr Barnardos, St James's Palace for Nat Children's Home Appeal 1989, Wigmore Hall for Jacqueline Du Pre Meml Appeal 1990, Gala Concert with Royal Liverpool Philharmonic Orch before HM The Queen 1991; overseas performances incl: Brahms Violin Concerto (Malta Festival) 1990, tour with Piers Lane to S America 1991, concertos and recitals in Paris, Prague, Germany, Cyprus, Canada, Greece, Zimbabwe, Hong Kong, China, Sultanate of Oman and Scandinavia; TV appearances incl: Highway (ITV), Little by Little (documentary with father, Yorkshire TV), recorded two movements of Mendelssohn Concerto (HTV), Royal Liverpool Philharmonic Gala Concert for HM the Queen (Granada TV); *Recordings* incl: Bruch and Dvorak Violin Concertos (with Royal Liverpool Philharmonic under Vernon Handley, EMI Classics for Pleasure) 1990, George Lloyd Sonatas for violin and piano (with Martin Roscoe, Albany) 1990, Vaughan Williams The Lark Ascending (with BBC Symphony Orch under Andrew Davis, WEA, Gramophone award nomination) 1990, Delius Double Concerto (with Raphael Wallfisch and Sir Charles Mackerras, EMI Eminence, Gramophone award nomination) 1991, Delius Violin Concerto 1991, Robert Saxton Violin Concerto (Collins Classics), Brahms and Sibelius Violin Concertos, Virtuoso Violin Disc (EMI Eminence), Arvo Part Disc (EMI Eminence) 1994, Rubbra Violin Concerto (Conifer, Gramophone award nomination) 1994, Walton Violin Concerto (Decca) 1995, French Violin Sonatas (EMI Eminence) 1995; *Recreations* theatre, languages, swimming, cooking; *Clubs* English Speaking Union; *Style*— Miss Tasmin Little; ✉ c/o Jilly Clarke, Harold Holt Ltd, 31 Sinclair Road, London W14 0NS (☎ 0171 603 4600, fax 0171 603 0019)

LITTLECHILD, Prof Stephen Charles; s of Sydney Littlechild, of Wisbech, and Joyce, *née* Sharpe; *b* 27 Aug 1943; *Educ* Wisbech GS, Univ of Birmingham (BCom), Stanford Univ, Northwestern Univ, Univ of Texas at Austin (PhD), Univ of California at Los Angeles; *m* 1 Aug 1975, Kathleen (d 1982), da of Charles T Pritchard; 2 s (Harry b 1978, Richard b 1980), 1 da (Elizabeth b 1976); *Career* Harkness fell Univ of Stanford 1965–67, sr res lectr Graduate Centre for Mgmnt Studies Birmingham 1970–72, prof of applied econs Aston Univ 1973–75, prof of commerce and head Dept of Industl Econs and Business Studies Univ of Birmingham 1975–89; visiting prof: Univ of New York, Univ of Stanford, Univ of Chicago, Virginia Poly 1979–80; memb: Monopolies and Mergers Cmmn 1983–89, ACORD 1987–89; advsr UK Govt on privatisation of BT, water and electricity; dir-gen Office of Electricity Regulation (Offer) 1989–; *Books* Operational Research for Managers (1977), Fallacy of the Mixed Economy (1978), Elements of Telecommunications Economics (1979), Energy Strategies for the UK (with K G Vaidya, 1982), Regulation of British Telecoms Profitability (1983), Economic Regulation of Privatised Water Authorities (1986), Austrian Economics (3 vols, ed, 1990), Operations Research in Management (with M F Shutler, 1991); *Recreations* genealogy; *Style*— Prof Stephen Littlechild; ✉ Office of Electricity Regulation, Hagley House, Hagley Road, Birmingham B16 8QG (☎ 0121 456 2100)

LITTLEFAIR, Henry George Peter (Harry); s of Bernard Littlefair, of York (d 1975), and Ellen Littlefair, *née* Houghton (d 1961); *b* 6 Feb 1931; *Educ* Ratcliffe Coll Leicester; *m* 9 Aug 1960, Mary Edith, da of Sydney Fryer Monkman, of York (d 1980); 2 s (Nicholas b 1962, Dominic b 1964); *Career* investmt mangr; vice chm Allied Dunbar Unit Tst 1986–88, md A D Unit Tst 1983–86 (dep md 1975–83); dir: Persimmon plc, Geared Income Investment Trust plc (chm), Metrotect Industries plc; *Recreations* philately, music, chess, walking; *Style*— Harry Littlefair, Esq; ✉ 24 The Old Mill, Wetherby, West Yorkshire LS22 6NB (☎ 01937 587863, fax 01937 587864)

LITTLEJOHN, Alistair George; s of James Davidson Littlejohn (d 1970); *b* 17 Feb 1935; *Educ* Aberdeen GS, Univ of Aberdeen (BScEng); *m* 1962, Mairwen Lloyd, da of Capt Henry Lloyd Jones (d 1971); 1 s, 1 da; *Career* civil engr; formerly dir Higgs and Hill Ltd; Liveryman Worshipful Co of Paviors; *Clubs* Eccentric, IOD; *Style*— Alistair Littlejohn, Esq; ✉ Harlyn, 14 Hempstead Lane, Potten End, Berkhamsted, Herts HP4 2QJ

LITTLEJOHN, Prof Gavin Stuart; *Educ* George Heriot's Sch Edinburgh, Univ of Edinburgh (BSc), Univ of Newcastle upon Tyne (PhD), Univ of Edinburgh (DSc); *Career* Cementation Co Ltd: sr geotechnical engr 1965–66, divnl liaison engr 1966–69, conslt Cementation Ground Engineering Ltd 1969–71; lectr Univ of Aberdeen 1971–76 (head Geotechnics Res Gp 1973–76); conslt Ground Anchors Ltd 1973–78; tech dir: The Cement Gun Co 1976–81, Losinger Systems (UK) Ltd 1979–84; dep md Colcrete Gp 1978–84 (tech dir 1976–84); prof of civil engrg Univ of Bradford 1985– (head Dept of Civil Engrg 1985–94); conslt: Colcrete Ltd 1985–86, GKN Foundations Ltd 1988–90, Keller Colcrete Ltd 1990–92, AMEC Civil Engineering Ltd 1992–, Parsons Brinckerhoff & Morrison Knudsen 1992–94; dir COLROK Joint Venture Tarbela Dam Pakistan 1979–82; visiting prof Univ of Newcastle 1980–83, govr Bradford GS 1985–87; external examiner: Portsmouth Poly 1981–84, Univ of Glasgow 1982–87, Univ of Newcastle 1983–86, Univ of Edinburgh 1987–89, UMIST 1989–91, Univ of Salford 1993–96; chm: Working Gp on Pre-stressed Ground Anchorages Fédération Internationale de la Précontrainte 1983–96, Steering Gp on Site Investigation 1991–, Organising Ctee for Int Conference on Ground Anchorages ICE 1995–97, Environmental Civil Engrg Ctee Science and Engrg Res Cncl 1993–94, Res Panel ISE 1993–94, Civil Engrg Panel for 1996 Res Assessment Exercise 1995–96; memb: Cmmn on Practical Construction Fédération Internationale de la Précontrainte 1983–96, Engrg Res Cmmn Science and Engrg Res Cncl 1993–94, Cmmn on Rock Grouting Int Soc of Rock Mechanics 1989–95, Res Panel ISE 1991–93, Anchor Ctee Post Tensioning Inst USA 1992–, Teaching Quality Assessment Panel Scottish Higher Educn Funding Cncl 1993; memb Ctee: Int Soc of Soil Mechanics and Fndn Engrg 1990–, British Standards Inst 1990–; memb Cncl: ISE 1991–94, ICE 1989–91 and 1992–95; assessor of mature candidiates ICE 1988–; FICE, FIStructE, FGS, FRSA, FEng 1993; *Style*— Prof G S Littlejohn, FEng; ✉ Department of Civil Engineering, University of Bradford, Bradford, W Yorks BD7 1DP (☎ 01274 383873, fax 01274 383888)

LITTLEJOHN, Joan Anne; da of Thomas Littlejohn (d 1950), and Joan, *née* Wynn (Mrs Edward G Shepherd); *b* 20 April 1937; *Educ* Mary Datchelor Girls Sch, RCM; *Career* freelance composer, poet, photographer and musicologist 1958–; postgrad study with Howells, Berkeley, Boulanger, Ruth Dyson and others; piano teacher Orpington GS 1958–59, admin staff RCM 1960–83, piano teacher Harrow 1972–73; asst to Br composers incl: Fricker, Howells, Hopkins, Poston; reassembled Howells Requiem 1980 and collated his MS sketches 1983; inducted memb Mozartgemeinde Vienna 1970s, memb Cncl Soc of Women Musicians 1970s, fndr memb RCM Staff Assoc 1976, chm RCM NALGO and London Music Colleges NALGO 1978–81, vice chm RCM Local Jt Ctee 1978–81; creative works (music) incl: La Mascarade de Jean de la Fontaine, The Heights of Haworth, Poems from Palgrave, 4 Sea Songs (words by J M Ritchie), 4 Lieder von F Schnabl, London Street Cries (cmmnd by Beth Boyd), St Juliot Cornwall (words by Rachel Pearse), Dreams of Anubis, Settings of Blake, Burns, De La Mare, Shakespeare, Hardy, choral scena The Bonny Earl of Murray (cmmnd by Antony Hopkins); creative works (poetry) incl: Poems for Free, In The Furrowed Field, Towards Exmoor, Bingo's Totleigh Diary, The Hearth, Hymn of the Interviewers, Grandad's Dinner, Autun, Legend; recorded 90 tunes for The Queen Mother's 90th Year; MSS and music deposited in The American Music Res Center Calif, BIRS London, Nat Library Vienna, Clarence House, Buckingham Palace and private collections, contrib (by invitation) to permanent exhibitions at The Int Museum of Peace and Solidarity Samarkand; fndr dir The Joan Littlejohn Archive (collection of MSS, letters, diaries, genealogy, memorabilia of mainly 20th century artists and personalities (destined for the nation) to be housed at The Devon Record Office by arrangement with The Nat Heritage Meml Fund); memb: Br Fedn of Music Festivals, IBC Advsy Cncl, PRS,

Women's Corona Soc, Brontë Soc, Bat Conservation Tst, Br Hedgehog Preservation Soc, River Taw Fisheries Assoc, World Parrot Tst, Poland and Poland Bantam Club, Partridge and Pencilled Wyandotte Club; UN Charter 50 patron 1994; in life fell American Biographical Inst Res Assoc 1983; World Decoration of Excellence medallion American Biog Inst 1989, first recipient IBC Medal Collection 1989 (for most distinguished biographies); recipient Howells' Composing Piano 1984; GRSM, LRAM; *Recreations* animals especially collies, canaries, pigeons, rare poultry, psittacines; *Style—* Miss Joan Littlejohn; ✉ Chanterhayes, Bow, nr Crediton, Devon EX17 6HR

LITTLEJOHN, William Hunter; s of William Littlejohn (d 1974), and Alice, *née* King (d 1984); *b* 16 April 1929; *Educ* Arbroath HS, Dundee Coll of Art (DA); *Career* artist; RSA 1973 (ARSA 1966), RSW, RGI; *Solo Exhibitions* The Scottish Gall 1963, 1967, 1972, 1977, 1984 and 1989, Univ of Aberdeen 1975, Univ of Leeds 1976, Peter Potter Gall 1978, The Loom Shop Gall 1980, 1983, 1985 and 1990, Kingfisher Gall 1993 and 1995; *Group Exhibitions* Contemporary Scottish Painting (Toronto) 1961, 20th Century Scottish Painting 1962, Contemporary Scottish Art (Reading Art Gall) 1963, Three Centuries of Scottish Painting (Nat Gall of Canada) 1968, Twelve Scottish Painters (tour USA and Canada) 1970, Art Spectrum (Aberdeen Art Gall) 1971, Painters In Parallel (Scottish Arts Cncl) 1978, Contemporary Art from Scotland (tour), Ten Scottish Painters (RA) 1986, The Scottish Collection (Fine Art Soc) 1989), Scottish Art (Hong Kong) 1994; *Work in Collections* Scottish National Gall of Modern Art, Scottish Arts Cncl, RSA, Edinburgh Civic Collection, Univ of Edinburgh, Univ of Aberdeen, Royal Bank of Scotland, Robert Fleming Holdings, Educational Inst of Scotland; *Awards* Guthrie Award RSA 1961, Cargill Prize RGI 1966 and 1990, Sir William Gillies Award RSW 1980, Alexander Graham Munro Award RSW 1993; *Style—* William Littlejohn, Esq, RSA; ✉ 16 Colvill Place, Arbroath, Tayside DD11 1RB (☎ 01241 874402)

LITTLEJOHNS, Douglas George; CBE (1991, OBE 1984); s of Gordon Augustus Littlejohns (d 1994), of Sittingbourne, Kent, and Margaret Goudie, *née* Smith; *b* 10 May 1946; *Educ* Borden GS, RNC Dartmouth, Univ of Reading (BSc), Warwick Univ Business Sch (MBA); *m* 1, 14 Nov 1970 (m dis 1987), Fiona, *née* Hilton; 1 s (Andrew b 1974), 2 da (Imogen b 1978, Diana b 1979); m 2, 4 June 1988, Deborah Anne, da of Captain Angus Andrew Nicol (d 1971); *Career* served RN until 1994; CO: HMS Osiris 1975–76, HMS Sceptre 1981–83, HMS London 1987–89; PSO to CDS 1989–91, Capt RNEC Manadon 1992–94; halls md Earls Court and Olympia Ltd 1994–96, chief exec offr Red Storm Entertainments Inc 1996–; dep chm Beeton Rumford Ltd 1995–96; Freeman City of London 1988, Younger Bro Trinity House 1989; CMath, FIMA 1995; *Recreations* cricket, golf, sailing, DIY, family; *Clubs* RN 1765 and 1785; *Style—* Douglas Littlejohns, Esq, CBE; ✉ Crawter Bank, Hachetty Way, Porlock, West Sussex TA24 8HZ; Red Storm Entertainments Inc, 114 MacKenan Drive, Suite 100, Cary NC 27511, USA (☎ 00 1 919 467 9700)

LITTLEMORE, Christopher Paul; s of Frederick Percival Littlemore, of Dunchurch Rd, Rugby, and (Edith) Marie, *née* Clarkson; *b* 8 March 1959; *Educ* Rugby, Univ of Manchester (BA, BArch); *m* 28 July 1984, Jane Evelyn, da of Derek Chalk, of Poulton, Gloucestershire; 1 s (Andrew b 1987), 1 da (Katharine b 1989); *Career* architect Ellis Williams Partnership Manchester 1980–81; The Charter Partnership: architect Bedford Office 1983–87, assoc dir 1986, dir Bournemouth Office 1987–, bd dir 1988; RIBA 1984; *Recreations* mountaineering, golf, watercolour painting, music; *Clubs* Midland Assoc of Mountaineers, Farrant Singers (Salisbury Cathedral); *Style—* Christopher Littlemore, Esq; ✉ The Charter Partnership Ltd, 2 St Stephens Court, 15–17 St Stephens Rd, Bournemouth BH2 6LA (☎ 01202 554625, fax 01202 294007, car 0836 260845)

LITTLER, Hon Mrs (Sarah Victoria); known as Sarah Long; da of 4 Viscount Long; *b* 1958; *m* 19 May 1990, George G Clegg Littler, er s of George Clegg Littler, and Mrs Frithjof Meidell-Andersen; 1 s (Alexander b 17 Jan 1996); *Career* gallery owner and art conslt; ptnr Long & Ryle Art International whose clients incl: Lloyd Thompson, McKinsey's & Co, Cazenove & Co, Kreditbank, Morgan Grenfell, Mitsubishi Corp PLC and London Underground; memb: Friends of the Tate, Friends of the Royal Academy, Royal Horticultural Soc; *Recreations* gardening, reading, music, visiting galleries and museums; *Clubs* Chelsea Arts; *Style—* Sarah Long; ✉ Long & Ryle Art International, 4 John Islip Street, London SW1P 4PX (☎ 0171 834 1434)

LITTLER, Brian Oswald; s of William Oswald Littler (d 1958), of London, and Mavis Pricilla, *née* Copping; *b* 22 Nov 1942; *Educ* St Dunstan's Coll, King's Coll London (BDS, MB BS); *m* 19 Feb 1972, Susan Elizabeth, da of Arthur Stent, of Wonersh, Surrey; 1 s (Adam Oswald b 20 Oct 1975), 2 da (Elizabeth Ann b 30 May 1978, Bryony Susan Jayne b 24 Oct 1984); *Career* conslt oral and maxillo-facial surgn to: The London Hosp, Whipps Cross Hosp, St Margaret's Hosp, Princess Alexandra Hosp Harlow, The London Independent Hosp, The Roding Hosp Redbridge; memb Inst of Advanced Motorists; FDS RCS 1969; *Recreations* sailing; *Style—* Brian Littler, Esq; ✉ Whipps Cross Hospital, Whipps Cross Rd, London E11 1NR (☎ 0181 539 5522)

LITTLER, Sir (James) Geoffrey; KCB (1985, CB 1981); s of James Edward Littler (d 1961), of Manchester, and Evelyn Mary Taylor; *b* 18 May 1930; *Educ* Manchester GS, Corpus Christi Coll Cambridge (BA); *m* 20 Sept 1958, Shirley, *qv*, da of Sir Percy Marsh, CSI, CIE (d 1969), of Dorchester-on-Thames, Oxfordshire; 1 s (Peter b 1967); *Career* HM Civil Serv: joined Colonial Office 1952, joined HM Treasy 1954, second perm sec (fin) HM Treasy 1983–88, chm Working Party 3 OECD 1985–88, chm Euro Community Monetary Ctee 1987–88; chm County NatWest Group Ltd 1991–92, dir NatWest Investment Bank Ltd 1989–90, dir National Westminster Bank plc 1991–92; currently sr advsr BZW Ltd; chm The Israel Fund plc, chm TR European Growth Trust plc, dir Montanaro UK Smaller Companies Investment Tst plc; hon fell Corpus Christi Coll Cambridge 1994; *Recreations* music, reading, travelling; *Clubs* Reform; *Style—* Sir Geoffrey Littler, KCB

LITTLER, George Gordon Clegg; s of George Clegg Littler, OBE, TD, of Ibiza, Spain, and Barbara Noble Meidell-Andersen, *née* Gordon, of Bergen, Norway; *b* 1 May 1950; *Educ* Bradfield, Coll of Law; *m* 1, 25 April 1981 (m dis 1986), Emma, da of Sir John Greville Stanley Beith, KCMG; m 2, 19 May 1990, Hon Sarah, da of Viscount Long; 1 s (Alexander George Richard Clegg b 17 Jan 1996); *Career* slr; ptnr Simmons & Simmons 1985– (joined 1981); memb Law Soc; *Recreations* theatre, contemporary art, association football; *Clubs* Brooks's; *Style—* George Littler, Esq; ✉ Simmons & Simmons, 21 Wilson Street, London EC2M 2TX (☎ 0171 628 2020, telex 888562, fax 0171 628 2070)

LITTLER, Lady; Shirley; da of Sir Percy Marsh, CSI, CIE (d 1969), of Dorchester-on-Thames, Oxon, and Joan Mary, *née* Beecroft (d 1972); *b* 8 June 1932; *Educ* Headington Sch Oxford, Girton Coll Cambridge (BA, MA); *m* 20 Sept 1958, Sir (James) Geoffrey Littler, KCB, *qv*; 1 s (Peter b 1967); *Career* princ HM Treasy 1960 (asst princ 1953), asst sec Prices and Incomes Bd (NBPI) 1969, sec to V and G Tbnl of Enquiry 1971, Home Office 1972; asst under sec of state: Broadcasting Dept Home Office 1978, Immigration and Nationality Dept Home Office 1981; dir gen IBA 1989–90 (dir of admin 1983, deputy dir gen 1986, ret 1991); chm: Gaming Bd for GB 1992–, Nat Advsy Body for the Confidential Enquiries into Stillbirths and Deaths in Infancy 1992–; FRSA 1988, MRTS; *Recreations* reading, history; *Style—* Lady Littler; ✉ c/o Coutts and Co, Campbell's Office, 440 Strand, London WC2R 0QS

LITTLER MANNERS, Judy; da of Sir Emile Littler (d 1985), and Lady Cora Littler, *née* Goffin; *b* 16 Oct 1952; *Educ* St Mary's Hall Brighton, Charters Towers Sch Bexhill-on-Sea, St Anne's Coll Oxford (MA); *m* 12 June 1982 (m dis 1990), David Peter Manners; 1 s (Max b 27 March 1983), 1 da (Marina b 6 Sept 1986); *Career* floor asst and asst floor mangr BBC Studio Mgmnt Dept 1975–78, prodn asst Drama in Europe Ltd and Derek Glynne Assocs 1978–79, producer MMA Presentations Ltd 1979–83, proprietor and chief exec Mum's The Word 1984–92; dir: British Amalgamated Theatres Ltd 1985–, The Night Company Ltd 1985–, GR Productions Ltd 1985–; non-exec dir Stratagem Group plc (formerly London Entertainments plc) 1987–93, memb Bd of Mgmnt Royal Hosp and Home Putney 1992–95 (chm Forget-me-not Ball 1988–92), hon treas The Actors' Charitable Trust; tstee: The Emile Littler Actors' Charitable Tst, The Emile Littler Fndn; patron Theatre in Trust; *Recreations* theatre, tennis, skiing; *Clubs* Hurlingham, The Harbour Club; *Style—* Mrs Judy Littler Manners; ✉ c/o Goodman Derrick & Co, 90 Fetter Lane, London EC4A 1EQ

LITTLEWOOD, Anthony George (Tony); s of George Kershaw Littlewood, of Sylvester House, Ashton-under-Lyne, and Sarah, *née* Rogers; *b* 3 Oct 1949; *Educ* Audenshaw GS, Nottingham Univ (BPharm); *m* 11 Dec 1982 (m dis 1992), Nikola Ann, da of Lance James du Lys Mallalieu (d 1973); 3 s (Russell b 1984, Guy b 1986, Harry b 1988); *Career* pharmacist; chm and md George Hinchliffe Ltd 1973–; chm Northern (chemists) Ltd 1981–, md Amchem (UK) Ltd 1995–; chm Local Pharmaceutical Ctee 1989–; non-exec dir Tameside Family Health Servs Authy 1990–; MRPharmS 1972, MIMgt 1980; *Recreations* tennis, golf, travel, (collecting) photographic, classic cars, flying light aircraft, endeavouring to solve sons' homework; *Clubs* Union (Ashton-under-Lyne), Ashton-under-Lyne Golf; *Style—* Tony Littlewood, Esq; ✉ Friezeland Grange, Greenfield, Saddleworth OL3 7LQ

LITTLEWOOD, Graham; s of Ernest Charles Littlewood (d 1960), and Ivy Lilian, *née* Masters (d 1978); *b* 19 Feb 1944; *Educ* Royal Liberty Sch Romford; *m* 30 Aug 1971, Marianne; 2 da (Catherine Ann b 22 March 1973, Jane Elizabeth b 9 June 1975); *Career* accountant; Bristow Burrell & Co 1960–67, Coopers & Lybrand 1967–69, gp fin controller Gazocean France 1969–71, ptnr Keens Shay Keens & Co 1973; Pannell Kerr Forster: joined 1978–, ptnr i/c Auditing Dept 1989–94, managing ptnr London 1994–95, ptnr i/c pension schemes and inward ivestmt 1995–; Freeman City of London 1983; FCA 1966; *Recreations* golf, reading; *Clubs* East India, Stapleford Abbotts Golf; *Style—* Graham Littlewood, Esq; ✉ Pannell Kerr Forster, New Garden House, Hatton Garden, London EC1N 8JA (☎ 0171 831 7393)

LITTLEWOOD, James; CB (1973); s of Thomas Littlewood (d 1930), of Royton, Lancs, and Sarah Jane, *née* Penhall (d 1967); *b* 21 Oct 1922; *Educ* Manchester GS, St John's Coll Cambridge (MA); *m* 9 Aug 1950, Barbara, da of Harry Shaw (d 1958), of Blackburn, Lancs; 2 s (David b 1955, Peter b 1957), 1 da (Pamela b 1953); *Career* enlisted Army 1942, cmmnd KORR, WWII serv India and Burma, transfd W Yorks Regt (later HQ 17 Indian Div 1945), Wingate's second campaign 1944, 17 Ind Div campaign 1945, Capt; Civil Serv: admin class 1947, HM Treasy 1947–67, seconded Cabinet Office 1955, transfd Dept for Nat Savings 1967, dir of savings 1972, ret 1981; *Recreations* golf, bridge; *Clubs* Barton on Sea Golf; *Style—* James Littlewood, Esq, CB

LITTMAN, Jeffrey James; s of Louis Littman (d 1981), of Edmonton, Middx, and Sarah (Sadie), *née* Coberman (d 1974); *b* 19 Feb 1943; *Educ* Latymer Sch Edmonton, St Catharine's Coll Cambridge (MA); *m* 20 March 1975, Sandra Lynne, da of David Kallman (d 1975), of NY; 2 da (Amanda, Léonie); *Career* ldr Mgmnt Gp Dept of Computing and Control Imperial Coll London; called to the Bar Middle Temple 1974; in practice Midland and Oxford circuit specialising in co disputes, insolvency and commercial litigation; writer, deviser and presenter the course on civil procedure for TV Law 1993; *Recreations* history, Jewish studies; *Style—* Jeffrey Littman, Esq; ✉ 2 Field Court, Gray's Inn, London WC1R 5BB (☎ 0171 405 6114, fax 0171 831 6112)

LITTMAN, Mark; QC (1961); s of Jack Littman (d 1963), and Lilian, *née* Rose; *b* 4 Sept 1920; *Educ* Owens Sch, LSE (BSc), Queen's Coll Oxford (MA); *m* 18 Sept 1965, Marguerite, da of Tyler Lamkin, of Monroe, Louisiana, USA; *Career* Lt RN 1941–46; called to the Bar Middle Temple 1947, in practice 1947–67 and 1979–, master of Bench 1971, master treas Middle Temple 1988, head of chambers; dep chm Br Steel Corp 1967–79; former dir: Burtons, Granada, Commercial Union (vice chm), British Enkalon, Amerada Hess (US), RTZ; memb Royal Cmmn Legal Servs 1976–79; *Clubs* Reform, Garrick, Oxford and Cambridge, Century (New York); *Style—* Mark Littman, Esq, QC; ✉ 12 Gray's Inn Square, London WC1R 5JP (☎ 0171 404 4866)

LITTON, Andrew; *Educ* Juilliard Sch New York; *Career* conductor; assoc conductor to Mstislav Rostropovich NSO Washington (formerly asst), debut with BBC Symphony Orch 1982, debut with RPO 1983; Bournemouth Symphony Orch: princ conductor and artistic advsr 1988–94, conductor laureate 1994–; music dir Dallas Symphony Orch 1994–; guest appearances with: all maj London orchs, English Chamber Orch, Scottish Chamber Orch, Royal Scottish National Orch, Oslo Philharmonic, Rotterdam Philharmonic, Czech Philharmonic, Orchestre Philharmonique de Monte Carlo, RAI Milan, RSO Berlin, l'Orchestre Suisse Romande, WDR Köln, Orchestre National de France, Czech Philharmonic, Chicago Symphony Orch, Los Angeles Philharmonic, Philadelphia Orch, Pittsburgh Symphony Orch and orchs of Minnesota, Montreal, Rochester, Toronto and Vancouver; 1994/5 season performances with: Israel Philharmonic Orch, Hessischer Rundfunk, Swedish Radio Orch, Gothenburg Symphony and Los Angeles Philharmonic (at Hollywood Bowl); opera debuts: Metropolitan Opera (Eugene Onegin, 1989), Royal Opera House (Trevor Nunn's Porgy and Bess, 1992), ENO (Falstaff, 1994); new prodn of Salome ENO 1996; *Recordings* incl: complete Tchaikovsky Symphonies (with Bournemouth Symphony Orchestra), all Rachmaninov Symphonies (with RPO), Mahler's Symphony No 1 and Songs of a Wayfarer, Elgar Enigma Variations, Bernstein The Age of Anxiety, Ravel and Gershwin piano concerti, Shostakovich Symphony No 10, Brahms Symphony No 1, Mahler Symphony No 5 (recorded live with Dallas Symphony Orch); *Style—* Andrew Litton, Esq; ✉ c/o IMG Artists Europe, Media House, 3 Burlington Lane, Chiswick, London W4 2TH (☎ 0181 233 5800, 0181 233 5917, fax 0181 233 5801)

LIU, David Tek-Yung; s of Pro Liu Tsu-Shya, of Sydney, Aust, and Mabel King, *née* Liang (d 1977); *b* 26 April 1941; *Educ* All Saints Bathurst NSW Australia, Univ of Sydney (MB BS), Univ of Sussex (MPhil); *m* 28 July 1976, Pamela Margaret, da of Arthur Heptinstall, of Surrey, England; 1 da (Natasha b 9 Sept 1981); *Career* res fell Univ of Sussex, lectr and res lectr Univ Coll London, sr lectr and hon conslt Univ of Nottingham 1989–, conslt Univ of Malaya 1989–91; co-fndr Embrace 1991; memb: Nottingham Charity Appeal for Pre-Natal Diagnosis, Birmingham and Midland Obstetric and Gynaecological Soc, jt MRC-RCOG Ctee Chorion Villus Sampling; FRCOG 1986, FRACOG 1992, DM Univ of Nottingham 1992; *Books* Thinking, Feeling (1987), Labour Ward Manual (1985), Chorion Villus Sampling (1987), Practical Gynaecology (1988); *Recreations* gardening, water sports, writing; *Clubs* Nottingham County Sailing; *Style—* David Liu, Esq; ✉ Department of Obstetrics & Gynaecology, City Hospital, Hucknall Road, Nottingham NG5 1PB (☎ 0115 969 1169, fax 0115 962 7670)

LIVELY, Penelope Margaret; OBE (1989); da of Roger Vincent Low, and Vera Maud Greer, *née* Reckitt; *b* 17 March 1933; *Educ* St Anne's Coll Oxford (BA); *m* 1957, Prof Jack Lively; 1 s (Adam), 1 da (Josephine); *Career* writer; book reviews and short stories in numerous magazines, various TV and radio scripts; former chm Soc of Authors (memb 1973–); memb: PEN 1985–, Arts Cncl Lit Panel 1990–92, Bd The British Library; Hon DLitt; FRSL; *children's books*: Astercote (1970), The Whispering Knights (1971), The Wild Hunt of Hagworthy (1971), The Driftway (1972), The Ghost of Thomas Kempe (Carnegie medal, 1974), The House in Norham Gardens (1974), Going Back (1975), Boy Without a Name (1975), A Stitch in Time (Whitbread award, 1976), The Stained Glass

Window (1976), Fanny's Sister (1976), The Voyage of QV66 (1978), Fanny and The Monsters (1978), Fanny and The Battle of Potter's Piece (1980), The Revenge of Samuel Stokes (1981), Fanny and the Monsters (three stories, 1983), Uninvited Ghosts (1984), Dragon Trouble (1984), Debbie and the Little Devil (1987), A House Inside Out (1987); *non-fiction*: The Presence of the Past (1976), Oleander, Jacaranda: A Childhood Perceived (1994); *fiction*: The Road to Lichfield (1977), Nothing Missing but the Samovar (Southern Arts Literary prize, 1978), Treasures of Time (Arts Cncl Nat Book award, 1979), Judgement Day (1980), Next to Nature, Art (1982), Perfect Happiness (1983), Corruption (1984), According to Mark (1984), Pack of Cards, stories 1978–86 (1986), Moon Tiger (Booker prize, 1987), Passing On (1989), City of the Mind (1991), Cleopatra's Sister (1993), Heat Wave (1996); *Style*— Ms Penelope Lively, OBE; ✉ c/o David Higham Associates, 5–8 Lower John Street, Golden Square W1R 4HA (☎ 0171 437 7888)

LIVENS, Leslie John Phillip; s of Lt Leslie Francis Hugh Livens (d 1981), of London, and Betty Livens; *b* 13 Dec 1946; *Educ* Wimbledon County Secdy Sch; *m* 3 Aug 1968, Carole Ann, da of Henry William Todd, of London; 1 s (Stephen b 1970), 1 da (Clare b 1972); *Career* ed and conslt ed Taxation Practitioner (Jl of Inst of Taxation) 1974–84; former ed: Tax Planning International, Financial Times World Tax Report, Review of Parliament; managing ed Butterworths Tax Books 1977–81; Moores Rowland (formerly Nevill & Co): taxation conslt 1981–83, ptnr 1983–, chm International Tax Group 1988–; on Br Acad of Experts' Register of Mediators 1991–, panellist on The City Disputes Panel 1995–; ATII 1972, ATTI 1983, MBAE 1989; memb: Offshore Inst 1995, Soc of Tst and Estate Practitioners 1995; *Publications* incl: Moores Rowland's Tax Guide (1982–87), Daily Telegraph Tax Guide (1987), Daily Telegraph Personal Tax Guide (1988), Debrett's International Offshore Finance (ed, 1992), Tolley's Valuation Handbook (1995); *Recreations* music, writing, walking, family; *Style*— Leslie Livens, Esq; ✉ Moores Rowland, Clifford's Inn, Fetter Lane, London EC4A 1AS (☎ 0171 831 2345, fax 0171 831 6123, telex 886504)

LIVERMORE, Karen; da of Joseph Livermore (d 1982), and Glenys, *née* Howard; *b* 12 Aug 1961; *Educ* Grays Sch, Thurrock Tech Coll; *Career* Drapers Record 1980–87, freelance journalist and stylist various cos and pubns for IPC Magazines and Sunday Mirror Magazine; Daily Star: fashion ed 1989–95, womans ed 1995–; *Style*— Miss Karen Livermore; ✉ Daily Star, 245 Blackfriars Rd, London SE1 9UX (☎ 0171 928 8000, fax 0171 922 7962)

LIVERPOOL, Archdeacon of; *see:* Metcalf, Ven Robert Laurence (Bob)

LIVERPOOL, 6 Bishop of (cr 1880) 1975–; Rt Rev David Stuart Sheppard; s of Stuart Sheppard (d 1937), and Barbara Sheppard (d 1983); *b* 6 March 1929; *Educ* Sherborne, Trinity Hall Cambridge (MA); *m* 1957, Grace, da of Rev Bryan Raymond Isaac; 1 da (Jenny); *Career* Nat Serv 2 Lt Royal Sussex Regt 1947–49; ordained: deacon 1955, priest 1956; curate St Mary's Islington 1955–57, warden and chaplain Mayflower Family Centre Canning Town 1957–69, bishop suffragan of Woolwich 1969–75; Hon LLD Univ of Liverpool 1981, Hon DTech Liverpool John Moores Univ 1987; Hon DUniv: Cambridge 1990, Exeter 1996; *Books* Parson's Pitch (1964), Built as a City (1974), Bias to the Poor (1983), The Other Britain (Dimbleby Lecture, 1984), Better Together (with Archbishop Derek Worlock, 1988), With Christ in the Wilderness (with Archbishop Derek Worlock, 1990), With Hope in Our Hearts (with Archbishop Derek Worlock, 1994); *Recreations* painting, following cricket (played for Sussex 1947–62, England 1950–63, Univ of Cambridge 1950–52), reading, gardening, bird watching, cooking, relaxing at home; *Style*— The Rt Rev the Bishop of Liverpool; ✉ Bishop's Lodge, Woolton Park, Liverpool L25 6DT; Church House, 1 Hanover St, Liverpool L1 3DW (☎ 0151 708 9480)

LIVERPOOL, Dean of; *see:* Walters, Very Rev (Rhys) Derrick Chamberlain

LIVERPOOL, 5 Earl of (UK 1905); Edward Peter Bertram Savile Foljambe; also Baron Hawkesbury (UK 1893) and Viscount Hawkesbury (UK 1905); s of Capt Peter George William Savile Foljambe (ka Italy 1944), and Elizabeth Joan, *née* Flint (who m 2, Maj Andrew Gibbs, MBE, TD, *qv*, and d 1993); *b* 14 Nov 1944; *Educ* Shrewsbury, Perugia Univ Italy; *m* 1, 29 Jan 1970 (m dis 1994), Lady Juliana Noel (Countess of Liverpool), da of 5 Earl of Gainsborough, *qv*; 2 s (Viscount Hawkesbury b 25 March 1972, Hon Ralph Foljambe b 24 Sept 1974); m 2, 26 May 1995, Marie-Ange, eldest da of Comte Géraud Michel de Pierredon; *Heir* s, Viscount Hawkesbury, *qv*; *Clubs* Turf, Pratt's; *Style*— The Rt Hon the Earl of Liverpool; ✉ House of Lords, London SW1 0PW

LIVERPOOL, Most Rev Archbishop of (RC) 1996–; Patrick Altham Kelly; s of John Kelly (d 1960), and Mary, *née* Altham (d 1989); *b* 23 Nov 1938; *Educ* Preston Catholic Coll, Venerable English Coll Rome, Pontifical Gregorian Univ Rome (PhL, STL); *Career* curate Lancaster Cathedral 1964–66, memb clery Archdiocese of Birmingham 1977, rector St Mary's Coll Oscott Birmingham 1979–84 (prof of dogmatic theology 1966–79), bishop of Salford 1984–96; sec Hierarchy Theology Cmmn 1967; prelate of honour to HH the Pope 1980–, consultor to the Pontificial Cmmn for Justice and Peace; *Recreations* reading, music, opera; *Style*— The Most Rev the Archbishop of Liverpool; ✉ Archbishop's House, 87 Green Lane, Mossley Hill, Liverpool L18 2EP (☎ 0151 722 2379)

LIVERSEDGE, Richard Lorton; s of Lt-Col John Ridler Liversedge (d 1968), of Fawke House, Sevenoaks, Kent, and Grace Evelyn Liversedge (d 1982); *b* 31 Aug 1940; *Educ* Tonbridge, London Hosp Dental Sch (BDS), London Hosp Med Coll (MB BS); *m* 28 Oct 1972, Jennifer Jane, da of John Hurrel Robertson, of Johannesburg, SA; 1 s (Dominic b 1974), 2 da (Annabel b 1975, Belinda b 1979); *Career* registrar London Hosp 1970–72 (house surgn 1968–69), sr registrar Royal Dental Hosp and St George's Hosp 1972–77; conslt maxillo-facial surgn: Middx Hosp 1977–89, Barnet Gp of Hosps 1977–; responsible for various surgical instrument innovations; winter sportsman (luge); winner Br Luge Champs 1971; Winter Olympics: represented GB Grenoble 1968, capt Sapporo 1972, capt Innsbruck 1976; pres Br Racing Toboggan Assoc 1972–; chm Med Ctee Fedn Internationale de Luge de Course 1972–, memb Med Ctee Br Olympic Assoc 1976–; Freeman City of London 1968, Liveryman Worshipful Co of Skinners 1977; FDS RCSEd 1971, FDS RCS 1972; *Recreations* luge, Cresta run, moto polo; *Clubs* St Moritz Toboganning; *Style*— Richard Liversedge, Esq; ✉ Oak Cottage, 117 Flaunden, Hertfordshire HP3 0PB (☎ 01442 833 047); Flat 1, 43 Wimpole St, London W1M 7AF (☎ 0171 935 7909)

LIVESAY, Adm Sir Michael Howard; KCB (1989); s of William Lindsay Livesay (d 1982), of Bishop Auckland, Co Durham, and Margaret Elenora Chapman Steel (d 1974); *b* 5 April 1936; *Educ* Acklam Hall GS Middlesbrough, RNC Dartmouth; *m* 8 Aug 1959, Sara, da of Dr Arthur Vivian House, of Bicester, Oxon; 2 da (Harriet b 1962, Georgia b 1964); *Career* joined RN 1952, trg appts 1954–57, cmmnd 1957, qualified aircraft direction specialist 1959, direction offr HMS Hermes and HMS Aisne, Fighter Direction Sch and 893 Naval Air Sqdn 1959–66; cmd: HMS Hubberston 1966–68, HMS Plymouth 1970–72; Capt Fishery Protection and Mine Counter Measures 1975–77, first CO HMS Invincible 1979–82, dir Naval Warfare 1982–84, Flag Offr Sea Trg 1984–85, asst chief Naval Staff 1986–88, Flag Offr Scotland and NI 1989–91, Second Sea Lord 1991–93; ret 1993; non-exec dir: Scottish Nuclear Ltd 1993–, Inter Exec Scotland Ltd 1994–; cmmr Northern Lighthouse Bd 1994– (vice chm 1995–), pres Royal Br Legion Scotland 1996–; CIMgt 1993, MInstD 1993; *Recreations* sailing, skiing, gardening, fishing, golf; *Clubs* Army and Navy, Royal Yacht Sqdn; *Style*— Adm Sir Michael Livesay, KCB; ✉ c/o Naval Secretary, Room 161 Victory Building, HM Naval Base, Portsmouth PO1 3LS

LIVESEY, Dr Anthony Edward; s of Joseph Livesey (d 1976), of Gt Harwood, Lancs, and Dorothy, *née* Birtwhistle; *b* 16 Jan 1953; *Educ* St Mary's Coll Blackburn Lancs, Univ of Dundee (BMSc, MB BCh); *m* 17 Aug 1974, Apolonia Marie, da of Jan Wachala, of Blackburn, Lancs; 2 s (Joseph John b 18 Jan 1980, David Michael b 12 Feb 1983); *Career* registrar psychiatry Manchester 1981–84, sr registrar child psychiatry Sheffield 1984–86, conslt child and adolescent psychiatry N Derbys DHA 1986–; dir of med affrs Community Health Care Servs (N Derbys) NHS Trust 1994–; memb Assoc for Psychiatric Study Adolescents; MRCPsych 1983; *Recreations* cycling, distance running, wind surfing, photography; *Style*— Dr Anthony Livesey; ✉ 31 Hartington Road, Millhouses, Sheffield S7 2LF (☎ 0114 236 0346); The Edmund Street Clinic, Edmund St, Chesterfield, Derbyshire (☎ 01246 451252)

LIVESEY, Bernard Joseph Edward; QC (1990); s of Joseph Augustine Livesey (d 1965), of Hatch End, Middx, and Marie Gabrielle, *née* Caulfield; *b* 21 Feb 1944; *Educ* Cardinal Vaughan Sch London, Peterhouse Cambridge (MA, LLB); *m* 25 Sept 1971, Penelope Jean, da of Samuel Walter Harper, of Slindon, W Sussex; 2 da (Sarah b 5 June 1973, Kate b 21 Aug 1977); *Career* called to the Bar Lincoln's Inn 1969, recorder 1987–; fell Int Acad of Trial Lawyers 1993; *Recreations* listening to music, gardening, bell ringing; *Style*— Bernard Livesey, Esq, QC; ✉ 2 Crown Office Row, Temple, London EC4Y 7HJ (☎ 0171 797 8000, fax 0171 797 8001)

LIVESEY, Dr David Anthony; s of Vincent Livesey (d 1963), of Derby, and Marie, *née* Parr (d 1983); *b* 30 May 1944; *Educ* Derby Sch, Imperial Coll London (BSc Eng), Christ's Coll Cambridge (PhD); *m* 30 Dec 1967, Sally Anne, da (Alfred) Noel Vanston; 1 s (Nathaniel James b 14 May 1970), 2 da (Ruth Laura b 6 April 1973, Harriet Sarah b 24 Oct 1980); *Career* Univ of Cambridge: res offr Dept of Applied Economics 1969–75, res fell Peterhouse 1971–74, official fell Emmanuel Coll 1974–91, bursar Emmanuel Coll 1983–91, univ lectr Dept of Engrg 1975–91, sec gen of the Faculties 1992–, professorial fell Emmanuel Coll 1992–; non-exec dir Addenbrooke's NHS Tst 1992–; ACGI; *Recreations* swimming, learning Welsh; *Style*— Dr David Livesey; ✉ 33 St Barnabas Road, Cambridge CB1 2BX (☎ 01223 364520); General Board of the Faculties, University of Cambridge, The Old Schools, Trinity Lane, Cambridge CB2 1TT (☎ 01223 332260, fax 01223 332277)

LIVESEY, Geoffrey Colin; OBE; *b* 21 Dec 1943; *m* 1, 1969 (m dis 1982), Elisa Jane Pullen; 2 s; m 2, 1985, Linda Ann Lowe; *Career* joined FCO 1962, second sec and vice-consul Abidjan 1977–81, vice-consul for Niger and Upper Volta 1981–83, first sec FCO 1982–85, first sec (commercial) and consul Havana 1985–89, first sec (mgmnt) Islamabad 1989–93, first sec FCO 1993–; *Recreations* squash, tennis; *Style*— Geoffrey Livesey, Esq, OBE; ✉ 6 Cullerne Close, Ewell Village, Surrey KT17 1XY; Foreign and Commonwealth Office, London SW1 (☎ 0171 270 2935)

LIVESEY, Rodger Charles; JP; s of Roland Livesey; *b* 19 June 1944; *Educ* Downing Coll Cambridge (MA); *m* 29 May 1972, Pat; 2 s (Matthew b 1974, Graham b 1979), 1 da (Caroline b 1977); *Career* md Security Pacific Hoare Govett Ltd 1976–88, dep chm Tokai Bank Europe PLC 1988–, chm W Hampton Ltd 1987–; dir: Securities and Futures Authy 1994–, Beds and Herts NHS Tst 1994–; gen cmmr of tax; Freeman City of London, Liveryman Worshipful Co of Actuaries; FIA; *Style*— Rodger Livesey, Esq, JP; ✉ 60 West Common, Harpenden, Herts AL5 2LD (☎ 01582 767527); Tokai Bank Europe plc, 1 Exchange Square, London (☎ 0171 638 6030, fax 0171 588 5875)

LIVESEY, His Hon Judge; Ronald John Dearden; QC (1981); s of John William Livesey (d 1952), of Southport, and Una Florence, *née* Williams; *b* 11 Sept 1935; *Educ* Malvern, Lincoln Coll Oxford; *m* 19 Aug 1965, Elizabeth Jane, *née* Coutts; 1 s (John William Allan), 1 da (Alexandra Jane); *Career* called to the Bar Lincoln's Inn 1962, bencher 1985; recorder 1981–92, circuit judge (Northern Circuit) 1992–, sr judge Sovereign Base Areas Cyprus 1996– (dep sr judge 1981); *Recreations* golf; *Clubs* Royal Birkdale Golf; *Style*— His Hon Judge Livesey, QC; ✉ c/o Northern Circuit Office, 15 Quay Street, Manchester M60 9FD

LIVESEY, Tony; s of John Livesey, of Nelson, Lancs, and Jean, *née* Comber (d 1977); *b* 11 Jan 1964; *Educ* SS John Fisher and Thomas More HS Colne Lancs, Nelson and Colne Coll; *m* Barbara, *née* Maley; 1 da (Megan Maley b 23 Aug 1994), 1 s (Angus Maley b 23 May 1996); *Career* jr reporter Nelson Leader 1983–86, writer news and features Gulf News Dubai 1986–87, reporter Lancs Evening Telegraph 1987–88; Sport Newspapers: successively sports reporter, sports ed, asst ed then dep ed Sunday Sport, launch ed News & Echo (since sold), managing ed Sunday and Daily Sport, ed Sunday Sport and gp managing ed 1993–95, gp ed-in-chief 1995–; NW Young Journalist of the Year 1988; *Books* 10 Years of Sunday Sport (1996); also author of a series of short children's stories (1986–87); *Recreations* reading, writing TV scripts, watching Burnley FC (often from behind the seat), after dinner speaking; *Style*— Tony Livesey, Esq; ✉ Sport Newspapers, 19 Great Ancoats Street, Manchester M60 4BT (☎ 0161 236 4466, fax 0161 228 6847)

LIVESLEY, Prof Brian; s of Thomas Clement Livesley (d 1980), and Stella Livesley (d 1980); *b* 31 Aug 1936; *Educ* King George V GS Southport Lancs, Univ of Leeds Med Sch (MB ChB, MRCP, DHMSA, MD (Lond), FRCP 1989); *m* 1, 1963, Beryl, *née* Hulme (d 1966); 1 s; m 2, 1969, Valerie Anne, *née* Nuttall; 2 da; *Career* house appts: Leeds Gen Infirmary 1961–62, Dist and Univ Hosps in Leeds, Manchester and Liverpool 1963–68; Harvey res fell King's Coll Hosp London 1969–72, conslt physician in geriatric med Lambeth, Southwark and Lewisham Health Authy 1973–87, Univ of London's prof of med in the elderly Charing Cross and Westminster Med Sch 1988–; clinical examiner in med Univ of London 1980–95 (sr clinical examiner 1990–95), examiner in med Worshipful Soc of Apothecaries 1987–94, examiner for dip in geriatric med RCP 1987–93; NW Thames regnl advsr on med for the elderly 1990–96; memb Med Cmmn on Accident Prevention 1984–89 (chm Home and Family Safety Cmmn 1988–89); govr: St Paul's Cray CE (controlled) Primary Sch Orpington 1986–87, Newstead Wood Sch for Girls Orpington 1987–92; Univ of London's Academic Cncl rep to Age Concern Bromley (chm 1992–93); KStJ 1994 (OStJ 1992), DG St John Ambulance 1994–96 (asst DG 1993–94); Freeman City of London 1975, Liveryman Worshipful Soc of Apothecaries (Yeoman 1975, memb Ct of Assts 1990); JP 1983–96; *Publications* investigations into aspects of the history, pathophysiology, biochemistry, psychology, epidemiology, sociology and education in med in our ageing society, book reviewer for professional jls; *Recreations* family, Christian culture study, marine and pond life, scuba diving; *Style*— Prof Brian Livesley; ✉ 4 Berger Close, Petts Wood, Kent BR5 1HR (☎ 01689 876694, fax 01689 896979); Chelsea and Westminster Hospital, Fulham Road, London SW10 9NH (☎ 0181 746 8063, fax 0181 746 8183)

LIVINGSTON, Dorothy Kirby; da of late Albert Paulus Livingston, and Margaret Alice, *née* Kirby; *b* 6 Jan 1948; *Educ* Central Newcastle HS, St Hugh's Coll Oxford (MA); *m* 11 Sept 1971, Julian, s of late Alfred Millar; 2 da (Katherine b 22 Jan 1983, Alice b 31 May 1986); *Career* Herbert Smith: articled clerk 1970–72, slr 1972–80, ptnr 1980–; memb: Law Soc 1979, City of London Slrs' Co 1979; vice chm Banking Law Sub Ctee and memb Competition Law Sub Ctee City of London Law Soc, chm St Hugh's Law Soc; *Publications include* Longmans Competition Law Sources (jtly 1991), FT Law and Tax: Competition Law and Practice (1995); *Recreations* gardening, photography, history; *Style*— Mrs Dorothy Livingston; ✉ Herbert Smith, Exchange House, Primrose Street, London EC2A 2HS (☎ 0171 374 8000, fax 0171 496 0043)

LIVINGSTON, Air Vice-Marshal Graham; s of Neil Livingston (d 1977), and Margaret Anderson, *née* Graham (d 1989), of Bo'ness, West Lothian; *b* 2 Aug 1928; *Educ*

Bo'ness Acad, Univ of Edinburgh (MB, ChB, DPH, DIH); *m* 1, 11 Nov 1953 (m dis 1968), Catherine Law; 1 s (Graham b 1955), 2 da (Jennifer b 1957, Catriona b 1959, d 1961); m 2, 19 June 1970, Carol Judith Palmer; 1 s (David b 1972), 1 da (Sara Jane b 1971); *Career* Med Offr RAF, flying stations N Ireland 1952–54, SMO RAF El Hamra Abyad Egypt 1954–55; GP 1956–57; SMO: RAF Lindholme 1958–60, RAF Honington 1960–62; postgrad Univ of Edinburgh 1962–63; SMO: RAF Laarbruch Germany 1963–66, RAF Coll Cranwell 1966–70; registrar RAF Hosp Cosford 1970, CO RAF IHMT Halton 1971, registrar TPMRAF Hosp Akrotiri Cyprus 1972–74; CO RAF Hosp: Cosford 1974–76, Wegberg Germany 1976–79; dep dir of med personnel and orgn MOD 1979–80, Air Cdre 1980, dep PMO Strike Cmd 1981–83; PMO: RAF Germany 1983–84, RAF Support Cmd 1984–89; conslt occupational health physician NW: Herts Health Authy 1989–94, Wycombe Health Authy 1991–94; Air Vice-Marshal 1984; Freeman City of London 1982; QHS 1985–89; MFCM 1974, MFOM 1981, FIMgt 1986, MFPHM 1990; *Recreations* golf, skiing, caravanning; *Clubs* RAF, Ashridge Golf; *Style*— Air Vice-Marshal Graham Livingston; ✉ c/o Lloyds Bank plc, Cox's and Kings Branch, PO Box 1190, 7 Pall Mall, London SW1Y 5NA

LIVINGSTON, Dr Martin Gerard; s of Arnold Louis Livingston, of Newton Mearns, Glasgow, and Joyce, *née* Sternstein; *b* 19 May 1953; *Educ* Hillhead HS Glasgow, Univ of Glasgow (MB ChB, MD); *m* 4 July 1974, Hilary Monica, da of Dr Basil Green, of Glasgow; 1 s (Richard Jack b 1983), 1 da (Judith Fiona b 1985); *Career* psychiatry rotation Southern Gen Hosp and Leverndale Hosp 1978–79; Univ of Glasgow: lectr Psychological Med Dept 1979–83, sr lectr and hon conslt psychiatrist 1983–; author of pubns on: rehabilitation in psychiatry, psychological impact of head injury and epilepsy on patients and their relatives, drug treatments in psychiatry; regnl advsr on psychiatric rehabilitation 1987–, chm Glasgow Psychiatric Speciality Ctee 1989–92; chm: Mental Health Unit Audit Ctee, Mental Health and Community Servs Tst R&D Ctee; pt/t cmmr Mental Welfare Cmmn 1994–; memb Collegium Internationale Neuropsychoparmacologicum (CINP), surgn Coll of Neuropsychopharmacology (ECNP); FRCPsych 1994 (MRCPsych 1980); *Books* Rehabilitation of Adults and Children with Severe Head Injury (contrib, 1989); *Recreations* reading, photography, classical music; *Style*— Dr Martin Livingston; ✉ 15 Ayr Road, Whitecraigs, Glasgow G46 6SB; University Department of Psychological Medicine, Gartnavel Royal Hospital, 1055 Great Western Road, Glasgow G12 0XH (☎ 0141 211 3920); Ward 1A, Gartnavel General Hospital, Great Western Rd, Glasgow G12 0YN (☎ 0141 211 3158)

LIVINGSTON, Roderick George; s of Hugh Livingston (d 1981), of Streetly, and Rhoda Margaret, *née* Mathieson; *b* 10 Dec 1944; *Educ* Shrewsbury, Univ of Aberdeen (BSc), Univ of Exeter (ADPA), Univ of Western Ontario; *m* 23 Sept 1974, Willma, da of William Watt (d 1977), of Edinburgh; 2 s (Alastair b 1976, Michael b 1981); *Career* admin asst UCW Aberystwyth 1970–72 (graduate asst 1969–70), asst sec Univ of Dundee 1975–78 (sr admin asst 1972–75); Univ of Strathclyde: asst sec 1978–81, asst registrar 1981–85, sr asst registrar 1985–88, sr asst registrar and faculty offr 1988–; pres Univ of Aberdeen Athletic Assoc 1967–68, sec Abertay Historical Soc 1975–78; UCCA: memb Cncl of Mgmnt 1982–93, memb Statistics Ctee 1986–93, dir of co 1982–95, memb Exec Ctee 1988–94; UCAS (following merger of UCCA and PCAS): memb Jt Advsy Bd 1992–93, memb Bd of Dirs 1993–; memb CVCP Steering Gp for the Review of the Nat Applications/Admissions Procedures 1994–; vice chm Glasgow Area Bd Young Enterprise Scotland 1993– (memb Scottish Bd 1993–), sec and treas Glasgow Quality Forum 1995– (sec 1994–95); memb: Scot Univs Cncl on Entrance 1987–90, Pubns and Schs Liaison Ctees; FSAScot 1963, ACIS 1972, FRSA 1996; *Recreations* castles, coins, rowing, sailing; *Clubs* Lansdowne, Leander; *Style*— Roderick Livingston, Esq; ✉ 51 Strathblane Rd, Milngavie, Glasgow G62 8HA (☎ 0141 956 3851); University of Strathclyde, McCance Building, 16 Richmond St, Glasgow G1 1XQ (☎ 0141 548 2387, fax 0141 552 0775, e-mail r.livingston@mis.strath.ac.uk)

LIVINGSTONE, Prof Ian; s of Donald Livingstone (d 1978), and Margaret Dunn Mackay, *née* Darling (d 1968); *b* 11 Oct 1933; *Educ* Univ of Sheffield (BA), Yale Univ (MA); *m* 8 Sept 1962, Grace Ida, da of Peter Watuwa (d 1983), of Mbale, Uganda; 1 s (John b 19 Nov 1966), 3 da (Shona b 19 June 1965, Edisa b 3 June 1973, Sia (twin) b 3 June 1973); *Career* dir economic res bureau Univ of Dar es Salaam 1968–71, reader in economics Univ of Newcastle upon Tyne 1971–78, prof of devpt economics Univ of East Anglia 1978–; research in Sub-Saharan Africa, Brazil, Laos, Vietnam, Cambodia 1990–; *Monographs* Economics for Eastern Africa (1968 and 1980), West African Economics (1969), Economics and Development (1970), Economic Policy for Development (1971), Agricultural Economics for Tropical Africa (1980), Development Economics and Policy (1981), Irrigation Economics in Poor Countries (1982), Approaches to Development Studies (1982), Rural Development, Employment and Incomes in Kenya (1986), Economics for West Africa (1987), The Marketing of Cocoa and Copra in Papua New Guinea (1989), Dams, Drought and Development in Brazil (1990); *Recreations* squash; *Style*— Prof Ian Livingstone; ✉ 6 Rosslare, Norwich NR4 6AW (☎ 01603 455624); School of Development Studies, University of East Anglia, Norwich NR4 7TJ (☎ 01603 456161, fax 01603 451999)

LIVINGSTONE, Ian Lang; OBE (1993); s of John Lang Livingstone, of Motherwell, and Margaret Steele, *née* Barbour (d 1982); *b* 23 Feb 1938; *Educ* Hamilton Acad, Univ of Glasgow (BL); *m* 30 March 1967, Diane, da of Frank Hales (d 1989), of Lytham St Annes; 2 s (Andrew b 1968, Gordon b 1970); *Career* conslt slr, Notary Public 1962; dir: Motherwell Enterprise Development Co 1983, Scotland West Bd TSB plc 1985, Glendale Homes (Strathclyde) Ltd, Islay Developments Ltd; chm: Motherwell FC 1973–87, Interchase Ltd, Lanarkshire Development Agency, Bowmere Properties Ltd, New Lanarkshire Ltd, Motherwell Coll Bd, Lanarkshire Health Bd 1993– (memb 1988–); hon pres: Motherwell Cons Assoc 1981–, Motherwell Utd YMCA, Motherwell Branch St Andrew's Ambulance Assoc; hon slr Dalziel HS Memorial Tst, memb Dalziel HS Bd 1990–, govr David Livingstone Meml Tst 1988–; *Recreations* golf, music; *Clubs* Motherwell Cons; *Style*— Ian Livingstone, Esq, OBE; ✉ Roath Park, 223 Manse Rd, Motherwell ML1 2PY (☎ 01698 253750, fax 01698 276730)

LIVINGSTONE, Jack; s of Harry Livingstone, of Southport, and Ruth, *née* Kaye; *b* 27 April 1934; *Educ* Ackworth Sch, King's Coll London; *m* 5 June 1963, Janice Vivienne, da of Lt Sidney Jeffrey Manson, of Salford, Manchester; 1 s (Terence b 1966), 2 da (Joanna b 1964 d 1978, Vanessa b 1970); *Career* sr aircraftsman 2 Tactical Force RAF, served Germany; dir London Scottish Bank plc; chm: J L Manson & Partners Ltd, Record Printing Ltd; involved with: Jewish Blind Soc, Central Br Fund, Brookvale for the Mentally Handicapped; memb: NW Ctee Nat Lottery Charities Bd, NW Ctee The Lord's Taverners; chm LCCC Youth Tst; *Recreations* tennis, bridge; *Style*— Jack Livingstone, Esq; ✉ London Scottish Bank plc, London Scottish House, 24 Mount Street, Manchester M2 3LS (☎ and fax 0161 839 9741, car tel 0831 116397)

LIVINGSTONE, Ken; MP (Lab) Brent East (majority 5,971); s of Robert Moffat Livingstone, and Ethel Ada Livingstone; *b* 17 June 1945; *Educ* Tulse Hill Comprehensive Sch, Philippa Fawcett Coll of Educn; *m* 1973 (m dis 1982), Christine Pamela Chapman; *Career* cncllr (Lab) GLC: Norwood 1973–77, Hackney North 1977–81, Paddington 1981–86; leader GLC 1981–86; memb Lab NEC 1987–89, MP (Lab) Brent E 1987–; vice pres Zoological Soc of London 1996– (memb Cncl 1994–); *Books* If Voting Changed Anything They'd Abolish It (1987), Livingstone's Labour (1989); *Recreations* gardening, cinema, science fiction; *Style*— Ken Livingstone, Esq, MP; ✉ House of Commons, London SW1A 0AA

LIVINGSTONE, Marco Eduardo; s of Leon Livingstone, of London, and Alicia Arce, *née* Fernández; *b* 17 March 1952; *Educ* Univ of Toronto (BA), Courtauld Inst of Art (MA); *Career* asst keeper of Br art Walker Art Gallery Liverpol 1976–82, dep dir Museum of Modern Art Oxford 1982–86, area ed 20th century The Dictionary of Art 1986–91 (dep ed 19th and 20th centuries 1987–91), UK advsr to Art Life Ltd Tokyo 1989–; freelance writer, ed and exhibition organiser; exhibitions organised incl: Patrick Caulfield retrospective (Liverpool and London) 1981, Jim Dine retrospective (Japanese tour) 1990–91, Pop Art (Royal Acad of Arts 1991, touring Cologne, Madrid and Montreal), Tom Wesselmann retrospective (Japanese tour) 1993, Hockney in California (Japanese tour) 1994, Duane Hanson retrospective (Montreal Museum of Fine Arts) 1994, Jim Dine: The body and its Metaphors (Japanese tour) 1996; memb: Soc of Authors 1980, Association Internationale des Critiques d'Art (AICA) 1992; *Books* Sheer Magic by Allen Jones (1979), David Hockney (1981, 3 edn 1996), Duane Michals (1985), R B Kitaj (1985, 2 edn 1992), David Hockney: Faces (1987), Pop Art (1990), Tim Head (1993), Jim Dine: Flowers and Plants (1994), Allen Jones Prints (1995); *Style*— Marco Livingstone, Esq; ✉ 36 St George's Avenue, London N7 0HD (☎ 0171 607 0282, fax 0171 607 8694)

LIVINGSTONE-LEARMONTH, John Christian; s of Lt-Col Lennox John Livingstone-Learmonth, DSO, MC (d 1988), and Nancy Winifred, *née* Wooler (d 1989); *b* 30 Oct 1950; *Educ* Eton, Univ of York (BA); *m* 13 Dec 1986, (Elizabeth) Fiona, da of Arthur Ivor Stewart-Liberty, MC (d 1990), of The Lee, Buckinghamshire; 1 s (Edward Miles Christian b 22 Sept 1988), 1 da (Marina Francesca b 4 May 1991); *Career* SA mktg offr James Buchanan and Co 1975–83, sr ptnr Livingstone Communication 1987–, dir City Decisions Ltd 1990–95; distinguished visitor to Miami; memb Circle of Wine Writers; *Books* The Wines of the Rhône (1978, 3 edn 1992); *Recreations* the turf, fishing, wine tasting and writing; *Clubs* Turf, Fox House; *Style*— John Livingstone-Learmonth, Esq; ✉ Livingstone Communication (☎ 0181 780 1202, fax 0181 789 2674)

LLAMBIAS, Douglas Ernest John; s of Ernest Llambias (d 1943), and Hilda, *née* Peat (d 1984); *b* 13 Nov 1943; *Educ* De La Salle Sch London; *m* 24 June 1984, Renée; 1 s by previous m (Damian Heathcote Jotham b 1971); *Career* CA; taxation specialist Arthur Andersen 1968–70, chm Douglas Llambias Associates PLC 1982– (md 1970), chm and chief exec The Business Exchange PLC 1984–, dir Murlen Ltd 1985, chm BEXBES plc; memb Cncl ICAEW; *Recreations* badminton, squash, wines; *Clubs* Reform, RAC; *Style*— Douglas Llambias, Esq; ✉ The Business Exchange PLC, 21 John Adam Street, London WC2N 6JG

LLANDAFF, Dean of; *see:* Rogers, Very Rev John

LLANDAFF, Bishop of 1985–; Rt Rev Roy Thomas Davies; s of William Hubert John Davies (d 1967), and Dilys Hannah, *née* Thomas (d 1991); *b* 31 Jan 1934; *Educ* St David's Coll Lampeter (BA), Jesus Coll Oxford (BLitt), St Stephen's House Oxford; *Career* ordained St David's Cathedral: deacon 1959, priest 1960; archdeacon of Carmarthen 1982–85, clerical sec The Governing Body Church in Wales 1983–85; *Recreations* walking, reading; *Clubs* Cardiff and County; *Style*— The Rt Rev the Bishop of Llandaff; ✉ Llys Esgob, Cathedral Green, LLandaff, Cardiff, South Glamorgan CF5 2YE (☎ 01222 562400)

LLEWELLIN, Rt Rev (John) Richard Allan; *see:* Dover, Bishop of

LLEWELLYN, Carl; s of Eryl D Llewellyn, of Hundleton, Pembroke, and Jean, *née* Harries; *b* 29 July 1965; *Educ* Pembroke Secdy Sch; *Career* national hunt jockey; turned professional 1986, winner Apprentice Championship setting record of 41 winners, rode Grand National winner Party Politics 1991; rep Br Jump Jockeys Team: Australia 1987 (series winners), Russia 1992; Pacemaker Jockey of the Year 1986–87; *Recreations* golf, water skiing, squash; *Style*— Carl Llewellyn, Esq; ✉ The Firs, Gainfield, Buckland, Faringdon, Oxon SN7 8QQ (☎ 01367 870254)

LLEWELLYN, David St Vincent (Dai); s and h of Sir Harry Llewellyn, 3 Bt, CBE, *qv*; *b* 2 April 1946; *Educ* Eton, Aix-en-Provence; *m* 15 March 1980 (m dis 1987), Vanessa Mary Theresa, da of Lt Cdr Theodore Bernard Peregrine Hubbard, and Lady Miriam Hubbard; 2 da (Olivia b 7 Oct 1980, Arabella b 1 Nov 1983); *Career* writer, broadcaster and impresario; Br Nat Export Cncl mission USA 1970, vice pres Nat Dog Owners' Assoc 1982, ldr Yugoslavian relief convoy 1992; club dir Dorchester Park Lane 1994–95; chevalier de l'Ordre des Coteaux de Champagne 1993; *Recreations* equestrian sports and wildlife conversation; *Clubs* Daniel's; *Style*— Dai Llewellyn, Esq; ✉ Suite 500, 2 Old Brompton Road, London SW7 3DQ (☎ 0171 413 9533)

LLEWELLYN, Prof David Thomas; s of Alfred George Llewellyn (d 1990), of Gillingham, Dorset, and Elsie Elizabeth, *née* Frith; *b* 3 March 1943; *Educ* William Ellis GS, LSE (BSc); *m* 19 Sept 1970, Wendy Elizabeth, da of Henry Cecil James, MM (d 1973); 2 s (Mark b 15 Aug 1972, Rhys b 18 Dec 1978); *Career* economist: Unilever NV Rotterdam 1964–65, HM Treasy 1965–68; lectr Univ of Nottingham 1968–73, economist IMF Washington 1973–76, prof of money and banking Loughborough Univ 1976– (head Dept of Economics 1980–90); chm Loughborough Univ Banking Centre 1985–, dir London Bd Halifax Building Soc 1986–93, memb Academic Bd Sundridge Park Mgmnt Centre 1990–, public interest dir Personal Investment Authority 1994–; conslt economist Harlow Butler Ueda 1989–; former conslt The World Bank, OECD, regulatory authorities, building socs and banks; occasional memb Bank of England Panel of Academic Conslts; memb Int Advsy Bd: European Banking Report Italian Bankers' Assoc 1994–, NCR Financial Systems Group, Productivity Mgmnt Int 1995–; memb Exec Bd Euro Fin Mgmnt Assoc; memb Editorial Bd Banking World 1978–84, managing ed Chartered Inst of Bankers Occasional Res Papers Series 1978–82; Bertil Danielsson Fndn visiting scholar Stockholm and Gothenburg Schs of Economics 1992; FCIB, FRSA; *Books* International Financial Integration (1980), Framework of UK Monetary Policy (1983), Regulation of Financial Institutions (1986), Evolution of British Financial System (1985), Reflections on Money (1990), Recent Developments in International Monetary Economics (1990), Surveys in Monetary Economics Vols 1 & 2 (with C Green, 1991), Competition or Credit Controls (Hobart Paper, 1991); *Recreations* boating, cooking, DIY, gardening, travel; *Style*— Prof David T Llewellyn; ✉ 8 Landmere Lane, Ruddington, Nottingham NG11 6ND (☎ 0115 921 6071); Department of Economics, Loughborough University, Loughborough, Leics (☎ 01509 222700)

LLEWELLYN, David Walter; CBE (1983); s of Eric Gilbert Llewellyn, and Florence May Llewellyn; *b* 13 Jan 1930; *Educ* Radley; *m* 1, 1955 (m dis 1985), Josephine Margaret Buxton; 3 s; m 2, Tessa Caroline Sandwith; *Career* cmmnd RE 1952; jt non-exec chm Llewellyn Management Services Ltd and other cos in the Llewellyn Gp 1953–, industl advsr to Min of Housing and Local Govt 1967–68; pres Joinery and Timber Contractors' Assoc 1976–77; chm: Nat Contractors' Gp of Nat Fedn of Bldg Trade Employers 1977, Bldg Regulations Advsy Ctee 1977–85; dep chm Nat Bldg Agency 1977–82, pres Chartered Inst of Bldg 1986–87; govr St Andrew's Sch Eastbourne 1966–78, tstee Queen Alexandra Cottage Homes Eastbourne 1973–95; Master Worshipful Co of Tin Plate Workers (Wire Workers) 1985; *Recreations* the use, restoration and preservation of historic vehicles; *Clubs* Reform, Devonshire (Eastbourne), Bentley Drivers'; *Style*— David Llewellyn, Esq, CBE; ✉ Coopers Cottage, Chiddingly, nr Lewes, E Sussex (☎ 01825 872447); Walter Llewellyn & Sons Ltd, 16–20 South Street, Eastbourne, East Sussex (☎ 01323 21300, telex 877213)

LLEWELLYN, Sir Henry Morton (Harry); kt (1956), 3 Bt (UK 1922), of Bwllfa, Aberdare, Glamorgan, CBE (1953, OBE Mil 1945), DL (Monmouthshire 1952); s of Sir David Richard Llewellyn, 1 Bt, (d 1940); suc bro, Sir Rhys Llewellyn, 2 Bt (d 1978); *b* 18 July 1911; *Educ* Oundle, Trinity Coll Cambridge (MA); *m* 1944, Hon Christine Llewellyn, da of 5 Baron de Saumarez (d 1969); 2 s (David (Dai) St Vincent Llewellyn, Roderic Victor Llewellyn, *qqv*), 1 da (Anna Christina (Mrs Christopher Elletson) b 1956); *Heir* s, David St Vincent Llewellyn b 2 April 1946; *Career* joined Warwickshire Yeo 1939, ME Staff Coll 1942, GSO2 8 Army 1942 (despatches twice), GSO1 21 Army Gp 1943–44 (US Legion of Merit); chm: C L Clay & Co Ltd (coal exporters and coal mine proprietors) 1936–47, Whitbread Wales Ltd 1958–74 (now pres), Davenco (Engineers) Ltd 1954–89, Wales Bd Eagle Star Insurance 1962–82, Wales Branch Nationwide Building Society Ltd 1974–86; dir: TWW Ltd 1958–68, Lloyds Bank (S Wales Region) 1963–82; memb Wales Tourist Bd 1969–75, chm Sports Cncl for Wales 1971–80; pres: Wales Branch IOD 1963–65, Inst of Marketing (Wales) 1965–67; dir Chepstow Racecourse Co Ltd 1952–; memb: Nat Hunt Ctee 1946– (steward 1948–50), Jockey Club 1969; riding 'Ego' came 2 Grand National 1936 and 4 1937, capt (riding 'Foxhunter') Br Show Jumping Team, winners Olympic Gold Medal Helsinki 1952, Fédération Equestre Internationale Gold Medal 1962; pres: Br Show Jumping Assoc 1967–69, Br Equestrian Fedn 1975–79, Royal Welsh Show 1985, Royal International Show 1990–92; memb Cncl World Wide Fund for Nature UK 1985–, chm Civic Tst for Wales; JP 1953–67, High Sheriff Monmouthshire 1966; Royal Humane Soc Medal for Life Saving 1956; fell Royal Inst for the Protection of Birds 1987; *Clubs* Jockey, Cavalry and Guards', Shikar; *Style*— Sir Harry Llewellyn, Bt, CBE, DL; ✉ Ty'r Nant, Llanarth, nr Raglan, Gwent NP5 2AR

LLEWELLYN, Dr (Graeme Ernest) John; s of Sir (Frederick) John Llewellyn (d 1988), and Joyce, *née* Barrett; *b* 13 Sept 1944; *Educ* Christchurch Boys' HS NZ, Scots' Coll Wellington NZ, Victoria Univ of Wellington (BA Economics and Law), Univ of Oxford (DPhil Economics); *m* 8 Dec 1990, Ruth, *née* Doncaster; 4 c (Frederic, Claire, Preston, Simon); *Career* researcher First National Bank of Boston 1966–67, research offr Dept of Applied Economics Univ of Cambridge 1970–74, fell St John's Coll Cambridge 1972–77, asst dir of research Faculty of Economics Univ of Cambridge 1974–77; OECD: head Economic Prospects Div 1978–86, dep dir Directorate for Social Affrs Manpower and Educn 1986–89, head Sec-Gen's Private Office 1989–94; Lehman Brothers: chief economist Europe 1995–96, global chief economist and md 1996–; sec Degree Ctee Faculty of Economics Univ of Cambridge 1974–77, memb Bd of Graduate Studies Univ of Cambridge 1976–77, dir of studies St John's Coll Cambridge 1976–77; temp dir of research Centro de Investigacion y Docencia Economicas Mexico City 1976–77, lectr Univ of Southern California Sch of Int Rels London 1976–77; memb Editorial Bd: OECD Economic Studies 1983–89, Economic Modelling 1983–93; memb: Conseil Scientifique Fondation Nationale des Sciences Politiques Paris 1986–94 (pt/t lectr in contemporary economic policy 1990–94), Comité Consultatif Observatoire Français des Conjonctures Economiques 1987–94; currently memb: Investment Ctee St John's Coll Cambridge, Advsy Bd of the Economics Prog RIIA London; *Publications* Economic Forecasting and Policy - The International Dimension (with S J Potter and L W Samuelson, 1985), Economic Policies for the 1990s (ed with S J Potter, 1991); author of numerous articles in economic jls and the press; *Recreations* photography, music, writing; *Style*— Dr John Llewellyn; ✉ Lehman Brothers Ltd, One Broadgate, London EC2M 7HA (☎ 0171 260 2272, fax 0171 260 2242, e-mail john_llewellyn@gbccmail.lehman.com)

LLEWELLYN, Rev (Richard) Morgan; CB (1992), OBE (1979, MBE 1976); s of Griffith Robert Poynz Llewellyn (d 1972), of Baglan Hall, Abergavenny, Gwent, and Bridget Margaret Lester, *née* Karslake (d 1980); *b* 22 Aug 1937; *Educ* Haileybury; *m* 24 Oct 1964, (Elizabeth) Polly Lamond, da of Lt-Col Francis Theodore Sobey, CBE, MC (d 1973), of Pine Lodge, Ilkley, Yorkshire; 3 s (Huw b 1967, Glyn b 1971, Robert b 1979), 2 da (Sally b 1967 d 1977, Kitty b 1981); *Career* cmmnd Royal Welch Fusiliers 1956, active serv in Malaya 1957 and Cyprus 1958–59, instr Army Outward Bound Sch 1962–63, Staff Coll 1970, mil asst to Chief of Gen Staff 1971–72, Bde Maj 39 Inf Bde 1974–76, cmd 1 Bn Royal Welch Fusiliers 1976–79, jr directing staff RCDS 1979–81, cmd Gurkha Field Force Hong Kong 1981–84, Dir Army Staff Duties MOD 1985–87, GOC Wales 1987–90, Chief of Staff HQ UK Land Forces 1990–91; Col Gurkha Tport Regt 1984–92, Col Queen's Own Gurkha Tport Regt 1992–93, Col The Royal Welch Fusiliers 1990; ret 1991 with rank of Maj Gen; ordained deacon 1993, ordained priest 1994, curate Brecon with Battle and Llanddew and minor canon of Brecon Cathedral 1993–95, chaplain Christ Coll Brecon 1995–; vice pres Soldiers' and Airmen's Scripture Readers Assoc; FIMgt; *Recreations* reading, hill walking, shooting; *Clubs* Army and Navy; *Style*— The Rev R M Llewellyn, CB, OBE; ✉ Llangattock Court, Llangattock, Crickhowell, Powys NP8 1PH

LLEWELLYN, Roderic Victor (Roddy); 2 s of Sir Harry Llewellyn, 3 Bt, CBE, *qv*, and Hon Lady Llewellyn, yr da of 5 Baron de Saumarez; *b* 9 Oct 1947; *Educ* Shrewsbury, Aix-en-Provence, Merrist Wood Agric Coll (Nat Cert of Horticulture, Surrey Co Cert in Landscape Construction); *m* 1981, Tatiana, da of Paul Soskin (d 1975), film producer; 3 da (Alexandra b 1982, Natasha b 1984, Rose-Anna b 1987); *Career* landscape designer, author, journalist and presenter; gardening corr: (Daily) Star 1981–86, Oracle 1982–83, Mail On Sunday 1987–; gardening presenter TV-am 1984, co-presenter The Gardening Roadshow (LWT) 1992 and 1993; assoc memb Inst of Horticulture (AIHort) 1995; *Books* Town Gardens (1981), Beautiful Backyards (1985), Water Gardens (1987), Elegance and Eccentricity (1989), Growing Gifts (1992), I Grew It Myself (1993); *Recreations* jig-saw puzzles; *Style*— Roddy Llewellyn, Esq; ✉ Old George House, Leafield, Nr Witney, Oxfordshire OX8 5NP (☎ and fax 01993 878700)

LLEWELLYN, Samson Evan (Sam); s of Bishop William Somers Llewellyn, of Leighterton, and Innis Mary, *née* Dorrien Smith; *b* 2 Aug 1948; *Educ* Eton, St Catherine's Coll Oxford (MA); *m* 1975, Karen Margaret Wallace; 2 s (William David b 1978, Martin Stephen b 1980); *Career* author; bass guitarist Spread Eagle 1971–72, ed Pan/Picador 1973–76, sr ed McClelland & Stewart Toronto Canada 1976–79; memb Ctee Hereford CPRE; *Books* Hell Bay (1980), The Worst Journey in the Midlands (1983), Dead Reckoning (1987), Great Circle (1987), Blood Orange (1988), Death Roll (1989), Pig in the Middle (1989), Deadeye (1990), Blood Knot (1991), Riptide (1992), Clawhammer (1993), Maelstrom (1994), The Rope School (1994), The Magic Boathouse (1994), The Iron Hotel (1996), Storm Force from Navarone (1996); *Recreations* sailing, building, accompanying Mrs Llewellyn on the guitar and banjo; *Clubs* Cruising Assoc; *Style*— Sam Llewellyn, Esq; ✉ c/o Andrew Hewson, John Johnson, Clerkenwell House, 45–47 Clerkenwell Green, London EC1R 0HT (☎ 0171 251 0125, fax 0171 251 2172)

LLEWELLYN, Timothy Charles David (Tim); s of Charles Gordon Llewellyn (d 1940), of Cardiff, and Betty Ella, *née* Field; *b* 6 June 1940; *Educ* XIV Sch Bristol, Monkton Combe Sch; *m* Feb 1964 (m dis 1972), Geraldine, *née* McCallan; 1 s (Alun Brendan b 2 April 1965); *partner* Deborah Anne Veronica Owen, *née* Lipton; 1 step da (Maccabee Szalwinska b 1978); *Career* reporter: Western Daily Press Bristol 1958–59, Barrie Examiner Barrie 1959–60, Toronto Telegram 1960–61; sub-ed: South Wales Echo Cardiff and Western Daily Press Bristol 1961, Press Assoc 1962–64, Globe and Mail 1964–66, Daily Sketch 1966; asst prodn team (Business Section) Sunday Times 1966, on staff prodn Times Business News 1967–71; BBC: chief sub/prodr 1971–73, newsroom 1973–76, corr Middle East 1976–80 and 1987–92 (East Africa 1980–82, foreign corr 1982–87); freelance 1992–; memb: RUSI, SOAS; *Recreations* permanent sloth punctuated by travel and desultory reading when unavoidable, talking; *Clubs* Travellers'; *Style*— Tim Llewellyn, Esq

LLEWELLYN, Timothy David; s of Graham David Llewellyn, and Dorothy Mary Driver; *b* 30 May 1947; *Educ* St Dunstan's Coll, Magdalene Coll Cambridge; *m* 1, 8 Aug 1970, Irene Sigrid Mercy, da of Sigurd Henriksen, of Copenhagen, Denmark; 1 s (Kristian b 1975); m 2, 9 Sept 1978, Elizabeth, da of Prof Mason Hammond, of Cambridge, Mass, USA; *Career* Sotheby's: dir 1974–94, md 1984–91, chief exec 1991–92, dep chm Sotheby's Europe 1992–94; currently dir The Henry Moore Fndn 1994–; chm: The Friends of the Courtauld Institute 1986–, The Henry Moore Sculpture Tst 1994–; memb Bd The Courtauld Inst 1991–, memb Int Cncl Villa I Tatti The Harvard Univ Center for Italian Renaissance Studies 1990–; Miny of Culture and Fine Arts of the People's Republic of Poland Order of Cultural Merit 1986; tstee The Elgar Fndn 1991–; fell the Ateneo Veneto Venice 1992–; *Recreations* music, fishing, travel; *Clubs* Brooks's; *Style*— Timothy D Llewellyn, Esq; ✉ 3 Cranley Mansion, 160 Gloucester Road, London SW7 4QF (☎ 0171 373 2333, fax 0171 244 0126); The Henry Moore Foundation, Dane Tree House, Perry Green, Much Hadham, Hertfordshire SG10 6EE (☎ 01279 843333, fax 01279 843647)

LLEWELLYN SMITH, Prof Christopher; s of John Clare Llewellyn Smith (d 1990), and Margaret Emily Frances, *née* Crawford; *b* 19 Nov 1942; *Educ* Wellington, New Coll Oxford (BA, DPhil); *m* 10 Sept 1966, Virginia, *née* Grey; 1 s (Caspar Michael b 24 Jan 1971), 1 da (Julia Clare b 2 Nov 1968); *Career* Royal Soc exchange fell Lebedev Inst Moscow 1967–68, fell Theoretical Studies Div CERN Geneva 1968–70, res assoc Stanford Linear Accelerator Centre (SLAC) Stanford California 1970–72, staff memb Theoretical Studies Div CERN Geneva 1972–74; St John's Coll Oxford: fell 1974–, lectr 1974–80, reader 1980–87, prof 1987–, chm of physics 1987–92; DG CERN Geneva (on leave of absence from Oxford) 1994–; FRS 1984; *Style*— Prof Christopher Llewellyn Smith, FRS; ✉ Director General, CERN, CH-1211 Geneve 23, Switzerland (☎ 00 41 22 767 2300)

LLEWELLYN-SMITH, Elizabeth Marion; CB (1986); da of John Clare Llewellyn Smith (d 1990), and Margaret Emily Frances, *née* Crawford; *b* 17 Aug 1934; *Educ* Christ's Hosp, Girton Coll Cambridge (BA, MA); *Career* govt serv Bd of Trade 1956, dep dir gen of Fair Trading 1982–87, dep sec DTI 1987–90; dir European Investment Bank 1987–90; princ St Hilda's Coll Oxford 1990–; memb: Research Ethics Ctee HSE, Business Appointments Panel DTI, Hebdomadal Cncl Univ of Oxford, Governing Body Rugby Sch; tstee Jacqueline du Pré Meml Appeal; hon fell Girton Coll Cambridge; *Style*— Miss Elizabeth Llewellyn-Smith, CB; ✉ St Hilda's College, Oxford OX4 1DY (☎ 01865 276884)

LLEWELLYN SMITH, HE Sir Michael John; KCVO (1996), CMG (1989); s of John Clare Llewellyn Smith (d 1990), and Margaret Emily Frances, *née* Crawford; *b* 25 April 1939; *Educ* Wellington, New Coll Oxford (BA), St Antony's Coll Oxford (DPhil); *m* 8 April 1967, Colette, da of Georges Gaulier (d 1979), of France; 1 s (Stefan Gregory b 1970), 1 da (Sophie Alexandra b 1971); *Career* cultural attaché Moscow 1973–75, first sec Br Embassy Paris 1976–77, cnsllr Athens 1980–83, head of Soviet Dept FCO 1985–87, min Paris Embassy 1988–91; ambass: Poland 1991–96, Greece 1996–; author; *Books* The Great Island - A Study of Crete (1965), Ionian Vision - Greece in Asia Minor 1919–22 (1983); *Clubs* Utd Oxford and Cambridge Univ; *Style*— HE Sir Michael Llewellyn Smith, KCVO, CMG; ✉ c/o Foreign and Commonwealth Office (Athens), King Charles Street, London SW1A 2AH (☎ 0171 270 2533)

LLEWELYN, *see:* Venables-Llewelyn

LLEWELYN, Desmond Wilkinson; s of Ivor Llewelyn (d 1930), of Newport, Gwent and Mia, *née* Wilkinson (d 1942); *b* 12 Sept 1914; *Educ* Radley, RADA; *m* 16 May 1938, Pamela Mary, da of Charles William Rivers Pantlin (d 1978); 2 s (Ivor b 1949, Justin b 1952); *Career* actor; joined Artists Rifles 1939, OCTU RMC Sandhurst 1939–40, cmmnd Royal Welch Fusiliers 1940, joined 1 Bn 1940, POW Germany 1940–45; in repertory Oxford Playhouse 1939, first appearance on TV 1939; plays incl: Golden Eagle, Spiders Webb; TV incl Follyfoot; films incl: Cleopatra, 15 James Bond films in the character of "Q"; *Recreations* gardening; *Clubs* Farmers; *Style*— Desmond Llewelyn, Esq; ✉ Osborn House, High Street, Bexhill on Sea, East Sussex TN40 2HA

LLEWELYN-DAVIES OF HASTOE, Baroness (Life Peer UK 1967), of Hastoe, Co Hertford; (Annie) Patricia Llewelyn Davies; PC (1975); da of C P Parry, of Prenton, Cheshire; *b* 16 July 1915; *Educ* Liverpool Coll Huyton, Girton Coll Cambridge; *m* 3 June 1943, Baron Llewelyn-Davies (Life Peer, d 1981); 3 da (Hon Melissa (Hon Mrs Curling) b 1 June 1945, Hon Harriet Lydia Rose b 7 Jan 1955, Hon Rebecca (Hon Mrs Daniel Rea) b 21 Dec 1957); *Career* sits as Lab Peer in Lords; temp administrative civil servant 1940–51, Parly candidate (Lab) 1951–60; dir Africa Educnl Tst 1960–69, chm Bd of Govrs Gt Ormond St Hosp for Sick Children 1967–69 (memb 1955–69); a Baroness in waiting to HM The Queen 1969–70; oppn dep chief whip House of Lords 1972, oppn chief whip 1973–74, capt of The Gentlemen at Arms and govt chief whip 1974–79, oppn chief whip 1979–82, princ dep chm Ctees House of Lords 1982–86, chm Lords' Euro Communities Select Ctee 1982–86; chm Women's Nat Cancer Control Ctee 1972–74, a dep speaker House of Lords 1986–; hon fell Girton Coll Cambridge 1978; *Style*— The Rt Hon the Lady Llewelyn-Davies of Hastoe, PC; ✉ Flat 15, 9–11 Belsize Grove, London NW3 4UU (☎ 0171 586 4060)

LLOYD, Prof Alan Brian; s of Howard Brinley Lloyd (d 1989), of Tredegar, Gwent, and Doris Marian, *née* Walsh; *b* 24 Sept 1941; *Educ* Tredegar GS, Univ Coll Swansea (BA), Queen's Coll Oxford (MA, DPhil); *m* 1, 14 Aug 1965, Caroline Barclay (d 1984), da of The Hon Julius McDonald Greenfield, CMG, of Rondebosh, SA; 2 s (Julian b 14 Aug 1966, Duncan b 19 Nov 1967), 1 da (Katherine b 28 Feb 1970); m 2, 30 Nov 1985, Patricia Elizabeth, da of Patrick Cyril Ward, of Llandaff, Cardiff; *Career* Univ of Wales Swansea: asst lectr 1967, sr lectr 1977, reader 1983, prof 1988–, dean of arts 1991–93, pro vice-chllr 1993–; memb Ctee of Egypt Exploration Soc, sometime memb Cncl Hellenic Soc; FSA 1987; *Books* Herodotus Book II (1975–88); The Tomb of Hetepka (with G T Martin, 1978), Ancient Egypt (with B Trigger et al, 1983), Erodoto Le Storie Libro II (1989), Saqqara Tombs I and II (with W V Davies et al, 1984 and 1990); *Style*— Prof Alan Lloyd; ✉ Department of Classics, University of Wales Swansea, Singleton Park, Swansea SA2 8PP (☎ 01792 205678)

LLOYD, Angus Selwyn; s of Selwyn Lloyd (d 1935), of Northiam, Sussex, and Elaine Mary, *née* Beck (d 1992); *b* 12 July 1935; *Educ* Charterhouse; *m* 12 Jan 1961, Wanda Marian, da of Raymond Davidson, of Melrose, Scotland; 3 s (James, Christopher, Richard), 2 da (Virginia, Philippa); *Career* Nat Serv 1954–55, 2 Lt 15/19 King's Royal Hussars (serv Malaya 1955); dir: Nathaniel Lloyd & Co (printers) 1956–63, Oscar & Peter Johnson Ltd (fine art dealers) 1963–81, Sealproof Ltd (textile proofing) 1973–; chm: Henri-Lloyd Ltd (textile mfrs) 1963–85, Craig-Lloyd Ltd (property) 1971–, Burlington Gallery Ltd (fine art/print dealers) 1979–, Burlington Paintings Ltd (fine art/picture dealers) 1984–; tstee: Albany Piccadilly 1967–, Charterhouse in Southwark 1962– (chm Tstees 1979–82); Freeman: City of London, Worshipful Co of Stationers and Newspaper Makers; *Recreations* golf; *Clubs* Royal St George's Golf (Sandwich, capt 1985), The Berkshire (capt 1978), Royal West Norfolk, Royal and Ancient Golf (St Andrews), Swinley Forest, Walton Heath, PGA Nat (USA), Old Marsh Golf (USA), Hon Co of Edinburgh Golfers; *Style*— Angus Lloyd, Esq; ✉ East Court, Beech Ave, Effingham, Surrey (☎ 01372 458111); Burlington Paintings Ltd, 12 Burlington Gardens, London W1X 1LG (☎ 0171 734 9984, fax 0171 494 3770)

LLOYD, Anthony Joseph (Tony); MP (Lab) Stretford (majority 11,137); *b* 25 Feb 1950; *Educ* Nottingham Univ, Manchester Business Sch; *m* Judith Lloyd; 1 s, 3 da; *Career* former university lectr; MP (Lab) Stretford 1983–; oppn spokesman on: tport 1988–89, employment 1988–92, training (employment and educn) 1992–94, the environment and London 1994–; cncllr Trafford DC 1979–84; *Clubs* West Indian Sports & Social, Stretford Ex-Serviceman's, Stretford Trades & Labour; *Style*— Tony Lloyd, Esq, MP; ✉ House of Commons, London SW1A 0AA (☎ 0171 219 3000)

LLOYD, Barbara Christine; da of Francis Kenneth Lloyd, of the Bahamas, and Herta Erica, *née* Menzler (d 1984); *b* 17 Aug 1946; *Educ* Putney HS for Girls, École Le Grand Verger Lausanne Switzerland, École Lemania Lausanne Switzerland, French Lycée London, Le Fleuron Florence Italy, Oskar Kokoschka Summer Acad Salzburg Austria; *Career* Marlborough Galleries 1967–90: shorthand typist and switchboard operator rising to registrar Marlborough Gallery NY, dir Marlborough Graphics 1979, subsequently dir Marlborough Fine Art London Ltd until 1990; responsible for exhibitions incl: all FIAC exhibitions Grand Palais Paris, Bill Brandt - A Retrospective, Brassai Secret Paris of the 30s, Irving Penn, Still Lives, Avigdor Arikha, Raymond Mason, Therese Oulton, Travelling Mason Retrospective; full time photographer 1990–; tstee: The Photographers Gallery London 1988– (chm 1994–), Save A Child Tst Divyachaya, Bombay and Calcutta, Children of India 1995; memb Patrons of New Art Acquisitions Sub-Ctee Tate Gallery 1996–97; *Books* The Colours of India (1988), Reflections of Spain (1992), The Colours of Thailand (1997); *Recreations* looking at and collecting art, opera, music, photography, reading, tennis, enjoying life; *Clubs* Arts, Dover Street, Chelsea Arts; *Style*— Miss Barbara Lloyd; ✉ c/o The Photographers Gallery, 5 Great Newport Street, London WC2

LLOYD, (David) Bernard; s of George Edwards Lloyd, and Lilian Catherine, *née* Thomas; *b* 14 Jan 1938; *Educ* Presteigne GS, Hereford HS; *m* 12 Oct 1968, Christine; 3 da (Claire b 1973, Joanne b 1975, Helen b 1975); *Career* Nat Serv RAPC; successively: various posts in local govt fin, internal auditor UCL, accountant UCH Med Sch; sec RCOG 1976–82 (accountant 1971–76), sec Nat Inst of Agric Engrg 1982–86, sec RCP and Faculty of Occupational Med 1986–; govr Roundwood Jr Sch 1980–89 (chm 1985–88), memb Mgmnt Ctee St Albans CAB 1983–94 (chm 1990–94), govr and chm Sir John Lawes Sr Sch 1986–87, memb Harpenden Town Cncl 1992–, dep Mayor Harpenden 1994, chm Harpenden Trust 1995–96; FCCA 1977; *Recreations* walking, garden; *Style*— Bernard Lloyd, Esq; ✉ 16 Hartwell Gardens, Harpenden, Herts AL5 2RW (☎ and fax 01582 761292); Royal College of Physicians, 11 St Andrews Place, Regents Park, London NW1 4LE (☎ 0171 935 1174, fax 0171 487 5218)

LLOYD, Dr Brian Beynon; CBE (1983); s of David John Lloyd (d 1951), of Menai Bridge, Anglesey, and Olwen, *née* Beynon (d 1974); *b* 23 Sept 1920; *Educ* Newport HS, Winchester, Balliol Coll Oxford (BA, MA, DSc); *m* 1949, Reinhild Johanna, da of Dr Karl Wilhelm Engeroff (d 1951), of Bad Godesberg, W Germany; 4 s (Thomas, Martyn, Brian and Owen (twins)), 3 da (Megan and Olwen (twins), Lucy); *Career* registered as conscientious objector 1941; Oxford Nutrition Survey: tech asst 1941, res asst 1943–46; pres Jr Common Room Balliol Coll Oxford 1941–42, chm Undergraduate Rep Cncl Univ of Oxford 1942; biochemist: SHAEF Nutrition Survey Gp Leiden Holland, Düsseldorf Germany 1945–46; Magdalen Coll Oxford: fell by examination in physiology 1948–52, by special election 1952–70, sr tutor 1963–64, vice pres 1967 and 1968, emeritus fell 1970–; chemist Laboratory of Human Nutrition, demonstrator and lectr in Physiology Univ of Oxford 1948–70 (sr proctor 1960–61), dir Oxford Poly (now Oxford Brookes Univ) 1970–80 (opened LLoyd Building 1984, hon fell 1991), dir Int Nutrition Fndn 1990–95, ret; table-maker with Owen LLoyd 1988–90; articles in physiological and biochemical jls on vitamin C, human respiration, blood gases and exercise; memb Advsy Cncl on Misuse of Drugs 1978–81; visiting physiologist NY 1963; Br Assoc for the Advancement of Sci: rep Ceylon 1959, rep Russia 1964, pres section I 1964–65, pres section X 1980; chm: govrs Oxford Coll of Technol 1963–69, CNAA Health and Med Servs Bd 1975–80, Oxford-Bonn Soc 1973–81, Oxford Mgmnt Club 1979–80, Health Educn Cncl 1979–82 (memb 1975–82), Oxford Gallery Ltd 1967–, Trumedia Study Oxford Ltd 1985–89, Trumedia Ltd 1989–, Pullen's Lane Assoc 1985–95; pres Oxford Poly Assoc 1984–89 (hon memb 1992); *Books* The Regulation of Human Respiration (jt ed, 1963), Cerebrospinal Fluid and the Regulation of Respiration (jt ed, 1965), Sinclair (jt ed, 1990); *Patent* Gas Analysis Apparatus (1960); *Recreations* Klavarskribo, Correggio, analysis of athletic records, slide rules, ready reckoners, round tables, home computing, soldering irons; *Style*— Dr Brian B Lloyd, CBE; ✉ High Wall, Pullen's Lane, Oxford OX3 0BX (☎ 01865 63353)

LLOYD, Christopher; s of Nathaniel Lloyd, OBE (d 1933), of Great Dixter, Northiam, Rye, E Sussex, and Daisy, *née* Field (d 1972); *b* 2 March 1921; *Educ* Rugby, King's Coll Cambridge (MA), Wye Coll London (BSc); *Career* author; asst lectr in decorative horticulture Wye Coll 1950–54, fndr nursery in clematis and unusual plants at family home Great Dixter 1954; Hon Doctorate Open Univ 1996; Victoria Medal of Honour RHS, memb RHS; *Publications* The Mixed Border (1957), Clematis (1965, revised 1977, revised with Tom Bennett 1989), Foliage Plants (1973), The Well Tempered Garden (1970), Shrubs and Trees for Small Gardens (1965), Gardening on Chalk and Lime (1969), Hardy Perennials (1967), The Well Chosen Garden (1985), The Adventurous Gardener (1985), The Year at Great Dixter (1987), The Cottage Garden (with Richard Bird, 1990), Garden Flowers From Seed (with Graham Rice, 1991), Christopher Lloyd's Flower Garden (1993), In My Garden (1993), Other People's Gardens (1995); *Recreations* music, walking, entertaining friends at Great Dixter, cooking; *Style*— Christopher Lloyd; ✉ Great Dixter, Northiam, Rye, E Sussex TN31 6PH

LLOYD, Christopher; LVO; s of Rev Hamilton Lloyd, of Litchfield, Hants, and Suzanne, *née* Moon; *b* 30 June 1945; *Educ* Marlborough, ChCh Oxford (BA, MA, BLitt); *m* 7 Oct 1967, (Christine Joan) Frances, da of George Henry Reginald Newth (d 1978), of Whitchurch, Hants; 4 s (Alexander b 1970, Benedict b 1972, Oliver b 1973, Rupert b 1980); *Career* asst curator pictures ChCh Oxford 1967–68; Dept of Western Art Ashmolean Museum Oxford: print room asst 1968, departmental asst 1969, asst keeper 1972–88; surveyor of the Queen's pictures 1988–; fell Villa I Tatti Florence (Harvard Univ) 1972–73, visiting res curator early Italian painting Art Inst Chicago 1980–81; FRSA; *Books* Art and Its Images (1975), A Catalogue of the Earlier Italian Paintings in the Ashmolean Museum (1977), Camille Pissarro (1980), A Catalogue of the Drawings by Camille Pissarro in the Ashmolean Museum (1980), The Journal of Maria Lady Callcott 1827–28 (1981), Camille Pissarro (1981), Dürer to Cézanne: Northern European Drawings from the Ashmolean Museum (1982), Impressionist Drawings from British Collections (1986), Catalogue of Old Master Drawings at Holkham Hall (1986), Studies on Camille Pissarro (ed and contrib, 1986), Woodner Collection Master Drawings (contrib, 1990), Henry VIII Images of A Tudor King (1990), The Queen's Pictures: Royal Collectors through the Centuries (1991), The Royal Collection. A Thematic Exploration of the Paintings in the Collection of Her Majesty The Queen (1992), Italian Paintings before 1600 in the Art Institute of Chicago (1993), Gainsborough and Reynolds: Contrasts in Royal Patronage (1994), The Queen's Pictures. Old Masters from the Royal Collection (1994), Masterpieces in Little: Portrait Minitures from the Collection of Her Majesty Queen Elizabeth II (1996); *Recreations* real tennis, theatre, music; *Clubs* Garrick; *Style*— Christopher Lloyd, Esq, LVO; ✉ Apartment 29B, St James's Palace, London SW1A 1BG (☎ 0171 839 5902); The Royal Collection, Stable Yard House, St James's Palace, London SW1A 1JR (☎ 0171 930 4832)

LLOYD, Clive Hubert; CBE (1992), AO (1985); s of Arthur Christopher Lloyd (d 1961), and Sylvia Thelma Lloyd; *b* 31 Aug 1944; *Educ* Fountain, Chatham HS Georgetown Guyana; *m* 11 Sept 1971, Waveney, *née* Benjamin; 1 s (Jason Clive b 15 June 1981), 2 da (Melissa Simone b 22 Feb 1974, Samantha Louise b 26 Jan 1976); *Career* clerk Georgetown Hosp 1960–66; cricketer; began career with Demarara CC Georgetown 1959, debut for Guyana 1963, first test match for the WI 1966, initial first class century 1966, played for Haslingden CC in the Lancs League 1967, played for Lancs CCC 1968–86 (capt 1981–84 and 1986), capt WI 1974–78 and 1979–85; scored over 30,000 runs incl 79 centuries during career, mangr WI tours to Australia, India and UK 1988–90, memb ICC Panel of Int Cricket Referees 1993; dir Red Rose Radio plc 1987–90, exec promotions offr Project Fullemploy 1987–89; memb: Cmmn for Racial Equality 1989–90, Sickle Cell Anemia Soc, Ctee Lancs CCC 1992, UK Sports Cncl 1995–; tstee: Fndn for Sports and the Arts, Danesford Tst, Help the Aged; voted Mancunian of the Year 1988 Manchester Jr C of C; Hon MA: Univ of Manchester, Univ of Hull; Hon BA: Lancashire Poly, Liverpool Poly; Hon Dr Univ of West Indies; OJ (Jamaica) 1985, OR (Guyana) 1985, OB (Barbados) 1986; *Books* Living for Cricket (with Tony Cazier), Clive Lloyd the Authorised Biography (with Trevor McDonald); *Style*— Clive Lloyd, Esq, CBE, AO; ✉ c/o Harefield Residential Care Home, Harefield Drive, Wilmslow, Cheshire SK9 1NJ (☎ and fax 01625 522371)

LLOYD, Prof David; s of Frederick Lewis Lloyd (d 1961), of Rhondda, Glam, and Annie Mary, *née* Wrentmore; *b* 26 Nov 1940; *Educ* Porth Co GS for Boys, Univ of Sheffield (BSc, DSc), Univ of Wales Cardiff (PhD); *m* 5 April 1969, Margaret, da of Thomas John Jones, of Criccieth, Gwynedd; 2 s (Alun Lewis b 4 Aug 1970, Siôn Huw b 19 Sept 1973); *Career* MRC res fell Univ Coll of S Wales and Monmouth 1967–69 (ICI res fell 1964–67); Univ Coll Cardiff (now Univ of Wales Cardiff): lectr in microbiology 1969–76, sr lectr 1976, reader 1976–78, personal chair 1978–, head Dept of Microbiology 1982–87, established chair holder 1982–; memb: Biochemical Soc 1961, Ctee S Wales Cancer Res Campaign, Ctee of Welsh Scheme for Med and Social Sci Res, Soc of Gen Microbiology 1980; *Books* The Mitochondria of Micro-organisms (1974), The Cell Division Cycle: Temporal Organization and Control of Cellular Growth and Reproduction (1982), Ultradian Rhythms in Living Systems: A Fundamental Inquiry into Chronobiology and Psychobiology (1992); *Recreations* music, cycling, tennis; *Style*— Prof David Lloyd; ✉ University of Wales Cardiff, Museum Ave, Cathays Park, Cardiff

LLOYD, David Alan; s of Dennis Herbert Lloyd, of Leigh-on-Sea, Essex, and Doris, *née* Renshaw; *b* 3 Jan 1948; *Educ* Southend HS; *m* 14 Dec 1972, Veronica Jardine, da of Maj Cochran Kirkwood MacLennan, MBE (d 1984); 1 s (Scott b 1975), 2 da (Camilla b 1979, Laura b 1981); *Career* former tennis player; memb Br Davis Cup Team 1973–82 (former capt), men's doubles semi-finalist Wimbledon (with J Paish) 1973; chm David Lloyd Leisure plc 1982–96 (national chain of 13 health and fitness clubs, stock market flotation 1993, sold to Whitbread plc 1995); non-exec dir: Snakeboard 1996–, Clubhaus 1996–; also operates Beckenham Golf Club and runs a tennis club in Portugal; tennis commentator ITV, Sky TV and BBC Radio; launched Slater Tennis Fndn (sponsorship and coaching scheme for young players) with J Slater 1986; former Entrepreneur of the Year; Freeman City of London 1985; *Recreations* golf; *Clubs* Wisley, London Open Golf, National Hunt Racing; *Style*— David Lloyd, Esq; ✉ Appletree Cottage, 12 Leys Rd, Oxshott, Surrey KT22 OQE (☎ 01372 842150); David Lloyd Associates, Sunbury International Business Centre, Brooklands Close, Windmill Road, Sunbury on Thames, Middx TW16 7DX (☎ 01932 787563)

LLOYD, David Antony Thomas; s of Arthur Thomas Lloyd, of West Bridgford, Notts, and Betty Jean, *née* Newcombe; *b* 26 Feb 1961; *Educ* Rushcliffe Comp Sch Nottingham; *Career* with Lloyd's Bank 1979–80, various on- and off-air appts rising to presentation co-ordinator Radio Trent 1980–87, gen mangr Leicester Sound 1989–91 (dep prog controller 1987–89), prog controller Lincs FM 1991–95, head of programming and advtg Radio Authy 1995–; Sony Radio Award 1988; *Recreations* collie dogs; *Style*— David Lloyd, Esq; ✉ The Radio Authority, 14/18 Great Queen Street, Holborn, London WC2B 5DG (☎ 0171 405 7062)

LLOYD, David Mark; s of Maurice Edward Lloyd (d 1988), and Roma Doreen, *née* Morgan (d 1958); *b* 3 Feb 1945; *Educ* Felsted, Brentwood Sch Essex, BNC Oxford (MA); *m* 30 Oct 1982, Jana, da of Karel Tomas (d 1980); 1 s (Mark b 1983), 1 da (Katie b 1985), 1 step s (Tom b 1976); *Career* BBC TV until 1986; ed: The Money Programme 1980–82, Newsnight 1982–83, 60 Minutes 1983–84, Breakfast Time 1984–86; sr commissioning ed news and current affairs Channel 4 1986–; Shell TV Award 1982, BAFTA nominations 1985, 1991 and 1995, Broadcast Magazine Commissioning Ed of the Yr 1995; *Recreations* cricket, golf, music, photography; *Style*— David Lloyd, Esq; ✉ Channel Four Television Corporation, 124 Horseferry Road, London SW1P 2TX (☎ 0171 396 4444)

LLOYD, Prof Geoffrey Ernest Richard; s of William Ernest Lloyd (d 1975), of London, and Olive Irene Neville, *née* Solomon; *b* 25 Jan 1933; *Educ* Charterhouse, King's Coll Cambridge (BA, MA, PhD); *m* 14 Sept 1956, Janet Elizabeth, da of Edward Archibald Lloyd (d 1978), of Paris, France; 3 s (Adam b 1957, Matthew b 1962, Gwilym b 1963); *Career* Nat Serv Intelligence Corps 2 Lt/Actg Capt; Cambridge: fell King's Coll 1957–89, univ asst lectr in classics 1965–67, univ lectr 1967–74, sr reader 1974–83, prof of ancient philosophy and sci 1983–; Bonsall prof Univ of Stanford 1981, Sather prof of classics California Univ (Berkeley) 1984, master Darwin Coll Cambridge 1989–; hon fell King's Coll Cambridge 1990; chm East Asian History of Sci Tst 1992–; fell Royal Anthropological Soc 1970; FBA 1983; *Books* Polarity and Analogy (1966), Aristotle The Growth and Structure of his Thought (1968), Early Greek Science (1970), Greek Science After Aristotle (1973), Hippocratic Writings (ed, 1978), Aristotle on Mind and the Senses (ed, 1978), Magic Reason and Experience (1979), Science Folklore and Ideology (1983), Science and Morality in Greco-Roman Antiquity (1985), The Revolutions of Wisdom (1987), Demystifying Mentalities (1990), Methods and Problems in Greek Science (1991), Adversaries & Authorities and Aristotelian Explorations (1996); *Recreations* travel; *Style*— Prof Geoffrey Lloyd, FBA; ✉ 2 Prospect Row, Cambridge CB1 1DU (☎ 01223 355970, fax 01223 335667)

LLOYD, Dr Geoffrey Gower; s of William Thomas Lloyd (d 1979), of Swansea, and Anne, *née* Davies (d 1993); *b* 7 June 1942; *Educ* Queen Elizabeth GS Carmarthen, Emmanuel Coll Cambridge (BA, MA, MB BChir, MD), Westminster Med Sch London, Inst of Psychiatry London (MPhil); *m* 19 Dec 1970, Margaret Hazel, da of Henry Doble Rose; 1 s (Richard Gower b 22 July 1977), 2 da (Alison Siân b 7 Nov 1972, Claire Rebecca b 16 July 1975); *Career* sr registrar Maudsley Hosp London 1974–76 (registrar 1970–73), lectr Inst of Psychiatry and King's Coll Hosp Med Sch London 1976–79; conslt psychiatrist: Royal Infirmary Edinburgh 1979–85, Royal Free Hosp London 1985–, Grovelands Priory Hosp London 1994–; ed Journal of Psychosomatic Research 1986–93; pres Section of Psychiatry Royal Soc of Medicine 1995–96; FRCPE 1981, FRCPsych 1984, FRCP 1988; *Books* Textbook of General Hospital Psychiatry (1991); *Recreations* golf, watching rugby football; *Clubs* Athenaeum, Royal Soc of Medicine, South Herts Golf, Pennard Golf; *Style*— Dr Geoffrey Lloyd; ✉ 148 Harley St, London W1N 1AH (☎ 0171 935 1207); home fax 0181 346 5090

LLOYD, Graham David; *b* 1 July 1969; *Career* professional cricketer; Lancashire CCC: debut 1988, awarded county cap 1992; highest score 132 v Kent 1992; memb England A Team to Aust 1992–93; *Style*— Graham Lloyd, Esq; ✉ Lancashire CCC, Old Trafford, Manchester M16 0PX (☎ 0161 848 7021)

LLOYD, Prof Howell Arnold; s of John Lewis Lloyd (d 1971), of Llanelli, S Wales, and Elizabeth Mary, *née* Arnold (d 1986); *b* 15 Nov 1937; *Educ* Queen Elizabeth GS Carmarthen, Univ Coll of Wales (BA), Jesus Coll Oxford (DPhil); *m* Sept 1962, Gaynor Ilid, da of Moses John Jones, of Mold, N Wales; 3 s (Jonathan, Timothy, Christian), 2 da (Susanna, Rebecca); *Career* fell Univ of Wales 1961–62; Univ of Hull: asst lectr in history 1962–64, lectr 1964–73, sr lectr 1973–82, reader 1982–85, prof 1985–, dean Sch of Humanities 1993–94, pro-vice chllr 1994–; fell commoner Churchill Coll Cambridge 1993

FRHistS 1975; *Books* The Gentry of South-West Wales, 1540–1640 (1968), The Relevance of History (with Gordon Connell-Smith, 1972), The Rouen Campaign, 1590–92 (1973), The State, France and the Sixteenth Century (1983), Charles Loyseau: A Treatise of Orders and Plain Dignities (ed, 1994); *Recreations* walking, swimming; *Style*— Prof Howell A Lloyd; ✉ 23 Strathmore Avenue, Hull HU6 7HJ (☎ 01482 851146); Department of History, The University of Hull, Hull HU6 7RX (☎ 01482 346311)

LLOYD, His Hon Judge Humphrey John; QC (1979); *Educ* Westminster, Trinity Coll Dublin (MA, LLB); *Career* called to the Bar Inner Temple 1963 (bencher 1985), recorder 1990–93, official referee of the High Ct 1993–; ed-in-chief: Building Law Reports 1977–93 (conslt ed 1993–), The International Construction Law Review 1984–; conslt ed Emden's Construction Law 1993–; *Style*— His Hon Judge Humphrey LLoyd, QC; ✉ St Dunstan's House, 133–137 Fetter Lane, London EC4A 1HD (☎ 0171 936 7437, fax 0171 936 7428)

LLOYD, Dr (David) Huw Owen; s of Dr David Owen Lloyd (d 1984), of Denbigh, Clwyd, and Dilys Lloyd; *b* 14 April 1950; *Educ* Westminster, Gonville and Caius Coll Cambridge (MA, MB BCh), Guy's Hosp Med Sch London (DRCOG); *m* 1973, Dr Mary Eileen Pike, da of William Arthur George Pike; 1 s (Dafydd b 17 July 1981), 3 da (Amy b 28 Dec 1976, Ceridwen b 4 April 1979, Bethan b 20 May 1986), 1 foster da (Stacy b 9 May 1979); *Career* house surgn in orthopaedics Guy's Hosp 1974–75, house physician Beckenham Hosp 1975, SHO in psychiatry Joyce Green Hosp Dartford 1975, trainee GP Taunton 1976–79, princ GP Cadwgan Surgery Old Colwyn Clwyd 1979–; currently memb: Clwyd Local Med Ctee, Bd of Dirs N Wales Alcohol Advsy Serv; currently chm: Clwyd MAAG, All Wales MAAG Chairpersons Ctee, Welsh Cncl RCGP (former Faculty rep), Mental Health Task Gp RCGP; memb BMA; FRCGP 1991 (MRCGP 1979); *Recreations* music, gardening, cooking, walking; *Style*— Dr Huw Lloyd; ✉ Cadwgan Surgery, 11 Bodelwyddan Avenue, Old Colwyn, Clwyd LL29 9NP (☎ 01492 515787, fax 01492 513270)

LLOYD, Sir Ian Stewart; kt (1986); s of Walter John Lloyd (d 1973), and Euphemia Craig Lloyd (d 1971), of Natal, SA; descended from Tudor Trevor (d 1048) and his w, Angharad, da of Hywel Dda, King of Wales; *b* 30 May 1921; *Educ* Michaelhouse Natal, Witwatersrand Univ, King's Coll Cambridge, Admin Staff Coll Henley; *m* 1951, Frances Dorward, da of Hon William Addison, CMG, OBE, MC, DCM (d 1966), of Salisbury, Rhodesia; 3 s; *Career* SA Air Force 1941–45, RAFVR 1945–49; econ advsr Central Mining Corpn 1949, dir Bri Comin plc and gp econ advsr (former head Res Dept) British Commonwealth Shipping Co 1956–83; dir Haldon Tst plc 1988–; pres: Cambridge Union, Section X The Br Assoc 1992; tstee: Kasanka Tst 1989–96, Educational Services Broadcasting Tst 1990–; MP (C): Portsmouth Langstone 1964–74, Havant and Waterloo 1974–83, Havant 1983–92; memb: UK delgn Cncl of Europe and WEU 1968–72, Select Ctee Sci and Technol 1970–79; chm: All-Pty Ctee on Info Technol 1979–87, Select Ctee on Energy 1979–89, Bd Parly Office for Sci and Technol 1988–92; pres Parly and Scientific Ctee 1990–92; *Books* Rolls Royce: The Growth of a Firm (Vol I), The Years of Endurance (Vol II), The Merlin at War (Vol III); *Recreations* sailing; *Clubs* Royal Yacht Sqdn, Army and Navy; *Style*— Sir Ian Lloyd

LLOYD, Illtyd Rhys; s of John Lloyd (d 1971), of Cwmafan, W Glamorgan, and Melvina Joyce, *née* Rees (d 1973); *b* 13 Aug 1929; *Educ* Port Talbot (Glan Afan) Co GS, UC Swansea (BSc, MSc, DipEd, DipStat); *m* 1955, Julia, da of David John Lewis (d 1951), of Pontyberem, Dyfed; 1 s (Steffan), 1 da (Catrin); *Career* RAF (Educn Branch) 1951–54, Flt Lt; second maths master Howard Sch for Boys Cardiff 1954–57, head Maths Dept Pembroke GS 1958–59, dep headmaster Howardian HS 1959–63; Her Majesty's Inspectorate: HM inspr 1964–71, staff inspr 1972–82, chief inspr (Wales) 1982–90; memb: Family Health Servs Authy S Glamorgan 1990–96 (vice chm 1992–96), Ind Schs Tbnl 1990–, Cncl Baptist Union of Wales 1990– (hon treas 1992–, vice pres 1995–96), Cncl Cardiff Theol Coll 1990– (chm 1995–), Cncl CEWC (Cymru) 1990–, Churches Educn Network (England and Wales) 1990–93, Governing Body Swansea Inst of HE 1991–95, Cncl FCC Wales 1992–, Churches Jt Educn Policy Ctee (England and Wales) 1993–, Educn Ctee FCFC 1994–; Cytun (Churches Together in Wales): memb Cncl 1992–, vice chm Fin Ctee 1995– (memb 1991–); chm: Governing Body Educn Resources Centre Aberystwyth Univ 1992–, Mgmt Ctee Glyn Nest Home 1992–; hon memb Gorsedd of Bards; hon fell Univ of Wales; *Recreations* walking; *Style*— Illtyd Lloyd, Esq; ✉ 134 Lake Road East, Roath Park, Cardiff CF2 5NQ

LLOYD, James Richard Beilby; s of James Beilby Lloyd, of Selsdon, Surrey, and Elsa Constance, *née* White; *Educ* Whitgift Middle Sch Croydon, Central Sch of Speech & Drama; *m* 1, 1957, Victoria Latham; 1 s (Timothy James b 1960), 1 da (Katherine Jane b 1963); m 2, 1972, Frances Mary Line; *Career* broadcaster; commenced career in theatre 1954–59; announcer: Tyne Tees Television 1959–60, ATV Midlands 1960–62; freelance broadcaster 1962–; progs incl: Wish You Were Here?, Television Club, Music from the People (BBC Radio 4), These Musical Islands (World Service), Folk on 2 (BBC Radio 2) 1970–; Folk Concert & Artist Management 1968–89; memb: Music Advsy Ctee Br Cncl 1985–, Steering Gp Nat Music Day 1991–93; dep chm Bd SE Arts 1992–93 (chm Music Panel 1988–91, memb Bd 1991); dir English Folk Dance & Song Soc 1985–86, tstee Nat Folk Music Fund 1995–; chm Friends of the Towner Art Gall Eastbourne 1991–93; Br Acad of Songwriters, Composers and Authors Gold Badge 1995; FRSA 1992; *Recreations* walking; *Style*— James Lloyd, Esq; ✉ BBC Radio 2, Broadcasting House, London W1A 1AA

LLOYD, (John) Jeremy; s of Lt-Col Eric Martin Lloyd, OBE (d 1970), of Long Crendon, Bucks, and Margaret, *née* Lees (d 1979); *Educ* Manchester GS; *m* 1970 (m dis 1972), Joanna, da of Maj James Lumley; *Career* scriptwriter: Dickie Henderson Show, Are You Being Served?, 'Allo 'Allo; writer and actor: Rowan and Martin's Laugh In; writer and performer: The Wonderful World of Captain Beaky, The Woodland Gospels; actor: Those Magnificent Men in their Flying Machines, Doctor in Clover, A Very Important Person, Murder on the Orient Express, We Joined the Navy; stage actor Robert and Elizabeth (musical); memb: Equity, Writers' Guild of America; *Books* The Further Adventures of Captain Dangerfield, The Continuing Adventures of Captain Dangerfield, Captain Beaky vols 1 and 2, Captain Cat and the Carol Singers; *Recreations* classic car collector; *Clubs* Annabel's; *Style*— Jeremy Lloyd, Esq

LLOYD, Jeremy William; s of late Maj-Gen Richard Eyre Lloyd, CB, CBE, DSO, of Lymington, Hants, and Gillian, *née* Patterson; *b* 19 Dec 1942; *Educ* Eton, Pembroke Coll Cambridge (MA), Harvard Business Sch (MBA); *m* 2 Sept 1966, Britta Adrienne, da of Alfred de Schulthess, of Geneva, Switzerland; 1 s (Adrian b 1979), 3 da (Tara b 1971, Bettina b 1975, Antonia b 1985); *Career* called to the Bar Middle Temple; formerly with Hill Samuel & Co, subsid dir London & Co Securities Bank 1971–72, dir Manufacturers Hanover Property Services Ltd 1973–81, dir James Capel Bankers Ltd 1982–87, sr mangr Hong Kong & Shanghai Banking Corporation 1982–; *Recreations* tennis, skiing; *Style*— Jeremy Lloyd, Esq; ✉ Hong Kong & Shanghai Banking Corporation Ltd, PO Box 199, 10 Lower Thames Street, London EC3R 6HH (☎ 0171 638 2366)

LLOYD, Dr Jill Patricia; da of Peter Brown (d 1984), of Dublin, and Patricia Irene, *née* Tucker; *b* 2 Aug 1955; *Educ* Wallington HS, Courtauld Inst of Art (BA, PhD), Free Univ Berlin; *m* 1989, Michael Henry Peppiatt, s of Edward George Peppiatt, and Elsa Eugene Schlaich; 1 da (Clio Patricia b 16 Feb 1991), 1 s (Alexander Michael b 23 April 1994); *Career* lectr in art history Univ Coll London 1981–88, sr ed Art International (Paris) 1989–90, ed-in-chief Art International (Paris) 1990–94, freelance writer and curator 1994–; regular contrib to: Art International, Art Monthly, Artscribe, The Burlington Magazine, the TLS; articles on early 20th century and contemporary art; essays in exhibitions catalogues incl: Primitivism and Modernity, an Expressionist Dilemma (Royal Academy) 1985, Franz Xaver Messerschmidt/Arnulf Rainer (ICA London) 1987, Gerhard Richter (Anthony D'Offay Gallery London) 1988, Bernhard Prinz (Serpentine Gallery London) 1988, Francis Bacon (Villa Malpensata, Lugano) 1993, Emil Nolde (Villa Malpensata, Lugano) 1994; awards: DAAD scholarship 1985, Br Cncl scholarship 1987, Paul Getty postdoctoral scholarship 1989; memb Int Art Critics' Assoc; *Books* German Expressionism, Primitivism and Modernity (1991, Nat Art Book Prize 1992); *Recreations* theatre and cinema; *Clubs* RAC; *Style*— Dr Jill Lloyd; ✉ Art International, 77 Rue des Archives, 75003 Paris, France (☎ 00 33 1 48048454, fax 00 33 1 48048200); 56 St James's Gardens, London W11 4RA (☎ and fax 0171 603 4353)

LLOYD, John David; s of John Alfred Lloyd (d 1981), and Lilian Mary, *née* Griffiths; *b* 1 Sept 1944; *Educ* SW Essex Sch of Art, London Coll of Printing (DipAD); *m* 24 May 1975, Julia Patricia, da of Geoffrey Earnest Maughan; 1 s (Adam John b 17 June 1978), 2 da (Elinor Jane b 27 May 1980, Anna Carol b 20 Dec 1981); *Career* apprentice designer Edwin Jones & Sons (printers) 1960–64; Allied International Designers: graphic designer 1968–75, jt head of graphic design 1972–75, corp identity projects incl ABN Bank, Delta Group, Nicholas International and Meneba (Netherlands); Lloyd Northover (merged with Citigate Design to form Lloyd Northover Citigate 1993): fndr 1975, currently creative dir, major corp identity projects incl ACAS, BAA, Barclays de Zoete Wedd, BNFL, British Biotech, BRS, Courtaulds, Dept of Employment, John Lewis, MTRC (Hong Kong), Nuclear Electric, Rover Group and TUC; other graphic design projects completed for RSC, British Rail and Reuters; visiting lectr in typographic design London Coll of Printing 1970–72, chm Br Design Export Gp 1983–85, external assessor and course advsr Information Graphics Trent Poly 1984–89 and Media Design and Production London Coll of Printing 1989–; exhibitions of Lloyd Northover work: The Design Centre 1980–81, D&AD Assoc 1981–83, Art Directors' Club of NY 1988; frequent speaker on design and identity mgmnt at confs and seminars; FCSD 1978, memb D&AD Assoc 1980; *Awards* Grand Prix in DBA/Mktg Design Effectiveness Awards for Courtaulds corp identity 1989, winner Amtico commercial interiors 1992 and finalist for BRS corp identity 1994, AEA Technology corp identity 1995, Banner (HMSO) corp identity 1996; *Style*— John Lloyd, Esq; ✉ Lloyd Northover Citigate Ltd, 8 Smart's Place, London WC2B 5LW (☎ 0171 430 1100, fax 0171 430 1490)

LLOYD, John Edbrooke; s of Arthur Llewellyn Lloyd (d 1935), and Laura Frances, *née* Edbrooke (d 1985); *b* 23 June 1928; *Educ* Royal Masonic Schs Bushey, Trinity Hall Cambridge (exhibitioner, MA, LLM), Manchester Business Sch; *m* 5 June 1954, Barbara Joan, da of Ralph Stock; 1 s (Anthony John Llewellyn b 15 Nov 1955), 3 da (Gillian Barbara b 8 Oct 1958, Jennifer Karen b 11 Aug 1962, Alison Claire b 1 Jan 1965); *Career* called to the Bar Middle Temple 1950, advocate and slr Drew & Napier Advocates and Solicitors Singapore and Kuala Lumpur 1950–65 (sr ptnr 1963–65), mil and UK Govt business mangr Bristol Engine Div Bristol Siddeley Engines Ltd/Rolls Royce Ltd 1966–75, fndr, precedent ptnr and md Rosemoor Holdings Ltd self-catering holiday business 1976–; chm: Pembrokeshire Health Authy 1992–95 (memb/non-exec dir 1984–), West Wales Health Cmmn 1994–95, Welsh Health Authorities' Chm's Ctee 1994–95; non-exec chm Cromwell Court Group of Assured Tenancy plc's 1988–94; non-exec dir and co sec: Tourism S and W Wales 1991–, Tall Ships Race Cncl (Wales) 1990–, Marketflare Ltd 1995–, Leisure and Tourism Logistics Ltd 1995–; chm Wales Assoc of Self-Catering Operators 1995– (chm Steering Ctee 1994–95); FIMgt 1979, FTS 1993; *Recreations* reading, historical and family research; *Style*— John E Lloyd, Esq; ✉ Rosemoor, Walwyns Castle, Haverfordwest, Pembrokeshire SA62 3ED (☎ 01437 781326); Tourism South & West Wales, Pembroke House, Charter Court, Enterprise Park, Swansesa SA7 9DB (☎ 01792 781212, fax 01792 781300)

LLOYD, John Eliot Fraser; s of Eliot Fraser Lloyd (d 1968), of London, and Bertha Mary, *née* Hackney (d 1989); *b* 17 Jan 1944; *Educ* Eton, Balliol Coll Oxford (BA), Manchester Business Sch (MBA); *m* 1, 18 Sept 1971 (m dis 1989), Penelope Anne, da of David Barrett Frost, of Essex; 1 s (Richard b 1981), 1 da (Harriet b 1978); m 2, 29 Sept 1989, Cathryn Gillian Knapp, da of John Nicholson, of Kent; *Career* trainee EMI 1965–69; Portals Group plc: commercial dir Houseman Ltd 1974–76, md Zerolit Ltd 1976–78, md ops Portals Ltd 1978–85, various other gp appts 1971–74 and 1985–90, gp fin dir 1990–93, gp md 1993–95; non-exec dir Hodder Headline PLC 1995–; *Recreations* music, skiing; *Style*— John Lloyd, Esq; ✉ c/o Hodder Headline PLC, 338 Euston Road, London NW1 3BH

LLOYD, Dr John Walter; OBE (1988); s of Maj Joseph Howell Lloyd (d 1939), of Llandeilo, Dyfed, and Kathleen May Zelie, *née* Nicholas (d 1986); *b* 26 Dec 1923; *Educ* Epsom Coll, The London Hosp; *m* 17 May 1969, Mary Frances, da of Flt Lt Stanley Rowland Lewis, of Ballater, Aberdeen; 3 s (Thomas Joe b 19 April 1971, William John Nicholas b 21 Aug 1972, John Henry b 24 Aug 1981), 1 da (Sarah Frances b 16 Aug 1974); *Career* Sqdn Ldr RAF med branch 1950–54 (MO i/c Air HQ Cyprus 1952–54), civilian MO RNCAF Germany 1954–56; conslt anaesthetist Radcliffe Infirmary Oxford 1962–89 (i/c intensive care 1962–66), dir Oxford Regnl Pain Unit 1970–89, now emeritus conslt to Radcliffe Infirmary and RAF; inventor of techniques of cryoanalgesia 1976 and Barbotage of CSF; memb Int Assoc for Study of Pain 1970–, vice pres Intractable Pain Soc of GB and Ireland 1983– (chm 1983–85); memb Cncl for the Preservation of Rural England (Oxon); hon MA Oxon 1978; MRCS, LRCP, DA, FFARCS(Eng) 1960, FRSM 1966; *Books* Oxford Textbook of Medicine (contrib), Headache (contrib), Current Controversies in Neurosurgery (contrib), Techniques of Neurolysis (contrib); *Recreations* squash, vintage cars; *Clubs* RAF, Frewin (Oxford); *Style*— Dr John Lloyd, OBE; ✉ Gate House, Mill Street, Eynsham, Oxon OX8 1JU (☎ 01865 881477, 01865 515036); Bays Hill, Llandeilo, Dyfed, South Wales (☎ 01558 822561); 23 Banbury Road, Oxford (☎ 01865 616036)

LLOYD, John Wilson; CB (1992); s of Dr Ellis Lloyd (d 1964), of Swansea, and Dorothy Wilcoxon, *née* Smith; *b* 24 Dec 1940; *Educ* Swansea GS, Clifton, Christ's Coll Cambridge (BA, MA); *m* 25 March 1967, Buddug (d 1996), da of Rev J D Roberts, of Caernarfon, Gwynedd; 2 s (Huw b 1972, Geraint b 1973), 1 da (Sarah b 1968); *Career* asst princ HM Treasy 1962–67 (private sec to Fin Sec 1965–67), successively princ HM Treasy, CSD then Welsh Office 1967–75 (private sec to Sec of State for Wales 1974–75); Welsh Office: asst sec 1975–82, under sec and princ establishment offr 1982–86, under sec Housing Health and Social Serv Gp 1986–88, dep sec 1988–; *Recreations* golf, walking, swimming; *Style*— John Lloyd, Esq, CB; ✉ Welsh Office, Cathays Park, Cardiff CF1 3NQ (☎ 01222 825111)

LLOYD, Kevin Reardon; s of Ellis Aled Lloyd (d 1969), of Derby, and Agnes Amelia; *b* 28 March 1949; *Educ* Bemrose GS Derby, East 15 Acting Sch; *m* Lesley Marcelle, da of Bernard Euan Upson; 4 s (Mark b 1 Jan 1970, James b 27 May 1979, Henry b 5 July 1982, Edward b 4 June 1988), 4 da (Sophie b 5 May 1972, Chloe b 4 Nov 1976, Poppy b 18 Oct 1980, Elly b 11 Jan 1991); *Career* actor; assoc actor memb Bristol Old Vic; *Theatre* incl: Funny Peculiar 1975, Breeze Block Park (both Liverpool Everyman) 1975, What the Butler Saw (Royal Court, West End) 1975, Ducking Out (Duke of Yorks, West End) 1980, Love Girl and the Innocent (RSC, Aldwych) 1981, The Foreigner (Albany); numerous seasons at: Nottingham Playhouse, Manchester Library Theatre, Crewe Theatre, Southampton and Sheffield; seasons with RSC; *Television* incl: The Jimmy Cricket Show, POSH, Z Cars, Blakes Seven, Sink or Swim, Farrington of the FO, Don't Wait Up, That's Showbusiness, Boon, The Collectors, Juliet Bravo, Spearhead, The Winning Streak, Misfits, Coronation Street, Minder, Auf Wiedersehen Pet, Dear John,

Shine on Harvey Moon, Dempsey and Makepiece, Midnite at the Starlite, Talent, Inadmissable Evidence, Noel Edmond's House Party, The Borgias, By the Sword Divided, The Bill; subject of This Is Your Life 1992; *Films* Britannia Hospital, Link, Billy the Kid and the Green Baize Vampire; *Awards* nominated Best Newcomer (Theatre) 1975, nominated Best Comedy Performance (for Dear John) 1986; *Recreations* all sports (mainly soccer, rugby, cricket and tennis), travelling, reading, relaxing; *Clubs* The Lord's Taverner's, Equity, Derby County Football; *Style*— Kevin Lloyd, Esq; ✉ c/o Saraband Associates, 265 Liverpool Road, Islington, London N1 1LX (☎ 0171 609 5313/4, fax 0171 609 2370)

LLOYD, Mark William; s of Keneth Charles Lloyd, of Bridgend, Mid Glam, and Ivy, *née* Jones; *b* 5 Feb 1963; *Educ* Ynysawdre Comp Sch, Swansea Coll of Art, North Essex Sch of Art; *m* Joanna Caroline, da of Daniel James Peter Ryan; 1 da (Emily Elizabeth b 22 Oct 1989), 1 s (William Henry b 14 Nov 1993); *Career* designer Michael Peters & Partners 1984–87 (included in Best of British Packaging 1988), designer rising to asst creative dir Coley Porter Bell and Partners 1987–91, design dir Smith & Milton Ltd 1991–92, creative dir Lloyd Ferguson Hawkins 1992–; *Style*— Mark Lloyd, Esq; ✉ Lloyd Ferguson Hawkins Brand Identity Consultants Ltd, 6a-10 Frederick Close, Stanhope Place, London W2 2HD (☎ 0171 706 8762)

LLOYD, Michael Raymond; *b* 20 Aug 1927; *Educ* Architectural Assoc Sch of Architecture (AADipl); *Career* chartered architect; dean and prof of architecture Faculty of Architecture Planning and Building Technol Kumasi Univ of Sci and Technol Ghana 1963–66; princ: Architectural Assoc Sch of Architecture 1966–71, Land Use Consultants London 1971–72; sr ptnr Sinar Associates Tunbridge Wells 1973–80; conslt head Hull Sch of Architecture UK 1974–77, sr lectr Development Planning Unit Univ Coll London 1976–79 (pt/t 1974–76), rector Bergen Sch of Architecture 1985–88; visiting prof and critic: Sch of Architecture Nat Univ of Costa Rica 1979–81, Sch of Architecture Univ of Baja California 1980, ITESO Guadalajara Mexico 1980; responsible for workshop Columbian Assoc of Schs of Architecture Bogota 1980; tech offr ODA Br Govt (advsr on higher educn to Univs of Central America) 1979–81; Norconsult International AS Oslo Norway 1981–93: coordinating architect and planner Al Dora Township Baghdad for State Organization of Housing Government of Iraq 1981–83, exec conslt for physical planning Buildings Div 1981–86, project mangr Al Qassim Comprehensive Regnl Development Plan for Miny of Municipal and Rural Affrs Kingdom of Saudi Arabia 1983–86, sr conslt Development Gp on Third World Housing 1987–93; chm Habitat Norway 1993–94, prof of int studies Oslo Sch of Architecture 1993–; extensive overseas work; author of: 14 papers on architectural and planning educn, 5 papers on housing, 7 reports for national govts, 2 books; external examiner Univs of: Edinburgh, Kuala Lumpur, Kumasi, Lund, Newcastle, Trondheim, Zaria, Oslo; external examiner Polytechnics of Central London and Hull; visiting lectr: Baghdad, Bogota, Canterbury, Edinburgh, Enugu, Guadalajara, Guanajuato, Helsinki, Jyvaskyla, Kingston, Kuala Lumpur, Lund, Mexico City, Mexicali, Newcastle, Oslo, Oxford, Santiago, Trondheim, Valparaiso, Zaria, Zurich; extensive involvement with: International Union of Architects, UNESCO, Br Cncl; memb numerous professional ctees 1966–; memb Ct RCA 1968–80; RIBA; memb: Norwegian Architects' Assoc, AA; *Style*— Michael Lloyd, Esq

LLOYD, Sir Nicholas Markley; kt (1990); *b* 9 June 1942; *Educ* Bedford Modern Sch, St Edmund Hall Oxford (MA), Harvard Univ; *m* 1; 2 s, 1 da; *m* 2, 23 May 1979, Eve Pollard, *qv*; 1 s (Oliver b 6 Aug 1980); *Career* dep ed Sunday Mirror 1980–82, ed Sunday People 1982–84, dir Mirror Gp 1982–84, ed News of the World Jan 1984–85, dir News Gp Newspapers 1985–96, ed Daily Express 1986–96; *Style*— Sir Nicholas Lloyd

LLOYD, Rt Hon Sir Peter Robert Cable; kt (1995), PC (1994), MP (C) Fareham (majority 24,141); s of David Lloyd (d 1991), and his 1 w, late Stella Lloyd; *b* 12 Nov 1937; *Educ* Tonbridge, Pembroke Coll Cambridge (MA); *m* 1967, Hilary Creighton; 1 s, 1 da; *Career* former mktg mangr United Biscuits; chm Bow Gp 1972–73, former ed Crossbow; Parly candidate (C) Nottingham W 1974 (both gen elections), MP (C) Fareham 1979–; sec Cons Parly Employment Ctee 1979–81, vice chm Euro Affrs Ctee 1980–81, PPS to Adam Butler as Min of State NI 1981–82, memb Select Ctee on Employment 1982, PPS to Sir Keith Joseph as Sec of State for Educn and Sci 1983–84, asst govt whip 1984–86, a Lord Cmmr of the Treasy (Govt whip) Oct 1986–88; Parly under sec: Dept of Social Security 1988–89, Home Office 1989–92; min of state Home Office 1992–94; *Style*— The Rt Hon Sir Peter Lloyd, MP; ✉ House of Commons, London SW1A 0AA (☎ 0171 219 3000)

LLOYD, Phyllida Christian; da of Patrick John Lloyd, of West Anstey, Devon, and Margaret, *née* Douglas-Pennant; *b* 17 June 1957; *Educ* Lawnside Sch Malvern, Univ of Birmingham; *Career* theatre director; Arts Cncl trainee dir Wolsey Theatre Ipswich 1985, prodns: Glengary Glen Ross, Hard Times Educating Rita; assoc dir Everyman Theatre Cheltenham 1986–87, prodns incl: Much Ado About Nothing, A Midsummer Night's Dream, Earth, Every Black Day, Woyzeck, Accidental Death of An Anarchist, Just Between Ourselves, What the Butler Saw; assoc dir Bristol Old Vic 1989, prodns: The Comedy of Errors, Dona Rosita The Spinster, A Streetcar Named Desire, Oliver Twist; Manchester Royal Exchange 1990–91, prodns: The Winter's Tale, The School for Scandal, Death and the King's Horseman, Medea; RSC prodns incl: The Virtuoso 1991, Artists and Admirers 1992; Royal Court prodns incl: Six Degrees of Separation 1992, Hysteria 1993; RNT prodns incl: Pericles 1994, What the Butler Saw 1994, The Way of the World 1995; The Donmar Warehouse: The Threepenny Opera 1994; *Opera* Opera North prodns incl: L'Étoile, La Bohème, Gloriana (also ROH), Medea; *Awards* incl John Fernald Award 1989; Olivier Award nominations: Best Dir (for Hysteria) 1994, Best Opera Prodn (for Gloriana) 1994; *Style*— Ms Phyllida Lloyd; ✉ c/o Annette Stone Associates, 9 Newburgh Street, London W1V 1LH (☎ 0171 734 0626, fax 0171 434 2014)

LLOYD, Reginald Arthur Harris; TD (1980, and clasp), DL (Shropshire 1979); s of Rev Richard Harris Lloyd (d 1952); *b* 24 Jan 1913; *Educ* Hull GS, Scarborough Coll; *m* 1946, Maureen, da of John Thelwall Salusbury (d 1946); 4 s, 1 da; *Career* Shropshire CC: cncllr 1961, vice chm 1977, chm 1981–85; head office mgmnt Sun Alliance London until 1973, ret; gen cmmr of taxes 1975–78; chm Bylaw (Ross) Ltd 1987; chm: Packwood Haugh Prep Sch Shropshire 1963–88, Shropshire Army Cadet League 1965–, Shropshire Agricultural Wages Ctee 1974–, W Mercia Police Authy 1989–93; govr: Church Stretton Sch, Shrewsbury Sch 1968–88; memb: Bd of Tstees and Exec Bd Ironbridge Gorge Museum Tst 1985–, Mgmnt Cncl W Midland Regnl Investment Tst 1985–; pres: Shropshire CPRE, Shropshire Assoc of Parish and Town Cncls 1984–91, Shrewsbury and Atcham Cons Assoc 1988–92; memb: Police Ctee Assoc of Co Cncls 1989–93, Shropshire Regimental Museum Appeal 1992–; govr RNIB Candover Hall Sch 1995–; *Recreations* fishing, walking; *Clubs* Carlton, MCC, Beaconsfield; *Style*— Reginald Lloyd, Esq, TD, DL; ✉ Acre Batch, Lower Wood, All Stretton, Shropshire SY6 6LG (☎ 01694 751233, fax 01694 751453)

LLOYD, Sir Richard Ernest Butler; 2 Bt (UK 1960), of Rhu, Co Dunbarton; o s of Maj Sir (Ernest) Guy Richard Lloyd, 1 Bt, DSO, DL (d 1987), and Helen Kynaston, *née* Greg (d 1984); *b* 6 Dec 1928; *Educ* Wellington, Hertford Coll Oxford (MA); *m* 6 June 1955, Jennifer Susan Margaret, er da of Brig Ereld Boteler Wingfield Cardiff, CB, CBE (d 1988), of Easton Court, nr Ludlow, Shropshire; 3 s ((Richard) Timothy Butler b 12 April 1956, Simon Wingfield Butler b 26 July 1958, Henry Butler b 22 Feb 1965); *Heir* s, (Richard) Timothy Butler Lloyd b 12 April 1956; *Career* former Capt Black Watch, Mil Serv Malaya 1947–49; banker; exec then dir Glyn Mills & Co 1952–70, chief exec Williams & Glyn's Bank 1970–78; Hill Samuel Bank Ltd: dep chm 1978–80 and 1991–95, dep chm and chief exec 1980–87, chm 1987–91; chm: Vickers plc 1992– (formerly dep chm), Argos plc 1995–; non-exec dir: Siebe plc 1988–, Simon Engineering plc; former memb: Industl Devpt Advsy Bd DTI, NEDC; memb Cncl CBI 1978–96, govr Ditchley Fndn; Freeman City of London 1964, Liveryman Worshipful Co of Mercers 1965, memb Guild of Freemen of Shrewsbury 1978; CIMgt, FCIB; *Recreations* fly-fishing, gardening, walking; *Clubs* Boodle's; *Style*— Sir Richard Lloyd, Bt; ✉ Sundridge Place, Sundridge, Sevenoaks, Kent TN14 6DD (☎ 01959 563599)

LLOYD, Robert Andrew; CBE (1991); s of Inspr William Edward Lloyd (d 1963), and May, *née* Waples; *b* 2 March 1940; *Educ* Southend HS, Keble Coll Oxford (MA), London Opera Centre; *m* 22 Feb 1964 (m dis 1989), Sandra Dorothy, da of Douglas Watkins; 1 s (Marcus b 1965), 3 da (Anna b 1966, Candida b 1969, Alice b 1973); *m* 2, 1992, Lynda Anne Hazell, *née* Powell; *Career* freelance opera and concert singer (bass), writer and broadcaster; Instr Lt RN 1962–65; civilian tutor Bramshill Police Staff Coll 1966–68; princ bass: Sadler's Wells Opera 1969–72, Royal Opera 1972–83; performed at numerous int venues incl: Royal Opera House Covent Garden, La Scala Milan, Metropolitan Opera NY, Paris Opera, Munich, Vienna Staatsoper, San Francisco Opera; recent performances incl: title role in André Tarkovsky prodn of Boris Godunov (Kirov Opera Leningrad), Simon Boccanegra (Metropolitan Opera), Magic Flute (Bastille Opera), Pelleas and Melisande (Metropolitan Opera); frequent broadcaster on radio and TV; memb: Exec Ctee Musicians' Benevolent Fund 1988–94, Conservatoires Advsy Gp HE Funding Cncl; pres Br Youth Opera 1989–94, visiting prof RCM 1996–; hon fell Keble Coll Oxford 1990; *Recordings* various audio and video incl: Parsifal, Don Carlos, Entführung aus dem Serail, Magic Flute, Handel's Messiah, Dream of Gerontius, Fidelio, The Damnation of Faust, Verdi Requiem, The Coronation of Poppea; *Films* Parsifal (Artificial Eye), 6 Foot Cinderella (BBC), Bluebeard's Castle (BBC, Prix Italia 1989); *Recreations* sailing, hill walking; *Clubs* Garrick; *Style*— Robert Lloyd, Esq, CBE; ✉ Lies Askonas Ltd, 6 Henrietta Street, London WC2 (☎ 0171 379 7700)

LLOYD, Robert Geoffrey; s of Robert Sydney Lloyd, MBE, of Llangefni, Gwynedd, and Joan Elizabeth, *née* Geerdts; *b* 20 April 1947; *Educ* Falcon Coll Rhodesia, Univ Coll Rhodesia; *Career* Capt Rhodesian Army 1973; sr registrar: Addenbrooke's Hosp Cambridge 1983–84, Norfolk and Norwich Hosp 1985–87; conslt in accident and emergency med Tameside Gen Hosp 1987–; memb Br Assoc Accident and Emergency Med; *Recreations* shooting, walking, reading; *Clubs* Anglesey Hunt; *Style*— Robert Lloyd, Esq; ✉ 12 Wellgate, Old Glossop, Derbyshire SK13 9RS (☎ 01457 469404); Tameside General Hospital, Ashton under Lyne, Lancashire OL6 9RW (☎ 0161 330 8373)

LLOYD, Simon Roderick; s of Desmond C F Lloyd (d 1978), and Amber, *née* Wallace-Barr; *b* 25 March 1947; *Educ* Wellington; *m* April 1972, Susan Margaret, *née* Cuthbert; 1 da (Rebecca Catherine b 1976), 1 s (Andrew James Wallace b 1978); *Career* trainee media planner/buyer Garland Compton Advertising 1966–74; Foote Cone & Belding Advertising: joined 1974, bd/media dir 1978–80, vice chm 1980–84, md 1984–86, dir of media Euro Region 1986–88; vice pres media Publicis FCB Europe (alliance of FCB and Publicis) 1988–89, chm Optimedia Europe (network of media planning/buying specialist cos owned by Publicis FCB Group) 1989–; MIPA, MIAA; *Recreations* sailing, cricket, walking, dogs, travel, almost any new experience!; *Clubs* MCC, Royal London Yacht, Seaview Yacht (Isle of Wight); *Style*— Simon Lloyd, Esq; ✉ Optimedia International Ltd, 84–86 Baker Street, London W1M 1DL (☎ 0171 935 0040, fax 0171 935 9412)

LLOYD, His Hon Judge Stephen Harris; s of Thomas Richard Lloyd (d 1951), and Amy Irene, *née* Harris (d 1971); *b* 16 Sept 1938; *Educ* Ashville Coll Harrogate, Univ of Leeds (LLB); *m* 2 June 1972, Joyce Eileen, da of Frederick Allen (d 1946); 2 step-da (Caroline Anne (Mrs Freuler) b 27 May 1958, Elizabeth Mary (Mrs Worsley) b 18 Feb 1962); *Career* Dale & Newbery Slrs: joined 1962, admitted slr 1965, ptnr 1968–85, sr ptnr 1985–95; recorder of the Crown Court 1993–95 (asst recorder 1989–93), circuit judge SE Circuit 1995 ; slr SW London Probation Service 1985–95; chm Nat Cncl for One Parent Families 1975 83, chm Mediation in Divorce 1986–90, chm Bd of Govrs Manor House Sch 1987–95; vice chm Bd St Peter's Nat Health Tst 1991–95; pres Ashvillian Soc 1993–94; memb Law Soc 1965–95; *Recreations* two 1930's motor vehicles, cottages in Yorkshire Dales, charity work, walking, music, entertaining; *Style*— His Hon Judge Stephen Lloyd; ✉ c/o Hove Court Centre, Landsdowne Road, Hove, East Sussex (☎ 01273 773841)

LLOYD, Thomas Owen Saunders; s of Maj John Audley Lloyd, MC, of Court Henry, Carmarthen, and (Mary Ivy) Anna, *née* Owen; *b* 26 Feb 1955; *Educ* Radley, Downing Coll Cambridge (MA); *m* 7 Nov 1987, (Christabel) Juliet Anne (d 1996), da of Maj David Harrison-Allen (d 1976), of Cresselly, nr Pembroke; *Career* slr, author; chm: Historic Bldgs Cncl for Wales 1992– (memb 1985–), Br Historic Bldgs Tst 1987–92, Pembrokeshire Historical Soc 1991–95, Buildings at Risk Tst 1992–; non-exec: dir Dyfed Family Health Servs Authy 1990–95 (chm Med and Dental Servs Ctees 1992–96), Wales Tourist Bd 1995–; memb Cadw - Welsh Historic Monuments Advsr Ctee 1992–; FSA 1991; *Books* The Lost Houses of Wales (1986, 2 edn 1989); *Style*— Thomas Lloyd, Esq, FSA; ✉ Freestone Hall, Cresselly, Kilgetty, Dyfed SA68 0SX (☎ and fax 01646 651493)

LLOYD, Hon Mr Justice; Hon Sir Timothy Andrew Wigram; kt (1996); s of Dr Thomas Wigram Lloyd (d 1984), and Margo Adela, *née* Beasley; *b* 30 Nov 1946; *Educ* Winchester, Lincoln Coll Oxford (exhibitioner, BA, MA); *m* 1978, Theresa Sybil Margaret, da of late Ralph Kenneth Holloway; *Career* called to the Bar Middle Temple 1970, bencher 1994, former head of chambers, QC 1986, Attorney Gen of the Duchy and Attorney and Serjeant within the Co Palatine of Lancaster 1993–96, judge of the High Ct of Justice (Chancery Div) 1996–; *Books* Wurtzburg & Mills, Building Society Law (15 edn, 1989); *Recreations* music, travel; *Style*— The Hon Mr Justice Lloyd; ✉ c/o Royal Courts of Justice, Strand, London WC2A 2LL

LLOYD, Ven (Bertram) Trevor; s of Bertram Lloyd, of Scole Norfolk, and Gladys, *née* Baker; *b* 15 Feb 1938; *Educ* Highgate Sch, Hertford Coll Oxford (scholar, BA, MA), Clifton Theol Coll Bristol; *m* 30 June 1962, (Margaret) Eldey, da of Frederick Butler (d 1990); 3 s (Christopher 1967, Jonathan b 1969, Peter b 1972 d 1985), 1 da (Hilary Kemp 1965); *Career* curate Christ Church Barnet 1964–69, vicar Holy Trinity Wealdstone 1970–84, priest i/c St Michael and All Angels Harrow Weald 1980–84, vicar Trinity St Michael Harrow 1984–89, archdeacon of Barnstaple 1989–, preb of Exeter Cathedral 1991–; area dean of Harrow 1977–82; chaplain to Gen Synod of C of E 1996–; memb: C of E Liturgical Cmmn 1981–, Gen Synod C of E 1990–, Central Bd of Fin C of E 1990–, Cncl for the Care of Churches 1993–, Standing Ctee Gen Synod 1996–, Gp for Renewal of Worship, Editorial Bd GROW-Alcuin Publications; *Publications* Informal Liturgy (1972), Institutions and Inductions (1973), The Agape (1973), Liturgy and Death (1974), Ministry and Death (1974), Lay Presidency at the Eucharist? (1977), Evangelicals Obedience and Change (1977), Anglican Worship Today (ed, 1980), Ceremonial in Worship (1981), Introducing Liturgical Change (1984), Celebrating Lent Holy Week and Easter (1985), Celebrating the Agape Today (1986), The Future of Anglican Worship (1987); *Recreations* hill walking, photography, swimming, caravanning, making things from wood; *Style*— The Ven Trevor Lloyd; ✉ Stage Cross, Whitemoor Hill, Bishop's Tawton, Barnstaple, Devon EX32 0BE (☎ 01271 75475, fax 01271 77934)

LLOYD, Ursula Elizabeth; da of Dr Jospeh D B Mountrose, of Wimpole St, London, and Maria, *née* Robinson; *b* 10 July 1943; *Educ* Francis Holland C of E Sch Clarence Gate London, Middx Hosp Med Sch (MB BS, LRCS, MRCP); *m* William Lloyd, s of

Roderick Lloyd; 2 da (Wendy b 28 Feb 1978, Anne b 6 Sept 1981); *Career* various trg posts Royal Marsden Hosp, Chelsea Hosp for Women and Queen Charlotte's Hosps; conslt obstetrician and gynaecologist: S London Hosp for Women 1982–87, St James' Hosp Balham 1987–89, St George's Hosp Tooting 1987–91, in private practice 1991–; Freeman City of London, Liveryman Worshipful Soc of Apothecaries; memb RSM, FRCOG; *Style*— Mrs Ursula Lloyd; ✉ Portland Hospital for Women, 209 Great Portland Street, London W1 (☎ 0171 935 3732, fax 0171 935 3732)

LLOYD, Wendy Anne; da of Geoffrey Hugh Lloyd, of Cambridge, and Irene Sylvia Lloyd; *b* 23 May 1969; *Career* writer, presenter, producer for television and radio, voice over artist; *Radio* credits incl: BBC Cambridge 1986–88, BBC GLR (Pop Life) 1988–91, BT's Music Service (Live Wire) 1988–89, BBC World Service, Radio Luxembourg 1992–93, Virgin Radio 1993–95, BBC Radio One (Clingfilm) 1995, Talk Radio 1996–; *Television* credits incl: Dial Midnight (LWT) 1993, The Little Picture Show (ITV) 1995; contrib: Channel One, GMTV; *Recreations* dress-making and home furnishings, gym, piano, skiing, theatre, live music, walking; *Style*— Miss Wendy Lloyd; ✉ c/o Fox Artist Management, Concorde House, 101 Shepherd's Bush Road, London W6 7LP (☎ 0171 602 8822, fax 0171 603 2352)

LLOYD-DAVIES, (John) Robert; CMG (1953); s of John Robert Davies (d 1971), of Muswell Hill, London, and Nellie Louise, *née* Wilson (d 1928); *b* 24 March 1913; *Educ* Highgate Sch, Oriel Coll Oxford (MA), Univ of Freiburg-im-Breisgau; *m* 1, 6 Feb 1943, Margery (d 1978), da of Maj William McClelland (ka 1918); 1 s (Peter Russell b 18 Nov 1943), 1 da (Virginia Mary b 9 March 1947); m 2, 19 June 1982, Grace, *née* Williams, wid of Frederick Reynolds II, of Bethesda, USA; *Career* Lt RNVR 1942–45; sr civil servant and memb of HM Dip Serv; private sec to Sir Thomas Phillips, KCB (Employment Dept) 1940; labour cnsllr HM Embassies Paris 1956–60 and Washington DC 1972–73; princ Trg Serv Agency 1973–77; pt/t teacher: Working Men's Coll London 1970–94, Inst for Learning in Retirement American Univ Washington DC 1987–; *Recreations* keyboard music (baroque and modern); *Clubs* Utd Oxford and Cambridge Univ; *Style*— Robert Lloyd-Davies, Esq, CMG; ✉ 59 Elm Park Court, Pinner, Middx HA5 3LL (☎ 0181 866 9526)

LLOYD-DAVIES, (Reginald) Wyndham; s of Dr Allan Wyndham Lloyd-Davies (d 1974), of Branksome Park, Poole, Dorset, and Muriel Constance, *née* Martin (d 1993); *b* 24 June 1934; *Educ* Rugby, Univ of London (MB, MS); *m* 1, 31 May 1958 (m dis 1981), Elizabeth Ann, da of Arthur Wesley Harding (d 1978); 2 da ((Susan) Vanessa Lloyd-Davies, MBE (Mil) b 1960, Fiona Caroline b 1964); m 2, 20 Aug 1983, Jill Black, *qv*, da of Austin Hemingsley (d 1969), of Dulwich; *Career* res urologist San Francisco Med Centre Univ of California 1969–70, conslt surgn Queen Victoria Hosp E Grinstead 1971–77, dep CMO Met Police 1983– (conslt surgn 1978–), sr conslt urologist St Thomas's Hosp 1986– (MRC res fell Dept of Surgery 1965, sr surgical registrar in urology 1966–69, conslt urologist 1970–86), clinical dir urology and lithotripsy Guy's and St Thomas' Hosp Tst 1993–, surgn King Edward VII Hosp for Offrs London 1994–; RSM: memb Cncl 1975–87, vice pres 1980, treas 1983–87; Urology Section RSM: memb Cncl 1991–92, pres elect 1990, pres 1991–92; author of numerous pubns on urological topics; Liveryman Worshipful Soc of Apothecaries 1974, Freeman City of London 1979; memb Br Assoc of Urological Surgns (memb Cncl 1980–83 and 1991–92), FRCS(Eng), FEBU, FRSM; *Recreations* shooting, fishing, stalking; *Clubs* Garrick; *Style*— Wyndham Lloyd-Davies, Esq; ✉ 53 Harley St, London W1N 1DD (☎ 0171 637 9411, fax 0171 636 4590); Matthews Cottage, Kingham, Oxon

LLOYD-DAVIS, Glynne Christian; s of Col G St G Lloyd-Davis (d 1956), and Daphne Mary, *née* Barnes (d 1995); *b* 9 March 1941; *Educ* St Paul's, Ealing Tech Coll, Royal Sch of Mines Univ of London, London Business Sch; *m* 20 April 1963, Dorothy Helen, da of Michael O'Shea (d 1991), of Aust; 1 s (Simon b 1966), 1 da (Sarah b 1964); *Career* chartered sec; asst sec The RTZ Corporation plc 1976–, dir subsid companies; sec The Mining Assoc of the UK 1987–; FCIS; *Recreations* reading, walking, sketching; *Clubs* Royal Over-Seas League; *Style*— Glynne Lloyd-Davis, Esq; ✉ Rentain Farmhouse, Chartham, Kent CT4 7JQ; RTZ Corporation plc, 6 St James's Square, London SW1Y 4LD (☎ 0171 753 2117, telex 24639)

LLOYD-EDWARDS, Capt Norman; RD (1971, and Bar 1980); s of Evan Stanley Edwards (d 1986), of Cardiff, and Mary Leah, *née* Lloyd (d 1977); *b* 13 June 1933; *Educ* Monmouth Sch, Quakers Yard GS, Univ of Bristol (LLB); *Career* Capt RNR, CO HMS Cambria, S Wales Div RNR 1981–84; slr; ptnr Cartwright Adams & Black 1960–93 (conslt 1993–); memb Cardiff City Cncl 1963–87 (dep Lord Mayor 1973–74, Lord Mayor 1985–86); chapter clerk Llandaff Cathedral 1975–90, Prior for Wales 1989–, pres Friends of Llandaff Cathedral 1990–, pres Friends of St John Parish Church Cardiff 1994–; memb Cncl BBC Wales 1987–90; chm: Wales Ctee Duke of Edinburgh Award 1980–96 (pres 1996–), Cardiff Festival of Music 1981–89, Nat Res Trg Cncl 1984–95, Glamorgan TA & VRA 1987–90; pres: S Glamorgan Scouts 1989–, Cardiff Branch Nat Tst, Wales Festival of Remembrance 1990–, Morgannwg Branch Br Red Cross 1994–; Lord Lt S Glamorgan 1990– (Vice Lord Lt 1986); ADC to HM The Queen 1984; fndr Master Welsh Livery Guild 1992–95; Hon Col 2 Bn Royal Regiment of Wales 1996–; GCStJ 1996 (KStJ 1988, OStJ 1983); *Recreations* music, gardening, table talk; *Clubs* Army & Navy, Cardiff & Co, United Services Mess; *Style*— Capt Norman Lloyd-Edwards, RD; ✉ Hafan Wen, Llantrisant Rd, Llandaff, Cardiff CF5 2PU (☎ 01222 578278); 36 West Bute St, Cardiff (☎ 01222 465959, fax 01222 480062)

LLOYD GEORGE, Hon Robert John Daniel; yr s of 3 Earl Lloyd George of Dwyfor, and his 1 w, Ruth Margaret, *née* Coit; *b* 13 Aug 1952; *Educ* Eton (King's scholar), Univ Coll Oxford (exhibitioner); *m* 1, 1977 (m dis 1991), Kim, o da of Carl Fischer, of New York City; 1 s (Richard Joseph b 1983), 1 da (Alice Margaret b 1987); m 2, 1992, Donna Jean, o da of John Archbold Hufty, of Palm Beach, Florida; 1 s (Alexander Gwilym b 16 Feb 1994), 1 da (Julia Frances b 1993); *Career* chm Lloyd George Management Ltd (Hong Kong); *Books* A Guide to Asian Stock Markets (1989), The East West Pendulum (1991), North South: An Emerging Markets Handbook (1994); *Style*— The Hon Robert Lloyd George; ✉ Lloyd George Management, 3808 One Exchange Square, Central Hong Kong (☎ 00 852 2845 4433, fax 00 852 2845 3911)

LLOYD GEORGE, Hon Timothy Henry Gwilym; s and h of, 3 Viscount Tenby, *qv*; *b* 19 Oct 1962; *Educ* Downside, Univ Coll of Wales Aberystwyth; *Style*— The Hon Timothy Lloyd George; ✉ Triggs, Crondall, nr Farnham, Surrey

LLOYD GEORGE OF DWYFOR, 3 Earl (UK 1945); Owen Lloyd George; DL (Dyfed); also Viscount Gwynedd (UK 1945); s of 2 Earl Lloyd George of Dwyfor (d 1968, s of the PM 1916–22) and his 1 w, Roberta, da of Sir Robert McAlpine, 1 Bt; *b* 28 April 1924; *Educ* Oundle; *m* 1, 1949 (m dis 1982), Ruth Margaret, da of Richard Coit (d 1960); 2 s, 1 da; m 2, 1982, (Cecily) Josephine (who m 1, 1957, as his 2 w, 2 Earl of Woolton, who d 1969; m 2, 1969 (m dis 1974), as his 2 w, 3 Baron Forres, who d 1978), er da of Sir Alexander Gordon Cumming, 5 Bt, MC (d 1939); *Heir* s, Viscount Gwynedd; *Career* Capt Welsh Gds 1942, serv 1944–45 in Italy; carried the sword at investiture of HRH The Prince of Wales, Caernarvon Castle 1969; underwriting memb of Lloyd's; memb Historic Buildings Cncl for Wales 1971–94; *Clubs* White's, Pratt's; *Style*— The Rt Hon the Earl Lloyd George of Dwyfor, DL; ✉ Ffynone, Boncath, Pembrokeshire SA37 0HQ; 47 Burton Court, Chelsea, London SW3 4SZ

LLOYD-HUGHES, Sir Trevor Denby; kt (1970); s of Elwyn Lloyd-Hughes (d 1969), of Dwygyfylchi, Penmaenmawr, and Lucy, *née* Denby (d 1960); *b* 31 March 1922; *Educ* Woodhouse Grove Sch, Jesus Coll Oxford (MA); *m* 1, 9 May 1950 (m dis 1971), Ethel Marguerite Durward (decd), da of late John Ritchie, of Bradford; 1 s (Richard b 1954), 1 da (Katherine b 1951); m 2, 18 May 1971, Marie-Jeanne, da of Marcel Moreillon, of Geneva, Switzerland; 1 s (decd), 1 da (Annabelle b 1971), 1 adopted da (Nammon b 1969, Thailand); *Career* served WWII Lt 75 (Shropshire Yeo) Medium Regt, RA Western Desert, Sicily and Italy (Staff Lt Welfare 6 Army Gp RA i/c welfare Trieste Italy 1945); asst inspr Taxes 1947–48; freelance journalist 1949; political corr: Liverpool Echo 1950, Liverpool Daily Post 1951–64; press sec to PM 1964–69, chief info advsr to Govt (dep sec Cabinet Office) 1969–70, int conslt in public affrs and chm Lloyd-Hughes Associates Ltd 1971–89; non-exec dir Trinity International Holdings 1978–91; ret; chm Circle of Wine Writers 1972–73 (memb 1961); FIMgt 1978, FInstD 1984; *Recreations* yoga, gardening, reading, travel, walking; *Clubs* Mossiman's (Belfry), Wellington; *Style*— Sir Trevor Lloyd-Hughes; ✉ Au Carmail, Labarrere, 32250 Montreal-du-Gers, France (☎ 00 33 62 29 45 31)

LLOYD JONES, (Richard) David; s of Richard Francis Lloyd Jones (d 1976), and Hester, *née* Ritchie (d 1985); *b* 10 May 1942; *Educ* Edgeborough Sch, Bradfield Coll, Architectural Assoc (AADipl); *m* 1971, Linda Barbara, da of Duncan John Stewart; *Career* Stillman and Eastwick-Field Architects 1964, National Building Agency 1966–72, RMJM Ltd (previously Robert Matthew Johnson-Marshall & Partners) 1972–91 (dir 1986, chm Design Group 1987); projects incl: HRH Prince of Wales' exhibition Vision of Britain at the Victoria and Albert Museum, NFU Mutual and Avon Insurance Group HQ, Auditorium Garsington Opera, Solar Offices Doxford International; princ David Lloyd Jones Associates 1991–, dir Studio E Architects Ltd 1994–; RIBA 1968 (memb London Regnl Cncl 1991–), FRSA 1990; *Recreations* sculpture, painting, tennis, travelling; *Clubs* Architectural Assoc, Royal Soc of Arts & Science; *Style*— David Lloyd Jones, Esq; ✉ 24 Liston Rd, London SW4 ODF; 28 Ghammar St, Gharb, Gozo, Malta; David Lloyd Jones Associates, Palace Wharf, Rainville Road, London W6 9HN (☎ 0171 385 7126, fax 0171 381 4995)

LLOYD-JONES, David Mathias; s of Harry Vincent Lloyd-Jones, and Margaret Alwyna, *née* Mathias; *b* 19 Nov 1934; *Educ* Westminster, Magdalen Coll Oxford (BA); *m* 23 May 1964, Anne Carolyn, da of Brig Victor Whitehead, of Montreal; 2 s (Gareth b 1966, Simon b 1968), 1 da (Vanessa b 1964); *Career* conductor; repetiteur with Royal Opera House Covent Garden 1959–60, chorus master and conductor New Opera Co 1961–64; freelance conductor engagements with: BBC, WNO, Scottish Opera; asst music dir Sadler's Wells ENO 1972–78, artistic dir Opera North 1978–90; many opera and concert engagements abroad, numerous recordings of Br and Russian music; ed original version of Mussorgsky's Boris Godunov 1974; published full score Gilbert and Sullivan's The Gondoliers 1983; trans: Eugene Onegin, Boris Godunov, The Queen of Spades, The Love of Three Oranges; Hon DMus Univ of Leeds; *Style*— David Lloyd-Jones, Esq; ✉ 94 Whitelands House, Cheltenham Terrace, London SW3 4RA (☎ and fax 0171 730 8695)

LLOYD-JONES, Prof Sir (Peter) Hugh Jefferd; kt (1989); s of Brevet Maj William Lloyd-Jones, DSO (d 1963, late Capt of Invalids Royal Hosp Chelsea), and Norah Leila, *née* Jefferd (d 1953); *b* 21 Sept 1922; *Educ* Westminster, Lycée Francais du Royaume Univ, Christ Church Oxford (MA); *m* 1, 30 July 1953 (m dis 1981), Frances Elizabeth, da of R H B Hedley; 2 s (Edmund b 1958, Ralph b 1960), 1 da (Antonia b 1962); m 2, 26 March 1982, Prof Mary Lefkowitz, da of Harold Rosenthal; *Career* 2 Lt Intelligence Corps, served India 1942, Capt 1944, demobbed 1946; fell Jesus Coll Cambridge 1948–54, lectr Univ of Cambridge 1952–54 (asst lectr 1950–52), fell and E P Warren praelector Corpus Christi Coll Oxford 1954–60, Regius prof of Greek Univ of Oxford, student Christ Church Oxford 1960–89; corresponding memb: Acad of Athens, American Acad of Arts and Scis, Nordrhein-Westfälische Akademie, Accademia di Letteratura Archeologia e Belle Arti Naples, Bayerische Akademie der Wissenschaften, American Philosophical Soc; Hon PhD Univ of Tel Aviv 1982, Hon DH Chicago Univ 1970; FBA 1966; *Books* The Justice of Zeus (1971, 2 edn 1983), Blood for the Ghosts (1982), Classical Survivals (1982), Supplementum Hellenisticum (with P J Parsons, 1983), Sophoclis Fabulae (with N G Wilson, 1990), Sophoclea (with N G Wilson, 1990), Academic Papers 2 vols (1990), Greek in a Cold Climate (1991), Sophocles (3 vols, 1994–96); *Recreations* cats, remembering old cricket; *Clubs* Utd Oxford and Cambridge; *Style*— Prof Sir Hugh Lloyd-Jones, FBA; ✉ 15 West Riding, Wellesley, Massachusetts 02181, USA (☎ 00 1 617 237 2212, fax 00 1 617 237 2246)

LLOYD-JONES, Robert (Bob); s of Robert Lloyd-Jones (d 1950), of Caernarvon, N Wales, and Edith May, *née* Hughes (d 1954); *b* 30 Jan 1931; *Educ* Wrekin Coll, Queens' Coll Cambridge (MA), Harvard Business Sch; *m* 9 June 1958 (m dis 1977), Morny Downer; 2 s (Ashley Paul b 8 June 1961, Alasdair Guy b 12 Feb 1966), 1 da (Sarah Louise (Mrs Hall) b 14 Oct 1962); *Career* Lt RN 1956–59; patent attorney Shell International 1959–62, head legal and licensing BTR Industrial Ltd 1962–64, dir (Woolmark) International Wool Secretariat 1964–71, PA to chm and export dir Schachenmayr Germany 1971–77; dir gen: Br Textile Employers Assoc 1977–81, Retail Consortium 1981–83, Brick Devpt Assoc 1984–94; dir Fedn Euro des Fabricants de Tuiles et de Briques 1984–94; conslt to corp mktg servs, conslt EEF; govr Cncl for Distributitive Trades 1982–84, fndr chm Nat Retail Trg Cncl 1982–84, memb Euro Trade Ctee DTI and chm of Nordic Countries 1994–; tstee Building Crafts and Conservation Tst; memb Mktg Ctee Sea Cadet Assoc; friend of: Royal Acad, Tate Gallery; Freeman and Liveryman Worshipful Co of Tylers and Bricklayers; FRSA; *Recreations* golf, tennis, squash, chess, travel, arts, reading, music; *Clubs* Lansdowne, Royal Birkdale Golf, Rye Golf, Liphook Golf (ctee memb), Formby Golf, Royal Ascot Tennis, RN Golfing Soc (match sec), China Golfing Soc, IOD; *Style*— R Lloyd-Jones, Esq; ✉ Mill Cottage, 10 High St, Odiham, Hampshire RG29 1LG (☎ and fax 01256 703008)

LLOYD-JONES, (Glyn) Robin; s of William Rice Lloyd-Jones (d 1980), and Esme Frances, *née* Ellis; *b* 5 Oct 1934; *Educ* Blundell's, Selwyn Coll Cambridge (MA), Jordanhill Coll of Educn; *m* 30 July 1959, Sallie, da of Cdr John Hollocombe, RN (d 1981); 1 s (Glyn b 1962), 2 da (Kally b 1965, Léonie b 1969); *Career* educn advsr 1972–89; writer; pres Scot Assoc of Writers 1981–86, vice pres (Scot) PEN Int 1991–, co-ordinator Scottish Forum for Devpt Educn in Schools; *Books* fiction incl: Where the Forest and the Garden Meet (1980), Lord of the Dance (winner BBC-Arrow First Novel competition, 1983), The Dreamhouse (1985), Fallen Angels (1992); other: Assessment from Principles to Action (with Elizabeth Bray, 1985), Better Worksheets (1986), Argonauts of the Western Isles (1989); *Radio Drama* Ice in Wonderland (Radio Times New Drama Script Award, 1992), Rainmaker (1995); *Recreations* mountaineering, sea-kayaking, chess, photography; *Style*— Robin Lloyd-Jones, Esq; ✉ 26 East Clyde St, Helensburgh G84 7PG (☎ 01436 672010, e-mail 100601.714@compuserve.com)

LLOYD LYONS, Bruno; s of Cyril Lloyd Lyons, and Kathleen Joan, *née* Webb; *b* 25 Jan 1942; *Educ* Henry Thornton GS; *m* 1, 1963 (m dis); 2 da (Sarah b 22 Aug 1972, Rebecca b 31 May 1969); m 2, 5 April 1986, Jennifer, da of Albert Cook; *Career* md Hartshorne Joyce Lloyd Lyons Ltd 1971–84, dir and dep chm Chetwynd Haddons Ltd 1984–89, chm Index Advertising Partnership Ltd 1989–90, vice chm Publicis Ltd 1990–93, chief exec The Lewes Consultancy Ltd 1993–; MIPA 1965; *Recreations* theatre, opera, horse racing, skiing; *Style*— Bruno Lloyd Lyons, Esq; ✉ The Lewes Consultancy Ltd, 29 Southover High Street, Lewes, East Sussex BN7 1HU (☎ 01273 477230, fax 01273 471120)

LLOYD MOSTYN, *see also:* Mostyn

LLOYD-MOSTYN, Dr Roger Hugh; s of Hugh Wynn Lloyd-Mostyn (d 1975), and Eileen Grace (decd); *b* 1 Dec 1941; *Educ* Lancing, Westminster Hosp Med Sch Univ of London; *m* 21 Jan 1967, Mary Frances, da of late Captain Edward Fothergill Elderton; 3 s (Christopher b 25 May 1968, James b 23 April 1970, David b 22 April 1981); *Career* house offr Westminster Hosp 1965–66, registrar King's Coll Hosp 1970–73, sr registrar Queen Elizabeth Hosp 1973–76, conslt physician Mansfield 1976–; fndr and chm of local orgn for cardio-pulmonary resuscitation trg; memb: BMA, Br Diabetic Assoc; FRCP 1983; *Recreations* swimming, gardening, music; *Style*— Dr Roger Lloyd-Mostyn; ✉ Kings Mill Hospital, Sutton-in-Ashfield, Notts (☎ 01623 22515)

LLOYD OF BERWICK, Baron (Life Peer UK 1993), of Ludlay in the County of East Sussex; Sir Anthony John Leslie Lloyd; kt (1978), PC (1984), DL (E Sussex 1983); s of Edward John Boydell Lloyd, of Little Bucksteep, Dallington, Sussex; *b* 9 May 1929; *Educ* Eton, Trinity Coll Cambridge; *m* 1960, Jane Helen Violet, da of C W Shelford, of Chailey Place, Lewes, Sussex; *Career* Nat Serv 1 Bn Coldstream Gds 1948; called to the Bar Inner Temple 1955, QC 1967, attorney-gen to HRH The Prince of Wales 1969–77, judge of the High Court of Justice (Queen's Bench Div) 1978–84, Lord Justice of Appeal 1984–93, Lord of Appeal in Ordinary 1993–; former memb Top Salaries Review Body; chm: Civil Serv Security Appeals Panel 1982–, Security Cmmn 1992–; pres Corporation of the Sons of the Clergy 1996–; memb Parole Bd 1983–84; chm Glyndebourne Arts Tst 1975–94, dir RAM 1979–; chm Chichester Diocesan Bd of Fin 1972–76; hon fell Peterhouse Cambridge 1981 (fell 1953); memb Ct of Assts Worshipful Co of Salters; *Clubs* Brooks's; *Style*— The Rt Hon Lord Lloyd of Berwick, PC, DL; ✉ Ludlay, Berwick, E Sussex (☎ 01323 870204); 68 Strand-on-the-Green, London W4 3PF (☎ 0171 994 7790)

LLOYD OF HIGHBURY, Baroness (Life Peer UK 1996), of Highbury in the London Borough of Islington; Dame June Kathleen Lloyd; DBE (1990); da of Arthur Cresswell Lloyd, MBE (d 1957), and Lucy Bevan, *née* Russell, BEM (d 1990); *b* 1 Jan 1928; *Educ* Royal Sch Bath, Univ of Bristol (MB ChB, MD), Univ of Durham (DPH); *Career* trg posts in medicine and paediatrics 1951–65 (Bristol, Oxford, Newcastle, Birmingham); Inst of Child Health London: sr lectr 1965–69, reader 1969–74, prof 1974–75; prof St George's Med Sch 1975–85; Nuffield prof of child health Univ of London 1985–92; scientific advsr Assoc of Medical Res Charities, chm Gene Therapy Advsy Ctee, past paediatric vice pres RCP; Hon DSc: Bristol 1991, Birmingham 1993; FRCP 1969, FRCPE 1990, FRCGP 1990; *Recreations* cooking, gardening; *Style*— The Rt Hon Lady Lloyd of Highbury, DBE; ✉ 37 Allingham Street, London N1 8NX

LLOYD PACK, Roger Anthony; s of Charles Lloyd Pack (d 1983), and Uli, *née* Pulay, of London; *b* 8 Feb 1944; *Educ* Bedales Sch, RADA; *partner* Jehane, da of David Markham; 1 da (Emily Lloyd b 29 Sept 1970), 3 s (Spencer b 4 Feb 1981, Hartley b 16 Nov 1984, Louis b 29 May 1988); *Career* actor; *Theatre* rep at Northampton, Coventry, Bromley, Leatherhead and season RSC; roles incl: Tartuffe in Tartuffe (Royal Exchange Manchester), Rocco in Snow Orchid (Gate Theatre), Etienne Plucheux in Flea in Her Ear (Old Vic), Kafka in Kafka's Dick (Royal Court), Waldemar in Deliberate Death of a Polish Priest (Almeida), Tim in Noises Off (Lyric, Savoy), Joey in The Homecoming (Garrick), Aston in the Caretaker (Shaw), Victor in One for the Road (Lyric); RNT: Chrysaldus in School for Wives, Juan in Yerma, Rosmer in Rosmersholm, The Garden of England, Osip Mandelstam in Futurists, Osip in Wild Honey, Will in Caritas; most recently incl: Fred in Party Time (Almeida), Oberon in A Midsummer Night's Dream (Haymarket Leicester), Albert Parker in When We Are Married (Savoy); *Television* incl: Newitt in Vicar of Dibley (ITV), Trigger in Only Fools and Horses (10 series, BBC), Phillips in Dandelion Dead (LWT), Fred in Party Time (Channel 4), Derek in Clothes in the Wardrobe (BBC), Quentin in Archer's Goon (6 episodes, BBC), Plitplov in The Gravy Train (2 series, Channel 4/Portman), David Irving in Selling Hitler (Euston Films), Mr Bean (Thames), Frankie in The Object of Beauty (BBC), Glendenning in The Contractor (BBC), Liz in The Naked Civil Servant (Thames), Sydney Bagley in Brassneck (BBC); *Films* incl: Fred in Young Poisoner's Handbook, piano teacher in Interview with a Vampire, Judge Haythorn in Princess Caraboo, Dr Butler in American Friends, Dr Pitman in Wilt, Geoff in The Cook, The Thief, His Wife & Her Lover 1984, Charles in The Go-Between, The Virgin Soldiers, Young Anthony Quinn in The Magus; *Awards* British Theatre Assoc Drama Awards Best Supporting Actor (for Wild Honey and One for the Road) 1984; *Recreations* tennis, chess, gardening, travelling, reading, music; *Clubs* Garrick, Soho House, Blacks; *Style*— Roger Lloyd Pack, Esq; ✉ c/o Kate Feast Management, 10 Primrose Hill Studios, Fitzroy Road, London NW1 8TR (☎ 0171 586 5502, fax 0171 586 9817)

LLOYD PARRY, Eryl; s of Capt Robert Parry (d 1974), of Caernarfon, and Megan, *née* Lloyd (d 1962); *b* 28 April 1939; *Educ* Caernarfon GS, St Peter's Coll Oxford (BA, Dip Public and Social Admin, MA); *m* 5 Aug 1967, Nancy Kathleen, da of Lt-Col Sir Richard Kenneth Denby (d 1986), of Ilkley; 3 s (Richard b 14 Jan 1969, Robert b 15 Dec 1970, Roland b 16 Jan 1979), 1 da (Helen b 16 May 1974); *Career* called to the Bar Lincoln's Inn 1966; in practice Northern Circuit 1966–92, pt/t chm Industl Tbnls 1977–92, vice pres Merseyside and Cheshire Rent Assessment Panel 1985–92, full-time chm Industl Tbnls (Manchester Region) 1992–; lay reader C of E; book reviewer for various pubns, one-act plays variously performed, poems variously published; memb: Amnesty Int, Prayer Book Soc; *Recreations* amateur dramatics, playwriting, cricket, reading; *Clubs* Liverpool Bar Cricket, Southport Dramatic, Sussex Playwrights, Sefton Theatre Company, Formby Theatre; *Style*— Eryl Lloyd Parry, Esq; ✉ Office of the Industrial Tribunals, 1 Union Court, Cook Street, Liverpool L2 4UJ (☎ 0151 236 9397)

LLOYD-ROBERTS, George Edward; s of George Charles Lloyd-Roberts (d 1986), of Cheyne Place, London, and Catherine Ann, *née* Wright; *b* 21 March 1948; *Educ* Gordonstoun, Univ of London (MSc); *m* 2 Aug 1969, Elizabeth Anne, da of Horace Edward Kenworthy, of Cork, Eire; 1 s (Henry b 1977), 1 da (Sophie b 1975); *Career* underwriter GE Lloyd-Roberts Syndicate 55 at Lloyd's, Lloyd's non-marine assoc 1986–92 (chm 1992), Lloyd's Solvency and Security 1987–89; Lloyd's Regulatory Bd 1993–96; *Recreations* running, riding, reading; *Style*— George Lloyd-Roberts, Esq; ✉ Lloyd's, Lime St, London (☎ 0171 623 7100)

LLOYD-ROBERTS, Dr Robert Edmund; TD (1972); o s of Richard Lloyd Roberts (d 1939), of Pinner, Middx, and Margaret Sarah Lloyd-Roberts, *née* Evans (d 1987); representative of a cadet branch of the ancient house of Nannau, N Wales, derived from the Princes of Powys; *b* 22 July 1925; *Educ* Merchant Taylors', St Thomas's Hosp (MB BS, MRCS, LRCP); *m* 2 July 1955, Elizabeth, yr da of Dr Mandale Byers (d 1923), of Mowhan House, Co Armagh, and St Anne's-on-Sea, Lancs (the Byers of Mowhan descend from the Byres of Coates, Scotland); 2 s (Richard b 1956, Meyrick b and d 1958), 2 da (Arabella b 1959, Sophia b 1963); *Career* Lt-Col RAMC TA (ret), DADMS 44 (Home Counties) Div TA 1962–67, CO 144 Field Ambulance RAMC(V) and SMO 44 Parachute Bde (V) 1969–73; hon treas Airborne Med Soc 1973–83; princ in gen med practice 1957–90; visiting med offr: Nunnery Fields Hosp 1957–90, Mount Hosp Canterbury 1985–89; med offr: Christ Church Coll 1962–90, St Edmund's Sch Canterbury 1986–90; local med advsr Med Advsy Serv Civil Serv Dept 1972–90, local chm War Pensions and Industl Injuries Med Bds DHSS; med examiner: insur cos, Br Red Cross Soc, etc; in attendance on HH Pope John Paul II at his visit to Canterbury Cathedral 29 May 1982; tstee Inst of Heraldic and Genealogical Studies; memb Br Geriatric Soc; former memb: Canterbury Police Advsy Ctee, Dist Gen Practitioners' Ctee; fndr: The Welsh Registry 1990, The Royal Third Dining Club 1990; FRSM; OStJ 1967; *Recreations* history, heraldry, genealogy, membership of various socs; *Clubs* Army and Navy, Kent and Canterbury (Canterbury); *Style*— Dr R E Lloyd-Roberts, TD; ✉ Plas Glanafon, Talybont, Merioneth, Gwynedd LL43 2AW; Longport House, 8 Longport, Canterbury, Kent CT1 1PE

LLOYD WEBBER, Sir Andrew; kt (1992); s of late William Southcombe Lloyd Webber, CBE, DMus, FRCM, FRCO, and late Jean Hermione, *née* Johnstone; *b* 22 March 1948; *Educ* Westminster, Magdalen Coll Oxford, RCM (FRCM 1988); *m* 1, 1971 (m dis 1983), Sarah Jane Tudor, *née* Hugill; 1 s, 1 da; m 2, 1984 (m dis 1990), Sarah Brightman; m 3, 1991, Madeleine Astrid; 2 s, 1 da; *Career* composer; columist Daily Telegraph; *Musicals* with lyrics by Timothy Rice: Joseph and the Amazing Technicolor Dreamcoat 1968 (revived 1973 and 1991), Jesus Christ Superstar 1970, Evita 1976 (stage version 1978); Jeeves (with lyrics by Alan Ayckbourn) 1975, Tell Me On Sunday (with lyrics by Don Black) 1980, Cats (based on poems by T S Eliot) 1981, Song and Dance (with lyrics by Don Black) 1982, Starlight Express (with lyrics by Richard Stilgoe) 1984, The Phantom of The Opera (lyrics by Richard Stilgoe and Charles Hart) 1986, Aspects of Love (with lyrics by Don Black and Charles Hart) 1989, Sunset Boulevard (with lyrics by Christopher Hampton and Don Black) 1993, By Jeeves (book and lyrics by Alan Ayckbourn) 1996, Whistle Down the Wind (premiere Washington DC, Dec 1996); prodr of many ventures incl: Cats 1981, Song and Dance 1982, Daisy Pulls It Off 1983, On Your Toes 1984, Starlight Express 1984, The Hired Man 1984, The Phantom of the Opera 1986, Lend me a Tenor 1988, Shirley Valentine 1989, Aspects of Love 1989, Joseph and the Amazing Technicolor Dreamcoat 1991, La Bête 1992, Sunset Boulevard 1993, By Jeeves 1996; *Film Scores* Gumshoe 1971, The Odessa File 1974; *Compositions* Variations 1978, Requiem Mass 1985, Amigos Para Siempre (Friends for Life) - official Olympic theme for 1992; *Awards* 6 Tony Awards, 4 Drama Desk Awards, 3 Grammy Awards, 5 Olivier Awards; numerous other awards incl: Triple Play Award ASCAP 1988, Praemium Imperiale Award 1995, Richard Rodgers Award 1996; cr a life peer 1997; *Publications* Evita (with Timothy Rice, 1978), Cats - the book of the Musical (1981), Joseph and the Amazing Technicolor Dreamcoat (with Timothy Rice, 1982), The Complete Phantom of the Opera (1987), The Complete Aspects of Love (1989), Sunset Boulevard - from movie to musical (1993); *Recreations* architecture, art; *Style*— Sir Andrew Lloyd Webber; ✉ c/o The Really Useful Group Limited, 22 Tower Street, London WC2H 9NS

LLOYD WEBBER, Julian; s of William Southcombe Lloyd Webber, CBE (d 1982), and Jean Hermione, *née* Johnstone (d 1993); bro of Andrew Lloyd Webber, *qv*; *b* 14 April 1951; *Educ* Westminster Under Sch, Univ Coll Sch, RCM, studied with Pierre Fournier (Geneva); *m* 1, 1974 (m dis 1989), Celia Mary, *née* Ballantyne; m 2, 1 July 1989, Zohra, *née* Mahmoud Ghazi; 1 s (David b 25 Feb 1992); *Career* cellist; UK debut Queen Elizabeth Hall London 1972, US debut Lincoln Centre NY 1980, debut with Berlin Philharmonic Orch 1984; has performed with all maj Br orchs and toured the USA, Canada, Germany, Holland, Africa, Bulgaria, Czechoslovakia, S America, Spain, Belgium, France, Scandinavia, Portugal and Australia; toured: Singapore and Japan 1986, Japan and Korea 1988, Singapore, Japan, Hong Kong, Taiwan 1990; first recordings of works by: Malcolm Arnold, Benjamin Britten, Frank Bridge, Gavin Bryars, Frederick Delius, Gustav Holst, Joaquin Rodrigo, Dmitri Shostakovich, Ralph Vaughan Williams; artistic dir Cellothon '88 South Bank Centre London, artistic dir Heart of England Music Festival 1994; winner Best British Classical Recording (for Elgar Cello Concerto) 1987; ARCM, FRCM 1994; *Books* incl: The Classical Cello (1980), The Romantic Cello (1981), The French Cello (1981), 6 pieces by Frank Bridge (1982), The Young Cellist's Repertoire Books 1, 2 & 3 (1984), Holst Invocation (1984), Vaughan Williams Fantasia on Sussex Folk Tunes (1984), Travels with My Cello (1984), Song of the Birds (1985), Recital Repertoire for Cellists (1986), Short Sharp Shocks (1990), The Great Cello Solos (1991), Cello Song (1993); *Recreations* countryside (especially British), reading horror stories; *Style*— Julian Lloyd Webber, Esq; ✉ IMG Artists Europe, Media House, 3 Burlington Lane, London W4 2TH (☎ 0181 233 5800, fax 0181 233 5801)

LLWYD, Elfyn; MP (Plaid Cymru) Merionnydd Nant Conwy (majority 4,613); s of late Huw Meirion Hughes, and Hefina Hughes; *b* 26 Sept 1951; *Educ* Llanrwst GS, Ysgol Dyffryn Conwy, UCW Aberystwyth, Coll of Law Chester; *m* 27 July 1974, Eleri, da of Huw and Jane Lloyd Edwards; 1 s, 1 da; *Career* admitted slr 1977, pres Gwynedd Law Soc 1990–91; MP (Plaid Cymru) Meirionnydd Nant Conwy 1992–; memb Parly Select Ctee on Welsh Affrs 1992–95, Parly whip (Plaid Cymru) 1995–; *Recreations* pigeon breeding, choral singing, rugby, fishing; *Style*— Elfyn Llwyd, Esq, MP; ✉ House of Commons, London SW1A 0AA (☎ 0171 219 5021/3555, fax 0171 219 2633)

LOACH, Kenneth Charles (Ken); s of John Loach (d 1973), of Nuneaton, and Vivien Nora, *née* Hamlin; *b* 17 June 1936; *Educ* King Edward VI Sch Nuneaton, St Peter's Coll Oxford (BA); *m* 17 July 1962, Lesley, da of William Leslie Ashton (d 1967); 3 s (Stephen b 1963, Nicholas b 1965, d 1971, James b 1969), 2 da (Hannah b 1967, Emma b 1972); *Career* film director; Golden Lion Award for Lifetime Achievement; Hon DLitt Univ of St Andrews; ACTT; *Films* incl: Up The Junction 1965, Cathy Come Home 1966, Poor Cow 1967, Kes 1969, Family Life 1971, Days of Hope 1975, The Price of Coal 1977, The Gamekeeper 1979, Black Jack 1979, Looks and Smiles 1981, Which Side Are You On? 1984, Fatherland 1986, The View from the Woodpile 1988, Hidden Agenda 1990, Riff-Raff 1991, Raining Stones 1993 (winner Jury Prize Cannes Film Festival 1993, winner Best Film Prize Evening Standard Film Awards 1994), Ladybird Ladybird 1994 (Best Actress Award for Crissy Rock, Critics' Award for Best Film Berlin Film Festival), Land and Freedom 1995, Felix (European Film of the Year Award 1995), Carla's Song 1996; *Recreations* watching football; *Style*— Ken Loach, Esq; ✉ c/o Judy Daish Associates, 2 St Charles Place, London W10 6EG (☎ 0181 964 8811, fax 0181 964 8966)

LOADER, Sir Leslie Thomas; kt (1987), CBE (1980); s of Edward Robert Loader (d 1963), of Southampton, and Ethel May, *née* Tiller (d 1966); *b* 27 April 1923; *Educ* Bitterne Park Sch, Bournemouth Coll, LSE; *m* 1, 27 April 1957, Jennifer Jane, *née* Pickering; 3 da (Melanie Susan (Mrs Loader-Pittams) b 18 Jan 1959, Katharine Lucy (Mrs Cledwyn) b 14 Oct 1961, Anna Victoria (Mrs Loader-Easton) b 10 Feb 1964); *Career* cmmnd Regt (now Royal Hampshire Regt), active serv Italy; company chm (ret); cncllr (C) Southampton City Cncl 1947–59, Parly candidate (C) Southampton Itchen 1955, memb Nat Union Exec Cons Pty 1969–76; chm: Southampton Young Cons 1947, Southampton Itchen Cons Assoc 1964–70, Southampton Cons Fedn 1966–70, Wessex Area Cons Pty 1972–75 (vice chm 1969–72), Ctee Southampton Cncl 1952 (proposed sale of cncl houses to tenants 1949), Swaythling Housing Soc 1975–83 (pres 1983–92), Wessex Body Scanner Appeal 1980–83; pres: Rotary Club of Bitterne and Woolston Housing Soc 1983– (fndr chm 1962–83), Eastleigh Cons Assoc; dir of charity Brendon Care Winchester 1979–83; former memb: Southampton and SW Hants Health Authy, Ct of Govrs Univ Coll Southampton and Univ of Southampton; memb Southampton Harbour Bd 1950–56, tstee Wessex Med Sch Tst 1983–86, hon life vice pres Wessex Area Cons Pty 1990; author of various articles on politics and housing; Freeman City of London, Liveryman Worshipful Co of Painter Stainers; *Clubs* Carlton; *Style*— Sir Leslie Loader, CBE

LOADES, Prof David Michael; s of Reginald Ernest Loades, and Gladys Mary, *née* Smith; *b* 19 Jan 1934; *Educ* Perse Sch Cambridge, Emmanuel Coll Cambridge (BA, MA, PhD, LittD); *m* 1, 18 Dec 1965 (m dis 1984), Ann Lomas, *née* Glover; m 2, 11 April 1987, Judith Anne, formerly Atkins; *Career* Nat Serv PO RAF 1953–55; lectr in political sci Univ of St Andrews 1961–63, reader Univ of Durham 1977–80 (lectr in history 1963–70, sr lectr 1970–77), prof of history Univ Coll N Wales 1980–96; FRHistS 1967, FSA 1984; *Books* Two Tudor Conspiracies (1965), The Oxford Martyrs (1970), Politics and the

Nation 1450–1660 (1974), The Reign of Mary Tudor (1979), The Tudor Court (1986), Mary Tudor - A Life (1989), Politics, Censorship and the English Reformation (1991), Revolution in Religion - The English Reformation 1530–1570 (1992), The Mid-Tudor Crisis 1545–1565 (1992), The Tudor Navy - An Administrative, Military and Political History (1992), Essays in European History 1953–1648 (1993), The Politics of Marriage; Henry VIII and his queens (1994), Essays on the Reign of Edward VI (1994), John Dudley; Duke of Northumberland (1996); *Recreations* scouting; *Style—* Prof David Loades, FSA; ✉ Four Seasons House, 102B Woodstock Road, Witney, Oxon OX8 6DY (☎ 01865 201615)

LOANE, (Simon Folliott) Warren Thomas Barton; DL (Co Fermanagh 1972); s of Simon Christopher Loane (d 1940), of Crocknacrieve, Enniskillen, NI, and Mildred Penelope Matilda, *née* Barton (d 1971); *b* 16 Aug 1920; *Educ* Portora Royal Sch; *m* 4 Aug 1955, (Heather Everina) Anne, da of Capt David Alexander Mackey (d 1986), of Crocknacrieve; 1 s (Charles b 14 Nov 1956), 1 da (Erica b 30 April 1959); *Career* farmer; dir and vice chm Ulster Wools 1970–93; dir: Ulster Wool Group 1981–, Ulster Wool and Farm Supplies 1981– (chm 1981–89); exec memb Ulster Farmers' Union 1945–76 (memb Cncl 1944–, fndr memb and former chm Fermanagh Branch), fndr memb N Fermanagh Gp Ctee 1951– (chm 1951–76); chm: Ulster Wool Growers 1980–92 (memb 1959–), NI Regnl Ctee Br Wool Mktg Bd 1987–93 (memb 1959–); memb Cncl Royal Ulster Agric Soc 1969–73, tstee Agric Res Inst for NI 1963–86, dir UK Wool Growers Fedn 1977–83, chm Mgmnt Ctee Irvinestown and Dist Attested Sales 1982–94 (memb 1959–94), memb Exec Ctee Ulster Agric Orgns Soc 1962–65; vice chm and fndn memb Western Educn and Library Bd 1973–85 and 1989–93, chm Library and Info Servs Cncl NI 1983–85 (memb 1980–85), memb Br Library Advsy Cncl 1984–85, memb Exec Ctee NI Assoc Educn and Library Bds 1984–85 and 1990–93; cncllr: Enniskillen RDC 1965–67, Fermanagh CC 1967–73 (chm Planning Ctee 1968–73, fndr memb and chm Museum Ctee 1969–73), Fermanagh DC 1985–93 (chm Planning Ctee); govr: Duke of Westminster HS 1975–, Enniskillen Collegiate Sch 1977–93 (vice chm 1983–90), Enniskillen HS 1981–93 (vice chm 1982–90); memb: Gen Synod Church of Ireland 1972–96 (memb Bd of Educn 1989–96), Exec Ctee Fermanagh Unionist Assoc 1981– (vice chm 1994–), Fermanagh and S Tyrone Unionist Cncl 1981– (exec memb 1985–), NI Rural Devpt Cncl 1991–95, Regnl Ctee Arts Cncl of NI 1991–93; dist cmmr of Scouts 1957–62, vice pres (later pres) Ballinamallard Young Unionists 1963–73; *Recreations* outdoor pursuits, genealogy, local history; *Style—* Warren Loane, Esq, DL; ✉ Crocknacrieve, Enniskillen, Co Fermanagh, Northern Ireland BT94 2EX (☎ 01365 388214)

LOBBENBERG, (John) Peter; s of Hans Lobbenberg (d 1955), and Annemarie, *née* Rabl (d 1971); *b* 12 Sept 1939; *Educ* Leighton Park Sch, Oriel Coll Oxford (MA); *m* 14 Dec 1969, Naomi, da of Ronald Green (d 1985); 1 s (David b 1971), 1 da (Anna b 1974); *Career* CA; sole practitioner, ptnr Clark Whitehill 1977–90, dir British Uralite plc 1984–88, chm Electronic Machine Co plc 1986–89; govr The Purcell Sch 1981–89; FAE; *Style—* Peter Lobbenberg, Esq; ✉ Peter Lobbenberg & Co, 74 Chancery Lane, London WC2A 1AA (☎ 0171 430 9300, fax 0171 430 9315)

LOCK, Barry David Stuart; s of John Albert Putnam Lock (d 1967), and Doris Nellie, *née* Amos (d 1975); *b* 28 July 1934; *Educ* Kings Sch Canterbury, Magdalen Coll Oxford (Mackinnon scholar, BCL, MA); *Career* admitted slr 1961; ptnr: Coward Chance 1964–87, Clifford Chance 1987–92; conslt Alsop Wilkinson (now Dibb Lupton Alsop) 1992–; City of London Slrs' Co prize, Travers Smith scholar, Clements Inn prize; *Recreations* music, the fine arts, collecting Chelsea-Derby porcelain; *Clubs* Athenaeum; *Style—* Barry Lock, Esq; ✉ 16 Morpeth Mansions, Morpeth Terrace, London SW1P 1ER (☎ 0171 233 5437); Dibb Lupton Alsop, 6 Dowgate Hill, London EC4R 2SS (☎ 0171 248 4141)

LOCK, (George) David; s of George Wilfred Lock (d 1943), and Phyllis Nita, *née* Hollingworth; *b* 24 Sept 1929; *Educ* Haileybury, Queens' Coll Cambridge (MA); *m* 1965, Ann Elizabeth, da of Sidney Harold Biggs; 4 s, 1 da; *Career* British Tabulating Co Ltd (now ICL) 1954–59, Save & Prosper Group Ltd 1959–69, American Express 1969–74, Private Patients Plan 1974–85 (md 1975–85); dir plan for active retirement Frizzell Insurance and Financial Services Ltd 1986–89; memb Bd of Mgmnt St Anthony's Hosp Cheam 1985–; dir: Home Concern for the Elderly 1985–96, Hosp Mgmnt Tst 1985–; sec Frizzell Fndn 1988–93; Freeman Worshipful Co of Barber Surgns; *Recreations* bridge, golf, music, entertaining, family activities; *Clubs* Piltdown Golf; *Style—* David Lock, Esq; ✉ Buckhurst Place, Horsted Keynes, W Sussex RH17 7AH (☎ 01825 790599)

LOCK, Prof David Peter; s of Arthur Lovering Lock, of Kent, and Kathleen Barbara, *née* Nash (d 1961); *b* 12 March 1948; *Educ* Sir Roger Manwood's GS, Nottingham Coll of Art and Design/Trent Poly (Dip Town and Country Planning); *m* 19 Sept 1970, Jeanette Anita, da of Frederick Charles Jones; 3 da; *Career* area planning offr Leicester City Cncl 1970–73 (asst branch sec Leicester City Branch NALGO 1971–73), planning aid offr Town & Country Planning Assoc 1973–78, planning mangr Milton Keynes Development Corporation 1978–81, assoc dir Conran Roche Ltd 1981–88, chm David Lock Associates Ltd 1988–, chief planning advsr DOE 1994–; memb Editorial Bd: Town & Country Planning Journal 1973–, Built Environment Quarterly 1975–, Urban Design Quarterly 1996–; chm: Milton Keynes Urban Studies Centre Ltd 1982–87, City Discovery Centre Ltd 1985–; visiting prof of town planning Univ of Central England in Birmingham 1988–; external examiner 1985–89: CNAA, Jt Centre for Urban Design, Oxford Poly; memb Cncl: RTPI 1975–80, Town & Country Planning Summer Sch 1974–79, Town & Country Planning Assoc 1978– (vice chm 1988–94); memb Urban Design Advsy Panel London Docklands Development Corporation 1990–94; memb: Town & Country Planning Assoc 1969, RTPI 1975, Land Use Soc 1980, Inst of Logistics 1993; FRSA 1993; *Publications* incl: Control and Urban Planning (contrib, 1973), Planning Aid (jtly, 1974), Environmental Impact Assessment (contrib, 1975), People and their Settlements (contrib, 1976), Growth and Change in the Future City Region (contrib, 1976), Why the Poor Pay More (jtly, 1977), Planning and the Future (contrib, 1977), New Towns in National Development (contrib, 1980), The Office of the Future (contrib, 1981), Property and Technology: the needs of Modern Industry (jtly, 1983), Riding the Tiger: Planning the South of England (1989), Alternative Development Patterns: New Settlements (jtly, 1993), On Track (contrib, 1994); *Recreations* history and geography, reading and research; *Style—* Prof David Lock; ✉ Department of the Environment, Room C13/03, 2 Marsham Street, London SW1P 3EB (☎ 0171 276 3502, fax 0171 276 6344); David Lock Associates Ltd, 50 North Thirteenth Street, Central Milton Keynes, Bucks MK9 3BP (☎ 01908 666276, fax 01908 605747)

LOCK, Lt Cdr Sir (John) Duncan; kt (1978); s of Brig-Gen F R E Lock, DSO; *b* 5 Feb 1918; *Educ* RNC Dartmouth; *m* 1947, (Alice) Aileen Smith (d 1982); 3 da; *Career* serv regular offr in RN 1931–58; WWII: Battle of the Atlantic, Norwegian and N African campaigns, Pacific War, Normandy and Anzio landings; farmed family estate in Somerset 1958–61; specialist in magnetic compasses Admty Compass Observatory 1961–83; cncllr: Eton RDC 1967–74, South Bucks Dist Cncl 1973– (chm 1985–87); chm: Bucks Branch RDC Assoc 1969–74, Bucks Branch Assoc of Dist Cncls 1974–91 (memb 1974–), Assoc of Dist Cncls of England and Wales 1974–79 (memb 1974–93); UK rep Cncl of Local and Regnl Authorities of Europe 1979–94, Local Authorities Mgmnt Servs and Computer Ctee 1981–86, chm Rep Body for England 1976–89; *Recreations* gardening, shooting; *Style—* Lt Cdr Sir Duncan Lock, RN; ✉ The Red Cottage, Ethorpe Close, Gerrards Cross, Bucks SL9 8PL (☎ 01753 882467)

LOCK, Dr Stephen Penford; CBE (1991); s of Wallace Henry Lock (d 1968), and Edith Mary Bailey (d 1991); *b* 8 April 1929; *Educ* City of London Sch, Queens' Coll Cambridge, St Bartholomew's Hosp (MA, MD, MSc); *m* 1955, Shirley Gillian, da of Edwin Walker; 1 s (decd), 1 da (Imogen); *Career* house physician St Bartholomew's Hosp and Central Middlesex Hosps, med offr RAF Command 1954–57, jr registrar London Hosp 1958, jr asst ed The Lancet 1959; registrar in pathology: Hosp for Sick Children Great Ormond St 1959–61, St Bartholomew's Hosp 1961–62; sr registrar in pathology Lewisham Hosp 1962–64, ed British Medical Journal 1975–91 (asst ed 1964–69, sr asst ed 1969–74, dep ed 1974–75), sr res assoc Royal Coll of Physicians 1991–92, res assoc Wellcome Inst of the History of Medicine 1992–; med corr BBC Overseas Service 1966–74; chm Int Gp on Medical Jl Style 1978; govr Brendoncare Fndn 1984–91; Offr Second Class White Rose of Finland; *Recreations* trying to learn Russian and the harpsichord; *Clubs* Royal Soc of Medicine; *Style—* Dr Stephen Lock, CBE; ✉ 3 Alde House, Alde House Lane, Aldeburgh, Suffolk IP15 5EE (☎ 01728 452411, fax 01728 454228); Wellcome Institute for the History of Medicine, 183 Euston Road, London NW1 2BE (☎ 0171 611 8888)

LOCK-NECREWS, John Ernest; JP (South Glamorgan); s of William Ernest Necrews (d 1982), and Mary Constance, *née* Lock (d 1987); *b* 30 Aug 1939; *Educ* Bridgend GS, Univ of Wales (DipArch); *m* 3 Jan 1978, Daphne, da of Maj Stanley Dickinson, of Cardiff; 1 s (Christian b 1979); *Career* chartered architect; md HLN Architects Ltd; architectural awards: Prince of Wales, Civic Tst, Times and RICS, Cardiff 2000, Lord Mayor's Civic; guest speaker on architectural conservation UNESCO World Congress Basle 1983; chm Central Branch Soc of Architects Wales 1981–82 (cncl memb 1974–82); ARIBA, ACIArb, FFB; *Recreations* golf, skiing, painting; *Clubs* Carlton, Cardiff and Co, Royal Porthcawl Golf, New (St Andrews); *Style—* John E Lock-Necrews, Esq, JP; ✉ Castle Edge, Llanblethian, Cowbridge, CF71 7JT; Westgate House, Womanby Street, Cardiff CF1 2UA (☎ 01222 798611)

LOCKE, Eur Ing (Harry) Brian; s of Henry William Locke (d 1982), of New Earswick, York, and Mary, *née* Moore (d 1972); *b* 28 May 1924; *Educ* Bootham Sch York, Imperial Coll London; *m* 1, 19 Feb 1949 (m dis 1974), Margaret Beven, da of Thomas William King (d 1962), of Barnet; 1 s (Richard b 28 March 1961), 3 da (Sarah (Mrs Watson) b 1 July 1952, Frances b 20 Jan 1954, Judith b 22 April 1958); m 2, 3 Jan 1976, Marie Patricia Jennings, *qv*; 1 step s (Michael b 18 July 1962); *Career* serv WWII as volunteer Friends Ambulance Unit 1942–46; Imperial Coll (City & Guilds Coll) 1946–48; chem engr Johnson Matthey Ltd Platinum Refinery 1948–49, mangr of plant labs Kestner Evaporator Ltd 1949–50, fuel engr and project mangr UK Oil-from-Coal Project Miny of Power 1950–58, Shape &c project mangr, LURGI study gp NCB 1958–65, mangr of industl chemistry and head of special projects and planning NRDC 1965–78, md Combustion Systems Ltd 1974–78, founder dir and now consulting engr Cadogan Consultants (int chartered consulting chemical engineers, energy management, process devpt, technol transfer, now the chemical engrg and energy arm of Rendel Palmer & Tritton) 1978–; dir: Formed Coke Ltd 1975–78, Electrolysis Energy Ltd 1979–83, Chem-Plant Stainless Ltd 1980–84, Locke Purandare Consultants (PVT) Ltd Bombay 1984–, Cadogan Management Ltd 1984–90 (chm 1984–88), Cadogan Services Ltd 1989–92; coal and energy specialist to UN Agencies, CEC, Br Cncl, ODA and other overseas bodies in places such as N Korea, Brazil, S Korea, India, Bulgaria, Alaska and China 1980–; business advsr Prince's Youth Business Tst 1994–; Melchett Award Design and Indust Assoc 1987, Special Award Inst of Energy 1987, Distinguished Serv Certificate BSI 1993; memb: Int Ctee Inst of Energy (chm Year Book Panel), Res and Technical Dirs Gp CBI, Low-Grade Coal Ctee World Energy Conf, CEBA Advsy Gp Royal Soc of Chemistry, Chemical Engrg and Fuel Technol Dept Liaison Ctee Univ of Sheffield, Tommorrow's Company Network RSA, Cncl The Black Sea Univ; fndr memb Cwlth Partnership on Technol Mgmnt Network (CPTM Ltd); hon advsr Int Soc for Educn Info Japan; founding hon sec Assoc for Design and Technol Educn; Old Centralians (now The City & Guilds Coll Assoc) The Imperial Coll Engrg Alumnus Assoc: hon sec 1981–90, pres 1991–92; Power Aid: founding hon treas 1990–96, memb Cncl 1990–; Freeman City of London 1984, Liveryman Worshipful Co of Engrs 1984; memb: The Club of Rome, Inst of Energy, Br Standards Instn (chm BS5845 Ctee thermal testing of boilers and fluid heaters), Assoc of Consltg Engrs, Br Nuclear Energy Soc, Inst of Materials, Br Assoc, Royal Instn, Inst of Advanced Motorists, Inst of Journalists, Acad of Experts; FIChemE 1948, FInstE 1953, FIGasE 1966, FInstD 1974, MConsE 1985, FCGI 1987, MAE 1988, FRSA 1990, fell World Acad of Art and Science 1993; *Books* Industrial Fuel Efficiency (annually 1957–85), Modern Motoring Handbook (annually 1959–82), Coal (jtly, 1965), Energy Users' Data Book (1985); several hundred professional papers, lectrs and reports incl: Thermal Processing of Biomass for Energy (UNIDO, 1990), Cleaner Use of Low-Grade Coal (UNIDO, 1991), UN - Changing Attitudes (1991), and other discussion papers of The British Association for The Club of Rome; *Recreations* Bentleys (memb Bentley Drivers' and Rolls-Royce Owners' (USA) Clubs), National Trust, silver, origins of thought, engineering history; *Clubs* Athenaeum (hon election sec), Royal Automobile (personal box 101), New Cavendish; *Style—* Eur Ing Brian Locke; ✉ Cadogan Consultants, Cadogan Grange, Bisley, Glos GL6 7AT (☎ 01452 770010, fax 01452 770058); Cadogan Consultants, 42 Kelvingrove Street, Glasgow G3 7RZ (☎ 0141 332 4153, fax 0141 331 1285)

LOCKE, John Christopher; s of Cdr Cyril Frederick Locke RN, of Aldwick, and Marjorie Alice Batt, *née* Collins; *b* 4 March 1947; *Educ* Pangbourne Coll, Regent Street Poly, Brixton Sch of Building, Northern Poly; *m* 1, 9 Aug 1969, (m dis 1989) Jacqueline Mercer, *née* Pamment; 2 s (Toby Jerome b 19 July 1971, Matthew Spencer b 9 Jan 1973); m 2, 15 Sept 1990, Maria Patricia, *née* Rogers; *Career* Prudential Assurance Co Ltd: trainee 1964–71, chartered surveyor 1971–80, regnl surveyor 1981–86 (S England 1981–84, Agency 1984–85, Property Mgmnt 1985–86), dir Estate Mgmnt UK 1987–88, div dir Estate Mgmnt Prudential Portfolio Mgrs Ltd 1989–91; chm Briggait Co Ltd 1987–90, dir City Aviation Insurance Tenancies 1989–90, dir Southbank Technopark Ltd 1985–91, (chm 1989–90), surveyor to Watling Street Properties 1989–90, chief exec NHS Estates 1991–; FRICS 1984 (ARICS 1971), Hon FIHospE 1992; *Recreations* opera, theatre, music, the arts, travel; *Style—* John Locke, Esq; ✉ NHS Estates, 1 Trevelyan Square, Boar Lane, Leeds, W Yorks LS1 6AE (☎ 0113 254 7000, fax 0113 2 547 299)

LOCKE, John Howard; CB (1984); s of Percy John Howard Locke, and Josephine Alice, *née* Marshfield; *b* 26 Dec 1923; *Educ* Hymers Coll Hull, Queen's Coll Oxford (MA); *m* 1948, Eirene Sylvia Sykes; 2 da (Diana, Imogen); *Career* MAFF 1945–65; under sec: Cabinet Office 1965–66, Miny of Tport 1966–68, Dept of Employment and Productivity 1968–71; dep sec Dept of Employment 1971–74, dir Health and Safety Exec 1975–83; chm Nat Examination Bd in Occupational Safety and Health 1986–92; *Recreations* hill walking, gardening, opera; *Style—* John Locke, Esq, CB; ✉ Old Box Trees, East Preston, Sussex BN16 1JP (☎ 01903 785 154)

LOCKE, Stephen; *b* 7 July 1944; *Educ* Bristol Cathedral Sch, Univ of Leicester (BSc), Univ of Oxford; *Career* natural history asst Curtis Museum Alton and Willis Museum Basingstoke 1966–68, dep dir Museum & Art Gallery Newport Gwent 1968–72, dir of Museums & Art Gallery and leisure offr Exeter City Cncl 1972–81, dir Area Museum Cncl for the SW 1981–88, dir Hampshire CC Museums Serv 1988–; Museums Assoc: dip 1972, memb Cncl and chm Educn Ctee 1979–82 and 1988–, princ examiner Museums dip 1979–81, FMA 1980, pres 1994–96; sec: S Western Fedn of Museums 1973–81, Exeter Festival 1975–81; memb: Cncl Devon Tst for Nature Conservation (and ed) 1979–82, Ctee of Area Museum Cncls 1981–88, Dartmoor Nat Park Ctee 1982–85, Duchy of Cornwall Wildlife and Landscape Advsy Gp 1983–90, Nat Tst Regnl Ctee for Devon and Cornwall 1985–88, Museums and Galleries Working Party on Professional Museum

Trg and Career Structure 1986–87, Somerset Arts Forum 1986–88, Bd Museum Trg Inst 1991–94, Nat Tst Southern Regnl Ctee 1991–; convenor Hampshire Museums Forum 1991–; external examiner Museum Studies Dept Univ of Leicester 1986–90; pres Hampshire Field Club and Archaeological Soc 1992–95; *Recreations* cultivating carnivorous plants, reading, gardening, walking, country pottery; *Style*— Stephen Locke, Esq; ✉ Hampshire County Council Museums Service, Chilcomb House, Chilcomb Lane, Winchester, Hants SO23 8RD (☎ 01962 846304, fax 01962 869836)

LOCKET, David Frank; s of late Frank Barton Locket, and Phyllis Jesie, *née* Lawson; *b* 29 June 1940; *Educ* Haileybury and ISC Hertford, Battersea Coll of Technol; *m* 1966, (Ingegerd) Christina, da of Ake Bontell, of Sweden; 1 s (Martin Frank b 1970), 1 da (Annicka Louise b 1972); *Career* Savoy Hotel (Strand Hotels) London 1972–78, catering mangr Anchor Hotels London 1978–83, md LMS (Consultants) Ltd 1983–; conslt Bowring Leisure Ltd; clerk Master Innholders Ltd; Freeman City of London 1973; FHCIMA; *Recreations* veteran cars, fishing, shooting, clocks; *Clubs* Veteran Car Club of GB (memb Ctee); *Style*— David F Locket, Esq; ✉ Pinecrest, Northdown Road, Woldingham, Surrey CR3 7AA (☎ 01883 653181)

LOCKETT, His Hon Judge Reginald; s of George Alfred Lockett, and Emma, *née* Singleton; *b* 24 June 1933; *Educ* Ashton-in-Makerfield GS, Univ of Manchester, Univ of London; *m* 1959, Edna, *née* Lowe; 1 s, 1 da; *Career* admitted slr 1955, asst coroner Wigan 1963–70, registrar Dist and Co Ct Manchester 1970–81, recorder Crown Ct 1978–81, circuit judge (Northern Circuit) 1981–; hon recorder of Preston 1996–; vice pres Boys Bde 1978– (dist pres NW 1973–90), lay reader C of E, co ed Butterworths Family Law Servs 1982–90, memb Co Ct Rule Ctee 1985–90; *Style*— His Hon Judge Lockett; ✉ The Law Courts, Openshaw Place, Ringway, Preston PR1 2LL

LOCKHART, *see also:* Sinclair-Lockhart

LOCKHART, Sheriff Brian Alexander; s of John Arthur Hay Lockhart, and Norah, *née* Macneil, of Quadrant Rd, Glasgow; *b* 1 Oct 1942; *Educ* Glasgow Acad, Glasgow Univ (BL); *m* 1967, Christine Ross, da of James B Clark, of Ayr; 2 s, 2 da; *Career* slr; ptnr Robertson Chalmers & Auld 1964–79; Sheriff: N Strathclyde 1979–81, Glasgow and Strathkelvin 1981–; *Recreations* fishing, golf, squash, family; *Clubs* Royal Scottish Automobile; *Style*— Sheriff Brian Lockhart; ✉ 18 Hamilton Ave, Glasgow (☎ 0141 427 1921); Sheriff Court, Glasgow (☎ 0141 429 8888)

LOCKHART, His Hon Judge Frank Roper; s of Clement Lockhart (d 1985), of Braithwell, Yorks, and Betsy, *née* Roper (d 1981); *b* 8 Dec 1931; *Educ* King Edward VI GS Retford, Doncaster GS, Univ of Leeds (LLB); *m* 5 Aug 1957, Brenda Harriett, da of Cyril Johnson (d 1985), of Woodlands, nr Doncaster; 1 s (John Michael Roper b 1961), 1 da (Jeanette Anne b 1959); *Career* slr; ptnr Jefferies Slrs 1965–88; chm: Social Security Tbnls 1970–88, Industl Tbnls 1983; recorder 1985–88, circuit judge (SE Circuit) 1988–; *Recreations* golf, squash; *Style*— His Hon Judge Frank R Lockhart; ✉ c/o South Eastern Circuit Office, New Cavendish House, 18 Maltravers Street, London WC2R 3EU (☎ 0171 936 7235)

LOCKHART, Geoffrey John Charles; s of George Arthur Lockhart (d 1961), of Christchurch, Hants, and Margaret Helen, *née* Sutton (d 1982); *b* 16 April 1926; *Educ* Truro Cathedral Sch; *m* 19 Feb 1960, Dodie Mary, da of John Walter Cooper (d 1958), of Brighton; 2 da (Juliet Caroline b 1963, Joanna Helen b 1964); *Career* CA; dir of several local cos; sr ptnr: Bland Fielden 1982–90, Scrutton Bland 1990–91 (ptnr 1965); memb Cncl ICAEW 1977–89, pres Assoc of Accounting Technicians 1985–86 (memb Cncl 1980–89); chm of govrs St Mary's Sch Colchester 1970–92, govr Colchester Inst 1989–; non-exec dir Essex Ambulance Serv 1990–95, pt/t memb VAT Tbnls 1991–, memb Essex North Valuation Tbnl 1992–96, cmmr of Inland Revenue 1993–; FCA; *Recreations* cricket, golf, gardening, reading, sport generally; *Clubs* MCC; *Style*— Geoffrey Lockhart, Esq; ✉ Chandlers, Nayland, Colchester, Essex CO6 4LA (☎ 01206 262617)

LOCKHART, Ian Stuart; s of Rev Prebendary Douglas Stuart Mullinger Lockhart (d 1983), and Hilda Mary, *née* Walker; *b* 9 Nov 1940; *Educ* Rugby, Clare Coll Cambridge (MA); *m* 30 Nov 1974, Rosanna, da of Capt Edward Hugh Cartwright, RN; *Career* admitted slr 1967; ptnr: Peake & Co 1969–89, Charles Russell 1989–; dir Wynnstay Properties plc and assoc cos 1972–; govr St Mary's Sch Wantage 1972–; memb Ctee St Marylebone Almshouses 1990–, tstee Historic Churches Preservation Tst 1993–; memb Ct of Assts Corp of The Sons of The Clergy 1972–, Liveryman Worshipful Co of Tylers & Bricklayers 1974; *Clubs* Athenaeum; *Style*— Ian S Lockhart, Esq; ✉ 9 Marlborough Hill, London NW8 0NN; c/o Charles Russell, 8/10 New Fetter Lane, London EC4A 1RS (☎ 0171 203 5000, fax 0171 203 0200)

LOCKHART-BALL, Hugh Frederick; s of Lt Cdr Alfred Ernest Ball, RN (d 1965), and Margaret Daphne, *née* Lockhart (d 1993); *b* 18 April 1948; *Educ* Sedbergh, Birmingham Sch of Architecture; *m* 1 April 1972 (m dis), Godelieve Antoinette; 1 s (Simon Hugh b 1976), 1 da (Amelia b 1979); *Career* architect; princ Lockhart-Ball Associates 1981–, vice-chm London Energy & Environment Group 1995– (chm 1983–95); offr UK Section of Int Solar Energy Soc 1984–95, memb Cncl S London Soc of Architects 1979–; former pres Rotary Club of Tooting 1986; *Recreations* conserving energy, sketching, reading, photography, building, jazz and blues, wine and food; *Style*— Hugh Lockhart-Ball, Esq; ✉ 934 Garratt Lane, London SW17 0ND (☎ 0181 767 6955, office 0181 672 1056, fax/modem 0181 767 9401, e-mail 100067.452@COMPUSERVE.COM)

LOCKHART-MUMMERY, Christopher John; QC (1986); s of Sir Hugh Evelyn Lockhart-Mummery, KCVO (d 1988), of Basingstoke, Hants, and Elizabeth Jean, *née* Crerar (d 1981); *b* 7 Aug 1947; *Educ* Stowe, Trinity Coll Cambridge; *m* 1, 4 Sept 1971 (m dis 1992), Hon Elizabeth Rosamund, da of Neil Patrick Moncrieff Elles, and Baroness Elles (Life Peer), of London; 1 s (Edward b 1975), 2 da (Clare b 1973, Alice b 1980); m 2, 4 Feb 1993, Mrs Mary-Lou Putley; *Career* called to the Bar Inner Temple 1971, bencher 1991, recorder of the Crown Ct 1994–, dep High Ct judge 1995–; currently head of chambers; *Books* specialist ed: Hill and Redman's Law of Landlord and Tenant (1973); *Recreations* fishing, gardening, opera; *Style*— Christopher J Lockhart-Mummery, Esq, QC; ✉ 78 Lansdowne Rd, London, W11 2LS (☎ 0171 221 8628); 4 Bream's Buildings, London EC4A 1AQ (☎ 0171 353 5835, fax 0171 430 1667)

LOCKHART OF THE LEE, Angus Hew; recognised as Chief of the Name Lockhart by The Lord Lyon 1957; s of late Maj Simon Foster Macdonald Lockhart of the Lee, and Ella Catriona Gordon; *b* 17 Aug 1946; *Educ* Rannoch Sch Perthshire, N of Scotland Coll of Agric; *m* 1970, Susan Elizabeth, da of Hon William Normand (d 1967), s of Baron Normand (Life Peer, d 1962), and Hon Mrs William Normand; 1 s, 1 da; *Career* landowner and land manager; memb: Standing Cncl of Scottish Chiefs, S W Ctee Scottish Landowners' Fedn; *Recreations* shooting, skiing; *Clubs* New (Edinburgh); *Style*— Angus Lockhart of the Lee; ✉ Newholm, Dunsyre, Lanark ML11 8NQ (☎ 01968 682254); Lee and Carnwath Estates, Estate Office, Carnwath, Lanark (☎ 01555 840273, fax 01555 840044)

LOCKLEY, Andrew John Harold; s of (Archdeacon) Dr Harold Lockley, of Quorn, Leicestershire, and Ursula Margarete, *née* Wedell (d 1990); *b* 10 May 1951; *Educ* Marlborough, Oriel Coll Oxford (Nolloth scholar, BA, MA); *m* 14 Sept 1974, Ruth Mary, da of (Laurence) John Vigor, of Bath, Avon; 2 s (Thomas Andrew b 1978, Philip Jonathan b 1981), 1 da (Naomi Jane Ursula b 1987); *Career* research scholar World Cncl of Churches 1973–75, articled clerk Messrs Kingsley Napley & Co London 1975–78; slr: Messrs Young & Solon London 1979–80, Messrs Meaby & Co London 1980–82; The Law Soc: sec Contentious Business Dept 1985–87 (asst sec 1982–85), dir of legal practice 1987–95, dir of corp and regional affrs 1995–96; head of professional servs Irwin Mitchell 1996–, conslt Dept of Law Univ of Sheffield 1996–, pt/t chm Special Educnl Needs Tribunal 1996–; memb: Cmmn of Efficiency in Criminal Courts 1986–94, CITCOM Advsy Ctee 1988–90, Information Technol and the Cts Ctee 1990–95; dir Solicitors Financial Services Ltd 1988–92; govr William Austin Sch Luton 1992–96; memb Law Soc 1979; *Books* Christian Communes (1976), The Pursuit of Quality - a guide for lawyers (ed, 1993); *Recreations* growing fruit and vegetables, swimming, travel, cooking, reading; *Style*— Andrew Lockley, Esq; ✉ Irwin Mitchell, St Peter's House, Hartshead, Sheffield S1 2EL (☎ 0114 276 7777, fax 0114 275 3306)

LOCKWOOD, Baroness (Life Peer UK 1978), of Dewsbury, Co W Yorkshire; Betty; DL (W Yorks); da of late Arthur Lockwood; *b* 22 Jan 1924; *Educ* Eastborough Girls' Sch Dewsbury, Ruskin Coll Oxford; *m* 1978, Lt-Col Cedric Hall (d 1988), s of late George Hall; *Career* sits as Lab Peer in House of Lords, memb Cncl of Europe and WEU 1992–94; Yorks regnl women's offr Lab Pty 1952–67, chief woman offr and asst nat agent Lab Pty 1967–75, chm Equal Opportunities Cmmn 1975–83, chm EEC Advsy Ctee on Equal Opportunities for Women and Men 1982–83; pres Birkbeck Coll Univ of London 1983–89; memb: Advtg Standards Authy Cncl 1983–92, Leeds Devpt Corp 1988–95; memb cncl: Univ of Bradford 1983– (pro-chllr 1988–, chm of cncl 1992–), Univ of Leeds 1985–91; chm Nat Coal Mining Museum for England 1995–; hon fell: UMIST (vice pres 1992–95), Birbeck Coll; Hon DLitt Univ of Bradford, Hon LLD Univ of Strathclyde 1985; *Clubs* Soroptimist Int; *Style*— The Rt Hon the Lady Lockwood, DL; ✉ 6 Sycamore Drive, Addingham, Ilkley, W Yorks LS29 0NY (☎ 01943 831098)

LOCKWOOD, David Stuart; s of Capt Ronald Arthur Lockwood, of Christchurch, Dorset, and Rachael, *née* Bamforth; *b* 15 May 1945; *Educ* Guthlaxton GS Leicester, Cambridge Sch of Art, Sch of Architecture Leicester, RIBA (DipArch); *m* 1, (m dis 1974); m 2, 25 May 1978, Marion Janice, da of Walter Glen Page (d 1974), of Sydney, Aust; *Career* Jr Leaders Regt RE 1960–63, RE 1963–66; architect; John Whisson and Ptnrs Newmarket 1966–67, Heaton and Swales Bury St Edmunds 1967–70, Gordon White and Hood Leicester 1973–74, Ivan P Jarvis and Assoc Leicester 1974–76; Cecil Denny Highton and Ptnrs London 1976–: assoc 1979, equity ptnr 1983, gp ptnr 1990, dir 1995; sr vice pres and dir of commercial architecture Hellmuth, Obata & Kassabaum Inc 1995–; RIBA, memb ARCUK 1974, assoc memb AIA 1994; *Recreations* sailing, skiing, architecture, ballet, cycling, squash; *Clubs* RAC, Christchurch Sailing; *Style*— David Lockwood, Esq; ✉ 4 Crown Reach, 145 Grosvenor Road, London SW1V 3JU (☎ 0171 976 6242); 23 Priory Quay, Quay Road, Christchurch, Dorset BH23 1DR (☎ 01202 481149); Cecil Denny Highton, Chartered Architects, Axtell House, 23/24 Warwick St, London W1R 6DH (☎ 0171 734 6831, fax 0171 734 0508); Hellmuth, Obata & Kassabaum Inc, Kent House, 14–17 Market Place, London W1N 7AJ (☎ 0171 634 2004, fax 0171 634 1987, e-mail DavidLockwood@HOK.COM)

LOCKWOOD, John William; s of Arthur William Lockwood, of Spridlington, nr Lincoln, and Heather, *née* Rogerson; *b* 24 Aug 1954; *Educ* Uppingham, UMIST (BSc); *m* 28 May 1982, Judith Ann, da of Patrick Henry Dickinson, of Gainsborough, Lincs; 2 s (George William b 5 March 1985, James Patrick Alexander b 21 Jan 1991), 1 da (Sarah Helen May b 2 Aug 1987); *Career* co dir: Castle Hill Holdings Ltd, Castle Square Developments Ltd, Castle Hill Developments Ltd, Lockwood Estates Ltd, Branston Potatoes Ltd; MFH Burton Hunt 1981–; *Recreations* hunting; *Style*— John Lockwood, Esq; ✉ Cammeringham Manor, Cammeringham, Nr Lincoln LN1 2SJ (☎ 01522 730342); Castle Hill Holdings Ltd, Scampton House, Scampton, Lincoln LN1 2SF (☎ 01522 730730, fax 01522 731777, car 0374 243783)

LOCKWOOD, Prof (Antony) Peter Murray; s of Sir John Francis Lockwood (d 1965), and Marjorie, *née* Clitheroe (d 1993); *b* 12 March 1931; *Educ* St Paul's, Trinity Coll Cambridge (BA, MA, PhD); *m* 24 Aug 1957, Kathleen May, da of Robert Marshall (d 1989); 2 s (David b 1960, Roger b 1964), 1 da (Christine (Mrs Leigh-Jones) b 1958); *Career* Nat Serv 1950–51; cmmnd RA 1950, served 42 LAA Regt; asst lectr Dept of Zoology Univ of Edinburgh 1957–59, res fell Trinity Coll Cambridge 1959–62, prof of marine biology Univ of Southampton 1980–96 (lectr 1962–68, sr lectr 1968–72, reader 1972–80, prof emeritus 1996–); hon zoological sec Soc for Experimental Biology 1969–73, chm Biological Cncl 1982–87 (hon sec 1976–80); memb: Bd Co of Biologists 1977–93, Aquatic Life Scis Grants Ctee NERC 1978–80, Advsy Ctee on Int Oceanographic Affrs NERC 1980–87, Cncl of Europe Evaluation Sub-Ctee on Programme for Postgrad Trg 1984–93; del to fourth ad hoc meeting on Trg Educn and Mutual Assistance UNESCO Cairo 1976 and Buenos Aires 1980, memb UNESCO interdisciplinary mission to Bahrain on AGU project 1983; FIBiol; *Books* Animal Body Fluids and Their Regulation (1963), Aspects of the Physiology of Crustacea (1968), The Membranes of Animal Cells (1971), The Physiology of Diving in Man and other Animals (with H V Hempleman, 1978); *Style*— Prof Peter Lockwood; ✉ 24 Merdon Avenue, Chandlers Ford, Hants SO53 1EJ (☎ 01703 254268); Department of Oceanography, SOC, University of Southampton, Southampton SO14 3ZH (☎ 01703 593640, fax 01703 593059)

LOCKYER, Bob; *b* 9 April 1942; *Career* dir and exec prodr of dance progs for BBC TV; worked with choreographers incl: Sir Frederick Ashton, Sir Kenneth MacMillan, Sir Peter Wright, Birgit Culberg; chair Dance UK 1982–92; dir dance video courses in: Australia 1990, NZ 1990 and 1993, Canada 1992, 1994 and 1996, various in UK; winner Royal Philharmonic Soc Award 1993; *Director* with Robert Cohan and London Contemporary Dance Co: Stabat Mater 1979, Forest 1980, Cell 1983, Nymphaes 1983; with Rambert Dance Co: Pulcinella 1988, Soldat 1989; others incl: Les Noces (Royal Ballet) 1978, Dance Masterclasses with Sir Frederick Ashton and Sir Peter Wright (both 1987); *Executive producer* numerous ballet relays incl: Sleeping Beauty (Royal Ballet) 1994, Mayerling (Royal Ballet) 1995; also exec prodr: Points in Space (BBC cmmn, winner Dir's dip Prague Int TV Festival) 1988, Strange Fish (DV8, winner Grand Prix at Prix Italia) 1994, Outside In (Grand Prix Prague Int TV Festival) 1995, *Writer* various ballet scenarios incl Corporal Jan (choreographed and directed by Peter Wright); *Recreations* walking, collecting and cooking; *Style*— Bob Lockyer, Esq; ✉ Studio Five, St Albans Studios, South End Row, St Albans Grove, London W8 5BT (☎ 0171 937 1230)

LODER, Edmund Jeune; s and h of Sir Giles Rolls Loder, 3 Bt, *qv*; *b* 26 June 1941; *Educ* Eton; *m* 1, 1966 (m dis 1971), Penelope Jane, da of Ivo Forde; 1 da (Gillian Marie (Mrs James D P Morgan) b 1968); m 2, 1992, Susan Warren, da of V W Warren Pearl, of Lindfield, Sussex; *Career* FCA; bloodstock breeder; *Style*— Edmund Loder, Esq; ✉ Eyrefield Lodge, The Curragh, Co Kildare

LODER, Sir Giles Rolls; 3 Bt (UK 1887), of Whittlebury, Northamptonshire, and of Leonardslee, Horsham, Sussex, JP (Sussex), DL (W Sussex 1977); s of Capt Robert Egerton Loder (ka 1917); suc gf, Sir Edmund Giles Loder, 2 Bt, 1920; *b* 1914; *Educ* Eton, Trinity Coll Cambridge (MA); *m* 1939, Marie Violet Pamela (OStJ), only da of Capt Bertram Hanmer Bunbury Symons-Jeune (d 1963); 2 s (Edmund Jeune b 1941, Robert Reginald b 1943); *Heir* s, Edmund Jeune Loder b 26 June 1941; *Career* serv 98 Surrey and Sussex Yeo Field Bde RA, 2 Lt 1935, Lt 1938; memb Horsham RDC 1947–68 (chm 1963–68), High Sheriff of Sussex 1948–49; vice pres Royal Horticulture Soc (VMH); *Recreations* horticulture, yachting; *Clubs* Royal Yacht Squadron (Cowes); *Style*— Sir Giles Loder, Bt, JP, DL; ✉ Ockenden House, Cuckfield, Haywards Heath, Sussex RH17 5LD

LODER, Hon Robert Beauclerk; CBE (1989); s of 2 Baron Wakehurst, KG; *b* 24 April 1934; *Educ* Eton, Trinity Coll Cambridge (BA); *m* 1973, Josette, da of Joseph Bromovsky, of Otmanach, Pischeldorf, Karnten, Austria; 2 s (Jan, Nicolai), 1 da (Nell); *Career* farmer

1966–; dir: Transcontinental Servs Gp NV 1970–86 (formerly Esperanza Ltd), Precious Metals Tst 1981–91; chm: Sheringham Hldgs Ltd 1982–95, Mental Health Fndn 1982–93; *Clubs* Beefsteak; *Style*— The Hon Robert Loder, CBE; ✉ 14 Ladbroke Grove, London W11 3BQ; Gas Works Studios, 155 Vauxhall Street, London Se11 5RH

LODER, Hon Timothy Walter; s and h of 3 Baron Wakehurst, *qv*, and Ingeborg Krumbholz-Hess (d 1977); *b* 28 March 1958; *Educ* Millfield; *m* 1987, Susan Elaine Hurst; *Style*— The Hon Timothy Loder; ✉ 26 Wakehurst Rd, London SW11 6BY

LODER-SYMONDS, Roderick Francis (Roddy); s of Brig Robert Guy Loder-Symonds, DSO, MC (ka 1945), of Three Chimneys, Heytesbury, Warminster, Wilts, and Mrs Merlin Audrey Houghton Brown, *née* Allen (d 1988); *b* 16 Nov 1938; *Educ* Radley, RAC Cirencester; *m* 20 July 1967, Caroline Anne, da of Cdr M F L Beebee (d 1988), of Womaston House, Presteigne, Radnorshire; 2 s (Robert b 31 Aug 1971, James b 28 May 1974), 1 da (Sacha b 19 Nov 1968); *Career* farmer Wellshead Farm Exford Somerset 1960–67, farmer Denne Mill Farm Womenswold Kent 1970–, asst surveyor Knight Frank and Rutley 1962–72, ptnr Strutt & Parker 1976– (joined 1973); churchwarden Womenswold Church 1970–82; chm: Farmers' Club 1976 (tstee 1994–), Parish Cncl 1978–86, Canterbury Farmers' Club 1982, Kent Branch CLA 1986–87; Bd memb Enteprise Agency E Kent 1985–; Liveryman Worshipful Co of Farmers; FRICS 1976; *Recreations* shooting and hunting; *Clubs* Farmers', Army and Navy; *Style*— Roddy Loder-Symonds, Esq; ✉ Denne Hill Farm, Womenswold, Canterbury, Kent CT4 6HD (☎ 01227 831203); Strutt & Parker, 2 St Margaret's St, Canterbury, Kent CT1 2TP (☎ 01227 451123, fax 01227 762509); 13 Hill St, London W14 8DL (☎ 0171 627 7282)

LÖDERER, Karl; s of Karl Löderer, of Austria, and Franziska, *née* Reschreiter; *b* 16 March 1939; *Educ* Realgymnasium Baden bei Wien, Hotelfachschule Lower Austria; *m* June 1966, Margaret; 1 s (James b 3 March 1967), 1 da (Franziska Maria b 19 Aug 1969); *Career* chef; apprentice 1952–55 (Hotel de France Schottenring Vienna, Restaurant Kerzenstuberl, Hotel Europa Karntnerstr, Drei Husaren Franziskanerplatz), chef de parti Hotel de France Sark Channel Islands 1957, chef de cuisine 1958–59 (La Sablonnerie Lyons France, Restaurant Mereguy, Restaurant Andron, Restaurant St Nectaire Manoir des Viginets Cap d'Antibes), chef and ptnr La Frégate St Peter Port Guernsey 1960–66, chef de cuisine Gravetye Manor E Grinstead 1966–78, chef and proprietor Manley's Storrington 1978– (awarded Michelin Star and also 4 rosettes from AA); awarded one of first Michelin Rosettes in UK at Gravetye Manor, top awards in all major food and hotel guides during time at Gravetye and presently at Manley's, orgn memb Master Chefs of GB; memb of Steering Committee of Master Chefs of GB 1984; *Recreations* opera-going, gardening, theatre; *Style*— Karl Löderer, Esq; ✉ Manley's, Manleys Hill, Storrington, West Sussex RH20 4BT (☎ 01903 742331)

LODGE, Anton James Corduff; QC (1989); *Educ* Univ of Cambridge (MA); *Career* called to the Bar Gray's Inn 1966, recorder; *Style*— Anton Lodge, Esq, QC; ✉ Park Court Chambers, 40 Park Cross Street, Leeds LS1 2QH

LODGE, Dr Brian Robert William; s of Bertram Hugh Cleverly Lodge (d 1967), of 10 the Vale, Golders Green, London, and Gwendolin Olive Theodosia, *née* Burford (d 1963); *b* 15 May 1925; *Educ* Univ Coll Sch Hampstead, London Hosp Med Sch (MRCS, LRCP); *m* 1, 15 Dec 1954, Kathleen Edith Peggy (d 1987), da of Ernest Herbert Fox (d 1951), of Bunwell, Norfolk; m 2, 16 Feb 1991, Lynn Mary, da of Leslie Keith Brown, of Burbage, Hinckley, Leics; 1 da (Rachel Elizabeth Margaret b 1991); *Career* temp conslt physician in geriatric med Utd Oxford Hosps and Oxford Regnl Hosp Bd 1965–71, conslt physician in geriatric and psychogeriatric med Leics Dist Health Authy 1971–92 (psychogeriatrician emeritus 1992), assoc lectr Univ of Surrey 1992–; formerly chm Specialist Planning Gp Mental Health Servs for the Elderly Mental Health Unit Leics Health Authy, formerly chm and later vice chm MIND Hinckley Leics; memb: Exec Ctee Age Concern Leics, Exec Ctee Br Assoc for Services to the Elderly (BASE) 1988–, Steering Gp for Quadruple Support for Dementia Hinckley Leics Health Authy; assoc memb Leics Housing Assoc 1991–, memb Mgmnt Ctee George Hythe House Quaker Housing Assoc 1992–; Health and Social Serv Jl Jt Care Award 1983; memb Br Geriatrics Soc, FRSM; *Publications* What's Happening to Grandad? (MIND, 1979), Choosing How to Live (MIND, 1979), Coping With Caring (MIND, 1983), Quadruple Support for Dementia (Scot Action on Dementia, jtly 1983), Use of Multidisciplinary Process by the Community Dementia Team (Scot Action on Dementia, jtly 1985), Living Well into Old Age (King's Fund, jtly 1986), Handbook of Mental Disorders In Old Age (Open Univ, 1988), Alternative Homes for People with Dementia (BASE, 1990), Whither Now? Planning Services for People with Dementia (BASE, 1991), Let's Go Wheelies (BASE, 1992); *Recreations* genealogy, books; *Style*— Dr Brian Lodge; ✉ 25 St George's Avenue, Hinckley, Leicestershire LE10 0TE

LODGE, Bubble; da of David Albert Ainley Lodge, of York, and Judith Anne, *née* Pennicard; *b* 24 May 1964; *Educ* Queen Margaret's Sch Escrick Park York, Bretton Hall Coll W Bretton, Univ of Leeds (BA); *Career* independent theatre producer and general manager; teacher special needs children 1982, admin and VIP host Nat Student Drama Festival Swansea 1985, co-organiser Nat Symposium of Youth Theatres Nottingham 1985, box office and co mangr Nat Student Theatre Co Edinburgh Festival 1985, first female asst mangr Stoll Moss Theatres (The London Palladium, Her Majesty's Theatre, Victoria Palace Theatre) 1986, exec dir Springboard Theatre Co 1988, house mangr The Globe Theatre, gen mangr The Theatre Comedy Co Ltd Shaftesbury Theatre 1988–91, chief exec Everyman Theatre Cheltenham 1992–94 (administrator 1991–92), temp gen mangr Palace Theatre and project fundraiser Sadlers Wells 1994–95; currently dir: Miller Lodge (prodn and gen mgmnt co), The Sound Company; memb ICFM; *Recreations* swimming, skiing, riding, dance, theatre; *Style*— Ms Bubble Lodge; ✉ 14 Richmond Avenue, London N1 0NF (☎ 0171 278 0889, fax 0171 278 1442); Rowancourt, Grantham Drive, York YO2 4TZ; business: 2 Lord Hills Road, London W2 6PD

LODGE, Prof David; s of Herbert Lodge, and Dorothy, *née* Moss; *b* 22 Sept 1941; *Educ* Weston Super Mare GS, Univ of Bristol (BVSc, PhD); *m* 1, 15 Feb 1964 (m dis), Susan, da of Sidney Hayling; 4 s (Marcus b 1964, Duncan b 1966, James b 1969, (Robert) Jolyon b 1971); m 2, 21 Oct 1995, Catherine Mary, da of Peter Sutton; 1 da (Josie Louise b 1993); *Career* jr fell and lectr Dept of Veterinary Surgery Univ of Bristol 1963–70, Wellcome Tst fell Dept of Physiology Animal Health Tst 1970–74; post doctoral res fell Aust Nat Univ 1974–79; Royal Veterinary Coll London: sr lectr 1979–84, prof of vet neuroscience 1984–91, prof of vet physiology and head of vet basic sciences 1989–91, currently head of CNS res Lilly Res Centre; currently: visiting prof of vet physiology Univ of London, hon prof of physiology Univ of Cardiff, Benjamin Meaker visiting prof Univ of Bristol; ed Neuropharmacology 1992–; memb Ctee Physiological Soc 1983–87; MRCVS 1963, DVA 1969; *Books* Excitatory Amino Acid Transmission (1987), Excitatory Amino Acids in Health and Disease (1988); *Recreations* rugby, running, skiing, coaching junior sport; *Style*— Prof David Lodge; ✉ Lilly Research Centre, Erl Wood Manor, Windlesham, Surrey GU20 6PH (☎ 01276 853417, fax 01276 853525)

LODGE, Prof David John; s of William Frederick Lodge, and Rosalie Marie, *née* Murphy; *b* 28 Jan 1935; *Educ* St Joseph's Acad Blackheath, UCL (John Oliver Hobbes scholar, BA, MA, John Morley medal, Quain Essay prize), Univ of Birmingham (PhD); *m* 15 May 1959, Mary Frances, da of Francis Jacob (d 1969); 2 s Stephen David b 1962, Christopher Adrian b 1966), 1 da (Julia Mary b 1960); *Career* Nat Serv RAC 1955–57; asst British Cncl Overseas Students Centre London 1959–60; Dept of English Univ of Birmingham: asst lectr 1960–62, lectr 1961–71, sr lectr 1971–73, reader in English lit 1973–76, prof of modern English lit 1976–87, hon prof of modern English lit 1987–; visiting assoc prof Univ of California Berkeley 1969, Henfield fell in Creative Writing UEA 1977, Whitney J Oates short term visiting fell Princeton Univ 1981, E J Pratt lectr Memorial Univ of St John's Newfoundland 1985, Lansdowne scholar Univ of Victoria BC 1986, Regents lectr Univ of California Riverside 1989; chm Booker Prize Judges 1989; has lectured and addressed conferences in Europe and further afield; hon fell: UCL 1982, Goldsmiths' Coll London 1992; FRSL 1976; *Novels* The Picturegoers (1960), Ginger You're Barmy (1962), The British Museum is Falling Down (1967), Out of the Shelter (1970), Changing Places: a Tale of Two Campuses (1975), How Far Can You Go (1980), Small World: an academic romance (1984), Nice Work (1988), Paradise News (1991), Therapy (1995); *Non-fiction* incl: Language of Fiction (1966), The Novelist at the Crossroads (1971), The Modes of Modern Writing (1977), Working With Structuralism (1981), Write On (1986), After Bakhtin (1990), The Art of Fiction (1992), The Practice of Writing (1996); *Stage and Screen* Between These Four Walls (with M Bradbury and J Duckett) 1963, Slap in the Middle (with M Bradbury, J Duckett and D Turner) 1965, Big Words - Small Worlds (Channel 4) 1987, Nice Work (BBC2 1989, Silver Nymph Award), The Writing Game (Birmingham Rep 1990, adapted for Channel 4 1995), The Way of St James (BBC1) 1993, Martin Chuzzlewit (adapted from Charles Dickens' novel, BBC2) 1994; *Style*— Prof David Lodge; ✉ Department of English, University of Birmingham, Birmingham B15 2TT

LODGE, Jane Ann; da of John Humphrey Lodge (d 1984), of York, and Marian, *née* Smith; *b* 1 April 1955; *Educ* Mill Mount GS York, Univ of Birmingham (BSc); *m* 2 July 1983, Anthony (Tony) John Borton, s of Reginal Aubrey Borton (d 1980), of Rugby; 1 s (John Aubrey b 1988), 2 da (Emma Jane b 1990, Victoria Mary b 1992); *Career* Touche Ross Birmingham: trainee accountant 1973, qualified 1976, ptnr 1986–; Birmingham & W Midlands Soc of Chartered Accountants: chm Young Chartered Accountants Gp 1986–88, memb Ctee 1987–, treas 1990–92, vice-pres 1992–93, dep pres 1993–94; Univ of Birmingham: memb Cncl 1986–91 and 1993–, pres Guild of Graduates 1987–88, memb Strategy Planning and Resources Ctee 1987–91; govr Arthur Terry Sch Sutton Coldfield Birmingham 1989–; FCA 1976; *Recreations* cookery, tapestry, golf; *Style*— Ms Jane Lodge; ✉ Deloitte & Touche, Colmore Gate, 2 Colmore Row, Birmingham B3 2BN (☎ 0121 200 2211)

LODGE, Prof Juliet; da of Arthur Robert Mayer, of New Malden, and Lenore, *née* Reppert; *Educ* Coombe Co Girls' Sch, CNAA (BA), Univ of Reading (MA, MPhil), Univ of Hull (PhD), DLitt (Reading 1992); *m* 1 da (Keri-Michèle b 1980), 2 s (David b 1981, Christopher b 1986); *Career* lectr in European and int politics Univ of Auckland NZ 1973–77 (tenured 1975–77), visiting fell Centre for Int Studies Dept of Int Relations LSE 1976–77; Univ of Hull: lectr in politics 1977–84, sr lectr in politics 1984–88, reader in EC politics 1988–91, prof of European politics 1991–96, Jean Monnet prof of European integration and co-dir EC Res Unit 1991–96; dir Centre for Euro Studies Univ of Leeds 1996–; NATO res fell 1992; visiting prof: Université Libre de Bruxelles, Vrije Universitet Brussel, Institut fü Studien Vienna 1996; convenor UK Political Studies Assoc Study Gp on the EC 1980–, exec memb Univ Assoc for Contemporary European Studies 1988–, dir Jean Monnet Gp of Experts on Enlargement and the 1966 Intergovernmental Conf; memb: Cncl for Europeanists NYC 1983–, Univs Assoc for Contemporary European Studies 1984–, Cncl European Consortium for Political Res (ECPR) 1985– (official rep to ECPR 1978–), Humberside TEC, Team Europe, ESRC Postgrad Ctee, ESRC Research Bd; awards: UK Woman of Europe 1991–92, European Woman of Europe 1992–93, European Woman of Achievement Award 1992; FRSA 1992; *Books* The European Policy of the SPD (1976), The New Zealand General Election of 1975 (co-author, 1978), The European Parliament and the European Community (co-author, 1978), The European Community and New Zealand (1982), Direct Elections to the European Parliament: A Community Perspective (co-author, 1982), Democratic Legitimacy and the EC (1991), The EC and the Challenge of the Future (1993), The 1994 Euro-Elections (1995), Internal Security and Judicial Cooperation After Maastricht (1996); ed numerous books and pubns; *Recreations* art, writing, laughing; *Clubs* Club of Rhodes; *Style*— Professor Juliet Lodge; ✉ Centre for European Studies, University of Leeds, Leeds LS2 9JT (☎ 0113 233 4441)

LODGE, Oliver Raymond William Wynlayne; eld s of Oliver William Foster Lodge (d 1955), of Upton St Leonards, Glos (eld s of late Sir Oliver Joseph Lodge), and Winifred (Wynlayne) (d 1922), only da of late Sir William Nicholas Atkinson; *b* 2 Sept 1922; *Educ* Bryanston, King's Coll Cambridge (MA); *m* 17 Oct 1953, Charlotte (d 1990), only da of Col Arthur Davidson Young, CMG (d 1938), of St Margaret's, Twickenham; 1 s (Oliver b 1957), 2 da (Victoria b 1955, (Elizabeth) Lucy b 1960); *Career* Royal Fus 1942; called to the Bar Inner Temple 1945, practised Chancery Bar 1945–74, admitted *ad eundem* Lincoln's Inn 1949, bencher 1973, treas 1995, regnl chm Industl Tbnls 1980–92 (perm chm 1975–80); memb: Bar Cncl 1952–56 and 1967–71, Supreme Ct Rules Ctee 1968–71; gen cmmr of Income Tax Lincoln's Inn 1983–90; *Recreations* walking, reading history; *Clubs* Garrick, Bar Yacht; *Style*— Oliver Lodge, Esq; ✉ Southridge House, Hindon, Salisbury, Wilts

LODGE, Sir Thomas; kt (1974); s of James Lodge (d 1936), of Sheffield; *b* 25 Nov 1909; *Educ* Univ of Sheffield; *m* 1940, Aileen (d 1990), da of James Corduff, of Co Donegal; 1 s, 1 da; *Career* ret medical practitioner; conslt radiologist United Sheffield Hospitals 1946–74; clinical lectr Univ of Sheffield 1963–66; former pres and Gold medallist RCR; *Books* Recent Advances in Radiology (6 edn 1979); *Clubs* RSM; *Style*— Sir Thomas Lodge; ✉ 46 Braemore Court, Kingsway, Hove, E Sussex BN3 4FG (☎ 01273 724371)

LOEFFLER, Frank; s of Ernst Loeffler (d 1967), and Bianka Klein, *née* Breitmann; *b* 21 Jan 1931; *Educ* Mill Hill Sch, Gonville and Caius Coll Cambridge, London Hosp Med Coll (MB BChir, FRCS, FRCOG); *m* 10 Aug 1958, Eva Augusta, da of Sir Ludwig Guttmann (d 1981), of High Wycombe and Aylesbury; 1 s (Mark b 15 April 1961), 2 da (Clare b 13 Dec 1959, Juliet b 26 June 1964); *Career* in private practice Harley St; conslt: Central Middlesex Hosp 1967–68, St Mary's Hosp W2 1968–96, Queen Charlotte's Hosp 1983–96; ed Br Jl of Obstetrics & Gynaecology 1973–80; memb Ctee on Safety of Medicines 1987–92; memb Cncl RCOG 1987–90; FRCS 1959, FRCOG 1973; *Recreations* tennis, sailing, skiing; *Clubs* Aldeburgh Yacht, Aldeburgh Golf, Royal Soc of Med; *Style*— Frank Loeffler, Esq; ✉ 86 Harley St, London W1N 1AE (☎ 0171 486 2966); St Mary's Hospital, Praed St, London W2 (☎ 0171 725 1045); Queen Charlotte's and Chelsea Hospital, Goldhawk Rd, London W6 (☎ 0181 748 4666)

LOEHNIS, Anthony David; CMG (1988); s of Cdr Sir Clive Loehnis, KCMG, RN (ret) (d 1992), and Rosemary, da of Hon Robert Ryder (ka 1917, s of 2 Earl of Harrowby, KG, PC, and Lady Mary Cecil, da of 2 Marqess of Exeter); *b* 12 March 1936; *Educ* Eton, New Coll Oxford, Harvard Univ; *m* 7 Aug 1965, Jennifer, da of Sir Donald Anderson; 3 s; *Career* with FCO until 1966; Schroder Wagg 1967–80, exec dir Bank of England 1981–89 (assoc dir 1980–81), dir S G Warburg Gp plc and vice chm S G Warburg & Co Ltd 1989–92; chm: The Baring Securities Emerging Markets Index Tracker Fund Ltd 1993–, HTR Japanese Smaller Companies Trust PLC 1993–, Matheson Lloyd's Investment Trust plc 1994–, The Knox D'Arcy Trust PLC 1996–; dir: UK-Japan 2000 Gp 1990–, St James's Place Capital plc 1993–, J Rothschild Assurance Holdings plc 1993–, J Rothschild International Assurance Holdings plc 1993–, Life Assurance Holding Corporation Ltd 1994–, Bank of Tokyo-Mitsubishi (UK) Ltd 1994–, Alpha Bank London Ltd 1994–, Tokyo-Mitsubishi International Ltd 1996–; chm Centre for Economic Policy Research 1990–; memb: Cncl of Mgmnt Ditchley Holdings Fndn 1992–, Governing Bd Br Assoc for Central and Eastern Europe 1994–, Cncl Baring Fndn 1994–; advsr Bank of

Tokyo-Mitsubishi Group London 1994–; dep chm Public Works Loan Commission 1996– (cmmr 1994); *Style—* Anthony Loehnis, Esq, CMG; ✉ Haughton House, Churchill, Oxon OX7 6NU

LOEWE, Prof Raphael James; MC (1943); s of Herbert Martin James Loewe (d 1940), of Cambridge, and Ethel Victoria, *née* Hyamson (d 1946); *b* 16 April 1919; *Educ* Dragon Sch Oxford, The Leys Sch Cambridge, St John's Coll Cambridge (MA); *m* 19 March 1952, Chloe, da of Mendel Klatzkin (d 1951), of London; 2 da (Elisabeth (Mrs Talbot) b 1953, Camilla b 1957); *Career* served The Suffolk Regt, 142 Regt RAC N African and Italian Campaigns, wounded in action 1940–45; lectr in Hebrew Leeds 1949, Bye fell Caius Coll Cambridge 1954, visiting prof Brown Univ Providence RI USA 1963–64, Goldsmid prof of Hebrew UCL until 1984 (formerly lectr then reader); author of numerous articles in learned jls and presentation vols; former Elder Spanish and Portuguese Jews' Congregation London; past pres: Soc for Old Testament Study, Jewish Historical Soc of England; FSA, fell Royal Asiatic Soc; *Books* The Position of Women in Judaism (1966), Encyclopaedia Judaica (contrib ed, 1971), Omar Khayyam (Hebrew version, 1982), The Rylands Haggadah (1988), Solomon ibn Gabirol (1989), The Barcelona Haggadah (contributing ed, 1992), History of Linguistics (contrib, 1994); *Recreations* travel, walking, translating English Latin & Hebrew poetry; *Style—* Prof Raphael Loewe, MC, FSA; ✉ 50 Gurney Drive, London N2 0DE (☎ 0181 455 5379)

LOEWENSTEIN-WERTHEIM-FREUDENBERG, Prince Rupert Ludwig Ferdinand zu; also Count von Loewenstein-Scharffeneck; s of Prince Leopold zu Loewenstein-Wertheim-Freudenberg (d 1974; of the family of mediatised Princes, title of Bavarian Prince conferred 1812, stemming from the morganatic marriage of Elector Palatine Friedrich I (d 1476) to Klara Tott, of Augsburg; Counts of HRE 1494, recreated Loewenstein-Scharffeneck 1875), and Countess Bianca Fischler von Treuberg; *b* 24 Aug 1933; *Educ* St Christopher's Letchworth, Magdalen Coll Oxford (MA); *m* 1957, Josephine Clare, da of Capt Montague Lowry-Corry (d 1977, gggs of 2 Earl Belmore) by his 1 w, Hon Mary Biddulph, yr da of 2 Baron Biddulph; 2 s (Prince Rudolf Amadeus b 1957, Prince Konrad Friedrich b 1958), 1 da (Princess Maria Theodora Marjorie b 1966); *Career* fin advsr, former merchant banker; CStJ; Knight of San Gennaro, Knight Grand Cross of Honour and Devotion SMO Malta (vice pres Br Assoc), Bailiff Grand Cross of Justice Constantinian Order of St George with collar (pres Br Assoc), Knight of Justice Order of St Stephen; *Recreations* music; *Clubs* Beefsteak, Boodle's, Buck's, Portland, Pratt's, White's; *Style—* Prince Rupert zu Loewenstein-Wertheim-Freudenberg; ✉ Petersham Lodge, River Lane, Richmond, Surrey TW10 7AG; Rupert Loewenstein Ltd, 2 King St, London SW1Y 6QL (☎ 0171 839 6454, fax 0171 930 4032)

LOFTHOUSE, Sir Geoffrey; kt (1995), JP (Pontefract 1970), MP (Lab) Pontefract and Castleford (majority 23,495); s of Ernest Lofthouse (d 1935), and Emma Lofthouse (d 1944); *b* 18 Dec 1925; *Educ* Featherstone Primary and Secondary Schs, Whitwood Tech Coll, Univ of Leeds; *m* 1946, Sarah (d 1985), da of Joesh Thomas Onions; 1 da; *Career* Manpower Office NCB 1964–70, personnel mangr NCB Fryston 1970–78; MP (Lab) Pontefract and Castleford Nov 1978–, memb Select Ctee on Energy, first dep chm of Ways and Means (dep Speaker of the House) 1992–; cncllr: Pontefract Borough DC 1962–74 (ldr 1969–74), Wakefield Metropolitan DC 1974–79 (first chm); FIPM 1984; *Books* A Very Miner MP (autobiography, 1986); *Recreations* rugby league, cricket; *Style—* Sir Geoffrey Lofthouse, JP, MP; ✉ 67 Carlton Crest, Pontefract, W Yorkshire (☎ 01977 704 275); House of Commons, London SW1A 0AA (☎ 0171 219 5133)

LOFTHOUSE, Marjorie Helen; MBE (1990); da of Ronald Douglas Minns (d 1968), of London, and Marjorie May, *née* Axford (d 1989); *b* 3 March 1943; *Educ* City of Bath Girls' Sch, Co of Stafford Trg Coll; *m* Ken Stephinson; 2 step da (Jacqueline, Joanne); *Career* broadcaster; formerly with HTV West; progs incl: Reports West, Here Today, Gallery; BBC: regular presenter of Pebble Mill at One (BBC 1), co-presenter Eating Out with Tovey (BBC 2), writer and narrator of many documentaries incl See for Yourself, presented The New Venturers series (BBC Scotland) 1990–91; radio: commenced bdcasting with Radio Metro Newcastle, presented Northern edn Woman's Hour (BBC Manchester and BBC Birmingham), developed Homeing-In, created Vintage Cider (two part biography of Laurie Lee), presented Enterprise (BBC Radio 4), presented numerous features and documentaries, created Romantic Strings series (BBC Radio 2), own music prog Prelude (BBC Radio 4) 1989–95, presenter Business on the Move (BBC Radio 5); prodn work BBC Radio 4 incl: Feet First, Hair Today, The Long Sleep, Timpson's England, Norfolk Men, Free for All, This Stately Home Business, The Big Day; presented Royal Show open air concert featuring Midland Concert Orch 1988, responsible for creating an annual competition to find Britain's most enterprising small businesses which were then featured on radio prog Enterprise 1984–91, runs workshops for corp trg; runner-up Sony Radio Awards for documentary Leslie 1986; co sec Stephinson Television; vice chair Greater Manchester Bd Prince's Youth Business Tst, pres Saddleworth Cancer Research Campaign; *Books* The New Adventurers; *Style—* Ms Marjorie Lofthouse, MBE; ✉ Stephinson Television, Saddleworth Station, Dobcross, Lancs OL3 5NS (☎ 01457 820820, fax 01457 820111)

LOFTHOUSE, Stephen; s of Harry Lofthouse (d 1980), and (Janet) Mary Hume Scott, *née* Fraser (d 1996); *b* 23 March 1945; *Educ* Tauntons GS, Univ of Manchester (BA, MA); *Career* res assoc Univ of Manchester 1968, lectr (later sr lectr) Manchester Poly 1969–72, lectr Manchester Business Sch 1972–75, dir Grade 10 Industs Assistance Cmmn Australia 1975, conslt Price Cmmn 1976–77, assoc Capel-Cure Myers 1977–83, sr exec James Capel and Co 1983–85, dir (then chm) James Capel Fund Managers Ltd (formerly James Capel International Asset Management Limited) 1985–92, dir (then chm) James Capel Unit Trust Management Ltd 1988–92, dir James Capel & Co Limited 1990–91, md James Capel Asset Management Ltd 1991–92; dir: Wardley Investment Services Ltd 1988–92 (non-exec), Wardley Global Selection SICAV 1991–92, Wardley Investment Services (Luxembourg) SA 1991–92; writer 1993–; *Books* Equity Investment Management (1994), Readings In Investments (1994), How to Fix your Finances (1996); numerous articles published in acad and professional jls; *Style—* Stephen Lofthouse, Esq; ✉ 4 North Several, London SE3 0QR (☎ and fax 0181 318 7132, e-mail SLofthouse@aol.com)

LOFTUS, Viscount; Charles John Tottenham; s and h of 8 Marquess of Ely, *qv*; *b* 2 Feb 1943; *Educ* Trinity Coll Sch Port Hope Ont, École Internationale de Genève, Toronto Univ (MA); *m* 1969, Judith Marvelle, da of Dr J J Porter of Calgary, Alberta, Canada; 1 adopted s (Andrew b 1973), 1 adopted da (Jennifer b 1975); *Heir* bro, Lord Timothy Tottenham; *Career* head of Dept of French Strathcona-Tweedsmuir Sch Calgary, Alberta; *Style—* Viscount Loftus; ✉ 1424 Springfield Place SW, Calgary, Alberta, T2W OY1 Canada

LOFTUS, John Michael; s of Donald Loftus, of 4 Hemmant Way, Gillingham, Beccles, Suffolk, and Jean, *née* Hockney; *b* 4 Dec 1952; *Educ* Woodbridge Sch Suffolk, Univ of Sheffield (BSc); *m* 1988, Marilyn Vera; 1 da (Naomi Elizabeth b 7 March 1990), 1 s (William Edward b 30 June 1994); *Career* slr, NP; ptnr Norton Peskett & Forward; clerk to: Lowestoft Charity Bd 1987–, Gen Cmmrs of Taxes (Lowestoft Div) 1989–; Henstead Parish Cncl: parish Cncllr 1990–, church warden 1989–; memb Soc of Tst and Estate Practitioners; *Recreations* running, gardening, cycling, camping, walking; *Style—* John Loftus, Esq; ✉ Keld House, The Street, Hulver, Beccles, Suffolk NR34 7UE (☎ 01502 476257); Norton Peskett & Forward, 148 London Road North, Lowestoft (☎ 01502 565146, fax 01502 515941)

LOGAN, Andrew David; s of William Harold Logan, of The Leys, Witney, Oxford, and Irene May, *née* Muddimer; *b* 11 Oct 1945; *Educ* Lord Williams's GS Thame, Burford GS Oxon, Oxford Sch of Architecture (DipArch); *Career* sculptor and artist; designer: Wolfy (Ballet Rambert London) 1987, Bastet (Sadler's Wells Royal Ballet) 1988; organiser Andrew Logan's Alternative Miss World nos 1–9 1972–95; opened Andrew Logan Museum of Sculpture Berriew Powys Wales 1991; *Exhibitions* incl: Biba's Sculpture Garden Goldfield 1974, Whitechapel Art Gallery 1976, Egypt Revisited Sand and Light Spectacular Super Tent Clapham Common 1978, Trigon-Graz Austria 1979, Goddesses exhbn Cwlth Inst London 1983, Henley Arts Festival, The Book Show, The Cylinder Gallery London 1984, Galactic Forest exhbn Functional Art Gallery, Los Angeles and Limelight Club NYC 1985, Galactic Forest exhbn Chicago, Daily Mail Ideal Home exhbn Arts Cncl Living Art Pavilion, Glass Sculpture exhbn Singapore 1986, Monuments and Music exhbn Botanical Gardens Rome, jewellery and sculpture exhibited Moscow 1989, Portraits (new works) Glasshouse London 1989, Wings Over Waves Angela Flowers 1990, Untamed Fashion Assembly jewellery incl in show Riga Latvia USSR, An Artistic Adventure Museum of Modern Art Oxford, Flowers East Gallery and The Old Library Cardiff 1991, Jewels Fantasy exhbn V&A Museum 1992, Millfield British 20th Century Sculpture exhbn 1992, Los Angeles Art Fair 1992, Bonham's Knightsbridge 1992, Cracked Mirrors - Very Nice (Festival Hall Craft Gallery London) 1993, Olympian Arts Centre exhbn London 1993, Monuments of Hope and Joy (display of Pegasus I and II Heathrow Airport) 1993, The Elements exhbn Concord Lighting London 1993, Museum of Sculpture Berriew Powys Wales (solo exhbn) 1994, exhbn of sculpture and jewels Northern Centre for Contemporary Art 1994, 101 Chairs exhbn South Bank Centre 1994, Fabulous Fakes and Flying Carpets (exhbn of sculpture and jewels) Bluecoat Display Centre Liverpool 1994, exhbn of Pegasus and jewels Roscarbery Ireland 1994, Elvis and Marilyn: 2 x Immortal Boston Mass (3 year travelling show throughout USA) 1994, Shining Through exhbn Crafts Cncl Islington 1995, The Happy Heart Show (exhbn of sculpture and jewels) Manchester City Art Galleries 1995; *Style—* Andrew Logan, Esq; ✉ The Glasshouse, Melior Place, London SE1 3QP (☎ 0171 407 6575, fax 0171 403 6820)

LOGAN, Colin Donald Campbell; s of Alistair Andrew Logan, of Heathfield, E Sussex, and Elisabeth Agnes, *née* Stephenson (d 1990); *b* 17 Feb 1938; *Educ* St Paul's, RMA Sandhurst; *Career* serv King's Regt Army 1957–77 (E Africa, Persian Gulf, Germany, Singapore, Hong Kong, NI), Staff Coll 1969–70, appts incl instr Far E Trg Centre and RMA Sandhurst, Bde Maj 48 Gurkha Inf Bde, ret 1977; asst sec Govt Secretariat Hong Kong 1977–80, chief exec Youth Hostels Assoc 1992– (joined 1981); tstee NCVO 1993–; memb: Devpt Ctee BTA, Exec Ctee Euro Union Fedn of Youth Hostel Assocs; MIMgt 1982; *Recreations* cricket, walking, swimming, sailing (but now landborne); *Style—* Colin Logan, Esq; ✉ Chief Executive, Youth Hostels Association (England and Wales), Trevelyan House, 8 St Stephen's Hill, St Albans, Herts AL1 2DY (☎ 01727 855215, fax 01727 844126)

LOGAN, David Brian Carleton; CMG (1991); s of Capt Brian Ewen Weldon Logan, RN (d 1995), of Linchmere, Surrey, and Mary, *née* Fass (d 1994); *b* 11 Aug 1943; *Educ* Charterhouse, Univ Coll Oxford (MA); *m* 4 March 1967, Judith Margaret, da of Walton Adamson Cole (d 1963); 2 s (Matthew b 1970, d 1988, James b 1976), 1 da (Joanna b 1968); *Career* Dip Serv 1965–; 3 sec (then 2 sec) Ankara 1965–69, private sec to Parly Under Sec of State for Foreign and Cwlth Affrs 1970–73, 1 sec UK Mission to the UN 1973–77, FCO 1977–82, cnsllr head of chancery and consul-gen Oslo 1982–85, head of Personnel Ops Dept FCO 1986–88; sr assoc memb St Antony's Coll Oxford 1988–89; min and dep head of mission Moscow 1989–92, asst under sec of state (Central and Eastern Europe) FCO 1992–93, asst under sec of state (Int Security) FCO 1994–95, min Washington 1995–; *Recreations* music, reading, sailing, tennis; *Clubs* Royal Ocean Racing, Hurlingham; *Style—* David B C Logan, Esq, CMG; ✉ c/o Foreign and Commonwealth Office (Washington), King Charles St, London SW1A 2AH (☎ 0171 270 2533)

LOGAN, Sir Donald Arthur; KCMG (1977, CMG 1965); s of Arthur Alfred Logan (d 1967), and Louise Anne Bradley (d 1984); *b* 25 Aug 1917; *Educ* Solihull; *m* 1957, Irène Jocelyne Angèle, da of Robert Everts, sometime Belgian Ambass to Madrid; 1 s, 2 da; *Career* served WWII RA; entered Dip Serv 1945: ambass Guinea 1960–62, cnsllr Paris 1964–70, ambass Bulgaria 1970–73, dep perm rep NATO 1973–75, perm leader UK Delgn to UN Conf on Law of the Sea 1976–77, ldr UK Delgn to Conf on Marine Living Resources of Antarctica 1978–80; dir GB East Europe Centre 1980–87; govr St Clare's Coll Oxford 1982– (chm Bd of Govrs 1984–93); dir Jerusalem and East Mission Trust Ltd 1980–96 (chm 1980–93), chm Friends of Bulgaria 1991–; *Clubs* Brooks's, RAC; *Style—* Sir Donald Logan, KCMG; ✉ 6 Thurloe St, London SW7 2ST (☎ and fax 0171 589 4010)

LOGAN, Nicholas John (Nick); s of John Andrew Peter Logan (d 1980), and Doris May, *née* Snell; *b* 3 Jan 1947; *Educ* Leyton GS London; *m* 1967, Julie, *née* Hillier; 2 s (Christian b 26 Feb 1968, Max b 6 Dec 1981), 1 da (Hallie b 10 March 1970); *Career* reporter West Essex Gazette and Walthamstow Guardian 1963–67, ed New Musical Express 1973–78 (writer 1967–73), fndr ed Smash Hits 1978–80, ed and publisher The Face 1980–90 and Arena 1986–90; editorial dir and publisher: The Face 1990–, Arena 1990–, Arena Homme Plus 1994–; chairperson's special award Br Soc of Magazine Editors 1987, Marcus Morris Award Periodical Publishers' Assoc 1990, Mark Boxer Award Br Soc of Magazine Editors 1994; *Style—* Nick Logan, Esq; ✉ The Face/Arena, Wagadon Ltd, 3rd Floor, Block A, Pine St, London EC1R 0JL (☎ 0171 837 7270, fax 0171 837 3906)

LOGAN, Russell James Vincent Crickard; s of John Stuart Logan, of Kent, and Joan Ena, *née* Solly; *b* 5 Oct 1942; *m* 1978, Gillian Enid, da of Charles Redfern; *Career* studio mangr Forces Broadcasting Servs Cyprus 1960–62, freelance theatrical work 1963–67, systems analyst IBM 1967–70, sr project mangr Twinlock Computer Services 1970–71, memb Bd Book Club Associates 1977–79 (fulfilment mangr 1971), fndr and sr ptnr Business Aid 1979–; chm and organiser annual DMA Database Mktg Seminar 1986–95, speaker trade confs and educn courses, advsr Br companies and charities; memb: DMA, IDM, ICFM, Crime Writers' Assoc; chm Database Mktg Ctee 1986–95; *Books* (all under pseudonym Russell James): Underground (1989), Daylight (1990), Payback (1991), Slaughter Music (1993), Count Me Out (1996); *Recreations* criminal research, travel to unlikely places; *Style—* Russell Logan, Esq; ✉ Business Aid, Penrose House, 30 Sydenham Rd, Cheltenham, Glos GL52 6EB

LOGAN, Rt Rev Vincent Paul; *see:* Dunkeld, Bishop of (RC)

LOGAN-SALTON, Maurice Highton Ekegren; s of Ivor Logan Assheton-Salton, of Cornwall, and Tora Ulla Margaretha, *née* Ekegren; *b* 2 Feb 1952; *Educ* Canford Sch, Univ of Durham, Teesside Poly (Dip SW, CQSW); *Career* local authy social worker 1973–87 and 1994–, factor Llanarth Ct 1988–91, co-prop Trebencyn Park Nursing Home 1989–91; author Monday Club policy paper Juvenile Crime 1984, campaigner for reduction in custody for young offenders, supporter of CHEs (community homes with educn) and the equivalent trg schs of N Ireland and former List D Schs of Scotland as spokesman for Monday Club Law and Order Ctee 1984–91, treas Univ of Durham Union Soc 1972–73; campaigner for repeal of Titles Deprivation Act (1917); memb: Ancient Monuments Soc, Irish Peers Assoc, Howard League for Penal Reform, ISTD (Inst for Study & Treatment of Delinquency); *Recreations* conservationist; *Style—* Maurice Logan-Salton, Esq; ✉ c/o 43 Falmouth Rd, Heaton, Newcastle upon Tyne NE6 5NS

LOGIE, John Robert Cunningham; s of Norman John Logie, TD (d 1972), of Aberdeen, and Kathleen Margaret Cameron, *née* Neill; *b* 9 Sept 1946; *Educ* Robert Gordons Coll, Trinity Coll Glenalmond, Univ of Aberdeen (MB ChB, PhD); *m* 1981, Sheila Catherine, da of James Pratt Will (d 1957), of Peterhead; 1 da (Joanna Catherine Neill b 1985), 1 s (David James Norman b 1989); *Career* med trg Aberdeen Royal Infirmary 1970–81 (house offr, lectr, registrar, sr registrar), conslt gen surgn Raigmore Hosp Inverness 1981–; FRCSEd 1974 (currently memb Cncl), FRCS 1975, FRCSGlas 1993; *Recreations* gardening, railway matters, rugby refereeing, ornamental waterfowl; *Style*— John R C Logie, Esq; ✉ The Darroch, Little Cantray, Culloden Moor, Inverness IV1 2EG (☎ 01463 792090); Raigmore Hospital, Inverness (☎ 01463 704000)

LOGIE, Nicholas; *b* 12 May 1950; *Educ* Yehudi Menuhin Sch, Royal Coll of Music, Musikhochschule Detmold Germany (German govt scholarship), BA (Open Univ), Conservatorio Santa Cecilia Rome (Italian govt scholarship); *m*; 2 c; *Career* viola player; with Vienna Symphony Orch 1973–78, Chilingirian String Quartet 1978–81, freelance 1981–; princ viola: London Mozart Players, Kent Opera Orch, Orch of the Age of Enlightenment; also performs with: Acad of St Martin in the Field, English Baroque Soloists, Gainsborough String Quartet; orch mangr: Kent Opera 1985–90, Glyndebourne Touring Opera 1990–; sr lectr Royal Northern Coll of Music 1989–; numerous recordings; *Style*— Nicholas Logie, Esq; ✉ Lotts End, Highgate, Forest Row, E Sussex RH18 5BE

LOGIER, Penelope Jane (Penny); da of Kenneth Charles Harry Whitworth, of Nottingham, and Barbara Joyce, *née* Tomlinson; *b* 16 Aug 1953; *Educ* Manning GS for Girls, Univ of Hull (BA); *m* 16 April 1977, Colin Douglas Alexander Logier, s of Stewart Alexander Logier; 1 s (Alexander William b 28 Jan 1989); *Career* graduate trainee IPC publishing 1975–76, gp head Harrison McCanns advtg agency 1977–79 (planner/buyer 1976–77), dep gp head J Walter Thompson 1979–81, assoc media dir Interlink (Lopex Group) 1981–82, media gp dir Grandfield Rork Collins 1982–86; media dir: Reay Keating Hamer 1986–91, Lansdown Conquest (formerly LansdownEuro) 1991–93; bd dir TMD Carat Advertising 1993–; MIPA 1979; *Clubs* Women's Advertising Club of London; *Style*— Mrs Penny Logier; ✉ TMD Carat Advertising Ltd, 172 Drury Lane, London WC2B 5QR (☎ 0171 611 8000)

LOGUE, Christopher; s of John Dominic Logue (d 1951), and Florence Mabel, *née* Chapman (d 1981); *b* 23 Nov 1926; *Educ* Portsmouth GS, Prior Park Coll Bath; *m* 1985, Rosemary Hill; *Career* writer, actor, Private Eye columnist; *Books* War Music: an Account of Books 16–19 of Homer's Iliad (1988), Kings: an Account of Books 1 and 2 of Homer's Iliad (1991), The Husbands: an Account of Books 3 and 4 of Homer's Iliad (1994); ed: The Children's Book of Comic Verse (1979), The Bumper Book of True Stories (1981), The Oxford Book of Pseuds (1983), Sweet and Sour: an Anthology of Comic Verse (1983), The Children's Book of Children's Rhymes (1986), Selected Poems (ed Christopher Reid, 1996); trans: Baal, The Seven Deadly Sins (1986), Bertold Brecht (1986); *Screenplays*: Professor Tucholsky's Facts (poem used as screenplay of animated film by Richard Williams, 1963), The End of Arthur's Marriage (music by Stanley Myers, dir Ken Loach, 1965), Savage Messiah (dir Ken Russell, 1972), Crusoe (with Walon Green, dir Caleb Deschanel, 1988); performing versions of War Music and Kings (with Alan Howard, dir Liane Aukin 1984 and 1991); *Clubs* The Groucho, The Hotsy Totsy (Ghent); *Style*— Christopher Logue; ✉ 41 Camberwell Grove, London SE5 8JA (☎ 0171 703 7853)

LOKER, John Keith; s of Denis Loker, of Pudsey, Yorks, and Irene May, *née* Threapleton (d 1968); *b* 15 Sept 1938; *Educ* Bradford Coll of Art and Design, RCA (Abbey minor travelling scholarship); *m* 1961 (m dis 1970), Eva, da of Alfred Kalnins; 2 s (Daniel Valdis b 1962, Simon Andris b 1965); *Career* artist; taught 1964–89: Manchester, Maidstone, Nottingham, Wolverhampton, Brighton, Portsmouth, Wimbledon, Chelsea, NE London, Middx; Nordstern Print Prize Royal Acad 1994; *Exhibitions* solo: studio exhbn London 1969, 1975 and 1986, Flowers Gallery 1970, 1973, 1975, 1978, 1980, 1982, 1983, 1985, 1988, 1990, 1992, 1993, 1994 and 1995, ICA 1970, Park Square Gallery Leeds 1975, 1978, Wetering Galerie Amsterdam 1978, 1980, 1982, 1986 and 1989, Arnolfini Gallery Bristol 1981, Newlyn Orion 1981, Cartwright Hall Bradford 1981, Newcastle Poly Gallery 1981, Galerie du Monde Hong Kong 1984, Watermans Arts Centre London 1992; numerous gp exhbns in UK and abroad; *Public Collections* Arts Cncl, Bradford City Art Gallery, British Cncl, Contemporary Art Soc, DOE, Dudley City Art Gallery, Ferens Art Gallery Hull, Hunterian Collection Glasgow, Leeds City Art Gallery, Manchester City Art Gallery, Power Inst of Fine Art Sydney, Rugby City Art Gallery, Tate Gallery, Van Reekumgalerie Apeldoorn, V&A, Wakefield City Art Gallery, Worcester City Art Gallery; *Commissions* Watmoughs Hldgs Bradford, Essex Gen Hospital, Stanhope Devpts for ITN Bldg (Norman Foster); *Publications* Thriding, Monogram - Arnolfini, Littered Ways; *Clubs* Chelsea Arts; *Style*— John Loker, Esq; ✉ Union Workhouse, Guilt Cross, Kenninghall, Norfolk NR16 2LJ (☎ 01953 681730); Angela Flowers Gallery, 199–205 Richmond Road, London E8 3NJ (☎ 0181 985 3333, fax 0181 985 0067)

LOMAS, Alfred (Alf); MEP (Lab) London North East (majority 57,085); s of Alfred Lomas; *b* 30 April 1928; *Educ* St Paul's Elem Sch Stockport, various further educnl estabs; *Career* former slr's clerk, radio telephony operator RAF and railway signalman; Lab Pty sec and agent 1959–65; political sec London Co-op 1965–79; MEP (Lab) London NE 1979–, ldr Br Lab Gp European Parliament 1985–87; *Style*— Alf Lomas, Esq, MEP; ✉ Suite 2, 2nd Floor, 78/102 The Broadway, Stratford, London E15 1NL (☎ 0181 519 8114)

LOMAS, Derek Frank; s of Derek Edward James Lomas, of 3 Whitewood Cottages, Eynsford, Kent, and Pauline Lomas, *née* Clements; *b* 10 Oct 1960; *Educ* Dartford West Kent Secdy Boys Sch, Medway Coll of Art and Design (DATEC Dip in Photography); *m* Sarah Ellen Kipps; 1 s (Edward); *Career* freelance photographer (editorial photography, mainly still life work for magazines incl: Vogue, Tatler, Elle, Marie Claire) 1989–; *Awards* AFAEP award for non-commissioned still-life 1989; memb Photographers Assoc 1989; *Recreations* walking, cinema, cooking, photography; *Style*— Derek Lomas, Esq; ✉ Derek Lomas Photography, (☎ 0171 622 0123)

LOMAS, Herbert; *b* 7 Feb 1924; *Educ* King George V Sch Southport, Univ of Liverpool (BA, MA); *Career* poet, translator and freelance writer; served WWII King's Liverpool Regt attached to Royal Garhwal Rifles (served Razmak Waziristan, Kohat NW Frontier Province) 1943–46; teacher of English Anargyrios Sch Spetsai Greece 1950–51, sr lectr Univ of Helsinki until 1965, princ lectr Borough Road Coll until 1982; poetry and articles published in: London Magazine, Encounter, The Spectator, The Hudson Review, Ambit and other journals; trans Medicine in Metamorphosis by Dr Martti Siirala; judge: Bennett Award 1987, Nat Poetry Competition 1989, Oxford Union Poetry Competition 1989, Aldeburgh Poetry Festival Prize 1990–94; *Awards* Guinness Poetry Competition 1961, runner up Arvon Fndn Poetry Competition 1980, Cholmondely Award for Poetry 1982, Poetry Book Society Biennial Award for Translation 1991, Finnish State Prize for Translation 1992; memb Finnish Acad, kt 1st Class Finnish Order of the White Rose; *Books* A Handbook of Modern English for Finnish Students (jtly, 1957), Chimpanzees are Blameless Creatures (1969), Who Needs Money? (1972), Private and Confidential (1974), Public Footpath (1981), Territorial Song (trans and ed, 1981), Fire in the Garden (1984), Letters in the Dark (1986), Contemporary Finnish Poetry (trans and ed, 1991), Trouble (1992), Wings of Hope and Daring (trans, 1992), Black and Red (trans, 1993), Narcissus in Winter (trans, 1994), The Year of the Hare (trans, 1995), Selected Poems (1995); *Style*— Herbert Lomas, Esq; ✉ North Gable, 30 Crag Path, Aldeburgh, Suffolk IP15 5BS

LOMAS, Jonathan; s of Grace Miriam Martha Hall, *née* Feesey (d 1988); *b* 30 April 1944; *Educ* Belmont Coll Bickington Devon, North Devon Coll Barnstaple, Poly SW (DipArch), Univ of Plymouth (Post Grad Dip in Architectural Conservation (with Commendation) 1994); *Career* RIBA Devon and Cornwall Soc of Architects travelling scholarship 1970, qualified architect 1973; ptnr Dyer Feesey Wickham 1976–; diocesan architect and ecclesiastical architect-surveyor Diocese of Exeter 1988, cmmnd architect to English Heritage 1988, architect to the Roman Catholic Diocese of Plymouth, conslt architect to the Nat Tst; memb: Exeter Diocesan Advsy Ctee 1980, Assoc for the Conservation of Historic Bldgs, Inst of Archaeology Univ of London, Devonshire Assoc Cncl of Management Devon Historic Bldgs Tst; rep on historic bldgs and specialist in the repair of ancient bldgs Society for the Protection of Ancient Bldgs 1973, tstee N Devon Athenaeum; RIBA/Arnold Sayers Commendation for House Design 1981, King of Prussia's Gold Medal for Architectural Repair 1992, N Devon Civic Soc Silver Award for Architectural Historic Repair 1994; RIBA 1973, FRSA 1973; *Books* Devon's Traditional Buildings (contrib, 1980), The Buildings of England Series: Devon (contrib, 1989), Transactions of the Devonshire Association (contrib); *Recreations* archaeology and local history, photography, travel, surfing, gardening with a keen interest in Japanese Gardens, steam railways; *Style*— Jonathan Lomas, Esq; ✉ Sheraton Cottage, Old Sticklepath Hill, Barnstaple, North Devon EX31 2BG (☎ 01271 78752); Dyer Feesey Wickham (Architects), 24 Castle Street, Barnstaple, Devon EX31 1DR (☎ 01271 45441)

LOMAS, Lisa; *née* Bellinger; *b* 9 March 1967; *m* Andrew Lomas; *Career* professional table tennis player; memb BFL Grove Club Market Drayton Shrops; honours incl: nat singles champion 1985, 1989 and 1994, nat doubles champion 8 times, Bronze medal Euro Championships (singles) Prague 1986, Silver medal Euro Championships (singles) Stuttgart 1992 Bronze medal Euro Championships (team) 1994; memb Eng squad World Championships 1991, memb GB squad Olympic Games Barcelona 1992; currently ranked number 1 in England (19th in Europe); *Style*— Mrs Lisa Lomas

LOMAX, Eric Sutherland; s of John Lomax (d 1950), and Elizabeth, *née* Sutherland (d 1942); *b* 30 May 1919; *Educ* Royal HS Edinburgh, Univ of Strathclyde; *m* 1, 20 Nov 1945, Agnes Scott, da of Alexander Dickson; 2 da (Linda May b 1946 (decd), Charmaine Carole b 1957), 1 s (Eric Scott b 1954 (decd)); m 2, 21 March 1983, Patricia Mary Wallace, da of Harry Barker; *Career* PO/PO Telephones Edinburgh 1936–39; served Br Army: UK, India, Malaya 1939–48 (POW Singapore and Burma-Siam Railway 1942–45, despatches 1946); Dept of Agriculture for Scotland Edinburgh 1948–49, Colonial Admin Serv Gold Coast W Africa 1949–55, various posts Indust Rels/Educn and Trg Scottish Gas Bd Edinburgh 1957–59, lectr in personnel mgmnt Univ of Strathclyde 1959–82; writer,broadcaster,conslt on mgmnt human resources 1959–; memb: Newcomen Soc for Study of History of Engrg and Technol, Soc of Authors, Scottish Far East POW Assoc (former pres); tstee Far East POW Funds; FRSA; *Books* A History of the Volta River Project (1953), Transport in the Northern Territories of the Gold Coast (1953), An Introductory Guide to Systematic Personnel Selection (1964), Human Factors in Communication (1967), The Management of Human Resources (1971), The Railway Man (1995, Esquire/Waterstone Non-Fiction Award 1995, PEN JR Ackerley Non-Fiction Award 1995, The Christopher Award NY 1995, shortlisted McVitie's Prize 1995, Scottish Writer of the Year, NCR Non-Fiction Award 1996); *Recreations* travel, antiques and antiquarian books, railway and canal historical research, Second World War in the Far East, research; *Style*— Eric Lomax, Esq; ✉ c/o Hilary Rubinstein, 61 Clarendon Road, London W11 4JE (☎ 0171 792 4282, fax 0171 221 5291)

LOMAX, Michael Acworth (Mike); s of Peter Francis George Lomax (d 1990), and Mary Rosamund Lomax; *b* 9 Jan 1943; *Educ* Downside Sch, Pembroke Coll Cambridge (BA); *m* (m dis); 2 s; *Career* grad trainee then mktg exec Foote Cone & Belding 1964–66, account exec Sharps Advertising 1966–69, account mangr McCann-Erickson 1969–70, Foster Turner & Benson 1970–75 (dir 1972–75), dir Streets Financial 1975–84, jt md Charles Barker City 1984–87, md First Financial Advertising/PR 1987–; IPA: finals tutor 1969–70, lectr Media Course 1970–71; memb: Media Representative Panel 1978–84, Mktg Panel 1984–85; lectr on fin mktg topics for various bodies incl Mktg Centre Europe, Inst for Int Res and MINTEL; memb Nat Appeals Ctee Cancer Res Campaign 1974–90, nat chm Cancer Youth Action 1978–83, chm Mktg Ctee Cancer Res Campaign 1987–90; MIPA 1967; *Recreations* golf (capt Fin Advtg Golfing Soc 1989–90), cooking, hill walking, reading, opera; *Clubs* Scribes West Int; *Style*— Mike Lomax, Esq; ✉ First Financial Advertising Ltd, 78 Cowcross St, London EC1M 6BP

LOMBARD, Louise; *b* 13 Sept 1970; *Career* actress; *Theatre* Katerina in The Brothers Karamazov (Royal Exchange Manchester), Helen Hayle in On Approval (dir Sir Peter Hall), Hilary in Now You Know (Hampstead) 1995; *Radio* Twentieth Century Vampire (BBC Radio 5), La Vie de Boheme (BBC) Noel Coward's Private Lives (BBC); *Television* Evangeline in The House of Eliott (3 series, BBC), Anna in Chancer II (Central), Lucy in A Black Velvet Gown (Worldwide TV), Jackanory (BBC), Casualty (BBC), Clarissa Calder in Bergerac (BBC), Perfect Scoundrels (TVS), The Bill (Thames), Shakers (BBC), Liz Shaw in Body Guards (Carlton), Lady Macbeth in Macbeth (BBC); *Film* Lucy in Angels, Twice Upon A Time, Wax Doll - Aids and Drug Abuse; *Style*— Ms Louise Lombard; ✉ ICM Ltd, Oxford House, 76 Oxford Street, London W1N 0AX (☎ 0171 636 6565, fax 0171 323 0101)

LOMER, Geoffrey John; CBE (1985); s of Frederick John Lomer, and Dorothy Lomer; *b* 5 Jan 1932; *Educ* St Austell GS Cornwall, Queens' Coll Cambridge (MA, open scholar); *m* 1, 1955, Pauline Helena, *née* May (d 1974); 1 s, 1 da; m 2, 1977, Antoinette Ryall; 1 step s, 1 step da; *Career* design engr EMI Research Laboratories Ltd 1953–57, head RF Div Broadcast Equipment Dept EMI Electronics Ltd 1957–63, head TV design team 1963–65, head transmitter Div Racal Communications Ltd, tech dir Racal-Mobilcal Ltd 1968–70, tech dir Racal Communications Ltd 1970–74, dir in charge Racal Communications Equipment Ltd 1974–76, dep md Racal-Tacticom Ltd 1976–77, tech dir Racal Electronics plc 1977–92, chm Racal Research Ltd 1979–92, chm Satellite Information Services Ltd 1993–, non-exec dir Vodafone Group plc 1993–; vice pres Inst of Electrical Engrs 1991–94; Hon DUniv Surrey 1994; FIEE 1975, FEng 1984; *Recreations* music, theatre; *Style*— Geoffrey Lomer, Esq, CBE, FEng; ✉ Ladiko, Little Croft Road, Goring-on-Thames, Reading RG8 9ER

LOMONOSSOFF, Dr George Peter; s of George Lomonossoff (d 1954), of Montreal, and Gertrude Margaret, *née*, Winkworth; *b* 15 Aug 1954; *Educ* Cambs HS for Boys, St John's Coll Cambridge (Lister scholar, BA, MA, PhD); *m* 11 July 1987, Kim Susan, da of late Remington Charles Chesher and Betty Chesher, *née* Read; 1 s (Michael George Remington b 8 Nov 1993), 1 da (Katherine Elizabeth Sumi b 26 Jan 1990); *Career* post doctoral fell MRC Lab of Molecular Biology Cambridge 1979–80, memb of staff John Innes Inst 1981– (fell 1980–81); short term EMBO fell 1982 and 1990; Fulbright scholarship to Cornell Univ 1987–88; achievements incl: determination of the genome structure of plant viruses, developing novel methods of producing virus resistant plants, and developing use of plant viruses as potential vaccines; numerous articles in scientific jls; memb: Soc for General Microbiology 1990, American Soc for Virology 1992; *Recreations* watching football, enjoying good food and drink; *Style*— Dr George Lomonossoff; ✉ Department of Virus Research, John Innes Centre, Colney Lane, Norwich NR4 7UH (☎ 01603 452571, fax 01603 456844)

LONDESBOROUGH, 9 Baron (UK 1850); Richard John Denison; s of 8 Baron Londesborough, TD, AMICE (d 1968, gs of Lord Albert Denison, *née* Conyngham, 2 s of 1 Marquess Conyngham), by his 2 w (Elizabeth) Ann, *née* Sale (d 1994); *b* 2 July 1959; *Educ* Wellington, Univ of Exeter; *m* 26 Sept 1987, Rikki, da of J E Morris, of Bayswater; 1 s (Hon James Frederick (Jack) b 4 June 1990), 1 da (Hon Laura Rose b 29 June 1992); *Heir* s, James Frederick b 4 June 1990; *Style*— The Rt Hon the Lord Londesborough; ✉ Edw Cottage, Aberedw, Powys

LONDON, Archdeacon of; *see:* Cassidy, Ven George Henry

LONDON, Prof David Robin; s of Zachariah London (d 1959), and Anne London (d 1985); *b* 17 July 1932; *Educ* Harrow, Oriel Coll Oxford (MA, Collection prize), St Thomas' Hosp Med Sch (BM BCh, DM, MRCP, Hadden prize); *m* 1957, Janet Rosemary, da of Otto Popper; 2 s (Nicholas b 1959, Jonathan b 1963), 2 da (Juliet b 1965, Rosamund b 1967); *Career* casualty offr, house physician then registrar St Thomas' Hosp 1958–62, registrar Westminster Hosp 1961–62, lectr then sr lectr St Thomas' Hosp Med Sch 1963–72, conslt physician Queen Elizabeth Hosp Birmingham 1972–92, registrar RCP 1992– (pro-censor then censor 1989–91); conslt advsr in med to Chief Med Offr 1983–92; ed Clinical Endocrinology 1975–78 (chm Editorial Bd 1989–93); treas Soc for Endocrinology 1981–85, pres Endocrine Section RSM 1986–87, chm Ctee of Mgmnt Clinical Sci 1986–87, chm Clinical Endocrinology Tst 1989–93, memb Birmingham HA 1988–91; MRC travelling fell 1965; Univ of Birmingham: hon prof 1985–, emeritus prof 1992–; Liveryman Worshipful Soc of Apothecaries 1962; FRCP 1973, FFPM 1995; *Recreations* music, gardening, travel, wine; *Clubs* Athenaeum, Buckland; *Style*— Prof David London; ✉ Middleton Cottage, Salwarpe, Droitwich, Worcestershire WR9 7JB (☎ 01905 774990); 38 Glebe Street, Chiswick, London W4 2BG (☎ 0181 747 1773); Royal College of Physicians, 11 St Andrews Place, Regents Park, London NW1 4LE (☎ 0171 935 1174, fax 0171 487 5218)

LONDON, John Frederick; s of Eric Horton London, MBE, of Bexhill-on-Sea, and Doris Emma, *née* Browning; *b* 17 Nov 1934; *Educ* Tonbridge; *m* 6 Oct 1962, Merrill Anne, da of Alfred Edward James Prior (d 1967), of Sevenoaks; 1 s (James b 8 Nov 1964), 2 da (Anne-Louise b 27 Oct 1967, Sally b 3 Aug 1969); *Career* Nat Serv 1953–54; Bank of England 1954–69, First Nat Bank of Boston London 1969–72, successively asst dir, dir then md Quin Cope Ltd (formerly Gerald Quin Cope and Co Ltd) 1972–89; fin dir Royal Artillery Museums, chm and pres Sevenoaks and Dist Mental Health Assoc 1962–79, chm Sevenoaks Dist Scout Cncl 1971–88; cncllr: Sevenoaks UDC 1959–62 and 1963–74 (chm 1970–71), Sevenoaks Town Cncl 1974– (Mayor of Sevenoaks 1974–75 and 1988–89); chm: Sevenoaks Cons Assoc 1992–96, Kent Co Cons Assoc 1994–96; memb Exec Ctee Nat Union of Cons and Unionist Assocs 1995–; *Recreations* sailing; *Style*— John London, Esq; ✉ 18 Knole Way, Sevenoaks, Kent TN13 3RS (☎ 01732 456327)

LONDON, Malcolm John; s of Frederick Albert John London (d 1977), of Ruislip, Middx, and Cicely Maud, *née* Boyce (d 1978); *b* 27 July 1938; *Educ* Bishopshalt Sch, LSE (BSc); *m* (m dis); *Career* ptnr: Cork Gully 1969–80, Coopers & Lybrand 1980–95; hon treas: Royal Concert 1985–95, Royal Musical Assoc 1981–95; hon sec City Arts Tst 1973–95, tstee Handel Inst 1987–, tstee Purcell Soc Tst 1981–, pres Insolvency Practitioners Assoc 1994; memb Cncl Soc of Insolvency Practitioners 1994–95; Freeman City of London 1989, memb Worshipful Co of Musicians 1989; FCA (ACA 1964), FIPA 1979; *Books* Tolley's Liquidation Manual (jtly, 1989), Tax Implications of Liquidations, Receiverships, Administration Orders and Voluntary Arrangements (jtly, 1989); *Recreations* all performing and visual arts; *Clubs* Arts; *Style*— Malcolm London, Esq; ✉ 76 Chenies Mews, London WC1E 6HX

LONDON, Bishop of 1995–; Rt Rev Richard John Carew Chartres; s of late Richard Arthur Carew Chartres, and Charlotte Ethel, *née* Day; *b* 11 July 1947; *Educ* Hertford GS, Trinity Coll Cambridge (MA), Cuddesdon Theol Coll, Lincoln Theol Coll (BD); *m* 1982, Caroline Mary, da of Alan McLintock, *qv*; 2 s (Alexander b 1986, Louis b 1991), 2 da (Sophie b 1988, Clio b 1993); *Career* master int sch Seville 1971, ordained 1973, curate Bedford St Andrew 1973–75, chaplain to the Bishop of St Albans 1975–80, Archbishop's chaplain 1980–84, vicar of St Stephen Rochester Row London 1984–92, bishop of Stepney 1992–95; six preacher Canterbury Cathedral 1991–; London area dir of ordinands 1985–92, Gresham prof of divinity 1986–92, Prelate of the Most Excellent Order of the British Empire 1995–; dean of HM's Chapels Royal 1996–; *Style*— The Rt Rev the Bishop of London; ✉ London House, 8 Barton Street, London SW1P 3NE (☎ 0171 222 8661)

LONEY, Francis Greville; s of Greville Groves Loney (d 1981), of Durban, S Africa, and Marjory Grace, *née* Redman (d 1995); *b* 11 Dec 1936; *Educ* St Charles' Coll Pietermaritzburg S Africa, Regent St Poly; *Career* photographer; formerly asst to Robert Gibb, freelance 1966–; photographic career has covered all aspects of advtg and editorial photography incl fashion, beauty, menswear, interiors, still life, celebrities, record sleeves, magazine covers, travel, theatre and the arts, press and society, landscapes, medical, portraits, children and animals, knitwear, charities and corporate; *Recreations* looking after sons and heirs Jasper and Justin (pedigree blue Burmese cats); *Style*— Francis Loney, Esq; ✉ Smiles Studio, Eardley House, 2 Uxbridge St, London W8 7SY (☎ 0171 727 2382, fax 0171 727 2386)

LONEY, Keith Edward; s of William Edward Loney (d 1977), of Yeovil, Somerset, and Marjorie Maud Rose Miles; *b* 16 Nov 1935; *Educ* King's Sch Bruton, Univ of London (LLM); *m* 1971, Valerie Elizabeth, da of Percy Arthur Stuttard (d 1977), of Purley, Surrey; 3 da (Alexandra b 1974, Victoria b 1976, Katherine b 1977); *Career* Royal Signals 1954–57, Cyprus 1955–56; CA 1962, called to the Bar Lincoln's Inn 1972; Br Insur Assoc 1966–85 (asst sec 1971, dep sec 1975), Assoc of Br Insurers 1985–93 (dep chief exec 1987–93), co sec Pool Reinsurance 1993–94, chief exec Centre for Insurance Studies 1994–; memb Hon Artillery Co; Freeman City of London 1959, Liveryman The Worshipful Co of Butchers 1960; *Recreations* swimming, travel; *Clubs* Lansdowne, Royal Society of Arts, Ward of Cordwainer; *Style*— Keith Loney, Esq; ✉ 4 Lyle Park, Sevenoaks, Kent TN13 3JX (☎ and fax 01732 457889)

LONG, Prof Adrian Ernest; s of Charles Long (d 1985), and Sylvia Evelyn Winifred, *née* Mills (d 1974); *b* 15 April 1941; *Educ* Royal Sch Dungannon, Queen's Univ of Belfast (BSc, PhD, DSc); *m* 18 March 1967, Elaine Margaret Long, da of James Thompson (d 1980); 1 s (Michael b 22 Feb 1971), 1 da (Alison b 18 Dec 1972); *Career* bridge design engr Toronto Canada 1967–68, asst prof Civil Engrg Dept Queen's Univ Kingston Canada 1968–71; Queen's Univ Belfast: lectr Civil Engrg Dept 1971–75, prof of civil engrg 1976–77, prof and head Civil Engrg Dept 1977–89, dean of Faculty of Engrg 1988–91, dir Sch of the Built Environment 1989–; visiting prof RMC Kingston Canada 1975–76, ed Jl of Engrg Structures 1985–94, visitor Tport and Road Res Lab 1989–92, co-ordinator of research PSAM Sub-Ctee EPSRC 1990–94, memb Civil Engrg Panel Research Assessment Exercise 1996; winner Royal Society/Esso Energy Award 1994; FICE 1982 (chm NI Assoc 1985–86, memb Cncl 1989–92), FEng 1989, FIStructE 1989 (chm NI Branch 1993–94); *Recreations* walking, church activities, travel; *Style*— Prof Adrian Long, FEng; ✉ Civil Engineering Dept, Queen's University, Belfast BT7 1NN (☎ 01232 245133 ext 4005, fax 01232 663754, telex QUBADM 74487)

LONG, Brian; s of Harry Long (d 1955), and Doris Long (d 1977); *b* 30 Aug 1932; *Educ* Hanson GS Yorks; *m* 29 Dec 1956, Joan Iris, da of Charles Eric Hoggard, of Huggate, Yorks; 2 s (Nigel b 10 Feb 1959, Gareth b 15 Jan 1962); *Career* qualified co sec 1953; International Computers and Tabulators Ltd 1955–65; joined Honeywell Ltd 1965, md Honeywell Information Systems Ltd 1978–86, memb Honeywell Advsy Cncl 1978–86, vice pres Honeywell Inc 1981–86, chief exec Honeywell Ltd 1986 (vice chm 1985), chm and chief exec Honeywell Bull Ltd (became Bull HN Information Systems Ltd) 1987, dir Bull SA of France 1987–92, chm Bull HN Information Systems Ltd (now Bull Information Systems Ltd) 1990, chm Zenith Data Systems 1990; memb Bd Nat Computing Centre (NCC) 1970–71, memb Indust Ctee Help the Aged 1988, tstee: ReAction Tst 1991–, Third Age Challenge Tst 1995; memb Cncl CBI 1992–; Freeman City of London 1987, fndr memb Worshipful Co of Information Technologists 1987; FInstD 1970, CIMgt 1987, MBCS 1987, FCIS 1988, FBCS 1989; *Recreations* walking, music, theatre; *Clubs* RAC; *Style*— Brian Long, Esq; ✉ Bull Information Systems Ltd, Computer House, Great West Road, Brentford, Middx TW8 9DH (☎ 0181 479 2675, fax 0181 479 2282)

LONG, HE Christopher William; CMG (1986); s of late Eric and May Long; *b* 9 April 1938; *Educ* King Edward's Sch Birmingham, Balliol Coll Oxford (Deakin scholar), Univ of Münster West Germany; *m* 1972, Patricia, da of late Dennis and May Stanbridge; 1 da, 2 s; *Career* served RN 1956–58; HM Dip Serv 1963–: FO 1963–64, Jedda 1965–67, Caracas 1967–69, FCO 1969–74, Budapest 1974–77, Belgrade 1977, cnsllr Damascus 1978–80, cnsllr and dep perm rep UK mission Geneva 1980–83, head of Near East and N Africa Dept FCO 1983–85, asst under sec of state FCO 1985–88; HM ambassador: to Switzerland 1988–92 (also accredited to Liechtenstein 1992), to Egypt 1992–95, to Hungary 1995–; *Style*— HE Mr Christopher Long, CMG; ✉ c/o Foreign and Commonwealth Office (Budapest), King Charles Street, London SW1A 2AH

LONG, Prof Derek Albert; s of Albert Long (d 1981), of Gloucester, and Edith Mary, *née* Adams (d 1983); *b* 11 Aug 1925; *Educ* Sir Thomas Rich's Sch Gloucester, Jesus Coll Oxford (MA, DPhil), Univ of Minnesota; *m* 8 Aug 1951, Moira Hastings, da of William Gilmore (d 1978), of Sheffield; 3 s (David b 1954, Richard b 1959, Andrew b 1962); *Career* fell Univ of Minnesota 1949–50, res fell spectroscopy Univ of Oxford 1950–55; Univ Coll Swansea 1956–66: lectr, sr lectr, reader in chemistry; Univ of Bradford: prof of structural chemistry 1966–92, prof emeritus 1992–, chm Bd Physical Scis 1976–79, dir Molecular Spectroscopy Unit 1982–88; OECD travelling fell Canada and USA 1964, Leverhulme res fell 1970–71; visiting prof: Reims, Lille, Bordeaux, Paris, Bologna, Florence, Keele; chm second int conf on Raman spectroscopy Oxford 1970, co-dir NATO Advanced Studies Inst Bad Windsheim 1982, memb Italian-UK mixed cmmn for implementation of cultural convention 1985, vice chm Euro Laboratory for Non-Linear Spectroscopy Florence 1986–92; fndr ed Jl of Raman Spectroscopy; Hon Docteur ès Sciences Reims 1979; FRCS, CChem; foreign memb Lincei Acad Rome 1979; *Books* Raman Spectroscopy (1977), Essays in Structural Chemistry (jt ed, 1971), Specialist Periodical Reports in Molecular Spectroscopy (jt ed vols 1–6, 1973–79), Non-Linear Raman Spectroscopy and its Chemical Applications (jt ed, 1982), Proceedings of the Eleventh International Conference on Raman Spectroscopy (jt ed, 1988), Sèvres Service des Arts Industriels in Tools and Trades Vol 9 (1997); around 200 sci papers in learned jls; *Recreations* collecting antique woodworking tools, history of science, Pembrokeshire; *Clubs* Utd Oxford and Cambridge Univ; *Style*— Prof Derek A Long; ✉ 19 Hollingwood Rise, Ilkley, West Yorkshire LS29 9PW (☎ and fax 01943 608472), Three Houses, Roch, Nr Haverfordwest, Pembrokeshire SA62 6JX (☎ 01437 710550); Structural Chemistry, University of Bradford, W Yorkshire BD7 1DP (☎ 01274 733466, fax 01274 305340)

LONG, Gerald; *b* 22 Aug 1923; *Career* Intelligence Corps 1943, posted ME 1943, cmmnd All-Arms Octu Acre, attached US army S of France invasion, served Number One Info Unit attached to Control Cmmn Germany, involved in activities connected with estab of free press, final rank Major, final post press offr N Rhine Westphalia; Reuters: corr in France Germany and Turkey 1950–60, asst gen mangr 1960–63, chief exec 1963–81, gen mangr 1963–73, md 1973–81; chm Visnews Ltd 1968–79, md Times Newspapers Ltd 1981–82, dep chm News International 1982–84; chm Exec Ctee Int Inst of Communications Ltd 1973–78, exec dir Journalists in Europe 1987–89, memb Design Cncl 1974–77; Commander Royal Order of the Phoenix (Greece) 1964, Grand Offr Order of Merit (Italy) 1973, Commander Order of Lion of Finland 1979, Chevalier Légion d'Honneur (France) 1979, Commander's Cross, Order of Merit (Germany) 1983; CIMgt (FIMgt 1978); *Recreations* cooking; *Style*— Gerald Long, Esq; ✉ 15 Rue d'Aumale, 75009 Paris, France (☎ 00 331 48 74 67 26); 15 Rue W K Ferguson, 14400 St Martin-des-Entrées (☎ 00 33 31 92 47 12)

LONG, Jeremy Paul Warwick; s of Ronald Walter Long, of Warwick, and Gwendolen Dorothy Long; *b* 24 March 1953; *Educ* Warwick Sch, Exeter Coll Oxford (MA); *m* Suzanne; 3 da; *Career* former chief exec Pavilion Services Ltd, dir BrightReasons Ltd, dep chief exec Mecca Leisure Group; currently chief exec Central London Training and Enterprise Council; FCA; *Recreations* tennis, theatre, cinema, skiing; *Style*— Jeremy Long, Esq; ✉ Central London Training, and Enterprise Council, 39 Victoria Street, London SW1 0UD (☎ 0171 314 0160, fax 0171 314 0161)

LONG, Martyn Howard; CBE (1991), DL; s of Victor Frederick Long (d 1993), and Dorothy Maud, *née* Lawrence; *b* 1933; *Educ* Univ Coll Sch London, Merrist Wood Agric Coll Surrey; *m* 4 Oct 1958, Veronica Mary Gascoigne, da of James Edward Bates (d 1952); 4 da (Helen b 1959, Maria b 1961, Samantha b 1965, Rosalind b 1969); *Career* Nat Serv RAF 1952–54; farmer 1949–85, dir of family firm; memb: W Sussex Area Health Authy 1973–77, SW Thames Regnl Health Authy 1980–81; chm: Mid-Downs Health Authy W Sussex 1981–94, Nat Assoc of Health Authorities 1988–90; vice chm Nat Assoc of Health Authys and Tsts 1990–93 (chm Health Authy Ctee 1990–93), chm Sussex Ambulance Service NHS Trust 1995–; chm E Grinstead Cons Assoc 1972–75; W Sussex CC: cncllr (C) 1973–93, chm Policy and Resources Ctee 1985–89, chm 1989–93; cncllr: E Sussex CC 1970–74, Cuckfield RDC 1972–74, Mid Sussex DC 1973–79; memb Assoc of CCs 1979–89, chm ACC Social Servs 1987–89, chm Br Homoeopathic Assoc 1993–95, memb Cncl & Instn King Edward VII Hosp Midhurst 1992–, tstee Mobility Tst 1993–; *Recreations* magic (assoc memb Inner Magic Circle with Silver Star); *Clubs* Farmers', Sussex; *Style*— Martyn Long, Esq, CBE, DL; ✉ Lunces Cottage, Church Lane, Wivelsfield, Haywards Heath, Sussex RH17 7RD (☎ 01444 471517)

LONG, Michael John; s of John Robert Long, and Annie Mabel, *née* Oates; *b* 15 March 1947; *Educ* King Edward VI GS East Retford, St John's Coll Cambridge (MA); *m* 23 Aug 1969, (Ursula) Christel, da of Alfred Kaempf (d 1944), of Wuerzburg, Germany; *Career* slr: Stephenson Harwood 1969–73, Donne Mileham & Haddock 1973–; memb Cncl Law Soc 1982–, senator JCI; treas Sussex Branch Cambridge Soc, tstee and sec Brighton Festival Tst; Liveryman Worshipful Co of Solicitors; *Books* Some Aspects of the Family Business (with D T Sparrow, 1979); *Recreations* Scotland, opera, theatre; *Clubs* United Oxford and Cambridge Univ; *Style*— Michael Long, Esq; ✉ Donne Mileham & Haddock, Frederick Place, Brighton, E Sussex BN1 1AT (☎ 01273 29833, fax 01273 739764)

LONG, 4 Viscount (UK 1921); Richard Gerard Long; CBE (1993); s of 3 Viscount Long, TD, JP, DL (d 1967); *b* 30 Jan 1929; *Educ* Harrow; *m* 1, 2 March 1957 (m dis 1984), Margaret Frances, da of Ninian Frazer; 1 s, 1 da (and 1 decd); m 2, 1984 (m dis 1990), Catherine Patricia Elizabeth Mier Woolf, da of Charles Terrence Miles-Ede, of Leicester; m 3, 19 June 1990, Helen Millar Wright Fleming-Gibbons; *Heir* s, Hon James Richard Long b 31 Dec 1960; *Career* The Wilts Regt 1947–49; vice pres Wilts Royal Br Legion; oppn whip 1974–79, Lord-in-Waiting (Govt whip) 1979–; Freeman City of London 1991; *Recreations* shooting, gardening; *Style*— The Rt Hon the Viscount Long, CBE; ✉ House of Lords, London SW1A 0PW

LONG, Dr Richard Glover; s of John Long (d 1978), of Higham, Kent, and Bridget, *née* Harrison; *b* 13 Aug 1947; *Educ* Canford Royal Free Hosp Sch of Med (MB BS, MD); *m* 12 Feb 1983, Anita Rosemary, da of Kenneth Eaton Wilson, of Aldridge, West Midlands; 1 s (Charles Matthew b 1983); *Career* hon sr registrar Hammersmith Hosp 1978–80, sr registrar St Thomas Hosp 1980–83, MRC travelling res fell San Francisco USA 1983, conslt gastroenterologist and clinical teacher Nottingham Hosp Med Sch 1983–; memb: Assoc of Physicians of GB and Ireland, Br Soc of Gastroenterology, American Gastroenterology Assoc, Med Res Soc; FRCP 1989; *Books* Radioimmunossay of Gut Regulatory Reptides (jt ed with S R Bloom, 1982); *Recreations* fly fishing; *Style*— Dr Richard Long; ✉ Coach House, Old Hall Drive, Widmerpool, Nottingham NG12 5PZ (☎ 0115 937 2467); City Hospital, Nottingham NG5 1PB (☎ 0115 969 1169); Park Hospital, Sherwood Lodge Drive, Arnold, Nottingham NG5 8RX (☎ 0115 967 0670)

LONG, Sarah; *see:* Littler, Hon Mrs (Sarah Victoria)

LONG, William John; s of Maj Richard Samuel Long, of Brook, Newport, IOW, and Mary, *née* Charrington; *b* 11 Nov 1943; *Educ* Woodbridge Sch; *m* 15 Jan 1969, Sarah Jane, da of Philip Barton Lockwood (d 1992); 2 s (Samuel b 18 April 1974, John b 8 April 1979), 1 da (Jane b 6 Feb 1972); *Career* ptnr: Laing & Cruickshank 1973–79, Milton Mortimer & Co 1982–86; dir: Lockwoods Food Ltd 1977–82, National Investment Group Ltd 1986–, Capel-Cure Myers Capital Management Ltd 1990–; underwriting memb Lloyd's; memb Earl Marshall's staff for state funeral of Sir Winston Churchill; MSI (memb Stock Exhange 1972); *Recreations* sailing, fishing, shooting and genealogy; *Style*— William Long, Esq; ✉ Coombe Fishacre House, Coombefishacre, Newton Abbot, Devon TQ12 5UQ (☎ 01803 812242); The Registry, Royal Mint Court, London EC3N 4EY; 35 Southernhay East, Exeter EX1 1NX (☎ 01394 76244, fax 01392 72161)

LONGAIR, Prof Malcolm Sim; *b* 18 May 1941; *Educ* Morgan Acad Dundee, Queen's Coll Univ of St Andrews (James Caird travelling scholar), Univ of Cambridge (James Clerk Maxwell scholar, MA, PhD); *m* Deborah Janet; 1 s (Mark Howard b 13 Sept 1976), 1 da (Sarah Charlotte b 7 March 1979); *Career* lectr Dept of Physics and visiting asst prof of radio astronomy California Inst for Advanced Study Princeton 1978, exchange visitor to USSR Space Res Inst Moscow (on 6 occasions) 1975–79, regius prof of astronomy Univ of Edinburgh 1980–90, dir Royal Observatory Edinburgh 1980–90, Astronomer Royal for Scotland 1980–90; visiting lectr: (in astronomy and astrophysics) Pennsylvania State Univ 1986, Univ of Victoria Canada; Regents fellowship Smithsonian Institution at Smithsonian Astrophysical Observatory Harvard 1990; Jacksonian prof of natural philosophy Univ of Cambridge 1991– (demonstrator Dept of Physics 1970–75, official fell and praelector Clare Hall 1971–80); memb: IUE Observatory Ctee 1975–78, Working Gp Euro Space Agency 1975–78, Interdisciplinary Scientists for the Hubble Space Telescope 1977–, Anglo Aust Telescope Bd 1982–87, Space Science Programme Bd 1985–88; chm: Space Telescope Advsy Panel 1977–84, Astronomy II (AII) Ctee 1979–80 (memb 1977–78), Millimetre Telescope Users Ctee 1979–83, Space Telescope Science Inst 1982–84; author of numerous scientific papers, has given numerous public lectures; Hon LLD Univ of Dundee 1982; FRAS, FRSE 1981; *Books* Observational Cosmology (co-ed J E Gunn and M J Rees, 1978), High Energy Astrophysics (1981), Theoretical Concepts in Physics (1984), Alice and the Space Telescope (1989), The Origins of Our Universe (1990), High Energy Astrophysics Vol 1 (1992); *Recreations* music, opera, art, architecture, golf; *Style*— Prof Malcolm Longair, FRSE; ✉ Cavendish Laboratory, University of Cambridge, Cambridge CB3 0HE (☎ 01223 337083)

LONGBOTHAM, Charles Norman; s of George Norman Longbotham (d 1949), and Alice Dillon Malcolm, *née* Campbell (d 1957); *b* 6 July 1917; *Educ* Portsmouth GS, HM Trg Ship Conway River Mersey; *m* 1, 1940, Eleanor Friedel, *née* Nairn-Allison (d 1972); 1 da (Joy Claire Allison (Mrs Claire Dalby) b 1944); *m* 2, 1979, Jeanie Mary Purefoy Campbell-Taylor, da of Rev John Goodacre; *Career* artist; apprentice at sea NZ Shipping Co Ltd 1935–37, engrg apprentice Messrs Mirrless Bickerton & Day Stockport 1939; offr RNR at sea and ashore 1940–45; professional modelmaker and dioramist 1946–69; modelmaking and design projects incl: Britain Can Make It exhbn Cncl of Industl Design 1946–47, Festival of Britain 1951, Brussels World Fair 1958, Shell Centre, London Airport, aircraft interiors for BOAC, Addenbrooke's Hospital, involved with design of QE2 exterior 1966; full-time watercolourist 1969–, numerous solo and gp exhbns (first solo exhbn FBA Galleries London 1965); RWS 1974 (ARWS 1969); *Style*— Charles Longbotham, Esq; ✉ 35 Owlstone Road, Newnham, Cambridge CB3 9JH (☎ 01223 357609); c/o Royal Watercolour Society, Bankside Gallery, 48 Hopton Street, Blackfriars, London SE1 9JH (☎ 0171 928 7521)

LONGBOTTOM, Charles Brooke; s of William Ewart Longbottom (d 1943); *b* 22 July 1930; *Educ* Uppingham; *m* Anita, da of Giulio Trapani; 2 da; *Career* called to the Bar Inner Temple, contested (C) Stockton on Tees 1955, MP (C) York 1959–66, PPS to Chllr of Duchy of Lancaster 1961–63; chm: Austin & Pickersgill Shipbuilders Sunderland 1966–72, A & P Appledore Ltd 1970–78, Seascope Holdings Ltd 1970–82, Seascope Shipping Ltd 1970–86, Illingworth Morris Pension Tstees Ltd 1990–94; dir: Henry Ansbacher Holdings plc, Henry Ansbacher & Co, Ansbacher Guernsey Ltd 1982–86, Kelt Energy plc 1987–95, MC Shipping Inc, Newman Martin & Buchan; memb: Gen Advsy Cncl BBC 1965–75, Community Rels Cmmn 1968–70; pt/t memb Bd of Br Shipbuilders, chm Acorn Christian Healing Tst; *Style*— Charles Longbottom, Esq; ✉ 66 Kingston House North, Princes Gate, London SW7

LONGDEN, Christopher John; s of John Stuart Longden (d 1994), of Sheffield, Yorkshire, and Daisy, *née* Heath; *b* 22 March 1955; *Educ* Granville Coll Sheffield, Blackpool Coll; *m* 31 March 1978, Carol, da of Bryan Pettinger; 2 s (Benjamin b 6 July 1981, James b 15 Feb 1984), 1 da (Jennifer b 31 March 1985); *Career* trainee mangr British Transport Hotels 1974–77, food and beverage mangr Hotel L'Horizon Jersey CI 1977–81, mangr Gleddoch House Hotel & Country Club Langbank 1981–85, md Gleddoch Hotels (incl Gleddoch House, Gleddoch Golf Club and Houstoun House Broxburn) 1985–91, exec gen mangr (pre-opening) Vermont Hotel Newcastle upon Tyne 1992–93, gen mangr Ballathie House Hotel Perthshire 1993–; Master Innholder 1986, Freeman City of London 1986; fell HCIMA 1974; *Recreations* yacht racing; *Style*— Christopher Longden, Esq; ✉ Ballathie House Hotel, Kinclaven, by Stanley, Perthshire PH1 4QN (☎ 01250 883268, fax 01250 883396)

LONGDEN, Sir Gilbert James Morley; kt (1972), MBE (Mil 1944); s of Lt-Col James Morley Longden, and Kathleen Morgan; *b* 16 April 1902; *Educ* Haileybury, Emmanuel Coll Cambridge (MA, LLB), Sorbonne; *Career* serv WWII with Durham LI, 2 Div and 36 Div in Burma Campaign; admitted slr 1927; sec ICI (India) Ltd 1930–38; contested (C) Morpeth 1945, MP (C) SW Herts 1950–74; UK del: Cncl of Europe 1953, XII and XIII Sessions of the UN 1957–58; *Books* A Conservative Philosophy (1947); jtly: One Nation (1950), Change is Our Ally (1954), A Responsible Society (1959), One Europe (1969); *Clubs* Brooks's; *Style*— Sir Gilbert Longden, MBE; ✉ 89 Cornwall Gardens, London SW7 4AX (☎ 0171 584 5666)

LONGDEN, John Charles Henry; s of Henry A Longden, FEng, of Woldingham, Surrey, and Ruth, *née* Gilliat; *b* 10 May 1938; *Educ* Oundle, Royal Sch of Mines Imperial Coll London; *m* 1965, Marion Rose, da of Dr W G S Maxwell; 1 da (Sarah b 1966), 2 s (Henry b 1969, Richard b 1971); *Career* British Coal Corporation (formerly National Coal Board): mining trainee 1960–63, various jr mgmnt posts 1963–67, mangr Welbeck Colliery Notts 1969–75 (dep mangr 1967–68), sr mining engr (planning and surveying) N Notts Area 1976–80, dep dir of mining S Midlands 1985 (chief mining engr 1980–85), dep dir of mining Notts 1986–88, dep operations dir HQ Eastwood 1988–89, actg area dir Notts and gp dir 1989–93, gp dir Midlands 1993–94; currently conslt mining engr; MIOSH, FEng 1992, fell Inst of Mining Engrs, FIMgt, FRSA; *Recreations* early motoring, sailing; *Clubs* Veteran Car Club of GB; *Style*— John Longden, Esq, FEng; ✉ Stonebank, Potter Lane, Wellow, Newark, Notts NG22 0EB (☎ 01623 861137)

LONGE, Laurence Peter; s of Robert John Longe, of Hollywood, W Midlands, and Ellen, *née* Mullally; *b* 9 Jan 1955; *Educ* St Thomas Aquinas' GS King's Norton; *m* 6 Sept 1980, Allyson Daphne, da of William Daniel Roberts; 1 s (Simon Laurence b 26 Nov 1986), 1 da (Rachel Allyson b 8 May 1992); *Career* Inland Revenue 1974–78, tax sr Dearden Farrow 1979–80, tax mangr KPMG Peat Marwick 1981–87; Baker Tilly: tax dir 1987–88, managing ptnr London Tax Dept 1988–91, managing ptnr Watford office 1991–96, nat managing ptnr 1996–; ATII 1981, ACA 1986; *Recreations* reading, listening to music, computer games; *Style*— Laurence Longe, Esq; ✉ Baker Tilly, Iveco Ford House, Station Road, Watford, Herts WD1 1TG (☎ 01923 816400, fax 01923 253402)

LONGE, Nicholas; s of late Lt Col Roland Bacon Longe, and Diana, *née* Hastings, of Hasketon Manor Lodge, Woodbridge, Suffolk; *b* 20 March 1938; *Educ* St Peter's Court, Harrow; *m* 14 March 1970, Julia Victoria, da of Maj David Arthur Peel, MC (ka 1944), and The Hon Sara Peel; 2 s (William b 1972, David b 1975); *Career* Sub Lt RN 1957–59; farmer; PE Consulting Gp Ltd 1968–73, dir Brook House Investmts Ltd 1985–89; memb Apple and Pear Devpt Cncl 1979–89 (chm Research Gp 1987–88), dir Kingdom Mktg Scheme 1980–89 (chm 1980–82), chm Museum of E Anglian Life 1980–96; High Sheriff of Suffolk 1984–85; Freeman: City of London, Worshipful Co of Fruiterers; *Recreations* sailing, sport, reading; *Clubs* Naval and Military; *Style*— Nicholas Longe, Esq; ✉ Hasketon Manor, Woodbridge, Suffolk; Grange Farm, Hasketon, Woodbridge, Suffolk (☎ 01473 735095)

LONGFIELD, Richard Lewis; s of John Longfield, OBE (d 1992), and Mary Lyon, *née* Waddell; *b* 2 Nov 1939; *Educ* Marlborough Coll, Trinity Coll Dublin (BA); *m* Felicity Laura, da of Alex Miller, of Straidarran, Co Londonderry; 1 s (Edward), 2 da (Onnalee (Mrs Hugo Cubitt), Shauna (Mrs John Garnett)); *Career* formerly head public affrs Shell UK oil; md: Longueville Energy, Longueville Communications; *Recreations* photography, golf, gardening, fishing; *Style*— Richard Longfield, Esq; ✉ The Old Rectory, Weston Patrick, Hampshire RG25 2NU; Longueville Energy (☎ 01256 862966, fax 01256 862973, e-mail 100410.2127@compuserve.comp)

LONGFORD, Countess of; Elizabeth; CBE (1974); da of late Nathaniel Bishop Harman, FRCS, and Katherine, *née* Chamberlain; *b* 30 Aug 1906; *Educ* Headington Sch Oxford, Lady Margaret Hall Oxford (MA); *m* 1931, Hon Francis Pakenham, 7 Earl of Longford, *qv*; 4 s (Thomas *qv*, Patrick, Michael, *qv*, Kevin, *qv*), 3 da (Lady Antonia Fraser, *qv*, Judith (Mrs Alexander Kazantzis), Lady Rachel Billington, *qv*), 1 da decd; *Career* author (as Elizabeth Longford and Elizabeth Pakenham); lectr WEA and univ extension lectr 1929–35; contested (Lab): Cheltenham 1935, Oxford 1950; candidate for King's Norton Birmingham 1935–43; memb Rent Tbnl Paddington and St Pancras 1947–54; tstee Nat Portrait Gallery 1968–78; memb: Advsy Cncl V&A Museum 1969–75, Advsy Bd Br Library 1976–79; vice-pres London Library 1983–; Hon DLitt Sussex 1970; FRSL; *Books* biographies incl: Victoria RI (James Tait Black Prize), Wellington (2 vols, Yorkshire Post Prize for vol I, condensed vol 1992), The Royal House of Windsor, Churchill, Byron, Wilfrid Scawen Blunt, The Queen Mother, Elizabeth R (1983); other books: Jameson's Raid (reprinted 1982), The Pebbled Shore (memoir, 1986), The Oxford Book of Royal Anecdotes (1989), Darling Loosy - Letters to Princess Louise (1991), Poets' Corner - An Anthology (1992), Royal Throne (1993); *Style*— The Rt Hon the Countess of Longford, CBE; ✉ Bernhurst, Hurst Green, E Sussex (☎ 0158 0860248); 18 Chesil Court, Chelsea Manor St, London SW3 (0171 352 7794)

LONGFORD, 7 Earl of (I 1785); Francis Aungier Pakenham; KG (1971), PC (1948); also Baron Longford (I 1756), Baron Silchester (UK 1821), Baron Pakenham (UK 1945); sits as Baron Pakenham; s of 5 Earl of Longford, KP, MVO (ka 1915), by his w, Lady Mary Julia Child-Villiers (d 1933, da of 7 Earl of Jersey); suc bro, 6 Earl, 1961; *b* 5 Dec 1905; *Educ* Eton, New Coll Oxford; *m* 1931, Elizabeth, Countess of Longford, CBE, *qv*, da of late Nathaniel Bishop Harman, FRCS; 4 s (Thomas *qv*, Patrick, Michael, *qv*, Kevin, *qv*), 3 da (Lady Antonia Fraser, *qv*, Judith (Mrs Alexander Kazantzis), Lady Rachel Billington, *qv*), 1 da decd; *Heir* s, Thomas Pakenham; *Career* sits as Labour peer in Lords; lord-in-waiting to HM 1945–46, Parly under sec of state for War 1946–47, Chllr of Duchy of Lancaster 1947–48, min of Civil Aviation 1948–51, first Lord of the Admty May-Oct 1951 and Lord Privy Seal 1964–65, sec of state for the colonies 1965–66, Lord Privy Seal 1966–68; chm Sidgwick & Jackson 1970–80; *Style*— The Rt Hon The Earl of Longford, KG, PC; ✉ Bernhurst, Hurst Green, East Sussex (☎ 0158 0860248); 18 Chesil Court, Chelsea Manor St, SW3 (☎ 0171 352 7794)

LONGHURST, Andrew Henry; s of Henry Longhurst, and Connie, *née* Evason; *b* 23 Aug 1939; *Educ* Glyn GS, Univ of Nottingham (BSc); *m* 1962, Margaret; 2 da, 1 s; *Career* Cheltenham & Gloucester Building Society: data processing mangr 1967–70, asst gen mangr (admin) 1970–77, dep gen mangr 1977–82, chief exec 1982–95; chief exec Cheltenham & Gloucester plc 1995–, dir: Lloyds Bank Plc 1995–, TSB Bank plc 1995–; memb: Cncl BSA 1985–, Nat House Building Cncl 1988–, Exec Ctee Metropolitan Assoc of Building Socs 1989–95, Exec Ctee Cncl of Mortgage Lenders 1989– (chm 1994), DTI Deregulation Task Force on Financial Servs 1993; dir Nat Waterways Museum Tst 1989–, pres Glos Operatic and Dramatic Soc 1990–; CIMgt, FBCS, FCIB; *Recreations* golf; *Style*— Andrew Longhurst, Esq; ✉ Cheltenham & Gloucester plc, Barnett Way, Gloucester GL4 3RL (☎ 01452 372372, fax 01452 373955)

LONGLEY, Adrian Reginald; OBE (1991); s of Evelyn Longley (d 1956), and Mary Anastasia, *née* Thompson (d 1962); *b* 27 Sept 1925; *Educ* Winchester, Trinity Coll Cambridge (MA); *m* 14 Dec 1957, Sylvia Margaret, da of Capt George Keith Homfray Hayter (d 1968); 3 da (Anne b 1959, Joanna b 1960, Melissa b 1963); *Career* Mil Serv Rifle Bde (A/Capt) served M East 1944–47; admitted slr 1959; Freshfields 1959–69, White Brooks and Gilman 1970–72; consit to NCVO, CPRE and other charities 1991– (legal advsr NCVO 1972–90); memb NCVO Ctees: on Malpractice in Fundraising for Charity, Report 1986, on Effectiveness and the Voluntary Sector, Report 1990; memb: Goodman Ctee on Charity Law and Voluntary Organisations 1974–76, Cncl L'Orchestre du Monde (Orchestra of the World) 1988; hon fell Inst of Charity Fundraising Managers; tstee: Cyril Wood Meml Tst, Menerva Educnl Tst, Russian Euro Tst; UK contrib Les Associations et Fondations en Europe: Régime Juridique et Fiscal 1990 and 1994; *Publications* contrib: Charity Finance Handbook (1992/93, 1993/94 and 1994/95), Charity Law & Practice Review (1992), ICSA Charities Administration Manual (1992/93), Charities: The Law & Practice (FT LAW & TAX, formerly Longmans, 1994, 1995, 1996 and 1997); *Recreations* music, reading, foreign travel; *Clubs* Royal Commonwealth Soc, Cavalry & Guards', MCC; *Style*— Adrian R Longley, Esq, OBE; ✉ Vijay Sharma Solicitors, 142 Buckingham Palace Road, London SW1W 9TR (☎ 0171 730 7322, fax 0171 730 4150); 7 Kersley St, London SW11 4PR (☎ 0171 924 5799)

LONGLEY, Mrs Ann Rosamund; da of Jack Dearlove (d 1967), of Sevenoaks, Kent, and Rhoda, *née* Billing; *b* 5 March 1942; *Educ* Walthamstow Hall Sch, Univ of Edinburgh (MA); *m* 12 Dec 1964, Stephen R Longley (d 1979), s of Cedric J Longley (d 1987), of Histon; 1 s (Justin b 25 Oct 1965), 2 da (Catherine b 20 Aug 1968, Emma b 14 May 1970); *Career* teacher: Toorak Coll Aust 1964–65, Choate Sch Conn USA 1968–73, Webb Sch California USA 1975–78; asst house mistress Peninsula C of E Sch Victoria Aust 1966–67; headmistress: Vivian Webb Sch California USA 1981–84, Roedean 1984–; Hon DUniv Sussex; fell ESU; FRSA; *Recreations* tennis, swimming, fishing, walking; *Style*—

Mrs Ann Longley; ✉ Roedean House, Roedean Sch, Brighton, E Sussex BN2 5RQ (☎ 01273 603181)

LONGLEY, Clifford; s of Harold Anson Longley, of Purley, Surrey, and Gladys, *née* Gibbs; *b* 1940; *Educ* Trinity Sch Croydon, Univ of Southampton (BSc (Eng)); *m*; 3 c; *Career* journalist; reporter: Essex and Thurrock Gazette 1961–64, Portsmouth Evening News 1964–67; The Times: reporter 1967–69, asst news ed 1969–71, feature writer 1971–72, religious affairs corr and columnist 1972–87, ldr writer 1984–92, religious affairs ed and columnist 1987–92, asst ed (leaders) 1990–92; The Daily Telegraph: columnist 1992–, ldr writer 1992–95, religious affairs ed 1994–95; columnist and contributing ed The Tablet 1994– (actg ed 1996); Univ of Oxford select preacher 1988, Hugh Kay meml lectr 1990; Br Press Awards Specialist Writer of the Year 1986; *Books* The Times Book of Clifford Longley (1991); *Recreations* music; *Style—* Clifford Longley, Esq; ✉ 24 Broughton Road, Orpington, Kent BR6 8EQ (☎ 01689 853189, fax 01689 811279)

LONGLEY, James Timothy Chapman; s of Alan Timothy Chapman Longley, of Haxby, nr York, and Avrill Ruth Nunn, *née* Midgley; *b* 21 May 1959; *Educ* Worksop Coll, Leeds Metropolitan Univ (BA); *Career* CA; Finnie and Co 1980–83, Arthur Andersen and Co 1983–85, Creditanstalt-Bankverein 1985–88, Touche Ross and Co 1988–89, The Wilcox Gp Ltd 1990, ptnr Chapman Longley CAs; dir: Fleet Management Group Ltd, Chapman Longley Ltd, White Horse Asset Management Ltd; FCA 1983; *Recreations* skiing, riding, tennis; *Clubs* Groucho; *Style—* James Longley, Esq; ✉ 33B Marryat Square, Fulham, London SW6 6UA (☎ 0171 493 4229); The Hoochie Coochie Club PLC, 10 White Horse Street, Mayfair, London W1Y 7LB (☎ 0171 493 4229, fax 0171 493 4239)

LONGLEY, Michael; JP (1974); s of Sir Norman Longley, KBE, DL (d 1994), of Crawley, W Sussex, and Dorothy Lilian, *née* Baker; *b* 23 July 1929; *Educ* Clifton, Brighton Tech Coll; *m* 24 Sept 1955, Rosemary, da of Walter Jackson (d 1968); 2 s (Julian Philip b 1957, James Christopher b 1959, d 1977); *Career* dir James Longley Holdings Ltd 1961–94; chm: Longley Developments 1961–94, James Longley and Co Ltd 1967–89, James Longley Enterprises Ltd 1976–94, Longley Freeholds Ltd 1979–94, Longley Properties Ltd 1981–94, Reigate Securities Ltd 1985–94; dir Compass Property Services Ltd 1992–; Freeman City of London 1950, Liveryman Worshipful Co of Armourers and Brasiers 1963; FCIOB 1980; *Recreations* gardening, ornithology, natural history, property speculation; *Style—* Michael Longley, Esq, JP; ✉ Home Farm House, Chelwood Vachery, Millbrook Hill, Nutley, Uckfield, East Sussex TN22 3HR (☎ 01825 712867)

LONGLEY, Michael; *b* 1939, Belfast; *Educ* Royal Belfast Academical Instn, Trinity Coll Dublin; *m* Edna Longley, the critic; 3 c; *Career* poet and writer; sometime teacher Dublin, London and Belfast, combined arts dir Arts Cncl of NI until 1991; author of numerous scripts for BBC Schools Dept, regular bdcaster; work has been the subject of four films incl The Corner of the Eye (RTE, BBC and C4); memb Aosdana, fndr memb Cultural Traditions Gp NI; FRSL; *Awards* Eric Gregory Award, British Airways Cwlth Poetry Prize, Whitbread Poetry Prize, Cholmondeley Award, others from Charitable Irish Soc of Boston, Irish American Cultural Inst and Ireland Funds of America; *Books* collections of poetry: No Continuing City (1969), An Exploded View (1973), Man Lying on a Wall (1976), The Echo Gate (1979), Poems 1963–1983 (1985, re-issued 1991), Gorse Fires (1991, winner Whitbread Prize for Poetry), The Ghost Orchid (1995, TS Eliot Award nominee 1996); ed: Causeway (on the Arts in Ulster), Under the Moon, Over the Stars (children's verse), Selected Poems of Louis MacNeice, Poems of W R Rodgers; *Style—* Michael Longley, Esq, FRSL; ✉ c/o Peters, Fraser & Dunlop, 503 The Chambers, Chelsea Harbour, Lots Road, London SW10 0XF (☎ 0171 344 1000)

LONGLEY, Peter; OBE (1993), DL (1991); s of Sir Norman Longley, CBE, DL (d 1994), and Dorothy Lilian Baker; *b* 28 July 1927; *Educ* Clifton; *m* 1954, Mary, da of Sidney Brittain (d 1974); 1 s (Robert b 1960), 2 da (Elizabeth b 1956, Alison b 1958); *Career* building contractor; chm: James Longley (Holdings) Ltd, Clayton House (Toc H) Crawley Ltd, The Longley Tst; dir: James Longley & Co Ltd 1961–87, BEC Pension Tstees Ltd, Amberley Chalk Pits Museum; pres Crawley Boys' Club, vice pres Sussex Assoc of Boys' Clubs; High Sheriff for County of West Sussex 1994–95; Liveryman Worshipful Co of Armourers and Brasiers; FRSA, FCIOB; *Clubs* Sussex; *Style—* Peter Longley, Esq, OBE, DL; ✉ Lackenhurst, Brooks Green, Horsham, W Sussex RH13 7JL; Longley House, East Park, Crawley, W Sussex (☎ 01293 561212)

LONGMAN, Lady Elizabeth Mary; *née* Lambart; er da of Field Marshal 10 Earl of Cavan, KP, GCB, GCMG, GCVO, CBE (d 1946), and Joan, Countess of Cavan, DBE (d 1976); *b* 16 Oct 1924; *m* 1949, Mark Frederic Kerr Longman (d 1972), 5 s of late Henry Kerr Longman, of Wildwood, Pyrford, Surrey; 3 da; *Career* bridesmaid at wedding of HM The Queen 1947; former dir The Fine Art Society plc (ret 1994), tstee Harrison Homes; *Recreations* gardening; *Style—* The Lady Elizabeth Longman; ✉ The Old Rectory, Todenham, Moreton-in-Marsh, Glos; 1–58 Rutland Gate, London SW7 (☎ 0171 581 1230)

LONGMAN, (James Edward) Ford; s of George Lewis Ernest Longman (d 1989), and Alice Lizzie Mary (d 1954); *b* 8 Dec 1928; *Educ* Watford GS, Birkbeck Coll Univ of London (BSc), Univ of Leeds; *m* 22 May 1954, Dilys Menai, da of Reginald Wilfred Richard Hunt (d 1972); 2 s (Jonathan b 1955, Richard b 1962), 3 da (Sarah b 1957, Rachel b 1960, Margaret b 1965); *Career* RAF Radar/Wireless Sch and Educn Branch 1947–49; Miny of Health, Bd of Control and Office Min for Sci 1949–62; hon sec Watford Cncl of Churches 1950–62 (lay preacher); asst dir Joseph Rowntree Meml Tst 1962–70; dir Yorks (Regnl) Cncl Social Serv, sec seven other regnl bodies 1970–75; hon sec Yorks Arts Assoc 1970–76, chm Yorks CSS 1967–70, sometime memb of ten Govt Ctees on Social Servs and Penal Matters (incl Ctee on Serv Overseas), memb Lord Chllr's Advsy Ctee on Crown Cts (NECCT), chm Bd HM Borstal Wetherby, conslt in social planning Govt of W Berlin and UNESCO, pioneered community devpt in Br, chm All-Pty Utd World Tst for Educn and Res, exec memb Nat Peace Cncl and NCSS, memb Yorks and Humberside Regnl Econ Planning Cncl 1965–72; jt fndr: Christian Industrial Leadership Schs, St Leonard's Housing Assoc, York Abbeyfield Soc, Regnl Studies Assoc, Community Devpt Tst 1968 (dir 1968–76); HM Inspr of Community Educn 1975–83; co cncllr N Yorks 1985–: dep ldr Lib Democrat Gp 1989–93, memb Exec Ctee Assoc of CCs 1993–95, currently chm Personnel Ctee, chm Appeals, dep chm Corp Policy Ctee; Parly candidate (Lib/SDP Alliance) Selby 1987; currently memb: Soc of Friends (Quakers), Methodist Church (local preacher), N Yorks Valuation Ct, Green Democrats, Lib Democrat Christian Forum, Yorkshire Provincial Cncl, N Yorks Police Authy, N Yorks Moors Nat Park Authy, Ripon Diocesan Bd of Social Responsibility; chm Ryedale Constituency Lib Democrats; govr Univ Coll Ripon and York St John, sometime govr twelve colls and schs; life fell and hon prof of community devpt Univ of Victoria; Hon DD, Hon LLD, Hon DPhil; FRAI; Baron Ordre Royal de la Couronne de Bohème, Knight Order of Holy Grail, Knight Cdr Lofsensichen Ursinius-orden, Knight Templar Order of Jerusalem; *Recreations* painting, gliding, reading, renovating historic buildings (with wife, restored Healaugh Priory 1981–86), writing; *Style—* Dr Ford Longman; ✉ Toby's Cottage, Slingsby, York YO6 7AH (☎ 01653 628402, fax 01653 628045)

LONGMAN, Peter Martin; s of Denis Martin Longman, of Somerset, and Mary Joy, *née* Simmonds (d 1977); *b* 2 March 1946; *Educ* Huish's Sch Taunton, Univ Coll Cardiff (BSc), Univ of Manchester (Drama); *m* 22 May 1976, Sylvia June, da of John Lancaster Prentice, of E Sussex; 2 da (Tania Louise b 1978, Natalie Therese b 1981); *Career* housing arts offr Arts Cncl GB 1969–78 (Fin Dept 1968–69), dep dir Crafts Cncl 1978–83, dir and sec Museums & Galleries Cmmn 1990–95 (dep sec 1983–84, sec 1984–90), dir The Theatres Trust 1995– (tstee 1991–95); conslt on arts, heritage and museums 1995–; sec working pty reports on: Trg Arts Administrators Arts Cncl 1971, Area Museum Cncls and Servs HMSO 1984, Museums in Scot HMSO 1986; memb: Arts Centres Panel Gtr London Arts Assoc 1981–83, Bd of Caryl Jenner Prodns Ltd (Unicorn Theatre for Children) 1983–87, Cncl Textile Conservation Centre Ltd 1983–, co-opted Bd Scot Museums Cncl 1986–95, British Tourist Authy Heritage Ctee 1991–95, Exec Ctee Cncl for Dance Educn and Trg 1996–, Advsy Ctee Art in Churches 1996–; FRSA 1989, Hon FMA 1995; *Recreations* discovering Britain, listening to music, looking at buildings; *Style—* Peter Longman, Esq; ✉ The Theatres Trust, 22 Charing Cross Road, London WC2H 0HR (☎ 0171 836 8591, fax 0171 836 3302)

LONGMORE, Hon Mr Justice; Hon Sir Andrew Centlivres; s of Dr John Bell Longmore (d 1973), of Shrewsbury, and Virginia Albertina, *née* Centlivres; *b* 25 Aug 1944; *Educ* Winchester, Lincoln Coll Oxford (MA); *m* 17 Oct 1979, Margaret Murray, da of Dr James McNair (d 1980), of Milngavie, Glasgow; 1 s (James Centlivres b 1981); *Career* called to the Bar Middle Temple 1966, bencher 1990; QC 1983, recorder of the Crown Ct 1992–93, judge of the High Court of Justice (Queen's Bench Div) 1993–; memb Bar Cncl 1982–85, chm Law Reform Ctee 1987–90; *Books* MacGillivray and Parkington Law of Insurance (co-ed, 6 edn 1975, 7 edn 1981, 8 edn 1988); *Recreations* fell-walking; *Style—* The Hon Mr Justice Longmore; ✉ Royal Courts of Justice, Strand, London WC2A 2LL

LONGMORE, Prof Donald Bernard; s of Bernard George Longmore (d 1992), of Sandwich, Kent, and Beatrix Alice, *née* Payne (d 1993); *b* 20 Feb 1928; *Educ* Solihull Sch, Guy's Hosp Med Sch (MB BS), Baylor Univ Texas, Univ of Texas, The London Hosp; *m* 2 April 1956, Patricia Christine Greig, da of Arthur Hardman Spindler (d 1984), of Bray on Thames, Berks; 3 da (Annabel b 1958, Juliet b 1959, Susan (Mrs Richard Smith) b 1962); *Career* Guy's Hosp: house appts 1953, jr lectr in anatomy 1954; surgical resident Baylor Univ Texas 1956–58, surgical registrar London Hosp 1958–59, sr registrar Middx Hosp 1960–61, lectr in surgery St Thomas' Hosp 1962–63, conslt Nat Heart Hosp 1963–83, dir Magnetic Resonance Unit Royal Brompton Hosp and Nat Heart Hosp 1983–93 (ret), currently dir Brompton MR Enterprises, chm and chief exec MR 3000 1993–, cardiac surgn and memb Britain's first heart transplant team; co fndr: Coronary Artery Disease Res Assoc (CORDA) (scientific advsr), The Heart Charity (formerly Heart); Hon Citizen State of Alabama 1994; personal chair Univ of London; Freeman the Co of Worldtraders 1993; LRCP, FRCSEd, FRCR, memb Br Inst Radiology; *Books* over 250 scientific pubns incl: Spare Part Surgery (1968), Machines in Medicine (1969), The Heart (1970), The Current Status of Cardiac Surgery (1975), Modern Cardiac Surgery (1978), Towards Safer Cardiac Surgery (1981); *Recreations* sailing, skiing; *Clubs* Royal Yacht Sqdn, Utd Hosps SC; *Style—* Prof Donald Longmore; ✉ Brompton MR Enterprises, 92 Fulham Road, Chelsea SW3 6HR (☎ 0171 581 9486, fax 0171 581 9475)

LONGRIGG, Roger Erskine; s of Brig Stephen Hemsley Longrigg, OBE, of Chancellor House, Tunbridge Wells (d 1979) and Florence Amy, *née* Anderson (d 1974); *b* 1 May 1929; *Educ* Bryanston Sch, Magdalen Coll Oxford (BA); *m* 20 July 1957, Jane Catherine, da of Capt Marcus Beresford Chichester, of Compton Chamberlyne, Wilts (d 1985); 3 da (Laura b 1958, Frances b 1961, Clare b 1963); *Career* entered army 1947, cmmnd Buffs 1948, demob 1949; joined TA 1952, Capt 1955; *Books* author of over 50 published books (pseudonyms incl Rosalind Erskine, Ivor Drummond, Laura Black, Domini Taylor); novels incl: High Pitched Buzz (1956), Daughters of Mulberry (1961), The Paper Boats (1965), The Desperate Criminals (1972), Bad Bet (1981), Mother Love (1983), Siege (1989); non fiction incl: The History of Horse Racing (1972), The History of Foxhunting (1975), The English Squire and His Sport (1977); *Recreations* trout fishing, painting; *Clubs* Brooks's, Pratt's; *Style—* Roger Longrigg, Esq; ✉ Orchard House, Crookham, Hampshire (☎ 01252 850333)

LONGSDON, (Robert) Shaun; s of late Wing Cdr Robert Cyril Longsdon, of Foxcote, Warwicks, and Evadne Lloyd, *née* Flower; *b* 5 Dec 1936; *Educ* Eton; *m* 19 Dec 1968, Caroline Susan, da of Col Michael Colvin Watson, OBE, MC, TD, of Barnsley, Gloucs; 3 s (James b 1971, Rupert b 1972, Charles b 1975), 1 da (Laura b 1983); *Career* reg Army Offr 1955–81; princ mil appts: Lt Col, mil asst (GSO1) to the Chief of Gen Staff 1975–77, CO 17/21 Lancers 1977–79, directing staff (GSO1 DS) NDC 1979–81; head of corp affairs Knight Frank & Rutley 1981–95, md Visual Insurance Protection Ltd 1995–; Clerk of the Cheque and Adjutant of the Queen's Body Gd of the Yeomen of the Guard 1993–, Col 17/21 Lancers 1988–93; govr RSC 1982–, chm Leonard Cheshire Home Gloucs 1995–; *Recreations* field sports; *Clubs* White's, Cavalry and Guards', Pratt's; *Style—* Col Shaun Longsdon; ✉ Southrop Lodge, Lechlade, Glos GL7 3NU (☎ 01367 850284, fax 01367 850377)

LONGSON, Dr Geoffrey John; s of late Arthur Walter Longson, and late Mary Margaret, *née* Pratt; *b* 1 Aug 1935; *Educ* Tiffin Sch Kingston upon Thames, Guy's Hosp Dental Sch (Open scholar, LDS, RCS (Eng), Newland Pedley prize), Univ of London BDS; *m* 1, Aug 1959, Dianne Frances Isaac; 1 s (Mark Frazer), 1 da (Tanya Clare Marie); m 2, Heather Jane Sutherland; 1 da (Olivia Jane Scott); *Career* dental surgn; in private practice Harley St and Fleet Hampshire; FRSM; fell: Int Acad of Implantology, Int Coll of Dentists; memb: American Acad of Gnathology, European Acad of Gnathology (pres); *Style—* Dr Geoffrey J Longson; ✉ 130 Harley St, London W1N 1AH (☎ 0171 636 6082, fax 0171 935 2385, car 0385 225075)

LONGSTAFF, Wilfred; s of Thomas Longstaff (d 1980), and Phoebe Alice Calvert, *née* Rain (d 1993); *b* 10 Dec 1931; *Educ* Tottenham Tech Coll, Northern Poly (DipArch); *m* 1 Aug 1959, Stephanie Maria, da of John Joseph Macken (d 1958); 2 s (Wilfred b 1960, David b 1961); *Career* RE Corpl served Cyprus and Egypt; chief architect Courage Eastern Ltd 1975–80, chartered architect in private practice 1983–; ARIBA; *Recreations* golf; *Clubs* Goring & Streatley Golf; *Style—* Wilfred Longstaff, Esq; ✉ 7 Cambrian Way, The Orchard, Calcot, Reading, Berkshire RG3 7DD (☎ 0118 941 9152, fax 0118 943 3041)

LONGWORTH, Dr Ian Heaps; CBE (1994); s of Joseph Longworth (d 1968), of Bolton, Lancs, and Alice, *née* Heaps (d 1961); *b* 29 Sept 1935; *Educ* King Edward VII Lytham, Peterhouse Cambridge (MA, PhD); *m* 27 Sept 1967, Clare Marian, da of Maurice Edwin Titford (d 1967), of Croydon; 1 s (Timothy b 1975), 1 da (Alison b 1978); *Career* Br Museum: asst keeper Dept of British and Medieval Antiquities 1963–69, keeper Dept of Prehistoric and Romano British Antiquities 1973–95 (asst keeper 1969–73); memb Ancient Monuments Bd for England 1977–84, chm Area Archaeological Advsy Ctee for NW England 1978–79; vice pres Soc of Antiquaries 1985–88 (fell 1966, sec 1974–80); memb Ancient Monuments Advsy Ctee 1991–94; *Books* Durrington Walls - Excavations 1966–68 (with G J Wainwright, 1971), Collared Urns of the Bronze Age in GB and Ireland (1984), Prehistoric Britain (1985), Catalogue of the Excavated Prehistoric and Romano British Material in the Greenwell Collection (with I A Kinnes, 1985), Archaeology in Britain Since 1945 (ed with J Cherry, 1986), Excavations at Grimes Graves Norfolk 1972–76 (contrib, 1988, 1991, 1992 and 1996); *Clubs* MCC; *Style—* Dr Ian Longworth, CBE; ✉ 2 Hurst View Rd, Croydon, Surrey CR2 7AG (☎ 0181 688 4960)

LONNEN, Ray; s of Herbert Stanley George Lonnen (d 1975), of Bournemouth, and Millicent Maud, *née* Jones; *b* 18 May 1940; *Educ* Stourfield Sch Bournemouth, Hampshire Sch of Drama Bournemouth; *children*; 2 s (Thomas b 6 Nov 1976, Rhys b 30 Jan 1986), 1 da (Amy b 30 Nov 1981); *Career* actor; *Theatre* nat tours: The Anniversary 1971,

How The Other Half Loves 1973, Rose (NZ) 1981; Same Time Next Year 1983, Murder By The Book 1985, Touch of Danger 1987; other credits incl: Wonderful Town (musical, West End) 1986–87, Bells Are Ringing (musical, Greenwich) 1988, Guys and Dolls (musical, Edinburgh) 1981, Run For Your Wife (West End) 1988, Having A Ball (West End) 1990, In Praise of Love (Apollo) 1995, Misfits (Manchester Royal Exchange) 1996; *Television* incl: Honey Lane (ATV) 1967–68, Melissa (BBC) 1974, Z Cars (BBC) 1975–76, Sandbaggers (YTV) 1978–80, Harry's Game (YTV, nominated Best Actor TV Times) 1982, The Brief (TVS) 1984, Yellowthread Street (YTV) 1989, Rich Tea and Sympathy (YTV) 1991, Cluedo, Heartbeat 1993, Harry, Crime Monthly 1994, Budgie the Little Helicopter (various voices) 1994, Expert Witness (LWT) 1995, Johnny and the Dead (LWT) 1995; *Recreations* cinema, music, travel, tennis; *Style—* Ray Lonnen, Esq; ✉ c/o Barry Langford, 17 Westfields Avenue, London SW13 0AT (☎ 0181 878 7148)

LONSDALE, Anne Mary; da of late Dr Alexander Charles George Menzies, of Harrow, Middx, and Mabel, *née* Griffiths; *b* 16 Feb 1941; *Educ* St Anne's Coll Oxford (BA (2), MA); *m* 1, 1962, Geoffrey Griffin (d 1962); m 2, 1964 (m dis 1994), Prof Roger Harrison Lonsdale; 1 s (Charles John b 1965), 1 da (Katharine Georgina b 1966); *Career* Univ of Oxford: teacher in classical Chinese Oriental Inst and St Anne's Coll 1965–71, Davis sr scholar and lectr in Chinese St Anne's Coll 1971–74, univ administrator 1974–90, dir External Rels Office 1990–93; sec-gen Central Euro Univ Budapest, Prague and Warsaw 1994–96, pres New Hall Cambridge 1996–; tstee: Inter-Univ Fndn 1988–, Cambridge Overseas Tst 1996–; chm UK Conf of Univ Admins 1991–93, jt chm Assoc of Univ Admins 1993–94, memb Steering Ctee Coimbra Gp of Euro Univs 1993–94, UK rep Cwlth Univs Study Abroad Consortium 1993–94, memb Advsy Bd Inter-Univ Centre Dubrovnik; Cavaliere dell'Ordine al Merito della Repubblica Italiana 1988; *Books* The Chinese Experience (contrib trans, 1978), University Administration in China (1983), The Government and Management of Indian Universities (1987); also author of reviews, contrib to encyclopedias in UK and Italy on Chinese topics; *Style—* Mrs Anne Lonsdale; ✉ New Hall, Cambridge CB3 0DF (☎ 01223 351721, fax 01223 352941)

LONSDALE, 7 Earl of (UK 1807); Sir James Hugh William Lowther; 8 Bt (GB 1764); also Viscount and Baron Lowther (GB 1797); s of Viscount Lowther (d 1949, er s of 6 Earl); suc gf 1953; *b* 3 Nov 1922; *Educ* Eton; *m* 1, 1945 (m dis 1954), Tuppina Cecily (d 1984), da of late Capt Geoffrey Henry Bennet; 1 s, 1 da; m 2, 1954 (m dis 1962), Hon Jennifer Lowther, da of late Maj the Hon Christopher William Lowther (himself s of 1 Viscount Ullswater); 1 s, 2 da; m 3, 1963, Nancy Ruth Stephenson, da of late Thomas Cobbs, of Pacific Palisades, Cal, USA; 1 s; m 4, 1975, Caroline Sheila, da of Sir Gerald Gordon Ley, 3 Bt, TD; 1 s, 1 da; *Heir* s, Viscount Lowther, *qv*; *Career* served WWII 1939–45 RAC and as Capt E Riding Yeo (despatches); memb: The Sports Cncl 1971–74, English Tourist Bd 1971–75; memb Ct of Assts Worshipful Co of Farmers; CIMgt, FRSA; *Clubs* Brooks's, Turf; *Style—* The Rt Hon the Earl of Lonsdale; ✉ Askham Hall, Penrith, Cumbria CA10 2PF (☎ 01931 712208)

LONSDALE, Prof Roger Harrison; s of Arthur John Lonsdale (d 1977), of Hornsea, Yorkshire, and Phebe, *née* Harrison; *b* 6 Aug 1934; *Educ* Hymers Coll Hull, Lincoln Coll Oxford (BA, DPhil); *m* 8 May 1964 (m dis 1994), Anne Mary, da of Alexander Charles Menzies, of Harrow; 1 s (Charles John b 5 July 1965), 1 da (Katherine Georgina b 16 Dec 1966); *Career* Nat Serv navigator RAF 1952–54; English Dept Yale Univ 1958–60, fell and tutor in English literature Balliol Coll Oxford 1963– (Andrew Bradley jr res fell 1960–63), prof of English literature Univ of Oxford 1992– (reader in English literature 1990–92); FRSL 1990, FBA 1991; *Books* Dr Charles Burney - A Literary Biography (1965); ed: The Poems of Gray, Collins and Goldsmith (1969), Vathek (by William Beckford, 1970), Dryden to Johnson (1971), The New Oxford Book of Eighteenth Century Verse (1984), The Poems of John Bampfylde (1988), Eighteenth Century Women Poets (1989); *Recreations* music, book collecting; *Style—* Prof Roger Lonsdale, FRSL, FBA; ✉ Balliol College, Oxford OX1 3BJ (☎ 01865 277755)

LOOKER, Roger Frank; *b* 20 Oct 1951; *Educ* Univ of Bristol (LLB); *Career* barr; dir Rea Brothers Ltd; *Recreations* rugby football; *Clubs* RAC, Harlequin Football (Chairman); *Style—* Roger Looker, Esq; ✉ Rea Brothers Ltd, Aldermans House, Aldermans Walk, London EC2M 3XR (☎ 0171 623 1155, fax 0171 623 2694)

LOOMES, Brian Robert; s of late Robert Loomes, and Dorothy, *née* Barrett; *b* 3 April 1938; *Educ* West Leeds HS, Univ of Leeds (BA); *m* 25 Jan 1966, Emily (Joy), da of late Robert Gartside, of Sheffield; 1 s (Robert b 1968); *Career* Civil Serv 1960–63, business 1963–66, self-employed as dealer in antique clocks 1966–; fell Soc of Genealogists; *Books* 20 titles on antique clocks incl: White Dial Clocks (1974), Watch and Clock Makers of the World (1976), Complete British Clocks (1978), Grandfather Clocks and their Cases (1985), Antique British Clocks Illustrated (1991), Antique British Clocks: A Buyer's Guide (1991), The Concise Guide to British Clocks (1992), The Concise Guide to Tracing Your Ancestry (1992), Bird Gardening (1992), Painted Dial Clocks (1994); *Recreations* horological research; *Style—* Brian Loomes, Esq; ✉ Calf Haugh Farmhouse, Pateley Bridge, via Harrogate, North Yorks (☎ 01423 711163)

LOPEZ, Paul Anthony; s of Anthony William Lopez, of Wolverhampton, and Lillian, *née* Rowley; *b* 22 Oct 1959; *Educ* Pendeford HS Wolverhampton, Univ of Birmingham (LLB); *m* 3 Nov 1984, Diana Douglas, da of Douglas Black (d 1982); 2 da (Antonia Charlotte Elizabeth b 10 May 1991, Miranda Annabelle Lucy b 22 Nov 1993); *Career* called to the Bar Middle Temple 1982, tenant St Ive's Chambers 1983– (ldr St Ive's Chambers' Personal Injuries Specialist Gp); memb: Midland and Oxford Circuit, Family Law Bar Assoc, Birmingham Family Law Bar Assoc, Personal Injury Bar Assoc, Birmingham Medico-Legal Soc, Shropshire Child Care Gp; *Recreations* horse riding, history, working; *Style—* Paul Lopez, Esq; ✉ 5 Rectory Drive, Weston-under-Lizard, Shropshire TF11 8QQ (☎ and fax 01952 850252); St Ive's Chambers, 9 Fountain Court, Steelhouse Lane, Birmingham B4 6DR (☎ 0121 236 0863/0929, fax 0121 236 6961)

LOPPERT, Max Jeremy; *b* 24 Aug 1946; *Educ* Hyde Park Sch Johannesburg, Univ of Witwatersrand Johannesburg (BA), Univ of York (BA); *m* Delayne, *née* Aarons; *Career* freelance music critic Venice and London 1972–76, teacher Oxford Sch Venice 1972, chief music and opera critic Financial Times 1980–96, assoc ed Opera Magazine 1986–; memb Critics' Circle London 1974; *Recreations* cooking, cinema, swimming, walking in Richmond Park, pottery; *Style—* Max Loppert, Esq; ✉ Opera, 1a Mountgrove Rd, London N5 2LU

LORAM, Vice Adm Sir David Anning; KCB (1979), CVO (1994, LVO 1957); s of John Anning Loram (d 1969), and Jessie Eckford, *née* Scott (d 1961); *b* 24 July 1924; *Educ* RNC Dartmouth, King's Dirk; *m* 1, 1958 (m dis 1981), Fiona, *née* Beloe; 3 s; m 2, 1983 (m dis 1990), Diana, *née* Keigwin; m 3, Sara, *née* Goodall; *Career* RN: served WWII, ADC to Govr Gen NZ 1946–48, equerry to HM The Queen 1954–57, flag offr Malta and NATO Cdr SE Med and Cdr Br Forces 1973–75, Cmdt Nat Def Coll 1975–77, Dep Supreme Allied Cdr Atlantic 1977–80; an extra gentleman usher to HM The Queen 1994– (a gentleman usher 1982–94); memb RN Cresta Team 1954–59, qualified signal offr and helicopter pilot; *Recreations* fishing; *Style—* Vice Adm Sir David Loram, KCB, CVO; ✉ Sparkford Hall, Sparkford, Somerset BA22 7LD (☎ 01963 440249)

LORD, Alan; CB (1972); s of Frederick Lord; *b* 12 April 1929; *Educ* Rochdale, St John's Coll Cambridge (BA, MA); *m* Joan; 2 da; *Career* entered Inland Revenue 1950 (private sec to Dep Chm and to Chm of the Bd 1952–54), HM Treasy 1959–62, princ private sec to First Sec of State (Rt Hon R A Butler) 1962–63, cmmr Inland Revenue 1969–73 (dep chm Bd 1971–73), princ finance offr to DTI (then to Depts of Indust, Trade, and Prices and Consumer Protection) 1973–75, second permanent sec (Domestic Econ) HM Treasy 1975–77; former exec dir Dunlop Holdings (md 1980, chief exec 1982–84), md Dunlop International Ltd 1978; dir: Allied-Lyons plc 1979–86, Bank of England 1983–86, Johnson Matthey Bankers 1985–86; dep chm and chief exec Lloyd's of London 1986–92; chm CBI Taxation Ctee 1979–81; memb Cncl of Mgmnt Henley Centre for Forecasting 1977–82, govr NIESR, pres Johnian Soc 1985–86; *Style—* Alan Lord, Esq, CB; ✉ Mardens, Hildenborough, Tonbridge, Kent

LORD, Geoffrey; OBE (1989); s of Frank Lord (d 1978), of Rochdale, and Edith, *née* Sanderson; *b* 24 Feb 1928; *Educ* Rochdale GS, Univ of Bradford (MA); *m* 15 Sept 1955, Jean; 1 s (Andrew Nicholas b 1962), 1 da (Karen Janet b 1959); *Career* Midland Bank Ltd (AIB) 1944–58, Gtr Manchester Probation Serv 1958–77 (dep chief probation offr 1974–77), sec and treas Carnegie UK Tst 1977–93; fndr tstee The Adapt Tst 1992–; memb Ctee Scottish Arts Cncl Lottery Ctee, chm Pollock Meml Missionary Tst, pres Centre for Environmental Interpretation, vice pres The Selcare Tst, tstee Home Start UK, chm Unemployed Voluntary Action Fund 1991–95; hon fell Manchester Metropolitan Univ 1987; FRSA 1985; *Books* The Arts and Disabilities (1981); *Recreations* arts; *Clubs* New (Edinburgh); *Style—* Geoffrey Lord, Esq, OBE; ✉ The Adapt Trust, Cameron House, Dunfermline, Fife KY12 7PZ (☎ 01383 623166, fax 01383 622149)

LORD, Graham John; s of Harold Reginald Lord, OBE (d 1969), of Beira, Mozambique, and Ida Frances, *née* McDowall (d 1966); *b* 16 Feb 1943; *Educ* Falcon Coll Essexvale Bulawayo Rhodesia, Churchill Coll Cambridge (BA); *m* 12 Sept 1962 (m dis 1990), Jane, *née* Carruthers; 2 da (Mandy b 1963, Kate b 1966); *partner* since 1988, Juliet, *née* Hayden; *Career* ed Varsity Cambridge 1964, reporter Cambridge Evening News 1964; Sunday Express: reporter 1965–69, literary ed 1969–92, launched Sunday Express Book of the Year Award 1987; Daily Telegraph columnist and arts correspondent 1993–94; The Times book reviewer and travel correspondent 1994–; ed Raconteur (short story quarterly) 1994–95; Lambourn parish cncllr 1983–87, vice chm Newbury Mencap 1982–88, chm Eastbury Poor's Furze Charity 1983–88, memb Sub Ctee W Berks Cons Assoc Exec 1985–88, cncllr Newbury DC 1985–87; *Books* Marshmallow Pie (1970), A Roof Under Your Feet (1973), The Spider and The Fly (1974), God and All His Angels (1976), The Nostradamus Horoscope (1981), Time Out Of Mind (1986), Ghosts Of King Solomon's Mines (1991), Just the One - The Wives and Times of Jeffrey Bernard (1992), A Party To Die For (1996); *Recreations* walking, music, reading; *Clubs* Chelsea Arts, Garrick, Useless Information Society; *Style—* Graham Lord, Esq; ✉ c/o Giles Gordon, Curtis Brown Ltd, 6 Ann Street, Edinburgh (☎ 0131 332 1993, fax 0131 315 2695)

LORD, His Honour John Herent; s of Sir Frank Lord, KBE, DL, JP (d 1974), and Rosalie Jeanette Herent, of Bruxelles (d 1981); *b* 5 Nov 1928; *Educ* Manchester GS, Merton Coll Oxford (MA); *m* 1959, June Ann, da of George Caladine (d 1969), and Ada Tomlinson (d 1992); 3 s; *Career* called to the Bar Inner Temple 1951; the jr of the Northern Circuit 1952, asst recorder Burnley 1971, recorder of Crown Ct 1972–78, circuit judge (Northern Circuit) 1978–93; *Recreations* photography, shooting, boating; *Clubs* Leander, St James's (Manchester); *Style—* His Honour John Lord; ✉ Three Lanes, Greenfield, Oldham, Lancashire (☎ 01457 872198)

LORD, John William; s of William James Lord (d 1970), and Bessie Maria, *née* Watkins (d 1995); *b* 28 May 1931; *Educ* Gravesend GS for Boys; *m* 28 April 1956, Patricia Jane, da of Maj Frank Palmer (d 1979); 3 s (David b 1964, Richard b 1966, Peter b 1971); *Career* Nat Serv RAF 1953–55; articled clerk MacIntyre Hudson and Co 1948–53, qualified CA, audit mangr Evans Fripp Deed and Co 1955–57, tax mangr Midgley Snelling and Co 1957–60, sr ptnr Carley and Co 1983– (mangr 1961, ptnr 1962–); dir and sec Gravesend Masonic Hall Co Ltd; former: pres of Gravesend Chamber of Trade, chm Gravesend Round Table; memb Assoc of Ex Round Tablers; FCA 1953, ATII 1962; *Recreations* golf, tennis, gardening; *Clubs* Mid Kent Golf; *Style—* John Lord, Esq; ✉ Lark Rise, Pondfield Lane, Shorne, nr Gravesend, Kent DA12 3LD; 8 Overcliffe, Gravesend, Kent DA11 0HJ (☎ 01474 569032, fax 01474 320410)

LORD, Michael Nicholson; MP (C) Suffolk Central (majority 16,031); s of John Lord, and Jessie, *née* Nicholson; *b* 17 Oct 1938; *Educ* Christ's Coll Cambridge (MA); *m* 1965, Jennifer Margaret, *née* Childs; 1 s, 1 da; *Career* formerly farmer, aboricultural conslt; Parly candidate Manchester Gorton 1979, MP (C) Suffolk Central 1983–; memb Select Ctee on Agric 1983–84, PPS to Rt Hon John MacGregor as Min of Agric, Fisheries and Food 1984–85 and as Chief Sec to the Treasy 1985–87, Parly del to Cncl of Europe and Western Euro Union 1987–91, memb Select Ctee for the Parly Cmmr for Admin (Ombudsman); cncllr: N Beds BC 1974–77, Beds CC 1981–83; pres Arboricultural Assoc 1989–95; *Recreations* golf, sailing, trees; *Style—* Michael Lord, Esq, MP; ✉ House of Commons, London SW1A 0AA (☎ 0171 219 3000)

LORD, Peter John; s of Godfrey Albert Lord, MBE (d 1985), of Welwyn Garden City, and Rose, *née* Clark (d 1983); *b* 1 Sept 1929; *Educ* Welwyn Garden City GS, The Architectural Assoc (AADipl); *m* 10 March 1956, (Dorothy) Shirley May, da of Reginald Munday (d 1973), of Hatfield; 1 da (Kathryn Jane b 8 Nov 1958); *Career* Nat Serv 1951–53, cmmnd RE and late AER; currently: conslt Austin-Smith: Lord architects, planners and designers (formerly sr ptnr), in practice The Lord Consultancy; recipient various awards incl: MOHLG, RIBA Nat and Regnl, Civic Tst, NW Regnl Energy; pres: Chartered Soc of Designers 1969, Int Cncl of Societies of Industl Design 1985–87, Assoc of Consultant Architects 1989–91; memb Construction Industry Cncl; hon memb: Industl Designers Soc of SA, Union des Designers En Belgique; memb Worshipful Co of Chartered Architects 1986; RIBA, FCSD, FRSA; *Books* The Concept of Professionalism in the Field of Design (1968); *Recreations* fishing, horology, ornithology, photography; *Style—* Peter Lord, Esq; ✉ Sperberry House, Coast Road, Cley-next-the-Sea, Norfolk NR25 7SA; Austin-Smith: Lord, 17 Bowling Green Lane, London EC1R 01BD (☎ 0171 251 6161, fax 0171 608 3409)

LORD, Rodney Arthur Lionel; s of Lionel Cornwallis Lord (d 1946), and Marjorie Agnes, *née* Webb-Jones; *b* 13 Jan 1946; *Educ* Christ's Hospital, Christ Church Oxford (MA); *m* 3 April 1971, Diana Mary, da of Neville Stanley Howarth, of Craglands, Clawthorpe, Burton, Carnforth, Lancs; 1 s (Simon b 1974), 1 da (Anna b 1977); *Career* fin writer Investors Review 1967–69, econs corr and columnist Daily Telegraph 1969–81, visiting res fell City Univ Business Sch 1981–82, special advsr HM Treasy 1983–86, econs ed The Times 1986–90, dir Privatisation International 1988–; *Books* Value for Money in Education (1984); *Recreations* sailing, music; *Style—* Rodney Lord, Esq; ✉ Privatisation International, Suite 404, Butlers Wharf Business Centre, 45 Curlew Street, London SE1 2ND (☎ 0171 378 1620, fax 0171 403 7876)

LORENZ, Andrew Peter Morrice; s of Hans Viktor Lorenz (d 1985), and Catherine Jesse Cairns, *née* James; *b* 22 June 1955; *Educ* Stamford Sch, Worcester Coll Oxford (Open Exhibitioner, MA, sports and arts ed Cherwell); *m* 1 Sept 1988, Helen Marianne, da of Brig John Malcolm Alway; 2 s (James Andrew George b 13 Jan 1994, Harry Alexander Lewis b 8 June 1995); *Career* successively graduate trainee, news reporter, labour reporter, educn corr then industl corr The Journal Newcastle 1978–82, business corr The Scotsman 1982–86, dep city ed The Sunday Telegraph 1988–89 (City reporter 1986–88); The Sunday Times: industl ed 1989–91, assoc business ed 1991–94, dep business ed 1994–95, business ed 1995–; *Books* A Fighting Chance - the revival and future of British industry (1989), Inside Rolls-Royce (1995); *Recreations* cricket, rugby, football, film; *Style—* Andrew Lorenz, Esq; ✉ The Sunday Times, 1 Pennington Street, London E1 9XN (☎ 0171 782 5768, fax 0171 782 5765)

LORENZ, Anthony Michael; s of Andre Lorenz (d 1986), and Mitzi Lorenz; *b* 7 Dec 1947; *Educ* Arnold House Sch, Charterhouse; *m* 1 Feb 1986, Suzanna Jane, da of Louis

Solomon; 1 s (David Alexander b 5 June 1986), 1 da (Charlaine Alexandra b 15 Nov 1978); *Career* sr ptnr Baker Lorenz Estate Agents; former chm Fund-raising Ctee Multiple Sclerosis Soc; *Recreations* flying, polo, shooting, skiing; *Clubs* Hurlingham, Knepp Castle Polo; *Style—* Anthony Lorenz, Esq; ✉ 25 Hanover Square, London W1R 0DQ (☎ 0171 409 2121, fax 0171 493 3812, telex 894113)

LORETTO, Denis Crofton; s of Cecil Rupert Loretto, MM (d 1976), of Belfast, and Violet Florence, *née* Walker; *b* 7 April 1936; *Educ* Royal Belfast Academical Inst; *m* 17 March 1960, (Margaret) Wilma, da of William Alexander Campbell (d 1986), of Belfast; 1 s (Timothy b 1961), 1 da (Angela b 1964); *Career* Cornhill Insurance: branch underwriter Belfast 1953–59, head office underwriter London 1959–62, branch supt Belfast 1962–72, asst branch mangr Belfast 1972–74, branch mangr Belfast 1974–81, div mangr Underwriting Head Office 1981–86, asst gen mangr Guildford 1986–93, gen mangr (Home) 1993–; dir: Trafalgar Insurance plc 1988, British Reserve Insurance Co Ltd 1988 (md 1989–), Cornhill Insur plc 1989, Allianz UK Ltd 1989; chm Pet Plan Healthcare plc 1996–; memb The Northern Ireland Partnership; Belfast city cncllr 1977–81; FCII 1961; *Recreations* walking, photography; *Style—* Denis Loretto, Esq; ✉ 107 Lower Rd, Fetcham, Leatherhead, Surrey KT22 9NQ (☎ 01372 453276); Cornhill Insurance, 57 Ladymead, Guildford, Surrey GU1 1DB (☎ 01483 568161, fax 01483 552707, telex 859383)

LORETTO, Prof Michael Henry; s of Carlo Claude Loretto (d 1963), of Caterham, Surrey, and Carrie, *née* Hill (d 1984); *b* 3 Dec 1930; *Educ* Caterham Sch, Univ of Sheffield (BMet); *m* 28 Aug 1955, Nita Margery (d 1994), da of Henry Hill, of Neath, S Wales; 2 s (Peter b 1959, David b 1962), 3 da (Anne b 1963, Frances b 1965, Catherine b 1969); *Career* res offr CSIRO Melbourne Aust 1955–62 and 1963–66; visiting fell: Cavendish Laboratory Cambridge UK 1962–63, Battelle Laboratory Columbus Ohio 1969–70; prof and IRC dir Univ of Birmingham 1989– (lectr 1966–70, sr lectr 1970–80, head Sch of Metallurgy and Materials 1988–89); memb Cncl Birmingham Metallurgical Assoc (past pres); FIM, FInstP; *Books* Defect Analysis in Electron Microscopy (1976), Electron Beam Analysis of Materials (1983); *Recreations* music, walking; *Style—* Prof Michael Loretto; ✉ 54 Selwyn Rd, Edgbaston, Birmingham B16 0SW (☎ 0121 454 3975); IRC in Materials for High Performance Applications, The University of Birmingham, Edgbaston, Birmingham B15 2TT (☎ 0121 414 5214, fax 0121 414 3441)

LORIMER, Sir (Thomas) Desmond; kt (1976); s of Thomas Berry Lorimer (d 1952), and Sarah Ann Lorimer (d 1970); *b* 20 Oct 1925; *Educ* Belfast Tech HS; *m* 1957, Patricia Doris, da of Ernest Samways; 2 da; *Career* CA 1948, in practice 1952–74; sr ptnr Harmood Banner Smylie & Co Belfast 1960; chm: Lamont Holdings plc 1973–96, Northern Bank Ltd 1985–, Northern Ireland Electricity 1991–94; dir: Ruberoid plc 1972–88, Irish Distillers plc 1986–, Old Bushmills Distillery 1986–, National Australia Bank (UK) Ltd 1993–; chm: Industl Devpt Bd for NI 1982–86, Ulster Soc of CAs 1960, NI Housing Exec 1971–75; memb Review Body on Local Govt in NI 1970; fell Inst of CAs in Ireland (pres 1968–69); *Recreations* gardening, golf; *Clubs* Carlton, Royal Co Down Golf, Royal Belfast Golf; *Style—* Sir Desmond Lorimer; ✉ Windwhistle Cottage, 6A Circular Road West, Cultra, Holywood, Co Down BT18 0AT (☎ 01232 423323)

LORIMER, Prof (Andrew) Ross; *b* 5 May 1937; *Educ* Uddingston GS, HS of Glasgow, Univ of Glasgow (MD); *m* 1963, Fiona, *née* Marshall; *Career* conslt physician and cardiologist Royal Infirmary Glasgow 1972–; memb: Assoc of Phyicians of the UK, Br Cardiac Soc; FRCP, FRCPGlas (memb Cncl), FRCPEd; *Books* Cardiovascular Therapy (1980), Preventive Cardiology (1990); *Style—* Prof Ross Lorimer; ✉ Royal Infirmary, Glasgow G4 0SF (☎ 0141 552 3535)

LORING, Anthony Francis; s of Brig Walter Watson Alexander Loring, CBE (d 1987), and Patricia Eileen, *née* Quirke; *b* 10 Oct 1954; *Educ* Ampleforth, Bedford Coll London (BA); *m* Elizabeth McClintock; 1 s, 1 da; *Career* admitted slr 1979; McKenna & Co: resident ptnr in Bahrain 1988–90, ptnr London 1990–; memb Law Soc; *Recreations* tennis, bridge, skiing; *Clubs* MCC, Oriental; *Style—* Anthony Loring, Esq; ✉ McKenna & Co, Mitre House, 160 Aldersgate Street, London EC1A 4DD (☎ 0171 606 9000)

LORISTON-CLARKE, Anne Jennifer Frances (Jennie); MBE (1979); da of Lt Col John Fitzherbert Symes Bullen, RHA (d 1966), of Charmouth, Dorset, and Anne Harris St John (d 1963); *b* 22 Jan 1943; *Educ* privately; *m* 27 Feb 1965, Anthony Grahame Loriston-Clarke, s of Capt Geoffrey Neame Loriston-Clarke, CBE, RN; 2 da (Anne Frances b 19 Jan 1966, Elizabeth Jane b 27 July 1970); *Career* horse breeder, equestrian dressage; winner: City of London Cup for Best Rider 1953–56, Jr Jumping Championships Richmond Royal Horse Show 1955, Pony Club Horse Trials Championship ; joined GB Dressage Team 1964; winner 6 World Cup qualifiers, Bronze medal World Dressage Championships (Goodwood) 1978; memb Br Olympic Team: Munich 1972, Montreal 1976, Los Angeles 1984, Seoul 1988; stud owner/mangr; developed The Catherston Stud, breeding competition Warmblood horses, pioneered the use of chilled and frozen semen in horses in the UK, author of 4 books and videos on dressage, longreining and training of young horses; NPSDip, Duke of Edinburgh Gold Award; FBHS; *Recreations* reading, writing, swimming, singing, walking the dog by bicycle; *Style—* Mrs Jennie Loriston-Clarke, MBE; ✉ Catherston Stud, Manor Farm, Hurstbourne Priors, Whitchurch, Hampshire RG28 7SE (☎ 01256 892045)

LORNE, Marquess of; Torquhil Ian Campbell; only s and h of 12 Duke of Argyll, *qv*; *b* 29 May 1968; *Educ* Cargilfield Sch Edinburgh, Glenalmond Coll Perthshire, RAC Cirencester (Dip Rural Estate Mgmnt); *Career* page of honour to HM The Queen 1981–83; asst land agent Buccleuch Estates Ltd Selkirk 1991–93; sales mangr Grosvenor House (Trust House Forte plc) 1994–96; marketing mangr Casella Far East Ltd Hong Kong 1996–; *Style—* Marquess of Lorne; ✉ Inveraray Castle, Inveraray, Argyll PA32 8XE

LOSOWSKY, Prof Monty Seymour; s of Myer Losowsky (d 1936), and Dora, *née* Gottlieb; *b* 1 Aug 1931; *Educ* Coopers' Company's Sch, Univ of Leeds (MB ChB, MD, MRCP); *m* 15 Aug 1971, Barbara; 1 s (Andrew b 1978), 1 da (Kathryn b 1973); *Career* res fell Harvard Med Unit Mass 1961–62, reader in med Univ Dept of Med Leeds Gen Infirmary 1966–69 (lectr 1962–64, sr lectr 1964–66), prof of med Univ Dept of Med St James's Univ Hosp Leeds 1969–96, dean Faculty of Med Univ of Leeds 1989–94; pres Br Soc of Gastroenterology 1993–94 (and memb of its Educn and Nominations Ctees 1992–94), convenor DHSS Gastroenterology Liaison Ctee 1982–85; memb: Leeds Eastern Health Authy 1981–89, Panel of Studies allied to Med Univ Grants Ctee 1982–88, Specialist Advsy Ctee on Gen (Internal) Med 1984–88, Systems Bd MRC Grants Ctee 1984–88, Br Digestive Fndn Sci and Res Awards Ctee 1987–90, Sci Advsy Ctee British Nutrition Fndn 1987–91, Yorkshire Regnl Health Authy 1989–90, Cncl of Deans of UK Med Schs 1989–94, Univs Hosps Assoc 1989–96, Gastroenterology Ctee RCP 1992–96, Univs Funding Cncl (and its Panel on Other Studies allied to Medicine) 1992–93; Ctee of Vice-Chllrs and Princs of Univs of the UK (CVCP): memb Med Advsy Ctee 1990–94, CVCP rep/alternate memb Dept of Health's NHS Mgmnt Exec Central Jt Planning Advsy Ctee (JPAC) 1989–94, CVCP rep Dept of Health's Jt Monitory Gp on Achieving a Balance 1990–92, CVCP rep/alternate memb Dept of Health's NHS Mgmnt Exec JPAC Gen Purposes Sub-Ctee 1990–93, CVCP alternate rep Dept of Health's NHS Mgmnt Exec JPAC Academic and Res Sub-Ctee 1993–94; Br Digestive Fndn: memb Exec Ctee 1992–94, memb Fund Raising Ctee 1992–93, memb Information Ctee 1992–93; chm of tstees Coeliac Tst 1983–95, memb Bd of Govrs The Coeliac Soc 1995–, chm HEFCE Panel of Studies Applied to Med 1995–96, Dept of Health NHS Mgmnt Exec memb of Working Gp on Undergraduate Med and Dental Educn and Res 1990–94, sci govr and cncl memb British Nutrition Fndn 1991–; memb GMC 1991–96; Freeman City of London 1954; memb RSM, FRCP 1969; *Books* Malabsorption in Clinical Practice (1974), The Liver and Biliary System (1984), The Gut and Systemic Disease (1983), Advanced Medicine (1983), Clinical Nutrition in Gastroenterology (1986), Gut Defences in Clinical Practice (1986), Gastroenterology (1988), Consensus in Clinical Nutrition (1994), Surgery of The Liver and Biliary Tract (2 edn, 1994); *Recreations* table tennis, watching cricket, medical memorabilia; *Style—* Prof Monty Losowsky; ✉ Southview, Ling Lane, Scarcroft, Leeds LS14 3HT (☎ 0113 289 2699)

LOTHIAN, Marchioness of; Antonella Reuss; *née* Newland; da of Maj-Gen Sir Foster Reuss Newland, KCMG, CB (d 1943), and Mrs William Carr (d 1986); *m* 1943, 12 Marquess of Lothian, *qv*; 2 s, 4 da; *Career* author, broadcaster, journalist; current affairs columnist Scottish Daily Express 1960–75, deviser and presenter various TV progs; vice pres Royal Coll of Nursing 1960–80, patron Nat Cncl of Women of GB, Ct patron RCOG, fndr and pres Woman of the Year Luncheon and Assoc; convener: Health Festival Assoc, Valiant for Truth Media Award; recipient UK Templeton Award 1992; fell Inst of Journalists, FRSA; *Books* Valentina. First Woman in Space; *Recreations* swimming, walking, music; *Clubs* Reform, Royal Soc of Arts, Press; *Style—* The Marchioness of Lothian; ✉ Tower Office, Jedburgh TD8 6NX, Scotland (☎ 01835 64023)

LOTHIAN, Lt-Col James Lambert; s of Maj James Lothian (d 1970), and Nancy Lambert, *née* Mactaggart (d 1982); *b* 21 Feb 1926; *Educ* Wellington, New Coll Oxford; *m* 1967, Jean Christine, da of Sir Arthur Clark, KCMG, CBE (d 1967); 2 da (Sarah Jane b 1968, Katherine Susan b 1973); *Career* 2 Lt RA 1946; served: India, Palestine, Egypt, Cyprus, Aden, Staff Coll Camberley 1957; Lt-Col 1968 cmmnd 42 Medium Regt RA 1968–70, Br instr W German Cmd and Staff Coll Hamburg 1970–73, ret 1975; PR dir Franklin Mint Limited 1982–92 (mangr 1975–82); German interpreter Civil Serv 1967; memb Mail Order Sub Ctee of Ctee of Advertising Practice 1987–92, Bd Br Direct Marketing Assoc 1990; MBIB 1970; *Recreations* breeding dachshunds, cabinet making; *Style—* Lt-Col James Lothian; ✉ Hollymead, Leigh Rd, Hildenborough, Kent TN11 9AH (☎ 01732 838619, fax 01732 838389)

LOTHIAN, 12 Marquess of (S 1701); Peter Francis Walter Kerr; KCVO (1983), kt SMO Malta, DL (Roxburghshire 1962); also Lord Newbottle (S 1591), Lord Jedburgh (S 1622), Earl of Lothian, Lord Ker of Newbattle (*sic*) (both S 1631), Earl of Ancram (1633), Viscount of Briene, Lord Ker of Newbottle, Oxnam, Jedburgh, Dolphinstoun and Nisbet (all S 1701), and Baron Ker of Kersheugh (UK 1821); s of Capt Andrew William Kerr, JP, RN (d 1929), and cous of 11 Marquess (d 1940); *b* 8 Sept 1922; *Educ* Ampleforth, ChCh Oxford; *m* 1948, Antonella (Marchioness of Lothian, *qv*), da of Maj-Gen Sir Foster Reuss Newland, KCMG, CB (d 1943), and Mrs William Carr, of Ditchingham Hall, Norfolk (d 1986); 2 s, 4 da; *Heir* s, Earl of Ancram, *qv*; *Career* Lt Scots Gds 1943; jt Parly sec Miny of Health April-Oct 1964; a lord-in-waiting to HM the Queen 1972–73; chm of Cncl Scottish Red Cross 1976–86; Lord Warden of the Stanneries and keeper of Privy Seal of Duke of Cornwall 1977–83; memb Queen's Body Guard for Scotland (Royal Co of Archers); FRSA; *Recreations* music; *Clubs* Boodle's, New (Edinburgh); *Style—* The Most Hon the Marquess of Lothian, KCVO, DL; ✉ 177 Cranmer Court, Whitehead's Grove, London SW3; Ferniehirst Castle, Jedburgh, Roxburghshire TD8 6NX (☎ 01835 864021); Melbourne Hall, Derby (☎ 01331 62163)

LOTT, Dame Felicity Ann Emwhyla; DBE (1996, CBE 1990); da of John Albert Lott, and Iris Emwhyla, *née* Williams; *b* 8 May 1947; *Educ* Pate's Girls GS Cheltenham, RHC Univ of London (BA), RAM (LRAM); *m* 1, 22 Dec 1973 (m dis 1982), Robin Mavesyn Golding; m 2, 19 Jan 1984, Gabriel Leonard Woolf, s of Alec Woolf; 1 da (Emily b 19 June 1984); *Career* opera singer, debut in The Magic Flute (ENO) 1975; princ appearances: ENO, Glyndebourne, Covent Garden, WNO, Scottish Opera, Paris, Brussels, Hamburg, Chicago, Munich, NY, Vienna, Milan, sang at Royal Wedding 1986; recordings for: EMI, Decca, Harmonia Mundi Chandos, Erato, Hyperion; patron New Sussex Opera; Hon DMus Univ of Sussex 1989, hon fell Royal Holloway Univ of London 1994; Chev dans l'Ordre des Arts et des Lettres (France) 1992; Hon DLitt Loughborough Univ 1996; FRAM; *Recreations* reading, gardening; *Style—* Dame Felicity Lott, DBE; ✉ c/o Lies Askonas Ltd, 6 Henrietta St, London WC2E 8LA (☎ 0171 379 7700, fax 0171 242 1831)

LOUBET, Bruno Jean Roger; s of Clement Loubet, of Libourne Gironde, France, and Mauricette, *née* Lacroix (d 1989); *b* 8 Oct 1961; *m* 27 Dec 1983, Catherine, da of Jacques Mougeol; 2 da (Laeticia b 4 Aug 1985, Laura Claire b 8 April 1987); *Career* lycée hotelier 1976–79; commis de cuisine: Hyatt Regency Brussels 1979–80, Restaurant Copenhague 1980–82; second maitre Nat French Navy and chef to the Admiral TCD Ouragan 1982, commis chef Tante Claire London 1982; head chef: Gastronome One Fulham 1982–85, Manoir aux Quat' Saisons Gt Milton 1985–86; chef mangr Petit Blanc Oxford 1986–88, chef Four Seasons Restaurant Inn On The Park 1988–93, chef/patron Bistro Bruno London 1993–, opened L'Odeon London 1995; awards: Young Chef of The Year Good Food Guide 1985, Acorn Award Caterer & Hotelkeeper 1988, Michelin Star 1990; memb Académie Culinaire de France GB 1990; *Publications* Bruno Loubet: Cuisine Courante (1991), Bistrot Bruno: Cooking from L'Odeon (1995); *Style—* Bruno Loubet, Esq; ✉ L'Odeon, 65 Regent Street, London W1R 7HH (☎ 0171 287 1400, fax 0171 287 1300)

LOUDEN, Rt Rev Mgr Stephen Henry; s of Joseph Henry Louden, and Sarah, *née* McNaughten; *b* 18 Nov 1941; *Educ* Upholland Coll, BA (Open), DipTh (CNNA), MTh (Oxon); *Career* ordained priest (Liverpool Dio) 1968; curate: All Saints Anfield 1968–73, St John's Kirkdale 1973–75, Our Lady's Formby 1975–78; Royal Army Chaplains Dept: TA cmmn 1972–78, reg army cmmn 1978, Dortmund Garrison 1978–79, 8 Inf Bde 1979–80, Münster Garrison 1980–82, Dhekelia Garrison 1982–84, RMA Sandhurst 1984–86, Berlin Inf Bde 1986–88, HQ NI 1988, Hong Kong 1988–90, sr chaplain RC HQ BAOR 1990–92, sr chaplain RC HQNI 1992–93, princ RC chaplain and VG (Army) 1993–; Prelate of Honour 1993; *Books* Chaplains in Conflict (1996); *Recreations* horology, photography, antiques, theology; *Clubs* Army and Navy; *Style—* Rt Rev Mgr Stephen Louden, VG; ✉ Principal RC Chaplain (Army), MOD Chaplains (Army), Trenchard Lines, Upavon, Pewsey, Wilts SN9 6BE (☎ 01980 615803, fax 01980 615800)

LOUDON, George Ernest; *b* 19 Nov 1942; *Educ* Christlijk Lyceum Zeist Holland, Balliol Coll Oxford (BA), Johns Hopkins Univ Washington DC (MA); *m* Angela; 1 s (b 1972), 1 da (b 1970); *Career* fin analyst Lazard Freres & CIE Paris 1967–68; project mgmnt: Ford Foundation NY and Jakarta 1968–71, McKinsey & Co Amsterdam 1971–76; Amsterdam-Rotterdam Bank NV Amsterdam: gen mangr New Issue and Syndicate Dept 1976–83, memb Bd of Managing Dirs responsible for Corporate and Int Banking 1986–88 (Investment Banking 1983–84, Treasy and Securities Trading 1984–86); currently dir: Geveke NV (Holland), Arjo Wiggins Appleton plc, Global Asset Management Ltd, Harrison/Parrott Ltd, Digital Collections Inc (USA), EASDAQ SA, EASD (Belgium), Galapagos Conservation Tst (also tstee); currently chm Helix Assocs Ltd; former dir: EBC Amro Bank Ltd, Banque Européenne pour L'Amerique Latine, Netherlands Joint Custodian Institute, Leveraged Capital Holdings NV, Netherlandse Trust Maatschapij, Oriental Art Magazine Ltd, M & G Group plc, M & G Ltd, Midland Bank plc 1988–92, MBSA (France), Amro International Asia Ltd; former vice chm: Amsterdam Stock Exchange, Samuel Montagu & Co Ltd; former treas Stichting 1986–88, former chief exec Midland Montagu 1988–92; former chm and chief exec: Midland Montagu (Holdings) Ltd, Trinkaus und Burkhardt (Germany), Euromobiliare (Italy); tstee: Tate Fndn, South Bank Fndn; former memb Cncl of Japan Festival 1990; currently memb: Acquisitions Ctee Museum of Modern Art of City of Amsterdam, Bd of Tstees Netherlands Royal Coll of Art, van den Berch van Heemstede Stichting; *Style*— George Loudon, Esq; ✉ 154 Brompton Road, London SW3 1HX (☎ 0171 581 1721)

LOUDON, James Rushworth Hope; s of Francis William Hope Loudon (d 1985), and Lady Prudence Katharine Patton, *née* Jellicoe; *b* 19 March 1943; *Educ* Eton, Magdalene Coll Cambridge (BA); *m* 17 May 1975, Jane Gavina, *née* Fryett; 2 s (Hugo John Hope b 1978, Alexander Guy Rushworth b 1980), 1 da (Antonia Louise Cameron b 1977); *Career* fin dir Blue Circle Industries PLC 1987– (joined 1977), non-exec dir Caldeonia Investments PLC 1995–; *Recreations* golf, tennis, cricket, opera; *Clubs* MCC, Rye Golf, Royal St George's Golf; *Style*— James Loudon, Esq; ✉ Olantigh, Wye, Ashford, Kent TN25 5EW (☎ 01233 812294); Blue Circle Industries PLC, 84 Eccleston Square, London SW1V 1PX (☎ 0171 828 3456, fax 0171 245 8169)

LOUDON, Prof Rodney; s of Albert Loudon (d 1965), and Doris Helen, *née* Blane (d 1980); *b* 25 July 1934; *Educ* Bury GS, Brasenose Coll Oxford (MA, DPhil); *m* 6 June 1960, Mary Anne, da of Eugene Philips; 1 s (Peter Thomas b 1964), 1 da (Anne Elizabeth b 1961); *Career* postdoctoral fell Univ of Calif Berkeley 1959–60, scientific civil servant RRE Malvern 1960–65, Bell Laboratories Murray Hill New Jersey 1965–66, prof of physics Essex Univ 1967– (reader 1966–67), BT Laboratories 1984 and 1989–95; visiting prof: Yale Univ 1975, Univ of Calif Irvine 1980, Ecole Polytechnique Lausanne 1985, Univ of Rome 1988 and 1996, Univ Libre de Bruxelles 1990; chm Bd of Eds Optica Acta 1984–87; Thomas Young Medal and Prize Inst of Physics 1987, Max Born Award of the Optical Soc of America 1992; fell Optical Soc of America 1994; FRS 1987; *Books* The Quantum Theory of Light (1973, 2 edn 1983), Scattering of Light by Crystals (with W Hayes, 1978), Introduction to the Properties of Condensed Matter (with D J Barber, 1989); *Style*— Prof Rodney Loudon, FRS; ✉ 3 Gaston Street, East Bergholt, Colchester, Essex CO7 6SD (☎ 01206 298550); Physics Department, Essex University, Colchester CO4 3SQ (☎ 01206 872880, fax 01206 873598, telex 98440 UNILIB G)

LOUDOUN, Maj-Gen Robert Beverley; CB (1973), OBE (1965); s of Robert Alexander Loudoun (d 1968), of Northwood, Middx, and Margaret Anne Homewood (d 1960); *b* 8 July 1922; *Educ* Univ Coll Sch London; *m* 1950, Audrey Olive, da of William Pearson Stevens (d 1976), of Dublin; 2 s (Steven, Robin); *Career* enlisted RM 1940, war serv Italy, Yugoslavia, post war serv Far East, Med, America, Caribbean, CO 40 Commando 1967–69, Brig UK Commandos 1969–71, Maj-Gen RM Trg 1971–75; chm Jt Shooting Ctee for GB 1977–82, dir Mental Health Fndn 1978–90; Rep Col Cmdt RM 1983–84, chm Br Southern Slav Soc 1989–95; Freeman City of London 1979, memb Guild of Freemen 1982–93; *Recreations* sport (spectator); *Clubs* Army and Navy; *Style*— Maj-Gen Robert Loudoun, CB, OBE; ✉ The Heathers, Bathampton Lane, Bathampton BA2 6SU (☎ 01225 484827)

LOUGHBOROUGH, Archdeacon of; *see:* Stanes, Ven Ian Thomas

LOUGHBOROUGH, Derek Ralph; *b* 5 March 1927; *Educ* Clark's Coll; *m* 1 Sept 1951, Hazel Hilda; 2 s (Martin b 1959, Andrew b 1964); *Career* RN 1945–47; joined Sun Life Assurance Society 1943–77 (mangr 1969), sec PO Insurance Society 1977–87, dir Lautro Ltd 1986–91; memb Formation Ctee PIA 1992; London Borough of Croydon: cncllr 1974–, chm Educn Ctee 1978–88, Mayor 1988–89, chm Environmental Health & Consumer Servs 1989–96, whip 1996–; ACII 1952, APMI 1977, MIMgt 1977; *Recreations* walking, photography; *Style*— Derek Loughborough, Esq; ✉ 45 Cheston Ave, Croydon CR0 8DE (☎ 0181 777 5583)

LOUGHRAN, James; s of James Loughran (d 1956), and Agnes, *née* Fox (d 1971); *b* 30 June 1931; *Educ* St Aloysius Coll Glasgow; *m* 1, 1961 (m dis 1983), Nancy Coggon; 2 s (Angus b 1965, Charles b 1966); m 2, 15 April 1985, Ludmila Navratil; *Career* conductor; first prize Philharmonia Competition 1961, assoc conductor Bournemouth Symphony Orch 1962–65; princ conductor: BBC Scottish Symphony Orch 1965–71, Hallé Orch 1971–83, Bamberg Symphony Orch 1979–83; conductor of princ orchs of Europe, USA, Japan and Aust; permanent guest conductor Japan Philharmonic Symphony Orchestra 1993–, chief conductor Aarhus Symphony Orchestra 1996; recordings with: London Philharmonic, BBC Symphony, Philharmonia, Hallé and Scottish Chamber Orch (Gold Disc EMI 1983); Liveryman Worshipful Co of Musicians; Hon DMus Univ of Sheffield; FRSAMD, FRNCM; *Recreations* travel, walking, golf; *Style*— James Loughran, Esq; ✉ 34 Cleveden Drive, Glasgow G12 0RX (☎ and fax 0141 337 2091)

LOUGHRAN, Rear Adm Terence William (Terry); *b* 27 March 1943; *Educ* Devonport HS, Britannia RNC Dartmouth; *m* 1, (m dis 1988); 2 da (Rebecca b 1968, Anna b 1973), 1 s (William b 1969); m 2, 1995, Philippa Mary Vernon; *Career* with RN; qualified rotary wing pilot 1967, flying instructor 1971, Canadian Forces Command and Staff Coll (Toronto) 1976, cmd 706 Naval Air Sqdn 1977, Office of Naval Sec MOD 1977–79, Cdr 1979, cmd HMS Phoebe 1980–81, Naval Plans MOD 1981–83, Exec Offr HMS Bristol 1983–84 and HMS Intrepid 1984–85, Capt 1986, cmd HMS Gloucester (concurrently cmd Armilla Patrol Arabian Gulf Task Unit) 1986–88, dir Int Affrs in Naval Staff Duties MOD 1988–90, dir Naval Manpower Planning 1990–92, cmd HMS Ark Royal and cmd Grapple Adriatic Task Group 1993–94, Rear Adm 1995, Flag Offr Naval Aviation 1995–; chm tstees: Fleet Air Arm Museum, Swordfish Heritage Tst; memb Rona Tst; memb Nautical Inst 1993; govr Countess Gytha Sch; *Publications* contrib RUSI Jl; *Recreations* sailing, motor cycling, spinning yarns; *Clubs* Naval, Blue Funnel Travellers (Newcastle); *Style*— Rear Adm Terry Loughran; ✉ FONA HQ, Yeovilton, Yeovil, Somerset BA22 8HL (☎ 01935 455501, fax 01935 455509)

LOUGHREY, (Stephen Victor) Patrick; s of Eddie Loughrey (d 1979), and Mary, *née* Griffin; *b* 29 Dec 1955; *Educ* Loreto Coll Milford Donegal, Univ of Ulster (BA), Queen's Univ Belfast (MA, PGCE); *m* 4 July 1978, Patricia, da of Thomas Kelly (d 1984); 1 s (Stephen b 26 Dec 1980), 2 da (Joanne b 26 Feb 1982, Christine b 10 June 1985); *Career* teacher St Colm's HS Draperstown 1978–84; BBC Northern Ireland: joined as prodr 1984, head of educnl bdcasting 1988–91, head of programmes 1991–, controller 1994–; memb: NI Curriculum Cncl, Hist Monuments Cncl, Advsy Ctee NI Arts Cncl; tstee Ulster Local History Tst Fund; *Books* Ordnance Survey of Ballinascreen (ed, 1981), The People of Ireland (ed, 1988); *Recreations* talking; *Style*— Patrick Loughrey, Esq; ✉ 7 The Willows, Coolshinney, Magherafelt, Northern Ireland (☎ 01648 33031, 01232 338442); BBC Northern Ireland, Broadcasting House, Ormeau Avenue, Belfast BT2 8HQ (☎ 01232 388000)

LOUGHTON, David Clifford; s of Clifford Loughton (d 1973) of Harrow, and Hazel Loughton; *b* 28 Jan 1954; *Educ* Roxeth Manor Sch Harrow Middlesex, Technical Colls in Harrow Watford and Southall; *m* 1986, Deborah, da of George Wellington; 1 s (Theodore David b 12 July 1990), 1 da (Georgina Anna b 12 July 1987); *Career* apprentice instrument technician Kodak Ltd 1970–74, asst hosp engr Hillingdon Area Health Authy 1974–76, hosp engr Herts Area Health Authy 1976–78, dir and gen mangr Ducost Ltd 1978–83, divnl mangr GEC Electrical Projects 1984–86, chief exec Walsgrave Hosp NHS Tst (now Walsgrave Hosps NHS Tst) 1986–; elected Midlands rep NHS Tst Fedn 1993–; memb: Inst of Health Services Mgmnt, Inst of Hosp Engrs, Inst of Plant Engrs; *Recreations* golf, country pursuits; *Style*— David Loughton, Esq; ✉ Blacon Cottage, Norton Lindsey, nr Warwick, Warwickshire CV35 8JN (☎ 0192 684 2070); Walsgrave Hospitals NHS Trust, Clifford Bridge Rd, Coventry, W Midlands CV2 2DX (☎ 01203 602020)

LOULOUDIS, Hon Mrs (Madeleine Mary); *née* Dillon; 4 but 3 survg da (twin) of 20 Viscount Dillon (d 1979); *b* 29 Oct 1957; *m* 4 March 1989, Leonard Constantine Louloudis, o s of Constantine Louloudis; 1 s (Constantine Michael b 15 Sept 1991), 1 da (Theodora Catherine Lily b 6 July 1993); *Career* asst private sec to HRH The Princess Royal 1988–; *Style*— The Hon Mrs Louloudis; ✉ Flat 2, 66 Westbourne Terrace, London W2 3UJ (☎ 0171 723 8816)

LOUSADA, Peter Allen; s of Air Cdre Charles Rochford Lousada, DL (d 1988), and Elizabeth, *née* Shaw; *b* 30 March 1937; *Educ* Epsom Coll; *m* 13 Oct 1962, Jane, da of Lt-Col Donald Gillmor (d 1972); 2 s (Toby b 1963, James b 1965), 1 da (Sarah b 1965); *Career* Nat Serv Flying Offr RAF, Canada & 61 Sqdn; vice pres Cadbury Beverages Europe 1987–92; dir: Schweppes International Ltd, Cadbury Beverages Ltd 1990–92; sr vice pres Cadbury Beverages 1992–; non-exec chm Hydrophane Ltd 1990–; pres Union of Euro Soft Drinks Assocs 1991–95; *Recreations* golf, fishing; *Clubs* RAF, Woburn Golf; *Style*— Peter A Lousada, Esq; ✉ Well Cottage, Bow Brickhill, nr Milton Keynes, Bucks MK17 9JU (☎ 01908 372186, fax 01908 366812)

LOUSADA, Sandra Reignier; da of Sir Anthony Baruh Lousada (d 1994), of Chiswick Mall, London W4, and his 1 w, Jocelyn Herbert, da of late Sir Alan Herbert, CH; *b* 29 June 1938; *Educ* St Paul's Girls' Sch, Regent St Poly; *m* 1 Jan 1965, Brian Richards, son of Alexander Hodgson Richards; 1 s (Sam b 12 June 1966), 1 da (Polly b 17 May 1968); *Career* asst photographer Scaioni Studios 1956–59; freelance photographer 1959–63 (work for magazines incl: Queen Magazine, Tatler, Nova, Brides, Vogue, Elle (Paris), Marie Claire (Paris), Vanity Fair, Mademoiselle and Glamour Magazines (Conde Naste) NY; work for English Stage Co (plays incl John Osborne's Luther and Wesker Trilogy); film work incl: The Loneliness of the Long Distance Runner, Tom Jones, The Charge of the Light Brigade; travelled and worked in USA, Japan, India and Russia; joined Whitecross Studios 1963–81, advtg work for agencies incl: J Walter Thompson, Ogilvy Benson & Mather, Collett Dickinson & Pearce; editorial work for most of main magazines and some publishers in London and New York; Susan Griggs Agency 1981–94, frequent travel to Europe and India; current photographic work incl portraits, children, crafts, fashion, health and beauty for number of London magazines, book publishers, design groups and advtg agencies; work for charities: Wellbeing (formerly Birthright), Great Ormond Street Hosp for Sick Children, Tommy Campaign, Peper Harow Fndn; *Awards* Silver award Assoc of Photographers 1988; *Style*— Ms Sandra Lousada; ✉ c/o Robert Montgomery and Partners, 3 Junction Mews, Sale Place, London W2 1PN (☎ 0171 439 1877, fax 0171 434 1144)

LOUTH, 16 Baron (I 1541); Otway Michael James Oliver Plunkett; s of 15 Baron (d 1950); *b* 19 Aug 1929; *Educ* Downside; *m* 1951, Angela Patricia, da of William Cullinane, of St Helier, Jersey; 3 s, 2 da; *Heir* s, Hon Jonathan Oliver Plunkett; *Style*— The Rt Hon the Lord Louth; ✉ Les Sercles, La Grande Piece, St Peter, Jersey

LOVAT, 16 Lord (S 1458–64); Simon Fraser; 25 Chief of Clan Fraser; *de facto* 16 Lord, 18 but for the attainder; also Baron Lovat (UK 1837), of Lovat, Co Inverness; er s of Hon Simon Augustine Fraser, Master of Lovat (d 1994), and Virginia, *née* Grose; suc gf 15 Lord Lovat, DSO, MC, TD 1995; *b* 13 Feb 1977; *Educ* Harrow; *Heir* bro, Hon Jack Fraser (Master of Lovat) b 22 Aug 1984; *Style*— The Rt Hon the Lord Lovat; ✉ Beaufort Lodge, Beauly, Inverness-shire

LOVE, Prof Andrew Henry Garmany; CBE (1995); s of Andrew Love (d 1976), of Ballymagee, Bangor, Co Down, and Martha, *née* Fleming (d 1981); *b* 28 Sept 1934; *Educ* Bangor Endowed Sch, Queen's Univ Belfast (BSc, MB BCh, BAO, MD); *m* 29 May 1963, Margaret Jean, da of William Stuart Lennox (d 1987); 1 s (Anthony W G b 24 Oct 1967); *Career* Queen's Univ Belfast: prof of gastroenterology 1977–83, dean of Faculty of Medicine 1981–86, prof of medicine 1983–; dir of educn and research Royal Victoria Hosp Belfast, censor RCP London; chm: Res Ctee Ulster Cancer Fndn, Advsy Ctee on Borderline Substances DHSS London, NI Cncl for Postgrad Med Educn, Review Bd for Overseas Doctors GMC; FRCP 1973, FRCPI 1973; Ulster Boys' Golf Champion 1952, Irish Amateur Golf Champion 1956; Gastroenterology, Tropical Diseases, Nutrition; *Recreations* riding, sailing; *Clubs* East India, Devonshire Sports, Royal Ulster Yacht; *Style*— Prof Andrew Love, CBE; ✉ The Glen Farm, Greyabbey, Co Down BT22 2LU (☎ 01247 788414); Department of Medicine, Queen's University Belfast, Institute of Clinical Science, Grosvenor Road, Belfast BT12 6BJ (☎ 01232 240503 ext 2707, fax 01232 329899, telex 747578 QUB MEDG)

LOVE, Heather Beryl; da of the late John Sydney Love, and Joyce Margaret, *née* Cracknell; *b* 17 Nov 1953; *Educ* Mayfield Sch Putney; 1 s (Matthew Paul Hodges b 1982); *Career* IPC Magazines: publicity mangr 1980, gp publicity mangr 1981, assoc publisher 1985, publisher 1988, publishing dir (Woman's Journal, Marie Claire, Options) 1988–; memb Nat Small Bore Rifle Assoc; *Recreations* pistol shooting, interior design, workaholic; *Style*— Miss Heather Love; ✉ Publishing Director, IPC Magazines, Kings Reach Tower, Stamford Street, London SE1 9LS (☎ 0171 261 5508, fax 0171 261 4277)

LOVE, Prof Philip Noel; CBE (1983); s of Thomas Love (d 1992), of Aberdeen, and Ethel, *née* Philip (d 1995); *b* 25 Dec 1939; *Educ* Aberdeen GS, Univ of Aberdeen (MA, LLB); *m* 1, 21 Aug 1963, Isabel Leah (d 1993), da of Innes Mearns (d 1991), of Aberdeen; 3 s (Steven b 1965, Michael b 1967, Donald b 1969); m 2, 15 April 1995, Mrs Isobel Pardey; *Career* advocate in Aberdeen 1963; princ Campbell Connon Slrs Aberdeen 1963–74 (conslt 1974–); Univ of Aberdeen: prof of conveyancing and professional practice of law 1974–92, dean Faculty of Law 1979–82 and 1991–92, vice princ 1986–90; vice-chllr Univ of Liverpool 1992–; memb Rules Cncl Ct of Session 1968–92, vice pres Scottish Law Agents' Soc 1970, chm Aberdeen Home for Widowers' Children 1971–92, local chm Rent Assessment Panel for Scotland 1972–92, Hon Sheriff Grampian Highlands and Islands 1978–; Law Soc of Scotland: memb 1963–, memb Cncl 1975–86, vice pres 1980–81, pres 1981–82; chm Grampian Med Ethical Ctee 1984–92, pt/t memb Scot Law Cmmn 1986–95, pres Aberdeen GS Former Pupils' Club 1987–88, tstee Grampian and Islands Family Tst 1988–92, memb Scot Univs Cncl on Entrance 1989–92, govr Inst of Occupational Med Ltd 1990–, chm Registers of Scot Customer Advsy Gp 1990–92, memb Butterworths Editorial Consultative Bd for Scot 1990–95, chm Scot Conveyancing and Executry Servs Bd 1991–96, chm The Mersey Partnership 1995–, tstee St George's Hall Tst 1996–, memb Cncl of Ctee of Vice-Chllrs and Princs (of the Univs of the UK) 1996–, chm Univs and Colls Employers Assoc; FRSA 1995, CIMgt 1996; *Recreations* rugby, formerly golf; *Clubs* New (Edinburgh), Athenaeum, Royal Aberdeen Golf; *Style*— Prof Philip N Love, CBE; ✉ The University of Liverpool, Senate House, Abercromby Square, Liverpool L69 3BX (☎ 0151 794 2003, fax 0151 708 7092)

LOVE, Robert Malcolm; s of Robert Love, of Paisley, Scotland, and Mary, *née* Darroch; *b* 9 Jan 1936; *Educ* Paisley GS, Univ of Glasgow (MA), Washington Univ St Louis; *Career* short serv cmmn Flt Lt Educn Branch RAF 1959–62; actor and dir numerous English rep theatres 1962–66, prodr TV drama Thames TV 1966–75; prodns incl: Public Eye, The Rivals of Sherlock Holmes, The Mind of Mr J G Reeder, Van der Valk, Frontier, Moody and Pegg; freelance TV prodr 1975–79, controller of drama Scottish TV 1979–; prodns incl: House on the Hill, City Sugar, Northern Lights, Taggart, Extras, The Steamie, The Advocates, Doctor Finlay, McCallum; govr Scottish Theatre Co 1981–87, visiting lectr in media studies Univ of Stirling 1986–, chm BAFTA Scotland 1987–92, drama chair Scottish Arts Cncl 1994–, govr Royal Scottish Acad of Music and Drama 1994–; memb RTS, fell Royal Scottish Acad of Music and Drama 1993; *Recreations* music, theatre, foreign travel, books, railway history; *Style*— Robert Love, Esq; ✉ Scottish Television plc, Cowcaddens, Glasgow G2 3PR (☎ 0141 332 9999, fax 0141 332 6982)

LOVEDAY, Mark Antony; s of George Arthur Loveday (d 1981), and Sylvia Mary, *née* Gibbs (d 1967); *b* 22 Sept 1943; *Educ* Winchester, Magdalen Coll Oxford (MA); *m* 1981, Mary Elizabeth, da of John Tolmie; 1 s (Samuel George b 15 June 1982), 1 da

(Lucy Sylvia Catherine b 9 Dec 1983); *Career* Cazenove & Co: joined 1966, corp fin ptnr 1974–, sr ptnr 1994–; Freeman City of London, Liveryman Worshipful Co of Skinners; MSI (memb Stock Exchange 1974); *Recreations* golf; *Clubs* Boodle's, Hurlingham, MCC; *Style*— Mark Loveday, Esq; ✉ Cazenove & Co, 12 Tokenhouse Yard, London EC2R 7AN (☎ 0171 588 2828)

LOVEGROVE, Ross; s of Herbert William John Lovegrove, BEM, of Penarth, S Glamorgan, and Mary Eileen Lovegrove; *b* 16 Aug 1958; *Educ* St Cyres Comp Sch Penarth, Cardiff Coll of Art & Design, Manchester Poly (BA), RCA (MDes); *partner* Miska Miller; 1 s (Roman S A Lovegrove); *Career* designer: Allied International Designers London 1978–82, Frogdesign Germany 1983–84 (projects incl: Apple Computers, Sony Walkman, AEG Telefunken and Louis Vuitton Luggage), Knoll International Paris 1984, Atelier De Nimes 1984–86 (freelance projects for Cacharel and Dupont), fndr ptnr Lovegrove & Brown 1987–90, fndr Lovegrove Studio X 1990– (clients incl: Knoll International, BA, Louis Vuitton, Parker Pens, Cacharel, Puma, Carrera, Hermes, Berol Pens, Cappellini SPA, Philips Eindhove, Form & Design, Connolly Leathers and Steuben Glass USA); winner: Oqqetti Per Domus award for the pocket disc camera and film cassette system 1984, first prize (product design) Creative Review Pantone Colour awards; work featured in various jls incl: Form, Design Week, L'Architecture D'Aujordhui, Elle, Harpers and Queen, Interior Design, Vogue, Casa Vogue, Domus, The Independent, Axis Japan, New Scientist; exhibitions incl: Designing for Britain or Abroad (London) 1985, Leading Edge (Tokyo) 1987, Mondo Materials (California) 1989–90, Synthetic Visions (V & A London) 1990, 91 Objects by 91 Designers (Gallery 91 NY) 1991, Razor Cheap Design, Current Observation (Lamp Gallery) 1992, Cappellini Arosio (Como Milan) 1992, FO8 Chair New British Furniture Design (The Fruitmarket Gallery Edinburgh) 1992; memb jury: Les 25 Objects Temoins des Annes 80 (for French product design) 1985, Interieur 90 Kortrijk Belgium 1990; pres Janus Des Etudients Paris 1991, visiting tutor Royal Coll of Art London; lectures: Aberdeen Sch of Architecture, Ravensbourne Poly Kingston, Kingston Poly, High Wycombe Sch of Furniture and Industl Design; TV and radio: Late Show BBC 2, The Changing Domestic Landscape (LBC Design Week interview with Ken Grange), Ross Lovegrove Industrial Designer (BBC Wales interview); *Style*— Ross Lovegrove, Esq; ✉ Lovegrove Design Consultants, 21 Powis Mews, London W11 1JN (☎ 0171 229 7104, fax 0171 229 7032); Lovegrove Studio X, 81 Southern Row, London W10 5AL (☎ 0181 968 4614)

LOVEJOY, Prof Derek Alfred Walter; s of J F Lovejoy (d 1952), and M Lovejoy (d 1975), *née* Stoner; *b* 16 Sept 1925; *Educ* St Olave's GS, Harvard Univ; *m* 5 Jan 1952, June, *née* Hotz; 1 s (Alan b 1956), 2 da (Davida b 1959, Vanessa b 1960); *Career* architect, landscape architect and town planner; chief landscape architect Crawley Devpt Corp 1956–58, dep head Dept of Architecutre and Town Planning South Bank Poly 1957–62; Derek Lovejoy and Partners: founding ptnr 1956, sr ptnr 1968–88); visiting prof of landscape architecture Univ of Sheffield 1986–; Int Fedn of Landscape Architects: memb Grand Cncl 1956–83, sec gen 1960–68, first vice pres 1980–83, chm Int Ctee 1990; Inst of Landscape Architects: convenor and first chm PR Ctee, convenor and first chm Res Ctee, chm of examiners 1964–68, pres 1971–73, rep Int Fedn of Landscape Architects at Earth Summit Rio de Janeiro 1992 and at UN 1994; Dept of Transport: memb Landscape Advsy Ctee for Trunk Roads 1969–90, chm Lighting Sub Ctee 1972–89, memb Service Area Sub Ctee 1971–81, Memb Urban Motorway Sub Ctee 1970–88; memb: Housing Awards Ctee DOE 1970–80, Natural Resources Ctee DOE 1970–, Planning Ctee CPRE 1970–76, UK Cncl Euro Architectural Heritage Year (1975) 1973–75, Planning Ctee Social Sci Res Cncl 1974–76, Cncl The Building Conservation Tst 1975–, Ctee USA Transportation Bd 1980–, Transportation Ctee Inst of Highways and Transportation, UK Ctee Int Cmmn for Monuments and Sites 1987–90, Awards Jury Sand and Gravel Assoc 1987–, Exec Ctee Fountain Soc 1988–, Advsy Ctee Devon Environmental Forum 1990–; county cmmr Surrey for Enterprise Neptune Campaign The Nat Tst 1968–70, memb Cncl The Tree Council 1970– (chm 1980), chm Jt Cncl for Landscape Industs 1972, tstee The Queen's Trees 1976–80, former vice chm and hon life assoc Professional Institutions Conservation Cncl 1980, environment assessor for Dodoma Tanzania United Nations Environment Programme 1983, vice pres Tst for Urban Ecology, former chm and memb Nat Cncl Int Tree Fndn, conslt to UN; memb Panel XVth World Congress Mexico (The Road within the Environment) 1975, vice pres Hong Kong International Congress on Urban Growth and the Environment 1994; chief assessor for competitions RIBA 1975– (occasional regnl chm RIBA Architecture Awards), occasional chm Regnl Awards Civic Tst, jt chm Tomorrows Towns (nat pubn); external examiner: MSc Rural and Regnl Resource Planning Univ of Aberdeen 1976, BA (Hons) Landscape Architecture Thames Poly 1976–84, MA Urban Design Oxford Poly 1977–80, BA (Hons) Landscape Architecture Kingston Univ 1993–; memb Validation Panel for Postgrad Dip in Landscape Architecture Univ of Central England 1994; memb Worshipful Co of Constructors 1978, memb Worshipful Co of Architects 1988, Freeman City of London 1978; FRIBA 1952, PPILA 1952, FRTPI 1953, FRSA 1970, FIHT 1980; *Books* Land Use And Landscape Planning (1975 and 80); *Recreations* work, travel, music; *Clubs* Architecture, Athenaeum, Directors; *Style*— Prof Derek Lovejoy; ✉ Hobtye, Church lane, Godstone, Surrey RH9 8BW (☎ and fax 01883 743331); 8–11 Denbigh Mews, Denbigh St, London SW1V 2HQ (☎ 0171 828 6392, fax 0171 630 6958)

LOVEKIN, Jonathan William; s of Barry William Lovekin, of Warwick, and Linda, *née* Pearson (now Mrs Lovekin-Smith); *b* 21 Nov 1964; *Educ* Licensed Victuallers' Sch, Medway Coll of Design; *m* 5 Sept 1992, Sanjana Yogeshwaree, da of Charles Harvey George Davis; 1 da (Lillie Laura b 15 Jan 1995); *Career* photographic asst (to Richard Mummery then John Wallace) 1984–87, freelance photographer working on various editorial and advtg assignments 1987–; Silver Award Assoc of Photographers 7th Awards, Best Still Life Graphis Photo '92 (Int Annual of Photography); memb Assoc of Photographers 1988; *Recreations* non-commissioned photography; *Style*— Jonathan Lovekin, Esq; ✉ 31–33 Shacklewell Street, London E2 7EG (☎ 0171 729 7072, fax 0171 739 7697)

LOVELACE, 5 Earl of (UK 1838); Peter Axel William Locke King; also Lord King, Baron of Ockham (GB 1725), and Viscount Ockham (UK 1838); s of 4 Earl of Lovelace (d 1964, seventh in descent from the sis of John Locke, the philosopher), and his 2 w, Manon Lis (d 1990), da of Axel Sigurd Transo, of Copenhagen, and widow of Baron Carl Frederik von Blixen Finecke; *b* 26 Nov 1951; *Educ* privately; *m* 1, 1980 (m dis 1989), Kirsteen Oihrig, da of Calum Kennedy of Leethland, Renfrewshire; m 2, 1994, Kathleen Anne Rose, da of Lem Smolders, of Milouka, Langwarrin, Australia; *Heir* none; *Style*— The Rt Hon the Earl of Lovelace; ✉ Torridon House, Torridon, Ross-shire

LOVELL, Alan Charles; s of William George Lovell (d 1984), of Andover, Hants, and Mary Kerr, *née* Briant (d 1970); *b* 19 Nov 1953; *Educ* Chafyn Grove Sch Salisbury, Winchester, Jesus Coll Oxford (MA, Lawn Tennis, Real Tennis and Rackets blues); *m* 10 July 1982, Hon Virginia, da of Baron Weatherill, PC, DL (Life Peer), *qv*; 2 da (Emma b 19 March 1985, Lucinda b 3 Oct 1986); *Career* articled clerk then CA Price Waterhouse 1976–80, The Plessey Company plc 1980–89, chief exec Conder Group plc 1992 (fin dir 1989–92), chief exec Costain Group plc 1995–97 (fin dir 1993–95); non-exec dir: Collett Dickenson Pearce Europe Ltd 1990, Abbotts Barton Group 1991–; non-exec memb Winchester Dist Health Authy 1990–93, non-exec dir Winchester and Eastleigh Healthcare Tst 1994–; memb Cncl Malvern Coll 1990–; International Real Tennis player 1975–87; FCA 1989 (ACA 1979); *Recreations* real and lawn tennis, gardening; *Clubs* All England Lawn Tennis, MCC, Queen's; *Style*— Alan Lovell, Esq; ✉ The Palace House, Bishop's Lane, Bishop's Waltham, Hants SO32 1DP (☎ 01489 892838); Costain Group plc, 111 Westminster Bridge Rd, London SE1 7UE (☎ 0171 705 8514, fax 0171 633 9210)

LOVELL, Sir (Alfred Charles) Bernard; kt (1961), OBE (1946); s of Gilbert Lovell; *b* 31 Aug 1913; *Educ* Kingswood GS, Univ of Bristol; *m* 1937, Mary Joyce Chesterman (d 1993); 2 s, 3 da; *Career* served Telecommunications Res Estab MAP 1939–45; prof of radio astronomy Manchester Univ 1951–80 (emeritus 1980–); fndr and dir Nuffield Radio Astronomy Laboratories Jodrell Bank 1945–81; pres: Royal Astronomical Soc 1969–71, British Assoc 1974–75; Hon Asst Worshipful Co of Musicians (Master 1986–87); Cdr Order of Merit (Poland) 1975; FRS 1955; *Books include* The Story of Jodrell Bank (1968), In the Centre of Immensities (1975), Emerging Cosmology (1981), The Jodrell Bank Telescopes (1985), Voice of the Universe (1987), Astronomer by Chance (1990), Echoes of War (1991); *Clubs* Athenaeum; *Style*— Sir Bernard Lovell, OBE, FRS; ✉ The Quinta, Swettenham, Cheshire (☎ 01477 571254); c/o University of Manchester, Nuffield Radio Astronomy Laboratories, Jodrell Bank, Macclesfield, Cheshire SK11 9DL (☎ 01477 571321, fax 01477 571618)

LOVELL, Dr Christopher Roland; s of Graham Ernest Lovell (d 1990), and Marion Gladys (d 1984); *b* 29 April 1950; *Educ* Bristol GS, Univ of Bristol (MD); *Career* sr registrar and tutor in dermatology Inst of Dermatology London 1978–84, conslt dermatologist Bath Health Dist 1985–; hon treas Dowling Club (formerly hon sec and hon pres), sec British Contact Dermatitis; regnl rep British Assoc of Dermatologists; treas Clinical Soc of Bath; FRCP, FRSM; *Books* Plants and the Skin (1993); *Recreations* cultivation and preservation of rare bulbs, music (mediaeval & renaissance recorder player); *Style*— Dr Christopher Lovell; ✉ Royal United Hospital, Combe Park, Bath BA1 3NG (☎ and fax 01225 824524)

LOVELL, Mary Sybilla; da of William George Shelton (d 1967), and Mary Catherine, *née* Wooley; *b* 23 Oct 1941; *Educ* Notre Dame Collegiate Liverpool, UCLA; *m* 1, 22 Oct 1960 (m dis 1977), Clifford C Lovell; 1 s (Graeme Robert b 1961); m 2, 11 July 1992, Geoffrey Alan Howard Watts (d 1995); *Career* author; fin controller Baron Instruments Ltd 1969–76; dir and co sec: Yachting Provence 1976–78, Baron Computers & Security Ltd 1978–80; mangr Tech Writing Div Tabs Ltd 1982–86; MFH New Forest Hounds 1988–89; vice-pres R S Surtees Soc 1981–; MIMgt 1973, FRGS 1994; *Books* A Hunting Pageant (1980), Cats as Pets (1981), Boys Book of Boats (1982), Straight on Till Morning (1986), The Splendid Outcast (ed, 1987), The Sound of Wings (1989), Cast No Shadow (1992), A Scandalous Life (1995); *Recreations* foxhunting, flying, sailing, travel, reading; *Clubs* Lansdowne, New Forest Hunt, Royal Over-Seas League, Soc of Authors, MFHA; *Style*— Mrs Mary S Lovell; ✉ Stroat House, Stroat, Glos NP6 7LR (☎ 01594 529330)

LOVELL-DAVIS, Baron (Life Peer UK 1974), of Highgate, in Greater London; Peter Lovell-Davis; s of William Lovell-Davis (d 1974), and Winifred Mary Lovell-Davis (d 1964); *b* 8 July 1924; *Educ* Christ's Coll Finchley, King Edward VI GS Stratford-on-Avon, Jesus Coll Oxford (MA); *m* 1950, Jean, da of Peter Foster Graham (d 1948); 1 s (Hon Stephen Lovell b 1955), 1 da (Hon Catherine Ruth b 1958); *Career* RAF Flt Lt pilot 1943–47; sits as Labour peer in Lords; md Central Press Features Ltd 1950–70, dir various newspaper & printing cos 1950–70; chm: Davis & Harrison Ltd 1970–73, The Features Syndicate Ltd 1971–74, Lee Cooper Licensing Ltd 1983–90, Pettifor Morrow & Assocs Ltd 1986–; memb Bd Cwlth Devpt Corp 1978–84, memb Bd London Consortium 1978–88; a Lord in Waiting to HM The Queen 1974–75, Parly under-sec of state Dept of Energy 1975–76; memb Islington Dist Health Authy 1982–85, tstee Whittington Hosp Academic Centre 1980–, vice pres YHA 1978–; *Recreations* industrial archaeology, aviation, inland waterways, bird-watching, walking; *Style*— The Rt Hon the Lord Lovell-Davis; ✉ 80 North Rd, Highgate, London N6 4AA (☎ 0181 348 3919)

LOVELL-PANK, Dorian Christopher; QC (1993); s of Christopher Edwin Lovell-Pank (d 1966), of Madrid, and Jean Alston de Oliva Day, *née* McPherson (d 1979), of Buenos Aires and Cape Town; *b* 15 Feb 1946; *Educ* Downside, Colegio Sarmiento Buenos Aires, LSE, Inns of Ct Sch of Law; *m* 1983, Diana, da of late Michael Cady Byford, and Sonia Byford, of Clare, Suffolk; 1 da (Frederica Sonia b 2 May 1986), 1 s (Michael Christopher John b 20 June 1987); *Career* called to Bar Inner Temple 1971; pupillage with Rt Hon Sir Leon Brittan, QC and Michael Worsley, QC; jr Mddx Bar Mess 1977–80, recorder 1989– (asst recorder 1985–89); memb: Gen Cncl of the Bar 1989–92, Panel of Chm of Police Discipline Appeal Tbnls 1991–, Ctee Criminal Bar Assoc 1989–, Int Bar Assoc 1993–, Human Rights Inst 1996–; *Recreations* travel, reading, swimming, things latin; *Clubs* Garrick, Hurlingham, Riverside, Annabel's; *Style*— Dorian Lovell-Pank, Esq, QC; ✉ 6 King's Bench Walk, Temple, London EC4Y 7DR (☎ 0171 583 0410, fax 0171 353 8791)

LOVELOCK, Sir Douglas Arthur; KCB (1979, CB 1974); s of late Walter Lovelock, and Irene Lovelock; *b* 7 Sept 1923; *Educ* Bec Sch London; *m* 1961, Valerie Margaret Lane; 1 s, 1 da; *Career* joined Treasy 1949, asst under sec (personnel) MOD 1971–72 (previously with Minys of Technol and Aviation Supply), DTI 1972–74; dep sec: Trade, Indust, Prices & Consumer Protection Depts 1974–77; chm: Bd Customs & Excise 1977–83, Civil Servs Benevolent Fund 1980–; First Church Estates Cmmr 1983–93; govr: Whitgift Sch 1986–, Trinity Sch 1986–, Old Palace Sch 1986– (chm of Govrs 1993–); *Style*— Sir Douglas Lovelock, KCB; ✉ The Old House, 91 Coulsdon Rd, Old Coulsdon, Surrey (☎ 017375 55211)

LOVERIDGE, Air Cdre David John; OBE (1981); s of Wing Cdr George Frederick Edmund Loveridge, OBE, of Melita, Middle Bourne, Farnham, Surrey, and Docie Annie, *née* West (d 1982); *b* 21 Oct 1937; *Educ* English Sch Cairo, Brockenhurst, RAF Coll Cranwell, RAF Staff Coll, Nat Def Coll; *m* 1 June 1963, Patricia (Poosie), da of Charles Perkins Garner (d 1971), of Burton Lazars, Melton Mowbray; 1 da (Sarah b 1964), 1 s (Simon b 1966); *Career* OC 230 Operational Conversion Unit 1977–79, Wing Cdr Strike Attack MOD Air Plans 1979–82, Station Cdr RAF Gatow Berlin 1982–85, dep dir Air Force Plans MOD 1985–87, Air Cdre flying trg 1987–89, dir trg (G) (RAF) 1990–91; bursar St Paul's Sch 1991–; FRAeS, FIMgt, MIPD; *Recreations* cycling, hill walking, sailing; *Clubs* RAF, Royal Fowey Yacht, Queenhithe Ward; *Style*— Air Cdre David Loveridge, OBE; ✉ Bursar, St Paul's School, Lonsdale Road, Barnes, London SW13 9JT (☎ 0181 748 5958)

LOVERIDGE, Sir John Henry; kt (1975), CBE (1964, MBE 1945); s of Henry Thomas Loveridge, and Vera Lilian Loveridge; *b* 2 Aug 1912; *Educ* Elizabeth Coll Guernsey, Caen Univ; *m* 1946, Madeleine Melanie, da of Eugene Joseph C M Tanguy; 1 s, 1 da; *Career* RAFVR 1954–59; called to the Bar Middle Temple 1950, advocate Royal Court of Guernsey 1951, bailiff of Guernsey 1973–82 (slr gen 1954–60, attorney-gen 1960–69, dep 1969–73), appeal judge Jersey 1974–82; KStJ 1980; *Clubs* Royal Guernsey Golf; *Style*— Sir John Loveridge, CBE

LOVERIDGE, Sir John Warren; kt (1988), JP (West Central Division 1963); s of Claude Warren Loveridge (d 1956), and Emilie Warren, *née* Malone (d 1954); *b* 9 Sept 1925; *Educ* St John's Coll Cambridge (MA); *m* 1954, Jean Marguerite, da of E J Chivers, of Devizes, Wilts; 3 s (Michael, Steven, Robert), 2 da (Amanda, Emma); *Career* sr ptnr of family business in educn, agric and property; Parly candidate (C) Aberavon 1951, contested Brixton (LCC) 1952; MP (C): Hornchurch 1970–74, Upminster 1974–83; memb: Parly Select Ctee on Expenditure, Gen Purposes Sub Ctee, Procedure Ctee; chm Cons Small Business Ctee 1979–83; memb Hampstead Borough Cncl 1953–59, treas and tstee

Hampstead Cons Assoc 1959–74; pres: Hampstead and Highgate Cons Assoc 1986–91, Upminster Cons Assoc 1992–; pres Gtr London Area Cons Assoc 1993–96 (vice pres 1984–93 and 1996–), vice pres Nat Cncl for Civil Protection (formerly Civil Def); chm Dinosaurs Club (former MPs) 1993–; Liveryman Worshipful Co of Girdlers; FRAS, FRAgS, MRIIA; *Books* Moving Forward: Small Businesses and the Economy (jt author), God Save the Queen (1981), Hunter of the Moon (1983), Hunter of the Sun (1984); *Recreations* painting, poetry, historic houses, shooting; *Clubs* Buck's, Carlton, Hurlingham; *Style—* Sir John Loveridge, JP; ✉ c/o The Private Office, 2 Arkwright Road, London NW3 6AD

LOVETT, David; *b* 1942; *Educ* Harvard Graduate Sch of Business (AMP); *m*; 2 s, 2 da; *Career* employed in heavy building materials industry 1964–; with Lafarge Corporation Canada 1968–92; Blue Circle Industries: Main Bd dir Blue Circle Industries plc 1992–, chief exec Blue Circle America 1992–95, chief exec Heavy Building Materials Int Gp 1995–, also responsible for Africa, Tech Servs Gp and Int Investments 1995–; *Recreations* skiing, golf, shooting, fishing; *Style—* David Lovett, Esq; ✉ Blue Circle Industries plc, 84 Eccleston Square, London SW1V 1PX (☎ 0171 828 3456, fax 0171 245 8169)

LOVETT, Ian Nicholas; s of Frederick Lovett, of Croydon, Surrey, and Dorothy Evelyn, *née* Stanley; *b* 7 Sept 1944; *Educ* Selhurst GS, Univ of Wales (BA); *m* 3 May 1969, Patricia Lesley; 2 da (Emma b 1977, Sophie b 1979); *Career* chief exec Dunbar Bank plc 1994– (md 1984–94); FCIB 1982; *Recreations* cricket; *Clubs* MCC; *Style—* Ian N Lovett, Esq; ✉ Dunbar Bank plc, 9 Sackville St, London W1A 2JP (☎ 0171 437 7844, telex 28300 ALLIED G)

LOVETT, Martin; OBE (1970); *b* 3 March 1927; *Educ* RCM; *m* 1950, Suzanne, *née* Rozsa; 1 s (Peter Sandor b 1955), 1 da (Sonia Naomi 1951); *Career* cellist of Amadeus Quartet 1947–1987; prof RAM; Hon DUniv York, Hon DMus London; Hon RAM; Grosses Verdienst Kreuz (Germany), Ehrenkreuz Fuer Kunst and Wissenschaft (Austria); FRSA; *Style—* Martin Lovett, Esq, OBE; ✉ 24 Redington Gdns, NW3 7RX (☎ 0171 794 9898); 5 Coastal Rd, Angmering-On-Sea, W Sussex 1BN 1SJ (☎ 01903 786900)

LOVICK, Peter Alan; s of Peter George Lovick (d 1953), and Dora Evelyn, *née* Elvidge; *b* 23 Jan 1928; *Educ* City of London Coll; *m* 14 July 1951, Shirley Georgina, da of Edward Duffin (d 1956); 1 da (Susan Caroline b 1963); *Career* dir: Bleichroder Bing & Co Ltd (Lloyd's brokers) 1965–69, Ropner Insurance Services 1969–72; Benfield Lovick Rees & Co Ltd: dir 1972–88, chm Underwriting Agencies Ltd 1980–89, chm Holdings Ltd 1984–88; dir: Bell & Clements Ltd 1984–95, Benfield Bell & Clements Ltd 1985–88; Liveryman Worshipful Co of Carmen; FCIB, FInstD; *Recreations* fine wine and food, MENSA, ecology, conservation; *Clubs* City of London; *Style—* Peter Lovick, Esq; ✉ Riverside, 67 Thorpe Bay Gardens, Thorpe Bay, Essex (☎ 01702 585449); Old Forge House, Thorington St, Stoke by Nayland, Suffolk (☎ 0120637 255)

LOVICK, (Elizabeth) Sara; da of Charles Trevor Lovick, of King's Walden, Herts, and Elizabeth Susan Hettie, *née* Phelps; *b* 3 Feb 1954; *Educ* North London Collegiate Sch Canons Edgware, Lady Margaret Hall Oxford (BA); *Career* admitted slr 1979; ptnr Cameron Markby Hewitt 1986–; Freeman Worshipful Co of Slrs 1989; memb: Law Soc, Common Law Inst of Intellectual Property; assoc memb: Chartered Inst of Patent Agents, The Inst of Trade Mark Agents; *Recreations* swimming, skiing, choral singing; *Style—* Miss Sara Lovick; ✉ Cameron Markby Hewitt, Sceptre Court, 40 Tower Hill, London EC3N 4BB (☎ 0171 702 2345, fax 0171 702 2303, telex 925779)

LOVILL, Sir John Roger; kt (1987), CBE (1983), DL (E Sussex 1983); s of Walter Thomas Lovill, and Elsie, *née* Page; *b* 26 Sept 1929; *Educ* Brighton Hove and Sussex GS; *m* 1958, Jacqueline, *née* Parker; 2 s, 1 da; *Career* SG Warburg 1951–55, dep gen mangr Securicor 1955–60; chm: Sloane Square Investments 1960–, Municipal Mutual Insurance 1993– (dir 1984–), Prime Health Ltd 1993–94; memb E Sussex CC 1967–89 (leader 1973–77); Assoc of Co Cncls: memb 1973–89, leader 1981–83, chm 1983–86; pres Sussex Assoc of Local Cncls 1987–; vice pres: Lewes Cons Assoc 1986–94, Nat Assoc of Local Cncls 1991–94; chm: Brighton Pavilion Cons Assoc 1958–60, Sussex Police Authy 1976–79 (memb 1973–81), Local Authys Conditions of Serv Advsy Bd 1978–83, Nationwide Small Business Property Tst 1989–95; *Recreations* opera, politics, marine paintings; *Style—* Sir John Lovill, CBE, DL; ✉ Narroway, Beddingham, nr Lewes, E Sussex

LOW, *see:* Morrison-Low

LOW, Alistair James; s of James Grey Low (d 1973), and Elsie Georgina, *née* Holden (d 1990); *b* 2 Aug 1942; *Educ* Dundee HS, Univ of St Andrews (BSc); *m* 30 Aug 1966, Shona Petricia, da of John Galloway Wallace, OBE, of Edinburgh; 2 s (John b 1970, Hamish b 1972), 1 da (Katharina b 1977); *Career* ptnr Duncan C Fraser and Co 1968–86, dir William M Mercer Ltd 1986–; chm General Ctee Royal & Ancient Golf 1991; FFA 1967; *Recreations* golf, skiing; *Clubs* Royal & Ancient Golf, Hon Co of Edinburgh Golfers, Gullane Golf, New (Edinburgh); *Style—* Alistair Low, Esq; ✉ Thornfield, Erskine Loan, Gullane, East Lothian; William M Mercer Ltd, Hobart House, 80 Hanover Street, Edinburgh (☎ 0131 226 4884)

LOW, Prof (Donald) Anthony; s of late Canon Donald Low, and Winifred, *née* Edmunds; *b* 22 June 1927; *Educ* Haileybury ISC, Univ of Oxford (MA, DPhil); *m* 1952, Isobel Smails; 1 s, 2 da; *Career* lectr then sr lectr Makerere Coll Univ Coll of E Africa 1951–58, fell then sr fell in history Res Sch of Social Sciences ANU 1959–64, founding dean of Sch of African & Asian Studies and prof of history Univ of Sussex 1964–72, dir Res Sch of Pacific Studies ANU 1973–75, vice chllr ANU 1975–82; Univ of Cambridge: former Smuts prof of the history of the Br Cwlth, pres Clare Hall 1987–94; PhD Cantab 1983; FAHA, FASSA; *Books* incl: Buganda in Modern History (1971), Lion Rampant (1973), Congress and the Raj 1917–47 (1977), Eclipse of Empire (1991); *Style—* Prof Anthony Low

LOW, Hon Charles Harold Stuart; s and h of 1 Baron Aldington, KCMG, CBE, DSO, TD, PC, DL, *qv*; bro of Hon (Priscilla) Jane Stephanie, see Hon Mrs Roberts, LVO; *b* 22 June 1948; *Educ* Winchester, New Coll Oxford, INSEAD; *m* 16 Sept 1989, Regine, da of late Erwin von Csongrady-Schopf; 1 s (Philip Toby Augustus b 1 Sept 1990), 2 da (Louisa Charlotte Patience and Marie-Therese Sophie Araminta (twins) b 8 July 1992); *Career* formerly with Citibank and Grindlays Bank; md Deutsche Bank AG London 1988–; chm: Euro Vocational Coll 1993–96, Centec 1995–; tstee Whitechapel Art Gallery Fndn 1992–96; Liveryman Worshipful Co of Grocers; *Clubs* Brooks's; *Style—* The Hon Charles Low; ✉ 59 Warwick Square, London SW1V 2AL; Deutsche Bank AG London, 6 Bishopsgate, London EC2P 2AT (☎ 0171 545 7509, fax 0171 545 7844)

LOW, Prof Donald Alexander; s of John Robertson Low, OBE, JP (d 1971), and Margaret Low (d 1987); *Educ* Univ of St Andrews (MA, BPhil), Pembroke Coll Cambridge (PhD); *m* 31 July 1965, Sheona Grant, da of Rev Malcolm A MacCorquodale; 1 s (Christopher Grant b 23 Jan 1969), 1 da (Kirsty Mary Lalage b 7 Oct 1971); *Career* lectr in English Univ of St Andrews 1965–72; Univ of Stirling: lectr in English 1972–82, reader 1982–90, prof 1990–; hon pres Int Burns Fedn 1989; FSA, FRSE 1985; *Books* Robert Burns: The Critical Heritage (ed, 1974), Thieves' Kitchen: The Regency Underworld (1982), The Songs of Robert Burns (ed, 1993), Robert Burns: Poems in Scots and English (1993); *Recreations* music, painting, travel; *Style—* Prof Donald Low, FRSE; ✉ Centre for Scottish Literature and Culture, University of Stirling, Stirling FK9 4LA (☎ 01786 73171)

LOW, Eur Ing Ernest; s of Rev Eli Ernest Low (d 1978), of Melbourne, Australia, and Rose Anna, *née* Kwan (d 1983); *b* 19 Jan 1927; *Educ* St James's Sch Calcutta, Univ of Hong Kong (BSc), City and Guilds Coll, Imperial Coll London (DIC); *m* 5 Sept 1959 (m dis 1984), Elizabeth, da of Dr Christopher William Lumley Dodd (d 1972), of Haywards Heath, Sussex; 1 s (Christopher b 31 Jan 1961, d 7 Dec 1971), 1 da (Alison b 1 Oct 1962); *Career* sr engr: Wimpey Central Laboratory 1954–57, Binnie & Ptnrs 1957–59; mangr of Site Investigation Div Marples Ridgway Ltd 1959–70; ptnr Low and Parsons Brown 1969–77, Low and Ptnrs Hong Kong (conslt engrs) 1976–88, conslt 1986–; dep chm Civil Div Hong Kong Instn of Engrs 1978–80, chm Hong Kong Branch CIArb 1980–82; memb: Ctee on Arbitration of the Hong Kong Law Reform Cmmn 1980–82, Cncl CIArb 1988–92; arbitrator on lists of: CIArb, pres Instn of Civil Engrs, pres Inst of Br Architects, Hong Kong Int Arbitration Centre, FIDIC, Euro Int Contractors, and others; chm Queenhithe Ward Club 1993–95; Liveryman of the Worshipful Co of Painter-Stainers 1973, Liveryman of the Worshipful Co of Arbitrators 1981; FICE 1968, FASCE 1969, FCIArb 1971, MConsE 1975; *Recreations* golf, oratorios, opera, reading; *Clubs* Carlton, City Livery, Hong Kong; *Style—* Eur Ing Ernest Low; ✉ 1302 Wing On Life Building, 22 Des Voeux Road Central, Hong Kong (☎ 00 852 2525 8367, fax 00 852 2810 6059); 60 Carlton Mansions, Randolph Ave, London W9 1NR (☎ 0171 328 2304, fax 0171 625 6628)

LOW, Dr Francis McPherson; s of Sir Francis Low (d 1972), of Camberley, Surrey, and Margaret Helen, *née* Adams (d 1991); *b* 6 May 1928; *Educ* Aitcheson Coll Lahore, Gordonstoun, Univ of Cambridge (MA, MB BChir), Univ of London (DMRD); *m* 7 Sept 1957, Juliet Frances Clarice, da of Dr Kenneth James Langlands Scott (d 1970); 3 s (Jonathan b 1961, Andrew b 1965, Alasdair b 1967), 1 da (Juliette b 1960); *Career* short service cmmn RAF Med Branch 1956–58; Flying Offr 1956, Flt Lt 1957, Sqdn Ldr 1958; med trg Cambridge and Bart's Hosp 1948–54; specialist trg: Radcliffe Infirmary Oxford 1960–64, King's Coll Hosp Denmark Hill London 1964–66; conslt radiologist W Middx Univ Hosp 1966–91, teacher Faculty of Med Univ of London 1980; Freeman City of London 1976, Liveryman Worshipful Soc of Apothecaries 1979; BMA 1955, FRCR 1975, FFR 1965; *Recreations* gardening, breeding Siamese cats; *Clubs* Hawks' (Cambridge); *Style—* Dr Francis Low; ✉ Langlands, Square Drive, Haslemere, Surrey GU27 3LP (☎ 01428 652961)

LOW, Robert Nicholas; s of Leslie Walter Low (d 1983), of Bath, and Agnes, *née* Walsh; *b* 15 Aug 1948; *Educ* St George's Coll Weybridge, Fitzwilliam Coll Cambridge (BA); *m* 1983, Angela, da of Monte Levin; 1 s (Daniel Reuben b 1 Oct 1984); *Career* journalist; teacher Univ of Chile La Serena 1970–72, journalist Birmingham Post and Mail 1973–77, The Observer 1977–93 (sub-ed, reporter, dep managing ed, sports ed, managing ed news, assoc ed features), freelance journalist and author 1993–94; dep ed Reader's Digest 1996– (sr ed 1994–96); *Books* The Kidnap Business (with Mark Bles, 1987), The Observer Book of Profiles (ed, 1991), La Pasionaria: The Spanish Firebrand (1992); *Recreations* watching cricket, playing tennis; *Clubs* Groucho, Middlesex CCC, Paddington Lawn Tennis, RAC; *Style—* Robert Low, Esq; ✉ 33 Canfield Gardens, London NW6 3JP (☎ 0171 624 9532, fax 0171 372 0182); Reader's Digest, 61 Curzon Street, London W1Y 7PE (☎ 0171 409 5785, fax 0171 408 0748)

LOW, Roger L; s of Dr Niels L Low, of USA, and Mary Margaret Low; *b* 29 Jan 1944; *Educ* Columbia Coll, Columbia Univ (AB), Wharton Graduate Sch of Fin and Commerce, Univ of Pennsylvania (MBA); *m* 1967, Helen Webster, da of Bates W Bryan, of Lookout Mountain, Tennesse, USA; 1 s, 1 da; *Career* 1 Lt US Marine Corps, served Vietnam; Drexel Burnham & Co 1971–75, vice pres Salomon Bros 1975–81, md Dean Witter Reynolds Overseas 1981–84, assoc dir Bear Stearns & Co 1984–; *Recreations* marathon running, skiing; *Clubs* St Anthony Hall (NYC); *Style—* Roger L Low, Esq; ✉ Bear Stearns International Ltd, 1 Canada Square, London E14 5AD (☎ 0171 516 6100)

LOW, William; CBE (1984), JP (1971); s of William Low (d 1957); *b* 12 Sept 1921; *Educ* Merchiston Castle Edinburgh; *m* 1949, Elizabeth Ann Stewart, *née* Sime; 2 s; *Career* Maj IA 1943–45; textile mfr; chm: Dundee Industrial Heritage Ltd 1984, Scottish Enterprise Tayside 1991–94; fell Scottish Cncl for Devpt and Indust 1988; Hon LLD Dundee 1993; CIMgt 1983–96; *Recreations* shooting, fishing, golf; *Clubs* Naval and Military, R & A; *Style—* William Low, Esq, CBE, JP; ✉ Herdhill Court, Kirriemuir, Angus DD8 5LG (☎ 01575 572215)

LOW-BEER, Dr Thomas Stephen; s of Walter Low-Beer (d 1954), and Alice Bettina, *née* Stadler (d 1991); *b* 25 Feb 1932; *Educ* Gordonstoun, Univ of Oxford Med Sch (MA), Middx Hosp Med Sch (BM, BCh); *m* 3 Sept 1965, Ann, da of Alexander Smith (d 1990); 2 s (Daniel Walter b 17 June 1969, Jacob b 11 Dec 1971); *Career* Nat Serv RAMC 1950–52; res fell Duke Univ USA 1967–69, lectr in med Univ of Bristol 1970–75, conslt physician, chm of med div and gastroenterologist Selly Oak Hosp Birmingham and sr clinical lectr Univ of Birmingham 1975–, conslt physician and gastroenterologist Wellington Hosp NZ 1985; contrib to several books; memb: Br Soc of Gastroenterology, American Gastroenterological Assoc, Br Assoc for Study of the Liver; tutor for visiting elective students Univ of Birmingham Med Sch; memb RSM, FRCP 1980; *Style—* Dr Thomas Low-Beer; ✉ University of Birmingham Hospital, NHS Trust Selly Oak, Birmingham B29 6JD (☎ 0121 627 1627)

LOWBRIDGE, Roy Thomas; s of Thomas Eric Lowbridge, of Barnsley, and Anni Sophie, *née* Sievers (d 1990); *b* 17 Oct 1950; *Educ* Kirk Balk Comp Hoyland, Barnsley Coll of Technol; *m* 25 Aug 1984, Caroline, da of John Pinder; 2 s (Thomas James b 7 April 1987, Joshua Alexander b 20 Feb 1989), 1 da (Amy Marie b 15 Feb 1985); *Career* engr; tech apprentice Newton Chambers Engineering Sheffield 1967–71, production and product devpt engr F Parramore Tools Sheffield 1972–77, jig and tool designer Record Tools Sheffield 1977–80, devpt mangr Ernest H Hill Ltd Sheffield until 1991 (design engr 1981–88), design engr Caradon PCL Ltd (formerly Pneumatic Components Ltd) Sheffield 1991–96, trg conslt RTL Consultancy 1996–; winner Br Design award 1990; *Recreations* playing guitar and piano; *Style—* Roy Lowbridge, Esq; ✉ RTL Consultancy, Tower House, 57 Haslewood Road, Newton Aycliffe, Co Durham DL5 4XF (☎ 01325 311678, fax 01325 320088)

LOWCOCK, Andrew Charles; s of Eric Lowcock, of Quarry Bank House, Styal, Wilmslow, Cheshire, and Elizabeth, *née* Kilner; *b* 22 Nov 1949; *Educ* Malvern, New Coll Oxford (MA); *m* 1, 14 Aug 1976 (m dis 1985), Patricia Anne, da of Emlyn Roberts; m 2, 7 Sept 1985, Sarah Elaine, da of Robert Edwards, of Quinton Lodge, Ditchling, Sussex; 2 s (Robert Charles b 24 Feb 1988, Edward George b 23 Jan 1990); *Career* called to the Bar Middle Temple 1973, in practice Northern circuit, asst recorder 1993–; govr The Ryleys Sch 1996–; *Recreations* music (princ timpanist Stockport Symphony Orchestra), cricket, theatre; *Clubs* Whicker Soc, Stockport Garrick Theatre, Lancashire CCC; *Style—* Andrew Lowcock, Esq; ✉ 28 St John St, Manchester M3 4DJ (☎ 0161 834 8418)

LOWE, Dr Christopher; s of Thomas Lowe (d 1971), of Maidenhead, Berkshire, and Hilda, *née* Moxham; *b* 15 Oct 1945; *Educ* Braywood C of E Sch, Windsor GS for Boys, Univ of Birmingham (BSc, PhD); *m* 14 Dec 1974, Patricia Margaret, da of late Albert Reed; 1 s (Alan Robert b 19 May 1979), 1 da (Andrea Elizabeth b 19 Oct 1981); *Career* postdoctoral res fell: Univ of Liverpool 1970–73, Univ of Lund Sweden 1973–74; sr lectr in biochemistry Univ of Southampton 1983–84 (lectr 1974–82), fndr dir Inst of Biotechnology Univ of Cambridge 1984–; dir: Affinity Chromatography Ltd 1988–, Environmental Sensors Ltd 1992–, Cambridge Sensors Ltd 1992–; 160 res publications, 20 patents, memb 12 editorial bds; Pierce Award (for outstanding contributions to the field of affinity chromatography) 1989; fell: Trinity Coll Cambridge 1984, Int Inst of Biotechnology 1987; *Books* Affinity Chromatography (1974), An Introduction to Affinity Chromatography (1979), Reactive Dyes in Protein and Enzyme Technology (1987),

Biosensors (1987); *Recreations* travel, antiques; *Style*— Dr Christopher Lowe; ✉ The Limes, Hempstead, Saffron Walden, Essex CB10 2PW (☎ 01799 599307); Institute of Biotechnology, University of Cambridge, Tennis Court Road, Cambridge CB2 1QT (☎ 01223 334160, fax 01223 334162)

LOWE, David Alexander; QC (1984); s of David Alexander Lowe (d 1986), and Rea Sadie Aitchison, *née* Bridges; *b* 1 Nov 1942; *Educ* Pocklington Sch York, St John's Coll Cambridge (scholar and exhibitioner, MA); *m* 19 Aug 1972, Vivian Anne, da of Eric John Langley; 3 s (Alexander Vivian b 4 June 1976, Mungo James b 28 Aug 1977, Felix Henry b 3 July 1981), 2 da (Francesca Victoria b 16 April 1979, Octavia Lucia b 21 Nov 1983); *Career* called to the Bar Middle Temple 1965, in practice Chancery Bar 1966–; pt/t supervisor in real property and equity for Cambridge Colls 1964–69; memb Chancery Bar Assoc (former memb Ctee); *Recreations* fine arts and antiques, historic houses, restoration of listed buildings; *Style*— David Lowe, Esq, QC; ✉ Wilberforce Chambers, 8 New Square, Lincoln's Inn, London WC2A 3QP (☎ 0171 306 0102, fax 0171 306 0095)

LOWE, His Hon Judge; David Bruce Douglas Lowe; s of Douglas Gordon Arthur Lowe, QC (Olympic Gold Medallist 800m 1924 and 1928, d 1981), and Karen, *née* Thamsen; *b* 3 April 1935; *Educ* Winchester, Pembroke Coll Cambridge; *m* 1; 1 s, 1 da; m 2, 1978, Dagmar, da of Horst Bosse (d 1972); 1 s, 3 da; *Career* prosecuting counsel to Dept of Trade 1975–83, recorder of the Crown Ct 1980–83, circuit judge (SE Circuit) 1983–; *Recreations* tennis, music; *Clubs* Hawks (Cambridge); *Style*— His Hon Judge Lowe; ✉ The Crown Court at Middlesex Guildhall, Broad Sanctuary, London SW1P 3BB

LOWE, Air Chief Marshal Sir Douglas Charles; GCB (1977, KCB 1974, CB 1971), DFC (1943), AFC (1946); s of John William Lowe (d 1970); *b* 14 March 1922; *Educ* Reading Sch; *m* 1944, Doreen Elizabeth, da of Ralph Henry Nichols (d 1952); 1 s, 1 da (Frances, m 1974, Hon Christopher Russell Bailey, *qv*); *Career* entered RAF 1940, Air Vice-Marshal 1970, Air Marshal 1973, AOC 18 Gp 1973–75, Controller of Aircraft MOD 1975–82, ADC to HM The Queen 1978–83, Chief of Defence Procurement 1982–83; dir: Rolls Royce Ltd 1983–92, Royal Ordnance 1984–87; chm: Mercury Communications Ltd 1984–85, Band Three Holdings Ltd 1986–91; *Style*— Air Chief Marshal Sir Douglas Lowe, GCB, DFC, AFC; ✉ c/o Lloyds Bank, 15 High Rd, Byfleet, Surrey

LOWE, (John) Duncan; CB (1995); s of John Duncan Lowe, of Kilwinning, and Davina, *née* Hunter; *b* 18 May 1948; *Educ* Hamilton Acad, Univ of Glasgow (MA, LLB); *m* 1 July 1971, Jacqueline, da of Stuart McGregor Egan; 2 s (Alastair b 2 March 1976, Donald b 12 Aug 1978); *Career* apprentice Biggart Lumsden & Co Slrs Glasgow 1971–73, Town Clerk's Office Ayr 1973–74; Fiscal Service: depute procurator fiscal Kilmarnock 1974–76, legal asst then sr legal asst Crown Office 1976–78, sr procurator fiscal depute Glasgow 1978–79, asst procurator fiscal Glasgow 1979–83, asst slr Crown Office 1983–84, dep crown agent Crown Office 1984–88, regnl procurator fiscal Lothian and Borders 1988–91, crown agent Scotland 1991–; memb Cncl Law Soc of Scotland 1988–90; *Recreations* golf, fishing; *Style*— Duncan Lowe, Esq, CB; ✉ Crown Office, 25 Chambers St, Edinburgh EH1 1LA (☎ 0131 226 2626, fax 0131 226 6910)

LOWE, Edwin Charles Ernest (Ted); MBE (1996); s of Ernest Lowe (d 1966), of Lambourn, Berks, and Gertrude, *née* Tame (d 1978); *b* 1 Nov 1920; *Educ* Lambourn C of E Sch; *m* 1, 1942 (m dis 1987); 1 da (Margaret Joan b 17 Aug 1945), 1 s (Michael Edwin b 28 Feb 1949); m 2, 1990, Jean Pamela, *née* Rich; *Career* snooker commentator; estimating and ratefixing in engrg 1937–46, gen mangr Leicester Square Hall London 1946–55, salesman to nat sales dir Allied Breweries 1955–80, non-exec dir Queens Moat Houses plc 1980–93; TV snooker commentator 1953–; devised: BBC Pot Black 1969, Pontins Festival of Snooker 1974, Pro/Celebrity Snooker 1975; fndr memb: Pro Snooker Players' Assoc, Billiards and Snooker Referees' Assoc; Grade A snooker referee; *Books* EP Sports - Snooker, Between Frames (autobiography), Snooker Characters; *Recreations* home, gardening, jazz music; *Style*— Ted Lowe, Esq, MBE

LOWE, Frank Budge; s of Stephen Lowe, and Marion Lowe; *b* 23 Aug 1941; *Educ* Westminster; *m*; 1 s (Hamilton Alexander), 1 da (Emma Rose); *Career* fndr, chm and chief exec offr The Lowe Group; dir Interpublic Group NY; *Style*— Frank Lowe, Esq; ✉ The Lowe Group, Bowater House, 68–114 Knightsbridge, London SW1X 7LT (☎ 0171 225 3434, fax 0171 584 0336)

LOWE, Prof Gordon; s of Harry Lowe (d 1968), and Ethel, *née* Ibbetson (d 1989); *b* 31 May 1933; *Educ* RCS Imperial Coll London (BSc, ARCS, Govrs prize and Edmund White prize, PhD, DIC), Univ of Oxford (MA, DSc); *m* 1 Sept 1956, Gwynneth, da of Harold Hunter; 2 s (Antony Stephen Hunter b 1964, Richard Christopher b 1966); *Career* Univ of Oxford: univ demonstrator 1959–65, Weir Jr Res Fell Univ Coll 1959–61, official fell and tutor in organic chemistry Lincoln Coll 1962–, lectr Dyson Perrins Laboratory 1965–88, sub rector Lincoln Coll 1986–89, Aldrichian Praelector in chemistry 1988–89, prof of biological chemistry 1989–; memb: Molecular Enzymology Ctee Biochemical Soc 1978–84, Biochemistry and Biophysics Ctee SERC 1979–82, Advsy Panel Biochemical Jl 1981–, Editorial Bd Bio-organic Chemistry 1983–, Oxford Enzyme Gp 1970–88, Oxford Centre for Molecular Sciences 1988–, Sectional Ctee 3 Royal Soc 1985–87 and 1995–, NY Acad of Sciences 1992–; Royal Soc of Chemistry Award for Stereochemistry 1992; FRSC 1981, FRS 1984, FRSA 1986; chm Medal for Enzyme Chemistry (RSC) 1983; *publications:* author of various reports and articles in learned jls; *Style*— Prof Gordon Lowe, FRS; ✉ 17 Norman Ave, Abingdon, Oxon OX14 2HQ (☎ 01235 523029); Dyson Perrins Laboratory, University of Oxford, South Parks Rd, Oxford OX1 3QY (☎ 01865 275649, fax 01865 275674); Lincoln College, Oxford OX1 3DR (☎ 01865 279782)

LOWE, Ian Charles; *b* 7 July 1953; *Educ* Sidney Sussex Coll Cambridge (MA); *m* 19 April 1980, Elizabeth Anne, *née* Eyre; *Career* admitted slr 1978, ptnr Berwin Leighton 1986– (currently head of Commercial Dept and IT Law Gp); memb City of London Slrs' Co; *Style*— Ian Lowe, Esq; ✉ Berwin Leighton, Adelaide House, London Bridge, London EC4R 9HA (☎ 0171 623 3144, fax 0171 623 4416)

LOWE, Prof James Stephen; s of James Stephen Lowe, of Leeds, and Mary Eileen, *née* Middleton (d 1991); *b* 25 June 1955; *Educ* St Thomas Aquinas GS Leeds, Univ of Nottingham (BMedSci, BM BS, DM, FRCPath); *m* 18 July 1979, Pamela Lynne, da of Robert Urie, of Garston Herts; 2 s (Nicholas b 1985, William b 1987); *Career* prof of neuropathology and hon conslt neuropathology Queen's Medical Centre NHS Tst 1986–; memb Editorial Bd: Neuropathology and Applied Neurobiology 1990–, Jl of Pathology 1990–, Neurodegeneration 1991–, Internet Medicine 1995–; examiner Royal Coll of Pathologists 1993–; memb: Pathological Soc of GB and Ireland, Neuropathological Soc, Int Acad of Pathologists; RCPath 1985; *Books* Histopathology (1985, 3 edn 1996), Pathology (ed, 1987), Clinical Dermatopathology (1990), Histology (1991, 2 edn 1996), Picture Tests in Histology (1992), Pathology (1994), Pathology Clinical Case Studies (1994); *CD-Roms* Pathology (multimedia, 1995), Basic Histopathology (1996); *Recreations* midi music; *Style*— Prof James Lowe; ✉ Department of Pathology, Nottingham University Medical School, Queens Medical Centre, Nottingham NG7 2UH (☎ 0115 970 9269, fax 0115 970 9759, e-mail James.Lowe@nottingham.ac.uk, world wide web http://www.ccc.nottingham.ac.uk/mpzjlowe/PathWWW.html)

LOWE, John; s of Frederick Lowe (d 1987), of New Tupton, Chesterfield, and Phyllis, *née* Turner (d 1988); *b* 21 July 1945; *Educ* Clay Cross Secondary Sch; *m* 30 July 1966, Diana, da of Jack Cuckson (d 1989), 1 s (Adrian b 14 April 1973), 1 da (Karen b 8 Feb 1975); *Career* professional darts player; England Capt; winner: fourteen World Open Championships, Embassy World Championship (incl 1993), World Masters, World Cup singles, News of the World, ten times Br pentathlon; played over one hundred times for England, first player to do a perfect game of 501 on TV 1985; memb Lord's Taverners; *Books* The Lowe Profile, The John Lowe Story, Darts The John Lowe Way; *Recreations* golf, motor sport, gardening, darts; *Clubs* Matlock Golf, London Rugby; *Style*— John Lowe, Esq; ✉ 5 Hayfield Close, Wingerworth, Chesterfield, Derbyshire S42 6QF (☎ 01246 203943, fax 01246 203943)

LOWE, John Christopher (Chris); s of Sir Edgar Lowe, KBE, CB (d 1992), and Mary McIlwraith, *née* Lockhart; *b* 25 Jan 1949; *Educ* Dragon Sch Oxford, Haileybury, Brasenose Coll Oxford (MA, CertEd); *m* 1975 (sep), Judith Anne Fielding; 1 s (Alexander b 3 Oct 1978), 1 da (Rebecca Anne b 11 Nov 1980); *Career* BBC: grad journalist trainee 1972–74, newsroom reporter 1974–76, political corr local radio and regnl TV 1976–81, news reporter network radio 1981–83, presenter Today (Radio 4) 1982–93, news reporter network TV 1983–86, presenter/reporter Newsnight (BBC2) 1986–89, presenter weekend TV news 1989–, presenter PM (Radio 4) 1993–; other programmes presented incl: Talking Politics, Breakfast News, One O'Clock News, Six O'Clock News; vice pres: Br Blind Sports, Middx Trust; *Recreations* sport (especially cricket, football and rugby), my children, a good book; *Clubs* Lord's Taverners, Middlesex CCC; *Style*— Chris Lowe, Esq; ✉ BBC, PM, Broadcasting House, Portland Place, London W1A 1AA (☎ 0171 927 4100)

LOWE, John Evelyn; s of late Arthur Holden Lowe; *b* 23 April 1928; *Educ* Wellington Coll, New Coll Oxford (MA); *m* 1; 2 s (Mark, Dominic), 1 da (Judith); m 2, Yukiko Nomura; 1 da (Miki); *Career* Sgt Instr RAEC 1947–49; Dept of Woodwork V & A Museum 1953–56, dep story ed Pinewood Studies 1956–57, asst to Dir V & A Museum (Dept of Ceramics 1957–61); dir City Museum and Art Gallery Birmingham 1964–69, fndr dir Weald and Downland Open Air Museum 1969–74; fndr princ West Dean Coll 1972–78; visiting prof Br cultural studies Doshisha Univ Japan 1979–81, full time writer 1982–, lit ed Kansai Time Out 1983–88; pres Midlands Museum Fedn 1967–69; memb: Exec Ctee Midlands Arts Centre for Young People 1964–69, Cncl Br Sch Rome 1968–70, Crafts Advsy Ctee 1973–78; Hofer-Hecksher Bibliographical lectr Harvard 1974; tstee: Sanderson Art in Indust Fund 1968–, Edward James Fndn 1972–73, Idlewild Tst 1972–78; asst ed Collins Crime Club 1953–54, fndr ed Faber Furniture Series 1954–56, conslt Seibu Tokyo 1968–78; own collection of Japanese arts and crafts given to Pitt Rivers Museum Univ of Oxford 1996; hon fell RCA 1988, FSA, FRSA; *Publications* Thomas Chippendale (1955), Cream Coloured Earthenware (1958), Japanese Crafts (1983), Into Japan (1985), Into China (1986), Corsica: A Traveller's Guide (1988), A Surrealist Life - Edward James (1991), A Short Guide to the Kyoto Archaeological Museum (1991), Glimpses of a Kyoto Life (1996); author of various articles on applied arts, foreign travel, social history and Japan; *Recreations* Japan, music, travel, book-collecting, reading; *Style*— John Lowe, Esq, FSA; ✉ Paillole Basse, 47360 Prayssas, France (☎ 00 33 53 68 86 45)

LOWE, (David) Mark; s of Capt Francis Armishaw Lowe, CBE, DSC, RN (d 1981), and Jean Christine, *née* Coates; *b* 17 June 1948; *Educ* Monkton Combe Sch, Univ of Kent (BA); *m* 15 Nov 1975, Christine Anne Elizabeth, da of Mostyn Thomas (d 1991); 2 da (Rebecca b 22 Aug 1978, Jessica b 5 Nov 1981); *Career* admitted slr 1974; asst slr Kidd Rapinet Badge 1974–75, ptnr Kingsley Napley 1976–80, ptnr and head of Litigation Dept Field Fisher Waterhouse 1980–; fndr memb Euro Cncl LCIA 1987; memb: Association Internationale des Jeunes Avocats, Soc of Construction Law, Int Cultural Exchange; supporting memb The London Maritime Arbitrators' Assoc; memb: British Polish Legal Assoc, Cwlth Lawyers' Assoc; ACIArb 1988; *Recreations* flying, music, squash, tennis; *Style*— Mark Lowe, Esq; ✉ Field Fisher Waterhouse, 41 Vine Street, London EC3N 2AA (☎ 0171 481 4841, fax 0171 488 0084)

LOWE, (Nicholas) Mark; QC (1996); s of John Lancelot Lowe (d 1970), of Colchester, and Ruthin, and Margaret Janet, *née* Hucklesby; *b* 17 June 1947; *Educ* Colchester Royal Grammar, Univ of Leicester (LLB); *m* 1975, Felicity Anne, da of David Vickery Parry-Williams (d 1950); 1 da (Kate Eleanor Ceridwen b 1978), 2 s (William John Felix b 1982, Samuel David Lancelot b 1983); *Career* called to the Bar Gray's Inn 1972; *Recreations* fishing, gardening, tennis, school sports from the touchline; *Clubs* Lawyers' Fishing; *Style*— Mark Lowe, Esq, QC; ✉ 2–3 Gray's Inn Square, Ground Floor, Gray's Inn, London WC1R 5JH (☎ 0171 242 4986, fax 0171 405 1166)

LOWE, Dr Martin John Brodie; *b* 10 April 1940; *Educ* Dunfermline HS, Univ of St Andrews (BSc, PhD); *m* 3 Dec 1966, Janet, *née* MacNaughtan; 3 s (Andrew David Nicoll b 27 Aug 1970, Robert Thomas MacNaughtan b 12 Nov 1975, Donald Martin Bryer b 10 June 1977), 1 da (Shona McArthur b 6 May 1972); *Career* offr (with serv in Tanzania and S India) British Cncl 1965–69; Univ of Strathclyde: admin asst 1969–71, asst registrar 1971–73, sec to Senate 1973–81; sec and registrar Univ of St Andrews 1981–89, sec to the Univ of Edinburgh 1990–; *Recreations* piping, hill walking, family interests; *Clubs* New (Edinburgh); *Style*— Dr Martin Lowe; ✉ Secretary to the University, University of Edinburgh, Old College, South Bridge, Edinburgh EH8 9YL (☎ 0131 650 2143, fax 0131 650 6532)

LOWE, Neville Henry; s of Henry Lee Lowe (d 1974), and Dorothy, *née* Hesketh (d 1993); *b* 28 Oct 1933; *Educ* Merchant Taylors', Northwood, Law Soc's Sch of Law; *m* 30 March 1959, Ruth Margaret, da of James George Ernest Turner (d 1975); 1 s (Justin Henry b 1966), 1 da (Fiona Ruth b 1962); *Career* slr; ptnr Heckford Norton & Co Slrs (Letchworth, Royston and Stevenage) 1962–66, sr ptnr Mooring Aldridge & Haydon (Bournemouth and Poole), and Aldridge Myers until 1984, dist registrar of High Ct and County Ct Registrar (Bournemouth and Poole) 1984–91, dist judge 1991–, recorder 1993–; former memb Bd Western Orchestral Soc Ltd (Bournemouth Symphony Orchestra); pres Bournemouth & District Law Soc 1977–78; Freeman: Merchant Taylors' Co 1980–, City of London 1980–; *Recreations* fishing, ancestral research, opera; *Style*— Neville H Lowe, Esq

LOWE, Philip Martin; s of late Leonard Ernest Lowe, and Marguerite Helen, *née* Childs; *b* 29 April 1947; *Educ* Reading Sch, St John's Coll Oxford (MA), London Graduate Sch of Business Studies (MSc); *m* 1, 1967 (m dis 1980), Gillian Baynton, *née* Forge; m 2, 1984, Nora Mai, *née* O'Connell; 2 s; *Career* Tube Investments Ltd 1968–73; EC Cmmn: joined 1973, asst to DG XVIII Credit and Investments 1979–82, memb Cabinet of EC Pres Thorn 1982–85, memb Cabinet of Cmmr Alois Pfeiffer 1985–86, asst to DG XXII Co-ordination of Structural Instruments 1986–87, head of unit for structural funds 1987–89, chef de cabinet to Cmmr Bruce Millan 1989–91, dir of rural devpt DG VI Agric 1991–93, dir Merger Task Force DG IV Competition 1993–94, chef de cabinet to Cmmr Neil Kinnock 1995–; *Recreations* music, theatre, running, hill walking; *Style*— Philip Lowe, Esq; ✉ Commission for the European Communities, Rue de la Loi 200, 1049 Brussels, Belgium

LOWE, Robson; s of John Boyd Lowe (d 1950); *b* 7 Jan 1905; *m* 1928, Winifred (d 1972); 2 da; *Career* philatelist (founded business 1920), publisher 1930–, auctioneer 1937– (merged with Christie's International 1980), dir Christie's; ed The Philatelist 1933–91; chm Expert Ctee British Philatelic Assoc 1941–65, philatelic advsr National Postal Museum 1964–; pres: Br Philatelic Fedn 1979–81, Cinderella Stamp Club 1985–, Postal History Soc 1986, Revenue Soc of GB 1990–; exposed: 1937 Coronation forgeries, 1953 Sperati forgeries, 1980 Gee-Ma forgeries; hon fell Royal Philatelic Soc; Order of the Postal Stone South Africa 1991; FRSA; *Books* Encyclopaedia of Empire Postage Stamps, Handstamps of the Empire, The British Postage Stamp, The Codrington Correspondence, The Lazara Correspondence, St Vincent (with J L Messenger), Waterlow

Die Proofs (with Colin Fraser), 16th Century Letters to Gratious Street London, Leeward Islands Stamps and Postal History, World War II US Service Letters; *Recreations* postal history, revenue stamps, writing; *Clubs* East India; *Style—* Robson Lowe, Esq; ✉ c/o East India Club, 16 St James's Square, London SW1 (☎ 0171 930 1000); St Cross, Bodorgan Rd, Bournemouth (☎ 01202 555150); Christie's, 8 King St, St James's, London SW1Y 6QT (☎ 0171 839 9060, fax 0171 839 1611, telex 916429)

LOWE, Ven Stephen Richard; *b* 3 March 1944; *Educ* Reading Sch, Birmingham Poly (BSc Univ of London), Ripon Hall Oxford; *m* Pauline Amy, *née* Richards; 1 s (Michael b 12 April 1969), 1 da (Janet b 7 Dec 1972); *Career* curate St Michael's Anglican Methodist Church Birmingham 1968–72, min in charge Woodgate Valley Conventional dist 1972–75, team rector East Ham 1975–88, hon canon Chelmsford Cathedral 1985–88, urban offr Chelmsford Diocese 1986–88, archdeacon of Sheffield 1988–; travelling fellowship Winston Churchill Meml Trust 1980, Pail Cadbury fell 1996; memb: BBC N Regnl Advsy Cncl 1993–95, Archbishop's Cmmn on the Organisation of the C of E 1994–96, Gen Synod; Bishop's liaison offr with HM Prison Serv Chaplaincy Dept 1993–, chair Sheffield Somalian Refugees Tst 1993–95; responsible for drawing up and implementation of Church Major Incident Plan following Hillsborough disaster; chm Diocesan Social Responsibility and Faith in City Ctees 1988–; memb Duke of Edinburgh's Study Conf 1989, tstee Church Urban Fund 1991– (chm Grants Ctee 1994–), church cmmr 1992– (memb Houses Ctee 1993–95, memb Bd of Govrs 1994–, memb Bishoprics Ctee 1996–); *Books* The Churches' Role in the Care of the Elderly (1969); *Recreations* watching football, travel, theatre, cinema, photography; *Clubs* Commonwealth Soc; *Style—* The Ven the Archdeacon of Sheffield; ✉ 23 Hill Turrets Close, Ecclesall, Sheffield S11 9RE (☎ 0114 235 0191); Diocesan Church House, 95–99 Effingham Street, Rotherham S65 1BL (☎ 01709 837548, fax 01709 837558)

LOWE, Dr Stuart Shepherd; s of Ian William Shepherd Lowe, of Chalfont St Giles, and Margaret Isobella, *née* Reid; *b* 27 April 1954; *Educ* St Nicholas GS Northwood Middx, St Mary's Hosp Med Sch London (MB BS, MRCS, LRCP); *m* 15 May 1976, Heather Donaldson, da of Thomas Oliver Donaldson Craig, of Surbiton, Surrey; 2 s (Matthew Shepherd, Simon Donaldson), 1 da (Emma Louise); *Career* sr house offr in anaesthetics Royal Sussex County Hosp Brighton 1978–79; rotation registrar in anaesthetics 1979–82: Charing Cross Hosp London, Nat Hosp for Nervous Diseases, Brompton Hosp London, Royal Surrey County Hosp Guildford; sr registrar in anaesthesia and intensive care 1982–85: Addenbrooke's Hosp Cambridge, Papworth Hosp, W Suffolk Hosp; conslt in anaesthesia and intensive care W Suffolk Hosp 1985–; vice chm W Suffolk Scanner Appeal, chm Div of Anaesthesia 1992–96; memb: Intensive Care Soc, Assoc of Anaesthetists of GB and I; FRCA 1981; *Recreations* golf; *Style—* Dr Stuart Lowe; ✉ Intensive Care Unit, West Suffolk Hospital, Hardwick Lane, Bury St Edmunds, Suffolk IP33 2QZ (☎ 01284 713000, fax 01284 701993)

LOWE, Sir Thomas William Gordon; 4 Bt (UK 1918), of Edgbaston, City of Birmingham; s of Sir Francis Reginald Gordon Lowe, 3 Bt (d 1986), and Franziska Cornelia Lanier, da of Siegfried Steinkopf, of Berlin; *b* 14 Aug 1963; *Educ* Stowe, LSE (LLB), Jesus Coll Cambridge (LLM); *Heir* bro, Christopher Francis Lowe b 25 Dec 1964; *Career* called to the Bar Inner Temple 1985, in practice at Chambers of Anthony Scrivener, QC; *Style—* Sir Thomas Lowe, Bt; ✉ 2–3 Gray's Inn Square, Ground Floor, Gray's Inn, London WC1R 5JH (☎ 0171 242 4986, fax 0171 405 1166)

LOWE, Veronica Ann; da of late Arthur Ernest Bagley, and Agatha Amy Annie, *née* Blackham (d 1978); *b* 29 June 1951; *Educ* King Edward VI GS for Girls Handsworth Birmingham, St Hugh's Coll Oxford (MA), Oxford Poly (Inst of Linguist exams), City of Birmingham Poly (slrs qualifying exams); *m* 2 Dec 1977, Ian Stanley Lowe, s of late Arnold Lowe; 1 da (Rhiannon Sara Amy b 21 Dec 1983); *Career* articled clerk with Messrs Ryland Martineau & Co (now Martineau Johnson) Birmingham 1976–78, admitted slr 1979, lectr in labour law Univ of Aston 1978–80, slr in private practice 1980–86, asst area dir Legal Aid Area No 8 1986–88, area dir Legal Aid Area No 6 1988–89, gp mangr (Midlands) Legal Aid Bd 1989–90, dir Slrs Complaints Bureau 1990–96, chief exec Valuation Office Agency Inland Revenue 1996–; memb Law Soc 1979; contrib to pubns on law for accountants and businessmen; *Recreations* cooking, eating and drinking, travel, reading, talking, writing unfinished novels, home life; *Style—* Mrs Veronica Lowe; ✉ Phoenix Cottage, 6 Rugby Road, Dunchurch, Warwicks CV22 6PE (☎ 01788 815861); Chief Executive's Office, Valuation Office Agency, New Court, Carey Street, London WC2A 2JE (☎ 0171 324 1155, fax 0171 324 1190)

LOWEN, David Travers; s of Norman Frederick Lowen, of Southgate, London, and Beatrice, *née* Dannell; *b* 20 June 1946; *Educ* Queen Elizabeth's GS Barnet, Emmanuel Coll Cambridge (MA); *m* 23 May 1970, Jennifer, da of Sqdn Ldr Leonard Durston, of Tipton St John, Devon; 1 s (James Cybranet b 1 May 1973), 1 da (Amy Lys b 15 Jan 1976); *Career* prodr and ed; economist NatWest Bank 1967–68, Kent Messenger 1968–71, Southern Television 1971–74, Westward Television 1974–77; Yorkshire Television: head of features 1977–92, dir of network prog devpt 1992–96, bd dir 1996–, dir of corp devpt Yorkshire Tyne Tees Television 1996–; dir: Chameleon Television 1992–, Sheffield Partnerships Ltd 1991–93, Walshys TV Facilities 1994–, Yorkshire Screen Cmmn 1994–; chm Leeds Media Initiative 1995–; vice chm Royal Television Soc 1994–96 (also chm Yorks Ctee), pres CIRCOM European Regional TV Assoc, ITV rep CIRCOM European TV Assoc; memb Ctee Emmanuel Coll Soc; *Books* Stay Alive with Eddie McGee (1979), Fighting Back: A Woman's Guide to Self-Defence (1983); *Recreations* cricket, birdwatching, horse racing; *Clubs* Lord's Taverners, Forty, Otley Cricket; *Style—* David Lowen, Esq; ✉ Yorkshire Television, TV Centre, Leeds LS3 1JS (☎ 0113 243 8283)

LOWENTHAL, Cecily; da of Samuel Stern, and Miriam, *née* Cohen; *Educ* SCEGGS Sydney NSW Aust (Betty Behan Meml Prize), Open Univ (BA); *m* Lawrence Lowenthal; 1 s (Andrew Simon b 15 May 1953), 1 da (Susan Elizabeth b 20 April 1951); *Career* freelance lectr and writer on art, Open Univ tutor 1985–86, guide Tate Gallery 1976–; fndr memb Patrons of New Art Tate Gallery; memb: ICOM 1980–, Contemporary Art Soc 1990– (hon sec); *Recreations* photography; *Style—* Mrs Cecily Lowenthal

LOWNDES, Rosemary Morley; da of Henry Vaughan Lowndes (d 1951), of Oxton, Cheshire, and Patricia, *née* Watts; *b* 20 Sept 1937; *Educ* Moreton Hall Shrops, Liverpool Coll of Art (BA); *m* 23 Oct 1975, Trevor Courtney Jones, s of William Jones (d 1978), of Caversham, Berks; 1 s (Simon Geoffrey b 30 Oct 1977); *Career* graphic designer, writer and illustrator with Claude Kailer; 46 childrens books incl: Make Your Own World of Christmas, Make Your Own History of Costume, Make Your Own World of Theatre, Make Your Own Noah's Ark, Make Your Own Victorian House, The Market, An Edwardian Album; designer for china and stationery; oil-painting exhibitions incl one man shows in: Paris, Deauville, Honfleur, London, Oxford, Chicago; FCSD 1976; *Recreations* opera, ballet; *Style—* Miss Rosemary Lowndes; ✉ 132 Tachbrook St, London SW1V 2ND (☎ 0171 834 5273), L'Observatoire Côte de Grace, Honfleur, Calvados, France

LOWNIE, Andrew James Hamilton; s of His Hon Ralph Hamilton Lownie, and Claudine, *née* Lecrocq; *b* 11 Nov 1961; *Educ* Fettes, Westminster, Magdalene Coll Cambridge (MA), Univ of Edinburgh (MSc), The Coll of Law Guildford; *Career* dir: John Farquharson Ltd literary agents 1986–88, Andrew Lownie literary agency 1988–, Denniston and Lownie Ltd 1991–93, Thistle Publishing; journalist; contrib: Spectator, The Times, Scotland on Sunday; tstee Iain MacLeod Award, former pres Cambridge Union Soc; Parly candidate (C) Monklands West 1992, vice chm Cons Gp for Europe 1992–95; FRSA, FRGS; *Books* The Edinburgh Literary Guide, North American Spies, John Buchan - The Presbyterian Cavalier, John Buchan's Poems (ed), John Buchan's Complete Short Stories (ed), The Scottish Short Stories of John Buchan (ed), Guy Burgess; *Recreations* music, outdoor pursuits; *Style—* Andrew Lownie, Esq; ✉ 122 Bedford Court Mansions, Bedford Square, London WC1B 3AH (☎ 0171 636 4917, fax 0171 436 1898)

LOWNIE, His Hon Judge Ralph Hamilton; s of James Hood Wilson Lownie (d 1961), of Edinburgh, and Jessie, *née* Aitken (d 1952); *b* 27 Sept 1924; *Educ* George Watson's Coll Edinburgh, Univ of Edinburgh (MA, LLB), Univ of Kent (PhD); *m* 12 Nov 1960, Claudine Theresa, da of Pierre Claude Lecrocq (d 1976), of Reims, France; 1 s (Andrew James Hamilton b 1961), 1 da (Solange Helen Hamilton b 1963); *Career* WWII RE 1943–47, served NW Europe; WS 1952, memb Faculty of Advocates 1959, called to the Bar Inner Temple 1962; in practice 1952–54, in Judicial and Legal Depts of Kenya Govt 1954–65, in Judicial Dept Bermuda Govt 1965–72, met stipendiary magistrate 1974–86, circuit judge (SE Circuit) 1986–95; *Style—* His Hon Ralph Lownie, WS

LOWRIE, Anthony Carmel (Tony); s of Vincent Lowrie (d 1988), of Rhodesia and SA (d 1988), and Gwendoline, *née* Stephens; *b* 24 March 1942; *Educ* Llewellyn HS N Rhodesia, RMA Sandhurst; *m* 1 Nov 1969, Liv Torill, da of Torbjon Ronningen; 1 s (Alexander Christian b 27 Jan 1975), 1 da (Louise Therese (twin) b 27 Jan 1975); *Career* Cadet Rhodesian Army 1960–62, 2 Lt Platoon Cdr Middx Regt, Lt Support Platoon Queen's Regt, Capt 10 PMO Gurkha Rifles cmdg support company, Maj 1/2 Gurkha Rifles cmdg C company; bd dir of Hoare Govett stockbrokers 1986–92 (trainee 1973, devpt of Asian Equity Sales, ptnr 1978–92, dir of Hoare Govett Asia, head of SE Asia Devpt Singapore), chm HG Asia Securities Ltd (formerly Hoare Govett International Securities) 1988–; dir: The SESDAQ Fund, The Scottish Asian Fund, The Thai Euro Fund, The Oriental Development Co Ltd, The Vietnam Frontier Fund, Oriental Smaller Companies Investment Trust; non-exec dir J D Wetherspoon; MSI; *Recreations* rugby, golf, tennis, skiing; *Clubs* London Capital, Walton Heath Golf, The Addington, Wisley Golf; *Style—* Tony Lowrie, Esq; ✉ 44 Egerton Crescent, London SW3 2ED (☎ 0171 589 5504); Glassenbury Cottage, Cranbrook, Kent (☎ 01580 713148); HG Asia Securities Ltd, 9th Floor, Moor House, 119 London Wall, London EC2Y 5ET (☎ 0171 814 6068/071 814 6000, fax 0171 256 9961, telex 919247)

LOWRIES, Hugh John; s of Ronald Hugh Lowries (d 1989), of Worthing, and Dorothy Edith, *née* Hansen; *b* 27 March 1947; *Educ* Great Walstead Sch, Steyning GS, Univ of Bristol (BA); *m* 1979, (Bridget) Zilla, da of Dr Herbert Henry Osborn; 3 s (Jeremy Hugh b 19 Feb 1986, Stephen Patrick b 9 June 1987, David William b 8 April 1989); *Career* Great Walstead Sch: asst master 1969, head of English 1970, house master of sr boys 1984, jt sr master 1989, dep head 1990, acting head 1991, headmaster 1992–; memb: Assoc of Christian Teachers 1974–, Inc Assoc of Preparatory Schs 1992–; *Recreations* reading (esp literature, history and theology), natural history, walking, cycling, sketching, church activities; *Style—* Hugh Lowries, Esq; ✉ Great Walstead School, Lindfield, Haywards Heath, West Sussex RH16 2QL (☎ 01444 483528, fax 01444 482122)

LOWRY, Baroness; Barbara Adamson Lowry; *née* Parker; QC (1975); da of Albert Parker, CBE (d 1980), and Lilian Maud, *née* Midgley (d 1972); *b* 30 April 1926; *Educ* St Helen's Northwood, Univ of London (BSc Econ); *m* 1, 1948, John Thornton Calvert, CBE (d 1987), s of Harry Thornton Calvert, MBE (d 1947); 1 s, 1 da; *m* 2, 10 June 1994, Baron Lowry, PC (Life Peer), *qv*; *Career* called to the Bar Middle Temple 1959 (bencher 1982), Bar of NI 1978 (QC 1978, hon bencher 1995); practice at Bar 1962–86; recorder: SE Circuit 1980, W Circuit 1992; memb Matrimonial Causes Rule Ctee 1983–86, full-time chm Industl Tbnl 1986–96 (pt/t chm 1974–86); Freeman City of London 1989; *Recreations* swimming, gardening, poetry; *Clubs* Royal Fowey Yacht, Sloane; *Style—* The Lady Lowry, QC; ✉ 4 Brick Court, Temple, London EC4 (☎ 0171 797 7766); 158 Ashley Gardens, London SW1P 1HW (☎ 0171 828 0530)

LOWRY, Sir John Patrick (Pat); kt (1985), CBE (1978); s of John McArdle Lowry; *b* 31 March 1920; *Educ* Wyggeston GS, LSE (BComm); *m* 1952, Sheilagh Davies; 1 s, 1 da; *Career* served WWII HM Forces, joined Engrg Employers Fedn (dir 1965–70); British Leyland 1970–81; chm ACAS 1981–87, mediator between Govt and unions in NHS dispute 1982; former memb: UK Employers' Delgn to ILO, Ct of Inquiry Grunwick Dispute 1977; pres Inst of Personnel Mgmnt 1987–89; chm: Nat Jt Cncl for Engrg Construction Indust 1987–, Univ Academics Salaries Ctee 1987–; CPIM, CIMgt; *Style—* Sir Pat Lowry, CBE; ✉ 31 Seaton Close, Lynden Gate, London SW15 3TJ (☎ 0181 785 6199)

LOWRY, Her Hon Judge Noreen Margaret (Nina); *née* Collins; da of John Edmund Collins, MC (d 1971), of Sway, Hants, and Hilda Grace, *née* Gregory (d 1985); *b* 6 Sept 1925; *Educ* Bedford HS, Univ of Birmingham (LLB); *m* 1, 25 March 1950 (m dis 1962), Edward Lucas, s of late Edward Walker Gardner, of Preston, Lancs; 1 s (Stephen b 15 May 1956), 1 da (Sally b 2 Oct 1953); m 2, 24 April 1963, His Hon Judge Richard John Lowry, *qv*; 1 da (Emma b 25 Nov 1964); *Career* called to the Bar Gray's Inn 1948, bencher 1995, practised as Miss Nina Collins, appointed metropolitan stipendiary magistrate 1967, memb Criminal Law Revision Ctee 1975, appointed circuit judge (SE Circuit) 1976; Hon LLD Univ of Birmingham 1992; *Recreations* theatre, travel; *Style—* Her Hon Judge Nina Lowry; ✉ Central Criminal Court, Old Bailey, London EC4M 7EH (☎ 0171 248 3277)

LOWRY, His Hon Judge Richard John; QC (1968); s of Geoffrey Charles Lowry, OBE, TD (d 1974), of Ham, Surrey, and Margaret Spencer, *née* Fletcher-Watson (d 1976); *b* 23 June 1924; *Educ* St Edward's Sch Oxford, Univ Coll Oxford (BA, MA); *m* 24 April 1963, Her Hon Judge Nina Lowry, *qv*, da of John Edmund Collins, MC (d 1971), of Sway, Hants; 1 da (Emma b 25 Nov 1964); *Career* enlisted RAF 1943, cmmnd and qualified as Pilot 1944, Gp Staff Offr 228 Gp India 1945, Flt Lt 1946; called to the Bar Inner Temple 1949, bencher 1977; memb Bar Cncl 1965–69, dep chm Herts QS 1968, recorder Crown Ct 1972–77, circuit judge (SE Circuit) 1977–, memb Home Office Advsy Ctee on Penal System 1972–77; *Recreations* theatre, swimming; *Clubs* Garrick, RAC, Vincent's (Oxford), Leander; *Style—* His Hon Judge Richard Lowry, QC; ✉ Central Criminal Court, Old Bailey, London EC4M 7EH (☎ 0171 248 3277)

LOWRY, Baron (Life Peer UK 1979), of Crossgar, Co Down; Robert Lynd Erskine Lowry; kt (1971), PC (1974), PC (NI 1971); s of William Lowry (Rt Hon Mr Justice Lowry, d 1949), and Catherine Hughes (d 1947), da of Rev R J Lynd, DD; *b* 30 Jan 1919; *Educ* Royal Belfast Academical Institution, Jesus Coll Cambridge (MA); *m* 1, 1945, Mary Audrey (d 1987), da of John Martin (d 1979), of Belfast; 3 da (Hon Sheila Mary (Hon Mrs Corrall) b 1950, Hon Anne Lynd (Hon Mrs McCoubrey) b 1952, Hon Margaret Ina b 1956); m 2, 10 June 1994, Barbara Adamson Calvert, QC, da of Dr Albert Parker, CBE (d 1980), of Northwood, Middx, and widow of John Thornton Calvert, CBE (d 1987); *Career* served WWII N Africa Royal Irish Fusiliers 1940–46, Maj, Hon Col TA Bn; called to the Bar NI 1947, QC (NI) 1956, High Court judge 1964; chm NI Constitutional Convention 1975; Lord Chief Justice of N Ireland 1971–88, Lord of Appeal in Ordinary 1988–94; hon bencher: Middle Temple 1973, King's Inns Dublin 1973; hon fell Jesus Coll Cambridge; *Recreations* golf, showjumping; *Clubs* Royal and Ancient (St Andrews), MCC, Army and Navy; *Style—* The Rt Hon the Lord Lowry, PC; ✉ White Hill, Crossgar, Co Down, NI (☎ 01396 830397)

LOWRY, Roger Clark; s of Henry Lowry (d 1972), and Evelyn Wilson Blair (d 1970); *b* 20 Sept 1933; *Educ* Campbell Coll Belfast, Queen's Univ Belfast (BSc, MB BCh); *m* 3 April 1964, (Dorothy) Joan, da of David Smith (d 1976); 4 s (Kevin, Michael, Peter, Alan), 1 da (Julie); *Career* assoc prof of med Univ of Tennessee 1976–77, conslt physician

Belfast City Hosp 1977–; chm NI Chest Heart and Stroke Assoc 1980–; involvement in interprovincial squash; memb: Br Thoracic Soc, BMA; FRCP, FRCPI; *Recreations* golf, squash, tennis; *Clubs* Royal Co Down Golf, Royal Belfast Golf; *Style*— Roger Lowry, Esq; ✉ Milecross House, 49 Belfast Rd, Newtownards, Co Down BT23 4TR (☎ 01247 813284); Belfast City Hospital, Lisburn Rd, Belfast BT9 7AB (☎ 01232 329241 ext 2812)

LOWRY, Suzanne; da of late C M Lowry, of Holywood, Co Down, NI, and Stella, *née* Davis; *Educ* Princess Gardens Sch Belfast, Trinity Coll Dublin (BA); *children* 1 s (Max Patrick b 1976); *Career* journalist; reporter Belfast Telegraph 1969, diary reporter Daily Mail 1970–71, woman's ed and feature writer The Guardian 1971–77; ed: Living Pages The Observer 1977–80, Look Pages Sunday Times 1981–83; cultural features ed International Herald Tribune 1986–88, chief Paris corr Daily and Sunday Telegraph 1988–; *Books* The Guilt Cage (1980), The Young Fogey Handbook (1984), The Princess in the Mirror (1984); *Recreations* reading, gardening, and moving house; *Clubs* Groucho; *Style*— Miss Suzanne Lowry; ✉ 242 rue de Rivoli, 75001 Paris, France (☎ 00 33 1 4260 3885, fax 00 33 1 4261 5291)

LOWSON, Sir Ian Patrick; 2 Bt (UK 1951), of Westlaws, Co Perth; s of Sir Denys Colquhoun Flowerdew Lowson, 1 Bt (d 1975), and Hon Lady Lowson; *b* 4 Sept 1944; *Educ* Eton, Duke Univ USA; *m* 1979, Mrs Tanya Theresa H du Boulay, da of Raymond F A Judge; 1 s, 1 da (Katherine Louisa Patricia b 1983); *Heir* s, Henry William Lowson b 10 Nov 1980; *Clubs* Boodle's, Pilgrims, Brook (New York); *Style*— Sir Ian Lowson, Bt; ✉ 23 Flood St, London SW3

LOWSON, Prof Martin Vincent; s of Alfred Vincent Lowson (d 1961), of Wraysbury, Bucks, and Irene Gertrude, *née* Thorp (d 1982); *b* 5 Jan 1938; *Educ* King's Sch Worcester, Univ of Southampton (BSc, PhD); *m* 4 Nov 1961, (Roberta) Ann, da of Max Pennicutt, of Emsworth, Hants; 1 s (Joff b 1965), 1 da (Sarah b 1967); *Career* apprentice Vickers Armstrong 1955–60, res student and asst Univ of Southampton 1960–64, head of applied physics Wyle Laboratories Huntsville USA 1964–69, Rolls Royce reader Loughborough Univ 1969–73, dir corp devpt Westland plc (formerly Westland Helicopters Ltd) 1979–86 (chief scientist 1973–79), prof of aerospace engrg Univ of Bristol 1986–; researcher and patentee in aerodynamics, acoustics, structures, and transport; FEng 1991, FRAeSoc, FASA, FAIAA; *Recreations* research, squash, music; *Style*— Prof Martin Lowson, FEng; ✉ Department of Aerospace Engineering, University of Bristol, Bristol BS8 1TR (☎ 0117 928 7694, fax 0117 925 1154)

LOWSON, Robert Campbell; s of George Campbell Lowson (d 1989), and Betty, *née* Parry; *b* 7 March 1949; *Educ* Gravesend GS, Brasenose Coll Oxford (BA); *m* 1973, Hilary May, da of Hubert Balsdon; 1 s (Andrew b 15 Nov 1980), 1 da (Judith b 18 Nov 1983); *Career* MAFF: joined 1970, under sec Agricultural Inputs, Plant Protection and Emergencies Gp 1994–95, min (agric) UK Perm Representation to the EU 1995–; *Style*— Robert Lowson, Esq; ✉ UK Representation, 6 Rond-Point Schuman, 1040 Brussels, Belgium (☎ 00 32 2 287 8254, fax 00 32 2 287 8228)

LOWTHER, Col Sir Charles Douglas; 6 Bt (UK 1824), of Swillington, Yorks; s of Lt-Col Sir William Guy Lowther, 5 Bt, OBE, DL (d 1982), and Grania Suzanne, *née* Douglas-Campbell; *b* 22 Jan 1946; *Educ* Winchester; *m* 1, 1969 (m dis 1975), Melanie Pensée FitzHerbert, da of late Roderick Christopher Musgrave; *m* 2, 1975, Florence Rose, da of late Col Alexander James Henry Cramsie, OBE, of O'Harabrook, Ballymoney, Co Antrim; 1 s (Patrick William b 1977), 1 da (Alice Rose b 1979); *Heir* s, Patrick William Lowther b 15 July 1977; *Career* served HM Forces 1965–93, Col; businessman and farmer; *Recreations* field sports, racing, travel; *Clubs* Cavalry and Guards'; *Style*— Col Sir Charles Douglas Lowther, Bt; ✉ c/o National Westminster Bank plc, 33 Lord Street, Wrexham, Clwyd LL11 1LP

LOWTHER, Viscount; Hugh Clayton Lowther; s and h of 7 Earl of Lonsdale, *qv*; *b* 27 May 1949; *m* 1, 1971, Pamela Colleen Middleton; m 2, 1986, Angela Mary, da of Capt Peter Wyatt, of Dartmouth, Devon; *Style*— Viscount Lowther; ✉ Lowther Estate Office, Lowther, Penrith, Cumbria CA10 2HH

LOWTHER, James; s of George Hugh Lowther, of Holdenby House, Northampton, and Sheila Rachel Isabelle, *née* Foster; *b* 27 Jan 1947; *Educ* Eton, Keble Coll Oxford (MA History); *m* Karen Healey, da of James Wallace; 2 da (Natasha Jane b 26 Nov 1988, Mamie Grace b 6 Aug 1994), 1 s (James William Dolfin b 29 Dec 1991); *Career* copywriter Hobson Bates & Partners 1968–71, creative gp head Wasey Campbell Ewald 1972–76, Saatchi & Saatchi 1977–95 (creative dir and dep chm 1991–95), fndr creative dir M&C Saatchi 1995–; dir BTA 1992–; memb Mktg Advsy Ctee Children in Crisis; memb: Historic Houses Assoc, Cncl for the Preservation of Rural England, Nat Tst, D&AD; *Awards* ITV Award for Best Cinema Commercial 1979 and for Best Commercial of the Yr 1992, 3 times Best Black & White Press Advertisement Campaign Press Awards, 2 times Best Poster of the Yr Campaign Poster Awards, 3 D&AD Silver Awards, 2 Silver and a Gold Cannes Int Advtg Festival, Ivor Novello Award (for composing advtg music for Schweppes), work incl in 100 Best Advertisements; *Books* The Copy Book (D&AD, contrib); *Recreations* listening to, playing and composing music; *Style*— James Lowther, Esq; ✉ M&C Saatchi Ltd, 34–36 Golden Square, London W1R 4EE (☎ 0171 543 4500, fax 0171 543 4535, mobile 0468 385100)

LOWTHER, Col Sir John Luke; KCVO (1997), CBE (1983), JP (1984); s of Col John George Lowther, CBE, DSO, MC, TD (d 1977), of Nortoft Grange, Northampton, and Lilah Challotte Sarah, *née* White (d 1976); 1st recorded Lowther Knight Sir Hugh Lowther 1250–1317; *b* 17 Nov 1923; *Educ* Eton, Trinity Coll Oxford (MA); *m* 21 Feb 1952, Jennifer Jane, da of Col J H Bevan, CB (d 1978); 1 s (Hugh b 1956), 2 da (Sarah b 1954, Lavinia b 1958); *Career* served King's Royal Rifle Corps 1942–47, NW Europe Capt; worked for Singer Machine Co USA 1949–51, md own manufacturing co 1951–60; dir Equitable Life Assurance Soc 1960–76; farmer 1960; memb Northamptonshire County Cncl 1970–84 (ldr of the Cncl 1977–81); High Sheriff 1971, DL 1977, Lord Lt and Custos Rotulorum of Northamptonsire 1984–; Hon Colonel: The Royal Anglian Regt (Northamptonshire) 1986–89, The Northamptonshire Army Cadet Force 1991–96; KStJ; *Recreations* shooting, countryman; *Clubs* Boodle's; *Style*— Col Sir John Lowther, KCVO, CBE, JP; ✉ Nortoft Grange, Guilsborough, Northampton NN6 8QB (☎ 01604 740289)

LOWTHER, Maurice James; s of James Lowther (d 1983), of Carnforth, Lancs, and Margaret Agnes Hind (d 1986); *b* 14 Sept 1926; *Educ* Lancaster Royal GS, Queen's Univ Belfast (BSc); *m* 1, 1 Nov 1947 (m dis 1976), Audrey Margaret, da of George Holmes (d 1979), of Belfast; 3 da (Anne, Valerie, Pamela); m 2, 1977, Dr Rachel Shirley Lloyd, da of Lt Cdr William F Hood (d 1980), of Handcross, Sussex; *Career* Capt RE 1944–48; md Newcastle and Gateshead Water Co 1971–86 non-exec dir 1986–90), non-exec dir Stanley Miller plc 1983–90; nat pres Inst of Water Engrs and Scientists 1980–81, nat chm Water Cos Assoc 1984–87 (vice pres 1987–), vice pres Water Aid (third world charity) 1991– (fndr dir 1981–91), chm Br Inst of Mgmnt Tyne and Wear 1973–75, govr Lancaster Royal GS 1982–; Freeman City of London, Liveryman Worshipful Co of Plumbers; Int Medal American Waterworks Assoc; FICE 1962, FIWES 1967, CIMgt 1986; *Recreations* fell walking, angling, beekeeping; *Clubs* National, Northern Counties (Newcastle-upon-Tyne); *Style*— Maurice Lowther, Esq; ✉ The Old Schoolhouse, Wall Village, Hexham, Northumberland (☎ 01434 681 660)

LOWY, Kurt; s of Bedrich Lowy (d 1959), of London, and Marie, *née* Gutmann; *b* 28 Dec 1919, (North Czechoslovakia); *Educ* GS, Prague Univ Metallurgical Chemistry; *m* 4 Nov 1945, Blanche Ellaine, da of Isaac Pack (ka 1941); 3 da (Michele b 1948, Arlene b 1951, Stephanie b 1958); *Career* Sgt Home Guard and Anti-Aircraft Battery 1940–44; md Denham & Morely Overseas 1968–73; JVC (UK) Ltd: md 1973–80, chm 1973–90, pres 1990–; life pres Vision Charity 1993–; *Clubs* IOD; *Style*— Kurt Lowy, Esq; ✉ 7 Fairgreen, Cockfosters, Hadley Woods, Herts EN4 0QS; Vision Charity, PO Box 30, East Horsley, Surrey KT24 6VX (☎ 0181 440 7212)

LOXDALE, Peter Alasdair; JP (N Cardiganshire 1992); s of Hector Alasdair Robert Loxdale, and Hilary Kathleen Ross, *née* Steen; *b* 21 Nov 1959; *Educ* Radley, Welsh Agric Coll Aberystwyth; *Career* farmer and land proprietor 1981–; pres Llanilar and N Cardiganshire Agric Soc 1987–, pres Llanilar FC 1990–; Country Landowners' Assoc: memb Welsh Ctee, memb Taxation Sub Ctee 1990–94, chm Dyfed Exec Ctee 1992– (vice chm 1990–92), memb Environment and Water Ctee 1995–, chm Farm Buildings Award Scheme Western Region 1995 and 1997; *Recreations* shooting; *Clubs* Farmers', Royal Over-Seas League; *Style*— Peter Loxdale, Esq, JP; ✉ Castle Hill, Llanilar, Aberystwyth, Cardiganshire (☎ 01974 241202, mobile 0836 657439)

LOY, (Francis) David Lindley; CBE (1997); s of Archibald Loy (d 1968), of Sheringham, Norfolk, and Sarah Eleanor, *née* Lindley (d 1967); *b* 7 Oct 1927; *Educ* Repton, CCC Cambridge (BA); *m* 28 Aug 1954, Brenda Elizabeth, da of William Henry Walker, of Strensall, York; 3 da (Sarah b 1958, Alexandra b 1960, Phillida b 1967); *Career* RN 1946–48; called to the Bar Middle Temple 1952, in practice North Eastern Circuit 1952–72, recorder Northern Circuit 1972; stipendiary magistrate: City of Leeds 1972–74, Leeds 1974–; recorder of the Crown Ct N Eastern Circuit 1983–; chm Soc of Provincial Stipendiary Magistrates 1990–96 (hon sec 1974–89); *Recreations* walking, reading, English history, travel; *Clubs* Leeds; *Style*— David Loy, Esq, CBE; ✉ 4 Wedgewood Drive, Roundhay, Leeds LS8 1EF; 14 The Avenue, Sheringham, Norfolk; Magistrates Room, Leeds District Magistrates Court, PO Box 97, Westgate, Leeds LS1 3JP (☎ 0113 245 9653)

LOYD, Sir Francis Alfred; KCMG (1965, CMG 1961), OBE (1954, MBE 1951); s of Maj A W K Loyd, Royal Sussex Regt; *b* 5 Sept 1916; *Educ* Eton, Trinity Coll Oxford (MA); *m* 1, 1946, Katharine (d 1981), da of Lt-Col S C Layzell, MC, of Kenya; 2 da; m 2, 1984, Monica, widow of Lt-Col C R Murray Brown, DSO, Royal Norfolk Regt; *Career* served WWII E Africa; dist offr Kenya 1939, private sec to Govr Kenya 1942–45, consul Mega Ethiopia 1945, dist cmmr 1947–55, provincial cmmr 1956, permanent sec govr's office 1962–63, HM Cmmr Swaziland 1964–68; dir London House for Overseas Graduates 1969–79; chm Oxfam Africa Ctee 1979–85; *Style*— Sir Francis Loyd, KCMG, OBE; ✉ 53 Park Road, Aldeburgh, Suffolk (☎ 01728 452478)

LOYD, Jeremy Charles Haig; s of Geoffry Haig Loyd, of Herefordshire, and Patricia, *née* Maclean; *b* 4 July 1954; *Educ* Pangbourne Coll; *m* 6 Oct 1983, Sally, da of Duncan Robertson, TD, JP (d 1988), of Beadlam, Yorkshire; *Career* Account exec Michael Rice and Co Ltd 1974–79; dir: RTI Productions Ltd 1976–80, Project Art Ltd 1978–, Carlton Television 1991–95, Carlton Music 1993–, chief exec offr Pickwick Group 1993–95, formerly md Capital Radio; dir: First Oxfordshire Radio Co 1988–, Channel KTV 1995–, Enterprise Radio Holdings 1995–96, ITFC Ltd 1995–, Capital Radio Investments Ltd and Capital Enterprises Ltd 1989–91, Wren Orchestra of London Ltd 1989–91, Devonair Ltd 1989–91; chm Direct Home Entertainment Ltd 1993–95; dep chm Blackwell Ltd 1996–; tstee Help A London Child 1987–91; *Recreations* fishing, sailing; *Clubs* Flyfishers'; *Style*— Jeremy Loyd, Esq; ✉ Blackwell Limited, Hythe Bridge Street, Oxford OX1 2ET (☎ 01865 792792)

LOYD, His Hon Judge; John Anthony Thomas; QC (1981); s of Leslie William Loyd (d 1981), of Colchester, and Joan Louisa, *née* Webb; *b* 18 July 1933; *Educ* Wycliffe Coll, Gonville and Caius Coll Cambridge (MA); *m* 23 May 1963, Rosaleen Iona, da of John Soloman (d 1959), of Little Baddow, Essex; 2 da (Antonia b 1964, Jocelyn b 1966 d 1986); *Career* called to the Bar Gray's Inn 1958, bencher 1994; circuit judge (official referee) 1990–; *Recreations* viticulture; *Style*— His Hon Judge Loyd, QC; ✉ Official Referees' Courts, St Dunstan's House, Fetter Lane, London EC4A 1HD (☎ 071 936 6408)

LOYD, Sir Julian St John; KCVO (1991, CVO 1979), DL (1983); s of Gen Sir Charles Loyd (d 1973), and Lady Moyra, *née* Brodrick (d 1982), da of 1 Earl of Midleton; *b* 25 May 1926; *Educ* Eton, Magdalene Coll Cambridge (MA); *m* 20 October 1960, Mary Emma, da of Sir Christopher Steel (d 1973); 1 s (Charles b 1963), 2 da (Alexandra Mary (Mrs Duncan Byatt) b 1961, Mary Rose (Mrs Ellis Whitcomb) b 1967); *Career* Coldstream Gds 1944–45; ptnr Savills 1955–64; Agent to HM The Queen at Sandringham 1964–91; chm King's Lynn and Wisbech NHS Trust 1992–94; FRICS 1958; *Recreations* fishing; *Clubs* Army and Navy; *Style*— Sir Julian Loyd, KCVO, DL; ✉ Perrystone Cottage, Burnham Market, King's Lynn, Norfolk (☎ 01328 730168)

LOYDEN, Edward; MP (Lab) Liverpool Garston (majority 12,279); s of Patrick Loyden, of Liverpool; *b* 3 May 1923; *Educ* Friary Elementary Sch, TUC educn courses, Nat Cncl of Lab Colls; *m* 1924, Rose Ann; 1 s, 2 da (1 da decd); *Career* merchant seaman 1938–46, port worker with Mersey Docks and Harbour Bd (Marine) 1946–74, dist and nat delegate to Docks and Waterways Trade Gp TGWU 1968–74; MP (Lab) Liverpool Garston 1974–79 and 1983– (TGWU sponsored); memb Lab Parly Ctees on: Foreign Affrs, Health, Transport; chair TGWU Sponsored MPs Parly Ctee 1991–; cncllr: Liverpool City Cncl 1960–74 and 1980–84 (elected 1959, dep ldr 1980), Liverpool Met Authy 1973–; pres Liverpool Trades Cncl and Lab Pty 1967–, chair Liverpool District Lab Pty 1986; *Style*— Edward Loyden, Esq, MP; ✉ 456 Queens Drive, Liverpool L4 8UA; House of Commons, London SW1A 0AA (☎ 0171 219 3000)

LOYN, David George; s of William George Grenville Loyn, and Elizabeth Margery, *née* Gent; *b* 1 March 1954; *Educ* Oundle, Worcester Coll Oxford (BA), Coll of Law London; *m* 1981, Estelle, da of Philip Daniel; 3 s (Thomas Jack b 18 Sept 1988, Christopher Mark b 19 Dec 1992, James Philip b 30 May 1995); *Career* reporter IRN/LBC 1979–87, currently S Asia corr BBC (joined 1987); Sony Award for Radio Reporter of the Year 1985; *Style*— David Loyn, Esq; ✉ 20 Malcha Marg, New Delhi 110001, India; BBC, Aifacs Building, 1 Rafi Marg, New Delhi 110001, India (☎ 00 91 11 335 5751); BBC News and Current Affairs, Television Centre, London W12 7RJ (☎ 0181 576 7690)

LOYN, Prof Henry Royston; s of Henry George Loyn (d 1939), of Cardiff, and Violet Monica, *née* Thomas (d 1987); *b* 16 June 1922; *Educ* Cardiff HS, Univ of Wales (BA, MA, DLitt); *m* 14 July 1950, Patricia Beatrice, da of Capt Richard Selwyn Haskew, OBE (d 1959), of Harpenden and London; 3 s (Richard Henry b 1951, John Andrew b 1954, Christopher Edward b 1958); *Career* Univ Coll Cardiff: asst lectr 1946–49, lectr 1949–61, sr lectr 1961–66, reader 1966–69, dean 1968–70, prof 1969–74, established chair of medieval history 1974–77, dean 1975–76, fell 1981, hon prof 1996; prof and head of dept Westfield Coll London 1977–86 (vice princ 1980–86, fell 1989); pres: Cardiff Naturalists Soc 1975–76, Glamorgan History Soc 1975–77, Hist Assoc 1976–79, St Albans and Herts Archaeology and Architecture Soc 1990–93; memb Ancient Monuments Bd for England 1982–84, pres Soc for Medieval Archaeology 1983–86, vice pres Soc of Antiquaries 1983–86, chm Fabric Advsy Ctee St Albans Abbey 1991–94, memb St Albans Abbey Res Ctee; FRHistS 1958, FSA 1968, FBA 1979; *Books* Anglo-Saxon England and The Norman Conquest (1962, 2 edn 1991), Norman Conquest (1965), Norman Britain (1966), Alfred The Great (1967), A Wulfstan MS (1971), The Reign of Charlemagne (1975), The Vikings in Britain (1977), Medieval Britain (1977), The Governance of England Vol 1 (1984), The Middle Ages: A Concise Encyclopedia (ed 1989), The Making of the English Nation (1991), Society and Peoples: Studies in the History of England and Wales c 600–1200 (1992), The Vikings in Britain (1995); gen intro to facsimile edn of Domesday Book (1987); *Recreations* natural history; *Clubs* Athenaeum; *Style*— Prof Henry Loyn; ✉ 4 Clinton Road, Penarth, S Glam CF64 3JB (☎ 01222 707584)

LUBBOCK, Emma Rachel (Hon Mrs Page); da of 3 Baron Avebury; *b* 16 April 1952; *Educ* Univ of Oxford (MA); *m* 1977, Michael Charles Page, s of Maj-Gen Charles E Page, CB, MBE, DL; 2 da (Sophie b 1982, Natasha b 1984); *Career* ptnr Price Waterhouse; FCA, ATII, MCA; *Style*— Miss Emma Lubbock; ✉ Price Waterhouse, Southwark Towers, 32 London Bridge Street, London SE1 9SY (☎ 0171 939 3000, fax 0171 378 0647); Lepe House, Exbury, Southampton, Hants

LUBBOCK, John David Peter; s of Michael Ronald Lubbock, MBE (d 1989), and Diana Beatrix, *née* Crawley (d 1976); *b* 18 March 1945; *Educ* Radley, Royal Acad of Music (GRSM); *m* 12 Feb 1977 (m dis), Eleanor, *née* Sloan; 2 s (Daniel, Patrick); m 2, 13 July 1991, Christine Cairns, *qv*; 2 s (Adam Thomas b 28 Nov 1991, Alexander Michael b 30 June 1993); *Career* fndr and conductor Orchestra of St John's Smith Square, music dir Belfast Philharmonic Soc; *Recreations* tennis, racquets, Royal tennis; *Style*— John Lubbock, Esq; ✉ 7 Warborough Road, Warborough, Oxon (☎ 01865 858210)

LUBBOCK, Hon Lyulph Ambrose Jonathan Mark; s and h of 4 Baron Avebury, *qv*, and his 1 w, Kina Maria, *née* O'Kelly de Gallagh; *b* 15 June 1954; *Educ* St Olave's GS, Univ of Birmingham (BSc); *m* 1977, Susan Carol, da of Kenneth Henry MacDonald, of Swanage, Dorset; 1 s (Alexander Lyulph Robert b 17 Jan 1985), 1 da (Vanessa Adelaide Felicity b 1983); *Career* business projects mangr Municipal Mutual Computing 1991–92; CFM Group Ltd (part of ICL): business mangr 1992–94, info technol conslt 1994–; Grad Inst of Physics; *Recreations* golf, astronomy; *Style*— The Hon Lyulph Lubbock; ✉ 53 Worlds End Lane, Orpington, Kent BR6 6AF

LUBRAN, Jonathan Frank; s of Prof Michael Lubran, of LA, California, and Avril Roslyn, *née* Lavigne; *b* 27 April 1948; *Educ* Bedales, Univ of Chicago (BA), Univ of Cambridge (Dip, PhD); *Career* investmt advsr Crown Agents for Overseas Govts 1979–80; md: Royal Bank of Canada Investment Management International 1980–88, Bankers Trust Investment Management Ltd 1988–94, Hypo Foreign & Colonial Institutional; former treas Crisis at Christmas, memb London Project Ctee Nat Art-Collections Fund 1977–88, dep warden Guild of Benefactors Corpus Christi Coll Cambridge 1996–; *Recreations* opera, theatre, antiques, swimming, photography; *Clubs* Brooks's, Hurlingham; *Style*— Jonathan Lubran, Esq; ✉ 129 Studdridge St, London SW6 3TD (☎ 0171 731 0048); Foreign & Colonial Management Ltd, Exchange House, Primrose Street, London EC2A 2NY (☎ 0171 628 8000, direct ☎ 0171 825 2126, fax 0171 625 2134)

LUCAN, 7 Earl of (I 1795); Sir Richard John Bingham; 13 Bt (S 1634); also Baron Lucan (I 1776) and Baron Bingham (UK 1934); patron of one living; s of 6 Earl, MC (d 1964, himself ggs of the Crimean War General who gave the order for the Charge of the Light Brigade) by his w Kaitlin, *née* Dawson (d 1985), paternal gda of 1 Earl of Dartrey; *b* 18 Dec 1934; *Educ* Eton; *m* 1963, Veronica Mary, da of late Maj Charles Moorhouse Duncan, MC; 1 s (Lord Bingham, *qv*), 2 da (Lady Frances b 30 June 1964, Lady Camilla b 24 Oct 1970); *Heir* s, Lord Bingham; *Career* former Lt Coldstream Gds; *Style*— The Rt Hon the Earl of Lucan; ✉ Whereabouts unknown since 7th November 1974

LUCAS, Prof Arthur Maurice; s of Joseph Alfred Percival Lucas (d 1985), of Colac, Victoria, and May Queen, *née* Griffin; *b* 26 Oct 1941; *Educ* Univ of Melbourne (BSc, BEd), Ohio State Univ (PhD); *m* 1970, Paula Jean, da of Geoffrey Ross Williams (d 1991); 1 da (Elizabeth Karen b 1974), 1 s (Arthur David b 1975); *Career* science/biology teacher Educn Dept of Victoria 1964–66, sr demonstrator in biology Flinders Univ of S Australia 1969–70 (demonstrator 1967–68), pt/t res assoc ERIC Analysis Center Ohio State Univ 1970–72, fndn lectr Educn Unit Warrnambool Inst of Advanced Educn 1973; Flinders Univ of S Australia: lectr in science educn 1974–75, sr lectr 1976–80, chm Sch of Educn 1977–79; KCL: prof of science curriculum studies 1980–, asst princ 1988–90, chm Res Strategy Ctee 1991–93, vice-princ (academic affairs) 1991–93, acting princ 1992–93, princ 1993–; memb Exec Ctee Field Studies Cncl 1987–93 and 1994–, vice-pres Cncl Zoological Soc of London 1993 (memb 1992–93); memb: SE Thames RHA 1993–94, Ctee for Public Understanding of Sci (COPUS) 1993–96; author and contrib to many pubns and jls; fell Australian Coll of Educn 1995 (memb 1973), FIBiol 1981, FKC 1992; *Clubs* Athenaeum; *Style*— Prof Arthur Lucas; ✉ King's College London, Cornwall House Annex, Waterloo Road, London SE1 8WA (☎ 0171 872 3434, fax 0171 872 3430, e-mail a.lucas@kcl.ac.uk)

LUCAS, Ven Brian Humphrey; CB (1993); s of Frederick George Humphrey Lucas (d 1977), of Port Talbot, W Glamorgan, S Wales, and Edith Mary, *née* Owen (d 1975); *Educ* Port Talbot Secdy GS, St David's Coll Lampeter (BA), St Stephen's House Oxford; *m* 23 July 1966, Joy, da of Roy Penn; 2 s (Mark Stephen b 19 March 1969, (Alan) Simon b 3 Dec 1971), 1 da (Helen Penelope b 30 April 1975); *Career* ordained: deacon 1964, priest 1965; asst curate: Llandaff Cathedral 1964–67, Parish of Neath 1967–70; RAF: cmmnd chaplain 1970, Halton 1970–71, St Mawgan 1971–72, Luqa Malta 1972–75, Honington 1975–77, Marham 1977–79, staff chaplain to Chaplain-in-Chief 1979–82, Akrotiri Cyprus 1982–85, sr chaplain RAF Coll Cranwell 1985–87, asst chaplain-in-chief Germany 1987–89 then RAF Support Cmd 1989–91, archdeacon and Chaplain-in-Chief RAF 1991–95, archdeacon emeritus 1996–; QHC 1988–95; canon emeritus of Lincoln 1995– (preb and canon 1991–95); rector of Claythorpe Fulbeck & Carlton Scroop 1996–; memb Gen Synod C of E 1991–95, vice pres Clergy Orphan Corp 1991–95; memb Cncl: RAF Benevolent Fund 1991–95, Bible Reading Fellowship 1991–95; memb British Museum Soc 1980; FRSA 1993; *Recreations* archaeology of Near and Middle East, watching rugby football, travel (avoiding tourist areas); *Clubs* RAF, Savage; *Style*— The Ven Brian Lucas, CB; ✉ Pen-y-Coed, 6 Arnhem Drive, Caythorpe, Lincolnshire NG32 3DQ

LUCAS, Christine Frances; da of John Hennessy (d 1969), and Ellen Alice, *née* Jones (d 1994); *b* 26 May 1944; *Educ* Our Lady's Convent Sch Cardiff, Cardiff Coll of Art, Ravensbourne Coll of Art & Design, Leicester Coll of Art & Design (DipAD); *m* 24 April 1971, John Lucas, s of Victor Lucas; *Career* asst knitwear designer Jaeger Co London 1966–70, design conslt for various men's and women's knitwear, leisurewear, swimwear, and loungewear companies 1970–80; Windsmoor Group 1980–90: successively designer Windsmoor & Planet knitwear, design team ldr on new design collections, product mangr, design co-ordinator, fndr and merchandise dir Précis petite collection; design dir Viyella Retail Div 1990–; winner Award for Excellence Coats Viyella Fashion Retail Div 1993; *Recreations* art, theatre, reading, travel, swimming; *Style*— Mrs Christine Lucas; ✉ Viyella Retail Division, Chesham House, 136 Regent Street, London W1R 6HJ (☎ 0171 200 2900, fax 0171 200 2977)

LUCAS, Christopher Tullis; CBE (1994); s of Philip Gaddesden Lucas, GM (d 1982), and Maise Hanson (d 1984); *b* 20 Dec 1937; *Educ* Winchester; *m* 14 July 1962, Tina, da of Dr E T Colville; 2 da (Katherine b 1964, Suzannah b 1966); *Career* Nat Serv 1956–58; Thomson McLintock and Co 1958–66, chief exec ICEM 1966–72, IBA 1972–74, first md Radio Forth Edinburgh 1974–77, sec and dir Royal Society for the encouragement of Arts Manufactures and Commerce (RSA) 1977–94, acting dir PROJECT 2001 1994–; non-exec dir RSA Examinations Bd 1987–94, sec Faculty of Royal Designers for Industry 1977–94; memb Inst of CAs of Scot 1964–94; currently govr: Berks Coll of Art and Design, Design Dimension Educational Tst Dean Clough; memb Tax Law Review Ctee Inst for Fiscal Studies; *Recreations* this and that; *Style*— Mr Christopher Lucas, CBE; ✉ 24 Montpelier Row, Twickenham, Middx TW1 2NQ (☎ 0181 892 6584)

LUCAS, (Henry) Cornel; s of John Lucas (d 1949), of London, and Mary Ann Elizabeth Lucas (d 1946); *b* 12 Sept 1923; *Educ* Regent St Poly, Northern Poly; *m* 30 Jan 1960, Jennifer Susan Lindem, da of Maj James Frederick Holman, CBE (d 1974), of Loraine, St Ives, Cornwall; 3 s (Jonathan b 3 May 1961, Frederick b 29 Sept 1965, Linus b 5 March 1979), 1 da (Charlotte Rosie Linden b 29 May 1976); *Career* RAF Photographic Sch Farnborough 1941–46; Denham/Pinewood Studios 1947–59, opened own film studio 1959; work in permanent collections of: Nat Portrait Gallery, Nat Museum of Photography, Museum of Photography Bradford, Royal Photographic Soc, Bath and Jersey Museum of Photography Jersey; memb BAFTA, FRPS, FBIPP; *Books* Heads and Tales (1988); *Recreations* music, painting, gardening; *Style*— Cornel Lucas, Esq; ✉ 57 Addison Road, London W14 8JJ (☎ 0171 602 3219)

LUCAS, Sir Cyril Edward; kt (1976), CMG (1956); s of Archibald Lucas (d 1970); *b* 30 July 1909; *Educ* Hull GS, Univ of Hull; *m* 1934, Sarah Agnes, da of Henry Alfred Rose; 2 s, 1 da; *Career* head Dept of Oceanography Univ of Hull 1942–48; entered Civil Serv 1948; dir fishery research in Scotland Dept of Agric and Fisheries for Scotland 1948–70; memb: Cncl for Scientific Policy 1969–70, Natural Environment Res Cncl 1970–78; FRSE 1939, FRS 1966; *Style*— Sir Cyril Lucas, CMG, FRS, FRSE; ✉ 16 Albert Terrace, Aberdeen (☎ 01224 645568)

LUCAS, Brig Frederick John; CBE (1984); s of Frederick Victor Lucas (d 1977), of London, and Mary Lois, *née* Heath (d 1990); *b* 15 April 1932; *Educ* Credon Secdy Sch London, Scottish Business Sch Univ of Strathclyde (Dip Mgmnt Studies); *m* 8 Feb 1961, Virginia Isabella Elliott, da of James Robertson Hastie, of Invergordon; 3 s (Lance b 1962, Clive b 1963, Adam b 1964); *Career* cmmnd 1951, asst dir Royal Pioneers MOD 1979–81, dir Pioneers BAOR 1982–84, dir Army Pioneers 1983–85, Hon Col Cmdt Royal Pioneers 1988–90; dist gen mangr Central Birmingham Health Authy 1985–86, ptnr Lucas Inns 1991–94; chm: Harwich Chamber of Trade and Commerce 1994–96, Harwich Consortium 1995–96; hon life memb Angestellten-Gewerkschaft 1983; *Recreations* work; *Clubs* Lansdowne; *Style*— Brig Frederick Lucas, CBE; ✉ c/o Lloyds Bank plc, 230 High Street, Dovercourt, Harwich, Essex CO12 3AY (☎ and fax 01255 503776)

LUCAS, Prof (George) Gordon; s of George Derrick Lucas, of Sturton-by-Stow, Lincs, and Florence Annie, *née* Bell; *b* 10 Oct 1933; *Educ* Lincoln Sch, Lincoln Tech Coll (ONC, HNC, IMechE endorsement), Coll of Aeronautics Cranfield (DCAe, now MSc), Loughborough Univ of Technol (PhD); *m* 11 Aug 1956, Mary Elizabeth, da of Samual Musgrave Ella; 2 s (Kevin John b 5 Nov 1961, Neal Edward George b 6 March 1965), 1 da (Carol Mary (Mrs Waterfield) b 14 Dec 1959); *Career* design engr Ruston & Hornsby Lincoln 1955–57 (apprentice 1950–55), design engr Lucas Gas Turbine Equipment Birmingham 1959–62; Univ of Loughborough: lectr 1962–73, sr lectr 1973–87, reader 1987–90, Ford prof of automotive engrg 1990–, dir Centre for Tport Engrg Practice 1980–87, dir MSc course in advanced automotive engrg 1987–; FIMechE 1982; *Books* The Testing of Internal Combustion Engines (with A B Greene, 1969), Road Vehicle Performance (1986); *Recreations* bridge; *Style*— Prof Gordon Lucas; ✉ Department of Transport Technology, University of Technology, Loughborough, Leics LE11 3TU (☎ 01509 223430, fax 01509 267613, e-mail g.g.lucas@lut.ac.uk)

LUCAS, Prof Ian Albert McKenzie; CBE (1977); s of Percy John Lucas (d 1970), and Janie Inglis Hamilton (d 1984); *b* 1 July 1926; *Educ* Clayesmore Sch, Univ of Reading (BSc), McGill Univ (MSc); *m* 20 Dec 1950, Helen Louise, da of Ernest Struban Langerman (d 1930), of SA; 1 s (Michael Ian b 27 Feb 1952), 2 da (Karen Elizabeth b 25 March 1953, Catherine Helen b 17 July 1967); *Career* lectr Harper Adams Agric Coll 1949–50, princ sci offr (formerly sci offr, then sr sci offr) Rowett Res Inst Aberdeen 1950–61, DSIR res fell Ruakura Res Station NZ 1957–58, prof of agric Univ Coll N Wales 1961–77, princ Wye Coll Univ of London 1977–88 (fell 1992); hon memb Br Cncl 1987, Hon DSc McGill Univ 1996; memb: Br Soc of Animal Prodn, Rural Educn and Devpt Assoc, RASE, Kent Co Agric Soc; FRAgS 1972, FIBiol 1978; *Recreations* sailing; *Clubs* Farmers', Canterbury Farmers', Hollowshore Cruising; *Style*— Prof Ian Lucas, CBE; ✉ Valley Downs, Brady Road, Lyminge, Folkestone, Kent CT18 8DU (☎ 01303 863 053)

LUCAS, Hon Ivor Thomas Mark; CMG (1980); 2 s of 1 Baron Lucas of Chilworth (d 1967); *b* 25 July 1927; *Educ* St Edward's Sch Oxford, Trinity Coll Oxford; *m* 1954, Christine Mallorie, twin da of Cdr A M Coleman, OBE, DSC, RN (d 1981); 3 s; *Career* served with RA; entered Dip Serv 1951, sometime dep high cmmr Kaduna Nigeria; cnsllr Copenhagen 1972–75, head Middle East Dept FCO 1975–79; ambass to: Oman 1979–81, Syria 1982–84; asst sec-gen Arab-Br C of C 1985–87; chm: Mgmnt Bd Centre for Near and ME Studies SOAS 1987–90, Anglo Omani Soc 1990–95, Editorial Bd Asian Affairs 1995– (memb 1994–); memb: Cncl Royal Soc for Asian Affrs 1988–94 (vice pres 1990–94), Central Cncl Royal Over-Seas League 1988–94 and 1996–; fell in Int Politics of the Middle East Univ of Cambridge Centre of Int Studies 1991–94; *Books* Politics and the Economy in Syria (contrib, 1987) Handbook to the Middle East (contrib, 1988), A Road to Damascus: Mainly Diplomatic Memoirs from the Middle East (1997); *Recreations* music, crosswords, scrabble; *Clubs* Commonwealth Tst, Royal Over-Seas League; *Style*— The Hon Ivor Lucas, CMG

LUCAS, Jeremy Charles Belgrave; s of Percy Belgrave Lucas, CBE, DSO, DFC, of London, and Jill Doreen, *née* Addison; *b* 10 Aug 1952; *Educ* Stowe, Pembroke Coll Cambridge (MA); *m* 4 Sept 1976, Monica Dorothea, *née* Bell; 2 s (Christopher b 1981, Timothy b 1984); *Career* slr Denton Hall and Burgin 1974–78; merchant banker Grenfell & Co Ltd 1978– (dir 1986–); *Recreations* tennis, golf; *Clubs* Royal West Norfolk Golf; *Style*— Jeremy Lucas, Esq; ✉ Morgan Grenfell & Co Ltd, 23 Great Winchester St, London EC2P 2AX (☎ 0171 588 4545)

LUCAS, Prof (William) John; s of Leonard Townsend Lucas, and Joan, *née* Kelly; *b* 26 June 1937; *Educ* Hampton GS, Univ of Reading (BA, PhD); *m* 30 Sept 1961, Pauline; 1 s (Ben b 28 June 1962), 1 da (Emma b 11 Dec 1964); *Career* asst lectr Univ of Reading 1961–64, visiting prof Univs of Maryland and Indiana 1967–68, reader in English studies Univ of Nottingham 1975–77 (lectr 1964–71, sr lectr 1971–75), dean Sch of Educn and Humanities Univ of Loughborough 1979–82 and 1988–96 (prof of English and drama and head of dept 1977–88), currently prof Dept of English and Media Studies Nottingham Trent Univ; Lord Byron visiting prof of English lit Univ of Athens 1984–85; advsy ed: Journal of European Studies, Victorian Studies, Critical Survey, Literature and History; gen and commissioning ed: Faber Critical Monographs, Merlin Press Radical Reprints; co-ed Byron Press 1965–82; regular contribs incl: Times Literary Supplement, Times Higher Educational Supplement, London Review of Books, New Statesman & Soc, The Listener, Poetry Review, BBC (Radios 3 and 4), Essays in Criticism, Cahiers Victoriens & Edourdiens; FRSA 1984; *Books* incl: Tradition and Tolerance in 19th Century Fiction (with David Howard and John Goode, 1966), The Melancholy Man: A Study of Dickens (1970 and 1980), Arnold Bennett: A Study of his Fiction (1974), The Literature of Change (1977), Modern English Poetry: from Hardy to Hughes (1986), Moderns & Contemporaries (1985), Modern English Poetry (1986), Essays on Heaney (1989), England & Englishness (1990), Dickens: The Major Novels (1992), John Clare (1994), Writing and Radicalism (1996); poetry: About Nottingham (1971), A Brief Bestiary (1972), Chinese Sequence (1972), The Days of the Week (1983), Studying Grosz on the Bus (1989), Flying to Romania: A Sequence in Verse and Prose (1992), One for the Piano: Poems (1997); *Style*— Prof John Lucas; ✉ 19 Devonshire Avenue, Beeston, Notts; Department of English and Media Studies, Nottingham Trent University, Burton Street, Nottingham NG1 4BU (☎ 0115 941 8418, fax 0115 948 4266)

LUCAS, John Randolph; s of Ven Egbert de Grey Lucas (Archdeacon of Durham, d 1958), and Joan Mary, *née* Randolph (d 1982); *b* 18 June 1929; *Educ* Dragon Sch, Winchester, Balliol Coll Oxford (scholar, BA, John Locke Prize); *m* 17 June 1961, Helen Morar, da of Adm Sir Reginald Portal, KCB, DSO (d 1983), of Savernake Lodge,

Marlborough; 2 s (Edward b 1962, Richard b 1966), 2 da (Helen b 1964, Deborah b 1967); *Career* fell: Corpus Christi Coll Cambridge 1956–59, Merton Coll Oxford 1953–56 and 1960–96; memb Archbishops' Cmmn on Christian Doctrine; chm Oxford Consumer Gp; pres Br Soc for the Philosophy of Sci 1991–93; FBA 1988; *Books* The Principles of Politics (1964), The Concept of Probability (1970), The Freedom of the Will (1970), A Treatise on Time and Space (1973), Democracy and Participation (1976), Freedom and Grace (1976), On Justice (1980), Space, Time and Causality (1985), The Future (1989), Spacetime and Electromagnetism (1990), Responsibility (1993), Ethical Economics (1996); *Style*— J R Lucas, Esq, FBA; ✉ Lambrook House, East Lambrook, South Petherton, Somerset TA13 5HW (☎ 01460 240413, e-mail john.lucas@merton.oxford.ac.uk)

LUCAS, Nigel David; s of Joseph Lucas (d 1986), of Purley, Surrey, and Dorothy Mary, *née* Collier (d 1995); *b* 14 May 1941; *Educ* Whitgift Sch, Westminster Hotel Sch; *m* 1, 19 Sept 1970, Linda Elisabeth (d 1979), da of Sidney Alfred Stanton (d 1972); 2 da (Sarah b 1973, Catherine b 1974); m 2, 5 May 1982, Janette Muriel, da of Harold Stanley Vian-Smith; 2 s (Matthew Peter b 12 Nov 1988, Andrew James (twin) b 12 Nov 1988); *Career* restaurateur and wine wholesaler; dir Castle Inn Ltd 1964–; memb: Hotel Catering and Institutional Mgmnt Assoc, Cookery and Food Assoc, Assoc Culinaire Française; people's warden St Mary the Virgin Chiddingstone; Freeman City of London 1983; *Recreations* family and home; *Style*— Nigel D Lucas, Esq; ✉ Withers, Chiddingstone, Edenbridge, Kent TN8 7AE (☎ 01892 870694); Castle Inn, Chiddingstone, Edenbridge, Kent TN8 7AH (☎ 01892 870247)

LUCAS, Peter William; s of William George Lucas (d 1993), of Bradford Abbas, Dorset, and Jose Mabel, *née* House; *b* 12 April 1947; *Educ* Foster's Sch Sherborne, Harrow Coll (DipM); *m* 10 June 1972, Gail, da of John Small (d 1983), of Camberley, Surrey; 1 s (James Peter William b 1981), 2 da (Zoe b 1978, Joanna b 1984); *Career* mktg dir Lyons Tetley Ltd 1978–84, md Foodcare Ltd 1984–85, princ The Marketing Department 1985–, managing ptnr Mappin Parry Lucas 1988–91; dir: Custom Management (UK) Ltd 1990–92, Kingsbourne Ltd 1990–95, Kingsbourne International Marketing Ltd 1995–; md Orange Development Ltd 1995–; chm: Bd Govrs Watlington CPS 1988–91, Watlington Primary Sch Tst 1990–; memb Mktg Soc 1980, FCIM 1987 (registered marketer 1996), FInstD 1989; *Recreations* shooting, fishing; *Style*— Peter Lucas, Esq; ✉ Clare Hill House, Pyrton, Watlington, Oxford OX9 5AX; office: 20 High Street, Watlington, Oxford OX9 5PY (☎ 01491 613366, fax 01491 613367, car 0836 288621)

LUCAS, Hon Simon William; s and h of 2 Baron Lucas of Chilworth; *b* 6 Feb 1957; *Educ* Univ of Leicester (BSc); *m* 21 Sept 1993, Fiona, yr da of Thomas Mackintosh, of Vancouver, BC, Canada; 1 s (John Ronald Muir b 1995); *Career* served with RE 1976–84; computer systems engr, geophysicist; *Style*— The Hon Simon Lucas; ✉ Vancouver, BC, Canada; c/o The Lord Lucas of Chilworth, House of Lords, London SW1A 0AA

LUCAS, Stephen Ralph James; s and h of Sir Thomas Edward Lucas, 5 Bt, *qv*; *b* 11 Dec 1963; *Educ* Wellington, Edinburgh Univ (BCom); *Style*— Stephen Lucas, Esq

LUCAS, Sir Thomas Edward; 5 Bt (UK 1887), of Ashtead Park, Surrey, and of Lowestoft, Co Suffolk; s of Ralph John Scott Lucas (ka 1941), late Coldstream Gds, gs of 1 Bt, and Dorothy (d 1985), da of H T Timson; *b* 16 Sept 1930; *Educ* Wellington, Trinity Hall Cambridge (MA); *m* 1, 1958, Charmian Margaret (d 1970), da of late Col James Stanley Powell; 1 s (Stephen Ralph James b 1963); m 2, 1980, Mrs Ann J Graham Moore; *Heir* s, Stephen Ralph James Lucas b 11 Dec 1963; *Career* engr, scientist, health management speaker and healer, co dir 1958–; advsr to EEC 1976–, UN, World Bank, public and private cos; sr tstee Inlight and Truemark Tsts 1996; practitioner The Hale Clinic London 1996, chm Medical Devices & Instrumentation Ltd 1996; *Recreations* mountains, people; *Style*— Sir Thomas Lucas, Bt; ✉ Shermans Hall, Dedham, Essex CO7 6DE (☎ 01206 323 506, fax 01206 322 737)

LUCAS OF CHILWORTH, 2 Baron (UK 1946); Michael William George Lucas; s of 1 Baron Lucas of Chilworth (d 1967, sometime Lord in Waiting to George VI and Parly Sec to Min of Transport), by his w Sonia (d 1979), da of Marcus Finkelstein, of Latvia; *b* 26 April 1926; *Educ* Peter Symonds Sch Winchester, Luton Tech Coll; *m* 1955 (m dis 1990), Anne-Marie, only da of Ronald William Buck, of Southampton; 2 s (Hon Simon William b 1957, Hon Timothy Michael b 1959), 1 da (Hon Rachel Ann (Hon Mrs Lucas-Wilder) b 1963); *Heir* s, Capt Hon Simon William Lucas b 6 Feb 1957; *Career* sits as Cons peer in House of Lords; served with Royal Tank Regt 1943–47; memb House of Lords Select Ctee on Sci and Technol 1980–83, a Lord in Waiting (Govt whip) 1983–84, Parly under sec of state Trade and Industry 1984–87, memb House of Lords Euro Communities Ctee 1987–93; UK delegate N Atlantic Assembly 1981–83 and 1988–; chm sub-ctee Civilian Affairs (OSCE and Civilian Security & Co-op Ctees); pres: League of Safe Drivers 1976–80, Inst of Tport Admin 1980–83; vice pres: Royal Soc for Prevention of Accidents 1980–, Inst of the Motor Indust 1992– (memb Cncl 1971–75); memb RAC Public Policy Ctee 1981–83 and 1988–, govr Churcher's Coll Petersfield 1984–96; LAE, FIMI, FInstTA, FIHT (Hon); *Clubs* RAC; *Style*— The Rt Hon the Lord Lucas of Chilworth

LUCAS OF CRUDWELL, 11 Baron (E 1663) and 8 Lord Dingwall (S 1609); Ralph Matthew Palmer; s of Anne Rosemary, Baroness Lucas of Crudwell (10 holder of the title) and Lady Dingwall (7 holder of the title in her own right) (d 1991), and Maj Hon Robert Jocelyn Palmer, MC (d 1991); *b* 7 June 1951; *Educ* Eton, Balliol Coll Oxford; *m* 1, 1978 (m dis 1995), Clarissa Marie, da of George Vivian Lockett, TD, of Stratford Hills, Stratford St Mary, Colchester; 1 s (Hon Lewis Edward b 1987), 1 da (Hon Hannah Rachel Elise b 1984); m 2, 1995, Amanda Atha; *Heir* s, Hon Lewis Edward Palmer b 7 Dec 1987; *Career* Lord in Waiting (Govt Whip) 1994–; Liveryman Worshipful Co of Mercers; *Style*— The Rt Hon the Lord Lucas of Crudwell; ✉ House of Lords, London SW1A 0PW

LUCAS-TOOTH, Sir (Hugh) John; 2 Bt (UK 1920); s of Sir Hugh Vere Huntly Duff Munro-Lucas-Tooth of Teananich, 1 Bt (d 1985), and Laetitia Florence, OBE (d 1978), er da of Sir John Ritchie Findlay, 1 Bt, KBE; *b* 20 Aug 1932; *Educ* Eton, Balliol Coll Oxford; *m* 1955, Hon Caroline Poole, er da of 1 Baron Poole, PC, CBE, TD (d 1993); 3 da; *Heir* cousin, James Lingen Warrand b 6 Oct 1936; *Clubs* Brooks's, Beefsteak; *Style*— Sir John Lucas-Tooth, Bt; ✉ 41 Lancaster Road, London W11 1QJ; Parsonage Farm, E Hagbourne, Didcot, Oxon OX11 9LN

LUCE, Rt Hon Sir Richard Napier; kt (1991), PC (1986), DL; s of Sir William Luce, GBE, KCMG (d 1977), and Margaret (d 1989), da of Adm Sir Trevelyan Napier, KCB; *b* 14 Oct 1936; *Educ* Wellington, Christ's Coll Cambridge; *m* 5 April 1961, Rose Helen, eldest da of Sir Godfrey Nicholson, 1 Bt (d 1991); 2 s (Alexander Richard b 1964, Edward Godfrey b 1968); *Career* Nat Serv Cyprus; dist offr Kenya 1960–62, former mangr Gallaher and Spirella Co (GB); Parly candidate (C) Hitchin 1970; MP (C): Arundel and Shoreham 1971–74, Shoreham 1974–92; PPS to Min for Trade and Consumer Affrs 1972–74, oppn whip 1974–75, oppn spokesman on foreign and Cwlth affrs 1977–79; FCO: Parly under sec 1979–81, min of state 1981–82 (resigned over invasion of Falkland Islands), re-appointed min of state June 1983–85; min for the arts and min of state Privy Cncl Office responsible for The Civil Serv Sept 1985–July 1990, ret from Parl April 1992; vice chllr Univ of Buckingham 1992–97; govr of Gibraltar 1997–; chm: Cwlth Fndn 1992–96, Atlantic Cncl of the UK; pres Voluntary Arts Network; non-exec dir Meridian Broadcasting Ltd, former non-exec dir Booker Tate Ltd; tstee Geographers A-Z Map Co; *Style*— The Rt Hon Sir Richard Luce, DL; ✉ The Convent, Gibraltar

LUCIE-SMITH, (John) Edward McKenzie; s of John Dudley Lucie-Smith, MBE (d 1943), and Mary Frances Maud, *née* Lushington (d 1982); *b* 27 Feb 1933; *Educ* King's Sch Canterbury, Merton Coll Oxford (BA, MA); *Career* Nat Serv RAF Flying Offr 1954–56; worked in advtg 1956–66, poet, art critic and freelance writer with contribs to The Times, Sunday Times, The Independent, The Mail on Sunday, The Listener, The Spectator, New Statesman, Evening Standard, Encounter, London Magazine, Illustrated London News; FRSL; *Books* A Tropical Childhood and Other Poems (1961), A Group Anthology (ed with Philip Hobsbaum, 1963), Confessions and Histories (1964), Penguin Modern Poets 6 (with Jack Clemo and George MacBeth, 1964), Penguin Book of Elizabethan Verse (ed, 1965), What is a Painting? (1966), The Liverpool Scene (ed, 1967), A Choice of Browning's Verse (ed, 1967), Penguin Book of Satirical Verse (ed, 1967), Towards Silence (1968), Thinking About Art (1968), Movements in Art since 1945 (1969), British Poetry since 1945 (ed, 1970), Art in Britain 1969–70 (with P White, 1970), A Primer of Experimental Verse (ed, 1971), French Poetry: The Last Fifteen Years (ed with S W Taylor, 1971), A Concise History of French Painting (1971), Symbolist Art (1972), Eroticism in Western Art (1972), The First London Catalogue (1974), The Well Wishers (1974), The Burnt Child (1975), The Invented Eye (1975), World of the Makers (1975), How the Rich Lived (with C Dars, 1976), Joan of Arc (1976), Work and Struggle (with C Dars, 1977), Fantin-Latour (1977), The Dark Pageant (1977), Art Today (1977), A Concise History of Furniture (1979), Super Realism (1979), Cultural Calendar of the Twentieth Century (1979), Art in the Seventies (1980), The Story of Craft (1981), The Body (1981), A History of Industrial Design (1983), Art Terms: An Illustrated Dictionary (1984), Art in the Thirties (1985), American Art Now (1985), The Male Nude: A Modern View (with François de Louville, 1985), Lives of the Great Twentieth Century Artists (1986), Sculpture Since 1945 (1987), The Self Portrait: A Modern View (with Sean Kelly, 1987), Art in the 1980's (1990), Art Deco Painting (1990), Fletcher Benton (1990), Latin American Art of the Twentieth Century (1993), Art and Civilization (1993), Wendy Taylor (1993), Race, Sex and Gender: issues in contemporary art (1994), Frink: a portrait (with Elizabeth Frink, 1994), John Kirby (1994), American Realism (1994), Art Today (completely new version, 1995), Visual Art in the 20th Century (1996), Albert Paley (1996); *Recreations* the auction rooms; *Style*— Edward Lucie-Smith, Esq; ✉ c/o Rogers Coleridge & White, 20 Powis Mews, London W11

LUCK, Victor Leonard; *b* 31 May 1947; *Educ* Bromley GS, Univ of Salford (BSc); *m* Jan 1970, Susan Lesley, *née* Jones; 2 da (Dominie Cara b 20 June 1974, Victoria Marie b 4 June 1976); *Career* Philips Industries 1967–69, Chrysler Corporation 1970–73, Ford of Europe 1973–74, Chrysler Corporation 1974–77; Coopers & Lybrand: joined 1977, managing ptnr Management Consultancy Servs 1993–; FCMA 1973, FIMC 1981; *Recreations* playing and watching soccer, modern history, travel; *Style*— Victor Luck, Esq; ✉ Coopers & Lybrand, 1 Embankment Place, London WC2N 6NN (☎ 0171 213 5173, fax 0171 213 3820)

LUCKE, Dr Jeremy N; s of Douglas Thurlow Lucke (d 1980), and Edith Ann Lucke (d 1990); *b* 18 Sept 1935; *Educ* Culford Sch, Univ of Bristol (BVSc, MRCVS, PhD); *m* 1961, Dr Vanda M Lucke, da of late Prof S K Kon; 1 da (Victoria Jane (Dr Mackle) b 1966), 1 s (Dr Thomas (Tom) William Lucke b 1967); *Career* formerly: veterinary surgn in gen practice, reader in veterinary surgery (anaesthesia) Univ of Bristol until 1983, staff Animals (Scientific Procedures) Inspectorate Home Office until 1994 (latterly superintending inspr); RCVS: memb Cncl 1982–, pres 1990–91, chm Specialisation and FE Ctee 1987–90, chm Educn Ctee 1991–93, chm Disciplinary Ctee 1996–, dir RCVS Charter Educn Tst; memb EC Advsy Ctee on Veterinary Trg 1991–, UK del Fedn of Veterinarians of Europe 1993–; memb BVA, FRSM; *Recreations* music, theatre, cinema, gardening, walking, wildlife; *Style*— Dr Jeremy N Lucke; ✉ The White House, Langford, Bristol BS18 7BD (☎ 01934 862341)

LUCKETT, Nigel Frederick; s of George Ward Luckett (d 1958), of Wolverhampton, and Marjorie Phyllis, *née* Jeffery (d 1974); *b* 27 Aug 1942; *m* 18 Sept 1965, Janet Mary, da of late Albert Edward Sadler; 2 s (Richard Stephen b 18 Nov 1971, David Nigel b 6 Feb 1981); *Career* articled clerk Ridsdale Cozens & Purslow Accountants Walsall, Birmingham Office Peat Marwick Mitchell & Co 1964–66; ptnr Thomson McLintock & Co 1970–87 (joined 1966), ptnr KPMG Peat Marwick (following merger) 1987–95; dep chm Benson Group plc 1995–; memb: Ctee Birmingham and West Midlands Soc of Chartered Accountants 1975–83, Soc of Tech Analysts 1988; ATII 1966, FCA 1975 (ACA 1964), MSI 1993; *Recreations* golf, classical music, antiques, walking, the technical analysis of securities; *Style*— Nigel Luckett, Esq; ✉ Englefield House, 108 White Hill, Kinver, Stourbridge, West Midlands DY7 6AU

LUCKHOO, Hon Sir Edward Victor; kt (1970), QC (Guyana 1965); s of Edward Alfred Luckhoo, OBE (d 1965); bro of Sir Lionel A Luckhoo, *qv*; *b* 24 May 1912; *Educ* Queen's Coll Guyana, St Catharine's Coll Oxford (BA); *m* 1981, Maureen, da of John Mitchell Moxlow (resides in Yorkshire); *Career* called to the Bar Middle Temple 1936, chllr and pres Ct of Appeal Guyana 1968–77; high cmmr for Guyana to India and Sri Lanka 1977–83; chm: Customs Tariff Tbnl 1954–56, Judicial Serv Cmmn in Guyana 1968–76, Honours Advsy Cncl of Guyana 1970–76; pres Guyana Bar Assoc 1953–60; memb: Municipal Cncl of Georgetown 1946, Exec Bd UNESCO 1983–87; rep Guyana: Caribbean Cncl of Legal Educn 1970–75, Cwlth Law Conf New Delhi 1977; Order of Roraima Guyana 1976; *Clubs* Georgetown Cricket; *Style*— Hon Sir Edward Luckhoo, QC

LUCKHOO, Sir Lionel Alfred; KCMG (1969), CBE (1962), QC (Guyana 1954); s of Edward Alfred Luckhoo, OBE (d 1965); bro of Hon Sir Edward V Luckhoo, *qv*; *b* 2 March 1914; *Educ* Queen's Coll Guyana; *m* Sheila Chamberlin; 2 s, 3 da; *Career* called to the Bar Middle Temple 1940; MLC 1947–52, memb State Cncl 1953–54, MEC 1955–57, min without portfolio 1955–57; high cmmr for Guyana in the UK 1966–70; ambass for Guyana and Barbados to Paris Bonn and the Hague 1967–70; ambass of Guyana to Venezuela 1970–72; private law practice 1972– (holds record as world's most successful advocate with 236 successful defences in murder cases); *Style*— Sir Lionel Luckhoo, KCMG, CBE, QC

LUCKHURST, Prof Geoffrey Roger; s of William Thomas Victor Luckhurst (d 1970), and Hilda Mary, *née* Flood; *b* 21 Jan 1939; *Educ* Sir Joseph Williamson's Mathematical Sch Rochester, Univ of Hull, Univ of Cambridge; *m* 3 July 1965, Janice Rita, da of Colin Jack Flanagan (d 1995), of Romsey, Hants; 2 da (Nicola Jane b 25 Jan 1970, Caroline b 15 July 1972); *Career* Univ of Southampton: lectr 1967–70, reader 1970–77, prof of chemistry 1977–, jr library curator 1996–; pres Int Liquid Crystal Soc 1992–96, chm Br Liquid Crystal Soc 1994–; FRSC 1982; *Style*— Prof Geoffrey Luckhurst; ✉ Department of Chemistry, University of Southampton SO17 1BJ (☎ 01703 593795, fax 01703 593781)

LUCKIN, (Peter) Samuel; s of Geoffrey Grimston Luckin (d 1986), of High Easter, nr Chelmsford, Essex, and Muriel Bessie, *née* Need (d 1962); *b* 9 March 1938; *Educ* Felsted Sch Essex; *Career* Nat Serv cmmnd Essex Regt 1956–58, platoon cdr BAOR; press aide for Rt Hon Edward Heath CCO 1960's, dep head of PR for Brewers' Soc 1970's, owner Sam Luckin Associates Surrey 1980–; memb: Bd of Mgmnt Ashridge Mgmnt Coll Assoc 1982–85, Cncl IPR 1989–91 and 1992–95 (chm Membership Ctee 1991, memb Bd of Mgmnt 1991), Surrey TEC NW Forum; chm Residents' Assoc, active with the Camberley Soc; FIPR 1990; *Recreations* swimming, jogging, theatre, management development, IPR events; *Clubs* Farmers', MCC; *Style*— Samuel Luckin, Esq; ✉ 13 Belmont Mews, Camberley, Surrey GU15 2PH (☎ 01276 61928, fax 01276 686922)

LUCY, *see:* Fairfax-Lucy

LUDBROOK, Michael Sydney; *b* 31 Oct 1942; *m* 1 (m dis); 1 s (James Michael b 1982), 3 da (Claudia Jane b 1976, Gemma Elizabeth b 1977, Hannah Penelope b 1979); m 2, 31 March 1989, Sarah Louise, *née* Long; 1 s (Harry b 1992); *Career* md: Warner Holidays

1985–87, Mecca Leisure Ltd 1981–90; jt md Mecca Leisure Group plc 1986–90; chm Mecca International 1986–90; former dir: Mecca Dancing, Mecca Scotland, Tiffany Productions Ltd; dir: Brightreasons Group PLC 1993–, Brightreasons Restaurants Ltd 1994–; chm Brightreasons International Ltd 1994–; dir Pavilion Services Group Ltd 1992–94; *Recreations* tennis; *Clubs* Groucho; *Style*— Michael S Ludbrook, Esq; ✉ Brightreasons International Ltd, Bakers House, 25 Bakers Road, Uxbridge, Middx UB8 1RG (☎ 01895 811911)

LUDDINGTON, Sir Donald Collin Cumyn; KBE (1976), CMG (1973), CVO (1974); s of Norman John Luddington; *b* 18 Aug 1920; *Educ* Dover Coll, Univ of St Andrews (MA); *m* 1945, Garry Brodie, da of Alexander Buchanan Johnston; 1 s, 1 da; *Career* WWII served KOYLI and RAC; Hong Kong Govt 1949–73: dist cmmr 1969–71, sec for home affrs 1971–73; high cmmr Western Pacific 1973–74, govr Solomon Islands 1974–76, chm Public Servs Cmmn Hong Kong 1977–78, cmmr Ind Cmmn Against Corruption Hong Kong 1978–80, ret; *Style*— Sir Donald Luddington, KBE, CMG, CVO; ✉ The Firs, Little Lane, Easingwold, York YO6 3AQ

LUDDINGTON, Gary Anthony Cluer; s of Anthony William Davey Luddington, of Thurlestone, Devon, and Mae Luddington; *b* 20 Feb 1946; *Educ* Brockenhurst GS, Univ of Cambridge (MA); *m* 1, 1968; 1 s (Thomas James b 11 Jan 1972), 1 da (Victoria Louise b 31 July 1970); m 2, 1978, Diana Elizabeth Parkinson, *née* Turnbull; 1 step s (Rufus Joseph b 1972), 1 step da (Clair Elizabeth b 1966); *Career* brand mangr: Beecham 1968–70, Warner Lambert 1970–72; mktg mangr Mars Confectionery 1972–77, md ATV Licensing 1977–79, mktg dir Carlsberg UK 1979–82, md Letraset UK 1982–83, mktg dir Guinness Brewing 1983–87, world wide gp mktg dir United Distillers Group 1987–89, md Norman Broadbent International 1989–; *Recreations* shooting, sailing, golf; *Style*— G Luddington, Esq; ✉ Norman Broadbent International, 65 Curzon Street, London W1Y 7PE (☎ 0171 629 9626)

LUDER, Ian David; s of Mark Luder, of Eastbourne, and Frances, *née* Stillerman; *b* 13 April 1951; *Educ* Haberdashers' Aske's, UCL (BSc(Econ)); *m* 21 Feb 1984, Elizabeth Jane, *née* Gledhill; 1 s (Nicholas Joseph b 27 Dec 1984), 1 da (Alice Rose b 2 Feb 1987); *Career* Arthur Andersen 1971–78: joined as articled clerk, subsequently tax sr then tax mangr 1975; ptnr MacIntyre Hudson CA's 1980–88, ptnr Arthur Andersen 1989–; cncllr Bedford Borough Cncl 1976–; chm: Policy Ctee 1988–93, Planning & Transport Ctee 1995–; FCA 1974, FTII 1974 (pres 1994–95), FRSA 1993; *Books* Tolleys Personal Tax and Investment Planning (ed), Simon's Taxes (contrib), Butterworths Tax and Remuneration Strategies; *Recreations* cricket, local politics, music; *Clubs* MCC, Bedford RUFC; *Style*— Ian Luder, Esq; ✉ 4 Orchard Close, Village Road, Bromham, Beds MK43 8HN (☎ 01234 822011); Arthur Andersen, 1 Surrey Street, London WC2R 2PS (☎ 0171 438 3915, fax 0171 438 2984)

LUDER, (Harold) Owen; CBE (1986); s of Edward Charles Luder (d 1981), and Ellen Clara, *née* Mason (d 1986); *b* 7 Aug 1928; *Educ* Sch of Architecture Regent St Poly, Sch of Architecture Brixton Sch of Bldg; *m* 1, 29 Jan 1951 (m dis 1989), Rose Dorothy (Doris), *née* Broadstock; 1 s (Peter Jonathan Owen b 6 Oct 1965, d 8 Dec 1965), 4 da (Jacqueline Kim b 3 May 1953, Kathryn Joy b 1954, Sara Jayne b 16 Oct 1966, Judith Amanda b 29 Jan 1968); m 2, 10 May 1989, Jacqueline Ollerton; *Career* Nat Serv RA 1946–48; qualified architect 1954, started own practice Owen Luder Ptnrship 1957, withdrew 1987 to develop new consultancy Communication In Construction; designed many bldgs UK and abroad 1954–87, environmental conslt NCB - Belvoir coal mines 1975–87; non-exec dir Jarvis PLC 1995–; various awards incl RIBA Bronze medallist 1963; pres: Norwood Soc 1981–92, RIBA 1981–83 and 1995– (hon treas 1975–78); vice pres Membership Communications 1989–90; columnist Building Magazine (Business Columnist of the Year 1985), contrib nat and tech press, radio and TV broadcaster; Arkansas Traveller 1971; ARIBA 1954, FRIBA 1967, FRSA 1984, MBAE 1992; *Recreations* writing, theatre, Arsenal FC, golf; *Clubs* RAC; *Style*— Owen Luder, Esq, CBE, PRIBA; ✉ 2 Smith Square, Westminster, London SW1P 3HS (☎ 0171 222 4737); Owen Luder Consultancy, 2 Smith Square, Westminster, London SW1P 3HS (☎ 0171 222 4737, fax 0171 233 0428)

LUDLAM, Dr Christopher Armstrong; *b* 6 June 1946; *Educ* Univ of Edinburgh (BSc, MB ChB, PhD); *Career* res fell MRC Univ of Edinburgh 1972–75, sr registrar Univ Hosp of Wales Cardiff 1975–78, lectr in haematology Univ of Wales 1979; Dept of Med Univ of Edinburgh 1980–: conslt haematologist, dir Edinburgh Haemophilia Centre, pt/t sr lectr; numerous publications on blood coagulation; FRCPE, FRCPath; *Style*— Dr Christopher Ludlam; ✉ Department of Haematology, Royal Infirmary, Edinburgh (☎ 0131 536 2122, fax 0131 536 2145)

LUDLOW, Christopher; s of Sydney Ludlow (d 1983), and Margaret Eleanor, *née* Barlee; *b* 7 Sept 1946; *Educ* King Edward VI Sch Macclesfield, London Coll of Printing (DipAD); *m* 7 Sept 1969 (m dis 1980), Louise Frances Heather, da of Claude Duchesne Janitsch; 1 s (Edward b 1972); *Career* graphic designer; assoc Stevenson Ward Macclesfield 1971–, ptnr Gray Design Associates 1974–, princ Henrion Ludlow & Schmidt 1981–; responsible for major corporate identities incl: Coopers & Lybrand, Amersham International, British Midland, London Electricity; responsible for orientation systems for: London Underground, Canary Wharf, Channel Tunnel Terminal Waterloo; conslt to various companies/instns incl: British Airports Authy, British Rail, KLM Royal Dutch Airlines, London Underground, Solvay, Univ of Leeds; author of articles in various design pubns; memb and int liaison offr American Soc of Environmental Graphic Designers, chm Sign Design Soc 1993–95; FCSD 1981, FRSA 1994; *Recreations* music, antique models; *Clubs* Naval & Military; *Style*— Christopher Ludlow, Esq; ✉ Henrion Ludlow & Schmidt, 12 Hobart Place, London SW1W 0HH (☎ 0171 235 5466, fax 0171 235 8637)

LUDLOW, Bishop and Archdeacon of 1994–; Rt Rev Dr John Charles Saxbee; *b* 7 Jan 1946; *Educ* Cotham GS Bristol, Univ of Bristol, Univ of Durham, Cranmer Hall Durham; *m*; 1 da; *Career* curate Emmanuel with St Paul Plymouth 1972–76, vicar St Philip Weston Mill Plymouth 1976–81, team vicar Central Exeter Team Miny 1981–87, dir SW Miny Trg Course 1981–92, preb Exeter Cathedral 1988–92, archdeacon of Ludlow 1992–; *Style*— The Rt Rev Dr John Saxbee, Bishop and Archdeacon of Ludlow; ✉ Bishop's House, Corvedale Road, Craven Arms, Shropshire SY7 9BT (☎ 01588 673571, fax 01588 673585)

LUDLOW, Michael Richard; s of Sir Richard Ludlow (d 1956), and Katharine, *née* Wood (d 1975); *b* 30 March 1933; *Educ* Rugby, Trinity Coll Oxford (MA); *m* 1, 1962 (m dis 1969), Prunella, *née* Truscott; 1s, 1 da; m 2, 31 Oct 1969, Diane, *née* Wright (d 1995); 2 da; m 3, 21 Dec 1996, Sheila, *née* Holmes, wid of Russell Pratt; *Career* Nat Serv 1951–52, jr under offr (Eaton Hall) Royal Welsh Fus, cmmnd 2 Lt Queen's Regt 1952, seconded to Sierra Leone Regt 1952 (trg offr), Lt N Staffs Regt TA 1952–54; admitted slr 1959, sr ptnr Beale & Co Slrs 1982–93 (ptnr 1965–93), ret; proprietor Michael Ludlow Mediations 1993–; chm London Branch Chartered Inst of Arbitrators 1993–95; Freeman: City of London 1987, Worshipful Co of Arbitrators 1987; memb Law Soc 1959–96; FCIArb 1983; *Books* Fair Charges? (1982); *Recreations* golf; *Clubs* Reform, Vincent's (Oxford), I Zingari, Grannies Cricket, Roehampton; *Style*— Michael Ludlow, Esq; ✉ 59 Christ Church Road, East Sheen, London SW14 7AN (business ☎ and fax 0181 876 4203, home ☎ 0181 876 4001)

LUDMAN, Harold; s of Nathan Ludman (d 1961), and Fanny Dinah, *née* Jerome (d 1936); *b* 23 Feb 1933; *Educ* Bradford GS, Sidney Sussex Coll Cambridge (MA), UCH Med Sch (MB BChir); *m* 1957, Lorraine, *née* Israel; 1 s (Peter Frederick b 1960), 1 da (Catherine Natalie b 1962); *Career* trained Cambridge, UCH Med Sch and KCH; conslt otolaryngologist: KCH 1965–94, Nat Hosp for Neurology and Neurosurgery 1967–; hon sr lectr Inst of Neurology; chm: Special Advsy Ctee in Otolaryngology 1988–91, Project Design Team Operating Theatres KCH until 1993, Future Med Policy Gp Nat Hosp Queen Square 1991–93; examiner: FRCS in Otolaryngology 1983–89, Intercollegiate Bd in Otolaryngology 1985–, Surgery MB BS (London) 1987–; chm Soc of Audiology Technicians 1967–75; pres: Section of Otology RSM 1985–86, BAOL 1990–93 (chm Special Advsy Ctee in Otolaryngology 1988–91); WJ Harrison Prize 1987, Walter Jobson-Horne Prize 1990; memb: BAOL, BMA, RSM; FRCS; *Books* Diseases of the Ear (5 edn, 1988), ABC of Otolaryngology (3 edn, 1993); also author of many chapters in other books and original pubns in learned jls on otology; *Recreations* reading, literature, philosophy, computers, theatre, music; *Style*— Harold Ludman, Esq; ✉ 149 Harley Street, London W1N 2DE (☎ 0171 935 4444)

LUESLEY, Dr David Michael; s of Michael James Joseph Luesley, of Wakefield, Yorkshire, and Elizabeth Montgomery, *née* Aitken (d 1970); *b* 14 Feb 1952; *Educ* Queen Elizabeth GS Wakefield, Downing Coll Cambridge, Univ of Birmingham Med Sch (MA, MB Ch, MD); *Career* reader in gynaecological oncology and hon conslt obstetrician and gynaecologist City Hosp Dudley Rd Univ of Birmingham; vice pres Br Soc for Colposcopy and Cervical Cytology; FRCOG 1993 (MRCOG 1980); *Recreations* rugby football, travel, photography, painting; *Clubs* Moseley RUFC; *Style*— Dr David Luesley; ✉ City Hosp, Maternity Department, Dudley Road, Birmingham (☎ 0121 554 3801)

LUETCHFORD, Robert Sellick; s of William Luetchford (d 1984), and Roma, *née* Lawrence; *b* 29 March 1949; *Educ* Harrow Co GS, Pembroke Coll Oxford (MA); *m* 7 Nov 1990, Nicola Christine, da of Michael Gilbert; *Career* International Computers Ltd 1971–74 (systems engr, systems conslt), Sperry Univac (UK) Ltd 1974–77 (mainframe sales exec, sr sales exec); Plessey Co Ltd: mktg mangr Plessey Microsystems Ltd 1977–79, asst to dir Plessey Corp Staff 1979–81, dir of planning and business devpt Plessey Office Systems Ltd 1981–84; Prudential Bache Securities: head of electronics res 1984–86, vice pres 1986, sr vice pres Corp Fin 1986; md Marshall Securities Ltd 1990– (dep chief exec 1986–90), non-exec chm Villiers Group plc 1991–; *Recreations* opera, classical music, fly fishing; *Style*— Robert Luetchford, Esq; ✉ Eastfields Farm, Melchbourne, Beds MK44 1BL (☎ 01234 709990); Marshall Securities Ltd, 99 Charterhouse Street, London EC1M 6HR (☎ 0171 490 3788, fax 0171 490 3787)

LUFF, Peter James; MP (C) Worcester (majority 6,152); s of Thomas Luff (d 1963), and Joyce, *née* Mills (d 1985); *b* 18 Feb 1955; *Educ* Licensed Victuallers' Sch Slough, Windsor GS, Corpus Christi Coll Cambridge (exhibitioner, MA); *m* May 1982, Julia Dorothy, da of Lt Cdr P D Jenks, RN; 1 s (Oliver Charles Henry b 10 Jan 1988), 1 da (Rosanna Amy b 29 Aug 1985); *Career* res asst to Rt Hon Peter Walker 1977–80, head of Private Office of Rt Hon Edward Heath 1980–82, asst md then md Good Relations Public Affairs Ltd 1980–87, special advsr to Sec of State for Trade and Indust 1987–89, sr conslt Lowe Bell Communications 1989–90, co sec Luff and Sons Ltd Windsor 1980–87, asst md Good Relations Ltd 1990–92; Parly candidate (C) Holborn and St Pancras 1987, MP (C) Worcester 1992–; memb Commons Select Ctee on: Welsh Affrs 1992–, Tport 1993–; PPS to: Min for Energy 1993–96, Lord Chllr 1996–; jt sec Cons Backbench Ctee on Transport 1992–93; MIPR; *Recreations* steam railways, going to musicals and theatre, being with my family; *Clubs* Worcestershire CCC, RAC; *Style*— Peter Luff, Esq, MP; ✉ House of Commons, London SW1A 0AA (☎ 0171 219 3000)

LUFF, Robert Charles William; CBE (1995); s of Robert Hill Luff (d 1955), and Ethel Maud Luff (d 1976); *b* 7 July 1914; *Educ* Bedford Modern Sch; *Career* served WWII Gordon Highlanders (India and Burma), Maj; underwriting memb Lloyd's 1961; life pres and tstee Cystic Fibrosis Res Tst, vice pres Nat Asthma Campaign; tstee: Brompton Hosp Adolescent and Adult Cystic Fibrosis Dept, Manton Charitable Tst, Gordon Highlanders Regtl Tst; pres: Br Scoliosis Res Fndn, Scarborough Ctee Br Heart Fndn, Scarborough Div St John Ambulance (fndr Robert Luff Foundation Benevolent Fund for St John Ambulance personnel); dir: Cystic Fibrosis Res Investmt Tst 1981–85 (chm 1985–86), Hammersmith Palais Ltd 1955–61, European Sports Promotions Ltd Empress Hall 1952–60, Crucial Enterprises Ltd, Crucial Films Ltd; chm: Beryl Evetts & Robert Luff Animal Welfare Trust Ltd, Robert Luff Foundation Ltd (controlling Futurist Light & Sound Ltd), Robert Luff Ltd, Robert Luff Plays Ltd (controlling John Tiller Schs of Dancing); impresario responsible for the promotion of all the Black and White Minstrel Show presentations in the West End (recognised in the Guinness Book of Records as longest running musical prodn); hon fell RVC, hon fell Animal Health Trust; OStJ, Hon FRCP, FInstD; *Clubs* RAC, Army and Navy, Highland Bde; *Style*— Robert Luff, Esq, CBE; ✉ 294 Earls Court Road, London SW5 9BB (☎ 0171 373 7003)

LUFFRUM, David John; s of Frederick George Luffrum (d 1970), and Gladys, *née* de Keyser (d 1994); *b* 14 Dec 1944; *Educ* Latymer Upper Sch; *m* 20 May 1967, Christine, da of Albert Walker; 2 s (Daniel b 6 Feb 1969, Russell b 18 July 1972); *Career* gp accountant London Borough of Ealing 1967–70, asst treas Thames Conservancy Board 1971–73, Thames Water Authority 1974–89 (princ budget offr, asst fin dir, head of fin, fin dir), gp dir fin and planning Thames Water plc 1989–; currently dir: TW Utilities Ltd, Isis Insurance Co Ltd; memb Cncl Univ of Reading; IPFA 1967; *Recreations* golf, piano; *Style*— David Luffrum, Esq; ✉ 2 Bluebell Drive, Burghfield Common, Reading, Berks RG7 3EF; Thames Water plc, 14 Cavendish Place, London W1M 0NU (☎ 0171 636 8686, fax 0171 833 6136)

LUFT, His Hon Arthur Christian; CBE (1988); s of Ernest Christian Luft (d 1962), and Phoebe Luft (d 1977); *b* 21 July 1915; *Educ* Bradbury Cheshire; *m* 1950, Dorothy, da of Francis Manley (d 1936); 2 s (Peter, Timothy); *Career* served RA and REME 1940–46; advocate Manx Bar 1940, HM Attorney Gen IOM 1973, HM Second Deemster (High Ct judge) 1974, HM First Deemster, Clerk of the Rolls and dep govr IOM 1980–88; memb: Legislative Cncl of IOM 1988–, Dept of Local Govt and Environment 1988–93, IOM Public Accounts Ctee 1988–, Ecclesiastical Ctee of Tynwald 1992–, Dept of Agric Fisheries and Forestry 1993–; chm: Criminal Injuries Compensation Tbnl 1975–80, Prevention of Fraud Investmts Act Tbnl 1975–80, Licensing Appeal Ct 1975–80, Tynwald Ceremony Arrangements Ctee 1980–88, IOM Income Tax Cmmrs 1980–88, IOM Arts Cncl 1992–, Diocesan Legislative Ctee; pres: Manx Deaf Soc 1975–, IOM Cricket Club 1980–; *Recreations* theatre, watching cricket, reading, gardening; *Clubs* Ellan Vannin, Manx Automobile; *Style*— His Hon Arthur C Luft, CBE, MLC; ✉ Leyton, Victoria Rd, Douglas, Isle of Man IM2 6AQ (☎ 01624 621048)

LUGG, (Herbert Kenneth) Michael; s of Reginald Lugg (d 1969), of Ryde, and Winifred Agnes, *née* Stuart; *b* 7 April 1934; *Educ* Ryde Sch Isle of Wight, Univ of London (BSc); *m* 22 July 1961, Valerie Dean, da of Maurice William Alfred Jacobs (d 1987); 1 da (Sarah b 1965); *Career* civil engr; graduate trainee Richard Thomas & Baldwins 1959–62, agent Bridgwater Bros (PWC) 1962–64, engr Shell Mex & BP 1964–73, mangr of retail engrg BP Oil 1973–78, engrg mangr BP Oil 1978–92, conslt 1992–; chm Assoc for Petroleum and Expolsives Admin (APEA) 1993–94; chm Grayshott Community Care 1992–, govr Ryde Sch 1982– (chm 1993), chm of govrs Bembridge Sch 1995–; *Recreations* concerts, theatregoing, classic sports cars, walking, gardening; *Style*— Michael Lugg, Esq; ✉ The Merrick, Tarn Rd, Hindhead, Surrey GU26 6TP (☎ 01428 606883, fax 01428 607365)

LUKE, 3 Baron (UK 1929); Arthur Charles St John Lawson Johnston; DL (Beds 1989); s of 2 Baron Luke, KCVO, TD (d 1996), and Barbara, da of Sir Fitzroy Hamilton Anstruther-Gough-Calthorpe, 1 Bt; *b* 13 Jan 1933; *Educ* Eton, Trinity Coll Cambridge (BA); *m* 1, 6 Aug 1959 (m dis 1971), Silvia Maria, da of Don Honorio Roigt, former

Argentine Ambass at The Hague; 1 s, 2 da (Hon Rachel Honoria (Hon Mrs Parrack) b 1960, Hon Sophia Charlotte (Hon Mrs Kirk) b 1966); m 2, 1971, Sarah Louise, da of Richard Hearne, OBE; 1 s (Hon Rupert Arthur b 1972); *Heir* s, Hon Ian James St John Lawson Johnston b 4 Oct 1963; *Career* art dealer; co cncllr Beds 1966–70 (chm of Staffing Ctee 1967–70), High Sheriff Beds 1969–70, cdr St John Ambulance Bde Beds 1985–90 (cmmr 1972–85); pres Nat Assoc of Warehouse-Keepers 1960–78; memb Ct: The Drapers Co 1993– (jr warden 1993), Corp of the Sons of the Clergy 1980–; KStJ; *Recreations* shooting, fishing; *Style*— The Rt Hon Lord Luke, DL; ✉ Odell Manor, Beds MK43 7BB (☎ 01234 720416, fax 01234 721311)

LUKE, Colin Rochfort; s of Donald Alfred Rochfort Luke, of Jersey, CI, and Mary Blanche, *née* Bennett; *b* 24 Jan 1946; *Educ* Bristol GS, Exeter Coll Oxford (MA, memb Univ fencing team, pres OU Film Soc, films ed Isis magazine); *m* 1, 1971 (m dis 1976), Sarah Moffat Hellings; m 2, 1978, Hon Felicity Margaret, da of Baron Crowther (Life Peer, d 1972); 2 s (Theodore Rochfort b 1979, Harley Rochfort b 1981), 1 da (Claudia Mary b 1983); *Career* director and producer; BBC: joined as trainee film ed 1967, film and studio dirs course 1969, prodr/dir 1969–79; formed own co Wobbly Pictures Ltd 1977 (renamed Mosaic Pictures Ltd 1989), freelance film dir 1979–, dir Document Films Ltd 1982, formed Document Television Ltd 1987; winner of numerous Adventure Film Awards; Freeman City of Louisville Kentucky 1963; fndr memb: BAFTA, Dirs Guild of GB; memb: PACT, RTS; *Television* progs for BBC 1969–79: The World About Us, The Romance of the Indian Railways (with James Cameron), A Desert Voyage (with Dame Freya Stark), Albion in the Orient (with Julian Pettifer), Black Safari, Take Six Girls-Israel, Taste for Adventure, Half Million Pound Magic Carpet, Diamonds in the Sky; as freelance dir/prodr: Nature Watch (ATV/TV) 1980, Towards an Unknown Land (with Dame Freya Stark) 1981, The Arabs (Channel Four) 1981, Britain at the Pictures (BBC) 1983, Duneriders (Channel Four) 1985, Heart of the Kremlin (Central/ITV Network) 1991, Will they Ring Tonight (BBC) 1993, A Change of Heart (BBC) 1993, Frontline Vietnam (Channel Four) 1993, The Making of Them (BBC) 1994, Apocalypse Then (BBC) 1994; exec prodr: Assignment Adventure (Channel 4) 1984–85, A Russia of One's Own (Channel 4) 1987, Frontline Doctors (BBC) 1991, Nomads (Channel 4) 1992, Captain Pedro and the Three Wishes (Channel Four); dir: The Golden Road (TBS) 1986–87, The Baltic Style (TBS) 1987, An Affair in Mind (BBC) 1987–88; series ed: Voyager (Central/ITV Network) 1988–89, The World of National Geographic (Central) 1988–89, Classic Adventure (BBC) 1991–92; series dir Russian Wonderland (BBC) 1995, United Kingdom (BBC) 1996; as prodr Quality Time (BBC) 1996, Birth of a Salesman (Channel Four) 1996; *Recreations* family, travel, cinema, politics; *Clubs* BAFTA; *Style*— Colin Luke, Esq; ✉ Mosaic Pictures Ltd, 8–12 Broadwick St, London W1 (☎ 0171 437 6514, fax 0171 494 0595)

LUKE, (William) Ross; s of Maj Hamish Galbraith Russell Luke TD, JP (d 1970), and Ellen Robertson Boyd, *née* Mitchell; *b* 8 Oct 1943; *Educ* Stowe; *m* 16 May 1970, Deborah Jacqueline, da of Derek John Gordon; 3 da (Alison b 1973, Kirstene b 1974, Victoria b 1978); *Career* CA 1968; sr ptnr Dukes CAs; vice pres London Scottish RFC 1995– (hon sec 1988–92); Met Police Commendation 1983; *Recreations* rugby football, squash; *Clubs* London Scottish Rugby FC; *Style*— Ross Luke, Esq; ✉ 105 Palewell Park, London SW14 8JJ (☎ 0181 876 9228); Dukes Chartered Accountants, 310 King St, London W6 0RR (☎ 0181 846 9644, fax 0181 741 4373)

LUM, Dr (Laurence) Claude; s of Samuel Lum (d 1954), and Florence, *née* Hill (d 1974); *b* 24 Jan 1916; *Educ* Adelaide HS, Univ of Adelaide (MB BS 1939), Univ of Cambridge (MA 1977); *m* 1, 1940 (m dis 1980), Mary Honora Carmody; m 2, Cynthia Anne, da of Edward Stratemeyer Adams; 1 s (Edward Stratemeyer b 10 Jan 1987), 1 da (Claudia Stratemeyer b 17 Feb 1983); *Career* med and surgical house physician Royal Adelaide Hosp 1939–40, War Serv Aust Army Med Corps SW Pacific 1941–46, med supt and flying doctor Alice Springs 1946–47, asst supt (med) Royal Adelaide Hosp 1949–50, conslt physician Ipswich Chest Clinic and Br Legion Sanatorium Nayland 1950–59; Papworth Hosp: physician i/c cardio-pulmonary bypass 1959–65, conslt physician 1959–81, regnl conslt in respiratory physiology 1962–81; conslt physician W Suffolk and Newmarket Gen Hosps 1971–80; memb Cncl Nat Assoc of Clinical Tutors 1965–81 (vice pres 1973–81), ex officio memb Cncl for Post Graduate Med and Dental Educn in England and Wales 1974–76, memb E Anglian Ctee for Post Graduate Med and Dental Educn 1965–81, vice pres RSM 1985–87 (pres Section Hypnosis and Pyschosomatic Med 1985–87); fndr memb Int Soc for Advancement of Respiratory Psychophysiology 1994 (ISARP award for outstanding contribs 1994); FRSM 1967, FRCP 1970 (MRCP 1948), FRACP 1973 (MRACP 1946); *Publications* Modern Trends in Psychosomatic Medicine (contrib, 1976), Pseudo-allergic Reactions (contrib, 1985), Behavioural and Psychological Approaches to Breathing Disorders (contrib, 1994); author of various papers on hyperventilation and the physiology of hypnosis; *Recreations* ocean racing and cruising, watercolour painting, music, opera, model railway construction; *Clubs* Ipswich Art, Royal Burnham Yacht; *Style*— Dr Claude Lum; ✉ Summerleas, Scotland Road, Dry Drayton, Cambs CB3 8BX (☎ 01954 780627)

LUMB, David John; s of George Spencer Lumb (d 1988), and Margaret Minnie, *née* Spencer (d 1995); *b* 25 July 1950; *Educ* Abbeydale GS, Leeds Sch of Architecture (Dip Arch); *m* Judith Margaret, da of James Sewell; 1 s (Daniel James b 1978), 2 da (Amy Elizabeth b 1980, Rachel Lucy b 1984); *Career* project architect Property Services Agency NE Region 1975–77; Fletcher Ross & Hickling: joined as architect 1977, assoc 1980–86, sr assoc 1986–88; md: Trevor Wilkinson Associates 1989–95 (joined as dir 1988), D Y Davies (York) 1995–96, ML Design Group (Northern) Ltd 1996–; chm Yorkshire Construction Indust Gp, vice chm RIBA Companies Ltd 1995–; RIBA 1980; *Awards* for Wistow Shaft site: Festival of Architecture Award 1984, Concrete Soc Commendation 1984, Civic Tst Award 1986; White Rose Award (for Riccall and Stillingfleet Shaft sites) 1986, Concrete Soc Commendation (for Doncaster Crown Ct) 1990, Craftmanship Award and Commendations (for York Crown Ct) 1991; *Recreations* reading newspapers; *Style*— David Lumb, Esq; ✉ Lumb ML Design Group, Mount House, 90 The Mount, York, N Yorks YO2 2AR

LUMLEY, Henry Robert Lane; s of Edward Lumley (d 1960), and Kathleen Agnew, *née* Wills (d 1978); *b* 29 Dec 1930; *Educ* Eton, Magdalene Coll Cambridge (MA); *m* 7 Oct 1959, Sheena Ann, da of Air Vice-Marshal Somerled Douglas MacDonald, CB, CBE, DFC (d 1979); 2 s (Peter b 1960, Robert b 1965); 1 da (Julia (Mrs Scott McKay) b 1962); *Career* insur broker; chm Edward Lumley Holdings Ltd 1986– (joined 1974); dir: Edward Lumley & Sons Ltd Lloyd's Brokers 1956–88, Lumley Corporation Ltd Aust 1974–89; vice pres Br Insur and Investmt Brokers' Assoc 1992– (chm 1990–92), memb Cncl Insur Brokers' Registration Cncl 1988–95; chm and md Windlesham Golf Management Ltd 1992–; *Clubs* East India, Windlesham Golf; *Style*— Henry Lumley, Esq; ✉ 99 Bishopsgate, London EC2M 3XD (☎ 0171 588 3188, fax 0171 588 3472)

LUMLEY, John Adrian; s of Thomas Lumley (d 1983), and Patience, *née* Henn Collins (d 1987); *b* 29 May 1942; *Educ* Eton, Magdalene Coll Cambridge (MA); *m* 14 June 1969, Catita, da of Hans Lieb (d 1959), of Algeciras, Spain; 1 s (Joshua b 1970), 2 da (Eliza b 1973, Olivia b 1981); *Career* Christie's (Christie, Manson & Woods Ltd); joined 1964, dir 1969–, jt dep chm 1993–96, jt vice-chm 1996–; memb Kent and E Sussex Regnl Ctee Nat Tst 1981–87; Liveryman Worshipful Co of Goldsmiths 1984; *Clubs* Brooks's; *Style*— John Lumley, Esq; ✉ Court Lodge, Egerton, Ashford, Kent (☎ 01233 756249); Christie's, 8 King St, London SW1 (☎ 0171 839 9060)

LUMLEY, Michael David; s of Thomas Henry Lumley (d 1969), and Annie Hudson Atkinson (d 1988); *b* 3 March 1943; *Educ* Thirsk Sch, Fitzwilliam Coll Cambridge (MA), Univ of Leicester (PGCE); *m* 29 March 1980, Margaret Frances Clare, da of Dr David Augustine Harper, OBE; 2 s (Thomas David Robert b 8 Aug 1981, Matthew Francis Michael b 31 Jan 1983), 1 da (Fiona Mary Clare b 16 Jan 1985); *Career* maths teacher John Mason HS Abingdon 1966–67, book ed Educational Systems Ltd 1967–68, researcher Centre for Educnl Television Overseas 1968; BBC TV: researcher/asst prodr Continuing Educn 1968–72, asst prodr Outside Bdcast Events 1972–77, prodr/exec prodr Outside Bdcasts 1977–82 (incl exec prodr and dir BBC TV coverage of Royal Wedding 1981), head of resource planning 1982–86, head of ops and gen mangr film 1986–88, controller of prodn resources 1989–91, controller of prodn 1991–93; controller of prodn resources (TV, Radio, News and Current Affrs) BBC Resources 1993–; FRTS 1996; *Recreations* family, walking; *Style*— Michael Lumley, Esq; ✉ BBC Resources, Television Centre, Wood Lane, London W12 7RJ (☎ 0181 576 7818, fax 0181 576 7030)

LUMLEY, Richard Edward Walter; er s of Edward Lumley Lumley (d 1960), and Kathleen Agnew, *née* Wills (d 1978); respective fndrs of the Edward Lumley Hall at the RCS of England (opened by HM The Queen 1954), and of Kathleen Lumley Coll Univ of Adelaide S Aust (opened 1969); *b* 7 July 1923; *Educ* Eton; *m* 1953, Josephine Mary, da of Dr F Melville Harvey, MC (d 1935), of St Mary's Hosp Paddington and of Montevideo; 3 s (Edward d 1955, John, Christopher), 5 da (Sarah (m Hon Charles Martyn-Hemphill, *qv*), Caroline, Astrid, Emma, Susan); *Career* served Coldstream Gds WWII, Capt; underwriting memb of Lloyd's 1944–; Edward Lumley & Sons Ltd: dir 1951–88, chm and md 1960–80, chm 1980–85; chm Edward Lumley & Sons (underwriting agencies) Ltd 1971–88; dir: Edward Lumley Holdings Ltd 1974– (chm 1974–85), Lumley Corporation Ltd Aust 1974–89; patron RCS; memb: Br Aust Soc, Cook Soc (chm 1992); *Recreations* family pursuits, walking in the country, skiing; *Clubs* Boodle's, Cavalry & Guards', East India & Devonshire, MCC, Berkshire Golf, Windlesham Golf; *Style*— Richard Lumley, Esq; ✉ Roundwood, Sunninghill Rd, Windlesham, Surrey GU20 6PP (☎ 01276 472337); Edward Lumley Holdings Ltd, 99 Bishopsgate, London EC2M 3XD (☎ 0171 588 3188)

LUMLEY, Viscount; Richard Osbert Lumley; s and h of 12 Earl of Scarbrough, *qv*; *b* 18 May 1973; *Style*— Viscount Lumley

LUMLEY-SAVILE, Hon Henry Leoline Thornhill; s of 2 Baron Savile, KCVO (d 1931), and hp of bro, 3 Baron; *b* 2 Oct 1923; *Educ* Eton; *m* 1, 1946 (m dis 1951), Presiley June, da of Maj G H E Inchbald; 1 s; m 2, 1961, Caroline Jeffie (d 1970), da of Peter Clive; m 3, 1972, Margaret Ann, da of Edward Matthew Phillips, and wid of Peter Alexander Bruce; 3 s (triplets b 1975); *Career* served with Grenadier Gds (wounded), demobbed 1947; *Clubs* White's, Buck's, Cavalry and Guards'; *Style*— The Hon Henry Lumley-Savile

LUMSDEN, Prof Andrew Gino Sita; s of Edward Gilbert Sita-Lumsden (d 1974), and Stella Pirie Lumsden (d 1980); *b* 22 Jan 1947; *Educ* Kingswood Sch Bath, St Catharine's Coll Cambridge (scholar, Frank Smart Prize for zoology, BA), Yale Univ (Fulbright Scholar), Univ of London (PhD); *m* 21 Nov 1970 (m dis), Anne Farrington, da of Paul Donald Roberg (d 1996); 2 da (Ailsa b 6 Oct 1979, Isobel b 24 Aug 1981); *Career* Guy's Hosp Med Sch: jr lectr in anatomy 1970–73, lectr 1973–79, sr lectr 1979–87; prof of developmental neurobiology Univ of London 1989– (reader in craniofacial anatomy 1987–89); int research scholar Howard Hughes Med Inst 1993–, visiting prof Miller Inst Univ of California at Berkeley 1994; FRS 1994; *Recreations* natural history, mechanical engineering; *Style*— Prof Andrew Lumsden, FRS; ✉ 12 Java Wharf, Shad Thames, London SE1 2YH; Department of Developmental Neurobiology, United Medical and Dental Schools, Guy's Hospital, London SE1 9RT (☎ 0171 955 4413, fax 0171 955 4886)

LUMSDEN, Andrew Michael; s of Sir David Lumsden, *qv*, of Soham, Cambs, and Sheila, *née* Daniels; *b* 10 Nov 1962; *Educ* Winchester Coll (music scholar), RSAMD, St John's Coll Cambridge (organ scholar, MA); *Career* organist; chorister New Coll Oxford, asst to Dr George Guest St John's Coll Cambridge; asst organist Southwark Cathedral 1985–88, sub-organist Westminster Abbey 1988–92 (played for memorial services for Lord Olivier and Dame Peggy Ashcroft and 50th anniversary of Battle of Britain), organist and master of the choristers Lichfield Cathedral 1992–; reg broadcaster on BBC radio and television; performances incl: LPO, English Chamber Orch, Busoni's Doktor Faust ENO 1990, recitals at Sydney, San Francisco, Budapest, Harare; recordings labels incl: Argo, Hyperion, Chandos, Virgin Classics, Nimbus; Nat Young Organist of the Year 1985, winner Manchester Int Competition 1986; ARCO 1979; *Recreations* travel, wine, flying; *Style*— Andrew Lumsden, Esq; ✉ 11 The Close, Lichfield, Staffs WS13 7LD (☎ and fax 01543 263306)

LUMSDEN, Sir David James; kt (1985); s of Albert Lumsden (d 1985), and Vera, *née* Tate (d 1980); *b* 19 March 1928; *Educ* Univ of Cambridge (MA, MusB, PhD); *m* 1951, Sheila Gladys, da of George Daniels; 2 s (Stephen, Andrew, *qv*), 2 da (Jennifer, Jane); *Career* fell and organist New Coll Oxford 1959–76, princ Royal Scottish Acad of Music and Drama Glasgow 1976–82, Royal Acad of Music London 1982–93; fell King's Coll London 1990; hon fell: Selwyn Coll Cambridge 1986, New Coll Oxford 1996; Hon DLitt Univ of Reading 1991; Liveryman Worshipful Co of Musicians; *Recreations* hill walking, reading, friends; *Style*— Sir David Lumsden; ✉ Melton House, Soham, Cambridgeshire CB7 5DB (☎ 01353 720100, fax 01353 720918)

LUMSDEN, Edward Gabriel Marr; s of Edward Gabriel Lumsden, of Ferndown, Dorset, and Isobel, *née* Dyker; *b* 4 July 1946; *Educ* Hampton GS, Westminster Hotel Sch (Nat Dip in Hotelkeeping and Catering); *Career* area mangr Truman Taverns 1980–81, dir and gen mangr Arden Taverns 1981–83, tied trade dir Drybroughs of Scotland 1983–86, innkeeper dir Truman Ltd 1986, innkeeper ops dir Watney Co Reid & Truman 1986–88, innkeeper dir Watney Truman 1989–91, md TW Guest Trust Ltd 1991–95, conslt to hosptitality indust 1995–; memb MENSA; memb Réunion des Gastronomes; FHCIMA, FCFA, FRSH, FIMgt, FBII, FInstD; *Recreations* travel, gastronomy, vintage motor cars, the arts; *Clubs* 190 Queen's Gate, Shark Angling Club of GB, Rugby Club of London; *Style*— Edward Lumsden, Esq; ✉ 68 Welley Road, Wraysbury, Middlesex TW19 5EP (☎ 01784 481502)

LUMSDEN, Ian George; s of James Alexander Lumsden, MBE, of Bannachra, by Helensburgh, Dunbartonshire, and Sheila, *née* Cross; *b* 19 March 1951; *Educ* Rugby, Corpus Christi Coll Cambridge (BA), Univ of Edinburgh (LLB); *m* 22 April 1978, Mary Ann, da of Maj Dr John William Stewart Welbon, of Cornwall; 1 s (Richard b 1984), 2 da (Sarah b 1986, Louise b 1989); *Career* ptnr Maclay Murray and Spens 1980– (trainee and asst slr 1974–78), asst slr Slaughter and May London 1978–80; memb: Law Soc of Scotland, Royal Faculty of Procurators; *Recreations* golf, shooting; *Clubs* New (Edinburgh), Prestwick Golf; *Style*— Ian Lumsden, Esq; ✉ The Myretoun, Menstrie, Clackmannanshire FK11 7EB (☎ 01259 761453); Maclay Murray and Spens, 3 Glenfinlas St, Edinburgh EH3 6AQ (☎ 0131 226 5196, fax 0131 226 3174 and 0131 225 9610, telex 727238 VINDEX)

LUMSDEN, (George) Innes; s of George Lumsden, MM (d 1982), and Margaret Ann Frances, *née* Cockburn (d 1992); *b* 27 June 1926; *Educ* Banchory Acad, Univ of Aberdeen (BSc); *m* 16 July 1958, Sheila, da of George Thomson (d 1965); 2 s (Graham b 1959, Richard b 1961), 1 da (Gillian b 1964); *Career* Geological Survey GB: geologist 1949, dist geologist S Scotland 1970, asst dir and sr offr Scotland 1980; dir Br Geological Survey 1985–87 (dep dir 1982–85); chm Recruitment Bds Civil Serv Cmmn 1988–91, sec W Euro Geological Surveys Standing Gp on Environmental Geology 1988–92 (chm

1984–87), conslt geologist 1991–; chm Recruitment Bds MOD 1992–; memb: Cncl Mgmnt Macaulay Inst Soil Res 1980–87, Engrg and Sci Advsy Ctee Derby Coll Higher Educn 1983–87, Geological Museum Advsy Panel 1985–87; FRSE 1967, MIGeol 1982, CGeol, FGS 1990; *Books* Geology and the Environment in Western Europe (ed, 1992); numerous papers on geological topics in official Geological Survey pubns and sci jls; *Recreations* music, theatre, sport, gardening; *Style*— G Innes Lumsden, Esq, FRSE; ✉ 3 Barn Close, Cumnor Hill, Oxford OX2 9JP (☎ 01865 864203)

LUMSDEN, Prof Keith Grant; s of Robert Sclater Lumsden (d 1964), of Bathgate, and Elizabeth, *née* Brow (d 1990); *b* 7 Jan 1935; *Educ* The Academy Bathgate, Univ of Edinburgh (MA), Stanford Univ (PhD); *m* 21 July 1961, Jean Baillie, da of Capt Kenneth Macdonald, MC (d 1962), of Armadale; 1 s (Robert Alistair Macdonald b 1964); *Career* Stanford Univ: instr Dept of Econs 1960–63, assoc prof Graduate Sch of Business 1968–75 (asst prof 1964–67), prof of econs Advanced Mgmnt Coll 1971–; res assoc Stanford Res Inst 1965–71, visiting prof of econs Heriot-Watt Univ 1969, academic dir Sea Tport Exec Programme 1984–, currently affiliate prof of econs INSEAD France and dir Edinburgh Business Sch; dir: Stanford Univ Conf RREE 1968, Econ Educn Project 1969–74, Behavioral Res Laboratories 1970–72, Capital Preservation Fund Inc 1971–75, Nielsen Engineering Research Inc 1972–75, Hewlett-Packard Ltd 1981–92; memb: American Econ Assoc Ctee on Econ Educn 1978–81, Advsy Cncl David Hume Inst 1984–; numerous articles in professional jls, creator of various softwear systems; Henry Villard Award 1994; FRSE 1992; *Books* The Free Enterprise System (1963), The Gross National Product (1964), International Trade (1965), New Developments in the Teaching of Economics, 1967), Microeconomics - A Programmed Book (with R E Attiyeh and G L Bach, new edn 1981), Economics - A Distance Learning Study Programme (1991); *Recreations* tennis, deep sea sports, fishing; *Clubs* Waverley Lawn Tennis, Squash, and Sports, Dalmahoy Golf and Country, Tantallon Golf, New; *Style*— Prof Keith Lumsden, FRSE; ✉ 40 Lauder Road, Edinburgh EH9 1UE (☎ 0131 667 1612); Edinburgh Business School, Heriot-Watt University, Riccarton, Edinburgh EH14 4AS (☎ 0131 451 3090, fax 0131 451 3002)

LUMSDEN, Prof (William Hepburn) Russell; s of William Lumsden, MC (d 1926), of Darlington, Co Durham, and Margaret Hepburn Russell, *née* Brown (d 1970); *b* 27 March 1914; *Educ* Univ of Glasgow (BSc, MB ChB), Univ of Liverpool (DTM, DTH), Univ of Glasgow (DSc, MD); *m* Pamela Kathleen, da of Cecil William Bartram; 2 s (John b 27 April 1949, James William Russell b 18 Sept 1953), 1 da (Margaret Alice Russell b 23 Nov 1947 d 1985); *Career* MRC fell in tropical med Dept of Parasitology and Entomology Liverpool Sch of Tropical Med 1938–41; Malaria Field Labs RAMC 1941–46: successively Lt (Entomologist), Maj (Malariologist) and CO (Lt-Col), served Egypt, Palestine, Syria, Transjordan, N African Campaign, Italian Campaign and India; MRC sr fell in tropical med Dept of Entomology London Sch of Hygiene and Tropical Med 1946–47; Yellow Fever (subsequently E African Virus) Res Inst Entebbe Uganda 1947–57: successively entomologist, epidemiologist, asst dir; dir E African Trypanosomiasis Res Orgn Tororo Uganda 1957–63, lectr Dept of Bacteriology Univ of Edinburgh Med Sch 1963–65, sr lectr Dept of Animal Health and head Applied Protozoology Res Unit Royal (Dick) Sch of Vet Studies Univ of Edinburgh 1965–68, visiting prof Dept of Parasitology Sch of Hygiene Univ of Toronto Canada Jan-March 1968, prof of med protozoology London Sch of Hygiene and Tropical Med 1968–79, hon res fell Univ of Dundee 1979–81, sr res fell Univ of Edinburgh 1981–89; memb: WHO Expert Advsy Panel on Parasitic Diseases (Trypanosomiasis) 1962–84, Cncl RZS Scot 1967–68, Cncl Scottish Branch Inst of Biol 1968–69, Cncl Royal Soc of Tropical Med and Hygiene 1969–73 and 1974–77 (pres Edinburgh Branch 1967–69), Trypanosomiasis Panel Miny of Overseas Devpt 1973–79, WHO Int Malaria Eradication Review Teams (Bangladesh) 1978, (Nepal) 1979, (Sri Lanka) 1980; FRSTM&H 1939, FRZS Scot 1966, FInstBiol 1966, FRSE 1968, FRCPEd 1972; *Books* Techniques with Trypanosomes (1973), Biology of the Kinetoplastida (vol 1 1976, vol 2 1979), Advances in Parasitology (sr ed vols 16–20, 1978–82); author of over 140 papers in scientific jls and contribs to textbooks; editing sec History of the Berwickshire Naturalists' Club 1988–92; *Recreations* hill walking; *Clubs* Edinburgh Univ Staff; *Style*— Prof W H R Lumsden, FRSE; ✉ 16a Merchiston Crescent, Edinburgh EH10 5AX, Scotland (☎ 0131 229 2702)

LUMSDEN OF CUSHNIE, David Gordon Allen d'Aldecamb; Baron of Cushnie-Lumsden (Co of Aberdeen); s of Maj Henry Gordon Strange Lumsden, The Royal Scots (d 1969), of Nocton Hall, Lincs, and Sydney Mary Elliott (d 1985), of Tertain, Co Carlow; *b* 25 May 1933; *Educ* Seafield Park Devon, Allhallows Devon, Bedford Sch, Jesus Coll Cambridge (MA); *Career* London Scottish TA; exec Br American Tobacco 1959–82 (served Africa, India, E Europe and Far East); Garioch Pursuivant of Arms 1986; dir: Heritage Porcelain Ltd, Heritage Recordings Ltd; co fndr: Castles of Scotland Preservation Tst 1985, Scot Historic Organs Tst 1991; pres 1745 Assoc and Scot Military History Soc 1991, memb Cncl The Royal Stuart Soc; convenor Monarchist League of Scotland 1993; memb Lloyd's 1985; FSAS 1984; Knight of Malta Honour and Devotion 1980, Knight of Justice Sacred Military Constantinian Order of St George 1978; *Books* The Muster Roll of Prince Charles Edward's Army 1745–46 (contrib, 1984); *Recreations* shooting, polo, rowing, sailing, architectural history, Scottish history, heraldry; *Clubs* Royal Northern & University (Aberdeen), Beefsteaks (Sublime Society), Pitt (Cambridge), Hawks' (Cambridge), Leander, Hidalgos (Madrid), Puffin's (Edinburgh); *Style*— David Lumsden of Cushnie; ✉ Keithick House, Couper Angus, Blairgowrie, Perthshire PH13 9NF (☎ and fax 01828 670532)

LUMSDEN OF THAT ILK AND BLANERNE, Patrick Gillem Sandys; s of Colin Cren Sandys-Lumsdaine (d 1967), of Scotland, and Joyce Dorothy, *née* Leeson; formerly Patrick Gillem Sandys Lumsdaine of Innergellie but recognised as Chief of the Name and Arms of Lumsden by Interlocutor of the Lord Lyon King of Arms 27 March 1985; *b* 15 Oct 1938; *Educ* Charterhouse; *m* 1966, Beverley June, da of Capt Ralph Ernest Shorter (d 1982); 2 s (Cren Lumsden Yr of that Ilk b 1968, James Ralph, now Sandys Lumsdaine of Innergellie b 1976), 1 da (Amy Patricia b 1969); *Career* East India merchant; dir: George Williamson & Co Ltd 1977, George Williamson (Assam) Ltd 1978, Williamson Magor & Co Ltd 1982, Williamson Tea Holdings plc 1989; *Recreations* golf; *Clubs* Oriental, Tollygunge; *Style*— Lumsden of that Ilk and Blanerne; ✉ Stapeley House, Hoe Benham, Newbury, Berks RG20 8PX (☎ 01488 608700); George Williamson & Co Ltd, 5 West Mills, Newbury, Berks RG14 5HG (☎ 01635 522088, fax 01635 551992, telex 846513 ROGAM G)

LUNAN, Dr (Charles) Burnett; s of Andrew Burnett Lunan, of Dalguise, Perthshire, and Jean Clarke, *née* Orr; *b* 28 Sept 1941; *Educ* Glasgow HS, Univ of Glasgow (MB ChB, MD); *m* 6 March 1973, Helen Russell, da of John Ferrie (d 1963); 2 s (Robert Ferrie b 1977, Donald John b 1979), 1 da (Kirsteen Burnett b 1974); *Career* lectr in obstetrics and gynaecology Univ of Aberdeen 1973–75, sr lectr in obstetrics and gynaecology Univ of Nairobi Kenya 1975–77, conslt in obstetrics and gynaecology Royal Infirmary and Royal Maternity Hosp Glasgow 1977–, WHO conslt in maternal and child health Bangladesh 1984–85 and 1988–89; pres Royal Medico-Chirurgical Soc of Glasgow 1991–92 (treas 1982–90, vice pres 1990–91); FRCOG 1983 (MRCOG 1970), FRCS 1985; *Recreations* gardening, photography, hill walking; *Style*— Dr Burnett Lunan; ✉ 1 Moncrieff Ave, Lenzie, Glasgow (☎ 0141 776 3227); Royal Maternity Hospital, Rottenrow, Glasgow (☎ 0141 211 5400)

LUNCH, John; CBE (1975), VRD (1965); s of Percy Valentine Lunch (d 1974), and Amy, *née* Somerville (d 1960); *b* 11 Nov 1919; *Educ* Roborough Sch Eastbourne; *m* 1, 6 Nov 1943, Joyce Barbara (d 1989), da of Arnold Basil O'Connell Clerke (d 1959); 2 s (Anthony John b 1945, Michael Richard b 1948); m 2, 14 Oct 1995, Fiona Charis Elizabeth Fleck, da of Arthur Axel Miller, MC (d 1981), wid of Peter Hugo Fleck (d 1975); *Career* Lt Cdr RNR 1940–69 (ret), served WWII Crete, Malta convoys, N Africa, Sicily D-Day, Atlantic convoys; Col (TA) Engr and Tport Staff Corps RE 1971–94 (ret); in business in City 1946–48; asst md Tokenhouse Securities Corp Ltd 1947, dir several cos; Br Tport Cmmn 1948–61, road and rail tport and ancillary businesses; PLA: joined 1961, dir of finance, also dir of commerce 1966, asst dir-gen (responsible docks and harbour) 1969, dir-gen and bd memb 1971–76; chm: Comprehensive Shipping Gp 1973–75, Transcontinental Air Ltd 1973–75; cncl memb: ICAEW 1970–77, CIT 1973–76; RNLI: memb Ctee of Mgmnt 1977–94, vice-pres 1987–94, life vice-pres 1994–, pres Hayling Island Station 1978–88, fndr chm Manhood Branch 1976, hon art advsr 1981–; Freeman City of London; court memb Worshipful Co of Watermen 1976–; Malta GC Commemorative Medal 1942–92; FCA, FCIT, FCIM, CIMgt, FRSA, Hon FIFF (pres 1972–73); *Recreations* sailing, art, opera, horse racing; *Clubs* Army and Navy, Itchenor Sailing (life memb); *Style*— John Lunch, Esq, CBE, VRD; ✉ Martins, East Ashling, Chichester, W Sussex PO18 9AX (☎ 01243 575252); 97A York Mansions, Prince of Wales Drive, London SW11 4BN (☎ 0171 622 8100)

LUND, Anthony Marling; s of Lt-Gen Sir Otto Lund, KCB, DSO (d 1956), and Margaret Phyllis Frances, *née* Harrison; *b* 24 Sept 1929; *Educ* Eton; *m* 1 Sept 1967, Sophie, da of Count Soumarokoff-Elston (d 1970), of London; 2 da (Tatiana b 1969, Anna Maria b 1970); *Career* 2 Lt 11 Hussars (PAO) 1948–49; assoc: Kuhn Loeb and Co NY 1952–59, Int Fin Corp Washington DC 1958–61; vice pres then ptnr/md: Kuhn Loeb and Co, Lehman Bros Kuhn Loeb Inc, Shearson Lehman Bros; chief exec EBC Amro Bank Ltd 1986–89, sr advsr Norinchukin International Ltd 1989–95; *Clubs* White's; *Style*— Anthony Lund, Esq

LUND, Bryan; s of Capt Clifford Lund (d 1989), and Vera, *née* Miller (d 1975); *b* 15 April 1938; *Educ* Royal Liberty GS Havering Essex; *m* 18 April 1964, Diana, da of Ernest Wilshaw (d 1986); 2 s (Mark b 1965, Paul b 1968), 1 da (Deborah b 1975); *Career* articled CA Hill Vellacott and Co 1954–59, Peat Marwick Cassleton Elliott 1960–62, gp audit mangr Touche Ross 1963–67, fin dir Norcros plc subsidiaries 1967–73, Euro fin dir Morton Thiokol Incorporated Chicago 1973–82; gp fin dir: Borthwicks plc 1982–87, Wonderworld plc 1987–; mgmnt conslt; independent memb Herts Police Authy 1995–; Freeman: City of London 1982, Worshipful Co of CAs 1982, Worshipful Co of Butchers 1984; FCA 1960; *Recreations* golf, motoring, water-skiing; *Clubs* RAC, Northwood Golf, High Performance; *Style*— Bryan Lund, Esq; ✉ 5 Wellesley Avenue, Northwood, Middlesex HA6 3HZ (☎ 01923 824268, fax 01923 840699)

LUND, Dr Charles Ames; s of (Henry) Charles Lund (d 1980), of Bebington, Cheshire, and (Sophia) Violet Iris, *née* Ames (d 1976); *b* 18 Aug 1942; *Educ* Birkenhead Sch, Univ of Liverpool (MB ChB), Univ of Aberdeen (Dip Psychotherapy); *m* 14 Feb 1968, Pauline, da of Arthur Morris Hunter, of Ponteland, Newcastle upon Tyne; 2 da (Sonia b 1969, Kathryn b 1974); *Career* sr house offr and registrar in psychiatry Sefton Gen Hosp Liverpool 1968–71 (house offr 1967–68), sr registrar in psychiatry Royal Southern Hosp Liverpool 1971–72; Univ of Aberdeen: Rowntree fell in psychotherapy 1972–73, lectr Mental Health Dept 1973–78; conslt psychotherapist Newcastle upon Tyne 1978–, dir of Newcastle Psychotherapy Course 1984–89, examiner for Membership Examination of RCPsych 1990–95; author of pubns in psychotherapy trg and gp therapy; memb: Northern Assoc for Analytical Psychotherapy Scot Assoc of Psycholanalytical Psychotherapists; FRCPsych 1987 (MRCPsych 1972); *Recreations* walking, gardening; *Style*— Dr Charles Lund; ✉ 92 Errington Rd, Darras Hall, Ponteland, Newcastle upon Tyne NE20 9LA (☎ 01661 872018); Regional Department of Psychotherapy, Claremont House, Royal Victoria Infirmary, Off Framlington Place, Newcastle upon Tyne NE2 4AA (☎ 0191 232 5131)

LUND, Prof Raymond Douglas; s of Henry Douglas Lund, and Rose, *née* Morgan; *b* 10 Feb 1940; *Educ* Bablake Sch Coventry, UCL (Bucknill scholar, BSc, PhD); *m* 1963, Jennifer Sylvia, da of Meredith W Hawes; 2 s (Benjamin Isambard b 3 Jan 1971, Simon Meredith b 26 July 1974); *Career* asst lectr then lectr Dept of Anatomy UCL 1963–66, res asst anatomy Univ of Pennsylvania 1966–67, asst prof of anatomy Stanford Univ Calif 1967–68, asst prof then prof of anatomy and neurosurgery Univ of Washington 1968–79, prof and head Dept of Anatomy Med Univ of S Carolina 1979–83, prof and head Dept of Neurobiology, Anatomy and Cell Science Univ of Pittsburgh 1983–91, prof and head Dept of Anatomy Univ of Cambridge 1992–95, Duke-Elder prof of Ophthalmology Inst of Ophthalmology 1995–; memb: Soc for Neuroscience 1970–, Assoc for Res in Vision and Ophthalmology 1983–; Herrick award American Assoc of Anatomists, MERIT award NIH; fell Clare Coll Cambridge 1992–95; FRS; *Books* Development and Plasticity of the Brain (1978); *Recreations* chamber music (LRAM); *Style*— Prof Raymond Lund, FRS; ✉ Institute of Ophthalmology, 11–43 Bath Street, London EC1V 9EL (☎ 0171 608 6800, fax 0171 608 6881)

LUND, Prof Valerie Joan; da of George Andrew Lund, and Joan, *née* Henry (d 1984); *b* 9 May 1953; *Educ* Charing Cross Hosp Med Sch London (MB BS, MRCS LRCP), Univ of London (MS); *Career* hon conslt: Royal Nat Throat Nose and Ear Hosp 1987–, Moorfields Eye Hosp 1990–; Inst of Laryngology and Otology: lectr in rhinology 1986–87, sr lectr 1987–93, reader 1993–95, prof 1995–; memb working parties: Int Consensus in Sinusitis 1993, Int Consensus in Rhinitis 1993–94, RCSEd Guidelines in Endoscopic Nasal Surgery 1993, RCS Working Pty on Minimal Access Therapy 1993; asst ed Jl of Laryngology and Otology; memb Editorial Bd: Rhinology, American Jl of Rhinology, Acta Oto-Rhino-Laryngologica Belgica, American Jl of Otolaryngology; Downs surgical travelling fell RSM 1985; Euro Rhonoligic Soc Special Prize 1986, Lionel Colledge fell RCS 1986, Br Academic Conf in Otolaryngology Scientific Exhbn Award 1987, George Davey Howell Meml Prize 1990; McBride Lecture Edinburgh 1993; memb: BMA, RSM (memb Cncl Section of Laryngology and Rhinology 1992), Euro Rhinologic Soc (treas 1992), Head and Neck Oncologists of GB, Euro Acad of Facial and Plastic Surgery (vice pres UK 1993), Otorhinolaryngological Research Soc, Br Assoc of Otolaryngologists (NE Thames rep 1993), Euro Soc of Head and Neck Radiologists, Collegium ORLAS 1990, American Rhinologic Soc 1992, American Triologic Soc 1993; scientific fell Zoological Soc of London; FRCS 1982 (memb Cncl 1994), FRCSEd 1993; *Books* Clinical Rhinology (with A Maran, 1990), Tumours of the Upper Jaw (with D F N Harrison, 1993); also author of various book chapters; *Recreations* cooking and eating; *Style*— Prof Valerie Lund; ✉ Institute of Laryngology and Otology, 330 Gray's Inn Road, London WC1X 8DA (☎ 0171 915 1497, fax 0171 833 9480)

LUNGHI, Cherie Mary; da of Allessandro Lunghi (d 1989), of London, and Gladys Corbett Lee (d 1996); *b* 4 April 1952; *Educ* Arts Educn Trust London, Central Sch of Speech and Drama; former partner, Roland Joffé; 1 da (Nathalie-Kathleen Lunghi-Joffé b 26 Aug 1986); *Career* actress; *Theatre* Irena in The Three Sisters and Lisa in Owners (Newcastle) 1973–74, Kate Hardcastle in She Stoops to Conquer (Nottingham Playhouse) 1974, Laura in Teeth'n'Smiles (Royal Court) 1975, Holiday (Old Vic) 1987, Ruth in The Homecoming (Comedy Theatre) 1991; RSC 1976–80: Hero in Much Ado About Nothing, Perdita in The Winter's Tale, Cordelia in King Lear, Destiny, Bandits, Celia in As You Like It, Saratoga, Viola in Twelfth Night; *Television* incl: The Misanthrope (BBC) 1978, 'Tis Pity She's A Whore (BBC) 1979, The Manhood of Edward Robinson (Thames) 1981, The Praying Mantis (Channel 4) 1982, Desert of Lies (BBC) 1983, Huis Clos (BBC) 1984, Much Ado About Nothing (BBC) 1984, Letters From an Unknown Lover (Channel 4)

1985, The Monocled Mutineer (BBC) 1985, The Lady's Not For Burning (Thames) 1987, The Manageress (Channel 4) 1988 and 1989, Put on by Cunning (TVS) 1990, Covington Cross (Reeves Entertainment and ABC TV), The Buccaneers (BBC); TV mini series: Master of the Game (US) 1983, Ellis Island (US) 1984, The Man Who Lived at The Ritz (US) 1988, The Strauss Dynasty (Austria) 1990; *Radio* Alice in Wonderland (BBC) 1965, Hedvig in The Wild Duck (BBC) 1965; *Films* Excalibur 1980, King David 1984, The Mission 1985, To Kill A Priest 1987, Jack and Sarah 1995, Frankenstein 1995; *Recreations* drawing and painting, going to the cinema and theatre, reading, walking, mothering; *Style—* Miss Cherie Lunghi; ✉ Peters Fraser & Dunlop Ltd, 503 The Chambers, Chelsea Harbour, Lots Road, London SW10 0XF (☎ 0171 352 4446, fax 0171 352 7356)

LUNN, Rt Rev David Ramsay; *see:* Sheffield, Bishop of

LUNN, Jonathan William Peter; s of Cecil Peter Lunn, and Eileen, *née* Smith; *b* 14 June 1955; *Educ* St John's Sch Leatherhead, Univ of Hull (BA), London Comtemporary Dance Sch; *m* 1979 (m dis 1985); *Career* dancer: Mantis 1980, Siobhan Davies & Dancers 1981, London Contemporary Dance Theatre (LCDT) 1981–91; assoc dir LCDT; choreography for LCDT: Wild Life Dung 1986, Hang Up 1987, Bottom's Dream 1988, Shift 1988, Doppelgänger 1989, Goes Without Saying 1989, Beneath the Skin 1990, The Blue Door 1990; other choreography incl: Movimento Para Uma Tela (Ballet Gulbenkian Lisbon) 1988, Mosaic (BBC TV) 1990, The Soldier's Tale (Henley Festival) 1991, Modern Living (dir and choreographer) 1992, Under Milk Wood (Bristol Old Vic), Pericles (RNT) 1994, In Other Words (Dance Portland Maine) 1994, Metaphorically Speaking (4D) 1994; res choreographer Cross-Cultural Dance Resources Arizona; travel and res award Arts Cncl and Rodin Fund 1992, Time Out Dance Award (for Modern Living) 1993, HKK Award 1993, Olivier Award nomination for Best Choreography (for Pericles) 1995; *Style—* Jonathan Lunn, Esq; ✉ 17 Highbury Terrace, London N5 1UP (☎ 0171 354 5108)

LUNN, (George) Michael; s of John Lunn (d 1969), of Edinburgh, and May, *née* Hope (d 1971); *b* 22 July 1942; *Educ* Kelvinside Acad Glasgow, Univ of Glasgow (BSc), Heriot Watt Univ (Dip Brewing); *m* 27 Aug 1971, Jennifer, da of John Burgoyne, of Glasgow; 3 s (Stuart b 17 Jan 1974, Jamie b 27 July 1978, Alexander b 18 March 1981); 1 da (Victoria b 11 Jan 1976); *Career* Lt RNR 1956–66; chm and chief exec The Whyte & Mackay Group plc until 1995, dir Gallaher Ltd until 1995, chm Wm Muir Ltd until 1995; proprietor Michael Lunn Associates 1995–; former dir Cncl Scotch Whisky Assoc, currently chm Glasgow Devpt Agency; *Recreations* golf, sailing, tennis; *Clubs* IOD, R & A Golf, Glasgow Gailes Golf; *Style—* Michael Lunn, Esq; ✉ Michael Lunn Associates, Fairmount, 17 Ledcameroch Road, Bearsden, Glasgow G61 4AB (☎ 0141 931 5566, fax/data coms 0141 931 5577)

LUNNON, Raymond John; s of William John Lunnon (d 1960), of High Wycombe, and Eliza, *née* White (d 1981); *b* 31 Oct 1927; *Educ* Royal GS High Wycombe, Regent St Poly, Inst of Child Health Univ of London (MPhil); *m* 1953, Eileen Vera da of Conrad Charles Norman MacKinnon; 1 s (Adrian John MacKinnon b 10 Dec 1960), 1 da (Jane Melanie MacKinnon b 1 Sept 1957); *Career* RN: joined 1945, draughtsman 1947–48; mechanical and optical instrument draughtsman 1943–45, asst med photographer Inst of Ophthalmology Univ of London 1948–52, lectr in clinical photography Inst of Dermatology St John's Hosp for Diseases of the Skin 1960–66 (head of Med Photography Dept 1952–66), dir of med illustration and sr lectr Inst of Child Health Univ of London/The Hospitals for Sick Children Special Health Authy 1966–89, curator Museum and Archive Serv Hosps for Sick Children 1989–, freelance conslt in med and other fields of audio visual communication; author of various scientific articles; awarded combined Royal Med Coll's medal 1959, Lancet trophy 1961 and 1986, Silver medal BMA film competition 1972, Norman K Harrison Gold medal 1978; FRPS 1959, FBIPP 1967, hon fell Inst of Med Illustrators 1988 (assoc 1969), Hon FRPS 1989; OStJ 1987; *Recreations* painting, drawing, golf, St John Ambulance Bde (pres High Wycombe Div); *Style—* Raymond Lunnon, Esq; ✉ Museum & Archive Service, Great Ormond Street Hospital for Children NHS Trust, Great Ormond St, London WC1N 3JH (☎ 0171 405 9200)

LUNT, Maj-Gen James Doiran; CBE (1964, OBE 1958); s of Brig Walter Thomas Lunt, MBE (d 1977), of Camberley, Surrey, by his w Archilles Cameron, *née* Dodd (d 1975); *b* 13 Nov 1917; *Educ* King William's Coll IOM, RMC Sandhurst; *m* 1940, Muriel Jessie, da of Albert Henry Byrt, CBE, of Bournemouth (d 1964); 1 s, 1 da; *Career* 2 Lt Duke of Wellington's Regt 1937, transferred 16/5 Lancers 1949; served: Burma Rifles 1939–42, Arab Legion 1952–55, Fedn Regular Army Aden 1961–64, chief of staff Contingencies Planning SHAPE 1968–70, Vice-Adj-Gen MOD 1970, Maj-Gen, ret 1972; Col 16/5 Queen's Royal Lancers 1975–80; fell and domestic bursar Wadham Coll Oxford 1973–83 (emeritus fell 1983–); author; FRGS, FRHistS; Hon MA Oxon; Order of Independence (Jordan) 1956, Order of South Arabia (1965); *Books* incl: Charge to Glory (1961), From Sepoy to Subedar (1970), Imperial Sunset (1981), Glubb Pasha (1984), Hussein of Jordan (1989); *Recreations* writing, flyfishing; *Clubs* Cavalry and Guards', Flyfishers'; *Style—* Maj-Gen James Lunt, CBE; ✉ Hilltop House, Little Milton, Oxon OX44 7PU (☎ 01844 279242)

LUPU, Radu; s of Meyer Lupu, and Ana, *née* Gabor; *b* 30 Nov 1945; *Educ* High Sch Brasov Romania, Moscow Conservatoire; *Career* concert pianist; London debut 1969, Berlin debut 1971, USA debut NY 1972; first prize: Van Cliburn Competition 1966, Enescu Competition 1967, Leeds Competition 1969; *Recordings* incl: Beethoven Piano Concertos (with Zubin Mehta and the Israel Philharmonic Orch), Mozart Sonatas for Violin and Piano (with Szymon Goldberg), Brahms Piano Concerto No 1 (with Edo de Waart and the London Philharmonic Orch), Mozart Piano Concerto K467 (with Uri Segal and the Eng Chamber Orch), various Beethoven and Schubert Sonatas (incl B Flat Sonata D960, Grammy Award 1995), Mozart and Beethoven Wind Quintets in E Flat, Mozart Concerto for 2 Pianos and Concerto for 3 Pianos transcribed for 2 pianos (with Murray Perahia and the Eng Chamber Orch), Schubert Fantasie in F Minor and Mozart Sonata in D for 2 Pianos (with Murray Perahia), Schumann Kinderszenen, Kreisleriana and Humoresque (Edison Award 1996); *Recreations* chess, bridge, history; *Style—* Radu Lupu, Esq; ✉ c/o Terry Harrison Artists Management, The Orchard, Market Street, Charlbury, Oxon OX7 3PJ (☎ 01608 810330, fax 01608 811331)

LURY, Adam Thomas; s of Prof Dennis Albert Lury (d 1981), and Margaret Antoinette Goldie, of London; *b* 11 July 1956; *Educ* Simon Langton GS, St Catherine's Coll Oxford (MA); *partner,* Claire Crocker; *Career* account exec then account supervisor Wasey Campbell Ewald 1978–81; Boase Massimi Pollitt: planner 1981–84, appointed to Bd 1985, gp planning dir 1986–87; jt managing ptnr HHCL and Partners (formerly Howell Henry Chaldecott Lury) 1987–; MIPA 1990; *Recreations* sculpture, consumer culture, Madonna fan; *Style—* Adam Lury, Esq; ✉ HHCL and Partners, Kent House, 14–17 Market Place, Great Titchfield Street, London W1N 7AJ (☎ 0171 436 3333)

LUSBY, John Martin; s of William Henry Lusby (d 1990), of Hull, and Florence Mary, *née* Wharam; *b* 27 April 1943; *Educ* Marist Coll Hull, Ushaw Coll Durham; *m* 1966, Clare, da of John Gargan (d 1957), of York; 1 s (James b 3 Sept 1969), 1 da (Sophie b 30 July 1973); *Career* entered NHS 1961; jr appointments: De la Pole Hosp Hull 1961–66, County Hosp York 1966–67, Kettering Gen Hosp 1967–68; admin asst Utd Sheffield Hosps 1968–70, dep hosp sec E Birmingham Hosp 1970–72, hosp sec Pontefract Gen Infirmary and Headlands Hosp Pontefract 1972–74, area gen admin Kirklees AHA 1974–76; Merton, Sutton and Wandsworth AHA(T): asst dist admin (Patient Servs) 1976–79, dist admin Wandsworth and E Merton Dist 1979–81; area admin Doncaster AHA 1981; Doncaster Health Authy: dist admin 1981–84, dist gen mangr 1984–90, exec dir 1990; Lothian Health Bd: gen mangr 1990–95, exec dir 1991–95 (memb 1990–91); chm Independent Review Panel NHS Complaints Procedure Northern and Yorkshire Region NHS Exec 1996–; tstee: Dementia Servs Devpt Centre Univ of Stirling 1991–95, The Scottish Dementia Appeal Tst 1994–95; memb: Scottish Cncl for Postgrad Med and Dental Educn 1992–95, Health Servs and Public Health Res Ctee (Scottish Office Home and Health Dept Chief Scientist Orgn) 1993–94; MHSM (AHA 1972), DipHSM 1972; *Recreations* music, reading, walking; *Style—* John Lusby, Esq; ✉ Kirkstone, Crabtree Green, Collingham, Wetherby, West Yorkshire LS22 5AB (☎ 01937 572600)

LUSCOMBE, Prof David Edward; s of Edward Dominic Luscombe (d 1987), of London, and Nora, *née* Cowell (d 1995); *b* 22 July 1938; *Educ* Finchley Catholic GS, King's Coll Cambridge (BA, MA, PhD, LittD); *m* 20 Aug 1960, Megan, da of John Richard Phillips (d 1967); 3 s (Nicholas b 1962, Mark b 1964, Philip b 1968), 1 da (Amanda b 1970); *Career* fell King's Coll Cambridge 1962–64, fell, lectr and dir of studies in history Churchill Coll Cambridge 1964–72; Univ of Sheffield: prof of medieval history 1972–95, Leverhulme personal research prof of medieval history 1995–, head Dept of History 1973–76 and 1979–84, dean of Faculty of Arts 1985–87, pro vice chllr 1990–94, chm Humanities Research Inst 1992–, dir Humanities Div Grad Sch 1994–; visiting prof: Royal Soc of Canada 1991, Univ of Connecticut at Storrs 1993; Leverhulme visiting European fell 1973, visiting fell All Souls Coll Oxford 1994; auditor Div of Quality Audit HE Quality Cncl 1994–95; vice pres Société Int L'Etude de la Philosophie Médiévale 1987–, chm Medieval Texts Editorial Ctee 1991–; hon sec Cambridge Univ Catholic Assoc 1968–70; memb: Governing Body St Edmund's House Cambridge 1971–84, Ctee Ecclesiastical History Soc 1976–79, Cncl Royal Historical Soc 1981–85, Ctee Soc for the Study of Medieval Languages and Literature 1991–96, Jt Supervisory Ctee of Br Acad and OUP for New Dictionary of Nat Biography 1992–, Cwlth Scholarship Cmmn 1994–96, Cncl Worksop Coll and Ranby House 1996–; British Acad: Raleigh lectr 1988, memb Cncl 1989–, pubns sec 1990–, memb Humanities Research Bd 1994–96, exchange visitor to Japan Acad 1996; FRHistS 1970, FSA 1984, FBA 1986; *Books* The School of Peter Abelard (1969), Peter Abelard's Ethics (1971), David Knowles Remembered (jtly, 1991); co-ed: Church and Government in the Middle Ages (1976), Petrus Abaelardus 1079–1142 (1980), D Knowles, The Evolution of Medieval Thought (1988); Cambridge Studies in Medieval Life and Thought (advsy ed 1983–88, gen ed 1988–); *Recreations* exercising a spaniel, using libraries, cricket, swimming; *Style—* Prof David Luscombe, FBA; ✉ Department of History, The University, Sheffield S10 2TN (☎ 0114 222 2559, fax 0114 278 8304, telex 547216 UGSHEF G)

LUSCOMBE, Rt Rev Lawrence Edward; s of Reginald John Luscombe (d 1970), and Winifred Luscombe; *b* 10 Nov 1924; *Educ* Kelham Theol Coll, King's Coll London, Univ of Dundee (MA, MPhil, PhD); *m* 1946, Dr Doris Carswell (d 1992), da of Andrew Morgan; 1 da; *Career* served WW II Indian Army, India and Burma (Maj); formerly chartered accountant, ptnr Watson Galbraith CAs Glasgow 1952–63; ordained: deacon 1963, priest 1964; rector St Barnabas Paisley 1966–71, provost of St Paul's Cathedral Dundee 1971–75, bishop of Brechin 1975–90; hon canon Trinity Cathedral Davenport Iowa 1983–; Primus of the Scottish Episcopal Church 1985–90; memb: Educn Ctee Renfrew CC 1967–71, Court Corp of the Sons of the Clergy 1985–, Tayside Regnl Health Bd 1989–93; chm: Edinburgh Theol Coll 1985–90, Governing Body Glenalmond Coll 1987–94; govr: Dundee Coll of Educn 1982–87, Lathallan Sch 1982–; CStJ; Hon LLD Univ of Dundee, Hon DLitt Geneva Theol Coll; hon res fell Univ of Dundee 1993–; FRSA, FSA (Scot); *Style—* The Rt Rev Lawrence Luscombe; ✉ Woodville, Kirkton of Tealing, by Dundee DD4 0RD (☎ 01382 380331)

LUSH, Christopher Duncan; CMG (1983); s of Eric Duncan Thomas Lush (d 1980), and Iris Lush (d 1988); *Educ* Sedbergh, Magdalen Coll Oxford (MA); *m* 1967, Marguerite Lilian, da of Frederick William Bolden (d 1975); *Career* barr 1953–59; asst legal advsr FO 1959–62, legal advsr then dep political advsr West Berlin 1962–66, first sec FO (later FCO) 1966–69, Amman 1969–71, cnsllr FCO 1971–73, Canadian Nat Def Coll 1973–74, Paris 1974–78, Vienna 1978–82, ambass to Cncl of Europe Strasbourg 1983–86, memb Euro Campaign for North South Awareness 1986–88, memb War Crimes Inquiry 1988; govr Br Inst of Human Rights 1988; fndr ed Human Rights Case Digest (1990); *Publications* The Relationship Between Berlin and the Federal Republic of Germany (International and Comparative Law Quarterly, 1965); *Clubs* Travellers'; *Style—* Christopher Lush, Esq, CMG; ✉ c/o Travellers' Club, 106 Pall Mall, London SW1Y 5EP

LUSH, David Michael; OBE (1992); s of Hyman Lush (d 1979), of London, and Bessie, *née* Tabor (d 1989); *b* 6 Feb 1931; *Educ* Poly Secdy Sch (Quintin Sch), Univ of London (BSc (Eng)); *m* 29 March 1962, Brenda Straus, da of Bernard Pappe (d 1946); 1 s (Dean Anthony b 18 Sept 1964); *Career* conslt electrical engr; Nat Serv RAOC 1950–51; graduate trainee Micanite and Insulators Co Ltd 1956–58, sr project engr Heating Investments Ltd 1958–60, sr sales engr then asst branch mangr (London and SE Regnl Office) Satchwell Control Systems Ltd 1961–69; Arup Associates/now Ove Arup and Partners: joined as specialist engr on M & E design problems 1970–71, tech dir Arup Research & Development 1971–93, dir Ove Arup and Partners 1993–94, conslt 1994–; external examiner BSc (Building Servs Engrg Degree) UMIST 1986–89, specialist advsr to House of Commons Environment Ctee (Indoor Pollution Enquiry) 1990–91; CIBSE: memb Cncl and Exec Bd, chm Technol Bd 1984–90, memb Chm's Ctee 1993, pres CIBSE 1993–94; chm: Four Professions' (comprising CIBSE, CIOB, RIBA, RICS) Energy Gp (now CIC Environment Ctee) 1987–90, CIC Task Gp on Environmental Issues 1991–92, CIRIA Environmental Forum Steering Gp (for Environmental Issues in Construction Study) 1991–92, BS7750 (Environmental Mgmnt Systems) Pilot Task Gp for Construction Indust 1992–93, CIC Regulations Advsy Panel 1995–; memb Advsy Ctee UKAS 1996–; memb Cncl: BSRIA 1990–, ERA 1990–96; memb Senate Engrg Cncl 1996–; author of numerous articles in learned jls, contrib various pubns and speaker at confs worldwide; CEng, MIEE 1969, FCIBSE 1985 (MCIBSE 1970), MACE 1993; *Recreations* bowls, bridge, family history, gardening, reading and travelling; *Style—* David Lush, Esq, OBE; ✉ c/o Engineering Council, 10 Maltravers Street, London WC2R 3ER

LUSH, Denzil Anton; s of Dennis John Lush, and Hazel June, *née* Fishenden (d 1979); *b* 18 July 1951; *Educ* Devonport HS Plymouth, UCL (BA, MA), Coll of Law Guildford, CCC Cambridge (LLM); *Career* admitted slr England and Wales 1978, slr and NP Scotland 1993; ptnr Anstey Sargent & Probert Slrs Exeter 1985–95, master Ct of Protection 1996–; former memb: Mental Health and Disability Ctee Law Soc, Steering Gp on Advance Directives BMA; pt/t chm Social Security Appeals Tbnls 1994–96; *Books* Cohabitation and Co-Ownership Precedents (1993), Elderly Clients - A Precedent Manual (1996), Enduring Powers of Attorney (4 edn, 1996); contrib: Encyclopaedia of Forms and Precedents Vols 26 (Minors) and 31 (Powers of Attorney), Atkin's Court Forms Vol 26 (Mental Health); *Recreations* supporting Plymouth Argyle FC and Somerset CCC; *Style—* Denzil Lush, Esq; ✉ Court of Protection, Stewart House, 24 Kingsway, London WC2B 6JX (☎ 0171 269 7300, fax 0171 404 1725, DX number DX 37965 Kingsway)

LUSH, Peter Maurice; s of Bernard Simeon Lush, of Middleton-on-Sea, Sussex, and Judy Adele, *née* Markham; *b* 19 April 1939; *Educ* Brighton Coll; *m* 1 (m dis), Cynthia, *née* Leslie-Bredée; m 2 (m dis), Peggy, *née* Gough; m 3, 3 Oct 1964, Lyn, da of Eyre Fitzgerald Massy (d 1970); 1 s (Jonathan Charles b 11 July 1966), 1 da (Amanda Lyn Geraldine b 18 Aug 1967); *Career* account dir Ogilvy & Mather advtg agency 1958–72, jt md Knight Keeley Ltd 1972–74, conslt TCCB 1988– (PR and mktg mangr 1974–87);

formed Peter Lush Ltd (PML) sports sponsorship and mktg conslts 1988; England cricket tour mangr: B team to Sri Lanka 1986, Aust (Ashes retained) 1986–87, World Cup in India and Pakistan 1987, Pakistan 1987, NZ 1988; Nehru Cup 1988, WI 1990, Aust and NZ 1990–91, Sussex jr squash champion 1957; *Recreations* cricket, golf; *Clubs* MCC, Old Brightonians, Sonning Golf; *Style—* Peter Lush, Esq; ✉ Dunmore, Holmemoor Dr, Sonning, Reading, Berks RG4 OTE (☎ 0118 969 3735, fax 0118 969 3202); TCCB, Lord's Cricket Ground, London NW8 8QZ (☎ 0171 286 4405, fax 0171 289 5619, telex 24462 TCCB G)

LUSHINGTON, Sir John Richard Castleman; 8 Bt (GB 1791), of South Hill Park, Berkshire; s of Sir Henry Edmund Castleman Lushington, 7 Bt (d 1988), and Pamela Elizabeth Daphne, *née* Hunter; *b* 28 Aug 1938; *Educ* Oundle; *m* 21 May 1966, Bridget Gillian Margaret, o da of late Col John Foster Longfield, of Knockbeg, Saunton, N Devon; 3 s (Richard Douglas Longfield b 1968, Greville Edmund Longfield b 1969, Thomas Robert Longfield b 1975); *Heir* s, Richard Douglas Longfield Lushington b 29 March 1968; *Career* mgmnt trg consult, ptnr MaST (Eastern), a memb of the MaST Orgn; Liveryman Worshipful Co of Grocers; *Style—* Sir John Lushington, Bt; ✉ The Glebe House, Henham, Bishop's Stortford, Herts

LUSIS, HE Janis (John); s of Arnolds Lusis (d 1993), and Lidija, *née* Liepins; *b* 2 June 1945; *Educ* Bloor Collegiate Inst Toronto, Univ of Toronto (BASc, MASc); *m* 1969, Mara, da of Aleksandrs Gugans; *Career* res and manufacturing positions to engrg and planning supt Canadian Industries Ltd 1972–84, dir Canadian ops Swift/Reichold Canada Ltd 1984–86, cnsllr legation of Latvia to Washington DC 1986–91, dir Admin Dept Miny of Foreign Affairs Riga 1992, Latvian ambass to the Ct of St James's 1992– (concurrently to Ireland 1993–); *Style—* HE Mr Janis Lusis; ✉ Embassy of Latvia, 45 Nottingham Place, London W1M 3FE (☎ 0171 312 0040, fax 0171 312 0042)

LUSTBADER, Eric Van; s of Melvin Harry Lustbader, of NYC, and Ruth, *née* Aaronson (d 1980); *b* 24 Dec 1946; *Educ* Stuyvesant HS NYC, Columbia Univ NYC; *Career* author 1979–; album ed/featured columnist Cash Box magazine USA 1969–72, asst to Pres/Dir of Int A&R Elektra Records USA 1972–74, dir of creative servs Dick James Music USA 1974–76, mangr of creative servs CBS Records 1977–79; *Books* The Sunset Warrior (1976), Doubleday/Berkley/Fawcett - Shallows of Night (1977), Dai-San (1978), Beneath an Opal Moon (1979), The Ninja (1980), Sirens (1982), Black Heart (1983), The Miko (1985), Jian (1986), Shan (1987), Zero (1988), French Kiss (1989), White Ninja (1990), Angel Eyes (1991), Black Blade (1992), The Kaisho (1993), Floating City (1994), Batman: the Last Angel (1994), Second Skin (1995), The Devil on Myrtle Ave (1995), The Immortal Unicorn (short story collection, 1995), The Singing Tree, David Copperfield's Tales of Illusion (short story collection, 1995), Dark Homecoming (1996), 16 mins, David Copperfields's Tales of the Impossible (short story collection, 1996); *Recreations* landscaping, pruning Japanese Maples; *Style—* Eric Van Lustbader, Esq; ✉ c/o Henry Morrison Inc, PO Box 235, Bedford Hills, NY 10507, USA (☎ 00 1 914 666 3600)

LUSTIG, Lawrence Barry; s of Ralph Lustig, of London, and Shelia Jeanette, *née* Bloom; *b* 17 Sept 1956; *Educ* Chingford HS; *m* 29 June 1984, Carol Ann, da of Ronald William Corless; 2 s (Joe Lawrence b 2 June 1988, Jack Ryan b 8 June 1992), 1 da (Laura Elizebeth b 20 March 1986); *Career* trainee photographer SKR Photos Int 1972–74, photographer Sporting Pictures UK 1974–79, freelance photographer 1980–86, staff photographer Daily Star 1986–; major sporting events covered incl World Cup football and World title boxing contests; Colour Sports Photographer of the Year 1990, Sports Picture of the Year from Royal Photographic Soc and Sports Cncl 1990; sports photographic awards from: Kodak, Ilford, BT, Fuji; memb: NUJ, Assoc of Int Press Sportees, Sports Writers' Assoc; fndr memb Fleet Street Sports Photographers' Assoc; *Recreations* football and boxing (non-participating); *Style—* Lawrence Lustig, Esq; ✉ The Daily Star, Express Newspapers, 245 Blackfriars Bridge Rd, London SE1 (☎ 0171 928 8000, car 0831 237 035)

LUSTIG, Robin Francis; s of Fritz Lustig, and Susan, *née* Cohn; *b* 30 Aug 1948; *Educ* Stoneham Sch Reading, Univ of Sussex (BA); *m* 24 Feb 1980, Ruth, da of Dr W B Kelsey (d 1986), of London; 1 s (Joshua b 1982), 1 da (Hannah b 1985); *Career* journalist; Reuters: Madrid 1971–72, Paris 1972–73, Rome 1973–77; The Observer: news ed 1981–83, Middle East corr 1985–87, asst ed 1988–89; journalist and broadcaster 1989–, presenter The World Tonight (BBC Radio 4); *Books* Siege: Six Days at the Iranian Embassy (jtly, 1980); *Recreations* reading newspapers, children; *Style—* Robin Lustig, Esq; ✉ 124 Dukes Ave, London N10 2QB (☎ 0181 883 3144)

LUTTRELL, Col Sir (Geoffrey) Walter Fownes; KCVO (1993), MC (1945), JP (Somerset 1961); s of Geoffrey Luttrell (d 1957), of Dunster Castle (which until recently had been in the Luttrell family's possession from 1375), and Alys, da of Rear Adm Walter Bridges, of Trewalla, Victoria, Aust; *b* 2 Oct 1919; *Educ* Eton, Exeter Coll Oxford; *m* 1942, Hermione Hamilton, da of late Capt Cecil Gunston, MC (er bro of Sir Derrick Gunston, 1 Bt), and Lady Doris Hamilton-Temple-Blackwood, da of 2 Marquess of Dufferin and Ava; *Career* served with: 15/19 King's Royal Hussars 1940–46, N Somerset Yeo 1952, Lt-Col 1955, Col 1987; Somerset: DL 1958, High Sheriff 1960, Vice Lord Lt 1968–78, Lord Lt 1978–94; memb Nat Parks Cmmn 1962–66, liaison offr Miny of Agric 1965–71; memb: SW Electricity Bd 1969–78, Wessex Regnl Ctee Nat Tst 1970–85; regnl dir Lloyds Bank 1972–83, memb University Grants Cmmn 1973–76, pres Royal Bath and West Show Soc 1982–83; Hon Col: 6 Bn Light Infantry 1977–87, Somerset ACF 1982–89; KStJ 1978; *Recreations* fishing, gardening; *Clubs* Cavalry and Guards'; *Style—* Col Sir Walter Luttrell, KCVO, MC, JP; ✉ Court House, East Quantoxhead, Bridgwater, Somerset TA5 1EJ (☎ 01278 741242)

LUTYENS, Mary; da of Sir Edwin Lutyens, OM, KCIE, PRA, the architect, and Lady Emily Lytton; sis of late Elisabeth Lutyens, the composer, and aunt of 4 Viscount Ridley, KG, *qv* and late Lord Ridley of Liddesdale (formerly Rt Hon Nicholas Ridley, MP); *b* 31 July 1908; *Educ* Queen's Coll London and abroad; *m* 1, 1930 (m dis 1945), Anthony Sewell (decd); 1 da (Amanda, b 1935, m John Pallant); m 2, 1945, Joseph Gluckstein Links, OBE, s of Calman Links; *Career* writer of fiction and of works on the Lyttons, Ruskin, Venice and Krishnamurti; FRSL; *Style—* Miss Mary Lutyens, FRSL; ✉ 8 Elizabeth Close, Randolph Avenue, London W9 1BN (☎ 0171 286 6674)

LUX, (Leslie) Brian; s of Sol Lux (d 1973), of London, and Marie, *née* Risch (d 1991); *b* 14 June 1932; *Educ* Bemrose GS Derby, Perse Sch Cambridge, Guy's Hosp Dental Sch London (LDSRCS, Boxing blue, London Hosps/Univ light welter champion); *m* 1; 1 s (Peregrine b 2 Feb 1960), 1 da (Naomi b 6 Oct 1962); m 2, 1989, Evelyn Gale, da of Micky Mosseley; *Career* RAF dentist 1957–59, asst dentist Huddersfield 1959–60, ptnr in dental practice Hale 1960–65, sole practitioner 1965–; memb GDC 1977–; monthly columnist The General Dental Practitioner; memb: Gen Dental Practitioners Assoc 1960 (past sec, chm and pres), American Dental Assoc 1988, Br Dental Implant Assoc 1990; *Recreations* sailing (own yacht), boxing (qualified ABA coach, fndr memb Sale West Amateur Boxing Club), writing (several articles and short stories published); *Clubs* Royal Welsh Yachting, RAF; *Style—* Brian Lux, Esq; ✉ 185 Hale Road, Hale, Altrincham, Cheshire WA15 8DG (☎ 0161 980 7485)

LUX, Jonathan Sidney; s of Martin Lux (d 1995), of Highgate, London, and Ruth, *née* Swager (d 1983); *b* 30 Oct 1951; *Educ* Abbotsholme Sch Rocester Staffs, Univ of Nottingham (LLB), Université d' Aix-Marseille; *m* 3 Sept 1979, Simone, da of Shalom Itah, of Israel; 1 s (Adam b 14 Jan 1986), 2 da (Ruth b 24 April 1981, Danielle b 24 Sept 1983); *Career* admitted slr 1977; ptnr Ince & Co 1983– (asst slr 1977–83), admitted slr Hong Kong 1986; speaker at various maritime law confs and author of various articles 1983–; supporting memb London Maritime Arbitrators' Assoc; memb Int Bar Assoc (chm Ctee A - Maritime and Tport Law), chm Ctee 2 Human Rights Inst; Freeman of City of London, Liveryman of Worshipful Co of Solicitors; memb Law Soc 1977, FCIArb, accredited mediator; *Books* The Law on Tug, Tow and Pilotage (jtly, 1982), The Law and Practice of Marine Insurance and Average (jtly, 1987), Classification Societies (1993), Bunkers (jtly, 1994); *Recreations* single seater motor racing (holder of RAC nat racing licence); *Style—* Jonathan Lux, Esq; ✉ Ince & Co, Knollys House, 11 Byward St, London EC3R 5EN (☎ 0171 623 2011, fax 0171 623 3225, telex 8955043 INCES G)

LUXMOORE, Rt Rev Christopher Charles; s of Rev William Cyril Luxmoore (d 1967), and Constance Evelyn, *née* Shoesmith (d 1979); *b* 9 April 1926; *Educ* Sedbergh, Trinity Coll Cambridge, Chichester Theological Coll; *m* 12 April 1955, Judith, da of Canon Verney Lovett Johnstone (d 1948); 4 s (Nicholas b 1956, Jonathan b 1957, Paul b 1960, Benedict b 1963), 1 da (Ruth b 1969); *Career* served Army (The Green Howards) 1944–47, ADC to GOC-in-C Bengal and Assam 1946–47; ordained deacon 1952, ordained priest 1953, asst curate St John the Baptist Newcastle upon Tyne 1952–55, vicar Newsham Blyth 1955–58, rector Sangre Grande Trinidad 1958–66, vicar Headingley Leeds 1967–81, memb Gen Synod C of E 1975–81, hon canon Ripon 1981, canon residentiary of Chichester Cathedral 1981–84, bishop of Bermuda and dean of Bermuda Cathedral 1984–89, archdeacon of Lewes and Hastings 1989–91; provost Southern Div Woodard Corporation 1989–96; asst Bishop of Chichester 1991–, canon emeritus Chichester Cathedral 1991–; *Recreations* opera, church history; *Style—* The Rt Rev Christopher Luxmoore; ✉ 42 Willowbed Drive, Chichester, W Sussex PO19 2JB (☎ 01243 784680)

LUXMOORE, Michael John; s of Edmund Luxmoore, of Staindrop Hall, Staindrop, Darlington, and Diana Jean, *née* Coote; *b* 5 April 1948; *Educ* Harrow, Trinity Coll Cambridge (MA); *m* 1, 28 April 1973 (m dis), Margaret Rosemary, da of late Surg Cdr John Graham More Nisbett, of The Drum, Gilmerton, Edinburgh; 2 s (Andrew b 1976, Jamie b 1979); m 2, 3 Dec 1988, Ann Dalrymple-Smith; *Career* admitted slr 1984; under sheriff County of Durham; dir Middleton Hall Ltd 1984–; *Recreations* fell running; *Clubs* Swaledale Outdoor; *Style—* Michael Luxmoore, Esq; ✉ High Bank Hse, Fremington, Richmond, N Yorks DL11 6AS (☎ 01748 884361)

LYALL, Eric; CBE; s of late Alfred John Lyall, of Essex, and Alice Amelia, *née* Jackson (d 1982); *b* 12 May 1924; *Educ* Chigwell Sch, King's Coll Cambridge; *m* 1952, Joyce, da of late Sydney Edward Smith; 1 s (Alexander); *Career* formerly: slr/ptnr Slaughter and May, dir Guinness Mahon; chm: AMP (UK) plc until 1994, Pearl Group plc until 1994, Rocla GB Ltd, Clarke Nickolls & Coombs plc until 1996; dir: AMP Asset Management plc until 1994, Lockton Developments plc until 1995; chm Letchworth Garden City Corporation (now Letchworth Garden City Heritage Fndn) until 1995; gen cmmr of income tax; *Recreations* stamp collecting, golf, medieval history; *Clubs* Oriental, City of London, MCC; *Style—* Eric Lyall, Esq, CBE; ✉ Riders Grove, Old Hall Green, Ware, Herts SG11 1DN (☎ 01920 821370)

LYALL, Dr Fiona Jane; MBE (1995), DL (Kincardine 1983); da of James Fraser (d 1984), and Christina Forbes (d 1983); *b* 13 April 1931; *Educ* Univ of Aberdeen (MB ChB, DPH); *m* 20 July 1957, Alan Richards Lyall, s of Alexander Lyall (d 1974); 1 s (Peter James Fraser b 9 Oct 1961), 1 da (Elizabeth Grace Hermione b 18 Oct 1958); *Career* GP Laurencekirk 1959–, dir Grampian TV plc 1980–; borough cncllr Laurencekirk, co cncllr Kincardineshire, regnl cncllr Grampian; *Recreations* skiing, provincial silver; *Style—* Dr Fiona Lyall, MBE, DL; ✉ Melrose Bank, Laurencekirk, Kincardineshire AB30 1AL (☎ 01561 377220)

LYALL, Gavin Tudor; s of Joseph Tudor Lyall, and Agnes Ann, *née* Hodgkiss (d 1989); *b* 9 May 1932; *Educ* King Edward VI Sch Birmingham, Pembroke Coll Cambridge (BA, MA); *m* 4 Jan 1958, Katharine Elizabeth Whitehorn, *qv*, da of Alan Drummond Whitehorn, MA (d 1980); 2 s (Bernard b 1964, John b 1967); *Career* author; RAF pilot 1951–53; journalist until 1963 (Picture Post, BBC TV, Sunday Times); chm Crime Writers' Assoc 1966–67; memb Air Tport Users' Ctee 1979–85 (hon conslt 1985–); author; *Books* 12 thriller/espionage titles, incl: The Secret Servant (1980), The Conduct of Major Maxim (1982), The Crocus List (1985), Uncle Target (1988), Spy's Honour (1993), Flight from Honour (1996); *Recreations* model making, cartooning; *Clubs* RAF, Detection; *Style—* Gavin Lyall, Esq; ✉ 14 Provost Road, London NW3 4ST (☎ 0171 722 2308)

LYALL, Michael Hodge; s of Alexander Burt Lyall, of Glenrothes, and Isabella Campbell, *née* Paterson; *b* 5 Dec 1941; *Educ* Buckhaven HS, Univ of St Andrews (MB ChB), Univ of Dundee (ChM); *m* 25 Dec 1965, Catherine Barnett, da of James Thomson Jarvie (d 1986), of Leven; 3 s (Grant Alexander b 18 Oct 1966, Stuart James Jarvie b 24 Jan 1968, Ewan Mark Stephen b 28 July 1969); *Career* conslt surgn Tayside Health Bd 1975–, hon sr lectr Univ of Dundee 1975–; fell Assoc of Surgns of GB and I; FRCS 1970; *Recreations* reading, rotary; *Clubs* Rotary of North Fife, Moynihan Chirurgical; *Style—* Michael Lyall, Esq; ✉ 26 Linden Avenue, Newport on Tay, Fife DD6 8DU (☎ 01382 543419); Ninewells Hospital & Medical School, Dundee (☎ 01382 60111)

LYALL GRANT, Maj-Gen Ian Hallam; MC (1944); s of Col Henry Frederick Lyall Grant, DSO (d 1958), of Aberdeen, and Ellinor Lucy Hardy (d 1951), of Cork; *b* 4 June 1915; *Educ* Cheltenham, RMA Woolwich, Gonville and Caius Coll Cambridge (MA); *m* 1951, Mary Jennifer, da of Norman Moore (d 1980); 1 s (Mark), 2 da (Sarah, Charlotte); *Career* cmmnd RE 1935, seconded Bengal Sappers and Miners 1938–46, served WWII 17 Indian Div Burma 1942–44, cmd 9 Para Sqdn 1951–52, cmd 131 AB Engr Regt 1955–56, DS JSSC 1957–58, Brig A/Q Aden 1962–64, Cmdt RSME 1965–67, Maj-Gen 1967, DQMG MOD 1967–70, ret 1970; Civil Serv DG Supply Co-ordination 1970–75; Col Cmdt RE 1972–77; chm Burma Campaign Fellowship Gp 1991–96; *Books* Burma: The Turning Point (1993); *Recreations* author-publisher, fishing, gemmology, travel, bridge; *Clubs* Naval and Military; *Style—* Maj-Gen Ian Lyall Grant, MC; ✉ 6 St Martin's Square, Chichester PO19 1NT

LYBURN, Andrew Usherwood (Drew); OBE (1995); s of Andrew Lyburn (d 1969), of Edinburgh, and Margaret Scott Glass (d 1988); *b* 16 Aug 1928; *Educ* Melville Coll, Univ of Edinburgh (MA); *m* 25 July 1958, Joan Ann (d 1994), da of Eric Stevenson (d 1975), of Edinburgh; 3 s (Andrew b 1960, Colin b 1962, Iain b 1967), 1 da (Fiona b 1974); *Career* RAF Flying Offr Cyprus 1954–56; actuary; Scottish Widows Fund 1949–54 and 1956–57, Confed Life Toronto 1957–59; Standard Life: Montreal 1959–65, Edinburgh 1965–91; consulting actuary to Scottish Transport Group 1970–; chm Cairn Petroleum Oil and Gas Ltd 1987–88, dir Dreamstar Properties Ltd 1989–94, conslt The Melrose Partnerships 1992–; chm Melville Coll Tst 1983–86; dir: Edinburgh Telford Coll 1992–95, The Royal Blind Asylum 1992–; vice pres Faculty of Actuaries 1987–91; memb: Occupational Pensions Bd 1982–, Cncl of St Dunstan's 1994–; FFA 1957, ASA (USA 1957), FCIA (Canada) 1965, FPMI 1976; *Recreations* bridge, golf, gardening, rugby, squash, hill walking; *Clubs* Bruntsfield Links Golfing Soc (Edinburgh), RAF; *Style—* Drew Lyburn, Esq, OBE; ✉ 4 Cumlodden Ave, Edinburgh EH12 6DR (☎ 0131 337 7580)

LYCETT, Andrew Michael Duncan; s of Peter Norman Lycett (d 1979), and Joanna Mary, *née* Day; *b* 5 Dec 1948; *Educ* Charterhouse, ChCh Oxford (MA); *m* 1981 (m dis 1989), Rita Diana Robinson; *Career* journalist and author; assoc ed New African, contrib ed GQ, contrib to The Times and other newspapers and magazines; FRGS; *Books* Gaddafi and The Libyan Revolution (with David Blundy, 1987), Ian Fleming (1995); *Recreations* travel, reading, cricket; *Clubs* RAC; *Style—* Andrew Lycett, Esq; ✉ c/o The

Times, 1 Pennington St, London E1 9XN; (home ☎ and fax 0171 328 4552, e-mail alycett@delphi.com)

LYCETT, Christopher Ronald (Chris); s of Eric Laybourn Lycett, MBE (d 1974), of the Isle of Man, and Thelma, *née* George (d 1987); *b* 3 Dec 1946; *Educ* Archbishop Tenison's GS Croydon, Ramsey GS IOM; *m* 6 June 1970, Anne, da of Richard Charles Frank Geary; 2 s (Daniel Christopher Laybourn b 15 March 1971, Nicholas Richard Charles Geary (Charlie) b 23 Dec 1981), 1 da (Sarah Anne Marie b 30 April 1974); *Career* BBC Radio 1: studio engr responsible for sight and sound simulcasts, prodr 1975–87, ed mainstream progs 1987–, head of music 1990–94, exec prodr live music 1995–; work as prodr incl: Live Aid 1986 (Sony Award), Nelson Mandela Concert 1988, Walters Weekly arts prog (Bdcasting Press Guild Award), Prince of Wales 40th Birthday Party, Prince's Tst Anniversary Concert Wembley; *Recreations* golf, walking, reading, theatre, music, cinema; *Style—* Chris Lycett, Esq; ✉ BBC Radio 1 FM, Egton House, London W1A 1AA (☎ 0171 765 3185, car 0850 740692)

LYCETT, Maj Michael Hildesley Lycett; CBE (1987); s of Rev Norman Lycett (d 1963), of East Dean, Sussex, and Ruth Edith, *née* Burns-Lindow (d 1965); *b* 11 Dec 1915; *Educ* Radley, Merton Coll Oxford; *m* 1, 4 Feb 1944, Moira Patricia Margaret (d 1958), da of Maj Norman Martin, CBE; 1 da (Anthea Theresa b 6 June 1954); m 2, 12 Oct 1959, Lady June Wendy Pelham, da of 5 Earl of Yarborough, MC (d 1948); *Career* Maj Royal Scots Greys 1935–47, served Palestine, Greece, Western Desert, Italy and Germany; md: Rhodesian Insurances Ltd 1949–61, Wright Deen Lycett Ltd Newcastle upon Tyne 1961–73, Lycett Browne-Swinburne & Douglas's Ltd (chm 1973–76); chm L B S and D (underwriting agents) 1976, dir L B S and D (Cumbria) Ltd; chm Morpeth Div Cons Assoc 1966–72; Parly candidate (C) Consett Co Durham 1981 and 1983; chm Cons Northern Area 1985–87; pres Northumbria Euro Constituency, former memb Cons Nat Exec and GP Ctees; govr and first chm exec Bernard Mizeki Schs 1959–61; MFH Tynedale Hunt 1975–77; *Recreations* Help Poland Fund, field sports, looking things up, writing rhymes; *Clubs* Cavalry and Guards', Pratt's, Boodle's, Northern Counties; *Style—* Maj Michael Lycett, CBE; ✉ West Grange, Scots Gap, Morpeth, Northumberland NE61 4EQ (☎ 01670 774662)

LYDDON, (William) Derek Collier; CB (1984); s of late Alfred Jonathan Lyddon, CBE, and Elizabeth Esther, *née* French (d 1942); *b* 17 Nov 1925; *Educ* Wrekin Coll, UCL (BA (Arch), DipTP); *m* 1949, Marian Louise Kaye, da of late Prof J K Charlesworth, CBE; 2 da; *Career* dep chief architect and planning offr Cumbernauld Devpt Corp 1962, chief architect and planning offr Skelmersdale Devpt Corp 1963–67, chief planning offr Scottish Devpt Dept 1967–85; pres Int Soc of City and Regnl Planners 1981–84; chm Planning Exchange; vice chm Edinburgh Old Town Renewal Tst, govr Edinburgh Coll of Art; hon prof Heriot-Watt Univ, hon fell Duncan of Jordanstone Coll Dundee; Hon DLitt Heriot-Watt 1981; FRGS, FRTPI, RIBA; *Style—* Derek Lyddon, Esq, CB; ✉ 31 Blackford Road, Edinburgh EH9 2DT (☎ 0131 667 2266)

LYDEKKER, Brig Richard Neville Wolfe; CBE (1976); s of Rev Neville Wolfe Lydekker (d 1956), of Sussex, and Sylvia Gwendolen, *née* Palmer (d 1970); descendant of Rev Gerrit Leydecker who presented the Petition of American Loyalists to King George III in 1782 before emigrating to England; *b* 7 May 1921; *Educ* Sherborne; *m* 25 March 1947, Margaret Julia Mary, da of Rev Canon Lionel Edward Lydekker (d 1973), of Bucks; 1 da (Elizabeth b 1955); *Career* cmmnd RA 1941, psc 1952, jssc 1959, serv WWII N Africa and Italy, cmd RA Regt Malaya and Borneo 1963–65, staff Strategic Reserve 1967–72, Dep QMG UK Land Forces 1972–74, dir MOD (Army Dept) 1974–76, ret; regnl organiser Army Benevolent Fund 1977–91; *Recreations* field sports, cricket; *Clubs* Army and Navy; *Style—* Brig Richard Lydekker, CBE; ✉ 26 Abbey Mews, Amesbury, Salisbury SP4 7EX (☎ 01980 624807)

LYE, Geoffrey Brian; s of James Douglas Lye, and Ruby Alma, *née* Cox; *b* 14 Oct 1949; *Educ* King Edward VI Sch Southampton, Gonville and Caius Coll Cambridge; *m* Linda May, da of George Arthur Muirhead; 2 da (Mary Elizabeth b 4 Sept 1975, Katherine Louise b 16 Nov 1978), 2 s (Charles Julian b 20 April 1982, Jonathan James b 29 Jan 1988); *Career* J Walter Thompson advtg agency 1972–74, General Foods 1974–80, gp dep chm Countrywide Porter Novelli Ltd 1980–, dir Sustainability Ltd 1995–; FRSA; *Style—* Geoffrey Lye, Esq; ✉ Countrywide Porter Novelli, Countrywide House, West Bar, Banbury, Oxon OX16 9SA (☎ 01295 272288, fax 01295 272170)

LYE, Richard Harold; s of Vincent Lye, and Agnes, *née* Ashurst; *b* 19 May 1947; *Educ* Bury GS, Univ of Manchester (BSc, MSc, PhD, MB ChB); *m* 15 Aug 1970, (Mary) Nanette, da of Dr John Randall Archibald; 5 s (Robert b 1973, James b 1974, Anthony b 1979, George b 1983, Matthew b 1986), 2 da (Helen (twin) b 1979, Catherine b 1988); *Career* conslt in neurosurgery 1982, reader in neurosurgery Univ of Manchester 1985–; FRCS 1976; *Style—* Richard Lye, Esq; ✉ Department of Neurosurgery, Manchester Royal Infirmary, Oxford Road, Manchester M13 9WL (☎ 0161 276 1234)

LYELL, 3 Baron (UK 1914); Sir Charles Lyell; 3 Bt (UK 1894), DL (Angus); s of Capt 2 Baron Lyell, VC, Scots Guards (ka 1943, VC awarded posthumously), and Sophie, *née* Trafford (whose family, of Wroxham Hall, Norfolk were a cadet branch of the Traffords now represented by the de Trafford Bts), whose mother was Lady Elizabeth Bertie, OBE, yst da of 7 Earl of Abingdon; *b* 27 March 1939; *Educ* Eton, Ch Ch Oxford; *Heir* none; *Career* 2 Lt Scots Gds 1957–59; CA; oppn whip House of Lords 1974–79, a lord in waiting (Govt Whip) 1979–84; memb Queen's Body Guard for Scotland (Royal Co of Archers); Parly under sec of state NI Office 1984–89; *Clubs* White's, Pratt's, Turf; *Style—* The Rt Hon the Lord Lyell, DL; ✉ Kinnordy House, Kirriemuir, Angus DD8 5ER (☎ 01575 72848); 20 Petersham Mews, Elvaston Place, London SW7 (☎ 0171 584 9419)

LYELL, Rt Hon Sir Nicholas Walter; kt (1987), PC (1990), QC (1980), MP (C) Mid-Bedfordshire (majority 25,138); s of Hon Mr Justice Maurice Legat Lyell (d 1975), and his 1 w, Veronica Mary, *née* Luard (d 1950); stepson of The Hon Lady (Katharine) Lyell; *b* 6 Dec 1938; *Educ* Stowe, Ch Ch Oxford (MA), Coll of Law; *m* 2 Sept 1967, Susanna Mary, da of Prof Charles Montague Fletcher, CBE (d 1995); 2 s (Oliver b 1 July 1971, Alexander b 8 Dec 1981), 2 da (Veronica b 8 May 1970, Mary-Kate b 5 March 1979); *Career* Nat Serv with RA 1957–59, 2 Lt 1957; with Walter Runciman & Co 1962–64; called to the Bar Inner Temple 1965, bencher 1986; in private practice London 1965–86, recorder of the Crown Ct 1985; MP (C): Hemel Hempstead 1979–83, Beds Mid 1983–; jt sec Constitutional Ctee 1979, PPS to Attorney Gen 1979–86, Parly under sec of state for Social Security DHSS 1986–87, Slr Gen 1987–92, Attorney Gen 1992–; chm Soc of Cons Lawyers 1985–86, vice chm BFSS 1983–86; Freeman City of London 1964, memb Ct of Assts Worshipful Co of Salters; *Recreations* gardening, drawing, shooting; *Clubs* Brooks's, Pratt's, Beefsteak; *Style—* The Rt Hon Sir Nicholas Lyell, QC, MP; ✉ House of Commons, London SW1A 0AA (☎ 0171 219 5142)

LYES, Jeffrey Paul; s of late Joseph Leslie Lyes, of Daventry, Northants, and Rose Mary Anne, *née* Harris; *b* 19 April 1946; *m* 5 Oct 1968, Jean, da of late John Armstrong, of Oxford; 2 da (Sarah b 1974, Julia b 1977); *Career* journalist United Newspapers 1963–69, exec Hertford PR 1969–71, news ed Heart of Eng Newspapers 1971–73, press and PR offr Thames Valley Police 1973–78; dir: Lexington International PR (J Walter Thompson) 1978–81, Granard Communications 1981–84 (dep md 1984), Good Relations Group plc 1985–86; md: Good Relations Technology 1985–86, Good Relations Corporate Communications 1986–87; md Good Relations Ltd 1987–89; chm: Good Relations Ltd 1989–95, chm Lowe Bell Good Relations Ltd 1995–; MIPR 1977, FIMgt 1985, FInstD 1988; *Recreations* motor yacht cruising; *Clubs* Reform; *Style—* Jeffrey Lyes, Esq; ✉ Lowe Bell Good Relations Ltd, 59 Russell Square, London WC1B 4HJ (☎ 0171 631 3434, fax 0171 631 1399)

LYGO, Adm Sir Raymond Derek; KCB (1977); s of Edwin Lygo; *b* 15 March 1924; *Educ* Ilford Co HS, Clarke Coll Bromley; *m* 1950, Pepper Van Osten, of USA; 2 s, 1 da; *Career* on staff The Times 1940; served RN 1942–78 (vice chief and chief of Naval Staff 1975–78); British Aerospace: md Hatfield/Lostock Div 1978–79, chief exec and chm Dynamics Gp 1980–82, memb Main Bd 1980, md 1983–86, chief exec 1986–89; chm Royal Ordnance 1987–88; aerospace def and industl conslt 1990–; dir James Capel Corporate Finance 1990–92, non-exec dir LET plc 1990–92, non-exec chm Rutland Trust 1991–; chm: TNT (Express) UK Ltd 1992–, TNT (Europe) Ltd 1992–; patron Nat Fleet Air Arm Assoc 1990–, pres Fleet Arm Offrs' Assoc 1990–; memb mgmnt review HM Prisons 1991; vice pres City Livery Club 1996–97 (vice chm 1995); Liveryman: Worshipful Co of Coachmakers and Coach Harness Makers, Worshipful Co of Shipwrights; hon fell Univ of Westminster; Hon FRAeS, CIMgt, FRSA, FPCL; *Clubs* Royal Naval & RAYC, IOD, City Livery; *Style—* Adm Sir Raymond Lygo, KCB; ✉ Barclays Premier Banking, 54 Lombard Street, London EC3P 3AH

LYLE, Alexander Walter Barr (Sandy); MBE (1987); s of Alex Lyle, and Agnes Lyle; *b* 9 Feb 1958; *Educ* Shrewsbury Secdy Sch; *m* 1 (m dis); 2 s (Stuart b 1983, James b 1986); m 2, 1989, (Brigitte) Jolande Huurman; 1 da ((Alexandra) Lonneke b 1993), 1 s (Quintin Tjeerd b 17 Jan 1995); *Career* professional golfer; amateur record: boys int 1972–75 (capt 1974–75), Midland boys champion 1972 and 1975, Shropshire and Herefordshire sr champion 1973 and 1975, triple co champion and champion of champions 1974, winner Carris Trophy 1975, Midland Open champion 1975, winner Brabazon Trophy 1975 and 1977, youth int 1975–77, memb Walker Cup Team 1977, memb Euro Mens Championship 1977; amateur victories in 1977: Youth Int, N of England Youths, Br Youth Int, Home Youth Int, Berkhamsted Trophy, Berks Trophy, Hants Hog; turned professional 1977; tournament victories: Nigerian Open 1978, Jersey Open 1979, Scottish Open 1979, Scandinavian Enterprise Open 1979, Euro Open 1979, Coral Classic 1980, French Open 1981, Lawrence Batley Int 1981 and 1982, Madrid Open 1983, Italian Open 1984, Lancome Trophy 1984, Kapulua Int 1984, Casio World Open 1984, Br Open Royal St George's 1985, Benson & Hedges Int 1985, Greater Greensborough Open 1986 and 1988, German Masters 1987, US Tournament Players' Championship 1987, Dunhill Br Masters 1988, Suntory World Match-Play 1988, Phoenix Open 1988, US Masters 1988, BMW Int Open 1991, Italian Open 1992, Volvo Masters 1992; memb Ryder Cup Team 1979, 1981, 1983, 1985 (winners), 1987 (winners); rookie of the year 1978, finished top order of merit 1979, 1980, 1985; proprietor public house Chesham; memb Golf Fndn, involved with Great Ormond St Hosp and children with leukemia; *Books* Learning Golf the Lyle Way (1986), Sandy Lyle Takes You Round the Championship Courses of Scotland; *Recreations* cars, motorcycles, aeroplanes, skiing, shooting; *Style—* Sandy Lyle, Esq, MBE; ✉ c/o Advantage International Ltd, The Limes, 123 Mortlake High Street, London SW1Y 8SN (☎ 0181 876 0044, fax 0181 876 4343)

LYLE, (Philip) Dominic; s of Robert Lyle, of Malveira, Portugal, and Helena, *née* Perks; *b* 6 March 1949; *Educ* Stonyhurst, Alliance Française, Université de Lausanne; *m* 5 Sept 1992, Vyvyan Lynne, *née* Mackeson; *Career* sales and mktg mangr Europe Tate & Lyle Refineries 1976–79; Cameron Choat & Partners: joined 1979, dir 1985–90, md 1990–91; dir Countrywide Communications (London) Ltd 1992–94, md Countrywide Porter Novelli (Brussels) 1994–; memb Mktg Soc, MIPR; *Recreations* opera, cooking; *Style—* Dominic Lyle, Esq; ✉ Countrywide Porter Novelli, 50 rue d'Arlon, 1000 Brussels, Belgium (☎ 00 32 2 280 1790, fax 00 32 2 280 1976, mobile 00 32 75703 183, e-mail dominic.lyle@countrywide.com)

LYLE, Sir Gavin Archibald; 3 Bt (UK 1929), of Glendelvine, Co Perth; s of Capt Ian Archibald de Hoghton Lyle (ka 1942), and Hon Lydia, *née* Yarde-Buller, da of 3 Baron Churston; suc gf, Col Sir Archibald Moir Park Lyle, 2 Bt, MC, TD, 1946; *b* 14 Oct 1941; *Educ* Eton; *m* 1967 (m dis 1985), Susan, o da of John Vaughan Cooper; 5 s (Ian Abram b 1968, Jake Archibald b 1969, Matthew Alexander b 1974, Joshua b 1979, Samuel b 1981), 1 da (Rachel b 1971); *Heir* s, Ian Abram Lyle b 25 Sept 1968; *Career* estate mangr; farmer; co dir; *Style—* Sir Gavin Lyle, Bt; ✉ Glendelvine, Caputh, Perthshire PH1 4JN

LYLE, Robert Arthur Wyatt; s of Maj Robert David Lyle (d 1989), and Irene Joyce, *née* Francis (d 1984); nephew of Lord Wyatt of Weeford, *qv*; *b* 5 May 1952; *Educ* Eton, Oriel Coll Oxford (MA); *m* 9 March 1991, Hon Teresa (Tessa) Ruth, da of Lord Mayhew (Life Peer) (d 1997); 1 s (Christopher Robert David Wyatt b 12 Feb 1992); *Career* dir: Cornwall Light & Power Co, NMG (Cornwall) Ltd, Cornish Spring Water Co, BPL Holdings Ltd; advsr Global Trade Insurance PTE Singapore; worldwide corr to China International Economic Consultants 1983–87, EC advsr to Russian Govt on investment insurance 1991–93; pres cornwall Branch Br Red Cross Soc, memb PCC St Keverne; owner Bonython Estate (one of four Lords of the Lizard); Liveryman Worshipful Co of Glass Sellers; *Recreations* travel, art, architecture; *Clubs* White's, MCC; *Style—* Robert Lyle, Esq; ✉ Bonython, Helston, Cornwall TR12 7BA (☎ 01326 240234, 01326 240550, fax 01326 240478, car 0831 104888)

LYLES, John; CBE (1987), JP (Dewsbury 1968); s of Percy George Lyles (d 1958), and Alice Maud Mary, *née* Robinson (d 1968); *b* 8 May 1929; *Educ* Giggleswick Sch, Leeds Univ (BSc); *m* 1953, Yvonne, da of G F Johnson (d 1954), of Waddesdon; 2 s (Jonathan, Christopher), 2 da (Jane, Anne); *Career* chm S Lyles plc until 1996; non-exec dir Hillards plc 1984–87; High Sheriff West Yorkshire 1985–86; chm: Yorkshire and Humberside CBI 1983–85, Yorks & Humberside Region Industry Year 1986; memb: Ct Univ of Leeds 1996– (memb Cncl 1988–96), Yorks Ctee Nat Tst 1988–, Cncl Northern Hort Soc 1992–; Hon Col King's Own Yorkshire Yeo 1996–; Lord-Lt W Yorks 1992– (DL 1987); *Recreations* gardening, photography, music, opera; *Style—* John Lyles, Esq, CBE, JP; ✉ 14 St Anne's Road, Leeds, W Yorkshire LS6 3NX (☎ 0113 224 9462, fax 0113 224 9463)

LYMBERY, Brian John; s of Dr John Graham Lymbery (d 1974), and Joyce Winifred, *née* Keen; *b* 1 March 1947; *Educ* Alun GS Mold Clwyd, Keble Coll Oxford (BA); *m* 1975 (m dis 1996), Susan Joan, da of Percy Sherratt (d 1992); 1 s (Matthew b 1976), 1 da (Jessica b 1979); *Career* lectr and librarian Mid-Western Tech Coll Auchi Nigeria 1969–70, exec sec The Prince of Wales Ctee Bangor 1971–76, dir The Prince of Wales Ctee Cardiff 1976–83, dep dir Civic Tst London 1983–87, exec dir UK 2000 1987–90, dir CSD 1990–; memb Indust Lead Body for Design 1990–, treas Bureau Euro Designers' Assoc 1992–94; memb Nat Cncl VSO 1979–90, tstee Tst for Urban Ecology 1981–92, memb Gen Advsy Cncl IBA 1983–88 (memb Ctee for Wales 1977–83), chm Soc for the Interpretation of Britain's Heritage 1984–85, memb Advsy Panel Centre for Environmental Interpretation Manchester Metropolitan Univ (formerly Manchester Poly) 1985–91, fndr chm Cncl for Occupational Standards and Qualifications in Environmental Conservation (COSQUEC) 1988–96, memb bd Environmental Training Organisation (ETO) 1995–; chm of govrs Gordonbrock Primary Sch London 1989–; FRSA 1981; *Recreations* enjoying opera, music, theatre and film, gardening, watching people; *Clubs* London Central YMCA; *Style—* Brian Lymbery, Esq; ✉ 31 St Donatt's Road, New Cross, London SE14 6NU; The Chartered Society of Designers, 32–38 Saffron Hill, London EC1N 8FH (☎ 0171 831 9777, fax 0171 831 6277)

LYMBERY, His Hon Robert Davison; QC (1967); s of Robert Smith Lymbery (d 1981), of West Wittering, Sussex, and Louise, *née* Barnsdale (d 1968); *b* 14 Nov 1920; *Educ* Gresham's, Pembroke Coll Cambridge (fndn exhibitioner, MA, LLB); *m* 1952, Pauline

Anne, da of Maj John Reginald Tuckett (d 1981), of Knebworth, Herts; 3 da (Carole, Sarah, Jane); *Career* served WWII 1940–46, cmmnd 1941, Maj Royal Tank Regt ME, Italy and Greece; called to the Bar Middle Temple 1949 (Harmsworth law scholar), practised Midland Circuit 1949–71, recorder Grantham 1965–71, chm Bedfordshire and Rutland Quarter Sessions 1961–71, circuit judge 1971–93, Common Serjeant in London 1990–93, Master of the Bench Middle Temple 1990; Freeman City of London 1983, Liveryman Worshipful Co of Cutlers 1992; *Recreations* retirement; *Clubs* Hawks (Cambridge); *Style*— His Hon Robert Lymbery, QC

LYMINGTON, Viscount; Oliver Henry Rufus Wallop; s and h of 10 Earl of Portsmouth, *qv*; *b* 22 Dec 1981; *Style*— Viscount Lymington

LYMPANY, Dame Moura; DBE (1992, CBE 1979); da of Capt John Johnstone, and Beatrice, *née* Limpenny; *b* 18 Aug 1916; *Educ* Belgium, England, Austria; *m* 1, 1944 (m dis 1950), Lt-Col Colin Defries; m 2, 1951 (m dis 1961), Bennet H Korn; 1 s (decd); *Career* concert pianist; first performance Mendelssohn's G Minor Concerto Harrogate 1929, won second prize Ysaye Int Pianoforte Competition Brussels 1938; performances given in USA, Canada, S America, Aust NZ, India and Europe; records made for: EMI, Decca, Olympia, HMV, Erato; Cdr Order of The Crown Belgium, Medal of Cultural Merit Portugal 1989, Chevalier des Arts et des Lettres France 1992, Decoration of Henry the Navigator (Portugal) 1996; FRAM 1948, FRCM 1995; *Style*— Dame Moura Lympany, DBE; ✉ Château Périgord 2, Monte Carlo, Monaco (☎ 00 337 93 307329, fax 00 337 93 509563)

LYNAM, Desmond Michael; s of Edward Lynam, and Gertrude Veronica, *née* Malone; *b* 17 Sept 1942; *Educ* Varndean GS Brighton, Brighton Business Coll (ACII); *m* 1965 (m dis 1974), Susan Eleanor, *née* Skinner; 1 s (Patrick); *Career* in insurance and freelance journalism until 1967; local radio reporter 1967–69, reporter, presenter and commentator BBC Radio 1969–78, presenter and commentator BBC TV Sport 1978– (incl Grandstand, Cwlth and Olympic Games, World Cup, Sportsnight and Wimbledon); former presenter Holiday (BBC TV); TV Sports Presenter of the Year (TV and Radio Industries Club) 1985, 1986, 1988 and 1992, Male TV Personality (Radio Times/Open Air) 1989, Best Sports Presenter of the Year (RTS Awards) 1995, Richard Dimbleby Award (BAFTA) 1995; *Publications* Guide to Commonwealth Games (1986), The 1988 Olympics (1988), The Barcelona Olympics 1992 (with Caroline Searle, 1992); *Recreations* golf, tennis, Brighton and Hove Albion FC, reading, theatre; *Style*— Desmond Lynam, Esq; ✉ c/o BBC TV, Room 5064, TV Centre, Wood Lane, London W12 7RJ (☎ 0171 225 6434)

LYNCH, Alan Russell; s of Stanley Benjamin (d 1967), and Lilian Ivy Moffett (d 1976); *b* 29 Dec 1936; *Educ* Christ's Hosp Sch, Guy's Hosp Univ of London (BDS); *m* 29 Dec 1959, Margaret, da of Dr Theodore Parkman, of Hastings, Sussex; *Career* house surgn Queen Victoria Hosp E Grinstead 1962, gen dental practice 1963–72, assistentenarzt Katharinen Hosp Stuttgart 1968, orthodontist in private practice 1972–; Liveryman Worshipful Soc of Apothecaries; *Recreations* sailing, skiing, music, forestry; *Clubs* Savage; *Style*— Alan R Lynch, Esq; ✉ 31 Queen Anne St, London W1M 9FB (☎ 0171 580 2786, fax 0171 436 7246); Pattendens Farm, Udimore Road, Broad Oak Brede, Rye, E Sussex TN31 6BU (☎ 01424 882423)

LYNCH, Dr Barry Andrew; s of Andrew Lynch, and Eileen, *née* O'Gara; *b* 20 Feb 1952; *Educ* Salford GS, Univ of St Andrews (BSc), Univ of Manchester (MB ChB); *Career* house offr Manchester Royal Infirmary and Univ Hosp of S Manchester 1977–78; BBC Wales: radio prodr 1978–82, TV prodr 1982–87, head of features and documentaries 1987–92; health corr Radio Times 1989–91; md Prospect Pictures Ltd 1992–; *Books* Don't Break Your Heart - All You Need to Know About Heart Attacks and How to Avoid Them (1987), The BBC Diet (1988), BBC Healthcheck (1989), The New BBC Diet (1990), The Complete BBC Diet (1994); *Clubs* Reform; *Style*— Dr Barry Lynch; ✉ Prospect Pictures Ltd, Prospect House, 150 Great Portland Street, London W1N 6BB (☎ 0171 636 1234, fax 0171 636 1236)

LYNCH, His Hon Judge; David; s of Henry and Edith Lynch; *b* 23 Aug 1939; *Educ* Liverpool Collegiate GS, Univ of London (LLB); *m* 1974, Ann Knights; 2 s; *Career* served RAF 1958–61; called to the Bar Middle Temple 1968, recorder 1988–90, circuit judge (Northern Circuit) 1990–; pres Mental Health Review Tbnls (restricted patients) 1991–; *Recreations* classical guitar music, golf; *Clubs* Caldy Golf; *Style*— His Hon Judge Lynch; ✉ The Queen Elizabeth II Law Courts, Derby Square, Liverpool L2 1XA (☎ 0151 473 7373)

LYNCH, James; s of Ronald F T Lynch, and Joy Ann, *née* Berry, of Seend, Wiltshire; *b* 12 July 1956; *Educ* Devizes Sch Wilts, Swindon Coll (graphic design dip); *m* 1977, Kate Mary, da of John Argent Armstrong; 2 s (Thomas Albert b 1978, Arthur James b 1982), 1 da (Alice Mary b 1980); *Career* artist; *Solo Exhibitions* incl: Linfield Galleries Bradford-on-Avon 1982 and 1983, Odette Gilbert London 1988, Maas Gallery London 1991, 1993 and 1995; *Gp Exhibitions* incl: RA Summer Shows annually 1984–89, Royal Soc of Painters in Watercolour 1986, Agnews London 1989 and 1990, Discerning Eye Mall Gallery 1991; *Awards* Elizabeth Greenshields Fndn Award 1983, RA Pimms Prize 1986, winner Adams/Spectator Painting Award 1993; *Commissions* incl Nat Tst and Folio Soc (illustrations for Wind in the Willows 1994); *Public Collections* Chatsworth Collection, Nat Tst Fndn for Art, Wessex Collection; *Recreations* cycling, saxophone, motorcycling; *Style*— James Lynch, Esq; ✉ The Dairy House, North Cadbury, Nr Yeovil, Somerset BA22 7DE (☎ 01963 440491); The Maas Gallery, 15a Clifford Street, London W1X 1RF (☎ 0171 734 2302, fax 0171 287 4836)

LYNCH, Paul Dominic Anthony; s of James Alphusos Lynch (d 1986), and Kathleen Mary, *née* Jenkin (d 1976); *b* 7 Feb 1946; *Educ* St Bede's Coll, Univ of Manchester Med Sch; *m* 1969 (m dis 1989), Carol Angela Walker; 1 s (Rory Daniel b 14 April 1978), 2 da (Tara Grace b 12 Sept 1972, Camilla Alexandra b 11 March 1976); *Career* dental surgeon; various appts and gen practice, now in sole private practice (Harley St, France, Geneva), specialist in advanced restorative dental surgery; *Recreations* active in sports, the arts; *Style*— Paul Lynch, Esq; ✉ 152 Harley St, London W1N 1HH (☎ 0171 935 8762, fax 0171 224 2574)

LYNCH, Philip F; *Educ* St Francis Coll NY (BSc); *Career* Lehman Brothers: joined in NY 1971, transferred London 1977, currently md Commodities Dept Lehman Brothers Inc and md Lehman Brothers Commodities Ltd until 1996; chief exec Exchange Clearing House (ECHO) 1996–; chm International Petroleum Exchange 1989–96, bd memb Securities and Futures Authority; former dir Assoc of Futures Brokers and Dealers, former dir Investors' Compensation Scheme Ltd, former chm London Chapter Futures Industry Assoc; *Style*— P F Lynch, Esq; ✉ Exchange Clearing House Ltd, 1 Harbour Exchange Square, London E14 (☎ 0171 971 5700)

LYNCH, Roderick Robertson (Rod); s of late Nanson Lynch, and Catherine, *née* Robertson; *b* 22 May 1949; *Educ* Perth Acad, Univ of Dundee (MA); *m* 1972, Christina, da of William Williams; 2 s (James b 1975, Alexander b 1980); *Career* served RAC 1966–67; various positions British Airways 1971–89, md Air Europe 1989–91, dir Forte Hotels 1991–93, chief exec BBC Resources Directorate 1993–; bd memb: Civil Aviation Authy 1993–, Nat Air Traffic Servs 1996–; *Recreations* watching rugby, military history, music, aviation; *Style*— Rod Lynch, Esq; ✉ BBC Resources Directorate, BBC White City, 201 Wood Lane, London W12 7TS (☎ 0181 752 5000)

LYNCH-BLOSSE, Gp Capt (Eric) Hugh; OBE (1952); s of Maj Cecil Eagles Lynch-Blosse (d 1966), and his 1 w Dorothy Delahaize, *née* Ouvry (d 1963); hp of kinsman, Sir Richard Hely Lynch-Blosse, 17 Bt; *b* 30 July 1917; *Educ* Blundell's, RAF Coll; *m* 1946, Jean Evelyn, da of Cdr Andrew Robertson Hair, RD, RNR (d 1965); 1 s (David Ian b 1950), 1 da (Valerie Jean (Mrs Irvine Cormack) b 1947), and 1 da decd (Fiona b 1955); *Career* served RAF 1935–67, POW 1941–45, Gp Capt; standards engr Rank Xerox 1969–74, sec Wyedean Tourist Bd and mangr Tourist Info Centre Ross on Wye 1974–80, ret; *Books* Wartime Memories from Newnham, Wings - and Other Things, Letters to my Grandson; *Clubs* RAF; *Style*— Gp Capt Hugh Lynch-Blosse, OBE; ✉ 17 Queens Acre, Newnham, Glos GL14 1DJ (☎ 01594 516 335)

LYNCH-BLOSSE, Sir Richard Hely; 17 Bt (I 1622), of Castle Carra, Galway; s of Sir David Edward Lynch-Blosse, 16 Bt (d 1971), and Elizabeth, *née* Payne; *b* 26 Aug 1953; *Educ* Welwyn Garden City, Royal Free Hosp Sch of Med Univ of London (MB BS, LRCP, MRCS); *m* 1976, Cara Lynne, only da of George Longmore Sutherland, of St Ives, Cambs; 2 da (Katherine Helen (Katy) b 1983, Hannah Victoria b 1985); *Heir* kinsman, (Eric) Hugh Lynch-Blosse, OBE, *qv*; *Career* med practitioner, short serv cmmn with RAMC 1975–85; MO Oxfordshire Army Cadet Force, advsr to Medivcine Group (publishing co), med offr to European Sch Culham, pres Royal Brit Legion Dorchester-on-Thames; memb: Oxford General Practice Primary Care Advsy Ctee, Medical Advsy Gp Healthcall plc Oxford; memb: BMA, Medical Defence Union, Soc of Ornamental Turner; DRCOG, MRCGP; *Recreations* shooting, ornamental turning, racquet sports; *Style*— Sir Richard Lynch-Blosse, Bt; ✉ The Surgery, Clifton Hampden, Oxon OX14 3EL

LYNCH-ROBINSON, Sir Dominick Christopher; 4 Bt (UK 1920), of Foxrock, Co Dublin; s of Sir Niall Bryan Lynch-Robinson, 3 Bt, DSC (d 1996), and Rosemary Seaton, *née* Eller; *b* 30 July 1948; *m* 1973, Victoria, da of Kenneth Weir, of Sale, Manchester; 1 s (Christopher Henry Jake b 1 Oct 1977), 1 da (Anna Elizabeth Seaton b 19 July 1973), 1 step da (Joselyn Cleare b 12 July 1969); *Heir* s, Christopher Henry Jake Lynch-Robinson b 1 Oct 1977; *Career* creative dir Bates Dorland (formerly BSB Dorland Advertising Ltd); *Style*— Sir Dominick Lynch-Robinson, Bt; ✉ Charnham Close, 26 Charnham Street, Hungerford, Berks; Bates Dorland, 121–141 Westbourne Terrace, London W2 6JR (☎ 0171 262 5077)

LYNDEN-BELL, Prof Donald; s of Lt-Col Lachlan Arthur Lynden-Bell, MC (d 1984), and Monica Rose, *née* Thring; *b* 5 April 1935; *Educ* Marlborough, Clare Coll Cambridge; *m* 1 July 1961, Ruth Marion, da of Dr D N Truscott, of Ely; 1 s (Edward Lachlan b 16 Dec 1968), 1 da (Marion Katharine b 10 April 1965); *Career* res fell Clare Coll and fell Cwlth (Harkness) Fund California Inst of Technol and Mt Wilson and Palomar Observatories 1960–62, dir of maths studies Clare Coll and asst lectr Univ of Cambridge 1962–65, SPSO Royal Greenwich Observatory Herstmonceux 1965–72, visiting prof Univ of Sussex 1970–72, dir Inst of Astronomy Cambridge 1972–77, 1982–87 and 1992–95, prof of astrophysics Univ of Cambridge and prof fell Clare Coll 1972–; pres: Cambridge Philosophical Soc 1982–84, RAS 1985–87 (Eddington Medal 1984, Gold Medal 1993); Brower Prize American Astronomical Soc 1990; Hon DSc Univ of Sussex 1987; foreign assoc: US Nat Acad of Sci 1990, Royal Soc of SA 1994; FRS 1978; *Recreations* hill walking; *Style*— Prof Donald Lynden-Bell, FRS; ✉ 9 Wellington Park Terrace, Belfast BT9 6DR (☎ 01232 683274); Institute of Astronomy (Cambridge University), The Observatories, Madingley Rd, Cambridge CB3 0DP (☎ 01223 337525, fax 01223 337523)

LYNDHURST, Nicholas; *Career* actor 1971–; *Theatre* incl: Harding's Luck (Greenwich), Trial Run (Oxford Playhouse), Black Comedy (tour), The Private Ear (tour), The Foreigner (Albery), Straight and Narrow (Wyndhams) 1992; also appeared in Royal Variety Performance (Theatre Royal Drury Lane) 1986; *Television* incl: Davy in Anne of Avonlea, Peter in Heidi, Tom Canty and Prince Edward in The Prince and the Pauper, Tootles in Peter Pan, Raymond in Going Straight (BBC), Adam in Butterflies (BBC), Philip in Father's Day (Granada), Tim in Fairies (BBC), Philip in Losing Her, Dobson in To Serve Them All My Days (BBC), Wilson in Spearhead, Rodney in Only Fools and Horses (BBC, 10 series), The Two of Us (LWT, 4 series), The Piglet Files (LWT, 3 series), Goodnight Sweetheart (BBC) 1994, Gulliver's Travels (Channel 4) 1996; *Films* Chalky in Bullshot and Gunbus; *Recreations* surfing, flying, diving; *Style*— Nicholas Lyndhurst, Esq; ✉ c/o Chatto & Linnit Ltd, Prince of Wales Theatre, Coventry Street, London W1V 7FE (☎ 0171 930 6677, fax 0171 930 0091)

LYNDON-SKEGGS, Andrew Neville; s of Dr Peter Lyndon-Skeggs, of Preston Candover, Hants, and June Angela, *née* Reid; *b* 10 Jan 1949; *Educ* Rugby, Magdalene Coll Cambridge; *m* 8 April 1972 (m dis); 2 da (Vanessa b 1975, Tessa b 1979); *Career* master and tstee Univ of Cambridge Drag Hunt 1968–71; chm Westbrook Property Developments Ltd 1981–, chm Town Pages Ltd 1995–; FRICS; *Recreations* stalking, hunting, fishing, skiing, gardening; *Clubs* Travellers'; *Style*— Andrew Lyndon-Skeggs, Esq; ✉ Westbrook House, Holybourne, Alton, Hants (☎ 01420 83244/541542, fax 01420 541322, car ☎ 0836 220633)

LYNDON SKEGGS, Barbara Noel; MBE (1990), JP (1966), DL (1988); da of late Philip Noel Rogers, of Hurstpierpoint, Sussex, and Beatrice, *née* Marillier; *b* 29 Dec 1924; *Educ* Queen Bertha's Sch Birchington Kent; *m* 1, 26 July 1943, (Griffith) Eric Carbery Vaughan Evans (d 1950), s of Brig-Gen Lewis Pugh Evans VC, CB, CMG, DSO, DL (d 1964); 2 s (Christopher b 5 Dec 1945, Roger b 23 June 1947); m 2, 8 April 1953, Michael Andrew Lyndon Skeggs, s of Dr Basil Lyndon Skeggs (d 1956); 2 da (Victoria (Mrs Bagge) b 28 April 1954, Marianne (Mrs Munro-Ferguson) b 11 Oct 1955); *Career* WRNS 1942–45; asst dir BRCS 1948–68; Northumberland CC: cncllr 1968–81, chm Health Ctee 1970–74, chm Social Servs 1974–81; memb Guild of City Freemen 1973, memb Northumberland DHA 1974–90 (vice chm 1987–90), FPC 1980–90, tax commissioner 1984–94; High Sheriff for Co of Northumberland 1994–95; Freeman City of London 1973; *Recreations* a baker's dozen grandmother; *Style*— Mrs M A Lyndon Skeggs, MBE, JP, DL; ✉ Dalgheal, Evanton, By Dingwall, Rossshire IV16 9XH (☎ 01949 830948)

LYNE, Air Vice-Marshal Michael Dillon; CB (1968), AFC (1943, and two bars 1947 and 1955), DL (Lincs 1973); s of Robert John Lyne (d 1943), and Ruth Walton, *née* Robinson (d 1952); *b* 23 March 1919; *Educ* Imperial Serv Coll, RAF Coll Cranwell; *m* 1943, Avril Joy, da of Lt-Col Albert Buckley, CBE, DSO* (d 1965), of Liverpool; 2 s (Peter, Roderic Lyne, CMG, *qv*), 2 da (Justine, Barbara); *Career* joined RAF 1937, Fighter Cmd 1939–43, flew Spitfire Battle of Dunkirk (wounded) 1940, merchant ship fighter unit 1941–42 (8 Atlantic convoys), trained and led first jet formation aerobatic team 1947, capt first jet aircraft flight (Canberra) from Europe to N America via 90 degrees N 1955, Air Attaché Moscow 1961–63, Cmdt RAF Coll Cranwell 1963–64, Air Vice-Marshal 1965, AOC No23 (Flying Trg) Gp 1965–67, Sr RAF Instr IDC 1967–69, Dir Gen RAF Trg 1969–71; past pres 54 Sqdn Assoc; vice pres: RAF Gliding Assoc, RAF Motor Sport Assoc; past vice pres: Old Cranwellian Assoc, Grantham Constituency Lib Democrats; sec Diocese of Lincoln 1971–76; *Recreations* photography, writing; *Clubs* RAF; *Style*— Air Vice-Marshal Michael Lyne, CB, AFC**, DL; ✉ 9 Far Lane, Coleby, Lincoln LN5 0AH (☎ 01522 810468)

LYNE, Roderic Michael John; CMG (1992); s of Air Vice-Marshal Michael Lyne, CB, AFC, DL, *qv*, of Coleby, Lincoln, and Avril Joy, *née* Buckley; *b* 31 March 1948; *Educ* Highfield Sch Liphook Hants, Eton, Univ of Leeds (BA); *m* 13 Dec 1969, Amanda Mary, da of Sir Howard Frank Trayton Smith, GCMG; 2 s (Jethro b 10 Nov 1971, Andrei b 31 May 1974), 1 da (Sasha b 7 Jan 1981); *Career* entered HM Dip Serv 1970, Br Embassy Moscow 1972–74, Br Embassy Senegal 1974–76; FCO: Eastern Europe and Soviet Dept 1976–78, Rhodesia Dept 1979, asst private sec to Foreign and Cwlth Sec 1979–82; UK mission to UN NY 1982–86, visiting res fell Royal Inst of Int Affrs 1986–87, head of Chancery and head of Political Section Br Embassy Moscow 1987–90, head of Soviet

Dept FCO 1990–91, head of Eastern Dept FCO 1992–92; private sec to PM 1993–96, dir Policy Devpt for CIS, Middle East and Africa British Gas plc 1996–; *Recreations* sport; *Style—* Roderic Lyne, Esq, CMG; ✉ c/o FCO, King Charles Street, London SW1

LYNER, Peter Edward; OBE (1991); s of Alfred Lyner, of Belfast, and Doreen Mary, *née* Devenney (d 1994); *b* 13 Oct 1942; *Educ* Royal Belfast Academical Inst, Univ of London (DPA); *m* 1964, Anne, da of Frederick Rogers (d 1974); 1 da (Anna Elizabeth b 1967), 1 s (Patrick Edward b 1970); *Career* librarian Belfast Public Library 1960–70, freelance journalist Irish Times until 1970; British Council: librarian Sudan 1970–73, librarian Yugoslavia 1973–76, inspr Mgmnt Servs Dept 1976–79, asst dir of educn Nigeria 1979–82, Russian language trg Univ of Strathclyde 1982–83, asst cultural attaché Moscow 1983–87, Bulgarian language trg SSEES 1987, cultural attaché Bulgaria 1987–90, dir Br Cncl N Ireland 1990–; ALA 1966, MIMgt 1981; *Books* Consignment of Ore (under pseudonym Peter Warden, 1983); *Recreations* music, writing, reading; *Style—* Peter Lyner, Esq, OBE; ✉ The British Council, 1 Chlorine Gardens, Belfast, BT9 5DJ (☎ 01232 666770, fax 01232 665242)

LYNK, Roy; OBE (1990); s of John Thomas Lynk (d 1950), and Ivy May Lynk (d 1980); *b* 9 Nov 1932; *Educ* Station Rd Higher Sch Notts, Univ of Nottingham (Cert Industl Rels); *m* 11 Nov 1978, Sandra Ann, da of William Watts (d 1949), and Harriet Watts; 3 s (Roy b 28 May 1968, John b 29 Nov 1972, Mark b 31 Aug 1971), 3 da (Lorraine b 12 June 1960, Carol b 1 Dec 1961, Dawn b 2 Dec 1964); *Career* RN 1948–50, TA 1956–68; miner British Coal 1947–79; NUM Nottingham Area: branch sec Sutton Colliery 1958–79, full time official 1979–83, fin sec 1983–85, gen sec 1985; UDM: gen sec Nottingham Section 1985–93, nat gen sec 1985–86, nat pres and sec 1987–93; asst area mangr Prince's Youth Business Tst 1994–96; conslt on human resource issues 1995–; memb: St John Ambulance Bde 1968–80, Euro Coal and Steel Ctee 1987–93, Industl Tbnls Nottingham 1992–, Bd The Coal Authy 1994–; dist cncllr Ashfield 1972–80; *Recreations* playing golf, watching football; *Style—* Roy Lynk, Esq, OBE; ✉ Columbia House, 143 Huthwaite Road, Sutton-in-Ashfield, Notts NG17 2HB (☎ 01623 513022)

LYNN, Archdeacon of; *see:* Foottit, Ven Anthony Charles

LYNN, Bishop of 1994–; Rt Rev David John Conner; s of William Ernest Conner (d 1989), and Joan Millington, *née* Cheek (d 1994); *b* 6 April 1947; *Educ* Erith GS, Exeter Coll Oxford (Symes exhibitioner, MA), St Stephen's House Oxford; *m* 10 July 1969, Jayne Maria, da of Lt-Col George E Evans, OBE; 2 s (Andrew David b 1970, Jonathan Paul b 1972); *Career* chaplain St Edward's Sch Oxford 1973–80 (asst chaplain 1971–73), team vicar Wolvercote with Summertown Oxford 1976–80, sr chaplain Winchester Coll 1980–86, vicar St Mary the Great with St Michaels Cambridge 1987–94, rural dean of Cambridge 1989–94; hon fell Girton Coll Cambridge 1995; *Recreations* reading and friends; *Style—* The Rt Rev the Bishop of Lynn; ✉ The Old Vicarage, Castle Acre, King's Lynn, Norfolk PE32 2AA (☎ 01760 755553, fax 01760 755085)

LYNN, Jonathan Adam; s of Dr Robin Lynn, of London, and Ruth Helen, *née* Eban; *b* 3 April 1943; *Educ* Kingswood Sch Bath, Pembroke Coll Cambridge (MA); *m* 1 Aug 1967, Rita Eleonora Merkelis; 1 s (Edward b 19 Oct 1973); *Career* director, writer and actor; Hon MA Univ of Sheffield; *Theatre* actor in repertory: Leicester, Edinburgh, Bristol Old Vic; West End (incl Fiddler on the Roof, 1967); artistic dir Cambridge Theatre Co 1977–81 (produced 42 prodns and directed over 20); London dir incl: The Glass Menagerie 1977, The Gingerbread Man 1977, The Unvarnished Truth 1978, Songbook 1979 (SWET and Evening Standard Awards for Best Musical, re-titled The Moony Shapiro Songbook for Broadway Prodn 1981), Anna Christie (RSC) 1979, Arms and the Man 1981, Pass The Butler 1981, A Little Hotel On The Side (NT) 1984, Jacobowski and the Colonel (NT) 1986, Three Men on a Horse (NT, Olivier Award for Best Comedy) 1987, Budgie 1988; company dir at NT 1986–87; *Television* as actor incl: Doctor in the House (series) 1970, The Liver Birds (series) 1972, My Brothers Keeper 1973 and 1974 (series, co-writer with George Layton), Barmitzvah Boy 1975, The Knowledge 1979, Outside Edge 1982, Diana 1984, as writer incl: Yes Minister 1980–82, Yes Prime Minister 1986–88 (with co-author Anthony Jay, BAFTA Writers' Award, Broadcasting Press Guild Award (twice), Pye Television Writers' Award (twice), Ace Award - best comedy writing on US cable TV, Special Award from The Campaign For Freedom of Information); TV dir: Smart Guys, Ferris Bueller (NBC TV pilots); *Film* as actor incl: Into The Night 1985, Three Men and A Little Lady 1990; screenplay The Internecine Project 1974; film as dir: Micks People (also wrote) 1982, Clue (also wrote) 1986, Nuns On The Run (also wrote, Golden Cane Award at Festival de Comedie Vevvey) 1989, My Cousin Vinny 1991, The Distinguished Gentleman 1991 (Environmental Media Award), Greedy 1993, Sgt Bilko 1995, Trial and Error 1997; *Books* A Proper Man (1976), The Complete Yes Minister (1984), Yes Prime Minister vol 1 (1986), vol 2 (with Antony Jay, 1987), Mayday (1993); *Recreations* changing weight; *Style—* Jonathan Lynn, Esq; ✉ c/o Peters Fraser and Dunlop, 5th Floor, The Chambers, Chelsea Harbour, Lots Road, London SW10 0XF (☎ 0171 344 1000, fax 0171 352 7356)

LYNN, Maurice Kenneth; *b* 3 March 1951; *Educ* Thornleigh Salesian Coll, Magdalen Coll Oxford (William Doncaster open scholar, Heath Harrison travelling scholar, MA); *Career* asst d'anglais École Normale Montpellier 1971–72; asst master: The Oratory Sch 1973–79, Radley Coll 1979–83; head of French Westminster Sch 1983–89, headmaster The Oratory Sch 1989–92; Westminster Sch: asst master 1992–95, head of modern languages 1995–; *Recreations* soccer, cycling, swimming, acting; *Style—* Maurice Lynn, Esq; ✉ Westminster School, 17 Dean's Yard, London SW1P 3PB (☎ 0171 222 2831)

LYNN, Michael David (Mike); *b* 18 July 1942; *m* 1965, Hilary, *née* Smyth; 1 da (Fiona b 1966), 1 s (Andrew b 1967); *Career* HMSO: joined 1960, dir Pubns Distribution 1980–83, dir of fin 1983–84, dir Print Procurement 1984–86, dir Gen IT & Supply 1986–87, DG Corp Servs 1987–89, dep chief exec 1989–95, controller and chief exec 1995–; *Style—* Mike Lynn, Esq; ✉ HMSO, St Crispins, Duke Street, Norwich NR3 1PD (☎ 01603 694200, fax 01603 695045)

LYNN, Prof Richard; s of Richard Lynn, and Ann Lynn; *b* 20 Feb 1930; *Educ* Bristol GS, King's Coll Cambridge (Passingham prize); *m* 1956 (m dis 1978), Susan Maher; 1 s, 2 da; m 2, 1989, Susan Lesley Hampson; *Career* lectr in psychology Univ of Exeter 1956–67; prof of psychology: Dublin Economic and Social Res Inst 1967–72, Univ of Ulster 1972–96 (prof emeritus 1996–); currently head Ulster Inst for Social Research; awarded US Mensa award for Excellence (for work on intelligence) 1985 and 1988; *Books* Attention Arousal and the Orientation Reaction (1966), The Irish Braindrain (1969), The Universities and the Business Community (1969), Personality and National Character (1971), An Introduction to the Study of Personality (1972), The Entrepreneur (ed, 1974), Dimensions of Personality (ed, 1981), Educational Achievement in Japan (1987), The Secret of the Miracle Economy (1991), Dysgenics (1997); author of various articles on personality, intelligence and social psychology; *Recreations* DIY, woodcutting; *Clubs* Northern Counties (Londonderry); *Style—* Prof Richard Lynn; ✉ Dunderg House, Coleraine, Co Londonderry, N Ireland

LYNN, Dame Vera Margaret; DBE (1975, OBE 1969); da of Bertram Welch, and Annie, *née* Martin; *b* 20 March 1917, East Ham; *Educ* Brampton Rd Sch East Ham; *m* 1941, Harry Lewis; 1 da (Virginia Penelope Ann); *Career* singer; with Ambrose Orch 1937–40, subsequently went solo, starred Applesauce (London Palladium) 1941, own radio show Sincerely Yours 1941–47; voted most popular singer Daily Express competition 1939, Forces' sweetheart WWII, toured Egypt, India, Burma 1944 (Burma Star 1985); subsequently: Tallulah Bankhead's Big Show (USA), London Laughs (Adelphi London), cabaret in Las Vegas, own TV show Vera Lynn Sings (BBC); numerous appearances over Europe, SA, Aust, NZ and Canada, 8 Command Performances, records incl Auf Wiederseh'n (over 12 million copies sold), first British artist to top American Charts; pres: Aust Variety Ladies' Assoc, RAFA, Y-Care Int Fund for Africa, London Taxi Drivers' Benevolent Fund, Young Concert Artists' Assoc, Local Women's Br Legion; first woman pres Printers' Charitable Corp; vice pres: Song Writers' Guild, Age Concern (memb Fund Raising Ctee); chm: Breast Cancer Tst Fund, Gilbert & Sullivan Tst Fund; vice chm Stars Orgn for Spastics, life govr Imperial Cancer Res Fund; Ivor Novello Award 1973, Show Business Personality Award Grand Order of Water Rats 1973, Music Publishers' Award and Songwriters of GB award 1974 and 1975, Woman of the World Award 1987, int ambass Variety Club Int 1987 (Humanitarian Award 1985); fndr Dame Vera Lynn Sch for Parents and Handicapped Children 1992, Master of Music City of London Univ 1992–; Freeman Cities of: London, Winnipeg (Canada), Melbourne (Aust), Cornerbrook (Newfoundland), Nashville (Tennessee); Hon LLD Meml Univ Newfoundland; fell Univ of E London 1990; Cdr of Orange Nassau (Holland) 1976; *Books* Vocal Refrain (autobiography, 1975), We'll Meet Again (jtly, 1989), Unsung Heroins (1990); *Recreations* gardening, painting, needlework, knitting; *Style—* Dame Vera Lynn, DBE

LYNNE, Elizabeth (Liz); MP (Lib Dem) Rochdale (majority 1,839); *b* 22 Jan 1948; *Educ* Dorking County GS; *Career* actress 1966–89 (numerous stage, TV, film and radio performances), freelance speech and voice conslt 1989–92; Parly candidate (Lib Alliance) Harwich 1987, MP (Lib Dem) Rochdale 1992–; Lib Dem spokesperson on: community care and homelessness for the North West 1990–92, social servs 1991–92; Lib Dem Parly spokesperson on: health and community care 1992–94, social security and disability 1994–; co-chair All Pty Gp on Breast Cancer, vice chair All Pty Gps on Manchester Airport, Child Support Agency Monitoring and Kashmir, sec All Pty Gp on Pensioners, memb numerous other all pty gps; chm Indonesian Co-ordination Gp Amnesty International 1972–79; memb Mgmnt Ctee: Rochdale Victim Support, Rochdale CAB; *Recreations* swimming, tennis, music, reading; *Style—* Liz Lynne, MP; ✉ House of Commons, London SW1A 0AA

LYNNE, Jeff; s of Philip Porter Lynne (d 1985), and Nancy, *née* Osborne (d 1988), of Birmingham; *b* 30 Dec 1947; *Educ* Alderlea Boys Sch Shard End Birmingham; *Career* producer, songwriter, singer and guitarist; band memb: Idle Race 1966–70, The Move 1970–72; formed: Electric Light Orchestra 1972–85 (toured America and Europe 1973–78, toured world 1978–82), The Traveling Wilbury's (with Roy Orbison, Bob Dylan, George Harrison and Tom Petty) 1988; writer, prodr, singer and guitarist of all ELO's records; albums incl: Eldorado (gold 1974), Face the Music (gold 1975), A New World Record (platinum 1976), Out of the Blue (quadruple platinum 1977, Nationwide Music Award/Album of the Year 1978), Discovery (double plantinum 1979), ELO's Greatest Hits (platinum 1980), Xanadu (film score, platinum 1980), Time (gold 1982); singles incl: Evil Woman (gold 1975, BMI Songwriters Award for 1,000,000 broadcasts in USA 1992), Livin' Thing (gold 1976), Telephone Line (gold 1977), Don't Bring Me Down (gold 1980), Xanadu (gold 1980, Ivor Novello Award for Best Film Theme Song 1981), Hold on Tight (gold 1982); co-prodr and co-writer Traveling Wilburys: Vol 1 (triple platinum 1988, Grammy Award 1989), Vol 3 (platinum 1991); solo album Armchair Theatre 1990; as prodr of other artists: co-prodr Cloud Nine (George Harrison, platinum 1987), prodr and co-writer Full Moon Fever (album, Tom Petty, triple platinum 1988), prodr and co-writer You Got It (Roy Orbison, platinum 1988), prodr and co-writer Into the Great Wide Open (Tom Petty, platinum 1991), co-prodr Free As a Bird (The Beatles, 1994), co-prodr Real Love (The Beatles, 1995); other major awards incl: Ivor Novello Award for contrib to British music 1979, Best Producer Rolling Stone Magazine 1989, Ivor Novello Award for outstanding contrib to British music 1996; memb: ASCAP, BASCA; *Recreations* computers, tennis; *Style—* Jeff Lynne, Esq

LYNTON, Prof Norbert Casper; s of Dr Paul Lynton (d 1974), and Amalie Christiane, *née* Lippert (d 1989); *b* 22 Sept 1927; *Educ* Douai Sch, Birkbeck Coll London (BA), Courtauld Inst (BA); *m* 1, 1949 (m dis 1968), Janet Mary, da of Henry Braid Irving; 2 s (Jeremy b 1957, Oliver b 1959); m 2, 3 May 1969, Sylvia Anne, da of Bernard Towning; 2 s (Thomas b 1970, Peter b 1973); *Career* lectr in history of art and architecture Leeds Coll of Art 1950–61, head Dept of Art History and Gen Studies Chelsea Sch of Art 1961–70 (previously sr lectr), dir of exhibitions Arts Cncl of GB 1970–75, visiting prof of history of art Open Univ 1975, prof of history of art Univ of Sussex 1975–89 (dean of Sch of Euro Studies 1985–88), visiting tutor in painting RCA 1989–92, currently involved in developing and organising exhibitions; recent exhibitions organised incl: Picturing People (Br Cncl, Kuala Lumpur, Hong Kong, Harare), Marc Vaux (NY), Victor Pasmore (NY), Ben Nicholson (Japan); written catalogues for exhibitions incl Henry Moore - The Human Dimension (Br Cncl and Henry Moore Fndn, Leningrad, Moscow, Helsinki) 1991; London corr Art International 1961–66, art critic The Guardian 1965–70, tstee Nat Portrait Gallery 1982–; chm Visual Art and Crafts Panel of SE Arts Assoc 1990–92; memb Assoc of Art Historians 1977; Hon FRCA 1993; *Books* incl: Paul Klee (1964), The Modern World (1968), The Story of Modern Art (2 edn, 1989), Looking at Art (1981), Looking into Paintings (jtly, 1985), Victor Pasmore, paintings and graphics 1980–92 (1992), Ben Nicholson (1993); *Style—* Prof Norbert Lynton; ✉ Flat 4, 14 Clifton Terrace, Brighton, E Sussex BN1 3HA (☎ 01273 328078)

LYON, Prof Christina Margaret; da of Edward Arthur Harrison, of Liverpool, and Kathleen Joan, *née* Smith; *b* 12 Nov 1952; *Educ* Wallasey HS for Girls, UCL (LLB, Maxwell Law prize); *m* 29 May 1976, Adrian Pirrie Lyon, s of Alexander Ward Lyon, of London; 1 s (David Edward Arandall b 8 July 1985), 1 da (Alexandra Sophie Louise b 5 Jan 1984); *Career* tutor and sometime lectr in law Faculty of Law UCL 1974–75; slr Bell & Joynson Liscard Wallasey Merseyside 1975–77; lectr in Law Faculty: Univ of Liverpool 1977–80, Univ of Manchester 1980–86 (sub-dean 1986); head Sch of Law Univ of Keele 1988–93 (prof of law and head Dept of Law 1986–93); prof of Common Law and head Dept of Law Faculty of Law Univ of Liverpool 1993– (dean Faculty of Law 1994–); Dr Barnardos Res Fellowship 1987–91; ed Journal of Social Welfare and Family Law 1984–, advsy ed Representing Children 1995–, pres N Staffs RELATE (marriage guidance) 1987–93 (memb Nat Exec Ctee 1991–94), ind memb Merseyside Children's Secure Accommodation Panel 1988–; memb ESRC Grants Bd 1988–91, memb Child Policy Review Gp NCB 1988–91, tstee, dir and chm IRCHIN, tstee and dir Schs Cncls (UK), vice chair Merseyside Guardians ad Libem Ctee 1993–; memb: Law Soc 1977, Soc of Public Teachers of Law 1977, Ctee of Heads of Univ Law Schs (and memb Exec Ctee 1989–); FRSA 1991; *Books* Matrimonial Jurisdiction of Magistrates Courts (1980), Cohabitation Without Marriage (1983), The Law of Residential Homes and Day Care Establishments (1984), Child Abuse (1990, 2 edn 1993), Atkins on Minors (1990), Butterworths Family Law Encyclopaedia (1990), Butterworths Family Law Handbook (1991), Living Away From Home (Barnardos, 1991), The Implications of the Children Act 1989 for Children with Disabilities (Barnardos, 1991), Butterworths Law and Practice relating to Children (1992), Atkins on Infants (vols 1 and 2, 1992), The Law relating to Children (Butterworths, 1993), Legal Issues Arising from the Care, Control and Safety of Children with Learning Disabilities who also Present Challenging Behaviour - Research Report and A Guide for Parents and Carers (Mental Health Foundation, 1994); *Recreations* tennis, opera, theatre, foreign travel, writing; *Style—* Prof Christina Lyon; ✉ Department of Law, Faculty of Law, University of Liverpool, PO Box 147, Liverpool L69 3BX (☎ 0151 794 2818, fax 0151 794 2829, telex 627095 UNILPL G, e-mail assl10@liv.ac.uk)

LYON, Capt Donald Stewart; s of Alexander Lyon (d 1969), of London, and Dorothy Elizabeth, *née* Tomlinson (d 1986); *b* 27 June 1934; *Educ* Goring Hall, King Edward VII Nautical Coll, Univ of London; *m* 27 June 1956, Marie Pauline, da of Walter Alfred Greenfield (d 1980); *Career* MN Offr Shell (cadet to chief offr) 1951–62; Inchcape Group 1962–73: gen mangr (prev asst) ME, dir and vice pres jt venture Incape/Canadian Pacific Canada; Thorn EMI Group 1977–82: dir AFA Minerva Ltd, chm overseas cos within gp; md Voith Engineering Ltd 1982–94 (ret), chm ABL Ltd 1993–; conslt to various cos; memb: Bahrain Soc, Anglo-Omani Soc; Freeman City of London 1974, Liveryman Honourable Co of Master Mariners; FInstD; *Recreations* squash; *Clubs* Special Forces, Oriental; *Style*— Capt Donald Lyon; ✉ Goldcrest, Badgers Holt, Hampers Lane, Storrington, West Sussex RH20 3ET

LYON, John Macdonald; *b* 12 April 1948; *Educ* Univ of Cambridge (MA); *m*; 2 c; *Career* Home Office: joined 1969, asst sec Ctee on the Future of Bdcasting 1974–77, sec Inquiry into Prison Disturbances 1990–91, head of Criminal Policy Dept 1994–; *Style*— John Lyon, Esq; ✉ Criminal Policy Department, The Home Office, 50 Queen Anne's Gate, London SW1H 9AT (☎ 0171 273 3000)

LYON, Dr John Stuart; s of Edwin Lyon (d 1947), and Isobelle Lydia, *née* Malkin (d 1973); *b* 14 April 1932; *Educ* King's Coll Taunton, St John's Coll Cambridge, Westminster Med Sch London (MA, MB BChir); *m* 4 Jan 1975, Christine Evelyn, da of John Edward Larner (d 1987); 1 s (Richard b 1977), 1 da (Annabelle b 1976); *Career* conslt psychiatrist Wessex RHA 1972; clinical teacher Univ of Southampton (ret 1993); clinical dir Adult Mental Health and unit med offr Basingstoke District; memb Ctees: RCPsych, Wessex RHA; involved with Mental Health Act Cmmn; memb: Mental Health Review Tbnls, Health Advsy Serv; pres Basingstoke MIND; non-exec dir and vice chm Loddon NHS Tst; MRCPsych, FRCPsych, MRCP, FRCP; *Books* Breast Cancer Management (contrib, 1977), Die Erkrangungen der Weiblichen Brustdrusse (contrib, 1982); *Recreations* photography, DIY (of necessity!); *Clubs* Basingstoke and Deane Rotary; *Style*— Dr John Lyon; ✉ Loddon NHS Trust, Clock Tower House, Park Prewett, Basingstoke, Hants RG24 9NA

LYON, Maj-Gen Robert; CB (1976), OBE (1964, MBE 1960); s of David Murray Lyon (d 1943), and Bridget, *née* Smith (d 1925); *b* 24 Oct 1923; *Educ* Ayr Acad; *m* 1, 1951, Constance Margaret (d 1982), da of Colin Gordon (d 1963); 1 s (David b 21 April 1953), 1 da (Melanie Jane (Mrs Manton) b 6 June 1957); m 2, 20 June 1992, Rosemary Jane, da of Gerald Hector Allchin; *Career* cmmnd A & SH 1943; served: Italy, Palestine, Egypt, Greece; transferred and regular cmmn RA 1947, 19 Field Regt BAOR 1947–53, instr Mons OCS 1953–56, 3 RHA Libya 1956, Staff Coll Camberley 1957, DAQMG 3 Div 1958–60, JSSC 1960, BC F Sphinx Battery 7 Para RHA ME 1961–62, GSO 1 ASD 2 MOD 1962–65; CO 4 Light Regt: Borneo (despatches), UK, Germany 1965–67; Brig CRA 1 Armd Div 1967–69, Imperial Def Coll 1970, dir operational requirements MOD 1971–73, Maj-Gen dir RA 1973–75, GOC SW Dist 1975–78, ret 1978; Col Cmdt RA 1976–; pres Army Hockey Assoc 1974–76; chm: Army Golf Assoc 1977–78, RA Cncl of Scotland 1984–90; memb: Lothian Territorial Assoc 1980–91, Offrs Assoc Scotland 1980–91; bursar Loretto Sch 1979–91; memb Exec Ctee: Ind Schs Bursars Assoc 1981–85, Ind Schs Info Serv (Scotland) 1988–90; HM cmmr Queen Victoria Sch Dunblane 1984–95; dir: Edinburgh Military Tattoo plc 1988–, Braemar Civic Amenities Tst 1986–88; regnl dir Scotland Mfrg Forum 1995–; memb Ctee Musselburgh Conservation Soc 1987–91; FIMgt (MBIM 1978, FBIM 1981); *Books* Irish Roulette; *Recreations* golf, gardening, writing; *Clubs* New (Edinburgh), Hon Co of Edinburgh Golfers, Craigendarroch Country; *Style*— Maj-Gen Robert Lyon, CB, OBE; ✉ Woodside, Braemar, Aberdeenshire (☎ and fax 01339 741667); November-April: Apt 6, La Punta, Avenida de Suecia, Los Cristianos, Arona, Tenerife, Canary Islands (☎ and fax 00 34 22 794592)

LYON, (Colin) Stewart Sinclair; s of Col Colin Sinclair Lyon, OBE, TD (d 1967), and Dorothy Winstanley, *née* Thomason (d 1946); *b* 22 Nov 1926; *Educ* Liverpool Coll, Trinity Coll Cambridge (MA); *m* 9 Aug 1958, Elizabeth Mary Fargus, da of Oliver Fargus Richards (d 1946); 4 s (Richard b 1959, Julian b 1961, Ian b 1962, Alistair b 1963), 1 da (Catherine b 1962); *Career* chief exec Victory Insurance Co Ltd 1974–76, dir and chief actuary Legal and General Assurance Society Ltd 1976–85, gp chief actuary Legal and General Group plc 1985–87 (dir and gen fin mangr 1980–87); dir: Lautro Ltd 1987–92, The Cologne Reinsurance Co Ltd 1987–, Aetna International (UK) Ltd 1988–91, Pearl Group PLC, UK Bd AMP and London Life 1991–, AMP (UK) plc 1994–; vice pres Br Numismatic Soc 1971– (pres 1966–70); dir: Disablement Income Gp 1984–94, City of Birmingham Touring Opera Ltd 1987–90; memb: Occupational Pensions Bd 1979–82, Inquiry into Provision for Retirement 1983–85; pres Inst of Actuaries 1982–84 (Gold medallist 1991); tstee: Ind Living Fund 1988–93, SE Music Tst 1994–; Sanford Saltus Gold medallist (Br Numismatic Soc) 1974; Freeman City of London, memb Worshipful Co of Actuaries 1984; FIA 1954, FSA 1972; *Books* Coinage in Tenth-Century England (with C E Blunt and B H I H Stewart, 1989); *Recreations* numismatics, amateur radio, music; *Clubs* Actuaries; *Style*— Stewart Lyon, Esq; ✉ Ardraeth, Malltraeth, Bodorgan, Anglesey LL62 5AW (☎ 01407 840273)

LYON, Thomas Stephen; s of Clifford Alexander Lyon (d 1962), and Felicia Maria Maximiliana, *née* Rosenfeld; *b* 26 Nov 1941; *Educ* Univ Coll Sch, Wadham Coll Oxford (MA), LSE (LLM); *m* 1971, Judith Elizabeth Jervis, da of Joseph Globe, of Toronto, Canada; 3 s (Edmund b 1971, Charles b 1973, Roger b 1974); *Career* slr; Woodham Smith Borradaile and Martin 1962–68, Berwin & Co 1968–70, Berwin Leighton 1970–; memb City of London Slrs' Co; *Recreations* books, music; *Clubs* Reform; *Style*— Thomas Lyon, Esq; ✉ 24 Denewood Rd, Highgate, London N6 4AJ (☎ 0181 340 0846); Fernlea, Redmire, Leyburn, N Yorks (☎ 01969 22776)

LYON, Victor Lawrence; s of Dr Jacqueline Beverley Lyon; *b* 10 Feb 1956; *Educ* Marlborough, Trinity Coll Cambridge (BA); *m* 4 Oct 1986, (Rosalind) Sara, da of late Anthony Compton Burnett; 2 s (Frederick James b 19 Feb 1990, Jonathan Henry b 22 Aug 1991); *Career* called to the Bar Gray's Inn 1980; *Recreations* tennis, golf, swimming; *Style*— Victor Lyon, Esq; ✉ Essex Court Chambers, 24 Lincoln's Inn Fields, London WC2A 3ED (☎ 0171 813 8000, fax 0171 813 8080, telex COMCAS G 888465)

LYON-DALBERG-ACTON, *see:* Acton

LYONS, Alastair David; *b* 18 Oct 1953; *Educ* Whitgift Sch Croydon, Trinity Coll Cambridge (MA); *m* Shauneen, *née* Rhodes; 1 s (Edward Alexander Rhodes b 1982), 2 da (Lucy Jane b 1984, Tabitha Sallyanne b 1993); *Career* articled clerk rising to asst audit mangr Price Waterhouse & Co CAs 1974–79, corp finance mangr N M Rothschild & Sons Ltd 1979; H P Bulmer Holdings plc: gp treas 1979–82, gp financial controller 1983–88, fin dir H P Bulmer Drinks Ltd and actg gp fin dir 1988–89; divnl dir corp fin Asda Group plc 1989–90, fin dir Asda Stores Ltd 1990–91; National and Provincial Building Society: fin dir 1991–94, chief exec 1994–96, chm N&P Life Assurance Ltd and N&P Unit Trust Management Ltd; md Insurance Div Abbey National plc 1996–; dir: Scottish Mutual Assurance plc 1996–, Abbey National Life plc 1996–, Commercial Union Underwriting Ltd 1996–; non-exec dir Benefits Agency 1994–; govr Giggleswick Sch; ATII, MCT; FCA; *Recreations* cycling, riding, hill walking, gardening, antiques; *Style*— Alastair Lyons, Esq; ✉ Abbey National plc, Provincial House, Bradford, W Yorks BD1 1NL (☎ 01274 842524, fax 01274 842387)

LYONS, Bernard; CBE (1964), JP (Leeds 1960), DL (Yorks W Riding 1971); s of S H Lyons, of Leeds; *b* 30 March 1913; *Educ* Leeds GS; *m* 1938, Lucy, da of Wilfred Hurst, of Leeds; 3 s, 1 da; *Career* dir, chm and md UDS Group Ltd 1954–82 (pres 1983–); memb Leeds City Cncl 1951–65; chm: Leeds Judean Youth Club 1955–70, Swarthmore Adult Educn Centre Appeal 1957–60, City of Leeds Audit Sub Ctee 1959–63, Yorks and NE Conciliation Ctee Race Relations Bd 1968–70; jt chm Leeds Branch Cncl of Christians and Jews 1955–60, hon life pres Leeds Jewish Rep Cncl 1960–; memb: Ct and Cncl Univ of Leeds 1953–58, Cmmn for Community Relations 1970–72, Govt Advsy Ctee on Retail Distribution 1970–76; Hon LLD Leeds 1973; *Books* The Thread is Strong (1981), The Narrow Edge (1985), The Adventures of Jimmie Jupiter (1988), Tombola (1995); *Recreations* farming, forestry, travel, writing; *Style*— Bernard Lyons, Esq, CBE, JP, DL; ✉ Upton Wood, Fulmer, Bucks SL3 6JJ (☎ 01753 662404)

LYONS, Derek Jack; s of Leslie Albert Lyons (d 1950), and Vera Violet Lyons (d 1988); *b* 5 Dec 1943; *Educ* Cranleigh; *m* 26 Feb 1982, Philippa Kate; 1 s (Robert), 1 step s (Stewart), 1 step da (Charlotte); *Career* Union Discount Co of London plc 1961–70, A C Goode Group of Co's Melbourne 1970–71, exec dir Union Discount Co of London 1983–95, md Union Discount Co Ltd 1991–95, dir Aitken Campbell & Co Ltd 1993–95; dir Roehampton Club Members Ltd 1991–; *Recreations* sport, walking, travelling; *Clubs* Roehampton, Jesters; *Style*— Derek Lyons, Esq; ✉ 8 Firs Avenue, East Sheen, London SW14 7NZ (☎ 0181 876 1151)

LYONS, Edward; QC (1974); s of Albert Lyons (d 1950), of Leeds, and Sarah, *née* Sellman; *b* 17 May 1926; *Educ* Roundhay Sch Leeds, Univ of Leeds (LLB); *m* 4 Sept 1955, Barbara, da of Alfred Katz (d 1972), of London; 1 s (John Adam b 1959), 1 da (Jane Amanda b 1961); *Career* served RA 1944–48, interpreter in Russian Br Control Cmmn Germany 1946–48; barr 1952, recorder of the Crown Ct 1972–, bencher Lincoln's Inn 1983–; MP: (Lab) Bradford E 1966–74, Bradford W 1974–81, (SDP) Bradford W 1981–83; PPS Treasy 1969–70, chm PLP Home and Legal Affrs Gps 1977–79, Parly spokesman SDP Home and Legal Affrs 1981–83, memb SDP Nat Ctee 1984–89; *Recreations* history, walking, opera; *Style*— Edward Lyons, Esq, QC; ✉ 4 Primley Park Lane, Leeds LS17 7JR (☎ 0113 268 5351); 59 Westminster Gdns, Marsham St, London SW1P 4JG (☎ 0171 834 1960); 4 Brick Court, Temple, London EC4Y 9AD (☎ 0171 797 8910, fax 0171 797 8929); 6 Park Sq, Leeds LS1 2LW (☎ 0113 245 9763, fax 0113 242 4395)

LYONS, Gary; s of Michael John Lyons, and Diane Rosemary, *née* Mills; *b* 21 June 1968; *Educ* Essington St John's Secdy Sch, Cheslyn Hay High; *m* 31 March 1990, Debbie Lane, da of David William Watkins; *Career* National Hunt jockey; amateur jockey in Point to Points (100 rides and 2 winners) 1984–87, turned professional 1987 (800 rides and 70 winners to date); *Recreations* racing, sleep with a little bit of squash; *Style*— Gary Lyons, Esq; ✉ 27 Beech Pine Close, Hednesford, Cannock, Staffs (☎ 01543 876740); c/o R Hollinshead, Lodge Farm, Upper Longdon, Nr Rugeley, Staffs (☎ 01543 490490)

LYONS, Isidore Jack; s of Samuel Henry Lyons (d 1958), of Leeds, and Sophia, *née* Niman; *b* 1 Feb 1916; *Educ* Leeds GS; *m* 21 Dec 1943, Roslyn Marion, da of Prof Dr Jacob Rosenbaum; 2 s (David Stephen, Jonathon Edward Lyons, *qv*), 2 da (Patricia Gail, Joanna Gaye); *Career* jt md: Alexandre Ltd 1953–73, Prices Trust Ltd 1955–80; dir: UDS Group 1955–80, Bain Capital Boston Mass 1984–87 (UK advsr 1981–87); chm: J Lyons, Chamberlayne & Co 1985–, J E London Properties Ltd 1987–, Natural Nutrition Co Ltd 1989–90; fin advsr Chamberlayne Macdonald Trust 1981–88, advsr Guinness Group PLC 1985–87; chm: LSO Trust 1961–91, Shakespeare Quad-Centenary Exhbn 1963–66, USA Bicentennial (cultural FO appt) 1974–76; fndr and chm Leeds Int Piano Competition 1964–65, dep chm Fanfare for Europe 1971–73, life tstee Shakespeare Birthplace Tst 1967, fndr and chm of tstees Sir Jack Lyons Charitable Tst; fndr Sir Jack Lyons Hall Univ of York Music Dept 1964, co-fndr Sir Jack Lyons Theatre Royal Acad of Music 1971, jt chm Henry Wood Rehearsal Hall London; memb: Ct Univ of York 1965, The Pilgrims 1967–; fndr memb World Wild Life 1001 Club 1970–; Freeman City of London; Hon DUniv York 1975, Hon FRAM 1973; *Recreations* tennis, swimming; *Style*— Isidore Jack Lyons; ✉ Chateau d'Oex 1837, Vaud, Switzerland

LYONS, Sir James Reginald; kt (1969), JP (Cardiff 1966); s of James Lyons (d 1968), and Florence Hilda Lyons (d 1951); *b* 15 March 1910; *Educ* Howard Gardens HS, Cardiff Tech Coll; *m* 1937, Mary Doreen, da of Thomas Alfred Fogg (d 1936); 1 s (Colin); *Career* served WW II Royal Tank Regt 1940–46; civil serv 1929–65; Cardiff City Cncl: cncllr 1949–58, Alderman 1958–74, Dep Lord Mayor 1966–67, Lord Mayor 1968–69; memb: Wales Tourist Bd 1951–72, BBC Wales; airport mangr Cardiff Airport 1954–75; chm and govr: De La Salle Sch, St Illtyds Coll 1955–91, Univ Coll Cardiff 1955–70; local govt offr 1965–75, co dir 1977–; assessor under Race Rels Act 1976, pres Welsh Games Cncl, pres Cardiff Hort Soc 1962–; memb Norfolk Ctee 1968; holder of Silver Acorn for Scouts; Gold Medal Fratres Scholarum Christian Romae (De La Salle Brothers) 1988; OStJ, KCSG 1975; *Recreations* rugby, all outdoor games; *Clubs* Cardiff Athletic; *Style*— Sir James Lyons, JP; ✉ 101 Minehead Ave, Sully, South Glamorgan, Wales CF64 5TL (☎ 01222 530403)

LYONS, Sir John; kt (1987); *b* 23 May 1932; *Educ* St Bede's Coll Manchester, Christ's Coll Cambridge (BA, Dip Ed, PhD, LittD); *m* 1959, Danielle Jacqueline Simonet; *Career* lectr in comparative linguistics SOAS of London 1957–61, lectr in gen linguistics Univ of Cambridge and fell Christ's Coll 1961–64, prof of gen linguistics Univ of Edinburgh 1964–76, prof of linguistics Univ of Sussex 1976–84 (pro vice chllr 1981–84), master Trinity Hall Cambridge 1984–; hon fell Christ's Coll Cambridge 1985; hon memb Linguistic Soc of America 1978; Docteur-ès-Lettres (Honoris Causa) Univ Cath de Louvain 1980; Hon DLitt: Univ of Reading 1986, Univ of Edinburgh 1988, Univ of Sussex 1990, Univ of Antwerp 1992; FBA 1973; *Books* Structural Semantics (1963), Psycholinguistics Papers (ed with R J Wales, 1966), Introduction to Theoretical Linguistics (1968), Chomsky (1970), New Horizons in Linguistics (1970), Semantics 1 and 2 (1977), Language and Linguistics (1980), Language, Meaning and Context (1980), Natural Language and Universal Grammar (1991), Linguistic Semantics (1995); *Style*— Sir John Lyons, FBA; ✉ Master's Lodge, Trinity Hall, Cambridge CB2 1TJ

LYONS, John; CBE (1986); s of Joseph Sampson Lyons (d 1989), and Henrietta, *née* Nichols (d 1984); *b* 19 May 1926; *Educ* St Paul's, Regent St Poly, Emmanuel Coll Cambridge (BA); *m* 25 March 1954, Molly; 4 c (Katherine Anna b 1958, Roderick Michael b 1960, Jane Rosalind b 1962, Matthew Jeremy b 1966); *Career* WWII RNVR 1944–46, Sub Lt Far Eastern Command; asst to mkt res mangr Vacuum Oil 1950; res offr: Bureau of Current Affrs 1951, PO Engrg Union 1952–57; dep gen sec IPCS 1966–73 (asst sec 1957–66); gen sec: Electrical Power Engrs Assoc 1973–91, Engrs and Mangrs Assoc 1977–91; memb: Exec Ctee Political and Econ Planning 1975–78, Nat Enterprise Bd 1976–79, Exec Ctee Industl Participation Assoc 1976–90, Cncl Policy Studies Inst 1978–81, Advsy Cncl for Applied R and D 1978–81, Court of Govrs LSE 1978–84, Bd of BT 1980–83, Engrg Cncl 1982–86 (fndr memb), Governing Body London Business Sch 1986–87; jt sec: Nat Jt Coordinating Ctee Electricity Supply Indust 1980–90, Nat Jt Negotiating Ctee Electricity Supply Indust 1980–86; sec Electricity Supply Trade Union Cncl 1976–91; chm: NEDC Working Party on Indust Trucks 1977–80, TUC Energy Ctee 1988–91; memb: TUC Gen Cncl 1983–91, Wilton Park Acad Cncl 1989–95, EC Econ and Social Ctee 1990–; hon memb Electrical Power Engrs' Assoc 1991, hon fell Inst of Incorporated Exec Engrs 1991; FRSA 1980; *Recreations* family, gardening, reading, music, golf, chess; *Style*— John Lyons, Esq, CBE; ✉ 305 Salmon Street, Kingsbury, London NW9 8YA

LYONS, John Trevor; s of Sir Rudolph Lyons, and Jeanette, *née* Dante; *b* 1 Nov 1943; *Educ* Leeds GS, Univ of Leeds (LLB); *m* 7 Sept 1969, Dianne Lucille, da of Geoffrey Saffer; 3 s (Alan b 1971, James b 1973, Benjamin b 1974); *Career* slr; ptnr Lyons & Dorsey; *Style*— John T Lyons, Esq; ✉ 140 Alwoodley Lane, Leeds LS17 7PP (☎ 0113

267 4575); Lyons & Dorsey, 20 East Parade, Leeds LS1 2BH (☎ 0113 243 3381, fax 0113 245 0559)

LYONS, Jonathon Edward; s of Isidore Jack Lyons, *qv*; *b* 1 May 1951; *Educ* Carmel Coll; *m* 30 Dec 1975, Miriam, da of Simon Djanogly (d 1980), of Geneva, Switzerland; 2 s (Jacob b 1976, Simon b 1980), 1 da (Deborah b 1983); *Career* exec sales Alexandra Ltd Leeds 1968–71, chief exec John David Mansworld Ltd 1971–89, ptnr International Investments Ltd 1978–, chief exec H Alan Smith Ltd 1983–85, dir JLC Ltd London 1986, jt chief exec JE London Properties Ltd 1988–, private investmt conslt Jonathon E Lyons & Co 1988–; dir: Britimpex Ltd Canada, Art Leasing Inc Canada, Johnson Fry plc (Jt Venture Property Div) 1994–; memb Ctee: Cons Industl Fund 1985–91, RMC, RAM; jt chm Hyde Park Ctee Central Br Fund 1975–80, tstee Sir Jack Lyons Charitable Tst 1986; rotarian Int Rotary Club 1995–; FInstD, memb FIMBRA; *Clubs* Carlton, IOD; *Style*— Jonathon E Lyons, Esq; ✉ 35 Loudoun Rd, St John's Wood, London NW8 (☎ 0171 624 7733); Chalet Emeraude, 1837 Chateau D'Oex, Switzerland; 8 Ledbury Mews North, Kensington, London W11 2AF (☎ 0171 229 9481, fax 0171 229 9229, car phone 0385 330033)

LYONS, (Andrew) Maximilian; s of Dennis John Lyons, CB, of Summerhaven, Gough Rd, Fleet, Hants, and Elizabeth Dora Maria, *née* Müller Haefliger; *b* 16 Jan 1946; *Educ* Queen Mary's GS Basingstoke, Brixton Sch of Bldg (graduate, DipArch); *m* 16 June 1983, Katherine Jane (Kate), da of Brig John Joseph Regan; 1 s (Shaun b 1984), 2 da (Rosalie b 1986, Charlotte b 1989); *Career* sr ptnr Lyons + Sleeman + Hoare architects 1974–; winner of: Euro Architectural Heritage Award 1974, Civic Tst Award 1988, 1992 and 1993, Br Cncl of Shopping Centres Award 1987 and 1992, Euro Cncl of Shopping Centres Award 1988, City Heritage Award of London 1988, Silver Jubilee Cup RTPI 1988, other environmental and design awards; RIBA 1974, FRSA 1993; *Recreations* sailing, shooting, walking; *Style*— Maximilian Lyons, Esq; ✉ School Lane House, School Lane, Ewshot, Farnham, Surrey GU10 5BN (☎ 01252 850222); Lyons + Sleeman + Hoare, Nero Brewery, Cricket Green, Hartley Wintney, Hook, Hampshire RG27 8QA (☎ 01252 844144, fax 01252 844800)

LYONS, Roger Alan; s of Morris Lyons (d 1990), of Hove, and Phyllis, *née* Lebof (d 1989); *b* 14 Sept 1942; *Educ* Christ's Coll Finchley, UCL (BSc(Econ)); *m* Kitty, *née* Horvath; 2 da (Sarah b 1973, Hannah b 1982), 2 s (Gideon b 1975, Joshua b 1986); *Career* ASTMS: regnl offr (North West) 1966–70, nat offr 1970–86, asst gen sec 1986–88 (until merger with TASS to form MSF); MSF: asst gen sec 1988–92, gen sec 1992–; memb TUC Gen Cncl, memb Exec Ctee Confedn of Shipbuilding and Engrg Unions, memb Monopolies and Mergers Cmmn 1995–; fell UCL 1996; *Recreations* supporting Arsenal; *Style*— Roger Lyons, Esq; ✉ 22 Park Crescent, London N3 2NJ (☎ 0181 346 6843); Manufacturing, Science and Finance Union, MSF Centre, 33–37 Moreland Street, London EC1V 8BB (☎ 0171 505 3011, fax 0171 505 3014)

LYONS, His Hon Judge; Shaun; s of Jeremiah Lyons (d 1978), and Winifred Ruth, *née* Doble; *b* 20 Dec 1942; *Educ* Portsmouth GS, Inns of Court Sch of Law; *m* 19 Dec 1970, Nicola Rosemary, da of Capt D F Chilton, DSC, RN; 1 s (Francis Daniel b 4 Jan 1972), 1 da (Victoria Clare b 26 Feb 1974); *Career* with RN 1961–92; Lt 1966, Lt Cdr 1974, called to the Bar Middle Temple 1975, Capt RN 1988 (Cdr 1981), chief naval judge advocate 1990–92, recorder of the Crown Court 1991–92 (asst recorder 1988–91), circuit judge (SE Circuit) 1992–, res judge Wood Green Crown Court 1995–; *Recreations* reading, gardening, walking; *Clubs* Army & Navy; *Style*— His Hon Judge Lyons; ✉ Wood Green Crown Court, Woodall House, Lordship Lane, London N22 4LF (☎ 0181 881 1400)

LYONS, Prof Terence John; s of Peter John Lyons, of Puddle, nr Lanlivery, Bodmin, Cornwall, and Christobel Valerie, *née* Hardie; *b* 4 May 1953; *Educ* Univ of Cambridge (BA), Univ of Oxford (DPhil); *m* 30 Aug 1975, (Christina) Barbara, da of Joseph Epsom; 1 s (Barnaby b 1981), 1 da (Josephine b 1983); *Career* jr res fell Jesus Coll Oxford 1979–81, Hedrick visiting asst prof UCLA 1981–82, lectr in mathematics Imperial Coll of Sci and Technol 1981–85; Univ of Edinburgh: Colin MacLaurin prof of mathematics 1985–93, head Dept of Mathematics 1988–91, hon prof 1993–; prof of mathematics Imperial Coll of Sci Technol and Med 1993–, sr fell EPSRC 1993–; FRSE 1987, FRSA 1990, FIMA 1991; *Recreations* cycling, swimming; *Style*— Prof Terence Lyons, FRSE; ✉ 4 Mark Terrace, The Drive, Wimbledon, London SW20 8TF (☎ and fax 0181 947 5198, e-mail t.lyons@ic.ac.uk)

LYONS, Thomas Colvill Holmes (Toby); s of Robert Henry Cary Lyons, of Powys, and Dorothy Joan Garnons Lyons; *b* 8 March 1937; *Educ* Harrow, Oriel Coll Oxford (MA); *m* 1, 17 July 1965 (m dis 1971), Heather Mary Menzies Forbes; 1 s (David b 1968), 1 da (Sophia b 1966); m 2, 3 June 1972, (Gwendolin) Frances, da of Col W D Gosling, TD, DL; 2 da (Kate b 1975, Annabel b 1976); *Career* RWF 1956–58 (TA 1958–69); admitted slr 1965, Linklaters & Paines 1964–66, Allen & Overy 1966–69, md Minster Tst Ltd 1973–91; dir: Minster Assets plc 1976–91, Tillshare plc 1984–90, Monument Oil & Gas plc 1984–91; chm R & J Hadlee Fine Art plc 1985–92; Liveryman Worshipful Co of Tinplate Workers (former memb Ct of Assts); memb Law Soc 1965; *Recreations* shooting, watersports, winter sports; *Style*— Toby Lyons, Esq; ✉ Hole Farm, Stansted, Essex CM24 8TJ

LYONS, Tony; s of Michael Lyons, of London, and Edith, *née* Morris; *b* 12 April 1947; *Educ* Tottenham GS, Univ of London (BA), Univ of Kent; *m* 30 July 1969, Alison, da of Simon MacLeod; 2 s (Matthew Michael Simon b 30 Nov 1973, Frazer Alexander David b 3 Nov 1981), 1 da (Jessica Jane b 23 May 1976); *Career* dep ed Planned Savings 1969–71, journalist Sunday Telegraph 1971–78, dep city ed The Observer 1978–81, owner public houses 1982–85, asst city ed Birmingham Post 1985–86, dir Buchanan Communications 1986–93, dir Tavistock Communications 1993–; *Recreations* good food, fishing, walking, films, relaxing; *Style*— Tony Lyons, Esq; ✉ Tavistock Communications Ltd, 1 Angel Court, London EC2R 7HX (☎ 0171 600 2288, fax 0171 600 5084)

LYONS, Hon William (Bill); s of Baron Lyons of Brighton (d 1978); *b* 1945; *m* 1, 1963 (m dis), Petra Deanna, da of William Tibble; 1 s (Kevin Oliver b 1964), 1 da (Teena Fern b 1967); m 2, 1986, Gillian Mary, da of Alfred Tullett; 1 da (Natasha Beatrice Holly b 1987), 1 s (Braham William Ash b 1990); *Career* writer: Z-Cars, Rooms, Juliet Bravo, Blake's 7, Gems, Marked Personal, Angels, Waggoners Walk, Eldorado; writer/storyliner/story ed East Enders; devisor/writer Working it Out; dir: HyVision, WRITinc; Writers' Guild of GB Award for Educnl Drama 1977; *Style*— The Hon William Lyons

LYSAGHT, Patrick James; s of late Horace James William Lysaght (bro of 6 Baron Lisle); hp to Barony of Lisle; *b* 1 May 1931; *Educ* Shrewsbury; *m* 1957, Mary Louise, da of late Lt-Col Geoffrey Reginald Devereux Shaw, and formerly w of Euan Guy Shaw-Stewart (later 10 Bt); 2 s, 1 da; *Career* former journalist and farmer; *Style*— Patrick Lysaght, Esq

LYSTER, Guy Lumley; DL (Essex 1975); s of Ronald Guy Lyster, OBE (d 1972), of Lances, Kelvedon, Essex, and Ada Erica, *née* Neal (d 1977); *b* 4 April 1925; *Educ* Winchester, Trinity Coll Cambridge (MA); *m* 10 May 1958, Gillian Rosemary, da of Michael Spencer Gosling (d 1979), of Parks Farm, Little Maplestead, Essex; 1 s (Anthony b 1960), 1 da (Sarah (Mrs Michael Retallack) b 1961); *Career* Grenadier Gds 1943–47: served NW Europe 1945, Capt 1946; Strutt & Parker Coval Hall Chelmsford: chartered surveyor 1952, assoc ptnr 1958, ptnr 1969, dep sr ptnr 1979, ret 1992; farmer and breeder of pedigree Charolais cattle 1967–; Master E Essex Foxhounds 1983–93, judge HIS, BSPS and Ponies of Br Panels; Freeman City of London, Liveryman Worshipful Co of Salters 1955; FRICS 1961, FCAAV 1961; *Recreations* hunting, shooting, cricket; *Clubs* Cavalry and Guards'; *Style*— Guy Lyster, Esq, DL; ✉ Rayne Hatch House, Stisted, Braintree, Essex CM7 8BY (☎ 01787 472087, fax 01787 476071)

LYSTER, Peter Haggard; s of Lionel Charles Lyster (d 1980), of Apps, Stock, Essex, and Avice Dorothy, *née* Haggard (d 1986); *b* 17 Nov 1934; *Educ* Marlborough; *m* 1967, Gillian Barbara, da of Sir Arthur John Grattan-Bellew, CMG, QC (d 1985); 1 s (Thomas), 2 da (Grania, Anna); *Career* former 2 Lt 11 Hussars; former Capt City of London Yeo; ptnr Wedd Durlacher Mordaunt & Co 1962–86; memb: Stock Exchange 1956, Cncl of Stock Exchange 1978–86; joint-master Meynell Foxhounds 1972–76; *Recreations* hunting, fishing; *Clubs* Cavalry and Guards', City of London; *Style*— Peter H Lyster, Esq; ✉ Little Chishill Manor, Royston, Herts (☎ 01763 838238)

LYSTER, Simon; s of John Neal Lyster, and Marjorie Aird, *née* Everard; *b* 29 April 1952; *Educ* Radley, Magdalene Coll Cambridge (MA, PhD); *m* 1990, Sandra Elizabeth Charity; 2 c; *Career* admitted slr England and Wales 1978, qualified New York attorney-at-law 1979; slr Slaughter and May 1976–78, prog offr Defenders of Wildlife (USA) 1979–81, sec Falkland Islands Fndn 1982–86, treaties offr WWF International and head of conservation policy WWF UK 1986–95, dir gen The Wildlife Trusts 1995–; *Books* International Wildlife Law (1985); *Recreations* tennis, cricket, birdwatching; *Style*— Simon Lyster, Esq; ✉ The Wildlife Trusts, 72–73 Wilton Road, London SW1V 1DE (☎ 0171 931 0744, fax 0171 931 0025)

LYTHALL, Basil Wilfrid; CB (1966); s of Frank Herbert Lythall (d 1969), of Kingswinford, Staffs, and Winifred Mary, *née* Carver (d 1953); *b* 15 May 1919; *Educ* King Edward's Sch Stourbridge, ChCh Oxford (MA); *m* 1942, Mary Olwen, da of Simon Dando (d 1980), of Wall Heath, W Midlands; 1 s (David); *Career* joined Royal Naval Scientific Serv 1940, asst dir Physical Res Admty 1957–58, dep chief scientist Admty Surface Weapons Estab 1958–60, first chief scientist Admty Underwater Weapons Estab 1960–64, chief scientist RN and memb Admty Bd Def Cncl 1964–78, dep controller of Navy for R & D 1964–71, dep controller Estabs and Res Procurement Exec MOD 1971–78; dir Saclant ASW Res Centre La Spezia Italy 1978–81; tstee Nat Maritime Museum 1974–80; chm: CORDA Policy Bd, Sema Group 1985–89; tech advsr MMC 1989 and 1990; memb Elmbridge Area Advsy Gp Surrey Youth and Continuing Educn Serv 1987–; *Recreations* sculpting, music, genealogy; *Style*— B W Lythall, Esq, CB; ✉ 48 Grove Way, Esher, Surrey KT10 8HL (☎ 0181 398 2958)

LYTHGOE, Joseph; s of Adam Lythgoe (d 1946), of Wigshaw Grange, Culcheth, Warrington, and Mary Elizabeth, *née* Leather; *b* 11 Aug 1922; *Educ* Ashton-in-Makerfield GS; *m* 1, 1948 (m dis 1989), Catherine Crompton, *née* Brooks; 1 s (David b 1954); m 2, 1990, Dorothy Deighton; *Career* served RCS 1941–46; chm and md Adam Lythgoe Ltd; fndr pres Country Guardian (opposing desecration of the countryside by wind-farms); *Recreations* restoration of rural economy, landscape conservation; *Clubs* Farmers', Warrington; *Style*— Joseph Lythgoe, Esq; ✉ Swinhoe House, Culcheth, Warrington WA3 4NH (☎ 01925 764106, fax 01925 767620)

LYTLE, Maj-Gen Simon William St John; CB (1995), DL (Hampshire 1996); *Educ* Sherborne, RMA Sandhurst; *m* Pam; 3 s; *Career* cmmnd Royal Irish Fusiliers 1960, served Libya, Germany and Sweden, Army Pilots' Course 1964, pilot Far E 1965–68, cmd Air Platoon Royal Irish Fusiliers 1968–69; transferred Army Air Corps 1969, psc 1973, cmd 658 Sqdn AAC Minden 1974–75, HQ BAOR 1976–77, staff offr Staff Coll 1978–81, cmd 1 Regt AAC Hildesheim 1981–83, Dep Dir Operational Requirements (Air) i/c operational requirements of all (AAC and RAF) battlefield helicopters 1983–86, Brig Cmdg Aviation BAOR 1986–89, rcds 1989, Dir of Army Recruiting 1989–92, Dir AAC 1992–Dec 1995, Dir Army Sport Control Bd 1996–; *Recreations* offshore sailing, tennis, bridge, disappointing golf; *Style*— Maj-Gen S W St J Lytle, CB, DL; ✉ Director, Army Sport Control Board, Clayton Barracks, Aldershot, Hants, GU11 2BG (☎ 01252 348568)

LYTTELTON, Hon Christopher Charles; s of 10 Viscount Cobham, KG, GCMG, GCVO, TD, PC (d 1977), and Elizabeth Alison, *née* Makeig-Jones; *b* 23 Oct 1947; *Educ* Eton; *m* 1973, Tessa Mary, da of Col Alexander George Jeremy Readman, DSO (d 1973); 1 s (Oliver b 1976), 1 da (Sophie b 1978); *Career* chm and chief exec NCL Investments Ltd (stockbrokers); *Recreations* gliding, cricket; *Clubs* MCC, Booker Gliding; *Style*— The Hon Christopher Lyttelton; ✉ 28 Abbey Gardens, London NW8 9AT; NCL Investments Ltd, 9–12 Basinghall St, London EC2V 5NS (☎ 0171 600 2801)

LYTTELTON, Humphrey Richard Adeane; descended from Humphrey Lyttelton who was executed for collaborating with Guy Fawkes in the Gunpowder Plot; *b* 23 May 1921; *Educ* Eton, Camberwell Art Sch; *Career* served WWII Grenadier Gds; former cartoonist London Daily Mail; jazz musician (trumpet, clarinet, tenor horn), bandleader, author, broadcaster and after-dinner speaker; trumpeter George Webb's Dixielanders 1947, formed The Humphrey Lyttelton Band (with Wally Fawkes on clarinet) 1948, solo visit to first Int Jazz Festival Nice 1948, early recordings made on own London Jazz label, signed recording contract with EMI and accompanied Sidney Bechet for Melodisc 1949, subsequent recordings for Parlophone Super Rhythm Style series incl Bad Penny Blues 1956, played series of London concerts alongside Louis Armstrong All Stars 1956, extended band to incl Joe Temperley, Tony Coe and Jimmy Skidmore (toured USA 1959), subsequent collaborations in Britain with Buck Clayton, Buddy Tate and singers Jimmy Rushing and Joe Turner, fndr Calligraph record label 1984; host The Best of Jazz (BBC Radio 2) for over 20 years, chm I'm Sorry I Haven't a Clue (BBC Radio 4) 1972–; Gold award Sony Radio Awards 1993; former regular contributor to Punch, The Field and BA Highlife magazines; pres Soc for Italic Handwriting 1991; Hon DLitt: Univ of Warwick 1987, Loughborough Univ 1988; Hon DMus: Univ of Durham 1989, Keele Univ 1992; *Books* incl: I Play As I Please (autobiography, 1954); *Recreations* birdwatching, calligraphy; *Style*— Humphrey Lyttelton, Esq; ✉ The Best of Jazz, BBC Radio 2, Broadcasting House, London W1A 1AA

LYTTELTON, Hon Richard Cavendish; s of 10 Viscount Cobham, KG, GCMG, GCVO, TD, PC (d 1977); *b* 1949; *Educ* Eton; *m* 1971, Romilly, da of Michael Barker; 1 s (Thomas), 1 da (May); *Career* md EMI Finland 1977–80, dir int ops EMI Records (UK) Ltd 1980–83, gp md EMI South Africa 1984–86, pres Capital Records-EMI of Canada 1986–88, pres EMI Classics 1988; *Recreations* music, shooting; *Style*— The Hon Richard Lyttelton; ✉ 5 Queen's Gate Place Mews, London SW7 5BG

LYTTLE, (James) Brian Chambers; OBE (1996); s of James Chambers Lyttle (d 1984), and Margaret Kirkwood, *née* Billingsley (d 1987); *b* 22 Aug 1932; *Educ* Bangor GS, Trinity Coll Dublin (scholar, BA, Brooke prize); *m* 2 Aug 1957, Mary Alma Davidson, da of John Campbell; 4 da (Valerie Ann b 6 Aug 1958, Amanda Mary b 14 Dec 1962, Margaret Susan b 30 Aug 1964, Heather Vanessa b 21 July 1968); *Career* NI Civil Serv: asst princ 1954–60, private sec to the Min of Commerce 1960–62, chief exec Enterprise Ulster 1972–75, dir NI Employment Serv 1975–77, dir NI Industl Devpt Orgn 1977–81, concurrently under sec Dept of Commerce later Dept of Econ Devpt 1977–84, under sec Dept of Fin and Personnel 1984–87, sec Probation Bd for NI 1987–; *Recreations* poetry, music, gardening; *Style*— Brian Lyttle, Esq, OBE; ✉ Probation Board for Northern Ireland, Belfast Headquarters, 80–90 North Street, Belfast BT1 1LD (☎ 01232 262400, fax 01232 262470)

LYTTON, 5 Earl of (UK 1880); Sir John Peter Michael Scawen Lytton; also Viscount Knebworth (UK 1880), 18 Baron Wentworth (E 1529), and 6 Bt (UK 1838); s of 4 Earl of Lytton; *b* 7 June 1950; *Educ* Downside, Univ of Reading; *m* 1980, Ursula, da of Anton Komoly, of Vienna; 2 s (Viscount Knebworth b 7 March 1989, Hon Wilfrid Thomas Scawen b 8 Jan 1992), 1 da (Lady Katrina b 1985); *Heir* s, Philip Anthony

Scawen, Viscount Knebworth b 7 March 1989; *Career* Inland Revenue Valuation Office 1975–81, Permutt Brown & Co 1982–86, Cubitt & West 1986–87, sole principal John Lytton & Co 1988–; chm Horsham Chamber of Commerce 1983–85, pres 1995–; pres: Newstead Abbey Byron Soc, Crawley and Horsham Hosp Tst Scanner Appeal; memb: Ctee Kent, Surrey and Sussex Branch CLA, CLA Cncl, CLA Executive, RICS Countryside Policies Panel 1996–; hill farmer; FRICS, ACIArb, IRRV; *Recreations* estate maintenance and management, DIY repairs, shooting, family history; *Style*— The Rt Hon the Earl of Lytton; ✉ Estate Office, Newbuildings Place, Shipley, Horsham, W Sussex RH13 7JQ (☎ 01403 741650)

LYTTON, Lady Madeleine; da of 3 Earl of Lytton, OBE (d 1951), and Rosa Alexandrine (Sandra), *née* Fortel (d 1980); *b* 28 Aug 1921; *Educ* Lisa Duncan Sch; *m*; 1 da (Eleonore, singer, b 7 June 1957); *Career* choreographer and lectr; early career incl: toured with Arts Cncl and Russian Opera and Ballet during WWII, recital Criterion Theatre London 1945, soloist Delphi Festival and Besançon Festival, choreographer Nîmes Festival; lecture series Art Life and Style of Isadora Duncan; lectr/guest numerous univs and cultural centres incl: London Contemporary Ballet 1978–79, Oudekapel de Jetty Roels Belgium 1981–83 and 1992, Comité National de Danse Paris 1982 and 1992, Sorbonne 1983, Brabant Conservatoire Tilburg Holland 1985, Oakland Univ Harvard Univ and American Dance Festival USA 1985, Institut des Sciences et des Belles Lettres France 1986, Café de la Danse Paris 1990, Gulbenkian Fndn Lisbon Portugal 1991, 3ieme Rencontres Européennes de l'Harmonie du Corps 1993, opening of Duncan Dance Research Centre Athens 1994; staged poetic montage Isadora Duncan - the Poem of her Life (Haute-Garonne Festival 1990); films: Isadora Duncan Yesterday and Today (1985), Movements of the Soul (1989); memb: Int Congress of Faculdade de Motricidade Humana Lisbon 1992, Comité National de Danse (UNESCO), Les Salons de Danse Paris, International Isadora Duncan Inst NY, American Biographical Inst; *Style*— Lady Madeleine Lytton; ✉ 4 rue des Hauts-Tillets, 92310 Sevres, France

LYTTON COBBOLD, Hon Henry Fromanteel; eldest s and h of 2 Baron Cobbold, *qv*; *b* 12 May 1962; *Educ* Eton, Univ of Kent (BA 1983); *m* 1987, Martha Frances, da of James Buford Boone, Jr, of Tuscaloosa, Alabama, USA; 1 s (Edward b 23 April 1992), 1 da (Morwenna Gray b 16 Aug 1989); *Style*— The Hon Henry Lytton Cobbold

LYVEDEN, 6 Baron (UK 1859); Ronald Cecil Vernon; s of 5 Baron Lyveden (d 1973); *b* 10 April 1915; *m* 1938, Queenie Constance, da of Howard Ardern; 3 s; *Heir* s, Hon Jack Leslie Vernon; *Style*— The Rt Hon the Lord Lyveden; ✉ 20 Farmer St, Te Aroha, NZ

LYWOOD, Jeremy Hugh Gifford; s of Gp Capt Geoffrey Edwin Gifford Lywood (d 1969), of Fittleworth, Sussex, and Joan Edith, *née* Hordern (d 1994); *b* 8 June 1934; *Educ* Charterhouse; *m* 3 Dec 1955, Elizabeth Anne, da of Col David Evans; 4 da (Sarah Gay Gifford b 20 Feb 1957, Amanda Clare Gifford b 16 Dec 1961, Joanna Elizabeth Gifford b 24 Dec 1963, Lucy Christian Gifford b 14 Aug 1975); 3 s (Rupert Charles Gifford b 14 May 1958, Simon James Gifford b 8 Feb 1960, Hugo Geoffrey Gifford b 14 Dec 1969); *Career* cmmnd 1 Bn King's Royal Rifle Corps 1952–54; progress chaser/buyer and PA to Sir Leonard Crossland Ford Motor Co 1954–60 (mgmnt trainee 1954–55), project mangr and local dir John Thompson Gp 1960–66, md Econheat 1966–68; Filtermist International plc (formerly Hoccom Developments): fndr md 1968, plc 1990, Queen's Award for Export 1990, pres 1993–; tax cmmr 1989–95, High Sheriff for Co of Shropshire 1994–95; *Recreations* sailing, hunting, shooting, fishing; *Style*— Jeremy Lywood, Esq; ✉ Ashford Court, Ashford Carbonell, Ludlow, Shropshire SY8 4DE (☎ 01584 831377); Filtermist International plc, Faraday Drive, Stourbridge Road, Bridgnorth, Shropshire WV15 5BA (☎ 01746 765361, fax 01746 766882, car 0385 550488)

M

MA, Yuzhen; *b* 1934, Beijing; *Educ* Beijing Inst of Foreign Languages; *m*; 1 s, 1 da; *Career* Chinese Dip Serv; memb staff Info Dept Miny of Foreign Affrs 1954–63, attache and third sec Burma 1963–69, dep div chief then div chief Info Dept Miny of Foreign Affrs 1969–80, first sec and cnsllr Ghana 1980–84, dir Info Dept Miny of Foreign Affrs 1984–88, consul-gen (with rank of ambass) Los Angeles 1988–91, ambass to Ct of St James 1991–96; *Style*— HE Mr Ma Yuzhen

MAAN, Bashir Ahmed; JP (1968), DL (Glasgow 1982); s of Chaudhry Sardar Khan Maan, of Village Maan, Gujranwala, Pakistan, and Hayat Begum Maan (d 1975); *b* 20 Oct 1926; *Educ* DB HS, Qila Didar Singh, Panjab Univ, MSc (Strathclyde) 1995; *m* (m dis); 1 s (Tariq Hassan), 3 da (Rashda Begum, Hanna Bano, Aalya Maaria); *Career* involved in struggle of Pakistan 1943–47, organized rehabilitation of refugees from India in Maan and surrounding areas 1947–48; emigrated to UK, settled in Glasgow 1953; fndr sec Glasgow Pakistan Social and Cultural Soc 1955–65 (pres 1966–69), memb Exec Ctee Glasgow City Lab Pty 1969–70, vice chm Glasgow Community Rels Cncl 1970–75, cncllr Glasgow City Corp 1970–75, magistrate City of Glasgow 1971–74, chm Glasgow Corp Police Ctee 1974–75 (vice chm 1971–74); memb: Nat Road Safety Ctee 1971–74, Scot Accident Prevention Ctee 1973–75, BBC Immigrant Prog Advsy Ctee 1972–80; convenor Pakistan Bill Action Ctee 1973, Parly candidate (Lab) E Fife 1974, pres Standing Conference of Pakistani Orgns in the UK and Eire 1974–77, police judge City of Glasgow 1974–75, cncllr City of Glasgow DC 1975–84, dep chm Cmmn for Racial Equality 1977–80, memb Scot Gas Consumer Cncl 1978–81, baillie City of Glasgow 1980–84, memb Gtr Glasgow Health Bd 1981–91, fndr and chm Scot Pakistani Assoc 1984–91 and 1993–, judge City of Glasgow District Cts, chm Strathclyde Community Relations Cncl 1986–93 and 1994–96, cncllr City of Glasgow Cncl 1995–, vice chm (chm Mgmnt Ctee) Glasgow Int Sports Festival Ltd 1987–89, govr Jordanhill Coll of FE 1987–91, memb Gen Advsy Cncl BBC 1991–95, baillie City of Glasgow 1996–; FRSA 1995; *Publications* The New Scots (The Story of Asians in Scotland); *Recreations* reading, golf; *Clubs* Douglas Park; *Style*— Bashir Maan, Esq, JP, DL; ✉ 8 Riverview Gardens, Flat 6, Glasgow G5 (☎ 0141 429 7689)

MAAS, Robert William; s of Richard Felix Maas (d 1948), of London, and Hilda Rose, *née* Gietzen; *b* 13 Feb 1943; *Educ* Gunnersbury GS; *Career* articled clerk Godwin & Taylor 1959–65, tax ptnr Stoy Hayward 1970–77 (tax sr 1965–70), proprietor Robert Maas & Co 1977–83; tax ptnr: Casson Beckman 1983–87, Blackstone Franks & Co 1987–; memb Editorial Bd Taxation; contrib of articles to various magazines and jls, lectr on a wide variety of tax topics; ICAEW: chm Tech Ctee Tax Faculty, chm Personal Tax Sub Ctee, memb Tax Faculty Ctee; memb Cncl and chm Tech Ctee IIT; former chm Small Practitioners Gp of Central London LSCA; FCA 1965, FTII 1965, AIIT 1992; *Publications* Tax Minimisation Techniques (4 edn, 1984), Taxation of Non-Resident Entertainers & Sportsmen (1987), Fringe Benefits (1987), Tax Planning for Entertainers (2 edn, 1987), Tax Planning for the Smaller Business (1990), Tolley's Anti-Avoidance Provisions (2 edn, 1991), Expat Investors Working and Retiring Abroad (1993), Taxation of Sportsmen and Entertainers (1993), Tolley's Property Taxes (9 edn, 1996), Tolley's Taxation of Employments (4 edn, 1995); *Recreations* reading, walking, pubs; *Clubs* Reform, St James's (Manchester); *Style*— Robert Maas, Esq; ✉ 76 Thirlmere Gardens, Wembley, Middlesex HA9 8RE (☎ 0181 904 0432); Blackstone Franks & Co, Barbican House, 26–34 Old St, London EC1V 9HL (☎ 0171 250 3300, fax 0171 250 1402)

MABBUTT, Gary Vincent; MBE (1994); s of Raymond William Mabbutt, of Bristol, and Avis Betty, *née* Blake (now Mrs Brown); *b* 23 Aug 1961; *Educ* Cotham GS Bristol; *Career* professional footballer; 147 appearances Bristol Rovers 1977–82 (debut v Burnley 1978); Tottenham Hotspur: joined 1982, debut v Luton Town 1982, capt 1987–, over 575 appearances; England caps: 11 youth (capt once), 7 under 21 (capt twice), 7 B (capt 5 times), 16 full 1982–92; capt Football League v League of Ireland 1990; honours: UEFA Cup winner's medal v Anderlecht 1984, FA Cup runners up medal v Coventry City 1987, FA Cup winner's medal v Nottm Forest 1991; *Books* Against All Odds (autobiography, 1990); *Style*— Gary Mabbutt, Esq, MBE; ✉ Tottenham Hotspur FC, 748 High Rd, Tottenham, London N17 OAP (☎ 0181 365 5000, (fax 01707 647399)

MABEY, Bevil Guy; CBE (1983); s of Guy Mabey (d 1951), and Madeline Johnson (d 1957); *b* 16 April 1916; *Educ* Tonbridge, Univ of Cambridge (MA); *m* 4 Oct 1947, June Penelope, da of Brig Cecil Herbert Peck, DSO, MC; 1 s (David b 1961), 5 da (Bridget Ann b 1949, Isabel Denise b 1950, Christine b 1954, Juliet b 1955, Fiona b 1965); *Career* cmmnd Royal Corps Signals 1939, RASC 1940–46, Maj, served France, N Africa, Italy, Yugoslavia, Greece; dir: Mabey Holdings Ltd, Mabey & Johnson Ltd, Mabey Securities Ltd, Fairfield-Mabey Ltd, Beachley Property Ltd; Freeman: City of London, Worshipful Co of Vintners; *Recreations* rowing, skiing, riding, golf, carpentry, bricklaying; *Clubs* Leander, London Rowing; *Style*— Bevil G Mabey, Esq, CBE; ✉ Mabey Holdings Ltd, Floral Mile, Twyford, Reading RG10 9SQ (☎ 0118 940 3921, fax 0118 940 3480, telex 848649 MABEY TG)

MABEY, Richard Thomas; s of Thomas Gustavus Mabey (d 1963), and Edna Nellie, *née* Moore (d 1993); *b* 20 Feb 1941; *Educ* Berkhamsted Sch, St Catherine's Coll Oxford (BA, MA); *Career* lectr in social studies Dacorum Coll of FE 1963–65, sr ed Penguin Books (Educn Div) 1966–73, freelance writer and broadcaster 1973–; columnist BBC Wildlife; reg contrib: Sunday Times, Independent, Modern Painters, Sunday Telegraph, Country Living, Times, Guardian, The Oldie, The Countryman; Leverhulme res fell 1983–84 and 1993–94; memb: Cncl Botanical Soc of the British Isles 1981–83, Nature Conservancy Cncl 1983–86, Cncl Plantlife 1989–, Advsy Cncl Open Spaces Soc; pres London Wildlife Tst 1982–92; dir: Common Ground 1988–, Learning Through Landscapes Tst 1990–; *Awards* Times Educnl Supplement Information Books Award 1977, New York Acad of Sciences Children's Book Award 1984, Whitbread Biography Award 1986; *Television* wrote and presented: The Unofficial Countryside (World About Us, BBC2) 1975, The Flowering of Britain (BBC2) 1980, A Prospect of Kew (BBC2) 1981, Back to the Roots (C4) 1983, White Rock, Black Water (BBC2) 1986, Postcards from the Country (BBC2) 1996; *Books* incl: Class (ed, 1967), Behind the Scene (1968), The Pop Process (1969), Food for Free (1972), Children in Primary School (1972), The Unofficial Countryside (1973), The Pollution Handbook (1973), The Roadside Wildlife Book (1974), Street Flowers (1976), Plants with a Purpose (1977), The Common Ground (1980), The Flowering of Britain (with Tony Evans, 1980), In a Green Shade (1983), Cold Comforts (1983), Oak and Company (1983), Second Nature (ed, 1984), The Frampton Flora (1985), Gilbert White (1986), The Gardener's Labyrinth (ed, 1987), The Flowering of Kew (1988), Home Country (1990), Whistling in the Dark (1993), The Wild Wood (with Gareth Lovett Jones, 1993), Landlocked (1994), The Oxford Book of Nature Writing (ed, 1995), Flora Britannica (1996); *Recreations* walking, birdwatching, food; *Clubs* Groucho; *Style*— Richard Mabey, Esq; ✉ c/o Richard Scott Simon, Sheil Land Associates, 43 Doughty St, London WC1N 2LF

MABEY, Simon John; *b* 29 Sept 1952; *Educ* City of London Sch, Clare Coll Cambridge (scholar, MA); *m* 9 May 1981, Carolyn Ann, *née* Crossman; 2 s (James b 1984, Richard b 1986), 2 da (Elizabeth b 1991, Victoria b 1993); *Career* CA Dixon Wilson & Co 1973–80; Smith & Williamson: joined 1980, ptnr 1981, currently managing tax ptnr, exec bd memb and chm Int Audit Ctee; dir: Smith & Williamson Securities 1981–, Smith & Williamson Trust Corporation Ltd 1986–; Westminster CC: memb 1982–90, chm Housing (private sector) Sub-ctee and vice chm Housing Ctee 1983–85, chm Social Servs Ctee 1985–89, Lord Mayor of Westminster (chm London Mayors' Assoc) 1989–90, dep high steward of Westminster 1989–90; Parly candidate (Cons) Knowsley North 1992, memb Cncl Assoc of Conservative Clubs Ltd 1993–; chm Bd of Tstees Charitable Tst City of Westminster 1989–90, govr Sherborne Sch for Girls 1994–; hon memb Worshipful Co of Master Mariners 1989–90; Freeman City of London 1981, Liveryman Worshipful Co of Bakers 1981; ATII 1976, FCA 1981 (ACA 1976); *Clubs* Carlton (hon sec Political Ctee 1992–), City Livery Club; *Style*— Simon Mabey, Esq; ✉ Smith & Williamson, 1 Riding House Street, London W1A 3AS (☎ 0171 637 5377, fax 0171 631 0741)

MABON, Rt Hon Dr (Jesse) Dickson; PC (1977); s of Jesse Dickson Mabon and Isabel Simpson, *née* Montgomery; *b* 1 Nov 1925; *Educ* schools in Cumbrae and Kelvinside; *m* 1970, Elizabeth Sarah, da of late Major William Victor Zinn (sometime princ ptnr W V Zinn & Associates, consulting engrs); 1 s; *Career* formerly in coalmining industry, journalist with Scottish Daily Record; MP (Lab and Co-op 1955–81, SDP 1981–83) Greenock 1955–74, Greenock and Port Glasgow 1974–83; Parly candidate Bute and N Ayrshire (Lab) 1951, Renfrewshire W (Lab and Co-op) 1955; jt Parly under sec Scotland 1964–67, min of state Scottish Office 1967–70, oppn spokesman Scotland 1970–72 (resigned frontbench over Labour's anti Common Market stance), min of state for Energy 1976–79; chm UK Labour Ctee for Europe 1974–76, Scottish PLP 1972–73 and 1975–76, fndr chm PLP Manifesto Gp 1974–76, pres European Movement 1975–76; memb: Cncl Europe 1970–72 and 1974–76, WEU Assembly 1970–72 and 1974–76; rejoined Lab Pty 1991; chm: Royal London Homoeopathic Hosp NHS Tst 1992–96, GEM Group of Companies 1984–; dep chm Cairn Energy plc 1991–96; pres Faculty of History of Medicine 1994–95, memb Energy Saving Tst 1992–96; Freeman City of London 1972, Liveryman Worshipful Soc of Apothecaries; FInstD, FInstPet, FRSA, FFHom; *Style*— The Rt Hon Dr J Dickson Mabon; ✉ 57 Hillway, London N6 6AD

MAC-FALL, Nigel James; s of Thomas Coulson Mac-Fall (d 1970), and Sylvia Dorothy, *née* Harriss (d 1987); *b* 27 April 1948; *Educ* Sch of Three Dimensional Design Ravensbourne Coll of Art and Design (BA), Sch of Furniture Design RCA (MA); *m* 11 May 1974, Shirley Anne, da of Ernest Chubb; 2 s (Julian James Chubb b 9 Jan 1976, Oscar Alexander James b 18 May 1981), 1 da (Rosina Sylvia Anne b 7 July 1977), 1 adopted da (Elaine Anne b 16 Aug 1968); *Career* furniture and product designer Planning Unit Ltd design and consultancy 1972–75, sr designer Supplies Div Property Services Agency 1975–78, ptnr, dir and head Dept of Three Dimensional Design Minale Tattersfield & Partners Ltd int design consultancy 1978– (i/c architecture, interiors, exhibition, product, furniture, signage, packaging and automotive); work incl: Heathrow Express, Hammersmith Station, BP Lubricants Packaging worldwide, Thorntons' Sweet Shops, Gucci Dining Room, Royal Armouries Museum Leeds (corp and exhbn design), Tetrapak UK (packaging), Viero Italy (machinery), FCO (Britannico exhbn Turin), English Heritage (Change of Heart exhbn RCA), Lend Lease - Bluewater Devpt (signage), Loctite worldwide (packaging), Northern Foods (interior design); *Recreations* family, swimming, cycling, sculpture, music, foreign travel; *Style*— Nigel James Mac-Fall, Esq; ✉ Minale Tattersfield & Partners Ltd, The Courtyard, 37 Sheen Rd, Richmond, Surrey TW9 1AJ (☎ 0181 948 7999, fax 0181 948 2435)

McADAM, Dr Elspeth Katharine; da of Prof Sir Ian McAdam, of Oxford, and Hrothgarde, *née* Gibson; *b* 16 Oct 1947; *Educ* Kenya HS, Newnham Coll Cambridge (MA), Middx Med Sch; *m* 1970 (m dis 1981), Prof (John) David Seddon, s of Eric Seddon (d 1950); 2 s (Michael David Indra b 10 May 1974, James Alexander b 28 April 1976); *Career* conslt child and adolescent psychiatrist 1987–, conslt Swedish Mental Health Services 1991–, dir Informetrics-Systemic Organisational Consultancy; memb MEDCAT; MRCPsych 1982; *Publications* Working Systemicly with Violence (1992); author of articles on: Cognitive Therapy with Children and Adolescents 1984–88, Systemic Social Constructionist Therapy 1995–96; *Recreations* tennis, golf, ecology, bird watching, gardening; *Style*— Dr Elspeth McAdam; ✉ 89 St Leonards Road, Norwich, Norfolk NR1 4JF (☎ and fax 01603 622440, e-mail 101364.3573@compuserve.com)

McADAM, James; CBE (1995); s of John Robert McAdam (d 1975), and Helen, *née* Cormack (d 1981); *b* 10 Dec 1930; *Educ* Lenzie Acad; *m* 4 Oct 1955, Maisie Una, da of Ernest James Holmes (d 1947); 2 da (Catherine Tryphena b 1956, Fiona Jane b 1961); *Career* Nat Serv RN 1949–50; J & P Coats Ltd: joined 1945, various overseas assignments 1953–61, fin dir Chile 1962–66, fin dir India 1966–70; fin dir Coats Patons (UK) 1972–75; Coats Patons plc: dir 1975, chief exec 1985, chm 1986, dep chm and chief ops offr Coats Viyella plc (following merger) 1986–91; exec chm Signet Group plc 1992–; non exec dir: Textile Pensions Trust 1985–96, London PO 1985–94, Scotia Holdings plc (formerly Efamol Holdings plc) 1991–; non-exec chm: F C Brown (Steel Equipment) Ltd 1991–, Bisley Office Equipment 1991–; chm: Br Clothing Indust Assoc 1991–, Br Knitting & Clothing Confedn 1991–, Br Apparel & Textile Confedn 1993–, Apparel, Knitting & Textiles Alliance 1994–; memb: Exec Ctee The Scottish Cncl Devpt & Indust 1989–, Trade Policy Forum DTI 1995–; FRSA, CIMgt, FInstD; *Recreations* theatre, gardening, travel; *Style*— James McAdam, Esq, CBE; ✉ Signet Group plc, 15 Stratton Street, London W1X 6NU (☎ 0171 495 2643)

McADAM, Prof Keith Paul William James; s of Sir Ian William James McAdam, OBE, and (Lettice Margaret) Hrothgarde, *née* Gibson (now Mrs Bennett); *b* 13 Aug 1945; *Educ* Prince of Wales Sch Nairobi Kenya, Millfield, Clare Coll Cambridge (MA, MB BChir), Middx Hosp Med Sch; *m* 27 July 1968, Penelope Ann, da of Rev Gordon

Charles Craig Spencer; 3 da (Karen, Ruth, Cheryl); *Career* house physician and house surgn Middx Hosp London 1969–70; sr house offr appts London: Royal Northern Hosp 1970–71, Brompton Hosp 1971–72, Royal Nat Hosp for Nervous Diseases 1972–73; lectr Inst of Med Res PNG 1973–75, Med Res Cncl travelling fellowship Nat Cancer Inst 1975–76, visiting scientist Nat Inst of Health Bethesda Maryland USA 1976–77, asst prof Tufts Univ Sch of Med Boston USA 1977–81, assoc prof New England Med Centre Boston USA 1982–84, Wellcome prof of tropical medicine London Sch of Hygiene and Tropical Med 1984–, physician Hosp for Tropical Diseases Camden & Islington Health Authy 1984–95, dir Medical Research Cncl Unit Fajara The Gambia 1995–; memb Med Advsy Bds: Br Cncl 1988–93, Br Leprosy Relief Assoc 1986–, The Leprosy Mission 1990–, MRC 1988–93, Wellcome Trust 1985–90, Beit Trust 1990–95; chief med offr conslt advsr 1989–95, expert advsr to House of Commons Soc Servs Ctee enquiry into AIDS 1987; FRSTM 1973, FRCP 1985; *Recreations* cricket, squash, tennis, skiing; *Clubs* MCC; *Style*— Prof Keith McAdam; ✉ Oakmead, 70 Luton Lane, Redbourn, Herts AL3 7PY; Department of Clinical Sciences, London School of Hygiene & Tropical Medicine, Keppel St, London WC1E 7HT; Medical Research Council Laboratories, Fajara, PO Box 273, Banjul, The Gambia, W Africa (☎ 00 220 495 442, fax 00 220 495 919, e-mail MRC@GAM.healthnet.org)

MACADAM, Sir Peter; kt (1981); s of Francis Macadam (d 1981), of Buenos Aires, and Marjorie Mary, *née* Browne (d 1984); *b* 9 Sept 1921; *Educ* Buenos Aires Argentina, Stonyhurst; *m* 1949, Ann, da of Eric Methven Musson; 3 da; *Career* gp chm BAT Industries Ltd 1976–82 (joined 1946), dir National Westminster Bank plc 1978–84, chm Libra Bank plc 1984–90; pres Hispanic and Luso Brazilian Cncls (Canning House) 1982–87; Hon FIMgt, FRSA 1975; *Clubs* Naval & Military; *Style*— Sir Peter Macadam; ✉ Layham Hall, Layham, nr Hadleigh, Suffolk IP7 5LE (☎ 01473 822137)

MACADAM, Thomas Storrar; s of John Johnston Macadam (d 1989), and Jean Cunningham, *née* Hudson (d 1982); *b* 14 Oct 1947; *Educ* Allan Glen's Sch Glasgow, Univ of Glasgow (BDS); *m* 11 Sept 1971, Dorothy Margaret, da of William Reilly; 2 s (Murray b 1 Sept 1973, Douglas b 10 Oct 1975); *Career* in gen dental practice Kirkintilloch Glasgow 1972–, visiting practitioner Glasgow Dental Hosp 1976–; memb GDC 1976–; Master Skinners' Co Glasgow 1987–88; *Recreations* golf, fishing, Partick Thistle FC (spectator); *Clubs* Saints and Sinners; *Style*— Thomas Macadam, Esq; ✉ 54 Cowgate, Kirkintilloch, Glasgow G66 1HN (☎ 0141 776 7413, fax 0141 578 0001)

McAFEE, Patrick John; s of John McAfee, and Maud O'Donnell, *née* Lynas (d 1979); *b* 25 May 1940; *Educ* Portora Royal Sch, Trinity Coll Dublin (MA); *m* 2 March 1979, Jane Greer, da of Prof W L J Ryan, of Dublin; 1 da (Clare Jane b 1982); *Career* banker; dir Morgan Grenfell & Co Ltd 1973–90, sr advsr Morgan Grenfell Group 1990–, chm Lochain Patrick insurance brokers 1990–; dir: The Cleveland Trust plc 1993–, Oryx International Growth Fund Ltd; chm Deutsch Morgan Grenfell (Ireland) Ltd; *Recreations* sailing, golf; *Clubs* Royal St George Yacht, Lahinch Golf, City of London, University (Dublin); *Style*— Patrick J McAfee, Esq; ✉ Morgan Grenfell & Co Ltd, 23 Gt Winchester St, London EC2P 2AX (☎ 0171 545 8000)

MACALDOWIE, (John) Kenneth; s of John Macaldowie (d 1984), and Mary Donald, *née* Main; *b* 24 June 1944; *Educ* Robert Gordon's Coll Aberdeen, Hillhead HS Glasgow; *m* 15 Oct 1968, Sheila, da of Dr George Leslie (d 1991); 2 s (Colin Neil b 12 Feb 1970, Keith Gary b 24 April 1973); *Career* accountant (latterly audit mangr) Cooper Brothers & Co until 1972 (apprentice 1962–67); BDO Stoy Hayward (formerly BDO Binder Hamlyn and Wyllie Guild & McIntyre): ptnr 1972–, managing ptnr Edinburgh 1992–95, chm Nat Partnership Ctee 1992–94; chm: Williamson & Wolfe 1980–, Salvation Army Housing Association (Scotland) Ltd 1992–; memb: Ct Glasgow Caledonian Univ 1985– (vice chm 1995–, chm Finance of the Ct 1988–), Bd of Govrs Kelvinside Acad 1987–95; hon treas YMCA Glasgow 1996–; elder Church of Scotland (Merrylea Parish Church) 1982–; Deacon Incorporation of Coopers of Trades House of Glasgow 1984–85, Liveryman Worshipful Co of Coopers 1985; Freeman: City of Glasgow 1977, City of London 1986; MICAS 1968 (memb examination bd 1982–90); *Recreations* tennis, gardening, reading, hillwalking, watching rugby and cricket; *Clubs* Western (Glasgow), Newlands Lawn Tennis, Hillhead Jordanhill Rugby; *Style*— Kenneth Macaldowie, Esq; ✉ Glenwood, 78 Langside Drive, Newlands, Glasgow G43 2ST (☎ 0141 637 5456); BDO Stoy Hayward, Ballantine House, 168 West George Street, Glasgow G2 2PT (☎ 0141 248 3761, fax 0141 332 5467)

McALEESE, Prof Mary Patricia; *née* Lenaghan; *b* 27 May 1951; *Educ* St Dominic's HS Belfast, Queen's Univ Belfast (LLB), Trinity Coll Dublin (MA), Inst of Linguistics (Dip in Spanish 1994); *m* 1976, Martin McAleese; 1 s (Justin b 6 April 1985), 2 da (Emma b 21 Sept 1982, Saramai b (twin) 6 April 1985); *Career* barrister-at-law: Inn of Ct NI 1974, King's Inns Dublin 1978; practising barrister Inn of Ct NI 1974–75, Reid prof of criminal law, criminology and penology Trinity Coll Dublin 1975–79, TV presenter/journalist RTE 1979–81, Reid prof of criminal law, criminology and penology Trinity Coll Dublin and pt/t presenter EUROPA (monthly current affairs prog) RTE 1981–87; The Queen's Univ Belfast: dir Inst of Professional Legal Studies 1987–, pro-vice chllr 1994–, sometime memb various univ ctees and bds incl Vice-Chllr's Ctee; non-exec dir: Northern Ireland Electricity plc, Channel 4 Television; memb British Cncl (Northern Ireland), univ rep Business in the Community; former fndr memb: Belfast Women's Aid, Irish Cmmn for Prisoners Overseas; former memb: Cncl for Social Welfare (Dublin), BBC Broadcasting Council for NI, Exec Ctee Focus Point for Homeless Young People (Dublin), Cmmn for Justice and Peace; memb: Int Bar Assoc (NI rapporteur), Inst of Advanced Legal Studies, European Bar Assoc, Irish Centre for European Law, Faculty of the Nat Inst of Trial Advocacy; hon pres NI Housing Rights Assoc; MIL 1994; *Publications* author of various articles, conference papers and dicussion documents; *Style*— Prof Mary McAleese; ✉ Queen's University Belfast, University Road, Belfast BT7 1NN

McALISTER, Michael Ian; s of S McAlister, CBE (d 1972), of Walton-on-Thames, Surrey, and Jessie Anne, *née* Smith (d 1991); *b* 23 Aug 1930; *Educ* St John's Coll Oxford (MA); *m* 1, 4 July 1953 (m dis 1984), Patricia Evans, of Sao Paulo, Brazil; 4 s (Richard, Peter, Sam, James), 3 da (Maureen, Carolyn, Emma); m 2, 2 June 1984, Elizabeth Anne, da of Louis and Marianne Hehn, of Hatfield Peverel, Chelmsford, Essex; *Career* Nat Serv Army 1949–51, Acting-Capt Intelligence Corps 1951, (MI8) Austria (BTA 3); articled clerk Price Waterhouse & Co 1954–58, private and fin sec HRH Duke of Windsor KG 1959–61, md Ionian Bank Tstee Co 1961–69, chm Slater Walker Securities (Australia) 1969–72, pres Australian Stock Exchanges 1972–75, Knight Int plc Chicago 1975–78, corporate planning dir Cluff Resources plc 1979–89, chm Int Dynamics Ltd 1989–91, dir Ionian Corporate Finance Ltd 1991–, md Tam Prog EBRD London 1993–; chm Woking Cons Assoc 1967–68, vice chm Braintree Cons Assoc 1990–93; ACA 1959, FCA 1969; *Recreations* carpentry and DIY; *Clubs* RAC; *Style*— Mr Michael McAlister; (☎ 01245 380158, fax 01245 382056)

McALISTER, Maj-Gen Ronald William Lorne; CB (1977), OBE (1968, MBE 1958); s of Col Ronald James Frier McAlister, OBE (d 1963), of Edinburgh, and Mrs Nora Ford Collins, *née* Prosser (d 1993); *b* 26 May 1923; *Educ* Sedbergh; *m* 25 Jan 1964, Sally Ewart, da of Dr Gordon King Marshall (d 1974), of Broadstairs, Kent; 2 da (Angela Frances b 15 May 1965, Caroline Jane b 14 Sept 1966); *Career* cmmnd 3 QAO Gurkha Rifles 1942, Adj 1/3 Gurkha Rifles Burma 1945 (despatches), 10 Gurkha Rifles 1948, Adj 2/10 Gurkha Rifles Malaya 1949–52 (despatches), instr Sch of Infantry Warminster 1952–55, Staff Coll 1956, Bde Maj Malaya 1957–58, Jt Serv Staff Coll 1961, asst sec Chiefs of Staff Ctee MOD 1962–64, CO 1/10 Gurkha Rifles 1965, Borneo 1966 (despatches), Hong Kong 1967, instr Jt Servs Staff Coll 1968, CO Berlin Infantry Bde 1968–71, Canadian Nat Def Coll 1971–72, exercise controller to UK Cs-in-C 1972–74, Maj Gen Bde of Gurkhas and Dep Cdr Hong Kong Land Forces 1975–77, ret 1977; bursar Wellesley House Prep Sch Broadstairs 1977–88; chm: Gurkha Brigade Assoc 1980–90, Buckmaster Memorial Home for Ladies Broadstairs 1983–; hon treas Royal St George's GC Sandwich 1991–96 (capt 1989); *Books* Bugle and Kukri Vol 2 (1986); *Recreations* golf, gardening; *Clubs* Army & Navy, Senior Golfers Soc; *Style*— Maj-Gen Ronald McAlister, CB, OBE; ✉ The Chalet, 41 Callis Court Rd, Broadstairs, Kent

McALISTER, William Harle Nelson; s of Flying Offr William Nelson (d 1940), and Marjorie Isobel, *née* McIntyre; *b* 30 Aug 1940; *Educ* St Edward's Sch Oxford, Univ Coll London (BA); *m* 1968 (m dis 1985), Sarah Elizabeth; 2 s (Daniel b 1969, Benjamin b 1977), 2 da (Leila b 1970, Alix b 1972); *Career* dir Almost Free Theatre 1968–72, dep dir Inter-Action Tst 1968–72, fndr dir Islington Bus Co 1972–77; dir: Battersea Arts Centre 1976–77, Sense of Ireland Festival 1980–; Bd dir London Int Theatre Festival 1983; chm for the Arts IT 82 Ctee 1982; co fndr Fair Play for Children 1974–75, advsr Task Force Tst 1972–74; tstee: Circle 33 Housing Tst 1972–75, Moving Picture Mime Tst 1978–80, Shape (Arts for the Disadvantaged) 1979–81; govr Holloway Adult Educn Inst 1974–76; dir: Inst of Contemporary Arts 1977–90, Creative Res Ltd 1988–91, Int House 1988; memb Cncl Africa Centre 1992–, cultural policy advsr Soros Fndns 1992–; memb: Ct RCA 1980–90, Bd World Circuit Arts 1995–; *Books* Community Psychology (1975), EEC and the Arts (1978); articles on arts policy; *Recreations* angling, tennis, travel; *Clubs* Chelsea Arts; *Style*— William McAlister, Esq; ✉ 151c Grosvenor Ave, London N5 2NH (☎ 0171 226 0205, fax 0171 226 7971)

McALLION, John; MP (Lab) Dundee E (majority 4,564); s of Joseph Alexander McAllion (d 1989), of Glasgow, and Norah Ellen, *née* McAloon (d 1996); *b* 13 Feb 1948; *Educ* St Augustine's Secdy Sch Glasgow, Univ of St Andrews (MA), Dundee Coll of Educn (PGCE); *m* 9 Oct 1971, Susan Jean, da of Alfred Godlonton; 2 s (Daniel James b 1 July 1976, Kevin John b 14 April 1978); *Career* teacher: St Saviour's HS Dundee 1973–78, Balgowan Sch Dundee 1978–82; res asst to Bob McTaggart MP 1982–86, convener Tayside Regnl Cncl 1986–87, MP (Lab) Dundee E 1987–; *Recreations* watching football, reading, five-a-side football, going to movies; *Style*— John McAllion, Esq, MP; ✉ 3 Haldane Street, Dundee DD3 0HP (☎ 01382 826678); 13 Cowgate, Dundee (☎ 01382 200329, fax 01382 322981 / 0171 219 5834)

McALLISTER, Arthur George; OBE (1995); s of John George McAllister (d 1971), of Beverley, and Ethel Mary McAllister (d 1962); *b* 31 July 1920; *Educ* Hull GS, St John's Coll York, Univ of Liverpool, Univ of Warwick (MEd); *m* 4 Dec 1943, Maud Ellen, da of Frederick W Hart; 3 da (Margaret, Janet, Gillian); *Career* headmaster Yapham CE Sch nr Pocklington 1953–57, headmaster Wrightington Hosp Sch nr Wigan 1957–64, headmaster Frank Merifield Sch Chesterfield 1964–68, princ Nat Star Centre Cheltenham 1969–70, fndr princ Hereward Coll Coventry 1970–83; sports admin; rugby player RAF 1940–45, athlete E Hull Harriers 1935–40 and 1949–53; hon coach and sec Northern Counties Athletic Assoc 1954–69, chm Br Amateur Athletics Bd 1975–80 (chm UK Coaching Ctee 1972–75), pres AAA 1986–91 (chm Gen Ctee 1982–86), pres Br Athletic Fedn 1991–96; *Books* An Approach to the Further Education of the Physically Handicapped (with J Panckhurst, 1980); *Recreations* athletics, gardening, table tennis, walking; *Style*— Arthur McAllister, Esq, OBE; ✉ British Athletic Federation, Edgbaston House, 3 Duchess Place, Hagley Rd, Edgbaston, Birmingham B16 8NM (☎ 0121 440 5000, fax 0121 440 0555)

McALLISTER, Ian Gerald; CBE (1996); s of Ian Thomas McAllister, and Margaret Mary, *née* McNally; *b* 17 Aug 1943; *Educ* Thornleigh Coll Bolton Lancs, UCL (BSc); *m* 7 Sept 1968, Susan Margaret Frances, da of Allan Alexander Gordon Mitchell; 3 s (Robert Ian Thomas b 1971, Douglas Peter b 1974, James Alexander b 1977), 1 da (Catherine Jessica b 1983); *Career* Ford Motor Co: graduate trainee finance 1964, fin analyst 1965–66, sr analyst Ford Europe 1966–68, supervisor Market Price Analysis Parts Ops 1968–70, P&A market planning mangr Parts Ops 1970–71, mangr market planning Parts Ops 1971–77, mangr Car Mktg Plans Sales and Mktg 1977–79, gen field mangr Eastern Dist Sales 1979–80, dir Parts Sales 1980–81, dir prodn and mktg Parts Ops 1981–83, dir Car Sales Ops 1983–84, dir Mktg Plans and Programs 1984–87, dir sales Ford Germany 1987–89, gen mktg mangr Lincoln Mercury Div USA 1989–91, chm and md Ford of Britain 1992– (md only 1991–92); dir Business in the Community 1992– (memb Cncl 1991–), vice pres Inst of Motor Indust 1992–, pres SMMT 1996–98 (memb Exec 1991–); memb: Advsy Cncl Imperial Coll Business Sch, Bd and Exec American Chamber of Commerce, Advsy Bd Victim Support, Bd Anglia Univ; *Recreations* gardening, golf, computer studies, running; *Style*— Ian McAllister, Esq, CBE; ✉ Ford Motor Company Limited, Eagle Way, Warley, Brentwood, Essex CM13 3BW (☎ 01277 253000, fax 01277 253349)

McALLISTER, John Brian; s of Thomas McAllister (d 1979), and Jane, *née* McCloughan; *b* 11 June 1941; *Educ* Royal Belfast Academical Instn, Queen's Univ Belfast (BA); *m* 1966, Margaret Lindsay, da of William Walker (d 1964), of Belfast; 2 da (Lynne b 1970, Barbara b 1972); *Career* civil servant 1964–88; princ: Dept of Educn (NI) 1971 (asst princ 1968, dep princ 1969), NI Info Serv 1973; dep sec: Dept of Educn (NI) 1980 (asst sec 1976, sr asst sec 1978), Dept of Fin (NI) 1983; under sec DOE (NI) 1985, chief exec Industl Devpt Bd NI 1986 (dep chief exec 1985); gp md CrestaCare Ltd 1988–93 (chief exec 1990–93), self-employed conslt 1993–94, chm Dromona Quality Foods 1993–95, chm James Anderson Ltd 1994–, chief exec Craegmoore Healthcare Ltd 1994–; *Recreations* family holidays, watching sport; *Clubs* Wolverhampton Wanderers; *Style*— John McAllister, Esq; ✉ Craegmoor Healthcare Ltd, Craegmoor House, 97 Friar Street, Droitwich, Worcestershire WR9 8EG (☎ 01905 795088, fax 01905 795095)

McALLISTER, Stephen Drummond; s of Henry McAllister, of Paisley, Renfrewshire, and Annie, *née* Gannon; *b* 16 Feb 1962; *Educ* Camphill HS Paisley; *Career* professional golfer; Scottish Masters 1987, Toyota Cup Denmark 1988, Atlantic Open Portugal 1990, Dutch Open 1990; amateur record: winner Lytham Trophy 1983, Scotland youth caps 1981–82, GB & Ireland youth cap 1982, 7 full Scotland caps 1983; memb Scotland Dunhill Cup team 1990; office clerk 1981–83; *Recreations* football, badminton, tennis, cars; *Style*— Stephen McAllister, Esq

McALLISTER, Victor Lionel; s of late Victor Lionel McAllister, and late Ethel Caroline McAllister; *b* 9 Oct 1941; *Educ* Sydney GS Aust, UCH (MB BS); *m* 22 April 1965, Pamela, da of Dr Denis Joel Johnson, MBE, TD (d 1982); 1 s (Peter Victor Lionel b 1970), 1 da (Karen Ann b 1967); *Career* conslt in admin charge neuroradiology Regnl Neurological Centre Newcastle Gen Hosp 1974– (clinical dir of neurosciences); invited lectr: Europe, India, Singapore, Aust; sec and treas Br Soc of Neuroradiologists 1982–86, memb Euro Soc of Neuroradiology, UK delegate (Br Soc of Neuroradiologists) to Euro Soc of Neuroradiologists 1992–96; LRCP, MRCS, DMRD, FRCR; *Books* Subarachnoid Haemorrhage (1986), Pyogenic Neurosurgical Infections (1991); author of over 60 pubns on all aspects neuroradiology; *Recreations* travel, badminton; *Clubs* Ponteland Lions, '62 (radiological); *Style*— Victor McAllister, Esq; ✉ Bermar, Horsley, Northumberland NE15 0NS (☎ 01661 853813); Department of Neuroradiology, Newcastle General Hospital, Westgate Road, Newcastle upon Tyne NE4 6BE (☎ 0191 273 8811 ext 22140, fax 0191 272 2641)

McALONAN, William Skilling; s of John McAlonan (d 1988), of Lanarks, and Margaret, *née* Black Skilling (d 1973); *b* 29 April 1929; *Educ* Wishaw HS, Nottingham Sch of Planning, Univ of Nottingham (MScEng); *m* 9 April 1955, Laura Elizabeth, da of

Thomas Ralph Burrows; 1 s (David John b 18 June 1966), 2 da (Elsa Jane b 1 Nov 1958, Kirsten Emma b 2 March 1962); *Career* Nat Serv cmmnd RE 1954–56; apprentice civil engr Lanark CC 1947–52, several appts to local govt 1952–69, dep city engr Stoke on Trent 1969–72, dep county surveyor Lanark CC 1972–75, dir of roads Strathclyde Region 1977–89 (dep dir 1975–77), conslt Babtie Group 1989–; chm Central & Southern Branch Inst of Highways and Transportation 1985–86, chm Glasgow & West Assoc Inst of Civil Engrs 1986–87; awarded AA Silver Medal 1986, visitor Tport Road Res Laboratory 1986–88, Br reporter Urban Roads PIARC Conf Brussels 1986, leader DTI Tech Mission to Aust and Japan 1988–; FIHT 1978, FICE 1979, FEng 1989; *Recreations* fishing, gardening, music; *Style*— William McAlonan, Esq, FEng; ✉ Brier Cottage, 88 Busby Road, Carmunnock, Glasgow G76 9BJ (☎ 0141 644 1315); Babtie Group, Consulting Engineers, 95 Bothwell St, Glasgow G2 7HX (☎ 0141 204 2511, fax 0141 226 3109)

McALOON, Patrick Joseph (Paddy); s of Thomas McAloon (d 1988), and Mary Veronica, *née* Nolan; *b* 7 June 1957; *Educ* Ushaw Coll Co Durham, Upholland Coll Lancs, Newcastle Poly (BA); *Career* singer and songwriter; formed Prefab Sprout with bro Martin whilst at sch, first record Lions in My Own Garden (on own label Candle Records) 1982, signed to Kitchenware Records and CBS 1983; albums: Swoon (1984, Gold), Steve McQueen (1985, Gold), From Langley Park to Memphis (1988, Gold), Protest Songs (1989, Silver), Jordan: the Comeback (1990, Gold), A Life of Surprises (1992, Gold); wrote The Gunman for Cher; *Awards* We Let the Stars Go (from Jordan: the Comeback) nominated for Ivor Novello Awards, Jordan: the Comeback nominated for BRITS, Steve McQueen voted among all time best albums in various American and Euro magazines, BAFTA nomination for Crocodile Shoes (tv series) 1995; *Recreations* musicals, movies, trying to imagine what it would have been like to overhear Leonard Bernstein and Stephen Sondheim writing "Something's Coming"; *Style*— Paddy McAloon, Esq; ✉ c/o Kitchenware Records, St Thomas St Stables, Newcastle upon Tyne (☎ 0191 230 1970, fax 0191 232 0262)

McALPINE, (Robert Douglas) Christopher; CMG (1967); s of Dr Archibald Douglas McAlpine, MBE (d 1981), and Elizabeth Meg, *née* Sidebottom (d 1941); *b* 14 June 1919; *Educ* Winchester, New Coll Oxford (MA); *m* 4 Dec 1943, Helen Margery Frances, da of Capt Astley Cannan (d 1934); 2 s (David b 1949, Robert b 1953), 2 da (Christine b 1944 d 1944, Sarah b 1946); *Career* WWII cmmnd Midshipman RNVR 1939, fighter pilot Fleet Air Arm 1941–44, demobbed as temp Lt 1946; Dip Serv 1946–69: FO 1946–47, asst private sec to Sec of State 1947–49, second sec then first sec Bonn High Cmmn 1949–52, FO 1952–54, Lima 1954–56, Moscow 1956–59, FO 1959–62, dep consul gen and cnsllr NYC 1962–65, cnsllr Mexico City 1965–68; ptnr and dir Baring Bros & Co Ltd 1969–79, non exec dir Horace Clarkson plc 1980–87; chm Tetbury Branch Royal Br Legion 1989–95; cncllr Tetbury Town Cncl 1987–91; Cdr Peruvian Order of Merit; *Recreations* sailing, golf; *Clubs* United Oxford & Cambridge Univ; *Style*— Christopher McAlpine, Esq, CMG

McALPINE, Kenneth; OBE (1997), DL (Kent 1976); s of Sir Thomas Malcolm McAlpine, KBE (d 1967), and Maud Dees (d 1969); *b* 21 Sept 1920; *Educ* Charterhouse; *m* 1955, Patricia Mary, da of Capt Francis William Hugh Jeans, CVO, RN (d 1968); 2 s; *Career* WWII Flying Offr RAFVR; dir: Sir Robert McAlpine & Sons Ltd 1941–91; chm McAlpine Helicopters Ltd 1969–; memb Construction Indust Trg Bd 1967–73, govr and dep chm Eastbourne Coll 1968–84, tstee Inst of Econ Affrs 1968–89, govr Royal Hosp of St Bartholomew 1972–74, proprietor Lamberhurst Vineyards 1972–95; High Sheriff Kent 1973–74; FRAeS; *Clubs* Royal Yacht Sqdn, Air Squadron; *Style*— Kenneth McAlpine, Esq, OBE, DL; ✉ The Priory, Lamberhurst, Kent TN3 8DS

McALPINE, Stewart; *b* 2 Jan 1937; *Career* dep md Barham Group Plc 1984–88; chm: SMA Group Ltd 1989–91, Smedley McAlpine Ltd 1960–91, IRB Group Ltd 1989–91, Cornwallis International Ltd 1992–93, Eagle Systems International Ltd 1993–95, Response Publishing Group plc 1993–; dir: Airship Industries Ltd 1984–91, International Business Communications (Holdings) Plc 1987–88, City of London PR Group Plc 1988–91, FCB Advertising Ltd 1991–92, SMcA Ltd 1991–, World Trade Magazines Ltd 1996–; *Style*— Stewart McAlpine, Esq; ✉ SMcA Ltd, 7 Mansion Gardens, London NW3 7NG (☎ and fax 0171 794 2120, mobile 0802 367586)

McALPINE, Hon Sir William Hepburn; 6 Bt (UK 1918), of Knott Park, Co Surrey; eldest s of Baron McAlpine of Moffat (Life Peer and 5 Bt; d 1990), and his 1 w, Ella Mary Gardner, *née* Garnett (d 1987); *b* 12 Jan 1936; *Educ* Charterhouse; *m* 1959, Jill Benton, o da of Lt-Col Sir Peter Fawcett Benton Jones, 3 Bt, OBE (d 1972); 1 s (Andrew William b 1960), 1 da (Lucinda Mary Jane b 1964); *Heir* s, Andrew William McAlpine b 22 Nov 1960; *Career* Life Guards 1954–56; dir: Sir Robert McAlpine Ltd 1959–, Newarthill plc 1977–, Turner & Newall plc 1983–91; chm Railway Heritage Tst 1985–; Liveryman Worshipful Co of Carmen; FRSE 1978, FRSA, FCIT; *Recreations* railway and transport preservation; *Clubs* Buck's, Garrick, Caledonian; *Style*— The Hon Sir William McAlpine, Bt, FRSE; ✉ 40 Bernard St, London WC1N 1LG (☎ 0171 837 3377, fax 0171 837 5209)

McALPINE OF WEST GREEN, Baron (Life Peer UK 1984), of West Green in the Co of Hampshire; (Robert) Alistair; 2 s of Baron McAlpine of Moffat (Life Peer and 5 Bt, d 1990); *b* 14 May 1942; *Educ* Stowe; *m* 1, 1964 (m dis 1979), Sarah Alexandra, da of late Paul Hillman Baron, of London W1; 2 da (Hon Mary Jane b 1965, Hon Victoria Alice b 1967); m 2, 1980, Romilly Thompson, o da of Alfred Thompson Hobbs, of Cranleigh, Surrey; 1 da (Skye b 1984); *Career* dir: Newarthill plc, George Weidenfeld Holdings Ltd 1975–83; vice pres Euro League of Econ Cooperation 1975– (treas 1974–75); hon treas: Euro Democratic Union 1978–88, Cons and Unionist Pty 1975–90 (dep chm 1979–83); dir: ICA 1972–73, T I Finance Ltd 1981–90 (chm 1985–90); vice chm Contemporary Arts Soc 1973–80; memb: Arts Cncl of GB 1981–82, Friends of V & A Museum 1976–91, Cncl British Stage Co 1973–75; tstee Royal Opera House Tst 1974–80; govr: Polytechnic of the South Bank 1981–82, Stowe Sch 1981–84; pres Br Waterfowl Assoc 1978–81 (patron 1981–); vice pres: Friends of Ashmolean Museum 1969–, Gtr London Arts Assoc 1971–77; pres The Medical Coll of St Bartholomew's Hosp 1993–; Liveryman Worshipful Co of Gunmakers; *Books* The Servant (1992), Journal of a Collector (1994), Letters to a Young Politician (1995); *Recreations* the arts, horticulture, aviculture, agriculture; *Clubs* Garrick, Pratt's, Weld (Perth, W Aust); *Style*— The Rt Hon the Lord McAlpine of West Green; ✉ c/o House of Lords, London SW1A OPW

MACAN, HE Thomas Townley; s of Dr Thomas Townley Macan, of Outgate, Ambleside, Cumbria (d 1985), and Zaida Bindloss, *née* Boddington; *b* 14 Nov 1946; *Educ* Shrewsbury, Univ of Sussex (BA, Pres of Union); *m* 1976, Janet Ellen, *née* Martin, of Hollidaysburg, Pennsylvania; 1 s (Nicholas b 1981), 1 da (Melissa b 1984); *Career* HM Dip Serv: UN Dept FCO 1969–71, Br Embassy Bonn 1971–74, Br Embassy Brasilia 1974–78, Maritime, Aviation and Environment Dept FCO 1978–81, press sec Br Embassy Bonn 1981–86, head Cwlth Coordination Dept FCO 1986–88, head Trg Dept FCO 1988–90, dep head of mission Br Embassy Lisbon 1990–94, ambass Vilnius 1995–; MIL 1992; *Recreations* boats, church architecture, walking; *Clubs* Naval, Island Cruising (Salcombe); *Style*— HE Mr Thomas Macan; ✉ c/o Foreign and Commonwealth Office (Vilnius), King Charles Street, London SW1A 2AH; British Embassy, 2 Antakalnio, 2055 Vilnius, Lithuania (☎ 00 370 2 222 070, fax 00 370 2 727 579)

McANALLY, Rear Admiral John Henry Stuart; LVO (1982); s of Arthur Patrick McAnally (d 1983), and Basil Hamilton Stuart, *née* Knight; *b* 9 April 1945; *Educ* Westminster Sch, Britannia RNC Dartmouth; *Career* with RN; Lt 1967, navigating and ops offr 6 warships incl US destroyer and Australian aircraft carrier 1968–78 (CO HMS Iveston 1973–75), navigation subspecialisation course HMS Dryad 1971, Lt Cdr 1975, RN Staff Coll (Director's Prize) 1978, 2 i/c HMS Birmingham 1978–79, Cdr 1979, navigating commander HMY Britannia 1980 and 1981, desk offr (size and shape of future RN) DN Plans MOD 1982–83, CO HMS Torquay and HMS Alacrity 1984–86, Capt 1987, Sixth Frigate Sqdn (CO HMS Ariadne and HMS Hermione) 1987–89, asst dir (role of future RN) DN Plans MOD 1989–91, RCDS 1992, Higher Command and Staff Course 1993, Cdre 1993, dir Naval Logistic Policy 1993, dep to Assistant Chief of Naval Staff 1994–95, Rear Adm 1996, Flag Offr Training and Recruiting 1996–; govr Portsmouth GS 1996; memb: Naval Review 1964, Nautical Inst 1975, Royal Inst of Navigation 1975, US Naval Inst (prize memb) 1978, RUSI 1978; MInstD 1995; *Recreations* golf, reading, jogging; *Clubs* Naval and Military, National Liberal, Coombe Wood, Hayling & Royal Mid Surrey Golf, Royal Naval & Royal Albert Yacht (Portsmouth); *Style*— Rear Admiral John McAnally, LVO; ✉ Trinity House, Anchor Gate Road, HM Naval Base, Portsmouth, Hants PO1 3NW; Naval Recruiting and Training Agency, Room 041, Victory Building, HM Naval Base, Portsmouth, Hants PO1 3LS (☎ 01705 727600, fax 01705 727615)

McANALLY, Mary B H; da of Patrick McAnally (d 1983), of Old Portsmouth, Hants, and Basil, *née* Knight; *b* 9 April 1945; *Educ* Tiffin Girls' Sch, Wimbledon Sch of Art; *m* 1979, Hugh Macpherson; *Career* researcher Man Alive BBC TV 1969; Thames Television: researcher and writer This Is Your Life 1970–71, prodr Money-Go-Round 1973–82, ed 4 What it's Worth (for Channel 4) 1982–90, creator and exec network prodr The Time - The Place 1987–92, head of features 1989–92; Meridian Broadcasting: controller of regnl progs and community affrs 1992–94, dir of progs 1994–95, dir of progs and prodn 1995–96, md and dir of progs 1996–; memb Nat Consumer Cncl 1987–, dir Southern Crimestoppers 1994–, dir Meridian Broadcasting Charitable Tst 1994–, dir Nat Consumer Cncl Services Ltd 1995–; international tennis player 1963–67, rep England and Surrey, competed Wimbledon Lawn Tennis Championships, former GB jr indoor champion (beating Virginia Wade in final); memb RTS 1980, FRSA 1989, memb Forum UK 1990; *Awards* incl: Freedom of Information Media Award 1989, San Francisco Gold Award, Santander Jury Prize, Glenfiddich Food Writer's Award, BMA Gold Award, Berlin Consumer Award, Monergy Award, New York Festival 1994; *Books* Buy Right (jtly, 1978); *Recreations* tennis, golf, painting; *Clubs* All England Lawn Tennis, Cumberland Tennis, Winchester Tennis, Le Touquet Tennis, Highgate Golf; *Style*— Ms Mary McAnally; ✉ Meridian Broadcasting Ltd, Television Centre, Northam Road, Southampton SO9 5HZ (☎ 01703 222555, fax 01703 712294)

MacANDREW, 3 Baron (UK 1959); Christopher Anthony Colin MacAndrew; er s of 2 Baron MacAndrew (d 1989); *b* 16 Feb 1945; *Educ* Malvern; *m* 1975, Sarah Helen, o da of Lt-Col Peter Hendy Brazier, of Nash Ct Farmhouse, Marnhull, Dorset; 1 s (Hon Oliver Charles Julian), 2 da (Hon Diana Sarah b 24 June 1978, Hon Tessa Deborah b 2 Aug 1980); *Heir* s, Hon Oliver Charles Julian MacAndrew b 3 Sept 1983; *Style*— The Rt Hon Lord MacAndrew; ✉ Hall Farm, Archdeacon Newton, Darlington, Co Durham (☎ 01325 462246)

McANDREW, Ian Christopher; *b* 20 Feb 1953; *Educ* Univ of Cambridge (MA); *m* 26 Aug 1978, Geraldine Baker; 2 da (Cathryn b 12 Jan 1985, Madeleine b 12 March 1989); *Career* Coopers & Lybrand 1975–88, fin and ops dir, co sec and compliance offr British and Commonwealth Merchant Bank plc 1988–92, fin dir Lawrence Graham 1992–; FCA (ACA 1978); *Style*— Ian McAndrew, Esq; ✉ 3 Frank Dixon Close, London SE21 7BD (☎ 0181 693 3592)

MacANDREW, Hon Nicholas Rupert; yr s of 2 Baron MacAndrew (d 1989); *b* 12 Feb 1947; *Educ* Eton; *m* 1975, Victoria Rose, da of George Patrick Renton, of Alton, Hants; 1 s, 2 da; *Career* Deloittes 1965–70, Schroders plc 1970– (gp md of finance, strategic planning and info technol 1991–); FCA 1970; *Style*— The Hon Nicholas MacAndrew; ✉ The Old Chapel, Greywell, Hook, Hampshire RG29 1BS (☎ 01256 702390); Schroders plc, 120 Cheapside, London EC2V 6DS (☎ 0171 382 6000, fax 0171 382 6878)

McANDREW, Nicolas; s of Robert Louis McAndrew (d 1981), and Anita Marian, *née* Huband (d 1996, aged 100); *b* 9 Dec 1934; *Educ* Winchester; *m* 20 Sept 1960, Diana Leonie Wood; 2 s (Charles Gavin b 14 Jan 1962, Mark James b 16 Feb 1964), 1 da (Fiona Catherine Mary b 16 June 1968); *Career* Nat Serv 1 Bn The Black Watch 1953–55 (active serv Kenya); articled clerk Peat Marwick Mitchell & Co 1955–61, qualified CA 1961; S G Warburg & Co Ltd: investmt mangr 1962–69, chm Warburg Investment Management 1975–78 (md 1969–75); md: NM Rothschild & Sons Ltd 1979–88, Rothschild Asset Management Ltd 1979–88, Murray Johnstone Ltd 1988– (chm 1992–); dep chm Burn Stewart Distillers plc 1990–, memb: Bd Highlands and Islands Enterprise 1993–, Liverpool Victoria Friendly Soc 1995–, North of Scotland Water Authy 1995–; memb Court of Assts Worshipful Co of Grocers (Master 1978–79); *Recreations* fishing, shooting, gardening; *Clubs* White's, City of London; *Style*— Nicolas McAndrew, Esq; ✉ Kilcoy Castle, Muir of Ord, Ross-shire IV6 7RX (☎ 01463 871393); Murray Johnstone Ltd, 7 West Nile St, Glasgow G1 2PX (☎ 0141 226 3131, fax 0141 204 0712)

MacARA, Dr Alexander Wiseman (Sandy); s of Rev Alexander MacAra (d 1992), and Marion Wiseman, *née* Mackay (d 1972); *b* 4 May 1932; *Educ* Irvine Royal Acad, Univ of Glasgow (Carnegie bursar, MB ChB), London Sch of Hygiene and Tropical Med (DPH (Lond), Hecht prize, Sir Wilson Jameson travelling scholar 1967); *m* 2 April 1964, Sylvia May, da of Edward Brodbeck Williams; 1 da (Alexandra Sarah b 1973), 1 s (James William b 1976); *Career* various hosp appts Glasgow Teaching Hosps 1958–60, GP experience Glasgow and London 1959–60, departmental med offr and sch med offr City and Co of Bristol 1960–63, hon community physician Bristol 1963–74; Univ of Bristol: lectr in public health 1963–73, sr lectr in community med and actg head of dept 1973–76, conslt sr lectr in public health med 1976–; hon regnl specialist in public health med: South and Western RHA 1976–96, Avon Health Authy 1996–; hon visiting conslt Bristol Royal Infirmary 1976–; conslt/temp advsr WHO 1970–, dir WHO Collaborating Centre in Environmental Health Promotion and Ecology 1989–; memb GMC 1979–; BMA: chm Jr Membs 1967, chm Public Health Conf 1979–84, chm Med Ethics Ctee 1982–89, chm Representative Body 1989–92, chm Cncl 1993–; sec-gen: Assoc of Schs of Public Health in Europe 1976–89, World Fedn for Teaching and Res in Public Health 1989–; treas Faculty of Public Health Med 1979–84; hon memb Hungarian Acad of Med Scis 1989, hon memb and Gold medallist Italian Soc of Hygiene, Preventative Med and Public Health 1991, hon life fell Soc of Public Health 1991; Doctor of Public Health (hc) and Gerasimos Alizivatos Prize Athens Sch of Public Health 1992, James Preston Meml Award 1993, Public Health Award Soc of Public Health 1994, John Kershaw Award 1995; Harben lectr 1996; FFCM 1973, FRIPHH 1973, fell BMA 1978, FRCGP (ad eundem) 1983, FFPHM 1989, FRCP 1991, FRSA 1995; *Books* Personal Data Protection in Health and Social Services (jtly, 1988), chapters in books and papers on epidemiology, public health, environmental health and medical ethics; *Recreations* reading, writing, music, gardening, church and human rights activities, rusty golf and tennis; *Clubs* Athenaeum, RSM; *Style*— Dr Sandy MacAra; ✉ Elgon, 10 Cheyne Road, Stoke Bishop, Bristol BS9 2DH (☎ 0117 968 2838, ☎ and fax 0117 968 4602); Department of Social Medicine, University of Bristol, Canynge Hall, Whiteladies Road, Bristol BS8 2PR (☎ 0117 928 9000, fax 0117 928 7204); British Medical Association, BMA House, Tavistock Square, London WC1H 9JP (☎ 0171 383 6100, fax 0171 383 6322)

McARDELL, John David; s of Patrick John McArdell (d 1988), and Elizabeth Frances, *née* Powling; *b* 25 Dec 1931; *Educ* Haberdashers' Aske's; *m* 22 Aug 1959, Margaret

Sylvia, da of George Lewis Cawley (d 1981); 2 da (Nicola Susan b 26 June 1964, Paula Frances b 19 Sept 1968); *Career* Nat Serv RAF Egypt 1950–52; dep md Ecclesiastical Insurance Group 1988– (mangr mktg and planning 1975–81, asst gen mangr 1985–88); dir: Aldwych Management Services Ltd, Blaisdon Properties Ltd, REI Investment Ltd Ireland, Heathfield Management Ltd, Allchurches Mortgage Company Ltd, Allchurches Life Assurance Ltd, EIO Trustees Ltd, CPS Ltd; memb: Insur Inst of London, Insur Golfing Soc of London; former pres Insur Inst of Gloucester, govr and dir Westonbirt Sch; Freeman City of London 1981; Liveryman: Worshipful Co of Insurers, Worshipful Co of Marketors; ACII 1957, FInstD 1980, FIMgt 1984, FCIM 1989, CI 1989; *Recreations* golf, bridge, rambling; *Clubs* IOD, City Livery, Wig and Pen; *Style—* John McArdell, Esq; ✉ Pen-Y-Bryn, Rodborough Common, Gloucs GL5 5BN (☎ 01453 873276); Beaufort House, Brunswick Rd, Gloucester (☎ 01452 28533, telex 43646)

McARDLE, Brian Thomas; s of John McArdle (d 1966), of Co Durham, and Mary, *née* McDonald; *b* 31 Jan 1948; *Educ* St Mary's Darlington, Univ of Newcastle upon Tyne (LLB); *m* 19 May 1973, Alison Jane, da of Edward William Knight, of Nottingham; 2 s (Joseph and Richard (twins) b 30 April 1992); *Career* slr; asst slr Molineux McKeag & Cooper Newcastle upon Tyne 1973–74; prosecuting slr: Northumbria Police Authy 1974–77, W Midlands Co Cncl 1977–86; chief crown prosecutor Inner London Crown Prosecution Serv 1987–93 (branch crown prosecutor 1986–87), chief crown prosecutor CPS E Midlands 1993–; memb: Prosecuting Slrs' Soc 1974–86, Law Soc 1973–; *Recreations* music, watching cricket; *Style—* Brian McArdle, Esq; ✉ Crown Prosecution Service, CPS East Midlands, 2 King Edward Court, King Edward Street, Nottingham, Notts NG1 1EL (☎ 0115 948 0480)

McARDLE, Colin Stewart; *b* 10 Oct 1939; *Educ* Jordanhill Coll Sch Glasgow, Univ of Glasgow (MB ChB, MD); *m* June Margaret Campbell, *née* Merchant; 2 s (Peter Alexander b 1975, Alan Douglas b 1982), 1 da (Kirsten Anne b 1977); *Career* sr registrar in surgery Western Infirmary Glasgow 1972–75 (Nuffield res fell 1971–72); conslt surgn: Victoria Infirmary Glasgow 1975–78, Dept of Surgery Royal Infirmary Glasgow 1978–96 (hon prof of surgery 1991); currently prof of surgery Univ of Edinburgh; author of papers on: breast, colon and stomach cancer, liver tumours, pain and postoperative pulmonary complications, shock, surgical sepsis and intensive care; FRCSEd 1968, FRCS 1969, FRCS Glasgow 1980, FRSM 1986; *Books* Surgical Oncology (1990); *Style—* Colin McArdle, Esq; ✉ 6 Collylinn Rd, Bearsden, Glasgow G61 4PN; University Department of Surgery, Western General Hospital, Edinburgh

McARDLE, John; s of John Joseph McArdle (d 1966), and Edeth, *née* Webster, of Liverpool; *b* 16 Aug 1949; *Educ* St Bede's Secdy Modern Sch, E15 Acting Sch Laughton Essex; *Career* actor; Hon memb NSPCC Cncl 1994; various credits BBC Radio Manchester; also appeared in Horses for Courses (Br Film Sch); *Theatre* began with various fringe cos in England and Wales; repertory: Liverpool Playhouse, Liverpool Everyman, Manchester Library Theatre, Contact Theatre, Forum Theatre, Oldham Coliseum, Bolton Octogan, Sheffield Crucible, Chester Gateway, Edinburgh Festival, Young Vic Theatre; *Television* for BBC incl: Thacker, Underbelly, Gallowglass (Barbara Vine series), Spender, Bambino Mio (Screen One) 1994, Skallergrig (Screen One) 1994, Seaforth 1994, Rich Deceiver 1994, Throwaways (Sch TV) 1996, Born to Run 1996; for Granada incl: Coronation Street, Strangers, Kavanagh QC 1995, Prime Suspect V 1996; other credits incl: Billy Corkhill in Brookside (Channel 4) 1986–91, Firm Friends (ITV), The Chief (police series, Anglia) 1994, Firm Friends II (Tyne Tees) 1994, Finney (ITV) 1994, Cracker (ITV) 1994, Wycliffe (HTV) 1995, Heartbeat (Yorkshire) 1995, Its Not Unusual (Sort and Curlies, Channel 4) 1995, In the Place of the Dead (LWT) 1995, And the Beat Goes On (Mersey) 1996; *Recreations* windsurfing, fell walking; *Style—* John McArdle, Esq; ✉ c/o Denis Lyne Agency, 108 Leonard Street, London EC2A 4RH (☎ 0171 739 6200, fax 0171 739 4101)

MacARTHUR, Brian Roger; s of S H MacArthur (d 1971), of Ellesmere Port, Cheshire, and Marjorie MacArthur (d 1993); *b* 5 Feb 1940; *Educ* Brentwood Sch, Helsby GS, Univ of Leeds (BA); *m* 22 Aug 1975, Bridget da of Nicholas Rosevear Trahair, of South Milton, Kingsbridge, South Devon; 2 da (Tessa b 1976, Georgina b 1979); *Career* educn corr The Times 1967–70, fndr ed The Times Higher Educnl Supplement 1971–76, exec ed The Times 1981–82, dep ed The Sunday Times 1982–84; ed: The Western Morning News 1984–85, Today 1985–86; exec ed The Sunday Times 1987–92, assoc ed (features) The Times 1992–; Hon MA Open Univ 1976; *Recreations* reading, France; *Clubs* Garrick; *Style—* Brian MacArthur, Esq; ✉ 25 Northchurch Road, London N1 4ED (☎ 0171 275 0277); The Times, 1 Pennington Street, London E1 9XG (☎ 0171 782 5801, fax 0171 782 5124)

McARTHUR, (Allan Robin) Dayrell; s of Alan John Dennis McArthur (d 1988), of Combe Hay, Bath, and Pamela Mary, *née* Henderson; *b* 28 June 1946; *Educ* Winchester; *m* 30 April 1977, Susan Diana, da of Christopher Cheshire, of Spain; 3 s (Alastair b 1979, Sam b 1981, Robert b 1985); *Career* Price Waterhouse 1965–69, McArthur Group Ltd 1969– (md 1971, chm 1987); pres Nat Assoc of Steel Stockholders 1986–88, pres Fédération Européenne du Négoce d'Acier (European Steel Trades Fedn) 1992–94; govr Univ of the West of England 1990–; Master Soc of Merchant Venturers of Bristol 1989–90; *Recreations* tennis, golf, cricket, rackets, music, theatre, skiing; *Clubs* MCC, Tennis & Rackets Assoc, Bristol and Clifton Golf; *Style—* Dayrell McArthur, Esq; ✉ Moorledge Farm, Chew Magna, Bristol (☎ 01275 332357); McArthur Group Ltd, Foundry Lane, Fishponds Trading Estate, Bristol BS5 7UE (☎ 0117 965 6242, fax 0117 958 3536)

McARTHUR, Gordon Borland; s of James Bennet McArthur (d 1985), of Easton Estate, Grantham, Lincs, and Helen Webster, *née* McRae (d 1971); *b* 28 Feb 1952; *Educ* various service and civilian schs in UK, Germany and Singapore, Kesteven Coll of FE Grantham; *m* 1974 (m dis 1992), Janet Sharpe; 1 s (James b 3 Nov 1974); *Career* sometime journalist Melton Mowbray Times then agency journalist London, ed Carrick Gazette and dep gp ed Galloway Gazette Group 1976–81; West Sound Radio: joined as duty ed 1981, head of news 1985–91, prog controller 1991–92, prog dir 1992–; *Style—* Gordon McArthur, Esq; ✉ Programme Director, West Sound Radio, Radio House, Holmston Road, Ayr KA7 3BE (☎ 01292 283662, fax 01292 262607)

MacARTHUR, Prof John Durno; s of Donald MacArthur (d 1936), of Harrow, Middlesex, and Isabel Norah, *née* Durno (d 1988); *b* 22 May 1934; *Educ* Reeds Sch, Caterham Sch, Univ of Reading, Univ of Oxford; *m* 11 July 1959, Anne Elliss, da of William Henry Hicks (d 1968), of Bexleyheath; 1 s (Andrew William b 1961), 2 da (Caroline Mary Anne b 1962, Juliet Claire b 1964); *Career* Nat Serv 1952–54, 2 Lt RASC 1953–54, serv Egypt; agric economist Kenya 1960–67, lectr UCNW Bangor 1967–72, visiting prof of agric and project econs Univ of Bradford 1995– (sr lectr 1972–87, prof 1988–95); conslt: IBRD, ODA, FAO, UNDP, UNIDO, CFC, CDC, CEU; fndr memb: SDP 1981, SLDP 1987 (Alliance candidate Elmet 1987); memb: Agric Econ Soc, Devpt Studies Assoc; *Books* Project Appraisal in Practice (co-author, 1976), Appraisal of Projects in Developing Countries (1988); *Recreations* golf, nature conservation, genealogy, bridge; *Style—* Prof John MacArthur; ✉ Development and Project Planning Centre, University of Bradford, Bradford BD7 1OP (☎ 01274 733466, fax 01274 385280, telex 51309 UNIBFD G)

McARTHUR, Dr Thomas Burns (Tom); s of Archibald McArthur (d 1967), of Glasgow, and Margaret Dymock Dow, *née* Burns (d 1986); *b* 23 Aug 1938; *Educ* Woodside Secdy Sch Glasgow, Univ of Glasgow (MA), Univ of Edinburgh (MLitt, PhD); *m* 30 March 1963, Fereshteh (d 1993), da of Habib Mottahedin, of Teheran, Iran; 1 s (Alan b 30 April 1970), 2 da (Meher b 11 Nov 1966, Roshan b 16 Nov 1968); *Career* 2 Lt offr instr RAEC 1959–62; educn offr: Depot the Royal Warks Regt, Depot the Mercian Bde; asst teacher Riland-Bedford Boys HS Sutton Coldfield Warks 1962–64, head of Eng Dept Cathedral and John Connon Sch Bombay India 1965–67, visiting prof Bharatiya Vidya Bhavan Univ of Bombay 1965–67, dir of studies Extra Mural Eng Language Courses Univ of Edinburgh 1972–79, assoc prof of Eng Université du Québec à Trois-Rivières Quebec Canada 1979–83; hon res fell Univ of Exeter 1992–; editor: English Today: The International Review of the English Language 1984–, The Oxford Companion to the English Language 1987–; memb Editorial Bd: International Journal of Lexicography 1988–, World Englishes Jl 1993–, LOGOS: The Professional Jl of the Book World 1994–; editorial advsr The Good Book Guide 1992–; conslt to: BBC, Bloomsbury, Collins, Longman, Chambers, Cambridge Univ Press, Good Book Guide, WHO, Henson International TV (creators of The Muppets), Govt of Quebec, Century Hutchinson, Macmillan, OUP, Time-Life Books; fndr memb and tutor Birmingham Yoga Club 1963, schs lectr and press offr Bombay Soc of Prevention of Cruelty to Animals (BSPCA) 1965–67, chm Scot Yoga Assoc 1977–79, co-chm Scots Language Planning Ctee 1978, memb Tech and Educnl Ctees Soc of Authors 1992–; numerous broadcasts BBC Eng by Radio (World Serv); *Books* Building English Words (1972), Using English Prefixes and Suffixes (1972), Using Compound Words (1972), A Rapid Course in English for Students of Economics (1973), Using Phrasal Verbs (1973), Collins Dictionary of English Phrasal Verbs and Their Idioms (with Beryl T Atkins, 1974), Learning Rhythm and Stress (with Mohamed Heliel, 1974), Using Modal Verbs (with Richard Wakely, 1974), Times, Tenses and Conditions (with John Hughes, 1974), Languages of Scotland (ed with A J Aitken, 1979), Longman Lexicon of Contemporary English (1981), A Foundation Course for Language Teachers (1983), The Written Word: A Course in Controlled Composition (books 1 and 2, 1984), Worlds of Reference: Lexicography, Learning and Language from the Clay Tablet to the Computer (1986), Understanding Yoga: A Thematic Companion to Yoga and Indian Philosophy (1986), Yoga and the Bhagavad-Gita (1986), Unitive Thinking: A Guide to Developing a More Integrated and Effective Mind (1988), The English Language as Used in Quebec: A Survey (ed, 1989), The Oxford Companion to the English Language (ed, 1992, abridged edn 1996); *Recreations* reading, television, walking, cycling, travel; *Style—* Dr Tom McArthur; ✉ 22–23 Ventress Farm Court, Cherry Hinton Rd, Cambridge CB1 4HD (☎ 01223 245934, fax 01223 241161, e-mail tmca@scotsway.demon.co.uk)

MacARTHUR CLARK, Judy Anne; da of Archibald Alastair Cameron MacArthur (d 1990), of Manchester, and Elinore Muriel, *née* Warde Fotheringhay; *b* 18 Nov 1950; *Educ* Orton GS Peterborough, Univ of Glasgow Coll of Vet Med (BVMS), RCVS (MRCVS 1973, Diplomate in Lab Animal Sci 1985, election to Specialist Register 1990); *m* 16 Feb 1991, David Wayne Clark, s of Robert Clark (d 1982), of Tell City, Indiana; 1 da (Sophie Katherine b 28 Aug 1991); *Career* gen vet practice Sussex 1973–74, vet advsr Univs Fedn for Animal Welfare 1974–76, pt/t hon lectr RVC London 1974–87, sr sientific offr Miny of Defence Porton Down 1976–82, head of lab animal sci Searle R&D High Wycombe 1983–86, dir of lab animal sci Pfizer Central Research Sandwich 1986–91, vet conslt JMC Consultancy Sandwich 1991–, dir REC Europe Ltd Margate 1992–; memb Cncl Section of Comparative Med RSM 1979–87; Br Lab Animals Vet Assoc (BLAVA): memb Cncl 1979–89, vice pres and pres 1983–89; RCVS: memb Cncl 1982–, chm Lab Animal Sci Bd 1990–, dir Charter 150 Prog 1990–, vice pres and pres 1991–94, rep Inst of Biology Accreditation Panel for Trg 1992–, chm Educn Ctee 1994–; Farm Animal Welfare Cncl (FAWC): memb 1993–, chm R&D Ctee 1994–; Biotechnology and Biological Scis Research Cncl (BBSRC): memb Planning and Resources Bd 1994–95, memb Cncl 1996–; memb Technology Liaison Ctee Inst for Animal Health Compton 1994–, memb Animal Production and Welfare Strategy Gp Silsoe Research Inst 1994– (chm 1996–); Animal Procedures Ctee (APC): memb 1994–, memb Primates Sub-ctee 1995–; chm Bill Hiddleston Award Fund Tstees 1985–92, vice pres Inst of Animal Technol (IAT) 1991–; Winston Churchill travelling fell USA and Canada 1982, Victory Medal Central Vet Soc BVA 1992, Pres's Award Vet Mktg Assoc 1993; approx 100 scientific pubns and invited presentations; memb: Assoc of Vet Teachers and Research Workers, Assoc of Veterinarians in Indust, BVA, BLAVA, Br Vet Zoological Soc, Euro Marmoset Research Gp, Fedn of Euro Lab Animal Sci Assocs, Lab Animal Sci Assoc, Primatological Soc of GB, Research Defence Soc, Univs Fedn for Animal Welfare, Vet Benevolent Fund; FRSM 1978; *Recreations* company of family and friends; *Clubs* Farmers', RSM; *Style—* Mrs Judy MacArthur Clark; ✉ REC Europe Ltd, Continental Approach, Westwood, Margate, Kent CT9 4JG (☎ 01843 232090, fax 01843 228875, mobile 0385 246002)

MACARTNEY, Dr (William John) Allan; MEP (SNP) NE Scotland (majority 31,227); s of Rev William Macleod Macartney, of Coupar Angus, Perthshire, and late Jessie Helen Inch, *née* Low; *b* 17 Feb 1941; *Educ* Elgin Acad, Univ of Tübingen, Univ of Marburg, Univ of Edinburgh (MA, PhD), Univ of Glasgow (BLitt); *m* 1963, (Jane Dorothy) Anne, da of late William Watchman Forsyth; 1 da ((Anna Helen) Jean (Dr Robertson) b 1964), 2 s (John William Forsyth b 1967, Andrew Allan Watchman b 1968); *Career* vol teacher Eastern Nigeria 1963–64, lectr in govt and admin Univ of Botswana, Lesotho and Swaziland 1966–74, res fell Univ of Edinburgh 1974–75, staff tutor in politics Open Univ Scotland 1975–94, MEP (SNP) NE Scotland 1994–; hon fell in politics Univ of Edinburgh 1984–; pres UN Assoc (Edinburgh) 1991–; memb: AUT 1975–, Political Sci Assoc (UK); *Books* Readings in Boleswa Government (1971), The Referendum Experience (1981), Islands of Europe (1983), Self-Determination in the Commonwealth (1988); *Recreations* music, languages, hill walking, vexillology; *Clubs* The St Andrew Society; *Style—* Dr Allan Macartney, MEP; ✉ North East Euro Centre, 70 Rosemount Place, Aberdeen AB25 2XJ (☎ 01224 623150, fax 01224 623160); European Parliament, Rue Belliard 97–113, 1040 Brussels, Belgium

MACARTNEY, Sir John Barrington; 6 Bt (I 1799), of Lish, Armagh; s of John Barrington Macartney (d 1951), and Selina, *née* Koch; suc uncle, Sir Alexander Miller Macartney, 5 Bt (d 1960); *b* 1917; *m* 1944, Amy Isobel Reinke (d 1978); 1 s (John Ralph b 1945); *Heir* s, John Ralph Macartney, *qv*; *Career* retired dairy farmer; *Style—* Sir John Macartney, Bt; ✉ 37 Meadow St, North Mackay, Queensland 4740, Australia

MACARTNEY, John Ralph; s and h of Sir John Barrington Macartney, 6 Bt, *qv*; *b* 1945; *m* 1966, Suzanne Marie Fowler, of Nowra, NSW; 4 da (Donna Maree b 1968, Karina Lee b 1971, Katherine Anne b 1974, Anita Louise b 1979); *Career* Petty Officer RAN (ret); teacher (head of dept) ACT Inst of TAFE; facilities mangr Mackay TAFE Qld Aust; *Style—* John Macartney Esq; ✉ 1 Kookaburra Street, Slade Point, Queensland 4740, Australia

MACASKILL, Ewen; s of John Angus MacAskill, of Erskine, Renfrewshire, Scotland, and Catherine, *née* MacDonald; *b* 29 Oct 1951; *Educ* Woodside Sch Glasgow, Univ of Glasgow (MA); *m* Anne, da of John Hutchinson; 3 s (Robbie b 19 Nov 1981, Andrew b 27 July 1984, Jamie b 29 Aug 1988); *Career* reporter Glasgow Herald 1974–77; journalist: Nat Bdcasting Cmmn of Papua New Guinea 1978–79, Reuters 1980, Scotsman 1981–83, China Daily Beijing 1984, Scotsman 1985, Washington Post (reporter) 1986; political ed Scotsman 1989–96 (journalist 1987), chief political corr The Guardian 1996–; *Awards* Scotland's Young Journalist of the Year 1974; *Books* Always A Little Further (1983); *Recreations* mountaineering, theatre; *Clubs* Junior Mountaineering Club of Scotland; *Style—* Ewen MacAskill, Esq; ✉ 11 Norman Avenue, St Margarets, Twickenham, Middx TW1 2LY (☎ 0181 891 0795); The Guardian, Press Gallery, House of Commons, Westminster SW1A 0AA (☎ 0171 219 3380)

MACASKILL, John Harry; s of John Macaskill (d 1981), and Nancy Love, *née* Mills (d 1963); *b* 13 Feb 1947; *Educ* Oundle, Univ of Nottingham (BA); *m* 11 May 1974, Gwyneth June, da of Ralph Herbert Keith Evers; 3 s (James b 6 Sept 1979, Robert b 1 Oct 1981, Sandy b 9 May 1985); *Career* ptnr Slaughter and May 1979–96 (articled clerk 1970–72, slr 1972–79); non-exec dir Skipton Building Society 1996–; Freeman City of London 1985, Liveryman The City of London Solicitors' Co 1985; memb Law Soc 1972; *Recreations* walking, sailing, Scottish history; *Clubs* Little Ship, RAC; *Style—* John H Macaskill, Esq

MACASKILL, Ronald Angus; s of Angus Duncan Macaskill, and Elsie Broadbridge, *née* Tosh; *b* 21 April 1947; *Educ* King's Coll Sch Wimbledon, King's Coll London (BSc, AKC), City Univ (MSc); *m* 6 Aug 1977, Irmgard Elisabeth, da of Heinrich Matthias Hinterstein, of Poysdorf, Austria; 1 s (Roald Ian b 6 May 1990), 2 da (Elisabeth Ann b 23 Aug 1981, Alexandra Jane b 15 Apr 83); *Career* mktg exec: Dynamit Nobel (UK) Ltd 1969–71, Macaskill Group 1971– (dir 1975–); memb: World Ship Soc, Farringdon Ward Club; sec Admty Ferry Crew Assoc; Freeman City of London 1978, Liveryman Worshipful Co of Blacksmiths 1978 (sec Social Ctee 1980–82, sec Fin Ctee 1982–83, sec Craft Ctee 1987–91, memb Ct 1996–); MIMgt 1970, FInstSMM 1979; *Recreations* skiing, swimming, ship modelling, photography; *Clubs* City Livery; *Style—* Ronald Macaskill, Esq; ✉ 41 The Gallop, Sutton, Surrey SM2 5RY (☎ 0181 643 7743); Macaskill Engineering Ltd, Forval Close, Mitcham, Surrey CR4 4NE (☎ 0181 640 7211, fax 0181 640 9411)

McATEER, Ian Henderson; s of William Henderson McAteer, of Mahé, Seychelles, and Juliette Angeline, *née* Mellon; *b* 17 Nov 1958; *Educ* Dollar Acad, Univ of Leeds (LLB); *m* 27 May 1989, Clare, da of late Philip Seymour Langridge; 2 s (Fergus Henderson b 23 Aug 1991, Rory Frederick b 14 Jan 1994); *Career* called to the Bar Gray's Inn 1982, practising until 1984; Saatchi & Saatchi Advertising London: joined 1984, bd dir 1989–92, gp account dir 1990–92; bd account dir and client servs dir Faulds Advertising Edinburgh 1992–96, fndr ptnr The Union 1996–; assoc memb D&AD, memb Mktg Soc; *Recreations* skiing, photography, reading; *Style—* Ian McAteer, Esq

McATEER, Jason; *b* 18 June 1971; *Career* professional footballer; clubs: Bolton Wanderers FC 1991–95, Liverpool FC 1995–; Rep of Ireland: 11 full caps, memb World Cup team 1994; *Style—* Jason McAteer, Esq; ✉ c/o Liverpool FC, Anfield Road, Anfield, Liverpool L4 0TH (☎ 0151 263 2361)

MACAULAY, Anthony Dennis; s of Dennis Macaulay, of Wakefield, W Yorks, and Frances, *née* Frain; *b* 15 Nov 1948; *Educ* Queen Elizabeth GS Wakefield, Keble Coll Oxford; *m* 7 Oct 1978, Dominica Francisca, da of Dr Henri Compernolle, of Bruges, Belgium; 1 s (Thomas b 29 March 1985), 2 da (Laura b 20 April 1983, Rosemary b 4 Oct 1987); *Career* admitted slr 1974; articled clerk/slr Biddle & Co 1971–75, asst slr Wilkinson Kimbers & Staddon 1975–77, ptnr Herbert Smith 1983– (asst slr 1977–83), sec to Panel on Take-overs and Mergers 1983–85; memb Law Soc; memb Worshipful Co of Slrs 1987; *Books* Butterworths Handbook of UK Corporate Finance (contrib, 1988); *Recreations* tennis, skiing, music, cooking, family; *Style—* Anthony Macaulay, Esq; ✉ Exchange House, Primrose St, London EC2A 2HS (☎ 0171 374 8000, fax 0171 496 0043, telex 886633)

McAULEY, David Anthony (Dave); MBE (1992); s of Donald Joseph McAuley, and Marion, *née* O'Neill; *b* 15 June 1961; *Educ* St Comgall's Secdy Sch, Larne Tech Coll; *m* 15 Sept 1983, Wendy, da of Omar Beggs; 1 da (Sacha b 12 June 1986); *Career* professional boxer; former memb St Agnes Club (amateur); amateur record: All-Ireland sr champion 1978–79, represented Ireland Euro Jr Championship 1979, 7 contests Ireland, Irish Flyweight champion 1980; turned professional 1983, won Br Flyweight title 1986 (relinquished title), challenged for WBA Flyweight title 1987 and 1988; Int Boxing Fedn Flyweight title: won v Duke McKenzie 1989, first defence 1989, second and third defences 1990, fourth and fifth defences (postwar Br record) 1991, lost v Rodolfo Blanco 1992; Br Boxing Bd of Control award for best contest (v Fidel Bassa) 1987, Texaco Sports Personality 1986, 1989, 1990; former employment: Kilroot Power Station 1978–83, chef 1983–89; *Recreations* clay pigeon shooting; *Style—* Dave McAuley, Esq, MBE; ✉ c/o B J Eastwood, Eastwood House, 2–4 Chapel Lane, Belfast (☎ 01232 238005)

McAULIFFE, Prof Charles Andrew; *b* 29 Nov 1941; *Educ* Univ of Manchester (BSc, DSc), Florida State Univ (MS), Univ of Oxford (DPhil); *m* 1 April 1967, Margaret Mary; 1 s ((Charles) Andrew b 30 Nov 1977), 2 da (Amy Noelle b 15 Oct 1972, Juliette Hilda b 12 Dec 1975); *Career* currently head Dept of Chemistry UMIST; memb Dalton Div Cncl RSC 1990–; FRSC; *Books* Transition Metal Complexes of Phosphine, Arsine and Antimony Ligands (with W Levason, 1978); *Style—* Prof Charles McAuliffe; ✉ The Coach House, 1 Pinewood, Bowdon, Cheshire WA14 3JG; Department of Chemistry, UMIST, Manchester M60 1QD (☎ 0161 236 3311)

MacAUSLAN, Harry Hume; s of John Mechan MacAuslan, and Helen Constance Howden, *née* Hume; *b* 2 Oct 1956; *Educ* Charterhouse, Univ of Manchester (BA); *m* 1981, Fiona Caroline, da of Brian Martin Boag; 2 s (Samuel Alexander b 9 Aug 1987, James Hume b 8 April 1989), 1 da (Clare Emily b 5 Jan 1985); *Career* advertising exec; mktg trainee De La Rue 1979–80; J Walter Thompson: joined as graduate trainee 1980, bd dir 1989–, head of account mgmnt 1993–; non-exec dir Sadler's Wells Trust Ltd 1995–; *Style—* Harry MacAuslan, Esq; ✉ J Walter Thompson, 40 Berkeley Square, London W1X 6AD (☎ 0171 499 4040)

McAVOY, Michael Anthony; s of Lt-Col John McAvoy, and Gertrude, *née* Gradidge (d 1962); *b* 31 July 1934; *Educ* Beaumont Coll, Lincoln Coll Oxford; *m* 1963, June Anne, da of Robert Harper; 1 da (Annabel Jane b 1966); *Career* Young & Rubicam Ltd: joined 1957, md Planned Public Relations Ltd 1965, chm Planned Public Relations 1970, chm GLH Marketing Ltd 1970, dir Young & Rubicam Holdings 1970, vice president Young & Rubicam International 1971, vice chm Burson Marsteller Ltd 1979–81; fndr and ptnr McAvoy Wreford & Associates 1981–84, vice chm McAvoy Wreford Bayley Ltd 1986–90 (dir 1984), vice chm McAvoy Bayley Ltd 1990–92, chm GCI Europe 1992–94, conslt 1995–; fndr chm PRCA 1969–72; memb IPRA, FIPR; *Recreations* golf; *Clubs* RAC; *Style—* Michael McAvoy, Esq; ✉ Middleton House, Milton Abbas, Blandford, Dorset DT11 0BS (☎ 01258 880333)

McAVOY, Thomas McLaughlin; MP (Lab and Co-op) Glasgow Rutherglen (majority 15,270); s of Edward McAvoy (d 1985), and Frances McLaughlin McAvoy (d 1982); *b* 14 Dec 1943; *Educ* St Columbkilles Jr Secdy Sch; *m* 1968, Eleanor Kerr, da of William Kerr, of Rutherglen, Glasgow; 4 s (Thomas b 1969, Michael b 1971, Steven b 1974, Brian b 1981); *Career* regnl cncllr Strathclyde 1982–87, MP (Lab and Co-op) Glasgow Rutherglen 1987–; oppn whip 1991–93 and 1996–; *Style—* Thomas McAvoy, Esq, MP; ✉ 9 Douglas Avenue, Rutherglen, Glasgow

MacBAIN, Gordon Campbell; s of John Ritchie Gordon MacBain (d 1966), and Dora, *née* Campbell; *b* 29 April 1938; *Educ* HS of Glasgow, Univ of Glasgow (MB ChB); *m* 9 July 1964, Margaret Janet, da of George Drummond Tait Wilson, of 13 Torphin Rd, Colinton, Edinburgh; 1 s (John b 1971), 1 da (Katharin b 1966); *Career* dir of surgery Southern Gen Hosp Glasgow 1974, chm Ross Hall Hosp Glasgow 1981; tstee Forum Arts Soc; FRCSEd 1966, FRCSGlas 1981 (memb Cncl); memb: BMA, Assoc of Surgns, Br Vascular Soc of GB and Ireland, Euro Vascular Soc; *Recreations* music, golf; *Style—* Gordon MacBain, Esq; ✉ Southern General Hospital, 1345 Govan Road, Glasgow G51 4TF (☎ 0141 201 1100)

McBAIN OF McBAIN, James Hughston; 22 Chief of Clan McBain (McBean); s of Hughston Maynard McBain of McBain (matriculated as Chief 1959, d 1977); *b* 1928; *Educ* Culver Mil Acad, Western Washington Coll, Univ of Arizona; *m* Margaret, *née* Stephenson; *Heir* s, Richard James b 1957; *Career* pres Scot Photo Shops Arizona 1962–; *Recreations* golf, Scottish history, Scottish country dancing; *Clubs* Royal Scottish Country Dance Soc; *Style—* James McBain of McBain; ✉ 7025 North Finger Rock Place, Tucson, Arizona 85718, USA

MacBEAN, Dr Ian Grant; CBE (1986); s of William Charles MacBean (d 1977), and Isabel Clara, *née* Haro; *b* 30 Sept 1931; *Educ* Highgate Sch, Imperial Coll London (PhD, BSc, DIC, ACGI); *m* 28 July 1956, Joan Annie, da of George Rowell (d 1989), of Alton, Hants; 3 da (Diane b 1961, Valerie b 1963, Judith b 1968); *Career* GEC plc: joined as devpt engr 1956, md Marconi Co Ltd 1985, subsequently chm GEC-Marconi Ltd until 1996, main bd dir GEC 1987–96, ret; FEng 1986, FIEE, CEng; *Recreations* golf, gardening, bridge, DIY; *Style—* Dr Ian MacBean, CBE, FEng

MACBEATH, John Thomson; s of Angus Macbeath (d 1982), of Inverness, and Christina Robertson, *née* Thomson; *b* 27 May 1938; *Educ* Inverness Royal Acad, Univ of Edinburgh (MB ChB); *Career* registrar in anaesthesia Edinburgh Royal Infirmary 1966–69, Reckitt res fell in anaesthesia Univ of Salford 1969–71, sr registrar in anaesthesia NW Region 1971–73, conslt in anaesthesia and intensive care Salford Health Authy 1973–, hon lectr in anaesthesia Univ of Manchester 1983– (faculty and coll tutor 1983–90); memb: Ctee Section of Anaesthesia Manchester Med Soc 1986–89, Coll of Anaesthetists of GB, Assoc of Anaesthetists of GB and I, Manchester Med Soc; *Recreations* opera, classical music, running; *Style—* John Macbeath, Esq; ✉ Department of Anaesthesia, Hope Hospital, Eccles Old Rd, Salford M6 8HD (☎ 0161 789 7373)

MACBETH, Dr Fergus Robert; s of Dr Ronald Graeme Macbeth (d 1992), and Margaret, *née* Macdonald (d 1983); *b* 5 Jan 1948; *Educ* Eton, Merton Coll Oxford, King's College Hosp Med Sch London (MA, BM BCh, DM); *Career* conslt in radiotherapy and oncology Beatson Oncology Cetnre Glasgow 1988–96, dir Clinical Support Unit for Wales 1996–, conslt oncologist 1996–; FRCR 1987, FRCP Glasgow 1989; *Style—* Dr Fergus Macbeth; ✉ Clinical Effectiveness Support Unit, Llandough Hospital, Denarth, South Glamorgan CF64 2XX (☎ 01222 716841, fax 01222 716242)

McBRIEN, Michael Patrick; s of Leo Patrick McBrien (d 1969), and Elizabeth Rosemary, *née* Phillips; *b* 4 July 1935; *Educ* Stonyhurst Coll, St Thomas's Hosp, Univ of London (MB BS); *m* 11 July 1964, Tessa Ann Freeland, da of Col Richard Bayfield Freeland (d 1980), of Beccles, Suffolk; 2 s (James b 2 May 1968, Rowan b 6 May 1972), 1 da (Emma b 12 March 1966); *Career* registrar in surgery: Southampton Hosp 1967–69, St Thomas' Hosp 1969–70; sr registrar and lectr in surgery St Thomas' Hosp 1970–73; sr conslt surgn: W Suffolk Gp of Hosps and St Edmund's Hosp 1973–; Hunterian prof RCS 1974, clinical teacher and examiner in surgery Univ of Cambridge; sec Ct of Examiners RCS 1992, med memb Pensions Appeal Tbnls 1996; MS 1973; memb: BMA 1960–, RSM 1960; FRCS 1968; *Books* Postgraduate Surgery (1986); *Recreations* tennis, golf, cricket, shooting, bridge, skiing, travel; *Clubs* RSM, MCC; *Style—* Michael McBrien, Esq; ✉ Stanton House, Norton, Bury St Edmunds, Suffolk IP31 3LQ (☎ 01359 230832, fax 01359 231266); West Suffolk Hospital, Hardwick Lane, Bury St Edmunds, Suffolk IP33 2QZ (☎ 01284 713165, fax 01284 712596)

McBRYDE, Prof William Wilson (Bill); s of William McBryde (d 1964), of Burntisland, Fife, and Marjory Wilson, *née* Husband (d 1991); *b* 6 July 1945; *Educ* Perth Acad, Univ of Edinburgh (LLB, LLD), Univ of Glasgow (PhD); *m* 1, 4 Nov 1972 (m dis 1982), Elspeth Jean Stormont Glover; 1 s (Donald b 5 March 1976), 1 da (Eileen b 23 Feb 1974); m 2, 12 April 1986, Joyce Margaret, da of Rev James Marcus Gossip (d 1985), of Edinburgh; 1 da (Helen b 23 June 1988); *Career* apprentice with Morton Smart Macdonald & Milligan WS 1967–70; admitted slr 1969; court procurator Biggart Lumsden & Co Glasgow 1970–72, lectr in private law Univ of Glasgow 1972–76, sr lectr in private law Univ of Aberdeen 1976–87, specialist Parly advsr to House of Lords Select Ctee on Euro Communities 1980–83, dean Faculty of Law Univ of Dundee 1989–90 (prof of Scots law 1987–, dep princ Univ 1991–92, vice princ 1992–94); dir Scot Univ Law Inst 1989–95; memb: Scot Consumer Cncl 1984–87, Scot Advsy Ctee on Arbitration 1986–, Insolvency Permit Ctee Inst of CA's of Scotland 1990–95, Advsy Panel on Security over Moveable Property DTI 1994–; Hon Sheriff Tayside, Central and Fife Dundee 1991–; FRSE 1994; *Books* Bankruptcy (Scotland) Act 1985 (1986), The Law of Contract in Scotland (1987), Petition Procedure in the Court of Session (2 edn, with N Dowie, 1988), Bankruptcy (1989, 2 edn 1995), Bankruptcy (Scotland) Act 1993 (1993); *Recreations* walking, photography; *Style—* Prof Bill McBryde, FRSE; ✉ Faculty of Law, The University, Dundee DD1 4HN (☎ 01382 223181, fax 01382 226905)

MacCABE, Prof Colin Myles Joseph; s of Myles Joseph MacCabe, and Ruth Ward MacCabe; *b* 9 Feb 1949; *Educ* St Benedict's Sch Ealing London, Univ of Cambridge (BA, MA, PhD), Ecole Normale Supérieure; *m* 2 s, 1 da; *Career* univ asst lectr in English Univ of Cambridge and coll lectr and fell King's Coll Cambridge 1976–81, prof of English Univ of Strathclyde 1981–85 (chm Dept of English Studies 1982–84), visiting fell Griffith Univ Brisbane 1981 and 1984, memb English Teaching Advsy Ctee for Br Cncl 1983–85 (Br Cncl lectr Shanghai Foreign Language Inst 1984), chm John Logie Baird Centre for Res in TV and Film Univ of Strathclyde 1985–91 (founding dir 1983–85), visiting prof in Programme for Literacy Linguistics Univ of Strathclyde 1985–91, Mellon visiting prof Univ of Pittsburgh 1985, head of prodn Br Film Inst 1985–89, prof of English Univ of Pittsburgh 1986–, criticism ed Critical Quarterly 1987–, head of res Br Film Inst 1989–, visiting prof Birkbeck Coll London 1992–; *Books* James Joyce and the Revolution of The World (1979), Godard: Images, Sounds, Politics (1980), The Talking Cure: Essays in Psychoanalysis and Language (ed, 1981), James Joyce: New Perspectives (ed 1982), Theoretical Essays: film, linguistics, literature (1985), The BBC and Public Sector Broadcasting (jt ed, 1986), High Theory Low Culture: Analysing Popular Television and Film (ed, 1986), futures for English (ed, 1987), The Linguistics of Writing (jt ed, 1988); *Recreations* eating, drinking, talking; *Style—* Prof Colin MacCabe; ✉ British Film Institute, Research Division, 21 Stephen Street, London W1P 1PL (☎ 0171 255 1444)

McCABE, John; CBE (1985); s of Frank McCabe (d 1983), and Elisabeth Carmen, *née* Herlitzius (d 1993); *b* 21 April 1939; *Educ* Liverpool Inst, Univ of Manchester (BMus), Royal Manchester Coll of Music (FRMCM), Hochschule für Musik Munich; *m* 1, (m dis 1973), Hilary Tann; m 2, 31 July 1974, Monica Christine, da of Jack Smith (d 1974); *Career* composer and pianist; res pianist Univ Coll Cardiff 1965–68, freelance music critic 1966–71, dir London Coll Music 1983–90; writer of operas, symphonies, concertos, choral and keyboard works, TV and film music; recent cmmnd works incl: Symphony No 4 Of Time and the River (BBC Symphony Orch and Melbourne Symphony Orch) 1995, Edward II (Stuttgart Ballet) 1995; numerous recordings incl 12 CD set complete piano works of Haydn; pres: Inc Soc Musicians 1982–83, Br Music Soc; memb Hon Cncl of Mgmnt RPS 1983–86, chm Assoc Professional Composers 1985–86, memb Gen Cncl and Donations Ctee Performing Rights Soc 1985–88; vice pres: Malvern Music Club, Luton Music Club; memb: Wigmore Hall Board 1987–90, Mechanical Copyright Protection Soc, Nat Tst of Scotland, WWF; FLCM, FRCM, Hon RAM, FRNCM 1986, FTCL 1989; *Books* BBC Music Guide: Bartok's Orchestral Music (1974), Haydn's Piano Sonatas (1986), Gollancz Musical Companion (contrib, 1973), Novello Short Biography: Rachmaninov (1974); *Recreations* cinema, books, cricket, golf, (watching) snooker, bonfires (playing); *Style—* John McCabe, Esq, CBE; ✉ c/o Novello & Co Ltd (Music Publishers), 8/9 Frith Street, London W1V 5TZ (☎ 0171 434 0066, fax 0171 287 6329)

MacCABE, Michael Murray; s of Brian Farmer MacCabe (d 1992), and Eileen Elizabeth Noel, *née* Hunter (d 1984); *b* 20 Nov 1944; *Educ* Downside, Lincoln Coll Oxford (1963–64);

m 1, 8 Aug 1969, Olga Marie (d 1985); 1 s (James Hunter b 1970), 1 da ((Alexandra) Kate b 1973); m 2, 23 July 1993, Gillian Rosemary; *Career* admitted slr 1969; managing ptnr: Freshfields 1985–90 (ptnr 1974–), Freshfields Paris 1981–84; dir Slrs Indemnity Mutual Insurance Association Ltd 1986–; Chelsea Arts Club Ltd 1992–; memb Ctee City of London Slrs Co; FRSA; *Recreations* fishing, painting; *Clubs* Boodle's; *Style*— Michael MacCabe, Esq; ✉ Freshfields, Whitefriars, Fleet St, London EC4

McCABE, Primrose Smith; da of Robert Scott (d 1978), of Uphall, W Lothian, and Jeannie McLaughlan, *née* Pollock (d 1962); *b* 21 Sept 1940; *Educ* Ayr Acad; *m* 25 June 1965, Ernest Henry Elfred McCabe; *Career* trainee Stewart Gilmour & Co, qualified CA 1963, various managerial positions leading to ptnr Deloitte Haskins & Sells Edinburgh 1981–87, in own practice The McCabe Partnership (formerly Primrose McCabe & Co) 1987–; dir: Dunfermline Building Society 1990–, Lothian and Edinburgh Enterprise Ltd 1995–; ICAS: memb Cncl 1987–, chm Gen Practice Ctee 1990–93, pres 1994–95; hon fell SCOTVEC 1994; *Recreations* dressmaking and dog walking; *Style*— Mrs Primrose McCabe; ✉ The McCabe Partnership, Regent House, Regent Centre, Linlithgow EH49 7HU (☎ 01506 842466, fax 01506 845090, mobile 0374 426349)

McCABE, Ven Trevor; RD; s of John Leslie McCabe (d 1981), of Falmouth, Cornwall, and Mary Ena McCabe (d 1990); *Educ* Falmouth GS, Univ of Nottingham (BA), Univ of Oxford (DipTh), Wycliffe Hall Oxford; *m* 1959, Mary, da of C H Thomas; 3 s (Jeremy b 7 June 1960, Stephen b 30 May 1963, Timothy b 3 June 1968), 1 da (Celia b 26 Jan 1965); *Career* curate Exeter Dio 1959–66, vicar of Capel Surrey 1966–71, chaplain of the Isles of Scilly 1971–81, residentiary canon Bristol Cathedral 1981–83, vicar of Manaccan, St Anthony and St Martin 1983–96, archdeacon of Cornwall 1996–; chaplain RNR 1963–, hon canon Truro Cathedral 1993–; memb Cornwall HA 1974– (vice chm until 1991), chm NHS Tst for Learning Disabilities 1991–; *Recreations* shrub gardening, Cornish local history; *Style*— The Ven the Archdeacon of Cornwall, RD; ✉ Archdeacon's House, 3 Knight's Hill, Kenwyn, Truro, Cornwall TR1 3UY (☎ 01872 72866, fax 01872 42102)

McCAFFER, Eur Ing Prof Ronald; s of John Gegg McCaffer (d 1984), and Catherine Turner, *née* Gourlay (d 1979); *b* 8 Dec 1943; *Educ* Univ of Strathclyde (BSc), Univ of Loughborough (PhD); *m* 13 Aug 1966, Margaret Elizabeth, da of Cyril Warner; 1 s (Andrew b 29 April 1977); *Career* design engr Babtie Shaw and Morton 1965–67; site engr: The Nuclear Power Gp 1967–69, Taylor Woodrow Construction 1969–70; Dept of Civil Engrg Univ of Loughborough: lectr 1970–78, sr lectr 1978–83, reader 1983–86, prof of construction mgmnt 1986–, head of dept 1987–93, dean Sch of Engrg 1992–97, sr pro-vice chllr 1997–; ed Engineering, Construction & Architectural Management 1994–, memb Engrg Construction Industry Trg Bd 1994–; FEng 1991, Eur Ing, FICE, FCIOB, MIMgt; *Books* Worked Examples in Construction Management (1986), Managing Construction Equipment (1991), Estimating and Tendering for Civil Engineering (1991), Modern Construction Management (1995), International Bid Preparation, International Bidding Case Study; *Style*— Eur Ing Prof Ronald McCaffer, FEng; ✉ Department of Civil Engineering, Loughborough University of Technology, Loughborough, Leicestershire LE11 3TU (☎ 01509 222600, fax 01509 223890, e-mail R.McCAFFER@LBORO.AC.UK)

McCAFFREY, Sir Thomas Daniel (Tom); kt (1979); s of William P McCaffrey; *b* 20 Feb 1922; *Educ* Hyndland Secdy Sch, St Aloysius Coll Galsgow; *m* 1949, Agnes Campbell Douglas; 2 s, 4 da; *Career* served WWII RAF; Scottish Office 1948–61, chief info offr Home Office 1966–71, press sec 10 Downing St 1971–72, dir Info Servs Home Office 1972–74, head of News Dept FCO 1974–76, chief of staff to Rt Hon James Callaghan, MP 1979–80 (his chief press sec when he was PM 1976–79), chief asst to Rt Hon Michael Foot, MP 1980–83; currently public affrs consltt; *Style*— Sir Tom McCaffrey; ✉ Balmaha, The Park, Great Bookham, Surrey (☎ 01372 54171)

McCAGUE, Martin; *b* 24 May 1969; *Career* professional cricketer; Kent CCC: debut 1991, awarded county cap 1992; England: memb team touring Aust 1994/95; played for W Aust 1990–92; Kent Player of the Year 1996; *Style*— Martin McCague, Esq; ✉ c/o Kent CCC, St Lawrence Ground, Canterbury, Kent CT1 3NZ (☎ 01227 456886)

McCAHILL, Patrick Gerard; QC (1996); s of John McCahill (d 1995), of Donegal, Ireland and Corby, Northants, and Josephine, *née* Conaghan; *Educ* Corby GS, St Catharine's Coll Cambridge (MA); *m* 8 Sept 1979, Liselotte Gabrielle Steiner; 2 da (Gabrielle Marie b 29 Nov 1980, Claire Elizabeth b 17 Aug 1984); *Career* supervisor St Catharine's Coll Cambridge, called to the Bar Gray's Inn 1975 (Bacon scholar, Atkin scholar), lectr St John's Coll Oxford 1975–78, asst dep coroner Birmingham and Solihull 1984–, barr King's Inns Dublin 1990, asst recorder 1993–; memb Ctee Midland Chancery and Commercial Bar Assoc; FCIArb 1992; *Style*— Patrick McCahill, Esq, QC; ✉ 2 Fountain Court, 1st Floor, Steelhouse Lane, Birmingham B4 6DR (☎ 0121 236 3882, fax 0121 233 3205)

McCALL, Christopher Hugh; QC (1987); yr s of late Robin Home McCall, CBE, and late Joan Elizabeth, *née* Kingdon; *b* 3 March 1944; *Educ* Winchester, Magdalen Coll Oxford (BA); *m* 20 June 1981, Henrietta Francesca, 2 da of Adrian Lesley Sharpe, of Trebetherick, N Cornwall; *Career* called to the Bar Lincoln's Inn 1966, second jr counsel to Inland Revenue in chancery matters 1977–87, jr counsel to HM Attorney-Gen in charity matters 1981–87; bencher Lincoln's Inn 1993; jt hon treas Barristers' Benevolent Assoc 1981–86; *Recreations* mountains, music, travel, Egyptomania; *Clubs* RAC, Leander, Alpine; *Style*— C H McCall, Esq, QC; ✉ One New Square Passage, Lincoln's Inn, London WC2A 3QQ (☎ 0171 405 2922)

McCALL, David Slesser; CBE (1988), DL (Norfolk 1992); s of Patrick McCall (d 1987), of Norwich, and Florence Kate Mary, *née* Walker; *b* 3 Dec 1934; *Educ* Robert Gordon Coll Aberdeen, Univ of Aberdeen; *m* 6 July 1968, (Lois) Patricia, da of Ernest Lonsdale Elder (d 1985), of Glasgow; *Career* Nat Serv RAF 1959–60; accountant Grampian TV Ltd 1961–68; Anglia Television: co sec 1968–76, dir 1970–, chief exec 1976–94, chm 1994–; chm TSMS Ltd (airtime sales co) 1994–, chm Greene King plc 1995–; fndr dir Channel 4 Television Co Ltd 1981–85; dir: British Satellite Broadcasting Ltd 1987–90, Independent Television News Ltd 1991–, Hodder & Stoughton 1992–93, Cosgrove Hall Films Ltd 1993–, Village Roadshow Ltd (Australia) 1994–, Satellite Information Services 1994–, Meridian Broadcasting Ltd 1994–, MAI plc 1994–96, MAI Media UK Ltd 1995–96; chm ITV Assoc 1986–88, hon vice pres Norwich City FC 1988–93, dir Eastern Advsy Bd National Westminster Bank 1988, pres Norfolk & Norwich C of C 1988–90 (vice pres 1984, dep pres 1986); chm: Norwich Playhouse 1992–, Norfolk & Norwich Millennium Bid Ltd 1996–; tstee CTBF 1995; RTS: fell 1988, vice pres 1992, hon pres E Anglia Centre 1993; MICAS 1958, CIMgt 1988, FRSA 1993; *Recreations* golf, tennis, skiing, soccer, travel; *Style*— David McCall, Esq, CBE, DL; ✉ Woodland Hall, Redenhall, Harleston, Norfolk IP20 9QW (☎ 01379 854442); Anglia House, Norwich, Norfolk NR1 3JG (☎ 01603 615151, fax 01603 623081, telex 97424, car 0860 703 016); Anglia Television Group Ltd, 48 Leicester Square, London WC2H 7FB (☎ 0171 389 8555, fax 0171 930 8499)

McCALL, John Armstrong Grice; CMG (1964); s of Rev Canon James George McCall (d 1954), of St Andrews, and Mabel Lovat Armstrong (d 1917); gggs of John McCall of Glasgow, one of fndrs of Thistle Bank in 1761; *b* 7 Jan 1913; *Educ* Glenalmond, Univ of St Andrews (MA), Univ of Cambridge; *m* 1951, Kathleen Mary, DL (Tweeddale 1987–), da of Arthur Clarke (d 1936); *Career* Colonial Admin Service (HMOCS) Nigeria 1936–67 (Class I 1956, Staff Grade 1958), chm Mid West Nigerian Corp 1966–67, asst chief admin offr East Kilbride Devpt Corp 1967–77, Scottish rep Exec Ctee Nigeria Br C of C 1977–88; memb: Panel Industl Tribunals (Scotland) 1972–74, Central Cncl Britain Nigeria Assoc 1983–88; gen sec for Scotland Royal Over-Seas League 1978–80, sec West Linton Community Cncl 1980–83; *Recreations* golf, walking; *Clubs* Caledonian, Royal and Ancient (St Andrews), Royal Over-Seas League (hon life memb); *Style*— J A G McCall, Esq, CMG; ✉ Burnside, W Linton, Scotland EH46 7EW (☎ 01968 660488)

McCALL, John Kingdon; s of Robin Home McCall (d 1991), CBE, of Winchester, and Joan Elizabeth, *née* Kingdon; *b* 28 July 1938; *Educ* Winchester; *m* 20 April 1963, Anne Margaret, da of Dr Harry Kirby Meller, MBE (d 1965); 2 s (Patrick b 1964, William b 1971), 1 da (Claire b 1966); *Career* slr; ptnr Freshfields 1969–93, seconded to Head of Legal Dept The Br Nat Oil Corpn 1976–79, sr res ptnr Freshfields NY 1983–87 and 1992–93, chm Int Bar Assoc's Section on Energy and Nat Resources Law 1988–90; *Recreations* real tennis, campanology, sea birds; *Clubs* Racquet and Tennis (NY); *Style*— John K McCall, Esq; ✉ Temple Barn, Capel, Surrey RH5 5HJ (☎ 01306 713238, fax 01306 713324)

McCALL, Sir (Charles) Patrick Home; kt (1971), MBE (1944), TD (1946); s of Charles William Home McCall, CBE (d 1958), and Dorothy Margaret, *née* Kidd; *b* 22 Nov 1910; *Educ* St Edward's Sch Oxford; *m* 1934, Anne (d 1991), da of late Samuel and Emily Brown, of Sedlescombe, Sussex; 2 s, 1 da; *Career* served WWII ADOS SEAC; admitted slr 1936; last clerk of the peace Lancs 1960–71, clerk of the CC 1960–72, clerk of the Lieutenancy Lancs 1960–74; *Recreations* walking, visiting art galleries, swimming, canoeing, travel, talking, drinking drams; *Style*— Sir Patrick McCall, MBE, TD; ✉ Craigshields, 13 Newall Terrace, Dumfries DG1 1LN (☎ 01387 253751)

McCALL, Robert Henry; s of William McCall (d 1937), and Anna Laurie (d 1937); *b* 15 Nov 1931; *Educ* Woodside Sr Secdy Sch Glasgow; *m* 4 Sept 1954, Grace, da of George Robinson (d 1958); 2 s (Laurie Allan b 1956, Roderick Robert b 1960); *Career* whisky broker and distiller; dir: Whyte & Mackay Group plc (parent company), Dalmore Whyte & Mackay Ltd, Whyte & Mackay Ltd, W & S Strong Ltd, Hay & Macleod Ltd, The Tomintoul-Glenlivet Distillery Ltd, Fettercairn Distillery Ltd, Jarvis Halliday & Co Ltd, Lycidas (109); *Recreations* golf, snooker, horse racing; *Clubs* Glasgow Golf; *Style*— Robert McCall, Esq; ✉ 20 Herries Road, Glasgow, Scotland G41 4DF (☎ 0141 423 4683); Whyte & Mackay Distillers Limited, Dalmore House, 310 St Vincent St, Glasgow G2 5RG (☎ 0141 248 5771, fax: 0141 221 1993)

McCALL-SMITH, Prof Alexander; *b* 24 Aug 1948; *Career* currently prof of med law Univ of Edinburgh and author; *Legal Books* Law and Medical Ethics (1984), Butterworths Medico Legal Encyclopaedia (1987), The Criminal Law of Botswana (1992), Scots Criminal Law (1992), The Duty to Rescue (1994), Introduzione allo Studio del Diritto Penale Scozzese (1995); *Children's Books* The White Hippo (1980), The Little Theatre (1981), The Perfect Hamburger (1982), On the Road (1987), Mike's Magic Seeds (1988), Alix and the Tigers (1988), Film Boy (1988), Uncle Gangster (1989), Suzy Magician (1990), Akimbo and the Elephants (1990), The Ice Cream Bicycle (1990), Jeffrey's Joke Machine (1990), The Five Lost Aunts of Harriet Bean (1990), Harriet Bean and the League of Cheats (1991), The Spaghetti Tangle (1990), Akimbo and the Lions (1992), Springy Jane (1992), The Princess Trick (1992), Calculator Annie (1992), The Doughnut Ring (1992), The Cowgirl Aunt of Harriet Bean (1993), Akimbo and the Crocodile Man (1993), Who Invented Peanut Butter (1993), My Chameleon Uncle (1993), Paddy and the Ratcatcher (1994), The Banana Machine (1994); *Adult Fiction* Children of Wax (1989), Heavenly Date (1995), Lions and Anthropologists (1996); *Clubs* Scottish Arts; *Style*— Prof Alexander McCall-Smith; ✉ 16A Napier Rd, Edinburgh EH10 5AY (☎ 0131 229 6083)

McCALLION, John; s of Robert Bernard McCallion, of London, and Patricia, *née* Furnston-Evans; *b* 4 Nov 1957; *Educ* Stanway Sch Colchester Essex, Colchester Inst of Technol (HND in Business Admin), Poly of Central London (Postgrad Dip in Mktg); *Career* product mangr/buyer Marks & Spencer plc (Head Office) 1984–88 (joined as grad trainee 1981), commercial mangr Texas Homecare plc 1989–90 (gp product mangr 1988–89), sr mktg mangr Pizza Hut (UK) Ltd 1990–91; mktg dir Red Star 1991–93, mktg dir Great Western Trains Co 1993–; MCIM, MIDM, memb Mktg Soc, MInstD; *Recreations* skiing, cinema, literature, squash, travel, cycling, golf; *Style*— John McCallion, Esq; ✉ 45 Marlow Road, Maidenhead, Berkshire SL6 7AQ (☎ 01628 36376); Great Western Trains Company, Milford House, 1 Milford Street, Swindon (☎ 01793 499413, fax 01793 499414)

MacCALLUM, Prof Charles Hugh Alexander; s of Alister Hugh McCallum (*sic*) (d 1955), of Perth, and Jessie MacLean, *née* Forsyth (d 1987); *b* 24 June 1935; *Educ* Hutchesons' GS Glasgow, Glasgow Sch of Architecture (BArch), MIT (MCP); *m* 27 Aug 1963, Andrée Simone, da of Rémond Jean René Tonnard (d 1986), of Brest, France; 2 da (Joëlle b 1964, Sophie b 1965); *Career* architect; Gillespie Kidd and Coia Glasgow 1957–67; Univ Coll Dublin Sch of Architecture: lectr 1970–73, exec dir 1973–74; own practice 1974–, prof of architectural design Univ of Wales 1985–94, prof of architecture Univ of Glasgow and head of Mackintosh Sch of Architecture 1994–; commissaire of the bicentenary exhibition on Louis Visconti (Paris) 1991; RIBA 1961, ARIAS 1986, FRSA 1993; *Books* Visconti (1791–1853) (1991); *Recreations* gardening, watercolours; *Style*— Prof Charles MacCallum; ✉ Flat 1, Italian Centre, 176 Ingram Street, Glasgow G1 1DN

McCALLUM, (Andrew) Graham Stewart; CBE (1975); s of H G McCallum (d 1975); *b* 1 April 1926; *Educ* Glenalmond, Pembroke Coll Oxford (MA); *m* 1952, Margaret; 1 da, 2 s; *Career* RAF 1944–47, Offr Pilot; Swire Group Far East and Aust 1950–78, pres John Swire & Sons (Japan) Ltd 1972–78, dir James Finlay plc 1979–91, exec dir John Swire & Sons Ltd 1979–88 (advsr to Bd 1988–94), chm Dunedin Japan Investment Trust PLC 1993–96; dir: Baillie Gifford Japan Trust PLC 1981–, Pacific Horizon Investment Trust PLC 1991–; chm: British C of C in Japan 1975–76, Japan Assoc 1982–88; exec vice chm Japan Festival 1991, dep chm Design Museum 1995–; *Recreations* golf, tennis; *Clubs* Royal Ashdown Forest Golf, Boodle's, Rye, St Enodoc; *Style*— Graham McCallum, Esq, CBE; ✉ Medleys Farm, High Hurstwood, nr Uckfield, E Sussex TN22 4AA (☎ 01825 732470, fax 01825 732222)

McCALLUM, Prof (Robert) Ian; CBE (1987); s of Charles Hunter McCallum (d 1958), and Janet Lyon, *née* Smith (d 1980); *b* 14 Sept 1920; *Educ* Dulwich, Guy's Hosp and Univ of London (MD, DSc); *m* 28 June 1952, Jean Katherine Bundy, da of Sir James Rögnvald Learmonth, KCVO, CBE (d 1967), of Edinburgh; 2 s (James b 1958, Andrew b 1966), 2 da (Helen b 1956, Mary b 1963); *Career* Rockefeller travelling fell USA 1953–54; Univ of Newcastle upon Tyne: reader in industl health 1962–81, prof of occupational health and hygiene 1981–85; hon consltt Inst of Occupational Med Edinburgh 1985–; chm Decompression Sickness Panel MRC 1982–85 (memb 1962–), ed Br Journal of Industl Med 1972–79, memb Advsy Ctee on Pesticides 1975–87; pres: Soc of Occupational Medicine 1979–80, Br Occupational Hygiene Soc 1983–84; hon consltt Br Army 1980–85, dean Faculty of Occupational Med RCP London 1984–86; FRCP London 1970, FFOM 1979, FRCPE 1985; *Recreations* gardening; *Clubs* RSM, Edinburgh Univ Staff; *Style*— Prof Ian McCallum, CBE; ✉ 4 Chessel's Court, Canongate, Edinburgh EH8 8AD (☎ 0131 556 7977); Inst of Occupational Medicine, Roxburgh Place, Edinburgh EH8 9SU (☎ 0131 667 5131)

McCALLUM, Ian Stewart; s of John Blair McCallum (d 1972), and Margaret Stewart, *née* Hannah (d 1989); *b* 24 Sept 1936; *Educ* Kingston GS; *m* 1, 26 Oct 1957 (m dis 1984), Pamela Mary, da of James Herbert Shave; 1 s (Andrew Stewart b 12 Sept 1958), 2 da (Sheila Anne (Mrs Curling) b 8 July 1960, Heather Jean (Mrs Drury) b 26 June 1963); m 2, 15 Sept 1984, Jean, da of Patrick Wittingstall Lynch, of Herpenden, Herts; 2 step da

(Michelle b 6 Feb 1971, Donna b 8 May 1974); *Career* Highland LI 1954–56, Eagle Star Insurance Co Ltd 1953–54 and 1956–58, FE Wright & Co 1958–63, M Clarkson Home Ltd 1963–68, exec sales mangr Save & Prosper Group Ltd 1968–95, sr sales mangr Allied Dunbar Assurance PLC 1995, ret; Mayor Woking BC 1976–77 (ldr 1972–76 and 1978–81, dep ldr 1981–84); hon vice pres Woking Cons Assoc 1976–, chm Assoc of DCs 1979–84 (ldr 1976–79); pres Woking Swimming Club 1977–84; vice chm: UK Steering Ctee on Local Authy Superannuation 1974–84, Standing Ctee Local Authys & the Theatre 1977–81, The Sports Cncl 1980–86; memb: Consultative Cncl on Local Govt Fin 1975–84, Local Authys Conditions of Serv Advsy Bd 1978–84, Cncl for Business & the Community 1981–84, Audit Cmmn 1983–86, Health Promotion Res Tst 1983–; LIA; *Recreations* swimming, jogging, walking, reading; *Style*— Ian McCallum, Esq; ✉ 5 Minters Orchard, Maidstone Rd, St Marys Platt, nr Sevenoaks, Kent TN15 8JQ (☎ 01732 883653)

MacCALLUM, Prof James Richard; s of Neil MacCallum (d 1972), and Anne, *née* MacKinnon (d 1993); *b* 3 May 1936; *Educ* Dumfries Acad, Univ of Glasgow (BSc, PhD, DSc); *m* 1961, Eleanor Margaret, *née* Thomson; 2 s (Richard Daniel b 1965, Philip James b 1971), 1 da (Kathryn Jane Mary b 1962); *Career* tech offr ICI Fibres Div 1961–62, ICI research fell Univ of Aberdeen 1962–63; Univ of St Andrews 1964–: successively lectr, sr lectr, reader, then prof of polymer chemistry, dean Faculty of Sci 1987–88, master United Colleges 1988–92, vice-princ 1992–96, pro-princ 1996–; FRSC, FRSE 1988; *Recreations* golf; *Clubs* Royal & Ancient (St Andrews); *Style*— Prof James MacCallum, FRSE; ✉ 9 Cairnsden Gardens, St Andrews, Fife KY16 8SQ; University of St Andrews, College Gate, North Street, St Andrews, Fife KY16 9AJ (☎ 01334 462546, fax 01334 462030)

MACCALLUM, Prof Norman Ronald Low; s of Neil Maccallum (d 1956), and Janet Jane, *née* Aitkenhead (d 1983); *b* 18 Feb 1931; *Educ* Allan Glen's Sch, Univ of Glasgow (BSc, PhD); *m* 23 June 1964, Mary Bentley, da of William Alexander (d 1977); 1 s (Andrew b 22 Aug 1971), 2 da (Moira b 24 July 1967, Catriona b 12 July 1969); *Career* Nat Serv RN 1955–57, Sub Lt RNVR 1956–61; Dept of Mechanical Engrg Univ of Glasgow: lectr 1957–61 and 1962–72, sr lectr 1972–82, reader 1982–92, prof 1992–96, hon sr research fell 1996–; performance engr Rolls-Royce Ltd 1961–62, conslt engr to various cos 1963–, expert witness in legal cases 1967–; pres Glasgow Univ Engineers Soc 1991–95, chm Glasgow Panel IMechE 1995–; numerous contribs to jls and confs; elder in local church Trinity Cambuslang (now Trinity St Paul's Cambuslang) 1967– (session clerk 1979–); FIMechE 1979 (memb 1968); *Recreations* singing; *Clubs* Royal Scottish Automobile; *Style*— Prof Norman Maccallum; ✉ 43 Stewarton Drive, Cambuslang, Glasgow, Scotland G72 8DQ (☎ 0141 641 3402); Department of Mechanical Engineering, University of Glasgow, Glasgow G12 8QQ (☎ 0141 339 8855 ext 4320, fax 0141 330 4343)

McCALMONT, Hugh Dermot; s of Maj Dermot Hugh Bingham McCalmont, MC (d 1968), of Mount Juliet, Thomastown, Co Kilkenny, and June Patteson, *née* Nickalls (d 1983); *b* 23 Jan 1942; *Educ* Uppingham; *m* 19 Aug 1963, Gillian Mary, da of Andrew Levins Moore, of Yeomanstown, Naas, Co Kildare; 1 s (Jamie b 20 June 1968), 1 da (Zara Jane (Hon Mrs Napier) b 28 July 1964); *Career* asst trainer to Bryan Marshall, Tom Jones and Paddy O'Gorman, leading amateur rider in England, Ireland and Kenya 1959–64, proprietor to D Gilbert and Sons Saddlers Newmarket (Royal Warrant Holders to HM The Queen and HM Queen Elizabeth The Queen Mother 1964–74), md Bloodstock and Gen Insurance 1968–74, fndr memb Bloodstock and Racehorse Industs Consideration 1974, breeder of race horses; memb Race Horse Owners' Cncl 1977–96; Freeman: City of London 1966, Worshipful Company of Saddlers; *Recreations* hunting, shooting, gardening, horseracing; *Clubs* Turf, Jockey Club Rooms; *Style*— Hugh McCalmont, Esq; ✉ St Agnes Cottage, Bury Road, Newmarket, Suffolk CB8 7BT (☎ 01638 662072); Yeomanstown Lodge, Naas, Co Kildare (☎ 00 353 458 97669); Tramuntana, Sa Coma, Andraitx 07150, Mallorca (☎ 00 3471 235199)

McCANCE, (John) Neill; s of Henry Bristow McCance, CBE (d 1977), and Frances May McCance (d 1976); the family has been involved in banking and the linen industry in Northern Ireland since early eighteenth century; John McCance was MP for Belfast 1835; *b* 6 Aug 1928; *Educ* Radley, Lincoln Coll Oxford MA; *Career* called to the Bar Inner Temple; stockbroker with Vickers da Costa Ltd 1954–86; memb: Stock Exchange 1955–88, Cncl of Stock Exchange 1982–84 (Cncl's Membership, Settlement Servs and Disciplinary Ctees); dir Worldwide Special Fund; dep chm Allside Asset Management Co Ltd 1986–94, investment mangr Rathbones 1994–; *Recreations* shooting, fishing, travel, music; *Clubs* Brooks's, 1900; *Style*— Neill McCance, Esq; ✉ Brook Farm, Bramley Road, Silchester, nr Reading, Berks RG7 2LJ; Rathbone Investment Management, University House, Lower Grosvenor Place, London SW1W 0EX (☎ 0171 630 5611, fax 0171 821 1437)

McCANDLESS, Air Vice-Marshal Brian Campbell; CBE (1990); s of Norman Samuel McCandless, and Rebecca, *née* Campbell; *b* 14 May 1944; *Educ* Methodist Coll Belfast, RAF Tech Coll Henlow (BSc), Univ of Birmingham (MSc Quality and Reliability), RAF Staff Coll; *m* 19 April 1967, Yvonne; 1 s (Robin); *Career* RAF 1962–; sr lectr in operational research and reliability engrg RAF Coll Cranwell 1972–76, OC Engrg Sqdn RAF Gibraltar 1976–78, electrical engr (Communications) No 11 Gp 1978–80, OC Engr Liaison Team 1980–81, Wing Cdr Communications RAF Support Cmd Signals HQ 1981–85, OC No 26 Signals Unit 1985–87, Gp Capt 1987, OC RAF Henlow 1987–89, dep chief Architecture and Plans Div NATO CIS Agency Brussels 1989–92, Air Cdre 1992, dir Cmd and Control Mgmnt Info Systems (RAF) 1992–93, dir Communications and Info Systems (RAF) 1993–95, Air Vice-Marshal 1996, Air Offr Communications and Info Systems and Air Offr cmdg Signals Units 1996–; CEng 1974, FIEE 1995; *Recreations* bridge, music, sailing, hillwalking; *Clubs* RAF; *Style*— Air Vice-Marshal Brian McCandless, CBE; ✉ Headquarters Logistics Command, Royal Air Force Brampton, Huntingdon, Cambs PE18 8QL (☎ 01480 52151 ext 6704)

McCANN, Christopher Conor; s of Noel McCann, and Katharine Joan, *née* Sultzberger; *b* 26 June 1947; *Educ* Downside, Clare Coll Cambridge (MA); *m* 1 June 1974, Merlyn Clare Winbolt, da of Dr Francis Lewis, of Bristol; 1 s (Edward), 2 da (Kate, Eleanor); *Career* Price Waterhouse and Co 1969–73, Barclays Merchant Bank 1973–82, sr vice pres Barclays Bank plc NY 1983–87, dir Natwest Ventures Ltd 1987–; non-exec dir: Aynsley Group Ltd 1988–92, Redifon Holdings Ltd 1988–94, Maritime Transport Services Ltd 1990–95, British World Aviation Ltd 1990–96, Capital Privée 1990–95, Living Well Health and Leisure Ltd 1994–96, Sheffield Forgemaster Ltd 1996–, Semcon Engineering 1996–; FCA 1969, ACIB 1978; *Recreations* skiing, sailing, travel; *Style*— Christopher McCann, Esq; ✉ 10 Lonsdale Sq, London N1 1EN (☎ 0171 607 8546); The Old Rectory, Ibberton, Dorset; Natwest Ventures Ltd, Fenchurch Exchange, 8 Fenchurch Place, London EC3M 4TE (☎ 0171 374 3503, fax 0171 374 3580)

McCANN, Peter Toland McAree; CBE (1977), JP (1967), DL (1977); s of Peter Toland McAree McCann, MSM (d 1943), of Glasgow, and Agnes Kennedy, *née* Waddell (d 1978); *b* 2 Aug 1924; *Educ* St Mungo's Acad Glasgow, Univ of Glasgow (BL); *m* 25 Nov 1958, Maura Eleanor Ferris, JP, da of Patrick Ferris (d 1959), of Causeway End, Lisburn, NI; 1 s (Peter Toland McAree b 13 Oct 1968); *Career* admitted slr 1947; cncllr Glasgow 1961, magistrate Glasgow 1962–66, Lord Provost of Glasgow 1975–77; NP, OStJ 1977; Medal of King Faisal Saudi Arabia 1976, three Golden Swords and one Silver Sword Saudi Arabia 1975–77; *Recreations* model soldiers, model aeroplanes, model railway, history, music; *Style*— Peter T McCann, Esq, CBE, JP, DL; ✉ Craig-en-Ross, Queen Mary Ave, Crosshill, Glasgow; Peter T McCann & Co, Solicitors, 90 Mitchell St, Glasgow (☎ 0141 221 1429 2725)

McCANNY, Prof John Vincent; s of Patrick Joseph McCanny, of Ballymoney, Co Antrim, and Kathleen Brigid, *née* Kerr; *b* 25 June 1952; *Educ* Dalriada GS Ballymoney Antrim, Univ of Manchester (BSc), New Univ of Ulster (DPhil); *m* 7 July 1979, Mary Bernadette (Maureen); 1 s (Damian Patrick b 28 June 1983), 1 da (Kathryn Louise b 4 Feb 1986); *Career* lectr in physics New Univ of Ulster 1977–78 (post-doctoral research fell Physics Dept 1978–79); Royal Signals and Radar Estab (RSRE): higher scientific offr 1979–82, sr scientific offr 1982–84, princ scientific offr 1984; Queen's Univ Belfast: info technol research lectr Dept of Electrical & Electronic Engrg 1984–87, reader 1987–88, prof of microelectronics engrg 1988–; dir Inst of Advanced Microelectronics in Ireland 1989–92, co-fndr (currently dir) Audio Processing Technology Ltd 1989, co-fndr (currently tech dir) Integrated Silicon Systems Ltd 1990; awards: NI Info Technol Award 1987/88, DTI Smart Award for Enterprise 1988, 1990 and 1995, NI Engrg Employers' Fedn Trophy (for research on DSP chips) 1993, research chosen by IT Advsy Bd and SERC (now EPSRC) as examples of new technological advances 1993, 1994 and 1995, Best Demonstration Award UK IT Conf 1994, Royal Acad of Engrg Silver Medal (for outstanding and demonstrated personal contrib to Br Engrg leading to market exploitation); CPhys 1982, FIEE, MIEEE 1988 (sr memb 1995), FInstP 1992 (MInstP 1982), FEng 1995, FRSA 1996; *Books* VLSI Technology and Design (jtly, 1987), Systolic Array Processors (jtly, 1989), VLSI Systems for DSP (jtly, 1991); 150 published tech papers in books, int jls and conf proceedings; 9 patents; *Recreations* golf, swimming, tennis, supporting Manchester Utd FC, watching sports (soccer, rugby, cricket), listening to music, photography, fine wine and good food; *Style*— Prof John McCanny, FEng; ✉ School of Electrical Engineering and Computer Science, The Queen's University of Belfast, The Ashby Building, Stranmillis Road, Belfast BT9 5AH (☎ 01232 335438, fax 01232 663992, e-mail j.mccanny@ee.qub.ac.uk)

McCARRAHER, His Hon David; VRD (1964); s of Colin McCarraher (d 1960); *b* 6 Nov 1922; *Educ* King Edward VI Sch Southampton, Magdalene Coll Cambridge; *m* 1950, Betty, *née* Haywood (d 1990); 2 da (Vera, Jane), 1 step s (*see* Hon Mrs McCarraher), 1 step da (Anne); *Career* WWII Indian Ocean NW Europe, Capt RNR 1969, CO Solent Div (HMS Wessex) 1969–72, ADC to HM The Queen 1972–73; called to the Bar Lincoln's Inn, ad eundum Western Circuit 1948–52, admitted slr 1955, recorder Crown Ct 1979–84, circuit judge (Western Circuit) 1984–95; *Recreations* family, golf, sailing; *Clubs* Stoneham Golf, Royal Naval Sailing Assoc, Naval; *Style*— His Hon David McCarraher, VRD

McCARTAN, Eamonn Gerard; s of John McCartan (d 1978), of Belfast, and Margaret, *née* Barrett; *b* 23 Jan 1953; *Educ* St Joseph's Teacher Trg Coll Belfast (BEd), Queen's Univ Belfast (Dip Advanced Study in Educn, Dip Mgmnt Studies, MBA); *m* 27 Dec 1976, Marian Francis, da of Patrick McFadden; 1 s (Kieran); *Career* PE teacher: St Mary's GS Belfast 1976–78, Sydney 1978–79, Christian Bros Secdy Sch Belfast 1979–80, St Mary's GS Belfast 1980–81; asst mangr Andersonstown Leisure Centre Belfast 1981–83, pa to Asst Dir of Leisure Servs Belfast CC 1983–84, administrator then asst dir of PE The Queen's Univ Belfast 1984–94, chief exec The Sports Council for NI Belfast 1994–; memb Community Relations Cncl; MCIM 1991, MIPM 1991, memb Inst of Leisure and Amenity Mgmnt 1992; *Recreations* skiing, golf, basketball, gardening, current/political affairs; *Clubs* Malone Golf; *Style*— Eamonn McCartan, Esq; ✉ The Sports Council for Northern Ireland, House of Sport, Upper Malone Road, Belfast BT9 5LA (☎ 01232 381222, fax 01232 682757, mobile 0860 331475)

McCARTER, Keith Ian; s of Maj Peter McCarter (d 1971), of Edinburgh, and Hilda Mary, *née* Gates; *b* 15 March 1936; *Educ* The Royal HS of Edinburgh, Edinburgh Coll of Art (DA); *m* 5 Jan 1963, Brenda Maude Edith, da of James A Schofield (d 1974), of Langley, Bucks; 1 s (Andrew Keith b 1968), 1 da (Alix-Jane b 1966); *Career* Nat Serv RA 1954–56; sculptor; primarily involved in architectural and landscaped situations; numerous cmmns incl: Ordnance Survey HQ Southampton 1967, Lagos Nigeria 1974, Wingate Centre City of London 1980, Goodmans Yard City of London 1982, 1020 19th Street Washington DC 1983, American Express Bank City of London 1984, Guy's Hosp NCC London 1986, Royal Exec Park NY 1986, Evelyn Gardens London 1987, London Docklands 1988, Midland Bank London 1989, Vogans Mill London 1989, Moody Gardens Galveston Texas USA (with Sir Geoffrey Jellicoe), Abbey Rd London 1991, Monks Cross York 1992, John Menzies HQ Edinburgh 1995; works in private collections world-wide; Sir Otto Beit medal RBS 1993; FRSA 1970, ARBS 1991; *Recreations* music, literature, beachcombing; *Clubs* Farmers'; *Style*— Keith McCarter, Esq; ✉ Ottermead, Church Rd, Great Plumstead, Norfolk NR13 5AB (☎ 01603 713001, fax 01603 717276)

McCARTHY, Arlene; MEP (Lab) Peak District (majority 49,307); da of John Joseph McCarthy, of Belfast, and June Florence McCarthy; *b* 10 Oct 1960; *Educ* The Friends' GS Lisburn NI, South Bank Poly (now Univ of the South Bank) (BA), Stuttgart Univ, Université de Clermont Ferrand, UMIST; *partner* Dr David Farrell; *Career* researcher and press offr to ldr Euro Parly Lab Pty 1990–91; Freie Universität Berlin: lectr, DAAD scholar, guest res fell 1991–92; head of Euro affairs Kirklees Metropolitan BC 1992–94, MEP (Lab) Peak District 1994–; *Publications* Changing States (jt ed, 1996); *Recreations* swimming, dancing, travel, foreign languages and music; *Style*— Ms Arlene McCarthy, MEP; ✉ Holmeleigh, 16 North Road, Glossop, Derbyshire SK13 9AS (☎ 01457 857300, fax 01457 867339)

McCARTHY, Dr Daniel Peter Justin; TD (1978, bar 1984 and 1990); s of Thomas Joseph McCarthy, GM (d 1988), and Margaret Mary Josephine, *née* Bowden; *b* 4 July 1939; *Educ* St Mary's Coll Crosby, Univ of Aberdeen (MB ChB), Coll of Law London; *m* 1977, Dr Bronwen Elizabeth Knight Teresa, da of Richard Knight Evans, of Wimbledon; 5 s (Oliver, Richard (twins), Simon, Philip, Nicholas); *Career* cmmnd 3 Bn The Gordon Highlanders 1964, MO 4 (V) Bn Royal Green Jackets 1982–, Maj RAMC (TA); called to the Bar Inner Temple 1978; med practitioner; HM dep coroner: City of London 1979–88, Inner W London 1980–; divnl surgn St John Ambulance, med offr Royal Home and Hosp at Putney 1986–91, medicolegal advsr to MOD (Navy) 1996; Freeman City of London 1975; Liveryman: Worshipful Soc of Apothecaries 1974, Worshipful Co of Scriveners 1996; memb: Coroners' Soc of Eng and Wales, Medico-Legal Soc, Soc of Doctors in Law; Knight Sovereign Military Order of Malta 1985, Donat of Justice (Malta) 1995; FSA Scot; Cross of Merit with Swords (pro merito melitensi) 1988, Knight Sacred Military Constantinian Order of St George 1994; *Recreations* beagling, music; *Clubs* Cavalry and Guards', Green Jackets; *Style*— Dr D P J McCarthy, TD; ✉ 23 Grandison Road, London SW11 6LS; 328 Clapham Rd, London SW9 9AE (☎ 0171 622 2006)

McCARTHY, David; s of John Francis McCarthy, of Coventry, Warwickshire, and Ivy Eileen, *née* Davies; *b* 27 Jan 1942; *Educ* Ratcliffe Coll Syston Leics, Univ of Birmingham (LLB); *children* 2 s (Gavin Stephen b 19 Feb 1972, Nicholas James b 17 May 1974); *Career* slr; articled with Wragge & Co Birmingham, ptnr Clifford Chance (formerly Coward Chance) 1978–94 (joined 1976); ptnr Cameron Markby Hewitt 1995–; conslt: Banco Ambrosiano Veneto SpA, Clifford Chance, MacKenzie Mills and other institutions; dir St George's Hill Residents Assoc Ltd; memb City of London Law Soc Company Law Sub-Ctee; *Recreations* fly fishing, tennis, cricket, books; *Clubs* Richmond Cricket, St George's Hill Tennis, Loch Achonachie Angling; *Style*— David McCarthy, Esq; ✉ Inishbeg, Cavendish Road, St George's Hill, Weybridge, Surrey KT13 0JX

McCARTHY, His Hon Judge; David Laurence; s of Laurence Alphonsus McCarthy (d 1979), of Solihull, and Vera May, *née* Protheroe (d 1982); *b* 7 April 1947; *Educ* St

Philip's GS Birmingham, ChCh Oxford (MA); *m* 2 May 1981, Rosalind Marguerite, da of Reginald Arthur Stevenson; 2 s (Charles Augustus Alexander Seraphim b 9 Aug 1983, Dominic Ambrose Emmanuel b 19 May 1986); *Career* called to the Bar Middle Temple 1970, recorder of the Crown Court 1992–95, circuit judge (Midland & Oxford Circuit) 1995–; *Recreations* science fiction, playing the organ; *Style*— His Hon Judge McCarthy; ✉ c/o The Circuit Administrator, Midland & Oxford Circuit, The Priory Courts, Bull Street, Birmingham B4 6DW

MacCARTHY, Fiona; da of Lt-Col Gerald MacCarthy (d 1943), and Yolande, *née* de Belabre; *b* 23 Jan 1940; *Educ* Wycombe Abbey Sch, Oxford Univ (MA); *m* 19 Aug 1966, David Mellor, OBE, *qv*, s of Colin Mellor (d 1970); 1 s (Corin b 1966), 1 da (Clare b 1970); *Career* design corr The Guardian 1961–69, women's ed Evening Standard 1969–71, critic The Times 1981–92, The Observer 1992–; hon fell: RCA London 1989, Centre for 19th Century Studies Univ of Sheffield; Hon DLitt Univ of Sheffield 1996; Royal Soc of Arts Bicentenary Medal 1987, Wolfson History Prize 1994; *Books* All Things Bright and Beautiful (1972), The Simple Life: C R Ashbee in the Cotswolds (1981), British Design since 1880 (1982), Eric Gill (1989), William Morris: a Life for our Time (1994); *Style*— Ms Fiona MacCarthy; ✉ The Round Building, Hathersage, Sheffield S30 1BA (☎ 01433 650220, fax 01433 650944)

McCARTHY, HE Nicholas Melvyn; OBE (1983); *b* 4 April 1938; *Educ* Queen Elizabeth's Sch Faversham, KCL (BA Modern Languages); *m* 1961, Gillian; 1 da (b 1963), 3 s (b 1964, 1968 and 1970); *Career* HM Dip Serv: vice-consul Saigon 1962–64, full time language student in Japanese then second sec (commercial) Tokyo 1965–70, Japan Desk FCO 1970–73, first sec (info) Brussels 1973–78, FCO 1978–81, first sec (commercial) and head of chancery Dakar 1981–84, FCO 1984–85, consul-gen Tokyo 1985, consul-gen and dir of trade promotion Osaka 1985–90, dep head of mission Brussels 1990–95, high cmmr Cameroon and non-resident ambass to Gabon, Central African Republic and Equatorial Guinea 1995–; *Recreations* golf, squash, tennis, Japanese pottery; *Clubs* Yaoundé Golf; *Style*— HE Mr Nicholas McCarthy, OBE; ✉ c/o Foreign and Commonwealth Office (Yaoundé), King Charles Street, London SW1A 2AH

McCARTHY, Rory Clement; s of Michael Joseph McCarthy, of Gable Lodge, The Bishop's Ave, London N2, and Marica, *née* Cortoubelides; *b* 25 June 1960; *Educ* St Benedict's Sch; *m* 1, 6 June 1987 (m dis 1991), Elizabeth Lucy, da of Keith Elliot Way, of Little Brook, Mid-Holmwood Lane, Dorking, Surrey; 1 s (Cameron Michael Gildart b 23 March 1989); m 2, 16 Jan 1992, Sally, da of late Maurice Clayton and former w of Charles Henry, Lord Settrington (now Earl of March and Kinrara); *Career* institutional sales exec W I Carr Sons and Co 1984–86, mangr Swiss Bank Corpn Int 1987–88, exec dir and head of global sales Asia Equity (UK) Ltd (formerly First Pacific Securities (UK) Ltd) 1988–, McCarthy Trading Ltd (formerly Siam Trading plc) 1992–; world record holder for: greatest descent by hang glider (34500 feet 19 June 1984), greatest freefall parachute altitude by a civilian (33400 feet from 35600 feet); *Recreations* hot air ballooning, aerobatics, skydiving; *Clubs* Annabel's; *Style*— Rory McCarthy, Esq; ✉ McCarthy Trading Ltd, 346 Kensington High Street, London W14 8NS (☎ 0171 371 6336)

McCARTHY, Shaun; *see:* Cory, Desmond

McCARTHY, Thomas Martin; s of Patrick McCarthy (d 1977), of Cappoquin, Co Waterford, Eire, and Helena, *née* Tobin (d 1979); *b* 6 March 1954; *Educ* St Anne's Cappoquin Co Waterford, Univ Coll Cork; *m* 22 July 1982, Catherine, da of T J Coakley, of Mallow, Co Cork; 1 s (Neil Patrick b 13 July 1988), 1 da (Kate Inez b 30 March 1985); *Career* librarian Cork City Libraries 1978–; former ed Poetry Ireland Review, currently poetry ed Stet Magazine; US lectr tour for Irish American Cultural Inst 1990, writer-in-res Combined Univs of Minneapolis St Paul US 1990; poet and author of: The First Convention (1978, Patrick Kavanagh Award 1977), The Sorrow-Garden (1981, Poetry Soc Alice Hunt Bartlett Award 1981), The Non-Aligned Storyteller (1984), Seven Writers in Paris (1989); novel: Without Powers (1991); winner annual American-Irish Fndn Literary Award 1984; hon fell Univ of Iowa 1978–79; memb Bd of Dirs Poetry of Ireland Soc; *Recreations* gardening, spreading political gossip; *Style*— Thomas McCarthy, Esq; ✉ Anvil Press Poetry, 69 King George St, London SE10 8PX (☎ 0181 858 2946)

McCARTHY, Baron (Life Peer UK 1975), of Headington in the City of Oxford; William Edward John McCarthy; s of Edward McCarthy; *b* 30 July 1925; *Educ* Holloway Court Sch, Ruskin Coll, Merton Coll and Nuffield Coll Oxford (MA, DPhil); *m* 1957, Margaret, da of Percival Godfrey; *Career* formerly worker in men's outfitters and clerk; lectr in industrial rels Univ of Oxford, res dir Royal Cmmn on Trade Unions and Employers Assocs 1965–68, fell Nuffield Coll Univ of Oxford and Templeton Coll 1969–, chm Railway Staff Nat Tribunal 1974–86; dir Harland & Wolff Ltd 1976–86, special cmmr Equal Opportunities Cmmn 1977–79; oppn spokesman (Lords) Employment 1983–; *Recreations* theatre, ballet, gardening; *Clubs* Reform; *Style*— The Rt Hon the Lord McCarthy; ✉ 4 William Orchard Close, Old Headington, Oxford (☎ 01865 62016)

MacCARTHY MÓR, The; Terence Francis McCarthy; also Prince of Desmond and Lord of Kerslawny; Chief of the Name and Head of the ancient Irish Royal House of Munster, Hereditary Head of the Niadh Nask (51st generation in unbroken male line descent from King Eoghan Mór (d AD 192) and heir male of King Donal IX MacCarthy Mór (d 1596), last regnant King of Desmond; in all this dynasty reigned for a period in excess of 1400 years); eldest surviving s of The MacCarthy Mór, and Harriet, eldest da of The Maguire of Fermanagh (d 1985), Chief of his Name and de jure Lord Enniskillen in the Jacobite Peerage as heir male of Brian Maguire, Lord Enniskillen (I 1628 and 1689); suc to the Chiefship 1980; *b* 1957; *Educ* privately, The Queen's Univ Belfast (BA (Hons) 1980, Queen's Fndn Scholarship, MA 1983); *Career* dir: Genealogical Services Ulster Historical Fndn 1983–86, Ulster Pedigrees 1986–90; chm Int Cmmn for Orders of Chivalry, patron Royal Clan MacCarthy Soc, chm Royal Clan MacCarthy Tst, tstee Clan Maguire Tst, memb Standing Cncl of Irish Chiefs and Chieftains, memb Royal Ulster Academy Assoc 1991, hon pres Cashel Heritage and Devpt Tst; patron: Royal Eoghanacht Soc, Cashel Arts and Heritage Soc, Cashel Writers' Circle; hon life memb: Heraldry Soc of USA 1995, Heraldry Soc of Zimbabwe 1995; memb Advsy Bd Heraldry Soc of Ireland 1983–, hon memb Int Bodguard Assoc 1995; Hon Col State of Alabama 1994, Col of Infantry State of South Carolina 1994; Hon Citizen: Covington Louisiana 1995, Foley Alabama 1995; Golden Branch Lit Award 1995, Int Medal Soc of the Sons of the American Revolution 1995; holder of several foreign orders including: Grand Offr of Skanderbeg (conferred by HM King Leka I of the Albanians), Knight Cdr Order of St Maurice and St Lazarus (conferred by HRH Crown Prince Victor Emmanuel of Italy), Knight of Justice Sacred Military Constantinian Order St George of Naples (conferred by HRH the Duke of Calabria), Order of St Michael of the Wing (conferred by HRH the Duke of Bragança), Knight Military Order of the Vitez (conferred by HIRH Archduke Jozef Arpad von Habsburg), Knight of the White Eagle and Grand Cordon of Polonia Restituta; *Books* One Thousand Royal and Noble Ancestors of the House of MacCarthy Mór (1988), The New Dictionary of Heraldry (all Irish sections, 1988), Historical Essays on the Kingdom of Munster (1994), Ulster Office 1552–1800: An Administrative History of the Irish Office of Arms from the Tudor Plantations to the Act of Union (1996), A History of The Niadh Nask (1996), The MacCarthys of Munster (1997); also author of numerous articles on heraldry, genealogy and Irish history; *Recreations* painting, writing, travel, music; *Style*— The MacCarthy Mór; ✉ El Minzah, 85 rue de la Liberté, Tangier, Morocco

McCARTNEY, Gordon Arthur; s of Arthur McCartney (d 1987), and Hannah, *née* Seel; *b* 29 April 1937; *Educ* Grove Park GS Wrexham; *m* 1, 23 July 1960 (m dis 1987), Ceris Isobel Davies; 2 da (Heather Jane b 11 April 1963, Alison b 6 Dec 1965); m 2, 26 March 1988, Wendy Ann Vyvyan, da of Sidney Titman; *Career* admitted slr 1959, chief exec Delyn Borough Cncl Clwyd 1974–81, sec Assoc of DCs 1981–91, co sec Local Govt Int Bureau 1988–91; dir National Transport Tokens Ltd 1984–91, md Gordon McCartney Associates 1991–, dir Leisure England Ltd 1993–; memb: Cmmn on the Legislative Process Hansard, Soc for Parly Govt 1991–93; hon fell Inst of Local Govt Studies Univ of Birmingham; *Recreations* music, gardening, cricket; *Clubs* MCC, Northants CCC; *Style*— Gordon McCartney, Esq; ✉ 33 Duck Street, Elton, Peterborough, Cambs PE8 6RQ (☎ 01832 280659, fax 01832 280002); 108 Frobisher House, Dolphin Square, London SW1 (☎ 0171 798 8777)

McCARTNEY, Ian; MP (Lab) Makerfield (majority 18,118); *b* 25 April 1951; *Career* Lab Pty organiser 1973–87, sec to Roger Scott, MP 1979–87; MP (Lab) Makerfield 1987–; memb Personal Social Servs Ctee and Select Ctee on Social Security 1988–92, oppn front bench spokesman on the NHS 1992–94, shadow min of state for employment 1994–; cncllr Wigan BC 1982–87; former chm All Pty Gps on: Home Safety, Child Abduction, Rugby League, Solvent Abuse; pres Wheelchair Fund; chm TGWU Parly GP 1989–91; memb: Wigan Family Practitioner Ctee 1984–86, Greater Manchester Fire and Civil Defence Authy 1986–87; TGWU sponsored; *Style*— Ian McCartney, Esq, MP; ✉ House of Commons, London SW1A 0AA (☎ 0171 219 3000)

McCARTNEY, Sir (James) Paul; kt (1997), MBE (1965); s of late James McCartney, of Allerton, Liverpool, and late Mary Patricia, *née* Mohin; *b* 18 June 1942; *Educ* Liverpool Inst; *m* 12 March 1969, Linda Louise, da of late Lee Eastman, of New York City; 1 s (James b 1977), 3 da (Heather b 1962, Mary b 1969, Stella b 1971); *Career* musician and composer; first group The Quarry Men 1957–59, Beatles formed 1960, first maj appearance Litherland Town Hall 1960, Please Please Me first Br No 1 1961, She Loves You cemented their success 1963, I Want to Hold Your Hand became the biggest selling Br single ever with worldwide sales of 15,000,000; 1963 appearances: UK, Sweden, Royal Variety Performance London; 1964 toured: UK, France, Sweden, Netherlands, Denmark, Hong Kong, NZ, Aust, Canada, USA; 1965 toured: UK, France, Spain, Italy, USA, Canada; other songs (with John Lennon) incl: Love Me Do, Can't Buy Me Love, I Saw Her Standing There, Eight Days A Week, All My Loving, Help!, Ticket To Ride, I Feel Fine, I'm A Loser, A Hard Day's Night, No Reply, I'll Follow The Sun, Yesterday, Eleanor Rigby, Yellow Submarine, All You Need Is Love, Lady Madonna, Hey Jude, We Can Work It Out, Day Tripper, From Me To You, Get Back, Paperback Writer, Hello Goodbye, Let It Be, The Long And Winding Road; Beatles albums: Please Please Me 1963, With The Beatles 1963, A Hard Day's Night 1964, Beatles For Sale 1964, Help! 1965, Rubber Soul 1965, Revolver 1966, Sgt Pepper's Lonely Hearts Club Band 1967, Magical Mystery Tour 1967, The Beatles (White Album) 1968, Yellow Submarine 1969, Abbey Road 1969, Let It Be 1970; Beatles films: A Hard Day's Night 1964, Help! 1965, Yellow Submarine 1968, Let It Be 1970; played live for last time together on roof of the Apple building London 1969; Beatles disbanded 1970; formed MPL group of cos, formed Wings 1971, returned to live work 1972, own TV special James Paul McCartney 1973, honoured by the Guinness Book of Records (Triple Superlative Award for sales of 100,000,000 albums 100,000,000 singles and as holder of 60 gold discs) making him the most successful popular music composer ever 1979, Wings disbanded 1981, performed at Bob Geldof's Live Aid concert 1985 and for The Prince's Trust concert 1986; tours incl: UK and Europe 1972–73, UK and Aust 1975, Europe and USA 1976, UK 1979, Europe, UK, Canada, USA and Brazil 1989–90, World tour 1993; albums incl: McCartney 1970, Ram 1971, Wildlife 1971, Red Rose Speedway 1973, Band On The Run 1973, Venus And Mars 1975, Wings At The Speed Of Sound 1976, Wings Over America 1976, McCartney II 1980, Tug Of War 1982, Pipes Of Peace 1983, Give My Regards To Broad Street 1984, Press To Play 1986, All The Best! 1987, CHOBA B CCCP 1988, Flowers In The Dirt 1989, Unplugged 1990, Tripping the Light 1992, Off the Ground 1993, Paul is Live 1993; Wings films: Rockshow 1981, Give My Regards To Broad Street 1984, Rupert And The Frog Song 1984 (won Best Animated Film BAFTA); film scores: The Family Way 1967, Live And Let Die (title song) 1973, Twice In A Lifetime (title song) 1984; singles with Ringo Starr and George Harrison: Free as a Bird 1995, Real Love 1996; winner numerous Grammy awards incl Lifetime Achievement award 1990; Ivor Novello awards: best ever selling UK single (Mull Of Kintyre) 1977, Int Achievement 1980, Int Hit of the Year (Ebony And Ivory) 1982, Outstanding Contrib to Music 1989; PRS special award for unique achievement in popular music; Freeman City of Liverpool 1984; Hon DUniv Sussex 1988; *Style*— Sir Paul McCartney, MBE; ✉ c/o MPL Communications Ltd, 1 Soho Square, London W1V 6BQ

McCARTNEY, Robert Law; QC (NI 1975), MP (UK Unionist) North Down (majority 2,892); s of William Martin McCartney, and Elizabeth Jane, *née* McCartney; *b* 24 April 1936; *Educ* Grosvenor GS Belfast, Queen's Univ Belfast (LLB); *m* 1960, Maureen Ann, *née* Bingham; 1 s, 3 da; *Career* admitted slr Supreme Ct of Judicature NI 1962, called to the Bar NI 1968; memb NI Assembly 1983–87; MP (UK Unionist) North Down 1995–; contested N Down as Ulster Unionist 1983 and as Real Unionist 1987; pres Campaign for Equal Citizenship 1986–88; *Publications* Liberty and Authority in Ireland (1985); *Recreations* reading (biography and military history), walking, sport (rugby and squash); *Style*— Robert McCartney, Esq, QC, MP; ✉ constituency office: 10 Hamilton Road, Bangor, Northern Ireland BT20 4LE (☎ 01247 272994, fax 01247 465037); House of Commons, London SW1A 0AA (☎ 0171 219 6590, fax 0171 219 0371)

McCAUGHAN, Prof Daniel Vincent; OBE (1993); s of Daniel Vincent McCaughan (d 1984), of Belfast, and Elizabeth Gabriel, *née* Erskine (d 1974); *b* 5 May 1942; *Educ* St Mary's GS Belfast, Queen's Univ Belfast (Sullivan and Lappin scholar, BSc, PhD, DSc); *m* 21 Aug 1968, Anne Patricia, da of John and Mary Kinsella; 1 s (Gareth John b 24 Aug 1970); *Career* memb Tech Staff Bell Laboratories Inc NJ USA 1968–74, sr princ scientific offr RSRE Malvern 1974–81, asst dir (components) GEC Hirst Res Centre Wembley 1981–86; tech dir: Marconi Electronic Devices Ltd and Electro-Optic Div EEV Ltd 1986–87, GEC Electronic Devices Ltd 1987–88; dir NI Telecommunications Engrg Centre Northern Telecom (NI) Ltd 1988–93, dir Univ and Scientific Relations BNR Europe 1993–94, dir External Affrs NT (NI) Ltd 1993–95, dir Nortel (NI) Ltd 1995–, dir External Res BNR World Trade 1994–95, chief scientist Bell Northern Research 1995–96, chief scientist Nortel Technology 1996–; professorial fell Queen's Univ of Belfast 1987– (visiting prof of microelectronics 1982–87); chm: Technol Bd for NI 1986–92, Bd Industl Res and Technol Unit of Dept of Econ Devpt 1992–93; memb Cncl Royal Acad of Engrg 1994–; FEng 1992, FIEE 1990, FInstP 1975, CPhys 1975, SMIEEE 1990, FInstD 1990; *Publications* tech chapters in numerous texts incl Handbook of Semiconductors; over 100 tech articles and 16 patents; *Recreations* antique glass, photography, fungi, gardening, hiking, amateur radio (call sign GI3RTS); *Clubs* Physical Society, Royal Belfast Golf; *Style*— Prof Daniel V McCaughan, OBE, FEng; ✉ Nortel (NI) Ltd, N Ireland Telecommunications Engineering Centre, Doagh Rd, Newtownabbey, Co Antrim BT36 6XA (☎ 01232 363500, fax 01232 363520)

McCAUGHREAN, Geraldine Margaret; da of Leslie Arthur Jones (d 1980), of Enfield, Middx, and Ethel, *née* Thomas; *b* 6 June 1951; *Educ* Enfield Co Sch for Girls, Christ Church Coll of Educn Canterbury (BEd); *m* 23 Nov 1988, John, s of William

McCaughrean (d 1964), of Aughton, Lancs; 1 da (Ailsa b 12 Dec 1989); *Career* Thames Television Ltd 1970–77, Marshall Cavendish Partworks Ltd 1977–89 (sec, sub-ed, staff writer); freelance writer 1989–; *Radio Play* Last Call (1991); *Books* 1001 Arabian Nights (1982), The Canterbury Tales (1984), A Little Lower than the Angels (1987, Whitbread Book of the Year, Katholischer Kindersbuchpreis Germany), A Pack of Lies (1988, Carnegie Medal, Guardian Children's Fiction Award), The Maypole (1989), St George and the Dragon (1989), El Cid (1989), Fires' Astonishment (1990), Vainglory (1991), The Odyssey (1993), Gold Dust (1993, Beefeater/Whitbread Children's Book of the Year), Stories from Shakespeare (1994), Plundering Paradise (1996); *Style—* Ms Geraldine McCaughrean; ✉ c/o David Higham Associates, 5–8 Lower John Street, Golden Square, London W1R 4HA (☎ 0171 437 7888, fax 0171 437 1072)

McCAUSLAND, Martin Patrick; s of Jack Patrick McCausland, and Audrey May, *née* Pomeroy; *b* 27 March 1961; *Educ* Hardye's GS Dorchester, Univ of Sheffield (BA); *m* 4 Sept 1988, Christine Dawn, *née* Burrows; *Career* articled clerk Chantrey Wood King CAs 1982–85, accountant Ernst & Young 1986–89; Carlton Communications plc: head office 1989–91, fin controller Carlton Television Ltd 1991–94, fin dir Carlton Television Ltd 1994, fin dir Carlton UK Productions Ltd 1995–; ACA 1985; *Style—* Martin McCausland, Esq; ✉ Carlton UK Productions, 35–58 Portman Square, London W1H 0NU (☎ 0171 486 6688, fax 0171 486 1132)

McCAVE, Prof (Ian) Nicholas; s of T T McCave (d 1941), and G M Langlois; *b* 3 Feb 1941; *Educ* Elizabeth Coll Guernsey, Hertford Coll Oxford (BA, MA, DSc), Brown Univ Providence USA (PhD); *m* 3 April 1972, Susan Caroline Adams, da of G de P Bambridge; 3 s (Thomas b 1973, Robert b 1975, Geoffrey b 1978), 1 da (Elise b 1981); *Career* NATO res fell Netherlands Inst voor Onderzoek der Zee 1967–69, reader Sch of Environmental Sci UEA 1976–78 (lectr 1969–76), adjunct scientist Woods Hole Oceanographic Institution 1978–86, Woodwardian prof of geology Univ of Cambridge 1985–, fell St John's Coll Cambridge 1986–; pres Scientific Ctee on Oceanic Res of the Int Cncl of Science Unions 1992–96; FGS 1963; *Books* The Benthic Boundary Layer (ed, 1976); *Style—* Prof Nicholas McCave; ✉ Dept of Earth Sciences, University of Cambridge, Downing St, Cambridge (☎ 01223 333400)

McCAWLEY, Leon Francis; s of Bernard McCawley, and Marian, *née* Sherwood; *b* 12 July 1973; *Educ* Chetham's Sch of Music Manchester, Curtis Inst of Music Philadelphia (Martin Musical Fund scholar, Myra Hess Award, Hattori Trust scholar); *Career* pianist; appeared with: CBSO under Sir Simon Rattle, BBC Philharmonic, LPO, RPO, Austrian Radio Orchestra and Vienna Symphony Orch; int tours: Japan (with Vienna Mozart Chamber Orch), New Zealand (with Auckland and Christchurch orch); festival appearances incl: Spoleto 1991–, Helsinki Summer Recital Series, Bath and Harrogate; debut BBC Proms with Bournemouth Symphony Orch and Andrew Litton 1995; 1995/6 season features: Int Piano Series South Bank, concerts with BBC Philharmonic, Royal Scottish National Orch, National Youth Orch of GB and tour with European Community Chamber Orch; debut recording of complete works for solo piano by Barber 1995; *Awards* piano section BBC Young Musician of the Year 1990, young soloist of the year LPO/Pioneer 1990, first National Power World Piano Competition 1992, 1st prize Ninth International Beethoven Piano Competition (Vienna) 1993, 2nd prize Leeds International Piano Competition 1993; *Recreations* travel, reading, languages, cooking; *Style—* Leon McCawley, Esq; ✉ c/o Harold Holt Ltd, 31 Sinclair Road, London W14 0NS (☎ 0171 603 4600, fax 0171 603 0019, telex 22339 HUNTER)

McCAWLEY, Michael John; s of Walter Alfred George McCawley (d 1979), and Audrey Mabel Uzielli Ellen McCawley; *b* 12 July 1938; *Educ* Colwyn Bay GS, Havering Tech Coll, Bromley Coll of Technol (Dip in Engrg Mgmnt); *m* Feb 1960, Teresa Mary, da of Owen Mervyn Vaughan-Jones; 2 s (Alan John b 2 Oct 1960, Neil Michael Owen b 13 July 1963); *Career* police cadet Met Police 1955–56; Nat Serv Royal Corps of Signals 1956–59; re-joined Met Police 1959, serv various divs and depts (latterly chief supt Croydon Div), ret 1989; office admin mangr Royal Horticultural Soc 1989–90; Cats Protection League: asst dir 1990–92, dep dir 1992–93, chief exec 1993–; memb Inst of Admin Mgmnt 1982, FIMgt 1988; *Recreations* tennis, gardening, walking; *Style—* Michael McCawley, Esq; ✉ Chief Executive, Cats Protection League, 17 Kings Road, Horsham, West Sussex RH13 5PN (☎ 01403 261947, fax 01403 218414)

McCLEAN, Prof (John) David; CBE (1994), Hon QC (1995); s of Maj Harold McClean (d 1983), of Prestbury, Cheshire, and Mabel, *née* Callow (d 1981); *b* 4 July 1939; *Educ* Queen Elizabeth GS Blackburn, Magdalen Coll Oxford (BA, BCL, MA, DCL); *m* 10 Dec 1966, Pamela Ann, da of Leslie Arthur Loader (d 1959), of Yeovil, Somerset; 1 s (Michael b 1969), 1 da (Lydia b 1972); *Career* Univ of Sheffield: lectr 1961–68, sr lectr 1968–73, prof 1973–, pro vice chllr 1991–96; visiting lectr Monash Univ 1968 (visiting prof 1978); lay vice pres Sheffield Diocesan Synod 1982–94; memb: Gen Synod 1970–, Crown Appts Cmmn 1977–87; vice chm House of Laity 1979–85 (chm 1985–95), chllr Dio of Sheffield 1992–; *Books* Legal Context of Social Work (1975, 2 edn 1980), Recognition of Family Judgments in the Commonwealth (1983), International Judicial Assistance (1992); co-author: Criminal Justice and the Treatment of Offenders (jtly, 1969), Defendants in the Criminal Process (1976), Shawcross and Beaumont on Air Law (4 edn, 1977), Dicey and Morris, the Conflict of Laws (10 edn 1980, 11 edn 1987, 12 edn 1993); *Recreations* detective fiction; *Clubs* RCS; *Style—* Prof David McClean, CBE, QC; ✉ 6 Burnt Stones Close, Sheffield S10 5TS (☎ 0114 230 5794); Faculty of Law, The University, Sheffield S10 2TN (☎ 0114 282 6754, fax 0114 272 1319)

McCLEAN, Richard Arthur Francis; s of Donald Stuart McClean (d 1959), and Marjory Kathleen, *née* Franks; *b* 5 Dec 1937; *Educ* Marlborough; *m* 29 Aug 1959, Janna, da of Eric Constantine Doresa; 1 s (Paul b 23 Sept 1962); 2 da (Lucinda b 27 June 1961, Philippa b 23 July 1966); *Career* Financial Times: joined Advertising Dept 1955, advertising dir 1974, appointed to the Bd 1977, mktg dir 1979, md Marketing, md Europe 1981, dep chief exec 1983–93; chief exec International Herald Tribune July 1993–; dir: Financial Times Group Ltd 1984, FT Business Information Ltd 1984, St Clements Press Ltd 1981, The Financial Times (Europe) Ltd 1978, Westminster Press Ltd 1986; *Recreations* golf, tennis; *Clubs* Garrick, Royal St George's Golf, Sunningdale Golf, MCC; *Style—* Richard McClean, Esq; ✉ International Herald Tribune, 181 Avenue Charles de Gaulle, 92521 Neuilly, Cedex, France (☎ 00 331 46 37 93 00)

McCLELLAN, Anthony; CBE (1991); s of James McClellan (d 1941), and Violet Mary, *née* Heenan (d 1974); *b* 12 April 1925; *Educ* Sedbergh, Clare Coll Cambridge; *m* 14 Jan 1958, Marie-Jose Alberte, da of Maurice Marie-Edouard Joriaux (d 1963); 1 s (James-Edward b 1 Dec 1961), 1 da (Beatrice Georgina Marguerite b 20 Aug 1963); *Career* RN Y Scheme 1943–44, transferred Army 1944, cmmnd KOSB, seconded 2 King Edward VII Own Gurkhas (The Sirmoor Rifles) 1945, demobbed as Capt 1947; HM Colonial Serv 1947, admin and JP N Nigeria 1949, ADC to Govr of Nigeria 1952, dist offr and magistrate Sarawak 1954, called to the Bar Inner Temple 1958, legal appts in commerce and indust 1959–73, princ legal advsr Cmmn of Euro Communities Brussels 1989–90 (legal advsr 1974), returned to practice at the Bar London 1990–95; life memb Univ of Cambridge Cons Assoc; *Recreations* exhibitions of art and antiques, National Trust, reading and travel; *Clubs* East India, Sirmoor, Sarawak Assoc; *Style—* Anthony McClellan, Esq, CBE; ✉ The Coach House, 6 Princes Road, Kew, Richmond, Surrey TW9 3HP

McCLELLAN, Col Sir (Herbert) Gerard Thomas; kt (1986), CBE (1979, OBE 1960), TD (1955), JP (City of Liverpool 1968), DL (Merseyside 1974, Lancs 1967–74); s of late George McClellan and Lillian, *née* Fitzgerald; *b* 24 Sept 1913; *m* 1939, Rebecca Ann (Nancy) (d 1982), da of late Michael and Ann Desforges; 1 s (Anthony George), 3 da (Mary Colette, Ann Winifred (Mrs Ann Welsh), Petra Clare (Mrs Russell Plant)); *Career* served WWII Loyal (N Lancs) Regt, Royal Regt of Artillery, London Irish Rifles RUR, served M East, N Africa, Italy (wounded, despatches), cmd 626 (Liverpool Irish) HAA Regt (RA, TA), 470 (3 W Lancs) RA TA 1955–60, County Cmdt W Lancs Army Cadet Force 1961–66; formerly vice chm and md: Vernons Trust Corporation, Vernons Finance Corporation, Vernons Insurance Brokers; dir Vernons Organisation; md Competition Management Services 1977–82; ret 1982; chm Intro Merseyside Ltd 1988–94; dir: JS Mortgage Corporation plc 1986–93, Richmond Storage and Transit Co (UK) Ltd 1990–93, Richmond Freight Services Ltd 1990–93; memb: TAVR Assoc W Lancs 1955–66 (vice-chm 1966–68), N W England & IOM 1968–70 (vice-chm 1970–75, chm 1975–79); former memb Liverpool City Cncl (Childwall Ward); govr: Archbishop Whiteside SM - St Brigid's High Sch 1961–91, Christ's Coll Liverpool 1962–69, St Mary's (Little Crosby) RC Primary Sch 1986–90, Sandown Coll Liverpool 1989–91; chm: Liverpool (Liverpool European) Cons Constituency Cncl 1978–84, Merseyside West European CCC 1984–85 (pres 1985–90); vice pres: Merseyside County Soldiers' Sailors' & Airmen's Assoc 1975–, Churchill Cons Club, Wavertree 1976–, The Liverpool Sch of Tropical Med 1987–92; memb: North West Area Cons Assoc 1971–90, The Nat Union of Cons and Unionist Exec Ctee 1982–87, Mabel Fletcher Tech Liverpool 1969–86 (chm Govrs 1971–86); pres: Wavertree Cons Assoc 1967–76 (chm 1962–67), Garston Cons Assoc 1979–90, Halewood Cons Club 1983–88, Crosby Cons Assoc 1986–89 (chm 1989–91); High Sheriff Merseyside 1980–81; FInstAM; *Clubs* Athenaeum (Liverpool), Army & Navy; *Style—* Col Sir Gerard McClellan, CBE, TD, JP, DL; ✉ Ince Blundell Hall, Ince Blundell, Merseyside L38 6JN (☎ 0151 929 2269, fax 0151 929 2188)

McCLELLAND, Prof (William) Grigor; CBE (1994); s of Arthur McClelland (d 1966), of Newcastle upon Tyne, and Jean, *née* Grigor (d 1966); *b* 2 Jan 1922; *Educ* Leighton Park Sch, Balliol Coll Oxford (MA); *m* 1946, Diana Avery, da of William Harold Close, of Hampstead; 2 s, 2 da; *Career* Friends Ambulance Unit 1941–46, md Laws Stores Ltd 1949–65 and 1978–85 (chm 1966–85), sr res fell Balliol Coll 1962–65, dir Manchester Business Sch 1965–77, prof of business admin Univ of Manchester 1967–77; ed: Quakers Visit China 1957, Journal of Management Studies 1963–65; dep chm Nat Computing Centre 1966–68; chm: Washington Devpt Corp 1977–88, EDC for the Distributive Trades 1980–84 (memb 1965–70), Tyne Tees Telethon Tst 1988–93, Tyne & Wear Fndn 1988–93, NE Regnl Advsy Panel Nat Lottery Charities Bd 1995–; memb: Consumer Cncl 1963–66, Econ Planning Cncl (Northern Region) 1965–66, IRC 1966–71, NEDC 1969–71, SSRC 1971–74, Northern Industl Devpt Bd 1977–86; tstee: Joseph Rowntree Charitable Tst 1956–94 (chm 1965–78), Anglo-German Fndn for the Study of Indust Soc 1973–79, Millfield House Fndn 1976–; govr: Nat Inst of Econ and Social Res, Leighton Park Sch 1952–60 and 1962–66; DL Tyne and Wear; MBA Univ of Manchester, Hon DCL Univ of Durham; FIGD, CIMgt; *Books* Studies in Retailing (1963), Costs and Competition in Retailing (1966), And a New Earth (1976), Washington: Over and Out (1988); *Recreations* walking, tennis, skiing; *Style—* Prof Grigor McClelland, CBE; ✉ 66 Elmfield Rd, Gosforth, Newcastle upon Tyne NE3 4BD

McCLELLAND, Dr (William) Morris; s of James McClelland, of Moodage, Tanderagee, Co Armagh, N Ireland, and May, *née* Johnston; *b* 22 June 1945; *Educ* Portadown Coll, Queen's Univ Belfast (MB BCh, BAO); *m* 14 Aug 1969; Margaret Christine, da of David Joseph Robinson, of Ballynagarrick, Gilford, Co Down, N Ireland; 1 s (Jamie b 8 April 1978), 2 da (Joanna b 7 May 1972, Sarah b 15 Jan 1976); *Career* chief exec NI Blood Transfusion Serv 1980–, hon conslt haematologist Royal Victoria Hosp Belfast 1980–; conslt advsr to: chief med offr NI 1986–, Overseas Devpt Admin 1988–; FRCPath; *Style—* Dr Morris McClelland; ✉ Northern Ireland Blood Transfusion Service, Belfast City Hospital, Lisburn Road, Belfast BT9 7TS (☎ 01232 321414, fax 01232 4390017)

McCLELLAND, Dr Richard Leeper (stage name Richard Leech); s of Herbert Saunderson McClelland (d 1953), of Dublin, and Isabella Frances, *née* Leeper (d 1963); *b* 24 Nov 1922; *Educ* Halleybury, Trinity Coll Dublin (BA, BAO, MB BCh); *m* 1, 28 Jan 1950, Helen Hyslop, *née* Uttley (d 1971); 2 da (Sarah Jane b 15 Jan 1952, Eliza b 3 June 1954); m 2, 27 June 1975, (Margaret) Diane, *née* Pearson; *Career* actor; house surgn and house physician Meath Hosp Dublin 1946; wrote column Doctor in the Wings in World Medicine 1968–83; dir Rocks Country Wines Ltd 1985–; *Theatre* incl: All My Sons 1948, The Lady's Not for Burning (London and Broadway) 1949, Relative Values 1950, No Other Verdict 1954, Uncertain Joy 1955, Subway in the Sky 1956, A Man for All Seasons 1960, Dazzling Prospect 1961, Cider with Rosie 1963, The Rt Hon Gentleman 1964, Horizontal Hold 1967, The Cocktail Party 1968, Whose Life Is It Anyway? (Savoy) 1979–81, My Friend Rudyard, A Kipling Recital; *Television* incl: Jane Eyre, The Gold Robbers, The Doctors, Barchester Chronicles, Smiley's People; *Films* incl: Dam Busters, A Night to Remember, Ice Cold in Alex, The Young Churchill, Gandhi, A Handful of Dust, The Shooting Party; *Books* How To Do It (1979), TCD Anthology (1945); *Recreations* bricklaying, cinematography, gardening; *Clubs* Garrick; *Style—* Dr Richard McClelland; ✉ 27 Claylands Rd, London SW8 1NX (☎ 0171 735 1678); Rocks Country Wines Ltd, Loddon Park Farm, New Bath Rd, Twyford, Berks (☎ 0118 934 2344)

MACCLESFIELD, Archdeacon of; *see:* Gillings, Ven Richard John

MACCLESFIELD, 9 Earl of (GB 1721); Richard Timothy George Mansfield Parker; also Viscount Parker of Ewelm, Co Oxford (GB 1721), Baron Parker of Macclesfield, Co Chester (GB 1716); s of 8 Earl of Macclesfield (d 1992), and Hon Valerie Mansfield (d 1994), da of 4 Baron Sandhurst, OBE; *b* 31 May 1943; *Educ* Stowe, Worcester Coll Oxford; *m* 1, 1967 (m dis 1985), (Tatiana) Cleone Anne, da of Maj Craig Wheaton-Smith, US Army, and his 1 w, *née* Princess Tatiana Wiasemsky; 3 da (Lady Tanya Susan b 1971, Lady Katharine Ann b 1973, Lady Marian Jane b (twin) 1973); m 2, 1986, Mrs Sandra Hope Mead, da of Sylvio Fiore, of Florida, USA; *Heir* bro, Hon David Jonathan Geoffrey Parker b 2 Jan 1945; *Style—* The Rt Hon the Earl of Macclesfield; ✉ Shirburn Castle, nr Watlington, Oxon OX9 5DL

McCLEVERTY, Prof Jon Armistice; s of John Frederick McCleverty (d 1948), and Agnes Elder, *née* Melrose (d 1973); *b* 11 Nov 1937; *Educ* Aberdeen GS, Fettes Coll Edinburgh, Univ of Aberdeen (BSc), Imperial Coll Univ of London (PhD); *m* 29 June 1963, Dianne Margaret, da of Ian William Barrack (d 1955); 2 da (Ashley b 1967, Roslyn b 1971); *Career* post doctoral fell (Fulbright scholar) MIT USA 1963–64, lectr and reader dept of chemistry Univ of Sheffield 1964–80; prof of Inorganic Chemistry: Univ of Birmingham 1980–90, Univ of Bristol 1990–; SERC: memb Chm's Ctee 1988–93 (chm 1990–93), chm Inorganic Chemistry Sub-Ctee 1988–90, memb Sci Bd 1990–93; chm Ctee of Heads of Univ Chemistry Depts 1989–91; Royal Soc of Chemistry: memb Int Ctee 1992–, chm 1993–; Euro Community: memb COST Tech Ctee for Chemistry 1991–95, chm Action D4 for Molecular Electronics 1991–95; chm Euro Research Cncl Chemistry Ctees (CERC 3) (memb 1990–93 and 1995–98); *Recreations* gardening, jazz, travel, food and wine, Scottish clan history; *Style—* Prof Jon McCleverty; ✉ School of Chemistry, University of Bristol, Cantocks Close, Bristol BS8 1TS

McCLINTOCK, Nicholas Cole; CBE (1979); s of Col Robert Singleton McClintock, DSO (d 1969), of Godstone, Surrey, and Mary Howard, *née* Elphinstone (d 1965); *b* 10 Sept 1916; *Educ* Stowe, Trinity Coll Cambridge (BA, MA, capt Univ fencing team); *m* 2 Sept 1953, Pamela Sylvia, da of Maj Rhys Clavell Mansel (d 1969), of Smedmore, Corfe Castle, Dorset; 2 s (Alexander b 1959, Michael b 1960), 2 da (Sylvia b 1954, Elizabeth b 1962); *Career* WWII cmmnd RA 1938–45 served Dunkirk, cmd 1 Field Batty final Burma

Campaign 1945; Col admin serv 1946–62; Northern Nigeria: private sec to Govr 1949–50, clerk to Exec Cncl Northern Region 1951–53, actg res Kano Province and res Bornu Province 1958–62; sec gen Order of St John 1968–81, sec Dorset Historic Churches Tst 1984–, chm Aidis Tst 1988–94; Freeman City of London 1981; KStJ 1968; *Books* Kingdoms in the Sand and Sun (1992); *Style*— Nicholas McClintock, Esq, CBE; ✉ Lower Westport, Wareham, Dorset BH20 4PR (☎ 01929 553252)

McCLOSKEY, Jane; da of Brian McCloskey, of Wolverhampton, W Midlands, and Hilda, *née* Blunn; *b* 10 March 1963; *Educ* Wolverhampton Girls' HS, Univ of Birmingham (BA); *Career* various media projects 1984–86 incl: author of Into the Labyrinth (networked children's drama series shown in UK, USA and Spain) for HTV West 1982, author of James and the Jailer (children's adventure series) for Beacon Radio 1983, author of Black Country Tales (local history feature) for BRMB Radio 1984–85, features writer for Select Magazine and Wolverhampton Post & Mail 1984–85; BBC 1986–92: researcher Pebble Mill at One, Pamela Armstrong and Reaching for the Skies (BBC 1 Network) 1986–87, successively asst prodr, studio dir then prodr Daytime Live (BBC 1 Network) 1988–90, prodr/studio dir Scene Today (BBC 1 Network) 1990, prodr People Today (BBC North), prodr/dir The Travel Show Guides (BBC North) and prodr BBC Election Night Special (BBC 1) and The Travel Show (BBC 2) 1991–92; freelance prodr 1993–94: series prodr Holiday Snaps and author of Holiday Snaps Brochure (GMTV), prodr Good Getaways (Carlton); head of features and prog devpt GMTV 1995–96 (head of features and entertainment 1994–95), dir of progs Westcountry Television 1996–; *Recreations* classical music, cookery, musical theatre; *Style*— Miss Jane McCloskey; ✉ Director of Programmes, Westcountry Television, Western Wood Way, Langage Science Park, Plymouth, Devon PL7 5BG (☎ 01752 333376, fax 01752 333379)

McCLOY, Dr Elizabeth Carol; da of Edward Bradley, of Guildford, Surrey, and Ada, *née* Entwisle; *b* 25 April 1945; *Educ* Guildford Co GS, Univ Coll Hosp UCL (BSc, MB BS), FRCP, FFOM; *m* 1969 (m dis 1989), Rory McCloy; 2 s (Liam James b 22 March 1972, Sean Michael b 22 Aug 1974); *Career* clinical asst (med) W Middx Univ Hosp 1972–83; Manchester Royal Infirmary: sr clinical med offr (occupational health) 1984–88, conslt in occupational med 1988–93; dir of occupational health and safety Central Manchester Healthcare Tst 1988–93, chief exec and dir Civil Service Occupational Health Service (now OHSA Ltd) 1993–96; memb Soc of Occupational Med (pres 1993–94); Peter Taylor medal; FRSM 1985, FRSA 1993; *Books* Hunter's Diseases of Occupations (contrib, 1988), Practical Occupational Medicine (jt ed, 1994), Oxford Textbook of Medicine (contrib, 1994); *Style*— Dr Elizabeth McCloy; ✉ c/o OHSA Ltd, 18–20 Hill Street, Edinburgh EH2 3NB (☎ 0131 220 4177, fax 0131 220 4183)

McCLUGGAGE, Dr John Robert (Jack); *b* 15 Nov 1940; *Educ* Queen's Univ Belfast (MB BCh, BAO); *m* (m dis); 1 c; *Career* princ GP Cherryvalley Belfast and pt/t clinical asst (dermatology) Ards Hosp Newtownards 1967–80, princ/sr lectr in gen practice Dept of Gen Practice Queen's Univ Belfast 1980–87, sec NI Cncl for Postgrad Med Educn 1987–93, chief exec/postgrad dean NI Cncl for Postgrad Med and Dental Educn 1993–; examiner for membership: RCGP 1984–90, Irish Coll of Gen Practitioners 1987–93; memb: Standing Ctee of Postgrad Deans 1987–, Conf of Postgrad Deans 1987–, Hosp Servs Sub-Ctee DHSS NI 1987–, Cncl GMC 1989– (concurrently memb Professional Conduct Ctee); author of various pubns in academic jls; memb BMA, fell Ulster Med Soc (vice pres 1994–95); FRCGP 1984, FRCPEd 1994, FRCP(Dublin) 1995; *Recreations* gardening, reading, music; *Style*— Dr Jack McCluggage; ✉ Apartment 2, Woodlodge, Croft Road, Holywood, Co Down BT18 0QB (☎ 01232 427032, office 01232 491731)

McCLUNE, Rear Adm (William) James; CB (1978); s of James McClune, MBE (d 1952); *b* 20 Nov 1921; *Educ* Foyle Coll, Queen's Univ Belfast, Univ of Birmingham (MSc); *m* 1953, Joan Elizabeth Symes, da of Albert Prideaux (d 1952); 1 s (James), 1 da (Bridget); *Career* radar offr RNVR 1941–47, CSO (engrg) to C-in-C Fleet 1976–78; live govr Monkton Combe Sch, life vice pres RNLI; *Recreations* sailing; *Clubs* Royal Naval and Royal Albert Yacht; *Style*— Rear Adm James McClune, CB; ✉ Harlam Lodge, Lansdown, Bath (☎ 01225 311748)

McCLURE, Prof John; s of Richard Burns McClure (d 1949), of Omagh, Co Tyrone, and Isabella McClure (d 1983); *b* 2 May 1947; *Educ* Queen's Univ Belfast (BSc, MD, BCh, BAO); *m* 26 June 1970, Sheena Frances, da of Alfred Henry Tucker (d 1973), of Belfast; 3 da (Sarah b 26 Oct 1971, Katy 13 Dec 1975, Emma 30 Jan 1978); *Career* trg posts in pathology Queen's Univ Belfast 1972–78, clinical sr lectr (also specialist and sr specialist tissue pathology) Inst of Med and Veterinary Sci and Univ of Adelaide S Aust 1978–83; Univ of Manchester: sr lectr and hon conslt histopathology 1983–87, Procter prof of pathology 1987–, assoc dean of undergrad med studies 1995–; clinical dir of laboratory med Central Manchester Healthcare Tst 1996–; MRCPath 1977, FRCPath 1989; *Style*— Prof John McClure; ✉ Department of Pathological Sciences, The Medical School, University of Manchester, Oxford Rd, Manchester M13 9PT (☎ 0161 275 5300, fax 0161 275 5567)

McCLURE, Rev Canon Timothy Elston (Tim); s of Kenneth Elston McClure, of Burton Bradstock, Dorset, and Grace Helen, *née* Hoar; *b* 20 Oct 1946; *Educ* Kingston GS, St John's Coll Durham (BA), Ridley Hall Cambridge; *m* 1 Aug 1969, Barbara Mary, da of Ven George John Charles Marchant; 1 s (Matthew Elston b 1 July 1970), 1 da (Naomi b 27 Nov 1973); *Career* curate Kirkheaton PC Huddersfield W Yorks 1970–73, mktg mangr Agrofax Labour Intensive Products Ltd Harrow Middx 1973–74, chaplain to Manchester Poly 1974–82, curate St Ambrose Chorlton-on-Medlock Manchester 1974–79, team rector Parish of Whitworth Manchester and presiding chaplain 1979–82, gen sec Student Christian Movement 1982–92, dir Churches' Cncl for Indust and Social Responsibility (ISR) Bristol, hon canon Bristol Cathedral and bishop's social and industl advsr 1992–, Lord Mayor's chaplain 1996–; non-exec chm Traidcraft plc 1990– (non-exec dir 1983–); memb: Industl Mission Assoc 1992, Anglican Assoc for Social Responsibility 1994; *Recreations* cooking, gardening, reading; *Style*— Canon Tim McClure; ✉ 7 South Road, Redland, Bristol BS6 6QP (☎ 0117 942 5264); ISR, St Nicholas House, Lawfords Gate, Bristol BS5 0RE (☎ 0117 955 7430, fax 0117 941 3252)

McCLURE FISHER, David Anthony; s of Douglas McClure Fisher, of Northwood, Middx, and Mary Margaret, *née* Haley; *b* 4 March 1939; *Educ* Tonbridge; *m* 30 Dec 1961, Lesley Carol, da of William Henry Chester-Jones (d 1971); 1 s (Duncan b 1964), 1 da (Joanna b 1968); *Career* md: Hogg Automotive Insurance Services Ltd 1984–94, Greyfriars Administration Services Ltd 1984–94, Hogg Insurance Brokers Ltd; dir: Hogg Group plc 1990–94, Bain Hogg Ltd 1994–95, IMC Insurance Services Ltd 1995–96; FCII, FInstD, FCIS, FBIIBA, FIMI; *Recreations* golf, bridge; *Clubs* Moor Park Golf; *Style*— D A McClure Fisher, Esq; ✉ Shelleys, Tag Lane, Hare Hatch, Berkshire RG10 9ST (☎ 0118 940 4149)

McCLUSKEY, Baron (Life Peer UK 1976), of Churchhill in District of City of Edinburgh; John Herbert McCluskey; QC (Scotland 1967); s of Francis John McCluskey (d 1961), of Edinburgh; *b* 12 June 1929; *Educ* St Bede's GS Manchester, Holy Cross Acad Edinburgh, Edinburgh Univ (Vans Dunlop Scholar, Harry Dalgety Bursar, MA, LLB); *m* 1956, Ruth, da of Aaron Friedland, of Manchester; 2 s (Hon (John) Mark b 1960, Hon David Francis b 1963), 1 da (Hon Catherine Margaret b 1962); *Career* advocate 1955, advocate-depute 1964, sheriff princ of Dumfries and Galloway 1973–1974, slr gen for Scotland 1974–79, senator of the Coll of Justice in Scotland 1984–; BBC Reith lectr 1986; Hon LLD Dundee 1989; *Books* Law, Justice and Democracy (1987), Criminal Appeals (1991); *Style*— The Rt Hon the Lord McCluskey; ✉ Ct of Session, Parliament Square, Edinburgh (☎ 0131 225 2595); 5 Lansdowne Crescent, Edinburgh EH12 5EQ (☎ 0131 225 6102, fax 0131 225 8213)

McCOLGAN, Elizabeth (Liz); *née* Lynch; MBE (1992); da of Martin Lynch, of Dundee, and Elizabeth, *née* Fearn; *b* 24 May 1964; *Educ* St Saviour's HS Dundee, Ricks Coll Idaho, Univ of Alabama; *m* 3 Oct 1987, Peter Conor McColgan, *qv*, s of Thomas McColgan, of Strabane, NI; 1 da (Eilish Karen b 25 Nov 1990); *Career* athlete; Gold medal 10,000m Cwlth Games 1986, UK 10,000m champion 1986, Silver medal World Cross Country Championships 1987, UK 5000m champion 1988, Grand Prix winner 5000m 1988, Silver medal 10,000m Olympic Games 1988, Silver medal 3000m Indoor World Championships 1989, UK 3000m champion 1989 and 1992, Bronze medal 3000m and Gold medal 10,000m Cwlth Games 1990, Gold medal 10,000m World Championships 1991, Bronze medal World Cross Country Championships 1991, winner NY Marathon 1991, winner Co Durham Cross Country Int 5000m 1991, winner IAAF World Half-Marathon Championship 1992, winner London Marathon (2hrs 27mins 54secs) 1996; world record holder 5000m on roads and indoor, world record holder 10,000m on roads, nat 5000m and 10,000m record holder; Sportswriters' Athlete of the Year 1988 and 1991, BBC Sports Athlete of the Year 1988, BBC Sports Personality of the Year 1991; granted Freedom of Tuscaloosa Alabama 1986; sports devpt offr Dundee CC; *Recreations* cooking, cinema, crosswords, my dogs; *Style*— Mrs Liz McColgan, MBE; ✉ c/o Park Associates Ltd, 6 George Street, Nottingham NG1 3BE (☎ 0115 948 3206, fax 0115 952 7203)

McCOLGAN, Peter Conor; s of Thomas McColgan, of Strabane, NI, and Maree, *née* O'Connor; *b* 20 Feb 1963; *Educ* Christian Brothers' Sch Omagh, Ricks Jr Coll Idaho, Univ of Alabama; *m* 3 Oct 1987, Liz McColgan, *qv*, da of Martin Lynch; 1 da (Eilish Karen b 25 Nov 1990); *Career* athletics competitor and coach; memb Dundee Hawkhill Harriers; achievements at 3000m steeplechase incl: semi-finalist World Championships Tokyo 1991, seventh Cwlth Games Edinburgh 1986, UK champion 1991, third AAA Championship 1991; holder N Ireland 3000m steeplechase record (8:27:93) Holland 1991; *Recreations* music, golf; *Style*— Peter McColgan, Esq; ✉ c/o Park Associates Ltd, 6 George Street, Nottingham NG1 3BE (☎ 0115 948 3206, fax 0115 952 7203)

McCOLL, Ian; CBE (1983); s of John McColl (d 1947), of Glasgow, and Sarah Isabella McColl (d 1968), of Bunessan, Isle of Mull; descends from the McColls of Mull; *b* 22 Feb 1915; *Educ* Hillhead HS Glasgow; *m* 1968, Brenda, da of Thomas McKean (d 1949), of Glasgow; 1 da (Elaine b 1970); *Career* served RAF WWII in air crew Coastal Cmd 202 Sqdn (despatches 1945); chm Scottish Express Newspapers Ltd 1975–82, dir Express Newspapers 1971–82; ed: Daily Express 1971–74, Scottish Daily Express 1961–71 (joined 1933); former memb: Press Cncl, Gen Assembly Bd of Pubns; vice pres Newspaper Press Fund 1981–; contested (Lib) Dumfries-shire 1945, Greenock 1950; former session clerk Sandyford-Henderson Meml Church of Scotland and former memb Presbytery of Glasgow and Synod of Clydesdale; chm: Media Div Cwlth Games (Scotland) 1986, Saints and Sinners Club of Scotland 1981; Bank of Scotland's Scottish Press Life Achievement Award 1993; memb Inst of Journalists; *Style*— Ian McColl, Esq, CBE; ✉ 12 Newlands Rd, Glasgow G43 2JB

McCOLL OF DULWICH, Baron (Life Peer UK 1989); Ian McColl; s of Frederick George McColl (d 1985), of Dulwich, and Winifred Edith, *née* Murphy (d 1984); *b* 6 Jan 1933; *Educ* Hutchesons' GS Glasgow, St Paul's, Univ of London (MB BS, MS); *m* 27 Aug 1960, Dr Jean Lennox, 2 da of Arthur James McNair, FRCS, FRCOG (d 1964), of London; 1 s (Dr Hon Alastair James b 25 July 1961), 2 da (Dr Hon Caroline Lennox b 19 Aug 1963, Hon Mary Alison b 9 Oct 1966); *Career* surgn to St Bartholomew's Hosp London and sub dean Med Coll 1967–71, prof of surgery at Guy's Hosp 1971–, dir surgery Guy's Hosp 1985–, chm Dept of Surgery United Med and Dental Schs of Guy's and St Thomas's Hosps 1987–; hon conslt surgn to British Army 1984–; Parly private sec to PM 1994–, dep speaker House of Lords 1994–; chm Bd of Govrs Mildmay Mission Hosp 1994– (pres 1985–94), vice chm Disablement Services Authy 1987–91; pres: Soc of Minimally Invasive Surgery 1991–94, Limbless Assoc (formerly Nat Assoc of Limbless Disabled), Assoc of Endo Surgns of Great Br and Ireland 1994–; vice pres John Grooms Soc for the Disabled; memb Cncl Royal Coll of Surgns 1986–94; Freeman City of London; Liveryman of Worshipful Co of Apothecaries 1979; Warden Worshipful Co of Barber Surgeons 1996 (Liveryman 1986, past memb Ct); FRCS, FACS, FRCSE; *Books* Intestinal Absorption in Man (jtly, 1975), NHS Data Book (jtly, 1983); *Recreations* forestry; *Style*— The Rt Hon the Lord McColl of Dulwich; ✉ 10 Downing Street, London SW1

McCOMB, Dr Janet Mary; da of Samuel Gerald McComb, of 3 New Forge Grange, Belfast, and Mary Clarke; *b* 22 Aug 1951; *Educ* Queen's Univ of Belfast (MB BCh, BAO, MD); *Career* clinical and res fell Harvard Med Sch and Massachusetts Gen Hosp 1983–86, conslt cardiologist Univ of Newcastle upon Tyne 1986– (sr lectr 1986–90); memb: Br Cardiac Soc, Br Pacing and Electrophysiology Gp, Assoc of Physicians; FRCP; *Style*— Dr J M McComb; ✉ Cardiac Department, Freeman Hospital, Newcastle upon Tyne NE7 7DN (☎ 0191 284 3111, fax 0191 213 1968)

McCOMB, Leonard; *b* 1930; *Educ* Manchester Sch of Art, Slade Sch of Art; *Career* artist; taught at various art colls (incl Oxford Poly Brookes Univ, RA, Slade, Goldsmiths and John Cass) 1960–89, fndr Sunningwell Sch of Art Oxon 1977, fndr Vincent Soc of Drawing 1990; destroyed most of work up to 1976; cmmnd through Art for Work to paint 3 oil paintings of Kennecott Utah (USA) copper mines for RTZ London offices 1995; keeper of the Royal Acad 1995–; RA 1990 (ARA 1987), fell Royal Soc of Painter Printmakers 1994; *Exhibitions* incl: Human Clay (Arts Cncl) 1976, British Painting 1952–77 (RA) 1977, British Art Show (Arts Cncl touring), Venice Biennale - Painters of the 80's 1980, British Scupture in the Twentieth Century (Whitechapel Art Gallery London) 1981, British Drawing Hayward Annual (Hayward Gallery) 1983, Leonard McComb Drawings, Paintings and Sculpture (Arts Cncl touring exhbn orgnd by Museum of Modern Art Oxford) 1983, Hard Won Image (Tate) 1984, Human Interest: 50 Years of British Art (Corner House Manchester) 1985, Representation Abroad (Hirschhorn Museum Washington DC) 1986, Flowers in the Twentieth Century (Stoke on Trent City Museum touring) 1986, Large Watercolours and Drawings (Raab Gallery Berlin) 1986, Viewpoint Selection of British Art (Museum of Modern Art Brussels) 1987, It's a Still Life (Plymouth City Museum and Art Gallery and tour) 1989, RA - Portraits Friends Room Exhbn 1989, various exhbns Gillian Jason Gallery London 1989–, Images of Paradise (Christie's London) 1990, The Discerning Eye (Mall Galleries London) 1992, The Sussex Scene (Hove and Eastbourne) 1993, Singer and Friedlander/Sunday Times watercolour competition (Mall Galleries) 1993, Drawings and Paintings (Browse & Darby London) 1993, Drawing on these Shores (mixed travelling exhbn) 1993–94, Browse and Darby Gallery London 1994, Open House exhbn (Kettles Yard Cambridge) 1995; *Public Collections* Arts Cncl, Birmingham City Art Gallery, British Cncl, Contemporary Arts Soc, Manchester Art Gallery, Swindon Art Gallery, Tate Gallery London, Univ of Cambridge, V&A, Worcester Museum and Art Gallery, Towner Art Gallery Eastbourne; cmmnd to produce tapestry design (woven at Edinburgh Weavers) for Boots Chemists Nottingham; *Awards* Jubilee Prize RA 1977, Korn Ferry Prize RA 1988, second prize Singer and Friedlander/Sunday Times watercolour competition 1993, second prize Singer & Friedlander/Sunday Times watercolour prize 1994; *Style*— Leonard McComb, Esq, RA; ✉ c/o Gilliam Jason Gallery, 42 Inverness Street, London NW1; Browse and Darby, 19 Cork Street, London W1X 2LP (☎ 0171 734 7984)

McCOMBE, Richard George Bramwell; QC (1989); s of Barbara Bramwell McCombe, *née* Bramwell (d 1969); *b* 23 Sept 1952; *Educ* Sedbergh, Downing Coll Cambridge (MA); *m* 1 (m dis 1986), m 2, 1986, Carolyn Sara, da of Robert Duncan Birrell, of Limpsfield, nr Oxted, Surrey; 1 s (Duncan b 4 April 1987), 1 da (Tamara b 20 Nov 1989); *Career* called to the Bar Lincoln's Inn 1975 (bencher 1996); first jr counsel to Dir Gen of Fair Trading 1987–89 (second jr counsel 1982–87), DTI inspr into the affrs of Norton Group plc (with J K Heywood, FCA) 1991–92 (report published 1993), recorder of the Crown Ct 1996– (asst recorder 1993–96); Attorney-Gen of the Duchy of Lancaster and Attorney and Serjeant within the County Palatine of Lancaster 1996–; memb: Ctee London section Old Sedberghian Club, Senate Inns of Ct and Bar Cncl 1981–86, Bar Cncl Ctees 1986–89 (chm Young Barristers' Ctee 1983–84), Bar Representation Ctee Lincoln's Inn 1992–96, Bar Cncl 1995– (vice chm Int Rels Ctee 1995–); head UK Delgn to the Cncl of the Bars and Law Socs of the EC; *Recreations* various sporting interests, travel, flying light aircraft; *Clubs* RAC, MCC, Lancs CCC, London Scottish FC, Harlequin FC; *Style*— Richard McCombe, Esq, QC; ✉ 13 Old Square, Lincoln's Inn, London WC2A 3UA (☎ 0171 404 4800, fax 0171 405 4267)

McCONACHIE, Neil Alexander; s of John and Margaret McConachie, of Lossiemouth; *b* 23 May 1950; *Educ* Fettes Coll Edinburgh, Robert Gordon's Univ Aberdeen (BSc), Univ of Strathclyde Glasgow (MSc); *m* 1974, Judy, da of Jack McLennan; 1 s (Iain b 1981), 1 da (Catriona b 1984); *Career* pharmacist: NHS 1974–75 and 1976–78, Wellcome Fndn 1976–78, DuPont 1982–95 (various posts UK and overseas); gen mangr Argyll and Clyde Health Bd 1995–; memb Royal Pharmaceutical Soc of GB 1975; *Recreations* golf, travel; *Clubs* MCC, Moray Golf; *Style*— Neil McConachie, Esq; ✉ Argyll and Clyde Health Board, Ross House, Hawkhead Road, Paisley PA2 7BN (☎ 0141 842 7200)

McCONNACHIE, (John Sneddon) Iain; s of John Meek McConnachie, of Sale, Greater Manchester, and Charlotte Sneddon, *née* Christie (d 1984); *b* 11 March 1956; *Educ* Sale GS, Lymm GS, Oxford Poly (HND), Huddersfield Poly (Dip Mktg Studies); *m* 9 June 1979, Shirley Diane, da of Norman George Burgess (d 1983); 1 da (Sara Anne b 2 Feb 1985); *Career* mkting asst Zockoll Group 1977–78, asst advertising mangr Baxter Travenol 1978–79, American Express 1979–88 (mktg exec, mktg mangr, mktg dir), vice pres sales and mktg Chase Manhattan Bank 1988–91, md Financial Marketing Consultancy Group 1991–92, head of direct distribution Legal and General plc 1992–93, md Financial Marketing Consultancy Group 1993–; MInstM 1989; *Recreations* golf, photography, shooting; *Clubs* Castle Royle Golf; *Style*— Iain McConnachie, Esq

McCONNELL, Anthony Sudlow; s of Roderick Hugh McConnell (d 1950), and Cynthia Mary, *née* Faulkner; *b* 23 June 1941; *Educ* Abbey Sch Ramsgate, Downside; partner, Philippa Mary Harrison; 3 da (Charlotte Ella b 29 May 1972, Lucy Hannah b 10 Jan 1981, Alice Georgina b 19 March 1982), 1 s (William Roderick b 5 June 1975); *Career* articled clerk Creasey Son & Wickenden Tunbridge Wells, qualified CA 1964, audit sr Elles Reeve & Co 1964–65, gp chief acct Heinemann Gp of Publishers 1966–77; fin dir: Leisure Circle 1977–83, Pan Books Ltd 1983–88, Random House 1988–89, Yellow Advertising Newspaper Gp 1989–92; gp fin dir Random House 1992–; FCA 1974 (ACA 1964); *Recreations* music, walking; *Style*— Anthony McConnell, Esq; ✉ Random House UK Ltd, 20 Vauxhall Bridge Road, London SW1V 2SA (☎ 0171 973 9651, fax 0171 233 6115)

McCONNELL, Baron (Life Peer UK 1995), of Lisburn in the County of Antrim; (Robert William) Brian McConnell; PC (N Ireland 1964); s of Alfred Edward McConnell (d 1963), 2 s of Sir Robert John McConnell, 1 Bt; *b* 25 Nov 1922; *Educ* Sedbergh, Queen's Univ Belfast (BA, LLB); *m* 1951, Sylvia Elizabeth Joyce, da of late Samuel Agnew, of Belfast; 2 s (Hon Richard Alfred b 1955, Hon Samuel James b 1958), 1 da (Hon Helen Elizabeth b 1964); *Career* called to the Bar NI 1948, MP (U) S Antrim, min home affrs NI Govt 1964–66, NI Parl 1951–68; pres: Industl Ct 1968–88, Euro Movement in NI 1992–95 (vice chm 1987–92); *Clubs* Farmers, Ulster Reform (Belfast); *Style*— The Rt Hon Lord McConnell, PC; ✉ 50a Glenavy Road, Lisburn, Co Antrim, Northern Ireland BT28 3UT

McCONNELL, Charlie Stephen; s of Charles Harold McConnell (d 1993), and Elsie Amelia, *née* Hogben; *b* 20 June 1951; *Educ* Huyton Hill Sch Ambleside, Granby Park Sch Harrogate, Harrogate Coll of Further Educn, City of Birmingham Poly (BA), Paisley Coll of Technol (MPhil); *m* 28 April 1995, Natasha, *née* Smirnova; 1 adopted s (Timor b 1978), 1 da (Holly Isadora b 1995); *Career* community worker Dobroyd Community Sch Calderdale 1974–75, res worker (community educn) Scottish Local Govt Res Unit 1975–77, lectr Clydebank Coll of Further Educn 1975–77, head post grad community educn course Dundee Coll of Educn 1977–84 (joined as lectr), sr policy devpt offr (consumer educn) Nat Consumer Cncl London 1984–87, dep dir Action Resource Centre London 1987–88, dir public affairs and Euro progs Community Devpt Fndn London 1988–93, exec dir Scottish Community Educn Cncl 1993–; nat sec UK Consumers' Congress 1985–87, vice pres Euro Social Action Network 1991–93; Parly candidate 1983; *Books* Community Worker as Politiciser of the Deprived (1977), Deprivation, Participation and Commmunity Action (et al, 1979), Community Education and Community Development (ed, 1982), Post 16: Continuing Education in Scotland (ed, 1984), Consumer Action and Community Development (ed, 1988), Towards a Citizen's Europe (ed, 1990), Community Development in Europe (ed, 1992), Community Development and Urban Regeneration (ed, 1993), Community Education in Scotland - The making of an empowering profession (ed 1995); *Recreations* fell walking; *Style*— Charlie McConnell, Esq; ✉ Scottish Community Education Council, Roseberry House, 9 Haymarket Terrace, Edinburgh EH12 5EZ (☎ 0131 313 2488, fax 0131 313 6800)

McCONNELL, Prof (James) Desmond Caldwell; s of Samuel David McConnell (d 1976), of Magheragall, NI, and Cathleen, *née* Coulter; *b* 3 July 1930; *Educ* Wallace HS Lisburn, Queen's Univ Belfast (BSc, MSc), Univ of Cambridge (MA, PhD); *m* 14 July 1956, Jean Elspeth, da of John Jackson Ironside (d 1975), of Wimborne, Dorset; 1 s (Craig b 1 July 1957), 2 da (Deirdre b 19 May 1959, Elspeth b 3 Nov 1960); *Career* Univ of Cambridge: demonstrator in Mineralogy 1955–60, lectr in mineralogy 1960–72, fell Churchill Coll 1962–82, reader in mineralogy 1972–82, Schlumberger/Cambridge res head of Rock Physics Dept 1983–86, extraordinary fell Churchill Coll 1983–87; emeritus prof of physics and chemistry of minerals Univ of Oxford 1995– (prof 1986–95); St Hugh's Coll Oxford: professorial fell 1986–95, hon fell 1995–; Humboldt Prize 1996; FRS 1987; *Books* Principles of Mineral Behaviour (with Andrew Putnis, 1980); *Recreations* choral singing, vernacular architecture; *Style*— Prof Desmond McConnell, FRS; ✉ 8 The Croft, Old Headington, Oxford OX3 9BU (☎ 01865 69100); Department of Earth Sciences, Parks Rd, Oxford (☎ 01865 272043)

McCONNELL, John; s of Donald McConnell (d 1982), and Enid, *née* Dimberline (d 1967); *b* 14 May 1939; *Educ* Borough Green Secdy Mod Sch Kent, Maidstone Coll of Art Kent (Nat Dip); *m* 1 March 1963, Moira Rose, da of William Allan Macgregor; 1 s (Sam b 20 Feb 1966), 1 da (Kate b 1 Feb 1969); *Career* designer; own practice 1963–74, co-fndr Face Photosetting 1967; ptnr Pentagram 1974–; D&AD Assoc President's Award for outstanding contrib to design 1985; ed Pentagram Papers 1975–; memb: PO Stamp Advsy Ctee, CNAA; RDI 1987; *Books* Living By Design (jtly, 1978), Ideas on Design (jtly, 1986); *Recreations* cookery, building; *Style*— John McConnell, Esq; ✉ 42 Bassett Rd, London W10 6JL (☎ 0171 912 0713); Pentagram Design Ltd, 11 Needham Rd, London W11 2RP (☎ 0171 229 3477, fax 0171 727 9932)

McCOOMBE, Gordon Malcolm; OBE (1989); s of Francis Herbert McCoombe (d 1928), and Dora Warren, *née* Brooke (d 1987); *b* 18 March 1929; *Educ* Royal Hospital Sch, various colls (ONC, HNC); *m* Dec 1954, Margaret Rose Compton; 2 da (Lynne Julie b 1955, Jill Lesley b 1958), 1 s (Andrew Malcolm b 1956, d 1984); *Career* RN Aircraft Artificer apprentice 1944–48, served RN 1948–59, A V Roe & Co (tech rep MOD trials of Vulcan Mark 2 bomber) 1959–65, served MOD 1965–89 (i/c flight trials numerous mil aircraft, head of Tornado engrg assessment and its engrg and armament section); memb Cncl: SLAET 1964–87 (pres 1986–87), RAeS 1987–95 (pres 1991–92); Engrg Cncl: memb Nominations Ctee 1983–, memb EGC5 1983–95 (chm 1994–95), memb Bd of Engrg Regulation 1994–, memb Senate 1996– Dec 1997; fell SLAET 1963 (memb 1958), MIMechE 1967, FRAeS 1987; *Publications* author of numerous classified flight trials reports 1965–89; *Recreations* travel, walking, gardening; *Style*— Gordon McCoombe, Esq, OBE; ✉ c/o Engineering Council, 10 Maltravers Street, London WC2R 3ER

McCORKELL, (Henry) Nigel Pakenham; s of Capt Barry Henry McCorkell (d 1948), and Nina Florence Kendal, *née* Gregory; *b* 9 Jan 1947; *Educ* Wellington Coll, City of London Poly; *m* 12 Sept 1973, Lesley Joan, da of Ernest Rowley, of Southwold, Suffolk; 1 s (Marcus b 1981), 2 da (Clare b 1975, Emma b 1977); *Career* CA; trained Thornton Baker 1968–72; fin dir KCA International plc 1977–78, asst divnl dir Nat Enterprise Bd 1979–81, fin dir FR Group plc 1981–83; Meggitt PLC: fin dir 1984–91, md 1991–95, dep chm 1995–96; currently chm Cork Industries Ltd; non-exec chm John Cleland & Sons Group Ltd; non-exec dir: The Microsystems Group plc 1984–88, Poole Hosp Tst 1991–, McKechnie plc 1993–; govr Bournemouth Univ (chm Fin Ctee); CIMgt; FCA; *Recreations* golf, skiing, fishing; *Clubs* MCC; *Style*— Nigel McCorkell, Esq; ✉ Cork Industries Ltd, 45 Berkeley Street, London W1A 1EB (☎ 0171 290 8356, fax 0171 290 8357)

MacCORKINDALE, Simon Charles Pendered; s of Gp Capt Peter Bernard MacCorkindale, OBE, and Gilliver Mary, *née* Pendered; *b* 12 Feb 1952; *Educ* Haileybury; *m* 1, 10 July 1976 (m dis), Fiona Elizabeth Fullerton, *qv*; m 2, 5 Oct 1984, Susan Melody (*see* Susan George), da of Norman Alfred George; *Career* actor, producer, writer and director; dir: Amy International Productions; memb: Dirs' Guild of America, Screen Actors' Guild, British Actors' Equity, American Equity, Acad of Motion Pictures Arts and Scis, The British Acad of Film & TV Arts; *Television* series incl: Manimal 1983, Falcon Crest 1984–86, Counterstrike 1990–93 (also prodr); films for TV incl: Jesus of Nazareth 1975, Quatermass 1978, Visitor from the Other Side 1980, The Manions of America 1980–81, Falcon's Gold 1982, Obsessive Love 1984, Sincerely Violet 1986, The House That Mary Bought (prodr/writer/dir), The Way to Dusty Death 1994, At The Midnight Hour 1995; *Films* incl: Juggernaut 1974, Road to Mandalay 1977, Death on the Nile 1977, The Riddle of the Sands 1978, The Quatermass Conclusion 1978, Cabo Blanco 1979, The Sword and the Sorcerer 1982, Jaws 3D 1983, Stealing Heaven (prodr) 1987, That Summer of White Roses (prodr and writer) 1988; *Recreations* tennis, skiing, music, writing, photography; *Clubs* St James's; *Style*— Simon MacCorkindale, Esq; ✉ Amy International Productions, PO Box 17, Towcester, Northants NN12 8YJ (☎ 01784 483131/3288, fax 01784 483812)

MacCORMACK, Prof Geoffrey Dennis; s of Capt Douglas Muns MacCormack (d 1946), and Kathleen Edith, *née* Peacock; *b* 15 April 1937; *Educ* Parramatta HS Sydney, Univ of Sydney (BA, LLB), Univ of Oxford (MA, DPhil); *m* 25 June 1965, Sabine Gabriele, da of Alfred Oswalt, of Frankfurt; 1 da (Catherine b 3 May 1970); *Career* prof of jurisprudence Univ of Aberdeen 1971–96; *Recreations* walking; *Style*— Prof Geoffrey MacCormack; ✉ 69 Don Street, Old Aberdeen, Aberdeen AB24 1UJ (☎ 01224 483784)

McCORMACK, Mark Hume; s of Ned Hume McCormack, and Grace Wolfe McCormack; *b* 6 Nov 1930; *Educ* Princeton Univ, William and Mary Coll (BA), Yale Univ Law Sch; *m* 1, 1954, Nancy Breckenridge; 2 s (Breck b 11 Dec 1957, Todd b 2 July 1960), 1 da (Leslie b 21 March 1966); m 2, 1 March 1986, Helen Elizabeth Nagelsen; *Career* Specialist 3 class Mil Police Corps; admitted Ohio Bar 1957, assoc in Arter Hadden Wykoff & Van Duzer 1957–63 (ptnr 1964); fndr pres (currently chm and chief exec offr) International Management Group 1962– (representing personalities in entertainment, classical music and sporting world, also organised the Pope's visit to GB 1982); commentator for televised golf; *Books* The World of Professional Golf (1967, 30 edn 1996), Arnie: The Evolution of a Legend (1967), The Wonderful World of Professional Golf (1973), What They Don't Teach You at Harvard Business School (1984), The Terrible Truth About Lawyers (1987), Success Secrets (1989), The 110 Per Cent Solution (1990), Hit The Ground Running (1993), Mark H McCormack on Negotiating (1995), Mark H McCormack on Selling (1995), Mark H McCormack on Managing (1995), Mark H McCormack on Communicating (1996); *Recreations* golf, tennis; *Clubs* Royal and Ancient Golf (St Andrews), Sunningdale Golf, Wentworth (Virginia Water), Annabel's; *Style*— Mark H McCormack, Esq; ✉ Chairman and Chief Executive Officer, International Management Group, Pier House, Strand on the Green, Chiswick, London W4 3NN (☎ 0181 233 5000, fax 0181 233 5001)

McCORMACK, Stephen John; s of Anthony McCormack, of Worthing, W Sussex, and Teresa, *née* Longworth; *b* 30 March 1957; *Educ* Worthing HS for Boys, Univ of Liverpool; *m* 13 Aug 1993, Eva Lopez i Ontiveros, da of Lluis Lopez i Paris, of Granollers, Barcelona; *Career* reporter Worthing Gazette and Herald 1979–81; BBC: reporter BBC Radio Stoke 1981–84, reporter then corr Parliamentary and Political Unit 1984–89, reporter BBC Radio News 1989–91, sports corr 1991–94, Berlin corr 1994; currently freelance broadcaster; *Recreations* squash, tennis, cricket; *Style*— Stephen McCormack, Esq; ✉ 38 Edith Road, London W14 9BB

MacCORMICK, Iain Somerled MacDonald; s of John MacDonald MacCormick (d 1961), of Glasgow, and Margaret Isobel, *née* Miller; bro of Prof Neil MacCormick, *qv*; *b* 28 Sept 1939; *Educ* Glasgow HS, Univ of Glasgow (MA); *m* 1, 31 March 1964 (m dis 1986), Micky Trefusis, da of Thomas Cogan Elsom (d 1974), of Inverness; 2 s (Angus b 1965, Duncan b 1966), 3 da (Marion b 1968, Annabel b 1970, Susan b 1976); m 2, 14 Sept 1988, Carole Burnett, da of George Edward Story, of Halifax; *Career* Capt Queen's Own Lowland Yeo (TA) 1957–67; asst princ teacher of history and econs Oban HS 1965–74; MP (SNP) Argyll 1974–79; sr nat account mangr British Telecommunications plc 1982–86, currently trade conslt The Bartering Co (UK) Ltd; cncllr Argyll and Bute Dist Cncl 1979–80, press offr SDP Scot 1982–84; *Recreations* rugby, sailing, local history; *Clubs* Brooks's; *Style*— Iain MacCormick, Esq

McCORMICK, John; s of Joseph McCormick (d 1977), and Roseann, *née* McNamara (d 1976); *b* 24 June 1944; *Educ* St Michael's Acad Irvine, Univ of Glasgow (MA, MEd); *m* 4 Aug 1973, Jean Frances, da of William Gibbons, of Kirkintilloch, Glasgow; 1 s (Stephen b 1980), 1 da (Lesley Anne b 1978); *Career* teacher St Gregory's Secdy Sch Glasgow 1968–70, educn offr BBC Sch Broadcasting Cncl for Scotland 1970–75, sr educn offr Scotland 1975–82, sec and head of info BBC Scotland 1982–87, sec of the BBC 1987–92, controller BBC Scot 1992–; memb: Glasgow Children's Panel 1972–77, Visiting Ctee Glenochil Young Offenders Instn 1979–85; vice-chm Youth-at-Risk Scotland 1985–92, chm Edinburgh Film Festival 1996– (memb Bd 1994–96), memb Ct Univ of Strathclyde 1996; *Style*— John McCormick, Esq; ✉ BBC, Broadcasting House, Glasgow G12 8DG (☎ 0141 330 2311, fax 0141 337 1674)

McCORMICK, John St Clair; *b* 20 Sept 1939; *Educ* St Paul's Cathedral Choir Sch, Sedbergh, Univ of Edinburgh Med Sch (MB ChB, FRCS); *m* 1964, Fiona Helen, *née* McLean; 2 s (Neil St Clair b 21 Oct 1967, Keith Graeme b 9 Feb 1972); *Career* conslt surgn: Dunfermline and W Fife Hosp 1974–79, Dumfries and Galloway Royal Infirmary 1979– (med dir 1994–); memb Cncl Royal Coll of Surgns of Edinburgh 1994–; memb Worshipful Co of Wax Chandlers and Tallow Makers 1963; memb: BMA 1964, Vascular Soc of GB and I 1976, Assoc of Surgns 1990; *Style*— John McCormick, Esq; ✉ Ivy

Cottage, Kirkpatrickdurham, Castle-Douglas DG7 3HG (☎ 01556 650245); Dumfries and Galloway Royal Infirmary, Bankend Road, Dumfries DG1 4AP (☎ 01287 246246 ext 3113)

MacCORMICK, Prof (Donald) Neil; s of John MacDonald MacCormick (d 1961), of Glasgow, and Margaret Isobel, *née* Miller; bro of Iain MacCormick, *qv*; *b* 27 May 1941; *Educ* HS Glasgow, Univ of Glasgow (MA), Balliol Coll Oxford (BA, MA), Univ of Edinburgh (LLD); *m* 6 Nov 1965 (m dis 1991), (Caroline) Karen Rona; 3 da (Janet b 1966, Morag b 1969, Sheena b 1971); m 2, 12 June 1992, Flora Margaret Milne; *Career* lectr in law Univ of St Andrews (Queen's Coll Dundee) 1965–67, fell Balliol Coll Oxford 1967–72, regius prof of public law and law of nature and nations Univ of Edinburgh 1972–; pres Soc of Public Teachers of Law 1983–84; memb: Broadcasting Cncl Scotland 1985–89, Nat Cncl SNP 1978–84, 1985–86 and 1989–94, ESRC 1995–; foreign memb Finnish Acad of Sciences and Letters 1974; memb Academia Europaea 1995; Hon LLD: Univ of Saarland 1994, Queen's Univ Kingston Ontario 1996; Juris Doctor hc Univ of Uppsala Sweden 1986; FRSE 1986, FBA 1986; *Books* The Scottish Debate (ed, 1970), Lawyers In Their Social Setting (ed, 1976), Legal Reasoning and Legal Theory (1978), HLA Hart (1981), Legal Right and Social Democracy (1982), An Institutional Theory of Law (with Ota Weinberger, 1986), The Legal Mind (ed with P Birks, 1986), Enlightenment, Rights and Revolution (ed with Z Barkowski, 1989), Interpreting Statutes (ed with R S Summers, 1991); *Recreations* piping, hill walking, sailing; *Clubs* Staff (Edinburgh); *Style*— Prof Neil MacCormick, FRSE, FBA; ✉ 19 Pentland Terrace, Edinburgh EH10 6HA (☎ 0131 447 7945); Centre for Law and Society, Faculty of Law, Univ of Edinburgh EH8 9YL (☎ 0131 650 2029, fax 0131 662 4902, telex 721442 UNIVED G, e-mail n.maccormick@ed.ac.uk)

McCORMICK, Sean Robert; s of late Lt-Col Robert McCormick, of Arundel, Sussex, and Letitia *née* Worsley; *b* 1 May 1950; *Educ* Alexandra GS Singapore, Chard Sch Somerset; *m* 22 Nov 1977, Zandra, da of Frederick William Hollick; 1 s (Liam b 1978), 1 da (Katy b 1984); *Career* Actg Pilot Offr RAF, aircrew trg RAF Henlow; assoc dir/broadcast Leo Burnett 1970–76, Kirkwood & Co advertising 1976–78, media dir and ptnr SJIP advertising 1978–84, dep md BBDO UK (formerly SJIP/BBDO), ptnr and bd account dir Horner Collis & Kirvan 1984, fndr ptnr Juler McCormick West 1987, communications devpt dir Geers Gross plc 1992, exec dir McCann Erickson 1993, managing ptnr Total Communication Partnership Ltd; dir: Fleet 2000 Ltd, Heritage Media Ltd, IMC Netwoek UK Ltd, Media Mats Ltd, Creative Midfield Ltd; *Recreations* motor racing, go karting, rugby, cricket, family life; *Clubs* BARC, RAC; *Style*— Sean McCormick, Esq; ✉ Windyridge, High Park Avenue, East Horsley, Surrey KT24 5DF

McCORQUODALE, Ian Hamilton; er s of Hugh McCorquodale, MC (d 1963), and Dame Barbara Cartland, DBE, *qv*; half-bro of Comtesse Raine de Chambrun, *qv*; *b* 11 Oct 1937; *Educ* Harrow, Magdalene Coll Cambridge; *m* 1970 (m dis 1993), Anna, *née* Chisholm; 2 da (Tara b 1971, Iona b 1973); *Career* former commercial and export mangr British Printing Corporation; chm Debrett's Peerage Ltd; ptnr Cartland Promotions 1976–; dir: Bellew Publishing Co Ltd, Camfield Estate Co Ltd, Cartland Productions Ltd, Castle Ashby Investments Ltd, Heritage Guides Ltd, Torrish Estates Co Ltd, Trio Publications Ltd; *Recreations* fishing, shooting, gardening, tennis; *Clubs* Boodle's, White's; *Style*— Ian McCorquodale, Esq; ✉ The Home Farm, Camfield Place, Hatfield, Hertfordshire AL9 6JE (☎ 01707 663014, fax 01707 663041)

McCORQUODALE, Lady (Elizabeth) Sarah Lavinia; *née* Spencer; eldest da of 8 Earl of Spencer, LVO, DL (d 1992), by his 1 w, Hon Frances Ruth Burke Roche, da of 4 Baron Fermoy; sis of Diana, Princess of Wales (*see* Royal Family); *b* 19 March 1955; *m* 1980, Neil Edmund McCorquodale, s of Alastair McCorquodale, and Rosemary, *née* Turnor, da of Lady Enid Vane (da of 13 Earl of Westmorland); 1 s (George b 1984), 2 da (Emily b 1983, Celia b 1989); *Career* extra lady-in-waiting to Diana, Princess of Wales; *Style*— The Lady Sarah McCorquodale; ✉ Grange Farm, Stoke Rochford, Grantham, Lincs NG33 3BD

McCOSH, Prof Andrew Macdonald; s of Rev Andrew McCosh (d 1970), of Dunblane, Scotland, and Margaret, *née* MacDonald (d 1968); *b* 16 Sept 1940; *Educ* Edinburgh Acad, Univ of Edinburgh (BSc), Univ of Manchester (MBA), Univ of Harvard (DBA); *children* 3 da; *Career* assoc prof of accounting Univ of Michigan 1966–71; prof of mgmnt accounting Manchester Business Sch 1971–85, prof of the orgn of industry and commerce Univ of Edinburgh 1986–95 (prof emeritus and univ fell in fin 1995–); MICAS 1963; *Books* Practical Controllership (1973), Management Decision Support Systems (1978), Developing Managerial Information Systems (1983), Organisational Decision Support Systems (1988); *Recreations* fishing, climbing, golf; *Clubs* Caledonian; *Style*— Prof Andrew McCosh; ✉ University of Edinburgh, 50 George Square, Edinburgh EH8 9JY (☎ 0131 650 3801, fax 0131 668 3053)

McCOSH OF HUNTFIELD, Lt Cdr Bryce Knox; JP (Lanark); s of Robert McCosh of Hardington, OBE, MC, WS, JP (d 1959), and Agnes Dunlop Knox; *b* 30 March 1920; *Educ* Loretto; *m* 1948, Sylvia Mary (d 1991, Lady of the Manors of Dacre, Dalemain and Barton, Patterdale and Martindale in the Co of Cumberland), da of Edward William Hasell of Dalemain, JP, DL (d 1972); 3 s (Edward b 1949, Robert b 1954, Andrew b 1955) and 1 s decd; *Career* Lt Cdr RNVR; WWII 1939–46 served: Atlantic, Channel Dieppe, Far East; formerly with Linen Thread Co, dir W & J Knox Ltd and others, sr ptnr S M Penney & Macgeorge stockbrokers (Glasgow, Edinburgh and London) 1956–76, hon pres Cncl Thistle Fndn; formerly: chm Thistle Tst, chm Biggar Museum Tst, dir Target Trust Managers (Scotland) Ltd, Rachan Investments Ltd; ret farmer; memb Royal Co of Archers (Queen's Body Guard for Scotland), Church of Scot Session Clerk; *Recreations* rural; *Style*— Lt Cdr Bryce McCosh of Huntfield, JP; ✉ Huntfield Estate Office, Biggar, Scotland ML12 6NA (☎ and fax 01899 220208); Dalemain Estate Office, Dacre, Penrith, Cumbria CA11 0HB (☎ 01768 486450, fax 01768 486223)

McCOURT, Graham Matthew; s of Matthew McCourt, of Wantage, Oxon, and Mary Elizabeth, *née* Major; *b* 17 Aug 1959; *Educ* Segsbury Secdy Modern Wantage; *m* 6 Jan 1985, Jane Deborah, da of John Dennis Manhood; 2 s (Thomas Matthew b 7 July 1985, Graham John b 3 April 1989); *Career* jockey; first ride Sept 1976, best season 1991/92 (102 winners), winner 921 races in Eng; winner: Breeders' Cup Chase America (richest steeple chase in world), Champion Hurdle and Gold Cup Steeple Chase; William Hill Golden Spurs Jockey of the Year 1990/91, Piper Hiedsick Jockey of the Year 1991/92; *Recreations* golf on a fine day, films on a rainy day; *Style*— Graham McCourt, Esq; ✉ Antwick Stud, Letcombe Regis, Wantage, Oxon OX12 9LH (☎ office 01235 764456, home 01235 764456, mobile 0374 870760)

McCOWAN, Rt Hon Lord Justice; Rt Hon Sir Anthony James Denys McCowan; PC (1989); s of John McCowan, MBE, of Georgetown, Br Guiana; *b* 12 Jan 1928; *Educ* Epsom, BNC Oxford; *m* 1961, Sue, da of Reginald Harvey, of Braiseworth Hall, Tannington, Suffolk; 2 s, 1 da; *Career* called to the Bar Gray's Inn 1951, QC 1972, recorder of the Crown Court 1972–81, judge of the High Court of Justice (Queen's Bench Div) 1981–89, presiding judge SE Circuit 1986–89 (ldr 1978–81), a Lord Justice of Appeal 1989–, Senior Presiding Judge of England and Wales 1991–95, bencher Gray's Inn 1980; memb: Parole Bd 1982–84, Crown Ct Rule Ctee 1982–88; *Style*— The Rt Hon Lord Justice McCowan; ✉ c/o Royal Courts of Justice, Strand, London WC2A 2LL

McCOWAN, David William Cargill; s of Sir David James Cargill McCowan, 2 Bt (d 1965); hp of bro, Sir Hew Cargill McCowan, 3 Bt, *qv*; *b* 28 Feb 1934; *m* 1 s (David b 1975), 1 da; *Style*— David McCowan, Esq

McCOWAN, Sir Hew Cargill; 3 Bt (UK 1934), of Dalwhat, Co Dumfries; s of Sir David James Cargill McCowan, 2 Bt (d 1965); *b* 26 July 1930; *Heir* bro, David William Cargill McCowan, *qv*; *Style*— Sir Hew McCowan, Bt

McCOWEN, Alec; CBE (1986, OBE 1972); *b* 26 May 1925; *Career* actor; *Theatre* Old Vic Co incl: Touchstone in As You Like It, Malvolio in Twelfth Night, Richard II, Mercutio in Romeo and Juliet, Antony and Cleopatra; RSC incl: Fool in King Lear, Comedy of Errors, The Representative, Elgar's Rondo 1993, The Tempest, The Cherry Orchard 1995; RNT incl: Double Bill, The Browning Version, Harlequinade, Equus (also NY), The Misanthrope (also NY), Fathers and Sons, Waiting For Godot, Dancing at Lughnasa (also Abbey Theatre Dublin, Phoenix Theatre); other prodn incl: Escapade, The Matchmaker, The Elder Statesman, Antony and Cleopatra (Ziefield Theatre NY), After the Rain (London and NY), Hadrian the Seventh (London and NY), The Philanthropist (London and NY), Pygmalion (Albery Theatre), Family Dance (Criterion), The Portage to San Cristobel of A.H. (Mermaid), The Cocktail Party (Bath and West End), St Mark's Gospel (Lamb's Theatre NY), The Heiress (Chichester Festival), Exclusive (Strand), A Single Man (Greenwich), Preserving Mr Panmure (Chichester), Caesar & Cleopatra (Greenwich), Someone to Watch Over Me (Hampstead and Booth Theatre NY) 1992; one man shows: Shakespeare, Cole and Co (Eng and America), Kipling (London and Broadway), St Mark's Gospel (Eng, America and Canada); dir: Definitely The Bahamas (Orange Tree Richmond), While The Sun Shines (Hampstead Theatre Club); *Television* incl: The Late Wife (LWT), Private Lives (BBC), Family Dance (ATV), Malvolio in Twelfth Night (BBC), Chorus in Henry V (BBC), All For Love (Granada), Mr Palfrey of Westminster (Thames), The Importance of Being Earnest (BBC), Dialogue in the Dark (BBC), Hunted Down (Thames), The War That Still Goes On (BBC), Maria's Child (BBC); *Film* incl: Frenzy, Travels With My Aunt, Stevie, Hanover Street, Never Say Never Again, The Assam Garden, Personal Services, Cry Freedom, The Age of Innocence 1992; *Awards* UK: Evening Standard Best Actor (Hadrian VII) 1968, Variety Club Best Actor (The Philanthropist) 1970 (The Misanthrope 1973 and The Portage to San Cristobel of A.H. 1982); USA: Tony nomination Best Actor (Hadrian VII) 1969 (also NY Drama League Award Best Actor 1969), Tony nomination Best Actor (The Philanthropist) 1971, Golden Globe nomination Best Actor (Travels With My Aunt) 1972, Tony nomination Best Actor (St Mark's Gospel) 1980; *Style*— Alec McCowen, Esq, CBE; ✉ c/o Conway van Gelder Robinson Ltd, 18–21 Jermyn Street, London SW1Y 6HP (☎ 0171 287 0077, fax 0171 287 1940)

McCOY, Hugh O'Neill; s of Hugh O'Neill McCoy, and Nora May, *née* Bradley; *b* 9 Feb 1939; *Educ* Dudley GS, Univ of London; *m* Margaret Daphne, da of Robert John Corfield; *Career* currently: md Horace Clarkson plc, chm H Clarkson & Co Ltd, vice chm Baltic Exchange; non-exec dir Gartmore Korea Fund plc; pres Inst of Chartered Shipbrokers 1992–94; specially elected memb Gen Cncl Lloyd's Register of Shipping; memb Cncl: Project Tst (Isle of Coll), United World Coll of the Atlantic; memb London Fundraising Ctee Missions to Seamen; hon vice pres Maritime Vol Serv; Freeman City of London, Liveryman Worshipful Co of Shipwrights; memb Lloyd's; FICS; *Style*— Hugh O'Neill McCoy, FICS; ✉ H Clarkson & Co Ltd, 12 Camomile St, London EC3A 7BP (☎ 0171 334 3125, fax 0171 626 4700)

McCOY, Sylvester; s of Percy James Kent-Smith (d 1943), and Molly Sheridan (d 1969); *b* 20 Aug 1943; *Educ* Blair's Coll Aberdeen, Dunoon GS; *m* Agnes, da of Tenn Verkaik; 2 s (Sam Kent-Smith b 19 Feb 1976, Joe Kent-Smith b 6 Nov 1977); *Career* actor; played Spoons with London Concert Orch at Barbican Hall; *Theatre* incl: Ken Campbell's Roadshow, theatre workshop with Joan Littlewood, title role in The Pied Piper (NT), Feste in Twelfth Night (Leicester), Tranio in The Taming of The Shrew and Pompey in Antony and Cleopatra (Haymarket), Stephano in The Tempest (Ludlow Festival), Puck in Benjamin Britten's A Midsummer Night's Dream (WNO), Asdak in Caucasian Chalk Circle (Young Vic), Androcles in Androcles and the Lion, Stan Laurel in Gone With Hardy (London and Toronto), Burt in I Miss My War, Satie in Adrian Mitchell's Satiesday Night, Bix in Hoagy Bix and Wolfgang Beethoven Bunkhaus, all the other parts in Can't Pay Won't Pay (Criterion), Pinnochio in Abracadabra (Lyric), Samuel in Pirates of Penzance (Drury Lane), Genie in Aladdin (Palace Theatre Manchester), The Devil in Temptation (Westminster Theatre), Good Robber in Babes in the Wood (Cambridge Arts), Count in Rajad Bolt's trans of Marriage of Figaro (Watford), The Government Inspector (Tricycle Theatre, Kilburn) 1994; *Television* incl: Vision On (BBC), Tiswas (Central TV), Big Jim and The Finger Club (BBC), Eureka (BBC), Starstrider (Granada), Dr Who (BBC), What's Your Story (BBC), Last Place on Earth (ITV); *Radio* incl: Big Jim and the Figaro Club, The Shiver Show, Play For Radio 3; *Films* incl: Dracula, The Secret Policeman's Ball, 3 Kinds of Heat; *Recreations* contemplating cycling, walking and yachting; *Clubs* Groucho; *Style*— Sylvester McCoy, Esq; ✉ Silvester Management, 122 Wardour Street, London W1V 3LA (☎ 0171 734 7232)

McCRACKEN, Guy; *Career* jt md i/c Food Div Marks and Spencer plc 1994– (previously exec dir foods); dir CORDA; *Style*— Guy McCracken, Esq; ✉ Marks and Spencer plc, Michael House, Baker Street, London W1A 1DN (☎ 0171 935 4422)

McCRACKEN, John Strachan; CBE (1986); s of Robert Ralston McCracken (d 1959), and Susan Dorian Strachan; *b* 5 July 1930; *Educ* Beath HS, Univ of Edinburgh (BSc); *m* 1, 1954, Margaret Boswell Smith (d 1984), da of George Allan Buchan (d 1961); 2 da (Margaret Anne b 1955, Suzanne b 1957), 1 s (Ralston b 1959); m 2, 1988, Moira Ann, da of late Eric Stein, of Westchester, USA; *Career* Lt RN 1953–56; IBM UK Ltd 1956; dir: IBM Scotland and N England 1980–85, Int Business Machines Ltd 1980–86, Scot Endeavour Trg 1983–85, Scot Nat Orch 1985–91, Scott Lithgow Ltd 1984–88, IBM Communications 1985–89, IBM UK Ltd 1986–89, Ewbank Preece 1988–91, Pan World Travel 1989–91; memb: Bd Scot Devpt Agency 1980–86, BR (Scotland) 1984–89; chm Exec Cncl Scot Business in the Community 1982–86; tstee: Nat Museums of Scot 1985–91, Soc of Scot Artists 1984–91; memb Cncl: Edinburgh Festival 1985–91, Scot Enterprise Fndn 1981–85, Scot Graduate Enterprise 1981–85; Liveryman Worshipful Co of Makers of Playing Cards; *Recreations* golf, art, music, cricket; *Clubs* Caledonian, Bruntsfield Links, MCC, New (Edinburgh), Hon Co of Edinburgh Golfers; *Style*— John S McCracken, Esq, CBE

McCRAE, Dr (William) Morrice; s of William Boyd McCrae (d 1982), of Kilmarnock, and Jean Alexandra, *née* Morrice; *b* 11 March 1932; *Educ* Kilmarnock Acad, Univ of Glasgow (MB ChB); *m* 28 March 1987, Jennifer Jane, da of John Graham (d 1985), of Aberdour, Fife; *Career* Capt RAMC 1955–57; Hall fell in med Univ of Glasgow; lectr in child health Univ of Glasgow, conslt physician Royal Hosp for Sick Children Edinburgh 1965; hon sr lectr Univ of Edinburgh, author of pubns on genetics and gastroenterology; ret; MB, MSc, FRCPE, FRCP Glasgow; *Recreations* gardening, history; *Clubs* New (Edinburgh), Scottish Art; *Style*— Dr Morrice McCrae; ✉ Seabank House, Aberdour, Fife KY3 1TY (☎ 01383 860452)

McCREA, Rev Dr (Robert Thomas) William; MP (UDUP) Mid-Ulster (majority 6,187); s of Robert Thomas McCrea, and Sarah Jane, *née* Whann; *b* 6 Aug 1948; *Educ* Cookstown HS, Theological Hall Free Pres Church of Ulster; *m* 25 June 1971, Anne Shirley, da of George McKnight (d 1983), of Rathfriland, Co Down; 2 s (Ian b 1976, Stephen b 1978), 3 da (Sharon b 1973, Faith b 1979, Grace b 1980); *Career* dist cncllr 1973– (chm 1977–81), memb NI Assembly 1982–85; MP (DUP) 1983–, DUP whip 1987–, spokesman on educn 1987–88, spokesman on health and social servs 1988–90, spokesman on security 1990–; gospel singer and recording artist (1 platinum, 3 gold and 1 silver discs), dir Daybreak Recordings Co; Hon DD 1989; *Recreations* riding;

Style— The Rev Dr William McCrea, MP; ✉ 11 Ballyronan Road, Magherafelt, Co Londonderry BT45 6BP (office ☎ 01648 32664, fax 01648 32035)

McCREA, Sir William Hunter; kt (1985); s of Robert Hunter McCrea (d 1956), of Chesterfield, and Margaret, *née* Hutton (d 1963); *b* 13 Dec 1904; *Educ* Chesterfield Sch, Trinity Coll Cambridge (MA, PhD, ScD), Göttingen Univ; *m* 1933, Marian Nicol Core (d 1995), da of Thomas Webster, JP (d 1939), of Edinburgh; 1 s (Roderick), 2 da (Isabella, Sheila); *Career* WWII Flt Lt Trg Branch RAFVR 1941–45, temp princ experimental offr Admty 1943–45; prof of mathematics: Queen's Univ Belfast 1936–44, Royal Holloway Coll London 1944–66; prof of astronomy Univ of Sussex 1966–72 (emeritus prof 1972–); pres: RAS 1961–63, Mathematical Assoc 1973–74; Freeman City of London 1988; FRSE 1931, MRIA 1938, FRS 1952; *Books* Relativity Physics (1935), Analytical Geometry of Three Dimensions (1942), Physics of the Sun and Stars (1950), Royal Greenwich Observatory (1975); *Style—* Sir William McCrea, FRS, FRSE; ✉ 87 Houndean Rise, Lewes, Sussex BN7 1EJ (☎ 01273 473296); Astronomy Centre, University of Sussex, Brighton BN1 9QH (☎ 01273 606755)

McCREDIE, Ian Forbes; OBE (1984); s of John Henry McCredie, and Diana, *née* Harris; *b* 28 Dec 1950; *Educ* Harvey GS, Churchill Coll Cambridge (MA); *m* 20 March 1976 (m dis 1997), (Katharine) Lucy, da of Sir Robert John Frank, 3 Bt (d 1987), of Reading; 1 s (James b 1981), 1 da (Alexandra ' 1983); *Career* diplomat; Br High Cmmn Lusaka 1976–79, Br interests section Tehran 1981–83, Br Embassy Copenhagen 1985–89, FCO 1989–92, counsellor UK Mission to UN New York 1992–96, FCO 1997–; *Recreations* squash, ballet, rollerblading, theatre, food and drink; *Clubs* Yale; *Style—* Ian McCredie, Esq, OBE; ✉ c/o FCO, King Charles St, London SW1A 2AH

McCRICKARD, Donald Cecil (Don); *b* 25 Dec 1936; *Career* fin, mktg and gen mgmnt appts until 1975; American Express Co 1975–83: chief exec American Express UK 1975–78, regnl vice pres American Express N Europe, ME and Africa 1978–79, sr vice pres American Express Corporate NY 1979–80, chief exec American Express Asia, Pacific and Australia 1980–83, dir American Express International Inc 1978–83; TSB Group plc 1983–92: chief exec UDT Holdings 1983–88, chief exec TSB Bank 1989–92, chief exec TSB Group 1990–92; chm Hill Samuel 1991–92, chm London Town plc 1995–; non-exec dir Carlisle Group plc 1993–96, non-exec dir National Counties Building Soc 1995–; non-exec chm TM Group Holdings plc 1996–; chm Barnet Enterprise Tst 1985–88; tstee: Crimestoppers Tst 1991–, Indust in Educn 1993–; FCIB; *Clubs* RAC; *Style—* Don McCrickard, Esq

MacCRINDLE, Robert Alexander; QC; s of Fergus R MacCrindle (d 1965), and Jean, *née* Hill (d 1976); *b* 27 Jan 1928; *Educ* Girvan HS, King's Coll London (LLB), Gonville and Caius Coll Cambridge (LLM); *m* 1959, Pauline Dilys, da of Mark S Morgan, of Berks; 1 s (Guy), 1 da (Claire); *Career* Flt Lt RAF 1948–50; called to the Bar Gray's Inn 1952 (bencher); in practice as commercial lawyer 1952–; memb Bar of Hong Kong, ptnr Shearman & Sterling NY, avocat au barreau de Paris; memb Royal Cmmn on Civil Liability; commercial and int arbitrator, memb City Disputes Panel; fell American Coll of Trial Lawyers; *Recreations* golf; *Clubs* Univ (NY); *Style—* R A MacCrindle, Esq, QC; ✉ 88 Ave de Breteuil, 75015 Paris, France (☎ 00 33 1 45 67 11 93); 114 Avenue de Champs-Elysées, 75008 Paris, France (☎ 00 33 1 53 89 7000)

McCRINDLE, Sir Robert Arthur; kt (1990); s of late Thomas Arthur McCrindle, of Girvan, Ayrs; *b* 1929; *Educ* Allen Glen's Coll Glasgow; *m* 1953, Myra, da of James P Anderson, of Glasgow; 2 s; *Career* MP (C): Billericay 1970–74, Brentwood and Ongar 1974–92; PPS to Min of State Home Office 1974, advsr to Br Caledonian Airways, conslt to Br Insur and Investmt Brokers' Assoc, chm Parly Aviation Gp; memb Select Ctees on: Trade and Indust 1983–87, Tport 1988–92; dir: Langham Life Assurance Co 1972–76, Worldmark Travel Ltd 1978–82, Hogg Robinson plc (non-exec) 1987–, M & G Assurance Group Ltd (non-exec), London & Edinburgh Insurance Group Ltd 1991–; chm: Cometco Ltd 1972–78, City Bond Storage plc 1986–91, Bradford and Bingley Building Society 1991–; *Style—* Sir Robert McCrindle; ✉ 26 Ashburnham Gdns, Upminster, Essex (☎ 01708 227152)

McCRIRRICK, Dr (Thomas) Bryce; CBE (1987); s of Alexander McCrirrick (d 1969), of Galashiels, Scotland, and Janet White, *née* Tweedie (d 1986); *b* 19 July 1927; *Educ* Galashiels Acad Scot, Heriot-Watt Univ Edinburgh, Regent St Poly London; *m* 1953, Margaret Phyllis, da of Walter Yates (d 1984); 3 s (Forbes Alexander b 1957, Alastair Bryce b 1959, Stuart Angus b 1963); *Career* BBC Radio Studio Centres Edinburgh, Glasgow and London 1943–46, served RAF 1946–49; BBC TV: joined 1949, engr i/c TV Studios 1963, head of engrg, TV recording and head Studio Planning and Installation Dept 1969, chief engr of radio bdcasting 1970, dir of engrg 1978–87 (asst dir 1971, dep dir 1976); currently non-exec business dir, conslt in UK and Far E 1987–; author of various tech papers on bdcasting engrg and mgmnt; tech assessor Clapham Junction Rail Accident Enquiry 1989; pres Soc of Electronic and Radio Technicians 1981–85 (vice pres 1979–80), vice pres IERE 1985–88, pres IEE 1988–89 (vice pres 1982–86, dep pres 1986–88, Hon FIEE); memb Cncl Royal Acad of Engrg 1989–92; govr Imperial Coll 1985–; Hon DSc Heriot-Watt Univ 1987 (memb Ct 1991–94); memb Senate Univ of London 1992–94; FRTS 1980, FEng 1981, FBKSTS 1982, FSMPTE 1989; *Recreations* skiing, theatre; *Style—* Dr Bryce McCrirrick, CBE, FEng; ✉ Surrey Place, Coach House Gardens, Fleet, Hampshire GU13 8QX (☎ 01252 623422)

McCRONE, Prof (Robert) Gavin Loudon; CB (1982); s of Robert Osborne Orr McCrone (d 1985), and Laura Margaret McCrone (d 1991); *b* 2 Feb 1933; *Educ* Stowe, St Catharine's Coll Cambridge (MA), Univ Coll of Wales Aberystwyth (MSc), Univ of Glasgow (PhD); *m* 27 June 1959, Alexandra Bruce Waddell, MBE; 2 s, 1 da; *Career* lectr Univ of Glasgow 1960–65, fell BNC Oxford 1965–70; Scottish Office: joined 1970, sec Indust Dept for Scotland 1980–87, sec Environment Dept 1987–92, chief economic advsr 1972–92; prof of applied economics Univ of Glasgow 1992–94; visiting prof Dept of Business Studies Univ of Edinburgh 1994–; memb Cncl: Royal Economic Soc 1977–82, Scottish Economic Soc 1982–91, ESRC 1986–89; memb Bd: Scottish Opera 1992–, Royal Infirmary of Edinburgh NHS Tst; hon fell Europa Inst 1992–; Hon LLD Univ of Glasgow 1986; FRSE 1982; *Books* The Economics of Subsidising Agriculture (1962), Agricultural Integration in Western Europe (1963), Scotland's Economic Progress 1951–60 (1965), Regional Policy in Britain (1969), Scotland's Future (1969), Housing Policy in Britain and Europe (with M Stephens, 1995); *Recreations* walking; *Clubs* United Oxford and Cambridge Univ; *Style—* Prof Gavin McCrone, CB, FRSE; ✉ Department of Business Studies, University of Edinburgh, 50 George Square, Edinburgh EH8 9JY (☎ 0131 650 4603, fax 0131 668 3053)

McCRORY, Glenn George; s of Brian McCrory, of Annfield Plain, Stanley, Co Durham, and Gloria, *née* Barrass; *b* 23 Sept 1964; *Educ* St Patrick's Dipton Co Durham, St Bede's Lanchester; *m* 1 June 1985, Amanda Teresa, da of Andrew Walsh, of Annfield Plain, Co Durham; 1 s (Joseph b 24 Oct 1990), 1 da (Victoria b 24 Nov 1985); *Career* boxer; formerly nat jr middleweight champion, young England rep (light-heavyweight), former undefeated British and Cwlth cruiserweight champion and IBF world cruiserweight champion; boxing commentator for Sky; made acting debut 1990; memb Equity; Boxing News Prospect of the Year 1985, Boxer of the Year 1989, NE Sports Personality 1989; *Recreations* sport, acting, reading; *Style—* Glenn McCrory, Esq; ✉ 35 Station Rd, Stanley, Co Durham

McCRUM, Michael William; CBE (1996); s of late Capt C R McCrum, RN, and Ivy Hilda Constance, *née* Nicholson; *b* 23 May 1924; *Educ* Sherborne, Corpus Christi Coll Cambridge (scholar, MA); *m* 1952, Christine Mary Kathleen, da of Sir Arthur fforde, GBE; 3 s, 1 da; *Career* WWII RN 1943–45 (Sub Lt RNVR 1943); asst master Rugby Sch 1948–50 (lower bench master 1949–50); Corpus Christi Coll Cambridge: fellow 1949, second tutor 1950–51, tutor 1951–62; headmaster: Tonbridge Sch 1962–70, Eton 1970–80; master Corpus Christi Coll Cambridge 1980–94; Univ of Cambridge: memb Council of the Senate 1955–58 and 1981–89, memb Gen Bd of Faculties 1957–62 and 1987–89, vice chllr 1987–89, memb Fin Bd 1985–89, chm Faculty Bd of Educn 1981–86 and 1990–93, chm Bd of Extra-Mural Studies 1982–86; chm: HMC 1974, Jt Educnl Tst 1984–87, GBA 1989–94 (dep chm 1982–89), Cathedrals Fabric Cmmn for England 1990–, Ind Schs Jt Cncl 1992–94; memb Governing Body Schools Cncl 1969–76; govr: Bradfield Coll 1956–62, Eastbourne Coll 1960–62, King's Sch Canterbury 1980–94, Sherborne Sch 1980–94, Oakham Sch 1981–85, United World Coll of the Atlantic 1981–94, Rugby Sch 1982–94; tstee: King George VI and Queen Elizabeth Fndn of St Catharine's Cumberland Lodge 1983–, Nat Heritage Meml Fund 1984–90; Hon Freeman Worshipful Co of Skinners 1980; Hon DEd Victoria BC 1989; Comendador de la Orden de Isabel la Católica (Spain) 1988; *Books* Select Documents of the Principates of the Flavian Emperors AD 68–96 (with A G Woodhead, 1961), Thomas Arnold - Headmaster (1989); *Clubs* Athenaeum, United Oxford & Cambridge University, East India, Devonshire, Sports and Public Schools, Hawks (Cambridge); *Style—* Michael McCrum, Esq, CBE; ✉ 32 Clarendon Street, Cambridge CB1 1JX (☎ 01223 353303)

McCRUM, (John) Robert; s of Michael William McCrum, of Cambridge, and Christine Mary Kathleen, *née* fforde; *b* 7 July 1953; *Educ* Sherborne, Corpus Christi Coll Cambridge (scholar, MA), Univ of Pennyslvania (Thouron fell); *m* 1, 1979 (m dis 1984), Olivia Timbs; m 2, 1995, Sarah Lyall; *Career* reader Chatto & Windus 1977–79, ed in chief Faber & Faber 1990–96 (editorial dir 1979–89), lit ed The Observer 1996–; *Books* In The Secret State (1980), A Loss of Heart (1982), The Fabulous Englishman (1984), The Story of English (non fiction, 1986, Peabody Award 1986, Emmy 1987), The World is a Banana (for children, 1988), Mainland (1991), The Psychological Moment (1992), Suspicion (1996); *Style—* Robert McCrum, Esq; ✉ The Observer, 119 Farringdon Road, London EC1R 3ER (☎ 0171 713 4445)

McCRYSTAL, Cal; s of Charles J McCrystal (d 1991), of Belfast, and Mary, *née* McKeown (d 1944); *b* 20 Dec 1935; *Educ* St Mary's Coll Dundalk, St Malachy's Coll Belfast; *m* 15 Oct 1958, Stella, da of John J Doyle; 3 s (Cal b 6 Aug 1959, Damien b 23 March 1961, Kieran b 18 Dec 1962); *Career* writer and journalist; reporter: Northern Herald Co Down 1955–56, Belfast Telegraph (also lab corr) 1956–64; Sunday Times 1964–89 (chief reporter, foreign corr, NY bureau chief, news ed, foreign features ed, dep foreign ed, sr foreign features and magazine writer); feature writer and columnist Independent on Sunday 1989–95, feature writer The Observer 1995–; runner-up Feature Writer of the Year Br Press Awards 1991, Mind Journalist of the Year 1994; *Books* Watergate: the full inside story (co-author, 1973); *Style—* Cal McCrystal, Esq; ✉ 94 Totteridge Lane, London N20 8JG (☎ 0181 445 6975); The Observer, 119 Farringdon Road, London EC1R 3ER (☎ 0171 287 2332)

McCRYSTAL, Damien Peter Adam Doyle; s of Cal C McCrystal, of London, and Stella Maris, *née* Doyle; *b* 23 March 1961; *Educ* Christ's Coll Finchley; *m* June 1990, Amanda, *née* Evans; 1 da (Jemima Cayley b 19 June 1995); *Career* news ed North London Advertiser Gp, dep ed PR Week, City corr London Evening Standard, asst City ed Today, City ed The Sun, freelance presenter What the Papers Say and Hard News, columnist New Law Journal, City Diary ed Daily Telegraph 1991–; *Style—* Damien McCrystal, Esq

McCUBBIN, Very Rev David; s of David McCubbin (d 1977), of Greenock, Strathclyde, and Annie Robertson Cram, *née* Young (d 1965); *b* 2 Nov 1929; *Educ* Finnart Sch Greenock, Greenock Acad, King's Coll London (AKC), St Boniface Coll Warminster; *Career* ordained Wells Cathedral: deacon 1955, priest 1956; curate Christ Church Frome 1955–57, curate Glastonbury Parish Church 1957–60; rector: Holy Trinity Dunoon 1960–63, St Peter's Kirkcaldy 1963–70, Wallsend Parish Church 1970–79 (surrogate Diocese of Newcastle 1970–79), St John's Aberdeen 1979–81, St Bride's Kelvinside Glasgow 1981–87, St Andrew's Millport 1987–94; provost and first canon Cumbrae Cathedral 1987–94 (hon canon 1994–), canon St John's Cathedral Oban 1987–94, synod clerk Diocese of Argyll and The Isles 1988–94; ed: Argyll & The Isles Diocesan Gazette 1960–63, Glasgow & Galloway Diocesan Gazette 1981–85; chm: Govrs Wallsend C of E Sch 1970–79, mangrs Wallsend C of E First Sch 1970–79, Prayer Book Soc (Scotland) 1988–91; tstee Cumbrae Cathedral and College 1994–; *Recreations* reading, music, walking; *Style—* The Very Rev David McCubbin; ✉ 137 Marlborough Avenue, Glasgow G11 7JE (☎ 0141 357 1553)

McCUE, Ian Roderick; s of John McCue, and Frances Mary, *née* Quantrill; *b* 24 May 1937; *Educ* Gravesend Tech Sch, SE London Tech Coll (HNC); *m* 1 April 1961, Stella Kathleen, da of Henry Battle; 1 s (Sean (decd)), 2 da (Jane b 1964, Sara b 1965); *Career* electrical engr; student apprentice Siemen Brothers Ltd 1953–59, co-fndr md Sarasota Automation Ltd 1966; dir: Sarasota Automation Inc USA 1978–90 (also pres), CEO Sarasota Technology plc 1982–88, Peek plc 1987–90; chm McCue plc 1990–; FIMgt, FID; *Recreations* sailing, flying, photography; *Clubs* The Field Club (Sarasota, Florida, USA), Royal Southern Yacht, Royal Southampton Yacht; *Style—* Ian R McCue, Esq; ✉ Parsonage Barn, Compton, Hampshire SO21 2AS (☎ 01962 713049)

McCULLOCH, James Russell; s of Dr John McCulloch, of Newlands, Glasgow, and Laura Patricia, *née* Russell; *b* 19 Nov 1954; *Educ* Glasgow Acad, Univ of Stirling (BA); *m* 16 Oct 1980, Sally Lindsay, da of Benjamin Butters; 3 da (Lindsay Anne b 17 July 1984, Victoria Jayne b 6 June 1986, Caroline Fiona b 12 April 1989); *Career* CA; articled clerk Coopers & Lybrand Glasgow 1976–79, audit mangr Coopers & Lybrand Houston Texas USA 1979–82, ptnr Speirs & Jeffrey 1985– (joined 1982); memb Stock Exchange 1985; memb Merchant House of Glasgow 1990; MICAS 1979; *Recreations* golf, squash, tennis, skiing; *Clubs* Glasgow Academical, Pollok Golf, Prestwick Golf; *Style—* James R McCulloch, Esq; ✉ 16 Calderwood Rd, Newlands, Glasgow G43 2RP (☎ 0141 637 1892)

McCULLOCH, Ken; s of Archie McCulloch, of Glasgow, and Kathleen McCulloch; *b* 7 Nov 1948; *Educ* Gresham's; *Career* hotelier; mgmnt trg British Transport Hotels 1965–69, mgmnt Stakis Hotels 1969–74, dir Chardon Hotels 1974–76; proprietor: Le Provencal Glagow 1976–, Charlie Parker's Glasgow 1976– and Edinburgh 1979–, Buttery Glasgow 1983–, Rogano Glasgow 1984–, One Devonshire Gardens 1986–; Mktg Award (British Airways) BBC Scotland 1991, Best Hotel in Scotland (Book of the Best) 1992, County Restaurant of the Year (Good Food Guide) 1992 and 1993, UK Hotelier of the Year 1993, Egon Ronay Hotel of the Year 1994, Michelin Star 1996; *Recreations* connoisseur of Scotland, cooking, Glasgow Rangers, motor racing; *Style—* Ken McCulloch, Esq; ✉ One Devonshire Gardens, Great Western Road, Glasgow G12 0UX (☎ 0141 339 2001, fax 0141 337 1663, car ☎ 0831 288131)

MacCULLOCH, Dr Malcolm John; s of William MacCulloch (d 1976), of Macclesfield, Cheshire, and Constance Martha, *née* Clegg; *b* 10 July 1936; *Educ* Kings Sch Macclesfield, Univ of Manchester (MB ChB, DPM, MD); *m* 1, 14 July 1962 (m dis 1975), Mary Louise, da of Ernest Sutcliffe Beton (d 1987), of Norwich; 1 s (Thomas Alistair b 1965), 1 da (Louise Elizabeth Mary b 1968); m 2, 24 Sept 1975, Carolyn Mary, da of Sqdn Ldr (William) Alan Walker Reid, of London; 2 da (Sarah Caroline b 1976, Sophie Isabel 1978); *Career* conslt child psychiatrist Cheshire 1966–67, lectr in child psychiatry and subnormality Univ of Birmingham 1967–70, sr lectr in psychiatry Univ of Liverpool 1970–75, sr princ med offr DHSS London 1975–79, med dir Park Lane Hosp Liverpool 1979–89, conslt WHO 1977–79, visiting prof of forensic psychiatry Toronto 1987–89, advsr in forensic psychiatry Ontario Govt 1987–92, sr res psychiatrist Ashworth Hosp Liverpool 1989–, sr med advsr Partnerships in Care Ltd 1994–; author of numerous pubns in professional jls; FRCPsych 1976; *Books* Homosexual Behaviour: Therapy and Assessment (1971), Human Sexual Behaviour (1980); *Recreations* music, golf, horse riding, inventing; *Style*— Dr Malcolm MacCulloch; ✉ 10 Abbotsford Rd, Blundellsands, Merseyside L23 6UX (☎ 0151 924 4989)

McCULLOCH, Dr Myra; da of Bryn Jones (d 1979), and Olwen Tegrudd Jones; *b* 19 April 1949; *Educ* Bedford Coll Univ of London (BSc), South Bank Poly (PGCE), Inst of Educn Univ of London (MSc(Econ)), Univ of Bristol (EdD); *m* (m dis); *Career* Haverstock Sch London NW1: asst teacher 1970–72, teacher 1972–73, head Dept of History and Social Scis 1973–76; pt/t temp lectr in social history City of London Poly 1977, research asst educn CNAA 1977–79; Bath Coll of HE: sr lectr in sociology 1979–83, princ lectr in educn 1983–84, head Faculty of Educn 1984–87; dep princ Bulmershe Coll 1987–89; Univ of Reading: head Dept of Educn Studies and Mgmnt 1989–92, dean Faculty of Educn and Community Studies 1992–95, pro-vice-chllr 1995–; pt/t lectr (hon title) Sch of Educn Univ of Bristol 1985–87; visiting prof Keene State Coll New Hampshire USA 1983, visiting lectr Sch of Educn Univ of Bristol 1994; memb Ed Bd: Jl of Teacher Training, Jl of Quality Assurance in Educn, Research in Post-Compulsory Educn; memb: Br Assoc for Teachers and Researchers in Overseas Educn, Br Educn Mgmnt Assoc, Br Sociological Assoc, Br Educational Research Assoc, Soc for Research in HE, Centre for the Study of Comprehensive Schs; govr: William Gray Jr Sch, Reading Adult Coll; FRSA 1992; *Books* School Experience in BEd/BEd(Hons) Degrees validated by the Council for National Academic Awards (1979), Improving Teacher Training? New Roles for teachers, schools and higher education (with Brian Fidler, 1994); also author of various book chapters and articles in learned jls; *Recreations* cooking, travel, detective fiction; *Style*— Dr Myra McCulloch; ✉ University of Reading, Bulmershe Court, Earley, Reading RG6 1HY (☎ 0118 9318865, fax 0118 9318873, e-mail emsmccul@reading.ac.uk)

McCULLOCH, Rt Rev Nigel Simeon; *see:* Wakefield, Bishop of

McCULLOUGH, Hon Mr Justice; Hon Sir (Iain) Charles Robert; kt (1981); *b* 1931; *Career* called to the Bar 1956, QC 1971, dep chm Notts Quarter Sessions 1969–71, recorder of the Crown Court 1971–81, judge of the High Court of Justice (Queen's Bench Div) 1981–; memb: Criminal Law Revision Ctee 1973–, Parole Bd 1984–86; *Style*— The Hon Mr Justice McCullough; ✉ c/o Royal Courts of Justice, Strand, London WC2A 2LL

McCULLOUGH, Dr John; s of Henry Christie McCullough, and Jessie, *née* Niven (d 1978); *b* 23 March 1949; *Educ* Model Sch Belfast, Paisley Coll of Technol, Portsmouth Poly (MSc, PhD); *m* 25 March 1971, Geraldine Mabel, da of Gerald Thomas Gardner; 1 s (Alexander b 1982), 2 da (Katherine b 1979, Eleanor b 1985); *Career* conslt engr (various appts in NI, Eng and Scot), expert witness in cases of litigation, arbitration and public inquiry in Scot, Eng and Netherlands; ptnr Hancox & Ptnrs 1982–88; dir: Rendel Hancox Ltd 1988–91, Rendel Palmer & Tritton (Scotland) Ltd 1991–; princ Cadogan Conslts 1992–; chm Scottish Region Inst of Energy 1984–85; CEng 1980, FInstE 1983, FIMechE 1986, Eur Ing 1988, MACE, MAE; *Recreations* music, walking, farming; *Clubs* Royal Over-Seas League; *Style*— Dr John McCullough; ✉ Dippany, Kilmacolm, Renfrewshire PA13 4TH (☎ and fax 01505 872895); Rendel Palmer & Tritton (Scotland) Ltd, 42 Kelvingrove St, Glasgow G3 7RZ (☎ 0141 332 4153, fax 0141 331 1285, DX 512229 Glasgow - Sandyford Place); Cadogan Consultants, 61 Southwark Street, London SE1 1SA (☎ 0171 928 8999, fax 0171 928 5566, mobile 0374 161033)

McCUTCHEON, Dr (William) Alan; s of William John McCutcheon (d 1978), of Bangor, Co Down, NI, and Margaret Elizabeth, *née* Fullerton (d 1987); *b* 2 March 1934; *Educ* Royal Belfast Academical Inst, Queen's Univ of Belfast (BA), pt/t univ study (MA, PhD); *m* 30 June 1956, Margaret, *née* Craig; 3 s (Patrick b 23 Feb 1961, Conor b 4 May 1963, Kevin b 21 Sept 1965); *Career* geography teacher Royal Belfast Academical Inst 1956–62, dir Survey of Indust Archaeology for Govt of NI 1962–68, keeper of technol and local history Ulster Museum Belfast 1968–77, dir Ulster Museum 1977–82, visiting teacher Glenalmond Coll 1984 and 1986, teacher (geography specialist) Ditcham Park Sch Petersfield Hants 1986–93; chm Historic Monuments Cncl NI 1980–85; memb: Malcolm Ctee on Regnl Museums in NI 1977–78, Jt Ctee Industl Archaeology NI 1981–85, Industl Archaeology Ctee Cncl for Br Archaeology 1981–85; FSA 1970, MRIA 1983; *Books* The Canals of the North of Ireland (1965), Railway History in Pictures-Ireland (Vol 1, 1969, Vol 2 1970), Wheel and Spindle - Aspects of Irish Industrial History (1977), The Industrial Archaeology of Northern Ireland (1980); contrib to many others, author of numerous articles and papers in professional jls; *Recreations* music, reading, travel, gardening; *Style*— Dr Alan McCutcheon, FSA; ✉ 25 Moira Drive, Bangor, Co Down BT20 4RW (☎ 01247 465519)

McCUTCHEON, Prof John Joseph; CBE (1994); s of James Thomson McCutcheon (d 1964), and Margaret, *née* Hutchison (d 1984); *b* 10 Sept 1940; *Educ* Glasgow Acad, St John's Coll Cambridge (scholar, MA, Wright's prize), Univ of Liverpool (PhD, DSc); *m* 1978, Jean Sylvia, *née* Constable; *Career* actuarial student Scottish Amicable Life Assurance Soc 1962–65, conslt actuary Duncan C Fraser & Co 1965–66, demonstrator Dept of Pure Mathematics Univ of Liverpool 1966–70, assoc prof Dept of Actuarial and Business Mathematics Univ of Manitoba 1970–72, dean Faculty of Science Heriot-Watt Univ 1995– (sr lectr 1972–75, prof of actuarial studies 1975–); FFA 1965 (pres 1992–94), FRSE 1993; *Books* An Introduction to the Mathematics of Finance (with W F Scott, 1986); author of papers in mathematics, actuarial science and demography; *Recreations* reading, opera, tennis, skiing; *Clubs* Colinton Lawn Tennis, Woodcutters' Cricket; *Style*— Prof John McCutcheon, CBE, FRSE; ✉ Department of Actuarial Mathematics and Statistics, Heriot-Watt University, Riccarton, Edinburgh EH14 4AS (☎ 0131 451 3202, fax 0131 451 3249)

McDERMID, Ven Norman George Lloyd Roberts; s of Rev Lloyd Roberts McDermid (d 1975), of Greystones, Bedale, and Annie, *née* Harrison (d 1966); *b* 5 March 1927; *Educ* St Peter's, York, St Edmund Hall Oxford (BA, MA), Wells Theol Coll; *m* 29 July 1953, Vera, da of Albert John Wood (d 1967), of Kirkby Overblow, Harrogate; 1 s (Nigel Lloyd b 1957), 3 da (Katherine Jane b 1954, Helen Sarah b 1959, Angela Mary b 1963); *Career* RN 1944–47; curate of Leeds 1951–56, vicar of Bramley Leeds 1956–64, rector Kirkby Overblow 1964–80, rural dean Harrogate 1977–83, vicar Knaresborough 1980–83, hon canon of Ripon Cathedral 1972–93, archdeacon of Richmond 1983–93, archdeacon and canon emeritus of Ripon 1993–; stewardship advsr: Ripon Diocese 1964–76, Bradford & Wakefield Diocese 1973–76; Church of England: memb General Synod 1970–93, memb C of E Pensions Bd 1972–79, church cmmr 1978–83, memb Bd Assets Ctee and Gen Purposes Ctee 1978–83, Exec Ctee Central Bd of Fin 1985–93, Redundant Churches Fund 1977–89; memb N Yorks Co Educn Ctee 1993–; tstee Yorks Historic Churches Tst 1993–; chm: House of Clergy Ripon Diocese 1982–93, Ripon Diocesan Bd of Finance 1988–92; *Recreations* church buildings, investment, gardens; *Clubs* Nat Lib; *Style*— The Ven Norman McDermid; ✉ Greystones, 10 North End, Bedale, North Yorkshire DL8 1AB (☎ 01677 422210)

MacDERMOT, Brian Hugh; s of Francis Charles MacDermot (d 1975), of Paris, and Elaine Orr MacDermot (d 1974); *b* 2 Dec 1930; *Educ* Downside, New Coll Oxford (MA); *m* 23 March 1985, Georgina Maria, da of Dayrell Gallwey, of Rockfield House, Tramore, Co Waterford; 1 s (Thomas Patrick b 16 March 1986), 1 da (Elaine Francesca b 19 Nov 1987); *Career* Lt Irish Guards 1952–55; memb Stock Exchange 1959–90, currently registered rep Panmure Gordon and Co (ptnr 1964–76), chm Mathaf Gallery Ltd; author of numerous contribs to jls; chm and tstee St Gregory Charitable Tst; former vice pres RAI, former cncl memb RGS; Hon Asst Worshipful Company of Bowyers (Master 1984–86); FRGS, FRAI; *Books* Cult of the Sacred Spear (1972); *Recreations* squash, tennis; *Clubs* Brooks's; *Style*— Brian MacDermot, Esq; ✉ Clock House, Rutland Gate, London SW7 1NY; Mathaf Gallery Ltd, 24 Motcomb St, London SW1X 8JU

McDERMOTT, Christopher James Ignatius; s of Michael McDermott, of Bodmin, Cornwall, and Christopha Veronica, *née* Birch; *b* 2 Nov 1959; *Educ* Royal GS High Wycombe, Christ's Coll Cambridge (open exhibitioner, MA); *m* 23 Aug 1995, Isobel Jane, da of David Hitchcock-Spencer, of London; *Career* exploration asst Amoco Europe & West Africa 1984–85, account exec ABS Communications 1986–87, gp head Reginald Watts Associates 1987–90; dir: Ruder Finn UK 1990–94, Shandwick Communications 1994–; MCIM 1996; *Recreations* literature, travel, diving, skiing; *Clubs* Three Per Cent; *Style*— Christopher McDermott, Esq; ✉ 1 Bedfordbury, Covent Garden, London WC2N 4DA (☎ 0171 240 3188); Shandwick Communications Ltd, 114 Cromwell Road, London SW7 4ES (☎ 0171 835 1001, fax 0171 373 4311, e-mail cmcdermott@shandwick.com)

MacDERMOTT, Rt Hon Lord Justice; Rt Hon Sir John Clarke; kt (1987), PC (1987); er s of Baron MacDermott, MC, PC (Life Peer, d 1979), and Louise Palmer, *née* Johnston; *b* 9 May 1927; *Educ* Campbell Coll Belfast, Trinity Hall Cambridge (BA), Queens Univ Belfast; *m* 1953, Margaret Helen, da of Hugh Dales (d 1935); 4 da (Helen b 1954, Anne b 1956, Janet b 1958, Gillian b 1959); *Career* called to the Bar Inner Temple and NI 1949, QC (NI) 1964, judge of High Court NI 1973, a Lord Justice of Appeal 1987–; *Recreations* golf; *Clubs* The Royal Belfast Golf; *Style*— The Rt Hon Lord Justice MacDermott; ✉ 6 Tarawood, Holywood BT18 0HS; The Royal Courts of Justice, Belfast BT1 3JF

McDERMOTT, Patrick Anthony; MVO (1972); s of Patrick J McDermott, of Belfast (d 1966), and Eileen, *née* Lyons (d 1990), of Cork; *b* 8 Sept 1941; *Educ* Clapham Coll London; *m* 1, 1963 (m dis), Patricia Hunter-Naylor; 2 s (Jeremy b 1967, Justin b 1970); m 2, 1976, Christa, da of Emil Herminghaus, of Krefeld, Germany; 2 s (Nicholas b 1977, Christian b 1981); *Career* joined FO (now FCO) 1960, Mexico City 1963, attaché UK delgn to UN 1966, vice consul Belgrade 1971, FCO 1973, second sec Bonn 1973, first sec Paris 1976, FCO 1979, HM consul gen W Berlin 1984–88, FCO 1988–90, cnsllr Paris 1990–95, head of Dept FCO 1995–; Freeman City of London 1986; *Style*— Patrick McDermott, Esq, MVO; ✉ c/o Foreign and Commonwealth Office, Downing Street, London SW1A 2AH

McDEVITT, Caroline Mary Margaret; da of John Peter Paul McDevitt, of Co Dublin, and Elizabeth-Anne, *née* Maher; *b* 6 Jan 1955; *Educ* St Victoire's Convent, St Martin's Sch of Art; *m* 1975 (m dis 1981), Richard Charles Burn Lyall, s of Richard Burn Lyall; *Career* draughtswoman on trg manuals for nuclear power stn engrs CEGB 1975–77, statistician's asst MOD 1977–78, sales asst Trident Television 1978–79, sales exec Westward Television 1979–81, sales exec rising to head of sales Grampian Television 1981–89 (joined at start of franchise), sales controller TVMM Saleshouse 1990–92, bd dir Westcountry Television 1992– (from start of franchise); memb various ITV Ctees 1991–; memb: Women's Advtg Club of London, RTS, Mktg Soc; *Recreations* golf, shooting, fishing, entertaining, theatre, ballet; *Clubs* Reform; *Style*— Caroline McDevitt, Esq; ✉ Westcountry Television Ltd, 48 Leicester Square, London WC2H 7LY (☎ 0171 736 7153, fax 0171 839 1512)

McDEVITT, Prof Denis Gordon; *b* 17 Nov 1937, Belfast; *Educ* Campbell Coll Belfast (scholar), The Queen's Univ Belfast (fndn entrance scholar, Hutchison-Stewart scholar, MB BCh, BAO, Gold medal in paediatrics, Smyth prize in surgery, MD, DSc), FRCPI, FRCP (London), FRCPEd, FFPM (UK); *m*; 3 c; *Career* jr hosp appts Royal Victoria and Belfast City Hosps (Queen's Univ Belfast) 1962–68, asst prof of med and conslt physician Christian Med Coll and Brown Meml Hosp Punjab N India 1968–71; Dept of Therapeutics and Pharmacology Queen's Univ Belfast: sr lectr 1971–76, reader 1976–78, prof of clinical pharmacology 1978–83; research assoc (on sabbatical) Dept of Med and Pharmacology Vanderbilt Univ Nashville Tennessee 1974–75; conslt physician Belfast City and Royal Victoria Hosps 1971–83; currently: prof of clinical pharmacology and dean Faculty of Med and Dentistry Univ of Dundee, hon conslt physician Dundee Teaching Hosps NHS Tst, civil conslt in clinical pharmacology RAF; chm: Assoc of Profs of Clinical Pharmacology 1990–93, Drugs and Meds Ctee Dundee Teaching Hosps NHS Tst 1994–; vice chm Meds Cmmn 1992–; memb: Ethics Ctee Inst of Aviation Med RAF 1988–, Selection Ctee Merck Int Fellowships in Clinical Pharmacology 1991–; dir Drug Development (Scotland) Ltd 1984–, tstee James Crooks Meml Fellowship 1984–; currently memb Editorial Bds: Pharmacology and Therapeutics, Pharmacoepidemiology and Drug Safety, Post-marketing Surveillance; numerous postgrad awards and prizes incl: Merck int fellowship in clinical pharmacology 1974, Smith Kline and French travelling prize for research in clinical pharmacology 1975 and Smith Kline and French fndn lecture 1977 (Br Pharmacological Soc), Graves' lectr (Royal Acad of Med in Ireland) 1977, hon memb Assoc of Physicians of GB and I 1988, Honyman Gillespie lecture (Edinburgh Med Coll) 1992; numerous memberships of professional assocs incl: American Soc for Clinical Pharmacology and Therapeutics, Assoc of Physicians of GB and I (pres 1987–88), Br Cardiac Soc, Br Hypertension Soc, Br Pharmacological Soc (chm Clinical Pharmacology Section 1985–88), Br Thoracic Soc, Harveian Soc of Edinburgh, Int Soc of Pharmacoepidemiology; FRSE 1996; *Style*— Prof Denis McDevitt, FRSE; ✉ Department of Pharmacology and Clinical Pharmacology, Ninewells Hospital, Dundee DD1 9SY (☎ 01382 632180)

McDIARMID, Alex; *b* 7 April 1944; *Educ* Birkenhead Coll of Technol, Inst of Gas Technol Chicago (W H Bennett Travelling Fellowship); *m* Mary; 2 da (Paula, Carol); *Career* early positions with Unilever plc, with North West Gas 1967–78, regnl distribution mangr Northern Gas 1978–82, dir of engrg Eastern Gas 1982–90, ops dir British Gas plc East Midlands 1990–94, ind conslt 1995–; pres Instn of Gas Engrs 1995–96 (memb Cncl 1986–), memb Senate Engrg Cncl; non-exec dir Eastern Region Technol Centre 1988–90, former memb E Mids Regnl Cncl CBI; sometime dir various engrg and mgmnt courses incl Instn of Gas Engrs courses Pembroke Coll Oxford and Univ of Salford; presenter tech and business papers at confs in USA, Europe, China, Aust and NZ; CEng, FIGasE (Silver Medal and SBGI Silver Medal), FIMgt; *Recreations* charity work in the community, rugby; *Clubs* Leicester RFC, Lions Club International (former pres); *Style*— Alex McDiarmid, Esq; ✉ c/o The Institution of Gas Engineers, 21 Portland Place, London W1N 3AF

MacDONAGH, Lesley Anne; da of Arthur George Payne, and Agnes Dowie, *née* Scott; *b* 19 April 1952; *Educ* Queen Elizabeth I Sch Wimborne, Coll of Law Guildford and London; *m* 1, 1975 (m dis 1985), John Belton; 1 da; m 2, 1987, Simon Michael Peter MacDonagh; 2 s; *Career* admitted slr 1976; a managing ptnr Lovell White Durrant 1995– (ptnr 1981–); Law Soc: memb Planning and Environmental Ctee 1988–95, memb Cncl 1992–, memb Policy Ctee 1996–; memb: Consultative Ctee Lands Tbnl 1991–95, Property Advsy Gp 1993–; tstee Citizenship Fndn 1991–, vice chm Environmental Ctee Knightsbridge Assoc 1991–; Liveryman Worshipful Co of Solicitors (memb Ct 1996–); *Recreations* family life, painting and drawing; *Style*— Mrs Lesley MacDonagh; ✉ Managing Partner, Lovell White Durrant, 65 Holborn Viaduct, London EC1A 2DY (☎ 0171 236 0066)

MacDONALD, Sheriff Alistair Archibald; s of James MacDonald (d 1984), and Margaret, *née* McGibbon (d 1947); *b* 8 May 1927; *Educ* Broughton Sch Edinburgh, Univ of Edinburgh (MA, LLB); *m* 1949, Jill, da of Sir Robert Russell (d 1972); 1 s (Ian b 1957), 1 da (Catriona b 1964); *Career* serv Army 1945–48; called to the Scottish Bar 1954;

Sheriff of Grampian Highland and Islands at Lerwick and Kirkwall 1961–92, memb Panel of Chm of the Social Security Appeal Tbnl 1992–, memb Panel of Chm of the Disability Appeal Tbnls 1992; DL of Shetland; Kt of the Equestrian Order of the Holy Sepulchre of Jerusalem; *Clubs* Royal Northern; *Style*— Sheriff Alistair MacDonald; ✉ West Hall, Ness of Sound, Lerwick, Shetland; 110 Nicolson St, Edinburgh

MACDONALD, His Hon Judge; Angus Cameron; s of Hugh Macdonald, OBE (d 1971), of Ravensden, Bedford, and Margaret Cameron, *née* Westley (d 1996); *b* 26 Aug 1931; *Educ* Bedford Sch, Trinity Hall Cambridge (MA); *m* 1956, Deborah Anne, da of John Denny Inglis, DSO, MC and Bar, JP (d 1976), of Oban, Argyll; 3 da (Deborah (Mrs Patrick Agnew), Sarah (Mrs Henry Bennett) (d 1994), Fiona (Mrs William Tricks)); *Career* Lt RA (TA) 1951–57; called to the Bar Gray's Inn 1955, resident magistrate Nyasaland Govt 1957–60, crown counsel and sr state counsel Nyasaland/Malawi Govt 1960–67, practised NE Circuit 1967–79, circuit judge (NE Circuit) 1979–, jr vice pres Cncl of HM Circuit Judges 1990; *Recreations* singing, shooting, fishing; *Clubs* Northern Counties (Newcastle upon Tyne); *Style*— His Hon Judge Macdonald; ✉ c/o North Eastern Circuit Office, 17th Floor, West Riding House, Albion Street, Leeds LS1 5AA

MACDONALD, Angus David; s of Surgn Capt Iain Macdonald, CBE (d 1976), of Strathtay, Perthshire, and Molly, *née* Barber (d 1983); *b* 9 Oct 1950; *Educ* Portsmouth GS, Jesus Coll Cambridge (MA), Univ of Edinburgh (BEd); *m* 10 April 1976, Isabelle Marjory, da of Maj John Ross, of Connel; 2 da (Mairi Catriona b 1982, Eilidh Iona b 1983); *Career* asst teacher Alloa Acad 1972–73, asst teacher Edinburgh Acad 1973–82, asst teacher King's Sch Paramatta NSW 1978–79, dep princ George Watson's Coll 1982–86 (head of geography 1982), headmaster Lomond Sch 1986–; *Recreations* outdoor recreation, piping, sport, gardening; *Style*— Angus Macdonald, Esq; ✉ Ashmount, 8 Millig St, Helensburgh, Argyll & Bute (☎ 01436 679204); Lomond School, 10 Stafford St, Helensburgh, Argyll & Bute (☎ 01436 672476)

MACDONALD, Angus John (Gus); s of Colin Macdonald (d 1966), and Jean, *née* Livingstone; *b* 20 Aug 1940; *Educ* Allan Glen's Sch Glasgow; *m* 7 Sept 1963, Alice; 2 da (Jean b 1965, Rowan b 1967); *Career* prodr, presenter and dir Granada TV 1967–85; Scottish Television plc: dir of progs 1985–90, md 1990–96, exec chm 1996–; chm ITV Broadcast Bd 1992–94; chm: TVMM (airtime sales house) 1992–93, Time Exchange 1993–94; dir GMTV; viewers' ombudsman Right to Reply programme (Channel 4) 1982–88; fndr chm Edinburgh Int TV Festival 1976, chm Cncl Edinburgh Film and TV Festival 1993–96, chm Edinburgh Int Film Festival 1994–96; hon jt chm BAFTA Scotland 1991–; govr Nat Film and TV Sch 1988–; visiting prof of film and media studies Univ of Stirling; Scottish Business Elite Award (voted by fellow chief execs in Scotland) 1993; FRSA, FRTS (vice pres 1994–); author; *Books* Victorian Eyewitness, Early Photography; *Recreations* visual arts, music, literature, sport; *Clubs* Reform, RAC; *Style*— Gus Macdonald, Esq; ✉ Scottish Television plc, Cowcaddens, Glasgow G2 3PR (☎ 0141 300 3000)

McDONALD, Antony Rycroft; s of Alexander McDonald, of Weston-Super-Mare, Avon, and Cicely Elaine, *née* Hartley; *b* 11 Sept 1950; *Educ* Monkton Coombe Sch Bath, Central Sch of Speech and Drama, Manchester Poly Sch of Theatre, Univ of Manchester; *Career* theatre designer and director; asst dir The Community and Schs; Co of The Welsh Nat Opera and Drama Co 1974–76; *Theatre* incl: Let's Make an Opera (Welsh Nat Opera) 1978, Jessonda (Oxford Univ Opera Soc) 1980, War Crimes (ICA) 1981, Degas (Ian Spink Dance Group and Channel 4) 1981, Dances from the Kingdom of the Pagodas (Royal Danish Ballet) 1982, Secret Gardens (Mickery Theatre Amsterdam) 1982, Insignifigance (Royal Court) 1982, Mrs Gauguin, Hedda Gabler (Almeida) 1984, Tom and Viv (Royal Court 1984, Public Theatre NY 1985), Orlando (Scottish Opera) 1985, Midsummer Marriage (Opera North), Bosendorfer Waltzes (Second Stride, Munich New Dance Festival) 1986, Dancelines (Channel 4) 1986, A Streetcar Named Desire (Crucible Sheffield) 1987, The Trojans (WNO, Opera North and Scottish Opera) 1987, Billy Budd (ENO) 1988, Hamlet (RSC) 1988, Mary Stuart (Greenwich) 1988, Heaven Ablaze in his Breast (Second Stride), As You Like It (Old Vic) 1989, Beatrice and Benedict (ENO) 1990, Berenice (RNT) 1990, Mad Forest (Royal Court and NT Bucharest) 1990, Richard II (RSC) 1990, Benvenuto Cellini (Netherlands Opera) 1991, Lives of the Great Poisoners (Second Stride) 1991, Hamlet (American Repertory Theatre Cambridge Mass) 1991, Marriage of Figaro (Aust Opera) 1992, The Seagull (American Rep Theatre Cambridge Mass) 1992, Touch Your Coolness to My Fevered Brown (Dutch Nat Ballet) 1992, Euridice (Musica Nel Chiostro Italy) 1992, Why Things Happen (Second Stride) 1992, Cherubin (Royal Opera House) 1994, Fearful Symmetries (Royal Ballet) 1994, Francesca Da Rimini (Bregenz Festival) 1994, Pelleas and Melisande (Opera North) 1995, Nabucco (WNO) 1995, Ebony Concerto (Royal Ballet), Nabucco (ROH) 1996, Pelleas and Melisande (Minnesota Opera) 1996, Orlando (Brooklyn Acad of Music) 1996, Now Langorous - Now Wild (Royal Ballet) 1996, Ariadne auf Naxos (Bavarian State Opera) 1996, A Midsummer Night's Dream (Metropolitan Opera NY) 1996; dir/designer: The Birthday Party (Glasgow Citizen's), Black Snow (American Rep Theatre Cambridge Mass) 1992, Orlando (Aix-en-Provence Festival) 1993, Wallenstein (RSC) 1993, Escape at Sea (Second Stride) 1993; *Style*— Antony McDonald, Esq; ✉ Loesje Sanders, 1 North Hill, Pound Square, Woodbridge, Suffolk IP12 1HH (☎ 01394 385260, fax 01394 388734)

MacDONALD, Calum; MP (Lab) Western Isles (majority 1,703); *Career* MP (Lab) Western Isles 1987–; *Style*— Calum MacDonald, Esq, MP; ✉ House of Commons, London SW1A 0AA (☎ 0171 219 3000)

MACDONALD, Charles Adam; QC (1992); s of Alasdair Cameron Macdonald, of Redlands Rd, Glasgow, and Jessie Catherine, *née* McCrow; *b* 31 Aug 1949; *Educ* The Glasgow Acad, New Coll Oxford (MA), Cncl of Legal Educn; *m* 17 June 1978, Dinah Jane, da of Ronald Manns, of Wargrave, Berkshire; 3 da (Kate, Anna, Elspeth); *Career* called to the Bar Lincoln's Inn 1972, practising in maritime and commercial law, asst recorder 1996; memb Commercial Bar Assoc, supporting memb London Maritime Arbitrators' Assoc; gen ed International Maritime Law; *Recreations* family life; *Style*— Charles Macdonald, Esq, QC; ✉ 4 Essex Court, Temple, London EC4Y 9AJ (☎ 0171 797 7970, fax 0171 353 0998, telex 8812528 ADROIT G)

MacDONALD, Dr (Isabelle Wilma) Claire; da of William Garland (d 1972), of Glasgow, and Barbara Sutherland, *née* MacDonald; *b* 6 Feb 1951; *Educ* Hutchesons Girls GS, Univ of Glasgow (BSc, MB ChB); *m* 28 April 1977, David John MacDonald, s of Alastair J MacDonald (d 1991), of Glasgow; 2 da (Jennifer b 21 Aug 1979, Elizabeth b 6 Dec 1982), 1 s (Alastair b 31 July 1991); *Career* Victoria Infirmary Glasgow: house offr in surgery 1975–76, registrar in pathology 1977–79, sr registrar 1979–81; house offr in medicine Stirling Royal Hosp 1976, sr house offr in pathology Western Infirmary Glasgow 1976–77, lectr in pathology Univ of Aberdeen 1981–84; Pontefract Gen Infirmary: conslt histopathologist 1984–, chm Div of Pathology 1989–92, dir Functional Unit of Pathology 1992–; FRCPath 1994 (MRCPath 1982); *Recreations* swimming, reading; *Clubs* Caledonian Soc, Con; *Style*— Dr Claire MacDonald; ✉ Pathology Department, Pontefract General Infirmary, Pontefract, W Yorks WF8 1PL (☎ 01977 600600)

MacDONALD, Colin Cameron; s of Capt Colin D C MacDonald (d 1993), and Ann, *née* Hough; *b* 13 July 1943; *Educ* Allan Glen's Sch Glasgow, Univ of Strathclyde (BA); *m* 1969, Kathryn Mary, da of Capt late Charles Campbell; 1 da (Sarah b 13 Nov 1973), 1 s (Finlay b 7 July 1975); *Career* Scottish Devpt Dept SO: asst res offr 1967–70, res offr 1970–71, sr res offr 1971–75, sr princ res offr 1975–81, chief res offr 1981–88, asst sec (Housing Div) 1988–91; asst sec Mgmnt Orgn Central Servs SO 1991–92, under sec and princ establishment offr SO 1992–; non-exec dir TSB Bank Scotland 1994–; *Recreations* tennis, fishing, music; *Style*— Colin MacDonald, Esq; ✉ The Scottish Office, 16 Waterloo Place, Edinburgh EH1 3DN (☎ 0131 244 3938, fax 0131 244 3896)

MACDONALD, David Cameron; s of James Fraser Macdonald, OBE (d 1977), and Anne Sylvia, *née* Hutcheson; *b* 5 July 1936; *Educ* St George's Sch Harpenden, Newport GS; *m* 1, 14 Feb 1968 (m dis 1980), Melody Jane, da of Ralph Vernon Coles, of Portland, Maine, USA; 2 da (Nancy Anne b 1969, Jessica Jean b 1972); m 2, 11 Nov 1983, Sally Anne Robertson, da of William Rodger, of Invercargill, NZ; 1 s (Hamish William b 1984), 1 da (Laura Mary Clare b 1987); *Career* Nat Serv 2 Lieut RA 1954–56, articled clerk then slr Slaughter and May 1956–64, dir and dep chm Hill Samuel & Co Ltd 1964–77 and 1979–80, chief exec and chm Antony Gibbs Holdings 1980–83, sr UK advsr Crèdit Suisse First Boston 1983–91; dir: Coutts & Co 1980–95, Sears plc 1981–, Bath & Portland Group plc (chm 1982–85), Merivale Moore plc 1985–, Pittards plc (chm 1985–); dir gen Takeover Panel 1977–79, chm Issuing Houses Assoc 1975–77, advsr to Sec of State for Trade and Indust on Upper Clyde shipbuilding crisis 1971; *Recreations* family, country pursuits, music; *Style*— David Macdonald, Esq; ✉ Lovel House, Upton Noble, Somerset BA4 6BA (☎ 01749 850572)

McDONALD, David Wylie; CMG (1978); s of William McDonald (d 1956), of Dundee, and Rebecca Wilkinson, *née* Wylie (d 1964); *b* 9 Oct 1927; *Educ* Harris Acad Dundee, Sch of Architecture Dundee Coll of Art (DA); *m* 3 July 1951, Eliza (Betty) Roberts, da of David Low Steele (d 1955), of Dundee; 2 da (Mairi Stewart (Mrs Bailey) b 22 Nov 1955, Fiona Margaret (Mrs Byrne) b 31 May 1959); *Career* mil serv Black Watch (RHR); architect with Gauldie Hardie Wright & Needham Dundee 1953, architect architectural office Public Works Dept Hong Kong 1955 (sr architect 1964, chief architect 1967, govt architect 1970, princ govt architect 1972), dir of bldg devpt 1973, dir of public works 1974, sec for lands and works 1981 (ret 1983); memb Cwlth Parly Assoc; former chm: Town Planning Bd, Devpt Progress Ctee, Lands and Works Conf; former memb: Legislative Cncl, Fin Ctee, Public Works Sub Ctee, Public Works Priorities Ctee, Land Devpt Policy Ctee, Hong Kong Housing Authy; former dir: Mass Transit Railway Corpn, Hong Kong Ind Estates Corpn, Ocean Park Ltd; former memb Cncl: Hong Kong Red Cross, Girl Guides Assoc, Hong Kong Housing Soc; tstee Scottish Tst for the Physically Disabled, memb Ctee Margaret Blackwood Housing Assoc; memb Mensa; Lorimer Meml prize 1950, City Corpn Design prize 1953, Silver Jubilee medal 1977; Fell Hong Kong Inst of Architects, RIBA, ARIAS; *Recreations* drawing, painting, calligraphy; *Clubs* Hong Kong (chm 1977), Royal Hong Kong Jockey; *Style*— David Wylie McDonald, Esq, CMG; ✉ Northbank, Backmuir of Liff, by Dundee DD2 5QU (☎ 01382 580483)

McDONALD, Sir Duncan; kt (1983), CBE (1976); s of Robert McDonald, and Helen, *née* Orrick; *b* 20 Sept 1921; *Educ* Dunfermline HS, Univ of Edinburgh (BSc); *m* 19 April 1955, Jane, da of John Guckian; 1 da (Jane Anne b 1956), 3 s (Kevan b 1958, Hamish b 1960, Niall b 1962); *Career* chief of Research, Devpt and Design Gp British Thomson Houston Company Rugby 1945–54; Bruce Peebles Industries Edinburgh: chief transformer designer 1954–59, chief engr 1959–62, dir 1960–62, md 1962–73, dir C A Parsons (following merger of Reyrolle Parson with Bruce Peebles Industries) 1969, dir Reyrolle Parsons Group 1973, chm and chief exec Reyrolle and Bruce Peebles Industries 1974–76, chief exec Reyroll Parsons Group 1976–77; Northern Engineering Industries plc (following merger of Reyrolle Parsons and Clarke Chapman): gp md 1977–80, chm and chief exec 1980–83, chm 1983–86, ret; IEE: John Hopkinson Premium, Cooper Hill War Meml Prize and Medal; Hon DSc Heriot-Watt Univ 1982, Hon DEng Univ of Newcastle upon Tyne 1984; hon fell Heriot-Watt Univ 1962, FRSE 1969, FEng 1980, Hon FIEE 1984, fell Scottish Cncl Devpt and Indust 1987; *Style*— Sir Duncan McDonald, CBE, FEng, FRSE; ✉ Duncliffe, 15 Kinellan Road, Edinburgh EH12 6ES (☎ 0131 337 4814)

MACDONALD, Dr Eleanor Catherine; OBE (1995, MBE 1945); da of Frederick William Macdonald (d 1959), and Frances Catherine, *née* Glover (d 1958); *b* 1 Sept 1910; *Educ* Woodford Sch Croydon, Univ of London (BA); *Career* WWII MOI and Security Serv 1939–45; fencing prof 1929–39 (1st woman to become Maître d'Armes de L'Académie d'Epée de Paris); Unilever: dir several subsid cos 1947–69; princ owner mgmnt and trg consultancy 1969–; author of numerous articles on staff devpt; fndr: Women in Mgmnt, 300 Gp; Hon DUniv Bradford 1989; memb RIIA, CIMgt, FRSA; *Books* incl: Live by Beauty, The Successful Secretary, Nothing by Chance; *Recreations* gardening, bird watching; *Style*— Dr Eleanor Macdonald, OBE; ✉ 4 Mapledale Ave, Croydon, Surrey CR0 5TA (☎ 0181 654 4659, fax 0181 656 0626)

MACDONALD, Euan Ross; s of Ian Somerled Macdonald (d 1958), and Elisabeth Barbara, da of Sir Marshall Warmington, 2 Bt; *b* 8 April 1940; *Educ* Marlborough, Trinity Coll Cambridge (BA Econ), Graduate Sch of Business Columbia Univ NY (MBA); *m* March 1965, (Jacqueline) Anne Gatacre Evelyn-Wright; 4 s (Iain Graham b 12 Oct 1966, Russell Ross b 19 May 1969, James Curtis (twin) b 19 May 1969, Dougal Evelyn b 7 May 1974); *Career* Lazard Brothers & Co Ltd 1963–74, first gen mangr International Financial Advisers Kuwait 1974–79, dir gen Ifabanque SA Paris 1979–82, S G Warburg & Co Ltd (dir 1982–, vice chm 1994), currently chm SBC Warburg (India) Bombay; work in Black Africa, India, Caribbean, Latin America, Russia and Eastern Europe carrying out fin and advsy contracts with sovereign and private sector clients; memb Worshipful Co of Clothworkers; *Style*— Euan Macdonald, Esq; ✉ SBC Warburg (India), Thomas Cook Building, 324 D N Road, Fort, Bombay, India

MacDONALD, Prof (Simon) Gavin George; s of Simon MacDonald (d 1967), of Edinburgh, and Jean Hogarth, *née* Thompson (d 1974); *b* 5 Sept 1923; *Educ* George Heriot's Sch, Univ of Edinburgh (MA), Univ of St Andrews (PhD); *m* 22 Oct 1948, Eva Leonie, da of Kurt Austerlitz (d 1929), of Breslau, Germany; 1 s (Neil b 1950), 1 da (Carolyn b 1954); *Career* jr sci offr RAE Farnborough 1943–46; lectr Univ of St Andrews 1948–57; sr lectr: Univ Coll of the WI 1957–62, Univ of St Andrews 1962–67; Univ of Dundee 1967–73: dean of sci 1970–73, vice princ 1974–79, prof of physics 1974–88; chm Bd of Dirs: Dundee Rep Theatre 1975–89, Fedn of Scottish Theatres 1978–80; convener Scottish Univ Cncl on Entrance 1976–82 (dep convener 1972–76, memb 1970); UCCA: convener Tech Ctee 1979–83, dep chm and convenor Fin and Gen Purposes Ctee 1983–89, convenor Stat Ctee 1989–93; FInstP 1958, FRSE 1973; *Books* Problems in General Physics (1967), Physics for Biology and Premedical Students (1970, 1975), Physics for the Life and Health Sciences (1975); *Recreations* bridge, golf, writing; *Clubs* Royal Commonwealth; *Style*— Prof Gavin MacDonald, FRSE; ✉ 10 Westerton Avenue, Dundee DD5 3NJ (☎ 01382 778692)

MACDONALD, 8 Baron (I 1776); Godfrey James Macdonald of Macdonald; JP (1976), DL (1986); Chief of the Name and Arms of Macdonald; s of 7 Baron Macdonald, MBE (d 1970); 3 Baron m 1803 Louisa Maria La Coast, natural da of HRH Duke of Gloucester (issue b before m succeeded to Bosville MacDonald btcy); *b* 28 Nov 1947; *Educ* Belhaven Hill Sch Dunbar, Eton; *m* 14 June 1969, Claire (Glenfiddich's 1982 Writer of the Year), eld da of Capt Thomas Noel Catlow, CBE, RN; 1 s (Hon Godfrey Evan Hugo Thomas b 24 Feb 1982), 3 da (Hon Alexandra Louisa (Hon Mrs Gunn) b 1973, Hon Isabella Claire b 1975, Hon Meriel Iona b 1978); *Heir* s, Hon Godfrey Macdonald of Macdonald; *Career* pres Royal Scottish Country Dance Soc 1970–73, memb Inverness CC 1970–75, tstee and memb Exec Ctee Clan Donald Lands Tst 1970–, vice convener Standing Cncl of Scottish Chiefs 1974–, memb of Skye and Lochalsh Dist Cncl 1975–83 (chm Fin Ctee 1979–83), chm Skye and Lochalsh Local Health Cncl 1978–80; memb

Highland Health Bd 1980–89; *Clubs* New (Edinburgh); *Style—* The Rt Hon Lord Macdonald; ✉ Kinloch Lodge, Isle of Skye (☎ 01471 833214)

MacDONALD, Prof (Donald) Gordon; RD (1976, and Bar 1986); s of Donald MacDonald (d 1981), of Milngavie, and Thelma Gordon, *née* Campbell (d 1975); *b* 5 July 1942; *Educ* Kelvinside Acad Glasgow, Univ of Glasgow (BDS, PhD); *m* 21 May 1966, Emma Lindsay (Linda), da of William Lindsay Cordiner (d 1961), of Coatbridge; 2 s (Lindsay b 1969, Alastair b 1972), 1 da (Katharine b 1968 d 1989); *Career* visiting assoc prof of oral pathology Univ of Illinois Chicago 1969–70, expert in forensic dentistry 1971–, hon conslt in oral pathology Glasgow 1974–, prof of oral pathology Univ of Glasgow 1991– (sr lectr 1974–82, reader 1982–91); vice pres Assoc of Head and Neck Oncologists of GB 1987–90 (sec 1983–87), speciality rep for oral pathology RCPath 1988–, pres Br Soc for Oral Pathology 1988–91; RNR: joined 1959, CO HMS Graham 1982–86, Capt and dir Plans, Personnel and Specialist Branches 1986–95, Cdre 1995–; Hon ADC 1996– (ADC 1991–93); MRCPath 1971, FRCPath 1985, FDSRCPSGlas 1986; *Books* Colour Atlas of Forensic Dentistry (1989); *Recreations* Royal Naval Reserve, golf, curling; *Clubs* Commonwealth Trust; *Style—* Prof D Gordon MacDonald, RD*; ✉ Glasgow Dental Hospital and School NHS Trust, 378 Sauchiehall St, Glasgow G2 3JZ (☎ 0141 211 9745, fax 0141 353 1593)

MacDONALD, Hamish Neil; s of John MacDonald (d 1977), of Glasgow, and Marion McKendrick, *née* Cuthbert; *b* 17 Aug 1933; *Educ* Glasgow HS, Univ of Glasgow (MB ChB), Univ of Leeds (PhD); *m* 16 Aug 1968, Rosemary Paterson, da of John Paterson (d 1982), of Campbeltown, Argyllshire; 1 s (Alasdair James b 13 Jan 1978), 1 da (Fiona Ann b 13 Jan 1978); *Career* Lt then Capt RAMC 1959–62, GSM (1960); asst res Hosp for Women of Maryland Baltimore USA 1963–64, res registrar Glasgow Royal Maternity Hosp 1964–66, sr registrar and tutor United Leeds Hosps 1966–68, conslt obstetrician gynaecologist and lectr United Leeds Hosps and Univ of Leeds 1968–72, conslt obstetrician gynaecologist and sr clinical lectr St James's Univ Hosp and Univ of Leeds 1972–93; med dir St James's Univ Hosp NHS Tst; memb: Incorporation of Hammerman of Glasgow, Grand Antiquity Soc, Gynaecological Visiting Soc of GB and Ireland; FRCOG; *Recreations* reading, walking, swimming, tennis; *Clubs* Chapel Allerton Lawn Tennis and Squash; *Style—* Hamish MacDonald, Esq; ✉ St James's University Hospital, Beckett Street, Leeds, West Yorkshire LS9 7TF (☎ 0113 243 3144)

MACDONALD, (J) Howard; *Career* with Royal Dutch Shell 1960–83 (various positions rising to gp treas), chm and chief exec Dome Petroleum Ltd Calgary 1983–88; National Westminster Bank plc: dir 1988–91, chm and chief exec County NatWest Ltd and NatWest Investment Bank Ltd 1988–91, chm County NatWest Ventures Ltd 1988–91; non-exec dir: The BOC Group plc 1991–, The Weir Group plc, McDermott International Inc, J Ray McDermott Inc; memb Advsy Ctee Energy International NV; CA, FCT; *Style—* J Howard Macdonald, Esq; ✉ The BOC Group plc, Chertsey Road, Windlesham, Surrey GU20 6HJ (☎ 01276 477222)

MACDONALD, Prof Hugh John; *b* 31 Jan 1940; *Educ* Univ of Cambridge (MA, PhD); *Career* lectr in music: Univ of Cambridge 1966–71, Univ of Oxford 1971–80; visiting prof of music Indiana Univ 1979, Gardiner prof of music Univ of Glasgow 1980–87, Avis Blewett prof of music Washington Univ St Louis 1987–; gen ed New Berlioz Edition 1967–; Szymanowski Medal (Poland); FRCM; *Books* Skryabin (1978), Berlioz (1982), Selected Letters of Berlioz (1995); *Style—* Prof Hugh Macdonald; ✉ Department of Music, Washington University, St Louis, MO 63130, USA (☎ 00 1 314 935 5519, fax 00 1 314 863 7231)

MACDONALD, Prof Ian; s of Ronald Macdonald, CBE, MC (d 1983), and Amy Elizabeth Macdonald (d 1965); *b* 22 Dec 1921; *Educ* Lancaster Royal GS, Univ of London and Guy's Hosp (MB BS, PhD, MD, DSc); *m* 1, 2 Feb 1946 (m dis 1980), Nora Patricia; 2 s (Graham b 1949, Peter b 1952), 1 da (Helen b 1961); m 2, 11 Aug 1980, Rose Philomena; *Career* RAMC 1946–48; Guy's Hosp: prof of applied physiology 1967–89, head Dept of Physiology 1977–89; memb Food Additives & Food Advsy Ctee MAFF 1977–86, pres Nutrition Soc 1980–83, vice pres Br Nutrition Fndn 1989– (chm 1985–87), chm joint WHO/FAO Expert Ctee on Dietary Carbohydrates 1980, memb Med Sub Ctee Br Olympic Assoc 1986–89, memb Cncl London Sports Med Inst 1986–91, chm Sports Nutrition Fndn 1991–95; Freeman: City of London 1967, Worshipful Soc of Apothecaries 1967; memb American Soc of Clinical Nutrition, FIBiol; *Books* ed: Effects of Carbohydrates on Lipid Metabolism (1973), Metabolic Effects of Dietary Carbohydrates (1986), Sucrose (1988); *Recreations* walking, DIY; *Style—* Prof Ian Macdonald; ✉ Hillside, Fountain Drive, London SE19 1UP (☎ 0181 670 3055)

McDONALD, Prof (William) Ian; s of William Allan Chapple McDonald (d 1962), of Christchurch, NZ, and Helen, *née* Leithead; *b* 15 March 1933; *Educ* St Andrew's Coll Christchurch NZ, Univ of Otago NZ (BMedSci, MB ChB, PhD); *Career* res fell Harvard Univ 1965–66; conslt physician: Nat Hosp for Neurology and Neurosurgery Queen Square 1966– (honorary 1974–), Moorfields Eye Hosp 1969– (honorary 1974–); prof of clinical neurology Inst of Neurology London 1974– (chm 1995–); visiting prof Univ of Düsseldorf 1990–; ed Brain jl 1991–; memb Med Res Advsy Ctee Multiple Sclerosis Soc; pres: European Neurological Soc 1994–95, Assoc of British Neurologists 1995; Liveryman Worshipful Soc of Apothecaries 1988; FRACP 1968, FRCP 1972, FRCOphth 1989; *Books* Diseases of the Nervous System (with A K Asbury and G McKhann, 1986), Multiple Sclerosis (with D H Silberberg, 1986); *Recreations* music; *Clubs* Garrick; *Style—* Prof Ian McDonald; ✉ Institute of Neurology, Queen Square, London WC1N 3BG (☎ 0171 829 8758, fax 0171 833 2823)

MACDONALD, Ian Alexander; QC (1988); s of Ian Wilson Macdonald (d 1989), of Gullane, E Lothian, and Helen, *née* Nicholson (d 1990); *b* 12 Jan 1939; *Educ* Glasgow Acad, Cargilfield Sch Edinburgh, Rugby, Clare Coll Cambridge (MA, LLB); *m* 1, 20 Dec 1968 (m dis 1977), Judith Mary, da of William Demain Roberts of Stockport, Cheshire; 2 s (Ian b 3 July 1970, Jamie b 25 Sept 1972); m 2, 12 Oct 1978 (m dis 1990), Jennifer, da of Roy Hall, of Grimsby, S Humberside; 1 s (Kieran b 17 Oct 1979); m 3, 31 Aug 1991, Yasmin Shahida, da of Mohammed Sharif, of Manchester; *Career* called to the Bar Middle Temple 1963, Astbury scholar 1962–65, jt head of chambers, lectr in law Kingston Poly 1968–72, sr legal writer and res conslt Incomes Data Servs 1974–80, pres Immigration Law Practitioners' Assoc 1984–, memb Editorial Advsy Bd Immigration and Nationality Law and Practice Journal; memb: SE Circuit, Euro Law Assoc, Criminal Bar Assoc, Admin Law Bar Assoc, Inquiry into Disappearance of Gen Humberto Delgado 1965; chm: Ind Inquiry into Racial Violence in Manchester Schs 1987–88, Inquiry into Funding of Caribbean House Hackney 1989–90; Grande Oficial Ordem Da Liberdade (Portugal) 1995; *Books* Race Relations and Immigration Law (1969), Race Relations - The New Law (1977), The New Nationality Act (with N J Blake 1982), Immigration Law and Practice (4 edn 1995), Murder in the Playground (1990); *Recreations* swimming, squash, watching football, reading; *Clubs* Cumberland Lawn Tennis; *Style—* Ian Macdonald, Esq, QC; ✉ 2 Garden Court, Temple, London EC4Y 9VL (☎ 0171 353 1633, fax 0171 353 4621)

MACDONALD, Prof Ian Grant; s of Douglas Grant Macdonald (d 1964), and Irene Alice, *née* Stokes (d 1995); *Educ* Winchester, Trinity Coll Cambridge (BA, MA), Oxford Univ (MA); *m* 31 July 1954, Margaretha Maria Lodewijk, da of René Van Goethem (d 1982); 2 s (Alexander b 1955, Christopher b 1957), 3 da (Catherine b 1959, Helen b 1959, Nicola b 1963); *Career* Nat Serv Rifle Bd 1947–49; asst princ and princ MOS 1952–57, asst lectr Univ of Manchester 1957–60, lectr Univ of Exeter 1960–63, fell and tutor in mathematics Magdalen Coll Oxford 1963–72, Fielden prof of pure mathematics Univ of Manchester 1972–76, prof of pure mathematics Queen Mary Coll Univ of London 1976–87 (emeritus 1987); FRS 1979; *Books* Algebraic Geometry: Introduction to Schemes (1968), Introduction to Commutative Algebra (with M F Atiyah, 1969), Spherical Functions on a Group of p-adic type (1972), Symmetric Functions and Hall Polynomials (1979, 2 edn 1995); *Style—* Prof I G Macdonald, FRS; ✉ 8 Blandford Avenue, Oxford OX2 8DY (☎ 01865 515373); School of Mathematical Sciences, Queen Mary and Westfield College, London E1 4NS

MACDONALD, Ian Hamish; OBE (1972); *b* 30 Dec 1926; *Educ* Inverness Royal Acad, Inverness Technical HS; *m* 1962, Patricia, da of James Lace; 1 da (Katie Fiona b 7 Jan 1967); *Career* currently dir AIB Group Nothern Ireland PLC and chm Clan Donald Lands Tst; RAFVR 1944, Queen's Own Cameron Highlanders 1945–48 (Hon Capt), Mercantile Bank 1948–59, Hong Kong and Shanghai Banking Corp 1959–83, exec dir and chm Hong Kong Bank of Canada 1981–83, gen mangr TSB Scotland 1983–86 and TSB Scotland PLC 1986–87; memb: Industl Soc 1984–87, Design Cncl 1985–88, Design Cncl Scot 1985–91, SCDI 1983–92, Scot Cncl Fndn 1983–92; dir: SSEB (now Scottish Power plc) 1985–92, TSB Group PLC 1986–87; memb Ct Univ of Edinburgh 1988–91; FCIBS, CIMgt, RSA; *Recreations* bridge, fishing, walking; *Clubs* New (Edinburgh), Oriental, Highland, Royal and Ancient, Hong Kong; *Style—* Ian Macdonald, Esq, OBE; ✉ Minewood Cottage, 11 Abercomby Drive, Bridge of Allan FK9 4EA (☎ 01786 832894, fax 01786 833254)

MACDONALD, Prof Ian Robert; s of Robert Harold Macdonald (d 1972), of Sutton, Surrey, and Jannette Wilhelmina, *née* Marang; *b* 4 May 1939; *Educ* Whitgift Sch, Univ of St Andrews (MA, Miller Prize), Univ of Aberdeen (PhD); *m* 21 April 1962, Frances Mary, da of James Ranald Alexander; 3 s (Bruce Ian b 10 May 1966, Andrew James b 14 April 1968, Graeme Alan b 6 Oct 1973); *Career* United Steel Cos Ltd 1961–64, postgraduate student 1964–65; Univ of Aberdeen: lectr in Spanish 1965–84, sr lectr 1984–90, prof in Spanish 1991–, convener Bd of Studies in Arts and Social Sciences 1989–92, dean Faculty of Arts and Divinity 1992–96, vice-princ 1995–, vice-princ (Strategic Planning) 1996–; *Books* Gabriel Miró: His Private Library and His Literary Background (1975), Gabriel Miró, El Obispo Leproso (ed, 1993); *Recreations* walking, digging, carpentry; *Style—* Prof Ian Macdonald; ✉ 47 North Deeside Road, Peterculter, Aberdeen AB14 0QL (☎ 01224 732284); Department of Spanish, King's College, University of Aberdeen, Aberdeen AB9 2UB (☎ 01224 272541, fax 01224 272562, e-mail i.r.macdonald@aberdeen.ac.uk)

MACDONALD, Dr James Stewart; s of Kenneth Stewart Macdonald (d 1959), of Mauritius and Perthshire, and Mary Janet, *née* McRorie (d 1991); *b* 11 Aug 1925; *Educ* Sedbergh, Univ of Edinburgh (MB ChB, DMRD); *m* 19 Oct 1951, Dr Catherine Wilton Drysdale, da of John Drysdale, CBE (d 1979), of Kuala Lumpur, Malaya and Perthshire; 2 s (Kenneth John Stewart, Murdo James Stewart); *Career* RAMC Maj 2 i/c 23 Para Field Ambulance 1952; asst radiologist St Thomas' Hosp London 1959–62; Royal Marsden Hosp: conslt radiologist 1962–85, vice chm Bd of Govrs 1975–82 (memb Bd 1967–82), dir Diagnostic X-ray Dept 1978–85; hon sr lectr Inst of Cancer Res 1966–85, teacher in radiology Univ of London 1966–85; contrib to numerous books and scientific jls on radiology of cancer; memb: Cncl Royal Coll of Radiologists 1968–73, numerous working parties MRC 1968–85, Ctee of Mgmnt Inst of Cancer Res 1969–82, Exec Ctee South Met Cancer Registry 1971–82, London Ctee Ludwig Inst for Cancer Res 1971–85; sec gen Symposium Ossium (London) Euro Assoc of Radiology 1968 (memb numerous ctees 1968–85); UK del for diagnostic radiology Union Européene des Medicins Specialistes 1972–81; appeals sec Duke of Edinburgh's Award Scheme (Perth and Kinross) 1986–88, chm Timber Growers UK (E of Scotland) 1988–91, dep chm Timber Growers UK (Scotland) 1991–94; memb: Exec Ctee Scottish Cncl Devpt and Indust 1991–94, Cncl Scottish Landowners' Fedn 1991–94, Cncl Rural Forum Scotland 1990–94; tstee Scottish Forestry Tst 1991–94; memb Br Inst of Radiology; FRSM, FRCPEd, FRCR, FRSA; *Recreations* field sports; *Clubs* Army & Navy; *Style—* Dr J S Macdonald; ✉ Darquhillan, Gleneagles, Auchterarder, Perthshire PH3 1NG (☎ 01764 662476)

McDONALD, Prof Janet Brown Inglis; da of Robert Inglis Caldwell (d 1987), and Janet Gilbert, *née* Lindsay (d 1987); *b* 28 July 1941; *Educ* Hutchesons' Girls' GS Glasgow, Royal Scottish Acad of Music and Drama pt/t, Univ of Glasgow (MA); *m* 1 July 1964, Ian James McDonald, s of James Murray McDonald (d 1947); 1 da (Katharine Lindsay b 14 April 1977); *Career* Univ of Glasgow: asst lectr Dept of English Literature 1965–66 (res fell 1963–65), lectr Dept of Drama 1966–79 (asst lectr 1966–68), prof of drama 1979–; chair: Drama Ctee Scottish Arts Cncl 1985–88 (also memb Cncl), Drama Theatre Bd CNAA 1982–85, Performing Arts Bd CNAA 1989–91, Standing Ctee of Univ Depts of Drama 1982–85, Bd of Citizens' Theatre Ltd 1991–; govr RSAMD 1982–94, memb Court Univ of Glasgow 1991–94; FRSAMD 1992, FRSE 1991; *Books* The New Drama 1990–1914 (1985), The Citizens' Theatre 1990 (with Claude Schumacher, 1991), Harley Granville Barker, An Edinburgh Retrospective (with Leslie Hill, 1993); *Style—* Prof Janet McDonald, FRSE; ✉ 61 Hamilton Drive, Glasgow G12 8DP (☎ 0141 339 0013); Department of Theatre, Film and Television Studies, University of Glasgow, Florentine House, 53 Hillhead Street, Glasgow G12 8QF (☎ 0141 330 5162, fax 0141 3304142)

MacDONALD, Maj-Gen John Donald; CB, CBE, DL; s of Col John MacDonald, OBE, of St Andrews, and Isabelle Brown Watt Brown; *b* 5 April 1938; *Educ* George Watson's Coll Edinburgh, RMA Sandhurst, RMCS Shrivenham, DSSC India, Nat Def Coll Latimer; *m* 31 March 1964, Mary, da of Dr Graeme Warrack, CBE, DSO, TD, DL; 2 da (Sarah b 1 Nov 1965, Caroline b 14 Feb 1967), 1 s (Neil Alisdair b 19 Sept 1968); *Career* cmmnd King's Own Scottish Borderers 1958, RASC 1963, Royal Corps of Tport 1976–78, cmd Armd Div Tport Regt BAOR 1978–80 (Lt-Col), exchange instructor Aust Army Cmd and Staff Coll 1980–82, head of personnel and logistics Armd Div BAOR 1983–86 (Col), head of personnel and offr for human resources MOD London 1987–88, distribution and tport dir 1 Br Corps BAOR 1988–91 (Brig), DG Tport and Movement (Distribution) Army 1991–93 (Maj-Gen); gen sec: jt secretariat Royal Br Legion Scotland, The Earl Haig Fund Scotland, Officers Assoc Scotland; chm Sportsmatch Scotland; memb Sports Cncl Scotand 1994–; Freeman City of London 1991, Liveryman Worshipful Co of Carmen 1991; FCIT 1988, FILDM 1990; *Recreations* travel, music, art, rugby (internationalist), athletics (internationalist), golf, skiing; *Clubs* Army and Navy, Royal and Ancient, Hon Co of Edinburgh Golfers; *Style—* Maj-Gen John MacDonald, CB, CBE, DL; ✉ Ormiston Hill, Kirknewton, W Lothian EH27 8DQ (☎ 01506 882180)

MacDONALD, John Grant; CBE (1989, MBE 1962); s of John Nicol MacDonald (d 1969), and Margaret, *née* Vasey (d 1977); *b* 26 Jan 1932; *Educ* George Heriot's Sch, NDC Latimer; *m* 5 Feb 1955, Jean, da of John Kenneth Kyle Harrison (d 1972); 1 s (Iain b 1959), 2 da (Margaret, Fiona); *Career* HM Armed Forces 1950–52; HM FS now Dip Serv 1949–92: Berne 1954–59, third sec Havana 1960–62, second then first sec (commerce) Lima 1966–71, Parly clerk FCO 1972–75, first sec (commerce) and head of Trade Promotion Section Washington 1975–79, head of Chancery Dhaka 1980–81, head of Chancery and HM Consul Bogota 1981–84, cnsllr FCO 1985–86, HM ambassador to Paraguay 1986–89, HM ambass to Panama 1989–92, head UK Delgn and dep head (policy) EC Monitor Mission Zagreb 1992–93, FCO 1993 (Cabinet Office 1994–95); *Recreations* travel, photography, swimming; *Clubs* Naval and Military, Royal Over-Seas League; *Style—* John G MacDonald, Esq, CBE; ✉ c/o Foreign and Commonwealth Office, King Charles Street, London SW1A 2AH

MacDONALD, John Grant; s of John William MacDonald (d 1985), of Kirkintilloch and Glasgow, and Jessie, *née* Grant (d 1992); *b* 20 May 1933; *Educ* Allan Glen's Sch

Glasgow, Univ of Strathclyde; *m* 30 March 1968, Ione Margaret, da of Melvyn Philip Bremer, JP (d 1977), of Lake Farm, Waverley, NZ; 1 da (Fiona b 5 March 1970); *Career* Nat Serv RAF 1959–61 serv Malaya and Singapore; with Sir Basil Spence London 1961–65, registered architect 1963 (ARIBA 1965), Garner Preston & Strebel 1965–66, directorate of devpt DOE 1966–73, in private practice 1973–; chm Andover Town Twinning Assoc 1977–78, pres Andover Chamber of Trade Commerce and Indust 1978–79, chm Central Hants Branch RIBA 1987–89, memb Cncl RIBA 1989–95; contrib DOE Review of Architects (Registration) Acts 1992; *Recreations* sailing, conversational French; *Style*— John G MacDonald, Esq; ✉ Chartered Architect, Russell Hse, 40 East St, Andover, Hants SP10 1ES (☎ 01264 324068)

MACDONALD, John Reginald; QC (1976); s of Ranald Macdonald, MBE (d 1959), and Marion Olive, *née* Kirkby (d 1981); *b* 26 Sept 1931; *Educ* St Edward's Sch Oxford, Queens' Coll Cambridge (MA); *m* 1958, Erica Rosemary, da of Lt-Col Eric Stanton (d 1987); 1 s (Toby b 1964), 1 da (Hettie b 1962); *Career* called to the Bar Lincoln's Inn 1955, bencher Lincoln's Inn 1985, in practice Chancery Bar specializing in human rights and constitutional cases 1957–; Parly candidate (Lib) Wimbledon 1966 and 1970, Parly candidate (Lib/Alliance) Folkestone & Hythe 1983 and 1987; chm Lib Dem Lawyers 1991–; *Recreations* cricket, theatre; *Clubs* MCC, National Liberal; *Style*— John Macdonald, Esq, QC; ✉ 12 New Square, Lincoln's Inn, London WC2A 3SW (☎ 0171 405 3808, fax 0171 831 7376)

MacDONALD, John William; s of John MacDonald (d 1984), and Anne, *née* Richards (d 1988); *b* 13 June 1938; *Educ* Boteler GS Warrington, NDC Latimer, Manchester Business Sch (dip); *m* 16 Jan 1960, Margaret Millam, da of James Burns; *Career* served RN 1957–59; HM Dip Serv: joined 1955, third sec Cairo 1960–64, third sec Tokyo 1964, Japanese language student 1964–66, second sec Tokyo 1967–69, FCO 1969–72, second sec Dhaka 1972–74, first sec Tokyo 1974–79, FCO 1979–80, seconded as head of Exports to Japan Unit DTI 1980–81, NDC Latimer 1981–82, first sec Dhaka 1982–83, first sec Dar es Salaam 1983–87, dep head Consular Dept FCO 1987–91, HM consul gen Shanghai 1991–94, ret; *Recreations* walking, golf, listening to music; *Clubs* Little Chalfont Golf; *Style*— John MacDonald, Esq; ✉ Cherry Orchard, Garden Reach, Chalfont St Giles, Bucks HP8 4BE (☎ 01494 763577)

McDONALD, Kenneth; *b* 24 May 1938; *Educ* George Heriot's Sch Edinburgh, Sch of Architecture Edinburgh Coll of Art (DipArch); *Career* architectural apprentice Basil Spence and Partners 1955–58; Reiach and Hall and associated companies: architect 1961–72, assoc 1972–89, ptnr 1989–93, dir 1993–; recent clients incl: Life Association of Scotland, Church Cmmrs of England, Standard Life, J Sainsbury, Lothian Health; lectr and ldr of discussion gps at practice and mgmnt courses Depts of Architecture Heriot-Watt Univ and Univ of Edinburgh and for Mgmnt Advsy Serv RIBA, jtly prepared and presented a design case study for Dept of Architecture and Bldg Sci Univ of Strathclyde; ARIBA 1962, FRIAS 1993 (ARIAS 1962); *Style*— Kenneth McDonald, Esq; ✉ Reiach and Hall Architects, 6 Darnaway Street, Edinburgh EH3 6BG (☎ 0131 225 8444, fax 0131 225 5079)

MACDONALD, Sir Kenneth Carmichael; KCB (1990), CB (1983); s of William Thomas Macdonald, and Janet Millar Macdonald; *b* 25 July 1930; *Educ* Hutchesons' GS, Univ of Glasgow (MA); *m* 1960, Ann Elisabeth Pauer; 1 s, 2 da; *Career* Nat Serv RAF 1952–54; MOD: entered 1954, dep under sec of state (Procurement Exec) 1980–84, dep under sec of state (Resources and Progs) 1985–88, second perm under sec of state 1988–90; chm: Raytheon Europe 1991–94, Cossor Electronics 1991–, Cncl of Voluntary Welfare Work 1993–, International Military Services Ltd 1993–, Raytheon UK 1995–; *Recreations* golf; *Style*— Sir Kenneth Macdonald, KCB; ✉ c/o Barclays Bank, 27 Regent Street, London SW1Y 4UB

McDONALD, Kevin; OBE (1996); s of Patrick McDonald (d 1966), and Teresa Mary McDonald (d 1976); *b* 20 Oct 1933; *Educ* Mexborough Schofield Tech Coll (City & Guilds Plumbing Sanitary and Domestic Engr); *m* 22 Jan 1988, Donna Brigitte, *née* Nunn; 1 s (Michael Francis b 14 March 1988), 1 da (Amie Mary b 1 July 1993); *Career* dir Hepworth Iron Co 1966–72; fndr chm and md: Bartol Plastics Ltd 1965–72, Macdee Plastics 1973–75, Polypipe plc 1980–; *Recreations* shooting, motor sport, fishing; *Clubs* Annabel's, Mark's; *Style*— Kevin McDonald, Esq, OBE; ✉ Polypipe plc, Broomhouse Lane, Edlington, Doncaster, S Yorkshire DN12 1ES (☎ 01709 770000, fax 01709 770001, telex 547353)

McDONALD, Dr (Edward) Lawson; s of late Charles Seaver McDonald, of London, and late Mabel Deborah, *née* Osborne; *b* 8 Feb 1918; *Educ* Felsted, Clare Coll Cambridge, Middx Hosp London (MD), Harvard Univ; *m* 1953 (m dis 1972), (Ellen) Greig, *née* Rattray; 1 s (James b 16 June 1956); *Career* WWII Surgn Lt RNVR served N Atlantic and Normandy campaigns 1943–46; asst Med Dept Peter Bent Brigham Hosp Boston Mass and res fell Harvard Univ 1952–53, Rockefeller travelling fell 1952–53, asst dir Inst of Cardiology Univ of London 1955–61; conslt cardiologist: London Hosp 1960–78, Nat Heart Hosp 1961–83, King Edward VII Hosp for Offrs London 1968–88, King Edward VII Hosp Midhurst 1970–92; hon conslt cardiologist Nat Heart Hosp 1983–, emeritus consulting cardiologist King Edward VII Hosp Midhurst 1992–; memb: Bd of Govrs Nat Heart and Chest Hosps 1975–82, Cncl Br Heart Fndn 1975–83; advsr Malaysian Govt; visiting lectr: Univs and Cardiac Socs in Europe, N and S America, China and USSR; St Cyres lectr 1966, Charles A Berns Meml lectr Albert Einstein Coll of Med NY 1973, 5 World Congress of Cardiology Souvenir Orator and Lectr's Gold medallist 1977; int fell Cncl on Clinical Cardiology American Heart Assoc, hon fell Turkish Med Soc; memb: Br Cardiac Soc (chm 1979), Assoc of Physicians of GB and I, American Heart Assoc, Italian Soc of Cardiology, Pakistan Cardiac Soc, Scientific Cncl Revista Portuguesa de Cardiologia, various cardiology socs in S America; fell American Coll of Cardiology, FRCP; Order of the Crown of Johore 1980; *Books* Medical and Surgical Cardiology (jtly, 1969), Very Early Recognition of Coronary Heart Disease (ed, 1977); *Recreations* art, skiing, mountain walking, sailing; *Style*— Dr Lawson McDonald; ✉ 9 Bentinck Mansions, Bentinck St, London W1M 5RJ (☎ 0171 935 7101)

MACDONALD, Morag (Mrs Walter Simpson); CBE (1993); da of Murdoch Macdonald Macdonald, of Glasgow, and Isobel, *née* Black; *b* 8 Feb 1947; *Educ* Bellahouston Acad Glasgow, Univ of Glasgow (LLB), Coll of Law London; *m* 12 Nov 1983, Walter Freeman Simpson, s of Vivian Simpson, OBE (d 1973); 1 da; *Career* called to the Bar Inner Temple 1974; The Post Office: joined 1968, various posts in telecommunications and corporate HQ 1969–79, PA to md Girobank 1980–81, seconded to DTI 1982, sec PO 1985–94 (dep sec 1983–85); memb Cncl and Mgmnt Ctee Indust and Parly Tst 1986–94; memb: Hon Soc The Inner Temple 1971, Cncl St George's Hosp Med Sch 1993–; FRSA 1990; *Recreations* walking, embroidery; *Style*— Miss Morag Macdonald, CBE

MACDONALD, Nigel Colin Lock; s of T W Macdonald, of Banstead, Surrey, and B E Macdonald, *née* Whitbourn; *b* 15 June 1945; *Educ* Cranleigh Sch; *m* Jennifer Margaret; 1 da (Genevieve Clare b 16 Dec 1985); *Career* articled clerk Thomson McLintock 1962–68, ptnr Ernst & Young (formerly Ernst & Whinney, previously Whinney Murray & Co) 1976–; dir British Standards Instn 1992–, chm James Lock & Co, pres Inst of Chartered Accountants of Scotland 1993–94; memb: Industl Devpt Advsy Bd, Review Panel Fin Reporting Cncl; MICAS 1968, FRSA 1993; *Clubs* RAC, City of London; *Style*— Nigel Macdonald, Esq; ✉ 10 Lynwood Road, Epsom, Surrey; Ernst & Young, 1 Lambeth Palace Road, London SE1 7EU (☎ 0171 931 3555, fax 0171 931 3807)

McDONALD, Dr Oonagh A; da of Dr H D McDonald; *Educ* Roan Sch for Girls Greenwich, E Barnet GS, King's Coll London (PhD); *Career* former philosophy lectr Bristol Univ; Parly candidate (Lab) Glos S Feb and Oct 1974, MP (Lab) Thurrock 1976–87; PPS to the chief sec to the Treasy 1977–79; oppn front bench spokesman on: defence 1981–83, Treasy and Civil Serv 1983–87; currently research and mgmnt conslt; memb Cncl Consumers' Assoc 1988–93; bd memb: Investors' Compensation Scheme 1991–, Securities and Investments Bd 1993–; Gwilym Gibbon res fell Nuffield Coll Oxford 1988–89; FRSA 1993; *Books* Parliament at Work (1989), The Future of Whitehall (1992); *Style*— Dr Oonagh McDonald; ✉ c/o The Securities and Investments Board, 2 Bunhill Row, London EC1Y 8SR (home ☎ 0181 940 5563)

McDONALD, Patrick John; s of Patrick McDonald, of Hepscott Manor, Morpeth, Northumberland, and Margaret, *née* Price; *b* 26 Sept 1962; *Educ* Northumberland Co Coll (Int Schoolboys Rugby); *m* 4 Aug 1984, Claire Alison, da of Brian Kell; 2 s (Samuel Patrick Donovan b 29 June 1987, Nathanial John Ryan b 11 March 1991), 1 da (Lois Amelia Kelly b 15 May 1993); *Career* chef de partie Granby Hotel Northumberland 1980–83, chef de partie then sr sous chef Grosvenor House Hotel 1983–84, sous chef Dorchester Hotel 1984–85, head chef Manor House Hotel Castle Combe Wilts 1985–87; exec chef: Ettington Park Hotel Stratford upon Avon 1987–88, Charingworth Manor Hotel Glos 1988–89; chef/patron Epicurean Restaurant 1991– (Stow on the Wold 1991–91, Evesham Rd Cheltenham 1991–94, 81 The Promenade Cheltenham 1994–); owner Waterloo Place (with Harvey Nichols) St James's London 1997–; dir: Designer Dinner Parties Ltd 1990–, Epicurean Restaurants Ltd 1994–; chef conslt Harvey Nichols PLC 1995–; *Awards* AA Best Newcomer of the Year Award 1990, Master Chef 1990, Good Food Guide Restaurant of the Year 1990, two AA Rosettes 1991, Egon Ronay Star 1991, Ackerman Clover Award 1991, three AA Rosettes 1993, Egon Ronay Rgnl Dessert of the Year 1993, Courvoisier Guide one of finest restaurants in world (by Lord Lichfield) 1993, Michelin Star 1994, two Egon Ronay Stars 1994, Good Food Guide County Restaurant 1994, four AA Rosettes 1995, Michelin Red M 1995; *Books* Simply Good Food (1997); *Recreations* shooting, fishing; *Style*— Patrick McDonald, Esq; ✉ Epicurean Restaurants Ltd, 81 The Promenade, Cheltenham, Glos GL51 1PJ (☎ 01242 222466, fax 01242 222474)

MACDONALD, Peter Cameron; DL (West Lothian 1987); s of Sir Peter George MacDonald, WS, JP, DL (d 1983), of Edinburgh, and Lady Rachel Irene, *née* Forgan (d 1990); *b* 14 Dec 1937; *Educ* Loretto, East of Scotland Coll of Agric (Dip Agric); *m* 2 Aug 1974, Barbara Helen, da of David Ballantyne, of Peebles; 2 step s (David Drimmie b 1964, Patrick Drimmie b 1967); *Career* farmer 1961–96; dir J Dickson & Son Gunmakers 1968–; Scottish Landowners Fedn: memb Cncl 1976–, convener 1985–88, chm Countryside Review Gp 1988, vice pres 1989; Scottish Landowners Fedn rep: Standing Conf on Countryside Sports 1985–, Scottish Ctee Game Conservancy 1988–, Ctee FACE (UK) 1991–, Steering Ctee The Code of Good Shooting Practice 1990–; memb: Cncl Blackface Sheepbreeders Assoc 1970–74, Pentland Hills Rural Land Mgmnt Gp 1977–84, West Lothian Countryside Advsy Ctee, West Lothian Dist Countryside Ctee 1978–81, Forth River Purification Bd 1979–87; dir Royal Highland Agric Soc of Scotland 1985; vice chm: Pentland Hills Regnl Park Consultative Ctee 1987–89, Pentland Hills Regional Park Advsy Ctee 1989–95; *Recreations* fishing, shooting, golf; *Clubs* Hon Co of Edinburgh Golfers; *Style*— Peter Macdonald, Esq, DL; ✉ Waterheads Farmhouse, Eddleston, Peeblesshire EH45 8QX (☎ and fax 01721 730229)

McDONALD, Hon Lord; Robert Howat McDonald; MC (1944); s of Robert Glassford McDonald (d 1965), of Paisley, Renfrew; *b* 15 May 1916; *Educ* John Neilson Inst Paisley, Glasgow Univ (MA, LLB); *m* 1949, Barbara, da of John Mackenzie, of Ross-shire; *Career* served WWII Maj NW Europe, KOSB (despatches); advocate 1946, QC 1956, Sheriff Ayr & Bute 1966–71, pres Industl Tbnl Scotland 1971–73, senator Coll Justice (Scottish Lord of Session with title Lord McDonald) 1973–89; *Clubs* New (Edinburgh); *Style*— The Hon Lord McDonald, MC; ✉ 5 Doune Terrace, Edinburgh

MACDONALD, Vice Adm Sir Roderick Douglas; KBE (1978, CBE 1966); s of late Douglas Macdonald, and Marjorie; *b* 25 Feb 1921, Java; *Educ* Fettes; *m* 1, 1943 (m dis 1980), Joan, da of Adm of the Fleet Sir Algernon Usborne Willis, GCB, KBE, DSO; 2 s (and 1 s decd); m 2, 1980, (Cynthia) Pamela Mary, da of Humphrey Ernest Bowman, CMG, CBE (d 1965), and sis of Sir Paul Humphrey Armytage Bowman, Bt, *qv*; formerly w of Rear Adm Josef Bartosik, CB, DSC, RN; *Career* entered RN 1939, served WWII Norway, Atlantic, Med, Eastern Fleet, N Sea and Normandy, served Cyprus 1957 (despatches), cmd Naval Forces Borneo 1965–66 (CBE), Vice Adm 1976, ADC to HM The Queen 1973, COS to C-in-C Naval Home Cmd 1973–76, COS Allied Naval Forces S Europe 1976–79; artist with regular one-man exhibitions London and Edinburgh 1979–, featured in Archibald's Dictionary of Sea Painters; chieftain Skye Highland Games; pres: Skye Piping Soc, Inverness Sea Cadet Unit; tstee Clan Donald Lands Trust; yr bro Trinity House; fell Nautical Inst (vice pres 1976–85); *Books* The Figurehead (1993); *Recreations* gardening, sailing; *Clubs* Caledonian, Royal Naval Sailing Assoc, Royal Scottish Pipers Soc; *Style*— Vice Adm Sir Roderick Macdonald, KBE; ✉ Ollach, Braes, Isle of Skye IV51 9LJ

MACDONALD, Roderick Francis; QC (Scot 1988); s of Finlay Macdonald (d 1991), and Catherine, *née* Maclean; *b* 1 Feb 1951; *Educ* St Mungo's Acad Glasgow, Univ of Glasgow (LLB Hons); *Career* admitted advocate 1975, advocate-depute (crown counsel) 1987–93, home advocate-depute (sr crown counsel) 1990–93; memb Criminal Injuries Compensation Bd 1995–, legal chm Pensions Appeal Tbnls for Scotland 1995–; *Style*— Roderick Macdonald, QC; ✉ 6A Lennox Street, Edinburgh EH4 1QA (☎ 0131 332 7240); Advocates' Library, Parliament House, Edinburgh EH1 1RF (☎ 0131 226 5071, fax 0131 225 3642, telex 727856 FACADVG)

MACDONALD, Ronald Robert; s of George Macdonald (d 1994), and Anne, *née* Chapman (d 1972); *b* 31 Dec 1927; *Educ* Hutchesons Boys GS, Univ of Glasgow (MB ChB, MD), Royal Coll of Obstetricians and Gynaecologists (MRCOG, FRCOG), Royal Coll of Surgeons Edinburgh (FRCSEd); *m* 17 Feb 1962, Joan, da of James Albert Raper (d 1994); 1 s (Robert Duncan b 1966), 1 da (Anne b 1963); *Career* Sqdn Ldr med branch RAF 1952–55 (despatches 1954); Hall fell Dept of Obstetrics and Gynaecology Univ of Glasgow 1958–60, sr lectr Dept of Obstetrics and Gynaecology Univ of Leeds 1962–, conslt obstetrician and gynaecologist Leeds 1963–93; memb: Euro Assoc of Gynaecologists and Obstetricians, BMA; *Books* Scientific Basis of Obstetrics and Gynaecology (ed 3 edn, 1985), European Journal of Obstetrics and Gynaecology (Br ed); *Recreations* golf, photography; *Clubs* Perinatal; *Style*— Ronald Macdonald, Esq; ✉ Glebe House, 5 Shaw Lane, Leeds LS6 4DH (☎ 0113 278 9471)

MACDONALD, Shelagh; *see:* Meyer, Shelagh

MacDONALD-BARKER, Anthony William; s of William Hector MacDonald-Barker, of Croxley Green, Herts, and Sylvia Gwendoline Ada, *née* Rollings (d 1990); *b* 18 May 1943; *Educ* Merchant Taylors' Northwood; *Career* Colgate-Palmolive 1964–67, Int Chem Co 1967–69, BPC Publishing 1969–71, chemicals trader LS Raw Materials Ltd 1972–75, sales mangr Pharmaceutical Div Intercity Chemicals Ltd 1976–77, sales dir Harbottle (Pharmaceuticals) Ltd 1978–92, proprietor Macbar (int trade conslts) 1992–; FIEx 1984; *Recreations* most sports especially cricket (player), football (spectator), music, theatre, travel, philately; *Clubs* Old Merchant Taylors' Soc, The Cricket Soc, The Forty Club; *Style*— Anthony MacDonald-Barker, Esq; ✉ 29a Chingford Ave, Chingford, London E4 6RJ (☎ and fax 0181 529 6054)

MACDONALD-BUCHANAN, Capt John; MC (1945), DL (Northants 1978); s of Sir Reginald Macdonald-Buchanan, KCVO, MBE, MC, DL (d 1981), and Hon Catherine Buchanan (d 1987), da of 1 Baron Woolavington; bro of (Alexander) James Macdonald-Buchanan; *b* 15 March 1925; *Educ* Eton, RMC; *m* 1, 3 Nov 1950 (m dis 1969), Lady Rose Fane, o da of 14th Earl of Westmorland (d 1948); 1 s (Alastair b 1960), 2 da (Fiona b 1954, Serena b 1956); m 2, 1969, Jill Rosamonde, o da of Maj-Gen Cecil Benfield Fairbanks, CB, CBE (d 1980), and former w of Maj Jonathan Salusbury-Trelawney (ggs of Sir William S-T, 10 Bt); 2 da (Kate b 1970, Lucy b 1972); *Career* 2 Lt Scots Gds 1943, served 1944–45 NW Europe, Malaya 1948–50, Capt 1948, ret 1952; High Sheriff Northants 1963–64, Vice Lord Lt Northants 1991–; sr steward of Jockey Club 1978–82 (steward 1969–72), memb Horserace Betting Levy Bd 1973–78; *Clubs* Turf, White's; *Style*— Capt John Macdonald-Buchanan, MC, DL; ✉ Cottesbrooke Hall, Northamptonshire NN6 8PQ (☎ 0160 124 732); 22 Cadogan Place, London SW1 (☎ 0171 235 8615)

MacDONALD BURNS, Dr David C; s of Lt-Col Evan MacDonald Burns (d 1956), and Enid, *née* Reynolds; *b* 24 Feb 1937; *Educ* Malvern, Univ of London (MB BS, LRCP, MRCS, FRCOG); *m* 9 Nov 1964 (m dis 1995), Janet, da of Dr John Smallpeice; 1 s (Richard), 1 da (Katherine); *Career* Royal Signals 1955–57; conslt venereologist Royal Free Hosp and HM Prison Holloway 1973–85, sr conslt in genito-urinary medicine Royal Free Hosp NHS Tst Hampstead 1985–; chm Hampstead Div BMA; fndr memb: Int AIDS Soc, Assoc Genito-Urinary Medicine; librarian ATDC (Austins 1930–39), pres Harveian Soc London 1996–; FRCOG; *Books* contrib: Gynaecological Enigmata (1981), Primary Care in Obstetrics and Gynaecology (1991); *Recreations* pre-war Austins, single malts, car keys; *Style*— Dr David MacDonald Burns; ✉ Malborough Department of STD, The Royal Free Hospital, Pond Street, Hampstead, London NW3 2QG (☎ 0171 830 2047)

MACDONALD LOCKHART OF THE LEE, Angus Hew; *see:* Lockhart of the Lee, Angus Hew

MACDONALD OF CLANRANALD, Ranald Alexander; *see:* Clanranald, Capt of

MACDONALD OF GWAENYSGOR, 2 Baron (UK 1949); Gordon Ramsay Macdonald; s of 1 Baron, KCMG, PC (d 1966), and Mary, *née* Lewis (d 1967); *b* 16 Oct 1915; *Educ* Upholland GS, Manchester Univ; *m* 6 May 1941, Leslie Margaret, da of John Edward Taylor, of Rainford, Lancs; 3 da; *Heir* none; *Career* served 1940–46 with RA, Maj GSO; joined Bd of Trade 1946; UK trade cmmr Australia 1947–53; md Tube Investments (Export) Ltd 1953–64; chief exec UK Operations Hayek Engineering (AG Zurich), Ferro Metal & Chemical Co, Satra Consultants (UK); *Style*— The Rt Hon Lord Macdonald of Gwaenysgor; ✉ c/o House of Lords, London SW1A 0PW

MACDONALD OF SLEAT, *see:* Bosville Macdonald of Sleat

MacDONALD ROSS, George; s of John MacDonald Ross, CBE, of London, and Helen Margaret, *née* Wallace; *b* 11 Nov 1943; *Educ* Mill Hill Sch, St Catharine's Coll Cambridge (MA); *m* 24 June 1974, (Margaret) Lynne Ross, da of Elwyn Chubb, of Cardiff; *Career* asst lectr in philosophy Univ of Birmingham 1969–72; Univ of Leeds: res fell in history and philosophy of sci 1972–73, lectr in philosophy 1973–88, sr lectr 1988–, head of Dept of Philosophy 1990–93, dean Faculty of Arts 1991–93; vice-princ and academic dean Univ Coll Scarborough 1994–96, hon fell Univ Coll Scarborough 1996–; chm Nat Ctee for Philosophy 1985–94; memb: Ctee Br Soc for the History of Philosophy, Cncl Royal Inst of Philosophy, Ctee Leibniz-Gesellschaft; pres: Leibniz Assoc, SAPERE; FRSA; *Books* Leibniz (1984); *Recreations* conviviality, bricolage, walking; *Style*— George MacDonald Ross, Esq; ✉ 1 Oakfield Terrace, Grove Lane, Leeds LS6 4EQ (☎ 0113 294 7379, fax 0113 294 7390); Department of Philosophy, University of Leeds, Leeds LS2 9JT (☎ 0113 233 3287, fax 0113 233 3265, e-mail georgemr@ucscarb.ac.uk or gm.ross@Leeds.ac.uk)

MacDONELL OF GLENGARRY, Air Cdre (Aeneas Ranald) Donald; CB (1964), DFC (1940); Hereditary 22 Chief of Glengarry, 12 Titular Lord MacDonell; eld s of Maj Aeneas Ranald MacDonell of Glengarry, CBE (d 1941), of Swanage, Dorset (*see* Burke's Landed Gentry, 18 edn, vol III), and Dorah Edith, *née* Hartford (d 1935); *b* 15 Nov 1913; *Educ* Hurstpierpoint Coll, RAF Coll Cranwell; *m* 1, 14 Oct 1940 (m dis 1972), Diana Dorothy (d 1980), da of Lt-Col Henry Richard Keane, CBE (d 1938), of Belleville House, Cappoquin, Co Tipperary; 2 s ((Aeneas) Ranald Euan (Younger of Glengarry) b 1941, (Colin) Patrick b 1946), 1 da (Lindsay Alice (Mrs Brian Cuthbertson) b 1947); m 2, 9 March 1973, Lois Eirene Frances, da of Rev Gerald Champion Streatfeild (d 1988), of Winchester, Hants; 1 s (James Donald of Scotus b 1974), 1 da (Penelope Lois b 1976); *Career* cmmnd Pilot Offr RAF 1934, No 54 (F) Sqdn 1934–36, seconded to Fleet Air Arm 1936 (Fleet Fighter Pilot); Flying Instr 1938, Sqdn Ldr Air Min 1939, Offr Cmdg No 64 Spitfire Sqdn 1940–41, POW 1941–45, War Cabinet Office (Wing Cdr) 1946–47, Chief Flying Instr RAF Coll Cranwell 1949–50; Air Cdre, Air Attaché Moscow 1956–58; Cmdt No 1 Initial Trg Sch 1959–60; dir Mgmnt and Work Study MOD 1960–64; ret 1964; mangr operational res, Constructors John Brown 1964–67; personnel mangr CITB 1967–73; head of Industl Dept Industrial Soc 1973–77; ptnr John Courtis & Ptnrs 1977–80; ret; memb Standing Cncl of Scottish Chiefs; tstee: Clan Donald Lands Tst, Finlaggan Tst, Invergarry Castle Tst; MBIM, FIWSP; *Recreations* bird watching, reading, writing; *Clubs* RAF; *Style*— Air Cdre Donald MacDonell of Glengarry, CB, DFC; ✉ Elonbank, Castle St, Fortrose, Ross-shire IV10 8TH (☎ 01381 620121)

McDONNELL, David Croft; JP; *b* 9 July 1943; *m* 9 Nov 1967, Marieke; 3 da (Emma, Sarah-Jane, Sophia); *Career* Bryce Hanmer & Co (became Thornton Baker 1964 then Grant Thornton 1971): articled clerk 1959–64, ptnr 1972, nat managing ptnr 1989; chm Bd of Tstees National Museums and Galleries on Merseyside 1995–; FCA (ACA 1965); *Recreations* sailing, motor racing (spectating), walking, mountaineering; *Style*— David McDonnell, Esq, JP; ✉ Grant Thornton, Grant Thornton House, Melton St, London NW1 2EP (☎ 0171 383 5100, fax 0171 383 4715)

McDONNELL, Prof James Anthony Michael (Tony); s of Michael Francis McDonnell, of Madeley, Nr Crewe, Cheshire, and Vera Phyllis, *née* Redding (d 1987); *b* 26 Sept 1938; *Educ* St Joseph's Coll Stoke on Trent, Univ of Manchester (BS, PLD); *m* 22 July 1961, Jean Mary, da of George Gordon (d 1976); 2 s ((Benedict) Michael b 27 Feb 1965, Roger James b 1 June 1971), 1 da (Louise Anne b 21 Aug 1962); *Career* res asst Nuffield Radio Astronomy Labs 1964–65, post-doctoral res assoc NASA Goddard Spaceflight Centre USA 1965–67; Univ of Kent: lectr in physical electronics 1967–72, sr lectr in electronics 1972–77, reader in space sciences 1977–85, prof of space physics and head of space sci 1985–; contrib to Planetary Science in Europe JAM McDonnell (Planetary and Interstellar Dust) 1980; various chapters of Advanced Space Res incl: Progress in Planetary Exploration 1981, Recent Researches into Solid Bodies and Magnetic Fields in the Solar System 1982, Cosmic Dust and Space Debris 1986; organiser and orater of welcome address Comet Nucleus Sample Return ESA Cornerstone Workshop Canterbury 1986; memb Ctee Space Astronomy and Radio Div SERC 1979–81; memb: UK Halley Watch Steering Ctee (later CHUKCC) 1983–87, Space Sci Prog Br Nat Space Centre 1988–; COSPAR: memb and sec Panel 3 C 1973–79, memb Sub-cmmn B1 ISC B 1982–86, exec memb ISC B 1984–88, chm ISC B 1988–, memb Organising Ctee IAU Cmmn 22 1979; memb: Meteoroid Shield Design Workshop ESA Comet Halley Mission 1981, ESA Lunar Polar Workshop 1981; govr Workshop on Planetology European Sci Fndn 1981, chm Organisation Ctee Symposium 6 COSPAR/IAU/IUTAM 1982, discipline specialist Int Halley Watch 1983, memb ESA/NASA Primative Bodies Study Team 1984; conslt: space station design USRA 1985, Comet nucleus sample return CNSR 1985–87, CAESAR assessment study 1986, VESTA phase A 1987; memb: Solar System Working Gp 1988–90, Rosetta Mission Definition Team ESA 1988; FRAS, FBIS 1987; *Books* Cosmic Dust (ed and co-author with John Wiley, 1978); *Recreations* tennis, woodwork; *Style*— Prof Tony McDonnell; ✉ Unit for Space Sciences, Physics Laboratory, University of Kent, Canterbury, Kent CT2 7NR (☎ 01227 459616, fax 01227 762616, telex 965449)

McDONNELL, John Beresford William; QC (1984); s of Beresford Conrad McDonnell (d 1960), and Charlotte Mary, *née* Caldwell (d 1981); *b* 26 Dec 1940; *Educ* City of London Sch, Balliol Coll Oxford (MA), Harvard Law Sch (LLM); *m* 3 Feb 1968, Susan Virginia, da of Wing Cdr Hubert Mortimer Styles, DSO (d 1942), and Audrey Elizabeth (now Lady Richardson); 2 s (Conrad b 1971, William b 1973), 1 da (Constance b 1975); *Career* called to the Bar Inner Temple 1968; Harkness fell 1964–66, Congressional fell American Political Sci Assoc 1965–66, Cons Res Dept 1966–69, HM Dip Serv 1969–71 (first sec, asst private sec to Sec of State 1970–71), in practice Chancery Bar 1972–; cncllr Lambeth BC 1968–69; Bencher Lincoln's Inn 1993; *Recreations* sculling; *Clubs* Athenaeum, London Rowing; *Style*— John McDonnell, Esq, QC; ✉ 17 Rutland Street, London SW7 1EJ (☎ 0171 584 1498, fax 0171 581 1731); office: 1 New Square, Lincoln's Inn, London WC2A 3SA (☎ 0171 405 0884, fax 0171 831 6109)

MacDONNELL, John Graham Randal; s of John Patrick Randal MacDonnell (d 1964), of Ilfracombe, and Vera Fuggle; *b* 15 Nov 1955; *Educ* Fortescue House Sch Twickenham (Shaftesbury Homes), Thames Valley GS, King Edward VI Sch Witley Surrey, Ealing GS, Newcastle upon Tyne Poly (BA); *m* Barbara Anne, da of William McBride, of Glasgow; 1 s (Graham Patrick Randal), 1 da (Lara Anne Siobhan); *Career* film ed BBC Scotland 1983–90; credits incl: Campus 1983, The Smith Boys 1983, A Kick Up The 80s 1984, The Visit 1984–88, Laugh - I Nearly Paid My Licence Fee 1985, The Master of Dundreich 1985, Naked Video 1986, Tutti Frutti (1987 BAFTA nomination, Kodak award), Arena - Byrne About Byrne 1988, The Justice Game 1989, Your Cheatin' Heart 1990; freelance film ed 1990–; credits: The Black Velvet Gown 1990 (NY Film & TV Festival Grand Award 1991), Accentuate the Positive 1991, The Blackheath Poisonings 1991–92, Blue Black Permanent 1992, Body and Soul 1992–93, Boswell and Johnson's Tour of the Western Isles 1993, Class Act 1993–94, Billy Connolly's World Tour of Scotland 1994, She's Out 1994–95, Class Act 1995, Silent Witness 1995–96; *Recreations* children, cinema, galleries, photography, television, reading, swimming, snooker, music; *Style*— John G R MacDonnell, Esq; ✉ 81 Bloxham Road, Banbury, Oxon OX16 9JS (☎ 01295 262391)

MacDONNELL OF THE GLENS, The Count Randal Christian Charles Augustus Somerled Patrick; s of The Count and 24 Chief Robert Jarlath Hartpole Hamilton MacDonnell of the Glens (d 1984), of 5 Longford Terr, Monkstown, Dublin, and his 2 w, The Countess MacDonnell of the Glens, *née* Una Kathleen Dolan; descent from Iain Mhóir MacDonnell, 2 s of John I Lord of the Isles and Princess Margaret, da of King Robert II of Scotland; *see* Burke's Irish Family Records 1976 and Burke's Peerage, Earl of Antrim (who descends from the yst s of 5 Chief and in the female line); f suc kinsman the 23 Chief (ka 1941); 19 Chief cr Bt 1872, dsp 1875; *b* 19 Aug 1950; *Educ* Stonyhurst, Trinity Coll, Dublin and the King's Inns, Dublin; *Heir* bro, Count Peter Martin Ignatius Laurence David Colla Hamilton MacDonnell; *Career* 25 chief Clan Donald S of Antrim; officially recognised Chief of the Name by the Chief Herald of Ireland (Gaelic patronymic "MacIain Mhóir") Lord of the Glens of Antrim; Count of the Holy Roman Empire (which title, created in the preceeding generation passed to the heirs male of the 1st Count in 1766); kt SMOM 1971; *Recreations* opera, ballet, rugby, polo, history, parties; *Style*— The Count Randal MacDonnell of the Glens; ✉ 94 Fisherman's Wharf, Dublin 4, Ireland

McDONOUGH, David Fergus; s of Alan James McDonough, of Eastbourne, Sussex, and Shirley Davis; *b* 7 June 1953; *Educ* Stowe, Merton Coll Oxford (MA); *m* 1, 1978, Caroline Eugénie, *née* Axford; m 2, 28 May 1992, Mrs Vanessa E L Reeves, da of Douglas Gent; *Career* personal asst to The Lord Feldman 1975–79, md McDonough Assocs Ltd 1979–90, sr conslt Lowe Bell Consultants 1990–; co-fndr and chm The October Club 1988–, memb Cncl of Mgmnt The Local Investment Fund 1995–, govr Queen Elizabeth's Fndn for Disabled People; Freeman City of London, Liveryman Worshipful Co of Merchant Taylors; FRSA; *Recreations* politics, reading, music, theatre, golf; *Clubs* White's, Lansdowne; *Style*— David McDonough, Esq; ✉ Lowe Bell Consultants, 7 Hertford St, Mayfair, London W1Y 8LP (☎ 0171 495 4044, fax 0171 491 2878)

McDOUGALL, Prof Bonnie S; da of William Morris McDougall (d 1990), and Ruth Constance, *née* Mather (d 1978); *b* 12 March 1941; *Educ* St George Girls' HS Sydney, Wollongong HS, Peking Univ, Univ of Sydney (MA, PhD, Univ medal); *m* Dec 1979, (Harry) Anders Hansson; 1 s ((Carl) Torkel b 30 April 1980); *Career* Univ of Sydney: Oriental librarian 1967–68, res fell 1970–71, lectr in Oriental studies 1972–76; Nuffield travelling scholar SOAS 1975, assoc Harvard Univ 1979–80 (res fell 1976–79), ed and translator Foreign Languages Press 1980–83, English teacher Coll of Foreign Affairs Peking 1984–86; prof of Chinese: Univ of Oslo 1987–90 (sr lectr 1986–87), Univ of Edinburgh 1990–; visiting lectr Harvard Univ 1977, 1978 and 1979; advsr Assoc of Chinese Translators and Interpreters in Scotland 1993–; memb: Amnesty International 1987–, Edgar Wallace Soc 1988–, PEN International 1989–92, Universities' China Ctee 1990– (memb Exec Cncl 1990–93), Cncl Br Assoc of Chinese Studies 1991– (pres 1995–), Bd Euro Assoc of Chinese Studies 1992–, Exec Ctee Scots Australia Cncl 1994–95; *Books* The Introduction of Western Literary Theories into China 1919–25 (1971), Paths in Dream: Selected Prose and Poetry of Ho Ch'i-fang (ed, 1976), Mao Zedong's Talks at the Yan'an Conference on Literature and Art (ed, 1980 and 1992), Notes from the City of the Sun: Poems by Bei Dao (ed, 1983), Popular Chinese Literature and Performing Arts in the People's Republic of China 1949–79 (ed, 1984), Bodong (ed, 1985), Waves (ed, 1985), The August Sleepwalker (ed, 1988), The Yellow Earth: A Film by Chen Kaige (1991); author of numerous papers in jls; *Recreations* travel, reading, walking; *Style*— Prof Bonnie S McDougall; ✉ Department of East Asian Studies, University of Edinburgh, 8 Buccleuch Place, Edinburgh EH8 9LW (☎ 0131 650 4227, fax 0131 651 1258)

MacDOUGALL, Sir (George) Donald Alastair; kt (1953), CBE (1945, OBE 1942); s of Daniel Douglas MacDougall (d 1929), and Beatrice Amy Miller (d 1954); *b* 26 Oct 1912; *Educ* Kelvinside Acad Glasgow, Shrewsbury, Balliol Coll Oxford (MA); *m* 1, 1937 (m dis 1977), Bridget Christabel, da of George Edward Bartrum; 1 s, 1 da; m 2, 1977, (Laura) Margaret (d 1995), da of George Edward Linfoot (d 1970), and formerly w of Robert Lowe Hall (later Baron Roberthall, d 1988); 2 step da; *Career* asst lectr Univ of Leeds 1936–39, economist; Winston Churchill's Statistical Branch 1939–45 and 1951–53; econ dir: OEEC Paris 1948–49, NEDO 1962–64; dir gen Dept of Econ Affairs 1964–68, head Govt Econ Serv and chief econ advsr HM Treasury 1969–73, chief econ advsr CBI 1973–84; chm EC Study Gp on Role of Public Fin in Euro Integration 1975–77; pres Royal Econ Soc 1972–74; Hon LLD Univ of Strathclyde, Hon LittD Univ of Leeds, Hon DSc Aston Univ; hon fell: Wadham Coll Oxford 1964– (fell 1945–50), Nuffield Coll Oxford 1967– (fell 1947–64), Balliol Coll Oxford 1992–; FBA; *Books include* The World Dollar Problem (1957), Studies in Political Economy (2 vols, 1975), Don and Mandarin: Memoirs of an Economist (1987); *Clubs* Reform; *Style*— Sir Donald MacDougall, CBE, FBA; ✉ Flat K, 19 Warwick Square, London SW1V 2AB (☎ 0171 821 1998)

McDOUGALL, Douglas Christopher Patrick; s of Patrick McDougall (d 1950), and Helen McDougall (d 1980); *b* 18 March 1944; *Educ* Edinburgh Acad, ChCh Oxford (MA);

m 4 June 1986, Hon Carolyn Jane, da of Baron Griffiths, MC, PC (Life Peer), *qv*; 2 da (Fiona Maria b 1987, Mary Helen b 1990); *Career* investmt mangr and ptnr Baillie Gifford & Co 1969 (sr ptnr 1989–); non-exec dir: IMRO 1987–, Provincial Insurance plc 1989–94, Baillie Gifford Japan Trust PLC 1989–, Pacific Horizon Trust plc 1992–; memb Investment Ctee Univ of Cambridge 1985–; chm: Exec Ctee Institutional Fund Mangrs Assoc 1994–96, Assoc of Investment Trust Companies 1995–; *Clubs* Brooks's, New (Edinburgh), City of London, Hon Co of Edinburgh Golfers; *Style*— Douglas McDougall, Esq; ✉ Linplum House, Haddington, E Lothian EH41 4PE (☎ 016O 810242); 1 Rutland Court, Edinburgh EH3 8EY (☎ 0131 222 4000, fax 0131 222 4099)

MACDOUGALL, Patrick Lorn; s of James Archibald Macdougall, WS (d 1982), and Valerie Jean, *née* Fraser; *b* 21 June 1939; *Educ* Schools in Kenya, Millfield, Univ Coll Oxford; *m* 1, 24 June 1967 (m dis 1982), Alison Noel, da of Herbert Charles Offer, MC (d 1991), of Cheshire; 2 s (Alasdair William Lorn b 1970, Thomas Hugh James b 1972); m 2, 15 April 1983, Bridget Margaret, da of Peter Scott Young (d 1988); 3 da (Laura Margaret Valerie b 1984, Nicola Elizabeth Bridget b 1987, Vanessa Emily Hope b 1990); *Career* called to the Bar Inner Temple 1962, mangr NM Rothschild & Sons 1967–70, chief exec Amex Bank (formerly Rothschild Intercontinental Bank) 1977–78 (exec dir 1970–77), exec dir Jardine Matheson Holdings 1978–85, chm and chief exec West Merchant Bank Ltd (formerly Standard Chartered Merchant Bank) 1990– (chief exec 1985–89); dir: Global Natural Resources Inc 1994–, Nuclear Electric plc 1994–96; FCA 1967, FRSA 1988; *Recreations* skiing, golf, opera, bridge; *Clubs* Hurlingham, The Wisley GC, Sotogrande CC (Spain), Shek-O CC (Hong Kong); *Style*— Patrick Macdougall, Esq; ✉ 40 Stevenage Road, London SW6 6ET (☎ 0171 736 3506); West Merchant Bank Ltd, 33–36 Gracechurch St, London EC3V OAX (☎ 0171 623 8711)

McDOWALL, David Buchanan; s of Angus David McDowall (d 1957), and Enid Margaret, *née* Crook; *b* 14 April 1945; *Educ* Monkton Combe Sch, RMA Sandhurst, St John's Coll Oxford (MA, MLitt); *m* 19 April 1975, Elizabeth Mary Risk, da of Dr John McClelland Laird; 2 s (Angus b 1977, William b 1979); *Career* Subaltern RA 1965–70; Br Cncl (Bombay, Baghdad & London) 1972–77, UNRWA 1977–79; writer (for adults and children); *Books* Lebanon - A Conflict of Minorities (1983), The Kurds (1985), The Palestinians (children's book 1986), The Palestinians (Minority Rights Gp 1987), The Spanish Armada (1988), An Illustrated History of Britain (1989), Palestine and Israel: The Uprising and Beyond (1989), The Kurds: A Nation Denied (1992), Europe and the Arabs: Discord or Symbiosis? (1992), Britain in Close-up (1993), The Palestinians: The Road to Nationhood (1994), A Modern History of the Kurds (1995), Richmond Park: the Walker's Historical Guide; *Style*— David McDowall, Esq; ✉ 31 Cambrian Rd, Richmond, Surrey TW10 6JQ (☎ 0181 940 3911)

MacDOWALL, Dr David William; s of William MacDowall (d 1944), of West Derby, Liverpool, and Lilian May, *née* Clarkson (d 1961); *b* 2 April 1930; *Educ* Liverpool Inst HS, Corpus Christi Coll Oxford (BA, MA, DPhil), Br Sch at Rome; *m* 21 June 1962, Mione Beryl, da of Ernest Harold Lashmar (d 1969), of Hinderton, Berkhamsted, Herts; 2 da (Sophie b 1965, Tara b 1968); *Career* Royal Signals: 2 Lt 1951–53, 2 Lt (TA) 1953, Lt (TA) 1956; asst keeper Dept Coins and Medals Br Museum 1956–60, princ Miny of Educn 1960–65; Univ Grants Ctee: princ 1965–70, asst sec 1970–73; master Univ Coll and hon lectr in classics, ancient history and oriental studies Univ of Durham 1973–78, dir N London Poly 1980–85 (asst dir 1979), chm Soc for S Asian Studies 1983–, assoc fell Centre for Research in East Roman Studies Univ of Warwick 1993–; conslt: OECD 1962 (also 1964 and 1966), UNESCO 1977 and 1978; hon treas: Royal Numismatic Soc 1966–73, Br Archaeological Assoc 1989–93; vice pres Br Archaeological Assoc 1993–, pres Royal Asiatic Soc 1994– (vice pres 1993–94); memb: Governing Body SOAS 1990–, Editorial Bd Numismatic Chronicle 1966–; hon sec Soc for Afghan Studies 1972–82; Barclay Head Prize for Ancient Numismatics Univ of Oxford 1953 and 1956, Medallist Associacion Numismatica Espanola 1964, Nelson Wright Medallist Numismatic Soc India 1974; corresponding memb: Istituto Italiano per il Medio ed Estremo Oriente 1986, American Numismatic Soc 1991; FRNS 1952, FRAS 1958, FSA 1960; *Books* Coin Collections - Their Preservation Classification and Presentation (1978), The Western Coinages of Nero (1979), The Roman Coins - Republic and Empire up to Nerva (Provinciaal Museum G M Kam at Nijmegen, XII, with A V M Hubrecht and W J A de Jong, 1991); *Recreations* travel, antiquities, photography, natural history, genealogy; *Clubs* Athenaeum; *Style*— Dr David MacDowall, FSA; ✉ Admont, Dancers End, Tring, Herts HP23 6JY

McDOWALL, Keith Desmond; CBE (1988); s of William Charteris McDowall (d 1941), of Croydon, Surrey, and Edna Florence, *née* Blake (d 1988), of Banstead, Surrey; *b* 3 Oct 1929; *Educ* Heath Clark Sch Croydon Surrey; *m* 1, 1957 (m dis 1985), Shirley Margaret Russell Astbury; 2 da (Clare Hamilton (Mrs Reid), Alison Ross (Mrs Dodson); m 2, 30 April 1988, Baroness Dean of Thornton-le-Fylde (Life Peer 1993), *qv*; *Career* Nat Serv RAF 1947–49; journalist 1946–55, journalist Daily Mail 1955–67 (indust ed London 1962–67); dir of info 1969–78: Bd of Trade, Dept of Econ Affrs, Home Office, Dept of Housing and Local Govt, N Ireland Office, Dept of Employment; dep dir gen CBI 1986–88 (dir of info 1981–86); conslt on public affrs and govt rels 1988–; *Recreations* sailing, golf; *Clubs* Reform, Royal Cornwall Yacht, Medway Yacht, South Herts Golf; *Style*— Keith McDowall, Esq, CBE; ✉ 2 Malvern Terrace, Islington, London N1 1HR

MacDOWELL, Prof Douglas Maurice; s of Maurice Alfred MacDowell (d 1973), and Dorothy Jean, *née* Allan (d 1980); *b* 8 March 1931; *Educ* Highgate Sch, Balliol Coll Oxford (MA, DLitt); *Career* classics master: Allhallows Sch 1954–56, Merchant Taylors' 1956–58; reader in Greek and Latin Univ of Manchester 1970–71 (asst lectr 1958–61, lectr 1961–68, sr lectr 1968–70), visiting fell Merton Coll Oxford 1969, prof of Greek Univ of Glasgow 1971–; FRSE 1991, FBA 1993; *Books* Andokides: On the Mysteries (1962), Athenian Homicide Law (1963), Aristophanes: Wasps (1971), The Law in Classical Athens (1978), Spartan Law (1986), Demosthenes: Against Meidias (1990), Aristophanes and Athens (1995); *Style*— Prof Douglas MacDowell, FRSE, FBA; ✉ Department of Classics, University of Glasgow, Glasgow G12 8QQ (☎ 0141 339 8855)

McDOWELL, Sir Eric Wallace; kt (1990), CBE (1982); s of Martin Wallace McDowell (d 1968), of Belfast, and Edith Florence, *née* Hillock (d 1974); *b* 7 June 1925; *Educ* Royal Belfast Academical Inst; *m* 24 June 1954, Helen Lilian, da of William Montgomery (d 1951), Belfast; 1 s (Martin b 11 Nov 1959), 2 da (Kathleen b 24 Jan 1958, Claire b 25 March 1964); *Career* WWII serv 1943–46; qualified CA 1948; ptnr Wilson Hennessey & Crawford 1952–73, sr ptnr in Belfast Deloitte Haskin & Sells 1980–85 (ptnr 1973–80); dir: NI Transport Holding Co 1971–74, Spence Bryson Ltd 1986–89, TSB Bank Northern Ireland plc 1986–92, Capita Management Consultants Ltd 1991– (chm 1992–), Shepherd Ltd 1992–, First Trust Bank 1992–96; memb: Advsy Ctee NI Central Investmt Fund for Charities 1975– (chm 1980–), NI Econ Cncl 1977–83, Industl Devpt Bd for NI 1982–91 (chm 1986–91), Broadcasting Cncl for NI 1983–86; memb: Exec Ctee Relate NI Marriage Guidance 1981– (chm 1992–96), Bd Tstees National Relate 1992–, Presbyterian Church in Ireland (trustee 1983–), Abbeyfield Belfast Soc (treas 1986–), Bd of Govrs Royal Belfast Academical Inst 1959– (chm 1977–86), Cncl Inst of CAs Ireland 1968–77 (pres 1974–75), Senate Queen's Univ of Belfast 1993–; pres Belfast Old Instonians Assoc 1993–94; Hon DSc Econ Queen's Univ of Belfast 1989; FCA 1957; *Recreations* current affairs, music & drama, foreign travel; *Clubs* Ulster Reform (Belfast), Royal Over-Seas League; *Style*— Sir Eric McDowell, CBE; ✉ Beechcroft, 19 Beechlands, Belfast BT9 5HU (☎ 01232 668771)

McDOWELL, Sir Henry McLorinan; KBE (1964, CBE 1959); s of John McDowell, and Margaret Elizabeth Bingham; *b* 10 Dec 1910; *Educ* Witwatersrand Univ, Queen's Coll Oxford, Yale Univ; *m* 1939, Norah Douthwaite (decd); 1 s, 1 da; *Career* served WWII 1 Bn N Rhodesia Regt; entered Colonial Serv 1938, sec Fed Treasy Rhodesia and Nyasaland 1959–63; chm Zimbabwe Bd Barclays Bank Int 1969–79; chllr Rhodesia/Zimbabwe Univ 1971–82; *Style*— Sir Henry McDowell, KBE; ✉ 2 Donne Ct, Burbage Rd, London SE24 9HH

McDOWELL, (Charles William) Michael; *b* 11 Feb 1928; *Educ* Huntingdon GS, UCL (BSc); *m* Audrey Diana; 1 s (Robert), 3 da (Sally Ann (Mrs Muir), Julie (Mrs Lloyd), Marion (Mrs Cook)); *Career* Public Works Dept Tanganyika 1951, sr engr Howard Humphreys & Sons 1958–62 (res engr 1954–56), dep res engr London CC 1956–58, princ and fndr M McDowell & Ptnrs 1963, sr ptnr M McDowell Co Partnership 1976–88, princ Engrg Disputes Servs 1988–; cncllr London Borough of Sutton 1968–74; IPHE: chm Met Centre 1972, memb Cncl 1973–87, pres 1982–83; memb Cncl CIWEM 1987–88; dir: Water Pollution Control Fedn 1986–89, Ciria 1988–90; chm Br Standard Clay Pipes; memb and leader: Euro Standards Delgn on Clay Pipes, Euro Standards Delgn on Sewerage and Drainage (outside buildings); Freeman City of London 1980, Liveryman Worshipful Co of Paviors 1980, Founder Master Company of Water Conservators 1988–90; FICE 1955, FIPHE 1956, FIHT 1958, FCIArb 1963, Hon FCIWEM 1988; *Recreations* veteran athletics; *Clubs* Ranelagh Harriers and Veterans Athletic, City Livery, United Wards; *Style*— Michael McDowell, Esq; ✉ 13 Gilhams Ave, Banstead, Surrey SM7 1QL (☎ 0181 394 1573, fax 0181 394 1864)

MacDUFF, Alistair Geoffrey; QC (1993); s of Alexander MacDonald MacDuff (d 1985), and Iris Emma, *née* Gardner; *b* 26 May 1945; *Educ* Ecclesfield GS nr Sheffield, LSE (LLB), Univ of Sheffield (LLM); *m* 1, 27 Sept 1969, Susan Christine (d 1991), da of Ronald David Kitchener, of Salthouse, Norfolk; 2 da (Karen b 1971, Jennifer b 1972); m 2, 9 July 1993, Katherine Anne, da of late Dr John Buckley, of Frampton on Severn, Glos; 1 da (Rebecca b 1995); *Career* called to the Bar Lincoln's Inn 1969, recorder of the Crown Ct 1987–; former chm local ward Lib Party; *Recreations* opera, theatre, golf, association football, collecting (and drinking) wine; *Clubs* Hendon GC, Economicals AFC; *Style*— Alistair MacDuff, Esq, QC; ✉ 13 Talbot Road, Highgate, London N6 (☎ 0181 245 9930); Devereux Chambers, Devereux Court, London WC2 (☎ 0171 353 7534, fax 0171 353 1724)

MACE, Brian Anthony; s of Edward Laurence Mace, and Olive, *née* Bennett; *b* 9 Sept 1948; *Educ* Maidstone GS, Gonville and Caius Coll Cambridge (MA); *m* 8 Sept 1973, Anne Margaret, *née* Cornford; *Career* Inland Revenue: admin trainee 1971–73, seconded to Secretariat Inflation Accounting Ctee 1974–75, princ 1975–82, asst sec 1982–90, under sec 1990–, currently dir Savings and Investment Div and Capital and Valuation Div; *Recreations* opera, Lieder, theatre, cricket; *Style*— Brian A Mace, Esq; ✉ Savings and Investment Division, Inland Revenue, South West Wing, Bush House, Strand, London WC2B 4RD (☎ 0171 438 6614, fax 0171 438 6766)

McEACHRAN, Colin Neil; QC (Scot 1981); s of Eric Robins McEachran (d 1974), and Norah Helen, *née* Bushe (d 1995); *b* 14 Jan 1940; *Educ* Glenalmond Coll, Merton Coll Oxford (MA), Univ of Glasgow (LLB), Univ of Chicago (JD); *m* 27 Sept 1967, Katherine Charlotte, da of K D D Henderson, CMG; 2 da (Katrina Emily b 24 Oct 1968, Juliet Helen b 27 Jan 1971); *Career* admitted advocate 1968, advocate depute 1974–77; pt/t pres Pension Appeal Tbnl of Scotland 1995–; memb Scottish Legal Aid Bd 1990–; chm Cwlth Games Cncl for Scotland 1995–; *Recreations* target shooting, hill-walking; *Style*— Colin McEachran, Esq, QC; ✉ 13 Saxe Coburg Place, Edinburgh EH3 (☎ 0131 332 6820)

MacECHERN, Gavin MacAlister; s of Dugald MacAlister MacEchern, and Diana Mary, *née* Body; *b* 7 March 1944; *Educ* Tonbridge; *m* 1972, Sarah Alison, da of late Eric and Cecil Walker, *née* Eaton-Evans; 3 da (Georgina b 1976, Tanya b 1978, Christina b 1981); *Career* admitted slr 1967; fndr shareholder and dir Arlington Securities Plc 1980–94, chm Mansford Holdings Plc 1995–; *Recreations* hunting, racing, skiing, shooting, tennis, golf; *Clubs* Brooks's, Turf, Wisley; *Style*— Gavin MacEchern, Esq; ✉ Southrop Manor, Glos; Mansford Holdings Plc, The Clockhouse, St Catherine's Mews, Milner Street, London SW3 2PX

McENERY, Peter Robert; s of Charles McEnery (d 1981), and Ada Mary Brinson McEnery; *b* 21 Feb 1940; *m* 1978; 1 da; *Career* actor; fndr memb and assoc artist with RSC; *Theatre* roles incl: Eugene in Look Homeward Angel (Phoenix) 1962, Rudge in Next Time I'll Sing to You (Criterion) 1963, Konstantin in The Seagull (Queens) 1964, Edward Gover in Made in Bangkok (Aldwych) 1986, Trigorin in The Seagull (Lyric) 1975; dir: Richard III (Nottingham) 1971, The Wound (Young Vic) 1972; *Television* Clayhanger 1976, The Aphrodite Inheritance 1979, The Jail Diary of Albie Sachs 1980, Japanese Style 1982, The Collectors 1986, The Mistress 1986, Witchcraft 1991; *Films* Tunes of Glory 1961, Victim 1961, The Moonspinners 1963, Entertaining Mr Sloane 1970; *Recreations* steam railway preservation, skiing, American football; *Style*— Peter McEnery, Esq; ✉ Dennis Selinger, ICM Ltd, Oxford House, 76 Oxford Street, London W1N 0AX (☎ 0171 636 6565, fax 0171 323 0101)

McENTEE, Peter Donovan; CMG (1978), OBE (1963); s of Ewan Brooke McEntee (d 1947), and Caroline Laura Clare, *née* Bayley (d 1949); *b* 27 June 1920; *Educ* Haileybury; *m* 1945, Mary Elisabeth, da of George Sheriff Sherwood (d 1956); 2 da (Carol, Bridget); *Career* HM Forces 1939–45, KAR (Maj); HM Overseas Civil Serv 1946–63 (dist cmmr, ret at princ Kenya Inst of Admin), first sec FCO 1963, Lagos 1964–67, served in Whitehall 1967–72, consul gen Karachi 1972–75, Govr and C-in-C Belize 1976–80; memb Cncl The Impact Fndn; *Recreations* music, reading, natural history; *Clubs* Royal Over-Seas League; *Style*— P D McEntee, Esq, CMG, OBE; ✉ Woodlands, Church Lane, Danehill, Sussex RH17 7EU (☎ and fax 01825 790574)

McEVOY, His Hon Judge; David Dand; QC (1983); s of David Dand McEvoy (d 1988), of Stevenston, Ayrshire, and Ann Elizabeth, *née* Breslin (d 1994); *b* 25 June 1938; *Educ* Mount St Mary's Coll, Lincoln Coll Oxford (BA); *m* 6 April 1974, Belinda Anne, da of Lt-Col Thomas Argyll Robertson, OBE, of Pershore, Worcs; 3 da (Alice b 1978, Louise b 1979, Isabella b 1984); *Career* 2 Lt The Black Watch (RHR) 1957–59, served Cyprus 1958; called to the Bar Inner Temple 1964, recorder of the Crown Ct 1979–96 (asst recorder 1977–79), circuit judge (Midland & Oxford Circuit) 1996–; *Recreations* racing, golf, fishing; *Clubs* Caledonian, Blackwell Golf; *Style*— His Hon Judge McEvoy, QC; ✉ 2 Fountain Court, Steelhouse Lane, Birmingham B4 (☎ 0121 236 3882)

McEWAN, Surgn Capt Alan; OBE (1977); s of Norman McEwan (d 1972), of Darnick, Melrose, and Ethel Maud, *née* Stanley (d 1983); *b* 20 Dec 1928; *Educ* Dollar Acad, Univ of Edinburgh (LRCP, LRCS, LRFPS); *m* 29 March 1963, Caroline Mary, da of Lt-Col Roderick Dillwyn Sims (d 1965), 2 s (Angus b 1964, Alistair b 1967); *Career* RN 1957, Royal Naval Hosp Haslar 1957–59, MO HMS Troubridge 1959–61, Infectious Disease Unit RN Hosp Haslar 1961–62, RA Med Coll Millbank 1962–63, Fleet MO S Atlantic and S American on C-in-C Staff Cape Town S Africa 1963–65, Admty Med Bd London 1965–67; Base MO HMS Tamar Hong Kong 1965–67; PMO: Polaris Base HMS Neptune Faslane Scotland 1969–72, HMS Tamar Hong Kong 1972–73; staff of Med Dir Gen London 1973–75, staff of med, dir gen dep dir med personnel and advsr in gen practice to RN 1975–77, dir of postgrad studies Inst of Naval Med Alverstoke Hants 1977–79, Surgn Capt 1977, voluntary ret 1979; OStJ 1977; res MO HM Tower of London 1979–89; med advsr: Financial Times 1980–, Booker plc 1980–, Int Wool Secretariat 1980–89, Goldman Sachs 1981–, Channel Four TV 1981–, Charles Barker Group 1985–, Total Oil Marine 1985–, John Swire & Sons Ltd, The Royal National Theatre; memb Scottish Int

Rugby Squad 1954–55 (played for Univ of Edinburgh, Melrose, Cooptimists, South of Scotland); hon med advsr SSAFA HQ London, memb Exec Ctee Forces Help Soc & Lord Roberts Workshops, med examiner in first aid St John Ambulance; former memb: Med Cncl Hong Kong 1967–69 and 1972–73, Gen Practice Advsy Ctee, Postgrad Cncl for Med Educn England and Wales 1974–79; Freeman City of London 1980, Liveryman Worshipful Co of Curriers 1980; FRSM 1973, MFCM 1977, FRCGP 1978, fell Med Soc of London 1980; *Recreations* golf, cricket, rugby; *Clubs* White's, Army & Navy, Berkshire GC, MCC, London Scottish RFC, Melrose RFC; *Style*— Surgn Capt Alan McEwan, OBE; ✉ 8 Wellington Rd, Hampton Hill, Middx (☎ 0181 977 6170); 107 Harley St, London W1 (☎ 0171 935 9463)

McEWAN, Geraldine; da of Donald McKeown, and Norah, *née* Burns; *b* 9 May 1932; *Educ* Windsor County Girls' Sch; *m* 1953, Hugh Percival Cruttwell; 1 s (Greg), 1 da (Claudia); *Career* actress; RSC 1956, 1958 and 1961, NT Co: 1965–71, 1980–81, 1983–84 and 1995–96; *Theatre* incl: The Rivals (NT, Evening Standard Award for Best Actress) 1983, Lie of The Mind (Royal Court) 1987, Lettice and Lovage (Globe) 1988–89, Hamlet (Riverside Studios) 1992, The Bird Sanctuary (Abbey Theatre Dublin) 1994, The Way of the World (RNT, Evening Standard Best Actress Award) 1995; as dir incl: As You Like It (Renaissance Co, Phoenix) 1988, Treats (Hampstead Theatre Club) 1989, Waiting for Sir Larry (Edinburgh Festival) 1990, Four Door Saloon (Hampstead Theatre Club) 1991, Keyboard Skills (Bush) 1993; *Television* incl: The Prime of Miss Jean Brodie 1977, L'Elegance 1982, The Barchester Chronicles 1983, Mapp and Lucia 1985–86, Oranges are Not the Only Fruit 1990 (BAFTA Best Actress Award), Mulberry 1992–93; *Films* incl: The Adventures of Tom Jones 1975, Escape from the Dark 1978, Foreign Body 1986, Henry V 1989, Robin Hood - Prince of Thieves 1991, Moses 1995; *Style*— Geraldine McEwan; ✉ c/o Marmont Management Ltd, Langham House, 308 Regent Street, London W1R 5AL (☎ 0171 637 3183, fax 0171 323 4798)

McEWAN, Ian Russell; s of Maj David McEwan, of Ash, Hants, and Rose Violet Lilian Moore; *b* 21 June 1948; *Educ* Woolverstone Hall Sch, Univ of Sussex (BA), Univ of E Anglia (MA); *m* 1982 (m dis), Penelope Ruth, da of Dennis Allen, of Lewes, Sussex; 2 s (William b 1983, Gregory b 1986), 2 step da (Polly b 1970, Alice b 1972); *Career* author; began writing 1970; Hon DLitt: Univ of Sussex 1989, UEA 1993; FRSL 1982; *Books* First Love, Last Rites (1975), In Between The Sheets (1978), The Cement Garden (1978), The Comfort of Strangers (1981), The Imitation Game (1981), Or Shall We Die? (1983), The Ploughman's Lunch (1985), The Child in Time (1987), The Innocent (1990), Black Dogs (shortlisted Booker Prize 1992), The Daydreamer (1994); *Films* The Ploughman's Lunch (1983), Last Day of Summer (1984), Sour Sweet (1989), The Innocent (dir by John Schlesinger, 1993), The Good Son (1993); *Style*— Ian McEwan, Esq; ✉ c/o Jonathan Cape Ltd, 20 Vauxhall Bridge Road, London SW1V 2SA (☎ 0171 973 9730)

McEWAN, Dr John Alexander; s of Duncan Watson McEwan (d 1980), of Bexhill-on-Sea, E Sussex, and Dr Mary McEwan, *née* Buck (d 1956); *b* 5 Feb 1929; *Educ* Sherborne, Univ of Cambridge (MA), The London Hosp (MB BChir); *m* 23 Aug 1958, Ishbel Margaret Maxwell, da of James Black (d 1973), of Strathclyde; 1 s (Ewan Duncan b 15 April 1960), 1 da (Islay Mary b 9 June 1962); *Career* Nat Serv RAF MO Egypt and Cyprus 1954–56; GP Southwark 1957–89, conslt in family planning KCH 1974–93, dir of GP studies KCH Med Sch 1976–81, jt dir Dept of Reproductive Med KCH 1989–93; currently hon conslt Dept of Family Planning and Reproductive Health Care Optimum-St Giles; memb: Clinical and Scientific Advsy Ctee Nat Assoc of Family Planning Doctors 1983–93, Camberwell Health Authy 1986–90, Fndn Bd Faculty of Family Planning and Reproductive Health Care RCOG 1993–95; chm: Brook Advsy Centres 1986–95, Jt Ctee on Contraception RCOG and RCGP 1989–93, Trg and Educn Ctee FFPRHC 1993–95; memb: BMA, RSM, NAFPD; FRCGP 1977, FRCOG ad eundem 1995, FFFP 1996; *Books* Handbook of Contraceptive Practice - DHSS (1974), Planning or Prevention (with P C L Diggory, 1976); *Recreations* sailing (medium distance cruising); *Clubs* Cruising Association; *Style*— Dr John McEwan; ✉ 21 Kennington Palace Court, Sancroft St, London SE11 5UL (☎ 0171 582 7346); Department of Family Planning and Reproductive Health Care, Optimum-St Giles, St Giles's Road, London SE5 7RN (☎ 0171 635 1112)

McEWAN, Mhairi; da of Edward McEwan, of Yorkshire, and Rose Helen, *née* Betts; *b* 5 July 1961; *Educ* St Michael's Sch Billingham, St Mary's Sixth Form Coll Middlesbrough, Univ of Leiceseter (BSc Psychology, Faculty of Sci prize); *m* 25 June 1988, Phillip Keague Bentley, s of Alan William Bentley; 1 da (Naomi Frances b 22 Jan 1992), 1 s (Guy Edward Keague b 29 April 1994); *Career* Lever Brothers Ltd UK 1982–89 (brand mangr 1982–86, nat account exec (sales) 1986–88, sr brand mangr 1988–89), market mangr Egypt Unilever Export Cairo 1989–92, Euro mktg mangr Lever Europe Paris 1992–94; vice pres mktg (Europe) Pepsi-Cola International Ltd London 1995–96, head of mktg Walkers Snacks Ltd (pt of Pepsi-Cola International) 1996–; memb: City Women's Network, Women in Mgmnt; FCIM 1995; *Recreations* horse-riding, skiing, tennis; *Style*— Ms Mhairi McEwan; ✉ Walkers Snacks Ltd, 1600 Arlington Business Park, Theale, Reading, Berks RG7 4SA (☎ 0118 930 6666, fax 0118 930 3152)

MacEWAN, Nigel Savage; s of Nigel Savage, and Ellen, *née* Wharton; *b* 21 March 1933; *Educ* Yale Univ (BA), Harvard Univ (MBA); *m*; 1 s (Nigel), 3 da (Alison, Pamela, Elizabeth); *Career* served USN 1955–57; assoc: Morgan Stanley & Co NYC 1959–62, White Weld & Co NYC 1962–63; vice pres R S Dickinson and Co Charlotte North Carolina 1963–68, chm Financial Consultants International Ltd Brussels 1965–68, ptnr then pres and dir White Weld & Co NYC 1968–78, sr vice pres and dir Merrill Lynch Pierce Fenner and Smith NYC 1978–87, chm Merrill Lynch Capital Partners Incorporated 1985–87, pres, chief exec offr and dir Kleinwort Benson N America Incorporated NYC 1987–93, dir Kleinwort Benson Aust Income Fund Inc 1987–; formerly pres and dir Kleinwort Benson Holdings Incorporated; formerly dir: Alex Brown Kleinwort Benson Reality Advisors Inc, Kleinwort Benson Ltd, Kleinwort Benson Group plc, Sharps Pixley Inc, Va Trading Corp, Supermarkets General, Amstar, Cellu-Craft, Sun Hung Kai International Ltd, Merrill Lynch International Ltd, Credit Suisse Whiteweld; chm NY Gp Securities Indust Assoc 1975–76; adj prof of business admin Univ of NY 1973–75, pres Tokeneke Tax Dist Darien 1978–80 (latterly treas); memb: Islesboro Sailors Museum Ctee 1994–, Islesboro Health Bd 1995–; memb Securities Indust Assoc (chm NY Gp 1975–76); *Clubs* Yale, Tokeneke, Wee Burn, Bond (NY), NY Yacht, Tarratine; *Style*— Nigel S MacEwan, Esq

McEWAN, Robin Gilmour; QC (Scot 1981); s of Ian Gilmour McEwan (d 1976), and Mary McArthur Bowman McEwan; *b* 12 Dec 1943; *Educ* Paisley GS, Univ of Glasgow (LLB, PhD); *m* 1973, Sheena, da of Stewart Francis McIntyre (d 1974); 2 da (Stephanie b 1979, Louisa b 1983); *Career* Sheriff of Lanark 1982–88, Sheriff of Ayr 1988–; temp judge Court of Session and High Court of Justiciary 1991–; *Recreations* golf; *Clubs* New (Edinburgh), Hon Co of Edinburgh Golfers, Prestwick Golf; *Style*— Robin McEwan, Esq, QC; ✉ Sheriff Ct, Ayr KA7 1DR (☎ 01292 268474)

McEWEN, Prof James; s of Daniel McEwen (d 1973), of Kinross, and Elizabeth Wells, *née* Dishington (d 1962); *b* 6 Feb 1940; *Educ* Dollar Acad, Univ of St Andrews (MB ChB); *m* 24 Oct 1964, Elizabeth May, da of late Andrew Archibald; 1 s (Daniel Mark b 6 May 1966), 1 da (Ruth Elizabeth b 24 Jan 1968); *Career* various trg posts in hosp and general practice Dundee 1963–65, asst med offr of health Dundee 1965–66, lectr Dept of Social and Occupational Med Univ of Dundee 1966–74, sr lectr Dept of Community Health Univ of Nottingham 1975–81, chief med offr Health Educn Cncl 1981–82, prof of community med KCL and dir of public health Camberwell Health Authy 1982–89, Henry Mechan prof of public health Univ of Glasgow 1989–; FFPHM, FFOM, FRCPGlas (memb Cncl); *Books* Coronary Heart Disease and Patterns of Living (jtly, 1979), Participation in Health (jtly, 1983), Measuring Health Status (jtly, 1986); *Style*— Prof James McEwen; ✉ Department of Public Health, University of Glasgow, 2 Lilybank Gardens, Glasgow G12 8RZ (☎ 0141 330 5013, fax 0141 330 5018)

McEWEN, Sir John Roderick Hugh; 5 Bt (UK 1953), of Marchmont, Co Berwick, and Bardrochat, Co Ayr; yr s of Sir Robert Lindley McEwen, 3 Bt (d 1980), and Brigid Cecilia, *née* Laver; suc bro, Sir James Francis Lindley, 4 Bt, 1983; *b* 4 Nov 1965; *Educ* Ampleforth, UCL; *Heir* cousin, Adam Hugo McEwen, b 9 Feb 1965; *Style*— Sir John McEwen, Bt; ✉ Polwarth Crofts, Greenlaw, Berwickshire TD10 6YR

McEWEN, John Sebastian; 6 s of Sir John Helias Finnie McEwen, 1 Bt (d 1962), of Marchmont, Berwickshire, Scotland, and Bridget Mary, *née* Lindley (d 1971); *b* 29 July 1942; *Educ* Eton, Trinity Coll Cambridge (MA); *m* 1975, Gillian Josephine, da of Dennis Martin Heeley; 2 s (David b 2 Nov 1977, Duncan Dundas b 3 May 1979); *Career* journalist and author; art critic The Sunday Telegraph 1990–; *Books* Howard Hodgkin - Forty Paintings 1973–84 (with David Sylvester) 1984, Paula Rego (1992, 2 edn, 1996), Glenkiln (with John Haddington, 1993), John Bellany (1994); *Clubs* Beefsteak, Green's; *Style*— John McEwen, Esq; ✉ 74 St Augustine's Road, London NW1 (☎ 0171 485 4386, fax 0171 284 4846)

McEWEN, Prof Keith Alistair; s of George Charles McEwen (d 1979), and Marjorie Anne, *née* Field (d 1991); *b* 11 Dec 1944; *Educ* Dr Challoner's GS Amersham, Pembroke Coll Cambridge (MA, PhD); *m* 20 May 1986, Ursula, da of Maximilian Steigenberger (d 1983); *Career* lectr in physics: Univ of Copenhagen 1970–73, Univ of Salford 1973–81; seconded as sr lectr to Institut Laue-Langevin Grenoble 1981–86, prof of experimental physics at Birkbeck Coll Univ of London 1986–; CPhys, FInstP 1989; *Recreations* music, walking, skiing; *Style*— Prof Keith McEwen; ✉ Department of Physics, Birkbeck College, University of London, Malet St, London WC1E 7HX (☎ 0171 631 6310, fax 0171 631 6220)

MACEY, Rear Adm David Edward; CB (1984); s of Frederick William Charles Macey (d 1978), of Strood, Kent, and Florence May, *née* Macey (d 1986); *b* 15 June 1929; *Educ* Sir Joseph Williamson's Mathematical Sch Rochester, Britannia RNC Dartmouth; *m* 1, 1958, Lorna Therese (d 1976), er da of His Hon Judge Oliver William Verner (d 1957); 1 s (Hugo), 1 da (Anna); m 2, 1982 (m dis 1994), Fiona Beloe, o da of Vice Adm Sir William Beloe, KBE, CB, DSC; *Career* RNC Dartmouth, Midshipman 1948, cruisers carriers and destroyers 1950–63, Cdr 1963, American Staff Coll 1964, Cdr RNC Dartmouth 1970, Capt 1972, Directorate Naval Plans 1972–74, RCDS 1975; dir: RN Staff Coll 1976–78, Naval Manpower 1979–81; ADC to HM the Queen 1981, Rear Adm 1981, Dep Asst Chief of Staff (Ops) Staff of the Supreme Allied Cdr 1981–84, ret; receiver gen Canterbury Cathedral 1984–, gentleman usher of the Scarlet Rod 1985–90, sec and registrar Order of the Bath 1990–, Archbishops' Cmmn on Cathedrals 1992–94; *Recreations* walking, cricket, cooking; *Clubs* MCC, Anglo-Belgian, Band of Brothers; *Style*— Rear Adm David Macey, CB; ✉ The Receiver General, Cathedral House, The Precincts, Canterbury, Kent CT1 2EH (☎ 01227 762862, fax 01227 762897)

MACEY, Air Vice-Marshal Eric Harold; OBE (1975); s of Harold Fred Macey (d 1989), and Katrina Macey (d 1981); *b* 9 April 1936; *Educ* Shaftesbury GS; *m* 1957, Brenda Ann, da of Frederick Tom Spencer Bracher (d 1983); 1 s (Julian b 1958); 1 da (Sharon b 1963); *Career* AOC and Cmdt RAF Coll Cranwell 1985–87, asst chief Def Staff (policy and nuclear) 1987–89, dir gen of trg RAF 1989–91; *Style*— Air Vice-Marshal Eric Macey, OBE; ✉ Ebblemead, Homington, Salisbury, Wilts SP5 4NL (☎ 01722 718565)

MACEY, Roger David Michael; s of late Eric Hamilton Macey, and Margaret Maria, *née* Newman; *b* 15 Nov 1942; *Educ* St Mary's Coll Ireland; *m* 1, 1970 (m dis 1995), Julie Elizabeth, da of John Everard Mellors, of Mount Eliza, Melbourne, Aust; 2 s (Jonathan b 20 April 1973, Giles b 25 May 1976); m 2, 1996, Barbara; *Career* dir: Wm Brandts Sons & Co (insur) Ltd 1972–76, P S Mossé & Ptnrs Ltd 1977–83, Macdonagh Boland Group 1989; non-exec dir: J Jackson & Partners Ltd 1975–76, P S Mossé Life & Pensions 1977–83, George Miller Underwriting Agencies Ltd 1977–86, Conquest Security Services PLC; md Macey Williams Ltd 1976–94, chm Macey Williams Insurance Services Ltd 1976–94, chm Macey Clifton Walters Ltd 1991–94, dir: Rollins Hudig Hall Ltd (following takeover of Macey Williams companies) 1994–96, Aon Risk Services Ltd (following name change) 1996–; memb Lloyd's 1974–; *Recreations* shooting, golf, tennis, horse racing; *Clubs* Turf, City of London; *Style*— Roger Macey, Esq; ✉ 2 Gonville House, Manor Fields, Putney, London SW15; Aon Risk Services Ltd, 16 St Helen's Place, London EC3A 6DE

McFADDEN, Jean Alexandra; CBE, JP, DL (City of Glasgow); *b* 26 Nov 1941; *Educ* Hyndland Sch, Univ of Glasgow (MA), Notre Dame Coll of Educn, Univ of Strathclyde (LLB); *Career* classics teacher various secdy schs Glasgow and Lanarkshire 1964–86, lectr in law Univ of Glasgow 1992–; Glasgow City Cncl (formerly Glasgow Corpn then Glasgow Dist Cncl): cncllr Cowcaddens Ward 1971–84, cncllr Scotstoun Ward following boundary change 1984–, convener Manpower Ctee 1975–77, opposition ldr 1977–79, ldr of the Cncl 1979–86 and 1992–94 (dep ldr 1990–92), hon city treas and convener Fin Ctee 1986–92, convener Glasgow City Cncl 1995–96, convener Social Strategy Ctee 1996–; memb: Scottish Economic Cncl 1993–96, Health Appointments Advsy Ctee 1994–; pres Convention of Scottish Local Authorities 1990–92; convener: Scottish Local Govt Info Unit, Scottish Local Authorities Mgmnt Centre; bd memb: Citizens Theatre, Glasgow Cultural Enterprises Ltd, GDA, Wild Cat Theatre, Mayfest; Depute Lord Lieutenant City of Glasgow 1992– (Vice Lord Lieutenant 1981–92); *Recreations* golf, hill walking, theatre-going; *Style*— Ms Jean McFadden, CBE, JP, DL; ✉ 16 Lansdowne Crescent, Glasgow G20 6NQ (☎ 0141 334 3522); Glasgow City Council, City Chambers, George Square, Glasgow G2 1DU (☎ 0141 287 4054)

MACFADYEN, Air Marshal Ian David; CB (1991), OBE (1984); Air Marshal Sir Douglas Macfadyen, KCB, CBE (d 1968), and Priscilla Alfreda, *née* Dafforn (now Mrs P A Rowan); *b* 19 Feb 1942; *Educ* Marlborough (capt shooting team), RAF Coll Cranwell (Sword of Honour); *m* 28 Jan 1967, Sally, da of Air Cdre Ernest Bruce Harvey; 1 s (Simon James Douglas b 19 Aug 1968), 1 da (Katherine Elizabeth b 28 April 1971); *Career* RAF Coll Cranwell 1960–63, 19 Sqdn 1965–68, ADC HQ RAF Strike Cmd 1969, flying instr Cranwell 1970–73, RAF Staff Coll 1973, 111 Sqdn 1974–75, Flt Cdr 43 Sqdn 1975–76, HQ 2 ATAF(PSO) 1976–79, cmd 29 Sqdn 1980–84, cmd 23 Sqdn 1984, MOD London 1984–85, cmd RAF Leuchars 1985–87, RCDS 1988, MOD 1988–90, COS then Cdr Br Forces Middle East Riyadh 1990–91, Asst Chief of Defence Staff Operational Requirements (Air Systems) 1991–94, DG Saudi Arabian Projects 1994–; pres RAF Clay Pigeon Shooting Assoc; Upper Freeman Guild of Air Pilots and Air Navigators; QCVSA 1974, FRAeS 1991 (MRAeS 1984); *Recreations* shooting, gliding, golf, photography, windsurfing, aviation history; *Clubs* RAF, Royal & Ancient; *Style*— Air Marshal Ian Macfadyen, CB, OBE

McFADYEN, Jock; s of James Lachlan McFadyen, of Carnoustie, Angus, and Margaret, *née* Owen; *b* 18 Sept 1950; *Educ* Renfrew HS, Chelsea School of Art (BA, MA); *m* 1, 1971 (m dis 1989), Carol Ann, *née* Hambleton; 1 s (James b 29 July 1972); m 2, 1991, Susie, *née* Honeyman; 1 da (Annie b 6 Feb 1993), 1 s (George b 23 June 1995); *Career* pt/t lectr Slade Sch of Art 1980–; designer The Judas Tree (Royal Opera House Covent Garden); *Exhibitions*: 25 solo exhibitions since 1978 incl: Acme Gallery, Blond Fine Art, National Gallery, Scottish Gallery, Camden Arts Centre; many mixed exhibitions in Europe and USA incl: Hayward Annual, John Moore's, Royal Academy, British Art Show, New

British Painting (USA), British Cncl Foreign Touring Shows; *Works in Public Museums* incl: National Gallery (residency), V & A, Imperial War Museum, Kunsthalle Hamburg, Manchester, Birmingham, Glasgow; *Commissions* incl: Arts Cncl purchase, National Gallery residency, Imperial War Museum Eastern Europe project; *Recreations* poodles, motorcycles; *Clubs* Vintage Japanese Motorcycle; *Style*— Jock McFadyen, Esq; ✉ 284 Globe Road, London E2 0NS (☎ 0181 983 3825)

McFADZEAN, Hon (Gordon) Barry; s of Baron McFadzean, KT (Life Peer; d 1996), and Eileen, *née* Gordon; *b* 14 Feb 1937; *Educ* Winchester, Christ Church Oxford; *m* 1, 1968 (m dis 1982), Julia Maxine, da of late Sir Max Dillon, of Sydney, NSW, Aust; 2 da; m 2, 1984, Diana Rosemary, yst da of late Sam Waters, of Norfolk; *Career* Nat Serv 2 Lt RA 1955–57; CA 1963; dir of various merchant banks 1964–85, exec dir S G Warburg & Co Ltd (Merchant Bankers) 1975–78, exec chm Corporate Advisory Partnership Ltd 1986–; *Recreations* music, theatre; *Clubs* Boodle's, City of London, Melbourne (Melbourne), Australian (Sydney); *Style*— The Hon Barry McFadzean; ✉ 108 The Butlers Wharf Building, 36 Shad Thames, London SE1 2YE (☎ 0171 357 7676)

McFALL, John; MP (Lab) Dumbarton (majority 6,129); s of John McFall, and Jean McFall; *b* 4 Oct 1944; *Educ* St Patrick's Sch Dumbarton, Paisley Coll of Technol, Open Univ (BA), Strathclyde Business Sch (MBA); *m* 1969, Joan, *née* Ward; 3 s (John, Gerald, Kevin), 1 da (Elaine); *Career* sch teacher 1974–87; MP (Lab) Dumbarton 1987–; former oppn whip (with responsibility for foreign affrs, defence and trade and indust) resigned post during Gulf War; former memb Select Ctee: on defence, on Sittings of the House; currently dep shadow sec of state for Scotland (with responsibility for indust, Highlands and Islands, fisheries and forestry, economic affrs, employment and trg, home affrs, tport and roads); currently memb: Information Ctee, Parly & Scientific Ctee (hon sec), Exec Ctee Parly Gp for Energy Studies; vice-chm Br/Italian Gp; sec: Retail Indust Gp, Roads Study Gp; jt sec Br/Peru Gp; treas: Br/Hong Kong Gp, Scotch Whisky Gp; *Recreations* golf, running, reading; *Style*— John McFall, Esq, MP; ✉ 14 Oxhill Rd, Dumbarton G82 4PG (☎ 01389 31437); House of Commons, London SW1A 0AA (☎ 0171 219 3521)

McFARLAND, Anthony Basil Scott; er s and h of Sir John Talbot McFarland, 3 Bt, TD, *qv*; *b* 29 Nov 1959; *Educ* Marlborough, Trinity Coll Dublin (BA); *m* 28 Oct 1988, Anne Margaret, 3 da of Thomas Kennedy Laidlaw, of Gernonstown, Slane, Co Meath; 1 da (Amelia Elizabeth b 13 Sept 1990), 2 s (Max Anthony b 13 July 1993, Rory John b 6 May 1996); *Career* exec: Ladbroke Group plc, Thompson T Line plc, Price Waterhouse; dir: Information and Imaging Systems Ltd, J T McFarland Holdings; ACA; *Recreations* tennis, rugby, skiing; *Style*— Anthony McFarland, Esq; ✉ 31 Walham Grove, London SW6

McFARLAND, Sir John Talbot; 3 Bt (UK 1914), of Aberfoyle, Co Londonderry, TD; s of Sir Basil Alexander Talbot McFarland, 2 Bt, CBE, ERD (d 1986), and Annie Kathleen, *née* Henderson (d 1952); *b* 3 Oct 1927; *Educ* Marlborough, Trinity Coll Oxford; *m* 5 March 1957, Mary Scott, eldest da of Dr William Scott Watson (d 1956), of Carlisle Place, Londonderry; 2 s (Anthony Basil Scott, Stephen Andrew John b 23 Dec 1968), 2 da (Shauna Jane (Mrs Andrew L H Gailey) b 11 Dec 1957, Fiona Kathleen (Mrs William Orme) b 1 Feb 1964); *Heir* s, Anthony Basil Scott McFarland b 29 Nov 1959; *Career* Capt RA (TA), Capt (RCT) 1962; memb Londonderry Co Borough Cncl 1955–69, High Sheriff Co Londonderry 1958, DL Londonderry 1962–82 (resigned), High Sheriff City of The Co of Londonderry 1965–67; memb North West HMC 1960–73, jt chm Londonderry & Foyle Coll 1976; chm: Lanes (Business Equipment) Ltd, J T McFarland Holdings; *Recreations* golf, shooting; *Clubs* Kildare and Univ, Northern Counties; *Style*— Sir John McFarland Bt, TD; ✉ Dunmore House, Carrigans, Lifford, Co Donegal, Republic of Ireland (☎ 00 353 74 40120, fax 00 353 74 40336)

MACFARLANE, Prof Alan Donald James; s of Maj Donald Kennedy Macfarlane (d 1976), and Iris, *née* Rhodes James; *b* 20 Dec 1941; *Educ* Dragon Sch, Sedbergh, Worcester Coll Oxford (MA, DPhil), LSE (MPhil), SOAS (PhD); *m* 1, 1966 (m dis), Gillian Ions; 1 da (Katharine b 1970); m 2, 1981, Sarah, *née* Tarring; *Career* Univ of Cambridge: lectr in social anthropology 1975–81, reader in hist anthropology 1981–, prof of anthropological science 1991–; fell King's Coll 1981– (sr res fell 1971–74); FRHistS 1967, FRAI 1970, FBA 1986; *Books* Witchcraft in Tudor and Stuart England (1970), The Family Life of Ralph Josselin (1970), Resources and Population (1976), The Diary of Ralph Josselin (ed, 1976), Reconstructing Historical Communities (1977), The Origins of English Individualism (1978), The Justice and the Mare's Ale (1981), A Guide to English Historical Records (1983), Marriage and Love in England (1986), The Culture of Capitalism (1987), Bernard Pignède, The Gurungs, A Himalayan Population of Nepal (ed and trans, 1993); *Recreations* gardening, second-hand book hunting, filming; *Style*— Prof Alan Macfarlane; ✉ 25 Lode Road, Lode, nr Cambridge CB5 9ER (☎ 01223 811976); King's College, Cambridge

MACFARLANE, Anne Bridget; da of Dr D W Griffith (d 1969), and Dr Grace Griffith (d 1971); *b* 26 Jan 1930; *Educ* Univ of Bristol (LLB); *m* 15 Feb 1957, J D Macfarlane; 2 da (Jessica, Deborah); *Career* admitted slr 1954; H M Land Registry 1966–75, registrar Bromley County Court 1975–82, Master of the Court of Protection 1982–95; contrib Atkins Court Forms 1983; *Recreations* collecting Victorian tiles; *Clubs* Law Soc; *Style*— Mrs A B Macfarlane

MACFARLANE, (John) Euan Caldwell; CBE (1990); *b* 5 Dec 1930; *Educ* Glasgow Acad, Univ of Strathclyde (formerly RCST); *m* Anita, *née* Beard; 2 s, 1 da; *Career* chm Cummins (UK) Ltd and Cummins Engine Co Ltd until 1992 (ret), Lloyd's Register Quality Assurance Ltd 1985 until 1992 (ret); memb English Industrial Estates Corp until 1994 (ret); chm: Barnard Castle Sch 1987, NHS Prescription Pricing Authy 1989; Cummins Engine Co Ltd winners of Queen's Award for Industry; CEng, FEng, CIMgt, FIMechE; *Recreations* golf, skiing, walking; *Clubs* Caledonian; *Style*— J C (Euan) Macfarlane, Esq, CBE, FEng; ✉ Willowfield, Darlington Rd, Barnard Castle, Co Durham DL12 8HN (☎ 01833 637511, fax 01833 631488)

MACFARLANE, Sir George Gray; kt (1971), CB (1965); s of John Macfarlane (d 1938), and Mary Knox Macfarlane (d 1933); *b* 8 Jan 1916; *Educ* Airdrie Acad, Univ of Glasgow (BSc), Dresden Technische Hochschule (DrIng); *m* 1941, Barbara Grant, da of Thomas Thomson (d 1947); 1 s, 1 da; *Career* scientist; Telecom Res Estab Malvern 1939–60, dep dir Nat Physical Laboratory 1960–62, dir Royal Radar Estab 1962–67, res controller Miny of Technol 1967–71, controller R & D Estabs and Res MOD 1971–76; memb: Bd PO 1978–81, Bd of Tstees Imperial War Museum 1978–86, NEB 1980–82, NRDC 1981–82, Br Technol Group 1982–85, Bd BT 1981–87; vice pres Royal Acad of Engrg 1978–80; Hon FIEE, FEng 1976 (fndr fell); *Recreations* walking, gardening; *Clubs* Athenaeum; *Style*— Sir George Macfarlane, CB, FEng; ✉ Red Tiles, Orchard Way, Esher, Surrey (☎ 01372 463778)

McFARLANE, Harry William; TD; s of Harry McFarlane (d 1986), and Ann Crammond, *née* Rew; *b* 21 July 1929; *Educ* Univ of St Andrews (MB ChB); *m* 4 Jan 1960, Zlata, da of Cedomir Dzinovic (d 1970); *Career* Med Branch RAF 1954–62, RAMC Vol 1979–; house surgn Royal Infirmary Huddersfield 1952–53, demonstrator in anatomy and lectr in physiology Univ of St Andrews 1956–59, surgical registrar Royal Infirmary Dundee 1959 (casualty offr 1953, house physician 1953–54, sr house offr in surgery 1954), surgical registgrar Aberdeen Gp of Hosps 1959–61, lectr in otorhinolaryngology Univ of Aberdeen 1963–65 (registrar in otorhinolaryngology 1961–62, sr registrar 1963–65); conslt otorhinolaryngologist 1965–: Derby Gp of Hosps 1965–94, Royal Sch for The Deaf Derby 1965–94, Midlands Asthma and Allergy Res Assoc 1970–94, Br Army 1983–94; med examiner industl deafness DHSS 1974– (med examiner war pensions 1970–); med advsr KRAF 1995–; examiner Midlands Inst of Otolaryngology 1966, auditor Derby Med Soc 1972–76 (treas 1968–72), bd memb and rep for Euro Soc for Ear Nose and Throat Advances in Children 1980, chm Res Ctee Midlands Asthma and Allergy Res Assoc 1985 (chm Ethical Ctee 1970); memb: Aberdeen Medico-Chirurgical Soc 1965, S Otolaryngological Soc 1963, Regnl Hosp Conslts and Specialists Assoc 1966, Midlands Visiting Gp in Otolaryngology 1968, Euro Working Gp in Paediatric Otolaryngology 1975, Nottingham Medico-Legal Soc 1987; tstee Amy Blurton Fund 1970–; FRCS 1961, FRCSEd 1961, FRSM 1966, FIMgt 1985, fell Joseph Soc 1987, FICS 1988, MInstD 1988; *Recreations* sailing, skiing, hillwalking; *Clubs* Rotary; *Style*— Harry McFarlane, Esq, TD

McFARLANE, Dr James Sinclair; CBE (1986); s of John Mills McFarlane (d 1959), and Hannah, *née* Langtry (d 1969); *b* 8 Nov 1925; *Educ* Manchester GS, Emmanuel Coll Cambridge (MA, PhD); *m* 31 March 1951, Ruth May, da of William Wallace Harden (d 1974); 3 da (Mary b 1952, Lucy b 1954, Joanna b 1959); *Career* ICI Ltd 1949–53, tech mangr and sales dir Henry Wiggin & Co Ltd 1953–69, chm and md Smith-Clayton Forge Ltd (GKN) 1969–76, md Garringtons Ltd (GKN) 1976–77, main bd dir GKN plc 1979–82, dir gen Engrg Employers' Fedn 1982–89; CEng, FIM, CIMgt; *Recreations* music; *Clubs* United Oxford and Cambridge Univ, Caledonian; *Style*— Dr James McFarlane, CBE; ✉ 24 Broad Street, Ludlow, Shropshire SY8 1NJ (☎ 01584 872495)

McFARLANE, John; OBE (1995); s of John McFarlane, of Dumfries, Scotland, and Christina Campbell (d 1976); *b* 14 June 1947; *Educ* Dumfries Acad, Univ of Edinburgh (MA), Cranfield Sch of Mgmnt (MBA); *m* 31 Jan 1970, Anne, da of Rev Fraser Ian MacDonald (d 1983), of Dumfries, Scotland; 3 da (Kirsty b 14 March 1976, Rebecca b 17 March 1979, Fiona b 18 March 1983); *Career* Ford Motor Co 1969–74, Citicorp 1975–93 (md Citibank NA (UK), chief exec offr Citibank International plc), gp exec dir Standard Chartered plc 1993–; non-exec dir: Capital Radio plc, Auditing Practices Bd, Cranfield Sch of Mgmnt, American C of C, Fin Law Panel, The London Stock Exchange 1989–91, The Securities Assoc 1989–91; MSI, FRSA, fell Hong Kong Inst of Bankers; *Recreations* business policy, Scottish affairs, art and music; *Style*— John McFarlane, Esq, OBE; ✉ Standard Chartered Bank, 1 Aldermanbury Square, London EC2V 7SB (☎ 0171 280 7033, fax 0171 280 7236)

MACFARLANE, Jonathan Stephen; s of William Keith Macfarlane (d 1987), and Pearl Hastings, *née* Impey; *b* 28 March 1956; *Educ* Charterhouse, Oriel Coll Oxford (MA); *m* 7 May 1983, Johanna Susanne, da of John Mordaunt Foster (d 1988); 1 s (David b 1988), 1 da (Laura b 1990); *Career* admitted slr 1980; ptnr Macfarlanes 1985– (corporate fin/mergers and acquisitions); *Clubs* Leander; *Style*— Jonathan Macfarlane, Esq; ✉ Macfarlanes, 10 Norwich Street, London EC4A 1BD (☎ 0171 831 9222, fax 0171 831 9607)

MacFARLANE, Murray Alexander; s of David Murray MacFarlane, of Scotland, and Olive Mary, *née* Hunter; *b* 6 May 1944; *Educ* Newport HS, Univ of Birmingham (MSc); *m* Jane Alexandra, *née* Allan; *Career* CA; articled clerk Walter Hunt & Co, Arthur Young & Co 1969–72, Coopers & Lybrand 1972–77, Commerical Union 1977–80, ptnr (CEWT/Fin Servs) Coopers & Lybrand 1984–; FCA, FIMC; *Recreations* riding, country life; *Clubs* IOD; *Style*— Murray MacFarlane, Esq; ✉ Coopers & Lybrand, 1 Embankment Place, London WC2N 6NN (☎ 0171 583 5000, fax 0171 212 4652)

MACFARLANE, Sir (David) Neil; kt (1988); s of Robert and Dulcie Macfarlane, of Yelverton, S Devon; *b* 7 May 1936; *Educ* Bancroft's Sch London; *m* 1961, June Osmond, er da of John King, of Somerset; 2 s, 1 da; *Career* Lt 1 Bn Essex Regt 1955–58, Capt RA 265 LAA TA 1959–69; cricketer Essex CCC 1952–56, Capt YA XI; with Shell Mex & BP 1959–74; Parly candidate: East Ham North 1970, Sutton & Cheam (by-election) 1972; MP (C) Sutton and Cheam Feb 1974–1992; dep arts min 1979–81; Parly under sec of state: DES 1979–81, for Sport 1981–85, DOE 1981–85; sec: Cons Greater London Membs, Cons Sports Ctee, Cons Energy Ctee; memb All-Pty Select Ctee on Sci and Technol; chm: Securicor Group plc, Rushman Lloyd International Ltd, Associated Nursing Services plc; dir: RMC plc 1988–, Bradford & Bingley Building Society, Zetters plc; capt Parly Golfing Soc, vice pres PGA European Tour; govr Sports Aid Fndn 1985–90; *Books* Politics and Sport (1986); *Recreations* golf; *Clubs* MCC, Essex CCC, Huntercombe Golf, Wentworth Golf, Harlequins RFC, Sunningdale Golf, Royal and Ancient Golf; *Style*— Sir Neil Macfarlane; ✉ Whitestacks, Pound Lane, Sonning on Thames, Berks (☎ 0118 969 4433); c/o Bradford & Bingley Building Society, Crossflatts, Bingley, West Yorkshire BD16 2UA (☎ 01274 555555)

MACFARLANE, Nicholas Russel; s of John Macfarlane, DL, and Pamela, *née* Laing; *b* 21 Feb 1952; *Educ* Cheam Sch, Radley, Univ of Lancaster (BA); *m* 25 July 1987, Elisabeth Anne, da of W David Crane, of Hallaughton; 1 s (James William Archibald b 7 Sept 1989), 1 da (Flora Emily Octavia b 11 Oct 1991); *Career* admitted slr 1977; ptnr Faithfull Owen & Fraser 1980 (amalgamated with Durrant Piesse 1985), currently ptnr specialising in intellectual property law Lovell White Durrant (amalgamated with Durrant Piesse 1988); Freeman Worshipful Co of Slrs; memb: Law Soc, Patent Slrs' Assoc; *Recreations* fishing, shooting; *Clubs* City of London; *Style*— Nicholas Macfarlane, Esq; ✉ Lovell White Durrant, 65 Holborn Viaduct, London EC1A 2DY (☎ 0171 236 0066, telex 887122 LWD G, fax 0171 248 4212)

MACFARLANE, Peter Froude; s of Archibald Macfarlane (d 1958), and Edith Decima Macfarlane; *b* 3 July 1938; *Educ* Woodhouse GS; *children* 2 da (Sarah Elizabeth b 1965, Claire Fiona b 1970); *Career* CA; sr auditor Coopers & Lybrand Nigeria 1961–65, asst gp accountant International Computers UK 1965–66, fin mangr (later dir) Kimberley-Clark UK USA Holland and Germany 1966–69, int controller and md BL Nigeria 1969–79 (treas London 1969–79); Rolls Royce 1979–91: treas, dir industl and marine, dir corp devpt, dir of fin; Allied Domecq plc (Allied-Lyons plc until 1994): fin dir 1991–94, chm Pedro Domecq and chm J Lyons & Co 1994–; chm Ultra Electronics; Liveryman Worshipful Co of Chartered Accountants; FCA, FCT; *Recreations* tennis, sailing, golf; *Style*— Peter Macfarlane, Esq; ✉ Allied Domecq plc, 24 Portland Place, London (☎ 0171 323 9000)

MACFARLANE, Prof Peter Wilson; s of Robert Barton Macfarlane (d 1965), of Glasgow, and Dinah, *née* Wilson; *b* 8 Nov 1942; *Educ* Hyndland Secondary Sch Glasgow, Univ of Glasgow (BSc, PhD); *m* 8 Oct 1971, Irene Grace, da of James Muir (d 1975), of Kirkintilloch; 2 s (Alan b 1974, David b 1977); *Career* Univ of Glasgow: asst lectr in med cardiology 1967–70, lectr 1970–74, sr lectr 1974–80, reader 1980–91, prof 1991–95, prof of electrocardiology 1995–; author and ed of various books and proceedings, res interest computers in electrocardiography, princ author of electrocardiogram analysis programme marketed worldwide; sec Int Soc of Electrocardiology, memb Br Cardiac Soc 1974; FBCS 1976, CEng 1990, FESC 1991, FRSE 1992; *Books* An Introduction to Automated Electrocardiogram Interpretation (1974), Computer Techniques in Clinical Medicine (1985), Comprehensive Electrocardiology (1989), 12–Lead Vectorcardiography (1995); *Recreations* jogging, playing the violin; *Style*— Prof Peter Macfarlane, FRSE; ✉ 12 Barrcraig Rd, Bridge of Weir, Strathclyde PA11 3HG (☎ 01505 614443); University Department of Medical Cardiology, Royal Infirmary, 10 Alexandra Parade, Glasgow G31 2ER (☎ 0141 211 5082, fax 0141 552 6114)

MACFARLANE, Maj-Gen William Thomson (Bill); CB (1981); s of James Macfarlane (d 1966), and Agnes Boylan (d 1970); *b* 2 Dec 1925; *m* 16 July 1955, Dr Helen Dora Macfarlane, da of The Rev Leonard Nelson Meredith (d 1976); 1 da (Christina b 22 July 1957); *Career* served Europe, Near, Middle and Far East theatres 1946–1981;

Cdr 16 Parachute Bde Signal Sqdn 1961–63, mil asst to C in C Far East Land Forces 1964–66, Cdr 1 Div HQ and Signal Regt Germany 1967–70, Cabinet Office Secretariat 1970–72, Cdr Corps Royal Signals Germany 1972–73, dir PR (Army) 1973–75, chief of staff UK Land Forces 1975–78, chief jt services liaison offr Br Forces Germany 1978–81, Col Cmdt Royal Signals 1980–85, ret; co dir, conslt, lectr; ops dir Hong Kong Resort Co Ltd 1981–84, admin Sion Coll 1984–93, chm and dir Citicare Co Ltd 1984–95, dir Compton Manor Estates Ltd 1990–; *Clubs* Naval and Military, Piccadilly; *Style*— Maj-Gen William T Macfarlane, CB; ✉ Colts Paddock, 24 Aveley Lane, Farnham, Surrey GU9 8PR

MACFARLANE OF BEARSDEN, Baron (Life Peer UK 1991), of Bearsden in the District of Bearsden and Milngavie; Sir Norman Somerville Macfarlane; KT (1996), kt (1982); s of Daniel Robertson Macfarlane (d 1985), and Jessie Lindsay, *née* Somerville (d 1975); *b* 5 March 1926; *Educ* High Sch of Glasgow; *m* 1953, Marguerite Mary, da of John Johnstone Campbell, of 17 Norwood Drive, Whitecraigs; 1 s (Hon Hamish b 26 Dec 1961), 4 da (Hon Fiona (Hon Mrs McNaught) b 17 Sept 1955, Hon Gail (Hon Mrs Allbutt) b 24 March 1957, Hon Marjorie (Hon Mrs Roberts) b 30 March 1960, Hon Marguerite b 14 July 1966); *Career* cmmnd RA; chm Macfarlane Group (Clansman) plc; chm: United Distillers plc 1987–96 (hon life pres 1996), United Distillers UK plc (formerly Arthur Bell Distillers plc), American Tst plc, The Fine Art Soc plc 1976–, Edinburgh Fund Managers plc; Guinness plc: chm non-exec dirs 1986–87, chm Guinness plc 1987–89, jt dep chm 1989–92; former dep chm Clydesdale Bank plc; dir: General Accident Fire and Life Assurance Corp plc until 1996, Glasgow C of C 1976–79, Scottish Nat Orch 1977–82, Third Eye Centre Glasgow 1978–81; former pres: Company of Stationers of Glasgow, Stationers Assoc of GB and Ireland, Glasgow HS Club; former memb Royal Fine Art Cmmn for Scotland, memb Scot CBI Cncl 1975–81, pres Royal Glasgow Inst of the Fine Arts 1976–87, govr Glasgow Sch of Art 1976–87, memb Bd Scot Devpt Agency 1979–87, memb Ct Univ of Glasgow 1980–88, vice-chm Scot Ballet 1983–87; Scot patron The Nat Arts Collections Fund, chm of govrs The HS of Glasgow 1979–92; tstee: Nat Heritage Memorial Fund, The Nat Galleries of Scot; chm Glasgow Devpt Agency (formerly Glasgow Action) 1985–93, hon vice-pres Glasgow Bn Boys Bde; Lord High Cmmr to the General Assembly of the Church of Scotland 1992 and 1993; underwriting memb Lloyd's of London; hon fell: Scotvec 1991, Glasgow Sch of Art 1992; Hon LLD: Strathclyde 1986, Glasgow 1988, Glasgow Caledonian 1993, Aberdeen 1995; Hon DUniv Stirling 1992, Hon Dr (HC) Univ of Edinburgh 1992; Hon FRIAS 1984, Hon RSA 1987, Hon RGI 1987, FRSE 1991, Hon FRCPS 1992; *Clubs* Royal Scottish Automobile, Glasgow Art, Glasgow Golf, New (Edinburgh); *Style*— The Rt Hon Lord Macfarlane of Bearsden, KT, FRSE; ✉ 50 Manse Road, Bearsden, Glasgow; office: Macfarlane Group (Clansman) plc, 21 Newton Place, Glasgow G3 7PY (☎ 0141 333 9666)

McFARLANE OF LLANDAFF, Baroness (Life Peer UK 1979), of Llandaff in Co of South Glamorgan; Jean Kennedy McFarlane; da of James McFarlane (d 1963), and Elina Alice McFarlane (d 1990); *b* 1 April 1926; *Educ* Howell's Sch Llandaff, Bedford and Birkbeck Colls London (MA, BSc); *Career* dir of educn Inst of Advanced Nursing Educn London 1969–71, sr lectr in nursing Dept of Social and Preventive Medicine Manchester Univ 1971–73, sr lectr and head Dept of Nursing Manchester Univ 1973–74, chm English National Bd for Nursing, Midwifery and Health Visiting 1980–83, prof and head Dept of Nursing Manchester Univ 1974–88; former memb: War Graves Cmmn, Royal Cmmn on NHS; memb Gen Synod of C of E 1990–; Hon DSc Ulster 1981, Hon DEd CNAA 1983, Hon FRCP 1990, Hon MD Liverpool 1990; SRN, SCM, FRCN; *Books* The Proper Study of the Nurse (1970), The Practice of Nursing Using the Nursing Process (1982); *Recreations* photography, walking, music, travel; *Style*— The Rt Hon the Lady McFarlane of Llandaff; ✉ 5 Dovercourt Ave, Heaton Mersey, Stockport, Cheshire; Department of Nursing, Univ of Manchester, Manchester M13 9PT

MacFARQUHAR, Prof Roderick Lemonde; s of late Sir Alexander MacFarquhar; *b* 2 Dec 1930, Lahore; *Educ* Fettes, Keble Coll Oxford (BA), Harvard Univ (AM), LSE (PhD); *m* 1964, Emily Jane, da of Dr Paul W Cohen, of New York; 1 s (Rory b 1971), 1 da (Larissa b 1968); *Career* Nat Serv 2 Lt; China specialist Daily Telegraph 1955–61, ed The China Quarterly 1959–68, reporter BBC Panorama 1963–64, co presenter BBC World Serv 24 Hours 1972–74 and 1979–80; Harvard Univ: prof of govt 1984–, dir Fairbank Centre for E Asian Res 1986–92, Leroy B Williams prof of history and political science 1990–; fell: Res Inst on Communist Affairs and E Asian Inst Columbia 1969, Royal Inst of Int Affairs 1971–74, Woodrow Wilson Int Centre for Scholars Washington DC 1980–81, American Acad of Arts and Sciences 1986–, Leverhulme Res Grant, Force Fndn Res Grant, Rockefeller Fndn Res Grant; MP (Lab) 1974–79; *Recreations* reading, travel, listening to music; *Style*— Prof Roderick MacFarquhar

McFETRICH, (Charles) Alan; s of Cecil McFetrich, OBE (d 1988), and Kathleen Margaret, *née* Proom; *b* 15 Dec 1940; *Educ* Oundle, Magdalene Coll Cambridge (MA); *m* 1, 25 March 1970 (m dis 1989); 2 s (Daniel Ross b 1974, Nicholas William (twin) b 1974), 1 da (Anna Louise b 1973); m 2, 3 Aug 1990, Janet Elizabeth Henkel, *née* Munro; *Career* student accountant Graham Proom & Smith 1959–61 and 1964–66; CA 1966; Deloitte Haskins & Sells: joined 1966, conslt 1968–73, conslt ptnr 1973–80, seconded as under sec Industl Devpt Unit Dept of Indust 1981–82, ops ptnr UK 1983–84, managing ptnr UK 1985–89; Coopers & Lybrand (formerly Coopers & Lybrand Deloitte): managing ptnr 1990–92, exec ptnr 1992–94, managing ptnr of external affairs 1994–96; memb IMC 1969, FCA 1976; *Recreations* gardening, theatre, reading; *Style*— Alan McFetrich, Esq; ✉ Carrick Pines, Castle Drive, St Mawes, Cornwall TR2 5DE

McGAHERN, Francis Jude Anthony (Frank); s of Francis McGahern (d 1977), and Susan, *née* McManus (d 1944); *b* 4 Nov 1943; *Educ* Presentation Coll; *m* Jan 1965, Mary Ellen, da of Michael Maher; 1 s (Mark b 20 Aug 1968), 3 da (Monica b 1 Oct 1965, Rachael b 12 Jan 1974, Rebecca b 12 Aug 1975); *Career* accountant; trainee Albright & Wilson (Chemicals) 1960–70, The Gas Cncl 1970–72; BBC: joined as engrg cost accountant 1972, successively head of engrg fin and costing servs, head of fin central servs, chief accountant Radio then fin controller Network Radio until 1995; dir and co sec Network Productions Ltd 1995–; fell CIMA (memb 1970); *Recreations* reading, swimming, home DIY, dinghy sailing; *Clubs* Savile; *Style*— Frank McGahern, Esq; ✉ Network Productions Ltd, 123 Lansdowne Way, London SW8 2NP (☎ 0171 498 8222, fax 0171 622 7988)

McGAHERN, John; s of Francis McGahern, and Susan, *née* McManus; *b* 12 Nov 1934; *Educ* Presentation Coll Carrick-on-Shannon, St Patrick's Dublin, Univ Coll Dublin; *m* 3 Feb 1973, Madeline; *Career* res fell Univ of Reading 1969–72, visiting prof Colgate Univ USA 1970–91, Br Northern Arts fell Univ of Newcastle upon Tyne and Univ of Durham 1974–76, visiting fell Univ of Dublin 1988; Hon LittD Univ of Dublin 1991; memb: Irish Acad of Letters, Aosdana; FRSL; Chevalier de L'Ordre des Arts et des Lettres 1989; *Books* The Barracks (1963), The Dark (1965), Nightlines (1971), The Leavetaking (1975), Getting Through (1978), The Pornographer (1980), High Ground (1985), The Rockingham Shoot (BBC TV, 1988), Amongst Women (1990), The Collected Stories (1992); play: The Power of Darkness (Abbey Theatre Dublin) 1991; *Style*— John McGahern, Esq; ✉ Faber and Faber, 3 Queen Square, London WC1N 3AU (☎ 0171 465 0045)

McGAIRL, Stephen James; s of John Lloyd McGairl (d 1979), of Chichester, and Lucy Hudson; *b* 18 Feb 1951; *Educ* Chichester HS, Worcester Coll Oxford (MA); *m* 24 May 1975, Madeleine, da of Christopher William Talbot Cox (d 1964), of Sidlesham; 4 s (Sam b 1977, Thomas b 1978, Joe b 1983, George b 1986); *Career* admitted slr 1976, admitted Conseil Juridique 1988, avocat 1992; Legal and Parliamentary Dept GLC 1974–77; Freshfields: joined 1977, ptnr 1984, Paris office 1986–92, head of CIS Practice Gp 1992–, head of Moscow office 1994–95; memb: Law Soc, City of London Slrs' Co, Société Française de Droit Aérien, CIS Panel of Br Invisibles, Unidroit study gp on int interests in mobile equipment; *Publications* contrib various professional jls relating to aviation, asset and project fin and business in Russia, memb Editorial Bd Central European; *Recreations* sailing, opera, classic cars; *Clubs* Cercle de l'Union Interalliée, Royal Automobile, Chichester Yacht; *Style*— Stephen McGairl, Esq; ✉ 65 Fleet Street, London EC4Y 1HS (☎ 0171 936 4000, fax 0171 832 7001)

McGANN, Paul; *Educ* Cardinal Allen GS Liverpool, RADA; *Career* actor; *Theatre* incl: title role in P B Shelley's Cain (Nottingham Playhouse) 1981, Finn in Trevor Griffiths' Oi For England (Royal Court Upstairs) 1982, Danny in Robert Walker's Yakety-Yak (Half Moon and Astoria) 1982, Tom in Howard Brenton's The Genius (Royal Court) 1983, Dennis in Joe Orton's Loot (Ambassador's) 1984, Frankie in Sam Shepard's A Lie of the Mind (Royal Court) 1987; *Television* for BBC incl: title role in Gaskin 1982, Mo in Give us a Break 1983, Toplis in The Monocled Mutineer 1986, Jack Worthing in The Importance of Being Earnest 1986, Colin in Drowning in the Shallow End 1989, The Hanging Gale 1995, Dr Who (TV film, in assoc with Universal) 1996; *Films* I in Withnail and I 1986, Lt Price in Empire of the Sun 1987, Raz in Streets of Yesterday 1988, Skrebensky in The Rainbow 1988, Pascoe in Dealers 1988, Harris in Paper Mask 1989, Photographer in Afraid of the Dark 1990, Golic in Alien III 1991; *Recreations* music, sport, travel; *Clubs* Liverpool FC; *Style*— Paul McGann, Esq; ✉ c/o Marina Martin Associates, 12–13 Poland Street, London W1V 3DE (☎ 0171 734 4818, fax 0171 734 4832)

McGAREL GROVES, Anthony Robin; s of Col Robin Jullian McGarel Groves, OBE, of Lymington, Hampshire, and Constance Morton, *née* Macmillan; *b* 7 Sept 1954; *Educ* Eton, Univ of Bath (BSc); *m* 16 Dec 1978, Ann Candace, da of Jack Dawes, of Ross on Wye, Herefordshire; *Career* Deloitte Haskins and Sells 1976–81, Kuwait Investmt Office 1981–94, assoc dir in charge of American investmts Hambro's Fund Management PLC 1994–; ACA; *Recreations* shooting, skiing, theatre, bridge, politics; *Style*— Anthony R McGarel Groves, Esq; ✉ Clapton Revel, Wooburn Moor, Buckinghamshire HP10 0NH; 1 America Square, 17 Crosswall, London EC3N 2LB

McGARRY, Ian Patrick; s of John McGarry (d 1957), of Lewes, and Jean Dearing (d 1973), of Steyning; *b* 27 Feb 1942; *Educ* Chichester HS for Boys, Lewes County GS; *m* 1964 (m dis), Christine, *née* Smith; 1 s (Andrew b 15 Dec 1971); *Career* Lab Pty constituency agent Putney 1964–76, gen sec British Actors' Equity Assoc 1991– (asst gen sec 1976–91); jt sec London Theatre Cncl and Provincial Theatre Cncl 1991–, memb Br Screen Advsy Cncl 1991–, vice pres Int Fedn of Actors 1992–, tstee Nat Music Day Tst, jt sec Jt Films Cncl; *Style*— Ian McGarry, Esq; ✉ British Actors' Equity Association, Guild House, Upper St Martin's Lane, London W1 (☎ 0171 379 6000)

McGARVEY, Alan; s of William Johnson McGarvey (d 1967), and Rosina, *née* Plane; *b* 22 June 1942; *Educ* Wallsend GS, Univ of Newcastle upon Tyne (BSc), Cranfield Sch of Mgmnt (MBA); *m* 11 Sept 1967, Eileen (d 1992); *Career* CA; Parsons 1958–64, Rio Tinto Zinc Ltd 1968–71, Decca Group 1972–76, MK Electric Ltd 1976–78, National Enterprise Bd 1978–82, Greater London Enterprise Bd 1982–86, Greater Manchester Economic Development Ltd 1987–90; ind specialist in industl devpt and restructuring 1990–93, Euro Cmmn (Phare) 1993–96, ind specialist in regional devpt and restructuring 1996–; memb Bd Northern Chamber Orchestra 1988–93, UK memb Advsy Cncl for Ctee for Industl Co-operation (EEC-ACP) Brussels; *Style*— Alan McGarvey, Esq; ✉ 11 Old Hall Mews, Bolton BL1 7PW (☎ 01204 840141, fax 01204 840723)

McGEACHIE, Daniel (Dan); OBE (1992); s of David McGeachie (d 1969), of Arbroath, and Jessie McGeachie; *b* 10 June 1935; *Educ* Arbroath HS; *m* 16 Jan 1962, Sylvia, *née* Andrew; 1 da (Fiona b 1964); *Career* Nat Serv 1953–55; journalist Scotland and Fleet St 1955–60, foreign corr (Africa) Daily Express 1960–65, parly corr then dip and political corr Daily Express 1965–75, UK political advsr to Conoco 1975–77, currently dir and gen mangr Govt and Public Affrs Conoco (UK) Ltd; cncl memb Indust and Parliament Tst, memb Parly Energy Studies Gp; *Clubs* Reform; *Style*— Dan McGeachie, Esq, OBE; ✉ 27 Hitherwood Drive, Dulwich, London SE19 1XA (☎ 0181 670 5546); Conoco (UK) Ltd, Park St, London W1Y 4NN (☎ 0171 408 6608)

McGEE, Prof James O'Donnell; s of Michael McGee (d 1981), and Bridget Gavin (d 1982); *b* 27 July 1939; *Educ* Univ of Glasgow (MB ChB, PhD, MD), Univ of Oxford (MA); *m* 26 August 1961, Anne McCarron Lee, da of Patrick Lee, of Cardonald, Glasgow; 1 s (Damon-Joel b 1969), 2 da (Leeanne b 1962, Sharon b 1964); *Career* lectr then sr lectr in pathology Univ of Glasgow 1967–75, prof and head Nuffield Dept of Pathology and Bacteriology Univ of Oxford 1975–, fell Linacre Coll Oxford 1975–, assoc fell Green Coll Oxford 1981–; dir UK Telepathology Co-ordinating Unit 1994–; distinguished visiting scientist Roche Inst of Molecular Biology Nutley NJ USA 1981 and 1989 (Med Res Cncl travelling fell 1969–70, visiting scientist 1970–71), Kattle Meml lectr Royal Coll of Pathologists 1981, guest lectr Royal Coll of Physicians of Ireland 1985, keynote lectr Med Res Inst SA 1994, special guest lectr Hellenic Pathology Congress Crete 1994; visiting prof: Univ of Baghdad 1976, Univ of Kuwait 1981 and 1983 (academic advsr 1984–), Univ of Witwatersrand SA 1994; academic advsr Hong Kong Medical Res Cncl 1990–; memb: Scientific and Grants Ctee Cancer Res Campaign UK 1978–93, Ctee on Safety of Meds Med Div UK 1984–90, Nat Cmmn (UK) Breast Screening Pathology 1989–; hon conslt Pathologist Oxford Health Authy 1975–; Bellahouston Gold Medal Univ of Glasgow 1973; FRCPath 1986 (MRCPath 1973), FRCP 1989; *Books* Biopsy Pathology of Liver (1980, 2 edn 1988), In Situ Hybridisation: Principles and Practice (1990, 2 edn 1995), Oxford Textbook of Pathology (vols 1, 2a and 2b, with P J Isaacson and N A Wright, 1992), Diagnostic Molecular Pathology (vols 1 and 2 with C S Herrington, 1992), The Macrophage (with C E Lewis, 1992), The NK Cell (with C E Lewis, 1992); *Recreations* talking with my family, swimming; *Style*— Prof James O'D McGee; ✉ University of Oxford, Nuffield Department of Pathology & Bacteriology, John Radcliffe Hospital, Headington, Oxford OX3 9DU (☎ 01865 220549, fax 01865 220078)

McGEECHAN, Ian Robert; OBE; s of Robert Matthew McGeechan (d 1969), and Hilda, *née* Shearer (d 1994); *b* 30 Oct 1946; *Educ* Moor Grange HS, West Park HS, Allerton Grange Comp, Carnegie Coll of Physical Educn; *m* 9 Aug 1969, Judith Irene, da of Thomas Fish (d 1976); 1 s (Robert James b 5 Nov 1978), 1 da (Heather Jane b 17 Aug 1983); *Career* rugby union national coach and former fly-half Scotland (32 caps); clubs: Headingley FC 1965–82 (300 appearances, capt 1972–73), Barbarians RFC 1973–78, Yorks CCC 1963–68 (played for second XI); Scotland: debut v NZ 1972, tour NZ 1975 (1 test appearance), capt 1977 and 1979, final game v France 1979, asst coach 1985–88, national coach 1988–93 (Grand Slam winners 1990, fourth place World Cup 1991); British Lions: toured SA 1974 (4 tests, won series 3–0, 1 drawn), toured NZ 1977 (4 tests), coach on tour of Aust 1989 (won series 2–1), coach World XV v New Zealand (for NZ rugby centenary) 1992, coach to New Zealand 1993 (lost series 1–2); dir: of rugby Northampton RFC 1994–, National Coaching Foundation 1995–; head of games Moor Grange HS 1968–72, head of humanities and year gp ldr Fir Tree Middle Sch 1972–90; trg mangr Scottish Life Assurance Company 1990–94; Rugby Writers: Robert Cherry trophy 1989, Pat Marshall trophy 1990; Coach of the Year: Rugby World 1989 and 1990, Br Inst of Sports Coaches 1990 and 1993; *Books* Scotland's Grand Slam (with Ian Robertson and M Cleary), So Close to Glory (1993 (British Lions tour of NZ));

Recreations caravanning, hill walking, family life, sailing, cricket; *Style*— Ian McGeechan, Esq, OBE

McGEEHAN, Prof Joseph Peter (Joe); s of Joseph Patrick James McGeehan, of Liverpool, and Rhoda Catherine, *née* Sleight (d 1989); *b* 15 Feb 1946; *Educ* Bootle GS for Boys, Univ of Liverpool (BEng, PhD); *m* 3 Oct 1970, Jean, da of Alan Lightfoot (d 1969); 2 da (Kathryn Anne b 13 July 1978, Sarah Jane b 12 Feb 1981); *Career* sr scientist Allan Clark Research Centre (Plessey Group Ltd) 1970–72; lectr then sr lectr Sch of Electrical Engrg Univ of Bath 1976–85; Univ of Bristol: first dir Centre for Communications Res 1987– (estab 1985), head Dept of Electrical and Electronic Engrg 1991– (chair in communications engrg 1985–); over 20 years res in spectrum efficient modulation techniques and systems; memb various nat and int ctees CCIR 1980–, memb ctee studying comparative modulation schemes for mobile radio Home Office 1980–82, advsr to first MOD/DTI Defence Spectrum Review Ctee, memb Accreditation Ctee and Pool of Assessors IEE 1985–, sometime memb various res ctees EPSRC and DTI/EPSRC Link Mgmnt Ctee in Personal Communication Systems; dir Science Research Fndn (formed by Univs of Bristol and Bath and UWE); memb Women's Academic Initiative Bristol; Wolfson Fndn rep Bd of Govrs John Cabot City Technol Coll Bristol; former memb and treas Friends of Bath HS; FRSA 1989, FIEE 1992, FEng 1994 *Awards* Mountbatten Premium (IEE) 1989, Neal Shepherd Award (IEEE, USA) 1990, Prince of Wales Award for Innovation 1992; *Publications* Radio Receivers (contrib, 1986); *Recreations* walking, music, cricket, cycling, theatre, reading, church; *Style*— Prof Joe McGeehan, FEng; ✉ Department of Electrical and Electronic Engineering, Queen's Building, University of Bristol, University Walk, Bristol BS8 1TR (☎ 0117 928 7721, fax 0117 925 5265, mobile 0374 940469)

McGEOCH, Vice Adm Sir Ian Lachlan Mackay; KCB (1969, CB 1966), DSO (1943), DSC (1943); s of L A McGeoch, of Dalmuir; *b* 26 March 1914; *Educ* Pangbourne, Univ of Edinburgh (MPhil); *m* 1937, Eleanor Somers, da of Rev Canon Hugh Farrie; 2 s, 2 da; *Career* joined RN 1932; Flag Offr: Scotland and NI 1968–70, Submarines 1965–67; Adm pres RNC Greenwich 1964–65; memb: Royal Co of Archers (Queen's Body Guard for Scotland) 1969–, Cncl White Ensign Assoc; tstee Imperial War Museum 1977–87; ed The Naval Review 1973–80, editorial dir Naval Forces 1980–83; dir Midar Systems Ltd; FNI; *Books* with Gen Sir John Hackett: The Third World War: a Future History (1978), The Third World War: The Untold Story (1982), An Affair of Chances (1991); *Clubs* Royal Yacht Sqdn, Royal Naval Sailing Assoc (past Cdre), Royal Cruising, Army & Navy; *Style*— Vice Adm Sir Ian McGeoch, KCB, DSO, DSC; ✉ c/o Coutts & Co, 440 Strand, London WC2R 0QS

McGEOUGH, Prof Joseph Anthony; s of Patrick Joseph McGeough (d 1982), of Stevenston, Ayrshire, and Gertrude, *née* Darroch (d 1975); *b* 29 May 1940; *Educ* St Michael's Coll Irvine, Univ of Glasgow (BSc, PhD), Univ of Aberdeen (DSc); *m* 12 Aug 1972, Brenda, da of Robert Nicholson, of Blyth, Northumberland; 2 s (Andrew b 1974, Simon b 1977), 1 da (Elizabeth b 1975); *Career* res demonstrator Univ of Leicester 1966, sr res fell Queensland Univ 1967, res metallurgist International R & D Ltd 1968–69, sr res fell Univ of Strathclyde 1969–72; Univ of Aberdeen: lectr 1972–77, sr lectr 1977–80, reader in engrg 1980–83; regius prof of engrg Univ of Edinburgh 1983– (head Dept Mechanical Engrg 1983–91), hon prof Nanjing Aeronautical and Astronautical Univ China 1992–, visiting prof Univ of Naples Federico II 1994; industl fell Sci and Engrg Res Cncl Royal Soc 1987–89; chm Coll Cncl Dyce Acad 1980–83, memb Tech Advsy Ctee Scot Centre Agric Engrg 1987–94, memb Engrg Res Bd Agric and Food Res Cncl 1992–94, hon pres Lichfield Sci and Engrg Soc 1988–89, chm Edinburgh and SE Scot Panel Inst of Mechanical Engrs 1988–91, chm Scottish Branch Inst of Mechanical Engrg 1993–95 (vice-chm 1991–93), pres Res Ctee on Electrophysical and Chemical Processes Int Coll of Prodn (CIRP) 1992–95; hon vice pres Univ of Aberdeen Athletics Assoc 1981–; various Scot Co AAA and universities Athletic Championship awards; FRSE 1990, FIMechE, FIEE (formerly FIProdE); *Books* Principles of Electrochemical Machining (1974), Advanced Methods of Machining (1988), section on Nonconventional Machining: Encyclopaedia Britannica (1987); ed in chief Processing of Advanced Materials 1991–94; CIRP ed Jl of Materials Processing Technology 1990–; *Recreations* walking, athletics; *Style*— Prof Joseph McGeough, FRSE; ✉ 39 Dreghorn Loan, Colinton, Edinburgh EH13 0DF (☎ 0131 441 1302); Department of Mechanical Engineering, University of Edinburgh, King's Buildings, Edinburgh EH9 3JL (☎ 0131 650 5682, fax 0131 667 3677, telex 727442 UNIVED G)

McGEOWN, Prof Mary Graham; CBE (1985); da of James Edward McGeown, of Lurgan, NI, and Sarah Graham, *née* Quinn; *b* 19 July 1923; *Educ* Lurgan Coll, Queen's Univ Belfast (MB, BAO, MD, PhD); *m* 1 Sept 1949 (Joseph) Maxwell Freeland (decd), s of Herbert Freeland (d 1982); 3 s (Peter b 1956, Mark b 1957, Paul b 1961); *Career* house physician Royal Victoria Hosp Belfast 1947–48, house offr Royal Belfast Hosp for Sick Children 1948; asst lectr: pathology Queen's Univ Belfast 1949–50, biochemistry Queen's Univ Belfast 1950–53; grantee MRC 1953–56, res fell Royal Victoria Hosp Belfast 1956–58, conslt nephrologist Belfast Hosps 1962–88, physician in admin charge Renal Unit Belfast City Hosp 1968–88, chm UK Transplant Mgmnt Ctee 1983–91; med advsr to NI Kidney Res Fund 1972–88 (patron 1988–), professorial fell Queen's Univ 1988–; memb: Assoc of Physicians Britain and Ireland, American Soc of Artificial Internal Organs, Int Soc of Nephrology, Irish Nephrological Soc (pres 1990–92), Ulster Med Soc (pres 1986–87); hon memb: Renal Assoc (pres 1983–86, hon treas 1986–89), Br Transplantation Soc (chm Supervisory Ctee on Organ Transplantation 1984–89, hon archivist 1988–), Euro Dialysis and Transplant Assoc, Euro Renal Assoc; Hon DSc New Univ of Ulster 1983, Hon DMSc Queen's Univ of Belfast 1991; FRCP, FRCPE, FRCPI; author of numerous articles and chapters on calcium metabolism, kidney diseases treatment, kidney transplantation; *Books* Clinical Management of Electrolyte Disorders (1983), Clinical Management of Renal Transplantation (1992); *Recreations* gardening, genealogy, history of transplantation, antiques; *Style*— Prof Mary McGeown, CBE; ✉ 14 Osborne Gardens, Belfast BT9 6LE (☎ 01232 669918); Department of Medicine, University Floor, Tower, Belfast City Hospital, Belfast BT9 7AB (☎ 01232 329241 ext 2963)

McGETTIGAN, Frank; *b* 1951; *m*; 4 c; *Career* Channel Four Television: dir and gen mangr (and main bd dir) 1988–, md subsid 124 Facilities Ltd, chair Channel Four New Media Group; dep chm: SKILLSET (bdcasting industry trg orgn), Central London TEC, Nat Film and TV Sch (and chm subsid Ealing Studios Ltd); *Style*— Frank McGettigan, Esq; ✉ Channel Four Television Corporation, 124 Horseferry Road, London SW1P 2TX (☎ 0171 396 4444, fax 0171 306 8356)

McGETTRICK, Prof Andrew David; s of Bartholomew McGettrick, of Glasgow, and Marion, *née* McLean; *b* 15 May 1944; *Educ* Univ of Glasgow (Jack Scholar, Thomas Russell Bursar, BSc), Univ of Cambridge (PhD, Dip in Computer Sci); *m* 27 Dec 1974, Sheila Margaret, da of Eugene Girot; 5 s (Peter 3 Dec 1975, Robert 27 June 1977, Andrew 13 Oct 1981, Rory 20 June 1984, Michael 20 Aug 1987), 1 da (26 Oct 1979); *Career* Univ of Strathclyde: reader Dept of Computer Sci 1982–84 (formerly lectr), personal prof 1984–86, prof 1986–, head Dept of Computer Sci 1984–90 and 1996–; chm Safety Critical Systems Ctee Inst of Electrical Engrs; ed-in-chief Jl of High Integrity Systems; govr Scottish Cncl for Educnl Technol; CEng, FBCS 1987, FIEE 1989, FRSE 1996; *Publications* over 110, selected books incl: Algol 68 - A First and Second Course (1978, reprinted 1980), The Definition of Programming Languages (1980), Program Verification using Ada (1982), Graded Problems in Computer Science (with P D Smith, 1983), Discrete Mathematics and uses in Computing, The Oxford Dictionary of Computer Science (1983, 2 edn 1985), Software Specification Techniques (ed with N Gehani, 1988), Concurrent Programming (ed with N Gehani, 1988); *Recreations* running, golf, squash; *Style*— Prof Andrew McGettrick, FRSE; ✉ 11 Coylton Road, Glasgow G43 2TA; University of Strathclyde, 26 Richmond Street, Glasgow G1 1XH (☎ 0141 552 4400 ext 3305, fax 0141 552 5330, e-mail adm@cs.strath.ac.uk)

McGHIE, Hon Lord; James Marshall; s of James Drummond McGhie (d 1970), and Jessie Eadie Bennie (d 1975); *b* 15 Oct 1944; *Educ* Perth Acad, Univ of Edinburgh; *m* 1968, Ann Manuel, da of Stanley Gray Cockburn (d 1982); 1 s (Angus b 1975), 1 da (Kathryn b 1983); *Career* admitted Faculty of Advocates; QC (Scot) 1983, advocate-depute 1983–86, pt/t chm Med Appeal Tbnls 1987–92, memb Criminal Injuries Compensation Bd 1992–96, chm Scottish Land Court and pres Lands Tbnl for Scotland 1996–; *Style*— The Hon Lord McGhie; ✉ 3 Lauder Rd, Edinburgh (☎ 0131 667 8325); Scottish Land Court, 1 Grosvenor Crescent, Edinburgh EH2 5ER (☎ 0131 225 3595)

MacGILLIVRAY, Dr (Barron) Bruce; s of John Alexander MacGillivray (d 1940), of SA, and Doreene Eleanore, *née* Eastwood (d 1974); *b* 21 Aug 1927; *Educ* King Edward VII Sch Johannesburg, Univ of Witwatersrand (BSc), Univ of Manchester, Univ of London (MB BS); *m* 7 Jan 1955, Ruth Marjorie, da of Albert Valentine (d 1965), of Cheshire; 2 s (John Bruce b 1955, Robert Alexander b 1962), 1 da (Carol Susan b 1957); *Career* house surgn and house physician Manchester Royal Infirmary 1955–56, res med offr Stepping Hill and Stockport Infirmary 1957–59, registrar and sr registrar Nat Hosp for Nervous Diseases 1959–64, res fell UCLA 1964–65, conslt physician in neurology and neurophysiology Royal Free Hosp 1965–92, conslt in neurophysiology Nat Hosp for Nervous Diseases 1971–92; Univ of London: dean Royal Free Hosp Sch of Med 1974–89, memb Senate 1980–89, pro vice chllr (med) 1985–87; memb Cncl: Sch of Pharmacy 1976–91, Br Postgrad Med Fedn 1984–88, St George's Hosp Med Sch 1994– (treas 1996–); author of various scientific pubns on neurophysiology, brain death and med computing; memb: Camden and Islington Area Health Authy 1976–82, NE Thames Regnl Health Authy 1982–86, Ctee of Vice Chllrs and Princs 1982–87, NHS Complaints Review Cmmn 1993–94; MRI, FRSM, FRSA, FRCP; *Recreations* flying, wood turning, photography; *Style*— Dr Bruce MacGillivray; ✉ 18 St Johns Ave, Putney, London SW15 2AA (☎ and fax 0181 788 5213)

McGILLYCUDDY OF THE REEKS, The (Mac Giolla Chuda); Richard Denis Wyer McGillycuddy; suc 1959; s of John Patrick, The McGillycuddy of The Reeks (d 1959), and Elizabeth Margaret, The Madam McGillycuddy of The Reeks; *b* 4 Oct 1948; *Educ* Eton, Aix en Provence; *m* 1984, Virginia Lucy, eld da of Hon Hugh Waldorf Astor, *qv*; 2 da (Tara b 1985, Sorcha b 1990); *Heir* cousin, Donough McGillycuddy b 1939; *Career* chm: Chelsea Green Ltd 1981–84, Figurehead Ltd 1981–83; *Recreations* motor-racing, reading; *Clubs* Pratt's; *Style*— The McGillycuddy of the Reeks

McGINN, Ambrose Somerville; s of John McGinn, of Ormskirk, Lancs, and Margaret Somerville, *née* O'Meara; *b* 18 Dec 1959; *Educ* Maricourt HS Sefton, Wigan Coll of Technol, UCL (BA Philosophy); *m* Diana, da of Richard Hanmer Hilton Jones; 1 s (Matthew Hanmer Somerville b 3 Sept 1993); *Career* graduate trainee Grand Metropolitan plc 1981–85, market sector mangr Unilever plc 1985–89; Abbey National plc: mktg mangr 1989–93, head of product mktg 1993–94, product dir 1994–95, mktg dir (lending and advtg) 1995–96, mktg dir and dir of retail savings 1996–; memb: Cncl ISBA, Consumer Fin Mgmnt Ctee Fin and Leasing Assoc, Consumer Affrs Ctee Br Bankers Assoc, Mktg Soc, Mktg Gp of GB; *Recreations* rural retreat reclamation; *Style*— Ambrose McGinn, Esq; ✉ Abbey National plc, 201 Grafton Gate East, Milton Keynes, Bucks MK9 1AN (☎ 01908 343275, fax 01908 343355)

McGIVERN, Eugene; s of James McGivern (d 1981), of Belfast, NI, and Eileen, *née* Dickie (d 1995); *b* 15 Sept 1938; *Educ* St Colman's Sch, St Mary's GS Belfast; *m* 1 Feb 1960, Teresa, da of Owen Doran, of Lurgan, NI; 2 s (Christopher b 1963, Nicholas b 1971), 1 da (Annette b 1961); *Career* Inland Revenue: joined 1955, on secondment as sec to Min of State (now Baroness White, *qv*) Welsh Office 1967–69, under sec 1986– (asst sec 1973); chm Mgmnt Ctee Cwlth Assoc of Tax Admins 1982–86, chm John Fisher Sch Purley 1985–86 (govr 1979–91); *Recreations* reading, gardening (if unavoidable); *Style*— Eugene McGivern, Esq; ✉ c/o Board of Inland Revenue, Somerset House, Strand, London WC2R 1LB (☎ 0171 438 6501)

McGLADDERY, (Joseph) Raymond; s of Joseph McGladdery (d 1946), and Margaret McGladdery (d 1983); *b* 28 May 1927; *Educ* Methodist Coll Belfast, Queen's Univ Belfast (BSc); *m* 31 March 1967, Ann Pitcairn, da of John Reekie (d 1982); 1 s (Joseph John); *Career* involved construction Carrington Power Station nr Manchester 1949 and i/c various projects NI 1950–58, a dep chief engr Durgapur Steelworks in W Bengal 1959–60, rep London consits i/c of first major construction project in Danakil Desert Ethiopa 1961–62; fndr McGladdery & Ptnrs 1962–; FIEI 1970, FICE 1973, MConsE 1974, FCIArb 1974, FIStructE 1975, FIHT 1975, FCIWEM 1987, Eur Ing 1989; *Style*— Raymond McGladdery, Esq; ✉ The Cottage, 43A Malone Park, Belfast BT9 6NL (☎ 01232 669734); McGladdery and Partners, Consulting Civil and Structural Engrs, 64 Malone Avenue, Belfast BT9 6ER (☎ 01232 660682)

MacGLASHAN, HE Maureen Elizabeth; CMG (1997); da of Kenneth MacGlashan (d 1967), and Elizabeth, *née* Elliott; *b* 7 Jan 1938; *Educ* Luton Girls HS, Girton Coll Cambridge (BA, LLM); *Career* HM Dip Serv: entered 1961, third later second sec HM Embassy Tel Aviv 1964–67, first sec and head of chancery E Berlin 1973–75, UK rep EEC Brussels 1975–77, Home Civil Serv 1977–82, cnsllr HM Embassy Bucharest 1982–85, asst dir Res Centre for Int Law Cambridge 1986–90, cnsllr HM Embassy Belgrade 1990, head of Western Euro Dept FCO 1991–92, resident chm Civil Service Selection Board 1992–95, HM ambass to The Holy See Rome 1995–; ASIL 1986, ILA (Br Section) 1986, BIICL; *Style*— HE Miss Maureen MacGlashan, CMG; ✉ c/o Foreign and Commonwealth Office (Rome), King Charles Street, London SW1A 2AH

McGLASHAN, Prof Maxwell Len; s of Leonard Day McGlashan (d 1969), of Greymouth, NZ, and Margaret Cordelia, *née* Bush (d 1985); *b* 1 April 1924; *Educ* Greymouth NZ Schs, Canterbury Univ Coll Christchurch NZ (BSc, MSc), Univ of Reading (PhD, DSc); *m* 15 Jan 1947, Susan Jane, da of Col Hugh Edward Crosse, OBE, MC, of Patoka, Hawkes Bay, NZ (d 1962); *Career* sr lectr in chemistry Canterbury Univ Coll NZ 1953 (asst lectr 1946–48, lectr 1948–53), reader in chemistry Univ of Reading 1961–64 (Sims Empire Scholar 1949–52, lectr 1954–61), prof of physical chemistry Univ of Exeter 1964–74, prof of chemistry and head Dept of Chemistry UCL 1974–89, emeritus prof Univ of London 1989–; ed Journal of Chemical Thermodynamics 1969–95; Cmmn on Physicochemical Symbols Terminology and Units: memb 1963–65, vice chm 1965–67, chm 1967–71; chm Interdivisional Ctee on Nomenclature and Symbols Int Union of Pure and Applied Chemistry 1971–76; memb: Metrication Bd 1969–80, Comité Consultatif des Unités (Metre Convention) 1969–; external memb Br Gas Res Ctee 1979–90, tstee Ramsay Meml Fellowships Tst 1982–96 (chm Advsy Cncl 1975–89); hon fell UCL 1991; FRSC 1962; *Books* Physicochemical Quantities and Units (2 edn, 1971), Chemical Thermodynamics (1979); *Recreations* Alpine climbing, theatre; *Clubs* Athenaeum, Swiss Alpine; *Style*— Prof Maxwell McGlashan; ✉ Patoka, Fairwarp, Uckfield, E Sussex TN22 3DT (☎ 01825 712172, fax 01825 713622); Department of Chemistry, University College London, 20 Gordon St, London WC1H 0AJ (☎ 0171 380 7451, fax 0171 380 7463)

McGLONE, Heather Margaret; da of Eric Vickers McGlone, of Brighton, and Margaret Gavin Lamond, *née* Russell; *b* 15 Feb 1957; *Educ* North London Collegiate Sch, SCEGGS Sydney Australia, Sydney Univ, Univ of Sussex (BA), Université de la Sorbonne, City

Univ London (Postgrad Dip in Journalism); *m* 3 Dec 1983, Louis Albert Francis Kirby, s of William and Anne Kirby; 2 da (Clementine Margaret Allegra b 10 April 1987, Iona Alice Eliza b 17 Feb 1990); *Career* Western Morning News and Evening Herald 1981–83, freelance journalist 1983–86; Daily Express: dep woman's ed 1986–88, woman's ed 1988–91, features ed 1991–93, asst ed features Oct 1993–Feb 1994, assoc ed Feb-Sept 1994, ed This Week magazine Sept 1994–June 1995, exec-ed June 1995–; *Recreations* theatre, ballet, art galleries, horse-riding; *Style*— Miss Heather McGlone; ✉ Daily Express, Ludgate House, 245 Blackfriars Road, London SE1 9UP (☎ 0171 922 7007)

McGONAGLE, Declan George; s of Stephen McGonagle, and Margaret, *née* White; *b* 15 Nov 1952; *Educ* St Columb's Coll Derry, Coll of Art Belfast (BA, higher dip in painting); *m* 28 July 1980, Mary Bernadette (Moira), da of Anthony Carlin; 2 s (Declan b 26 Sept 1984, Paul b 2 March 1987); *Career* lectr in fine art Regnl Tech Coll 1976–78, organiser Orchard Gallery Derry 1978–84, dir of exhibitions ICA London 1984–86, visual arts organiser Derry 1986–90, dir Irish Museum of Modern Art Dublin 1990–; Sunday Tribune Visual Arts award 1987; *Recreations* politics, reading, piano; *Style*— Declan McGonagle, Esq; ✉ Irish Museum of Modern Art, Kilmainham, Dublin 8, Ireland (☎ 00 353 1 6718666, fax 00 353 1 6718695)

McGONIGAL, Christopher Ian; s of Maj H A K McGonigal, MC (d 1963), of Beverley, E Yorks, and Cora, *née* Bentley (d 1946); *b* 10 Nov 1937; *Educ* Ampleforth, CCC Oxford (MA); *m* 28 Sept 1961, (Sara) Sally Ann, da of Louis David Mesnard Fearnley Sander (d 1975); 3 s (Dominic b 1962, Gregory b 1967, Fergus b 1969), 1 da (Alice b 1964); *Career* slr 1965; Coward Chance: asst slr 1965–68, ptnr 1969–87, sr litigation ptnr 1972–79, sr resident ptnr ME 1979–83, sr litigation ptnr 1983–87; slr Hong Kong 1981; Clifford Chance: jt sr litigation ptnr 1987–92, sr litigation ptnr 1992–95, ptnr Contentious Business 1995–; recorder of the Crown Court 1995– (asst recorder 1989–95); Freeman Worshipful Co of Slrs 1972; *Recreations* local history, gardening, walking; *Style*— Christopher McGonigal, Esq; ✉ Sandhurst Farm, Clayhill Road, Lamberhurst, Kent TN3 8AX (☎ 01892 890595); Clifford Chance, 200 Aldersgate Street, London EC1A 4JJ (☎ 0171 600 1000, fax 0171 600 5555, telex 887847 LEGIS G)

McGOUGH, Roger Joseph; OBE (1997); *b* 9 Nov 1937; *Educ* St Mary's Coll Liverpool, Hull Univ (BA, CertEd); *Career* poet; fell of poetry Univ of Loughborough 1973–75, writer-in-residence Western Aust Coll of Advanced Educn Perth 1986; vice pres The Poetry Soc 1996 (memb Exec Cncl 1989–93); hon prof Thames Valley Univ 1993; *Poetry* The Mersey Sound (with Adrian Henri and Brian Patten, 1967), In the Glassroom (1976), Holiday on Death Row (1979), Summer with Monika (1978), Waving at Trains (1982), Melting into the Foreground (1986), Selected Poems (1989), Blazing Fruit (1990), You At The Back (1991), Defying Gravity (1992); wrote and appeared in Thames TV prog Kurt Mungo BP and Me (BAFTA Award, 1984), wrote poems for and presented Channel Four TV prog The Elements 1992 (Royal Television Award); for children: The Great Smile Robbery (1983), Sky in the Pie (1983), The Stowaways (1986), Noah's Ark (1986), Nailing the Shadow (1987), An Imaginary Menagerie (1988), Helen Highwater (1989), Counting by Numbers (1989), The Lighthouse That Ran Away (1991), My Dad's a Fire-eater (1992), Another Custard Pie (1993), Lucky (1993), Stinkers Ahoy! (1995), The Magic Fountain (1995), Sporting Relations (1996), The Kite and Caitlin (1996); *Clubs* Chelsea Arts (chm 1984–86, tstee 1993–); *Style*— Roger McGough, Esq, OBE; ✉ c/o Peters, Fraser & Dunlop, 5th Floor, The Chambers, Chelsea Harbour, London SW10 0XF

McGOURTY, Christine Marina; da of Thomas McGourty, of Perth, Scotland, and Marina, *née* Farrants; *b* 22 Nov 1965; *Educ* Barrhead HS Glasgow, Univ of Edinburgh (BSc), UCW Cardiff (postgrad dip in journalism); *m* 3 Aug 1996, Andrew Walpole; 1 s (Benjamin Thomas Walpole b 13 Dec 1995); *Career* journalist; news corr Nature: London 1988–89, Washington 1989; technol corr Daily Telegraph 1989–95, technol corr BBC News 1995–; memb Assoc of Br Sci Writers 1988; *Recreations* singing, swimming, travelling, reading, learning languages; *Style*— Ms Christine McGourty; ✉ BBC Television Centre, Room 7083, Wood Lane, London W12 7RJ (☎ 0181 576 4144, fax 0181 749 9016)

McGOWAN, Prof David Alexander; s of George McGowan, MBE (d 1979), of Portadown, Co Armagh, and Annie Hall, *née* Macormac (d 1994); *b* 18 June 1939; *Educ* Portadown Coll, Queen's Univ Belfast (BDS, MDS), Univ of London (PhD); *m* 21 June 1968, (Vera) Margaret, da of James Macauley, of Closkelt, Co Down; 1 s (Andrew), 2 da (Anna, Marion); *Career* lectr in dental surgery Queen's Univ Belfast 1968, sr lectr in oral and maxillofacial surgery London Hosp Med Coll 1970–77; University of Glasgow: prof of oral surgery 1977–, post grad advsr in dentistry 1977–90, dean of dental educn 1990–95, memb Senate 1995–; dean Dental Faculty RCPSG 1989–92, currently: chm Nat Dental Advsy Ctee (Scotland), memb and vice chm Exec GDC, memb EC Advsy Ctee on the Training of Dental Practitioners; FDSRCS 1964, FFDRCSI 1966, FDSRCPSG 1978; *Books* An Atlas of Minor Oral Surgery (1989), The Maxillary Sinus (1993); *Recreations* music, dog-walking; *Style*— Prof David McGowan; ✉ Glasgow Dental Hospital & School, 378 Sauchiehall Street, Glasgow G2 3JZ (☎ 0141 211 9650, fax 0141 211 9834)

McGOWAN, Frankie (Mrs Peter Glossop); *Educ* Notre Dame HS, Poly of Central London; *m* 27 March 1971, Peter Glossop; 1 s (Tom b 28 Dec 1973), 1 da (Amy b 8 May 1977); *Career* journalist and author; Evening News 1970–73, freelance 1973–85, assoc ed Woman's Journal 1985–86, asst ed Sunday Mirror 1986–87, launch ed and ed New Woman 1988–90, ed-in-chief and relaunch ed People Magazine 1990–91, launch ed and ed Top Santé 1993–94, columnist Good Housekeeping 1996–; publicity conslt for ROC (research into ovarian cancer); *Books* Ellie (1993), Women returning to work (1993), The Things We Do For Love (with John McGowan, 1993), Out There (1994), Unfinished Business (1996); *Style*— Ms Frankie McGowan; ✉ c/o A M Heath & Co, 79 St Martin's Lane, London WC2N 4AA

McGOWAN, 3 Baron (UK 1937); Harry Duncan Cory McGowan; s of 2 Baron McGowan (d 1966), and Carmen (d 1996), da of Sir (James) Herbert Cory, 1 Bt, JP, DL; *b* 20 July 1938; *Educ* Eton; *m* 1962, Lady Gillian Angela Pepys, da of 7 Earl of Cottenham (d 1968); 1 s, 2 da; *Heir* s, Hon Harry John Charles McGowan b 23 June 1971; *Career* ptnr Panmure Gordon & Co 1971– (currently dir and head of corp fin); non-exec dir Wessex Water plc 1994–; *Clubs* Boodle's, Jockey; *Style*— The Rt Hon the Lord McGowan; ✉ 12 Stanhope Mews East, London SW7 (☎ 0171 370 2346); Highway House, Lower Froyle, Alton, Hants (☎ 01420 22104)

McGOWAN, Ian Duncan; s of Alexander McGowan (d 1989), and Dora, *née* Sharp; *b* 19 Sept 1945; *Educ* Liverpool Inst, Exeter Coll Oxford (BA); *m* 30 Oct 1971, Elizabeth Ann, da of David Weir; 2 da (Catherine b 22 March 1977, Margaret b 22 July 1978); *Career* Nat Library of Scotland: asst keeper 1971–78, keeper (catalogues and automation) 1978–88, sec of the library 1988–90, librarian 1990–; chm National Preservation Advsy Ctee 1994–, vice pres Scottish Library Assoc 1996–; *Clubs* New (Edinburgh); *Style*— Ian McGowan, Esq; ✉ 23 Blackford Road, Edinburgh EH9 2DT (☎ 0131 667 2432); National Library of Scotland, George IV Bridge, Edinburgh EH1 1EW (☎ 0131 226 4531, fax 0131 220 6662)

McGOWAN, Jeff; s of Percy McGowan (d 1988), and Hilda Ethel, *née* Wade (d 1994); *b* 29 Sept 1944; *m* 1, 3 Sept 1965 (m dis 1980), Marjorie, da of Andrew McClure; 2 s (Paul Wade b 8 Dec 1967, Derry Wade 24 April 1971); m 2, 19 Dec 1981, Marilyn Elizabeth, da of Geoffrey Grieg Duncan; 2 da (Alexandra Clare b 20 March 1986, Victoria Rose b 30 June 1992), 1 s (William James b 9 April 1990); *Career* trainee journalist with weekly newspapers in Widnes, St Helens and Merseyside 1959–61, journalist Lancashire Evening Telegraph Blackburn 1961–65, journalist rising to dep news ed Daily Express 1965–78, news ed Daily Star 1978–88, asst ed new launch The Post 1988, ed Daily Sport 1993– (asst ed 1989–93); originated annual Gold Star Award for bravery heroism and acts of kindness Daily Star 1980; *Recreations* gardening (memb Heald Green Horticultural Soc), poultry-keeping; *Clubs* Liverpool Press; *Style*— Jeff McGowan, Esq; ✉ Sport Newspapers Ltd, 19 Great Ancoats Street, Manchester M60 4BT (☎ 0161 236 4466, fax 0161 236 4535)

McGOWAN, Sheriff John; s of Arthur McGowan (d 1993), of Kilmarnock, and Bridget, *née* McCluskey; *b* 15 Jan 1944; *Educ* St Joseph's Acad Kilmarnock, Univ of Glasgow (LLB); *m* 16 April 1966, Elise, da of Owen Peter Smith; 2 s (Kenneth Owen b 6 May 1967, Christopher John b 27 March 1970); *Career* legal apprenticeship 1965–67, qualified slr 1967, sheriff of Glasgow and Strathkelvin 1993– (temp sheriff 1986–93); chm DHSS Appeal Tbnl 1980–86, memb Cncl Law Soc of Scot 1982–85; *Recreations* theatre, concerts, reading, playing golf and tennis, swimming and curling; *Style*— Sheriff John McGowan; ✉ 19 Auchentrae Crescent, Ayr KA7 4BD (☎ 01292 260139); Sheriff Court House, 1 Carlton Place, Glasgow G5 9DA

McGOWAN, Prof Margaret Mary; da of George McGowan, and Elizabeth, *née* McGrail; *b* 21 Dec 1931; *Educ* Stamford HS for Girls, Univ of Reading (BA, PhD); *m* Prof Sydney Anglo; *Career* lectr in French: Univ of Strasbourg 1955–57, Univ of Glasgow 1957–64; Univ of Sussex: lectr in French 1964–66, reader 1966–74, prof 1974–, dean Sch of European Studies 1977–80, sr pro vice chllr 1992– (pro vice chllr 1981–86 and 1989–92); Una lectr Univ of California Berkeley 1980; pres Assoc of Professors of French 1981–82; vice-pres British Acad 1996–; memb Soc of Renaissance Studies; Freedom City of Tours 1988; FBA 1993; *Books* L'Art du Ballet de Cour (1963), Montaigne's Deceits (1974), Ideal Forms in the Age of Ronsard (1985), Moy qui me voy (1989); *Recreations* sport, music; *Style*— Prof Margaret McGowan, FBA; ✉ University of Sussex, Falmer, Brighton BN1 9QN (☎ 01273 678210, fax 01273 678335)

McGRADY, Edward Kevin; MP (SDLP) Down South (majority 6,342); s of late Michael McGrady, of Downpatrick, and Lillian, *née* Leatham; *b* 3 June 1935; *Educ* St Patrick's Downpatrick; *m* 6 Nov 1959, Patricia, da of William Swail; 2 s (Jerome, Conaill), 1 da (Paula); *Career* ptnr MB McGrady & Co CA and insur brokers; Downpatrick Urban Dist Cncl: cncllr 1961–73, chm 1964–73; Down Dist Council: cncllr 1973–89, chm 1974, 1976, 1978 and 1981; fndr memb and first chm SDLP 1970–71; memb Northern Ireland Assembly 1973–74 and 1982–86, NI Convention 1975, min for co-ordination NI Exec 1974, SDLP chief whip 1975–; MP (SDLP) Down South 1987– (also contested 1979, 1983 and 1986); chm: Down Regnl Museum 1981–89, Jobspace NI Ltd 1985–93, Down/Chicago Link 1991–93; memb: Bd of Dirs Down/Chicago Link Ltd, NI Affairs Select Ctee, SDLP's team to Forum for Peace and Reconciliation, front bench SDLP's team at Multi-Party Talks, NI Forum for Political Dialogue May 1996 - July 1996 (resigned); FCA (ACA); *Recreations* gardening, walking, ancient monuments, choral music; *Style*— Edward McGrady, Esq, MP; ✉ Constituency Office, 32 Saul Street, Downpatrick, Co Down BT30 6AQ (☎ 01396 612882)

McGRAIL, Prof Sean Francis; *b* 5 May 1928; *Educ* Univ of Bristol (Harry Crook scholar, BA), Univ of London Inst of Archaeology, Univ of London (PhD), Campion Hall Oxford (MA), Univ of Oxford (DSc); *m* 28 July 1955, (Ursula) Anne Yates; 1 s (Hugh Fergus b 29 Jan 1958), 3 da (Frances Joanna b 26 May 1956, Mary Ursula b 9 March 1960, Catherine Clare b 29 March 1963); *Career* RN: cadet to Lt Cdr (qualified as Master Mariner) 1946–68, pilot Fleet Air Arm 1952–68 (cmd 849 Sqdn 1962–63); National Maritime Museum: asst keeper (archaeology) Dept of Ships 1972, head Dept of Archaeology of Ships 1973–76, chief archaeologist and head Archaeological Res Centre 1976–86 (dep keeper 1976–80, keeper 1980–86); prof of maritime archaeology Inst of Archaeology Univ of Oxford 1986–93; visiting prof: Univ of Southampton 1991–, Danish Nat Museum's Centre for Maritime Archaeology Roskilde 1994, Centre for Maritime Studies Univ of Haifa Israel 1995; memb Cncl: Prehistoric Soc 1980–83, Soc of Antiques 1983–86; memb: Dept of National Heritage Advsy Ctee on Historic Wrecks 1975–, Exec Ctee Mary Rose Tst 1980–86, Egyptian Antiques Orgn's Ctee on Establishment of a Nat Maritime Museum in Alexandria 1985–86, Academic Advsy Ctee of States of Guernsey Ancient Monuments Ctee 1985–; vice chm Tst for Preservation of Oxford Coll Barges 1987–93, excavations on prehistoric and medieval sites (Norway, Denmark, Orkney, Ireland, Britain) 1974–; FSA 1981, MIFA 1983; *Books* Sources and Techniques in Boat Archaeology (ed, 1977), Logboats of England and Wales (1978), Medieval Ships and Harbours in Northern Europe (ed, 1979), Rafts, Boats and Ships (1981), Aspects of Maritime Archaeology and Ethnography (ed, 1984), Ancient Boats in NW Europe (1987), Seacraft of Prehistory (ed 2 edn, 1988), Maritime Celts, Frisians and Saxons (ed, 1990), Medieval Boat and Ship Timbers from Dublin (1993); National Maritime Museum Archaeological Series (ed, 1977–86), Studies in Maritime Archaeology (1997); *Style*— Prof Sean McGrail, FSA; ✉ Institute of Archaeology, 36 Beaumont Street, Oxford OX1 2PG (☎ 01865 278240)

McGRATH, Rev Dr Alister Edgar; s of Edgar Parkinson McGrath, of Co Down, and Annie Jane, *née* McBride; *b* 23 Jan 1953; *Educ* Wadham Coll Oxford (MA), Linacre Coll Oxford, Merton Coll Oxford (DPhil, BD), St John's Coll Cambridge; *m* 1980, Joanna Ruth, da of John Stuart Collicutt; 1 s (Paul Alister b 1981), 1 da (Elizabeth Joanna b 1983); *Career* curate St Leonard's Church Wollaton Nottingham 1980–83, research lectr Univ of Oxford 1993–, research prof of theol Regent Coll Vancouver Canada 1993–, princ Wycliffe Hall Oxford 1995– (lectr 1983–95); Hon DD Virginia Theological Seminary 1996; *Books* Intellectual Origins of The Reformation (1987), The Genesis of Doctrine (1990), Encyclopaedia of Modern Christian Thought (1993), Christian Theology (1994); *Recreations* walking, wines; *Style*— The Rev Dr Alister McGrath; ✉ Wycliffe Hall, Oxford OX2 6PW (☎ 01865 274200, fax 01865 274215, e-mail mcgrath@ermine.ox.ac.uk)

McGRATH, Anthony Charles Ormond; s of Patrick Anthony Ormond McGrath, MC, TD (d 1988), of Southwater, Sussex, and Eleanor Mary Howard, *née* Horsman; *b* 10 Nov 1949; *Educ* Worth Abbey Sch, Univ of Surrey (BSc); *m* 20 July 1974, Margaret Mary, da of Capt William Arthur Usher, RN (d 1959), of Painswick; 1 s (Thomas b 21 Aug 1978), 1 da (Philippa b 20 Nov 1980); *Career* Deloitte Haskins & Sells 1971–76, Baring Brothers International Ltd (formerly Baring Brothers & Co Limited) 1976– (dir 1984–); non-exec dir W & F C Bonham & Sons Ltd 1987–90; memb Nat Cncl CBI (memb Cos Ctee 1996–), memb London Regnl Cncl CBI 1994–; non-exec memb Br Standards Inst Quality Assurance Bd 1986–90; FCA 1974; *Clubs* Flyfishers; *Style*— Anthony McGrath, Esq; ✉ Baring Brothers International Ltd, 60 London Wall, London EC2M 5TQ (☎ 0171 767 1040, fax 0171 767 7222)

McGRATH, Sir Brian Henry; KCVO (1993, CVO 1988); s of William Henry McGrath, and Hermione Gioja McGrath; *b* 27 Oct 1925; *Educ* Eton; *m* 1959, Elizabeth Joan Bruce, *née* Gregson-Ellis (d 1977); 2 s, 1 step da; *Career* served Irish Guards 1943–46, Lt; Cannon Brewery Co 1946–48; Victoria Wine Co: joined 1948, dir 1949, chm 1960–82; chm Grants of St James's Ltd, dir Allied Breweries Ltd (later Allied-Lyons plc) 1970–82, chm Broad Street Securities 1983–92, treas to HRH The Duke of Edinburgh 1984–95 (asst private sec, then private sec 1982–92); Yr Bro Trinity House 1993–; MW; *Recreations* golf, tennis, shooting; *Clubs* Boodle's, White's; *Style*— Sir Brian McGrath, KCVO

McGRATH, Prof (John Christie) Ian; s of John (Jack) Christie McGrath, of Barrhead, Strathclyde, and Margaret Gilmore Cochrane, *née* Murray (decd); *b* 8 March 1949; *Educ* John Neilson Instn, Univ of Glasgow (BSc, PhD); *m* 25 June 1970, Wilma, da of late John

Nicol; 1 s (Nicolas John b 13 Aug 1974), 1 da (Katie Isabella b 8 Jan 1981); *Career* Wellcome interdisciplinary res fell Dept of Pharmacology and Univ Dept of Anaesthesia Glasgow Royal Infirmary Univ of Glasgow 1973–75; Inst of Physiology Univ of Glasgow: lectr 1975–83, sr lectr 1983–88, reader 1988–89, titular prof 1989–91, regius prof, head Dept of Physiology 1991–93, head of Biomedical Sci Gp 1991–93, co-dir Clinical Research Initiative in Heart Failure 1994–; memb: SERC Case Panel 1981–82, Ctee Physiological Soc 1988–; memb Editorial Bd: Br Jl of Pharmacology 1984–91, Pharmacological Review 1989–, Jl of Cardiovascular Pharmacology 1988–, Jl of Vascular Res 1991–; Pfizer Award for Biology 1983; memb: Br Pharmacological Soc 1975 (Sandoz Prize 1980), Physiological Soc 1978; *Publications* articles in academic jls; *Recreations* travel, running, eating and drinking, politics (memb Labour Party); *Style*— Prof Ian McGrath; ✉ Co-Director, Clinical Research Initiative in Heart Failure, West Medical Building, University of Glasgow, Glasgow G12 8QQ (☎ 0141 330 4483, fax 0141 337 1651, mobile 0850 502553, e-mail imcgrath@biomed.gla.ac.uk)

McGRATH, John Brian; *b* 20 June 1938; *Educ* Brunel Univ (BSc); *m* Sandy McGrath; 1 s (Paul b 17 Aug 1971), 1 da (Lucy b 19 April 1969); *Career* various appts 1956–81 with UKAEA, National Coal Board, Ford Motor Co, Jaguar Cars and Stone-Platt Ltd, chief exec Compair Ltd 1984 (md Construction and Mining Div 1982–83); Grand Metropolitan group: gp dir Watney Mann & Truman Brewers Ltd 1985, chm and md Grand Metropolitan Brewing 1986, jt md responsible for GrandMet Brewing, International Distillers & Vintners Ltd, IDV UK and Heublein 1988–91, chm and chief exec International Distillers & Vintners Ltd 1992–95 (md and chief operating offr 1991–92), gp chief exec Grand Metropolitan plc 1996–; non-exec dir Cookson plc 1993–; first chm The Portman Group (promoting responsible use of alcohol); chm The Scotch Whiskey Assoc; Freeman City of London; *Style*— John McGrath; ✉ Grand Metropolitan plc, 8 Henrietta Place, London W1M 9AG (☎ 0171 518 5445, fax 0171 518 4642)

McGRATH, Dr John Neilson; s of John McGrath (d 1977), of Aberdare, Mid Glamorganshire, and Agnes Louisa Jones (d 1989); *b* 16 May 1941; *Educ* St Benedict's Sch Ealing, Univ Coll Cardiff (BSc, PhD), RNC Greenwich (MSc); *m* 14 April 1970, Zena Gladys, da of Norman William Haysom, of Portsmouth, Hants; 2 s (James 1971, Paul 1973); *Career* Lt 1967, Lt Cdr 1971, Cdr 1979, Capt 1986, trg cdr Career Trg HMS Sultan 1979–82, head of materials technol RNEC 1982–86, Capt 1986, head of manpower computer systems HMS Centurion 1987–89, dean RNEC Manadon Plymouth 1990–93, Welsh dir The Open Univ 1993–; Welsh épée champion 1965, Welsh foil champion 1970; vice chm Grange Gp of Schs 1979–82; memb: Technician Educn Cncl Maritime Studies Ctee 1979–82, Devon Sci and Technol Regnl Orgn 1984–86, Ct of Govrs Univ of Wales 1994–; CEng, FIM 1991, FIMarE 1988; *Recreations* fencing, gardening, book collecting; *Style*— Dr John McGrath; ✉ Welsh Director, The Open University, 24 Cathedral Road, Cardiff CF1 9SA (☎ 01222 397911)

McGRATH, John Peter; s of John Francis McGrath (d 1986), and Margaret McCann (d 1985); *b* 1 June 1935; *Educ* Alyn GS Mold Clwyd, St John's Coll Oxford; *m* 1962, Elizabeth, da of Sir Hector Ross MacLennan (d 1978); 2 s (Finn b 1966, Daniel b 1968), 1 da (Kate b 1979); *Career* writer and dir; artistic dir 7:84 Theatre Co England and Scotland 1971–88; dir Channel Four Television Corporation 1989–95; writer of: over 40 plays (performed and many published), over 20 TV and film screenplays, numerous poems and songs (performed and published), libretto Behold The Sun (opera by Alexander Goehr); dir of numerous films and TV progs and prodr with Freeway Films (own co); Judith E Wilson visiting fell in theatre Univ of Cambridge 1978–79 and 1989–90; memb Cncl: IPPA 1986–90, PACT 1991–92, BAFTA 1993–; *Books* A Good Night Out (1979), The Bone Won't Break (1990), Six-Pack (!996); *Style*— John McGrath, Esq; ✉ c/o Freeway Films, 67 George Street, Edinburgh EH2 2JG (☎ 0131 225 3200, fax 0131 225 3667); c/o Freeway Films, 33A Pembroke Square, London W8 6PD (☎ 0171 937 9114, fax 0171 937 3938)

McGRATH, Paul; *b* 4 Dec 1959; *Career* professional footballer (defender); clubs: Manchester Utd 1981–90 (FA Cup winners 1985), transferred Aston Villa FC 1989–96 (signing fee of £400,000), transferred Derby County FC 1996–; honours with Aston Villa: runners-up League Championship 1989 and 1993, winners Coca Cola Cup 1994 and 1996; PFA Player of the Year 1992/93; Republic of Ireland: over 70 full caps, memb World Cup squad 1994; *Style*— Paul McGrath; ✉ Derby County FC, Baseball Ground, Shaftesbury Crescent, Derby DE3 8NB

MacGREGOR, Alastair Rankin; QC (1994); s of Alexander MacGregor, and Anne, *née* Neil; *b* 23 Dec 1951; *Educ* Glasgow Acad, Univ of Edinburgh, New Coll Oxford (MA); *m* 21 Feb 1982, Rosemary Alison, da of Ralph Trevor Kerslake; 1 s (James b 13 June 1984), 1 da (Martha b 5 Jan 1989); *Career* called to Bar Lincoln's Inn 1974, in practice London; *Style*— Alastair R MacGregor, Esq, QC; ✉ One Essex Court, Temple, London EC4Y 9AR (☎ 0171 583 2000, fax 0171 583 0118)

McGREGOR, Rev Alistair Gerald Crichton; QC (Scot 1982), WS (1965); s of James Reid McGregor, CB, CBE, MC (formerly Capt and perm under-sec of state at WO, d 1985), and Dorothy Janet, *née* Comrie (d 1979); *b* 15 Oct 1937; *Educ* Charterhouse, Pembroke Coll Oxford (BA), Univ of Edinburgh (LLB), New Coll Univ of Edinburgh (BD); *m* 7 Aug 1965, Margaret Dick, da of David Jackson Lees, of Edinburgh; 2 s (James b 1969, Euan b 1973), 1 da (Elizabeth b 1970); *Career* Nat Serv Intelligence Corps 1956–58; admitted slr 1965, advocate 1967; standing jr counsel to: Queen's and Lord Treasurer's Remembrancer 1976, Scot Home and Health Dept 1978, Scot Devpt Dept 1979; clerk to Ct of Session Rules Cncl 1974, temporary sheriff 1984–86; chm: Family Care Inc 1983–88, Discipline Ctee Potato Mktg Bd; sec Barony Housing Assoc Ltd 1973–83; dir: Apex (Scotland) Ltd 1989–, Kirk Care Housing Association Ltd 1994–; elder Church of Scot 1967–86, minister N Leith Parish Church Edinburgh 1987–; memb Faculty of Advocates 1967; *Recreations* squash, tennis, swimming; *Clubs* Edinburgh University Staff; *Style*— The Rev Alistair McGregor, QC, WS; ✉ 22 Primrose Bank Rd, Edinburgh EH5 3JG (☎ 0131 551 2802); 1A Madeira Place, Leith, Edinburgh 6 (☎ 0131 553 7378)

McGREGOR, Dr Angus; s of Dr William Hector Scott McGregor (d 1989), of Mickleton, Glos, and Dr Olwen May Richards (d 1967); *b* 26 Dec 1926; *Educ* Solihull Sch, Univ of Cambridge (MA, MD), Univ of Liverpool (DPH); *m* 14 Apr 1951, May Bridget, da of Peter Burke (d 1967), of Birr, Ireland; 1 da (Catherine b 1963); *Career* RAMC: Lt 1951, Capt 1952, GP 1953, asst MOH Chester 1954–56; dep MOH: Swindon 1957, Hull 1958–65; MOH and Port MO Southampton 1965–74, dist community physician E Dorset 1964–79, regnl MO W Mids RHA 1979–88, ret 1988; visiting prof Univ of Keele 1988–95; FFCM 1973, FRCP 1986, FRSA 1986; *Books* Disciplining and Dismissing Doctors in the NHS (with T Bunbury, 1988), and contributions to various med jls; *Recreations* piano; *Clubs* Royal Over-Seas League; *Style*— Dr Angus McGregor; ✉ 4 Meon Close, Upper Quinton, Stratford upon Avon CV37 8SX (☎ 01789 720863)

MACGREGOR, Sir Edwin Robert; 7 Bt (UK 1828), of Savile Row, Middlesex; s of Sir Robert James McConnell Macgregor, 6 Bt, MM (d 1963), and Annie Mary, *née* Lane (d 1990); *b* 4 Dec 1931; *Educ* Univ of British Columbia (BA Sc 1955, MA Sc 1957); *m* 1, 1952 (m dis 1981), Margaret Alice Jean, da of Arthur Peake, of Haney, BC, Canada; 2 s (1 decd), 2 da (Valerie Jean b 1956, Jessie Elizabeth Marlene b 1963); m 2, 1982, Helen Linda Herriott; *Heir* s, Ian Grant Macgregor b 22 Feb 1959; *Career* dep min of Lands and Parks Provincial Govt BC Canada until 1992, ret; *Style*— Sir Edwin Macgregor, Bt; ✉ 6136 Kirby Rd, RR3, Sooke, BC V0S 1N0, Canada

MACGREGOR, Elizabeth Ann; da of Rt Rev Gregor Macgregor, Bishop of Moray, Ross and Caithness, *qv*, and Elizabeth Jean Macgregor, of Inverness; *b* 16 April 1958; *Educ* Stromness Acad Orkney, Univ of Edinburgh (MA), Univ of Manchester (post grad museums studies dipl); *m* 30 July 1988, Peter Simon Jenkinson; *Career* curator Scottish Arts Cncl Travelling Gallery 1980–84, art offr Arts Cncl of GB 1984–89, dir Ikon Gallery Birmingham 1989–; judge Turner Prize 1995; memb: Visual Arts & Galleries Assoc 1985, The Lunar Soc 1991, Women in Business Assoc 1991; memb Bd: Public Art Devpt Tst, Kokuma Dance Theatre; tstee Pier Art Centre Orkney; FRSA; *Style*— Ms Elizabeth A Macgregor; ✉ Ikon Gallery, 58–72 John Bright Street, Birmingham B1 1BN (☎ 0121 643 0708, fax 0121 643 2254)

McGREGOR, Prof Gordon Peter; s of William Arthur Kenney McGregor (d 1976), of Horfield, Bristol, and Mary Aloysius, *née* O'Brien (d 1978); *b* 13 June 1932; *Educ* St Brendan's Coll Bristol, Univ of Bristol (BA), Univ of East Africa (MEd), Univ of Sussex (DPhil); *m* 10 Aug 1957, Jean Olga, da of William Henry Thomas Lewis (d 1984), of New Tredegar, Gwent; 3 da (Clare b 1958, Helen b 1962, Fiona b 1963); *Career* Flying Offr RAF (Educn Branch) 1953–56; asst master: Worcester Coll for the Blind 1956–59, King's Coll Budo Uganda 1959–63, lectr in English language Makerere Univ Uganda 1963–66; Univ of Zambia: sr lectr in educn 1966–68, reader and head of Dept of Educn 1968–69, prof of educn 1970; princ: Bishop Otter Coll Chichester Sussex 1970–80, Univ Coll of Ripon and York St John 1980–95; prof of educn Univ of Leeds 1991–95, emeritus prof 1995–; writer for: Times Higher Education Supplement, Church Times, Univs Quarterly, PNEU Journal; memb: Nat Cmmn UNESCO 1983–86, Voluntary Sector Consultative Cncl for Higher Educn 1985–88, Bd of Nat Advsy Body for Higher Educn 1986–88; chm Cncl of Church and Associated Colleges 1990–95; memb: York Dist Health Authy 1982–86, Ct Univ of York, Ct Univ of Hull; vice chm Bd of Govrs Theatre Royal York; Hon DLitt Ripon Coll Wisconsin USA 1986; Hon DHumLitt: York Coll Pennsylvania 1993, Union Coll New York 1996; *Books* King's Coll Budo: The First Sixty Years (1967), Educating the Handicapped (1967), English for Education? (1968), Teaching English as a Second Language (1970), English in Africa (1971), Bishop Otter College and Policy for Teacher Education 1839–1980 (1981), A Church College for the 21st Century? 150 Years of Ripon and York St John (1991), Towards True Education (1994); *Recreations* literature, theatre, music, swimming, travel, writing; *Style*— Prof Gordon McGregor; ✉ Hollyhocks, High St, Selsey, West Sussex (☎ 01243 602680)

MacGREGOR, Prof Graham A; s of Prof A B McGregor (d 1964), and Sybil, *née* Hawkey (d 1974); *b* 1 April 1941; *Educ* Marlborough, Trinity Hall Cambridge (MA, MB BChir), Middx Hosp; *m* 2 Nov 1968, Christiane, da of Maurice Bourquin (d 1956), of Switzerland; 1 s (Christopher b 5 Sept 1973), 2 da (Annabelle b 16 Nov 1970, Vanessa b 6 April 1972); *Career* dir Blood Pressure Unit (former sr lectr) Charing Cross and Westminster Med Sch 1979–89, prof of cardiovascular medicine and dir Blood Pressure Unit St George's Hosp Med Sch 1989–; FRCP 1982; *Books* Salt Free Diet Book (1985, 2 edn 1991), Hypertension in Practice (1987, 2 edn 1995); *Style*— Prof Graham MacGregor; ✉ Blood Pressure Unit, Department of Medicine, St George's Hospital Medical School, Cranmer Terrace, London SW17 0RE (☎ 0181 725 2848, fax 0181 725 2989)

MACGREGOR, Rt Rev Gregor; *see:* Moray, Ross and Caithness, Bishop of

McGREGOR, Harvey; QC (1978); s of William Guthrie Robertson McGregor, and Agnes, *née* Reid; *b* 25 Feb 1926; *Educ* Inverurie Acad, Scarborough Boys' HS, Queen's Coll Oxford (BA, BCL, MA, DCL), Univ of Harvard (Dr of Juridical Sci); *Career* Nat Serv 1944–48, Flying Offr; called to the Bar Inner Temple 1955, bencher 1985, head of chambers; Bigelow teaching fell Univ of Chicago 1950–51, visiting prof NY Univ and Rutgers Univ 1963–69, conslt to Law Cmmn 1966–73, warden New Coll Oxford 1985–; memb Editorial Bd Modern Law Review 1986– (memb Editorial Ctee 1967–86); ind chm London and Provincial Theatre Cncl 1992– (dep ind chm 1971–92), tstee Oxford Union Soc 1977–, pres Harvard Law Sch Assoc of UK 1981–, fell Winchester Coll 1985–, memb Acad European Private Lawyers 1994–; *Books* McGregor on Damages (15 edn, 1988), International Encyclopaedia of Comparative Law (contrib, 1972), articles in legal journals; *Recreations* music, theatre, travel; *Clubs* Garrick; *Style*— Harvey McGregor, Esq, QC; ✉ The Warden's Lodgings, New College, Oxford OX1 3BN (☎ 01865 279501, fax 01865 279590); Gray's Inn Chambers, Gray's Inn, London WC1R 5JA; 4 Paper Buildings, Temple, London EC4Y 7EX (☎ 0171 353 3366, fax 0171 353 5778)

McGREGOR, Prof Sir Ian Alexander; kt (1982), CBE (1968, OBE 1959); s of John McGregor (d 1945), of Cambuslang, Lanarkshire, and Isabella, *née* Taylor (d 1974); *b* 26 Aug 1922; *Educ* Rutherglen Acad, St Mungo Coll of Med Glasgow (LRCPE, LRCSE, LRFPS Glas); *m* 30 Jan 1954, Nancy Joan, da of Frederick Herbert Small (d 1968), of Mapledurham, Oxfordshire; 1 s (Alistair b 1956), 1 da (Lesley b 1957); *Career* Capt RAMC 1946–48, served Palestine (despatches); scientific staff MRC 1949–84, Human Nutrition Res Unit 1949–53, dir MRC Laboratories Gambia W Africa 1954–73, head Laboratory for Tropical Community Studies Nat Inst for Med Res 1974–77, dir MRC Laboratories Gambia 1978–80, MRC external staff at Univ of Liverpool 1981–84, visiting prof Univ of Liverpool at Liverpool Sch of Tropical Med 1981–94; memb: WHO Advsy Panel on Malaria 1960–, MRC Tropical Med Res Bd 1975–77 and 1981–83, Cncl of Liverpool Sch of Tropical Med 1982–95; pres Royal Soc of Tropical Med and Hygiene 1983–85, chm WHO Expert Ctee on Malaria 1985–89; memb Cncl Royal Soc 1985–87 (chm Med Sciences Res Ctee 1988–94, chm Ctee for Sci in Developing Countries 1988–94, chm Third World Science Ctee 1994–96), memb Editorial Bd Annals of Tropical Paediatrics 1989–, conslt Malaria Vaccine Devpt Prog US Agency for Int Devpt 1988–94; Chalmers medal of Royal Soc of Tropical Med and Hygiene 1963, Stewart Prize in Epidemiology of BMA 1971, Darling Fndn medal and prize of WHO 1974, Laveran medal of Soc de Pathologie Exotique de Paris 1983, Glaxo prize for Med Writing 1989, Mary Kingsley medal Liverpool Sch of Tropical Med 1994; Fred Soper lectr American Soc of Tropical Med and Hygiene 1983, Heath Clark lectr London Sch of Hygiene and Tropical Med 1983–84 (memb Ct of Govrs 1987–93), Henry Cohen History of Med lecture Univ of Liverpool 1989, Albert Norman meml lecture Inst of Med Lab Scis 1992, Manson oration Royal Soc of Tropical Med and Hygiene 1994; hon memb: American Soc of Tropical Med and Hygiene 1984, Br Soc for Parasitology 1988–; Hon LLD Univ of Aberdeen 1983, Hon DSc Univ of Glasgow 1984; DTM & H, MRCP, FRCP, FFCM, FRS, FRSE 1987, Hon FRCPS (Glasgow) 1984, Hon FRSTM & H 1995; *Publications* Malaria - The Principles and Practice of Malariology (ed jtly, 1988); author of numerous papers on tropical diseases and related subjects; *Recreations* ornithology, fishing, travel; *Clubs* Royal Society of Medicine; *Style*— Prof Sir Ian McGregor, CBE, FRS, FRSE; ✉ Greenlooms House, Homington, Salisbury, Wilts SP5 4NL (☎ 01722 718452)

MACGREGOR, Ian Grant; s & h of Sir Edwin Robert Macgregor, 7th Bt, *qv*; *b* 22 Feb 1959; *Style*— Ian Macgregor, Esq; ✉ 3886 King's Road, East Bay, Nova Scotia, Canada B0A 1H0

MacGREGOR, Sir Ian Kinloch; kt (1986); s of Daniel MacGregor and Grace, *née* Maclean; *b* 21 Sept 1912; *Educ* George Watson's Coll Edinburgh, Hillhead High Sch Glasgow, Glasgow Univ (BSc), Univ of Strathclyde (Dip Royal Coll Sci & Technol, LLD); *m* Sibyl, *née* Spencer (d 1996); 1 s (Ian), 1 da (Elizabeth (Mrs Bates)); *Career* chm and chief exec Amax Inc 1966–77 (hon chm 1977–82), dep chm BL Ltd 1977–80, ptnr Lazard Frères & Co New York 1978–90, pres Int C of C 1978, chm and chief exec British Steel Corp 1980–83, chm British Coal 1983–86; chm Trst House Forte Inc (USA) 1987–90; Hon LLD, Hon DEng, Hon DSc; AIMMPE (medallist), FIMechE; Chev Legion d'Honneur (France) 1974; *Books* The Enemies Within (1986); *Recreations* fishing, gardening, reading; *Clubs* RAC, Brooks's; *Style—* Sir Ian MacGregor; ✉ Apt 78, One Hundred Pond Street, Cohasset, MA 02025, USA; 21 Mt Wyndham Drive, Hamilton Parish, Bermuda CR04

MacGREGOR, Joanna Clare; da of Alfred MacGregor, of North London, and Angela, *née* Hughes; *b* 16 July 1959; *Educ* South Hampstead Sch for Girls, New Hall Cambridge (BA), Royal Acad of Music (recital dip, Gold medallist), Van Cliburn Inst Texas (masterclasses with Jorge Bolet); *m* 19 Sept 1986, Richard Williams; 1 da (Miranda (decd)); *Career* pianist; appeared as soloist with RPO, LSO, Eng Chamber Orch (tours to Bermuda and USA incl Carnegie Hall), BBC Symphony Orch, BBC Orch Scot, City of London Sinfonia, Nat Youth Orch (Proms 1990), London Mozart Players, BBC Symphony Orch, Rotterdam Philharmonic, CBSO, Orch of St John's, Dutch Radio Orch, Berlin Symphony Orch; soloist Last Night of the Proms 1996; Br Cncl tours: Senegal, Sierra Leone, Zimbabwe, The Phillipines, Norway, New Zealand, South Africa, Sweden, Germany, Singapore; premiered works by Br composers incl: Michael Finnissy, Gary Carpenter, Alasdair Nicolson, Hugh Wood and Harrison Birtwistle; recordings incl: American Piano Classics (1989), Satie Piano Music, Britten Piano Concerto (with Eng Chamber Orch and Steuart Bedford), Barber/Ives Sonatas, Scarlatti Sonatas, Bach Art of Fugue, Nancarrow Canons and pieces by Ravel, Bartok, Debussy and Messiaen; composer Br music for theatre and TV prodns incl: Cheek By Jowl, Oxford Stage Co, C4; organised Platform Festival of New Music ICA 1991–93; artistic dir Sound Circus Bridgewater Hall Manchester 1996; author of fantasy play based on Erik Satie's writings (BBC Entry Prix d'Italia 1990, Sony Awards entry 1991); radio presenter BBC Radio 3; TV presenter: BBC Omnibus, BBC Masterclass, Young Musician of the Year, Strings Bow and Bellows (BBC series); FRAM, FTCL, Hon FRAM; *Style—* Ms Joanna MacGregor; ✉ David Sigall, Ingpen and Williams, 14 Kensington Court, London W8 5DN (☎ 0171 937 5158, fax 0171 938 4175)

McGREGOR, John Cummack; s of John Alexander McGregor, OBE, of Edinburgh, and Isobel Millar, *née* Cummack; *b* 21 April 1944; *Educ* Paisley GS, Univ of Glasgow (Rainey bursary, BSc, MB ChB, John Hunter medal, David Livingston prize); *m* 22 July 1972, Moira, da of Gordon Imray; 1 da (Trudy Isabel b 1 Aug 1973), 1 s (Alan John Alexander b 26 March 1975); *Career* jr hosp posts in med Royal Alexander Infirmary Paisley then in surgery Western Infirmary Hosp Glasgow 1969–70, Hall fell Professorial Dept of Surgery Western Infirmary Glasgow 1970–71, registrar in gen surgery Stobhill Hosp Glasgow and locum registrar in plastic surgery Canniesburn Glasgow 1971–76, SHO/registrar in plastic surgery Nottingham City Hosp 1975–77, registrar in plastic surgery Canniesburn Glasgow 1977–78, sr registrar in plastic surgery Bangour Hosp nr Edinburgh 1978–80, conslt plastic surgn Bangour Edinburgh and St John's Hosps W Lothian 1980–; Sir Ernest Finch research prize Trent RHA 1977; memb: Br Assoc of Plastic Surgns, Br Assoc of Aesthetic Plastic Surgns, Int Soc of Aesthetic Plastic Surgns; FRCS 1974, FRCSEd 1983; *Books* contrib chapters: Advances and Technical Standards in Neurosurgery (Resconstructive Surgery of the Head) (1981), Essential Surgical Practice (1988); author of over 50 pubns in med jls on various topics incl burns, pressure sores, breast surgery, compound leg injuries, skin cancer, plastic surgery audit and sport injuries; *Recreations* golf, tennis, watching football and rugby, keeping budgerigars, collecting cacti, writing medical articles; *Clubs* Bruntsfield Golf (Edinburgh), Royal Burgess Golf (Edinburgh); *Style—* John McGregor, Esq; ✉ c/o BUPA Murrayfield Hospital, 122 Corstorphine Road, Edinburgh EH12 6UD (☎ 0131 334 0363, fax 0131 334 7338); St John's Hospital at Howden, Howden, Livingston, W Lothian EH54 6PP (☎ 01506 419666)

MacGREGOR, Rt Hon John Roddick Russell; OBE (1971), PC (1985), MP (C) Norfolk South (majority 17,565); s of late Dr N S R MacGregor, of Shotts; *b* 14 Feb 1937; *Educ* Merchiston Castle Sch Edinburgh, Univ of St Andrews, King's Coll London; *m* 1962, Jean Dungey; 1 s, 2 da; *Career* univ admin 1961–62; former chm: Fedn of Univ Cons & Unionist Assocs, Bow Gp; first pres Cons and Christian Democratic Youth Community; editorial staff New Society 1962–63, special asst to PM 1963–64, Cons Res Dept 1964–65, head of Ldr of Oppn's Private Office 1965–68; with Hill Samuel 1968–79 (dir 1973–79); MP (C) Norfolk S Feb 1974–, oppn whip 1977–79, a Lord Cmmr of the Treasy (Govt whip) 1979–81, Parly Under Sec for Trade and Indust with responsiblity for small businesses 1981–83, Min of State for Agric Fisheries and Food 1983–85, Chief Sec to the Treasy 1985–87, Min for Agric Fisheries and Food 1987–July 1989, Sec of State for Educn July 1989–Nov 1990, Lord Pres of the Council and Leader of the Commons Nov 1990–92, Sec of State for Transport 1992–94; non-exec chm Hill Samuel Bank 1994–96; non-exec dir: Associated British Foods plc 1994–, Slough Estates PLC 1995–, Unigate plc 1996–; vice pres Assoc of County Cncls 1995–, memb Cncl King's Coll London 1996–; Hon LLD Univ of Westminster 1995; *Recreations* opera, gardening, travel, conjuring; *Style—* The Rt Hon John MacGregor, OBE, MP; ✉ House of Commons, London SW1A 0AA

MACGREGOR, His Hon John Roy; s of Charles George McGregor, of Jamaica and New York (d 1914), and Amy Lilla Isabelle, *née* Green (d 1962); *b* 9 Sept 1913, Brooklyn, NY; *Educ* Bedford Sch; *Career* WWII RA 1939–46, served ME (POW), RA (TA) and SAS (TA) 1950–61, Maj; called to the Bar Gray's Inn 1939, dep chm Cambs QS 1967–71, recorder 1972–74, legal assessor to Gen Optical Cncl 1972–74, hon recorder Margate 1972–79, circuit judge 1975–87; vice pres Clan Gregor Soc 1985–; *Clubs* Special Forces; *Style—* His Hon John Macgregor; ✉ Nether Gaulrig, Yardley Hastings, Northampton NN7 1HD (☎ 01604 696861)

MacGREGOR, (Robert) Neil; s of Alexander Rankin MacGregor, and Anna Neil; *b* 16 June 1946; *Educ* Glasgow Acad, New Coll Oxford, Ecole Normale Supérieure Paris, Univ of Edinburgh, Courtauld Inst of Art; *Career* memb Faculty of Advocates Edinburgh 1972, lectr in history of art and architecture Univ of Reading 1976, ed Burlington Magazine 1981–86, dir Nat Gallery 1987–; Hon Doctorate: Univ of York 1992, Univ of Edinburgh 1994; *Style—* Neil MacGregor, Esq; ✉ The National Gallery, Trafalgar Square, London WC2N 5DN (☎ 0171 839 3321)

McGREGOR, Peter; s of Peter McGregor (d 1977), of Altafearn, Kames, Argyll, and Margaret Thomson, *née* McAuslan (d 1992); *b* 20 May 1926; *Educ* Cardiff HS, Univ of Birmingham, LSE (BSc); *m* 4 Sept 1954, Marion Edith Winifred, da of Herbert Thomas Downer (d 1974), of Cardiff; 1 s (Iain Peter b 1955), 1 da (Fiona Janet b 1958); *Career* mangr Ferranti Ltd 1950–74 (gen mangr Power Div 1970–74); dir: Industrie Elettriche di Legnano (Italy) 1970–74, Oxford Univ Business Summer Sch 1972 (memb Steering Ctee 1974–79); sec gen Anglo-German Fndn for the Study of Industrial Soc 1974–80, industl dir (dep sec) Nat Econ Devpt Office 1980–84, dir gen Export Gp for Constructional Industs 1984–91, assoc dir Corp Renewal Associates Ltd 1988–92, sr ptnr McGregor & Associates 1988–96, conslt to EGCI 1991–94; former industl advsr to the Lib Pty, memb Konigswinter Conf Steering Ctee 1975–90, hon treas Anglo-German Assoc 1978–91; elder and hon treas St Columba's Church Oxford; FRSA, FIEE, CEng, FIMgt, MCIM, CIMfgE; *Recreations* gardening, walking, listening to music, sailing, reading, writing; *Clubs* Athenaeum, Caledonian; *Style—* Peter McGregor, Esq; ✉ c/o Caledonian Club, 9 Halkin Street, London SW1X 7DR

MacGREGOR, Susan Katriona (Sue); OBE (1992); da of Dr James MacWilliam MacGregor, and late Margaret, *née* MacGregor; *b* 30 Aug 1941; *Educ* Herschel Sch Cape Town; *Career* programme presenter S African Broadcasting Corp 1962–67, BBC radio reporter (World at One, PM, World this Weekend) 1967–72; presenter BBC Radio 4: Woman's Hour 1972–87, Today 1985–; Hon DLitt Nottingham; Hon MRCP, FRSA; *Recreations* theatre, cinema, skiing; *Style—* Ms Sue MacGregor, OBE; ✉ c/o BBC, London W1A 1AA (☎ 0171 765 5566)

McGREGOR OF DURRIS, Baron (Life Peer UK 1978), of Hampstead in Greater London; Oliver Ross McGregor; s of late William McGregor; *b* 25 Aug 1921; *Educ* Worksop Coll, Univ of Aberdeen, LSE; *m* 1944, Nellie, da of Harold Weate, of Manchester; 3 s (Hon William Ross b 1948, Hon Alistair John b 1950, Hon Gregor Weate b 1952); *Career* sits as Lib Dem peer in House of Lords; chm: Forest Philharmonic Orchestra, Advertising Standards Authy 1980–91, Press Complaints Commission 1991–95; pres: Nat Cncl for One Parent Families 1975–91, Nat Assoc of Citizens Advice Bureaux 1981–87; prof of social instns Univ of London 1964–85, head of Dept of Sociology Bedford Coll 1964–77, jt dir Rowntree Legal Research Unit 1966–85, dir Centre for Socio-Legal Studies Univ of Oxford 1972–75, fell Wolfson Coll Oxford 1972–75; ind tstee Reuters 1984–, chm Reuters Founders Share Co 1987–, hon memb Int Fedn of Newspapers Publishers 1984–; hon fell LSE 1977–, Hon LLD Univ of Bristol 1986; *Clubs* Garrick; *Style—* The Rt Hon Lord McGregor of Durris; ✉ Far End, Wyldes Close, London NW11 7JB (☎ 0181 458 2856, fax 0181 455 3309)

MacGREGOR OF MacGREGOR, Brig Sir Gregor; 6 Bt (GB 1795), of Lanrick, Co Perth; 23 Chief of Clan Gregor; s of Capt Sir Malcolm MacGregor of MacGregor, 5 Bt, CB, CMG, JP, DL, RN (d 1958), and Hon Gylla Rollo, OBE (d 1980), sis of 12 Lord Rollo; *b* 22 Dec 1925; *Educ* Eton; *m* 8 Feb 1958, Fanny, o da of Charles Hubert Archibald Butler, of Newport, Essex, sometime High Sheriff for that county; 2 s (Malcolm Gregor Charles b 1959, Ninian Hubert Alexander b 1961); *Heir* s, Maj Malcolm Gregor Charles MacGregor of MacGregor, yr, *qv*; *Career* served WWII Scots Gds, Palestine 1947–48, Malaya 1950–51, Borneo 1965; Staff Coll Course 1960; Jt Servs Staff Coll 1965; cmd 1 Bn Scots Gds 1966–69, Br Liaison Offr US Army Inf Centre 1969–71, Col 'A' Recruiting HQ Scotland 1971, Lt-Col cmdg Scots Gds 1971–74; def and mil attaché Br Embassy Athens 1975–78, cmd Lowlands 1978–80, ADC to HM The Queen 1979; Grand Master Mason of Scotland 1988–93; memb Royal Co of Archers (Queen's Body Guard for Scotland); *Clubs* Pratt's, New (Edinburgh); *Style—* Brig Sir Gregor MacGregor of MacGregor, Bt; ✉ Bannatyne, Newtyle, Angus PH12 8TR (☎ 0182 85 314); R-5 Buttonwood Bay, 96000 Overseas Highway, Key Largo, Florida 33037–2124 (☎ 00 1 305 852 5740)

MacGREGOR OF MacGREGOR, YOUNGER, Maj Malcolm Gregor Charles; s and h of Brig Sir Gregor MacGregor of MacGregor, 6 Bt, and Fanny MacGregor of MacGregor, *née* Butler; *b* 23 March 1959; *Educ* Eton; *m* 8 Oct 1988, Cecilia Margaret Lucy, er da of Sir Ilay Campbell of Succoth, 7 Bt; *Career* Maj Scots Gds, chief of staff 51 Highland Bde, served Hong Kong, NI, BAOR and UK; memb Royal Co of Archers (Queen's bodyguard for Scotland); FRGS; *Recreations* travel, photography, tennis; *Clubs* Cavalry & Guards', Royal Perth; *Style—* Malcolm MacGregor of MacGregor, younger; ✉ Bannatyne, Newtyle, Angus PH12 8TR (☎ 01828 650 314)

McGRIGOR, Sir Charles Edward; 5 Bt (UK 1831), of Campden Hill, Middx; DL (Argyll and Bute); s of Lt-Col Sir Charles Colquhoun McGrigor, 4 Bt, OBE (d 1946), and Amabel Caroline, *née* Somers-Cocks (d 1977); Sir James McGrigor, 1 Bt, KCB, was Dir-Gen of the Army Med Dept for thirty-six years and three times Lord Rector of Marischal Coll Aberdeen; *b* 5 Oct 1922; *Educ* Eton; *m* 7 June 1948, Mary Bettine, da of Sir Archibald Charles Edmonstone, 6 Bt (d 1954), of Duntreath Castle, Blanefield, Stirlingshire; 2 s (James Angus Rhoderick Neil b 19 Oct 1949, Charles Edward b 7 Aug 1959), 2 da (Lorna Gwendolyn b 18 Feb 1951, Kirstie Rowena Amabel (Mrs Rory John MacLaren) b 3 Feb 1953); *Heir* s, James Angus Rhoderick Neil McGrigor b 19 Oct 1949, *qv*; *Career* 2 Lt Rifle Bde 1942, Capt 1943, served in N Africa and Italy (despatches); ADC to HRH The Duke of Gloucester, KG 1945–47 (Australia and England); memb Royal Co of Archers (Queen's Body Guard for Scotland); Exon of the Queen's Body Guard of Yeomen of the Guard 1970–85; vice-pres and memb Ctee of Mgmnt RNLI (former dep chm); former convenor Scottish Lifeboat Cncl; *Recreations* fishing, gardening; *Clubs* Prestwick Golf; *Style—* Sir Charles McGrigor, Bt, DL; ✉ Upper Sonachan, by Dalmally, Argyll PA33 1BJ (☎ 01866 833229)

McGRIGOR, James Angus Rhoderick Neil; s and h of Sir Charles Edward McGrigor, 5 Bt, *qv*; *b* 19 Oct 1949; *Educ* Eton; *m* (m dis), Caroline F, da of late Jacques Roboh, of Paris; 2 da (Sibylla b 1988, Sarah b 1989); *Career* farmer; memb Royal Company of Archers (Queen's Body Guard for Scotland); *Recreations* fishing, shooting, travel, music, cinema; *Clubs* Turf, Chelsea Arts, White's; *Style—* James McGrigor, Esq; ✉ Ardchonnel House, by Dalmally, Argyll PA33 1BW; 10 Sydney Street, London SW3

McGROUTHER, Prof (Duncan) Angus; *b* 3 March 1946; *Educ* Univ of Glasgow (MB ChB, MD), Univ of Strathclyde (MSc); *Career* Cruden med res fell Bioengineering Unit Univ of Strathclyde 1972–73, sr registrar in plastic surgery Canniesburn Hosp Glasgow 1976–78 (registrar 1975–76), assistentartz Klinikum rechts der Isar Munich 1978, hon clinical lectr Univ of Newcastle upon Tyne 1978–80; conslt plastic surgn: Northern RHA Shotley Bridge Gen Hosp 1979–80, Canniesburn Hosp Glasgow 1981–89; asst ed Journal of Hand Surgery 1987; examiner in anatomy Royal Coll of Physicians and Surgns of Glasgow; Br Assoc of Plastic Surgns: memb 1978, sec Sr Registrars Travelling Club 1978–79, memb Educn and Res Ctee 1982–84 (chm 1988–), memb Editorial Bd Br Journal of Plastic Surgery 1981–83, memb Cncl 1986–89; Br Soc for Surgery of the Hand: memb 1980, memb Cncl 1983–85, memb Editorial Bd 1983–85; Int Fedn of Socs for Surgery of the Hand: memb Flexor Tendon Injuries Ctee, memb Res Ctee, chm Dupuytren's Disease Ctee; chm Div of Plastic and Maxillofacial Surgery 1986–, chair plastic and reconstructive surgery UCL (newly created, funded by Phoenix Appeal) 1989–; FRCS 1973, FRCS Glasgow 1973; *Publications* contrib: Cleft Lip and Palate, Oral Surgery (1986), Microanatomy of Dupuytren's Contracture, Dupuytren's Disease (1986), Dupuytren's Disease, Methods and Concepts in Hand Surgery (1986), Surgery of the Thumb (with D A C Reid, 1986), Principles of Hand Surgery (with F D Burke and P Smith, 1989); author of numerous papers on hand and limb reconstructive surgery; *Recreations* skiing; *Style—* Prof D Angus McGrouther; ✉ Department of Plastic and Reconstructive Surgery, University College London, The Rayne Institute, University St, London WC1E 6JJ

McGUCKIAN, John Brendan; s of Brian McGuckian (d 1967), of Ardverna, Cloughmills, Ballymena, and Pauline, *née* McKenna; *b* 13 Nov 1939; *Educ* St McNissis Coll Garrontower, Queen's Univ of Belfast (BSc); *m* 22 Aug 1970, Carmel, da of Daniel McGowan, of Pharis, Ballyveeley; 2 da (Breige b 1977, Mary Pauline b 1989), 2 s (Brian b 1972, John b 1981); *Career* chm: Cloughmills MFG Co 1967–, Ulster TV plc 1991–; dir: Munster & Leinster Bank 1972–, Allied Irish Bank plc 1976–, Harbour GP Ltd 1978–, Aer Lingus plc 1979–84, Unidare plc 1987–, Irish Continental Group plc 1988–; memb: Derry Devpt Cmmn 1968–71, Laganside Corp 1988–92; chm: Int Fund for Ireland 1990–93, Northern Ireland Industrial Devpt Bd 1991–; pro chllr Queen's Univ Belfast 1990–; *Style—* John B McGuckian, Esq; ✉ Ardverna, Cloughmills, Ballymena (☎ 01265 638692); Lisgoole Abbey, Culkey, Enniskillen; 1 Ballycregagh Rd, Cloughmills, Ballymena (☎ 01265 38121, fax 01265 38122)

McGUCKIAN, Maeve Therese Philomena (Medbh); da of Hugh Albert McCaughan, of Belfast, and Margaret, *née* Fergus; *b* 12 Aug 1950; *Educ* Fortwilliam Convent GS Belfast, Queen's Univ Belfast (open scholar, BA, MA, Dip Ed, TC); *m* June 1977, John McGuckian, s of John McGuckian; 3 s (John Liam b 23 April 1980, Hugh Oisin b 6 July 1982, Fergus Joseph Gregory b 20 March 1985), 1 da (Emer Mary Charlotte Rose b 23 Aug 1989); *Career* teacher of Eng Fortwilliam Convent Belfast and St Patrick's

Coll Belfast, writer in residence Queen's Univ Belfast, lectr in Eng St Mary's Trg Coll Belfast, visiting fell Univ of Calif Berkeley 1991, writer in residence New Univ of Ulster Coleraine 1995–; Irish memb Aosdana; *Awards* winner Nat Poetry Competition, Alice Hunt Bartlett Award, Rooney Prize for Lit, Gregory Award 1980, winner Cheltenham Poetry Prize; *Books* incl: Single Ladies (1980), Portrait of Joanna (1980), The Flower Master (1982), Venus and the Rain (1984), On Ballycastle Beach (1988), Two Women - Two Shores (1988), Marconi's Cottage (1991), Captain Lavender (1994); *Style*— Mrs Medbh McGuckian; ✉ c/o Henry Raddie, Downview Avenue, Antrim Road, Belfast BT15 4EZ

McGUFFIN, Prof Peter; s of Capt William Brown McGuffin, RD (d 1994), of Seaview, IOW, and Melba Martha, *née* Burnison; *b* 4 Feb 1949; *Educ* Leeds Univ Med Sch (MB ChB), Univ of London (PhD); *m* 11 July 1972, Dr Anne Elizabeth Farmer, da of Alfred Lesly Farmer; 1 s (Liam b 1976), 2 da (Catrina b 1975, Lucy b 1978); *Career* house offr then registrar St James' Univ Hosp Leeds 1972–77, registrar then sr registrar Bethlem Royal and Maudsley Hosps London 1977–79, MRC fell and lectr Inst of Psychiatry London 1979–82, visiting fell Washington Univ of St Louis MO 1981–82, MRC sr clinical fell, hon conslt and sr lectr Inst of Psychiatry and KCH London 1982–86, prof and head of dept of psychological med Univ of Wales Coll of Med; memb Neurosciences Bd MRC; FRCP 1988 (MRCP 1976), FRCPsych 1990 (MRCPsych 1978); *Books* The Scientific Principles of Psychopathology (with Shanks and Hodgson, 1984), A Psychiatric Catechism (with Greer, 1987), Schizophrenia: The Major Issues (with Bebbington, 1988), The New Genetics of Mental Illness (with Murray, 1991), Seminars in Psychiatric Genetics (with Owen, O'Donovan, Thapar and Gottesman, 1994); *Clubs* Vale of Glamorgan Riding; *Style*— Prof Peter McGuffin; ✉ Dept of Psychological Medicine, University of Wales College of Medicine, Heath Park, Cardiff CF4 4XN (☎ 01222 743241, fax 01222 747839, e-mail McGuffin@Cardiff.ac.uk)

McGUFFOG, John Lee; s of Capt Donald McGuffog, of Grayshot, Surrey, and Ethel Mary, *née* Lee; *b* 18 Aug 1945; *Educ* Wallington GS; *m* 1, 1971 (m dis 1976), Patricia Anne White; m 2, 6 March 1978, Penelope Jayne, da of Philip Gordon Lee (d 1995); 1 da (Charlotte b 21 Feb 1979); *Career* surveyor 1963–, qualified chartered auctioneer 1968, chief surveyor Leonard W Cotton & Ptnrs 1969; Mann & Co (estate agents): joined 1972, dir 1975, chm commercial div 1985; main bd dir: Countrywide Surveyors Ltd 1988–, Countrywide Commercial 1994–; memb Cranleigh and Dist Round Table 1978–86, chm Cranleigh and Dist 41 Club 1991–92; memb City Owls (promoted by Worshipful Co of Chartered Surveyors), govr Farlington Sch Horsham 1993–; ARVA 1969, FRICS 1976, ACIArb 1979; *Recreations* fishing; *Clubs* Fernfell; *Style*— John McGuffog, Esq; ✉ c/o Countrywide Commercial, Steward House, Commerical Way, Woking, Surrey (☎ 01483 722256, fax 01483 756 229, car 0860 174521)

McGUINNESS, Anne Marie; da of Roland McGuinness, of Belfast, and Eileen, *née* Fitzpatrick; *b* 29 Oct 1954; *Educ* St Dominic's HS Belfast, Queen's Univ Belfast (MB BCh, BAO); *m* 10 March 1984, James William Park, s of James Boyd Park (d 1989), of Braintree, Essex; 2 s (Oscar Boyd b 1988, Hugo Blair b 1991); *Career* sr house offr/anatomy prosector Queen's Univ Belfast 1980–81, former registrar in surgery Royal Victoria Hosp Belfast (jr house offr 1979) and Ulster Hosp Dundonald Belfast, registrar in surgery Ards Hosp Newtownards Co Down 1982–84, conslt Royal Free Hosp 1987–96, clinical dir in A&E UCH London 1996–; memb: BMA 1979, Br Assoc for Accident and Emergency Med 1986, Br Trauma Soc 1989, Br Assoc of Clinical Anatomists 1995; FMS (London) 1986, FRCSEd 1983, fndr fell Faculty of Accident and Emergency Med 1993; *Recreations* swimming, music, art; *Style*— Ms Anne McGuinness; ✉ Accident & Emergency Department, University College Hospital, Gower Street, London WC1E 6AU

McGUINNESS, Maj-Gen Brendan Peter; CB (1986); s of Bernard McGuinness; *b* 26 June 1931; *Educ* Mount St Mary's Coll, Staff Coll Camberley, RCDS; *m* 1968, Ethne Patricia Kelly; 1 s (Peter b 18 Nov 1969), 1 da (Nicola b 7 March 1972); *Career* Borneo (despatches 1966), Brig RA 1975, GOC Western Dist 1983–86; govr City Technol Coll Kingshurst; consultant; *Clubs* Army and Navy; *Style*— Maj-Gen B P McGuinness, CB; ✉ The Old Rectory, 14 Whittington Road, Worcester WR5 2JU (☎ 01905 360102)

McGUINNESS, Rt Rev James Joseph; *see:* Nottingham, Bishop of (RC)

McGURK, Dr Harry; *b* 23 Feb 1936; *Educ* Sch of Social Studies Univ of Glasgow (dipl in social work), Univ of Strathclyde (BA, PhD); *Career* probation offr Edinburgh 1961–63, relief mangr Educn Authy of E Nigeria 1963–64, tutor in introductory psychology Univ of Strathclyde 1968–71, visiting lectr in developmental psychology New Sch of Social Res NYC 1971–72, visiting res fell Infant Lab Educnl Testing Serv Princeton New Jersey 1971–72; Univ of Surrey: lectr in child devpt and developmental psychology 1972–76, sr lectr Dept of Psychology 1976–86, acting head Dept of Psychology 1984–85, prof of developmental psychology 1986–90; Univ of London: prof of developmental psychology 1990–94, dir Thomas Coram Research Unit Inst of Educn 1990–94, emeritus prof of developmental psychology Thomas Coram Research Inst 1994–; dir Australian Inst of Family Studies 1994–; visiting prof: Inst of Child Devpt Univ of Minnesota Minneapolis 1981, 1982 and 1985, La Trobe Univ Melbourne 1988, Autonoma Univ of Madrid 1989–, Univ of Seville 1989–; memb Senate Univ of Surrey 1973–77 and 1988–90, Inst of Educn Univ of London: memb Senate 1990–94, memb Res Bd 1990–92, memb Jt Planning Ctee Senate and Cncl 1991–94; memb Editorial Bd for Developmental Psychology Lawrence Erlbaum Associates 1988–, conslt psychologist Burwood Park Sch for the Deaf Walton-on-Thames Surrey; author of numerous articles, pubns and papers, esp on childhood developmental psychology; pres Int Soc for the Study of Behavioural Devpt 1996–; memb: British Psychological Soc 1971–80 (sec and fndr memb Developmental Psychology Section 1972–74, memb Scientific Affairs Bd 1975–79), Int Soc for the Study of Behavioural Devpt 1971– (gen sec 1975–81, memb Exec Ctee 1983–90), Soc for Res in Child Devpt 1972–, hon princ psychologist Mid Downs Area Health Authy 1983–; FBPsS 1980 (memb Cncl 1981–84, chm Developmental Psychology Section 1982–84 (memb Ctee 1981–84, memb Exec Ctee 1988–90), FRSM 1994; *Style*— Dr Harry McGurk; ✉ Australian Institute of Family Studies, 300 Queen Street, Melbourne, Vic 3000, Australia (☎ 00 613 9214 7807, fax 00 613 9214 7840)

McGURK, John C; *b* 12 Dec 1952; *m* Karen; 1 s (Josh), 1 da (Chloe); *Career* dep ed Sunday Mail 1987–89, ed Sunday Sun Newcastle 1989–91, dep ed Scottish Daily Record 1991–94, ed Edinburgh Evening News 1995–; *Style*— John McGurk, Esq; ✉ Evening News, 20 North Bridge, Edinburgh EH1 1YT (☎ 0131 225 2468, fax 0131 225 7302)

MACH, David Stefan; s of Joseph Mach, of Methil, Fife, Scotland, and Martha, *née* Cassidy; *b* 18 March 1956; *Educ* Buckhaven HS, Duncan of Jordanstone Coll of Art Dundee (Duncan of Drumfork travelling scholar, Dip in Art, Post Dip in Art, Pat Holmes Meml prize, SED minor and major prizes), RCA (MA, Royal Coll drawing prize); *m* 25 Aug 1979, Lesley June, da of William Ronald White; *Career* professional sculptor 1982–; exhibitions incl: British Sculpture '83 (Hayward Gallery London) 1983, Fuel for the Fire (Riverside Studio London) 1986, A Hundred and One Dalmations (Tate Gallery London) 1988, Five Easy Pieces (Barbara Toll Fine Art NY) 1989, Here to Stay (The Tramway Glasgow) 1990, Out of Order (Kingston-upon-Thames Surrey) 1990, David Mach Sculpture (Ujazdowski Castle Center for Contemporary Art Warsaw) 1993, Fully Furnished (Museum of Contemporary Art San Diego) 1994, David Mach New Drawings (Jill George Gallery London) 1995, David Mach (Galerie Andata/Ritorno Geneva) 1995; video Clydeside Classic (Channel 4) 1990; one of two Br reps at Sao Paolo Biennale 1987, one of three Scottish reps at Venice Biennale 1990; nominated for Turner prize 1988; cmmns incl Peter Gabriel's US project 1992; winner City of Glasgow Lord Provost Prize 1992; *Recreations* television, film, music; *Clubs* Chelsea Arts; *Style*— David Mach, Esq; ✉ 64 Canonbie Rd, Forest Hill, London SE23 3AG (☎ 0181 699 1668)

MacHALE, Joseph Patrick; s of Seamus Joseph MacHale, and Margaret Mary, *née* Byrne (d 1982); *b* 17 Aug 1951; *Educ* Ampleforth, Queen's Coll Oxford (MA); *m* 28 Feb 1981, Maryann, da of Rear Adm David Dunbar-Nasmith, CB, DSO; 3 s (Henry b 1983, Martin b 1986, Thomas b 1990), 1 da (Laura b 1985); *Career* with Price Waterhouse 1973–78, qualified CA 1976; joined J P Morgan Inc 1979, sr vice pres Morgan Guaranty Tst 1986–89, md J P Morgan & Co Inc NY 1989–; FCA 1978; *Clubs* Brooks's; *Style*— Joseph MacHale, Esq; ✉ The Old House, Wonston, Winchester, Hants SO21 3LS

McHARDY, David Keith; s of Charles Stuart McHardy (d 1956), and Mary Isabella, *née* Laverick; *b* 29 Aug 1950; *Educ* Lord Wandsworth Coll Long Sutton Hampshire, PCL Univ of London (LLB); *m* Barbara Lillian, da of Donald Farley (d 1956); 2 s (Alexander b 27 Sept 1981, Nicholas b 31 July 1984), 1 da (Susannah b 6 June 1992); *Career* admitted slr 1978; ptnr Hutchins & Co 1979–; Slrs Family Law Assoc: chm Legal Aid Working Pty 1987–89 (memb 1985–89), nat chm 1989–91; memb Legal Aid Area Ctee Legal Aid Bd; memb: Law Soc, Justice; chm Hackney and E London Family Mediation Serv; lectr; dep district judge Princ Registry of the Family Div London; *Recreations* tennis, golf, West Essex Golf; *Clubs* Connaught; *Style*— David McHardy, Esq; ✉ Hutchins & Co, 85 Lower Clapton Rd, London E5 0NP (☎ 0181 986 3911, fax 0181 986 8252)

McHARDY-YOUNG, Dr Stuart; s of John McHardy-Young (d 1974), of Twickenham, Middx, and Violet Collin; *b* 20 Feb 1936; *Educ* St Paul's, Guy's Hosp Univ of London (MD, MB BS), Stanford Univ California USA; *m* 9 Sept 1961, Margaret Elizabeth, da of William Alan Cash (d 1949), of Eaglescliffe, Co Durham; 1 da (Catherine b 19 April 1978); *Career* post doctoral fell Stanford Univ Med Sch California 1967–68, sr lectr and hon conslt physician Guy's Hosp Med Sch 1970–72; conslt physician and endocrinologist: Central Middx Hosp 1972–93, Royal Nat Throat Nose and Ear Hosp 1973–, Royal Masonic Hosp London 1982–96; subdean St Mary's Hosp Med Sch London 1983–88; hon clinical sr lectr UCL 1973–; memb Br Diabetic Assoc, chm NW Thames Regnl Med Manpower Cmmn (memb Central Ctee), former univ memb Brent Health Authy; memb: BMA, RSM; *Recreations* golf, travel; *Clubs* Royal Mid-Surrey Golf; *Style*— Dr Stuart McHardy-Young; ✉ 20 Belmont Rd, Twickenham, Middx TW2 5DA; 2 Hillview, Uplopers, Bridport, Dorset; 106 Harley St, London W1 (☎ 0171 935 2797); Central Middlesex Hospital, London NW10

MACHELL, Dr Richard John; s of Richard Greville Kenneth Machell (d 1951), of Plymouth, and Muriel, *née* Harvey; *b* 3 Sept 1946; *Educ* Queen's Coll Taunton, Univ of London (MB BS, MRCS LRCP); *m* 10 May 1969, Elizabeth Joan Walter, da of John Ambrose Walter Reed (d 1950), of Feniton, Devon; 1 s (Jonathan b 9 May 1970), 2 da (Claire b 28 May 1971, Isabel b 12 April 1977); *Career* house offr Guy's Hosp 1969–70, sr house offr Univ of Southampton Hosps 1970–73, registrar Addenbrooke's Hosp Cambridge 1973–76, lectr in medicine Univ of Cambridge 1976–80, conslt physician and gastroenterologist The Royal Cornwall Hosp 1980–; memb Br Soc of Gastroenterology 1977, chm Cornwall Gastrointestinal Cancer Appeal 1987–; Hon MA Univ of Cambridge 1977; FRCP 1990; *Books* Cimetidine in the 1980s (1981); *Recreations* tennis, wind surfing, gardening; *Clubs* BSG; *Style*— Dr Richard Machell; ✉ The Royal Cornwall Hospital, Treliske, Truro, Cornwall (☎ 01872 74242)

MACHIN, (Edward) Anthony; QC (1973); s of Edward Arthur Machin (d 1958), of Finchley, London, and Olive Muriel, *née* Smith (d 1980); *b* 28 June 1925; *Educ* Christ's Coll Finchley, New Coll Oxford (BCL, MA); *m* 1953, Jean Margaret, da of Reginald McKanna (d 1972), of Epsom; 2 s (Timothy, Christopher), 1 da (Anna); *Career* Vinerian law scholar 1950, Tancred student 1950, Cassel scholar 1951; called to the Bar Lincoln's Inn 1951; recorder Crown Ct 1976–90, judge Cts of Appeal of Jersey and Guernsey 1988–95; *Recreations* music, sailing (Kasta Loss), languages; *Clubs* Bar Yacht; *Style*— Anthony Machin, Esq, QC; ✉ Strand End, Strand, Topsham, Exeter (☎ 01392 877992, fax 01392 876532)

MACHIN, Arnold; OBE (1965); s of late William James Machin, of Stoke-on-Trent; *b* 1911; *Educ* Stoke Sch of Art, Derby Sch of Art, RCA (Silver medal, travelling scholar for sculpture); *m* 1949, Patricia, da of late Lt-Col Henry Newton; 1 s; *Career* artist and sculptor; tutor RCA 1951–58, master of sculpture Royal Acad Sch 1958–67; sculptures incl: St John the Baptist and The Annunciation (bought by the Tate Gallery), Spring (a large terracotta bought by the Chantrey Bequest for the Tate Gallery); designer: new coin effigy 1964 and 1967 (decimal coinage), definitive issue of postage stamp 1967, Silver Wedding commemorative crown 1972, Silver Jubilee commemorative crown 1977; FRBS 1955, RA 1956 (ARA 1947); *Recreations* music, garden design; *Style*— Arnold Machin, Esq, OBE, RA; ✉ 4 Sydney Close, London SW3; Garmelow Manor, nr Eccleshall, Staffs

MACHIN, David; s of Lt Cdr Noel Percy Machin, RN (d 1977), of Las Palmas, Canary Islands, and Joan Evelyn Hildige (d 1959); *b* 25 April 1934; *Educ* Sunningdale Sch Berks, Eton, Trinity Coll Cambridge (MA); *m* 8 June 1963, Sarah Mary, da of Col William Alfred Chester-Master, DL (d 1963), of Cirencester, Glos; 2 da (Georgina (Mrs Hugo Gerrard) b 1964, Alice (Mrs Mark Been) b 1966); *Career* Nat Serv 1952, 2 Lt Welsh Gds served UK & Egypt; publisher's ed and literary agent William Heinemann Ltd and Gregson & Wigan Ltd 1957–68, ptnr A P Watt & Son 1968–70, dir Jonathan Cape Ltd 1970–78, gen sec Soc of Authors 1978–81, md The Bodley Head Ltd 1981–87; under treas Gray's Inn 1989–, vice chm Hammersmith Democrats 1988–89, chm of tstees Inns of Ct Gainsford Tst 1992–; *Recreations* reading, walking; *Clubs* Garrick; *Style*— David Machin; ✉ 5 Gray's Inn Square, London WC1R 5AZ (☎ 0171 405 8164); 20 Lansdown Crescent, Bath BA1 5EX

MACHIN, Prof (George) Ian Thom; s of Rev George Seville Machin (d 1950), of Stockport, Cheshire, and Mary Dunsmore Brown, *née* Thom (d 1981); *b* 3 July 1937; *Educ* Silcoates Sch Wakefield, Jesus Coll Oxford (MA, DPhil); *m* 2 April 1964, Dr Jane Margaret Pallot, da of Reginald Charles Pallot (d 1971), of Jersey, CI; 2 s (Jonathan b 1965, Raoul b 1969), 1 da (Anna b 1967 d 1981); *Career* asst lectr then lectr in history Univ of Singapore 1961–64, lectr in modern history Univ of St Andrews 1964–67; Univ of Dundee: lectr in modern history 1967–75, sr lectr 1975–82, reader 1982–89, prof of Br history 1989–, head History Dept 1992–95; sometime examiner Univs of Cambridge, St Andrews, Aberdeen, Hull, Leicester, Sussex and Stirling; memb History Panel Scottish Univs Cncl on Entrance 1990–94, Univs memb History Panel Scottish Examination Bd 1996–, observer History Panel Scottish Examination Bd 1991–94; treas Dundee Branch Historical Assoc 1981–92 (pres 1992–95); FRHistS 1965; *Books* The Catholic Question in English Politics 1820 to 1830 (1964), Politics and the Churches in Great Britain 1832 to 1868 (1977), Politics and the Churches in Great Britain 1869 to 1921 (1987), The Liberal Governments 1905–15 (1991), Disraeli (1995); *Recreations* the arts, hill-walking, photographing historic signposts; *Style*— Prof Ian Machin; ✉ 50 West Road, Newport on Tay, Fife DD6 8HP (☎ 01382 543371); Department of Modern History, The University, Dundee DD1 4HN (☎ 01382 344514, fax 01382 345506)

MACHIN, Stephen James; s of Maj John Machin, of Sheffield, Yorks, and Edna, *née* Young; *b* 9 Nov 1954; *Educ* King Edward VII Sch Sheffield, Univ of Cambridge (MA, LLB); *m* W Joanna Claire, *née* Spurway; 2 s (Alexander Peter b 22 April 1980, James Edward Spurway b 29 Dec 1995), 1 da (Susannah Helen b 22 April 1982); *Career* admitted slr 1980, ATII 1982, ptnr Ashurst Morris Crisp 1987– (currently head Tax Dept); *Recreations* cricket, golf, Sheffield Wednesday FC, music, playing piano; *Clubs* Roehampton, Lyneham Golf, Stellenbosch Golf; *Style*— Stephen Machin, Esq;

✉ Ashurst Morris Crisp, Broadwalk House, 5 Appold St, London EC2A 2HA (☎ 0171 638 1111, fax 0171 972 7990, telex 887067, car 0831 420352)

McHUGH, Daniel Anthony; *b* 14 Feb 1956; *m* 3 Sept 1990, Daphne; *Career* chief financial offr Lehman Brothers Ltd 1991–; dir: Lehman Brothers Securities 1987–, Lehman Brothers Gilts Ltd 1987–, Lehman Brothers Nominees Ltd 1988–, Lehman Brothers Money Brokers Ltd 1988–, Lehman Brothers Holdings Ltd 1988–, Lehman Brothers UK Holdings plc 1988–, SLB Mortage Backed Securities (No 1) Ltd 1989–, Pamco (UK) Ltd 1989–, Lehman Brothers Ltd 1990–, Messels Service Co 1990–, Lehman Brothers International (Europe) 1990–, Shearson American Express Ltd 1991–, E F Hutton & Co (London) Ltd 1991–, E F Hutton & Co (Securities) Ltd 1991–, E F Hutton International (UK) Ltd 1991–, Platform Mortage Ltd 1993–; *Style*— Daniel A McHugh, Esq; ✉ Lehman Brothers Ltd, One Broadgate, London EC2M 7HA (☎ 0171 260 2162, fax 0171 260 2941/2842)

McHUGH, James; CBE (1989); s of Edward McHugh (d 1962), and Martha, *née* Smith (d 1948); *b* 4 May 1930; *Educ* Carlisle GS, various colls, Sheffield C of C Prize in Mgmnt Studies; *m* 1953, Sheila, da of James Cape; 2 da (Janet Elisabeth (Mrs Hoskin) b 21 April 1955, Kathlyn Joan (Mrs Kaiser) b 20 Sept 1958); *Career* Nat Serv Army; articled pupil in gas industry 1947, various tech and engrg appts in Northern and E Midlands Gas Bds (prodn engr 1967, dir of engrg W Midland Gas Bd 1971), dir of ops British Gas Corporation 1975 (memb Bd 1979), md prodn and supply and exec dir British Gas plc 1986–91, chm British Pipe Coaters Ltd 1991–95, dir United Kingdom Accreditation Service 1995–; dir Lloyd's Register Quality Assurance 1985–; memb: Meteorological Ctee MOD 1981–85, Engrg Cncl 1989–92; Gold Medal Inst of Gas Engrs (pres 1986–87), pres Inst of Quality Assurance 1992–; Freeman City of London, Liveryman Worshipful Co of Engrs; foreign memb Engrg Acad of St Petersburg; FIMechE, FIGasE, FIQA, FInstPet, CIMgt, FRSA, FEng 1986; *Recreations* mountaineering, dinghy sailing; *Clubs* RAC, Royal Anglo-Belgian; *Style*— James McHugh, Esq, CBE, FEng; ✉ Institute of Quality Assurance, 61 Southwark Street, London SE1 1SB (☎ 0171 401 7227)

McHUGH, Patrick; s of Capt B McHugh (d 1982), and Majorie Ann, *née* Mahoney; *b* 2 June 1952; *Educ* Mount St Mary's Coll, KCL (BSc(Eng)), Cheltenham Poly (Dip in Mgmnt Studies); *m* 31 Jan 1975, Henrietta Theresa Maria, da of Dr Hugh Francis Devlin; 1 s (Thomas Charles b 19 May 1981), 2 da (Alice Florence Henrietta Rose b 19 June 1984, Beatrice Lily Henrietta Rosamond b 8 Oct 1991); *Career* project engr (thermal, hydraulic and nuclear energy) CCM Sulzer (France) 1973–76; R A Lister (Hawker Sideley Group) 1976–82: successively prodn control mangr, product gp mangr (diesel assembly and test), mktg mangr (Belgium) and prodn mangr (diesel assembly, test and press shop); Coopers & Lybrand: conslt in mfrg and distribution mgmnt 1982–86, ptnr (engrg and technol industs) 1986–95; princ EDS 1995; vice pres A T Kearney 1995–; chm Media Group; memb: Br Operations Management Soc 1983, House of Lords Select Ctee on Science and Technol 1990, Mgmnt Consultants Assoc 1990, Cncl Fndn for Science and Technol 1991, Br Assoc for Science and Technology 1992, Tomorrow's Company Enquiry, Action for Engineering Task Force; fndr memb Guild of Mgmnt Consultants 1993, hon moorings offr Treaddur Bay Sailing Club; CEng 1976, MIMgt 1978, FIMechE 1993, ACA 1994, FRSA; *Books* Business Process Re-engineering (with H J Johansson, A J Pendlebury and W A Wheeler III, 1993), The Chain Imperative (with Paul Hannon, 1994), Beyond Business Process Reengineering (with Giorgio Merli and W A Wheeler III, 1995); *Clubs* Trearddur Bay Sailing, Arts; *Style*— Patrick McHugh, Esq; ✉ 20 Dulwich Common, London SE21 7EX (☎ 0181 693 2728); Ty Llwyd, Inland Sea Valley, Anglesey, Gwynedd, Wales (☎ 01407 741717); A T Kearney, Landsdowne House, Berkeley Square, London W1X 5DH (☎ 0171 468 8000, fax 0171 468 8001)

McHUGO, (Christopher) Benedict; s of Christopher Lawrence McHugo (d 1987), and Doris May, *née* Bellringer; *b* 11 July 1949; *Educ* John Fisher Sch Purley, Wadham Coll Oxford (MA); *m* 25 March 1995, Ananda, *née* Sithravadivel; *Career* Peat Marwick Mitchell 1971–76 (qualified CA 1974), called to the Bar Middle Temple 1978, Br Insurance Assoc 1980–85, taxation mangr Assoc of Br Insurers 1988–; memb: The Catenian Assoc, BACFI; FCA (ACA 1974); *Recreations* travel, languages, cooking; *Style*— Benedict McHugo, Esq; ✉ Association of British Insurers, 51 Gresham Street, London EC2V 7HQ (☎ 0171 600 3333, fax 0171 696 8999)

McILHENEY, Barry Wilson; s of David Parker McIlheney (d 1979), of Belfast, and Muriel, *née* Wilson; *b* 13 May 1958; *Educ* Belfast Royal Acad, Trinity Coll Dublin (BA), City Univ London (Dip of Journalism); *m* 16 March 1991, Lola, da of Francis Borg; 1 s (Francis Salvador David b 5 June 1992), 1 da (Mary Sophia b 9 March 1996); *Career* reporter London Newspaper Group 1984–85, reviews ed Melody Maker 1985–86, ed Smash Hits 1986–88; managing ed: Empire 1992–94 (ed 1989–91), Premiere 1992–94; md EMAP Metro 1995–; awards: Feature Writer of the Year 1985, EMAP Ed of the Year 1987 and 1991, PPA Magazine of the Year 1991, PPA Consumer Magazine Ed of the Year 1993; memb Br Soc of Magazine Editors 1986; *Recreations* sport, cinema, travel, eating, drinking, history; *Clubs* Irish, Academy Sports, Cliftonville Golf (hon); *Style*— Barry McIlheney, Esq; ✉ EMAP Metro, Mappin House, 4 Winsley Street, London W1N 7AR (☎ 0171 312 8124, fax 0171 312 8148)

McILLMURRAY, Dr Malcolm Barron; s of Joseph McIllmurray, and Margot, *née* Jordon; *b* 7 Dec 1945; *Educ* Taunton's Sch Southampton, London Hosp Med Coll (MB BS, MRCP), Univ of Nottingham (DM); *m* 27 July 1968, Geraldine Mary, da of Dr Daniel Gerard O'Driscoll (d 1992); 2 s (Daniel Joseph Barron b 1971, Matthew James Barron b 1975), 2 da (Joanna Maria (Mrs Kelly) b 1969, Naomi Jane b 1977); *Career* lectr in therapeutics Univ of Nottingham and hon sr registrar in gen med Nottingham City Hosp 1973–78, Macmillan conslt in med oncology and palliative care Royal Lancaster Infirmary and Westmorland Gen Hosp Kendal 1994– (conslt physician and med oncologist 1978–94); nat Lederle bronze awarded to Lancaster cancer servs 1991, Ernest Finch lectr Univ of Sheffield 1992, Paul Harris fell Rotary Club of GB 1993; fndr tstee N Lancs and Lakeland Continuing Care Tst 1981–, fndr chm CancerCare - North Lancs and South Lakeland 1984–, med dir St John's Hospice Lancaster 1985–; govr Bentham Sch; FRCP 1985; *Books* ABC of Medical Treatment (contrib, 1979), Essential Accident and Emergency Care (contrib, 1981); author of numerous articles in learned jls; *Style*— Dr Malcolm McIllmurray; ✉ Royal Lancaster Infirmary, Ashton Road, Lancaster LA1 4RT

McILROY, Ian; *b* 28 Dec 1947; *Educ* Glasgow Sch of Art (DA); *m* Diane Elizabeth, *née* Murray; 1 s (Sean b 30 June 1983); *Career* designer; worked for: J & P Coats and William Collins 1972–79, Tayburn Design Group 1979–81; formed McIlroy Coates 1981, formed EH6 Design Consultants 1992; recent clients incl: Kwik-Fit, The Nat Galleries of Scotland, The Design Cncl, The Clydesdale Bank; awards incl: Design Annual Award of Excellence 1984, D&AD Awards 1980, 1982, 1983 and 1990, Br Letterhead Awards 1981 and 1985, Scottish Designer of the Year runner up 1984, Scottish Annual Report prize 1988 and 1989; visiting lectr in graphic design Duncan of Jordanstone Coll of Art Dundee; FCSD 1991, memb D&AD Assoc 1980; *Style*— Ian McIlroy, Esq; ✉ EH6 Design Consultants Ltd, 19 Silvermills Court, Edinburgh EH3 5DG (☎ 0131 558 3383, fax 0131 556 1154)

McILVANNEY, William Angus; s of William Angus McIlvanney (d 1955), of Kilmarnock, and Helen Crawford, *née* Montgomery; *b* 25 Nov 1936; *Educ* Kilmarnock Acad, Univ of Glasgow (MA); *m* 1961 (m dis 1982), Moira Watson; 1 da (Siobhan Janet b 17 June 1967), 1 s (Liam Angus b 8 April 1970); *Career* writer; Irvine Royal Acad: asst teacher of English 1960–65, special asst 1965–68, princ teacher of English 1970–72; housemaster Ravenspark Acad 1969–70, tutor to US students Grenoble 1970–71, asst headmaster Greenwood Acad 1973–78; writer in residence: Univ of Strathclyde 1972–73, Univ of Aberdeen 1981–82; TV presenter BBC Scotland 1979–81 and 1993–; *Awards* Geoffrey Faber Meml Award 1966, Scottish Arts Cncl Publication Award 1968, Whitbread Prize 1975, Silver Dagger 1977 and 1983, Edgar Allan Poe Special Award 1977 and 1983, The People's Prize Glasgow Herald 1990 and 1992, Scottish Arts Cncl Award 1991, BAFTA Scottish Award 1991; *Novels* Remedy is None (1966), A Gift From Nessus (1968), Docherty (1975), Laidlaw (1977), The Papers of Tony Veitch (1983), The Big Man (1985), Strange Loyalties (1991); *Poetry* The Longships in Harbour (1970), Landscapes and Figures (1973), These Words - Weddings and After (1983), In Through the Head (1988); *Short Stories* Walking Wounded (1989); *Non-Fiction* Surviving the Shipwreck (1991); *Style*— William McIlvanney, Esq

McILWAIN, Alexander Edward; CBE (1985); s of Edward Walker McIlwain (d 1974), of Aberdeen, and Gladys Edith, *née* Horne; *b* 4 July 1933; *Educ* Aberdeen GS, Univ of Aberdeen (MA, LLB); *m* 14 July 1961, Moira Margaret, da of William Kinnaird (d 1951), of Aberdeen; 3 da (Karen b 5 March 1963, Shona b 6 Feb 1967, Wendy b 17 March 1969); *Career* Lt RCS 1957–59; dist prosecutor Hamilton 1975–76 (burgh prosecutor 1967–75), dean Soc of Slrs Hamilton and Dist 1981–83, Hon Sheriff of S Strathclyde Dumfries and Galloway at Hamilton 1981– (chm Hamilton Sheriff Ct Project 1991–), Temp Sheriff 1984–; sr ptnr Leonards (slrs) Hamilton 1984–, WS 1985; sec Lanarkshire Scout Assoc 1967–81, chm Lanarkshire Scout Area 1981–91, memb Lanarkshire Health Bd 1981–91, hon memb American Bar Assoc 1983–, pres Law Soc of Scotland 1983–84, memb Central Advsy Ctee on JP's 1985–, chm Legal Aid Central Ctee 1985–87; memb: Scout Cncl 1986–, Supreme Ct Ctee Scottish Legal Aid Bd 1987–93; pres Temp Sheriffs' Assoc 1995– (vice pres 1993–95); SSC 1966; *Recreations* gardening, reading, listening to music; *Style*— A E McIlwain, Esq, CBE, WS; ✉ 7 Bothwell Rd, Uddingston, Glasgow (☎ 01698 813368); Leonards, 133 Cadzow St, Hamilton, Strathclyde (☎ 01698 457313)

MacILWAINE, David Robin; s of Robin MacIlwaine, and Anne MacIlwaine (d 1967); *b* 16 Dec 1947; *Educ* Rydens Sch Walton upon Thames, Univ of Leicester (BA); partner, Rose Gray; 1 s (Dante MacIlwaine Gray b 1973), 3 step c (Hester Gray b 1963, Lucy Gray b 1964, Ossie Gray b 1965); *Career* Christies Contemporary Art 1986–89, sculpture dir Berkeley Square Gallery 1989–96, ind art conslt 1996–; *Recreations* sculpting; *Style*— David MacIlwaine, Esq; ✉ 7 Plympton Street, London NW8 8AB (☎ and fax 0171 258 1780)

McILWRAITH, Dr George Robert; s of Alexander Herd McIlwraith (d 1971), of Ruislip, Middx, and Kathleen Joan, *née* Heaton; *b* 15 July 1941; *Educ* Merchant Taylors', Univ of St Andrews (MB ChB); *m* 24 July 1982, Isabel Margaret, da of Harry Jack Manwaring (d 1988), of Collier St, Marden, Kent; 1 s (Harry Alexander b 1987); *Career* various jr appts in UK hosps; asst prof of internal med Pulmonary Div Univ of Michigan Med Sch USA 1979–80, conslt physician Maidstone Dist Hosps 1981–; author of pubns, chapters, papers and articles on cardiological and respiratory med matters; memb: Br Thoracic Soc, Br Geriatric Soc, Euro Respiratory Soc; FRCP 1988; *Style*— Dr George McIlwraith; ✉ Noah's Ark Farmhouse, East Sutton Rd, Headcorn, Ashford, Kent TN27 9PS (☎ 01622 891278); The Maidstone Hospital, Hermitage Lane Barming, Maidstone, Kent (☎ 01622 729000)

McINDOE, Very Rev John Hedley; s of William McIndoe (d 1969), of Kilcreggan, Dunbartonshire, and May, *née* Hedley (d 1972); *b* 31 Aug 1934; *Educ* Greenock Acad, Univ of Glasgow (MA, BD, Wylie fellowship), Hartford Theol Seminary Connecticut (STM); *m* 1960, Evelyn Kennedy, da of Rev Thomas K Johnstone; 3 da (Margot Evelyn b 13 May 1962, Sheila Elizabeth b 12 April 1964, Jennifer Anne b 29 Oct 1967); *Career* ordained to Miny of Church of Scotland by Presbytery of Paisley 1960; asst min Paisley Abbey 1960–63; min: Park Church Dundee 1963–72, St Nicholas Parish Lanark 1972–88, St Columba's Pont St London 1988–; hon chaplain London Scottish Regt 1988–, govr Royal Scottish Corp London 1988–; moderator Gen Assembly Church of Scotland 1996–97 (convener Ctee on Church and Nation 1980–84); *Recreations* film and theatre; *Clubs* Caledonian; *Style*— The Very Rev John McIndoe; ✉ St Columba's Church of Scotland, Pont Street, London SW1X 0BD (☎ 0171 584 2321)

McINDOE, William Ian (Bill); CB (1978); s of John McIndoe, MM (d 1982); *b* 11 March 1929; *Educ* Sedbergh, Corpus Christi Coll Oxford; *m* 1, 1954, Irene Armour Mudie (d 1966); 3 c; m 2, 1971, Jamesanna Smart, *née* MacGregor; *Career* Nat Serv 2 Lt RHA 1951–53; HM Dip Serv: joined 1953, served in Canberra and Salisbury 1956–62, private sec to Sec of State 1962–63, private sec to Sec of Cabinet then asst sec Cabinet Office 1963–66, Scottish Office 1966–76 (under sec 1971); dep sec: Cabinet Office 1976–79, DOE 1979–86; dep chm Housing Corp 1986–90; *Recreations* golf; *Clubs* New (Edinburgh); *Style*— Bill McIndoe, Esq, CB; ✉ Speedyburn House, Station Road, Gifford, E Lothian EH41 4QL (☎ 01620 810363)

McINNERNY, Tim; s of William Ronald McInnerny, and Mary Joan, *née* Gibbings; *b* 18 Sept 1956; *Educ* Marling Sch Stroud Glos, Univ of Oxford (BA); *Career* actor; *Theatre* performances incl: Lorenzaccio Story (Edinburgh Festival), Freddie in Pygmalion (Glasgow Citizens), Lyssipus in The Maid's Tragedy (Glasgow Citizens), Derek in Once A Catholic (Leicester Haymarket), Keith in Local Affairs, Laertes in Hamlet, Sir Benjamin in School for Scandal (Leicester Haymarket), Paul in Valued Friends (Hampstead), Frankenfurter in The Rocky Horror Show (Piccadilly); Royal Exchange Manchester: Clitandre in The Misanthrope, Gately in PVT Wars, Charlie in The Detective Story, Billy Bibbett in One Flew Over The Cuckoos Nest, Mick in The Caretaker, Orsino in Twelfth Night, The Kid in The Unseen Hand, Roy in Lone Star; NT: Waiter in The Government Inspector, Andrew May in Pravda, Hamlet in Hamlet; *Television* incl: Blackadder, Blackadder II, Blackadder Goes Forth, Edge of Darkness, Sherlock Holmes, A Very British Coup, Shadow of the Noose, August Saturday, The Comic Strip Presents; *Films* John Morgan in Wetherby, Sven in Erik The Viking, 101 Dalmations; *Recreations* acting; *Style*— Tim McInnerny, Esq; ✉ c/o Caroline Dawson Associates, Apartment 9, 47 Courtfield Road, London SW7 4DB (☎ 0171 370 0708, fax 0171 835 1403)

MacINNES, Archibald; CVO (1977); s of Duncan MacInnes (d 1987), of Gourock, and Catherine, *née* MacDonald (d 1970); *b* 10 April 1919; *Educ* Kirkcudbright Acad, Royal Tech Coll Glasgow; *m* 10 June 1950, Nancey Elizabeth (d 1976), da of Alec Blyth (d 1958), of Wivenhoe; 1 s (Duncan John b 1955), 2 da (Morag Catherine b 1951, Fiona Margaret b 1960); *Career* Scotts Shipbuilding and Engrg Co Greenock 1938–45, HMOCS Nigeria 1945–59; WO: cmd works offr Gibraltar 1959–63, supt engr Southern Cmd Wilton 1963–64; supt engr MPBW Bristol 1964–68, cmd works offr DOE Germany 1968–72, dir London Region PSA 1972–79, under sec 1973, conslt planning inspr DOE 1980–89; CEng, FIMechE, FIMgt; *Recreations* fishing, shooting, golf, rugby supporter; *Clubs* Civil Service, Salisbury RFC, High Post Golf; *Style*— Archibald MacInnes, Esq, CVO; ✉ New House, Lower Rd, Homington, Salisbury SP5 4NG (☎ 01722 718336)

MacINNES, Hamish; OBE (1980), BEM (1965); s of Duncan MacInnes, of Gourock, Renfrewshire (d 1987), and Catherine, *née* MacDonald (d 1967); *b* 7 July 1930; *Educ* Gatehouse of Fleet Public Sch; *Career* writer, mfr, advsr on films and mountain rescue; designer: mountain rescue stretchers (used internationally), first all metal ice axe, terodactyl climbing tools; dir Glencoe Productions; dep ldr Everest SW Face Expedition 1975 (taken part in 20 other expeditions to various parts of the world), special advsr to BBC and feature films in many countries, author of 20 books, fndr and hon pres Search and Rescue Dog Assoc, former pres Alpine Climbing Gp, former ldr Glencoe Mountain

Rescue Team, hon memb Scottish Mountaineering Club, former hon dir Leishman Res Laboratory; Hon DSc Univ of Aberdeen 1988, Heriott Watt Univ 1992; Hon LLD Univ of Glasgow; *Style*— Hamish MacInnes, Esq, OBE, BEM; ✉ Achnacone, Glencoe, Argyll (☎ 018552 258)

McINNES, Sheriff John Colin; QC (Scot 1989); s of Ian Whitton McInnes (d 1976), of Cupar, Fife, and Lucy Margaret, *née* Wilson; *b* 21 Nov 1938; *Educ* Cargilfield Sch Edinburgh, Merchiston Castle Sch Edinburgh, Brasenose Coll Oxford (BA), Univ of Edinburgh (LLB); *m* 6 Aug 1966, Elisabeth Mabel, da of Hugh Royden Neilson, of Kelso, Roxburghshire; 1 s (Ian b 1969), 1 da (Iona b 1972); *Career* 2 Lt 8 RTR 1956–58, Lt Fife and Forfar Yeo Scottish Horse TA 1958–64; advocate in practice Scottish Bar 1963–72, dir R Mackness & Co Ltd 1963–70, tutor Univ of Edinburgh 1964–72, chm Fios Group Ltd (continental quilt manufacturers) 1970–72; Parly candidate (C) Aberdeen N 1964; memb Ct Univ of St Andrews 1983–91, chm Fife Family Conciliation Serv 1988–90; vice pres: Security Serv Tbnl 1989–, Intelligence Serv Tbnl 1994–; Sheriff: Lothians and Peebles 1973–74, Tayside Central and Fife 1974–; pres The Sheriff's Assoc 1995–; Hon LLD St Andrews 1994; *Books* Divorce Law and Practice in Scotland; *Recreations* fishing, shooting, skiing, photography; *Style*— Sheriff John McInnes, QC; ✉ Sheriff's Chambers, Sheriff Court House, Tay Street, Perth PH2 8NL (☎ 01738 620546, fax 01738 623601)

MacINNES, Keith Gordon; CMG (1984); s of Kenneth Lionel MacInnes, CBE (d 1989), and Helen, da of Sir (Archibald) Douglas Gordon, CIE (d 1966); *b* 17 July 1935; *Educ* Rugby, Trinity Coll Cambridge (MA); *m* 1, 1966 (m dis 1980), Jennifer Anne Fennell; 1 s (Alexander b 1970), 1 da (Francesca b 1968); m 2, 9 March 1985, Hermione Ann Felicity Pattinson, 2 step s (Kyle b 1968, Rupert b 1970); *Career* diplomat; HM Forces 1953–55, FO 1960, 3 later 2 sec Buenos Aires 1961, FO 1984 (1 sec 1965), private sec to Perm Under Sec CO 1965, 1 sec (info) Madrid 1968, FCO 1970, cnsllr and head of Chancery Prague 1974, cnsllr and head of Chancery Geneva 1977, also dep perm rep 1979, head of Info Dept FCO 1980, asst under sec of state (princ fin offr) FCO 1983, ambass to the Philippines 1987–92, UK permanent rep (with personal rank of ambass) to Organisation for Economic Cooperation and Devpt Paris 1992–95, ret; *Recreations* bridge, chess, golf, tennis; *Clubs* Liphook Golf; *Style*— Keith MacInnes, Esq, CMG; ✉ c/o Foreign & Commonwealth Office, King Charles Street, London SW1A 2AH

McINROY, Alan Roderick; s of Charles Alan McInroy (d 1932), of St Mary's Tower, Birnam, Perthshire, and Marjory, *née* Walford (d 1981); *b* 6 June 1920; *Educ* Loretto, Hertford Coll Oxford; *m* 6 Jan 1966, Daphne Eileen Wells, da of Sir Eric Weston (d 1976), of The Manor, Moreton Pinkney, Northants; *Career* RA served ME 1940–42, Italy (POW) 1942–43, Germany (POW) 1943–45, Palestine 1946–48; ptnr Scott-Moncrieff Thomson & Shiells CA 1953–59, mangr American Trust Ltd 1959–69, md Edinburgh Fund Managers plc 1969–84, chm McInroy & Wood Ltd 1986–, dir Noble Grossart Holdings Ltd; chm Haddington Citizens' Advice Bureau 1983–88; memb Soc Investmt Analysts 1963; MICA 1951; *Recreations* golf, music; *Clubs* New (Edinburgh), Hon Co of Edinburgh Golfers, Club de Golf Valderrama (Spain); *Style*— Alan McInroy, Esq; ✉ Muirfield Green, Gullane, East Lothian EH31 2EG (☎ 01620 842175)

MACINTOSH, Alexander James; s of Edward Hyde Macintosh, CBE (d 1970), of Kirkhill, Inverness-shire, and Doreen O'Hara, *née* Cross; *b* 5 Oct 1931; *Educ* Stowe, Trinity Coll Cambridge (MA); *m* 12 June 1965 (m dis 1994), Jane Wigham, da of Michael Finch Wigham Richardson (d 1988), of Wiltshire; 2 s (Jonathan b 1968, Marcus b 1970); *Career* cmmnd Seaforth Highlanders 1950; numerous directorships incl: The Port of London Authority 1980–92, Cunard Steam Ship Co plc and subsidiaries 1985–91, Associated Container Transportation (Australia) Ltd and subsidiaries 1974–91, Ellerman Group Ltd 1987–91, Heavylift Cargo Airlines Ltd 1985–91, Gen Cncl of British Shipping Ltd 1987–91, British Shipping Federation Ltd 1987–91, Ben Line Containers Ltd 1987–91, H E Moss & Co Ltd 1987–91, International Transport Ltd (owned Port of Tilbury) 1992–95; memb Tst Devpt Bd Horton Gen Hosp Banbury Oxfordshire 1991–92; govr Stowe Sch Buckingham 1991–, chm Stowe Sch Educnl Servs Ltd 1996–; *Recreations* country pursuits; *Style*— Alexander Macintosh, Esq; ✉ 29 Richborne Terrace, London SW8 1AS (☎ 0171 735 4399)

McINTOSH, Anne Caroline Ballingall; MEP (C) Essex North and Suffolk South (majority 3,633); da of Dr A B McIntosh, and G L McIntosh, *née* Thomson; *b* 20 Sept 1954; *Educ* Harrogate Coll, Univ of Edinburgh (LLB); *m* 19 Sept 1992, John Harvey; *Career* postgraduate studies Univ of Aarhus Denmark 1977–78, trainee EC Competition Directorate Brussels 1978, legal advsr Didier & Assocs Brussels 1979–80, trained Scottish Bar 1980–82, admitted Faculty of Advocates Edinburgh 1982, advocate Euro Community Law Office Brussels 1982–83, political advsr Euro Democratic Gp (EDG) Euro Parliament 1983–89; MEP (C): Essex N E 1989–94, Essex N and Suffolk S 1994–; Br Conservative spokesman Euro Parliament: Tport Ctee 1992–, Rules of Procedure Ctee 1992–94; memb Euro Parliament Delegation with: Norway 1989–94 (chm 1994–95), Poland 1994–; memb: Social Affrs Ctee 1992–94, Women's Rights Ctee 1992–94; substitute memb: Legal Affrs Ctee 1989–, Jt Parly Ctee with EEA 1995–; asst EDG whip 1989–92, elected to Bureau Br Section EPP 1994–; memb Exec Cncl Br Conservative Assoc Belgium 1987–89; pres Anglia Enterprise in Europe; memb: Chllr's Cncl Anglia Poly Univ, Governing Bd Writtle Coll; *Recreations* swimming, reading, cinema; *Clubs* Carlton, Royal Overseas League; *Style*— Ms Anne McIntosh, MEP; ✉ constituency office: The Old Armoury, 3 Museum Street, Saffron Walden, Essex CB10 1JN (☎ and fax 01799 523631); European Parliament, Rue Belliard 97, 1047 Brussels, Belgium (☎ 00 322 284 7239, fax 00 322 284 9239)

McINTOSH, (Alastair) Bruce; s of Robert Ian Fanshawe McIntosh (d 1988), of Budleigh Salterton, Devon, and Jane, *née* Rought; *b* 25 Feb 1958; *Educ* Winchester, Univ of Cambridge (MA); *m* 1991, Sophia Mary, da of Lt-Col Sir Blair Aubyn Stewart-Wilson, KCVO, *qv*, of London; 3 da (Lily b 5 Jan 1993, Kitty b 24 April 1994, Tarn b 21 Dec 1995); *Career* SG Warburg Group plc 1984–89, dir John Govett and Co Ltd 1989–90; dir: Perpetual Portfolio Management Ltd 1990–, Perpetual UK Smaller Companies Investment Trust plc 1995–; *Style*— Bruce McIntosh, Esq; ✉ The Hyde, Ewelme, Wallingford, Oxon OX10 6HP (☎ 01491 835025)

MACINTOSH, Catherine Ailsa (Kate); MBE 1987; s of Ronald Hugh Macintosh, OBE, and Bertha, *née* Holt (d 1978); *b* 2 July 1937; *Educ* Rudolf Steiner Sch Edinburgh, Sch of Arch Edinburgh Sch of Art (DipArch), Warsaw Poly (Br Cncl scholarship); *partner* since 1968, George Bernard Finch; 1 s (Sean Alisdair Finch Macintosh b 1971); *Career* architect; Lennart Bergstrom (Stockholm office) 1962–63, Klaus Bremmer (Copenhagen) 1963, Toivo Korhonen (Helsinki office) 1963–64, Denys Lasden 1964–65 (working on Nat Theatre project), London Borough of Southwark 1964–68 (designed Dawsons Heights Dulwich), London Borough of Lambeth 1968–72 (designed Leigham Court Rd Sheltered Housing), Arup Associates 1972 (worked on Kensington and Chelsea Depot), Ahrends Burton & Koralek 1972–74 (designed holiday devpt St Raphael), East Sussex Co Architects 1974–86 (team ldr and project architect for Halton Fire Station Hastings, Maresfield Fire Brigade Trg HQ Maresfield, Thornwood Old Persons Home and Sheltered Housing Bexhill, Preston Rd Family Centre Brighton, Fire Brigade Communications Centre Lewes and Battle Langton Primary Sch), Hampshire Co Architects 1986–95 (sr architect designing Rushmoor Fire Station, Priory Sch Sports Hall and Music Suite, Solent Infants Sch and Audleys Close Centre for severely handicapped adults), in private practice as Finch Macintosh Architects Winchester 1995–; Civic Tst commendations for Maresfield Fire Brigade Trg HQ, Preston Road Family Centre Brighton and Lewes Fire Brigade Communications Centre; Rushmoor Civic Design Award for Rushmoor Fire Station; Portsmouth Soc Award: for best bldg and best landscaping 1993 (Priory Sch Sports Hall and Music Suite), for best bldg 1995 (Solent Infants Sch); sometime tutor/visiting lectr/external examiner various Schs of Arch; vice chm Architects and Engrs for Social Responsibility 1991– (fndr chair when Architects for Peace 1980–91); sec Sussex Heritage Tst 1978–84; RIBA 1965 (memb Cncl, vice pres 1971, subsequently first chair Women's Architect Gp, currently vice pres for public affrs); *Books* Sussex after the Bomb (jtly, 1984); *Recreations* yoga, painting, theatre, walking; *Style*— Miss Kate Macintosh, MBE; ✉ Finch Macintosh Architects, Osborne Place, 11 West End Terrace, Winchester, Hants SO22 5EN (☎ 01962 855240, fax 01962 852227)

McINTOSH, David Angus; s of Robert Angus McIntosh, of Scotland, and Monica Joan Sherring, *née* Hillier; *b* 10 March 1944; *Educ* Selwood Co Sch Frome Somerset; *m* 14 Sept 1968, Jennifer Mary, da of Jack Dixon, of Mill Hill, London; 2 da (Sarah Alison b 1973, Louise b 1978); *Career* clerk Ames Kent & Rathwell Somerset, articled clerk Davies Arnold Cooper 1964, admitted slr 1968, sr ptnr Davies Arnold Cooper 1976– (ptnr 1968); Int Bar Assoc: chm ctee on Consumer Affrs, Advtg, Unfair Competition and Product Liability, chm Disaster Litigation Worldwide Prog Strasbourg; Law Soc: memb various working parties on reform and admin of civil law, memb Jt Working Ctee of the Senate of the Bar and Law Soc (made recommendations to Lord Chllr on proposed US/UK Reciprocal Enforcements Convention and allied jurisdictional matters), memb Supreme Ct Procedure Ctee 1994–, memb Cncl 1996–; US Int Assoc of Defense Counsel: memb Excess and Reinsurance Product Liability Litigation Ctee, memb Toxic and Hazardous Substances Litigation Ctee; Freeman City of London, Liveryman Blacksmiths Co, memb City of London Slrs Co; memb: Int Bar Assoc, Law Soc, US Int Assoc of Defense Counsel, Def Res and Trial Lawyers Assoc of America, Professional Liability Underwriters Assoc, Law Soc of England and Wales; CIArb; *Books* regular contributor to legal, insurance, and pharmaceutical journals, memb Editorial Bd The Litigator; *Recreations* family, golf, fitness; *Clubs* Chigwell Golf, La Manga Golf, Barbican Health, City Livery; *Style*— David McIntosh, Esq; ✉ Davies Arnold Cooper, 6–8 Bouverie St, London EC4Y 8DD (☎ 0171 936 2222, fax 0171 936 2020)

MACINTOSH, Dr Farquhar; CBE (1982); s of John Macintosh (d 1938), of Elgol, Isle of Skye, and Kate Ann, *née* Mackinnon (d 1975); *b* 27 Oct 1923; *Educ* Portree HS Skye, Univ of Edinburgh (MA), Univ of Glasgow (DipEd); *m* 19 Dec 1959, Margaret Mary Inglis, da of James Inglis, of Peebles (d 1965); 2 s (John James, Kenneth Donald), 2 da (Ann Mary, Ailsa Kate); *Career* Sub Lt RNVR 1944–46; history teacher: Greenfield Jr Secdy Sch Hamilton 1951–52, Glasgow Acad 1953–59; princ teacher of history Inverness Royal Acad 1959–62; headmaster: Portree HS 1962–66, Oban HS 1967–72; rector Royal HS Edinburgh 1972–89; contributor: The Times Educnl Supplement Scotland, The Scotsman, The Herald; memb: Skye Hosps Bd of Mgmnt 1963–66, Oban Hosps Bd of Mgmnt 1968–72, Aberdeen Coll of Educn Governing Body 1961–66, Jordanhill Coll of Educn Glasgow 1967–72 (chm 1970–72), Highlands and Islands Devpt Consultative Cncl 1965–82 (chm Educn Sub Ctee 1968–82), Broadcasting Cncl for Scotland 1975–79, Ct Univ of Edinburgh 1976–91; chm: Highlands and Islands Education Tst 1973–, Scot Assoc for Educnl Mgmnt and Admin 1979–82, Scot Examination Bd 1977–90, Sch Broadcasting Cncl Scot 1980–85, Sabhal Mor Ostaig (Gaelic Coll) 1991–, Euro Movement (Scottish Cncl) 1996– (chm Educn Ctee 1993–96); govr: St Margaret's Sch Edinburgh, The Royal Blind Sch Edinburgh; Hon DLitt Heriot-Watt Univ 1980, Hon Dr Univ of Edinburgh 1992; memb: Headmasters' Conference, Headmasters' Assoc of Scot, Scot History Soc, An Comunn Gaidhealach; FEIS 1970, FScotvec 1990; *Recreations* hill-walking, travel, Gaelic; *Clubs* Rotary (Murrayfield-Cramond), East India; *Style*— Dr Farquhar Macintosh, CBE; ✉ 12 Rothesay Place, Edinburgh EH3 7SQ (☎ 0131 225 4404)

McINTOSH, Genista Mary; *b* 23 Sept 1946; *Educ* Hemel Hempstead GS, Univ of York (BA); *m* 30 Jan 1971 (m dis 1990), Neil Scott Wishart McIntosh; 1 s (Alexander b 22 Dec 1975), 1 da (Flora b 25 April 1979); *Career* dir Marmont Management Ltd 1984–86; Royal Shakespeare Company: casting dir 1972–77, planning controller 1977–84, sr admin 1986–90, assoc prodr 1990; exec dir Royal Nat Theatre 1990–96, chief exec Royal Opera House 1997–; chair S E London Common Purpose; memb: Advsy Panel on Dance and Drama Br Cncl, Bd Young Vic Theatre; FRSA; *Style*— Ms Genista McIntosh; ✉ Royal Opera House, Covent Garden, London WC2E 9DD (☎ 0171 240 1200, fax 0171 379 7057)

McINTOSH, Ian Alexander Neville; s of Alexander McIntosh (d 1990), of Heaton, Bradford, W Yorks, and Marie Josephine, *née* Lester (d 1994); *b* 24 Sept 1938; *Educ* Bradford GS, Univ of Edinburgh (MA); *m* 26 June 1965, Gillian Mary Sophia, da of Harold John Cropp (d 1984); 1 s (Angus b 15 June 1975), 1 da (Fiona b 3 June 1971); *Career* Armitage & Norton 1959–63, Coopers & Lybrand 1963–69; Samuel Montagu & Co Ltd 1969–: dir 1972–, dep chief exec and head of corp fin 1989–96, vice chm 1996–; non-exec dir IMI plc 1989–; memb Quotations Ctee of London Stock Exchange; Liveryman Worshipful Co of Goldsmiths; FCA 1963; *Recreations* golf, tennis; *Clubs* MCC, Ashridge Golf, RAC; *Style*— Ian McIntosh, Esq; ✉ HSBC Samuel Montagu, Vintners Place, 68 Upper Thames Street, London EC4V 3BJ (☎ 0171 336 9301, fax 0171 336 4533)

McINTOSH, Vice Adm Sir Ian Stewart; KBE (1973, MBE 1941), CB (1970), DSO (1944), DSC (1942); s of Alexander James McIntosh (d 1973), of Melbourne, Aust; *b* 11 Oct 1919; *Educ* Geelong GS; *m* 1943, Elizabeth Rosemary (d 1995), da of Albert Henry Rasmussen, of Aalesund, Norway; 3 s (Donald, Jamie, Rory), 1 da (decd); *Career* joined RN 1938, Capt 1959, Rear Adm 1968, dir-gen Weapons (Naval) MOD 1969–70, Vice Adm 1970, dep CDS (Operational Requirements) MOD 1970–73, ret; conslt Alexander Hughes and Assocs 1973–78; *Style*— Vice Adm Sir Ian McIntosh, KBE, CB, DSO, DSC; ✉ 19 The Crescent, Alverstoke, Hants

McINTOSH, John Charles; OBE (1996); s of Arthur McIntosh, and Betty, *née* Styche; *b* 6 Feb 1946; *Educ* Ebury Tech Sch, Shoreditch Coll, Univ of Sussex (MA); *Career* London Oratory Sch: asst master 1967–71, dep headmaster 1971–77, headmaster 1977–; memb: Headmasters' Conf 1986–, Nat Curriculum Cncl 1990–93, Educn Gp Centre for Policy Studies 1982–, Educn Unit Advsy Cncl Inst of Econ Affairs 1988–, Catholic Union of Gt Britain 1978–, Health Educn Cncl 1985–88; govr: St Philip's Prep Sch London, Oratory Primary Sch London; FRSA; *Recreations* playing the organ, ballet, opera; *Clubs* Athenaeum, East India; *Style*— John McIntosh, Esq, OBE; ✉ 75 Alder Lodge, River Garden, Stevenage Road, London SW6 6NR (☎ 0171 385 4576, fax 0171 610 0834); The London Oratory School, Seagrave Road, London SW6 1RX (☎ 0171 385 0102, fax 0171 381 3836, car 0831 464889)

McINTOSH, Kinn Hamilton; MBE (1988); da of Robert Aeneas Cameron McIntosh (d 1978), and Violet Jessie, *née* Kinnis (d 1988); *b* 20 June 1930; *Educ* Waverley Sch Huddersfield Yorkshire, Greenhead HS; *Career* detective novelist as Catherine Aird; asst treas World Assoc of Girl Guides and Girl Scouts 1978–84, chm UK Fin Ctee Girl Guides Assoc 1975–80 and 1983–87, chm Crime Writers Assoc 1990–91; Hon MA Univ of Kent at Canterbury 1985; *Books* The Religious Body (1966), A Most Contagious Game (1967), The Complete Steel (1969), Henrietta Who? (1968), A Late Phoenix (1971), His Burial Too (1973), Slight Mourning (1975), Parting Breath (1978), Some Die Eloquent (1979), Passing Strange (1981), Last Respects (1982), Harms's Way (1984), A Dead Liberty (1986), The Body Politic (1990), A Going Concern (1993), Injury Time (1994), After Effects (1996); non-fiction (ed): Sturry - The Changing Scene (1972), Fordwich - The Lost Port (1975), Chislet and Westbere - Villages of the Stour Lathe (1979), Hoath and Herne

· The Edge of the Forest (with H E Gough, 1985), In Good Faith (1995); *Recreations* bridge; *Clubs* The English-Speaking Union; *Style*— Miss Kinn McIntosh, MBE

McINTOSH, Sir Malcolm Kenneth; kt (1996); s of Kenneth Stuart McIntosh, and Valerie, *née* Mackenzie; *b* 14 Dec 1945; *Educ* Australian Nat Univ (BSc, PhD); *m* 1971, Margaret, *née* Stevens; 3 s, 1 da; *Career* res scientist Aust Weapons Res Estab 1970–72, Aust Army 1972–74, Aust Econ Minys 1974–82, Aust Dept of Def 1982–90, sec Aust Dept of Indust Technol and Commerce 1990–; Chief of Defence Procurement MOD 1991–; *Style*— Sir Malcolm McIntosh; ✉ Ministry of Defence, Main Building, Horseguards Avenue, London SW1A 2HB (☎ 0171 218 6304)

McINTOSH, Sir Ronald Robert Duncan; KCB (1975, CB 1968); s of Dr Thomas Steven McIntosh, and Christina Jane McIntosh; *b* 26 Sept 1919; *Educ* Charterhouse, Balliol Coll Oxford; *m* 1951, Doreen Frances, only da of Cdr Andrew MacGinnity, of Frinton-on-Sea, Essex, and Margaret MacGinnity; *Career* served MN WWII; joined BOT 1947, under sec 1963–64, dep under sec of state DEA 1966–68, dep sec Cabinet Office 1968–70; dep sec: Employment 1970–72, Treasy 1972–73; dir gen NEDO and memb NEDC 1973–77; chm APV plc 1982–89 (dep chm 1981); dir: S G Warburg Ltd, Foseco plc, London & Manchester Group plc 1978–90; chm Danish-UK C of C 1989–92, chm Br Healthcare Consortium for former Soviet Union 1989–; memb Cncl CBI 1980–90; Hon DSc Aston Univ 1977; FRSA, CBIM; *Clubs* Royal Thames Yacht; *Style*— Sir Ronald McIntosh, KCB; ✉ 24 Ponsonby Terrace, London SW1P 4QA (☎ 0171 821 6106, fax 0171 834 3740)

McINTOSH, Thomas Lee; s of John Christian McIntosh (d 1967), of Washington DC, and Mildred White (d 1953); *b* 3 Dec 1938; *Educ* Juilliard Sch of Music (BSc, MSc); *m* 30 Sept 1982, Miranda Harrison Vincent, da of Vincent Booth Reckitt (d 1975), of Otley, Yorks; *Career* conductor and music dir London City Chamber Orch 1973–; artistic dir: E Anglian Summer Music Festival 1978–, Penang Malaysia Music Festival 1986 and 1987, Opera Anglia 1989–, Artsanglia Ltd 1988–; princ guest conductor Canton Symphony Orch 1994; contributing ed eighteenth century symphonic music for Garland Symphony Series; Arrangements for Orch of the following: Valentine Waltzes (George Antheil), Rag Suite (various composers), Flower Rag Suite (Scott Joplin); FRSA; *Recreations* gardening, theatre; *Clubs* Civil Service; *Style*— Thomas McIntosh, Esq

McINTOSH OF HARINGEY, Baron (Life Peer UK 1982), of Haringey in Gtr London; Andrew Robert McIntosh; s of late Prof Albert William McIntosh, OBE, (d 1994), and Helena Agnes (Jenny), *née* Britton (d 1989); *b* 30 April 1933; *Educ* Haberdashers' Aske's Hampstead Sch, Royal GS High Wycombe, Jesus Coll Oxford (MA), Ohio State Univ; *m* 1962, Prof Naomi Ellen Sargant, *qv*, da of Thomas Sargant, OBE, JP (d 1988), and Marie, *née* Hlouskova; 2 s (Hon Francis Robert b 1962, Hon Philip Henry Sargant b 1964); *Career* memb Hornsey Borough Cncl 1963–65, memb Haringey Borough Cncl 1964–68; chm: Market Res Soc 1972–73 (pres 1995–), Assoc for Neighbourhood Cncls 1974–80; memb GLC for Tottenham 1973–83, ldr GLC oppn 1980–81; House of Lords: chm Computer Sub Ctee 1984–92, princ Lab oppn spokesman on home affairs 1992– (on educn and sci 1985–87, on environment 1987–92), dep ldr of the opposition 1992–; IFF Research Ltd: md 1965–81, chm 1981–88, dep chm 1988–95, dir 1995–; chm Fabian Soc 1985–86; *Style*— The Rt Hon the Lord McIntosh of Haringey; ✉ 27 Hurst Avenue, London N6 5TX (☎ 0181 348 1874, fax 0181 348 4641)

McINTOSH OF HARINGEY, Baroness; *see:* Sargant, Prof Naomi Ellen

MACINTYRE, Charles Edward Stuart; s of John Macintyre (d 1978), and Mary, *née* Agnew; *b* 13 Feb 1932; *Educ* Priory GS Shrewsbury; *m* 28 June 1956, Barbara Mary, da of William Abley (d 1959); 3 da (Sarah (Mrs Garratt) b 10 April 1957, Ruth b 30 March 1958, Jane b 23 May 1963); *Career* dir and gen mangr Heart of England Building Soc 1983–92, chm Jephson Housing Association Ltd 1993–; pres Coventry Centre Building Soc's Inst; FCBSI 1969, FCIB; *Recreations* sport; *Style*— Charles Macintyre, Esq; ✉ Merrywood, Hampton-on-the-Hill, Warwick CV35 8QR (☎ 01926 492766)

McINTYRE, Sir Donald Conroy; kt (1992), CBE (1985, OBE 1975); s of George McIntyre, and Hermyn, *née* Conroy; *b* 22 Oct 1934; *Educ* Mount Albert GS New Zealand, Auckland Teachers Trg Coll, Guildhall Sch of Music London; *m* 29 July 1961, Jill Redington, da of Norton Mitchell, DFC (d 1989), of Barnstaple, Devon; 3 da (Ruth Frances b 1965, Lynn Hazel b 1967, Jenny Jane b 1971); *Career* int opera singer, bass baritone; debut UK Welsh Nat Opera 1959; princ bass: Sadler's Wells Opera 1960–67, Royal Opera House Covent Garden 1967–, Bayreuth Festival 1967–84; frequent int guest appearances: Metropolitan (NY), Vienna, Munich, Hamburg, Paris, Buenos Aires, La Scala (Milan), Berlin, Sydney and more; princ roles incl: Wotan and Wanderer (The Ring), Dutchman (Flying Dutchman), Telramund (Lohengrin), Amfortas, Klingsor and Gurnemanz (Parsifal), Kurwenal (Tristan and Isolde), Hans Sachs (Die Meistersinger), Barak (Die Frau Ohne Schatten), Golaud (Pelleas and Melisande), Pizzaro and Rocco (Fidelio), Kasper (Der Freischutz), Scarpia (Tosca), Macbeth (Macbeth), Nick Shadow (Rake's Progress), Count (Figaro), Cardillac (Cardillac), Shakloviti (Khovanshina); numerous concert appearances worldwide; appeared as: Hans Sachs in Die Meistersinger (first ever staged prodn of this opera in NZ) 1990, Balstrode in Peter Grimes (Munich) 1991–92, Boris in Lady Macbeth of Mtsensk 1993; video films incl: Der Fliegende Hollander 1975, Electra 1979, Bayreuth Centenary Ring 1981, Die Meistersinger 1984; recording incl: Pelleas and Melisande, The Messiah, Beethoven's Ninth Symphony, Damnation of Faust, Il Trovotore, Oedipus Rex, The Ring, Parsifal; winner: Fidelio medal (Assoc of Int Dirs of Opera) 1989, NZ Commemoration award 1990; life memb Auckland Choral Soc; *Recreations* swimming, tennis, farming, walking; *Style*— Sir Donald McIntyre, CBE; ✉ c/o Ingpen and Williams Ltd, 14 Kensington Court, London W8 5DN

MACINTYRE, Donald John; s of Kenneth MacKenzie Campbell Macintyre (d 1988), and Margaret Rachel, *née* Freeman; *b* 27 Jan 1947; *Educ* Bradfield Coll, Christ Church Oxford (BA), Univ Coll Cardiff (Dip in Journalism); *children* 1 s (James b 18 August 1979); *Career* journalist The Sunday Mercury 1971–75, industl corr The Daily Express 1975–77, labour corr The Times 1977–83; labour ed: The Sunday Times 1983–85, The Times 1985–86, The Independent 1986–87; political ed: The Sunday Telegraph 1987–89, The Sunday Correspondent 1989–90, The Independent on Sunday 1990–93, The Independent 1993–96; chief political commentator The Independent 1996–; *Books* Talking About Trade Unions (1980), Strike (co-author, 1985); *Style*— Donald Macintyre, Esq; ✉ The Independent, 1 Canada Square, Canary Wharf, London E14 5DL (☎ 0171 293 2000, fax 0171 334 0082)

MacINTYRE, Prof Iain; s of John MacIntyre (d 1954), of Tobermory, Mull, and Margaret Fraser Shaw (d 1967), of Stratherick, Inverness; *b* 30 Aug 1924; *Educ* Jordanhill Coll Sch Glasgow, Univ of Glasgow (MB ChB), Univ of London (PhD, DSc); *m* 14 July 1947, Mabs Wilson, da of George Jamieson (d 1951), of Largs, Ayrshire; 1 da (Fiona Bell b 1953); *Career* Royal Postgraduate Med Sch: prof of endocrine chemistry 1967–82, dir Endocrine Unit 1967–89, chm Academic Bd 1986–89, dir Dept of Chemical Pathology 1982–89, emeritus prof 1989; research dir William Harvey Research Inst St Bartholomew's and the Royal London Sch of Med and Dentistry Queen Mary and Westfield Coll London 1995– (assoc dir 1991–95), conslt chem pathologist Hammersmith and Queen Charlotte's Hosps; memb: Hammersmith and Queen Charlotte's Health Authy 1982–90, Br Postgraduate Fedn Central Academic Cncl 1983–89; vice pres Eng Chess Assoc; Gairdner Int Award Toronto 1967, Elsevier Award for Distinguished Res 1992, Paget Fndn Award 1995; Hon MD Turin Univ 1985; FRCPath 1971 (MCRPath (fndr memb) 1965), FRCP 1977 (MRCP 1969), FRS 1996; *Recreations* tennis, chess; *Clubs* Athenaeum, Queen's, Hurlingham; *Style*— Professor Iain MacIntyre, FRS; ✉ Great Broadhurst Farm, Broad Oak, Heathfield, E Sussex TN21 8UX (☎ 01435 883515, fax 01435 883611, e-mail calc@broadoak.demon.co.uk); William Harvey Research Institute, Charterhouse Square, London EC1M 6BQ (☎ 0171 982 6168, fax 0171 982 6162, e-mail calc@chs-whri-o3.mds.qmw.ac.uk)

MACINTYRE, Iain Melfort Campbell; s of late John Macintyre, of Edinburgh, and Mary, *née* Campbell; *b* 23 June 1944; *Educ* Daniel Stewart's Coll Edinburgh, Univ of Edinburgh (MB ChB, MD); *m* 8 April 1969, Tessa Lorna Mary, da of Rev Basil E R Millar; 3 da (Carol Anne Mary b 13 Nov 1969, Alison Jane b 5 Jan 1972, Lucy Nicola b 13 Oct 1975); *Career* trained in surgery Edinburgh and Durban SA; lectr in surgery Univ of Edinburgh 1974–78, locum prof of surgery Univ of Natal SA 1978–79, conslt surgn with administrative responsibility Gen Surgical Unit Leith Hosp Edinburgh 1979–85, conslt surgn Gen Surgical and Gastro-Intestinal Unit Western General Infirmary Edinburgh 1985– (conslt with administrative responsibility Surgical Review Office); chm Lister Postgraduate Inst 1995– (asst dir of studies 1991–95); memb Nat Med Advsy Ctee 1991–94; RCSEd: examiner 1979–, examiner Intercollegiate Bd in Gen Surgery 1994–, memb Educn and Sci Ctee 1987–91, memb Editorial Bd 1991–, memb Educn and Trg Bd 1994–95, memb Cncl 1990–; Cncl of Europe fell 1990, Continuing Med Educn fell in minimally invasive surgery 1992; memb: Assoc of Surgns of GB and I, Assoc of Endoscopic Surgns of GB and I; FRCSEd 1973; *Books* Venous Thrombo-Embolic Disease (ed with C V Ruckley, 1975), Endoscopic Surgery for General Surgeons (ed and contrib, 1995); *Recreations* golf, flying light aircraft, reading, music; *Clubs* Moynihan Chirurgical, Aesculapians, Clouston, Bruntsfield Links Golfing Soc; *Style*— Iain Macintyre, Esq; ✉ 20 Lygon Road, Edinburgh EH16 5QB (☎ 0131 466 0095); General Surgical and Gastro-Intestinal Unit, Western General Hospital, Crewe Road, Edinburgh EH4 2XU (☎ 0131 537 1549)

McINTYRE, Ian James; s of Hector Harold McIntyre (d 1978), of Inverness, and Annie Mary Michie (d 1979); *b* 9 Dec 1931; *Educ* Prescot GS Lancs, St John's Coll Cambridge (MA, pres Cambridge Union), Coll of Europe Bruges; *m* 24 July 1954, Leik Sommerfelt, da of Benjamin Vogt (d 1970), of Kragerø, Norway; 2 s (Andrew James, Neil Forbes), 2 da (Anne Leik, Katharine Elspeth); *Career* Nat Serv cmmnd Intelligence Corps; writer and broadcaster; BBC: current affrs talks prodr 1957–59, ed At Home and Abroad 1959–60, mgmnt trg organiser 1960–61, bdcasting contract 1970–76; controller: Radio 4 1976–78, Radio 3 1978–87; assoc ed The Times 1989–90; prog servs offr ITA 1961–62, dir of info and res Scot Cons Central Office Edinburgh 1962–70; author of book reviews for The Times and The Independent; Parly candidate (Cons) Roxburgh, Selkirk and Peebles gen election 1966; *Books* The Proud Doers (1968), Words (1975), Dogfight: the Transatlantic Battle over Airbus (1992), The Expense of Glory: A Life of John Reith (1993), Dirt & Deity: A Life of Robert Burns (1995); *Recreations* walking, swimming, gardening; *Clubs* Cambridge Union, Beefsteak; *Style*— Ian McIntyre, Esq; ✉ Spylaw House, Newlands Avenue, Radlett, Herts WD7 8EL (☎ 01923 853532)

McINTYRE, James Archibald; CBE (1995, OBE 1989), JP (1973); s of John Marshall McIntyre (d 1977), of Stranraer, and Isabella Fraser, *née* Kirkpatrick (d 1969); *b* 2 Sept 1926; *Educ* Stranraer HS, Strathallan Sch, Queen's Coll Oxford, West of Scotland Agric Coll; *m* 2 April 1953, Hilma Wilson, da of James Archibald Lachlan Brown; 2 da (Helen Nicol b 7 Nov 1954, Karen Kirkpatrick b 18 Nov 1962), 1 s (James Ian b 24 March 1957); *Career* Univ of Oxford short army course, cmmnd 12th Royal Lancers 1946; W of Scotland Agricultural Coll 1948–49, farm mangr for Earl of Stair 1952–56, farm owner 1956–91; chm Dumfries and Galloway Health Bd 1985–95 (memb 1973–); dir: NFU Mutual Insurance Soc 1983–93, Dumfries and Galloway Enterprise Co 1991–; OStJ 1979; pres NFU Scotland 1969–70 (memb Cncl 1962–72), memb Scottish Landowners' Fedn; *Recreations* curling, watching rugby; *Clubs* Farmers'; *Style*— James McIntyre, Esq, CBE, JP; ✉ Glenorchy, Broadstone Road, Stranraer DG9 0EU (☎ 01776 702450); Dumfries and Galloway Health Board, Nithbank, Dumfries DG1 2SD (☎ 01387 41802, fax 01387 52375)

McINTYRE, Very Rev Prof John; CVO (1985); s of John Clark McIntyre, of Bathgate, and Annie McIntyre; *b* 20 May 1916; *Educ* Bathgate Acad, Edinburgh Univ (MA, BD, DLitt); *m* 1945, Jessie, da of William Buick, of Coupar Angus; 2 s, 1 da; *Career* ordained 1941, min Fenwick Parish 1943–45; St Andrews Coll Univ of Sydney: prof of systematic theol 1946–56, princ 1950–56, hon fell 1991–; prof of divinity Edinburgh Univ 1956–86, princ warden Pollock Halls of Residence 1960–71, princ New Coll and dean Faculty of Divinity Edinburgh Univ 1968–74, acting princ and vice-chllr Edinburgh Univ 1973–74 and 1979, dean Order of Thistle 1974–89; chaplain to HM The Queen in Scotland 1975–86, extra chaplain 1974–75 and 1986–, moderator Gen Assembly of Church of Scotland 1982; Hon DHL College of Wooster Ohio 1983, Hon DD Glasgow Univ 1961, Dr (honoris causa) Edinburgh Univ 1987; FRSE 1977 (memb Cncl 1979–82, vice pres 1983–86); *Books* St Anselm and His Critics (1954), The Christian Doctrine of History (1957), On the Love of God (1962), The Shape of Christology (1966), Faith, Theology and Imagination (1987), The Shape of Soteriology (1992), Theology After the Storm (1996); *Style*— The Very Rev Prof John McIntyre, CVO, FRSE; ✉ 22/4 Minto St, Edinburgh EH9 1RQ (☎ 0131 667 1203)

McINTYRE, John; s of John McIntyre, of E Kilbride, and Jean, *née* Geddes; *b* 6 July 1961; *Educ* Claremont HS; *Career* photographer; former: factory labourer, hotel worker, copy boy with Glasgow Herald, George Outram & Co and Evening Times; *Awards* Amateur Photographer of the Year Glasgow District 1985, first prize Brooke Bond Nat Photographic Competition 1991, first prize (Features) Fuji UK Press Awards 1992, runner up (Features) Fuji Press Awards 1993, runner up Colab Ltd Children at Play Competition 1993; *Recreations* running in the marathon; *Clubs* Scottish Photographic Soc, Calderglen Harrier; *Style*— John McIntyre, Esq; ✉ 5 Glen Dessary, St Leonards, East Kilbride, Glasgow G74 2AQ (☎ 013552 39753)

McINTYRE, Keith Thomas; s of Gordon Leslie McIntyre, of Edinburgh, and Sheila, *née* McDonald; *b* 22 Dec 1959; *Educ* Trinity Acad Secdy Sch Edinburgh, Dundee Coll of Art (Drumfolk travelling scholar, Farquar Reid travelling scholar), Barcelona Paper Workshop; *m* 30 Dec 1983, Sheenagh Margaret Patience; 2 s (Lewis Cathcart b 22 Oct 1987, Casey John b 4 Sept 1991); *Career* artist; solo exhibitions: Shore Gallery Leith 1982, 369 Gallery Edinburgh 1984 and 1986, Compass Gallery Glasgow 1985, Pittenweem Arts Festival Fife 1985, Raab Galerie Berlin 1987, Raab Gallery London 1988, The Paintings for Jock Tamson's Bairns (Tramway Theatre Glasgow and Raab Gallery London) 1990, Pittencrieff House Museum Dunfermline 1995, Northern Print Gallery N Shields 1996, Galerie Christian Dam Copenhagen 1996; group exhibitions incl: Saltire Soc Edinburgh 1982, Clare Hall Cambridge 1984 and 1986, Five Contemporary Scottish Artists (Leinster Fine Art London) 1985, Open Circle (Schweinfurt Exhibition Germany) 1986, De Brakke Gallery Amsterdam 1987, The Lion Rampant: New Scottish Painting and Photography (Artspace San Francisco) 1988, Scottish Myths (Scot Gallery Edinburgh) 1990, Galerie Bureaux & Magasins Ostend Belgium 1991, Divers Memories (Pitt Rivers Museum Oxford); public collections incl: Aberdeen Art Gallery, BBC, Dundee Coll of Commerce, Scot Nat Gallery of Modern Art, W Sussex CC; arts projects incl: visual dir Jock Tamson's Bairns (Tramway Theatre Glasgow) 1989–90, jt film venture (with Timothy Neat and John Berger) 1990; pt/t teacher in fine art Glasgow Sch of Art 1984–89, sr lectr in painting Univ of Northumbria at Newcastle 1993–; artistic dir Songs for the Falling Angel (requiem for Lockerbie air crash victims, Edinburgh Int Festival) 1991, exhibition of paintings for Songs for the Falling Angel (Kelvingrove Art Gallery

Glasgow) 1991/92; visual art dir: Rites (with Scottish Chamber Orch, Briggait Glasgow) 1993, Legend of St Julian (with Communicado, Traverse Theatre, Edinburgh Int Festival) 1993; awards: Hospitalfield scholar Arbroath 1981, RSA Carnegie 1982, RSA William Gillies 1983, Elizabeth Greenshields 1983, first prize Scottish Drawing Competition 1993; *Style*— Keith McIntyre, Esq; ✉ Department of Fine Art, Squires Building, University of Northumbria at Newcastle (☎ 0191 227 4935)

McINTYRE, Malcolm; s of Stanley Archibald Lovell McIntyre (d 1995), of Purley, Surrey, and Mary, *née* MacGregor; *b* 28 May 1934; *Educ* Roke Sch; *m* 17 May 1958, Avis Joan, da of Robert Leonard Winwood (d 1968), of New Malden, Surrey; 2 s (Simon Timothy b 1959 d 1962, Paul Timothy b 1963), 2 da (Claire Louise b 1961, Kate Lucy b 1965); *Career* PA to Maj-Gen Robert Urquhart GOC in C Br Troops Austria 1952–54; journalist and ed 1954–70; jt md Kingsway PR (later Saatchis) 1970–83, md Malcolm McIntyre & Partners 1983–93; UK rep Champagne Industry's governing body 1975–93; tstee Help the Homeless; Chevalier de l'Ordre du Merite Agricole France 1996; *Books* Home Extensions; *Recreations* golf; *Clubs* RAC; *Style*— Malcolm McIntyre, Esq; ✉ McIntyre Consultants, 391 City Road, London EC1V 1NE (☎ 0171 278 7333)

MACINTYRE, Malcolm Valentine Strickland; s of Donald George Frederick Wyville Macintyre, RN, DSO, DSC (d 1981), and Monica Josephine Clifford Rowley, da of Roger Walter Strickland (descended in the sr line of Strickland of Sizergh Castle, Westmorland); f Capt Donald Macintyre was famous U-boat hunter in WWII, f's great uncle Lt-Gen Donald Macintyre raised the 4th Gurkhas and won VC, ggf Gen John Macintyre also served in Indian Army in Madras Artillery; gf Maj-Gen Donald Macintyre served in 2nd and commanded 4th Gurkhas; *b* 5 Nov 1942; *Educ* Ampleforth; Luton Coll of Technol (HND Mech Engrg); *m* 22 Feb 1969, Lesley Winifred, da of Leslie Donald Brown (d 1961); 1 s (Donald Malcolm Macintyre 1970); *Career* chief exec Plysu plc 1993– (dir 1981–); *Recreations* dog breeding and training, flying (PPL); *Style*— Malcolm V S Macintyre; ✉ Cedarbrook, Lower Dean, Huntingdon, Cambs PE18 0LL; Plysu plc, Station Road, Woburn Sands, Milton Keynes, Bucks MK17 8SE (☎ 01908 582311, fax 01908 585265)

McINTYRE, Prof Michael Edgeworth; s of Archibald Keverall McIntyre, and Anne Hartwell McIntyre; *b* 28 July 1941; *Educ* King's HS Dunedin NZ, Univ of Otago NZ (sr sci scholar, BSc, Robert Jack prize, NZ Inst of Chemistry prize), Trinity Coll Cambridge (Cwlth scholar, PhD); *m* 1968, Ruth Hecht; 2 step s, 1 step da; *Career* asst lectr in mathematics Univ of Otago NZ 1963, postdoctoral fell Woods Hole Oceanographic Inst 1967, postdoctoral res assoc Dept of Meteorology MIT 1967–69, res fell St John's Coll Cambridge 1968–71; Dept of Applied Mathematics and Theoretical Physics Univ of Cambridge: asst dir of res in dynamical meteorology 1969–72, lectr 1972–87, reader in atmospheric dynamics 1987–93, prof of atmospheric dynamics 1993–; co-dir Cambridge Centre for Atmospheric Sci 1992–; EPSRC sr res fell 1992–; sr visiting fell Japan Soc for the Promotion of Sci 1984; sr conslt: Science and Technology Corporation Hampton Virginia 1987–, Jet Propulsion Laboratory Pasadena Calif 1991–; project scientist UK Univs' Global Atmospheric Modelling Prog 1987– (memb Sci Steering Gp 1990–); memb: Editorial Bd Jl of Fluid Mechanics 1969–80, Int Cmmn for Meteorology of the Upper Atmosphere 1979–89, Atmospheric Sci Ctee NERC 1989–94, Strateole Scientific Steering Ctee 1992–, World Climate Res Prog SPARC Gravity Wave Ctee 1994–; vice pres Catgut Acoustical Soc 1978–83, memb New Violin Family Steering Ctee Royal Coll of Music 1976–80; Adams prize Univ of Cambridge 1981; FRMetS 1969, memb Academia Europaea 1989, fell American Meteorological Soc 1991 (Carl-Gustaf Rossby Res medal 1987), FRS 1990; *Publications* author of numerous papers in professional jls incl Jl of Fluid Mechanics, Quarterly Jl RMetSoc and Jl of the Atmospheric Sciences; *Recreations* music, gliding; *Style*— Prof M E McIntyre, FRS; ✉ 98 Windsor Rd, Cambridge CB4 3JN; Department of Applied Mathematics and Theoretical Physics, Silver St, Cambridge CB3 9EW (☎ 01223 337871, secretary's ☎ 01223 337870, fax 01223 337918)

McINTYRE, Prof Neil; s of John William McIntyre (d 1986), of Ferndale, Mid Glamorgan, and Catherine, *née* Watkins; *b* 1 May 1934; *Educ* Porth Co Sch for Boys, King's Coll London (BSc), King's Coll Hosp Med Sch (MB BS, MD); *m* 3 Sept 1966, Wendy Ann, da of Wing Cdr Richard Kelsey (ret), of Southwold, Suffolk; 1 s (Rowan b 1969), 1 da (Waveney b 1968); *Career* MRC travelling fellowship Mass Gen Hosp and Harvard Med Sch USA 1966–68, hon conslt Royal Free Hosp; Royal Free Hosp Sch of Med: sr lectr in med 1968–73, reader in med 1973–78, clinical sub-dean 1976–80, prof of med 1979–, chm Dept of Med 1983–93, vice dean 1993–95; dir of med educn Med Sch UCL and Royal Free Hosp 1993–95; sec MRS 1972–77; Freeman City of London, Liveryman Worshipful Soc of Apothecaries; FRCP 1972; *Books* The Problem Orientated Medical Record (1979), Lipids and Lipoproteins (1990), Oxford Textbook of Clinical Hepatology (1991); *Recreations* golf, photographing medical statues; *Clubs* Athenaeum, Highgate Golf; *Style*— Prof Neil McIntyre; ✉ 20 Queenscourt, Wembley, Middx HA9 7QU (☎ 0181 902 2751); University Department of Medicine, Royal Free Hospital, Pond Street, London NW3 2QG (☎ 0171 794 0500 ext 3969, fax 0171 830 2321)

McINTYRE, Patrick; s of Patrick Owen McIntyre (d 1986), of Winnipeg, Manitoba, Canada, and Elizabeth May, *née* Gair (d 1985); *b* 18 June 1936; *Educ* St Paul's Coll Winnipeg, Open Univ (BA); *m* 27 June 1957, Margaret Inger (d 1990), da of Robert Jarman (d 1954); 1 s (Patrick), 1 step s (David), 1 step da (Hilary Patricia); *Career* Royal Winnipeg Ballet 1946–56, American Ballet Theatre 1957–58, West End Theatre (West Side Story) 1958–60, ten West End prodns 1960–83, numerous feature films and TV series 1960–83, house mangr Old Vic Theatre 1983–96; direction and choreography: RSC Stratford, LA Light Opera, Gaiety Theatre Dublin, various Br provincial theatres; memb Cncl for Dance Educn and Trg 1996–; memb: AGMA, AGVA, ACTRA, American and Br Equity; *Recreations* walking, reading, travel; *Style*— Patrick McIntyre, Esq; ✉ Flat 1, 29 Palmeira Square, Hove, Sussex BN3 2JP (☎ 01273 735701)

McINTYRE, Dr Robert Douglas; s of John Ebenezer McIntyre (d 1961), of Edinburgh, and Catherine Campbell, *née* Morison (d 1961); *b* 15 Dec 1913; *Educ* Hamilton Acad, Daniel Stewart Coll, Univ of Edinburgh (MB ChB), Univ of Glasgow (DPH); *m* 11 Sept 1954, Letitia Sarah, *née* MacLeod; 1 s (John Douglas b 21 Sept 1959); *Career* area conslt chest physician Stirlingshire 1951–79, hon conslt Stirling Royal Infirmary 1978–; Scot Nat Pty: MP Motherwell & Wishaw 1945, chm 1948–56, pres 1958–80; Parly candidate: Motherwell & Wishaw 1950, Perth and E Perthshire 1951, 1955, 1959 and 1964, West Stirlingshire 1966 and 1970, Stirling Burgh's (by election 1971, gen election Feb and Oct 1974), Euro election Mid Scotland & Fife 1979; memb Univ Ct Univ of Stirling 1967–75 and 1979–88 (chllrs assessor 1979–88), memb Stirling Town Cncl 1957–75 (hon treas 1958–64), provost 1967–75; Hon DUniv Stirling; Freeman Royal Burgh of Stirling, fell Scot Cncl; *Recreations* sailing; *Clubs* Scottish Arts, Stirling County; *Style*— Dr Robert McIntyre; ✉ 8 Gladstone Place, Stirling (☎ 01786 473456)

MACINTYRE, William Ian; CB (1992); s of Robert Miller Macintyre, CBE (d 1991), of Uckfield, E Sussex, and Florence Mary, *née* Funnell; *b* 20 July 1943; *Educ* Merchiston Castle Sch, Univ of St Andrews (MA); *m* 2 Sept 1967, Jennifer Mary, da of Sir David Bruce Pitblado, KCB, CVO, and Edith Mary, *née* Evans, of London; 1 s (Jonathan b 13 Sept 1974), 2 da (Emma b 22 March 1969, Victoria b 6 Dec 1971); *Career* BP Co Ltd 1965–72, ECGD 1972–73; Dept of Energy (now part of DTI): Oil Div 1973–77, seconded ICFC 1977–79, asst sec Gas Div 1979–1983, dir gen Energy Efficiency Office 1983–87, under sec Electricity Div 1987–88, under sec Electricity Div B 1988–91, under sec Coal Div 1991–94, head of Telecommunications Div 1994–95, head of Communications and Information Industries Directorate 1996–; govr: Shene Sch 1982–86, East Sheen Primary Sch 1974–92; warden parish of Mortlake with East Sheen 1991–95; *Style*— William Macintyre, Esq, CB; ✉ Dept of Trade and Industry, 151 Buckingham Palace Road, London SW1W 9SS (☎ 0171 215 1839)

McIVER, Malcolm; SSC; s of late Donald John McIver, and Jean Begg, *née* Macdonald (d 1958); *b* 9 March 1935; *Educ* The Nicolson Inst Stornoway, Univ of Glasgow (MA, LLB); *m* 15 April 1960, Margaret, da of Alexander Wilson Fox Elliot; 1 s (Calum Alexander b 10 July 1967); *Career* apprentice slr Baird Smith Barclay & Muirhead and Maclay Murray & Spens 1955–58, slr Crawford Herron & Cameron 1958–59, slr Peter Morris & McTaggart 1959–60, ptnr Crawford Herron & Cameron 1960–73, ptnr Bird Semple & Crawford Herron 1973–87, sr ptnr Bird Semple 1991– (ptnr 1987–); chm Rodime plc 1991–; tutor in jurisprudence Univ of Glasgow 1960–85; chm Royal Scottish Acad of Music and Drama 1993–, dep chm Accounts Cmmn 1994– (memb 1988–); memb Incorporation of Hammermen Glasgow; memb: Law Soc in Scotland 1958, Royal Faculty of Procurators in Glasgow 1960; FInstPet, FRSA; *Recreations* sailing, music; *Clubs* Western (Glasgow), RSAC, Royal Western Yacht; *Style*— Malcolm McIver, Esq, SSC; ✉ Bird Semple, 249 West George Street, Glasgow G2 4RB (☎ 0141 221 7090, fax 0141 204 1902)

McIVOR, Rt Hon (William) Basil; OBE (1991), PC (NI 1971); s of Rev Frederick McIvor (d 1968), and (Elizabeth) Lilly, *née* Dougan (d 1972); *b* 17 June 1928; *Educ* Methodist Coll Belfast, Queen's Univ Belfast (LLB), Lincoln's Inn; *m* 3 Jan 1953, (Frances) Jill, *qv*, da of late Cecil Reginald Johnston Anderson, of Lisburn, NI; 2 s (Jonathan, Timothy), 1 da (Jane); *Career* called to the Bar NI 1950, presiding magistrate 1974–93, MP (UU) Larkfield NI Parly 1969, min of Community Relations NI 1971–72, memb (UU) for S Belfast NI Assembly 1973–75, min Educn NI 1974; govr Campbell Coll 1975– (chm 1983); fndr memb and chm: Fold Housing Assoc NI 1976–, Lagan Coll (the first purposely designed integrated RC and Protestant Sch in NI) 1981–; *Recreations* music, gardening, golf; *Clubs* Royal Over-Seas League; *Style*— The Rt Hon Basil McIvor, OBE; ✉ Larkhill, 98 Spa Road, Ballynahinch, Co Down (☎ 01238 563534)

McIVOR, Ian Walker; s of William Walker McIvor, of Worsley, Manchester (d 1986), and Susannah, *née* Glover (d 1990); *b* 19 Jan 1944; *Educ* Worsley HS, Bolton Inst, London Univ (LLB); *m* 16 Sept 1969, Patricia Wendy, da of Harry Blackhurst Swift, of Caerphilly, South Wales; 1 s (Andrew Walker b 1977), 4 da (Helen b 1970, Rachel b 1971, Caroline b 1974, Joanne b 1984); *Career* AVR 2 Kings Regt OTC 1966–68; called to the Bar Inner Temple 1973 (Marshall Hall Tst Award and Pupillage Scholarship), head of Chambers 1977–; *Recreations* golf, swimming, walking, DIY; *Clubs* Heald Green, Didsbury and Holyhead Golf; *Style*— Ian W McIvor, Esq; ✉ 38 Framingham Rd, Brooklands, Sale, Cheshire M33 3SH (☎ 0161 962 8205); 334 Deansgate, Manchester (☎ 0161 834 3767, fax 0161 839 6868)

McIVOR, Dr James; s of James McIvor, of Troon, Ayrshire, and Ann Donaldson, *née* Hunter; *b* 23 Sept 1936; *Educ* Glasgow Acad, Univ of Glasgow (BDS, MB ChB, FDS RCS, FRCR); *m* 1966 (m dis 1988), Elizabeth Ann Gibbon; 1 s (Martin James b 4 Feb 1972), 1 da (Claire Elizabeth b 14 June 1975); *Career* jr house offr Glasgow Royal Infirmary 1963–64; registrar in oral surgery: Eastman Dental Hosp London 1964–65, Queen Mary's Hosp Roehampton 1965–66; registrar in radiology: Westminster Hosp London 1966–67, King's Coll Hosp London 1968–69; conslt radiologist: Hillingdon Hosp Uxbridge Middlesex 1970–76, Charing Cross Hosp 1976–; in private radiological practice Harley St 1980–97, head of X-Ray Eastman Dental Inst 1985–, chief of service (general radiology) Hammersmith Hosps NHS Tst 1985–; author or jt author over 50 scientific papers in med jls 1965–; memb Editorial Bd two med jls, chm DDR Examination Bd RCR 1990–95; fell Cardiovascular and Interventional Radiological Soc of Europe 1992–; *Books* Diagnostic Radiology (contrib, 1986 and 1991), Maxillofacial Injuries (contrib, 1994), Radiology for Surgeons (1997); *Recreations* fringe theatre, moderate exercise, gossip; *Style*— Dr James McIvor; ✉ 39 Rosedew Road, London W6 9ET (☎ 0181 748 1854); Charing Cross Hospital, Fulham Palace Rd, London W6 8RF (☎ 0181 846 1234); Eastman Dental Institute, Gray's Inn Rd, London WC1 8LD

McIVOR, (Frances) Jill; CBE (1994), QSM (NZ 1993); da of Cecil Reginald Johnston Anderson (d 1956), of Lisburn, Co Antrim, and Frances Ellen, *née* Henderson (d 1978); *b* 10 Aug 1930; *Educ* Methodist Coll, Lurgan Coll, Queen's Univ Belfast (LLB); *m* 1953, Rt Hon William Basil McIvor, *qv*; 2 s (Jonathan, Timothy), 1 da (Jane); *Career* Queen's Univ Belfast: asst librarian (law) 1954–55, tutor in legal res Law Faculty 1965–74; editorial staff NI Legal Quarterly 1966–76, librarian Dept of Dir of Public Prosecutions 1977–79; memb Gen Dental Cncl 1979–91, chm Lagan Valley Regnl Park Ctee 1984–89 (memb 1975–89); memb: Lay Panel Juvenile Ct 1976–77, IBA 1980–86, Ulster Countryside Ctee 1984–89, Fair Employment Agency 1984–89, Fair Employment Cmmn 1990–91; called to the Bar NI 1980; memb: Bd Cooperation North 1987–90, NI Advsy Ctee Br Cncl 1987–, Home Sec's Advsy Panel on Community Radio 1985–86; chm: Ulster NZ Tst 1987–, Bd of Visitors Queen's Univ Belfast 1988– (memb Ethics Research Ctee 1996–), EGSA (Educnl Guidance Serv for Adults) 1988–89; memb and dep chm Radio Authy 1990–94; NI Parly Ombudsman and Cmmr for Complaints 1991–96, NI hon consul for NZ 1996–; FRSA 1988; *Publications* Irish Consultant, Manual of Law Librarianship (contrib, 1976), Elegantia Juris: selected writings of F H Newark (ed, 1973), Chart of the English Reports (new edn, 1982); *Recreations* gardening, New Zealand; *Clubs* Royal Over-Seas League; *Style*— Mrs Jill McIvor, CBE, QSM; ✉ Larkhill, Spa Road, Ballynahinch, Co Down BT24 8PP (☎ 01238 563534, fax 01846 648098)

MACK, Anthony George (Tony); s of Anthony Mack (d 1991), of Bognor, Sussex, and Joyce Agnes, *née* Smith; *b* 10 Dec 1948; *Educ* Imberhorne Sch; *m* 17 Feb 1979, Sally Frances, da of Frank Frederick Legg, of Sussex; 2 s (Alastair b 1981, Freddy b 1986), 1 da (Holly b 1982); *Career* Air London International plc (formerly Air London Ltd): dir 1970, md 1979, chm and md 1989–; FFA, AMRAeS; *Recreations* sailing, squash, skiing; *Clubs* Hamble River Sailing; *Style*— Tony Mack, Esq; ✉ Air London International plc, Platinum House, Gatwick Rd, Crawley, Sussex RH10 2RP (☎ 01293 549555, fax 01293 536810, telex 87671)

MACK, Hazel Mary; da of Peter Nevard Perkins (d 1992), of 6 Keswick Ave, Loughborough, Leics, and Elizabeth, *née* Walker; *b* 4 April 1952; *Educ* Loughborough HS for Girls, Univ of Exeter (BA); *m* 19 May 1977, Brian Mack, s of Frank Mack (d 1982); *Career* co sec Morgan Grenfell & Co Ltd 1987–90 (joined 1980), dir Mergers and Acquisitions Unit Willis Corroon PLC 1990–; ACIS; *Recreations* cooking, gardening, fly fishing, swimming; *Style*— Mrs Hazel Mack; ✉ Pounce Hall Cottage, Sewards End, nr Saffron Walden, Essex CB10 2LE (☎ 01799 527740); Willis Corroon PLC, Ten Trinity Square, London EC3P 3AX (☎ 0171 975 2329, fax 0171 488 8562, telex 882141 WILLIS G)

MACK, Dr (Brian) John; s of Harold Brian Mack, of Belfast, and Joan Alexandra, *née* Kelly; *b* 10 July 1949; *Educ* Campbell Coll Belfast, Univ of Sussex (BA, MA), Merton Coll Oxford (DPhil); *m* 1976, Caroline Helen Claire, da of Rev Dr Daniel T Jenkins; 1 da (Katy b 12 Oct 1985), 1 s (Samuel b 13 Feb 1989); *Career* Dept of Ethnography British Museum: research asst 1976–77, asst keeper 1977–91, keeper 1991–; memb: Advsy Cncl NACF, Bd W African Museums Programme, Bd for Academy Sponsored Insts and Socs British Academy; govr Powell-Cotton Museum Kent; winner NACF Award for Images of Africa exhibition 1991; FRAI 1976, FSA 1994; *Publications* African Textiles (with J Picton, Craft Advsy Cncl Book of the Year, 1979, 2 edn 1989), Zulus (with J Picton, 1980), Culture History in the Southern Sudan (with P T Robertshaw, 1982), Ethnic Sculpture (with M D McLeod, 1984), Madagascar, Island of the Ancestors (1986), Ethnic

Jewellery (1988), Malagasy Textiles (1989), Emil Torday and the Art of the Congo 1900–1909 (1990); African Textile Design (with C Spring, 1991), Masks, the Art of Expression (1994); also author of articles and reviews in learned jls; *Recreations* museums, galleries, walking; *Clubs* Machynlleth Golf (Powys); *Style*— Dr John Mack; ✉ Museum of Mankind, 6 Burlington Gardens, London W1X 2EX (☎ 0171 323 8024, fax 0171 323 8013)

McKANE, Christopher Hugh; s of Leonard Cyril McKane, MBE, of Lingfield, Surrey, and (Eleanor) Catharine, *née* Harris; *b* 13 July 1946; *Educ* Marlborough, New Coll Oxford (MA); *m* 31 Oct 1970, Anna Rosemary, da of George Paul Henshell (d 1984); 3 da (Camilla b 1977, Sophie b 1979, Felicity b 1981); *Career* journalist: The Oxford Times 1968–71, The Birmingham Post 1971–74; The Times: joined 1974, chief home sub ed 1982–86; The Independent: dep home ed 1986–88, picture ed 1988–92, night ed 1992–94; The Times: joined 1994, night ed 1995–; Freeman City of London, Liveryman Worshipful Co of Stationers and Newspaper Makers; *Recreations* bonsai, wine, running; *Style*— Christopher McKane, Esq; ✉ The Times, 1 Pennington Street, London E1 9XN (☎ 0171 782 5000)

McKANE, Prof William; s of Thomas McKane (d 1964), and Jemima, *née* Smith (d 1957); *b* 18 Feb 1921; *Educ* Univ of St Andrews (MA, Football blue), Univ of Glasgow (MA, PhD, DLitt); *m* 3 July 1952, Agnes Mathie, da of James Howie (d 1973), of South Fergushill, Ayrshire; 3 s (Thomas b 15 May 1953, James b 8 July 1956, William b 4 May 1966), 2 da (Ursula b 22 Jan 1959, Christina b 20 March 1963); *Career* RAF 1941–45; sr lectr in Hebrew Univ of Glasgow 1965 (asst lectr 1953); Univ of St Andrews: prof of Hebrew and Oriental languages 1968–90 (emeritus prof 1990–), dean Faculty of Divinity 1973–77; foreign sec Soc for Old Testament Study 1981–86 (pres 1978), princ St Mary's Coll St Andrews 1982–86; Burkitt medal of Br Acad for distinguished work in biblical studies 1985; Min Church of Scot; DD (Honoris Causa) Univ of Edinburgh 1984; FRAS 1957, FBA 1980, FRSE 1983; *Books* I and II Samuel (1963), Prophets and Wise Men (1965), Proverbs: A New Approach (1970), Jeremiah 1–25 International Critical Commentary (1986), Studies in the Patriarchal Narratives (1979), Selected Christian Hebraists (1989), A Late Harvest (1995), Jeremiah 26–52 International Critical Commentary (1996); *Recreations* walking; *Clubs* Royal and Ancient (St Andrews); *Style*— Prof William McKane, FBA; ✉ 51 Irvine Cres, St Andrews, Fife KY16 8LG (☎ 01334 73797); St Mary's Coll, St Andrews, Fife KY16 9JU (☎ 01334 76161)

MACKANESS, James; DL (Northants 1984); s of John Howard Mackaness, of Northampton, and Majorie, *née* Andrews; *b* 6 Feb 1945; *Educ* Millfield, RAC Cirencester; *m* 7 Jan 1972, Susan, da of Harold Pike; 1 da (Louise Mackaness b 1973), 1 s (Oliver James b 1975); *Career* md A J Mackaness Ltd (family firm); dir Mixconcrete Holdings Plc 1981–83; High Sheriff of Northants 1995–96; memb St John Ambulance 1974–, chm St John Cncl for Northants 1982–; govr: St Andrew's Hosp 1987–, Three Shires Hosp 1995–; tstee Mackaness Family Charitable Tst 1994–; CStJ 1982; *Recreations* hunting, shooting, skiing; *Clubs* Northampton County; *Style*— James Mackaness, Esq, DL; ✉ A J Mackaness Ltd, Billing House, The Causeway, Great Billing, Northampton NN3 9EX (☎ 01604 409096, fax 01604 407222)

MACKARNESS, Simon Paul Richard; TD (1980); s of Peter John Coleridge Mackarness, TD, of Petersfield, Hants, and Torla Frances Wedd, *née* Tidman; *b* 10 Sept 1945; *Educ* Portsmouth GS, Univ of Bristol (BA); *m* 9 Dec 1978, Diana, da of Dr Lewis MacDonald Reid, MC (d 1978); 1 s (Daniel b 1982), 1 da (Louise b 1981); *Career* Capt Royal Signals on RARO; admitted slr 1970, sr ptnr Mackarness & Lunt; memb Law Soc; *Recreations* amateur dramatics, motorcycling; *Style*— Simon Mackarness, Esq, TD; ✉ 6 Bepton Down, Petersfield, Hants GU31 4PR (☎ 01730 265111, fax 01730 267994)

McKAY, Maj-Gen Alexander Matthew; CB (1975); s of Colin McKay (d 1977), of Vancouver, Canada, and Ann McKay (d 1979); *b* 14 Feb 1921; *Educ* RN Dockyard Sch, Portsmouth Poly; *m* 1949, Betty Margaret, da of George Lee, of London; 1 s (Andrew), 1 da (Fiona), (1 da decd); *Career* serv WWII DEME (Army) 1942–75 (despatches twice), Palestine, Malaya, (Maj-Gen); chm Stocklake Hldgs plc 1975–87; pres Winchester Div SSAFA 1988–, memb ASME sec Inst of Mech Engrs 1976–87, pres Itchen Valley Royal British Legion 1996– (vice pres 1992–96); Freeman City of London 1984; FEng 1984, FIMechE, FIEE, FRSE 1985; *Recreations* flyfishing, gardening, restoring antique furniture; *Style*— Maj-Gen Alexander McKay, CB, FEng, FRSE; ✉ Church Cottage, Martyr Worthy, Nr Winchester SO21 1DY (☎ 01962 779339)

MACKAY, Andrew James; MP (C) Berkshire East (majority 28,680); s of Robert James MacKay, and Olive Margaret MacKay; *b* 27 Aug 1949; *Educ* Solihull; *m* 1975, Diana Joy Kinchin; 1 s, 1 d; *Career* ptnr Jones MacKay & Croxford Estate Agents 1974–, dir Birmingham Housing Industs Ltd 1975–83; chm Solihull Young Cons 1971–74, vice chm Solihull Cons Assoc 1971–74, chm Britain in Europe Meriden Branch 1975; MP (C): Birmingham Stechford March 1977–79, Berkshire E 1983–; memb Cons Party Nat Exec 1979–82, sec of Cons Back Bench Foreign Affrs Ctee 1984–86; PPS to: Sec of State for NI 1986–89, Sec of State for Defence 1989–92; asst Govt whip 1992–93, a Lord Cmmr of the Treasury (Govt whip) 1993–95, Vice-Chamberlain of HM Household (Govt whip) 1996, Treasurer of HM Household (dep chief whip) 1996–; *Recreations* golf, squash; *Clubs* Berkshire Golf, Aberdovey Golf; *Style*— Andrew MacKay, Esq, MP; ✉ House of Commons, London SW1A 0AA (☎ 0171 219 4109)

McKAY, Andy; s of James Gardner McKay (d 1993), of Birmingham, and Jean Margaret, *née* Oliver; *b* 23 May 1961; *Educ* Light Hall GS, Solihull Tech Coll, Maidstone Coll of Art (BA); *m* 18 May 1991, Antoinette, da of Richard Michael O'Byrne; 1 da (Molly Jean b 18 March 1993); *Career* advtg art dir: Boase Massimi Pollitt 1983–87, Aspect Hill Holliday 1987–89; Simons Palmer Denton Clemmow & Johnson: art dir 1989, head of art 1992, jt creative dir 1995–; recipient various advtg indust awards; *Recreations* subscriber to 2000 AD; *Style*— Andy McKay, Esq; ✉ Creative Director, Simons Palmer Clemmow Johnson Ltd, 19–20 Noel Street, London W1V 3PD (☎ 0171 287 4455, fax 0171 734 2658)

MACKAY, Prof Angus Iain Kenneth; s of Neil Angus Roderick Mackay, and Mary, *née* Macaulay; *b* 28 Aug 1939; *Educ* Royal HS Edinburgh, Univ of Edinburgh (MA, PhD); *m* 10 Jan 1963, Linda, da of Carlo Volante; 1 s (Angus John b 10 Sept 1964), 1 da (Anne Marie b 20 April 1967); *Career* asst lectr Univ of Reading 1962–66; Univ of Edinburgh: joined 1966, lectr, sr lectr, reader then prof; FRHistSoc, FBA; *Books* incl: Spain in the Middle Ages - From Frontier to Empire 1000–1500, Money Prices and Politics in Fifteenth-Century Castile (1981), Society, Economy and Religion in Late Medieval Castile (1987), Medieval Frontier Societies (jt ed, 1989), The Impact of Humanism on Western Europe (jt ed, 1990); *Recreations* reading; *Style*— Prof Angus Mackay, FBA; ✉ History Department, William Robertson Building, George Square, Edinburgh EH8 9JY (☎ 0131 664 5162)

MACKAY, Dr Angus Victor Peck; s of Victor Mackay (d 1982), of Edinburgh, and Christine, *née* Peck (d 1985); *b* 4 March 1943; *Educ* George Heriot's Sch Edinburgh, Univ of Edinburgh (BSc, MB ChB), Univ of Cambridge (MA, PhD); *m* 1969, Elspeth Margaret Whitton, da of Thomas Norris; 2 s (Jason b 20 Nov 1970, Aidan b 31 March 1978), 2 da (Ashley b 20 June 1972, Zoe b 17 Jan 1983); *Career* undergraduate trg in pharmacology and med Univ of Edinburgh 1962–69, house offr Med/Surgical Professorial Unit Edinburgh Royal Infirmary 1969–70, graduate trg Univ of Cambridge 1970–73 (MRC jr res fell and supervisor in pharmacology Trinity Coll Cambridge and hon registrar Fulbourn Hosp Cambridge), MRC clinical res fell MRC Brain Metabolism Unit Edinburgh, hon registrar in psychiatry Royal Edinburgh Hosp and hon lectr Dept of Pharmacology Edinburgh 1973–76, hon sr registrar Edinburgh Royal Infirmary 1976, sr clinical scientific staff memb and latterly dep dir MRC Neurochemical Pharmacology Unit Cambridge and lectr in pharmacology Trinity Coll Cambridge 1976–80; currently: physician supt Argyll and Bute Hosp, conslt psychiatrist, clinical dir and Tst med offr Argyll and Bute NHS Tst and Macintosh lectr in psychological med Glasgow 1980–, hon conslt Cambridge Area Health Authy and hon lectr Dept of Psychiatry Cambridge 1980–; UK rep Conf on Psychiatric Hosp Orgn and Mgmnt WHO 1983; memb: Res Ctee Mental Health Fndn 1981–88, Working Gp on Guidelines for Clinical Drug Evaluation WHO 1984–89, Ctee on Safety of Meds Dept of Health 1983–; chm: Multidisciplinary Working Pty on Research into Care of the Dementing Elderly Chief Scientist Orgn 1986–87, Working Gp on Mental Illness Servs in Scotland CRAG/SCOTMEG 1992–96, External Reference Gp Scottish Health Dept 1996–; memb Health Policy Bd Scotland 1996–; author of over 70 pubns; Keith Medal and Meml Lecture RSA 1974; FRCPEd 1989 (MRCP 1986), FRCPsych 1993 (MRCPsych 1976); *Recreations* sailing, rowing, rhododendrons; *Clubs* Ardrishaig Boat, American Rhododendron Soc; *Style*— Dr Angus Mackay, Esq; ✉ Tigh An Rudha, Ardrishaig, Argyll (☎ 01546 603272); Argyll and Bute Hospital, Lochgilphead, Argyll PA31 8LD (☎ 01546 602323, fax 01546 602606)

MACKAY, Charles Dorsey; s of Brig Kenneth Mackay, CBE, DSO (d 1974), and Evelyn Maud, *née* Ingram (d 1982); *b* 14 April 1940; *Educ* Cheltenham, Queens' Coll Cambridge (MA), INSEAD (European Institute of Business Administration) (MBA); *m* 11 July 1964, Annmarie, da of Fritz Joder (d 1978); 2 s (Hugo b 1965 d 1981, Caspar b 1971), 1 da (Romola b 1966); *Career* The British Petroleum Co Ltd: commercial apprentice 1957–59, univ apprentice 1959–62, mktg asst 1962–63, sales supervisor Algeria 1963–65, commercial dir Burundi/Rwanda/Zaire 1965–68, seconded to INSEAD 1968–69; McKinsey & Co Inc London/Paris/Amsterdam/Dar es Salaam: conslt 1969–71, jr engagement mangr 1971–72, sr engagement mangr 1972–76; Pakhoed Holding NV Rotterdam: dir Paktrans Div 1976–77, chm 1977–81; Chloride Group plc: dir 1981–86, chm Chloride Overseas 1981–85, chm Chloride Power Electronics 1985–86; Inchcape plc: dir 1986–96, chm Inchcape (Hong Kong) Ltd 1986–87, chm and chief exec Inchcape Pacific Ltd (Hong Kong) 1987–91, gp chief exec 1991–96, dep chm 1995–96; non-exec dir: The Hongkong and Shanghai Banking Corporation Ltd (Hong Kong) 1986–92, Union Insurance Society of Canton Ltd (Hong Kong) 1986–91, HSBC Holdings plc 1991–, Midland Bank plc 1992–93, British Airways plc 1993–96; non-exec dep chm Thistle Hotels plc 1996–, non-exec chm DSL Defence Systems Ltd 1996–; second vice chm Hong Kong Gen C of C 1989–91 (memb 1987–91); memb: Gen Ctee Br C of C in Hong Kong 1987–91, Cncl Hong Kong Trade Devpt Cncl 1989–91, Bd Hong Kong Community Chest 1990–91; *Recreations* travel, tennis, skiing, classical music, opera, chess; *Clubs* Hong Kong; *Style*— Charles Mackay, Esq

MACKAY, His Hon Judge; David Ian; s of David Mackay (d 1982), and Jessie Beazley, *née* Johnston, of Higher Tranmere, Birkenhead; *b* 11 Nov 1945; *Educ* Birkenhead Sch, Brasenose Coll Oxford (MA, William Hulme Open scholar); *m* 1974, Mary Elizabeth, only da of Mr and Mrs N Smith, of Batley, Yorks; 2 da (Emily Jane b 1980, Harriet Louise b 1984), 1 s (James Hugh b 1981); *Career* called to the Bar Inner Temple 1969 (Duke of Edinburgh scholar, Profumo scholar, pupillage prize), practised at Liverpool (N Circuit) 1970–92, recorder 1989–92 (asst recorder 1986–89), circuit judge ((Northern Circuit) Official Referee's business) 1993–; legal memb Mental Health Review Tbnl 1988–92; chm Govrs Birkenhead Sch 1991– (govr 1979–); *Recreations* history, transport, travelling in France; *Clubs* Athenaeum (Liverpool); *Style*— His Hon Judge Mackay; ✉ Queen Elizabeth II Law Courts, Derby Square, Liverpool L2 1XA (☎ 0151 473 7373)

MACKAY, Prof Donald; *b* 27 Feb 1937; *Educ* Univ of Aberdeen (MA); *Career* prof of political economy Univ of Aberdeen 1971–76; Heriot Watt Univ: prof of economics 1976–82, professorial fell 1982–91, currently hon prof; econ conslt to Sec of State for Scotland 1971–, chm Scottish Enterprise; fndr dir and chm Pieda, dir Grampian Holdings; currently: govr NIESR, memb Scottish Econ Cncl; industl arbitrator ACAS 1974–93; formerly: ind memb Bd S Scotland Electricity, memb Sea Fish Indust Authy, vice pres Edinburgh C of C, memb Cncl Royal Econ Soc, memb Cncl Scottish Econ Soc; author various pubns on labour market and regnl economics; hon LLD Univ of Aberdeen 1994, DUniv Univ of Stirling 1994; FRSE; *Style*— Prof Donald Mackay, FRSE; ✉ Scottish Enterprise, 120 Bothwell Street, Glasgow G2 7JP

MacKAY, Prof Sir Donald Iain; kt (1996); s of William MacKay (d 1980), and Rhona, *née* Cooper; *b* 27 Feb 1937; *Educ* Dollar Acad, Univ of Aberdeen; *m* 31 July 1961, Diana Marjory, da of Maj George Raffan (d 1980); 1 s (Donald Gregor b 1969), 2 da (Deborah Jane b 1964, Paula Clare b 1967); *Career* prof of political economy Univ of Aberdeen 1971–76, professorial fell Heriot-Watt Univ 1982–91 (prof of econs 1976–81); chm Pieda plc planning, economic and devpt conslts 1975–, dir Grampian Holdings 1987–; chm Scottish Enterprise 1993–; econ conslt to Sec of State for Scot 1971–; memb: Sea Fish Indust Authy 1981–87, S of Scot Electricity Bd 1985–88, Scot Econ Cncl 1985–; govr NIESR; FRSE 1987; *Books* Geographical Mobility and the Brain Drain (1970), Local Labour Markets and Wage Structures (1970), Labour Markets Under Different Employment Conditions (1971), Men Leaving Steel (1971), The Political Economy of North Sea Oil (1975), British Employment Statistics (1977); *Recreations* tennis, golf, bridge, chess; *Style*— Prof Sir Donald MacKay, FRSE; ✉ Pieda, 10 Chester St, Edinburgh EH3 7RA (☎ 0131 225 5737, fax 0131 225 5196)

MACKAY, Eileen Alison (Mrs A Muir Russell); CB; da of Alexander William Mackay, OBE (d 1967), of Dingwall, Ross-shire, Scotland, and Alison Jack, *née* Ross (d 1982); *b* 7 July 1943; *Educ* Dingwall Acad, Univ of Edinburgh (MA); *m* 19 Aug 1983, (Alastair) Muir Russell, *qv*, s of Thomas Russell (d 1988), of Glasgow; *Career* res offr Dept of Employment 1965–72; princ: Scottish Office 1972–78, HM Treasy 1978–80; policy advsr Central Policy Review Staff Cabinet Office 1980–83; The Scottish Office: asst sec 1983–88, under sec Housing Gp Environment Dept 1988–92, chm Castlemilk Urban Partnership 1988–92, princ fin offr 1992–96; non-exec dir: Moray Firth Maltings plc 1988–, Royal Bank of Scotland plc 1996–, Edinburgh Investment Trust 1996–; chm Standing Advsy Ctee on Trunk Road Assessment 1996–; memb Scottish Screen Interim Bd 1996; *Recreations* reading, gardening, holidays in France; *Clubs* New (Edinburgh), Royal Soc of Arts, Royal Cwlth Soc; *Style*— Miss Eileen Mackay, CB; ✉ Royal Bank of Scotland plc, 36 St Andrew Square, Edinburgh EH2 2YB (☎ 0131 556 8555, fax 0131 557 6565)

MACKAY, Sir (George Patrick) Gordon; kt (1966), CBE (1962); s of Rev Adam Mackay, BD (d 1931), and Katie Forrest, *née* Lawrence (d 1918); *b* 12 Nov 1914; *Educ* Univ of Aberdeen (MA); *m* 1954, Margaret Esmé, da of Christopher John Martin (d 1948); 1 s, 2 da; *Career* gen mangr East African Railways and Harbours 1961–64; World Bank: 1965–71, consultant 1971–73, dep dir 1974–75, dir 1975–78; memb Bd of Crown Agents 1980–82; OStJ 1964; *Clubs* Nairobi; *Style*— Sir Gordon Mackay, CBE; ✉ Well Cottage, Sandhills, Brook, Surrey GU8 5UP (☎ 01428 682549, fax 01428 685051)

McKAY, Hilary Jane; da of Ronald Damms, of Boston, Lincs, and Mary Edith, *née* Hampton; *b* 12 June 1959; *Educ* Boston Girls' HS, Univ of St Andrews (BSc); *m* 13 Aug 1982, Kevin Kerr McKay; 1 s (James Rufus (Jim) b 8 Jan 1993); *Career* writer; *Books* The Exiles (1991, jt winner Guardian Children's Fiction Award 1992), The Exiles At Home (1993, overall winner Smarties Prize for Children's Literature 1994), Dog Friday (1994), The Amber Cat (1995), The Zoo in the Attic (1995); *Recreations* reading, gardening, darning Panda; *Style*— Mrs Hilary McKay

MACKAY, Dr (Edward) Hugh; s of Hector Mackay (d 1971), of Rugby, Warwickshire, and Marjorie Rose, *née* Rolfe; *b* 10 Aug 1941; *Educ* Lawrence Sheriff Sch Rugby, Univ of Bristol (MB ChB); *m* Sept 1962, Valerie, da of Albert Cyril Ellenger (d 1961); 2 s (Andrew b 1965, Colin b 1968); *Career* registrar in pathology Frenchay Hosp Bristol 1970–72, clinical tutor in pathology Radcliffe Infirmary Oxford 1972–78, conslt histopathologist Leicester Gen Hosp 1978–; ACP: memb Cncl, pres East Mercia Branch; memb: BMA, RSPB, Leicester Caledonian Soc; FRCPath 1986; *Recreations* trout fishing, bird watching, sketching; *Clubs* Leicester Med Soc; *Style—* Dr Hugh Mackay; ✉ 68 Leicester Rd, Markfield, Leicestershire LE67 9RE (☎ 01530 243770); Leicester General Hospital, Gwendolen Rd, Leicester LE5 4PW (☎ 0116 249 0490)

MACKAY, (Douglas) Ian; QC (Scot 1993); s of Walter Douglas Mackay (d 1982), of Inverness, and Carla Marie Anna, *née* Fröhlich (d 1974); *b* 10 Aug 1948; *Educ* Inverness HS, Univ of Aberdeen (LLB); *m* Susan Anne, da of William Nicholson; 1 da (Julie Anne b 2 Aug 1970), 2 s (Garry Ian b 28 July 1973, Andrew William Nicholas b 20 Feb 1986); *Career* admitted Faculty of Advocates 1980; *Recreations* Scottish art and antiques, travel, shooting and gundogs, browsing in auction sales; *Style—* Ian Mackay, Esq, QC; ✉ St Ann's House, Lasswade, Midlothian EH18 1ND (☎ 0131 660 2634, fax 0131 654 1600); Mount Pleasant Farm, by Fortrose, Ross-shire (☎ 01381 620888); c/o Advocates' Library, Parliament House, Edinburgh EH1 1RF (☎ 0131 226 5071)

MACKAY, Ian Stuart; s of Rev Gordon Ernest Mackay (d 1991), of Adelaide, Aust, and Sylvia Viola Dorothy, *née* Spencer (d 1975); *b* 16 June 1943; *Educ* Kearsney Coll Bothas Hill Natal SA, Univ of London (MB BS); *m* 1, 11 May 1968 (m dis), Angela; 1 s (Angus b 1971), 1 da (Fiona b 1972); m 2, 4 Sept 1981, Madeleine Hargreaves, *née* Tull; 1 da (Antonia b 1982), 1 step da (Charlotte b 1971); *Career* conslt ENT surgn Charing Cross Hosp and Brompton Hosp, hon sr lectr in rhinology Inst of Laryngology and Otology, hon sr lectr Cardiothoracic Inst Univ of London; jt ed Rhinology Volume in Scott-Brown's Otolaryngology, contrib section on rhinoplasty to Smith's Operative Surgery; pres elect Br Assoc of Otolaryngologists; memb RSM, FRCS; *Style—* Ian S Mackay, Esq; ✉ 55 Harley Street, London W1N 1DD (☎ 0171 580 5070)

MACKAY, Dr James Alexander; s of William James Mackay (d 1981), and Minnie Somerville, *née* Matheson (d 1990); *b* 21 Nov 1936; *Educ* Hillhead HS Glasgow, Univ of Glasgow (MA, DLitt); *m* 1, 24 Sept 1960 (m dis 1972), Mary Patricia, *née* Jackson; 1 s (Alastair Andrew b 29 July 1967), 1 da (Fiona Elizabeth b 5 April 1963); m 2, 9 Oct 1972 (m dis 1992), Joyce May Greaves; m 3, 11 Dec 1992, Renate Friederike, *née* Finlay-Freundlich; *Career* Nat Serv Lt RA Guided Weapons Range Hebrides 1959–61; asst keeper i/c philatelic collections Dept of Printed Books British Museum 1961–71, full-time writer 1972–; philatelic columnist The New Daily 1962–67, columnist Collecting Wisely 1967–72, philatelic and numismatics columnist Financial Times 1972–85 (columnist 1967–72), ed-in-chief IPC Stamp Encyclopedia 1968–72; ed: Burns Chronicle 1977–91, Burnsian 1986–89, Postal History Annual 1978–90, Coin and Medal Bulletin 1990–91, Antiques Today 1992–93, Coin News Yearbook 1993–, Medal News Yearbook 1994–, Stamp Yearbook 1996–; publisher of books on postal history 1976–90, contrib to over 100 periodicals worldwide on philately, numismatics and applied and decorative arts 1959–; tstee James Currie Meml Tst 1988–, sec Burns-Gaelic Tst 1992–; chm Advsy Bd International Burns Suppers Ltd 1992–; Spellman Fndn Silver-Gilt medal for philatelic lit 1982, 1986 and 1990, Thomas Field award for servs to Irish philately 1982; *Books* 160 incl: A Guide to the Uists (1961–67), Commonwealth Stamp Design (1965), Modern Coins (1969), Airmails 1870–1970 (1971), The World of Classic Stamps (1972), Turn of the Century Antiques (1974), Robert Bruce, King of Scots (1974), Rural Crafts in Scotland (1976), Encyclopaedia of World Stamps (1976), Dictionary of Western Sculptors in Bronze (1977), Stamp Collecting (1980), Numismatics (1982), The Burns Federation 1885–1985 (1985), The Complete Works of Robert Burns (ed, 1986, 2 edn 1991), The Complete Letters of Robert Burns (ed, 1987, 2 edn 1991), History of Dumfries (1990), Coin Collecting (1991), Making Money Made Simple (with Noel Whittaker, 1991), Burns (1992, Scottish Book of the Year 1993), Kilmarnock (1992), Coin Facts and Feats (1992), Vagabond of Verse: A Life of Robert W Service (1995), William Wallace: Brave Heart (1995), Allan Pinkerton: The Eye Who Never Slept (1996), Michael Collins (1996); *Recreations* travel, learning languages, playing the piano, photographing post offices; *Style—* Dr James Mackay; ✉ 67 Braidpark Drive, Giffnock, Glasgow G46 6LY (☎ 0151 633 5422)

McKAY, Dr John Henderson; CBE (1987), DL (Edinburgh 1988); s of Thomas Johnstone McKay (d 1956), of Pumpherston, Midlothian, and Patricia Madeleine, *née* Henderson (d 1986); *b* 12 May 1929; *Educ* West Calder HS, Open Univ (BA, PhD); *m* 8 Feb 1964, Catherine Watson, da of William Middleton Taylor (d 1968), of Edinburgh; 1 s (Ewen b 1969), 1 da (Charis b 1965); *Career* Nat Serv RA 1950–52, gunner UK and Far East; Customs & Excise 1952–85; Lord Provost of Edinburgh 1984–88, JP Edinburgh 1984, Lord Lt Edinburgh 1984–88; chm Edinburgh Int Festival Soc 1984–88, co-chm Edinburgh Mil Tattoo 1984–88, convener Business Ctee of Gen Cncl Univ of Edinburgh 1992–96; cncllr Royal Caledonian Hort Soc 1974–77 and 1984–88 (sec and treas 1988–92, vice pres 1993–96); chm: Scottish Working People's History Tst 1992–, Edinburgh Quartet Tst 1995–; Dr hc Univ of Edinburgh 1989; *Recreations* golf, gardening; *Clubs* Lothianburn Golf; *Style—* Dr John McKay, CBE, DL; ✉ 2 Buckstone Way, Edinburgh EH10 6PN (☎ 0131 445 2865)

McKAY, Michael J (Mike); s of James Lyon McKay (d 1980), of Birmingham, and Mary Florence, *née* Meek; *b* 26 March 1943; *Educ* Great Barr Sch Birmingham; *m* 1969, Patricia Ann, da of Horace Leggett; 2 c (Katie, Sean (twins) b 30 March 1970); *Career* reporter various newspapers 1960–68 (incl Gloucestershire Echo, Sheffield Telegraph, Daily Mirror); BBC Radio News: Manchester 1968–70, reporter on The World at One, PM, News Desk and news bulletins London 1970–72; with BBC Televison News 1972–, covered Turkish War in Cyprus, the Troubles in Northern Ireland, Chad rebellion, Red Brigades' kidnap and murder of Aldo Moro in Italy, Papal visits to Poland, Ireland and France, Iran-Iraq war, US Embassy siege in Iran, miners' strike in N of England; BBC North of England correspondent 1989–, covered Strangeways Prison riot, Hillsborough football ground disaster, Lockerbie and M1 aeroplane crashes, James Bulger search and murder trial; RTS Home News Award for coverage of Strangeways riot 1990; *Recreations* walking, theatre, cinema, golf, books, travel; *Style—* Mike McKay, Esq; ✉ BBC Broadcasting Centre, Woodhouse Lane, Leeds, W Yorkshire LS2 9PX (☎ 0113 244 1188)

MACKAY, Neil Douglas Malcolm; s of Gp Capt Malcolm Bruce Mackay (d 1971), and Josephine Mary, *née* Brown (d 1965); *b* 28 Aug 1939; *Educ* Loretto; *m* 10 May 1969, Frances Sarah, da of Lt-Col Claude Dudgeon van Namen (d 1991); 2 s (Loudon b 1971, Rory b 1982), 2 da (Kirsty b 1973, Lorna b 1976); *Career* Lt RA BAOR; merchant banker; Indust Reorganisation Corporation 1967–68; Lazard Bros & Co Ltd: asst dir 1974–78, exec dir 1979–93, md 1987–91, non-exec dir 1994–; non-exec dir of other cos incl: Tridant Group Printers Ltd 1974–79, R & AG Crossland Ltd 1975–78, Hadson Petroleum International plc 1981–86, Aaronite Group plc 1983–86, Lamont Holdings PLC 1993–, Incepta Group plc 1994–; *Recreations* bridge, shooting, tennis; *Clubs* Hurlingham; *Style—* Neil D M Mackay, Esq

McKAY, Neil Stuart; s of Roy McKay (d 1989), and Alison Maud, *née* Dent; *b* 19 Feb 1952; *Educ* Dame Allan's Boys' Sch Newcastle upon Tyne; *m* 17 Aug 1978, Deirdre Mary, da of Patrick Francis McGinn; 2 s (Sean Francis b 6 Jan 1981, Joseph Anthony b 8 Oct 1983); *Career* clerical offr trainee Univ of Newcastle HMC 1970–72, asst hosp sec Dunston Hill Hosp Gateshead 1972–74, admin asst Gateshead AHA 1974–75, hosp admin Dryburn Hosp Durham 1975–76, commissioning offr St George's Hosp London 1978–80 (asst sector admin 1976–78), planning admin Wandsworth Health Authy 1980–82, hosp admin Springfield Hosp London 1982–85, gen mangr Doncaster Royal Infirmary 1985–88, gen mangr Northern Gen Hosp Sheffield 1988–91, chief exec Northern Gen Hosp NHS Tst 1991–96, regional dir Trent Regional Office NHS Executive 1996–; DipHSM; *Recreations* family pursuits, reading, sport (including following Sunderland AFC); *Style—* Neil McKay, Esq; ✉ NHS Executive Trent, Fulwood House, Old Fulwood Road, Sheffield S10 3TH (☎ 0114 263 0300, fax 0114 282 0367)

MACKAY, Prof Norman; s of Donald Mackay (d 1937), of Glasgow, and Catherine, *née* Macleod (d 1957); *b* 15 Sept 1936; *Educ* Govan HS, Univ of Glasgow (MB ChB, MD); *m* 10 Feb 1961, (Grace) Violet, da of Charles McCaffer (d 1959), of Kilwinning; 2 s (Ronald b 8 Sept 1967, Donald b 30 Dec 1970), 2 da (Susan b 28 July 1962, Violet b 24 July 1964); *Career* hon conslt physician Victoria Infirmary Glasgow 1989– (conslt 1973–89), dean of postgrad med and prof of postgrad med educn Univ of Glasgow 1989–; Royal Coll of Physicians and Surgeons Glasgow: hon sec 1973–83, visitor 1992–94, pres 1994–; hon sec Conf of Royal Med Colls and Faculties in Scotland 1982–91; pres Southern Med Soc 1989–90; hon: FACP, FRACP, FCPC; FRCP, FAMS, FRCPGlas, FRCPE, FRCSEd, FRCGP, FCPSP; *Recreations* soccer, golf, gardening; *Style—* Prof Norman Mackay; ✉ 4 Erskine Ave, Dumbreck, Glasgow G41 5AL (☎ 0141 427 0900); Department of Postgraduate Medical Education, The University, Glasgow G12 8QQ (☎ 0141 339 3786, fax 0141 330 4526)

MACKAY, Peter; CB (1993); s of John Swinton Mackay, FRCS (d 1993), of Kinnoir, Aberdeenshire, and Patricia May, *née* Atkinson (d 1976); *b* 6 July 1940; *Educ* Glasgow HS, Univ of St Andrews (MA); *m* 29 Aug 1964, Sarah White, da of Reginald White Holdich (d 1992), of Cherry Burton, East York; 1 s (Andrew), 2 da (Elspeth, Sally); *Career* teacher Kyogle HS NSW Aust 1962–63, asst princ Scottish Office 1963, princ private sec to Sec of State of Scotland Rt Hon Gordon Campbell, MC and Rt Hon William Ross, MBE 1973–75, Nuffield Travelling fell (Canada, Aust, NZ) 1978–79, seconded dir Scotland Manpower Servs Cmmn 1983–85; under sec: Dept of Employment 1985–86, Scottish Educn Dept 1987–89 (responsible for further and higher educn arts and sport); princ estab offr Scottish Office 1989, sec and chief exec Scottish Office Industry Dept 1990–95; exec dir Advanced Mgmnt Programme in Scotland 1995–; non-exec dir: Wise Group Glasgow 1995–, British Linen Bank Group 1996–; memb: Univ Ct Napier Univ Edinburgh 1995–, Bd Scottish Agric Coll 1995–, Monopolies and Mergers Cmmn 1996–; tstee Scottish Maritime Museum 1996–, patron Nat Museums of Scotland 1996–; Hon LLD Robert Gordon Univ Aberdeen 1996; *Recreations* high altitudes and latitudes, climbing, sea canoeing, sailing, tennis; *Clubs* Clyde Canoe, Lothian Sea Kayak, Scottish Arctic; *Style—* Peter Mackay, Esq, CB; ✉ 6 Henderland Rd, Edinburgh EH12 6BB (☎ and fax 0131 337 2830); c/o Scottish Financial Enterprise, 91 George Street, Edinburgh EH2 3ES (☎ 0131 225 6990, fax 0131 220 1353)

MACKAY, Shena; da of Benjamin Carr Mackey, of Ardrossan, and Morag, *née* Carmichael; *b* 6 June 1944; *Educ* Tonbridge Girls' GS, Kidbrooke Comp; *m* 1964 (m dis), Robin Francis Brown; 3 da (Sarah Frances b 11 March 1965, Rebecca Mary b 21 Aug 1966, Cecily Rose b 15 May 1969); *Career* author; awarded: Arts Cncl grants 1970s, travelling scholarship Soc of Authors 1986, Fawcett prize 1987, Scottish Arts Cncl Book award 1992 and 1994; memb: PEN, ALCS, The Writers' Guild, London Arts Bd; *Books* Dust Falls on Eugene Schlumburger (1964), Toddler on the Run (1964), Music Upstairs (1965), Old Crow (1967), An Advent Calendar (1971), Babies in Rhinestones (1983), A Bowl of Cherries (1984), Redhill Rococo (1986), Dreams of Dead Women's Handbags (1987), Dunedin (1992), The Laughing Academy (1993), Such Devoted Sisters (ed, 1993), Collected Stories (1994), The Orchard on Fire (1996); *Style—* Shena Mackay; ✉ Rogers Coleridge & White Ltd, 20 Powis Mews, London W11 1JN (☎ 0171 221 3717, 0171 229 9084)

McKAY, William Robert; CB (1996); s of William Wallace McKay (d 1987), of Edinburgh, and Margaret Halley Adamson, *née* Foster; *b* 18 April 1939; *Educ* Trinity Acad Leith, Univ of Edinburgh (MA); *m* 28 Dec 1962, Rev Margaret Muriel McKay, da of Eric Millard Bellwood Fillmore, OBE (d 1995), of Bexhill on Sea, Sussex; 2 da (Catriona Margaret (Mrs Benedict Curtis) b 4 March 1967, Elspeth Mary (Mrs Timothy Sagar) b (twin) 4 March 1967); *Career* Dept of the Clerk of the House of Commons 1961–, clerk Scot Affrs Ctee 1971–74 and 1979–81, sec House of Commons Cmmn 1981–84, princ clerk Fin Ctees 1985–87, sec Public Accounts Cmmn 1985–87; jt clerk Br-Irish Inter-Parly Body 1989–94, clerk of the Jls 1987–91, clerk of Public Bills 1991–94, clerk asst 1994–; interim clerk designate Scot Assembly 1978; *Books* Erskine May's Private Journal 1883–86 (ed, 1984), Mr Speaker's Secretaries (1986), Clerks in the House of Commons 1363–1989 a Biographical List (1989), Observations, Rules and Orders (ed, 1989); *Recreations* living on Coll; *Style—* William McKay, Esq, CB; ✉ 1 Howe Hall Cottages, Littlebury Green, Saffron Walden, Essex CB11 4XF; Lochan a'Bhaigh, Isle of Coll, Argyll; House of Commons, London SW1A OAA

MACKAY-DICK, Maj Gen Iain C; MBE; *Educ* Sherborne, RMA Sandhurst; *m* 1971, Carolynn; 3 da (Alexandra b 1972, Georgina b 1975, Olivia b 1979); *Career* cmmnd Scots Gds 1965, served as Platoon Cdr 1 Bn Scots Gds Borneo, platoon instr Gds Depot Pirbright 1967–69, Mortar Platoon Cdr 2 Bn Münster 1969–70, served Windsor and N Ireland 1970–71, JDSC 1971, Adj 1 Bn 1971 (served Windsor, N Ireland and Germany), Co Cdr 2 Bn until 1974 (served Pirbright and N Ireland), Adj New Coll Sandhurst 1974–76, Army Staff Coll course 1976–78, Co Cdr 2 Bn Scots Gds Münster 1978–79, Bde Maj (COS) 3 Infantry Bde Portadown 1979–81, 2 i/c 2 Bn Scots Gds 1981–82 (served Falklands War), memb Directing Staff Army Staff Coll 1982–84, CO 2 Bn 1984–86 (served Cyprus), Cmdt Jr Div Staff Coll 1986–88, Higher Cmd and Staff Course Staff Coll 1989, CO 11 Armd Bde Minden 1989–91, Dep Mil Sec (A) MOD London 1991–92, GOC 1 Armd Div Germany 1992–93, Cdr Br Forces Falkland Is 1993–94, GOC London Dist and Maj Gen cmdg Household Div 1994–; memb Guards Golfing Soc; FIMgt; *Recreations* military history, walking, all forms of sport (Army squash champion 1971); *Clubs* Cavalry and Guards, Edinburgh Angus, Jesters; *Style—* Maj Gen I C Mackay-Dick, MBE; ✉ HQ Household Division, Horse Guards, Whitehall, London SW1A 2AX (☎ 0171 414 2331, fax 0171 414 2462)

MACKAY OF ARDBRECKNISH, Baron (Life Peer UK 1991), of Tayvallich in the district of Argyll and Bute; John Jackson MacKay; PC (1996); s of Jackson MacKay (d 1964), of Tayvallich, Argyll, and Jane, *née* Farquharson; *b* 15 Nov 1938; *Educ* Univ of Glasgow (BSc, DipEd); *m* 1961, Sheena, da of James Wagner (d 1963), of Bishopton, Renfrewshire; 2 s (Hon David Ferguson b 1967, Hon Colin James b 1969), 1 da (Hon Fiona Jackson b 1964); *Career* former head Maths Dept Oban HS; MP (C): Argyll 1979–83, Argyll and Bute 1983–87; PPS to George Younger as Sec of State for Scotland 1982; Parly under sec of state Scot Office with responsibility for: Health and Social Work 1982–85, Health Social Work and Home Affrs 1985–86, Educn Agric and Fisheries 1986–87; chief exec Scot Cons Pty 1987–90, chm Sea Fish Industry Authority 1990–93; memb until 1993: Select Ctee on the European Communities, Sub-Ctee B of EC Ctee on Energy, Industry & Tport, Delegated Powers Scrutiny Ctee; a Lord in Waiting (Govt whip) 1993–94, under-sec of state for transport 1994, min of state DSS 1994–; *Recreations* fishing, sailing; *Style—* The Rt Hon Lord Mackay of Ardbrecknish, PC; ✉ Innishail, 51 Springkell Drive, Pollokshields, Glasgow G41 4EZ (☎ 0141 427 5356)

MACKAY OF CLASHFERN, Baron (Life Peer UK 1979), of Eddracchillis in the District of Sutherland; James Peter Hymers Mackay; PC (1979); s of James Mackay (d 1958); *b* 2 July 1927; *Educ* George Heriot's Sch Edinburgh, Univ of Edinburgh, Trinity Coll Cambridge; *m* 1958, Elizabeth Gunn Hymers, da of D D Manson; 1 s (Hon James b 1958), 2 da (Hon Elizabeth Janet (Hon Mrs Campbell) b 1961, Hon Shona Ruth b 1968); *Career* advocate 1955, QC Scot 1965; sheriff principal Renfrew and Argyll 1972–74, vice dean Faculty of Advocates 1973–76, dean 1976–79; cmmr Northern Lighthouses 1975–84, pt/t memb Scottish Law Cmmn 1976–79, dir Stenhouse Holdings Ltd 1976–77, memb Insur Brokers' Registration Cncl 1977–79; Lord Advocate of Scotland 1979–84, Lord of Session 1984–85, Lord of Appeal in Ordinary 1985–87, Lord Chllr 1987–; Elder Bros Trinity House 1990; chllr Heriot-Watt Univ 1991–; Hon LLD: Dundee 1983, Edinburgh 1983, Strathclyde 1985, Aberdeen 1987, St Andrews 1988, Cambridge 1989; Hon Dr of Laws Coll of William and Mary 1989; hon fell: Trinity Coll Cambridge 1979, Girton Coll Cambridge 1989, Univ of Newcastle upon Tyne 1990, Univ of Birmingham; Hon Freeman Worshipful Co of Woolmen; fell Int Acad of Trial Lawyers 1979, hon FTII 1983, FRSE 1984, hon FICE 1989, hon FRCSEd 1989, hon FRCPEd; *Clubs* New (Edinburgh); *Style*— The Rt Hon the Lord Mackay of Clashfern, PC; ✉ House of Lords, London SW1A 0PW

MACKAY OF DRUMADOON, Baron (Life Peer UK 1995), of Blackwaterfoot in the District of Cunninghame; Donald Sage Mackay; PC (1996), QC (Scot 1987); s of Rev Donald George Mackintosh Mackay (d 1991), of Edinburgh, and Jean Margaret, *née* McCaskie, of Edinburgh (d 1994); *b* 30 Jan 1946; *Educ* George Watson's Boys Coll Edinburgh, Univ of Edinburgh (LLB, LLM), Univ of Virginia (LLM); *m* 5 April 1979, Lesley Ann, da of late Edward Waugh; 2 da (Hon Caroline b 7 Sept 1980, Hon Diana b 19 Aug 1982), 1 s (Hon Simon b 20 Jan 1984); *Career* apprentice slr Davidson & Syme CS Edinburgh 1969–71, slr Allan McDougall & Co SSC Edinburgh 1971–76, called to the Scottish Bar 1976, advocate depute 1982–85, Slr Gen for Scotland 1995, Lord Advocate for Scotland 1995–; memb Criminal Injuries Compensation Bd 1989–95; *Recreations* golf, Isle of Arran; *Clubs* Western (Glasgow); *Style*— The Rt Hon Lord Mackay of Drumadoon, PC, QC; ✉ 39 Hermitage Gardens, Edinburgh EH10 6AZ (☎ 0131 447 1412); Crown Office, 25 Chambers Street, Edinburgh EH1 1LA (☎ 0131 226 2026); Lord Advocate's Chambers, 2 Carlton Gardens, London SW1Y 5AA (☎ 0171 210 1030)

McKEAN, Prof Charles Alexander; s of John Laurie McKean, of Glasgow, and Nancy Burns, *née* Lendrum; *b* 16 July 1946; *Educ* Fettes Coll Edinburgh, Univ of Bristol (BA); *m* 18 Oct 1975, Margaret Elizabeth, da of Mervyn Yeo, of Cardiff; 2 s (Andrew Laurie b 1978, David Alexander b 1981); *Career* ed London Architect 1970–75; architectural corr: The Times 1977–83, Scotland on Sunday 1988–90; RIBA: London regnl sec 1968–71, Eastern regnl sec 1971–79, projects offr Community Architecture and Industl Regeneration 1977–79; sec and treas RIAS 1979–94, prof of architecture and head of sch Duncan of Jordanstone Coll Univ of Dundee 1994–; memb Exhibitions Panel Scottish Arts Cncl 1980–83, dir Workshops and Artists Studios Ltd 1980–85, sec to the RIAS Hill House Tst 1979–82, tstee Thirlestane Castle Tst 1983–, memb Environment and Town Planning Ctee The Saltire Soc 1984–85, memb Advsy Cncl for the Arts in Scotland 1985–88; currently memb Cncl Architectural Heritage Soc of Scotland, convenor Buildings Ctee Nat Tst for Scotland, former vice chm Charles Rennie Mackintosh Soc, former memb Advsy Ctee Edinburgh Common Purpose; Architectural Journalist of the Year 1979 and 1983, Building Journalist of the Year 1983, RSA Bossom Lecture 1986; hon memb The Saltire Soc 1990; Hon DLitt RGU 1994; FRSA 1978, FSA (Scot) 1983, Hon FRIBA 1990, Hon FRIAS 1994; *Books* London 1981 (1970), Modern Buildings in London 1965–75 (with Tom Jestico, 1975), Living over the Shop (1976), Battle of Styles (with David Atwell, 1976), Funding the Future (1977), Fight Blight (1977), An Outine of Western Architecture (jtly, 1980), Architectural Guide to Cambridge and East Anglia since 1920 (1980), Edinburgh - an Illustrated Architectural Guide (1982), Dundee - an Illustrated Introduction (with David Walker, 1984), Stirling and the Trossachs (1985), The Scottish Thirties (1987), The District of Moray (1987), Central Glasgow (with Prof David Walker and Prof Frank Walker), Banff and Buchan (1990), For a Wee Country (1990), Edinburgh - Portrait of a City (1991), Dundee (with Prof D Walker, 1993), West Lothian (with Richard Jacques, 1994); *Clubs* Scottish Arts; *Style*— Prof Charles McKean; ✉ 10 Hillpark Rd, Edinburgh EH4 (☎ 0131 336 2753); Duncan of Jordanstone College, University of Dundee, 13 Perth Road, Dundee DD1 4HT (☎ 01382 345260)

McKEAN, Douglas; CB (1977); s of Alexander McKean (d 1962), of Enfield, and Irene Emily, *née* Ofverberg (d 1980); *b* 2 April 1917; *Educ* Merchant Taylors', St John's Coll Oxford (MA); *m* 1, 6 June 1942, Anne (d 1994), da of Roger Clayton (d 1954), of Riding Mill, N'mberland; 2 s (Robert b 1944, Andrew b 1948); m 2, 8 Sept 1995, Joyce, wid of Alan Beslee; *Career* Civil Serv: princ WO 1947–49, HM Treasy 1949–77 (asst sec 1956–62, under sec 1962–77, on loan to DOE 1970–72); dir Agric Mortgage Corp 1978–87; dep sec Central Bd of Fin C of E 1978–83, tstee Irish Sailors and Soldiers Land Tst 1980–, govr Whitelands Coll Roehampton 1984–89; *Books* Money Matters - A Guide to the Finances of The Church of England (1987); *Recreations* mountain walking; *Clubs* Utd Oxford and Cambridge Univ; *Style*— Douglas McKean, Esq, CB; ✉ 66 Graeme Road, Enfield, Middlesex EN1 3UT (☎ 0181 363 5438)

McKEAN, Lorne; da of Lt Cdr J A H McKean, RN (d 1981), and Beatrice Blanche Mowbray *née* Bellairs (d 1991); *b* 16 April 1939; *Educ* Elmhurst Ballet Sch, Guildford Art Sch, Royal Acad Schs; *m* 7 Nov 1964, Edwin John Cumming Russell, s of Edwin Russell; 2 da (Rebecca b 21 Jan 1966, Tanya b 25 April 1968); *Career* sculptor; public and large works include: A A Milne memorial London Zoo Bear Club, Shearwaters Richmond, Arctic Terns Chester Business Park, Willoughby House Fountain Richmond, Girl and the Swan Reading, Herons Thames Water Authy Reading, Osprey Fountain Greenwich Connecticut USA, Great Swan Great Swan Alley EC2, Swan Fountain Horsham; equestrian and horse sculptures: HRH Prince Philip on his polo pony, HM The Queen's personal Silver Wedding gift to her husband, Prince Charles on polo pony Pans Folly, John Pinches International Dressage Trophy, Galoubet French show jumping stallion, pony series for Royal Worcester Porcelain, racehorses Troy and Snurge; portraits include: the late Lord Salisbury (Hatfield House), Sir Michael Redgrave, HRH the late Prince William of Gloucester, the Earl of Lichfield televised for portrait series, HM The Queen, Drapers' Hall and RHHT; FRBS 1968; *Recreations* animals; *Style*— Miss Lorne McKean; ✉ Lethendry, Polecat Valley, Hindhead, Surrey GU26 6BE (☎ 01428 605655)

McKEAN, Roderick Hugh Ross (Roddy); *b* 13 March 1956; *Educ* The HS of Dundee, Univ of Edinburgh (LLB Hons); *Career* articled clerk W & J Burness, WS 1978–80; admitted slr 1980; asst slr: Maclay Murray and Spens 1980–84, Lovell White & King 1984–88; ptnr Lovell White Durrant 1988–; memb: Law soc, Law Soc of Scotland; *Recreations* skiing, tennis, yachting, riding, golf; *Clubs* Royal London Yacht, Royal Corinthian Yacht, Woking Golf; *Style*— Roddy McKean, Esq; ✉ Lovell White Durrant, 65 Holborn Viaduct, London EC1A 2DY (☎ 0171 236 0066, fax 0171 248 4212, telex 887122)

MacKEAN, His Hon Judge Thomas Neill; s of Andrew Neill MacKean (d 1979), of Southampton, and Mary Dale, *née* Nichol (d 1974); *b* 4 March 1934; *Educ* Sherborne, Trinity Hall Cambridge (BA); *m* 20 Oct 1962, Muriel Sutton, da of late Rev Gwynne Hodder; 4 da (Sarah b 15 Aug 1963, Elizabeth b 30 Nov 1964, Jane b 14 July 1966, Margaret b 2 Jan 1972); *Career* articled to Messrs White & Leonard Slrs London 1954–57, ptnr Hepherd Winstanley & Pugh Slrs Southampton 1960–93 (sr ptnr 1988–93), recorder W Circuit 1992–93, circuit judge (Western Circuit) 1993–; HM coroner Southampton & New Forest 1990–93; pres: Hampshire Incorporated Law Soc 1985, Southern Rent Assessment Panel & Tbnl 1983–88; *Style*— His Hon Judge MacKean

MACKECHNIE, John Allan; s of Allan Mackechnie (d 1986), and Christina Johan, *née* Mackenzie (d 1985); *b* 19 Aug 1949; *Educ* Hyndland Sr Secdy Sch, Glasgow Sch of Art (DA), Faculty of Art & Design Brighton Poly; *m* 28 June 1976, Susan Shirley, da of William Ian Burnett; 1 da (Kirsty Joanne Louise b 25 Feb 1978); *Career* printmaker; printmaking asst: Faculty of Art & Design Brighton Poly 1972–73, Faculty of Art & Design Newcastle Poly 1973–76; Glasgow Print Studio: etching technician 1978–79, workshop mangr 1980–82, dir 1983–95; visitng lectr to art colls throughout UK; memb Soc of Scottish Artsists 1984– (memb Ctee 1989), memb Advsy Bd Bradford Int Print Biennale 1990–91, memb Steering Ctee Glasgow Art Fair, memb Ctee Glasgow Visual Art Forum, advisor on printmaking to Northern Regn over last ten years, major contrib to Glasgow's yr as 1990 European city of Culture through exhbns and artists exchanges and projects; *Exhibitions* incl: Young Generation (Norrkoping Museum Sweden) 1974, Epinal Biennale France 1975, Bradford Int Print Biennale 1976, 30 Contemporary Printmakers (Arnolfini Gallery Bristol) 1976, World Print Competition (Museum of Modern Art San Francisco) 1977, Impressions (Scottish Arts Cncl tour) 1978, Scottish Print Open (touring UK and Australia) 1980, solo exhbn Third Eye Centre Glasgow 1981, solo exhbn Richard Demarco Gallery Edinburgh 1981, Northern Printmakers (Gallery F15 Norway) 1982, Ljubljana Print Biennale Slovenia 1983, New Scottish Prints (touring Scotland, USA and Canada) 1983, Photography in Printmaking Glasgow Print Studio 1983, solo exhbn Edinburgh Printmakers Workshop 1983, Scottish Prints Open tour 1984, Society of scottish Artists 1984 and 1985, The Clyde Exhibition Glasgow Print Exhibition 1986; *Awards* Glasgow Educnl Tst award 1971, Northern Arts major award 1976 and 1978, Scottish Arts Cncl travel award 1982, Arts Cncl Incentive Funding award for Glasgow Print Studio 1989; *Public Collections* incl: Scottish Arts Cncl, Hunterian Museum & Art Gallery, Museum of Modern Art San Francisco, Norrkoping Museum Sweden, Aberdeen Art Gallery, Br Cncl, V&A, Kelvingrove Museum and Art Gallery; *Recreations* the visual arts, golf; *Style*— John Mackechnie, Esq; ✉ Glasgow Print Studio, 22 King Street, Glasgow G1 5QP (☎ 0141 552 0704, fax 0141 552 2919)

McKEE, Dr Angus Hugh; s of William Bissett McKee, of Glasgow, and Alice, *née* Ingram (d 1995); *b* 12 Feb 1946; *Educ* Buckhaven HS, Univ of Edinburgh (BSc, MB ChB); *m* 18 Oct 1980, Ruth Fraser, da of Alec McBain (d 1978), of Douglas, Lanarkshire; *Career* sr registrar in anaesthetics (former sr house offr, registrar) W Infirmary Glasgow 1972–77, conslt anaesthetist Stobhill Hosp Glasgow 1977–; church elder and covenanter ldr W Glasgow New Church; FRCA 1974; *Recreations* hill walking, preaching; *Style*— Dr Angus McKee; ✉ 526 Anniesland Rd, Glasgow G13 1YA (☎ 0141 954 1992); Stobhill General Hospital, Balornock Rd, Glasgow (☎ 0141 201 3000)

McKEE, Maj Sir (William) Cecil; kt (1959), ERD (1945); s of W B McKee; *b* 13 April 1905; *Educ* Methodist Coll, Queen's Univ Belfast; *m* 1932, Florence Ethel Irene Gill; 1 da; *Career* served WWII RA; estate agent; Lord Mayor of Belfast 1957–59, JP Belfast 1957; Hon LLD Queen's Univ Belfast; KStJ; *Style*— Maj Sir Cecil McKee, ERD, JP; ✉ 250 Malone Rd, Belfast, N Ireland (☎ 01232 666979)

McKEE, His Hon Judge; John; RD (1968, and Bar 1972), QC (1974); s of Frank McKee (d 1980), and Mollie, *née* Millar (d 1994); *b* 18 May 1933; *Educ* Strathallan Sch Scotland, Queen's Univ Belfast (BA, LLB); *m* 1962, Annette, da of W Howard Wilson (d 1957); 2 s, 1 da; *Career* RNR 1952–73, Lt-Cdr; called to the Bar: NI 1960 (sr barr 1974), Middle Temple 1971, King's Inns Republic of Ireland 1975; chm UK Delgn to CCBE 1979–81, Co Court judge NI 1981–, bencher Inn of Ct NI 1995–; pres: Industl Tbnls NI 1981–89, Industl Ct NI 1981–89; *Recreations* golf; *Clubs* Ulster Reform (Belfast), Royal County Down Golf, Royal Portrush Golf, Ringladdy Cruising; *Style*— His Hon Judge McKee, QC; ✉ c/o Northern Ireland Court Service, Windsor House, Bedford Street, Belfast BT2 7LT

McKEE, Prof (James Clark St Clair) Sean; s of James Roy Alexander McKee (d 1996), and Martha (Martie) Beattie, *née* Chalmer; *b* 1 July 1945; *Educ* George Watson's Coll Edinburgh, Univ of St Andrews (class medal, Duncan medal, BSc), Univ of Dundee (PhD), Univ of Oxford (MA, DSc); *m* 1970 (m dis 1996), Hilary Ann Frances, da of William Bidgood; *partner* Joyce Lloyd; *Career* National Cash Register fell Univ of Dundee 1970–72, lectr in numerical analysis Univ of Southampton 1972–75; Univ of Oxford: CEGB sr research fell 1975–79, co-ordinator univ consortium for industl numerical analysis 1979–86; head of mathematics and statistics Unilever Research Colworth and prof of industl mathematics Univ of Strathclyde 1986–88, prof of mathematics Univ of Strathclyde 1988–; fell Hertford Coll Oxford 1975–86; ed: IMA Jl of Mathematics Applied to Business and Industry, Mathematical Engrg in Industry, Applied Mathematics and Computation, Applied Mathematical Modelling, Fasciculi Mathematici; Inst of Mathematics and its Application (IMA): fell, memb Cncl, chm Scottish Branch; fndr memb and memb Cncl Euro Consortium for Mathematics in Industry (ECMI); memb: US Soc for Industl and Applied Mathematics, Edinburgh Mathematical Soc, Sociedade Brasilieira de Matemática Applicada e Computacional, American Mathematical Soc; FRSE 1996; *Books* Industrial Numerical Analysis (1986), Vector and Parallel Computing (1989), Artificial Intelligence in Mathematics (1990); also author proceedings the Third European Conference on Mathematics in Industry (1990); *Recreations* golf, gardening, hill walking, squash; *Clubs* Royal Soc of Edinburgh; *Style*— Prof Sean McKee, FRSE; ✉ North Craighall Farm, Jackton, Nr East Kilbride, Scotland G75 8RR; Department of Mathematics, University of Strathclyde, Glasgow G1 1XH (☎ 0141 552 4400 ext 3671)

McKEE, Dr William James Ernest; s of John Sloan McKee (d 1974), of Pontefract, Yorks, and Annie Emily *née* McKinley (d 1971); *b* 20 Feb 1929; *Educ* Queen Elizabeth's Wakefield, Trinity Coll Cambridge (BA, MA, MB BChir, MD, LRCP, MRCS), Queen's Coll Oxford, The Radcliffe Infirmary; *m* Josée, da of Francis James Tucker (d 1975), of Cardiff; 3 da (Jennifer b 1958, Katherine b 1963, Fiona b 1971); *Career* Nat Serv RAF Educn Serv 1947–49; clinical and res hosp appts 1952–61, community med appts with London RHB 1961–69, sr admin MO Liverpool RHB 1969–74; regnl MO: Mersey RHA 1974–76, Wessex RHA (regnl med advsr) 1976–89; contrib to med jls on various subjects; memb: Hunter Working Pty on the Future Arrangements for Med Admin and Public Health in the NHS 1972–73, Sec of State's Advsy Ctee on the Application of Computing Sci to Med and the NHS 1973–76; chm Jt Liaison Ctee for Health Serv Boundary Reorganisation in Met Co of Merseyside 1974; memb: Cncl for Postgrad Med Educn (Eng and Wales) 1975–85, Bd of Faculty of Med Univ of Southampton 1976–89; chm Working Pty to Review Health Serv Policy for the Mentally Handicapped in Wessex 1978, memb DHSS Advsy Ctee on Med Manpower Planning 1982–85, chm Eng Regnl Med Offrs 1984–86, UK med rep to Hosp Ctee of the EEC 1985–89, memb DHSS Jt Planning Advsy Ctee 1985–89, head UK delgn to Hosp Ctee of EEC 1988 and 1989, conslt various State Bds and Depts of Health 1989–; QHP 1987–90; FFCM 1972; *Recreations* fly fishing, golf; *Style*— Dr William McKee; ✉ Morningdale, 22A Bereweeke Ave, Winchester, Hants SO22 6BH (☎ 01962 861369)

McKEE, William Stewart; *Educ* Bangor GS, Queen's Univ Belfast (BSc), Ulster Poly (Dip in Mgmnt Studies, MBA); *m* Ursula Catherine; 1 da (Catherine b 1 April 1987), 1 s (William b 27 June 1990); *Career* VSO teacher W Africa 1970–71, student Queen's Univ Belfast 1971–75, summer vacational student Conservation Branch NI Dept of the

Environment 1973, 1974, 1975 and 1976, clerical offr Belfast City Cncl 1975–76, nat admin trainee NI Staffs Cncl for the Health and Social Servs 1976–78, sr admin offr Lisburn Health Centre and Dist Offices Eastern Health & Social Servs Bd 1978–79, units admin Daisy Hill Hosp Southern Health & Social Servs Bd 1979–82; Eastern Health & Social Servs Bd: units admin Ulster Hosp 1982–84, gp admin Musgrave Park Hosp 1984–88, gp admin Royal Gp of Hosps 1988–90, unit gen mangr Royal Gp of Hosps 1990–92, chief exec Royal Gp of Hosps and Dental Hosp HSS Tst 1992–; former chm NI Div Inst of Health Servs Mgmnt; memb Business Strategy Gp Business in the Community and Belfast City Partnership Bd; *Style*— William S McKee, Esq; ✉ Chief Executive, Royal Group of Hospitals Trust, Royal Victoria Hospital, Grosvenor Road, Belfast BT12 6BA (☎ 01232 894755, fax 01232 240899)

McKELL, Iain Spiers; s of Joseph Duncan McKell, and Gwendoline Helen McKell; *b* 18 April 1957; *Educ* Clifton, Exeter Coll of Art and Design (SIAD dip); *Career* fashion, advertising and editorial photographer since 1981, commercials director since 1993; early career as seaside photographer (summer holidays) 1975–79, subsequent experience in record sleeve photography 1982; fashion and portrait cmmns for Italian and English Vogue (Most Promising Newcomer 1982), ID and The Face, portrait cmmns for The Sunday Times and Observer magazines; subjects incl Madonna (her first magazine cover), Gilbert & George, Bob Hoskins, Sinead O'Connor, Boy George, Jilly Cooper, Tom Sharp, Jeremy Irons and Sir John Gielgud; photographic advtg campaigns incl: Red Stripe 1986, Holsten Export 1988, Vladivar Vodka and Corona Lemonade 1990, Levis (UK and Europe) 1991, Philip Morris (Germany) and Dunhill 1992; other work incl: photographer and creative dir for Pineapple Fashion 1988–90, direction of Post Modern links for MTV (USA, UK and Europe) 1990; solo and gp exhbns incl: Skinheads (Camera Obscura, Germany) 1981, Iain McKell Live (Open Day Studio Show) 1984, Iain McKell Live and Five Years of The Face 1985, Fashion and Surrealism (V&A Museum) 1987, Creative Future Awards (cmmnd by Direction magazine) 1988, BA sponsored exhbn (touring NY, Chicago, Los Angeles, Hong Kong, Tokyo and Sydney) 1989, Magnificent Seven 1992; memb: AFAEP, NUJ; *Recreations* skiing, photography, drawing, writing; *Clubs* Soho House; *Style*— Iain McKell, Esq; ✉ c/o Robert Montgomery & Partners, 3 Junction Mews, London W2 (☎ 0171 439 1877)

McKELLEN, Sir Ian Murray; kt (1991), CBE (1979); s of Denis Murray McKellen (d 1964), of Bolton, Lancs, and Margery Lois, *née* Sutcliffe (d 1952); *b* 25 May 1939; *Educ* Wigan GS, Bolton Sch, St Catharine's Coll Cambridge (BA, hon fell 1982); *Career* actor and director since 1961; dir: Liverpool Playhouse 1969, Watford and Leicester 1972, A Private Matter (Vaudeville) 1973, The Clandestine Marriage (Savoy) 1975; assoc dir RNT; pres Marlowe Soc 1960–61, memb Cncl Equity 1971–72, Cameron Mackintosh prof of contemporary theatre Univ of Oxford 1991; Hon DLitt: Nottingham 1989, Aberdeen 1993; *Theatre* first stage appearance A Man for all Seasons (Belgrade Theatre Coventry) 1961, Arts Theatre Ipswich 1962–63, Nottingham Playhouse 1963–64, first London stage appearance A Scent of Flowers 1964 (Duke of York's (Clarence Derwent Award)); RNT incl: Much Ado About Nothing (at Old Vic) 1965, Venice Preserv'd, Wild Honey (also Los Angeles & NY (Olivier Award, Plays and Players Award)) 1986–87, Coriolanus 1984–85 (London Standard Award), Kent in King Lear and title role in Richard III 1990 (Olivier Award (assoc prodr for world tour 1990–91)), Napoli Milionaria 1991, Uncle Vanya 1992, Richard III (USA tour) 1992; as assoc dir prodr and performer: The Duchess of Malfi, The Real Inspector Hound with The Critic, The Cherry Orchard (Paris and Chicago), Bent 1990 (also Garrick); RSC incl: Dr Faustus (Edinburgh Festival and Aldwych) 1974, Marquis of Keith (Aldwych) 1974–75, King John (Aldwych) 1975, Too Good to be True (Aldwych and Globe) 1975, Romeo and Juliet, The Winter's Tale, Macbeth 1976–77 (Plays and Players Award 1976), Pillars of the Community (SWET Award 1977), Days of the Commune, The Alchemist (SWET Award 1978); prodr RSC tour 1978: Three Sisters, Twelfth Night, Is There Honey Still for Tea, Iago in Othello (The Other Place, Stratford and Young Vic 1989, BBC TV (Evening Standard and London Critics' Award)); Acting Shakespeare tours: Israel, Norway, Denmark, Sweden 1980, Spain, NYC (Drama Desk Award) 1983, San Francisco, Washington DC, Los Angeles, Olney, Cleveland, San Diego, Boston (Elliot Norton Award) 1987, Playhouse London 1987–88; Actors Company (fndr memb): Ruling The Roost, 'Tis Pity She's a Whore (Edinburgh Festival) 1972, Knots, Wood-Demon (Edinburgh Festival) 1973 and with King Lear (Brooklyn Acad of Music, Wimbledon Theatre season) 1974; other roles incl: A Knight Out (Lyceum Theatre, NYC, South Africa and UK tour), The Recruiting Officer, A Lily in Little India (St Martin's), Man of Destiny/O'Flaherty VC (Mermaid), Their Very Own and Golden City (Royal Court) 1966, The Promise (Fortune, also Broadway) 1967, White Lies/Black Comedy (Lyric), Richard II 1968 (Prospect Theatre Co (revived with Edward II Edinburgh Festival UK and Euro tours)), Chips with Everything (Cambridge Theatre Co) 1971, Hamlet 1971 (Cambridge, Br and Euro tours), Ashes (Young Vic) 1975, Words, Words, Words (solo recital, Edinburgh and Belfast Festivals) 1976, Acting Shakespeare (Edinburgh and Belfast Festivals) 1977, Bent 1979 (Royal Court, Criterion (SWET Award 1979)), Amadeus 1980–81 (Broadhurst NY (Drama Desk, NY Drama League, Outer Critics' Circle and Tony Awards)), Short List (Hampstead) 1983, Cowardice (Ambassadors) 1983, Henceforward (Vaudeville) 1988; *Television* since 1966 incl: Walter 1982 (RTS Performance Award 1982), Walter and June 1983, Countdown to War 1989, And the Band Played On 1992 (Emmy nomination 1994), Cold Comfort Farm 1994; *Films* since 1968 incl: A Touch of Love, The Promise, Alfred the Great, Priest of Love, Scarlet Pimpernel, Plenty, Zina, Scandal 1988, The Ballad of Little Jo 1992, I'll Do Anything 1992, Last Action Hero 1993, Six Degrees of Separation 1993, The Shadow 1993, Jack and Sarah 1994, Restoration 1994, Richard III 1995, Rasputin (Emmy Award nomination 1996) 1995, Amy Foster 1996, Bent 1996; *Style*— Sir Ian McKellen, CBE; ✉ c/o ICM Ltd, Oxford House, 76 Oxford Street, London W1N 0AX (☎ 0171 636 6565, fax 0171 323 0101); c/o ICM, 8942 Wilshire Boulevard, Beverly Hills, CA 90211–1934, USA (☎ 001 310 550 4000, fax 001 310 550 4100)

McKELVEY, Air Cdre John Wesley; CB (1969), MBE (1944); s of Capt John Wesley McKelvey, of Enfield, Middx (d 1939), and Emily Francis Louisa, *née* Milsted (d 1976); *b* 25 June 1914; *Educ* Enfield Central Sch, RAF Aircraft Apprentice; *m* 13 Aug 1938, Eileen Amy, da of John Charles Carter, of Enfield (d 1968); 2 s (John b 1943, d 1969, Michael b 1944); *Career* Fighter Cmd 1932–38, cmmnd 1941 (Eng branch), served Egypt, Syria, Iraq, Bomber Cmd 1939–45, OC Air Miny Manpower Res Unit 1945–47, OC Air Miny Servicing and Devpt Unit 1947–49, RAF Staff Coll 1949; engr duties: FEAF 1949–52, HQ Bomber Cmd 1952–54; Jt Servs Staff Coll Latimer 1954, OC no 60 Maintenance Unit 1954–56; sr tech SO: HQ no 19 Gp 1956–57, Task Force Grapple Christmas Is 1957–59; sr air SO HQ no 24 Gp 1959–62, dep dir of intelligence (tech) 1962–64, dir aircraft and asst attaché Defence Res Devpt Br Embassy Washington DC 1964–66, AO Wales and Cmdt RAF St Athan 1966–69, ret 1969; sec appeals RAF Benevolent Fund 1970–79; MRAeS 1967, CEng 1968; *Recreations* bowls, gardening; *Clubs* RAF; *Style*— Air Cdre John McKelvey, CB, MBE; ✉ Inchmerle, 19 Greensome Drive, Ferndown, Dorset BH22 8BE (☎ 01202 894464)

McKELVEY, William; MP (Lab) Kilmarnock and Loudoun (majority 6,979); *b* 1934; *Educ* Morgan Acad, Dundee Coll of Technol; *m*; 2 s; *Career* former full-time union official, memb Dundee City Cncl, joined Lab Pty 1961; MP (Lab): Kilmarnock 1979–83, Kilmarnock and Loudon 1983–; sponsored by AUEW; chm Select Ctee on Scottish Affrs; *Style*— William McKelvey, Esq, MP; ✉ 41 Main Street, Kilmaurs, Ayrshire; House of Commons, London SW1A 0AA (☎ 0171 219 3000)

McKENNA, Charles; s of John George McKenna (d 1987), and Bernadette, *née* Conney; *b* 9 April 1954; *Educ* St Bede's GS Lanchester Co Durham, Univ of Durham (BA); *m* 30 May 1986, Alison Jane, da of John Fearn; *Career* admitted slr 1978; ptnr Allen & Overy 1985– (articled clerk, asst slr 1978–85), seconded as legal advsr in Quotations Dept The Stock Exchange 1981–82; Freeman Worshipful Co of Slrs 1986; memb Law Soc 1978; *Recreations* sport, travel; *Style*— Charles McKenna, Esq; ✉ Allen & Overy, One New Change, London EC4M 9QQ (☎ 0171 330 3000, fax 0171 330 9999)

McKENNA, David; CBE (1967, OBE 1946, MBE 1943); s of Rt Hon Reginald McKenna (d 1943), and Pamela Margaret, *née* Jekyll (d 1943); *b* 16 Feb 1911; *Educ* Eton, Trinity Coll Cambridge (BA, MA); *m* 4 April 1934, Lady Cecilia Elizabeth Keppel, da of 9 Earl of Albemarle, MC (d 1979); 3 da (Miranda (Mrs John Villiers) b 10 Aug 1935, Primrose (Mrs Christopher Arnander) b 9 May 1937, Sophia b 11 June 1944); *Career* WWII RE Capt 1939, Maj 1942, Lt-Col 1944 Transportation Serv Iraq, Turkey, India, Burma; London Passenger Tport Bd 1934–39 and 1946–55, asst gen mangr Southern Region BR 1955–61, chief commercial offr HQ 1962, gen mangr S Region 1963–68, memb bd BR 1968–76 (pt/t memb bd 1976–78); dir Isles of Scilly Steamship Co 1976–92; chm: Govrs of Sadler's Wells 1962–76, Bach Choir 1968–76 (memb 1934–76); memb Dover Harbour Bd 1969–80, vice pres RCM 1980 (memb Cncl 1946); Liveryman Worshipful Co of Musicians; FRCM, FCIT (pres 1972); Commandeur de l'Ordre Nationale du Mérite (France) 1974; *Recreations* music; *Clubs* Brooks's, Royal Cornwall Yacht; *Style*— David McKenna, Esq, CBE; ✉ Rosteague, Portscatho, Truro, Cornwall TR2 5EF (☎ 01872 580346)

McKENNA, Paul William; s of William Joseph McKenna, of Enfield, Middx, and Joan Brenda, *née* Garner; *b* 8 Nov 1963; *Educ* St Ignatius Coll Enfield, PhD in clinical hypnosis; *Career* hypnotist, entertainer and television presenter; disc jockey: Radio Caroline 1984, breakfast show Chiltern Radio 1985–87, Capital Radio 1988–91, BBC Radio 1 1991–92; first hypnotic show 1986, appeared at numerous major venues incl Royal Albert Hall 1992, TV debut Paul McKenna's Hypnotic Show (special then series, Carlton) 1993, series The Hypnotic World of Paul McKenna (Celador Productions and Paul McKenna Productions for Carlton/ITV Network) 1994–, presenter Network First factual prog Paul McKenna's Hypnotic Secrets (Man Alive Group and Paul McKenna Productions for Carlton) 1995, series The Paranormal World of Paul McKenna (Man Allive Group and Paul McKenna Productions for Carlton) 1996, special The World's Funniest Hypnotist (ABC) 1996; also recorded set of audio and video hypnotherapy tapes; chm Br Cncl of Professional Stage Hypnotists 1990–92, memb Fedn of Ethical Stage Hypnotists (FESH); *Awards* TRIC Celebrity Award for New Talent of the Year 1994, Capital Radio Best London Show award for Paul McKenna's Hypnotic Show 1994; *Books* The Hypnotic World of Paul McKenna (1993), Paul McKenna's Hypnotic Secrets (1996); *Style*— Paul McKenna, Esq; ✉ PO Box 5514, London W8 4ZY

McKENNA, Virginia Anne; da of Terence Morell McKenna (d 1948), and Anne-Marie (Anne de Nys, the music composer), *née* Dennis (who m (2) Jack Drummond Rudd and (3) Sir Charles Richard Andrew Oakeley, 6 Bt, and d 1993); *b* 7 June 1931; *Educ* Herschel Capetown SA, Herons Ghyll Horsham, Central Sch of Speech and Drama; *m* 1 1954 (m dis 1957), Denholm Mitchell Elliot, CBE (d 1992), the actor; m 2, 19 Sept 1957, William Inglis Lindon (Bill) Travers, MBE (d 1994), the actor, s of William Halton Lindon Travers (d 1966); 3 s (William Morrell Lindon b 4 Nov 1958, Justin McKenna Lindon b 6 March 1963, Daniel Inglis Lindon b 27 Feb 1967), 1 da (Louise Annabella Linden b 6 July 1960); *Career* actress and writer; co-fndr The Born Free Fndn (formerly Zoo Check Charitable Tst) 1984; patron: Elizabeth Fitzroy Homes, Slade Centre, Dorking Operatic Soc, Plan International UK (formerly World Family), Dorking Hospice Homecare, Earthkind (formerly Crusade), Children of the Andes 1991, Wildlife Aid 1991, The Surrey Badger Protection Soc 1996; Freeman City of Houston Texas 1966; *Theatre* incl: season Old Vic 1955–56, The Devils 1961, Beggars Opera 1963, A Little Night Music 1976, The King and I (SWET Award for Best Musical Actress), Hamlet (RSC) 1984; *Films* incl: The Cruel Sea 1952, A Town Like Alice 1954 (Academy Award for Best Actress), Carve Her Name With Pride (Belgian Prix Femina) 1957, Born Free (Variety Club Award for Best Actress) 1964, Ring of Bright Water 1968; *Television* incl: Romeo and Juliet (Best Actress Award ITV) 1955, Passage to India 1965, The Deep Blue Sea 1974, Cheap in August; *Books* On Playing with Lions (with Bill Travers), Some of my Friends have Tails, Beyond the Bars (jt ed and jt author), Headlines from the Jungle (anthology of verse, co-ed, 1990), Into the Blue (1992); audio book of The Butterfly Lion (by Michael Morpurgo); *Recreations* reading, travelling, gardening; *Style*— Miss Virginia McKenna; ✉ The Born Free Foundation, Coldharbour, Surrey RH5 6HA (☎ 01306 712091, fax 01306 713350)

MACKENZIE, *see:* Muir Mackenzie

MACKENZIE, Angus Alexander; s of Kenneth Mackenzie (d 1958), of Drumine, Gollanfield, Inverness-shire, and Christina, *née* Mackinnon (d 1966); *b* 1 March 1931; *Educ* Inverness Royal Acad, Univ of Edinburgh; *m* 31 March 1959, Catherine, da of Murdo Maclennan (d 1971), of Sand Gairloch, Ross-shire; 1 da (Margaret Jane b 1960); *Career* Nat Serv RAF 1955–57; qualified CA 1955, own practice 1961–; currently sr ptnr Angus Mackenzie & Co Inverness; chm Highland Gp Riding for the Disabled Assoc, sec and treas Highland Field Sports Fair, chm Highland Hospice 10 Anniversary Appeal Ctee; MICAS 1955; *Recreations* shooting, stalking, hill walking, and gardening; *Clubs* Highland Inverness; *Style*— Angus Mackenzie, Esq; ✉ Tigh-An-Allt, Tomatin, Inverness-shire (☎ 01808 511270); Redwood, 19 Culduthel Rd, Inverness (☎ 01463 235353, fax 01463 235171)

McKENZIE, Dr Christopher Gurney; s of Benet Christopher McKenzie (d 1984), and Winifred Grace, *née* Masterman (d 1984); *b* 3 Jan 1930; *Educ* Douai Sch, Univ of London (MB BS); *m* 12 Oct 1963, Barbara Mary Kinsella, da of James Quirk (d 1983); 2 s (James b 1966, Richard b 1972), 1 da (Caroline b 1964); *Career* Nat Serv in Dental Branch RAF (Flt Lt) 1953–55; Maj RAMC (Sr Specialist Surgery) 1967–70; conslt in clinical oncology Hammersmith Hosp, sr lectr Royal Postgrad Med Sch 1974–95, ret; hon conslt: St Mary's Hosp Paddington, the Central Middlesex Hosp; LDSRCS 1951, FRCS 1962, DMRT 1972, FRCR 1974; *Books* author of many articles and chapters on med subjects; *Recreations* sailing, opera; *Clubs* Cruising Assoc; *Style*— Dr Christopher G McKenzie

MACKENZIE, Colin; s of Hector Colin Beardmore Mackenzie, of Thame, Oxon, and Frances Evelyn, *née* Purkis; *b* 4 Nov 1945; *Educ* Eastbourne Coll; *m* 19 Oct 1968, Fiona Maureen, *née* Barr; 2 da (Rebecca Ann b 7 April 1975, Elizabeth Fiona b 21 Dec 1976); *Career* chartered surveyor; Hampton & Sons: Mayfield E Sussex 1974–80, Sevenoaks Kent 1980–85, Country House Dept London 1985–87, md Country House and Estates Depts 1987–; FRICS, FSVA; *Recreations* fishing, shooting; *Style*— Colin Mackenzie, Esq; ✉ Hamptons, 6 Arlington Street, St James's, London SW1A 1RB (☎ 0171 493 8222, fax 0171 491 3541, car 0836 269758)

McKENZIE, Dr Dan Peter; s of William Stewart McKenzie, and Nancy Mary McKenzie; *b* 21 Feb 1942; *Educ* Westminster, King's Coll Cambridge (BA, MA, PhD); *m* 5 June 1971, Indira Margaret; 1 s (James Misra b 3 April 1976); *Career* Univ of Cambridge: sr asst in res 1969–75, asst dir of res 1975–79, reader in tectonics 1979–84, currently Royal Soc res prof Dept of Earth Scis; Hon MA Univ of Cambridge 1966; memb Royal Soc 1976, foreign assoc US Nat Acad of Scis 1989; Balzan Prize of Int Balzan Fndn (with F J Vine and D H Matthews, 1981), Japan Prize Sci and Technol Fndn of Japan (with W J Morgan and X Le Pichon, 1990), Royal Medal of the Royal Soc 1991; *Publications* author of various papers in learned journals; *Recreations* gardening; *Style—* Dr Dan McKenzie; ✉ Bullard Laboratories, Madingley Road, Cambridge CB3 0EZ

McKENZIE, Justice Donald Cameron Moffat; s of John McKenzie (d 1975), of Perth, and Jessie Cameron Creelman, *née* Moffat (d 1989); *b* 3 March 1934; *Educ* St Ninian's Cathedral Sch, Balhousie Boys' Sch, Perth Commercial Sch, Queen's Coll; *m* 29 June 1967, Patricia Janet, da of Ernest Russell Hendry (d 1974), of Dundee; 2 da (Alison b 1968, Evelyn b 1972); *Career* accountant Trinity Coll Glenalmond 1966–70, bursar Corp of High Sch Dundee 1970–80; co cncllr magistrate social work and health convener Perth 1971–75, co cncllr Perth and Kinross 1971–75, justice District Court 1975; estate factor Pitlochry Estate Tst 1980, govr Dundee Coll of Educn, dir R Dundee Instn for the Blind; capt Soc of High Constables; memb: Justices Ctee, Prison Visiting Ctee; OStJ 1978; fell Inst of Fin Accountants 1976, FFA, FIMgt 1980; *Recreations* rifle shooting, cricket, music; *Style—* Justice Donald McKenzie; ✉ Balnacraig, Moulin, Pitlochry, Perths (☎ 01796 472591, Pitlochry Estate Office ☎ 01796 472114)

MacKENZIE, Hector Uisdean; s of George Campbell MacKenzie (d 1986), and Williamina Budge, *née* Sutherland (d 1957); *b* 25 Feb 1940; *Educ* Portree HS Isle of Skye, Leverndale Sch of Nursing, W Cumberland Sch of Nursing (Lindsay Robertson Gold Medal, RGN, RMN); *m* 1961 (m dis 1991), Anna Roberston Morrison, da of George Morrison; 3 da (Catriona b 20 Aug 1961, Ishbel Georgina, Morag Sutherland (twins) b 23 April 1963), 1 s (David Hector b 15 Jan 1973); *Career* student nurse Leverndale Hosp Glasgow 1958–61, asst lighthousekeeper Clyde Lighthouses Trust 1961–64, staff nurse W Cumberland Hosp Whitehaven 1966–69 (student nurse 1964–66); COHSE: regnl sec Yorks and E Midlands 1970–74 (asst regnl sec 1969–70), national offr 1974–83, asst gen sec 1983–87, gen sec 1987–93; associate gen sec UNISON 1993– (following merger of COHSE, NUPE and NALGO); co sec UIA (Insurance) Ltd 1996–; *Recreations* work, reading, aviation; *Style—* Hector MacKenzie, Esq; ✉ UNISON, Unison Centre, 1 Mabledon Place, London WC1H 9AJ (☎ 0171 388 2366, fax 0171 383 7218)

MACKENZIE, Lady Jean; *née* Leslie; CBE (1991); da of 20 Earl of Rothes (d 1975); *b* 26 Aug 1927; *m* 26 April 1949, Roderick Robin Mackenzie, s of Capt Roderick Kilgour Mackenzie (d 1937); *Career* chm: Nat Assoc of Youth Clubs 1959–65, Physically Handicapped & Able Bodied (PHAB) 1961–80 (fndr), Royal UK Beneficient Assoc 1985–91; *Style—* The Lady Jean Mackenzie, CBE; ✉ Kingfisher House, Ampfield, Romsey, Hants SO51 9BT

MACKENZIE, Gen Sir (John) Jeremy George; KCB (1992), OBE (1982); s of Lt-Col John William Elliot Mackenzie, DSO, QPM (d 1990), and Valerie Margaret, *née* Dawes; *b* 11 Feb 1941; *Educ* Duke of York Sch Nairobi Kenya; *m* 12 April 1969, Elizabeth Lyon (Liz), da of Col George Leftwich Wertenbaker, USAF (d 1986); 1 s (Edward John George b 17 May 1976), 1 da (Georgina Elizabeth b 8 July 1978); *Career* cmmnd 1 Bn Queen's Own Highlanders 1961, CO Queen's Own Highlanders 1979–82, Instr Staff Coll Camberley 1982–83, Col Army Staff Duties 2 MOD 1983, Cmd 12 Armd Bde (as Brig) 1984–87, Dep Cmdt Staff Coll Camberley 1987–89, Maj-Gen 1989, Cmdt Staff Coll Camberley 1989, GOC 4 Armd Div 1989–91, Lt-Gen 1991, cmd 1 British Corps Bielefeld 1991–92, cmd ACE NATO Rapid Reaction Corps (ARRC) Oct 1992–Dec 1994, Dep Supreme Cdr Allied Powers Europe (DSACEUR) Dec 1994–; memb Queen's Body Guard for Scotland (Royal Co of Archers) 1986–; Col Cmdt AGC 1992–, Col The Highlanders Regt 1994–; pres: Servs Branch Br Deer Soc, Combined Servs Winter Sports Assoc; *Recreations* shooting, fishing, watercolour painting; *Clubs* Army & Navy, Ferrari Owners'; *Style—* Gen Sir Jeremy Mackenzie, KCB, OBE; ✉ c/o Lloyds Bank, Cox & King's, PO Box 1190, 7 Pall Mall, London SW1Y 5NA

MACKENZIE, Rear Adm (David) John; CB (1983); s of David Mackenzie (d 1950), and Alison Walker, *née* Lawrie; *b* 3 Oct 1929; *Educ* Cargilfield Sch Edinburgh, RNC; *m* 1965, Ursula Sybil, da of Cdr Ronald Hugh Balfour, RN; 2 s (David, Alastair), 1 da (Rachel); *Career* joined RN cadet 1943–47, Midshipman 1947–48, Sub Lt 1950–51, Lt 1951–59, Lt Cdr 1959–65, promoted Cdr 1965, exec offr HMS Glamorgan 1965–67, Cdr Sea Trg 1967–70, CO HMS Hermione 1971, promoted Capt 1972, CO HMS Phoenix 1972–74, Capt F8 HMS Ajax 1974–76, dir Naval Equipment 1976–78; CO HMS: Blake 1978–79, Hermes 1979–80; promoted Rear Adm 1981; Flag Offr Gibraltar 1981–83; ret 1983; pres King George's Fund for Sailors (Scotland) 1996–; dir Atlantic Salmon Trust 1985–; fell Nautical Inst (former vice pres); memb Queen's Body Guard for Scotland (Royal Co of Archers); *Recreations* shooting, fishing; *Clubs* New (Edinburgh); *Style—* Rear Adm John Mackenzie, CB; ✉ Atlantic Salmon Tst, Moulin Pitlochry, Perthshire (☎ 01796 473439)

MACKENZIE, John Alexander Hugh Munro; s of John Mackenzie of Mornish, *qv*, and Eileen Louise Agate, *née* Shanks; *b* 16 Aug 1953; *Educ* Eton, Corpus Christi Coll Oxford; *Career* called to the Bar 1976; chm and md Sloane Graphics Ltd 1987–; dir: Tace plc 1981–91, SEET plc 1983–, London and Northern Group plc 1985–87, Kenneth Mackenzie Holdings Ltd 1988–, Justunit Ltd 1988–; Freeman: City of London 1975, Worshipful Co of Merchant Taylors; *Recreations* reading, smoking; *Clubs* Vincent's (Oxford), Wig & Pen; *Style—* John Mackenzie, Esq; ✉ SEET plc, Essex Hall, Essex Street, London WC2R 3JD (☎ 0171 836 9261, fax 0171 836 4859)

McKENZIE, John Cormack; s of William Joseph McKenzie and Elizabeth Frances Robinson; *b* 21 June 1927; *Educ* St Andrew's Coll, Trinity Coll Dublin (MA, MAI), Queen's Univ Belfast (MSc), Tadzhikistan Univ (DSc); *m* 1954, Olga Caroline Cleland; 3 s, 1 da; *Career* civil engr: McLaughlin & Harvey, Sir Alexander Gibb & Partners 1946–48; asst lectr Queen's Univ Belfast 1948–50; civil engr and md Edmund Nuttall Ltd 1950–82 (dir 1967–82), chm Nuttall Geotechnical Services Ltd 1967–82, dir British Wastewater Ltd 1978–82, md Thomas Telford Ltd 1982–90, dir H R Wallingford Ltd 1990–95; prem sec Inst of Civil Engrs 1982–90, vice pres Register of Engrs for Disaster Relief 1985–, sec gen WFEO 1987–, foreign sec Royal Acad of Engrg 1988–92, dep chm UK Ctee Int Decade for Natural Disaster Reduction 1989–92; pres Beaconsfield Advsy Centre 1978–; FEng 1984, FICE, FIEAus, FIEI, FRSA; *Publications* Research into Some Aspects of Soil Cement (1952), Engineers: Administrators or Technologists? (1971), Construction of the Second Mersey Tunnel (1972), Civil Engineering Procedure (3 edn, 1979), Mitigation of Wind Induced Disasters (1994), The Contribution of Engineers to the UN International Decade of Natural Disaster Reduction (1994), Sustainable Development and the Maintenance of Economic Viability (1994), Developments in the Application of Environmental Engineering and Sustainable Development (1994), Europe - Continuing Wealth Creation and Sustainable Development for Future Generations (1995), Continuing Wealth Creation and Sustainable Development for Future Generations (1995), International Application of Ethics for Engineers (Paris, 1996), To Save the World as We Know It (Buenos Aires, 1996), Accreditation (Beusnos Aires, 1996); *Recreations* philately, collecting ancient pottery, climbing; *Clubs* Athenaeum; *Style—* John McKenzie, FEng; ✉ 20 Ledborough Lane, Beaconsfield, Bucks HP9 2PZ (☎ 01494 675191)

McKENZIE, Prof John Crawford; s of Donald Walter McKenzie (d 1978), and Emily Beatrice, *née* Stracey (d 1992); *b* 12 Nov 1937; *Educ* LSE (BSc), Bedford Coll London (MPhil), Univ of London Inst of Educn (PGCE); *m* 5 Aug 1960, Ann; 2 s (Simon Andrew b 28 Feb 1964, Andrew John b 10 March 1966); *Career* princ: Ilkley Coll 1978, Bolton Inst of Higher Educn 1981; rector Liverpool Poly 1984; The London Institute: rector 1986–96, govr and dir of int devpt 1996–; visiting prof Univs of London and Newcastle; dir various cos; Chev dans l'Ordre des Arts et des Lettres (France) 1992; *Books* Changing Food Habits (ed, 1964), Our Changing Fare (ed, 1966), The Food Consumer (ed, 1987); *Recreations* collecting antiquarian books; *Clubs* Athenaeum, Chelsea Arts, Royal Society of Medicine; *Style—* Prof John McKenzie; ✉ The London Institute, 65 Davies Street, London W1Y 2AA (☎ 0171 495 3222)

McKENZIE, Julia Kathleen (Mrs Jerry Harte); da of Albion James Jeffrey McKenzie (d 1970), of Enfield, Middx, and Kathleen, *née* Rowe; *b* 17 Feb 1942; *Educ* Tottenham Co Sch, Guildhall Sch of Music and Drama; *m* 1972, Jerry Harte, s of Carl Harte; *Career* actress and director; FGSM 1985; *Theatre* West End and New York performances incl: Cowardy Custard, Miriam in Outside Edge, Lily Garland in On the Twentieth Century, Hobson's Choice, Schweyk in the Second World War, Miss Adelaide in Guys and Dolls (NT, winner Best Actress Variety Club and The Soc of West End Theatre Awards 1982), Sally in Follies, The Witch in Into the Woods, Company, Promises Promises, Mame, Side by Side (by Sondheim); Alan Ayckbourn plays incl: Norman Conquests, Ten Times Table, Communicating Doors), Woman in Mind (winner Best Actress London Evening Standard Awards 1986); Mrs Lovett in Sweeney Todd (RNT, winner Best Actress in a Musical Olivier Awards) 1994; theatre dir: Stepping Out (Duke of York's Theatre), Steel Magnolias (Lyric Theatre), Just So (Watermill Theatre Newbury), Merrily We Roll Along (staged concert, 1988), Putting it Together (NY and London); *Television* incl: Fame is the Spur, Dear Box Number, Those Glory Glory Days, Blott on the Landscape, Absent Friends, Hotel du Lac, Adam Bede, Hester in Fresh Fields and French Fields (voted Favourite Comedy Performer TV Times Viewers' Poll 1985, 1986, 1987 and 1989); *Films* incl: Gillian in Shirley Valentine, Mrs Jarley in Old Curiosity Shop; *Style—* Ms Julia McKenzie; ✉ c/o April Young Limited, 11 Woodlands Road, Barnes, London SW13 0JZ (☎ 0181 876 7030, fax 0181 878 7017)

MacKENZIE, Kenneth John; CB (1996); s of Capt John Donald MacKenzie (d 1967), of Milngavie, Dunbartonshire, and Elizabeth Pennant Johnston, *née* Sutherland (d 1985); *b* 1 May 1943; *Educ* Birkenhead Sch, Pembroke Coll Oxford (BA, MA), Stanford Univ California (AM); *m* 3 Sept 1975, Irene Mary, da of William Ewart Hogarth (d 1947), of Mayfield, Paisley, Renfrewshire; 1 s (John b 1977), 1 da (Mary b 1979); *Career* asst princ Scot Home & Health Dept 1965–70, private sec to Jt Parly Under Sec of State Scot Office 1969–70; princ: Regnl Devpt Div Scot Office 1970–73, Scot Educn Dept 1973–77; Civil Serv fell: Downing Coll Cambridge 1972, Dept of Politics Univ of Glasgow 1974–75; princ private sec to Sec of State for Scotland 1977–79; asst sec: Scot Econ Planning Dept 1979–83, Scot Office Fin Div 1983–85; princ fin offr Scot Office 1985–88, under sec Scot Home and Health Dept 1988–91, sec Scot Office Agriculture and Fisheries Dept 1992–95 (under sec 1991–92), dep sec Econ and Domestic Affairs Secretariat Cabinet Office 1995–; memb Agriculture and Food Research Cncl 1992–94, memb Biotechnology and Biological Sciences Research Cncl 1994–95; St Cuthbert's Parish Church Edinburgh: session clerk 1971–91, convenor Congregational Bd 1991–95; memb Edinburgh Civil Serv Dramatic Soc 1966– (hon pres 1989–95); *Style—* Kenneth MacKenzie, Esq, CB; ✉ Cabinet Office, 70 Whitehall, London SW1A 2AS (☎ 0171 270 0240, fax 0171 270 0057)

McKENZIE, Kenneth Stevenson; *b* 18 June 1953; *Educ* Trinity Sch Croydon, Univ of Exeter; *m* 1985, Jane Helen Bowden; 2 da (Jennifer 1985, Alice b 1989), 1 s (James b 1987); *Career* admitted slr 1978; Davies Arnold Cooper: joined 1978, litigation ptnr 1986–, currently jt head Litigation Dept; specialism incl insurance, reinsurance and professional indemnity; memb Law Soc 1978; *Publications* Chubb Directors & Officers Liability Guide on How to Minimise Risk (jtly); also author numerous articles; *Style—* Kenneth McKenzie, Esq; ✉ Davies Arnold Cooper, 6–8 Bouverie Street, London EC4Y 8DD (☎ 0171 936 2222, fax 0171 936 2020)

McKENZIE, Master; Michael; QC (1991); s of Robert McKenzie (d 1992), of Brighton, and Kitty Elizabeth, *née* Regan (d 1985); *b* 25 May 1943; *Educ* Varndean GS Brighton; *m* 19 Sept 1964, Peggy Dorothy, da of Thomas Edward William Russell, of Heathfield, E Sussex; 3 s (Justin Grant b 31 May 1968, Gavin John b 28 April 1971, Jamie Stuart b 14 Jan 1977); *Career* called to the Bar Middle Temple 1970, bencher Middle Temple 1993; dep clerk of the peace Middx Quarter Sessions 1970–72, dep courts admin Middx Crown Court 1972–73, courts admin NE Circuit (Newcastle) 1974–79, clerk of the Central Criminal Court 1979–84, dep circuit admin SE circuit 1984–86, asst registrar Court of Appeal Criminal Div 1986–88, Queen's Coroner and Attorney and Master of the Crown Office; registrar: of Criminal Appeals, of Courts Martial Appeal Court 1988–; Freeman City of London 1979; hon fell Univ of Kent 1991; FRSA 1990, memb NY Acad of Sci 1992; *Books* Butterworths Rules of Court (ed), Criminal Court Practice; *Recreations* Northumbrian stick dressing, fell walking, shooting; *Style—* Master McKenzie, QC; ✉ Royal Cts of Justice, Strand, London WC2A 2LL (☎ 0171 936 6108, fax 0171 936 6900)

MACKENZIE, Michael Philip Uvedale Rapinet; s of Brig M R Mackenzie, DSO (d 1985), of Mayfield, Sussex, and Vivienne, *née* Price; *b* 1937; *Educ* Downside, Lincoln Coll Oxford; *m* 1966, Jill, da of Charles Foweraker Beckley, of Chislehurst, Kent; 1 s (William b 1966), 1 da (Elizabeth b 1970); *Career* United Biscuits plc 1966–86; prodn dir of various businesses 1974–83, md DS Crawford Bakeries 1983–86; DG Food and Drink Fedn; FRSA 1988; *Clubs* Travellers; *Style—* Michael Mackenzie, Esq; ✉ Ebony Cottage, Ebony, nr Tenterden, Kent TN30 7HT; Food & Drink Federation, Catherine St, London WC2B 5JJ

MACKENZIE, Robert Stephen; s of Brig (Frederick) Stephen Ronald Mackenzie, OBE (d 1981), and Daphne Margaret, *née* Jickling (d 1993); *b* 12 Nov 1947; *Educ* Radley, RMA Sandhurst; *m* 24 Mar 1973, Amanda Clare, da of Lt Cdr Richard John Beverley Sutton; 1 s (Rupert b 1982), 1 da (Emily b 1977); *Career* serv Queen's Royal Irish Hussars; Allied Lyons 1978, md Badger Inns 1984– (dir 1983–); dir: Hall and Woodhouse, Heavitree Inns 1991–; *Recreations* riding; *Style—* Robert Mackenzie, Esq; ✉ Northfield House, Todber, Sturminster, Newton, Dorset (☎ 01258 820269); Badger Inns, The Brewery, Blandford, Dorset (☎ 01258 451462, fax 01258 451462, car 0468 145520)

MACKENZIE, Dr Sir Roderick McQuhae; 12 Bt (NS 1703), of Scatwell, Ross-shire; s of Capt Sir Roderick Edward François McQuhae Mackenzie, 11 Bt, CBE, DSC (d 1986), and Marie Evelyn Campbell, *née* Parkinson (d 1993); *b* 17 April 1942; *Educ* Sedbergh, King's Coll London, St George's Hosp (MB BS, MRCP (UK), FRCP (C), DCH); *m* 1970, Nadezhda (Nadine), da of Georges Frederic Leon Schlatter, Baron von Rorbas, of Buchs-K-Zurich, Switzerland; 1 s (Gregory Roderick McQuhae b 1971), 1 da (Nina Adelaïda b 1973); *Heir* s, Gregory Roderick McQuhae Mackenzie b 8 May 1971; *Recreations* classical music (violin, viola), riding (3–day eventing), skiing, wind-surfing; *Style—* Dr Sir Roderick Mackenzie, Bt; ✉ 2431 Udell Rd, Calgary NW, Alberta, Canada T2N 4H4

MACKENZIE, Ruth; OBE (1995); da of Kenneth Mackenzie, of Paris, and Myrna Blumberg, of London; *b* 24 July 1957; *Educ* South Hampstead HS, Sorbonne (dip), Newnham Coll Cambridge (MA); *Career* co fndr, dir and writer Moving Parts Theatre Co 1980–82, dir of Theatre in the Mill Univ of Bradford 1982–84, artistic dir Bradford Multicultural Festival Bradford Met Cncl 1983–84, drama offr with responsibility for theatre writing Arts Cncl of GB 1984–86, head of strategic planning South Bank Centre 1986–90, exec dir Nottingham Playhouse 1990–; chm Paines Plough Theatre Co, bd memb Dance 4, Exec Ctee Memb Common Purpose; memb: Arts Cncl Touring Bd and Lottery Bd, British Cncl Dance and Drama Panel; Hon DLitt Nottingham Trent Univ, Hon fell Univ of Nottingham; FRSA 1992; *Recreations* work; *Style—* Ms Ruth Mackenzie, OBE; ✉ Nottingham Playhouse, Wellington Circus, Nottingham NG1 5AF (☎ 0115 947 4361, fax 0115 947 5759)

MACKENZIE, Sheriff (Colin) Scott; DL (Western Isles 1975); s of Colin Scott Mackenzie (d 1971), of Stornoway, and Margaret Sarah Tolmie (d 1993); *b* 7 July 1938; *Educ* Nicolson Inst Stornoway, Fettes, Univ of Edinburgh (BL); *m* 1966, Christeen Elizabeth Drysdale, da of William McLauchlan (d 1968), of Tong, Isle of Lewis; *Career* admitted slr 1960; procurator fiscal Stornoway 1969–92, sheriff Grampian Highland and Islands at Kirkwall and Lerwick 1992–; clerk to the Lieutenancy 1974–92, dir Harris Tweed Assoc Ltd 1979–95, Vice Lord-Lt Western Isles 1984–92, memb Cncl Law Soc of Scotland 1985–92 (convenor Criminal Law Ctee 1991–92), kirk elder 1985, convener Church and Nation Ctee Presbytery of Lewis 1990–92, convenor Study Gp on Young People and the Media for General Assembly of the Church of Scotland 1991–93; FSA (Scot) 1995; *Recreations* fishing, boating, travel, amateur radio (GM7 RD0), private flying; *Clubs* RSAC (Glasgow), New (Edinburgh), Royal Northern and Univ (Aberdeen); *Style—* Sheriff C Scott Mackenzie, DL; ✉ Middlebank, Bells Road, Lerwick, Shetland (☎ 01595 695808); High Toft, Berstane Road, Kirkwall, Orkney (☎ 01856 876790); Park House, Matheson Rd, Stornoway, Western Isles (☎ 01851 702008); Sheriff Court House, King Erik St, Lerwick, Shetland ZE1 0HD

McKENZIE, Dr Sheila Agnes; da of Capt Raymond K McKenzie (d 1980), of Dollar, Scotland, and Agnes Muirhead, *née* Steel (d 1978); *b* 5 June 1946; *Educ* Dollar Acad, Univ of Edinburgh; *Career* conslt paediatrician Queen Elizabeth Hosp for Children London E2; regnl paediatric advsr Br Paediatric Assoc (RCP) 1988–95, advsr to Tushinskya Children's Hosp Moscow; MD, FRCP 1989, FRCPE; *Recreations* hill-walking, cultivation of old roses, photography; *Style—* Dr Sheila McKenzie; ✉ 69 Gordon Rd, London E18 1DT (☎ 0181 505 7481); An Sithean, Bonar Bridge, Sutherland (☎ 01863 766461); Queen Elizabeth Hospital for Children, Hackney (☎ 0171 739 8422)

MACKENZIE, Ursula Ann; Ian Alexander Ross Mackenzie, of Great Massingham, Norfolk, and Phyllis, *née* Naismith; *b* 11 Dec 1951; *Educ* Malvern Girls' Coll, Westlake Sch for Girls LA (ESU exchange scholar), Univ of Nottingham (BA, PhD); *children* 1 s (Matthew James Johnson b 1 Sept 1987); *Career* lectr in English and American literature Univ of Hong Kong 1976–79, International Scripts Literary Agency 1979–80, rights mangr Granada Publishing 1981–84; Transworld Publishers: editorial and rights mangr Bantam Press, editorial and rights dir 1985–88, publishing dir 1988–95, publisher of hardback books 1995–; *Style—* Ms Ursula Mackenzie; ✉ Transworld Publishers Ltd, 61–63 Uxbridge Road, London W5 5SA (☎ 0181 579 2652, fax 0181 579 5479)

MACKENZIE-GREEN, John Garvie; s of Jack Green (d 1990), of Malvern, Worcs, and Moira, *née* Garvie; *b* 28 April 1953; *Educ* Malvern, Guilford Law Sch; *m* 1976, Tessa Mary, *née* Batten; 2 s (Henry, William), 1 da (Claire); *Career* dir Fielding Insurance Holdings 1976–86, chm Heath Fielding Insurance Broking 1986–, gp md C E Heath plc 1990– (dir 1986–); MBIBA; *Recreations* sailing, skiing, rural gardening, shooting; *Clubs* Lloyds, HAC, Royal Western; *Style—* John Mackenzie-Green, Esq; ✉ C E Heath plc, 133 Houndsditch, London EC3A 7AH (☎ 0171 234 4000, fax 0171 234 4140)

MACKENZIE OF GAIRLOCH, *see:* Inglis of Glencorse

MACKENZIE OF MORNISH, John Hugh Munro; s of Lt-Col John Munro Mackenzie of Mornish, DSO, JP, Military Knight of Windsor (d 1964), of Henry VIII Gateway, Windsor Castle, and Etheldreda Henrietta Marie, *née* Taaffe (d 1965); The Mornish branch of the Mackenzie Clan are direct male descendants of the ancient feudal Barons of Kintail, chiefs of the Mackenzie Clan through the Mackenzies of Gairloch and the Mackenzies of Letterewe; *b* 29 Aug 1925; *Educ* Edinburgh Acad, Loretto, Trinity Coll Oxford (MA), Hague Academy of Int Law, Inns of Ct Law Sch, McGill Univ Montreal; *m* 20 June 1951, Eileen Louise Agate, da of Alexander Shanks, OBE, MC (d 1965); 5 s (John Alexander Hugh Munro, *qv*, b 1953, Charles b 1956, Cristin b 1959, Kenneth b 1961, d 1984, James b 1966), 1 da (Catriona b 1952); *Career* served Army 1942–47, Capt The Royal Scots (Royal Regt); War Serv: Europe, 1 KOSB, A Co, 9 Bde, 3 Inf Div (despatches, certs of gallantry), Far E HQ Allied Land Forces SE Asia and HQ Ceylon Army Cmd, Staff Capt Mil Sec's Branch; HM Guard of Honour Balmoral 1946, HQ 3 Auto Aircraft Div 1946–47, GSO III; Harmsworth law scholar Middle Temple 1950, called to the Bar Middle Temple 1950; trainee Utd Dominions Tst, legal asst Estates Dept ICI Ltd 1951; Hudson's Bay scholar 1952–53; buyer ICI 1953–54, co sec and legal advsr Trubenised (GB) Ltd and Assoc Cos 1955–56, gp devpt offr Aspro-Nicholas Ltd 1956–57, Knitmaster Holdings 1957, formed Grampian Holdings Ltd (mangr and sec) 1958 (md 1960); chm: London and Northern Group plc 1962–87, Tace plc 1967–91, SEET plc (formerly Scottish English and European Textiles plc) 1969–96, Pauling plc 1976–87, Goring Kerr plc 1983–91; eight Queen's Awards for Export won by gp cos; memb Worshipful Co of Farmers; FRSA, FIMgt; *Recreations* opera, bridge, shooting, fishing, field sports; *Clubs* Royal Automobile, Royal Scots (Edinburgh), New (Edinburgh); *Style—* John Mackenzie of Mornish; ✉ Mortlake House, Vicarage Rd, London SW14 8RU; Scaliscro Lodge, Uig, Isle of Lewis HS2 9EL; Shellwood Manor, Leigh, Surrey RH2 8NX; SEET plc, 16 Maddox Street, London W1R 1PL (☎ 0171 629 6759)

McKENZIE SMITH, Ian; OBE (1992); s of James McKenzie Smith (d 1977), of Aberdeen, and Mary, *née* Benzie (d 1989); *b* 3 Aug 1935; *Educ* Robert Gordon's Coll Aberdeen, Gray's Sch of Art Aberdeen (DA), Hospitalfield Coll of Art Arbroath; *m* 3 April 1963, Mary Rodger, da of John Fotheringham (d 1990); 2 s (Patrick John b 8 Aug 1966, Justin James b 4 Feb 1969), 1 da (Sarah Jane b 5 Jan 1965); *Career* artist; educn offr Cncl of Industl Design Scottish Ctee 1963–68, dir Aberdeen Art Gallery and Museums 1968–89, city arts and recreation offr City of Aberdeen 1989–96; sec Royal Scottish Acad 1991– (treas and dep pres 1990–91); memb: Scottish Arts Cncl 1970–77, Scottish Museums Cncl 1980–87, Nat Heritage Scottish GP 1983–, Nat Tst for Scotland Curatorial Ctee, Cncl Nat Tst for Scotland; tstee Scottish Sculpture Workshop; external assessor: Glasgow Sch of Art 1982–86, Duncan of Jordanstone Coll of Art 1982–86; govr: Edinburgh Coll of Art, Robert Gordon Univ Aberdeen; Hon LLD Aberdeen 1991; RSW 1981 (pres 1988–), FRSA 1973, FSS 1984, FMA 1988, FSA Scotland 1970; *Work in Permanent Collections* Scottish Nat Gallery of Modern Art, Scottish Arts Cncl, Arts Cncl of NI, Contemporary Art Soc, Aberdeen Art Gallery and Museums, Glasgow Art Gallery and Museums, Perth Art Gallery, Abbott Hall Art Gallery Kendal, Hunterian Museum Glasgow, Nuffield Foundation, Carnegie Tst, Strathclyde Educn Authy, Lothian Educn Authy, Edinburgh District Cncl, Royal Scottish Acad, DOE, Robert Fleming Holding, IBM; *Awards* Inst of Contemporary Prints Award 1969, RSA Guthrie Award 1971, RSA Gillies Award 1980, ESU Thyne scholarship 1980; *Clubs* Royal Northern (Aberdeen); *Style—* Dr Ian McKenzie Smith, OBE; ✉ 70 Hamilton Place, Aberdeen AB15 5BA (☎ and fax 01224 644531)

MACKENZIE-STUART, Baron (Life Peer UK 1988), of Dean in the City and County of Edinburgh; Alexander John Mackenzie Stuart; s of Prof Alexander Mackenzie Stuart, KC (d 1935), and Amy Margaret, er da of John Reid Dean, of Aberdeen; *b* 18 Nov 1924; *Educ* Fettes, Sidney Sussex Coll Cambridge (BA, hon fell 1977), Univ of Edinburgh (LLB); *m* 1952, Anne Burtholme, da of late John Sidney Lawrence Millar, WS, of Edinburgh; 4 da (Hon Amanda Jane (Hon Mrs Hay) b 29 April 1954, Hon Katherine Anne b 13 June 1956, Hon Laura Margaret b 27 March 1961, Hon Judith Mary (Hon Mrs Aspinall) b 14 May 1964); *Career* served RE 1942–47 (T/Capt 1946); admitted Faculty of Advocates 1951, QC (Scot) 1963, Keeper of the Advocates Library 1970–72; Standing Jr Counsel: Scottish Home Dept 1956–57, Inland Revenue in Scotland 1957–63; Sheriff-Princ of Aberdeen, Kincardine and Banff 1971–72, a senator of the College of Justice in Scotland (as Hon Lord Mackenzie Stuart) 1972, judge of the Court of Justice European Communities Luxembourg 1972–84 (pres 1984–88); govr Fettes Coll 1962–72; hon bencher: Middle Temple 1978, King's Inn Dublin 1983; hon memb Soc of Public Teachers of Law 1982, hon prof Collège d'Europe Bruges 1974–77; Hon DUniv Stirling 1973; Hon LLD: Exeter 1978, Edinburgh 1978, Glasgow 1981, Aberdeen 1983, Cambridge 1987, Birmingham 1988; awarded: Grand-Croix de l'Ordre Grand-Ducal de la Couronne de Chêne Luxembourg 1988, Prix Bech for servs to Europe 1989; FRSE 1991; *Books* Hamlyn Lectures - The European Communities and the Rule of Law (1977); A French King at Holyrood (1995); articles in legal publications; *Recreations* collecting; *Clubs* Athenaeum, New (Edinburgh); *Style—* The Lord Mackenzie-Stuart, FRSE; ✉ 7 Randolph Cliff, Edinburgh EH3 7TZ; Le Garidel, Gravières, 07140 Les Vans, France

McKEON, Andrew John; s of Kenneth McKeon, of Manchester, and Maurine, *née* Ilsley; *b* 22 Sept 1955; *Educ* William Hulme's GS Manchester, St Catharine's Coll Cambridge (scholar, BA); *m* 1989, Hilary, da of Rev G Neville; 1 s (Christopher b 26 Feb 1990), 1 da (Sarah b 28 Nov 1991); *Career* Dept of Health: joined 1976, various positions rising to private sec to Sec of State for Health 1988–90; currently head Primary Care NHS Executive; *Style—* Andrew McKeon, Esq; ✉ NHS Executive, Quarry House, Quarry Hill, Leeds LS2 7UE (☎ 0113 254 5811, fax 0113 254 6346)

McKEOWN, Allan John; s of Albert Victor McKeown (d 1977), and Edith Mabel Alice, *née* Humphries (d 1970); *b* 21 May 1946; *Educ* Beal GS for Boys; *m* 27 Dec 1983, Tracey Ullman, *qv*; 1 da (Mabel Ellen b 2 April 1986), 1 s (John Albert Victor b 6 Aug 1991); *Career* TV commercials prodr 1970, md James Garratt Ltd TV advtg prodn co 1971, md JGP Ltd London and NY 1972–73, fndr British Lion Productions Ltd and conslt Shepperton Studios 1973, chief exec Pembridge Productions 1974–76, in US 1976–79, fndr WitzEnd Productions Ltd (with Dick Clement and Ian La Frenais) 1979; SelecTV PLC: chief exec (following reverse takeover by WitzEnd) 1988–95, exec chm 1995–, fndr SelecTV subsids Alomo Productions (with Laurence Marks, *qv*, and Maurice Gran, *qv*) 1988, Clement La Frenais Productions (with Dick Clement and Ian La Frenais) 1989; co-fndr, dir of comedy programming and main bd dir Meridian Broadcasting 1991–; SelecTV group progs incl: Auf Wiedersehen Pet (exec prodr for WitzEnd, BAFTA Award nominated), Lovejoy (exec prodr for WitzEnd, US Cable Acad Award nominated), Tracey Ullman Takes On New York (exec prodr, Emmy nominated), Birds of a Feather (Alomo), Love Hurts (Alomo), Pie in the Sky (WitzEnd); memb: RTS, Acad of Television Arts and Sciences, BAFTA; *Recreations* golf, running, French food; *Clubs* Sunningdale Golf, Royal Dornoch Golf, Riviera Country; *Style—* Allan McKeown, Esq; ✉ SelecTV PLC, 6 Derby Street, London W1Y 7HD (☎ 0171 355 2868, fax 0171 495 3310)

McKEOWN, Dermot William; s of Ronald Hubert McKeown, of Dungannon, and Rosemary, *née* McMorran; *b* 16 Aug 1954; *Educ* Royal Sch Dungannon, Univ of Edinburgh (MB ChB); *m* 23 July 1976, (Margaret Janet) Laurie, da of Samuel Clinton, of Strathaven; 1 s, 2 da; *Career* SHO, registrar then sr registrar in anaesthetics Edinburgh 1978–84, sr registrar in anaesthesia and intensive care Flinders Med Centre SA 1985, conslt in anaesthesia and intensive care Royal Infirmary of Edinburgh 1986–; FFARCS 1981; *Style—* Dermot McKeown, Esq; ✉ 3 Merchiston Gardens, Edinburgh, Scotland EH10 5DD (☎ 0131 337 5967)

McKEOWN, John Wilson; s of John McKeown, and Sarah, *née* Black; *b* 17 April 1950; *Educ* Royal Belfast Academic Inst, Christ's Coll Cambridge (MA); *m* Lynn Fennah; 1 s (Christopher William John b 7 Aug 1983), 1 da (Rachel Sara Louise b 2 April 1978); *Career* formerly: dir Ind Coope Ltd, md Ind Coope & Allsopp Ltd, md Ansells Ltd; currently md Allied Domecq Inns (largest pub chain in UK); *Recreations* sport, politics; *Style—* John McKeown, Esq; ✉ Allied Domecq plc, 24 Portland Place, London W1N 4BB (☎ 0171 323 9000)

McKEOWN, Prof Patrick Arthur (Pat); OBE (1991); s of Robert Matthew McKeown (d 1978), and Bessie Augusta, *née* White (d 1993); *b* 16 Aug 1930; *Educ* Cambridge GS, Bristol GS, Cranfield Inst of Technol (MSc); *m* 1954, Mary Patricia, da of Donald S B Heath, of Bristol; 3 s (Alistair Jonathan b 1957, Jeremy Patrick b 1960, Nicholas William b 1963); *Career* student apprentice Bristol Aircraft Co 1951–54 (nat state scholar 1954), Coll of Aeronautics Cranfield 1954–56, works and tech dir Société Genevoise d'Instruments de Physique 1964–68 (joined 1956), dir Cranfield Unit for Precision Engrg 1968–95, prof of precision engrg Cranfield Inst of Technol (now Cranfield Univ) 1974–95 (emeritus prof 1995), chm Cranfield Precision Engineering Ltd 1992–96 (fndr chm and chief exec 1987–92), dir Pat McKeown and Associates (conslts in advanced mfrg, precision engrg and nanotechnology) 1995–; non-exec dir Control Techniques plc 1989–94; hon visiting prof Nanjing Aeronautical Inst People's Republic of China 1985, visiting prof of mechanical engrg Univ of California Berkeley March 1994; int advsr GINTIC Inst of Mfrg Technol Singapore 1991–; memb: Evaluation Ctee Nat Bureau of Standards USA 1980–86, Advanced Mfrg Technol Ctee DTI 1982–86, RCA Visiting Ctee 1984–87, UK Nanotechnology Strategy Ctee DTI/SERC 1987–94; pres CIRP (int acad for prodn engrg res) 1989–90; Fulbright prof of mechanical engrg Univ of Wisconsin Madison 1982, F W Taylor medal USA Soc of Mfrg Engrs 1983, Thomas Hawksley Gold medal IMechE 1987; Hon DSc: Univ of Connecticut 1996, Cranfield Univ 1996; FEng 1986, FIMechE, FIEE, Chartered Fell American Soc of Mfrg Engrs USA; *Recreations* music, theatre, walking; *Style—* Prof Pat McKeown, OBE, FEng; ✉ 37 Church End, Biddenham, Bedfordshire MK40 4AR (☎ 01234 267678, fax 01234 262560); School of Industrial and Manufacturing Science, Cranfield University, Cranfield, Bedfordshire MK43 0AL (☎ 01234 754024, fax 01234 752159)

McKERN, Leo Reginald; AO (1983); s of Norman Walton McKern (d 1969), of Sydney, and Vera Martin (d 1971); two McKern bros migrated to Sydney from Limerick (McKern Printing Works) in 1864; *b* 16 March 1920; *Educ* Sydney Technical HS; *m* 9 Nov 1946, Joan Alice (Jane Holland, actress), da of late Joseph Southall; 2 da (Abigail b 1955, Harriet b 1964); *Career* actor; engrg apprentice 1935–37, served AIF (Corp Engrs) 1940–42; first appearance Metropolitan Theatre Sydney (amateur) 1943, arrived England 1946; *Theatre* incl: The Miser, Arts Cncl tours, Nottingham Repertory Theatre, Love's Labour's Lost, She Stoops to Conquer, Hamlet, Old Vic New Theatre 1949, Feste in Twelfth Night (re-opening of Old Vic Theatre 1950), Bartholomew Fair, Henry V 1951, Merry Wives of Windsor, Electra, The Wedding, King Lear; Shakespeare Memorial Theatre Australian and NZ tour 1953: Iago in Othello, Touchstone in As You Like It, Glendower and Northumberland in Henry IV Pt 1; Stratford Season 1954: Ulysses in Troilus and Cressida, Grumio in Taming of the Shrew, Quince in A Midsummer Night's Dream, Friar Lawrence in Romeo and Juliet; Toad in Toad of Toad Hall (Prince's Theatre) 1954, Big Daddy in Cat on a Hot Tin Roof (Aldwych) 1958; title role in Rollo (Strand) 1959, the Common Man in a Man for All Seasons (Globe) 1960, Thomas Cromwell in A Man for All Seasons (Anta Theatre, NY) 1961; last season at Old Vic 1962–63: Peer Gynt, The Alchemist, Othello; title role in Volpone (Garrick) 1971; Melbourne Theatre Co 1971, Adelaide Festival (best actor); Shylock in The Merchant of Venice (Oxford Playhouse) 1973, title role in Uncle Vanya (Royal Exchange Manchester) 1978, Crime and Punishment, Rollo 1980, Boswell for the Defence 1989–90 (London, Melbourne, Sydney, Hong Kong Festival (best performance Victorian Green Room Award), Hobson's Choice (Chichester, Lyric) 1995; dir The Shifting Heart (Duke of York's) 1959; *Film* over 30 appearances incl: Murder in the Cathedral, A Man for all Seasons, Ryan's Daughter, The French Lieutenant's Woman, Travelling North, On Our Selection (Aust) 1994; *Television* appearances incl: King Lear, Monsignor Quixote, Rumpole of the Bailey (ITV series 1977–, Best TV Series Award 1984), The Master

Builder, The Last Romantics (BBC film on Sir Arthur Quiller-Couch), Veterans (BBC film, 1992), A Foreign Field (BBC) 1993; *Awards* Best Actor Award Montreal Film Festival and Australian Film Inst 1987, Best Actor (Film) Critics' Circle 1988; *Books* Just Resting (memoirs, 1983); *Recreations* sailing, photography, travel; *Clubs* The Sloane; *Style—* Leo McKern, Esq, AO; ✉ c/o Barclays, 211/213 Banbury Rd, Oxford OX2 7HH; c/o Richard Hatton Ltd, 29 Roehampton Gate, London SW15 5JR (☎ 0181 876 6699, fax 0181 876 8278)

MACKERRAS, Sir (Alan) Charles MacLaurin; kt (1979), CBE (1974); s of Alan Patrick Mackerras (d 1973), and Catherine Brearcliffe (d 1977); *b* 17 Nov 1925; *Educ* Sydney GS Aust, NSW Conservatorium of Music Aust, Acad of Music Prague; *m* 1947, Helena Judith, da of Frederick Bruce Wilkins (d 1961); 2 da; *Career* staff conductor Sadler's Wells Opera 1948–54, princ conductor BBC Concert Orch 1954–56, first conductor Hamburg State Opera 1966–69, musical dir ENO 1970–77, chief guest conductor BBC Symphony Orch 1976–79, associate artist ENO 1980–, chief conductor Sydney Symphony Orch 1982–85, princ guest conductor Royal Liverpool Philharmonic Orch 1985–87, musical dir Welsh Nat Opera 1987–92 (conductor emeritus 1992); princ guest conductor: Scottish Chamber Orch 1992–95 (conductor laureate 1995–), San Francisco Opera 1993–97, Royal Philharmonic Orch 1993–, Czech Philharmonic Orch 1997–; Hon DMus: Univ of Hull 1990, Univ of Nottingham 1991, Univ of York 1994, Masaryk Univ of Brno 1994, Griffith Univ Brisbane 1994; LRAM 1969, FRCM 1987; *Style—* Sir Charles Mackerras, CBE; ✉ 10 Hamilton Terrace, London NW8 9UG (☎ 0171 286 4047, fax 0171 289 5893)

McKERRELL OF HILLHOUSE, Charles James Mure; Baron of Dromin, Hereditary Keeper of Cashel; s of Capt Robert James Mure McKerrell of Hillhouse (d 1964), and Winifred Scott, *née* Walkinshaw; matric arms Ct of the Lord Lyon 1973, recognised by the Lord Lyon as McKerrell of Hillhouse and 15th head of the name, also recorded arms Genealogical Office Dublin Castle and recognised as 15th head of the name by Chief Herald of Ireland; *b* 23 Jan 1941; *Educ* Cranleigh; *m* 2 Jan 1991, May Weston Cochrane, da of Matthew Cochrane White (d 1967); *Career* Chancellor to The MacCarthy Mór, *qv*, Hereditary Niadh Nask and Chancellor of the Niadh Nask (an ancient Gaelic Irish Knightly Order), OStJ, Kt Order of St Michael of the Wing, Kt Cdr Order of Polonia Restituta; founder memb Heraldry Soc of Ireland; memb: Royal Celtic Soc, Royal Stuart Soc, Heraldry Soc of Scotland, Internat Commn for Orders of Chivalry; FSA(Scot); *Style—* McKerrell of Hillhouse; ✉ Magdalene House, Lochmaben, Dumfries DG11 1PD (☎ 01387 810439)

McKERROW, Colin William; s of William Henry McKerrow, MC (d 1976), and Phyllis Mary Livingstone, *née* Robinson (d 1980); *b* 22 Jan 1934; *Educ* The Downs Sch Colwall, Eastbourne Coll; *Career* trainee Royal Insurance Co plc 1951–58, stockbroker 1958–91, fund mangr Ely Fund Managers Ltd 1991–; dir Derby County FC plc 1983–94; MSI (memb Stock Exchange 1966); FRMetS; *Recreations* watching football, cricket, bridge, travel, oenology, ornithology; *Clubs* MCC, Hurlingham, Caledonian; *Style—* Colin McKerrow, Esq; ✉ 6 Thornton Road, Wimbledon, London SW19 4NE (☎ 0181 946 6195); Ely Fund Managers Ltd, Audrey House, Ely Place, London EC1N 6RY (☎ 0171 404 5333, fax 0171 404 5747)

McKERROW, June; da of Alexander Donald McKerrow, and Lorna McKerrow; *b* 17 June 1950; *Educ* Brunel Univ (MPhil); *Career* local govt housing 1967–71, housing mangr Paddington Churches Housing Assoc 1971–76, dep dir Church Army Housing 1977–80, dir Stonham Housing Assoc 1980–92, dir The Mental Health Fndn 1992–; memb Nat Cncl of Nat Fedn of Housing Assocs 1982–90, tstee and vice chair Shelter 1985–93, fndr memb Homeless Int 1987–93; tstee: Charity Projects 1992–96, Cherwell Housing Tst Oxford 1992–; *Style—* Ms June McKerrow; ✉ Director, Mental Health Foundation, 37 Mortimer Street, London W1N 7RJ (☎ 0171 580 0145)

MACKESON, Sir Rupert; 2 Bt (UK 1954), of Hythe, Co Kent; s of Brig Sir Harry Ripley Mackeson, 1 Bt (d 1964); *b* 16 Nov 1941; *Educ* Harrow, Trinity Coll Dublin (MA); *m* 22 July 1968 (m dis 1972), Hon Camilla Margaret, da of Baron Keith of Castleacre (Life Peer); *Career* Capt RHG, ret 1968; author of numerous books as Rupert Collens; *Books* incl: A Look at Cecil Alin Dogs and Hounds, Snaffles Life and Works, 25 Legal Luminaries from Vanity Fair, 50 Cheltenham Gold Cups; *Style—* Capt Sir Rupert Mackeson, Bt; ✉ c/o The Cecil Aldin Book Co, The Parade, Marlborough, Wiltshire SN8 1BR

MACKESON-SANDBACH, Ian Lawrie; s of Capt Lawrie Mackeson-Sandbach (d 1984), of Caerllo, Llangernyw, Clwyd, and Geraldine, *née* Sandbach; *b* 14 June 1933; *Educ* Eton, Univ of New Brunswick; *m* 6 May 1967, Annie Marie, da of J M G Van Lanschot (d 1983), of S'Hertogenbosch, Netherlands; 4 da (Antoinette b 1969, Sara b 1970, Louise b 1973, Megan b 1976); *Career* Lt Welsh Gds emergency reserve 1952–57; md France Fenwick Ltd 1969–75, dir Demerara Co Ltd 1969–76, chief exec Ernest Notcutt Group Ltd 1976–82; chm Crown Estate Paving Cmmn 1983 (cmmr 1974); Provincial Grand Master N Wales 1990; Liveryman: Worshipful Co of Grocers, Worshipful Co of Insurers; memb Inst of Fire Engrs 1960; *Recreations* shooting, fishing; *Clubs* Boodle's, Pratt's, Royal St George's (Sandwich); *Style—* Ian Mackeson-Sandbach, Esq; ✉ 20 Hanover Terrace, Regent's Park, London NW1 4RJ; Maesol, Llangernyw, Denbighshire LL22 8UA; Sir John Lyon House, 5 High Timber Street, Upper Thames Street, London EC4V 3LE (☎ 0171 248 4931, fax 0171 402 6390)

MACKEY, Prof James Patrick; s of Peter Mackey (d 1976), and Esther Josephine, *née* Morrissey (d 1991); *b* 9 Feb 1934; *Educ* Mount St Joseph Coll, Nat Univ of Ireland (BA), Pontifical Univ Maynooth (LPh, BD, STL, DD), Queen's Univ Belfast (PhD); Univs of: London, Oxford, Strasbourg; *m* 25 Aug 1973, (Hanorah) Noelle, da of Nicholas Aloysius Quinlan, of City View, Leamy St, Waterford, Ireland; 1 da (Ciara b 9 Oct 1974), 1 s (James b 28 Jan 1976); *Career* Queen's Univ Belfast 1960–66 (asst lectr and lectr in philosophy 1963–66), lectr in theology St John's Coll Waterford 1966–69, visiting assoc prof Catholic Univ of America 1968, Univ of San Francisco 1969–79 (assoc prof and prof of systematic and philosophical theology 1973–79), visiting prof Univ of California Berkley 1974, Thomas Chalmers prof of theology Univ of Edinburgh 1979– (dean Faculty of Divinity 1984–88, dir of Graduate Sch 1995–), visiting prof Dartmouth Coll NH USA 1989, visiting prof Univ of San Francisco 1990, convener and chair Int Conf on Cultures of Europe Derry 1991; writer and presenter: The Hall of Mirrors (Channel Four) 1984, Perspectives (BBC Belfast) 1986–87, The Gods of War (Channel Four) 1987; ed Studies in World Christianity 1995–; memb Catholic Theologic Soc GB; *Books* The Modern Theology of Tradition (1962, 1963), Life and Grace (1966), Tradition and Change in the Church (1968), Contemporary Philosophy of Religion (1968), Morals, Law and Authority: Sources and Attitudes in the Church (ed, 1969), The Church, Its Credibility Today (1970), The Problems of Religious Faith (1972), Jesus the Man and the Myth (1979), The Christian Experience of God as Trinity (1983), Religious Imagination (ed, 1986), Modern Theology: A Sense of Direction (1987), New Testament Theology in Dialogue (with J D G Dunn, 1987), An Introduction to Celtic Christianity (ed, 1989), The Cultures of Europe: The Irish Contribution (ed, 1993), Power and Christian Ethics (1994); *Recreations* sailing; *Clubs* Edinburgh Univ, Saint Brendan's Cruising, Port Edgar Yacht; *Style—* Prof James Mackey; ✉ 10 Randolph Crescent, Edinburgh EH3 7TT (☎ 0131 225 9408); Clonea, Dungarvan, Co Waterford, Ireland; Faculty of Divinity, University of Edinburgh, New College, Mound Place, Edinburgh EH1 2LX (☎ 0131 650 8907)

McKIBBIN, Prof Brian; s of William McKibbin (d 1971), and Elizabeth, *née* Wilson (d 1984); *b* 9 Dec 1930; *Educ* Roundhay Sch Leeds, Univ of Leeds (MB ChB, MD), Univ Coll Oxford, Univ of Illinois (MS); *m* Pamela Mary, da of John Charles Francis Pask (d 1965); 2 s (Alexander b 1964, Hugh b 1967); *Career* Nat Serv Capt RAMC 1957–58; sr lectr and head Dept of Orthopaedics Univ of Sheffield 1966–72, prof of traumatic and orthopaedic surgery Univ of Wales Coll of Med 1972–93 (prof emeritus 1993); pres: Br Orthopaedic Res Soc 1973–75, Br Orthopaedic Assoc 1987–88; memb Cncl RCS; FRCS 1960; *Books* Recent Advances in Orthopaedics (vol 2, vol 3, 1979, vol 4, 1981); *Style—* Prof Brian McKibbin; ✉ The Orchard, Peterston-super-Ely, Cardiff, South Glamorgan CF5 6LH

MACKIE, Charles Gordon; TD (1945), DL (1985); s of Capt Charles Gordon Stewart Mackie, OBE (d 1966), of Angus, and Gertrude Irvine Mackie (d 1946); *b* 19 March 1916; *Educ* Harrow, St John's Coll Oxford (MA); *m* 5 May 1945, Margaret Georgina (Peggy), da of Maj Frederick Ernest Koebel, DSO (d 1940), of Chudleigh, Devon; 1 s (Alexander b 1946), 2 da (Mary b 1953, Sally b 1958); *Career* cmmnd 2 Lt 7 Bn Argyll and Sutherland Highlanders 51 Highland Div TA 1938, served France 1939–40 (wounded, despatches), Capt 1941, 8 Army 1941–42; serv: N Africa, Sicily, Italy; Europe 1944 (wounded), invalided out 1945; Stewarts & Lloyds 1937–67: trainee 1937–39, mangr London City office 1953; asst md Stanton Ironworks Ltd (subsid) 1956, md Stanton & Staveley Ltd (subsid) 1962, subsequently chm and md Stanton & Staveley Ltd; dir: Stewarts & Lloyds 1964–67, Tubes Div British Steel Corporation 1967–78; chm: Shanks & McEwan Ltd 1978–81, Booth International Ltd 1979–82; treas Univ of Nottingham 1982–93 (cncl memb 1962–93); gen cmmr of income tax 1960–91; High Sheriff Nottinghamshire 1977–78; Hon LLD Univ of Nottingham 1992; OStJ 1967; *Recreations* shooting, fishing, golf; *Clubs* Carlton; *Style—* Charles Mackie, Esq, TD, DL

MACKIE, David Lindsay; s of Alastair Cavendish Lindsay Mackie, CBE, DFC, of London, and Rachel, *née* Goodson; *b* 15 Feb 1946; *Educ* St Edmund Hall Oxford (BA, MA); *m* 1, 13 Feb 1971 (m dis 1986); 2 s (James b 1974, Edward b 1976), 1 da (Eleanor b 1978); m 2, 6 Dec 1989, Phyllis, da of Robert Gershon, of NYC; *Career* admitted slr 1971, ptnr Allen & Overy 1975–, recorder Crown Court 1992, Higher Court advocate (civil and criminal) 1994–; chm Product Liability Advertising and Unfair Competition Ctee Int Bar Assoc 1987–91, memb Civil and Family Ctee Judicial Studies Bd 1991–96; author various pubns; FCIArb; *Recreations* climbing; *Style—* David Mackie, Esq; ✉ Allen & Overy, One New Change, London EC4M 9QQ (☎ 0171 330 3000, fax 0171 330 9999)

MACKIE, (William) Denis Grenville; DL (Co Antrim 1994); s of (William) Grenville Mackie (d 1994), of Cloughmills, Co Antrim, and Constance Beatrice, *née* Rodden (d 1981); *b* 10 Sept 1934; *Educ* Shrewsbury; *m* 23 April 1960, Susannah, da of Bernard Dixon (d 1983), of Pampisford, Cambs; 2 s (Alastair b 15 March 1963, Peter b (twin) 1963), 1 da (Caroline (Mrs John Ogden) b 1961); *Career* dir: James Mackie and Sons Ltd Belfast (and Hldgs) 1968–77, Robert McCalmont and Co Ltd Belfast 1968–83; md Lissanoure Farms Ltd Co Antrim 1969–, non-exec dir Strand Spinning Co Belfast 1977–90; memb: Co Antrim Jury Bursay Ctee, BASC NI Advsy Cncl 1990; High Sheriff Co Antrim 1979; *Recreations* skiing, country pursuits, sailing; *Clubs* Ulster Reform (Belfast), Royal NI Yacht; *Style—* Denis Mackie, Esq, DL; ✉ Lissanoure, Loughguile, Cloughmills, Co Antrim, NI (☎ 01265 641471, fax 01265 641727)

MACKIE, James Campbell Stephen; s of Prof John Duncan Mackie, CBE, MC, LLD (d 1978), and Cicely Jean, *née* Paterson (d 1976); *b* 1 Oct 1926; *Educ* Charterhouse, Univ of Glasgow, New Coll Oxford (MA); *m* 1951, Margaret Pamela Daphne Moore, da of late Maj Hugh King, Seaforth Highlanders, MC and Bar; 4 s (Alexander b 1952, Hugh b 1956, Simon b 1960, Tobias b 1964), 1 da (Miranda b 1962); *Career* served RM 1944–47, NW Europe 1945, cmmnd 1946, Sub Lt Malayan RNVR 1955–58; HM Overseas Civil Serv Malaya 1950–59 (decorated by Malayan Govt AMN 1959); sec: Liverpool Cotton Assoc Ltd 1960–61, Cattle Food Trade Assoc 1965–71; DG Grain and Feed Trade Assoc 1973–91 (sec gen 1971–73), non-exec dir Corn Exchange Company Ltd 1975–78; memb: Cncl London C of C and Indust 1974–91 (memb Commercial Court Ctee 1975–91), Haslemere Ctee of Action Res for the Crippled Child (chm 1992–94), Haslemere Town Cncl 1991–, Waverley BC 1995–; Mayor of Haslemere 1993–94; chm Cons and Unionist Assoc: Grayswood Branch 1965–73 and 1976–83, Farnham Div 1976–83; pres: SW Surrey Cons Assoc 1987–93 (vice pres 1984), Haslemere Branch Cons Assoc 1987–; vice pres Haslemere Hockey Club 1988–; memb PCC All Saints Church Grayswood 1994; Freeman City of London 1990, memb Ct of Assts Worshipful Co of Arbitrators 1992; FCIArb 1992; *Publications* A Short History of All Saints Church, Grayswood (1996); *Recreations* photography, history, antiques, dogs, reading, travelling; *Clubs* Farmers'; *Style—* James C S Mackie, Esq; ✉ Weald Mount, Hill Rd, Haslemere, Surrey GU27 2JP (☎ 01428 643833)

MACKIE, Dr Neil; CBE (1996); s of William Fraser Mackie (d 1979), of King's Gate, Aberdeen, and Sheila Roberta, *née* Taylor (d 1973); *b* 11 Dec 1946; *Educ* Aberdeen GS, Royal Scot Acad of Music and Drama (DipMusEdRSAMD, DipRSAMD), RCM (fndn scholar, ARCM (Hons)); *m* 1973, Kathleen Mary, da of William Livingstone (d 1972); 2 da (Alison Kathleen b 1980, Elinor Sheila b 1983); *Career* international concert singer (tenor); RCM: prof of singing 1985–, head of vocal studies 1994–; Gulbenkian fellowship, Caird scholar, Munster scholar; London recital debut Wigmore Hall 1972, London concert debut with Eng Chamber Orch under Raymond Leppard 1973; world premières incl: Unpublished Songs by Britten, Hans Werner Henze's Three Auden Settings, several Kenneth Leighton works incl Symphony No 3, many cmmnd works by Scottish composers; works especially written for him by Peter Maxwell Davies: The Martyrdom of St Magnus (title role), The Lighthouse (role of Sandy), Into the Labyrinth (solo cantata for tenor and orch), A Solstice of Light; CStJ 1996 (OStJ 1987); Hon DMus Univ of Aberdeen 1993; FRSA 1991, FRSAMD 1992, FRSE 1996; *Recordings* numerous on EMI, Decca, Philips, Chandos, Deutsche Grammophon, Unicorn-Kanchana, Accent, Abbey Records; *Awards* runner up Gramophone Solo Voice Recording of the Year for Britten Tenor, Horn and Strings (with Scottish Chamber Orch) 1989, Grammy Award 1993; *Recreations* reading, charity work and occasional gardening; *Clubs* Athenaeum; *Style—* Dr Neil Mackie, CBE, FRSE; ✉ 70 Broadwood Avenue, Ruislip, Middlesex HA4 7XR (☎ 01895 632115, fax 01895 625765); Lies Askonas Ltd, 6 Henrietta St, London WC2E 8LA (☎ 0171 379 7700, fax 0171 242 1831); Royal College of Music, Prince Consort Road, London SW7 2BS (☎ 0171 589 3643, fax 0171 589 7740)

MACKIE, Dr Peter Howard; s of Dr Lawrence Percival Mackie (d 1988), of Wellesbourne, Warwick, and Elizabeth Bates, *née* Pedlow; *b* 13 Oct 1947; *Educ* Cheltenham Coll, Hertford Coll Oxford (MA, BM BCh); *m* 14 July 1973, Joanna Jane, da of John Henry McGhee, TD (d 1987), of Kineton, Warwick; 4 da (Sarah b 1975, Julia b 1978, Diana b 1980, Rachel b 1986); *Career* house physician Harefield Hosp 1973, house surgn Cheltenham Gen Hosp 1973–74, sr house offr and registrar Bristol Royal Infirmary 1974–76, hon tutor Univ of Bristol 1974–76, res registrar Queen Elizabeth Hosp Birmingham 1976–77, lectr Dept of Immunology Univ of Birmingham 1977–79, sr registrar haematology John Radcliffe Hosp Oxford 1979–82, conslt haematologist E Berks Dist 1982–, chm Div of Medicine E Berks Dist 1989–93, dir Lab Servs Heatherwood and Wexham Park Hosps Tst 1992– (chm Med Staff Ctee 1993–95); memb: Windsor and Dist Organists' Assoc 1984–94, Ancient Soc of Coll Youths 1970–; FRCPath 1993 (MRCPath 1981), FRCP 1995 (MRCP 1978); *Recreations* music, bellringing, gardening; *Style—* Dr Peter Mackie; ✉ Westbury, Duffield Lane, Stoke Poges, Bucks SL2 4AH (☎ 01753 645510, fax 01753 550109)

MacKIE, Prof Rona McLeod; da of Prof J Norman Davidson, FRS (d 1972), of Bearsden, Glasgow, and Morag, *née* McLeod; *b* 22 May 1940; *Educ* Laurel Bank Sch, Univ of Glasgow (MB, ChB, MD); *m* 1, 1962 (m dis); 1 s (Douglas b 1965), 1 da (Alison b 1963); m 2, 16 April 1994, Prof Sir James Whyte Black, FRS, *qv*; *Career* hon conslt dermatologist Gtr Glasgow Health Bd 1978– (conslt dermatologist 1973–78), prof of dermatology Univ of Glasgow 1978–; vice-pres Nat Eczema Soc, pres Br Assoc of Dermatologists; FRCP Glasgow 1978, FRSE 1983, FRCPath 1984, FRCP London 1985, FIBiol 1988; DSc Glasgow 1994; *Books* Clinical Dermatology - An Illustrated Textbook (1981), Eczema and Dermatitis (1983), Malignant Melanoma (ed, 1983), Current Perspectives in Immunodermatology (ed, 1984), Milne's Dermatopathology (ed, 1984), Clinical Dermatology An Illustrated Textbook (1986), Skin Cancer (1989); *Recreations* skiing, music especially opera, gardening; *Style*— Prof Rona MacKie, FRSE; ✉ Department of Dermatology, Robertson Building, University of Glasgow, Glasgow G12 8QQ (☎ 0141 339 8855 ext 4006, fax 0141 330 4008, telex 777070 UNIGLA)

MACKIE, Sheila Gertrude (Mrs R Fenwick-Baines); da of James Watt Bell Mackie (d 1968), and Edna Irene, *née* Watson (d 1989); *b* 5 Oct 1928; *Educ* Durham HS, King Edward VII Sch of Art Newcastle upon Tyne, Univ of Durham (BA); *m* 3 Aug 1967, Robert Fenwick-Baines, s of Albert Baines; 1 s (James Alastair b 1970), 1 da (Anneliese b 1969); *Career* head Dept of Art Consetts Sch 1950–82, occasional lectr Sunderland Coll of Art and lectr numerous art socs, artistic advsr Bertam Mills Circus 1950s-60s; artist and illustrator; princ artist J R S Lourenco & Co Ltd 1991–; work in The Royal Collection; exhbns at the Royal Acad and and RSA, shows in London and provinces, solo show Durham Gallery April-May 1994; five cmmnd works for Derwentside DC; *Publications* incl: Adventure in Glides Garden (with Terri Le Guerre, 1979), The Great Seasons (with David Bellamy, 1980), The Mouse book (with David Bellamy, 1982), Lindisfarne - the Cradle Island (with Magnus Magnusson, 1984), Beowulf (with Magnus Magnusson and Julian Glover, 1987); in preparation: The Wanderer (with Michael Cronin and Charlton Heston), The Dragons Hoard, Beowulf's Treasure; *Style*— Miss Sheila Mackie; ✉ Hoddington Oaks, Spa Grounds, Shotley Bridge, Consett, Co Durham DH8 0TN (☎ 01207 505025)

MACKIE, (John) Stuart; s of Norman Frederic Mackie (d 1956), of Halifax, and Mary, *née* Rushworth (d 1976); *b* 12 March 1933; *Educ* Sowerby Bridge GS, Univ of Sheffield (DipArch); *m* 3 Aug 1957, Elsie, da of William Breeden, of Ashton under Lyne; 1 s (Robin Jonathan b 1964), 1 da (Amanda Lauren b 1958); *Career* RE 1955–57, served Germany and Cyprus; chartered architect, ret 1995; chm RIBA: Teesside Branch 1975–76, Northern Regn 1978–79, Housing Advsy Gp 1982–95; memb Cncl: ARCUK 1982–89, RIBA 1981–91; past-pres Teesside and Dist C of C and Indust; chm Stockton on Tees City Challenge Ptnrship; *Recreations* travel, photography; *Style*— Stuart Mackie, Esq; ✉ 15 Spring Hill, Welbury, Northallerton, N Yorks (☎ 01609 882453)

MACKIE OF BENSHIE, Baron (Life Peer UK 1974), of Kirriemuir, Co Angus; George Yull Mackie; CBE (1971), DSO (1944), DFC (1944), LLD (1982); s of Maitland Mackie, OBE, LLD, and bro of Baron John-Mackie (d 1994) and Sir Maitland Mackie, CBE, JP (d 1996); *b* 10 July 1919; *Educ* Aberdeen GS, Aberdeen Univ; *m* 1, 1944, Lindsay Lyall (d 1985), da of Alexander Sharp, advocate, of Aberdeen, and Isabella Sharp, OBE; 3 da (Hon Lindsay Mary (Hon Mrs Rusbridger) b 1945, Hon Diana Lyall (Hon Mrs Hope) b 1946, Hon Jeannie Felicia (Hon Mrs Leigh) b 1953) (and 1 s decd); m 2, 29 April 1988, Jacqueline, widow of Andrew Lane and da of Col Marcel Rauch, Legion d'Honneur and Croix de Guerre; *Career* serv WWII Bomber Cmd; farmer 1945–89; chm Mackie Yule & Co, Caithness Glass Ltd 1966–85, Caithness Pottery Co, Benshie Cattle Co; rector Univ of Dundee 1980–83; MP (Lib) Caithness & Sutherland 1964–66; Parly candidate (Lib) Angus S 1959, Euro Parly candidate Scotland NE 1979; chm Scot Lib Pty 1965–70; chm Land & Timber Services Ltd 1986–88; Lib spokesman House of Lords on: Devolution, Agriculture, Scotland; memb: Parly Assembly Cncl of Europe 1986–, Western Euro Union 1986–; pres Scottish Lib Pty until 1988 (became SLD); Hon LLD 1982; *Recreations* golf, shooting; *Clubs* Garrick, Farmers', RAF; *Style*— Rt Hon Lord Mackie of Benshie, CBE, DSO, DFC; ✉ Cortachy House, by Kirriemuir, Angus (☎ 01575 540229)

MacKIERNAN, Most Rev Francis Joseph; *see:* Kilmore, Bishop of (RC)

MACKILLIGIN, HE David Patrick Robert; CMG (1994); s of Robert Springett Mackilligin, CMG, OBE, MC (d 1972), and Patricia Margaret, *née* Waldegrave (d 1975); *b* 29 June 1939; *Educ* Winchester Coll, Pembroke Coll Oxford (MA, Capt of Boats); *m* 1976, Dr Gillian Margaret Zuill Walker, da of Dr James Zuill Walker, of Glasgow; 2 da (Lucy Charlotte Anne b 16 Jan 1979, Shona Elizabeth b 9 Sept 1980); *Career* HM Dip Serv; joined CRO 1961, on temp duty Salisbury (now Harare) as private sec to High Cmmr Lord Alport 1962, third later second sec Pakistan 1962–66, asst private sec to Sec of State Cwlth Office 1966–68, private sec to Min without Portfolio 1968, UN Dept 1969, dep cmmr Anguilla 1969–71 (actg cmmr on various occasions), first sec Ghana 1971–73, head of Chancery and consul Cambodia (chargé d'affaires on various occasions) 1973–75, press offr FCO 1975–76, W African Dept FCO 1976–80, cnsllr (commercial and aid) Indonesia 1980–85, NATO Defence Coll Rome 1985–86, cnsllr (economic and commercial) and dir of trade promotion in Aust 1985–90, high cmmr Belize 1991–95, govr Br Virgin Islands 1995–; *Recreations* walking and swimming in remote places, visiting ruins, literature, theatre, cinema, cats, second hand bookshops; *Clubs* United Oxford and Cambridge Univ, Commonwealth Tst; *Style*— HE Mr David Mackilligin, CMG; ✉ c/o Foreign and Commonwealth Office (Tortola), King Charles Street, London SW1A 2AH

MACKILLIGIN, Robert Guy Walter; MC (1944, and bar 1945); s of late Hector Rennie Mackilligin; *b* 11 Oct 1918; *Educ* Charterhouse, Camborne Sch of Mines; *m* 1949, Daphne Gwendoline, *née* Cooper; 3 da; *Career* serv WWII 51 Highland Div RA 1939–46; petroleum engr Shell International Petroleum Co Ltd 1946–53, mangr Shell International Co Ltd 1954–73, exec dir Bisichi Mining plc 1974–, chm Dragon Markets Ltd 1984–; *Recreations* genealogy, gardening, ornithology; *Style*— Robert Mackilligin, Esq, MC; ✉ Walnut Tree Cottage, Woodlands, Pembury Rd, Tunbridge Wells (☎ 01892 530392); Bisichi Mining plc, 8–10 New Fetter Lane, London EC4A 1NQ (☎ 0171 415 5000)

McKILLOP, Prof James Hugh; s of Dr Patrick McKillop (d 1979), of Coatbridge, and Dr Helen Theresa McKillop, *née* Kilpatrick; *b* 20 June 1948; *Educ* St Aloysius' Coll Glasgow, Univ of Glasgow (BSc, MB ChB, PhD); *m* 17 Aug 1973, Caroline Annis, da of Charles Allen Oakley, CBE (d 1993), of Glasgow; 2 da (Beth b 1977, Jenny b 1981); *Career* Harkness fellowship Stanford Univ 1979 and 1980, Muirhead prof of med Univ of Glasgow 1989– (lectr 1977–82, sr lectr 1982–89); treas Scottish Soc of Experimental Med 1982–87; Br Nuclear Med Soc: cncl memb 1985–94, hon sec 1988–90, pres 1990–92; memb Exec Ctee Euro Assoc of Nuclear Med 1995– (congress pres 1997); chm: Intercollegiate Standing Ctee on Nuclear Med 1995–, ARSAC Ctee Dept of Health 1996– (memb 1988–, vice chm 1989–95); ed Nuclear Medicine Communications 1991–; FRCPGlas 1985, FRCPEd 1990, FRCP 1992, FRCR 1994; *Books* Atlas of Technetium Bone Scans (with D L Citrin, 1978), Imaging in Clinical Practice (with A G Chalmers and P J Robinson, 1988), Clinician's Guide to Nuclear Medicine: Benign and Malignant Bone Disease (with I Fogelman, 1991); *Recreations* cricket, opera, reading; *Clubs* Royal Soc of Med; *Style*— Prof James McKillop; ✉ 18 Beaumont Gate, Glasgow G12 9ED (☎ 0141 339 7000); University Department of Medicine, Royal Infirmary, Glasgow G31 2ER (☎ 0141 211 4675, fax 0141 552 2953)

MACKINLAY, Andrew; MP (Lab) Thurrock (majority 1,172); *b* 1949; *Educ* Salesian Coll Chertsey (DMA), ACIS; m; 3 c; *Career* MP (Lab) Thurrock 1992–; sec All Pty: Poland Gp, Manx Gp; memb TGWU; ACIS; *Style*— Andrew Mackinlay, Esq, MP; ✉ House of Commons, London SW1A 0AA (☎ 0171 219 3000)

MACKINLAY, Col Hamish Grant; LVO (1979); s of James Johnstone Mackinlay (d 1988), of Tillicoultry, Clackmannanshire, and Margaret Keir, *née* Grant; *b* 11 March 1935; *Educ* Dollar Acad, RMA Sandhurst; *m* 25 Jan 1964, Elizabeth (Elspeth) Paul Gray, da of The Rev Peter Bryce Gunn (d 1979), of Ancrum, Roxburghshire; 1 s (Jamie b 1966), 1 da (Diana b 1969); *Career* cmmnd RCS 1955, sr seconded offr State of Qatar 1976–79, SO Army Staff Duties MOD 1979–82, dep head Mil Mission to HRH the Crown Prince of Saudi Arabia 1982–86, def and mil attaché Cairo 1986–88, dep govr HM Tower of London 1989–95; sec The Friends of Norwich Cathedral 1995–, non-exec dir Royal British Legion Attendants Co 1995–; FIMgt, FRSA; *Clubs* Royal Commonwealth Soc; *Style*— Col Hamish Mackinlay, LVO; ✉ 12 The Close, Norwich NR1 4DH (☎ 01603 622625)

MACKINLAY, (Jack) Lindsay; *b* 24 Jan 1936; *m* 30 Sept 1961, Catherine Elizabeth (Elise); 1 s (Graham b 1966), 1 da (Carolyn b 1968); *Career* dir Rowntree Mackintosh plc 1973–89; chm: Bradford & Bingley Building Society 1995–, RPC Group Plc; non-exec dir Argos plc; FCA 1959, FCMA 1968, FIMgt; *Recreations* golf, sailing, music; *Style*— Lindsay Mackinlay, Esq; ✉ The Cottage, Skelton, York YO3 6XX; Bradford & Bingley Building Society, Crossflatts, Bingley, West Yorkshire BD16 2UA (☎ 01274 555555)

McKINLAY, Peter; s of Peter McKinlay (d 1991), and Mary Clegg, *née* Hamill; *b* 29 Dec 1939; *Educ* Campbeltown GS, Univ of Glasgow (MA); *m* 28 Sept 1963, Anne, da of David and Jane Rogerson Thomson; 2 s (Alasdair Rogerson b 31 Jan 1966, Fraser b 3 Jan 1975), 1 da (Shelagh b 13 Oct 1967); *Career* asst postal controller GPO HQ Edinburgh 1963–67; SO: asst princ 1967–70, princ 1970–77 (incl private sec to the Min of State, Rt Hon Bruce Millan), asst sec 1977–88, dir Scottish Prison Serv 1988–91; chief exec Scottish Homes 1991–; *Recreations* family, friends, garden, television, reading, food, drink; *Clubs* Machrihanish Golf; *Style*— Peter McKinlay, Esq; ✉ Scottish Homes, Thistle House, 91 Haymarket Terrace, Edinburgh EH12 5HE (☎ 0131 313 0044, fax 0131 313 4527)

MacKINLAY MacLEOD, Michael John; s of John MacKinlay MacLeod (d 1991), of Worcs, and Dorothy Rule, *née* MacFarlane (d 1975); *b* 2 Oct 1935; *Educ* Eton, Pembroke Coll Cambridge, RAC Cirencester; *m* 1, 17 May 1958 (m dis 1966), Sandra Elizabeth, da of late Lt-Col Alister Maynard, MBE; 3 s (Torquil b 1959, Jocelyn b 1961, Caspar b 1963); m 2, 14 Feb 1967, Pamela Dawn, da of late Hugh Nicholas Charrington; 1 s (Euan b 1970), 2 da (Emma b 1967, Iona b 1971); *Career* Lt Grenadier Gds, Capt Ayrshire (ECO) Yeomanry; shipping Baltic Exchange London, Redheads Tyne; ship mangr H Hogarth and Sons Glasgow; antiques business London & Broadway Worcs; farmer Scotland and Worcs, branch chm CLA 1987–90; memb: Wychavon DC, Agric Land Tribunal (Midlands Area); vice chm W Midlands Agric Forum; AICS; Freeman City of London, Liveryman Worshipful Co of Shipwrights; memb Lloyd's; *Recreations* shooting; *Clubs* Pratt's, Farmers', Union & County (Worcs); *Style*— Michael MacKinlay MacLeod, Esq; ✉ Garnstone House, Weobley, Herefordshire HR4 8QP (☎ 01544 318943, fax 01544 318197)

McKINNELL, Ian Hayes; s of Neil Hayes McKinnell (d 1990), of Newcastle-upon-Tyne, and Olga, *née* Smith; *b* 6 Nov 1954; *Educ* Penistone GS Yorkshire, Barnsley Sch of Art and Crafts, Faculty of Art & Design Brighton Poly (BA Hons); *partner* Elizabeth Heaney; 1 s (Albert Meredith Heaney McKinnell b 24 May 1994); *Career* photographic technician for various cos in Brighton and Newcastle 1976–79, exhibition designer Dove Cottage Trust Grasmere Cumbria 1980–81, self-employed photographer 1981–; solo exhibitions: Still Life (Spectro Arts Centre Newcastle-upon-Tyne and tour) 1980, Recent Work (Special Photographers Co Gallery London and tour) 1990; gp exhibitions incl: Br Int Print Biennale Bradford, Northern Young Contemporaries Manchester, 6th and 7th Assoc of Photographers Tour, Royal Photographic Soc's Annual Exhibition Bath 1990 and 1994, Against the Grain Camerawork London 1990; memb Assoc of Photographers 1987; *Books* One Day and 1/30th of a Second in Edinburgh (1979); *Recreations* travel, work; *Style*— Ian McKinnell, Esq; ✉ 9 Bristol House, 80a Southampton Row, London WC1B 4BB (☎ 0171 631 3017, fax 0171 404 2026)

MacKINNON, Alastair Marr; s of Hector Allan MacKinnon (d 1990), of Aberdeen, Scotland, and Edith Patterson, *née* Marr; *b* 25 Feb 1960; *Educ* Glenrothes HS Fife, Univ of Edinburgh (LLB, BD), Dartmouth Coll New Hampshire USA; *Career* asst St Cuthbert's Parish Church and St John's Scottish Episcopal Church Edinburgh 1985–87, dir St Cuthbert's Educn Centre 1985–87, tutor in Christian ethics and practical theology Univ of Edinburgh 1988–89; freelance journalist and writer; Scottish corr Church Times London 1990–, religious affairs corr Scotland on Sunday 1990–91; contrib: Crucible, Theology; conslt to Centre for Theology and Public Issues Univ of Edinburgh 1991–96; dir: Crime Prevention Educn Project (W Lothian) 1991–, Drug and Alcohol Project (W Lothian) 1991–96; memb Official Visiting Ctee Polmont HMY01 1996–; *Recreations* modern visual art, cooking, badminton; *Clubs* Univ of Edinburgh Staff; *Style*— Alastair M MacKinnon, Esq

McKINNON, (David) Douglas; s of John McKinnon (d 1957), and Margaret Douglas McGregor (d 1963); *b* 18 July 1926; *Educ* Stirling HS, Univ of Glasgow (BSc); *m* 1960, Edith June, da of Edward Fairful Kyles (d 1942); 1 s, 2 da; *Career* asst Maths Dept Univ of Glasgow 1946–48, pres Faculty of Actuaries 1979–81, memb Cncl Int Actuarial Assoc 1972–89 (UK sec 1975–89); gen mangr and actuary Scottish Mutual Assurance Society 1982–90 (dir 1981–91); dir: Scottish Mutual Assurance plc 1992–96, Scotsure Insurance Co Ltd 1991–, Church of Scotland Insurance Co Ltd 1992–; pres Falkirk Bn the Boys Bde 1972–77, chm Church of Scotland Tst 1991–96 (vice chm 1984–89), memb Church of Scotland Assembly Cncl 1987–96, chm Assoc Scottish Life Offices 1988–89, memb Bd Assoc of Br Insurers 1988–90; FFA, CMath, FIMA; *Recreations* golf; *Clubs* Western (Glasgow); *Style*— Douglas McKinnon Esq; ✉ Kinburn, 4 Carronvale Rd, Larbert, Stirlingshire FK5 3LZ (☎ 01324 562373)

MacKINNON, Neil; *b* 17 May 1955; *Educ* Waterloo GS Seaforth, Univ of Liverpool (BA(Econ)), Univ of Southampton (MSc Economics & Econometrics); *Career* economist; with HM Treasury 1982–86, currently chief economist and chief currency strategist Citibank NA; memb American Economic Assoc 1989; *Books* The Sterling Money Market (with M Dowding, foreword by Sir Douglas Wass, 1989), Gilts - Facing the Challenge (with D Corrigan, 1990), Economics - A Guide for the Financial Markets (with Paula Neal, 1992), The Financial Times Guide to Global Investing (contrib, 1995); *Style*— Neil MacKinnon, Esq; ✉ Citibank NA, 336 Strand, London WC2R 1HB (☎ 0171 500 1000)

McKINNON, Warwick Nairn; s of His Hon Judge Neil Nairn McKinnon (d 1988), of Purley, Surrey, and Janetta Amelia, *née* Lilley (d 1989); *b* 11 Nov 1947; *Educ* King's Coll Sch Wimbledon, Christ's Coll Cambridge (MA); *m* 29 July 1978, Nichola Juliet, da of David Alan Lloyd, of Limpsfield, Surrey; 1 s (Rory b 1981), 1 da (Kirsty b 1982); *Career* called to the Bar Lincoln's Inn 1970; ad eundum SE Circuit, recorder of the Crown Court 1995–; *Publications* WordPerfect 5.1 for the Criminal Lawyer; *Recreations* tennis, gardening, computers, opera; *Style*— Warwick McKinnon, Esq; ✉ Queen Elizabeth Building, Temple, London EC4Y 9BS

MacKINNON OF MacKINNON, Madam; Anne Gunhild MacKinnon; da of Alasdair Neil Hood MacKinnon of MacKinnon (d 1983), 37 Chief of Clan Fingon (MacKinnon); suc father as 38 Chief; *b* 13 Feb 1955; *Educ* Badminton Sch Bristol, St

Loyes Sch of Occupational Therapy (Dip of Occupational Therapy); *m* 1981, Allan; 2 s (Andrew b 1982, Robert b 1985); *Career* occupational therapist Somerset Hosps and Social Services 1976–; NVQ assessor, occupational therapist clinical supervisor; memb Br Assoc of Occupational Therapists; *Style—* Madam MacKinnon of MacKinnon; ✉ 16 Durleigh Rd, Bridgwater, Somerset TA6 7HR

MacKINNON OF MacKINNON, Lt-Col Ian Kroyer; yr s of Cdr Arthur Avalon MacKinnon of MacKinnon, OBE, RN (d 1964), 36 Chief of Clan MacKinnon, of Charity Acre, Pilgrims Way, Hollingbourne, Kent, and Gunhild, *née* Kroyer (d 1946); er bro Alasdair Neil Hood MacKinnon, 37 Chief of Clan MacKinnon (d 1983); *b* 8 Oct 1929; *Educ* Wellington, RMA Sandhurst; *m* 1 Jan 1955, Joanna Eileen, er da of Capt Sir Robert William Stirling-Hamilton, 12 Bt, JP, DL (d 1982); *Career* cmmnd Queen's Own Cameron Highlanders 1950; served with 1 Bn in: Tripoli, Canal Zone, Austria 1950–53; Depot Camerons Inverness 1953–56, 1 Bn in Malaya, Aden and Dover 1956–59, Adjt 4/5 Bn Queen's Own Cameron Highlanders (TA) Inverness 1959–61, staff appt HQ Land Forces Hong Kong 1961–63, Trg Maj Univ of St Andrews 1964–65, 1 Bn Queen's Own Highlanders (Seaforth and Camerons) Osnabrück and Berlin 1965–66, staff appt HQ Highland Div and Dist Perth 1966–68, 1 Bn Queen's Own Highlanders (2 i/c) Edinburgh and Sharjah 1968–71, HQ BAOR DAMS 1971–73, staff appt HQ Dir of Inf Warminster 1973–76, Lt-Col 1976, cmd Scottish Inf Depot Bridge of Don Aberdeen 1976–79, cmdt Stanford Trg Area Thetford Norfolk 1979–84, ret 1984; regnl sec Norfolk and Suffolk CLA 1985–94; fndr chm: Breckland Group, Norfolk Wildlife Tst; *Recreations* shooting, gardening; *Style—* Lt-Col Ian MacKinnon of MacKinnon; ✉ Little Breck House, 4 Trenchard Crescent, Watton, Norfolk IP25 6HR (☎ 01953 883139)

MACKINTOSH, Dr Alan Finlay; s of Dr Finlay George Mackintosh (d 1989), and Eileen Ormsby, *née* Johnson; *b* 14 Jan 1948; *Educ* Oundle, King's Coll Cambridge (BA), Westminster Med Sch (MD BChir); *m* 16 Feb 1974, Susan Patricia, da of Col Claude Hugo Macdonald Hull (d 1979); 1 s (Nicholas b 14 April 1982), 1 da (Clare b 18 April 1979); *Career* med registrar: Brighton 1975–76, King's Coll Hosp London 1976–77; sr cardiology registrar Cambridge 1978–81, conslt cardiologist St James's Univ and Killingbeck Hosp Leeds 1981–, sr lectr Univ of Leeds 1991– (lectr 1981–91); treas Br Cardiovascular Intervention Soc 1987–93, chm Jt Royal Colls and Ambulance Services Liaison Ctee 1995–; FRCP, FESC; *Books* The Heart Disease Reference Book (1984), Case Presentations in Heart Disease (1985, 2 edn 1992); *Recreations* horse racing, tennis, opera; *Style—* Dr Alan Mackintosh; ✉ 15 Charville Gardens, Shadwell, Leeds LS17 8JL (☎ 0113 273 7293); St James's University Hospital, Beckett Street, Leeds LS9 7TP (☎ 0113 243 3144)

MACKINTOSH, Anthony Robert Kilgour (Tony); s of Philip Kilgour Mackintosh, of Five Ashes, Sussex, and Beryl Ada, *née* Brodie; *b* 15 June 1943; *Educ* Brighton Hove and Sussex GS, Hertford Coll Oxford (MA); *m* 21 Oct 1967, Barbara Dorothy, da of Thomas Fox; 3 s (Julian b 1970, Alastair b 1971, Jonathan b 1975); *Career* exec Br Petroleum Co 1965–71; dir: Wood Mackenzie & Co Ltd 1984–86 (ptnr 1976–84, oil analyst 1972–76), Hill Samuel Bank Ltd 1986–89, Laing and Cruickshank 1990, Henderson Crosthwaite 1993–95; *Recreations* chess, bridge, golf, reading; *Clubs* Utd Oxford and Cambridge Univ, Highgate Golf; *Style—* Tony Mackintosh; ✉ 3 North Hill, London N6 4AB (☎ 0181 340 4984)

MACKINTOSH, Sir Cameron Anthony; kt (1996); *b* 17 Oct 1946; *Educ* Prior Park Coll Bath, Central Sch of Speech and Drama (1 year); *Career* theatre producer; began work as cleaner, stagehand and later asst stage mangr Theatre Royal Drury Lane, work with Emile Littler (dep stage mangr 110 In The Shade, Palace Theatre) 1966 and Robin Alexandar 1967; chm Cameron Mackintosh Ltd 1981–; hon fell St Catherine's Coll Oxford; *Theatre* London prodns incl: Little Women 1967, Anything Goes (Savile Theatre) 1969, Trelawney of the Wells 1972, The Card (Queens' revival Watermill Theatre Newbury 1992) 1973, Winnie the Pooh 1974 and 1975, The Owl and the Pussycat Went to See 1975, Godspell 1975, 1977 and 1979, Side By Side By Sondheim 1976, Oliver! 1977–80, 1983 and 1994, My Fair Lady 1979, Gingerbread Man 1979 and 1980, Oklahoma! 1979, Tomfoolery (London and NY) 1980, Jeeves Takes Charge 1981, Cats (also worldwide) 1981, Song and Dance (West End and Broadway) 1982, Blondel 1983, Little Shop of Horrors 1983, Abbacadabra 1983, The Boyfriend 1984, Les Miserables (Barbican, Palace and worldwide) 1985, The Phantom of the Opera (Her Majesty's) 1986, Cafe Puccini 1986, Follies (Shaftesbury) 1987, Miss Saigon (Theatre Royal Drury Lane and worldwide) 1989, Just So 1990, Five Guys Named Moe (and worldwide) 1990, Putting It Together 1992, Moby Dick 1992, Carousel 1993, Martin Guerre 1996; *Style—* Sir Cameron Mackintosh; ✉ Cameron Mackintosh Ltd, 1 Bedford Square, London WC1B 3RA (☎ 0171 637 8866, fax 0171 436 2683, telex 266164 CAMACK)

MACKINTOSH, Dr Colin Edward; s of Colin Mayne Mackintosh (d 1974), and Mary Victoria, *née* Pitcairn; *b* 10 Jan 1936; *Educ* Melville Coll Edinburgh, Univ of Edinburgh (MB ChB); *m* 1965 (m dis 1984); 2 da (Sarah b 29 June 1969, Celia b 1 March 1973); *Career* house surgical and physician appts Leith Hosp and Edinburgh Royal Infirmary 1959–62, surgical sr house offr and registrar Kirkaldy Hosp and Edinburgh Royal Infirmary 1962–64, registrar then sr registrar in diagnostic radiology Nat Hosp for Nervous Diseases Royal Free Hosp 1964–70, visiting assoc prof of radiology Univ of Southern Calif 1970–71, conslt radiologist Royal Free Hospital 1971–; contrib to British Journal of Hospital Medicine 1976–82, fndr of London Imaging Centre (first computerised tomogram clinic in the W End 1980), first person to run a private mobile CT scanner 1982; Rohan Williams medal; FRSM, FRCR; *Recreations* writing, music; *Style—* Dr Colin Mackintosh; ✉ 50 Harley Street, London W1N 1AD (☎ 0171 255 1889)

MACKINTOSH, Hon Graham Charles; s of 2 Viscount Mackintosh of Halifax (d 1980), and Gwyneth, *née* Gledhill; *b* 12 March 1964; *Educ* The Leys Sch, Univ of Newcastle upon Tyne (BSc), Coll of Estate Mgmnt, Univ of Reading; *m* March 1994, Anjella Ruth, yr da of Bryan Fisher, of Tenbury Wells, Worcs; *Career* chartered surveyor; *Recreations* cricket, golf, tennis, swimming, hockey, squash; *Clubs* E India, MCC, Annabel's, Groucho; *Style—* The Hon Graham Mackintosh; ✉ The Mill House, Cuddesdon, nr Wheatley, Oxon OX44 9HQ

McKINTOSH, His Hon Judge Ian Stanley; s of Herbert Stanley McKintosh (d 1975), of Cranford Ct, Chester; *b* 23 April 1938; *Educ* Leeds GS, Exeter Coll Oxford (MA); *m* 2 Sept 1967, (Alison) Rosemary, da of Kenneth Blayney Large, of Erlestoke, Wilts; 2 s (Edward b 1970, William b 1975), 1 da (Alexandra b 1972); *Career* serv RAF UK and Germany 1957–59; admitted slr 1966, Slr's Dept New Scotland Yard 1966–68, private practice 1969–88, dep circuit judge 1976–81, recorder of the Crown Ct 1981–88, circuit judge (Western Circuit) 1988–; chm Swindon Branch of Stonham Housing Assoc, memb of Stonham Housing Assoc, memb of SW Legal Aid Area Local Gen and Area Appeals Ctees 1970–89; *Recreations* family, cricket, sailing, rowing, talking; *Clubs* MCC, XL; *Style—* His Hon Judge Ian McKintosh; ✉ The Castle, Exeter, Devon EX4 3TH

MACKINTOSH OF HALIFAX, 3 Viscount (UK 1957); Sir (John) Clive Mackintosh; 3 Bt (UK 1935); s of 2 Viscount Mackintosh of Halifax, OBE, BEM (d 1980, whose f was head of the Mackintosh confectionery manufacturers), by his 2 w, Gwynneth, *see* Viscountess Mackintosh of Halifax; *b* 9 Sept 1958; *Educ* The Leys Sch, Oriel Coll Oxford (MA); *m* 1, 1982 (m dis 1993), Elizabeth, *née* Lakin; 2 s (Hon Thomas Harold George b 8 Feb 1985, Hon George John Frank b 24 Oct 1988); m 2, 12 June 1995, Mrs Claire Jane Wishart, yr da of Stanislaw Nowak; *Heir* s, Hon Thomas Harold George Mackintosh b 8 Feb 1985; *Career* chartered accountant; ptnr Price Waterhouse; pres Oxford Univ Cons Assoc 1979; sits as Cons in House of Lords; FCA; *Recreations* cricket, golf, bridge; *Clubs* MCC, RAC; *Style—* The Rt Hon the Viscount Mackintosh of Halifax; ✉ House of Lords, London SW1A 0PW

McKIRDY, John Langlands; s of Alexander Watson McKirdy (d 1972), of Glasgow, and Agnes, *née* Langlands; *b* 13 Sept 1931; *Educ* Queens Park Sch Glasgow; *m* 28 Sept 1955, Isobel Fawkes, da of Andrew Brownlee; 4 da (Susan Janet b 14 Nov 1956, Fiona Ann b 27 Oct 1957, Lesley Jane b 14 May 1960, Alison Lynn b 10 Dec 1962); *Career* Nat Serv RAF 1951–53; agency inspr Scottish Amicable 1955–60 (actuarial student 1948–55), life supt Yorkshire Insurance Co 1960–63; Noble Lowndes & Partners Glasgow: joined as conslt 1963, regnl life dir Scot 1967, regnl life dir London 1969, memb Bd 1972, asst new business dir Noble Lowndes Personal Fin Servs 1973, new business dir 1976, dep md 1978, md 1979, dep chief exec Noble Lowndes & Partners Ltd 1987, dep chm 1990–91; dir: Aitchison & Colegrave Ltd, Fame Computers Ltd; *Recreations* golf, bridge; *Clubs* Caledonian, Tandridge Golf; *Style—* John McKirdy, Esq; (☎ 01883 625154)

McKITTRICK, David; s of Frey McKittrick (d 1987), of Belfast, and Rita, *née* Hegarty; *b* 10 Aug 1949; *m* 1978, Patricia, da of P J Hackett, of Coalisland, Co Tyrone; 2 da (Kerry b 1979, Julie b 1981); *Career* reporter East Antrim Times 1971–73; Irish Times: reporter Belfast 1973–76, Northern ed 1976–81, London ed 1981–85; journalist BBC Belfast 1985–86, Ireland corr The Independent 1986–; sometime Ireland corr: Sunday Times, Economist, Le Monde; contrib: Fortnight, Listener, New Statesman, Hibernia, Boston Globe, San Francisco Examiner, New York Times; numerous TV bdcasts; co-recipient Christopher Ewart-Biggs meml prize 1989, Irish media award for reporting on Ireland for a pubn abroad 1987, runner-up Reporter of the Year Br Press Awards 1987; memb: NUJ 1971, Exec Br-Irish Assoc; *Books* Despatches from Belfast (1989), Endgame (1994), The Nervous Peace (1996), The Fight for Peace (with Eamonn Maille, 1996); *Style—* David McKittrick, Esq; ✉ Ireland Correspondent, The Independent, 1 Canada Square, Canary Wharf, London E14 5DL (☎ 0171 293 2000, fax 0171 293 2435)

McKITTRICK, Neil Alastair; s of Ian James Arthur McKittrick, OBE (d 1987), and Mary Patricia McKittrick, JP, *née* Hobbs; *b* 1 Jan 1948; *Educ* King's Sch Ely Cambs, Univ of London (LLB), The Coll of Law Guildford; *m* 31 May 1975, Jean, da of Mark Armstrong, of Low Bentham, N Yorks; 1 s (Mark Alastair b 1976), 1 da (Lucinda Mary b 1980); *Career* articled clerk then asst slr Cecil Godfrey & Son Nottingham 1967–73, prosecuting slr Notts 1973–77; clerk to the Justices: Darlington 1977–81, E Herts 1981–86, N Cambs 1986–89; stipendiary magistrate Middx Cmmn Area of Greater London 1989–; recorder of the Crown Ct 1996–; memb: Advsy Gp Magistrates' Trg Courses Univ of Cambridge 1989–96, Brent Magistrates' Cts Ctee 1990–96, Middx Area Probation Ctee 1990–; special licensing ed Justice of the Peace Reports 1983–, ed Justice of the Peace 1985–89, ed Jl of Criminal Law 1990–; memb Law Soc 1972; *Books* Wilkinson's Road Traffic Offences (ed jtly, 13–17 edns, 1987–95); *Recreations* writing, walking, swimming; *Clubs* Reform; *Style—* Neil McKittrick, Esq; ✉ Magistrates' Courts Brent, Church End, 448 High Road, London NW10 2DZ (☎ 0181 451 7111)

MACKLEY, Eur Ing Frank Rainsford; yr s of Capt John Thomas Mackley (d 1960), of Kingsmead, Maudlyn Lane, Steyning, W Sussex, and Louise Matilda, *née* Brown (d 1930); *b* 13 Nov 1923; *Educ* Shoreham GS, Brighton Tech Coll; *m* 18 Jan 1947 (m dis 1965), Peggy, da of Walter Hamblin (d 1957), of Hangleton Road, Hove, East Sussex; 2 s (b 1949 and 1950); *Career* port construction and repair gp RE HQ No 5 1942–47; articled pupil civil and structural engrg 1939–42, engrg asst 1947–50, res engr West Africa 1950–53, sr asst engr 1953–56, contracts mangr and engr 1956–60, chief design engr 1960–62, dir chief engr and consulting engr 1962–81, co chm 1981–, currently chm J T Mackley & Co Ltd civil engrg contractors Henfield W Sussex; involved with devpt of various S Coast ports incl Shoreham Harbour; chm: Southern Assoc ICE 1971–72, Maritime & Waterways Engrg Bd ICE 1976, 1977 and 1981, Piling Gp 1976–77; memb Cncl ICE 1974–77 and 1981–83; supervising engr for Reservoirs Act 1975 (Sec of State for the Environment appointee); author of sundry tech papers incl Amphibious Air Cushion Duo Platforms to ICE (awarded Webb prize 1974 and S G Brown award Royal Society 1976); FICE 1956, FInstW 1961, MIWEM 1963, memb Société des Ingénieurs et Scientifiques de France 1965, FCIArb 1971, FEng 1984, FRSA 1986, Eur Ing 1992; *Books* Piles & Foundations (contrib, 1981); *Style—* Eur Ing Frank Mackley, FEng; ✉ 45 Broomfield Rd, Henfield, West Sussex BN5 9UD; No 177, Alle 10, Domaine Marin de Grimaud, 83310 Grimaud, Var, France; Bankside House, Henfield Rd, Small Dole, Henfield, West Sussex BN5 9XQ (☎ 01273 492212, fax 01273 494328)

MACKLEY, HE Ian Warren; CMG (1989); s of Harold William Mackley (d 1973), and Marjorie Rosa Sprawson, *née* Warren; *b* 31 March 1942; *Educ* Ardingly Coll; *m* 1, 9 Nov 1968 (m dis 1988), Jill Marion, da of Frank Saunders (d 1955); 3 s (Jonathan b 1970, Nicholas b 1973, Christopher b 1983); m 2, Jan 1989, Sarah Anne, da of John Churchley; 1 s (Richard b 1991), 1 da (Elizabeth b 1989); *Career* FO: entered 1960, third sec Br Embassy Saigon 1963, asst private sec Min of State 1967; second sec 1968, Br High Cmmn Wellington NZ 1969, first sec 1972; FCO 1973, Br High Cmmn New Delhi 1976, FCO 1980, seconded to ICI 1982; cnsllr 1984, dep head UK Delgn to CDE Stockholm, chargé d'affaires Br Embassy Kabul Afghanistan 1987, dep high cmmr Canberra 1989, head of training FCO 1993–96, high cmmr Ghana (concurrently non-resident ambass to Republic of Togo) 1996–; pres and capt Kabul Golf and Country Club 1988–89; *Recreations* golf; *Style—* HE Mr Ian W Mackley, CMG; ✉ c/o FCO (Accra), King Charles Street, London SW1A 2AH

MACKLIN, David Drury; CBE (1989), DL (Devon 1991); s of (Laurence) Hilary Macklin, OBE (d 1969), of Wendens Ambo, Essex, and Alice Dumergue, *née* Tait (d 1977); *b* 1 Sept 1928; *Educ* Felsted, St John's Coll Cambridge; *m* 23 July 1955, Janet, da of Alastair MacNaughton Smallwood (d 1985), of Uppingham; 4 s (Alan Drury, Simon Andre, Alastair Jeremy, Adrian Roger); *Career* asst slr: Coward Chance and Co 1954–56, Warwicks CC 1956–61, Devon CC 1961–67 (asst clerk 1967–69); dep clerk Derbys CC 1969–73; chief exec: Lincs CC 1973–79, Devon CC 1979–88; chm Community Council of Devon; memb: Boundary Cmmn for England, Devon & Cornwall Housing Assoc; *Recreations* golf, sailing, bird watching, travelling; *Clubs* Hawks', Exeter Golf and Country; *Style—* David Macklin, Esq, CBE, DL; ✉ Randolls, Victoria Rd, Topsham, Exeter, Devon EX3 0EU (☎ 01392 873160)

MACKLIN, Peter Richard; s of Lt-Col P H Macklin, OBE (d 1976), and Joan Elizabeth, *née* Butcher, of Yelverrton, Devon; *b* 1 April 1946; *Educ* Wellington, Durham Univ (BA); *m* 21 Aug 1971, Pamela Adele, da of A F Plant Jr, of Washington DC, USA; 3 s (Andrew b 1974, Jonathan b 1977, Christopher b 1981); *Career* slr Clifford Turner 1971–76, ptnr Freshfields 1979– (departmental managing ptnr Property Dept 1986–91); memb Cncl Br Property Fedn; memb: Worshipful Co of Slrs, Law Soc; *Recreations* family, opera, exploration; *Clubs* Malden Golf; *Style—* Peter Macklin, Esq; ✉ Whitefriars, 65 Fleet St, London EC4Y 1HT (☎ 0171 936 4000, fax 0171 248 3487/8/9, telex 889292)

MACKRELL, Judith Rosalind (Mrs S P Henson); da of Alexander George Mackrell, of Surrey, and Margaret Elizabeth, *née* Atkinson; *b* 26 Oct 1954; *Educ* Sutton HS, Univ of York (BA), Univ of Oxford (DPhil); *m* Simon Peter Henson, s of Peter Henson; 2 s (Frederick Juan b 12 Feb 1990, Oscar Henson b 17 Dec 1992); *Career* pt/t lectr in English literature: Oxford Poly, Lincoln and St Anne's Coll Oxford, City Lit London 1981–85; freelance dance writer 1984– (work published in Vogue, Tatler, Dance Theatre Journal); dance corr: The Independent 1986–94, The Guardian 1994–; broadcasts incl: Dance International BBC TV, South Bank Show, Radio 3, Radio 4 and World Service; hon fell

Laban Centre London 1996; *Books* British New Dance (1991); *Recreations* family, travel, reading, food, music; *Style*— Ms Judith Mackrell; ✉ 73 Greenwood Road, London E8 1NT (☎ 0171 249 5553)

MACKRELL, Keith Ashley Victor; s of Henry George Mackrell (d 1967), of Romsey, Hants, and Emily Winifred Jesse Mackrell (d 1972); *b* 20 Oct 1932; *Educ* Peter Symonds Sch Winchester, LSE (BSc Econ); *m* 20 Feb 1960, June Mendoza; 1 s (Ashley b 1961), 3 da (Elliet b 1956, Kim b 1958, Lee b 1961); *Career* RAF Flying Offr 1953–55; dir: Cope Allman International 1977–86, Shell International 1977–91, Private Investment Corp for Asia (PICA) 1980–84, Shell Pensions Tst Ltd 1983–94, Standard Chartered PLC 1991–, Rexam plc (formerly Bowater plc) 1991–, Regalian Properties PLC 1991–, Fairey Group PLC 1993–, British Gas plc 1994–; govr LSE 1991–, chm Enterprise LSE; memb: Int Advsy Cncl East-West Centre Honolulu 1985, Cook Soc; Hon LLD Nat Univ of Singapore; MIOD 1977, CIMgt; *Clubs* Hurlingham; *Style*— Keith Mackrell, Esq; ✉ British Gas plc, The Adelphi, John Adam Street, London WC2N 6JT (☎ 0171 269 4846)

MACKSEY, Kenneth John; MC (1944); s of Henry George Macksey (d 1949), and Alice Lillian, *née* Nightingall (d 1972); *b* 1 July 1923; *Educ* Goudhurst Sch for Boys; *m* 22 June 1946, (Catherine Angela) Joan, da of Thomas Henry Little (d 1967); 1 s (Andrew b 1949), 1 da (Susan b 1947); *Career* enlisted RAC 1941, cmmnd from Sandhurst 141 Regt RAC (The Buffs), transferred RTR 1946, various regtl and staff, appts Army Staff Coll 1956, ret Maj 1968; mil historian; dep ed Purnell's History of the Second and First World War, conslt Canadian Army with task of writing tactical instructional manuals in form of novels; Clash series 1981–91; fndr and vice chm Beaminster Sports Assoc, memb Beaminster Town Cncl 1973–84, vice chm Dorset Local Cncls Assoc 1983–85; *Books* incl: The Shadow of Vimy Ridge, Afrika Korps, Guinness Book of Tank Facts and Feats, The Guinness History of Land Warfare, Kesselring: the Making of the Luftwaffe, The Tanks 1945–75, History of the Royal Armoured Corps 1914–75, First Clash, The Guinness History of Sea Warfare, The Tank Pioneers, Guderian, Panzer-General, Technology in War, Godwin's Saga, Military Errors of World War II, Tank Versus Tank, The Penguin Encyclopedia of Modern Warfare, The Penguin Encyclopedia of Weapons and Military Technology, The Hitler Options, From Triumph to Tragedy; *Recreations* umpiring ladies hockey, listening to music; *Style*— Kenneth Macksey, Esq, MC; ✉ Whatley Mill, Beaminster, Dorset DT8 3EN (☎ 01308 862321)

MACKWORTH, Cdr Sir David Arthur Geoffrey; 9 Bt (GB 1776), of The Gnoll, Glamorganshire; s of Vice Adm Geoffrey Mackworth, CMG, DSO (d 1952), 5 s of 6 Bt; suc uncle, Sir Harry Llewellyn Mackworth, 8 Bt, CMG, DSO, 1952; *b* 13 July 1912; *Educ* Farnborough Sch Hants, RNC Dartmouth; *m* 1, 1941 (m dis 1971), Mrs Mary Alice (Molly) Robinson-Smith (d 1993), da of late Thomas Henry (Harry) Grylls, of London; 1 s (Digby John b 1945); m 2, 1973, Beryl Joan, former w of late Ernest Henry Sparkes, and 3 da of late Pembroke Henry Cockayn Cross; *Heir* s, Digby John Mackworth b 2 Nov 1945; *Career* joined RN 1926, served HMS Eagle and HMS Suffolk 1939–45, Cdr 1948; naval advsr to Dir of Guided Weapon R & D Miny of Supply 1945–50, ret 1956; *Clubs* Royal Ocean Racing, Royal Naval Sailing Assoc, Royal Yacht Sqdn; *Style*— Cdr Sir David Mackworth, Bt, RN; ✉ 36 Wittering Rd, Hayling Island, Hants (☎ 01705 464085)

MACKWORTH, Digby John; s and h of Sir David Arthur Geoffrey Mackworth, 9 Bt, *qv*, and his 1 w, Mary Alice (Molly), *née* Grylls (d 1993); *b* 2 Nov 1945; *Educ* Wellington; *m* 1971, Antoinette Francesca, da of Henry James McKenna (d 1992); 1 da (Octavia b 1977); *Career* former Lt Aust Army Aviation Corps in Malaysia and Vietnam; helicopter pilot: Bristow Helicopters Iran 1972–77, British Airways Helicopters North Sea, China and India 1977–89; currently airline pilot British Airways Heathrow; MRIN, MRAeS; *Style*— Digby Mackworth, Esq; ✉ Blagrove Cottage, Fox Lane, Boars Hill, Oxon OX1 5DS (☎ and fax 01865 735543, e-mail 72016.314@compuserv.com)

MACKWORTH, Rosalind; CBE (1994); da of Rev Albert Walters (d 1963), and Alma, *née* Richards (d 1985); *b* 10 Aug 1928; *Educ* Moorfields Sch, Saxenholme Sch Southport, Queen's Univ Belfast (BA), Girton Coll Cambridge (MA); *m* 2 July 1960, Richard Charles Audley Mackworth, s of late Air Vice Marshall Philip Mackworth, CB, CBE; 2 da (Julia Kathleen b 27 June 1968, Victoria Alma Louise b 17 Feb 1971); *Career* articled clerk, admitted slr 1955, asst then ptnr Gregory Rowliffe Slrs 1955–67; ptnr: Mackworth & Co 1968–82, Mackworth Rowland 1982–; cmmr Social Fund for Great Britain and Social Fund for N Ireland 1987–95; memb: Value Added Tax Tribunals, Law Soc; *Recreations* restoring an old house; *Style*— Mrs Rosalind Mackworth, CBE; ✉ Mackworth Rowland, 3 Zenobia Mansions, Queen's Club Gardens, London W14 9TD (☎ 0171 385 4996)

MACKWORTH-YOUNG, Lady Iona Sina; *née* Lindsay; da of 29 Earl of Crawford and (12 of) Balcarres; *b* 10 Aug 1957; *Educ* Univ of Edinburgh (MA); *m* 1983, Charles Gerard Mackworth-Young, s of Sir Robin Mackworth-Young, GCVO, *qv*; 1 s (Robin Gerard Lindsay b 6 Oct 1994), 2 da (Rose Bettina Natalie b 1987, Constance Ruth Sina b 1990); *Career* art historian; asst curator: Exhibitions Print Room Windsor Castle 1982–84, Drawing Dept Fogg Art Museum 1984–86; *Style*— The Lady Iona Mackworth-Young; ✉ 18 The Chase, London SW4 0NH

MACKWORTH-YOUNG, Sir Robert Christopher (Robin); GCVO (1985, KCVO 1975, CVO 1968, MVO 1961); s of Gerard Mackworth-Young, CIE (d 1965; s of Sir (William) Mackworth Young, KCSI, himself 3 s of Sir George Young, 2 Bt, by Susan, da of William Mackworth-Praed and sis of Winthrop MP, the MP and poet); *b* 12 Feb 1920; *Educ* Eton, King's Coll Cambridge; *m* 1953, Helen Rosemarie, da of Werner Charles Rudolf Aue (d 1978), of Menton, France; 1 s (Charles Gerard, m Iona see Lady Iona Mackworth-Young, da of 29 Earl of Crawford); *Career* serv RAFVR as Sqdn Ldr UK, ME, Normandy; Foreign Serv 1948–55; dep librarian Windsor Castle 1955–58, librarian and asst keeper The Queen's Archives 1958–85, librarian emeritus to HM The Queen 1985–; *Recreations* music, skiing, electronics; *Clubs* Roxburghe; *Style*— Sir Robin Mackworth-Young, GCVO; ✉ c/o Barclays Bank, 61 Cheap Street, Sherborne, Dorset DT9 3BB

MACLACHLAN, Alistair Andrew Duncan; s of Alexander Syme MacLachlan (d 1974), and Amy Louise Pennington, *née* Anderson; *b* 14 March 1946; *Educ* Perth Acad, Univ of Strathclyde (BA); *m* 9 Aug 1968, Alison Mary Simpson, da of James Love, of Dundee; 2 s (Laurie b 3 July 1975, Greg b 26 June 1977); *Career* asst rector Keith GS 1974–78 (princ teacher of business studies and economics 1971–74); depute rector Elgin HS 1978–82, rector Forres Acad 1983–; memb Scottish Consultative Ctee on the Curriculum, memb Bd Moray Badenoch and Strathspey Local Enterprise Co 1996–; sometime chm Elgin Squash Club, exec sec and treas Keith Show; FRSA; *Recreations* music, reading, keeping fit; *Style*— Alistair MacLachlan, Esq; ✉ 82 Duncan Drive, Elgin IV30 2NH (☎ 01343 542193); Forres Acad, Burdsyard Rd, Forres IV36 0DG (☎ 01309 672271)

McLACHLAN, Gordon; CBE (1967); s of Gordon McLachlan (d 1946), of Leith, and Mary Thomson, *née* Baird; *b* 12 June 1918; *Educ* Leith Acad, Univ of Edinburgh (BComm); *m* 17 Feb 1951, (Monica) Mary, da of Nevill Alfred Malcolm Griffin; 2 da (Katrina Mary (Kirstie) b 19 March 1958, Tessa Anne b 17 Dec 1961); *Career* RNVR 1939–46, gunnery specialist 1943–46; accountant Edinburgh Corp 1946–48, dep treas NW Met Regnl Hosp Bd 1948–53, asst dir (fin) Nuffield Fndn 1953–55, sec accountant ed Nuffield Prov Hosp Tst 1955–86; memb various official ctees of Miny Health; memb Inst of Med of the Nat Acad of Sciences Washington DC 1974–, hon fell RCGP 1978; Hon LLD Birmingham 1977; FCA 1947; *Publications* What Price Quality: The NHS in Review (1990), A History of The Nuffield Provincial Hospitals Trust 1940–1990 (1992); *Recreations* reading, theatre, rugby football; *Clubs* Caledonian; *Style*— Gordon McLachlan, Esq, CBE; ✉ 95 Ravenscourt Rd, London W6 0UJ (☎ 0181 748 8211)

McLACHLAN, John James; s of William McLachlan (d 1980), of Birkenhead, and Helen, *née* Duffy; *b* 28 Aug 1942; *Educ* Rock Ferry High GS Cheshire; *m* 24 Sept 1966, Heather Joan, da of George Smith (d 1975), of Heswall; 1 s (Alexander b 4 Jan 1975), 1 da (Deborah b 19 Feb 1972); *Career* mgmnt accountant Norwest Construction 1966–67, investmt analyst Martins Bank Trust Co 1967–69, investmt res mangr Barclays Bank Trust Co 1969–71, dep investmt mangr 1971–74, investmt mangr British Rail Pension Fund 1974–83, dir pensions investmt 1983–84, investmt mangr Reed International plc 1984–88, investmt dir United Friendly Insurance plc and United Friendly Group plc 1988–; dir: United Friendly Unit Trust Managers Ltd 1993, United Friendly Asset Management plc 1993; former chm Investmt Ctee Nat Assoc of Pension Funds; former memb: Panel on Take Overs and Mergers, Institutional Shareholders Ctee; non-exec dir: Iceland Group plc, Iceland Frozen Foods Pensions Ltd, Ushers Holdings Ltd 1994, Usher of Trowbridge plc 1994, GT Income Growth Trust plc, Schroder Ventures International Investment Trust plc (chm); AIIMR, FCA, FRSA; *Recreations* squash, watching cricket and soccer, reading; *Style*— John McLachlan, Esq; ✉ United Friendly Insurance plc, 42 Southwark Bridge Rd, London SE1 9HE (☎ 0171 800 8505, fax 0171 800 8150, telex 8813953)

McLACHLAN, Peter John; OBE (1983), DL (Belfast 1992); s of Rev Dr H J McLachlan, of Sheffield, and Joan Dorothy Hall (d 1979); gf Dr H McLachlan, historian, author of many historical books, prof of Hellenistic Greek at Univ of Manchester; *b* 21 Dec 1936; *Educ* Magdalen Coll Sch, Queen's Coll Oxford (MA); *m* 1965 (m dis 1992), Gillian Mavis, da of John Christopher Lowe (d 1985); 2 da (Heather b 1967, Fiona b 1969); *Career* admin trainee Miny of Fin NICS 1959–62, admin Nat Youth Orchestra of GB 1962–65 and 1966–70, PA to chm of IPC 1965–66, Cons Res Dept 1970–72, exec dir Watney & Powell Ltd 1972–73, Unionist memb S Antrim in NI Assembly 1973–75, gen mangr S H Watterson Engineering 1975–77, jt md Ulster Metalspinners Ltd 1976–77, projects mangr Peace by Peace Ltd 1977–79, sec Peace People Charitable Tst 1977–79, chm Community of The Peace People 1978–80; fndr chm: NI Fedn of Housing Assocs 1976–78, Belfast Improved Houses Ltd 1975–81 (memb Ctee 1975–); memb: Ctee Lisnagarvey Housing Assoc Ltd 1977–90, The Corrymeela Community 1975–, Admin Cncl Royal Jubilee Tsts 1975–82, NI Projects Tst 1977–87; chm NI Peace Forum 1980–82; vice chm: NI Hospice Ltd 1981–91, Gulbenkian Advsy Ctee on Community Work 1978–81; gen sec Belfast Voluntary Welfare Soc 1980–86, chief exec Bryson House 1995– (dir 1986–95), fndr ctee memb Belfast Civic Tst 1981–, memb Cncl Children's Community Holidays 1982–85, memb Exec Ctee NI Children's Holiday Scheme 1982–85 (tstee 1982–), chm Dismas House 1983–87 (memb Ctee 1983–89), presenter BBC Street Corner (Community Action programme) 1983–86; memb: Min's Advsy Ctee on Community Work 1982–84, Min's Advsy Ctee on Personal Social Services 1984–88, Exec Ctee NI Chest Heart & Stroke Assoc 1982–85, Bd of Visitors HM Prison Maghaberry 1986–90 (dep chm 1987–89, chm 1989), Ctee Belfast Common Purpose 1992–; tstee: Buttle Tst 1987–, Anchor Tst 1987–91, Victoria Homes Tst 1989–, Cecil King Meml Fndn 1993–; hon sec NI Fedn Victims' Support Scheme 1983– (chm 1995–), vice chm Victim Support UK 1988–90 (memb Cncl 1987–94), fndr ctee memb NI Conflict and Mediation Assoc 1986–94; dir: Belfast Community Radio Ltd 1989–, Community Network Ltd 1989–, North City Training Ltd 1989–, Partnership Care (West) Ltd 1994–; non-exec dir Eastern Health and Social Services Bd 1991–94, Lagan Watersports Ltd 1994–; memb MRC 1995–; chm: Belfast Branch Carers Nat Assoc 1991–96, Forum for Community Work Educn 1992–94, Belfast Hills Regnl Park 1992–, Fellowship of Reconciliation (NI) 1991–, Thanksgiving Square Belfast 1995–; UK Eisenhower fell 1986; *Recreations* piano playing, mountain walking, conservation; *Clubs* Cwlth Tst, New Cavendish; *Style*— Peter McLachlan, Esq, OBE, DL; ✉ 9 Ashburne Mews, Belfast, N Ireland BT7 1SF (☎ 01232 325602); Bryson House, 28 Bedford St, Belfast BT2 7FE (☎ 01232 325835)

macLACHLAN, Simon; MBE (1983); s of Geoffrey Cheasty macLachlan (d 1965), of Ipswich, and Violet Edith Gasgoigne (d 1990); *b* 17 Dec 1934; *Educ* Downside Sch; *m* 11 May 1963, Julie, da of John Mannering (d 1985), of River, Kent; 2 s (Justin b 1964, Luke b 1965), 2 da (Martha b 1967, Hannah b 1972); *Career* 2 Lt Queens Own Royal West Kent Regt 1953–55, seconded 5 Bn Kings African Rifles 1953–54 (served in Kenya, despatches), Lt 4/5 BN Queens Own Royal West Kent Regt (TA) 1955–62; admitted slr 1959, ptnr Clifford-Turner 1964, assigning ptnr Co Dept 1980–87, ptnr Clifford Chance 1987–93 (head of corp practice 1987–91); non-exec dir: Mid Kent Holdings plc 1991–, Nelson Hurst plc 1993–, Hiscox Select Insurance Fund plc 1993–; chm: Capital Markets Forum Int Bar Assoc 1991–93, Cranbrook and District CAB 1994–, New Islington and Hackney Housing Assoc 1967–83, Kent Rural Community Cncl 1994–; ind memb Kent Police Authy (and chm Audit Ctee) 1995–; tstee Circle 33 Housing Tst 1978–93, memb: Law Soc 1959, Int Bar Assoc 1979 (memb SBL Cncl 1991–93); *Books* Life After Big Bang (1987); *Recreations* gardening, tennis; *Clubs* RAC; *Style*— Simon macLachlan, Esq, MBE; ✉ Sissinghurst Place, Sissinghurst, Cranbrook, Kent TN17 2JP (☎ 01580 712863, fax 01580 719410)

McLAGGAN, Murray Adams; JP (Mid Glamorgan 1968); s of Sir John Douglas McLaggan, KCVO (d 1967), and Elsa Violet, *née* Adams (d 1987); *b* 29 Sept 1929; *Educ* Winchester, New Coll Oxford (MA); *m* 1959, Jennifer, da of Robert Iltyd Nicholl (d 1966); 2 s (John Hector Nicholl b 1961, Rory James Murray b 1964), 1 da (Iona Jane Helen b 1966); *Career* 2 Lt RA 1948–50, served Hong Kong; called to the Bar Lincoln's Inn 1955; student and tutor in law ChCh Oxford 1957–66; farmer; High Sheriff 1978–79, Lord-Lt Mid Glamorgan 1990– (DL 1982); formerly chm: Glamorgan Naturalists Tst, Timber Growers Assoc S Wales, Historic Houses Assoc Wales, Regnl Advsy Ctee (Wales Conservancy) Forestry Cmmn, Nat Tst Ctee for Wales; chm: Gen Cmmrs for Income Tax (Brigend Div), Wales Regnl Flood Def Ctee Environment Agency; memb: Environment Agency Advsy Ctee for Wales, Parly Boundary Cmmn for Wales 1980–, S Wales Police Authy 1988–90; *Recreations* bibliophily, dendrology, amateur operatics; *Style*— Murray McLaggan, Esq, JP; ✉ Merthyr Mawr House, Bridgend, Mid Glamorgan CF32 0LR (☎ 01656 652038, fax 01656 648100)

McLAREN, Dr Alexander Clark (Alex); s of Douglas Clark McLaren (d 1953), of Hobart, Tasmania, and Ruby, *née* Jones (d 1964); *b* 24 Aug 1928; *Educ* Hutchins Sch Hobart, Univ of Tasmania (BSc), Univ of Cambridge (PhD, ScD); *m* 1955, Jeanette Helen, *née* Thompson; 1 s (Duncan Alexander Clark b 1961), 1 da (Susan Jane Clark b 1958); *Career* sr res scientist Central Res Laboratories ICI Melbourne 1957–62, reader in physics Monash Univ 1969–85 (sr lectr 1962–69), professorial fell Res Sch of Earth Sciences ANU Canberra 1985–91 (also Res Sch of Chemistry 1985–90); prof Res Sch of Earth Sciences ANU Canberra 1992–93 (ret 1993, visiting fell Faculty of Engrg 1994–95), visiting fell Res Sch of Earth Sciences ANU 1996–; hon res assoc Dept of History Univ of Tasmania 1993–94; visiting scientist Inst of Geophysics and Planetary Physics UCLA 1966, sr visiting fell Dept of Geology Univ of Manchester 1975, professeur invité Université de Rennes France 1982, visiting fell Electron Microscope Centre Univ of WA 1984, participating guest Lawrence Livermore Nat Laboratory USA 1992; memb Advsy Bd Physics and Chemistry of Minerals jl 1977–; memb Tasmanian Historical Res Assoc 1959, FAIP 1966; *Books* Transmission Electron Microscopy of Minerals and Rocks (1991); *Recreations* music, photography, Tasmanian history, bush-walking; *Style*— Prof

Alex McLaren; ✉ Research School of Earth Sciences, Australian National University, Canberra, ACT 0200, Australia (☎ 00 61 6 2492494, fax 00 61 6 2798253, e-mail Alexander.McLaren@anu.edu.au); 59 Ambalindum Street, Hawker, ACT 2614, Australia (☎ 00 61 6 2543343)

McLAREN, (Dame) Dr Anne; DBE (1993); *b* 26 April 1927; *Educ* Univ of Oxford (MA, DPhil); *m* 1952, Donald Michie; 1 s (Jonathan b 1957), 2 da (Susan b 1955, Caroline b 1959); *Career* memb Scientific Staff of Agric Res Cncl's Unit of Animal Genetics Edinburgh 1959–74, dir Mammalian Devpt Unit MRC 1974–92, memb Scientific Staff of Wellcome/CRC Inst of Cancer and Developmental Biology Cambridge 1992–; memb: Govt Ctee on Human Fertilisation and Embryology 1982–84, Voluntary (Interim) Licensing Authy for Human Fertilisation and Embryology 1985–91, Human Fertilisation and Embryology Authy 1990–; FRS 1975 (foreign sec 1991–, first women offr), FRSE 1971, FRCOG 1987; memb Polish Academy of Sciences 1988; *Books* Mammalian Chimeras (1976), Germ Cells and Soma (1981); *Style*— Dr Anne McLaren, DBE, FRS, FRSE; ✉ Wellcome/CRC Institute, Tennis Court Road, Cambridge CB2 1QR

McLAREN, Hon (Henry) Charles; s and h of 3 Baron Aberconway, *qv*; *b* 26 May 1948; *Educ* Eton, Sussex Univ (BA); *m* 1981, Sally Ann, yr da of Capt Charles Nugent Lentaigne, RN (d 1981), of Hawkley Place, Hawkley, Liss, Hants, and formerly w of Philip Charles Bidwell; 1 s (Charles Stephen b 27 Dec 1984), 1 da (Emily b 1982), and 1 step s (Alex b 1975); *Style*— The Hon Charles McLaren

McLAREN, Hon Christopher Melville; s of 2 Baron Aberconway, CBE (d 1953); *b* 15 April 1934; *Educ* Eton, King's Coll Cambridge (MA); *m* 1973, Jane Elizabeth, da of James Barrie; 1 s (Robert Melville b 1974), 1 da (Lara Jane Christabel b 1976); *Career* Nat Serv Army in Malaya; called to the Bar; formerly with Baker Perkins Engineers, currently business conslt, chm Systems C Ltd; memb Kensington & Chelsea Borough Cncl 1974–86; S Bank Univ (formerly S Bank Poly): chm of govrs 1989–, chllr 1992–; dep chm Ctee of Univ Chairmen 1993–; English Speaking Union: govr 1992–, hon treasurer 1996–; *Recreations* travel, hillwalking, skiing, gardening, music, tennis; *Clubs* Boodle's; *Style*— The Hon Christopher McLaren; ✉ 31 Upper Addison Gardens, London W14 8AJ (☎ 0171 602 1983, fax 0171 371 2730)

MACLAREN, Deanna; *née* Bullimore; *b* 4 Feb 1944; *m* 1, 1965, Patrick Maclaren; m 2, 1974, Michael Godfrey; m 3, 1987, Nicholas Kent; *Career* author, journalist, broadcaster and public speaker; presenter The Single Life (C4); *Books* Little Blue Room (1974), The First of all Pleasures (1975), Dagger in the Sleeve (1979), Your Loving Mother (1983); non-fiction: The Single File, How to Live Alone and Like It; *Recreations* opera, gardening, exploring London, Nice and Paris; *Clubs* Chelsea Arts, Club 2000; *Style*— Ms Deanna Maclaren; ✉ 22 Cromwell Ave, Highgate, London N6 5HL

McLAREN, (George William) Derek; s of Thomas George McLaren, of Eldon Lee, Ormiston Gardens, Melrose, Scotland, and Davina Siddis (d 1982); *b* 21 Nov 1934; *Educ* Galashiels Acad; *m* 1, 7 June 1958 (m dis 1987), Marjory Watt, da of Robert McInnes (d 1981), of Edinburgh; 2 s (Roger b 1960, Angus b 1962), 1 da (Fay (Mrs Thom) b 1964); m 2, 12 Aug 1988 (m dis 1996), Waltraud, da of Fritz Loges (d 1975), of W Germany; *Career* Nat Serv RAMC 1953–55; mangr Theodore Hamblin Ltd 1963–68, md A Schmied UK Ltd 1975–; dir Eyecare Information Service 1993–; chm: Optical Frame Importers' Assoc 1980–90, Optical Info Cncl 1988–90; memb Cncl: Fedn of Mfrg Opticians, Assoc of Br Dispensing Opticians; tstee: Vision Aid Overseas 1993–, Renata Campbell Tst 1991–; Freeman City of London 1980, Liveryman and Court Asst Worshipful Co of Spectacle Makers 1982; FBDO 1956, FInstD 1981, MIMgt 1980; *Recreations* gardening, antique restoring, reading; *Clubs* City Livery; *Style*— Derek McLaren, Esq; ✉ A Schmied UK Ltd, 333 High Rd, London N22 4GZ (☎ 0181 889 9997, fax 0181 889 2782)

MACLAREN, Derek Anthony Ewen; s of late John Ewen Maclaren, and Sylvia Castriot, *née* Mayne; *b* 19 Jan 1925; *Educ* Cranbrook, Sydney Univ (BE); *m* 1951, Pamela Ann, da of late Harold William and Caroline Patricia Miller; 2 s (Anthony b 1954, John b 1958), 1 da (Anne b 1964); *Career* Sub-Lt Royal Australian Navy 1943–47; dir: PA Consulting Services Pty Ltd 1966–70, PA International Consulting Services Ltd 1971–85, PA Holdings Ltd 1982–85, Critchley plc 1984–, CSL Ltd 1987–89; chm: PA Computers and Telecommunications 1976–83, Imperial Software Technology Ltd 1984–88, Videologic plc 1985–96; Stock Exchange: memb Information Services Bd 1987–89, memb Trading Markets Managing Bd 1990–91; memb: Computing Servs Assoc Cncl 1975–76, CSERB 1976–78; memb Advsy Bd: Information Systems & Technol for the Post Office 1986–88, BR 1985–90, Syntech 1986–92; FIMC, MInstD; *Recreations* history, historic buildings, gardening, skiing; *Clubs* Union (Sydney); *Style*— Derek Maclaren, Esq; ✉ The Manor House, West Coker, Somerset BA22 9BJ (☎ 0193 586 2646); Flat 2, 27 The Little Boltons, London SW10 9LL (☎ 0171 373 8330)

MACLAREN, Lady Edith Huddleston; *née* Abney-Hastings; da of Countess of Loudoun (d 1960); co-heiress to the Baronies of Botreaux, Stanley and Hastings; *b* 1925; *m* 1947, Maj David Kenneth Maclaren; 2 s (Norman Angus b 1948, Rory John b 1950); *Style*— The Lady Edith Maclaren; ✉ Ard Daraich, Ardgour, by Fort William, Inverness-shire PH33 7PA (☎ 01855 841 248)

MacLAREN, Iain Ferguson; s of Dr Patrick Duncan MacLaren (d 1967), of Edinburgh, and Sheenac MacInnes, *née* Ferguson; *b* 28 Sept 1927; *Educ* The Edinburgh Acad, Fettes Coll, Univ of Edinburgh (MB ChB); *m* 23 June 1967, Fiona Barbara, da of George Mills Heptonstall (d 1945), of Wood Ditton, Newmarket, Cambridgeshire; 1 s (Patrick b 1972), 1 da (Catriona b 1970); *Career* Nat Serv Capt RAMC and RMO 1 Bn XX The Lancashire Fusiliers 1950–52; fell in surgical res Hahnemann Med Coll and Hosp Philadelphia Pennsylvania USA; conslt surgn: Deaconess Hosp Edinburgh 1967–85, The Royal Infirmary Edinburgh 1974–92, Leith Hosp Edinburgh 1985–87; hon clinical teacher Dept of Clinical Surgery Univ of Edinburgh 1970–92; chm Scottish Triple Qualification Bd of Mgmnt 1984–89, vice pres RCS(Ed) 1983–86 (memb Cncl 1972–92, hon sec 1972–77, convener Examinations Ctee 1990–94); sec Gen Cncl Univ of Edinburgh 1993; Liveryman Worshipful Soc of Apothecaries of London 1989; chm Clan MacLaren Soc 1968–91, chieftain Clan Labhran 1991; Hon Pipe-Maj Royal Scot Pipers' Soc 1960–62, hon sec The Aesculapian Club 1978–; pres: The Old Fettesian Assoc 1990–92, Harveian Soc of Edinburgh 1988, Moynihan Chirurgical Club 1992; FRCSEd 1955, FRCS 1960, FRCPE 1995; *Recreations* music, reading; *Clubs* New (Edinburgh); *Style*— Iain MacLaren, Esq; ✉ 3 Minto Street, Edinburgh EH9 1RG (☎ 0131 667 3487); The Royal College of Surgeons of Edinburgh, (☎ 0131 556 6206, fax 0131 557 6406)

McLAREN, Ian Alban Bryant; QC (1993); s of Alban McLaren (d 1972), and Doris Martha, *née* Hurst; *b* 3 July 1940; *Educ* Sandbach Sch, Blackpool GS, Univ of Nottingham (LLB); *m* 7 Sept 1964, Margaret, da of Alfred George Middleton; 2 s (Andrew James McLaren, FRCS, b 28 Feb 1967, Mark Ian b 29 Aug 1968), 1 da (Dr Rachel Margaret b 28 Dec 1970); *Career* called to the Bar Gray's Inn 1962 (Entrance scholar, Mackaskie scholar), law tutor Univ of Nottingham 1962–64, in practice at the Bar in Nottingham 1962–, recorder of the Crown Ct 1996– (asst recorder 1992); *Recreations* wine, photography, gardening; *Style*— Ian McLaren, Esq, QC; ✉ Ropewalk Chambers, 24 The Ropewalk, Nottingham NG1 5EF (☎ 0115 947 2581, fax 0115 947 6532)

McLAREN, Sir Robin John Taylor; KCMG (1991, CMG 1982); s of Robert Taylor McLaren (d 1981), of Richmond, Surrey, and Marie Rose, *née* Simond; *b* 14 Aug 1934; *Educ* Ardingly Coll Sussex, St John's Coll Cambridge (scholar, MA); *m* 5 Sept 1964, Susan Ellen (Sue), da of Wilfrid Byron Hatherly (d 1988), of Little Rissington, Glos; 1 s (Duncan b 1973), 2 da (Emma (Mrs Nigel Davies) b 1965, Jessica (Mrs Robert Ramsay) b 1966); *Career* Nat Serv Sub Lt RN 1953–55; joined FO 1958, Chinese language student Hong Kong 1959–60, third sec Peking 1960–61, FO 1962–64 (asst private sec to Lord Privy Seal 1963–64), second (later first sec) Rome 1964–68, asst political advsr Hong Kong 1968–69, FCO 1970–75 (dep head Western Orgns Dept 1974–75), cnsllr and head Chancery Copenhagen 1975–78; FCO: head Hong Kong and Gen Dept 1978–79, head Far Eastern Dept 1978–81; political advsr Hong Kong 1981–85, HM ambass to Philippines 1985–87, asst under sec of state Asia 1987–90, sr Br rep Sino-Br Jt Liaison Gp 1987–89, dep under sec of state Asia/Americas 1990–91, HM ambass to China 1991–94, ret; dir: Govett Oriental Trust PLC, INVESCO Asia Trust PLC, Batey Burn Ltd Hong Kong 1995–; *Recreations* music, walking; *Clubs* United Oxford and Cambridge Univ, Hong Kong; *Style*— Sir Robin McLaren, KCMG; ✉ c/o United Oxford & Cambridge University Club, 71 Pall Mall, London SW1Y 5HD

MACLAREN, HE the Hon Roy; s of Wilbur MacLaren (d 1971), and Ann MacLaren (d 1986); *b* 26 Oct 1934, Vancouver; *Educ* Univ of British Columbia (BA), Univ of Cambridge (MA), Univ of Toronto (MDiv); *m* Alethea; 2 s (Ian, Malcolm), 1 da (Vanessa); *Career* Canadian diplomat; Canadian Dip Serv 1957–69 (served Hanoi, Saigon, Prague, Geneva, UN NY and Ottawa), dir of public affrs Massey-Ferguson Ltd 1969–73, pres Ogilvy and Mather (Canada) Ltd 1974–76, chm Canadian Business Media Ltd 1977–93; dir: Deutsche Bank (Canada) Ltd, London Insurance Group, Royal LePage Ltd; elected memb Parl (Etobicoke N) 1979, 1980, 1988 and 1993, Parly sec (energy mines and resources) 1980–82, min of state (fin) 1983, min of nat revenue 1984, min for int trade 1993–96; high cmmr to the Ct of St James's 1996–; Hon DSLitt Toronto; *Publications* Canadians in Russia, Canadians on the Nile, Canadians Behind Enemy Lines, Honourable Mentions; *Clubs* White's, Rideau (Ottawa), Toronto (Toronto), Royal Canadian Yacht (Toronto); *Style*— HE the Hon Roy MacLaren; ✉ Canadian High Commission, 1 Grosvenor Square, London W1X 0AB (☎ 0171 258 6328, fax 0171 258 6303)

McLAUCHLAN, Derek John; s of Frederick William McLauchan, of Bristol (d 1974), and Nellie, *née* Summers (d 1996); *b* 5 May 1933; *Educ* Queen Elizabeth's Hosp Bristol, Univ of Bristol (BSc); *m* 21 Aug 1960, Dr Sylvia June, da of Sidney George Smith; 2 da (Rosemary Jane b 21 Aug 1964, Juliet Sara b 1 Oct 1966); *Career* British Aircraft Corp 1954–66, Euro Space Technol Centre Holland 1966–70, Marconi Space and Def Systems 1970–76, engrg dir ICL 1976–88, md Renishaw Res Ltd 1988–89; CAA Nat Air Traffic Servs Ltd: DG (projects and engrg) 1989–91, chief exec and memb Bd 1991–; memb Bd Architecture Project Managements Ltd 1996– (non-exec chm 1994–96); memb: Cncl The Air League 1994–, Advsy Bd Inst of Geodesy Univ of Nottingham 1994–; author various pubns on satellites, computers, air traffic control; awarded RAeS Simms Prize 1996 (for paper on Air Traffic Control 2000); CEng 1988, FIEE 1989, FRAeS 1993; *Recreations* music, theatre, walking; *Style*— Derek McLauchlan, Esq; ✉ National Air Traffic Services Ltd, CAA House, 45–59 Kingsway, London WC2B 6TE (☎ 0171 832 5772, fax 0171 832 6368)

McLAUCHLAN, Prof Keith Alan; s of Frederick William McLauchlan (d 1972), and Nellie, *née* Summers (d 1996); *b* 8 Jan 1936; *Educ* Queen Elizabeth's Hosp Bristol, Univ of Bristol (BSc, PhD, W E Garner prize for chemistry), Univ of Oxford (MA); *m* 23 Aug 1958, Joan Sheila, da of Howard Dickenson; 1 s (Gavin Ian b 4 June 1962), 1 da (Christine Anne b 4 Aug 1964); *Career* post doctoral fell Nat Research Cncl Ottawa 1959–60, sr res fell then sr scientific offr Nat Physical Laboratory 1960–65; Univ of Oxford: lectr 1965–94, reader in physical chemistry 1994–96, prof of chemistry 1996–; fell Hertford Coll Oxford 1965–; visiting prof: Tata Inst Bombay 1986, Univ of Konstanz 1990; memb: Editorial Bd Chemical Physics Letters 1991–95, Exec Editorial Ctee Molecular Physics 1993–, Gen Bd Oxford 1993–; pres Int EPR Soc 1993–96 (Silver medal 1994); FRS 1992; *Books* Magnetic Resonance (1972); author of 170 pubns and reviews in scientific jls; *Recreations* skiing, walking, reading, listening to music, gardening, watching cricket; *Style*— Prof Keith McLauchlan, FRS; ✉ Physical Chemistry Laboratory, South Parks Road, Oxford OX1 3QZ; Hertford College, Catte Street, Oxford (☎ 01865 275424, fax 01865 275410)

McLAUCHLAN, Dr Sylvia June; da of Sydney George Smith (d 1979), and Muriel May, *née* Treweek (d 1987); *b* 8 June 1935; *Educ* High Sch for Girls Chichester, Univ of Bristol (MB ChB), Univ of Manchester (MSc); *m* 6 Aug 1960, Derek John Alexander McLauchlan, s of Frederick William McLauchlan; 2 da (Rosemary Jane b 21 Aug 1964, Juliet Sara b 1 Oct 1966); *Career* house surgn and physician Bristol Royal Infirmary 1959–60, GP Bristol 1960–66, med offr Dept of Public Health Portsmouth 1970–76, clinical med offr Macclesfield 1976–77, Community Med Dept NW RHA 1977–86, Public Health Dept SW Thames RHA 1986–91, dir of public health Ealing Health Authy 1991–93, dir-gen The Stroke Association 1993–; memb BMA 1959, FFPHM 1989; *Recreations* theatre, gardening, cooking; *Clubs* New Cavendish; *Style*— Dr Sylvia McLauchlan; ✉ Director General, Stroke Association, CHSA House, Whitecross Street, London EC1Y 8JJ (☎ 0171 490 7999, fax 0171 490 2686)

McLAUGHLIN, Eleanor Thomson; JP (1975); da of Alexander Craig, and Helen, *née* Thomson; *b* 3 March 1938; *Educ* Broughton Sch; *m* 1959, Hugh McLaughlin; 1 s (Michael b 8 Dec 1967), 2 da (Eleanor b 26 Aug 1961, Maureen b 7 Jan 1963); *Career* memb (Lab) Edinburgh DC 1974– (dep chm 1984–88), Lord Provost and Lord Lieutenant of Edinburgh 1988–92; chm: Edinburgh Festival Soc 1988–92, Edinburgh Military Tattoo Ltd 1988–; *Recreations* Shetland lace knitting, gardening, Alpine plants; *Style*— Eleanor McLaughlin; ✉ 28 Oxgangs Green, Edinburgh EH13 9JS (☎ 0131 445 4052); Edinburgh District Council, City Chambers, High St, Edinburgh EH1 1PL (direct ☎ 0131 225 2424, fax 0131 220 1494)

McLAUGHLIN, Richard Terence Pike; *b* 28 May 1942; *Educ* Sherborne, Emmanuel Coll Cambridge (MA), Univ of Leeds (MSc); *Career* Ove Arup & Partners 1964–65, Sir Alexander Gibb & Partners 1967–72, Bertlin & Partners 1972–74, BP International 1974–83, exec bd dir George Wimpey 1983–92, independent mgmnt conslt and lectr 1993–; FICE, FIStructE; *Recreations* tennis, rock climbing, bridge; *Clubs* Queen's; *Style*— Richard McLaughlin, Esq; ✉ 52 Canonbury Park North, London N1 2JT (☎ 0171 226 9443, fax 0171 226 8597)

MACLAURIN, Robert Allister Charles; s of (Allister) James Maclaurin, and Mary, *née* Boniface; *b* 12 June 1961; *Educ* Edinburgh Coll of Art; *Career* artist; *Solo Exhibitions* incl: Mercury Gallery Edinburgh 1987, 369 Gallery Edinburgh 1989, Berkeley Square Gallery London 1990, The Fruitmarket Gallery Edinburgh 1991, Benjamin Rhodes Gallery London 1991 and 1993, Edinburgh Printmakers Gallery 1993, Vardy Gallery Univ of Sunderland 1993, Kirkaldy Art Gallery & Museum 1994, Durham Art Gallery 1994, Glasgow Print Studio 1995; *Group Exhibitions* incl: New Scottish Painting (Art in General NY) 1988, Chicago International Art Exposition 1988–89, Athena Awards Exhibition (Barbican Art Gallery London) 1988–89, International Weeks of Painting (Slovenia, touring exhibition of former Yugoslavia) 1989–90, Scottish Art Since 1900 (Scottish Nat Gallery of Modern Art Edinburgh, Barbican Art Gallery London) 1989–90, The Int FIAR Prize Exhibition (touring to Milan, Rome, Paris, London, LA, NY) 1991–92, LA Art Fair 1991, Chicago Int Art Exposition 1991; work in the collection of: Edinburgh City Art Centre, Contemporary Art Soc, Scottish Nat Gallery of Modern Art, Fleming's Holdings, Coopers & Lybrand, Phillips Petroleum (London), The Standard Life Assurance Company, McKenna and Co, Scottish Art Cncl, Unilever, Pearl Assurance, Tetrapak, Hewlett Packard, Pioneer International Australia; *Awards* John Kinross scholar RSA Florence 1984, Turkish Govt scholar 1984–85, Br Cncl travel grant 1988,

Scottish Arts Cncl bursary 1988, Durham Cathedral Artist in residence 1993–94, Dunmoochin Fndn Studio Aust 1995–96, Sir Robert Menzies fellowship Aust 1995; *Style*— Robert Maclaurin, Esq; ✉ c/o Jason & Rhodes Gallery, 4 New Burlington Place, London W1X 1SB (☎ 0171 434 1768/9, fax 0171 287 8841)

MacLAURIN OF KNEBWORTH, Baron (Life Peer UK 1996), of Knebworth in the County of Hertfordshire; Sir Ian Charter MacLaurin; kt (1989), DL (Herts 1992); s of Arthur George MacLaurin (d 1989), and Evelina Florence, *née* Bott (d 1970); *b* 30 March 1937; *Educ* Malvern; *m* 25 March 1960, Ann Margaret, da of Edgar Ralph Collar (d 1968); 1 s (Hon Neil Ralph Charter b 1966), 2 da (Hon Fiona Margaret (Hon Mrs Archer) b 1962, Hon Gillian b 1964); *Career* Nat Serv RAF Fighter Cmd 1956–58; Tesco PLC: first co trainee 1959, memb Bd 1970, md 1973, dep chm 1983, chm 1985–97; non-exec dir: Enterprise Oil PLC 1984–90, Guinness PLC 1986, National Westminster Bank plc 1990–, Gleneagles Hotels PLC 1992–; currently chm UK Sports Cncl; pres Inst of Grocery Distribution 1989–92; govr Malvern Coll; memb Save The Children Fund Commerce and Indust Ctee, Stock Exchange Advsy Ctee 1988–91; chllr Univ of Hertfordshire 1996–; Freedom City of London 1981, Liveryman Worshipful Co of Carmen 1982; Hon DPhil Univ of Stirling 1987; Hon FCGI 1992; FRSA 1986, FInstM 1987; *Recreations* golf; *Clubs* MCC; *Style*— The Rt Hon Lord MacLaurin of Knebworth, DL; ✉ c/o Tesco PLC, Tesco House, Delamare Road, Cheshunt, Herts EN8 9SL (☎ 01992 632222, fax 01992 627033)

MACLAY, 3 Baron (UK 1922); Sir Joseph Paton Maclay; 3 Bt (UK 1914); DL (Renfrewshire 1986); s of 2 Baron Maclay, KBE (d 1969); *b* 11 April 1942; *Educ* Winchester; *m* 1976, Elizabeth, da of George Buchanan, of Pokataroo, NSW; 2 s, 1 da; *Heir* s, Hon Joseph Paton Maclay b 6 March 1977; *Career* md: Denholm Maclay Ltd 1970–83, Triport Ferries Mgmnt 1975–83, Denholm Maclay Offshore Ltd 1976–83; dir: Milton Shipping 1970–83, Br Steamship Short Trades Assoc 1976–83, N of England Protection & Indemnity Assoc 1978–83, Denholm Ship Management (Holdings) Ltd 1990–93; gp mktg exec Acomarit Group 1993–, dir Altnamara Shipping plc 1994–; md Milton Timber Servs Ltd 1984–89, chm Scottish branch Br Sailors Soc 1979–81, vice chm Glasgow Shipowners & Shipbrokers Benevolent Assoc 1982–83; *Recreations* gardening, fishing; *Clubs* Western; *Style*— The Rt Hon Lord Maclay, DL; ✉ Duchal, Kilmacolm, Renfrewshire (☎ 0150 587 2255)

MACLAY, Michael William; s of William Paton Maclay, and late Janette Kiddie Maclay; *b* 14 July 1953; *Educ* Churchers Coll Petersfield, Trinity Coll Cambridge (sr scholar, MA), Univ of Freiburg FRG; *m* Dec 1980, Elfi, da of Adam Lunkenheimer; 1 s (Christopher b 1986), 1 da (Catriona b 1983); *Career* FCO 1976, Br High Cmmn Lagos 1977–79, second later first sec UK Mission to UN NY 1980–83, Southern Africa Dept FCO 1983–84, researcher, reporter and prodr Weekend World (LWT) 1984–88, policy ed The Sunday Correspondent 1988–90, prodr 'War in the Gulf' (LWT) and prodr/dir 'Special Enquiry' on peace in the ME 1991, asst ed The European 1991–93, special advsr to the Foreign Sec 1993–95, special advsr to Crl Bildt High Rep Bosnia 1995–; *PS* Multi-Speed Europe? The Community Beyond Maastricht (Chatham House, 1992), Maastricht Made Simple (ed, 1993); *Recreations* music, sport, family; *Clubs* United Oxford and Cambridge Univ; *Style*— Michael Maclay, Esq; ✉ 23 Disraeli Road, London W5 5HS (☎ 0181 579 2739); Foreign and Commonwealth Office, London SW1A 2AH (☎ 0171 270 2112)

MACLEAN, Prof Allan B; s of Bruce H Maclean, of Auckland, NZ, and Marie F, *née* Mackie; *b* 8 Feb 1947; *Educ* Univ of Otago NZ (BMedSc, MB ChB, DipObst, MD); *m* Mary R, *née* Callanan; 2 da (Nicola b 19 March 1975, Fiona b 4 Aug 1977), 2 s (Simon b 16 April 1981, Allan b 10 Dec 1986); *Career* sr lectr Christchurch Clinical Sch of Med Christchurch NZ 1980–85, sr lectr Dept of Midwifery Univ of Glasgow and conslt obstetrician and gynaecologist Queen Mother's Hosp and Western Infirmary Glasgow 1985–92, prof of gynaecology and head of dept Royal Free Hosp Sch of Med 1992–; FRCOG 1990 (MRCOG 1978); *Books* Clinical Infection in Obstetrics and Gynaecology (1990); *Recreations* rowing and rugby, the life and works of Robert Burns; *Style*— Prof Allan Maclean; ✉ Department of Gynaecology, Royal Free Hospital School of Medicine, Rowland Hill Street, London NW3 2PF (☎ 0171 794 0500)

McLEAN, Prof André Ernest Michael; s of Dr Fritz Fraenkel (d 1943), of Mexico, and Hildegard Maria, *née* Leo; *b* 5 Jan 1931; *Educ* Christ's Hosp, Univ of Oxford, UCL (BM BCh, PhD); *m* 1, Oct 1956 (m dis 1992), Dr Elizabeth Kathleen Hunter, da of Donald Hunter (d 1978); 2 s (Thomas b 1958, Adam b 1960), 2 da (Angela b 1961, Martha b 1965); m 2, Alison Lamb; 2 s (James, Andrew (twins) b 1992); *Career* Colonial Med Serv 1960–63; assoc prof Chicago Med Sch 1964–65, memb scientific staff MRC Jamaica and Carshalton 1965–67, prof of toxicology Univ of London 1980–; author of papers on human malnutrition and relation between diet and toxicity of drugs and chemicals; chm Br Toxicology Soc 1987–88, former memb ctees on food additives, pesticides, and Ctee on Safety of Medicines for Dept of Health, conslt toxicologist on chemicals and pharmaceuticals; FRCPath; *Recreations* canoe, gardening; *Style*— Prof André McLean; ✉ Toxicology Laboratory, Department Medicine (Clinical Pharmacology), University College London, 5 University St, London WC1 (☎ and fax 0171 209 6194, e-mail AMCLEAN@UCL.AC.UK)

McLEAN, Bruce; *b* 1944; *Educ* Glasgow Sch of Art, St Martin's Sch of Art; *Career* artist; solo exhibitions incl: King for a Day (Nova Scotia Coll of Art Gallery 1970 and Tate Gallery 1972), The Object of Exercise? (The Kitchen NY Rosi McLean) 1978, Chantal Crousel Paris 1981, Modern Art Galerie Vienna 1982, DAAD Gallery Berlin 1983, Whitechapel 1983, Tate Gallery 1985, Arnolfini Gallery Bristol 1990; selected group exhibitions incl: Five Young Artists (ICA) 1965, The British Avant Garde (Cultural Centre NY) 1971, Lives and Annual Exhibition (Hayward) 1979, Performance Symposium (Centre Georges Pompidou) 1979, A New Spirit in Painting (Royal Acad) 1981, British Sculpture in the Twentieth Centre (Whitechapel) 1981, New Art (Tate) 1983, An International Survey of Recent Painting and Sculpture (MONA NY) 1984, British Art in the Twentieth Century (Royal Acad) 1987, Twenty Years of British Sculpture (Lettovre) 1988, Great British Art Show (Glasgow) 1990; performance artist and memb Nice Style 1965–; performance work incl: Inteview Sculpture (with Gilbert & George, London) 1969, Sorry! A Minimal Musical in Parts (with Rosi McLean, Hayward) 1979, Simple Manners and Physical Violence (Tate, Riverside Studios and Kunstmuseum Dusseldorf) 1985, A Ball is Not a Dancing School (Whitechapel) 1988, Vertical Balcony (Arnolfini Gallery Bristol, Henry Moore Sculpture Tst Studio Halifax and Tramway Glasgow) 1990; designer Soldat (Rambert Dance Co) 1989; work in the collections of: Arts Cncl of GB, Br Cncl, Contemporary Arts Soc, Saatchi Collection, Nat Museum of Modern Art Osaka, South Bank Centre, Canary Wharf, BR, Tate, Van Abbemuseum Eindhoven, V & A, Nat Museum of Scotland, Scottish National Museum of Modern Art Edinburgh; *Style*— Bruce McLean, Esq; ✉ c/o Anthony D'Offay Gallery, 9/21/23 Dering Street, New Bond Street, London W1R 9AA (☎ 0171 499 4100, fax 0171 495 4443)

McLEAN, Colin; CMG (1977), MBE (1964); s of late Dr L G McLean; *b* 10 Aug 1930; *Educ* Fettes, St Catharine's Coll Cambridge; *m* 1953, Huguette Leclerc; 1 s, 1 da; *Career* Kenya admin 1955–64; Dip Serv 1964, cnsllr Oslo 1977–81, head Trade Rels and Export Dept FCO 1981–83, high cmmr Uganda 1983–86, UK perm rep to Cncl of Europe (with rank of ambass) 1986–90, ret; *Style*— Colin McLean, Esq, CMG, MBE; ✉ 28 The Heights, Foxgrove Road, Beckenham, Kent BR3 2BY

MACLEAN, Colin William; s of Percy Kenneth Maclean (d 1975), and Elsie Violet, *née* Middleton (d 1986); *b* 19 June 1938; *Educ* William Hulmes GS, Univ of Liverpool (MVSc, FRCVS, William Hunting awards); *m* 19 Sept 1959, Jacqueline Diana, da of Frederick Brindley; 2 da (Antonia Karen b 12 Feb 1962, Nicola Janine b 20 Dec 1963); *Career* vet surgn 1961–66; Unilever Ltd: chief vet advsr 1966–72, mangr pig breeding 1972–74, md Farm Mark Ltd and Masterbreeders Ltd 1974–80, gen mangr (South) BOCM Silcock Ltd 1980–83; dep md and dir product devpt Glaxo Animal Health Ltd 1983–88, DG Meat and Livestock Cmmn 1992– (tech dir 1988–92); fndr memb and pres Pig Veterinary Soc (memb 1966), past pres Br Cattle Veterinary Assoc; memb: Royal Counties Veterinary Assoc 1975 (past chm), RASE 1988; *Recreations* squash, rugby, football; *Clubs* Farmers'; *Style*— Colin Maclean, Esq; ✉ Meat and Livestock Commission, PO Box 44, Winterhill House, Snowdon Drive, Winterhill, Milton Keynes MK6 1AX (☎ 01908 677577, fax 01908 609221)

MACLEAN, Donald Michael (Don); s of Charles George Ezra Maclean (d 1985), of Birmingham, and Rosina, *née* Field (d 1990); *b* 11 March 1943; *Educ* St Philip's GS Birmingham, Birmingham Theatre Sch (Dip Speech & Drama), Univ of Warwick (BA); *m* 11 Feb 1967, Antoinette, da of Thomas Auguste Roux; 1 s (Rory Gregor b 24 June 1972), 1 da (Rachel Heather b 19 March 1969); *Career Theatre* London Palladium Seasons 1970 and 1974, Blackpool Summer Seasons 1970, 1972 and 1976, various command performances incl Queen Mother's 90th birthday celebration; *Television* Crackerjack (BBC) 1972–77, Black & White Minstrels (BBC) 1974–77, Cheapest Show on the Telly (BBC) 1979, Mouthtrap (Anglia) 1985, First Letter First (BBC) 1993; *Radio* Keep it Maclean 1980–84, Maclean up Britain 1981, Good Morning Sunday (BBC Radio 2) 1990–; *Books* Maclean Up Squash (1986), Smiling Through (biography, 1996); *Recreations* playing squash, flying my light aircraft, watching my son play rugby; *Style*— Don Maclean, Esq; ✉ Good Morning Sunday, BBC Radio 2, New Broadcasting House, Oxford Rd, Manchester M60 1SJ

MACLEAN, Sir Donald Og Grant; kt (1985); s of Maj Donald Og Maclean, OBE, MC (d 1974), of Dalnabo, Crieff, and Margaret, *née* Smith (d 1972); *b* 13 Aug 1930; *Educ* Morrison's Acad Crieff, Heriot-Watt Univ; *m* 11 Jan 1958, Muriel (d 1984), da of Charles Giles (d 1972), of Newcastle upon Tyne; 1 s (Donald b 1962), 1 da (Fiona b 1960); *Career* Nat Serv RAMC 1952–54; ophthalmic optician (optometrist) in practice 1963–: Edinburgh, Newcastle upon Tyne, Perth, Ayr; chm: Ayr Constituency Assoc (C) 1971–75, W of Scotland Area Cncl SCUA 1977–79; pres SCUA 1983–85, vice chm Scottish Cons Pty 1989–91 (dep chm 1985–89); chm: Ayrshire Medical Support Ltd, Bell Hollingworth Ltd 1996–; elder Church of Scotland, former memb Local Transport Users Consultative Ctee, former chm SW Scotland AOP and Local Optical Ctee, former pres W Highland Steamer Club; Freeman City of London 1987, Liveryman Worshipful Co of Spectacle Makers 1989; Dean of Guildry of the Guildry of the Royal Burgh of Ayr 1993–95; FBOA, FBCO; *Recreations* photography, reading, seeking suicidal trout; *Style*— Sir Donald Maclean; ✉ Dun Beag II, 22 Woodend Rd, Alloway, Ayrshire KA7 4QR; J Rusk (Opticians), 59 Newmarket St, Ayr KA7 1LL (☎ 01292 262630)

McLEAN, Sir Francis Charles; kt (1967), CBE (1953, MBE 1945); s of Michael McLean; *b* 6 Nov 1904; *Educ* Univ of Birmingham (BSc); *m* 1930, Dorothy Blackstaffe; 1 s, 1 da; *Career* chief engr Psychological Warfare Div SHAEF 1943–45, dir of engrg BBC 1963–68 (dep chief engr 1952–60, dep dir 1960–63); chm: BSI Telecommunications Industry Standards Ctee 1960–77, Royal Cmmn on FM Broadcasting in Aust 1972; dir Oxley Developments 1971–; *Style*— Sir Francis McLean, CBE; ✉ Greenwood Copse, Tile Barn, Woolton Hill, Newbury, Berks RG15 (☎ 01635 253583)

MACLEAN, Gordon Hector; s of Lt-Col Norman George Maclean (d 1975), ex Cmmr of Colonial Police, and Katherine Emily, *née* Scott (d 1977); *b* 30 June 1932; *Educ* Bedford Sch, Univ of the Witwatersrand, Johannesburg (BArch 1955); *m* 5 Sept 1959, Heather (d 1984), da of Donald Graham (d 1983); 2 s (Angus b 1960, Donald b 1962), 1 da (Jane b 1965); *Career* architect; conslt Murray Ward & Partners (chartered architects); FRIBA 1970 (ARIBA 1957); *Recreations* music, philately; *Style*— Gordon Maclean, Esq; ✉ 12B Daleham Gardens, Hampstead, London NW3 5DA (☎ 0171 431 2975); Murray Ward & Partners, 1 Heddon St, Piccadilly, London W1R 8HT (☎ 0171 439 9774, fax 0171 494 3250)

MACLEAN, Vice Adm Sir Hector Charles Donald; KBE (1962), CB (1960), DSC (1941), JP (Norfolk 1963), DL (Norfolk 1977); s of Capt Donald Charles Hugh MacLean, DSO, Royal Scots (d 1909), and Gwendoline Katherine Leonora, *née* Hope (ggggda of 1 Earl of Hopetoun); *b* 7 Aug 1908; *Educ* Wellington; *m* 1933, Opre, da of late Capt William Geoffrey Vyvyan, Royal Welsh Fus; 1 s, 2 da; *Career* joined RN 1926, served WWII, Rear Adm 1958, Vice Adm 1960, ret 1962; *Style*— Vice Adm Sir Hector MacLean, KBE, CB, DSC, JP, DL; ✉ Deepdale Old Rectory, Brancaster Staithe, King's Lynn, Norfolk (☎ 0148521 210281)

McLEAN, His Hon Judge Ian Graeme; s of Lt Gen Sir Kenneth Graeme McLean, KCB, KBE (d 1987), and Daphne Winifred Ashburner, *née* Steele (d 1979), of Melrose; *b* 7 Sept 1928; *Educ* Aldenham Sch, Christ's Coll Cambridge (MA); *m* 23 Feb 1957, Eleonore Maria, da of Gebhard Gmeiner, of Bregenz, Austria; 2 da (Elisabeth b 23 Dec 1957, Fiona b 5 March 1959); *Career* Intelligence Corp 1946–48; called to the Bar Middle Temple 1951, practice in London and W Circuit 1951–55, crown counsel Northern Nigeria 1955–59, sr lectr and head of Legal Dept Inst of Admin Northern Nigeria 1959–62, advsr Native Cts 1959–62, practice in London and SE Circuit 1962–70, pt/t dep chm London QS 1968–70, pt/t dep recorder Oxford 1968–70, pt/t adjudicator under the Immigration Acts 1968–70, metropolitan stipendiary magistrate 1970–80, circuit judge (Western Circuit) 1980–; admitted Faculty of Advocates Edinburgh 1985; author of a number of books on the criminal law; *Recreations* travel, languages; *Style*— His Hon Judge McLean; ✉ Combined Court Centre, London Road, Southampton

MacLEAN, Dr Ian Hamish; *b* 9 Oct 1947, Bishop's Stortford, Herts; *Educ* King's Coll Choir Sch Cambridge (choral scholar), Felsted Sch Essex, Mid-Essex Tech Coll Chelmsford, Univ of St Andrews, Univ of Dundee (MB ChB); *m* Anne; 2 c; *Career* RAF flying scholarship 1964; house offr (gen surgery then gen med) Cumberland Infirmary Carlisle 1972–73, sr house offr (accident and emergency) Hexham Gen Hosp Northumberland 1973, MO Support Ships MAFF (Iceland Support Op) 1973–74, sr house offr (accident and emergency) Hexham Gen Hosp 1974, locum GP Longtown and Kirkoswald Cumbria 1974, sessional MO Nat Blood Transfusion Serv 1975, registrar in community med Durham and Gateshead AHAs 1975–77, sr registrar in community med N Tyneside and Northumberland AHAs 1977–80, conslt in public health med Borders Health Bd 1980–89, chief admin MO and dir of public health Dumfries and Galloway Health Bd 1989–, hon sr clinical lectr in public health Univ of Glasgow; chm: COPPISH Project Bd, SIGN Working Gp; vice chm Scottish Directors of Public Health; memb: Health Servs and Public Health Ctee, CHI/UPI Project Bd, Scottish Public Health Forum; FFCM 1989 (MFCM 1982); *Publications* author of published papers in learned periodicals; *Recreations* music (especially modern jazz), photography, art, sailing and boatbuilding, gliding and powered flying (PPL), model making, fishing, shooting, gardening, practical engineering (mechanical and civil), restoration of a ruinous mansion house built by Thomas Rickman; *Style*— Dr Ian MacLean; ✉ Dumfries and Galloway Health Board, Nithbank, Dumfries DG1 2SD (☎ 01387 241860)

McLEAN, James Yuille (Jim); s of Thomas McLean, of Lanarkshire, and Annie, *née* Yuille; *b* 2 Aug 1937; *Educ* Larkhall Acad; *m* Doris, da of Robert Aitken; 2 s (Colin Thomas b 21 Sept 1962, Gary Robert b 10 Oct 1968); *Career* former professional football player and manager; former player: Hamilton Academical, Clyde, Dundee FC, Kilmarnock; former coach Dundee; Dundee Utd: mangr 1971–93, chm 1989–; Scot League Cup 1980 and 1981, Premier Division champions 1982–83, runners up UEFA Cup 1987; former rep Glasgow Select; former joiner; Freeman City of Dundee 1993; *Recreations* golf, bowls, tennis; *Style*— Jim McLean, Esq; ✉ Dundee Utd FC, Tannadice Park, Dundee (☎ 01382 832202, fax 01382 89398)

McLEAN, John Alexander Lowry; QC (1974); s of John McLean (d 1969), and Phoebe Jane Bowditch (d 1975); *b* 21 Feb 1921; *Educ* Methodist Coll, Queen's Univ Belfast (LLB), Inn of Court of NI; *m* 1950, Diana Elisabeth (d 1986), da of Dr S B Boyd Campbell, MC, MD, FRCP (d 1971); 1 s (Simon), 2 da (Jane (Mrs P S Ward), Sara); *Career* served WWII Intelligence Corps 1943–47, NW Europe 1944–45, Rhine Army 1945–47; barr NI 1949, asst sec NI Supreme Ct and private sec to LCJ of NI 1956–66, perm sec NI Supreme Ct 1966–79 (princ sec to LCJ 1979–93), clerk of the Crown for NI 1966–93, under treas Inn of Ct of NI 1966–; chm and memb Wages Cncls 1950–94; memb Cncl Irish Legal History Soc; *Clubs* Royal Cwlth Soc; *Style*— John A L McLean, Esq, QC; ✉ 24 Marlborough Park South, Belfast BT9 6HR (☎ 01232 667330); Lifeboat Cottage, Cloughey, Co Down BT22 1HS (☎ 01247 771313)

MACLEAN, John Robert; DL (Moray 1987); s of Cdr Hugh Chapman Maclean, JP, DL, RN (d 1973), of Westfield House, and Sylvia Louise Radford, *née* Boase; *b* 24 May 1951; *Educ* Blairmore Sch, Milton Abbey Sch; *m* 12 Jan 1979, Veronica Mary Lacy, da of Evelyn Hubert-Powell (d 1985), of Mayfield, Sussex; 1 s (Hugh Charles b 8 May 1984), 2 da (Charlotte Louise b 19 Jan 1982, Anastasia Mary b 18 Sept 1986); *Career* Mons Offr Cadet Sch 1971, cmmnd Queen's Own Highlanders, served Germany, NI and Canada 1971–73, trg offr Scottish Inf Depot Edinburgh 1973–75, served Germany, Belize, UK and NI 1975–77, ret Lt 1977; chm Elgin Branch Earl Haig Fund; memb Ctee Moray War Veterans; memb Royal Co of Archers (Queen's Body Guard of Scotland); *Recreations* shooting, tennis, golf; *Clubs* Army and Navy; *Style*— John Maclean, Esq, DL; ✉ Westfield House, nr Elgin, Moray, Scotland (☎ 01343 547308, fax 01343 551340)

McLEAN, John Talbert; s of late Talbert McLean, of Arbroath, and Dorothy, *née* Gladhill; *b* 10 Jan 1939; *Educ* Reform Street Sch Kirriemuir, Arbroath HS, Univ of St Andrews, Courtauld Inst Univ of London (BA); *m* 1964, Janet Alison, da of Edward Backhouse Norman; *Career* teacher of art history: pt/t Chelsea Sch of Art 1966–74, UCL 1974–78; teacher of painting Winchester Coll of Art 1978–82, visiting tutor in painting at many art schs in GB, Canada and USA; solo exhibitions incl: Talbot Rice Art Centre (Univ of Edinburgh) 1975, 1985 and 1994, House Gallery London 1978, Nicola Jacobs Gallery London 1980, Art Placement Saskatoon Canada 1981, Art Space Galleries Aberdeen 1982, Byck Gallery Louisville Kentucky USA 1983, Martin Gerrard Gallery Edmonton Canada 1984, Dept of Architecture (Univ of Edinburgh) 1986, Kapil Jariwala Gallery London 1987, Jariwala-Smith Gallery NY USA 1988, Francis Graham Dixon Gallery London 1988, 1989, 1991/92 and 1994, Edinburgh Coll of Art 1989; paintings in public collections incl: Tate Gallery, Scot Nat Gallery of Modern Art, Arts Cncl of GB, Scot Arts Cncl, Br Cncl, DOE, Federated Union of Black Artists S Africa, Glasgow Museums and Galleries, Hunterian Collection Univ of Glasgow, City Art Centre Edinburgh; paintings in corporate collections worldwide; maj work incl cmmn for three large paintings for Pollock Halls Univ of Edinburgh 1971, and five large paintings for Scottish Equitable Edinburgh 1996; *Awards* Arts Cncl award 1974, Arts Cncl maj award 1980, Br Cncl travel award 1981, 1984 and 1993, Lorne award 1992/93; *Style*— John McLean, Esq; ✉ Francis Graham-Dixon Gallery, 17–18 Great Sutton St, London EC1V ODN (☎ 0171 250 1962, fax 0171 490 1069)

MACLEAN, Maj Hon Sir Lachlan Hector Charles; 12 Bt (NS 1631), of Dowart and Morvaren, Argyllshire; 28 Chief of Clan Maclean; DL (1993 Argyll and Bute); o s of Baron Maclean, KT, GCVO, KBE, PC (Life Peer and 11 Bt, d 1990), and (Joan) Elizabeth, *née* Mann; *b* 25 Aug 1942; *Educ* Eton; *m* 1966, Mary Helen, eldest da of William Gordon Gordon, of Lude, Blair Atholl, Perthshire; 2 s (Malcolm Lachlan Charles b 1972, Andrew Lachlan William b 1979), 2 da (Emma Mary (Mrs Giovanni Amati) b 1967, Alexandra Caroline b 1975), and 1 da decd; *Heir* s, Malcolm Lachlan Charles Maclean b 20 Oct 1972; *Career* Maj Scots Gds (ret); *Style*— Maj the Hon Sir Lachlan Maclean, Bt, DL; ✉ Arngask House, Glenfarg, Perthshire

MACLEAN, Lowry Druce; s of Ian Albert Druce Maclean, and Diana Futvoye, *née* Marsden-Smedley (d 1979); *b* 22 July 1939; *Educ* Eton, Pembroke Coll Cambridge (MA), Massachusetts Inst of Technol (prog for sr execs); *m* 1966, Frances Anne, da of Henry Crawford (d 1967), of USA; 2 s, 1 da; *Career* dir: Karastan Inc 1970–72, John Crossley & Sons Ltd 1972–79; chm: John Smedley Ltd 1991–, Tomkinsons plc 1991– (gp chief exec 1979–91); The Wesleyan Assurance Society: jt md 1991–92, md 1992–, vice chm 1993–; govr Worcester Coll of HE 1987–; *Clubs* Lansdowne; *Style*— Lowry Maclean, Esq; ✉ The Pound, Old Colwall, Gt Malvern, Worcs WR13 6HG (☎ 01684 540426); The Wesleyan Assurance Society, Colmore Circus, Birmingham B4 6AR (☎ 0121 200 3003)

McLEAN, Peter Standley; CMG (1985), OBE (1965); s of Maj William McLean (d 1961), and Alice, *née* Standley (d 1993); *b* 18 Jan 1927; *Educ* King Edward's Sch Birmingham, Wadham Coll Oxford (MA); *m* 23 Jan 1954, Margaret Ann, da of Richard Henry Minns (d 1967); 2 s (Iain b 1957, Alistair b 1964), 2 da (Fiona b 1955, Catriona b 1962); *Career* Lt 15/19 King's Royal Hussars 1946–48; perm sec for planning Uganda 1963–65 (joined Colonial Serv Uganda 1951), asst sec ODA FCO 1975–79 (memb 1965–87, princ 1965–75), min and perm rep to UN Food and Agric Orgn Rome 1980–85; *Recreations* watercolour painting, watching sport; *Style*— Peter McLean, Esq, CMG, OBE; ✉ 17 Woodfield Lane, Ashtead, Surrey KT21 2BQ (☎ 01372 278146)

McLEAN, Philip Alexander; CMG (1994); s of William Alexander McLean (d 1978), of Oxton, Wirral, Cheshire, and Doris, *née* Campbell (d 1987); *b* 24 Oct 1938; *Educ* King George V Sch Southport, Keble Coll Oxford (BA, MA); *m* 17 Sept 1960, Dorothy Helen, da of Robert Norman Kirkby (d 1984), of Malvern, Worcs; 2 s (Nicholas Alexander b 1963, Patrick Campbell b 1967), 1 da (Alison Elisabeth b 1964); *Career* Nat Serv RAF 1956–58; mgmnt trainee then jr exec in various sales, prodn and engrg mgmnt positions paper and packaging co 1961–65, overseas area mangr consumer goods co 1965–68; HM Dip Serv: entered 1968, second then first sec Euro Integration Dept FCO 1969–70, first sec La Paz Bolivia 1970–74, head of section E Africa Dept FCO 1974–76, dep dir Br Trade Devpt Office NY and head of industl mktg 1976–80, cnsllr and consul-gen Algiers 1981–83, overseas inspr 1983–85, head S America Dept FCO 1985–88, consul-gen Boston USA 1988–91, min and dep head of mission Peking 1991–94, ambass Cuba 1994–; dean Consular Corps Boston 1989–91, chm New England Br Business Assoc 1988–91; Hon LLD American Int Coll 1991; *Recreations* hill walking, Haydn, wines and food; *Clubs* United Oxford & Cambridge Univ, St Botolph (Boston), Club of Odd Volumes (Boston); *Style*— Philip McLean, Esq, CMG; ✉ c/o Foreign & Commonwealth Office (Havana), King Charles St, London SW1A 2AH

MacLEAN, Hon Lord; Ranald Norman Munro MacLean; s of John Alexander MacLean (d 1992), of Inverness, and Hilda Margaret Lind, *née* Munro; *b* 18 Dec 1938; *Educ* Fettes, Univ of Cambridge (BA), Univ of Edinburgh (LLB), Yale Univ (LLM); *m* 21 Sept 1963 (m dis 1993), Pamela, da of Prof Allan Dawson Ross, of London (d 1982); 3 s (Fergus Ranald b 1970, Donald Ross b 1972, 1 s decd); 1 da (Catriona Joan b 1967); *Career* called to Scottish Bar 1964, QC 1977; advocate-depute 1972–75, home advocate-depute 1979–82; memb: Cncl on Tbnls 1985–90 (chm Scottish Ctee), Scottish Legal Aid Bd 1986–90; Senator of the Coll of Justice 1990–; chm of govrs Fettes Coll 1996–; *Recreations* hill walking, Munro collecting, swimming; *Clubs* New (Edinburgh), RSAC (Glasgow); *Style*— The Hon Lord MacLean; ✉ 38 Royal Terrace, Edinburgh EH7 5AH; Court of Session, Parliament House, Parliament Square, Edinburgh EH1 1RQ

MACLEAN, Sir Robert Alexander; KBE (1973), kt (1955), DL (Renfrewshire 1970); s of Andrew Johnston Maclean, JP (d 1924); *b* 11 April 1908; *Educ* Glasgow HS; *m* 1938, Vivienne Neville (d 1992), da of Capt Bertram Walter Bourke, JP (ka 1915), and half sis of Eileen, Countess of Mount Charles; 2 s (Charles, Robin), 2 da (Caroline, Gillian); *Career* CA; chm Scottish Ctee Cncl of Industl Design 1949–58, regnl controller (Scot) Bd of Trade 1944–46; memb: Export Cncl for Europe 1960–64, Br Nat Export Cncl 1966–70; chm: Scottish Industl Estates Corp 1955–72, Scottish Exports Ctee; pres Glasgow C of C 1956–58, chm Cncl of Scottish C of C 1960–62, pres Assoc of British C of C 1966–68, dir Norwich Union Insurance Group, hon pres Stoddard Carpets Ltd and assoc cos; Hon LLD Glasgow Univ 1973; CStJ 1975; FRSA, CIMgt; *Recreations* golf, fishing; *Clubs* Carlton; *Style*— Sir Robert Maclean, KBE, DL; ✉ South Branchal Farm, Bridge of Weir, Renfrewshire PA11 3SJ

McLEAN, (John David) Ruari; CBE (1973), DSC (1943); s of John Thomson McLean (d 1962), of Stranraer, and Isabel Mary Ireland (d 1958); *b* 10 June 1917; *Educ* Dragon Sch Oxford, Eastbourne Coll; *m* 1945, Antonia Maxwell, da of Dr Henry George Carlisle, MD (d 1995), of Heswall; 2 s (David, Andrew), 1 da (Catriona); *Career* RNVR served Atlantic, N Sea and SE Asia as Ordinary Seaman, Sub Lt then Lt 1940–45; typographer; fndr ptnr Rainbird McLean Ltd 1951–58, hon typographic advsr HM Stationery Office 1966–80; tstee Nat Library of Scot 1981; Croix de Guerre (France) 1941; *Books* Modern Book Design (1958), Victorian Book Design (1963, revised edn 1972), Magazine Design (1969), Jan Tschichold, Typographer (1975), The Thames & Hudson Manual of Typography (1980, reprinted 1992, 1994 and 1996), The Last Cream Bun (1984), Benjamin Fawcett, Engraver and Colour Printer (1988), Nicolas Bentley drew the pictures (1990), Typographers on Type (1995), The New Typography (by Jan Tschichold, trans 1995); *Clubs* New (Edinburgh), Double Crown (pres 1971); *Style*— Ruari McLean, Esq, CBE, DSC; ✉ Pier Cottage, Carsaig, Isle of Mull PA70 6HD (☎ and fax 01681 704216)

McLEAN, Prof Sheila Ann Manson; da of William Black, of Dunblane, and Bethia, *née* Manson; *b* 20 June 1951; *Educ* Glasgow HS for Girls, Univ of Glasgow (LLB, MLitt, PhD); *m* 1976 (m dis 1987), Alan McLean; *Career* Area Reporter to the Children's Panel Strathclyde Regl Cncl 1972–75; Univ of Glasgow: lectr Dept of Forensic Medicine 1975–89, sr lectr Sch of Law 1989–90, Int Bar Assoc prof of law and ethics in med 1990–; dir Inst of Law and Ethics in Med Univ of Glasgow 1985– (co-dir with Prof K C Calman, *qv* 1985–87); rapporteur generale XXth Colloquy on Euro Law Cncl of Europe 1990; visiting researcher Univ of Otago New Zealand 1983; Sec of State appointee to UK Central Cncl for Nursing, Midwifery and Health Visiting; memb: Audit Ctee World Assoc of Medical Law, SHEFC, Advsy Gp to Data Protection Registrar, Broadcasting Cncl for Scotland, Sectional Ctee Philosophy, Theology and Law Royal Soc of Edinburgh; memb Ed Bd: Int Jl of Medical Practice and Law, Medical Law Int, Bulletin of Medical Ethics; tstee: Scottish Civil Liberties Tst, Joyce Watson Meml Fund Re-Solv; FRSA 1996, FRSE 1996; *Books* Medicine, Morals and the Law (co-author, 1983, reprinted 1985), A Patient's Right to Know: Information Disclosure, the Doctor and the Law (1989); edited books: Legal Issues in Medicine (1981), Human Rights: From Rhetoric to Reality (co-editor, 1986), The Legal Relevance of Gender (jt ed, 1988), Legal Issues in Human Reproduction (1989), Law Reform and Human Reproduction (1992), Compensation for Personal Injury: An International Perspective (1993), Law Reform and Medical Injury Litigation (1995), Law and Ethics in Intensive Care (1996), Death, Dying and the Law (1996), Contemporary Issues in Law, Medicine and Ethics (1996); also author of numerous book chapters and articles in learned jls; *Recreations* playing guitar, singing, music, literature; *Clubs* Lansdowne; *Style*— Prof Sheila McLean, FRSE; ✉ School of Law, The University, Glasgow G12 8QQ (☎ 0141 330 5577, fax 0141 330 4698, e-mail PROF.S.McLEAN@law.gla.ac.uk)

MACLEAN, William James; s of John Maclean (d 1962), Master Mariner, of Harbour House, Inverness, and Mary Isabella, *née* Reid (d 1978); *b* 12 Oct 1941; *Educ* Inverness Royal Acad, HMS Conway, Grays Sch of Art Aberdeen (DA); *m* 18 Aug 1968, Marian Forbes, da of David Leven, of Fife, Scotland; 2 s (John b 1973, David b 1981), 1 da (Miriam b 1971); *Career* schoolteacher (art) Fife County 1970–79; prof of fine art Duncan of Jordanstone Coll Univ of Dundee 1981–; numerous exhibitions in UK and abroad, incl retrospective Talbot Rice Gall Edinburgh 1992; works in public collections incl: British Museum, Fitzwilliam Museum Cambridge, Scottish National Gallery of Modern Art Edinburgh, Kelvingrove Art Gallery Glasgow; memb SSA, assoc Royal Scot Acad 1978, FSA (Scot) 1981; Scottish Educnl Tst award 1973, Scottish Art Cncl Visual Arts award 1979, Royal Scottish Acad Gillies award 1988; RSA 1991; *Style*— William Maclean, Esq

MACLEAN-BRISTOL, Maj Nicholas Maclean Verity; OBE (1994), DL (Argyll and Bute 1996); s of Arnold Charles Verity Bristol (d 1984), of Wotton, Surrey, and Lillias Nina Maclean, *née* Francis-Hawkins; *b* 25 May 1935; *Educ* Wellington, RMA Sandhurst; *m* 2 April 1965, Hon Lavinia Mary Hawke, da of 9 Baron Hawke (d 1985); 3 s (Charles Bladen b 1967, Alexander Stanhope b 1970, Lauchlan Neil b 1974); *Career* 2 Lt KOSB 1955, Malaya 1955–58, Lt 1957, ADC GOC 52(L) Inf Div and Lowland Dist 1958–60, Berlin 1960–61, Capt 1961, Aden 1962–64, Radfan 1964, Borneo 1965, GSO3 19 Inf Bde, GSO3 MOD (AT2) 1966–68, Maj 1968, Trg Maj 1 51 Highland 1970–72; proprietor Breacachadh Builders and Contractors 1983–; dir The Project Tst 1972–95 (fndr 1967, dir 1968–70, vice chm 1970–72), jt fndr West Highland and Island Historical Research Ltd 1972; FSA (Scot); *Books* Hebridean Decade: Mull, Coll and Tiree 1761–1771 (1982), The Isle of Coll in 1716 (1989), Warriors and Priests: The Clan Maclean 1300–1570 (1995); *Recreations* farming, Hebridean history, wine; *Clubs* Army & Navy, New (Edinburgh); *Style*— Major Nicholas Maclean-Bristol, OBE, DL; ✉ Breacachadh Castle, Isle of Coll, Argyll PA78 6TB (☎ 01879 230353); The Project Trust, Isle of Coll, Argyll (☎ 01879 230444, fax 01879 230357, telex 777325G)

MACLEAN OF DOCHGARROCH, yr, Very Rev Allan; s of Rev Donald Maclean of Dochgarroch, of Hazelbrae House, Glen Urquhart, and Loraine, *née* Calvert; *b* 22 Oct 1950; *Educ* Dragon Sch, Trinity Coll Glenalmond, Univ of Edinburgh, Cuddesdon Coll Oxford, Pusey House Oxford; *m* 29 Jan 1990, Anne Cameron Cavin, wid of David Lindsay (d 1983); 1 s (Hector Allan Cameron b 26 July 1991), 1 da (Augusta Jane Murray b 29 Oct 1992), 1 step s (David Lindsay b 1983); *Career* ordained: deacon 1976, priest 1977; chaplain St Mary's Cathedral Edinburgh 1976–81, rector Holy Trinity Dunoon 1981–86, examining chaplain to Bishop of Argyll and the Isles 1983–, provost of St John's Cathedral Oban 1986–; vice pres and chm of cncl Clan Maclean Assoc 1982–94, pres Int Clan Maclean Assoc 1994–; editor: Clan Maclean 1975–85, Argyll and the Isles 1984–93; *Books* Telford's Highland Churches (1989); *Recreations* topography, history, genealogy, architecture; *Clubs* New, Puffins (both Edinburgh); *Style*— The Very Rev Allan Maclean of Dochgarroch, yr; ✉ The Rectory, Ardconnel Terrace, Oban, Argyll PA34 5DJ (☎ 01631 562323); 3 Rutland Sq, Edinburgh EH1 2AS (☎ 0131 228 6036)

MACLEAN OF DUNCONNEL, Sir Charles Edward; 2 Bt (UK 1957), of Dunconnel, Co Argyll; 16 Hereditary Captain and Keeper of Dunconnel in the Isles of the Sea; s of Sir Fitzroy Hew Maclean of Dunconnel, 1 Bt, KT, CBE (d 1996); *b* 31 Oct 1946; *Educ* Eton, New Coll Oxford; *m* 1986, Deborah, da of Lawrence Young, of Chicago; 3 da (Margaret Augusta b 1986, Katharine Alexandra b 1988, Charlotte Olivia b 1991); *Heir* bro, (Alexander) James Maclean b 1949; *Books* Island on the Edge of the World, The

Wolf Children, The Watcher, Scottish Country, Romantic Scotland, The Silence; *Style*— Sir Charles Maclean of Dunconnel, Bt; ✉ Inverglen, Strachur, Argyll

MACLEAN OF DUNCONNEL, Hon Lady (Veronica Nell); da of 14 Lord Lovat (and 16 but for the attainder) KT, GCVO, KCMG, CB, DSO, TD (d 1933); *b* 1920; *m* 1, 1940, Lt Alan Phipps, RN (d 1943); 1 s, 1 da; m 2, 1946, Sir Fitzroy Hew Maclean of Dunconnel, 1 Bt, KT, CBE (d 1996); 2 s; *Books* Crowned Heads - Conversations with Twenty Monarchs (1993); *Style*— The Hon Lady Maclean of Dunconnel; ✉ Strachur House, Argyll

MacLEARY, Alistair Ronald; s of Donald Herbert MacLeary (d 1984), of Inverness, and Jean Spiers, *née* Leslie (d 1973); *b* 12 Jan 1940; *Educ* Inverness Royal Acad, Coll of Estate Mgmnt, Edinburgh Coll of Art (DipTP), Univ of Strathclyde (MSc); *m* 6 May 1967, Mary-Claire Cecilia (Claire), da of James Leonard (d 1976), of Livingston; 1 s (Roderic b 1976), 1 da (Kate b 1984); *Career* asst Gerald Eve & Co chartered surveyors 1962–65, asst to dir Murrayfield Real Estate Co Ltd 1965–67, asst and partner Wright and Partners Surveyors 1967–76, MacRobert prof of land economy Univ of Aberdeen 1976–89; memb: Lands Tbnl Scotland 1989–, Natural Environment Res Cncl 1988–91, Govt Ctee of Inquiry into the Acquisition and Occupancy of Agricultural Land (The Northfield Ctee 1977–79); pres planning and devpt div RICS 1984–85; chm: Bd of Educn Cwlth Assoc Surveying and Land Econ 1980–90, Watt Ctee on Energy Working Gp on Land Resources 1977–79; hon fell Cwlth Assoc of Surveying and Land Economy (CASLE) 1992; FRICS, FRTPI, FRSA, FIMgt; *Books* Property Investment Theory (with N Nanthakumeran, 1988), National Taxation for Property Management and Valuation (1990); *Recreations* shooting, skiing, hill walking; *Clubs* Royal Northern & Univ (Aberdeen); *Style*— Alistair MacLeary, Esq; ✉ St Helens, St Andrews Rd, Ceres, Fife KY15 5NQ (☎ 0133 482 8862); Lands Tribunal for Scotland, 1 Grosvenor Crescent, Edinburgh

MACLEAY, Very Rev John Henry James (Ian); s of James Macleay (d 1932), and Charlotte Isabella, *née* Kilgour (d 1932); *b* 7 Dec 1931; *Educ* Trinity Coll Glenalmond, St Edmund Hall Oxford (MA); *m* 14 Jan 1970, (Jane) Jean Speirs, da of James Cuthbert (d 1964); 1 s (James b 1971), 1 da (Mairi b 1971); *Career* ordained: deacon 1957, priest 1958; curate St John's E Dulwich 1957–60, rector St Michael's Inverness 1962–70 (curate 1960–62), priest i/c St Columba's Grantown-on-Spey with St John the Baptist Rothiemurchus 1970–78, rector St Andrew's Fort William 1978–, canon Inverness Cathedral 1977–78, canon Oban Cathedral and synod clerk Dio of Argyll and the Isles 1980–87, dean of Argyll and the Isles 1987–; *Recreations* reading, fishing, visiting old buildings; *Style*— The Very Rev the Dean of Argyll; ✉ St Andrew's Rectory, Parade Rd, Fort William PH33 6BA (☎ 01397 702979)

MacLEHOSE OF BEOCH, Baron (Life Peer UK 1981), of Beoch in the District of Kyle and Carrick and of Victoria in Hong Kong; Sir (Crawford) Murray MacLehose; KT (1983), GBE (1976, MBE (Mil) 1946), KCMG (1971, CMG 1964), KCVO (1975), DL (Ayr and Arran 1983); s of Hamish A MacLehose, and Margaret Bruce, *née* Black; *b* 16 Oct 1917; *Educ* Rugby, Balliol Coll Oxford; *m* 1947, Margaret Noël, da of Sir (Thomas) Charles Dunlop, TD, JP, DL (d 1960), of Doonside, Ayrshire, and Elfrida, *née* Watson (whose mother was Ernestine, da of Ernest Slade and gda of Gen Sir John Slade, 1 Bt); 2 da (Hon Mrs Wedgwood, Hon Mrs Sandeman); *Career* joined Colonial Serv Malaya 1939; served WWII Lt RNVR; joined Foreign Serv 1947 (later FO, then FCO, and seconded to CRO), served Hankow, FO, Prague, Wellington and Paris; princ private sec to Foreign Sec 1965–67; ambass: Vietnam 1967–69, Denmark 1969–71; govr and C-in-C Hong Kong 1971–82 (political advsr with rank of cnsllr 1959–63); dir National Westminster Bank 1983–88; chm: Scottish Tst for the Physically Disabled, Margaret Blackwood Housing Assoc, SOAS 1983–92; a vice-pres GB China Centre 1992– (pres 1983–92); Hon LLD: Univ of York, Univ of Strathclyde, Univ of Hong Kong; hon fell SOAS; KStJ 1972; *Clubs* Athenaeum, New (Edinburgh); *Style*— The Rt Hon the Lord MacLehose of Beoch, KT, GBE, KCMG, KCVO, DL; ✉ Beoch, Maybole, Ayrshire (☎ 01655 883114)

McLEISH, Alexander (Alex); s of Alexander N McLeish (d 1981), and Jane (Jean), *née* Wylie; *b* 21 Jan 1959; *Educ* Barrhead HS, John Neilson HS Paisley; *m* 8 Dec 1980, Jill Moira, da of Daniel Taylor, of Aberdeen; 2 s (Jon Alexander b 28 May 1981, Jamie Daniel b 6 Aug 1985), 1 da (Rebecca Lisa b 7 July 1989); *Career* professional footballer; Aberdeen FC: Euro Cup Winners' Cup medal, Super Cup medal, five Scot Cup wins, two League Cup wins, three championship medals; transferred as player/manager Motherwell FC 1994; 77 caps Scotland; involved in local charities; *Books* Don of an Era (1988); *Recreations* tennis, cinema, golf; *Style*— Alexander McLeish, Esq; ✉ Motherwell Football Club, Fir Park, Fir Park Street, Motherwell ML1 2QN

McLEISH, Duncan; s of James McLeish (d 1932), and Dorothy Maud McLeish (d 1982); *b* 16 July 1927; *Educ* Univ Coll Sch Hampstead, St Catharine's Coll Cambridge (Kitchener scholar); *m* 29 July 1950, Jeanne Helen, da of Geoffrey Goodyear; 3 s (Richard James b 3 July 1952, Andrew Philip b 3 July 1959, Charles Anthony b 2 April 1962), 1 da (Susan Mary b 20 May 1954); *Career* cmmnd RN 1948–51; ed The National Builder and The House-Builder & Estate Developer monthly jls 1951–56, chm and md McLeish Associates Ltd London 1960–82, pres Underwood Jordan McLeish Associates Inc NY 1969–82; dir: Inside Canada Public Relations Ltd Ontario 1974–82, Inside Europe Public Relations Ltd London 1976–82, Grigsmore Ltd Ipswich 1982–87; ind PR conslt 1987–; Braintree Cons Assoc: fndr chm 1971–75, pres 1976–78, chm Constituency All-Pty Gp for Britain in Europe 1975; vice chm S Suffolk Constituency Cons Assoc 1987–89; govr Port Regis Sch Dorset (chm Fin and Gen Purposes Ctee) 1969–75; IPR: memb 1962, fndr chm City and Fin Gp 1975, memb Cncl 1984–87, fell 1986; PRCA: memb Bd of Mgmnt 1973, treas 1974, chm 1981; memb NFU; *Recreations* farming, gardening, walking, music; *Clubs* Farmers'; *Style*— Duncan McLeish, Esq; ✉ Vale Farm, East Bergholt, Colchester, Suffolk CO7 6SA (☎ and fax 01206 298356)

McLEISH, Henry Baird; MP (Lab) Fife Central (majority 10,578); s of Harry McLeish, of Kennoway, Fife, and Mary, *née* Baird (d 1985); *b* 15 June 1948; *Educ* Buckhaven HS, Heriot-Watt Univ (BA); *m* 16 March 1968, Margaret (d 1995), da of Walter Drysdale; 1 s (Niall b 1 March 1974), 1 da (Clare b 29 May 1976); *Career* res offr Dept of Social Work Edinburgh Corp 1973–74; planning offr: Fife CC 1974–75, Dunfermline DC 1975–87; MP (Lab) Fife Central 1987–; pt/t lectr/tutor Heriot-Watt Univ 1973–86, pt/t employment consultancy work 1984–87; *Style*— Henry McLeish, Esq, MP; ✉ Constituency Offfice, Unit 14A, Hanover Court, North Street, Glenrothes, Fife KY7 5SB (☎ 01592 755540, fax 01592 610325); House of Commons, London SW1A 0AA

McLEISH, Iona Jacqueline Carol; da of Gordon Alaster McLeish (d 1984), and Jacqueline, *née* Constantinou (d 1993); *b* 18 Dec 1952; *Educ* Pelham Sch for Girls, Wimbledon Sch of Art; *children* 2 s (Rory Alaster McLeish-Lambeth b 12 Dec 1988, Archie Robert McLeish-Lambeth b 25 April 1990); *Career* theatre designer; *Prodns* incl: Arturo Ui (Half Moon) 1978, Merchant of Venice (Young Vic) 1978, Hamlet (New Half Moon) 1979, Pal Joey (Albery) 1980, New Anatomies (Women's Theatre Group) 1981, Alarms (Riverside) 1987, Heresies (RSC) 1987, Medea (Lyric Hammersmith) 1988, Savannah Bay (Foco Novo) 1989, Entertaining Mr Sloane (Derby Playhouse) 1989, For the Love of a Nightingale (RSC) 1989, The Caretaker (Sherman) 1990, My Mother Said I Never Should (Chichester) 1990, Eden Cinema (Theatre Off Stage) 1991, Configurations (Shobana Jeyasingh Dance Co) 1992, From the Mississippi Delta (Talawa Theatre) 1993, India Song (Theatr Clwyd) 1993, The Old Ladies (Greenwich) 1994, House of Mirth (Cambridge Theatre Co) 1995, Women of Troy (RNT) 1995; *Awards* London Theatre Award 1987; *Recreations* music, gardening; *Style*— Ms Iona McLeish; ✉ 43 Helix Road, London SW2 2JR (☎ 0181 674 5753); Framework, The Foundry, 156 Blackfriars Road, London SE1 8EN (☎ 0171 721 7158, fax 0171 721 7159)

McLEISH, Kenneth; s of John McLeish, of Victoria, Canada, and Stella, *née* Tyrrell; *b* 10 Oct 1940; *Educ* Bradford GS, Worcester Coll Oxford (BMus, MA); *m* 30 May 1967, Valerie; 2 s (Simon b 27 Dec 1968, Andrew b 9 Sept 1970); *Career* schoolmaster 1963–75; posts at: Watford GS 1963–68, Bedales Sch 1969–73; author, translator and broadcaster; *Publications* (over 80) incl for adults: The Theatre of Aristophanes (1980), Penguin Companion to the Arts in the 20th Century (1984), Listener's Guide to Classical Music (jtly with V McLeish, 1985), Shakespeare's Characters (1987, 2 edn 1991), Bloomsbury Good Reading Guide (1988 - biannually), Good Books Start Here (1992), Guide to Human Thought (ed, 1993), Crucial Classics (jtly with V McLeish, 1994), Myth (1996), The Greek Myths (Folio Soc, ed, 1996), Key Thinkers (ed, 1997); for children: Oxford First Companion to Music (jtly with V McLeish, 1979), Children of the Gods (1984), Collins Illustrated Encyclopaedia of Famous People (jtly with V McLeish, 1990); trans performed on stage, TV and radio incl: The Serpent Son (BBC TV 1979), Philoctetes (Cheek by Jowl, 1988), Electra (RSC London, 1990), Peer Gynt (Royal Nat Theatre, 1990), Medea (Royal Exchange Theatre, 1991), Pig in a Poke (Oxford Stage Co. 1992), The Great Highway (Gate, 1993), Jeppe of the Hill (Gate, 1994), Lysistrata (Contact, 1994), School for Wives (English Touring Theatre, 1995), Agamemnon's Children (Gate, 1995), Women of Troy (Royal Nat Theatre, 1995), Hedda Gabler (English Touring Theatre, 1996), Medea (Opera North, 1996), The Belle Vue (Actors' Touring Company) 1996, Orpheus (Actors' Touring Company, 1997); *Recreations* listening to music, gardening; *Style*— Kenneth McLeish, Esq; ✉ c/o A P Watt Ltd, 20 John St, London WC1N 2DR (☎ 0171 405 6774)

MACLEISH, Martin; s of Cyril Hubert Macleish (d 1986), and Kathleen Josephine, *née* McCoy; *b* 1 Sept 1955; *Educ* St Ignatius Coll Enfield Middx; *m* 18 April 1981, Shirley Teresa, da of Sidney Gilbert Rodrigues, of Sydney, Aust; 2 s (Mark b 8 March 1983, Michael b 18 Feb 1986); *Career* fndr dir Kensington Publications Ltd (int reference book and magazine publishers for Cwlth Secretariat and numerous int orgns); *Books* VIP Guide to London 1995–96 and 1996–97, The Australian Bicentenary 1788–1988, The Commonwealth Ministers Reference book 1996–97; *Recreations* tennis, golf, travel; *Style*— Martin Macleish, Esq; ✉ Kensington Publications Ltd, 111 Southwark Street, London SE1 0JF (☎ 0171 717 0077, fax 0171 717 1026, telex 936012)

McLELLAN, Prof David Thorburn; s of Robert Douglas McLellan (d 1973), and Olive May, *née* Bush; *b* 10 Feb 1940; *Educ* Merchant Taylors', St John's Coll Oxford (BA, MA, DPhil); *m* 1 July 1967, Annie, da of André Brassart; 2 da (Gabrielle b 8 Nov 1968, Stephanie b 8 May 1970); *Career* Univ of Kent: lectr 1966–70, sr lectr in politics 1970–75, prof of political theory 1975–; visiting prof State Univ of NY 1969, visiting fell Indian Inst of Advanced Study Simla 1970; *Books* The Young Hegelians and Karl Marx (1969), Marx before Marxism (1970), Karl Marx: The Early Texts (1971), Marx's Grundrisse (1971), The Thought of Karl Marx (1971), Marx (1971), Karl Marx: His Life and Thought (1973), Engels (1977), Karl Marx: Selected Writings (1977), Marxism after Marx (1980), Karl Marx: Interviews and Recollections (1983), Marx: The First Hundred Years (ed, 1983), Karl Marx: The Legacy (1983), Ideology (1985), Marxism: Selected Texts (ed, 1987), Marxism and Religion (1987), Simone Weil: Utopian Pessimist (1990), Unto Caesar: The Political Relevance of Christianity (1992), Religion in Public Life (ed, 1993), Politics and Christianity (1995), Political Christianity: A Reader (1997); *Style*— Prof David McLellan; ✉ 13 Ivy Lane, Canterbury, Kent CT1 1TU (☎ 01227 463579); Eliot College, University of Kent, Canterbury, Kent CT2 7NS (☎ 01227 764000)

McLELLAN, Gamon Paul Averre; s of Eric Arthur McLellan (d 1965), and Emily Joyce, *née* Sadler; *b* 30 Oct 1949; *Educ* Brighton Coll, Keble Coll Oxford (MA), Patriarchal Inst for Patristic Studies Thessaloniki Greece; *m* Dr Bengisu Rona, lectr in Turkish Studies SOAS; *Career* freelance journalist and ed Political & Economic Weekly Ankara 1976–78, asst ed Arab Month Magazine London 1979; BBC World Service: head BBC Turkish Serv and E Mediterranean commentator on other BBC servs 1979–88, dep head BBC Central European Servs 1988–92, head BBC Arabic Serv 1992–; *Style*— Mr Gamon McLellan; ✉ BBC Arabic Service, PO Box 76, Bush House, Strand, London WC2B 4PH (☎ 0171 257 2534, fax 0171 836 2264, e-mail Gamon.McLellan@bbc.co.uk)

MACLELLAN, Ian David; s of Maj Henry Crawford Maclellan, MBE, TD, of Walton-on-the-Hill, Surrey, and Daphne Loya, *née* Taverner; *b* 21 Feb 1948; *Educ* Sherborne, Cranfield Business Sch (MBA); *m* 29 Aug 1974, Maja Ursula, da of Dr Hans Schaschek, of Weinheim, Germany; 1 s (Henry b 1983), 1 da (Kirstin b 1980); *Career* public co dir; gp md Ibstock plc until 1996, dir Higgs & Hill plc, dir Howden Group plc; FCA; *Recreations* shooting, horses; *Style*— Ian D Maclellan, Esq; ✉ Wormleighton Grange, nr Leamington Spa, Warwickshire CV33 0XJ (☎ 01295 770334); Lutterworth House, Lutterworth, Leics (☎ 01455 553071)

MacLELLAN, Maj-Gen (Andrew) Patrick Withy; CB (1981), CVO (1989), MBE (1964); s of Kenneth MacLellan (d 1981), and Rachel Madeline, *née* Withy (d 1979); *b* 29 Nov 1925; *Educ* Uppingham; *m* 1954, Kathleen Mary, da of Capt Robert Armstrong Bagnell (d 1969), of Hindhead; 1 s (Ian), 2 da (Fiona, (twin) Diana); *Career* cmmnd Coldstream Gds 1944; serv Palestine, N Africa, Egypt, Germany, DAA and QMG 4 Gds Bde Gp 1958–59, mil asst to Chief of Def Staff (Adm of the Fleet Earl Mountbatten of Burma) 1961–64, instr Staff Coll Camberley 1964–66, GSO1 (plans) Far East Cmd 1966–67, CO 1 Bn Coldstream Gds 1968–70, Col GS Near East Land Forces 1970–71, Cdr 8 Bde 1971–72, RCDS 1973, dep cdr and COS London Dist 1974–77, pres Regular Cmmns Bd 1978–80; govr HM Tower of London and Keeper of the Jewel House 1984–89, memb (Walbrook Ward) Ct of Common Cncl City of London 1989– (chm Police Ctee 1995–); memb Ctee Royal Humane Soc, vice pres Offrs' Assoc, memb Advsy Cncl Women's Tport Serv (FANY); Freeman: City of London, Co of Watermen and Lightmen of the River Thames; Liveryman Worshipful Co of Fletchers (currently Upper Warden); Chevalier de la Légion d'Honneur 1960; FIMgt 1970; *Clubs* White's, Pratt's, Walbrook Ward (chm 1995); *Style*— Maj-Gen Patrick MacLellan, CB, CVO, MBE; ✉ c/o Bank of Scotland, 38 Threadneedle St, London EC2P 2EM

MacLENNAN, HE David Ross; s of David Ross MacLennan (d 1980), and Agnes, *née* McConnell; *b* 12 Feb 1945; *m* Margaret, *née* Lytollis; 2 da (b 1964 and 1966); *Career* HM Dip Serv: joined FO 1963, MECAS 1966–69, third then second sec Aden 1969–71, FCO 1972–75, first sec UK Delgn OECD Paris 1975–79, first sec Abu Dhabi 1979–82, asst head N America Dept FCO 1983–84, seconded to EC Brussels 1984–85, cnsllr and dep head of mission Kuwait 1985–89, dep high cmmr Cyprus 1989–90, HM consul gen Jerusalem 1990–93, head Africa Dept (Equatorial) FCO and cmmr Br Indian Ocean Territory 1994–96, HM ambass Lebanon 1996–; *Style*— HE Mr David MacLennan; ✉ c/o Foreign & Commonwealth Office (Beruit), King Charles Street, London SW1A 2AH

MACLENNAN, Prof Duncan; s of James Dempster Maclennan (d 1968), of Mull, and Mary Mackechnie, *née* Campbell; *b* 12 March 1949; *Educ* Allan Glen's Secdy Sch Glasgow, Univ of Glasgow (MA, Silver Medal and univ essay prize Royal Scottish Geographical Soc, pres Geographical Soc, MPhil); *m* 1971 (sep 1989); 1 s (John Campbell b 14 July 1975), 1 da (Marjory Kate b 21 Sept 1977); *Career* res fell Univ of Glasgow 1974–76, lectr in economics Univ of Aberdeen 1976–79; Univ of Glasgow: lectr in applied econ 1979–84, dir Centre for Housing Res 1984–96, prof of applied economics 1985–88, prof of urban studies 1988–90, Mactaggart prof of economics and finance 1991–; Susman visiting prof Wharton Business Sch Univ of Pennsylvania 1989, Regents prof Univ of Calif 1996; dir ESRC Prog on Cities 1996–, exec chm Joseph Rowntree Area Regeneration Steering Gp 1996–; memb: Bd Scottish Homes 1989–, European Urban Inst 1992–, Co-ordinating Ctee European Housing Res Network 1989–; economic advsr: housing Joseph Rowntree Fndn 1991–95, Duke of Edinburgh's second inquiry into British Housing 1990–91; chm Care and Repair (Scotland) 1989–93; FRSA 1993; *Books* Regional Policy: Past Experiences and New Directions (ed, 1979), Housing Economics (1982), Neighbourhood Change (1986), The Housing Authority of the Future (ed, 1992), Housing Finance (ed, 1993); *Recreations* gardening (or at least digging holes), slimming, watching rugby, enjoying Glasgow; *Style*— Prof Duncan Maclennan; ✉ 3 Glenburn Road, Bearsden, Glasgow G61 4PT (☎ 0141 942 1394); Centre for Housing Research, University of Glasgow, 25 Bute Gardens, Glasgow G12 8RS (☎ 0141 339 8855 ext 4615, fax 0141 330 4983)

MacLENNAN, Moray Alexander Stewart; s of Brig Donald Ross MacLennan, of Edinburgh; *b* 29 Aug 1961; *Educ* Fettes, Christ's Coll Cambridge (scholar, MA); *m* Helen, da of Neil Chaffey; *Career* Saatchi & Saatchi Advertising: joined 1983, bd dir 1988, md 1994–95 (resigned); jt chief exec M&C Saatchi Ltd 1995–; *Recreations* golf, rugby, cooking; *Style*— Moray MacLennan, Esq; ✉ M&C Saatchi Ltd, 34–36 Golden Square, London W1R 4EE (☎ 0171 543 4500, fax 0171 543 4501)

McLENNAN, Peter Robert; s of Jack McLennan (d 1985), and Dorothy, *née* Walker; *b* 8 March 1946; *Educ* Edmonton Co GS, Middx Poly, Enfield Coll; *m* 29 July 1972, Vivien Joy, da of Kenneth William West; *Career* md: Metal Supplies Ltd 1982–89, Boustead Industs Ltd 1986–; dir Boustead plc 1989–; memb Wicken Bonhunt PCC; *Recreations* gardening, architecture, travel; *Style*— Peter McLennan, Esq; ✉ Boustead plc, 14–15 Conduit St, London W1R 9TG (☎ 0171 491 7674, fax 0171 493 6647)

MACLENNAN, Robert Adam Ross; MP (Lib Dem) Caithness and Sutherland (majority 5,365); s of Sir Hector Maclennan (d 1978), by his 1 w, Isabel, *née* Adam; *b* 26 June 1936; *Educ* Glasgow Acad, Balliol Coll Oxford, Trinity Coll Cambridge, Columbia Univ NY; *m* 1968, Helen, wid of Paul Noyes, and da of Judge Ammi Cutter, of Cambridge, Mass; 1 s, 1 da, 1 step s; *Career* called to the Bar 1962; MP (Lab until 1981, SDP 1981–88, now Lib Dem) Caithness and Sutherland 1966–; PPS to Cwlth Affrs Sec 1967–69 and to Min without Portfolio 1969–70, oppn spokesman on Scottish Affrs 1970–71, on Def 1971–72, Parly under sec for prices and consumer protection 1974–79, memb Commons Public Accounts Ctee 1979–, oppn spokesman on foreign affrs 1979–80, SDP spokesman on agric 1981–87, SDP spokesman on home & legal affrs 1983–87, ldr of the SDP 1987–88, Lib Dem spokesman on home affrs and nat heritage 1988–94, Lib Dem pres and spokesman on constitutional affrs and nat heritage 1994–; *Recreations* theatre, music and visual arts; *Clubs* Brooks's; *Style*— Robert Maclennan, Esq, MP; ✉ House of Commons, London SW1A 0AA (☎ 0171 219 6553)

MacLENNAN, Prof William Jardine; s of Alexander MacLennan (d 1975), and Mary Sinclair Angus (d 1986); *b* 11 Feb 1941; *Educ* Hutchesons' Boys GS, Univ of Glasgow (MB ChB, MD); *m* 9 Aug 1969, Fiona Hannah, da of Hugh Campbell, of Mount Florida, Glasgow; 2 s (Peter b 1974, Richard (twin) b 1974); *Career* jr hosp and univ post in Glasgow 1964–71, sr lectr in geriatric med Univ of Southampton 1971–80, sr lectr then reader in geriatric med Univ of Dundee 1980–86, prof of geriatric med Univ of Edinburgh 1986–96; chm of tstees Dementia Servs Devpt Centre Stirling, memb Cncl for Professions Supplementary to Medicine; FRCP (Glasgow, Edinburgh, London); *Books* The Elderly (with A N Shephard and I H Stevenson, 1984), Bone Disease in the Elderly (with C R Paterson, 1984), Medical Care of the Elderly (with M R P Hall and M D W Lye, 2 edn, 1986, 3 edn, 1993), Metabolic and Endocrine Problems in the Elderly (with N R Peden, 1989), Old Age (1990), Infections in Old Age (1994); *Recreations* reading, hillwalking, model ship building; *Style*— Prof William MacLennan; ✉ 26 Caiystane Ave, Fairmilehead, Edinburgh (☎ 0131 445 1755)22

MacLENNAN OF MacLENNAN, Ruairidh Donald George; 35 Chief of Clan MacLennan; o s of Ronald George MacLennan of MacLennan (d 1989), 34 Chief of Clan MacLennan, and Margaret Ann, *née* MacLennan (d 1993); *b* 22 April 1977; *Educ* Inverness Royal Acad, Fettes, Heriot-Watt Univ; *Career* head chorister St Andrew's Episcopal Cathedral Inverness, pipe major Fettes Coll Pipe Band; *Recreations* reading, music, canoeing, fishing, Duke of Edinburgh's Award (Bronze, Silver and Gold), Scottish country dancing; *Style*— The MacLennan of MacLennan; ✉ The Old Mill, Dores, Inverness IV1 2TR

MacLEOD, Alexander Joseph; s of Arthur Norman MacLeod (d 1967), and Florence Ellen Feltoé, *née* Cameron; *b* 24 Jan 1934; *Educ* Christ's Coll GS NZ, Univ of NZ (BA Hons); *m* 1956, Gabriella Terezia Borbala, da of Zoltan Vági; *Career* news compiler NZ Broadcasting Serv 1955–56, cmmnd offr Royal NZ Armd Corps 1956–59, leader and feature writer NZ Herald 1959–61, def corr The Scotsman Edinburgh 1961–63 (dip corr 1963–66), freelance broadcaster (BBC current affairs programmes) 1962–67, ed NZ Listener 1967–72, freelance writer and broadcaster 1972–74, presenter Twenty Fours Hours (BBC World Service) 1973–84, dip ed The Scotsman 1974–85, ed Round Table Quarterly Journal of Int Affairs 1976–79, presenter The World Tonight (BBC Radio 4) 1983–, dep foreign ed Sunday Times London 1985–86 (foreign ed 1987–88), columnist Scotland on Sunday Edinburgh 1988–, contrib ed Foreign Affairs BBC Radio 1988–90, Br Isles corr The Christian Science Monitor Boston USA 1988–; pres NZ Inst of Int Affairs 1970–72; *Recreations* music, reading history, foreign travel, gentle walking; *Style*— Alexander MacLeod, Esq; ✉ c/o BBC Radio 4, Broadcasting House, London W1A 1AA

McLEOD, Dr Andrew Alasdair; s of Andrew Frederick McLeod, OBE, of Bathford, Nr Bath, Somerset, and Janet Mary, *née* Comline; *b* 21 Jan 1948; *Educ* King Edward's Sch Bath, St Catharine's Coll Cambridge (BA, MA, MB BChir, MD), FRCP; *m* 3 Sept 1983, Sharon (m dis 1994), da of Wallace Redpath, of Appleton Park, Cheshire; 2 da (Anna Louise b 26 May 1989, Katharine Sîan b 2 Feb 1991); *Career* assoc Faculty of Med Duke Univ Med Center N Carolina 1983 (Br Heart Fndn and American Heart Assoc fell 1981–83), conslt cardiologist King's Coll and Dulwich Hosps 1984–88, conslt cardiologist and physician Poole Gen Hosp Dorset 1988–; memb: Cncl Action on Smoking and Health, Rehabilitation Ctee Coronary Prevention Gp, Cncl Br Cardiac Soc; FRCP; *Recreations* golf, sailing, classical guitar, music; *Clubs* Parkstone Yacht, Royal Motor Yacht, Parkstone Golf; *Style*— Dr Andrew McLeod; ✉ Poole General Hospital, Longfleet Rd, Poole, Dorset BH15 2JB (☎ 01202 665511 ext 2572, fax 01202 442754)

MacLEOD, Dr Calum Alexander; CBE (1991); s of Rev Lachlan Macleod (d 1966), of Glenurquhart, and Jessie Mary Morrison (d 1970); *b* 25 July 1935; *Educ* Nicolson Inst Stornoway, Glenurquhart HS, Univ of Aberdeen (MA, LLB); *m* 21 July 1962, Elizabeth Margaret, da of David Davidson (d 1973), of Inverness; 2 s (Allan b 1966, David b 1968), 1 da (Edythe b 1972); *Career* Nat Serv 2 Lt RAEC; ptnr Paull & Williamsons (advocates) Aberdeen 1964–80; chm: Abtrust Scotland Investment Co PLC 1986–, Grampian TV PLC 1993– (dep chm 1982), Britannia Building Society 1994– (dep chm 1993–94); dep chm Scottish Eastern Investment Trust plc 1988–; dir: Aberdeen Bd Bank of Scotland 1980–, Bradstock Group PLC 1994–, Macdonald Hotels PLC 1995–; dir Caledonian Res Fndn 1990–94; chllr's assessor Univ of Aberdeen 1979–90; memb: White Fish Authy 1973–80, North of Scot Hydro-Electric Bd 1976–84, Highlands and Islands Devpt Bd 1984–91; chm: Robert Gordon's Coll 1981–94, Harris Tweed Assoc 1984–93, Scot Cncl of Ind Schs 1991–, Grampian Health Bd 1993– (memb 1991); Hon LLD Univ of Aberdeen 1986; memb Law Soc of Scotland 1958, FInstD 1982; *Recreations* golf, music, travel, reading; *Clubs* Royal Northern, Royal Aberdeen Golf, Nairn Golf; *Style*— Dr Calum MacLeod, CBE; ✉ Grampian Television PLC, Queen's Cross, Aberdeen AB9 2XJ (☎ 01224 846600, fax 01224 846805)

McLEOD, Sir Charles Henry; 3 Bt (UK 1925), of The Fairfields, Cobham, Surrey; s of Sir Murdoch Campbell McLeod, 2 Bt (d 1950), and Susan, *née* Whitehead (d 1964); elder bro Roderick Campbell McLeod ka, Salerno, 1943; *b* 7 Nov 1924; *Educ* Winchester; *m* 5 Jan 1957, (Anne) Gillian (d 1978), 3 da of late Henry Russell Bowlby, of London; 1 s (James Roderick Charles b 1960), 2 da (Belinda Ann (Mrs Shaker) b 1957, Nicola (Mrs Bampfylde) b 1958); *Heir* s, James Roderick Charles McLeod b 26 Sept 1960; *Career* DipIBrew, MSI; *Recreations* shooting; *Clubs* MCC, I Zingari, Free Foresters, Jesters; *Style*— Sir Charles McLeod, Bt; ✉ Coombe Green Cottage, Lea, Malmesbury, Wiltshire SN16 9PF

McLEOD, Prof David; s of Norman McLeod (d 1985), and Anne, *née* Heyworth (d 1994); *b* 16 Jan 1946; *Educ* The GS Burnley Lancs, Univ of Edinburgh (MB ChB, BSc); *m* 16 Dec 1967, Jeanette Allison; 1 s (Euan b 1972), 1 da (Seona b 1974); *Career* conslt ophthalmic surgn Moorfields Eye Hosp 1978–88, conslt advsr in ophthalmology to the RAF 1984–, prof of ophthalmology Univ of Manchester 1988–, hon conslt ophthalmic surgn Royal Eye Hosp Manchester 1988–; FRCS 1974, FCOphth 1988; *Recreations* walking, golf; *Clubs* Bramall Park Golf Bramhall Cheshire; *Style*— Prof David McLeod; ✉ Royal Eye Hospital, Oxford Road, Manchester M13 9WH (☎ 0161 276 5620)

MACLEOD, Dr Donald MacRae; s of Allan Martin MacLeod, of Glen House, Carloway, Isle of Lewis, and Margaret MacLeod; *b* 19 Oct 1956; *Educ* Nicolson Inst Stornoway, Univ of Aberdeen (MB ChB); *m* 19 April 1986, Moira Catherine, da of Thomas Anderson, of Marykirk; 1 s (Allan b 1987), 2 da (Alice b 1989, Elizabeth b 1992); *Career* lectr London Hosp Med Coll 1986–88, visiting assoc Duke Univ Med Centre Durham N Carolina USA 1988–89, conslt in anaesthetics Aberdeen Royal Infirmary 1989–; hon sr lectr Univ of Aberdeen; FFARCSI 1986; *Recreations* sailing, golf; *Clubs* Banff Sailing, Royal Aberdeen Golf; *Style*— Dr Donald Macleod; ✉ Westwood House, Kinellar, Aberdeen; Aberdeen Royal Infirmary, Aberdeen, Scotland (☎ 01224 681818)

MacLEOD, Duncan James; CBE (1986); s of Alan Duncan MacLeod, of Skeabost, Isle of Skye (ka Sicily 1943), and Joan Nora Paton, *née* de Knoop (d 1991); *b* 1 Nov 1934; *Educ* Eton; *m* 14 June 1958, Joanna, da of Samuel Leslie Bibby, CBE, DL, of Villans Wyk, Headley, Surrey (d 1985); 2 s (Alan Hamish b 1959, Charles Alasdair b 1961), 1 da (Davina b 1965); *Career* CA 1958; ptnr Brown Fleming & Murray (now Ernst & Young) 1960–89; dir: Bank of Scotland 1973–91, Scottish Provident Institute 1976–, The Weir Group plc 1976–, Harry Ramsden's plc 1989–, Motherwell Bridge Holdings Ltd 1990–; chm Scot Industl Devpt Advsy Bd 1989– (memb 1980–), memb Scot Tertiary Educn Advsy Cncl 1985–87; *Recreations* golf, shooting, fishing; *Clubs* Western (Glasgow), Prestwick Golf, Royal and Ancient, MCC; *Style*— Duncan J MacLeod, Esq, CBE; ✉ Monkredding House, Kilwinning, Ayrshire KA13 7QN (☎ 01294 52336, fax 01294 58465)

McLEOD, Fraser Neil; s of James McLeod, of Cuffley, Herts, and Mary, *née* Yuill; *b* 13 July 1951; *Educ* Hertford GS, St Bartholemew's Hosp Med Coll (MB BS); *m* 16 April 1983, Angela Mary, da of Thomas Campbell, of Purley, Surrey; 1 s (David Paul Christopher b 13 Feb 1989), 1 da (Madeleine Kate b 17 June 1994); *Career* lectr in obstetrics and gynaecology and pioneer in test tube baby devpt Royal Free Hosp 1981–83, sr registrar in obstetrics and gynaecology Southmead Hosp Bristol 1983–85, conslt obstetrician and gynaecologist Frenchay and Southmead Hosps Bristol 1985–; local treas BMA, examiner RCOG, sec Hey Groves Med Soc, fndr memb Br Soc for Gynaecological Endoscopy; MRCOG 1980, MRCS; *Recreations* golf; *Clubs* Berkshire Golf, Henbury Golf; *Style*— Fraser McLeod, Esq; ✉ 7 Percival Rd, Clifton, Bristol BS8 3LE (☎ 0117 974 1396)

MACLEOD, Iain; s of Alexander Macleod (d 1978), and Mary Ann Macleod (d 1989), of Isle of Lewis, Scotland; *b* 27 May 1956; *Educ* Nicolson Inst; *m* June 1989, Evridika, da of Benjamin Lapshov, of Sofia, Bulgaria; 2 s (Alexander b 1990, Andrew b 1991); *Career* started journalism with Stornoway Gazette, freelanced for The Scotsman, The Times and others; Daily Telegraph: sports news corr 1990–93, athletics corr 1993– (specialises in int sports politics); has covered all major events incl soccer World Cup and European Champiobships, European and World Athletic Championships, Olympic Summer and Winter Games; for many years a specialist in European soccer; highly commended Olympic sports writer Br Sports Journalism Awards 1992; given observer status Press Cmmn IOC 1994; memb: Br Athletic Writers Assoc (vice-chm 1995–97), Sports Writers Assoc of GB, AIPS (Int Sports Journalist Assoc); *Recreations* Italian opera, classical music, travel, wine, politics, history of the 20th century; *Style*— Iain Macleod, Esq; ✉ The Daily Telegraph, 1 Canada Square, Canary Wharf, London E14 5DT (☎ 0171 538 6383)

MACLEOD, Prof Iain Alasdair; s of Donald MacLeod (d 1976), of Achiltibuie, Ross-shire, and Barbara Mary, *née* Mackenzie (d 1977); *b* 4 May 1939; *Educ* Lenzie Acad, Univ of Glasgow (BSc, PhD); *m* 18 Nov 1967, Barbara Jean, da of Allen Daven Booth (d 1973), of Salmon Arm, Br Columbia, Canada; 1 s (Alastair b 1976), 1 da (Mairi b 1975); *Career* structural engr: Crouch and Hogg Glasgow 1960–62, H A Simons Vancouver Canada 1966–67; structural res engr Portland Cement Assoc USA 1967–69, lectr Dept of Civil Engrg Univ of Glasgow 1969–73 (asst lectr 1962–66), prof and head of Dept of Civil Engrg Paisley Coll of Technol 1973–81, prof of structural engrg Univ of Strathclyde 1981–; vice pres IStructE 1989–90, memb Standing Ctee on Structural Safety; FIStructE, FICE; *Books* Analytical Modelling of Structural Systems (1990); *Recreations* sailing, mountaineering, skiing; *Style*— Prof Iain MacLeod; ✉ Department of Civil Engineering, University of Strathclyde, 107 Rottenrow, Glasgow G4 0NG (☎ 0141 552 4400 ext 3275, fax 0141 552 0062)

McLEOD, Sir Ian George; kt (1984), JP (1977); s of George McLeod; *b* 17 Oct 1926; *Educ* Kearsney Coll Natal, Natal Univ; *m* 1950, Audrey Davis; 2 da; *Career* md EDP Servs Computer Bureau 1964–; dir Seeboard plc 1989– (memb bd SE Electricity Bd 1983–89); chm: Croydon Central Cons Assoc 1973–76, Greater London Area Conservatives 1981–84; memb Nat Union Exec Ctee Conservative Pty 1974–84; ACIS; *Clubs* Carlton, MCC; *Style*— Sir Ian McLeod, JP

McLEOD, James Roderick Charles; s and h of Sir Charles Henry McLeod, 3 Bt, *qv*; *b* 26 Sept 1960; *m* 20 Jan 1990, Helen M, er da of Capt George T Cooper, OBE, RN, of Lilliput, Poole, Dorset; 1 s (Rory b 7 July 1994), 1 da (Alexandra b 10 Jan 1992); *Style*— James McLeod, Esq

MacLEOD, James Summers; s of Charles MacLeod (d 1982), and Margaret, *née* Summers (d 1986); *b* 3 Aug 1941; *Educ* Dumfries Acad, Univ of Glasgow (LLM); *m* Sheila, da of late George Stromier; 1 da (Fiona b 1968), 2 s (Niall b 1971, Roderick b 1976); *Career* Univ of Edinburgh: lectr 1965–68, prof Dept of Accounting and Business Method 1986–; lectr Heriot-Watt Univ 1968–71; Ernst & Young (formerly Arthur Young McClelland Moores & Co): joined 1971, ptnr 1973–; insurance ed Simons Taxes; CA (Scotland) 1965; FInstT 1971; *Books* Taxation of Insurance Business (1988); *Recreations* bridge, piano, music, gardening, political biography; *Clubs* New; *Style*— James MacLeod, Esq; ✉ 2 Bonaly Road, Edinburgh EH13 0EA (☎ 0131 441 4144); Ernst & Young, 10 George Street, Edinburgh EH2 2DZ (☎ 0131 226 6400, fax 0131 247 5286)

MACLEOD, Dr John Alasdair Johnston; DL (Western Isles 1979); s of Dr Alexander John Macleod, OBE (d 1979), of Lochmaddy, and Dr Julia Parker, *née* Johnston (d 1989); *b* 20 Jan 1935; *Educ* Lochmaddy Sch, Nicolson Inst Stornoway, Keil Sch Dumbarton,

Univ of Glasgow (MB ChB); *m* 4 Nov 1972, Lorna, da of Dr Douglas Ian Ferguson (d 1994), of Winterbourne Down, nr Bristol; 2 s (Alasdair Ian b 1974, Torquil John b 1979), 1 da (Elizabeth Jane b 1975); *Career* Temp Actg Sub Lt RNVR 1957–59; jr hosp posts Glasgow and London 1963–70, RMO and sr registrar Middx London 1970–72, GP Isle of N Uist 1973–, examing offr DHSS 1973–, med offr Lochmaddy Hosp 1974–, Admty surgn and agent 1974–91, local med offr 1974–; non-exec dir Olscot Ltd 1969–93; visiting prof Dept of Family Med Univ of N Carolina; memb: N Uist Highland Gathering, N Uist Angling Club, Scandinavian Village Assoc; vice chm Western Isles Local Med Ctee 1991–93 (sec 1977–91); author of various articles and papers on isolated gen practise within the NHS; memb Western Isles Advsy Ctee on JPs 1985–; memb: BMA, World Orgn of Nat Colls Academique of Family Practice (memb Ctee on Rural Practice); FRCGP, FRSM; *Recreations* promoting Western Isles, time-sharing, arboriculture, writing; *Clubs* Western and Highland; *Style*— Dr John A J Macleod, DL; ✉ Tigh-na-Hearradh, Lochmaddy, Isle of North Uist, Western Isles HS6 5AE (☎ 01876 500224, fax 01876 500877)

MACLEOD, Dr Malcolm Robert; s of Robin Macleod, of Inverness, and Mary, *née* Hossack; *b* 26 Aug 1965; *Educ* Loretto Sch Musselburgh, Univ of Edinburgh (pres Students' Union, BSc, MBChB); *m* 26 June 1992, Lindsay Dorothy Greig Thomson, da of James Thomson; 1 s (Calum Alexander Thomson b 10 Sept 1995); *Career* med house offr Eastern Gen Hosp Edinburgh; Western Gen Hosp Edinburgh: neurosurgical house offr, SHO in med 1992–94; sr SHO Falkirk & District Royal Infirmary 1994–95, MRC clinical training fell Dept of Pharmacology Univ of Edinburgh 1995–, hon clinical fell Dept of Clinical Neurosciences Western Gen Hosp Edinburgh 1995–; rector and chm Univ Ct Univ of Edinburgh 1994–; MRCP 1994; *Recreations* juggling, hill walking, political history; *Style*— Dr Malcolm Macleod; ✉ Rector's Office, University of Edinburgh, 12 Buccleuch Street, Edinburgh (☎ 0131 650 4027, e-mail Malcolm.Macleod@ed.ac.uk)

MacLEOD, Hon Sir (John) Maxwell Norman; 5 Bt (UK 1924), of Fuinary, Morven, Co Argyll; er s of Very Rev Baron MacLeod of Fuinary, MC, DD (Life Peer and 4 Bt, d 1991), and Lorna Helen Janet, *née* MacLeod (d 1984); *b* 23 Feb 1952; *Educ* Gordonstoun; *Heir* bro, Hon Neil David MacLeod b 1959; *Style*— The Hon Sir Maxwell MacLeod, Bt; ✉ Fuinary Manse, Loch Aline, Morven, Argyll

McLEOD, Michael Alastair; s of Robert David McLeod (d 1976), of Surrey, and Iris May, *née* Hocking; *b* 19 Jan 1935; *Educ* Falmouth GS, Christ Coll Brecon; *m* 1957, Joan Patricia Joyce, da of Phillip Charles Mitchell (d 1968), of Cornwall, and Violet Hughes (d 1961); 2 da (Anne b 23 Aug 1959, Fiona b 29 July 1964); *Career* trainee JH Snellgrove & Partners Cornwall 1951–57; Langdon & Every: asst Singapore 1957–58, office mangr Kuala Lumpur 1958–61, assoc Kuala Lumpur 1961–63, ptnr Kuala Lumpur 1963–69, ptnr London 1970–88; jt sr ptnr Davis Langdon & Everest 1988–93, sr ptnr Davis Langdon Arabian Gulf 1988–93 (dir associated cos in Italy, Aust, Germany 1988–93), ret 1993; conslt 1993–; govr: Cranleigh Sch 1981–, St Catherine's Sch Bramley 1983; FRICS 1966 (ARICS 1957); *Recreations* golf, sailing, gardening, music; *Style*— Michael McLeod, Esq; ✉ The Pheasantry, Hascombe, Surrey GU8 4BT (☎ 01483 273079, fax 01483 273405)

MACLEOD, Nigel Ronald Buchanan; QC (1979); s of Donald Macleod (d 1956), and Katie Ann Buchanan Macleod; *b* 7 Feb 1936; *Educ* Wigan GS, Ch Ch Oxford (MA, BCL); *m* 1966, Susan Margaret; 1 s (Alasdair b 1968), 1 da (Victoria b 1972); *Career* Nat Serv RAF 1954–56; called to the Bar Gray's Inn 1961, asst cmmr Boundary Cmmn for England 1981–84, recorder Crown Court 1981–; dep High Ct judge 1992–; bencher Gray's Inn 1993; vice chm Planning and Environment Bar Assoc 1994–; *Recreations* walking, sailing; *Style*— Nigel Macleod, Esq, QC; ✉ The Start, Start Lane, Whaley Bridge, Derbyshire (☎ 01663 732732); 4 Breams Buildings, London EC4A 1AQ (☎ 0171 353 5835, fax 0171 430 1677)

MacLEOD, Norman; *b* 26 April 1938; *Career* DHSS until 1968; Scottish Office: various positions 1968 92, chief exec Pensions Agency 1992–; *Recreations* golf, Gaelic language and song; *Clubs* Ratho Park Golf; *Style*— Norman MacLeod, Esq; ✉ Scottish Office Pensions Agency, St Margaret's House, 151 London Road, Edinburgh EH8 7TG (☎ 0131 244 3211, fax 0131 244 3579)

MacLEOD, Sheriff Principal Norman Donald; QC (Scot 1986); s of Rev John MacLeod (d 1989), and Catherine Mullen, *née* Macritchie (d 1939); *b* 6 March 1932; *Educ* Mill Hill, George Watson's Boys' Coll, Edinburgh Univ, Oxford Univ; *m* 1957, Ursula Jane, da of George Herbert Bromley, of Inveresk, Midlothian (d 1982); 2 s (Ian b 1959, Patrick b 1963), 2 da (Catriona b 1960, Johanna b 1964); *Career* passed advocate 1956, Colonial Serv dist offr and crown counsel 1957–64, sheriff of Lanarkshire at Glasgow (subsequently sheriff of Glasgow and Strathkelvin) 1967–86; sheriff princ of Glasgow and Strathkelvin 1986–; visiting prof Strathclyde Univ; *Recreations* gardening, sailing; *Style*— Sheriff Principal Norman D MacLeod, QC; ✉ Calderbank, Lochwinnoch, Renfrewshire PA12 4DJ (☎ 01505 843 340); Sheriff Principal's Chambers, Sheriff Court of Glasgow and Strathkelvin, 1 Carlton Place, Glasgow G5 9DA (☎ 0141 429 8888)

MACLEOD OF BORVE, Baroness (Life Peer UK 1971), of Borve, Isle of Lewis; Evelyn Hester Macleod; *née* Blois; JP (Middx 1955), DL (Gtr London 1977); da of Rev Gervase Vanneck Blois (d 1961, yst s of Sir John Blois, 8 Bt, DL), and Hon Hester Pakington, da of 3 Baron Hampton; *b* 19 Feb 1915; *Educ* Lawnside Gt Malvern; *m* 1, 1937, Mervyn Charles Mason (ka 1940), s of Alwyne Humfrey-Mason, JP, formerly of Foxley Manor, Malmesbury and Necton Hall Norfolk; m 2, 1941, Rt Hon Iain Norman Macleod, PC, MP (d 1970), s of Dr Norman Macleod, of Isle of Lewis; 1 s (Hon Torquil Anthony Ross b 1942), 1 da (Hon Diana Hester (Hon Mrs Heimann) b 1944); *Career* sits as Cons in House of Lords; memb IBA 1972–76; chm: Nat Gas Consumers Cncl 1972–77, Nat Assoc League of Hosp Friends 1976–85 (pres 1985–89); memb Parole Bd 1977–81; govr Queenswood Sch 1977–85; tstee Nat Assoc of Widows 1976–; co-fndr and life pres of charity for single homeless Crisis at Christmas; tstee Attle Meml Fndn 1980–90; memb: Ethical Ctee Abbey Life 1989–95, Ct Middlesex Univ 1995–; *Recreations* family, music, conservation; *Style*— The Rt Hon the Baroness Macleod of Borve, JP, DL; ✉ Luckings Farm, Coleshill, Amersham, Bucks HP7 0LS (☎ 01494 725158)

MacLEOD OF MacLEOD, John; s of Capt Robert Wolrige Gordon, MC; officially recognised in the name of Macleod of MacLeod, Yr, by decree of Lyon Court 1951; suc maternal grandmother Dame Flora MacLeod of MacLeod, DBE, 1976, as Chief of Clan MacLeod; *b* 10 Aug 1935; *Educ* Eton; *m* 1, 1961, Drusilla Mary, da of Sebastian Lewis Shaw (d 1994), actor; m 2, 1973, Melita, da of Duko Kolin, of Sofia, Bulgaria; 1 s (Hugh b 1973), 1 da (Elena b 1977); *Heir* s, Hugh Magnus b 1973; *Style*— John MacLeod of MacLeod; ✉ Dunvegan Castle, Isle of Skye

McLINTOCK, (Charles) Alan; s of Charles Henry McLintock (d 1947), and Charlotte Alison, *née* Allan (d 1971); *b* 28 May 1925; *Educ* Rugby; *m* 1955, Sylvia Mary, da of George Foster Taylor (d 1969); 1 s, 3 da; *Career* CA; sr ptnr KMG Thomson McLintock (later KPMG Peat Marwick McLintock, KPMG Peat Marwick) 1982–87 (ptnr 1954–87); pres Woolwich Building Society 1995– (chm 1984–95); chm: Allchurches Trust Ltd 1986–, AJ's Family Restaurants Ltd 1987–96, Govett Strategic Investment Trust plc 1975–94, Central Bd of Fin Church of Eng 1992–; dir: National Westminster Bank plc 1979–90, Ecclesiastical Insurance Group plc 1972–93 (also chm), M & G Group plc 1982–94, Royal Artillery Museums Ltd 1996–; tstee Church Urban Fund; chm Governing Body Rugby Sch 1988–95 (vice chm 1984–88, memb 1973–95), chm Governing Body Westonbirt Sch 1991– (memb 1977–); memb Cncl Univ of London 1987–; *Recreations* music, family life; *Clubs* Army and Navy; *Style*— Alan McLintock, Esq; ✉ The Manor House, Westhall Hill, Burford, Oxon OX18 4BJ (☎ 01993 822276); Woolwich Building Society, 88 Fleet Street, London EC4Y 1PJ (☎ 0171 638 3722, fax 0171 936 3587)

McLINTOCK, Sir Michael William; 4 Bt (UK 1934), of Sanquhar, Co Dumfries; s of Sir William Traven McLintock, 3 Bt (d 1987), and his 1 w, Andrée, *née* Lonsdale-Hands; *b* 13 Aug 1958; *Heir* bro, Andrew Thomson McLintock b 2 Dec 1960; *Style*— Sir Michael McLintock, Bt

McLOUGHLIN, Kevin; *b* 17 July 1952; *Educ* Xaverian Coll, Univ of Sheffield (MA); *m* 16 Dec 1978, Sheila Mary McLoughlin; 1 s (Daniel b 27 July 1980), 1 da (Jessica b 14 Sept 1984); *Career* admitted slr 1978; memb Law Faculty Bd Univ of Sheffield; ptnr Dibb Lupton Alsop Solicitors; *Style*— Kevin McLoughlin, Esq; ✉ 98 Riverdale Road, Ranmoor, Sheffield S10 3FD (☎ 0114 230 7350); Dibb Lupton Alsop, Fountain Precinct, Balm Green, Sheffield S1 1RZ (☎ 0345 262728, fax 0114 272 5030)

McLOUGHLIN, Patrick; MP (C) Derbyshire West (majority 18,769); *Career* MP (C) Derbyshire W 1986–; a Lord Cmmr HM Treasy (Govt whip) 1996–; *Style*— Patrick McLoughlin, Esq, MP; ✉ House of Commons, London SW1A 0AA (☎ 0171 219 3000)

McLUCAS, William Philip; s of James McLucas, of South Queensferry, and Jean Violet, *née* Stobie (d 1986); *b* 12 Feb 1955; *Educ* Daniel Stewarts Coll Edinburgh, Scottish Coll of Textiles Galashiels; *m* 25 March 1976, Blyth Agnes, da of late Thomas Russell McLaren; 1 s (James Thomas William b 19 June 1982), 1 da (Camilla Charlotte Blyth b 28 July 1984); *Career* investmt analyst Scottish Amicable Life Assurance Soc 1967–77, moneybroker UDISCO Brokers Ltd 1977–78; stockbroker: Laurence Prust & Co (London) 1978–80, Jackson Graham Moore & Ptnrs (Sydney) 1980–84; ceo Waverley Mining Finance plc 1995–; dir Mining (Scotland) Ltd; chm: Montagu Gold NL, Perseverance Corp Ltd, Monkton Hall Mineworkers Ltd; non-exec dir: Kingstream Resources NL (all Australian cos), Dia-Dem Resources (Canadian Co); memb: Assoc of Mining Analysts 1981, Scottish Young Business Group 1990–, Scottish Ski Club 1993, DHO 1994; *Recreations* skiing, sailing, travel; *Style*— William McLucas, Esq; ✉ Waverley Mining Finance plc, 13 Charlotte Square, Edinburgh EH2 4DJ (☎ 0131 225 1551, fax 0131 225 1550, portable 0836 638912)

MACLURE, Sir John Robert Spencer; 4 Bt (UK 1898), of The Home, Whalley Range, nr Manchester, Co Palatine of Lancaster; s of Lt-Col Sir John William Spencer Maclure, 3 Bt, OBE (d 1980), and Elspeth King, *née* Clark (d 1991); *b* 25 March 1934; *Educ* Winchester; *m* 26 Aug 1964, Jane Monica, da of late Rt Rev Thomas Joseph Savage, Bishop of Zululand and Swaziland; 4 s (John Mark b 1965, Thomas Stephen b 1967, Graham Spencer b 1970, Stephen Patrick Ian b 1974); *Heir* s, John Mark Maclure b 27 Aug 1965; *Career* 2 Lt KRRC 2 Bn BAOR 1953–55, Lt Royal Hants Airborne Regt TA; asst master Horris Hill 1955–66 and 1974–78; teacher: NZ 1967–70, St Edmund's Hindhead 1971–74; headmaster Croftinloan Sch 1978–92; Dip IAPS; *Clubs* MCC, Royal and Ancient Golf, Royal North Devon Golf; *Style*— Sir John Maclure, Bt; ✉ Wild Goose Cottage, Gooseham, Morwenstow, Bude, N Cornwall (☎ 01288 331584)

MACLURE, (John) Mark; s and h of Sir John Robert Spencer Maclure, 4 Bt, and Jane Monica, *née* Savage; *b* 27 Aug 1965; *Educ* Winchester; *m* 17 Aug 1996, Emily Jane, da of Peter Frean, of Cothal, Aberdeenshire; *Career* former stockbroker with: Statham Duff Stoop 1984–85, Sheppards & Chase 1985–88, Panmure Gordon & Co 1988–91; with Business Pursuits Event Management 1992–; *Recreations* sailing, skiing, soccer, tennis, squash; *Clubs* MCC; *Style*— Mark Maclure, Esq; ✉ The Stable House, Caversfield, Bicester, Oxon OX6 9TQ

MACLURE, (John) Stuart; CBE (1982); s of Hugh Seton Maclure (d 1967), of Highgate, London, and Berth Lea, *née* Hodge (d 1948); *b* 8 Aug 1926; *Educ* Highgate Sch, Christ's Coll Cambridge (MA); *m* 8 Sept 1951, (Constance) Mary, da of Alfred Ernest Butler (d 1962), of Fulbrook, Burford, Oxon; 1 s (Michael b 1952), 2 da (Mary b 1957, Clare b 1962); *Career* Sub Lt RNVR 1946–47; editorial trainee The Times 1950, reporter The Times Educnl Supplement 1951–54; ed: Education 1954–69, The Times Educnl Supplement 1969–89; JRMT Distinguished visiting fell Policy Studies Inst 1989–90, assoc fell Univ of Warwick Centre for Educn and Indust 1991–94; hon fell: Sheffield Hallam Univ (formerly Sheffield Poly), Westminster Coll, Coll of Preceptors; Hon DUniv Open Univ 1990; FRSA; *Books* Educational Documents England and Wales 1816 to present day (ed, 1965–86), A Hundred Years of London Education (1970), Educational Development and School Building 1945–1973 (1984), Education Re-Formed (1988), Missing Links (1991), Learning to Think, Thinking to Learn (ed, 1991); *Recreations* golf, bridge; *Clubs* MCC; *Style*— Stuart Maclure, Esq, CBE; ✉ 109 College Rd, Dulwich, London SE21 7HN (☎ 0181 693 3286)

McLYNN, Francis James (Frank); *b* 29 Aug 1941; *Educ* John Fisher Sch Purley, Wadham Coll Oxford (open scholar, BA, MA), UCL Inst of Latin American Studies (MA, PhD); *Career* author; asst dir Bogota and Colombia Br Cncl 1969–71 (joined 1968), Parry fell Buenos Aires Argentina 1971–72, Alistair Horne res fell St Antony's Coll Oxford 1987–88, now full time author; winner Cheltenham Prize for Literature 1985; FRHistS 1987, FRGS 1987; *Books* France and The Jacobite Rising of 1745 (1981), The Jacobite Army in England (1983), The Jacobites (1985), Invasion: From The Armada To Hitler (1987), Charles Edward Stuart (1988), Crime and Punishment in Eighteenth Century England (1989), Stanley: The Making of An African Explorer (1989), Burton: Snow Upon The Desert (1990), Of No Country (1990), Stanley: Sorcerer's Apprentice (1991), From The Sierras To The Pampas (1991), Hearts of Darkness (1992), Fitzroy Maclean (1992), Robert Louis Stevenson (1993), Jung: A Biography (1995); *Style*— Frank McLynn, Esq; ✉ c/o Random House, 20 Vauxhall Bridge Road, London SW1

McMAHON, Sir Brian Patrick; 8 Bt (UK 1817); s of Sir (William) Patrick McMahon, 7 Bt (d 1977); *b* 9 June 1942; *Educ* Wellington, Wednesbury Tech Coll (BSc 1964); *m* 1981 (m dis 1991), Kathleen Joan, da of late William Hopwood; *Heir* bro, Shaun Desmond McMahon, *qv*; *Career* AIM; *Style*— Sir Brian McMahon, Bt; ✉ Oak Ridge, School Road, Thorney Hill, Bransgore, Christchurch, Dorset BH23 8DS

MacMAHON, Brian Sean; s of Gerard MacMahon (d 1962), of Dublin, and Mary, *née* Coughlan (d 1983); *b* 3 April 1938; *Educ* Terenure Coll Dublin; *m* 1, 18 Sept 1961 (m dis 1977), Una Mary, da of Bernard Egan (d 1953), of Dublin; 2 s (Gerard b 1965, Cormac b 1967), 2 da (Cara b 1962, Niamh b 1964); m 2, 17 Dec 1983, Colleen Jean, da of Harry Harbottle, of Bristol; *Career* Irish Pensions Tst Dublin 1955–72, pension fund mangr Allied-Lyons Pension Fund 1973–82, dir gp pensions BET plc 1996– (gp benefits exec 1982–96); pres Occupational Pensions Advsy Serv (OPAS) 1993– (vice pres 1992–93), vice pres Nat Assoc of Pension Funds 1993–95 (chm 1991–93), memb Cncl Pensions Mgmnt Inst 1981–85; fell Pensions Mgmnt Inst; FRSA; *Recreations* golf, cricket, theatre; *Clubs* Bristol and Clifton Golf; *Style*— Brian MacMahon, Esq; ✉ BET Pensions, PO Box 278, Bristol BS99 5BH (☎ 0117 907 4888, fax 0117 927 6551)

McMAHON, Sir Christopher William (Kit); kt (1986); *b* 10 July 1927; *Educ* Melbourne GS, Univ of Melbourne, Magdalen Coll Oxford; *m* 1, 1956, Marion Kelso; 2 s; m 2, 1982, Alison Braimbridge; *Career* fell and economics tutor Magdalen Coll Oxford 1960–64; Bank of England: advsr 1964, advsr to the govrs 1966–70, exec dir 1970–80, dep govr 1980–85; Midland Bank plc: gp chief exec 1986–91, dep chm 1986–87, chm 1987–91; chm: Coutts Consulting Group plc 1992–, Pentos plc 1993–95 (dir 1991–); dir: Hong Kong and Shanghai Banking Corp 1987–91, Eurotunnel plc 1987–91, Taylor Woodrow plc 1991–, Royal Opera House 1991–, Angela Flowers Gallery, Aegis plc 1992–, Newspaper Publishing plc 1992–94, FI Group plc 1994–; hon fell UCNW; FInstM;

Style— Sir Kit McMahon; ✉ Taylor Woodrow plc, 4 Dunraven Street, London W1Y 3FG (☎ 0171 629 1201, fax 0171 493 1066)

MACMAHON, Clare; *Educ* Methodist Coll, Queen's Univ Belfast (Hugh Wisnom scholar, BSc); *Career* sci mistress Bartrum Gables Kent 1946–47, biology mistress John Bright FS Llandudno 1947–48, schs organiser & guide lectr Belfast Museum and Art Gallery 1948–52, sr lectr Stranmillis Coll Belfast 1957–59 (lectr 1952–57), vice-princ Leeds Day Training Coll (now James Graham Coll) 1959–63, Stranmillis Coll Belfast: vice-princ 1963–82, dep princ 1982; pro-chllr The Queen's Univ Belfast 1987–; chm: Fire Authy for NI 1979–81 (memb 1973), Civil Serv Cmmr 1985–93, Memb Ctee Int Fedn of Univ Women 1986–93 (memb 1980–93), NI Regional Ctee RSPB 1987–93; Ulster Cancer Fndn 1969–94: successively fndn memb, vice chm, chm then pres; memb Gen Consumer Cncl for NI 1985–; MIBiol 1973 (memb Ctee NI Branch 1978); *Style*— Miss Clare Macmahon; ✉ Pro-Chancellor, Queen's University of Belfast, University Road, Belfast BT7 1NN

MacMAHON, Dr Douglas Graham; s of Kenneth Graham Macmahon (Sqdn Ldr), and Stella Miriam, *née* Coster; *b* 1 Jan 1951; *Educ* Latymer Upper Sch, King's Coll Hosp Univ of London (MB BS); *m* 5 Jan 1974, Pauline Angela, da of Roger Mitchell; 2 s (Richard Graham b 3 June 1978, Michael James b 18 May 1980); *Career* conslt physician (special responsibility for the elderly) 1979–, med dir 1991–95, hon sr lectr Univ of Plymouth; special interests: the elderly, Parkinson's disease, cerebrovascular disease, rehabilitation; sr registrar John Radcliffe Hosp and Radcliffe Hosps Oxford, registrar Stoke Mandeville, sr house offr Portsmouth, house physician King's Coll Hosp; memb: Exec Ctee Br Geriatrics Soc 1987–90 (currently chm Policy Ctee), RCP Geriatrics Ctee, Cncl of Mgmnt Parkinson's Disease Soc UK (chm Nurse Steering Gp), Exec Bd Age Concern Cornwall; MRCS, LRCP 1973, MRCP 1976, FRCP 1991; *Books* Care of the Elderly (dep ed), Geriatric Medicine; chapters in various textbooks; *Style*— Dr Douglas MacMahon; ✉ Alma Manor, 66 Highertown, Truro, Cornwall TR1 3QD (☎ 01872 72260); Camborne-Redruth Hospital, Barncoose Terrace, Redruth, Cornwall TR15 3ER (☎ 01209 881631, fax 01209 881715)

McMAHON, Hugh R; MEP (Lab) Strathclyde West (majority 25,023); *Career* MEP (Lab) Strathclyde W 1984–; *Style*— Hugh R McMahon, Esq, MEP; ✉ constituency office: 9 Low Road, Paisley PA2 6AQ (☎ 0141 889 9990, fax 0141 889 4790)

McMAHON, Linda Ann; da of Richard Burtonshaw Martin, and Mary Ann Smith, *née* Paterson; *b* 12 June 1954; *m* 29 July 1989, Gerald John McMahon, s of James McMahon; 1 da (Rosie Jessica, Mary b 9 July 1994); *Career* fencer; memb Br Fencing Team 1977–88, nat devpt offr Amateur Fencing Assoc 1988–93, mangr Br Women's Team for Olympic Games Barcelona 1992; Olympic Games competitor: Moscow 1980, LA 1984, Seoul 1988; competitor 9 World Championships (finalist 1982), Bronze medallist Euro Championships 1983, Br Champion 1976, 1982, 1983, 1985 and 1987; memb Amateur Fencing Assoc; Churchill fell 1978; *Recreations* squash, cycling, golf; *Style*— Mrs Linda McMahon; ✉ Baron's Gate, 33–35 Rothschild Rd, London W4 5HT (☎ 0181 742 3032, fax 0181 742 3033, telex 8956058 CLPRG)

McMAHON, Shaun Desmond; s of Sir (William) Patrick McMahon, 7 Bt (d 1977); h to Btcy of bro, Sir Brian Patrick McMahon, 8 Bt, *qv*; *b* 29 Oct 1945; *Educ* Wellington Coll; *m* 1, 1971, Antonia Noel, da of Antony James Adie, of Rowington, Warwicks; m 2, 1985, Jill Rosamund, yr da of Dr Jack Cherry, of 44 Park Road, Abingdon, Oxon; 2 s (Patrick John Westropp b 7 Feb 1988, Charles Beresford b 19 July 1989); *Style*— Shaun McMahon Esq; ✉ Dendron, Old Vineyard Road, Constantia, Cape Town, South Africa

McMAHON, Rt Rev Thomas; *see:* Brentwood, Bishop of (RC)

McMANNERS, Prof Rev John; s of Rev Canon Joseph McManners (d 1975), and Ann Marshall (d 1979); *b* 25 Dec 1916; *Educ* Univ of Oxford (BA), Univ of Durham (DipTheol), Univ of Oxford (DLitt); *m* 27 Dec 1951, Sarah Carruthers Errington, da of William Carruthers (d 1952); 2 s (Joseph Hugh b 9 Dec 1952, Peter John b 9 Jan 1958), 2 da (Helen b 28 Feb 1955, Ann b 22 June 1961); *Career* WWII 2 Lt Royal Northumberland Fusiliers 1940; First Bn Royal Northumberland Fusiliers: platoon cdr, co second in cmd, adjutant; Maj GSO II 210 Br Liaison Unit (Greek Mission) 1943; fell and chaplain St Edmund Hall Oxford 1948–56, prof of history Univ of Tasmania 1956–59, prof of European history Univ of Sydney 1959–66, professorial fell All Souls Coll Oxford 1965–66, prof of history Univ of Leicester 1967–72, Regius prof of ecclesiastical history and canon of Christchurch Univ of Oxford 1972–84, fell and chaplain All Souls Coll Oxford 1984–, directeur d'études associé École Pratique des Hautes Études Paris 1980–81; Wolfson literary prize 1981; tstee Nat Portrait Gallery 1970–78, memb Doctrinal Cmmn C of E 1978–82; Hon DLitt Univ of Durham 1984; fell Aust Acad of Humanities 1970, FRHistS 1956, FBA 1978; Offr of the Royal Order of King George I of the Hellenes 1945, Cdr dans l'Ordre des Palmes Académiques 1991; *Books* French Ecclesiastical Society under the Ancien Regime: a Study of Angers (1960), Lectures on European History 1789–1914: Men, Machines and Freedom (1966), The French Revolution and the Church (1969), Church and State in France 1870–1914 (1972), Death and The Enlightenment (1981), Oxford Illustrated History of Christianity (1990); *Recreations* tennis; *Style*— Prof the Rev John McManners, FBA; ✉ All Souls College, Oxford OX1 4AL (☎ 01865 279 368)

McMANUS, Prof John; s of Eric Stanley McManus (d 1986), of Harwich, Essex, and Jessie Amelia, *née* Morley (d 1991); *b* 5 June 1938; *Educ* Harwich Co HS, Imperial Coll London (Watts Medal, BSc, PhD), Univ of Dundee (DSc); *m* 31 July 1965, (Jean) Barbara, da of David Kenneth Beveridge; 2 s (Steven b 21 Dec 1968, Neil b 21 July 1972), 1 da (Kay b 6 Dec 1974); *Career* lectr Univ of St Andrews 1964–67 (asst 1963–64); Univ of Dundee: lectr 1967–72, sr lectr 1972–80, reader 1980–88; prof Univ of St Andrews 1993– (reader 1988–93); formerly memb Senate Univ of Dundee; memb Univ of St Andrews: Senate, Ct 1991–95; pres: Cupar Choral Assoc 1970–79, Cupar Amateur Opera 1979–91, Estuary and Coastal Servs Assoc 1995–98; memb: Aquatic Atmospheric Physical Scis Ctee Natural Environment Research Cncl 1971–76, Bd Nature Conservancy Cncl (Scotland) 1990–91, Bd Scottish Natural Heritage SE Region 1991–, BSI Ctee on Sedimentation 1991–, Geological Conservation Review Panel Jt Nature Conservancy Cncl 1993–94; MInstEnvSci 1973, MIGeol 1979, FRSE 1980; *Books* Developments in estuary and coastal study techniques (ed jtly, 1989), Geomorphology and Sedimentology of Lakes and Reservoirs (ed jtly, 1993); *Recreations* making music; *Style*— Prof John McManus, FRSE; ✉ Department of Geology, University of St Andrews, St Andrews, Fife KY16 9ST (☎ 01334 463948, fax 01334 463949, e-mail jm@purds.st-and.ac.uk)

McMANUS, Richard Brian; s of Michael Mansley McManus (d 1982), and Margaret, *née* Davison; *b* 15 March 1956; *Educ* Huddersfield New Coll, Jesus Coll Oxford (BA), INSEAD (MBA); *m* 1, 1978 (m dis 1983), Susan Mary; m 2, 10 Sept 1991, Diana Catherine, da of R J L Breese, of Northwood, Middx; 1 da (Sophie Alexandra b 24 Dec 1992), 1 s (Frederick John b 6 Aug 1994); *Career* mgmnt conslt: Proctor & Gamble 1977–80 (mktg), Johnson & Johnson 1980–82 (business devpt), Boston Consulting Gp (after MBA) 1984–86; md: First Research 1987–, First Europe 1988–; *Recreations* skiing, jogging, theatre, travelling; *Clubs* Beaujolais, IOD; *Style*— Richard McManus, Esq; ✉ 44 Upham Pk Rd, Chiswick (☎ 0181 994 1980); business: (☎ 0181 747 4054, fax 0181 747 3969)

McMASTER, Gordon James; MP (Lab and Co-op) Paisley S (majority 9,549); s of William McMaster, and Alison, *née* Maxwell; *b* 13 Feb 1960; *Educ* Johnstone HS, Langside Coll, W of Scotland Agric Coll, Jordanhill Coll of Educn; *Career* foreman gardener Renfrew DC 1980 (apprentice gardener 1976–77, student W of Scotland Agric Coll 1977–80), sr lectr in horticulture Langside Coll 1986–89 (lectr 1980–86), co-ordinator Growing Concern (Strathclyde) 1989–90; MP (Lab and Co-op) Paisley S 1990–; sec All-Pty Disablement Gp 1992–95, Scottish Oppn whip 1992–95, asst to chief whip 1995–, frontbench spokesperson on disabled people's rights 1996–; chm Co-op Gp of MP's and Peers 1994–95 (vice-chm 1993–94); memb Euro Standing Ctee A; memb Select Ctees on: Procedure 1991–95, Standing Orders 1992–95, Broadcasting 1992–93; special interests: housing, Euro affairs, econ devpt, elderly and disability, Scottish affairs; Renfrew DC: memb 1984–91, dep ldr 1987–88, ldr 1988–90; chm Johnstone Community Cncl 1982–84 (elected memb 1980); vice-chm All-Pty gardening club; Freedom City of Houston Mo USA; MIHort; *Recreations* reading, writing, gardening; *Clubs* United Services (Johnstone), St Peter's (Glenburn); *Style*— Gordon McMaster, Esq, MP; ✉ The Gatehouse, 22 Neilston Road, Paisley PA2 6LN (☎ 0141 848 9004, fax 0141 848 0754)

McMASTER, Paul; s of Dr James McMaster (d 1987), of Liverpool, and Sarah Lynne McMaster; *b* 4 Jan 1943; *Educ* Liverpool Coll, Univ of Liverpool (MB ChB), Univ of Cambridge (MA); *m* Aug 1969, Helen Ruth, da of Derek Bryce; 2 s (Michael Robert b 1971, Richard Benjamin b 1978), 1 da (Amanda Helen b 1974); *Career* conslt surgn; sr lectr dept of surgery Cambridge 1976–80, tutor Trinity Hall Cambridge 1978–80, dir Liver Transplant Services Queen Elizabeth Hosp Univ of Birmingham 1980–; memb: Cncl Nat and Int Transplantation Soc 1991–, Euro Soc Organ Transplantation (pres 1992–93); FRCS 1970; *Style*— Paul McMaster, Esq; ✉ 13 St Agnes Road, Moseley, Birmingham B13 (☎ 0121 449 5600); The Liver Unit, The Queen Elizabeth Hospital, University of Birmingham, Edgbaston, Birmingham (☎ 0121 472 1311, fax 0121 414 8133)

McMASTER, Peter; CB (1991); s of Peter McMaster (d 1965), and Ada Nellie, *née* Williams (d 1966); *b* 22 Nov 1931; *Educ* Kelvinside Acad Glasgow, Royal Mil Coll of Sci Shrivenham; *m* 23 Dec 1955, Catherine Ann, da of William Rosborough (d 1968); 1 s (Peter), 1 da (Morag); *Career* Mil Serv: Royal Mil Acad Sandhurst 1950–52, RE 1952–70, ret Maj; called to the Bar Middle Temple 1969; dir gen Ordnance Survey 1985–91 (joined 1970), memb Lord Chllr's Panel of Ind Insprs 1991–; visiting prof Univ of Kingston 1991–93; memb Cncl: Br Cartographic Soc 1975–92, RGS 1990–93; FRICS 1971, FIIM 1990; *Recreations* foreign travel, walking; *Style*— Peter McMaster, Esq, CB; ✉ Hillhead, Stratton Rd, Winchester, Hampshire SO23 0JQ (☎ 01962 862684)

McMICHAEL, Prof Andrew James; s of Sir John McMichael, FRS (d 1993), and Sybil Eleanor, *née* Blake (d 1965); *b* 8 Nov 1943; *Educ* St Paul's, Gonville and Caius Coll Cambridge (BA, MA), St Mary's Hosp Medical School (MB BChir); *m* 12 Oct 1968, Kathryn Elizabeth, da of Capt Alexander Alfred Cross, MBE, of The Old Smithy Cottage, Whittonditch, Ramsbury, Wiltshire; 2 s (Hamish b 1973, Robert b 1982), 1 da (Fiona b 1971); *Career* MRC clinical res prof of immunology Nuffield Dept of Medicine Univ of Oxford 1982– (Wellcome sr fell in clinical science 1977–79, lectr 1979–82), fell Trinity Coll Oxford 1982–; memb: Scientific Ctee Cancer Res Campaign 1986–88, Systems Bd MRC 1987–91, AIDS Steering Ctee MRC 1988–94; FRCP 1985; FRS 1992; *Books* Monoclonal Antibodies in Clinical Medicine (ed 1981), Leucocyte Typing III, White Cell Differentiation Antigens (ed 1987); *Recreations* walking, reading; *Style*— Prof Andrew McMichael, FRS; ✉ Institute of Molecular Medicine, John Radcliffe Hospital, Oxford (☎ 01865 222336)

McMICHAEL-PHILLIPS, (William) James (Jim); s of William James Phillips (d 1982), of Edinburgh, and Mary Jane, *née* Sneddon (d 1983); *b* 17 March 1934; *Educ* George Heriot's Sch Edinburgh; *m* 1, 12 Aug 1957, Fleming (d 1981), da of James McKinnel McMichael (d 1982), of Lochmaben, Dumfriesshire; 2 s (Scott b and d 1961, James b 1962), 1 da (Danielle b 1966); m 2, 4 Oct 1982, Laura Teresa, da of Valtiero Bertonesi (d 1988), of La Spezia, Italy; *Career* cmmnd RA 1952–54, RA (TA) 1954–57; dir 1969–72: John Newbould & Son Ltd Bradford, Arthur Davy & Son Ltd Sheffield, Sunblest Bakeries Ltd Sheffield; regnl gen mangr Associated Dairies Ltd Leeds 1972–78; gp gen mangr Milk Gp Co-operative Society Ltd 1978–93; dir: Southern Co-op Ltd 1983–94, Hyde Dairies Ltd 1984–94; chm English Butter Marketing Co Ltd 1993–94; vice pres EEC Advsy Ctee on Milk and Milk Products 1982–94, pres Dairy Trade Fedn 1987–89 and 1993–94; currently ind memb Greater Manchester Police Authority; MCIM, FRSA; *Recreations* badminton, reluctant gardener; *Style*— Jim McMichael-Phillips, Esq; ✉ 15 Westfield Road, Cheadle Hulme, Cheshire SK8 6EH (☎ and fax 0161 485 2118)

McMICKING, Maj David John; LVO (1966); s of Maj-Gen Neil McMicking, CB, CBE, DSO, MC, DL (d 1963), of Eastferry, Dunkeld, Perthshire, and Margaret Winifred, *née* Landale (d 1989); *b* 29 April 1939; *Educ* Eton, RMA Sandhurst, Univ of Strathclyde (MSc); *m* 6 June 1970, Janetta Ellen Dorothea, da of Lt-Col Douglas Alwyn Charles Wood-Parker, OBE, DL (d 1968), of Keithick, Coupar Angus, Perthshire; 1 s (Alexander b 6 April 1981), 1 da (Susannah b 12 Jan 1978); *Career* cmmnd Black Watch 1960, Equerry to HM Queen Elizabeth The Queen Mother 1963–66 (Extra Equerry 1993–), Adj Black Watch 1968–70, Staff Offr MOD 1970–72, Co Cdr Black Watch in Hong Kong 1972–73, ret 1973; business exec personnel John Menzies 1973–86, md Somerton Guns 1986–95, outplacement conslt Caledonian Career Consultants 1992–; life memb: Nat Tst for Scotland, Nat Arts Collection Fund 1986–, RSPB, Br Assoc for Shooting and Conversation, Scottish Wildlife Tst, Br Deer Soc; exec memb: Earl Haig Fund, Offrs Assoc Scotland; memb: Queen's Body Guard for Scotland (Royal Co of Archers), Worshipful Co of Merchants of Edinburgh 1984; FBIM 1982, MIPM 1985; *Recreations* shooting; *Clubs* White's, Pratt's, New (Edinburgh); *Style*— Maj David McMicking, LVO; ✉ 10 Albert Terrace, Edinburgh EH10 5EA (☎ 0131 447 6192); Needs, Alyth, Blairgowrie, Perthshire (☎ 01575 582337)

MACMILLAN, Hon Adam Julian Robert; s of Viscount Macmillan of Ovenden (Rt Hon Maurice Macmillan, d 1984), and Katharine, Viscountess Macmillan of Ovenden, DBE, *qv*; *b* 21 April 1948; *Educ* Eton, Univ of Strasbourg; *m* 1982, Sarah Anne Mhuire, yr da of late Dr Brian MacGreevy, of London; 2 s (Frederick b 1990, another b 1995), 2 da (Sophia b 1985, Alice b 1987); *Career* dir Chinese Gourmet Partnership Ltd 1981–94; tstee: Harold Macmillan Tst 1986–, One Plus One (formerly Marriage Res Centre) 1989–; patron: Order of Malta Volunteers 1980–, Br Nepalese Otology Soc 1988–; Schuman medal 1980; *Recreations* shooting, fishing; *Clubs* Carlton, Pratt's; *Style*— The Hon Adam Macmillan; ✉ 20 The Little Boltons, London SW10 9LP

MACMILLAN, Dr Alexander Ross; s of Donald Macmillan (d 1975), and Johanna, *née* Ross (d 1973); *b* 25 March 1922; *Educ* Tain Royal Acad; *m* 17 June 1961, Ursula Miriam, da of Edwin Grayson (d 1975); 2 s (David b 1964, Niall b 1966), 1 da (Alexandra b 1962); *Career* WWII Corpl RAF 1942–46 (despatches 1945); banker 1938–87; chief gen mangr Clydesdale Bank PLC 1971–82 (dir 1974–87); dir: Caledonian Applied Technol plc 1982–87, Highland North Sea Ltd 1982–, Highland Deephaven 1982–, John Laing plc 1982–86, Radio Clyde Ltd 1982–93, Radio Clyde Holdings plc 1991–93, Scottish Development Finance Ltd 1982–92, Martin Black plc 1983–85, Kelvin Technol Development 1984–86, First Northern Corporate Finance Ltd 1983–87, Wilsons Garage Co (Argyll) Ltd 1987–94, Wilsons Fuels Ltd 1987–94, EFT Gp plc 1987–93, Balmoral Gp Ltd 1988–93, North of Scotland Radio Ltd 1989–93, Nemoquest Ltd 1990–96, Gilmorehill Power Management Ltd 1993–96; chm Nat House Building Cncl (Scot) 1982–1988; dir HS of Glasgow 1979–92, memb Court Univ of Glasgow 1980–86 (Hon Dr Univ of Glasgow 1989); Freeman Royal Burgh of Tain 1975; FCIB Scot 1942, CIMgt 1980; *Recreations* golf; *Clubs* Killermont Glasgow; *Style*— Dr Alexander R Macmillan; ✉ 16 Ledcameroch Rd, Bearsden, Glasgow G61 4AB (☎ 0141 942 6455, 0141 943 0606)

McMILLAN, Colin Bernard; s of Michael McMillan, of Grenada, W Indies, and Maria McMillan; *b* 12 Feb 1966; *Educ* Warren Comp Sch; *m* 2 June 1992, Sue; 2 da (Keisha b 1988, Amber b 1993); *Career* professional boxer (featherweight); amateur career: Port of London Authy champion 1984, London ABA champion 1985–88, Nat ABA finalist 1987 and 1988 (semi-finalist 1985); turned professional 1989; professional career: former WBO Featherweight champion 1991, former Commonwealth Featherweight champion 1992, Br Featherweight champion 1992 and then May 1996; memb Olympic team 1988; engr BT; gen sec Professional Boxers' Assoc; *Recreations* music; *Style*— Colin McMillan, Esq; ✉ c/o Professional Boxers' Association, Francis House, Francis Street, London SW1P 1DE (☎ 0171 630 7486, fax 0171 630 8820)

McMILLAN, Rev Monsignor Donald Neil; s of Daniel McMillan (d 1942), and Mary Cameron, *née* Farrell (d 1951); *b* 21 May 1925; *Educ* St Brendan's Coll Bristol, Prior Park Coll Bath, Oscott Coll Sutton Coldfield, Open Univ (BA 1995); *Career* Army Chaplain 1951–81: BAOR 1961–63, 1966–68, 1975–77, Middle East 1956–59, 1968–70, E Africa 1961, Far East 1952–55, Princ RC Chaplain and Vicar Gen (Army) MOD 1977–81; ordained priest Diocese of Clifton 1948; curate: Bath 1948–49, Gloucester 1949–51, Taunton 1951; parish priest: St Augustine's Gloucester 1981–85, St Teresa's Bristol 1985–86, St Nicholas Winchcombe 1986–; Prelate of Honour 1977; *Recreations* walking, reading; *Clubs* Army and Navy; *Style*— The Rev Monsignor Donald McMillan; ✉ St Nicholas Presbytery, Chandos St, Winchcombe, Glos GL54 5HX (☎ 01242 602412)

MACMILLAN, Prof (John) Duncan; s of Prof William Miller Macmillan (d 1974), and Mona Constance Mary, *née* Tweedie, of Dorchester on Thame, Oxon; *b* 7 March 1939; *Educ* Gordonstoun, Univ of St Andrews (MA), Univ of London (Academic Dip), Univ of Edinburgh (PhD); *m* 5 June 1971, Vivien Rosemary, da of Canon W T Hinkley, of Alnwick, Northumberland; 2 da (Christina Rachel b 1973, Annabel Kate b 1976); *Career* Dept of Fine Art Univ of Edinburgh: lectr 1974–83, sr lectr 1983–88, reader 1988–94, personal chair history of Scottish art 1994–; curator Univ of Edinburgh Galleries & Collections 1988–, dir Talbot Rice Gall, art critic The Scotsman 1994–; chm Edinburgh Galleries Assoc, memb Euro Community Ctee for Cultural Cooperation, convener Univ Museums Gp, memb Cncl Edinburgh Festival Soc; hon keeper of portraits RCSEd; Hon RSA, FRSA; *Books* Gavin Scobie (1984), Painting in Scotland - The Golden Age (1986), Scottish Art 1460–1990 (1990, Scottish book of the year Saltire Soc), Symbols of Survival - The Art of Will MacLean (1992), The Paintings of Steven Campbell (1993), Scottish Art in the Twentieth Century (1994); *Recreations* walking; *Style*— Prof Duncan Macmillan; ✉ 20 Nelson Street, Edinburgh, Scotland EH3 6LJ (☎ 0131 556 7100); Talbot Rice Gallery, The University of Edinburgh, Old College, S Bridge, Edinburgh (☎ 0131 650 2212, telex 27442 UNIVED P)

MACMILLAN, Sir (Alexander McGregor) Graham; kt (1983); s of James Orr Macmillan (d 1961), of Glasgow, and Sarah Dunsmore, *née* Graham (d 1952); *b* 14 Sept 1920; *Educ* Hillhead HS Glasgow; *m* 1947, Christina Brash, da of Robert Brash Beveridge, of Glasgow; 2 s (Alistair b 1948, Donald b 1956), 2 da (Janie b 1950, Catriona b 1955); *Career* govr Leeds GS 1968–75, dir Scot Cons Pty 1975–84, dir M & P Financial Services 1984–88 (chm 1986–88), chm Mid Anglian Enterprise Agency 1988–92 (govr 1987–); exec sec YorCan Communications Ltd 1989–94; memb Tport Users' Consultative Ctee for Eastern England 1987–95; *Recreations* fishing, watching cricket and rugby; *Style*— Sir Graham Macmillan; ✉ 46 Crown St, Bury St Edmunds, Suffolk IP33 1QX (☎ 01284 704443)

McMILLAN, Prof James Francis; s of John McMillan (d 1995), and Hannah, *née* McManus; *b* 10 March 1948; *Educ* St Mirin's Acad Paisley (Sch Dux), Univ of Glasgow (MA), Balliol Coll Oxford (DPhil); *m* 8 April 1989, Donatella, da of Roberto Fischer; *Career* temp lectr Univ of Glasgow 1972–73, lectr Dept of History Univ of York 1973–92, prof of Euro history Univ of Strathclyde 1992–; exchange prof California State Univ Long Beach USA 1987–88; convenor Scottish Catholic Historical Assoc 1996; FRSE 1996; *Books* Housewife or Harlot: the Place of Women in French Society 1870–1940 (1981), Dreyfus to De Gaulle: Politics and Society in France 1898–1969 (1985), Napoleon III (1991), Twentieth Century France: Politics and Society 1898–1991 (1992); *Recreations* opera, theatre, concerts, cinema, walking, travel; *Style*— Prof James McMillan, FRSE; ✉ History Department, University of Strathclyde, McCance Building, 16 Richmond Street, Glasgow G1 1XQ (☎ 0141 548 2731, fax 0141 552 8509)

MacMILLAN, Lt-Gen Sir John Richard Alexander; KCB (1988), CBE (1979, OBE 1973); s of Gen Sir Gordon MacMillan, KCB, KCVO, CBE, DSO, MC, DL (d 1986), and Marian, *née* Blakiston Houston (d 1991); *b* 8 Feb 1932; *Educ* Eton, Trinity Coll Cambridge (MA, Rowing blue, double sculls Olympic Games 1952); *m* Belinda, da of Lt-Col Richard H Lumley Webb, MC (d 1984), of Tunstall House, Sittingbourne, Kent; 1 s (Gordon John b 1967), 2 da (Elizabeth Mary (Mrs Toomey) b 1966, Diana Belinda b 1971); *Career* cmmnd A&SH 1953, CO 1 Gordon Highlanders 1971–73, Cdr 39 Infantry Bde 1977–78, GOC Eastern Dist 1982–85, GOC Scotland 1988–91; self employed fruit farmer 1991–; chm Princess Louise's Hosp Erskine, exec chm Scottish Conservation Projects Tst, HM cmmr Queen Victoria Sch, memb Bd Assoc for Int Cancer Research; *Recreations* most; *Style*— Lt-Gen Sir John MacMillan, KCB, CBE; ✉ c/o Northern Bank, 9 Donegall Square North, Belfast BT1 5GJ

McMILLAN, (Duncan) Lindsay; s of late Duncan Alexander McMillan, and Phyllis Enrica, *née* Spencer; *b* 9 May 1940, Pretoria, SA; *Educ* St Stithian's Coll Johannesburg, Univ of Stellenbosch Cape Province, Witwatersrand Univ Johannesburg (BSc, MB BCh); *m* Ceinwen Mair, da of late Dr Idwal James Mathias; 1 s (Duncan Rhydian b 15 June 1977), 1 da (Katrin Alexandra b 23 July 1979); *Career* former geophysical geologist for the Hans Merensky Tst Northern Cape in the Kalahari Desert; registrar/hon lectr (obstetrics and gynaecology) Royal Free Hosp London 1974–77, sr registrar/hon lectr (obstetrics and gynaecology) Mill Road Maternity Hosp Liverpool, The Women's Hosp Liverpool and Liverpool Maternity Hosp 1977–81, conslt (obstetrics and gynaecology) Whipps Cross Hosp London 1981– (chm Dept of Obstetrics and Gynaecology 1989–91), hon sr lectr St Bartholomew's Hosp and Univ of London 1993–; special interest in minimal access surgery in gynaecology and in pre-malignant and malignant diseases and their medical and surgical treatment; treas Br Soc of Gynaecological Endoscopy; memb: Int Soc for Gynaecologic Endoscopy, Br Soc of Colposcopy and Cervical Pathology, Euro Soc of Gynaecological Hysteroscopy and Laparoscopy, RSM (memb Ctee Obstetric and Gynaecology Div); FRCOG; *Recreations* skiing, mountaineering, theatre, music; *Style*— Lindsay McMillan, Esq; ✉ 17 Wimpole Street, London W1M 7AD (☎ 0171 631 0914, fax 0171 323 9126)

McMILLAN, Moira Teresa; da of Austin Damer, of Surrey, and Sheila, *née* Griffin; *b* 6 April 1949; *Educ* Holy Trinity GS Bromley, Univ of Southampton (BSc); *m* William (Bill) McMillan, *qv*; 1 da (Hannah Katy b 30 Nov 1988); *Career* research and mfrg Duracell UK 1970–76; Chemical Industries Assoc 1976–90: co-author Directory of Chemicals/Tech Exec, UK rep on Euro and int ctees (WHO and FAO), head of int trade representing indust to EEC Cmmn and GATT 1982, ldr various trade missions overseas; dir Paintmakers Association of GB Ltd 1990–93, dir British Coatings Federation Ltd 1993– (incorporating Paintmakers Assoc and Soc of Br Printing Ink Mfrs and representing Wallcovering Mfrs Assoc); FRSA 1993; *Recreations* skiing, swimming; *Clubs* Royal Society of Medicine; *Style*— Mrs Moira McMillan; ✉ British Coatings Federation Ltd, James House, Bridge Street, Leatherhead, Surrey KT22 7EP (☎ 01372 360660, fax 01372 376069)

McMILLAN, Dr Nigel Charles; s of Ian McInnes McMillan (d 1980), and Joan Muriel McMillan, *née* Winchester; *b* 13 May 1950; *Educ* Loretto, Univ of Glasgow (MB ChB); *m* 24 March 1976, Linda Jean Douglas, da of Sqdn Ldr Archibald McDougall, of Giffnock, Glasgow; 1 s (Christopher b 1978), 1 da (Lorna b 1981); *Career* GP S Glasgow 1976–78, conslt radiologist to Western Infirmary Glasgow 1983– (registrar then sr registrar in radiology 1978–83); clinical dir diagnostic radiology West Glasgow Hosps Univ NHS Tst 1993–; FRCR 1982, MRCPG 1995; *Recreations* choral music, golf, skiing; *Style*— Dr Nigel McMillan; ✉ 5 Woodburn Road, Glasgow, Scotland G43 2TN (☎ 0141 637 1441)

McMILLAN, William (Bill); s of Edward McMillan (d 1975), of Ayrshire, and Agnes Conway (d 1979); *b* 11 Jan 1929; *Educ* Ayr Acad, Royal Tech Coll, Univ of Glasgow; *m* 1, 26 Aug 1950 (m dis), Sheila Hallett; 2 s (Ian William b 1955, Neil David b 1960); m 2, Moira McMillan, *qv*; 1 da (Hannah Katy b 30 Nov 1988); *Career* joined Standard Telephones & Cables (ITT) as res (later press rels) mangr 1955, PR mangr BSI 1963–65, princ scientific offr Miny of Technol 1965–68, mangr public affrs Assoc of Br Pharmaceutical Indust; dir of info: Chemical Indust Assoc 1973–83, UKAEA 1983–88; sec gen Assoc Européenne des Producteurs d'Acides Gras (APAG) Brussels 1988–92; FRSM; *Books* The Role and Place of the Chemical Industry in Europe (cmmnd by UN, 1982), numerous tech scientific articles; *Recreations* music, skiing; *Style*— Bill McMillan, Esq; ✉ Woodgate, Moat Lane, Cowden, Kent TN8 7DP (☎ 01342 850116)

MACMILLAN, Very Rev Dr William Boyd Robertson; s of Robert Macmillan (d 1953), and Annie Simpson, *née* Machattie (d 1989); *b* 3 July 1927; *Educ* Royal HS Edinburgh, Univ of Aberdeen (MA, BD, DD); *m* 22 Aug 1962, Mary Adams Bisset, da of Donald Bisset Murray (d 1974); *Career* RN 1946–48; parish min: St Andrews Bo'ness 1955–60, Fyvie 1960–67, Bearsden (South) 1967–78, St Mary's Dundee 1978–93; moderator Presbytery of Dumbarton 1976–77, convenor Bd of Practice and Procedure and convenor of Assembly Arrangements C of S 1984–88, chaplain in ordinary to HM the Queen in Scotland 1988–, moderator Gen Assembly of the Church of Scotland 1991–92; chm of Dirs HS of Dundee 1993–, chm Murray Home; sr chaplain Sea Cadet Corps; memb: Exec Cncl Scottish Veterans' Assoc (pres 1993–), Scottish Church Soc, Church Serv Soc; tstee Scottish Nat War Meml 1994–; Hon LLD Univ of Dundee 1990; Freeman of Dundee 1991; prelate Order of St John (Scotland) 1993; *Recreations* golf, stamp collecting, reading; *Clubs* New (Edinburgh); *Style*— The Very Rev Dr William Macmillan; ✉ 3/5, Craigend Park, Edinburgh, Scotland EH16 5XY

MacMILLAN OF MacMILLAN AND KNAP, George Gordon; s of Gen Sir Gordon Holmes Alexander MacMillan, KCB, KCVO, CBE, DSO, MC (d 1986), of Finlaystone, Langbank, Renfrewshire, and Marian, *née* Blakiston-Houston, OBE (d 1991); *b* 20 June 1930; *Educ* Eton, Trinity Coll Cambridge (MA), Univ of Strathclyde; *m* 2 Sept 1961, (Cecilia) Jane, da of Capt Arthur Rushworth Spurgin, IA (d 1934); 3 s (Arthur Gordon b 29 July 1962, Richard Anthony b 30 Dec 1963, d 1985, Malcolm James b 30 June 1967); *Career* teacher Wellington Coll 1953–63, lectr in religious knowledge Trinity Coll Toronto 1963–64, lectr in religious studies Bede Coll Durham 1965–74; currently self-employed and owner of small estate with historic house and garden open to the public; elder Langbank Church of Scotland; *Recreations* garden-tending, making small structures; *Style*— George MacMillan of MacMillan and Knap; ✉ Finlaystone, Langbank, Renfrewshire PA14 6TJ (☎ 01475 540285)

MACMILLAN OF OVENDEN, Katherine, Viscountess; Hon Dame Katharine Margaret Alice Macmillan; *née* Ormsby-Gore; DBE (1974); da of 4 Baron Harlech, KG, GCMG, PC (d 1964); *b* 4 Jan 1921; *m* 1942, Rt Hon Maurice Victor Macmillan, PC, MP (Viscount Macmillan of Ovenden, d 1984), s of 1 Earl of Stockton (d 1986); 3 s (one of whom 2 Earl of Stockton, *qv*, and 1 s decd), 1 da; *Career* vice-chm Cons Pty 1968–71; *Style*— Katharine, Viscountess Macmillan of Ovenden, DBE; ✉ 9 Warwick Sq, London SW1 (☎ 0171 834 6004)

McMILLAN-SCOTT, Edward Hugh Christian; MEP (C) Yorkshire North (majority 7,072); s of Walter Theodore Robin McMillan-Scott, and Elizabeth Maud Derrington Hudson; *b* 15 Aug 1949; *Educ* Blackfriars Sch Llanarth Raglan Monmouthshire, Blackfriars Sch Laxton Corby, Exeter Tech Coll; *m* 1972, Henrietta Elizabeth Rumney, da of Richard Derrington Mogridge Hudson, of Bristol, Avon; 2 da (Lucinda b 1973, Arabella b 1976); *Career* tour dir in Europe, Africa, USSR 1968–75; private exec then Parly conslt 1976–84, political advsr Falkland Islands Govt London Office 1983–85, MEP (C): York 1984–94, Yorkshire North 1994–; *Clubs* St Stephens Constitutional; *Style*— Edward McMillan-Scott, MEP; ✉ Wick House Farm, Wick, Pershore, Worcs WR10 3NU (☎ 01386 552366, fax 01386 556038); European Parliament, 97 Rue Belliard, Brussels 1040, Belgium

McMINN, Dr Alexander (Alex); JP (Merseyside 1972); s of William Edward Blanchard McMinn, and Sara, *née* Bird; *b* 12 Dec 1932; *Educ* Liverpool Collegiate Sch, Inst of Med Laboratory Sciences Liverpool Univ Centre; *m* 18 Aug 1956, Kathleen Frances, da of Arthur Rannard; 2 da (Helen b 1961, Fiona b 1964); *Career* princ lectr in med scis Liverpool Poly 1968–72; educn advsr: WHO Geneva 1972–84, UN Econ Cmmn for Europe 1984–85; exec dir Int Assoc for Med Scis 1982–88, chief exec Health Manpower Services Ltd 1984–88, chm and chief exec Athena Training International 1988–; chm Vocational Guidance Assoc UK 1985–92; dir: Diagnostic Services Ltd 1984–, Santé International, Merseyside Vocational Servs 1985–94; chm Southport & Formby NHS Tst 1993–95; hon sr lectr Dept of Int Community Health Liverpool Sch of Tropical Med 1985–, assoc prof of health care Univ of N Carolina USA; conslt in med educn for numerous govts and int orgns 1972–; memb Cncl Univ Coll of Ajman UAE 1988–, conslt in health care Kingdom of Saudi Arabia 1992–; educn and trg advsr St John Ambulance Assoc; memb: Tst Merseyside Christian Youth Camps 1970–, Educn and Trg Ctee Merseyside Chamber of Trade 1986–92; Medal of the Cncl of Europe fell Inst of Biomedical Scis 1955, FRSM, MIBiol 1964, CBiol, FRSA 1993; *Books* Training Medical Laboratory Technicians (1975), Design of Competency Based Curricula for Health Workers (1984); *Recreations* watersports, playing the organ; *Clubs* Athenaeum (Liverpool, pres 1991–92); *Style*— Dr Alex McMinn, JP; ✉ Athena Training International, Crosby House, Church Street, Merseyside L20 1AF (☎ 0151 933 6072, fax 0151 944 1559, car 0831 440818)

McMULLAN, Rt Rev Gordon; *see:* Down and Dromore, Bishop of

McMULLAN, His Hon Michael Brian; s of Joseph Patrick McMullan (d 1967), of Bournemouth, and Emma Frances, *née* Burton; *b* 15 Nov 1926; *Educ* Taunton's Sch Southampton. The Queen's Coll Oxford (MA); *m* 1960, Rosemary Jane Margaret, da of Stanley Halse de Lossy de Ville; 2 da (Philippa Anne (Mrs Rogerson) b 26 May 1961, Gillian Frances (Mrs Cubey) b 15 Aug 1962), 1 s (Dr Patrick John de Ville McMullan b 13 Dec 1963); *Career* Nat Serv Army 1946–48; served Gold Coast/Ghana Colonial Admin Serv 1949–60 (political admin Ashanti, Miny of Fin Accra and Ghana Agric Devpt Corp), freelance journalism 1960–61; called to the Bar Gray's Inn 1960, in practice SE Circuit 1961–80, recorder 1979–80, circuit judge (SE Circuit) 1980–95, ret; *Clubs* United Oxford & Cambridge University; *Style*— His Hon Michael McMullan; ✉ c/o The Law Courts, Woodall House, Lordship Lane, Wood Green, London N22

McMULLEN, Jeremy John; QC (1994); s of John E McMullen, and Irene, *née* Gardner; *b* 14 Sept 1948; *Educ* William Hulme's GS Manchester, Brasenose Coll Oxford, LSE, Inns of Court Sch of Law; *m* 1973, Debbie, *née* Cristman; 1 s (Ben b 1976), 1 da (Katy b 1979); *Career* called to the Bar Middle Temple 1971; assoc attorney NY 1972–73, General and Municipal Workers' Union 1973–84, barr 1984–; chair: Industrial Law Soc 1989–93 (memb Ctee 1978–), Employment Law Bar Assoc 1994–95; pt/t chm Industrial Tbnl, memb Employment Lawyers' Assoc 1993–; *Books* Rights at Work, Employment Law, Employment Tribunal Procedure; *Clubs* Reform, West London Trade Union; *Style*— Jeremy McMullen, Esq, QC; ✉ Old Square Chambers, 1 Verulam Buildings, Gray's Inn, London WC1R 5LQ (☎ 0171 831 0801, fax 0171 405 1387)

McMURRAY, Dr Cecil Hugh; s of late Cecil Edwin McMurray, and Margaret Napier, *née* Smyth; *b* 19 Feb 1942; *Educ* Royal Belfast Academical Inst, Greenmount Agric Coll, Queen's Univ Belfast (BSc, BAgr), Univ of Bristol (PhD); *m* 3 Jan 1967, (Isabel) Ann, da of C A Stuart, of Belfast; 2 s (Alan, Trevor), 1 da (Rebecca); *Career* res fell Harvard Univ Cambridge Mass USA 1970–72, head of biochemistry Vet Res Labs Dept of Agric for NI 1972–84; joint appt as prof of food and agric chemistry Queen's Univ Belfast and dep CSO Dept of Agric for NI 1985–88, CSO Dept of Agric for NI 1988–; memb: Bd Northern Ireland Public Sector Enterprises Ltd, Bd Agricultural Systems Directorate, Biotechnologies and Biological Scis Res Cncl, Advsy Ctee on Microbiological Safety, Governing Body Rowett Res Inst Aberdeen; tstee Agric Res Inst for NI; Salzburg fell 1983; FRSC 1981, FIFST 1987; *Publications* contrib: CIBA Fndn Symposia number 79 copper also number 101 Biology of Vitamin E, Trace Elements of Man and Domestic Animals Vol 5, and 6 Int Conference on Production Disease of Farm Animals, Selenium in Biology and Medicine; Detection Methods for Irriated Food (ed with others, 1996); also author of over 100 other scientific communications; *Recreations* photography, walking; *Style*— Dr Cecil McMurray; ✉ Department of Agriculture for Northern Ireland, Dundonald House, Upper Newtonwards Road, Belfast BT4 3SB (☎ 01232 524635, fax 01232 525002, telex 74578 DEPAGR-G)

McMURRAY, David Bruce; CFM (1974, Bar 1984); s of James McMurray, CBE (d 1950), and Kathleen Mary, *née* Goodwin; *b* 15 Dec 1937; *Educ* Loretto, Pembroke Coll Cambridge (BA, MA); *m* 25 Aug 1962, Antonia Alexandra, da of Lt Cdr A D S Murray (d 1988); 3 da (Georgina b 1963, Philippa b 1968, Suzannah b 1973); *Career* Nat Serv 1956–58, 2 Lt the Royal Scots 1957–58; asst master: Stowe Sch 1961; Fettes Coll: asst master 1964, head of English Dept 1968, house master 1972; headmaster: Loretto 1976, Oundle 1984–; memb Edinburgh Festival Cncl 1981–84; FRSA 1989; *Recreations* golf, diving, theatre; *Clubs* MCC, East India, Devonshire, Sports & Public Sch, New (Edinburgh); *Style*— David McMurray, Esq, CFM; ✉ Cobthorne, West St, Oundle, Peterborough PE8 4EF (☎ 01832 272251); Oundle Sch, Oundle, Peterborough PE8 4EN (☎ 01832 273536, fax 01832 74448)

McMURTRIE, Simon Nicholas; s of Anthony William Stratton McMurtrie, and Sally, *née* Bateson; *b* 20 Feb 1966; *Educ* Radley, Univ of Birmingham (BA); *m* 8 Aug 1992, Virginia, *née* Jagger; 1 da (Anna Charlotte b 22 Dec 1994); *Career* William Heinemann Ltd 1988, Mandarin Paperbacks 1989, Euro sales mangr Octopus Publishing 1990, publishing dir Mitchell Beazley and Miller's Publications 1991, publishing dir Reed Illustrated Books 1992–93, md De Agostini Editions 1993–95, chief exec De Agostini UK (incl Orbis) 1995–; publishing conslt Harvard University Press 1989–; non-exec dir Hunter and Foulis Ltd 1993–; *Recreations* organist; *Style*— Simon McMurtrie, Esq; ✉ De Agostini UK, Griffin House, 161 Hammersmith Road, London W6 8SD (☎ 0181 600 2000, fax 0181 748 1607)

McNAB, Harry; OBE (1977), JP (Glasgow, 1971); s of John McNab (d 1980), of Glasgow, and Margaret Helen, *née* Higginbotham (d 1980); *b* 14 Nov 1924; *Educ* Whitehill Sr Secdy Sch Glasgow, RSAMD, LTCL; *m* Emily Mary, da of late George Archibald Falconer; *Career* served RAF 1943–47; trainee journalist Glasgow Herald/Evening Times and Scottish Newspaper Services 1940–43, general mangr Cossar Press Glasgow 1948–54, md John Cossar Ltd 1957–83 (dir and co sec 1954–57); dir: Radio Glasgow Ltd 1971–74, Govan Trades Ltd 1971–84, Advertising Standards Bd of Fin Ltd 1975–88; sales and mktg dir: James Paton Ltd Paisley 1983–87, J & J Cook Ltd Paisley 1983–87, Clyde Publishing Ltd 1987–91; chm: Strathclyde News Holdings Ltd 1971–83, Scottish Newsprint Users' Assoc 1975–84, Q96 FM Ltd Paisley 1991–; pres: Scottish Newspapers Proprietors' Assoc 1974–76, Glasgow Master Printers' Assoc 1976–78, Soc of Master Printers of Scotland 1979–81, YMCA Glasgow 1983–; press offr (Scotland) Variety Club of Great Britain 1991–; *Books* History of Govan Weavers' Society (1956); *Recreations* music, books, wine, walking; *Clubs* Govan Rotary; *Style*— Harry McNab, Esq, OBE, JP; ✉ Kittochpark, 2 Dalkeith Avenue, Dumbreck, Glasgow G41 5BQ (☎ 0141 427 3566); Q96 FM Ltd, 26 Lady Lane, Paisley PA1 2LG (☎ 0141 887 9630, fax 0141 887 0963)

McNAB, John Stanley; s of Robert Stanley McNab (d 1974), and Alice Mary, *née* Sawyers (d 1965); *b* 23 Sept 1937; *m* 1 (m dis 1977), Carol; 2 da (Lesley Anne b 12 Oct 1965, Jacqueline Carol Davey b 19 July 1968); m 2, 30 Jan 1980, Jacqueline; *Career* Nat Serv RE 1956–58; Port of London Authority: joined as jr clerical offr 1954, various accountancy appts rising to docks accountant Upper Docks 1971, md PLA (Thames) Stevedoring Ltd (formerly Thames Stevedoring (1965) Ltd) 1973, dir Upper Docks 1974, memb Bd 1978–92, exec dir manpower (formerly jt dir) 1978–82, dir docks ops 1982–83, dir Tilbury 1983–87, dir Port of London Authority 1987–92; chief exec Port of Tilbury London Ltd 1992–95; chm London Port Employers' Assoc 1978–89, memb Nat Dock Lab Bd 1978–89; former memb: Exec and Mgmnt Ctees Nat Assoc of Port Employers, Nat Jt Cncl for Port Tport Indust; govr Thurrock Tech Coll 1988– (chm Fin and Gen Purposes Ctee); Freeman: City of London 1988, Worshipful Co of Watermen and Lightermen of the River Thames 1989; FCCA, FCIT, MIMgt, FRSA; *Recreations* walking the dogs, swimming, tennis, DIY; *Style*— John McNab, Esq; ✉ 2 Spinnaker Drive, Heybridge Basin, Maldon, Essex CM9 4UG (☎ 01621 852166, mobile 0976 323444)

MACNAB OF MACNAB, Hon Mrs (Diana Mary); *née* Anstruther-Gray; DL (Fife 1992); er da of Baron Kilmany, PC, MC, JP, DL (Life Peer; d 1985), and Monica Helen Anstruther-Gray, OBE, DL, *née* Lambton (d 1985); *b* 16 June 1936; *m* 11 April 1959, James Charles Macnab of Macnab (The Macnab), *qv*); 2 s (James William Archibald b 1963, Geoffrey Charles b 1965), 2 da (Virginia Mary (Mrs Richard Fyffe) b 1960, Katharine Monica b 1968); *Career* chm Scotland's Gardens Scheme 1983–91 (hon vice-pres 1991–), memb Exec Ctee National Tst for Scotland, pres Central and North Fife Preservation Soc; *Style*— The Hon Mrs Macnab of Macnab, DL; ✉ Leuchars Castle Farmhouse, Leuchars, St Andrews, Fife KY16 0EY (☎ 01334 838777)

MACNAB OF MACNAB (THE MACNAB), James Charles Macnab of Macnab; 23 Chief of Clan Macnab; eldest s of Lt-Col James Alexander Macnabb, OBE, TD (d 1990, *de jure* 21 Chief), of Bramerton St, Chelsea, and his 1 w, Ursula, *née* Barnett (d 1979); suc great unc, Archibald Corrie Macnab of Macnab, CIE (*de facto* 22 Chief) 1970; *b* 14 April 1926; *Educ* Radley, Ashbury Coll Ottawa; *m* 11 April 1959, Hon Diana Mary Anstruther-Gray (*see* Hon Mrs Macnab of Macnab); 2 s, 2 da; *Heir* s, James William Archibald Macnab of Macnab, yr, b 22 March 1963; *Career* RAF 1944, Scots Gds 1944–45, Lt Seaforth Highlanders 1945–48, Capt Seaforth Highlanders (TA) 1960–64; asst then dep supt Fedn of Malaya Police 1948–57; mangr and owner Kinnell Estate and farms 1957–78, sr conslt Hill Samuel Investment Services Ltd 1982–92; memb: Western Dist Cncl of Perthshire 1961–64, Perth and Kinross Jt County Cncl 1964–75, Central Regnl Cncl 1978–82; memb Royal Co of Archers (Queen's Body Guard for Scotland); JP Perthshire 1968–75 and Stirling 1975–86; *Clubs* New (Edinburgh); *Style*— The Macnab; ✉ Leuchars Castle Farmhouse, Leuchars, St Andrew's, Fife KY16 0EY (☎ 01334 838777)

MACNAGHTEN, Sir Patrick Alexander; 11 Bt (UK 1836), of Bushmills House, Co Antrim; s of Sir Antony Macnaghten, 10 Bt (d 1972), and Magdalene, *née* Fisher; *b* 24 Jan 1927; *Educ* Eton, Trinity Coll Cambridge; *m* 1955, Marianne, da of Dr Eric Schaefer, of Cambridge; 3 s (Malcolm Francis b 1956, Edward Alexander b 1958, David Charles b 1962); *Heir* s, Malcolm Francis Macnaghten b 21 Sept 1956; *Career* ret project mangr Cadbury Schweppes plc; *Style*— Sir Patrick Macnaghten, Bt; ✉ Dundarave, Bushmills, Co Antrim BT57 8ST

McNAIR, Archibald Alister Jourdan (Archie); s of Donald McNair (d 1975), and Janie, *née* Jourdan (d 1970); *b* 16 Dec 1919; *Educ* Blundells; *m* 1954, Catherine Alice Jane, da of John Fleming (d 1947), of Barraghcore, Kilkenny, Ireland; 1 s (Hamish Lindsay), 1 da (Camilla Margaret (Mrs Mair)); *Career* chm: Mary Quant Group 1955–88, Thomas Jourdan plc 1971–88, TPI Corp Ltd 1988–90; dir City & Capital Hotels plc 1986–92; *Recreations* fruit farming, chess, carving wood; *Style*— Archie McNair, Esq; ✉ c/o Coutts & Co, 440 Strand, London WC2R 0QS

McNAIR, 3 Baron (UK 1955); Duncan James McNair; s of 2 Baron McNair (d 1989); *b* 26 June 1947; *Educ* Bryanston; *m* 1; 1 s (Hon Thomas John b 1972), 1 da (Hon Victoria b (twin) 1972), 1 adopted da (Charlotte b 1968); m 2, Hannah Margaret Elizabeth; 1 step s (Sean b 1968); *Heir* bro, Hon William Samuel Angus McNair b 19 May 1958; *Career* chm Emission Control Systems Int, chm DMCK Consultants 1996–; vice chm Parly Waterways Gp (Canals) 1994–, fndr memb Cncl for Human Rights and Religious Freedom 1996, memb Exec Ctee Euro Parly Intercultural Ctee 1996–; memb Sub Ctee for Environment House of Lords Select Ctee on EC 1990–92, memb All Party Parly Gp on Race and Community 1994–95; memb Drugs Misuse Gp 1991–; special interests: human rights, educn, drug abuse prevention, religious freedom, environment; *Style*— The Rt Hon the Lord McNair; ✉ House of Lords, Westminster, London SW1A OPW

McNAIR, Sylvia; da of George Becker McNair (d 1979), of Mansfield, Ohio, and Marilou, *née* Smith; *Educ* Wheaton Coll (BA), Univ of Indiana (MMus); *m* 12 April 1986, Hal France, s of Harold France; *Career* soprano; San Francisco Opera Apprenticeship Program 1982, Glyndebourne debut 1989, Covent Garden debut 1989; appeared at venues incl: Carnegie Hall NY, San Francisco, Detroit, Atlanta, St Louis, Washington, LA, Lyon, Strasbourg, Berlin, Vienna, Glyndebourne; performed with orchs incl: Chicago Symphony, Berlin Philharmonic, City of Birmingham Symphony, Monteverdi Choir and Orch; worked with conductors incl: Seiji Ozawa, Sir George Solti, Sir Neville Marriner, Simon Rattle, Bernard Haitink, Claudio Abbado, John Eliot Gardiner; *Performances* incl: Pamina in The Magic Flute (Santa Fe, Deutsche Oper Berlin, Vienna State Opera), Ilia in Idomeneo (St Louis, Lyon, Strasbourg, Euro tour with Monteverdi Choir and Orch, Royal Opera House Covent Garden 1989, Salzburg Festival 1990), Susanna in The Marriage of Figaro (Netherlands Opera, Vienna State Opera), Hero in Beatrice and Benedict (St Louis), Morgana in Alcina (St Louis), Anne Truelove in The Rake's Progress (Glyndebourne 1989); *Style*— Ms Sylvia McNair; ✉ c/o Lies Askonas Ltd, 6 Henrietta Street, London WC2E 8LA (☎ 0171 379 7700)

McNAIR SCOTT, Simon Guthrie; s of Thomas Michael McNair Scott, of St Peter, Jersey, CI, and Susannah, *née* Hodges (d 1993); *b* 12 May 1960; *Educ* Eton, Univ of Exeter (BA); *m* 1, 1988 (m dis 1991), Hon Camilla Birgitta, *née* Davidson, da of 2 Viscount Davidson; m 2, 8 Sept 1995, Natasha Jane, da of Alexander Stevenson (d 1994); *Career* film and TV freelance location mangr 1982–; recent credits incl: The Camomile Lawn 1991, MacGyver 1993, Judge Dredd 1994, Mission: Impossible 1995; advsr London Film Cmmn 1996; *Recreations* golf, surfing; *Clubs* Hurlingham, Brooks's; *Style*— Simon McNair Scott, Esq; ✉ The Old Rectory, Lesnewth, Boscastle, North Cornwall PL35 0HR (☎ 01840 261730)

McNAIR-WILSON, Sir Patrick Michael Ernest David; kt (1989), MP (C) New Forest (majority 20,405); s of Dr Robert McNair-Wilson, of Lyndhurst, Hants; bro of Sir (Robert) Michael McNair-Wilson (d 1993); *b* 28 May 1929; *Educ* Eton; *m* 1953, Diana Evelyn Kitty Campbell, da of Hon Laurence Methuen-Campbell (d 1970, s of 3 Baron Methuen); 1 s, 4 da; *Career* conslt; MP (C): Lewisham W 1964–66, New Forest 1968–; PPS to Min for Tport Indust DOE 1970–74, oppn front bench spokesman on energy 1974–76, chm Jt Lords and Commons Select Ctee on Private Bill Procedure 1987–; ptnr Ferret Public Relations & Govt Affairs, dir Photo-Me International Plc; *Recreations* pottery, flying, photography; *Style*— Sir Patrick McNair-Wilson, MP; ✉ House of Commons, London SW1A 0AA

McNALLY, Eryl Margaret; MEP (Lab) Beds and Milton Keynes (majority 33,209); da of Llywelyn Williams MP (d 1965), and Elsie, *née* Macdonald (d 1976); *b* 11 April 1942; *Educ* Newbridge GS Gwent, Univ of Bristol (BA), UC Swansea (PGCE); *m* 15 Aug 1964, James Frederick McNally, s of James McNally; 1 da (Helena Mary b 14 Feb 1967), 1 s (Gavin Richard b 6 Dec 1968); *Career* teacher of modern languages at various schs and colls 1964–84, advsy work Bucks CC 1985–93, freelance sch inspector 1993–94; MEP (Lab) Beds and Milton Keynes 1994–; cncllr: Watford Rural DC 1972–74, Three Rivers DC 1973–77, Herts CC 1986–95; Parly candidate W Herts 1992; memb Nat Assoc of Language Advsrs; *Recreations* reading, world music, learning languages; *Clubs* Co-op Party, TGWU; *Style*— Ms Eryl McNally, MEP; ✉ 146 Abbots Road, Abbots Langley, Herts WD5 0BL (☎ 01923 264525)

McNALLY, Gordon Louis; VRD; s of William McNally (d 1988), of Bexhill-on-Sea, Sussex, and Alice Lina, *née* Allbutt (d 1987); *b* 26 June 1924; *Educ* St Mary's Commercial Sch Hornsey; *m* 1, 4 Jan 1947 (m dis 1982), Marie Alice Doreen, *née* Upton; 2 s (Graham b 1947, Ross b 1958), 2 da (Alison b 1952, Heather b 1956); m 2, 31 May 1985, Sylvia Anne-Marie, da of Idris Henry Lowe, of Perth, W Aust; *Career* Lt Cdr RNVR and RNR 1943–71, served HM Ships N Sea, Atlantic, Pacific, Ceylon, organised repatriation Far East Allied POWs and internees; Yuills Ltd: joined 1940, co sec 1954, md 1965; Exchange Travel Group: md 1958, chm (following purchase from Yuills Ltd) 1972; pioneered tourism in Malta, Gibraltar and Cyprus 1960, pioneered lowering Aust NZ-UK air fares and formed ANZEFA which was first to charter Boeing 747 1965–67, pioneered franchising in travel indust 1984; memb Nat Cncl ABTA 1965–72; ind Parly candidate: Hastings and St Leonards 1979, Hastings and Rye 1983; fndr VOTES (Victims of the Establishment System) 1997; fell Inst of Travel and Tourism 1965, CIMgt 1985; *Recreations* swimming, exotic horticulture; *Style*— Gordon McNally, Esq, VRD; ✉ Kingsbrook Consultancy, 2nd and 3rd Floors, 22 Robertson Street, Hastings, East Sussex TN34 1HL (☎ and fax 01424 772847)

McNALLY, Kevin Robert; s of Robert Gerard McNally, of Wedmore, Somerset, and Margaret June, *née* Sperring; *b* 27 April 1956; *Educ* Central GS Birmingham, RADA (Ronson Award, Bancroft Award); *ptnr* Stevie Harris; 1 step s (Peter), 1 da (Rachel b 7 Nov 1988); *Career* actor; also writes for TV under name Kevin Sperring (with Bernard Dempsey); *Theatre* incl: Birmingham Repertory Theatre 1972–73, Not Quite Jerusalem and Prayer For My Daughter (Royal Ct); NT 1979–80: Lark Rise, The Passion, Dispatches, The Iceman Cometh; Loose Ends (Hampstead), Pistols and Airbase (The Arts), Andromache (Old Vic), Scenes from an Execution (with Almeida Co); West End theatre incl: Extremities (Duchess), Glengarry Glen Ross (Mermaid), Hidden Laughter (Vaudeville); *Television* for BBC incl: Commitments, Poldark, I Claudius, Duchess of Duke Street, Diana, Thin Air, Dream Baby, Tygo Road, The Common Pursuit; Praying Mantis (Channel 4), A Brother's Tale (Granada), The Contract (YTV), The Paradise Run (Thames), Hard Cases (Central), Act of Will (Tyne Tees), Jekyll and Hyde (LWT), Full Stretch (Meridian); *Films* incl: The Spy Who Loved Me, The Long Good Friday, Inside Man, Enigma, The Antagonists, Not Quite Jerusalem, The Berlin Affair, Cry Freedom, The Hangover; *Recreations* golf; *Clubs* Carlton Snooker, Groucho's; *Style*— Kevin McNally, Esq; ✉ c/o Stephen Hatton Management, 1a Shepperton House, 83–93 Shepperton Road, London N1 3DF (☎ 0171 359 3593, fax 0171 354 2189)

McNALLY, Peter Joseph Deane; s of Gp Capt Patrick John McNally, of Marlow, Bucks, and Mary Deane, *née* Outred; *b* 16 March 1933; *Educ* Stonyhurst; *m* 1, 1956 (m dis 1960), Mary B Gardiner; 1 da (Joanna b 1957); m 2, 3 March 1969, Edmée Maria, da of Egon Carmine del Sasso, of Estaplatz, Vienna, Austria; 2 s (Alexis b 1970, Markus b 1972); *Career* exec dir: LWT 1969–93, LWT (Holdings) plc 1976–93; past non-exec dir: Hutchinson Ltd, Independent TV Publications Ltd; past chm: Company of Designers plc, The Listener Ltd; currently non-exec dir: Arcadian International plc, Logitron Holdings plc; currently chm: Sunspot Tours Ltd, Production Finance and Management Ltd; underwriter at Lloyd's; FCA (ACA 1955); painter; first solo exhbn The Osborne Studio Gallery Cork St London 1997; *Recreations* fishing, shooting, skiing, tennis, bridge; *Clubs* Boodle's, Hurlingham; *Style*— Peter McNally, Esq; ✉ 1 Elthiron Road, London SW6 4BN (☎ 0171 731 5066)

McNALLY, Baron (Life Peer UK 1995), of Blackpool in the County of Lancashire; Thomas (Tom) McNally; s of John Patrick McNally (d 1982), and Elizabeth May McNally (d 1982); *b* 20 Feb 1943; *Educ* Coll of St Joseph Blackpool, UCL (BSc); *m* 1, 1970 (m dis 1990), Eileen Isobel, da of Thomas Powell, of Dumfries, Scotland; m 2, 1990, Juliet, da of George Lamy Hutchinson, of Swansea, S Wales; 2 s (Hon John b 15 June 1990, Hon James George b 7 Aug 1993), 1 da (Hon Imogen b 28 Oct 1995); *Career* asst gen sec the Fabian Soc 1966–67, vice pres NUS 1966–67, int sec Lab Party HQ 1969–74 (researcher 1966–77); political advsr: to Foreign and Cwlth Sec 1974–76, to PM (head of Political Office 10 Downing St) 1976–79, currently to Paddy Ashdown; MP (Lab until 1981, whereafter SDP) Stockport South 1979–83, memb House of Commons Trade and Indust Select Ctee 1979–83; public affrs advsr, head of public affrs Hill and Knowlton (UK) Ltd PR conslts 1987–93, vice chm Shandwick Consultants Ltd PR conslts 1996– (dir of public affrs 1993–96); memb Fed Exec Lib Democrats 1987–; fell UCL 1995; *Recreations* watching sport, reading political biographies; *Style*— The Rt Hon Lord McNally; ✉ Shandwick Consultants Ltd, Aldermary House, 10–15 Queen Street, London EC4N 1TX (☎ 0171 329 0096, fax 0171 919 9073)

McNAMARA, Dr John Francis; s of Francis McNamara (d 1978), of Bolton, Lancs, and Olivia, *née* Whittingham (d 1982); *b* 18 July 1945; *Educ* Worsley-Wardley GS, Univ of Leeds; *m* 19 Dec 1981, Olwen, da of Richard Fellows, of Altrincham, Cheshire; 1 s (James Declan b 23 Oct 1983), 1 da (Katherine Jane b 16 March 1985); *Career* sr MO Br Nuclear Fuels Risley Nuclear Power Centre 1979–83, occupational health physician City of Salford 1983–87, conslt physician in occupational med Halton General Hosp Runcorn and W Cheshire NHS Tst Chester 1986–, conslt occupational physician and dir of occupational med Univ Hosp of S Manchester 1992–; occupational physician Steripak Pharmaceuticals Runcorn Cheshire 1987–; memb: BMA 1971, Soc of Occupational Med 1977, Chester and N Wales Med Soc 1986, Cncl Assoc of Nat Health Occupational Physicians 1986; hon clinical lectr in occupational med Univ of Manchester 1993–; LLM Univ of Wales 1994; LRCP 1970, MRCS 1970, MRCGP 1975, MRCP 1979 (collegiate memb London and Edinburgh 1979), MFOM (RCP) 1983, MFFP (RCOG) 1993, FRCP (Glasgow) 1994; *Books* The Patient with Respiratory Problems (contrib, 1989); *Recreations* bridge, swimming, walking, history, scripophily; *Style*— Dr John McNamara; ✉ Upway, Parkhill Road, Hale, Altrincham, Cheshire WA15 9JX (☎ 0161 980 5054); Occupational Health Unit, Fielden House, University Hospital of South Manchester, Nell Lane, West Didsbury, Manchester M20 2LR (☎ and fax 0161 291 4603)

McNAMARA, (Joseph) Kevin; MP (Lab) Hull North (majority 15,384); s of Patrick McNamara, of Liverpool; *b* 5 Sept 1934; *Educ* St Mary's Coll Crosby, Hull Univ (LLB); *m* 1960, Nora, da of John Jones, of Warrington; 4 s, 1 da; *Career* former lectr in law Hull Coll of Commerce and head History Dept St Mary's GS Hull; MP (Lab): Hull North 1966–74 and 1983–, Kingston-upon-Hull Central 1974–83; sec of state for econ affrs 1967–69, PPS to min without portfolio 1969–70, chm PLP NI Gp 1974–79, oppn front bench spokesman on defence and disarmament 1982–87, chief oppn spokesman on Northern Ireland 1987–94, shadow spokesperson for the Civil Serv 1994–95 (resigned); formerly: chm Select Ctee on Overseas Devpt, memb Select Ctee on Foreign Affairs, memb Cncl of Europe and NATO Parly Assembly; sec TGWU Parly Gp, vice pres League Against Cruel Sports; *Style*— Kevin McNamara, Esq, MP; ✉ 145 Newland Park, Hull, East Yorkshire HU5 2DX (☎ 01482 448170); House of Commons, London SW1A 0AA

McNAMARA, Steve Shaun; s of Edward McNamara, of Hull, and Christine, *née* Bilton; *b* 18 Sept 1971; *Educ* South Holderness HS; *m* 15 July 1995, Michaela, da of Brian Jeffery; 1 da (Stacey b 19 July 1986); *Career* rugby league player; clubs: Hull RLFC 1989–96, Bradford Bulls RLFC 1996–; England schoolboy capt; GB: under 21's 5 appearances (capt twice), full debut v France 1991, memb touring team Australia and NZ 1992; played England: v Wales 1995, v France 1995; bricklayer 1987–92, commercial rep 1992–; *Recreations* golf and fishing; *Style*— Steve McNamara; ✉ c/o Bradford Bulls RLFC, Odsal Stadium, Bradford BD6 1BS

McNAUGHT, His Hon Judge; John Graeme; s of Charles William McNaught (d 1955), and Isabella Mary McNaught (d 1969); *b* 21 Feb 1941; *Educ* King Edward VII Sch Sheffield, The Queen's Coll Oxford (MA); *m* 1966, Barbara Mary, da of George Rufus Smith (d 1961); 2 s, 1 da; *Career* called to the Bar Gray's Inn 1963; in practice Western circuit, recorder 1981–87, circuit judge (Western Circuit) 1987–; *Style*— His Hon Judge McNaught; ✉ c/o Swindon Crown Court, Islington Street, Swindon (☎ 01793 614848)

McNAUGHTON, John Ewen; OBE (1985), JP; s of Alastair McNaughton (d 1968), and Anne Corries Campbell (d 1967); *b* 28 May 1933; *Educ* Cargilfield, Loretto; *m* 4 Sept 1956, Jananne Ogilvy, da of Lt-Col Percy Ewen Clunes Honeyman (d 1945); 2 s (Malcolm b 1957, Allan b 1959), 2 da (Carolyn b 1961, Fiona b 1964); *Career* farmer; memb: Panel of Agric Arbiters 1973–, Red Deer Cmmn 1975–92, Br Wool Mktg Bd 1975–, Nat Farmers' Union of Scot, Scottish Agric Arbiters' Assoc; chm Scotch Quality Beef and Lamb Assoc 1981–, former chm Nat Sheep Assoc; elder Church of Scot; FRAgS; *Recreations* yachting, stalking, woodwork; *Clubs* Farmers', Royal Highland Yacht; *Style*— John McNaughton, Esq, OBE, JP; ✉ Inverlochlarig, Balquhidder, Lochearnhead, Perthshire FK19 8PH (☎ 01877 384232, fax 01877 384695)

MACNAUGHTON, Sir Malcolm Campbell; kt (1986); s of James Hay Macnaughton (d 1951), and Mary Robieson, *née* Hogarth (d 1954); *b* 4 April 1925; *Educ* Glasgow Acad, Univ of Glasgow (MB ChB, MD); *m* 26 April 1955, Margaret-Ann, da of William Boyd Galt, of Glasgow; 2 s (Graham b 1958, Torquil b 1964), 3 da (Jane b 1960, Gillian b 1965, Jennifer (twin) b 1965); *Career* Capt RAMC 1949–51; lectr in obstetrics and gynaecology Univ of Aberdeen 1957–61, sr lectr Univ of St Andrews 1961–66, hon sr lectr Univ of Dundee 1966–69, prof emeritus and sr res fell Dept of Obstetrics and Gynaecology Univ of Glasgow 1990– (Muirhead prof 1969–90); memb Warnock Ctee 1982–84, govr Glasgow Acad; memb Incorporation of Fleshers Glasgow 1944; Hon LLD Univ of Dundee 1988; FRCOG (pres 1984–87), FRCPG, FRSE 1984; *Books* Combined Text Book of Obstetric Gynaecology (1976), Medical Gynaecology (1984); *Recreations* fishing, golf, walking; *Clubs* Glasgow Academical; *Style*— Sir Malcolm Macnaughton; ✉ 15 Boclair Road, Bearsden, Glasgow G61 2AF (☎ 0141 211 4702, fax 0141 942 1909); Department of Obstetrics & Gynaecology, Queen Elizabeth Building, 10 Alexandra Parade, Glasgow G31 2ER (☎ 0141 552 3535, fax 0141 553 1367)

McNAY, Michael George; s of Harold Edward McNay (d 1978), of Darlington, Co Durham, and Eleanora McNay, *née* Yanischek (d 1989); *b* 7 March 1935; *Educ* Lawrence Royal Mil Sch India, Queen Elizabeth GS Darlington Co Durham, Balliol Coll Oxford; *m* 1, 1957 (m dis 1972), Marian Alison Milne; 1 s (Ross b 1966), 1 da (Lois b 1963); m 2, 1974, Susan Pilkington; 1 da (Anna b 1979); *Career* reporter Bedfordshire Times 1958–62, sub ed Oxford Mail 1962–63; The Guardian 1963–: sub ed 1963, northern arts critic 1964–70, ed arts page 1970–75, dep features ed 1975–78, asst ed (front page) 1978–; awarded Southern Arts Literary Prize 1981; *Books* East Malling - Portrait of a Kentish Village (1980), Red Guide to Kent (1989); *Recreations* cooking; *Style*— Michael McNay, Esq; ✉ The Guardian, 119 Farringdon Rd, London EC1R 3ER (☎ 0171 278 2332)

McNEANY, Kevin Joseph; s of Bernard Joseph McNeany, of Keady, Co Armagh, and Mary Christina, *née* McDonnell; *b* 10 April 1943; *Educ* St Patrick's Coll Armagh, Queen's Univ Belfast (BA), Univ of London, Univ of Manchester; *m* 1 Aug 1968 (m dis 1985), Christine, da of Stephen McNulty; 2 s (Matthew Ciaron b 1971, Myles Anthony b 1986); *Career* teacher: St Paul's Sch Lurgan Co Armagh 1964–66, Corpus Christi Sch Leeds 1966–68; lectr: Kitson Coll Leeds 1968–70, Southport Tech Coll 1970–73, Wythenshawe Coll Manchester 1973–77; co-fndr (with Christine McNeany 1972), md and chief exec Nord Anglia Education plc (formerly Nord-Anglia International) 1977–; fndr: British School of Warsaw Poland 1992, British Int Sch of Moscow 1994, English Sch Prague 1995; *Recreations* walking, cycling; *Clubs* National Liberal; *Style*— Kevin McNeany, Esq; ✉ Ridge Park, 32 Bramhall Park Rd, Bramhall, Cheshire SK7 3JN (☎ 0161 439 2563); 10 Eden Place, Cheadle, Cheshire SK8 1AT (☎ 0161 491 4191, fax 0161 491 4409)

McNEE, Sir David Blackstock; kt (1978), QPM (1975); s of John McNee; *b* 23 March 1925; *Educ* Woodside Sr Secdy Sch Glasgow; *m* 1952, Isabella Hopkins; 1 da; *Career* dep chief constable Dunbartonshire 1968–71; chief constable: Glasgow 1971–75, Strathclyde 1975–77; cmmr Metropolitan Police 1977–82; memb Air Safety Review Ctee Br Airways 1982–87, advsr to Chm Br Airways 1982–87; dir: Clydesdale Bank 1982–93, Fleet Holdings 1983–86, Forte (formerly Trusthouse Forte) 1983–93, Control Technology (UK) Ltd 1986–93; chm: Integrated Security Systems 1985–90, Clyde Publishing Ltd 1987–89, Clyde Helicopters 1988, M R Memex Ltd 1988, Wrightson Wood Associates Ltd 1991; non-exec chm Scottish Express Newspapers 1983–92; pres: Nat Bible Soc of Scotland, Royal Life Saving Soc UK 1982–89; hon vice pres Boys' Bde, patron Scottish Motor Neurone Disease Assoc; Freeman City of London; CIMgt; KStJ 1991 (CStJ); *Clubs* Caledonian, Naval (life memb); *Style*— Sir David McNee, QPM; ✉ M R Memex Ltd, 2 Redwood Court, Peel Park, East Kilbride G74 5PF (☎ 01355 233804)

MACNEE, (Daniel) Patrick; s of Daniel Macnee (d 1952), of Lambourn, Berks, and Dorothea Mary Henry, BEM (d 1985, niece of 13 Earl of Huntingdon); *b* 6 Feb 1922; *Educ* Summerfields, Eton; *m* 1, Nov 1942 (m dis 1956), Barbara Douglas; 1 s (Rupert b 1947), 1 da (Jennifer b 1950); m 2, April 1965 (m dis 1968), Kate Woodville; m 3, Feb 1988, Baba Sekerley, *née* Majos de Nagyzsenye; *Career* actor; served WWII 1942–46: Sub Lt HMS Alfred (Offrs' Trg Sch nr Brighton) 1942, Royal Naval Coll Greenwich 1943, 1 MTB Flotilla 1943, 1 Lt 1944, demobbed 1946; Long Service Medal, Atlantic Medal; memb: Palm Springs Youth Centre, Palm Springs Opera Guild; Freedom of Filey Yorks 1962, Freedom of City of Macon Georgia 1985; *Theatre* over 150 stage appearances incl: Sleuth (Broadway) 1972–73, Killing Jessica (West End) 1986–87; *Television* incl: The Avengers 1960–69, Alfred Hitchcock presents, Dial M For Murder, Thriller, Columbo, For The Term of his Natural Life, Murphy's Law, Dick Francis Stories, Ray Bradbury Theatre 1991, The Golden Years of Sherlock Holmes 1990, Superforce 1991, PS I Luv U 1991, The Hound of London 1991, Dream On and Murder She Wrote 1992, Coach 1993, Kung Fu 1993, Thunder in Paradise 1993, Mysteries, Magic and Miracles (series) 1994–95; *Film* incl: The Life and Death of Colonel Blimp 1942, Hamlet 1948, The Elusive Pimpernel 1950, Scrooge 1951, Battle of the River Plate 1956, Les Girls 1957, Incense for the Damned (US: Bloodsuckers) 1970, Mr Jericho 1970, Matt Helm 1975, King Solomon's Treasures 1976, Sherlock Holmes in New York 1976, Battlestar Galactia 1979, The Sea Wolves 1980, The Howling 1981, This is Spinal Tap 1983, A View to a Kill 1984, Shadey 1984, Waxworks 1988, The Chill Factor 1988, The Lobster Man From Mars 1988, The Masque of the Red Death 1989, Eye of the Widow 1989, Scared Silly 1990, Waxwork II 1991; *Recordings* incl: reading Jack Higgins stories on audio cassette 1994; Kinky Boots recorded with Honor Blackman 1964 (reached no 5 in the Top 40 singles Dec 1990); *Awards* incl: Variety Club of GB Jt TV Personality of the Year Award (with Honor Blackman) 1963, Straw Hat Award (NY) 1975, Golden Camera Award (Berlin), Air Safety Award From the Admin of the Federal Airway Administration (Washington DC); *Books* Blind In One Ear (autobiography, 1988); *Recreations* tennis, reading, conversing with friends, swimming, walking; *Style*— Patrick Macnee, Esq; ✉ c/o Michael Whitehall Ltd, 125 Gloucester Road, London SW7 4TE (☎ 0171 244 8466, fax 0171 244 9060)

McNEECE, John; s of Francis McNeece (d 1967), and Mary Frances, *née* Ferguson (d 1990); *b* 27 Oct 1939; *Educ* Glasgow Sch of Art (DA); *m* 1, 1964 (m dis), Margaret Josephine Fleming; 2 s (Adrian b 1965, Mark b 1968); m 2, 6 May 1980, Norma Margaret Lewis Zunterstein; *Career* interior design conslt; Keppie Henderson & Ptnrs 1963–64, J L Gleave & Ptnrs 1964–65; currently chm & chief exec McNeece (ptnr and dir 1963–); cruise ship projects: Sovereign of the Seas (Royal Caribbean Cruises) 1988, Crown Odyssey (Royal Cruise Line) 1988, Horizon (Celebrity Cruises) 1991, Cunard Princess and Cunard Countess (Cunard Line) 1991, Zenith (Celebrity Cruises) 1992, refit Queen Elizabeth 2 (Cunard Line) 1994, Oriana (P&O Cruises) 1995, Century (Celebrity Cruises) 1995; current projects: Galaxy & Mercury (Celebrity Cruises), Black Watch (Fred Olsen Line), New Build (Renaissance Cruises); nat design award Br Inst of Interior Designers 1988; Freeman City of London 1989, Liveryman Worshipful Co of Gardeners 1989, Freeman Worhshipful Co of Shipwrights 1996; FCSD 1970 (memb Cncl 1993, hon sec 1994–96), FBID 1970; *Recreations* golf, shooting, swimming, music, walking, writing; *Clubs* Carlton, Caledonian; *Style*— John McNeece, Esq; ✉ McNeece, 3 Angel Square, Islington High Street, London EC1V 1NY (☎ 0171 837 1225, fax 0171 837 1233)

McNEIL, Lady; Barbara Jessie; da of Percy Stuart Turner (d 1944), and Laura Beatrice Cowley (d 1967); *b* 7 Jan 1915; *Educ* Wimbledon Sch; *m* 1939, Sir Hector McNeil, CBE (d 1978); 1 s, 1 da; *Career* fndr pres Motor Neurone Disease Assoc; *Recreations* gardening, tapestry, foreign languages; *Style*— Lady McNeil; ✉ Bramber, St George's Hill, Weybridge, Surrey (☎ 01932 848484)

McNEIL, (Thomas) David; s of late Thomas McNeil, and late Beryl, *née* Rowe; *b* 30 Jan 1944; *Educ* Southland Boys' HS New Zealand; *m* 17 March 1973, Elizabeth, *née* Gossling; 1 s (James b 2 Aug 1976), 2 da (Helen b 22 May 1980, Melissa b 19 May 1986); *Career* announcer, then TV scriptwriter and journalist New Zealand Broadcasting Corp 1961–65, editorial asst Int Planned Parenthood Fedn London 1967–68, radio newswriter, then sub-ed and newsreader Swiss Broadcasting Corp 1968–69, BBC World Service Newsroom London 1969–72; radio correspondent BBC: Middle East (Beirut) 1972–75, New York 1975–78, S Africa (Johannesburg) 1978–80, London 1980–82, Israel (Jerusalem) 1982–85, Washington 1985–93; freelance radio presenter and univ lectr; *Style*— David McNeil, Esq; ✉ The Old Coach House, Fornham St Martin, Bury St Edmunds, Suffolk IP31 1SR (☎ 01824 704362)

MacNEIL, Ian Breckenridge; s of Robert B W MacNeil, of New York, and Rosemarie, *née* Copland; *b* 5 Feb 1960; *Educ* Croydon Sch of Art (Dip), Trinity Coll Connecticut (BA); *Career* stage designer; repertory work incl: prodn for Derby Playhouse, Contact Theatre Manchester, Cheltenham Everyman, Duke's Lancaster, Dublin Grand Opera; Gate Theatre London: Jerker 1990, Pioneers in Ingolstadt 1991, Crackwalker; Royal Court: Talking in Tongues, Death and the Maiden; RNT: An Inspector Calls 1992 (Olivier Award Best Designer 1993, Critics' Circle Award 1993, Drama Desk Award New York 1994), Machinal (Critics' Circle Award 1994) 1993; most recently Ariodante

(ENO) 1995, Enter Achilles (DV8 Physical Theatre) 1995, Tristan and Isolde (ENO) 1996; *Style*— Ian MacNeil, Esq; ✉ c/o 6 Windmill Street, London (☎ 0171 255 1362, 0171 631 4631)

McNEIL, Ian Robert; JP (1968); s of Robert McNeil (d 1969), and Doris Mary, *née* Henderson (d 1987); *b* 14 Dec 1932; *Educ* Brighton Coll; *m* 6 July 1963, Ann, da of Rev Evan Harries Rees; 2 da (Mary Ann b 21 June 1964, Janet Elizabeth (Libby) b 20 Aug 1966); *Career* Cooper Brothers CAs 1956–58, ptnr Nevill Hovey Gardner CAs (became Rowland Nevill, now Moores Rowland) 1958–; pres S Eastern Soc of CAs 1979–80; ICAEW: vice pres 1989–90, dep pres 1990–91, pres 1991–92, memb Cncl until 1996; dep chm Financial Reporting Cncl 1991–92 (memb Takeover Panel 1991–92); memb Lord Chllr's Advsy Ctee on Legal Educn and Conduct 1994–; Freeman City of London; Liveryman: Worshipful Co of Curriers (Master 1994), Worshipful Co of CAs; FCA 1965 (ACA 1955); *Recreations* gardening, walking, travel; *Clubs* Athenaeum; *Style*— Ian McNeil, Esq, JP; ✉ Lancasters, West End Lane, Henfield, W Sussex BN5 9RB (☎ 01273 492606); Moores Rowland, Nile House, PO Box 1034, Nile St, Brighton, E Sussex BN1 1JB (☎ 01273 324411, fax 01273 779172)

MACNEIL OF BARRA, The; Prof Ian Roderick Macneil of Barra; Chief of Clan Macneil; s of Robert Lister Macneil of Barra, of Kisimul Castle, Isle of Barra (d 1970), and Kathleen Gertrude Metcalf Macneil (d 1933); *b* 20 June 1929; *Educ* Scarborough Sch, Univ of Vermont (BA), Harvard Univ (LLB); *m* 1952, Nancy Carol, da of James Tilton Wilson, of Ottawa, Canada; 2 s, 1 da (and 1 s decd); *Heir* s, Roderick Macneil, yr of Barra b 1954; *Career* Lt US Army 1951–53, Army Res 1950–69; prof Cornell Law Sch Ithaca NY 1959–72 and 1974–76, visiting prof Faculty of Law Univ Coll Dar-es-Salaam Tanzania 1965–67, visiting prof of law Duke Univ 1970–71, prof of law and memb Centre For Advanced Studies Univ of Virginia 1972–74, Ingersoll prof of law Cornell 1976–80, Wigmore prof of law Northwestern Univ 1980–; visiting fell: Univ of Edinburgh 1978, 1979 and 1987, Univ of Oxford 1979; Braucher visiting prof of law Harvard Univ 1988–89; author, arbitrator, legal conslt; *Recreations* tennis; *Style*— The Macneil of Barra; ✉ Kisimul Castle, Isle of Barra (☎ 0187 14300); Flat 6, 95 Grange Loan, Edinburgh EH9 2ED (☎ 0131 667 6068)

McNEILL, Cameron Alastair; s of Albert William McNeill, of Newbury, Berks, and Elizabeth, *née* Kelly; *b* 25 March 1958; *Educ* Christ's Hosp, Pembroke Coll Oxford (BA); *Career* dir: Barclays De Zoete Wedd Ltd 1986–89, Barclays De Zoete Wedd Capital Markets Ltd 1986–89, Ebbgate Holdings Ltd 1986–89; md Oxford Technical Systems Ltd 1986– (dir 1983), exec dir Fuji International Finance plc 1991–; memb Ad Hoc Swaps Ctee Bank of England 1988–89; *Clubs* United Oxford and Cambridge Univ; *Style*— Cameron McNeill, Esq; ✉ c/o Messrs Druces and Attlee, Salisbury House, London Wall, London EC2M 5PS (☎ 0171 638 9271)

McNEILL, James Walker; QC (Scot 1991); s of James McNeill, and Edith Anna Howie, *née* Wardlaw; *b* 16 Feb 1952; *Educ* Dunoon GS, Univ of Cambridge (MA), Univ of Edinburgh (LLB); *m* 1986, Katherine Lawrence, da of William Crocket McDowall; 2 s (Thomas Howie b 1987, Andrew Hodge b 1988), 1 da (Christina Jane Crocket b 1992); *Career* advocate 1978; standing jr counsel to: Dept of Tport in Scot 1984–88, Inland Revenue in Scot 1988–91; memb Cncl Scottish Universities Law Institute Ltd 1993–; *Recreations* music, hillwalking, golf, sailing, travel; *Clubs* New (Edinburgh), Isle of Colonsay Golf; *Style*— James McNeill, Esq, QC; ✉ 28 Kingsburgh Road, Edinburgh EH12 6DZ

McNEILL, Prof John; s of Thomas McNeill (d 1972), of Edinburgh, and Helen Lawrie, *née* Eagle (d 1984); *b* 15 Sept 1933; *Educ* George Heriot's Edinburgh, Univ of Edinburgh (BSc, PhD); *m* 1, 29 July 1961 (m dis 1990), Bridget Mariel, da of Paul Winterton; 2 s (Andrew Thomas b 1964, Douglas Paul b 1966); m 2, 6 April 1990, Dr Marilyn Lois James; *Career* asst lectr then lectr Dept of Agric Botany Univ of Reading 1957–61, lectr Dept of Botany Univ of Liverpool 1961–69, sr res scientist Biosystematics Res Inst Canada Ottawa 1977–81 (res sci when formerly known as Plant Res Inst 1969–77), prof and chm Dept of Biology Univ of Ottawa Canada 1981–87, Regius Keeper Royal Botanic Garden Edinburgh 1987–89, dir and pres Royal Ontario Museum Toronto Canada 1991–97 (assoc dir curatorial 1989–90, actg dir 1990–91); concurrently: dir George R Gardiner Museum of Ceramic Art Toronto, pres Royal Ontario Museum Fndn; prof Dept of Botany Univ of Toronto, adjunct prof Dept of Biol Univ of Ottawa 1991; pres: Biological Cncl of Canada 1986–87 (vice-pres 1984–86), Canadian Cncl of Univ Biology Chairmen 1984–85 (vice-pres 1983–84); treas Int Organization for Systematic and Evolutionry Biology 1996–; exec memb Int Union of Biological Sci 1985–88 and 1991–94, admin of fin Int Assoc of Plant Taxonomy 1987–93 (cncllr 1981–87 and 1993–); author of numerous scientific papers and reports; memb 15 scientific socs; *Books* Phenetic and Phylogenetic Classification (ed with V H Heywood, 1964), Grasses of Ontario (with W G Dore, 1980), The Genus Atriplex in Canada (with I J Bassett et al, 1983), International Code of Botanical Nomenclature (adopted 1981, jt ed, 1983), International Code of Botanical Nomenclature (adopted 1987, jt ed, 1988, translations in French, German and Japanese), Preliminary Inventory of Canadian Weeds (with C W Crompton, A E Stahevitch and W A Wojtas, 1988), Flora of North America (Vols I and II, jt ed, 1993, Vol III, jt ed, 1997), International Code of Botanical Nomenclature (adopted 1993, jt ed, 1994, French, German and Slovakian trans 1995), International Code of Nomenclature for Cultivated Plants (jt ed, 1995); *Style*— Prof John McNeill; ✉ Royal Ontario Museum, 100 Queen's Park, Toronto, Ontario M5S 2C6, Canada (☎ 00 1 416 586 5639, fax 00 1 416 586 8044, e-mail johnm@rom.on.ca)

McNEILL, Dr Peter Grant Brass; QC (Scot 1988); s of William Arnott McNeill (d 1973), and Lillias Philips, *née* Scrimgeour (d 1980); *b* 3 March 1929; *Educ* Hillhead HS Glasgow, Morrison's Acad Crieff, Univ of Glasgow (MA (Hons Hist), LLB, PhD); *m* 1959, Matilda Farquhar; 1 s (Angus), 3 da (Christian, Morag, Katrina); *Career* called to the Scottish Bar 1956; Hon Sheriff Substitute of Lanarkshire and of Stirling, Clackmannan and Dumbarton 1962, standing jr counsel to Scottish Devpt Dept (Highways) 1964, advocate depute 1964; sheriff of: Lanarkshire (later Glasgow and Strathkelvin) at Glasgow 1965, Lothian and Borders at Edinburgh 1982–96, ret; temp sheriff 1996; chm: Review Bd Chinook Helicopter Accident 1988, Scottish Legal History Gp 1990–, Cncl Stair Soc 1990–; memb Cncl Scottish Records Advsy Cncl 1989–95; *Books* Balfour's Practicks (ed, 1962–63), An Historical Atlas of Scotland c400–c1600 (jt ed, 1975), Adoption of Children in Scotland (2 edn, 1986); legal and historical articles in: Juridicial Review, Scots Law Times, Glasgow Herald, Encyclopaedia Britannica; *Recreations* legal history, gardening, bookbinding; *Style*— Dr Peter G B McNeill, QC; ✉ 31 Queensferry Road, Edinburgh EH4 3HB

McNEISH, Prof Alexander Stewart; s of Dr Angus Stewart McNeish (d 1964), and Minnie Howieson, *née* Dickson (d 1992); *b* 13 April 1938; *Educ* Glasgow Acad, Univ of Glasgow (MB ChB), Univ of Birmingham (MSc); *m* 4 March 1963, Joan Ralston, da of William Hamilton (d 1970); 2 s (Alistair Stewart b 1964, Iain Alexander b 1968), 1 da (Fiona Hamilton b 1966); *Career* fndn prof of child health Univ of Leicester 1976–80; Univ of Birmingham: Leonard Parsons prof of paediatrics and child health and dir Inst of Child Health 1980–95, dean Faculty of Medicine and Dentistry 1987–92; dir MRC Clinical Scis Centre Royal Postgrad Med Sch London 1995–96, warden St Bartholomew's and Royal London Med and Dental Sch and vice-principal Queen Mary and Westfield Coll London 1997–; dir of R&D W Midlands Regnl Health Authy 1992–95; memb: GMC 1985–95, Central Birmingham Health Authy 1987–91; non-exec dir S Birmingham Health Authy 1991–92; pres Euro Soc for Paediatric Gastroenterology and Nutrition 1984–87; FRCP 1977, FRCP (Glasgow) 1985; *Recreations* golf, music, gardening; *Clubs* Athenaeum, Blackwell Golf, Southerness Golf; *Style*— Prof Alexander McNeish; ✉ 128 Westfield Road, Birmingham B15 3JQ; Drumbuie, Kirkbean, Dumfries and Galloway; The London Hospital Medical College, Turner Street, London E1 2AD

MacNICOL, Dr David Dewar; s of Malcolm MacNicol (d 1970), and Kathleen Jean, *née* Dewar; *b* 25 Dec 1939; *Educ* Hutchesons' Boys' GS, Univ of Glasgow (BSc, PhD, DSc); *Career* post doctoral DSIR research fell Univ of Oxford 1965–66; Univ of Glasgow: lectr in chemistry 1966–76, sr lectr 1976–82, reader 1982–; exec ed Comprehensive Supramolecular Chemistry (Vols 1–11) 1996; FRSE 1996; *Recreations* numismatics, photography, angling; *Style*— Dr David MacNicol, FRSE; ✉ Department of Chemistry, University of Glasgow, Glasgow G12 8QQ (☎ 0141 330 5289, fax 0141 330 4888)

McNICOL, Duncan; s of Alfred McNicol (d 1989), of Isle of Skye, and Joan, *née* Fox; *b* 18 March 1952; *Educ* Cranford Sch, London Coll of Printing (HND in creative photography); *m* 21 June 1975, Margaret, da of Albert Frederick Bradberry; 2 s (Ross b 13 Nov 1979, Ewan b 27 June 1981); *Career* photographic asst 1973–76, own studio (advtg and design photography) 1976–; pt/t photographic teacher London Coll of Printing 1976–79; main advtg clients incl: Citroen, Rover, Barclays Bank, Nat Westminster, Kit Kat, Armitage Shanks, De Beers, Br Telecom, Royal Mail, Royal Insurance, Spanish Tourist Bd, Scottish Tourist Bd, Du Pont, Compuserve, Polaroid, BICC, Tarmac; memb Assoc of Photographers 1977, memb RPS; *Awards* Assoc of Photographers Awards 1987, 1989, 1995 and 1996, Assoc of Photographers Gold Award 1994, Communication Arts Award (USA) 1994, John Kobal Awards 1996; finalist: Epica Awards 1993, Cannes Ad Awards 1993; *Recreations* photography, walking, theatre, cycling, art galleries; *Style*— Duncan McNicol, Esq; ✉ Costers Mill, West Lavington, Midhurst, West Sussex GU29 0EN (☎ 01730 812219, fax 01730 812252)

MacNICOL, Ian Duncan Robertson; s of Maj Duncan Cowan MacNicol (d 1969), and Ethel Margaret, *née* Blanch (d 1976); *b* 25 Aug 1943; *Educ* Fettes, Royal Agric Coll Cirencester; *m* 11 May 1974, Adel Jean, da of Richmond Noel Richmond-Watson, of Potterspury, Northants; 2 s (Charles b 1 Sept 1980, George b 9 Feb 1983), 2 da (Arabella b 24 Aug 1976, Catherine b 6 June 1978); *Career* currently dir: G C & F C Knight Ltd, Premier Livestock Auctions, Barnham Broom plc; former tstee Game Conservancy, former chm Norfolk Branch CLA; currently: dep pres CLA (memb Cncl), memb Cncl Royal Agric Soc; chm Bd of Govrs: Astley Primary Sch, Beeston Hall Sch, Tudor Hall Sch; chm Stody Parish Cncl; High Sheriff of Norfolk 1996–97; FRICS; *Recreations* country pursuits; *Clubs* White's, Farmers'; *Style*— Ian MacNicol, Esq; ✉ Stody Lodge, Melton Constable, Norfolk NR24 2EW (☎ 01263 860254); Stody Estate Office, Melton Constable, Norfolk (☎ 01263 860572)

MACNICOL, Malcolm Fraser; s of Rev Robert (Roy) Simpson Macnicol (d 1986), of Edinburgh, and Eona Kathleen; *b* 18 March 1943; *m* 30 Sept 1972, Anne Morag; 2 s (Sean Malcolm Fraser b 1979, Calum Alexander Ruaridh b 1983), 1 da (Sarah Anne Marie b 1977); *Career* conslt orthopaedic surgn, regnl advsr in orthopaedic surgery S E Scot, sr lectr; treas: RCSEd, Special Advsy Ctee in Orthopaedic Surgery; memb: Shaw Report team, Br Orthopaedic Assoc, Br Assoc for Surgery of the Knee, Br Soc for Children's Orthopaedic Surgery; *Books* Basic Care of The Injured Hand (1984), Aids To Orthopaedics (1984), The Problem Knee (1986, 2 edn 1995), Children's Orthopaedics and Fractures (1994), Colour Atlas and Text of Osteotomy of the Hip (1995); *Recreations* tennis, squash, painting; *Clubs* Scottish Arts; *Style*— Malcolm Macnicol, Esq; ✉ The Red House, 1 South Gillsland Road, Edinburgh EH10 5ED (☎ 0131 447 9104); Princess Margaret Rose Orthopaedic Hosp, Frogston Road West, Edinburgh (☎ 0131 536 4600); Royal Hospital for Sick Children, Sciennes Road, Edinburgh EH9 (☎ 0131 536 0000)

McNISH, Althea Marjorie; da of Joseph Claude McNish (d 1964), of Port of Spain, and Margaret Bourne (d 1977); *Educ* Port of Spain (by father and others), London Coll of Printing (NDD (Special), Illustration prize), Central Sch of Art and Crafts, Royal Coll of Art (DesRCA); *m* 20 Aug 1969, John Saul Weiss, s of Woolf Weiss (d 1994), of London; *Career* freelance designer 1957–; exhibitions incl: Inprint 1964–71, Design Cncl USA and Sweden 1969, London 1970 and 1975–80, USA 1972, Design-In (Amsterdam) 1972–74, The Way We Live Now (V & A London) 1978, Indigo Lille 1981–82, Cwlth Festival Art Exhibition (Brisbane) 1982, Designs for British Dress and Furnishing Fabrics (V & A London) 1986, Make or Break (Henry Moore Gallery London) 1986, Surtex NY 1987, Ascher (V & A London) 1987; commissioned by Ascher and Liberty's 1957, designs for mfrs worldwide; visiting lectr: Central Sch of Art and Crafts and other colls and polys 1960–, USA 1972, Italy, W Germany and Slovenia 1985–; advsy tutor furnishing and surface design London Coll of Furniture 1972–90, external assessor for educnl and professional bodies incl CSD and CNAA 1966–, memb jury for Leverhulme scholarships 1968; judge: Portuguese textile design competition Lisbon 1973, Living Design Awards 1974, Carnival Selection Panels Arts Cncl of GB 1982–83; designer: special features Daily Mail Ideal Home Exhibition 1966–78, for sec gen of the Cwlth 1975, bedlinen collection Courtaulds 1978, for BR Bd 1978–81, for London Office of High Cmmr of Trinidad and Tobago 1981, for Fede Cheti Milan 1987–91, murals and hangings for passenger liners Nordic Empress 1990 and Monarch of The Seas 1991; advsr on exhibition design for Govt of Trinidad and Tobago Cwlth Inst 1982–84; memb: Bd Design Cncl 1974–81, Selection Panels for Design Awards and Design Index 1968–80, Selection Panel Jubilee Souvenir 1976 and Royal Wedding Souvenir 1981, CNAA Fashion and Textiles Design Bd 1975–78, Governing Body Portsmouth Coll of Art 1972–81, London Local Advsy Ctee IBA 1981–90, Formation Ctee ILEA London Inst 1985; CSD: assessor and examiner 1966–, vice pres 1977–78, memb Cncl and Ctees 1958–90; FCSD, FSIA 1968 (MSIA 1960); Chaconia Gold Medal of the Repub of Trinidad and Tobago 1976, Scarlet Ibis Award of the Office of the High Cmmr for the Repub of Trinidad and Tobago London 1993; *Publications* textile designs produced in many countries and published in many jls and books incl: Decorative Art, Studio Books (1960, 1961 and 1962), Designers in Britain (1972), Did Britain Make It, Design Council (1986), Fabrics and Wallpapers (Bell and Hyman, 1986), Ascher (1987), Fabrics and Wallpapers: Design sources and Inspirations (Ebury Press, 1991), The House of Liberty (Thames and Hudson, 1992), The Caribbean Artists Movement 1966–72 (New Beacon Books, 1992); *Recreations* skiing, travelling, music, gardening; *Clubs* Soroptimist; *Style*— Ms Althea McNish

MACNIVEN, Hugh Campbell; s of Hugh Macniven, MBE (d 1960), of Glasgow, and Georgina May, *née* Fraser (d 1992); *b* 24 April 1942; *Educ* Glasgow Acad, Univ of Glasgow (MA); *m* 2 May 1966, Jacqueline, da of Georges Stanislaus Suder; 2 da (Isabelle b 1970, Catriona b 1974); *Career* dir Butler Dennis & Garland Ltd 1976, md The Publicity Department 1981; FInstD; *Recreations* opera, book collecting; *Style*— Hugh Macniven, Esq; ✉ The Publicity Department, 2 Fairfield Villas, Henrietta Rd, Bath BA2 6LT (☎ 01225 466062, fax 01225 448708)

MacNULTY, Christine Avril; da of William Arthur Ralph (d 1975), of The Brook House, Egerton, Lancs, and Marjorie Holland, *née* Hale; *b* 22 April 1945; *Educ* Bolton Sch, Univ of London, George Washington Univ Washington DC; *m* 26 Aug 1972, (William) Kirk MacNulty Jr, s of Brig-Gen William K MacNulty; *Career* systems analyst Plessey Radar Ltd 1967–69, sr memb staff International Research & Technology Corporation 1969–72, ptnr Many Futures 1972–76, conslt Progs Analysis Unit 1976–78, program mangr Europe Strategic Environment Centre SRI International 1978–82, conslt Int Res Inst on Social Change 1982–84, md Taylor Nelson Applied Futures 1984–88, chief exec Applied Futures Ltd 1988–, pres Applied Futures Inc 1993–; lectr: Univ of Bradford, Admin Staff Coll, Ashridge Management Coll, Brunel Univ, The Industl Soc,

Nat Defense Univ, Naval War Coll, Air War Coll, Industl Coll of the Armed Forces; memb Inst for Transitional Dynamics; FRSA 1989; *Books* Industrial Applications of Technological Forecasting (jtly, 1971), The Future of the UK 2010 (jtly); author of numerous articles on scenario devpt, social change and forecasting; *Recreations* sailing, cooking, philosophy, psychology, comparative mythology; *Style*— Mrs Christine MacNulty; ✉ 1600 S Eads Street, Apt 10345, Arlington, VA 22202, USA; Applied Futures Inc, 2101 Crystal Plaza Arcade, No 233, Arlington, VA 22202, USA (☎ 00 703 521 5416, fax 00 202 895 2915, e-mail Futures@delphi.com)

McNULTY, Dermot Anthony; s of William J McNulty (d 1970), of River Forest, Illinois, USA, and Margaret, *née* Reigh; *b* 11 March 1949; *Educ* Marquette Univ USA (BA); *m* 11 June 1977, Paula, *née* Gaber; *Career* PR account dir Burson Marsteller London 1977–81, sr vice pres and md Burson Marsteller Hong Kong 1981–87, exec vice pres Burson Marsteller NY 1987–89; exec vice pres Shandwick North America NY 1989–90; Shandwick plc: dir of int mktg 1990–91, chief operating offr 1991–94, chief exec 1994–; *Recreations* golf, tennis, travel, reading; *Style*— Dermot McNulty, Esq; ✉ Shandwick plc, 61 Grosvenor Street, London W1X 9DA (☎ 0171 408 2232, fax 0171 493 8163)

McNULTY, Mark; *b* 25 Oct 1953, Zimbabwe; *children* 1 s (Matthew b 1985), 1 da (Catherine b 1988); *Career* professional golfer 1977–; Euro tour tournament victories incl: Gtr Manchester Open 1979, German Open 1980, 1987, 1990 and 1991, Portuguese Open 1986, Four Stars Nat Pro-Celebrity 1987, Dunhill Br Masters 1987, Cannes Open 1988 and 1990, Benson & Hedges Mixed Team Championship 1988, Monte Carlo Open 1989, BMW Int Open 1994, Sun Dutch Open, Dimension Data Pro-Am; winner of 27 other tournaments; *Recreations* piano, fine arts, Koi fish; *Style*— Mark McNulty, Esq; ✉ c/o IMG, Pier House, Strand on the Green, Chiswick, London W4 3NN (☎ 0181 233 5000, fax 0181 233 5001)

McPARTLIN, Sheriff Noel; s of Michael Joseph McPartlin, of Galashiels (d 1955), and Ann, *née* Dunn (d 1978); *b* 25 Dec 1939; *Educ* Galashiels Acad, Univ of Edinburgh (MA, LLB); *m* 10 July 1965, June Anderson, da of David Anderson Whitehead, of Stirling (d 1961); 3 s (Simon b 1970, Guy b 1972, Donald b 1982), 3 da (Alison b 1966, Diana b 1967, Julia b 1979); *Career* slr 1964–76, advocate 1976; Sheriff: Grampian Highland and Islands at Peterhead and Banff 1983–85, Elgin 1985–; *Recreations* country life; *Clubs* Elgin; *Style*— Sheriff Noel McPartlin; ✉ Sheriff Court, Elgin

MacPHAIL, Sir Bruce Dugald; kt (1992); s of Dugald Ronald MacPhail; *b* 1 May 1939; *Educ* Haileybury, Balliol Coll Oxford, Harvard Business Sch; *m* 1, 1963, Susan Mary (d 1975), da of late Col T Gregory, MC, TD; 3 s; m 2, 1983, Caroline Ruth Grimston, o da of Capt Tatlock Hubbard, MC, RA, and former w of David Dangar Henry Honywood Curtis-Bennett; *Career* articled Price Waterhouse 1961–65, with Hill Samuel & Co 1967–69; fin dir Sterling Guarantee Trust 1969–74; md: Town & City Properties Ltd 1974–76, Sterling Guarantee Trust 1976–85, Peninsular and Oriental Steam Navigation Co 1985– (dir 1983–); also dir various P & O SNCo subsids; govr Royal Ballet Sch 1982–; Univ of Oxford: chm Cncl Templeton Coll 1992–95 (memb 1986–), tstee Balliol Coll 1991–, non-exec chm various BES Schemes Balliol Coll and Magdalen Coll 1993–, Barclay fell Templeton Coll 1995–; life govr and memb Cncl Haileybury 1992, tstee Sir Jules Thorn Charitable Trust 1994–; FCA; *Style*— Sir Bruce MacPhail; ✉ Peninsular & Oriental Steam Navigation Co, 79 Pall Mall, London SW1Y 5EJ (☎ 0171 930 4343, fax 0171 930 8572)

MACPHAIL, Sheriff Iain Duncan; QC (Scotland, 1989); s of Malcolm John Macphail (d 1988), of Edinburgh, and Mary Corbett Duncan (d 1973); *b* 24 Jan 1938; *Educ* George Watson's Coll, Univ of Edinburgh (MA), Univ of Glasgow (LLB); *m* 1970, Rosslyn Graham Lillias, da of Edward John Campbell Hewitt, TD, of Edinburgh; 1 s (David b 1973), 1 da (Melissa b 1977); *Career* admitted to Faculty of Advocates 1963, practising advocate Scotland 1963–73, Faulds fell in law Univ of Glasgow 1963–65; lectr in evidence and procedure: Univ of Strathclyde 1968–69, Univ of Edinburgh 1969–72; extra advocate-depute 1973; Sheriff of: Glasgow and Strathkelvin (formerly Lanarkshire) 1973–81, Tayside, Central and Fife at Dunfermline and Alloa 1981–82, Lothian and Borders at Linlithgow 1982–88, Edinburgh 1988–89 and 1995–; chm Scottish Assoc for the Study of Delinquency 1978–81, memb Scottish Law Cmmn 1990–94; Hon LLD Univ of Edinburgh 1992; *Books* The Law of Evidence of Scotland (1979), Evidence (1987), Sheriff Court Practice (1988); *Clubs* New (Edinburgh); *Style*— Sheriff I D Macphail, QC; ✉ Sheriff Court House, 27 Chambers Street, Edinburgh EH1 1LB (☎ 0131 225 2525, fax 0131 225 2288)

MacPHAIL, Ian Angus Shaw; s of Robert Shaw MacPhail (d 1938), and Edith Hadden (d 1968); *b* 11 March 1922; *Educ* Grays Sch of Art Aberdeen (Dip Graphic Design); *m* 1, 1943 (m dis 1948), Armorel Davie; 1 da (Diana); m 2, 12 March 1951, Michal Hambourg, da of Mark Hambourg; 1 s (Robert); *Career* RAF 1940–43; asst music controller ENSA 1944–46, asst music dir Arts Cncl 1946–52, publicity dir Dexion Ltd 1952–58, dir Greenway Advsy Serv 1958–60, PR conslt Brewers Soc 1960–61, DG World Wildlife Fund (UK) 1961–67, chief info offr Arthur Guinness Son & Co Ltd (conslt in communications) 1968–79; Euro co-ordinator Int Fund for Animal Welfare 1976–92, tstee Tiger Tst 1992, chm Young Peoples Tst for Nature Conservation 1990–96, govr Brathay Hall Tst; hon PR advsr: Fauna Preservation Soc, Nat Assoc for Gifted Children; former chm PR Ctee Royal Soc for the Prevention of Accidents; ed: You and the Theatre, You and the Opera, English Music 1200–1750, Dexion Angle, Good Company, World Wildlife News; lectr to: publicity and Rotary clubs, schs, tech colls, univs, HM prisons and borstals, women's socs; graphic designer (responsible for prodn supervision of publicity): eight coronation concerts at the Royal Festival Hall, third congress Int Assoc of Gerontology, jt metallurgical socs meeting in Europe, house style and literature World Wildlife Fund, first World Conf on Gifted Children; Orden den Sol Cdr (Order of the Sun Peru) 1985, Kt rder of the Gold Ark (Netherlands); MSIA, FIPR 1970; *Books* You and the Orchestra (1948), Birdlife of Britain and Europe (1977); *Recreations* ornithology, music, poetry; *Clubs* Savile, Wig and Pen; *Style*— Ian MacPhail, Esq; ✉ 35 Boundary Rd, St John's Wood, London NW8 0JE (☎ 0171 624 3535, fax 0171 624 9358)

McPHEE, George McBeth; s of late George Hugh McPhee, and of late Daisy, *née* Clyne; *b* 10 Nov 1937; *Educ* Woodside Sch, Royal Scot Acad of Music, Univ of Edinburgh (BMus); *m* 22 July 1961, Margaret Ann, da of Robert Scotland (d 1951); 1 s (Colin b 1964), 2 da (Catriona b 1966, Susan b 1969); *Career* asst organist St Giles' Cathedral Edinburgh 1959–63, dir of music Paisley Abbey 1963–, lectr in music Royal Scot Acad of Music and Drama 1963–, visiting prof of organ St Andrews Univ; numerous performances, recordings, broadcasts and appearances; special commissioner Royal Sch of Church Music, adjudicator/examiner Assoc Bd Royal Schs of Music, chm Paisley Int Organ Festival; memb ISM 1965, hon fell Royal Sch of Church Music 1991; *Recreations* golf; *Clubs* Royal Troon Golf; *Style*— George McPhee, Esq, MBE; ✉ 17 Main Road, Castlehead, Paisley PA2 6AJ (☎ 0141 889 3528)

MACPHERSON, Sheriff Alexander Calderwood (Sandy); Sheriff (South Strathclyde Dumfries and Galloway at Hamilton, 1978); s of Alexander Macpherson (d 1982), and Jean McCulloch, *née* Calderwood; *b* 14 June 1939; *Educ* Glasgow Acad, Univ of Glasgow (MA, LLB); *m* 1963 (m dis 1985), Christine Isobel, *née* Hutchison; 2 s (Alan b 1965, Duncan b 1967); *Career* admitted slr 1962; in practice until 1978, pt/t asst Law Faculty Univ of Glasgow 1962–66, pt/t lectr Law Faculty Univ of Strathclyde 1966–78, a sheriff of S Strathclyde, Dumfries and Galloway at Hamilton 1978–; *Recreations* bagpipe playing, psychotherapy, the theatre; *Clubs* RSAC (Glasgow), Glasgow Art, Royal Scot Pipers' Soc; *Style*— Sheriff A C Macpherson; ✉ Hamilton Sheriff Court, Hamilton, Lanarks ML3 6AA (☎ 01698 282 957)

MACPHERSON, Angus John; s of Lt Archibald Norman Macpherson, RN, of Itchen Abbas, Hants, and Joan Margaret, *née* Backhouse; *b* 17 March 1953; *Educ* Stowe, Pembroke Coll Cambridge (MA); *m* 14 Aug 1982, Anne Louise Felicity, da of Capt Edward Morton Barford, of Godalming, Surrey; 1 s (William Archibald b 19 March 1988), 2 da (Eloise Isobel b 5 Jan 1985, Myrtle Maud b 30 Jan 1991); *Career* called to the Bar Inner Temple 1977, in practice SE circuit; *Recreations* tennis, Scottish history, cooking; *Clubs* Lansdowne; *Style*— Angus Macpherson, Esq; ✉ The Granary, Lane End, Nr Owslebury, Winchester, Hants SO21 1JU (☎ 01962 777624); 5 Bell Yard, London WC2A 2JR (☎ 0171 333 8811)

MACPHERSON, Donald Charles; s of Donald Hugh Macpherson (d 1947), of Calcutta, India, and Hilda Mary, *née* Pulley (d 1952); *b* 3 Jan 1932; *Educ* Winchester; *m* 3 May 1962, Hilary Claire, da of Lt-Col Norman Standish, MBE (d 1988), of Port Elizabeth, SA; *Career* Nat Serv 2 Lt Black Watch 1950–52; mangr Thomson & Balfour Ltd 1952–57, sr ptnr Fielding Newson Smith & Co 1985 (joined 1957, ptnr 1961), md County NatWest Ltd 1989– (exec dir 1986–89), chm NatWest Markets Corporate Finance Ltd 1994– (dir 1989–, dep chm 1993–94); *Recreations* collecting, ballet, opera; *Style*— Donald Macpherson, Esq; ✉ 28 Campden Hill Square, London W8 7JY (☎ 0171 727 8292); NatWest Markets Corporate Finance Ltd, 135 Bishopsgate, London EC2M 3UR (☎ 0171 375 5000, fax 0171 628 7098)

MACPHERSON, Ewen Cameron Stewart; s of G P S Macpherson (d 1981), and Elizabeth Margaret Cameron, *née* Smail; *b* 19 Jan 1942; *Educ* Fettes Coll Edinburgh, Queens' Coll Cambridge (MA), London Business Sch (MSc); *m* 1982, Laura Anne, da of 5 Baron Northbrook (d 1991); 2 s (James b 25 Oct 1983, George b 27 Nov 1985); *Career* rep Massey-Ferguson (Export) Ltd 1964–68, various appointments ICFC (now 3i Group plc) from 1970; 3i Group plc: memb Exec Ctee 1985–, fin dir 1990–92, chief exec 1992–; dir: Scottish Power plc 1996–, M&G Group PLC 1996–; govr NIESR 1993–; *Recreations* gardening, sailing, vintage motor cars; *Clubs* City of London, Caledonian, Royal Lymington Yacht; *Style*— Ewen Macpherson, Esq; ✉ 3i Group plc, 91 Waterloo Rd, London SE1 8XP (☎ 0171 928 3131, fax 0171 928 0058)

MACPHERSON, Fiona; *Educ* Univ of St Andrews; *m* Adrian Bailey; 1 s, 1 da; *Career* formerly with: DC Thomson Dundee, IPC Magazines, Queen Magazine; also formerly in contract publishing; currently ed Harpers & Queen; *Style*— Ms Fiona Macpherson; ✉ Harpers & Queen, National Magazine House, 72 Broadwick Street, London W1V 2BP (☎ 0171 439 5340, fax 0171 439 5506)

MACPHERSON, (John Hannah) Forbes; CBE (1983); s of John Hannah Macpherson (d 1942), of Glasgow, and Anne Hicks, *née* Watson (d 1976); *b* 23 May 1926; *Educ* Glasgow Acad, Merchiston Castle Sch; *m* 1959, Margaret Graham, da of Robert Roxburgh (d 1957), of Glasgow; 1 s (John b 1972); *Career* Sub Lt RNVR 1943–47; Wilson Stirling & Co (subsequently part of Touche Ross & Co): articled clerk 1947–49 (chartered accountant 1949), ptnr 1956–86; chm: TSB Bank Scotland 1984–94, Scottish Mutual Assurance Society 1985–96; dep chm Hill Samuel Bank Ltd 1991–94; non-exec dir: TSB Group plc 1985–94, Scottish Metropolitan Property plc 1986–96, PCT Group plc 1992–96; chm: Glasgow Jr C of C 1965, Scot Industl Estates Corp 1972, Irvine Devpt Corp 1976, Glasgow Opportunities Enterprise Tst 1983–89, Glasgow Action 1985, Glasgow Devpt Agency 1992–95; pres Glasgow C of C 1980; memb: Prince and Princess of Wales Hospice, Merchants House of Glasgow (Lord Dean of Guild); chm of Ct Univ of Glasgow, DUniv (hc) 1996; govr Merchiston Castle Sch 1988; OStJ 1980; *Recreations* travel, gardening, reading; *Clubs* East India, Western (Glasgow); *Style*— J H Forbes Macpherson, Esq, CBE; ✉ 16 Collylinn Rd, Bearsden, Glasgow G61 4PN (☎ 0141 942 0042)

MACPHERSON, Hon Ian David Patrick; s and h of 2 Baron Strathcarron, *qv*; *b* 31 March 1949; *Style*— The Hon Ian Macpherson; ✉ Flat 1, 26 Old Church Street, London SW3 5BY

MACPHERSON, Prof Ian Richard; s of George Macpherson (d 1974), of Aberdeen, and Violet Alice, *née* Warwick (d 1974); *b* 4 Jan 1934; *Educ* Aberdeen GS, Univ of Aberdeen (MA), Univ of Manchester (PhD); *m* 7 Aug 1959, Sheila Constance, da of Capt John Turner (d 1949), of Heaton Mersey; 2 s (David John b 21 Feb 1962, Peter Jeremy b 24 Jan 1964); *Career* temp lectr Univ of Manchester 1959–60; lectr Univ of Wales at Aberystwyth 1960–64; Univ of Durham: lectr 1964–72, sr lectr 1972–75, reader 1975–80, prof of Spanish 1980–93, emeritus prof 1993–; hon res fell QMW Coll London 1993–; visiting prof Univ of Wisconsin Madison 1970–71; pres: Assoc of Hispanists of GB and I 1986–88, Br-Spanish Mixed Cmmn 1986–90; corresponding memb The Hispanic Soc of America 1986–, Socio de honor Asociación Hirpánica de Literatura Medieval 1995–; Comendador de la Orden de Isabel la Catolica (Spain) 1986; *Books* Juan Manuel - Libro de los estados (with R B Tate, OUP 1974, Castalia 1991), Spanish Phonology: Descriptive and Historical (1975), Juan Manuel Studies (1975), The Manueline Succession: The Poetry of Don Juan Manuel II and Dom Joao Manuel (1979), Juan Manuel: A Selection (1980), Federico Garcia Lorca: Yerma (with Jacqueline Minett, 1987), The Age of the Catholic Monarchs 1474–1516: Literary Studies in Memory of Keith Whinnom (with Alan Deyermond, 1989); *Recreations* books, tennis, bridge, Europe; *Style*— Prof Ian Macpherson; ✉ Department of Hispanic Studies, Queen Mary and Westfield College, University of London, Mile End Rd, London E1 4NS (☎ 0171 975 5062, fax 0181 980 5400)

McPHERSON, James Alexander Strachan; CBE (1982), JP (Banff & Buchan); s of Peter John McPherson (d 1953), and Jeannie Geddie, *née* Strachan (d 1969); *Educ* Banff Acad, Univ of Aberdeen (MA, BL, LLB); *m* 4 Aug 1960, Helen Marjorie, da of Capt Jack Perks, CBE, DSC (d 1973), of Kibworth, Beauchamp, Leics; 1 s (Ewan John b 1961), 1 da (Lesley Anne b 1963); *Career* Nat Serv cmmnd Lt RA 1952–54; conslt Alexander George & Co slrs Macduff, memb Macduff Town Cncl and Banff CC 1958–75, convener Banff CC 1970–75, provost of Macduff 1972–75, chm Public Protection Ctee Grampian Regnl Cncl 1974–86 (memb Cncl 1974–90); Lord-Lt of Grampian Region (Banffshire) 1987–, Hon Sheriff Grampian Highland and Islands at Banff 1972–; govr Scottish Police Coll 1974–86, chm Banff and Buchan JP Advsy Ctee 1987–; memb: Grampian Health Bd 1974–82, Police Advsy Bd for S 1974–86, Post Office Users' Nat Cncl for Scot 1976–80, Scottish Slr's Discipline Tbnl 1990–95, Ct Univ of Aberdeen 1993–; FSA (Scot); *Recreations* reading, local history, swimming; *Clubs* Town and County (Banff), Duff House Royal Golf, The Royal Northern & University (Aberdeen); *Style*— James McPherson, Esq, CBE, FSA, JP; ✉ Dunalastair, Macduff, Banffshire AB44 1XD (☎ 01261 832377); 24 Shore Street, Macduff, Banffshire (☎ 01261 832201, fax 01261 832350)

McPHERSON, Dr James Paton (Pat); OBE (1987); s of David Robb McPherson (d 1974), of Dundee, and Georgina Watt, *née* Dunbar (d 1969); *b* 9 July 1916; *Educ* Dundee HS; *m* 7 March 1942, Muriel Stewart, da of Stewart Finlay Anderson (d 1948), of Dundee; *Career* RAF Air Sea Rescue 1941–46; pres Wright Health Group Ltd; chm: Walter D Watt and Co Ltd, Drug Development (Scot) Ltd; dir Abbey National Building Soc (Scottish bd) 1981–87, chm Dundee Indust Assoc; govr of fin and memb Ct Univ of Dundee 1982–90, vice chm Tenovus Tayside; former pres: Rotary Club of Dundee, Assoc of Dental Manufacturers & Traders of the UK 1960–61; former dir Dundee Crematorium Ltd, Paul Harris Fellowship Award 1992, memb Ctee The Malcolm Sargent Cancer Fund for Children (Dundee Ctee), life govr The Imperial Cancer Res Fund, memb Bobby Jones

Memorial Tst; JP, Cmmr of Taxes 1983–91; LLD Univ of Dundee 1986; MInstD; *Recreations* golf; *Clubs* Rosemount, Gleneagles Golf; *Style—* Dr Pat McPherson, OBE; ✉ Mylnefield House, Invergowrie, Dundee, Scotland DD2 5EH (☎ 01382 360360); Wright Health Group Ltd, Kingsway West, Dundee, Scotland DD2 3QD (☎ 01382 833866, fax 01382 811042)

MACPHERSON, Sir (Ronald) Thomas Stewart; kt (1992), CBE (1967), MC (1943, and 2 Bars 1944 and 1945), TD (1960), DL (Gtr London 1972); 5 s of Sir (Thomas) Stewart Macpherson, CIE (d 1949), of Newtonmore, Inverness-shire, and Helen (d 1976), er da of Rev Archibald Borland Cameron, of Edinburgh; bro of 1 Baron Drumalbyn, cous of 15 Earl of Kinnoull and 2 Baron Strathcarron, *qqv*; *b* 4 Oct 1920; *Educ* Cargilfield, Fettes, Trinity Coll Oxford (MA, Athletics blue); *m* 1953, Jean Henrietta, yst da of David Butler-Wilson, of Alderley Edge, Cheshire; 2 s, 1 da; *Career* cmmnd Queen's Own Cameron Highlanders 1939; served WWII: Scot Commando, parachutist (POW 1941–43), Maj 1943 (despatches); formerly chm cos in Aust and USA; chm Mallinson-Denny Group 1980–82 (joined William Mallinson & Sons Ltd 1948, md Mallinson-Denny 1967–81); dir: Transglobe Expedition Ltd 1976–83, Brooke Bond Group 1981–82, Birmid Qualcast plc (and chm) 1982–88, Scottish Mutual Assurance Society 1982–91, Nat Coal Bd 1983–86, C H Industrials plc 1983–91, Cosmopolitan Textile Co Ltd (and chm) 1983–91, Webb-Bowen International Ltd 1984–94, English Architectural Glazing Ltd 1985–, New Scotland Insurance 1986–93, TSB Scotland 1986–91, Boustead plc 1986–, Kymmene UK Holdings PLC 1986–96, Caledonian Paper PLC 1987–96, Keller Group plc 1990–, Fitzwilton (UK) PLC 1990–, Société Generale merchant bank 1991–93, Truswal Timber UK Ltd 1991–93, Global Satellite Communications (Scotland) PLC 1991–92, The Education Exchange Ltd 1994–, Fitzwilton Finance (UK) PLC 1996–; chm: Allstate Reinsurance Co Ltd 1983–96, Employment Conditions Abroad Ltd 1983–93, Karablue Ltd 1985–96, Karablue Equipment Ltd 1987–96, Owl Creek Investments plc 1989–91, Internet Network Services (UK) Ltd 1995–, Wineworld London PLC 1995–, Annington Homes PLC 1996–; London advsr Sears Roebuck & Co 1984–, memb Int Advsy Bd Bain & Co 1987–; memb: Cncl CBI (past chm London and SE Region, memb Pres's City Advsy Bd), Ctee on Invisible Exports 1982–85, Scot Cncl for Devpt and Indust, Steering Bd Univ of Strathclyde 1980–85; chm Cncl London C of C 1980–82 (vice pres 1982–), chm Nat Employers Liaison Ctee for Vol Res Forces 1986–92; chm Assoc of British C of C 1986–88, pres Assoc of Euro Chambers of Commerce 1992–94 (hon pres 1995–); govr Fettes Coll 1984–92, pres Achilles Club 1981–, fndn tstee Acad of Euro Law Germany 1993–, vice patron Ulysses Tst for Res Forces 1993–; memb Queen's Body Guard for Scotland (Royal Co of Archers); High Sheriff Gtr London 1983–84; memb: Worshipful Co of Dyers (memb Ct of Assts 1982–, Prime Warden 1985–86), Worshipful Co of Carpenters; Chev de la Légion d'Honneur, Croix de Guerre (2 Palms and Star); FRSA, FIMgt; *Recreations* fishing, shooting, modern languages, squash, outdoor sport (former Univ of Oxford and London Scot rugby player, Univ of Oxford and Mid-Surrey hockey player and Scot Int athlete); *Clubs* New (Edinburgh), Hurlingham, MCC; *Style—* Sir Thomas Macpherson, CBE, MC, TD, DL; ✉ 27 Archery Close, London W2 2PN (☎ 0171 262 8487); Craigdhu, Newtonmore, Inverness-shire PH20 1BS (☎ 01528 544200)

MACPHERSON, Tim John; s of Charles Jaffrey Macpherson, of Kingsbridge, S Devon, and Barbera, *née* Pratt; *b* 11 Sept 1962; *Educ* Kingsbridge Comp Sch, Kingsbridge Sixth Form Coll, S Devon Art Coll; *m* 29 May 1993, Lesley Ann, da of David Waters; *Career* asst photographer Prudence Cuming Associates fine art photographers Dover St London 1983–89, asst to Ben Rice people photographer London 1989–90, freelance asst photographer 1990–92 (worked with Jillian Edelstein, Dave Gamble, Frank Herholdt, Duncan McNicol, Bob Miller and Michael Joseph), photographer 1992–; editorial cmmns incl: Sunday Times, Observer, ES and GQ Mazagines, Sunday Telegraph; other assignments for indust, design and advtg; memb Assoc of Photographers; *exhibitions* Icons, Idols & Heroes 1992 and Portrait 1994 (Association Gallery), National Portrait Gallery; *awards* Individual Image & Portfolio award Assoc of Photographers Assistants Awards 1991, Individual Image Silver medal RPS 135th Int Print Exhbn 1991, represented Britain at Kodak Euro Panorama of Young Photography Arles France 1992, winner Individual Image Assoc of Photographers Eleventh Awards 1993, American Communication Arts Award 1995; *Recreations* travel, photography; *Style—* Tim MacPherson, Esq; ✉ 6 Appollo Studios, Charlton Kings Road, London NW5 2SB (☎ 0171 482 3032)

MACPHERSON-FLETCHER OF BALAVIL, Allan William; s of Rev John Fletcher (d 1990), of Edinburgh, and Elizabeth, *née* Stoddart (d 1966); nephew of Mrs H E Brewster-Macpherson of Balavil (d 1990); assumed additional surname of Macpherson 1990; *b* 27 July 1950; *Educ* Trinity Coll Glenalmond, Univ of Aberdeen (BSc); *m* 30 Oct 1976, Marjorie, da of George Daniel (d 1984), of Aberdeen; 1 s (James b 1979), 1 da (Elizabeth-Anne b 1978), 3 step s (Antony Sherlock b 1965, Michael Sherlock b 1966, Nicholas Sherlock b 1973); *Career* mangr McLaren Marine Queensland Aust 1973–75, proprietor Balavil Estate 1975–, dir Badenoch Land Management Ltd 1975–, mangr Bell-Ingram Sporting Dept 1987–89, sporting estate conslt Hamptons 1989–95 (dir E Midlands, Northern and Scottish region), Highland conslt Strutt and Parker 1996–; dir and govr Butterstone School Holdings Ltd 1988–93, ed Scottish and African Sporting Gazettes 1996–, dir Highland Vernacular Bldgs Tst, pres Kingussie Sheep Dog Trial Assoc; memb Brenchley Vineyards Carriage Driving Team World Championships Poland 1995, Br nat champions Windsor 1995; memb: Northern Meeting Soc, Scottish Landowners' Fedn, Game Conservancy; *Recreations* shooting, stalking, fishing, skiing, sailing, travel, wine; *Clubs* The Highland; *Style—* Macpherson-Fletcher of Balavil; ✉ Balavil, Kingussie, Inverness-shire (☎ 01540 661413, fax 01540 662021); 13 Sandend, Portsoy, Banffshire

MACPHERSON OF CLUNY (AND BLAIRGOWRIE), Hon Sir William Alan Macpherson of Cluny (Cluny Macpherson); kt (1983), TD (1965); 27 Chief of the Clan Macpherson; s of Brig Alan David Macpherson of Cluny-Macpherson, DSO, MC (d 1969), and Catharine Richardson Macpherson (d 1967); *b* 1 April 1926; *Educ* Wellington Coll, Trinity Coll Oxford (MA); *m* 27 Dec 1962, Sheila McDonald, da of Thomas Brodie (d 1979), of Edinburgh; 2 s (Alan Thomas b 8 Oct 1965, James Brodie b 5 June 1972), 1 da (Anne b 10 Nov 1963); *Heir* s, Alan Macpherson, yr of Cluny b 1965; *Career* Capt Scots Gds 1944–47, Lt-Col 21 SAS Regt (TA) 1962–65, Hon Col 21 SAS 1983–90; called to the Bar Inner Temple 1952, bencher 1978; QC 1971, recorder of the Crown Court 1971, judge of the High Court of Justice (Queen's Bench Div) 1983–96, presiding judge Northern Circuit 1984–88; hon memb Northern Circuit 1987; memb Royal Co of Archers (Queen's Body Guard for Scotland) 1976 (Brig 1989); govr Royal Scottish Corp (vice pres 1989); hon fell Trinity Coll Oxford 1991; *Recreations* golf, fishing, rugby football; *Clubs* Caledonian, Special Forces, Highland Soc of London (pres 1991–94), London Scottish Football (pres 1972–79), Blairgowrie Golf, Denham Golf; *Style—* The Hon Sir William Macpherson of Cluny, TD; ✉ Newton Castle, Blairgowrie PH10 6SU

MACPHERSON OF DRUMOCHTER, 2 Baron (UK 1951); (James) Gordon Macpherson; JP (Essex 1961); s of 1 Baron (d 1965), and Lucy (d 1984), da of Arthur Butcher; *b* 22 Jan 1924; *Educ* Wells House Malvern, Loretto; *m* 1, 1947, (Dorothy) Ruth (d 1974), da of late Rev Henry Coulter, of Bellahouston, Glasgow; (1 s decd), 2 da; m 2, 1975, Catherine Bridget, only da of Dr Desmond MacCarthy, of Brentwood; 1 s, 2 da (Hon Jennifer b 1976, Hon Anne b 1977); *Heir* s, Hon James Anthony Macpherson b 27 Feb 1979; *Career* served with RAF 1941–46; chm Godron Macrobin (Insurance) Ltd, chm and md Macpherson Train & Co Ltd (Food & Produce Importers and Exporters), chm A J Macpherson & Co (Bankers); memb: Cncl of London C of C 1958, Exec Ctee of W India Ctee 1959 (dep chm 1971, chm 1973), Cncl E Euro Trade Cncl 1969–72; fndr chm and patron Br Importers Confedn 1972–; chief Scottish Clans Assoc London 1972–74; memb Essex Magistrates' Cts Ctee 1974–75, dep chm Brentwood Bench 1972; govr Brentwood Sch 1970–75; hon game warden for the Sudan 1974; Freeman: City of London 1969, Worshipful Co of Butchers 1969; landowner (grouse, deer and salmon, with farming); Fell Royal Entomological Soc, FZS, FRSA; *Recreations* shooting, fishing, gardening; *Clubs* Boodle's; *Style—* The Rt Hon the Lord Macpherson of Drumochter, JP; ✉ Kyllachy, Tomatin, Inverness-shire IV13 7YA (☎ 01808 511212)

MACPHERSON OF PITMAIN, (Michael) Alastair Fox; 17 Sr Chieftain of the Clan Macpherson; s of Stephen Marriott Fox (d 1971), of Surrey, and Margaret Gertude Macpherson of Pitmain; *b* 17 Dec 1944; *Educ* Haileybury, Magdalene Coll Cambridge (MA Law); *m* 10 June 1972, Penelope Margaret, da of Frederick William Birkmyre Harper (d 1977), of Oxon; 2 s (Alexander b 5 Feb 1976, Charles b 8 May 1980), 1 da (Isabella b 3 July 1973); *Heir* s, Alexander Macpherson, yr of Pitmain; *Career* admitted slr 1971; ptnr Ashurst Morris Crisp slrs 1974–; non-exec dir: Smith & Nephew plc 1986–, Johnson Fry plc 1987–89, Thomas Jourdan plc 1987–; memb Cncl White Ensign Assoc 1995–, vice chm Clan Macpherson Assoc; *Recreations* golf, fishing, shooting, rhododendrons; *Clubs* Boodle's, Queen's, Hurlingham, MCC; *Style—* Alastair Macpherson of Pitmain, Esq; ✉ 58 Luttrell Ave, Putney, London SW15 6PE (☎ 0181 788 1812); Achara House, Duror of Appin, Argyll (☎ 01631 740262); Ashurst Morris Crisp, Broadwalk House, 5 Appold Street, London EC2A 2HA (☎ 0171 638 1111, fax 0171 972 7990)

MACPHIE, Maj-Gen Duncan Love; s of Donald Macphie (d 1967), of Glasgow, and Elizabeth Adam, *née* Gibson; *b* 15 Dec 1930; *Educ* Hutchesons' Sch Glasgow, Univ of Glasgow (MB ChB); *m* 11 July 1957, Isobel Mary (Mollie), da of Archibald James Jenkins (d 1985), of Stirling; 1 s (Ruary James b 26 March 1964), 2 da (Morven Elizabeth b 29 May 1959, Catriona Mary b 24 Oct 1966); *Career* RMO IRS 1958–61, RMO 3 RHA 1963–66, CO BMH Dharan and SMO British Gurkha L of C 1970–72, CO 24 Field Ambulance RAMC 1972–74, CO BMH Munster 1974–76, ADMS 4 Armoured Div 1976–80, ADG AMDI MOD 1980–83, CO QEMH Woolwich 1983–85, Chief Med Plans Branch SHAPE 1985–87, Cdr Med BAOR 1987–90, ret as Maj-Gen; exec dir St John Ambulance London 1994–95 (med dir 1993–94); QHS 1985–90, Col Cmdt RAMC 1990–95; OStJ; memb BMA; *Recreations* gardening, reading, classical music, watching rugby; *Style—* Maj-Gen Duncan Macphie

McQUAID, Dr James; CB (1997); s of James McQuaid (d 1981), and Brigid, *née* McDonnell (d 1988); *b* 5 Nov 1939; *Educ* Christian Brothers' Sch Dundalk, Univ Coll Dublin (BEng), Jesus Coll Cambridge (PhD), Nat Univ of Ireland (DSc); *m* 17 Feb 1968, Catherine Anne, da of Dr James John Hargan (d 1988), of Rotherham; 2 s (James Benedict b 1968, Martin Hargan b 1971), 1 da (Fiona Catherine b 1969); *Career* graduate engr apprentice Br Nylon Spinners Ltd 1961–63; Safety in Mines Res Estab: sr res fell 1966–68, sr sci offr 1968–72, princ sci offr 1972–78; dir Safety Engrg Laboratory 1980–85 (dep dir 1978–80), res dir Health and Safety Exec 1985–92, dir Strategy and Gen Div and chief scientist 1992–96, dir Science and Technology and chief scientist 1996–; CEng, MIMechE 1972, FIMinE 1986, FEng 1991; *Recreations* model engineering, ornamental turning, industrial archaeology; *Clubs* Athenaeum; *Style—* Dr James McQuaid, CB, FEng; ✉ 61 Pingle Rd, Sheffield, S Yorks S7 2LL (☎ 0114 236 5349); Health and Safety Executive, Rose Court, 2 Southwark Bridge, London SE1 9HS (☎ 0171 717 6497)

MACQUAKER, Donald Francis; CBE (1991); s of Thomas Mason Macquaker MC (d 1979), of Brae of Auchendrane by Ayr, and Caroline Bertha Floris Macquaker (d 1983); (gf Sir Thomas, fndr Royal Samaritan Hosp for Women Glasgow); *b* 21 Sept 1932; *Educ* Winchester, Trinity Coll Oxford (MA), Univ of Glasgow (LLB); *m* 9 Jan 1964, Susan Elizabeth, da of William Archibald Kay Finlayson (d 1969); 1 da (Diana b 1965), 1 s (Charles b 1968); *Career* farmer, landowner and slr; ptnr T C Young & Son Glasgow 1957–93, conslt 1993–96; memb (later vice chm) bd of mgmnt Glasgow Royal Maternity Hosp 1965–74; chm: Gtr Glasgow Health Bd 1983–87 (convenor Fin Ctee 1973–83), Common Servs Agency Scot Health Serv 1987–91; dir: Lithgows Ltd 1987–, The Prince and Princess of Wales Hospice Glasgow 1991–94; *Recreations* shooting, fishing, gardening; *Clubs* Western (Glasgow), Western Meeting (Ayr), Leander (Henley); *Style—* Donald Macquaker, Esq, CBE; ✉ Blackbyres, by Ayr KA7 4TS (☎ 01292 441088)

McQUARRIE, Sir Albert; kt (1987); s of Algernon Stewart McQuarrie (d 1955), and Alice Maud Sharman (d 1961); *b* 1 Jan 1918; *Educ* Highlanders Acad Greenock, Greenock HS, Royal Coll of Sci and Technol Univ of Strathclyde (MSE, PEng 1945); *m* 1, 1945, Roseleen McCaffery (d 1986); 1 s (Dermot Hugh Hastings, producer/dir TV); m 2, 1989, Rhoda Annie Gall; *Career* served in HM Forces 1939–45, Offr RE; chm: A McQuarrie & Son (Great Britain) Ltd 1946–88, Sir Albert McQuarrie & Associates Ltd 1988–; vice chm Clan McQuarrie Assoc 1980–; dir: Hunterston Development Co 1989–, British American Corporation 1991–, Prooftask Ltd 1993–; conslt Bredero Projects Ltd 1975–; former Dean of Guild Gourock Town Cncl, chm Fyvie/Rothienorman/Monquitter Community Cncl 1975–79; Parly candidate (C): Kilmarnock 1966, Caithness and Sutherland 1974, Banff and Buchan 1987; Euro Parly candidate Highlands and Islands 1989; MP (C): Aberdeenshire E 1979–83, Banff and Buchan 1983–87; chm British/Gibraltar All Pty Gp 1979–87, vice chm Cons Fisheries Sub Ctee 1979–87; sec: Scottish Cons Back Bench Ctee 1985–87, Scotch Whisky All Pty Gp 1979–87; memb Speaker's Panel of Chairmen 1986–87; memb Select Ctees: on Scottish Affrs 1979–83, on Agriculture 1983–85, on Private Bill Procedure 1987; memb Cncl Soc of Engrs 1978–87; chm Cunningham South Cons Assoc 1991–92, vice chm Ayr Cons Assoc 1992–96, patron N Tayside Cons Assoc 1996; hon memb Cwlth Parly Assoc, hon vice pres Gibraltar Assoc of Euro Rights 1996–; hon pres: Banff and Buchan Cons and Unionist Assoc 1989–, Gourock Hort Soc 1993– (hon vice pres 1954–93); patron Ardgowan Hospice Greenock; FRSH 1952; Freeman City of Gibraltar 1982; KSJ 1991; *Recreations* golf, bridge, music, soccer, swimming, horticulture; *Clubs* Lansdowne, Western (Ayr), Royal Scottish Automobile (Glasgow), Marine Highland (Troon); *Style—* Sir Albert McQuarrie; ✉ Crimond, Balcomie Crescent, Troon, Ayrshire KA10 7AR

MacQUEEN, Prof Hector Lewis; s of John MacQueen, of Damnaglaur, and Winifred, *née* McWalter; *b* 13 June 1956; *Educ* George Heriot's Sch Edinburgh, Univ of Edinburgh (LLB, PhD); *m* 29 Sept 1979, Frances Mary, da of Robert Young, of Dalkeith; 2 s (Patrick b 1984, Jamie b 1987), 1 da (Sarah b 1982); *Career* Univ of Edinburgh: lectr in law 1979–91, assoc dean Faculty of Law 1987–90, sr lectr 1991–94, reader 1994, prof of private law 1994–; visiting prof Cornell Univ 1991; exec dir The David Hume Inst Edinburgh 1992–; ed Edinburgh Law Review 1996–; *Books* New Perspectives in Scottish Legal History (ed, 1984), Centenary - Heriot's FP Cricket Club 1889–1989 (1989), Copyright, Competition and Industrial Design (1989, 2 edn 1995), The College of Justice and Other Essays by R K Hannay (ed, 1991), Studying Scots Law (1993), Common Law and Feudal Society in Medieval Scotland (1993), Scots Law into the 21st Century (ed, 1996); *Recreations* cricket, things Scottish, walking; *Clubs* Edinburgh Univ Staff, Heriots FP Cricket; *Style—* Prof Hector MacQueen; ✉ 47 Falcon Gardens, Edinburgh EH10 4AR (☎ 0131 447 3043); University of Edinburgh, Department of Private Law, Old College, South Bridge, Edinburgh EH8 9YL (☎ 0131 650 2060, fax 0131 662 4902, telex 727442 UNIVED G, e-mail Hector.L.MacQueen@ed.ac.uk)

MacQUEEN, Prof John; s of William Lochhead MacQueen (d 1963), of Springboig, Glasgow, and Grace Palmer, *née* Galloway (d 1983); *b* 13 Feb 1929; *Educ* Hutchesons' GS, Univ of Glasgow (MA), Christ's Coll Cambridge (BA, MA); *m* 22 June 1953, Winifred Wallace, da of Wallace McWalter (d 1979), of Calderwood, East Kilbride; 3 s (Hector b 1956, Angus b 1958, Donald b 1963); *Career* PO, Flying Offr RAF 1954–56; asst prof Washington Univ St Louis Missouri USA 1956–59; Univ of Edinburgh: lectr 1959–63, Masson prof 1963–71, dir Sch of Scottish Studies 1969–88, prof of Scottish lit 1971–88 (now emeritus), endowment fell 1988–92, hon fell Faculty of Arts 1992–95; Hon DLitt Nat Univ of Ireland 1985; FRSE 1992; *Books* St Nynia (1961, revised edn 1990), Robert Henryson (1967), Ballattis of Luve (1970), Allegory (1970), Progress and Poetry (1982), Numerology (1985), The Rise of the Historical Novel (1989), Scotichronicon 3 and 4 (with W W MacQueen, 1989), Humanism in Renaissance Scotland (ed, 1990), Scotichronicon 1 and 2 (with W W MacQueen, 1993), Scotichronicon 5 and 6 (with W W MacQueen and D E R Watt, 1995); *Recreations* walking, reading, music, casual archaeology, astronomy; *Clubs* Scottish Arts, University Staff (Edinburgh); *Style—* Prof John MacQueen, FRSE; ✉ Slewdonan, Damnaglaur, Drummore, Stranraer, Wigtownshire DG9 9QN (☎ 01776 840637)

McQUEEN, John; s of late Dr Leonard George McQueen, and Mira Milstead, *née* Birch; *b* 20 May 1942; *Educ* Rugby, Trinity Coll Cambridge, St Thomas's Hosp Med Sch (MA, MB BChir); *m* Dorothy, da of Gilbert Dyke; 5 da (Katy b 1968, Deborah b 1971, Philippa b 1977, Sarah b 1984, Laura b 1987); *Career* sr registrar Queen Charlotte Hosp and Chelsea Hosp, currently clinical dir and conslt obstetrician gynaecologist Bromley Hosps NHS Trust; author of various papers on obstetrics, gynaecology and the menopause; memb Int Menopause Soc; Liveryman Worshipful Soc of Apothecaries, Freeman City of London; FRCS 1972, FRCOG 1985 (memb 1973); *Recreations* travel, golf; *Clubs* London Obstetric, Gynaecological Soc; *Style—* John McQueen, Esq; ✉ Downs View, Heritage Hill, Keston, Kent BR2 6AU (☎ 01689 859058); Beckenham Hospital, Croydon Rd, Beckenham, Kent BR3 3QL (☎ 0181 289 6684)

MacRAE, HE Sir (Alastair) Christopher Donald Summerhayes; KCMG (1993, CMG 1987); s of Dr Alexander Murray MacRae (d 1969), of Edge, Glos, and Dr Grace Maria Lynton Summerhayes MacRae; *b* 3 May 1937; *Educ* Rugby, Lincoln Coll Oxford (BA), Harvard Univ (Henry fell in int rels); *m* 1963, Mette, da of Svend Willert; 2 da (Christina b 1963, Pia b 1967); *Career* midshipman RN 1956–58; HM Dip Serv: CRO 1962, third later second sec Dar es Salaam 1963, MECAS 1965, Beirut 1967, first sec FCO 1968, first sec and head of Chancery Baghdad 1970, first sec and head of Chancery Brussels 1972, special unpaid leave to the Cmmn of EC 1976, ambass Libreville 1978–80, non-resident ambass to São Tomé and Principe 1979–80, head of W African Dept FCO 1980–83, non-resident ambass to Chad 1982–83, cnsllr and head of Chancery Paris 1983–87, min and head of Br Interests Section Tehran 1987, visiting fell IISS 1987–88, Support Serv Scrutiny FCO 1988, on loan to Cabinet Office 1988–91; high cmmr: Lagos (concurrently non-resident ambass to Benin) 1991–94, Islamabad 1994–; Hon MA Univ of Oxford 1988; memb IISS 1987; *Recreations* exploring Provençe; *Style—* HE Sir Christopher MacRae, KCMG; ✉ c/o FCO (Islamabad), King Charles Street, London SW1A 2AH

McRAE, Frances Anne; *née* Cairncross; da of Sir Alec (Alexander Kirkland) Cairncross, KCMG, *qv*; *b* 30 Aug 1944; *Educ* Laurel Bank Sch Glasgow, St Anne's Coll Oxford (MA), Brown Univ Rhode Island USA (MA); *m* 10 Sept 1971, Hamish McRae, *qv*; 2 da (Isabella Frances b 28 July 1977, Alexandra Barbara Mary b 5 Dec 1979); *Career* staff memb: The Times 1967–69, The Banker 1969, The Observer 1970–73, The Guardian (economics corr 1973–81, ed women's page 1981–84); The Economist: Br ed 1984–89, environment ed 1989–94, media ed 1994–; non-exec dir Prolific Group 1988–89, memb Bd Alliance and Leicester Building Society 1990–; memb: Economics Ctee SSRC 1972–76, Newspaper Panel Monopolies Cmmn 1973–80, Cncl Royal Economic Soc 1980–85, Inquiry into Br Housing 1984–85, Cncl Inst for Fiscal Studies 1995–; hon treas Nat Cncl for One Parent Families 1980–83, tstee Kennedy Meml Tst 1974–89, memb Sch Teachers' Review Body 1992–93, govr NIESR 1995–; hon fell St Anne's Coll Oxford; *Books* Capital City (with Hamish McRae, 1971), The Second Great Crash (with Hamish McRae, 1973), The Guardian Guide to the Economy (1981), Changing Perceptions of Economic Policy (1981), The Second Guardian Guide to the Economy (1983), Guide to the Economy (1987), Costing the Earth (1991), Green Inc (1995); *Recreations* home life; *Style—* Mrs Hamish McRae; ✉ c/o The Economist, 25 St James's Street, London SW1A 1HG (☎ 0171 830 7025)

McRAE, Hamish Malcolm Donald; s of Donald Barrington McRae (d 1980), and Barbara Ruth Louise (Jasmine), *née* Budd; *b* 20 Oct 1943; *Educ* Fettes, Trinity Coll Dublin (BA); *m* 10 Sept 1971, Frances McRae, *qv*, da of Sir Alexander Kirkland (Alec) Cairncross, KCMG, *qv*; 2 da (Isabella Frances b 28 July 1977, Alexandra Barbara Mary b 5 Dec 1979); *Career* graduate trainee Liverpool Post 1966–67, asst ed then dep ed The Banker 1967–72, ed Euromoney 1972–75, fin ed The Guardian 1975–89, business and city ed The Independent 1989–91 (assoc ed 1991–); Harold Wincott Young Fin Journalist of the Year 1971, Harold Wincott Fin Journalist of the Year 1979; *Books* Capital City: London as a Financial Centre (with Frances Cairncross, 1973, current edn 1991), The Second Great Crash: how the oil crisis could destroy the world economy (with Nihon Keisai Shimbun, 1975), Japan's Role in the Emerging Global Securities Market (1985), The World In 2020: Power, Culture and Property - a vision of the future (1994); *Recreations* skiing and walking; *Style—* Hamish McRae, Esq; ✉ Associate Editor, The Independent, 1 Canada Square, Canary Wharf, London E14 5DL (☎ 0171 293 2000, fax 0171 293 2435)

MACRAE, Dr John Esmond Campbell; CMG (1986); s of Col Archibald Campbell Macrae, IMS (d 1961), and Euretta Margaret, *née* Skelton (d 1967); *b* 8 Dec 1932; *Educ* Sheikh Bagh Sch Srinagar Kashmir, Fettes, Christ Church Oxford (open scholar, MA, PhD), Princeton Univ; *m* 8 Sept 1962, Anne Catherine Sarah, da of late Joseph Strain; 4 s (Marcus Campbell b 14 Aug 1965, Angus James Campbell b 16 Jan 1968, Rory Lucien b 16 June 1970, Gavin Alan Nicholas b 16 Oct 1971); *Career* FO (later FCO): joined 1959, 2 sec Tel Aviv 1960, 2 sec Djakarta April-Oct 1964, 1 sec Vientiane Oct 1964–66, N African Dept FO until 1967, Central Dept until 1969, Central and S African Dept until 1972, UK Mission to the UN (dealing with social affairs, population and outer space) 1972–75, cnsllr (sci and technol) 1975–80, head Cultural Rels Dept FCO 1980–85, RCDS 1985, ambass to Senegal (accredited also to Mali, Mauritania, Guinea, Guinea (Bissau) and Cape Verde) 1985–90, ambass to Morocco (accredited also to Mauritania) 1990–92; Order of the Lion (Senegal); *Recreations* travel, music, tinkering, picnicking; *Style—* Dr John Macrae, CMG; ✉ Les Aires, 26110 Mirabel Aux Baronnies, France

McRAE, (Stuart) Neil; s of Max Harvey McRae (d 1990), of George, S Africa, and Vivienne Blanche Rosemary, *née* Lewin (d 1990); *b* 23 June 1939; *Educ* Diocesan Coll Cape Town, Univ of the Witwatersrand (BA); *m* 24 June 1961, Joyce Rowena, da of Arthur Breeze Carr; 3 da (Fiona Jane b 1965, Louise Mary b 1967, Caroline Anne b 1970); *Career* md Reader's Digest Association Ltd 1986–, chm David and Charles plc 1990–; chm Periodical Publishers Assoc 1992–93; dir: Reader's Digest (Ireland) Ltd, Victoria House Publishing Ltd, Berkeley Magazines Ltd, Reader's Digest (Family Insurance Services) Ltd; *Recreations* dinghy sailing, book collecting; *Clubs* Lansdowne; *Style—* Neil McRae, Esq; ✉ Reader's Digest Association Ltd, 61 Curzon Street, London W1Y 7PE (☎ 0171 409 5707, fax 0171 409 5754)

MACRAE, Col Sir Robert Andrew Alexander Scarth; KCVO (1990), MBE (1953), JP (1975); s of Robert Scarth Farquhar Macrae, CIE, CBE (d 1926), of Grindelay, Orphir, Orkney, and Beatrix Reid, *née* McGeoch (d 1970); *b* 14 April 1915; *Educ* Lancing, RMC Sandhurst; *m* 7 June 1945, Violet Maud, da of Walter Scott MacLellan (d 1959) of Edinburgh; 2 s (Christopher b 1948, Malcolm b 1956); *Career* cmmnd 2 Lt Seaforth Highlanders 1935, served BEF 1940 (POW); active service NW Europe 1940–45 (despatches), Korea 1952–53, Kenya 1953–54, Col 1963 ret 1968; farmer; memb: Orkney CC 1970–74, Orkney Islands Cncl 1974–78; vice chm: Orkney Hosp Bd 1971–74, Orkney Health Bd 1974–79; Hon Sheriff Grampian Highlands and Islands 1974, Hon Col 2 Bn 51 Highland Volunteers 1979–83; Lord-Lt Orkney 1972–90 (DL 1946, Vice Lord-Lt 1967); Freeman of Orkney 1990; *Recreations* sailing, gardening; *Clubs* New (Edinburgh), Army & Navy, Puffins; *Style—* Col Sir Robert Macrae, KCVO, MBE, JP, DL; ✉ Grindelay, Orphir, Orkney KW17 2RD (☎ 01856 811228); Binscarth Farms, Orkney

McRAE, Prof Thomas Watson; s of Thomas Watson McRae (d 1976), of Edinburgh, and Catherine Hawthorn, *née* Galloway (d 1971); *b* 16 Sept 1932; *Educ* Royal HS Edinburgh, LSE (BSc); *m* 26 March 1960, Helen Elizabeth, da of Emlyn Thomas (d 1952), of Peterborough; 1 s (Paul David Watson b 19 July 1963), 2 da (Julie Clare b 21 Dec 1961, Cathleen Margaretta b 26 Feb 1966); *Career* Nat Serv Lt KAR Kenya and Uganda 1955–57; sr auditor Price Waterhouse London 1957–58, systems analyst and lectr IBM Career London 1958–61, PD Leake res fell LSE 1961–63, lectr in accounting and finance Univ of Hull 1964–67, lectr Manchester Business Sch 1967–69, prof of business admin Witwatersrand Univ Business Sch Johannesburg SA 1969–71, prof of fin (now prof of personal fin) Univ of Bradford Mgmnt Centre 1972–; memb Bank of England Ctee on Training for the Fin Insts 1973–75; MICAS 1965; *Books* Introduction to Business Computer Programming (1966), Analytical Management (1969), Computers and Accounting (1972), Foreign Exchange Management (1981), The Uses of Statistical Sampling in Internal Auditing (1983), Introduction to Personal Financial Planning (1994), International Business Finance (1996); *Recreations* microcomputing, travel, hill-walking; *Style—* Prof Thomas McRae; ✉ 12 Warlbeck, Kings Road, Ilkley, West Yorkshire LS29 9RH (☎ 01943 607071); Bradford University Management Centre, Emm Lane, Bradford, W Yorks (☎ 01274 384393, fax 01274 546866, telex 51309 UNIBFD G)

MACREADY, Sir Nevil John Wilfrid; 3 Bt (UK 1923), of Cheltenham, Co Gloucester; CBE (1983); s of Lt-Gen Sir Gordon Nevil Macready, 2 Bt, KBE, CB, CMG, DSO, MC (d 1956); *b* 7 Sept 1921; *Educ* Cheltenham, St John's Coll Oxford (MA); *m* 1949, Mary, o da of Sir (John) Donald Balfour Fergusson, GCB (d 1963); 1 s (Charles Nevil b 1955), 3 da (Caroline Elisabeth (Mrs Clive F Tucker) b 1950, Sarah Diana Mary b 1953, Anna Louise b 1963); *Heir* s, Charles Nevil Macready b 19 May 1955; *Career* served RA 1942–47, Staff Capt 1945; BBC Euro Serv 1947–50, Mobil Oil Co Ltd 1952–85 (md 1975); pres: Royal Warrant Holders' Assoc 1979–80, Inst of Petroleum 1980–82; chm: Crafts Cncl 1984–91, Horseracing Advsy Cncl 1986–93, Mental Health Fndn 1993–; dep chm Br Horseracing Bd 1993–95; tstee V & A Museum 1985–95; *Clubs* Boodle's, Jockey (Paris); *Style—* Sir Nevil Macready, Bt, CBE; ✉ The White House, Odiham, Hants RG29 1LG (☎ 01256 702976)

MacRORY, Avril; da of Patrick Simon MacRory, of Dublin, and Elizabeth, *née* Flynn; *b* 5 April 1956; *Educ* Sion Hill Dublin, Univ Coll Dublin (BA); *m* 9 Sept 1983, Valentine John Griffin, s of Valentine John Griffin (d 1987), of Dublin, Ireland; 1 s (Sam b 31 March 1985); *Career* TV prodr and dir Radio Telefis Eireann (RTE) 1979–86, head of variety 1986–88, commissioning ed (music) Channel 4 TV 1988–93, head of music progs BBC TV 1993–; fndr memb Centre for Performing Arts Dublin; memb ITPA 1985, pres International Music Centre Vienna 1989–98; memb: BAFTA, RTS; *Recreations* music, cinema, sailing; *Clubs* United Arts (Dublin, affiliated Chelsea Arts Club), Irish Club of GB (bd memb); *Style—* Mrs Avril MacRory; ✉ Room EG05, BBC Music and Arts, East Tower, Television Centre, Wood Lane, London W12 7RJ

MACRORY, Henry David; s of Sir Patrick Arthur Macrory (d 1993), of Walton-on-the-Hill, Surrey, and Marjorie Elizabeth, *née* Lewis; *b* 15 Dec 1947; *Educ* Westminster, Univ of Kent (BA); *m* 4 April 1972, Janet Carolyn, da of Henry James Potts; 1 s (David b 1985), 2 da (Julia b 1978, Caroline b 1980); *Career* reporter Kent Messenger 1969–72; Sunday Express 1972–: reporter 1972–79, political columnist 1979–83, asst ed 1983, exec ed 1990, acting ed 1991, dep ed 1994–; Daily Star: political ed 1993, currently asst ed; *Style—* Henry Macrory, Esq; ✉ Daily Star, Ludgate House, 245 Blackfriars Road, London SE1 9UX (☎ 0171 928 8000, fax 0171 620 1656)

MACRORY, Prof Richard Brabazon; s of Sir Patrick Arthur Macrory (d 1993), of Walton-on-the-Hill, Surrey, and Marjorie Elizabeth, *née* Lewis; *b* 30 March 1950; *Educ* Westminster, ChCh Oxford (MA); *m* 6 Oct 1979, Sarah Margaret, da of Bernard Christian Briant, CVO, of Aldeburgh, Suffolk; 2 s (Sam b 1980, Robert b 1983); *Career* called to the Bar Gray's Inn 1974; legal advsr FOE Ltd 1975–78; Imperial Coll Centre for Environmental Technol: lectr in environmental law 1980–89, reader 1989–91, prof 1991–94, prof of environmental law 1996–; dir Environmental Change Unit Univ of Oxford and professorial fell Linacre Coll 1994–95, supernumerary fell Linacre Coll 1996–; ed Jl of Environmental Law; specialist advsr House of Commons Select Ctee on the Environment, standing counsel Cncl for Protection of Rural England 1981–92, first chm UK Environmental Law Assoc 1986–88, specialist advsr House of Lords Select Ctee on the EC (Environment Subctee) 1992 and 1996, specialist advsr House of Commons Select Ctee on the Environment 1989–; memb: Royal Cmmn on Environmental Pollution 1991–, UK Nat Advsy Ctee on Eco-labelling 1990–91, Expert Panel UK Inter-Agency Ctee on Global Environmental Change 1995–96; chm Merchant-Ivory Film Prodns Ltd 1992–; *Books* Nuisance (1982), Water Law: Principles and Practice (1985), Water Act 1989 (1989), Bibliography of European Community Law (1995); author of numerous articles in learned jls; *Recreations* reading, board games, films; *Style—* Prof Richard Macrory; ✉ Imperial College Centre for Environmental Technology, 48 Princes Gardens, London SW7 2PE (☎ 0171 594 9303, fax 0171 594 9304, e-mail r.macrory@ic.ac.uk); Brick Court Chambers, 15–19 Devereux Court, London WC2R 3JJ (☎ 0171 583 0777, fax 0171 583 9401)

McSHANE, Ian David; s of Henry McShane, of Manchester, and Irene, *née* Cowley; *b* 29 Sept 1942; *Educ* Stretford GS Leeds, RADA; *m* 1 (m dis), Suzan Farmer; m 2 (m dis), Ruth Post; 1 s (Morgan b 7 July 1974), 1 da (Kate b 18 April 1970); m 3, 30 Aug 1980, Gwendolyn Marie, da of Claude Humble; *Career* actor; memb: BAFTA, Acad of Motion Picture Arts and Sciences, Screen Actors' Guild, Directors' Guild; *Theatre* West End: The Glass Menagerie 1965, Loot 1966, The Promise 1967 (also on Broadway); Los Angeles: As You Like It 1979, Betrayal 1983, Inadmissable Evidence 1985; *Television* incl: Jesus of Nazareth, Wuthering Heights, Whose Life Is It Anyway?, Evergreen, The Letter, Marco Polo, AD, War and Remembrance, Dallas, Lovejoy, Columbo, The Young Charlie Chaplin, Madson; *Films* incl: The Wild and the Willing 1962, The Battle of Britain 1968, If It's Tuesday This Must Be Belgium 1969, Villain 1971, Sitting Target 1972, Cheaper to Keep Her 1977, Exposed 1984, Torchlight 1986; *Style—* Ian McShane, Esq; ✉ c/o ICM Ltd, Oxford House, 76 Oxford Street, London W1N 0AX (☎ 0171 636 6565, fax 0171 323 0101)

McSHARRY, Brendan John; MBE (1994); s of Charles Patrick McSharry (d 1976), and Emily Annie, *née* Poundall (d 1983); *b* 25 July 1949; *Educ* St James RC HS, Univ of Wales (BA), Univ of Exeter (PGCE), Univ of Leeds (MA), Univ of Cambridge (DTEFL); *Career* exec offr staff trg Dept of Employment 1972–74, English teacher Folk Univ Örebro/Karlstadt 1975–77; British Council: English teacher Milan 1977–79, asst dir of studies Milan 1979–81, asst dir of teacher trg studies 1982–85, dir Chiang Mai Thailand 1985–87, dir of studies Baghdad 1987–89, mangr and ODA poject mangr English teaching in secdy schs Quito 1989–92, dir Milan 1992–95, dir Yemen 1995–; speaker on educnl methodology at various int confs; memb Int Sonnenberg Assoc of GB 1973; *Recreations* reading, running (completed Singapore marathon 1984); *Style*— Brendan McSharry, Esq, MBE; ✉ The British Council, As-Sabain St No 7, PO Box 2157, Sana'a, Yemen

McSHARRY, Carmel; da of John Francis McSharry (d 1962), of London, and Christina, *née* Harvey (d 1968); *Educ* St Vincent's Continuation Sch Westminster, RADA (Silver Medal); *m* 1949; 1 s (Sean Michael b 18 Sept 1954), 2 da (Desna Anne b 17 Aug 1950, Thérèse Frances b 16 Aug 1952); *Career* actress; *Theatre* Edith Westmore in The Linden Tree (Duchess), Janet in The Anatomist (Westminster), Mrs Prizborski in The Ring of Truth (Savoy), Bertha in Boeing Boeing (Apollo), Miss Tipdale in Not Now Darling (Strand), Bodice in Lear (Royal Court), Mother in Far From the City (Royal), Mother in Tibetan Inroads (Royal), Mother in Artists and Admirers (Riverside), Mother in Love on the Dole (Royal Exchange Manchester), Woman in Mary Rose (Shaw), Wife in Rafferty's Chant (Mermaid), Kath in Entertaining Mr Sloane (Grand Swansea), Mother in Glass Menagerie (Watford Palace), Mother in Saved (Watford Palace), Stand Up Comic in Not Waving (Traverse), Jackie Bast in Howard's End (New), Mrs Birley in An Inspector Calls (Windsor), Vera Swift in Straight and Narrow (Wyndhams and Aldwych), Marvin's Room (Comedy Theatre) 1993, Mrs Bedwin in Oliver (London Palladium) 1994, Mrs Gogan in The Plough and the Stars (RNT) 1996; *Television* Biddy in Love of Mike (ATV), Nancy in Oliver Twist (BBC), Kipling (series, BBC), Z Cars (BBC), Armchair Theatres (Granada), Mrs Bently in To Encourage the Others (BBC), Aunt Mary in Bluebell (BBC), Beryl in Beryl's Lot (Yorks), Sharon & Elsie (BBC), Wish Me Luck (LWT), Mother in The Liver Birds (BBC), Mrs Hollingberry in In Sickness and In Health (BBC), Mother in Oy Vey Maria (BBC), Circle of Deceit (LWT), The Deep Blue Sea 1994; *Radio* Woman in All That Fall (BBC World Service); *Film* Mother in All Coppers Are..., The Witches, Mary in Little Lord Fauntleroy; *Awards* Manchester Evening News Drama Award (Best Actress in a Visiting Prodn for Straight and Narrow) 1992; *Style*— Ms Carmel McSharry; ✉ c/o Chatto & Linnit Ltd, Prince of Wales Theatre, Coventry Street, London W1V 7FE (☎ 0171 930 6677, fax 0171 930 0091)

MACTAGGART, Sir John Auld; 4 Bt (UK 1938), of King's Park, City of Glasgow; s of Sir Ian (John) Auld Mactaggart, 3 Bt (d 1987), and Rosemary, *née* Williams (d 1992); *b* 21 Jan 1951; *Educ* Shrewsbury, Trinity Coll Cambridge (MA); *m* 1, 1977 (m dis 1990), Patricia, yst da of late Maj Harry Alastair Gordon, MC; m 2, 18 May 1991, Caroline, yst da of Eric Charles Williams, of Esher, Surrey; 2 s (Jack Auld b 11 Sept 1993, Sholto Auld b 16 Dec 1996), 1 da (Kinvara May b 18 Feb 1992); *Heir* s, Jack Auld Mactaggart b 11 Sept 1993; *Career* chartered surveyor; chm: Central and City Holdings, Western Heritable Investment Co Ltd; dir of property cos; dir Scottish Ballet; FRICS; *Clubs* Boodle's, Argyllshire Gathering; *Style*— Sir John Mactaggart, Bt; ✉ Ardmore House, Ardtalla Estate, Islay, Argyll; 74 South Audley Street, London W1Y 5FF (☎ 0171 491 2948, fax 0171 629 0414)

MacTAGGART, Dr Kenneth Dugald; s of Iain MacTaggart, BEM, of Glasgow, and Isabel Paton, *née* Dow; *b* 15 April 1953; *Educ* Allan Glen's Sch Glasgow, Paisley Coll of Technol (BA), Univ of Aston (PhD); *m* 16 March 1985, Caroline, da of Henry McNicholas, of Finchley, London; 2 da (Laura Ann b 1989, Catriona Patricia b 1991); *Career* doctoral res Univ of Aston 1976–80; journalist, publisher and ed Export Times London 1980–84, ed Property International London 1984–87, dir Inc Newsletters London 1987–88, sr economist Highlands and Islands Devpt Bd 1988–91, dir of strategy Highlands & Islands Enterprise 1995– (head of economics 1991–95); memb Nat Tst Scot, Mountain Bothies Assoc; chm Old Astonians Mountaineering Club; *Books* Technical Innovation in Industrial Production (1984); *Recreations* piano, photography, mountaineering, writing; *Clubs* TAF, Glasgow; *Style*— Dr Kenneth MacTaggart; ✉ The Sutors, 28 Broadstone Park, Inverness IV2 3LA (☎ 01463 233717); Highlands & Islands Enterprise, Bridge House, 20 Bridge St, Inverness IV1 1QR (☎ 01463 244278, fax 01463 244351)

MacTAGGART, Air Vice-Marshal William Keith; CBE (1976, MBE 1956); s of Duncan MacTaggart (d 1947), of Islay, and Marion Winifred, *née* Keith (d 1988); *b* 15 Jan 1929; *Educ* Aberdeen GS, Univ of Aberdeen (BSc); *m* 1, 30 July 1949 (m dis 1977), Christina Carnegie, da of James Geddes (d 1974), of Aberdeen; 1 s (Alan b 26 May 1954), 2 da (Carol b 24 March 1950, Shelagh b 23 April 1952); m 2, (m dis 1994), 9 Sept 1977, Barbara Smith Brown, da of Adm Stirling P Smith (d 1977); 1 step da (Carolyn b 12 June 1957); m 3, 22 Feb 1995, Kathleen Mary Wilkie, da of William Booth, of Aberdeen; *Career* cmmnd RAF 1949, Engr Offr/Pilot 1949–70, Gp Capt and OC RAF Newton 1971, Air Cdre and dir of air armament MOD (PE) 1973, RCDS 1977, Air Vice-Marshal and vice pres Ordnance Bd 1978 (pres 1978–80); dep chm Tomash Holdings Ltd 1980–84, md MPE Ltd 1984–89, ret 1989; CEng 1965, FIMechE 1973, FRAeS 1974, FIMgt 1978; *Recreations* music, travel, reading; *Clubs* RAF; *Style*— Air Vice-Marshal W MacTaggart, CBE; ✉ Croft Stones, Lothmore, Helmsdale, Sutherland KW8 6HP

McTAGUE, (George) Peter; s of George McTague, and (Eileen) Norah, *née* McCarthy; *b* 22 Feb 1951; *Educ* St Michael's Coll Leeds, The Grammar Sch Harrogate; *m* 19 April 1980, Hilary Anne, da of Bernard Cheshire; 3 s (Richard William b 7 May 1982, Nicholas Michael b 22 Aug 1984, Patrick George b 15 Jan 1988); *Career* chain store mgmnt and personnel appts (latterly trg offr) The Littlewoods Organisation Ltd 1970–77; Stylo PLC: gen mangr then commercial dir Stylo Barratt Shoes Ltd 1977–83, md Pennywise Discount Stores 1983–85; ops and property dir Comet Group PLC 1985–91, dir Merry Hill Centre Mountleigh Group PLC 1991–92, md NORWEB Retail 1992–; *Style*— Peter McTague, Esq; ✉ 3 Kent Road North, Harrogate, North Yorkshire HG1 2EX; NORWEB PLC, Manchester Road, Bolton BL3 2SW (☎ 01204 376403)

MacTHOMAS OF FINEGAND, Andrew Patrick Clayhills; o s of Capt Patrick Watt MacThomas of Finegand (d 1970), and Elizabeth, *née* Clayhills-Henderson (d 1995), of Invergowrie, Angus; suc f 1970 as 19 Chief of Clan MacThomas; *b* 28 Aug 1942; *Educ* St Edward's Sch Oxford; *m* 1985, Anneke Cornelia Susanna, o da of Mr and Mrs A Kruyning-van Hout, of The Netherlands; 1 s (Thomas b 1987), 1 da (Amy b 1989); *Heir* s, Thomas David Alexander MacThomas, yr of Finegand; *Career* head of public affairs Barclays plc 1989–; memb Standing Cncl of Scottish Chiefs; pres Clan MacThomas Soc; FSA (Scot); *Recreations* young family, tennis; *Clubs* Hurlingham; *Style*— Andrew MacThomas of Finegand; ✉ Barclays plc, 54 Lombard Street, London EC3P 3AH

MACVE, Prof Richard Henry; s of Alfred Derek Macve, of Buckhurst Hill, Essex, and Betty Lilian, *née* Simmons; *b* 2 June 1946; *Educ* Chigwell Sch Essex, New Coll Oxford (scholar, MA), LSE (MSc); *m* 28 July 1973, Jennifer Jill, da of Leslie Charles Wort; 2 s (Thomas Charles b 25 March 1980, Arthur James b 5 March 1985), 1 da (Joanna Catherine b 16 Sept 1977); *Career* Peat Marwick Mitchell London 1968–74 (articled clerk, sr accountant, asst mangr), internal auditor seconded to MOD 1973–74, lectr in accounting LSE 1974–78, Julian Hodge prof of accounting and head of Dept of Accounting and Fin Univ of Wales Aberystwyth 1978–96, prof of accounting LSE 1996–, visiting assoc prof of accounting Rice Univ Houston Texas 1982–83; memb Cncl ICAEW 1986–93, chm Conf of Profs of Accounting 1990–92, memb Bd UK CEED 1993–, academic advsr to Research Bd ICAEW 1994–; ICAEW (first place intermediate examination 1969, second place final pt one 1970, first place final pt two 1971); FCA 1979 (ACA 1972); *Publications* A Conceptual Framework for Financial Accounting and Reporting (1981), A Survey of Lloyd's Syndicate Accounts (2 edn, 1993), Accounting for Marketable Securities in The Financial Services Industry (1991), Accounting Principles for Life Insurance (1995); *Recreations* sailing, riding, mountain walking; *Clubs* Royal Over-Seas League, Aberystwyth Boat; *Style*— Prof Richard Macve; ✉ Bronwydd, 3 Trefor Rd, Aberystwyth, Ceredigion SY23 2EH (☎ 01970 624586); Department of Accounting and Finance, London School of Economics, London WC2A 2AE (☎ 0171 955 6138, fax 0171 955 7420)

McVITTIE, John Bousfield; s of Brig Arthur Bousfield McVittie, OBE (d 1976), and Valerie Florence, *née* Crichton (d 1994); *b* 9 April 1943; *Educ* Radley, Selwyn Coll Cambridge (MA), Stanford Business Sch (MBA); *m* 4 Sept 1971, Jane Elizabeth, *née* Hobson; 2 da (Clare, Amy); *Career* md Privatbanken Ltd 1984–87, sr vice-pres and gen mangr First Interstate Bank of California 1987–89, md John Charcol Commercial 1989–92, ptnr Royal Trust Bank 1992–96, gen mangr Tengra Ltd 1996–; Freeman: City of London 1969, Worshipful Co of Clothworkers 1974; *Recreations* skiing, tennis; *Clubs* Queen's, Pembroke Tennis; *Style*— John McVittie, Esq; ✉ 72 Scarsdale Villas, London W8 6PP (☎ 0171 937 8926); Tengra Ltd, 9 Cheapside, London EC2V 6AD (☎ 07000 836472)

McWHINNIE, Prof William Robin; s of William Clark McWhinnie (d 1961), and Mary Gabrielle, *née* Birch; *b* 10 July 1937; *Educ* Chislehurst and Sidcup GS, QMC (BSc, PhD, DSc); *m* 19 Jan 1961, Vinitha Lilamani, da of Prof Joseph Lionel Christie Rodrigo, CMG (d 1972); 2 s (Dr Sean Lakshman William b 1964, Neil Rohan Clark b 1965); *Career* Aquinas Univ Coll Sri Lanka 1960–62, Queen Elizabeth Coll Univ of London 1962–67; Aston Univ: reader 1967–73, prof 1973–, pro vice chllr 1974–76, dir of univ relations 1987–88; author of over 180 scientific papers; CChem FRSC, FRSA, CIChemE; *Recreations* the arts (especially opera); *Style*— Prof William McWhinnie; ✉ 22 Widney Manor Road, Solihull, West Midlands B92 3JQ (☎ 0121 359 3611 ext 4738); Head of Chemistry, Department of Chemical Engineering and Applied Chemistry, Aston University, Aston Triangle, Birmingham B4 7ET (☎ and fax 0121 359 4094, telex 336997 UNIAST G)

McWHIRTER, Prof John Graham; s of Francis David McWhirter (d 1982), of Newry, Co Down, and Elizabeth, *née* Martin (d 1984); *b* 28 March 1949; *Educ* Newry HS, Queen's Univ Belfast (Fndn scholar, BSc Maths, Purser research student, PhD); *m* 17 Aug 1973, Avesia Vivianne Wolfe; 1 da (Lindsey Joy b 17 Jan 1977), 1 s (Colin Francis b 13 Nov 1979); *Career* DRA Malvern: higher scientific offr 1973–77, sr scientific offr 1977–80, princ scientific offr 1980–86, sr princ scientific offr 1986–96, dep chief scientific offr and head Signal Processing Gp 1996–; visiting prof Electrical Engrg Dept Queen's Univ Belfast 1986–; chm and proceedings ed IMA Int Conf on Mathematics in Signal Processing 1988 and 1992, memb Cncl IMA 1996–, fndr memb Signal Processing Sub Gp IEE 1987–92, Euro Program chm Int Conf on Systolic Arrays 1989, memb IT Panel UK Technol Foresight Programme 1994, Euro Program chm Int Symposium on Computer Arithmetic IEEE 1995, memb EPSRC Peer Review Coll for IT (Communications) 1995–; author of over 100 research papers, inventor and co-inventor 27 UK, Euro, US and Canadian patents; CMath, FIMA 1988, FIEE 1994, FEng 1996; *Awards* Northern Ireland Info Technol Award Br Computer Soc (jtly with J V McCanny) 1987, J J Thomson Premium IEE (jtly) 1990, J J Thomson Medal IEE (for research on systolic arrays) 1994; *Recreations* swimming for exercise, building and flying radio controlled model gliders; *Clubs* Malvern Soaring Association; *Style*— Prof John McWhirter, FEng; ✉ Defence Research Agency, St Andrew's Road, Malvern, Worcs WR14 3PS (☎ 01684 895384, fax 01684 896502, e-mail mcwhirter@signal.dra.hmg.gb)

McWHIRTER, Norris Dewar; CBE (1980); s of William McWhirter; er twin brother of Ross McWhirter (killed 1975, co-fndr and ed of Guinness Book of Records); *b* 12 Aug 1925; *Educ* Marlborough, Trinity Coll Oxford (MA); *m* 1, 1957, Carole (d 1987), da of George Eckert; 1 s, 1 da; m 2, 1991, Tessa Mary, da of late Joseph D Pocock; *Career* former sports corr (athletics Scotland) Observer and Star; BBC Olympic commentator: radio 1952–56, TV 1960–72; memb Sports Cncl 1970–74; dir Guinness Publishing Ltd 1954–96 (md 1954–76), co-fndr and ed Guinness Book of Records 1954–86; co-presenter: Record Breakers (with late Roy Castle) BBC 1972–94, Guinness Hall of Fame (with David Frost) 1986–; dir: McWhirter Twins Ltd, Gieves plc 1972–95; chm: Freedom Assoc 1983–, Referendum First Campaign 1991–; tstee Police Convalescent and Rehabilitation Tst; chm: Hampden Trust, Wiltshire Branch RNLI, Ross McWhirter Fndn; pres Nat Union of Track Statisticians; Parly candidate (C) Orpington 1964 and 1966; *Books* Guinness Book of Records (380 edns in 38 languages, 81 million sales), Dunlop Book of Facts (1964–73), Guinness Book of Answers, Ross - Story of a Shared Life; *Recreations* family tennis, hunting in libraries, watching athletics and rugby; *Clubs* Carlton, Achilles, Vincent's (Oxford); *Style*— Norris McWhirter, Esq, CBE; ✉ c/o Guinness Publishing Ltd, 33 London Rd, Enfield, Middlesex EN2 6DJ (☎ 0181 367 4567)

McWILLIAM, Jillian; MBE (1988); da of Herbert McWilliam, of Preston, Lancs, and Mabel Harwood, *née* Harrison; *b* 17 Nov 1946; *Educ* Ashton-on-Ribble Secdy Sch, Elizabeth Gaskell Coll (DipEd); *m* 28 Sept 1979, Geoffrey Michael Lee, s of Percy John Lee (d 1977), of Flamstead, Herts; *Career* mktg dir Bejam 1987–88, head corp affrs Iceland Frozen Foods plc 1989–, currently broadcaster; memb Inst Home Economics; *Books* 7 cookery books on freezing and microwave cooking; *Recreations* cooking, reading, gardening; *Style*— Miss Jillian McWilliam, MBE; ✉ Adelaide Cottage, Common Road, Studham, nr Dunstable, Beds (☎ 01582 873214); Iceland Group plc, Second Avenue, Deeside Industrial Park, Deeside, Clwyd CH5 2NW (☎ 01244 830100, fax 01244 814531)

McWILLIAM, John David; MP (Lab) Blaydon (majority 13,343); s of Alexander McWilliam, and Josephine McWilliam; *b* 16 May 1941; *Educ* Leith Acad, Heriot-Watt Univ, Napier Coll of Science and Technol; *m* 1965, Lesley Mary Catling; 2 da; *Career* engr Post Office, treas City of Edinburgh 1973–74, cmmr Local Authy Accounts in Scotland 1974–78; MP (Lab) Blaydon 1979–; memb: Bd of Scottish Cncl for Technical Educn 1973–80, Speaker's Panel of Chairmen 1987–; vice chm: Pitcom 1987–, Space Ctee 1988–; *Style*— John McWilliam, Esq, MP; ✉ House of Commons, London SW1A 0AA

McWILLIAM, Sir Michael Douglas; KCMG (1996); s of Douglas McWilliam (d 1969), of Oakridge Lynch, Glos, and Margaret, *née* Leach (d 1992); *b* 21 June 1933; *Educ* Cheltenham Coll, Oriel Coll Oxford (BA), Nuffield Coll Oxford (MA, BLitt); *m* 1960, Ruth, da of Dr Friedrich Arnstein; 2 s (Robert b 1962, Martin b 1964); *Career* Treasy Kenya 1958–62, Samuel Montagu & Co 1962–66; The Standard Bank (subseq Standard Chartered Bank): joined 1966, a gen mangr 1973, gp md 1983–88; dir Sch of Oriental and African Studies Univ of London 1989–96; chm Superannuation Arrangements for Univ of London 1990–, memb Bd Commonwealth Devpt Corp 1990–, chm Royal African Soc 1996– (memb Cncl 1979–91, vice pres 1991–96), chm Royal Commonwealth Soc 1996– (dep chm 1982–91); dir: Shanghai Fund 1992–, Bangladesh Fund 1994–, Simba Fund 1995–; pres Cheltenham Coll Cncl 1988–92 (memb 1977–92); *Clubs* Commonwealth Trust; *Style*— Sir Michael McWilliam, KCMG; ✉ 82 Portland Place, Apartment W, London W1N 3DH (☎ 0171 636 3186)

McWILLIAMS, Dr Donald Michael; s of Owen John (d 1974), of Dublin, and Josephine, *née* Murphy (d 1981); *b* 23 June 1929; *Educ* Blackrock Coll Dublin, Prior Park Coll Bath, Trinity Coll Dublin (MA, MB BCh, BAO, BA); *m* 12 Aug 1956 (m dis 1976), (Josephine) Valerie Mary, da of Ronald Shepherd, OBE; 2 s (Michael Owen b 1957, (Ronald) Nigel b 1957), 1 da (Wendy Jane b 1958); m 2, 15 June 1978, Anne Norah, *née* Oldershaw; *Career* conslt anaesthetist Royal Berkshire Hosp 1961– (sr registrar 1959–61); chm: Social Serv Berkshire CC, E Berkshire AHA 1982–90; memb Assoc of

Anaesthetists; FFARCS; *Recreations* ornithology, porcelain, music; *Clubs* Royal St George Yacht, Phyllis Court; *Style—* Dr Donald McWilliams

McWILLIAMS, Sir Francis; GBE (1992); s of J J McWilliams, of Edinburgh, and Mary, *née* McSherry; *b* 8 Feb 1926; *Educ* Holy Cross Acad Edinburgh (higher leaving certificate), Univ of Edinburgh (BSc); *m*, Winifred, *née* Segger; 2 s (D F b 24 Nov 1951, Michael b 25 July 1955); *Career* engr various Local Authys and Contractors 1945–53, town engr Petaling Jaya Devpt Corp Malaysia 1954–64, consulting civil and structural engr F McWilliams and Assocs Kuala Lumpur 1964–76, student Inns of Court Sch of Law 1976–78, called to the Bar Lincoln's Inn 1978–79, int arbitrator 1979–, bencher Lincoln's Inn; pres: Instn of Incorporated Exec Engrs 1994–, British/Southern Slav States Law Soc; vice pres British/Malaysian Soc; master Worshipful Co of Arbitrators 1984–85, sheriff City of London 1988–89, master of the Worshipful Co of Engineers 1990–91, dep lt City of London 1992, Lord Mayor of London 1992–93, Master of the Worshipful Co of Loriners 1995–96, Liveryman Worshipful Co of Plaisterers; chm Centre for Economic and Business Res, vice chm Trustees of the Fndn for Manufacturing and Indust; memb: Hon Co of Edinburgh Golfers, Panel of Arbitrators (Kuala Lumpur, Cairo, Hong Kong, British Columbia), Bd East of Scotland Water; dir HSBC (Malaysia); Hon DCL City Univ 1992, Hon DEng Univ of Kingston 1993, Dr (hc) Univ of Edinburgh 1994; Hon FICE 1993 (memb Panel of Arbitrators), FCIArb, FEng 1991, FCGI; Pingat Jasa Kebaktian Serv Medal Malaysia 1964, Dato' Seri Selera Order of the Royal Datos Selangor Malaysia 1973, Order du Merite of Senegal, Order of Independence (class III) UAE, Grande Oficial da Ordem do Infante Dom Henrique of Portugual, KStJ, KSG; *Recreations* golf, skiing; *Clubs* Royal Selangor, City Livery; *Style—* Sir Francis McWilliams, GBE, FEng; ✉ 85 North Road, Hythe, Kent (☎ 01303 216800)

MADDEN, Anne; *Educ* Chelsea Sch of Art; *m* Louis le Brocquy; 2 s; *Career* artist; solo exhibitions: Leicester Galleries London 1959, 1961 and 1967, Dawson Gallery Dublin 1960, 1964, 1968, 1970 and 1974, New Gallery Belfast 1964, New Art Centre 1970, 1972, 1974, 1978 and 1990, Oxford Gallery Oxford 1970, Gimpel Weitzenhoffer Gallery NY 1970, Demarco Gallery Edinburgh 1971, Ulster Museum Belfast 1974, Galerie Darthea Speyer Paris 1976 and 1979, Taylor Galleries Dublin 1979, 1982 and 1987, The Arts Cncl of NI Belfast 1979, Galerie Le Dessin Paris 1978 and 1980, Fondation Maeght Saint-Paul France 1983, The Bank of Ireland Dublin 1984, Wexford Arts Centre Ireland 1984, Galerie Maeght Barcelona 1985, Galerie Joachim Becker Cannes 1985, Armstrong Gallery NY 1986, Galerie Jeanne Bucher Paris 1989, The Kerlin Gallery Dublin 1990 and 1992, New Art Centre London 1990, R H A Gallagher Gallery Dublin 1991, Crawford Municipal Gallery Cork 1992, Galerie Sapone 1993; gp exhibitions: The Mirror and the Square (Burlington Galleries London) 1951, The Irish Exhibition of Living Art (Dublin) 1952, Art '65 (American Express Pavilion NY World Fair) 1965, Quatrième Biennale de Paris (representing Ireland) 1965, Modern Irish Painters (CIE Ulster Museum Belfast) 1966, Modern Irish Painting (Helsinki, Gothenburg, Norrköping, Stockholm) 1969, An Oireachtas (Dublin) 1970 and 1988, The 8th International Biennial Exhibition of Prints (Tokyo) 1973, Irish Directions (touring) 1974–75, ICA (Boston Mass) 1974–75, Salon de Montrouge (Paris) 1982, ROSC 84 (Dublin) 1984, CNAC (Nice) 1985, A Propos de Dessin (Galerie Adrian Maeght Paris) 1987, Prestige du Fonds Regional d'Art Contemporain (Provence France) 1989, Modern Masters (Musée Jacquemart André Paris) 1989, The Nat Self Portrait Collection (Crawford Municipal Art Gallery Cork and Nat Gallery Dublin) 1990, Les Abstractions Autour des Années 1970–80, Museum of Modern Art and Contemporary Art Nice 1990; public collections possessing work incl: Contemporary Arts Society London, The Gulbenkian Fndn Portugal, The Arts Council of Ireland, The Arts Council of NI, The Arts Council of GB, The Hugh Lane Municipal Gallery of Modern Art Dublin, The J H Hirshhorn Museum and Sculpture Garden Washington D C, Contemporary Irish Arts Society, Musée d'Art Moderne de la Ville de Paris, La Fondation Maeght France, Musée Picasso Antibes, Musée d'Art Moderne et d'Art Contemporain; *Style—* Ms Anne Madden; ✉ c/o New Art Centre, 41 Sloane Street, London SW1X 9LU

MADDEN, Adm Sir Charles Edward; 2 Bt (UK 1919), of Kells, Co Kilkenny; GCB (1965); s of Adm of the Fleet Sir Charles Edward Madden, 1 Bt, GCB, OM, GCVO, KCMG (d 1935), and Constance Winifred (d 1964), yst da of Sir Charles Cayzer, 1 Bt, of Gartmore; *b* 15 June 1906; *m* 1942, Olive (d 1989), da of late George Winchester Robins, of Caldy, Cheshire; 1 da (Roseann (Mrs John R Beddington) b 1945); *Heir* n, Peter John Madden b 1942; *Career* joined RN 1920, WWII served HMS Warspite (despatches) and HMS Emperor (despatches); chief of Naval Staff NZ 1953–55, naval ADC to HM The Queen 1955, C-in-C Plymouth 1959–62, Adm 1961, C-in-C Home Fleet and Eastern Atlantic 1963–65, ret 1965; tstee Nat Maritime Museum 1968 (chm 1972–77), chm Royal Nat Mission to Deep Sea Fishermen 1971–81, chm Standing Cncl of the Baronetage 1975–77; Vice Lord Lt (Gtr London) 1969–82; *Clubs* Arts; *Style—* Adm Sir Charles Madden, Bt, GCB; ✉ 21 Eldon Rd, London W8 (☎ 0171 937 6700)

MADDEN, Maxwell Francis (Max); MP (Lab) Bradford West (majority 9,502); s of George Francis Leonard Madden, and Rene Frances Madden; *b* 29 Oct 1941; *Educ* Lascelles Secdy Mod Sch, Pinner GS; *m* 1972, Sheelagh Teresa Catherine, *née* Howard; *Career* journalist: E Essex Gazette, Tribune, Sun, Scotsman; Br Gas Corpn press and info offr; MP (Lab): Sowerby Feb 1974–79, Bradford W 1983–; dir of publicity Lab Pty 1979–83, oppn front bench spokesman on health and social security 1983–84; *Recreations* fishing; *Style—* Max Madden, Esq, MP; ✉ House of Commons, London SW1A 0AA

MADDEN, Michael; s of John Joseph Madden (d 1978), and Mary Ann, *née* Donnelly (d 1993); *b* 14 Jan 1937; *Educ* St Illtyds Coll Cardiff Wales, London Sch of Economics (BSc); *m* 27 Feb 1960, Patricia Margaret, da of Charles Gaspa, of Cliftonville, Kent; 2 s (Simon Jude b 1960, Stephen Paul b 1964), 1 da (Alison Maria b 1962); *Career* asst gen mangr Moscow Narodny Bank Ltd 1966–68 (economic advsr 1959–66), gen mangr First National Finance Corporation Ltd 1968–70, md Exim Credit Management Consultants Ltd 1971–76, exec dir Standard Chartered Merchant Bank Ltd 1977–86, dir Standard Chartered Merchant Bank Holdings 1984–86, md Standard Chartered Merchant Bank Ltd 1986, chief exec Standard Chartered Export Finance Ltd 1987–88, gen mangr Standard Chartered Bank 1987–88; currently non-exec dep chm and conslt (Int Ops) Afribank Nigeria plc; non-resident conslt: IBRD (World Bank) Washington, FAO (Investmt Centre) Rome, International Trade Centre, UNCTAD Geneva; FRSA; *Recreations* rugby football, gardening, writing; *Clubs* Reform, Overseas Bankers'; *Style—* Michael Madden, Esq; ✉ 16 Wolsey Rd, Moor Park, Herts HA6 2HW (☎ 01923 826767)

MADDEN, Nicholas Paul; s of Dr (Cyril) Paul Madden (d 1958), of Romford, Essex, and Barbara Joan, *née* Sykes; *b* 12 June 1950; *Educ* Haileybury, Brasenose Coll Oxford (MA, BM BCh); *m* Su-Anna Margaret, *née* Boddy; 1 s (Christopher Paul b 6 Feb 1987), 1 da (Katherine Anna b 15 Sept 1988); *Career* house surgn Bart's and house physician Rochford Gen Hosp 1975, SHO A/E Dept Bart's and resident med offr Wellington Hosp 1976, temporary lectr in anatomy Bart's Med Coll 1977–78, SHO in paediatric surgery Great Ormond Street Hosp for Sick Children 1978, SHO in gen and oncological surgery Royal Marsden Hosp 1978–79, SHO in gen surgery Stoke Mandeville Hosp 1979–80, registrar in gen surgery and urology Luton and Dunstable Hosp 1980–82, registrar in paediatric surgery and urology Alder Hey Children's Hosp Liverpool 1982–85, res fell in paediatric surgery Inst of Child Health 1985–87, locum consIt paediatric surgn Leeds General Infirmary and St James's Univ Hosp Leeds 1990–91 (sr registrar in paediatric surgery 1987–91), consIt paediatric surgn: Chelsea and Westminster Hosp 1991–, St Mary's Hosp 1992–; memb: RSM 1991, British Assoc of Paediatric Surgns 1992 (prize 1987); FRCS 1980; author of numerous pubns in med jls; *Recreations* skiing, swimming, watching cricket; *Style—* Nicholas Madden, Esq; ✉ 15 Bridgefield Road, Cheam, Surrey SM1 2DG (☎ 0181 661 7528); Department of Paediatric Surgery, Chelsea and Westminster Hospital, Fulham Road, London SW10 9NH (☎ 0181 746 8696, fax 0181 746 8644)

MADDICOTT, Dr John Robert Lewendon; s of Robert Maddicott (d 1990), and Barbara, *née* Lewendon (d 1996); *b* 22 July 1943; *Educ* Cheltenham GS, King Edward's Sch Bath, Worcester Coll Oxford (MA, DPhil); *m* 1965, Hilary, da of Thomas Owen; 2 da (Philippa b 1968, Sarah b 1972); *Career* asst lectr Univ of Manchester 1967–69; Exeter Coll Oxford: fell and tutor in modern history 1969–, sub-rector 1988–90; visiting prof Univ of South carolina 1983; jt ed English Historical Review 1990–; FRHistS, FSA, FBA 1996; *Books* Thomas of Lancaster, 1307–1322 (1972), The English Peasantry and the Demands of the Crown, 1294–1341 (1975), Law and Lordship: Royal Justices as Retainers in Thirteenth and Fourteenth Century England (1978), Simon de Montfort (1994); *Recreations* hill-walking, book-collecting, poetry; *Style—* Dr John Maddicott, FSA, FBA; ✉ Exeter College, Oxford OX1 3DP (☎ 01865 279621, fax 01865 279630)

MADDISON, Prof Peter John; s of John Maddison, of London, and Renée, *née* Le Mesurier; *b* 12 Dec 1945; *Educ* St Albans Sch, Pembroke Coll Cambridge, St Bartholomew's Med Sch (MA, MB BChir, MD); *m* 17 Feb 1968, Merle Chadburn, da of late Denby Bamford, CBE, of Little Barrow, Cheshire; 1 s (Christopher); *Career* fell in rheumatology and immunology Stake Univ of New York at Buffalo 1974–77, asst prof of med 1977–79, conslt rheumatologist Royal Nat Hosp for Rheumatic Diseases Bath 1979–88; Univ of Bath: prof of bone and joint med 1988–96, dean Sch of Postgraduate Med 1989–95; chm and res dir Bath Inst of Rheumatic Diseases until 1996, res and educn dir Royal Nat Hosp for Rheumatic Diseases 1991–92; conslt rheumatologist Gwynedd Hosps Tst 1996–; Greenberg scholar Oklahoma Medical Res Fndn USA 1992–93, Heberden Roundsman British Soc for Rheumatology 1994; author of over 200 scientific articles, reviews and chapters; med sec of the Arthritis and Rheumatism Cncl 1990–93, chm Wessex R & D Grants Ctee 1993–96, memb Advsy Bd Nat Osteoporosis Soc; FRCP 1986, memb British Soc of Rheumatology; *Books* Rheumatological Medicine (with P A Dieppe, M Doherty and D G Macfarlane, 1985), The Skin In Rheumatic Diseases (with C L Lovell and G Campion, 1989), Rheumatology Examination and Injection Techniques (with M Doherty, J D Perry, C W Hutton and B L Hazelman, 1992), Oxford Textbook of Rheumatology (ed, with D A Isenberg, P Woo and D N Glass, 1993); *Recreations* cooking, music, golf; *Style—* Prof Peter Maddison; ✉ Bryn Selar, Glan Conwy, Colwyn Bay LL28 5SL (☎ 01492 572126); Ysbyty Gwynedd, Bangor, Gwynedd LL57 2PW (☎ 01248 384384)

MADDISON, Roger Robson; s of Ralph Robson Maddison (d 1943), and Ethel Daisy, *née* Smith; *b* 15 July 1929; *Educ* Dulwich Coll, Univ of Cambridge (MA); *m* 1, 1954 (m dis 1975), Christine Elizabeth, *née* Fulljames; 2 s (Patrick James Robson b 1959, Timothy Paul Robson b 1963), 1 da (Vivien Mary b 1956); m 2, Sara Caroline, da of Arthur Geoffrey Howland-Jackson, MBE; *Career* slr; sr ptnr Knapp-Fishers (Westminster) 1980–83, sr ptnr Baldocks (Guildford) 1984–90; memb Law Soc; *Recreations* golf, tennis, music, gardening; *Clubs* Worplesdon Golf; *Style—* Roger Maddison, Esq; ✉ 59 Quarry St, Guildford, Surrey (☎ 01483 573 303)

MADDOCK, Diana; MP (Lib Dem) Christchurch (majority 16,427); *b* 19 May 1945; *Educ* Brockenhurst GS, Shenstone Teacher Trg Coll; *Career* ESL teacher Extra Mural Dept Stockholm Univ 1969–72; MP (Lib Dem) Christchurch 1993–; Lib Dem spokesperson on: housing, the family and women's issues; vice chm All Pty Parly: Warm Houses Gp, Homelessness and Housing Need Gp, Building Socs Gp; *Recreations* travel, music and reading; *Clubs* National Liberal; *Style—* Ms Diana Maddock, MP; ✉ House of Commons, London SW1A 0AA (☎ 0171 219 3000)

MADDOCKS, His Hon Judge; Bertram Catterall; s of His Hon George Maddocks (d 1980), of Southport, Lancs, and (Harriet) Mary Louisa, *née* Day; *b* 7 July 1932; *Educ* Rugby, Trinty Hall Cambridge (scholar, MA Law); *m* 13 June 1964, Angela Vergette, da of Michael Leetham Forster, of Aughton; 2 s (Jeremy Christopher Catterall b 8 Dec 1965, Jolyon Simon Napoleon (Jo) b 4 Jan 1989), 1 da (Lucinda Jane Vergette (Cindy) b 8 Aug 1987); *Career* Nat Serv 2 Lt RA 1951; called to the Bar Middle Temple 1956 (Harmsworth scholar), pt/t chm VAT Tbnls 1977–90, recorder 1983–90, circuit judge (Northern Circuit) 1990–; memb Lincoln's Inn; Capt Duke of Lancaster's Own Yeomanry (TA) 1958–67; *Recreations* real tennis, lawn tennis, skiing, bridge; *Clubs* Queens, Manchester Tennis & Racquet, Northern Counties (Newcastle upon Tyne); *Style—* His Hon Judge Maddocks; ✉ Moor Hall Farm, Prescot Road, Aughton, Lancashire L39 6RT

MADDOCKS, Fiona Hamilton; da of William Hunter Maddocks, and Dorothy Christina, *née* Hill; *b* 1 June 1955; *Educ* Blackheath HS London, Royal Coll of Music, Newnham Coll Cambridge (MA); *m* 1, 1989 (m dis), Robert Cooper; 2 da; m 2, 1995, Tom Phillips, RA, *qv*; *Career* teacher of Eng lit Istituto Orsoline Cortina D'Ampezzo Italy 1978, art publisher Medici Soc 1979, news trainee rising to sr prodr LBC 1980–82, launch ed Comment (Channel 4) 1982, regular contrib to The Times 1983–86, asst commissioning ed Music (Channel 4) 1985, journalist, music ed and feature writer Independent 1986–91, fndr ed BBC Music Magazine 1992–; freelance writer various pubns, TV and radio; winner BP Arts Journalism Press Award 1990, various awards for BBC Music Magazine; assoc Newnham Coll 1985–; *Style—* Miss Fiona Maddocks; ✉ c/o BBC Worldwide, 80 Wood Lane, London W12 0TT

MADDOCKS, Sir Kenneth Phipson; KCMG (1958, CMG 1956), KCVO (1963); s of Arthur P Maddocks (d 1957); *b* 8 Feb 1907; *Educ* Bromsgrove Sch, Wadham Coll Oxford; *m* 1, 1951, Elnor Radcliffe (d 1976), da of Sir E John Russell, OBE, FRS (d 1965); m 2, 1980, Patricia Josephine, *née* Hare Duke, wid of Sir George Mooring, KCMG; *Career* HMOCS; civil sec Northern Region Nigeria 1955–57, dep govr 1957–58, actg govr Northern Region Nigeria 1956 and 1957, govr and C-in-C Fiji 1958–63, dir and sec East Africa and Mauritius Assoc 1964–69; KStJ; *Recreations* gardening; *Clubs* Cwlth Tst; *Style—* Sir Kenneth Maddocks, KCMG, KCVO; ✉ 11 Lee Rd, Aldeburgh, Suffolk IP15 5HG (☎ 01728 453443)

MADDOCKS, Rt Rev Morris Henry St John; s of Rev Canon Morris Arthur Maddocks (d 1953), and Gladys Mabel, *née* Sharpe; *b* 28 April 1928; *Educ* St John's Sch Leatherhead, Trinity Coll Cambridge, Chichester Theol Coll; *m* 1955, Anne, da of late William Oliver Miles; *Career* Nat Serv 2 Lt RASC; curate: St Peter's Ealing 1954–55, St Andrew's Uxbridge 1955–58; vicar: Weaverthorpe Helperthorpe and Luttons Ambo 1958–61, St Martin-on-the-Hill Scarborough 1961–71; suffragan bishop of Selby 1972–83; hon asst bishop: Diocese of Bath and Wells 1983–87, Diocese of Chichester 1987–; prebendary of Bracklesham in Chichester Cathedral 1992–; chm of Churches Cncl for Health and Healing 1982–85 (joint chm 1975–82), advsr to the Archbishops of Canterbury and York for the Miny of Health and Healing 1983–95; joint fndr (with wife) of Acorn Christian Healing Tst 1983; *Books* The Christian Healing Ministry (1981), The Christian Adventure (1983), Journey to Wholeness (1986), A Healing House of Prayer (1987), Twenty Questions About Healing (1988), The Vision of Dorothy Kerin (1991); *Recreations* walking, gardening, music; *Clubs* Army and Navy; *Style—* The Rt Rev Morris Maddocks; ✉ 3 The Chantry, Cathedral Close, Chichester, West Sussex PO19 1PZ (☎ 01243 788888)

MADDOCKS, Dr Peter Dobell; s of Thomas Frederick Maddocks (d 1976), and Enid Margaret Dobell Newton, *née* Colson; *b* 16 Feb 1935; *Educ* Berkhamstead Sch, Univ of

London, Middlesex Hosp Med Sch (MB, BS, MRCP, DPM, FRCPsych); *m* 6 June 1959, Dr (Williamina Thelma) Astrid, da of Dr William Frederick Twining McMath; 4 s (Mark b 1961, Jeremy b 1962, William b 1965, Giles b 1967); *Career* sr house offr St Luke's Woodside Hosp 1960, casualty med offr Middlesex Hosp 1961, med registrar Sr Helier Hosp Carshalton 1962–64, sr registrar St Thomas' Hosp 1966–69, currently conslt psychiatrist Heatherwood and Wexham Park NHS Tst; memb: Slough Dist Assoc for Mental Health, Maidenhead Assoc for Mental Health; RCPsych: memb Cncl 1993–, chm Chiltern & Thames Valley Div 1995–; *Recreations* travel, windsurfing; *Style*— Dr Peter Maddocks; ✉ 47 Alma Rd, Windsor, Berks (☎ 01753 851551); Department of Psychiatry, Wexham Park Hospital, Slough, Berkshire (☎ 01753 634212)

MADDOX, Bronwen Maria; da of John R Maddox, and Brenda, *née* Murphy; *b* 7 May 1963; *Educ* St Paul's Girls' Sch London, Westminster, St John's Coll Oxford (BA); *Career* venture capital analyst Charterhouse Bank 1985–86, Bd dir Kleinwort Benson Securities and head Media Res Team 1986–91; Financial Times: reporter 1991–, ldr writer 1994–, ed People/Observer column 1995–; Br Press Award for Maxwell teams investigation; *Style*— Ms Bronwen Maddox; ✉ Financial Times, One Southwark Bridge, London SE1 9HL (☎ 0171 873 4073)

MADDOX, Sir John Royden; kt (1995); s of A J Maddox, of Swansea, and M E Maddox; *b* 27 Nov 1925; *Educ* Gowerton Boys Co Sch, ChCh Oxford, King's Coll London; *m* 1, Nancy Fanning (d 1960); 1 s, 1 da; m 2, 1960, Brenda Power, *née* Murphy; 1 s, 1 da; *Career* writer and bdcaster; asst lectr then lectr theoretical physics Univ of Manchester 1949–55, sci corr The Guardian 1955–64, affiliate Rockfeller Inst NY 1962–63, asst dir Nuffield Fndn and co-ordinator Nuffield Fndn sci teaching project 1964–66, md Macmillan Jls Ltd 1970–72, dir Macmillan & Co Ltd 1968–73, chm Maddox Ltd 1972–74, dir Nuffield Fndn 1975–80; ed Nature 1966–73 and 1980–95; memb: Royal Cmmn on Environmental Pollution 1976–78, Genetic Manipulation Advsy Gp 1976–80, Br Library Advsy Cncl 1976–81, Cncl on Int Devpt 1977–79; chm Cncl Queen Elizabeth Coll 1980–85, memb Cncl King's Coll London 1985–, memb Crickadarn and Gwendwr CC (Powys) 1991–; *Books* The Spread of Nuclear Weapons (with Leonard Beaton, 1962), Revolution in Biology (1964), The Doomsday Syndrome (1972), Beyond The Energy Crisis (1975); *Clubs* Athenaeum; *Style*— Sir John Maddox; ✉ 9 Pitt St, London W8 4NX (☎ 0171 937 8981)

MADDOX, Ronald Arthur; s of Harold George Maddox, and Winifred Maddox; *b* 5 Oct 1930; *Educ* Herts Coll of Art and Design, London Coll of Printing and Graphic Art; *m* 1958, Camilla Farrin (d 1995); 2 s; *Career* Nat Serv Air Miny Design Unit RAF 1949–51; graphic artist and art dir various advtg agencies London 1951–61, in private practice as artist, illustrator and conslt designer 1962– (cmmnd by nat and multinational cos, govt depts, local authys, TV and publishers); designer Br postage stamps and philatelic material 1972–; stamp issues designed incl: Village Churches, Historic Buildings, Urban Renewal, Industrial Archaeology; designer Landscape of Britain series Royal Mail aerogrammes, work widely reproduced as illustrations for books, calendars, prints and cards; exhibitions incl: Mall Galleries, Royal Acad, Bankside Galleries; works in the collections of: HM Queen Elizabeth the Queen Mother, 10 Downing St, Sultanate of Oman, Nat Tst, PO, DOE, Barclays Bank, BP, Shell, John Laing, Mobil Oil; winner Prix de l'Art Philatelique 1987, Winsor and Newton RI awards 1981 and 1991, Rowland Hilder RI Award 1996 (for outstanding landscape painting); memb Mgmnt Bd Fedn of Br Artists; Royal Inst of Painters in Water Colours: memb 1959, vice pres 1979, pres 1989–; hon memb: Pastel Soc, Soc of Architect Artists, Fedn of Canadian Artists, United Soc of Artists, Soc of Graphic Artists, Campine Assoc of Watercolours Belgium; Hon RWS 1990, FCSD, FSAI, FRSA; *Recreations* compulsive drawing, walking, cycling, gardening; *Style*— Ronald Maddox, Esq; ✉ Herons, 21 New Rd, Digswell, Welwyn, Herts AL6 0AQ (☎ 01438 714884)

MADDRELL, Geoffrey Keggen; s of Capt Geoffrey Douglas Maddrell (d 1975), of Port Erin, IOM, and Barbara Mary Maddrell; *b* 18 July 1936; *Educ* King William's Coll Isle of Man, Corpus Christi Coll Cambridge (MA), Columbia Univ New York (MBA); *m* 12 Oct 1964, Winifred Mary Daniel, da of Frank Dowell Jones (d 1984), of St Asaph, Clwyd; 2 s (Paul b 1965, Michael b 1971), 1 da (Siân b 1966); *Career* Lt Parachute Regiment 1955–57; Shell Int Petroleum 1960–69; dir Bowater Corp 1978–86, chief exec Tootal Group plc 1986–91; chm: ProShare 1994– (chief exec 1991–94), Glenmorangie plc, LDV Ltd, Westbury plc, Ivory and Sime ISIS Trust plc, Manx and Overseas plc; dir Transport Development Group plc; pt/t Civil Service cmmr 1992–96; govr UMIST; *Recreations* running, golf; *Clubs* Serpentine Running, Rowany Golf; *Style*— Geoffrey Maddrell, Esq; ✉ 28 Sussex St, London SW1V 4RL

MADDRELL, (Alan) Lester; s of Capt Stanley Taubman Maddrell, of Colby, IOM, and Sylvia, *née* Leece; *b* 20 Feb 1944; *Educ* King William's Coll IOM; *m* 26 March 1966, Diana Mary, da of Arthur Fallows Tate (d 1984), of Douglas, IOM; 2 s (Richard b 1975, Alan b 1976), 2 da (Tania b 1974 (decd), Stephanie b 1987); *Career* admitted slr 1971; dep co prosecuting slr Gloucestershire 1977–80, HM coroner for the Cheltenham dist of Gloucestershire 1988–, dep traffic cmmr 1996–; *Recreations* family; *Style*— Lester Maddrell, Esq; ✉ 70 Bournside Rd, Cheltenham GL51 5AH; Lester Maddrell & Co, 109 Promenade, Cheltenham GL50 1NW (☎ 01242 514000, fax 01242 226575)

MADDRELL, Dr Simon Hugh Piper; s of Hugh Edmund Fisher Maddrell (d 1969), farmer, and Barbara Agnes Mary, *née* Chamberlin (d 1996), photographer; *b* 11 Dec 1937; *Educ* Peter Symonds' Sch Winchester, St Catharine's Coll Cambridge (scholar, MA, PhD, ScD); *m* 1, Anna, *née* Myers; 1 da (Penelope Jane b 21 Feb 1962), 3 s (Robin Charles Fisher b 17 Jan 1965, Joseph Timothy b 19 June 1968, Samuel James b 2 Jan 1971); m 2, Katherine Mona, *née* Mapes; *Career* Nat Res Cncl of Canada postdoctoral res fell Dalhousie Univ Halifax Canada, SRC/NATO postdoctorate res fell Dept of Zoology Cambridge 1964–65, open (prize) res fell Gonville & Caius Coll Cambridge 1964–68, currently investments manager The Company of Biologists Ltd (fin sec 1965–), res assoc Univ of Mass Amherst 1967, fell and coll lectr Gonville & Caius Coll Cambridge 1968–, sr scientific offr ARC Unit of Invertebrate Chemistry & Physiology Dept of Zoology Cambridge 1972, res assoc Dept of Zoology Univ of Br Columbia Vancouver 1974 and 1975, princ scientific offr ARC Unit of Invertebrate Chemistry & Physiology Dept of Zoology Cambridge 1972–78, sr princ scientific offr (individual merit promotion) AFRC Unit of Insect Neurophysiology and Pharmacology Dept of Zoology Cambridge 1978–90, hon reader in comparative physiology Univ of Cambridge 1990–; Centenary Yr Scientific Medal Zoological Soc of London 1976; FRS 1981; *Recreations* golf, gardening, art and architecture, wine, travel, photography; *Style*— Dr Simon Maddrell, FRS; ✉ The Company of Biologists Ltd, Department of Zoology, Downing Street, Cambridge CB2 3EJ (fax 01223 353980, e-mail SHPM100@HERMES.CAM.AC.UK)

MADEL, Sir (William) David; kt (1994), MP (C) Bedfordshire South West (majority 21,273); s of William R Madel (d 1975), and Eileen Madel; *b* 6 Aug 1938; *Educ* Uppingham, Keble Coll Oxford (MA); *m* 1971, Susan Catherine, da of Lt Cdr Hon Peter Carew, RN (ret); *Career* former advertising exec; memb Bow Gp Cncl 1966–67; MP (C): Bedfordshire South 1970–83, Bedfordshire South West 1893–; PPS to jt Parly under secs of state for defence and to min of state for defence 1973–74, chm Cons Parly Educn Ctee 1983–85; *Style*— Sir David Madel, MP; ✉ 120 Pickford Rd, Markyate, Herts

MADEN, Prof (Barry) Edward Howorth; s of late Harold Maden, of Windermere, and Kathleen, *née* Cope; *b* 5 Nov 1935; *Educ* Uppingham, Trinity Hall Cambridge, King's Coll Hosp Med Sch (MA, MB BChir, PhD), Univ of Glasgow (DSc, 1992); *m* 1, 16 July 1960 (m dis 1989), Regina; 1 s (Christopher b 1961), 1 da (Jill b 1963); m 2, 22 Aug 1992, Sybil; *Career* res assoc Albert Einstein Med Coll NY 1967–69; Univ of Glasgow: lectr Dept of Biochemistry 1969–72, sr lectr 1972–76, reader 1976–83; visiting scientist Dept of Embryology Carnegie Inst of Washington Baltimore USA 1977–78, Johnston prof of biochemistry Univ of Liverpool 1983–, William Evans visiting fell Univ of Otago NZ 1990; tstee Drummond Tst for Nutrition, memb Biochemical Soc Awards Ctee, author of 80 scientific articles, reviews, chapters, incl contrib to: Journal of Molecular Biology, Biochemical Journal, Nature and Proceedings of the Royal Soc; FRSE 1978; *Books* contrib to: Cell Biology in Medicine (1972), Ribosomes (1974), Transmethylation (1978), Classic Rock (1978), The Cell Nucleus (vol 10, 1982), The Nucleolus (1983), Chromatography and Modification of Nucleosides (part b, 1989); *Recreations* mountaineering and hill-walking (completed Scottish Munros 1990); *Clubs* Alpine, Climbers', Scottish Mountaineering; *Style*— Prof Edward Maden, FRSE; ✉ 25 Gwydrin Road, Liverpool L18 3HA (☎ 0151 722 0290); University of Liverpool, School of Biological Sciences, Life Sciences Building, Liverpool L69 3BX (☎ 0151 794 4350, fax 0151 794 4349)

MADGWICK, Sandra Elizabeth; da of Kenneth Edward Madgwick, and Shirley Anne, *née* Cross; *b* 7 March 1963; *Educ* The Royal Ballet Sch; *Career* ballet dancer; *Performances incl* 80 birthday anniversary of Sir Frederick Ashton, Lise in La Fille Mal Gardée, Aurora in Petipa's The Sleeping Beauty, Swanhilda in Peter Wright's Coppelia, Vicky Hobson in David Bintley's Hobson's Choice, Girl in Sir Frederick Ashton's The Two Pigeons, Gerda in David Bintley's The Snow Queen, Sir Kenneth MacMillan's Quartet; *Style*— Miss Sandra Madgwick

MADGWICK, Timothy; s of Arthur William Madgwick, of Pembury, Kent, and Daisy May, *née* Jones (d 1990); *b* 31 May 1943; *Educ* Huntley's Secdy Sch for Boys Tunbridge Wells, Beckenham Sch of Art, Ravensbourne Coll of Art and Design, RCA; *m* 1965, Edwina Patricia, da of Air Cdre Victor A Hatcher; 1 s (Justin Lawrence b 1969), 1 da (Anna Frances b 1971); *Career* designer Robert Matthew Johnson-Marshall & Partners 1967–75 (sr designer/furniture designer working on projects for Univ of York, Asian Inst of Technol Thailand, Br Embassy Bangkok, Preston Guild Hall and Hillington Civil Centre 1973–75), in own practice Tim Madgwick Design (architectural, interior, landscape and furniture design consultancy/UK, Repub of Ireland and France) 1975–; projects incl: design of facilities for the disabled Enham/Papworth Industries 1985–87, design and construction of Intelligent House Cambridge 1988–90; winner N Herts Civic Award for Design Excellence 1978 and 1983; memb: Business Club Univ of Cambridge 1994–, Cambridge C of C and Indust 1994–; CSD: memb Cncl 1989–93, area chm 1988–92, regnl chm 1992–; MSIAD 1968; *Recreations* hill walking, furniture making, art working, travel; *Style*— Timothy Madgwick, Esq; ✉ Tim Madgwick Design; (☎ 01366 728062)

MADOC, Ruth Llewellyn (Mrs John Jackson); *b* 16 April 1943; *Educ* RADA; *m* John Jackson; 1 s (Rhys), 1 da (Lowri); *Career* actress; began career with Black and White Minstrel Show; numerous guest appearances for charity nationwide; *Television* incl: Gladys Pugh in Hi-De-Hi (BAFTA Award nomination), Hunters Walk, Lloyd George, The Morecambe and Wise Show, Blankety Blank, Give Us A Clue, Whose Baby, Tell the Truth, This is Your Life, Through the Keyhole, Oliver's Travels, Agatha Christie's Pale Horse (Zenith), The Famous Five, Royal Variety Shows (four appearances), presenter Songs of Praise; *Theatre* incl: Man of La Mancha (Piccadilly), Under Milk Wood, Irma in Irma La Douce, Letty in Something's Afoot, Mixed Feelings, Maria in Twelfth Night (Regent's Park Open Air), Bless the Bride (Sadler's Wells) 1988, Touch and Go (Opera House Jersey) 1988, Rose in Gypsy, Helen in A Taste of Honey (Grand Theatre Swansea), Find the Lady (Salisbury, Eastbourne and Jersey) 1990, guest appearance in Night of a Hundred Stars (London Palladium) 1990, Steel Magnolias (Leatherhead) 1992, Phantom of the Opera (Japan and Manila) 1992, Pickwick (tour) 1994–95, Madame Rowlands in The Dark Stranger (King's Head) 1995; pantomine work incl: various principal boy roles, Babes in the Wood 1987, Robinson Crusoe (Theatre Royal Plymouth) 1988, Fairy Fruit of The Forest (Swansea Grand); *Film* incl: Fiddler on the Roof, The Prince and the Pauper, Under Milk Wood; *Style*— Ms Ruth Madoc; ✉ 1 Euston Street, Huntingdon, Cambs PE18 6QR (☎ 01480 434728, fax 01480 450262)

MADOCKS, John Edward; CBE (1965, MBE 1956), DL (Notts 1978); s of Sidney George Robert Madocks (d 1935), of Lichfield, and Ada Jane, *née* Edwards (d 1936); *b* 14 March 1922; *Educ* King Edward VI Sch Lichfield, Univ of Birmingham (BA), Univ of London; *m* 1945, Jessica (Peta) Kinross, da of Andrew Davidson (d 1939); 1 s (Rodney John Davidson b 1952), 1 da (Susan Catherine b 1954); *Career* served WWII, Europe and ME, Maj Airborne Forces; perm sec HMOCS 1946–65; bursar Univ of Nottingham 1967–87; dir ATV Network Ltd 1979–81, chm East Midlands Bd Central Independent Television plc 1982–92; memb Regnl Bd BR (London Midland) 1979–90; memb: E Midlands Economic Planning Cncl 1975–79, Prince's Youth Business Tst, Nottingham Devpt Enterprise; tstee Djanogly City Tech Coll, govr Nottingham Girls' HS, chm Notts Economic Planning Forum 1980–82, nat chm Assoc of Br Chambers of Commerce 1980–82 (also vice pres), co rep Royal Jubilee Tsts 1976–86; pres: Nottinghamshire Hospice, East Midlands Quality Club; High Sheriff of Nottinghamshire 1988–89; *Recreations* books, arts, sport; *Style*— John Madocks, Esq, CBE, DL

MAEHLER, Prof Herwig Gustav Theodor; s of Ludwig Maehler (d 1945), and Lisa, *née* Meyer (d 1989); *b* 29 April 1935; *Educ* Katharineum GS Lübeck, Univ of Hamburg (PhD), Univ of Tübingen, Univ of Basel, Univ of Oxford (Br Cncl Scholar); *m* 1963, Margaret, da of Eric Anderson; 2 da (Alexandra b 17 Oct 1978, Olivia b 14 July 1980); *Career* research asst: Univ of Hamburg 1962–63, Hamburg Univ Library 1963–64; keeper of Greek papyri Egyptian Museum W Berlin 1964–79, habilitation Free Univ Berlin 1975, visiting research fell Inst of Advanced Studies in the Humanities Univ of Edinburgh 1977, prof of papyrology Univ Coll London 1981– (reader 1979–81); memb: Egypt Exploration Soc 1979–, Hellenic Soc 1980–; corresponding memb German Archaeological Inst 1979–; FBA 1986; *Books* Die Auffassung des Dichterberufs (1963), Die Handschriften der St Jacobi-Kirche Hamburg (1967), Urkunden römischer Zeit (1968), Bakchylides, Lieder und Fragmente (1968), Bacchylides, Carmina cum fragmentis (1970), Pindarus, Part I (1971, 8 edn 1987), Papyri aus Hermupolis (1974), Pindarus, Part II (1975, new edn 1989), Die Lieder des Bakchylides (2 vols, 1982), Greek Bookhands of the Early Byzantine Period (with G Cavallo, 1987); *Recreations* chamber music (viola), horse riding; *Style*— Prof Herwig Maehler, FBA; ✉ Department of Greek and Latin, University College London, Gower Street, London WC1E 6BT (☎ 0171 380 7490, fax 0171 209 2324)

MAGAN, George Morgan; s of Brig William Morgan Tilson Magan, CBE; *b* 14 Nov 1945; *Educ* Winchester; *m* 1972, Wendy Anne, da of Maj Patrick Chilton, MC; 2 s (Edward b 1975, Patrick b 1984), 1 da (Henrietta b 1977); *Career* merchant banker; tstee: Royal Opera House Covent Garden, London Philharmonic Orch; FCA; *Clubs* Royal Yacht Squadron, Turf, Boodle's, The Brook (NY), Kildare St and Univ (Dublin); *Style*— George Magan, Esq; ✉ 32 Queen Anne's Gate, London SW11 9AB (☎ 0171 233 1400, fax 0171 222 4978)

MAGEE, Bryan; s of Frederick Magee; *b* 12 April 1930; *Educ* Christ's Hosp, Lycée Hôche Versailles, Keble Coll Oxford (MA), Yale; *m* 1954 (m dis), Ingrid Söderlund; 1 da; *Career* writer, critic and broadcaster; formerly: columnist The Times, drama critic The Listener; music critic for numerous pubns 1959–; Parly candidate (Lab) Mid Beds 1959 and 1960, MP Leyton (Lab until 1982, Ind Lab 1982, SDP 1982–83); lectr in philosophy Balliol Coll Oxford 1970–71, visiting fell All Souls Coll Oxford 1973–74, hon sr fell in the history of ideas King's Coll London 1984–94, visiting prof King's Coll London 1994–, academic visitor LSE 1994–96; visiting fell: Wolfson Coll Oxford 1993–94 (visiting scholar 1991–93), New Coll Oxford 1995; memb Arts Cncl (chm Music Advsy Panel) 1993–94; memb Cncl: Critics' Circle 1975– (pres 1983–84), Ditchley Fndn 1982– (govr 1979–); judge: Evening Standard Opera Award 1973–84, Laurence Olivier Opera Award 1990–91 and 1993–95, Royal Philharmonic Soc Annual Opera Award 1991–97; pres Edinburgh Univ Philosophy Soc 1987–88; Silver Medal RTS 1978; fell: Queen Mary and Westfield Coll 1989 (QMC 1988), Royal Philharmonic Soc 1990; hon fell Keble Coll Oxford 1994; *Books* Crucifixion and Other Poems (1951), Go West Young Man (1958), To Live in Danger (1960), The New Radicalism (1962), The Democratic Revolution (1964), Towards 2000 (1965), One in Twenty (1966), The Television Interviewer (1966), Aspects of Wagner (1968 and revised, ed 1988), Modern British Philosophy (1971), Popper (1973), Facing Death (1977), Men of Ideas (1978), The Philosophy of Schopenhauer (1983, revised edn 1997), The Great Philosophers (1987), On Blindness (1995); *Recreations* music, theatre; *Clubs* Garrick, Savile; *Style*— Bryan Magee, Esq; ✉ 12 Falkland House, Marloes Rd, London W8 (☎ 0171 937 1210)

MAGEE, Christopher Douglas; s of Douglas David Magee, of Farnham, Surrey, and Eva Mary, *née* Pope; *b* 3 Nov 1945; *Educ* George Abbott Sch Guildford, Guildford Coll of Technol, Univ of Reading (OND, HND, MSc); *m* 4 May 1985, Carol Elizabeth, da of Alan Boocock, of Bispham, Blackpool, Lancs; 2 da (Laura Victoria b 27 May 1986, Sarah Eve b 7 April 1988); *Career* mangr Jeddah W S Try International Ltd 1979, commercial exec W S Try Ltd 1984, gen mangr Barlow Turnkey Contracts Ltd 1986, md George Kemp Stroud & Co Ltd 1989 (dir 1988); dir Oxfordshire Building Safety Assoc Ltd 1990; chm Southern Region Practice Ctee Chartered Inst of Building, memb Ctee Chartered Inst of Bldg Guildford Centre (chm 1987), nat bd memb Chartered Building Company Scheme; FCIOB 1981, FIMgt 1982; *Recreations* keeping fit, photography; *Style*— Chris D Magee, Esq; ✉ 45 Abbots Ride, Farnham, Surrey GU9 8HZ (☎ 01252 723743); George Kemp Stroud & Co Ltd, Aldershot, Hants GU11 3YY (☎ 01252 20339, fax 01252 333924, car 0831 595915)

MAGEE, Ian; *b* 9 July 1946; *Educ* St Michael's Coll Leeds, Univ of Leeds (BA); *Career* DSS (formerly DHSS): joined 1969, private sec to Min for Social Security 1976–78, seconded to Enterprise Unit Cabinet Office 1984–86, dep to Dir of Personnel 1986–89, dir Southern Territory Benefits Agency 1990–93, chief exec Information Technology Services Agency 1993–; non-exec dir Laing Management Contracting 1989–91; memb Advsy Bd: Lancaster Univ Sch of Mgmnt, KPMG 'Impact'; *Recreations* sport, family, reading; *Clubs* MCC; *Style*— Ian Magee, Esq; ✉ Information Technology Sevices Agency, 4th Floor, Verulam Point, Station Way, St Albans, Herts AL1 5HE (☎ 01727 815838, fax 01727 833740)

MAGENTA, Duchesse de; Hon Amélie Margaret Mary; da of Capt Humphrey Drummond of Megginch, MC, and Baroness Strange, *qqv*; *b* 2 July 1963; *Educ* Heathfield, Dundee Coll of Commerce, London Poly, Lycée Viticole de Beaune; *m* 4 May 1990, as his 2 w, Philippe, 4 Duc de Magenta, 8 Marquis de MacMahon, s of Maurice, 3 Duc de Magenta, 7 Marquis de MacMahon (d 1954); 1 s (Maurice de MacMahon b 30 March 1992), 1 da (Pélagie b 24 June 1990); *Recreations* gardening, long baths, Mills & Boon, chocolate; *Style*— Mme la Duchesse de Magenta; ✉ Château de Sully, 71360 Epinac, Saone-et-Loire, France (office ☎ 00 333 85 82 01 08, fax 00 333 85 82 92 54); Megginch Castle, Errol, Perthshire

MAGGIORA, Rosa Maria; da of Louis Sebastian Maggiora (d 1973), of London, and Geraldine, *née* White; *b* 29 Oct 1963; *Educ* St Annes Convent London, Battle Abbey Sussex, Kingston Coll, Manchester Poly, Central Sch of Art, Int American Art Sch Paris; *Career* film and theatre designer; *Theatre* as asst designer incl: Theatre de Complicite (RNT), L'Opera de Chambre, Tramway (Glasgow), 7.84 Theatre Co, The Gate Theatre, Theatre de Gennevilliers (Paris), The Westling School, Opera Circus; as designer incl: Women of no Importance (Greenwich Festival), Venus and Adonis, Happy Days (both Glasgow Citizens' Theatre), How to Cook a Wolf (BAC), Party Girls (Theatre Royal Stratford East), Easter (RSC) 1995, Crocodile Looking at Birds (Lyric Studio) 1995, Making the Future (regnl tour and Young Vic); *Film* incl: Crime Punishment (winner Best Short Film 1993), A Stiff Drink 1995; *Style*— Ms Rosa Maggiora; ✉ c/o agent, Clare Vidal Hall, 28 Perrers Road, London W6 0EZ (☎ 0181 741 7647, fax 0181 741 9459); Edwin Shirley Productions Ltd, Three Mills Island Studios, Three Mill Lane, London E3 3DU (☎ 0171 363 0033, fax 0171 363 0034)

MAGGS, Air Vice-Marshal William Jack; CB (1967), OBE (1943); s of Frederick Wilfrid Maggs (d 1959), and Hilda Lilian Marguerite Maggs (d 1914); *b* 2 Feb 1914; *Educ* Bristol GS, St John's Coll Oxford (MA); *m* 1940, Margaret Grace, da of Thomas Liddell Hetherington (d 1975); 1 s, 1 da; *Career* joined RAF 1939, Air Vice-Marshal 1967; served WWII in UK, N Africa, Sicily, Italy; sr staff offr RAF Maintenance Cmd 1967–69; official fell and domestic bursar Keble Oxford 1969–77, emeritus fell Keble Coll 1981–; govr Bristol GS 1970–89; *Recreations* golf, gardening; *Clubs* RAF; *Style*— Air Vice Marshal William Jack Maggs, CB, OBE; ✉ No 7 The Spindlers, Church St, Kidlington, Oxon OX5 2YP (☎ 01865 373139)

MAGILL, John Walter; s of Walter Magill (d 1969), and Margaret Bartle; *b* 11 March 1944; *Educ* Merchant Taylors' Sch Crosby; *m* 30 Jan 1971, Gillian Irene, da of William Hanna; 2 s (Christopher John b 17 April 1976, Alistair William b 5 Oct 1981); *Career* ACA 1968; Touche Ross (now Deloitte & Touche): ptnr 1975–, ptnr i/c Local Govt Audit 1983–, ptnr and nat dir Accounting and Auditing 1985–93, nat dir Risk Mgmnt 1993–, memb Bd of Ptnrs 1984–; memb Auditing Practices Bd 1994–; FCA; *Style*— John Magill, Esq; ✉ Deloitte & Touche, Hill House, 1 Little New Street, London EC4A 3TR (☎ 0171 936 3000, fax 0171 353 9820)

MAGINNIS, Ken Wiggins; MP (UU) Fermanagh and South Tyrone (majority 14,113); s of Gilbert Maginnis (d 1974), of Dungannon, and Margaret Elizabeth Wiggins (d 1984); *b* 21 Jan 1938; *Educ* Royal Sch Dungannon, Stranmillis Teacher Trg Coll Belfast; *m* 1961, Joy Stewart, da of Herbert Moneymore (d 1976), and Jeannie Moneymore; 2 s (Stewart b 1963, Steven b 1971), 2 da (Gail b 1964, Grainne b 1969); *Career* Ulster Special Constabulary 1958–65, UDR 1970–81 (RMA Sandhurst, Co Cdrs Course Warminster, Maj 1972); teacher: Cookstown Secdy Sch 1959–60, Drumglass Primary Sch Dungannon 1960–66; princ Pomeroy Primary Sch 1966–82; MP (UU) Fermanagh and S Tyrone 1983–; memb: House of Commons Select Ctee on Def 1984–85, Southern Health and Social Servs Bd 1989–91, Armed Forces Bill 1990–91, Southern Health and Social Servs Cncl 1991–93, N Ireland Affairs 1994–; elected to NI Forum 1996–; memb: Dungannon DC 1981–93, Northern Ireland Assembly 1982–86; memb Assembly's: Fin and Personnel Ctee (dep chm 1982–86), Security and Home Affairs Ctee (chm 1982–86); vice pres UU Cncl, memb Exec UU Party (spokesman on defence, and home affrs); memb Bd: Tyrone Economic Devpt Initiative (TEDI), Fermanagh Businesss Initiative; Parly advsr RUC Fedn, chm Moygashel Community Devpt Assoc; *Publications* McGimpsey & McGimpsey v Ireland (1989), Witness for the Prosecution (1993); author of various articles in national newspapers; *Clubs* Army & Navy; *Style*— Ken Maginnis, Esq, MP; ✉ House of Commons, London SW1A 0AA (☎ 0171 219 3000)

MAGNUS, Alan Melvyn; s of Norman Alexander Magnus, and Mimi, *née* Folkson; *b* 31 Aug 1938; *Educ* Sir George Monoux GS, Worcester Coll Oxford (MA), Coll of Law; *m* 25 Nov 1962, Judith Sophia, da of Sidney Sack (d 1987); 2 s (Adrian b 1963, Brian b 1966), 1 da (Tina b 1968); *Career* admitted slr 1964; head co and commercial branch legal dept NCB 1973–87; ptnr D J Freeman 1987–; jt treas Reform Synagogues of GB 1988–91, chm Friends of Progressive Judaism in Israel and Europe 1993–95, fndr and first sec The Mining and Mineral Law Gp 1994–96, treas Euro Region WUPJ 1995–; Freeman City of London 1988; memb Law Soc 1963; *Publications* Investment Agreements in - A Practioners Guide to Venture Capital Law (1991), Property Joint Ventures - Structures and Precedents (ed, 1993), The Career of Rabbi in the Progressive Movements - RSGB and ULPS (1993), Partnership Arrangements and Joint Ventures in Local Government Precedents and Procedures (1996); *Recreations* Alpine walking, opera, ballet, music; *Style*— Alan M Magnus, Esq; ✉ 84 Holders Hill Rd, Hendon, London NW4 1LN (☎ 0181 346 1941); D J Freeman, 1 Fetter Lane, London EC4A 1BR (☎ 0171 583 5555, fax 0171 583 3232, telex 894579, e-mail AMM@DJFREEMAN.CO.UK)

MAGNUS, Sir Laurence Henry Philip; 3 Bt (UK 1917), of Tangley Hill, Wonersh, Co Surrey; s of Hilary Barrow Magnus, TD, QC (d 1987), and Rosemary Vera Anne, *née* Masefield; suc unc, Sir Philip Magnus-Allcroft, 2 Bt (d 1988); *b* 24 Sept 1955; *Educ* Eton, Christ Church Oxford (MA); *m* 1983, Jocelyn Mary, eldest da of Robert Henry Foster Stanton; 2 s (Thomas Henry Philip b 1985, Edmund Robert Hilary b 1991), 1 da (Iona Alexandra b 1988); *Heir* s, Thomas Henry Philip Magnus b 30 Sept 1985; *Career* Samuel Montagu & Co Ltd: gen mangr Singapore branch 1984–88, exec dir and dep head UK Corp Fin 1988–95; dir Phoenix Securities Limited 1995–; *Recreations* fishing, reading, hill walking; *Clubs* Millennium; *Style*— Sir Laurence Magnus, Bt; ✉ Flat 8, 44 Lower Sloane Street, London SW1W 8BP; Phoenix Securities Limited, 1 Laurence Pountney Hill, London EC4R 0EU (☎ 0171 638 2191, fax 0171 638 0707)

MAGNUSSON, Magnus; Hon KBE (1989); s of Sigursteinn Magnússon (d 1982), of Edinburgh, and Ingibjörg, *née* Sigurdardóttir (d 1983); *b* 12 Oct 1929; *Educ* The Edinburgh Acad, Jesus Coll Oxford (BA, MA); *m* 30 June 1954, Mamie, da of John Baird (d 1945), of Rutherglen, Glasgow; 2 s (Siggy b 1961, d 1973, Jon b 1965), 3 da (Sally Magnusson, *qv* b 1955, Margaret b 1959, Anna b 1960); *Career* journalist and broadcaster; reporter (latterly asst ed) Scottish Daily Express 1953–61, chief features writer and asst ed The Scotsman 1961–68; presenter many BBC TV and radio progs incl: Tonight 1964–65, Chronicle (fndr memb and chief presenter) 1966–83, Mastermind 1972–97, BC: The Archaeology of the Bible Lands, Vikings!, Pebble Mill at One, Living Legends, Personal Pursuits, Current Account, All Things Considered, Landlord or Tenant - A View of Irish History, Birds For All Seasons; co-translator BBC Radio 4 serial The Tree of Strife from Njal's Saga 1994; ed: The Bodley Head Archaeologies, Popular Archaeology 1979–80; lord rector Univ of Edinburgh 1975–78, fndr chm Scot Churches Archaeological Heritage Tst 1978–85, tstee Nat Museums of Scot 1985–89, pres RSPB 1985–90, memb UK Ctee for Euro Year of the Environment 1987; chm: Stewards York Archaeological Tst, Scot Youth Theatre 1976–78, Ancient Monuments Bd for Scot 1981–89, Nature Conservancy Cncl for Scot 1991 (chm Scot Advsy Ctee 1990–91), Scot Office Departmental Working Party on the Cairngorms 1991–92; chm Scottish Natural Heritage 1992–; hon vice pres: Age Concern Scotland, RSSPCC; winner: Scot TV Personality of the Year 1974, Iceland Media Award 1985, Medlicott Medal Historical Assoc 1989; hon fell Jesus Coll Oxford; Hon DUniv: Edinburgh 1978, York 1981, Strathclyde 1993, Paisley 1993; FSA (Scot) 1974, FRSE 1980, FRSA 1983, Hon FRIAS 1987, FSA 1991, fell Royal Scot Geographical Soc 1991; Knight Cdr of the Order of the Falcon (Iceland) 1986 (Knight 1975); *Publications* Introducing Archaeology (1972), Viking Expansion Westwards (1973), The Clacken and the Slate (Edinburgh Academy 1824–1974, 1974), Hammer of the North (1976, 2 edn Viking Hammer of the North 1980), BC: The Archaeology of the Bible Lands (1977), Landlord or Tenant? a view of Irish History (1978), Iceland (1979), Vikings! (1980, 1992), Magnus on the Move (1980), Treasures of Scotland (1981), Lindisfarne: The Cradle Island (1984), Iceland Saga (1987); *Translations* (with Hermann Pálsson): Njal's Saga (1960), The Vinland Sagas (1965), King Harald's Saga (1966), Laxdaela Saga (1969); (all by Halldor Laxness): The Atom Station (1961), Paradise Reclaimed (1962), The Fish Can Sing (1966), World Light (1969), Christianity Under Glacier (1973); (by Samivel) Golden Iceland (1967); *Contributor* The Glorious Privilege (1967), The Future of the Highlands (1968), Strange Stories, Amazing Facts (1975), Pass the Port (1976), Book of Bricks (1978), Chronicle (1978), Discovery of Lost Worlds (1979), Pass the Port Again (1981), Second Book of Bricks (1981); *Editor* Echoes in Stone (1983), Reader's Digest Book of Facts (1985), Chambers Biographical Dictionary (1990), The Nature of Scotland (1991); *Recreations* reading, wildlife; *Style*— Magnus Magnusson, Esq, KBE, FRSE, FSA; ✉ Blairskaith House, Balmore-Torrance, Glasgow G64 4AX (☎ 01360 620226, fax 01360 620444)

MAGNUSSON, Sally Anne; da of Magnus Magnusson, *qv*, and Mamie, *née* Baird; *b* 11 Oct 1955; *Educ* Laurel Bank Sch Glasgow (dux), Univ of Edinburgh (MA); *m* 9 June 1984, Norman Arthur Stone, s of Rev Arthur Stone; 4 s (Jamie Magnus b 15 Dec 1985, Sigurdur Gordon b 21 Feb 1988, (Ian Arthur) Ross b 19 Sept 1991, Magnus Jack b 20 May 1995), 1 da (Anna Lisa b 2 Jan 1990); *Career* graduate trainee Thomson Regional Newspapers (incl The Scotsman), reporter The Scotsman 1978–81, news/feature writer Sunday Standard Glasgow 1981–83; BBC: reporter Current Account BBC Scotland 1983, presenter Sixty Minutes (BBC1) 1983–84, presenter London Plus (BBC1) 1984–85, presenter Breakfast Time (BBC1) 1985–89, occasional presenter Songs of Praise (BBC1) and other progs, presenter Breakfast News (BBC1) 1994–; T S Murray Award as trainee journalist, Scottish Feature Writer of the Year 1981; *Books* The Flying Scotsman (1981), Clemo: A Love Story (1986), A Shout in the Street (1991); *Style*— Ms Sally Magnusson; ✉ c/o Sue Freathy, Curtis Brown Group Ltd, 4th Floor, Haymarket House, 28–29 Haymarket, London SW1Y 4SP (☎ 0171 396 6600)

MAGONET, Rabbi Prof Jonathan David; s of Capt Alexander Philip Magonet (d 1978), and Esther, *née* Slonims (d 1972); *b* 2 Aug 1942; *Educ* Westminster, Middlesex Hosp Med Sch Univ of London (MB BS), Leo Baeck Coll (Rabbinic ordination), Univ of Heidelberg (PhD); *m* 10 May 1974, Dorothea Elsa Martha, da of Gerhardt Foth; 1 s (Gavriel b 4 May 1978), 1 da (Avigail b 28 April 1981); *Career* lectr and head of Dept of Bible Studies Leo Baeck Coll 1974–85, princ Leo Baeck Coll 1985–, prof of Hebrew and Biblical Studies 1996–, scholar in residence Dept of Jewish Educn Univ of Tel Aviv 1990–91, visiting prof Kirchliche Hochschule Wuppertal (Summer Semester) 1992, 1993 and 1995; vice-pres World Union for Progressive Judaism 1985–; memb Editorial Bd European Judaism 1978–, co-ed European Judaism 1992–; *Books* Form and Meaning: Studies in Literary Techniques in the Book of Jonah (1976), Forms of Prayer: Vol 1 Daily and Sabbath Prayerbook (co-ed with Lionel Blue, 1977), Forms of Prayer: Vol III Days of Awe Prayerbook (co-ed with Lionel Blue, 1985), The Guide to the Here and the Hereafter (co-ed with Lionel Blue, 1988), A Rabbi's Bible (1991), How To Get Up When Life Gets You Down: A Companion and Guide (co-ed with Lionel Blue, 1992), Bible Lives (1992), The Little Blue Book of Prayer (co-ed with Lionel Blue, 1993), A Rabbi Reads the Psalms 1994, Forms of Prayer: Vol II Pilgrim Festivals (co-ed with Lionel Blue, 1995), Kindred Spirits: A Year of Readings (co-ed with Lionel Blue, 1995), Jewish Explorations of Sexuality (ed, 1995); *Style*— Rabbi Prof Jonathan Magonet; ✉ Leo Baeck College, 80 East End Rd, London N3 2SY (☎ 0181 349 4525, fax 0181 343 2558)

MAGORIAN, Michelle Jane; da of William Magorian, and Gladys Freda Evans (d 1975); *b* 6 Nov 1947; *Educ* Kilbreda Coll Victoria Aust, Convent of the Cross Hants, Rose Bruford Coll of Speech and Drama, L'Ecole Internationale de Mime Paris; *m* 18 Aug 1987, Peter Keith Venner, s of Albert Keith Venner; 2 s (Tom b 5 March 1989, George b 23 Sept 1993); *Career* writer, entertainer; in rep since 1970, one woman show touring Italy and UK 1980, one woman show The Pact 1993–; memb: Soc of Authors, PEN; *Books* Goodnight Mister Tom (1981, lyrics for stage musical 1992, broadcast Radio 5),

Back Home (1985, made into TV film 1989, dramatised for Radio 4 1995), Waiting For My Shorts To Dry (1989), Who's Going to Take Care of Me? (1990), Orange Paw Marks (1991), A Little Love Song (1991), In Deep Water (a collection of short stories, 1992), Cuckoo in the Nest (1994); short stories incl six anthologies; *Style*— Ms Michelle Magorian

MAGOS, Adam László; s of László Aurel Pal Magos, of London, and Eva Maria, *née* Banjamin; *b* 26 Sept 1953, Budapest; *Educ* Whitgift Sch Haling Park S Croydon Surrey, King's Coll London (BSc), King's Coll Hosp Sch of Med London (MB BS, MD, MRCOG); *m* Anne Cyprienne, *née* Coburn; 3 s (Tiarnan Adam b 5 Aug 1985, Siadhal László b 16 March 1987, Abban Zoltan b 24 April 1990); *Career* clinical lectr and hon sr registrar Nuffield Dept of Obstetrics and Gynaecology John Radcliffe Hosp Oxford 1986–90, sr lectr and hon conslt Academic Dept of Obstetrics and Gynaeocology Royal Free Hosp Sch of Med 1990–91, conslt obstetrician and gynaecologist and hon sr lectr Univ Dept of Obstetrics and Gynaecology Royal Free Hosp 1991–, conslt gynaecologist King Edward VII's Hosp for Offrs London 1992–; treas Br Soc for Gynaecological Endoscopy 1989–92; memb: Advsy Bd Euro Soc for Hysteroscopy 1990–, Working Gp on New Technol in Endoscopic Gynaecological Surgery RCOG 1993–94, Editorial Bd Gynaecological Endoscopy 1993– (ed 1990–93); author of over 100 pubns in peer review jls and chapters in books; Syntex Award (Int Soc of Reproduction Med) 1988, hon memb Aust Soc of Gynaecological Endoscopy 1994; memb: Blair Bell Research Soc 1982, Euro Soc of Hysteroscopy 1988; fndr memb: Br Soc for Gynaecological Endoscopy 1989, Soc of Minimally Invasive Therapy 1990; *Style*— Adam Magos, Esq; ✉ University Department of Obstetrics and Gynaecology, The Royal Free Hospital, Pond Street, Hampstead, London NW3 2QG (☎ 0171 431 1321, fax 0171 431 1321); King Edward VII's Hospital for Officers, 10 Beaumont Street, London W1N 2AA (☎ 0171 486 4411, fax 0171 224 4417)

MAGUIRE, Adrian Edward; s of Joseph Maguire, of Kilmessan, Co Meath, and Philomena Maguire (d 1995); *b* 29 April 1971; *Educ* Kilmessan Nat Sch, Trim Vocational Sch; *m* 1995, Sabrina; 1 da (Shannon b 1996); *Career* racehorse jockey; achievements incl: champion pony race rider 1986, champion point-to-point rider 1990–91, champion conditional jockey 1991–92; major races won: Cheltenham Gold Cup, Irish Grand Nat (youngest ever winning jockey), Galway Plate, Imperial Cup, Greenalls Gold Cup, Queen Mother Champion Chase (Cheltenham), King George VI Chase (Kempton Park), Triumph Hurdle and Cathcort Chase (both Cheltenham); records: most point-to-point winners in a season, most winners in a season for a conditional jockey (71) 1991–92; *Recreations* squash, watching TV; *Style*— Adrian Maguire, Esq; ✉ c/o The Jockey Club (Jockey Section), 42 Portman Square, London W1H 0EM

MAGUIRE, Dr Anne; da of Richard Patrick Maguire (d 1971), and Ruth Alice, *née* Glencross (d 1963); *Educ* London Sch of Med for Women Royal Free Hosp (MB BS), CG Jung Inst Zurich (Dip in Analytical Psychology); *Career* dermatological trg St John's Hosp for Diseases of the Skin Guy's Hosp and Univ Coll Hosp 1956–57, in private practice Harley St; author of various papers; Ratclyffe Crocker travelling fellowship Univ Coll Hosp 1964; memb: Br Assoc of Dermatologists, St John's Dermatological Soc, Int Assoc of Internal Med, Int Assoc for Analytical Psychologists; FRCP, FRSM; *Books* Hauterkrankungen als Botschaften der Seele (1991), Vom Sinn der kranken Sinne (1993), The Seven Deadly Sins (published in German, 1996); *Style*— Dr Anne Maguire; ✉ 17 Wellington St, St John's, Blackburn BB1 8AF (☎ 01254 59910); 23 Harley St, London W1N 1DA (☎ 0171 436 5262)

MAGUIRE, Air Marshal Sir Harold John; KCB (1966, CB 1958), DSO (1946), OBE (1949); s of Michael Maguire, of Maymooth, Ireland, and Harriette, *née* Warren; *b* 12 April 1912; *Educ* Wesley Coll, Trinity Coll Dublin; *m* 1940, Mary Elisabeth, da of George Wild, of Dublin; 1 s, 1 da; *Career* joined RAF 1933, served WWII, Gp Capt 1950, Air Cdre 1958, Air Vice-Marshal 1960, SASO Far East Air Force 1962–64, asst CAS (Intelligence) 1964–65, dep CDS (Intelligence) 1965–68, Air Marshal 1966, ret RAF 1968; dir-gen Intelligence MOD 1968–72; dir Commercial Union Assur Co 1975–82 (political and economic advsr 1972–79); chm cncl of Offrs' Pension Soc 1974–84; Freeman City of London 1978, Liveryman Guild of Air Pilots and Air Navigators 1978; *Clubs* RAF; *Style*— Air Marshal Sir Harold Maguire, KCB, DSO, OBE; ✉ c/o Lloyds Bank, 7 Pall Mall, London SW1

MAGUIRE, Sheriff Principal John Joseph; QC (Scot, 1990); s of Robert Maguire (d 1954), solicitor, of Glasgow, and Julia, *née* Long (d 1986); *b* 30 Nov 1934; *Educ* St Ninian's HS Kirkintilloch, St Mary's Coll Blairs, Pontifical Gregorian Univ (PhL), Univ of Edinburgh (LLB); *m* 23 April 1962, Eva, da of Thomas O'Hara, of Tralee; 2 s (Andrew Sean b 22 Jan 1964, Gordon Patrick b 3 Jan 1968), 2 da (Julia Mary b 8 June 1965, Aisling Elizabeth b 9 Sept 1969); *Career* called to the Bar 1958, standing jr to Miny of Public Bldgs & Works 1962–68, sheriff at Airdrie 1968–79, sheriff at Glasgow 1973–90, sheriff principal of Tayside, Central and Fife 1990–; pres Sheriffs Assoc 1988–90 (sec 1982–87), memb Departmental Ctee on Alternatives to Prosecution 1977–82, Scottish rep Int Union of Judges 1984–87; chairman Northern Light Houseboard 1995; chm: St Philip's List D Sch 1969–77, Caldervale Dist Scouts 1975–85; chm and co-fndr PHEW charity for the mentally handicapped 1984–90; *Recreations* reading, travel (by train, if possible); *Clubs* New (Edinburgh); *Style*— Sheriff Principal John Maguire, QC; ✉ Sheriff Principals Chambers, Perth Sheriff Court, Tay Street, Perth PH2 8NL (☎ 01738 620546, fax 01783 623601)

MAGUIRE, Mairead; da of Andrew and Margaret Corrigan; *b* 27 Jan 1944; *Educ* St Vincent's Primary Sch Falls Road Belfast, Miss Gordon's Commercial Coll Belfast; *m* 1981, Jackie Maguire; 2 s (John Francis b 1982, Luke b 1984), 3 step c (Mark, Joanne, Marie Louise); *Career* initiator of Peace Movement in NI, jt fndr Community of the Peace People, chm Peace People 1980–81, hon life pres Peace People; winner numerous honours and awards; jt recipient Nobel Peace Prize 1976; winner: Norwegian People's prize, Carl-Von-Ossietzky medaille for Courage Berlin 1976; special honouree: UN Women of Achievement programme 1978, American Acad of Achievement; winner Pacem in Terris (Peace and Freedom award) Davenport Iowa 1990, Hon Dr Yale Univ; co fndr Ctee for the Administration of Justice, former volunteer Legion of Mary (work with prisons and prisoners); previously employed as confidential sec to md A Guinness Son & Co (Belfast) Ltd; *Recreations* swimming, music; *Style*— Mrs Mairead Maguire; ✉ 224 Lisburn Road, Belfast BT9 6GE, Northern Ireland (office ☎ 01232 663465, fax 01232 683947, e-mail peacepeople@gn.apc.org.)

MAGUIRE, Robert Alfred; OBE (1983); s of Arthur Maguire (d 1950), of London, and Rose Lilian, *née* Fountain (d 1986); *b* 6 June 1931; *Educ* Bancroft's, The Architectural Assoc Sch of Arch (AA Dipl); *m* 1, 6 Aug 1955 (m dis 1978), Robina Helen, da of Robert Finlayson; 4 da (Susan b 1956, Rebecca b 1958, Joanna b 1960, Martha b 1963); m 2, 26 Oct 1982, Alison Margaret, da of George Marshall Mason, of Henley-on-Thames; *Career* bldgs ed Architects' Jl 1954–59, private architectural practice 1956–, ptnr Robert Maguire and Keith Murray 1959–89; chm: Maguire & Co 1989–, Maguire and Co International 1990–, Maguire Glynn Miller Ltd 1991–95; most important works incl: St Paul's Church Bow Common London 1959 (listed Grade II Star), Trinity Coll Oxford extensions 1965, student village Stag Hill Ct Univ of Surrey 1969; comp wins incl: extensions Magdalen Coll Oxford 1975, Kindertagesstatte Berlin-Kreuzberg 1983, extensions Pembroke Coll Oxford 1986, visitor centre Chepstow Castle 1986, extensions Worcester Coll Oxford 1988; also bldgs in Cathedral Precinct for King's Sch Canterbury 1975–86; Surveyor of the Fabric to St George's Chapel Windsor Castle 1975–87, head of Dept of Architecture Oxford Poly (now Oxford Sch of Architecture) 1976–85; RIBA 1953, FRSA 1984; *Books* Modern Churches of the World (1963); *Recreations* sailing, growing sub-tropical fruits; *Style*— Robert Maguire, Esq, OBE; ✉ South Weston Cottage, South Weston, Thame, Oxon OX9 7EF (☎ 01844 281262); Cortijo Pepe Pedro, Pago de Sarja, Cómpeta, Málaga, Spain; 104 High St, Thame, Oxon OX9 3DZ (☎ 01844 217373, fax 01844 216846)

MAHADOO, Babooram; s of late Bhahannoo Mahadoo, of Mauritius, and late Gangabye, *née* Rama, of Mauritius; *b* 8 July 1936; *Educ* RC Aided Sch Mauritius, Windsor Coll Mauritius (dip in social studies, sociology degree, dip in journalism); *m* 18 Aug 1963, Jaywantee, *née* Hurree; 1 da (Brinda b 17 Feb 1965), 1 s (Rajiv b 15 Aug 1966); *Career* Mauritian diplomat; secdy sch teacher Mauritius: Windsor Coll 1960–65, Eden Coll 1966–86; pres Religious and Socio-Cultural Orgns 1966–81; asst sec Parti Socialiste Mauricien 1981, elected memb Legislative Assembly for Vacoas-Floreal 1982, min of arts, culture and leisure 1983–86, fndr memb Militant Socialist Militant Party 1983, min of local govt 1986–88, Parly private sec under the aegis of the PM 1988–92, high cmmr for Mauritius to the Ct of St James's 1992–96, non-resident ambass extraordinary and plenipotentiary to the Holy See 1992–96, non-resident ambass extraordinary and plenipotentiary to Sweden, Norway, Denmark and Finland 1993–96; *Books* The Eternal Legacy; *Recreations* reading, swimming, jogging and football; *Style*— Mr Babooram Mahadoo

MAHAFFY, Sarah Georgiana; da of Rupert Mahaffy, of London, and Victoria, *née* Ponsonby (d 1995); *b* 21 July 1952; *Educ* Francis Holland Sch, St Hugh's Coll Oxford (BA); *m* W H Baker; 1 s (Charles), 1 da (Sophia); *Career* editorial asst Methuen Educational 1974–75, Macmillan Publishers 1975–84, fndr md Boxtree 1986–96, md Pan Macmillan 1996–; *Recreations* theatre, food, reading, family; *Style*— Miss Sarah Mahaffy; ✉ 28 Cassland Rd, London E9 7AN; The Old Rectory, Scremby, nr Spilsby, Lincs; Pan Macmillan, 25 Eccleston Place, London SW1 (☎ 0171 881 8000)

MAHAPATRA, Dr Sasi Bhusan; s of late Nila Kantha Mahapatra, and late Moti Mahapatra; *b* 2 Nov 1935; *Educ* BC HS Ranpur Orissa India, Ravenshaw Coll Cuttack Orissa India, SCB Med Coll and Utkal Univ Orissa India (MB BS, DPM); *m* 1 Oct 1963, Maureen Rose, da of late William Henry Piggott; 1 s (Timothy Martin), 2 da (Sonjeeta Krishna, Rachelle Elizabeth); *Career* house offr and house surgn SCB Med Coll Cuttack Orissa 1958–59, med offr Manmunda Health Centre Orissa India 1959–61; sr registrar in psychiatry 1964–66: Runwell Hosp Wickford Essex (sr house offr and registrar 1961–64), St Clements Hosp, The London Hosp; conslt psychiatrist Univ of Leeds 1976– (lectr 1966–70, sr lectr and hon conslt 1970–76), conslt psychiatrist and sr clinical lectr St James's Hosp Univ Hosp 1976–94, dir of psychiatry servs Leeds Eastern Health Authy 1986–90, med dir Harrogate Clinic 1990–, hon conslt psychiatrist Leeds Community and Mental Health Serv Tst Leeds 1994–, Lord Chllr's Medical Visitor 1995–; memb N Yorks AHA 1971–76, sub dean RCPsych 1977–82; chm: NE Div RCPsych 1984–88, Sub Ctee of Overseas Psychiatry Trainees 1976–84; FRCP 1982, FRCPsych; *Books* Antidepressive Drugs - Side-Effects of Drugs (1972), Deafness and Mental Health (1972), Psychosomatic Aspects of Coronary Artery Disease - Psychosomatic Medicine (1973), Problems of Language in Examinations for Foreign Psychiatrists (1974), Short Term Effects of Antidepressive Drugs and Placebo (1975), Schizophrenic Language (ed, 1976), Handbook for Psychiatric Inceptors and Trainees (ed, 1980); *Recreations* cricket, gardening, sailing, music, skiing, photography; *Style*— Dr Sasi Mahapatra; ✉ Woodlands Grange, Woodlands Drive, Apperley Bridge, Bradford BD10 0NX (☎ 0113 250 6854); Glebe House, 5 Shaw Lane, Leeds 6 (☎ 0113 278 9472); BUPA Hospital, Jackson Avenue, Roundav, Leeds LS8 1NT (☎ 0113 269 3939); Harrogate Clinic, 23 Ripon Road, Harrogate HG1 2JL (☎ 01423 500599)

MAHER, Hon Mrs (Sarah Jane); *née* Lawson; da of Lt-Col 5 Baron Burnham, JP, DL (d 1993); *b* 7 Oct 1955; *Educ* Heathfield; *m* 1, 1982 (m dis 1991), Michael Ian Grade, *qv*; m 2, 1992, David Patrick Maher; *Career* slr Macfarlanes 1976–80, agent Curtis Brown 1980–82, vice-pres Devpt TV D L Taffner Ltd 1982–84, pres Taft Entertainment/Lawson Group 1985–87; md: Lawson Productions Ltd 1987–95 and 1996–, md Anglia Television Entertainment Ltd 1995–96; *Style*— The Hon Mrs Maher (professionally known as Sarah Lawson); ✉ 5 Sussex Mews East, London W2 2TS; Newton Park, Wicklow, Co Wicklow, Ireland

MAHER, Stephen Francis; s of Francis John Maher, of Harrow, Middlesex, and Bridget Rita, *née* Dillon; *b* 19 Feb 1961; *Educ* The John Lyon Sch Middlesex, Balliol Coll Oxford (exhibitioner, MA, Coolidge Pathfinder award); *m* 23 Sept 1989, Sarah Jane, da of Adrian George Beckett; 1 da (Sophie Elizabeth b 10 March 1992), 1 s (Edward Archie Francis b 3 Dec 1994); *Career* advtg graduate account trainee Allen Brady & Marsh Ltd 1983; account mangr: ABM 1984–86, Abbott Mead Vickers SMS Ltd 1986–88; account dir AMV 1988–89; Simons Palmer Denton Clemmow & Johnson Ltd: account dir 1989–90, bd account dir 1990–93, head of account mgmnt 1993; md Maher Bird Associates Ltd 1994–; *Recreations* music, guitar, reading, travel, skiing, football, photography, film, Corgi/Dinky car collecting, family; *Style*— Stephen Maher, Esq; ✉ Maher Bird Associates Ltd, Academy House, 161–167 Oxford Street, London W1R 1TA (☎ 0171 287 1718, fax 0171 287 0197)

MAHER, His Hon Judge; Terence; s of John Maher (d 1954), and Bessie Maher; *b* 20 Dec 1941; *Educ* Burnley GS, Univ of Manchester (LLB); *m* 4 Sept 1965 (m dis 1983); 2 da (Catherine Helen b 1971, Elizabeth Jane b 1972); *Career* met stipendiary magistrate 1983–95, chm Inner London Youth Court and Family Proceedings Court, recorder of the Crown Court until 1995, circuit judge (SE Circuit) 1995–; *Recreations* reading, walking, travel; *Clubs* Frewen (Oxford); *Style*— His Hon Judge Maher; ✉ Wood Green Crown Court, Woodall House, Lordship Lane, London N22 5LF

MAHER, Terence Anthony (Terry); s of Herbert Maher (d 1978); *b* 5 Dec 1935; *Educ* Xaverian Coll Manchester; *m* 1960, Barbara, da of Dr Franz Greenbaum (d 1961); 3 s (Nicholas b 1960, Anthony b 1962, Jeremy b 1964); *Career* with: Carborundum Co Ltd 1961–69, First National Corp 1969–72; fndr, chm and chief exec Pentos plc 1972–93; chm: Dillons Bookstores 1977–93, Athena International 1980–93, Ryman 1987–93, The Chalford Publishing Co Ltd 1994–; fndr and chm Maher Booksellers Ltd 1995–; fndr tstee Lib Dems 1988–, tstee Photographers Gallery 1994–; FCCA (1970, ACCA 1960), FRSA 1988; *Books* Counterblast (co-author, 1965), Effective Politics (co-author, 1966), Against My Better Judgement (1994); *Recreations* skiing, reading, walking, tennis, bridge; *Clubs* Savile; *Style*— Terry Maher, Esq; ✉ 33 Clarence Terrace, London NW1 4RD

MAHLER, Prof Robert Frederick; s of Dr Felix Mahler (d 1959), of London, and Olga, *née* Lowy (d 1989); *b* 31 Oct 1924; *Educ* Edinburgh Acad, Univ of Edinburgh (BSc, MB ChB); *m* 13 June 1951, Maureen, da of Horace Calvert (d 1963), of Dublin; 2 s (Graeme, Brian); *Career* Sqdn Ldr RAF Med Branch 1949–51; res fell Harvard Univ 1956–58, reader in med Guy's Hosp London 1958–66, prof of med Univ of Wales 1966–79; visiting prof: Univ of Indiana 1962–63, Stockholm 1976–77; physician Clinical Res Centre Harrow 1979–90; ed Jl of RCP 1987–94; FRCP (London) 1963, FRCP (Edinburgh) 1963; *Recreations* opera, theatre, music, watching rugby; *Clubs* RSM; *Style*— Prof Robert Mahler; ✉ 14 Manley Street, London NW1 8LT (☎ 0171 586 1198)

MAHON, Alice; MP (Lab) Halifax (majority 478); *Career* MP (Lab) Halifax 1987–; *Style*— Mrs Alice Mahon, MP; ✉ 2 West Parade, Halifax, West Yorkshire HX1 2TA (☎ 01422 331102, fax 01422 381577)

MAHON, His Hon Judge; Charles Joseph; *b* 16 Aug 1939; *Career* circuit judge (Northern Circuit); *Style*— His Hon Judge Mahon; ✉ c/o Northern Circuit Office, 15 Quay Street, Manchester M60 9FD

MAHON, Sir (John) Denis; kt (1986), CBE (1967); s of John FitzGerald Mahon (d 1942), 4 s of Sir W Mahon, 4 Bt, and Lady Alice Evelyn Browne (d 1970), da of 5th Marquess of Sligo; *b* 8 Nov 1910; *Educ* Eton, ChCh Oxford (MA); *Career* art historian; tstee Nat Gallery 1957–64 and 1966–73, memb Advsy Panel Nat Art Collections Fund 1975; specialist on 17th century painting in Italy and has notable collection (exhibited Nat Gallery Feb-May 1997); has long campaigned for fiscal measures to encourage support from private individuals for art galleries and museums; memb Ctee of the Biennial Exhibitions at Bologna Italy; awarded: medal for Benemeriti della Cultura 1957, Archiginnasio d'Oro City of Bologna 1968, Serena medal for Italian Studies Br Acad 1972; elected Academico d'Onore Clementine Acad Bologna 1964; corresponding fell Accad Raffaello Urbino 1968, Deputazione di Storia Patria per le provincie di Romagna 1969, Ateneo Veneto 1987; Hon Citizen Cento 1982, Hon Student ChCh Oxford 1996; Hon DLitt: Newcastle 1969, Oxford 1994; FBA 1964; *Publications* Studies in Seicento Art and Theory (1947), Mostra dei Carracci, Catalogo critico dei Disegni (1956, 1963), Poussiniana (1962), Catalogues of the Mostra del Guercino (Dipinti 1968, Disegni 1969), The Drawings of Guercino in the Collection of HM The Queen at Windsor Castle (with N Turner, 1989), Catalogues of exhibitions in 1991–92 in celebration of 4 centenary of Guercino's birth: Bologna/Cento (paintings), Bologna (drawings), Frankfurt (Schirn Kunsthalle, paintings), Washington (Nat Gallery of Art, paintings); contrib: Actes of Colloque Poussin (1960), Friedlaender Festschrift (1965), Problemi Guardeschi (1967), I Dipinti del Guercino (conslt to Luigi Salerno, 1988); author of numerous articles, especially on Caravaggio and Poussin, in art historical periodicals incl: Apollo, The Art Bulletin, The Burlington Magazine, Gazette des Beaux Arts, Art de France, Commentari, Paragone, Zeitschrift für Kunstwissenschaft; collaborated in compilation of catalogues raisonnés of many exhibitions incl: Artists in 17th Century Rome (London 1955), Italian Art in Britain (Royal Academy 1960), L'Ideale Classico dei Seicento in Italia (Bologna 1962), Omaggio al Guercino (Cento 1967); *Style*— Sir Denis Mahon, CBE, FBA; ✉ 33 Cadogan Square, London SW1X 0HU (☎ 0171 235 7311, 0171 235 2530)

MAHON, Sean Patrick Lauritson; s of John Patrick Mahon (d 1983), of Sheffield, and Peggy Lauritson, *née* Bines (d 1978); *b* 16 April 1946; *Educ* Ratcliffe Coll Leics; *m* 14 Sept 1968, Pauline Kathleen, da of Eric Reginald Starling; 1 s (Sean Ciaran b 15 June 1971), 3 da (Victoria Amanda b 4 Oct 1972, Siobhan Katherine b 3 April 1975, Anne Marie b 3 Nov 1983 d 1986); *Career* articled clerk Smith Holloway and Clarke Sheffield 1964–69, CA 1969; Coopers & Lybrand: joined 1969, secondment to Montreal and Chicago 1973–74, ptnr Sheffield 1976, memb Nat Audit Ctee 1983, memb Audit Bd (following merger) 1989, currently chm North (former ptnr i/c Sheffield 1989), memb Managing Bd; chm: Sheffield CAs Students Soc 1979–84, Sheffield CAs Tech Advsy Ctee 1982–87; memb: Accreditation Bd ICAEW 1982–88, Tech Advsy Ctee ICAEW 1984–87; pres: Sheffield & Dist Soc of CAs 1990–91, Irish Soc of Sheffield & District 1982–87; memb Univ of Sheffield Careers Advsy Bd 1982–88, dir S Yorks Met Ambulance and Paramedics Trust 1991–, chm Fin Ctee Boys' Clubs of S Yorks 1984–; capt: Sheffield RFC Colts, Yorkshire Rugby Colts; England U21 trialist; FCA (ACA 1969); *Recreations* fishing trout, salmon and pike in Ireland, clay pigeon shooting; *Clubs* Sheffield, Abbeydale RFC, Abbeydale Golf; *Style*— Sean Mahon, Esq; ✉ Coopers & Lybrand, 1 East Parade, Sheffield S1 2ET (☎ 0114 272 9141, fax 0114 275 2573)

MAHON, Col Sir William Walter; 7 Bt (UK 1819), of Castlegar, Co Galway; s of Sir George Edward John Mahon, 6 Bt (d 1987), and his 1 w, Audrey Evelyn (d 1957), da of Dr Walter Jagger; *b* 4 Dec 1940; *Educ* Eton; *m* 20 April 1968, Rosemary Jane, yr da of late Lt-Col Michael Ernest Melvill, OBE, of The Old Manse, Symington, Lanarkshire; 1 s, 2 da (Annabel Jane (Mrs Richard Amphlett) b 1970, Lucy Caroline b 1972); *Heir* s, James William Mahon b 29 Oct 1976; *Career* Irish Gds 1959–92, served Germany, Malaysia, Hong Kong, Pakistan, Spain; memb HM Bodyguard of the Hon Corps of Gentlemen at Arms 1993–; fundraiser for Cancer Relief Macmillan Fund; *Recreations* shooting, travel, history, collecting; *Clubs* Army and Navy, White's; *Style*— Col Sir William W Mahon, Bt

MAHONEY, Dennis Leonard; s of late Frederick Mahoney; *b* 20 Sept 1950; *Educ* W Hatch Tech HS; *m* 1 (m dis), Julia McLaughlin; 1 s, 1 da; m 2, 1988, Jacqueline Fox; 1 s, 2 da; *Career* broker; dep chm Sedgwick Forbes North America 1982 (md 1979), chm Alexander Howden Ltd 1984–94, dep chm Alexander Howden Group Ltd 1994–; *Recreations* skiing, shooting; *Style*— Dennis L Mahoney, Esq; ✉ Alexander Howden Group Ltd, 8 Devonshire Square, London EC2M 4PL (☎ 0171 623 5500, fax 0171 621 1511, telex 920625 HOWDEN G)

MAHONEY, Rev Prof John Aloysius (Jack); SJ; s of Patrick Mahoney (d 1966), and Margaret Cecilia, *née* Doris (d 1994); *b* 14 Jan 1931; *Educ* Our Lady's HS Motherwell, St Aloysius' Coll Glasgow, Univ of Glasgow (MA), Pontifical Gregorian Univ Rome (LicPhil, LicTheol, DTheol); *Career* ordained Jesuit priest 1962; lectr in moral and pastoral theology Heythrop Coll: Oxon 1967–70, London 1970–86 (princ 1976–81); F D Maurice prof of moral and social theology KCL 1986–93; founding dir Business Ethics Res Centre KCL 1987–93; dean Faculty of Theology Univ of London and Faculty of Theol and Religious Studies KCL 1990–92; Dixons prof of business ethics and social responsibility London Business Sch 1993–; Martin D'Arcy meml lectr Campion Hall Oxford 1981–82; Mercers' Sch meml prof of commerce Gresham Coll London 1987–93; memb Int Theol Cmmn Rome 1974–80; memb Int Study Gp on Bioethics Int Fedn of Catholic Univs 1984–93; pres Catholic Theol Assoc 1984–86; founding ed Business Ethics, A European Review 1992–; domestic chaplain to Lord Mayor of London 1989–90; CIMgt 1993, FRSA; *Books* Seeking the Spirit (1981), Bioethics and Belief (1984), The Making of Moral Theology (1987), The Ways of Wisdom (1987), Teaching Business Ethics in the UK, Europe and USA (1990), Business Ethics in a New Europe (ed, 1992); *Style*— The Rev Prof Jack Mahoney, SJ; ✉ Farm Street Church, 114 Mount Street, London W1Y 6AH (☎ 0171 493 7811); London Business School, Sussex Place, Regent's Park, London NW1 4SA (☎ 0171 706 6872, fax 0171 258 3720)

MAHONY, Stephen Dominic Patrick; s of Dermot Cecil Mahony, of Cork, Ireland, and Kate, *née* O'Neill; *b* 3 March 1956; *Educ* Ampleforth, Keble Coll Oxford (MA); *m* 15 July 1983, Lucinda Margaret Ann, da of late Maj Donald Struan Robertson; 1 s (Dermot b 16 Nov 1988), 1 da (Caroline b 3 May 1987); *Career* Citibank NA 1977–82, Swiss Bank Corp International Ltd 1982–88 (exec dir 1986–88), head of eurosecurities and swaps Istituto Bancario San Paolo di Torino London 1989–91, dir A Boursot & Co Ltd wine merchants 1992–, dir of investment mgmnt Batten & Co 1996–; memb Ctee of Constance Fund Royal Soc of Br Sculptors 1991–; *Books* The Muskerry Book of Hunting Fiction (ed, 1992), Borrower Briefings (1993), International Guide to Government Securities and Derivatives (1994), Understanding Options (1996), Using Options (1996), Mastering Government Securities (1996); *Clubs* Chelsea Arts; *Style*— Stephen Mahony, Esq; ✉ Broadclose House, Babcary, Somerton, Somerset TA11 7ED (☎ 01458 223318, fax 01458 223999)

MAHY, Dr Brian Wilfred John; s of Wilfred John Mahy (d 1966), of Guernsey, CI, and Norah Lilian, *née* Dillingham (d 1968); *b* 7 May 1937; *Educ* Elizabeth Coll Guernsey, Univ of Southampton (BSc, PhD), Univ of Cambridge (ScD, MA); *m* 1, 27 Aug 1959 (m dis 1986), Valerie Elaine, da of John Victor Pouteaux, of Guernsey; 2 s (Alex b 1964, Tim b 1966), 1 da (Penny b 1970); m 2, 29 Oct 1988, Penny Mary, da of Robert William Cunningham (d 1987), of Swansea, S Wales; *Career* Univ of Cambridge: asst dir of res in virology 1965–80, Huddersfield lectr in special pathology 1980–84, fell Wolfson Coll 1966–84; dir: Animal Virus Res Inst 1984–89, Div of Viral and Rickettsial Diseases Centers for Disease Control and Prevention Atlanta Georgia 1989–; vice pres Int Union of Microbiological Socs (past chm Virology Div); memb: American Soc of Virology, American Soc for Microbiology, Soc for General Microbiology; fell Infectious Diseases Soc of America; *Recreations* violin, gardening; *Style*— Dr Brian W J Mahy; ✉ Steele Cobb House, 2632 Fox Hills Drive, Decatur, Ga 30033, USA (☎ 00 1 404 728 0564, fax 00 1 404 728 0032); Division of Viral & Rickettsial Diseases, Centers for Disease Control and Prevention, 1600 Clifton Rd, Atlanta, Ga 30333, USA (☎ 00 1 404 639 3574, fax 00 1 404 639 3163)

MAIDEN, (James) Dennis; s of James William Maiden (d 1971), of Parkgate, Yorkshire, and Elsie, *née* Brotherton (d 1982); *b* 28 June 1932; *Educ* Wath-upon-Dearne GS; *m* 4 June 1953, Irene, da of Benjamin Harris (d 1976), of Rotherham, Yorkshire; 1 s (Jonathan b 1962), 1 da (Sally b 1959); *Career* engrg conslt Husband and Co 1958–63, chief engr British Shoe Corporation 1963–67; CITB: devpt mangr 1967–73, gen mangr 1973–76, dir of trg 1976–85, chief exec 1985–90; dir gen Fedn of Master Builders 1990–; tstee the Leonard Cheshire Fndn 1986–91; pres: Norfolk Outward Bound Assoc, King's Lynn branch BIM; Freeman City of London 1988, Liveryman Worshipful Co of Constructors 1990, Liveryman Worshipful Co of Plumbers 1989; CEng, MIMechE 1960, CIMgt 1966, MIPM 1969, FFB 1987; *Recreations* golf, gardening, theatre; *Clubs* RAC, Hunstanton Golf; *Style*— Dennis Maiden, Esq; ✉ Micklebring, Church Lane, Bircham, King's Lynn, Norfolk PE31 6QW (☎ 01485 578336); 203 Gilbert House, Barbican, London (☎ 0171 588 6019); Federation of Master Builders, 14–15 Great James St, London WC1N 3DP (☎ 0171 242 7583, fax 0171 404 0296)

MAIDMENT, Francis Edward (Ted); s of Charles Edward, and late Olive Mary Maidment; *b* 23 Aug 1942; *Educ* Pocklington Sch York, Jesus Coll Cambridge (scholar); *Career* housemaster Lancing 1975–81 (asst master 1965–81); headmaster: Ellesmere Coll Shropshire 1982–88, Shrewsbury 1988–; *Recreations* singing, medieval history, modest tennis; *Style*— Ted Maidment, Esq; ✉ Shrewsbury School, Shropshire SY3 7BA (☎ 01743 344537)

MAIDMENT, Dr Susan Rachel; da of Peter Elman, of Jerusalem, Israel, and Frances, *née* Tuckman; *b* 15 Feb 1944; *Educ* South Hampstead HS for Girls, LSE (LLB, LLM), Univ of Keele (LLD); *children* 1 s (Adam b 1973), 2 da (Alice b 1971, Eleanor b 1980); *Career* called to the Bar Lincoln's Inn 1968, lectr in law Univ of Bristol 1967–70, sr lectr in law Univ of Keele 1970–84, practising barr 1984–; *Books* Child Custody and Divorce (1984); *Style*— Dr Susan Maidment; ✉ 1 King's Bench Walk, Temple, London EC4 (☎ 0171 583 6266)

MAIDSTONE, Viscount; Daniel James Hatfield Finch Hatton; s and h of 16 Earl of Winchilsea; *b* 7 Oct 1967; *m* 18 June 1996, Shelley Amanda, da of Gordon Gillard, of The Garden House, The Park, Yeovil, Somerset; *Style*— Viscount Maidstone

MAIDSTONE, Bishop of 1992–; Rt Rev Gavin Hunter Reid; s of Arthur William Reid (d 1971), and Jean Smith, *née* Guthrie (d 1977); *b* 24 May 1934; *Educ* Roan Sch Greenwich, QMC and King's Coll London (BA); *m* 1959, Mary Eleanor, da of Herbert Arthur Smith; 2 s (Stephen Clive Guthrie b 24 Aug 1961, Stuart Andrew John b 26 March 1963), 1 da (Catherine Fiona (Mrs Reid-Jones) b 26 March 1966); *Career* ordained deacon Chelmsford Cathedral 1960, asst curate St Paul's E Ham 1960–63, curate i/c St John & Matthew S Hornchurch 1963–66, publications sec Church Pastoral Aid Soc 1966–71, editorial sec United Soc for Christian Literature 1971–74, hon curate St John's Worksop 1972–92, conslt missioner Church Pastoral Aid Soc 1990–92 (sec for evangelism 1974–90); seconded as: nat dir Mission England 1982–85, project dir Mission 89 1988–89; elected proctor (Guildford Dio) Gen Synod 1985–92; memb: Gen Synod Standing Ctee 1989–92, Bd for Mission and Unity (later Bd for Mission) 1986–92; chm Archbishops' Advsy Gp for the Millennium 1995–; *Books* The Gagging of God (1969), The Elaborate Funeral (1972), A New Happiness (1974), To Be Confirmed (1977), Good News to Share (1979), Starting out Together (1981), To Reach a Nation (1987), Beyond Aids (1987); co-author and ed of several other publications; *Recreations* golf, sailing, bird watching, photography; *Style*— The Rt Rev the Bishop of Maidstone; ✉ Bishop's House, Pett Lane, Charing, Ashford, Kent TN27 0DL (☎ 01233 712950, fax 01233 713543)

MAILE, Nigel Kingsley; s of David G Maile, of Canterbury, Kent, and Suzanne Mary, *née* Derham; *b* 4 Sept 1955; *Educ* Mill Hill Sch, Hatfield Poly; *m* 19 Oct 1985, Julia Eileen, da of Cdr John E Hommert, of Rowland's Castle, Hants; 1 da (Caroline Beatrice b 21 Feb 1993); *Career* chartered accountant Spicer & Oppenheim 1977–82, gp fin dir Bartle Bogle Hegarty (advtg agency) 1982–; ACA 1982; *Recreations* golf, walking, motorcycling; *Style*— Nigel Maile, Esq; ✉ Rowland's Castle, Hants PO9 6AF (☎ 01705 412483); Bartle Bogle Hegarty Ltd, 60 Kingly Street, London W1R 6DS (☎ 0171 734 1677, fax 0171 437 3666)

MAIN, Rev Prof Alan; TD (1982); s of James Emslie Walker Main, and Mary Ann Ross, *née* Black; *b* 31 March 1936; *Educ* Robert Gordon's Coll Aberdeen, Univ of Aberdeen (MA, BD, PhD), Union Theol Seminary NY (STM); *m* 30 July 1960, Anne Louise, da of Alexander Swanson, of Thurso, Caithness (d 1959); 2 da (Katherine b 1 April 1964, Lesley Anne b 20 Dec 1965); *Career* cmmnd chaplain RACHD 1971, with 153(H) Artillery Support Regt RCT(V) 1971–92; parish minister Chapel of Garioch Aberdeenshire 1963–70, chaplain Univ of Aberdeen 1970–80, moderator Presbytery of Aberdeen 1984–85 (Garioch 1969–70), prof of practical theology Christ's Coll Aberdeen 1980– (provost Faculty of Divinity 1990–93, master Christ's Coll 1992–); sr advsr in religious bdcasting Grampian TV 1977–87; chm: Grampian Marriage Guidance Cncl 1978–82, Cruse 1980–84, NE Cncl on Disability 1982–85, Jt Ethical Ctee Univ of Aberdeen and Grampian Health Bd 1992–; memb Assembly Cncl Church of Scotland 1982–87, memb Int Acad of Practical Theology 1992–; govr Robert Gordon's Coll Aberdeen 1988–; *Books* Worship Now II (ed, 1989), One Man's Ministry (ed, 1993), But Where Shall Wisdom Be Found (ed, 1995); *Recreations* golf, music; *Style*— The Rev Prof Alan Main, TD; ✉ Kirkfield, Barthol Chapel, Inverurie, Aberdeenshire AB51 8TD (☎ 01651 806602); Department of Divinity with Religious Studies, King's College, University of Aberdeen (☎ 01224 272380/5)

MAIN, Prof Brian George McArthur; s of George McArthur Main, of Buckhaven, Fife, and Margaret Welsh, *née* Currie; *b* 24 Aug 1947; *Educ* Univ of St Andrews (BSc), Univ of California Berkeley (MBA, MA, PhD); *m* 4 July 1980, June Marks Lambert, da of James S Lambert; 2 s (Christopher b 23 June 1985, Simon b 4 July 1988), 1 da (Alice b 11 March 1992); *Career* prodn planning assoc and mangr Eli Lilly 1971–72, reader in economics Univ of Edinburgh 1983–87 (lectr 1976–83); prof of economics: Univ of St Andrews 1987–91, Univ of Edinburgh 1991–; memb Cncl Scottish Economic Soc 1982–91; *Recreations* running, fishing; *Style*— Prof Brian Main; ✉ University of Edinburgh, Department of Economics, Edinburgh, Scotland EH8 9JY (☎ 0131 650 8360, fax 0131 668 4514)

MAIN, Donald Alexander; *b* 13 Jan 1935; *Educ* Morgan Acad Dundee, Univ of St Andrews; *m* Sara Anne Elizabeth; 3 c; *Career* trainee CA 1952–57, commercial mangr Vickers plc Germany 1958–64, mangr CPC Inc Scandinavia 1964–69, fin dir (international) British Leyland 1969–72, fin mangr (Europe) Mars Inc 1972–76, fin dir Alcan Aluminium (UK) Ltd 1976–78, md (Alcan Sheet) Alcan Aluminium 1979–81, gp fin dir Forte plc 1981–; also currently dir: The Savoy Hotel plc, Gardner Merchant

Services Group, Funding for Homes Ltd; memb Accounting Standards Bd, memb Cncl and treas Univ of Surrey; MICAS 1958; *Recreations* golf, music, travel; *Style*— Donald Main, Esq; ✉ Mahogany Hall, The Common, Chipperfield, Herts WD4 9BX; Forte plc, 166 High Holborn, London WC1V 6TT (☎ 0171 836 7744)

MAIN, Air Vice-Marshal John Bartram; CB (1996), OBE (1979, MBE 1977); s of Wing Commander James Taylor Main, OBE (d 1980), and Nellie Ethel, *née* Toleman; *Educ* Portsmouth GS, Univ of Birmingham (BSc); *m* 1965, Helen Joyce, da of Ronald E Lambert; 2 da (Susan Elizabeth b 29 Sept 1966, Julie Patricia b 21 March 1969); *Career* cmmnd Engr Branch RAF 1960, RAF Tech Coll Henlow 1964; served: RAF Benson 1964–66, RAF Hiswa Aden 1966–67, RAF Thorney Island 1967–70, Directorate of Scientific and Tech Intelligence 1970–74; OC No 33 Signals Unit Cyprus 1974–77, OC RAF Digby 1977–79, RAF Staff Coll Bracknell 1979–80, RAF Signals Engrg Estab Henlow 1980–83, head of Tech Intelligence (Air) 1983–87, RCDS 1986, Dep Cmd Aerosystems Engr 2 HQ Strike Cmd 1987–88, Cmdt RAF Signals Engrg Estab and Air Cdre Signals HQ RAF Support Cmd 1988–89, Dir of Cmd Control, Communication and Info Systems (Policy & Operational Requirements) 1989–93, Dir Gen of Support Servs (RAF) 1993–94, Air Offr Communications and Info Systems and Air Offr Cmdg Signals Units 1994–96; mil dir Matra Marconi Space UK Ltd 1996–; CEng 1968, FIEE 1983, FRAeS 1984, Fell Inst of Electronics and Electrical Incorporated Engrs (FIEIE) 1991; *Recreations* gardening, cycling, tennis, windsurfing, sailing and reading; *Clubs* Royal Air Force; *Style*— Air Vice-Marshal John Main, CB, OBE; ✉ Matra Marconi Space UK Ltd, Anchorage Road, Portsmouth, Hampshire PO3 5PU

MAIN, His Hon John Roy; QC (1974); s of Alfred Charles Main (d 1968); *b* 21 June 1930; *Educ* Portsmouth GS, Hotchkiss Sch USA, BNC Oxford; *m* 1955, Angela de la Condamine, da of Robert William Home Davies (d 1970); 2 s (Christopher b 11 March 1961, Anthony (twin) b 11 March 1961), 1 da (Bridget (Mrs Hobson) b 3 June 1958); *Career* Lt RNR; called to the Bar Inner Temple 1954; memb Special Panel Tport Tbnl 1970–76, dep chm IOW Quarter Sessions 1971, recorder Crown Court 1972–76, circuit judge (SE Circuit) 1976–95; pres Tport Tbnl 1996–; govr Portsmouth GS 1988–; *Recreations* walking, gardening, music; *Style*— His Hon J R Main, QC; ✉ 4 Queen Anne Drive, Claygate, Surrey KT10 0PP (☎ 01372 466380)

MAIN, Sir Peter Tester; kt (1985), ERD (1964); s of Peter Tester Main (d 1977), of Aberdeen, and Esther Paterson, *née* Lawson (d 1968); *b* 21 March 1925; *Educ* Robert Gordon's Coll Aberdeen, Univ of Aberdeen (MB ChB, MD); *m* 1, 13 May 1952, Dr Margaret Fimister (d 1984), da of Thomas William Tweddle (d 1952); 2 s (Lawson Fimister b 16 Feb 1953, Gerald Peter b 5 Oct 1957), 1 da (Jennifer Marjory (Mrs Shilton) b 26 June 1955); m 2, 13 Dec 1986, May Hetherington Anderson, *née* McMillan; *Career* Lt-Col RAMC (AER); The Boots Co: joined 1957, dir of res 1968, dir 1973–85, vice-chm 1980–81, chm 1982–85; dir: W A Baxter & Sons Ltd 1985–91, John Fleming & Co Ltd 1985–89; govr Henley Mgmnt Coll 1983–86; memb: NEDC 1984–85, Scottish Health Servs Policy Bd 1985–88; chm Inveresk Research International 1986–89; dir Scottish Devpt Agency 1986–91, memb Univ of Aberdeen Devpt Tst 1987–, chm Grantown Heritage Tst 1987–91; Hon LLD Aberdeen 1986; FRCPE 1982, CIMgt 1978; *Recreations* fishing, Scottish music; *Style*— Sir Peter Main, ERD; ✉ Ninewells House, Chirnside, Duns, Berwickshire TD11 3XF (☎ 01890 818191)

MAINDS, Allan Gilfillan; s of Capt George Gordon Gilfillan Mainds, and Helen Northgate, *née* Woodhouse; *b* 15 Dec 1945; *Educ* Berkhampsted Sch; *m* 1, 17 July 1982 (m dis 1987), Hon Veronica Mary Addington, da of Viscount Sidmouth; m 2, 11 April 1992, Lavinia Marion, da of Christopher and Celia Prideaux; 2 da (Polly b 1994, Harriet b 1996); *Career* admitted slr 1972; called to the Bar Inner Temple 1977, recorder of the Crown Ct 1996–; *Recreations* flying light aircraft and gliding, rowing and sculling; *Clubs* London Rowing; *Style*— Allen Mainds, Esq; ✉ Chambers of James Hunt, Esq, QC, 36 Bedford Row, London WC1R 4JH (☎ 0171 421 8000)

MAINELLI, Michael R; s of Michael R Mainelli, and Katherine E, *née* Smith; *b* 19 Dec 1958; *Educ* Harvard Univ (Martin Marietta scholar, BA), Trinity Coll Dublin, LSE (DPhil); *children* 1 s (Nicholas b 7 Oct 1989); *Career* researcher Harvard Laboratory for Computer Graphics and Spatial Analysis 1977–81; Petroconsultants Group: Geodat project dir Petroconsultants Ltd 1979–82, general mangr Petroconsultants (CES) Ltd 1982–85; pres ISF Inc 1985–86, sr mangr Arthur Andersen & Co Management Consultants 1986–87, ptnr (BDO Consulting) BDO Binder Hamlyn 1988–94, ptnr Arthur Andersen & Co 1994–95; dir: Whale Conservation Inst 1994–, Z/Yen Ltd 1995–; corp devpt dir Defence Evaluation & Research Agency (DERA) MOD 1995–; memb: Strategic Planning Soc 1990 (dir 1995–), Ed Bd Journal of Strategic Change 1990–; MInstPet 1986, MInstD 1988, MBCS 1989, MIMC 1990; author of numerous pubns in learned jls; *Recreations* sailing; *Clubs* Royal Corinthian Yacht, Harvard; *Style*— Michael Mainelli, Esq; ✉ 1 Upbrook Mews, London W2 3HG; Z/Yen Ltd, 5–7 St Helen's Place, London EC3A 6AU (☎ 0171 562 9562, fax 0171 628 5751)

MAINES, (James) Dennis; s of late Arthur Burtonwood Maines, and Lilian Maines,*née* Carter; *b* 26 July 1937; *Educ* Leigh GS, City Univ (BSc); *m* 15 Oct 1960, Janet Enid, da of late Percy Kemp; 3 s (Stephen, Christopher, Daniel); *Career* joined RSRE (formerly RRE) Malvern 1956: scientific offr 1960, head Guided Weapons Optics and Electronics Gp 1981–83, head Microwave and Electro-optics Gp 1983; head Sensors Electronic Warfare and Guided Weapons GP ARE Portsdown 1984, dep dir (weapons) RAE 1986–88, dir gen Guided Weapons and Electronic Systems MOD (PE) 1988–95, dir gen Command Info Systems MOD 1995–; FIEE, CEng; *Books* Surface Wave Filters (contrib 1977), more than 30 pubns in learned jls; *Recreations* sailing, cricket, squash, painting, gardening, car restoration; *Style*— Dennis Maines, Esq; ✉ MOD (PE), Abbey Wood, CEDAR No 127, PO Box 702, Bristol BS1 7DU

MAINGARD DE LA VILLE-ÈS-OFFRANS, Sir (Louis Pierre) René; kt (1982), CBE (1961); s of Joseph René Maingard de la Ville-ès-Offrans (d 1956), and Véronique, *née* Hugnin (d 1969); *b* 9 July 1917; *Educ* St Joseph's Coll, Royal Coll of Mauritius, Business Trg Corp London; *m* 1946, Marie Hélène Françoise, da of Sir Philippe Raffray, CBE, QC (d 1975); 3 da (Catherine, Anne, Sophie); *Career* served WWII RAF Fighter Cmd 131 and 165 Sqdn 1939–45; chm De Chazal du Mée Assocs Ltd, chm and md Rogers & Co Ltd 1948–82; chm: Mauritius Steam Navigation Co Ltd 1964, Mauritius Portland Cement Co Ltd 1960–, Mauritius Molasses Co Ltd 1968–, United Docks Ltd 1960–; dir: Mauritius Commercial Bank Ltd 1956–, The Anglo-Mauritius Assurance Co, Indian Ocean Bulk Carriers Ltd; consul for Finland in Mauritius 1957–83, Order of the White Rose Finland 1973; *Recreations* golf, fishing, boating; *Clubs* Dodo, Mauritius Turf; *Style*— Sir René Maingard de la Ville-ès-Offrans, CBE; ✉ De Chazal Du Mée Associates Ltd, PO Box 799, Port Louis, Mauritius (☎ 00 230 208 7923, fax 00 230 208 0086, telex 4417 DDC)

MAINI, Sir Amar Nath; kt (1957), CBE (1953, OBE 1948); s of Nauhria Ram Maini, of Nairobi; *b* 31 July 1911; *Educ* Govt Indian Sch Nairobi, LSE, Middle Temple; *m* 1935, Ram Saheli Mehra (d 1982); 2 s; *Career* first mayor of Kampala 1950–55, min of Corporations and Regnl Communications Uganda 1955–58, min of Commerce and Indust 1958–61, speaker E African Central Legislative Assembly 1961–67, dep chm Kenya Broadcasting Corporation 1962–63; formerly: advocate High Cts of Uganda and Kenya, pres Central Cncl Indian Assocs Uganda, dep chm Uganda Electricity Bd; *Clubs* The Reform; *Style*— Sir Amar Maini, CBE; ✉ 55 Vicarage Rd, East Sheen, London SW14 8RY (☎ 0181 878 1497)

MAINWARING, Richard Charles; s of Henry Charles Richard Mainwaring, and Ann Findley, *née* Hobbs; *b* 4 June 1953; *Educ* Avonhurst Sch Bristol; *m* 15 Nov 1980, Josephine Ann, da of Kenneth Wiltshire; 1 da (Eleanor Louise), 1 s (Samual Alexander); *Career* Br barefoot waterskiing speed record 72 mph 1978 (entry in Guiness Book of Records still current); most successful Euro and Br barefoot waterskier ever: 6 times Euro champion (1983, 1984, 1985, 1986, 1987 and 1989), 11 times Br champion 1984–95, capt Br Barefoot Waterski Team 1985–88; world record jump 90.3 ft (27.5m) set Lakeside London 1994; Br record holder for jump, tricks & jump and Veterans' Div slalom; current ranking: No 1 in Britain, No 13 in world; Freedom Tell City Indiana (USA tour 1979); *Clubs* Keuka Waterski; *Style*— Richard Mainwaring, Esq; ✉ White Hart House, Fairford, Gloucestershire GL7 4NH (☎ 01285 711022, fax 01285 711033)

MAIR, Alexander; MBE (1968); s of Charles Meston Mair (d 1968), and Helen, *née* Dickie (d 1969); *b* 5 Nov 1922; *Educ* Skene Central Sch, Sch of Accountancy Glasgow; *m* 7 Aug 1953, Margaret Isobel Gowans, da of John Rennie (d 1955); *Career* RAC 1943–47, 3 Carabiniers 1944–47, served in India and Burma; chief accountant Bydand Industrial Holdings 1956–60; Grampian TV: co sec 1961–70, dir 1967, chief exec 1970–87; dir: ITN 1978–87, TV Times 1975–87; chm RGIT Ltd 1988–; pres: Aberdeen C of C 1989–91, Royal Northern and Univ Club 1984–85; chm Aberdeen Int Football Festival 1981–90; memb Aberdeen Airport Users' Ctee 1978–, govr Robert Gordon's Coll Aberdeen 1987–; FCMA, FRTS, FRSA; *Recreations* skiing, golf, gardening; *Clubs* Royal Northern and University (Aberdeen), Royal Aberdeen Golf; *Style*— Alexander Mair, Esq, MBE; ✉ Ravenswood, 66 Rubislaw Den South, Aberdeen AB2 6AX (☎ 01224 317619)

MAIR, Alexander Stirling Fraser (Alistair); MBE (1987), DL (Perth and Kinross 1993); *b* 1935, Aberdeenshire; *Educ* Robert Gordon's Coll Aberdeen, Univ of Aberdeen (BSc); *m*; 4 s, 1 da; *Career* short serv cmmn RAF 1960–62, tech offr Central Work Study Unit Air Miny; Rolls Royce Ltd Glasgow 1957–71 (graduate apprentice rising to shop control mangr and product centre mangr), md Caithness Glass Ltd Wick 1971–75, mktg dir Worcester Royal Porcelain Co 1975–77; Caithness Glass plc: md 1977–91, cmmnd new factory Perth 1979, led MBO 1984, chm 1991–, led second MBO 1993; non-exec dir: Grampian Television plc 1986–, Crieff Hydro Ltd 1994– (chm 1996–); CBI: memb Scot Cncl 1981–92, memb Cncl 1985–, chm Scot 1989–91, memb Pres's Ctee 1990–91, chm Regnl Chairmen's Ctee 1990–91; pres Br Glass Manufacturers Confedn 1997– (dep pres 1994–96); govr Morrison's Acad Crieff 1985– (chm 1996–), cmmr Queen Victoria Sch Dunblane 1992–, memb Ct Univ of Aberdeen 1993–; chm Crieff and Dist Aux Assoc (Richmond House) 1993–; vice chm Cons and Unionist Party Scotland 1992–93 (memb Scot Business Gp 1989–93); FRSA 1986; *Clubs* RSAC (Glasgow); *Style*— Alistair Mair, Esq, MBE, DL; ✉ Dungora, Crieff, Perthshire PH7 4AG (☎ 01764 652191)

MAIR, Antony Stefan Romley; s of John Mair, MBE (d 1971), of Hill House, Surley Row, Caversham, Berks, and Marie Justine Antoinette, *née* Bunbury; *b* 27 Dec 1946; *Educ* Reading Sch, Magdalen Coll Oxford (BA, MA); *Career* slr; chm Mgmnt Ctee Holman Fenwick and Willan 1987–88 (joined 1976, ptnr 1979), ptnr Stephenson Harwood 1988–; memb: Law Soc, IBA; Freeman City of Oxford 1975; *Recreations* theatre, gardening; *Style*— Antony Mair, Esq; ✉ Stephenson Harwood, One St Paul's Churchyard, London EC4 (☎ 0171 329 4422, fax 0171 606 0822, telex 886789 SHSPC G)

MAIR, Prof (William) Austyn; CBE (1969); s of Dr William Mair (d 1968), of London, and Catharine Millicent, *née* Fyfe (d 1966); *b* 24 Feb 1917; *Educ* Highgate Sch, Clare Coll Cambridge (BA, MA); *m* 15 April 1944, Mary Woodhouse, da of Rev Christopher Benson Crofts (d 1956); 2 s (Christopher b 1945, Dr Robert Mair, FEng, *qv* b 1950); *Career* engrg pupil Rolls-Royce Ltd 1939–40; cmmnd Pilot Offr RAF (Tech Branch) 1940, attached to Royal Aircraft Estab 1940–46, released from serv Sqdn Ldr 1946; dir Fluid Motion Laboratory Univ of Manchester 1946–52; Univ of Cambridge: fell Downing Coll 1953–83 (hon fell 1983), Francis Mond prof of aeronautical engrg 1952–83 (emeritus prof 1983), head Engrg Dept 1973–83; Hon DSc Cranfield 1990; FRAeS 1954, FEng 1984; *Books* Aircraft Performance (with D L Birdsall, 1992); *Style*— Prof Austyn Mair, CBE, FEng; ✉ 7 The Oast House, Pinehurst, Grange Road, Cambridge CB3 9AP (☎ 01223 350137)

MAIR, Dr Robert James; s of Prof (William) Austyn Mair, CBE, FEng, *qv*, of Cambridge, and Mary Woodhouse, *née* Crofts; *b* 20 April 1950; *Educ* Leys Sch Cambridge, Clare Coll Cambridge (MA, PhD); *m* 19 Sept 1981, Margaret Mary Plowden, da of Rt Hon Sir Patrick O'Connor, *qv*; 1 da (Julia b 29 May 1984), 1 s (Patrick b 13 May 1986); *Career* asst engr (later sr engr) Scott Wilson Kirkpatrick & Partners London & Hong Kong 1971–82 (seconded to Univ of Cambridge researching tunnelling in soft ground 1976–79); dir Geotechnical Consulting Group (specialising in geotechnical engrg) 1983–; Royal Acad of Engrg visiting prof Univ of Cambridge; Br Geotechnical Soc Prize 1981, ICE Unwin Meml lectr 1992, Bishop medal 1994; FICE 1990, FEng 1992; *Books* Pressuremeters - Use and Interpretation (with D M Wood, 1987); *Clubs* Hurlingham; *Style*— Dr Robert J Mair, FEng; ✉ 21 Beauclerc Road, London W6 0NS (☎ 0181 741 1201); Director, Geotechnical Consulting Group, 1a Queensberry Place, London SW7 2DL (☎ 0171 581 8348, fax 0171 584 0157)

MAIRANTS, Ivor; s of Solomon Mairants (d 1933), of London, and Sara Thema, *née* Kopa (d 1975); *b* 18 July 1908; *Educ* Raine's Foundation Sch London; *m* 18 Oct 1931, Lily, da of Aaron Schneider (d 1962), of London; 1 s (Stuart b 1938), 1 da (Valerie b 1933); *Career* guitarist; Roy Fox's Band 1932–37, Ambrose's Band 1938–43, Geraldo's Orchestra 1940–52, guitar conslt to Boosey and Hawkes Ltd 1950–60, estab Central Sch of Dance Music London 1950–59, estab Ivor Mairants Musicentre London 1959, Mantovani's Orchestra 1963–77, Manuel and His Music of the Mountains 1962–78, Melody Maker poll winner 1944–46, 1950–51 and 1953–54; composer of numerous guitar works (incl The Great Jazz Guitarists); subject of Focus on Ivor Mairants (Zodiac cassette, 1990); memb: Musician's Union, Performing Right Soc, Br Acad of Song Writers Composers and Authors, Guitar Fndn of America; Freeman: City of London 1987, Worshipful Co of Musicians 1989; memb Guild of Freemen 1989; fell Inst of Arts and Letters Switzerland 1957; BASCA Gold Badge of Merit 1994; *Books* My Fifty Fretting Years (autobiography, 1980), Three Jazz Sonatas for Solo Guitar (1996); *Recreations* swimming, travel, walking; *Clubs* Coda (vice chm); *Style*— Ivor Mairants, Esq; ✉ 4 Hollies End, Mill Hill Village, London NW7 2RY (☎ 0181 959 3136); Ivor Mairants Musicentre, 56 Rathbone Place, London W1P 1AB (☎ 0171 636 1481/2)

MAIRS, Raymond John; s of David Mairs (d 1991), of Co Antrim, and Susan Elizabeth, *née* Colvin (d 1978); *b* 15 Aug 1951; *Educ* Ballyclare HS, Queen's Univ Belfast (BSc, Dip Arch); *m* 6 Aug 1976, Carol Jean Ruth, da of Neville Arthur Ginn, of Co Antrim; 3 da (Rachel Ruth b 1981, Rebecca Ann b 1985, Jessica Elizabeth b 1989); *Career* architect, fish farmer; private practice 1978, ptnr Mairs & Wray 1979–92, Raymond J Mairs Chartered Architects 1992–; memb RSUA Housing Ctee 1985–86; chm: Br Trout Assoc 1988–90, Euro Gp of Fédération Européenne de la Salmoniculture 1988–93, Southern Trout Co-op 1993–95; dir Northern Ireland Seafoods Ltd 1993–, dir NI Food and Drink Assoc 1996–; rapporteur Aqua-Culture Working Gp of Fisheries Advsy Ctee to Euro Cmmn 1989–92, dir Southern Trout Co-operative Ltd 1993–95, memb Health Promotion Agency N Ireland 1990–, memb BBC NI Agric Advsy Ctee 1994–; *Style*— Raymond J Mairs, Esq; ✉ Glen Oak House, Crumlin BT29 4BW (☎ 01849 423172); Raymond J Mairs Chartered Architects, Glen Oak Mills, Crumlin BT29 4XL (fax 01849 422434)

MAISEY, Prof Michael Norman; *b* 10 June 1939; *Educ* Caterham Sch Surrey, Guy's Hosp Med Sch (BSc, MB BS, MD); *m* 2 c; *Career* Guy's Hospital: house physician March 1964, casualty offr June 1964, house surgeon 1964–65; sr house offr in medicine New Cross Hosp 1965; house physician in: chest diseases Brompton Hosp, rheumatology

Hammersmith Hosp; registrar: in neurology Brook Gen Hosp 1967, in gen med Guy's Hosp 1969–70 (endocrinology and radioisotopes 1967–69); fell Nuclear Medicine Johns Hopkins Hosp USA 1970–72; Guy's Hosp: sr registrar gen med 1970–72, consIt physician in nuclear med and endocrinology 1973–83, clinical dir Radiological Service, consIt physician in nuclear med, consIt physician to Thyroid Clinic, currently med dir Guy's Hosp; prof of radiological sciences United Med & Dental Schs of Guy's and St Thomas's Hosps, dir Guy's & St Thomas's Hosp Clinical PET Centre, jt med dir Guy's and St Thomas' Hosp Tst 1993–; hon consIt in nuclear medicine and endocrinology to the Army, chm Guy's Hosp Unit Mgmnt Bd 1991–93, examiner Soc of Radiographers Diploma in Nuclear Medicine 1976–, pres British Nuclear Medicine Soc 1978–80 (sec 1976–78), visiting prof Nuclear Medicine Toronto 1976, chm SAC (Nuclear Medicine) of JCHMT 1982–84, visiting exchange prof Johns Hopkins Hosp Baltimore 1985–, visiting lectr Forces Inst of Cardiology Pakistan 1987, visiting prof Shanghai Univ Hosp 1988; memb: Scientific Ctee on Euro Nuclear Med Congress 1989, Editorial Bd Nuclear Medicine Communications and Euro Jl of Nuclear Med; memb: BIR, British Nuclear Medicine Soc, Euro Nuclear Med Soc, American Soc of Nuclear Med, Thyroid Club, EORTC Thyroid Cancer Gp; MRCS, LRCP, FRCR, FRCP; *Books* Nuclear Medicine - A Clinical Introduction (1980), An Altas of Normal Skeletal Santigraphy (with J J Flannagan, 1985), An Altas of Nuclear Medicine (with I Fogelman, 1988, 2 edn 1994), Clinical Nuclear Medicine (ed with K E Britton, D L Gilday, 1983, 2 ed 1992), numerous articles in various learned jls; *Style*— Prof Michael Maisey; ✉ Guy's Hospital, St Thomas Street, London SE1 9RT (☎ 0171 955 4531, fax 0171 955 4532, e-mail m.maisey@umds.ac.uk)

MAISNER, Air Vice-Marshal Alexander (Aleksander); CB (1977), CBE (1969), AFC (1955); s of Henryk Maisner (d 1943), and Helene Anne, *née* Brosin (d 1959); *b* 26 July 1921; *Educ* High Sch and Lyceum Czestochowa Poland, Warsaw Univ; *m* 1946, Mary, da of O R Coverley (d 1958); 1 s, 1 da; *Career* War Serv Polish Artillery and Polish AF, joined RAF 1946, DSD RAF Staff Coll, CO RAF Seletar, asst cmdt RAF Coll Cranwell, ret as dir gen Personnel Mgmnt 1977; personnel exec Reed International Ltd 1977–82; govr Shiplake Coll 1978–96; pres of Polish AF Assoc 1982–; dir Indust and Parliament Tst 1984–1987; Cdr's Cross with Star Order of Polonia Restituta 1990, Cdr Order of Merit (Poland) 1992; *Recreations* reading, gardening; *Clubs* RAF; *Style*— Air Vice-Marshal Alexander Maisner, CB, CBE, AFC; ✉ c/o Lloyds Bank, 1 Reading Rd, Henley-on-Thames, Oxon RG9 1AE

MAITLAND, Colin Neil; s of Col Otis Edward Maitland, MBE (d 1977), of Surrey, and Margaret Joan, *née* Haslehurst (d 1955); *b* 7 July 1940; *Educ* Old Buckenham Hall Norfolk, Embley Park Romsey Hants, Univ of Southampton; *m* 30 Sept 1967, Judy, da of Col Howard Watson Wright; 2 s (Mark Otis b 1976, Sam Ragen b 1980), 1 da (Kate Margaret b 1978); *Career* offr RM 1958–69; NOP 1969–70, Louis Harris 1970–71, res mangr Leo Burnett LPE 1971–73; md: EyesCan 1973–83, ISIS Research PLC 1984–; chm Embley Park Sch 1969–90; *Books* New Product Launch Planner (1988), Colins Guides (China, Taiwan, Vietnam, Philippines) (1994), Positioning Research (1996); *Style*— Colin Maitland, Esq

MAITLAND, Sir Donald James Dundas; GCMG (1977, CMG 1967), kt (1973), OBE (1960); s of Thomas Douglas Maitland, and Wilhelmina Sarah Dundas; *b* 16 Aug 1922; *Educ* George Watson's Coll Edinburgh, Univ of Edinburgh (MA); *m* 1950, Jean Marie, da of Gordon Young; 1 s, 1 da; *Career* served WWII ME India and Burma in Royal Scots and Rajputana Rifles; served Foreign Serv (later Dip Serv) 1947–80: in Amara, Baghdad, dir MECAS Lebanon 1956–60, Cairo 1963–65, head News Dept FO 1965–67, princ private sec 1967–69, ambass Libya 1969–70, chief press sec 10 Downing St 1970–73, ambass and perm UK rep UN 1973–74 and EEC 1975–79, dep under-sec FCO 1974–75, dep perm under-sec FCO 1979–80, perm under-sec Dept Energy 1980–82, ret 1982; govt dir Britoil 1983–85; dir: Slough Estates 1983–92, Northern Engineering Industries 1986–89; advsr to British Telecom 1985–86; chm: UK Ctee World Communications Year 1983, Ind Cmmn for World-Wide Telecommunications Devpt 1983–85, Christians for Europe (now Charlemagne Inst) 1984–; memb Cwlth War Graves Cmmn 1983–87, dep chm IBA 1986–89; pres: Bath Inst for Rheumatic Diseases 1986–94, Federal Trust for Educn and Res 1987–; chm: Health Educn Authy 1989–94, Think Net Cmmn 1990–95; govr Westminster Coll Oxford 1990– (chm 1994–); Hon LLD Bath 1995; *Books* Diverse Times - Sundry Places (autobiography, 1996); *Recreations* hill-walking, music; *Style*— Sir Donald Maitland, GCMG, OBE; ✉ Murhill Farm House, Limpley Stoke, Bath BA3 6HH (☎ 01225 723157)

MAITLAND, Viscount; Ian Maitland; The Master of Lauderdale; s and h of 17 Earl of Lauderdale; *b* 4 Nov 1937; *Educ* Radley, Brasenose Coll Oxford (MA); *m* 27 April 1963, Ann Paule, da of Geoffrey B Clark, of London; 1 s, 1 da; *Heir* s, Master of Maitland, *qv*; *Career* Lt RNR 1963–73; has held various appts in mfrg industry; National Westminster Bank Plc: joined 1975, asst regnl mangr N Africa 1985, regnl mangr N Africa 1986, regnl mangr Middle East 1989, sr regnl mangr Africa and Middle East 1991–95; dir Maitland Consultancy Services Ltd 1995–; marketing advsr LSE 1995–; chm Tachbrook St Residents' Assoc, chm Pimlico Fedn of Residents' Assocs; memb The Queen's Body Guard for Scotland (Royal Co of Archers); *Recreations* sailing, photography; *Clubs* Royal Ocean Racing, New (Edinburgh); *Style*— Viscount Maitland; ✉ 150 Tachbrook St, London SW1V 2NE

MAITLAND, The Master of; Hon John Douglas Peter Maitland; s and h of Viscount Maitland, *qv*; *b* 29 May 1965; *Educ* Emanuel Sch, Radley, Durham Univ (BSc); *Style*— The Master of Maitland

MAITLAND, Lady (Helen) Olga; *née* Maitland; MP (C) Sutton and Cheam (majority 10,756); elder da of 17 Earl of Lauderdale, *qv*; *b* 23 May 1944; *Educ* Sch of St Mary and St Anne Abbots Bromley, Lycée Francais de Londres; *m* 18 April 1969, Robin William Patrick Hamilton Hay, *qv*, s of William Reginald Hay, of Mapperley, Nottingham; 2 s (Alastair b 1972, Fergus b 1981), 1 da (Camilla b 1975); *Career* former trainee reporter: Fleet St News Agency, Blackheath and District Reporter; reporter and columnist Sunday Express 1967–91, freelance journalist 1991–; fndr and chm: Families for Defence 1983–; Parly candidate (C) Bethnal Green & Stepney 1987, MP (C) Sutton and Cheam 1992–; memb: Select Ctee for Educn, All Party Br Ctee; sec to Cons Backbench Ctee NI and Defence and sec to Yugoslav Parly Gp; nominated for UN Media Peace Prize 1983; *Publications* Margaret Thatcher: the first ten years (1989); contrib: Peace Studies in Our Schools (1985), Political Indoctrination in Our Schools; *Recreations* theatre, travel; *Style*— The Lady Olga Maitland, MP; ✉ House of Commons, London SW1A 0AA

MAITLAND-CAREW, Hon Gerald Edward Ian; DL (Roxburgh, Ettrick and Laurderdale 1990); yr s of 6 Baron Carew, CBE (d 1994); name changed to Maitland-Carew by deed poll 1971; *b* 28 Dec 1941; *Educ* Harrow; *m* 1972, Rosalind Averil, da of Lt-Col Neil Hanning Reed Speke, MC; 2 s, 1 da; *Career* 2 Lt 15/19 Hussars 1961, Capt 1965, formerly ADC to GOC 44 Div Dover, Castle; memb the Queen's Body Guard for Scotland (The Royal Co of Archers) 1978; elected memb the Jockey Club 1987, chm: Lauderdale Hunt 1979–, Musselburgh Racecourse 1994–; *Clubs* Cavalry & Guards', White's; *Style*— The Hon Gerald Maitland-Carew, DL; ✉ Thirlestane Castle, Lauder, Berwickshire (☎ 01578 722 254, fax 01578 718 749)

MAITLAND-MAKGILL-CRICHTON, *see:* Crichton

MAITLAND SMITH, Geoffrey; s of Philip John Maitland Smith (d 1989), of Ramsden Heath, Billericay, Essex, by his w Kathleen, *née* Goff; *b* 27 Feb 1933; *Educ* Univ Coll Sch London; *m* 3 May 1986, Lucinda Enid, da of Lt-Col Gerald Owen Whyte (d 1994); *Career* chm: Sears plc 1985–June 1995 (dir 1971–95, chief exec 1978–88), Selfridges 1985–93, Mallett plc 1986–89, Hammerson plc 1993– (dir 1990–), W & FC Bonham and Sons Ltd 1996–; dir: Asprey plc 1980–93, Courtaulds plc 1983–90, Central Independent Television plc 1983–85, Imperial Group plc 1984–86, Midland Bank plc 1986– (dep chm 1992–), HSBC Holdings plc 1993–96; chm: Cncl Univ Coll Sch London 1987–96, Britain's 1996 Olympic Appeal 1994; memb: Film Reporting Cncl 1990–, Appeal Cncl Police Convalescence & Rehabilitation Tst 1993–, Appeal Advsy Gp Royal Coll of Surgns 1993–; hon chm Intercontinental Gp of Dept Stores 1990–; Liveryman Worshipful Co of Gardeners; FCA, CIMgt 1981; *Recreations* opera; *Style*— Geoffrey Maitland Smith, Esq; ✉ Hammerson plc, 100 Park Lane, London W1Y 4AR (☎ 0171 887 1000)

MAITLAND-TITTERTON, Col David Henry Sandford Leslie; s of Maj David Maitland-Titterton, TD (Herald Marchmont, d 1989), of Moberty, Airlie, and Mary Etheldritha Audrey Leslie (d 1988); *b* 4 Jan 1933; *Educ* Campbell Coll Belfast, Mons OCS, RMA Sandhurst, JSSC; *m* 23 April 1963, Rinalda Malvina, da of Sqdn Ldr The Hon Greville Baird (ka 1941); 1 s (Rupert Seymour Aulin Leslie b 1965), 1 da (Shân Gelda Jane b 1968); *Career* 2 Lt NIH (TA) 1952, 2 Lt 12 L 1954, GSOI US Army Armour Sch Fort Knox 1968, CO 9/12 Royal Lancers 1972, GSOI Br Army Trg Team Sudan 1974, GSOI (PE) 1977, Cmd Kuwait Liaison Team 1978, Col M3 (MOD) 1981, Defence Naval Military and Air Attache Damascus and Beirut 1985–86, Dep COS (Army) HQ 1 Gp 1986, ROI Chief Inspr Range Safety Inspection Team (Army) 1989–; memb CPRE 1989; Order of Two Niles Sudan 1980; *Recreations* country pursuits, history, engineering; *Clubs* Civil Service; *Style*— Col David Maitland-Titterton; ✉ Rimes Gigot, Baughurst, Hants RG26 5LW (☎ 0118 981 5098)

MAITLIS, Prof Peter Michael; s of Jacob J Maitlis (d 1987), and Judith, *née* Ebel (d 1985); *b* 15 Jan 1933; *Educ* Hendon Co GS, Univ of Birmingham (BSc), Univ of London (PhD, DSc); *m* 19 July 1959, Marion da of Herbert Basco (d 1977); 3 da (Niccola b 1963, Sally b 1965, Emily b 1970); *Career* asst lectr Univ of London 1956–60, Fulbright fell Cornell Univ 1960–61, res fell Harvard Univ 1961–62, prof McMaster Univ Hamilton Canada 1967–72 (asst prof 1962–64, assoc prof 1964–67), prof of inorganic chem Univ of Sheffield 1972–; fell Alfred P Sloan Fndn (USA) 1968–70, EWR Steacie Prize (Canada) 1971, RSC medallist (UK) 1981, Tilden lectr 1979, Sir Edward Frankland lectr (UK) 1984, RSC Mond lectr (UK) 1996–97; various offices in RSC (pres Dalton Div 1984–86), chm SERC Chemistry Ctee 1985–88, memb BBC Sci Consultative Gp 1988–93; FRS 1984 (memb Cncl 1991–93), FRSC; *Books* The Organic Chemistry of Palladium (Vols 1 & 2 1971); res papers in various chemistry jls; *Recreations* travel, swimming, theoretical fruit-growing; *Style*— Prof Peter Maitlis, FRS; ✉ Department of Chemistry, University of Sheffield, Sheffield S3 7HF

MAJOR, Christopher Ian; s of Edward Richard Major, of Friar's Cliff, Dorset and Audrey Yvonne, *née* Beardmore; *b* 14 June 1948; *Educ* Kingston GS, Wadham Coll Oxford (MA); *m* 19 Aug 1972, Susan Fenella, da of Harry Morrison Kirton (d 1984); *Career* slr 1973; ptnr: Lovell, White & King 1979–88, Lovell White Durrant 1988–; memb: Worshipful Co Slrs 1974, Law Soc of England & Wales 1973, Int Bar Assoc 1979, American Bar Assoc 1981, American Arbitration Assoc 1981; *Recreations* tennis; *Style*— Christopher Major, Esq; ✉ Lovell White Durrant, 65 Holborn Viaduct, London EC1A 2DY (☎ 0171 236 0066, fax 0171 236 0084)

MAJOR, Dr Edward; s of Morgan Major, of Llangynwyd, Bridgend, Mid Glamorgan, and late Nancy, *née* Jenkins; *b* 26 Nov 1948; *Educ* Maesteg GS, London Hosp Med Coll (MB BS); *m* 9 March 1974, Heather Gillian, da of Christopher Bevil Spiller, of Ipswich; 2 s (Euan Thomas, Huw Edward), 1 da (Sarah Ann); *Career* sr registrar Hosp for Sick Children Gt Ormond St 1979, sr lectr and consIt in anaesthetics London Hosp 1979–84 (sr registrar 1978–79), consIt in anaesthesia and intensive therapy Morriston Hosp Swansea 1984–; chm Intensive Care Soc 1989–91 (memb Cncl 1984–91, meetings sec 1987–89); memb Coll of Anaesthetists; *Books* Hazards and Complications of Anaesthesia (2 ed with T H Taylor, 1993); *Recreations* sailing; *Clubs* Mumbles Yacht; *Style*— Dr Edward Major; ✉ Heddfan, 23 Tavistock Road, Sketty, Swansea SA2 0SL; Intensive Therapy Unit, Morriston Hospital, Swansea SA6 6NL (☎ 01792 703472)

MAJOR, Eric Patrick; s of Reginald Charles Major (d 1982), of Walthamstow, London, and Katherine Teresa, *née* Weir (d 1986), of Leigh-on-Sea, Essex; *b* 25 June 1937; *Educ* William Morris Tech Sch, SW Essex Tech Coll (Essex cross country champion); *m* 1961, Patricia Leonora Mary, da of Leo Francis Ring (d 1983); 3 da (Perpetua b 30 April 1962, Felicity b 6 Oct 1963, Lucy b 29 Nov 1969), 1 s (Paul b 10 March 1965); *Career* Nat Serv RAF 1956–58; publicity mangr Frederick Muller Publishers 1958, publicity dir Collins Publishing 1968–75; Hodder & Stoughton: dep md 1975–78, md Gen Div 1978–91, dep publisher 1991–93; Hodder Headline Group PLC (merged with Hodder & Stoughton): md Religious Books 1993–96, publisher 1993–96, dir Hodder Headline Gp PLC 1993–96; md Doubleday Publishing 1996–; *Recreations* sailing, mountaineering, athletics, gardening and sleeping; *Clubs* Savile, Essex Yacht; *Style*— Eric Major, Esq; ✉ Doubleday Publishing, 1540 Broadway, New York, NY 10036, USA (☎ 00 1 212 3546500, fax 00 1 212 7828911)

MAJOR, The Rt Hon John; PC (1987), MP (C) Huntingdon (majority 36,230); s of Thomas Major (d 1963), actor (real name Abraham Thomas Ball), and his 2 w, Gwendolyn Minnie, *née* Coates (d 1970); *b* 29 March 1943; *Educ* Rutlish GS; *m* 1970, Norma Christina Elizabeth, da of Norman Wagstaff (ka 1945); 1 s (James b 1975), 1 da (Elizabeth b 1972); *Career* sr exec Standard Chartered Bank plc 1965–79; joined Conservative Party 1960, various offices Brixton Cons Assoc 1960–69 (chm 1970–71), memb Lambeth Borough Cncl 1968–71 (chm Housing Ctee 1970–71), dir Warden Housing Assoc 1974–82; parly candidate (C) St Pancras N (Camden) 1974 (both elections); MP (C): Huntingdonshire 1979–83, Huntingdon 1983–; jt sec Cons Party Parly Environment Ctee 1979–81, parly consIt Guild of Glass Engravers 1979–83, pres Eastern Area Young Conservatives 1983–85; PPS to Mins of State Home Office 1981–83, asst Govt whip 1983–84, a Lord Cmmr of the Treasury (Govt whip) 1984–85, parly under sec of state for social security 1985–86, min of state for social security and the disabled 1986–87, chief sec to the Treasury June 1987–July 1989, sec of state for foreign and Cwlth affrs July-Oct 1989, Chancellor of the Exchequer Oct 1989–Nov 1990, Prime Minister, First Lord of the Treasury and Min for the Civil Service 28 Nov 1990– (resigned as leader of Cons Pty June 1995, re-elected July); AIB; *Recreations* reading, watching opera, cricket, soccer and rugby; *Clubs* Carlton; *Style*— The Rt Hon John Major, MP; ✉ 10 Downing Street, London SW1A 2AA

MAJUMDAR, Bish; s of Pran Kumar Majumdar (d 1949), of Calcutta, and Sudha, *née* Sengupta; *b* 20 Jan 1944; *Educ* Univ of Calcutta (MB, BS), Univ of London (DLO); *m* 19 Jan 1979, Sutapa Majumdar, da of Kalyan Sengupta (d 1954); 2 da (Selina b 26 Jan 1983, Mita b 27 Nov 1985); *Career* registrar Dept of ENT Surgery: Univ Hosp of Wales 1974–76, W Infirmary Glasgow 1976–78; sr registrar: Sheffield Hosps 1978–80, Univ Hosps Nottingham 1980–82; consIt ENT surgn Derbys Royal Infirmary 1982–; clinical teacher otolaryngology Univ of Nottingham; memb: Portmann Fndn (Bordeaux), Euro Acad of Rhinology, Otolaryngolgy Res Soc, Br Assoc of Otolaryngology, Midland Inst of Otology, Euro Acad of Facial Surgery; FRCSEd, FRCS, FRSM, FICS (USA); *Recreations* swimming, golf, travel; *Style*— Bish Majumdar, Esq; ✉ 478 Burton Rd, Derby DE23 6AL (☎ 01332 371209); Derbyshire Royal Infirmary, Department of Otolaryngology, London Rd, Derby (☎ 01332 254659)

MAKAROVA, Natalia; *b* 1940, Leningrad; *Educ* Vaganova Sch Leningrad; *m* 1976, Edward Karkar; 1 s (Andrusha b 1 Feb 1978); *Career* ballet dancer and choreographer, also actress; with Kirov Ballet 1959–70, defected in London and joined American Ballet Theater (ABT) 1970 (but invited to dance with Kirov in Leningrad again in 1989, first ever Russian artistic exile so invited); guest artist with numerous int ballet cos incl: Royal Ballet, Paris Opera Ballet, National Ballet of Canada, Stuttgart Ballet, Royal Danish Ballet, English National Ballet (formerly London Festival Ballet), Bejart's Ballet of the 20th Century, Roland Petit's Ballet de Marseille; *Roles* with American Ballet Theater incl: debut in Giselle 1970, Tudor's Dark Elegies, Lilac Garden, Pillar of Fire and Romeo and Juliet, various by Balanchine, Robbins and Tetley; with Royal Ballet incl: Swan Lake, Giselle, Sleeping Beauty, Les Sylphides, Manon, Song of the Earth, Concerto, Cinderella, A Month in the Country, Voluntaries, Dances at a Gathering, Serenade, Elite Syncopations, Rituals, Checkmate, Les Biches and Romeo and Juliet; works created for her incl: Robbins' Other Dances, Ashton's Rossignol, Tetley's Sacre du Printemps and Contradance, a MacMillan Pas de Deux with Donald MacLeary, Neumeier's Epilogue, Petit's Blue Angel; others incl: Onegin (Evening Standard Award 1985), La Bayadere, The Firebird, Don Quixote, Coppèlia, La Fille Mal Gardee, Notre Dame de Paris, Carmen, Cranko's Romeo and Juliet, La Sylphide, Jullitta Messina in Fellini (première, Rome Opera House) 1995; *Productions staged* The Kingdom of the Shades from La Bayadere (for American Ballet Theater) 1974, full length prodn of La Bayadere with reconstructed last act (for ABT 1980, Royal Swedish Ballet and Royal Ballet 1989, Teatro Colon Buenos Aires 1992, La Scala Milan 1992), Swan Lake (for London Festival Ballet) 1988; *Television* ballet prodns incl: Swan Lake, Giselle, Romeo and Juliet, La Bayadere, The Leningrad Legend, excerpt from Swan Lake in reunion with Kirov Ballet 1988; other progs and series: Ballerina (BBC) 1987, In a Class of Her Own (Channel 4), Assoluta (BBC), Natasha (BBC), Makarova Returns (documentary on return to the Kirov Ballet) 1989, Great Railway Journeys St Petersburg to Tashkent (documentary on the Bolshoi Express for BBC) 1994; *Theatre* On Your Toes (musical comedy, Broadway, winner Tony award for best actress in a musical and seven other awards, later in West End, winner Olivier Award) 1983–84, Tovarich (Chichester Festival Theatre then West End) 1991; *Books* A Dance Autobiography (1979); chapter St Petersburg to Tashkent (in Great Railway Journeys, 1994); *Style*— Ms Natalia Makarova; ✉ c/o Mrs Jean Diamond, London Management, 2–4 Noel Street, London W1V 3RB (☎ 0171 987 9000, fax 0171 287 3036)

MAKEHAM, Peter Derek James; s of Derek James Stark Makeham, and Margaret Hélene Wilmott, *née* Carter; *b* 15 March 1948; *Educ* Chichester HS, Univ of Nottingham (BA), Univ of Leeds (MA); *m* 1972, Carolyne Rosemary, *née* Dawe; 1 s (William b 6 June 1979), 3 da (Sophie b 12 Nov 1980, Isabelle b 11 Oct 1982, Abigail b 5 Dec 1984); *Career* economist Dept of Employment 1971–82, seconded as economist Unilever 1982–83, speechwriter to Chllr and Chief Sec HM Treasy 1983–84, as economist Enterprise Unit Cabinet Office 1984–85, head Employment Policy Dept of Employment 1985–87, DTI 1987–90; Dept for Education and Employment (formerly Dept of Employment): head Fin Servs 1990–91, head Business Servs 1991–92, dir Strategy and Employment Strategy 1992–95, dir Employment and Adult Trg DfEE 1995–; *Style*— Peter Makeham, Esq; ✉ DfEE, Sanctury Buildings, Great Smith Street, London SW1P 3BT (☎ 0171 925 5573)

MAKEPEACE, John; OBE (1988); s of Harold Alfred Smith (d 1957), of Fenny Compton, Warwicks, and Gladys Marjorie, *née* Wright (d 1996); *b* 6 July 1939; *Educ* Denstone Coll Staffs; *m* 1 (m dis); m 2, 3 Dec 1984, Jennifer Moores, da of Harry Brinsden; *Career* furniture designer and maker; teacher Birmingham Educn Authy 1959–62, dir Farnborough Barn Ltd (subsequently John Makepeace Ltd) 1963–; dir: The Parnham Tst (charitable educnl tst) 1977–, Parnham Coll 1977–; memb Crafts Cncl 1972–77; Liveryman Worshipful Co of Furniture Makers 1977, tstee Victoria and Albert Museum 1988–90; FCSD 1975, FIMgt 1986, FRSA; *Clubs* Farmers'; *Style*— John Makepeace, OBE; ✉ Parnham House, Beaminster, Dorset DT8 3NA (☎ 01308 862204)

MAKEPEACE-WARNE, Maj-Gen Antony; CB (1992), MBE (1972); s of Keith Makepeace-Warne (d 1981), and Nora, *née* Kelstrup (d 1977); *b* 3 Sept 1937; *Educ* Taunton Sch, Open Univ (BA); *m* 22 Oct 1966, Jill Estelle, da of Eric Ivor Wadham Seath (d 1992), of Whitstable, Kent; 2 da (Annelie b 19 Sept 1970, Victoria b 20 May 1974); *Career* cmmnd King's Own Yorkshire Light Infantry 1960, served Malaya, Germany, Aden, Berlin; Staff Coll Camberley 1970, 2 Bn Light Infantry 1971–72, Bde Maj 24 Airportable Bde 1972–74, instr Staff Coll 1975–77, CO 1 Bn Light Infantry 1977–80, served Hong Kong, Ireland, Cyprus; Col ASD 2 MOD UK (Army) 1980–82, Cdr Berlin Infantry Bde 1982–84, RCDS 1985, ACOS HQ UKLF 1986–88, GS Study of Individual Trg Orgn 1988–89, Cmdt Jt Serv Def Coll 1990–92; Dep Col Light Infantry (Somerset and Cornwall) 1987–89, Col Light Infantry 1990–92; dir Army Museums Ogilby Tst 1996–; *Publications* Exceedingly Lucky - A History of the Light Infantry 1968–1993 (1993), The British Army Today and Tomorrow (1993), Brassey's Companion to the British Army (1995); *Clubs* Army and Navy; *Style*— Maj-Gen Antony Makepeace-Warne, CB, MBE; ✉ c/o LLoyds Bank (Cox's and King's), 7 Pall Mall, London SW1Y 5NA

MAKGILL, Hon Diana Mary Robina; CVO (1990, LVO 1983, MVO 1971); da (by 1 m) of 12 Viscount of Oxfuird; *b* 4 Jan 1930; *Educ* Strathcona Lodge Sch Vancouver Island BC Canada; *Career* ceremonial offr Protocol Dept FCO 1961–90, protocol conslt 1990–; vice chm: Women of the Year Luncheon, Stalls Ctee Int Social Servs Spring Fair; memb Int Ctee: Operation Raleigh 1990–, Action on Addiction 1990–; conslt to Princess Helena Coll, Dean of Westminster's rep on Cncl of Queen Anne's Sch Caversham 1994–, govr St John and St Mary Primary Sch Hindon Wilts; hon steward of Westminster Abbey 1977–; Freedom of the City of London 1989; Jubilee Medal 1977; Order of Star of Afghanistan 1971, Order of the White Rose of Finland 1969, Order of the Sacred Treasure of Japan 1971, Order of Al Kawkab of Jordan 1966, Order of Independence of the United Arab Emirates 1989; *Recreations* riding, reading, gardening; *Style*— The Hon Diana Makgill, CVO; ✉ Clouds Lodge, E Knoyle, nr Salisbury, Wilts SP3 6BE (☎ and fax 01747 830260)

MAKGILL CRICHTON MAITLAND, Maj John David; s of Col Mark Edward Makgill Crichton Maitland, CVO, DSO, DL, JP (d 1972), of Wilton, Salisbury, Wilts; *b* 1925; *Educ* Eton; *m* 1, 1954, Jean Patricia (d 1985), da of Maj-Gen Sir Michael Creagh, KBE, MC (d 1970), of Salisbury, Wilts; 1 s, 1 da; m 2, 1987, Mary Ann Vere Curzon, *née* Ogilvy, widow of Capt James Quintin Curzon (d 1986); *Career* Grenadier Gds 1944–57, Temp Maj 1952, ret 1957 as Capt (Hon Maj); Lord-Lieut Renfrewshire 1980–94 (DL 1962, Vice-Lord Lieut 1972); *Clubs* Turf, Puffins, MCC; *Style*— Maj J D M Crichton Maitland; ✉ Daluaine, Rhynie, Huntly, Aberdeenshire AB54 4WA (☎ 01464 861638)

MAKIN, Prof Brian; s of Clifford Makin (d 1985), of Sheffield, and Edith Ivy, *née* Rogers; *b* 28 Dec 1935; *Educ* High Storrs GS Sheffield, Univ of Southampton (BSc, PhD); *m* 12 Dec 1959, Hazel, da of Major Jack Phillips; 3 s (Paul Brian b 12 May 1964, Andrew Philip b 15 May 1966, Darren Keith b 3 Feb 1970); *Career* project engr W G Pye and Co Ltd Cambridge 1964–66, lectr Dept of Electrical Engrg Univ of Southampton 1966–74; Univ of Dundee: Watson-Watt prof of electrical engrg and head Dept of Electrical Engrg 1974–87, prof Dept of Applied Physics and Electrical and Mechanical Engrg 1987–; FIEE 1980, FInstP 1985, FRSE 1993; *Recreations* gardening, fishing, walking; *Clubs* Rotary Claverhouse Dundee; *Style*— Prof Brian Makin, FRSE; ✉ Department of Applied Physics and Electronic Engineering, University of Dundee, Dundee DD1 4JB (☎ 01382 344394, fax 01382 202830)

MAKIN, (Norman) Christopher; s of Windsor Makin, of Huddersfield, and Kathleen Mary, *née* Dyson; *b* 7 July 1943; *Educ* King James GS Huddersfield; *m* 9 Aug 1969, Gillian, da of Eric Reginald Mitton; 1 da (Rebecca Jane b 3 May 1977); *Career* chartered accountant; ptnr Charles F Beer & Co 1971–87, ptnr Revell Ward Chartered Accountants 1987– (head of litigation support); princ double bass Leeds Symphony Orch; FCA 1969, FIMgt 1978, FAE 1994; *Style*— N Christopher Makin, Esq; ✉ Well Cottage, 39 Water Royd Lane, Mirfield, West Yorkshire WF14 9SF (☎ 01924 495888); Revell Ward, Chartered Accountants, Airedale House, 77 Albion St, Leeds LS1 5HT (☎ 0113 245 1483, fax 0113 242 6124, car 0836 635676)

MAKIN, John Beverley; s of William Makin (d 1983), of Ottershaw, Surrey, and Helen, *née* Southern (d 1980); *b* 28 Feb 1937; *Educ* Kingston GS; *m* 4 Oct 1969, Alicia Jane, da of Gordon Edward Fairclough, of Weybridge, Surrey; 3 s (Andrew b 1975, Alex b 1980, Stephen b 1983); *Career* assoc ed Motoring News 1960, ed Cine Camera 1960–63 (formerly asst ed), Parker PR 1963–67, chm IH Publications 1967–77 (formerly md), dep chief exec Adgroup 1977–81, dir Dewe Rogerson 1982–, md Dewe Rogerson Corporate Publications 1992–; Br Assoc of Communicators in Business: fell 1966, nat chm 1973–74, chm of senate 1984–87, pres 1996–; *Books* A Management Guide to House Journals (1970); *Recreations* walking, bridge, golf; *Clubs* RAC; *Style*— John Makin, Esq; ✉ Easter Cottage, Wrens Hill, Oxshott, Surrey (☎ 01372 843516); Dewe Rogerson Ltd, 3 1/2 London Wall Buildings, London Wall, London EC2M 5SY (☎ 0171 378 0002)

MAKINSON, John Crowther; s of Kenneth Crowther Makinson (d 1974), and Phyllis Georgina, *née* Miller; *b* 10 Oct 1954; *Educ* Repton, Christ's Coll Cambridge (exhibitioner, MA); *m* Virginia Clare, da of Dr John Macbeth; 2 da (Emma Violet b 13 April 1990, Lucy India b 3 Dec 1991); *Career* journalist Reuters (London, Paris and Frankfurt) 1976–79, ed Lex Column and head of companies section Financial Times 1979–86, vice chm Saatchi & Saatchi (US) Holdings 1986–89, fndr ptnr Makinson Cowell investor relations conslts 1989–94, md The Financial Times Ltd 1994–96, fin dir Pearson plc 1996–; *Recreations* music, theatre, travel; *Clubs* Groucho; *Style*— John Makinson, Esq; ✉ Pearson plc, 3 Burlington Gardens, London W1X 1LE (☎ 0171 411 2305, fax 0171 411 2329)

MAKOWER, Peter; s of Anthony Makower, (d 1984), of London, and Sylvia Evelyn, *née* Chetwynd; *b* 12 Sept 1932; *Educ* Westminster, Trinity Coll Cambridge (MA), The Poly Regent St (DipArch), UCL (DipTP); *m* 20 Aug 1960, Katharine, da of James Haworthe Paul Chadburn, MBE, of London; 2 s (Andrew b 1961, Timothy b 1965), 1 da (Mary b 1963 d 1979); *Career* RE 1951–56, architect and town-planner on staff of Frederick Gibberd & Partners 1959–82 and Chapman Taylor Partners 1982–85, in practice Peter Makower Architects and Planners 1985–; memb: London Diocesan Synod, Hammersmith and Fulham Deanery Synod; C of E reader; FRIBA; MRTPI; *Style*— Peter Makower, Esq; ✉ Peter Makower Architects and Planners, 1 Lillian Road, London SW13 9JG (☎ 0181 563 8326, fax 0181 563 8327)

MAKSYMIUK, Jerzy; *b* 1936; *Educ* Warsaw Conservatory (studied violin, piano and conducting); *Career* conductor; winner Paderewski Piano Competition 1964; fndr Polish Chamber Orch, princ conductor Polish National Radio Orch 1975–77, conductor laureate BBC Scottish Symphony Orch 1993– (chief conductor 1984–93); has also worked with numerous other orchs incl: BBC Welsh, BBC Philharmonic, CBSO, Bournemouth Sinfonietta, LSO, LPO, The Philharmonia, Orchestre National de France, Ensemble Orchestral de Paris, Ensemble de Grenoble, Tokyo Metropolitan Symphony, Israel Chamber Orch, English National Opera (debut conducting Don Giovanni 1990, then Die Fledermaus 1993), Cracow Philharmonic Orch, Hallé Orch, Orchestre de Toulouse, Royal Liverpool Philharmonic, Prague Symphony Orch, New Zealand Symphony Orch, Winterthur Orchestra, Iceland Symphony Orchestra; conducted various world premières incl: Macmillan's The Confession of Isobel Gowdie (later recorded, Gramophone Contemporary Music Award 1993), Robin Holloway Violin Concerto (with BBC Philharmonic); Hon DLitt Univ of Strathclyde 1990; *Recordings* incl Medtner Piano Concerti Nos 2 and 3 (with BBC Scottish Symphony Orch, Gramophone Best Concerto Award 1992), works by Grieg (with BBC Scottish Symphony Orch), works by Rachmaninov (with Nat Symphony Orch of Ireland); *Style*— Jerzy Maksymiuk, Esq; ✉ c/o Natalie Cruse, IMG Artists Europe, Media House, 3 Burlington Lane, Chiswick, London W4 2TH (☎ 0181 233 5828, fax 0181 233 5801)

MALAHIDE, Patrick; *b* 24 March 1945; *Educ* Douai Sch, Univ of Edinburgh; *Career* actor; *Theatre* Bristol Old Vic incl: The Tempest, The Cherry Orchard, King Lear, Accidental Death of an Anarchist, Clandestine Marriage, Uncle Vanya; Birmingham Rep incl: The Crucible, The Wedding Feast; Traverse incl: The Android Circuit, Every Good Boy Deserves Favour; Royal Court incl: Operation Bad Apple, In the Ruins; other credits incl: Judgement (Liverpool), Cockups (Manchester Exchange), Map of the Heart (Globe); *Television* incl: The Standard, Love Lies Bleeding, Dying Day, Minder, Black Adder, Pickwick Papers, The Russian Soldier, The December Rose, The Singing Detective, After the War, The Franchise Affair, Inspector Morse, Lovejoy, A Doll's House, The Blackheath Poisonings, The Secret Agent, Force of Duty, The Inspector Alleyn Mysteries, Middlemarch, Deacon Brodie; *Films* incl: The Killing Fields, Comfort and Joy, A Month in the Country, December Bride, A Man of No Importance, Two Deaths, Cutthroat Island, Til There was You, The Long Kiss Goodnight; *Screenplays* writer The Writing on the Wall (BBC 1) 1996; *Recreations* sailing, walking; *Clubs* Irish, Royal Fowey Yacht; *Style*— Patrick Malahide, Esq; ✉ c/o ICM Ltd, Oxford House, 76 Oxford Street, London W1N 0AX (☎ 0171 636 6565, fax 0171 323 0101)

MALAND, David; s of Rev Gordon Albert Maland (d 1978), and Florence Maude, *née* Bosence; *b* 6 Oct 1929; *Educ* Kingswood Sch Bath, Wadham Coll Oxford; *m* 23 March 1953, Edna, *née* Foulsham; 2 s (Oliver b 1957, Nicholas b 1959); *Career* Nat Serv, Flying Offr RAF 1951–53; asst master Brighton GS 1953–56, sr history master Stamford Sch 1957–66, headmaster Cardiff HS for Boys 1966–68, headmaster Denstone Coll 1969–78, high master Manchester GS 1978–85; memb Ctee of Headmasters Conf 1977–79 and 1982–84; called to the Bar Gray's Inn 1986, in chambers Lamb Bldg Temple 1987–88, 1 Garden Court 1989–95; *Books* Europe in the Seventeenth Century (1966), Culture and Society in Seventeenth Century France (1971), Europe in the Sixteenth Century (1975), Europe at War 1600–1650 (1981); *Clubs* Athenaeum; *Style*— David Maland, Esq; ✉ Windrush, Underhill Lane, Westmeston, nr Hassocks, West Sussex (☎ 01273 844783)

MALCOLM, Alastair Richard; QC (1996); s of late Colin Ronald Malcolm; *b* 20 Oct 1947; *Educ* Eton, New Coll Oxford; *m* 1971, Elizabeth Anne, da of Edward Wilfred George Joicey-Cecil; 2 s; *Career* called to the Bar Inner Temple 1971; *Recreations* shooting, country pursuits; *Style*— Alastair Malcolm, Esq, QC; ✉ 1 Paper Buildings, 1st Floor, Temple, London EC4Y 7EP (☎ 0171 831 3833)

MALCOLM, Derek Elliston Michael; s of J Douglas Malcolm (d 1967), and Dorothy Vera, Elliston-Taylor (d 1964); *b* 12 May 1932; *Educ* Eton, Merton Coll Oxford (BA); *m* 1, 1962 (m dis 1966), Barbara, *née* Ibbott; 1 da (Jaqueline b 1962); m 2, 1994, Sarah, *née* Gristwood; *Career* amateur rider Nat Hunt 1951–53, actor 1953–56, drama critic Gloucestershire Echo Cheltenham 1956–62; The Guardian: features sub-ed and writer 1962–69, racing corr 1969–71, film critic 1971–; film critic Cosmopolitan 1974–96; dir London Int Film Festival 1984–86, govr BFI 1989–92; pres: Int Film Critics 1991– (chm UK Section 1982–), Critics Circle UK 1980, British Fedn of Film Socs 1993–; Int Publishing Co's Critic of the Yr 1972; *Books* Robert Mitchum (1984); *Recreations* cricket, tennis, squash, music; *Style*— Derek Malcolm, Esq; ✉ 28 Avenue Road, Highgate,

London N6 5DW (☎ and fax 0181 348 2013); The Dower House, Hull Place, Sholden, Kent CT14 0AQ (☎ 01304 364614)

MALCOLM, Devon Eugene; s of Albert Malcolm, and late Brendalee Malcolm; *b* 22 Feb 1963, Kingston, Jamaica; *Educ* St Elizabeth Tech HS, Richmond Coll, Derby Coll; *m* 1989, Jennifer; *Career* professional cricketer; formerly played league cricket for Sheffield Works and Sheffield Utd; with Derbyshire CCC 1984– (awarded county cap 1989); England: became eligible 1987, over 20 test matches 1989–, 4 one day ints, best test performances 10 for 137 v W Indies Port of Spain 1990, 9 for 57 v S Africa 1994; tours: Eng to W Indies 1989/90, Eng to Aust 1990/91, Eng A to Bermuda and W Indies 1991/92, Eng to India and Sri Lanka 1992/93, W Indies 1993/94, Aust 1994/95 and S Africa 1995/96; *Recreations* music, swimming; *Style—* Devon Malcolm, Esq; ✉ c/o Derbyshire CCC, County Ground, Nottingham Road, Derby DE2 6DA (☎ 01332 383211)

MALCOLM, Dugald; CMG (1966), CVO (1964), TD (1945); s of Maj-Gen Sir Neill Malcolm, KCB, DSO (d 1953), and Angela Malcolm (d 1930); *b* 22 Dec 1917; *Educ* Eton, New Coll Oxford (MA); *m* 22 June 1957, Patricia Anne, wid of Capt Peter Atkinson Clarke (killed 1944), da of late Gilbert Gilbert-Lodge; 2 da (Anne (Mrs Carpenter) b 1943, Helen (Mrs Whittow) b 1962); m 2, Margaret Roy, da of late Rev R P R Anderson; *Career* Argyll & Sutherland Highlanders (Territorial Cmmn) 1939, discharged as wounded 1945; HM Dip Serv: Lima, Bonn and Seoul 1945–57, HM Vice-Marshal of the Dip Corps 1957–65, ambass Luxembourg 1966–70, ambass Panama 1970–74, min Holy See 1975–77; Freeman Worshipful Co of Fishmongers; *Clubs* Boodle's, Brooks's; *Style—* Dugald Malcolm, Esq, CMG, CVO, TD; ✉ 3 South Cuil, Duror of Appin, Argyll PA38 4DA (☎ 0163 174234)

MALCOLM, George John; CBE (1965); s of George Hope Malcolm, and Johanna, *née* Brosnahan; *b* 28 Feb 1917; *Educ* Wimbledon Coll, Balliol Coll Oxford (MA, BMus), RCM; *Career* musician; master of the cathedral music Westminster Cathedral 1947–59 (trained boys' choir for which Benjamin Britten wrote Missa Brevis), now mainly harpsichordist, pianist and conductor; numerous tours and recordings as soloist and with chamber ensembles in Europe, USA and Far East; conducted English Chamber Orch BBC Proms 1996; hon fell Balliol Coll Oxford 1966; Hon DMus Sheffield 1978; Hon RAM 1961, FRCM 1974, Hon FRCO 1988; Papal Knight of the Order of St Gregory the Great 1970; *Style—* George Malcolm, Esq, CBE; ✉ 99 Wimbledon Hill Rd, London SW19 7QT; c/o Harold Holt Ltd, 31 Sinclair Rd, London W14 0NS (☎ 0171 603 4600, fax 0171 603 0019, telex 22339 Hunter G)

MALCOLM, Col Sir James William Thomas Alexander; 12 Bt (NS) 1665, of Balbedie and Innertiel, Co Fife; DL (Surrey 1991); s of Lt-Col Aarthur William Alexander Malcolm, CVO (d 1989), and Hester Mary, *née* Mann (d 1992); suc kinsman, Sir David Peter Michael Malcolm, 11 Bt (d 1995); *b* 15 May 1930; *Educ* Eton, RMA Sandhurst; *m* 1955, Gillian Heather, only c of Elton Henry Humpherus, of Kennards, Leigh, Kent; 2 s (Alexander James Elton b 1956, Robin William b 1958), 2 da (Julia Mary (Mrs Julian Spurling) b 1960, Annabel Heather (Mrs Patrick Toyne Sewell) b 1967); *Heir* s, Lt Col Alexander James Elton Malcolm b 30 Aug 1956; *Career* cmd 1 Bn Welsh Gds 1970–72, cmd Welsh Regt of Foot Gds 1972–76; appeals dir Br Heart Fndn 1976–89, High Sheriff of Surrey 1991–92; *Recreations* golf; *Clubs* MCC, Royal St George's Golf, Berkshire Golf; *Style—* Col Sir James Malcolm, Bt, DL; ✉ Thatchers Barn, Worplesdon, Guildford, Surrey GU3 3RD (☎ 01483 232281)

MALCOLM, (Thomas) Neil Carmichael; s of Robert Malcolm (d 1983), and Janet Irene, *née* Carmichael; *b* 1 Sept 1938; *Educ* HS of Stirling, Univ of Glasgow; *m* 30 Sept 1967, Kay Donnet, da of John Donnet Anderson; 2 da (Susan b 1968, Victoria b 1971), 1 s (Colin b 1975); *Career* CA; sr ptnr Macfarlane Gray 1967–; memb Tax Practice Ctee Inst of CAs of Scotland; treas: Allan Park South Church of Scotland 1971–, Stirling GC 1977–; FCCA, FSAS; *Recreations* golf, squash, tennis, hill walking; *Clubs* Stirling Golf, Stirling Lawn Tennis and Squash, Rotary of Stirling; *Style—* T N C Malcolm, Esq; ✉ 26 Snowdon Place, Stirling FK8 2JN (☎ 01786 475975); Macfarlane Gray, 15 Gladstone Place, Stirling FK8 2NX (☎ 01786 451745, fax 01786 472528)

MALDEN, Aubrey Dicken; s of Peter James Malden, of Chiswick, London, and Marie Roselyn, *née* Clarke; *b* 7 Nov 1949; *Educ* Fowey Sch Cornwall, Ealing Sch of Art London; *m* 24 Sept 1983, Veronika Susan, da of Horst Max Schneider (d 1979), of Johannesburg, SA; *Career* fndr memb Craton Lodge & Knight New Product Development Consultancy London 1973–79, gp head J Walter Thompson Brussels 1979–80; creative dir and memb Bd Ogilvy & Mather: Brussels 1980–82, Johannesburg 1982–87; currently md McCann-Erickson Scotland; Clio and NY Festival awards for TV work, radio & print work, other awards for print, TV, and radio; assoc memb IOD, chmb Scottish Mktg Soc, MIPA; *Recreations* shooting, rugby, squash, fishing; *Style—* Aubrey Malden, Esq; ✉ 8 Rosehall Place, Haddington, Scotland; McCann Erickson Scotland, Marine Drive, Edinburgh (☎ 0131 336 1733)

MALDEN, Charles Christopher; s of Christopher Edward Scott Malden (d 1956), and Helen Margaret, *née* Thwaites (d 1976); *b* 27 Aug 1932; *Educ* Stowe (capt 1 XV), Kings Coll Cambridge (MA, coll rugby capt); *m* 1957, Elizabeth Ann, *née* Willday; 4 da (Lucinda Josephine b 1960, Alexandra Louise b 1964, Christina Grace b 1969, Georgia Kate b 1972); *Career* 2 Lt Rifle Bde 1951–53, 21 SAS (Artists) TA 1953–60; jt head Windlesham House Sch 1957–94 (founded by gggf 1837, first and largest co educnl ind boarding sch since 1967); co fndr and tstee Jt Educnl Trust 1972–; co fndr (with wife) The Malden Theatre 1988; govr: Lancing Coll 1972–89, Cranleigh Sch 1976–88, Stowe Sch 1974–92; memb IAPS 1959–94, cncl memb and memb Exec Ctee Boarding Schs Assoc (memb 1965–94); *Recreations* creating a cliff garden - Lands End, creating an arboretum - W Sussex; *Clubs* Greenjackets; *Style—* Charles Malden, Esq; ✉ Clidga Cottage, Sennen, Lands End TR19 7AX (☎ 01736 871344)

MALDEN, Viscount; Frederick Paul de Vere Capell; s and h of 10 Earl of Essex; *b* 29 May 1944; *Educ* Skerton Boys' Secdy Sch, Lancaster Royal GS, Didsbury Coll of Educn, N Sch of Music; *Career* acting head teacher Marsh Co Jr Sch 1974–77; head teacher Cockerham C of E Sch 1979–81; i/c pastoral care curriculum devpt and music Skerton Co Primary Sch Lancaster 1981–90, dep head teacher Skerton CP Sch 1990–95; patron Morecambe Philharmonic Choir; LLCM (TD), ALCM, FRSA, ACP; *Recreations* travel, music; *Style—* Viscount Malden

MALDONADO VÁSCONEZ, HE (Luis) Patricio; s of Nicolas Augusto Maldonado (d 1966), and Leonor, *née* Vásconez, of Quito, Ecuador; *b* 10 Aug 1932; *Educ* Colegio Montufar Quito, Universidad Central del Ecuador Quito; *m* 14 May 1955, Delia, da of Eduardo Samaniego; 2 s (Patricio b 26 Feb 1958, Nicolas b 25 Nov 1961), 2 da (Maria b 13 Feb 1956, Delia b 19 May 1961); *Career* Ecuadorian diplomat; Admin Dept: Miny of Foreign Affrs Quito 1952–53, Consulate of Ecuador Miami 1953–57; vice consul Los Angeles 1957–60; second sec: Washington DC 1960–61, Miny of Foreign Affrs 1961–62; ceremonial head Presidential House Quito 1962–63; first sec: Miny of Foreign Affrs 1963–64, London 1964–69; Miny of Foreign Affrs: cnsllr 1969–70, head of Min's Cabinet 1970–71, dir of Int Economic Politics Dept 1971–72; chargé d'affaires Madrid 1975–76 (cnsllr 1972–75); Miny of Foreign Affrs: cnsllr and dir of Info and Press Dept 1976–77, min 1977–78, dir of Personnel Dept 1978; chargé d'affaries Belgrade 1978–79, min Washington DC 1979–82; Miny of Foreign Affrs: min and dir of Treaty Dept 1982–83, ambass and gen dir of tech co-operation and economic promotion 1983–85; ambass: Managua 1985–86, Seoul Korea 1986–90; gen dir of protocol Miny of Foreign Affrs 1990–91, advsr from Miny of Foreign Affrs to Nat Congress 1991–93, ambass to Ct of St James's 1993–; Comendador de la Orden Isabel la Católica (Spain), Gran Oficial de la Orden de Mayo (Argentina); Gran Cruz: de la Orden Bernardo O'Higgins (Chile), de la Orden Servicio Diplomático de la República de Corea; *Recreations* football, basketball; *Style—* HE Senor Patricio Maldonado; ✉ 7 Trevor Square, London SW7 1DT (☎ 0171 581 2386); Ecuadorian Embassy, Flat 3B, 3 Hans Crescent, London SW1X OLS (☎ 0171 584 1367, fax 0171 823 9701)

MALE, David Ronald; CBE (1991); s of Ronald Male (d 1963), of Worthing, and Gertrude, *née* Simpson (d 1946); *b* 12 Dec 1929; *Educ* Aldenham; *m* 6 June 1959, Mary Louise, da of Rex Powis Evans, of St Albans; 1 s (James b 1964), 2 da (Sarah b 1962, Charlotte b 1966); *Career* Nat Serv 2 Lt RA 1948–49; Gardiner & Theobald: ptnr 1960–79, sr ptnr 1979–91, conslt 1992–; RICS: memb Gen Cncl 1976–93, pres quantity surveyors Divnl Cncl 1977–78, pres 1989–90; memb: Bd of Dirs Building Centre 1970–80, Govt Construction Panel 1973–74; memb Econ Devpt Cncl for Bldg 1982–86, chm Commercial Buildings Steering Group 1984–88; MCC: memb Ctee 1984–95 and 1996–, chm Estates Sub Ctee 1984–94; govr Aldenham Sch 1974–93, pres Old Aldenhamian Soc 1986–89, non-exec dir London & Bristol Developments plc 1985–91; memb Bd of Mgmnt Cancer Relief Macmillan Fund 1992–, memb Bd of Govrs The Wilson Centre Cambridge 1993–; church cmmr 1989–93; Freeman City of London 1961, Liveryman Worshipful Co Painter-Stainers 1961–93, Hon Asst Worshipful Co of Chartered Surveyors (memb Ct 1977–90, Master 1984–85); ARICS 1954, FRICS 1964; *Recreations* opera, ballet, lawn tennis, real tennis, golf; *Clubs* Boodle's, Garrick; *Style—* David Male, Esq, CBE; ✉ Inkpen House, Inkpen, Hungerford, Berkshire RG17 9DS (☎ 01488 668793, fax 01488 668871); 6 Bowland Yard, Kinnerton St, London SW1X 8EE; Gardiner & Theobald, 32 Bedford Square, London WC1B 3EG

MALEK, Ali; QC (1996); s of Ali Akbar Malek, and Irene, *née* Johnson; *b* 19 Jan 1956; *Educ* Bedford Sch, Keble Coll Oxford (MA, BCL); *m* Sept 1989, Francesca Shoucair; 2 da (Rokhsan Nesa b 18 July 1991, Mithra b 25 May 1993); *Career* called to the Bar Gray's Inn 1980 (Cynthia Terry Entrance Award and Malcolm Hilberry Award), specialist in commercial law; memb Commercial Bar Assoc; *Recreations* running, skiing, golf, music; *Clubs* Vincent's (Oxford); *Style—* Ali Malek, Esq, QC; ✉ 3 Verulam Buildings, Gray's Inn, London WC1R 5NT (☎ 0171 831 8441, fax 0171 831 8479, mobile 0836 607075)

MALEM, Keir David; s of David Malem, of Greatstone, Kent, and Angela, *née* Wells; *b* 15 May 1965; *Educ* Southlands Comp Sch; *Career* fashion designer; fndr ptnr Whitaker Malem 1988–; launched new line of male and female leather torsos (with Adel Roostein) 1995; lectr in fashion various colls of art and design; special assignments incl: body sculptures for re-opening of Bauhaus Dessau, outfit for Naomi Campbell in Vauxhall advertising campaign 1993; cmmns for: Mick Jagger, Cher, Pamela Anderson, Gloria Estefan, Janet Jackson, Jerry Hall, Bono; film cmmns incl: Mortal Kombat 1995, The Changeling 1995; Unlaced Grace (Banbury Museum and nat touring exhbn) 1994–95; *Recreations* film and soundtrack collecting, swimming, cooking, gardening; *Style—* Keir Malem, Esq; ✉ Whitaker Malem, Top Floor, Candid Studios, 3 Torrens Street, Angel, Islington, London EC1V 1NQ (☎ 0171 278 6332, fax 0171 278 6332)

MALET, Sir Harry Douglas St Lo; 9 Bt (GB 1791), of Wilbury, Wilts; JP; s of Sir Edward William St Lo Malet, 8 Bt, OBE (d 1990), and (Maria Johana) Benedicta (d 1979), da of Baron Wilhelm von Maasburg, of Vienna; *b* 26 Oct 1936; *Educ* Downside, Trinity Coll Oxford (BA); *m* 28 Aug 1967, Julia Gresley, da of Charles Harper, of Perth, W Australia; 1 s (Charles Edward St Lo); *Heir* s, Charles Edward St Lo Malet b 30 Aug 1970; *Career* late Queen's Royal Irish Hussars; *Style—* Sir Harry Malet, Bt, JP; ✉ Wrestwood, RMB 184, Boyup Brook, W Aust 6244, Aust

MALIM, Rear Adm Nigel Hugh; CB (1971), LVO (1960), DL (1987); s of John Charles Malim, MBE (d 1957), and Brenda Stirling, *née* Robinson (d 1973); *b* 5 April 1919; *Educ* Weymouth Coll, RN Engrg Coll Plymouth, RNC Greenwich; *m* 6 Sept 1944, Moonyeen Maureen Ogilvy, da of Capt William Edmund Maynard, DLI (d 1926); 2 s (Jeremy b 1945, Timothy b 1957), 1 da (Marquita b 1953); *Career* special entry cadet RN 1936, HMS Manchester 1940–42, HMS Norfolk 1942–43, HMS Jamaica 1945–47, staff RNEC 1948–50, HMS Triumph 1954–56, Admty 1956–58 (1951–54), HM Yacht Britannia 1958–60, dist overseer Scotland 1960–62, dep dir Marine Engrg 1962–65, IDC 1966, Capt RNEC 1967–69, CSO (T) to C in C Western Fleet 1969–71; md Humber Graving Dock & Engineering Co Ltd 1972–82, chm Association Western Euro Shiprepairers 1982–86; Lincoln Cathedral: memb Preservation Cncl 1985–, chm Fabric Cncl 1985–91; *Recreations* gardening, sailing; *Clubs* RNSA, Royal Ocean Racing; *Style—* Rear Adm Nigel Malim, CB, LVO, DL; ✉ The Old Vicarage, Caistor, Lincoln LN7 6UG (☎ 01472 851275)

MALIN, Prof Stuart Robert Charles; s of Cecil Henry Malin (d 1968), and Eleanor Mary, *née* Howe; *b* 28 Sept 1936; *Educ* Royal GS High Wycombe, King's Coll London (BSc), Univ of London (PhD, DSc); *m* 30 March 1963, Irene, da of Frederick Alfred Saunders (d 1989), of Polegate, Sussex; 2 da (Jane b 1966, Rachel b 1969); *Career* Royal Greenwich Observatory Herstmonceux: asst experimental offr 1958–61, scientific offr 1961–65, sr scientific offr 1965–70, princ scientific offr 1970–76; Cape observer Radcliffe Observatory SA 1963–65, visiting scientist Nat Center for Atmospheric Res USA 1969; Inst of Geological Scis Herstmonceux and Edinburgh: sr princ scientific offr (individual merit) 1976–81, head Geomagnetism Unit 1981–82; Green scholar Scripps Inst Oceanography USA 1981, visiting prof Dept of Physics and Astronomy UCL 1983–; head: Dept of Astronomy and Navigation Nat Maritime Museum 1982–88, Mathematics Dept Dulwich Coll 1988–91 and 1992–94, Haberdashers' Aske's Hatcham Coll 1991–92; prof of geophysics Bosphorus Univ Turkey 1994–, conslt Rahmi M Koc Museum Turkey 1995–, visiting prof Cairo Univ 1996–; assoc ed Quarterly Jl of The Royal Astronomical Soc 1988–91, ed Geophysics Jl Int 1996–; 1961, FInstP 1971, CPhys 1985; *Books* The Greenwich Meridian (with C Stott, 1984), Spaceworks (with C Stott, 1985), The Planets (1987), Stars Galaxies and Nebulae (1989), The Story of the Earth (1991); *Recreations* croquet, clocks; *Clubs* RAS; *Style—* Prof Stuart Malin; ✉ 30 Wemyss Rd, Blackheath, London SE3 0TG (☎ 0181 318 3712); Bogazici Universitesi, Kandilli Observatory and Earthquake Research Institute, 81220 Cengelköy, Istanbul, Turkey (☎ 00 90 216 308 0525 ext 389, fax 00 90 216 332 1711, e-mail malin@boun.edu.tr)

MALINOWSKI, Antoni Pawel; s of Wojciech Janusz Malinowski (d 1981), of Warsaw, and Krystyna Gąssowska; *b* 13 June 1955, Warsaw; *Educ* Acad of Fine Art Warsaw, Chelsea Coll of Art; *Career* artist; *Solo Exhibitions* Künstlerhaus Hamburg 1985, The Drawing Room installation London 1986, Galerie Wilma Tolksdorf Hamburg 1987 and 1988, Life Drawing installation and performance Chisenhale Gallery London 1987, Provisional Statements on the Rights of the Citizen installation Angel Studios London 1988, Mario Flecha Gallery London 1989, The Showroom London 1990, Galeria Dziekanka Warsaw 1991, Galerie Marie-Louise Wirth Zürich 1993, Gimpel Fils Gallery London 1993 and 1995; *Gp Exhibitions* incl: National Review of Life Art (Riverside Studios London) 1987, Open Futures (Ikon Gallery Birmingham) 1988, Whitechapel Open London 1989, 1990 and 1992, What is a Gallery (Kettles Yard Cambridge) 1990, Jesteśmy (Zachęta Warsaw) 1991, New Voices (Br Cncl show Brussels) 1992, EC Young Painters (Seoul Korea), Moving into View - Recent British Painting (Royal Festival Hall and tour) 1993, Recent CAS Aquisitions (Museum of Modern Art Oxford) 1994, Recent Contemporary Art Soc Purchases (Butler Gallery Kilkenny Castle) 1995, London Stories (GE Gallery, Winterthur Switzerland) 1995; *Work in Public Collections* Arts Cncl, Br Cncl, Tate Gallery, CAS; *Style—* Antoni Malinowski, Esq; ✉ c/o Gimpel Fils, 30 Davies Street, London W1Y 1LG (☎ 0171 493 2488, fax 0171 629 5732)

MALINS, Julian Henry; QC (1991); s of Rev Peter Malins, and Joan, *née* Dingley; *b* 1 May 1950; *Educ* Greenways Sch Codford St Mary Wilts, St John's Sch Leatherhead Surrey, BNC Oxford (MA, Boxing blue); *m* 1 July 1972, (Catherine) Joanna Wilson, da of John Henry Pearce; 3 da (Annabel b 1977, Cressida b 1979, Miranda b 1984); *Career* called to the Bar Middle Temple 1972; memb: Ct Common Cncl, Gen Cncl of the Bar; Freeman City of London 1979; *Style*— Julian Malins, Esq, QC; ✉ Brick Court Chambers, 15–19 Devereux Court, London WC2R 3JJ (☎ 0171 583 0777, fax 0171 583 9401, telex 892687 IBRICK G)

MALLABY, Sir Christopher Leslie George; GCMG (1996, KCMG 1988), GCVO (1992); s of Brig A W S Mallaby, CIE, OBE (ka 1945), and Margaret Catherine, *née* Jones; *b* 7 July 1936; *Educ* Eton, King's Coll Cambridge (BA); *m* 1961, Pascale, da of Francois Thierry-Mieg, of Paris; 1 s (Sebastian b 1964), 3 da (Emily b 1967, Julia b 1971, Charlotte b 1972); *Career* HM Dip Serv: entered 1959, Moscow Embassy 1961–63 and 1975–77, first sec Berlin 1966–69; dep dir Br Trade Devpt Office (NY) 1971–74; head of: Arms Control & Disarmament Dept FCO 1977–79, E Euro and Soviet Dept 1979–80, Planning Staff 1980–82; min Bonn 1982–85, dep sec Cabinet 1985–87, ambass Bonn 1988–92, ambass Paris 1993–96, ret; a tstee Tate Gallery 1996–; *Recreations* fishing, reading, travel; *Clubs* Brooks's, Beefsteak; *Style*— Sir Christopher Mallaby, GCMG, GCVO; ✉ c/o FCO, King Charles Street, London SW1A 2AH

MALLALIEU, Baroness (Life Peer UK 1991), of Studdridge in the County of Buckinghamshire; Ann Mallalieu; QC (1988); da of Sir (Joseph Percival) William Mallalieu (d 1980), and Harriet Rita Riddle, *née* Tinn; *b* 27 Nov 1945; *Educ* Holton Park Girls' GS Wheatley Oxon, Newnham Coll Cambridge (MA, LLM); *m* 1979, as his 2 w, Timothy Felix Harold Cassel, QC, *qv*, eldest s of His Honour Sir Harold Felix Cassel, 3 Bt, TD, QC, *qv*; 2 da (Hon Bathsheba Anna b 1981, Hon Cosima Ione Harriet b 1984); *Career* called to the Bar Inner Temple 1970, bencher 1992; recorder 1985–94; oppn spokesman on home affrs and legal affrs House of Lords 1991–; chm: Independent Cncl of the Ombudsman for Corp Estate Agents 1993–, Suzy Lamplugh Tst 1996–; first woman pres Cambridge Union Soc 1967, hon fell Newnham Coll Cambridge 1991; *Recreations* hunting, sheep, reading poetry; *Style*— The Baroness Mallalieu, QC; ✉ House of Lords, London SW1

MALLALIEU, Huon Lancelot; s of Sir Edward Lancelot Mallalieu, QC, MP (d 1979), and Betty Margaret Oxley, *née* Pride (d 1993); *b* 11 Aug 1946; *Educ* Dragon Sch Oxford, Harrow, Trinity Coll Oxford (MA); *m* 11 Dec 1982, Fenella Jane, *née* Rowse; 1 s (Joshua, b 25 Sept 1990), 1 da (Ilaira b 4 June 1988); *Career* cataloguer for Christies 1969–73; writer and journalist 1973–; contrib: The Times, Country Life, The Sunday Telegraph, The Antiques Trade Gazette, The Oldie; ed Watercolours and Drawings Magazine 1986–91, property ed Country Life 1989–90, saleroom writer Country Life 1990–; ctee memb two maj antique fairs; memb: Cncl for the Care of Churches 1992–, Ctee London Library 1994–, Advsy Ctee Lambeth Palace Chapel 1996–; *Books* incl: Crome, Cotman and The Norwich School (1974), The Dictionary of British Watercolour Artists (3 vols 1976, 1979, 1990), How To Buy Pictures (1984), Understanding Watercolours (1985), The Illustrated History of Antiques (gen ed, 1991), Antiques Roadshow A - Z of Antiques Hunting (ed, 1995); *Recreations* helicopters, writing novels, cartoons; *Style*— Huon Mallalieu, Esq; ✉ 100 Mortimer Road, London N1 4LA

MALLARD, Prof John Rowland; OBE (1992); s of John Edward Mallard (d 1947), of Northampton, and Margaret Gwendoline, *née* Huckle (d 1958); *b* 14 Jan 1927; *Educ* Northampton Town and County Sch, Univ Coll Nottingham (BSc), Univ of Nottingham (PhD, DSc); *m* 6 June 1958, Fiona MacKenzie Murdoch, da of Robert Murdoch Lawrance (d 1934), of Aberdeen; 1 s (John b 1959), 1 da (Katriöna b 1964); *Career* asst physicist Liverpool Radium Inst 1951–53, head Dept of Physics Hammersmith Hosp 1958–63 (physicist 1953–58), reader in bio-physics Postgrad Med Sch and St Thomas's Hosp Med Sch London 1963–65, dir of med physics Grampian Health Bd and prof of med physics Univ of Aberdeen 1965–92 (now emeritus); Julio Palacios lectr Lisbon 1974, Silvanus Thompson medal Br Inst of Radiolgy 1981 (Barclay prize 1976), Otto Glasser lectr Cleveland USA 1982, Royal Soc Wellcome Fndn prize and Gold medal 1984, Free Enterprise special award Aims for Industry 1984, George Van Hevesy medal Euro Soc for Nuclear Med 1985, Euro Workshop of Nuclear Magnetic Resonance in Med award 1987, Commemoration lectr Univ of Osaka Japan 1987, Sr Scientist Merit award Int Union of Physical and Engrg Sci in Med 1988 (fndr pres 1980–85), Royal Soc Mullard prize and medal 1990, Barclay medal Br Inst of Radiology 1991, Norman Veall Prize Br Nuclear Medicine Soc 1995; memb: Equipment Res Ctee Sec of State for Scotland 1973–77 (Bio-Engrg Study Gp 1969–72, Bio-Med Res Ctee 1973–77), Bds MRC 1975–86, UK Nat Ctee for Bio-Physics 1977–85, Admin Radioactive Substances Advsy Ctee DHSS 1982–85; chm UK Nat Ctee for Med Physics 1975–88 (sec 1965–75), cmmr Int Cmmn of Radiation Units and Measurements 1985–94; Hon DSc: Univ of Hull 1994, Univ of Nottingham 1996; hon fell Australian Coll of Physical Scis applied to Med 1978; hon memb: RCR 1966, Br Nuclear Med Soc; FIPSM 1951 (pres 1970–73, hon fell 1993), FInstP (CPhys) 1960, FIEE (CEng) 1962, FRSE 1972, FRCPath 1974, BES 1975 (pres 1975–76), FEng 1993; *Books* contrib: Radioisotopes in Medical Diagnosis (1971), Progress in Nuclear Medicine (1972), NMR Imaging (1983), Modern Microscopies (1989), Scientific Europe (1990), Twentieth Century Physics (1995); *Recreations* handicrafts including jewellery making; *Style*— Prof John Mallard, OBE, FRSE, FEng; ✉ 121 Anderson Drive, Aberdeen AB15 6BG (☎ 01224 316204); Department of Bio-Medical Physics & Bio-Engineering, University of Aberdeen and Grampian Health Board, Foresterhill, Aberdeen AB9 2ZD (☎ 01224 681818 ext 52499, fax 01224 685645, telex 73458 UNIABN G)

MALLET, John Valentine Granville; s of Sir Victor Alexander Louis Mallet, GCMG, CVO (d 1969), and Christiana Jean (Peggy), *née* Andreae (d 1984); bro of Philip Louis Victor Mallet, *qv*; *b* 15 Sept 1930; *Educ* Winchester, Balliol Coll Oxford (BA); *m* 6 Sept 1958, Felicity Ann, da of (Philip Thurstane Richard) Ulick Basset, of Beaupré, Glamorgan; 1 s (Hugo Thurstane Victor Ulick b 1962); *Career* Nat Serv Intelligence Corps, temp Lt Trieste Security Office 1949–50; Ceramics and Works of Art Dept Sotheby & Co 1955–62; keeper Dept of Ceramics V & A 1976–89 (asst keeper 1962–76, sec Advsy Cncl 1967–73); Prime Warden Ct of Assts Fishmongers Co 1983–84 (memb of Ct 1970–); memb: Exec Ctee Nat Art Collection Fund 1989–, Wissenschaftlicher Beirat of the Ceramica-Stiftung (Basel) 1990–, Arts Advsy Panel Nat Tst 1996–; guest scholar J Paul Getty Museum Los Angeles 1993; hon fell Balliol Coll Oxford 1992; FRSA, FSA; *Books* various articles and reviews on ceramics; *Recreations* tennis; *Clubs* Brooks's; *Style*— J V G Mallet, Esq

MALLET, Philip Louis Victor; CMG (1980); s of Sir Victor Alexander Louis Mallet, GCMG, CVO (d 1969), and Christiana Jean, *née* Andreae (d 1984); descended from Jacques Mallet du Pan, chronicler of the French Revolution; bro of John Valentine Granville Mallet, *qv*; *b* 3 Feb 1926; *Educ* Winchester, Balliol Coll Oxford (BA); *m* 1953, Mary Moyle Grenfell, da of Rev Granville William Borlase (d 1953); 3 s (James, Stephen, Victor); *Career* HM Dip Serv (ret); high cmmr Guyana, non-res ambass Suriname 1978–82; *Clubs* Brooks's; *Style*— Philip Mallet, Esq, CMG; ✉ Wittersham House, Wittersham, Kent TN30 7ED (☎ 01797 270238)

MALLET, Victor John; s of Philip Louis Victor Mallet, and Mary Moyle Grenfell, *née* Borlase; *b* 14 May 1960; *Educ* Winchester, Merton Coll Oxford (BA); *Career* journalist; with Reuters in London, Paris, Johannesburg and Cape Town 1981–86; Financial Times: Africa correspondent 1986–88, Middle East correspondent 1988–91, SE Asia correspondent 1992–94, dep features ed 1995–; *Style*— Victor Mallet, Esq; ✉ The Financial Times, 1 Southwark Bridge, London SE1 9HL (☎ 0171 873 3000)

MALLETT, John; s of K J H Mallett, of Lincoln, and Dr V A Skinner; *b* 28 May 1970; *Educ* Millfield, West London Inst, Univ of Bath; *Career* rugby union player; over 50 appearances Bath RFC 1991–; honours with Bath: Courage League Champions 1996, winners Pilkington Cup 1996; England: capt Colts Student World Cup, 1 full cap v Western Samoa World Cup 1995; mktg asst Contemporary Leisure plc 1991–93, devpt offr and PE master Marlborough Coll 1995–; *Recreations* golf; *Style*— John Mallett, Esq; ✉ c/o Bath Rugby Club, The Recreation Ground, Bath

MALLETT, Prof Michael Edward; s of Edward Campbell Mallett (d 1990), of Little Roods, Gamblesby, nr Penrith, Cumbria, and Mary Florence, *née* Thompson; *b* 14 July 1932; *Educ* St Edward's Sch Oxford, Worcester Coll Oxford (BA, MA, DPhil); *m* 3 June 1961, Patricia Berenice, da of Ivor George Sullivan (d 1955); 2 s (Lucien b 1976, Cyprian b 1978); *Career* Nat Serv RA 1951–52, 2 Lt 1952; asst prof of history Univ of Manitoba 1960, asst dir and librarian Br Sch at Rome 1962; Univ of Warwick: lectr 1967–71, sr lectr 1971–74, reader 1974–78, prof of history 1978–; memb Exec Ctee Venice in Peril Fund; FRSL 1970, FRHistS 1977; *Books* The Florentine Galleys in the 15th Century (1967), The Borgias (1969), Mercenaries and Their Masters: Warfare in Renaissance Italy (1974), The Military Organisation of a Renaissance State: Venice 1400–1617 (with J R Hale, 1984), Lettere di Lorenzo de' Medici, vols V and VI (1990); *Style*— Prof Michael Mallett; ✉ 2 Lansdowne Circus, Leamington Spa, Warwickshire CV32 4SW (☎ 01926 425529); Department of History, University of Warwick, Coventry CV4 7AL (☎ 01203 523487)

MALLETT, Michael John; s of Albert William Mallett (d 1972); *b* 14 Dec 1931; *Educ* Devonport HS Plymouth, Penzance; *m* 1956, Joan Barbara, *née* Ayre; 1 s, 2 da; *Career* ptnr Noel Lewis & Co Liverpool 1957–60; James Neill Holdings Ltd: sec 1960, dir corp devpt 1970, dep chief exec 1974; chm: Ayre Mallett & Co Ltd 1960–, Radio Hallam Ltd 1979–90, Girobank plc (NE Regnl Bd) 1985–90, Yorks Radio Network plc 1987–90, Andionics Ltd 1987–90, Coated Electrodes International 1988–90; chm and chief exec Neill Tool Group Ltd 1981, chm and md Neill Tools 1981–83, exec dir James Neill Holdings plc 1983–84, dep chm TT Group plc 1984–95 (non-exec dir 1995–); chm: Record Holdings plc 1985–, Rediffusion Holdings (Singapore) Private Limited 1989–96, Rediffusion Communication Private Ltd 1989–96, Rediware Marketing Singapore Private Limited 1989–96, Multimedia Investments plc 1993–; dir: Unisheff Ventures Ltd 1984–92, Viking Radio Ltd 1987–90, Bradford Community Ltd 1987–90, Sheffield Academic Press Ltd 1988–, Yorkshire Venture Capital Ltd 1989–96, 3T Productions Ltd 1991–; chm: Yorks and Humberside Regnl Cncl CBI 1979–81, Nat Cncl CBI 1979–95, Econ and Fin Policy Ctee CBI 1982–88, Accounting Standards Ctee 1982–89, Sheffield Dist Soc Chartered Accountants (pres 1986–87); memb Cncl ICAEW 1995–; Master Co of Cutlers in Hallamshire 1978–79; Liveryman: Worshipful Co of Cutlers, Worshipful Co of CAs; FCA; *Recreations* horses, reading; *Clubs* Army & Navy; *Style*— Michael Mallett, Esq; ✉ 106 Ivy Park Rd, Sheffield, S Yorks S10 3LD (☎ 0114 230 5166)

MALLETT, Timmy; s of Rev Michael Mallett, and Nan Mallett; *b* Marple, Cheshire; *Educ* Univ of Warwick (BA); *Career* children's television personality, actor, prodr/director; disc jockey: BBC Radio Oxford 1977–81, Radio Luxembourg 1981, Piccadilly Radio Manchester 1982–87; television presenter: BBC Schools TV 1983, Wide Awake Club/Wacaday (TV-am) 1983–92, Utterly Brilliant (ITV) 1989–91, Around the World in 80 Seconds (Children's Channel) 1993–94; prodr and presenter: Way to Go (GMTV) 1996, Timmy Towers (ITV) 1997; currently dir Brilliant TV; numerous other TV and radio appearances; pantomime and theatre incl: Biker Mice from Mars (tour) 1995, Aladdin in Aladdin (Swindon) 1995–96; Dick in Dick Whittington Northampton 1994–95; Sony DJ of the Year Award 1984, TV Times Children's Personality of the Year 1991; other activities incl: presenting record-breaking radio show of 75 hours 1981, presenting Piccadilly Radio show from bath of custard, sitting on every seat at Manchester Utd and Manchester City football grounds for charity 1985; *Records* (as Bombalurina) incl: single Itsy Bitsy Teeny Weeny Yellow Polka Dot Bikini (reached UK No 1 summer 1990, only person to host and be top of Network Chart), single Seven Little Girls Sitting in the Back Seat (Top 20 1990), album Huggin' an' a-Kissin'; *Videos* incl: The Utterly Brilliant Magic Box, The Utterly Brilliant Paint Box; *Books* How to be Utterly Brilliant, The Utterly Brilliant History of the World; *Recreations* painting, cycling, pinball, bell ringing, rowing, football (Oxford Utd), collecting spectacles (over 150 pairs); *Style*— Timmy Mallett, Esq; ✉ c/o John Miles Organisation, Cadbury Camp Lane, Clapton-in-Gordano, Bristol BS20 9SB (☎ 01275 854675, fax 01275 810186)

MALLICK, Prof Netar P; s of Dr Bhawani Mallick (d 1964), of Blackburn, Lancs, and Shanti Devi, *née* Talwar (d 1986); *Educ* Queen Elizabeth Sch Blackburn, Univ of Manchester (BSc, MB ChB); *m* 11 July 1960, Mary, da of Albert Wilcockson (d 1977), of Brough, E Yorkshire; 3 da (Andrea b 1964, Naomi b 1966, Paula b 1968); *Career* conslt physician Dept of Renal Med Manchester Royal Infirmary 1973 (sr lectr med 1972–73); vice chm Blackburn Hyndburn Ribble Valley Health Authy 1985–90; prof in renal med Univ of Manchester 1994–; pres: Manchester Lit and Philosophical Soc 1985–87, Renal Assoc of GB and I 1989–92; chm Registry Ctee Euro Renal Assoc 1991–94; FRCP 1976, FRCPEd 1992; *Books* Renal Disease in General Practice (1979), Case Presentations in Renal Medicine (1983); *Style*— Prof Netar Mallick; ✉ Department of Renal Medicine, Manchester Royal Infirmary, Oxford Rd, Manchester M13 9WL (☎ 0161 276 4111, fax 0161 273 4834)

MALLIN, Anthony Granville; s of Frederick Granville Mallin (d 1986), and Phyllis May Mallin; *b* 26 May 1955; *m* 1989, Marie-Louise; 2 da (Josephine Louise b 4 Dec 1990, Annabelle Marie b 18 Oct 1995), 1 s (Frederick Harry b 15 April 1993); *Career* vice chm Hambros Bank Ltd 1994–, dir Hambros plc 1995–; vice chm Leaseeurope 1994–; chm: Equipment Leasing Assoc 1992–, Finance & Leasing Assoc 1993–; dir East London Youth & Minorities Activities Ltd (charity); *Recreations* rowing, golf, opera; *Clubs* Lea Rowing (pres), Leander; *Style*— Anthony Mallin, Esq; ✉ Hambros Bank Ltd, 41 Tower Hill, London EC3N 4HA (☎ 0171 865 1424, fax 0171 702 9825, mobile 0836 205434)

MALLIN, Rev Canon Stewart Adam Thomson; s of George Garner Mallin (d 1976), of Melville View, Lasswade, Midlothian, and Elizabeth, *née* Thomson (d 1949); *b* 12 Aug 1924; *Educ* Lasswade Secdy Sch, Coates Hall Theol Coll Edinburgh; *Career* ordained: deacon 1961, priest 1962; precentor Inverness Cathedral 1961–64, itinerant priest for the Diocese 1964–68, priest i/c St Peter and The Holy Rood Thurso and rector St John the Evangelist Wick 1968–77, canon Inverness Cathedral 1974, rector St James the Great Dingwall and St Anne's Strathpeffer 1977, dean Moray Ross and Caithness 1983–91 (synod clerk 1981–83), hon canon Inverness Cathedral and res priest St Paul's Strathnairn 1991–; memb: Co of the Servants of God, St John Assoc of Scotland Highland Branch, Rotary Club of Dingwall (former pres); hon memb Royal Br Legion Thurso Caithness (Communication USA Caithness) Unit 1971–77; exec memb Ross and Cromarty Cncl (on Alcohol, of Voluntary Serv); chaplain Dingwall Acad; OStJ (Priory of Scotland) 1995; *Recreations* gardening, music, travel; *Style*— The Rev Canon Stewart Mallin; ✉ St Paul's Parsonage, Croachy, Strathnairn, Inverness IV1 2UB (☎ 0180 852 1397)

MALLINCKRODT, George Wilhelm; *see:* Von Mallinckrodt, Georg Wilhelm

MALLINSON, Anne Mary; da of David Butler Wilson, MC (d 1961), of Alderley Edge, Cheshire, and Dorothy Catherine, *née* Bunn; *b* 20 Aug 1930; *Educ* Acton Reynold Shropshire, Edinburgh Coll of Domestic Sci; *m* 4 June 1955, Terence Stuart Mallinson,

CBE, DL, MA, s of Col Sir Sidney Mallinson, CBE, DSO, MC, JP, DL (d 1981), of Woodford Green, Essex; 3 s (Lawrence Stuart b 4 Sept 1957, Michael David Stuart b 22 April 1959, Roland Arthur Stuart b 13 July 1966), 1 da (Sheila Mary Anne b 24 May 1961); *Career* memb Westminster City Cncl 1974–; magistrate: N Westminster 1966–89, City of London 1969–89; Lord Mayor of Westminster 1986–87, Westminster rep London Tourist Bd 1980–85; memb: Paddington & North Kensington DHA 1983–85, Governing Cncl London Institute 1989–93, Central London Valuation Tbnl 1990–; vice chm Divert Tst 1993–; chm: Tower Hamlets DHA 1988–90, Bd of Govrs St James and St Michael's C of E Primary Sch 1988–90 (memb 1975–); govr Malborough Coll 1974–87; chm: Beauchamp Lodge Settlement 1981–86 (memb 1965), Bd of Tstees The Montessori Centre 1988–; govr St Mary Hosp 1985–89; memb: Delegacy Imperial Coll of Sci Technol and Med 1989, Ctee of Mgmnt Inst of Child Health 1992–; Liveryman City of London 1993 (Freeman 1963), Freeman Worshipful Co of Gardeners 1987; Order GDR 1987, Commendatore Repubblica Italiana 1988, Dame Chevalier de L'Ordre des Coteaux de Champagne 1987; *Recreations* hill walking, design, gardening, meeting people; *Clubs* Aldeburgh Yacht, English Speaking Union; *Style*— Mrs Terence Mallinson, JP; ✉ 28 Albion St, London W2 2AX (☎ 0171 262 1717, fax 0171 706 2266)

MALLINSON, Anthony William; s of Stanley Tucker Mallinson, of Bury St Edmunds, Suffolk (d 1955), and Dora Selina, *née* Burridge (d 1960); f was 2 s of Sir William Mallinson, 1 Bt, of Walthamstow, the fndr of William Mallinson & Sons Ltd, timber merchants, later part of the Mallinson-Denny Group; hp to kinsman Sir William James Mallinson, 5 Bt; *b* 1 Dec 1923; *Educ* Marlborough, Gonville and Caius Coll Cambridge (BA, LLM); *m* 30 April 1955, Heather Mary, da of Thomas Arthur Mansfield Gardiner (d 1950); *Career* Army 1943–47, Maj RA Europe and India; admitted slr 1951; sr ptnr Slaughter and May 1984–86 (ptnr 1957–86); dir: Baring Stratton Investment Trust plc 1986–94, Morgan Grenfell Asset Management Ltd 1986–91; slr to Worshipful Co of Fishmongers 1964–86, chm Cinematograph Films Cncl 1973–76, hon legal advsr Accounting Standards Ctee 1982–86; memb: Cncl Section on Business Law Int Bar Assoc 1984–90, London Bd Bank of Scotland 1985–93, Exec Ctee Essex CCC 1986–92, Financial Services Tbnl 1988–97, Financial Reporting Review Panel 1991–95; Liveryman Worshipful Co of Fishmongers; *Recreations* sport watching (principally cricket), reading; *Clubs* MCC; *Style*— Anthony Mallinson, Esq; ✉ 15 Douro Place, London W8 5PH (☎ 0171 937 2739)

MALLINSON, Dr Christopher Niels; s of Lawrence Mallinson (d 1960), and Thea Ruth, *née* Bergmann (d 1990); *b* 29 Oct 1935; *Educ* Cheltenham, King's Coll Cambridge (VIII Henley), Guy's Hosp; *m* 1966, Helen Gillian, da of J Noel Bowen; 2 da (Polly Jane b 1973, Sarah b and d 1976), 1 s (William (twin) b and d 1976); *Career* house physican Guy's Hosp, house surgn W Middlesex Hosp, sr house offr Guy's Neurosurgical Unit, registrar then sr registrar Guy's Hosp, res fell Pennsylvania USA; conslt physician and clinical tutor Greenwich Dist Hosp, lectr in physiology Guy's Hosp Med Sch 1969–79, conslt physican Lewisham Hosp 1979; fndr memb and memb Ctee Pancreatic Soc of GB and Ireland (pres 1987–88), pres Gastroenterology Sub Ctee European Union of Med Specialists, memb Br Soc of Gastroenterology 1965; FRCP 1973; *Publications* Report of Royal College of Physicians Working Party on Communications in Medicine, Psychiatric Complications of Organic Disease (ed, RCP); *Recreations* garden design, painting, opera, conversation; *Clubs* Garrick; *Style*— Dr Christopher Mallinson; ✉ 134 Harley St, London W1N 1AH (☎ 0171 935 4849)

MALLINSON, Michael Heathcote; CBE (1995); s of Reynold Heathcote Mallinson (d 1970), of Chalford, Glos and Beatrice Maud *née* Butt (d 1978); *b* 17 Sept 1934; *Educ* Marlborough; *m* 9 Aug 1958, Audrey, da of Lt-Col Frank Clifford Arnold, of Belmont, Surrey; 1 s (Matthew Frank Heathcote b 1964); *Career* RA 1953–55, 2 Lt 1954; chartered surveyor Prudential Assurance Co 1955–80, property dir and chief surveyor Prudential Portfolio Managers Ltd 1985–90 (jt chief surveyor 1981–85); pres Br Property Fedn 1989–90 (memb 1984–); memb: Cmmn for the New Towns 1986–, Property Advsy Gp DOE 1985–88; govr South Bank Univ (formerly South Bank Poly) 1986–; dir: Property and Professional Services Ltd 1990–94, Small Business Property Investment (London) Ltd; FRICS 1960; *Recreations* music, gardening, walking; *Style*— Michael Mallinson, Esq, CBE; ✉ Chelston, Guildford Rd, Chobham, Surrey (☎ 01276 858720)

MALLON, Rt Rev Monsignor Joseph Laurence; s of John Mallon, and Mary, *née* O'Neill; *b* 8 Aug 1942; *Educ* St Nathy's Coll, St Kieran's Coll; *Career* ordained priest Diocese of Salford 1966; curate: St Joseph's Bury 1966–67, St Anne's Stretford 1967–73; RAChD: commissioned 1973, various postings UK and overseas as sr chaplain 1982–89 (chaplain 1973–82), princ RC chaplain and vicar general (Army) MOD 1989–93; parish priest St Anne's Ancoats Manchester 1993–; Prelate of Honour 1989; *Recreations* recreational mathematics, bridge, The Times crossword, owns a set of golf clubs (a squash racquet and some fishing rods) but has the strength of character to overcome guilt feelings about their non use; has reservations about: dog owners, children in groups of more than three, curry lunches; *Style*— The Rt Rev Monsignor Joseph Mallon; ✉ St Annes House, Cuthers Street, Ancoats, Manchester M4 7EQ

MALLON, Seamus; MP (SDLP) Newry and Armagh (majority 7,091); s of Francis Patrick Mallon (d 1969), of Markethill, Armagh, and Jane, *née* O'Flaherty (d 1965); *b* 17 Aug 1936; *Educ* Abbey GS Newry, St Mary's Coll of Educn Belfast; *m* 22 June 1964, Gertrude Cora, da of Edward Cush, of Armagh; 1 da (Orla b June 1969); *Career* headmaster St James's PS Markethill 1960–73; memb: Armagh DC 1973–86, NI Assembly 1973–74, NI Convention 1975–76, Irish Senate 1982, New Ireland Forum 1983–84; MP (SDLP) Newry and Armagh 1986–, memb House of Commons Select Ctee on Agric 1986–92, memb Br-Irish Inter-Parly Body 1990–; Humbert Summer Sch Peace Prize 1988; *Recreations* golf, angling, landscape painting; *Clubs* Challoner; *Style*— Seamus Mallon, Esq, MP; ✉ 5 Castleview, Markethill, Armagh (☎ 01861 551555); House of Commons, Westminster SW1A 0AA (☎ offices: 0171 219 3000, 01861 526800, 01396 67933)

MALLOWS, Surgn Rear Adm (Harry) Russell; s of Harry Mallows (d 1953), of Martock, Somerset, and Amy, *née* Law (d 1941); *b* 1 July 1920; *Educ* Wrekin Coll, Christ's Coll Cambridge (MA, MD), Univ of London (DPH); *m* 1942, Rhona Frances, da of William Christopher Wyndham-Smith, of Patagonia, Argentina; 1 s (Richard), 2 da (Robin, Bryony); *Career* served Home, Med and Far E Cmds RN 1946–77, Surgn Rear Adm; house physician Wellhouse Hosp Barnet and Royal N Hosp Holloway, sr med advsr Shell International Petroleum Co Ltd 1977–85; QHP 1974–77; FFOM, FFPHM, DIH; CStJ 1976; *Recreations* music, travel; *Style*— Surgn Rear Adm Russell Mallows; ✉ Chesters, 1 Shear Hill, Petersfield, Hants GU31 4BB

MALMESBURY, 6 Earl of (GB 1800); William James Harris; TD (1944) and two clasps; also Baron Malmesbury (GB 1788) and Viscount Fitzharris (GB 1800); s of 5 Earl of Malmesbury, JP, DL (d 1950, gn of 3 Earl, who d 1889, having been sec of state for foreign affrs and Lord Keeper of the Privy Seal); 1 Earl was last to be created in the GB Peerage (three days before the Union with Ireland), he had previously been sent in 1794, as a special envoy to Brunswick, to negotiate the marriage between Princess Caroline and the future George IV; *b* 18 Nov 1907; *Educ* Eton, Trinity Coll Cambridge (MA); *m* 1, 1932, Hon Diana Claudia Patricia (Maria) Carleton (d 1990), da of 2 and last Baron Dorchester, OBE (d 1963); 1 s (James), 2 da (Sylvia, Nell); m 2, 14 March 1991, Margaret Fleetwood, OBE (1992), JP, DL (d 1994), yst da of late Col Robert William Pigott Clarke Campbell-Preston, and widow of Capt Raymond Alexander Baring (d 1967); m 3, July 1996, Bridget Graham, wid of Capt Peter Hawkings; *Heir* s, Viscount FitzHarris; *Career* serv Royal Hampshire Regt (TA) 1928–46; a Gold Staff Offr at Coronation of King George VI; professional surveyor RICS; chm Hants CLA 1954–56, personal liaison offr to Min of Agric SE Region 1958–64, chm Hants Agric Exec Ctee 1959–67, dir Mid Southern Water Co 1961–78; Official Verderer of the New Forest 1966–74; JP Hants 1949–82, DL 1957–60, Vice Lord Lt Southampton Co 1960–73, Lord Lt and Custos Rotulorum of Hampshire and Isle of Wight 1973–83; Hon Col 65 Signal Regt 1959–66 and Hon Col 2 Bn Wessex Regt 1970–73; memb Ct of Assts Worshipful Co of Skinners (Master 1952–53); KStJ; ARICS; *Recreations* rural life, sailing, working and training labradors, travel; *Clubs* Royal Yacht Sqdn (vice cdre 1971–78); *Style*— The Rt Hon the Earl of Malmesbury, TD, JP, DL; ✉ The Ford, Deptford Lane, Greywell, Hook, Hampshire RG29 1BA (☎ 01256 703223)

MALONE, (Peter) Gerald; MP (C) Winchester (majority 8,121); s of Peter Andrew Malone and Jessie Robertson Ritchie Malone, of Glasgow; *b* 21 July 1950; *Educ* Aloysius Coll, Univ of Glasgow (MA, LLB); *m* 1981, Anne Scotland, da of William Blyth, of Edinburgh; 2 s (Andrew Blyth, Peter), 1 da (Jane); *Career* slr; MP (C): Aberdeen S 1983–87, Winchester 1992–; PPS to Parly Under Secs of State Dept of Energy 1985, PPS to Sec of State DTI 1985–86, asst govt whip 1986–87, dep chm Cons Party 1992–94, min of state Dept of Health 1994–; dir of Euro affrs Energy and Environmental Center Harvard Univ 1987–90, ed The Sunday Times Scotland 1989–90 (now editorial conslt); *Recreations* opera, music; *Clubs* Winchester Conservative; *Style*— Gerald Malone, Esq, MP; ✉ House of Commons, London SW1A 0AA (☎ 0171 219 2634)

MALONE, Rt Rev Vincent; s of Louis Malone (d 1974), of Liverpool, and Elizabeth, *née* McGrath (d 1972); *b* 11 Sept 1931; *Educ* St Francis Xavier's Coll Liverpool, St Joseph's Coll Upholland, Univ of Liverpool (BSc), Univ of Cambridge (CertEd, DipEd); *Career* chaplain Notre Dame Training Coll Liverpool 1955–59, asst priest St Anne's Liverpool 1960–61, asst master Cardinal Allen GS Liverpool 1961–71, chaplain Univ of Liverpool 1971–79, admin Liverpool Metropolitan Cathedral 1979–89, aux bishop of Liverpool and titular bishop of Abora 1989–; memb Nat Bd Catholic Women-Episcopal Liaison, chm Higher Educn Ctee RC Bishops' Conf of England and Wales; FCP 1967; *Style*— The Rt Rev Vincent Malone; ✉ 17 West Oakhill Park, Liverpool L13 4BN (☎ 0151 228 7637, fax 0151 475 0841)

MALONE-LEE, Michael Charles; CB (1995); s of Dr Gerard Brendan Malone-Lee, of Pinner, Middx, and Theresa Marie Germaine Malone-Lee; *b* 4 March 1941; *Educ* Stonyhurst, Campion Hall Oxford (MA Classics); *m* Claire Frances, da of Canon C M Cockin; 2 s (John b 1975, Francis b 1980); *Career* Civil Serv: joined 1968, princ private sec to Sec of State for Social Servs 1976–79, area admin City & East London AHA 1979–81, dist admin Bloomsbury Health Authy 1982–84, under sec and dir of personnel DHSS HQ 1984–87, princ fin offr Home Office 1987–89, dep sec and dir of corp affrs NHS Mgmnt Exec Dept of Health 1990–93, head Policy Gp Lord Chllr's Dept 1993–95, ret; vice chllr Anglia Polytechnic Univ Sept 1995–; memb Inst of Health Serv Mgmnt; *Recreations* running, natural history, anything French; *Style*— Michael Malone-Lee, Esq, CB; ✉ Anglia Polytechnic University, Bishop Hall Lane, Chelmsford, Essex CM1 1SQ (☎ 01245 493131, fax 01245 495419)

MALONEY, Michael Anthony Gerard; s of Gp Capt Gerard Maloney, of London, and Pamela Maloney; *b* 19 June 1957; *Educ* Ampleforth, LAMDA; *Career* actor; jt winner Alec Clunes Award LAMDA; *Theatre* RSC incl: Prince Hal in Henry IV Parts 1 and 2, Romeo in Romeo and Juliet, title role in Derek; other credits incl: Taking Steps (Lyric Theatre), Benjamin Britten in Once in a While the Odd Thing Happens (NT), title role in Peer Gynt (Cambridge), Two Planks and a Passion (Greenwich), Alice's Adventures Underground (RNT); *Television* for BBC: Starlings (first prize Monte Carlo), Telford's Change, The Bell, Falkland in The Rivals, Relatively Speaking, Love On A Branch Line; other credits incl: Dominic in What if it's Raining (Channel 4), William Boot in Scoop (LWT), Indiana Jones Chronicles (Lucas Films); *Films* incl: Dauphin in Henry V, Rosencrantz in Hamlet, Leonardo in La Maschera, Truly Madly Deeply, Ordeal By Innocence, Sharma and Beyond, In the Bleak Midwinter, Othello; *Style*— Michael Maloney, Esq; ✉ Markham & Froggatt, 4 Windmill St, London W1 (☎ 0171 636 4412)

MALPAS, Prof James Spencer; s of Tom Spencer Malpas (d 1972); *b* 15 Sept 1931; *Educ* Sutton Co GS, Bart's Univ of London, Univ of Oxford; *m* 1957, Joyce May, da of Albert Edward Cathcart (d 1962); 2 s; *Career* emeritus prof of med oncology Bart's Univ of London, dir Imperial Cancer Res Fund Unit of Med Oncology, conslt physician Bart's, dean Med Coll 1969–72; asst registrar RCP 1975–80, vice pres Med Coll 1987–93, sr physician Bart's 1993–; pres Assoc of Cancer Physicians 1994–; Master of the London Charterhouse 1996–; *Recreations* skiing, sailing, history, painting, travel; *Clubs* Little Ship; *Style*— Prof James Malpas; ✉ Master's Lodge, Charterhouse, London EC1M 6AN

MALPAS, (John) Peter Ramsden; s of A H Malpas (d 1942), and E N E D Malpas, *née* Gledhill (d 1992); *b* 14 Dec 1927; *Educ* Winchester, New Coll Oxford (MA); *m* 10 May 1958, Rosamond Margaret, da of R J Burn, RA (d 1984), of Chiswick, London; 3 s (Simon b 1959, David b 1962, Johnny b 1965); *Career* Lt RB served India and UK 1946–48; commercial asst Imperial Chemical Industries 1951–55, Chase Henderson & Tennant Stockbrokers 1956–58; Paribas Quilter Securities (formerly Quilter Goodison, previously Quilter & Co): joined 1959, dep sr ptnr and chm 1983–87; dir: Penny & Giles International 1988–92, West Wittering Estates plc; hon treas Royal Hosp for Neuro-disability, memb Ctee Friends of Templeton Coll Oxford, tstee Living Again (formerly Devpt Tst for Young Disabled); memb Stock Exchange 1961–88; *Recreations* skiing, walking, sailing, the arts; *Clubs* Itchenor Sailing, Ski Club of GB; *Style*— Peter Malpas, Esq; ✉ 48 Berwyn Rd, Richmond, Surrey TW10 5BS (☎ 0181 878 2623)

MALPAS, Robert; CBE (1976); s of Cheshyre Malpas (d 1962), and Louise Marie Marcelle, *née* Boni (d 1984); *b* 9 Aug 1927; *Educ* Taunton Sch, St George's Coll Buenos Aires, King's Coll Univ of Durham (BSc); *m* 30 June 1956, Josephine, da of Leslie James Dickenson (d 1982); *Career* main bd dir ICI 1975–78 (joined 1948), pres Halcon International Corporation USA 1978–82, memb Bd and md BP plc 1983–89; chm: PowerGen (one of successor cos to CEGB) 1988–90, Cookson plc 1991–, Eurotunnel plc (jtly) 1996– (non-exec dir 1987–, co chm Eurotunnel 1996); non-exec dir: BOC plc 1981–96, Repsol SA (Spain); chm: LINK (the DTI business HEI initiative) 1987–93, NERC 1993–96; pres Soc of Chem Indust 1988–89, memb Cncl of Indust and Higher Educn; Hon DUniv: Surrey 1986, Loughborough 1985, Newcastle 1991, Bath 1991; fell Westminster Univ (formerly Central London Poly) 1988; FEng 1978, FIMechE, FIChemE, FIMatH; Order of Civil Merit (Spain) 1968; *Recreations* music, sport, opera; *Clubs* RAC London, Mill Reef (Antigua), The River (New York); *Style*— Robert Malpas, Esq, CBE, FEng; ✉ 2 Spencer Park, London SW18 2SX; Cookson Group plc, 130 Wood Street, London EC2V 6EQ (☎ 0171 606 4400, fax 0171 600 4281)

MALSBURY, Angela Mary; da of late Reginald Malsbury, and Madge Meagan, *née* Stenson; *b* 5 May 1945; *Educ* Loughborough HS for Girls, Kibworth Beauchamp GS, RCM; *m* 1965, David Robin Pettit; 1 s (Timothy Nicholas David b 1967); *Career* clarinettist; Wigmore Hall debut 1968, Royal Festival Hall debut with London Mozart Players 1976; princ clarinettist London Mozart Players, prof of clarinet RAM; memb: Albion Ensemble, Primavera Ensemble, De Saram Clarinet Trio, London Winds, Musicians of the Royal Exchange; also plays with: Acad of St Martin in the Fields, London Sinfonietta, Nash Ensemble; Mozart Meml Prize, Hon RAM; *Recordings* incl: Mozart's 13 Wind Serenade (variously with London Mozart Players, Acad of St Martin's and Albion Ensemble), Mozart's Clarinet Quintet (with Coull Quartet), Mozart's Clarinet Concerto (with London Mozart Players), Prokovieff's Overture on Yiddish Themes,

Mississippi 5 (with Albion Ensemble); *Recreations* swimming, walking, cooking, art; *Style*— Ms Angela Malsbury; ✉ c/o John Wright, The Wheelhouse Barn, Marwell Farm Ringmore, nr Kingsbridge, S Devon TQ7 4HF (☎ 01548 810716, fax 01548 810026)

MALTBY, Colin Charles; s of George Frederick Maltby, MC, and late Dorothy Maltby; *b* 8 Feb 1951; *Educ* George Heriot's Sch Edinburgh, King Edward's Sch Birmingham, Christ Church Oxford (MA, MSc), Stanford Business Sch; *m* 1983, Victoria Angela Valerie, da of late Paul Guido Stephen Elton; 1 s (Matthew b 1989), 2 da (Lorna b 1976, Katherine b 1986); *Career* merchant banker; pres Oxford Union 1973, chm Fedn of Cons Students 1974–75; dir: Kleinwort Benson (ME) EC 1983–84, Kleinwort Benson Investment Management Ltd 1984–95, Banque Kleinwort Benson SA 1985–95 (chm 1993), Kleinwort Benson Group plc 1989–95; chief exec Kleinwort Benson Investment Management Ltd 1988–95, chm Kleinwort Overseas Investment Trust plc 1992–96; dir Fuji Investment Trust Management KK 1993–95, chief investment offr Equitas Reinsurance Ltd 1996–; memb Tomorrow's Company Inquiry Team 1993–95; FRSA, MRI, MSI; *Recreations* music, theatre, curiosity; *Style*— Colin Maltby, Esq; ✉ 51 Addison Avenue, London W11 4QU

MALTBY, John Newcombe; CBE (1988); s of Air Vice-Marshal Sir Paul Copeland Maltby, KCVO, KBE, CB, DSO, AFC, DL (d 1971), and Winifred Russell, *née* Paterson (d 1993); *b* 10 July 1928; *Educ* Wellington, Clare Coll Cambridge; *m* 28 July 1956, Lady Sylvia Veronica Anthea Harris, er da of 6 Earl of Malmesbury, TD; 1 s (William John b 5 Sept 1959), 2 da (Caroline Jane b 14 May 1957, Sophia Louise (Mrs Alexander Ross) b 11 Nov 1963); *Career* chm: Burmah Oil plc 1983–90, Dover Harbour Board 1989–, UKAEA 1990–93, Harrisons & Crosfield plc 1991–94; *Recreations* history, sailing, gardening; *Clubs* Brooks's, Royal Yacht Squadron; *Style*— John Maltby, Esq, CBE; ✉ Broadford House, Stratfield Turgis, Hook, Hants RG27 0AS

MALTHOUSE, Eric James; s of James William Malthouse (d 1961), of Whitchurch, Cardiff, and Florence Dorothy, *née* Alder (d 1971); *b* 20 Aug 1914; *Educ* King Edward VI Sch Aston, Birmingham Coll of Arts and Crafts; *m* 24 July 1942, Anne May, da of late William Gascoigne (d 1982), of High Row, Haswell, Durham; 1 s ((Jonathan) Paul Gascoigne b 14 June 1952), 2 da (Penelope b 19 May 1944, Diana b 29 April 1948); *Career* WWII serv RAC 1940–42 (invalided out); artmaster Salt High Schs Saltaire Shipley 1938–43, asst lectr (later sr lectr) Cardiff Coll of Art 1944–73, ret; artist; exhibited first painting Royal Birmingham Soc of Artists 1931; mural paintings at: Wales Gas Helmont House, Penlyan Hostel Univ Coll Cardiff, L G Harris & Co Ltd Bromsgrove; exhibitions incl: Ten Year Retrospective 1959, Growth of Two Paintings 1963, New Vision Gallery (paintings) 1965, AIA (small paintings) 1969, Bangor Art Gallery (paintings and prints) 1970, Oxford Gallery 1971, Exeter Univ 1975, A Family Affair Sherman Theatre 1981, Recent Paintings and a Selection of Prints Oriel Welsh Arts Cncl Gallery Cardiff 1981 work in collections incl: Nat Museum of Wales, Welsh Art Cncl, Swansea Art Gallery, Newport Art Gallery, Bath Art Gallery, Bristol Art Gallery, V & A, Tate, Univ of Cardiff, Univ of Aberystwyth, Univ of Swansea, Univ of Exeter, Univ of Glasgow, Oxford CC, Glamorgan CC, Somerset CC; fndr memb: S Wales Gp 1949, Watercolour Soc Wales 1959; fndr 56 Gp Wales 1956 (resigned 1970); Welsh Arts Cncl Prize for best designed book Ancestor Worship by Emyr Humphreys 1971; memb: Print Makers Cncl 1971, Royal Cambrian Acad; RWA; *Recreations* gardening, walking, jazz, chamber music, opera; *Style*— Eric Malthouse, Esq; ✉ 56 Porth-Y-Castell, Barry, South Glamorgan CF62 6QE (☎ 01446 749380)

MALTZ, Dr Milton Beer; s of Prof Jayme Maltz, of Porto Alegre, Brazil, and Matilde, *née* Beer; *b* 2 Oct 1954; *Educ* Porto Alegre HS Brazil, Shawnee Mission S HS Kansas City (grad dip), Univ of Med Porto Alegre Rio Grande Do Sul Brazil (MD), Bart's Hosp Univ of London (Br Cncl scholar, dip in gen med, MPhil), Univ of London and St Bartholomew's Med Coll; *Career* formerly casualty student offr Accident and Emergency Hosp Porto Alegre Brazil; Bart's London: sr house offr in gen med 1984–85, hon cardiac registrar Dept of Cardiology 1985–88, clinical asst in cardiology 1988–90; dir Clinical Res Prog in Cardiology St George's Hosp London 1990–92; currently in private practice Harley St, chm Medical Centre Cardiac Research Ltd; med and nursing staff teacher for MB and GP trg on specialised courses, author of numerous med articles for learned jls, invited speaker at numerous int cardiac meetings; offr surgn St John Ambulance Prince of Wales District London; fell in gen med Univ of Med Porto Alegre Brazil 1984; *Books* The Clinical Evaluation on Angina Pectoris of a Calcium Antagonist - Tiapamil; *Recreations* tennis; *Clubs* Angela Bexton Tennis; *Style*— Dr Milton Maltz; ✉ 48 Harley Street, London W1N 1AD (☎ 0171 323 9292 and 0171 580 3145, fax 0171 323 5297)

MALVERN, 3 Viscount (UK 1955); Ashley Kevin Godfrey Huggins; s of 2 Viscount Malvern (d 1978), and Patricia Margery, *née* Renwick-Bower; *b* 26 Oct 1949; *Heir* unc, Hon (Martin) James Huggins; *Style*— The Rt Hon the Viscount Malvern

MALVERN, John; s of Harry Ladyman Malvern, CBE (d 1982), of Cookham, and Doreen, *née* Peters; *b* 3 Oct 1937; *Educ* Fettes, Univ of London (BSc), London Hosp (MB BS); *m* 10 July 1965, Katharine Mary Monica, da of Hugh Guillebaud (d 1958), of Marlborough; 1 s (James b 1977), 2 da (Susan (Lady Wilmot) b 1966, Joanna b 1969); *Career* conslt obstetrician Queen Charlotte's Hosp 1973, conslt gynaecologist Chelsea Hosp for Women and hon sr lectr Inst of Obstetrics and Gynaecology 1973–; pres Obstetrics and Gynaecology Section RSM 1990; examiner: RCOG, Central Midwives Bd, Univs of London, Liverpool, Manchester, Benghazi, Colombo, Khartoum and Hong Kong; hon treas and offr RCOG 1991– (memb Cncl 1977–83 and 1987–90), chm Academic Gp Inst of Obstetrics and Gynaecology 1986–88, pres Queen Charlotte's Hosp Dining Club, Fothergill Club 1991; memb: Central Manpower Ctee 1981–84, Gynaecological Visiting Soc, Int Continence Soc (fndr memb), Blair Bell Res Soc; Liveryman Worshipful Soc of Apothecaries; FRCSEd, FRCOG, FRSM; *Books* The Unstable Bladder (ed jtly, 1989), Turnbull's Obstetrics (contrib, 1995), Gynaecology by Ten Teachers (contrib, 1995), Lecture Notes on Gynaecology (ed jtly, 1996); various pubns on urogynaecology and obstetrics; *Recreations* wine tasting, Chinese ceramics, travel; *Clubs* RSM, Hurlingham; *Style*— John Malvern, Esq; ✉ 30 Roedean Crescent, Roehampton, London SW15 5JU (☎ 0181 876 4943); 82 Harley St, London W1 (☎ 0171 636 2766, fax 0171 631 5371)

MAMATSASHVILI, HE Teimuraz; s of David Mamatsashvili (d 1969), of Tbilisi, Georgia, and Maria, *née* Robakidze; *b* 10 Nov 1942; *Educ* Georgian Politechnical Inst Tbilisi, Acad of Foreign Trade Moscow; *m* 1967, Arkhangelskaya Irina; 2 da (Tamara b 1968, Natia b 1977); *Career* Georgian diplomat; sr engr: Scientific Inst of Metrology Tbilisi 1965–70, Trade Representation of the USSR in Australia (Canberra) 1973–77; sr engr, vice dir then dir Foreign Trade Orgn ('Licensintorg') Moscow 1977–89, Foreign Trade Orgn ('Licensintorg') rep Trade Representation of the USSR in Japan (Tokyo) 1989–92, min Ctee of Foreign Economic Rels Georgia 1992–93, Georgian ambass to the Ct of St James's 1995–; bd memb Black Sea Countries Economic Co-operation Cncl Turkey 1992–93, Georgian rep Int Maritime Orgn London 1995–; govr European Bank; *Style*— HE Mr Teimuraz Mamatsashvili; ✉ Embassy of the Republic of Georgia, 45 Avonmore Road, London W14 8RT (☎ 0171 603 5226, fax 0171 603 5325)

MAMDANI, Prof Ebrahim; s of Hassanali Mamdani (d 1965), of Tanzania, and Fatmabai Mamdani; *b* 1 June 1942; *Educ* Karimjee Government Sch Tanga Tanzania, Coll of Engrg Poona (BE), Queen Mary Coll London (MSc, PhD); *m* Oct 1968, Virginia Anne, da of V Edward Perkins; 1 s (Geoffrey Asif b 18 March 1976), 1 da (Caroline Sahira b 30 Oct 1978); *Career* Dept of Electrical Engrg Queen Mary Coll London: joined as lectr 1968, reader 1976, personal chair in electronics 1984–95; Nortel/Royal Acad of Engrg chair in Telecommunications Strategy and Services Imperial Coll London 1995–; visiting prof Tokyo Inst of Technol 1977 (summer); seconded to British Telecom Research Laboratories 1988–89; FIEE 1982, FIEEE (USA) 1993, FEng 1994; *Books* Fuzzy Reasoning and its Applications (co-ed, 1981), Non-Standard Logics for Automated Reasoning (co-ed, 1988); *Recreations* computing: multi-media, cooking, conversation; *Style*— Prof Ebrahim Mamdani, FEng; ✉ 31 Roding Drive, Kelvedon Hatch, Brentwood, Essex CM15 0XA (☎ 01277 374772); Department of Electrical and Electronic Engineering, Imperial College, Exhibition Road, London SW7 2BT (☎ 0171 594 6316, fax 0171 823 8125, e-mail e.mamdani@ic.ac.uk)

MAMED-KULIYEV, HE Mahmud; *b* 15 Oct 1949, Ganja, Azerbaijan; *Educ* Dept of Law Azerbaijan State Univ; *m*; 3 c; *Career* Azerbaijanian diplomat; lectr in law Azerbaijan State Univ 1972–74, various positions Government Serv 1974–92, vice pres Commercial Bank 1992–93, dep foreign min of foreign affrs 1993–, ambass to the Ct of St James's 1994–; MP 1995–; *Style*— HE Mr Mahmud Mamed-Kuliyev; ✉ Embassy of the Azerbaijan Republic, 1 Kensington Court, London W8 5DL (☎ 0171 938 3412, fax 0171 937 1783)

MAMUJEE, Dr Abdullah; s of Mulla Mamujee Nurbhai (d 1947), and Khatijabai, *née* Alibhai (d 1942); *b* 10 Oct 1934; *Educ* Univ of Poona (MB, BS); *m* 15 Dec 1966, Dr Nalini Mamujee, da of Vaikunth Gopal Shanbhag (d 1980); 1 s (Salil b 5 Nov 1969), 1 da (Anila b 10 June 1968); *Career* surgical registrar Ashford Hosp Middx, surgical registrar Poplar Hosp London, conslt and sr lectr in surgery Univ of Dar es Salaam Tanzania, conslt and head of Accident and Emergency Dept Ipswich Hosp 1978, chm Cncl of Racial Equality, memb Bd of Visitors Hollesly Bay Young Offenders Inst; RSM, BMA; FRCSEd; FFAEM; *Recreations* reading, writing; *Style*— Dr Abdullah Mamujee; ✉ Springfields, 151 The Street, Rushmere St Andrew, Ipswich, Suffolk IP5 7DG (☎ 01473 272269); Accident and Emergency Department, Ipswich Hospital, Heath Rd, Ipswich, Suffolk (☎ 01473 712233)

MANASSEH, Leonard Sulla; OBE (1982); *Educ* Cheltenham Coll, AA Sch of Architecture; *Career* pilot Fleet Air Arm 1943–46; asst architect: CRE N London, Guy Morgan & Partners 1941; on teaching staff AA and Kingston Sch of Art 1941, asst architect Architects Dept Herts CC 1943–48, sr architect Stevenage Development Corporation 1948–50, fndr Leonard Manasseh & Partners (became Leonard Manasseh Partnership) 1950; AA: on teaching staff Sch of Architecture 1951–59, Cncl memb 1955–66, pres 1964–65; memb Cncl: Industrial Design 1965–68, British Sch at Rome 1976–83, National Trust 1977–91; pres Franco-British Union of Architects 1978–79, pres Royal West of England Acad 1989–94 (memb 1972–); chm Ctee Dulwich Picture Gallery 1988–93 (surveyor 1987–93), dep chm Chatham Historic Dockyard Tst 1991 (tstee 1984), RA nominee Bd of Govrs Dulwich Schools Fndn 1987–94; winner Festival of Britain Competition 1950; RA 1979 (ARA 1976), FRIBA 1964 (ARIBA 1941, memb Cncl 1968–70 and 1976–82, hon sec 1979–81), FCSD 1965, FRSA 1967; *Style*— Leonard Manasseh, Esq, OBE, RA; ✉ 6 Bacon's Lane, Highgate Village, London N6 6BL

MANATON, John Westacott; s of William Alfred Westacott Manaton, and Linda Maud, *née* Townsend; *b* 10 Jan 1926; *Educ* Dulwich, Downing Coll Cambridge (BA); *m* 23 June 1951, Mavis June, da of Frederick George Langton (d 1959), of Dartford, Kent; 1 da (Gillian Clare b 15 May 1964); *Career* Fleet Air Arm RN 1945–47; Lt Inns of Court Regt and 3/4 Co of London Yeo (Sharpshooters) TA; Royal Exchange Assurance 1947–51, Legal & General Assurance Society Ltd 1951–56, Canada Life Assurance Co Ltd 1956–59, Scottish Provident Institution 1959–63, pensions mangr National Mutual Life Association of Australasia Ltd 1964–67, gen mangr (UK) Swiss Life Insurance and Pension Co 1967–89, chm Westacott & Manaton Ltd 1977–90, non-exec dir Maidstone Priority Care NHS Tst 1991–; Freeman City of London 1980, Liveryman Worshipful Co of Actuaries 1980; AIA, FPMI; *Recreations* sailing (yachtmaster); *Clubs* United Oxford and Cambridge Univ, Little Ship, RNSA, Alleynian SS; *Style*— John Manaton, Esq; ✉ 2 Blair Drive, Sevenoaks, Kent TN13 3JR (☎ 01732 458528)

MANCE, Hon Mr Justice; Hon Sir Jonathan Hugh; kt (1993); s of Sir Henry Stenhouse Mance (d 1981), and Joan Erica Robertson, *née* Baker; *b* 6 June 1943; *Educ* Charterhouse, Univ Coll Oxford (MA); *m* 26 May 1973, Dame Mary Howarth Arden, DBE (Hon Mrs Justice Arden), *qv*, da of Lt-Col Eric Cuthbert Arden (d 1973); 1 s (Henry b 1982), 2 da (Abigail b 1976, Jessica b 1978); *Career* called to the Bar Middle Temple 1965, QC 1982, judge of the High Court of Justice (Queen's Bench Div) 1993–; dir Bar Mutual Indemnity Fund Ltd 1988–94; chm Banking Appeal Tbnls 1992–93; *Recreations* tennis, music, languages; *Clubs* Cumberland Lawn Tennis; *Style*— The Hon Mr Justice Mance; ✉ Royal Courts of Justice, Strand, London WC2A 2LL

MANCHESTER, 12 Duke of (GB 1719); Angus Charles Drogo Montagu; also Baron Kimbolton (E 1620) and Earl of Manchester (E 1626, cr three days after Charles I's coronation); s of 10 Duke, OBE (d 1977; himself tenth in descent from the 2 Earl of Manchester, a Parly Cdr in the Great Rebellion, being Cromwell's immediate superior at Marston Moor) and his 1 w, Nell Vere, *née* Stead (d 1966); suc bro, 11 Duke (d 1985); *b* 9 Oct 1938; *Educ* Gordonstoun; *m* 1, 1961 (m dis 1970), Mary Eveleen, da of Walter Gillespie McClure, of Geelong, Vic, Australia; 2 s, 1 da; m 2, 1971 (m dis 1985), Diane Pauline, da of Arthur Plimsaul, of Wimborne, Dorset; m 3, 27 Jan 1989, Mrs Ann-Louise Bird, da of Dr Alfred Butler Taylor, of Cawthorne, S Yorkshire; *Heir* s, Viscount Mandeville, *qv*; *Career* business conslt; pres and patron The Duke's Tst; *Recreations* golf; *Style*— His Grace the Duke of Manchester; ✉ House of Lords, Westminster, London SW1A 0PW

MANCHESTER, Archdeacon of; *see:* Harris, Ven (Reginald) Brian

MANCHESTER, Bishop of 1993–; Rt Rev Christopher John Mayfield; *b* 1935; *Educ* Sedbergh, Gonville and Caius Coll Cambridge (MA), Linacre House Oxford (dip in theol), Cranfield Inst of Technol (MSc); *Career* lectr St Martin-in-the-Bullring Birmingham 1967–71 (curate 1963–67), vicar of St Mary Luton 1971–80, rural dean of Luton 1974–80, archdeacon of Bedford 1980–85, suffragan bishop of Wolverhampton 1985–93; *Recreations* cricket, walking; *Style*— The Rt Rev the Bishop of Manchester; ✉ Bishopscourt, Bury New Road, Manchester M7 4LE (☎ 0161 792 2096, fax 0161 792 6826)

MANCHESTER, Dean of; *see:* Riley, Very Rev Kenneth Joseph

MANCROFT, 3 Baron (UK 1937); Sir Benjamin Lloyd Stormont Mancroft; 3 Bt (UK 1932); s of 2 Baron Mancroft, KBE, TD (d 1987); *b* 16 May 1957; *Educ* Eton; *m* 20 Sept 1990, Emma L, eldest da of Tom Peart, of Kensington; 1 s (Hon Arthur Louis Stormont b 3 May 1995), 1 da (Hon Georgia Esme b 25 April 1993); *Heir* s, Hon Arthur Louis Stormont Mancroft b 3 May 1995; *Career* chm: Scratch 'n' Win Lotteries Ltd 1995–, Inter Lotto (UK) Ltd 1995–, Transfer Technologies (UK) Ltd; dep chm Phoenix House Housing Assoc 1990–; patron: Patsy Handy Tst 1991–, Sick Dentists' Tst 1991–; chm: Addiction Recovery Fndn 1989–, Drug and Alcohol Fndn 1995–; vice chm Br Field Sports Soc 1992–; jt master Vale of White Horse Hunt 1987–89; memb Bd Mentor Fndn (Geneva); exec: Assoc of Cons Peers 1989–94, Nat Union of Cons Assocs 1989–94; *Style*— The Rt Hon the Lord Mancroft; ✉ House of Lords, London SW1

MANDELSON, Peter Benjamin; MP (Lab) Hartlepool (majority 8,782); s of George Norman Mandelson (d 1989), and the Hon Mary Joyce Mandelson, *née* Morrison; *b* 21 Oct 1953; *Educ* Hendon Sr HS, St Catherine's Coll Oxford (BA); *Career* chm Br Youth Cncl 1977–80, cncllr Lambeth BC 1979–82, prodr Weekend World London Weekend TV 1982–85, dir of campaigns and communications Lab Pty 1985–90, MP (Lab) Hartlepool 1992–; *PS* The Blair Revolution - Can New Labour Deliver (co-author, 1996); *Recreations* countryside, collecting objects, swimming; *Style*— Peter Mandelson, Esq, MP; ✉ House of Commons, London SW1A 0AA (☎ 0171 219 4607)

MANDER, Sir Charles Marcus; 3 Bt (UK 1911), of The Mount, Tettenhall, Co Stafford; s of Maj Sir Charles Arthur Mander, 2 Bt, TD, JP, DL (d 1951), and Monica Claire, *née* Cotterell (d 1963); *b* 22 Sept 1921; *Educ* Eton, Trinity Coll Cambridge; *m* 1945, Maria Dolores Beatrice, da of Alfred Edmund Brödermann (d 1923), of Gross Fontenay, Hamburg; 2 s ((Charles) Nicholas b 1950, Francis Peter Edward b 1952), 1 da (Penelope Anne Mary (Mrs Simon J Loder) b 1946); *Heir* s, (Charles) Nicholas Mander b 23 March 1950; *Career* served WWII, Capt Coldstream Gds; dir: Mander Bros Ltd 1948–58, Headstaple Ltd 1976, Arlington Securities (chm 1976–82, dep chm 1982–83); chm London & Cambridge Investments Ltd 1984–91; underwriting memb Lloyd's 1956–92; High Sheriff Staffs 1962; Liveryman Worshipful Co of Fishmongers; *Recreations* yachting, shooting, music; *Style*— Sir Charles Mander, Bt; ✉ Little Barrow, Moreton-in-Marsh, Glos (☎ 01451 830265, fax 01451 830791)

MANDER, David Charles; s of Alan Mander, of Warwicks, and Muriel Betty, *née* Whiteman (d 1975); *b* 16 April 1938; *Educ* Wrekin Coll Salop, Univ of Birmingham (LLB); *m* Elizabeth Ann, da of late F W Thorn, of Coventry; 2 s (Philip James b 1964, Nicholas David b 1967), 1 da (Charlotte Louise b 1972); *Career* slr; sr ptnr Mander Hadley & Co Solicitors; dir Warwicks Law Soc Ltd 1969–96; memb Cncl: Warwicks Law Soc (sec 1969–72), Birmingham Law Soc 1972–80; memb Cncl The Law Soc for constituency of: W Midlands W Mercia and Welsh Marshes 1980–89, Coventry and Warwickshire 1989–96; chm: Coventry Diocesan Tstees 1985–96, Law Soc Indemnity Insur Ctee 1986–87, Law Soc Trg Review Ctee 1994–96; dir Solicitors Indemnity Fund Ltd 1987–96 (chm 1987–89); memb Ct Univ of Warwick; Freeman City of Coventry; *Recreations* golf, music; *Style*— David C Mander, Esq; ✉ Whitestitch House, Great Packington, Nr Meriden, Warwickshire CV7 7JW (☎ 01676 522362); Mander Hadley & Co, 1 The Quadrant, Coventry CV1 2DW (☎ 01203 631212, fax 01203 633131)

MANDER, His Hon Judge Michael Harold; s of Elisha Harold Mander, of Cumberland (d 1984), and Ann, *née* Moores (d 1960); *b* 27 Oct 1936; *Educ* Workington GS, Queen's Coll Oxford (MA); *m* 6 Aug 1960, Jancis Mary, da of Rev Charles William Dodd (d 1974), of Eaton Constantine; *Career* RA 2 Lt 1955–57; slr 1963–72; called to the Bar Inner Temple 1972; in practice Birmingham 1972–85, asst recorder 1982–85; dep chm of Agric Lands Tbnl 1983–85; circuit judge (Midland and Oxford Circuit) 1985–; *Recreations* life under the Wrekin; *Clubs* Wrekin Rotary (hon memb), Magic Circle; *Style*— His Honour Judge Michael Mander; ✉ Garmston, Eaton Constantine, Shrewsbury SY5 6RL (☎ 01952 510288, fax 01952 510067)

MANDER, Michael Stuart; s of James Charles Stuart Mander (d 1974), and Alice Patricia Mander (d 1964); *b* 5 Oct 1935; *Educ* Tonbridge, Hackley NY; *Career* dir: Times Newspapers Ltd 1971–80, International Thomson Organisation plc 1983–86, Thomson Directories 1983–; chm and chief exec: Thomson Information Services Ltd 1985–86, Hill Samuel & Co Ltd 1987–96; dir Close Brothers Coporate Finance Ltd 1996–; chm: MAID plc 1988–, National Readership Surveys Ltd 1990–93; dir: Southnews plc 1989–, BLCMP (Library Services) Ltd 1993–; vice pres Periodical Publishers' Assoc, chm Inst of Directors 1993– (memb Cncl 1974–); Liveryman Worshipful Co of Marketors; FCIM, FRSA; *Recreations* sailing, skiing, golf; *Clubs* Royal Southern Yacht, Royal Wimbledon Golf; *Style*— Michael Mander, Esq; ✉ 41 Rivermill, Grosvenor Rd, London SW1V 3JN (☎ 0171 821 9651); Close Brothers Corporate Finance Ltd, 12 Appold Street, London EC2A 2AA (☎ 0171 426 4000, fax 0171 426 4385)

MANDER, (Charles) Nicholas; s and h of Sir Charles Marcus Mander, 3 Bt, *qv*; *b* 23 March 1950; *Educ* Downside, Trinity Coll Cambridge (MA); *m* 1972, Karin Margareta, da of Gustav Arne Norin (d 1985), of Stockholm, Sweden; 4 s ((Charles) Marcus Septimus Gustav b 1975, Benedict Edward Arthur b 1977, Hugo Richard Theodore b 1981, Fabian Edmund Quintin b 1987), 1 da (Sarra Mary b 1973); *Career* co dir (various publishing, educnl, land and overseas property devpt cos); farming, holiday cottages and forestry; Lloyd's underwriter 1972; fndr ptnr of Mander Portman Woodward (private tutors) in Kensington 1973; Liveryman Worshipful Co of Fishmongers; opening house to public at Owlpen, a Tudor manor house and garden 1974–; fndr dir Alan Sutton Publishing Ltd 1976–86; *Recreations* humane letters and arts, conversation, conservation, dreaming; *Clubs* Boodle's; *Style*— Nicholas Mander, Esq; ✉ Owlpen Manor, nr Dursley, Gloucs GL11 5BZ (☎ 01453 860261, fax 01453 860819); Finca La Katria, Mijas, Málaga

MANDEVILLE, Viscount Alexander Charles David Drogo Montagu; s and h of 12 Duke of Manchester, *qv*; *b* 11 Dec 1962; *m* 1992, Wendy Dawn, da of Michael Buford, of Arnheim Hill, Calif, USA; 1 s (Alexander, Lord Kimbolton b 13 May 1993); *Career* pres Global Atlantic Investments and Summit Investments Turks and Caicos Is BWI; *Style*— Viscount Mandeville; ✉ 17138 Von Karman Avenue, Irvine, CA 92712, USA

MANDEVILLE, Sharon; da of Frank Edward James Alldis, of Woking, Surrey, and Joan Doreen, *née* Clarke; *b* 7 Nov 1954; *Educ* Cert in Mktg, Dip in Mktg; *children* 1 s (Joshua b 18 Nov 1995); *Career* Barclays Bank 1971–: dist mktg mangr London Northern Region 1984–87, direct mktg mangr rising to mktg communications mangr Business Sector 1987–90, head of mktg communications 1993–96, head of communications Business Sector 1996–; MCIM 1993, founder MIDM 1994; *Recreations* cooking, keep fit; *Style*— Ms Sharon Mandeville; ✉ Barclays Bank plc, Longwood Close, Westwood Business Park, Coventry CV4 8JN (☎ 01203 532483, fax 01203 532497, mobile 0850 748579)

MANDUCA, Charles Victor Sant; s of Victor John Sant Manduca (d 1989), and Ethel Florence, *née* Johnson (d 1960); *b* 21 Nov 1954; *Educ* Harrow, UCL (LLB); *Career* admitted slr 1979; ptr Lovell White Durrant (formerly Durrant Piesse) 1983–; Freeman Worshipful Co of Slrs 1988; memb: Law Soc, London Slrs Litigation Assoc; *Recreations* golf, gardening, antique clocks; *Clubs* Wentworth Golf, Lansdowne; *Style*— Charles Manduca, Esq; ✉ 65 Holborn Viaduct, London EC1A 2DY (☎ 0171 236 0066, fax 0171 248 4212, telex 887122)

MANDUCA, Paul Victor Sant; s of Victor Sant Manduca (d 1989), and Elisabeth, *née* Johnson (d 1960); *b* 15 Nov 1951; *Educ* Harrow, Hertford Coll Oxford (MA); *m* 1982, Dr Ursula, da of Edmund Vogt, of Jollenbeck, nr Bielefeld, W Germany; 2 s (Mark b 1983, Nicholas b 1988); *Career* chm Touche Remnant Hldgs 1989–92 (vice chm 1987–89), dep gp md Henderson Administration PLC (following takeover of Touche Remnant) 1992–94, chief exec Threadneedle Asset Management 1994–; dir: Clydesdale Investment Trust 1987–88, TR Smaller Companies Investment Trust plc 1987–, Allied Dunbar Assurance plc 1994–, Eagle Star Holdings 1994–, Gresham Trust 1994–; md TR Industrial and General plc 1986–88; chm TR High Income plc 1989–94; chm Assoc of Investment Trust Cos 1991–93 (Takeover Panel 1991–93); memb Investment Ctee Univs Superannuation Scheme 1993–; Freeman of the City of London 1988, Liveryman Worshipful Co of Bakers 1989; *Recreations* golf, squash, shooting; *Clubs* Wentworth, Princes', Lansdowne; *Style*— Paul Manduca, Esq; ✉ 54 Brompton Square, London SW3 2AG (☎ 0171 584 3987)

MANFORD, Bruce Robert James; s of John Julian Manford, of Stanmore, Middx, and Ruth, *née* Heldmann; *b* 21 March 1957; *Educ* Haberdashers' Aske's, Keele Univ (BA); *m* 1992, Frances, *née* Turay; *Career* admitted slr 1981; ptnr Lawrence Graham 1988–96, legal advsr Tamoil Group 1996–; memb Law Soc 1981; *Clubs* RAC; *Style*— Bruce Manford, Esq; ✉ Tamoil Services S.A.M., 17 Avenue des Spélugues, Complexe Métropole, MC 98000, Monaco (☎ 00 377 93 15 69 00, fax 00 377 93 15 69 67)

MANGHAM, Maj-Gen (William) Desmond; CB (1978); s of Lt-Col William Patrick Mangham (d 1973), and Margaret Mary, *née* Donnachie (d 1965); *b* 29 Aug 1924; *Educ* Ampleforth; *m* 1960, Susan, da of Col Henry Brabazon Humfrey (d 1964); 2 s (Mark b 1962, Benedict b 1971), 2 da (Catherine b 1965, Louisa b 1966); *Career* 2 Lt RA 1943, served India, Malaya 1945–48, BMRA 1 Div Egypt 1955, staff HQ ME, Cyprus 1956–58, instr Staff Coll Camberley and Canada 1962–65, OC 3 Regt RHA 1966–68, Cdr RA 2 Div 1969–70, RCDS 1971, COS 1 Br Corps 1972–74, GOC 2 Div 1974–75, VQMG MOD 1976–79; Col Cmdt: RA 1979; RHA 1983; dir of the Brewers' Soc 1979–90; memb: Fndn Ctee Gordon's Sch, Advsy Governing Body Ampleforth Coll; *Recreations* shooting, golf; *Clubs* Army & Navy; *Style*— Maj-Gen Desmond Mangham, CB; ✉ Redwood House, Woolton Hill, nr Newbury, Berks RG20 9UZ (☎ 01635 253460)

MANGHAM, Prof Iain Leslie; *b* 23 Nov 1936; *Educ* Bretton Hall (Teaching Cert), Univ of London (BSc(Econ)), Univ of Leeds (PhD); *m* Olive Margaret; 1 s (Alasdair b 1966), 1 da (Catriona b 1969); *Career* sr lectr Swinton Day Trg Centre, dep dir Dept of Management Studies Univ of Leeds, area dir (Italy, Southern Europe, Middle East) Eli Lilly Int Corp, head Sch of Management Studies Univ of Bath; AFBPsS, CPsychol; *Books* T-Groups: A Survey of Research (1971), Interactions and Interventions in Organizations (1978), The Politics of Organizational Change (1979), Exploring Participation (1981), Organization Development in Transition: Evidence of an Evolving Profession (1982), Power and Performance in Organizations: An Exploration of Executive Process (1986), Organizations as Theatre: A Social Psychology of Dramatic Appearances (1987), Organization Analysis and Development: A Social Construction of Organizational Behaviour (1987), Effecting Organizational Change: Further Explorations of the Executive Process (1988), The Doing of Managing (1991); *Recreations* theatre, walking, cycling, music; *Style*— Prof Iain Mangham; ✉ School of Management, University of Bath, Claverton Down, Bath BA2 7AY (☎ 01225 826687)

MANGNALL, Richard Anthony; JP (S Westminster 1986); s of Col (Anthony) Derek Swift Mangnall, OBE, TD, of Bradley Court, Chieveley, Berks, and (Cynthia) Mary, *née* Foster (later Lady FitzGerald); *b* 27 Nov 1942; *Educ* Douai Abbey Berks; *m* 25 March 1975, Maureen Patricia, da of Lawrence Donnelly (d 1965), of Delhi, India; *Career* Sant & Co Loss Adjusters 1962–74, dir Tyler & Co (Adjusters) Ltd 1989– (ptnr 1974–), chm Proteus Open Space Management Ltd 1993–; elected underwriting memb Lloyd's 1978, pres The Insurance Adjusters Assoc 1987–89 (assoc 1967, fell 1972), pres Chartered Inst of Loss Adjusters, memb Lime St Ward Club; memb Ctee of Magistrates Inner London 1994–96; Freeman: City of London 1989, Worshipful Co of Fletchers 1989; FCILA 1992, ACIArb, FInstD; *Recreations* sailing; *Clubs* Royal London Yacht, Royal Ocean Racing, Royal Southern Yacht; *Style*— Richard Mangnall, Esq, JP; ✉ Clarendon Lodge, 7 Clarendon Place, London W2 2NP; 1 Norton Folgate, London E1 6DB (☎ 0171 377 0282, fax 0171 377 6355, car ☎ 0860 242 966); Domaine de la Crouzille, 24390 Hautefort, France (☎ 00 33 53 50 54 65)

MANGOLD, Thomas Cornelius (Tom); s of Dr Fritz Mangold (d 1957), and Dorothea Stephanie Mangold (d 1986); *b* 20 Aug 1934; *Educ* Dorking GS; *children* 3 da (Sarah b 1965, Abigail b 1975, Jessica b 1979); *Career* served RA BAOR; Sunday Mirror 1958–62, Daily Express 1962–64; reporter: BBC TV News 1964–70, BBC TV current affrs and several investigative documentaries 1970–76, BBC TV Panorama 1976–; *Books* The File on the Tsar (co-author, 1976), The Tunnels of Cu Chi (co-author 1985), Cold Warrior (1991); *Recreations* reading, writing, playing blues harmonica; *Style*— Tom Mangold, Esq; ✉ c/o BBC TV, White City, London W12 7TS (☎ 0181 752 7100)

MANHIRE, Dr Adrian Ross; s of Kenneth Croyden Manhire, of Norwich, and Ida, *née* Fielding; *b* 28 March 1945; *Educ* City of Norwich Sch, King Edward VI Sch Norwich, Univ of London (MB BS, BSc); *m* 13 Nov 1982, Eileen Margaret, da of Walter Le May, DFC, of Bishopton, Renfrewshire; *Career* conslt radiologist City Hosp Nottingham 1984–; memb MENSA 1981, FRCR 1983, FRCP 1996 (MRCP 1976); *Recreations* skiing, squash, badminton, photography; *Style*— Dr Adrian Manhire; ✉ 4 Eagle Close, Beeston Fields Drive, Beeston, Nottingham NG9 3DY (☎ 0115 922 2475); Department of Radiology, City Hospital, Nottingham (☎ 0115 969 1169)

MANKOWITZ, Wolf; s of Solomon Mankowitz, and Rebecca Mankowitz; *b* 7 Nov 1924; *Educ* East Ham GS, Downing Coll Cambridge (MA); *m* 1944, Ann Margaret Seligmann; 3 s (Gered, Daniel, Ben) and 1 s decd (Jonathan Adam d 1992); *Career* Univ of New Mexico: adjunct prof of English 1982–86, adjunct prof of theatre arts 1987–88; hon consul Republic of Panama in Dublin 1971; author; *Exhibitions* mixed media: Davis Gallery Dublin 1991, Grosvenor Gallery London 1994; *Plays incl* Belle (musical, 1961), Pickwick (musical 1963, revived 1993), Passion Flower Hotel (musical, 1965), Samson and Delilah (published as The Samson Riddle, 1978), Casanova's Last Stand (1980), Iron Butterflies (1986); *Films* Make Me an Offer (1954), A Kid for Two Farthings (1954), The Bespoke Overcoat (1955), Expresso Bongo (1960), The Millionairess (1960), The Long and The Short and The Tall (1961), The Day the Earth Caught Fire (1961), The Waltz of the Toreadors (1962), Where The Spies Are (1965), Casino Royale (1967), The Assassination Bureau (1969), Bloomfield (1970), Black Beauty (1971), Treasure Island (1972), The Hebrew Lesson (and dir, 1972), The Hireling (1973), Almonds and Raisins (1984); *Television* Dickens of London (1976); *Books* novels: Make Me An Offer (1952), A Kid for Two Farthings (1953), Laugh Till You Cry (1955), My Old Man's a Dustman (1956), Cockatrice (1963), The Biggest Pig in Barbados (1965), Penguin Wolf Mankowitz (1967), Raspberry Reich (1979), Abracadabra! (1980), The Devil in Texas (1984), Gioconda (1987), The Magic Cabinet of Professor Smucker (1988), Exquisite Cadaver (1990), A Night With Casanova (1991); short stories: The Mendelman Fire (1957), The Blue Arabian Nights (1973), The Day of the Women and the Night of the Men (fables, 1977); biographies: Dickens of London (1976), The Extraordinary Mr Poe (1978), Mazeppa (1982); miscellaneous: Wedgwood (a history, 1957), 12 Poems (poetry, 1971); *Recreations* sleeping, making collages; *Style*— Wolf Mankowitz, Esq; ✉ The Bridge House, Ahakista, Co Cork

MANKTELOW, Rt Rev Michael Richard John; s of Sir (Arthur) Richard Manktelow, KBE, CB (d 1977), of Dorking, and (Edith) Helen Saxby (d 1965); *b* 23 Sept 1927; *Educ* Whitgift Sch Croydon, Christ's Coll Cambridge (BA, MA), Chichester Theol Coll; *m* 1966, Rosamund, da of Alfred Mann, of Penrith; 3 da (Helen b 1967, Elizabeth b 1969, Katharine b 1971); *Career* served RN 1948–51; ordained: deacon 1953, priest 1954; curate Boston Lincs 1953–57, chaplain Christ's Coll Cambridge 1957–61, chaplain and sub warden Lincoln Theol Coll 1961–66; vicar: Knaresborough 1966–73, St Wilfrid's Harrogate 1973–77; rural dean Harrogate 1972–77; bishop of Basingstoke 1977–93, canon residentiary of Winchester Cathedral 1977–91 (vice dean 1987–91); asst bishop: of Chichester 1994–, in Europe 1994–; pres: Anglican and Eastern Churches Assoc 1980–, Assoc for Promoting Retreats 1982–87; *Books* Forbes Robinson: Disciple of Love (ed, 1961); *Recreations* walking, reading, music; *Style*— The Rt Rev Michael Manktelow; ✉ 2 The Chantry, Canon Lane, Chichester, W Sussex PO19 1PZ (☎ 01243 531096)

MANLEY, Dr Brian William; CBE (1994); s of Gerald William Manley (d 1950), of Eltham, London, and Ellen Mary, *née* Scudder (d 1965); *b* 30 June 1929; *Educ* Shooter's Hill GS, Univ of London, Woolwich Poly (BSc), Imperial Coll (DIC); *m* 1 May 1954, Doris Winifred, da of Alfred Dane (d 1966), of Eltham, London; 1 s (Gerald b 1958), 1 da (Susan b 1955); *Career* RAF 1947–49; Mullard Res Laboratories 1954–68, commercial gen mangr Mullard Ltd 1971–75; md: Pye Business Communications Ltd 1975–77, TMC Ltd 1977–82, Philips Data Systems Ltd 1979–82; gp md Philips Business Systems 1980–83, chm and md MEL Defence Systems 1983–86, dir for telecommunications def electronics and res Philips Electronic & Associated Industries Ltd 1983–87; chm: AT&T Network Systems (UK) Ltd 1986–89, Pye Telecommunications Ltd 1984–87, BYPS Communications Ltd 1989–91; managing ptnr Manley Moon Associates 1988–, chm Moondisks Ltd 1994–; pres: Telecommunications Engrg & Mfrg Assoc 1985–86, Inst of Electrical Engrs 1991–92, Inst of Physics 1996–; memb: Cncl Inst of Employment Studies 1986–, Exec Ctee Nat Electronics Cncl 1986–88, NEDO Ctee on Info Technol 1982–85, Police Scientific Devpt Ctee Home Office 1972–74, Cncl Engrg Trg Authy 1990–91, Bd Teaching Company Scheme 1996–; Univ of Sussex: memb Cncl 1990–, dep chm 1992–94, chm of Cncl 1995–, sr pro-chllr 1995–; chm Univ of Greenwich Industl Liaison Bd 1990–96, memb Cncl Loughborough Univ 1988–96; sr vice pres Royal Acad of Engineering 1994–96 (vice pres 1992–94), memb Senate Engrg Cncl; govr Univ of Greenwich 1993–95; author of numerous published papers on electronics and communications; represented England in swimming 1947–50; Centenary fell Thames Poly (now Univ of Greenwich) 1991, Hon DSc Loughborough Univ 1995; FInstP 1967, FIEE 1974, FEng 1984, FIProdE 1990, FCGI 1990; *Recreations* swimming, walking, gardening; *Style*— Dr Brian Manley, CBE, FEng; ✉ Hopkins Crank, Ditchling Common, Sussex BN6 8TP (☎ 01444 233734); Manley Moon Associates, St John's Innovation Centre, Cowley Rd, Cambridge CB4 4WS (☎ 01223 421033)

MANLEY, Ivor Thomas; CB (1984); s of Frederick Stone, and Louisa Manley; *b* 4 March 1931; *Educ* Sutton HS Plymouth; *m* 1952, Joan Waite; 1 s, 1 da; *Career* entered Civil Serv 1951; princ: Miny of Aviation 1964–66, Miny of Technol 1966–68; private sec to: Rt Hon Anthony Wedgwood Benn 1968–70, Rt Hon Geoffrey Rippon 1970; princ private sec to Rt Hon John Davies 1970–71, asst sec Dept of Trade and Industry 1971–74, princ estab offr Dept of Energy 1974–78, under sec Atomic Energy Div 1978–81; dep sec: Dept of Energy 1981–87, Dept of Employment 1987–91; conslt 1991–; memb: UKAEA 1981–86, Br Tourist Authy 1991–95, gp reviewing the future of the Royal Parks 1991–96; tstee The Volunteer Centre UK 1992–; *Style*— Ivor Manley, Esq, CB; ✉ 28 Highfield Ave, Aldershot, Hants GU11 3BZ (☎ and fax 01252 22707)

MANN, David William; s of William James Mann (d 1966), of Trimley Saint Mary, Suffolk, and Mary Ann, *née* Bloomfield (d 1987); *b* 14 June 1944; *Educ* Felixstowe County GS, Jesus Coll Cambridge (BA, MA); *m* 29 June 1968, Gillian Mary, da of Rev David Emlyn Edwards (d 1978), of Felixstowe, Suffolk; 2 s (Richard b 1972, Edward b 1975); *Career* computing systems conslt; CEIR (UK) Ltd (now EDS-Scicon) 1966–69; Logica plc: joined on its formation 1969, mangr conslt 1971, mangr Advanced Systems Div 1972, dir Advanced Systems Gp 1976, md UK ops 1979, dep gp md 1982, md and chief exec 1987–93, dep chm 1993–94; non-exec dir: Industrial Control Services Group plc 1994–, Room Underwriting Systems Ltd 1996–, Druid Group plc 1996–; non-exec chm: Cambridge Display Technology Ltd 1995–, Flomerics Group plc 1995–; exec chm Charteris Ltd 1996–; pres Br Computer Soc 1994–95; memb: Engrg Cncl 1993–95, sr warden Worshipful Co of Info Technologists 1996–97; CEng, CIMgt, FInstD; *Recreations* gardening, walking, skiing, golf; *Style*— David Mann, Esq; ✉ Theydon Copt, Forest Side, Epping, Essex CM16 4ED (☎ 01992 575842, fax 01992 576593)

MANN, Dr Felix Bernard; s of Leo William Mann (d 1956), and Caroline Lola Mann (d 1985); *b* 10 April 1931; *Educ* Shrewsbury, Malvern, Christ's Coll Cambridge, Westminster Hosp; *m* 1986, Ruth Csorba von Borsai; *Career* fndr Medical Acupuncture Soc (pres 1959–80), first pres Br Medical Acupuncture Soc 1980; awarded Deutscher Schmerzpreis 1995; *Books* Acupuncture - The Ancient Chinese Art of Healing (2 edn, 1971), The Treatment of Disease by Acupuncture (1963), The Meridians of Acupuncture (1964), Atlas of Acupuncture (1966), Acupuncture - Cure of Many Diseases (1971), Scientific Aspects of Acupuncture (1977), Textbook of Acupuncture (1987), Reinventing Acupuncture (1992); *Recreations* walking in the countryside; *Clubs* RSM; *Style*— Dr Felix Mann; ✉ 15 Devonshire Place, London W1N 1PB (☎ 0171 935 7575)

MANN, Geoffrey Horton; s of Stanley Victor Mann (d 1986), of Coventry, and Dorothy, *née* Horton (d 1964); *b* 12 May 1938; *Educ* Warwick Sch, Univ of Liverpool (BArch), RIBA (MCD); *m* 28 Dec 1963, Meg, da of Francis Richard Evans, of Denton, Manchester; 4 da (Katherine b 1964, Clare b 1966, Rachel b 1968, Shelley b 1972); *Career* architect; W S Hattrell & Ptnrs Manchester 1963–70, equity ptnr Renton Howard Wood Levin Ptnrship 1980– (joined 1970); responsible for commercial bldgs incl Beaufort House, St Katharine's Dock, County Hall, Battersea Power Station and Ludgate; memb: children's charities, Coventry City FC, Bodmin & Wenford Railway; ARCUK 1965, ARIBA 1965; *Recreations* Coventry City FC, railways; *Clubs* Coventry City; *Style*— Geoffrey Mann, Esq; ✉ 41 Charles St, Berkhamsted, Herts HP4 3DQ (☎ 01442 864707); Saughtree Railway Station, Roxburghshire; Renton Howard Wood Levin Partnership, 77 Endell St, London WC2 (☎ 0171 379 7900, fax 0171 836 4881, telex 896691 TLXIR G Renhow, car 0831 327663)

MANN, (Francis) George; CBE (1983), DSO (1944), MC (1943); s of Capt Francis Thomas Mann (d 1964; 3 s of Sir Edward Mann, 1 Bt who was chm of Mann Crossman & Paulin, and of Brandon's Putney Brewers), and Enid Agnes, *née* Tilney; *b* 6 Sept 1917; *Educ* Eton, Pembroke Coll Cambridge (BA); *m* 1949, Margaret Hildegarde, *née* Marshall Clark (d 1995); 3 s (Simon, Richard, Edward), 1 da (Sarah); *Career* served WWII Scots Gds (wounded); dir: Mann Crossman and Paulin, Watney Mann, Watney Mann and Truman Brewers 1946–77; non-exec dep chm Extel Group 1980–87 (dir 1977–87); Middx CCC: first played 1937, capt 1948–49, pres 1983–91; captained England: SA 1948–49, NZ 1949; chm: Test and County Cricket Bd 1978–83, Cricket Cncl 1983; *Clubs* MCC (pres 1984–85); *Style*— George Mann, Esq, CBE, DSO, MC; ✉ Great Farm House, West Woodhay, Newbury, Berks RG20 0BP

MANN, Jane Robertshaw; da of Jack Mann (d 1990), of Southport, and Jean, *née* Dixon; *b* 20 May 1955; *Educ* Nottingham HS for Girls, Univ of Manchester (BA); *m* 24 April 1982, Robert Klevenhagen, s of Dr Stan Klevenhagen; *Career* Leo Burnett Ltd 1976–86, Michael Peters Group 1986–90, fndr ptnr Dragon International (mktg and design co) 1991–; *Style*— Ms Jane Mann; ✉ Dragon International Consulting Ltd, 137 Blenheim Crescent, London W11 2EQ (☎ 0171 229 6090, fax 0171 229 4014)

MANN, Jessica D E (Jessica D E Thomas); da of Dr F A Mann, CBE (d 1991), of London, and Eleonore, *née* Ehrlich (d 1980); *b* 13 Sept 1937; *Educ* St Paul's, Newnham Coll Cambridge (MA), Univ of Leicester (LLB); *m* 1 July 1959, Prof A Charles Thomas, CBE, s of D W Thomas (d 1959), of Cornwall; 2 s (Richard b 1961, Martin b 1963), 2 da (Susanna b 1966, Lavinia b 1971); *Career* writer and journalist; memb: Carrick DC 1972–78, Cornwall AHA 1976–78, Industl Tbnls 1977–, SW RHA 1979–84, Med Practices Ctee 1982–87, Cornwall FPC 1985–88; DOE planning inspector 1992–93; chair: OFWAT (South West) 1993–, Network 200 SW Ltd 1995–; *Books* A Charitable End (1971), Mrs Knox's Profession (1972), The Only Security (1973), The Sticking Place (1974), Captive Audience (1975), The Eighth Deadly Sin (1976), The Sting of Death (1978), Deadlier than the Male (1981), Funeral Sites (1982), No Man's Island (1983), Grave Goods (1985), A Kind of Healthy Grave (1986), Death Beyond The Nile (1988), Faith Hope and Homicide (1991), Telling Only Lies (1992), A Private Inquiry (1996); *Style*— Ms Jessica Mann; ✉ Lambessow, St Clement, Cornwall TR1 1TB (☎ 01872 72980, fax 01872 225417)

MANN, John Frederick; s of Frederick Mann (d 1972), and Hilda Grace *née* Johnson (d 1992); *b* 4 June 1930; *Educ* Poole and Tavistock GS, Univ of Oxford (MA), Univ of Birmingham; *m* 30 July 1966, Margaret, da of Herbert Frederick Moore, of Bridlington, Yorks; 1 s (David John b 6 Dec 1971), 1 da (Susan Margaret b 6 March 1970); *Career* Nat Serv RAF 1949–50; asst educn offr Essex CC 1965–67, dep educn offr Sheffield City Cncl 1967–78, sec Schools Cncl for Curriculum and Examination 1978–83, dir of educn London Borough of Harrow 1983–88; educn conslt since 1988 to various bodies incl: London Boroughs of Harrow and Camden, KPMG, ATL, Br Cncl, Govt of Chile; vice chm Soc of Educn Conslts 1994–95 (sec 1991–94); lay assessor Dept of Health, memb Nat Tst; hon fell: Sheffield City Poly 1979, Coll of Preceptors 1986; FRSA; *Books* Education (1979), Chapters in Education Administration (1988), Life & Death of Schools Council (1985), Highbury Fields School (1994); *Recreations* local history, theatre, writing; *Style*— John Mann, Esq; ✉ 109 Chatsworth Rd, London NW2 4BH (☎ 0181 459 5419)

MANN, Martin Edward; QC (1983); s of S E Mann and M F L Mann, *née* Wakely; *b* 12 Sept 1943; *m* Jacqueline Harriette; 2 da (Daya Lucienne, Estelle Imogen); *Career* called to the Bar Gray's Inn 1968, recorder 1991–, dep judge of the High Ct (Chancery); *Recreations* numerous; *Clubs* Garrick; *Style*— Martin Mann, Esq, QC; ✉ 24 Old Buildings, Ground Floor, Lincoln's Inn, London WC2A 3UJ (☎ 0171 404 0946, fax 0171 405 1360)

MANN, Rt Hon Sir Michael; kt (1982); s of Adrian Bernard Mann, CBE, and Mary Louise, *née* Keen; *b* 9 Dec 1930; *Educ* Whitgift, King's Coll London (LLB, PhD); *m* 1, 1957 (m dis 1988), Jean Marjorie, *née* Bennett; 2 s; m 2, 22 Dec 1989, Audrey, wid of Lt Cdr H Umpleby, RN; *Career* called to the Bar Gray's Inn 1953; bencher 1980, pt/t legal asst FO 1954–56; law lectr LSE 1957–64 (asst lectr 1954–57), jr counsel Land Cmmn 1967–71, QC 1972, recorder of the Crown Court 1979–82, judge of the High Court of Justice 1982–88, a Lord Justice of Appeal 1988–95, ret; inspr Vale of Belvoir Coal Inquiry 1979–80; fell King's Coll London 1984; *Books* (ed jtly) Dicey, Dicey & Morris, Conflict of Laws (7 edn 1957, 8 edn 1967 to 10 edn 1980); *Clubs* Athenaeum; *Style*— The Rt Hon Sir Michael Mann; ✉ c/o Royal Courts of Justice, London WC2A 2LL

MANN, Rt Rev Michael Ashley; KCVO (1989); s of late Herbert George Mann, and Florence Mary *née* Kelsey, MBE (d 1950); *b* 25 May 1924; *Educ* Harrow, RMC Sandhurst, Wells Theol Coll, Harvard Business Sch (AMP); *m* 1, 25 June 1949, Jill Joan (d 1990), da of Maj Alfred Jacques (d 1960), of Thanet; 1 s (Capt Philip Ashley Mann, 1 Queen's Dragoon Gds b 1 Aug 1950 ka 1975), 1 da (Dr Elizabeth Mann b 22 Aug 1950); m 2, 25 May 1991, Elizabeth Margaret, da of Maj-Gen Roger Gillies Ekin, CIE, and widow of Rt Rev (George) Christopher Cutts Pepys, Bishop of Buckingham; *Career* 1 King's Dragoon Gds, served Italy 1943–44, Greece 1944–45, ME 1945, Palestine 1945–46, Capt 1945, Maj 1945; Colonial Admin Serv Nigeria 1946–55; ordained 1957, curate Newton Abbot 1957–59; vicar: Sparkwell 1959–62, Christ Church Port Harcourt 1962–67; dean Port Harcourt Social and Industl Project 1963–67, home sec Missions to Seamen 1967–69, canon Norwich Cathedral 1969–73 (vice-dean 1971–73), Bishop of Dudley 1973–76; Dean of Windsor, Domestic Chaplain to HM The Queen, Register of the Order of the Garter 1976–89; Prelate of the Ven Order of St John of Jerusalem 1990–; nat chaplain Royal British Legion 1985–; dep chm Tstees: Imperial War Museum 1980–96, Army Museums Ogilby Tst 1984–95; tstee: Br Library 1990–93, Army Records Soc 1991–; cmmr Royal Hosp Chelsea 1983–90, chm Friends Nat Army Museum, govr Harrow Sch 1976–91 (chm 1980–88); CIMgt; KStJ; *Books* A Particular Duty, A Windsor Correspondence, And They Rode On, China 1860, Some Windsor Sermons, Survival or Extinction, History of The Queen's Dragoon Guards, History of the Trucial Oman Scouts; *Recreations* military history; *Clubs* Cavalry and Guards'; *Style*— The Rt Rev Michael Mann, KCVO; ✉ Lower End Farm Cottage, Eastington, Northleach GL54 3PN (☎ and fax 01451 860767)

MANN, Prof (Colin) Nicholas Jocelyn; s of Colin Henry Mann (d 1987), of Mere, Wilts, and Marie-Elise, *née* Gosling; *b* 24 Oct 1942; *Educ* Eton, King's Coll Cambridge (MA, PhD); *m* 27 June 1964, Joelle, da of Pierre Emile Bourcart (d 1982), of Geneva; 1 s (Benedict Julian b 1968), 1 da (Olivia Sophie b 1965); *Career* res fell Clare Coll Cambridge 1965–67, lectr Univ of Warwick 1967–72, visiting fell All Souls Coll Oxford 1972, fell and tutor Pembroke Coll Oxford 1973–90 (emeritus fell 1991), dir Warburg Inst and prof of the history of the classical tradition Univ of London 1990–; memb Cncl: Museum of Modern Art Oxford 1984–92 (chm 1988–90), Contemporary Applied Arts 1994– (chm 1996–), Royal Hollway Coll London 1996–; tstee Cubitt Artists 1996–; FBA 1992, fell Euro Medieval Acad 1993; *Books* Petrarch Manuscripts in the British Isles (1975), Petrarch (1984), A Concordance to Petrarch's Bucolicum Carmen (1984); *Recreations* yoga, sculpture; *Style*— Prof Nicholas Mann, FBA; ✉ Warburg Institute, Woburn Square, London WC1H 0AB (☎ 0171 580 9663, fax 0171 436 2852)

MANN, Patricia Kathleen Randall (Mrs Pierre Walker); OBE (1996); da of Charles Alfred Mann (d 1986), of Westcliff-on-Sea, Essex, and Marjorie Lilian, *née* Heath; *b* 26 Sept 1937; *Educ* Clifton HS for Girls, Bristol; *m* 23 June 1962, Pierre George Armand Walker, s of Thomas George Walker (d 1969), of Paris and London; 1 da (Lucy b 26 June 1965); *Career* J Walter Thompson Co Ltd: joined as copywriter 1959, dir of public affrs and vice pres international 1981–; dir: Woolwich Building Society 1983–96, UK Centre Econ and Environmental Devpt 1984–, Valor plc (now Yale & Valor plc) 1985–90, British Gas plc 1995–; memb: Cncl Advertising Standards Authy 1973–86, Cncl Nat Advertising Benevolent Soc 1973–77, Awards Nomination Panel Royal TV Soc 1974–78, Cncl Brunel Univ 1976–86 (memb Ct 1976–), Gas Consumers Cncl 1981–90, Monopolies and Mergers Cmmn (pt/t) 1984–93, MAFF Food Advsy Ctee 1986–, Kingman Ctee Enquiry Teaching of English 1987, EC Commerce and Distribution Ctee 1989–, Senior Salaries Review Body 1994–; govr: CAM Educnl Fndn 1971–77, Admin Staff Coll Henley 1976–92; ed Consumer Affairs 1974–; Hon DUniv Brunel Univ 1996; FIPA 1966, FCAM 1979, CIMgt 1986, FRSA 1989; *Recreations* word games; *Clubs* Reform, Women's Advertising London; *Style*— Miss Patricia Mann, OBE; ✉ c/o J Walter Thompson Company Ltd, 40 Berkeley Square, London W1X 6AD (☎ 0171 499 4040, fax 0171 493 8432)

MANN, Sir Rupert Edward; 3 Bt (UK 1905), of Thelveton Hall, Thelveton, Norfolk; s of Edward Charles Mann, DSO, MC (d 1959), and great nephew of Sir (Edward) John Mann, 2 Bt (d 1971); *b* 11 Nov 1946; *Educ* Malvern; *m* 1974, Mary Rose, da of Geoffrey Butler, of Cheveley Cottage, Stetchworth, Newmarket, Suffolk; 2 s (Alexander, William); *Heir* s, Alexander Rupert Mann, b 6 April 1978; *Career* farmer; *Clubs* Norfolk, MCC; *Style*— Sir Rupert Mann, Bt; ✉ Billingford Hall, Diss, Norfolk (☎ 01379 740314)

MANN, Vernon; s of Victor Cecil Mann (d 1977), of Berkeley, Glos, and Violet Gwendoline, *née* Rummells; *b* 5 May 1945; *Educ* Lydney GS, Stroud Coll; *m* 1977, Avril Rosalind, da of David Ockleford Hiley; 2 s (Anthony Victor b 6 Jan 1985, Arron Lee b 9 May 1988); *Career* indentureship Gloucestershire Citizen 1963, prodr ABC News Perth W Australia 1966–70; reporter: Channel 7 Sydney 1970, HTV West Bristol and HTV Wales Cardiff 1971, UPI Audio and IRN 1973; ITN: joined as writer 1973, prodr/reporter 1973–80 (incl Rhodesia, Lebanon, Iran, USA), foreign ed 1980–83, Washington news ed 1984, foreign corr 1985–90 (incl Afghanistan, China (expelled 1989), Romania, Lebanon, Ireland), West Country corr 1990–93, gen corr 1993–; RTS Home News Award 1986 (for report on escaped IRA terrorist); *Recreations* cycling, food, wine, family; *Clubs* Out of Town (Carpenters Arms, Stanton Wick, Avon); *Style*— Vernon Mann, Esq; ✉ Independent Television News Ltd, 200 Gray's Inn Road, London WC1X 8XZ (☎ 01761 452248, mobile 0410 459620, pager 01426 277798)

MANNERS, Crispin Luke; s of Norman Donald Manners, of Windlesham, Surrey, and Noeline Mary, *née* Blake (d 1994); *b* 2 Aug 1957; *Educ* Ranelagh GS Bracknell Berkshire, Bedford Coll London (BSc); *m* 18 Aug 1979, Judith Ann, da of Peter Simpson; 2 s (Matthew b 1 July 1981, Philip b 12 May 1985); *Career* salesman CPC UK Limited 1978–80; The Argyll Consultancies plc: exec asst to Chm 1980, account dir 1984, md

1987, chief exec 1989–; MIPR, FInstD; *Clubs* Camberley Heath Golf (Surrey); *Style*— Crispin Manners, Esq; ✉ The Argyll Consultancies PLC, Central House, 75–79 Park Street, Camberley, Surrey GU15 3PT (☎ 01276 675566, fax 01276 678380)

MANNERS, Prof Gerald; s of George William Wilson Manners (d 1964), and Louisa Hannah, *née* Plumpton (d 1979); *b* 7 Aug 1932; *Educ* Wallington Co GS, St Catharine's Coll Cambridge (MA); *m* 1, 11 July 1958 (m dis 1982), Anne, *née* Sawyer; 1 s (Christopher Winslow b 24 Oct 1962), 2 da (Carolyn Jarvis b 16 Jan 1961, Katharine b 26 April 1967); m 2, 11 Dec 1982, Joy Edith Roberta, *née* Turner; 1 s (Nicholas Robert b 12 May 1985); *Career* Nat Serv Flying Offr RAF 1955–57; lectr in geography UC Swansea 1957–67; UCL: reader in geography 1967–80, prof of geography 1980–; visiting scholar Resources for the Future inc Washington DC 1964–65; visiting fell: Harvard-MIT Jt Center for Urban Studies 1972–73, Aust Nat Univ 1991; Location of Offices Bureau 1970–80, SE Econ Planning Cncl 1971–79; specialist advsr to: House of Commons Select Ctee on Energy 1980–92, House of Lords Select Ctee on Sustainable Devpt 1994–95; vice pres Sadler's Wells Fndn 1995– (govr 1978–95, chm govrs 1986–95); chm: Estate Ctee City Parochial Fndn 1987– (memb Central Governing Body 1977), City Parochial Fndn 1996–; FRGS, MIBG, FRSA, MBIEE; *Books* Geography of Energy (1964), South Wales in the Sixties (1964), Changing World Market for Iron Ore (1971), Spatial Policy Problems of the British Economy (1971), Minerals and Man (1974), Regional Development in Britain (1974), Coal in Britain (1981), Office Policy in Britain (1986); *Recreations* music, dance, theatre, walking; *Style*— Prof Gerald Manners; ✉ 338 Liverpool Road, London N7 8PZ (☎ 0171 607 7920); University College London, Gower St, London WC1E 6BT (☎ 0171 387 7050)

MANNERS, Hon John Hugh Robert (Willie); s and h of 5 Baron Manners, *qv*; *b* 5 May 1956; *Educ* Eton; *m* 8 Oct 1983, Lanya Mary Patrica (Lala), da of late Dr H E Heitz, and Mrs Ian Jackson, and step da of Ian Jackson; 2 da (Harriet Frances Mary b 29 July 1988, Catherine Mary Patricia b 18 Sept 1992); *Career* admitted slr 1980; ptnr Macfarlanes 1986– (currently in charge insurance litigation, landlord and tenant litigation and defamation); *Recreations* riding, shooting; *Clubs* Pratt's, Boodle's, City; *Style*— The Hon Willie Manners; ✉ 14 North Ripley, Avon, nr Christchurch, Dorset BH23 8EP (☎ 01425 672249); 10 Norwich Street, London EC4A 1BD (☎ 0171 831 9222, fax 0171 831 9607)

MANNERS, 5 Baron (UK 1807); John Robert Cecil Manners; s of 4 Baron Manners, MC, JP, DL (d 1972, himself ggs of 1 Baron, who was in his turn 5 s of Lord George Manners-Sutton, 3 s of 3 Duke of Rutland, KG), by his w Mary Edith (d 1994), twin da of Rt Rev Lord William Gascoyne-Cecil, DD, 65 Bishop of Exeter and 2 s of 3 Marquess of Salisbury, the Cons PM; *b* 13 Feb 1923; *Educ* Eton, Trinity Coll Oxford; *m* 1949, Jennifer Selena (d 1996), da of Stephen Fairbairn (whose w Cynthia was gggda of Sir William Arbuthnot, 1 Bt); 1 s, 2 da; *Heir* s, Hon John Hugh Robert Manners; *Career* joined RAFVR, Flying offr 1942, Fl Lt 1944; slr of the Supreme Ct 1949; Official Verderer of the New Forest 1983–93; *Clubs* Brooks's; *Style*— The Rt Hon the Lord Manners; ✉ Sabines Avon, Christchurch, Dorset BH23 7BQ (☎ 01425 672317)

MANNERS, (Arthur Edward) Robin; s of Arthur Geoffrey Manners (d 1989), and Betty Ursula Joan, *née* Rutter (d 1972); *b* 10 March 1938; *Educ* Winchester, Trinity Hall Cambridge; *m* 22 Oct 1966, Judith Mary, da of Lt-Col Francis William Johnston, MBE, of The Old Steading, Berkhamsted, Hertfordshire; 2 s (George b 1968, Richard b 1970); *Career* 2 Lt 10 Royal Hussars 1956–58, Maj Staffordshire Yeo 1958–68; dir Bass plc 1983–93 (joined 1961), self-employed 1993– (holds 2 non-exec directorships); *Recreations* golf, tennis, shooting, fishing, gardening, skiing; *Clubs* Cavalry and Guards'; *Style*— Robin Manners, Esq; ✉ The Old Croft, Bradley, Stafford ST18 9EF

MANNING, HE David Geoffrey; CMG (1992); s of John Robert Manning, and Joan Barbara Manning; *b* 5 Dec 1949; *Educ* Ardingly Coll, Oriel Coll Oxford (open history scholar, BA), Johns Hopkins Sch of Advanced Int Studies Bologna Italy (postgrad scholar); *m* 1973, Dr Catherine Manning, da of Dr W Parkinson; *Career* HM Dip Serv: joined FCO 1972, third later second sec Warsaw 1974–76, second later first sec New Delhi 1976–80, E Euro and Soviet Dept FCO 1980–82, Policy Planning Staff FCO 1982–84, first sec (political internal) Paris 1984–88, cnsllr on loan to Cabinet Office 1988–90, cnsllr and head of Political Section Moscow 1990–93, head of Eastern (formerly Soviet) Dept FCO 1993–94, head of Policy Planning Staff FCO 1994–Nov 1995 (concurrently Br rep on ICFY Contact Gp on Bosnia April-Oct 1994), ambass to Israel Nov 1995–; *Style*— HE Mr David Manning, CMG; ✉ c/o Foreign & Commonwealth Office, (Tel Aviv), King Charles Street, London SW1A 2AH

MANNING, (Everard Alexander) Dermot Niall; s of Col Frederick Everard Beresford Manning, Indian Med Serv (d 1987), and Elizabeth Robina, *née* Webber; *b* 20 Feb 1949; *Educ* Rossall Sch Lancs, The Middx Hosp Med Sch London (MB BS); *m* 1 Aug 1981, Ann Ming Choo, da of Pak Shoon Wong, of Kuala Lumpur, Malaysia; 1 s (Edward b 1985), 1 da (Catherine b 1988); *Career* registrar in obstetrics and gynaecology: St Helier Hosp Surrey 1981–83, The Middx Hosp London 1983–85; sr registrar in obstetrics and gynaecology The Middx Hosp and Central Middx Hosp London 1985–87, conslt and clinical dir of obstetrics and gynaecology Central Middx Hosp NHS Trust and hon clinical sr lectr St Mary's Hosp Med Sch 1987–; Br Soc for Colposcopy and Cervical Pathology FBI; FRCOG 1995 (MRCOG 1982), forum memb RSM 1985; *Recreations* photography, gemmology and jewellery; *Clubs* Wine Soc; *Style*— Dermot Manning, Esq; ✉ Central Middlesex Hospital NHS Trust, Acton Lane, Park Royal, London NW10 7NS (☎ 0181 453 2410/2407, fax 0181 453 2408)

MANNING, Prof Geoffrey; CBE (1986); s of Jack Manning, and Ruby Frances, *née* Lambe; *b* 31 Aug 1929; *Educ* Tottenham GS, RCS Imperial Coll London (BSc, PhD, ARCS, DIC); *m* 9 Sept 1951, Anita Jacqueline Davis; 2 s (Howard b 3 March 1953, Ian b 25 March 1956), 1 da (Karen b 20 Dec 1959); *Career* Nat Serv Sgt Educn Corps RAF 1948–49; asst lectr in physics Royal Coll of Science 1953–55; res physicist: English Electric Company 1955–56, Canadian Atomic Energy Agency 1956–58, California Inst of Technol 1958–59; princ scientific offr AERE 1959–66; Rutherford Laboratory: sr princ scientific offr 1966–69, dep dir 1969–79, head High Energy Physics Div 1969–75 (dep head 1968–69), head Atlas Computing Div 1975–79; project leader Construction of the Spallation Neutron Source 1977–81, dir Rutherford in Rutherford Appleton Laboratories 1979–81, computing co-ordinator SERC 1980–84, dir Rutherford Appleton Laboratory 1981–86, chm Active Memory Technology Ltd (now Cambridge Parallel Processing Ltd) 1986–92, dir Recognition Research 1991–94, conslt UKERNA 1991–93, hon scientist Rutherford Appleton Laboratory 1993–, visiting scientist Fermi Nat Accelerator Laboratory USA 1994–95; memb: Ordnance Survey Sci and Technol Advsy Ctee 1986–89, Bd of Visitors Physics Dept Imperial Coll London 1987–92, Civil Service Individual Merit Promotion Panel 1988–89, IT Advst Bd DTI/SERC 1991–92 (memb 1988–92, chm Systems Architecture Ctee 1991–92, chm Parallel & Novel Architecture Sub-Ctee); visiting prof Dept of Physics & Astronomy UCL 1987; author of over 40 articles in scientific jls; FInstP 1984, MBCS 1989; *Recreations* squash, skiing, golf; *Style*— Dr Geoffrey Manning, CBE; ✉ 38 Sunningwell Village, Abingdon, Oxon OX13 6RB

MANNING, Dr Geoffrey Lewis; s of Issac Harold Manning (d 1960), and Florence Hilda, *née* Tomlin (d 1983); *b* 21 Sept 1931; *Educ* Rossall Sch Fleetwood Lancs, Univ of Birmingham (BDS, MB ChB); *m* 15 Sept 1978, Patricia Margaret (Maggie), da of Frederick Wilson (d 1986), of Trentham; 1 da (Kate Elizabeth b 27 Aug 1980); *Career* Nat Serv, Capt RADC Wuppertal BAOR Germany 1954–56; house offr N Staffs Royal Infirmary 1961–63; sr registrar in oral surgery 1964–68: Central Middx Hosp, Mount Vernon Hosp Northwood Middx; exchange res Parkland Memorial Hosp Dallas 1967, conslt oral surgn N Staffs Hosp 1968–93; chm N Staffs Hosp Centre NHS Tst 1992–; dir Stoke City FC 1984–90 (MO 1987–), chm Med Advsy Ctee 1985–91, memb N Staffs DHA 1985–91; fell: Br Assoc of Oral and Maxillo-facial Surgns, Oral Surgery Club of GB (pres 1986); FDSRCS(Eng) 1964, FRCS(Ed) 1986; *Recreations* squash, gardening; *Clubs* Trentham Golf Staffordshire, British Pottery Manufacturers Fedn; *Style*— Dr Geoffrey Manning; ✉ The Old Hall, Haughton, Stafford ST18 9HB (☎ 01785 780273)

MANNING, Graham Ralph; s of James William Manning (d 1974), of Chelmsford, Essex, and Daisy Maud, *née* Warren; *b* 4 June 1943; *Educ* Chelmsford Tech HS; *m* 29 Sept 1966, Barbara, da of Cyril Alfred Burrough (d 1979), of Bradford; 2 s (James 1973, John 1978), 1 da (Joanne 1971); *Career* trainee CA Longcrofts 1960–66, qualified CA 1966, supervisor Deloitte Haskins & Sells Montreal 1966–69, ptnr Buzzacott & Co 1970–79 (mangr 1969–70); ptnr: McNally Manning & Co Ipswich 1979–83, Manning Hilder & Girling Ipswich 1983–; ACA; *Recreations* sailing, books, paintings; *Style*— Graham Manning, Esq; ✉ 16a Falcon St, Ipswich IP1 1SL (☎ 01473 2599 84, fax 01473 2599 88)

MANNING, Dr Jane Marian; OBE (1990); da of Gerald Manville Manning (d 1987), of Norwich, and Lily, *née* Thompson (d 1989); *b* 20 Sept 1938; *Educ* Norwich HS, Royal Acad of Music (GRSM, LRAM, ARCM), Scuola Di Canto Cureglia Switzerland; *m* 24 Sept 1966, Anthony Edward Payne, s of Edward Alexander Payne (d 1958), of London; *Career* int career as soprano concert singer; London debut 1964, more than 300 world premieres, regular appearances in leading halls and festivals, Brussels Opera 1980, Scottish Opera 1978, numerous tours of Aust, NY debut 1981, first BBC broadcast 1965 (over 300 since), numerous recordings incl Messiaen Song Cycles; visiting prof: Mills Coll Oakland California 1981, 1983 and 1986, Royal Coll of Music 1995–; hon prof Keele Univ 1996–99; visiting lectr: Harvard Univ, Stanford Univ, Princeton Univ, Yale Univ, Cornell Univ, Univ of York, Univ of Cambridge, Univ of Durham; vice pres Soc for the Promotion of New Music, chm Nettlefold Festival Tst, fndr and artistic dir Jane's Minstrels Ensemble 1988; memb: Exec Ctee Musicians Benevolent Fund; received special award composers Guild of GB 1973; Hon DUniv York 1988; FRAM 1984, ISM, memb SPNM; *Books* New Vocal Repertory (1986, reissued 1993, Vol II 1996), A Messiaen Companion (contrib, 1995); *Recreations* cinema, theatre, swimming, ornithology, reading; *Style*— Dr Jane Manning, OBE; ✉ 2 Wilton Square, London N1 3DL (☎ 0171 359 1593, fax 0171 226 4369); 7 Park Terrace, Upperton Rd, Tillington, nr Petworth, W Sussex GU28 9AE

MANNING, Patrick John Mannes (Paddy); s of Col Francis James Manning, TD, of Wiveliscombe, Somerset, and Sarah Margaret, *née* Jenkins; *b* 16 July 1940; *Educ* Downside, RMA Sandhurst; *m* 19 April 1986, Sally Gail, da of Maj Jeremy Green, of Bideford on Avon, Warwicks; 2 s (Francis James Daniel b 5 March 1990, Jeremy Patrick Augustus b 31 March 1992), 1 da (Charlotte b 1987); *Career* Lt 4/7 Royal Dragoon Gds 1961–64, Royal Yeo 1965–72; stockbroker Laurence Keen & Gardner 1965–70; dir: Charles Barker City Ltd 1970–80, PR McCann Erickson 1981–84, St James PR Ltd 1984–; hon PR advsr The Br Cwlth Ex-Servs League; MIPR 1974; *Recreations* shooting, opera; *Clubs* Cavalry and Guards'; *Style*— Paddy Manning, Esq; ✉ 49 Breer St, London, SW6 3HE; St James Public Relations, 4 Bedford Square, London WC1B 3RA (☎ 0171 436 4101, fax 0171 436 4164)

MANNING-COX, Andrew Richard; s of Frederick Cox, of Kinver, Staffs, and Beatrice Maud, *née* Brown; *b* 23 April 1956; *Educ* Peter Symonds' Sch Winchester, Univ of Cambridge (MA); *m* 31 Oct 1987, Janet Elaine, da of Eric Binns, of Bramhall, Cheshire; *Career* admitted slr 1980; ptnr Wragge & Co 1985; sec Birmingham Branch Cambridge Soc; memb Law Soc 1980, NP 1992; *Recreations* riding, walking, country pursuits; *Style*— Andrew Manning-Cox, Esq; ✉ Wragge & Co, 55 Colmore Row, Birmingham B3 2AS (☎ 0121 233 1000, fax 0121 214 1099)

MANNINGHAM-BULLER, Hon James Edward; er s and h of 2 Viscount Dilhorne, *qv*; *b* 20 Aug 1956; *Educ* Harrow, Sandhurst; *m* 4 May 1985, Nicola Marion, eldest da of Sven Mackie (d 1986); 1 s (Edward John b 25 Jan 1990), 1 da (Camilla Mary b 1 July 1992); *Career* Capt Welsh Gds 1976–84; TA OC The North Irish Horse; Lloyd's Broker: Stewart Wrightson Surety and Specie Ltd 1984–86, Gibbs Hartley Cooper Ltd 1986–89; insur conslt Heritage Insurance Services 1990–; *Recreations* shooting, gardening; *Clubs* Pratt's; *Style*— The Hon James Manningham-Buller; ✉ Ballymote House, Downpatrick, Co Down (☎ 01396 612244, fax 01396 612111)

MANNINGS, William Anthony; s of William Edward Mannings (d 1965), of Claverton Down, Bath, and Helena Mary, *née* Stoffels (d 1961); *b* 2 Sept 1930; *Educ* King Edward Sch Bath; *m* 1 June 1957, June, da of Albert Edward Hill (d 1955), of Bath; *Career* Nat Serv Fleet Air Arm RN 1948–50; former chm G Mannings and Sons Ltd, former ptnr JW Knight and Son, dir Fred Daw Garden Centre Trowbridge 1980– (Bath 1975), dir M & C Holdings Ltd 1981–, chm Bath Investment and Building Society 1984–; govr King Edward's Sch Bath 1983–, pres Bath Golf Club 1988–90 (capt 1962); gen cmmr of Income Tax Bath 1992–; *Recreations* golf; *Clubs* Bath Golf; *Style*— William Mannings, Esq; ✉ Byfield, Winsley, Bradford on Avon, Wilts BA15 2HW (☎ 01225 723799)

MANNION, David Victor; s of Francis Victor Mannion, and Irene Joan, *née* Brocklehurst (d 1991); *b* 5 Nov 1950; *Educ* Long Eaton GS Derbyshire; *m* Jennifer, da of Ilya Andrusyk; 1 s (Ronald b 29 Dec 1983); *Career* reporter: Long Eaton Advertiser 1967–70, Raymonds News Agency 1970–74, Leicester News Service 1974–75; journalist/bdcaster: Radio Trent 1975–77, ATV Birmingham 1977–79; Independent Television News: dep news ed 1979–81, news ed 1981–83, ed Lunchtime News 1983–86, dep ed and mangr Channel Four News 1986–88, assoc ed 1988–91, ed ITN progs on ITV 1991–95; ed GMTV 1995–96, independent news consultant 1996–; memb: BAFTA, RTS, Int Press Inst, Guild of Editors, PROGRESS (pressure gp in support of legal embryo research); *Awards* BAFTA News Award 1991, 1993 and 1994 (also nominated 1990); *Recreations* tennis, music, travel; *Style*— David Mannion, Esq

MANNION, Rosa; da of Patrick Anthony Mannion, of Crosby, Liverpool, and Maria, *née* MacGregor; *b* 29 Jan 1962; *Educ* Seafield GS Crosby, Royal Scottish Acad of Music and Drama (BA, RSAMD); *m* 13 July 1985, Gerard McQuade, s of Michael McQuade, of Cardonald, Glasgow; 2 s; *Career* opera singer; studied with Patricia Boyer Kelly, professional debut in L'Elisir d'Amore with Scottish Opera 1984, princ soprano Scottish Opera 1984–86; debuts: Edinburgh Festival 1985 (with Scottish Nat Orch), Buxton Festival 1986, ENO 1987 (as Sophie in Der Rosenkavalier), Glyndebourne Festival 1988 (as Konstanze in Die Entführung aus dem Serail), Wigmore Hall 1988; other performances incl: Magnolia in Show Book (Opera North at Royal Shakespeare Theatre Stratford) 1990, Pamina in Die Zauberflöte (with Israeli Philharmonic Orchestra Tel Aviv) 1991; winner Scottish Opera Int Singing Competition 1988, finalist Luciano Pavarotti Singing Competition 1985; *Recreations* tennis, swimming, reading; *Style*— Ms Rosa Mannion; ✉ IMG Artists Europe, Media House, 3 Burlington Lane, London W4 2TH (☎ 0181 233 5800, fax 0181 233 5801)

MANOR, Prof James Gilmore; s of James Gilmore Manor, of Lakeland, Florida, and Ann Jones Manor; *b* 21 April 1945; *Educ* Yale Univ (BA), Univ of Sussex (DPhil); *m* July 1974, Brenda, da of Sydney Cohen; 1 s (Hugh Benjamin b 16 March 1989); *Career* asst lectr Chinese Univ of Hong Kong 1967–69, tutor SOAS London 1973–75, asst prof Yale Univ 1975–76, lectr Univ of Leicester 1976–85, prof of government Harvard Univ 1985–87, fell Inst of Devpt Studies Univ of Sussex 1987–, dir and prof of Cwlth politics

Inst of Cwlth Studies Univ of London 1994–; research fell: Australian Nat Univ 1974, MIT 1982; memb Senate Univ of Leicester 1980–84; memb Bd: Inst of Latin American Studies, British Documents on the End of Empire Project, Amsterdam Sch of Social Science Research, Centre for the Advanced Study of India Univ of Pennsylvania; conslt to: Ford Fndn, World Bank, OECD, UN Capital Devpt Fund, British, Dutch and Swedish govts; *Books* Political Change in an Indian State (1977), Transfer and Transformation: Political Institutions in the New Commonwealth (co-ed, 1983), Sri Lanka in Change and Crisis (ed, 1984), The Expedient Utopian: Bandaranaike and Ceylon (1989), States or Markets (co-ed, 1992), Rethinking Third World Politics (ed, 1992), Power, Poverty and Poison: Disaster and Response in an Indian City (1993), Nehru to the Nineties: The Changing Office of Prime Minister in India (ed, 1994); *Recreations* reading, theatre; *Style*— Prof James Manor; ✉ Institute of Commonwealth Studies, University of London, 28 Russell Square, London WC1B 5DS (☎ 0171 580 5876, fax 0171 255 2160, e-mail j.manor@sas.ac.uk)

MANS, Keith Douglas Rowland; MP (C) Wyre (majority 11,664); s of Maj Gen Rowland Spencer Noel Mans, CBE, of Milford on Sea, Hants, and Violet, *née* Sutton; *b* 10 Feb 1946; *Educ* Berkhamsted Sch, RAF Coll Cranwell, Open Univ (BA); *m* 19 Aug 1972, Rosalie Mary, da of J McCann (d 1977), of Liverpool; 2 da (Louise b 5 Nov 1980, Emma b 6 May 1986), 1 s (David b 9 Sept 1982); *Career* former Flt Lt RAF, served UK, Germany, Malta, Cyprus and Malaya; formerly central buyer for electronics John Lewis Ptnrship; MP (C) Wyre 1987–, memb House of Commons Select Ctee on the Environment 1987–91, sec Cons Aviation Ctee 1987–90, memb Select Ctee on Defence 1995–; PPS to: Min of State for Health 1990–92, Sec of State for Health 1992–95, Sec of State for Nat Heritage 1995; chm: Parly Environment Group 1993–, Parly Aerospace Group 1994–; cncllr New Forest DC 1983–87 (sometime dep ldr); sch govr 1984–87; memb Royal United Servs Inst for Def Studies 1965; *Recreations* flying; *Clubs* Army and Navy, RAF; *Style*— Keith D R Mans, Esq, MP; ✉ House of Commons, London SW1A 0AA (☎ 0171 219 6334/3436)

MANS, Maj-Gen Rowland Spencer Noel; CBE (1971, OBE 1966, MBE 1956); s of Thomas Frederick Mans (d 1954), of Bispham, Lancs, and May Frances, *née* Seigenberg (d 1975); *b* 16 Jan 1921; *Educ* Surbiton GS, RMC Sandhurst; *m* 6 Jan 1945, Veeo Ellen, da of Frank Sutton (d 1951), of Southampton; 3 s (Keith b 1946, Mark b 1955, Lance b 1957); *Career* WWII Queen's Royal Regt and King's African Rifles 1939–45, Maj served: E Africa, Madagascar, Palestine, ME, Far East, Canada; Queen's Royal Regt 1939–76, regtl and staff appts 1945–69, Col, Cdr Aldershot A/GOC SE Dist, Brig, D/Dir Personnel Servs 1972–73, Dir Mil Assistance Office 1973–76, Maj-Gen, Col Queen's Regt 1978–83; UK assoc Burdeshaw Ltd (USA) 1988–94, articles for jls in UK and USA; co cncllr Hants 1984–89, pres New Forest Cons Assoc 1984–87; Freeman City of London; Knight Cdr: Dannebrog (Denmark) 1983, Orange Nassau (Netherlands) 1983; *Books* Canada's Constitutional Crisis (1978); *Recreations* writing, gardening; *Clubs* Army and Navy, Royal Lymington Yacht, Victory Services; *Style*— Maj-Gen Rowley Mans, CBE; ✉ Ivy Bank Cottage, Vinegar Hill, Milford-on-Sea, Hants (☎ 01590 643982)

MANSEL, Sir Philip; 15 Bt (E 1622), of Muddlescombe, Carmarthenshire; s of Sir John Philip Ferdinand Mansel, 14 Bt (d 1947), and Hannah, *née* Rees; *b* 3 March 1943; *Educ* Grosvenor Coll Carlisle, Carlisle GS; *m* 24 Aug 1968, Margaret, o da of Arthur Docker, of Hainings Gate, Moorhouse, Carlisle; 2 s (John Philip b 1982, Richard James b 31 July 1990), 1 da (Nicol b 1978); *Heir* s, John Philip Mansel b 19 April 1982; *Career* chm and md Eden-Vale Engineering Co Ltd; FInstSMM; *Style*— Sir Philip Mansel, Bt; ✉ 2 Deyncourt Close, Darras Hall, Ponteland, Northumberland NE20 9RP

MANSEL LEWIS, Sir David Courtenay; KCVO (1995), JP (1969); s of Charlie Ronald Mansel Lewis (d 1960), and Lillian Georgina (d 1982), da of Sir Courtenay Warner, 1 Bt; *b* 25 Oct 1927; *Educ* Eton, Keble Coll Oxford (MA); *m* 1953, Lady Mary, da of 3 Earl of Wharncliffe; 1 s, 2 da; *Career* Welsh Gds 1946–49, Lt 1948, RARO; High Sheriff Carmarthenshire 1965, DL 1971, HM Lt Camarthenshire 1973–74, HM Lt Dyfed 1974–79, Lord Lt Dyfed 1979–; pres: W Wales TAVRA 1979–90, Mid and W Wales TAVRA 1990–95, Wales TAVRA 1995–, Wales ACF 1995–; patron Carmarthenshire Royal Br Legion 1974, fndr pres Llanelli Branch Welsh Guards Assoc 1974–, pres Dyfed SSAFA 1986–; patron Dyfed Branch Br Red Cross Soc; pres: Dyfed Branch Magistrates' Assoc 1979–, St John Cncl for Dyfed, Carmarthenshire Assoc of Boy Scouts, Carmarthen/Cardigan Branch CLA 1979–91, Dyfed Branch CLA 1991–; chm: S West Wales Div Royal Forestry Soc 1963–93, S Wales Woodlands 1969–85; patron Carmarthenshire Wildfowlers Assoc 1976–, pres Dyfed Wildlife Tst 1987–; patron Carmarthenshire Fedn of Young Farmers' Clubs; memb: Ct of Govrs UCW Aberystwyth 1974–, Cncl Nat Museum of Wales 1987–91 (memb Ct 1974–); formerly memb: Music Ctee Wales Arts Cncl, Bd Welsh Nat Opera; formerly pres Swansea Philharmonic Choir; pres: Burry Port Operatic Soc, Llanelli Art Soc 1956–, Heart of Wales Line Travellers Assoc 1993–; fndr chm Carmarthen-Cardigan Ctee Sail Trg Assoc 1968–, pres Burry Port RNLI 1982–, regnl chm Sail Trg Assoc S Wales 1985–, fndr Cdre and pres Burry Port Yacht Club 1966–, patron Tall Ships Cncl of Wales 1991; KStJ; *Recreations* sailing (yacht 'Wendy Woo'), music; *Clubs* RYS, Lansdowne, Cruising Assoc; *Style*— Sir David Mansel Lewis, KCVO, JP; ✉ Stradey Castle, Llanelli, Dyfed SA15 4PL (☎ 01554 774626); 53 New Rd, Llanelli, Dyfed (☎ 01554 773059)

MANSELL, Gerard Evelyn Herbert; CBE (1977); s of Herbert Goodinge Mansell, of Paris (d 1968), and Anne Marie Lintz (d 1985); *b* 16 Feb 1921; *Educ* Lycée Hoche Versailles, Lycée Buffon Paris, Ecole Libre des Sciences Politiques Paris, Chelsea Sch of Art London (Nat Dip in Design); *m* 1956, Diana Marion, da of Roland Crichton Sherar, of Burnham Market, Norfolk; 2 s; *Career* WWII 1940–46 (despatches), Royal Norfolk Regt and Durham LI, served Western Desert, Sicily, NW Europe; intelligence staff offr 50 Div and 8 Corps (Maj); joined BBC Euro Serv 1951, controller Radio 4 and music programme BBC 1965–69, dir of programmes BBC Radio 1970–71, md external broadcasting BBC 1972–80, dep DG BBC 1977–80; hon visiting fell Graduate Centre for Journalism City Univ 1992–; chm: Br Ctee for Journalists in Europe 1977–95, Int Cncl for Journalists in Europe 1977–95, Jt Advsy Ctee for Trg of Radio Journalists 1981–87, Communications Advsy Ctee UK Nat Cmmn for UNESCO 1983–85, New Hampstead Garden Suburb Tst 1984–90 and 1992–93, Friends of UNESCO 1986–87, CNAA; memb: Exec Ctee GB-China Centre 1986–96 (vice chm 1987–96), Franco-British Cncl 1990–, Sandford St Martin Tst 1991–; govr Falmouth Coll of Arts 1988–, chm Burgh House Trust Hampstead 1995–; Sony Gold Award for Services to Radio 1988; French Croix de Guerre 1944; FRSA; *Books* Tragedy in Algeria (1961), Let Truth be Told (1982); *Style*— Gerard Mansell, Esq, CBE; ✉ 15c Hampstead Hill Gardens, London NW3 2PH

MANSELL, Nigel Ernest James; OBE (1991); *b* 8 Aug 1953; *Educ* Hall Green Bilateral, Matthew Bolton Poly, Solihull Tech Coll, N Birmingham Poly (HND); *m* 19 April 1975, Rosanne Elizabeth, da of Walter Denis Perry; 2 s (Leo James b 4 Jan 1985, Greg Nigel b 8 Nov 1987), 1 da (Chloe Margaret b 16 Aug 1982); *Career* former motor racing driver; began car racing 1976, winner Br Fusegear Championship 1977, memb Unipart March Dolomite Formula 3 team 1979, memb Ralt-Honda Formula 2 team 1980; Formula 1: first grand prix Austria 1980, memb Lotus team 1981–84, memb Canon-Williams team 1985–88 and 1991, memb Ferrari team 1989–90, memb Williams-Renault team 1992; left grand prix racing to join Newman Haas Indy Car team (USA) 1993, rejoined Formula 1 (Williams-Renault team, part time) 1994 (winner Australian grand prix 1994), memb McLaren team 1995; achievements incl: driven in over 175 grands prix, first win Grand Prix of Europe Brands Hatch 1985, total 30 wins, winner World Drivers' Championship 1992 (runner-up 1986, 1987 and 1991); records held: 17 fastest laps on various circuits, 15 consecutive front row grid positions 1987, only driver to win first 5 races of a grand prix season 1992, most grand prix wins in a season, beat Stirling Moss's English record of 16 grands prix wins 1990, beat Jackie Stewart's Br record with 28th grand prix win Silverstone 1992, Indy Car World Series champion 1993 (only driver to win 'back to back' Formula 1 and Indy Car World Championships); BBC Sports Personality of the Year 1986 and 1992 (third 1993), Br Racing Drivers' Club award 1989 and 1991; Hon DEng Univ of Birmingham 1993; former laboratory technician then prodn mangr Lucas Aerospace, former sr sales engr Tractor Div Girling; *Recreations* flying both planes and helicopters, golfing, shooting, running, cycling, swimming, Red Arrows; *Style*— Nigel Mansell, Esq, OBE; ✉ c/o Nicki Dance, Woodbury Park Golf and Country Club, Woodbury Castle, Woodbury, Exeter EX5 1JJ (☎ 01395 233382)

MANSELL-JONES, Richard Mansell; s of Arnaud Milward Jones (d 1964), of Carmarthen, and Winifred Mabel, *née* Foot (d 1978); *b* 4 April 1940; *Educ* Queen Elizabeth's Carmarthen, private tuition, Worcester Coll Oxford (MA); *m* 30 June 1971, Penelope Marion, yr da of Maj Sir David Henry Hawley, 7 Bt (d 1988); *Career* articled clerk and investigation sr Price Waterhouse & Co 1963–68, mangr corp fin N M Rothschild & Sons Ltd 1968–72; Brown, Shipley & Co Ltd: dir 1972–88, dep chm 1984–88, chm 1992; J Bibby & Sons PLC: dir 1978–, dep chm 1987, chm 1988–; also chm: Brown Shipley Development Capital Ltd, Finanzauto SA, Sociedade Tecnica de Equipmentos e Tractores SA; dir: Barlow Ltd (exec) 1988–, Brown Shipley Holdings plc 1984–93, Barr & Wallace Arnold Trust plc 1984–93, Fitzmaurice Management Ltd (non-exec), Standard Bank London Ltd (non-exec); tstee Shaw Tst; memb SFA, FCA, FRSA; *Clubs* Boodle's, City, Oriental; *Style*— Richard Mansell-Jones, Esq; ✉ J Bibby & Sons PLC, 16 Stratford Place, London W1N 9AF (☎ 0171 629 6243)

MANSELL-MOULLIN, Michael; s of Sqdn Ldr Oswald Mansell-Moullin (d 1964), and Mary Bagott, *née* Green; *b* 8 Oct 1926; *Educ* St Edward's Sch Oxford, Jesus Coll Cambridge (MA, DIC); *m* 17 May 1969, Marion Elizabeth, da of Capt R L Jordan RN (d 1988); 1 s (David b 1972), 1 da (Jenny Melissa b 1976); *Career* Capt RE India & Pakistan 1944–49; chief hydrologist Binnie & Ptnrs (Consulting Engineers) 1959–69, ind conslt hydrologist UK and Int 1970–; fndr and pres Br Hydrological Soc 1983–85 (hon life memb); companion ICE, MCIWEM, FRGS; *Publications* contrib leading scientific jls on water resources and hydrological subjects; *Recreations* sailing, hill walking, woodwork; *Clubs* Bosham Sailing; *Style*— Michael Mansell-Moullin, Esq; ✉ Old Hatch, Lower Farm Rd, Effingham, Surrey KT24 5JL (☎ 01372 452672)

MANSER, (Peter) John; CBE (1992); s of Lt-Col Peter Robert Courtney Manser (d 1944), and Florence Delaplaine, *née* Ismay (d 1983); *b* 7 Dec 1939; *Educ* Marlborough; *m* 31 May 1969, Sarah Theresa Stuart (Tessa), *née* Todd; 2 da; *Career* CA; Robert Fleming group: with Brown Fleming & Murray 1959–66, dir Robert Fleming & Co Ltd 1967–75, md Jardine Fleming & Co Ltd 1975–79, chief exec Save & Prosper Group Ltd 1979–88, chm Robert Fleming Holdings Ltd 1997– (gp chief exec 1990–97); dir: Capital Shopping Centre PLC, Fleming Enterprise Investment Trust; dir Securities and Investmts Bd 1986–93, chm London Investment Banking Assoc 1994–; memb Cncl Cancer Res Campaign; Freeman City of London, Liveryman Worshipful Co of Grocers; FCA 1976; *Recreations* gardening, shooting, walking; *Clubs* Boodle's, City of London, MCC; *Style*— John Manser, Esq, CBE; ✉ 1 Airlie Gardens, London W8 7AJ (☎ 0171 792 3193); Robert Fleming Holdings Ltd, 25 Copthall Ave, London EC2R 7DR (☎ 0171 638 5858, fax 0171 588 7219, telex 297451)

MANSER, Jonathan; s of Michael John Manser, of Chiswick, and Dolores Josephine, *née* Bernini; *b* 15 Jan 1955; *Educ* Westminster, Univ of Cambridge (MA, memb Boat Race crew 1976 and 1977), South Bank Poly (Dip Arch); *m* 1983, Sarah Christiane, da of Air Vice Marshal W V C Crawford-Compton, DSO, DFC; 2 da (Olivia Bianca Imogen b 1986, Claudia Augusta Marie-Claire b 1989); *Career* architect; Foster Associates 1974, Hulme Chadwick & Partners 1977–78, Renton Howard Wood Levine 1980–82, Chapman Taylor Partners 1982–83, self-employed sole practitioner 1983–85, dir Manser Associates 1986–; winner award for Hilton Hotel Heathrow Airport, RIBA and Steel Award for Southampton Airport; RIBA, memb Civic Tst; also former int yachtsman; memb Br team: Onion Patch Cup 1978, Admiral's Cup 1979, Southern Cross Cup 1979; second place 6 metre class Euro Cup 1985, winner 6 metre class World Championships 1986; *Clubs* Hawks, Groucho, Archetypals; *Style*— Jonathan Manser, Esq; ✉ Manser Associates, Bridge Studios, Hammersmith Bridge, London W6 9DA (☎ 0181 741 4381, fax 0181 741 2773)

MANSER, Michael John; CBE (1993); s of Edmund George Manser (d 1971), and Augusta Madge, *née* Bonell (d 1987); *b* 23 March 1929; *m* 1953, Dolores Josephine, da of Isadore Bernini; 1 s (Jonathan), 1 da (Victoria); *Career* Nat Serv RE, Staff Capt; chartered architect, fndr (currently chm) Manser Associates 1961; pres RIBA 1983–85, cncllr AA 1971–72; memb: Cncl RIBA 1979–81 Cncl RSA 1985–91, LT Design Policy Ctee; architectural awards: two Civic Tst Awards, Civic Tst Commendation, Euro Heritage Year Award, DOE Commendation for Good Design in Housing, Steel Award and Steel Award Commendation, outright winner Harrow Heritage Tst Award, two RIBA Awards, two RIBA Regnl Awards, RIBA Award Commendation, RCFA/Sunday Times Building of the Yr Award, British Construction Industry Award; architectural journalism, radio and TV; chm Art in Workplace Awards 1995–; memb: Cncl Nat Tst 1992–95, Royal West of England Acad; RIBA, Hon FRAIC, RA 1995; *Recreations* home, garden, books, music, walks, boats (Amadeus); *Clubs* Brooks's; *Style*— Michael Manser, Esq, CBE, RA; ✉ Morton House, Chiswick Mall, London W4 2PS; Manser Associates, Bridge Studios, Hammersmith Bridge, London W6 9DA (☎ 0181 741 4381)

MANSER, Paul Robert; s of Bob Manser, and Margaret, *née* Rubinstein; *b* 27 March 1950; *Educ* Eltham Coll, Univ of Warwick (BA); *m* 28 July 1972, Lindy, da of Harry Myers; 2 s (Nicolas b 19 June 1981, Edward b 18 Feb 1983); *Career* admitted slr 1977: currently ptnr Taylor Joynson Garrett; memb Law Soc; *Recreations* tennis, photography, music, books; *Style*— Paul Manser, Esq; ✉ Taylor Joynson Garrett, Carmelite, 50 Victoria Embankment, London EC4Y 0DX (☎ 0171 353 1234)

MANSERGH, Capt Michael Cecil Maurice; CBE; s of Adm Sir Maurice James Mansergh, KCB, CBE (d 1966), Chief of Staff to Allied Naval C-in-C, Expeditionary Force for invasion of Normandy (responsible for naval planning 'Overlord'), 5 Sea Lord, C-in-C Plymouth, by his wife, Violet Elsie (d 1983), da of late Bernard Hillman; ggs of James Mansergh (d 1905), Pres Inst of Civil Engrs; *b* 12 Aug 1926; *Educ* RNC Dartmouth, jssc, War Coll; *m* 10 March 1956, Margaret Jean, da of Bernard Howell Cameron Hastie (d 1981); 2 s (Robert b 1957, Michael b 1959), 1 da (Penelope b 1963); *Career* RN 1940, qualified gunnery and air weapons, Cdr 1961, RNAS Lossiemouth 1966–68, Naval Staff 1968–69, Capt 1969, Naval Asst to Chief of Fleet Support 1969–72, Queen's Harbourmaster Plymouth 1972–73, Cmdg Offr HMS Excellent and Phoenix 1974–76, Vice Pres Admty Interview Bd 1976–79, Naval asst to Naval Sec 1979–82; FIMgt (formerly FBIM) 1970; *Clubs* Lyme Regis Golf; *Style*— Capt Michael Mansergh, CBE, RN; ✉ Cothayes, Whitchurch Canonicorum, Bridport, Dorset DT6 6RH

MANSFIELD, Prof Averil O; *b* 21 June 1937; *Educ* Blackpool Collegiate Sch, Univ of Liverpool (MB ChB, ChM); *m*; *Career* formerly: lectr in surgery Univ of Liverpool, conslt surgn and hon sr lectr in surgery United Liverpool Hosps, conslt surgn Hillingdon and Hammersmith Hosps and St Mary's Hosp London; currently: prof of vascular surgery and dir Academic Surgical Unit St Mary's Hosp London, sr lectr in vascular surgery Royal Postgraduate Med Sch (Hammersmith Hosp), hon conslt in paediatric surgery/vascular surgery Hosp for Sick Children Great Ormond Street; postgraduate sub-dean St Mary's Hosp Med Sch 1987–91; RCS: memb Cncl 1990–, chm Ct of Examiners 1990–92; pres elect Section of Surgery RSM 1996–97; chm: Intercollegiate Bd in Gen Surgery 1992–95, Fedn of Surgical Speciality Assocs 1993–95; memb: Audit Ctee Euro Carotid Stroke Surgery Trial, Steering Ctee Asymptomatic Carotid Surgery Trial; Moynihan fell Assoc of Surgns of Great Britain and I, Hunterian prof, Arnott demonstrator and Kinmonth lecture RCS, Hon FRACS and Syme orator RACS 1996; memb: Assoc of Surgns of GB and I (pres 1992–93), Vascular Surgery Soc (pres elect 1996–97), Surgical Res Soc, Euro Soc of Vascular Surgery; Hon MD Univ of Liverpool 1994; FRCSEd 1966, FRCS 1967; *Style*— Prof Averil O Mansfield; ✉ Director, Academic Surgical Unit, Imperial College School of Medicine, St Mary's Hospital, 10th Floor, Queen Elizabeth The Queen Mother Wing, South Wharf Road, London W2 1NY (☎ 0171 725 1301, fax 0171 725 1810)

MANSFIELD, David James; s of Wilfred Victor Leonard Mansfield (d 1972), and Helen, *née* Preston; *b* 12 Jan 1954; *m* 15 Sept 1979, Alison Patricia, da of Gerald Frederick Hedley Pullin; 2 s (James William Robert b 1983, Edward Nicholas Jack (Ned) b 1994), 1 da (Clare Amy Frances b 1986); *Career* sales and sr mktg exec Scottish and Grampian TV 1977–80, mktg gp head and gen sales mangr Scottish TV 1981–84; Thames TV: mktg controller 1985–87, sales and mktg controller 1987–90, dep sales dir 1990–92; gp commercial dir Capital Radio plc 1993–; chm Capital Group Studios; Bd dir: Media Sales and Marketing (wholly owned subsid of Capital Radio plc) until 1996, Radio Advertising Bureau, Independent Radio News; *Recreations* fly fishing, contemporary music, art deco china; *Style*— David Mansfield, Esq; ✉ 16 Sudbrooke Rd, London SW12 8TG; Capital Radio plc, Euston Tower, Euston Road, London NW1 3DR (☎ 0171 608 6080, fax 0171 387 2345)

MANSFIELD, Gp Capt Eric Arthur; s of Edward Arthur Mansfield (d 1980), and Violet Mary, *née* Ricketts (d 1973); *b* 14 April 1932; *Educ* Southend HS, Univ of Cambridge (MA), RAF Tech Coll, Univ of Southampton (MSc); *m* 2 Jan 1954, Marion, da of Alfred Charles Byrne (d 1975); 1 s (Russell b 27 Jan 1956), 1 da (Penelope b 10 June 1958); *Career* apprentice RAF 1949, cmmnd 1953, pilot wings 1958, jr appts fighter and bomber units, MOD 1963, HQ SAC (USAF) 1966, HQ Strike Cmd 1969, RAF Cottesmore 1972, HQ RAF Germany 1974, HQ 18 GP 1978, MOD 1981, HQ AfSouth 1984, HQ RAF Support Cmd 1986; freelance conslt; Freeman City of London; CEng, MRAeS; *Recreations* squash, skiing, rough shooting, photography, philately; *Clubs* RAF; *Style*— Gp Capt Eric Mansfield; ✉ 33 Chalgrove End, Stoke Mandeville, Buckinghamshire (☎ 01296 613792)

MANSFIELD, Eric Harold; s of Harold Goldsmith Mansfield (d 1959), and Grace, *née* Phundt (d 1924); *b* 24 May 1923; *Educ* St Lawrence Coll Ramsgate, Trinity Hall Cambridge (MA, ScD); *m* 1, 1947 (m dis 1973), Mary Ola Purves Douglas; 2 s, 1 da; m 2, 1974, Eunice Lily Kathleen Shuttleworth-Parker; *Career* Royal Aerospace Estab: dep chief sci offr 1967–80, chief sci offr (individual merit) 1980–83; memb cncl Royal Soc 1977–78; visiting prof Univ of Surrey 1984–90; James Alfred Ewing Gold Medal for engrg research 1991, Royal Medal Royal Society 1994; FRS, FEng 1976 (fndr fell), FRAeS, FIMA; *Books* Bending and Stretching of Plates (1964, 2 edn 1989); Bridge: The Ultimate Limits (1986); *Recreations* bridge, palaeontology, snorkelling; *Style*— Dr Eric Mansfield, FRS, FEng; ✉ Manatoba, Dene Close, Lower Bourne, Farnham, Surrey GU10 3PP (☎ 01252 713558)

MANSFIELD, Vice Adm Sir (Edward) Gerard Napier; KBE (1974), CVO (1981); s of Vice Adm Sir John Maurice Mansfield, KCB, DSO, DSC (d 1949), and Alice Talbot Napier (d 1979); *b* 13 July 1921; *Educ* RNC Dartmouth; *m* 1943, Joan Worship, da of late Cdr John Byron, DSC and Bar; 2 da; *Career* joined RN 1935, serv WWII in destroyers and combined ops (despatches), Capt 1959, Rear Adm 1969, sr naval memb Directing Staff IDC 1969–70, Flag Offr sea Trg 1971–72, Vice Adm 1972, Dep Supreme Allied Cdr Atlantic 1973–75, ret; chm Assoc of RN Offrs' Cncl 1975–86; memb Admin Cncl Royal Jubilee Tsts 1978–82, chm Operation Raleigh 1984–89; Liveryman Worshipful Co of Shipwrights; *Recreations* golf, gardening; *Clubs* Army and Navy; *Style*— Vice Adm Sir Gerard Mansfield, KBE, CVO; ✉ White Gate House, Heath Lane, Ewshot, Farnham, Surrey GU10 5AH (☎ 01252 850325)

MANSFIELD, Hon Guy Rhys John; QC (1994); s and h of 5 Baron Sandhurst, DFC; *b* 3 March 1949; *Educ* Harrow, Oriel Coll Oxford (MA); *m* 1976, Philippa St Clair, da of late Digby Everard Verdon-Roe, of Le Cannet, France; 1 s (Edward James b 12 April 1982), 1 da (Alice Georgina b 4 Feb 1980); *Career* called to the Bar Middle Temple 1972, recorder 1993–; vice-chm Legal Aid & Fees Ctee Gen Cncl of the Bar 1995–; *Recreations* cricket; *Clubs* Leander, MCC; *Style*— The Hon Guy Mansfield, QC; ✉ 1 Crown Office Row, London EC4Y 7HH (☎ 0171 797 7500, fax 0171 797 7550)

MANSFIELD, Michael; QC; s of Frank Le Voir Mansfield (d 1960), of London, and Marjorie, *née* Sayer (d 1977); *b* 12 Oct 1941; *Educ* Highgate Sch, Univ of Keele (BA); *m* 1, 28 Sept 1965 (m dis 1992), Melian, da of Lt Cdr Bordes; 3 s (Jonathan, Leo, Keiran), 2 da (Anna, Louise); m 2, 31 Dec 1992, Yvette Vanson; 1 s (Frederic); *Career* called to the Bar Gray's Inn 1967, estab chambers Tooks Ct 1984; Hon LLD: South Bank Univ 1994, Univ of Keele 1995, Univ of Hertfordshire 1995; hon fell Univ of Kent; memb TGWU, hon memb NUM; *Style*— Michael Mansfield, Esq, QC; ✉ 14 Tooks Ct, Cursitor St, London EC4A 1JY (☎ 0171 405 8828)

MANSFIELD, Sir Peter; kt (1993); s of Sidney George Mansfield (d 1966), of Lambeth, London, and Rose Lilian, *née* Turner (d 1985); *b* 9 Oct 1933; *Educ* William Penn Sch Peckham, QMC London (BSc, PhD); *m* 1 Sept 1962, Jean Margaret, da of Edward Francis Kibble (d 1972), of Peckham, London; 2 da (Sarah Jane b 1967, Gillian Samantha b 1970); *Career* Nat Serv RASC 1952–54; res assoc Univ of Illinois USA 1962–64; Univ of Nottingham: lectr, sr lectr then reader 1964–79, prof of physics 1979–94, prof emeritus 1994; sr res visitor Max Planck Inst for Med Res Heidelberg Germany 1971–72, pres Soc of Magnetic Resonance in Med 1987–88; Gold Medal Soc of Magnetic Resonance in Med 1982, Gold Medal and Prize Royal Soc Wellcome Fndn 1984, Duddell Medal and Prize Inst of Physics 1988, Sylvanus Thompson Medal Br Inst of Radiology 1988, Euro Workshop Trophy Euro Soc of Magnetic Resonance in Med and Biology 1988, Antoine Béclère Medal for Radiology 1989, Royal Soc Mullard Medal 1990, ISMAR Prize Int Soc of Magnetic Resonance 1992, Barclay Medal Br Inst of Radiology 1993, first Silver Plaque Euro Soc of Magnetic Resonance in Med and Biology 1993, Gold Medal Euro Assoc of Radiology 1995, Garmisch-Partenkirschen Prize for Magnetic Resonance Imaging 1995, Rank Prize 1997; Dr (hc) Univ of Strasbourg 1995, DSc (hc) Univ of Kent 1996; fell QMC London 1987; hon fell: Royal Coll of Radiology 1992, Inst of Physics 1996; hon memb: Br Inst of Radiology 1993, Soc of Magnetic Resonance Imaging 1994; FRS 1987, fell Soc of Magnetic Resonance 1994; *Books* NMR Imaging in Biomedicine (with P G Morris, 1982), NMR Imaging (ed with E L Hahn, 1990), MRI in Medicine (ed, 1995); *Recreations* languages, walking, flying (PPL and PPL(H)); *Style*— Sir Peter Mansfield, FRS; ✉ Magnetic Resonance Centre, Department of Physics, University of Nottingham, University Park, Nottingham NG7 2RD (☎ 0115 951 4740, fax 0115 951 5166, telex 37346 UNINOT G)

MANSFIELD, Sir Philip Robert Aked; KCMG (1984, CMG 1973); s of Philip Theodore Mansfield (d 1975); *b* 9 May 1926; *Educ* Winchester, Pembroke Coll Cambridge; *m* 1953, Elinor, da of Dr Burtis Russell MacHatton (d 1959), of USA; 2 s (Adrian, Humphrey); *Career* WWII Lt Grenadier Gds 1944–47; Sun Insurance Office 1949–50, Sudan Political Serv Equatoria Province 1950–55; Dip Serv: Addis Ababa, Singapore, Paris, Buenos Aires; cnsllr and head Rhodesia Dept FCO 1969–72, Royal Coll Def Studies 1973, cnsllr and head of chancery 1974–75, dep high cmmr Nairobi 1976, asst under sec of state FCO 1976–79, ambass and dep perm rep to the UN 1979–81, ambass to the Netherlands 1981–84; consIt: Rank Xerox 1987–95, BPB Industs 1987–95; *Recreations* birdwatching, tree planting, cooking; *Clubs* Cwlth Trust; *Style*— Sir Philip Mansfield, KCMG; ✉ Palmer's Farm, St Breward, Bodmin, Cornwall PL30 4NT (☎ 01208 850460)

MANSFIELD, Prof Roger; s of Arthur George Mansfield (d 1985), and Edith, *née* Leggett (d 1985); *b* 18 Jan 1942; *Educ* Kingston GS, Gonville and Caius Coll Cambridge (BA), Wolfson Coll Cambridge (MA, PhD); *m* 24 July 1969, Hélène Marie Louise, da of René Rica, of Quimper, France; 2 da (Marie-Anne (Mrs Ian Mackie) b 1972, Stephanie b 1977); *Career* student apprentice and res engr Stewarts and Lloyds Ltd Corby 1960–66; FME teaching fell Dept of Engrg Univ of Cambridge 1966–68, visiting lectr Yale Univ 1968–69, sr res offr London Business Sch 1969–73, lectr in industl sociology Imperial Coll 1973–76, prof of business admin Univ of Wales Cardiff Business Sch 1976–; head of dept: Business Admin and Accountancy UWIST 1977–85, Business and Economics UWIST 1985–87; dir Cardiff Business Sch 1987–, dep princ UWIST 1985–88, pro-vice-chllr Univ of Wales Cardiff 1996–; chm Br Acad of Mgmnt 1993–, vice chm Cncl of Univ Mgmnt Schs 1988–92; dir S Glamorgan Trg and Enterprise Cncl 1989–94; FRSA; *Books* Managers in Focus: the British Manager in the Early 1980s (with M J F Poole, 1981), Organizational Structures and National Contingencies (1983), Frontiers of Management Research and Practice (1989); *Recreations* gardening; *Clubs* Cardiff and County; *Style*— Prof Roger Mansfield; ✉ 64 Bishops Road, Whitchurch, Cardiff CF4 1LW (☎ 01222 617381); Cardiff Business School, University of Wales, Aberconway Building, Colum Drive, Cardiff CF1 3EU (☎ 01222 874417, fax 01222 874419, telex 497368)

MANSFIELD AND MANSFIELD, 8 Earl of (GB 1776 and 1792); William David Mungo James Murray; JP (Perth and Kinross 1975), DL (1980); also Lord Scone (S 1605), Viscount Stormont (S 1621), Lord Balvaird (S 1641); hereditary keeper of Bruce's Castle of Lochmaben; s of 7 Earl of Mansfield, JP, LL (d 1971, whose family were long the owners of Robert Adam's neo-classical Kenwood; Lord Mansfield is sixth in descent from the bro of the celebrated Lord Chief Justice and 1 Earl who was Alexander Pope's 'silver-tongued Murray'), and Dorothea (d 1985), da of Hon Sir Lancelot Carnegie, GCVO, KCMG, 2 s of 9 Earl of Southesk; *b* 7 July 1930; *Educ* Wellesley House, Eton, ChCh Oxford; *m* 19 Dec 1955, Pamela Joan, da of Wilfred Neill Foster, CBE; 2 s (Viscount Stormont b 17 Oct 1956, Hon James b 7 June 1969), 1 da (Lady Georgina b 10 March 1967); *Heir* s, Viscount Stormont, *qv*; *Career* Nat Serv Lt Scots Gds 1949–50 (Malaya); called to the Bar 1958; practising barrister until 1971; dir General Accident Fire & Life Assurance Corp and numerous cos 1972–79 and 1985–; memb Br Delgn to Euro Parliament 1973–75; oppn front bench spokesman in the House of Lords 1975–79; min of state: Scottish Office 1979–83, NI Office 1983–84; first cmmr and chm The Crown Estate 1985–95; chm Historic Houses Assoc Scotland 1976–79; vice pres Wildfowl & Wetlands Tst; pres: Scottish Assoc of Boys' Clubs 1976–79, Fédération des Associations de Chasse de l' Europe 1977–79, Royal Scottish Country Dance Soc 1977–; Hon Sheriff Perth 1974; Hon MRICS 1993; *Clubs* Turf, White's, Pratt's, Beefsteak; *Style*— The Rt Hon the Earl of Mansfield and Mansfield, JP, DL; ✉ Scone Palace, Perthshire PH2 6BE (☎ 01738 551115, fax 01738 552588)

MANSON, Alexander Reid; CBE (1989); s of Capt Alexander Manson (d 1965), of Old Meldrum, Aberdeenshire, and Isobel, *née* Reid, MBE (d 1985); *b* 2 Sept 1931; *Educ* Robert Gordon's Coll Aberdeen, N of Scotland Coll of Agric (DipAg); *m* 29 May 1957, Ethel Mary, da of Robert Philip (d 1980), of Strichen; 1 s (Alexander), 2 da (Anne, Lesley); *Career* fndr chm Aberdeen Beef & Calf Ltd 1962, chm Buchan Meat Producers Ltd 1982–92 (joined 1968), pres Scottish Agricultural Organisation Society Ltd 1986–89, Beef Advsy Ctee Brussels 1986–96, pres Fedn of Agric Co-operatives (UK) Ltd 1990–91; dir Animal Data Centre 1992–95, tstee Plunkett Fndn Oxford 1977–91; memb: Meat & Livestock Cmmn 1986–95, Williams Ctee Bd of Enquiry 1989; chm Old Meldrum Sports Ctee 1971–75 (memb 1955–82), memb Old Meldrum Town Cncl 1960–65, gen cmmr of Income Tax 1991–; FRAgS 1995 (ARAgS 1993); *Recreations* golf, shooting and conservation, bird watching; *Clubs* Farmers'; *Style*— Alexander Manson, Esq, CBE; ✉ Kilblean, Old Meldrum, Inverurie, Aberdeenshire AB51 0DN (☎ and fax 01651 872226)

MANTEL, Hilary Mary (Mrs Gerald McEwen); da of Henry Thompson (took name of step f, Jack Mantel), and Margaret Mary, *née* Foster; *b* 6 July 1952; *Educ* Harrytown Convent Romiley Cheshire, LSE, Univ of Sheffield (BJur); *m* 1972, Gerald McEwen, s of Henry McEwen; *Career* author; film critic The Spectator 1987–90, writer of columns and criticism in a wide range of newspapers and magazines 1987–; Shiva Naipaul meml prize 1987, Winifred Holtby prize 1990, Cheltenham Festival lit prize 1990, Southern Arts lit prize 1991, Sunday Express Book of the Year award 1992, Hawthornden Prize 1996; FRSL 1990; *Novels* Every Day is Mother's Day (1985), Vacant Possession (1986), Eight Months on Ghazzah Street (1988), Fludd (1989), A Place of Greater Safety (1992), A Change of Climate (1994), An Experiment in Love (1995); *Recreations* watching cricket; *Style*— Hilary Mantel, FRSL; ✉ c/o Bill Hamilton, A M Heath & Co, 79 St Martin's Lane, London WC2N 4AA (☎ 0171 836 4271, fax 0171 497 2561)

MANTELL, Brian Stuart; s of Sidney Mantell (d 1988), of Chigwell, Essex, and Anne, *née* Goldstein (d 1981); *b* 14 Jan 1935; *Educ* Co HS Ilford, Univ of London (MB BS, MRCP); *m* 15 Aug 1971, Dr Janet Mantell, da of Maurice Share (d 1963), of Kingston, Surrey; 1 s (David b 1974), 1 da (Rachel b 1977); *Career* conslt in radiotherapy and oncology: The Royal London Hosp 1970–, London Chest Hosp 1971–; chm Regnl Radiotherapy Advsy Ctee and regnl postgraduate advsr NE Thames NHS Regn 1990–94; memb BMA, past treas Radiotherapists Visiting Soc of GB and Scandinavia; RSM 1961, FFR 1967, FRCR 1975, FRCP 1990; *Recreations* reading, swimming, travel; *Clubs* RSM; *Style*— Dr Brian Mantell; ✉ The Royal London Hospital, London E1 1BB (☎ 0171 377 7690); 10 Ferrings, College Rd, Dulwich, London SE21 7LU (☎ 0181 693 8141)

MANTELL, Hon Mr Justice; Hon Sir Charles Barrie Knight; kt (1990); s of Francis Christopher Knight Mantell, and Elsie Mantell; *b* 30 Jan 1937; *Educ* Manchester GS, Univ of Manchester (LLM); *m* 1960, Anne Shirley; 2 da; *Career* Nat Serv RAF 1958–61; called to the Bar Gray's Inn 1960, in practice Manchester and London 1961–82, recorder of the Crown Ct 1978–82, QC 1979, judge of the Supreme Ct Hong Kong 1982–85, circuit judge 1985–90, bencher Gray's Inn 1990, judge of the High Ct of Justice (Queen's Bench Div) 1990–, sr presiding judge Western Circuit 1995– (presiding judge 1993–96); *Recreations* reading, watching cricket; *Style*— The Hon Mr Justice Mantell; ✉ c/o Royal Courts of Justice, Strand, London WC2A 2LL

MANTON, 3 Baron (UK 1922); Joseph Rupert Eric Robert Watson; DL (Humberside 1980); s of 2 Baron Manton, JP (d 1968), by his 1 w Alethea (d 1979), da of Col Philip Langdale, OBE, and gggda of 17 Baron Stourton; *b* 22 Jan 1924; *Educ* Eton; *m* 1951, Mary Elizabeth, twin da of late Maj T D Hallinan; 2 s, 3 da; *Heir* s, Hon Miles Ronald Marcus Watson; *Career* joined Army 1942, Lt Life Gds 1943, transferred 7 (QO) Hussars 1951, Capt, ret 1956; sr steward Jockey Club 1982–85, former Jockey Club representative on Horserace Betting Levy Bd 1970–75, former gentleman rider (won 130 Nat Hunt races and Point to Points 1947–64); landowner, farmer, race horse owner; *Clubs* Jockey, White's; *Style—* The Rt Hon the Lord Manton, DL; ✉ Houghton Hall, Sancton, York (☎ 01430 873234)

MANTON, Michael George; s of Brig Lionel Manton, DSO, OBE (d 1961), and Joan Eileen Ross, *née* Gifford (d 1978); *b* 10 Feb 1927; *Educ* Stowe, Trinity Coll Cambridge (entrance exhibitioner, BA); *m* 1 (m dis 1978), Ilne du Plessis; 1 s (Christopher John b 1954), 1 da (Jennifer Jane b 1958, decd); m 2, 1982, Margaret Davies; *Career* mercantile asst India 1948–51, London mangr Indian advtg agency 1951–53, dir W S Crawford Ltd 1961–64 (joined 1953), jt fndr ptnr Kingsley Manton & Palmer Ltd 1964–75, chief exec Kimpher Group 1975–77, jt fndr ptnr and chm Manton Woodyer & Ketley 1977–80, fndr consultancy practice 1980; chm: Assoc of Media Independents 1981–86, Direct Mail Sales Bureau plc 1982–91; vice chm TMD Advertising Holdings plc (Carat UK Ltd from 1991) 1988–94 (non-exec dir 1985–94); FIPA; *Recreations* sailing slowly in Eastern Mediterranean, listening to classical music, putting off writing books; *Clubs* Little Ship; *Style—* Michael Manton, Esq; ✉ 4 Dunollie Place, London NW5 2XR (☎ 0171 485 2569); Carat UK Ltd, New London House, 172 Drury Lane, London WC2B 5QR (☎ 0171 611 7654, fax 0171 344 0300)

MANWARING, Michael John; s of Randle Gilbert Manwaring, of Newick, Sussex, and Betty, *née* Rout; *b* 7 Sept 1946; *Educ* Christ Coll Brecon, Imperial Coll London (BEng); *m* Dec 1977, Annabelle, da of Praxidus Fernandes; 4 da (Nina Joanna b 12 May 1980, Lara Sophia b 13 Oct 1983, Maya Louise b 15 Sept 1986, Priya Grace b 21 April 1993); *Career* KMP Partnership Ltd advtg agency: joined 1969, dir 1976, client services dir 1978, dep md 1982–84; dep chm WCRS 1989–94; memb: Mktg Soc 1992, D&AD 1993; MIPA 1990; *Recreations* tennis, photography, Indian culture/art; *Clubs* MCC, Glyndebourne, Queen's Tennis; *Style—* Michael Manwaring, Esq

MANZONI, Michael Victor; s of Sir Herbert Manzoni (d 1972), of Birmingham, and Lilian, *née* Davies (d 1988); *b* 4 Sept 1928; *Educ* Rugby, Univ of Cambridge (MA Mech Scis); *m* 1957, Julia Mary, da of John Wait; 1 da (Susan Louise b 1958), 3 s (John Alexander b 1960, Charles Peter b 1963, James Edward b 1965); *Career* indentured pupil PLA 1949–51, various engrg trg in Canada 1952–54; R M Douglas Construction Ltd: joined 1954, dir 1964, md 1982, dep chm 1990–91, ret; dir Robert M Douglas Holdings plc 1978–91; currently non-exec dir Francis Graves Ltd; memb Engrg Cncl 1988–; FICE 1970, FRSA 1988; *Recreations* offshore cruising; *Clubs* Royal Thames Yacht, Edgbaston Golf, Barnt Green Sailing; *Style—* Michael Manzoni, Esq; ✉ Moss House, 27 Twatling Road, Barnt Green, Birmingham B45 8HY (☎ 0121 445 3072)

MAPLE, District Judge Graham John; s of Sydney George Maple, of Croydon, and Thelma Olive, *née* Winter; *b* 18 Dec 1947; *Educ* Shirley Secdy Modern Sch Croydon, John Ruskin GS Croydon, Bedford Coll London (LLB); *m* 30 March 1974, Heather Maple, JP, da of James Anderson; 2 s (Andrew John b 30 March 1978, Christopher James b 18 March 1980); *Career* Lord Chancellor's Dept 1968, chief clerk Divorce Registry 1981–86, establishment offr 1986–89, sec Family Div 1989–91, district judge Principal Registry of the Family Div High Ct of Justice 1991–; memb: Outer London Family Court Servs Ctee 1991–95, Outer London Family Forum 1995–; churchwarden St Mildred's Parish Church Tenterden Kent 1992–; *Books* Practioner's Probate Manual (jt ed 21 edn, 1979), Holloway's Probate Handbook (ed 8 edn, 1987), Rayden and Jackson on Divorce (co ed 13–16 edn, 1979–91); *Recreations* steam and model railways, Roman Britain; *Style—* District Judge Maple; ✉ Principal Registry of the Family Division, Somerset House, Strand, London WC2R 1LP

MAPLES, John; *b* 22 April 1943; *Educ* Marlborough, Univ of Cambridge (MA), Harvard Business Sch; *m* Jane; 1 s (Tom), 1 da (Rose); *Career* called to the Bar 1965; self-employed lawyer and businessman 1965–83 (USA and WI 1967–78); MP (Cons) Lewisham W 1983–92, PPS to Chief Sec to the Treasy 1987–90, economic sec to Treasy 1990–92, jt dep chm Cons Pty 1994–95; chm and chief exec Saatchi & Saatchi Government Communications Worldwide 1992–96, chm Rowland Sallingbury Casey; Liveryman Worshipful Co of Vintners; *Style—* John Maples, Esq

MAPLES, (Charles James) Julian; s of Charles John Maples (d 1973), and Renee Lolita Elisabeth Gordon, *née* Clark, of Cooden, Sussex; *b* 26 Jan 1949; *Educ* St Peter's Sch Seaford, Harrow, Univ of Liverpool (LLB); *m* 1972, Anne-Francoise, da of B B W Bromley, of Crowborough, Sussex; 2 s (Charles James b 30 Sept 1978, John Henry b 10 June 1984); *Career* Theodore Goddard: articled clerk 1971, ptnr 1980–, head Banking Gp 1985–; memb: Worshipful Co of Fletchers, Worshipful Co of Weavers, City of London Solicitors Co, Law Soc; *Recreations* shooting, sailing; *Style—* Julian Maples, Esq; ✉ Lower Parrock House, Hartfield, East Sussex (☎ 01342 822666, fax 01342 825601); Theodore Goddard, 150 Aldersgate Street, London EC1A 4EJ (☎ 0171 606 8855, fax 0171 606 4390)

MAPLESON, Prof William Wellesley; s of Francis Mapleson (d 1959), of Amersham, Bucks, and Amy Kathleen, *née* Parsons (d 1968); *b* 2 Aug 1926; *Educ* Dr Challoner's GS Amersham Bucks, Univ Coll Durham (BSc, PhD, DSc); *m* 10 July 1954, Gwladys Doreen, da of William Horatio Wood (d 1981), of Cardiff; 1 s (Roger b 1963), 1 da (Jenny b 1955); *Career* Nat Serv instr in radar Flying Offr RAF 1947–49; Coll of Med Univ of Wales: lectr 1952–65, sr lectr 1965–69, reader 1969–73, prof of physics of anaesthesia 1973–91, emeritus prof and conslt Dept of Anaesthetics 1991–; Pask Certificate of Honour AAGBI 1972, Faculty Medal Royal Coll of Anaesthetists 1981, Dudley Buxton Medal Royal Coll of Anaesthetists 1992; hon memb Brazilian Soc of Anaesthesiology 1983, hon memb Assoc of Anaesthetists of GB and I 1991, Hon FRCA; FInstP, FIPSM; *Books* Automatic Ventilation of the Lungs (jtly, 3 edn, 1980); *Recreations* theatre-going, walking; *Style—* Prof William Mapleson; ✉ Dept of Anaesthetics, University of Wales College of Medicine, University Hospital of Wales, Cardiff CF4 4XN (☎ 01222 743110, fax 01222 747203)

MAPPLE, Andrew (Andy); s of Roy Boardman Mapple, of Preston, and Janet, *née* Marquis; *b* 3 Nov 1962; *Educ* Carr Hill HS Kirkham Lancs; *m* 17 Oct 1987, Deena, *née* Brush, also water skier; *Career* professional water skier; began competing 1976, memb Br team 1981; Gold medal Slalom World Championships 1981–82, current slalom world champion, world professional slalom champion 1987–, US Masters champion 6 times; world record holder slalom 1989–, world professional record holder; memb Team O'Brien; *Recreations* golf, motorsports, cycling, triathlon, cars; *Style—* Andy Mapple, Esq; ✉ c/o British Water Ski Federation, 390 City Road, London EC1V 2QA

MAR, Countess of (31 holder of S Earldom *ab initio*, before 1114); Margaret; *née* of Mar; also Lady Garioch (an honour originally held together with the ancient territorial Earldom of Mar; holder of Premier Earldom of Scotland by date (the oldest peerage in the Br Isles); the predecessors of the original Earls of Mar were Mormaers of Mar in pre-feudal Scotland, long before the term 'Earl' came to be used; maintains private offr-of-arms (Garioch Pursuivant); da of 30 Earl of Mar (d 1975), and Millicent Mary Lane, *née* Salton (d 1993); *b* 19 Sept 1940; *Educ* Lewes County GS for Girls Sussex; *m* 1, 1959 (m dis 1976), Edwin Noel of Mar (recognised in surname 'of Mar' by Warrant of the Lord Lyon 1969), s of Edwin Artiss; 1 da (Lady Susan Helen, Mistress of Mar, *qv*, b 31 May 1963); m 2, 1976, John (also recognised in the surname 'of Mar' by Warrant of Lord Lyon 1976), s of Norman Salton; m 3, 1982, John Henry Jenkin, MA(Cantab), LRAM, FRCO, ARCM, s of William Jenkin, of Hayle, Cornwall; *Heir* da, Mistress of Mar; *Career* British Telecom sales superintendent until 1982; patron: Dispensing Doctors' Assoc, Worcester Mobile Disabled Group, Gulf Veterans' Assoc; lay memb Immigration Appeals Tbnl; chm ELECT, pres Elderly Accommodation Counsel; Laurent Perrier/Country Life Parliamentarian of the Year 1996; *Recreations* gardening, painting, interior decoration, pig and goat keeping; *Style—* The Rt Hon the Countess of Mar; ✉ St Michael's Farm, Great Witley, Worcester WR6 6JB

MAR, Mistress of; Lady Susan Helen; *née* of Mar; da of Countess of Mar, *qv*, 31 holder of S Earldom, by her 1 husb Edwin Artiss (later 'of Mar'); *b* 31 May 1963; *Educ* Kidderminster HS for Girls, Christie Coll Cheltenham; *m* 10 June 1989, Bruce Alexander Wyllie; 2 da (Isabel Alice b 10 Sept 1991, Frances Alexandra b 1 Nov 1994); *Style—* Mistress of Mar; ✉ Firethorn Farm Cottage, Plough Lane, Ewhurst Green, Cranleigh, Surrey GU6 7SG (☎ 01483 275733)

MAR AND KELLIE, 14 and 16 Earl of (S 1565, 1619); James Thorne Erskine; DL (Clackmannan, 1991); also Lord Erskine (S 1426), Baron Erskine of Dirletowne (*sic* as stated by The Complete Peerage, S 1604), and Viscount of Fentoun and Lord Dirletoun (S 1619); also Hereditary Keeper of Stirling Castle; s of Maj the 13 Earl of Mar (and 15 of) Kellie, JP (d 1993), and Pansy Constance, OBE, JP, *née* Thorne (d 1996); *b* 10 March 1949; *Educ* Eton, Moray House Coll of Educn Edinburgh (Dip Social Work, Dip Youth & Co Work), Inverness College (Certificate in Bldg); *m* 1974, Mary Irene, yr da of Dougal McDougal Kirk (d 1992), of Edinburgh; 5 step c; *Heir* bro, Hon Alexander David Erskine b 1952; *Career* Pilot Offr RAuxAF Regt 1979–82, Flying Offr 1982–86 (2622 Highland Sqdn), memb RNXS 1985–89; page of honour to HM The Queen 1962–63; community serv volunteer York 1967–68, youth and community worker Craigmillar 1971–73; social worker: Sheffield 1973–76, Elgin 1976–77, Forres 1977–78, Aviemore 1979, HM Prison Inverness 1979–81, Inverness West 1981, Merkinch 1982; supervisor Community Serv by Offenders Inverness 1983–87, memb Visiting Ctee HM Young Offenders Inst Glenochr; bldg technician 1989–91; project worker SACRO Central IPP Falkirk 1991–93; canoe and small boat builder 1993–94; estate mangr; Liveryman Worshipful Co of Cordwainers; sits as a Scottish Lib Dem peer in the House of Lords; *Recreations* open canoeing, Alloa Tower, cycling, gardening, elder of Church of Scotland, railways; *Clubs* Farmers'; *Style—* The Earl of Mar and Kellie; ✉ Erskine House, Kirk Wynd, Clackmannan, Scotland FK10 4JF (☎ 01259 212438)

MARA, Rt Hon Ratu Sir Kamisese Kapaiwai Tuimacilai; GCMG (1983), KBE (1969, OBE 1961), PC (1973); *b* 13 May 1920; *Educ* Central Med Sch Fiji, Sacred Heart Coll NZ, Otago Univ NZ, Wadham Coll Oxford (MA), LSE (Dip); *m* 1951, Adi Lady Lala Mara; 3 s (1 s decd), 5 da; *Career* MLC Fiji 1953–, MEC 1959–61, prime minister of Fiji 1970–94, president and Commander in Chief of Fiji 1994–, Chancellor of the Order of Fiji 1995, hereditary high chief of the Lau Islands; hon fell Wadham Coll Oxford 1971, hon fell LSE 1986; Hon Dr of Laws Univ of Guam 1969, Hon Dr of Laws Otago Univ NZ 1973, Hon Dr of Laws Univ of New Delhi 1975, Hon Dr of Political Science Yonsei Univ Republic of Korea 1978, Hon Dr of the USP Du 1980, Hon Dr of Law Tokai Univ Japan 1980, Hon Dr of Law Univ of Papua New Guinea 1982; KStJ; *Style—* The Rt Hon Ratu Sir Kamisese Mara, GCMG, KBE; ✉ Government House, Suva, Fiji

MARA, Prof Timothy Nicholas (Tim); *b* 27 Sept 1948; *Educ* Epsom and Ewell Sch of Art, Wolverhampton Poly (DipAD), Royal Coll of Art (MA); *Career* artist; lectr in printmaking: Nat Coll of Art & Design 1976–78, Brighton Poly 1978–79; princ lectr in printmaking Chelsea Sch of Art London 1980–90, prof of printmaking Royal Coll of Art 1990–; visiting lectr at numerous art schs and colls incl RCA, Slade, Ruskin, Central, Newcastle Poly 1976–; external examiner: Nat Coll of Art & Design Dublin 1983–87, Falmouth Sch of Art 1984–87, Staffordshire Poly 1988–91, Glasgow Sch of Art 1988–91, Limerick Coll of Art 1990–93; artist in residence Br Sch at Rome 1984; work in the collections of: V&A, Arts Cncl of GB, Br Cncl, Tate Gallery, Brooklyn Mus NY, Nat Art Gall Wellington NZ, Wakefield Art Gallery Bath, Rank Xerox, BBC, IBM, J Walter Thompson, Collett Dickinson Pearce; *Exhbns* solo incl: ICA London 1976, Project Arts Centre Dublin 1977, Wolverhampton Municipal Art Gallery 1977, Thumb Gallery 1980, David Hendrik's Gallery Dublin 1981, Angela Flowers Gallery London 1988, Drumcroon Arts Centre Wigan 1988, The Black Prints Flowers East London 1990, Flowers East 1992 and 1996, The Graphic Studio Dublin 1992; recent gp exhibitions incl: The Ties That Bind, The Family in Contemporary Art Univ of Strathclyde Glasgow and tour 1987–88, Leicestershire CC Exhibition Loughborough 1988, Figuratively Speaking Bankside Gallery London 1989, Angela Flowers 20 Year Anniversary Exhibition Barbican Arts Centre 1989–90, European exhibition of large format prints Guinness Hop Store Dublin 1991, 11 Norwegian Int Print Biennale Fredrikstad 1995, 21 Int Biennale of Graphic Art Ljubljana Slovenia 1995, numerous other international exhibitions; *Awards* Stowells Trophy, BA Art Award, RCA Major travelling scholarship, New Contemporaries award; *Clubs* Chelsea Arts; *Style—* Prof Tim Mara; ✉ Royal College of Art, Kensington Gore, London SW7 2EU (☎ 0171 590 4425, fax 0171 590 4438)

MARAN, Prof Arnold George Dominic; s of John Maran (d 1969), of Edinburgh, and Hilda, *née* Mancini (d 1984); *b* 16 June 1936; *Educ* Daniel Stewart's Coll Edinburgh, Univ of Edinburgh (MB ChB, MD); *m* 25 April 1962, Anna Marie Terese; 1 s (Charles Mark Damien b 1965), 1 da (Dr Nicola Jane b 1963); *Career* currently prof of otolaryngology Univ of Edinburgh; author of over 130 scientific papers; vice pres RCSEd, past pres Laryngology Section RSM; FRCSEd 1963, FACS 1974, FRCP 1988, FRCS 1991, Hon FDSRCS 1994; *Books* Clinical Otolaryngology (1964, 2 edn 1972), Head and Neck Surgery (1969, 2 edn 1993), Clinical Rhinology (1990); *Recreations* music, golf, travel; *Clubs* New (Edinburgh), Royal & Ancient Golf (St Andrews); *Style—* Prof Arnold Maran; ✉ 15 Cluny Drive, Edinburgh (☎ 0131 447 8519); 2 Double Dykes Rd, St Andrews (☎ 013347 2939); 14 Moray Place, Edinburgh (☎ 0131 225 8025)

MARAN, Stephen; *Career* md Lloyds and Scottish Finance (now Lloyds Bowmaker) until 1984 (joined 1969); Lloyds Abbey Life plc: gp fin dir and dep md until 1991, chief exec 1991–; dir Lloyds Bank plc 1994–; MICAS; *Style—* Stephen Maran, Esq; ✉ Lloyds Abbey Life plc, 205 Brooklands Road, Weybridge, Surrey KT13 0PE (☎ 01932 850888, fax 01932 856343)

MARANZANO, Alexander Mario (Alex); s of Michele Luciano Maranzano, and Iole, *née* Iannamico; *b* 27 Nov 1943; *Educ* Royal Coll of Art (MD), Camberwell Coll of Art (NDD); *m* 14 Sept 1968, Rosemary Jean, da of Dennis Norman Licence; 3 s (Damian Paul b 27 Sept 1970 d 1989, Michael Anthony b 15 May 1976, James William b 25 May 1979), 1 da (Sonia Elisa b 13 May 1972); *Career* designer; Minale Tattersfield & Partners Ltd: joined 1968, ptnr and dep md 1983, md 1988–; Gold award for Fox corp identify design NY 1976, Silver award Designers and Arts Dirs Club London for Heathrow subways 1978, designed Central TV symbol 1982, Most Outstanding Graphics Silver award for PO applied design 1984, designed concept for Br Airports Exhbn in Museum of Modern Art NY; memb Exec Ctee Designers and Art Dirs Club 1985–87; FCSD; *Style—* Alex Maranzano, Esq; ✉ Minale Tattersfield & Partners Ltd, The Courtyard, 37 Sheen Rd, Richmond, Surrey TW9 1AJ (☎ 0181 948 7999, fax 0181 948 2435, telex 8953130)

MARBER, Patrick; *b* 19 Sept 1964; *Educ* Wadham Coll, Univ of Oxford; *Career* writer, actor and director; *Theatre* as dir: 1953 (Almeida), Dealer's Choice (RNT and Vaudeville), Blue Remembered Hills (RNT); *Television* as writer and actor for BBC2 incl: The Day Today, Paul Calf Video Diary, Knowing Me Knowing You, the BAFTA Award winning 3 Fights 2 Weddings and a Funeral; as writer and dir for BBC2 incl: The Curator, After Miss Julie; *Awards* for Dealers Choice: Evening Standard Award for Best Comedy 1995, Writer's Guild Award for Best West End Play 1995; *Publications* Dealer's Choice (1995), After Miss Julie (1996); *Style—* Patrick Marber, Esq; ✉ c/o Alan Brodie Representation, 211 Piccadilly, London W1N 9LD (☎ 0171 917 2871, fax 0171 917 2872)

MARCALL, (Raymond) George; s of George James Marcall, of Southport, and Martha, *née* Douglas; *b* 16 Feb 1950; *Educ* Maghull GS Lancs, Univ of Nottingham, Thames Poly (BSc); *m* 14 June 1975, Rosamond, da of Clifford Denis Brinded; 2 da (Joanna Louise b 25 July 1978, Elizabeth Ellen b 7 Sept 1980), 1 s (Robert James George b 24 March 1986); *Career* Marks & Spencer plc 1973–86: successively commercial mgmnt trainee, departmental mangr then asst mangr 1973–80, systems analyst Computer Servs Dept (Head Office) 1981–82, subsequently assigned to Sales Promotion/Mktg Dept, successively mangr Photographic Dept, creative servs mangr (head of all design areas), controller of divnl display teams, mktg mangr all products, mktg mangr Food Div/Mktg Div 1982–86; gp sales and mktg/bd dir Airtours plc 1986–96; non-exec dir Yates Brothers Wine Lodges PLC, non-exec chm Foto Processing Ltd; FInstTT, memb Mktg Soc; *Recreations* squash, jogging, all aspects of the theatre and music; *Clubs* Tytherington Leisure; *Style—* George Marcall, Esq

MARCELL, Philip Michael; s of Stanley Marcell (d 1972), and Mabel Isobel Thomas, *née* Coe; *b* 21 Aug 1936; *Educ* Wimbledon Coll, BRNC Dartmouth, RNC Greenwich, Univ of London (LLB), Cambridge (postgrad res); *m* 22 Dec 1962, Lucina Mary, da of Capt Ernest May (d 1978); 1 s (Andrew b 1967), 3 da (Susannah b 1964, Virginia b 1965, Harriet b 1973); *Career* RN cadet BRNC Dartmouth 1952–54, Midshipman 1955, Sub Lt 1956, Lt 1958, Lt Cdr 1966, Cdr 1972; dir Jardines Insurance Brokers 1980 (co sec 1978–), chief exec American Reinsurance Co (UK) Ltd 1983; chm: Continental Reinsurance London, Continental Reinsurance Corp (UK) Ltd 1986–93, Unionamerica Insurance Co Ltd 1986–, London Insurance and Reinsurance Market Assoc (LIRMA (successor body to ROA)) 1995– (memb Cncl 1991–); memb Exec Ctee Reinsurance Offices Assoc (ROA) 1985–90; Freeman Worshipful Co of Chartered Secs and Admins (memb Ct of Assts); FIFA 1977, MIMgt 1978, FCIS 1987; *Recreations* squash, sailing; *Clubs* Utd Oxford & Cambridge; *Style—* Philip Marcell, Esq; ✉ Weavers End, Church Lane, Haslemere, Surrey GU27 2BJ (☎ 01428 651421); London Underwriting Centre, 3 Minster Court, Mincing Lane, London EC3R 7DD (☎ 0171 617 5952, fax 0171 617 5993, telex 883148)

MARCH, Lionel John; o s of Leonard March, and Rose March; *b* 26 Jan 1934; *Educ* Hove GS for Boys, Magdalene Coll Cambridge (state scholar, DipArch, MA, ScD); *m* 1 (m dis); 1 s (Ben b 1964), 2 da (Candida b 1961, Talitha b 1966); m 2, 23 July 1984, Maureen Mary Vidler; 1 step s (Ben b 1964), 2 step da (Anna b 1968, Sarah b 1969); *Career* Nat Serv Sub-Lt RN 1953–55; Harkness fell (Cwlth Fund) Jt Centre for Urban Studies Harvard Univ and Mass Inst of Technol 1962–64; Univ of Cambridge: res offr Estate Mgmnt Advsy Serv 1961–62, asst lectr Dept of Architecture 1966–67, dir Centre for Land Use and Built Form Studies 1969–73, lectr Dept of Architecture 1968–69 and 1973–76; prof Dept of Systems Design Faculty of Engrg Univ of Waterloo Ontario 1974–76; prof of design and head of design discipline Faculty of Technol Open Univ 1976–81; rector and vice provost RCA London 1981–84, prof Grad Sch of Architecture and Urban Planning Univ of Calif LA 1984–94 (vice chm and head Architectural Prog 1985–90), prof of design Sch of the Arts and Architecture UCLA 1994–; chm Bd of Dirs Applied Research of Cambridge Ltd Cambridge 1969–73, vice pres Applied Research of Cambridge (Canada) Ltd Toronto 1975–77, govr Imperial Coll of Sci and Technol 1981–84, memb Center for Medieval and Renaissance Studies UCLA 1992–; gen ed (with Sir Leslie Martin) Cambridge Urban and Architectural Studies 1970–, fndr ed Environment and Planning Series B Int Jl of Architectural and Design Science 1974–; fell Inst of Mathematics and its Applications 1979, FRSA 1979, fell RCA 1981; *Books* Whitehall: A Plan for the Government and National Centre (with Sir Leslie Martin, 1965), The Geometry of Environment (with Philip Steadman, 1971), Urban Space and Structures (ed with Sir Leslie Martin, 1972), The Architecture of Form (ed, 1976), R M Schindler - Composition and Construction (ed with Judith Sheine, 1993); *Style—* Mr Lionel March; ✉ The How House, 2422 Silver Ridge Avenue, Silver Lake, Los Angeles, Calif 90039, USA (☎ 00 1 213 661 7907)

MARCH, Prof Norman Henry; s of William Henry March, and Elsie May, *née* Brown; *b* 9 July 1927; *Educ* King Edward VII GS Coalville Leicester, King's Coll London (BSc, PhD); *m* 23 April 1949, (Margaret) Joan (d 1994), da of George Hoyle; 2 s (Peter Henry b 1 May 1951, Anthony John b 29 March 1953); *Career* prof of physics Univ of Sheffield 1961–72, prof of theoretical solid-state physics Imperial Coll London 1972–77; Univ of Oxford: Coulson prof and head Dept of Theoretical Chemistry 1977–94, professorial fell Univ Coll 1977–94, prof emeritus 1994–; former chm: Condensed Matter Physics Ctee Inst of Physics London, Advsy Ctee on Condensed Matter Int Centre for Theoretical Physics Trieste Italy; Hon DTech Chalmers Univ Gothenburg Sweden 1980; *Books* The Many-Body Problem in Quantum Mechanics (with W H Young and S Sampanthar, 1967), Liquid Metals (1968), Theoretical Solid State Physics (with W Jones, 1973), Self-Consistent Fields in Atoms (1974), Orbital Theories of Molecules and Solids (1974), Atomic Dynamics in Liquids (with M P Tosi, 1976), Collective Effects in Solids and Liquids (with M Parrinello, 1983), The Theory of the Inhomogeneous Electron Gas (with S Lundqvist, 1983), Coulomb Liquids (with M P Tosi, 1984), Amorphous Solids and the Liquid State (with M P Tosi, 1985), Chemical Bonds Outside Metal Surfaces (1986), Crystalline Semiconducting Materials and Devices (with P N Butcher and M P Tosi, 1986), The Single Particle Density in Physics and Chemistry (with B M Deb, 1987), Order and Chaos in Nonlinear Physical Systems (with S Lundqvist and M P Tosi, 1988), Electrons in Metals and Alloys (with J A Alonso, 1989), Liquid Metals - Concepts and Theory (1990), Chemical Physics of Liquids (1990), Electron Density Theory of Atoms and Molecules (1991), Chemical Physics of Free Molecules (with J F Mucci, 1993), Atoms and Molecules in Intense External Fields (with L S Cederbaum and K C Kulander, 1996); *Recreations* music, chess; *Style—* Prof Norman March; ✉ 6 Northcroft Rd, Egham, Surrey TW20 0DU

MARCH, Peter Reginald; s of Edwin Charles March (d 1987), of Bristol, and Alice Gladys, *née* Cave (d 1988); *b* 23 March 1940; *Educ* Bristol GS, Redland Coll, Univ of Bristol (ACE, DipEd); *m* 25 Aug 1962, Christine Ann, da of Ernest William Clark (d 1973), of Poole, Dorset; 2 s (Andrew b 1965, Daniel b 1972), 2 da (Alison b 1967, Rachel b 1974); *Career* contrib ed Aircraft Illustrated 1968–96; Careers Res and Advsy Centre 1972, princ careers advsr Co of Avon 1974–87, managing ed RAF Benevolent Funds IAT Publishing 1987–; freelance aviation broadcaster; aviation correspondent HTV West 1989–; chm Air Display Assoc UK 1994; ed: Air Display International 1987–92, RAF Yearbook, USAF Yearbook, Fighter Command Yearbook; contrib ed Air World International 1995–96; dir PRM Aviation Photo Library; *Books* 17+ Decisions - Your Choice Beyond School, Military Aircraft Markings (1978–95), Preserved Aircraft (1980), Confederate Air Force (1991), Civil Airliner Recognition (1991, 1993 and 1995), Desert Warpaint (1991), Combat Aircraft Recognition (1991), Light Aircraft Recognition (1992 and 1995), Brace by Wire to Fly by Wire (1993), International Air Tattoo 93 (1993), Royal Air Force Almanac (1994), International Air Tattoo 94 (1994), The Real Aviation Enthusiast II (1995), Hawk Comes of Age (1995), International Air Tattoo Silver Jubilee (1996); *Recreations* private flying, photography; *Style—* Peter March, Esq; ✉ PO Box 46, Westbury-on-Trym, Bristol BS9 1TF (☎ 0117 968 5193, fax 0117 968 3928)

MARCH AND KINRARA, Earl of; Charles Henry Gordon Lennox; o s and h of 10 Duke of Richmond and (4 Duke of) Gordon; *b* 8 Jan 1955; *Educ* Eton; *m* 1, 1976 (m dis 1989), Sally, da of late Maurice Clayton, and Mrs Dennis Irwin; 1 da (Lady Alexandra b 1985); m 2, 30 Nov 1991, Hon Janet Elizabeth Astor, da of 3 Viscount Astor (d 1966); 2 s (Charles Henry, Lord Settrington b 20 Dec 1994, Hon William b 29 Nov 1996); *Style—* Earl of March and Kinrara; ✉ Goodwood, Chichester, Sussex PO18 0PX

MARCHANT, Ian; s of Derek William Marchant, of Crawley, and Rosemary, *née* Bode; *b* 9 Feb 1961; *Educ* Trinity Sch Croydon, Univ of Durham (BA Econ); *m* Elizabeth Helen; 1 da (Sarah Elizabeth b 4 Dec 1990), 1 s (James Richard b 18 Aug 1994); *Career* with Coopers & Lybrand 1983–92 (seconded Dept of Energy 1989–90); Southern Electric plc: head of corp fin planning 1992–95, chief exec SE Power Generation 1995–96, gp fin dir 1996–; ACA 1983; *Recreations* golf, watching sport, travelling, reading; *Style—* Ian Marchant, Esq; ✉ Southern Electric plc, Westacott Way, Littlewick Green, Maidenhead, Berkshire SL6 3QB (☎ 01628 584611, fax 01628 584408, mobile 0385 111426)

MARCHANT, Leonard; s of Henry Marchant (ka 1945), of Cape Town, and Kathleen Marchant; *b* 23 Oct 1929; *Educ* St Joseph's Coll Cape Town, St Martin's Sch of Art, Central Sch of Art and Design; *Career* artist, specialist in mezzotint engraving; lectr in etching Fine Art Dept Central Sch of Art & Design London 1963–83; RE; *Solo exhibitions* Argus Gallery Cape Town 1950 and 1957, Lidchi Gallery Johannesburg 1957, Angela Flowers Gallery London 1975, The Pigeonhole London 1977 and 1980, Hogarth Galleries Sydney 1983, New Metropole Art Centre Folkestone 1985, Shrewsbury Sch 1986 and 1993, Pretoria Museum 1988, Michaelis Univ of Cape Town 1988, Hurlingham Gallery Chelsea 1989, Ludlow Assembly Rooms 1994; *Group exhibitions* incl: Royal Soc of Wood Engravers exhbn Craft Centre London 1962, Soc of Painter Etchers and Engravers (now Royal Soc of Painter Etchers) exhbns 1963, 1964, 1985, 1987, 1988, 1990 and 1994, Royal Academy Summer Exhibition 1970, 1971, 1972, 1974, 1982, 1984, 1989 and 1995, Bradford City Art Gallery 1966 and 1967, Printmakers' Council exhbns 1970 (touring) and 1972, Br Cncl Br Printmakers Exhbn 1968–70, International Contemporary Mezzotints London then Park Square Gallery Leeds 1974, Still Life - A New Life (Harris Museum and Art Gallery Preston then touring) 1985, 9th Int Biennale Bradford 1986, The Print Show (Angela Flowers Gallery London) 1986, Art in Bloomsbury (St George's Crypt London) 1988, Royal Soc of Painter Etchers and Engravers Moscow and Leningrad Exhbn 1989, Chelsea Arts Club Centennial Exhbn (Smiths Gallery London) 1991, Christmas Exhbn Waterman's Gallery Lndon 1992; *Collections* work in public collections incl: V&A, Museum of Contemporary Art Skopje Yugoslavia, Nat Gallery of S Africa Cape Town, Museum of Fine Art Boston Mass, Br Cncl, Arts Cncl, Bradford Museum, Univ of Southampton, Churchill Coll Cambridge, Ulster Museum, Birmingham Art Gallery, Whitworth Art Gallery Manchester; *Awards* Stet Prize Florence Biennale 1970, Grocers' fell Br Sch at Rome 1975, Christie's Contemporary Art Prize for best print in RE exhbn 1986; *Clubs* Chelsea Arts; *Style—* Leonard Marchant, Esq; ✉ Radnor House, Pountney Gardens, Belle Vue, Shrewsbury, Salop SY3 7LU (☎ 01743 367096)

MARCHANT, Peter James; s of Clifford James Marchant, of Bexhill, Sussex, and Vivian Breta, *née* Sargent; *b* 7 Sept 1943; *Educ* Bexhill GS for Boys, Portsmouth Poly (HND); *m* 4 Oct 1969, Angela May, da of Walter Sydney Foster; 1 s (Christopher James b 28 Aug 1970), 1 da (Helen Elizabeth b 10 July 1973); *Career* engr BBC Television Recording Dept 1966–69 (tech trainee BBC 1962–66), asst chief engr Centre for Educnl Television Overseas 1969; ITN: maintenance engr with special responsibility for intro of colour 1969–74, supervisory engr responsible for Television Standards conversion 1974–76, memb Mgmnt Team 1976–89, dep dir of engrg 1986–89; chief engr BBC Television 1989–94, chief engr (television) National Transcommunications Ltd (NTL) 1994–96, chief engr Channel Four Television Corporation 1996–; CEng, RTS, FIEE; *Recreations* flying (PPL), long distance road running, German language, playing the organ and piano; *Clubs* RAF Henlow Flying Club, N Herts Road Runners; *Style—* Peter Marchant; ✉ Channel Four Television Corporation, 124 Horseferry Road, London SW1P 2TX (☎ 0171 396 4444, fax 0171 306 8350)

MARCHWOOD, 3 Viscount (UK 1945); Sir David George Staveley Penny; 3 Bt (UK 1933); also Baron Marchwood (UK 1937); s of 2 Viscount Marchwood, MBE (d 1979), and Pamela, *née* Colton Fox; *b* 22 May 1936; *Educ* Winchester; *m* 1964, Tessa Jane, da of Wilfred Francis Norris, of Lurgashall, W Sussex; 3 s (Hon Peter, Hon Nicholas b 1967, Hon Edward b 1970); *Heir* s, Hon Peter George Worsley Penny b 8 Oct 1965; *Career* 2 Lt, Royal Horse Gds (The Blues) in UK and Cyprus 1955–57; former dir of various cos in Cadbury Schweppes Gp; md Moët & Chandon (London) Ltd; dir other cos in Moët Hennessy Gp; *Recreations* real tennis, shooting, racing; *Clubs* White's, Twelve, MCC; *Style—* The Rt Hon the Viscount Marchwood; ✉ Filberts, Aston Tirrold, nr Didcot, Oxon (☎ 01235 850386); 5 Buckingham Mews, London SW1 (☎ 0171 828 2678)

MARCUS, Steven David; s of Gerald Marcus, of Bushey, Herts, and Joan Kasmir; *b* 5 Oct 1951; *Educ* Merchant Taylors', Univ of Nottingham (BSc); *m* 5 Sept 1979, Madeleine, da of Godfrey Lee; *Career* Grant and Partners 1973–76 (jr negotiator, sr negotiator), Jones Lang Wootton 1976–78, assoc Allsop & Co 1978–84, ptnr then exec dir Druce & Co 1984–92 sr ptnr Marcus & Co 1992–; FRICS (prof assoc 1979); *Style—* Steven Marcus, Esq; ✉ Marcus & Co, Canons House, 7 Handel Close, Canons Drive, Edgware, Middx HA8 7QZ (☎ 0181 952 3636, fax 0181 952 6633)

MARDER, His Hon Judge; Bernard Arthur; QC (1977); s of Samuel Marder (d 1977), of St Annes-on-Sea, and Marie, *née* Solomons (d 1986); *b* 25 Sept 1928; *Educ* Bury GS, Univ of Manchester (LLB); *m* 1953, Sylvia Levy, MBE; 2 c; *Career* called to the Bar Gray's Inn 1952, principally practising in planning and local govt, recorder 1979–83, circuit judge (SE Circuit) 1983–; pres Lands Tbnl 1993–; chm: Richmond Parish Lands Charity, Tstees Richmond Museum; memb Bd Orange Tree Theatre; hon fell ISVA 1994; *Recreations* music (especially opera), theatre, video-editing; *Clubs* Royal Over-Seas League; *Style—* His Hon Judge Marder, QC; ✉ Lands Tribunal, 48–49 Chancery Lane, London WC2A 1JR (☎ 0171 936 7204, fax 0171 404 0896)

MAREK, Dr John; MP (Lab) Wrexham (majority 6,716); *b* 24 Dec 1940; *Educ* King's Coll London (BSc, PhD); *m* 1964, Anne, da of R H Pritchard; *Career* lectr in applied mathematics Univ Coll Wales Aberystwyth 1966–83; MP (Lab) Wrexham 1983–; oppn front bench spokesman on health 1985–87, oppn front bench spokesman on Civil Service and Treasy matters 1987–92; memb Int Astronomical Union; *Style—* Dr John Marek, MP; ✉ House of Commons, London SW1A 0AA (☎ 0171 219 6347); office (☎ 01978 364334)

MARENBON, Dr John Alexander; s of Arthur Marenbon (d 1984), of London, and Zena, *née* Jacobs; *b* 26 Aug 1955; *Educ* Westminster, Trinity Coll Cambridge (MA, PhD); *m* 1981, Sheila Margaret Mary, da of Arthur C Lawlor; 1 s (Maximus John Arthur b 10 Dec 1989); *Career* Trinity Coll of Cambridge: res fell 1978–79, fell and dir of studies in English 1979–, British Acad res reader 1991–93; memb Schs Examination and Assessment Cncl (SEAC) 1992–93; *Books* From the Circle of Alcuin to the School of Auxerre (1981), Early Medieval Philosophy (1983), Later Medieval Philosophy (1987), Aristotle in Britain during the Middle Ages (1996), The Philosophy of Peter Abelard (1997); *Style—* Dr John Marenbon; ✉ Trinity College, Cambridge CB2 1TQ (☎ 01223 338524)

MARGADALE, Maj 2 Baron (UK 1964); James Ian Morrison; TD (1963), DL (Wilts 1977); s of 1 Baron Margadale, TD (d 1996), and Margaret Esther Lucy, *née* Smith, da of 3 Viscount Hambleden (d 1980); bro of Hon Sir Charles Andrew Morrison, DL, *qv*, Hon Mary Anne Morrison, DCVO, *qv*, and Rt Hon Sir Peter Morrison (d 1995); ggs of James Morrison who purchased much of the property at present owned; *b* 17 July 1930; *Educ* Eton, RAC Cirencester; *m* 1952, Clare, da of Anthony Lister Barclay, of Broad Oak End, Hertford; 2 s (Hon Alastair John b 1958, Hon Hugh b 1960), 1 da (Hon Fiona Elizabeth (Viscountess Trenchard) b 1954); *Heir* s, Hon Alastair John Morrison b 4 April 1958; *Career* 2 Lt Life Gds 1949–50, Maj Royal Wilts Yeo; farmer, landowner and co dir; Wilts Co cncllr 1955 and 1973–77, alderman 1969, High Sheriff Wilts 1971; pres W Wilts (Westbury) Cons Assoc 1972–84 (chm 1967–71); chm: Tattersalls Ctee 1969–80, Wilts CLA 1978–81; Hon Col: A (Royal Wilts Yeo) Sqdn Royal Yeo RAC TA 1982–89, (Royal Wilts Yeo) Sqdn Royal Wessex Yeo 1982–89, Royal Wessex Yeo RAC TA 1984–89; memb: Queen's Body Guard for Scotland (Royal Company of Archers); *Recreations* racing, field sports; *Clubs* White's, Jockey; *Style*— Maj the Rt Hon Lord Margadale, TD, DL; ✉ Hawking Down, Hindon, Salisbury, Wilts (☎ 01747 820234); Estate Office, Fonthill Bishop, Salisbury SP3 5SH (☎ 01747 820246); Islay Estate Office, Bridgend, Islay, Argyll PA44 7PB (☎ 01496 810221)

MARGESSON, 2 Viscount (UK 1942); Francis Vere Hampden Margesson; s of 1 Viscount, PC, MC (d 1965, whose mother was Lady Isabel Hobart-Hampden, JP, 3 da of 7 Earl of Buckinghamshire); *b* 17 April 1922; *Educ* Eton, Trinity Coll Oxford; *m* 1958, Helena, da of late Heikki Backstrom, of Oulu, Finland; 1 s, 3 da; *Heir* s, Maj the Hon Richard Francis David Margesson, *qv*; *Career* late ADC to Govr Bahamas, dir Thames & Hudson Publications Inc of N Y; Sub-Lt RNVR 1942–45; info offr Br Consulate-Gen N Y 1964–70; *Style*— The Rt Hon the Viscount Margesson; ✉ Ridgely Manor, Box 245, Stone Ridge, New York, NY 12484, USA

MARGESSON, Maj the Hon Richard Francis David; s and h of 2 Viscount Margesson; *b* 25 Dec 1960; *Educ* St Paul's Sch New Hampshire USA, Eton, Exeter Univ; *m* 15 Dec 1990, Wendy Maree, da of James Hazelton, of Kempsey, NSW, Australia; 1 da (Isabel b 28 June 1995); *Career* cmmnd Coldstream Guards 1983; *Clubs* Cavalry and Guards'; *Style*— Maj the Hon Richard Margesson

MARGETSON, Sir John William Denys; KCMG (1986, CMG 1979); s of Very Rev W J Margetson (d 1946), and Marion, *née* Jenoure (d 1937); *b* 9 Oct 1927; *Educ* Blundell's, St John's Coll Cambridge (choral scholar, MA); *m* 1963, Miranda, da of Sir William Coldstream, CBE; 1 s (Andrew b 1965), 1 da (Clare b 1967); *Career* Lt Life Gds 1947–49; dist offr Colonial Serv Tanganyika 1951–60 (private sec to Govr 1956–57); Dip Serv 1960–87: The Hague 1962–64, speech writer for Rt Hon George Brown MP 1966–68, head of chancery Saigon 1968–70, seconded to Cabinet Secretariat 1971–74; head of chancery UK Delgn to NATO 1974–78, ambass Vietnam 1978–80, seconded to MOD as sr civilian instr Royal Coll of Def Studies 1980–82, ambass and dep perm rep UN NY 1983–84, pres UN Trusteeship Cncl 1983–84, ambass Netherlands 1984–87; dir John S Cohen Fndn 1988–93; chm: Royal Sch of Church Music 1988–94, Foster Parents Plan (UK) 1988–90, Yehudi Menuhin Sch 1990–94, Jt Ctee London Royal Schs of Music 1991–94; patron Suffolk Int Trade Gp 1988–90, jt pres Suffolk and SE Cambridgeshire 1992 Club 1988–90; tstee: Fitzwilliam Museum Tst 1990–, Ouseley Tst 1991–; Gentleman Usher of the Blue Rod 1992–; special rep of Sec of State for Foreign and Cwlth Affrs 1994–; FRSCM, Hon RCM; *Recreations* music and the arts; *Clubs* Brooks's; *Style*— Sir John Margetson, KCMG

MARGO, David Philip; s of Gerald Margo, of Bexleyheath, Kent, and Rene, *née* Goldstein; *b* 14 May 1951; *Educ* Chislehurst and Sidcup GS for Boys; *m* 14 Nov 1976, Lezley Susan (d 1991), da of Maurice and Helen Kaye, of Bournemouth, Dorset; 1 s (Alexi Nicholas b 1981), 2 da (Jodi Rochelle b 1980, Kerri Miriam b 1984); *Career* admitted slr 1975; ptnr Forsyte Saunders Kerman (formerly Saunders Sobell Leigh & Dobin); memb Law Soc; *Recreations* bridge, swimming; *Style*— David Margo, Esq

MARGRETT, David Basil; s of Basil Stanley Margrett, of Yelverton, Devon, and Kathleen Hilda Nellie, *née* Hayter; *b* 25 Oct 1953; *Educ* Plymouth Poly; *m* 15 March 1985, Pauline Annette, da of Donald Lowe; 2 s (Charles, Richard); *Career* gp chief exec Lowndes Lambert Group Holdings plc 1995–; *Style*— David Margrett, Esq; ✉ 60 Deansway, E Finchley, London N2 0JE; Lowndes Lambert Group Holdings plc, Lowndes Lambert House, Friary Court, Crutched Friars, London EC3N 2NP (☎ 0171 560 3552, fax 0171 560 3551)

MARGRIE, Prof Victor Robert; CBE (1984); s of Robert Margrie, of London, and Emily Miriam, *née* Corbett; *b* 29 Dec 1929; *Educ* Southgate Co GS, Hornsey Sch of Art (NDD, ATD); *m* 1955 (sep 1988), Janet, *née* Smithers; 3 da (Joanna b 19 Oct 1959, Kate b 26 Dec 1961, Miriam b 10 Sept 1963); *Career* own workshop 1952–71, pt/t teaching London Colls of Art and Design 1952–56, head of ceramics and sculpture Harrow Sch of Art 1956–71 (fndr studio pottery course 1963), solo exhibitions Crafts Centre of GB (now Contemporary Applied Arts) 1964, 1966 and 1968, prof RCA 1984–85; prof Univ of Westminster 1992–96; studio potter, critic and teacher 1985–; external advsr Univ of the W of England: Dept of Ceramics 1987–, Nat Video and Electronic Archive of the Crafts 1993–; external advsr: Goldsmiths' Coll London 1989–93, Sch of Fine Art Cardiff Inst of Higher Educn 1991–93; memb Bd Studies in Fine Art Univ of London 1989–94; memb Faculty of Visual Arts Banff Centre for the Arts Alberta 1988–, sec Crafts Advsy Ctee 1971–77, dir Crafts Cncl 1977–84; memb: Advsy Cncl Victoria and Albert Museum 1979–84, Ctee for Art and Design CNAA 1981–84, Fine Art Advsy Ctee Br Cncl 1983–86, UK Nat Cmmn UNESCO 1984–85; govr Loughborough Coll of Art and Design 1984–92, memb Craft Initiative Gulbenkian Fndn 1985–89; memb: Craftsmen Potters Assoc 1960–89, Int Acad of Ceramics 1971, FCSD 1975; *Books* contrib: Europaischt Keramik Seit 1950–79 (1979), Oxford Dictionary of Decorative Arts (1975), Lucie Rie (1981); assoc ed Studio Pottery 1993–; *Recreations* cooking; *Style*— Prof Victor Margrie, CBE; ✉ Bowlders, Doccombe, Moretonhampstead, Devon TQ13 8SS (☎ 01647 440264)

MARINO, Joseph Robert; s of late Joseph Etiene Marino, and Gladys, *née* Brown; *b* 6 Oct 1946; *Educ* Newall Green Sch, TEC Dip in Economics; *m* (Mary Rose) Elaine, *née* Campbell; 2 da (Michelle b 25 Sept 1973, Claire b 31 May 1976); *Career* W J Brookes Old Trafford Gtr Manchester 1968–74, Jesse Oldfield Old Trafford Gtr Mancester 1975–79, gen sec Bakers, Food and Allied Workers' Union 1979– (memb Exec Cncl 1972–79); *Recreations* cricket (memb CCC), reading, music, walking, Sherlock Holmes studies; *Clubs* Victoria (Westminster); *Style*— Joseph Marino, Esq; ✉ Bakers, Food and Allied Workers' Union, Stanborough House, Great North Road, Stanborough, Welwyn Garden City, Herts AL8 7TA (☎ 01707 269501, fax 01707 261570)

MARJORIBANKS, Sir James Alexander Milne; KCMG (1965, CMG 1954); s of Rev Thomas Marjoribanks of that Ilk, DD (d 1947); *b* 29 May 1911; *Educ* Edinburgh Acad, Univ of Edinburgh (MA), Univ of Strasbourg; *m* 1936, Sonya Patricia Stanley Alder (d 1981); 1 da; *Career* HM Dip Serv 1934–71: asst under sec of state FCO 1962–65, ambass to EEC Euro Atomic Energy Community and ECSC 1965–71; dir The Distillers' Co 1971–76; chm Scot in Europe 1979–90; vice-pres Scottish Cncl (devpt and indust) 1971–83; governing memb Inveresk Res Fndn 1979–89; Europe Medal 1973; *Recreations* mountaineering; *Clubs* Scot Mountaineering, New (Edinburgh); *Style*— Sir James Marjoribanks, KCMG; ✉ 13 Regent Terrace, Edinburgh, Scotland EH7 5BN (☎ 0131 556 3872)

MARK, Jan Marjorie; da of Colin Dennis Brisland, and Marjorie, *née* Harrow; *b* 22 June 1943; *Educ* Ashford County GS, Canterbury Coll of Art; *m* 1 March 1969 (m dis 1989), Neil John Mark; 1 s (Alexander b 1974), 1 da (Isobel b 1969); *Career* freelance writer 1975–, writer fell Oxford Poly 1982–84; *Awards* Penguin/Guardian Award 1975, Library Assoc Carnegie Medal 1976 and 1983, Rank/Observer Award 1982, Angel Award for Fiction 1983 and 1987; *Books* Thunder & Lightnings (1976), The Ennead (1978), Divide and Rule (1979), Aquarius (1982), Feet (1983), Handles (1984), Zeno Was Here (1987), Enough is Too Much Already (1988), A Can of Worms (1990), The Hillingdon Fox (1991), Great Frog and Mighty Moose (1992), The Oxford Book of Children's Stories (1993), They Do Things Differently There (1994), A Fine Summer Knight (1995); *Recreations* gardening; *Style*— Ms Jan Mark; ✉ 98 Howard Street, Oxford OX4 3BG (☎ 01865 727702); c/o David Higham Associates Ltd, 5–8 Lower John Street, Golden Square, London W1R 4HA (☎ 0171 437 7888, fax 0171 437 1072)

MARK, (John) Richard Anthony; s of John Mark, and Dorothy, *née* White; *b* 20 Jan 1946; *Educ* Clifton, Magdalene Coll Cambridge (MA); *m* 1, 30 Sept 1972 (m dis 1979), Angela Mary, da of Jeffrey Holroyd; 1 s (James b 1975), 1 da (Clare b 1973); *m* 2, 31 March 1983, Diane Virginia, *née* Roberts; 1 da (Isabel b 1985); *Career* Peat Marwick Mitchell & Co 1967–73, British Linen Bank 1973–77, currently md banking NationsBank Europe (formerly Panmure Gordon Bankers Ltd); FCA 1970, MSI 1993; *Style*— Richard Mark, Esq; ✉ NationsBank, 35 New Broad Street, London EC2M 1NH (☎ 0171 638 8888)

MARK, Sir Robert; GBE (1977), kt (1973), QPM (1965); s of John Mark (d 1962); *b* 13 March 1917; *Educ* William Hulme's GS Manchester; *m* 1941, Kathleen Mary, da of William Leahy (d 1977); 1 s (Christopher), 1 da (Christina); *Career* served WWII RAC, Maj, NW Europe 1942–47; chief constable Leicester 1957–67, cmmr London Met Police 1972–77 (dep cmmr 1968–72); dir Phoenix Assurance Co 1977–85, chm Forest Mere Ltd 1978–91, dir Control Risks Ltd 1979–87; Dimbleby TV Lecture 1973; govr and memb Admin Bd Corps of Commissionaires 1977–86; visiting fell Nuffield Coll Oxford 1970–78 (MA 1971); Hon LLM Leicester 1967, Hon DLitt Loughborough 1976; Hon LLD: Manchester 1978, Liverpool 1978; KStJ 1977; *Publications*Policing a Perplexed Society (1977), In the Office of Constable (1978); *Style*— Sir Robert Mark, GBE, QPM; ✉ Esher, Surrey KT10 8LU

MARKESINIS, Prof Basil Spyridonos; s of Spyros Markesinis, former Prime Minister of Greece, and Ieta Markesinis; *b* 10 July 1944; *Educ* Univ of Athens (LLB, DIur), Univ of Cambridge (Yorke prize, MA, PhD, LLD), DCL (Oxon); *m* 5 Sept 1970, Eugenie, da of late George Trypanis; 1 da (Julietta b 6 July 1971), 1 s (Spyros George b 30 Jan 1976); *Career* asst prof Law Faculty Univ of Athens 1965–68; Univ of Cambridge: res fell Churchill Coll 1970–73, fell of Trinity Coll and dir of studies in law 1974–86, univ lectr 1974–86; Denning prof of comparative Law Univ of London 1986–93 (dep dir Centre for Commercial Law Studies Queen Mary & Westfield Colls), prof of European private law UCL 1993–95, fndr and dir Centre for European Law Studies and prof of European law Univ of Oxford 1995–; prof of Anglo-American private law Univ of Leiden 1986–, fndr and dir Leiden Inst of Anglo-American Law; visiting prof Univ of Paris I & II 1982–83, Francqui visiting prof Univ of Ghent 1989–90, professore a contrato Univ of Siena 1985–86; visiting prof: Cornell Law Sch (fall terms) 1981–84, Univ of Michigan Ann Arbor (fall term) 1986, Univ of Texas at Austin (fall terms) 1985 and 1987–94; called to the Bar Gray's Inn 1973 (bencher 1991), advocate to the Supreme Ct Athens 1976–86; memb: Int Acad of Comparative Law 1987, American Law Inst 1989, Institut Canadien d'Etudes Juridiques Supérieures 1990; membre actif Cour d'Arbitrage et de Conciliation Paris 1991; corresponding memb Unidroit 1992; corresponding fell: Royal Belgian Acad 1990, Royal Netherlands Acad of Arts and Sciences 1995; fell Acad of Athen 1994; Atkin lectr Reform Club 1989, Shimihzu lectr LSE 1991, Cohen lectr Hebrew Univ of Jerusalem 1993; Hon DIur Univ of Ghent 1989, Leverhulme fell 1981; Offr Order of Merit (FDR) 1992, Offr Ordre Nationale des Palmes Académiques (France) 1992, Cavaliere Ufficiale del Ordine al Merito (Republic of Italy) 1995, Chevalier dans l'Ordre National de la Légion d'Honneur 1995, Humboldt Forschungspreise 1995; *Books* The Mother's Right to Guardianship According to the Greek Civil Code (1968), The Theory and Practice of Dissolution of Parliament (1972), The English Law of Torts - A Comparative Introduction (1976), An Outline of the Law of Agency (co-author, 1979, 3rd edn 1990), Tortious Liability for Unintentional Harm in the Common Law and the Civil Law Vol I & II (co-author vol I and II, 1982), Tort Law (co-author, 1984, 3rd edn 1994), La Réparation du Préjudice Corporel (co-author, 1985), The German Law of Torts - A Comparative Introduction (1986, 3rd edn 1994), The Gradual Covergence - Foreign Ideas, Foreign Influences on English Law on the Eve of the 21st Century (ed and contrib, 1994), Bridging the Channel (ed and contrib, 1996), The German Law of Contract and Restitution (co-author, 1997); author of numerous articles in US, Belgian, British, Canadian, French, German, Greek and Italian law jls; *Recreations* painting, music, archaeological digging; *Style*— Prof Basil Markesinis; ✉ Faculty of Laws, St Cross Building, St Cross Road, Oxford OX1 3UL (☎ 01865 281610, fax 01865 281611); Middleton Stoney House, Middleton Stoney, Bicester, Oxfordshire (☎ 01869 343560)

MARKEY, Air Vice-Marshal Peter Desmond; s of Althorpe Hazel Christopher Markey, and Marjorie Joyce, *née* Thomas; *b* 28 March 1943; *Educ* RAF Coll Cranwell, Open Univ (BA 1980), Cranfield Univ (MSc 1994); *m* 1966, Judith Mary Widdowson; 1 s, 1 da; *Career* cmmnd supply offr RAF 1964, served Singapore, France and UK until 1981, Nat Def Coll 1981–82, HQ Strike Cmd 1982–83, HQ AFCENT The Netherlands 1983–85, MoD Carlisle 1986–88, station cdr Carlisle 1988–89, RCDS 1990, Central Staff MoD 1991, Dept of AMSO 1991, HQ Logistics Cmd 1994, dir gen of Support Mgmnt RAF 1995–; author of various papers and contribs to learned jls; *Recreations* running, mountain walking, caravanning; *Clubs* RAF; *Style*— Air Vice-Marshal Peter Markey, OBE; ✉ Headquarters Logistics Command, Royal Air Force Brampton, Huntingdon, Cambs PE18 8QL (☎ 01480 52151 ext 6502, fax 01480 413563)

MARKHAM, Sir Charles John; 3 Bt (UK 1911), of Beachborough Park, Newington, Kent; s of Sir Charles Markham, 2 Bt (d 1952); *b* 2 July 1924; *Educ* Eton; *m* 1949, Valerie, o da of Lt-Col E Barry-Johnston, of Kenya; 2 s ((Arthur) David b 1950, Richard Barry b 1954), 1 da (Elizabeth-Anne (Mrs Peter J Bateman) b 1958); *Heir* s, (Arthur) David Markham; *Career* served WWII 1943–47, Lt 11 Hussars (despatches); MLC Kenya 1955–60; KStJ; *Style*— Sir Charles Markham, Bt; ✉ PO Box 42263, Nairobi, Kenya

MARKHAM, (Arthur) Geoffrey; s of Col Frank Stanley Markham (d 1978), of Huddersfield, and Emma Woodhouse, *née* Spurr (d 1983); *b* 27 Sept 1927; *Educ* Giggleswick Sch, Univ of Leeds (LLB); *m* 26 Sept 1959, Patricia, da of John James Holliday (d 1935), of Barnsley, Yorks; 1 s (Jonathan b 1962), 1 da (Sarah b 1966); *Career* admitted slr 1949, sr ptnr Raley and Pratt Barnsley 1967–89, conslt Raleys Barnsley 1990–; chm Soc Security Appeal Tribunal 1981–95; historian; memb Law Soc 1949–; *Books* Woolley Hall, The Historical Development of a Country House (1979); *Recreations* reading, writing, music, freemasonry, gardening; *Style*— Geoffrey Markham, Esq; ✉ Petwood House, Woolley, Wakefield WF4 2JJ (☎ 01226 382495); 5 Regent St, Barnsley S70 2EF (☎ 01226 211111, fax 01226 211112)

MARKHAM, Dr Gillian Christine; da of Harry Markham, of Plympton St Maurice, nr Plymouth, and Irene Mary, *née* Aspinwall; *b* 22 Dec 1948; *Educ* Plympton GS, Univ of Liverpool Med Sch (MB ChB, DObstRCG, DMRD, FRCR); *m* Oct 1972, James North Johnson, s of late Edwin Johnson; 1 da (Katharine Sarah Markham b 2 Oct 1987), 1 s (Charles Henry North b 15 Jan 1990); *Career* house offr Clatterbridge Hosp Wirral, obstetrics and gynaecology house offr Broadgreen 1971–72, paediatrics house offr Myrtle Street Children's Hosp 1972, radiological trg course Univ of Liverpool and on Mersey rotation 1972–77, conslt radiologist Whiston and St Helens Hosps 1977–, clinical lectr Dept of Radio-Diagnosis Univ of Liverpool 1978–; memb: Liverpool Med Instn 1970 (hon sec 1984–87, vice pres 1988), Med Women's Fedn Exec 1978–94 (treas 1983–89, pres 1993–94), Editorial Bd Medical Woman 1986–91, GMC 1994– (dep chm Assessment Referral Ctee 1996–); regnl educnl advsr RCR 1990–94; BMA: hon sec Mersey Conslts and Specialists Ctee 1995–, memb Central Conslt Specialists Ctee 1989–, memb Career Progress of Doctors Ctee 1993–, memb Radiological Sub-ctee 1993–; *Recreations* listening to music (particularly opera), choral singing, travel, sports (formerly county tennis, University badminton/squash and swimming), family activities; *Clubs* Reform; *Style*—

Dr Gillian Markham; ✉ Talgarth, 66 View Road, Rainhill, Prescot, Merseyside L35 0LS (☎ 0151 426 4306); Whiston Hospital, Prescot, Merseyside L35 5DR (☎ 0151 430 1265, fax 0151 430 1626); 35 Rodney Street, Liverpool, Merseyside L1 9EN (☎ 0151 708 7410, fax 0151 708 6950)

MARKHAM, Jane Frances; da of Keith Markham, of Somerset, and Rosemary Anne, *née* Aste; *b* 11 June 1957; *Educ* Weirfield Sch Taunton, Taunton Sch, LAMDA (teacher's dip), London Coll of Printing, Middx Poly; *partner* Bill Broomfield; *Career* sec, res and PA London Weekend TV and Capital Radio 1981–83, bdcaster AA Roadwatch Unit 1983–85, reporter Newsbeat BBC Radio 1 1985–89, newsreader Breakfast Time and London Plus BBC TV 1985–89; Fox FM: head of news and dep prog controller 1989–91, presenter and ed Fox Report (winner Sony Radio Awards best daily news prog 1991); sr prodr Danny Baker's Morning Edition BBC Radio 5 1992–93, freelance broadcaster/prodr 1993, presenter Classic FM 1994–; memb: NUJ, Equity; *Style—* Ms Jane Markham; ✉ c/o Unique Broadcasting Company, 50 Lisson Street, London NW1 5DF

MARKHAM, Richard; s of Charles Roberts Markham, of Grimsby, and Marion Edna, *née* Willows; *b* 23 June 1952; *Educ* Wintringham GS Grimsby, RAM London; *Career* concert pianist; London début as soloist with Eng Chamber Orch under Raymond Leppard (Queen Elizabeth Hall) 1974, has toured internationally with David Nettle, *qv*, (Nettle-Markham Piano Duo), also with Raphael Wallfisch (cello) and Burlington Piano Trio; solo and piano duo performances at: Royal Festival Hall, Royal Albert Hall, Barbican Hall and at various major festivals incl BBC Proms; ARAM 1983; *Recordings* incl: works by Kabalevsky, Stravinsky and Rachmaninov (with Raphael Wallfisch on cello) 1976, Stravinsky's Rite of Spring and Petrushka (with David Nettle) 1984, Holst's The Planets 1985, Dyson's The Blacksmiths (with RCM Chamber Choir and RPO, 1987), Elgar's From the Bavarian Highlands 1987, Holst's Folksongs and works by Delius and Grainger 1988, Scenes from (Bernstein's) West Side Story (arranged and performed with David Nettle), Grainger's Fantasy on (Gershwin's) Porgy and Bess and Bennett's Four Piece Suite 1988, Rossini's Petite Messe Solennelle (with soloists Field, Owens, Barham and Tomlinson and CBSO chorus) 1990, South of The Border - Latin American Songs with Jill Gomez (with two pianos and NPO, 1990), Saint-Saens' Carnival of Animals (with Aquarius, 1991), Nettle and Markham in England 1993, Arnold's Concerto for Piano Duet 1993, Concerto for Two Pianos 1994, Nettle and Markham in France 1995; *Awards* Nora Naismith Scholarship 1969–72, prizewinner Geneva Int Competition 1972, Countess of Munster Musical Tst Awards 1973 and 1974, Frederick Shinn Fellowship 1975, Gulbenkian Fndn Fellowship 1976–78, Music Retailers Assoc Award for Best Chamber Music Record 1985; *Recreations* travelling, theatre, playing cards, swimming, naturism; *Clubs* ISM, RAM; *Style—* Richard Markham, Esq; ✉ The Old Power House, Atherton Street, London SW11 2JE (☎ and fax 0171 738 2765)

MARKHAM, Sarah Anne Judith; da of Leonard Markham, of Tithe Farm, Renhold, Bedfordshire, and Margaret Elizabeth, *née* Joyce; *b* 25 July 1962; *Educ* Bedford High Sch, Oxford and County; *Career* Shuttleworth Coll staff 1981–88, Christie's Old Master Picture Dept 1988–93, Sotheby's Old Master Paintings Dept 1993–95, art dealer 1995–; *Recreations* riding, travelling, wildlife conservation; *Clubs* The Farmers'; *Style—* Miss Sarah Markham; ✉ Tithe Farm, Renhold, Bedfordshire MK41 0LX (☎ 01234 771364, fax 01234 772337)

MARKING, Giles; s of Frank I Marking, of Wareham, Dorset, and Anne, *née* Percival; *b* 26 Dec 1947; *Educ* Duncan Hall Norfolk, Architectural Assoc Sch of Architecture (AADipl), Univ of Washington (MArch); *m* 11 Sept 1971, (Margaret Judith) Stacy, da of Canon R Patteson Stacy-Waddy, of Hindhead, Surrey; 1 da (Havana b 6 March 1972); *Career* designer Francisco and Jacobus NY 1967–68, film designer Maizin Wycoff NY 1968–70, graphic designer Inst of Contemporary Arts 1971–74, lectr in architecture Univ of Washington 1975–76, visiting prof Univ Metropolitana Mexico City 1980, currently dir and sr conslt Fitch plc (joined as md 1976); FCSD; *Books* Emergency Housing in Peru - Architectural Design; *Recreations* travel, sheep farming, India and cricket; *Style—* Giles Marking, Esq; ✉ 5 Mercer St, Covent Garden, London WC2 (☎ 0171 240 2345); The Manor, Toller Whelme, Beaminster, Dorset (☎ 01308 862339); Fitch plc, No 1 New Oxford Street, London WC1 (☎ 0171 208 8000)

MARKING, Sir Henry Ernest; KCVO (1978), CBE (1969), MC (1944); s of Isaac Marking; *b* 11 March 1920; *Educ* Saffron Walden GS, UCL; *Career* served WWII Sherwood Foresters (N Africa, ME, Italy); admitted slr 1948; asst slr BEA 1949 (chief exec 1964–72, chm 1971–72); memb Bd: BOAC 1971–72, BA 1971–80 (md 1972–76, dep chm 1972–77); chm: Br Tourist Authy 1977–85 (memb bd 1969–77), Carreras Rothmans 1979–85, Rothmans (UK) Ltd 1985–86; dir: Barclays International Ltd 1978–86, Rothmans International plc 1979–86; tstee The Leonard Cheshire Fndn 1962–95; CRAeS, FCIT, FIMgt; *Clubs* Reform; *Style—* Sir Henry Marking, KCVO, CBE, MC; ✉ 6A Montagu Mews North, London W1H 1AH

MARKOVA, Dame (Lilian) Alicia; DBE (1963, CBE 1958); da of Arthur Tristman Marks and Eileen Barry; *b* 1 Dec 1910; *Career* Diaghilev's Russian Ballet Co 1925–29, Rambert Ballet Club 1931–34, Vic-Wells Ballet Co 1933–35, Markova-Dolin Ballet Co 1935–37, Ballet Russe de Monte Carlo 1938–41, Ballet Theatre USA 1941–46, co fndr and prima ballerina Festival Ballet 1950–51, Br prima ballerina assoluta; guest prima ballerina: La Scala Milan 1956, Buenos Aires 1952, Royal Ballet 1953 and 1957, Royal Danish Ballet 1955, Festival Ballet 1958 and 1959; guest appearances at Metropolitan Opera House New York 1952, 1953–54, 1955, 1957, 1958; vice pres Royal Acad of Dancing 1958–, dir Metropolitan Opera Ballet 1963–69; guest prof: Royal Ballet Sch 1973–, Paris Opera Ballet 1975, Australian Ballet Sch 1976; prof of Ballet and Performing Arts College-Conservatory of Music Univ of Cincinnati 1970–; govr Royal Ballet 1973–; pres: London Ballet Circle 1980–, All England Dance Competition 1983–, Arts Educnl Schs 1984–, London Festival Ballet (now English Nat Ballet) and Sch 1986–; BBC series Markova's Ballet Call 1960, Masterclass BBC2 1980; Queen Elizabeth II Coronation award Royal Acad of Dancing 1963, Special Award Evening Standard Ballet, Opera and Classical Music Awards 1995, Woman of Distinction Award 1995; Hon DMus: Leicester 1966, East Anglia 1982; prof Yorkshire Ballet Seminars 1975–; int conslt 1990–; *Books* Giselle and I (1960), Markova Remembers (1986); *Style—* Dame Alicia Markova, DBE; ✉ c/o Royal Ballet School, London W14 9DE

MARKS, Bernard Montague; OBE (1984); s of Alfred Marks (d 1942), and Elizabeth Marks (d 1972); *b* 11 Oct 1923; *Educ* Highgate, Imperial Coll London; *m* 11 Oct 1956, Norma Delphine (d 1990), da of Jack Renton (d 1972); 2 s (Nicholas b 1952, Stephen b 1959); *Career* chm and md Alfred Marks Bureau Group of Cos 1946–84 (life pres 1984–); memb Equal Opportunities Cmmn 1984–85; vice chm (later chm) Fedn of Personnel Serv 1965–69 and 1973–82; *Recreations* bridge, golf; *Clubs* St George's Hill Golf; *Style—* Bernard Marks, Esq, OBE; ✉ Flat G, 29 Eaton Square, London SW1W 9DF

MARKS, David Norman; s of Alex Marks, of London, and Edna, *née* Dufman; *b* 13 Feb 1953; *Educ* Orange Hill GS Edgware Middx, LSE (BSc Econ); *m* 22 June 1975, Selina Rachael, da of Michael Sharpe, of London; 2 s (Daniel b 1980, James b 1982); *Career* accountant; Arthur Andersen 1974– (tax ptnr 1984); FCA 1978, ATII 1979; *Books* Practical Tax Saving (jtly, 1984), Tax Digest on Share Incentive Schemes for Institute of Chartered Accountants in England and Wales (1994), Profit-Related Pay (jtly, 1995); *Recreations* theatre, music; *Style—* David Marks, Esq; ✉ Arthur Andersen, 1 Surrey St, London WC2R 2PS (☎ 0171 438 3429, fax 0171 438 3004)

MARKS, Dennis Michael; s of Samuel Marks, of Hove, East Sussex, and Kitty, *née* Ostrovsky; *b* 2 July 1948; *Educ* Haberdashers' Aske's, Trinity Coll Cambridge (BA); *m* 12 Oct 1992, Sally Hilary Groves; 1 da (Gabriella Nicole b 14 June 1974), 1 s (Benjamin Adam b 27 Feb 1979); *Career* various posts in teaching, research and acting 1969–70, freelance researcher, dir and prodr 1970–77, prodr BBC Music and Arts (series prodr Arena Art and Design, dir numerous documentaries for Omnibus, Arena and others) 1975–78, fndr (with Barrie Gavin and Tony Staveacre) BBC Bristol Arts Unit (various prodns for BBC) 1978–81, co-fndr Third Eye Productions (work for BBC, Granada and Channel 4) 1981–85, ed Music Features BBC TV 1985–88, asst head Music and Arts Dept BBC TV 1988–91, head of Music Programmes BBC TV 1991–93, gen dir ENO 1993–; regular arts journalism contribs to New Statesman, The Listener, Time Out, Opera Now and others 1970–; pres IMZ Int Music Centre Vienna 1989–92, dep chm Arts Cncl Film and Video Panel 1990–93 (memb Contemporary Music Panel 1976–79), tstee London Opera Festival; *Awards* Int EMMY 1987, Italia Prize 1989; *Books* Great Railway Journeys of the World (contrib, 1981), Repercussions (contrib, 1985); *Recreations* cooking, travel; *Style—* Dennis Marks, Esq; ✉ General Director, English National Opera, London Coliseum, St Martin's Lane, London WC2N 4ES (☎ 0171 836 0111)

MARKS, Geoffrey Robert; s of Nathan Marks (d 1985), and Lily, *née* Bargroff; *b* 22 Dec 1941; *Educ* Arnold Sch Blackpool, Lancaster Gate Coll of Law London (G H Charlesworth scholar, George Hadfield prize); *m* 1967, Rachel, *née* Stemmer; 2 s (Daniel Richard b 1971, John Edward b 1974), 1 da (Karen Ilana b 1969); *Career* articled clerk then ptnr A H Howarth & Co Manchester (later Howarth Goodman & Co) 1964–74; ptnr: Maurice Rubin & Co 1974–85, Halliwell Landau 1985–; former co cncllr then chm Mgmnt Ctee Gtr Manchester CC (now abolished); memb Law Soc 1963; ACIArb; *Recreations* the study of ancient and contemporary Hebrew, politics, theatre, family, friends; *Clubs* Manchester Anglers' Assoc; *Style—* Geoffrey Marks, Esq; ✉ Hilton House, Bland Rd, Prestwich, Manchester M25 8WL (☎ 0161 773 6092); Halliwell Landau, St James's Court, Brown St, Manchester M2 2JF (☎ 0161 835 3003, fax 0161 835 2994, car 0585 571211)

MARKS, Prof Isaac Meyer; s of Moshe Nahman Marks (d 1979), of Cape Town, and Anna Marks (d 1981); *b* 16 Feb 1935; *Educ* Univ of Cape Town (MB ChB, MD), Univ of London (DPM); *m* 14 Oct 1957, Shula Eta, *qv*, da of Chaim Winokur (d 1957), of Cape Town; 1 da (Lara b 1963), 1 s (Rafi b 1965); *Career* prof of experimental psychopathology Int of Psychiatry London, conslt psychiatrist Royal Bethlem Maudsley Hosp London; former pres Assoc of Behavioural Clinicians; former chm: Br Assoc of Behavioural Psychotherapy, European Assoc of Behavioural Therapy; FRCPsych 1971; *Books* inter alia: Living with Fear (1978), Fears Phobias and Rituals (1987); *Recreations* theatre, gardens, hiking; *Style—* Prof Isaac Marks; ✉ Institute of Psychiatry, London SE5 8AF (☎ 0171 919 5411 ext 3365, fax 0171 703 5796)

MARKS, Dr John Henry; s of Lewis Myer Marks (d 1960), and Rose, *née* Goldbaum (d 1986); *b* 30 May 1925; *Educ* Tottenham Co GS, Univ of Edinburgh (MB ChB, MD, DObstRCOG); *m* 17 June 1954, Shirley Evelyn, da of Alic Nathan, OBE (d 1988); 1 s (Richard), 2 da (Helen, Laura); *Career* Capt RAMC 1949–51; house physician and surgn Wembley Hosp 1948–49, sr house offr obstetrics St Martin's Hosp Bath 1951–52; clinical asst dermatology: Barnet Gen, Mount Vernon, Wat Gen Hosps; trainee asst 1952–53, asst GP 1953–54, GP Borehamwood 1954–89; med dir Nat Med Examination Network (Definitech Ltd); chm Cncl BMA 1984–90; memb Herts CC Health Ctee, chm Herts Exec Cncl 1971–74; memb: GMC 1979–84 and 1989–94, Standing Med Advsy Ctee 1984–90; MRCGP 1959, FRCGP 1975; *Recreations* modern British postal stamps, medical politics, walking, gardening; *Style—* Dr John Marks; ✉ Brown Gables, Barnet Lane, Elstree, Herts WD6 3RQ (☎ and fax 0181 953 7687)

MARKS, Jonathan Clive; QC (1995); s of Geoffrey Jack Marks, of Beechlands, Rotherfield Road, Henley-on-Thames, and Patricia Pauline, *née* Bowman (d 1995); *b* 19 Oct 1952; *Educ* Harrow, Univ Coll Oxford (BA); *m* 1, 18 Dec 1982 (m dis 1991), Sarah Ann Russell; 1 s (David b 1986), 1 da (Freya b 1988); m 2, 30 Oct 1993, Clementine Medina Cafopoulos, da of Panayiotes and Catherine Cafopoulos, of Athens; 1 da (Lara b 1996); *Career* called to the Bar Inner Temple 1975; in practice Western circuit; visiting lectr in advocacy: Univ of Malaya Kuala Lumpur 1985 and 1989–91, Univ of Mauritius 1988, Sri Lanka Law Coll 1992; fndr memb SDP 1981, Euro Parly candidate for Cornwall and Plymouth 1984; Parly candidate: Weston-Super-Mare 1983, Falmouth and Camborne 1987; memb Lib Democrat Ctee for England 1988–89; Freeman: City of London 1975, Worshipful Co of Pattenmakers; *Recreations* skiing, tennis, theatre, food, wine, travel; *Clubs* RAC; *Style—* Jonathan Marks, Esq, QC; ✉ Tythrop Park, Kingsey, Buckinghamshire HP17 8LT (☎ 01844 291310, fax 01844 291102); 4 Pump Court, Temple, London EC4Y 7AN (☎ 0171 353 2656, fax 0171 583 2036)

MARKS, Laurence; s of Bernard Marks (d 1975), and Lily, *née* Goldberg (d 1969); *b* 8 Dec 1948; *Educ* Holloway County Sch London, Guildhall Sch of Music; *m* 1 June 1988, Brigitte Luise, da of Friedrich Ludwig Ernst Kirchheim; 1 step s (Daniel Joel Kahn b 28 Feb 1968); *Career* trainee journalist Thomson Regional Newspapers, reporter N London Weekly Herald, Sunday Times and current affrs prog This Week (Thames TV) until 1980, television scriptwriter 1980–; creator and writer (with Maurice Gran, *qv*): Holding the Fort 1979–82, Roots, Shine on Harvey Moon 1982–85 and 1995–, Roll Over Beethoven, Relative Strangers, The New Statesman 1987–91, Birds of a Feather 1989–, Snakes and Ladders, So You Think You've Got Troubles, Get Back, Love Hurts 1991–93, Wall of Silence (film) 1993, Goodnight Sweetheart 1994–, Mosley 1997, Unfinished Business 1997; fndr (with Maurice Gran and Allan McKeown) Alomo Productions 1988 (now part of SelecTV PLC); chm Pipesmoking Cncl of Great Britain, Pipesmoker of the Year 1990; Freeman City of London 1992, Liveryman Worshipful Co of Tobacco Blenders and Briar Pipe Makers 1994; *Awards* Silver Medal Int Film and TV Festival NY for Relative Strangers 1985, Int Emmy for The New Statesman 1988, BAFTA Best Comedy Award for The New Statesman 1990, Mitsubishi TV Sitcom of the Year for Birds of a Feather 1991, Mitsubishi TV Drama of the Year for Love Hurts 1991, BAFTA Writer's Award (jtly with Maurice Gran) 1992; *Books* Moorgate - The Anatomy of a Disaster (1976), Ruth Ellis - A Case of Diminished Responsibility (1977), Holding the Fort (with Maurice Gran, 1981), The New Statesman Scripts (with Maurice Gran, 1992), Dorien's Diary (with Maurice Gran, 1993); *Recreations* music (saxophone player), reading, English churches, tennis, medieval German, Chinese literature, the study of Freud, Jung and Breuer, British politics; *Clubs* Reform, St James's, Arsenal Supporters'; *Style—* Laurence Marks, Esq; ✉ Alomo Productions Ltd, 45 Fouberts Place, London W1V 2DN (☎ 0171 434 3060, fax 0171 494 1421)

MARKS, Martin; s of Harry Marks (d 1988), of Harrogate, and Sarah, *née* Zissling (d 1988); *b* 4 May 1931; *Educ* Roundhay Sch Leeds; *m* 1, 27 March 1955 (m dis 1975), Judith Joyce, da of late Saul Bloom; 2 da (Debora Susan b 27 Sept 1957, Joanne Carol b 1 May 1960); m 2, 3 April 1979, Anne Kushner, da of late Hyman Teper; 2 da (Caroline Nadia b 26 June 1958, Amanda Jane b 18 June 1960); *Career* articled to J Barrett 1949–54; Nat Serv RAPC (attached to Manchester Regt) 1955–57; sr asst J C Kirk & Son (chartered accountants) Leeds 1957–61; ptnr: Vice Marks & Co Leeds (later Vice Marks Stead & Co) 1961–86, Pannell Kerr Forster (specialising in gen small/medium private co advice and corp fin) 1986–92 (conslt 1992–); dir The Independent Financial Partnership Ltd 1994–; FCA (ACA 1955); *Recreations* football, bridge, history, family, travel and climatology; *Style—* Martin Marks, Esq; ✉ 15 Swan Court, York Road, Harrogate, North Yorkshire HG1 2QH (☎ 01423 526580 and 01423 523311)

MARKS, Prof Richard Charles; s of Maj William Henry Marks (d 1982), and Jeannie Eileen, *née* Piggott (d 1979); *b* 2 July 1945; *Educ* Berkhamsted Sch, QMC (BA), Courtauld Inst of Art, Univ of London (MA, PhD); *m* 19 July 1970, Rita, da of Charlie Spratley; *Career* researcher Corpus Vitrearum Ctee Br Acad 1970–73 (currently Ctee memb), asst keeper Dept Medieval and Later Antiquities Br Museum 1973–79, keeper Burrell Collection and asst dir Glasgow Museums and Art Galleries 1979–85, dir Royal Pavilion Art Gallery and Museums Brighton 1985–92; prof Centre for Medieval Studies Univ of York 1992–; pres Int Bd Corpus Vitrearum 1995–, memb Conservation Ctee Care of Churches, vice-pres Soc of Antiquaries 1991–94; tstee Stained Glass Museum, York Glaziers Tst, River and Rowing Museum; Liveryman Worshipful Co of Glaziers & Painters of Glass 1990; FSA 1977; *Books* British Heraldry (jtly, 1978), The Golden Age of English Manuscript Painting (jtly, 1980), The Burrell Collection (jtly, 1983), Burrell: Portrait of a Collector (1983 and 1988), The Glazing of the Collegiate Church of the Holy Trinity Tattershall (1984), The Souvenir Guide to the Burrell Collection (1985), Sussex Churches and Chapels (jtly, 1989), Stained Glass in England during the Middle Ages (1993); *Recreations* opera, parish churches, travelling in the Levant, cricket, rowing; *Clubs* MCC, Clydesdale Rowing; *Style*— Prof Richard Marks; ✉ Flat 3, The King's Manor, University of York, York YO1 2EP; Hillcroft, 11 Stewkley Road, Soulbury, Beds LU7 0DH; Centre for Medieval Studies, The King's Manor, University of York, York YO1 2EP (☎ 01904 433919, fax 01909 433918, e-mail RCM1@York.ac.uk)

MARKS, Prof Ronald; s of Isadore Marks (d 1966), and Jessie Marks (d 1991); *b* 25 March 1935; *Educ* St Marylebone GS, Guy's Hospital Med Sch (BSc, MB BS); *m* 1 (m dis 1978); 2 da (Louise Anne b 17 March 1962, Naomi Suzanne b 1 Jan 1965); m 2, 11 Nov 1978, Hilary, *née* Venmore; *Career* MO short service cmmn 1960, med div Queen Alexander Mil Hosp 1961–63, specialist in dermatology Br Mil Hosp Munster W Germany 1963–65; sr lectr Inst of Dermatology and conslt dermatologist St John's Hosp for Diseases of the Skin London 1971–73; Univ of Wales Coll of Med Cardiff: sr lectr in dermatology Dept of Med 1973, reader 1977, personal chair in dermatology 1980, established chair in dermatology 1990; hon conslt in dermatology Univ Hosp of Wales 1973; author, ed, jt ed or contrib numerous papers in scientific jls, co-ed The Jl of Dermatological Treatment; lit award Soc of Cosmetic Chemists NY USA 1985; pres Br Cosmetic Dermatology Gp 1994, hon chm Br Assoc of Univ Teachers of Dermatology, hon chm Skin Charity to Advance Res, hon pres Int Soc for Bioengineering and the Skin; Freeman City of Besançon 1983; FRCP 1977 (memb 1964), FRCPath 1985; *Publications* jt ed and/or contrib to numerous books incl: Common Facial Dermatoses (1976), Investigative Techniques in Dermatology (ed, contrib, 1979), Psoriasis (1981), Acne (1984), Skin Diseases in Old Age (1987), The Sun and Your Skin (1988), Acne and Related Disorders (jt ed, contrib, 1989), Retinoids In Cutaneous Malignancy (1991), Eczema (1992), Sun Damaged Skin (1992), The Environmental Threat to the Skin (1992), Clinical Signs and Procedures in Dermatology (1993), Roxburgh's Common Skin Diseases (16th edn, 1993), Skin Therapy (1994); *Recreations* visual art of the 19th and 20th centuries, playing squash; *Style*— Prof Ronald Marks; ✉ Department of Dermatology, University of Wales College of Medicine, Heath Park, Cardiff CF4 4XN (☎ 01222 742885, fax 01222 762314)

MARKS, Prof Shula Eta; OBE (1996); da of Chaim Winokur (d 1957), of Cape Town, and Frieda, *née* Sack; *b* 14 Oct 1938; *Educ* Univ of Cape Town (BA), Univ of London (PhD); *m* 31 March 1957, Isaac Meyer Marks, *qv*, s of Moshe Nahman Marks (d 1979), of Cape Town; 1 s (Rafi b 26 Jan 1965), 1 da (Lara b 22 Jan 1963); *Career* Univ of London: lectr in history of Africa jtly at Inst of Cwlth Studies and SOAS 1963–76, reader in history of Southern Africa 1976–84, dir Inst of Cwlth Studies 1983–93, prof of Cwlth history 1984–93, prof of history of Southern Africa SOAS 1993–; conslt WHO 1977–80, chair World Univ Southern African Scholarships Ctee 1981–92, govr Inst of Devpt Studies Univ of Sussex 1988–91, memb Advsy Cncl on Public Records 1989–94, memb Cncl Soc for Protection of Sci and Learning 1983– (chair 1993–), memb Governing Body Queen Elizabeth House Oxford 1991–94, memb Cwlth Scholarships Cmmn 1992–; Hon DLitt Univ of Cape Town 1994; FBA 1995; *Books* Reluctant Rebellion: An Assessment of the 1906–08 Disturbance in Natal (1970), Economy and Society in Preindustrial Society (ed jtly, 1980), Industrialisation and Social Change in South Africa (ed jtly, 1982), Ambiguities of Dependence in South Africa: Class, Nationalism and the State in Twentieth Century Natal (1986), The Politics of Race, Class and Nationalism in Twentieth Century South Africa (ed jtly, 1987), Not Either an Experimental Doll: The Separate Worlds of Three South African Women (1987), Divided Sisterhood: Race Class and Nationalism in the South African Nursing Profession (1994); *Recreations* theatre, cinema; *Style*— Prof Shula Marks, OBE, FBA; ✉ School of Oriental and African Studies, Thornhaugh Street, London WC1H 0XG (☎ 0171 637 2388, fax 0171 436 3844)

MARKS, Hon Simon Richard; only s and h of 2 Baron Marks of Broughton, *qv*; *b* 3 May 1950; *Educ* Eton, Balliol Coll Oxford; *m* 1982, Marion, only da of Peter F Norton, of the Azores; 1 s (Michael b 13 May 1989), 2 da (Miriam Ann b 1983, Susannah Elizabeth b 1986); *Style*— The Hon Simon Marks; ✉ c/o Michael House, Baker St, London W1

MARKS, Victor James (Vic); s of Harold George Marks (d 1989), and Phyllis Joan, *née* Farthing; *b* 25 June 1955; *Educ* Blundell's, St John's Coll Oxford (BA, cricket blue, rugby fives half blue); *m* 9 Sept 1978, Annabelle Margaret, *née* Stewart; 2 da (Amy Tamsin b 27 Nov 1979, Rosie b 8 Nov 1987); *Career* cricket correspondent; professional cricketer: Somerset CCC 1974–89 (capt 1988–89), 6 test matches England 1982–84 (35 one day ints 1980–88); teacher Blundell's 1978–80, cricket corr The Observer 1990–, contrib BBC's Test Match Special 1990–, dir The Cricketer magazine 1990–; *Books* Somerset CCC Scrapbook (1984), Marks out of XI (1985), TCCB Guide to Better Cricket (1987), Ultimate One Day Cricket Match (1988), Wisden Illustrated History of Cricket (1989), My Greatest Game - Cricket (with Bob Holmes, 1994); *Recreations* golf; *Style*— Vic Marks, Esq

MARKS, Prof Vincent; s of Lewis Myer Marks (d 1960), of London, and Rose, *née* Goldbaum (d 1986); *b* 10 June 1930; *Educ* Tottenham Co Sch, BNC Oxford, St Thomas's Hosp Med Sch; *m* 10 Feb 1957, Averil Rosalie, da of Maurice Sherrard (d 1965), of London; 1 s (Lewis b 27 Jan 1961), 1 da (Alexandra b 9 Sept 1959); *Career* sr lectr in chem pathology Univ of London 1961–62, conslt chem pathologist Epsom 1962–70; Univ of Surrey: prof of clinical biochemistry 1970–95, dean Faculty of Sci 1980–83, head Dept of Biochemistry 1986–89, prof emeritus 1995–, dean of med 1996–; dir: Clifmar Associates Ltd 1985–, Quatro Biosystems Ltd 1988–, Biostat Ltd 1990–; fndr memb and former vice chm Healthwatch; non-exec dir Mid Surrey Health Authy 1990–95; vice pres RCPath 1989–92, pres Assoc of Clinical Biochemists 1989–91; FRCPE 1957, FRCPath 1963, FRCP 1969, MAE 1993; *Books* Scientific Foundations of Clinical Biochemistry Vol 1 and 2 (1978 and 1983), Hypoglycaemia (2 edn 1981); *Recreations* conversation; *Clubs* Athenaeum; *Style*— Prof Vincent Marks; ✉ EIHMS, Stirling House, University of Surrey, Guildford GU2 5RF (☎ 01483 450326, fax 01483 503106)

MARKS OF BROUGHTON, 2 Baron (UK 1961); Michael Marks; s of 1 Baron Marks of Broughton, sometime chm and jt md Marks & Spencer (d 1964), by his w Miriam (d 1971), sis of Joseph Edward Sieff (Hon Pres of M & S), and late Baron Sieff (Life Peer, who m (the first) Lord Marks of Broughton's sis) and aunt of Baron Sieff of Brimpton; *b* 27 Aug 1920; *Educ* St Paul's, CCC Cambridge; *m* 1, 1949 (m dis 1958), Ann Catherine, da of Maj Richard James Pinto, MC; 1 s (Hon Simon Richard b 1950), 2 da (Hon Naomi Anne (Hon Mrs Wölffer) b 1952, Hon Sarah Elizabeth (Hon Mrs Radomir) b 1953); m 2, 1960 (m dis 1965), Helene, da of Gustave Fischer; m 3, 1976 (m dis 1985), Toshiko Shimura; m 4, 1988 (m dis), Liying Zhang; m 5, 1994, Marina Sakalis; *Heir* s, Hon Simon Richard Marks, *qv*; *Style*— The Rt Hon Lord Marks of Broughton; ✉ Michael House, Baker St, W1

MARKWICK, Stephen Douglas; s of Douglas Wilfred Markwick (d 1995), and Ruth Mildred, *née* George; *b* 20 Aug 1947; *Educ* Lindisfarne Coll Ruabon N Wales, Ealing Hotel Catering Sch (Nat Dip); *m* 1972, Judy Elizabeth, *née* Pursall; 2 da (Claire Elizabeth b 1974, Zoë Jane b 1975); *Career* chef; Br Tport Hotels 1970–74, worked for George Perry-Smith (formerly of Hole-in-the-Wall Bath) Carved Angel Dartmouth and Riverside Helford Cornwall 1974–80, prop/chef Bistro Twenty-One Bristol 1980–87, prop/chef Markwicks Bristol 1989–; Good Food Guide Bistro of the Year, Independent Restaurant of the Year; *Recreations* cricket and rugby (now confined to spectating), eating and drinking (wines); *Style*— Stephen Markwick, Esq; ✉ Markwicks, 43 Corn Street, Bristol BS1 1HT (☎ 0117 926 2658)

MARLAND, (Peter) Michael; CBE (1977); s of Albert Marland (d 1977), of London; *b* 28 Dec 1934; *Educ* Christ's Hosp, Sydney Sussex Coll Cambridge (BA, MA); *m* 1, 1955, Eileen (d 1968); 4 s (Edgell b 1956 d 1990, Oliver b 1959, Timothy b 1962, Benjamin Peter b 1967), 1 da (Folly b 1956); m 2, 1972 (m dis 1977), Rose; m 3, 11 Feb 1989, Linda; 1 s (Matthew b 1990); *Career* teacher: Der Halephagen Oberschule Hamburg 1957–58, Simon Langton GS Canterbury 1958–61; head of English Abbey Wood Sch London 1961–64, head of English then dir of studies Crown Wood Sch London; headmaster: Woodberry Down Sch London 1971–79, North Westminster Sch (London's first multi-campus sch) 1980–; hon prof of educn Univ of Warwick 1980–92; chm: Nat Textbook Reference Library, Royal Opera House Advsy Cncl, AIDS and the Tutor Working Pty; memb: Ethical Implications of AIDS Study Gp, Inst of Med Ethics, Technol Educn Project, Educn and Human Devpt Ctee ESRC, Cwth Inst Educn Ctee, Faculty of Community Med, Nat Assoc of Arts in Educn, City of Westminster Arts Coll; FRSA 1991; *Books* Education for the Inner City (1980), Departmental Management (1981), Sex Differentiation and Schooling (1983), Meetings and Partings (1984), Short Stories for Today (1984), School Management Tasks (1985), New Directions in Pastoral Care (1985), The Tutor and the Tutor Group (1990), Marketing the School (1991), Craft of the Classroom (1993), Leadership in the Secondary School: Portraits of Headship (1994), Scenes from Plays (1996); numerous other editions and papers; gen ed Longman Imprint Books (Heinemann Sch Mgmnt Series); *Recreations* reading, music; *Style*— Michael Marland, Esq, CBE; ✉ 22 Compton Terrace, London N1 2UN; North Westminster Community School, Marylebone Lower House, Penfold Street, London NW1 6RX (☎ 0171 262 8000, fax 0171 224 9226)

MARLAND, Paul; MP (C) Gloucestershire West (majority 4,958); s of Alexander Marland, and Elsa May, *née* Lindsey; *b* 19 March 1940; *Educ* Gordonstoun, Trinity Coll Dublin; *m* 1, 1965 (m dis 1983), Penelope Anne Barlow; 1 s, 2 da; m 2, 1984, Caroline Anne Rushton; *Career* farmer; worked with Hopes Meal Windows 1964, London Press Exchange 1965–66; MP (C) Gloucs W 1979–, jt PPS to Hon Nicholas Ridley as fin sec to the Treasy and Jock Bruce-Gardyne as econ sec to the Treasy 1981–83, PPS to Rt Hon Michael Jopling as Min of Agric 1983–86; memb Agricultural Select Ctee 1986–, chm Cons Backbench Agric Ctee 1989–; *Clubs* Boodle's; *Style*— Paul Marland Esq, MP; ✉ Ford Hill Farm, Temple Guiting, Cheltenham, Glos; House of Commons, London SW1A 0AA (☎ 0171 219 3000)

MARLAND, Ross Crispian; s of John Marland (d 1988), and Sylvia, *née* Norris; *b* 17 Aug 1940; *Educ* Stamford Sch, RNC Dartmouth, UCL (LLM, Dip Air and Space Law); *m* 23 Oct 1965, (Daphne Mary) Virginia, da of Brig William Hugh Denning Wakely (d 1979); 1 s (Timothy b 27 July 1970), 1 da (Lavinia b 22 Sept 1974); *Career* graduated RNC Actg Sub Lt 1961, transfd RAF PO 1963, No 1 Advanced Navigation Sch flying offr 1964, Flt Lt 1966, jt servs warfare course 1968, Jr Cmd and Staff Sch 1973, Flt Cdr Jt Air Reconnaissance and Intelligence Centre 1973–79; called to the Bar Inner Temple 1975, in practice 1979–81; dir: International Insurance Services Ltd 1981–87, Airclaims Insurance Services Ltd 1987–91; mangr Tech Servs Div British Aviation Insurance Group 1991–; memb: Bd Int Court of Air and Space Arbitration, Ctee Inter Pacific Aviation Law Assoc, Aerospace Ctee Inter Pacific Bar Assoc, Royal Aeronautical Soc, Air Law Gp; lectr Chartered Inst Insur Studies; memb: Huntingdon Cons Club, Bar Assoc Commerce Finance and Indust, Aviation Law Assoc of Australia and NZ; MRIN 1973, MRAeS 1982, ACIArb 1984; *Recreations* salmon and trout fishing, equestrian sports; *Clubs* RAF; *Style*— Ross Marland, Esq; ✉ 84 East Hill, Wandsworth, London SW18 2HG (☎ 0181 870 6893, fax 0181 874 5964); British Aviation Insurance Group, Fitzwilliam House, 10 St Mary Axe, London EC3A 8EQ (☎ 0171 369 2244, fax 0171 369 2800, telex 887938 AVGEN G, e-mail Rossm@BAIG7.demon.co.uk)

MARLBOROUGH, 11 Duke of (E 1702); John George Vanderbilt Henry Spencer-Churchill; JP (Oxon 1962), DL (1974); also Baron Spencer (E 1603), Earl of Sunderland (E 1643), Baron Churchill of Sandridge (E 1685), Earl of Marlborough (E 1689), Marquess of Blandford (E 1702), Prince of the Holy Roman Empire (1704), and Prince of Mindelheim (1705, cr of the Emperor Joseph); s of 10 Duke of Marlborough (d 1972), by his 1 w, Hon Alexandra Cadogan, CBE, da of Viscount Chelsea and gda of 5 Earl Cadogan, KG; *b* 13 April 1926; *Educ* Eton; *m* 1, 1951 (m dis 1960), Susan Mary, da of Michael Charles St John Hornby (d 1987), of Pusey House, Berks, by his w Nicolette (d 1988), da of Capt Hon Cyril Ward, MVO, RN, 5 s of 1 Earl of Dudley; 1 s, 1 da (and 1 s decd); m 2, 1961 (m dis 1971), Mrs Tina (Athina) Livanos (d 1974), da of Stavros G Livanos, of Paris, and formerly w of Aristotle Onassis (d 1975); m 3, 1972, (Dagmar) Rosita (Astri Libertas), da of Count Carl Ludvig Douglas (d 1961); 1 s (Lord Edward b 1974), 1 da (Lady Alexandra b 1977) (and 1 s decd); *Heir* s, Marquess of Blandford, *qv*; *Career* proprietor of Blenheim Palace, said to be England's largest domestic bldg and one of the masterpieces of Sir John Vanbrugh; formerly Capt Life Gds to 1953; chm: Martini & Rossi Ltd 1979–96, London Paperweights Ltd; pres: Thames and Chilterns Tourist Bd 1974–, Oxon Assoc for Young People, Oxon CLA 1978–; former Oxon ccllr; memb House of Lords Bridge Team in match against Commons 1982; dep pres Nat Assoc Boys' Clubs; pres: Sports Aid Fndn (Southern Area) 1981; Oxfordshire Branch SSAFA 1977; Oxford United Football Club 1975; hon vice-pres Football Assoc 1959; cncl memb Winston Churchill Memorial Tst 1966–; memb Forte Cncl 1993–; *Clubs* White's, Portland; *Style*— His Grace the Duke of Marlborough, JP, DL; ✉ Blenheim Palace, Woodstock, Oxon OX20 1PS (☎ 01993 811666, fax 01993 813107); 1 Shepherd's Place, Upper Brook St, London W1 (☎ 0171 629 7971)

MARLER, David Steele; OBE (1985); s of Steele Edward Marler (d 1961), and Dorothy Eliza, *née* Vickery; *b* 19 March 1941; *Educ* Brighton Hove & Sussex GS, Merton Coll Oxford (open postmastership, BA, MA); *m* 17 Aug 1963, Belinda Mary, da of Harold William Handisyde (d 1974); 2 s (Blake David b 1964, Edmund Henry b 1968); *Career* British Council: joined 1962, seconded to SOAS 1962–63, asst rep Bombay 1963, regnl offr India 1967, dep rep Ethiopia 1970, rep Ibadan 1974, dir Policy Research Dept 1977, rep Cyprus 1980, seconded to SOAS 1984, Nat Univ Singapore 1985, rep China 1987, controller Asia Pacific & Americas Div 1990–92, dir Turkey 1993–; *Recreations* sailing, flying, walking, reading; *Clubs* Changi Sailing (Singapore), Cyprus Aero; *Style*— David Marler, Esq, OBE; ✉ The British Council, 10 Spring Gardens, London SW1A 2BN (☎ 0171 389 4786, fax 0171 839 6347, telex 8952201 BRICON G)

MARLER, Dennis Ralph Greville; s of Greville Sidney Marler (d 1952), and Ivy Victoria, *née* Boyle (d 1977); *b* 15 June 1927; *Educ* Marlborough; *m* 11 June 1952, Angela, da of Harold Cann Boundy, of Putney; 1 s (Timothy b 1957), 1 da (Melanie b 1955); *Career* Lt 2 Bn Royal Lincs Regt 1945–48, served in Palestine (MELF); chm Capital & Counties plc 1985–90 (md 1969–85); pres Br Property Fedn 1983–84, chm Falcon Property Tst 1988–95; Freeman of City of London, memb Ct Worshipful Co of Merchant Taylors; FRICS 1969, CIMgt, FRSA; *Recreations* reading, golf, travel; *Clubs* Royal Thames Yacht, Roehampton, St Enodoc Golf; *Style*— Dennis Marler, Esq; ✉ Stoptide, Rock, Cornwall PL27 6JZ (☎ 01208 862141)

MARLESFORD, Baron (Life Peer UK 1991), of Marlesford in the County of Suffolk; Mark Shuldham Schreiber; DL (Suffolk 1991); s of John Shuldham Schreiber, AE, DL (d 1968), of Marlesford Hall, Woodbridge, Suffolk, and Constance Maureen, *née* Dent (d 1980); *b* 11 Sept 1931; *Educ* Eton, Trinity Coll Cambridge (MA); *m* 1969, Gabriella Federica, da of Conte Teodoro Veglio di Castelletto d'Uzzone; 2 da (Hon Nicola Charlotte b 1971, Hon Sophie Louisa b 1973); *Career* Nat Serv Coldstream Gds, 2 Lt; Fisons Ltd 1957–63, Conservative Res Dept 1963–67, dir Conservative Party Public Sector Research Unit 1967–70, special advsr HM Govt 1970–74, special advsr to leader of the Opposition 1974–75, editorial conslt The Economist 1974–91 (Parly lobby correspondent); chm Baring Taiwan Fund 1994–; dir: Eastern Group plc 1989–95, Times Newspapers Holdings Ltd (ind nat dir) 1991–, Mitsubishi Corporation International NV 1990–; advsr John Swire & Sons 1992–; memb: Countryside Cmmn 1980–92, Rural Devpt Cmmn 1985–93; chm CPRE 1993–; *Clubs* Pratt's; *Style*— The Rt Hon Lord Marlesford, DL; ✉ Marlesford Hall, Woodbridge, Suffolk IP13 0AU; 5 Kersley St, London SW11 4PR

MARLING, Sir Charles William Somerset; 5 Bt (UK 1882), of Stanley Park and Sedbury Park, Co Gloucester; s of Lt-Col Sir John Stanley Vincent Marling, 4 Bt, OBE (d 1977); *b* 2 June 1951; *Educ* Harrow; *m* 1979, Judi P, da of Thomas W Futrille, of Sunningdale; 3 da (Georgina Katharine b 1982, Aimy Frances b 1984, Laura Beatrice b 1990); *Heir* none; *Clubs* White's, Chelsea Arts; *Style*— Sir Charles Marling, Bt

MARLOW, Antony Rivers (Tony); MP (C) Northampton North (majority 3,908); s of late Maj Thomas Keith Rivers Marlow, MBE, RE, and late Beatrice Nora, *née* Hall; *b* 17 June 1940; *Educ* Wellington, RMA Sandhurst, St Catharine's Coll Cambridge; *m* 1962, Catherine Louise Howel, *née* Jones (d 1994); 3 s, 2 da; *Career* served Army 1958–69; mgmnt conslt 1969–79; Parly candidate: Normanton Feb 1974, Rugby Oct 1974; MP (C) Northampton N 1979–, memb Select Ctee on Euro Legislation; Cons whip temporarily withdrawn over opposition to govt's euro policies 1994–95; *Clubs* Spencer Working Men's; *Style*— Tony Marlow Esq, MP; ✉ House of Commons, London SW1A 0AA

MARLOW, David Ellis; *b* 29 March 1935; *m* Margaret; 1 da (Jenny); *Career* CA; articled clerk with practice assoc with (and now part of) KPMG Peat Marwick; 3i Group plc: joined 1960, responsible for regnl orgn 1975–88, chief exec 1988–92, ret; dir: Brixton Estate plc, Brunner Mond Holdings plc, Trinity International Holdings plc; memb Slrs' Disciplinary Tbnl; *Recreations* playing tennis, playing the piano, the organ and the cello, skiing and walking in the Alps; *Clubs* Athenaeum, Cercle de l'Union Interalliée; *Style*— David Marlow, Esq; ✉ The Platt, Elsted, Midhurst, W Sussex GU29 0LA

MARLOW-THOMAS, Piers John Derrick; s of Michael John Marlow-Thomas (d 1983), of Leics, and Angela Claire, *née* Hignett; *b* 11 Oct 1957; *Educ* Pangbourne Coll, RMA Sandhurst; *m* 1984, Julia Mary, da of Maj B H Heaton, MC, OBE, of Mold, Clwyd; 2 s (Oliver John Basil b 23 April 1987, Charles Michael Adrian b 4 May 1993), 1 da (Amelia Daisy Bronwyn b 20 April 1993); *Career* served The Life Gds 1977–85; Bass plc 1985–88, Charles Barker plc 1989–92, mktg dir Hill & Knowlton UK 1992–95, dir business devpt Richards Butler 1995–; MInstD; *Recreations* sailing, shooting, fishing, skiing; *Clubs* Cavalry and Guards', City, Household Div Yacht; *Style*— Piers Marlow-Thomas, Esq; ✉ The Mill, West Hendred, nr Wantage, Oxon OX12 8RJ; Richards Butler, Beaufort House, 15 St Botolph Street, London EC4A 4EA

MARMOT, Prof Michael Gideon; s of Nathan Marmot, of Sydney, Australia, and Alice, *née* Weiner; *b* 26 Jan 1945; *Educ* Univ of Sydney Australia (BSc, MB BS), Univ of California Berkeley (MPH, PhD); *m* 8 Sept 1971, Alexi, da of Bernard Ferster; 2 s (Andre b 1982, Daniel b 1986), 1 da (Deborah b 1992); *Career* Univ of Sydney: student fell in cardiovascular pharmacology 1965–66, res med offr Royal Prince Alfred Hosp 1969, fell in thoracic med 1970, travelling fell Postgraduate Med Fndn 1971–72; lectr Dept of Biomedical and Environmental Health Sciences Univ of California Berkeley 1975–76, sr lectr (formerly lectr) in epidemiology London Sch of Hygiene and Tropical Med 1976–85; UCH and Middlesex Sch of Med: prof 1985–, fell Faculty of Public Health Med (formerly Faculty of Community Med) 1989 (memb 1984); hon conslt Med Div Univ Coll Hosp 1980–84; London Sch of Hygiene and Tropical Medicine: prof of epidemiology 1990–, dir Int Centre for Health and Society 1994–, MRC research prof 1995–; memb: Medical Aspects of Food Policy Ctee, CMO's Working Gp on Health of the Nation Dept of Health, Coronary Prevention Gp, Royal Cmmn on Environmental Pollution 1995–; *Books* Mortality of Immigrants to England and Wales (1984), Coronary Heart Disease Epidemiology (1992); *Style*— Prof Michael Marmot; ✉ Department of Epidemiology and Public Health, UCL Medical School, 1–19 Torrington Place, London WC1E 6BT (☎ 0171 391 1680, fax 0171 813 0280)

MAROT, Marc Etienne; s of Col Pierre Etienne Marot, MBE, of Shennington, Nr Banbury, and Gwendolin May, *née* Handley; *b* 5 May 1959; *m* 2 Sept 1989, Jacqueline; 2 s (Luc Etienne b 7 Nov 1990, Christian Roland b 17 June 1995); *Career* sometime A & R and talent scout; md: Blue Mountain Music Publishing (copyrights incl U2 and Bob Marley) 1984–86, Island Music Publishing 1986–90, Island Records Ltd (bought by Polygram Records 1990) 1990–; bands on Island Records label incl: Pulp, The Cranberries, PJ Harvey, Tricky, The Orb, US, Stereo MCs; *Recreations* music, gardening, computers and computing; *Style*— Marc Marot, Esq; ✉ Island Records, 22 St Peters Square, London W6 9NW (☎ 0181 910 3333, fax 0181 741 0206, e-mail marc@channel.co.uk)

MAROWITZ, Charles; s of Harry Julius Marowitz, of Lithuania, and USA, and Tillie, *née* Rosencrantz; *b* 26 Jan 1934; *Educ* UCL, Central Sch Speech and Drama, London Acad Music and Dramatic Art, Sorbonne; *m* 1, 1976 (m dis 1980), Julia; m 2, 14 Dec 1982, Jane Windsor, da of Rear Adm David John Allsop, RN, of Ipswich; *Career* US Army 1952–54; dir In-Stage 1958–62, co-dir RSC Experimental Gp 1966–67, co-artistic dir London Traverse Co 1967–68, artistic dir Open Space Theatre 1968–80, assoc dir LA Theater Center 1982–89; artistic dir: Malibu Stage Co 1990–, Texas Stage Co 1994–; West Coast corr The Times 1980–, drama critic LA Herald Examiner 1989, West Coast theatre columnist Theater Week Magazine 1989–; memb: International PEN, Sons of Judas Macabeas, Schmendrick Soc of Gtr LA County, Dramatists Guild, The Writers Guild of America; Order of the Purple Sash (Denmark) 1974; *Books* Method as Means (1964), Confessions of a Counterfeit Critic (1973), The Marowitz Shakespeare (1980), Sex Wars (1986), Potboilers (1986), Prospero's Staff (1987), Burnt Bridges (1990), Recycling Shakespeare (1991), Directing the Action (1991), Alarums and Excursions (1996); *Recreations* balling; *Clubs* Putzvaytiks; *Style*— Charles Marowitz, Esq; ✉ 3058 Sequit Drive, Malibu, Calif 90265, USA (☎ 00 1 310 456 5060, fax 00 1 310 456 8170)

MARPER, (William) John; s of Ronald Marshall Marper, of Saltburn, and Caroline, *née* Jarville; *b* 9 Dec 1946; *Educ* Sir William Turners Sch; *m* 12 Dec 1976, Maureen Ann, da of Henry Pullen, of Eastbourne; *Career* CA; Charles Barker Group 1972–77, vice pres Citicorp 1977–85, dir ANZ Merchant Bank 1985–89, exec dir The Co-operative Bank plc 1989–; FCA, MSI; *Recreations* tennis, English literature; *Style*— John Marper, Esq; ✉ 1 Balloon St, Manchester M60 4EP (☎ 0161 832 3456)

MARPLES, Stuart Arthur; *b* 29 Aug 1948; *m*; 2 c; *Career* various health service admin posts 1966–78, unit administrator Rotherham Dist Gen Hosp 1978–85, unit gen mangr Bournemouth Acute Unit 1985–92, chief exec Royal Bournemouth and Christchurch Hosps NHS Tst 1992–; memb Professional Qualification Sub-Ctee and associated ctees Inst of Health Serv Mgmnt; inspr King's Fund Organisational Audit; AHSM; *Recreations* soccer, swimming, golf, reading, family; *Style*— Stuart Marples, Esq; ✉ Royal Bournemouth and Christchurch Hospitals NHS Trust, Royal Bournemouth Hospital, Castle Lane East, Bournemouth, Dorset BH7 7DW (☎ 01202 303626, fax 01202 704077)

MARQUAND, Prof David Ian; s of Rt Hon Hilary Marquand (d 1972), and Rachel Eluned, *née* Rees (d 1996); *b* 20 Sept 1934; *Educ* Emanuel Sch, Magdalen Coll Oxford, St Antony's Coll Oxford, Univ of California Berkeley; *m* 12 Dec 1959, Judith Mary, da of Dr Morris Reed, of London; 1 s (Charles b 1962), 1 da (Ruth b 1964); *Career* Nat Serv RAF 1952–54; leader writer The Guardian 1959–62, res fell St Antony's Coll Oxford 1962–64, lectr in sch of social studies Univ of Sussex 1964–66; MP (Lab) Ashfield 1966–77; PPS to: Min of Works 1966–67, Min of Overseas Devpt 1967–69; Br delegate to Cncl of Europe and WEU Assemblies 1970–73, chief advsr European Cmmn Brussels 1977–78; prof of contemporary history and politics Univ of Salford 1978–91; Univ of Sheffield: prof of politics 1991–96, dir of Political Economy Research Centre 1993–96, visiting prof 1996–; princ Mansfield Coll Oxford 1996–; jt ed The Political Quarterly 1987–97; chm High Peak SDP 1981–82 and 1987–88, pres High Peak SLD 1988–91; memb: Nat Ctee SDP 1981–88, Policy Ctee SLD 1988–90; FRHistS 1986, FRSA 1992; *Books* Ramsay MacDonald (1977), Parliament for Europe (1979), European Elections and British Politics (with David Butler, 1981), John Mackintosh on Parliament and Social Democracy (ed, 1982), The Unprincipled Society (1988), The Progressive Dilemma (1991); *Recreations* walking, listening to music; *Style*— Prof David Marquand; ✉ Mansfield College, Oxford OX1 3TF (☎ 01865 270999)

MARQUIS, Simon John; s of Henry Derek Marquis, of Harpenden, Herts, and Margaret, *née* Parish; *b* 3 May 1953; *Educ* Lancing, Peterhouse Cambridge (MA); *m* 1 May 1993, Nicola Jane Horner, da of Capt Richard Bates, RN; 1 s (Edward James Richard b 7 July 1994), 2 step da (Sophie, Clio); *Career* Benton & Bowles advtg 1975–80, Allen Brady Marsh advtg 1980–83, md Burkitt Weinreich Bryant Clients & Co Ltd 1990–92 (media dir 1983–90), editorial dir Marketing magazine 1993–; FIPA; *Recreations* golf, skiing, birds, drawing; *Style*— Simon Marquis, Esq; ✉ Marketing, Haymarket Publishing, 174 Hammersmith House, London W6 7JP (☎ 0171 413 4382, fax 0171 413 4504)

MARR, Andrew William Stevenson; s of William Donald Marr, and Valerie, *née* Stevenson, of Longforgan, Perthshire; *b* 31 July 1959; *Educ* Dundee HS, Craigflower Sch Fife, Loretto, Trinity Hall Cambridge (MA, exhibitioner); *m* Aug 1987, Jackie Ashley, *qv*, da of Lord Ashley of Stoke, CH, PC, *qv*; 1 s (Harry Cameron b 5 July 1989), 2 da (Isabel Claire b 4 Oct 1991, Emily Catherine b 3 Nov 1994); *Career* trained TRN Newcastle upon Tyne 1981; The Scotsman: trainee 1982, gen reporter then business reporter 1983–85, Parly corr 1985–86; political corr and Whitehall corr The Independent 1986–87, political ed The Scotsman 1988, political ed The Economist 1989–92, ed The Independent 1996– (chief political commentator 1992–96); winner Columnist of the Year Br Press Awards 1995; *Books* The Battle for Scotland (1992), Ruling Britannia (1995); *Recreations* whining and dining; *Clubs* Buffers, St James's, Pinks, The Reaction; *Style*— Andrew Marr, Esq; ✉ The Independent, 1 Canada Square, Canary Wharf, London E14 5DL (☎ 0171 293 2000, fax 0171 293 2435)

MARR, Prof Geoffrey Vickers; s of John Marr (d 1971), and Florrie, *née* Vickers; *b* 30 Jan 1930; *Educ* Darlington Queen Elizabeth GS, Univ of Manchester (BSc, DSc), Univ of Reading (PhD); *m* 3 July 1954, Jean, da of John Robert Tebb; 2 s (Peter John b 1956, Richard Nigel b 1961), 1 da (Kathryn Janet b 1958); *Career* fell Dept of Physics Univ of Western Ontario 1954–57, lectr Dept of Physics McGill Univ Montreal 1957–59, physicist Atomic Power Div English Electric 1959–61, fell, lectr then reader in physics J J Thomson Laboratory Univ of Reading 1961–81; Univ of Aberdeen: prof of natural philosophy and head of Dept of Physics 1981–89, prof (pt/t) Dept of Engrg 1989–1990, emeritus prof 1990–; current res interests incl photoionization of molecules, physics of thin films and synchrotron radiation source (in association with Daresbury Laboratory CLRC); FInstP 1963, CPhys 1986, FRSE 1986, FRSA 1988; *Books* Photoionization Processes in Gases (1967), Plasma Spectroscopy (1968), Handbook on Synchrotron Radiation Vol 2 (ed, 1987); *Recreations* walking, painting, beekeeping; *Style*— Prof Geoffrey Marr, FRSE; ✉ The Long House, Low Row, nr Richmond, N Yorks DL11 6NE (☎ 01748 886452)

MARR, John; s of Harry Needham Marr, of Manchester, and Harriet Constance, *née* Portwood; *b* 7 March 1946; *Educ* Doncaster GS, Univ of Manchester (BComm); *m* 15 April 1972 (m dis 1993), Caroline Anne, da of David Cowan, of Stockport; 1 s (Richard b 23 March 1985), 2 da (Victoria b 18 Oct 1978, Jessica 3 Feb 1981); *Career* commercial apprentice Mather and Platt 1964–69, investment mangr Co Operative Insur Soc 1969–73; Charterhouse Tilney Securities (formerly Tilney and Co) Stockbrokers: investment analyst 1973–77, ptnr 1977–86, dir 1986–; underwriter Lloyds of London 1987; ACIS 1969, ASIA 1970, FCCA 1970, memb Stock Exchange 1976; *Recreations* squash, cricket, fine wine, vintage cars; *Clubs* Liverpool Racquet, Yorks County Cricket; *Style*— John Marr, Esq; ✉ 17 Deva Terrace, off Dee Lane, Chester CH3 5AJ (☎ 01244 347268); Charterhouse Tilney Securities, Royal Liver Building, The Pier Head, Liverpool L3 1NY (direct ☎ 0151 472 5570, fax 0151 472 5557 ext 273)

MARR, Lindsay Grigor David; s of Grigor Wilson Marr (d 1986), and Linda Grace, *née* Sergeant; *b* 14 Sept 1955; *Educ* The Perse Sch, Gonville and Caius Coll Cambridge (MA); *m* 23 Feb 1991, Susan Ann, *née* Scott; 1 s (Andrew b 1992); *Career* admitted slr 1981; Freshfields: articled clerk 1979–81, asst slr 1981–87, ptnr 1987–; Freeman City of London Slrs' Co 1988; memb The Law Soc; *Recreations* reading, music, golf, sailing; *Style*— Lindsay Marr, Esq; ✉ 39 Broad Lane, Hampton, Middlesex TW12 3AL (☎ 0181 979 0517); 65 Fleet St, London EC4Y 1HS (☎ 0171 936 4000, fax 0171 832 7001)

MARR-JOHNSON, His Hon Judge Frederick James Maugham; s of Kenneth Marr-Johnson (d 1986), and Hon Diana Julia, *née* Maugham, da of 1 Viscount Maugham; *b* 17 Sept 1936; *Educ* Winchester, Trinity Hall Cambridge (MA); *m* 26 March 1966, Susan, da of Maj R P H Eyre, OBE (d 1982); 1 s (Thomas b 30 Sept 1966), 1 da (Rachel b 27 May 1969); *Career* Nat Serv RN 1955–56, midshipman RNVR; called to the Bar Lincoln's Inn 1962, recorder Crown Ct 1986–91, circuit judge (SE Circuit) 1991–; Liveryman Worshipful Co of Merchant Taylors; *Recreations* sailing; *Clubs* Royal Yacht Sqdn; *Style*— His Hon Judge Marr-Johnson; ✉ 33 Hestercombe Avenue, London SW6 5LL (☎ 0171 731 0412); Clerkenwell County Court, 33 Duncan Terrace, Islington, London N1 8AN

MARRACK, Rear Adm Philip Reginald; CB (1979); s of Capt Philip Marrack, RN (d 1955), and Annie Kathleen, *née* Proud (d 1992); *b* 16 Nov 1922; *Educ* Eltham Coll, RNEC; *m* 1954, Pauline Mary, da of Charles Haag (d 1938); 2 da (Claire, Philippa); *Career* war serv Atlantic and Mediterranean, Naval Offr, 8 appointments at sea in surface ships and submarines, 5 other appointments in shore estabs and MOD (incl dir Naval Ship Production MOD 1974–77, dir Dockyard Production and Support MOD 1977–81), ret 1981; specialist in engrg and submarines; *Recreations* trout and salmon fishing, viticulture; *Style*— Rear Adm Philip Marrack, CB

MARRE, Lady; (Romola) Mary; *née* Gilling; CBE (1979); da of Aubrey John Gilling (d 1952), of Chelmsford, Essex, and Romola Marjorie, *née* Angier (d 1989); *b* 25 April 1920; *Educ* Bedford Coll for Women, Univ of London (BA); *m* 24 Dec 1943, Sir Alan

Samuel Marre, KCB (d 1990); 1 s (Andrew), 1 da (Kate); *Career* served ATS 1942–45, Jr Cdr, psychologist No 41 (ATS) WOSB; asst principal (temp) Miny of Health 1941–42, organiser W Hampstead Citizens' Advice Bureau 1962–65, dep gen sec Camden Cncl of Social Service 1965–73, advsr on community health cncls to DHSS 1974–75, chm advsy gp on hosp services for children with cancer in N Western Region 1979; memb: Milk Marketing Bd 1973–82, Lord Chancellor's Advsy Ctee on Legal Aid 1975–80; memb then chm BBC and IBA Central Appeals Advsy Ctee 1980–86; chm Volunteer Centre 1973–78, dep chm Royal Jubilee Tsts 1981–89, tstee City Parochial Fndn 1975–89 (vice chm 1989–93); memb Cncl: Charity Projects 1984–92, Middx Hosp Ethics Ctee 1988– (now jt UCL/UCHL); chm: Ctee on Future of Legal Profession 1986–88, Cmmn of Enquiry into Human Aids to Communication 1990–92, Dist Ethics Ctee Camden and Islington Health Authy 1993–; pres Barnet Voluntary Service Cncl; *Recreations* gardening, embroidery, meeting friends, family life; *Style*— Lady Marre, CBE; ✉ 27 Edmunds Walk, London N2 0HU (☎ 0181 883 4420)

MARRIN, John Wheeler; QC (1990); *Educ* Univ of Cambridge (MA); *Career* called to the Bar Inner Temple 1974; asst recorder of the Crown Court 1993–; *Style*— John Marrin, Esq, QC; ✉ Keating Chambers, 10 Essex Street, London WC2R 3AA (☎ 0171 240 6981, fax 0171 240 7722)

MARRINER, Andrew Stephen; s of Sir Neville Marriner, the conductor; *b* 25 Feb 1954; *Educ* King's Coll Cambridge (chorister), King's Sch Canterbury, New Coll Oxford, Hochschule für Musik Hannover; *m* 1988, Elisabeth Anne, *née* Sparke; 1 s (Douglas Lawrence b 11 Oct 1989); *Career* solo chamber and orchestral clarinettist; freelance 1977–84, princ clarinet LSO 1985–, princ clarinet Acad of St Martin-in-the-Fields 1986–; solo and concert appearances at venues incl Royal Festival Hall, Barbican Hall, various in Paris, Berlin, Vienna, USA, Far East and Australia; concerto work with conductors incl Sir Neville Marriner, Sir Colin Davis, Leonard Bernstein, Mstislav Rostropovich, Michael Tilson Thomas and Richard Hickox; visiting prof RAM; Hon RAM 1994; *Recordings* with Acad of St Martin-in-the-Fields incl: Schubert Octet (Chandos), Beethoven Octet (Philips), Spohr Octet and Nonet (Philips), Mozart Divertimenti (Philips), Weber Concerti (Philips); others incl: Mozart Clarinet Quintet (Classics for Pleasure), Mozart Clarinet Concerto (CFP), Schubert Octet (with Chilingrian, EMI); *Recreations* family, cricket; *Clubs* Lord's Taverners; *Style*— Andrew Marriner, Esq; ✉ 67 Cornwall Gardens, London SW7 4BA; c/o Ingpen & Williams Ltd, 14 Kensington Court, London W8 5DN (☎ 0171 937 5158)

MARRINER, Neville George; s of Kenneth George James Marriner (d 1980), and Sadie Kathleen, *née* Burn; *b* 6 March 1949; *Educ* Spotswood Coll New Plymouth NZ; *m* 3 Feb 1973, Maureen Elizabeth, da of Ronald John Bulcraig; 2 s (Christopher George Anderson b 20 June 1981, Andrew James b 3 Nov 1983); *Career* press photographer; photographic staff Taranaki Daily News NZ 1966–69, Auckland Star 1969, Nat Serv RNZA 1970–71, Evening Post Wellington 1971, chief photographer Christchurch Press 1972–75 (covered Cwlth Games for subsequent book 1973), with sport and gen press agency London 1975–76, freelance photographer for Times, Sunday Express and Daily Mail 1976–78, staff photographer Daily Mail (news, sport and fashion) 1978–; NZ Press Photographer of the Year 1973; ARPS 1988; *Recreations* motor racing (chm BCV8 competition register 1986–90); *Clubs* MG Car; *Style*— Neville Marriner, Esq; ✉ Daily Mail, Northcliffe House, 2 Derry St, London W8 5TT (☎ 0171 938 6373, fax 0181 398 9156)

MARRIOTT, *see:* Smith-Marriott

MARRIOTT, Gareth John; s of Trevor John Marriott, of Holme Pierrepont, Nottingham, and Muriel, *née* Haynes; *b* 14 July 1970; *Educ* Brunts Upper Sch Mansfield, South Notts Coll of Further Educn; *Career* canoeist; competes in white water slalom single man canoe class; debut 1982, jr int debut 1985, sr int debut 1987; achievements incl: Gold medal Jr World Championships Spain 1988, sixth World Championships USA 1989, fourth World Cup 1990, Br champion 1990 and 1991, Gold medal World Cup 1991, Bronze medal World Championships (3–man team) 1991, Silver medal World Cup 1992, Silver medal Olympic Games Barcelona 1992, World Club Champion 1994 and 1995, fourth Olympic Games Atlanta 1996; first ever Br canoeing medal at Olympics; Nottinghamshire Amateur Sportsperson of the Year 1991–92; *Recreations* skiing, mountain biking, surfing, water skiing, go-karting; *Style*— Gareth Marriott, Esq; ✉ c/o British Canoe Union, Adbolton Lane, West Bridgford, Nottingham NG2 5AS (☎ 0115 982 1100, fax 0115 982 1797)

MARRIOTT, Martin Marriott; s of Rt Rev Philip Selwyn Abraham, Bishop of Newfoundland, Canada (d 1956), and Elizabeth Dorothy Cicely, *née* Marriott (d 1975); *b* 28 Feb 1932; *Educ* Lancing, New College Oxford (MA); *m* 10 Nov 1956, Judith Caroline Gurney, da of Lt-Col Michael Ronald Lubbock, MBE (d 1989), of Toronto, Canada; 1 s (Charles), 2 da (Virginia (Mrs O'Conor), Rebecca); *Career* educn officer RAF 1956–59; teacher: Heversham GS 1959–66, Haileybury College 1966–76; headmaster Canford Sch 1976–92; chm: Headmasters' Conf 1989, Steering Ctee of the Bloxham Project 1985–91; lay canon of Salisbury Cathedral 1993–; *Recreations* grandchildren, sailing, golf, walking, gardening; *Clubs* East India; *Style*— Martin Marriott, Esq; ✉ Morris' Farm House, Baverstock, nr Dinton, Salisbury, Wilts SP3 5EL (☎ 01722 716874)

MARS-JONES, Hon Sir William Lloyd; kt (1969), MBE (1945); s of Henry Mars Jones, of Denbighshire; *b* 4 Sept 1915; *Educ* Denbigh Co Sch, Univ Coll of Wales at Aberystwyth (LLB), St John's Cambridge (BA); *m* 1947, Sheila Cobon; 3 s; *Career* WWII Lt Cdr RNVR; called to the Bar 1941, QC 1957, dep chm Denbighshire QS 1962–68; recorder: Birkenhead 1959–65, Swansea 1965–68, Cardiff 1968–69; High Ct judge (Queen's Bench) 1969–90, presiding judge Wales & Chester Circuit 1971–75; inspector Home Office inquiry into allegations against Metropolitan Police Offrs 1964, memb Home Sec's Advsy Cncl on Penal System 1966–68; pres N Wales Arts Assoc 1976–, treas Gray's Inn 1982; pres: Univ Coll of N Wales Bangor 1983–94, Univ Coll of Wales Aberystwyth Old Students Assoc 1987–88, London Welsh Tst 1989–93; Hon LLD Univ Coll Wales; *Clubs* Garrick; *Style*— Sir William Mars-Jones, MBE; ✉ c/o Royal Courts of Justice, Strand, London WC2

MARSDEN, Andrew Guy; s of Flt Lt Geoffrey Ansdell Marsden, DFC, of Egmont House, Darley, Harrogate, N Yorks, and Margaret Jean, *née* Furniss; *b* 6 Aug 1953; *Educ* Monkton Combe Sch, Pembroke Coll Oxford (MA); *Career* called to the Bar Middle Temple 1975, memb SE circuit; in practice: Colchester, Norwich, Ipswich 1977–; patron Acorn Villages Mistley Home for Mentally Handicapped, organist Church of Holy Innocents Lamarsh Essex, memb Kelvedon Singers; *Recreations* historical vocal recordings, architecture, singing; *Clubs* United Oxford and Cambridge; *Style*— Andrew Marsden, Esq; ✉ Little Gables, Lamarsh, Bures, Suffolk (☎ 01787 227054); East Anglian Chambers, 53 North Hill, Colchester, Essex CO1 1PY (☎ 01206 572756, fax 01206 562447); 57 London Street, Norwich NR2 1HL (☎ 01603 572756); 5 Museum Street, Ipswich, Suffolk IP1 1HA (☎ 01473 214481)

MARSDEN, Andrew Kendall; s of Frank Marsden, of Shipley, Yorks, and Jeane Mary, *née* Kendall; *b* 24 May 1948; *Educ* Woodhouse Grove Sch, Univ of Leeds; *m* 20 March 1976, Alberta (Abe), *née* Maloney; 2 da (Stephanie Jane b 1980, Jennifer Kay b 1984); *Career* conslt accident and emergency med Pinderfields Gen Hosp Wakefield 1979–92, chm Resuscitation Cncl UK 1984–88, med dir St John Ambulance Assoc 1988–93, conslt med dir Scottish Ambulance Service; author pubns on accident and emergency med; memb Bd Immediate Med Care, RCSE, latterly police surgn (expert in medico legal case reporting); memb: Br Assoc Accident and Emergency Medicine, Br Assoc Immediate Care, Emergency Med Res Soc, World Assoc Emergency and Disaster Med; *Books* Care of the Acutely Ill and Injured (1982), Save A Life - An Instructors Guide (1986), Textbook of Accident & Emergency Medicine (1989), Resuscitation for the Citizen (1989), First Aid Manual (1992); *Recreations* fell walking, music; *Style*— Andrew Marsden, Esq; ✉ 9 Eglinton Crescent, Edinburgh EH12 5DD (☎ 0131 225 1870)

MARSDEN, Prof (Charles) David; s of Brig Charles Moustaka Marsden, CBE (d 1982), and Una Maud, *née* Bristow; *b* 15 April 1938; *Educ* Cheltenham, St Thomas' Hosp Med Sch Univ of London MB BS, DSc, MRCPsych, FRCP); *m* 1, 1961, Jill Slaney Bullock; 2 s, 3 da; m 2, 1979, Jennifer Sandom; 3 da; *Career* St Thomas's Hosp: house physician 1964, house surgn 1964–65, res fell Dept of Med 1965–66, lectr in med (neurology) 1966–68; house physician Nat Hosp for Nervous Diseases 1968–70, sr lectr in neurology Inst of Psychiatry 1970–72, locum conslt neurologist King's Coll Hosp 1970–72, hon lectr Inst of Neurology 1970–72, prof of neurology and head Univ Dept of Neurology Inst of Psychiatry and King's Coll Hosp Med Sch 1972–87, conslt neurologist Maudsley & Bethlem Royal Hosps 1972–87, conslt neurologist King's Coll Hosp and Cane Hill Hosp 1978–87, hon conslt neurologist Guy's Hosp 1983–, prof of neurology and head Univ Dept of Clinical Neurology Inst of Neurology Nat Hosp for Neurology and Neurosurgery 1987–, hon dir MRC Human Movement and Balance Unit; numerous invited lectures and visiting professorships worldwide; ed: Jl of Neurology Neurosurgery and Psychiatry 1977–87, Movement Disorders 1986–; memb numerous other editorial bds of med jls incl Brain 1991–, author of various med papers and books; memb: Parkinson's Disease Soc (memb Cncl 1984–92), Assoc of Br Neurologists (memb Cncl 1980–84), World Fedn of Neurology (memb Cncl on Extrapyramidal Diseases 1977–), Br Neuropathological Soc, MRC (memb Neuroscience Bd and Cncl 1983–91), RSM, MRS, The Harveian Soc, Physiological Soc, Pharmacological Soc, Psychopharacological Soc, Assoc of Pysicians, World Fedn of Neurology, Int Brain Res Orgn (memb Cncl 1979–83), American Neurological Assoc 1977, American Acad of Neurology 1982, Societe Francaise de Neurologie, The Spanish Soc of Neurology, Italian Soc of Neurology 1987, Fulton Soc 1989; FRS 1983 (memb Cncl 1991–94); *Clubs* Athenaeum; *Style*— Prof David Marsden, FRS; ✉ Institute of Neurology, The National Hospital for Neurology and Neurosurgery, 23 Queen Square, London WC1N 3BG (☎ 0171 837 3611)

MARSDEN, Gordon; s of George Henry Marsden, of Stockport, and Joyce, *née* Young; *b* 28 Nov 1953; *Educ* Stockport GS, New Coll Oxford (scholar, MA, Gibbs prize in history), Warburg Inst Univ of London, Kennedy Sch of Govt Harvard Univ (Kennedy scholar in politics/int rels); *Career* tutor and lectr Open Univ 1977–, public affrs/PR conslt 1980–85 (public affrs advsr Eng Heritage 1984–85), conslt ed New Socialist 1989–90, ed History Today 1985–; chm Young Fabians 1979–80, memb Fabian Soc Res Ctee, nat judge UK Conservation Fndn Awards 1995–; Parly candidate (Lab) Blackpool South 1992, prospective Parly candidate 1997 gen election; memb: Assoc of Br Eds 1986–, Bd Inst of Historical Res 1994–; FRSA 1995; *Books* Victorian Values? Personalities and Perspectives in Nineteenth-Century Society (ed, 1990), The History Debate (contrib, 1990), Holland's War Against Hitler (contrib, 1991); *Recreations* swimming, choral and early music, theatre, medieval culture and travel; *Style*— Gordon Marsden, Esq; ✉ History Today, 20 Old Compton Street, London W1V 5PE (☎ 0171 439 8315)

MARSDEN, John David; s of John Noel Marsden, of Manchester, and Mary Marsden; *b* 3 March 1970; *Educ* St Mary's RC HS Astley Gtr Manchester, RNCM; *Career* tenor; Bayreuth Festival Chorus 1991–92, princ Royal Opera House 1993–95, princ ENO 1995–; *Recreations* food, drink, music, travel; *Style*— John Marsden, Esq; ✉ English National Opera, London Coliseum, St Martin's Lane, London WC2N 4ES (☎ 0171 836 0111)

MARSDEN, Sir Nigel John Denton; 3 Bt (UK 1924), of Grimsby, Co Lincoln; s of Sir John Denton Marsden, 2 Bt (d 1985), and Hope, *née* Llewelyn; *b* 26 May 1940; *Educ* Ampleforth; *m* 1961, Diana Jean, er da of Air Marshal Sir Patrick Hunter Dunn, KBE, CB, DFC, *qv*; 3 da (Lucinda Ann b 1962, Rose Amanda b 1964, Annabel Juliet b 1968); *Heir* bro, Simon Neville Llewelyn Marsden, *qv*; *Career* self employed gardener; *Recreations* walking, family, countryside pursuits; *Style*— Sir Nigel Marsden, Bt; ✉ 1 Grimsby Rd, Waltham, Grimsby, South Humberside DN37 0PS

MARSDEN, Rear Adm Peter Nicholas; s of Dr James Pickford Marsden (d 1977), and Evelyn Holman (d 1970); *b* 29 June 1932; *Educ* Felsted; *m* 12 Oct 1956, Jean Elizabeth, da of Cdr J H Mather, DSO, VRD, RNVR (d 1957); 2 s (James b 1957, Jonathan b 1960), 1 da (Joanna b 1963); *Career* RN 1950–88, dir Fleet Supply Duties Div MOD 1980–81, Cdre Admty Interview Bd 1983–85, sr naval memb Directing Staff RCDS 1985–88; exec dir 21st Century Trust 1989–92, chm Isle of Wight Gardens Tst 1994–; *Recreations* beagling, gardening, golf; *Style*— Rear Adm Peter Marsden; ✉ c/o National Westminster Bank, Standishgate, Wigan, Lancs WN1 1UJ

MARSDEN, Simon Neville Llewelyn; yr s of Sir John Denton Marsden, 2 Bt (d 1985); hp of bro, Sir Nigel John Denton Marsden, 3 Bt, *qv*; *b* 1948; *Educ* Ampleforth, Sorbonne; *m* 1, 1970 (m dis 1978), Catherine Thérèsa, yr da of late Brig James Charles Windsor-Lewis, DSO; m 2, 1984, Caroline, yst da of John Stanton, of Houghton St Giles, Walsingham, Norfolk; 1 s (Tadgh Orlando Denton b 25 Dec 1990), 1 da (Skye Atalanta b 24 Feb 1988); *Career* author and photographer; collections in: V & A, Getty Museum California; *Books* In Ruins (The Once Great Houses of Ireland) (1980), The Haunted Realm (Ghosts, Witches and other Strange Tales) (1986), Visions of Poe (1988), Phantoms of the Isles (1990), The Journal of a Ghosthunter (1994); *Style*— Simon Marsden, Esq; ✉ The Presbytery, Hainton, Lincoln LN3 6LR (☎ and fax 01507 313646)

MARSDEN, (James) Stuart; s of James Herbert Marsden (d 1969), and Constance Hilda Naylor (d 1970); *b* 20 Dec 1930; *Educ* William Hulmes Sch Manchester; *m* 22 June 1957, Eileen Kinloch, da of Reginald Wilkinson (d 1928), of Ormskirk; 1 s (Richard James Nicholas b 16 July 1961), 1 da (Jill Karen (Mrs Walsh) b 14 March 1958); *Career* Martins Bank 1948–50; Nat Serv RAF, Flying Offr 1950–52; articled to W H Robinson Manchester 1952, British Waterways 1955–57, currently conslt (former practice chm) Edmund Kirby Architects and Surveyors (joined 1957); chm Merseyside & Isle of Man Branch RICS 1980; memb Liverpool C of C & Indust (memb Planning and Strategy Ctee (chm 1989–91)), memb Bd and chm Harbour Housing Gp Riverside Housing Assoc, memb Ctee Dale Farm for the Mentally Handicapped (chm 1985), tstee and memb Cncl of Management Norton Priory Museum Tst Assoc; FRICS 1957; *Recreations* sailing, skiing, tennis, gardening; *Clubs* Oriental; *Style*— Stuart Marsden, Esq; ✉ Edmund Kirby, India Buildings, Water Street, Liverpool L2 0TZ (☎ 0151 236 4552, fax 0151 236 4024)

MARSDEN, William; CMG (1991); s of Christopher Alexander Marsden (d 1989), of The Vineyard, Saffron Walden, Essex, and (Margaret) Ruth, *née* Kershaw (d 1970); *b* 15 Sept 1940; *Educ* Winchester, Lawrenceville Sch USA, Trinity Coll Cambridge (MA), Univ of London (BSc); *m* 19 Sept 1964, Eileen Ursula (Kaia) Collingham; 1 s (Thomas Alexander b 16 Jan 1970), 1 da (Inge Katharine b 29 July 1966); *Career* third sec UK Delgn to NATO Paris 1964–66, second sec Rome Embassy 1966–69, seconded as asst to Gen Mangr Joseph Lucas Ltd 1970, first sec and cultural attaché Moscow Embassy 1976–79, asst head Euro Community Dept FCO 1978–81, cnsllr UK Representation to the EEC Brussels 1981–85, head E African dept FCO and cmmr Br Indian Ocean Territory 1985–88, ambass to Costa Rica (concurrently non-resident ambass to Nicaragua) 1989–92, min (trade) Washington Embassy 1992–94, asst under-sec (Americas) FCO 1994–; Freeman: City of London 1967, Worshipful Co of Grocers 1967; MIMgt; *Style*— William Marsden, Esq, CMG; ✉ c/o Foreign and Commonwealth Office, London SW1A 2AH

MARSDEN-SMEDLEY, Christopher; s of Basil Futuoye Marsden-Smedley, OBE (d 1964), and Hester Harriott, *née* Pinney (d 1982); *b* 9 Feb 1931; *Educ* Harrow, Univ Coll London (BA); *m* 7 Dec 1957, Susan Penelope, da of Sir James Granville Le Neve King, Bt, TD (d 1989); 2 s (Timothy Charles b 19 Feb 1959, Philip John b 11 May 1961), 1 da (Catherine Penelope b 8 May 1964); *Career* architect; sr ptnr Nealon Tanner Partnership 1990–96 (ptnr 1961–96); High Sheriff for Co of Avon 1994–95; chm Bristol Age Care 1988–, pres Bristol Commercial Rooms 1988, hon sec Bristol Civic Soc 1966–71, govr Fairfield Sch 1969–75 (chm 1972–75); FRIBA 1969 (ARIBA 1959); *Publications* Burrington - Church and Village (1991); *Recreations* architecture, painting, travel, charitable organisations; *Style*— Christopher Marsden-Smedley, Esq; ✉ Church Farm, Burrington, nr Bristol BS18 7AD (☎ 01761 462481)

MARSH, Alan James; s of James Alfred Leonard Marsh, of Castlemain, Avondale Rd, St Leonards-on-Sea, Sussex, and Grace Maud, *née* Weller (d 1985); *b* 26 Aug 1929; *Educ* Colfes GS, ChCh Oxford (MA); *m* 1, 28 Dec 1957 (m dis 1974), Ingrid Hilma Elizabet, da of Nils Areskog (d 1977), of Kalmar, Sweden; 1 s (Neil b 4 Aug 1959), 1 da (Caroline b 27 Oct 1961); m 2, 11 July 1975, Joanna Maud, da of Brig Bertram Edward Lionel Burton, CBE (d 1976), of Uckfield, Sussex; *Career* Lt 4 RTR 1952–54; Metal Box Co 1954–61, mangr Corporate Strategy Div PA Int Mgmnt Conslts 1961–71, gp fin dir Revertex Chemicals Ltd 1971–80, exec dir Midland Montagu Ventures 1980–89, chm Aegis Corporate Strategy Ltd 1989–96; Freeman City of London, Liveryman Worshipful Co of Gold and Silver Wire Drawers; FCMA 1966, FCT 1978, MIMC 1963, FRSA; *Recreations* sailing, golf; *Clubs* United Oxford and Cambridge Univ, Royal Corinthian YC, Royal Burnham YC; *Style*— Alan Marsh, Esq; ✉ Fairway Cottage, Creeksea Lane, Burnham on Crouch, Essex CM0 8PH (☎ 01621 783539)

MARSH, Alan John Scott; s of Reginald John Marsh, and Vera Kathleen, *née* Wood; *b* 1 Nov 1936; *Educ* Charterhouse, Coll of Estate Mgmnt London; *m* 3 Nov 1962, Pamela Mary, da of Albert Edward White, of Eastbourne; 2 da (Caroline b 1963, Nicola b 1965); *Career* Ford Motor Co 1960–72, gen sales mangr Austin Morris 1972–75, fleet sales dir Leyland Cars 1975–77, regnl dir Leyland Int 1977–78, serv dir Rover Triumph 1978–79, sales and mktg dir Toyota (GB) Ltd 1979–84, md IMC Belgium 1984–85, chm Toyota (GB) Ltd 1992–94 (md and chief exec 1986–92), dir Inchcape plc 1992–94, vice chm Toyota Motor Europe Marketing and Engineering SA 1994–; FInstD; *Recreations* motoring, sport, boating; *Clubs* RAC; *Style*— Alan Marsh, Esq; ✉ Toyota Motor Europe Marketing and Engineering SA, Avenue du Bourget 60, Bourgetlaan 60, B1140 Brussels, Belgium (☎ 00 32 2 745 2006, fax 00 32 2 745 2008)

MARSH, Dr Barbara Elizabeth; JP (Shropshire 1969), DL (Shropshire 1993); da of John Watson (d 1965), of St Helens, Lancs, and Elizabeth, *née* Burrows (d 1987); *b* 3 July 1931; *Educ* Cowley Girls' GS, Univ of London (BSc), Univ of Birmingham (PhD); *m* 1 April 1958, (George) Eric Marsh, s of Richard George Marsh, of Newport, Shropshire; 3 s (Andrew b 1958, Stephen b 1961, Piers b 1963), 1 da (Fiona b 1967); *Career* demonstrator King's Coll Newcastle 1956–57, lectr St Helen Tech Coll 1957–58, teacher Adams GS Newport 1959–60; non-exec memb: Midlands Electricity Bd 1984–89, Shropshire Health Authy 1990–93; chm Royal Shrewsbury Hosps Tst 1993–; memb: Industl Tbnl, Cncl on Tbnls 1977–84, Roskill Ctee on Fraud 1984–86, W Mercia Police Authy 1989–93; memb Shropshire CC 1964– (vice chm 1981–85); former memb Exec and chm Educn Ctee Assoc of CCs, former chm Area Manpower Bd for Shropshire, former vice pres Nat Inst of Adult Continuing Educn; cmmr Rural Devpt Cmmn 1991–; *Recreations* dabbling; *Clubs* Farmers'; *Style*— Dr Barbara Marsh, JP, DL; ✉ The Old Smithy, Chetwynd Aston, Newport, Shropshire TF10 9LJ

MARSH, (Graham) Barrie; s of Ernest Heaps Marsh (d 1983), of Birkdale, Southport, and Laura Greenhalgh, *née* Baucher; *b* 18 July 1935; *Educ* Loughborough GS, Univ of Liverpool (LLB); *m* 5 April 1961, Nancy, da of Leslie Herbert Smith (d 1984), of Anstey, Leicester; 1 s (Peter James b 1962), 2 da (Susan Nancy b 1964, Caroline Judith b 1966); *Career* Nat Serv with RASC 1957–59; admitted slr 1967; pres Liverpool Publicity Assoc 1980; chm: Merseyside Chamber of Commerce and Indust 1984 86, Radio City plc 1988–; nat chm Young Slr Gp Law Soc 1975; pres: Liverpool Law Soc 1978–79, Slrs Disciplinary Tbnl 1988–; Belgian Consul in Liverpool; FRIA; *Books* Employer and Employee (3 edn, 1989); *Recreations* hill walking, golf, bird watching; *Clubs* Liverpool Racquet, Anglo-Belgian (London); *Style*— Barrie Marsh, Esq; ✉ Calmer Hey, Benty Heath Lane, Willaston, South Wirral L64 1SA (☎ 0151 327 4863); Mace & Jones, 19 Water St, Liverpool L2 0RP (☎ 0151 236 8989, fax 0151 227 5010)

MARSH, (John) Colin Trafford; s of Frank Edward Marsh (d 1975), and Celia, *née* Trafford; *b* 9 Sept 1931; *Educ* St Michael's Sch Limpsfield Surrey, apprentice cabinet maker 1947–50, Kingston Sch of Art; *m* 1, 1958 (m dis 1965), Susan; 2 da (Nicolette, Michelle); m 2, 1975, Sarah Josephine, da of John Arthur Whale; 1 s (Henry Benjamin b 1980), 1 da (Laura Alice b 1977); *Career* airframe fitter RAF 1950–52; cabinet maker and design asst Ian Audsley Furniture 1954–55, self-employed furniture maker 1956–59, Baderlex Engineering Ltd 1959–62; designer: Adron Duckworth Associates 1962–63, Planning Unit Design Consultants 1963–75 (dir 1971–75); fndr freelance design consultancy 1975–; formerly sessional lectr in furniture design various institutions, sr lectr High Wycombe Coll of Art and Design 1978–79, assoc lectr Ravensbourne Coll of Design and Communication 1985–; chm Product Gp and memb Cncl Chartered Soc of Designers 1988–90 (membership assessor 1984–); FCSD (MCSD 1975); *Recreations* sailing, vintage sports cars; *Clubs* Yarmouth Sailing; *Style*— Colin Marsh, Esq; ✉ 13 Kent Rd, East Molesey, Surrey KT8 9JZ (☎ 0181 979 4177, fax 0181 979 4177)

MARSH, David John; s of Harry Cheetham Marsh (d 1979), of Solihull, Warwickshire, and Florence, *née* Bold (d 1990); *b* 2 Nov 1936; *Educ* Leeds GS, Merton Coll Oxford (MA); *m* 26 May 1962, Hilary Joy, da of Edwin Leslie Pitt (d 1993), of Tetbury, Glos; 1 s (Nigel b 1966), 2 da (Carole b 1963, Rowena b 1965); *Career* admitted slr 1961, ptnr Wragge & Co Slrs 1963–92, ptnr Lenchwick Management Services 1992–; dir Marla Tube Fittings Ltd 1965–, chm Bd of Tstees United Industries plc gp pension schemes 1992–; memb Law Soc 1961; *Recreations* sport, travel, wine, food; *Style*— David Marsh, Esq; ✉ Lenchwick House, Lenchwick, nr Evesham, Worcs WR11 4TG (☎ and fax 01386 442451)

MARSH, Dr David Max; s of Joseph Richard James Maximilian Marsh (d 1985), and Dorothy, *née* Pemberton; *b* 29 April 1934; *Educ* King George V Sch Southport, Gonville and Caius Coll Cambridge (BA, MB BChir, MFOM); *m* 7 Nov 1959, Jennifer Margaret, da of Robert Samuel Heaton (d 1977); 2 s (Simon b 24 Nov 1960, Nigel b 4 July 1962), 1 da (Fiona b 25 Jan 1964); *Career* GP 1961–, employment med advsr Health and Safety Exec 1973–; English golf champion 1964 and 1970, English int golf 1956–72, capt England golf 1968–71, capt GB golf 1973–75; chm Rules of Golf Ctee Royal and Ancient Golf Club 1988–90; former chm Everton Football Club; pres: Lancashire Union of Golf Clubs 1985, Eng Golf Union 1988; MFOM; *Recreations* golf, soccer; *Clubs* Southport and Ainsdale Golf, Formby Golf, Royal and Ancient (Capt 1990–91), Ormskirk Golf, Royal Worlington and Newmarket Golf, Royal Over-Seas League; *Style*— Dr David Marsh; ✉ 26 Blundell Drive, Southport, Merseyside PR8 4RG (☎ 01704 65639); 63 Henlow Ave, Kirkby, Liverpool L32 9RN (☎ 0151 549 2212)

MARSH, Eric Morice; s of Frederick Morice Marsh (d 1970), of Carnforth, Lancs, and Anne, *née* Leigh; *b* 25 July 1943; *Educ* The Abbey Sch Fort Augustus Inverness-shire Scotland, Courtfield Catering Coll Blackpool, Lancs (Nat Dip Hotelkeeping & Catering); *m* 2 Sept 1968, Elizabeth Margaret, da of John (Jack) Lowes, of Macclesfield, Cheshire; 2 s (Andrew Paul b 4 Aug 1969, Christopher Simon b 5 July 1974), 2 da (Erika Louise b 26 Oct 1971, Lucy Anne b 4 Aug 1982); *Career* student Hotel Sch 1960–63, stagiare George V Hotel Paris 1964–65, trainee The Dorchester 1965–68, asst mangr Royal Lancaster 1969–73, dir and gen mangr Newling Ward Hotels Ltd 1973–75, tenant Cavendish Hotel Chatsworth Estate 1975–; md: Paludis Ltd (trading as Cavendish Hotel) 1975–, Cavendish Aviation Ltd; pt/t lectr Sheffield Hallam Univ, occasional contribs to professional pubns; memb Catholic Church Fin Ctee, Co-ordinator Ctee Neighbourhood Watch, dep chm Br Aerobatics Assoc, memb Ctee Br Hospitality Assoc; memb Inst of Advanced Motorists, MInstM; *Recreations* collection of fine art, aviation (aerobatics), distance running; *Style*— Eric Marsh, Esq; ✉ Cavendish Hotel, Baslow, Derbys DE45 1SP (☎ 01246 582311); Paludis Ltd, Baslow, Derbys DE45 1SP (☎ 01246 582311, fax 01246 582312, car 0836 587 690, telex 547150 CAVTEL G)

MARSH, Baroness; Hon Felicity Carmen Francesca; da of Baron McFadzean of Kelvinside (Life Peer, d 1992), and his 1 w, Isabel McKenzie, *née* Beattie; *b* 26 April 1946; *Educ* St Paul's Girls' Sch, SOAS (BA in Japanese); *m* 1979, as his 3 w, Baron Marsh, *qv*; *Career* investment analyst/portfolio mangr Robert Fleming 1974–79, asst vice pres Rowe Price-Fleming Int Inc 1979–81, dir Mannington Mgmnt Servs Ltd 1982–; memb Bd Cmmn for the New Towns 1992–; *Books* Japanese Overseas Investment - The New Challenge (1983), Japan's Next Export Success: The Financial Services Industry (1986); *Recreations* Oriental antiques, classic cars, windsurfing, photography; *Style*— The Lady Marsh; ✉ c/o Lloyds Bank Ltd, Covent Garden, London W1

MARSH, Dr Francis Patrick (Frank); s of Horatio Septimus Marsh, of Leeds, Yorks, and Violet Mabel Constance, *née* Murphy; *b* 15 April 1936; *Educ* Gonville and Caius Coll Cambridge (BA, MB BChir, MA), London Hosp Med Coll Univ of London, MRCP, FRCP; *m* 31 Aug 1963, Pamela Anne Campbell, da of Richard Campbell Bradbury (d 1963), of London; 1 s (Nicholas b 1966), 2 da (Penelope b 1964, Alexandra b 1971); *Career* The Royal London Hosp: house offr 1960–61, registrar in med 1963–65, res fell Med Unit Med Coll 1965–67, lectr Med Coll 1967–70, sr lectr in med 1970–, conslt physician 1971–, dean of med studies Med Coll 1990–95 (memb Cncl of Govrs Med Coll 1990–95, memb Academic Bd Med Coll 1990–); SHO Kent and Canterbury Hosp 1961–62, registrar in med Royal Free Hosp 1962–63; chm NE Thames Regnl Med Advsy Ctee 1986–90; memb: Exec Ctee Renal Assoc 1983–87, Central Ctee for Hosp Med Servs 1984–87, Jt Formulary Ctee Br Nat Formulary 1986–, Special Advsy Ctee on Renal Disease, Jt Ctee on Higher Med Trg 1986–90, Jt Academic Ctee City of E London Confedn for Med and Dentistry 1991–95, Bd of Faculty of Basic Med Scis Queen Mary and Westfield Coll 1992–95; memb: Euro Renal Assoc, BR Transplant Soc, Int Soc of Nephrology, Royal Society of Medicine, Royal Society of Apothecaries; *Books* incl: Urology (contrib, 1976), Price's Textbook of Medicine (contrib, 1978), Oxford Textbook of Medicine (contrib, 1982, 1987), Postgraduate Nephrology (ed, 1985), Hutchisons Clinical Methods (contrib, 1975, 1980, 1984, 1989 and 1996), Drugs and the Kidney (contrib, 1990); author of numerous original papers on renal diseases; *Recreations* music, sailing, skiing; *Clubs* Blizard; *Style*— Dr Frank Marsh; ✉ 28 Highfield Drive, Bromley, Kent BR2 0RX (☎ 0181 460 6295); Eastnor Cottage, East Dean, Chichester, West Sussex PO18 0JA (☎ 01243 811239); The Royal London Hospital, Whitechapel, London E1 1BB (☎ 0171 377 7367, fax 0171 377 7003)

MARSH, Frederick Oliver; *b* 13 Sept 1925; *Educ* Regent St Poly (Dip Mgmnt Studies); *Career* Capt Royal Berks Regt, demobbed 1948; chm and md Winton-Smith (Foods) Ltd 1964–74, princ Marsh Business Servs 1974–; mktg conslt: UN Agency (ITC UNCTAD WTO 1978–93, Helsinki Sch of Econs 1984–; chm Royal Aero Club 1995– (vice chm 1977–82), vice pres Fedn Aeronautique Internationale 1982–90 (pres Membership Ctee 1990–), pres Europe Airsports 1988–95; Br Air Racing champion 1972, winner Duke of Edinburgh Trophy for Formula Air Racing 1972 and 1976; FAI Tissandier Dip 1978, OM World Aerospace Educn Orgn 1985, Royal Aero Club Silver medal 1989; Freeman City of London 1962, Liveryman Worshipful Co of Butchers 1962; FIMgt 1970, memb Central Cncl for Physical Recreation 1992; *Books* The Market for Pet Products in Europe (1990, re-written 1992), The Marsh Guide to Business Customs, Conventions and Etiquette (1992), A Survey of European Markets for Handicrafts (1994); *Recreations* air sport, painting, travel, Scottish dancing; *Clubs* Naval & Military, Royal Aero; *Style*— Frederick Marsh, Esq; ✉ 36 Edwardes Square, London W8 6HH (☎ and fax 0171 603 3133)

MARSH, Gordon Victor; s of Ven Wilfred Carter Marsh (d 1931), of Devil's Lake, North Dakota, USA, and Rosalie Marsh (d 1947); *b* 14 May 1929; *Educ* The Coll and Commonwealth GSs Swindon Wilts, Keble Coll Oxford (MA), Sloan Business Sch Cornell Univ USA; *m* 13 June 1959, Millicent, da of Christopher Thomas Rowsell (d 1959); 1 s (Richard b 1960), 1 da (Susan (Mrs Barr) b 1961); *Career* RAF PO personnel selection branch 1947–49; dep sec United Cardiff Hosps 1960–65, dep sec and house govr St George's Hosp 1965–72, admin and sec Bd of Govrs UCH 1972–74, area admin Lambeth Southwark and Lewisham Area Health Authy (teaching) 1974–82, dep health serv cmmr for Eng Scot and Wales 1982–89; memb Cncl NAHA 1979–82, vice chm Assoc of Chief Admins of Health Authys 1980–82; memb: Advsy Bd Coll of Occupational Therapists 1974–95, various working parties concerned with med ethics, Police Complaints Authority 1989–96; chm Trelawn Mgmnt Ctee of Richmond Fellowship 1970–83; wandsman, guide and hon sec of congregation St Paul's Cathedral 1980–, memb RSM, FHSM 1964; *Recreations* gardens and gardening, music; *Clubs* United Oxford and Cambridge Universities; *Style*— Gordon Marsh, Esq; ✉ Springwater, St Lucian's Lane, Wallingford OX10 9ER (☎ 01491 836660

MARSH, Capt John; CBE (1987); s of Arthur Frank Marsh (d 1953), of Cheam, Surrey, and Doris Evelyn, *née* Dabbs; *b* 23 Aug 1932; *Educ* Epsom Coll, St John's Coll Cambridge (MA); *m* 12 April 1958, Margaret Hilda, da of Eric William Beresford Brailey (d 1977), of Fremington, Devon; 2 s (Jonathon b 1961, Nigel b 1964); *Career* cmmnd RN 1954, Cdr 1968, Staff of Saclant Norfolk VA USA 1972, HMS Ark Royal 1975, RN Sch of Meteorology and Oceanography 1977, Capt 1978, Staff of Saceur Belgium 1979, Staff of CinC Fleet 1982, dir naval oceanography and meteorology MOD London 1985, Chief Naval Instr Offr 1986; dir Int Toga Project Office World Meteorological Orgn Geneva Switzerland 1987–94; *Recreations* bridge, music, walking; *Style*— Capt John Marsh, CBE; ✉ Overton House, Queen Camel, Yeovil, Somerset BA22 7NG (☎ 01935 850172)

MARSH, Ven Dr (Francis) John; s of William Frederick Marsh (d 1979), of Bromley, Kent, and Helena Mary, *née* Petley (d 1979); *b* 3 July 1947; *Educ* Beckenham and Penge GS, Univ of York (BA, DPhil), Selwyn Coll Cambridge (CertTheol), Oak Hill Theol Coll London, ARCO, ARCM, ATCL; *m* 20 July 1974, Gillian, da of Derek John Popely, of York; 2 da (Joanna Clare b 1979, Victoria Ruth b 1986); *Career* curate: St Matthew Cambridge 1975–78, Christ Church Pitsmoor Sheffield 1979–81; memb staff St Thomas' Crookes Sheffield 1981–85, vicar Christ Church S Ossett 1985–96, rural dean of Dewsbury 1993–96, proctor in convocation 1990–96, archdeacon of Blackburn 1996–; *Recreations* music, dog-walking; *Style*— The Ven the Archdeacon of Blackburn; ✉ 19 Clarence Park, Blackburn, Lancs BB2 7FA (☎ 01254 262571, fax 01254 263394)

MARSH, Prof John Stanley; CBE (1993); s of Stanley Albert Marsh (d 1973), and Elsie Gertrude, *née* Powell (d 1969); *b* 5 Oct 1931; *Educ* George Dixon GS Birmingham, St John's Coll Oxford (MA); *m* 20 Sept 1958, Kathleen Edith, da of Eric Arthur Casey (d 1982); 1 s (Peter b 1967), 1 da (Christine b 1969); *Career* Nat Serv RAF 1950–52; Univ of Reading 1956–77: res economist, lectr, sr lectr, reader, prof of agric economics 1984–, dean agric 1986–89, dir Centre for Agric Strategy; prof of agric economics Univ of Aberdeen 1977–84; author of numerous articles and pubns on agric related topics; sec

Agric Economics Soc 1969–84; memb: Potato Mktg Bd 1979–84, SWP Food and Drink Mfrg 1990–92; chm Agric Wages Bd 1990–; FRSA 1978, FRAgS 1993, FRASE 1991; *Books* A Preliminary Study of the Small Dairy Farm and the Small Farm Scheme (1960), The National Association of Corn and Agricultural Merchants and the Merchant's Future (1967), A Future for European Agriculture (jtly, 1971), CAP: UK Priorities, European Opinion (1976), L'Ordre Alimentaire Mondial (contrib, 1982), The Human Food Chain (contrib, 1989), The Changing Role of the Common Agricultural Policy (jtly, 1991); *Recreations* photography, caravanning; *Clubs* Farmers'; *Style*— Prof John Marsh, CBE; ✉ 15 Adams Way, Earley, Reading, Berks RG6 2UT (☎ 0118 986 8434); Department of Agricultural Economics and Management, University of Reading, 4 Earley Gate, Whiteknights Rd, P O Box 237, Reading, Berkshire RG6 2AR (☎ 0118 931 8970, fax 0118 975 6467, telex 847813 RULIBG)

MARSH, June Margaret; da of Frederick John Palmer (d 1981), of Cheshunt, Hertfordshire, and Ivy Margaret, *née* Tate; *b* 3 July 1948; *Educ* King Harold Sch Waltham Abbey Essex, London Coll of Fashion; *m* Graham John Marsh, s of late Frederick John Marsh; *Career* fashion ed: Woman's Own 1974–78, Evening News 1979–80, TV Times 1980–81; ed Browns magazine 1980–81, fashion and beauty ed Options 1981–86, tutor St Martin's Sch of Art 1986–; contrib ed: Sunday Times, Times, Evening Standard, Vogue, Observer, Sunday Express Magazine, New Woman, Company Magazine, The Daily Telegraph; fashion ed: Country Life 1989–91, Daily Mail 1995–; memb NUJ; *Recreations* reading, writing, painting; *Style*— Mrs June Marsh; ✉ Daily Mail, Northcliffe House, 2 Derry Street, London W8 (☎ 0171 938 6171); 6 Hyde Vale, Greenwich, London SE10 8QH (☎ 0181 691 0568)

MARSH, Laurie Peter; s of Davis Marsh (d 1991); *b* 23 Oct 1930; *Educ* Perse Sch Cambridge; *m* 1, 1961 (m dis); 1 s, 2 da; m 2, 2 June 1995; *Career* md L P Marsh Properties Ltd 1958–, John Laurie & Co Ltd 1961–64, jt md English Property Corporation 1965–70, chm and chief exec Intereuropean Properties Ltd (formerly Tigon Group) 1969–, merged with Assoc Communications Corporation 1979, dir ACC 1979–; chm and chief exec: Town and District Properties Ltd, Laurie Marsh Group, Laurie Marsh Consultants, International Heritage Corporation Ltd and others 1980–; chm Cole Kitchenn Ltd (theatrical prodn mangrs and prodrs); fin and commercial conslt to: Urban Space Holdings Ltd, Urban Space Management Ltd; chm of and conslt to national charities; *Recreations* theatre, travel, music, literature; *Style*— Laurie Marsh, Esq; ✉ Laurie Marsh, 30 Grove End Rd, London NW8 9LJ (☎ 0171 289 6081, fax 0171 286 9907); 244 East 48th St, New York 10017, USA; Les Montels Lunas, Herault, France

MARSH, Prof Leonard George; OBE (1992); s of Ernest Arthur Marsh, and Anne Eliza, *née* Bean; *b* 23 Oct 1930; *Educ* Ashford GS, Borough Road Coll London Inst of Educn, Univ of Leicester, Univ of York; *m* 20 Aug 1953, Ann Margaret, da of Thomas Francis Gilbert (d 1979); 1 s (David Richard b 1964), 1 da (Carol Ann b 1956); *Career* lectr St Paul's Coll Cheltenham 1963–65, princ lectr and head Postgrad Primary Educn Dept Goldsmiths' Coll London 1965–74, princ Bishop Grosseteste Coll Lincoln 1974–96; visiting lectr: Bank St Coll NY, Virginia Cwlth Univ; former conslt OECD Portugal, educnl conslt Teacher Trg Project Botswana 1981, specialist tour India for Br Cncl; memb: Gen Advsy Cncl IBA 1977–82, N Lincs AHA 1984–90, School Curriculum and Assessment Authy 1993–; chm Nat Assoc for Primary Educn 1981–83; hon prof Univ of Hull 1987–; Hon DLitt Univ of Hull; Hon FCP; *Books* Let's Explore Mathematics Books 1–4 (1964–67), Children Explore Mathematics (1967, 3 edn 1969), Exploring the Metric World (1970), Let's Discover Mathematics Books 1–5 (1971–72), The Guinness Mathematics Book (1980), Alongside the Child in the Primary School (1970), Being a Teacher (1973); *Recreations* photography, theatre going, films; *Clubs* Athenaeum; *Style*— Prof Leonard Marsh, OBE; ✉ Broomfields, The Meadow, Chislehurst, Kent BR7 6AA (☎ and fax 0181 467 6311)

MARSH, Prof Paul Rodney; s of Harold Marsh, of Bournemouth, Dorset, and Constance, *née* Miller; *b* 19 Aug 1947; *Educ* Poole GS, LSE (BSc Econ), London Business Sch (PhD); *m* 13 Sept 1971, Stephanie Beatrice, da of Mark Simonow, of London; *Career* systems analyst: Esso Petroleum 1968–69, Scicon 1970–71; London Business Sch 1974–: Bank of England res fell 1974–85; Centre for Mgmnt Devpt: non exec dir 1984–91, prof of mgmnt & fin 1985–, memb Governing Body 1986–90, faculty dean 1987–90, dep princ 1989–90, dir masters prog in finance 1993–; non exec dir M&G Investmt Mgmnt 1989–, dir Hoare Govett Indices Ltd 1991–; govr Examinations Bd Securities Inst; author of numerous pubns on corporate fin and investmt mgmnt in: Journal of Finance, Journal of Financial Economics, Managerial Finance, Harvard Business Review, Journal of the Institute of Actuaries, Research in Marketing, The Investment Analyst, Long Range Planning; memb CBI task force on City-Indust relationships 1986–88; exec ctee memb Br Acad of Mgmnt 1986–89; memb: Euro Fin Assoc, American Fin Assoc; *Books* Cases in Corporate Finance (1988), Managing Strategic Investment Decisions (1988), Accounting for Brands (1989), Short-Termism on Trial (1990), The HGSC Smaller Companies Index (1996); *Recreations* gardening; *Style*— Prof Paul Marsh; ✉ London Business School, Sussex Place, Regents Park, London NW1 4SA (☎ 0171 262 5050, fax 0171 724 7875, e-mail pmarsh@lbs.lon.ac.uk)

MARSH, Peter Dudley; s of Dudley Graham Marsh (d 1969), of Canterbury, and Norah Marion *née* Wacher (d 1974); *b* 16 Feb 1926; *Educ* Dulwich, St John's Coll Hurstpierpoint, Univ of Edinburgh, Sch of Architecture Canterbury Coll of Art; *m* 1, 18 Aug 1949, June, *née* Saxby (d 1969); 2 s (Richard b 1957, Jonathan b 1961), 1 da (Anne Crouch b 1953); m 2, 23 May 1970, Valerie (d 1994), da of Charles Alfred Williams (d 1983); 1 s (Henry b 1977); *Career* architect in private practice 1952–, Surveyor to the Fabric Canterbury Cathedral 1969–91; chm: Canterbury Branch RIBA 1969, Cathedral Architects Assoc 1984–87; pres Rotary Club of Dover 1973, memb Tech Sub Ctee Euro Cathedrals Assoc 1986–, chm Fabric Advsy Ctee Rochester Cathedral; vice chm Bd of Govrs Kent Inst of Art and Design; Freeman City of London, Liveryman Worshipful Co of Masons 1978; memb EASA, ARIBA 1953, FSA 1982; *Recreations* bee keeping; *Style*— Peter Marsh, Esq, FSA; ✉ The Old Stables, Canterbury Road, Lydden, Kent CT15 7EP (☎ 01304 822022)

MARSH, Baron (Life Peer UK 1981), of Mannington, Co Wilts; Richard William Marsh; kt (1976), PC (1966); s of William Marsh, of Belvedere, Kent; *b* 14 March 1928; *Educ* Jennings Sch Swindon, Woolwich Poly, Ruskin Coll Oxford; *m* 1, 1950 (m dis 1973), Evelyn Mary, da of Frederick Andrews, of Southampton; 2 s (Hon Andrew b 1950, Hon Christopher b 1960); m 2, 1973, Caroline Dutton (d 1975); m 3, 1979, Hon Felicity Carmen Francesca, *qv*, o da of Baron McFadzean of Kelvinside (Life Peer, d 1992); *Career* health servs offr Nat Union of Public Employees 1951–59; memb Clerical and Admin Whitley Cncl for Health Serv 1953–59; MP (L) Greenwich 1959–71; memb Nat Exec Fabian Soc; jt parly sec Miny of Labour 1964–65, Miny of Technol 1965–66, min of Power 1966–68, min of Tport 1968–70; chm: Br Railways Bd 1971–76, Br Iron and Steel Consumers' Cncl until 1983, Lee Cooper Licensing Services, Lee Cooper plc 1982–88, Newspaper Publishers' Assoc 1976–90, TV-AM (pt/t) 1983–84, Mannington Management Services Ltd, Lopex plc, Laurentian Financial Group plc 1989–, China and Eastern Investment Trust (Hong Kong) 1987–, British Income & Growth Tst; dir Imperial Life of Canada (Toronto) 1984; *Clubs* Reform; *Style*— The Rt Hon the Lord Marsh, PC; ✉ House of Lords, London SW1A 0PW

MARSH, Steven Andrew; s of Melvyn Graham Marsh, of Walderslade, Chatham, Kent, and Valerie Ann, *née* Box; *b* 27 Jan 1961; *Educ* Walderslade Secdy Sch for Boys, Mid Kent Coll of Higher and Further Educn; *m* 27 Sept 1986, Julie Ann, da of Robert Colin Wilson; 1 s (Christian James Robert b 20 Nov 1990), 1 da (Hayley Ann b 15 May 1987); *Career* professional cricketer; Kent CCC: debut 1982, awarded county cap 1986, vice capt 1991–96, capt 1996; 2 one day ints England A v Sri Lanka 1991; jt world wicket-keeping record 8 catches in an innings v Middlesex 1991 (scored 108 not out in same match); *Recreations* golf, watching sport on TV, Chelsea FC, music; *Style*— Steven Marsh, Esq; ✉ Kent CCC, St Lawrence Ground, Old Dover Rd, Canterbury, Kent CT1 3NZ (☎ 01227 456886)

MARSH, Thérèse Virginia (Terry); da of Rear Adm John Anthony Bell, CB, of Taunton, and Eileen Joan, *née* Woodman; *b* 3 Dec 1946; *Educ* St Joseph's Convent London, Norfolk Catholic HS Virginia USA, Gumley House Isleworth, Univ of Liverpool (BEd), Univ of Surrey (MSc); *m* 1968 (m dis 1980), Michael Frederick Marsh, s of Francis Joseph Marsh; 2 da (Suzanna Joan b 14 Nov 1970, Caroline Margaret b 7 Jan 1972); *Career* mathematics teacher Trinity HS Trinidad 1970, princ Ifold Nursery Centre Sussex 1972–76, financial controller Marsh Developments Guildford 1976–77, assoc lectr in statistics Univ of Surrey 1977–78; BBC: researcher BBC Educn 1979–80, asst prodr BBC Children's TV 1980–83, prodr BBC Continuing Educn 1986–89 (asst prodr 1984–86), exec prodr BBC School TV 1989–90, head of BBC School TV 1990–92, head bi-media BBC School Progs 1992–95; vice pres programming Sci-Fi Europe 1995–; memb: DTI Task Force Action for Engineering, Women in Film and TV 1995; govr Digby Stuart Coll Roehampton Inst; winner Times Technology Programme Award for Micro Live, City of Basle Award for Sex Education; memb RTS 1988; *Recreations* community theatre, dancing; *Style*— Ms Terry Marsh

MARSHALL, Albert Selwyn; MBE (1968); s of Albert Marshall (d 1978), of Barrow, Bury St Edmunds, Suffolk, and Ethel, *née* Andrews; *b* 26 Sept 1934; *Educ* Dartford West Co Sch; *m* 1, 19 March 1960, Joan Margaret (d 1985), da of Victor Percy Lashwood, of Newport Pagnell; 1 s (Trevor Keith b 19 June 1961), 1 da (Julie Carina b 8 Aug 1963); m 2, 19 July 1988, Marion Rose, *née* Wilmott; *Career* diplomat; FO 1955–61, communications offr UK mission to UN NY 1961–64, archivist Br Embassy Prague 1964–65, immigration offr Br High Cmmn Kingston Jamaica 1965–68, FCO 1968–72, admin offr Br Embassy Addis Ababa Ethiopia 1972–75, Br vice consul Belgrade Yugoslavia 1976–77, HM vice consul Tokyo Japan 1977–81, FCO 1981–86, first sec Br Embassy Washington USA 1986–90, HM consul Br Embassy Tel Aviv Israel 1990–94, ret; *Recreations* ice skating, gardening, cycling, cricket; *Style*— Albert Marshall, Esq, MBE; ✉ 4 Tansy Close, Merrow Park, Guildford, Surrey GU4 7XN (☎ 01483 454377)

MARSHALL, Alexander Badenoch; *b* 31 Dec 1924; *Educ* Glenalmond, Worcester Coll Oxford (MA); *m* 1961, Mona; 2 s, 1 da; *Career* served WWII RNVR; with P&O Group in India and UK 1947–79 (chief exec 1972–79); chm: Commercial Union Assurance Co plc 1983–90 (dir 1970–90), Bestobell plc 1979–85, The Maersk Co Ltd 1986–93 (dir 1980–96), RBC Holdings (UK) Ltd 1988–95; dir and vice chm The Boots Co plc 1980–91, dir Royal Bank of Canada 1985–95; pres UK Chamber of Shipping 1994–95; Liveryman Worshipful Co of Shipwrights; *Style*— Alexander Marshall, Esq; ✉ Crest House, Woldingham, Surrey CR3 7DH

MARSHALL, Andrew Paul; s of Michael David Marshall, of Lowestoft, Suffolk, and Doris Constance, *née* Greaves; *b* 27 Aug 1954; *Educ* Lowestoft Co GS, Borough Rd Coll Isleworth, Inst of Educn London (BEd); *partner* Mark Laidler; *Career* freelance screenwriter; contrib Week Ending (BBC Radio) during mid-1970's; *Work* with David Renwick, *qv*: 47 episodes of The Burkiss Way (Radio 4); for LWT: End of Part One (Harlequin Award), Whoops Apocalypse (NY International Film and TV Festival Award, RTS Award 1981), Hot Metal (Emmy nomination); for BBC TV: Alexei Sayle's Stuff (3 series) 1989–91 (International Emmy, Broadcasting Press Guild Award, Writers' Guild Award), If You See God, Tell Him; others incl: The Steam Video Company (Thames), Whoops Apocalypse (film, ITC), Wilt (film, Rank/LWT); stage play Angry Old Men 1995; as solo writer: Sob Sisters (CTV) 1989, several episodes Poirot (LWT) 1991, 2point4 children (BBC, 6 series) 1990–95, Health & Efficiency (BBC) 1993–94, Dad 1996–97; *Books* The Burkiss Way, Whoops Apocalypse; *Recreations* feature animation, architecture, modern art, classic television, nets: compuserve; *Clubs* Soho Place; *Style*— Andrew Marshall, Esq; ✉ Roger Hancock Limited, 4 Water Lane, London NW1 8NZ (☎ 0171 267 4418)

MARSHALL, Sir Arthur Gregory George; kt (1974), OBE (1948), DL (Cambs 1968); s of David Gregory Marshall, MBE (d 1942), and Maude Edmunds, *née* Wing (d 1931); *b* 4 Dec 1903; *Educ* Tonbridge, Jesus Coll Cambridge (MA, Athletics blue); *m* 1931, Rosemary Wynford (d 1988), da of Marcus Dimsdale (d 1918); 2 s, 1 da; *Career* chm and md Marshall of Cambridge (Engineering) Ltd 1942–89 (joined garage co of Marshall (Cambridge) Ltd 1926, estab aircraft co now Marshall of Cambridge (Aerospace) Ltd 1929), life pres Marshall of Cambridge (Holdings) Ltd 1990–; High Sheriff of Cambs and Isle of Ely 1967–70; chm Aerodrome Owners' Assoc 1964–65; memb: Air Cadet Cncl 1951–59 and 1965–76, Advsy Cncl on Technol 1967–70; Liveryman Guild of Air Pilots and Air Navigators; Hon Old Cranwellian 1979, Hon Companion RAeS 1980, hon fell Jesus Coll Cambridge 1990; Hon DSc Cranfield Univ 1992, Hon LLD Cantab 1996; companion Air League 1996; Olympic Team reserve 1924; Order of Istiqlal 1st Class (Jordan) 1990; *Books* The Marshall Story: A Century of Wheels and Wings (1994), No 104 (City of Cambridge) Squadron Air Training Corps: The First Fifty-Six Years 1939–1994 (1995); *Recreations* flying; *Clubs* RAF (hon memb 1969), Hawks (Cambridge); *Style*— Sir Arthur Marshall, OBE, DL; ✉ Horseheath Lodge, Linton, Cambridge CB1 6PT (☎ 01223 891318); Marshall of Cambridge (Aerospace) Ltd, Airport Works, Newmarket Rd, Cambridge CB5 8RX (☎ 01223 373737)

MARSHALL, Arthur Stirling-Maxwell; CBE (1986, OBE 1978); s of Victor Stirling-Maxwell Marshall (d 1941), of Edinburgh, and Jeannie Theodora, *née* Hunter (d 1971); *b* 29 Jan 1929; *m* 1, 25 Dec 1955, Eleni (d 1969), da of Panagiotis Kapralos (d 1946), of Athens, Greece; 1 s (John b 1958), 2 da (Jeannie b 1956, Anna b 1957); m 2, 14 Aug 1985, Cheryl Mary, da of Desmond Hookens, of Madras, India; 1 da (Christina b 1988), 1 step s (Lionel b 1974), 2 step da (Suzanne b 1972, Margaret b 1973); *Career* FO 1959, ME Centre for Arab Studies Lebanon 1959–61, political offr Bahrain 1961–64, registrar HBM Ct for Bahrain 1961–64, attache Br Embassy Athens 1964–67, second sec Br Embassy Rabat Morocco 1967–69, first sec Br High Cmmn Nicosia Cyprus 1970–75 (formerly second sec), first commercial sec Br Embassy Kuwait 1975–79, dep Br high cmmr Southern India 1979–83, cnsllr Br Embassy Kuwait 1983–85, Br ambass People's Democratic Repub of Yemen 1986–89, ret 1989; *Recreations* nature, music; *Style*— Arthur Marshall, Esq, CBE; ✉ 147 Highbury Grove, London N5 1HP

MARSHALL, (Herbert) Brian; s of Charles Ridings Marshall, MBE (d 1974), of Doncaster, and Phyllis Enid Marshall (d 1995); *b* 2 March 1935; *Educ* Bradfield, Univ of Leeds (LLB); *m* 1 Feb 1964, Jillian Lloyd, da of Owen Tunnicliffe (d 1972), of Bessacarr, Doncaster; 1 s (Timothy Noel b 2 Jan 1965), 1 da (Juliet Anne Lloyd b 24 Feb 1967); *Career* admitted slr 1959, NP, clerk to the Tax Commissioners Conisborough Div; chm Doncaster Racecourse Club; memb Law Soc; *Recreations* horse racing, snooker, travel; *Clubs* St George's (Doncaster, pres); *Style*— Brian Marshall, Esq; ✉ Canterbury, 3 Alderson Drive, Bennetthorpe, Doncaster DN2 6BZ (☎ 01302 323869); Hill House Chambers, 7 Regent Terrace, South Parade, Doncaster, South Yorkshire DN1 2EJ (☎ 01302 366831, fax 01302 329718)

MARSHALL, Christopher James; s of Geoffrey Gordon Marshall, and Mary Beatrice, *née* Try (d 1986); *b* 24 Sept 1959; *Educ* John Lyon Sch Harrow, Univ of Reading (BA), Goldsmiths Coll London (MMus); *m* 31 Aug 1985, Wendy Jane, da of Leslie Thompson;

2 s (William James b 1987, Edward Gabriel b 1991); *Career* BBC 1981–; Music Dept Radio Three: prodr 1985–88, sr prodr 1988–90, chief prodr 1990–; *Recreations* reading 20th century fiction, riding, cooking; *Style*— Christopher Marshall, Esq; ✉ BBC Broadcasting Centre, Pebble Mill Road, Birmingham B5 7QQ (☎ 0121 414 8630)

MARSHALL, Sir Colin Marsh; kt (1987); s of Marsh Edward Leslie Marshall, and Florence Mary Marshall; *b* 16 Nov 1933; *Educ* Univ Coll Sch Hampstead; *m* 1958, Janet Winifred, da of John Cracknell; 1 da (Anna (Mrs Simon Birkett)); *Career* Orient Steam Navigation Co 1951–58; Hertz Corporation: joined as mgmnt trainee (Chicago and Toronto) 1958, gen mangr (Mexico) 1959–60, asst to Pres (NY) 1960, gen mangr (UK) 1961–62, gen mangr (UK, Netherlands and Belgium) London 1962–64; Avis Inc: regnl mangr and vice pres (Europe 1964–66, Europe and ME 1966–69, worldwide 1969–71), exec vice pres and chief operating offr (NY), pres 1975, chief exec 1976, co chm 1979 (following takeover by Norton Simon Inc of which he became exec vice pres 1979); dir and dep chief exec Sears Holdings plc 1981–83; British Airways plc: chief exec 1983–95, dep chm 1989–93, chm 1993–; chm Inchcape plc 1995–, dep chm British Telecommunications plc 1996– (dir 1995–); dir: HSBC Holdings plc (non-exec) 1993–, Midland Bank Group until 1994, Grand Metropolitan plc 1988–95, IBM UK Holdings Ltd until 1995, US Air 1993–96, Qantas Airways 1993–, NY Stock Exchange 1994–; pres CBI 1996–; chm London First (formerly London Inward) Ctee 1993–, memb Int Advsy Bd British-American Business Cncl 1994– (chm 1994–96), dep chm Fin Reporting Cncl 1996–; dir Women's Econ Devpt Team Business in the Community (BIC); vice pres Advtg Assoc, pres CIM 1991–96, co-fndr and chm The Mktg Cncl 1995–96; memb: Cncl IOD, Exec Ctee IATA; bd dir Br American C of C; tstee: Duke of Edinburgh Cwlth Study Conf, RAF Museum; vice chm World Travel and Tourism Cncl; Liveryman Guild of Air Pilots and Air Navigators, Liveryman Worshipful Co of Information Technologists; *Recreations* tennis, skiing; *Clubs* Queen's; *Style*— Sir Colin Marshall; ✉ Chairman, British Airways Plc, Head Office (S214), Speedbird House, PO Box 10, Heathrow Airport London, Hounslow, Middx TW6 2JA (☎ 0181 759 5511, telex 8813983)

MARSHALL, David; MP (Lab) Glasgow Shettleston (majority 14,834); *b* 7 May 1941; *Educ* Larbert, Denny and Falkirk High Schs, Woodside Sr Secondary Sch; *m* 1968, Christina; 2 s, 1 da; *Career* joined Lab Pty 1962, memb TGWU, former Lab Pty organiser for Glasgow, cncllr Glasgow Corp 1972–75, vice chm Gtr Glasgow Passenger Tport Authy, regnl cncllr Strathclyde 1974–79 (chief whip, chm Manpower Ctee), former chm Manpower Ctee of the Convention of Scottish Local Authorities (COSLA), former memb LACSAB; MP (Lab) Glasgow Shettleston 1979–; memb: Select Ctee on Scottish Affairs 1981–83, Select Ctee on Tport 1985– (chm 1987–92), Liaison Ctee 1987–92; sec Scottish Labour MPs 1981–, chm PLP Tport Ctee 1987–, co-chm Parly Advsy Cncl for Tport Safety (PACTS) 1991–; sponsored Solvent Abuse (Scotland) Act 1983; *Recreations* music, gardening; *Style*— David Marshall, Esq, MP; ✉ 32 Enterkin St, Glasgow G32 7BA (☎ 0141 778 8125); House of Commons, London SW1A 0AA (☎ 0171 219 5134)

MARSHALL, (Andrew) David Michael Creagh; s of Andrew Harold Marshall (d 1970), of London, and Brenda Medlicott, *née* Massy; *b* 6 Sept 1954; *Educ* King's Coll Sch Wimbledon, Merton Coll Oxford (MA); *m* 19 March 1983, Jill Francesca, da of Laurence Duval Merreywether, of Harrogate; 1 s (Andrew b 1988), 1 da (Cicely b 1987); *Career* called to the Bar Lincoln's Inn 1981; memb Cncl Soc for Computers and Law 1987–92; various reviews and articles on technology and the law; *Style*— David Marshall, Esq; ✉ 3 Paper Buildings, Temple, London EC4Y 7EU (☎ 0171 797 7000, fax 0171 797 7100, e-mail DavidMarshall@msn.com)

MARSHALL, Sir Denis Alfred; kt (1982); s of late Frederick Herbert Marshall, and Winifred Mary Marshall; *b* 1 June 1916; *Educ* Dulwich; *m* 1, 1949, Joan Edith, *née* Straker (d 1974); 1 s; m 2, 1975, Jane, *née* Lygo; *Career* WWII cmmnd XX The Lancashire Fusiliers 1939, served India and Burma (Maj) 1940–45, slr 1937; ptnr Barlow Lyde & Gilbert 1949–83 (conslt 1983–); memb: Cncl Law Soc 1966–86 (vice-pres 1980, pres 1981–82), Insur Brokers Registration Cncl 1979–91, Criminal Injuries Compensation Bd 1982–90; memb Cncl FIMBRA 1986–90; Liveryman City of London Solicitors' Co; *Recreations* sailing (yacht 'Turtledove of Mersea'); *Clubs* Naval and Military, Royal Dart Yacht; *Style*— Sir Denis Marshall; ✉ Redways, Warfleet Rd, Dartmouth, South Devon TQ6 9BZ; Beaufort House, 15 St Botolph St, London EC3A 7NJ (☎ 0171 247 2277, telex 887249 G)

MARSHALL, Dr Enid Ann; da of Rev John Marshall (d 1945), of Whitehills, Banff, and Lizzie, *née* Gilchrist (d 1975); *b* 10 July 1932; *Educ* Whitehills Jr Secdy, Banff Acad, Bell-Baxter Sch Cupar, Univ of St Andrews (MA, LLB, PhD); *Career* apprentice slr Pagan & Osborne WS Cupar 1956–59, lectr in law Dundee Coll of Technol 1959–72; Univ of Stirling: lectr in business law 1972–74, sr lectr in business law 1974–77, reader in business law 1977–94, reader in Scots Law Research Unit 1994–; ed: Arbitration Section The Journal of Business Law 1976–, Scottish Law Gazette 1983–; chm Social Security Appeal Tbnl Stirling and Falkirk 1984–; memb: Law Soc of Scotland 1959, Scot Law Agents Soc 1960; FRSA 1984, ARICS 1986, ACIArb 1988; *Books* incl: The Companies (Floating Charges and Receivers) (Scotland) Act 1972 (1972), Scottish Cases on Contract (1978, 2 edn 1993), Scottish Cases on Agency (1980), Scottish Cases on Partnerships and Companies (1980), General Principles of Scots Law (1971, 6 edn 1995), Scots Mercantile Law (1983, 2 edn 1992), Gill on Arbitration (ed, 3 edn 1983), Oliver and Marshall's Company Law (12 edn 1994); *Recreations* animal welfare, veganism; *Style*— Dr Enid A Marshall; ✉ 24 Easter Cornton Rd, Stirling FK9 5ES (☎ 01786 478865); Edenbank, 1 Dermoch Drive, Dunblane, Perthshire FK15 9JH (☎ 01786 823117); University of Stirling, Stirling FK9 4LA (☎ 01786 473171 or 01786 467285, fax 01786 467308, international fax 44 786 467308)

MARSHALL, Ernest Harold; s of Ernest Marshall (d 1931), of Chadwell Heath, and Annie Beatrice, *née* Lefever (d 1967); *b* 29 Nov 1924; *Educ* Rayleigh Sr Sch, Shrewsbury, Univ of Bonn, Univ of Tehran; *m* 21 July 1954, Christine Louise Harrad, of Thundersley, Essex; 2 s (Ian b 22 July 1960, Nicholas b 16 Dec 1964); *Career* RAF Polish Sqdn 1942–47; dir Sedgwick Group 1960–81, underwriter Lloyd's 1969–, conslt 1981–, dir SE Essex Tech Coll 1989–91; St John Ambulance: pres Rayleigh Div 1984–91, dep pres Essex 1993–94, chm Cncl Essex 1994– (memb 1986–); pres Rochford Constituency Cons Assoc 1986–89; OStJ 1988; Freeman City of London 1980, Liveryman Worshipful Co of Insurers 1981–, hon prof Tehran Univ 1976; vice pres Insurance Inst London 1978–, memb IBRC 1981–, memb CIB 1974–81; Pilsudski Medal (Poland) 1944; *Books* Construction and Erection Insurance (1978 and 1985), Directors' and Officers' Liability (1986); *Recreations* travel, fine arts; *Style*— Ernest Marshall, Esq; ✉ Beverley Lodge, Great Wheatley Road, Rayleigh, Essex SS6 7AP (☎ 01268 775156, fax 01268 776919)

MARSHALL, Dr Geoffrey; s of Leonard William Marshall (d 1953), and Kate, *née* Turner (d 1961); *b* 22 April 1929; *Educ* Arnold Sch Blackpool, Univ of Manchester (BA, MA), Univ of Glasgow (PhD); *m* 10 Aug 1957, Patricia Anne Christine, da of Edward Cecil Woodcock (d 1988), of Oxford; 2 s (David b 1962, Stephen Edward b 1967); *Career* res fell Nuffield Coll Oxford 1955–57, provost The Queen's Coll Oxford 1993– (fell and praelector 1957–93), Andrew Dixon White visiting prof Cornell Univ 1985–, delegate OUP 1987–92; memb Oxford City Cncl 1964–74, Sheriff City of Oxford 1970–71; FBA 1970; *Books* Parliamentary Sovereignty and the Commonwealth (1957), Police and Government (1965), Constitutional Theory (1971), Constitutional Conventions (1986), Ministerial Responsibility (1989); *Recreations* squash; *Style*— Dr Geoffrey Marshall, FBA; ✉ The Queen's College, Oxford OX1 4AW

MARSHALL, Dr (Frank) Graham; s of Frank Marshall, of Bournemouth, and Vera, *née* Barker; *b* 28 March 1942; *Educ* W Bridgford GS, Univ of Birmingham (BA), Univ of Nottingham (PhD); *m* 10 July 1965, Patricia Anne, da of Thomas Leonard Bestwick, of Nottingham; 2 s (Stephen James b 1967, David Edward b 1971), 1 da (Anne-Marie b 1969); *Career* RSRE (MOD) Malvern 1966–80 (sr princ sci offr 1975–80), seconded to HM Dip Serv as sci and technol cnsllr Br Embassy Tokyo 1980–82, md Plessey Electronic Systems Research (later Plessey Research) 1982–87, tech dir Plessey Naval Systems Ltd 1987–90, gp res and devpt dir Colt Group Ltd 1990–; IEEE Best Paper award (jtly) 1973, Wolfe award (jtly) 1973; FIEE 1984; *Publications* numerous papers on electronic signal processing devices in various jls; *Recreations* country hobbies, electronic projects; *Style*— Dr Graham Marshall; ✉ Colt Group Ltd, New Lane, Havant, Hants PO9 2LY (☎ 01705 491401)

MARSHALL, Prof (Ian) Howard; s of Ernest Ewart Marshall (d 1977), and Ethel, *née* Curran; *b* 12 Jan 1934; *Educ* Dumfries Acad, Aberdeen GS, Univ of Aberdeen (MA, BD, PhD), Univ of Cambridge (BA), Univ of Göttingen; *m* 25 March 1961, Joyce Elizabeth, da of Frederick John Proudfoot (d 1971); 1 s (Neil), 3 da (Morag, Aileen, Alison); *Career* asst tutor Didsbury Coll Bristol 1960–62, methodist min Darlington 1962–64, prof of New Testament Exegesis Univ of Aberdeen 1979– (lectr 1964–70, sr lectr 1970–77, reader 1977–79), dean Faculty of Divinity Univ of Aberdeen 1981–84; Hon DD Asbury 1996; *Books* Eschatology and the Parables (1963, 1978), Pocket Guide to Christian Beliefs (1963, 1978, 1989), The Work of Christ (1969, 1994), Kept by the Power of God (1969, 1975, 1995), Luke: Historian and Theologian (1970, 1989), The Origins of New Testament Christology (1976), New Testament Interpretation (ed 1977, 1979), The Gospel of Luke (New International Greek Testament Commentary, 1978), I Believe in the Historical Jesus (1977), The Epistles of John (New International Commentary on the New Testament, 1978), Acts (Tyndale NT Commentaries, 1980), Last Supper and Lord's Supper (1980), Biblical Inspiration (1982, 1995), 1 and 2 Thessalonians (New Century Bible, 1983), Christian Experience in Theology and Life (ed, 1988), Jesus The Saviour (1990), I Peter (IVP New Testament Commentary Series, 1991), The Theology of the Shorter Pauline Letters (with K P Donfried, 1992), The Acts of the Apostles (New Testament Guides, 1992), The Epistle to the Philippians (1993); *Recreations* reading, walking, gardening, music; *Style*— Prof I Howard Marshall; ✉ Department of Divinity with Religious Studies, University of Aberdeen, Aberdeen AB9 2UB (☎ 01224 272388, fax 01224 273750, telex 73458)

MARSHALL, Rev Canon Hugh Phillips; s of Dr Leslie Phillips Marshall, MC, TD (d 1979), late of RAMC, and Dr Catherine Mary Marshall (d 1982); *b* 13 July 1934; *Educ* Marlborough, Sidney Sussex Coll Cambridge (MA), Lincoln Theol Coll; *m* 22 Sept 1962, Diana Elizabeth, da of late Capt Charles Gosling, RN; 1 s (Philip b 1971), 3 da (Catherine b 1963, Ruth b 1965, Anna b 1967); *Career* served RN 1952–54; curate St Stephen with St John Westminster 1959–65, vicar St Paul Tupsley Hereford 1965–74, vicar and rector St Mary Wimbledon 1974–87, rural dean of Merton 1979–85, vicar St Peter and St Paul Mitcham 1987–90, chief sec Gen Synod Advsy Bd of Ministry 1990–96, vicar St Mary Wendover Bucks 1996–, priest-in-charge St Michael Halton Bucks 1996–; commissary to Bishop of Matabeleland 1988–, canon emeritus Southwark Cathedral 1990– (hon canon 1989–90), hon canon St John's Cathedral Bulawayo 1996–; govr various CE schs 1965–87, chm of govrs Priory CE Middle Sch Merton 1976–90, chm of govrs Benedict County First Sch Mitcham 1987–90, chm Betty Rhodes Fund 1995– (hon treas 1989–95); civic chaplain London Borough of Merton 1978–79 and 1989–90; *Recreations* DIY, gardening, cooking, travel; *Style*— The Rev Canon Hugh Marshall; ✉ The Vicarage, 34 Dobbins Lane, Wendover, Aylesbury, Bucks HP22 6DH (☎ 01296 622230)

MARSHALL, Hugh Thomas Christopher; s of Maj R W Marshall (decd), and Elizabeth, *née* Woods (decd); *Educ* SE Essex Sch of Art Barking (Dip in Graphics NDD Illustration (SL), Illustration prizes), RCA (Royal scholar, ARCA), travelling scholarship Germany 1957; *m* 1952, Anne, *née* Martin; 3 s; *Career* illustrator/designer 1960–; designed and edited audio-visual film strips for American co 1969–73; designed: Bulls Blood Wine posters 1976–78, new symbols for Blue Circle Cement 1984 (shortlisted BBC Design awards 1987), exhibits for Museum of Natural Science Taiwan and King David Tower Jerusalem 1989, exhibits for a desert museum Oman 1994 (opened 1995); RCA: designed and edited Newsletter 1985–91, memb Ct 1991–93; conslt ASB Gallery (on the Herbert Bayer exhibition) 1985 (also compiler of press release), conslt designer Letts Educational (producing extensive series of titles of classics and modern classics) 1993–, conslt Nosâavi Visual Communications (on corp ID) 1994–95; *Awards* Silver Medal IGI of America (for Rank Xerox drawings) 1986, Studio Magazine Awards (for Wine Soc designs 1988, for exhibition work in Jerusalem 1989), 12 Biennale of Graphic Design 1986, 14 Biennale of Graphic Design 1990; *Exhibitions* Brno Czechoslovakia 1986 and 1990, Vancouver Canada 1986, Paperpoint London 1986, Berthold Centre Toronto 1988–89, Self Image (Israel Museum Jerusalem) 1989, Self Image (Design Museum) 1991, 6 Annual Typographic Circle (CSD) 1991, Private Pursuits and Public Problems (RCA) 1993, Hugh Marshall and his Special Design Unit (Wroclaw, Poland) 1995, 1 Int Triennial of Stage Posters Sofia '95 Bulgaria 1995; illustration/graphics tutor Southend Sch of Art 1958–68, deviser first year design syllabus Sch of Photography Paddington Coll 1979–80, visiting lectr Barnet Coll 1980–81 (conslt lectr and advsr on industl contact 1983–84), lectr and deviser first year course on type/sign/symbol Canterbury Coll of Art 1981–87 (produced feasibility study for MA course 1986), visiting lectr Croydon Coll of Art 1986–87, external tutor Central Sch of Art 1987–88, visiting lectr Art Dept Richmond on Thames Coll 1987–89, head Special Design Unit (Graphics) Kingston University 1990–96, conslt on research prog ICOGRADA 1996–; memb Liaison Panel Croydon Coll of Art (chaired by Martin Lambie-Nairn, *qv*) 1988–90; lectr on the Bauhaus, modern graphics and typography, conductor of instructional tours at various colls and for Friends of the V & A; memb Membs Ctee ICA 1971–74, fndr FORUMS for Assoc of Illustrators 1975; CSD: memb Graphics Gp Panel 1985–, memb Educn and Trg Bd 1986–88, memb Assessment Panel 1991–; memb: Typographic Circle, Art & Architecture 1985, Design and Indust Assoc 1985–91, Soc for the Protection of Ancient Bldgs 1985; FCSD 1984; *Books* Art Directing Photography (1989); *Recreations* collecting tin boxes, objets trouvés, old keys, driftwood sculpture, fossils and looking after an old Alfa Romeo Guilietta, travelling (Europe, Jerusalem, Canada, Hong Kong, Japan and USA), classical music of the 16th, 17th and 20th centuries; *Style*— Hugh Marshall; ✉ 36 Stanhope Gardens, London SW7 5QY (☎ 0171 373 2890)

MARSHALL, James; MP (Lab) Leicester South (majority 9,440); *b* 13 March 1941; *Educ* Sheffield City GS, Leeds Univ; *m* 1, Shirley, *née* Ellis; 1 s, 1 da; m 2, 1986, Susan, *née* Carter; 1 da; *Career* Parly candidate Harborough 1970, MP (Lab) Leicester S Oct 1974– (also contested Feb 1974), asst Govt whip 1977–79; oppn spokesman on: home affrs 1982–83, Northern Ireland 1988–92; memb Br Delgn to the Cncl of Europe and WEU; cncllr: Leeds City Cncl 1965–68, Leicester City Cncl 1971–76; *Style*— James Marshall, Esq, MP; ✉ House of Commons, London SW1A 0AA (☎ 0171 219 3000)

MARSHALL, James Charles; s of James Charles Marshall (d 1964), of London, and Beatrice Fanny, *née* Wingrove (d 1984); *b* 29 July 1923; *m* 1, 1942 (m dis 1971), Violet Elizabeth, da of Samuel Wheeler Dover; 1 s (Terry b 15 March 1944); m 2, 1975 (m dis 1982), Irene, *née* Philips; 1 da (Victoria b 18 Aug 1971); m 3, 27 July 1985, Nancy Elizabeth, da of George William Noel Kilpin, of Aspley Guise; *Career* professional musician and singer, then drummer, dance, band leader and drum teacher 1949–60; md: Jim Marshall & Son 1960–63, J & T Marshall Ltd 1963–66, Marshall Amplification Plc

1964–, Marshall Music 1966–80; mfr of Marshall Amplification and winner Queen's award for Export Achievement 1984 and 1992; handprints in Rock Wall of Fame Sunset Boulevard Hollywood; vice pres: London Fedn of Boys' Clubs, Bucks Assoc of Youth Clubs; chm Variety Club of GB Youth Clubs Ctee, former pres Bedfordshire Youth Assoc, ctee memb MacIntyre Homes Milton Keynes, memb Variety Club of GB; companion Grand Order of Water Rats; Freeman City of London; *Style*— James Marshall, Esq; ✉ Marshall Amplification plc, Denbigh Rd, Bletchley, Milton Keynes MK1 1DQ (☎ 01908 375411, fax 01908 376118)

MARSHALL, (John) Jeremy Seymour; s of Edward Pope Marshall (d 1983), of Truro, Cornwall, and Nita Helen, *née* Seymour; *b* 18 April 1938; *Educ* Sherborne, New Coll Oxford (MA); *m* 20 July 1962, Juliette Anne, da of (Archibald) Donald Butterley (d 1957), of Leicester; 1 s (Simon b 1965), 2 da (Sarah b 1964, Anna b 1971); *Career* Nat Serv Lt Royal Signals 1956–58; Wiggins Teape 1962–64, Riker Laboratories 1964–67, CIBA Agrochems 1967–71, Hanson plc 1971–87; md: Dufaylite Developments Ltd 1971–76, SLD Olding Ltd 1976–79; chief exec: Lindustries Ltd 1979–86, Imperial Foods Ltd 1986–87, BAA plc 1987–89, De La Rue plc 1989–; non-exec dir: John Mowlem & Co plc 1991–, Camelot Group plc 1993–, BTR plc 1995–; tstee Design Museum 1996–; CIMgt, FCIT; *Recreations* tennis, squash, skiing, shooting; *Clubs* RAC; *Style*— Jeremy Marshall, Esq; ✉ Willow House, Bourn, Cambridge CB3 7SQ; De la Rue plc, 6 Agar Street, London WC2N 4DE (☎ 0171 836 8383)

MARSHALL, Prof John; CBE; s of James Herbert Marshall, and Bertha, *née* Schofield; *b* 16 April 1922; *Educ* Thornleigh Coll Bolton, Univ of Manchester (MB ChB, MD, DSc); *m* 9 Oct 1946, (Margaret) Eileen, da of Albert Hughes (d 1937), of Unionville, Pennsylvania, USA; 2 s (Michael John, Christopher John), 3 da (Patricia Mary, Mo Lin Cecilia, Catherine Ann); *Career* Lt-Col RAMC 1949–51; sr lectr Univ of Edinburgh 1954–56; Univ of London: reader in neurology 1956–71, prof 1971–87, dean Inst of Neurology 1982–87, emeritus prof 1987–; chm Disability Living Allowance Advsy Bd 1982–93 (memb 1978–93); chm Nat Soc for Epilepsy 1992–95; memb: Assoc of Br Neurologists 1954, Assoc of Physicians 1956; Auenbrugger medal Univ of Graz (1983); *Books* Management of Cerebrovascular Disease (1965), Planning for a Family (1965), The Infertile Period (1969), Love One Another (1995); *Recreations* walking, gardening; *Style*— Prof John Marshall, CBE; ✉ 203 Robin Hood Way, London SW20 0AA (☎ 0181 942 5509)

MARSHALL, Capt John Andrew; LVO (1979); s of Rt Rev Guy Marshall, MBE (d 1979), and Dorothy Gladys, *née* Whiting (d 1975); *b* 14 Dec 1937; *Educ* St John's Sch Leatherhead Surrey, RNCs Dartmouth and Manadon; *m* 15 Jan 1966, Vivien Mary, da of Kenneth James Robertson, DSC (ka 1943); 1 s (Rory Jerome), 2 da (Peta Sophie, Morva Anna); *Career* RN served HMS Ulster 1958–59, HMS Albion 1963–65, HMS Dolphin 1965, HMS Cachalot 1965–68, RNC Dartmouth 1968, RNC Greenwich 1968–69, HMS Renown 1970–72, HMS Forth and HMS Defiance 1972–74, Royal Dockyard Devonport 1974–77, Royal Yacht 1977–79, naval attaché Moscow 1984–85, MOD 1979–82, 1985–88 and 1990–91, Capt RNEC 1988–90, conslt 1991–93; CEng, FIMechE, FIMarE; *Recreations* sailing, estate, design for energy leanness, management; *Style*— Capt John Marshall, LVO; ✉ Royal Navy, Wilmington House, Wilmington, Polegate, East Sussex BN26 5SJ (☎ and fax 0323 870445)

MARSHALL, John Leslie; MP (C) Hendon South (majority 12,047); s of Prof William Thomas Marshall (d 1975), of Glasgow, and Margaret Ewing Marshall (d 1994); *b* 19 Aug 1940; *Educ* Glasgow Acad, Univ of St Andrews (MA); *m* 1978, Susan Elizabeth, da of David Spencer Mount, JP, of Petham, Kent; 2 s (William b 1979, Thomas b 1982); *Career* lectr in economics Univ of Aberdeen 1966–70; stockbroker; ptnr Carr Sebag & Co 1979–82; Kitcat & Aitken: assoc memb 1982–83, ptnr 1983–86, dir investment res 1986–90; conslt: Carr Kitcat & Aitken 1990–93, London Wall Equities (now Mees Pierson Securities) 1993–; dir Beta Global Emerging Markets Investment Trust plc 1990–; MEP (EDG) London N 1979–89, MP (C) Hendon S 1987–; PPS: to Min of State for Social Security 1989–90, to Sec of State for Social Security 1990–92, to Ldr of House of Commons 1992–95; memb Health Select Ctee; chm: Br Israel Parly Gp, Anglo-Israel Assoc; conslt Bus and Coach Cncl; ACIS; *Recreations* spectator sports, theatre, bridge; *Clubs* Carlton, MCC, Middlesex CCC; *Style*— John Marshall, Esq, MP; ✉ House of Commons, London SW1A 0AA (☎ 0171 219 6327)

MARSHALL, His Hon Judge Laurence Arthur; s of Reginald Herbert Marshall (d 1981), of Eastbourne, and Nora, *née* Curtis; *b* 1 June 1931; *Educ* Ardingly Coll, King's Coll London; *m* 1, (m dis 1979), Marian Charlotte, *née* Mowlem Burt; 2 s (Piers Simon Curtis b 27 Dec 1961, Thomas Edward Curtis b 23 Aug 1965), 2 da (Candida Lucy Elizabeth b 3 March 1963, Eloise Catherine b 27 March 1969); m 2, Gloria Elizabeth, da of Lt-Col C R H Kindersley, DSO, MC; *Career* called to the Bar 1957, in practice 1957–91, circuit judge (SE Circuit) 1991–; *Recreations* building; *Clubs* Royal London Yacht; *Style*— His Hon Judge Laurence Marshall; ✉ The Old Post Office, Stourton, Shipston on Stour, Warwickshire CV36 5HG (☎ 01608 686363)

MARSHALL, Margaret Anne (Mrs Graeme Davidson); *née* Marshall; *b* 4 Jan 1949; *Educ* Stirling HS, Royal Scottish Acad of Music and Drama; *m* 25 March 1970, Graeme Griffiths King Davidson; 2 da (Nicola b 19 Nov 1974, Julia b 29 Dec 1977); *Career* soprano; first prize Munich Int Festival 1974; concert and opera appearances at numerous international venues incl: Royal Opera House Covent Garden, La Scala Milan, Vienna Staatsoper, Frankfurt Opera, Salzburg Festival, Florence, Hamburg, Cologne; winner Gulliver Award for Performing Arts in Scotland 1992; has made numerous recordings; *Recreations* skiing, squash, tennis, cooking, golf; *Clubs* Gleneagle Country; *Style*— Miss Margaret Marshall; ✉ c/o Allied Artists Agency, 42 Montpelier Square, London SW7 1JZ (☎ 0171 589 6243, fax 0171 581 5269)

MARSHALL, Mark Anthony; CMG (1991); s of Prof T H Marshall (d 1981), of Cambridge, and Nadine, *née* Hambourg; *b* 8 Oct 1937; *Educ* Westminster, Trinity Coll Cambridge (BA); *m* 29 Aug 1970, Penelope Lesley, step da of George Seymour (d 1987), of Powick, Worcester; 2 da (Charlotte Dorothea b 1973, Frances Margaret b 1975); *Career* Dip Serv 1958–93; cnsllr: Tripoli 1979–80, Damascus 1980–83; ambass Yemen Arab Republic 1987–93; *Recreations* golf, fell walking; *Style*— M A Marshall, Esq, CMG; ✉ The Old Farm, Skelwith Fold, Ambleside LA22 0HT

MARSHALL, Sir (Robert) Michael; kt (1990), DL (W Sussex 1990), MP (C) Arundel (majority 19,863); s of Robert Ernest Marshall (d 1988), of Hathersage, Derbyshire, and Margaret Mary Marshall (d 1983); *b* 21 June 1930; *Educ* Bradfield Coll, Harvard Univ (MBA), Stanford Univ; *m* 1972, Caroline Victoria Oliphant, da of Alexander Oliphant Hutchison (d 1973), of Upper Largo, Fife; 2 step da; *Career* cricket commentator BBC 1954–69; md (Bombay) Calcutta Branch United Steel (India) Ltd 1960–64 (mangr 1954–58), commercial dir Workington Iron & Steel Co Ltd 1964–67, md Head Wrightson Export Co Ltd 1967–69, mgmnt conslt Urwick Orr & Partners Ltd 1969–74; MP (C) Arundel Feb 1974–, Parly under sec of state for indust 1979–81; Parly advsr to: Br Aerospace and Cable & Wireless 1982–, Williams Holdings 1987–; pres Cncl of the Inter-Parliamentary Union 1991–; Hon DL New England Coll 1982; *Books* author/ed 9 books incl Jack Buchanan, Gentleman and Players; *Recreations* cricket commentating, golf, theatre, writing and travel; *Clubs* Garrick, Lord's Taverners, R & A, MCC, Goodwood Golf; *Style*— Sir Michael Marshall, DL, MP; ✉ Old Inn House, Slindon, Arundel, W Sussex; House of Commons, London SW1A 0AA (☎ 0171 219 4046)

MARSHALL, Michael John; DL (Cambridgeshire 1989); s of Sir Arthur Gregory George Marshall, OBE, DL, *qv*, and Rosemary Wynford, *née* Dimsdale (d 1988); *b* 27 Jan 1932; *Educ* Eton, Jesus Coll Cambridge (MA, Rowing blue, rep GB in Euro championships 1955); *m* 1, 1960 (m dis 1977), Bridget Wykham Pollock; 2 s, 2 da; m 2, 1979, Sibyl Mary Walkinshaw, *née* Hutton; 2 step s; *Career* RAF pilot 1950–52; Marshall of Cambridge (Engineering) Ltd: joined 1955, dep chm and md 1964–90; chm and chief exec Marshall of Cambridge (Holdings) Ltd 1990–; dir Eastern Electricity Bd 1971–77; chm BL Cars Distributor Cncl 1977 and 1983 (memb 1975–84); vice pres: IMI 1980–, Engrg Employers Fedn 1993–; chm Cambs Manpower Ctee 1980–83; vice chm Cambs Youth Involvement Ctee Silver Jubilee Fund 1977–78, chm Cambridge Olympic Appeal 1984, memb Ely Cathedral Restoration Appeal Co Ctee 1987–, pres Cambridge Soc for the Blind 1989–92, chm Prince's Tsts' Cambs Appeal Ctee 1991–92; chm Civilian Ctee 104 (City of Cambridge) Sqdn ATC 1975–, chm Beds and Cambs Wing ATC 1987–93, memb Air Cadet Cncl 1994–; High Sheriff of Cambridgeshire 1988, Vice Lord-Lt of Cambridgeshire 1992–; Freeman City of London, Liveryman Guild of Air Pilots and Air Navigators; IEng, FRAeS, FRSA, FIMI; *Recreations* flying, sailing, countryside; *Clubs* RAF, Hawks' (Cambridge); *Style*— Michael Marshall, Esq, DL; ✉ Marshall of Cambridge (Holdings) Ltd, The Airport, Cambridge CB5 8RX (☎ 01223 373737, fax 01223 324224)

MARSHALL, Nigel Bernard Dickenson; s of Norman Dickenson Marshall (d 1958), of The Old Rectory, Lea, Gainsborough, and (Gertrude) Olga, *née* Pumfrey (d 1991); *b* 9 April 1935; *Educ* Rugby, Queens' Coll Cambridge (MA, LLM); *Career* slr Herbert Smith & Co London 1961–63; ptnr: Underwood and Co London 1964–90, Miller and Co Cambridge 1969–88; sole practitioner 1990–; clerk: St Edward's Parochial Charity Cambridge 1967–90, The Great St Mary's Charity Cambridge 1967–71, The Wray Jackenett Merrill & Elie Charity Cambridge 1971–72; sec Cambridge and District Trade Protection Assoc 1967–86; *Recreations* gardening; *Clubs* Boodle's, United Oxford and Cambridge Univ, Univ of Cambridge Pitt, City Univ, Oriental; *Style*— Nigel Marshall, Esq; ✉ The Old Rectory, Lea, Gainsborough, Lincs DN21 5JA (☎ 01427 612783); 50 Rawlings Street, London SW3 2LS (☎ 0171 584 0194)

MARSHALL, Paul Roderick Clucas; s of Alan Marshall, of London, and Mary Sylvia Clucas Hanlin; *b* 2 Aug 1959; *Educ* Merchant Taylors', St John's Coll Oxford (BA), INSEAD (Louis Frank scholar, MBA); *m* 1986, Sabina Perrini de Balkany, da of Giorgio Perrini; 1 s (Winston Aubrey Aladar b 20 Dec 1987), 1 da (Giovanna Mary Ilus b 2 Oct 1990); *Career* int trainee Germany and Switzerland then foreign exchange dealer London Lloyds Bank International 1981–84; Mercury Asset Management Group plc: joined 1985, dir i/c Continental European equity investmts Warburg Asset Management 1989, dir Mercury Asset Management plc 1995–; research asst to Charles Kennedy MP 1984, Parly candidate (SDP/Lib Alliance) Fulham 1987, chm City Lib Dems 1994, memb Exec Ctee Lib Dem Business Liaison Gp 1995; *Recreations* family, history, soccer (Manchester United), tennis, music; *Style*— Paul Marshall, Esq; ✉ Mercury Asset Management plc, 33 King William Street, London EC4R 9AS (☎ 0171 280 2301, fax 0171 280 2820)

MARSHALL, Sir Peter Harold Reginald; KCMG (1983, CMG 1974); s of Reginald Henry Marshall; *b* 30 July 1924; *Educ* Tonbridge, Corpus Christi Coll Cambridge; *m* 1, 1957, Patricia Rendell Stoddart (d 1981); 1 s, 1 da; m 2, 16 Sept 1989, Judith, *née* Miller, wid of E W F Tomlin; *Career* diplomat; asst dir Treasy Centre for Admin Studies 1964–66, cnsllr UK Mission Geneva 1966–69, cnsllr and head of chancery Paris 1969–71, head of Fin Relations Dept FCO 1971–73, asst under sec of state FCO 1973–75, UK rep to Econ and Social Cncl of UN 1975–79, ambass and UK perm rep to Office of UN and other int orgns Geneva 1979–83, dep cwlth sec-gen (Econ) 1983–88; hon fell Corpus Christi Coll Cambridge; chm Cwlth Tst (and Royal Cwlth Soc) 1989–92, pres Queen Elizabeth House Oxford 1990–94, memb Bd of Govrs English Speaking Union 1984–90, tstee King George VI and Queen Elizabeth Fndn of St Catharine's 1986–; memb Cncl: Overseas Devpt Inst 1989–, VSO 1990–95; memb Exec Ctee Pilgrims of GB 1986–, chm Jt Cwlth Socs Cncl 1993–; hon fell Univ of Westminster 1992; *Books* The Dynamics of Diplomacy (1989), United Kingdom-United Nations (contrib, 1989); *Clubs* Travellers'; *Style*— Sir Peter Marshall, KCMG; ✉ 26 Queensdale Road, London W11 4QB (☎ 0171 229 1921)

MARSHALL, Peter Izod; s of Charles Marshall (d 1987), of Buxton, Derbyshire, and Gwendoline Anne, *née* Parker (d 1989); *b* 16 April 1927; *Educ* Buxton Coll; *m* 4 Aug 1955, Davina Mary, da of Ernest Hart (d 1980), of Grappen Hall, Cheshire; 1 s (David Bruce b 4 Feb 1960), 1 da (Helen Elizabeth (Mrs Le Houx) b 21 Feb 1957); *Career* commercial dir EMI Electronics Ltd 1962–67, fin dir Norcros plc 1967–77, dir and dep chief exec Plessey Co plc 1977–87, chm Ocean Group plc 1987–, chm Plessey Pension Trust Ltd, dep chm Astec (BSR) plc; memb Jarrett Ctee on Br Univs; LRAM 1945, FCA 1955, CIMgt 1986, FInstD 1986; *Recreations* music, swimming, golf; *Clubs* Les Ambassadeurs, Wentworth (Surrey); *Style*— Peter Marshall, Esq; ✉ Moyns, Christchurch Rd, Virginia Water, Surrey (☎ 01344 842118, fax 01344 842046); Ocean House, The Ring, Bracknell, Berkshire RG12 1AN (☎ 01344 302000, fax 01344 710031)

MARSHALL, Peter James; CMG (1996); s of George Aubrey Marshall (d 1958), and Joan, *née* Gibson; *b* 25 June 1944; *Educ* Ripon GS Yorkshire; *m* 1 Oct 1966, Roberta, da of Frederick George Alfred Barlow; 1 s (Neil b 26 July 1967), 3 da (Nicola b 21 March 1969, Lisa b 28 Feb 1972, Claudia b 1 Feb 1974); *Career* HM Dip Serv; Miny of Aviation 1963–64, Cwlth Rels Office 1964–65, seconded to Cwlth Secretariat 1965–67, Br High Cmmn Malta 1967–70, vice-consul (commercial) Johannesburg 1970, second sec (commercial/info) Kaduna 1970–74, vice-consul (commercial) San Francisco 1974–79, first sec FCO 1979–83, dep high cmmr Malta 1983–88, first sec FCO 1988–90, dep head News Dept FCO 1990–94, ambass Algeria 1995–Oct 1996 (cnsllr, consul gen and dep head of Mission then chargé d'affaires Algiers 1994–95), consul gen Atlanta Georgia USA 1997–; *Recreations* tennis, bridge, gardening, photography, grandchildren; *Style*— Peter Marshall, Esq, CMG; ✉ c/o Foreign and Commonwealth Office (Atlanta), King Charles Street, London SW1A 2AH (☎ 00 1 404 524 5856, fax 00 1 404 524 3153)

MARSHALL, Sir Robert Braithwaite; KCB (1971, CB 1968), MBE (1945); s of Alexander Halford Marshall, and Edith Mary, *née* Lockyer; *b* 10 Jan 1920; *Educ* Sherborne, CCC Cambridge; *m* 1945, Diana Elizabeth Westlake; 1 s, 3 da; *Career* WWII served FO; chm Nat Water Cncl 1978–82, fndr and first chm Wateraid Tst 1981–82 (memb Cncl 1983–93, a vice pres 1993), second perm sec Dept of Environment 1973–78, indust sec DTI as second perm sec 1970–73 (dep sec 1966–70, under sec 1964–66); served Ministries: Works, Aviation, Power, Technology; private sec to sec of Cabinet 1950–53; chm Liberal Party's Trade & Indust Panel 1984–86; *Style*— Sir Robert Marshall, KCB, MBE; ✉ 1 Shatcombe, Uploders, Bridport, Dorset DT6 4NR (☎ 01308 485348)

MARSHALL, Roger Michael James; s of James Edward Frederick Marshall (d 1979), and Jeanne, *née* Warren; *b* 20 Aug 1948; *Educ* Truro Sch, LSE (BSc); *m* 4 May 1974, Margaret Elizabeth, da of John Macpherson, of The Manor House, Abbotskerswell, Devon; 2 da (Charlotte Emily b 1977, Anabelle Verity b 1978), 1 s (Oliver George b 1991); *Career* Price Waterhouse: articled 1970, ptnr 1981–; FCA (ACA 1973); *Recreations* sailing, bridge, reading, skiing; *Style*— Roger Marshall, Esq; ✉ Price Waterhouse, 32 London Bridge St, London SE1 9SY

MARSHALL, Prof Sir (Oshley) Roy; kt (1974), CBE (1968); s of Fitz Roy Marshall, and Corene Carmelita Marshall; *b* 21 Oct 1920; *Educ* Harrison Coll Barbados, Pembroke Coll Cambridge, Univ Coll London; *m* 1945, Eirwen Lloyd; 1 s, 3 da; *Career* vice chllr Univ of Hull 1979–85, head of enquiry into immigration serv for Cmmn on Racial Equality until 1981; called to the Bar 1947, prof of law, head Dept of Law Univ of Sheffield 1956–69 (visiting prof 1969–79), prof of law and dean of Law Faculty Univ of

Ife Nigeria 1963–65, vice chllr Univ of WI 1969–74; chm Cwlth Educn Liaison Ctee 1974–81 and Cwlth Legal Cooperation Ctee 1975, vice-chm Governing Body Cwlth Inst 1980–81, memb Police Complaints Bd 1977–81; chm: Cwlth Standing Ctee on Student Mobility 1982–94, Bd of Govrs Hymers Coll 1985–89; exec chm Cncl for Educn in the Cwlth 1985–91, chm Review Ctee on the Cave Hill Campus of the Univ WI 1986, constitutional commn on the Turks and Caicos Islands 1986, memb Bd of Govrs The Commonwealth of Learning 1989–91; High Commissioner for Barbados in London 1989–91; *Clubs* Royal Cwlth Soc; *Style*— Prof Sir Roy Marshall, CBE; ✉ Kirk House, Kirk Croft, Cottingham, N Humberside HU16 4AU (☎ 01482 847413, fax 01482 876709)

MARSHALL, Sally Christine; da of Maj John Trevor Marshall (d 1985), of Broadstone, Dorset, and Marjorie Kathleen, *née* Cooke; *b* 19 Oct 1949; *Educ* Mountford House West Hallam Derbys, Clifton Hall Nottingham, Univ Coll of Wales Aberystwyth (BScEcon); *Career* investmt mangr Hill Samuel 1972–80, Henderson Adminstration Group 1980–94, institutional mktg dir Hill Samuel Investment Management Ltd 1994–; Freeman City of London; *Recreations* golf, skiing, travel; *Clubs* Roehampton, Broadstone GC, Dorset; *Style*— Miss Sally Marshall; ✉ 4 Putney Common, London SW15 1HL; Hill Samuel Investment Management Ltd, 10 Fleet Place, London EC4M 7RH (☎ 0171 203 3054)

MARSHALL, Dr William Jasper; s of Edward Alwin Marshall (d 1986), of Tenterden, Kent, and Lorna Alice, *née* Jeffery (d 1988), of Bromley, Kent; *b* 1 April 1944; *Educ* St Dunstan's Coll, St Catherine's Coll Oxford (MA), Univ of London (PhD, MB BS, MSc); *m* 1, (m dis 1991), Anne Katharine Stewart; 2 da (Eleanor Ruth b 24 Nov 1970, Harriet Lorna Mary b 13 Aug 1973); m 2, Wendy Rowena French, *née* Morgan-Jones; *Career* sr lectr and hon conslt in chemical pathology King's Coll Sch of Med and Dentistry 1980–; asst registrar RCPath 1996–; memb: Assoc of Clinical Biochemists, BMA, Soc of Authors (chm Med Writers' Gp 1994–95); FRCP 1993 (MRCP 1979), FRCPath 1992 (MRCPath 1980), FRCPE 1996; *Books* Illustrated Textbook of Clinical Chemistry (1988, 3 edn 1995), Clinical Chemistry, an Illustrated Outline (1991), Intensive Care and Clinical Biochemistry (with P Gosling and M Clapham, 1994), Clinical Biochemistry: Metabolic and Clinical Aspects (with S K Bangert, 1995), Primary Care and Laboratory Medicine (with J Hooper, G McCreanor and P Myers, 1996); *Recreations* distance running, writing, gardening, reading detective stories; *Clubs* Players Theatre; *Style*— Dr William Marshall; ✉ Department of Clinical Biochemistry, King's College School of Medicine and Dentistry, London SE5 9PJ (☎ 0171 346 3275, fax 0171 737 7434)

MARSHALL-ANDREWS, Robert Graham; QC (1987); s of Robin Marshall-Andrews (d 1986), and Eileen Norah Marshall-Andrews (d 1996); *b* 10 April 1944; *Educ* Mill Hill Sch, Univ of Bristol (LLB); *m* Gillian Diana; 1 da (Laura b 1971), 1 s (Tom b 1973); *Career* called to the Bar Gray's Inn 1967 (bencher 1996); Parly candidate (Lab) Medway 1992 and 1996; tstee: George Adamson Wildlife Tst, Geffrye Museum; former chm Grey Court Sch; *Books* Palace of Wisdom (novel, 1989); *Clubs* Druidston (Pembrokeshire); *Style*— Robert Marshall-Andrews, Esq, QC; ✉ 4 Paper Buildings, Ground Floor, Temple, London EC4Y 7EX (☎ 0171 353 3366, fax 0171 353 5778, mobile 0860 271773)

MARSHALL-CLARKE, Geoffrey; s of Colin Marshall Clarke, of Rowan Drive, Kilburn, Derbyshire, and Irene, *née* Allsop; *b* 2 Oct 1952; *Educ* Swanwick Hall GS, Univ of Nottingham (LLB); *m* 25 Oct 1975, Susan Joy, da of Kenneth Norman Sansom, of Pentire Crescent, Newquay, Cornwall; 1 s (Alexander b 18 June 1985), 1 da (Holly b 18 July 1987); *Career* graduate trainee Boots The Chemist 1973–75, brand mangr Ranks Hovis McDougall 1975–76, mktg mangr Br Aluminium 1976–78, md Print Promotions and Publicity 1978–82, chm Koster Marshall-Clarke plc 1982–; fndr memb SDP, memb Lib Democrats; memb: IOD 1980, Inst of Mgmnt 1984, The Mktg Soc 1988, SPCA Ctee 1988–92; *Recreations* golf, squash, reading, music; *Clubs* Y; *Style*— Geoffrey Marshall-Clarke, Esq; ✉ Lye Green Cottage, Lycrome Rd, Lye Green, nr Chesham, Bucks (☎ 01494 774465); The Koster Marshall-Clarke Consultancy, Claridge House, 200 High Street, Berkhamsted, Herts HP4 3AP (☎ 01442 875941, fax 01442 866459, mobile tel 0831 694570)

MARSHAM, Julian Charles; s of Col Peter Marsham, MBE (s of Hon Sydney Marsham, yst s of 4 Earl of Romney), and Hersey, da of Maj Hon Richard Coke (3 s of 2 Earl of Leicester, KG, JP, DL, by his 2 w, Hon Georgina Cavendish, da of 2 Baron Chesham); hp of kinsman, 7 Earl of Romney; *b* 28 March 1948; *Educ* Eton; *m* 1975, Catriona, da of Robert Christie Stewart CBE, TD (nephew of Sir Christopher Lighton, 8 Bt, MBE); 2 s (David b 1977, Michael b 1979), 1 da (Laura b 1984); *Career* land agent; farmer; *Recreations* shooting, fishing, silviculture, gardening; *Style*— Julian Marsham, Esq; ✉ Gayton Hall, King's Lynn, Norfolk PE32 1PL (☎ 01553 636259, estate office 01553 636292)

MARSLAND, Prof David; s of Ernest Marsland (d 1991), of Leavesden Green, Herts, and Fay, *née* Savoury (d 1993); *b* 3 Feb 1939; *Educ* Watford GS, Christ's Coll Cambridge (scholar, BA, MA), LSE, Brunel Univ (PhD); *Career* Dept of Sociology Brunel Univ 1964–88 (lectr, sr lectr, dir postgrad studies, prof assoc), prof of social res West London Inst of Higher Educn 1989–95, prof of social scis Brunel Univ 1995–; asst dir The Social Affairs Unit London 1981–89; dir Centre for Evaluation Res 1989–; special advsr to Parly Social Security Ctee 1993–95; memb: Social Scis Bd UNESCO 1983–86, Social Scis Ctee CNAA 1987–92; formerly memb EC Social Res Assoc and hon gen sec Br Sociological Assoc; first Thatcher Award winner for contribs to analysis of freedom 1991; memb: BSA 1964, SRA 1985; MIMgt 1987, FRSH 1990, FRSA 1992; *Books* Seeds of Bankruptcy (1988), Cradle to Grave (1989), Understanding Youth (1993), Work and Employment (1994), Self-Reliance (1995), Welfare or Welfare State? (1996); *Recreations* reading and writing poetry, music, theatre; *Style*— Prof David Marsland; ✉ Director, Centre for Evaluation Research, Lancaster House, Borough Road, Isleworth, Middx TW7 5DU (☎ 0181 891 0921)

MARSLEN-WILSON, Prof William David; s of David William Marslen-Wilson (d 1983), and Pera, *née* Funk; *b* 5 June 1945; *Educ* St John's Coll Oxford (BA), MIT (PhD); *m* 1982, Lorraine Komisarjevsky Tyler; 2 da (Eliza and Lydia), 1 s (Jack); *Career* asst prof Dept of Behavioural Scis Univ of Chicago 1973–78, scientific assoc Max-Planck-Institut für Psycholinguistik Nijmegen 1977–82, univ lectr Dept of Experimental Psychology Univ of Cambridge 1982–84, co-dir Max-Plank-Institut für Psycholinguistik Nijmegen 1985–87, sr scientist MRC Applied Psychology Unit Cambridge 1987–90, prof of psychology Birkbeck Coll Univ of London 1990–; Sloan fell MIT 1980–81, visiting prof Univ of Southern California LA 1989–90, visiting prof Univ of Arizona 1994–95, hon dir Beijing Normal Univ 1995–; fell Academia Europeae 1996, FBA 1996; *Publications* author of numerous articles in learned jls, conference proceedings and book chapters; *Style*— Prof William Marslen-Wilson, FBA; ✉ Department of Psychology, Birkbeck College, Malet Street, London WC1E 7HX (☎ 0171 631 6207, fax 0171 631 6312, e-mail w.marslen-wilson@psychology.bbk.ac.uk)

MARSTON, (Jeffery) Adrian Priestley; s of Maj J E Marston, DSO, MC (d 1945), and Doreen, *née* Norris (d 1980); *b* 15 Dec 1927; *Educ* Marlborough, Magdalen Coll Oxford (MA, DM, MCh), St Thomas's Hosp Med Sch London; *m* 17 July 1951, Sylvie Colin; 2 s (John b 24 Feb 1960, Nicholas b 4 Jan 1963), 1 da (Joanna b 24 Sept 1954); *Career* Nat Serv Lt RAMC, then Capt 1954–57; surgical registrar and sr registrar St Thomas's Hosp 1960–65, sr lectr in surgery Faculty of Clinical Sci Univ Coll London 1965–; conslt surgn: The Middx Hosp 1968–92, Royal Northern Hosp 1970–85, UCH 1985–92; vice pres RCS 1991–92, chm Senate of Royal Colls of Surgns Euro Ctee, memb Jt Consultatants Ctee 1993–; dean RSM 1995– (hon treas 1993–95); pres: Vascular Surgical Soc of GB and Ireland 1985, Assoc of Surgns of GB and Ireland 1986; memb d'honneur Association Française de Chirurgie 1986, soc de honor Asociación Espanola de Cirujanos 1987; Hon MD Nice 1986; FRCS 1958; *Books* Intestinal Ischaemia (1976), Contemporary Operative Surgery (1979), Visceral Artery Reconstruction (1986), Splanchnic Ischemia and Multiple Organ Failure (1989); author of numerous papers on vascular surgery and gastroenterology; *Recreations* literature, languages, travel, music; *Clubs* Hurlingham; *Style*— Adrian Marston, Esq; ✉ 4 Hereford Square, London SW7 4TT (☎ 0171 373 7678)

MARSTON, David Charles; s of Reginald Charles Moor Marston (d 1991), and Catherine Ann, *née* Romanes; *b* 22 March 1955; *Educ* Cheam Sch, Shrewsbury, Univ of Newcastle on Tyne (BA); *Career* Deloittes (now part of Coopers & Lybrand) 1976–80 (articled clerk then CA), under sec Auditing Practices Ctee ICAEW 1980–82, audit mangr Grant Thornton 1982–84, Citicorp Group 1984– (fin controller of various subsids, now Euro group compliance offr); memb Fin Reporting Ctee ICAEW 1990–; Liveryman Worshipful Co of Gardeners 1980; FCA 1989 (ACA 1979); *Recreations* tenor in church choir, scout leader; *Style*— David Marston, Esq; ✉ Citibank NA, Cottons Centre, Hays Lane, London SE1 (☎ 0171 500 2161)

MARSTON, Dr Geoffrey; s of Arthur Marston (d 1982), of Newark, Notts, and Mabel, *née* Binns (d 1996); *b* 17 March 1938; *Educ* Magnus GS Newark Notts, UCL (LLB, LLM, PhD); *Career* mgmnt trainee Assoc Br Maltsters Export Co Ltd 1960–62, project offr Australian public serv Canberra 1962–67, sr lectr in Law Australian Nat Univ of Canberra 1967–70, attaché de recherches Graduate Inst of Int Studies Geneva 1970–73, fell Sidney Sussex Coll and lectr in Law Cambridge Univ 1973–; called to the Bar Middle Temple 1993; *Books* The Marginal Seabed: United Kingdom Legal Practice (1981); *Recreations* mountain walking, beachcombing, photography, traditional jazz; *Clubs* Athenaeum; *Style*— Dr Geoffrey Marston; ✉ Sidney Sussex College, Cambridge CB2 3HU (☎ 01223 338800, fax 01223 338884)

MARTELL, Vice Adm Sir Hugh Colenso; KBE (1966, CBE 1957), CB (1963); s of Engr Capt Albert Arthur Green Martell, DSO (d 1951), and Susan, da of William Colenso; *b* 6 May 1912; *Educ* Edinburgh Acad, RNC Dartmouth; *m* 1, Marguerite Isabelle, da of Sir (Rudolph) Dymoke White, 2 Bt (d 1968); 5 s, 1 da; m 2, Margaret, da of Maj A R Glover (d 1979); 2 s, 6 da; *Career* joined RN 1926, serv WWII (despatches), Russian Convoys and Pacific, Capt 1952, ADC to HM, Overall Operational Cdr Nuclear Tests in Montebellos NW Australia 1957, Rear Adm 1962, Dir Gen Naval Recruiting 1964–65, Admiral Cmdg Reserves, Vice Adm 1965, Chief Allied Staff NATO Forces Mediterranean, Aegean and Black Sea 1965–67, ret; dir: Derritron Electronics Ltd, Reslosound Ltd, City and Military Personnel Consultants and Directors' Secretaries Ltd; chm Bury Manor Schs Tst Ltd; govr: Dorset House Sch, Manor House Sch; *Recreations* yachting; *Clubs* Royal Naval, RN Sailing Assoc; *Style*— Vice Adm Sir Hugh Martell, KBE, CB

MARTEN, Lt Cdr George Gosselin; LVO (1985, MVO 1950), DSC (1942); s of Vice Adm Sir Francis Arthur Marten, KBE, CB, CMG, CVO (d 1950), and Phyllis Raby, *née* Morgan; *b* 28 Dec 1918; *Educ* RNC Dartmouth; *m* 25 Nov 1949, Hon Mary Anna Marten, OBE, DL, *qv*, *née* Sturt, da of 3 Baron Alington (ka 1940); 1 s (Napier b 1959), 5 da (Victoria b 1950, Charlotte b 1952, Georgina b 1953, Amabel b 1954, Sophia b 1962); *Career* served in destroyers WWII, in cmd HMS Wilton 1943–45 (despatches 3 times); equerry to HM King George VI 1948–50, High Sheriff of Dorset 1962; *Recreations* forestry, bloodstock breeding; *Clubs* Turf; *Style*— Lt Cdr George Marten, LVO, DSC; ✉ Crichel, Wimborne, Dorset BH21 5DT

MARTEN, (Richard) Hedley Westwood; s of Capt Lewis Westwood Marten (ka 1944), and Kathleen, *née* Ogston (d 1988); n of Rt Hon Sir Neil Marten, MP, Min for Overseas Devpt 1979–83, and gn of Sir Henry Marten, KCVO, Provost of Eton and personal tutor to HM The Queen; *b* 24 Jan 1943; *Educ* Winchester, Magdalene Coll Cambridge (MA); *m* 30 July 1971 (m dis 1983), Fiona Mary, da of George William Carter Sinclair, and sis of Sir Clive Sinclair, *qv*; 2 s (Benedict b 9 Sept 1976, Alexander b 24 July 1978), 1 da (Laura b 19 April 1973); *Career* called to the Bar Lincoln's Inn 1966; in practice Chancery Bar 1968–, head of Chambers 1995–; Chancery Bar rep Bar Cncl 1990–96; *Recreations* playing Bach, cricket and chess; *Clubs* Brooks's, Butterflies Cricket; *Style*— Hedley Marten, Esq; ✉ 3 New Square, Lincoln's Inn, London WC2 (☎ 0171 405 5577, fax 0171 404 5032)

MARTEN, Hon Mrs (Mary Anna Sibell Elizabeth); OBE (1980), DL (Dorset 1989); da of 3 Baron Alington (ka 1940), and Lady Mary Ashley Cooper (d 1936), da of 9 Earl of Shaftesbury; *m* 25 Nov 1949, Lt Cdr George Gosselin Marten, LVO, DSC, *qv*; 1 s, 5 da; *Career* tstee Br Museum 1985–; High Sheriff of Dorset 1989; *Style*— The Hon Mrs Marten, OBE, DL; ✉ Crichel, Wimborne, Dorset BH21 5DT

MARTIN, Prof Alan Douglas; s of Frederick Charles Martin (d 1979), and Emily May, *née* Berkley (d 1990); *b* 4 Dec 1937; *Educ* Eltham Coll, UCL (BSc, PhD); *m* 4 April 1964, Rev Penny Elizabeth Martin, da of William Eric Leggett Johnson, BEM (d 1985); 1 s (Robert b 4 April 1967), 2 da (Rebecca b 30 March 1966, Rachel b 23 March 1974); *Career* res assoc: Univ of Illinois 1962–63, Rutherford Laboratory 1963–64; Univ of Durham: lectr, sr lectr, reader, prof 1964–; CPhys, FInstP; *Books* Elementary Particle Theory (with T D Spearman, 1970), Quarks and Leptons (with F Halzen, 1984), Hadron Interactions (with P D B Collins, 1984), Particle Physics and Cosmology (jtly, 1989); *Recreations* tennis, walking, music; *Style*— Prof Alan Martin; ✉ 26 Telford Close, High Shincliffe, Durham DH1 2YJ (☎ 0191 386 1742); Department of Physics, University of Durham, Durham City DH1 3LE (☎ 0191 374 2162, fax 0191 374 3848)

MARTIN, Alan Frederick Joseph Plunkett; s of Dr Hugh Thomas Plunkett Martin, of Bournemouth, and Sylvia Mary, *née* Gilbert; *b* 22 Aug 1951; *Educ* Realgymnasium Basel Switzerland, Univ of Basel; *m* 19 May 1979, Rita Maria, da of Walter Gasser, of St Gall, Switzerland; 3 da (Stephanie b 1980, Felicity b 1983, Dominique b 1986); *Career* Swiss Bank Corporation: Basel 1975–77 and 1979–80, NY 1981; Credit Commercial de France Paris 1978, exec dir Swiss Bank Corporation London 1986– (joined 1981); *Recreations* family, gardening, skiing, photography; *Style*— Alan Martin, Esq; ✉ Compton Water, Fairmile Park Road, Cobham, Surrey KT11 2PG (☎ 01932 863504); Swiss Bank House, 1 High Timber Street, London EC4V 3SB (☎ 0171 711 2545, fax 0171 711 4359, telex 887434)

MARTIN, Barrie Stuart Meredyth; s of James William Meredyth Martin, of Mayfield, E Sussex and formerly of Shanghai and Hong Kong, and Joyce Stuart, *née* Bidwell; *b* 18 Aug 1941; *Educ* Shanghai Br Sch, St John's Beaumont, Beaumont Coll, Trinity Coll Dublin (BA, LLB); *Career* articled clerk to Sir Charles Russell Bt, ptnr Charles Russell and Co, asst slr Sprott and Sons, sr ptnr Rix and Kay slrs (currently conslt); memb Law Soc; *Recreations* tennis, travel; *Clubs* The Sloane; *Style*— Barrie Martin, Esq; ✉ Rix and Kay, 84 High St, Heathfield, East Sussex TN21 8JG (☎ 01435 865211, fax 01435 866822); Postmill Cottage, Argos Hill, Rotherfield, E Sussex TN6 3QF

MARTIN, Brian William; s of Cecil William Martin, of Southend on Sea, Essex, and Annie Elizabeth, *née* Bradley (d 1986); *b* 26 June 1937; *Educ* Southend HS, Hertford Coll Oxford (MA, DipEd), Univ of Leicester (PhD); *m* 22 Dec 1965, Margaret Louise, da of Kenneth Maidment, of Oxford and Auckland, NZ; 2 s (Barnaby b 1972, Felix b 1974), 2 da (Sophie b 1971, Laura b 1980); *Career* cmmnd RAEC 1958–60; head of English Magdalen Coll Sch Oxford (housemaster and archivist) 1961–, awarder Oxford and Cambridge Schs Examination Bd 1965–, inspr of schs OFSTED 1993–, assoc ed New Dictionary of National Biography 1994–; lectr in modern English lit: New Coll Oxford 1974–76, Pembroke Coll 1976–83; tutor Oxford and Berkeley Univ prog 1971–78, tutor and lectr Univ of Massachusetts Oxford prog 1980–85, res lectr Hertford Coll Oxford 1985; book critic and occasional columnist The Times, book critic Daily Telegraph, Independent, Financial Times and Spectator 1980–, various contribs to learned jls; vice pres Eng Schs Hockey Assoc 1970; *Books* John Keble - Priest, Professor and Poet (1976), John Henry Newman - His Life and Work (1982, revised edn 1990), John Henry Newman (ed, 1986), Volume 4 Nineteenth Century Macmillan Anthology of English Literature (ed, 1989); *Recreations* lawn tennis, real tennis; *Clubs* Theological Wine; *Style*— Brian Martin, Esq; ✉ 4 Chalfont Road, Oxford OX2 6TH

MARTIN, Cary John; s of John Martin, of Manchester, and Joan Molly Wilson, *née* Skinner; *b* 22 Aug 1956; *Educ* William Hulme's GS Manchester, Univ of Birmingham (MA, BA), Christ's Coll Cambridge; *m* 23 Sept 1978, Ruth Lilian, da of Arthur Henry George Amy, of Bristol; *Career* exec Mori 1979–85; Dewe Rogerson: joined 1985, dep chief exec 1989–95, chief exec 1995–; hon res fell UCL; *Publications* A Demotic Land Lease from Philadelphia (Jl of Egyptian Archaeology Vol 72, 1986); *Recreations* Egyptology; *Style*— Cary Martin, Esq; ✉ 14 Collingham Place, London SW5 0PZ (☎ 0171 373 6773); Dewe Rogerson, 3 1/2 London Wall Buildings, London Wall, London EC2M 5SY (☎ 0171 638 9571, fax 0171 638 7091)

MARTIN, Charles Edmund; s of Flt Lt Charles Stuart Martin, RAFVR (ka 1944), of Newcastle upon Tyne, and Sheila, *née* Richardson; *b* 19 Sept 1939; *Educ* Lancing, Selwyn Coll Cambridge (MA), Univ of Bristol (PGCE); *m* 6 Aug 1966, Emily Mary, da of Ernest Franklin Bozman, MC (d 1968), of Cambridge; 1 s (Joseph Ernest), 1 da (Charlotte Mary); *Career* VSO Sarawak 1958–59, asst master Leighton Park Sch Reading 1964–68, sixth form master and day housemaster Sevenoaks Sch Kent 1968–71, dep headmaster and head of English Pocklington Sch York 1971–80; headmaster: King Edward VI Camp Hill Boys' Sch Birmingham 1980–86, Bristol GS 1986–; memb SHA 1980–; HMC: memb 1986–, sec SW Div 1992, chm 1993, memb Central Ctee 1992–93; *Recreations* walking, theatre, travel; *Clubs* E India, Public Schs; *Style*— Charles Martin, Esq; ✉ The Grammar School, University Rd, Bristol BS8 1SR (☎ 0117 973 6006, fax 0117 946 7485)

MARTIN, Christopher John William; s of William Joseph Martin (d 1942), of Potters Bar, and Kathleen Emily Martin (d 1982); *b* 13 Feb 1939; *Educ* Seaford Coll, KCL (LLB), Merton Coll Oxford; *m* 29 June 1963, Felicity Mary, da of Gp Capt Alfred Weston (d 1985), of Kilkenny; 2 s (Dominic b 1964, Jonathan b 1970), 1 da (Diana b 1966); *Career* account exec Lintas in London and Barcelona 1961–64; BBC TV 1964–91: documentary prodr, dir and ed Omnibus, ed Arts Features, ed Design and Architecture; films incl: A Life of Christ (with Malcolm Muggeridge), City of Towers (with Christopher Booker), Triumph of the West (with John Roberts), Sir Joshua - Artist of the Portrait, A Vision of Britain and The Earth in Balance (with HRH The Prince of Wales), Charles - Public Role Private Man (1994); dir CM Productions 1994–95, Network First (Carlton TV, 1996); *Books* In the Secret Garden - Autumn with the Ruralists (1991); *Recreations* walking; *Style*— Christopher Martin, Esq; ✉ The Old Rectory, Bleddfa, Knighton, Powis, Wales (☎ 01547 81658)

MARTIN, Christopher Sanford; s of Geoffrey Richard Rex Martin (d 1986), of London, and Hazel, *née* Matthews (d 1996); *b* 23 Aug 1938; *Educ* Westminster, Univ of St Andrews (MA); *m* 30 March 1968, (Mary) Julia, da of Dr John Parry Evans, of Colwyn Bay, N Wales; 1 s (William Drake b 1971), 1 da (Katharine Mary b 1969); *Career* Nat Serv 2 Lt 2/10 PMO Gurkha Rifles 1957–59; asst master and house master Westminster Sch 1963–78, asst master Philips' Acad Exeter New Hampshire USA 1966; headmaster: Bristol Cathedral Sch 1979–90, Millfield School 1990–; chm: SW Div HMC 1987, Choir Schs' Assoc 1987–89, HMC/SHA Working Pty on Teacher Supply 1987–91; memb Educn Panel Privy Cncl 1986–, fndr Textbooks for Africa Project 1987; *Recreations* skiing, sailing; *Style*— Christopher Martin, Esq; ✉ Millfield School, Street, Somerset BA16 0YD (☎ 01458 442291, fax 01458 447276)

MARTIN, David; s of Edward Sydney Morris Martin, of Exeter, and Dorothy Mary, *née* Cooper; *b* 11 Feb 1952; *Educ* Worthing HS for Boys, St John's Coll Cambridge; *m* 24 Aug 1991, Ruth Kathryn, da of Terence Colin Howells; 1 da (Abigail Ruth b 10 May 1994); *Career* ptnr Herbert Smith 1986– (asst slr 1979–86, tax slr 1979–); memb Religious Soc of Friends; *Recreations* reading, walking; *Style*— David Martin, Esq; ✉ Firbank House, 83 South End Road, London NW3 2RJ (☎ 0171 794 4619); Herbert Smith, Exchange House, Primrose St, London EC2A 2HS (☎ 0171 374 8000, fax 0171 496 0043, telex 886633)

MARTIN, Rev Prof David Alfred; s of Frederick Martin (d 1979), and Rhoda Miriam, *née* Davey (d 1981); *b* 30 June 1929; *Educ* Richmond and E Sheen GS, Westminster Coll Oxford (DipEd), LSE (BSc, PhD); *m* 1, 12 April 1953 (m dis 1957), Daphne Sylvia (d 1973), da of Arthur Treherne (d 1970); 1 s (Jonathan Paul b 25 March 1956); m 2, 30 June 1962, Bernice, da of Frederick William Thompson (d 1956); 2 s (Izaak David b 4 May 1965, Magnus Aidan b 25 Jan 1971), 1 da (Jessica Heloise b 8 April 1963); *Career* Nat Serv 1948–50; sch teaching 1952–59, lectr Univ of Sheffield 1961–62; LSE: lectr 1962–67, reader 1967–71, prof of sociology 1971–89, prof emeritus 1989–; Scurlock prof Southern Methodist Univ Dallas 1986–90; visiting prof: King's Coll London 1989–92, Univ of Boston 1991–95, Univ of Lancaster 1993–; Sarum lectr Univ of Oxford 1994–95, Gunning lectr Univ of Edinburgh 1997; pres Int Assoc for Sociology of Religion 1975–83; ordained: deacon 1983, priest 1984; hon asst Guildford Cathedral 1983– (non-stipendiary priest 1984); vice pres: Prayer Book Soc 1980–92, London Soc for Study of Religion 1974–93; select preacher Univ of Cambridge; fell Japanese Soc for the Promotion of Sci 1978–79; memb: UK UNESCO Ctee 1982–83, UK Advsy Ctee Encyclopaedia Britannica 1986–; chm Cncl for Academic Autonomy 1988–90; hon fell Westminster Coll Oxford 1992; *Books* Pacifism (1965), A Sociology of English Religion (1967), The Religious and the Secular (1971), A General Theory of Secularization (1978), The Breaking of the Image (1980), Tongues of Fire (1990), Reflections on Sociology and Theology (1996), The Forbidden Revolutions (1996), Does Christianity Cause War? (1997); *Recreations* piano accompaniment; *Style*— The Rev Prof David A Martin; ✉ Cripplegate Cottage, 174 St John's Rd, Woking, Surrey (☎ 01483 762134); LSE, Aldwych, London, WC2 (☎ 0171 405 7686, fax 0171 242 0392, telex 24655 BLPES G)

MARTIN, David John Pattison; MP (C) Portsmouth South (majority 242); s of John Besley Martin, CBE (d 1982), and Muriel, *née* Pattison; *b* 5 Feb 1945; *Educ* Kelly Coll Tavistock, Fitzwilliam Coll Cambridge (BA); *m* 8 Jan 1977, Basia Constance, da of Tadeusz Dowmunt; 1 s (Henry b 1985), 4 da (Naomi b 1978, Melissa b and d 1980, Francesca 1981, Charis b 1983); *Career* called to the Bar Inner Temple, in practice 1969–76; MP (C) Portsmouth S 1987–, PPS to Rt Hon Alan Clark as min of state for defence procurement 1990, PPS to Rt Hon Douglas Hurd as sec of state for foreign and Cwlth affrs 1990–94; dir Martins Caravan Co and assoc co until 1990; *Recreations* music, golf; *Clubs* Hawks; *Style*— David Martin, Esq, MP; ✉ House of Commons, London SW1A 0AA

MARTIN, David MacLeod; s of Allan MacLeod Martin (d 1976), and Jessie McCurdie, *née* Harris (d 1974); *b* 30 Dec 1922; *Educ* Govan HS, Glasgow Sch of Art (Dip Art); *m* 30 July 1951, Isobel Agnes Fowlie, da of George Frances Fowlie Smith (d 1972); 4 s (Brian b 4 Aug 1954, Allan b 26 Sept 1956, Kenneth b 21 July 1960, Derek b 30 Sept 1966); *Career* served WWII Sgt RAF 1943–46; teacher and princ teacher Hamilton GS 1973–83; painter 1983–; annual exhibitions: RSA, RSW, RGI (RA 1984); numerous group shows incl: Lynn Stern Assoc London, London 20th Century Art Fair, Miami Art Fair; one man shows: Glasgow, Edinburgh, Perth, Greenock & Stone Gallery Newcastle, Thackery Gallery London 1992 and 1994, John Martin of London 1995, Fosse Gallery Stow on the Wold 1995; work in numerous private and public collections incl: The Fleming Collection London, Credit Lyonnaise London, The Earl of Moray, Lord Goold, Lord MacFarlane, Lady MacKay, Scottish Arts Cncl; work cmmnd by Lord Bute for Bute Fabrics, special award of merit Robert Colquhoun Meml art prize Kilmarnock 1974, prizewinner Friends of the Smith Gallery Stirling 1981, May Marshall Brown Award RSW 1984, EIS Purchase Prize 1986, prizewinner Hamilton museum exhibiton 1988, £1,000 prizewinner The Laing Collection art competition 1990 and 1993, David Cargill Award (RGI 1995); cncl memb RGI, cncl memb RSW (past vice president); memb: SSA 1949 (hon memb 1992), RSW 1961, RGI 1981, SAAC (Scottish Artists and Artist Craftsmen) 1992; *Recreations* gardening, period ship modelling, music; *Style*— David M Martin, Esq; ✉ The Old Schoolhouse, 53 Gilmour St, Eaglesham, Glasgow G76 0LG (☎ 01355 303308)

MARTIN, David Weir; MEP (Lab) Lothians (majority 37,207); s of William Martin and Marion Weir; *b* 26 Aug 1954; *Educ* Liberton HS, Heriot Watt Univ (BA); *m* 1979, Margaret Mary, *née* Cook; 1 s, 1 da; *Career* former stockbroker's asst and animal welfare campaigner; memb Lab Pty 1975–, Lothian regnl cncllr Inch/Gilmerton 1982; MEP (Lab) Lothian 1984–, ldr Br Lab Gp Euro Parl 1987–89, vice-pres Euro Parl 1989–; memb: Tport and Gen Workers' Union, General and Municipal Boilermakers', Fabian Soc, Anti-Apartheid Movement; memb Parly Inst Ctee; vice-pres: Int Inst for Democracy, Advocates for Animals, Nat Playbus Assoc; *Books* Traditional Industrial Regions of the European Community (report), Bringing Common Sense to the Common Market - A Left Agenda for Europe (pamphlet, 1988), The Democratic Deficit (chapter in A Claim of Right for Scotland, ed by Owen Dudley Edwards), European Union and the Democratic Deficit (pamphlet, 1990), Europe - An Ever Closer Union (1991), Refreshing the Parts (contrib), The Intergovernmental Conferences in the Context of Parliament's Strategy for European Union (4 reports on Maastricht), Towards a Wider, Deeper, Federal Europe (pamphlet, 1992), European Union - The Shattered Dream? (pamphlet, 1993); *Recreations* reading, sport; *Style*— David Martin, Esq, MEP; ✉ 4 Lothian Street, Dalkeith, Edinburgh EH22 1DS (☎ 0131 654 1606, fax 0131 654 1607)

MARTIN, Prof Derek Humphery; s of Alec Gooch Martin (d 1986), of Eastbourne, and Winifred, *née* Humphery (d 1991); *b* 18 May 1929; *Educ* Hitchin GS, Eastbourne GS, Univ of Nottingham (BSc, PhD); *m* 7 July 1951, Joyce Sheila, da of William Samuel Leaper (d 1973), of Eastbourne; 1 s (Richard Jonathan b 1960), 1 da (Elizabeth Jane b 1962); *Career* prof of physics Queen Mary Coll London 1967–94 (lectr 1954–63, reader 1963–67, dean Faculty of Sci 1968–70); memb Bd: Athlone Press 1973–83, IOP Publications Ltd 1985–94; ed Advances in Physics 1974–85; senator Univ of London 1980–87, hon sec Inst of Physics 1984–94; memb: SRC Astronomy, Space and Radio Bd 1975–78, Royal Greenwich Observatory Estab Ctee 1977–80, Br Nat Ctee for Radioscience 1983–88, Ct Univ of Essex 1986–, Br Nat Ctee for Physics 1987–90, Sc Unions Ctee Royal Soc 1994–; Metrology Award Nat Physical Laboratory 1983, K J Button Prize Int Soc for Optical Engrg 1992; hon fell Queen Mary and Westfield Coll London 1996; FInstP 1969, CPhys 1985; *Books* Magnetism in Solids (1967), Spectroscopic Techniques (1967); *Clubs* Athenaeum; *Style*— Prof Derek Martin; ✉ Hermanus, Hillwood Grove, Brentwood, Essex CM13 2PD (☎ 01277 210546); Queen Mary and Westfield College, Mile End Rd, London E14 NS

MARTIN, Eamonn Thomas; s of Albert Fredrick Martin (d 1972), and Margarita Filamena, *née* O'Donnell; *b* 9 Oct 1958; *Educ* Fryerns Comp, Barking Coll of Technol/North East London Poly (HNC); *m* 28 Sept 1985, Julie Teresa, da of Malcolm Hull; 2 da (Lydia Lauren b 5 July 1986, Rosie Louise b 29 Jan 1989), 1 s (Eamonn Christopher b 15 April 1993); *Career* athlete; English schoolboy: cross country champion 1973, 1500 metres champion 1975; represented English schs at int level 1975; memb Basildon Athletic Club 1975–; nat sr cross country champion 1984 and 1992; AAA's: 5,000 metres champion 1988, 1990 and 1991, 10,000 metres champion 1989 and 1992; IAAF 5,000 metres champion 1988; Cwlth Games Gold medallist 10,000 metres 1990, winner London Marathon 1993, winner Chicago marathon 1995; memb Olympic squad 1984, 1988 and 1992, represented GB at World Cross Country Championships six times; Br record holder 10,000 metres (27m 23.06 secs); employed at Research and Devpt Centre Ford Motor Co Essex; *Recreations* following most sports, cars; *Style*— Eamonn Martin, Esq

MARTIN, Edward Charles; *b* 2 Sept 1932; *Educ* Alderman Newton's GS Leicester 1941–44, Henry Mellish GS Nottingham 1944–48, Nottingham Coll of Art and Design (pt/t); *m* 1958, Audrey Elizabeth, *née* Eite; 1 da (Alison Wendy b 1967); *Career* Nat Serv 1950–52 Prov Marshal Branch RAF Police; Marshall and Co Ltd (photographers and printers) 1948–50, Nottingham Coll of Art and Crafts, studio and location asst Vogue Studios London 1954–55, F R Logan Ltd Birmingham 1955–57, teacher Birmingham Coll of Art and Crafts 1956–57, lectr in photography Birmingham Coll of Art and Crafts Birmingham Poly 1957–74 (head of Sch of Photography 1967–74), course ldr Trent/Derby Dip Course in Creative Photography 1974–; sec: IBP E Midlands Gp Assts and Students Gp 1949–50, Nottingham Coll of Art and Crafts Students Union 1950–52, IBP W Midlands Gp 1956–70, Communication Studies Course Devpt Ctee Trent Poly 1974–75; chm: Soc for Photographic Educn UK 1973–74, Creative Arts Course Devpt Ctee Trent Poly 1974–76, Assoc Examining Bd Photography Advsy Ctee 1987–89 (memb 1983–89); memb: Assoc Teachers of Photography (fndr) 1963, Mgmnt Ctee Soc Photographic Educn UK 1973–80, EEC Working Pty on Photographic Educn Brussels 1969; vice chm Assoc Examining Bd Visual Arts Advsy Ctee 1987–89; numerous papers on photography; memb NUJ, FBIPP; *Recreations* garden designing and maintenance; *Style*— Edward Martin, Esq; ✉ Lambley Lane, Burton Joyce, Nottinghamshire NG14 5BN; Dept of Visual and Performing Arts, The Nottingham Trent University, Burton St, Nottingham NG1 4BU (☎ 0115 948 6479, fax 0115 948 6403, telex 377534 Polnot G)

MARTIN, Evelyn Fairfax (Eve); OBE (1994); da of Kenneth Gordon Robinson (d 1970), of Liverpool, and Beatrice, *née* Munro; *b* 12 Aug 1926; *Educ* Belvedere Sch Liverpool, Huyton Coll Liverpool, Mrs Hoster's Secretarial Coll London; *m* 24 Sept 1949, Dennis William Martin, s of William Henry Martin; 4 da (Carolyn Ann b 10 June 1952, Lindsay Claire b 5 Jan 1953, Fiona Elizabeth b 11 Sept 1955 d 1964, Philippa Lee b 27 Nov 1962); *Career* private sec I M Marsh Coll of PE 1949–51, sch sec Trinidad 1950–53, foster parent 1960–80; chm: Battered Wives Hostel 1980–81, Calderdale Well Women's Centre 1982–86, Calderdale Community Health Cncl 1982–84; Nat Cncl of Women of GB: nat pres 1986–88, co sec 1992–; ldr Women's Health & Screening Delgn 1985–91, co-chair Women's Nat Cmmn 1991–93; FRSA; *Recreations* gardening, animals, travelling, friends; *Clubs* Univ Women's; *Style*— Mrs Eve Martin, OBE; ✉ 32 Clifton Rd, Halifax, W Yorkshire HX3 0BT (☎ and fax 01422 360438); National Council of Women of Great Britain, 36 Danbury Street, Islington, London N1 8JU

MARTIN, (Thomas) Geoffrey; s of Thomas Martin (d 1973), Belfast, NI, and Sadie Adelaide, *née* Day (d 1991); *b* 26 July 1940; *Educ* Newry GS, Queen's Univ Belfast; *m* 6 July 1968, Gay Madeleine Annesley, da of Herbert Annesley Brownrigg, of Bognor Regis; 1 s (Thomas), 3 da (Bluebell, Poppy, Gabriella); *Career* pres NUS 1966–68, dir Shelter 1972–73, dip staff Cwlth Secretariat 1973–79, head Euro Cmmn Office NI 1979–85, head of Press and Info Serv EC SE Asia 1985–87, head of external relations Euro Cmmn Office London 1987–94, head Euro Cmmn Representation in the UK 1994–; *Recreations* running; *Clubs* Travellers'; *Style*— Geoffrey Martin, Esq; ✉ 64 Mortlake Rd, Kew, Richmond TW9 4AS (☎ 0181 876 3714); 8 Storeys Gate, London SW1P 3AT (☎ 0171 973 1979)

MARTIN, Geoffrey; s of late James Martin, and Agnes, *née* Woods; *b* 14 Aug 1953; *Educ* Ballymena Boys' Sch; *m* Susannah, *née* Forte; 1 s (Paul James b 22 June 1977), 2 da (Suzanne b 16 May 1975, Catherine Elizabeth b 25 Nov 1989); *Career* journalist Ballymena Guardian 1973–76; sports ed: Newbury Weekly News 1978–79 (journalist 1976–79), Berks and Bucks Observer 1979–83; ed Windsor Observer 1983–84, ed in chief Berks and Bucks Observer Group 1984–90 (winner several awards for editorial excellence in newspapers), ed Belfast News Letter 1990– (UK Press Gazette Regional Free Journalist of the Year 1992, Newspaper Soc Journalist of the Year 1993); contrib BBC and Ind Radio and ed various sports instruction books; fndr Slough and Windsor Cancer Screening Charity 1985; *Recreations* keen golfer, sports (especially soccer (Chelsea FC fan)), rock and classical music, good books, fine wines; *Style*— Geoffrey Martin, Esq; ✉ Belfast News Letter, 45–46 Boucher Crescent, Belfast, Northern Ireland BT12 6QY (☎ 01232 680000, fax 01232 664412)

MARTIN, Geoffrey Haward; CBE (1986); s of Ernest Leslie Martin (d 1967), of Colchester, and Mary Hilda, *née* Haward (d 1987); *b* 27 Sept 1928; *Educ* Colchester Royal GS, Merton Coll Oxford (MA, DPhil), Univ of Manchester; *m* 12 Sept 1953, Janet Douglas, da of Douglas Hamer, MC (d 1981), of Sheffield, and Enid Hope, *née* Porter (d 1986); 3 s (Christopher b 1957, Patrick b 1963, Matthew b 1963), 1 da (Sophia b 1961); *Career* prof of history Univ of Leicester (formerly Univ Coll of Leicester) 1973–82 (lectr 1952–66, reader 1966–73), keeper of Public Records 1982–88, visiting prof Carleton Univ Ottawa 1958–59 and 1967–68, visiting res fell Merton Coll Oxford 1971, sr visiting fell Loughborough Univ of Technol 1987–, distinguished visiting prof of history Univ of Toronto 1989, sr res fell Merton Coll Oxford 1990–93, res prof Univ of Essex 1990–, Leverhulme Emeritus Res fell 1989–91; chm: Br Records Assoc 1981–92, Cwlth Archivists Assoc 1984–88; hon visiting fell Sch of Library Archive and Info Studies UCL; memb Royal Cmmn on Historical Monuments (England) 1987–94, miembro Distinguido del Sistema Nacional de Archivos Mexico 1988, govr Museum of London 1989–95; vice pres: Br Records Assoc, Cumberland and Westmorland Archaeological Soc, Essex Archaeological Soc, Assoc of Genealogists and Record Agents; chm Humanities Arts and Design Res Degrees Sub-Ctee Cncl for Nat Acad Awards 1987–92; hon memb Int Cmmn for the History of Towns 1988–; winner Besterman medal (Library Assoc) 1972; Hon DUniv Essex 1989; FSA 1975, FRHistS 1958 (vice pres 1984–88), FGSM 1996; *Books* The Story of Colchester (1959), The Town: A Visual History (1961), The Royal Charters of Grantham (1963), Bibliography of British and Irish Municipal History (with Sylvia McIntyre, 1972), Ipswich Recognizance Rolls (1973), The Dublin Merchant Guild Roll (with Philomena Connolly, 1992), Portsmouth Royal Charters 1194–1974 (1995), Knighton's Chronicle 1337–96 (1995); *Recreations* fell-walking, gardening; *Clubs* Utd Oxford and Cambridge Univ, RCS; *Style*— Prof G H Martin, CBE, FSA; ✉ Flat 27, Woodside House, Wimbledon, London SW19 7QN (☎ 0181 946 2570)

MARTIN, Prof Geoffrey Thorndike; s of Albert Thorndike Martin (d 1947), and Lily, *née* Jackson (d 1964); *b* 28 May 1934; *Educ* Palmer's Sch Grays Thurrock, UCL (BA), CCC Cambridge, Christ's Coll Cambridge (MA, PhD, LittD); *Career* Lady Wallis Budge res fell in Egyptology Christ's Coll Cambridge 1966–70; UCL: lectr in Egyptology 1970–78, reader in Egyptian archaeology 1978–87, prof of Egyptology (Ad Hominem) 1987, Edwards prof of Egyptology 1988–93 (prof emeritus 1993); field dir jt Egypt Exploration Soc and Leiden Museum expdn in Egypt 1975–; memb Ctee Egypt Exploration Soc, corresponding memb German Archaeological Inst 1982; FSA 1975; *Books* Egyptian Administrative and Private-Name Seals (1971), The Royal Tomb at El-Amarna (vol 1 1974, vol 2 1989), The Tomb of Hetepka (1979), The Sacred Animal Necropolis at North Saqqara (1981), Canopic Equipment in the Petrie Collection (with V Raisman, 1984), Scarabs, Cylinders and other Ancient Egyptian Seals (1985), The Tomb Chapels of Paser and Raia (1985), Corpus of Reliefs of the New Kingdom (vol 1 1987), Excavations in the Royal Necropolis at El-Amarna (with A El-Khouly, 1987), The Memphite Tomb of Horemheb (1989), The Hidden tombs of Memphis (1991), Auf der Suche nach dem verlorenen Grab (German ed, 1994), A Bibliography of the Amarna Period (1991), The Tomb of Tia and Tia (1997); *Recreations* travel, English history, book collecting; *Style*— Prof Geoffrey Martin; ✉ c/o Department of Egyptology, Institute of Archaeology, University College London, Gower St, London WC1E 6BT (☎ 0171 387 7050)

MARTIN, District Judge Geoffrey William; OBE (1992); s of late Bertie Philip Martin, of Suffolk, and Marion, *née* Bonney (d 1968); *b* 9 Nov 1935; *Educ* Framlingham Coll, St John's Coll Cambridge (MA); *m* 1, 1959, Patricia, *née* Jones; 2 da (Jane Elizabeth b 7 Dec 1960, Jill Marion b 9 June 1962); m 2, Marie Turner; *Career* district offr and magistrate Tanganyika 1959–62, admitted slr 1966, private practice (litigation) 1966–77, registrar co ct and district 1977–86, puisne judge Tonga 1986–88, chief justice Tonga 1988–91, pt/t judge Vanuatu Ct of Appeal 1988–95, pt/t judge Western Samoa Ct of Appeal 1990, district judge 1992–, pt/t chief justice St Helena 1992–, pt/t judge of appeal Tonga 1994–, pt/t judge Falkland Islands 1996–; memb: Law Soc, Cwlth Magistrates and Judges' Assoc; *Recreations* sailing, tennis, golf, books, music, travel; *Style*— District Judge Geoffrey Martin, OBE; ✉ Leicester County Court, 90 Wellington Street, Leicester LE1 6ZZ

MARTIN, Sir George Henry; kt (1996), CBE (1988); s of Henry Martin (d 1967), and Bertha Beatrice, *née* Simpson (d 1948); *b* 3 Jan 1926; *Educ* St Ignatius Coll, Bromley County Sch, Guildhall Sch of Music; *m* 1, 3 Jan 1948 (m dis 1966), Sheena Rose, *née* Chisholm; 1 s (Gregory Paul b 1957), 1 da (Alexis Jane b 1953); m 2, 24 June 1966, Judy (Lady Martin, *qv*), da of late Kenneth Lockhart Smith; 1 s (Giles Henry Blake b 1969), 1 da (Lucie Annabel b 1967); *Career* Fleet Air Arm 1944–46; BBC (6 months) 1950, EMI 1950–65, record prodr and head of Parlophone Records, fndr and chm Air Studios (merged with Chrysalis 1974) 1965–, fndr Air Studios Montserrat W Indies 1979, main bd dir Chrysalis plc 1985–, chm Heart 106.2FM (subsid of Chrysalis) 1995–; original sponsor Brit Sch for Performing Arts, professional patron Salford Coll for Performing Arts; Hon DMus Berklee Coll of Music Boston Mass 1989, Hon MA Salford Univ Coll 1992; *Books* All You Need Is Ears (1979), Making Music (1983), Summer of Love - The Making of Sgt Pepper (1993); *Recreations* music, design, boats, snooker; *Clubs* Oriental; *Style*— Sir George Martin, CBE; ✉ Air Studios, Lyndhurst Hall, Lyndhurst Road, Hampstead, London NW3 5NG (☎ 0171 794 0660, fax 0171 794 0623)

MARTIN, Glenn Philip; s of Walter Philip, and Eileen Denton, *née* Savage; *b* 11 Feb 1949; *Educ* Kings Coll Sch Wimbledon, Wadham Coll Oxford (BA); *m* 4 July 1970, Beryl, da of Albert Darby, of Sale; 3 s (Christopher, Alastair, Nicholas), 1 da (Sarah); *Career* dir operations Swiss Bank Corpn 1995– (dir banking ops 1990); *Recreations* squash, tennis; *Clubs* City Swiss; *Style*— Glenn Martin, Esq; ✉ Hatchetts, Westerham Road, Limpsfield, Surrey RH8 0SW (☎ 01883 723685); Swiss Bank House, 1 High Timber St, London EC4V 3SB (☎ 0171 711 2694, fax 0171 329 8700)

MARTIN, Ian Alexander; *b* 1935; *Educ* Univ of St Andrews (MA), ICA Scotland (CA); *Career* Grand Metropolitan plc: chm and chief exec Watney Mann & Truman Brewers 1982 (joined 1979), GrandMet main bd dir 1985–94, gp md and chief operating offr 1991–93, dep chm 1993–94; chm and chief exec Glenisla Group Ltd 1994–; non-exec dir: Unigate plc (chm) 1995–, Granada Group plc, House of Fraser plc, Cities in Schools; int cnsllr Centre for Strategic and Int Studies, int tstee Duke of Edinburgh's Award Assoc; Liveryman Worshipful Co of Brewers; Freeman City of London; MICAS; *Clubs* Buck's, Carlton; *Style*— Ian Martin, Esq; ✉ Glenisla Group Ltd, 3 St James's Square, London SW1Y 4JU (☎ 0171 839 2820, fax 0171 839 2877)

MARTIN, Ian James; s of Alfred James Martin, and Eileen Joan Martin; *b* 14 June 1952; *Educ* Univ of Essex (BA); *m* Theresa Mary; 1 s (Maximillian Joseph b May 1988), 1 da (Kerensa May b Aug 1981); *Career* Arthur Andersen & Co (London and S America) 1973–85, fin dir County NatWest then NatWest Investment Bank 1985–87, chief operating offr Baring Securities Ltd 1987–93, gp md Union PLC (formerly Union Discount plc) 1993–; non-exec dir Pointon York Group plc 1993–; numerous published articles and speaking engagements; SFA 1988–93: dir, chm Securities Capital Ctee, memb Exec Ctee, head Int Policy; MSI, FCA (memb Business Law and Banking Ctees), FRSA; *Books* Accounting In The Foreign Exchange Market (1987, 2 edn 1993); *Style*— Ian Martin, Esq; ✉ Union PLC, 39 Cornhill, London EC3V 3NU (☎ 0171 623 1020, fax 0171 626 9069)

MARTIN, Ian Robert; s of William Otway Martin (d 1985), of Wallington, and Marion Weir, *née* Gillespie (d 1976); *b* 29 Dec 1935; *Educ* Wallington Co Sch, Ch Ch Oxford (BA, MA); *m* 1 Aug 1964, Susan, da of Neville Joseph Mountfort (d 1992), of Olton, Solihull; 3 s (Andrew, Roger, Alan), 1 da (Sally); *Career* Nat Serv RN 1954–56; current affrs and feature progs incl Face to Face BBC TV 1959–68; Thames TV: exec prodr documentaries 1968–70, ed This Week 1971, exec prodr features 1972–75, controller features educn and religion 1976–85, head of documentaries 1986–87, head of music and theatre 1988–92; chief exec HD Thames and The High Definition Company 1992–; exec prodr many major documentaries and specials incl: St Nicolas 1977, The Gospel According to St Mark 1979, Swan Lake 1980, first Br fund-raising Telethon 1980, Rigoletto 1982, The Mikado 1987, Jessye Norman's Christmas Symphony 1987, Martin Luther King - The Legacy 1988, In From the Cold? Richard Burton 1988, Twelfth Night 1988, Xerxes 1989, The Midsummer Marriage 1989, The Tailor of Gloucester 1989, Una Stravaganza dei Medici 1990, La Bayadere 1991, Mozart at Buckingham Palace 1991, The Return of Columbus (in HDTV) 1992, D W Griffith: Father of Film 1993, The Lillehammer Winter Olympics (in HD) 1994, World Figure Skating Championships (in HD) 1995, Les Miserables (HD) 1995; chm Cncl Vision 1250, pres HIPA 1250; govr Isleworth & Syon Sch, memb Kensington Area Synod; BAFTA (former chm TV and Awards Ctees); *Books* From Workhouse to Welfare (1969); *Recreations* collecting puzzles and quotations; *Style*— Ian Martin, Esq; ✉ 83 Wood Lane, Isleworth, Middx TW7 5EG (☎ 0181 560 4584); HD Thames, Pinewood Studios, Pinewood Road, Iver, Bucks SL0 0NH (☎ 01753 657100, fax 01753 656698)

MARTIN, James Brown; s of James Brown Martin, of Larbert, Scotland, and Anne, *née* Cuthill; *b* 6 Dec 1953; *Educ* Larbert HS, Heriot-Watt Univ (BA), Moray House Coll of Educn; *m* 20 Sept 1975, (Grace) Anne, da of Charles McNaughton, of Perth; 1 s (Alan James b 23 April 1987), 1 da (Amy Thomson b 1 Sept 1984); *Career* teacher in modern studies and econs Falkirk HS; The Educational Institute of Scotland: field offr 1979–84, asst gen sec 1984–88, gen sec 1988–95; memb: Exec Bd Forth Valley Enterprise, Exec Ctee Scot Cncl for Devpt and Indust, Gen Cncl Scot TUC (chm Educn and Trg Ctee), Exec Bd Euro Trade Union Ctee for Educn, Exec Bd Educn Int; vice pres Educn Int (Europe); *Recreations* golf, Hibernian FC; *Style*— James Martin, Esq

MARTIN, Jeremy Tobin Wyatt; s of Albert Wyatt (Toby) Martin (d 1986), and Joan Elizabeth, *née* Hallett (d 1982); *b* 27 March 1943; *Educ* Sherborne, Downing Coll Cambridge (MA); *m* 17 May 1969, Penelope Ann, da of Ronald Owen Jenkins, of Guildford; 2 da (Amanda Juliet b 1972, Sally Wyatt b 1974); *Career* admitted slr 1967, sr ptnr Trowers & Hamlins; dir: Daniel Thwaites plc, Longstop Showlag Management Ltd, Strikegold Ltd, Thwaites Inns Ltd; chm Manuplastics Ltd; memb: Macular Disease Soc, Law Soc; *Recreations* gardening, walking, fishing, horse racing; *Style*— Jeremy Martin, Esq; ✉ Beechfield, 54 Warren Rd, Guildford GU1 2HH (☎ 01483 562934); Trowers & Hamlins, 6 New Square, Lincoln's Inn, London WC2A 3RP (☎ 0171 831 6292, fax 0171 831 8700, telex 21422)

MARTIN, Jessica Cecelia Anna Maria Thérèse; da of Placido Martin, of London, and Mary Bernadette, *née* Maguire; *b* 25 Aug 1962; *Educ* St Michael's Convent GS London, Westfield Coll Univ of London (exhibitioner, BA); *Career* actress; awarded scholarship UCLA; *Pantomime* Cinderella (De Montfort Hall Leicester 1985, The Palace Manchester 1987), Aladdin (The Grand Wolverhampton) 1986, The Wizard of Oz (Theatre Royal Plymouth) 1988; *Theatre* nat tour with Rory Bremner 1987, Babes in Arms (Regents Park) 1988, Me and My Girl (Adelphi Strand (nat tour 1993)) 1989–91, The Case of the Dead Flamingo Dancer (Thorndike Theatre Leatherhead) 1991, Curtain Up (Edinburgh Festival) 1992, Shakers (Nottingham Playhouse) 1994, The Card (Regents Park) 1994, Lonely Hearts (Oxford Fire Station) 1995, Something for the Boys and Leave it to Me (Barbican lost musicals season) 1995, Swingtime Canteen (King's Head) 1995, Mack and Mabel (Piccadilly) 1996, Blame It On My Youth (Jermyn Street) 1996, I Can Get It For You Wholesale (Barbican lost musicals season); *Television* Spitting Image 1985, Copycats 1985, And There's More 1985, Bobby Davro on the Box 1985, Bobby Davro's TV Weekly 1986, Summertime Special 1986, Tarby and Friends 1986, Royal Variety Show 1987, Bobby Davro's Christmas Annual 1987, Dr Who 1988, A Night of a Hundred Stars 1990, Tonight at 8.30 (BBC) 1991, Gibberish (BBC) 1992; *Radio* The Big Broadcast of 1991 (BBC Radio 2) 1991, Where Are You (Radio 5) 1992, Full Steam A-Hudd (Radio 2) 1995, Ned Sherrin's Review of Revues (Radio 2) 1996; *Style*— Miss Jessica Martin; ✉ c/o Sara Randall, Saraband Associates, 265 Liverpool Road, London N1 1LX (☎ 0171 609 5313, fax 0171 609 2370)

MARTIN, (Leonard) John; VRD (1969); s of Leonard A Martin (d 1983), and Anne Elizabeth, *née* Scudamore (d 1975); *b* 20 April 1929; *Educ* Ardingly Coll; *m* 3 March 1956, Elisabeth Veronica, da of David Samuel Jones, MBE (d 1968); 1 s (Christopher John b 15 July 1958), 1 da (Rosemary Elisabeth Scudamore b 12 May 1960); *Career* Nat Serv Navy 1949–50, Sub Lt RNVR, ret Lt Cdr RNR 1975; R Watson & Sons: joined 1952, qualified actuary 1954, ptnr 1957, sr ptnr 1983–93; pres Inst of Actuaries 1992–94; chm: Assoc of Conslt Actuaries 1985–87, Occupational Pensions Jt Working Gp 1986–87, Consultative Gp of Actuaries in EEC 1988–91; dep chm Occupational Pensions Bd 1988–92, non-exec dir NPI (formerly National Provident Institution) 1993–; Liveryman: Guild of Air Pilots and Air Navigators, Worshipful Co of Actuaries; FIA 1954, FPMI 1958, FSS 1958; *Recreations* singing, sailing and flying; *Clubs* Naval; *Style*— John Martin, Esq, VRD; ✉ R Watson & Sons, Watson House, London Rd, Reigate, Surrey (☎ 01737 241144, fax 01737 241496, telex 946070)

MARTIN, His Hon Judge; John Alfred Holmes; QC (1989); s of Very Rev Dr Alfred Martin (d 1986), of Belfast, and Doris Muriel, *née* McRitchie; *b* 31 May 1946; *Educ* Royal Belfast Academical Instn, Queen's Univ Belfast (LLB, Dip Law, capt Univ Boat Club 1966–67); *m* 20 Aug 1983, Barbara Elizabeth Margaret, da of Rev Thomas Kyle (d 1995); 1 adopted s (Peter b 1991); *Career* called to the NI Bar 1970, called to the Bar Gray's Inn 1974 (Bar of Republic of Ireland 1975), in practice 1970–88, called to the Inner Bar of NI (QC) 1989, County Ct judge 1990– (dep County Ct judge 1983–88), Crown Ct judge 1990–, the Recorder of Londonderry 1993–94, additional judge for County Ct Civ of Belfast 1994–, hon sec Cncl of HM Co Ct Judges in Northern Ireland 1995–; pt/t lectr in matrimonial practice and procedure NI Inn of Ct 1977–80, chm of Industrial Tbnls 1988–89 (pt/t chm 1981–88), memb NI Bar Cncl 1983, asst dist electoral area cmmr 1984, vice pres Industrial Tbnls and Fair Employment Tbnl 1990; vice pres Irish Amateur Rowing Union (also chm Ulster Branch) 1978–79, int rowing umpire 1977–86, jury memb and umpire rowing events of Olympic Games 1980 and Cwlth Games 1986; *Recreations* rowing, hill walking, gardening, reading; *Clubs* Ulster Reform, Leander; *Style*— His Hon

Judge Martin, QC; ✉ County Court Office, Old Townhall Building, 80 Victoria Street, Belfast BT1 3FA

MARTIN, John Cecil; s of Cecil Walter Martin (d 1939), of School House, Lydd, Kent, and Mabel Emma, *née* Harvey (d 1957); *b* 14 Jan 1927; *Educ* Simon Langton GS Canterbury Kent, De Havilland Aeronautical Tech Sch Hatfield Herts; *m* 1, 15 Aug 1953 (m dis 1979), Marjorie Stella, da of Frank Simpson (d 1989); 1 s (Roderick b 7 Feb 1958), 1 da (Helen b 14 Aug 1954); m 2, 30 May 1980, Barbara Jean, *née* Watkins; *Career* chief design engr (equipment and furnishings) Hawker Siddeley Aviation Hatfield 1967–80; BAe 146: dep project designer 1980–82, project designer 1982–87, chief designer 1987–88, chief design engr 1988–89; chief designer Special Projects Airlines Div BAe 1989, aviation conslt BP International Ltd 1989–92, ind aviation conslt 1989–93, ret 1994; CEng, FRAeS 1970; *Recreations* watching cricket, music, woodwork, gardening; *Clubs* Kent CCC; *Style*— John C Martin, Esq; ✉ White Timbers, 89a Sandpit Lane, St Albans, Herts AL1 4BJ

MARTIN, Vice Adm Sir John Edward Ludgate; KCB (1972, CB 1968), DSC (1943); s of Surgn Rear Adm W L Martin, OBE; *b* 10 May 1918; *Educ* RNC Dartmouth; *m* 1942, Rosemary Deck; 2 s, 2 da; *Career* RN: served in WWII, Capt 1957, Cdr Br Forces Caribbean Area 1962–63, Rear Adm 1966, Flag Offr ME 1966–67 (despatches), Cdr Br Forces Gulf 1967–68, dir gen Personnel Servs and Trg (Navy) 1968–70, Vice Adm 1970, Dep Supreme Allied Cdr Atlantic 1970–73, ret; Lt Govr and C-in-C of Guernsey 1974–80; FNI (pres 1975–78); *Style*— Vice Adm Sir John Martin, KCB, DSC; ✉ c/o Army and Navy Club, 36 Pall Mall, London SW1Y 5JG

MARTIN, John Hadlow; JP (Macclesfield 1979); s of Norman Hadlow Martin (d 1988), of Sidmouth, Devon, and Irene Priscilla, *née* Thomas (d 1994); *b* 11 Aug 1931; *Educ* Minchenden Sch N London, Univ of Liverpool, FDSRCS, DOrthRCS; *m* 13 July 1957, (Winifred Elizabeth) Myfanwy, da of Osborn Vernon Whitley Jones (d 1986), of Deganwy, N Wales; 3 s (Timothy b 1960, Nicholas b 1962, Julian b 1964); *Career* Capt RADC 1959–62, dental specialist BMH Singapore; lectr Univ of St Andrews 1962–70, conslt dental surgn Edinburgh 1970–72, conslt orthodontist Leighton Hosp Cheshire 1972–96, visiting conslt IOM 1980–, hon lectr Univ of Liverpool 1980–96; memb: BDA, BOS, EOS; *Recreations* sailing; *Clubs* RYA, MCA, NWCC; *Style*— John Martin, Esq, JP; ✉ Hafod, Marl Edge, Prestbury, Cheshire SK10 4BT (☎ 01625 828353)

MARTIN, John Joseph Charles; s of Benjamin Martin, and Lucille Martin; *b* 25 Nov 1940; *Educ* Latymer Upper; *m* 1979, Frances, *née* Oster; 1 s (James b 1982), 1 da (Lucy b 1980); *Career* Illustrated Newspapers 1960–63, Planned Public Relations 1963–68, Martin Dignum Assocs 1969, chm Welbeck Golin/Harris Communications Ltd 1988– (joined 1969, dir 1972, chief exec 1984); FIPR 1994 (MIPR 1968); *Recreations* painting, tennis; *Style*— John Martin, Esq; ✉ 53 Hampstead Way, Hampstead Garden Suburb, London NW11 (☎ 0181 455 8482); Welbeck Golin/Harris Communications Ltd, 43 King St, Covent Garden, London WC2E 8RJ (☎ 0171 836 6677, fax 0171 836 5820, telex 263291)

MARTIN, Prof John Powell; s of Bernard Davis Martin (d 1986), and Grace Edith Martin (d 1976); *b* 22 Dec 1925; *Educ* Leighton Park Sch Reading, Univ of Reading (BA), LSE (Dip Soc Admin), Univ of London (PhD); *m* 1, 11 July 1951 (m dis 1981), Sheila Isabel, da of Stuart Feather (d 1985); 3 s (Andrew b 1953, Lawrence b 1955, Stuart b 1957); m 2, 16 Sept 1983, Joan Margaret, *née* Higgins; *Career* lectr LSE 1952–59, asst dir of res Inst of Criminology Cambridge 1960–66, fell King's Coll Cambridge 1964–67; Univ of Southampton: prof of sociology and social admin 1967–87, prof of social policy 1987–89, res prof 1989–92, prof emeritus 1992–; visiting prof of social policy Univ of Manchester 1992–; academic advsr Police Trg Cncl 1990–; memb and vice chm Bd of Visitors HM Prison Albany 1967–78; memb: IOW Health Authy 1974–90, Jellicoe Ctee on Bds of Visitors 1974–75, Hants Probation Ctee 1975–92, Raison Ctee on Local Monitoring of Prison Estabs 1994–95; *Books* Social Aspects of Prescribing (1957), Offenders as Employees (1962), The Police: A Study in Manpower (with Gail Wilson, 1969), The Social Consequences of Conviction (with D Webster, 1971), Violence and the Family (ed, 1978), Hospitals in Trouble (1984), Licensed to Live (with J B Coker, 1985), Probation Motor Projects in England and Wales (with D Webster, 1994); *Recreations* sailing, woodwork; *Clubs* Lymington Town Sailing; *Style*— Prof John Martin; ✉ 3 Gordon Place, Withington, Manchester M20 3LD (☎ and fax 0161 434 4602); Department of Social Policy and Social Work, University of Manchester, Manchester M13 9PL

MARTIN, John Sinclair; CBE (1977); s of Joseph Heber Martin, JP (d 1974), of Ely, Cambs, and Mary Sinclair, *née* McDade; *b* 18 Sept 1931; *Educ* Leys Sch Cambridge, St John's Coll Cambridge (BA, DipAg, MA); *m* 2 July 1960, Katharine Elisabeth, da of Rev George Barclay (d 1953), of Glasgow; 3 s (William b 1961, David b 1963, Robert b 1965), 1 da (Clare b 1967); *Career* farmer; chm Ely Local Branch NFU 1963, memb Gt Ouse River Authy 1970–74; chm: Anglian Water Gt Ouse Drainage Ctee 1984–89, NRA Anglian Regnl Flood Def Ctee 1989–; vice pres Assoc of Drainage Authys 1986–, memb Bd Anglian Water 1988–89, chm Regnl Panel MAFF 1981–86, memb ARC 1968–78; High Sheriff of Cambs 1985; *Recreations* fell walking; *Clubs* Farmers'; *Style*— John Martin, Esq, CBE; ✉ Denny Abbey, Waterbeach, Cambridge CB5 9PQ (☎ 01223 860282)

MARTIN, John Vandeleur; QC (1991); s of Col Graham Vandeleur Martin, MC, of Salisbury, Wilts, and Margaret Helen, *née* Sherwood; *b* 17 Jan 1948; *Educ* Malvern, Pembroke Coll Cambridge (MA); *m* 7 Dec 1974, Stephanie Johnstone, da of Maj Michael Johnstone Smith, MC, of Bedford; 2 s (Timothy b 1979, Nicholas b 1985), 1 da (Josephine b 1983); *Career* called to the Bar Lincoln's Inn 1972; in practice Chancery Bar: Northern Circuit 1973–81, London 1981–; dep high court judge 1993–; Freeman City of London 1969, Liveryman Worshipful Co of Drapers 1973; *Recreations* opera, walking; *Style*— John Martin, Esq, QC; ✉ Wilberforce Chambers, 8 New Square, Lincoln's Inn, London WC2A 3QP (☎ 0171 306 0102, fax 0171 306 0095)

MARTIN, Jonathan Arthur; OBE (1995); s of Arthur Martin (d 1977), of Gravesend, Kent, and Mabel Gladys, *née* Bishop (d 1969); *b* 18 June 1942; *Educ* Gravesend GS, St Edmund Hall Oxford (MA); *m* 4 June 1967, Joy Elizabeth, da of Cecil William Fulker, OBE (d 1970), of Rickmansworth, Herts; 2 s (Stewart John Edmund b 1969, Andrew Robert Jonathan b 1972); *Career* BBC 1964–: gen trainee 1964–65, prodn asst Sportsview and Grandstand 1965–69, prodr Sportsnight 1969–74, ed Sportsnight and Match of the Day 1974–79, exec prodr Wimbledon Tennis Coverage 1979–81, exec prodr Grand Prix 1977–80, exec prodr Ski Sunday 1978–80, managing ed Sport 1980–81, head of TV Sport 1981–87, head of TV Sport and Events Group 1987–; vice chm Sports Experts Euro Broadcasting Union (EBU) 1984–; *Recreations* watching sport, watching television, golf, skiing; *Clubs* Harewood Downs Golf; *Style*—Jonathan Martin, Esq, OBE; ✉ Arkle, Valentine Way, Chalfont St Giles, Bucks HP8 4JB; BBC Television, Television Centre, Wood Lane, London W12 7RJ (☎ 0181 225 6174)

MARTIN, Lady; Judy Gordon; da of Kenneth Robert Lockhart Smith (d 1978), of Green Tye, Much Hadham, Herts, and Iris Opal Gordon, *née* Blake (d 1979); *b* 13 Nov 1928; *Educ* Bedford Sch, St James Secretarial Coll; *m* 24 June 1966, Sir George Henry Martin, CBE, *qv*, s of Henry Martin (d 1967); 1 s (Giles b 9 Oct 1969), 1 da (Lucie b 9 Aug 1967); *Career* EMI Abbey Rd Studios 1948, sec to Oscar Preuss 1948–55, PA to George Martin, head Parlophone Records 1955–65, fndr memb Air Records 1965 (merged with Chrysalis 1974), ret to raise family 1967, co-fndr Air Studios Montserrat 1969; *Recreations* gardening, reading, travel; *Clubs* Oriental; *Style*— Lady Martin

MARTIN, Jurek; OBE (1997); *b* 22 Feb 1942; *Educ* Royal GS Worcester, Hertford Coll Oxford (BA); *m* 1 da; *Career* journalist; Financial Times: NY bureau chief 1970–72, foreign news ed 1973–75, US ed Washington DC 1975–81, Far East ed Tokyo 1982–86, foreign ed FT London 1986–92, US ed 1992–; visiting fell Univ of South Carolina 1981–82, ed Europe magazine Washington DC 1981–82; broadcaster: BBC World Service, Voice of America, numerous radio and TV stations in US; *Recreations* eating, drinking, tennis, golf, Sumo wrestling and the modern Japanese diet, baseball; *Style*— Jurek Martin, Esq, OBE; ✉ US Editor, The Financial Times, 1225 Eye Street, Suite 810, Washington DC 20005

MARTIN, Kevin Joseph; s of James Arthur Martin (d 1961), of Coventry, and Ivy Lilian, *née* Reeson (d 1986); *b* 15 June 1947; *Educ* Cotton Coll North Staffs; *m* 7 Oct 1971, Maureen Dympna, da of Kevin James McCormack; 2 s (James Roland b 21 Oct 1975, Richard Thomas b 3 Oct 1977); *Career* admitted slr 1970, ptnr Mackintosh & Co Birmingham 1972–79 (joined 1970), fndr and sr ptnr K J Martin & Co 1979–; Law Society: memb Young Slrs' Gp 1978–82, memb Cncl 1996–, chm Campaign for New Leadership 1996–; co-proprietor (with wife) Davenport Lodge Sch Coventry 1986–; Freeman City of Coventry 1970; memb Law Soc 1970; *Recreations* golf, skiing, watching cricket, rugby, classical music, literature; *Clubs* Ladbrook Park Golf, Coventry and North Warwickshire Cricket, Warwickshire CCC, Drapers' (Coventry); *Style*— Kevin Martin, Esq; ✉ K J Martin & Co, 217 Station Road, Balsall Common, Coventry, West Midlands CV7 7FE (☎ 01676 535050, fax 01676 535129, e-mail alert@kjmartin.u-net.com)

MARTIN, Kit; s of Prof Sir John Leslie Martin, of Gt Shelford, nr Cambridge, and Sadie, *née* Speight; *b* 6 May 1947; *Educ* Eton, Jesus Coll Cambridge (MA, DipArch); *m* 1, 24 Oct 1970 (m dis 1978), Julia Margaret, da of Dr Peter Dennis Mitchell, of Bodmin, Cornwall; m 2, 15 Sept 1980, Sally Martha, da of Sqdn Ldr Edwin Hector Gordon Brookes, AFC (d 1947), of Laxton, Northants; 1 da (Amy Victoria b 17 Sept 1992); *Career* ptnr Martin & Weighton 1969–76, chm Kit Martin Historic Houses Rescue Ltd (formerly Lucca Wines Ltd) 1974–; responsible for rescue, restoration and conversion of various important listed bldgs incl: Dingley Hall, The Hazells, Gunton Park, Cullen House, Keith Hall, Callaly Castle, Tyninghame House, Burley; memb Historic Bldgs Cncl for Scotland 1987–; dir Historic Buildings Rescue Ltd 1993–; tstee Save Europe's Heritage 1994–; *Publications* incl: The Country House - To Be or Not To Be, Jamaica's Heritage: An Untapped Resource; *Recreations* skiing, squash, private flying, landscape gardening; *Style*— Kit Martin, Esq; ✉ Park Farm, Gunton Park, Hanworth, Norfolk NR11 7HL (☎ 01263 761202)

MARTIN, Prof Sir Laurence Woodward; kt (1994), DL (Tyne and Wear 1987); s of Leonard Martin (d 1983), and Florence Mary, *née* Woodward (d 1987); *b* 30 July 1928; *Educ* St Austell GS, Christ's Coll Cambridge (MA), Yale (MA, PhD); *m* 18 Aug 1951, Betty, da of William Parnall (d 1958); 1 s (William Martin b 1962), 1 da (Jane Martin b 1959); *Career* Flying Offr RAF 1948–50; instr political sci Yale Univ 1955–56, asst prof of political sci MIT 1956–61, assoc prof of Euro diplomacy Sch of Advanced Int Studies Johns Hopkins Univ 1961–64, Woodrow Wilson prof of int politics Univ of Wales 1964–68 (dean Faculty of Social Sci 1966–68), prof of war studies King's Coll London 1968–77, vice chllr Univ of Newcastle upon Tyne 1978–90; chief exec Royal Inst of Int Affrs 1991–97; *Books* The Anglo-American Tradition in Foreign Affairs (with Arnold Wolfers, 1956), Peace without Victory: Woodrow Wilson and British Liberalism (1958), Neutralism and Non-Alignment (1963), The Sea in Modern Strategy (1966), America and The World (jtly 1970), Arms and Strategy (1973), Retreat from Empire (jtly 1973), Strategic Thought in the Nuclear Age (ed 1979), The Two-Edged Sword: Armed Force in the Modern World (1982), Before The Day After (1985), The Changing Face of Nuclear Warfare (1987); *Style*— Prof Sir Laurence Martin, DL; ✉ Royal Institute of International Affairs, Chatham House, St James's Square, London SW1Y 4LE (☎ 0171 957 5700, fax 0171 957 5710)

MARTIN, Prof Sir (John) Leslie; kt (1957); s of late Robert Martin, FRIBA, of Manchester; *b* 17 Aug 1908; *Educ* Univ of Manchester (MA, PhD); *m* 1935, Sadie (d 1992), da of Dr Alfred Speight; 1 s (Kit), 1 da (Susan); *Career* practising architect; architect to LCC 1953–56 (dep architect 1948–53), prof of architecture Univ of Cambridge 1956 (emeritus prof 1973–); Slade prof of fine arts Oxford 1965–66, visiting prof Yale 1973–74, Lethaby prof RCA 1981, emeritus fell Jesus Coll Cambridge 1976 (fell 1956, hon fell 1973); bldgs designed for: Univs of Cambridge, Oxford, Leicester and Hull, RSAMD Glasgow, Gallery of Modern Art Gulbenkian Fndn Lisbon; scheme design Royal Concert Hall Glasgow; Royal Gold medal RIBA 1973, tstee's medal RIBA Architecture Awards Tst 1991, Centenary Award Architects Journal 1995; Hon LLD Univs of: Leicester, Hull, Manchester; Hon LittD Cambridge, Hon DUniv Essex; Hon FRSAMD Glasgow; Cdr Order of Santiago da Espada Portugal; RA 1986; FRIBA; *Style*— Prof Sir Leslie Martin, RA; ✉ The Barns, Church St, Great Shelford, Cambridge CB2 5EL (☎ 01223 842399)

MARTIN, Lionel; s of Max Rosenthal, and Renée, *née* Marks; *b* 9 Aug 1950; *Educ* Quintin Sch; *m* 20 July 1975, Carole, da of Michael Packer; 3 da (Carly b 1978, Joanna b 1981, Lily b 1987); *Career* CA; ptnr Martin Greene Ravden; ACA 1973, FCA 1983, FCCA 1983; *Recreations* tennis, music (incl professional writing); *Clubs* The David Lloyd Slazenger Racquet; *Style*— Lionel Martin, Esq; ✉ 55 Loudoun Road, St John's Wood, London NW8 0DL (☎ 0171 625 4545, fax 0171 625 5265, car ☎ 0836 209 962, telex 21338 MARTIN G)

MARTIN, Michael Charles; s of Charles Stanley Martin (d 1979), and Muriel, *née* Mudd (d 1965); *b* 7 April 1933; *Educ* Malvern, Univ of Loughborough (BSc); *m* 1, 2 May 1964 (m dis 1988), Katharine Valentine, da of Thomas Arthur Saul, of Skegness, Lincs; 1 s (Charles Thomas b 3 May 1967), 1 da (Arabella Katharine b 15 March 1966); m 2, 26 Sept 1988, Helen Gillard, *née* Coleman (d 1988); *Career* 2 Lt REME 1956–58, served Germany; chm CS Martin Group of Cos, dep chm Louis Newmark plc, former chm Leicester Branch IOD and Inst of Prodn Engrs, memb Leicester C of C; govr Sports Aid Fndn E Midlands, pres Leics Lawn Tennis Assoc 1985–88, hon sec and treas Soc of Lawn Tennis Referees 1973–93; Liveryman Worshipful Co of Makers of Playing Cards 1967; Worshipful Co of Framework Knitters: Liveryman 1962, memb Ct of Assts 1977, Master 1988–89; FInstD 1961, CEng 1968, MIEE 1968, CIMgt 1987; *Recreations* tennis, rugby referee, holiday golf, sailing; *Clubs* RAC; *Style*— Michael Martin, Esq; ✉ The Paddocks, Hungarton, Leics LE7 9JY (☎ and fax 0116 259 5230)

MARTIN, Dr Michael Frederick Roy; s of Frederick Roy Martin, of Bournemouth, and Elsie Winifred Martin; *b* 29 March 1949; *Educ* Clifton, Jesus Coll Cambridge (MA, MB BChir), St Bartholomew's Hosp Med Sch; *m* 18 Aug 1973, Ann Teresa, da of Joseph O'Neill (d 1974); 1 s (Andrew Michael b 24 Oct 1987), 3 da (Gemma b 7 Aug 1975, Leana b 11 Nov 1977, Rebecca b 16 May 1981); *Career* house offr St Bartholomew's Hosp 1973, md registrar Royal Cornwall Hosp 1977, sr registrar in rheumatology Leeds 1980, conslt rheumatologist St James's Univ Hosp Leeds 1984, author of papers on prostaglandin E in various peripheral vascular diseases 1979–85; memb: Nat Tst, Royal Northern Horticultural Soc, Br Soc for Rheumatology 1980; FRCP 1991 (MRCP 1978); *Recreations* sailing, squash, marathon running, gardening; *Clubs* Ripon Sailing, Ashville Coll Sports Centre; *Style*— Dr Michael Martin; ✉ 26 Duchy Rd, Harrogate, N Yorkshire HG1 2ER (☎ 01423 509307); St James's University Hospital, Beckett St, Leeds LS9 7TF (☎ 0113 243 3144)

MARTIN, Michael John; MP (Lab) Glasgow Springburn (majority 14,506); s of Michael Martin, and Mary Martin; *b* 3 July 1945; *Educ* St Patrick's Boys' Sch Glasgow; *m* 1966,

Mary McLay; 1 s, 1 da; *Career* Rolls Royce (Hillington) AUEW shop steward 1970–74, trade union organiser 1976–79; MP (Lab) Glasgow Springburn 1979–, PPS to Rt Hon Denis Healey MP 1980–83, chm Scottish Grand Ctee 1987–, memb Speaker's Panel of Chairmen 1987–, memb Select Ctee on House of Commons Servs; memb Coll of Pipers; *Recreations* playing and listening to the Scottish pipes; *Style*— Michael J Martin, Esq, MP; ✉ 144 Broomfield Rd, Balornock, Glasgow G21 3UE

MARTIN, Millicent; da of William Martin (d 1970), of Florida, and Violet, *née* Bedford (d 1946); *b* 8 June 1934; *Educ* Heath Park HS, Italia Conti Stage Sch; *m* 26 Sept 1977, Marc Alexander; *Career* actress and singer; *Theatre* recent work incl: Follies, 42nd Street, Shirley Valentine, Two Into One, Noises Off, Sondheim's Side by Side, The Cemetary Club, The Rise and Fall of Little Voice, Love Julie; *Television* incl: Moon & Son (series), LA Law, Downtown, That Was The Week That Was, Newhart, Hardball, Murphy Brown, Coach, Upper Hand; *Recreations* cooking, animals, aerobics; *Style*— Miss Millicent Martin; ✉ c/o London Management, 2–4 Noel Street, London W1V 3RB (☎ 0171 287 9000, fax 0171 287 3036)

MARTIN, (Roy) Peter; MBE (1970); s of Walter Martin (d 1959), and Annie Mabel, *née* Cook (d 1966); *b* 5 Jan 1931; *Educ* Highbury Co Sch, Birkbeck Coll London (BA, MA), Univ of Tübingen; *m* 1, 31 March 1951 (m dis 1960), Marjorie Patricia Anne Peacock; m 2, March 1960 (m dis 1977), Joan Drumwright; 2 s (Adam b 1963, James b 1964); m 3, 11 April 1978, Catherine Mary Sydee; *Career* Nat Serv RAF educn branch 1949–51; Br Cncl: offr 1960–83, cultural attaché Br Embassy Budapest 1972–73, cultural cnsllr Br Embassy Tokyo 1979–83; freelance author and critic 1983–; memb: BAFTA, Crime Writers' Assoc, Mystery Writers of America, and other socs; *Books* Japanese Cooking (with Joan Martin, 1970); as James Melville: The Wages of Zen (1979), The Chrysanthemum Chain (1980), A Sort of Samurai (1981), The Ninth Netsuke (1982), Sayonara, Sweet Amaryllis (1983), Death of a Daimyo (1984), The Death Ceremony (1985), Go Gently Gaijin (1986), The Imperial Way (1986), Kimono For A Corpse (1987), The Reluctant Ronin (1988), A Haiku for Hanae (1989), A Tarnished Phoenix (1990), The Bogus Buddha (1990), The Body Wore Brocade (1992), Diplomatic Baggage (1994), The Reluctant Spy (1995); as Hampton Charles: Miss Seeton, By Appointment (1990), Advantage Miss Seeton (1990), Miss Seeton at the Helm (1990); *Recreations* music, books; *Clubs* Travellers', Detection; *Style*— Peter Martin, Esq, MBE; ✉ c/o Curtis Brown, 4th Floor, Haymarket House, 28–29 Haymarket, London SW1Y 4SP (☎ 0171 396 6600)

MARTIN, Peter; s of John Francis Martin, and Teresa, *née* Slattery; *b* 13 June 1948; *Educ* Newport HS for Boys, Wimbledon Coll, Worcester Coll Oxford (MA), Stanford Business Sch California (Stanford Executive Program); *m* 1977, Alexandra, *née* Ingram; 2 da (Clare b 15 April 1986, Julia b 21 Sept 1988); *Career* TV journalist 1970–76: variously News at Ten (ITN), Weekend World (LWT), Granada Reports (Granada TV); writer and asst ed The Economist 1976–83, managing ed/exec prodr Business Times NY 1983–84, editorial dir then md Economist Intelligence Unit 1985–87; Financial Times 1988–: features ed then fin ed until 1995, ed int edn 1995–; *Publications* Arabian Peninsula (survey for The Economist, 1978), Wall Street (survey for The Economist, 1981), After the Crash (research study for Economist Intelligence Unit, 1987), How to Survive and Prosper in a Recession (1991); *Style*— Peter Martin; ✉ International Edition, Financial Times, 1 Southwark Bridge, London SE1 9HL (☎ 0171 873 3000, fax 0171 873 3076, e-mail peter.martin@ft.com)

MARTIN, Maj-Gen Peter Lawrence de Carteret; CBE (1968, OBE 1964); s of late Col Charles de Carteret Martin; *b* 15 Feb 1920; *Educ* Wellington, RMC Sandhurst; *m* 1, 1949 (m dis), Elizabeth Felicia, da of the late Col C M Keble, OBE; 1 s, 1 da; m 2, 1973 (sep 1984), Valerie Elizabeth, *née* Brown; 2 step s; *Career* DPS (Army) 1971–74, Col the 22 (Cheshire) Regt 1971–78, Col Cmdt Mil Provost Staff Corps 1972–74; head of admin Smith & Williamson 1976–86; pres Lady Grover's Hospital Fund for Offrs' Families 1989– (chm 1975–85, vice-pres 1985–89); memb: Nat Exec Ctee Forces Help Soc 1975–96, Gen Ctee Ex-Servs Mental Welfare Soc 1977–92, Ctee Br Friends of Normandy 1992–; servs liaison offr Variety Club of GB 1976–86, dir Utd Women's Homes Assoc 1981–94, nat pres Normandy Veterans Assoc 1995– (nat vice pres 1989–95), chm The Spirit of Normandy Trust 1994–; FIMgt 1980; *Recreations* golf, skiing, walking, reading; *Clubs* Army & Navy; *Style*— Maj-Gen Peter Martin, CBE; ✉ 17 Station St, Lymington, Hants SO41 3BA (☎ and fax 01590 672620)

MARTIN, Richard Alfred; s of Alfred Martin (d 1986), and Margaret Emma, *née* Portch; *b* 30 June 1946; *Educ* Wandsworth GS; *m* 20 Sept 1969, Judith Ann, da of Leslie Frederick Green, of London; 1 s (Steven b 1979), 2 da (Joanne b 1972, Claire b 1975); *Career* trainee dealer William H Hart & Co 1965–66, business devpt exec Castrol Ltd 1966–71, market devpt mangr Courage Ltd 1971–73, chief exec Marketing Improvements Group plc 1973–; chm: Marketing Improvements Research Ltd, Marketing Improvements Learning Ltd 1973–; church warden St Dunstan with St Thomas Willesden Episcopal Area; memb Mktg Soc; *Recreations* the theatre, reading, tennis, chess; *Style*— Richard Martin, Esq; ✉ Marketing Improvements Group plc, 17 Ulster Terrace, Regents Park Outer Circle, London NW1 4PJ (☎ 0171 487 5811, fax 0171 935 4839, telex 299 723 MARIMPG)

MARTIN, Richard Lionel; TD (1965); s of Alfred John Martin (d 1948), and Ellen Mary, *née* Warren (d 1981); *b* 18 June 1932; *Educ* Churchers Coll Petersfield, Architectural Assoc Sch of Architecture London; *m* 13 Sept 1958, Gillian Mary, da of Lesley Vivian Taylor, of Weybridge, Surrey; 3 s (Nigel Peter b 1962, Richard John b 1964, David James b 1966); *Career* Nat Serv 1950–52; Royal Hampshire Regt: cmmnd 2 Lt 1951 served 1 Bn, TA (V), promoted Lt 1952, serv 4 TA Bn and 4/5 (TA) Bn, promoted Capt 4/5 (TA) 1954, Capt 4/5 (TA) Bn Cameronian Scot Rifles 1964–67, ret 1967; London CC Architects Dept 1957–63 (worked on Crystal Palace Sports Centre and Queen Elizabeth Concert Hall, Haywood Gallery), Scott Brownrigg & Turner Architects and Planning Conslts 1963–86; ptnr: SBT Advisory Services 1986–94, Martin & McKibbin Chartered Architects 1994–; Structural Steel Design award 1972; Freeman City of London 1978, Liveryman Worshipful Co of Arbitrators 1981; RIBA 1961, ARIAS 1964, FCIArb 1973, FFB 1976, MSCL 1985, MBAE 1988 (memb Cncl 1993), FBAE 1990; *Recreations* classical music; *Clubs* Wig and Pen; *Style*— Richard Martin, Esq, TD; ✉ Colesons, South Hay, Binsted, Hants (☎ 01420 473237); Martin & McKibbin, Chartered Architects, 20 York Buildings, London WC2N 6JU (☎ 0171 839 6996, fax 0171 839 6243)

MARTIN, Prof Robert Bernard; s of Morris Carl Martin (d 1947), of Davenport, Iowa, and Margaret, *née* Cratsenberg (d 1972); *b* 11 Sept 1918, La Harpe, Ill; *Educ* Univ of Iowa (AB), Harvard Univ (AM, Swaine scholarship), Univ of Oxford (BLitt, Fulbright scholar); *Career* Princeton Univ: instructor in English 1951–55, asst prof 1955–60, assoc prof 1960–66, prof 1966–75, prof emeritus of English 1975–; visiting prof Victorian Centre Univ of Leicester 1978, Citizens' prof of English Univ of Hawaii 1981–82 and 1984–88 (prof emeritus of English 1988–); fell: American Cncl of Learned Socs 1966–67, Guggenheim Fndn 1971 and 1983–84, Rockefeller Res Center Bellagio Italy 1979; Mellon fell Nat Humanities Center 1988–89, sr fell Nat Endowment for the Humanities 1976–77; hon vice pres Tennyson Soc 1988–; citation New Jersey Writers' Conf 1986, Christian Gauss Award for Literary Scholarship Phi Beta Kappa 1981, Heinemann Award RSL 1981; DLitt Oxford 1987, Hooker distinguished prof McMaster Univ 1992; FRSL 1981; *Books* A Companion to Victorian Literature (with T M Parrott, 1955), Charles Kingsley's American Notes (ed, 1958), The Dust of Combat - A Life of Charles Kingsley (1959), Enter Rumour - Four Early Victorian Scandals (1962), Victorian Poetry - Ten Major Poets (ed, 1964), The Accents of Persuasion - Charlotte Brontë's Novels (1966), The Triumph of Wit - A Study of Victorian Comic Theory (1974), Tennyson, The Unquiet Heart (1980, Duff Cooper Award for Biography 1981, James Tait Black Award for Biography 1981), With Friends Possessed - A Life of Edward FitzGerald (1985), Gerard Manley Hopkins - A Very Private Life (1991); author of four novels under pseudonym Robert Bernard and numerous reviews and articles in NY Review of Books, TLS, London Review of Books, The Spectator and other jls; *Recreations* music, gardens, architecture; *Style*— Prof R B Martin, FRSL; ✉ 8 Walton Street, Oxford OX1 2HG (☎ 01865 514515); c/o Curtis Brown, 4th Floor, Haymarket House, 28–29 Haymarket, London SW1Y 4SP (☎ 0171 396 6600)

MARTIN, Robert Logan (Roy); QC (Scot 1988); s of late Robert Martin, MC, of The Willows, Crosbie Wood, Paisley, and Janet Johnstone, *née* Logan; *b* 31 July 1950; *Educ* Paisley GS, Univ of Glasgow (LLB); *m* 9 Nov 1984, Fiona Frances, da of John Roxburgh Bingham Neil, of St Ives, NSW, Aust; 1 s (Robert John Neil b 12 Aug 1987), 2 da (Camilla Nancy Neil b 25 Sept 1988, Phoebe Logan Neil b 2 Sept 1991); *Career* slr 1973–76, admitted to Faculty of Advocates 1976, memb Sheriff Courts Rules Cncl 1981–84, standing jr counsel to Dept of Employment (Scotland) 1983–84, advocate-depute 1984–87, admitted to Bar of NSW 1987, called to the Bar Lincoln's Inn 1990; pt/t chm Industl Tbnls 1991–, chm Scottish Planning, Local Govt and Environmental Bar Gp 1991–96; hon sec Wagering Club 1982–91; affiliate RIAS 1995; *Recreations* shooting, skiing, modern architecture, vintage motoring; *Clubs* New (Edinburgh); *Style*— Roy Martin, Esq, QC; ✉ Hardengreen House, by Eskbank, Dalkeith, Midlothian (☎ 0131 660 5997); Advocates' Library, Parliament House, Edinburgh (☎ 0131 226 5071); 1 Serjeants' Inn, London EC4Y 1NH (☎ 0171 583 1355)

MARTIN, Stanley William Frederick; CVO (1992, LVO 1981), JP (Inner London 1993); s of Stanley Martin (d 1976), of Walmer, Kent, and Winifred Rose Kilburn (d 1976); *b* 9 Dec 1934; *Educ* Bromley GS, Univ Coll Oxford (MA); *m* 3 Sept 1960, Hanni Aud, da of Aage Valdemar Johannes Hansen (d 1957), of Copenhagen, Denmark, and Oda Maja Valborg Nielsen (d 1989); 1 s (Nicholas b 1962), 1 da (Birgit b 1964); *Career* mil serv 2 Lieut RASC 1953–55; entered CRO 1958, asst private sec to Sec of State 1959–62; first sec: Canberra 1962–64, Kuala Lumpur 1964–67; Planning Staff and Personnel Dept FCO 1967–70, seconded to CSD (CSSB) 1970–71, asst marshal Dip Corps 1972–81, first asst marshal Dip Corps 1981–92, assoc head Protocol Dept FCO 1986–92, ret Dip Serv 1992, protocol advsr FCO 1993–; Extra Gentleman Usher to The Queen 1993–; visiting prof Univ of Westminster 1987–; diplomatic conslt Hyde Park Hotel 1993–, advsr The Consular Corps of London 1993–; memb: Ctee London Diplomatic Assoc 1972–, Cncl The Oxford Soc 1993–, Cncl Toynbee Hall 1996–; tstee The Attlee Fndn 1993–, vice patron Apex Tst 1995–; Freeman City of London 1988; Companion Order of Distinguished Serv (Brunei) 1992; FRSA 1985; contrib to Jl of Orders and Medals Res Soc, Jl of Royal Over-Seas League; *Publications* Royal Service: History of Royal Victorian Order, Medal and Chain (jtly, 1996); *Recreations* collecting books, manuscripts and obituaries, historical research and writing, walking, siestas; *Clubs* Royal Over-Seas League (memb Central Cncl 1982–); *Style*— Stanley Martin, Esq, CVO, JP; ✉ 14 Great Spilmans, London SE22 8SZ (☎ 0181 693 8181)

MARTIN, Stella; da of James Shepherd (d 1979), and Kathleen Ivy, *née* Batten; *b* 10 Dec 1953; *Educ* The Hulme GS for Girls Oldham, Camborne GS for Girls Cornwall, Univ of Nottingham Medical Sch (BMedSci, BM, BS); *m* 16 May 1981, John Douglas Martin; *Career* crime writer (as Stella Shepherd); various posts as hospital dr (main specialty radiotherapy): Derby, Nottingham, Braintree, Manchester (DMRO); memb: Crime Writers' Assoc, BMA, Richard the Third Soc; *Books* Black Justice (1988), Murderous Remedy (1989), Thinner than Blood (1991), A Lethal Fixation (1993), Nurse Dawes is Dead (1994), Something in the Cellar (1995), Embers of Death (1996); *Recreations* choral singing, piano playing, badminton; *Style*— Dr Stella Martin; ✉ Jacintha Alexander Associates, 47 Emperor's Gate, London SW7 4HJ (☎ 0171 373 9258, fax 0171 373 4374)

MARTIN, Stephen Alexander; MBE (1994); s of James Alexander Martin, of Bangor, Co Down, NI, and Mamie, *née* Weir; *b* 13 April 1959; *Educ* Bangor GS, Univ of Ulster (BA); *m* 13 April 1987, Dorothy Esther Elizabeth, da of William Edwin Armstrong, of Belmont, Belfast; 1 s (Patrick Armstrong b 14 Nov 1991), 1 da (Hannah Rebecca b 18 Jan 1996); *Career* hockey player; Bronze medallist World Champions Trophy 1984 (vice capt), Bronze medallist Olympic Games LA 1984, Silver medallist World Champions Trophy 1985, Gold medallist Olympic Games Seoul 1988, 6th Olympic Games Barcelona 1992 (capt); 94 Caps GB 1983–92, 135 Caps Ireland 1980–91 (capt 1984–85, Euro Cup 1983, 1987 and 1991 and World Cup 1990, total 229 most capped player in GB and Ireland), World Champions Trophy 1984–92; played Ulster 1980–91; Sports Cncl administrator and sports broadcaster; memb: Br Assoc of Sports Med/Sci, Programme Ctee NI Inst of Coaching 1985–88, Br Olympians Club, Br Inst of Sports Coaches; *Recreations* hockey, golf; *Clubs* Newry Olympic Hockey, Donaghadee Golf, Holywood 87; *Style*— Stephen Martin, Esq, MBE; ✉ 5 The Coaches, Brown's Brae, Holywood, Co Down, NI BT18 0LE (☎ 01232 421338)

MARTIN, Stephen Graham Balfour; s of Graham Hunter Martin (d 1985), and Ragna, *née* Balch-Barth; *b* 21 Oct 1939; *Educ* Tonbridge; *m* 1, 1966 (m dis 1969), Angela Wood; 1 s (Diccon Carl Henry b 1967); m 2, 27 Nov 1976, Elizabeth Mary, da of Dennis John Ward, of Chatteris; 2 da (Charlotte Louise Elizabeth b 1978, Olivia Rose Ragna b 1993); *Career* chm and md: Intermail Holdings Ltd, Home Shopping Club Ltd; dir: Fineline Printing Ltd, Strategic Marketing Databases Ltd, Common Cause Ltd; Liveryman Worshipful Co of Armourers and Brasiers; FIWC, DipDM; *Recreations* fishing, shooting, gardening; *Clubs* In & Out, Flyfishers'; *Style*— Stephen Martin, Esq; ✉ Manor Farm House, Chilton Foliat, Hungerford, Berks RG17 0TJ; Intermail Ltd, 10 Fleming Road, Newbury, Berks RG13 2DE (fax 01635 41678)

MARTIN, Stephen Harcourt (Steve); s of Robert Harcourt Martin, of Maidstone, and Joan Winifred, *née* Carpenter; *b* 4 Sept 1952; *Educ* Haywards Heath GS, Univ of Hull; *m* 1987, Amanda Suna; 1 s (Thomas Harcourt b 1984), 1 da (Ruth Mary b 1991); *Career* nursing asst Dela Pole Psychiatric Hosp Humberside 1973–74; Welsh Office: exec offr Town and Country Planning 1974–77, admin trainee and higher exec offr Indust Dept 1977–79, private sec to Perm Sec 1979–81, princ Housing Div 1985–87 (Health Dept 1981–85), asst sec Health and Social Servs Dept 1987–92, dir Educn Dept 1992–; *Recreations* music, reading, Welsh language; *Style*— Steve Martin, Esq; ✉ Welsh Office, Crown Buildings, Cathays Park, Cardiff CF1 3NQ (☎ 01222 823207, fax 01222 825524)

MARTIN, Timothy Charles (Tim); s of Godfrey Martin (d 1975), of Findon, Sussex, and Nancy Cordelia, *née* Orrom; *b* 17 May 1951; *Educ* Worthing HS, King's Coll Cambridge (BA, MA); *m* 31 March 1984, Sarah, da of Arthur James Moffett, FRCS, of Cooksey Green, Worcs; 2 s (Alexander Dods b 19 Aug 1985, Charles Murray b 15 Jan 1988); *Career* admitted slr 1977, Allen and Overy 1975–79, dir (corp fin) Hill Samuel and Co 1986–87 (joined 1979), dir (corp fin) Barclays de Zoete Wedd Ltd 1988–; *Recreations* tennis, gardening, opera; *Clubs* Lansdowne; *Style*— Tim Martin, Esq; ✉ Barclays de Zoete Wedd Ltd, Ebbgate House, Swan Lane, London EC4R 3TS (☎ 0171 623 2323, fax 0171 956 4663)

MARTIN, Valerie Ann (Val); da of William Herbert Bennett (d 1996), of Purley, Surrey, and Ann Georgina, *née* Hon (d 1977); *b* 15 Oct 1951; *Educ* King George V Sch Hong Kong, Girton Coll Cambridge (MA); *m* July 1973, Professor Benjamin Raymond Martin; 2 s (Paul b 3 June 1980, David b 10 Sept 1985), 1 da (Sarah b 5 Dec 1982);

Career teacher VSO W Africa 1973–75, NHS nat admin trainee Manchester 1975–77, unit administrator New Cross Hosp London 1978–82, project mangr for reorganisation and merger of Guy's and Lewisham Health Dist 1982–83, dep unit general mangr Guy's Hosp London 1983–85, mangr Dist Industl Servs Lewisham and N Southwark Health Authy 1988–89, project mangr for NHS trust status application for Guy's and Lewisham NHS Trust 1989–91, gen mangr Lewisham and Hither Green Hosps 1991–93, chief exec Lewisham Hosp NHS Trust 1993–; memb S London TEC; MHSM, FRSA; *Recreations* reading, swimming, enjoying life; *Style*— Mrs Val Martin; ✉ The Lewisham Hospital NHS Trust, Lewisham High Street, London SE13 6LH (☎ 0181 333 3283, fax 0181 333 3282)

MARTIN, Dr Vivian Max; s of Martin Martin, of Melbourne, Australia, and Rachel, *née* Godfrey; *b* 9 Oct 1941; *Educ* Monash Univ Aust (MB BS), RCP (MRCP); *m* Dec 1967, Penelope Georgina, da of Leon Samuels; 2 s (Simon James b 22 Nov 1971, Nicholas Giles b 23 Dec 1973); *Career* jr RMO Launceston Gen Hosp Tasmania 1968, sr RMO Sutherland Dist Hosp Sydney 1969–70, sr RMO Queen Victoria Meml Hosp Melbourne 1970–71; SHO Royal Free Hosp 1972–73, registrar Whittington Hosp 1973–76; sr registrar UCH 1976–81; conslt rheumatologist: St Albans City Hosp 1981–82, QEII Hosp, Welwyn Garden City 1981–82, Cromwell Hosp 1982–, UCH 1983–84, Manor House Hosp 1991–; conslt physician PPP Med Centre 1985–94; memb: BMA, RSM, Br Soc for Rheumatology, RCP, Int Back Pain Soc; *Publications* author of articles in various learned journals; *Style*— Dr Vivian Martin; ✉ 38 Devonshire Place, London W1N 1PE (☎ 0171 486 2365, fax 0171 224 0034); Cromwell Hospital, Cromwell Rd, London SW5 OTU (☎ 0171 460 2000, fax 0171 460 5555)

MARTIN, William Edward (Bill); s of Joseph Edward Martin (d 1987), of Upminster, Essex, and Pamela Maud, *née* Ruse; *b* 10 March 1951; *Educ* Beal Essex, Univ of Exeter (BA), Univ of Wales (MSc); *m* 28 Aug 1976, Yvette Mary, da of James Geard McBrearty (d 1976); 1 s (Samuel b June 1978), 1 da (Anna b May 1980); *Career* economist DTI 1973–81, advsr Central Policy Review Staff Cabinet Office 1981–83; UBS Ltd: joined UBS Phillips & Drew 1983, chief economist UBS until 1996, md of economic research 1996–; advsr Treasy and Civil Serv Select Ctee 1986–; memb Royal Economics Society; *Books* The Economics of the Profits Crisis (ed 1981); *Recreations* theatre, art; *Style*— Bill Martin, Esq; ✉ 186 Norsey Road, Billericay, Essex CM11 1DB (☎ 01277 634194); UBS Ltd, 100 Liverpool Street, London EC2M 2RH (☎ 0171 901 3501)

MARTIN, William Wylie Macpherson (Bill); s of Ian Alistair Macpherson (d 1985), of Glasgow, and Lettia, *née* Wylie; *b* 9 Nov 1938; *Educ* Glasgow; *m* Janet Mary, da of Maj Bruce Anthony Olley (d 1981), and Jeanne, *née* Blackburn; 1 s (Angus), 3 da (Meran, Alison, Melanie); *Career* songwriter: Puppet on a String (first Br songwriter to win Eurovision Song Contest), Congratulations, My Boy, The Water Babies, Shanga-lang and 50 other top ten songs; music publisher: Sky, Van Morrison, Bay City Rollers, BA Robertson, Billy Connolly; record producer: Billy Connolly, Bay City Rollers, Elkie Brooks; Variety Club Silver Heart award for servs to charity; Freeman: City of London 1981, City of Glasgow 1987; Liveryman Worshipful Co of Distillers; *Recreations* golf; *Clubs* RAC (past capt Golf Club), Annabel's, St George's Hill; *Style*— Bill Martin, Esq; ✉ Love This Music Limited, Hundred House, 100 Union Street, London SE1 0NL (☎ 0171 928 4444, fax 0171 928 0920)

MARTIN ALEGI, Lynda Margaret; da of George Watt (d 1990), and Dorothy May, *née* Humphreys; *b* 7 March 1952; *Educ* Woodford County HS, Newnham Coll Cambridge (MA), Université Libre de Bruxelles - Institut D'Etudes Européenes (License Spécial en Droit Européen); *m* 6 Jan 1989, Peter Alegi; *Career* Baker & McKenzie: articled clerk 1975–77, asst slr 1977–81, ptnr 1981–, ptnr i/c EC, Competition and Trade Dept 1989–, memb Professional Devpt Ctee 1989–93; memb: Competition Panel CBI 1990–, Law Ctee IOD 1993–95, Competition Ctee Int C of C UK 1995–; ed Competition Law chapter Encyclopaedia of Information Technology Law (Sweet & Maxwell) 1989–; numerous articles and speeches on Euro and competition law issues; memb: Law Soc 1977, Slrs' Euro Gp 1977; *Recreations* Italian hill towns, wine and gardens; *Style*— Ms Lynda Martin Alegi; ✉ Baker & McKenzie, 100 New Bridge Street, London EC4V 7JA (☎ 0171 919 1000, fax 0171 919 1999, mobile 0802 203604)

MARTIN-JENKINS, Christopher Dennis Alexander; 2 s of Lt-Col Dennis Frederick Martin-Jenkins, TD (d 1991), of Cranleigh, Surrey, and Dr Rosemary Clare Martin-Jenkins, *née* Walker; *b* 20 Jan 1945; *Educ* Marlborough, Univ of Cambridge (BA, MA); *m* 1971, Judith Oswald, da of Charles Henry Telford Hayman (d 1950), of Brackley; 2 s (James b 1973, Robin b 1975), 1 da (Lucy b 1979); *Career* BBC sports broadcaster 1970–, cricket corr 1973–80 and 1984–91, ed The Cricketer 1981–91 (dep ed 1967–70), cricket corr Daily Telegraph 1991–; played cricket for Surrey second XI and MCC; *Books* author of various books on cricket; *Recreations* cricket, golf, tennis; *Clubs* MCC and many other CCs, W Sussex Golf; *Style*— Christopher Martin-Jenkins, Esq; ✉ Daily Telegraph, 1 Canada Square, Canary Wharf, London E14 5DT

MARTIN-JENKINS, David Dennis; eldest s of Lt-Col Dennis Frederick Martin-Jenkins, TD (d 1991), of Cranleigh, Surrey, and Dr Rosemary Clare Martin-Jenkins, *née* Walker; *b* 7 May 1941; *Educ* Kingsmead, Meols, St Bede's Eastbourne, Marlborough; *m* 24 June 1967, Anthea, da of Arthur Milton de Vinny (d 1983); *Career* dir: JW Cameron and Co Ltd 1972–82, Ellerman Lines plc 1974–82, Tollemache and Cobbold Breweries Ltd 1976–82; chm MN Offrs Pension Fund Investmt Ctee 1976–82; dir: Primesight Plc 1984–, National Home Loans Holdings plc 1985–95, Capital and Regnl Properties plc 1986–95; tstee John Ellerman Fndn 1991–; treas: Lurgashall PCC, Shipwrecked Mariners' Soc 1995–; FCA 1965, FCT 1979; *Recreations* sport (Tranmere Rovers and Liverpool FC's), politics (Lib Democrat), hill walking (climbed Mera Peak (21200ft) Nepal 1986, Aconcagua (22,835ft) Argentina 1993, Pisco (18,867ft) Peru 1996), the countryside; *Clubs* Lancashire CCC; *Style*— David Martin-Jenkins, Esq; ✉ Jobson's Cottage, Jobson's Lane, Haslemere, Surrey GU27 3BY (☎ and fax 01428 707294)

MARTIN-QUIRK, Howard Richard Newell; s of George Donald Martin, of Dorset, and Nelly Katie, *née* Newell; *b* 8 Aug 1937; *Educ* Lancing, Christ's Coll Cambridge (MA), UCL (BSc (Arch), MSc); *m* 1, 4 Jan 1964, Sally Anne (d 1976), da of Ernest Davies, former MP, of London; m 2, 1 Oct 1976, Mary Teresa, da of Dudley C Quirk, JP; 1 s (Inigo b 1989); *Career* architect & architectural historian, author, princ lectr Kingston Univ Sch of Architecture 1970–, ptnr Martin Quirk Assocs 1983–, chief oenologist Chiddingstone Vineyards Ltd 1984–94; external examiner Univ of N London, visiting prof DEI Coll Thessaloniki Greece; *Recreations* music, chess, squash rackets, gardening, wine; *Clubs* Architectural Assoc, Soc of Architectural Historians, Victorian Soc, Ecclesiological Soc, Wagner Soc, EVA; *Style*— H R N Martin-Quirk, Esq; ✉ The Old Coach Road, Chiddingstone, Edenbridge, Kent TN8 7BH (☎ and fax 01892 870235); Kingston University (☎ 0181 547 2000); Martin-Quirk Associates (☎ and fax 01892 870235)

MARTINDALE, Air Vice-Marshal Alan Rawes; CB (1984); s of late Norman Martindale, and late Edith, *née* Rawes; *b* 20 Jan 1930; *Educ* Kendal GS, Univ Coll Leicester (BA); *m* 1952, Eileen Alma Wrenn; 3 da; *Career* cmmnd RAF 1951, Cmd Supply Offr RAF Germany 1972–74, dir Supply Mgmnt MOD Harrogate 1974–75 (dep dir 1971–72), RCDS 1976, Air Cdre Supply and Movements RAF Support Cmd 1977, dep gen mangr NATO Multi-Role Combat Aircraft Mgmnt Agency 1978–81, dir Supply Policy (RAF) MOD 1981–82, DG Supply (RAF) 1982–84; dist gen mangr Hastings Health Authy 1985–90, census area mangr S Kent and Hastings 1990–91, chm Battle Festival 1991–96; *Recreations* gardening, golf; *Clubs* RAF; *Style*— Air Vice-Marshal Alan Martindale, CB; ✉ Taylors Cottage, Mountfield, Robertsbridge, E Sussex TN32 5JZ

MARTINDALE, Richard John; s of Eric Martindale (d 1970), of Hindley, nr Wigan, and Margaret Joyce, *née* Whiteside (d 1993); *b* 25 Oct 1950; *Educ* Bolton Sch, Univ of Sheffield (LLB); *m* 1, 5 Aug 1971 (m dis 1992), Jackie Avril, da of Philip Watkin Edwards; 4 s (Nicholas Jolyon b 16 April 1977, Timothy George b 8 Aug 1978, Alastair James b 16 July 1982, Justin Matthew b 31 Aug 1984); m 2, 18 June 1994, Carole Mary, da of George Harold Ellicock; *Career* Hill Dickinson Davis Campbell (formerly Hill Dickinson & Co) Liverpool: articles until 1974, ptnr 1979, specialist in commercial law; chief examiner in shipping law RSA 1980–84; memb Law Soc 1974–, Slrs Euro GP; *Recreations* music, in particular choral singing, reading, dinghy sailing, walking; *Style*— Richard Martindale, Esq; ✉ Pant Farmhouse, Pant, Marford, Clwyd LL12 8SE (☎ 01978 855228); Hill Dickinson Davis Campbell, Pearl Assurance House, Derby Square, Liverpool L2 9XL (☎ 0151 236 5400, fax 0151 236 2175)

MARTINEAU, His Hon Judge David Nicholas Nettlefold; s of Frederick Alan Martineau (d 1990) of Chobham, Surrey, and Vera Ruth, *née* Naylor; *b* 27 March 1941; *Educ* Eton, Trinity Coll Cambridge (MA, LLB); *m* 20 Jan 1968, Elizabeth Mary, da of Maurice James Carrick Allom (d 1995), of Ightham, Kent; 1 s (Luke b 27 March 1970), 1 da (Alice b 8 June 1972); *Career* called to the Bar Inner Temple 1964, recorder 1986–94 (asst recorder 1982), circuit judge (SE Circuit) 1994–; memb Nat Exec Ctee Cystic Fibrosis Res Tst 1989–; *Recreations* skiing, water-skiing, windsurfing, music, wine, food; *Clubs* Hawks, MCC; *Style*— His Hon Judge David Martineau; ✉ 37 Bedford Gardens, London W8 7EF (☎ 0171 727 7825); Snaresbrook Crown Court, 1 English Grounds, off Battlebridge Lane, London SE1 2HU

MARTINEAU, (Alan) Denis; s of Col Sir Wilfrid Martineau, MC, TD (d 1964), of Edgbaston, Birmingham and Upper Coscombe, Temple Guiting, nr Cheltenham, Glos, and Elvira Mary Seton, *née* Lee Strathy (d 1982); *b* 5 April 1920; *Educ* West House Sch, Rugby, Trinity Hall Cambridge (MA); *m* 5 July 1952, Mollie, da of John Lewis Davies, MBE (d 1987), of St Brides Major, Glamorgan; 3 s (Jeremy, Peter b 1956, Charles b 1961); *Career* Army 1940–46, cmmnd Royal Warwickshire Regt 1941, served as Capt in ME, N Africa and Italy; admitted slr 1950; ptnr Ryland Martineau & Co 1954–84, NP; vice consul for Portugal 1964–75; memb Birmingham City Cncl 1961–91 (Lord Mayor 1986–87); dir: City of Birmingham Symphony Orch 1961–91 (chm 1968–74), Birmingham Repertory Theatre 1976–91, Birmingham Botanical Gardens 1985–; chm: Cncl of Order of St John W Mids 1987–93, Birmingham Civic Soc 1988–94, George Henry Collins Charity 1988–; tstee various charitable tsts; pres Birmingham Bach Soc 1987–; jt pres Birmingham Festival Choral Soc, vice pres SENSE in the Midlands; vice patron Birmingham Co Royal Br Legion, patron Birmingham Festival of Remembrance 1991–; memb: Law Soc 1952, Soc of Provincial Notaries 1965; OStJ 1988; *Recreations* music, Birmingham history, the country, watching sport; *Style*— Denis Martineau, Esq; ✉ 10 Vicarage Rd, Edgbaston, Birmingham B15 3ES (☎ 0121 454 0479); Pike Cottage, Upper Coscombe, Temple Guiting, Glos GL54 5SB (☎ 01386 584524)

MARTINEAU, (Elizabeth) Jane; da of Rupert William Hammond, CBE (d 1986), of Sussex, and Camille Sylvia, *née* Longmore; *b* 27 March 1951; *Educ* Cheltenham Ladies' Coll; *m* 7 Aug 1982, John Denis Martineau (d 1990), s of Charles Herman Martineau, of Fife; 2 s (Robert b 1985, Edward b 1987); *Career* admitted slr 1974; currently conslt (former ptnr) Clyde & Co; non-exec dir Ealing DHA 1991–93; memb Law Soc; *Recreations* walking, tennis, cooking, music; *Style*— Mrs Jane Martineau; ✉ Clyde & Co, 51 Eastcheap, London EC3M 1JP (☎ 0171 623 1244, fax 0171 623 5425, telex 884886)

MARTINEZ, Dylan John; s of Raul Osmar Martinez, of Buenos Aires, Argentina, and Penelope Margarita, *née* Woolcock; *b* 5 July 1969; *Educ* Coll of FE Oxford, Coll of Art and Technol Newcastle, Newcastle Poly; *m* Alice Helen Louisa, *née* Dunhill; *Career* freelance photographer for music press (New Musical Express, Sounds, etc) and record companies 1989, subsequently joined Select Photo Agency working on cmmn for Time, Newsweek, Der Spiegel and Business Week International, later worked through Sygma Photos (concurrently working for The Sunday Mirror newspaper and magazine) until 1991, staff photographer Reuters 1994– (full-time contract stringer 1991–94); winner News Photographer of the Yr and runner-up Photographer of the Yr Picture Eds Guild 1993, highly commended UK Press Gazzette Photographer of the Yr 1993; *Recreations* jazz music, holidays; *Style*— Dylan Martinez, Esq; ✉ UK Picture Desk, Reuters, 85 Fleet Street, London EC4P 4AJ (☎ 0171 542 7949)

MARTLEW, Eric Anthony; MP (Lab) Carlisle (majority 3,108); *b* 3 Jan 1949; *Educ* Harraby Sch, Carlisle Technical Coll; *m* Elsie, *née* Duggan; *Career* formerly lab technician then personnel mangr Nestlé; MP (Lab) Carlisle 1987–, shadow defence spokesman (RAF) 1992–95, oppn whip 1995–; chm T&GWU Parly Gp; memb Carlisle City Cncl 1972–74, memb Cumbria CC 1973–88 (chm 1983–85), memb Carlisle HA then East Cumbria HA 1975–88 (chm 1977–79); *Recreations* photography, fell walking, local history; *Style*— Eric Martlew, Esq, MP; ✉ House of Commons, London SW1A 0AA (☎ 0171 219 3000)

MARTON, Capt Christopher; s of Henry Brooks Marton (d 1978), and Eileen, *née* Moon (d 1980); *b* 18 Aug 1939; *Educ* Eccles HS, Liverpool Tech Coll (Masters Cert of Competency); *m* 14 Jan 1969, Margaret Christine, da of Henry Clarence Broughton (d 1972); 2 s (Andrew Christopher b 1 June 1969, Robert Charles b 3 Oct 1971); *Career* apprentice MN 1956–60, MN Offr 1960–72; master: hydrographic survey ship 1972–73, offshore supply vessels 1973–74; marine surveyor and conslt 1974–; memb: Cncl Naval Club London, PCC; Freeman City of London 1981, Liveryman Worshipful Co of Loriners 1982; *Recreations* cricket, shooting, squash, gardening; *Clubs* Lighthouse, Rugby, Lancs CCC, City Livery; *Style*— Capt Christopher Marton; ✉ 10 Church Green, Milton Ernest, Bedford MK44 1RH; Noble Denton Europe Ltd, Noble House, 131 Aldersgate St, London EC1A 4EB (☎ 0171 606 4961, fax 0171 606 5035, telex 885 802)

MARTONMERE, 2 Baron (UK 1964) John Stephen Robinson; s of Hon Richard Anthony Gasque Robinson (d 1979), and Hon Mrs (Wendy Patricia) Robinson; gs of 1 Baron Martonmere, GBE, KCMG, PC (d 1989); *b* 10 July 1963; *Educ* Lakefield Coll Sch, Seneca Coll; *Heir* bro, David Alan Robinson b 15 Sept 1965; *Style*— The Rt Hon Lord Martonmere; ✉ 390 Russell Hill Rd, Toronto, Ontario, Canada M4V 2V2 (☎ 416 485 3077)

MARTYN, John Reid; s of Ernest John Martyn (d 1970), of Ealing, and Evelyn Isobel, *née* Reid (d 1973); *b* 16 June 1944; *Educ* Ealing GS for Boys, Univ of Exeter (BA); *m* 4 Aug 1967, Frances Howell, da of Cyril Howell Williams; 1 s (Gareth John b 4 Sept 1974), 1 da (Charis Jane b 15 Sept 1977); *Career* with Ford Motor Co 1965–80, with BICC plc 1980–84 (gp fin dir 1983–84), gp fin dir The Littlewoods Organisation plc 1984–87, gp fin dir Dalgety plc 1987–97; non-exec dir Lloyds Abbey Life plc 1993–, non-exec (link) dir The Littlewoods Organisation 1996–; vol for various charities; FICMA; *Recreations* gardening, golf; *Style*— John Martyn, Esq; ✉ Redcroft, Stanville Rd, Cumnor Hill, Oxford (☎ 01865 862740); Dalgety plc, 100 George St, London W1H 5RH (☎ 0171 486 0200)

MARTYN, (Anthony) Nigel; s of Alfred Horace Martyn, of St Austell, Cornwall, and Delphia June, *née* Marks; *b* 11 Aug 1966; *Educ* Penrice Comp St Austell; *m* 17 Aug 1987, Amanda Tamblyn, da of Christopher Edwin Bailey; 1 s (Thomas Anthony b 5 Nov 1992); *Career* professional footballer; Bristol Rovers 1987–89 (debut Aug 1987 v Rotherham, 124 appearances); Crystal Palace 1989–96: joined for a fee of £1m, debut Nov 1989 v Tottenham Hotspur, over 250 appearances, runners-up FA Cup v

Manchester Utd 1990, winners Zenith Data Systems Cup v Everton 1991, Division 1 Championship medal 1993/94; joined Leeds United 1996–; England: 11 under 21 caps, 6 B caps, 3 full caps, memb squad Euro Championship Sweden 1992; office clerk Smith and Treffry Coal Merchants 1983–87, plastics mixer Holmbush Plastics 1987; *Recreations* golf, cricket, most other sports; *Style*— Nigel Martyn, Esq; ✉ Leeds United Football Club, Elland Road, Leeds LS11 0ES (☎ 01532 716037, fax 01532 706560)

MARTYN, (Charles) Philip; s of James Godfrey Martyn (d 1970), of London, and Kathleen Doris, *née* Crawford; *b* 17 July 1948; *Educ* St Dunstans Coll London, Univ of Exeter (LLB); *Career* slr: Coward Chance London 1972–77, Clifford Turner 1977–79; jt gen mangr Sumitomo Bank Ltd London 1988– (joined 1979); tstee Waldorf Sch SW London; memb Law Soc; *Recreations* studying Rudolf Steiner's work, gardening, Bach; *Style*— Philip Martyn, Esq; ✉ The Sumitomo Bank Ltd, Temple Ct, 11 Queen Victoria St, London EC4N 4TA (☎ 0171 786 1017, fax 0171 236 0049)

MARTYN, (Charles) Roger Nicholas; s of Rev Charles William Martyn (d 1956), Clerk in Holy Orders, of Aylsham, Norfolk, and Doris Lilian, *née* Batcheller (d 1989); *b* 10 Dec 1925; *Educ* Charterhouse, Merton Coll Oxford (MA); *m* 24 Sept 1960, Helen Ruth, da of Samuel Frank Everson, of Camberley, Surrey (d 1981); 2 s (Nicholas b 1963, Christopher b 1965), 1 da (Sarah b 1962); *Career* 60 Rifles KRRC 1944–47; admitted slr 1952; ptnr: Sherwood & Co (Parly agent) 1954–60, Lee Bolton & Lee 1961–73; Master of the Supreme Ct 1973–95, pt/t memb Immigration Appeal Authy 1991–95; *Recreations* sailing, walking, horology, book-binding; *Clubs* Thames Barge, Salcombe Yacht; *Style*— Roger Martyn, Esq; ✉ 29 St Albans Road, London NW5 1RG

MARTYN-HEMPHILL, Hon Charles Andrew Martyn; s of 5 Baron Hemphill, *qv*; *b* 8 Oct 1954; *Educ* Downside, St Benet's Hall Oxford; *m* 1985, Sarah J F, eld da of Richard Edward Walter Lumley, *qv*, of Windlesham, Surrey; 1 s (Richard Patrick Lumley b 17 May 1990), 3 da (Clarissa Mary b 1986, Amelia Rose b 1988, Marina Olivia Astrid b 22 Oct 1992); *Career* dir: Morgan Grenfell Investment Management, Morgan Grenfell Asset Management 1994–; *Recreations* sailing, skiing, shooting, hunting; *Clubs* White's; *Style*— The Hon Charles Martyn-Hemphill; ✉ 78 Streathbourne Road, London SW17 8QY (☎ 0181 672 2536); Morgan Grenfell Asset Management Ltd, 20 Finsbury Circus, London EC2M 1NB (☎ 0171 256 7500)

MARTYR, Peter McCallum; s of John Walton Martyr, and Jean Wallace Robertson, *née* McCallum; *b* 31 March 1954; *Educ* Clifton, Univ of Wales (LLB); *m* 27 May 1978, Carol Frances, da of Donald Edgar Busby; 1 s (Luke b 26 Dec 1985), 1 da (Laura b 7 Nov 1988); *Career* admitted slr 1979, ptnr Norton Rose 1985– (specialising in insurance, int and marine litigation); Freeman Worshipful Co of Solicitors 1979; *Recreations* swimming, collector's motor cars, music; *Style*— Peter Martyr, Esq; ✉ Norton Rose, Kempson House, Camomile Street, London EC3A 7AN (☎ 0171 283 6000, fax 0171 283 6500)

MARU, Rajesh Jamnadass; s of Jamnadass Maru (d 1995), and Prabhavati, *née* Galoria; *b* 28 Oct 1962; *Educ* Rooks Heath HS Harrow, Pinner Sixth Coll; *m* 21 Sept 1991, Amanda Jane, da of Ronald and Judith Lock; 2 s (Christopher Patrick b 21 Jan 1993, Daniel James b 7 Jan 1996); *Career* professional cricketer; North London Poly 1975–79, Brondersbury 1980–83, Middlesex CCC 1980–83, Hampshire CCC 1984– (awarded county cap 1986); England: schs under 15 1977–78 (capt 1978), 2 test matches Young England v W Indies 1979–80, 3 test matches Young England v India 1980; represented MCC v Middlesex 1986, MCC tour of Leeward Islands 1992, MCC tour of Bangkok Malaysia Singapore and India 1995; County Championship and Gillette Cup winners Middlesex 1980; voted Most Promising English Schoolboy Cricket Soc 1978, Hampshire Young Player of the Year 1986; coaching: NCA qualified advanced cricket coach, coached in NZ 1985–87, ran private coaching sch 1988, coach to W of England Schs under 14 1990, NCA staff coach; *Recreations* golf, squash, swimming, tennis, badminton; *Style*— Rajesh Maru, Esq; ✉ Hampshire CCC, Northlands Rd, Southampton, Hampshire (☎ 01703 333788)

MARUNCHAK, Alexander (Alex); s of Ivan Marunchak, of Westminster, and Paraskewia, *née* Korpesio; *b* 31 May 1951; *Educ* St Marylebone GS London, Kilburn Poly; *m* 1, 1976 (m dis 1978), Susan Tatarczuk; m 2, 1982, Jennifer Hickman; 2 s; *Career* journalist; Slough Observer 1977–79, Middlesex Chronicle 1979–80, Evening Echo 1980–81; News of the World: joined 1981, crime reporter 1983–85, chief crime reporter 1985–87, dep news ed 1987–91, news ed 1992–95, asst ed (news) 1995–; chm: N Westminster Young Libs 1979–81, Ukrainian Soc 1981–82; contested (Lib) Westminster City Cncl 1981; *Recreations* politics, reading, langugages (speaks Ukrainian and Russian); *Clubs* National Liberal; *Style*— Alex Marunchak, Esq; ✉ News of the World, 1 Virginia St, London E1 9XR (☎ 0171 782 4000, fax 0171 583 9504)

MARWICK, Prof Arthur John Brereton; s of William Hutton Marwick, and Maeve Cluna, *née* Brereton; *b* 29 Feb 1936; *Educ* George Heriot's Sch Edinburgh, Univ of Edinburgh (MA, DLitt), Balliol Coll Oxford (BLitt); *children* 1 da; *Career* asst lectr in history Univ of Aberdeen 1959–60, lectr in history Univ of Edinburgh 1960–69, prof of history Open Univ 1969–, dean and dir of studies in arts Open Univ 1978–84, visiting prof in history State Univ of NY at Buffalo 1966–67, visiting scholar Hoover Inst and visiting prof Stanford Univ 1984–85, directeur d'études invité l'Ecole des Hautes Etudes en Sciences Sociales Paris 1985, visiting prof Rhodes Coll Memphis Tennessee 1991, visiting prof Univ of Perugia 1991; FRHistS; *Books* The Explosion of British Society (1963), Clifford Allen (1964), The Deluge (1965, 2 edn 1991), Britain in the Century of Total War (1968), The Nature of History (3 edn, 1989), War and Social Change in the Twentieth Century (1974), The Home Front (1976), Women at War 1914–1918 (1977), Class: Image and Reality in Britain, France and USA since 1930 (1980, 2 edn 1990), Illustrated Dictionary of British History (ed 1980), British Society since 1945 (1982, 3 edn 1996), Britain in Our Century (1984), Class in the Twentieth Century (ed 1986), Beauty in History: Society Politics and Personal Appearance c 1500 to the Present (1988), Total War and Social Change (ed, 1988), The Arts, Literature and Society (ed, 1990), Culture in Britain since 1945 (1991); *Clubs* Open Univ Football and Tennis; *Style*— Prof Arthur Marwick; ✉ 67 Fitzjohns Ave, Hampstead, London NW3 6PE

MARWOOD, Roger Paul; s of Kenneth Ian Marwood (d 1988) and Blanche Greenberg (d 1980); *b* 23 July 1947; *Educ* Cheltenham GS, Univ of London (MB BS, MSc, Water Polo double purple); *m* 21 Feb 1976, Suzanne Christine, da of Francis Brown; 1 s (Joseph Roger George b 31 Oct 1984), 2 da (Rebecca Alice Georgina b 25 March 1978, Sophie Christine Blanche b 30 Dec 1979); *Career* sr registrar in obstetrics and gynaecology St Mary's Hosp 1980–82 (registrar 1975–80); conslt in obstetrics and gynaecology Chelsea & Westminster Hosp 1982–, conslt gynaecologist to King Edward VII Hosp 1985–; memb Worshipful Co of Apothecaries 1985; contrib to numerous jls on clinical obstetrics and gynaecology; vice pres RSM, FRCOG 1989 (MRCOG 1977); *Recreations* opera, skiing, pinball machines, swimming; *Clubs* Garrick; *Style*— Roger Marwood, Esq; ✉ 96 Harley St, London W1; Chelsea & Westminster Hospital, Fulham Road, London SW10 (☎ 0171 637 7977 and 0171 746 8218, fax 0171 486 2022 and 0181 846 7998)

MARX, Enid Crystal Dorothy; da of Robert J Marx; *b* 20 Oct 1902; *Educ* Roedean Sch, Central Sch of Arts & Crafts, RCA Painting Sch; *Career* designer of: handblock printed textiles (1925–39), wood engraving and autolithography pattern papers, book jackets, book illustration and decorations, trademarks, printed and woven furnishing fabrics, wallpapers, ceramics, plastics, PO stamps (definitive 1952, Christmas 1976); works in public collections incl: V & A, Musée des Arts Décoratifs, Boston Museum, Scottish Arts Cncl, Sheffield Arts Cncl; regular lectr on textiles and folk art, articles and bdcasts on aspects of industl design in numerous countries; memb: Nat Register of Industl Designers Central Inst of Art and Design, Bd of Trade Design Panel on Utility Furniture, Soc of Wood Engravers; RDI 1944, sr fell RCA 1987 (fell 1982), FRSA, FSIAD; *Books* English Popular and Traditional Art (jtly, 1947), English Popular Art (with Margaret Lambert 1951, 2 edn 1988); author and illustrator of 12 books for children; *Recreations* study of popular art in different countries, gardening; *Style*— Ms Enid Marx; ✉ The Studio, 39 Thornhill Road, Barnsbury Square, London N1 1JS (☎ 0171 607 2286)

MARYON DAVIS, Dr Alan Roger; s of Cyril Edward Maryon Davis (d 1994), of Osterley, Middx, and Hilda May, *née* Thompson (d 1995); *b* 21 Jan 1943; *Educ* St Paul's, St John's Coll Cambridge (MA, MB BChir), St Thomas' Hosp Med Sch, LSHTM (MSc); *m* 14 March 1981, (Glynis) Anne, da of Dr Philip Trefor Davies (d 1970) of Hartlepool; 2 da (Jessica b 1983, Elizabeth b 1985); *Career* med conslt, writer and broadcaster; clinical med 1969–74, community and preventive med 1974–, chief MO Health Educn Cncl 1984–87, hon sr lectr in community med St Mary's Hosp Med Sch 1985–89, hon specialist in community med Paddington and N Kensington Health Authy 1985–88, conslt in public health med W Lambeth Health Authy (now Lambeth, Southwark and Lewisham Health Authy) 1988–, sr lectr in public health med Utd Med and Dental Schs Guy's and St Thomas' Hosps 1988–; regular med columnist for Woman magazine; MRCP 1972, FFCM 1986, FRIPH 189, FRSM 1995; *Radio* BBC Radio 4 series: Action Makes the Heart Grow Stronger 1983, Back in 25 Minutes 1984, Not Another Diet Programme 1985, Cancercheck 1988; *Television* BBC series: Your Mind in Their Hands 1982, Save a Life 1986, Bodymatters 1985–89, Ruby's Health Quest 1995, The Body-Clock Diet 1996; *Books* Family Health & Fitness (1981), Bodyfacts (1984), Diet 2000 (with J Thomas, 1984), How to Save a Life (with J Rogers, 1987), Pssst a Really Useful Guide to Alcohol (1989), Cholesterol Check (1991), The Good Health Guide (1994); *Recreations* relaxing in the Yorkshire Dales, singing in the group 'Instant Sunshine'; *Style*— Dr Alan Maryon Davis

MASCARENHAS, HE John Philip; *b* 14 April 1938; *Educ* King's Coll Seychelles, Bournville Coll Birmingham, York Tech Coll; *m* 25 Feb 1978, Janet, da of William Spears; 1 da (Alice b 24 Oct 1983); *Career* Nat Serv RCS 1955–58; radio and TV bdcasting trg Senegal 1960–61, prodr Radio Senegal and Voice of Kenya 1962–67; staff African Savings Credit Assoc of Kenya 1968–70, youth and community ldr Waltham Forest 1972–76, chief exec offr Immigration Dept Seychelles 1977, chief welfare offr Seychelles 1978–79, successively princ sec of youth and community PR, of int affrs then of environment Seychelles 1979–92, Seychelles high cmmr to Ct of St James's 1992–; memb Central Ctee Seychelles People's Progressive Front (chm People's Assembly) 1980–86, chm Rent Bd, Nat Sports Cncl and Seychelles Nat Olympic Ctee 1982–87; Knight of Redemption of Africa Liberia, Chev de l'Ordre du Merite Senegal; Dr (hc) American Language Center UCLA 1984; *Recreations* rambling, swimming, fishing, basketball, football; *Style*— HE Mr John Mascarenhas; ✉ Seychelles High Commission, 111 Eros House, Baker Street, London W1M 1FE (☎ 0171 224 1660, fax 0171 487 5756, car 0836 253763)

MASCHLER, Thomas Michael; s of Kurt Leo Maschler; *b* 16 Aug 1933; *Educ* Leighton Park; *m* 1970, Fay Goldie (the writer on restaurants Fay Maschler), da of Arthur Coventry (d 1969); 1 s (Benjamin Joseph b 1974), 2 da (Hannah Kate b 1970, Alice Mary b 1972); *Career* publisher; chm Jonathan Cape 1970– (editorial dir 1960, md 1966); prodn asst André Deutsch 1955, ed MacGibbon & Kee 1956–58, fiction ed Penguin Books 1958–60; *Recreations* tennis, skiing; *Style*— Thomas Maschler Esq; ✉ 18 Lennox Gardens, London SW1; Jonathan Cape Ltd, Random House, 20 Vauxhall Bridge Road, London SW1V 2SA

MASDIN, Dr (Edward) Guy; s of Frank Masdin (d 1986), and Marjorie Mary, *née* Clark (d 1980); *b* 9 May 1936; *Educ* Ecclesfield GS, Univ of Sheffield (BSc, PhD, univ first XI cricket); *m* 21 June 1958, Beryl Monica, da of George Barnes; 2 s (Robert Howard b 1962, Philip Carl b 1970), 2 da (Kay Judith b 1964, Linda Ruth b 1966); *Career* div head Shell Research Ltd 1966–73, tech mktg mangr Shell Coal International 1973–81, head Res Planning and Co-ordination Shell International Petroleum Co 1981–91; dir: Shell Research Ltd 1981–91, Shell Recherches 1981–91; res mgmnt conslt 1991–; past pres Inst of Energy, memb Ct and Cncl Univ of Reading, tstee Wokingham Cricket Club; FInstE, FIChemE, FBIM, FEng 1986; *Recreations* golf, gardening, cricket; *Clubs* Athenaeum, Berks CCC, North Hants Golf; *Style*— Dr Guy Masdin, FEng; ✉ 2 Martins Drive, Wokingham, Berkshire RG41 1NY (☎ 0118 978 5880)

MASEFIELD, Sir Peter Gordon; kt (1972); s of Dr (William) Gordon Masefield, CBE, JP, MRCS, LRCP, DPM, sometime Hon Gen Sec BMA, by his w Marian Ada, da of Edmund Lloyd-Owen, of New York; *b* 19 March 1914; *Educ* Westminster, Chillon Coll Switzerland, Jesus Coll Cambridge; *m* 1936, Patricia Doreen, da of Percy Rooney; 3 s, 1 da; *Career* former aircraft designer, pilot and aviation journalist; war corr, advsr to Lord Beaverbrook as Lord Privy Seal and sec War Cabinet Ctee on Post War Civil Air Tport 1943–45, first civil air attaché Br Embassy Washington DC 1945–47, dir gen of long term planning and projects Miny of Civil Aviation 1947–48; md: BEA 1949–55, Bristol Aircraft Ltd 1955–60; dir Beagle Aviation Finance Ltd 1962–71; dir Pressed Steel Co 1960–68; chm: British Airports Authy 1965–71, Beagle Aircraft Ltd 1968–70 (md 1960–68), Project Management Ltd 1972–89; dir: Worldwide Estates Ltd 1972–89, Nationwide Building Society 1973–80; dir Caledonian Airways Group 1978–87 (dep chm British Caledonian Airways 1972–87), dir London Transport 1973–82 (chm 1980–82); past pres: Inst of Road Tport Engrs, Royal Aeronautical Soc, Chartered Inst of Tport, numerous charitable tsts; pres: Duxford Aviation Soc 1970–, Br Assoc of Aviation Conslts 1973–93, Croydon Airport Soc, Brooklands Museum Tst 1994– (chm 1987–93); memb numerous aviation socs; memb Cncl Royal Aero Club (chm Aviation Ctee 1960–65, chm 1968–70); chm Bd of Govrs Reigate GS 1979–91; govr Ashridge Mgmnt Coll 1981–91, pres Reigate Soc 1991–; Hon DSc Cranfield 1977, Hon DTech Loughborough 1977; Freeman City of London, Liveryman Guild of Air Pilots and Air Navigators; hon fell: American Inst of Aeronautics and Astronautics, Canadian Aeronautics and Space Inst; US Aerospace Golden Eagle Award 1991; Hon FRAeS, FCIT, CIMechE, CIMgt, CEng; *Books* To Ride the Storm (1982); *Recreations* reading, writing, gardening; *Clubs* Athenaeum, Royal Aero, Nat Aviation (Washington); *Style*— Sir Peter Masefield; ✉ Rosehill, Doods Way, Reigate, Surrey RH2 0JT (☎ 01737 242396)

MASEFIELD, HE (John) Thorold; CMG (1986); s of Dr Geoffrey Bussell Masefield, and (Mildred) Joy Thorold, *née* Rogers; *b* 1 Oct 1939; *Educ* Dragon Sch Oxford, Repton, St John's Coll Cambridge (MA); *m* 18 Aug 1962, Jennifer Mary, da of Rev Dr Hubert Carey Trowell, OBE; 2 s (Nigel Anthony b 26 March 1964, Roger Francis b 24 Dec 1970), 2 da (Sally Clare b 18 Dec 1966, Helen Rachel b and d Aug 1968); *Career* Dip Serv: joined Cwlth Relations Office 1962; private sec to Permanent Under Sec 1963–64, second sec Br High Cmmn Kuala Lumpur 1964–65, second sec Br Embassy Warsaw 1966–67, FCO 1967–69, first sec UK Delgn to Disarmament Conf Geneva 1970–74, dep head Policy Planning Staff FCO 1974–77, dep head Far Eastern Dept FCO 1977–79, cnsllr and consul gen Br Embassy Islamabad 1979–82, head of Personnel Serv Dept FCO 1982–85, head of Far Eastern Dept FCO 1985–87, fell Center for Int Affairs Harvard Univ 1987–88, memb Civil Serv Selection Bd 1988–89, Br high cmmr to United Republic of Tanzania 1989–92, asst under sec of state FCO for Southern Asia and the Pacific 1992–94, high cmmr Nigeria (concurrently non-resident ambass to Chad and to Benin) 1994–June 1997, govr and C-in-C Bermuda June 1997–; *Recreations* fruit and vegetables; *Clubs* Royal Cwlth Soc; *Style*— HE Mr Thorold Masefield, CMG; ✉ until June 1997: c/o

FCO (Lagos), King Charles Street, London SW1A 2AH; after June 1997: Government House, Bermuda

MASERI, Prof Attilio; s of Adriano Maseri, and Antonietta Maseri; *b* 12 Nov 1935; *Educ* Cividale (Udine) Licenza Liceo Classico, Med Sch of Padua (MD), postgrad bds in cardiology and nuclear med, Med Sch Univ of Pisa; *m* 30 July 1960, Countess Francesca Maseri Florio di Santo Stefano; 1 s (Filippo (decd)); *Career* Univ of Pisa: intern Med Clinic 1960–62, Euratom res fell 1962–65, asst prof Dept of Med 1967–70, Docenza in Patologia Medica 1968, Aiuto Istituto Patologia Medica 1970–79, prof of Cardiopulmonary Pathophysiology 1970–79, prof of patologia Speciale Medica 1977–79, Cattedra di Fisiopatologia Cardiocircolatoria 1979; res fell Columbia Univ NY 1965–66, Johns Hopkins Univ 1966–67; head Coronary Res Gp Laboratory of Clinical Physiology of Nat Res Cncl Pisa 1970–79, Sir John McMichael prof of cardiovascular med Royal Postgrad Med Sch Univ of London 1979–91, dir of cardiology Hammersmith Hosp 1979–91, prof of cardiology and dir Inst of Cardiology Catholic Univ of the Sacred Heart Rome Italy 1991–; visiting professorships incl: Mount Sinai Sch of Med NY 1977, Cedars-Sinai Med Center LA 1984, Vanderbilt Univ Nashville 1986, Baylor Coll of Medicine Houston 1991, Favaloro Fndn Univ of Buenos Aires 1993, Health Sciences Center Univ of Virginia 1994; Laurence H Green lectr Brigham and Women's Hosp Boston 1994; memb Editorial Bd: Circulation, Jl of the American Coll of Cardiology, New England Jl of Medicine; FRCP, FACC; memb: Assoc of Physicians of GB & Ireland, Med Res Soc, Br Cardiac Soc, Italian Soc of Cardiology, American Heart Assoc (hon fell Cncl on Clinical Cardiology 1982), Academic Cncl Inst of Sports Med; foreign memb Royal Acad of Med Belgium; George von Heresy Prize for Nuclear Med (World Congress of Nuclear Med Tokyo) 1974, James B Herrick Heart Award (Int Congress of Cardiovascular Diseases Las Vegas) 1979, lifetime memb Johns Hopkins Soc of Scholars 1980, commendatoré (Italy) 1990, King Falsal International Prize for Med 1992; *Books* Ischemic Heart Disease: A Rational Basis for Clinical Practise and Clinical Research (1995), numerous book chapters and articles in learned jls, ed of various books of proceedings; *Recreations* tennis, skiing, sailing; *Clubs* Queens; *Style*— Prof Attilio Maseri; ✉ Institute of Cardiology, Policlinico A Gemelli, Largo A Gemelli 8, 00168 Rome, Italy (☎ 00 39 6 305 1166, fax 00 39 6 305 5535)

MASHAM OF ILTON, Baroness (Life Peer UK 1970), of Masham in N Riding, Co Yorkshire; Susan Lilian Primrose Cunliffe-Lister (Countess of Swinton); DL (N Yorkshire 1991); da of Maj Sir Ronald Norman Sinclair, 8 Bt, and Reba Inglis, later Mrs R H Hildreth (d 1985); *b* 14 April 1935; *Educ* Heathfield Ascot, London Poly; *m* 8 Dec 1959, 2 Earl of Swinton, *qv* (works under title Baroness Masham of Ilton); 1 s, 1 da (both adopted); *Career* sits as Independent peer in House of Lords; pres N Yorks Red Cross 1963, patron 1989; pres Yorks Assoc for Disabled; memb Bd of Visitors for Wetherby Borstal 1963–94 (now Young Offenders Inst); pres Spinal Injuries Assoc, late memb Peterlee and Newton Aycliffe Corpn; vice pres: Coll of Occupational Therapists Action for Dysphasic, Hosp Saving Assoc; patron: Disablement Income Group, Adults (DIA), Int Spinal Res Tst; pres: The Psoriasis Assoc, The Registration Cncl of Scientists in Health Care, Countrywide Workshops Charitable Tst, League of Friends of Harrogate Hospitals, Inst of Welfare Offrs; memb: Parly All Pty Disablement Gp Drug Misuse Ctee (vice chm), Parly Gps on Children, Alcohol Misuse, Breast Cancer, Food and Health, Skin and Epilepsy, Penal Affairs Gp; vice chm Parly AIDS Ctee; memb cncl Winston Churchill Tst; memb/govr Ditchley Fndn; dir Assoc for Prevention of Addiction; patron Yorks Faculty of GPs; vice-pres and patron of numerous other organisations; memb: Yorks RHA 1982–90, Family Health Services Authy N Yorks 1990–96, Gen Advsy Cncl of BBC until 1991; chm: Home Office Ctee on Young People, Alcohol and Crime, Cncl London Lighthouse; patron Phoenix House (Drug Rehabilitation Centres); Freeman Borough of Harrogate 1989; Hon MA: York 1985, Open Univ 1985; Hon LLD: Leeds 1988, Teesside 1993; Hon DSc Ulster 1990, Hon DLitt Keele 1993; hon fell: Royal Coll of GPs 1981, Bradford & Ilkley Community Coll 1988; *Recreations* swimming, breeding Highland ponies, gardening; *Style*— Baroness Masham of Ilton, DL; ✉ Dykes Hill House, Masham, Ripon, Yorks HG4 4NS (☎ 01765 689241); 46 Westminster Gardens, Marsham Street, London SW1P 4JG (☎ 0171 834 0700)

MASKALL, Michael Edwin; s of Leslie George Maskall (d 1968), and Alice Rose, *née* Hare (d 1984); *b* 26 Oct 1938; *Educ* Brentwood Public Sch; *m* (m dis 1987); 2 s (Andrew James b 6 March 1963, Jake Alexander b 17 April 1971), 2 da (Louise Claire b 6 March 1963, Michelle Amanda b 30 Sept 1965); *Career* CA 1961; Price Waterhouse: ptnr 1976–, ptnr i/c int tax and trade Price Waterhouse 1985–, currently dir business devpt Europe; FCA 1971; *Books* International Taxation Management And Strategy (1985), European Trends In Taxation Towards 1992 (1988); *Recreations* skiing, model making; *Clubs* Pickwick (Orsett, Essex); *Style*— Michael Maskall, Esq; ✉ Director of Business Development, Price Waterhouse Europe, No 1 London Bridge, London SE1 9QL (☎ 0171 939 5851, fax 0171 939 4660)

MASKELL, John Michael; s of Horace Maclean Maskell (d 1985), and Kathleen Muriel, *née* Hatton (d 1990); *b* 26 March 1942; *Educ* Winchester, Peterhouse Cambridge (MA, LLB); *m* 1, 6 Aug 1966 (m dis 1982), Elisabeth Joan (d 1986), da of Montagu Ralph Threlkeld Edwards (d 1983); 1 s (Paul Nicholas John b 18 Oct 1973), 1 da (Jane Elisabeth b 26 March 1971); m 2, 7 Jan 1992, Margaret Joy, da of Norman Leslie Upton (d 1982); *Career* admitted slr 1966; ptnr: Norton Rose 1971–93, Shaw and Croft 1993–95; marine arbitrator; chm London Arbitrators' Assoc Supporting Membs 1980–84, pres Aldgate Ward Club 1986–87, memb Marine Arbitrators' Assoc; *Recreations* bridge, war games, music; *Clubs* MCC; *Style*— John Maskell, Esq; ✉ Justice Wood, Wheelers Hill, Little Waltham, Chelmsford, Essex (☎ 01245 362456); c/o Mammoet Shipping BV, Third Floor, 5 St Helens Place, London EC3A 6AU (☎ 0171 588 9444, fax 0171 588 9458)

MASON, Air Vice-Marshal (Richard) Anthony (Tony); CB (1988), CBE (1982); s of William Mason (d 1971), and Maud, *née* Jenkinson (d 1978); *b* 22 Oct 1932; *Educ* Bradford GS, Univ of St Andrews (MA), Univ of London (MA); *m* 17 Nov 1956, Margaret Sneddon da of Alexander McNab Stewart, MBE, of Burntisland, Fife; 2 da (Alice Lindsay b 21 Sept 1957, Pamela Anne b 17 Aug 1959 d 1985); *Career* RAF: cmmnd 1956, USAF War Coll 1971, RAF Staff Coll 1972; dir: Defence Studies 1976–82, Personnel (Ground) 1982–84; Air Sec 1986–89 (dep 1985–86); Leverhulme Airpower res dir Fndn for Int Security 1989–94, memb Bd Brassey UK Ltd 1989–; Univ of Birmingham: visiting sr fell 1989–96, prof of aerospace policy 1996–; head SBAC Eurofighter Info Unit 1992–94; external doctoral examiner in Defence Studies 1986–: Univ of Oxford, Univ of Cambridge, Univ of London; visiting fell: Conflict Studies Centre RMA Sandhurst, Mosher Defence Inst Texas; memb Advsy Bd Smithsonian Inst Washington DC; pres Cheltenham Branch RAF ASSOC 1987; memb: IISS 1966, RUSI 1966; *Books* History of RAF Staff College (1972), Readings in Airpower (1978), Airpower in the Next Generation (1979), The Royal Air Force Today and Tomorrow (1982), Airpower in the Nuclear Age (1983/5), British Airpower in the 1980s (1984), War in the Third Dimension (1986), The Soviet Air Force (1986), Airpower: an Overview of Roles (1987), To Inherit the Skies (1990), Air Power: A Centennial Appraisal (1994); *Recreations* music, gardening; *Clubs* RAF; *Style*— Air Vice-Marshal Tony Mason, CB, CBE; ✉ c/o Lloyds Bank, Montpellier, Cheltenham, Glos GL50 1SH

MASON, Lt Col Colin Rees; TD (1982); s of Clifford Harold Mason (d 1970), and Ann, *née* Jones; *b* 19 Aug 1943; *Educ* Gwent Coll, St Julian's HS Newport, Univ of Wales Aberystwyth (BA), Harvard Graduate Sch of Business (OPM), Magdalene Coll Cambridge (MPhil); *m* 22 Aug 1968, (Grace) Angela, da of Ernest Alan St Helier Tweney (d 1979); 1 s (Richard Colin St Helier b 12 Oct 1970), 1 da (Penelope Jane St Helier b 19 March 1974); *Career* Lt-Col Royal Regt of Wales (TA), served Gulf War 1991, CO Pool of Public Info Offrs TA 1990–93; began bdcasting in USA while post grad researcher Rice Univ Texas in 1960s; formerly bdcaster with: Ulster TV, BBC Local Radio; PA and dir Natural History TV Unit BBC until 1974, prog dir Swansea Sound 1974–79, asst md Standard Broadcasting 1979; fndr md Chiltern Radio plc 1980–95, dep chm Choice FM Group 1995–; dir Network News (Radio) Ltd 1991–96; dir Milton Keynes Chamber of Commerce and Indust 1984–91; *Recreations* rowing, riding; *Clubs* Army and Navy, Reform; *Style*— Lt Col Colin Mason, TD; ✉ Hall End House, Hall End, nr Wootton, Bedfordshire MK43 9HJ (☎ and fax 01234 766123)

MASON, Prof Sir David Kean; kt (1992), CBE (1987); s of George Hunter Mason (d 1983), of Glasgow Rd, Paisley, and Margaret MacCulloch Kean (d 1975); *Educ* Paisley GS, Glasgow Acad, Univ of St Andrews (LDS, BDS), Univ of Glasgow (MB ChB, MD); *m* 3 June 1967, Judith Anne, da of John Campbell Armstrong (d 1979), of Belfast, NI; 2 s (Michael b 1971, Andrew b 1979), 1 da (Katie b 1974); *Career* hon conslt dental surgn Gtr Glasgow Health Bd 1965–92, prof of oral med Univ of Glasgow 1967–92 (dean of dental educn 1980–90); pres Gen Dental Cncl 1989–94; Hon DChD Univ of Wales 1991, Hon LLD Univ of Dundee 1993, Hon FFDRCSI 1988, Hon FDS RCPSGlas 1990, Hon FRCSEd 1995; *Recreations* golf, tennis, gardening, enjoying countryside pleasures; *Clubs* Royal and Ancient Golf (St Andrews), Royal Scottish Automobile, Kilmacolm Golf, Elie Golf House; *Style*— Prof Sir David Mason, CBE; ✉ Greystones, Houston Road, Kilmacolm, Renfrewshire, PA13 (☎ 0150 587 2001); Glasgow Dental Hospital and School NHS Trust, 378 Sauchiehall Street, Glasgow G2 3JZ (☎ 0141 211 9724)

MASON, David Peter; s of Michael Henry Mason (d 1982), and Dorothy Margaret, *née* Sturdee; *b* 13 Aug 1951; *Educ* Eton; *m* 1980, Monique Agnès, *née* Juranville; 3 da (Natalie b 1981, Catherine b 1984, Chantal b 1989), 1 s (Michael b 1991); *Career* offr 1 Bn Welsh Guards 1970–78, seconded to Desert Regt Sultan of Oman's Armed Forces 1974–76 (Sultan's Bravery Medal 1975), Transglobe expedition 1979–82, High Sheriff for Co of Oxfordshire 1994–95; *Books* Shadow Over Babylon (1993), Little Brother (1996); *Recreations* travel, shooting, skiing; *Clubs* Beefsteak, Turf, Shikar; *Style*— David Mason, Esq

MASON, Debbie; da of Maurice Bayliss, of Paris and Cap Martin, and Jane, *née* Mitchelmore (d 1984); *b* 9 Jan 1962; *Educ* St George's Sch Ascot Berks; *Career* formerly freelance prodr; credits incl: Memory Palace (film-based multimedia event for Spanish Expo '92), Horse Opera (TV opera set in Wild West, composed by Stewart Copeland), Silent Night (one-off drama for Channel 4, written by Steve Berkoff), Red Hot and Blue (90 minute music special to raise awareness and money for AIDS), Wired (20 hours of music programming for Channel 4, Granada International and Showtime in USA), co-deviser Win A Wedding (game show bought by Scandinavia and Greece and currently being piloted by HBO Independent Productions in US); currently md Kudos Productions; memb: Seminar Ctee Women in Film and TV, Advsy Ctee Edinburgh Int TV Festival; *Recreations* football and clubbing; *Clubs* Soho House, Union; *Style*— Ms Debbie Mason; ✉ Kudos Productions Ltd, 12–14 Argyll Street, London W1V 1AB (☎ 0171 287 0097, fax 0171 734 9204, mobile 0802 321688, e-mail Lady@ Kudospd.demon.co.uk)

MASON, Derek S; CBE (1986), JP (1977); *b* 1934, Dennistoun, Glasgow; *Educ* Allan Glen's Sch, Royal Tech Coll (pt/t); *m* 3 July 1958, Jeanette (Jean) Miller, da of Samuel Whitehill; 2 s (Douglas b 4 Sept 1959, Andrew b 30 April 1966), 1 da (Hilary b 29 May 1962); *Career* Nat Serv RAF 1952–54; qualified quantity surveyor; sr ptnr John Baxter Dunn and Gray (joined 1952); chm: Scottish Jr Branch RICS 1966–67, Scottish Branch Faculty of Bldg 1995–; dir SCOTVEC 1993–, chm W Glasgow Hosps Univ NHS Tst 1996–; cnclr (Cons): Glasgow Corp 1970 and 1972–75, Glasgow Dist Cncl 1974–84; memb Cncl of Mgmnt Scottish Special Housing Assoc 1979–89 (dep chm 1980–81, chm 1981–89), govr Hutchesons' Educnl Tst 1972– (vice chm 1987–), memb Glasgow Shawlands Rotary Club, elder and mangr Newlands S Parish Church; FRICS 1970 (ARICS 1960), FFB 1987; *Recreations* watching football, reading, politics and current affairs; *Style*— Derek S Mason, Esq, CBE, JP; ✉ 77 Newlands Road, Glasgow G43 2JP (☎ 0141 649 2665); West Glasgow Hospitals University NHS Trust, Administration Building, Western Infirmary, Dumbarton Road, Glasgow G11 6NT (☎ 0141 211 2907, fax 0141 211 1920)

MASON, Donald David; s of Robert Mason, of Upton Wirral, and Mary, *née* Davies; *b* 25 June 1938; *Educ* Ruthin Sch N Wales, Fitzwilliam House Cambridge (MA, LLM); *m* 28 Sept 1963, Joyce, da of George Henry Griffiths; 1 s (Ian Stuart b 1 July 1970), 1 da (Susan Caroline b 22 Jan 1966); *Career* Batesons & Co Liverpool (merged with Alsop Stevens 1967, now Alsop Wilkinson): articled clerk 1960–63, asst slr 1963–67, ptnr 1967–; chm Liverpool Sch of Tropical Med 1987–93; memb: Law Soc 1963, Liverpool Law Soc 1963, Soc of Trust and Estate Practitioners; *Recreations* reading, music, rugby league (listening and watching); *Clubs* Artists (Liverpool); *Style*— Donald Mason, Esq; ✉ Alsop Wilkinson, India Buildings, Liverpool L2 0NH (☎ 0151 227 3060, fax 0151 236 9208)

MASON, Sir Frederick Cecil; KCVO (1968), CMG (1960); s of Ernest Mason (d 1966), and Sophia Charlotte, *née* Dodson (d 1953); *b* 15 May 1913; *Educ* City of London Sch, St Catharine's Coll Cambridge (BA); *m* 1941, Karen, da of Christian Rorholm (d 1968), of Denmark; 2 s, 1 da (and 2 da decd); *Career* entered Consular Serv 1935; serv: Antwerp, Paris, Belgian Congo, Faroes, Panama, Chile, Oslo, FO, Bonn, Athens, Tehran; head Econ Rels Dept FO 1960–64, under sec Miny of Overseas Devpt and Cwlth Rels Office 1965–66; ambass: Chile 1966–70, to UN Geneva 1971–73, ret; dir New Ct Natural Resources 1973–83, UK memb Int Narcotics Control Bd 1974–77, chm Anglo-Chilean Soc in London 1979–83; *Recreations* ball games, walking, bird watching, painting; *Clubs* Canning; *Style*— Sir Frederick Mason, KCVO, CMG; ✉ The Forge, Church St, Ropley, Hants SO24 0DS (☎ 01962 772285)

MASON, Gary; s of Wylie Mason, of NY, USA, and Lillian, *née* Read; *b* 15 Dec 1962; *Educ* St Joseph's Sch, St Thomas Moore Sch, Cardinal Manning Sch; *Career* former professional boxer; formerly memb Wandsworth Amateur Boxing Club; professional debut v Al Malcolm 1984 (1st round win), winner Br Heavyweight Title v Hughroy Currie 1989, successful defence v Jess Harding 1989, 35 consecutive wins (longest unbeaten record of any British heavyweight) until defeated by Lennox Lewis 1991, retired due to eye injury 1991; granted manager's licence Br Boxing Bd of Control 1991, occasional boxing commentator for BBC and Sky TV; rugby league player London Crusaders 1992, fndr World Armwrestling Consortium 1992; proprietor jewellery and sports retailing outlets; *Recreations* cricket, soccer, baseball; *Style*— Gary Mason, Esq

MASON, Brig Harvey Christopher; *b* 22 Dec 1932; *Educ* Rothesay Acad, Univ of Glasgow (MB ChB), London (DTM & H); *m* 27 Dec 1957, Rosemary Elizabeth, *née* Fisher; 2 s (Christopher b 27 Feb 1960, Jon b 8 July 1962), 1 da (Ailie b 5 June 1965); *Career* serv in Korea, W Germany Cyprus; cmd advsr in GP BAOR 1977–80 and 1985–87, dir of Army GP 1988–91; Hon Surgn to HM the Queen 1989; memb BMA; Montefiore medal 1971; OStJ 1987; FMS London, FRCGP (1977, MRCGP 1972); *Recreations* food, wine, opera, reading, cats; *Style*— Brig Harvey Mason; ✉ Mytilus House, 75 Brown St, Salisbury, Wilts SP1 2BA (☎ 01722 337705)

MASON, Prof Haydn Trevor; s of Herbert Thomas Mason (d 1973), of New Hedges, nr Tenby, Dyfed, and Margaret Ellen, *née* Jones (d 1973); *b* 12 Jan 1929; *Educ* Greenhill GS Tenby, Univ Coll of Wales Aberystwyth (BA), Middlebury Coll Vermont USA (AM

1951), Jesus Coll Oxford (DPhil); *m* 1, 5 Feb 1955 (m dis 1982), Gretchen; 1 s (David b 24 March 1961), 1 da (Gwyneth b 8 April 1964); m 2, 14 Sept 1982, Adrienne Mary, da of Alfred Barnes, of Sutton Coldfield; 1 step da (Kate b 26 Nov 1968); *Career* Nat Serv 1951–53, 2 Lt RASC 1952; instr in French Princeton Univ USA 1954–57, lectr Univ of Newcastle 1960–63, reader Univ of Reading 1965–67 (lectr 1964–65), prof Univ of E Anglia 1967–79, prof Université de Paris-III (Sorbonne Nouvelle) 1979–81, prof Univ of Bristol 1981–94, emeritus prof 1994–; pres: Assoc of Univ Profs of French 1981–82, Soc of French Studies 1982–84, Br Soc for Eighteenth Century Studies 1984–86, Int Soc for Eighteenth Century Studies 1991–95; dir Voltaire Fndn Univ of Oxford 1977– (chm 1989–93); chm Clifton and Hotwells Improvement Soc 1994–; Officier dans L'Ordre des Palmes Académiques 1985, Médaille d'Argent de la Ville de Paris 1989; *Books* Pierre Bayle and Voltaire (1963), Voltaire (1975), Voltaire: A Biography (1981), French Writers and their Society 1715–1800 (1982), Cyrano de Bergerac: L'Autre Monde (1984), Voltaire: Candide (1992); ed: Marivaux: Les Fausses Confidences (1964), Voltaire: Zadig and Other Tales (1971), Essays Presented in Honour of W H Barber (with R J Howells, A Mason and D Williams, 1985), Myth and its Making in the French Theatre: Studies Presented to W D Howarth (with E Freeman, M O'Regan and S W Taylor, 1988), The Impact of the French Revolution on European Consciousness (with W Doyle, 1989), Voltaire: Candide (1995); *Recreations* walking, crosswords, gardening; *Style*— Prof Haydn Mason; ✉ 11 Goldney Avenue, Bristol BS8 4RA (☎ 0117 973 5767)

MASON, Sir (Basil) John; kt (1979), CB (1973); s of John Robert Mason (d 1937); *b* 18 Aug 1923; *Educ* Fakenham GS, Univ Coll Nottingham (BSc, DSc); *m* 1948, Doreen Sheila Jones; 2 s (Barry b 1955, Nigel b 1962); *Career* served WWII, Flt Lt RAF; prof of cloud physics Imperial Coll London 1961–65, dir gen Meteorological Office 1965–83; perm rep of the UK at the World Meteorological Orgn 1965–83 (memb Exec Ctee 1966–75 and 1977–83), treas and sr vice pres The Royal Soc 1976–86, pro chllr Univ of Surrey 1980–85, dir UK/Scandinavian Acid Rain Prog 1983–90, sr advsr Centre for Environmental Technology Imperial Coll London 1991–; pres: Royal Meteorological Soc 1968–70, Inst of Physics 1976–78, Br Assoc 1982–83, Nat Soc for Clean Air and Environmental Protection 1989–91, Assoc for Sci Educn 1992–93; UMIST: pres 1986–94, chllr 1994–; memb Advsy Bd Res Cncls 1983–86, chm Coordinating Ctee for Marine Sci and Technol 1987–91; FRS (1965); *Recreations* music, walking, foreign travel; *Style*— Sir John Mason, CB, FRS; ✉ 64 Christchurch Rd, East Sheen, London SW14 7AW (☎ 0181 876 2557)

MASON, Sir John Charles Moir; KCMG (1980, CMG 1976); o s of Charles Moir Mason, CBE (d 1967), and Madeline Mason; *b* 13 May 1927; *Educ* Manchester GS, Peterhouse Cambridge (MA); *m* 1954, Margaret Newton, da of Noel David Vidgen (d 1971); 1 s, 1 da; *Career* Lt XX Lancashire Fusiliers 1946–48, Capt Royal Ulster Rifles Korea 1950–51; joined HM Foreign Serv 1952, third sec FO 1952–54, sec & private sec to Ambass Br Embassy Rome 1954–56; second sec: Warsaw 1956–59, FO 1959–61; first sec (commercial Damascus 1961–65), first sec & asst head of dept FO 1965–68, dir of trade devpt and dep consul-gen New York 1968–71, head Euro Integration Dept FCO 1971–72, seconded as under sec ECGD 1972–75, asst under sec state (econ) FCO 1975–76, ambass to Israel 1976–80, Br high cmmr to Australia 1980–84; chm: Lloyds Bank NZA Sydney 1985–90, Thorn EMI (Australia) 1985–94, VSEL (Australia) 1985–92, Spencer Stuart Bd of Advice Sydney 1985–96, Prudential Corporation Australia 1987–92, Prudential Finance 1987–90, Prudential Funds Management 1987–92, Lloyds International 1985–90, Multicon 1987–91, North Shore Heart Research Fndn 1987–92, Pirelli Cables Australia 1993– (dir 1987–); dir: Wellcome Australia 1985–90, Fluor Daniel (Australia) 1985–93, Churchill Meml Tst 1985– (dep chm 1995–), Nat Bank of New Zealand 1985–90, Cancer Cncl of NSW 1993–, Duke of Edinburgh Award 1996–; public memb: Australian Press Cncl 1992–, Professional Conduct Ctee Bar Cncl of NSW 1992–, Law Soc of NSW 1993–; *Clubs* Union (Sydney); *Style*— Sir John Mason, KCMG; ✉ 147 Dover Rd, Dover Heights, NSW 2030, Australia (☎ and fax 00 612 9371 7863)

MASON, John Muir; MBE (1987); s of James William Mason, Sheriff Clerk, of Wigtown (d 1962), and Tomima Watt, *née* Muir (d 1972); *b* 21 Jan 1940; *Educ* Kirkwall GS, Orkney, Douglas Ewart HS Newton Stewart, Univ of Edinburgh (BL); *m* 25 Jan 1967, Jessica Hilary Miller, da of John Groat (d 1981) of Stronsay, Orkney Islands; 1 s (James Muir Angel b 1969), 2 step s (Peter John Chalmers b 1960, Rognvald Inkster Chalmers b 1963); *Career* slr; sr ptnr Waddell & Mackintosh Slrs Troon, md J D C Pubns Ltd, dir private cos; princ conductor and musical dir The Strings of Scotland and The Scottish Fiddle Orchestra; chm The Rev James Currie Memorial Tst, life govr Imp Cancer Res Fund, tstee Niel Gow Memorial Tst; deacon Incorporation of Skinners and Glovers Trades House of Glasgow; *Recreations* music, history; *Style*— John Mason, Esq, MBE; ✉ 27 Victoria Dr, Troon, Ayrshire (☎ 01292 312796); 36 West Portland St, Troon, Ayrshire (☎ 01292 312222)

MASON, Keith Edward; s of Arthur Ernest Mason (d 1982), and Nellie Louise, *née* Hawkes; *b* 3 May 1943; *Educ* Westminster GS; *m* 11 Feb 1964 (m dis 1988) Jacqueline Claire, da of Robert W Mitcham; 3 s (Sean b 9 March 1965, Nicholas b 11 Feb 1967, Stuart b 24 March 1974), 1 da (Jacqueline b 22 Aug 1968); *Career* asst mangr admin Bank of London and S America 1971–72, head of data processing Lloyds and Bolsa Int 1972–73; C Hoare & Co: head of data processing 1974–77, head of accounts 1977–83, mangr admin 1983–87, gen mangr 1987–; *Recreations* rowing, reading, music; *Clubs* London Rowing, Leander; *Style*— Keith Mason, Esq; ✉ 119 Kenilworth Court, Lower Richmond Rd, Putney, London SW15 1HA (☎ 0171 788 3434), C Hoare & Co, 37 Fleet St, London EC4P 4DQ (☎ 0181 353 4522, fax 0181 353 4521, telex 24622)

MASON, Prof (John) Kenyon French; CBE (1973); s of Air Cdre John Melbourne Mason, CBE, DSC, DFC (d 1955), and Alma Ada Mary, *née* French (d 1983); *b* 19 Dec 1919; *Educ* Downside, Univ of Cambridge (MA, MD), Univ of Edinburgh (LLD); *m* 14 Jan 1943, Elizabeth Hope (d 1977), da of Trevor Latham (d 1960); 2 s (Ian b 1944, Paul b 1947); *Career* RAF: Sqdn MO 1943–47, pathologist trg 1948, conslt in pathology and offr i/c Dept of Aviation and Forensic Pathology RAF Inst of Pathology 1955–73, ret Gp Capt 1973; Univ of Edinburgh: regius prof of forensic med 1973–85, hon fell Faculty of Law 1985–; pres Br Assoc in Forensic Med 1982–84; King Haakon VII Freedom Medal (Norway) 1945; FRCPath, FRSE; *Books* Human Life and Medical Practice (1988), The Courts and the Doctor (co-author, 1990), Forensic Medicine, An Illustrated Reference (1993), Law and Medical Ethics (co-author, 4 edn 1994), Forensic Medicine for Lawyers (3 edn 1995), Medico-legal Aspects of Reproduction and Parenthood (2 edn 1997), The Pathology of Trauma (ed, 3 edn 1997); *Clubs* RAF; *Style*— Prof Kenyon Mason, CBE, FRSE; ✉ 66 Craiglea Drive, Edinburgh EH10 5PF (☎ and fax 0131 447 2301); Faculty of Law, Old College, South Bridge, Edinburgh EH8 9YL (☎ 0131 650 2051, fax 0131 662 4902)

MASON, Michael Aidan; s of Kenneth Albert Mason, of Emsworth, Hants, and Marjorie Evelyn, *née* Edwards; *b* 5 March 1947; *Educ* Lancing, St Edmund Hall Oxford (MA); *Career* news ed Gay News 1972–81, presenter Bookshelf (LBC Radio) 1975–76, dir Kenneth Mason Publications 1976–, co-fndr and ed Capital Gay 1981–; Freeman Worshipful Co of Skinners; *Books* Dinghy Sailing (1966); *Style*— Michael Mason, Esq; ✉ Stonewall Press Ltd, 1 Tavistock Chambers, Bloomsbury Way, London WC1A 2SE (☎ 0171 242 2750); Kenneth Mason Publications, Dudley House, North St, Emsworth, Hants

MASON, Michael Hugh; *b* 1 April 1934; *Educ* Wrekin Coll; *m* 5 Feb 1959, Barbara Anne, da of John Birtles; 2 s (1 decd), 2 da; *Career* joined T B Cooke & Co stockbrokers 1955, memb Stock Exchange 1958, ptnr Charles W Jones & Co stockbrokers 1959–75, ptnr Tilney & Co (following merger with Charles W Jones) 1975, sr ptnr Tilney & Co 1984–86, chm Charterhouse Tilney 1986–96, dir Charterhouse plc 1986–93; memb Cncl Int Stock Exchange 1982–86; *Recreations* skiing, motor cruising, golf; *Clubs* Formby Golf, Huntercombe Golf, Royal Thames Yacht; *Style*— Michael Mason, Esq

MASON, Monica Margaret; da of Richard Mason, and Mrs E Fabian; *b* 6 Sept 1941; *Educ* Johannesburg, Royal Ballet Sch; *m* 1968, Austin Bennet; *Career* Royal Ballet Co: joined 1958, princ dancer 1968, asst to Sir Kenneth Macmillan 1980, asst to princ choreographer 1980–84, princ repetiteur 1985, asst to dir 1988–, asst dir 1991–; Hon Doctorate Univ of Surrey 1996; *Style*— Miss Monica Mason

MASON, Patrick Damian Stuart; s of Dr Adair Stuart Mason, of Havering, and Rosemary Ann, *née* Kelly; *b* 16 April 1951; *Educ* St Augustine's Ramsgate, Downside, Central Sch of Speech and Drama (Dip); *Career* theatre director; asst dir Abbey Theatre Dublin 1972–73, lectr in performance studies Univ of Manchester 1974–77 (drama fell 1973–74), res dir Abbey Theatre Dublin 1977–80, assoc artist Gate Theatre Dublin 1986–; currently artistic dir Abbey Theatre Dublin and freelance theatre dir Ireland, UK and USA; freelance opera dir: Wexford Festival Opera, Opera North, Israeli Opera, Welsh Nat Opera, English Nat Opera; awards: Best Director Harvey's Irish Theatre Awards (3 times), Sunday Tribune Arts Award, Sunday Independent Arts Award, nominated Best Director Olivier Awards, Best Director Tony Awards, Drama Desk and Outer Circle Awards NY; memb: Irish Actors Equity, Soc of Stage Directors and Choreographers NY; *Publications* The Way to Keep Him (by Arthur Murphy, ed); *Recreations* piano, hill walking; *Style*— Patrick Mason, Esq

MASON, His Hon (George Frederick) Peter; QC (1963); s of George Samuel Mason (d 1966), of Keighley, and Florence May Mason (d 1965); *b* 11 Dec 1921; *Educ* Lancaster Royal GS, St Catharine's Coll Cambridge (BA, MA); *m* 1, 30 Dec 1950 (m dis 1977), Faith Maud, *née* Bacon; 2 s (Jonathan b 18 Nov 1952, Michael b 1 April 1962), 3 da (Pippa b 25 July 1951, Melodie b and d 1957, Alison b 17 Oct 1960); m 2, 6 March 1981, Sara Lilian, da of Sir Robert Ricketts, 7 Bt, *qv*, of Minchinhampton, Glos; *Career* WWII cmmnd 78 Medium Regt RA (Duke of Lancaster's Own Yeomanry), Staff Capt RA 13 Corps ME and Italy; barr 1947, dep chm Agric Land Tbnl W Yorks and Lancs 1962, dep chm West Riding Qtr Sessions 1965; recorder of York 1965, circuit judge 1970–87, sr judge Snaresbrook Crown Ct 1974–81, judge Central Criminal Ct 1982, sr judge Inner London Crown Ct 1983–87; lay memb Cncl Assoc of Futures Brokers and Dealers 1987–91, ind memb Bd of Securities and Futures Authy 1991–93, lay dir Int Petroleum Exchange 1993–; Freeman City of London 1977, Liveryman Worshipful Co of Wax Chandlers 1981; FCIArb 1986; *Recreations* walking, cycling, carpentry, music; *Clubs* Athenaeum, Hawks' (Cambridge); *Style*— His Hon Peter Mason, QC; ✉ Lane Cottage, Amberley, Glos GL5 5AB (☎ 01453 872412, fax 01453 878557); 11 King's Bench Walk, Temple, London EC4 (☎ 0171 353 3337, fax 0171 583 2190)

MASON, Richard Graham; s of Arthur Ernest Mason (d 1988), and Catherine Mary, *née* Boakes (d 1964); *b* 21 June 1944; *Educ* Wilson's GS Camberwell London; *m* 2 Sept 1967, Lynda Miriam Mary, da of Frederick William Tothill (d 1983); 1 s (Andrew Philip b 1970), 1 da (Karen Elizabeth b 1973); *Career* Bank of England: Exchange Control Dept 1965–79, sec City EEC Ctee 1980–84, sec City Capital Markets Ctee 1980–84, sec City Taxation Ctee 1980–82; dir of UK Operations British Invisibles (formerly British Invisible Exports Cncl) 1992–93 (exec dir 1984–91, sec and treas 1982–84); treas: Chertsey PCC 1969–82 and 1987–89, Chertsey Jt Church Cncl 1980–87, Runnymede Deanery Synod 1989–, Bread Street Ward Club 1989– (chm 1991–92), Runnymede District Scout Cncl 1994–; memb: CBI Export Promotion Ctee 1984–89, London C of C International Ctee 1984–93, Br Tourist Authy Devpt Ctee 1984–93, Guildford Diocesan Bd of Fin 1989–95, Governing Body United Wards' Club of the City of London 1991–96; advsr publicity and mktg Chertsey Museum 1995–, advsr press rels Surrey Museums Consultative Ctee 1996–; Freeman City of London 1992; ACIB 1966, MIEx 1987; *Recreations* walking; *Clubs* Bankers; *Style*— R G Mason, Esq; ✉ Betoncroft, 21a Abbey Rd, Chertsey, Surrey KT16 8AL (☎ 01932 564773)

MASON, The Rev Canon Richard John; s of Vice Adm Sir Frank Trowbridge Mason, KCB (d 1988), of Hurstpierpoint, W Sussex, and Dora Margaret, *née* Brand (d 1993); *b* 26 April 1929; *Educ* Shrewsbury; *Career* clerk in Holy Orders, asst curate Bishop's Hatfield Herts 1958–64, domestic chaplain to the Bishop of London 1964–69, vicar of Riverhead Kent 1969–73, vicar of Edenbridge Kent 1973–83, archdeacon of Tonbridge 1977–95, min of St Luke Sevenoaks 1983–95, ret; *Recreations* watching cricket; *Style*— The Rev Canon Richard Mason; ✉ 61 Nelson Road, Ipswich, Suffolk IP4 4DU (☎ 01473 726350)

MASON, Prof Roger Maxwell; *b* 24 Oct 1940; *Educ* Welsh Nat Sch of Med Univ Coll Cardiff (MB BCh, PhD), MD (London) 1983; *m*; *Career* house physician Professorial Med Unit Cardiff Royal Infirmary 1965–66, house surgn St David's Hosp Cardiff 1966, MRC jr research fell Biochemistry Dept UC Cardiff 1966–69, lectr in biochemistry Univ of Nottingham Med Sch 1969–73, visiting scientist Nat Inst of Health Bethesda USA 1978–79, sr lectr in biochemistry Charing Cross Hosp Med Sch 1973–83; Charing Cross and Westminster Med Sch: reader in biochemistry 1983–88, prof of biochemistry 1988–, head Dept of Biochemistry 1992– (acting head 1983–84); visiting prof Dogliotti Coll of Med Univ of Liberia W Africa (sponsored by Inter-Univ Cncl) 1977, guest worker Dept of Biochemistry Monash Univ Melbourne Aust (Wellcome-Ramaciotti research travel grant) 1981; author of numerous scientific pubns on connective tissues and their diseases; Lettsomian lectr Med Soc of London 1995; memb: Br Connective Tissue Soc (chm 1992–96), Biochemical Soc, Research Defence Soc; FRSA, fell Med Soc of London; *Style*— Prof Roger Mason; ✉ Department of Biochemistry, Charing Cross and Westminster Medical School, Fulham Palace Road, London W6 8RF (☎ 0181 846 7047, fax 0181 846 7099, e-mail r.mason@cxwms.ac.uk)

MASON, Prof Sir Ronald; KCB (1980); s of David John Mason (d 1950) and Olwen, *née* James (d 1992); *b* 22 July 1930; *Educ* Quakers Yard, Univ of Wales (BSc), Univ of London (PhD, DSc); *m* 1, 1952, Pauline Pattinson; 1 s (decd), 3 da; m 2, 1979, Elizabeth Rosemary, da of Maj Theodore Walpole Grey-Edwards (d 1993); *Career* prof of inorganic chemistry Univ of Sheffield 1963–71, prof of chemistry Univ of Sussex 1971–86 (pro vice chllr 1977–78); chief sci advsr MOD 1977–83, UK rep on UN Bd on Disarmament Matters 1984–92; memb: Advsy Bd Res Cncl 1977–83, SRC 1971–75; visiting prof of int rels UCW 1985–93, many visiting professorships in USA, Canada, France, Israel, NZ and Aust; chm Hunting Engineering Ltd 1987–88 (dep chm 1985–87), dir Thom UK Holdings 1987–90; pres BHRA 1987–94; chm: BHR Group 1989–95, Br Ceramic Res Ltd 1990–96 (dir 1988), Eng Tech Ctee DTI 1990–93, UCL Hosps 1992–, Science Applications Int (UK) Ltd 1993–96; Hon Ancien NATO Def Coll 1991; DSc (hc) Univ of Wales 1987, DSc (hc) Univ of Keele 1993; fell: Univ of Wales Cardiff 1981, UCL 1995; hon fell: Polys of Wales 1988, IMechE 1996; CChem, FRS, FIM (pres 1995–96), FRSC; *Recreations* cooking and stirring; *Clubs* Athenaeum; *Style*— Prof Sir Ronald Mason, KCB, FRS; ✉ Chestnuts Farm, Weedon, Bucks HP22 4NH; British Ceramics Research Ltd, Penkhull, Stoke-on-Trent, Staffs (☎ 01782 45431); UCL Hosps, St Martin's House, 140 Tottenham Court Road, London (☎ 0171 380 9634)

MASON, Prof (John) Stanley; s of George Mason, of Wigan, and late Grace, *née* Vaughan; *b* 30 Jan 1934; *Educ* Wigan GS, Univ of Nottingham (BSc), CNAA (PhD); *m* 3 July 1957, Florence, da of Thomas Carter; 2 s (David John b 23 Sept 1963, Andrew George b 2 Aug 1965); *Career* grad employee National Coal Bd 1958–60 (apprentice then underground employee 1950–54), mathematics master Leeds GS 1960–63; Lt RN 1963–66 (served on HMS Corunna and RNC Manadon); maths master Bolton Sch 1966–67, sr lectr in engrg Liverpool Poly 1967–68, sr res fell Univ of Nottingham 1968–69, princ lectr and head Div of Thermodynamics/Fluid Mechanics Liverpool Poly 1969–73, head Dept of Engrg then dean Faculty of Technol Thames Poly 1973–87, depute dir Glasgow Coll of Technol 1987–88, princ and vice-chllr Glasgow Caledonian Univ 1992– (princ Glasgow Poly 1988–92); memb Res Ctee and Ctee for Science Technol CNAA 1973–83, chm Engrg Bd CNAA 1979–83 (memb 1973–83), memb LINK Steering Gp 1990–, memb Cncl SERC 1990–; awarded Silver Plate by USA Powdershow Int for servs to bulk solids handling technol res and educn 1985, awarded Bulk Solids Handling Shield UK IMechE 1987; MIMinE 1958, CEng, FIMechE 1974, FIMarE 1974; *Recreations* travel, sport, meeting people, conversation; *Style*— Prof Stanley Mason; ✉ Glasgow Caledonian University, Cowcaddens Road, Glasgow G4 0BA (☎ 0141 331 3113, fax 0141 331 3008)

MASON, (James) Stephen; CB (1988); s of Albert Wesley Mason (d 1966), and Mabel, *née* Topham (d 1979); *b* 6 Feb 1935; *Educ* Windsor County GS, Brasenose Coll Oxford (MA, BCL); *m* 1961, Tania Jane, da of Edward Warner Moeran; 2 da (Jane Emma b 24 April 1962, Sarah Pymonie b 30 May 1963), 1 s (Nicholas Adam b 23 Aug 1966); *Career* called to the Bar Middle Temple 1953, barr 1961–67; Office of the Parliamentary Counsel: sr asst 1973–75, dep parly counsel 1975–80, parly counsel 1980–94, counsel to the Speaker 1994–; *Recreations* reading, walking, playing the piano; *Style*— Stephen Mason, Esq, CB; ✉ House of Commons, London SW1A 0AA (☎ 0171 219 3776)

MASON, Stephen Maxwell; s of Harold Geoffrey Mason (d 1986), and Ursula, *née* Habermann; *b* 19 May 1949; *Educ* Bradford GS, Gonville and Caius Coll Cambridge (MA); *m* 26 March 1976, Judith Mary, da of Hebbert, of Ilkley; 2 da (Fiona b 1979, Nicola b 1985), 1 s (Alistair b 1981); *Career* slr; ptnr Mason Bond, Leeds, ed Travel Law Jl; author of numerous articles on package holiday law including Don't Shoot the Tour Operator (1983), Holiday Damages - The Gravy Train Slows Down (1987), Holiday Law (jtly, 1995); *Recreations* writing, travel by train; *Clubs* Law Soc; *Style*— Stephen Mason, Esq; ✉ King Charles House, Leeds LS1 6LA (☎ 0113 242 4444, fax 0113 246 7542)

MASON, Terence Harold (Terry); s of Harold Henry Mason, of Walsall, W Mids, and Winifred May, *née* Sadler; *b* 7 July 1941; *Educ* Queen Mary's GS Walsall; *m* 25 Sept 1971, Beryl, da of Albert Ernest Hughes, of Claverley, Shrops; *Career* articled clerk Herbert Pepper & Rudland Chartered Accountants Walsall 1957–64, audit mangr Peat Marwick Mitchell CAs Birmingham 1964–66, gp fin dir Tarmac Plc Wolverhampton 1986–97 (other fin posts 1966–86), ret; FCA 1964; *Recreations* golf, theatre; *Style*— Terry Mason, Esq; ✉ Stratton Ct, Long Common, Claverley, Shropshire; Tarmac plc, Hilton Hall, Essington, Wolverhampton WV11 2BQ (☎ 01902 307 407, fax 01902 307 408, telex 338544)

MASON, Timothy Ian Godson; s of Ian Godson Mason (d 1992), and Muriel Marjorie Berkeley, *née* Vaile, of Alverstoke, Hants; *b* 11 March 1945; *Educ* St Alban's Sch Washington DC USA, Bradfield Coll Berks, ChCh Oxford (BA, MA); *m* 1975, Marilyn Ailsa, da of Frederic George Williams (d 1969), of Wellington, NZ; 1 da (Grace b 1979), 1 s (Giles b 1982); *Career* asst admin Oxford Playhouse 1966–67, asst to Peter Daubeny World Theatre Season London 1967–69; admin: Ballet Rambert 1970–75, Royal Exchange Theatre Manchester 1975–77; dir: Western Aust Arts Cncl 1977–80, Scottish Arts Cncl 1980–90; conslt to Arts Cncl and Office of Arts and Libraries 1990–91, chief exec London Arts Bd 1991–95, dir Museums & Galleries Cmmn 1995–; memb BBC Gen Advsy Cncl 1990–; *Recreations* arts, family; *Style*— Timothy Mason, Esq; ✉ 30 Chatsworth Way, London SE27 9HN; Museums & Galleries Commission, 16 Queen Anne's Gate, London SW1H 9AA (☎ 0171 233 4200, fax 0171 233 3686)

MASON, Timothy John Rollit (Tim); s of late John Milton Rollit Mason, and late Ailsa Mary, *née* Garland; *b* 23 July 1957; *Educ* Stowe, Univ of Warwick (BA); *m* Laura Gillian; 3 da, 1 s; *Career* successively trainee Walls Meat Co, asst product mangr then product mangr Unilever 1979–82; Tesco Stores Ltd: joined 1982, successively product mangr, mktg mangr, controller product mktg, assoc dir (devpt and mgmnt Healthy Eating prog), trading dir, regnl md 1990–93, mktg ops dir Tesco Stores Ltd 1993–95, Main Bd mktg dir Tesco plc 1995–; *Recreations* golf, tennis; *Style*— Tim Mason, Esq; ✉ Tesco plc, Tesco House, Delamare Road, Cheshunt, Herts EN8 9SL (direct ☎ 01992 644117, direct fax 01992 644752)

MASON, Tony; s of George Donald (d 1982), and Hattie, *née* Mockett (d 1986); *Educ* Lancaster Royal GS, MCAM, FIMI; *m* Susan; 1 da (Emma); *Career* early career training with various advtg and mktg agencies; former co-driver in Ford works team, winner numerous events incl RAC Rally (with Roger Clark) 1972, later appointed competition co-ordinator with Ford, export dir Mill Accessory Group 1975, fndr own accessory co 1979, contracted to commentate on Lombard RAC Rally and joined Top Gear as a presenter (both with BBC) 1987, also contracted as occasional presenter for Channel 9 TV Aust, fndr Tony Mason Motorsport (distributing motor sport products), regular contrib to numerous other pubns, presenter on Top Gear Motorsport (BBC), fndr Tony Mason Associates (PR, TV and Motorsport consultancy) 1992; after dinner speaker (with over 1000 appearances); *Books* author of 4 books incl Rallying (with Stuart Turner); *Style*— Tony Mason, Esq; ✉ Tony Mason Associates, Southlands House, 61 Hightown Road, Banbury, Oxon OX16 9BE (☎ 01295 276100, fax 01295 276111)

MASON, William Ernest; CB (1983); s of Ernest George Mason (d 1975), and Agnes Margaret Mason, *née* Derry (d 1986); *b* 12 Jan 1929; *Educ* Brockley GS, LSE (BSc); *m* 1959, Jean; da of Charles John Bossley (d 1961); 1 s (Robert b 31 Dec 1966), 1 da (Jane b 5 Jan 1962); *Career* Miny of Food 1949–54; MAFF 1954: princ 1963, asst sec 1970, under sec 1975, Fisheries sec 1980, dep sec (Fisheries and Food) 1982–89; non-exec dir Allied Domecq plc (Allied-Lyons plc until 1994) 1989–, conslt to food and drink industs 1989–; FIGD, Hon FIFST; *Recreations* music, reading, gardening, British painting; *Clubs* Reform; *Style*— William Mason, Esq, CB; ✉ 82 Beckenham Place Park, Beckenham, Kent BR3 2BT (☎ 0181 650 8241); Allied-Domecq plc, 24 Portland Place, London W1N 4BB (☎ 0171 323 9000)

MASON OF BARNSLEY, Baron (Life Peer UK 1987), of Barnsley, S Yorkshire; Roy Mason; PC (1968); s of late Joseph Mason, of Carlton, nr Barnsley; *b* 18 April 1924; *Educ* Carlton and Royston Elementary Schs, LSE; *m* 1945, Marjorie, da of Ernest Sowden, of Royston, W Riding; 2 da (Hon Susan Ann (Hon Mrs Duke) b 1947, Hon Jill Diane (Hon Mrs Martin) b 1955); *Career* former coal miner 1938–53; MP (Lab) Barnsley 1953–83, Barnsley Central 1983–87; oppn spokesman Def and Post Office 1960–64; min of state BOT 1964–67; min Def Equipment 1967–68, postmaster-gen 1968, min Power 1968–69; pres BOT 1969–70; oppn spokesman Civil Aviation Shipping Tourism Films & Trade 1970–74; sec of state: Def 1974–76, NI 1976–79; oppn spokesman Agric Fish & Food 1979–; former NUM official; chm: Yorks Gp Labour MPs, Miners Gp of Labour MPs, Prince's Youth Business Tst of S Yorks 1985–, Barnsley Business and Innovation Centre; DUniv Hallam Univ Sheffield 1993; *Style*— The Rt Hon Lord Mason of Barnsley, PC; ✉ 12 Victoria Avenue, Barnsley, S Yorks

MASON-PEARSON, Sara Ann; da of John Vernon Henry Franklin, of Robertsbridge, E Sussex, and Jeanette Marguerite, *née* Webster; *b* 1 Aug 1953; *Educ* Rosary Priory Convent; *m* 4 Oct 1974, Jonathan Stuart Mason-Pearson, s of Eric Mason-Pearson; 2 da (Chloe Ann b 15 March 1978, Clementine Sara b 29 Nov 1985), 1 s (Charlie Jon Eric b 29 Oct 1979); *Career* jr sub Sunday Telegraph 1970–74, PR account exec Odhams & Gunn 1974–76, bd dir Durden-Smith Communications 1978–80 (PR account mangr 1976–78), fndr ptnr The SPA Partnership 1980– (sold to Yellowhammer plc 1989, reacquired 1990); *Recreations* keeping hens, making large bonfires; *Style*— Mrs Sara Mason-Pearson; ✉ The SPA Partnership, 3 Bedfordbury, Covent Garden, London WC2N 4BP (☎ 0171 240 7711, fax 0171 240 3311)

MASSAM, (Arthur) David Wright; s of Arthur Greenwood Massam (d 1989), of Southport, Lancashire, and Emily, *née* Wright (d 1945); *b* 18 Nov 1934; *Educ* King George V Sch Southport, Univ of Manchester (MPS), Univ of London (LLB); *m* 1957 (m dis 1970), Angela, da of Joseph Smith (d 1986), of Southport, Lancashire; 1 s (Nigel Robin b 1961), 1 da (Melinda Jane b 1958); *Career* Nat Serv RAMC 1956–58; C F Thackray Ltd 1958–70; Datapharm Publications Ltd: exec dir 1980–92, dir 1993–; sec Assoc of the Br Pharmaceutical Indust 1982–92 (joined 1970), dir Prescription Medicines Code of Practice Authy 1993–; memb: Advsy Cncl on Misuse of Drugs, Poisons Bd, Standing Pharmaceutical Advsy Ctee 1982–94; Freeman: Worshipful Soc of Apothecaries 1993, City of London 1994; memb Hon Soc of the Inner Temple 1968, fell Royal Pharmaceutical Soc of GB 1980 (memb 1956); *Recreations* history, reading; *Clubs* Reform; *Style*— David Massam, Esq; ✉ 80A Westbury Road, Finchley, London N12 7PD (☎ 0181 446 1037); Prescription Medicines Code of Practice Authority, 12 Whitehall, London SW1A 2DY (☎ 0171 930 9677, fax 0171 930 4554)

MASSER, Patrick Kenneth (Pat); s of Arnold Kenneth Masser, of York, and Muriel Olive, *née* Benson (d 1985); *b* 19 Feb 1931; *Educ* St Peter's York; *m* 28 March 1964, Margaret Joan Boyle, da of Alexander Moig, of Cupar, Fife; *Career* trainee hotel mangr BT Hotels 1951–57 (The Midland Hotel Manchester, The Queen's Hotel Leeds, Welcombe Hotel Stratford on Avon, Tregenna Castle Hotel St Ives, Gleneagles Scotland, Lotti Hotel Paris, Charing Cross London); asst mangr: Great Western Royal Hotel London 1957–58, Midland Hotel Manchester 1958–60; staff mangr Gleneagles Hotel Scotland 1960–62; dep mangr: North British Hotel Edinburgh 1962–64, Adelphi Hotel Liverpool 1964–66; gen mangr: Queen's Hotel Birmingham 1966, Lockalsh Hotel Kyle of Lochalsh 1967, Royal Victoria Hotel Sheffield 1968–73, Adelphi Hotel Liverpool 1973–75; ops mangr BT Hotels Ltd London 1975–77; gen mangr: North British Hotel Glasgow 1977–82, Marine Highland Hotel Troon 1982–85, Savoy Hotel Blackpool 1985–88, Ruskin Hotel Blackpool 1988–90; md Associated Business Consultants 1991–93; govr: Sheffield Poly, Glasgow Coll of Food Technol, Liverpool Coll of Craft & Catering, Blackpool & Fylde Coll, Ayr Tech Coll; chm Blackpool Community Services Tst; Leading Citizen of the Year 1996; Master Innholder 1977, Winston Churchill fellowship 1987; Freeman City of London 1978; memb: RIPH&H, Cookery & Food Assoc, UK Bartenders' Guild, Northern Guild of Toastmasters, Guild of Sommeliers, La Chaine de Rotisseurs, NW Tourist Bd; FHCIMA, BHA; *Recreations* cricket, rugby, athletics, swimming, charitable activities and local authority projects; *Clubs* RAC, London & Scotland, Yorkshire County Cricket, St Anne's Conservative; *Style*— Pat K Masser, Esq; ✉ Clifton House, 155 Clifton Drive, Starr Gate, Blackpool FY4 1RU (☎ 01253 47864); Associated Business Consultants, Hotel & Catering, Clifton House, 155 Clifton Drive, Starr Gate, Blackpool FY4 1RU (☎ 01253 47864, fax 01253 752687)

MASSEREENE AND FERRARD, 14 & 7 Viscount (I 1660 & 1797); John David Clotworthy Whyte-Melville Foster Skeffington; also Baron of Loughneagh (I 1660), Baron Oriel of Collon (I 1790), and Baron Oriel of Ferrard (UK 1821, which sits as); o s of 13 Viscount Massereene and Ferrard (d 1992), and Annabelle Kathleen, *née* Lewis; *b* 3 June 1940; *Educ* Millfield, Inst Monte Rosa; *m* 1970, Ann Denise, da of Norman Rowlandson (d 1967); 2 s (Hon Charles b 1973, Hon Henry William Norman Foster Clotworthy b 1980), 1 da (Hon Harriette Denise Margaretta Eileen b 1975); *Heir* s, Hon Charles John Foster Clotworthy Whyte Melville Skeffington b 7 Feb 1973; *Career* served Grenadier Gds 1959–61; dir: Shirlstar Container Tport Ltd, Broad Abandonment Research; chm: Atkin Grant & Lang (Gunmakers), R M Walkden & Co Ltd; stockbroker with M D Barnard & Co Ltd; *Recreations* shooting, vintage cars, history; *Clubs* Turf, Pratt's; *Style*— The Rt Hon the Viscount Massereene and Ferrard; ✉ Knock, Isle of Mull, Argyll; Scarisdale House, New Rd, Esher, Surrey KT10 9PS (☎ 01372 465468)

MASSEY, Daniel Raymond; s of Raymond Hart Massey (d 1983), and Gladys Allen Whitney (the actress Adrianne Allen); *b* 10 Oct 1933; *Educ* King's Coll Cambridge (MA); *m* 1 (m dis), Adrienne Corri; m 2 (m dis), Penelope Wilton; 1 da (Alice Linden Pearl b 1977); *Career* actor; served 2 Lt Scots Guard 1951–53; *Theatre* incl: The Happiest Millionaire (Cambridge) 1958, Make Me an Offer (Haymarket), The School for Scandal (Haymarket), The Rivals, The Importance of Being Earnest (Haymarket), Bloomsbury (Phoenix), Don Juan Comes Back From The War (NT), Macbeth (NT), Jack Tanner in Man and Superman (SWET Award for Actor of the Year 1981), Twelfth Night (RSC), Measure for Measure (RSC), The Time of Your Life (RSC) 1983, Waste 1985, Breaking the Silence 1985, Follies (Shaftesbury) 1987, Doll's House 1989, Hector in Heartbreak House (Yvonne Arnaud Guildford and Haymarket) 1992, Don Armado in Love's Labour's Lost (RSC) 1993, Burgoyne in Devil's Disciple (RNT) 1994, Taking Sides 1995 (Chichester Festival, Criterion (Olivier Award nomination for Best Actor 1995, Variety Club Stage Actor of the Year 1995, jtly London Critics' Circle Award 1995)); *Televison* incl: The Golden Bowl, Roads to Freedom, Good Behaviour (BBC), Intimate Contact (Central), Inspector Morse, Nobody Here but us Chickens (Central), G.B.H. (Channel 4) 1991; *Films* incl: Girls At Sea 1957, The Queen's Guard 1960, Go To Blazes 1962, Moll Flanders 1966, Star 1968 (Best Supporting Actor Hollywood Golden Globe Awards 1968), The Cat and the Canary 1978, Escape to Victory 1981, Stalin (HBO) 1991, In the Name of the Father 1993; *Recreations* golf, reading, travel, classical music; *Style*— Daniel Massey, Esq; ✉ c/o Julian Belfrage Associates, 46 Albemarle Street, London W1X 4PP (☎ 0171 491 4400, fax 0171 493 5460)

MASSEY, Doreen Elizabeth; da of Jack Hall (d 1989), of Darwen, Lancs, and Mary Ann, *née* Sharrock (d 1973); *Educ* Darwen GS, Univ of Birmingham (BA, DipEd, vice pres Student Union, Hockey and Cricket blues), Univ of London (MA); *m* Dr Leslie Massey, s of James York Massey, of Conisbrough, Yorks; 3 c (Elizabeth Caitlin b 1969, Owen John b 1971, Benjamin James b 1973); *Career* family planner; grad serv overseas Gabon 1962–63, Springside Sch Philadelphia USA 1967–69, Pre-Sch Play Group Assoc 1973–77, Walsingham Sch 1977–83, advsr Inner London Educn Authy 1983–85, mangr Young People's Prog Health Educn Authy 1985–87, dir The Family Planning Assoc 1989–94 (dir of educn 1987–89), independent conslt in health skills and sexual health; memb numerous voluntary orgns, primary sch govr; speaker, bdcaster and writer on family planning and sex educn; FRSA; *Books* Sex Education: Why, What and How (1988), Sex Education Sourcebook (1994), Lovers' Guide Encyclopaedia (conslt ed, 1996); *Recreations* theatre, cinema, opera, reading, art and design, vegetarian cookery, travel, walking, yoga; *Style*— Mrs Doreen E Massey; ✉ 9 Kyrle Road, London SW11 6BD (☎ and fax 0171 207 3723)

MASSEY, Paul Christopher; s of Clifford Joseph Massey (d 1991), and Janine Linda, *née* Melvyn; *b* 5 Oct 1963; *Educ* William Ellis Sch Highgate London, Hinchley Wood Sch Surrey; *Career* press photographer; staff photographer specialising in: news Evening Standard 1980–86, news, features and fashion London Daily News 1987, news, fashion and features Daily Mirror 1987–90, fashion and features The European 1990–91 (chief photographer); freelance photographer for Times Magazine, Sunday Times Magazine, Night and Day magazine The Mail on Sunday and all UK and numerous foreign magazines 1992–; special assignments incl: travelled on board Canada Maritime for 3 months in Transatlantic Yacht Race for Evening Standard 1984, travelled through

Kyber Pass and Hindu Kush with Imran Khan for The Times, several visits to India filming with Goldie Hawn; Ilford Photography Awards: Social Award 1981, Ilford Award 1982–85, 1987, 1990 and 1991, Photographer of the Year 1988, Features Photographer of the Year 1993; Nikon Arts Photographer of the Year 1993, 1994 and 1995, British Press Awards Arts Photographer of the Year 1993 and 1994; memb: Press Photographers' Assoc, NUJ; *Publications* contrib to several books and calenders; *Recreations* travel, interior design, tennis, cricket; *Style—* Paul Massey, Esq; ✉ c/o The Picture Desk, The Mail on Sunday, Northcliffe House, 2 Derry Street, Kensington, London W8 5TS (☎ 0171 938 6000)

MASSEY, Ray John Thomas; s of Kenneth Edwin Massey (d 1988), of Taunton, Somerset, and Dorothy May, *née* Brooks; *b* 26 Sept 1951; *Educ* Ladymead Secdy Sch Taunton, Somerset Coll of Art, Medway Coll of Art and Technol; *m* (sep), Annie, da of Maurice Geay, of Pessac, France; 2 s (Jethro b 6 Jan 1978, Jean-Michel b 24 Feb 1983); *Career* asst photographer 1970–71, freelance photographer 1972–; numerous exhbns incl: Assoc of Photographers London, JIP Arles France, IIP Ireland; proprietor Primary Colour Laboratory; life memb Assoc of Photographers; *Recreations* travel, swimming, photography; *Clubs* BSAC, Porsche Owners'; *Style—* Ray Massey, Esq; ✉ Horton-Stephens, 9 Lyme Street, London NW1 0EH (☎ 0171 485 2082, fax 0171 267 7590)

MASSEY, Raymond (Ray); s of David Massey, of Newcastle upon Tyne, and Elizabeth Irene, *née* Jeffrey (d 1987); *b* 7 June 1960; *Educ* Walbottle Grammar Northumberland, Univ of Warwick (Lord Rootes fndn scholar, Deutscher Akademischer Austauschdienst Stipendium, BA); *Career* journalist and author; Coventry Evening Telegraph 1982–87 (reporter, industl corr, feature writer and diarist, China corr); educn corr Press Association 1988–90 (news reporter PA 1987–); Daily Mail: educn corr 1990–95, motoring corr 1995–; FRSA; *Books* Parent Power (1993); *Recreations* thinking about keep-fit, travel; *Style—* Ray Massey, Esq; ✉ The Daily Mail, Northcliffe House, 2 Derry St, London W8 5TT (☎ 0171 938 6102/6000, fax 0171 937 5287)

MASSEY, Dr Roy Cyril; s of Cyril Charles Massey (d 1966), of Birmingham, and Beatrice May, *née* Morgan (d 1987); *b* 9 May 1934; *Educ* Moseley GS Birmingham, Univ of Birmingham (BMus); *m* 22 Feb 1975, Ruth Carol Craddock, da of Frederick George Grove (d 1958), of Fron-y-Gog, Machynlleth, Montgomeryshire; *Career* organist: St Alban's Conybere St Birmingham 1953–60, St Augustine's Edgbaston Birmingham 1960–65, Croydon Parish Church 1965–68; warden Royal Sch of Church Music Addington Palace Croydon 1965–68, conductor Birmingham Bach Soc 1966–68, organist and master of the choristers Birmingham Cathedral 1968–74, dir of music King Edward's Sch Birmingham 1968–74, organist and master of the choristers Hereford Cathedral 1974–, conductor Three Choirs Festival and Hereford Choral Soc 1974–; memb Cncl: RCO, Royal Sch of Church Music; fell St Michael's Coll Tenbury 1979–88; chm Hereford Competitive Music Festival, pres Incorporated Assoc of Organists 1991–93; Hon DMus Canterbury 1991, FRSCM 1972, FRCO 1956, ARCM 1954; *Recreations* the countryside, walking the dog on the Malvern hills, motoring; *Clubs* Conservative (Hereford); *Style—* Dr Roy Massey; ✉ 1 College Cloisters, Cathedral Close, Hereford HR1 2NG (☎ 01432 272011); The Cobbles, Stretton Grandison, Ledbury, Herefordshire HR8 2TW

MASSEY, Rupert John Candide; s of Zenke Stefan, of Warsaw, Poland, and Sonia Mary Massey (d 1978); *b* 21 Nov 1945; *Educ* Clayesmore Sch Dorset, Balliol Coll Oxford (BA); *m* 6 Jan 1984, Kate Miranda, da of Philip Rae-Scott, of Richmond, Surrey; 3 s (Thomas Jack b 14 Dec 1985, Jacob Jonathan b 23 Aug 1988, Joel Peter (twin) b 23 Aug 1988); *Career* warden youth and community centre S London 1968–72, called to the Bar Inner Temple 1972, barr-at-law; broadcasting journalist; contrib to: Granada TV, Capital Radio, BBC Radio 4, Thames ITV and nat press; performer and actor: Clockwise 1986, Intimate Contact (Zenith) 1987, Life Story (BBC TV) 1987, Battalion 1988, Moon & Son (BBC TV) 1991; guest speaker Cranworth Law Soc Downing Coll Cambridge 1991, guest speaker various univs and colls incl St Thomas' Hosp Postgrad Med Sch Dept of Psychiatry and Bournemouth Univ Dept of Media Production and Studies; hon legal and policy advsr Fedn of Small Businesses, pres Bd YMCA (Winton); memb: NUJ, Br Equity, BAFTA, BECTU, Hon Soc of Inner Temple London; *Recreations* deep sea sailing/cruising, all water sports, youth & community work, work with young offenders, psychology; *Clubs* Cruising Assoc; *Style—* Rupert Massey, Esq; ✉ 141 Sheen Road, Richmond upon Thames, Surrey TW9 1YJ (☎ 0181 940 3672); Barristers' Chambers, Eaton House, 4 Eaton Rd, Branksome Park, Poole, Dorset BH13 6DG (☎ 01202 766301, fax 01202 766301)

MASSEY, (Charles) Trevor; OBE (1992); s of Roland Massey (d 1973), of Higham, nr Barnsley, S Yorkshire, and Vera, *née* Hemmingway; *b* 3 May 1934; *Educ* Queen Elizabeth GS Wakefield, Univ of Leeds (BSc); *m* Enid, da of William Cyril Herbert (d 1972); 2 s (Brynnen David b 1960, Adrian Paul b 1962), 1 da (Angela Dawn b 1963); *Career* mining engr; British Coal (formerly NCB): colliery mangr 1969–72, prodn mangr 1972–74, chief mining engr Doncaster Area 1974–77, dep dir S Yorkshire Area 1977–81, i/c Selby Project N Yorks Area 1981–85, head Tech Dept 1985–91, head Supply and Contracts Dept 1991–92; conslt Health Serv Contracts 1993–; memb Int Ctee of Coal Res 1985–93, dir IEA Coal Res 1988–93; Inst of Mining Engrs: vice pres 1990–91, pres 1992–93, hon treas 1994–; FIMinE, FEng 1990; *Recreations* gardening, bee keeping; *Style—* Trevor Massey, Esq, OBE, FEng; ✉ Vissitt Manor, Hemsworth, Pontefract, West Yorkshire WF9 4PN (☎ and fax 01977 611388)

MASSEY, William Greville Sale; QC (1996); s of Lt Col Patrick Massey, MC, of Arawai House, Liss, Hants, and Bessie Lee, *née* Byrne (d 1978); *b* 31 Aug 1953; *Educ* Harrow, Hertford Coll Oxford (BA); *m* 2 Dec 1978, Cecilia D'Oyly, da of Daniel Edmund Awdry, TD, DL, of The Old Manor, Beanacre, Melksham, Wilts; 3 s (Patrick William Edmund b 31 July 1983, Richard Daniel Hugh b 8 May 1985, Edmund Greville Robert b 12 June 1990); *Career* called to the Bar Middle Temple 1977; memb: Chancery Bar Assoc, Revenue Bar Assoc; *Books* Potter and Monroe's Tax Planning with Precedents (jtly 9 edn), Encyclopaedia of Forms and Precedents (contrib); *Recreations* skiing, gardening, bookbinding, chess; *Style—* William Massey, Esq, QC; ✉ Pump Court Tax Chambers, 16 Bedford Row, London WC1R 4EB (☎ 0171 414 8080, fax 0171 414 8099)

MASSIE, Allan Johnstone; s of Alexander Johnstone Massie, of Banchory, Aberdeenshire, and Evelyn Wilson, *née* Forbes; *b* 16 Oct 1938; *Educ* Drumtochty Castle, Glenalmond, Trinity Coll Cambridge (BA); *m* 22 June 1973, Alison Agnes Graham, da of Robert Scott Langlands, of Kelso, Roxburghshire; 2 s (Alexander, Louis), 1 da (Claudia); *Career* school master Drumtochty Castle 1960–71, TEFL Rome 1972–75; author, journalist and playwright; princ fiction reviewer The Scotsman 1975–, TV critic The Sunday Standard 1981–83; columnist: Glasgow Herald 1985–88, Sunday Times Scotland 1987–91, The Daily Telegraph 1991–; plays incl: Quintet in October, The Minstrel and The Shirra 1989; winner: Frederick Niven Prize for the Last Peacock 1981, Fraser of Allander Award Critic of the Year 1982, Scottish Arts Cncl Book Awards 1982 and 1986, The Scotsman, Scottish Book of the Year 1990; memb Scottish Arts Cncl 1989; FRSL 1982; *Books* Change and Decay in All Around I See (1978), The Last Peacock (1980), The Death of Men (1981), The Caesars (1983), Portrait of Scottish Rugby (1984), One Night in Winter (1984), Augustus (1986), Byron's Travels (1987), A Question of Loyalties (1989), Glasgow (1989), The Hanging Tree (1990), Tiberius (1991), The Sins of the Father (1991), Caesar (1993), These Enchanted Woods (1993); *Recreations* reading, watching rugby, cricket, attending my daughter at Pony Club and other equestrian events, walking the dogs; *Clubs* Academy, Selkirk RFC; *Style—* Allan Massie, Esq; ✉ Thirladean House, Selkirk TD7 5LU (☎ 01750 20393)

MASSIE, Herbert William (Bert); OBE (1984); s of Herbert Douglas Massie, of Liverpool, and Joan Lucy, *née* Roberts; *b* 31 March 1949; *Educ* Sandfield Park Special Sch Liverpool, Portland Trg Coll for the Disabled Mansfield, Hereward Coll Coventry, Liverpool Poly (BA), Manchester Poly (CQSW); *Career* Wm Rainford Ltd 1968–68, West Cheshire Newspapers Ltd 1968–70, Liverpool Assoc for the Disabled 1970–72, Disabled Living Fndn 1977, dir The Royal Assoc for Disability and Rehabilitation (RADAR) 1990– (joined 1978); memb: Mgmnt Ctee Disabled Drivers Assoc 1968–71, Careers Serv Advsy Cncl for Eng 1979–83, Exec Ctee OUTSET 1983–91, Access Ctee for Eng 1984–93, Disabled Persons Tport Advsy Ctee 1986–, BR Advsy Gp on Disabled People 1986–94, Nat Advsy Cncl on Employment of People with Disabilities 1991–, nat Disability Cncl 1996–, Ind Cmmn on Social Justice 1993–94, DSS Panel of Experts on Review of Incapacity Benefit 1994, Cabinet Office Working Gp on Equal Opportunities in the Sr Civil Serv 1994–95; vice chm: Assoc of Disabled Professionals 1986–94 (memb Exec Ctee 1979–), Vol Cncl for Handicapped Children 1985–93 (memb 1980–93), Tripscope 1989– (memb 1986–); tstee: BEAMA Fndn for Disabled People 1990– (sec 1986–90), Ind Living Fund 1990–93; patron Disabled Living Servs Manchester 1990–, UK nat sec Rehabilitation Int 1993– (dep vice pres for Euro 1996–); FRSA 1988, MInstM 1990; *Publications* Work and Disability 1977 (with M Greaves, 1979), Employers Guilde to Disabilities (with M Hettle, 1982, 2 edn 1986), Aspects of the Employment of Disabled People in the Federal Republic of Germany (1982), Day Centres for Young Disabled People (jtly, 1984), Travelling with British Rail (1985), Wheelchairs and their Use (with J Weyers, 1986), Choosing a Wheelchair (with J Male, 1990), Seat Belts and Disabled People (with J Isaacs, 1990), Social Justice and Disabled People (1994); *Style—* Bert Massie, Esq, OBE; ✉ 4 Moira Close, London N17 6HZ (☎ 0181 808 0185); Director, The Royal Association for Disability and Rehabilitation, 12 City Forum, 250 City Road, London EC1V 8AF (☎ 0171 250 3222, fax 0171 250 0212, mobile 0860 927665)

MASSIMO OF ROCCASECCA DEI VOLSCI, Prince (Title of Papal and Italian Royal Decree 31 March 1932) Stefano Shaun Francesco Filippo Gabriel Charles James; Don Stefano, Prince of Roccasecca dei Volsci; s of Prince Vittorio Massimo and his 2 wife Dawn Addams, the film actress; *b* 10 Jan 1955, London; *Educ* Collegio San Giuseppe de Merode Rome, Collegio alla Querce Florence; *m* 1973 (m dis 1996), Atalanta Edith, da of Maj Ivan Foxwell, and Lady Edith Sybil, *née* Lambart (d 1996), gda of 9 Earl of Cavan, KP, PC, DL; 3 s (Don Valerio b 1973, Don Cesare b 1977, Don Tancredi b 1986); *Heir* Don Valerio Massimo; *Career* photographer; *Clubs* Circolo degli Scacchi, (Rome); *Style—* Prince Massimo of Roccasecca dei Volsci; ✉ c/o National Westminster Bank, Bloomsbury Way, London WC1A 2TS

MASSINGBERD, Hugh John Montgomery-; s of John Michael Montgomery-Massingberd, of Cookham, Berks, formerly of Gunby, Lincs, and Marsali Winlaw, *née* Seal; *b* 30 Dec 1946; *Educ* Harrow, Law Soc's Coll of Law; *m* 1, 1972 (m dis 1979), Christine Martinoni; 1 s (Luke b 1977), 1 da (Harriet b 1974); m 2, 1983, Caroline, er da of Sir Hugh Ripley, 4 Bt, *qv*; *Career* author; gave up place reading history at Selwyn Coll Cambridge to join editorial staff of Burke's Peerage publications (asst ed 1968–71, ed 1971–83), assoc ed The Field 1984–86; The Daily Telegraph: obituaries ed 1986–94, television critic 1994–96; former memb: Cncl Assoc of Genealogists and Record Agents, Research Ctee Historic Houses Assoc; *Books* The Monarchy (1979), The British Aristocracy (with Mark Bence-Jones, 1979), The London Ritz (with David Watkin, 1980, revised 1989), The Country Life Book of Royal Palaces, Castles and Homes (with Patrick Montague-Smith, 1981), Diana - The Princess of Wales (1982), Heritage of Royal Britain (1983), Royal Palaces of Europe (1984), Blenheim Revisited (1985), Her Majesty The Queen (1986), Debrett's Great British Families (1987), The Field Book of Country Homes and their Owners: Family Seats of the British Isles (1988), Great Houses of England and Wales (with Christopher Simon Sykes, 1994); also edited Burke's Landed Gentry (1972), Burke's Guide to The Royal Family (1973), Burke's Presidential Families of the USA (1975, 2nd edn 1981), Burke's Irish Family Records (1976), Burke's Family Index (1976), Burke's Royal Families of the World (Vol I 1977, Vol II 1980), Burke's Guide to Country Houses (Vol I 1978, Vol II 1980, Vol III 1981), Lord of the Dance: A Moncreiffe Miscellany (1986), The Daily Telegraph Record of the Second World War (1989), A Guide to the Country Houses of the North West (1991), The Disintegration of a Heritage (1993), The Daily Telegraph Book of Obituaries: A Celebration of Eccentric Lives (1995), The Daily Telegraph Second Book of Obituaries: Heroes and Adventurers (1996); contrib to The Sunday Telegraph, The Spectator, Literary Review, Harpers & Queen, The Field, etc, lectures and broadcasts too humorous to mention; *Recreations* hanging around stage-doors and unsaddling enclosures; *Clubs* I Zingari, Butterflies Cricket; *Style—* Hugh Massingberd, Esq; ✉ 31 Hyde Park Square, London W2 2NW (fax 0171 706 7221)

MASSINGHAM, David Charles; s of Derek George Massingham (d 1976), and Margaret Catherine, *née* Callaghan; *b* 26 June 1959; *Educ* Dame Alice Owens GS, Laban Centre for Movement and Dance (BA, Advanced Performance Certificate); *Career* choreographer; fndr/dancer Geographical Duvet 1984–86, dancer Transitions 1986, fndr dir/choreographer/dancer Adventures in Motion Pictures 1986–88, choreographer int course for choreographers and composers 1988, fndr David Massingham Dance 1989, choreographer in res Northern Arts 1995; major works incl: Companion Pieces 1989, The Immortals 1990, Cradle 1994, With the Company We Keep 1994, Hinterland 1996; theatre incl: The Tempest (RNT), The Red Balloon (Birmingham Rep), Cabaret (Newcastle Live Theatre); Bonnie Bird Award 1992; *Recreations* motorcycling; *Style—* David Massingham, Esq; ✉ David Massingham Dance, Dance City, Peel Lane, Off Waterloo Street, Newcastle-upon-Tyne NE1 4DW (☎ 0191 261 0505, fax 0191 230 0486)

MASSY, Hon David Hamon Somerset; s and h of 9 Baron Massy, *qv*; *b* 4 March 1947; *Educ* St George's Coll Weybridge; *Career* serving with Merchant Navy; *Style—* The Hon David Massy

MASSY, 9 Baron (I 1776); Hugh Hamon John Somerset Massy; s of 8 Baron (d 1958); *b* 11 June 1921; *Educ* Clongowes Wood Coll, Clayesmore Sch; *m* 1943, Margaret Elizabeth, da of late John Flower; 4 s, 1 da; *Heir* s, Hon David Hamon Somerset Massy, *qv*; *Career* serv 1940–45 War, Private RAOC; *Style—* The Rt Hon the Lord Massy; ✉ 88 Brooklands Rd, Cosby, Leicester

MASTER, (Humphrey) Simon Harcourt; s of Humphrey Ronald Master, of Thetford, Norfolk, and Rachel Blanche, *née* Plumbly (d 1989); *b* 10 April 1944; *Educ* Ardingly, Univ de La Rochelle; *m* 3 May 1969, Georgina Mary, da of Sir Brian Caldwell Cook Batsford (d 1991), of Winchelsea, E Sussex; 2 s (Nicholas Harcourt b 1973, Matthew Harcourt b 1976); *Career* sr ed: Pan Books Ltd 1966–69, B T Batsford Ltd 1969–70; Pan Books Ltd: editorial dir 1970–73, publishing dir 1973–79, managing dir 1980–87; chief exec Random House UK Ltd 1987–89, exec vice pres int Random House Inc 1989–91, dep chm Random House Group 1989–, exec chm Arrow Books 1990–92, exec chm Random House Gen Books Div 1992–; dir HMSO 1990–95; Publishers Assoc: memb Cncl 1989–95, vice pres 1995–96, pres 1996–97; *Recreations* reading, golf, classic cars, gardening; *Clubs* Groucho, Sherborne Golf; *Style—* Simon Master, Esq; ✉ 13 Patten Rd, London SW18 3RH (☎ 0181 874 2204); Random House, 20 Vauxhall Bridge Rd, London SW1V 2SA (☎ 0171 973 9000, fax 0171 233 6115)

MASTERMAN, His Hon Judge; Crispin Grant; s of Osmond Janson Masterman (d 1988), of Gerrards Cross, Bucks, and Anne, *née* Bouwens; *b* 1 June 1944; *Educ* St

Edward's Sch Oxford, Univ of Southampton (BA); *m* 3 Jan 1976, Margaret Elizabeth Clare, da of Robert Fletcher (d 1967), of Cardiff; 1 s (Kerrin b 25 Oct 1979), 2 da (Claudia b 21 Sept 1977, Laura b 9 Aug 1982); *Career* cmmnd RAFVR 1967 PO; called to the Bar Middle Temple 1971, recorder of the Crown Court 1988–95, circuit judge (Wales & Chester Circuit) 1995–; FCIArb 1991; *Recreations* family and friends; *Style—* Crispin Masterman, Esq; ✉ 28 South Rise, Llanishen, Cardiff, South Glamorgan CF4 5RH (☎ 01222 754072)

MASTERS, Rt Rev Brian John; *see:* Edmonton, Bishop of

MASTERS, Dr Christopher; s of Wilfred Masters, and Mary Ann Masters; *b* 2 May 1947; *Educ* Richmond GS, King's Coll London (BSc, AKC), Univ of Leeds (PhD); *m* 1971, Gillian Mary; 2 da; *Career* res chemist Shell Research BV Amsterdam 1971–77, PA to MD Shell Chemicals UK 1977–78, corp planner Shell UK 1978–79; Christian Salvesen PLC: business devpt mangr 1979–81, dir of planning Merchants Refrigerating Company USA (following takeover by Christian Salvesen) 1981–83, md Christian Salvesen Seafoods 1983–85, md Industl Servs Div 1985–89, main bd dir 1987–, chief exec 1989–; non-exec dir: British Assets Trust, Scottish Widows, Scottish Chamber Orch Tst, Scottish Opera; memb Scottish Higher Educn Funding Cncl; chm Young Enterprise Scotland; FRSE 1996; *Recreations* wines, music, opera; *Style—* Dr Christopher Masters, FRSE; ✉ Christian Salvesen PLC, 50 East Fettes Avenue, Edinburgh EH4 1EQ (☎ 0131 559 3600)

MASTERS, Dame Sheila Valerie (Dame Sheila Noakes); DBE (1996); da of Albert Frederick Masters, of Eltham, London, and Iris Sheila, *née* Ratcliffe; *b* 23 June 1949; *Educ* Eltham Hill GS, Univ of Bristol (LLB); *m* 3 Aug 1985, (Colin) Barry Noakes, s of Stuart Noakes, of Brenchley; *Career* KPMG: joined 1970, ptnr 1983–; seconded to: HM Treasy as accounting/commercial advsr 1979–81, Dept of Health as fin dir on NHS Mgmnt Exec 1988–91; non-exec dir Court of the Bank of England 1994; elected to: London Soc of CAs 1984–88, Cncl ICAEW 1987; memb: Ctee of Enquiry MAFF 1988, Mgmnt Bd of Inland Revenue 1992, NHS Policy Bd 1992–95, Private Fin Panel 1993; cmmr of Public Works Loan Bd 1995; FCA, ATII; *Books* Tolley's Stamp Duties (1980); *Recreations* skiing, horse-racing, opera, early classical music; *Style—* Dame Sheila Masters, DBE; ✉ Church House, High St, Goudhurst, Kent TN17 1AJ (☎ 01580 211427, fax 01580 212244); KPMG, 1 Puddle Dock, Blackfriars, London EC4V 3PD (☎ 0171 311 3190, fax 0171 311 2925)

MASTERSON, David Napier; s of Philip Bursell Edwin Masterson (d 1985), of Upminster, Essex, and Pamela, *née* Napier; *b* 20 June 1959; *Educ* Brentwood Sch Essex, City of London Poly; *m* 19 May 1994, Adèle Deborah, *née* Kean; *Career* Kingston Smith Chartered Accountants: trainee 1977–81, ptnr 1988–; memb Audit Registration Ctee ICAEW 1991–; FCA 1991 (ACA 1981); *Recreations* golf, squash, skiing; *Clubs* Greenford Rotary (hon treas), Soc of Old Brentwoods; *Style—* David N Masterson, Esq; ✉ Kingston Smith, Devonshire House, 146 Bishopsgate, London EC2M 4JX (☎ 0171 377 8888, fax 0171 247 7048)

MASTERSON, (Margaret) Valerie (Mrs Andrew March); CBE (1988); da of Edward Masterson, and Rita McGrath; *Educ* Holt Hill Convent, studied in London and Milan on scholarship with Edwardo Asquez; *m* 1965, Andrew John March; 1 s ((Edward) Jason b 13 May 1969), 1 da (Caroline Louisa b 13 Aug 1973); *Career* opera and concert singer; prof of singing at the Royal Acad of Music and at Trinity Coll of Music 1992–; debut Landestheater Salzburg; appearances with D'Oyly Carte Opera, Glyndebourne Festival Opera, ENO, Royal Opera House Covent Garden; has appeared at numerous major opera houses incl: Paris, Aix En Provence, Toulouse, NY (Metropolitan and Carnegie Hall), Munich, Madrid, Geneva, Barcelona, Milan, San Francisco, Chicago, Chile, Brazil; leading roles in: La Traviata, Le Nozze di Figaro, Manon, Faust, Alcina, Die Entfhrung, Julius Caesar, Rigoletto, Romeo and Juliet, Carmen, Count Ory, Mireille, Louise, Idomeneo, Les Dialogues des Carmelites, The Merry Widow, Xerxes, Orlando; recordings incl: La Traviata, Elisabetta, Regina d' Inghliterra, Der Ring des Nibelungen, The Merry Widow, Kismet, Song of Norway, Julius Caesar Scipione, several Gilbert and Sullivan; broadcasts regularly on radio and TV; pres Br Youth Opera, hon pres Rossini Soc Paris; awarded Soc of West End Theatre Award 1983; FRCM 1992, Hon RAM 1993; *Recreations* tennis, swimming, ice skating; *Style—* Ms Valerie Masterson, CBE; ✉ c/o Music International, 13 Ardilaun Rd, Highbury, London N5 2QR

MASUDA, Yosuke; s of Kazuo Masuda (d 1957), of Tokyo, and Miyoko, *née* Hamada (d 1983); *b* 27 April 1946; *Educ* Waseda Sch, Waseda Univ Tokyo (BSc), QMC London (LLB); *m* 16 Feb 1975, Yuriko, da of Yoshiaki Ohnari, dir of Miny of Int Trade and Indust Tokyo; 1 s (Christopher Toshihiro b 1977), 2 da (Alison Nobuko b 1980, Margaret Takako b 1988); *Career* structural engr Kumagai Gumi Co Ltd 1969, asst project mangr Hong Kong Mass Transit Railway 1976–79, md Kumagai Gumi UK Ltd 1985, assoc dir Kumagai Co Ltd Tokyo 1988–94; MP Japan 1995–; called to the Bar Middle Temple 1984; memb: Japanese C of C UK, Anglo Japanese Assoc; fell QMC London; memb Japanese Inst of Civil Engrs; *Books* Pneumatic Caisson Design (1975), Pleasant Gentlemen of the Opera (1993), The Legacy Hunter (1994), Romantic Story in Kyoto (1995); *Recreations* theatre, travel, classical music, fishing, riding; *Clubs* Reform; *Style—* Yosuke Masuda, Esq; ✉ 4–18–4 Numabukuro, Nakano-ku, Tokyo, Japan (☎ 00 81 3 3386 3959, fax 00 81 3 3385 6133); House of Councillors, 2–1–1 Nagata-cho, Chiyoda, Tokyo, Japan (☎ 00 81 3 3508 8303, fax 00 81 3 5512 2303)

MATES, James Michael; s of Michael Mates, MP, *qv*, and Mary Rosamund, *née* Paton; *b* 11 Aug 1961; *Educ* Kings Coll Sch, Marlborough, Farnham Coll, Univ of Leeds (BA); *m* Fiona Margaret, da of John Standish Bennett; 1 s (Leo James de Vars b 4 Nov 1991), 1 da (Flora Katherine b 3 March 1994); *Career* ITN: joined as grad trainee 1983, Tokyo corr 1989–91, N of England corr 1991–92, Moscow corr 1992–93, diplomatic ed 1993–; *Recreations* water sports, bridge; *Style—* James Mates, Esq; ✉ ITN Ltd, 200 Gray's Inn Road, London WC1X 8XZ (☎ 0171 430 4130)

MATES, Michael John; MP (C) East Hampshire (majority 29,165); s of Claude Mates; *b* 9 June 1934; *Educ* Salisbury Cathedral Sch, Blundell's, King's Coll Cambridge; *m* 1, 1959 (m dis 1980), Mary Rosamund Paton; 2 s, 2 da; m 2, 1982, Rosellen, da of W T Bett, of West Wittering, W Sussex; 1 da; *Career* army offr 1954–74 (Royal Ulster Rifles, Queen's Dragoon Gds RAC, Maj 1967, Lt-Col 1973); MP (C): Petersfield Oct 1974–1983, E Hants 1983–; min of state Northern Ireland Office 1992–93 (resigned); chm: All Party Anglo-Irish Gp 1979–92, Select Ctee on Defence 1987–92 (memb 1979–92), Cons Home Affrs Ctee 1987–88 (vice chm 1979–87); memb Intelligence and Security Ctee 1994–; vice chm Cons NI Ctee 1979–81 (sec 1974–79), sec 1922 Ctee 1987–88; Liveryman Worshipful Co of Farriers 1975 (Master 1986); *Style—* Michael Mates, Esq, MP; ✉ House of Commons, London SW1A 0AA

MATHER, Sir (David) Carol Macdonell; kt (1987), MC (1944); s of Loris Emerson Mather, CBE (d 1976) and Leila Gwendoline, *née* Morley; yr bro of Sir William Mather, CVO, OBE, MC, TD, DL, *qv*; *b* 3 Jan 1919; *Educ* Harrow, Trinity Coll Cambridge; *m* 1951, Hon Philippa Selina Bewicke-Copley, da of 5 Baron Cromwell; 1 s (Nicholas), 3 da (Selina, Rose, Victoria); *Career* joined Welsh Gds 1940, WWII served Commandos, SAS, LO to Montgomery, Palestine 1946–48; Asst Mil Attaché Athens 1953–56, WO 1957–61, Mil Sec E Cmd 1961–62, ret as Lt-Col 1962; CRD 1962–70, Parly candidate Leicester NW 1966, MP (C) Esher 1970–87, oppn whip 1975–79; Lord Cmmr of the Treasy 1979–81, vice chamberlain of HM's Household 1981–83, comptroller 1983–86; *Books* Aftermath of War (1992); *Clubs* Brooks's; *Style—* Sir Carol Mather, MC; ✉ Oddington House, Moreton-in-Marsh, Glos

MATHER, Graham Christopher Spencer; MEP (Cons) Hampshire N and Oxford (majority 9,194); er s of Thomas Mather, and Doreen Mather; *b* 23 Oct 1954; *Educ* Hutton GS, New Coll Oxford (Burnet law scholar, MA); *m* 18 Sept 1981 (m dis 1995), Fiona Marion McMillan, er da of Sir Ronald Bell, QC, MP (d 1982); 2 s (Oliver James William b 20 June 1987, Alexander Richard Christopher b 30 March 1991); *Career* slr and subsequently conslt Cameron Markby 1978–80; Inst of Dirs: asst to DG 1980–83, head of Policy Unit 1983–86; Inst of Econ Affrs: dep dir 1987, gen dir 1987–92; pres European Policy Forum 1992–, visiting fell Nuffield Coll Oxford 1992–; vice pres: Strategic Planning Soc 1993–, Assoc of Dist Cncls 1994–; Parly candidate (C) Blackburn 1983; MEP (C) Hampshire N and Oxford 1994–; radio and TV broadcaster, contributor to The Times and various jls; memb: MMC 1989–94, Westminster City Cncl 1982–86, Cncl Small Business Research Tst, HM Treasy Working Pty on Freeports 1983; *Clubs* Oxford and Cambridge; *Style—* Graham Mather, Esq, MEP; ✉ European Policy Forum, 20 Queen Anne's Gate, London SW1H 9AA (☎ 0171 222 0579, fax 0171 233 1953)

MATHER, Howard Stephen Gilchrist; s of T Mather, and M D Mather; *b* 10 July 1957; *Educ* Hutton GS, New Coll Oxford; *Career* admitted slr 1982; ptnr Corporate Fin and Co Law Simmons & Simmons 1986–; memb Standing Ctee on Co Law Law Soc 1995–; FRGS; *Recreations* antiquarian book collecting, chess, travel, Morgans; *Style—* Howard Mather, Esq; ✉ Simmons & Simmons, 21 Wilson Street, London EC2M 2TY (☎ 0171 628 2020, fax 0171 628 2070, telex 888562 SIMMON G)

MATHER, Prof Paul Michael; s of Albert Mather (d 1953), of Bolton, Lancs, and Catherine, *née* Faulkner (d 1980); *b* 27 Jan 1944; *Educ* Thornleigh Coll Bolton, Selwyn Coll Cambridge (BA, MA), Univ of Nottingham (PhD); *m* 3 Jan 1970, Rosalind Mary, da of Roland Trench-Smith (d 1986), of Axminster, Devon; 4 s (Charles b 1971, William b 1974, James b 1976, John Paul b 1981), 1 da (Tamsin b 1972); *Career* lectr Univ of Manchester 1969, prof of geographical info systems The Univ of Nottingham 1988– (lectr 1970, sr lectr 1981); chm The Remote Sensing Soc 1989–92 (vice-pres 1992–); Hon ARICS, FRGS, FRSS; *Books* Computational Methods of Multivariate Analysis (1976), Computers in Geography (1976), Computer Processing of Remotely-Sensed Images (1987), Computer Applications in Geography (1991), Terra-1: Understanding the Terrestrial Environment (ed, 1992), Geographical Information Handling - Research and Applications (ed, 1993), Remote Sensing Data Systems and Networks (ed, 1995); *Recreations* travel, walking, reading, opera, music, choral singing; *Style—* Prof Paul M Mather; ✉ 33 Willow Road, W Bridgford, Nottingham NG2 7AY (☎ 0115 923 5469); Dept of Geography, The University of Nottingham, University Park, Nottingham NG7 2RD (☎ 0115 951 5430, fax 0115 951 5249, telex 37346, e-mail Paul.Mather@nottingham.ac.uk)

MATHER, Richard Martin (Rick); s of Richard John Mather (d 1993), and Opal, *née* Martin (d 1995); *Educ* Dept of Urban Design Architectural Assoc London, Sch of Architecture and Allied Arts Univ of Oregon; *Career* architect; princ Rick Mather Architects 1973–; projects incl: Sch of Educn, Sch of Information Systems and the Climatic Res Unit UEA Norwich (Architectural Design Award 1984 and RIBA Award 1988), La Lumière Building London (RIBA Award 1992), ZENW3 Restaurant London (Evening Standard Best Restaurant Design Award 1987), Studio Drama Centre, Constable Terrace (RIBA Award 1994 and Civic Tst Award 1995) and Nelson Ct UEA Norwich, ARCO Bldg Keble Coll Oxford (RIBA Award 1996), All Glass Structure Hampstead (RIBA Nat Award 1994), Nat Maritime Museum Greenwich; conslt architect: Architectural Assoc 1978–92, UEA 1988–94, Univ of Southampton 1996–; teacher 1967–88: Bartlett Univ Coll London, Univ of Westminster, Architectural Assoc London, Harvard Grad Sch of Design; RIBA external examiner 1986–: Univ of Cambridge, Univ of Westminster, De Montfort Univ, Univ of Central England, Mackintosh Sch of Architecture Glasgow, Univ of Ulster; numerous exhbns and lectrs; memb Cncl Architectural Assoc London 1992–96; books on work: Zen Restaurants Architecture in Detail (1992, Phaidon), Urban Approaches A Blueprint Monograph (1993); *Recreations* gardens, food, skiing; *Style—* Rick Mather; ✉ Rick Mather Architects, 123 Camden High Street, London NW1 7JR (☎ 0171 284 1727, fax 0171 267 7826)

MATHER, Sir William Loris; kt (1968), CVO (1986), OBE (1957), MC (1945), TD (and 2 Clasps 1949), DL (Cheshire 1963); s of Loris Emerson Mather, CBE (d 1976), and Gwendoline Leila, *née* Morley (d 1976); elder bro of Sir Carol Mather, MC, *qv*; *b* 17 Aug 1913; *Educ* Oundle, Trinity Coll Cambridge (MA); *m* 1937, Eleanor, da of Prof R H George (d 1979), of Providence, Rhode Island; 2 s (Rev William Mather, Peter), 2 da (Gillian (Mrs Pattinson), Jennifer (Mrs Murray)); *Career* serv WWII, Cheshire Yeo and IRTR, Palestine, Lebanon, Syria, Iraq, Iran, Western Desert, Italy, Belgium, Holland, Germany, instr Staff Coll Camberley 1943–44, cmd Cheshire Yeo 1954–57, Dep Cdr 23 Armd Bde TA 1957–60, Col; ADC to HM The Queen 1961–66; chm: Mather & Platt Ltd 1960–78, CompAir Ltd 1978–83, Neolith Chemical Co Ltd 1983–87, Advanced Manufacturing Technology Centre 1985–88; dir: District Bank, National Provincial Bank and National Westminster Bank 1960–84 (chm Northern Bd), Br Steel Corporation (regnl dir) 1968–73, Manchester Ship Canal Co 1970–85, Wormald International Ltd 1977–78, Imperial Continental Gas Assoc 1980–83; chm: NW Econ Planning Cncl 1968–75, IOD 1979–82; pres: Manchester C of C and Indust 1964–66, Br Pump Makers' Assoc 1977–79, Manchester Guardian Soc for Protection of Trade 1971–85, Gtr Manchester E Scouts 1972–94, Br Mech Engrg Confedn 1974–79, Assoc of Colls of Higher and Further Educn 1975–76, Manchester Univ Inst of Sci and Technol 1976–85, Civic Tst for the NW 1980–90 (chm 1961–80), Econ League 1990–93 (chm for the NW 1982–90), Manchester YMCA 1982–91 (chm 1958–82); memb Cncl Duchy of Lancaster 1977–85; High Sheriff Cheshire 1969–70, Vice Lord-Lt Cheshire 1975–90; hon fell Manchester Coll of Art and Design 1967, hon fell UMIST 1986, hon memb Town Planning Inst 1977; Hon DEng Liverpool 1980, Hon LLD Manchester 1983; CEng, CIMgt, FRSA; *Recreations* field sports, golf; *Clubs* Leander; *Style—* Sir William Mather, CVO, OBE, MC, TD, DL; ✉ Whirley Hall, Macclesfield, Cheshire SK10 4RN (☎ and fax 01625 422077)

MATHERS, James Irvine; s of James Cuthbert Mathers, of 4 Dalhousie Gdns, Bishopbriggs, Glasgow, and Jean Benton, *née* Cobb; *b* 26 Sept 1947; *Educ* Lenzie Acad, Univ of Strathclyde (BSc, DMS); *m* 12 July 1970, Janis Chalmers, da of Douglas Bell (d 1959), of Glasgow; 1 s (Craig b 1973), 1 da (Lynne b 1975); *Career* analyst and programmer Singer Sewing Machines 1968–74, sr systems analyst Hepworth Tailoring 1974–79, sr systems analyst Consolidated Pneumatic Tool Co 1979–80; Hydro Electric: systems mangr 1980–89, computer ops mangr 1989–93, IT Services Manager 1993–; elder Church of Scot; MIMgt 1988; *Style—* James Mathers, Esq; ✉ 68 Newburgh Drive, Bridge of Don, Aberdeen (☎ 01224 820606); Hydro Electric, Ashgrove Road West, Aberdeen AB9 2NY (☎ 01224 287287)

MATHESON, Alasdair Burnett; OBE (1991); s of Chief Constable Alexander John Matheson, MBE (d 1963), of Aberdeen, and Elizabeth Rose, *née* Burnett (d 1994); *b* 18 June 1940; *Educ* Aberdeen GS, Univ of Aberdeen (MB ChB); *m* 15 July 1969, Moira, da of William Salmond MacFarlane (d 1975), of Friockheim; *Career* Aberdeen Royal Infirmary: house offr in med and surgery 1964–65, sr registrar 1975–77, conslt in accident and emergency care 1977–; lectr in physiology Univ of Newcastle upon Tyne 1966, demonstrator in anatomy Univ of Aberdeen 1967, registrar in surgery Cumberland Infirmary Carlisle 1970–73; med memb Royal Med Benevolent Fund Aberdeen, memb Aberdeen Medico-Chirurgical Soc, former chm: Scot Ctee Hosp Med Servs, Grampian Area Ctee Hosp Med Servs; FRCSEd 1972, founding fell Faculty of Accident and Emergency Med 1993; *Books* Pye's Surgical Handicraft (contrib 22 edn, 1992), The

Pathology of Trauma (contrib 2 edn, 1993); *Recreations* trout fishing, curling, model engineering, architecture; *Style*— Alasdair Matheson, Esq, OBE; ✉ The Accident and Emergency Department, Aberdeen Royal Infirmary, Foresterhill, Aberdeen AB25 2ZN (☎ 01224 681818, fax 01224 840718)

MATHESON, Alexander (Sandy); OBE (1990), JP (Western Isles 1972), DL (Western Isles 1994); s of Dr Alexander Matheson (d 1978), of Stornoway, Isle of Lewis, and Catherine Agnes, *née* Smith (d 1986); *b* 16 Nov 1941; *Educ* Nicolson Inst Stornoway, Robert Gordon Tech Coll Aberdeen; *m* 29 March 1965, Irene Mary, da of Alex Davidson; 2 s (Alexander b 2 Sept 1966, Donald Roderick b 9 Nov 1972), 2 da (Isobel Mary b 27 Nov 1969, Irene Louise Catherine b 26 March 1975); *Career* apprentice pharmacist Davidson & Kay Ltd (qualified 1965); Roderick Smith Ltd: superintendent pharmacist 1965–, md 1967–82, chm 1967–; memb: Stornoway Town Cncl 1967–75 (provost 1971–75), Stornoway Tst Estate 1967– (chm 1971–81), Stornoway Pier and Harbour Cmmn 1968– (chm 1971–72 and 1991–), Ross and Cromarty CC 1967–75; fndr chm Western Isles Devpt Fund 1972–; memb: Western Isles Health Bd 1974– (chm 1993–), Western Isles Cncl 1974–90 (convener 1982–90); pres Islands Cmmn of Conf Peripheral Maritime Regions of Europe 1987–91; dir: Western Isles Enterprise 1991–95, Harris Tweed Assoc 1991–94 (now Harris Tweed Authy, memb 1995–), Callanish Ltd 1993–; memb Stornoway Branch RNLI 1974– (chm 1974–79 and 1994–); Hon Sheriff of the Western Isles 1972, Vice Lt of the Western Isles 1994; memb: Royal Pharmaceutical Soc of GB 1965, Royal Soc of Health 1965, Inst of Pharmacy Mgmnt Int 1968; FRPharmS 1993; *Recreations* local history, genealogy, European and Islands travel; *Clubs* Royal Scottish Automobile (Glasgow); *Style*— Sandy Matheson, Esq, OBE, JP, DL; ✉ 33 Newton Street, Stornoway, Isle of Lewis HS1 2RW, Scotland (☎ 01851 702082); Roderick Smith Ltd, 52 Point Street, Stornoway, Isle of Lewis HS1 2XF, Scotland (☎ 01851 702082, fax 01851 706644)

MATHESON, Angus William; s of Angus McQueen Matheson (d 1979), and Jean Beith, *née* McNeil (d 1995); *b* 12 Jan 1937; *Educ* King's Park Sr Secdy Sch; *m* 6 July 1962, Irene Brown, da of Walter McPhee Fleming (d 1991); 1 s (Robin Guy b 21 Aug 1965), 1 da (Lisa Jane b 19 June 1968); *Career* articled clerk Mackie & Clark CAs Glasgow 1955–61 (didn't qualify), auditor/accountant Whinney Murray & Co Glasgow 1961–64, asst to Head of Investmt Dept Whinney Murray & Co 1964–65, head of Investmt Dept Campbell Neill & Co stockbrokers Glasgow 1965–68, investmt analyst rising to asst investmt mangr Coats Patons plc 1968–80, pensions investmt mangr Coats Viyella plc 1980–94 (formerly Coats Patons plc until merger with Vantona Viyella plc 1986), md Bothwell Asset Management Ltd 1989–94; independent investmt advsr Strathclyde Pension Plan 1994–; assoc dir Bestrustees plc 1995–, memb Market Advsy Panel Tradepoint Financial Networks Plc 1995–; Nat Assoc of Pension Funds: vice chm Investmt Ctee 1990–92, chm Investmt Ctee 1992–94, vice pres 1994–96; assoc Inst of Investmt Mgmnt and Res 1968, chm Strathaird Investments Ltd 1964–; FRSA 1992; *Recreations* gardening, countryside, art, photography, music, reading; *Clubs* Western (Glasgow), Royal Scottish Automobile, The Oil Club, West of Scotland Business Club; *Style*— Angus W Matheson, Esq; ✉ 16 Arkleston Road, Paisley, Renfrewshire PA1 3TF (☎ and fax 0141 889 3613)

MATHESON, Duncan; QC (1989); *Educ* Trinity Coll Cambridge (MA, LLM); *Career* called to the Bar Inner Temple 1965, bencher 1994; in practice SE Circuit, recorder of the Crown Ct 1985–; standing jr counsel to the Law Soc in legal aid matters 1981–89; *Style*— Duncan Matheson, Esq, QC; ✉ 1 Crown Office Row, Temple, London EC4Y 7HH (☎ 0171 797 7500, fax 0171 797 7550)

MATHESON, Sir (James Adam) Louis; KBE (1976, MBE 1944), CMG (1972); s of William Matheson (d 1927), and Lily Edith Matheson (d 1951); *b* 11 Feb 1912; *Educ* Bootham Sch York Eng, Manchester Univ (BSc, MSc), Birmingham Univ (PhD); *m* 1937, Audrey Elizabeth, 3 s; *Career* Capt Home Guard Eng; prof of civil engrg Melbourne Univ 1947–50, Beyer prof of engrg Manchester Univ 1951–59, vice-chllr Monash Univ 1960–76, chllr Papua New Guinea Univ of Technol 1973–75, chm Australian Sci and Technol Cncl 1975–76, chm Newport Review Panel 1977; Kernot Meml Medal 1970, P N Russell Meml Medal 1977; Hon DSc Hong Kong; Hon LLD: Manchester, Monash, Melbourne; Hon FICE, Hon FIEAust, FTS, FEng 1980; *Books* Hyperstatic Structures (Vol I 1959, Vol II 1960), Still Learning (1980); *Recreations* music, woodcraft; *Style*— Sir Louis Matheson, KBE, CMG, FEng; ✉ 26/166 West Toorak Rd, South Yarra, Vic 3141, Australia (☎ 00 61 3 9866 4957)

MATHESON, Stephen Charles Taylor (Steve); CB (1993); s of Robert Walter Matheson (d 1962), of Aberdeen, and Olive, *née* Lovick; *b* 27 June 1939; *Educ* Aberdeen GS, Univ of Aberdeen (MA); *m* 23 Jan 1960, Marna Rutherford, da of James Alexander Burnett (d 1958), of Aberdeen; 2 s (Paul b 16 March 1961, Scott b 4 July 1966); *Career* HM inspr of taxes 1961–70, princ Bd of Inland Revenue 1970–75; private sec: to Paymaster Gen 1975–76, to Chllr of the Exchequer 1976–77; asst sec Bd of Inland Revenue 1977, project mangr Computerisation of PAYE Project 1977–84, under sec 1984, dir of information technol Inland Revenue 1984–88, dep sec and DG (mgmnt) Inland Revenue 1989–94, dep chm Bd of Inland Revenue 1993–, dep chm (Policy and Compliance) 1994–; Hon DBA De Montfort Univ 1994; FBCS (pres 1991–92); *Books* Maurice Walsh, Storyteller (1985); *Recreations* cooking, cards, reading; *Style*— Steve Matheson, Esq, CB; ✉ Inland Revenue, Somerset House, London WC2R 1LB (☎ 0171 438 6789, fax 0171 438 7444)

MATHESON OF MATHESON, Maj Sir Fergus John; 7 Bt (UK 1882), of Lochalsh, Co Ross; yr s of Gen Sir Torquhil George Matheson, 5 Bt, KCB, CMG (d 1963), and Lady Elizabeth Keppel, ARRC (d 1986), da of 8 Earl of Albemarle; suc bro, Sir Torquhil Alexander Matheson of Matheson, 6 Bt, DL (d 1993); *b* 22 Feb 1927; *Educ* Eton; *m* 17 May 1952, Hon Jean Elizabeth Mary Willoughby, da of 11 Baron Middleton, KG, MC; 1 s (Lt-Col Alexander Fergus Matheson, yr of Mathesopn, Coldstream Gds b 1954, m 1983, *see* Michael Oswald, CVO), 2 da (Elizabeth Angela Matilda (Mrs Martin C Thompson) b 1953, Fiona Jean Lucia (Mrs Andrew T Kendall) b 1962); *Heir* s, Lt-Col Alexander Fergus Matheson, yr of Matheson b 1954; *Career* serv 1 and 3 Bns Coldstream Gds 1945–64: Palestine, N Africa, Germany, Adjt Mons OCS 1952–55, one of HM Body Guard of Hon Corps of Gentlemen at Arms 1979–, Standard Bearer 1993–; *Clubs* Army & Navy; *Style*— Maj Sir Fergus Matheson of Matheson, Bt; ✉ The Old Rectory, Hedenham, Norfolk NR35 2LD (☎ 01508 482218)

MATHEW, Dr Christopher George Porter; s of Gother Donaldson Porter Mathew, QC (d 1984), of Port Elizabeth, SA, and Evelyn Mary, *née* O'Connor; *b* 7 Sept 1949; *Educ* St Andrew's Coll Grahamstown SA, Univ of Cape Town (BSc), Univ of Port Elizabeth (BSc), Univ of London (PhD, MRCP); *m* Denise, da of Charles Manning; *Career* sr biochemist Provincial Hosp Port Elizabeth 1972–77, PhD student Inst of Cancer Research London 1977–80, S African Med Research Cncl trg fell Dept of Biochemistry St Mary's Hosp London 1980, sr biochemist Univ of Cape Town 1981–82, specialist (med sci) Univ of Stellenbosch SA 1983–86, team ldr Section of Human Cancer Genetics Inst of Cancer Research Sutton Surrey 1986–89, dir SE Thames Regnl DNA Lab and hon sr lectr Div of Med and Molecular Genetics United Med and Dental Schs of Guy's and St Thomas's Hosps London 1989–; Ranbaxy Sci Fndn visiting prof All-India Inst of Med Scis New Delhi 1995; memb Ctee on Clinical Genetics RCP 1994–; MRCPath (memb Cncl and chm Genetics Speciality Advsy Ctee 1993–); memb: Clinical Genetics Soc, Clinical Molecular Genetics Soc, Euro Soc of Human Genetics, Human Genome Orgn; *Recreations* golf, cycling, theatre, cinema; *Style*— Dr Christopher Mathew; ✉ South East Thames Regional DNA Laboratory, Paediatric Research Unit, 8th Floor Guy's Tower, Guy's Hospital, London SE1 9RT (☎ 0171 955 4653, fax 0171 955 4644)

MATHEW, John Charles; QC (1977); s of Sir Theobald Mathew, KBE, MC (d 1964), of 7 Cranley Mansions, London SW7, and Phyllis Helen, *née* Russell (d 1982); *b* 3 May 1927; *Educ* Beaumont; *m* 6 Sept 1952, (Jennifer) Jane, da of Reginald Bousfield Lagden, OBE, MC (d 1944), of Calcutta; 2 da (Sally (Mrs Jamieson) b 17 March 1956, Amanda b 13 Oct 1958); *Career* RN 1945–47; called to the Bar Lincoln's Inn 1949; jr prosecuting counsel to Crown at Central Criminal Ct 1959 (sr Prosecuting Counsel 1964), bencher Lincoln's Inn 1972, head of chambers; *Recreations* golf, tennis, bridge, backgammon; *Clubs* Garrick; *Style*— John Mathew, Esq, QC; ✉ 47 Abingdon Villas, London W8 6XA (☎ 0171 937 7535); 5 Paper Buildings, Temple, London EC4 (☎ 0171 583 6117, fax 0171 353 0075)

MATHEW, Robert Knox (Robin); QC (1992); s of Robert Mathew, TD, MP (d 1966), and Joan Leslie, *née* Bruce (d 1989); *b* 22 Jan 1945; *Educ* Eton, Trinity Coll Dublin (BA); *m* 13 Sept 1968, Anne Rosella, da of Brig Robert Elliott, RA; 1 da (Juliet Alexa Liberty); *Career* journalist 1967–75; called to the Bar 1974, asst boundary cmmr 1993; *Recreations* country pursuits, racing; *Clubs* Boodle's; *Style*— Robin Mathew, Esq, QC; ✉ Church Farm, Little Barrington, nr Burford, Oxford OX18 5TE (☎ and fax 01451 844311); 5 Bell Yard, London WC2A 2JR (☎ 0171 333 8811, fax 0171 333 8831)

MATHEW, Theobald David; s of Robert Mathew (d 1954), and Joan Alison (d 1996), da of Sir George Young, Bt, MVO; *b* 7 April 1942; *Educ* Downside Abbey, Balliol Coll Oxford (MA); *Career* Green staff offr at Investiture of HRH Prince of Wales 1969, Rouge Dragon Pursuivant of Arms 1970, Windsor Herald of Arms 1978–; dep treas College of Arms; OStJ 1986; *Recreations* sailing, cricket, music, sketching; *Clubs* Athenaeum, MCC, Middlesex CCC; *Style*— Theobald Mathew, Esq; ✉ 76 Clifton Hill, London NW8 0JT (☎ 0171 624 8448)

MATHEWS, Dr John Alan; s of Henry Alexander Mathews, and Dora, *née* Apley; *b* 19 June 1934; *Educ* Haberdashers' Aske's, Jesus Coll Cambridge, Guy's Hosp Med Sch (MA, MD, FRCP); *m* 14 July 1957, Wendy, da of Jack Dewhurst; 1 s (Colin David b 1960), 2 da (Gillian Anne b 1962, Catherine Jane b 1972); *Career* dir of specialty and conslt physician Dept of Rheumatology Guy's and St Thomas' Hosp Tst London 1970–; sometime memb Cncl Br Assoc for Rheumatology; sec: Heberden Soc, Br Assoc for Rheumatology and Rehabilitation; past pres Rheumatology and Rehabilitation Section RSM; *Style*— Dr John A Mathews; ✉ 6 Longwood Drive, Roehampton, London SW15 5DL (☎ 0181 789 7831); Department of Rheumatology, St Thomas' Hospital, London SE1 7EH (☎ 0171 928 9292 ext 2171); Churchill Clinic, 80 Lambeth Rd, London SE1 7PW (☎ 0171 928 5633)

MATHEWS, Michael Robert; s of George Walter Mathews, of London, and Betty, *née* Willcox; *b* 3 Nov 1941; *Educ* Uppingham, King's Coll Cambridge (hon scholar, MA); *m* 19 March 1966, Ann Rosemary, da of David Watson Gieve, OBE; 2 s (Robert George b 12 Oct 1969, Stephen Charles b 1 Jan 1973), 1 da ((Caroline) Lucy b 27 Aug 1976); *Career* Coward Chance (became Clifford Chance 1987): articled clerk 1963–66, asst slr 1966–71, ptnr 1971–; Broderip prize Law Soc 1966, City of London Solicitors Co prize 1966; Liveryman City of London Solicitors Co; memb: Cncl Law Soc 1995– (dep vice pres 1996–97), Ctee City of London Law Soc (vice pres 1992–95); *Recreations* walking, watching good cricket; *Style*— Michael Mathews, Esq; ✉ Clifford Chance, 200 Aldersgate Street, London EC1A 4JJ (☎ 0171 600 1000, fax 0171 600 5555)

MATHEWSON, David Carr; s of H Douglas C Mathewson (d 1980), and Evelyn, *née* Carr; *b* 26 July 1947; *Educ* Daniel Stewarts Coll Edinburgh, Univ of St Andrews (BSc, capt athletics team), Wits Business Sch Johannesburg; *m* 23 Sept 1972, Janet, da of late James N McIntyre; 1 s (Ewan b 3 July 1981), 1 da (Emily b 4 Aug 1983); *Career* articled clerk Deloittes Edinburgh 1972, with Williams Glyn & Co London 1972–76, various sr appts Nedbank Group Johannesburg 1976–85; Noble Grossart Ltd merchant bankers: joined 1985, asst dir 1987–89, dir 1989–; also dir: Quicks Group plc 1991–, Rodime plc 1992–, various private cos; MICAS 1972; *Recreations* golf, skiing, gardening, family interests; *Clubs* Bruntsfield Links Golfing Soc, New Golf (St Andrews), New (Edinburgh), Johannesburg Country; *Style*— David Mathewson, Esq; ✉ Dalveen, 7 Barnton Park, Edinburgh EH4 6JF (☎ 0131 336 3214); Noble Grossart Ltd, 48 Queen Street, Edinburgh EH2 3NR (☎ 0131 226 7011, fax 0131 226 6032)

MATHEWSON, Dr George Ross; CBE; s of George Mathewson, of Perth, by his w Charlotte Gordon, *née* Ross; *b* 14 May 1940; *Educ* Perth Acad, Univ of St Andrews (BSc, PhD), Canisius Coll Buffalo NY (MBA); *m* 1966, Sheila Alexandra Graham, da of Eon Bennett (d 1975), of Bridge of Earn, Perth; 2 s; *Career* asst lectr Univ of St Andrews 1964–67; with Bell Aerospace (Buffalo, NY) in res and devpt and avionics engrg 1967–72, joined ICFC Edinburgh 1972 (area mangr Aberdeen 1974, asst gen mangr and dir 1979), chief exec and memb Scottish Devpt Agency 1981–87; The Royal Bank of Scotland Group plc: dir of strategic planning and development 1987–90, dep gp chief exec 1990–92, gp chief exec 1992–; Hon LLD Dundee 1983; FRSE 1988, FCIB (Scot) 1994, CEng, MIEE, CIMgt; *Recreations* rugby, golf, business; *Clubs* New (Edinburgh); *Style*— Dr George Mathewson, CBE; ✉ 29 Saxe Coburg Place, Edinburgh EH3 5BP; The Royal Bank of Scotland Group plc, 42 St Andrew Square, Edinburgh EH2 2YE (☎ 0131 523 2672, fax 0131 558 3741)

MATHEWSON, Dr Hew Byrne; s of Alexander Mackechnie Mathewson, of Elie, Fife, and Dorothy Wightman, *née* Reid; *b* 18 Nov 1949; *Educ* HS of Glasgow, Univ of Glasgow (BDS), Univ of Wales Cardiff (LLM), DGDP (UK), FDS RCS (Edinburgh); *m* 1971, Lorna Anne Marshall, da of George S McConnachie; 1 da (Elizabeth b 1977), 1 s (Andrew b 1980); *Career* assoc dental surgn: Glidden and Archibald Wishaw 1974, Atkins & Cox Canterbury 1975–77; sr ptnr Mathewson & Thomason dental practice Edinburgh 1977–; regnl gen practice vocational trg advsr for SE Scotland 1988–96, dental postgrad advsr for SE Scotland 1987–, asst dir of dental studies Univ of Edinburgh 1987–; BDA: pres E of Scotland branch 1985–86, Scottish sec 1985–90, memb Scottish Gen Dental Servs Ctee 1981–85 and 1991– (chm 1991–97), memb Gen Dental Servs Ctee 1991–, memb Exec 1991–, chm Sick Dentist Mgmnt Gp 1990–; memb: Dental Ctee Scottish Cncl for Postgrad Med and Dental Educn 1987–, Dept of Health SO Advsy Gp on NHS Complaints 1995–96, GDC 1996–; scientific advsr British Dental Jl 1992–; chm Peggy's Mill Assoc 1986–88; memb: BDA 1970, Royal Odonto Chirurgical Soc of Scotland 1986, Faculty of Gen Dental Practioners RCS 1992, Faculty of Dental Surgery RCS (Edinburgh) 1995; *Recreations* carpentry, geriatric tennis, hill walking (mostly in valleys); *Clubs* Edinburgh Sports; *Style*— Dr Hew Mathewson; ✉ Mathewson & Thomason, 182 St John's Road, Edinburgh EH12 8BE (☎ 0131 334 2704, fax 0131 312 7026)

MATHIAS, (Jonathan) Glyn; s of Roland Mathias, of Brecon, and Mary Annie, *née* Hawes; *b* 19 Feb 1945; *Educ* Llandovery Coll, Jesus Coll Oxford (MA), Univ of Southampton (MSc); *m* 1, 1970, Sian, *née* Davies (d 1989); 1 s (Mathew b 1971), 1 da (Megan b 1975); m 2, 1993, Barbara, *née* Pike; *Career* reporter South Wales Echo 1967–70, reporter BBC Southampton 1970–73; ITN: political corr 1973, home affrs corr 1979–81, political ed 1981–86, asst ed 1986–91, controller of public affrs 1991–93, chief political corr 1993–94; political ed BBC Wales 1994–; chm Parly Lobby 1985; memb RTS; *Books* Europe or the Open Sea? (jtly, 1971), Televising Democracies (contrib, ed by Bob Franklin, 1992); *Recreations* sailing, cycling, walking; *Clubs* Reform; *Style*— Glyn Mathias, Esq; ✉ Pendragon, Trerhyngyll, Cowbridge, Vale of Glamorgan CF71 7TN (☎ 01446 773444); BBC Wales, Broadcasting House, Llandaff, Cardiff CF5 2YQ (☎ 01222 572888, fax 01222 552973)

MATHIAS, Julian Robert; s of Anthony Robert Mathias (d 1973), and Cecily Mary Agnes, *née* Hughes; *b* 7 Sept 1943; *Educ* Downside, Univ Coll Oxford (MA); *Career* mangr Hill Samuel and Co Ltd 1964–71, ptnr Buckmaster and Moore 1971–81, dir Foreign and Colonial Management Ltd 1981–95, dir BZW Investment Management Ltd 1995–96; *Recreations* wine tasting, bridge, golf, shooting; *Clubs* Boodle's, City of London, Berkshire Golf; *Style—* Julian Mathias, Esq; ✉ 8 Grove Court, Drayton Gardens, London SW10 9QY (☎ 0171 373 2725, and 01225 448508)

MATHIAS, Dr Peter; CBE (1984); s of John Samuel Mathias (d 1960), and Marion Helen, *née* Love; *b* 10 Jan 1928; *Educ* Colston's Hosp, Jesus Coll Cambridge (BA, MA), Harvard Univ, LittD (Oxon) 1985, DLitt (Cantab) 1987; *m* 5 April 1958, (Elizabeth) Ann, da of Robert Blackmore (d 1979), of Bath; 2 s (Sam b 3 March 1959, Henry b 15 May 1961), 1 da (Sophie b 25 July 1964); *Career* Univ of Cambridge: history lectr 1955–68, res fell Jesus Coll 1952–55 (hon fell 1987), fell and dir of history studies Queens' Coll 1955–68 (tutor 1957–68, hon fell 1987), sr proctor 1965–66; Univ of Oxford: Chichele prof of econ history and fell All Souls Coll 1969–87, curator Bodleian Library 1972–87; Master Downing Coll Cambridge 1987–95 (hon fell 1995); visiting prof: Toronto Univ 1961, Delhi Univ 1967, California Univ Berkeley 1967, Pennsylvania Univ 1972, Columbia Univ (Virginia Gildersleeve prof) 1972, Johns Hopkins Univ 1979, Natal Univ 1980, Australian National Univ 1981, Geneva Univ 1986, Leuven Univ 1990, San Marino Univ 1990, Waseda 1996; hon pres Int Econ History Assoc 1978– (pres 1974–78); vice pres: Royal Historical Soc 1975–80, Business Archives Cncl 1980–84 and 1995– (chm 1967–72, pres 1984–95), Int Inst of Econ History Datini Prato Italy 1987–, Econ History Soc 1992– (hon treas 1968–88, pres 1989–92); hon treas: Econ History Soc 1967–88, Br Acad 1979–89; chm: Int Advsy Ctee Univ of Buckingham 1979–84, Advsy Panel for History of Med Wellcome Tst 1980–88, Friends of Kettle's Yard 1990–, Nat Advsy Cncl Br Library 1994– (memb Humanities and Social Scis Advsy Cncl 1990–94); memb: Advsy Bd for the Res Cncls 1983–89, Round Table Cncl of Indust and Higher Educn 1989–93, Beirat Wissenschaftskolleg Berlin 1992–; memb Syndicate Fitzwilliam Museum Cambridge 1987–, chm Fitzwilliam Museum Enterprises Ltd 1990–; Hon LittD: Univ of Buckingham 1985, Univ of Hull 1992, Univ of Warwick 1995, de Montfort Univ 1995; Hon DLitt Univ of Birmingham 1988; memb: Econ History Soc 1951, Academia Europaea 1989; foreign memb: Royal Danish Acad 1982, Royal Belgian Acad 1988; FRHistS 1972, FBA 1977; *Books* The Brewing Industry in England 1700–1830 (1959), English Trade Tokens (1962), Retailing Revolution (1967), The First Industrial Nation (1969, 1983), The Transformation of England (1979), Science and Society (ed and contrib, 1972), The First Industrial Revolutions (ed with J A Davis and contrib, 1989), Innovation and Technology in Europe (ed with J A Davis and contrib, 1991), L'Economia Britannica dal 1815–1914 (1994); *Recreations* travel; *Style—* Dr Peter Mathias, CBE, FBA; ✉ Bassingbourn Mill, Mill Lane, Bassingbourn, Royston SG8 5PP (☎ and fax 01763 248708); Downing College, Cambridge CB2 1DQ (☎ 01223 334800)

MATHIAS, Sean Gerard; s of John Frederick Mathias (d 1983), of Swansea, and Anne Josephine Patricia, *née* Harding; *b* 14 March 1956; *Educ* Bishop Vaughan Comprehensive Swansea; *Career* director and writer; as playwright: Cowardice (starring Ian McKellen) 1983, Infidelities (Edinburgh Fringe Festival - Perrier Pick of the Fringe Award (transferred to Donmar Warehouse and Boulevard Theatre)) 1985, Prayer for Wings (Edinburgh Fringe Festival - Fringe First Award (dir Joan Plowright)) 1985, Poor Nanny (King's Head) 1989, adapted The Lost Language of Cranes by David Leavitt (BBC, WNET Playhouse series USA (Golden Gate Award Best Television Drama, nominated Radio Times Best Screenplay 1992)); as dir: Acting Shakespeare (Ian McKellen's one-man show on Broadway), A Prayer for Wings (Bush Theatre), Infidelities (Boulevard Theatre) 1986, Exceptions (New End Theatre), The Bed Before Yesterday (int tour starring Sheila Hancock), Talking Heads (Theatre Royal), Noel and Gertie (nat tour and season at Duke of York) 1991, Ghosts (Sherman Theatre), Design for Living (Donmar Warehouse) 1994 (transferred to West End (Evening Standard Drama Award for Best Dir 1994 and Critics' Circle Award for Best Dir 1995)), Indiscretions 1995 (Les Parent Terribles (Barrymore Theatre New York starring Kathleen Turner, 9 Tony Award nominations incl Best Dir 1995)); Royal National Theatre: Bent 1991 (City Limits Best Rival of the Year Award), Uncle Vanya (5 Olivier Award nominations incl Best Dir 1992), Les Parents Terribles (Evening Standard Drama Award for Best Dir 1994 and Critics' Circle Award for Best Dir 1995, 7 Olivier Award nominations incl Best Dir 1994)), A Little Night Music (starring Judi Dench) 1995; film Bent 1996 (starring Clive Owen, Lothaire Bluteau, Ian McKellen, Mick Jagger); *Books* Manhattan Mourning (1988); *Style—* Sean Mathias, Esq; ✉ c/o Judy Daish Associates Ltd, 2 St Charles Place, London W10 6EG (☎ 0181 964 8811, fax 0181 964 8966)

MATHIESON, (John) George; CBE (1982), TD (1964), DL (1977); *b* 15 June 1932; *Educ* George Watson Coll Edinburgh, Univ of Glasgow (LLB); *m* 1958, Shirley Bidder, *née* Clark; 1 s (John George b 30 Oct 1959), 1 da (Elspeth Catherine b 13 Feb 1962); *Career* slr; Nat Serv Royal Artillery 1950–51; articled McGrigor Donald Slrs Glasgow, articled Maclay Murray & Spens, ptnr Clark Oliver Dewar & Webster Slrs 1959 (joined 1957), chm Thorntons WS (successor firm) 1990–; chm: Scottish Slrs' Discipline Tbnl 1982–90, Independent Tbnl Service 1990–, Earl Haig Fund Arbroath 1980–, Royal Br Legion Arbroath 1983–, Scottish Wildlife Tst (Dundee & Angus Branch) 1970–75, Angus Jubilee Ctee 1975–77; Scottish dir Woolwich Building Society 1975–; TA: Cmdg Offr The Highland Regt RA 1964–66, Col Highlands 1972–76, ADC (TA) to HM The Queen 1975–80, chm Highland TAVRA 1976–82; Hon Col 105 (Scottish) Air Def Regt (RA) (V) 1986–91, hon pres Angus Bn Boys' Bde 1985–; Hon Sheriff Arbroath 1994–; *Recreations* shooting, golf, gardening; *Clubs* New (Edinburgh); *Style—* George Mathieson, Esq, CBE, TD, DL; ✉ Thorntons WS, Brothockbank House, Arbroath, Angus DD11 1NJ (☎ 01241 872683, fax 01241 871541)

MATHIESON, Ian Douglas; s of Robert James Mathieson (d 1958), of Harrow, and Violet Lilian, *née* Jones (d 1981); *b* 1 Oct 1942; *Educ* Harrow Weald GS, Coll of Estate Mgmnt Univ of London (BSc), UCL (DipTP); *m* 19 Aug 1967, Lesley, da of Jack Stanley Glass, of Pinner; 2 s (Mark James b 1973, John Robert b 1977); *Career* chartered surveyor in local govt and private practice until 1973, md Commercial Union Properties Ltd 1984– (property investmt mangr 1974–80, dir 1980–), dep md Commercial Union Asset Management Ltd 1987–; memb Wycombe Dist Health Authy 1983–93; memb Teesside Devpt Corp 1990–, memb South Bucks NHS Tst 1993–; Freedom City of London 1986; FRICS 1975 (ARICS 1967); *Clubs* RAC, Royal Over-Seas League; *Style—* Ian Mathieson, Esq; ✉ Commercial Union Properties Ltd, Schomberg House, 80–82 Pall Mall, London SW1Y 5HF (☎ 0171 283 7500, ext 23558, fax 0171 930 3844)

MATHIESON, William Allan Cunningham; CB (1970), CMG (1955), MBE (1945); s of Rev William Miller Mathieson (d 1935), of Scotland, and Elizabeth Cunningham, *née* Reid (d 1957); *b* 22 Feb 1916; *Educ* Dundee HS, Univ of Edinburgh (MA), King's Coll Cambridge; *m* 18 May 1946, Elizabeth Frances, da of Henry Marvell Carr, RA, RP (d 1970), of London; 2 s (Alexander b 1947, Rhoderick Henry b 1951); *Career* RA 1940–45, Maj Europe; Colonial Office 1939–45, asst sec 1949, cnsllr colonial affrs, Br Mission to the UN New York 1951–54, head E Africa Dept Colonial Office 1955–58, min of educn, labour and lands Govt of Kenya 1958–60, under sec Dept of Tech Co-Operation 1961–64, min of Overseas Devpt 1964, dep sec 1968–75, sr conslt UN Devpt Prog New York 1976–81, memb Exec Bd UNESCO 1968–74; memb Bd of Tstees Int Wheat and Maize Improvement Centre Mexico 1976–86, memb and chm Bd of Tstees Int Serv for Nat Agric Res The Hague 1979–84, memb Governing Cncl Int Centre of Insect Physiology and Ecology Nairobi 1983–89; hon fell African Acad of Sciences 1989; *Recreations* gardening, angling, photography, archaeology, travel; *Style—* William Mathieson, Esq, CB, CMG, MBE; ✉ 13 Sydney House, Woodstock Rd, Bedford Park, London W4 1DP (☎ 0181 994 1330)

MATSON, Malcolm John; s of Gp Capt Jack Norman Matson (d 1991), and Wynne Ruth, *née* Parker, of Sherborne, Dorset; *b* 4 Oct 1943; *Educ* Strodes Sch, Trinity Coll of Music, Univ of Nottingham (BA), Harvard (MBA); *m* 1, 1969 (m dis 1988), Judith Helen Wellby, da of Arthur Kenneth Colley (d 1986); 2 s (Thomas Daniel Blandford b 5 Feb 1975, Henry Samuel Quarrington b 21 Dec 1977), 1 da (Cecilia Elspeth Adean b 26 Feb 1980); m 2, 6 Aug 1991, Alexandra Mary, da of William Alexander Noble; *Career* J Walter Thompson 1966–69, Winston Churchill fell 1969, mgmnt conslt 1972–84, gen commercial mangr Westland Helicopters Ltd 1978–81, conslt MMG Patricof (venture capital) 1982–84, fndr and chm Nat Telecable Ltd 1984–; fndr and chm: City of London Telecommuncations Ltd 1988–92, Telecable One Ltd 1994; chm: Chester Square Ltd 1994, Elm House Christian Communications Ltd; memb Cncl PITCOM (Parly IT Ctee); lay reader St Michael's Church Chester Square; Freeman City of London 1967, Alderman City of London (Bread St Ward) 1994–, memb Ct of Assts Worshipful Co of Coopers (Upper Warden 1991), Liveryman Worshipful Co of Glass Sellers 1988; FIMgt 1982; *Recreations* music, motor cycling, thinking, chocolate; *Clubs* City Livery; *Style—* Malcolm Matson, Esq; ✉ 9 The Postern, London EC2Y 8BJ (☎ 0171 628 5998)

MATSON, Richard Tullis; s of Robert Lancelot Matson (d 1986), of The Twemlows, Whitchurch, Shropshire, and Helen Rosemary, *née* Hanson; *b* 24 Sept 1942; *Educ* Uppingham, Royal Agric Coll Cirencester; *m* 9 May 1964, Petronella Vyvyan Anne, da of Lt-Col R F P Eames, TD (d 1987), of Cotley, Chard, Somerset; 2 s (Edward, Tullis), 1 da (Sarah); *Career* farmer and stud owner; vice pres Royal Agric Soc of England 1984– (hon treas 1977–91), chm of Govrs Harper Adams Agric Coll; first Geoffrey Cragghill Scholarship RAC Cirencester 1991; *Recreations* hunting, shooting, stalking; *Clubs* Farmers'; *Style—* Richard Matson, Esq; ✉ Twemlows Hall, Whitchurch, Shropshire SY13 2EZ (☎ 01948 663239, fax 01948 663836, car 0860 526768)

MATTHEW, Brian; s of Joseph Samuel Matthew (d 1971), of Coventry, and Doris Mary, *née* Cleaver (d 1985); *b* 17 Sept 1928; *Educ* Bablake Sch Coventry, RADA; *m* 1951, Pamela Dorothy, *née* Wickington; 1 s (Christopher b 1954); *Career* actor and broadcaster; commenced career doing stage and rep work 1951–52, broadcaster Radio Nederland Hilversum 1953–54, announcer and prodr BBC Radio 1955–60, freelance work for BBC Radio, Radio Luxembourg and ABC TV 1960–; pop music progs incl: Saturday Club, Easy Beat, Thank Your Lucky Stars (TV); other progs incl: Roundabout, Late Night Extra!, Album Time, Round Midnight; returned to theatre 1990, played Justice Shallow in Merry Wives (Chichester), Pa in Snoo Wilson's Lynchville, UK tour of Daisy Pulls It Off 1991, produced reading of Christmas Carol with own co, appeared in pantomime Cinderella (Leatherhead), Beyond Reasonable Doubt 1992–93, Abanazar in Aladdin, fndr memb Fairplay Productions (touring as Nag in Endgame and at Arts Theatre London), Charles Dickens in These Garish Lights (Haymarket and tour 1996–97) 1995; regular prog Sounds of the Sixties voted most popular music prog for third successive year, Sony Award 1996; *Books* Trad Mad, Stage Right, Where I Came In (autobiography); *Recreations* sailing; *Style—* Brian Matthew, Esq; ✉ 1 Roseneath Close, Chesfield Hill, Orpington, Kent BR6 7SR

MATTHEW, Christopher Charles Forrest; s of Leonard Douglas Matthew (d 1984), of Wells-next-the-Sea, Norfolk, and Doris Janet Matthew (d 1988); *b* 8 May 1939; *Educ* King's Sch Canterbury, St Peter's Coll Oxford (MA); *m* 19 Oct 1979, Wendy Mary, da of Kenneth Henry Whitaker (d 1987), of Tilford, Surrey; 2 s (Nicholas b 1980, William b 1982), 1 step da (Charlotte b 1970); *Career* journalist; columns incl: Punch, Vogue, The Daily Telegraph, The Observer; *Radio* chm Something to Declare, The Travelling Show, presenter Points of Departure, Invaders, Plain Tales from the Rhododendrons, Cold Print, A Nest of Singing Birds, contrib Fourth Column; *TV* scripts for The Good Guys (LWT/Havahall Pictures Ltd); *Publications* The Times Travel Guide (ed 1972–74), A Different World: Stories of Great Hotels (1974), Diary of a Somebody (1978), Loosely Engaged (1980), The Long-Haired Boy (1980, adapted for TV as A Perfect Hero, 1991), The Crisp Report (1981), Three Men in a Boat (annotated edn with Benny Green, 1982), The Junket Man (1983), How to Survive Middle Age (1983), Family Matters (1987), The Amber Room (1995); *Recreations* skiing, sailing, golfing, walking in the country with a dog; *Clubs* Garrick, Aldeburgh Yacht, Aldeburgh Golf; *Style—* Christopher Matthew, Esq; ✉ 35 Drayton Gardens, London SW10 9RY (☎ 0171 373 5946)

MATTHEW, Prof (Henry) Colin Gray; s of Henry Johnson Scott Matthew, and Joyce Mary, *née* McKendrick; *b* 15 Jan 1941; *Educ* Sedbergh, ChCh Oxford (MA, DPhil); *m* 17 Dec 1966, Sue Ann, da of Clarence William Curry, of Indianapolis, USA; 2 s (David Hamish Curry b 26 April 1968, Oliver James Gray b 25 July 1973), 1 da (Lucy Ellyn b 21 Nov 1969); *Career* educn offr (IIA) Tanzanian CS 1963–66, lectr in Gladstone studies ChCh Oxford 1970–94, student of ChCh Oxford 1976–78, fell and tutor in modern history St Hugh's Coll Oxford 1978–, prof of modern history Univ of Oxford 1992–; ed New Dictionary of National Biography 1992–; literary dir Royal Historical Soc 1984–89; FRHistS 1973; FBA 1991; *Books* The Liberal Imperialists (1973), The Gladstone Diaries, Vols 3–14 (1974–94), Gladstone 1809–1874 (1986), Gladstone 1875–1898 (1995); *Recreations* second hand book buying, fishing; *Style—* Prof Colin Matthew, FBA; ✉ St Hugh's College, Oxford OX2 6LE (☎ 01865 274900)

MATTHEW, Philip Gregory; s of William Percival Matthew (d 1956), and Winifred Edith, *née* Wilding; *b* 7 Nov 1940; *Educ* St Dunstan's Coll; *m* 1 (m dis); m 2, 28 Nov 1994, Susan Margaret, da of William Ronald Hanworth, of Stansfield, Suffolk; *Career* articled clerk Cooper & Cooper London 1958–63, qualified CA 1964 (Robert Fletcher prize and Plender prize ICAEW 1961); Martin & Acock: joined 1964, ptnr 1974–96, conslt 1996–; treas: Norfolk Lib Dems 1991–94, Mid Norfolk Lib Dems 1995–; memb English Cncl of the Lib Dems 1993–94, chm S Norfolk Lib Dems 1988–90 (vice chm 1991–93); memb Bd of Mgmnt Wherry Housing Assoc 1996–; FCA (ACA 1964); *Recreations* politics, photography, computers, driving Audi Quattros; *Clubs* Audi; *Style—* Philip Matthew, Esq; ✉ The Old Prince of Wales, Prince of Wales Road, Upton, Norfolk NR13 6BW

MATTHEW-WALKER, Robert; s of Samuel Walker (d 1964), of Eltham, and Mary Elizabeth Walker; *b* 23 July 1939; *Educ* St Olave's GS, Goldsmiths' Coll, London Coll of Music, London Coll of Printing; *m* 27 Dec 1969, Lynn Sharon, da of Kenneth Herbert Alfred Andrews (d 1981), of Bromley, Kent; 1 s (Paul b 1971); *Career* Nat Serv RASC 1959–62; private composition study with W Darius Milhaud Paris 1962–63, co sec Thom and Cook Ltd 1963–70, head of Classical Dept CBS Records UK 1971–74, dir mktg CBS Records 1974, dir of masterworks Europe CBS 1974–75, head of Classical Dept RCA Records 1975–78, fndr Chandos Records Ltd 1979–80, fndr Phoenix Records 1982–87, ed Music and Musicians Int 1984–88; dir classical music: Filmtrax plc 1986–88, AVM Records (UK) 1988–90, Allied West Entertainments Ltd 1989–91; md: Grayways Ltd 1989–91, Alfred Lengnick & Co Ltd 1989–91; first performances of compositions incl: Sonata for String Orch Tehran Orch 1976, Piano Trio Cardiff Festival 1978, Sinfonia Solemnis RNCM 1981, Sinfonia Magna For Organ Cologne Cathedral 1984, Christ On The Road to Emmaus City of London Festival 1988; prodr of over 120 records, awarded Grand Prix Du Disque of Academie Charles Cros Paris (for Sonatas for String Quartet by Brian Ferneyhough) 1980; memb: PRS, Critics' Circle; *Books* Rachmaninoff - His Life and Times (1980), Muhammad Ali - His Fights In The Ring (1978), Elvis Presley - A

Study in Music (1979), Simon and Garfunkel (1984), David Bowie - Theatre of Music (1985), Madonna (1989), The Keller Column (1990), The Symphonies of Robert Simpson (1990), A Composer and the Gramophone - Alun Hoddinott on Record (1993), The Recordings of Edvard Grieg (1993), Edvard Grieg (1993), New World Music (1994), Heartbreak Hotel - The Life and Music of Elvis Presley (1995), Havergal Brian (1995), Cincinnati Interludes (1995); *Recreations* history, politics; *Clubs* National Liberal; *Style*— Robert Matthew-Walker; ✉ 1 Exford Road, London SE12 9HD (☎ 0181 857 1582)

MATTHEWMAN, His Hon Judge; Keith Matthewman; QC (1979); s of Lt Frank Matthewman (d 1976), and Elizabeth, *née* Lang (d 1985); *b* 8 Jan 1936; *Educ* Long Eaton GS, UCL (LLB); *m* 1962, Jane, da of Thomas Maxwell (d 1957); 1 s; *Career* called to the Bar Middle Temple 1960; commercial asst (Int Div) Rolls Royce Ltd 1961–62; in practice at the Bar 1962–83 (Midland Circuit, later Midland-Oxford Circuit), recorder Crown Ct 1979–83, circuit judge (Midland and Oxford Circuit) 1983–; memb: Heanor UDC 1960–63, Ctee of the Cncl of Her Majesty's Circuit Judges 1984–89, Notts Probation Ctee 1986–, Mental Health Review Tbnl (Trent Region) 1992–, Parole Bd 1996–; 12 weekly television appearances in Crimestalker (Central) 1993; *Recreations* gardening, reading; *Clubs* Beeston Fields Golf; *Style*— His Hon Judge Matthewman, QC; ✉ Nottingham Crown Court, Nottingham NG1 7EJ

MATTHEWS, Christopher Wynne (Chris); s of Heilwynne James Matthews (d 1968), and Evelyn Christian, *née* Brodie; *b* 31 Oct 1955; *Educ* Royal HS Edinburgh, Univ of Newcastle upon Tyne (BA); *Career* Arthur Andersen & Co 1977–82, fin dir Grass Roots Partnership 1982–85, Valin Pollen 1985–88, chief exec Shandwick Consultants 1993– (joined 1988); *Recreations* sailing, skiing, motorcycling; *Style*— Chris Matthews, Esq; ✉ Shandwick Consultants Ltd, Aldermary House, 10–15 Queen Street, London EC4N 1TX (☎ 0171 329 0096, fax 0171 919 9883)

MATTHEWS, Dr Colin Herbert; s of Herbert Henry Matthews (d 1975), of London, and Elsie Lilian; *b* 13 Feb 1946; *Educ* Univ of Nottingham (BA, MPhil), Univ of Sussex (DPhil); *m* 29 Oct 1977, Belinda Mary, da of Maj-Gen R E Lloyd, CB, CBE, DSO (d 1991), of Lymington; 1 s (Daniel b 1978), 2 da (Jessica b 1972, Lucy b 1980); *Career* composer; lectr Univ of Sussex 1971–72 and 1976–77; more than sixty compositions since 1968 incl: orchestral Fourth Sonata (1974), Night Music (1977), Landscape (1981), Cello Concerto (1984), Monody (1987), Cortège (1989), Broken Symmetry (1991), Memorial (1993), Cello Concerto (1996), Renewal (1996); assoc composer London Symphony Orch 1991–; S Nat Orchestra Ian Whyte award 1975, Park Lane Gp Composer award 1983; dir Holst Estate and Fndn 1973–, memb Cncl and Exec Soc for Promotion of New Music 1981–93 and 1994–, tstee Britten Pears Fndn and dep chm Britten estate 1983–, memb Exec Cncl Aldeburgh Fndn 1984–93, patron Musicians against Nuclear Arms 1986–, dir NMC Recordings 1988–, dir Performing Right Soc 1992–95; *Style*— Dr Colin Matthews; ✉ c/o Faber Music Ltd, 3 Queen Square, London WC1N 3AU (☎ 0171 278 7436, fax 0171 837 8668, telex 299633 FABER G)

MATTHEWS, His Hon Judge; (William) David; s of Edwin Kenneth William Matthews (d 1970), of Hereford, and Bessie, *née* Raiswell (d 1994); *b* 19 Nov 1940; *Educ* Wycliffe; *m* 4 Sept 1965, Pauline Georgina May, da of Percival James Lewis; 2 s (Alastair Charles David b 14 Feb 1967, Duncan Kenneth Craig b 30 Jan 1970); *Career* admitted slr 1964, ptnr Messrs T A Matthews Slrs (articled clerk 1959–64); recorder of the Crown Court 1990, circuit judge (Midland and Oxford Circuit) 1992–; memb Law Soc 1964; pres Herefordshire Breconshire and Radnorshire Incorporated Law Soc 1987–88; *Recreations* farming, walking, cricket, boating; *Clubs* New Quay Yacht; *Style*— His Hon Judge Matthews; ✉ Queen Elizabeth II Law Courts, Newton Street, Birmingham B4 6QQ (☎ 0121 236 9751)

MATTHEWS, Dr Geoffrey Vernon Townsend; OBE (1986); s of Geoffrey Tom Matthews (d 1943), of Northwood, Middx, and Muriel Ivy Matthews (d 1984); *b* 16 June 1923; *Educ* Bedford Sch, Christ's Coll Cambridge (MA, PhD); *m* 1, 6 July 1946 (m dis 1961), Josephine, da of Col Alured Charles Lowther O'Shea Bilderbeck, of Bexhill-on-Sea; 1 s (Vincent Anthony b 1951), 1 da (Rosalind Josephine b 1953); m 2, 2 Jan 1964 (m dis 1978), Janet, da of William Kear, of Sevenoaks; m 3, 26 Jan 1980, Mary Elizabeth, da of William Evans, of Vancouver; 1 s (Alexander William Geoffrey b 1983), 1 da (Catriona Elizabeth b 1981); *Career* Flt Lt and Sci Offr RAFVR 1943–46, serv operational res sections (Bomber Cmd, SE Asia Cmd, Air Miny); dep dir and dir of res and conservation Wildfowl Tst Slimbridge 1955–88, special lectr Univ of Bristol 1956–88, hon professorial fell Univ Coll Cardiff 1970–90, dir Int Waterfowl Res Bureau 1969–88, author of numerous papers on bird migration/orientation and wetland and waterfowl conservation; vice pres Br Ornithologists Union 1972–75 (union medal 1980), pres Assoc for the Study of Animal Behaviour 1971–74; memb: Advsy Ctee on Birds Nature Conservancy Cncl 1978–90, Anglo-Soviet Environmental Protection Agreement 1976–80, Severn Barrage Ctee Dept of Energy 1978–81; EEC advsr on conservation of wild birds 1976–85, chm Environmental Advsy Panel Severn Tidal Power Gp 1987–89, memb many other ctees; corresponding fell American Ornithologists Union 1969, corresponding memb Swiss Soc for Bird Study 1975; RSPB medal 1990; FIBiol; Officier De Orde Van De Gouden Ark (Netherlands) 1987; *Books* Bird Navigation (1955, 2 edn 1968, German edn 1971), The Ramsar Convention on Wetlands: its history and development (1993, German edn 1993, Japanese edn 1995), also author of chapters in a number of multi-authored books; *Recreations* listening to music, collecting biological stamps, collecting fossils, DIY; *Clubs* Victory; *Style*— Dr Geoffrey Matthews, OBE; ✉ Uplands, 32 Tetbury St, Minchinhampton, Stroud, Glos GL6 9JH (☎ 01453 884 769)

MATTHEWS, Jeffery Edward; s of Henry Edward Matthews (d 1960), and Sybil Frances, *née* Cooke (d 1951); *b* 3 April 1928; *Educ* Alleyn's, Brixton Sch of Building (NDD); *m* 12 Sept 1953, (Sylvia Lilian) Christine (d 1994), da of Cecil Herbert William Hoar (d 1974); 1 s (Rory b 1956), 1 da (Sarah Jane b 1958); *Career* graphic designer J Edward Sander 1949–52, pt/t tutor 1952–55, lettering and calligraphy assessor SIAD 1970–; designs for the PO: decimal 'To Pay' labels 1971, font of numerals for definitive stamps 1981, new range of colours for stamps 1987; stamps: United Nations 1965, British Bridges 1968, definitives for Scotland, Wales, NI and IOM 1971, Royal Silver Wedding 1972, 25th Anniversary of the Coronation 1978, London 1980, 80th Birthday of the Queen Mother 1980, Christmas 1980, Wedding of Prince Charles and Lady Diana Spencer 1981, Quincentenary of the College of Arms 1984, 60th Birthday of the Queen 1986, Wedding of Prince Andrew and Sarah Ferguson 1986, Order of the Thistle Tercentenary of Revival 1987, 150th Anniversary of The Penny Black 1990; also: first day covers, postmarks, presentation packs, souvenir books and posters; designer featured in film Picture to Post 1969; other work includes: title banner lettering and coat of arms Sunday Times 1968, cover design and lettering for official programme Royal Wedding 1981, The Royal Mint commemorative medal Order of the Thistle 1987, official heraldry and symbols HMSO, hand-drawn lettering COI, calligraphy, packaging, promotion and book binding designs, logotypes, brand images and hand-drawn lettering; for various firms incl: Unicover Corp USA, Harrison & Sons Ltd, Metal Box Co, John Dickinson, Reader's Digest Association Ltd, Encyclopaedia Britannica International Ltd, ICI, H R Higgins (Coffee-Man) Ltd; work exhibited in A History of Bookplates in Britain and at V & A Museum 1979; Citizen & Goldsmith of London (Freedom by patrimony) 1949; FCSD 1978, FRSA 1987, AIBD 1951; *Books* Designers In Britain (contrib 1964, 1971), 45 Wood-Engravers (contrib, 1982), Royal Mail Year Book (contrib, 1984, 1986, 1987); *Recreations* furniture restoration, playing the guitar, gardening, DIY; *Style*— Jeffery Matthews, Esq

MATTHEWS, Prof John Burr Lumley (Jack); s of Dr John Lumley Matthews (d 1971), of Leamington Spa, and Susan Agnes, *née* Burr (d 1990); *b* 23 April 1935; *Educ* Warwick Sch, St John's Coll Oxford (MA, BSc, DPhil); *m* 28 July 1962, Jane Rosemary, da of Eric Goldsmith (d 1946); 1 s (Roderic John b 1964), 2 da (Susan Jane b 1966, Eleanor Mary b 1971); *Career* Nat Serv 15/19 King's Royal Hussars 1953–55 (served Germany and Malaya); sr scientific offr Oceanographic Laboratory Edinburgh 1964–67, visiting prof Univ of Br Columbia 1977–78, prof of marine biology Univ of Bergen Norway 1978–84 (sr lectr 1967–78), hon prof Univ of Stirling 1988–; sec Scottish Assoc for Marine Science 1988– (dep dir 1984–88, dir 1988–96), dir Dunstaffnage Marine Laboratory NERC 1989–94; memb Ctee for Scotland Nature Conservancy Cncl 1989–90, memb SW Region Bd Scottish Natural Heritage 1991– (dep chm 1994–), memb Bd and Academic Cncl Univ Highlands Islands Project 1994–; sec: Int Assoc of Biological Oceanography 1994–, MARS Network of Euro Marine Stations 1994–; tstee Int Sch Bergen 1980–84; FRSE 1988, FRSA 1989; *Books* Freshwater on the Sea (jt ed), author of numerous scientific articles in professional jls; *Recreations* gardening, country winemaking, pethau cymreig; *Style*— Prof Jack Matthews, FRSE; ✉ Grianaig, Rockfield Rd, Oban, Argyll PA34 5DH (☎ 01631 562734); Dunstaffnage Marine Laboratory, PO Box 3, Oban, Argyll PA34 4AD (☎ 01631 562244, fax 01631 565518)

MATTHEWS, Dr John Duncan; CVO (1989); s of Joseph Keith Matthews (d 1956), of Grayrigg, Tyrells Wood, Surrey, and Ethel, *née* Chambers (d 1978); *b* 19 Sept 1921; *Educ* Shrewsbury, Univ of Cambridge (BA), Univ of Edinburgh (MB ChB); *m* 12 Oct 1945, Constance Margaret, da of Dr James Moffat (d 1975), of Glendevon, West Cornforth, Co Durham; 2 s (Graeme b 1948, Christopher b 1952); *Career* RAMC: 1946–48, TA 1951–62, Col TARO; FRCPE 1958; conslt physician Royal Infirmary Edinburgh 1956–86, hon sr lectr Univ of Edinburgh 1956–86, private practice 1956–88, CMO Scottish Provident Inst 1970–88, vice pres RCPEd 1982–85; chm and memb various NHS and BMA ctees, played cricket for Scotland 1951–58; Holyroodhouse: High Constable 1961–91, Moderator of High Constables and Guard of Hon 1987–89; *Recreations* fishing, gardening, golf; *Clubs* Edinburgh Medical Angling, Grange Cricket, Luffness and Bruntsfield Golf; *Style*— Dr John Matthews, CVO; ✉ 3 Succoth Gardens, Edinburgh EH12 6BR (☎ 0131 337 2636)

MATTHEWS, John Waylett; s of Percy Victor Matthews (d 1970), and Phyllis Edith, *née* Waylett; *b* 22 Sept 1944; *Educ* Forest Sch; *m* 27 May 1972, Lesley Marjorie, da of Alastair Herbert Menzies Halliday; 2 s (Jonathan b 1975, Edward b 1977), 1 da (Anna b 1981); *Career* Dixon Wilson & Co 1962–69, NM Rothschild and Sons 1969–71, dir County NatWest Ltd 1971–88, dep chief exec offr Beazer plc 1988–91 (dep chm 1982–91), chief exec offr Indosuez Capital Ltd 1991–94; chm: Ludgate Group Ltd 1991–, Crest Nicholson plc 1996– (non-exec dir 1992–); non-exec dir: Perry Group plc 1979–, Mithras Investment Trust 1992–94, Ulster Investment Bank Ltd 1988–91, Granville & Co 1995–, Regus Business Centre BV 1995–, Mercury Holdings plc 1996–; FCA; *Recreations* golf, tennis, shooting, bridge; *Clubs* City of London, Royal Automobile, Bath Golf, Crail Golf, Chigwell Golf; *Style*— John Matthews, Esq; ✉ Limpley Crest, Limpley Stoke, Bath BA3 6JW (☎ 01225 723354); Ludgate Group Ltd, 111 Charterhouse Street, London EC1M 6AA (☎ 0171 253 2252, fax 0171 253 4717)

MATTHEWS, Kenneth Joseph (Ken); MBE; s of Joseph Harold Matthews (d 1988), of Sutton Coldfield, West Midlands, and Florence, *née* Brain (d 1984); *b* 21 June 1934; *Educ* Moor End Lane Secdy Modern Sch Birmingham; *m* 12 Aug 1962, Sheila Iris, da of Harry James Eyre; 1 s (Ian Kenneth b 10 July 1966); *Career* former international athlete; Royal Sutton Coldfield Walking Club 1955; 10 AAA titles 2 miles and 7 miles; 16 major appearances incl: Gold medal 20 km walk World Walking Championships Lugano 1961 and 1963, Gold medal 20 km walk Euro Championships Belgrade 1962, Gold medal 20 km walk Olympic Games Tokyo 1964 (also competed Rome 1960); records: world 5 mile walk 1960, world 10 mile walk 1964, Br 6 to 15 miles 1964, Br and Cwlth 20 km 1964, Br and Cwlth 1 hour walk 1964, UK 2 hour walk 1964, UK and Cwlth 7 mile walk 1964; *Recreations* cycle time trials; *Style*— Ken Matthews, Esq, MBE

MATTHEWS, Michael Gough; s of late Cecil Gough Matthews, and Amelia Eleanor Mary Matthews; *b* 12 July 1931; *Educ* Chigwell Sch, Royal Coll of Music; *Career* pianist, teacher and adjudicator of int piano competitions; RCM: dir Junior Dept and prof of piano 1972–75, registrar 1975, vice dir 1978–84, dir 1985–93; dip of honour and prize Chopin Int Piano Competition 1955, Italian Govt scholarship 1956, Chopin fellowship Warsaw 1959; dir Assoc Bd of the Royal Schs of Music; tstee: Ballantine's Music Fndn, Prince Consort Fndn 1993; hon vice pres Governing Ctee Royal Choral Soc, hon dir The Royal Music Fndn Inc; chm Awards Ctee Musicians' Benevolent Fund 1994; memb: Nat Youth Orchestra, Royal Philharmonic Soc, Mgmnt Bd London Int String Quartet Competition, Music Study Group EEC, Comité d'Honneur Presence de L'Art Paris, Cncl Purcell Tercentenary Tst; vice pres: Royal College of Organists, Nat Youth Choir, Herbert Howells Soc; music conslt: Jaguar Cars 1995, HM The Sultan of Oman 1995; Hon FLCM 1976, Hon RAM 1979, ARCO, ARCM, FRCM 1972, FRSAMD 1986, Hon GSM 1987, FRSA, FRNCM 1991; *Recreations* gardening; *Clubs* Athenaeum; *Style*— Michael Gough Matthews, Esq; ✉ Laurel Cottages, South Street, Mayfield, East Sussex TN20 6DD (☎ and fax 01435 873065); 16 Brompton Park Crescent, London SW6 1SN (☎ 0171 381 6004)

MATTHEWS, Neil Howard; s of Howard Matthews, and Gwyneth, *née* Davies; *b* 2 Aug 1948; *Educ* Duffryn GS, Port Talbot Welsh Sch of Architecture Cardiff (BSc, BArch); *m* 29 July 1972, Averil Susan, da of Ronald Abbott (Flt-Offr RAF), of 132 Bolgoed Rd, Pontardulais, W Glam; 1 da (Lydia Dee Matthews b 1978), 1 s (Jack Timothy Rhys Matthews b 1986); *Career* architect and developer; princ Neil H Matthews Assoc; md: Rhodethorn Developments Ltd 1987–, Gower Marine Ltd 1994–; RIBA; played rugby: Bridgend, Glam Wanderers, Llanelli, Aberavon; 1967 swimmer of the year BLDSA (selected GB team Scheld Swim Holland, Welsh Schools 100m freestyle champion), Wales under 21 water polo team 1967, John Williams prizewinner WSA 1972; *Recreations* squash, swimming, sailing; *Style*— Neil Matthews, Esq; ✉ Frongelli House, Llanedi, Pontardulais, Swansea SA4 1YR (☎ 01792 883251, fax 01792 884062); 2 Station Rd, Pontardulais, Swansea

MATTHEWS, Sir Peter Alec; kt (1975), Hon AO (1980); s of Maj Alec Matthews, and Elsie Lazarus Barlow; *b* 21 Sept 1922; *Educ* Shawnigan Lake Sch Vancouver Island, Oundle; *m* 1946, Sheila Bunting; 4 s, 1 da; *Career* served RE 1940–46, Maj; joined Stewarts and Lloyds Ltd 1946 (dir of res and tech devpt 1962), memb for R & D BSC 1968–70 (dep chm 1973–76); chm Vickers plc 1980–84 (md 1970–79); dir: Lloyds Bank 1974–91 (chm Central London Regnl Bd 1978–90), British Electric Traction plc 1976–87, Pegler-Hattersley plc 1977–87 (chm 1979–87), Sun Alliance & London Insurance 1979–89, Cookson Group (formerly Lead Industries Group) 1980–90, Hamilton Oil Great Britain 1981–90, Lloyds and Scottish 1983–86; chm Armed Forces Pay Review Body 1984–89; memb: Top Salaries Review Body 1984–89, BOTB 1973–77, Export Guarantees Advsy Cncl 1973–78, NRDC 1974–80, Engrg Industs Cncl 1976–84 (chm 1980–84), Advsy Cncl for Applied R & D 1976–80, Status Review Ctee ECGD 1983–84; pres: Sino-Br Trade Cncl 1983–85, Engrg Employers' Fedn 1982–84; hon fell UCL 1982 (chm Cncl 1980–89); FRSA; *Recreations* sailing, gardening; *Clubs* Royal Yacht Squadron (Cowes); *Style*— Sir Peter Matthews, AO; ✉ Chalkwell, Nether Wallop, Stockbridge, Hants SO20 8HE (☎ 0264 782136)

MATTHEWS, Sir Peter Jack; kt (1981), CVO (1978), OBE (1974), QPM (1970), DL (Surrey 1981); s of Thomas Matthews; *b* 25 Dec 1917; *Educ* Blackridge Public Sch W Lothian; *m* 1944, Margaret, da of Cecil Levett; 1 s; *Career* WWII, Flt Lt and pilot RAF;

with Met Police 1937–65 (seconded to Cyprus 1955), chief constable Surrey 1968–82 (E Suffolk 1965–67, Suffolk 1967–68); chm Home Office Standing Ctee on Police Dogs 1978–81; int pres Int Police Assoc 1966–70 (Br pres 1964–70), pres Assoc of Chief Police Offrs (Eng and Wales) 1976 (seconded to Royal Hong Kong Police 1981), i/c Br Study Team in Singapore 1982; lectures of major incident procedures given to police forces: Royal Hong Kong, Singapore, Royal Bahamas, Canada, USA; also lectured to: BMA, BASICS, Airline Trg Assocs, International Military Services Ltd; specialist advsr Def Select Ctee House of Commons 1983–92; ACPO rep of Interpol 1977–80; hon memb BASICS; pres Woking Branch Air Crew Assoc 1988–; CIMgt; kt 1981; *Clubs* RAF; *Style—* Sir Peter Matthews, CVO, OBE, QPM, DL

MATTHEWS, Peter Jeffrey; s of Arthur Robert Matthews (d 1977), of Wembley, Middlesex, and Rosina Louise, *née* Saulez (d 1984); *b* 29 July 1942; *Educ* Ealing Tech Coll, Ealing Sch of Art (DipAD); *m* 2 April 1977, Caroline, da of Maj John Harvey Moore, OBE, ISO, of Kemp Town, Brighton, Sussex; 1 s (Ross b 1978), 1 da (Chloë b 1980); *Career* craftsman demonstrator RCA 1962–65, sr lectr Wimbledon Sch of Art 1966–; exhibitions: RWS Gallery London 1961, British Printmakers in the 60s touring USA 1966, Galerie Unicorn Copenhagen 1978, Ljubljana Print Biennale 1985, British Prints State Publishing Gallery Moscow 1989, Int Print Biennale Varna Bulgaria 1989, Int Print Biennale Maastricht 1994, Foreign Press Assoc London 1996, New Acad Gallery London 1996; work in public collections incl: V and A Museum London, Bibliotheque Royale Brussels, Br Cncl, Albertina Museum Vienna; fell Royal Soc of Painter Printmakers 1985; *Clubs* Royal Soc of Painter Printmakers; *Style—* Peter Matthews, Esq; ✉ 1 Manor Road, London SW20 9AE; Chez Blanchard, Charente, France; Wimbledon School of Art, Merton Hall Rd, Wimbledon, London SW19 (☎ 0181 540 0231)

MATTHEWS, Peter John; s of William John Matthews (d 1990), of Norwich, and Pamela Mary, *née* Butt; *b* 6 Jan 1945; *Educ* Uppingham; *m* 1 Nov 1969, Diana Joan, da of John Randell; 2 s (John Paul b 22 Dec 1972, Michael Robert b 1 Nov 1975); *Career* Arthur Guinness Son & Co Ltd 1963–: information offr Guinness 1975–77, dir Guinness Publishing 1989–96 (gen mangr 1977–80, editorial dir 1980–84), conslt ed Guinness Book of Records 1996– (sports ed 1982–91, ed 1991–95); media info mangr for athletics Olympic Games Atlanta 1996; chief announcer Athletics Commonwealth Games 1970, athletics commentator ITV 1985– (BBC Radio 1975–85), ed Int Athletics Annual 1985–; *Books* Guinness Book of Athletics Facts and Feats (1982), Official Book of the 1986 Commonwealth Games (1986), Guinness Encyclopaedia of Sports Records and Results (1987, 1990, 1993 and 1995), Cricket Firsts (with Robert Brooke, 1988), Who's Who in British Athletics (1990), Guinness International Who's Who of Sport (1993), All-Time Greats of British Sport (with Ian Buchanan, 1995); *Style—* Peter Matthews, Esq; ✉ 10 Madgeways Close, Great Amwell, Ware, Herts SG12 9RU (☎ 01920 870434); Guinness Publishing, 33 London Road, Enfield, Middlesex EN2 6DJ (☎ 0181 367 4567, fax 0181 366 7849)

MATTHEWS, Richard Bonnar; CBE (1971), QPM (1965); s of Charles Richard Matthews (d 1960), of Worthing, and Beatrice Alexandra, *née* Bonnar (d 1975); *b* 18 Dec 1915; *Educ* Stowe; *m* 1 Jan 1943, Joan Emily, da of Basil Worsley (d 1978), of Henstridge, Somerset; 2 da (Miranda b 22 Jan 1944, Rosemary b 23 Dec 1946); *Career* WWII serv Lt RNVR 1939–45; Met Police 1936–54, asst chief constable E Sussex 1954–56; chief constable: Cornwall and Isles of Scilly 1956–64, Warwickshire 1964–76; chm Traffic Ctee Assoc of Chief Police Offrs 1973–76, memb Williams Ctee on obscenity and film censorship 1977–79, chm Bds for Civil Serv cmmn 1979–85; *Recreations* fishing, skiing, gardening; *Clubs* Naval; *Style—* Richard Matthews, Esq, CBE, QPM; ✉ Smoke Acre, Great Bedwyn, Marlborough, Wiltshire SN8 3LP (☎ 01672 870584)

MATTHEWS, Sir Stanley; kt (1965), CBE (1957); s of late Jack Matthews; *b* 1 Jan 1915; *Educ* Wellington Sch Hanley; *m* 1, 1935 (m dis 1975), Elizabeth Hall, da of J Vallance; 1 s, 1 da; m 2, 1975, Gertrud (Mila) Winterova; *Career* professional footballer: Stoke City FC 1931–47, Blackpool FC 1947–61 (FA Cup winners 1953), Stoke City FC 1961–65; Footballer of the Year 1947 and 1965, European Player 1957; gen mangr Port Vale FC 1965–68; 54 England caps (11 goals) 1935–57; pres Stoke City FC; Freeman City of Stoke-on-Trent 1963, FIFA Gold Merit Order 1992; *Books* The Stanley Matthews Story (1960), Stanley Matthews (biography, 1989); *Recreations* golf, tennis; *Clubs* Nat Sporting; *Style—* Sir Stanley Matthews, CBE; ✉ c/o Stoke City Football Club, Victoria Ground, Stoke-on-Trent

MATTHEWS, Stephen George; s of George William Matthews, of Exeter, and Eileen Mary, *née* Lount (d 1957); *b* 1 Feb 1946; *Educ* Torquay GS; *m* Diana Lynne Matthews; 1 s (Richard b 3 Oct 1975), 2 da (Victoria b 23 Jan 1974, Emily b 8 Nov 1981); *Career* journalist: N Devon Journal Herald 1966–71, BBC Radio 1971–72; Westward TV 1972–80: reporter, news ed, ed, prodr, presenter, rising to head of news and current affrs; ed TVS 1980–82; HTV West: head of news and current affrs 1982–92, dir of progs 1992–95, md (progs) 1995–; *Recreations* flying, sailing; *Style—* Stephen Matthews, Esq; ✉ Red Gables, Silver St, Chew Magna, Bristol BS18 8RE (☎ 0117 933 2285); HTV West Ltd, Television Centre, Bath Road, Bristol BS4 3HG (☎ 0117 972 2150, fax 0117 972 3100)

MATTHEWS, Suzan Patricia; QC (1993); da of Sidney Herbert Clark (d 1965), of Guildford, and Susan Hadnett, *née* Mathews (d 1983); *b* 5 Dec 1947; *Educ* Univ of Bradford (BSc); *m* 1970, Anthony Robert Matthews, s of Frederick Russell Matthews; 1 s (Robert Jonathan Richard b 1977); *Career* called to the Bar Middle Temple 1974; in practice in chambers: Bradford 1974–79, Guildford 1979–; recorder of the Crown Court 1995– (asst recorder 1991–95), asst boundary cmmr 1992–; chm: Ctees of Investigation MAFF 1994–, The Valley Trust; rep London & SE Regn Gas Consumers Cncl 1987–96, memb Criminal Injuries Compensation Appeals Panel 1996–; *Recreations* historical research, gardening, music and messing about on boats; *Style—* Mrs Suzan Matthews, QC; ✉ Guildford Chambers, Stoke House, Leapale Lane, Guildford, Surrey GU1 4LY (☎ 01483 39131, fax 01483 300542)

MATTHEWS, Tim John; s of Kenneth James Matthews, of Kingston, S Devon, and Vera Joan, *née* Fittall; *b* 24 June 1951; *Educ* Plymouth Coll, Peterhouse Cambridge (exhibitioner, BA); *m* Sally Vivien, da of William Tudor Davies; 2 s (Tom Alexander b 14 Sept 1984, James Osborn Louie b 5 Sept 1987); *Career* DHSS: admin trainee 1974, private sec to perm sec 1978–80, princ 1980–84; dist gen administrator Bloomsbury Health Authy 1984–85, gen mangr The Middx Hosp Div Bloomsbury Health Authy 1985–88, dist gen mangr Maidstone Health Authy 1988–91, dist gen mangr W Lambeth Health Authy and chief exec St Thomas' Hosp 1991–93, chief exec Guy's and St Thomas' Hosp NHS Trust 1993–; dir Central London Trg and Enterprise Cncl 1996–; tstee Kent Community Housing Trust 1991–94; MHSM 1985, FRSA 1993; *Style—* Tim Matthews, Esq; ✉ Guy's and St Thomas's Hospital Trust, St Thomas Street, London SE1 9RT (☎ 0171 955 4164, fax 0171 955 4844)

MATTHEWS-MAXWELL OF SLEICHAM AND SEUM THE YR, Maj Christopher Ranulph George St John; TD (1979 and Clasps 1985 and 1991); 26 Lord of Mounton and Lord of the Manors of Cophill, Langham Parva, Merton and Wolton; formerly patron of two livings; s of Lt-Col Alastair Arthur Charles St John Matthews-Maxwell, 25 Lord of Mounton (d 1958), and Georgina Muriel, *née* Buchanan-Dunlop-Reay (d 1953); *b* 28 June 1945; *Educ* King's Sch, RMA Sandhurst, Univ of Durham, Newcastle and Exeter; *m* 1983, Bronwen Nicola Grendon, *née* Grendon-Jones (late Maj QARANC); *Career* cmmnd Army 1967, transferred to T&AVR 1970, Maj 1980, HAC 1981; Mil Marshal of the City of London; company dir and farmer; owner of Mounton and Cophill Estates, chm S Northumberland Area YFC 1970–71; memb: Centre for Mgmnt in Agric, CLA, NFU, Northern MBA Working Gp 1986–88; chm BIM Mgmnt Res Gp North; govr RNLI, non-exec dir Northumberland Family Health Services Authy, assoc memb Northumberland DHA; dep chm: Northern Regnl Ctee for Employment of Disabled Persons, Northumberland Co Branch Cncl for Protection of Rural England; memb: Countryside Movement, Sr Med Appts Bd Northern and Yorks RHA, NHS National Pharmaceutical Appeals Ctee, Northern Regnl Bd Anchor Housing Assoc, Anchor Trust, Northern Regnl Bd Guardian Housing Assoc Ltd, Occupational Pensions Advsy Serv, Br Nuclear Forum, Northern Regnl Employers Forum, NE Human Resources Forum; lay memb Diocesan Bd of Educn Adjudication Panel; Knight of Justice Hospitaller Order of St John of Jerusalem 1983; Freeman City of London, Liveryman Worshipful Co of Meadmakers; FCIS, CDipAF, DipMM, MIPM, MITD, MIMgt, FRSA, FSA(Scot); *Recreations* hunting, shooting, skiing, sailing, equestrian sports; *Clubs* Constitutional, Army and Navy, Royal Over-Seas League, Prince Albert Brussels; *Style—* Maj Christopher Matthews-Maxwell of Sleicham and Seum The Yr; ✉ Royal Bank of Scotland, Grey St, Newcastle upon Tyne

MATTISON, John Eric; s of Alfred James Mattison (d 1973), of Lingwood, Norfolk, and Mildred Edith, *née* Temperley (d 1974); *b* 12 Aug 1940; *Educ* City of Norwich Sch, LSE (BSc); *m* March 1964, Margaret Jane, da of Patrick Malervy; 3 s (John Patrick b 17 March 1965, James Gerard b 24 July 1966, Nicholas Frank b 30 Nov 1970); 2 da (Sally Jane b 22 March 1968, Catherine Temperley b 5 Sept 1975); *Career* fin journalist 1962–70: Investors' Chronicle, Evening Standard, Sunday Times; dir: McLeish Associates 1970–80, Lopex Public Relations 1980–85, Hill & Knowlton 1985–88; chief exec Burson-Marsteller Financial 1988–93, dir Shandwick Consultants 1993–95; chm Mattison Public Relations 1995–; Freeman Borough of Alnwick Northumberland 1956; *Books* Bluffer's Guide to Finance (1968); *Recreations* golf, sailing; *Style—* John Mattison, Esq

MATTOCK, John Clive; s of late Raymond Jack Mattock, of Sidmouth, E Devon, and Eva Winifred Zoë, *née* Ward; *b* 21 Jan 1944; *Educ* Dartford GS; *m* 1985, Susan, da of Richard Clulow, of 97 Upper Mealines, Harlow, Essex; 2 s (Anthony b 1986, Christopher b 1988); *Career* stockbroker; ptnr Fiske and Co 1975–88; dep chm: Carlisle Group plc 1985–90, Peak Tst Ltd 1988, Corporate Services Group plc 1989; dir: Stalwart Assurance Group plc 1986–89, Takare plc 1986–89, Ellis and Partners Ltd 1991–; FCA 1967; *Recreations* tennis, squash; *Clubs* Bexley Lawn Tennis (vice pres), Limpsfield Lawn Tennis, Penshurst Amateur Dramatic Soc; *Style—* J C Mattock, Esq; ✉ Beacon Platt, Dormansland, Lingfield, Surrey RH7 6RB; Ellis and Partners, Talisman House, The Courtyard, East Park, Crawley, W Sussex RH10 6AS (☎ 01293 517744)

MATTOCK, Prof John Nicholas; s of Gilbert Arthur James Mattock (d 1970), of Horsham, Sussex, and Margaret Kathleen, *née* Gale; *b* 6 Jan 1938; *Educ* Christ's Hosp, Pembroke Coll Cambridge (MA, PhD); *Career* Drapers res fell Pembroke Coll Cambridge 1963–65, prof of Arabic and Islamic studies Univ of Glasgow 1987– (lectr 1965, sr lectr 1976); ed Jl of Arabic Literature and Studies in Arabic Literature 1970–; pres UEAI 1990–94; memb BRISMES (fell 1973); *Books* Arabic Technical and Scientific Texts (6 vols, 1965–78); *Recreations* food and wine, tennis, golf; *Clubs* Royal and Ancient Golf (St Andrews); *Style—* Prof John Mattock; ✉ Dept of Arabic and Islamic Studies, University of Glasgow, Glasgow G12 8QQ (☎ and fax 0141 330 5586)

MAUCHLINE, Lord; Michael Edward Abney-Hastings; assumed by deed poll 1946 surname of Abney-Hastings; s of Countess of Loudoun, and (first husb) Capt Walter Strickland Lord; h to Earldom of mother; *b* 22 July 1942; *Educ* Ampleforth; *m* 1969, Noelene Margaret, da of W J McCormick; 2 s (Hon Simon Michael b 1974, Marcus William b 1981), 3 da (Hon Amanda Louise b 1969, Hon Lisa Maree b 1971, Hon Rebecca Lee b (twin) 1974); *Heir* s, Hon Simon Michael Abney-Hastings b 1974; *Style—* Lord Mauchline; ✉ 74 Coreen St, Jerilderie, NSW 2716, Australia

MAUD, Hon Sir Humphrey John Hamilton; KCMG (1993, CMG 1982); s of Baron Redcliffe-Maud (Life Peer; d 1982), and Jean, *née* Hamilton (d 1993); *b* 17 April 1934; *Educ* Eton, King's Coll Cambridge, Nuffield Coll Oxford; *m* 1963, Maria Eugenia Gazitua; 3 s; *Career* Nat Serv Coldstream Gds 1953–55; instr in classics Univ of Minnesota 1958–59; joined FO 1959, Madrid 1961–63, Havana 1963–65, FCO 1966–67, seconded to Cabinet Office 1968–69, Paris 1970–74, sabbatical at Nuffield Coll Oxford studying economics 1974–75, head of financial rels FCO 1975–79, min Madrid 1979–82, ambass Luxembourg 1982–85, asst under-sec of state (int economic affairs and trade rels) FCO 1985–88, high cmmr Nicosia 1988–90, ambass Buenos Aires 1990–93; Cwlth dep sec-gen (economic and social) 1993–; *Recreations* music, golf, bird watching; *Clubs* Utd Oxford and Cambridge Univ; *Style—* The Hon Sir Humphrey Maud, KCMG; ✉ 31 Queen Anne's Grove, Bedford Park, London W4 1HW (☎ 0181 994 2808)

MAUDE, Rt Hon Francis Anthony Aylmer; PC (1992); yr s of Baron Maude of Stratford-upon-Avon, TD, PC (Life Peer; d 1993) and Barbara Elizabeth Earnshaw, *née* Sutcliffe; *b* 4 July 1953; *Educ* Abingdon Sch, Corpus Christi Coll Cambridge (BA); *m* 1984, Christina Jane, yr da of A Peter Hadfield, of Copthorne, Shrewsbury; 2 s (Henry Peter Angus b 10 Sept 1990, Alastair Timothy Charles b 17 March 1994), 3 da (Julia Elizabeth Barbara b 26 Dec 1986, Cecily Mary Anne b 29 July 1988, Lydia Helen Grace b 28 Feb 1996); *Career* called to the Bar Inner Temple 1977 (Law scholarship, Forster Boulton Prize), barr in chambers of Sir Michael Havers, QC, MP (later Lord Havers); memb Westminster City Cncl 1978–84, MP (C) Warwickshire N 1983–92; PPS to Hon Peter Morrison as Min of State for Employment 1984–85, a Govt whip 1985–87; parly under sec of state: for corporate and consumer affrs DTI 1987–88, for corporate affrs 1988–89; min of state FCO 1989–90, financial sec to the Treasy 1990–92; advsr to Hongkong and Shanghai Banking Corp on bid for Midland Bank 1992, a dir of corporate finance (head of Privatisation Unit) Salomon Brothers International 1992–93, head of privatisation and an md Morgan Stanley 1993–; non-exec dir Asda Group plc 1992–; chm HM Govt Deregulation Task Force 1994–, chm of Govrs Abingdon Sch 1994–; *Recreations* skiing, cricket, music, opera; *Style—* The Rt Hon Francis Maude; ✉ Morgan Stanley International, 25 Cabot Square, Canary Wharf, London E14 4QA (☎ 0171 425 8000)

MAUDE-ROXBY, Richard Gay; s of John Henry Maude-Roxby; *b* 7 June 1947; *Educ* Dauntseys Sch; *m* 1971, Lynda Helena Marjorie, *née* Sanders; 3 c; *Career* dir: buying and mktg Budgen Limited 1978–82, Budgen Ltd 1982–86, Booker Food Services 1986–89, Booker Cash & Carry 1989–93, Booker Belmont Wholesale 1993–; non-exec dir Courthaven; Liveryman Worshipful Co of Skinners; *Recreations* shooting, fishing; *Style—* Richard Maude-Roxby, Esq; ✉ Red House Farm, Watery Lane, Beachampton, Milton Keynes, Bucks (☎ 01908 569161)

MAUDSLAY, John Rennie; s of Maj Sir Rennie Maudslay, GCVO, KCB, MBE (d 1988), and Jane Ann, *née* McCarty; *b* 26 May 1953; *Educ* Eton; *m* 12 April 1986, Alexandra, da of Dr William Lothian, of Shoreham, Kent; 3 da (Georgina b 1987, Sophia b 1989, Fenella b 1992); *Career* memb Lloyd's 1979; ptnr Barder & Marsh 1988–96; dir: Barder & Marsh Ltd 1992–96, M J Tullberg & Co Ltd 1992–94; Freeman City of London, Liveryman Worshipful Co of Mercers 1980; *Recreations* shooting, fishing; *Clubs* White's; *Style—* John Maudslay, Esq

MAUDSLAY, Richard Henry; s of Cecil Winton Maudslay (d 1969), and Charity Magdalen, *née* Johnston (d 1995); *b* 19 Nov 1946; *Educ* Christ's Hosp Horsham, Univ of Edinburgh (BSc); *m* 3 Aug 1968, Rosalind Elizabeth, da of James Slater Seville; 2 da (Diana Elizabeth b 29 Jan 1973, Helen Catherine b 4 Sept 1974); *Career* graduate trainee Scottish Electrical Trg Scheme 1968–69, systems analyst Parsons Peebles Ltd 1969–71, systems mangr Reyrolle Belmos Ltd 1971–72, systems and programming mangr Parsons Peebles Ltd 1972–74, prodn mangr Parsons Peebles Power Transformers 1974–78, general mangr Transformadores Parsons Peebles de Mexico 1978–85; md: NEI Parsons Ltd 1985–92, Rolls-Royce Industrial Power Group 1992– (memb Bd Rolls-Royce plc 1994–); FEng 1994, FIEE; *Recreations* music; *Clubs* Royal Overseas; *Style—* Richard Maudslay, Esq, FEng; ✉ Rolls-Royce Industrial Power Group, NEI House, Gosforth, Newcastle upon Tyne NE3 3SB (☎ 0191 284 3191, fax 0191 284 4482)

MAUGHAN, Air Vice-Marshal Charles Gilbert; CB (1976), CBE (1970), AFC (1960); s of Charles Alexander (d 1964), of London, and Magdalene Maria, *née* Tacke (d 1979); *b* 3 March 1923; *Educ* Sir George Monoux GS, Harrow Co Sch; *m* 14 June 1947, Pamela Joyce, da of late Cecil Wicks, of London; 1 s (David b 24 Nov 1953), 1 da (Susan b 12 July 1950); *Career* Fleet Air Arm (Swordfishes, Albacores, Seafires) 1942–46, joined RAF 1949, CO 65 Sqdn (Hunters) 1958, won Daily Mail Air Race London-Paris 1959, CO 9 Sqdn (Vulcans) 1964; Station Cdr: RAF Honnington (Victors) 1964, RAF Waddington (Vulcans) 1965; Gp Capt Ops HQ Bomber Cmd 1967, Air Attaché Bonn 1970, AI Admin Strike Cmd 1974, Sr ASO Strike Cmd 1975, ret RAF 1978; gen sec Royal Br Legion 1978–83, inspr on panel of ind insprs DOE and Tport 1983–93; Chevalier Legion d'Honneur France 1960; *Recreations* walking, travel, theatre; *Style—* Air Vice-Marshal Charles Maughan, CB, CBE, AFC; ✉ Whitestones, Tresham, Wotton under Edge, Glos GL12 7RW

MAULEVERER, (Peter) Bruce; QC (1985); s of Maj Algernon Arthur Mauleverer, of Poole, Dorset (d 1979), and Hazel Mary, *née* Flowers (d 1983); *b* 22 Nov 1946; *Educ* Sherborne, Univ of Durham (BA); *m* 7 Aug 1971, Sara, da of Dr Michael Hudson-Evans, of St Maughans, Monmouth, Gwent; 2 s (Edward b 1972, Barnaby b 1974), 2 da (Harriet b 1977, Clementine b 1982); *Career* called to the Bar Inner Temple 1969, bencher 1993, head of chambers; recorder of the Crown Court 1985–; hon sec gen Int Law Assoc 1986–93 (vice chm 1993); *Recreations* sailing, skiing; *Style—* Bruce Mauleverer, Esq, QC; ✉ 4 Pump Ct, Temple, London EC4Y 7AN (☎ 0171 353 2656, fax 0171 583 2036)

MAUNDER, Prof Leonard; OBE (1977); s of Thomas George Maunder (d 1975), and Elizabeth Ann Maunder, *née* Long (d 1985); *b* 10 May 1927; *Educ* Bishop Gore GS Swansea, Univ Coll Swansea (BSc), Univ of Edinburgh (PhD), MIT (ScD); *m* 1958, Moira Anne, da of Edwin George Hudson (d 1977); 1 s (David), 1 da (Joanna); *Career* instr and asst prof MIT 1950–54, Aeronautical Res Lab US Air Force 1954–56, lectr Univ of Edinburgh 1956–61; Univ of Newcastle upon Tyne: prof of mech engrg 1967–92 (prof of applied mechanics 1961, prof emeritus 1992–), dean of Faculty of Engrg 1973–78; chm: SRC/DTI Working Pty for the Teaching Co Scheme 1974–77 (chm Mgmnt Ctee 1977–85), SRC Engrg Bd 1976–80, Advsy Cncl on R & D Dept of Energy 1981–92; memb: NRDC 1976–81, Cncl Br Technol Gp 1981–92; dep chm Newcastle Hosps Mgmnt Ctee 1971–73, memb Newcastle Dist Health Authy 1973–91; pres: Int Fedn for the Theory of Machines & Mechanisms 1976–79, Engrg Br Assoc for the Advancement of Sci 1980; vice pres Inst of Mech Engrs 1976–81; Christmas lectr Royal Inst 1983; memb Advsy Cncl on Sci Technol 1987–93; hon fell Univ Coll of Swansea 1989, hon foreign memb Polish Soc of Applied Mechanics 1984; FEng 1981; *Books* Gyrodynamics and its Engineering Applications (with R N Arnold, 1961), Machines in Motion (1986), numerous papers in the fields of applied mechanics; *Style—* Prof Leonard Maunder, OBE, FEng; ✉ Old Forge Building, The University of Newcastle upon Tyne, Newcastle NE1 7RU (☎ 0191 222 6200, fax 0191 222 7153)

MAUNDERS, Prof Keith Terrence; s of Roy Keith Maunders, of Newport, Gwent, and Hilda Violet, *née* Brett; *b* 11 Sept 1939; *Educ* Newport High Sch, Univ of Hull (BSc); *m* 26 July 1969, Julie, da of James E Mantle, of Leeds; 2 da (Helen b 1976, Hannah b 1980); *Career* prof of business fin and accounting Univ of Leeds 1978–89, prof of accounting Univ of Hull 1989–; assoc dean Tel Aviv Int Sch of Mgmnt 1996–; visiting prof: Univ of Texas 1985, Univ of Sydney 1986, Aust Nat Univ 1989; gen sec Br Accounting Assoc; FCCA; *Books* Accounting Information Disclosure and Collective Bargaining (1977), Corporate Social Reporting (1987); *Recreations* birdwatching; *Style—* Prof Keith Maunders; ✉ Dept of Accounting, University of Hull, Hull HU6 7RX (☎ 01482 466391, fax 01482 466377, telex 592530 UNIHUL G)

MAUNDRELL, John William; s of Rev Canon Wolseley David Maundrell, of Chichester, West Sussex, and Barbara Katharine, *née* Simmons (d 1985); *b* 27 Sept 1955; *Educ* Winchester, Courtauld Inst of Art Univ of London (BA); *m* 31 Oct 1987, Hazel, da of Francis Walter Monck; 1 s (William Frederick b 22 Nov 1991), 1 da (Alexandra Katharine b 30 Sept 1989); *Career* articled clerk Deloitte Haskins & Sells 1979–82, qualified chartered accountant 1982, asst dir County Bank Ltd/County NatWest 1986–87 (joined 1982), dir Gilbert Eliott Corporate Finance Ltd 1989–90 (asst dir 1987–89), dir Rea Brothers Limited 1991–93; co sec Hobson plc 1994–96, dir Cruden Bay plc 1996–; ACA; *Recreations* mountaineering, swimming, tennis; *Style—* John Maundrell, Esq; ✉ Tanglewood, 6 Hall Close, Henham, nr Bishop's Stortford, Hertfordshire CM22 6AU

MAUNG, Hla; *b* 8 Nov 1932; *Educ* Univ of Yangon (BA), Vanderbilt Univ USA (MA, dip in devpt economics); *m*; 6 c; *Career* Myanman diplomat; Miny of Planning and Fin: admin offr 1955–60, asst dir 1960–67, dep dir 1967–72, DG 1972–80 and 1980–84; exec dir Asian Development Bank 1981–83 (alternate exec dir 1978–80); Myanman ambass to: Philippines 1984–87, Belgrade 1987–92, Ct of St James's 1992–96 (concurrently non-resident ambass to Norway and Sweden 1993–96, non-resident ambass to Denmark 1994–96); delgn and conf experience incl: World Bank and AID Loan Negotiation Meeting USA 1973, Annual World Bank Meeting Kenya 1973, Philippines 1976 and USA 1977; holder of various titles and awards; *Style—* U Hla Maung

MAUNSELL, Michael Brooke; s of Capt Terence Augustus Ker Maunsell, RN (d 1972), of Walton on Thames, Surrey, and Elizabeth, *née* Brooke (d 1974); *b* 29 Jan 1942; *Educ* Monkton Combe Sch, Gonville and Caius Coll Cambridge (MA, LLB); *m* 1, 7 Aug 1965 (m dis 1986), Susan Pamela, da of George Cruickshank Smith (d 1969), of Attenborough, nr Nottingham; m 2, 8 Aug 1986, (Caroline) Harriet Maunsell, OBE, da of Prof Geoffrey Sharman Dawes, CBE, of Oxford; *Career* solicitor; ptnr: Lovell White & King 1971–88, Lovell White Durrant 1988– (jt managing ptnr 1993–); tstee Highgate Cemetery Charity 1988–95; Liveryman Worshipful Co of Slrs 1980; memb Law Soc 1967; *Recreations* walking, watching birds, opera, travelling; *Style—* Michael Maunsell, Esq; ✉ Lovell White Durrant, 65 Holborn Viaduct, London EC1A 2DY (☎ 0171 236 0066, fax 0171 248 4212)

MAURICE, Clare Mary; *née* Rankin; da of Antony Colin Deans Rankin, of Manton, Marlborough, Wiltshire, and Barbara, *née* Vernon; *b* 25 Feb 1954; *Educ* Sherborne Sch for Girls, Univ of Birmingham (LLB); *m* 20 Dec 1980, Ian James Maurice, s of Douglas Creyke Maurice (d 1968); 2 da (Anna b 10 Mar 1987, Kate b 8 Oct 1989); *Career* admitted slr 1978; Allen & Overy: articled 1976, asst slr 1978, ptnr 1985–, grad recruitment ptnr 1994–; special tstee Bart's and St Mark's Hosps 1994–; *Recreations* theatre, travel; *Clubs* Reform; *Style—* Mrs Clare Maurice; ✉ 33 Norland Square, London W11 4PU (☎ 0171 221 0962); Allen & Overy, One New Change, London EC4M 9QQ (☎ 0171 330 3000, fax 0171 330 9999)

MAURICE, Dr Rita Joy; da of Albert Newton Maurice (d 1943), and Florence Annie, *née* Dean (d 1971); *b* 10 May 1929; *Educ* East Grinstead Co Sch, UCL (BSc, PhD); *Career* lectr in economic statistics UCL 1951–58; statistician then chief statistician Miny of Health and Central Statistical Office 1959–72; head Economics and Statistics Div DTI 1972–77; dir of statistics Home Office 1977–89; memb Cncl Royal Statistical Soc 1978–82, memb Parole Bd 1991–94, memb Advsy Ctee Retail Prices Index 1992–94; *Style—* Dr Rita Maurice; ✉ 10 Fairfax Place, Swiss Cottage, London NW6 4EH (☎ 0171 624 5797)

MAURICE-WILLIAMS, Robert Stephen; s of Dr Hubert Cecil Maurice-Williams, OBE (d 1981), of Southampton, and Eileen Florence, *née* Lauder; *b* 14 June 1942; *Educ* Winchester, Pembroke Coll Cambridge (BA, MA, MB BChir), St Thomas' Hosp Med Sch; *m* 9 Sept 1968, Elizabeth Anne, da of Dr Swithin Pinder Meadows, of London; 1 s (Julian Robert Cecil b 1979), 3 da (Francesca Clare Louise b 1971, Harriet Elizabeth Anne b 1974, Vanessa Christina Alice b 1982); *Career* registrar in neurosurgery Guy's Maudsley Neurosurgical Unit 1971–73, sr registrar in neurosurgery St Bartholomew's Hosp 1973–77, conslt neurosurgn Brook Hosp 1977–80, sr conslt neurosurgn The Royal Free Hosp 1980–; papers on surgery and physiology of the central nervous system; ed British Journal of Neurosurgery 1992–, memb Ct of Examiners Royal Coll of Surgns of England 1992–; fell Hunterian Soc 1980; FRCS 1971, FRCP 1990 (MRCP 1973); *Books* Spinal Degenerative Disease (1981), Subarachnoid Haemorrhage (1988); *Recreations* walking; *Clubs* The Athenaeum, Pitt (Cambridge); *Style—* Robert Maurice-Williams, Esq; ✉ Royal Free Hospital, Regional Neurosurgical Unit, London NW3 2QG (☎ 0171 794 0500 ext 3356/3357); Neurosurgical Unit, Wellington Hospital, London NW8 9LE (☎ 0171 722 1224)

MAVOR, Prof John; s of Gordon Hattersley Mavor (d 1967), and Wilhelmina Baillie, *née* McAllister; *b* 18 July 1942; *Educ* Bromley Tech HS, City Univ (BSc), Univ of London (PhD, DSc); *m* 1968, Susan Christina, da of Alfred Ethelbert Colton; 2 da (Helen McAllister b 1969, Louise McAllister (twin)); *Career* electronics engr AEI Research Laboratories 1964–65, product engr Texas Instruments Ltd 1968–70, sr electronics engr Emihus Microcomponents Ltd 1970–71; Univ of Edinburgh: lectr in electronic engrg 1971–79, reader 1979–80, Lothian chair of microelectronics 1980–85, head Dept of Electrical Engrg 1984–89, chair of electrical engrg 1986–94, dean Faculty of Science and Engrg 1989–94; Napier Univ: prof 1994–, princ and vice chllr 1994–; FInstP 1981, FIEE 1982, FIEEE 1989, FRSE 1989, FEng 1994; *Books* MOST Integrated Circuit Engineering (1973), Introduction to MOS LSI Design (1983); *Recreations* walking, steam railways; *Clubs* New (Edinburgh); *Style—* Prof John Mavor, FEng, FRSE; ✉ 8 Heriot Row, Edinburgh EH3 6HU (☎ 0131 556 7003); Principal's Office, Napier University, Craiglockhart Campus, 219 Colinton Road, Edinburgh EH14 1DJ (☎ 0131 455 4600/4601, fax 0131 455 4570)

MAVOR, Michael Barclay; CVO (1983); s of William Ferrier Mavor, of Melton Park, Newcastle upon Tyne, and Sheena Watson, *née* Barclay (d 1995); *b* 29 Jan 1947; *Educ* Loretto, St John's Coll Cambridge (MA); *m* 20 Aug 1970, (Jane) Elizabeth, da of Albert Sucksmith (d 1958), of Lima, Peru; 1 s (Alexander b 31 Oct 1981), 1 da (Veronica b 5 Oct 1977); *Career* Woodrow Wilson fell Northwestern Univ Evanston Illinois USA 1969–72, asst master Tonbridge Sch 1972–78, course tutor for The Open Univ 1974–76; headmaster: Gordonstoun 1979–90, Rugby Sch 1990–; *Recreations* fishing, golf, painting, theatre; *Clubs* Hawks'; *Style—* Michael Mavor, Esq, CVO; ✉ Rugby School, Rugby, Warwickshire CV22 5EH (☎ 01788 543465, fax 01788 579745)

MAVROGORDATO, Peter; s of Nicolas Mavrogordato and Nol, *née* Dineen (d 1989); *b* 5 April 1943; *Educ* Elstree, Eton, RAC Cirencester; *m* Hosanna, da of Paul Henry Mills Richey DFC; *Career* chartered surveyor; ptnr Warmingtons 1971–; FRICS; *Recreations* everything; *Style—* Peter Mavrogordato, Esq; ✉ Warmingtons, Stevington, Bedford MK43 7QF (☎ 01234 823661, fax 01234 822625)

MAVROSKOUFIS, Dr Filippos; s of Simeon Mavroskoufis, of Thessaloniki, Greece, and Leontia, *née* Vassilakaki; *b* 15 Aug 1952; *Educ* Thessaloniki HS Greece, Dental Sch Aristotelion Univ of Thessaloniki (DDS), Univ Coll London (MSc, PhD), Univ of Lund Malmö Sweden; *m* 25 May 1985, Janice Gibson, da of John Sailes Clark; 1 s (Simeon b 30 July 1985), 2 da (Antigoni b 15 July 1989, Elektra b 19 Aug 1991); *Career* Univ Coll Hosp: registrar Prosthetics Dept Dental Sch 1977–78, registrar Community Med Dept 1978–79, involved in teaching of prosthetic dentistry and treating of patients Dental Sch 1977–83; in general practice: pt/t 1981–83, full-time 1983–; in Harley St 1988–; presented 3 scientific papers to Dental Confs of Euro Prosthodontic Assoc, published 6 scientific papers in Dental Journals of Europe and America; memb: Br Soc for Study of Prosthetic Dentistry 1977, Euro Prosthodontic Assoc 1977, General Dental Practitioners Assoc 1989, Hellenic Soc of Professional People and Scientists in GB, Hellenic Med Soc in GB, Macedonian Soc of GB; *Recreations* basketball, swimming, stamp collecting, cooking, debating; *Clubs* YMCA; *Style—* Dr Filippos Mavroskoufis; ✉ 22 Mercers Road, London N19 4PJ (☎ 0171 272 7694); 44 Harley St, London W1N 1AD (☎ 0171 255 1492)

MAW, (John) Nicholas; s of Clarence Frederick Maw (d 1967), and Helen, *née* Chambers (d 1950); *b* 5 Nov 1935; *Educ* Wennington Sch Wetherby Yorks, RAM; *m* Nov 1960 (m dis 1976), Karen Graham; 1 s (Adrian Lindsay), 1 da (Natasha Helen von Sternberg); *Career* composer of operas, symphonic works, instrumental, chamber and choral music; tutor in composition: RAM 1962–64, Univ of Exeter 1972–74; visiting prof of composition: Yale Univ USA 1984, 1985 and 1989, Boston Univ USA 1986; prof of music Milton Avery Graduate Sch for the Arts Bard Coll USA 1990; Lili Boulanger Meml Prize 1959, Midsummer Prize City of London 1980, Koussevitsky Award 1990, Sudler International Wind Band Prize 1992; memb (and formerly chm) Assoc of Professional Composers; FRAM 1973; *Style—* Nicholas Maw, Esq; ✉ c/o Faber Music, 3 Queen Square, London WC1N 3AU (☎ 0171 278 7436)

MAWER, Philip John Courtney; *b* 30 July 1947; *Educ* Hull GS, Univ of Edinburgh (MA), Univ of London (external dip in public admin); *m* 1972, Mary Ann, *née* Moxon; 1 s, 2 da; *Career* sr pres Student Representative Cncl 1969–70; Home Office: joined 1971, private sec to Min of State 1974–76, princ 1976–83 (Nuffield and Leverhulme travelling fell 1978–79), sec Lord Scarman's Inquiry into Brixton Disturbances 1981, asst sec/head of industl rels Prison Dept 1984–87, princ private sec to Home Sec 1987–89, under sec Cabinet Office 1989–90; sec gen Gen Synod C of E 1990–; FRSA 1991; *Recreations* family and friends; *Style—* Philip Mawer, Esq; ✉ Secretary General of the General Synod of the Church of England, Church House, Great Smith Street, London SW1P 3NZ (☎ 0171 222 9011)

MAWHINNEY, Rt Hon Dr Brian Stanley; PC (1994), MP (C) Peterborough (majority 5,376); s of Stanley Mawhinney; *b* 26 July 1940; *Educ* Royal Belfast Academical Inst, Queen's Univ Belfast (BSc), Univ of Michigan (MSc), Univ of London (PhD); *m* 1965, Betty Louise Oja; 2 s, 1 da; *Career* asst prof of radiation res Univ of Iowa 1968–70; lectr and sr lectr Royal Free Hosp Sch of Med 1970–84; memb: MRC 1980–83, Gen Synod 1985–90; pres Cons Trade Unionists 1987–90; Parly candidate (C) Stockton-on-Tees Oct 1974, MP (C) Peterborough 1979–; PPS to: Barney Hayhoe as Min of State Treasury 1982–84, Rt Hon Tom King as Sec of State for Employment then NI 1984–86; Parly under sec of state NI Office 1986–90; min of state: for N Ireland 1990–92, Dept of Health 1992–94; sec of state for tport 1994–95, chm Cons Pty 1995–, Cabinet min without portfolio 1995–; *Style—* The Rt Hon Dr Brian Mawhinney, MP; ✉ House of Commons, London SW1A 0AA (☎ 0171 219 6205)

MAWREY, Richard Brooks; QC (1986); s of Philip Stephen Mawrey, of Benson, Oxon, and Alice Brooks, *née* Blezard; *b* 20 Aug 1942; *Educ* Rossall Sch, Magdalen Coll Oxford (Eldon law scholar, BA, MA), Gray's Inn (Albion Richardson scholar); *m* 18 Sept 1965, Gillian Margaret, da of Francis Butt (d 1985); 1 da (Eleanor Frances b 1977); *Career* barr; called to the Bar Gray's Inn 1964; lectr in law: Magdalen Coll Oxford 1964–65, Trinity Coll Oxford 1965–69; recorder Crown Court 1986– (asst recorder 1982–86), dep High Ct judge 1994–; co-fndr and tstee Historic Gardens Fndn; *Books* Computers and the Law (1988); *Recreations* opera, history, cooking; *Style*— Richard B Mawrey, Esq, QC; ✉ 2 Harcourt Buildings, Temple, London EC4Y 9DB (☎ 0171 583 9020, fax 0171 583 2686)

MAWSON, David; OBE (1990), JP (Norwich 1972), DL (Norfolk 1986); s of John William Mawson (d 1964), of Keri Keri, NZ, and Evelyn Mary, *née* Bond; *b* 30 May 1924; *Educ* Merchant Taylors', Wellington Coll NZ, Auckland Univ NZ, Kingston-upon-Thames Coll of Art; *m* 1951, Margaret Kathlyn, da of Charles Joseph Norton (d 1942), of Norwich, Norfolk; 1 s (Iain), 1 da (Diana); *Career* architect 1953– (to Norwich Cathedral 1977–90), conslt Feilden & Mawson 1990– (ptnr 1956–90); Norfolk Soc (CPRE): chm 1971–76, vice pres 1976–96, pres 1996–; chm: Br Assoc of Friends of Museums 1973–89 (vice pres 1989–), Friends of Norwich Museums 1985–, Norfolk Professional Firms Group 1994–; fndr and chm Norfolk Gardens Tst 1988–91 (vice pres 1991–); fndr pres World Fedn of Friends of Museums 1975–81; pres: Norfolk Club 1986, Norfolk Assoc of Architects 1977–79 (memb 1952–95), Costume and Textile Assoc for Norfolk Museums 1989–; hon treas Heritage Co-ordination Gp 1980–86, memb Ctee of Nat Heritage 1973–90; tstee: Norfolk Historic Buildings Tst 1975–90, Theatre Royal Norwich 1991–; govr Wymondham Coll 1991–; FSA, RIBA; *Recreations* yachting, photography; *Clubs* Norfolk (Norwich); *Style*— David Mawson, Esq, OBE, JP, DL, FSA; ✉ Gonville Hall, Wymondham, Norfolk NR18 9JG (☎ 01953 602166)

MAWSON, Dr David Charles; s of Richard Mawson, and Alice Margaret, *née* Greenhalgh; *b* 8 April 1947; *Educ* Aldenham, UCH London (MB BS, DPM); *m* 3 Oct 1970, Mina Mawson; 2 s (Benjy b 1971, Ben b 1977), 1 da (Laura b 1980); *Career* conslt forensic psychiatrist Broadmoor Hosp and sr lectr Inst of Psychiatry 1981–86; med dir: Moss Side Hosp 1986–89, AMI Stockton Hall 1989–91; ind practice in forensic psychiatry 1991–93, conslt forensic psychiatrist Broadmoor Hosp 1993– (also curently dir of Med Servs); author of chapters and articles on general and forensic psychiatry; DPM 1976, FRCPsych 1989 (MRCPsych 1976); *Style*— Dr David Mawson; ✉ Broadmoor Hospital, Crowthorne, Berks RG11 7EG

MAWTUS, Michael John; s of Richard John Mawtus, of York, and Eileen Mawtus (d 1980); *b* 11 Feb 1947; *Educ* BSc; *m* 16 Feb 1974, Ann, da of John Evans; 2 da (Emma Jane b 25 Sept 1983, Samantha Mary b 12 June 1985); *Career* dir of channel strategy IBM Europe, Middle E and Africa 1991–93; IBM UK Ltd: dir of distribution and mktg 1993–96, main bd dir 1994–; central mangr distribution and channels IBM Europe, ME and Africa 1996–; memb Bd American C of C; supporter Business in the Community; FRSA 1995, FCIM 1996; *Recreations* golf, fly fishing; *Clubs* Windlesham Golf; *Style*— Mike Mawtus, Esq; ✉ IBM United Kingdom Ltd, New Square, Bedfont Lakes, Feltham, London TW14 8HB (☎ 0181 818 4107, fax 0181 818 5386, mobile 0802 224414, e-mail gbibm936@ibmmail)

MAX, Robert Ian; s of Michael G Max, and Wendy, *née* Segal; *b* 7 Feb 1968; *Educ* St Paul's Sch Barnes, RAM (GRSM, DipRam, LRAM), RNCM (post graduate dip), Julliard Sch New York USA; *m* 21 March 1993, Zoë Solomon; *Career* cellist; winner: Euro Music for Youth Cello Competition Brussels 1984, Int Young Concert Artists Tst competition (strings section) 1989; solo concert performances in UK, USA, Germany, Austria, Belgium, Denmark and France; as cellist of Barbican Piano Trio: recording for ASV 1989 and 1994, toured Denmark, France, Italy, Bulgaria, USA, Russia, S America, Far East and UK; broadcasts incl BBC Radio 3, French TV and BBC World Service; chm Music Aid 1992–95; musical dir: Nonesuch Orchestra 1993–96, Zemel Choir 1994–; recording for Olympia; asst musical dir Pro Corda, plays 'Saveuse' Stradivarius Cello of 1726; *Recreations* cooking Indian food, reading, walking, gardening, skiing; *Style*— Robert Max, Esq; ✉ 5 Asmuns Hill, London NW11 6ES (☎ and fax 0181 458 2839)

MAXEY, Peter Malcolm; CMG (1982); *b* 26 Dec 1930; *Educ* Bedford Sch, CCC Cambridge; *m* 1, 1955 (m dis 1978), Joyce Diane Marshall; 2 s, 2 da; m 2, 1978, Christine Irene Spooner; *Career* entered Foreign Serv 1953, seconded to Lazard Bros 1971–72, cnsllr CSCE Delgn Geneva 1973, head UN Dept FCO 1974–77, cnsllr Dublin 1977, loaned to Cabinet Office as under-sec 1978–81, ambass GDR 1981–84, ambass & dep perm rep to UN (New York) 1984–86; editorial dir Global Analysis Systems 1986–88; *Style*— Peter Maxey, Esq, CMG

MAXFIELD, Ron; *b* 11 July 1962; *Educ* Oak Park Comp Havant Hants, Southdowns Tech Coll Purbrook Hants (City & Guilds); *Career* second chef Royal Corinthian Yacht Club Cowes June-Oct 1980, second chef Devils Punch Bowl Hotel Hindhead 1980–81, jr commis rising to sr commis London Hilton Int Park Lane 1981–84, chef de partie Waterside Inn Bray Berks 1984–86, head chef Cliveden 1988– (second sous chef 1986–87, sr sous chef 1987–88); memb: Academie Culinaire de France, Craft Guild of Chefs; Master Chef of GB; *Awards* Silver Award McDougalls Catering Awards 1983, finalist Restaurateurs Assoc Young Chef of the Year 1987, third Egon Ronay Br Pork Chefs Competition 1992, winner 30 under 30 Acorn Awards 1992, Michelin Star (Waldo's Restaurant Cliveden Hotel) 1992, Good Hotel Guide César Award 1995, Egon Ronay Guide Kitchen of the Year Award and County Dessert of the Year 1995, Egon Ronay Guide highest rated hotel 1995 and 1996, Egon Ronay Guide star (Waldo's Restaurant) 1995, Hotel & Caterer Magazine Hotel of the Year Award 1996, Egon Ronay Guide Hotel of the Year 1996; *Style*— Ron Maxfield, Esq; ✉ Cliveden, Taplow, Berkshire SL6 0JF (☎ 01628 668561, fax 01628 661837)

MAXLOW-TOMLINSON, Paul Christian; s of John Maxlow-Tomlinson, and Marjorie Maude, *née* Muhlenkamp; *b* 24 Oct 1931; *Educ* Cranleigh, Trinity Coll Dublin, Wadham Coll Oxford (MA); *m* 1, 1 Nov 1959 (m dis 1962), Jeanette McDonald; m 2, 28 June 1969 (m dis 1994), Anne, da of Charles Trench Stewart; 1 s (Charles Henry b 29 July 1974), 1 da (Claudia Lucy b 6 March 1972); m 3, 6 Feb 1994, Julia Berkkan, *née* Pipe-Wolferstan; *Career* cmmnd Queen's Royal Regt 1950–52; Mercantile Credit Co: Zimbabwe 1956–62, London 1962–63, NI 1963–64; Grand Circle Travel Co 1965–68; admitted slr 1971, currently sr ptnr Stones Slrs (joined 1972); chm Ski Club of GB 1982–87 (memb Cncl 1978–82); memb: Devon Probation Ctee 1983–86, Exec Cncl Br Acad of Forensic Sciences 1987–90; Br rep Legal Ctee Federation Internationale de Ski 1988–96, arbitrator Int Court of Arbitration for Sport Lausanne Switzerland 1995–; fndr memb and chm Oakfields Project (ex-prisoners' hostel in Exeter), dir Omnijuris (consortium of Euro lawyers) 1992–95; memb Law Soc (memb Childrens Panel 1987–); author of various articles on international skiing law; MBAE 1995; *Recreations* skiing, shooting, fishing, painting; *Clubs* Garrick, Ski Club of GB; *Style*— Paul Maxlow-Tomlinson, Esq; ✉ Northernhay Place, Exeter, Devonshire EX4 3QQ (☎ 01392 51501, fax 01392 57007)

MAXMIN, Dr (Hiram) James (Jim); s of Henry W Maxmin (d 1992), of USA, and Louise, *née* Strousse (d 1977); *b* 26 Sept 1942; *Educ* Cheltenham HS, Grinnell Coll Iowa (BA), Fitzwilliam Coll Cambridge, King's Coll London (PhD); *m* 1987, Prof Shoshana Zuboff; 1 s (Jacob b 1995); 3 s (Peter b 1972, Jonathan b 1977, Ben b 1983) and 2 da (Kate b 1971, Chloe b 1992) from previous m; *Career* trainee Unilever Ltd 1968–69, Lever Bros 1969–71, dir Unilever Orgn 1971–73, mktg dir Volvo Concessionaires UK 1975–78, jt chm and md Volvo UK 1978–83, dir Thorn EMI plc 1983–92, chm and chief exec Thorn Home Electronics 1983–92, pres Thorn EMI inc (USA) 1983–92, chief exec Laura Ashley plc 1991–94, chm Informate Associates 1994–, chm and managing ptnr Global Brand Development Ltd; non-exec dir: Geest plc 1993–, BAA PLC 1994–, Dawson International Plc 1995–, Streamline Inc 1995–, ABM Ltd 1996–; former offr SMMT; lectr at business coll, fund raiser Fitzwilliam Coll Cambridge, involved in local educn initiatives; FIMI 1983, CIMgt 1985; *Recreations* rugby, fishing, swimming; *Style*— Dr Jim Maxmin; ✉ Flat 14, 51 Iverna Gardens, London W8 6TP (☎ 0171 937 2858); Lake Field Farm, Morang Cove Rd, Nobelboro, Damiscrotta 04555, Maine, USA (☎ 00 1 207 832 4781)

MAXTON, John Alston; MP (Lab) Glasgow Cathcart (majority 8,001); s of John Maxton, and Jenny Maxton; *b* 5 May 1936; *Educ* Lord Williams' GS Thames, Univ of Oxford; *m* Christine Maxton; 3 s; *Career* joined Lab Pty 1970, MP (Lab) Glasgow Cathcart 1979–; oppn spokesman on: health, local govt and housing in Scotland 1985–87, Scotland 1987–92; memb: Scottish Select Ctee 1981–83, Public Accounts Ctee 1983–84, Nat Heritage Select Ctee 1992–; memb Speaker's Panel of Chairmen 1994–; *Style*— John Maxton, Esq, MP; ✉ House of Commons, London SW1A 0AA (☎ 0171 219 3000)

MAXTONE GRAHAM, Robert Mungo; s of Anthony James Oliphant Maxtone Graham (d 1971), of Cultoquhey, Crieff, Perthshire, and Joyce Anstruther (d 1953, 'Jan Struther' author of 'Mrs Miniver'); the Maxtone of Cultoquhey line is traced back to 1410 (see Burke's LG, 18 edn, Vol III, 1972); *b* 6 May 1931; *Educ* USA, Stowe, Trinity Coll Cambridge (MA), Univ of Edinburgh; *m* 1962, Claudia Eva Elizabeth Page-Phillips, da of Frederick Tannert (d 1980), of Bickley, Kent; 1 da (Ysenda Maxtone-Smith, *qv*, b 1962), and 1 step da (Livia (Mrs Sevier) b 1958); *Career* Nat Serv cmmnd Scots Gds 1949–51 served Malaya; advocate of the Scots Bar 1956, legal assoc Royal Town Planning Inst, planning inspr DOE 1980–, fndr and proprietor Malthouse Arcade Hythe Kent; *Recreations* genealogy, book-collecting, photography; *Style*— Robert Maxtone Graham, Esq; ✉ 6 Moat Sole, Sandwich, Kent (☎ 01304 613270, fax 01304 615436); 8 Atholl Crescent Lane, Edinburgh 3 (☎ 0131 228 3338); 55 rue des Teinturiers, Avignon, France (☎ 90865292)

MAXTONE GRAHAM, Ysenda; *see:* Maxtone-Smith, Ysenda May

MAXTONE-SMITH, Ysenda May; da of Robert Mungo Maxtone Graham, *qv*, of Sandwich, Kent; *b* 31 Dec 1962; *Educ* The King's Sch Canterbury, Girton Coll Cambridge (MA); *m* 14 Aug 1993, Michael James Smith (who upon marriage adopted by deed poll surname of Maxtone-Smith), s of David Smith, JP, of Keyworth, Notts; 2 s (Toby Robert b 2 July 1994, Charles Mungo b 8 Oct 1996); *Career* as Ysenda Maxtone Graham, freelance journalist writing for The Express, Sunday Telegraph, Evening Standard, Daily Mail, Church Times, Harpers and Queen, Tatler and others; *Books* The Church Hesitant, a Portrait of the Church of England Today (1993), Without a Guide (contrib, 1996); *Recreations* singing, bicycling, drawing; *Style*— Mrs Ysenda Maxtone-Smith; ✉ 1 Avalon Road, London SW6 2EX (☎ 0171 736 8710, fax 0171 736 2757)

MAXWELL, (Wellwood George) Charles; s of Maj George Cavendish Maxwell, of Hartley Wintney, Hants, and Margaret, *née* Bishop; *b* 27 June 1952; *Educ* Stowe; *m* 15 Sept 1977, Anne, da of Rear Adm Bryan Cecil Durant, CB, DSO, DSC (d 1983); 1 s (George b 4 April 1981), 1 da (Eloise b 18 Nov 1983); *Career* dir: Finsbury Distillery Co 1981 (md 1986), JE Mather & Sons Ltd 1983, Matthew Clark & Sons (Holdings) plc 1988–92; former md Old Chelsea Distillers Ltd 1992; Freeman City of London 1974, Liveryman Worshipful Co of Distillers 1974; *Recreations* shooting, motor racing, rough gardening, wine, music, stamp collecting; *Clubs* Cavalry and Guards', BARC; *Style*— Charles Maxwell, Esq; ✉ Squirrels, Kennel Lane, Frensham, Surrey

MAXWELL, Donald; s of Kenneth M MacAlpine, of Perth, Scotland, and Margaret MacAlpine; *b* 12 Dec 1948; *Educ* Perth Acad, Univ of Edinburgh (MA); *Career* baritone; Scottish Opera 1976–82: John Noble bursary, debut 1977, title-role in Barbiere di Siviglia, Sharpless in Madama Butterfly, Enrico in Lucia di Lammermoor, Zurga in Les Pecheurs de Peries, Ipparco in L'Egisto, Shiskov in From the House of the Dead; WNO 1982–85: Renato in Un Ballo in Maschera, Shishkov, Marcello in La Boheme, Don Carlos in Ernani, Rigoletto, Iago in Otello, The Count in Le Nozze di Figaro, title-role in Falstaff, Golaud in Pelleas & Melisande; freelance 1985–; Royal Opera House debut 1987; performances at Royal Opera House incl: The English Archer in The King Goes Forth to France (Br premiere), The Herald in Lohengrin, Kothner in Die Meistersinger von Nurnberg, Alidoro in La Cenerentola, Gunther in Götterdämerung; ENO: Yeletsky in The Queen of Spades, title-role in Il Barbiere di Siviglia, Wozzeck, Leander in L'Armour des Trois Oranges; Opera North: Riccardo in I Puritani Germont in La Traviata, Escamillo in Carmen, Pizarro in Fidelio, title-role in Der Fliegende Hollander, Scarpia in Tosca; other performances incl Berg's Lulu (BBC Proms) 1996; numerous appearances in UK festivals and in foreign operas incl Paris, Vienna, NY, Tokyo, Milan and Buenos Aires; regular contribs to radio and TV operas; memb Music Box; recordings incl: Carmina Burana, Kismet, Amahl and The Night Visitors, Bitter Sweet, The Student Prince, Le Nozze di Figaro, Noye's Fludde, The Song of Norway; *Recreations* railways, travel; *Style*— Donald Maxwell, Esq; ✉ Music International, 13 Ardilaun Rd, Highbury, London N5 2QR (☎ 0171 359 5183, fax 0171 226 9792)

MAXWELL, Glyn Meurig; s of Dr James Maxwell, and Mary Buddug, *née* Powell; *b* 7 Nov 1962; *Educ* Stanborough Sch Welwyn Garden City, Worcester Coll Oxford (exhibitioner, BA), Boston Univ Mass USA (scholarship, MA); *Career* editorial asst W H Allen & Co Plc 1989, poet and freelance ed/writer 1989–; writing fell Nanyang Technological Univ Singapore 1995, visiting writer Amherst Coll Mass USA 1996, writer-in-residence Univ of Warwick 1997–; contrib to various magazines and jls UK and USA incl: TLS, London Review of Books, Vogue, Spectator, The Independent, The Independent on Sunday, The Sunday Times, Poetry Review, The New Yorker, Atlantic Monthly, Manhattan Review, Massachusetts Review, Partisan Review; included on New Br Poets tour of UK 1990; prizewinner Arvon Int Poetry Competition 1989, third prize Nat Poetry Competition 1989, winner Eric Gregory award 1991, Somerset Maugham Travel prize 1992, shortlisted for Sunday Times Young Writer of the Year 1990 and 1992; *Books* Tale of the Mayor's Son (Poetry Book Soc choice 1990, shortlisted for John Llewellyn Rhys Meml Prize 1990), Out of the Rain (Poetry Book Soc recommendation 1992, shortlisted Whitbread Poetry Prize 1992), Gnyss the Magnificent (1993), Blue Burneau (1994, shortlisted Whitbread First Novel Prize 1994), Rest for the Wicked (1995, shortlisted Whitbread Poetry Prize and T S Eliot Prize 1995); work incl in various anthologies incl: Poetry with an Edge (1988), Poetry Book Society Anthology (1988, 1990 and 1991), Soho Square (1991), New Writing (1991 and 1992), Penguin Modern Poets 3 (1995); *Plays* The Heart in Hiding (1995), Wolfpit (1996), Broken Journey (1996); *Recreations* amateur acting and directing, soccer; *Style*— Glyn Maxwell, Esq; ✉ 75 Oxford Gardens, London W10 5UL (☎ 0181 960 6960)

MAXWELL, (Charles) James Stuart; s of Charles Chalmers Maxwell, and Mary Stuart, *née* Sheppard; *Educ* Sherborne; *m* 9 April 1983, Joanna Augustine Lewis, da of H J L Osbourn; 2 s (Charles Thomas Osbourn b 21 April 1987, Alexander Sheppard b 14 June 1992), 1 da (Lucy Stuart Osbourn b 29 Sept 1988); *Career* journalist: Haymarket Publishing Ltd 1975–78, Daily Mail 1978; sr conslt: Comark Europe Brussels 1979–80, Shandwick 1980–82; chief exec Scope:Communications Group 1995–97 (fndr md 1983–95), chief exec offr Scope Ketchum Communications (following merger with Ketchum PR) 1997–; Freeman City of London, memb Worshipful Co of Merchant Taylors; MInstD; *Recreations* cricket, tennis, shooting, rugby; *Clubs* Boodle's, MCC, Harlequins, Hurlingham, Lord's Taverners; *Style*— James Maxwell, Esq; ✉ Scope Ketchum Communications, Tower House, 8–14 Southampton St, London WC2E 7HA (☎ 0171 379 3234, fax 0171 240 7729)

MAXWELL, John; *Career* Rank Xerox Ltd 1967–82, Grand Metropolitan plc 1983–86, chief exec Provincial Group 1986–92, fin dir then chief exec BPB Industries plc 1992–93, corp devpt dir Prudential Corporation plc 1994–96, dir gen Automobile Association

Group 1996–; FCA; *Style*— John Maxwell, Esq; ✉ Automobile Association, Fanum House, Basing View, Basingstoke, Hants RG21 4EA

MAXWELL, John Frederick Michael; s of late Lt Frederic Michael Maxwell (RIN), of Sidcup, Kent, and Mabel Doreen, *née* Turner; *b* 20 May 1943; *Educ* Dover Coll, New Coll Oxford (MA); *m* 1, 1964 (m dis 1986), Jennifer Mary; 1 s (Edward b 1967) 1 da (Alice b 1966); m 2, 1 Sept 1986, Jayne Elizabeth, da of George Douglas Hunter (d 1984), of Birmingham; *Career* called to the Bar Inner Temple 1965, Midland and Oxford Circuit, recorder of the Crown Court; chm: Birmingham Karma Ling Buddhist Centre, vice chm Rokpa Birmingham (aid to the homeless); tstee: Samye Ling Tibetan Centre Eskdalemuir Dumfriesshire, Holy Island (Buddhist and Interfaiths retreats), Rokpa Tst (aid to Tibet, relief of poverty, therapy, educn and promotion of Buddhism), Trangu Rimpoche Tst (Buddhist Centre Oxford); *Recreations* music, yachting; *Clubs* Royal Yachting Assoc, Old Gaffers Assoc, Gravesend Sailing; *Style*— John F M Maxwell, Esq; ✉ Grey Walls, 1131 Warwick Rd, Solihull, W Midlands B91 3HQ (☎ 0121 705 2670); 4 Fountain Ct, Steelhouse Lane, Birmingham B4 6DR (☎ 0121 236 3476, fax 0121 200 1214)

MAXWELL, Sir Michael Eustace George; 9 Bt (NS 1681), of Monreith, but does not yet appear on the Official Roll of the Baronetage; o s of Maj Eustace Maxwell (d 1971), and Dorothy Vivien (Dodo), *née* Bellville; suc unc, Capt Sir Aymer Maxwell, 8 Bt, 1987; *b* 28 Aug 1943; *Educ* Eton, Univ of London; *Heir* unascertained; *Career* chartered surveyor; currently running Monreith Estate and holiday accommodation; ARICS; *Style*— Sir Michael Maxwell, Bt; ✉ Monreith House, Port William, Newton Stewart, Scotland DG8 9LB (☎ 0198 87 248); 56 Queensmill Rd, London SW6 (☎ 0171 385 6163)

MAXWELL, Richard; QC (1988); s of Thomas Maxwell (d 1957), and Kathleen Marjorie, *née* Truswell (d 1979); *b* 21 Dec 1943; *Educ* Nottingham HS (scholar), Hertford Coll Oxford (state scholar and Baring scholar, MA); *m* 10 Sept 1966, Judith Ann, da of Hedley Vincent Iliffe, of Breaston, Derby; 2 s (Richard Alexander b 1971, Thomas Daniel b 1973), 2 da (Karen Laetitia b 1968, Catharine Antonia b 1969); *Career* called to the Bar Inner Temple 1968, recorder of the Crown Ct 1992–, head of chambers; *Recreations* squash, flyfishing, water colours, walking, half-marathon, malt whisky, wine; *Clubs* Nottingham Services; *Style*— Richard Maxwell, Esq, QC; ✉ Ropewalk Chambers, 24 The Ropewalk, Nottingham NG1 5EF (☎ 0115 947 2581); Doughty Street Chambers, 11 Doughty Street, London WC1N 2PG (☎ 0171 404 1313)

MAXWELL, Dr Robert James; CBE (1993), JP (1971); s of Dr George Barton Maxwell, MC (d 1972), and Cathleen Maxwell, *née* Blackburn; *b* 26 June 1934; *Educ* Leighton Park Sch Reading, New Coll Oxford (BA, MA), Univ of Pennsylvania (MA), LSE (PhD); *m* 1960, Jane, da of Geoffrey FitzGibbon, JP, of Dursley Gloucestershire; 3 s (Patrick, Benedict, Geoffrey), 2 da (Catherine, Favell); *Career* Lt Cameronians (Scot Rifles) 1952–54; asst mangr Union Corp 1958–66, princ McKinsey and Co 1966–75, admin Special Tstees for St Thomas' Hosp London 1975–80, sec/chief exec King's Fund 1980–; chm Leighton Park Sch Reading; govr: Nat Inst of Social Work, United Med and Dental Sch, Lewisham NHS Tst, Med Def Union; tstee Joseph Rowntree Fndn; hon memb: RCP, Assoc of Anaesthetists; Hon FRCGP; Hon DUniv Brunel, Hon DLitt Univ of West of England; *Recreations* walking, poetry; *Clubs* Brooks's; *Style*— Dr Robert Maxwell, CBE, JP; ✉ Pitt Court Manor, N Nibley, Dursley, Glos (☎ 01453 542942); King's Fund, 11–13 Cavendish Square, London W1M 0AN (☎ 0171 307 2487, fax 0171 307 2803)

MAXWELL, Prof Thomas Jefferson (Jeff); *b* 7 Oct 1940; *Educ* Silcoates Sch, Univ of Edinburgh (BSc, PhD); *Career* animal husbandry advsy offr E of Scotland Coll of Agric 1967–70, princ scientific offr Hill Farming Research Orgn 1975–79 (sr scientific offr Animal Studies Dept 1971–75), livestock research offr Victorian Dept of Agric Australia (secondment) 1979–80, head Animal Production Dept Hill farming Research Orgn 1981–87, dir Macaulay Land Use Research Inst 1987–; chief exec Macaulay Research and Consultancy Servs Ltd 1995–; Scottish Cashmere Producers' Assoc: chm 1986–88, memb Cncl and dir 1988–93; vice-chm Research Bd Scientific Advsy Ctee (formerly Scottish Natural Heritage) 1992–; memb: Cncl Br Soc of Animal Production 1976–79, Sec of State's Hill Farming Advsy Ctee 1987–, Sci Research and Devpt Bd Nature Conservation Cncl (Scotland) 1990–92, Cncl Aberdeen Research Consortium 1992– (chm Land Mgmnt and Environmental Scis Research Centre 1992–), Steering Ctee for a Euro Environmental Inst 1994–, Plant and Soil Dept Users Liaison Ctee Univ of Aberdeen 1995–, Bd Euro Environmental Mgmnt Inst Ltd Aberdeen 1996–; conslt to Min of Agric Lesotho (ODA sponsored) 1991; tstee Macaulay Development Tst 1995–; hon prof of land use systems Univ of Aberdeen, hon research fell Univ of Edinburgh; FRSGS 1995, FRSE 1996; *Publications* numerous contribs to learned jls; *Style*— Prof Jeff Maxwell, FRSE; ✉ Macaulay Land Use Research Institute, Craigiebucker, Aberdeen AB15 8QH (☎ 01224 318611, fax 01224 324880)

MAXWELL DAVIES, Sir Peter; kt (1987), CBE (1981); s of Thomas Maxwell Davies, and Hilda Maxwell Davies; *b* 8 Sept 1934; *Educ* Leigh GS Salford, Univ of Manchester (MusB), Royal Manchester Coll of Music; *Career* composer and conductor; studied with Goffredo Petrassi in Rome 1957, dir of music Cirencester GS 1959–62, Harkness fellowship Grad Sch Princeton Univ (studying with Roger Sessions, Milton Babbitt and Earl Kim) 1962–64; fndr and co-dir (with Harrison Birtwistle) The Pierrot Players 1967–71, fndr and artistic dir The Fires of London 1971–87, fndr and artistic dir St Magnus Festival Orkney Islands 1977–86 (pres 1986–), artistic dir Dartington Hall Summer Sch of Music 1979–84, assoc composer/conductor Scottish Chamber Orch 1985–, conductor/composer BBC Philharmonic Orch Manchester 1992–; assoc composer/conductor Royal Philharmonic Orch 1992–, composer laureate Scottish Chamber Orch 1994–; visiting Fromm prof of composition Harvard Univ 1985; pres: Schools Music Assoc 1983–, North of England Educn Conf Chester 1985, Composers' Guild of GB 1986–, Nat Fedn of Music Socs 1989–, Cheltenham Arts Festivals 1994–, Soc for Promotion of New Music 1995–; major retrospective festival (28 works) South Bank Centre London 1990; hon memb Guildhall Sch of Music and Drama 1981, hon memb Royal Philharmonic Soc 1987, hon fell Royal Incorporation of Architects in Scotland 1994; Hon DMus: Edinburgh 1979, Manchester 1981, Bristol 1984, Open Univ 1986, Glasgow 1993, Durham 1994; Hon LLD: Aberdeen 1981, Warwick 1986; Officier dans L'Ordre des Arts et des Lettres (France) 1988; memb Royal Swedish Acad of Music 1993; FRNCM 1978, hon RAM 1978, FRSAMD 1994, FRCM 1994; *Awards* Cobbett Medal for services to chamber music 1989, First Award Assoc of British Orchs (ABO) 1991, Gulliver Award for the Performing Arts in Scotland 1991, Nat Fedn of Music Socs Charles Groves Award for outstanding contrib to Br music 1995, Royal Philharmonic Soc Award for large-scale composition (for Symphony No 5) 1995; *Works* incl Sonata (for trumpet and piano) 1955, Alma redemptoris mater (for ensemble) 1957, O Magnum Mysterium (for SATB chorus) 1960, Revelation and Fall (for soprano and ensemble) 1966, Missa super L'Homme Arme (for speaker and ensemble) 1968, Worldes Blis (for orch) 1969, Eight Songs for a Mad King (music theatre work for ensemble) 1969, Taverner (opera in two acts) 1970, Stone Litany (for mezzo soprano and ensemble) 1973, Symphony No 1 1976, The Martyrdom of Saint Magnus (chamber opera) 1976, The Two Fiddlers (opera for children to perform) 1978, Salome (ballet in two acts) 1978, Solstice of Light (for tenor, SATB chorus and organ) 1979, Cinderella (pantomime opera for children to perform) 1979, Symphony No 2 (for orch) 1980, Brass Quintet 1981, Into the Labyrinth (for tenor and orch) 1983, An Orkney Wedding with Sunrise (for orch) 1985, Violin concerto (for violin and orch) 1985, Strathclyde Concerto No 1 for oboe and orch 1986, Resurrection (opera) 1987, The Great Bank Robbery (music theatre work for children to perform) 1989, Symphony No 4 1989, Caroline Mathilde (ballet in two acts) 1990, Ojai Festival Overture (for orch) 1991, Strathclyde Concerto No 5 (for violin, viola and string orch) 1991, Strathclyde Concerto No 6 (for flute and orch) 1991, Strathclyde Concerto No 7 (for double bass and orch) 1992, The Turn of the Tide (for orch) 1992, Strathclyde Concerto No 8 (for bassoon and orch) 1993, A Spell for Green Corn: The MacDonald Dances (for orch) 1993, Symphony No 5 1994, Cross Lane Fair (for orch) 1994, Strathclyde Concerto No 9 (for six woodwind instruments and string orch) 1994, The Beltane Fire (choreographic poem for orch) 1995, The Three Kings (for chorus, orch and soloists) 1995, The Doctor of Myddfai (cmmnd Welsh National Opera 50th Anniversary season), Symphony No 6 (London premiere BBC Proms with RPO 1996), Strathclyde Concerto No 10: Concerto for orch 1996; *Style*— Sir Peter Maxwell Davies, CBE; ✉ c/o Mrs Judy Arnold, Flat 3, 50 Hogarth Road, London SW5 0PU (☎ 0171 370 1477/2328, fax 0171 373 6730)

MAXWELL-HYSLOP, Sir Robert John (Robin); kt (1992); s of late Capt A H Maxwell-Hyslop, GC, RN, of Prideaux House, Par, Cornwall; *b* 6 June 1931; *Educ* Stowe, ChCh Oxford (MA); *m* 1968, Joanna Margaret, er da of late Thomas McCosh, of Pitcon, Dalry, Ayrshire; 2 da; *Career* Capt TARO RA; Rolls-Royce Aero Engines 1954–60; Parly candidate N Derby (C) 1959, MP (C) Tiverton Nov 1960–92; chm Br-Brazilian Parly Gp; memb: Trade and Indust Select Ctee 1971–92, Standing Orders Ctee 1977–92, Procedure Select Ctee 1978–92; non-exec dir Ugland International Holdings plc; hon assoc Br Veterinary Assoc; *Style*— Sir Robin Maxwell-Hyslop; ✉ 4 Tiverton Road, Silverton, nr Exeter, Devon EX5 4JQ

MAXWELL-IRVING, Alastair Michael Tivey; s of Reginald Tivey (d 1977), of Warwickshire, and Barbara Annie Bell Irving (d 1988); *b* 1 Oct 1935; *Educ* Lancing Coll, Univ of London (BSc (Eng)), Univ of Stirling; *m* 21 Sept 1983, Esther Mary, da of Rev James Hamilton, formerly of Auchterhouse, Angus; *Career* chartered engr: English Electric Co 1960–64, Annandale Estates 1966–69, Weir Pumps Ltd 1970–91; quality conslt 1992–94; architectural and historical writer and archaeologist; sometime hon asst Royal Cmmn on Ancient and Historical Monuments Scotland; memb: Dumfries and Galloway Antiquarian Soc, Hawick Archaeological Soc, Stirling Field and Archaeological Soc, Clackmannan Field Soc, Antiquarian Horological Soc; fndr memb and sec BIM Central Scotland 1975–79, community cncllr (treas) Logie 1984–; CEng 1973, MIEE 1972, MIMgt 1974, AMICE 1970, FSA Scot 1967; *Publications incl* The Irvings of Bonshaw (1968), The Irvings of Dumfries (1968), Early Firearms and their Influence on the Military And Domestic Architecture of the Borders (1974), Cramalt Tower (1982), Borthwick Castle (1982), Hoddom Castle (1989), Lochwood Castle (1990), The Castles of Buittle (1991), Torthorwald Castle (1993), Scottish Yetts and Window-Grilles (1994); *Recreations* architecture and history of the Border towers of Scotland, archaeology, family history and genealogy, art and architecture of Tuscany, horology, heraldry, photography, gardening; *Style*— Alastair Maxwell-Irving, Esq; ✉ Telford House, Blairlogie, Stirling FK9 5PX (☎ 01259 761721)

MAXWELL-LAWFORD, Nicholas Anthony; OBE (1986); s of Capt F Maxwell-Lawford MBE (k rail accident 1937), of Achimota Coll Accra, Gold Coast, and Ruth Claire, *née* Jerred; *b* 8 Nov 1935; *Educ* Stonyhurst Coll, GWEBI Coll of Agric, S Rhodesia (Dip AG), Harvard Business Sch; *m* 8 Sept 1962, Mary Susan, da of Richard Fauconburg Bellasis (d 1964), of Rioki, Kiambu, Kenya; 1 s (Richard b 1965), 3 da (Helena b 1967, Frances b 1970, Antonia b 1973); *Career* Nat Serv Devonshire Regt 1955 and seconded KAR 1955–56, ADC & private sec to HE The Govr of Nyasaland Sir Robert Armitage, KCMG, MBE, 1959–61; joined Barclays Bank Ltd: various appts 1961–69, local dir for branches local head office 1969–73, local dir Lombard St local head office 1973–75, asst gen mangr Barclays Bank International 1976, res dir Barclays Bank SA (Paris) 1977, advsy dir SW Regnl Office 1987–94; dir: Valtare Ltd, Devon & Exeter Steeplechases Ltd; tstee: Angela Gallagher Meml Fund, West of Eng Sch for Children with Little or No Sight; Freeman City of London 1965, Liveryman Drapers Co 1968; Kt of Grace and Devotion Sov Order of Malta 1977, City of Paris Medal in Silver-Gilt 1986; *Style*— Nicholas Maxwell-Lawford, Esq, OBE; ✉ The Old Rectory, Buckerell, Honiton, Devon EX14 OEJ (☎ 01404 850332); c/o Buzzacott & Co, 4 Wood Street, London EC2V 7JB

MAXWELL-SCOTT, Sir Dominic James; 14 Bt (E 1642), of Haggerston, Northumberland; er s of Sir Michael Fergus Constable Maxwell-Scott, 13 Bt (d 1989), and Deirdre Moira, *née* McKechnie; *b* 22 July 1968; *Educ* Eton, Univ of Sussex; *Heir* bro, Matthew Joseph Maxwell-Scott b 27 Aug 1976; *Style*— Sir Dominic Maxwell-Scott, Bt; ✉ c/o 10 Evelyn Mansions, Carlisle Place, London SW1

MAXWELL-SCOTT, Dame Jean Mary Monica; DCVO (1984, CVO 1969); da of Maj-Gen Sir Walter Maxwell-Scott, 1 and last Bt, CB, DSO, DL (d 1954), and Mairi, *née* MacDougall; ggggda of Sir Walter Scott; *b* 8 June 1923; *Educ* Couvent des Oiseaux Westgate-on-Sea; *Career* VAD Red Cross nurse 1941–46; lady-in-waiting to HRH Princess Alice Duchess of Gloucester 1959–; *Clubs* New Cavendish; *Style*— Dame Jean Maxwell-Scott, DCVO; ✉ Abbotsford, Melrose, Roxburghshire TD6 9BQ

MAY, Hon Mr Justice; Hon Sir Anthony Tristram Kenneth May; kt (1991); s of Dr Kenneth Sibley May (d 1985), and Joan Marguérite, *née* Oldaker (d 1985); *b* 9 Sept 1940; *Educ* Bradfield, Worcester Coll Oxford (MA); *m* 4 May 1968, Stella Gay, da of Rupert George Pattisson (d 1976); 1 s (Richard b 1974), 2 da (Charmian b 1971, Lavinia b 1972); *Career* called to the Bar Inner Temple 1967; QC 1979, recorder of the Crown Court 1985–91, bencher Inner Temple 1985; cmmr Savings and Investment Bank Public Enquiry Isle of Man 1990; judge of the High Court of Justice (Queen's Bench Div) 1991–; chm Guildford Choral So 1980–91 (vice pres 1991–); *Publications* Keating on Building Contracts (6 edn, 1995); *Recreations* gardening, music, books; *Style*— The Hon Mr Justice May; ✉ Royal Courts of Justice, Strand, London WC2A 2LL

MAY, Prof Brian Albert; s of Albert Robert May (d 1986), and Eileen, *née* May; *b* 2 June 1936; *Educ* Faversham GS, Aston Univ (BSc); *m* 2 Aug 1961, Brenda Ann, da of Norman Smith; 3 s (Christopher b 15 March 1964, Timothy b 1965, Jeremy b 1967); *Career* Nat Serv Craftsman REME Kenya and Malaya 1954–56; design engr Massey Ferguson 1962–63; Silsoe Coll: lectr and sr lectr 1963–72, head Dept of Agric Engrg 1972–75, head of coll 1976–87; Cranfield Inst of Technol: prof of agric engrg 1975–92, dean of faculty 1976–87, prof emeritus 1992; head Cranfield Rural Inst 1987–91; ind devpt advsr 1991–; ed The Agricultural Engineer 1970–75; chm Br Agric Educn and Trg Servs 1984–86, pres Inst of Agric Engrs 1984–86, dir Br Agric Export Cncl 1985–88, memb Br Cncl Agric and Veterinary Advsy Ctee 1985–91, memb Br Cncl Engrg and Technol Ctee 1991–93, dir Bd Br Soc for Res in Agric Engrg; FIAgrE, FRAgs, MASAE, FEng 1990; *Books* Power on the Land (1975); *Recreations* reading, photography, people; *Clubs* Farmers'; *Style*— Prof Brian May, FEng; ✉ 23 Spencer Square, Ramsgate, Kent CT11 9LA (☎ and fax 01843 580746)

MAY, Brian Harold; s of Harold May, and Ruth May; *b* 19 July 1947; *Educ* Hampton GS, Imperial Coll London (BSc); *m*; 1 s (Jimmy), 2 da (Louisa, Emily); *Career* guitarist and songwriter; formed first band "1984" 1964; co-fndr: Smile 1968, Queen 1970– (with Freddie Mercury (d 1991), Roger Taylor, *qv*, John Deacon, *qv*); *Albums* incl: Queen (1973, Gold), Queen II (1974, Gold), Sheer Heart Attack (1974, Gold), A Night at the Opera (1975, Platinum), A Day at the Races (1976, Gold), News of the World (1977, Gold), Jazz (1978, Gold), Live Killers (1979, Gold), The Game (1980, Gold), Flash Gordon Original Soundtrack (1980, Gold), Greatest Hits (1981, 9 times Platinum), Hot Space (1982, Gold), The Works (1984, Platinum), A Kind of Magic (1986, double Platinum), Live Magic (1986, Platinum), The Miracle (1989, Platinum), Queen at the Beeb (1989), Innuendo

(1991, Platinum), Greatest Hits Two (1991), Made In Heaven (1995); other albums: Gettin' Smile (earlier recordings of Smile, 1982), Starfleet Project (Brian May & Friends, 1983), Back to the Light (solo, 1993); number 1 singles: Bohemian Rhapsody 1975 and 1991, Under Pressure 1981, Innuendo 1991; numerous tours worldwide, performed at Live Aid Concert Wembley Stadium 1985; voted Best Band of the Eighties ITV/TV Times 1990, Br Phonographic Indust award for Outstanding Contribution to Br Music 1990; *Style*— Brian May, Esq; ✉ Duck Productions Ltd, PO Box 141, Windlesham, Surrey GU20 6YW (☎ 01344 875448)

MAY, David Oliver; s of John Oliver May (d 1960), and Joan, *née* Harrison; *b* 1 March 1935; *Educ* Wellington, Univ of Southampton; *m* March 1960, Baroness Catherine, da of Baron Van Den Branden De Reeth (d 1966); 2 s (Brian, Dominic), 1 da (Georgia); *Career* Nat Serv Sub Lt RN 1954–55; chm: Berthon Boat Co Ltd, Lymington Marina Ltd, Newmil Garage, Lymington Marine Garage, Nat Boat Shows 1986–88; tstee Br Marine Inds Fedn 1988; dir: Marina Mutual Insurance Association Ltd, Transatlantic Capital Ltd; Liveryman Worshipful Co of Shipwrights; FRINA 1964, CEng; *Recreations* yacht racing, sailing, shooting; *Clubs* Royal Thames Yacht, Royal Ocean Racing, RN, Royal Lymington Yacht, Royal London Yacht, Island Sailing; *Style*— David Oliver May, Esq; ✉ Berthon Boat Co Ltd, The Shipyard, Lymington, Hants SO41 3YL

MAY, Derwent James; s of Herbert Alfred May (d 1982), and Nellie Eliza, *née* Newton (d 1959); *b* 29 April 1930; *Educ* Strodes Sch Egham, Lincoln Coll Oxford (MA); *m* 22 Sept 1967, Yolanta Izabella, da of Tadeusz Sypniewski, of Lodz, Poland (d 1970); 1 s (Orlando James b 1968), 1 da (Miranda Izabella b 1970); *Career* theatre and film critic Continental Daily Mail Paris 1952–53, lectr English Univ of Indonesia 1955–58, sr lectr in English lit Univs of Warsaw and Lodz Poland 1959–63, ldr writer TLS 1963–65, lit ed The Listener 1965–86, lit and arts ed The Sunday Telegraph 1986–90, contrib of nature notes to The Times 1981–, ed Élan (the arts magazine of the European) 1990–91; The Times: Euro arts ed 1992, feature writer 1993–; memb Booker Prize Jury 1978, memb Hawthornden Prize Ctee 1987–; *Books* The Professionals (1964), Dear Parson (1969), The Laughter in Djakarta (1973), A Revenger's Comedy (1979), Proust (1983), The Times Nature Diary (1983), Hannah Arendt (1986), The New Times Nature Diary (1993), Feather Reports (1996); ed: Good Talk: An Anthology from BBC Radio (1968), Good Talk 2 (1969), The Music of What Happens: Poems from The Listener 1965–80 (1981); *Recreations* birdwatching, opera; *Clubs* Beefsteak, Garrick; *Style*— Derwent May, Esq; ✉ 201 Albany St, London NW1 4AB (☎ 0171 387 0848)

MAY, Douglas; *b* 24 April 1931; *Career* ed-in-chief Bedford Div Westminster Press 1967–73, md and chief exec Cheshire Co Newspapers 1975–87 (md designate 1973–74); dir: Piccadilly Radio plc Manchester 1975–95, Signal Radio Stoke-on-Trent 1982–; conslt Messenger Group Warrington 1987–92; chm Guild of Br Newspaper Eds London and Home Counties Region 1970; pres: North West Newspaper Soc 1982–83, Newspaper Society Cncl London 1982–87; *Style*— Douglas May, Esq; ✉ 3 Highcroft, Minchinhampton, Glos GL6 9BJ

MAY, Douglas Anthony Roland; s of late Roland John May, of Guildford, Surrey, and late Amy Doreen, *née* Hall; *b* 14 Nov 1940; *Educ* Woking Boys' GS; *m* 1, 30 Dec 1961 (m dis 1977), Jill Margaret Lane; 1 s (Timothy b 1968), 1 da (Joanna b 1971); m 2, 6 Oct 1979, Jacqueline Diane, da of Sydney Albert Norman Humphries; 2 s (Oliver b 1981, Thomas b 1982); *Career* Legal and General Assurance Society Ltd 1961–68, Crawfurd Beck and Amos Ltd 1968–71, Graham How and Co Insurance Brokers Ltd 1971–82 (life pensions dir 1972, md 1976–82), md Hinton Hill Life and Pensions Consultants 1982–88, chm of all fin servs Hinton Hill Group 1988–90, md Pendleton May Financial Services Ltd 1990–; dir: Pendleton May Insurance Brokers Ltd 1990–, Retirement Planning Services Ltd 1984–, St Pancras Building Society 1990–93; leader Guildford Borough Cncl 1982–87 (memb 1973–95), Mayor of Guildford 1994–95; chm: Yvonne Arnaud Theatre Tst 1983–88 (tstee 1976–), Yvonne Arnaud Theatre Management Ltd 1988– (dir 1979–), Guildford Arts Cncl; ACII, FBIIBA, MLIA(Dip); *Recreations* breeding and showing Jacob sheep; *Clubs* Vanbrugh, Guildford Co; *Style*— Douglas May, Esq; ✉ Monkshatch Cottage, Compton, Guildford, Surrey GU3 1DL (☎ 01483 810229); Pendleton May Financial Services Ltd, Anchor House, Station Row, Shalford, Guildford, Surrey GU4 8BY (☎ 01483 39922, fax 01483 37552, mobile 0385 750106)

MAY, Douglas James; QC (Scot 1989); s of Thomas May (d 1977), of Edinburgh, and Violet Mary Brough Boyd or May (d 1995); *b* 7 May 1946; *Educ* George Heriot's Sch Edinburgh, Univ of Edinburgh (LLB); *Career* advocate 1971, temp sheriff 1990, dep social security cmmr 1992–93, social security cmmr Child Support Cmmn 1993–; Parly candidate (C): Edinburgh E Feb 1974, Glasgow Cathcart 1983; capt Scottish Univs Golfing Soc 1990, pres Edinburgh Photographic Soc 1996; memb Faculty of Advocates, ARPS; *Recreations* golf, photography, travel, concert going; *Clubs* Bruntsfield Links Golfing Soc, Scottish Arts; *Style*— Douglas May, Esq, QC; ✉ Office of the Social Security Commissioners, 23 Melville Street, Edinburgh EH3 7PW (☎ 0131 225 2201)

MAY, Evelyn Jane; da of Henry May (d 1980), and Jane Bonner, *née* Brown; *b* 16 Jan 1955; *Educ* Glasgow HS for Girls, Univ of Glasgow (BDS), Univ of Wales (MScD), FDS RCPS (Glasgow), DOrthRCS (Eng); *Career* postgrad student in orthodontics Welsh Nat Sch of Med Cardiff 1981–83, registrar in orthodontics Raigmore Hosp Inverness 1983–84, sr registrar in orthodontics Glasgow Dental Hosp 1984–88 (house offr, sr house offr, then registrar 1977–81), conslt Middlesbrough Gen Hosp 1988–; memb: Br Orthodontist Soc, Conslt Orthodontists Gp, BDA, Craniofacial Soc of GB; *Clubs* Soroptimist International of GB and NI; *Style*— Miss Evelyn May; ✉ Middlesbrough General Hospital, Ayresome Green Lane, Middlesbrough, Cleveland TS5 5AZ (☎ 01642 854259, fax 01642 824727)

MAY, Geoffrey John; s of James Ebrey Clare May (d 1986), of London, and Eleanor Isobel, *née* Tate (d 1989); *b* 7 May 1948; *Educ* Eltham Coll London, Fitzwilliam Coll Cambridge (MA, PhD); *m* 5 Jan 1974, Sarah Elizabeth, da of Stanley George Felgate (d 1986), of Chislehurst; 2 s (Timothy b 1976, Daniel b 1980); *Career* Chloride Group plc 1974–82, Hawker Siddeley Group (BTR plc) 1982–90 and 1991–, dir Tungstone Batteries Ltd 1982–88, dir and gen mangr Hawker Fusegear Ltd 1988–90, dir Caparo Industries plc, md Barton Abrasives Ltd 1990–91, dir R&D Hawker Batteries Group 1991–; CEng 1978, FIM 1987; *Recreations* skiing, gardening, sailing; *Style*— Geoffrey May, Esq; ✉ Troutbeck Hse, 126 Main St, Swithland, Loughborough, Leics LE12 8TJ (☎ 01509 890547); Hawker Batteries Ltd, Market Harborough, Leics LE16 9E2 (☎ 01858 410900, fax 01858 434447, telex 34305 TUNGST G)

MAY, James Nicholas Welby; s of Richard Percy, and Caroline Rosemary Welby, *née* Jack; *b* 21 Feb 1949; *Educ* Sherborne, Univ of Southampton (BSc), Coll of Law; *m* 19 May 1979, Diana Mary Tamplin; 2 s (b 18 Nov 1983 and 4 May 1986); *Career* called to the Bar Lincoln's Inn 1974; prog officer UN Environmental Prog Nairobi 1976–77, res officer IUCN Bonn 1977–78, legal officer and co sec Friends of the Earth Ltd 1978–79, head of legal servs NFU 1980–89, DG British Retail Consortium 1989–97, DG UK Offshore Operators' Association 1997–; memb: Cncl Nat Retail Trg Cncl 1989–94, Bd EuroCommerce, Bd Distributive Occupational Standards Cncl 1994–; MIMgt, MInstD; FRSA; *Recreations* skiing, tennis, squash, travel; *Style*— James May, Esq; ✉ Director General, UK Offshore Operators' Association, 3 Hans Crescent, London SW1X 0LN (☎ 0171 589 5255)

MAY, Hon Jasper Bertram St John; s and h of 3 Baron May, *qv*; *b* 24 Oct 1965; *Educ* Harrow; *Style*— The Hon Jasper May

MAY, Air Vice-Marshal John Anthony Gerard; CB (1995), CBE (1993); s of late Anthony Frederick May, and late Beatrice Mary, *née* Niblett; *b* 12 Nov 1941; *Career* joined RAF 1961, flying trg then flying instr RAF Linton-on-Ouse 1966, served with Nos 56, 5 and 19 Sqdns, Staff Coll Camberley 1977, Chief Flying Instr RAF Coll Cranwell 1979, Stn Cdr RAF Binbrook 1984–86, Dep Dir of Air Defence MOD 1986–88, Air Cdre Policy & Plans HQ RAF Support Cmd 1990–92, Sr Air Staff Offr Strike Cmd and AOC No 38 Gp 1993–94, Air Offr Trg and AOC Trg Gp at Personnel & Trg Cmd 1994–97; QCVSA 1971; *Recreations* Alpine skiing, classic cars; *Clubs* RAF; *Style*— Air Vice-Marshal John May, CB, CBE; ✉ HQ RAF Personnel and Training Command, RAF Innsworth, Gloucester GL3 1EZ (☎ 01452 712612)

MAY, Rt Hon Sir John Douglas; kt (1972), PC (1982); s of E A G May (d 1942), of Shanghai; *b* 28 June 1923; *Educ* Clifton, Balliol Coll Oxford (MA); *m* 1958, Mary, da of Sir Owen Morshead, GCVO, KCB, DSO, MC; 2 s, 1 da; *Career* served WWII Lt (SpSc) RNVR; called to the Bar Inner Temple 1947, master of the Bench 1972, treas 1993, QC 1965, recorder of Maidstone 1971, ldr SE Circuit 1971, high ct judge (Queen's Bench) 1972–82, presiding judge Midland & Oxford Circuit 1973–77, lord justice of appeal 1982–89, appointed to conduct Inquiry into Guildford and Woolwich Bombings 1989; memb Parole Bd 1977–80 (vice chm 1980); chm: Inquiry into Prison Servs 1978–79, Univ Commissioners 1989–95; memb Royal Cmmn on Criminal Justice 1991–93; pres Clifton Coll 1987–93; *Clubs* Vincent's (Oxford); *Style*— The Rt Hon Sir John May; ✉ Lindens, Sturminster Newton, Dorset DT10 1BU (☎ 01258 473321)

MAY, 3 Baron (UK 1935); Sir Michael St John May; 3 Bt (1931); s of 2 Baron (d 1950), by his 2 w Ethel; *b* 26 Sept 1931; *Educ* Wycliffe Coll, Magdalene Cambridge; *m* 1, 1958 (m dis 1963), Dorothea Catherine Ann, da of Charles McCarthy; m 2, 1963, Jillian Mary, da of Albert Edward Shipton; 1 s, 1 da (Hon Miranda b 17 Oct 1968); *Heir* s, Hon Jasper Bertram St John May, *qv*; *Career* late Lt Royal Corps of Signals; *Style*— The Rt Hon the Lord May; ✉ Gautherns Barn, Sibford Gower, Oxfordshire

MAY, (William) Nigel; s of Flt Lt (William) David May, of 70 Chaldon Way, Coulsdon, Surrey, and (Evelyn) Christine, *née* Pike; *b* 24 May 1950; *Educ* Whitgift Sch, Univ of Nottingham (BA), Univ of Cambridge (Dip); *Career* called to the Bar Inner Temple 1974; currently working in criminal practice, prosecution and def, grade three prosecutor for Crown Prosecution Serv; fndr memb of present chambers in 1984, appointed pt/t judge-advocate in Courts Martial 1994; *Recreations* reading, skiing, walking, music; *Style*— Nigel May, Esq; ✉ 33 Bedford Row, London WC1R 4JH (☎ 0171 242 6476)

MAY, Peter N J; *Career* md Charterhouse Tilney Securities Ltd 1993– (joined Charterhouse Bank 1982); *Style*— Peter May, Esq; ✉ Charterhouse Tilney Securities Ltd, 1 Paternoster Row, St Paul's, London EC4M 7DH (☎ 0171 522 3779, fax 0171 246 2139)

MAY, His Honour Judge Richard George; s of G W May, of Ware, Herts, and Phyllis May (d 1989); *b* 12 Nov 1938; *Educ* Haileybury, Selwyn Coll Cambridge (BA, LLB); *m* Radmila, da of J D A Barnicot, OBE; 2 da, 1 s; *Career* Palled to the Bar Inner Temple 1965, practised on S Eastern Circuit and later on Midland and Oxford Circuit, recorder 1985, circuit judge (Midland and Oxford Circuit) 1987–; *Books* Criminal Evidence (1986, 3 edn 1995); *Clubs* Savile; *Style*— His Hon Judge Richard May; ✉ c/o Midland & Oxford Circuit Office, The Priory Courts, 33 Bull Street, Birmingham B4 6DW

MAY, Prof Sir Robert McCredie; kt (1996); s of Henry Wilkinson May, of Sydney, Australia; *b* 8 Jan 1936; *Educ* Sydney Boys' Sch, Sydney Univ (BSc, PhD); *m* 3 Aug 1962, Judith, da of Jerome Feiner, of New York, USA; 1 da (Naomi Felicity b 25 March 1966); *Career* Gordon Mackey lectr in applied mathematics Harvard Univ 1959–61 and 1966, prof of physics Sydney Univ 1962–72, prof of astrophysics California Inst of Technol 1967; prof of plasma physics: UKAEA Lab Culham 1971, Magdalen Coll Oxford 1971, Inst for Advanced Study Princeton 1972, King's Coll Res Centre Cambridge 1976; visiting prof Imperial Coll London 1975–88, Class of 1877 prof of zoology Princeton Univ 1973–88, Royal Soc res prof Oxford Univ and Imperial Coll London 1988–95 (leave of absence 1995–); chief scientific advsr to UK Govt and head of Office of Sci and Technol 1995–; pres British Ecological Soc 1991–93; memb: NRC, Sci-Advsy Cncl for WWF (US) 1978, Int Whaling Cmmn 1978–82, US Marine Animals Cmmn 1979–, Governing Bd Soc of Conservation Biologists 1985–88, Advsy Bd Inst for Sci Info 1986–; chm Bd of Tstees Natural History Museum 1994–99 (tstee 1989–94); tstee: WWF (UK) 1990–94, Nuffield Fndn 1993–, Royal Botanic Gardens Kew and Wakehurst Place 1991–94; Rockefeller scholar Italy 1986; Hon Degrees: Univ of London 1989, Uppsala Univ 1990, Yale Univ 1993, Univ of Edinburgh 1994, Heriot-Watt Univ 1994, Sydney Univ 1995; fell American Acad of Arts and Sciences 1977, Aust Acad of Sciences 1991, foreign memb US Nat Acad of Sciences; FRS 1979; *Books* Stability and Complexity in Model Ecosystems (1973, 2 edn 1974), Theoretical Ecology: Principles and Applications (ed 1976, 2 edn 1981), Population Biology of Infectious Diseases (ed with R M Anderson, 1982), Exploitation of Marine Communities (ed, 1984), Perspectives in Ecological Theory (ed with J Roughgarden and S A Levin, 1989), Population Regulation and Dynamics (ed with M P Hassell, 1990), Infectious Diseases of Humans (with R M Anderson, 1991), Large Scale Ecology and Conservation Biology (ed with P J Edwards and N R Webb, 1994), Extinction Rates (ed with J H Lawton, 1995); *Recreations* running, tennis; *Style*— Professor Sir Robert May, FRS; ✉ Department of Zoology, University of Oxford, South Parks Rd, Oxford OX1 3PS (☎ 01865 271170, fax 01865 310447)

MAY, Roger; s of Fred May (d 1967), and Agnes Doreen, *née* Abrahams (d 1971); *b* 12 June 1931; *Educ* High Storrs GS Sheffield; *m* 1, 14 March 1953 (m dis 1973); 2 s (Paul b 1958, Jonathan b 1962); m 2, 1973, (Margaret) Yvonne; *Career* slr; former justices' clerk: Barry, Cowbridge, Penarth; former dep High Ct and dep Co Ct dist judge; *Recreations* photography, travel; *Style*— Roger May, Esq; ✉ Hillcrest, Quarhouse, Brimscombe, Stroud, Gloucestershire GL5 2RR

MAY, Simon Philip Walter; s of Walter May (d 1963), and Marianne Louise, *née* Liedtke; *b* 9 Aug 1956; *Educ* Westminster, ChCh Oxford (MA), Birkbeck Coll London (BA); *Career* Euro affrs advsr to Rt Hon Douglas Hurd MP 1977–79, foreign affrs advsr to Rt Hon Edward Heath 1979–83, memb Cabinet of Vice Pres EEC Cmmn 1983–85, co fndr Action Ctee Europe 1985–86, dir Northern Telecom Europe 1986–88, chief exec Mondiale Ltd 1988–92, conslt in telecommunications 1992–; dir Whatman plc 1994–; *Books* The European Armaments Market and Procurement Cooperation (1988); *Recreations* music, walking; *Style*— Simon May, Esq; ✉ 129 Riverview Gardens, London SW13 9RA (☎ 0181 748 6920, fax 0181 741 0953)

MAY, Stephen Charles; s of Paul May, CBE (d 1996), and Dorothy Ida, *née* Makower (d 1961); *b* 5 Sept 1937; *Educ* Berkhamsted Sch, ChCh Oxford (MA); *m* 2 June 1977, Jeannette de Rothschild (d 1980), da of Frederick Ernest Bishop (d 1940); *Career* Nat Serv 2 Lt RA 1956–58; John Lewis Partnership: joined 1961, md Edinburgh 1973–75, md Peter Jones 1975–77, dir of personnel 1978–92, gen inspr 1992–; *Recreations* skiing, tennis, travel; *Clubs* Vanderbilt; *Style*— Stephen May, Esq; ✉ The John Lewis Partnership, 171 Victoria St, London SW1E 5NN (☎ 0171 828 1000, ext 6166)

MAYALL, David William; s of Arthur William Mayall, of Derby, and Pamela, *née* Bryant; *b* 19 July 1957; *Educ* Repton, Univ of Cambridge (MA); *m* 22 June 1985, Wendy Madeleine, da of Peter Black of Douglas, IOM; 1 s (James b 13 April 1988), 1 da (Sophie b 31 May 1990); *Career* called to the Bar Gray's Inn 1979, pt/t immigration adjudicator 1993–; *Recreations* bridge, tennis, golf; *Style*— David Mayall, Esq; ✉ Highstone House, 148 Totteridge Lane, Totteridge, London N20 8AJ; Francis Taylor Building, Temple, London EC4Y 7BY (☎ 0171 353 7768)

MAYALL, Prof James B L; *b* 14 April 1937; *Educ* Sidney Sussex Coll Cambridge (open scholar, BA); *Career* Nat Serv 2 Lt Queen's Own Nigeria Regt 1955–57; Sir John Dill fell Princeton Univ 1960–61, asst princ Board of Trade 1961–63, Treasy Centre for Admin Studies 1963–64, first sec (econ) Br High Cmmn New Delhi 1964–65, princ Bd of Trade 1965–66; LSE: lectr Int Relations Dept 1966–75, sr lectr 1975–83, reader 1983–91, rep Inter-Univ Ctee for Study on Africa 1984–, prof and convenor of Int Relations Dept 1991–94; visiting lectr: Univ of New Brunswick 1976–77, Univ of Capetown 1977–78; visiting prof of govt Dartmouth Coll New Hampshire 1982, 1984, 1989, 1990, Centre for Political Studies Jawaharlal Nehru Univ New Delhi 1988; assoc ed Survey and Documents on Int Affairs RIIA 1968–72; convenor: S Africa Study Gp RIIA 1990–, research project on Int Soc after the Cold War (funded by Ford Foundation) 1993–95; chm Steering Ctee and Ed Bd LSE Centre for Int Studies 1991 (memb 1975); memb: Cncl RIIA 1992–, Exec Ctee Br Int Studies Assoc 1981–85 and 1987–88, Research Ctee Int Africa Inst 1986–88, Editorial Ctee Ethnic and Racial Studies 1989–94, Nations and Nationalism 1994–; *Books* Documents on International Affairs, 1962 (ed with D C Watt and Cornelia Navari, 1971), Current British Foreign Policy (3 vols ed with D C Watt, 1970, 1971, 1972), Africa: The Cold War and After (1971), A New International Commodity Regime (ed and contributor with Geoffrey Goodwin, 1979), The End of the Post War Era: Documents on Great Power Relations, 1968–75 (ed and introduced with Cornelia Navari, 1981), The Community of States (ed, 1982), Nationalism and International Society (1990); author of articles in various political jls; *Style—* Prof James Mayall; ✉ Centre for International Studies, London School of Economics and Political Science, Houghton Street, London WC2A 2AE (☎ 0171 955 7400 (direct), 0171 405 7686, fax 0171 955 7556, telex 24655 LSELON G)

MAYALL, Richard Michael (Rik); s of John Mayall, and Gillian Mayall; *b* 7 March 1958; *Educ* Univ of Manchester; *m* Barbara, *née* Robbin; 2 da (Rosemary Elizabeth, Bonnie), 1 s (Sidney Richard); *Career* comedian, actor and writer; *Theatre* incl: Nick in The Common Pursuit (Phoenix) 1988, Vladimir in Waiting for Godot (Gielgud Theatre) 1991–92, Khelstakov in The Government Inspector, Sean Bourke in Cell Mates (Albery) 1995; *Television* incl: Rick in The Young Ones (originator and co-writer, 2 series, BBC) 1982 & 1984, The Comic Strip Presents (Channel Four) 1983–84 & 1992, George's Marvellous Medicine (5 episodes, Jackanory, BBC) 1985, Alan B'Stard in The New Statesman (4 series, YTV) 1987–88, 1990 & 1994, Grim Tales (2 series, Initial for Central) 1990, Bottom (3 series, BBC) 1990, 1992 & 1994, Rik Mayall Presents (2 trilogies of films, Granada TV) 1992–94, Wham Bham Strawberry Jam! (BBC) 1995, Alan B'Stard in The Alan B'Stard Interview with Brian Walden (SelecTV for BBC) 1995; *Films* incl: SAS Commander in Whoops Apocalypse 1982, title role in Drop Dead Fred (Working Title) 1990, Wyatt Earp in Horse Opera (Initial for Channel Four) 1992, Ian in Remember Me (Talisman Films/Channel Four) 1996, Marty in Bring Me the Head of Mavis Davis (Goldcrest/The Mission) 1996; voices for animations incl: Tom Thumb in World of Peter Rabbit & Friends - Tale of Two Bad Mice (TVC for F Warne & Co) 1994, Toad in The Wind in the Willows (TVC for Carlton) 1995, The Robber King in The Snow Queen (Martin Gates Prodns) 1995, Prince Froglip in The Princess & The Goblin (Siriol Animations), Hero Baby in How to be a Little Sod (BBC) 1995, Young William Tell in Oscar's Orchestra 1996; *Live Stand Up* incl: Comic Strip 1982, Kevin Turvey & Bastard Squad 1983, Rik Mayall Ben Elton Andy De La Tour (UK tour & Edinburgh Fringe) 1983, Rik Mayall & Ben Elton 1984–85, Rik Mayall & Ben Elton (Aust tour) 1986, Rik Mayall & Andy De La Tour 1989–90, Rik Mayall & Ben Elton 1992, Rik Mayall & Adrian Edmondson (UK tour) 1993, Rik Mayall & Adrian Edmondson (70 dates, UK tour) 1995, Rik Mayall & Adrian Edmondson (UK tour) 1997; *Awards* for The New Statesman: Int Emmy Award 1989, BAFTA Best New Comedy 1990, Int Film & Festival and TV Festival of New York 1991, Special Craft Gold Medal Best Performer/Narrator; Comedy Awards Best New Comedy for Bottom 1992, British Comedy Awards Best Comedy Actor for Rik Mayall Presents 1993; *Style—* Rik Mayall, Esq; ✉ c/o Ms Aude Powell, The Brunskill Management Ltd, Suite 8A, 169 Queen's Gate, London SW7 5HE (☎ 0171 581 3388, 01768 881430, fax 01768 881850)

MAYBURY, Neil Martin; s of Leonard Albert Maybury (d 1992), of Harborne, Birmingham, and Kathleen Margaret, *née* Howse (d 1982); *b* 25 Aug 1943; *Educ* King Edward's Sch Birmingham, Univ of Birmingham (LLB); *m* 10 May 1980, Sally Elizabeth, da of Kenneth Carroll, of Streetly, W Midlands; 3 s (Thomas Charles b 1983, Toby George b 1986, Henry Giles b 1992), 1 da (Natasha Poppy b 1987); *Career* admitted slr 1969; asst slr Clifford-Turner & Co London 1969–72, ptnr Pinsent & Co (merged with Simpson Curtis to form Pinsent Curtis May 1995) 1975–95, ptnr Dibb Lupton Broomhead 1995–; dir: Securemethod Ltd, Tantell Ltd; sec: Wemtech Ltd, Mid Shires Hotels Ltd; memb: Cncl Soc for Computers and Law 1979–88, Fedn Against Software Theft Legal Advsy Gp, Technol Ctee Birmingham Law Soc; memb Law Soc; *Books* Guide to The Electronic Office (with Keith James, 1988); *Recreations* tennis, squash, flying, gardening, classic cars, skiing, opera; *Clubs* Edgbaston Priory, Wig & Pen, Edgbaston Golf; *Style—* Neil Maybury, Esq; ✉ Dibb Lupton Broomhead, Windsor House, Temple Row, Birmingham B2 5LF (☎ 0121 200 5009, fax 0121 200 5042)

MAYBURY, Air Cdre Peter Lawrence; s of Lysander Montague Maybury (d 1971), of Portsmouth, and Florence Edna, *née* Kaines (d 1989); *b* 10 Aug 1928; *Educ* Sherborne, Univ of Cambridge, UCH (MA, MB BChir); *m* 18 Sept 1954, Helen Lindsay Livingstone, da of Daniel Wills (d 1946), Res Cmmn Central Johore; 2 da (Nicola Helen b 1956, Karen Peta b 1958); *Career* qualified med practitioner 1952; joined RAF Med Branch 1954, Air Cdre served UK, RAF Germany, Libya, Cyprus; dep princ MO HQ RAF Germany 1967–70, cmdg health MO HQ Strike Cmd 1975–78, dir of health and res MOD 1980–82 (dep dir 1978–80), ret 1982; RAF Central Med Estab London: sr med offr, dep pres Central Med Bd 1982–94, ret 1994; FFCM, FFPHM, MFOM; *Recreations* gardening, walking, sailing; *Clubs* RAF; *Style—* Air Cdre Peter Maybury; ✉ Puddledock Garden, Clay Hall Lane, Acton, Sudbury, Suffolk (☎ 01787 377092)

MAYDON, Peter John; *Career* Reckitt & Colman plc: joined 1963, various sr mgmnt posts in UK, Australia, Africa and Pakistan, main bd dir 1980–, currently gp dir supply; *Style—* Peter Maydon, Esq; ✉ Reckitt & Colman plc, One Burlington Lane, London W4 2RW (☎ 0181 994 6464)

MAYER, Dr Christopher Norman; s of George Emanuel Mayer, of Bath, Avon, and Margaret, *née* Jones; *b* 30 Aug 1954; *Educ* City of Bath Boys Sch Avon, Welsh Nat Sch of Med Cardiff (MB BCh); *m* 12 Sept 1981, Joanna Paget, da of Michael James Lock, of Arundel, Sussex; 1 s (Humphrey b 2 Sept 1991), 3 da (Alice b 25 July 1984, Annabel b 9 Feb 1986, Felicity b 30 July 1988); *Career* sr registrar Dept of Psychiatry St George's Hosp London 1983–86, conslt psychiatrist W Suffolk Hosp Bury St Edmunds 1986–, med dir Alcohol Treatment Prog Dukes Priory Hosp Chelmsford 1992–, convenor Approved Visits for Royal Coll of Psychiatrists 1994–; pubns incl papers on anorexia nervosa; TV appearances incl: The Purchase and Importation of Camels from North Africa (BBC 2), The Crisis of British Public Conveniences (Channel 4); patron W Suffolk Relate; MRCPsych 1983; *Recreations* digging in the garden, 19th Century literature; *Style—* Dr Christopher Mayer; ✉ Cattishall Farmhouse, Great Barton, Bury St Edmunds, Suffolk IP31 2QT (☎ 01284 787340); West Suffolk Hospital, Hardwick Lane, Bury St Edmunds, Suffolk IP33 2QZ (☎ 01284 713592)

MAYER, Prof Colin Peter; s of Harold Charles and late Anne Louise Mayer, of London; *b* 12 May 1953; *Educ* St Paul's, Oriel Coll Oxford (MA), Wolfson Coll Oxford (MPhil), Harvard Univ (Harkness fell, DPhil Oxon); *m* Annette Patricia, da of Annesley Haynes; 2 da (Ruth Sarah b 21 Oct 1984, Hannah Claire b 21 July 1987); *Career* HM Treasy 1976–79, fell in economics St Anne's Coll Oxford 1980–86, prof of corporate fin City Univ Business Sch 1987–92, prof of economics and finance Univ of Warwick 1992–94, prof of mgmnt studies and dep dir Sch of Mgmnt Studies Univ of Oxford 1994–; Houblon Norman fell Bank of England 1989–90, hon fell St Anne's Coll Oxford; *Books* European Financial Integration (with A Giovannini, 1991), Capital Markets and Financial Intermediation (with X Vives, 1993), Hostile Takeovers: Defence, Attack and Corporate Governance (with T Jenkinson, 1994); *Recreations* piano playing, jogging, reading philosophy and science; *Style—* Prof Colin Mayer; ✉ Wadham College, University of Oxford, Oxford OX1 3PN (☎ 01865 277900)

MAYER, Laurence David Joseph (Laurie); *Educ* Univ of Essex (BA); *m* 1971, Jill; 2 s (Nicholas and Simon); *Career* asst press offr New Scotland Yard 1968–70; TV and radio bdcaster; prodr/presenter Rush Hour breakfast prog BBC Radio London 1970–73, presenter/reporter Newsbeat BBC Radio 1 1973–79, BBC TV reporter Nationwide, 60 Minutes and Six O'Clock News 1979–88; BBC TV presenter: South East at Six, One O'Clock News, Six O'Clock News, NewsView and Summaries 1988–89, Breakfast News 1989–93, Around Westminster 1991–93; presenter Sky World News 1993–; RTS Award for Home News 1985; *Style—* Laurie Mayer, Esq; ✉ Sky News, 6 Centaurs Business Park, Grant Way, Isleworth, Middx TW7 5QD (☎ 0171 705 3000)

MAYER, Thomas (Tom); CBE (1985); s of Hans Mayer (d 1967), and Jeanette, *née* Gumperz (d 1956); *b* 17 Dec 1928; *Educ* King's Sch Harrow, Regent St Poly (BSc); *m* 1975, Jean Patricia, da of John Ernest Frederick Burrows, of Dagenham; 1 s (Peter), 1 da (Helen); *Career* md Marconi Communication Systems Ltd 1969–81, chm and md Thorn EMI Electronics Ltd 1981–86, dir Soc of Br Aerospace Cos Ltd 1984–90, chief exec Thorn EMI Technology Group 1986–89, chm Thorn EMI Electonics 1986–90; dir: Babcock Thorn 1986–90, Thorn EMI plc 1987–90, Devonport Management Ltd 1990–, Eurodis Electron plc 1991–; chm: Eldonray Ltd 1990–, Holmes Protection Group Inc 1990–91, ITT Defence Ltd 1993–; memb Nat Electronics Cncl; FEng 1987, FIEE, FRTS; *Clubs* Ellesborough Golf; *Style—* Tom Mayer, Esq, CBE, FEng; ✉ 1590 AD, Burton Lane, Monks Risborough, Buckinghamshire HP27 9JF

MAYES, Ian; QC (1993); yr s of Harold and Beatrice Mayes; *b* 11 Sept 1951; *Educ* Highgate Sch, Trinity Coll Cambridge; *m* 1986, Shirley Ann, da of Reginald Bothroyd; 2 s (Oliver Tobias b 31 Oct 1988, Theo Alexander b 9 Feb 1992); *Career* called to the Bar Middle Temple 1974 (Harmsworth scholar), Dept of Trade Inspection London Capital Group Ltd 1975–77, standing counsel to Inland Revenue 1983–93; memb Justice Ctee on Fraud, chm Disciplinary Ctee Lloyd's of London; *Recreations* skiing, scuba diving, paintings and pots; *Style—* Ian Mayes, Esq, QC; ✉ 3 (North) King's Bench Walk, Temple, London EC4Y 7HR (☎ 0171 797 8600, fax 0171 797 8699)

MAYES, Rt Rev Michael Hugh Gunton; *see:* Kilmore, Elphin and Ardagh, Bishop of

MAYFIELD, Rt Rev Christopher John; *see:* Manchester, Bishop of

MAYHEW, Baroness; Cicely Elizabeth; da of George Shaw Ludlam (d 1970), of Zimbabwe, and Lily Hyde, *née* Darwent (d 1987); *b* 16 Feb 1924; *Educ* Sheffield HS, Cheltenham Ladies' Coll, Lady Margaret Hall Oxford (University Gerrans scholar, BA); *m* 1949, Baron Mayhew (Life Peer (d 1997)); 2 s (Hon David Francis b 1951, Hon (Christopher) James b 1959), 2 da (Hon Teresa Ruth (Hon Mrs Lyle) b 1953, Hon Judith Emily Anne b 1955); *Career* linguist GCHQ 1944–45, PATRA 1945, asst princ HM Treasy 1946–47, HM Dip Serv 1947–49 (served London, Belgrade and Geneva); VSO: sometime selector, memb Exec Ctee and memb Cncl; memb Civil Serv Selection Bds in various capacities 1970–93, memb Parole Bd 1984–87; govr The Froebel Sch London 1987–95; memb: Bach Choir 1953–91 (sometime ctee memb, vice chm 1983–90), Nat Tst; *Publications* What is Titoism? (pamphlet, 1951), occasional published articles; *Recreations* hill walking, travel, gardening, choral singing; *Style—* The Rt Hon the Lady Mayhew

MAYHEW, Kenneth (Ken); s of Albert Chadwick Mayhew (d 1967), and Alice, *née* Leigh; *b* 1 Sept 1947; *Educ* Manchester GS, Worcester Coll Oxford (MA), LSE (MSc); *m* 1 (m dis 1982), Margaret, *née* Humphreys; 1 da (Rowena Kate b 1978); m 2, 1990, Gillian Alexandra, da of Arthur Alexander McGrattan, of Belfast; 1 s (Alexander Chadwick b 1991); *Career* economist; economic asst HM Treasy 1970–72; res offr: Queen Elizabeth House Oxford 1972, Inst of Econs Oxford 1972–81; fell Pembroke Coll Oxford 1976–, econ dir NEDO 1989–90; assoc ed Oxford Review of Economic Policy; *Books* Pay Policies for the Future (ed with D Robinson, 1983), Improving Incentives for the Low Paid (ed with A Bowen, 1990), Reducing Regional Inequalities (ed with A Bowen, 1991), Providing Health Care (ed with A McGuire and P Fenn, 1991), Britain's Training Deficit (ed with R Layard and G Owen, 1994); *Recreations* travel, literature; *Clubs* Reform; *Style—* Ken Mayhew, Esq; ✉ 49 Hamilton Rd, Oxford OX2 7PY (☎ 01865 510977); Pembroke College, Oxford OX1 1DW (☎ 01865 276434, fax 01865 276418)

MAYHEW, The Rt Hon Sir Patrick Barnabas Burke; kt (1983), PC (1986), QC (1972), MP (C) Tunbridge Wells (majority 17,132); s of (Alfred) Geoffrey Horace Mayhew, MC (d 1985), of Sevenoaks Weald, Kent, and Sheila Margaret Burke, *née* Roche; *b* 11 Sept 1929; *Educ* Tonbridge, Balliol Coll Oxford (MA); *m* 15 April 1963, Jean Elizabeth, 2 da of John Gurney, *qv*, of Walsingham Abbey, Norfolk; 4 s (James b 1964, Henry b 1965, Tristram b 1968, Jerome b 1970); *Career* served 4/7 Royal Dragoon Gds, Capt (Nat Serv and AER); called to the Bar Middle Temple 1956, bencher 1982; Parly candidate (C) Camberwell and Dulwich 1970, MP (C) Tunbridge Wells Feb 1974–; vice chm Cons Home Affrs Ctee and memb Exec 1922 Ctee 1976–79, Parly under sec for employment 1979–81, min of state Home Office 1981–83, Slr-Gen 1983–87, Attorney-Gen 1987–92, sec of state for Northern Ireland 1992–; pres: Tonbridge and Tunbridge Wells Dist MENCAP, Tunbridge Wells Constitutional Club, Kilndown CC; vice pres: Tunbridge Wells RFC, Goudhurst CC; Liveryman Worshipful Co of Skinners; *Recreations* sailing, country pursuits; *Clubs* Pratt's, Beefsteak, Garrick, Tunbridge Wells Constitutional; *Style—* The Rt Hon Sir Patrick Mayhew, QC, MP; ✉ House of Commons, London SW1A 0AA

MAYHEW-SANDERS, Sir John Reynolds; kt (1982); s of Jack Mayhew-Sanders (d 1982); *b* 25 Oct 1931; *Educ* Epsom Coll, RNC Dartmouth, Jesus Coll Cambridge (MA); *m* 1958, Sylvia Mary (d 1995), da of George S Colling (d 1959); 3 s, 1 da; *Career* RN 1949–54; formerly with Mayhew-Sanders CAs and with PE Consulting Group Ltd; John Brown & Co Ltd: dir 1972–83, chief exec 1975–83, chm 1978–83); chm Heidrick & Struggles 1985–87, chief exec Samuelson Group plc 1987–88; non-exec dir: Rover Group plc 1980–88, Dowty Group plc 1982–86; memb: Cncl of Engrg Employers' Fedn 1977–80, BOTB 1980–83, BBC Consultative Gp Industl & Business Affrs 1981–83; chm Overseas Project Bd 1980–83, pres Br-Soviet C of C 1983–88; govr Sadler's Wells Fndn 1983–89, dir Sadler's Wells Tst, chm New Sadler's Wells Opera Co; FCA, CIMgt; FRSA; *Recreations* fishing, shooting, music, astronomy; *Style—* Sir John Mayhew-Sanders; ✉ Earlstone House, Burghclere, Newbury, Berks RG20 9HN (☎ 01635 278288)

MAYNARD, Prof Alan Maynard; s of Edward Joseph Maynard, of W Kirby, Wirral, Merseyside, and Hilda Marion, *née* McCausland; *b* 15 Dec 1944; *Educ* Calday Grange GS W Kirby Merseyside, Univ of Newcastle upon Tyne, Univ of York (BPhil); *m* 22 June 1968, Elizabeth Mary, da of Kevin Joseph Shanahan, of Edinburgh; 2 s (Justin b 11 Feb 1970, John b 24 Oct 1971), 2 da (Jane b 31 July 1974, Samantha b 8 Nov 1976); *Career* asst lectr and lectr in economics Univ of Exeter 1968–71, prof of economics and founding dir Centre for Health Economics Univ of York 1981–95 (lectr in economics 1971–76, sr lectr and dir Graduate Prog in Health Economics 1976–83), sec Nuffield

Provincial Hosps Tst 1995–96; visiting lectr: Italy, NZ, Sweden; non-exec dir York NHS Tst Hosp 1991–; memb: York Health Authy 1982–91, ESRC 1983–86 (memb Human Behaviour and Devpt Ctee 1988–89), MRC Health Servs Res Ctee 1986–92, chm Evaluation Panel for Fourth Med and Health Res Prog Euro Cmmn 1990; memb: Royal Econ Soc, Soc for the Study of Addiction, Royal Society of Medicine; over 150 articles in jls; *Books* Health Care in the European Community (1976), Public Private Mix for Health (ed with G McLachlan, 1982), Controlling Legal Addictions (ed with D Robinson and R Chester, 1989), Preventing Alcohol and Tobacco Problems (ed with P Tether, 1990), Competition in Health Care: Reforming the NHS (ed, with A J Culyer and J Posnett); *Recreations* reading, walking, current affairs and cricket; *Clubs* RSM, Royal Cwlth Soc; *Style*— Prof Alan Maynard; ✉ c/o Karen Bloor, Department of Health Sciences, University of York, Heslington, York YO1 5DD

MAYNARD, Bill; *b* 8 Oct 1928; *Educ* Kibworth GS; *Career* actor; *Theatre* The Entertainer (Edinburgh), Loot, Semi Detached, The Caretaker, Cat on a Hot Tin Roof (Derby), Harvey, The Odd Couple, A Face for All Occasions, Crete and Sergeant Pepper (Royal Court), Die Fledermaus (Opera North), Strippers (Phoenix), When we are Married (Whitehall Theatre), Annie, The Creation and God in The Passion (Dartford and Malvern), A Man for all Seasons (Swansea), Hobson's Choice; *Television* Yorkshire: Oh No It's Selwyn Froggitt, Bill Maynard in Person, The Gaffer; Granada: The Life of Riley, Paper Roses, Coronation Street; BBC: Kisses at Fifty, Till Death Do Us Part, Trinity Tales, Spotlight, Filipina Dreamgirls; Worzel Gummidge (Southern), The Inheritors (HTV), Tales of the Unexpected (Anglia), Juno and the Paycock (STV), Minder (Euston), The Tale of Little Pig Robinson (TVS), Heartbeat (YTV); *Films* incl: various Carry On... and Confessions Of..., Bless this House, Man About the House, Robin and Marion, All Things Bright and Beautiful, Oddball Hall, Hear my Song; *Recreations* lying down; *Style*— Bill Maynard, Esq; ✉ c/o Richard Stone Partnership, 25 Whitehall, London SW1A 2BS (☎ 0171 839 6421)

MAYNARD, (Henry) Charles Edward; s of Henry Maynard, of Coleshill, Bucks, and Diana Elizabeth, *née* Lee; *b* 10 Feb 1941; *Educ* Bryanston, Imperial Coll London (BSc); *m* 17 March 1984, Susan Marjorie, da of Edward George Hedges Barford; 2 da (Catherine Anna b 1 May 1986, Rebecca Jane b 28 April 1989); *Career* ptnr Moores Rowland CA's 1969 (ptnr i/c London Office 1979–85, vice chm Moores Rowland Int 1987–91, chm 1991–); memb Worshipful Co of CA's in England and Wales; FCA 1962; *Recreations* golf, tennis, skiing, sailing, Victorian watercolours; *Clubs* Hurlingham, Royal West Norfolk Golf; *Style*— Charles Maynard, Esq; ✉ Moores Rowland, Clifford's Inn, Fetter Lane, London EC4 1AS (☎ 0171 831 2345, fax 0171 831 6123)

MAYNARD, Prof Geoffrey Walter; s of Walter F Maynard, and Maisie, *née* Bristow; *b* 27 Oct 1921; *Educ* Univ of London, LSE (BSc(Econ)), Univ of Wales (PhD); *m* 1949, Marie Lilian, *née* Wright; 2 da (Joanna b 1956, Victoria b 1961); *Career* taught at several univs in UK and USA; at various times conslt: FCO, World Bank, Harvard Univ Devpt Advsy Serv; held advsy posts to number of developing countries incl Argentina and Liberia; ed Bankers' Magazine 1968–72, dep chief econ advsr HM Treasy 1976–77 (under sec 1972–74), vice pres and dir of econs Europe and Middle East Chase Manhattan Bank 1977–86 (econ conslt 1974), econ conslt Investcorp International Ltd 1986–; memb Econ Affrs Ctee Econ and Soc Res Cncl 1982–85, govr Inst of Development Studies Univ of Sussex 1984–91, govr Inst of Fiscal Studies 1987–; *Books* princ books incl: Economic Development and the Price Level (1961), A World of Inflation (jtly, 1976), The British Economy Under Mrs Thatcher 1979–87 (1988); *Recreations* walking; *Clubs* Reform; *Style*— Prof Geoffrey Maynard; ✉ Flat 219, Queens Quay, 58 Upper Thames St, London EC4

MAYNARD, John David; s of Albert William Henry Maynard (d 1968), of Surrey, and Ellen Hughes-Jones (d 1970); *b* 14 May 1931; *Educ* Whitgift Sch, Charing Cross Hosp London (MB BS, Gold medal Clinical Medicine and Surgery, FRCS (England), MS (London)); *m* 1, 13 Aug 1955 (m dis 1971), Patricia Katharine, da of C W F Gray (d 1985), of Sutton, Surrey; 2 s (Andrew b 1959, Nicholas b 1962), 2 da (Sarah b 1956, Julia b 1962); m 2, 23 June 1972, Gillian Mary, da of H F Loveless, of Milford-on-Sea, Hampshire; 1 s (Timothy b 1976); *Career* Capt RAMC 1956; lectr in anatomy London Hosp 1958–59, sr conslt surgn Guy's Hosp London 1967–, dir of the Pathology of Museums Guy's and St Thomas's Med Schs 1969–, teacher Univ of London 1963–, hon sr lectr in surgery Guy's Hosp 1992–; hon conslt surgn St Luke's Hosp for the Clergy 1990–; surgical tutor: RCS 1967–76, Guy's Hosp Med Sch 1967–76; sr examiner of surgery Univ of London 1962–85, examiner of surgery Soc of Apothecaries 1962–70; chm The Salivary Gland Tumour Panel England 1970–90, RCS advsr on surgical services to HM Prison Serv 1995–, memb Cncl Royal Soc of Med 1996–, surgical advsr to Dir of Museums Royal Coll of Surgns 1996–; author of various papers on diseases of salivary glands; Hunterian prof RCS 1963; Liveryman The Worshipful Soc of Apothecaries 1962; memb: BMA 1954, Med Soc of London 1961, The Chelsea Clinical Soc 1962; scientific FZS 1956, FRSM 1958; fell: Assoc of Surgeons 1967, The Hunterian Soc 1985; *Books* Surgery (jtly, 1974), Surgery of Salivary Glands in Surgical Management (1984, 1988), Contemporary Operative Surgery (1979), Carcinoma of Salivary Glands in Head & Neck Oncology (1991), Text Book and Colour Atlas of Diseases of Salivary Glands (contrib chapters on Parotid Surgery, 1995); *Recreations* golf, hill walking, photography; *Clubs* Carlton; *Style*— John D Maynard, MS, FRCS; ✉ 14 Blackheath Park, London SE3 9RP (☎ 0181 852 6766); Mountsloe, Frogham, Fordingbridge, Hants SP6 2HP (☎ 0142565 3009); Guy's Hospital, London SE1 9RT (☎ 0171 955 4359); 97 Harley St, London W1N 1DF (☎ 0171 935 4988, fax 0171 935 6617)

MAYNARD, Matthew Peter; s of Kenneth Maynard (d 1984), of Menai Bridge, N Wales, and Anne Patricia, *née* Buckley; *b* 21 March 1966; *Educ* Ysgol David Hughes Menai Bridge Anglesey; *m* 27 Sept 1986, Susan Lloyd, da of Eifion Owen Jones; 1 s (Thomas Lloyd b 25 March 1989), 1 da (Ceri Lloyd b 5 Aug 1993); *Career* professional cricketer; represented Welsh Schs under 15's; Glamorgan CCC: debut 1985, awarded county cap 1987, 225 first class appearances; 4 test caps England, memb squad Ashes series 1993, memb team touring W Indies 1993/94; scorer of Glamorgan's fastest ever 50 in 14 minutes, youngest Glamorgan player to be capped and to score a century; 5 Benson & Hedges Gold awards, 4 NatWest Gold awards, Cricket Writers' Club Young Cricketer of the Year 1988; *Recreations* golf, squash, family; *Style*— Matthew Maynard, Esq; ✉ c/o Glamorgan CCC, Sophia Gardens, Cardiff CF1 9XR (☎ 01222 343478)

MAYNARD, Air Chief Marshal Sir Nigel Martin; KCB (1973, CB 1971), CBE (1963), DFC (1942), AFC (1947); s of Air Vice-Marshal Forster Herbert Martin Maynard, CB, AFC (d 1976); *b* 28 Aug 1921; *Educ* Aldenham; *m* 1946, Daphne, da of Griffith Llewellyn (d 1972); 1 s, 1 da; *Career* served WWII RAF, Gp Capt 1958, ADC to HM The Queen 1961–65, Air Cdre 1965, Air Vice-Marshal 1968, Cmdt Staff Coll Bracknell 1968–70, Air Cdr Far East 1970–71, Air Marshal 1972, Dep C-in-C Strike Cmd 1972, C-in-C RAF Germany and Cdr 2 Allied Tactical Air Force 1973–76, Air Chief Marshal 1976, C-in-C Strike Cmd 1976–77, ret; *Recreations* travel; *Clubs* Naval and Military, RAF, MCC; *Style*— Air Chief Marshal Sir Nigel Maynard, KCB, CBE, DFC, AFC; ✉ Manor House, Piddington, Bicester, Oxon OX6 0QB (☎ and fax 01844 238270)

MAYNE, Prof David Quinn; s of Leslie Harper Mayne (d 1963), and Jane, *née* Quin; *b* 23 April 1930; *Educ* Christian Brothers Coll Boksburg SA, Univ of The Witwatersrand SA (BSc, MSc), Univ of London (PhD, DSc); *m* 16 Dec 1954, Josephine Mary, da of Joseph Karl Hess (d 1968); 3 da (Susan Francine (Mrs Leung) b 9 March 1956, Maire Anne b 16 July 1957, Ruth Catherine b 18 April 1959); *Career* lectr Univ of the Witwatersrand 1950–54 and 1957–59, R & D engr Br Thomson Houston Co Rugby 1955–56; Imperial Coll London: lectr 1959–67, reader 1967–71, prof of control theory 1971–91, head of Electrical Engrg Dept 1984–88, currently prof emeritus Dept of Electrical and Electronic Engrg; res fell Harvard 1971; prof emeritus Dept of Electrical and Computer Engrg Univ of Calif at Davis 1991–; FIEE 1980, FIEEE 1981, FRS 1985, FEng 1987; *Books* Differential Dynamic Programming (1970); *Recreations* walking, cross country skiing; *Style*— Prof David Mayne, FRS, FEng; ✉ Department of Electical and Electronic Engineering, Imperial College of Science, Technology and Medicine, London SW7 2BT

MAYNE, John Fraser; CB (1986); s of John Leonard Mayne (d 1982), and Martha Laura, *née* Griffiths (d 1993); *b* 14 Sept 1932; *Educ* Dulwich, Worcester Coll Oxford (BA); *m* 10 May 1958, Gillian Mary, da of Leonard Arthur Key (d 1955); 1 s (Jonathan Leonard b 1964), 1 da (Catharine Hilary b 1965); *Career* Nat Serv RTR Subaltern 1951–53; Air Miny 1956–64, HM Treasy 1964–67, Cabinet Office and Central Policy Review Staff 1970–73, asst under sec of state (Air Staff) MOD 1976–78 (asst private sec to Sec of State 1968–70, private sec to Sec of State 1975–76), princ establishments and fin offr NI Office 1979–81, dir gen of mgmnt Audit MOD 1981–83, dep sec Cabinet Office MPO 1984–86, princ establishments and fin offr Dept of Health 1986–90 (DHSS 1986–89); non-exec memb Hampstead Health Authy 1990–93; mgmnt conslt PA Consulting Group 1990–95; memb Public Policy Unit 1990–, dir Carnegie Young People Initiative 1995–; memb Cncl RUSI 1986–89, tstee Nat Aids Tst; Freeman City of London 1983; *Recreations* music, fell walking, cooking, work; *Style*— John Mayne, Esq, CB; ✉ Hazlefield House, Auchencairn, Castle Douglas DG7 1RF (☎ 01556 640351); 2 Ashley Gardens, Ambrosden Avenue, London SW1P 1QD (☎ 0171 838 5059)

MAYNE, Very Rev Michael Clement Otway; KCVO (1996); s of Michael Ashton Otway Mayne (d 1933), and Sylvia Clementina, *née* Lumley Ellis; *b* 10 Sept 1929; *Educ* King's Sch Canterbury, Corpus Christi Coll Cambridge (BA, MA); *m* 16 Oct 1965, Alison Geraldine, da of Henry Erskine McKie (d 1985); 1 s (Mark b 1968), 1 da (Sarah b 1966); *Career* Nat Serv Pilot Offr RAF 1949–51; asst curate St John the Baptist Harpenden 1957–59, domestic chaplain to Bishop of Southwark 1959–65, vicar Norton Letchworth 1965–72, head religious progs BBC Radio 1972–79, vicar Great St Mary's (Univ Church) Cambridge 1979–86, dean of Westminster 1986–Dec 1996, dean Order of the Bath 1986–Dec 1996, ret; select preacher: Univ of Cambridge 1988, Univ of Oxford 1989 and 1993; chm of Govrs Westminster Sch 1986–96, memb Cncl St Christopher's Hospice 1988–, tstee King George VI and Queen Elizabeth Fndn of St Catherine's Cumberland Lodge 1992–, chm Sandford St Martin Tst 1993–; *Books* Prayers for Pastoral Occasions (1982), Encounters (ed, 1985), A Year Lost and Found (1987), From Power to Partnership (ed 1991), This Sunrise of Wonder (1995); *Recreations* theatre, books, bird watching, silence; *Style*— The Very Rev Michael Mayne, KCVO; ✉ 37 St Mark's Road, Salisbury, Wilts SP1 3AY

MAYNE, Dr Richard John; s of John William Mayne, of London, and Kate Hilda, *née* Angus; *b* 2 April 1926; *Educ* St Paul's, Trinity Coll Cambridge (MA, PhD); *m* 1, 1954, Margaret Ellingworth Lyon; m 2, 1970, Jocelyn Mudie, da of William James Ferguson, of London; 2 da (Zoë, Alice); *Career* writer and broadcaster; served Royal Signals 1944–47; Leverhulme Euro scholar and Rome corr New Statesman 1953–54, asst tutor Cambridge Inst of Educn 1954–56; official: Euro Coal and Steel Community Luxembourg 1956–58, EEC Brussels 1958–63; PA to Jean Monnet 1963–66; Encounter: Paris corr 1966–71, co-ed 1985–90, contributing ed 1990–91; dir Federal Tst for Educn and Res 1971–73, head of UK Offices Cmmn of the Euro Communities 1973–79 (special advsr 1979–80); film critic: Sunday Telegraph 1987–89, The European 1990–; visiting prof Univ of Chicago 1971, hon professorial fell UCW Aberystwyth 1986–89; memb Cncl: RIIA, Federal Tst for Educn and Research; memb: Franco-British Cncl, Broadcasting Ctee Soc of Authors; *Books* The Community of Europe (1962), The Institutions of the European Community (1968), The Recovery of Europe (1970), The Europeans (1972), Europe Tomorrow (ed, 1972), The New Atlantic Challenge (ed, 1975), The Memoirs of Jean Monnet (trans 1978, Scott-Moncrieff prize 1979), Postwar: the Dawn of Today's Europe (1983), Western Europe: a Handbook (ed, 1986), Federal Union: the Pioneers (1990), Europe: a History of its People (trans 1990), Illustrated History of Europe (trans 1993), A History of Civilizations (trans 1993); *Recreations* travel, fell walking, sailing (Flying Falcon); *Clubs* Groucho, Les Misérables (Paris); *Style*— Dr Richard Mayne; ✉ Albany Cottage, 24 Park Village East, Regent's Park, London NW1 7PZ (☎ 0171 387 6654)

MAYNE, William; s of William Mayne (d 1992), and Dorothy, *née* Fea (d 1964); *b* 16 March 1928; *Career* writer 1950–; author of ca 90 stories for children; Library Assoc medal 1957, Guardian Children's Book Award 1993; *Recreations* baking, typesetting; *Style*— William Mayne, Esq; ✉ c/o David Higham Associates, 5–8 Lower John St, Golden Square, London W1R 4HA

MAYO, Benjamin John; s of Dr Frank Mayo, of Fawley, Hampshire, and Gladys Margaret, *née* Mason; *b* 8 Nov 1944; *Educ* Churchers Coll Petersfield, Univ of Birmingham (BSc); *m* 1973, Hon Christine Mary Plumb, da of Lord Plumb, DL, MEP, *qv*; 3 da (Katharine Elizabeth b 28 Jan 1977, Sarah Louise b 14 Nov 1979, Stephanie Caroline b 9 April 1983); *Career* project mgmnt support Matthew Hall Engineering 1965–66; ICI: joined as graduate trainee 1966, Plastics Div Dumfries (maintenance, process devpt, plant mgmnt) 1967–74, sr process engr ICI Plastics Welwyn Garden City 1975–77, prodn mangr ICI Hillhouse Works Fleetwood 1978–79, process engrg mangr Welwyn Garden City 1980–81, prodn mangr Dumfries Works 1982–83, works mangr Oil Works Billingham 1984–85, chief engr (NE) Engrg Dept Billingham 1986–87, ops dir ICI Imagedata 1988–90, research and technol dir ICI Films Wilton 1993– (ops dir 1991–92); memb Cncl Inst of Chemical Engrg 1990–93 (chm Professional Devpt Ctee); FIChemE 1990, FEng 1993; *Recreations* squash, lawn tennis, real tennis, piano; *Style*— Benjamin Mayo, Esq, FEng; ✉ The Garth, Kirby Lane, Gt Broughton, North Yorkshire TS9 7HH (☎ 01642 712214); Research and Technology Director, ICI Films, PO Box 90, Wilton, Middlesbrough, Cleveland TS90 8JE (01642 432883)

MAYO, Col (Edward) John; OBE (1976); s of Rev Thomas Edward Mayo, JP (d 1973), of Axminster, Devon, and Constance Muriel, *née* Knibb (d 1991); *b* 24 May 1931; *Educ* King's Coll Taunton; *m* 1961, Jacqueline Margaret Anne, MBE (d 1993), da of Brig Charles Douglas Armstrong, CBE, DSO, MC (d 1985); 1 s (Charles); *Career* cmmnd RA 1951, served Malta, N Africa, Malaya, W Germany; cmd 17 Trg Regt and Depot RA 1972–75, Col Gen Staff HQ BAOR 1979–83, ret; DG Help the Aged 1983–; tstee: Helpage India 1985, Helpage Kenya 1985, Helpage Sri Lanka 1986, Helpage International 1994, Global Cancer 1996, Ex Services Mental Welfare 1996; FRSA; *Recreations* gardening, fishing, fine arts, travel, swimming; *Clubs* Army and Navy, MCC, Special Forces, Woodroffe's; *Style*— Col John Mayo, OBE; ✉ Sehore House, Tekels Ave, Camberley, Surrey GU15 2LB (☎ 01276 29653, fax 01276 670425); Help the Aged, St James's Walk, Clerkenwell, London EC1R 0BE (☎ 0171 253 0253)

MAYO, John William; s of Malcolm Guy Mayo (d 1968); *b* 8 Oct 1920; *Educ* St Paul's; *m* 1959, Susan Margaret; 3 s, 1 da; *Career* Capt RA (UK, Ceylon, India); admitted slr 1947; Linklaters & Paines slrs: joined 1947, ptnr 1952, sr ptnr 1980–85; exec dir SBC Warburg 1985–96 (formerly S G Warburg & Co Ltd); non-exec dir: Wellington Underwriting Holdings Ltd, Wellington Underwriting Agencies Ltd, Rothmans International BV; Hon FRCGP 1979; *Recreations* bridge, golf; *Clubs* Royal Wimbledon

Golf, Hunstanton Golf, Ealing RFC; *Style*— John Mayo, Esq; ✉ 38 Marryat Rd, Wimbledon, London SW19 5BD (☎ 0181 946 1537); The Mill Cottage, 41 Peddars Way North, Ringstead, Hunstanton, Norfolk PE36 5JP (☎ 01485 25391)

MAYO, 10 Earl of (I 1785); Terence Patrick Bourke; also Baron Naas (I 1776) and Viscount Mayo (I 1781); s of Hon Bryan Longley Bourke (d 1961), and nephew of 9 Earl (d 1962); *b* 26 Aug 1929; *Educ* St Aubyns Rottingdean, RN Coll Dartmouth; *m* 1, 1952 (m dis 1987), (Margaret) Jane Robinson (d 1992), only da of Gerald Joseph Cuthbert Harrison, DL (d 1954), of Wetheral, Cumbria; 3 s (Lord Naas, *qv*, Hon Patrick Antony b 1955, Hon Harry Richard b 1960); m 2, 1987, Sally Anne, only da of F G Matthews, of Bampton, Oxon; 1 s (Hon James Edward Maurice b 1986); *Heir* s, Charles Diarmuidh John Bourke, Lord Naas, *qv*; *Career* Lt RN 1952, served Suez 1956; Solo Aerobatic Displays, Farnborough 1957; md Irish Marble Ltd Merlin Park Galway; memb Lib Pty 1963–65, stood for Dorset S as Lib candidate 1964; memb Gosport Borough Cncl 1961; *Style*— The Rt Hon the Earl of Mayo; ✉ Château d'Arlens, Couloumé Mondebat, 32160 Plaisance-du- Gers, France

MAYOCK, John Paul; s of Vincent Mayock, of Hoyland, Barnsley, and Edna Mayock; *b* 26 Oct 1970; *Educ* Kirk Balk Sch Barnsley, Barnsley Sixth Form Coll, Staffordshire Univ; *Career* athlete (1500m runner); clubs: Rockingham 1982–91, Barnsley 1991–93, Cannock and Stafford 1993–; coached by Peter Elliot and Peter Watson; former winner English schs cross country and track championships; achievements incl: Silver medal 5000m Euro Jr Championships Varazdin 1989, Gold medal 5000m World Student Games Sheffield 1991, Silver medal 3000m Euro Indoor Championships Genoa 1992, fourth 5000m European Cup Birmingham 1994, third 1500m Commonwealth Games Canada 1994, 11th 1500m final Olympic Games Atlanta 1996; ranked: top 10 1500m (world) 1995, number 3 mile (world) 1996, number 1 1500m/mile (Br, UK) 1995 and 1996; currently pt/t sports promotions offr and computer res offr; *Recreations* socialising, cinema, driving, reading; *Style*— John Mayock, Esq; ✉ 3 Lilleshall Way, Western Downs, Stafford, Staffs ST17 9FD (☎ 01785 226423)

MAYOR, His Hon Judge Hugh Robert; QC (1986); s of George Mayor, of Fulwood, Preston, and Grace Mayor; *b* 12 Oct 1941; *Educ* Kirkham GS, St John's Coll Oxford (MA), Univ of Leicester (MA); *m* 1970, Carolyn Ann, da of Gp Capt Dennis Raymond Stubbs, DSO, DFC, OBE, of Sutton, Norfolk (d 1973); 1 s (Nicholas Dennis Robert b 1973), 1 da (Sally Jane b 1975); *Career* lectr Univ of Leicester 1964–68, called to the Bar Gray's Inn 1968, in practice Midland and Oxford Circuit 1968–92, recorder of the Crown Ct 1982–92, circuit judge (Midland and Oxford Circuit) 1992–; *Recreations* history, photography; *Style*— His Hon Judge Mayor, QC; ✉ Crown Court, Leicester, Leics

MAYOR, (Frederick) James; s of Fred Hoyland Mayor (d 1973), and Pamela Margaret, *née* Colledge (d 1994); *b* 20 March 1949; *Educ* Charterhouse; *m* 1978, Viviane Martha Cresswell, da of John Leigh Reed (d 1982); 2 da (Louisa Harriett Cresswell b 1981, Alice Marina Pamela b 1984); *Career* asst: Galerie Louise Leiris Paris 1968, Perls Galleries NY 1968, Impressionist Painting Dept Sothebys's London 1969, i/c Contemporary Painting Dept Parke-Bernet Inc NY 1969–72; chm The Mayor Gallery Ltd London 1980– (md 1973–); memb Exec Ctee Soc of London Art Dealers 1981–88; *Recreations* cooking, painting and gardening; *Clubs* Buck's, The Travellers' (Paris), Racehorse Owners' Association, Chelsea Arts; *Style*— James Mayor, Esq; ✉ The Mayor Gallery Ltd, 22A Cork Street, London W1X 1HB (☎ 0171 734 3558, fax 0171 494 1377)

MAYOR, Susan; da of Fred Hoyland Mayor (d 1973), and Pamela Margaret, *née* Colledge; *b* 1 March 1945; *Educ* French Lycée London; *m* 9 July 1975, Prof J Mordaunt Crook, s of Austin Mordaunt Crook (d 1967); *Career* Christies: joined 1964, dir 1984, currently head of textiles; memb Ctee: Costume Soc 1975, Fan Circle Int 1975–; *Books* Collecting Fans (1980), Letts Guide to Collecting Fans (1991); *Recreations* travelling; *Style*— Miss Susan Mayor; ✉ 55 Gloucester Ave, London NW1 7BA (☎ 0171 485 8280); Christie's South Kensington, 85 Old Brompton Rd, London SW7 3LD (☎ 0171 581 7611, fax 0171 584 0431, telex 922061)

MAYR-HARTING, Dr Henry Maria Robert Egmont; s of Herbert Mayr-Harting (d 1989), of Vienna, and Anna, *née* Münzer (d 1974); *b* 6 April 1936; *Educ* Douai Sch, Merton Coll Oxford (Amy Mary Preston Read scholar, MA, DPhil); *m* 1968, Caroline Mary Humphries, da of Dr Thomas H Henry; 1 s (Felix b 1969), 1 da (Ursula b 1972); *Career* asst lectr and lectr in medieval history Univ of Liverpool 1960–68; Univ of Oxford: fell and tutor in medieval history St Peter's Coll 1968–, lectr in medieval history Merton Coll 1976–, Slade prof of fine art 1987–88, reader in medieval history 1993–; visiting fell Peterhouse Cambridge 1983, Brown Fndn fell Univ of the South Tennessee 1992; FBA 1992; *Books* The Acta of the Bishops of Chichester 1075–1207 (1965), The Coming of Christianity to Anglo-Saxon England (1972, 3 edn 1991), Ottonian Book Illumination: An Historical Study (2 vols, 1991); *Recreations* music (especially playing keyboard instruments), watching cricket; *Style*— Dr Henry Mayr-Harting, FBA; ✉ St Peter's College, Oxford OX1 2DL (☎ 01865 278907)

MAYS, Colin Garth; CMG (1988); s of William Albert Mays (d 1982), and Sophia May Mays, *née* Pattinson (d 1972); *b* 16 June 1931; *Educ* Acklam Hall Sch, St John's Coll Oxford (MA); *m* 1956, Margaret Patricia, da of Philemon Robert Lloyd (d 1993), and Gladys Irene Lloyd, *née* Myers, of Marske by Sea, Cleveland; 1 s (Nicholas Robert b 1964); *Career* HM Dip Serv: FO 1955–56, Sofia 1956–58, Baghdad 1958–60, UK Delgn to the Conf of the 18 Nation Ctee on Disarmament Geneva 1960, Bonn 1960–65, FCO 1965–69, Prague 1969–72, FCO 1972–77 (head of Info Admin Dept 1974), commercial cnsllr Bucharest 1977–80, seconded to PA Management Consultants Ltd 1980–81, overseas inspr Dip Serv 1981–83; Br high cmmr: Seychelles 1983–86, The Bahamas 1986–91; bursar The Yehudi Menuhin Sch 1991–; Liveryman Worshipful Co of Painter Stainers; *Recreations* sailing, travel; *Clubs* Travellers'; *Style*— Colin Mays, Esq, CMG; ✉ The Yehudi Menuhin School, Stoke d'Abernon, Cobham, Surrey KT11 3QQ

MAYS-SMITH, Alan Alfred Michael; DL (East Sussex 1996); s of Lt Col Robert Shankland Mays-Smith, MBE (d 1980), of Iden, Rye, E Sussex, and Brenda Mary Hilda, *née* Rickett (d 1990); *b* 26 April 1933; *Educ* Eton, Trinity Coll Cambridge (BA, rowing blue); *m* 19 Nov 1963, Rosemary, da of Kenneth Richard Ellson; 3 da (Charlotte b 24 Sept 1965, Alexandra b 28 June 1968, Antonia b 14 May 1970), 1 s (Simon b 30 Sept 1971); *Career* Nat Serv 2 Lt Rifle Bde 1951–53; various appts Unilever plc latterly as gen sales mangr Indonesia Unilever 1956–63, bd/mktg dir James Burrough Ltd (distillers of Beafeater Gin) 1967–88 (mktg mangr 1964–67); conslt: James Burrough Boat Race Sponsorship 1988–95, Merrydown Wine Company 1992–; past memb Exec Cncl Wine and Spirit Benevolent Soc; organiser: Oxford and Cambridge Univ Boat Race 1966–83, Cambridge Blues Dinner 1980–94; steward Henley Royal Regatta, pres Eton Vikings Club 1987–91; govr Bede's Sch E Sussex; High Sheriff of E Sussex 1995–96; memb Ct of Assts Worshipful Co of Clothworkers, Liveryman Worshipful Co of Watermen and Lightermen of the River Thames; *Recreations* reading, shooting, gardening, classical music, singing; *Clubs* Army and Navy, Leander, Hawks'; *Style*— Alan Mays-Smith, Esq, DL; ✉ Bryckden Place, Waldron, Heathfield, E Sussex TN21 0RD (☎ 01435 863094)

MAYS-SMITH, (Robert) Martin; s of Lt-Col Robert Shankland Mays-Smith, MBE (d 1980), of Rye, Sussex, and Brenda Mary Hilda, *née* Rickett; *b* 17 Nov 1930; *Educ* Eton, Trinity Coll Cambridge; *m* 1, 22 June 1963, Jennifer Joan (d 1989), da of Capt Eustace Makins (d 1968), of Dereham, Norfolk; 3 da (Kate b 6 March 1964, Henrietta b 17 Jan 1966, Arabella b 10 July 1970); m 2, 7 Feb 1992, Lady Elizabeth Maria, *née* Guinness, sis of 3 Earl of Iveagh, and formerly w of David Hugh Lavallin Nugent; *Career* Irish Guards 1949–51; Bank of England 1954–63, local dir Oxford Barclays Bank 1968–69 (joined 1963); md: William Brandt & Sons & Co Ltd 1969–72, Nat & Grindlays Bank 1970–72; dir: Kleinwort Benson Ltd 1972–89 (banking dir 1972–84, head Banking Div 1984–87), Kleinwort Benson Group plc 1984–89; chm: Empire Stores Ltd until 1994, First National Finance Corp plc until 1995, Norwich & Peterborough Building Soc, Morland & Co; memb Governing Body of Ripon Coll Cuddesdon, govr Mary Hare GS for the Deaf; Liveryman Worshipful Co of Clothworkers; FCIB 1983; *Recreations* life in the country (especially fishing), music (especially opera); *Clubs* Boodle's, Beefsteak, Flyfishers', Leander; *Style*— Martin Mays-Smith, Esq; ✉ Chaddleworth House, Chaddleworth, Newbury, Berks RG20 7EB (☎ 01488 638209, fax 01488 638341)

MEACHER, Michael Hugh; MP (Lab) Oldham West (majority 8,333); s of George Hubert Meacher (d 1969), of Berkhamsted, Herts; *b* 4 Nov 1939; *Educ* Berkhamsted Sch, New Coll Oxford; *m* 1, 1962 (m dis 1987), Molly Christine, da of William Reid, of Grayshott, Surrey; 2 s, 2 da; m 2, 1988, Lucianne, da of William Craven, of Gerrards Cross, Bucks; *Career* joined Lab Pty 1962, sec Danilo Dolci Tst 1964, lectr in social admin Univ of York 1966–69 and LSE 1970; MP (Lab) Oldham W 1970–; Parly under sec of state: Dept of Indust 1974–75, DHSS 1975–76, Dept of Trade 1976–79; memb Treasy Select Ctee 1980–83, chm Select Ctee on Lloyd's Bill 1982, contested Lab dep leadership election 1983, elected to Shadow Cabinet 1983, memb NEC Oct 1983–; chief oppn spokesman on: health and social security 1983–87, employment 1987–89, social security 1989–92, devpt and co-operation 1992–93, Citizen's Charter 1993–94, Tport 1994–95, employment 1995–96, environmental protection 1996–; author; *Books* Taken for a Ride (1972), Socialism with a Human Face (1982), Diffusing Power: the Key to Socialist Revival (1992); *Style*— Michael Meacher, Esq, MP; ✉ 34 Kingscliffe Gardens, London SW19

MEACHIN, Penelope Jane (Penny); da of George Ernest Meachin, of Auckland, NZ, and Elizabeth Mary, *née* Tootle; *b* 15 Aug 1958; *Educ* Kelston Girls' HS, Auckland Technical Inst; *partner* Martyn Taylor; *Career* fashion designer; early career as flamenco dancer, later trained as electrician working in NZ; began jewellery design business 1983, formed Zebra womenswear label 1985, renamed Gamble and Tootle 1988, fndr ptnr Idol (wholesaling internationally) 1990–; *Recreations* flamenco, yoga, travel; *Style*— Ms Penny Meachin; ✉ Idol, 15 Ingestre Place, Soho, London W1R 3LP (☎ and fax 0171 439 8537)

MEAD, Anthony Frederick John; s of Frederick James Mead (d 1978), of Carshalton, Surrey, and Doris Kathleen, *née* Sharratt (d 1990); *b* 4 May 1941; *Educ* Trinity Sch Croydon, Univ of Hull (BSc); *m* 29 July 1972, Alison Margaret, da of George Melvin Ward (d 1996); 2 s (Christopher Frederick James b 9 Dec 1976, Andrew Melvin John b 31 Dec 1978), 1 da (Katharine Mary Louise b 1 July 1981); *Career* articled clerk Lewis Bloom & Co 1963–66, sr mangr Coopers & Lybrand 1967–78, internal auditor AFIA Worldwide Insurance 1978–79, ptnr and insur indust specialist Rowley Pemberton Roberts & Co (became Pannell Kerr Forster 1981) 1980– (mangr 1979–80); FCA 1967, FCMA 1993; *Recreations* family, sch govr; *Style*— Anthony Mead, Esq; ✉ Pannell Kerr Forster, New Garden House, 78 Hatton Garden, London EC1N 8JA (☎ 0171 831 7393, fax 0171 405 6736)

MEAD, Anthony John; RD (1986); s of James Reginald Mead, JP (d 1984), and Muriel Violet, *née* Johnston (d 1993); *b* 3 Feb 1942; *Educ* Wrekin Coll; *m* 25 March 1988, June, da of Sydney Thomas Farrington, DFC (d 1981); *Career* RNR Lt 1971, Lt Cdr 1979; CA; articles Foster and Stephens Birmingham 1960–64, Touche Ross and Co Birmingham 1964–65, ptnr Daffern and Co Coventry 1965–75, princ Mead and Co Kenilworth and Kingswear 1976–; memb NEC 1995–96, vice chm Nat Taxation Legal and Fin Ctee Engrg Industries Assoc 1995–96 (memb 1974–96); memb Cncl Univ of Warwick 1984–87, tstee 29th May 1961 Charitable Tst, chm Saving our Seabirds Appeal, clerk Kingswear Parish Cncl 1987–93, memb Kingswear Parish Cncl 1993–95 (vice chm 1994–95), HM Coastguard Auxiliary Serv 1991–92, memb Port of Dartmouth Royal Regatta Ctee 1994, govr Kingswear County Primary Sch 1993– (chm 1996–); FCA; *Recreations* walking, sea fishing; *Clubs* Royal Naval Sailing Assoc, Kingswear RFC (treas), Dartmouth Yacht (treas); *Style*— Anthony J Mead, Esq, RD; ✉ Stoneleigh House, Higher Contour Road, Kingswear, Dartmouth, Devon TQ6 0DE (☎ and fax 01803 752468)

MEAD, Richard Barwick; s of Thomas Gifford Mead, MBE, of Storrington, W Sussex, and Joyce Mary, *née* Barwick (d 1990); *b* 18 Aug 1947; *Educ* Marlborough, Pembroke Coll Cambridge (MA); *m* 25 June 1971, Sheelagh Margaret, da of James Leslie Thom, of Ludlow, Shropshire; 2 s (Timothy b 1973, Rupert b 1977), 1 da (Nicola b 1975 d 1976); *Career* audit supervisor Arthur Young 1969–73, corporate fin exec Brandts Ltd 1973–75, dir and head Corporate Fin Dept Antony Gibbs and Sons Ltd 1975–83, dir corporate fin Credit Suisse First Boston Ltd 1983–85, ptnr and nat dir corporate fin Ernst & Young 1985–94, independent fin advsr 1994–, non-exec dep chm Inventure Holdings Limited 1995–; non-exec dir: Tom Cobleigh plc 1995–, Hills Electrical Holdings plc 1996–; FCA 1972, MSI 1993; *Recreations* gardening, history, music, family; *Style*— Richard Mead, Esq; ✉ Shambles, Watts Cross, Hildenborough, Tonbridge, Kent TN11 9NB (☎ 01732 832858, fax 01732 834291)

MEADE, Richard John Hannay; OBE (1974); s of John Graham O'Mahony Meade, JP, DL, of Maran Hassa, Itton, Chepstow, Gwent, and Phyllis Brenda, *née* Watts; *b* 4 Dec 1938; *Educ* Lancing, Magdalene Coll Cambridge; *m* 11 May 1977, Angela Dorothy, da of Lt Charles Richard Farquhar, MC, DL (d 1980), of Cubley Lodge, Ashbourne, Derbyshire; 3 s (Charles b and d 1979, James b 1981, Harry b 1983), 1 da (Lucy b 1985); *Career* Nat Serv 1958–60, cmmnd 11 Hussars (Prince Albert's Own); competed internationally for 25 years in Three-day Eventing; rep GB: four Olympic Games, five World Championships, six Euro Championships 1963–82; Olympics: team gold Mexico 1968, team gold Munich 1972, individual gold 1972; World Championships: individual silver Burghley 1966, individual silver Punchestown 1970, team gold Punchestown 1970, team silver Burghley 1974, team gold Luhmühlen 1982; Euro Championships: team silver Moscow 1965, team gold Punchestown 1967, team gold Burghley 1971, team bronze Kiev 1973, team gold Horsens Denmark 1981; also rep GB at alternative Olympics Fountainebleau 1980, won Burghley 1964, Badminton 1970 and 1982; memb Three-Day Event Ctee Int Equestrian Fedn (FEI) 1977–80, chm Northern Euro Gp of Nations and memb Bureau FEI; pres Br Equestrian Fedn 1989–92; chm: Br Horse Fndn, Mark Davies Injured Riders Fund 1988–94; churchwarden St James's Church W Littleton; Yeoman Worshipful Co of Saddlers 1972, Hon Freeman Worshipful Co of Loriners 1975; *Books* Fit for Riding (1984); *Recreations* shooting, skiing; *Style*— Richard Meade, Esq, OBE

MEADEN, Sonia Irene; da of Marshal Coneley, of Lowestoft, Suffolk, and Irene, *née* Bowles; *b* 27 Nov 1936; *Educ* Oswestry Girls' HS Salop, Kidderminster GS Worcs; *m* 1, 1954 (m dis 1960), Henry Charles; 2 da (Gail b 1956, Deborah b 1959); m 2, 1962 (m dis 1964), Raymond Peagram; m 3, 1966, Brian Meaden, s of Thomas Meaden (d 1982); 2 da (Emma b 1969, Cass b 1972); *Career* nat vice pres (first lady) Br Amusement Catering Trades Assoc 1987– (pres (first lady) 1985–87), chm (first lady) Nat Amusement Cncl 1987–, dir and chm (first lady) Amusement Trades Exhibition Co 1988–; memb George Thomas Fellowship; tstee: The Grand Order of Lady Ratlings, BACTA Charitable Tst 1989– (chm 1989–96); dir Cornwall Tourist Bd 1992–94, vice chm West Country Tourist Bd 1996– (dir 1992–); *Recreations* boating, theatre, travel; *Style*— Mrs Sonia Meaden; ✉ Weststar Holidays Ltd, 8 Abbey Court, Eagle Way, Sowton, Exeter EX2 7HY (☎ 01392 447788, fax 01392 445202)

MEADER, Peter John; s of Leonard Charles Meader (d 1990), and Brenda Edith, *née* Richardson (d 1969); *b* 1 Sept 1940; *Educ* Univ Coll Sch; *m* 6 Oct 1969, Féodor Bryana, da of Theodore Edmund Longfield; 1 s (James Edmund b 8 Aug 1973), 2 da (Helen Lesley b 7 August 1970, Susan Clare (twin) b 8 Aug 1973); *Career* articled clerk Messrs Gibson Harris & Turnbull 1957–64; Deloitte Plender Griffiths (now Coopers & Lybrand): joined 1964, seconded to Lagos Nigeria as ptnr 1976–80, ptnr London 1980, opened Croydon office 1984 (currently ptnr i/c); FCA 1974, MInstD 1984; *Recreations* golf, reading; *Clubs* RAC; *Style*— Peter Meader, Esq; ✉ Coopers & Lybrand, Melrose House, 42 Dingwall Road, Croydon, Surrey CR0 2NE (☎ 0181 681 5252, fax 0181 760 0897)

MEADES, Jonathan Turner; s of John William Meades (d 1981), of Salisbury, Wilts, and Marjorie Agnes (Bunty), *née* Hogg (d 1993); *b* 21 Jan 1947; *Educ* King's Coll Taunton, Univ of Bordeaux, RADA; *m* 1, 15 Sept 1980 (m dis), Sally Dorothy Renée, da of Raymond Brown (d 1996); 2 da (Holly b 7 May 1981, Rose (twin) b 7 May 1981); m 2, 1 June 1988, Frances Anne, da of Sir William Bentley; 2 da ((Eleanor) Lily b 31 Dec 1986, (Evelyn) Coral b 15 April 1993); *Career* journalist, writer and TV presenter 1971–; contrib to: Books and Bookman, Time Out, Curious, The Observer, Architects Jl, Sunday Times, Harpers & Queen, Literary Review, Tatler, A La Carte, The Times, The Independent, Sunday Correspondent, Evening Standard, magazines in Canada and USA; ed Event 1981–82, pt/t memb editorial staff Tatler 1982–87; TV series incl: The Victorian House (1987), Abroad in Britain (1990), Further Abroad (1994), Jerrybuilding (1994), Even Further Abroad (1996); *Awards* Glenfiddich Awards 1986, 1990 and 1995, Essay Prize Paris Int Art Film Festival 1994; *Books* This is Their Life (1979), An Illustrated Atlas of The World's Buildings (1980), Filthy English (1984), Peter Knows What Dick Likes (1989), Pompey (1993); *Scripts* L'Atlantide (dir Bob Swaim, 1993); *Recreations* buildings, mushrooms, sloth; *Clubs* Groucho; *Style*— Jonathan Meades, Esq; ✉ c/o 1 Pennington Street, London E1 9XN (☎ 0171 782 5843)

MEADOW, Prof Sir (Samuel) Roy; kt (1997); s of Samuel Tickle Meadow (d 1980), of Wigan, Lancs, and Doris Marion, *née* Peacock (d 1984); *b* 9 June 1933; *Educ* Wigan GS Bromsgrove, Worcester Coll Oxford (BA, MA), Guy's Hosp Med Sch (BM BCh); *m* 1 Sept 1962 (m dis 1974), Gillian Margaret, da of Sir Ian Maclennan, KCMG (d 1985), of Richmond; 1 s (Julian Robert Ian b 1963), 1 da (Anna Jane b 1965); m 2, 14 Aug 1978, Marianne Jane, *née* Harvey; *Career* Lt RA 1951–53; jr med posts 1960–67, sr res fell MRC Inst of Child Health Birmingham 1967–68; St James's Univ Hosp Leeds: sr lectr and conslt paediatrician 1970–80, inaugural prof and head of Dept of Paediatrics and Child Health 1980–; pres: Br Paediatric Assoc 1994–96 (chm Academic Bd 1990–94), Coll of Paediatrics and Child Health 1996–; ed Archives of Disease in Childhood 1979–87; published reports Meadows Syndrome One 1968 and Meadows Syndrome Two (Munchausen Syndrome By Proxy) 1977; memb and chm Assoc of Child Psychology and Psychiatry 1983–84, memb Ctee Safety of Med 1987–90; MRCP, FRCP, DRCOG, DCH; *Books* Lecture Notes on Paediatrics (1973), Bladder Control and Enuresis (1973), The Child and His Symptoms (1978), Recent Advances in Paediatrics (ed, 1983–86), Paediatric Kidney Disease (ed, 1992), ABC of Child Abuse (ed, 1996); *Recreations* gardening; *Style*— Prof Sir Roy Meadow; ✉ Weeton Grange, Weeton, Leeds LS17 0AP (☎ 01423 734234, fax 01423 734726); Department of Paediatrics & Child Health, University of Leeds, St James's University Hospital, Leeds LS9 7TF (☎ 0113 243 3144 ext 5657, fax 0113 283 6811)

MEADOWS, Prof Bernard William; s of William A F Meadows, and Ethel; *b* 19 Feb 1915; *Educ* Norwich Sch, Norwich Sch of Art, RCA; *m* 1939, Marjorie, *née* Payne; 2 da (Julia, Anthea); *Career* sculptor 1947–; lectr Chelsea Sch of Art 1947–60, prof of sculpture RCA 1969–80 (emeritus 1960); works incl in the collections of: V&A, British Museum, Metropolitan Museum NY, Guggenheim Museum NY, Tate Gallery; various public and private collections in Europe and America; memb Royal Fine Art Commission 1971–76; ARCA 1947; *Style*— Prof Bernard Meadows; ✉ 34 Belsize Grove, London NW3 4TR (☎ 0171 722 0772)

MEADOWS, Prof (Arthur) Jack; s of Flt Sgt Arthur Harold Meadows (d 1971), and Alice, *née* Elson (d 1962); *b* 24 Jan 1934; *Educ* New Coll Oxford (MA, DPhil), UCL (MSc); *m* 6 Dec 1958, (Isobel) Jane Tanner, da of Stanley Charles Bryant (d 1937); 1 s (Michael b 1962), 2 da (Alice b 1960, Sally b 1962); *Career* Nat Serv Lt Intelligence Corps 1952–54; Univ of Leicester 1966–86: lectr, sr lectr, prof 1972–86, head Depts Astronomy and History of Sci; head Primary Communications Res Centre 1976–86, head Office Humanities Communication 1983–86, prof Dept of Info and Library Studies Univ of Loughborough 1986– (dean Educn and Humanities 1991–94, pro-vice-chllr 1995–96); author of sixteen books and approximately 200 res papers; hon vice pres Library Assoc 1995; Hon DSc City Univ 1995; FInstP 1983, FLA 1989, FInfSc 1987; *Recreations* sleeping; *Style*— Prof Jack Meadows; ✉ 47 Swan St, Seagrave, Leics LE12 7NL (☎ 01509 812557); Department of Information and Library Studies, Loughborough University of Technology, Loughborough, Leics LE11 3TU (☎ 01509 223082, fax 01509 223053)

MEADOWS, Dr John Christopher; s of Dr Swithin Pinder Meadows (d 1993), and Doris Steward, *née* Noble; *b* 25 March 1940; *Educ* Westminster, Univ of Cambridge (BA, MB BChir, MD); *m* 9 July 1966, Patricia, da of the late John Appleton Pierce, of IOM; 2 s; *Career* former conslt neurologist St George's Hosp, conslt neurologist King Edward VII Hosp, hon neurologist Newspaper Press Fund; FRCP; *Recreations* gardening, walking, travelling, reading; *Style*— Dr John C Meadows; ✉ c/o 143 Harley St, London W1N 1DJ (☎ 0171 935 1802)

MEADOWS, Pamela Catherine; da of Sidney James Meadows, and Hilda Catherine, *née* Farley; *b* 9 Jan 1949; *Educ* Kenya HS Nairobi, Univ of Durham (BA), Birkbeck Coll (MSc); *m* 26 Aug 1975, Paul Andrew Ormerod; 1 s (Andrew Whitworth b 3 Sept 1982); *Career* res offr 1972–74 (res asst 1970–71) NIESR; Home Office Economic Planning Unit: sr econ asst 1974–77, econ advsr 1977–78; Dept of Employment: econ advsr 1978–79, seconded to OECD 1979–80, econ advsr 1980–84, princ Manpower Policy Div I 1984–85, econ advsr Employment Market Res Unit 1985–87, head of Economics Branch (sr econ advsr) 1988–90, head of Educn and Skills Analysis Branch (sr econ advsr) 1990–91, head of Labour Market Briefing and Labour Market Analsis Branch (sr econ advsr) 1991–92, chief econ advsr and dir Economics Res and Evaluation Div 1992–93; dir PSI 1993–; memb: Advsy Bd Univ of Warwick Industl Rels Res Unit, Cncl Public Finance Fndn, Advsy Bd North London Common Purpose, Cncl UK Evaluation Soc, Editorial Bd Prospect; tstee Employment Policy Inst; FRSA; *Books* British Economic Policy 1960–1974 (contrib, 1978), The United Kingdom Economy (contrib, 1976), Women and Employment (1981), National Survey of 1980 Graduates and Diplomates Methodological Report (with Julia Field, 1987), The London Labour Market (with Hilary Cooper and Richard Bartholemew, 1988), Work out - or work in (ed, 1996); numerous articles in other pubns; *Style*— Ms Pamela Meadows; ✉ Policy Studies Institute, 100 Park Village East, London NW1 3SR (☎ 0171 468 0468, fax 0171 388 0914)

MEADOWS, William Robert; CBE (1993), DL (Somerset 1989); s of William de Warenne Meadows (d 1974), of Norfolk, and Marianne Alice, *née* Stokes (d 1930); *b* 10 Aug 1926; *Educ* Sherborne, Corpus Christi Coll Cambridge; *m* 8 Nov 1960, Alison Rosemary, da of Sir Austin Anderson (d 1973), of Surrey; 1 s (William b 1972), 2 da (Victoria b 1962, Marianne b 1963); *Career* Lt RM Commandos 1944–47, served Europe, Far East; glass engraver and lectr; memb Baltic Exchange 1951–68; Somerset CC: chm Educn Ctee 1981–83, chm Cncl 1983–85; chm: Exmoor Nat Park Ctee 1987–89, Somerset Co Cadet Ctee 1987–90; pres Taunton Constituency Cons Assoc 1991–94; *Recreations* gardening, painting, fishing; *Style*— William R Meadows, Esq, CBE, DL; ✉ Wayside House, North Street, Milverton, Taunton, Somerset TA4 1LG

MEADS, John David; s of Arnold David Meads (d 1978), and Marian, *née* Hill, of Tewin, Herts; *b* 1 Oct 1951; *Educ* Alleyne's Sch Stevenage, Corpus Christi Coll Cambridge (MA); *m* Sept 1988, Janette, da of Hugh Streener, of Widdrington, Northumberland; 1 s (David Hugh b April 1991); *Career* Br Assoc of Colliery Mgmnt: res offr 1973–75, asst to gen sec 1975–78, regnl organising sec (Scotland and NE England) 1978–89, gen sec 1989–94; prospective Parly candidate (Lab) Rutland and Melton; *Recreations* croquet, politics; *Style*— John Meads, Esq; ✉ Castle View, 17 Main Street, Redmile, Leics NG13 0GA (☎ 01949 842426, fax 01949 842426)

MEADWAY, (Richard) John; s of Norman Pardey Meadway (d 1957), of Arundel, Sussex, and Constance, *née* Parker; *b* 30 Dec 1944; *Educ* Collyer's Sch Horsham, Peterhouse Cambridge (MA), Univ of Edinburgh (PhD), Univ of Oxford (MA); *m* 23 March 1968, Rev Dr Jeanette Valerie, da of Stephen George Partis (d 1984), of Long Clawson, Leics; 2 da (Eleanor Anne b 1974, Margot Elizabeth b 1977); *Career* asst princ Miny of Technol 1970, private sec to Min for Trade and Consumer Affrs 1973–74, princ Dept of Prices and Consumer Protection 1974–76, private sec to PM 1976–78; asst sec: Dept of Trade Int Trade Policy Div 1979–83, DTI Vehicles Div 1983–86, DTI Mgmnt Servs Div 1987–89; under sec DTI Overseas Trade Div 2 1989–94, under sec DTI Export Control and Non-Proliferation Div 1994–96, UK govr IAEA 1994–96; *Recreations* reading, travel; *Clubs* Reform; *Style*— John Meadway, Esq; ✉ 4 Glebe Avenue, Woodford Green, Essex IG8 9HB (☎ 0181 491 6040)

MEAKIN, Henry Paul John; s of Wing Cdr Henry John Walter Meakin, DFC and bar, RAF (d 1989), of Harare, Zimbabwe, and Elizabeth Wilma, *née* Fairbairns; *b* 2 Jan 1944; *Educ* Plumtree Sch Rhodesia; *m* 2 Jan 1971, Vicki Lynn, da of Maurice James Bullus (d 1990), of Hilltop Hall, Pannal, Harrogate, N Yorks; 2 s (Oliver b 1975, Harry b 1980), 1 da (Katie b 1972); *Career* exec dir Pensord Press Ltd 1970–74; chm: Aspen Communications 1979–85 (md 1975–78), Aspen Communications PLC 1985–, GWR Group PLC 1988–, Classic FM plc 1991–93; fndr dir Wiltshire Radio plc 1981–85, dir GWR Radio 1985–87, dir Chiltern Radio plc (following takeover by GWR Group) 1995–; memb Cncl Wine Guild of the UK; FRSA; *Recreations* tennis, golf, music; *Style*— Henry Meakin, Esq; ✉ Aspen Communications PLC, Aspen House, Thomas St, Cirencester, Gloucs GL7 2AX (☎ 01285 652176, fax 01285 656620)

MEALE, (Joseph) Alan; MP (Lab) Mansfield (majority 11,724); s of Albert Henry Meale (d 1986), and Elizabeth, *née* Catchpole; both parents trade union shop stewards; *b* 31 July 1949; *Educ* Ruskin Coll Oxford, Sheffield Hallam Univ; *m* 15 March 1983, Diana, da of Lt Cdr John Gillespy, RN (ret); *Career* nat employment devpt offr (Home Office funded) 1977–79, asst to Ray Buckton as Gen Sec ASLEF 1979–83, Parly and political advsr to Michael Meacher MP 1983–88; MP (Lab) Mansfield 1987–, PPS to John Prescott as Dep Ldr of Lab Pty 1994–; memb Parly Select Ctees on: Euro Legislation 1988–90, Home Affrs 1990–92; vice chm Employment Ctee PLP 1987–, chm Parly Beer Club 1994–; memb: War Pensions Bd 1990–, SSAFA Bd 1990–94; author; journalist of various publications; *Recreations* reading; *Clubs* Mansfield Labour, Bellamy Road and Mansfield Woodhouse Working Men's, Mansfield Town FC; *Style*— Alan Meale, Esq, MP; ✉ 5 Clumber Street, Mansfield, Notts NG18 1NT; House of Commons, London SW1A 0AA (☎ 0171 219 3000)

MEARS, Rt Rev John Cledan; s of Joseph Mears (d 1972), of Aberystwyth, and Anna Lloyd Mears (d 1968); *b* 8 Sept 1922; *Educ* Ardwyn GS Aberystwyth, Univ Coll of Wales Aberystwyth (BA, MA), Wycliffe Hall Oxford; *m* 1949, Enid Margaret, da of James Tudor Williams (d 1952), of Glamorgan; 1 s (Wyn b 1950), 1 da (Eleri b 1955); *Career* ordained: deacon 1947, priest 1948; curate: Mostyn 1947–49, Rhosllannerchrugog 1949–55; vicar of Cwm 1955–58, lectr St Michael's Coll Llandaff and Univ of Wales Cardiff 1959–73 (chaplain 1959–67, sub warden 1967–73), vicar of St Mark's Gabalfa 1973–82, bishop of Bangor 1983–92; clerical sec Governing Body Church in Wales 1977–82, hon canon of Llandaff Cathedral 1981–82; author of articles on: eucharistic sacrifice, prayers for the dead, comparative religion, marriage and divorce, trinity and creation; *Recreations* hill walking, long distance paths; *Style*— The Rt Rev John Mears; ✉ Isfryn, 25 Avonridge, Thornhill, Cardiff CF4 9AU (☎ 01222 615505)

MEARS, Patrick Michael; s of Alex Benjamin Albert Mears, of Henley-on-Thames, and Moira Denise, *née* Buzetti; *b* 19 Jan 1958; *Educ* Henley GS, LSE (LLB); *m* 1, 27 Aug 1983, Carol Lucia (d 1987), da of Carl William Anders (d 1965), of Rochester, NY; 1 da (Elizabeth Helen Carol b 8 Sept 1987); m 2, 7 Dec 1995, Rachel Elizabeth, da of Prof M S Anderson, of Highgate, London; *Career* admitted slr 1982; ptnr Allen & Overy 1988– (currently head of Taxation Dept); Freeman Worshipful Co of Slrs; memb Law Soc; *Recreations* parenting, bridge, squash, theatre; *Clubs* Dulwich Squash Rackets; *Style*— Patrick Mears, Esq; ✉ Allen & Overy, One New Change, London EC4M 9QQ (☎ 0171 330 3000, fax 0171 330 9999)

MEARS, Roger Malcolm Loudon; s of Dr K P G Mears, of Vancouver Island, Canada, and Dr Eleanor Mears, *née* Loudon (d 1992); *b* 15 Feb 1944; *Educ* City of London Sch, Corpus Christi Coll Cambridge (MA, DipArch); *m* 4 Nov 1978, Joan Adams, *née* Speers; 3 da (Emily b 1981, Rebecca b 1983, Jessica b 1986); *Career* princ Roger Mears Architects (specialising in historic bldgs and conservation); work incl: Tudor House Cheyne Walk, The Ham Wantage, Church of St Simon and St Jude at Llanddeusant Carmarthenshire; memb Ctee Soc for the Protection of Ancient Bldgs; RIBA; *Recreations* chamber music (viola player), watermills, walking; *Style*— Roger Mears, Esq; ✉ Roger Mears Architects, 2 Compton Terrace, London N1 2UN (☎ 0171 359 8222, fax 0171 354 5208)

MEATH, 14 Earl of (I 1627); Anthony Windham Normand Brabazon; also Baron Ardee (I 1616), and Baron Chaworth (UK 1831), in which title he sits in House of Lords; s of 13 Earl, CB, CBE (d 1949), by his w Lady Aileen Wyndham Quin (da of 4 Earl of Dunraven); *b* 3 Nov 1910; *Educ* Eton, RMC Sandhurst; *m* 30 July 1940, Elizabeth Mary, da of Capt Geoffrey Vaux Salvin Bowlby, Royal Horse Gds (ka 1915); 2 s, 2 da; *Heir* s, Lord Ardee; *Career* ADC to Govr Bengal 1936, Capt Grenadier Gds 1938, Maj 1941, wounded 1943, ret 1946; *Style*— The Rt Hon the Earl of Meath; ✉ Killruddery, Bray, Co Wicklow, Ireland

MEATH, Bishop (RC) of 1990–; Most Rev Michael Smith; s of John Smith, and Bridget Fagan, of Liss, Oldcastle, Co Meath; *b* 6 June 1940; *Educ* St Finian's Coll Mullingar, Lateran Univ Rome; *Career* ordained 1963; *Style*— The Most Rev the Bishop of Meath; ✉ Bishop's House, Dublin Road, Mullingar, Co Westmeath, Ireland (☎ 00 353 44 48841/42038, fax 00 353 44 43020)

MECKLER, Nancy; da of Herman Meckler, of Florida, and Lillian, *née* Brodksy; *b* 26 April 1941; *Educ* Antioch Coll Ohio USA (BA), NY Univ; *m* 20 June 1969, David Aukin, s of late Charles Aukin; 2 s (Daniel Max b 23 Nov 1970, Jethro James b 8 Jan 1976); *Career* freelance director; artistic dir Freehold Theatre Co 1968–72; productions incl: Antigone (John Whiting Award), Duchess of Malfi, Genesis, Beowulf, Mary, Mary; other credits incl: Action (Royal Court Upstairs) 1973, Kiss Me Kate (Oxford Playhouse Co) 1974, Action and Killer's Head (American Place NY) 1975, Susanna Andler (Leicester Haymarket) 1975, Dusa, Fish, Stas and Vi (Hampstead & West End transfer) 1976, Curse of the Starving Class (Royal Court) 1977, Pennywhistle (Hampstead) 1978, Twelfth Night (Young Vic) 1978, Daughters of Men (Hampstead) 1979, The Tax Exile (Bush Theatre) 1979, Uncle Vanya (Hampstead) 1979, Dusa, Fish, Stas and Vi (NY) 1980, Buried Child (Hampstead) 1980, Saint Joan (Cambridge Theatre Co) 1981, Who's Afraid of Virginia Woolf? (NT) 1981, The Workshop (Long Wharf USA) 1982, Dreyfus

(Hampstead) 1982, The Hard Shoulder (Hampstead & West End transfer) 1982, The Communication Cord (Hampstead) 1983, Sufficient Carbohydrate (West End transfer) 1983; prodns for Leicester Haymarket (Main House) 1984–87: The Cherry Orchard, A Midsummer Night's Dream, Macbeth; prodns for Leicester Haymarket (Studio Co) 1984–87: Medea, The Bald Prima Donna, The Phoney Physician, Baal, The Hypochondriac, Electra, Orestes, My Sister In This House (also tour and Hampstead); also directed Low Level Panic (Royal Court Upstairs and Lyric Hammersmith Studio) 1988; artistic dir Shared Experience Theatre: The Bacchae (tour Edinburgh Festival and Lyric Hammersmith Studio) 1988, True West (Boulevard) 1989, Abingdon Square (Soho Poly and Cottesloe) 1989, Heartbreak House (Derby Playhouse, Singapore, Riverside Studios) 1989, The Birthday Party (tour, Belfast Festival) 1990, Sweet Sessions (The Place) 1991, Anna Karenina (UK tour, Tricycle, Prague, Helsinki, Malaysia and Singapore) 1992–93, Trilby and Svengali (UK tour, Cockpit) 1992–93; memb Directors' Guild; *Recreations* tennis; *Style*— Ms Nancy Meckler; ✉ c/o Casarotto Ramsay Ltd, National House, 4th Floor, 60–66 Wardour Street, London W1V 3HP (☎ 0171 287 4450, fax 0171 287 9128)

MEDAWAR, His Hon Judge; Nicholas Antoine Macbeth; QC (1984); s of late Antoine Nicolas Medawar, and Annie Innes Logie Tulloch, *née* Macbeth; *b* 25 April 1933; *Educ* Keswick Sch, Trinity Coll Dublin (BA, LLB); *m* 1, 1962 (m dis 1977), Joyce Catherine, *née* Crosland-Boyle; 1 s (Anthony Crosland b 1962), 1 da (Zohara Dawn b 1966 (decd)); m 2, 1977, (Caroline) Mary Medawar, the author, da of late Harry Samuel Collins; *Career* Nat Serv 1957–59, cmmnd RASC, served UK and Cyprus; called to the Bar Gray's Inn 1957, a legal assessor Gen Optical Cncl 1984–87, recorder 1985–87, circuit judge (SE Circuit) 1987–; memb Ethnic Minorities Advsy Ctee to Judicial Studies Bd 1993–96; *Recreations* walking; *Style*— His Hon Judge Medawar, QC; ✉ Snaresbrook Crown Court, Hollybush Hill, Snaresbrook, London E11 1QW

MEDFORTH-MILLS, Dr (Leslie) Robin; s of Cyril Mills, and Nora, *née* Medforth; *b* 8 Dec 1942; *Educ* Univ of Durham (BA, PhD); *m* 24 Sept 1983 (m dis 1991), HRH Princess Helen of Roumania, 2 da of HM King Michael of Roumania, GCVO; 1 s (Nicholas Michael de Roumanie b 1 April 1985), 1 da (Elisabetta Karina de Roumanie b 4 Jan 1989); *Career* third world devpt conslt: Nigeria 1964–67, Sudan 1967–71, Ghana 1971, Sierra Leone 1972–74, Sudan (Int Lab Orgn) 1974–81, UN Fund for Population Activities 1981–87; sr res fell Centre for Overseas Res and Devpt Univ of Durham 1987–90; conslt UN Children's Fund (UNICEF) Geneva 1987–91, resident project offr N W Somalia UNICEF 1992–94, UNICEF co-ordinator Northern Iraq 1994–; *Recreations* genealogy, antique silver, calligraphy; *Clubs* Athenaeum; *Style*— Dr Robin Medforth-Mills; ✉ Flass Hall, Esh Winning, Durham DH7 9QD (☎ 0191 373 0466, fax 0191 373 2466)

MEDHURST, Brian; s of Eric Gilbert Medhurst (d 1983), and Bertha May Medhurst (d 1989); *b* 18 March 1935; *Educ* Godalming GS, Trinity Coll Cambridge (MA); *m* 1960, Patricia Anne, da of Bernard Charles Beer (d 1982); 2 s, 1 da; *Career* The Prudential Assurance Co Ltd: investmt mangr 1975–80, jt chief investmt mangr 1981–82, gen mangr 1982; md Int Div Prudential Corporation plc 1984–94; dir: Prudential Nominees Ltd 1981–94, Prudential Assurance Co Ltd 1981–94, Prudential Corporation plc 1985–94, Prudential Corporation Canada 1985–94, Prudential Life of Ireland Ltd 1985–94, Maricourt Ltd 1985–94, Jackson National Life Insurance Co 1986–94, Brooke Holdings Inc 1986, Brooke Life Insurance Co 1986–94, Chrissy Corporation 1986–94, Prudential Vita Spa 1990–94, Prudential Assurance Co Singapore (Pte) Ltd 1990–94, Prudential Property Services Ltd 1990–94, Prudential Leven NV 1991–94, Prudential Annuities Ltd 1992–94, The Prudential Group Assurance Company of England (Canada) 1992–94, The Prudential Life Assurance Company of England 1992–94; chm Br Insur Assoc Investmt Protection Ctee until 1982; FIA 1962 (memb Cncl 1982–87); *Recreations* windsurfing, golf, piano duets, tree felling; *Clubs* North Hants Golf, Yelverton Golf; *Style*— Brian Medhurst, Esq; ✉ Woodcroft, Yelverton, Devon PL20 6HY (☎ 01822 853337)

MEDLAM, Charles Samuel; s of Wilfrid Gaston Medlam, of Eastcombe, Glos, and Virginia Medlam; *b* 10 Sept 1949; *Educ* Winchester, Salzburg Mozarteum, Vienna Acad, Paris Conservatoire; *m* 1978, Ingrid, da of Günther Seifert; 1 s (Lukas b 31 Dec 1985), 1 da (Hannah b 8 July 1988); *Career* dir London Baroque 1978–; ensemble has appeared at numerous festivals and venues worldwide incl Salzburg, Bath, Stuttgart, Innsbruck, Vienna and Utrecht; regular tours to USA and Japan; *Recordings* over 20 CDs of baroque chamber music for EMI and Harmonia Mundi (France); *Recreations* literature, classics; *Style*— Charles Medlam; ✉ Brick Kiln Cottage, Hollington, Newbury, Berks RG20 9XX (☎ 01635 254331, fax 01635 253629)

MEDLAND, Prof Anthony John (Tony); s of Reginald George (d 1989), of Newton Abbot, Devon, and Phyllis Mary, *née* Battershill (d 1989); *b* 13 July 1940; *Educ* Highweek Sch Newton Abbot, Torquay Tech Coll, Brunel Coll Acton (Dip Technol); *m* 5 June 1965, Beryl Denise, da of David Gynn (d 1974), of Forestgate, London; 1 s (Paul David b 1972), 1 da (Clare Catherine b 1969); *Career* patent engr Westland Aircraft Ltd 1963–64 (gen engrg apprenticeship 1957–63), stress engr Westland Helicopters Ltd 1963–64, post grad res student UCL 1964–67, sr res and devpt engr (mechanical) Cambridge Consultants Ltd 1967–70, MOD/SERC res fell Hatfield Poly, sr res and devpt engr PATS Centre Int 1977–78, prof in computer aided design Brunel Univ 1985–94 (lectr and sr lectr 1978–85), dir The Centre for Geometric Modelling and Design, prof of design engrg Univ of Bath 1995–; FIMechE 1990 (MIMechE 1973); *Books* The Computer-Based Design Process (1986, 2 edn 1992), CADCAM in Practice (with Piers Burnett, 1986), Principles of CAD - A Coursebook (with G Mullineux, 1988); *Style*— Prof Tony Medland; ✉ School of Mechanical Engineering, University of Bath, Claverton Down, Bath BA2 7AY (☎ 01225 826158, fax 01225 826928)

MEDLAND, David Arthur; s of James William Medland (d 1986), and Merle Ermyntrude, *née* Rotchell (d 1994); *b* 23 Sept 1946; *Educ* St Paul's Sch Darjeeling India; *m* (m dis 1979), Patricia Ann, da of Timothy Wood (d 1971); 1 s (Christopher James b 25 Dec 1968); *Career* CA; Robson Rhodes: joined 1965, asst mangr 1973, mangr 1974, sr mangr 1976, ptnr 1979–, memb Exec Ctee 1990–92; seconded as asst dir Serious Fraud Office 1993–96; FCA 1979 (ACA 1971); *Books* The Unlisted Securities Market - A Review; *Recreations* pianist, theatre, golf; *Style*— David A Medland, Esq; ✉ Robson Rhodes, 186 City Rd, London EC1V 1NU (☎ 0171 251 1644, fax 0171 250 0801, telex 885734)

MEDLEY, George Julius; OBE (1989); s of Brig Edgar Julius Medley, DSO, OBE, MC (d 1972), and Norah, *née* Templer; *b* 2 Aug 1930; *Educ* Winchester, Wye Coll Univ of London (BSc, full purple for Athletics 1951), London Business Sch; *m* 4 Sept 1952, Vera Frances, da of George Brand (d 1980); 1 s (Patrick Jonathan Julius b 1956), 1 da (Alexandra Isobel Frances b 1957); *Career* fruit farmer 1952–56, mangr Chem Dept Harrisons & Crosfield Colombo 1956–63 (mercantile asst 1956–58), dir Fisons (Ceylon) Ltd 1958–63, tech devpt mangr Tata Fison Industries Ltd (Bangalore) 1963–64, gen mangr Tata Fison Industries Ltd (Bombay) 1964–68, sales mangr Western Hemisphere Fisons International Ltd (London) 1968–70, overseas mangr Fisons Agrochemical Div (Cambridge) 1970–72, md Glaxo Laboratories India Ltd 1973–77 (dep md 1972–73); dir WWF UK (World Wide Fund for Nature) 1978–93, dir Edward Jewson Services to Charity Ltd 1993–, chm Alexis Produtions Ltd 1994–; tstee: Farming & Wildlife Trust Ltd 1983–93, Falklands Islands Fndn 1984–91; memb Bd Int Inst Environment and Devpt 1989–93, fndr memb Inst of Charity Fundraising Mangrs 1983– (chm 1984–86), memb Radioactive Waste Mgmnt Advsy Ctee to Min of State Dept of Environment 1991–, UK Ecolabelling Bd 1995–; hon treas: Wiltshire Markets Soc Ltd 1993–, Wiltshire Wildlife Tst 1994–; chm London Business Sch Alumni Assoc 1970–72, vice pres Orgn Pharmaceutical Prodrs of India 1973–77; FRSA 1989, FIMgt 1977, fell Inst Charity Fundraising Mangrs 1988; Officer Order of the Golden Ark (Netherlands) 1993; *Books* Long Range Planning (contrib, 1987 and 1992); *Recreations* gardening, DIY; *Style*— George Medley, Esq, OBE; ✉ Hoddinotts House, Tisbury, Salisbury, Wilts SP3 6QQ (☎ 01747 870677, fax 01747 870677)

MEDLICOTT, Michael Geoffrey; s of late Geoffrey Henry Medlicott, of Hythe, Kent, and late Beryl Ann, *née* Burchell; *b* 2 June 1943; *Educ* Downside (scholar), Lincoln Coll Oxford (scholar, MA); *m* 8 Sept 1973, Diana Grace, da of Brian Fife Fallaw, of Gosforth, Northumberland; 1 s (Oliver), 3 da (Charlotte, Annabel, Flora); *Career* dir Europe P & O 1983–86 (gen mangr fleet 1975–80, gen mangr Europe 1980–83), md P & O Air Holidays 1980–86, dir P & O Travel 1980–84, md Swan Hellenic 1983–86, chief exec Br Tourist Authority 1986–93; Delta Air Lines Inc: vice pres (Europe) 1993–96, vice pres (Europe and Asia) 1996–; pres Delta Air Lines Moscow 1996–; memb: Cncl of Mgmnt Passenger Shipping Assoc 1983–86, Bd of Mgmnt Heritage of London Tst 1986–, Br Travel Educn Tst 1986–93, Tidy Britain Gp 1986–, Bd London Tourist Bd 1992–93, Advsy Panel Languages Lead Body 1990–93, Advsy Cncl Univ of Surrey Tourist Mgmnt Dept 1991–, Bd Gatwick Handling 1995–, Bd Deltair Investments UK Ltd 1995–, Lesteris Ltd 1995–; hon memb Univ Centre Hellenic and Euro Studies (Piraeus) 1994–; chm: Planning Ctee Euro Travel Cmmn 1990–92, Euro Travel Cmmn 1992–93, Date (Moscow) 1996–; Queen Mother's Birthday Awards for Environmental Improvement 1993 and 1995; FRSA, CRAeS; *Recreations* philately, gardening, tennis; *Clubs* Royal Philatelic Soc; *Style*— Michael Medlicott, Esq; ✉ Delta Air Lines Inc, 25 Buckingham Gate, London SW1E 6LD (☎ 0171 932 8310, fax 0171 931 7400)

MEDLYCOTT, Sir Mervyn Tregonwell; 9 Bt (UK 1808), of Ven House, Somerset; s of late Thomas Anthony Hutchings Medlycott (d 1970), 2 s of Sir Hubert Medlycott, 7 Bt, of Edmondsham House, Dorset, and Cecilia Mary Eden, da of late Maj Cecil Harold Eden, of Cranborne, Dorset; suc unc, Sir (James) Christopher Medlycott, 8 Bt (d 1986); *b* 20 Feb 1947; *Heir* none; *Career* genealogist; Somerset and Dorset Family History Soc: fndr 1975, hon sec 1975–77, chm 1977–84, pres 1986–; memb Assoc of Genealogists and Record Agents (AGRA), FSG; *Clubs* East India, Devonshire, Sports and Public Schools; *Style*— Sir Mervyn Medlycott, Bt; ✉ The Manor House, Sandford Orcas, Sherborne, Dorset DT9 4SB (☎ 01963 220206)

MEDWAY, Lord; (John) Jason Jasper Gathorne-Hardy; s and h of 5 Earl of Cranbrook, *qv*; *b* 26 Oct 1968; *Style*— Lord Medway; ✉ 7 Woodfall Street, Chelsea, London SW3 4DJ

MEDWIN, Michael Hugh; adopted s of Dr Mary Jeremy, OBE, and Ms Clopton-Roberts; *b* 18 July 1927; *Educ* Canford, Inst Fischer Montreux Territet Lac Leman Switzerland; *m* 1960 (m dis 1970), M B Sunny Back; *Career* theatre, television, film actor and producer; fndr ptnr (with Albert Finney) Memorial Films Limited 1965–; currently chm David Pugh Ltd; *Theatre* roles incl: Man and Superman, The Rivals, Love for Love, Duckers and Lovers, Alfie, St Joan of the Stockyards, Weapons of Happiness, Volpone, The Madras House, What The Butler Saw, Lady from the Sea, There's a Girl in my Soup, The Division Belle; plays produced incl: Spring and Port Wine 1965, A Day In The Death of Joe Egg 1967, Joe Egg 1968, Forget-Me-Not Lane 1972, Chez Nous 1974; plays co-produced with Robert Fox incl: Another Country, Interpreters, Orphans; *Television* roles incl: The Army Game, The Love of Mike, Three Live Wires, Shoestring, The Ronnie Corbett Show, Minder, Boon; *Film* roles incl: The Courtneys of Curzon Street, Boys in Brown, An Ideal Husband, Charlie Moon, The Steel Helmet, Man on the Beach, Twenty Four Hours to Kill, The Longest Day, Rattle of a Simple Man, Countess of Hong Kong; films produced incl: Charlie Bubbles 1966, If.... 1968, Spring and Port Wine 1969, Gumshoe 1971, O Lucky Man 1972, Alpha Beta 1973, Law and Disorder 1974, Memoirs of a Survivor 1981; *Awards* Evening Standard Drama Desk Award Best Play of the Year Joe Egg 1968, Best Comedy of the Year Privates on Parade 1978 (co-prodr); *Recreations* golf, skiing; *Clubs* Royal & Ancient Golf, Sunningdale Golf; *Style*— Michael Medwin, Esq; ✉ c/o Peters Fraser & Dunlop Ltd, 503 The Chambers, Chelsea Harbour, Lots Road, London SW10 0XF (☎ 0171 352 4446, fax 0171 352 7356)

MEECHIE, Brig Helen Guild; CBE (1986); da of John Strachan Meechie (d 1994), of Walderslade, Kent, and Robina Guild, *née* Robertson (d 1980); *b* 19 Jan 1938; *Educ* Morgan Acad Dundee, Univ of St Andrews (MA); *Career* cmmnd WRAC 1960, served UK, Cyprus and Hong Kong 1961–76, UK and Germany 1977–82, dir WRAC 1982–86, ADC to HM The Queen 1986 (hon ADC 1982–86), Hon Col Tayforth Univs OTC 1986–91, memb RCDS 1987, dir Army Serv Conditions 1988–89, dep DG Personnel Servs Army 1989–91, ret; Dep Col Cmdt AGC 1993–; govr Royal Sch Hampstead 1984–91; memb: Cncl Union Jack Club 1988–91, Nat Exec Ctee Forces Help Soc and Lord Roberts Workshops 1988–91; Freeman City of London 1983; Hon LLD Univ of Dundee 1986; CIMgt 1986; *Recreations* golf, gardening, music, travel; *Style*— Brig Helen Meechie, CBE; ✉ 28 London Road, Amesbury, Wilts SP4 7DY

MEEHAN, Anthony Edward (Tony); s of the late Edward Joseph Meehan, of 8 Highburgh Rd, Glasgow, and Mary, *née* Whelan; *b* 24 Aug 1943; *Educ* St George's Westminster London; *m* 24 Oct 1975, Linda Jane, da of John Alexander Portugal Stone, of Vancouver Island, BC; 1 s (Michael Anthony b 1980), 1 da (Claire Louise b 1982); *Career* md Tony Meehan and Assocs Ltd 1976–, chief exec and md TMA Communications 1985–; former chm IPR Scottish Gp 1987–89 (chm Educn Ctee 1984–87, vice chm 1985–87), chm SPRCA; visiting prof Glasgow Caledonian Univ, fell Strathclyde Inst; chm Scottish Soc of Epicureans; Master Deacon Inc of Weavers, Freeman City of Glasgow; memb BAFTA; FIPR (memb Cncl 1993–96), FRSA; *Clubs* The Western, Scottish Soc of Epicureans; *Style*— Prof Tony Meehan; ✉ Moorhouse, Old Mugdock Rd, Strathblane, Stirlingshire (☎ 0141 333 1551, fax 0141 333 1661)

MEEK, Charles Innes; CMG (1961); s of Charles Kingsley Meek, DSc (d 1965), and Margery Helen, *née* Hopkins (d 1960); ggf Gen Sir Thomas Gordon was one of well-known twins with identical careers, the other Gen Sir John Gordon; *b* 27 June 1920; *Educ* King's Sch Canterbury, Magdalen Coll Oxford (demy scholar, MA); *m* 1947, Nona, da of Charles Corry Hurford (d 1955); 2 s (Innes, Kingsley), 1 da (Sheena); *Career* 2 Lt A and SH 1940–41; Colonial Admin Serv Tanganyika 1941, head Civil Serv 1961, perm sec to PM, sec to Cabinet, chm White Fish Authy 1973 (chief exec 1962), ret 1982; chm Nautilus Consultants 1986–88; FRSA (1963); *Recreations* travel, bridge, gardening, The Spectator crossword; *Clubs* Royal Over-Seas League; *Style*— Charles Meek, Esq, CMG; ✉ Mariteau Cottage, German St, Winchelsea, Sussex TN36 4ES (☎ 01797 226408)

MEEK, Prof John Millar; CBE (1975); s of Alexander Meek (d 1972), of W Kirby, Wirral, and Edith, *née* Montgomery (d 1976); *b* 21 Dec 1912; *Educ* Monkton Combe Sch Bath, Univ of Liverpool (BEng, DEng), Univ of California Berkeley; *m* 18 July 1942, Marjorie, da of Bernard Ingleby (d 1957), of Sale, Cheshire; 2 da (Rosalind b 1945, Sara b 1947); *Career* res engr Met-Vickers Electrical Co Ltd Trafford Park 1934–38 and 1940–45, prof of electrical engrg Univ of Liverpool 1946–78; pres IEE 1968–69, memb IBA 1969–74; Hon DSc Univ of Salford 1971; FIEE 1954, FInstP 1956, FEng 1976 (fndr fell); *Books* The Mechanism of the Electric Spark (1941), Electrical Breakdown of Gases (1953), High-Voltage Laboratory Technique (1953); *Recreations* golf, gardening, theatre; *Style*— Prof John Meek, CBE, FEng; ✉ 4 The Kirklands, W Kirby, Wirral (☎ 0151 625 5850)

MEEK, Marshall; CBE (1989); s of Marshall Meek (d 1955), of Auchtermuchty, Fife, and Grace Robertson, *née* Smith (d 1970); *b* 22 April 1925; *Educ* Bell Baxter HS Cupar Fife, Univ of Glasgow (BSc); *m* 2 March 1957, Elfrida Marjorie, da of William George Cox (d 1946), of Purley, Surrey; 3 da (Hazel Valerie b 1960, Ursula Katherine b 1962, Angela Judith b 1966); *Career* chief naval architect and dir Ocean Transport & Trading Ltd 1967–78 (joined 1953), head of ship technol British Shipbuilders 1979–84, dep chm British Maritime Technology 1984–86, conslt naval architect 1986–; visiting prof in naval architecture: Univ of Strathclyde 1972–83, UCL 1983–86; JP Liverpool 1977–78; past pres NE Coast Inst of Engrs & Shipbuilders 1984–86, pres RINA 1990–93, master elect Faculty of Royal Designers for Indust 1996; dir Centre for Advanced Indust 1996; memb: Cncl RSA, DSAC, Marine Safety Agency Res Ctee, Tech Ctee Lloyd's Register of Shipping, Gideons Int UK; chm: NE Coast Engrg Tst 1994–96, NE Region RSA 1992–, Argonautics Maritime Technologies Ltd 1995–; tstee Northumberland and Newcastle Police Court Mission Fund 1990–; Hon RDI (RSA) 1986; FEng 1990, FRINA, FIMarE, FRSA; *Books* contrib numerous tech papers to learned jls; *Recreations* garden; *Clubs* Caledonian; *Style*— Marshall Meek, Esq, CBE, RDI, FEng; ✉ Coppers, Hillside Road, Rothbury, Northumberland NE65 7PT (☎ and fax 01669 621403)

MEEKE, (Robert) Martin James; *Educ* Allhallows Sch, Univ of Bristol (LLB); *Career* called to the Bar Gray's Inn 1973, currently head of chambers; *Style*— Martin Meeke, Esq; ✉ Colleton Chambers, Colleton Crescent, Exeter EX2 4DG (☎ 01392 274898, fax 01392 412368)

MEERS, Jeffrey (Jeff); s of James Meers, of London, and Marie Ellen, *née* Hugkulstone; *b* 10 Feb 1953; *Educ* Ashford Co GS, Univ of Nottingham (BSc); *m* June 1981, Yvette, da of Pleun Veldhoen, of Holland; 2 s (James b 5 July 1982, David b 22 Oct 1983); *Career* psychologist RN (MOD) 1975; account planner Boase Massimi Pollitt advtg 1976–81 (award winning ads for Courage Best Bitter, John Smith's Yorkshire Bitter), dir WCRS 1981–85 (award winning ads for BMW, Carling Black Label, Bergasol), dir Leagas Delaney 1985–87 (award winning ads for Nationwide Building Soc), vice chm DFSD Bozell Group and md Bozell UK (pan Euro responsibility incl Unisys Advertising) 1987–94, pres International Data Group IMS Europe, Middle East and Africa 1994–; IPA Advtg Effectiveness Award 1982 and 1994 (Global and Europe Awards); fndr ptnr MAID Systems Ltd, chm Ashford Sports Club Ltd; memb Mktg Soc, MIPA; *Books* Advertising Effectiveness (contrib, 1982); *Recreations* golf, cricket and hockey (former Surrey Schs and Middx Colts Cricket Teams, 1st XI Cricket and Hockey captain), skiing, opera; *Clubs* Ashford Manor Golf, Ashford Sports; *Style*— Jeff Meers, Esq; ✉ International Data Group IMS Europe, Middle East and Africa, Church House, 18 Church Street, Staines, Middlesex TW18 4EP (☎ 01784 210210, fax 01784 210201, internet jeff_meers@idg.com)

MEERS, Nicholas Raymond Beaghen (Nick); s of Peter Rupert Neame Meers, of Cheltenham, and Rachel Barbara, *née* Beaghen; *b* 16 May 1955; *Educ* Bryanston, W of England Sch of Art Bristol, Guildford Sch of Photography (dip), W Surrey Coll of Art & Design; *Career* photographer; numerous editorial and advtg cmmns (landscape, architectural, etc) 1978–; photographs have appeared on various book jackets, magazine front covers, calendars, postcards and in numerous magazines incl: National Trust, Country Life, Country Living, Gardens Illustrated, Period Living, In Britain, Heritage, Landscape, Illustrated London News, American Vogue, Fast Lane, Observer, Individual Homes, Mail on Sunday, Sunday Times, Guardian, Telegraph Weekend Magazine; memb Assoc of Photographers; *Photographic Books* Amsterdam (1978), Paris (1978), California (1978), Los Angeles (1979), Orchids (Hawaii, 1979), Holland (1979), Wisconsin, USA (1979), Ohio, USA (1979), National Parks of California (1979), Israel the Promised Land (1980), Barbados (1980), Cayman Islands (1980), Bahamas (1980), Puerto Rico (1980), Parish Churches of England (1980), Senegal, West Africa (1981), Ivory Coast, West Africa (1981), Ireland and her People (1981), Ferrari (California, 1982), Porsche (California, 1982), The National Parks of Canada (1982), San Francisco (1983), Gardens of Britain (1985), New Shell Guide to South & Mid-Wales (with Wynford Vaughan-Thomas, 1986), New Shell Guide to the Channel Islands (1986), Christopher Wray's Guide to Decorative Lighting (with Barty Phillips, 1986), New Shell Guide to Oxfordshire & Berkshire (1987), The Spirit of the Cotswolds (with Susan Hill, 1987), New Shell Guide to Gloucestershire, Hereford & Worcester (1988), New Shell Guide to Sussex (1989), Enigmatic England (with Sue Seddon, 1989), Panoramas of English Gardens (with David Wheeler, 1990), Panoramas of England (with Adam Nicolson, 1991), Panoramas of English Villages (1992); *Recreations* panoramic photography, kite flying, astrocartography; *Style*— Nick Meers; (☎ and fax 0181 767 3053)

MEGAHEY, Leslie; s of Rev Thomas Megahey (d 1975), and Beatrice, *née* Walton; *b* 22 Dec 1944; *Educ* Elm Grove Belfast, King Edward VI Lichfield, Pembroke Coll Oxford; *Career* dir, writer prodr of film drama and documentary; ed Omnibus 1979–81; film prodns incl: Schalcken the Painter 1979, Cariani and the Courtesans 1987, Duke Bluebeard's Castle 1988, The Hour of the Pig 1993; theatre prodn Jack 1994; head of music and arts BBC TV 1988–91; *Style*— Leslie Megahey, Esq; ✉ c/o Peters Fraser & Dunlop, The Chambers, Chelsea Harbour, London SW10 OXF (☎ 0171 344 1000, fax 0171 352 7356)

MEGAHY, Thomas; MEP (Lab) Yorkshire South West (majority 59,562); s of Samuel Megahy, and Mary Megahy; *b* 16 July 1929; *Educ* Wishaw HS, Ruskin Coll Oxford, Coll of Educn (Tech) Huddersfield, Univ of London (BSc, Dip Econ and Political Sci, Dip FE Leeds); *m* 1954, Jean, *née* Renshaw; 3 s; *Career* former railway worker and lectr; MEP (Lab) Yorkshire SW 1979–; vice pres Euro Parl 1987–89; memb: Social Affrs Ctee, Employment and the Working Environment Ctee, Tport and Tourism Ctee, Hungarian Delgn; *Style*— Thomas Megahy, Esq, MEP; ✉ 6 Lady Heton Grove, Mirfield, W Yorks WF14 9DY; constituency office: 3 Burton Street, Wakefield, West Yorkshire WF1 2DD (☎ 01924 382396, fax 01924 366851)

MEGARRY, Rt Hon Sir Robert Edgar; kt (1967), PC (1978); s of Robert Lindsay Megarry, OBE, LLB (d 1952), of Belfast and Croydon, Surrey, and Irene Marion (d 1929), da of Maj-Gen Edgar Clark; *b* 1 June 1910; *Educ* Lancing, Trinity Hall Cambridge (MA, LLD); *m* 1936, Iris, da of Elias Davies, of Neath, Glamorgan; 3 da; *Career* slr 1935–41; Miny of Supply: princ 1940–44, asst sec 1944–46; called to the Bar Lincoln's Inn 1944, in practice at Chancery Bar 1946–67; book review ed and asst ed Law Quarterly Review 1944–67; asst reader in equity Inns of Ct 1946–51 (reader 1951–71), memb Lord Chllr's Law Reform Ctee 1952–73, QC 1956, bencher Lincoln's Inn 1962 (and treas 1981), High Ct judge 1967–85, vice-chllr High Ct Chancery Div 1976–81, vice-chllr Supreme Ct 1982–85; the visitor: Univ of Essex 1983–90, Clare Hall Cambridge 1984–88; chm: Friends of Lancing Chapel 1969–93, Cncl of Law Reporting 1972–87, Comparative Law Section of Br Inst of Int and Comparative Law 1977–88; memb Advsy Cncl on Public Records 1980–85, pres Lancing Club 1974–; hon fell Trinity Hall Cambridge 1973–; Hon LLD: Hull, Nottingham, London, The Law Soc of Upper Canada; Hon DUniv Essex 1991; FBA 1970; *Books* The Rent Acts (1939), A Manual of the Law of Real Property (1946), Miscellany-At-Law (1955), The Law of Real Property (with Prof H W R Wade, QC, 1957), Lawyer and Litigant in England (The Hamlyn Lectures, 1962), Arabinesque-at-Law (1969), A Second Miscellany-At-Law (1973); *Recreations* heterogeneous; *Style*— The Rt Hon Sir Robert Megarry; ✉ 5 Stone Buildings, Lincoln's Inn, London WC2A 3XT (☎ 0171 242 8607); Institute of Advanced Legal Studies, Charles Clore House, 17 Russell Square, London WC1B 5DR (☎ 0171 637 1731, fax 0171 436 9613)

MEGAW, Rt Hon Sir John; kt (1961), CBE (1956), TD (1951), PC (1969); 2 s of Hon Mr Justice Megaw (d 1947), of Belfast; *b* 16 Sept 1909; *Educ* Royal Academical Inst Belfast, St John's Coll Cambridge, Harvard Law Sch; *m* 1938, Eleanor Grace Chapman; 1 s, 2 da; *Career* served WWII, Col RA; called to the Bar Gray's Inn 1934, QC 1953 (NI 1954), recorder Middlesbrough 1957–61, high ct judge (Queen's Bench) 1961–69, pres Restrictive Practices Ct 1962–68, lord justice of appeal 1969–80, chm Ctee of Inquiry into Civil Serv Pay Dispute 1981–82; Hon LLD Queen's Univ Belfast 1968, Hon DSc Univ of Ulster 1990; hon fell St John's Coll Cambridge, Legion of Merit (US) 1946; *Style*— The Rt Hon Sir John Megaw, CBE, TD; ✉ 14 Upper Cheyne Row, London SW3

MEGSON, Raymond James; s of Roderick Kevin Megson, and Margaret Elizabeth, *née* Welsh; *b* 4 Sept 1945; *Educ* North Sydney HS, Douglas Ewart HS, Univ of Edinburgh (LLB); *m* 11 Oct 1976, Kim Frances, da of Norman McCreadie; 3 s (Jason b 1977, Calum b 1983, Gregor b 1985), 1 da (Paula b 1978); *Career* slr/advocate, SSC, NP, last pres The Faculty of Procurators of Midlothian, admitted one of the first slr-advocates Scotland 1993; former rugby player at centre: Edinburgh Wanderers, Scottish Co-optimists, Edinburgh Dist; rugby referee Scottish Int Panel: England v Japan 1986, Wales v England 1987, Ireland v Wales 1988, Ireland v Italy 1988, Namibia v France 1990 (2 tests), Italy v Holland 1990, Italy v Romania 1990, Wales v England 1991, Hong Kong 7s finals 1991 and 1993, Aust v NZ 1991, England v Wales 1992, France v Argentina 1992, World Cup 7s 1993, France v Italy 1994, Wales v Ireland 1995, New Zealand v Australia 1995, New Zealand v S Africa 1996; *Recreations* golf, rugby, tennis; *Clubs* Edinburgh Wanderers, Mortonhall Golf, Mortonhall Tennis; *Style*— Raymond J Megson, Esq; ✉ 22 Cluny Drive, Edinburgh (☎ 0131 447 2343); Grindlay St Ct, Edinburgh (☎ 0131 228 2501, fax 0131 228 5554)

MEHAFFEY, Rt Rev James; *see:* Derry and Raphoe, Bishop of

MEHTA, Dr Atul Bhanu; *b* 14 Jan 1954; *Educ* Battersea GS, Jesus Coll Cambridge (MA, MB BChir), King's Coll Hosp Univ of London (MD, MRCP, MRCPath); *m* 23 May 1981, Kokila; 1 da (Avani b 6 Sept 1986); *Career* Royal Postgrad Med Sch and Hammersmith Hosp 1981–86: registrar, sr registrar, MRC res fell; conslt haematologist Royal Free Hosp 1986–; author of various res papers on haematological diseases and their treatment; *Style*— Dr Atul Mehta; ✉ Dept of Haematology, Royal Free Hospital, Pond St, London NW3 2QG (☎ 0171 794 0500 ext 3264, fax 0171 431 4537)

MEHTA, Bharat; s of Maganlal Jinabhai Mehta (d 1971), and Rattanben Mehta; *b* 5 March 1956; *Educ* Shenfield Sch Essex, Plymouth Poly (BA), UCL (MSc); *m* 29 Sept 1990, Sally Ann, da of Reginald Chambers; 2 c (Kriyaa Uma b 30 Sept 1991, Puja Kavita b 10 Nov 1993); *Career* research asst MRC UCH Med Sch 1979–80, community worker Pensioners Link 1981–83, policy offr NCVO 1983–87, princ offr for vol orgns London Borough of Waltham Forest 1987–89, chief exec National Schizophrenia Fellowship 1994– (dir of devpt 1989–94); *Recreations* hockey, squash, swimming; *Clubs* Southgate Adelaide Hockey; *Style*— Bharat Mehta, Esq; ✉ 18 Kelvin Avenue, Palmers Green, London N13 4TG (☎ 0181 888 9873); Chief Executive, National Schizophrenia Fellowship, 28 Castle Street, Kingston upon Thames, Surrey KT1 1SS (☎ 0181 547 3937, fax 0181 547 3862, mobile 0836 571025)

MEHTA, Dr (Sukhdev) Thomas; s of Dr Ramji Das Mehta (d 1956), of New Delhi, India, and Basanti Devi Mehta (d 1976); *b* 8 July 1927; *Educ* Univ of Calcutta (MB BS); *m* 20 Sept 1964, Pauline Phyllis; 1 s (Anil b 1965), 1 da (Anita Jane b 1968); *Career* conslt anaesthetist Burnley Gp of Hosps 1968–; author of articles on anaesthetics and related topics; examinership Pt III F C Anaesthetics of GB and Ireland, chm Extended Training Advsy Body Lancashire Ambulance Serv, memb NW Regnl Higher Awards Ctee, fell Overseas Doctors' Assoc 1986; memb: Assoc of Anaesthetics of GB and Ireland, Intensive Care Soc, Intractable Pain Soc, History of Anaesthesia Soc; FFARCS; *Books* A Concise Guide to Treatment of Cardiac Arrest (1984); *Recreations* research, photography, reading; *Style*— Dr Thomas Mehta; ✉ Burnside, 11 Reedley Drive, Burnley, Lancashire BB10 2QZ (☎ 01282 619408)

MEHTA, Zubin; *Educ* Vienna Musikakademie (studied with Hans Swarawsky); *Career* conductor, debut Vienna 1958; asst conductor Royal Liverpool Philharmonic Orchestra, musical dir for life Israel Philharmonic Orchestra; musical dir: Montreal Symphony Orch 1960–64, Los Angeles Philharmonic Orch 1961–78, NY Philharmonic Orch 1978–91 (longest ever holder of post, over 1000 public concerts); recent work incl: Live from Lincoln Centre (for TV), Pension Fund Concert (with Daniel Barenboim), New Year's Eve Concert (with June Anderson), Mozart Bicentennial Celebration, Salute to Carnegie Hall (with Isaac Stern) 1990, Bartok's Piano Concerto No 2 (with Andras Schiff) 1993; tours with NY Philharmonic incl: Argentina and the Dominican Repub 1978, Europe 1980 and 1988, US and Mexico 1981, S America 1982, US 1983, Asia 1984 and 1989, Europe and Israel 1985, Latin America 1987, Soviet Union (incl jt concert in Gorky Park Moscow with State Symphony Orchestra of Soviet Miny of Culture) 1988; advsr to Maggio Musicale Fiorentino, frequent guest conductor for maj orchs and opera cos; numerous recordings with NY Philharmonic incl: Mahler's Symphony No 5, Holst's The Planets, Sibelius Symphony No 2 and Finlandia, Stravinsky's La Sacre du Printemps and Symphony in Three Movements, Gershwin Collection (incl Rhapsody in Blue, An American in Paris and excerpts from Porgy and Bess), Paine's Symphonies Nos 1 and 2, Overture to As You Like It, Dvořák's Violin Concerto (with Midori), Domingo at the Philharmonic; recordings with Berlin Philharmonic incl: Richard Strauss' Alpine Symphony, Bartók's Concerto for Orchestra, Miraculous Mandarin Suite and Violin Concertos Nos 1 and 2 (with Midori); recordings with Israel Philharmonic incl: Chopin's Piano Concertos Nos 1 and 2 (with Murray Parahia), Fauré Schoenberg and Sibelius settings of Pelléas et Mélisande; *Awards* first prize Int Conductors Competition Liverpool 1958, Padma Bhusham of Indian Govt (Order of the Lotus), Gold medal from Pope Paul VI, commendation from PM Golda Meir for contrib to the cultural life of Israel, Commendatore Repub of Italy 1976, Nikisch Ring (bequeathed by Karl Boehm), Vienna Philharmonic Ring of Honor; hon citizen of Tel Aviv; *Style*— Zubin Mehta, Esq; ✉ Lies Askonas Ltd, 6 Henrietta St, London WC2E 8LA (☎ 0171 379 7700, fax 0171 242 1831, telex 921 194 ASKONA G)

MEIKLE, Alan; CBE (1987); s of Malcolm Coubrough Meikle, MC (and Bar) (d 1947), of Wick Grange, Pershore, Worcs, and Mary Alma, *née* Fletcher (d 1985); *b* 22 March 1928; *Educ* St Michael's Coll Tenbury Wells, Pangbourne Coll Berks, Birmingham Sch of Architecture (Dip Arch); *m* 1, 30 Aug 1958, Marjorie Joan (d 1981), da of Arundel Spencer Clay (d 1982); 2 s (Stewart b 1959, Robert b 1960), 1 da (Grace b 1963); m 2, 22 Oct 1988, Barbara Joan Zienau, *née* Warland; *Career* midshipman RNR 1945–46; furniture designer Herts CC 1952–55, asst architect Notts CC 1955–71, co property offr Hereford and Worcs CC 1982–88 (co architect 1971–82); designer of sports centres, schools, libraries and other public bldgs; advsr Audit Cmmns: DES, NEDO; chm Assoc Heads of Co Property Depts 1986; RIBA 1953 (head Clients' Advsy Serv 1989–91, memb Cncl 1977–83, vice pres 1980–81); *Recreations* sailing, sculpture, furniture design; *Style*— Alan Meikle, Esq, CBE

MEINERTZHAGEN, Sir Peter; kt (1980), CMG (1966); yst s of Louis Ernest Meinertzhagen (d 1941), and Gwynedd, da of Sir William Llewellyn, GCVO, PRA; *b* 24 March 1920; *Educ* Eton; *m* 1949, Dido, da of late (William) Jack Pretty, of Cranleigh, Surrey; 1 s (Simon b 1950), 1 da (Tana (Mrs Knyvett)); *Career* serv WWII Maj Europe and Far East (despatches); gen mangr Cwlth Devpt Corp 1973–85, dir Booker Tate Ltd 1988–95, chm Booker Tate Pension Tstees Ltd 1996–; Croix de Guerre 1944; *Clubs*

Muthaiga Country (Nairobi); *Style*— Sir Peter Meinertzhagen, CMG; ✉ Mead House, Ramsbury, Wilts SN8 2QP (☎ 01672 520715)

MEINS, Paul Godfrey; s of John Callaghan Meins (d 1985), and Doris, *née* Green; *b* 3 March 1944; *Educ* London Nautical Sch, Univ of London (BSc), Cranfield Univ (MBA); *m* 4 Sept 1988, Lorna Margaret, da of Albert Francis Grosse; 1 da (Emily Lucy Sarah b 17 Oct 1989), 1 s (Richard Alexander b 23 Nov 1991); *Career* apprentice Bacon & Woodrow 1965–71, jt actuary Old Mutual Life Assurance Co 1971–74; ptnr i/c of actuarial consulting Coopers & Lybrand 1975–96; actuarial conslt 1996–; FIA 1969, ASA 1977, FPMI 1985, FRSA 1993, MAE 1996; *Recreations* sailing; *Clubs* Gallio; *Style*— Paul Meins, Esq; ✉ 2 Suters Cottages, Diamond Terrace, Greenwich, London SE10 8QN (☎ and fax 0181 691 3133)

MEIRION-JONES, Prof Gwyn Idris; s of Maelgwyn Meirion-Jones, of Manchester (d 1989), and Enid, *née* Roberts (d 1962); *b* 24 Dec 1933; *Educ* N Manchester GS, King's Coll London (BSc, MPhil, PhD); *m* 1 April 1961, Monica, da of George Havard, of Winchester (d 1961), and Marion, *née* Milson (d 1976); *Career* Nat Serv RAF 1954–56; schoolmaster 1959–68, lectr in geography Kingston Coll of Technol 1968; London Guildhall Univ (formerly Sir John Cass Coll, then City of London Poly): sr lectr in geography 1969, head of geography 1970–89, prof 1983–89, Leverhulme res fell 1985–87, emeritus prof 1989–; currently visiting prof of archaeology Univ of Reading; author and conslt on historic bldgs; author of papers on scientific, archaeological and ethnological jls; Ancient Monuments Soc: cncl memb 1974–79 and 1983–94, hon sec 1976–79, vice pres 1979–, ed 1985–94; Br Assoc for the Advancement of Science: sec 1973–78, memb Cncl 1977–80, memb Gen Ctee 1977–83, recorder 1978–83, pres Archaeology and Anthropology Section 1992–93; ed Medieval Village Res Gp 1978–86, memb Royal Cmmn on the Historical Monuments of England 1985–97, pres Surrey Domestic Bldgs Res Gp 1986–91 (hon vice pres 1991–), memb Advsy Ctee on Buildings and Domestic Life Welsh Folk Museum 1991–95; hon corr memb Société Jersiaise 1980–, corr memb Compagnie des Architectes en Chef des Monuments Historiques 1989–; FSA 1981; *Books* La Maison Traditionnelle (1978), The Vernacular Architecture of Brittany (1982), Aimer les Châteaux de Bretagne (with Prof Michael Jones, *qv*, 1991, also English and German edns), Les Châteaux de Bretagne (with Prof Michael Jones, 1992), Manorial Domestic Buildings in England and Northern France (1993), La Ville de Cluny et ses Maisons (XIe-XVe siècles) (jlty, 1997), Historic Buildings and Dating by Dendrochronology (1997); *Recreations* food, wine, music, walking, swimming; *Clubs* Athenaeum; *Style*— Prof Gwyn Meirion-Jones, FSA; ✉ 11 Avondale Rd, Fleet, Hampshire GU13 9BH (☎ and fax 01252 614300, mobile 0374 946075); Department of Archaeology, University of Reading, Reading RG6 6AA

MEISENKOTHEN, Walter Anton; s of Walter Meisenkothen (d 1981), and Marion Justina Anne, *née* Frankel; *b* 20 Sept 1946; *Educ* River Dell HS New Jersey, Fairleigh Dickinson Univ (Academic Excellence awrd, BSc); *m* 5 March 1976, Judith, da of Francis Hopkins; *Career* tax mangr Arthur Andersen Miami and New York 1968–75, corp tax dir IMS International 1975–78; ptnr Arthur Andersen 1982–; bd memb and chm Taxation Ctee American Chamber of Commerce 1990–; memb: American Inst of Certified Public Accountants, Florida Inst of Certified Public Accountants; *Recreations* golf; *Clubs* Cirencester Golf, Burford Golf; *Style*— Walter Meisenkothen, Esq; ✉ Arthur Andersen, 1 Surrey Street, London WC2R 2PS (☎ 0171 438 3600, fax 0171 831 1133)

MELBOURN, John William; CBE (1993); *b* 1937; *Career* National Westminster Bank PLC: dir 1989–96, chief exec gp risk until 1994, dep gp chief exec 1994–96; non-exec dir: 3i Group plc 1990–, Tesco PLC 1996–, National Westminster Bank PLC 1996–; chm Lombard North Central PLC 1996–; pres Chartered Inst of Bankers 1995–96 (dep chm 1994–95); FCIB; *Style*— John Melbourn, Esq, CBE; ✉ Lombard North Central PLC, Lombard House, 3 Princess Way, Redhill, Surrey RH1 1NP; c/o National Westminster Bank plc, 41 Lothbury, London EC2P 2BP (☎ 0171 726 1000)

MELCHETT, 4 Baron (UK 1928); Sir Peter Robert Henry Mond; 4 Bt (UK 1910); s of 3 Baron Melchett (d 1973, gs of 1 Baron, better known as Sir Alfred Mond, first chm of ICI and min of Health 1921–22); *b* 24 Feb 1948; *Educ* Eton, Pembroke Coll Cambridge, Keele Univ; *Career* sits as Lab peer in House of Lords; at LSE and Addiction Res Unit 1973–74; a lord in waiting (govt whip) 1974–75, Parly under-sec of state DOI 1975–76, min of state NI Office 1976–79; chm: Working Pty on Pop Festivals 1975 76, Community Indust 1979–85, Greenpeace UK 1986–88, Greenpeace Japan 1995–; pres Ramblers' Assoc 1981–84; exec dir Greenpeace UK 1988–; *Style*— The Rt Hon the Lord Melchett; ✉ The House of Lords, London SW1A 0PW

MELDRUM, Keith Cameron; CB (1995); s of Dr Walter James Meldrum (d 1971), and Eileen Lydia, *née* Freckelton; *b* 19 April 1937; *Educ* Uppingham, Royal Sch of Veterinary Studies Univ of Edinburgh (B Veterinary Med and Surgery, Dip Veterinary State Med, MRCVS); *m* 1, 3 March 1962, (m dis 1980), Rosemary Ann, da of Maj Jack Aikman Crawford (d 1988); 2 s (James Aikman b 1966, Andrew William b 1968), 1 da (Janet Marina b 1964); m 2, 11 Aug 1982, Vivien Mary; *Career* in gen practice as veterinary surgn Scunthorpe Lincs 1961–63, veterinary offr MAFF Oxford 1963–72, divnl veterinary offr MAFF Tolworth 1972–75, MAFF divnl veterinary offr Leamington Spa 1975–78, dep regnl veterinary offr Nottingham 1978–80, regnl veterinary offr Tolworth 1980–83, asst chief veterinary offr 1983–86, dir of veterinary field servs 1986–88, chief veterinary offr 1988–; *Recreations* competitive target rifle shooting, outdoor activities; *Clubs* North London Rifle, Farmers'; *Style*— Keith Meldrum, Esq, CB; ✉ Ministry of Agriculture, Fisheries and Food, Government Buildings, Hook Rise South, Tolworth, Surbiton, Surrey KT6 7NF (☎ 0181 330 8050, telex 22203 AHSURB, fax 0181 330 6872)

MELFORD, Dr David Austin; OBE (1990); s of Austin Melford (d 1971), of London, and Jessie, *née* Winter (d 1971); *b* 16 Oct 1927; *Educ* Hall Sch Hampstead, Charterhouse, Clare Coll Cambridge (MA, PhD, ScD); *m* 3 Sept 1955, Amanda Patricia, da of Leonard Farrar (Cdr RN, d 1959); 1 s (Mark Austin b 29 April 1969), 1 da (Clare Amanda b 14 June 1973); *Career* Army Serv 1946–48, cmmnd 2 Lt Royal Signals; TI fell Cavendish Laboratory Cambridge 1955–57; TI Group: res scientist TI Research Laboratories 1957–68, design and devpt Scanning Electron Probe Microanalyser, chief metallurgist and head of Metallurgy Div 1968–79, dir of res and dep gen mangr 1979–87; materials res conslt 1987–, Royal Acad of Engrg visiting prof Dept of Materials Sci and Metallurgy Univ of Cambridge 1994–; former: memb Engrg Bd SERC, chm Materials Advsy Ctee DTI, memb Cncl, memb Standing Ctee on Engrg and assessor SERC Cncl Royal Acad of Engrg; Hadfield medallist 1975, Pfeil medallist 1976, Platinum medallist 1993 Inst of Materials (former vice pres, memb Cncl and memb Exec Ctee); author of numerous contribs to learned jls esp jl of Inst of Metals; FEng 1984, FIM, MInstP; *Recreations* writing, instrument making, gardening and the pursuit of trout; *Clubs* MCC; *Style*— Dr David Melford, OBE, FEng; ✉ Clare College, Cambridge

MELGUND, Viscount; (Gilbert) Timothy George Lariston Elliot-Murray-Kynynmound; s and h of 6 Earl of Minto, OBE, *qv*; *b* 1 Dec 1953; *Educ* Eton (BSc); *m* 30 July 1983, Diana Barbara, da of Brian S L Trafford, of Tismans, Rudgwick, W Sussex; 3 s (Gilbert b 1984, Lorne b and d 1986, Michael b 1987), 1 da (Clare Patricia b 1991); *Heir* s, Hon Gilbert Francis Elliot-Murray-Kynynmound b 15 Aug 1984; *Career* Lt Scots Gds 1972–76; memb Royal Co of Archers (Queen's Body Guard for Scotland); ARICS; *Clubs* White's; *Style*— Viscount Melgund

MELIA, Dr Terence Patrick; CBE (1993); s of John Melia (d 1975), and Kathleen, *née* Traynor (d 1984); *b* 17 Dec 1934; *Educ* Sir John Deanes GS Northwich, Univ of Leeds (PhD); *m* 21 May 1976, Madeline, da of Arthur Carney (d 1975); 1 da (Alexandra b 1980); *Career* tech offr ICI Ltd 1961–64, lectr and sr lectr Univ of Salford 1964–70, princ N Lindsey Coll of Technol 1970–74; HM inspr of schs 1974–92: regnl staff inspr NW 1982–84, chief inspr higher educn 1985–91, sr chief inspr 1991–92; chief inspr Further Educn Funding Cncl 1993–96; visiting prof Leeds Metropolitan Univ 1993–; FRSC, FRSA, CChem; *Recreations* golf, gardening; *Clubs* Berkhamsted Golf; *Style*— Dr Terence Melia, CBE; ✉ Further Education Funding Council, Sheriffs Orchard, Greyfriars Road, Coventry CV1 3PJ

MELLAART, James; s of Jacob Herman Jan Mellaart (d 1972), of Kasteel Mheer, Holland, and Apollonia Dingena, *née* Van Der Beek (d 1934); *b* 14 Nov 1925; *Educ* Gymnasiums The Hague and Maastricht Holland, UCL (BA); *m* 23 April 1954, (Meryem) Arlette, da of Kadri Cenani, OBE (d 1984), of Istanbul; 1 s (Alan b 1955); *Career* archaeologist; asst dir Br Inst of Archaeology Ankara Turkey 1959–61 (scholar and fell 1951–58), specialist lectr Istanbul Univ 1961–63, lectr in Anatolian archaeology Inst of Archaeology Univ of London 1964–91; excavations: Beycesultan (with S Lloyd) 1954–59, Hacilar 1957–60, Çatal Hüyük 1961–63 and 1965; FSA 1964, FBA 1980; *Books* Beycesultan (excavation reports with Seton Lloyd, Vol I 1962, Vol II 1965), Earliest Civilisations of The Near East (1965), The Chalcolithic and Early Bronze Ages in The Near East and Anatolia (1966), Çatal Hüyük, A Neolithic Town in Anatolia (1967), Excavations at Hacilar (1970), The Neolithic of the Near East (1975), The Archaeology of Ancient Turkey (1978), The Goddess from Anatolia, II, Çatal Hüyük and Anatolian Kilims (1989), Beycesultan (vol III.2, with Ann Murray, 1995); *Recreations* music (Baroque and Gaelic), art (Celtic and Turkish), geology, ancient history; *Style*— James Mellaart, Esq, FSA, FBA; ✉ 12–13 Lichen Court, 79 Queen's Drive, London N4 2BH (☎ 0181 802 6984)

MELLAR, Gordon Hollings; s of George Herbert Mellar (d 1962), and Gladys, *née* Hollings (d 1990); *b* 15 Oct 1935; *Educ* High Storrs GS Sheffield, Trinity Coll Cambridge (MA); *m* 17 Aug 1963, Ann Mary, da of Herbert Bates (d 1961); 1 s (Toby b 21 March 1972), 1 da (Sadie b 8 June 1969); *Career* Nat Serv cmmnd RAF (pilot trg) 1954–56, Flying Offr (pilot) No 616 S Yorks Sqdn RAuxAF 1956–57; dir Centrax Ltd 1977– (mechanical engr 1959–, dir Gas Turbine Div 1976–); marker and referee Newton Abbot Squash Club; memb: Mid Devon Cycling Club, Newton Abbot Photographic Club; FIMechE; *Recreations* squash, cycling, photography, golf; *Style*— Gordon Mellar, Esq; ✉ Centrax Ltd, Newton Abbot, Devon TQ12 4SQ (☎ 01626 53342, 01626 52251, fax 01626 52250, telex 42935 CENTRX G)

MELLERS, Prof Wilfrid Howard; OBE (1982); s of late Percival Wilfrid Mellers, and Hilda Maria, *née* Lawrence; *b* 26 April 1914; *Educ* Leamington Coll, Downing Coll Cambridge (BA, MA), Univ of Birmingham (DMus), City Univ (DPhil); *m* 1, 1940 (m dis), Vera Muriel, da of late Gustavus Hobbs; m 2, March 1950 (m dis), Peggy Pauline Lewis; 3 da (Judith, Olivia Caroline, Sarah); m 3, 17 July 1980, Robin Stephanie Hildyard, *née* Spicer; *Career* professional composer (over 50 published compositions); tutor and supervisor Downing Coll Cambridge 1945–48, staff tutor in music Extra Mural Dept Univ of Birmingham 1948–60; visiting prof of music: Univ of Pittsburgh USA 1960–63, City Univ 1981–, Univ of Keele 1981–; emeritus prof Univ of York 1982 (founding head of Dept of Music 1964–81); formerly visiting prof of music at numerous American Univs incl Andrew Mellon visiting prof Tulane Univ USA; author of numerous pubns in reference books and encyclopaedia; fell Sonneck Soc USA 1984; FGSM 1981; *Books* incl: François Couperin and the French Classical Tradition (1950, enlarged edn 1987), Man and his Music (various edns, various languages 1957–87), Music in a New Found Land: Themes and Developments in the History of American Music (1964), Twilight of the Gods: the Beatles in Retrospect (1973), Bach and the Dance of God (1980), Beethoven and the Voice of God (1983), Vaughan Williams and the Vision of Albion (1989), Percy Grainger (1992), Francis Poulenc (1993); *Style*— Prof Wilfrid Mellers, OBE; ✉ Oliver Sheldon House, 17 Aldwark, York YO1 2BX (☎ 01904 638686)

MELLING, John Kennedy; s of John Robert Melling (d 1948), of Westcliff-on-Sea, Essex, and Ivy Edith May, *née* Woolmer (d 1982); *b* 11 Jan 1927; *Educ* Thirsk Sch Westcliff, Westcliff HS for Boys; *Career* CA; lectr, author, broadcaster, playwright and historian; drama and literary critic: The Stage 1957–90, Fur Weekly News 1968–73; ed: The Liveryman Magazine 1970–75, Black Dagger series 1986–91; Crime Writers' Assoc: memb Ctee 1985–88, ed Handbook 1989, CWA Award for Outstanding Servs; int life vice pres American Fedn of Police, elected to US Chiefs of Police Nat Drug Task Force 1991; Knight Grand Cross Order of St Michael the Archangel of the Nat Assoc of Chiefs of Police USA; govr Corp of the Sons of the Clergy; memb: BAFTA 1960, Mystery Writers of America; memb Ct of Assts Worshipful Co of Poulters (Master 1980–81), memb Worshipful Cos of Bakers, Farriers and Constructors; FCA, FFB, FRSA, FTII, MCFA, OMAA; *Books* incl: Discovering Lost Theatres, Discovering London's Guilds and Liveries (5 edn), Alchemy of Murder, Gwendoline Butler: Inventor of the Women's Police Procedural, Murder Done To Death, Scaling the High C's (with John Brecknock); *Plays* incl: George....from Caroline, The Gilded Cage; *Clubs* City Livery; *Style*— John Kennedy Melling, Esq; ✉ 85 Chalkwell Ave, Westcliff-on-Sea, Essex SS0 8NL; 44a Tranquil Vale, Blackheath, London SE3 0BD; 9 Blenheim St, New Bond St, London W1Y 9LE (☎ and fax 0171 499 2519, ☎ 0171 499 7249)

MELLING, Joseph Anthony (Joe); s of John Gerard Melling (d 1989), of Preston, Lancashire, and Monica, *née* Clifton; *b* 18 June 1946; *Educ* Preston Catholic Coll; *m* Patricia Mary, da of Thomas Gornall; 3 da (Sarah Louise b 28 Oct 1973, Jane Elizabeth b 9 May 1975, Louisa Clare b 9 May 1979); *Career* journalist; acting sports ed Blackburn Times 1967, sport and news reporter Lancashire Evening Post 1968 (trainee news reporter 1965); Daily Express: sport sub ed Manchester 1969, NE area sports writer 1972–78, Midlands sports reporter 1978–80, dep chief football writer 1980–83; football ed Mail On Sunday 1986– (chief football writer 1983); Sports Reporter of the Year (1986), special award of distinction for coverage of Hillsborough disaster; chm Football Writers' Assoc 1987–88, 1991–92, 1992–93 and 1996–97; *Books* United To Win (biography of Ron Atkinson, 1984), Kerry (biography of Kerry Dixon, 1986); *Recreations* walking, gourmet eating, wine collecting; *Style*— Joe Melling, Esq; ✉ The Mail On Sunday, Northcliffe House, 2 Derry St, Kensington, London (☎ 0171 938 7075, fax 0171 937 4115, car 0836 273030)

MELLINGER, Lucas Emmanuel Matthias; s of Dr Frederick Mellinger (d 1970), of Los Angeles, USA, and Eva, *née* Schlesinger (d 1959); *b* 9 July 1921; *Educ* Bunce Court Sch, Northern Poly (DipArch); *m* 27 Sept 1957 (m dis 1987), Janet Elizabeth, da of Sidney Kybert (d 1964); 1 s (Simon b 1964), 1 da (Karina b 1959); *Career* Corpl RE 1940–46; architect, planning conslt, design conslt; planning offr Notts Co Cncl 1948–50, chief tech and res asst Wells Wintemute Wells Coates 1950–53, in private practice 1953–; former conslt to: Br Film Inst, Cinematograph Exhibitors' Assoc, Film Prodn Assoc; architect of exhibitions, trade fairs and restaurants incl: Hatchetts (Piccadilly), The Sands (Bond St), Dukes (Duke St), Xenon Nightclub (Piccadilly); conslt to housing assocs, charitable tsts, church authys and Leisure indust; patentee of furniture sets for sedentary work, window fitting and water saving sanitary fitting; three times winner Institutions Int Design award; FRIBA, FRTPI, FCSD, FRSA; *Publications* No One is Eccentric (1992), Housing the Communtiy - 2000 (Cities, April 1994); *Recreations* armchair philosophy, politics; *Clubs* Private; *Style*— Lucas E M Mellinger, Esq; ✉ 60 Richmond Hill Court, Richmond, Surrey TW10 6BE (☎ 0181 940 8255)

MELLIS, Capt David Barclay Nairne; DSC (1941); s of Rev David Barclay Mellis Mellis (Lt 1 Bn Seaforth Highlanders 1915–19 Mesopatamia (twice wounded); d 1961), of Edinburgh, and Margaret Blaikie, *née* MacKenzie (d 1970); *b* 13 June 1915; *Educ* RNC Dartmouth, RNC Greenwich; *m* 13 April 1940, Anne Patricia (d 1994), da of Lt-Col Walter Stuart Wingate-Gray, MC (d 1977); 1 s (Patrick Mellis, *qv* b 1943), 2 da (Matilda b 1941, Charlotte b 1952); *Career* cadet RN 1929; served HMS: Malaya 1932, York 1934, Gallant 1936–37; Lt 1937, navigation specialist 1938, Persian Gulf and China HMS Bideford 1938–39; served HMS's Malcolm, Worcester and Mackay (Portsmouth and Harwich) 1940–41 (despatches (Dunkirk) 1940), Manchester 1942, Rotherham (Eastern Fleet) 1942–43; Staff Cdre D Eastern Fleet 1943–45, Lt Cdr 1945, Staff HMS Dryad 1945–47, Fleet Navigating Offr East Indies HMS Norfolk 1947–49, First Lt HMS Dryad 1949–51, Cdr 1951, in cmd HMS Redpole 1951–52, Admty 1952–54, in cmd HMS St Kitts 1954–55, 2 i/c and Exec Offr HMS Centaur 1955–56, Staff C-in-C Med as Asst Capt of the Fleet (Suez War) 1956–58, Capt 1958, jssc 1958, Br Naval Attaché Athens and Tel Aviv 1959–61, in cmd HMS Puma Captain 7 Frigate Sqdn (S Atlantic and S America) 1961–63, Capt HMS Dryad 1963–65, COS to C-in-C Med and as COMEDSOUEAST (NATO appt) 1965–67, Cdre 1965–67, ret 1967; Comptroller Duart Castle Mull 1967–68, Admty Approved Master (Warship Trials) 1969–79; jt fndr: Royal Naval Pipers Soc 1951, Royal Naval Club Argyll 1969; Cdre Western Isles Yacht Club 1975–81, tstee Royal Highland Yacht Club; Younger Brother Trinity House, Elder Church of Scotland; *Recreations* gardening, arguing, reading history and political biography; *Clubs* New (Edinburgh), Royal Scottish Pipers Soc; *Style*— Capt David Mellis, DSC, RN; ✉ High Water, Aros, Isle of Mull, Argyll PA72 6JG (☎ 01680 300370)

MELLIS, Margaret; da of Rev David Barclay Mellis (d 1961), and Margaret Blaikie, *née* MacKenzie (d 1970); *b* 22 Jan 1914; *Educ* Queen Margaret's PNEU Sch Edinburgh, Edinburgh Coll of Art (DA, MacLaine Watters medal for colour, Andrew Grant postgrad award, travelling scholarship, 2 year fellowship); *m* 1, 1938, Adrian Stokes (the writer), s of Durham Stokes; 1 s (Telfer b 1940); m 2, Francis Davison (the collagist), s of George Davison; *Career* artist; studied in Paris, Spain and Italy, worked Euston Road Sch London, lived and worked St Ives Cornwall then Cap d'Antibes France, currently based Suffolk; *Solo Exhibitions* AIA Gallery London 1958, Scottish Gallery Edinburgh 6 1959, UEA 1967, Bear Lane Gallery Oxford 1968, Grabowski Gallery London 1969, Richard Demarco Gallery Edinburgh 1970, Univs of Stirling and Exeter 1970, Basil Jacobs Gallery London 1972, Compass Gallery Glasgow 1976, Pier Art Centre Orkney 1982, New '57 Gallery Edinburgh 1982, Redfern Gallery London 1987, 1990 and 1994, Aldeburgh artist in residence Aldeburgh Festival Exhibition 1991, Gainsborough House Museum 1992; *Group Exhibitions* incl: Waddington Galleries 1959–62, John Moores Liverpool Exhibition 4 and 5 1963 and 1965, Edinburgh Open 100 1967, Painting in Cornwall 1945–55 (New Art Centre London) 1977, The Women's Art Show 1550–1970 (Castle Museum Nottingham) 1982, Objects (recent acquisitions, V & A) 1978, Pier Gallery Collection Exhibition (Tate Gallery), St Ives 1939–64 (Tate Gallery) 1985, Art Since 1900 (Scottish Nat Gallery of Modern Art and Barbican London) 1989, Glasgow's Great British Art Exhibition (McLellan Galleries) 1990, New Gallery of Modern Art Glasgow 1996, Bede Gallery Jarrow (with Francis Davison) 1996; *Work in Collections* incl: Tate Gallery, V & A, Kelvin Grove Museum and Art Gallery Glasgow, Nuffield Fndn, Sztuki W Lodzi Museum Poland, Scottish Nat Gallery of Modern Art Edinburgh, Pier Collection Orkney, Scottish Arts Cncl, Arts Cncl of GB, Graves Collection Sheffield, Sainsbury Centre Norwich, Gallery of Modern Art Glasgow, Norwich Castle Museum 1996; *Recreations* music, reading, dancing, walking, ballet, opera, cinema; *Style*— Miss Margaret Mellis; ✉ Redfern Gallery, 20 Cork St, London W1X 2HL (☎ 0171 734 1732/0578, fax 0171 494 2908)

MELLIS, Patrick David Barclay Nairne; s of Capt David Mellis, DSC, RN, *qv*, and Anne Patricia, *née* Wingate-Gray (d 1994); *b* 14 May 1943; *Educ* Loretto, Univ of Glasgow (BSc Naval Architecture); *m* 26 Nov 1969, Elizabeth Jane Workman, *née* Carslaw; 2 da (Rosemary Anne Nairne b 14 Nov 1975, Catherine Fiona Nairne b 25 April 1977), 1 s (Robert Barclay Nairne b 13 May 1980); *Career* student apprentice Alex Stephens & Sons (shipbuilders) Glasgow 1961–66 (design draughtsman 1966–68); naval architect: Litton Industries Mississippi USA 1968–70, A Darden & Sons (constructors) New Orleans USA 1970–72, International Offshore Services London 1972–74; project mangr P & O Three Quays 1974–83, marine dir Seaforth Maritime Ltd Aberdeen 1983–89, project mangr Saudi Arabian Oil Co Saudi Arabia 1990–96, md P & O Three Quays 1996–; memb Br Maritime League; memb Instn of Engrs and Shipbuilders in Scotland 1962, MRINA 1962, assoc memb Soc of Naval Architects and Marine Engrs USA 1972; *Recreations* squash, golf, sailing; *Style*— Patrick Mellis, Esq; ✉ 1 Avenue Road, Bishop's Stortford, Herts CM23 5NS (☎ 01279 652127); Three Quays Marine Services Ltd, 12–20 Camomile Street, London EC3A 7AS (☎ 0171 929 2299, fax 0171 929 1650)

MELLISH, Baron (Life Peer 1985), of Bermondsey in Greater London; Robert Joseph Mellish; PC (1967); s of John Mellish, of Deptford, London; *b* 3 March 1913; *Educ* St Joseph's RC Sch Deptford; *m* 1938, Anne Elizabeth, da of George Warner, of Bermondsey; 4 s (Hon Robert, Hon David, Hon Paul, Hon Stephen); *Career* served WWII as Lance-Corpl then rose to Maj RE SE Asia; left school at 14, worked as clerk in docks, joined TGWU 1929, organiser of dockers 1938–40; MP (Lab 1946–82, Ind Lab 1982): Bermondsey Rotherhithe 1946–50, Bermondsey 1950–74, Southwark Bermondsey 1974–82; PPS to First Lord of Admty then to Min for Pensions then to Min of Supply 1950–51, jt Parly sec Miny of Housing 1964–67, min for Public Bldgs and Works 1967–69, Parly sec to the Treasy (Govt chief whip) 1969–70 and 1974–76 (oppn chief whip 1970–74); vice chm London Docklands Devpt Corp 1981–84; Papal Knight Order of St Gregory the Great 1959; *Style*— The Rt Hon Lord Mellish, PC; ✉ c/o House of Lords, London SW1A 0PW

MELLITT, Prof Brian; s of John Mellitt (d 1990), of Preston, UK, and Nelly, *née* Heaney; *b* 29 May 1940; *Educ* Preston GS, Univ of Loughborough (BTech), Imperial Coll London (DIC); *m* 30 Dec 1961, Lyn, da of Edward Waring, of Preston; 1 s (John Edward b 1967), 1 da (Anna Jane b 1969); *Career* design engr (Electric Traction) English Electric 1956–66, sr lectr Huddersfield Poly 1966–68, sr princ scientific offr Res Div British Railways Bd 1968–71; Univ of Birmingham: lectr 1971, sr lectr 1981, prof 1983, head Undergraduate Sch 1983, head Electrical Engrg and Electronics Dept 1985, dean Faculty of Engrg 1987–88, hon prof 1989; head Power Electronics and Traction Gp 1971–88 (conslt engr to various railways incl LUL, Hong Kong MTRC, Singapore MRTC, CIE, Metro Madrid), engrg dir London Underground 1989–95, dir engrg and prodn Railtrack plc 1995–; hon ed IEE Proceedings - Electric Power Applications 1978–; Leonardo da Vinci Award Italian Industl Design Assoc 1989; Hon DTech Univ of Loughborough 1991; FIEE 1978 (vice pres 1996–), FIMechE 1986, FIRSE 1984, FEng 1990; *Books* Computers in Railway Operations (ed, 1987), Computer Applications in Railway Operations (ed, 1990); *Recreations* bridge; *Clubs* Athenaeum; *Style*— Prof Brian Mellitt, FEng; ✉ Railtrack plc, 40 Bernard Street, London WC1N 1BY (☎ 0171 344 7116, fax 0171 344 7220)

MELLON, Sir James; KCMG (1989, CMG 1979); *b* 25 Jan 1929; *Educ* Univ of Glasgow; *m* 1, 1956, Frances Murray (d 1976); 1 s, 3 da; m 2, 1979, Mrs Philippa Shuttleworth, *née* Hartley; *Career* joined FO 1963, commercial cnsllr E Berlin 1975–76, head of Trade Rels and Export Dept FCO 1976–78, high cmmr Ghana and ambass to Togo 1978–83, ambass to Denmark 1983–86, consul gen New York 1986–89; chm: Scottish Homes 1989–96, Thamesmead Town 1993–96, RTM (Radio Thamesmead) 1993–96, Regent Pacific Corporate Finance 1991–; *Style*— Sir James Mellon, KCMG; ✉ Regent Pacific Corporate Finance, 39 St James's Street, London SW1A 1JQ (☎ 0171 316 0007)

MELLOR, Christopher John; s of John Whitaker Mellor (d 1987), and Mary, *née* Thompson (d 1970); *b* 3 March 1949; *Educ* Dovecliffe GS Burton upon Trent; *m* 6 Dec 1969, Mavis Ann, da of Thomas Twiselton; 3 da (Faye Elizabeth Mary b 22 Nov 1972, Katie Louise b 14 Nov 1975, Alison Jane 9 Feb 1978); *Career* various posts in local govt finance in Staffs and Glos 1967–79; Anglian Water Authy (privatised to become Anglian Water PLC 1989): joined as sr accountant 1979, princ accountant then head of financial planning until 1990, gp fin dir 1990–; non-exec dir Addenbrooke's NHS Hosp Tst 1993–; IPFA 1977; *Recreations* running, golf, reading, watercolours; *Style*— Christopher Mellor, Esq; ✉ Anglian Water plc, Ambury Road, Huntingdon, Cambridgeshire PE18 6NZ (☎ 01480 443257)

MELLOR, David; OBE (1981); s of Colin Mellor (d 1970), and Ivy Mellor (d 1975); *b* 5 Oct 1930; *Educ* Sheffield Coll of Art, Royal Coll of Art (hon fell 1966), Br Sch at Rome; *m* 1966, Fiona, da of Col Gerald Heggart MacCarthy (d 1943); 1 s, 1 da; *Career* designer, manufacturer and retailer; conslt DOE 1963–70, chm Design Cncl Ctee of Inquiry into Standards of Design in Consumer Goods in Britain 1982–84, chm Crafts Cncl 1982–84, tstee V & A Museum 1983–88; Royal Designer for Industry 1962; Hon DLitt Univ of Sheffield 1986; *Style*— David Mellor, Esq, OBE; ✉ The Round Building, Hathersage, Sheffield S30 1BA (☎ 01433 650220, fax 01433 650944)

MELLOR, Prof David Hugh; s of Sydney David Mellor, and Ethel Naomi, *née* Hughes; *b* 10 July 1938; *Educ* Pembroke Coll Cambridge (BA), Univ of Minnesota (MS), Univ of Cambridge (PhD, ScD, MEng); *Career* tech offr ICI Central Instruments Laboratories 1962–63; Univ of Cambridge: asst lectr in philosophy 1965–70, lectr in philosophy 1970–83, reader in metaphysics 1983–86, prof of philosophy 1986–; Philosophy Faculty Univ of Cambridge: librarian 1970–76, chm Bd and Degree Ctee 1976–78 and 1991–93 (sec 1981–85), dir Graduate Studies 1988–90; pres Cambridge Assoc of Univ Teachers 1976–78; Univ of Cambridge: memb Cncl of the Senate 1976–78, memb Library Syndicate 1976–78, memb Bd of Graduate Studies 1989–93, chm History and Philosophy of Sci Syndicate 1980–83, memb General Bd of the Faculties 1995–98; official fell Pembroke Coll Cambridge 1966–70 (Draper's res fell 1964–66); dir Studies in Philosophy: Pembroke Coll 1964–83, Downing Coll 1966–83, Trinity Hall 1982–83; Darwin Coll: fell 1971–, vice-master 1983–87; external examiner in philosophy: Univ of Khartoum 1978–79, Univ of Warwick 1978–80, Univ Coll of N Wales Bangor 1982–84; visiting fell in philosophy Aust Nat Univ Inst Advanced Study 1975, Radcliffe Tst Fell in Philosophy 1978–80, visiting prof of philosophy Univ of Auckland 1985; pres: Br Soc for Philosophy of Sci 1985–87, Aristotelian Soc 1992–93; memb: Cncl Royal Inst of Philosophy 1987–, Exec Ctee Mind Assoc 1982–86; FBA 1983; *Books* The British Journal for The Philosophy of Science (ed, 1968–70), Cambridge Studies in Philosophy (ed, 1978–82), Australasian Journal of Philosophy (memb Editorial Bd, 1977–89), The Matter of Chance (1971), Science, Belief and Behaviour (ed, 1980), Prospects for Pragmatism (ed, 1980), Real Time (1981), Matters of Metaphysics (1991), Ways of Communicating (ed, 1991), The Facts of Causation (1995); *Recreations* theatre; *Style*— Prof D H Mellor; ✉ 25 Orchard St, Cambridge CB1 1JS (☎ and fax 01223 564724, e-mail DHM11@CAM.AC.UK)

MELLOR, The Rt Hon David John; PC (1990), QC (1987), MP (C) Putney (majority 7,526); s of Douglas H Mellor; *b* 12 March 1949; *Educ* Swanage GS, Christ's Coll Cambridge (LLB); *m* 1974 (m dis 1996), Judith Mary, da of Prof Edward Hall, of Upper Beeding, W Sussex; 2 s (Anthony, Frederick); *Career* chm Univ of Cambridge Assoc 1970; called to the Bar Inner Temple 1972; Parly candidate (C) W Bromwich E Oct 1974, MP (C) Putney 1979–; PPS to Francis Pym as Ldr of the House 1981; Parly under sec state: for energy 1981–83, Home Office 1983–86; min of state: Home Office 1986–87, FCO 1987–88, for health 1988–89, Home Office 1989–90, Privy Cncl Office (Min for the Arts) 1990; chief sec to the Treasury 1990–92, sec of state for Nat Heritage April-Sept 1992; columnist the Guardian 1992–95, book reviewer the Daily Telegraph, contrib to various newspapers; host 6.06 phone-in show (Radio Five Live, BBC Radio Personality of the Year 1995 Variety Club Awards) 1992–, presenter Vintage Years (BBC Radio 3), host Soapbox (BBC Radio 4); judge: Sony Radio Awards 1993, Whitbread Literary Prize 1993, Sunday Express Award for Fiction; chm Panel of Judges Science Book Awards 1994; chm Sports Aid Fndn 1993–, a govr Nat Youth Orchestra; hon assoc Br Vet Assoc 1986, tstee Richmond Theatre, memb Cncl Nat Youth Orchestra, former dep chm London Philharmonic Tst, former memb Bd ENO; FZS; *Style*— The Rt Hon David Mellor, QC, MP; ✉ House of Commons, London SW1A 0AA

MELLOR, His Hon Judge; David John; s of John Robert Mellor, of IOM, and Muriel, *née* Field; *b* 12 Oct 1940; *Educ* Plumtree Sch Southern Rhodesia (Zimbabwe), King's Coll London (LLB); *m* 21 May 1966, (Carol) Mary, da of David Morris Clement, CBE, of Sutton, Surrey; 2 da (Freya Mary Asquith b 1968, Annabelle Elizabeth Asquith b 1972); *Career* called to the Bar Inner Temple 1964, recorder of the Crown Ct 1986–89, circuit judge (SE Circuit) 1989–, princ judge in civil matters for Cambridgeshire, Norfolk and Suffolk 1991–; *Clubs* Norfolk; *Style*— His Hon Judge Mellor; ✉ Norwich Combined Court Centre, Bishopgate, Norwich NR3 1UR (☎ 01603 761776)

MELLOR, Derrick; CBE (1984); s of William Mellor, and Alice, *née* Hirst; *b* 11 Jan 1927; *m* 4 Feb 1954, Kathleen, *née* Hodgson; 2 s (Simon David b 1959, Michael John b 1962), 1 da (Helen Lucy b 1960); *Career* Army 1945–49; BOT 1950–57; Trade Cmmn Serv 1958–64: Kuala Lumpur and Sydney; Dip Serv 1961–: Malaysia, Australia, Denmark, Venezuela; ambass Paraguay 1979–84, ret 1984, re-employed FCO 1984–; occasional lectr SOAS, S American project dir GAP Int Youth Exchange; *Recreations* golf, tennis; *Clubs* Royal Cwlth, Travellers'; *Style*— Derrick Mellor, Esq, CBE; ✉ Summerford Farm, Withyham, E Sussex TN7 4DA (☎ 01892 770826); Foreign and Commonwealth Office, King Charles Street, London SW1A 2AH

MELLOR, Hugh Salisbury; s of Wing Cdr Harry Manners Mellor, MVO (ka 1940), and Diana Marion, *née* Wyld; *b* 16 March 1936; *Educ* Harrow, Christ Church Oxford (MA); *m* 6 Feb 1966, Sally, da of Flt Lt Clive Newton Wawn, DFC, RAF, of Victoria, Australia; 2 s (Nicholas Hugh b 29 May 1967, Andrew Harry Clive b 3 Jan 1970), 1 da (Sari b 14 July 1972); *Career* Nat Serv 2 Lt Coldstream Gds 1954–56; asst dir Morgan Grenfell & Co Ltd 1968 (joined 1960), exec Dalgety plc (formerly Dalgety Ltd) 1970–90 (bd memb 1968); dir: Pearl Group plc (formerly Australian Mutual Provident Society) 1979–94, Burmah Castrol plc (previously Burmah Oil plc) 1984–97, Bank of NZ (London) 1983–89, Meghraj Bank Ltd 1987–, Harrisons & Crosfield plc 1991–, Govett Oriental Investment Trust plc 1994–; fell RSPB, fell Br Tst for Ornithology; *Recreations* ornithology, entomology; *Style*— Hugh Mellor, Esq; ✉ Blackland Farm, Stewkley, Leighton Buzzard, Beds LU7 0EU

MELLOR, Ronald William; CBE (1984); s of William Mellor (d 1941), of Highgate, London, and Helen Edna, *née* Thomson (d 1952); *b* 8 Dec 1930; *Educ* Highgate Sch, King's Coll London (BSc); *m* 1 Sept 1956, Jean, da of Albert Sephton, of Rainhill; 1 s (Andrew John b 3 March 1961), 1 da (Ann Margaret b 10 July 1958); *Career* cmmnd 2 Lt Royal Artillery 1950, Capt Royal Artillery TA 1956; Ford Motor Company: mangr of Cortina product planning 1964, mangr of truck product planning 1965, chief res engr 1969, chief engine engr 1970, chief body engr Ford Werke AG W Germany 1974, vice pres of car engrg Ford of Europe Inc 1975–87, dir Ford Motor Company Ltd 1983–87; memb Bd of Govrs Anglia Poly Univ 1993–; Freeman City of London 1991, Liveryman Worshipful Co of Carmen 1991; FIMechE 1980 (memb Cncl 1985–87, chm Automobile Div 1986–87, sec 1987–93), FEng 1983; *Recreations* yachting; *Style*— Ronald Mellor, Esq, CBE, FEng; (☎ and fax 01245 400208)

MELLOR, Simon John; s of Raymond Mellor, and Phyllis, *née* Canter; *b* 10 Sept 1954; *Educ* Univ of Bristol (BSc); *m* 3 Feb 1990, (Carolyn) Mary, da of Ewen Langford; 2 da (Phoebe b 23 April 1991, Imogen b 12 July 1993), 2 step s (Dominic b 18 Nov 1975, Thomas b 23 June 1977); *Career* Saatchi & Saatchi Company plc: asst to Chm 1976–78, corp devpt mangr 1978–84, assoc dir 1984–, dir Main Bd 1985, dep chief exec offr Communications Div 1988, responsible for co's corp communication 1990, commercial dir Saatchi & Saatchi Advertising Worldwide 1991–94; gp commercial dir Blenheim Group Plc 1994–96, managing ptnr Humana International 1996–; Freeman City of London, memb Worshipful Co of Clockmakers; *Recreations* theatre, cinema, soccer, cricket; *Style*— Simon Mellor, Esq; ✉ Humana International, 14 Fulwood Place, London WC1V 6HZ (☎ 0171 831 9225, fax 0171 831 1225)

MELLORS, Prof Colin; s of George Mellors, and Phyllis, *née* Buxton; *b* 2 June 1949; *Educ* Firth Park GS Sheffield, Univ of Sheffield (BA, MA), Univ of Bradford (PhD); *Career* tutor Univ of Sheffield 1971–73, lectr in politics Univ of Southampton 1973–74; Univ of Bradford: lectr 1974–84, sr lectr 1984–94, dean Faculty of Social Scis 1992–94, prof 1994–, pro-vice-chllr 1994–; former tutor Open Univ and educn advsr NALGO; currently advsr and analyst BBC Political Unit; FRSA; *Books* British MP (1978), Promoting Local Authorities in the EC (1986), Local Government in the Community (jtly, 1987), Political Parties and Coalitions in European Local Government (jtly, 1988), EC Regional Policy (jtly, 1989), Training for Europe (ed, 1992), Language Training and Services for Business (ed, 1993), Managing without a Majority (1996); also author of numerous reports and articles in learned jls; *Recreations* photography, fell walking; *Style*— Prof Colin Mellors; ✉ University of Bradford, Bradford, West Yorkshire BD7 1DP (☎ 01274 383816, fax 01274 385720, e-mail C.Mellors@Bradford.ac.uk)

MELLOWS, Prof Anthony Roger Mellows; TD (1969); s of Laurence Beresford Mellows (d 1984), and Margery Phyllis, *née* Winch; *b* 30 July 1936; *Educ* King's Coll London (LLB, BD, LLM, PhD, LLD); *m* 1973, Elizabeth Angela Mellows (CStJ), da of Ven Benjamin George Burton Fox, MC, TD (d 1978); *Career* admitted slr, sr ptnr Alexanders Easton Kinch 1962–96, prof of the law of property London Univ 1974–90 (emeritus prof 1990); dir: Lord Rayleigh's Farms Inc 1980–89, Strutt and Parker (Farms) Ltd 1985–91; Liveryman City of London Solicitors' Co; GCStJ 1991 (KStJ 1988); chllr Order of St John 1991– (registrar 1988–91); *Books* Taxation for Executors and Trustees (1967, 6 edn 1984), Taxation of Land Transactions (1973, 3 edn 1982), The Law of Succession (1970, 4 edn 1983), The Modern Law of Trusts (jt 1966, 5 edn 1983); *Clubs* Athenaeum; *Style*— Prof Anthony Mellows, TD; ✉ 22 Devereux Court, Temple Bar, London WC2R 3JJ

MELLY, (Alan) George Heywood; s of Francis Heywood, and Edith Maud Melly; *b* 17 Aug 1926; *Educ* Stowe; *m* 1, 1955 (m dis 1962), Victoria Vaughan; 1 da; m 2, 1963, Diana Margaret Campion Dawson; 1 s, 1 step da; *Career* AB RN 1944–47; asst in London Gallery 1948–50; professional jazz singer, TV critic and film scriptwriter; with John Chilton's Feetwarmers 1974–; Critic of the Year IPC Nat Press Awards 1970; pres Br Humanist Assoc 1972–74; *Books* incl: I Flook (1962), Owning Up (1965), Revolt into Style (1970), Flook by Trog (1970), Rum Bum and Concertina (1977), The Media Mob (with Barry Fantoni, 1980), Tribe of One: Great Naive and Primitive Painters of the British Isles (1981), Mellymobile (1982), Scouse Mouse (1984), It's All Writ Out for Ye - the life and work of Scottie Wilson (1984), Paris and The Surrealists (with Michael Woods, 1991); *Recreations* trout fishing, singing and listening to 1920s blues, collecting modern painting; *Clubs* Colony Room, Chelsea Arts; *Style*— George Melly, Esq; ✉ 33 St Lawrence Terrace, London W10 5SR

MELMOTH, Graham; *m* Jenny; 2 s; *Career* early career with BOC, Fisons and Letraset; Co-operative Wholesale Society Ltd (CWS): joined 1975, sec 1976, chief exec 1996–; chm Ringway Development plc; pres International Co-operative Alliance (ICA); *Recreations* co-operative history and ideas, opera, theatre; *Style*— Graham Melmoth, Esq; ✉ Co-operative Wholesale Society Ltd, PO Box 53, New Century House, Manchester M60 4ES (☎ 0161 834 1212, fax 0161 833 1383)

MELROSE, Margaret Elstob; *née* Jackson; DL (Cheshire 1987); da of Samuel Chantler Jackson (d 1978), of Prestbury, Cheshire, and Annie Young, *née* Arnot (d 1978); *b* 2 May 1928; *Educ* Howell's Sch Denbigh, Girton Coll Cambridge (Drapers' Co Scholarship); *m* 19 June 1948 (m dis), Kenneth Ramsay Watson, s of late Albert Watson; assumed surname of Melrose by deed poll; 1 da (Joanne b 1953); *Career* vice consul for the Lebanon for N Eng, Scot and NI 1963–67; Cheshire CC: cncllr (Cons) 1967–, chm 1984–85 and 1986–87, sec Cons Gp 1973–75 and 1987–92, dep Cons whip 1975–77 and 1992–94, Cons chief whip 1977–83 and 1994–; cncllr: Macclesfield RDC 1968–74, Nether Alderley Parish Cncl (currently chm) 1968; gen cmmr of taxes Salford and N Manchester 1985–; chm: NW Regnl Children's Planning Ctee 1977–81, Bd of Govrs Crewe and Alsager Coll of Higher Educn 1978–88, Tatton Park Mgmnt Ctee 1985–, Manchester Airport Consultative Ctee 1986–, Cheshire Rural Community Cncl 1988–, Crewe and Alsager Coll of Higher Educn Inc Bd 1990–92 (vice chm 1988–90); vice chm David Lewis Centre for Epilepsy 1993– (dir 1989–), govr Manchester Met Univ 1993–; vice pres: Cheshire Agric Soc 1985– (lady patroness 1996–97), Ploughing and Hedgecutting Soc 1986–, Reaseheath Tst 1992–; memb Runcorn New Town Devpt Corp 1975–81, pres Macclesfield Constituency Cons Assoc 1988–95, vice chm Tatton Constituency Cons Assoc 1995–; memb Miny of Tport Sleep Res Steering Gp 1990–93, memb ESU 1995–; N of Eng Woman of the Year 1985, Cheshire Woman of the Year 1986; *Recreations* golf, sailing, horses, bridge, country life; *Clubs* Wilmslow Golf, Cheshire County; *Style*— Mrs Margaret Melrose, DL; ✉ The Coach House, Stamford Rd, Alderley Edge, Cheshire SK9 7NS (☎ 01625 585629, fax 01625 590647); County Hall, Chester CH1 1SG (☎ 01244 602424, telex 61347, DX no 19986, fax 01244 603800)

MELSOM, Andrew John; s of Maj John George Melsom, and Anne Sabine Rowbotham, *née* Pasley; *b* 1 Feb 1953; *Educ* Uppingham; *m* 2 Feb 1980, Melanie Clare, da of Maj Derek Hague, MC (d 1965); 2 s (Harry George b 8 Aug 1984, Jack Andrew b 25 Aug 1987, d 1988), 2 da (Edwina Lily b 11 Aug 1989, Cecily Kate b 23 Jan 1992); *Career* with Foote Cone and Belding 1971, dir J Walter Thompson 1982, founding ptnr BMP Business (Advertising) 1985; fndr Agency Insight (Search and Selection) 1994; author/dir Best of the Fringe Theatrical Revue Duke of York's Theatre 1976, memb Cncl of Management The Fndn for the Study of Infant Deaths; *Books* Are you there Moriarty? (Debrett's, 1979), Play it Again Moriarty (Debrett's, 1980), Codes of Advertising Practice Ctee (CAP) (1994); *Recreations* tennis, film; *Style*— Andrew J Melsom, Esq; ✉ South House, Ham, Marlborough, Wilts SN8 3RB (☎ 01488 668987, fax 01488 668912)

MELVILLE, (Richard) David; s of Col Robert Kenneth Melville, of London, and Joan Emerton, *née* Hawkins (d 1996); *b* 22 April 1953; *Educ* Wellington, Pembroke Coll Cambridge (MA); *m* 31 Oct 1981, Catharine Mary, da of late Hon William Granville Wingate, QC, of Heathfield, E Sussex; 1 s (Thomas Wingate b 29 Aug 1985), 1 da (Emma Rose b 21 July 1987); *Career* called to the Bar Inner Temple 1975; *Recreations* sailing; *Clubs* Royal Corinthian Yacht, Bar Yacht; *Style*— David Melville, Esq; ✉ 39 Essex St, London WC2R 3AT (☎ 0171 353 4741, fax 0171 353 3978)

MELVILLE, Prof David; s of Frederick George Melville (d 1981), and Mary, *née* Smith; *b* 4 April 1944; *Educ* Clitheroe Royal GS, Univ of Sheffield (BSc, PhD), Columbia Univ NYC (NASA scholarship, Dip in Space Physics); *children* 2 da (Ruth Helen b 27 July 1971, Jane Cathryn b 17 Nov 1973), 1 s (Richard Sean b 20 Oct 1975); *Career* Univ of Southampton: ICI res fell 1968, lectr in physics 1968–78, sr lectr in physics 1978–84; Lancashire Poly: prof and head Sch of Physics and Astronomy 1985–86, asst dir 1986–89, vice-rector 1989–91; vice-chllr Middlesex Univ 1992–96 (dir when Middlesex Poly 1991–92), chief exec Further Educn Funding Cncl 1996–; visiting researcher: CNR Italy 1974 and 1976, ICI plc 1975; visiting prof: Univ of Parma Italy 1974–79, Oporto Univ Portugal 1984; FInstP 1978; *Recreations* sailing, hill walking, skiing; *Clubs* IOD; *Style*— Prof David Melville; ✉ Rosebell Cottage, 12 Cross Street, Winchester, Hants SO23 8SZ; The Further Education Funding Council, Cheylesmore House, Quinton Road, Coventry CV1 2WT (☎ 01203 863192, fax 01203 863199)

MELVILLE, Sir Harry Work; KCB (1958); s of Thomas Melville (d 1973); *b* 27 April 1908; *Educ* George Heriot's Sch Edinburgh, Univ of Edinburgh (DSc, PhD), Trinity Coll Cambridge (PhD); *m* 1942, Janet Marian Cameron; 2 da; *Career* sci advsr Miny of Supply 1940–43, supt Radar Res Station 1943–45; prof of chemistry: Univ of Aberdeen 1940–48, Univ of Birmingham 1948–56; chief sci advsr for Civil Defence Midlands Region 1952–56, sec to Privy Cncl for Scientific and Industl Res 1956–65, chm SRC 1965–67, princ Queen Mary Coll London 1967–76, memb Parly and Scientific Ctee 1971–75; FRS, FRSE 1937; *Style*— Sir Harry Melville, KCB, FRS, FRSE; ✉ Norwood, Dodds Lane, Chalfont St Giles, Bucks (☎ 012407 872222)

MELVILLE, James; *see:* Martin, (Roy) Peter

MELVILLE, Nigel Edward; s of Maj E K L Melville (d 1991), and P D Melville; *b* 5 June 1945; *Educ* Sedbergh, Trinity Coll Oxford (MA), London Business Sch (MSc); *m* 15 Aug 1970, Maria Hadewij, *née* Van Oosten; 1 s (Christopher Patrick b 8 Dec 1978), 1 da (Sophie Olivia b 15 Dec 1980); *Career* with Baring Brothers rising to dir responsible for int corp fin 1974–95; currently ptnr Melville Partners; FCA; *Recreations* tennis, golf, skiing, flying; *Clubs* Hurlingham, Vanderbilt, Leckford Golf; *Style*— Nigel Melville, Esq; ✉ Melville Partners, 65 Duke Street, London W1M 6AJ (☎ 0171 495 3150, fax 0171 495 8990, e-mail 101736.1415@compuserve.com)

MELVILLE, 9 Viscount (UK 1802); Robert David Ross Dundas; also Baron Duneira (UK 1802); only s of Hon Robert Maldred St John Melville Dundas (ka 1940, yr s of 7 Viscount); suc uncle 1971; the 2 Viscount was First Lord of the Admty (1812–27 and 1828–30) and an enthusiast for Arctic exploration; Melville Sound is named after him; *b* 28 May 1937; *Educ* Cargilfield Sch, Wellington; *m* 23 July 1982, Fiona Margaret, da of late Roger Kirkpatrick Stilgoe, of Derby House, Stogumber, Taunton; 2 s (Robert b 1984, James David Brouncker b 19 Jan 1986); *Heir* s, Hon Robert Henry Kirkpatrick Dundas b 23 April 1984; *Career* served in Scots Gds (Nat Serv), Reserve Capt Scots Gds, Lt Ayrshire Yeo (TA); cncllr and dist cncllr Midlothian; pres Lasswade Civic Soc, tstee Poltonhall Community Assoc; *Recreations* shooting, fishing, golf, chess; *Clubs* Turf, Cavalry and Guards', Midlothian County, House of Lords Motor, Bonnyrigg and Dist Ex-Serviceman's (pres); *Style*— Capt Rt Hon the Viscount Melville; ✉ Norfolk House, 39 Portmore Park Road, Weybridge, Surrey; 3 Roland Way, London SW7 (☎ 0171 370 3553)

MELVILLE, Sir Ronald Henry; KCB (1964, CB 1952); s of Henry Edward Melville (d 1976), of Whitacre, Bengeo, Hertford; *b* 9 March 1912; *Educ* Charterhouse, Magdalene Coll Cambridge; *m* 1940, Enid Dorcas Margaret, da of late Harold Godfrey Kenyon, of Ware, Herts; 2 s, 1 da; *Career* entered Civil Serv 1934, asst under sec of state Air Miny 1946–58, dep under sec of state 1958–60, dep under sec of state War Office 1960–63, second perm under sec of state MOD 1963–66, perm sec Miny of Aviation 1966–71, attached Civil Serv Dept 1971–72, ret; dir Westland Aircraft 1974–82; dir Electronic Components Indust Fedn 1972–81; chm: Nat Rifle Assoc 1972–84, Jt Shooting Ctee for GB 1985–88; *Clubs* Brooks's; *Style*— Sir Ronald Melville, KCB; ✉ The Old Rose and Crown, Braughing, Ware, Herts

MELVILLE-ROSS, Timothy David (Tim); s of Lt Cdr Antony Stuart Melville-Ross, DSC, RN (ret) (d 1993), and Anne Barclay Fane, *née* Gamble; *b* 3 Oct 1944; *Educ* Uppingham, Portsmouth Coll of Technol (Dip); *m* 19 Aug 1967, Camilla Mary Harlackenden, da of Lt-Col Richard Harlackenden Cawardine Probert, of Bures, Suffolk; 2 s (Rupert b 1971, James b 1972), 1 da (Emma b 1975); *Career* chief exec Nationwide Building Society 1985–94; DG Institute of Directors 1994–; dir Monument Oil & Gas plc; memb Greenbury Ctee on executive remuneration 1995; *Recreations* reading, bridge, walking, the countryside, family; *Style*— Tim Melville-Ross, Esq; ✉ Little Bevills, Bures, Suffolk CO8 5JN (☎ 01787 227424); Institute of Directors, 116 Pall Mall, London SW1Y 5ED (☎ 0171 839 1233, fax 0171 930 1949)

MELVIN, Peter Anthony Paul; s of Charles George Thomas Melvin (d 1959), and Elsie, *née* Paul (d 1983); *b* 19 Sept 1933; *Educ* St Marylebone GS, Poly Sch of Architecture (DipArch); *m* 23 April 1960, Muriel, da of Col James Cornelis Adriaan Faure (d 1984); 2 s (Jeremy Paul b 1964, Stephen James b 1967), 1 da (Joanna Claire b 1962); *Career* architect; fndr ptnr Melvin Lansley & Mark until 1995, ptnr Atelier MLM 1995–; awards: RIBA Bronze medal for offices, vicarage and parish hall Tring 1975, Civic Tst awards for Tankerfield Place and Old Garden Court St Albans and violin workshop for W Hill & Sons; projects incl: Civic Centres Hemel Hempstead and Amersham, Emmanuel Church Guildford, HQ for Sir William Halcrow & Partners Swindon; RIBA: chm Eastern Region 1974–76, memb Cncl 1977–83 and 1985–88, vice pres 1982–83 and 1985–87; visiting fell Natal Sch of Architecture 1983; visiting tutor Dept of Architecture Univ of Dundee 1991–92; external examiner: Univ of Dundee 1993–, South Bank Univ 1994–; memb RIBA visiting bds to South Africa validating the Schs of Architecture at Univs of Capetown, Witwatersrand, Natal, the Orange Free State and Port Elizabeth 1995 and 1996; FRIBA 1971, FAE, FRSA; *Recreations* music, walking, sketching, looking; *Clubs* Arts; *Style*— Peter Melvin, Esq; ✉ Woodlands, Beechwood Drive, Aldbury, Tring, Hertfordshire HP23 5SB (☎ 01442 851211); Atelier MLM, Woodlands, Beechwood Drive, Aldbury, Tring, Hertfordshire HP23 5SB (☎ and fax 01442 851518)

MELZACK, Harold; s of Lewis Melzack (d 1938), and Celia, *née* Eisenstark (d 1987); *b* 6 Feb 1931; *Educ* Christ's Coll London, Coll of Estate Management; *m* 22 June 1954, June, da of Leonard Lesner, of London; 2 da (Gillian b 1957, Susan b 1960); *Career* chartered surveyor; jt founding sr ptnr Smith Melzack 1961 (currently sr conslt), former chm Br Numismatic Trade Assoc; Freeman: City of London, Worshipful Co of Chartered Surveyors; memb American Soc of Real Estate Cnsllrs; hon sec Lamda Alpha; FCIArb; *Recreations* golf, numismatics, historic documents, bridge; *Clubs* Arts, Hartsbourne Golf and Country, Bushey; *Style*— Harold Melzack, Esq; ✉ Smith Melzack, Sackville House, 40 Piccadilly, London W1V 0HQ (☎ 0171 393 4000, fax 0171 393 4114); Warnford Court, 29 Throgmorton Street, London EC2N 2AT

MELZER, (Arthur) David; OBE (1994); s of Albert Cecil Melzer (d 1982), of Brisbane, Australia, and Winifred Le Machond (d 1982); *b* 24 Aug 1932; *Educ* Brisbane Boys GS, Univ of Queensland (BSc, Dip Phys Ed); *m* 1957, Shirley Grace, da of William Tab Rooney, of Brisbane, Australia; 4 s; *Career* geologist; Premier Oil plc: dir 1982–97, exec offr Tech and Resource Devpt 1997–; md David Melzer Pty Ltd (Australia), chm Austral Communications (UK); *Recreations* walking, swimming, tennis; *Clubs* Oriental, Tanglin, Broome Park Country; *Style*— David Melzer, Esq, OBE; ✉ 24 Thorndon Hall, Ingrave, Essex CM13 3RJ (☎ 01277 812046); Premier Oil plc, 23 Lower Belgrave Street, London SW1W 0HR (☎ 0171 730 1111, fax 0171 730 4690)

MENAUL, Christopher; s of Stewart William Blacker Menaul (d 1987), and Helene Mary, *née* Taylor; *b* 25 July 1944, Cambridge, UK; *Educ* Hurstpierpoint Coll, St Catharine's Coll Cambridge; *m* 4 Feb 1989, Kathleen Elizabeth Mackie; *Career* film and television drama director; recent credits incl: Precious Bane (with Janet McTeer and John McEnery, BBC) 1989, Nice Work (with Warren Clarke and Haydn Gwynne, BBC) 1989, Prime Suspect (with Helen Mirren, Granada) 1991, A Dangerous Man - T E Lawrence

After Arabia (with Ralph Fiennes and Dennis Quilley) 1992, Fatherland (with Rutger Hauer and Miranda Richardson, HBO) 1994, Feast of July (with Embeth Davidtz, Merchant Ivory prodn) 1995; *Awards* for Precious Bane: nominated Best Single Drama RTS Awards 1989, winner Public Jury Prize Best Fiction Film Télévision Rencontres Européennes de Reims 1990; for Nice Work: Best Drama Serial RTS Awards 1989, nominated BFI TV Award 1990; for Prime Suspect: Best Drama Serial BAFTA 1991, Best Drama Broadcasting Press Guild Awards 1991, Best Drama Serial RTS Awards 1991, Best Drama and Best Mini Film Awards Banff Festival 1992, winner Golden Plaque Chicago Int Film Festival; for A Dangerous Man: Int Emmy Best Drama 1992; for Fatherland: Golden Globe nomination for Best Film; *Style*— Christopher Menaul, Esq; ✉ c/o Peters, Fraser & Dunlop Ltd, 503/4 The Chambers, Chelsea Harbour, London SW10 0XF (☎ 0171 344 1043); Creative Artists' Agency, 9830 Wilshire Boulevard, Beverley Hills, Calif 90212–1825 (☎ 00 1 310 288 4545)

MENDEL, Renée; da of Oscar Mendel (d 1940), of Hamburg, Germany, and Sophie Mendel (d 1946); *b* 22 Sept 1908; *Educ* Hamburg Lichtwark Schule; *Career* sculptor, studied with Ernesto de Fiori in Berlin and under Pablo Garfallo in Paris; exhibitions and subjects incl: Salon d'Automne Paris 1934, Lord Beaverbrook (Royal Academy) 1942, H E Jean Maisky 1943, Sir Laurence Olivier, Renee Asherson in Henry V (sculpture for the home, exhibited by Heals Department Store), The Beatles (Camden Arts Centre, sold at Sotheby's 1980) 1967, Idi Amin (Royal Exchange) 1977, James Joyce (wood carving, Nat Portrait Gallery) 1987, Dr H Winsley-Stolz, GP (bronze portrait head) 1989, Yassir Arafat and The Liquidator (Ben Uri Art Soc) 1993, The Art Show Alexander Palace (4 Exhibits) 1994; *Recreations* television (current affairs), keeping fit, travels; *Style*— Miss Renée Mendel; ✉ 27 Onslow Gardens, Muswell Hill, London N10 3JT

MENDELOW, Prof (Alexander) David; s of Harry Mendelow, of Johannesburg, and Ruby, *née* Palmer; *b* 19 May 1946; *Educ* Univ of Witwatersrand SA (MB BCh, PhD); *m* 2 s (Trevor Neil b 1971, Robert Kevin b 1974), 1 da (Toni Andrea b 1969); *Career* registrar in neurosurgery Univ of Witwatersrand and Johannesburg Hosp 1970–76, sr registrar Univ of Edinburgh 1977–79, sr lectr Univ of Glasgow 1980–86, prof of neurosurgery Univ of Newcastle upon Tyne 1987–; author of articles in scientific journals and books on head injury and stroke; memb: Royal Soc of Medicine, Soc of Br Neurosurgeons, Surgical Res Soc; convenor Br Neurosurgery Res Group; FRCSEd 1974; *Books* Fibre Systems of the Brain and Spinal Cord (1981); *Recreations* sailing; *Style*— Prof A David Mendelow; ✉ Department of Surgery (Neurosurgery), University of Newcastle, Regional Neurosciences Centre, Newcastle General Hospital, Westgate Road, Newcastle upon Tyne NE4 6BE (☎ 0191 273 8811, fax 0191 256 3267)

MENDELSOHN, (Heather) Leigh; da of Maurice Raymond Mendelsohn (d 1989), and Hazel Frances, *née* Keable; *b* 20 Feb 1946; *Educ* Fleetwood GS, Rothwell GS, Pudsey GS; *Career* trainee journalist R Ackrill Ltd Harrogate 1965–69, dep ed Action Desk Western Mail Cardiff 1969–71, dep Women's Page ed Daily Record Glasgow 1971–73, fashion ed Reveille London 1973–74, contract foreign corr The Sun Amsterdam 1975, freelance current affairs researcher 1976, PR conslt Market-Link PR 1976–78, fndr dir Phoenix PR 1978–; memb: NUJ, PRCA (memb Bd, chm Public Affrs Ctee); *Recreations* tennis, swimming, archery, gardening; *Style*— Ms Leigh Mendelsohn; ✉ Phoenix Public Relations, 105–107 Farringdon Rd, London EC1R 3BT (☎ 0171 833 8487, fax 0171 833 5726)

MENDELSOHN, Martin; s of Arthur Mendelsohn (d 1961), and Rebecca, *née* Caplin (d 1975); *b* 6 Nov 1935; *Educ* Hackney Downs Sch; *m* 20 Sept 1959, Phyllis Linda, da of late Abraham Sobell; 2 s (Paul Arthur b 1962, David Edward b 1964); *Career* admitted slr 1959; Adlers Solicitors: ptnr 1961–90, sr ptnr 1984–90, conslt 1990–92; ptnr MPM Consultancy 1990–92, ptnr Jaques & Lewis (now Eversheds) Solicitors 1992–; visiting prof of franchising and dir of the Centre for Franchise Research City Univ Business Sch, legal conslt Br Franchise Assoc; Int Bar Assoc: fndr chm Int Franchising Ctee of Section on Business Law, chm Membership Ctee 1988–92; warden Kenton Synagogue 1976–78, hon slr to various charitable instns; Freeman City of London 1964; Liveryman: Worshipful Co of Solicitors, Worshipful Co of Arbitrators; memb: The Law Soc, Int Bar Assoc, American Bar Assoc; FCIArb, FRSA; *Books* Obtaining A Franchise (for DTI 1977), Comment Negocier une Franchise (jtly, 1983), International Franchising - An Overview (ed, 1984), The Ethics of Franchising (1987, 2 edn 1995), How to Franchise your Business (jtly, 1989), How to Franchise Internationally (1989), The Journal of International Franchising and Distribution Law (ed), Franchising and the Block Exemption Regulation (jtly, 1991), The Guide to Franchising (5 edn 1992), Franchising in Europe (ed, 1992), Franchising and Business Development (A Study for the ILO Geneva) (1993), Franchising (jtly, 1995), Franchisor's Manual (2 edn 1996), How to Evaluate a Franchise (6 edn 1996); contrib and lectr to pubns and audiences worldwide; *Recreations* cricket, philately; *Clubs* MCC; *Style*— Martin Mendelsohn, Esq; ✉ 9 Sandown Court, Marsh Lane, Stanmore, Middlesex HA7 4HZ (☎ and fax 0181 954 9384, mobile 0385 396217); Eversheds, Senator House, 85 Queen Victoria Street, London EC4V 4JL (☎ 0171 919 4500, fax 0171 919 4919)

MENDELSON, Prof Maurice Harvey; QC (1992); s of William Maizel Mendelson (d 1959), of London, and Anne, *née* Aaronson; *b* 27 Aug 1943; *Educ* St Marylebone GS, New Coll Oxford (MA, DPhil); *m* 26 Dec 1968, Katherine Julia Olga, da of late Bertalan Kertesz, of London; 2 da (Charlotte b 1 Nov 1972, Rachel b 15 Sept 1974); *Career* called to the Bar Lincoln's Inn 1965, in practice 1971–; lectr in law King's Coll London 1968–74, fell and tutor in law St John's Coll Oxford 1975–86, prof of int law UCL 1987–; memb Exec Cncl Br Branch Int Law Assoc; *Recreations* painting, the arts, riding, swimming; *Clubs* Athenaeum; *Style*— Prof Maurice Mendelson, QC; ✉ Faculty of Laws, University College London, Bentham House, 4 Endsleigh Gardens, London WC1H OEG (☎ 0171 391 1428, fax 0171 387 9597); 2 Hare Court, Temple, London EC4Y 7BH (☎ 0171 583 1770, fax 0171 583 9269)

MENDELSON, Paul Anthony; s of Monty Mendelson (d 1992), of Pinner, Middx, and Yetta, *née* Dresner; *b* 6 April 1951; *Educ* Newcastle Royal GS, Glasgow HS, Harrow Co GS, Emmanuel Coll Cambridge (MA), Lancaster Gate Coll of Law; *m* 31 March 1974, Michal Zipora, da of Armand Safier; 2 da (Zoë Rachel b 17 April 1976, Tammy Polly b 3 Feb 1978); *Career* freelance TV writer; articled Gasquet Metcalf & Walton slrs 1973, trainee copywriter rising to creative gp head Ogilvy & Mather advtg agency 1973–80, dep creative dir Wasey Campbell Ewald 1980–82, creative gp head Dorland Advertising 1982–88, creative dir Capper Granger 1988–90, full-time freelance TV writer 1990–; creator and writer: May to December (BBC comedy series, nominated Best Comedy Series BAFTA 1990), So Haunt Me (BBC comedy series), Under the Moon (BBC); writer: Pigsty (BBC Children's TV), In the Matter of Isabel (film project in devpt); winner advtg awards incl: Cinema, TV and Best Radio Commercial and Best Radio Campaign (for Don't Drink and Drive) 1980, D&AD 1982, Best Media Commercial Clio 1982, Best Radio Commercial (food) Clio 1986; judge on various panels incl London Int Advtg Awards, British Comedy Awards; memb Writers' Guild 1991; *Recreations* walking, theatre, collecting Broadway musical recordings, carpentry, family; *Clubs* Groucho; *Style*— Paul A Mendelson, Esq; ✉ c/o Alan Brodie Representation, 211 Piccadilly, London W1V 9LD (☎ 0171 917 2871, fax 0171 917 2872)

MENDES, Samuel Alexander (Sam); s of James Peter Mendes, of London, and Valerie Hélène, *née* Barnett; *b* 1 Aug 1965; *Educ* Magdalen Coll Sch Oxford, Peterhouse Cambridge (scholar, BA); *Career* artistic director; asst dir Chichester Festival Theatre 1987–88, artistic dir Chichester Festival Theatre Tent 1988, artistic dir Minerva Studio Theatre Chichester 1989 (prodns incl Summerfolk and Love's Labours Lost), freelance dir, currently artistic dir Donmar Warehouse; *Theatre* prodns incl: London Assurance (Chichester and Haymarket) 1989, The Cherry Orchard (Aldwych) 1989, Troilus and Cressida (RSC, Swan) 1990, Kean (Old Vic and Toronto) 1990, Plough and the Stars (Young Vic) 1991, The Alchemist (RSC, Swan) 1991, The Sea (RNT) 1991, The Rise and Fall of Little Voice (RNT and Aldwych, Olivier and Evening Standard Awards) 1992, Richard III (RSC regnl and world tour) 1992, Assassins (Donmar Warehouse, Critics' Circle Award) 1992, Translations (Donmar Warehouse) 1993, The Tempest (RSC, RST) 1993, Cabaret (Donmar Warehouse and Carlton TV) 1993, The Birthday Party (RNT) 1994, Glengarry Glen Ross (Donmar Warehouse) 1994, Oliver! (London Palladium) 1994, The Glass Menagerie (Donmar Warehouse and Comedy) 1995, Habeas Corpus (Donmar Warehouse) 1996; *Awards* winner of Hamburg Shakespeare Scholarship 1989, London Critics' Circle Most Promising Newcomer Award 1989, Olivier Award for Best Director (for Company and The Glass Menagerie) 1996; *Recreations* watching and playing cricket; *Style*— Sam Mendes, Esq; ✉ c/o Donmar Warehouse, Earlham Street, London WC2H 9LD

MENDONÇA, Dennis Raymond; s of Walter Mendonça, and Adelaide, *née* De Souza; *b* 9 Oct 1939; *Educ* Med Coll Bombay (MB BS, MS), Univ of London (retraining), FRCS; *m* 1, 8 Dec 1966 (m dis 1993), Dr Lorna Maria Mendonca, da of late Joaquim Noguer; 2 s (Neil Dennis b 25 July 1967, Nolan Andrew b 2 Sept 1971), 1 da (Nicola Maria b 3 Dec 1969); m 2, 19 March 1994, Judith Mary (barr), da of late Dr Cyril Lynch; *Career* surgn in England 1967–; sr house surgn Farnborough Kent, registrar Ashford Folkstone and Dover, sr registrar for ENT Sheffield and Leicester, sr registrar Univ of Toronto (sabbatical year), conslt ENT surgn Queen Mary's Univ Hosp London 1975–, private practice Harley St; memb: Med Protection Soc, Br Assoc of Otolaryntology, GMC; FCPS (India) 1966; *Recreations* playing the piano, accordion, guitar and tennis; *Style*— Dennis R Mendonça, Esq; ✉ 2 Roedean Crescent, Roehampton, London SW15 5JU (☎ and fax 0181 878 7271); 138 Harley St, London W1N 1AH (☎ 0171 486 9416); Queen Mary's University Hospital, Roehampton Lane, London SW15 5PN (☎ 0181 789 5124, fax 0181 789 3099)

MENDOZA, June Yvonne; da of John Morton, and Dot, *née* Mendoza; *Educ* Lauriston Girls' Sch Melbourne, St Martin's Sch of Art; *m* Keith Mackrell; 1 s (Ashley), 3 da (Elliet, Kim, Lee); *Career* portrait painter; work for governments, regiments, med, academia, theatres, literature and sport; exhibited in public and private int collections; portraits incl: HM The Queen, HRH The Prince of Wales, HRH The Princess of Wales, HM Queen Elizabeth The Queen Mother, The Princess Royal, Margaret Thatcher, The Most Rev the Rt Hon Archbishop of Canterbury, Corazon Aquino (former pres of the Philippines), Vigdis Finnbogadottir (pres of Iceland), Ratu Sir Kamisese Mara (PM of Fiji), Sir John Gorton (former PM of Australia); gp portraits incl: House of Commons in Session, Cncl Royal Coll of Surgns, Australian House of Representatives; continuing series of musicians incl: Yehudi Menuhin, Georg Solti, Joan Sutherland, Paul Tortelier; memb: Royal Soc of Portrait Painters, Royal Inst of Oil Painters; Hon DLitt: Univ of Bath 1986, Loughborough Univ 1994; Officer of the Order of Australia 1989; *Style*— Miss June Mendoza; ✉ 34 Inner Park Rd, London SW19 6DD

MENEVIA, Bishop of (RC) 1987–; Rt Rev Daniel Joseph Mullins; s of Timothy Mullins (d 1968), of Kilfinane, Co Limerick, and Mary, *née* Nunan; *b* 10 July 1929; *Educ* Mount Melleray, St Mary's Aberystwyth, Oscott Coll, Univ Coll of S Wales and Monmouth (BA); *Career* ordained priest 1953; curate: Barry 1953–56, Newbridge 1956, Bargoed 1956–57, Maesteg 1957–60; asst chaplain to Univ Coll Cardiff 1964–68, vicar gen Archdiocese of Cardiff 1968, auxiliary bishop 1970–87; chm Ctee for Catechetics, memb Ct of Govrs Univ Coll Swansea, pres Catholic Record Soc; fell Univ Coll Cardiff, hon fell St David's Univ Coll Lampeter; *Recreations* golf, walking; *Style*— The Rt Rev the Bishop of Menevia; ✉ 79 Walter Road, Swansea, West Glamorgan SA1 4PS (☎ 01792 650534); Curial Offices, Diocese of Menevia, 115 Walter Road, Swansea, West Glamorgan SA1 5RE (☎ 01792 644017)

MENHENNET, Dr David; CB (1991); s of Thomas William Menhennet (d 1970), of Redruth, Cornwall, and Everill Waters, *née* Nettle (d 1992); old Cornish families, both sides; *b* 4 Dec 1928; *Educ* Truro Sch Cornwall, Oriel Coll Oxford (BA), Queen's Coll Oxford (MA, DPhil); *m* 29 Dec 1954, Audrey, da of William Holmes (d 1958), of Accrington, Lancs; 2 s (Mark b 1956, Andrew b 1958); *Career* librarian House of Commons 1976–91 (dep librarian 1967–76, joined 1954); gen ed House of Commons Library Documents Series 1972–90; chm Bibliographic Servs Advsy Ctee Br Library 1986–92, memb Exec Ctee Friends of the Nat Libraries 1991–96; visiting fell Goldsmiths' Coll Univ of London 1990–; FRSA 1966; Liveryman Worshipful Co of Stationers & Newspaper Makers 1990; *Books* Parliament in Perspective (with J Palmer, 1967), The Journal of the House of Commons: A Bibliographical and Historical Guide (1971), The House of Commons in the Twentieth Century (contrib, 1979), The House of Commons Library: a History (1991); *Recreations* country walking, gardening, lecturing, family history, visiting old churches; *Clubs* Athenaeum; *Style*— Dr David Menhennet, CB; ✉ 50 Kelsey Lane, Beckenham, Kent BR3 3NE

MENIN, Rt Rev Malcolm James; *see:* Knaresborough, Bishop of

MENKES-SPANIER, Suzy Peta; da of Edouard Gerald Lionel Menkes (d 1943), and Betty Curtis, *née* Lightfoot; *b* 24 Dec 1943; *Educ* Brighton and Hove HS, Newnham Coll Cambridge (BA, MA); *m* 23 June 1969, David Graham Spanier, s of Eric John Spanier (d 1973); 3 s (Gideon Eric Lionel b 26 Sept 1971, Joshua Edward Graham b 11 Nov 1973, Samson Curtis b 3 Oct 1978), 1 da (Jessica Leonie Salome b 24 May 1977, d 1977); *Career* jr reporter The Times London 1966–69, fashion ed The Evening Standard 1969–77, women's ed Daily Express 1977–80; fashion ed: The Times 1980–87, The Independent 1987–88, International Herald Tribune 1988–; Freeman of Milan 1987; *Books* The Knitwear Revolution (1983), The Royal Jewels (1985), The Windsor Style (1987), Queen and Country (1992); *Recreations* family life; *Style*— Mrs Suzy Menkes-Spanier; ✉ International Herald Tribune, 181 Avenue Charles de Gaulle, 92521 Neuilly, France (☎ 00 33 1 41 43 93 41, fax 00 33 1 41 43 93 38)

MENSFORTH, Sir Eric; kt (1962), CBE (1945), DL (South Yorks 1971); s of Sir Holberry Mensforth, KCB, CBE (d 1951); *b* 17 May 1906; *Educ* Altrincham HS, Univ Coll Sch, King's Coll Cambridge (MA); *m* 1934, Betty, JP (d 1996), da of late Rev Picton W Francis; 3 da (Elizabeth, Rosemary, Susan); *Career* dir, chm and pres Westland Aircraft Ltd, dep chm John Brown and Co Ltd, dir Boddy Industries Ltd; chm Governing Body Sheffield Poly 1969–75, gen treas Br Assoc for Sci 1971–76; Vice Lord Lt S Yorks 1974–81; Master Co of Cutlers in Hallamshire 1965–66, Liveryman Worshipful Co of Coachmakers & Coach Harness Makers; FEng 1976; *Publications* Extracts from the records of the Cutlers' Company, Family Engineers, Clogs to Clogs; *Clubs* Alpine, RAC; *Style*— Sir Eric Mensforth, CBE, DL, FEng; ✉ 42 Oakmead Green, Woodcote Side, Epsom, Surrey KT18 7JS (☎ 01372 742313)

MENTER, Sir James Woodham; kt (1973); s of late Horace Menter, and late Jane Anne, *née* Lackenby; *b* 22 Aug 1921; *Educ* Dover GS, Peterhouse Cambridge (MA, PhD, ScD); *m* 1947, Marjorie Jean, da of late Thomas Stodart Whyte-Smith, WS; 2 s, 1 da; *Career* treas and vice pres Royal Soc 1972–76, princ Queen Mary Coll London Univ 1976–86; dir: Tube Investmts Res Laboratories 1961–68, Tube Investmts 1965–86, Br Petroleum Co 1976–87, Steetley Co 1981–85; memb Ct Univ of Stirling 1987–95; FRS, Hon FRSE; *Style*— Sir James Menter, FRS; ✉ Carie, Kinloch Rannoch, by Pitlochry, Perthshire

MENTETH, *see:* Stuart-Menteth

MENUHIN, Baron (Life Peer UK 1993), of Stoke D'Abernon in the County of Surrey; Sir Yehudi Menuhin; OM (1987), KBE (1965); s of Moshe Menuhin (d 1988), and Marutha Menuhin, *née* Sher (d 1996, aged 100); *b* 22 April 1916, NY; *Educ* privately; *m* 1, 1938, Nola Ruby Nicholas, of Australia; 1 s (Hon Krov), 1 da (Hon Zamira Benthall); m 2, 1947, Diana Rosamond Gould; 2 s (Hon Gerard, Hon Jeremy); *Career* violinist and conductor; début with San Francisco Orch aged 7; gave over 500 concerts during WWII; artistic dir Bath Festival for 10 years and fndr Bath Festival Orch; fndr: Yehudi Menuhin Sch Surrey 1963, Int Menuhin Music Acad Gstaad (venue of summer Festival since 1956), Live Music Now (a charitable orgn); fndr and conductor Asian Youth Orch, princ guest conductor English String Orch; pres: Euro String Teachers' Assoc, Young Musicians' Symphony Orch, Musicians' Int Mutual Aid Fund; UNESCO: former pres (served full term of six years) Int Music Cncl, ambass of goodwill 1992–; pres and assoc conductor RPO and Hallé Orch; sr fell RCA, hon fell and pres Trinity Coll of Music; hon doctorates incl: Oxford (1962), St Andrews (1963), Queen's Belfast (1965), London (1969), Cambridge (1970), Ottawa (1975), Sorbonne (1976); Hon Freeman Worshipful Co of Musicians; Epée D'Academicien (Academie de Beaux Arts 1988); awards and honours for WWII, humanitarianism and music incl: Croix de Lorraine (Fr), Ordre de la Couronne and Ordre de Léopold (Belgium), Order of Merit (FDR), Nehru Peace Prize (for raising famine funds) India 1968, Buber-Rosenzweig Medaille (Gesellschaften für Christlich-Jüdische Zusammen-Arbeit) Bonn 1990; medals of Cities of Paris New York and Jerusalem, Cobbett medal Worshipful Co of Musicians, Gold and Mozart medals Royal Philharmonic Soc 1962 and 1965, Gold medal Canadian Music Cncl 1975, Albert medal RSA 1981, Una Vita Nella Musica Italy 1983, Brahms medal Hamburg 1987, Brahms Orden Hamburg 1988, Gold medal Univ of Cordoba 1990, Glenn Gould prize Canada 1990; Yehudi Menuhin and Luciano Berio Wolf prize 1991; *Publications* incl: Menuhin Music Guides, Unfinished Journey (autobiography, awarded Peace Prize of German Book Fedn), Music of Man (also CBC TV series), Conversations with Menuhin (with Robin Daniels), The King, the Cat and the Fiddle (for children, with Christopher Hope), Life Class; *Clubs* Athenaeum, Garrick; *Style*— The Rt Hon the Lord Menuhin, OM, KBE; ✉ c/o Sym Music Co, 110 Gloucester Avenue, London NW1 8JA (☎ 0171 586 5958, fax 0171 730 0150)

MENZIES, (Iain) Alasdair Graham; s of Maj Ian Menzies (1979), of London, and Alice, *née* Stoettinger; *b* 7 Jan 1952; *Educ* Eton, Sorbonne Univ; *m* 1974, Sandra Francoise, da of Cyril Bertram Mills; 3 s (Alexander Graham, Andrew Ian Graham, Jonathan Harwood Graham); *Career* md Merrill Lynch 1984–88 (sales exec 1971–80, dir 1980–84), dir Schroder Securities 1988–91, dir James Capel & Co Ltd 1991–; *Recreations* skiing, classic cars; *Clubs* White's, Annabel's; *Style*— Alasdair Menzies, Esq; ✉ James Capel & Co Ltd, Thames Exchange, 10 Queen Street Place, London EC4R 1BL (☎ 0171 336 2324, fax 0171 621 0639)

MENZIES, Duncan Adam Young; QC (Scot 1991); s of Douglas William Livingstone Menzies (d 1977), of Edinburgh, Margaret Adam, *née* Young; *b* 28 Aug 1953; *Educ* The Edinburgh Acad, Cargilfield Sch, Glenalmond (scholar), Wadham Coll Oxford (scholar, MA), Univ of Edinburgh (LLB); *m* 31 March 1979, Hilary Elizabeth McLauchlan, da of Col T R R Weston, OBE, TD; 2 s (Jamie Douglas Adam b 1985, Ruaraidh Duncan McLauchlan b 1988); *Career* admitted Faculty of Advocates 1978, standing jr counsel to Admiralty Bd 1984–91, memb Faculty ADR Panel 1991–, temp sheriff 1996–; Parly candidate (C): Midlothian 1983, Edinburgh Leith 1987; chm Ptarmigan Wines 1979–89; *Recreations* shooting, golf, wine, gardening; *Clubs* New (Edinburgh), Hon Co of Edinburgh Golfers; *Style*— Duncan Menzies, Esq, QC; ✉ Leaston House, Humbie, East Lothian EH36 5PD (☎ 01875 833219, fax 01875 833348); Advocates' Library, Parliament House, Edinburgh EH1 1RF (☎ 0131 226 5071, fax 0131 225 3642, car 0831 526330)

MENZIES, Ian William; s of Adam Menzies (d 1946), of Muirhead, Glasgow, and Margaret McDermid Stewart, *née* Colvin (d 1961); *b* 30 Dec 1927; *Educ* Coatbridge Sch Strathclyde, Royal Tech Coll Glasgow (BSc), Univ of London (LLB); *m* 1, 3 May 1952, June Alice (d 1978), da of Joseph Mullard (d 1951), of Liverpool; 3 da (Margaret b 1952, Sheena b 1955, Alison b 1957); m 2, 8 Oct 1983, Dr Monica Patricia Hunter, da of Thomas Burrows (d 1995), of Swansea; 3 step da (Nicola b 1963, Francesca b 1965, Lizette b 1972); *Career* Nat Serv 2 Lt RAEC 1947–49, 2 Lt RE RARO 1949–82; res engr Kuwait 1954–56, ptnr Menzies & Durkin Zambia 1956–59, res engr Ghana 1960–62, ptnr Charles Weiss & Ptnrs 1975–87, dir Charles Weiss Partnership Ltd 1987–95, conslt Ernest Green Partnership Ltd 1995–; chm Chartered Inst Arbitrators 1991–92; govr W Kent Coll; Freeman City of London, Liveryman Worshipful Co of Arbitrators; FICE, MIStructE, FCIArb, FRSA; *Recreations* armory, genealogy, cosmology; *Style*— Ian Menzies, Esq; ✉ Ernest Green Partnership Ltd, 63 Croydon Road, London SE20 7TS (☎ 0181 659 9040, fax 0181 676 9515)

MENZIES, Dr John Barrie; s of late Henry John Menzies, of Sibsey, Boston, Lincs, and late Eva Ellen Menzies; *b* 7 Nov 1937; *Educ* Univ of Birmingham (BSc, PhD), City Univ (Dip CU); *m* 2 Sept 1961, Ann, da of late Frank Naylor; 2 s (Ian Anthony b 17 Nov 1963, Robert John b 4 Aug 1965), 1 da (Theresa Margaret b 4 Oct 1962); *Career* dir Geotechnics and Structures Gp Building Res Estab DOE 1982–1990 (joined 1962), ptnr Andrews Kent & Stone Consltg Engrs 1990–92; hon prof of engrg Univ of Warwick 1988–; vice chm Construction and Building Standards Ctee BSI 1990–91; chm: EC Task Gp on Actions 1985–90, Eurocode for Actions Sub Ctee Euro Ctee for Standardisation 1990–; memb Standing Ctee on Structural Safety 1988–91 (sec 1991–); pres Br Masonry Soc 1989, vice chm Br Gp Int Assoc for Bridge and Structural Engrg; IStructE: hon treas 1988–89, hon sec 1989–90; FIStructE 1977, FEng 1989; *Recreations* travel, good food and wine, swimming, walking; *Style*— Dr John B Menzies, FEng; ✉ 42 Sheepcot Lane, Garston, Watford, Hertfordshire WD2 6DT (☎ 01923 675106); Engineering Conslt (☎ 01923 675106, fax 01923 680695)

MENZIES, John Maxwell; s of John Francis Menzies (d 1940), and Cynthia Mary, *née* Graham (d 1988); *b* 13 Oct 1926; *Educ* Eton; *m* 4 June 1953, Patricia Elinor Trevor, yst da of Cdr Sir Hugh Trevor Dawson, 2 Bt, CBE (d 1976); 4 da (Miranda Jane (Mrs Jenkinson) b 1954, Sarah Jane (Mrs Speke) b 1955, Cynthia Emma (Mrs Harrison) b 1958, Katherine Patricia (Mrs Slater) b 1960); *Career* Lt Grenadier Gds 1945–48; chm: John Menzies plc 1952–, Ivory & Sime Enterprise Capital PLC (formerly Independent Investment Co plc) 1983– (dir 1973–), Atlantic Assets Trust 1983–88 (dir 1973–78), Rocky Mountains Oil & Gas Ltd 1980–85, Personal Assets Trust plc 1981–92, Bank of Scotland plc 1984–94, Guardian Royal Exchange plc 1984–, Guardian Royal Exchange Assurance 1985–, Malcolm Innes Gallery Ltd 1989–; dir: Scottish American Mortgage Co 1959–63, Standard Life Assurance Co 1960–63, Vidal Sassoon Inc 1969–80, Nimslo International Ltd 1970–85, Gordon & Gotch plc 1970–85, Ivory & Sime plc 1980–83, Kames Dairies Ltd 1995–; tstee: Newsvendors Benevolent Instn (pres 1968–74), Nat Library of Scotland 1991–; memb: Berwickshire CC 1954–57, Royal Co of Archers (Queen's Body Guard for Scotland); landowner (2600 acres); *Recreations* farming, shooting, reading, travel; *Clubs* Beefsteak, Boodle's, New (Edinburgh); *Style*— John Menzies, Esq; ✉ Kames, Duns, Berwickshire TD11 3RD (☎ 01890 840202); John Menzies plc, 108 Princes St, Edinburgh EH2 3AA (☎ 0131 225 8555, fax 0131 226 3752)

MENZIES, Sir Peter Thomson; kt (1972); s of John Caithness Menzies (d 1918), and Helen, *née* Aikman; *b* 15 April 1912; *Educ* Musselburgh GS, Univ of Edinburgh (MA); *m* 1, 1938, Mary McPherson Alexander (d 1992), da of late John Turner Menzies, and Agnes, *née* Anderson; 1 s (Ian), 1 da (Cecilia); m 2, 1994, Muriel, da of late Harold McKee Langton and Ethel, *née* Miles; *Career* dep chm ICI 1967–72 (joined 1939, dir 1956–72); chm Imperial Metal Industs 1964–72 (joined 1962); dir: Commercial Union Assurance Co 1962–1982, Nat West Bank 1968–82; chm: Electricity Cncl 1972–77, London Exec Ctee Scottish Cncl (devpt and indust) 1977–82; gen treas and vice pres Br Assoc for the Advancement of Sci 1981–86; *Clubs* Caledonian; *Style*— Sir Peter Menzies; ✉ 9 Fern Grove, Welwyn Garden City, Herts AL8 7ND (☎ 01707 327234)

MENZIES, (Rowan) Robin; s of Capt George Cunningham Paton Menzies, DSO (d 1968), and Constance Rosabel, *née* Grice Hutchinson; *b* 30 Oct 1952; *Educ* Stowe, Trinity Coll Cambridge (BA); *Career* ptnr Baillie Gifford and Co (investmt mangrs); *Style*— Robin Menzies, Esq; ✉ 1 Rutland Court, Edinburgh EH3 8EY (☎ 0131 222 4000, fax 0131 222 4488)

MENZIES-WILSON, William Napier; CBE (1985); s of James Robert Menzies-Wilson (d 1977), of Fotheringhay Lodge, Nassington, nr Peterborough, and Jacobine Joanna Napier, *née* Williamson-Napier (d 1955); *b* 4 Dec 1926; *Educ* Winchester, New Coll Oxford (MA), Northwestern Univ Chicago; *m* 25 July 1953, Mary Elizabeth Darnell, da of Ralph Juckes, MC (d 1982), of Fiddington Manor, nr Tewkesbury, Glos; 2 s (Charles Napier b 1957, James Ralph b 1959), 1 da (Gillian Elizabeth b 1960); *Career* Lt Rifle Bde 1945–47; dir Stewarts & Lloyds Ltd 1964 (joined 1950), dir supplies & tport British Steel Corporation 1968–72; chm: Ocean Transport and Trading plc 1980–87 (dir 1972–80), Edinburgh Tankers plc, Forth Tankers plc, Celtic Tankers plc; dir NFC plc 1986–95; chm Help The Aged 1987–95; *Recreations* gardening, shooting, golf; *Clubs* Hon Co of Edinburgh Golfers; *Style*— William Menzies-Wilson, Esq, CBE; ✉ Last House, Old, nr Northampton NN6 9RJ (☎ 01604 781346, fax 01604 781036, London ☎ 0181 994 4793)

MERCER, Prof Alan; s of Harold Mercer (d 1954), of Stocksbridge, and Alice Ellen, *née* Catterall; *b* 22 Aug 1931; *Educ* Penistone GS, Univ of Cambridge (MA, Dip Math Stat), Univ of London (PhD); *m* 7 Aug 1954, Lillian Iris, da of Charles Frederick Pigott (d 1988), of Penistone; 2 s (Jonathan Andrew Timothy b 1959, Nicholas Anthony Julian b 1961); *Career* NCB 1954–56, UKAEA 1956–62, Armour and Co Ltd 1962–64; Univ of Lancaster: joined 1964, prof of operational research 1968–, chm Sch of Mgmnt and Organisational Sciences 1982–85; memb: Central Lancs Devpt Corp 1971–85, NW Econ Planning Cncl 1973–79, Mgmnt and Industl Rels Ctee SSRC 1972–76 and 1980–82; chm: employers side of Whitley Cncl for New Towns Staff 1979–89 (memb 1971–), Indust and Employment Ctee ESRC 1984–87 (vice chm 1982–84), Warrington and Runcorn Devpt Corp 1986–89 (memb 1985–); memb Operation Res Soc 1955; *Books* Operational Distribution Research (jtly, 1978), Implementable Marketing Reseach (1991), European Journal of Operational Research (jt ed); *Recreations* travel, walking, sport; *Style*— Prof Alan Mercer; ✉ South Cottage, Calton, Airton, Skipton, N Yorks BD23 4AD (☎ 01729 830542); The Management School, Lancaster University, Bailrigg, Lancaster LA1 4YX (☎ 01524 593864, fax 01524 844885, telex 65111 LANCUL G)

MERCER, Dr (Robert) Giles Graham; s of Leonard Mercer (d 1961), of Langholm, Dumfriesshire, and Florence Elizabeth, *née* Graham; *b* 30 May 1949; *Educ* Austin Friars Sch Carlisle, Churchill Coll Cambridge (MA), St John's Coll Oxford (DPhil); *m* 2 March 1974, Caroline Mary, da of Alfred Harold Brougham (d 1983), of Tackley, Oxfordshire; 1 s (Edward b 1977); *Career* head of history Charterhouse Sch 1974–76, asst princ MOD 1976–78, dir of studies and head of history Sherborne Sch 1979–85; headmaster: Stonyhurst Coll 1985–96, Prior Park Coll Bath 1996–; FRSA 1983; *Books* The Teaching of Gasparino Barzizza (1979); *Recreations* swimming, art, music, reading; *Clubs* Athenaeum, Public Schools, E India; *Style*— Dr Giles Mercer; ✉ Kent House, Prior Park College, Bath BA2 5AH (☎ 01225 835353, fax 01225 835753)

MERCER, Prof Ian Dews; CBE (1996); s of Eric Baden Royds Mercer (d 1955), of Herongate, Wombourn, Staffs, and Nellie Irene, *née* Dews; *b* 25 Jan 1933; *Educ* King Edward's Sch Stourbridge, Univ of Birmingham (BA); *m* 1, 7 July 1957 (m dis 1976), Valerie Jean, da of late Eric Hodgson; 4 s (Jonathan b 1958, Benjamin b 1961, Thomas b 1963, Daniel b 1966); m 2, 10 Dec 1976, Pamela Margaret Gillies, da of Maj Thomas Waldy Clarkson; *Career* Nat Serv Sub-Lt RNR 1954–56; warden Slapton Ley Field Centre Kingsbridge Devon 1959–68, lectr St Luke's Coll Exeter 1968–70, co conservation offr Devon CC 1970–73, chief offr Dartmoor Nat Park Authy 1973–90, chief exec Countryside Cncl for Wales 1990–96; sec gen Assoc of Nat Park Authorities 1996–; prof of rural conservation practice Univ of Wales 1991–; pres: Field Studies Cncl, Devon Wildlife Tst, Devonshire Assoc 1983, Assoc of Countryside Rangers 1986–93; chm Regnl Advsy Ctee W England Forestry Cmmn 1987–90, chm Devon Rural Community Cncl 1996–; memb: England Ctee Nature Conservancy Cncl 1977–87, Gen Advsy Ctee BBC 1981–86, Br Ecological Soc, Landscape Res Gp, Devon and Cornwall Ctee Nat Tst, Inland Waterways Amenity Advsy Cncl 1995–; govr Univ of Plymouth 1996–; Hon LLD Exeter 1994, Hon DSc Plymouth 1995; *Books* Nature Guide to South West England, Conservation in Practice (contrib, 1973), Environmental Education (contrib, 1974), National Parks in Britain (contrib, 1987); *Recreations* golf, painting, birdwatching, watching sons play rugby; *Style*— Prof Ian Mercer, CBE; ✉ Ponsford House, Moretonhampstead, Newton Abbot, Devon TQ13 8NL (☎ 01647 440612)

MERCER, (Andrew) Philip; s of Maj Laurence Walter Mercer (d 1951), of Huntingtower, Perthshire, and Josephine Madeline, *née* Moran; *b* 24 Aug 1937; *Educ* Stonyhurst, Univ of Edinburgh (BArch); *m* 2 Oct 1965, Alexandra Margaret, da of Capt John Cyril Dawson, of Sussex; 2 da (Claudia Alexandra b 1977, Portia Andrea b (twin) 1977); *Career* chartered architect; princ of architectural practice 1969– (specialising in planning and restoration in Central London and historic bldgs in Scot); ARIBA; *Recreations* skiing, yachting, tennis, travelling; *Style*— Philip Mercer, Esq; ✉ Hillslap Tower, Roxburghshire; 79 Bedford Gardens, London W8 7EF

MERCER, Roger James; s of Alan James Mercer, and Patricia, *née* Hicks; *b* 12 Sept 1944; *Educ* Harrow Co GS, Univ of Edinburgh (MA); *m* 28 March 1970, Susan Jane, da of (William) Stephen Fowlie: 1 s (Andrew James b 3 Dec 1981), 1 da (Katherine Jane b 26 Aug 1975); *Career* inspr of ancient monuments Dept of the Environment 1969–74; Dept of Prehistoric Archaeology Univ of Edinburgh: lectr in archaeology 1974–82, reader in archaeology 1982–90, actg head of dept 1983–87; sec Royal Cmmn on the Ancient and Historical Monuments of Scotland 1990–; Br Acad/Br Gas reader 1990; vice pres: Prehistoric Soc 1987–91 (treas 1972–76), Soc of Antiquaries of Scotland 1988–92 (treas 1977–87), Cncl for Br Archaeology 1991–94; external examiner Univs of Durham, Birmingham, Cambridge, Newcastle and York; FSA(Scot) 1969, FSA 1976, MIFA, FRSE; *Books* Hambledon Hill - A Neolithic Landscape (1981), Grimes Graves Excavations 2 vols (1981), The Excavation of a Neolithic Enclosure Complex at Carn Brea, Illogan, Cornwall (1981), Causewayed Enclosures (1990); *Recreations* music, reading; *Clubs* New (Edinburgh); *Style*— Roger Mercer, Esq, FSA, FRSE; ✉ 4 Old Church Lane, Duddingston, Edinburgh EH13 3PX; Royal Commission on the Ancient and Historical Monuments of Scotland, John Sinclair House, 16 Bernard Terrace, Edinburgh EH8 9NX (☎ 0131 662 1456)

MERCER, Terence; s of Sydney Agnew Mercer (d 1971), of N Yorks, and Mollie, *née* Lewis (d 1971); *b* 4 Sept 1931; *Educ* Ermysteds GS Skipton Yorks, Leeds Coll of Commerce; *m* 21 Nov 1959, Frances Karene, da of Col Francis Henry Jordan, DSO, MC (d 1975); 2 s (Nicholas Justin b 1962, Simon Jonathan Jordan de Suakville b 1965); *Career* cmmnd Army, served MELF 1954–56, AER 1956–59; chm Tattersall Advertising Ltd Harrogate 1971–; memb Cncl: Audit Bureau of Circulations 1991–93, Ripon Cathedral Tst Appeal, Ripon Diocesan Synod 1970–73, Nat Tst Fountains Abbey Appeal 1984–85; hon publicity advsr: Save the Children Fund, Yorks North Cons Euro Constituency Cncl

1981–83, IAM, ROSPA, Noise Abatement Soc; hon life memb Friends of Harrogate and District Museums 1989; fndr benefactor of The Mercer Gallery Harrogate; FZS, FRSA, MIPA; *Recreations* field sports, charity work, sketching, politics; *Style*— Terence Mercer, Esq; ✉ Low Bridge House, Markington, Harrogate, North Yorkshire HG3 3PQ (☎ 01765 677393); Tattersall Advertising Ltd, Harrogate, North Yorkshire HG1 5LL (☎ 01423 504676, fax 01423 508092)

MERCER, Dr Wendy Sara; da of Charles William Mercer (d 1976), of Castletown, Isle of Man, and Thelma Margaret Hawkins (formerly Mercer), *née* Higgins; *b* 23 Dec 1956; *Educ* Bedford Coll London (BA, MA), Univ of London (PhD), Sch of Educn Univ of Durham (PGCE), Heidelberg Univ; *Career* French teacher Greycoat Sch Westminster 1979–80, lectr Université de Paris X (Nanterre) 1981–83, visiting lectr in French Bedford Coll London 1983–84, visiting lectr Royal Holloway and Bedford New Coll London 1984–85 and 1988–91, pt/t visiting lectr in French Buckingham Univ 1984–85, lectr Ecole Normale Supérieure Fontenay-aux-Roses 1985–87, pt/t chargée de cours Ecole Nationale de Statistique et d'Administration Economique 1985–87, pt/t res asst UCL 1987–88, British Acad Postdoctoral Res Fellowship RHBNC and UCL 1988–91, lectr Dept of French UCL 1991–; Medaille d'honneur Ville de Pontarlier 1992; *Books* Xavier Marmier (1808–1892) - Un Fils de Pontarlier Célèbre dans le Monde, Jane Osborn - Drama by Léonie d'Aunet (ed), Voyage d'une Femme au Spitzberg (ed, by Léonie D'Aunet); *Style*— Dr Wendy Mercer; ✉ Department of French, University College London, Gower Street, London WC1E 6BT (☎ 0171 387 7050)

MERCER, Dr William Leslie (Les); s of Edward Mercer, of Horwich, Lancs, and Louisa, *née* Meadows; *b* 7 Oct 1932; *Educ* Wigan GS, Univ of Leeds (BSc, PhD); *m* 14 Aug 1954, Barbara Ann, da of Reginald Platt; 2 s (Andrew David b 10 Aug 1955, Geoffrey Ian b 20 June 1959); *Career* res engr GEC/SC Atomic Energy Gp (later UPC, then APC); British Gas plc (and predecessor bodies): joined 1965, station dir Engrg Res Station 1978–88, dir Research Resources 1988–93, ret; pres: Inst of Gas Engrs 1984–85, Inst of Metals 1990–92; sen Engrg Cncl 1997–; FIM 1972, FIGasE 1979, FEng 1985; *Recreations* technology, the open air, travel, photography, bridge; *Style*— Dr Les Mercer, FEng; ✉ 6 Rowthorn Drive, Solihull, West Midlands B90 4ST

MERCER NAIRNE, Lord Robert Harold; s of 8 Marquess of Lansdowne, PC; *b* 1947; *Educ* Gordonstoun, Univ of Kent at Canterbury (BA), Univ of Washington Graduate Sch of Business Admin (MBA), PhD; *m* 1972, Jane Elizabeth, da of Lt-Col Lord Douglas Gordon; 2 s, 1 da; *Career* md Blackman Martin Group 1972–82, self-employed 1982–83, Univ of Washington 1983–89, managing tstee Meikleour Tst 1989–; memb River Tay Flood Steering Gp 1990–94; elder Church of Scotland 1990–; hon lectr Univ of Dundee 1992–; Liveryman Worshipful Co of Fishmongers; FIMgt; *Style*— Lord Robert Mercer Nairne; ✉ Kinclaven Church House, Kinclaven, by Stanley, Perth PH1 4QW

MERCHANT, Piers Rolf Garfield; MP (C) Beckenham (majority 15,285); s of Garfield Frederick Merchant, of Nottingham, by his w Audrey Mary Rolfe-Martin; *b* 2 Jan 1951; *Educ* Nottingham HS, Univ of Durham (MA); *m* 1977, Helen Joan, da of James Frederick Albert Burrluck, of Colchester; 1 s (Rolf b 9 Oct 1991), 1 da (Alethea); *Career* news ed The Journal 1980–82 (joined as reporter 1973), ed Conservative Newsline 1982–84; Parly candidate Newcastle Central 1979; MP: Newcastle Central (after boundary change) 1983–87, Beckenham 1992–; PPS to Rt Hon Peter Lilley Sec of State for Social Security 1992–; dir of corp publicity Northern Engineering Industries plc 1987–90, dir of public affrs The Advertising Association 1990–92; co-chm Freeflow of Info Ctee Int Parly Gp 1986–89, vice chm All-Party Parly Ctee on AIDS 1987; *Recreations* DIY, electronics, genealogy; *Clubs* Sr Common Room of Univ Coll Durham; *Style*— Piers Merchant, Esq, MP; ✉ House of Commons, London SW1 1AA (☎ 0171 219 6314, e-mail MERCHANTMP@AOL.com)

MERCIER, Sheila Betty; da of Herbert Dobson Rix (d 1966), and Fanny Nicholson; *b* 1 Jan 1919; *Educ* French Convent Hull, Hunmanby Hall E Yorks, Randle Ayrton Coll of Drama Stratford on Avon; *m* 26 March 1951, Peter Edward Alexander Mercier, s of Capt Charles Jerome Andrew Nicholas Mercier, of London; 1 s (Nigel David b 6 Dec 1954); *Career* actress; WWII LACW WAAF Signals 1941–44, section offr, asst adj and adj 1944–46; post-war played all over the country with various Repertory Theatre as leading lady, next eleven years spent at the Whitehall Theatre with brother Sir Brian Rix (now Lord Rix), has spent the last twenty three years playing Annie Sugden in the Yorkshire TV soap opera Emmerdale Farm (now Emmerdale); memb Cons Assoc; *Style*— Mrs Sheila Mercier; ✉ 16 Oakfield, Hawkhurst, Kent TN18 4JR (☎ 01580 754 718)

MEREDITH, David Wynn; s of John Ellis Meredith (d 1981), of Aberystwyth, Dyfed, and Elizabeth, *née* Jones; *b* 24 May 1941; *Educ* Ardwyn GS Aberystwyth, Normal Coll Bangor Gwynedd (Univ of Wales Teaching Dip); *m* 23 March 1968, Luned, da of Prof Emeritus Alun Llywelyn Williams; 3 c (Owain Llywelyn b 11 Feb 1969, Elin Wynn b 6 Jan 1971, Gruffydd Seimon Morgan b 7 Feb 1974); *Career* specialist teacher Welsh Cardiff Educn Authy 1961–65, mid-Wales mangr then advtg and sales exec Wales Tourist Bd 1965–68, head of press and PR HTV Cymru/Wales 1968–89, fndr dir STRATA (PR co) 1989–90, estab David Meredith PR 1990–95, head of press and PR S4C Television 1995–; reg contrib to radio and TV in Wales; presenter in Eng and Welsh HTV: Pwy Fase'n Meddwl (quiz series), Gair o Wlad y Sais (lit prog), Arlunwyr (art series); memb: Royal Welsh Show Publicity Ctee 1969–, Welsh Ctee Live Music Now 1990–, Mktg Bd Nat Eisteddfod of Wales 1990–, Presbyterian Church of Wales Publicity Ctee; fell PR Soc of Wales 1984 (former chm); *Books* Michelangelo (Life and Work), Rembrandt (Life and Work); Congrinero (for children), Anturiaethan Fôn Fawr a Bili Bach (for children, with Owain Meredith); *Recreations* pottering on the farm, visiting art galleries and growing trees; *Style*— David Meredith, Esq; ✉ Head of Press, Corporate and Public Relations, S4C, Parc Ty Glas, Llanishen, Caerdydd CF4 5GG (☎ 01222 747444, fax 01222 741457)

MEREDITH, George Hubbard; s of George Thomas Meredith (d 1959), of Birmingham, and Ivy Lilian, *née* Hubbard (d 1972); *b* 16 Jan 1943; *Educ* Marlborough; *m* 9 April 1983, Wendy, da of Frank David Gardiner, of Yeovil, Devon; 1 s (John b 1991), 2 da (Claire b 1984, Jane b 1986); *Career* called to the Bar Gray's Inn 1969; in practice: London 1970–72, Exeter 1972– (head of Chambers 1975–90); dep district judge 1991–95; hon sec and librarian Exeter Law Library Soc, chm tstees Belmont Chapel; *Recreations* family life, reading, photography, hill walking; *Style*— George Meredith, Esq; ✉ 33 Southernhay East, Exeter, Devon (☎ 01392 55777, fax 01392 412021, DX 8353)

MEREDITH-HARDY, Michael Francis; s of late Howard Meredith-Hardy; *b* 12 May 1923; *Educ* Eton, Pembroke Coll Cambridge; *m* 1955, Penelope Jane Meredith-Hardy, OBE, JP, *qv*, da of late Hon Bartholomew Pleydell-Bouverie, OBE, s of 6 Earl of Radnor and late Lady Doreen Pleydell-Bouverie, da of 6 Earl of Donoughmore; 4 s; *Career* joined 5 Royal Inniskilling Dragoon Gds 1942, Maj 1947, Capt City of London Yeo TA, Staff Offr London Armd Div TA 1948–55; barr 1951–76; chm: Nat Insur Appeal Tbnl DHSS 1967–95, Nat Insur Appeal Tbnl Dept of Employment 1967–95, Appeal Bd Road Traffic Act 1972–91; examiner High Ct of Justice 1969–89, immigration appeal adjudicator Immigration Appeals Authy 1980–94; High Sheriff of Hertford 1980; *Recreations* painting; *Style*— Michael Meredith-Hardy, Esq; ✉ Radwell Mill, Baldock, Herts SG7 5ET (☎ 01462 730242)

MEREDITH-HARDY, Penelope Jane; OBE (1995), JP (Herts 1973); da of late Hon Bartholomew Pleydell-Bouverie, s of 6 Earl of Radnor and late Doreen Pleydell-Bouverie, da of 6 Earl of Donoughmore; *b* 4 Nov 1932; *m* 1955, Michael Francis Meredith-Hardy, *qv*, s of late Howard Meredith-Hardy; 4 s; *Career* memb: Supplementary Benefits Tbnl 1972–89, Stevenage Drugsline 1975–82, Herts Link Scheme 1983–, Herts Caretrusts 1986–, Herts Probation Ctee 1978– (chm 1987–93), Central Probation Cncl 1989–95 (chm Ct and Community Ctee 1990–95); tstee Herts Alcohol Problems and Advice Serv 1996–, chm Herts branch Magistrates Assoc 1996–; *Style*— Mrs Penelope Meredith-Hardy, OBE, JP; ✉ Radwell Mill, Baldock, Herts SG7 5ET (☎ 01462 730242)

MEREDITH-HARDY, Richard; s of Michael Francis Meredith-Hardy, *qv*, of Baldock, Herts, and Penelope Jane Meredith-Hardy, *qv*, *née* Pleydell-Bouverie; *b* 23 Aug 1957; *Educ* Eton, Birmingham Poly; *m* 5 Dec 1987, Nicola Louise, da of Hugh Morgan Lindsay Smith, of Downham Market, Norfolk; 1 s (Hugo b 11 Jan 1994), 2 da (Alexandra b 29 Dec 1990, Isobel b 23 Oct 1992); *Career* property developer, farmer, explorer; organiser of safaris to Africa 1980 and 1981; microlight aircraft pilot; achievements: first flight from London to Capetown 1985–86, Steve Hunt Meml Trophy winner 1986 and 1988, Br Nat champion 1987, 1988 and 1990, Gold Colibri winner 1988, Euro individual and team champion 1988–91, World Cup champion 1989–90, World individual champion 1990–92, memb World Champion Team 1990–94, Spanish nat champion 1991, team awarded Royal Aero Club's Britannia Trophy 1991, 3 world speed records FAI Class R1 1991–95, Light Aviation Navigation Award Royal Inst of Navigation 1995; pilot camera-ship: Running High (C4) 1990, Dacron Eagles (BBC 1) 1992; sec Assoc of Microlight Professionals 1992–, memb Cncl British Microlight Aircraft Assoc 1994–; *Recreations* flying; *Clubs* AMP, BMAA, Royal Aero; *Style*— Richard Meredith-Hardy, Esq; ✉ Radwell Lodge, Baldock, Herts SG7 5ES (☎ 01462 834 776)

MEREDITH HARDY, Simon Patrick; s of Patrick Talbot Meredith Hardy (d 1986), of Bembridge, IOW, and Anne, *née* Johnson; *b* 31 Oct 1943; *Educ* Eton; *m* 26 July 1969, Hon Joanna Mary, da of Baron Porritt, GCMG, GCVO, CBE (Life Peer); 2 s (Henry Patrick b 1975, George Peter b 1978); *Career* cmmnd LG 1964, ADC to HE The Govr Gen of NZ 1967–68, left army 1969; stockbroker; formerly ptnr Wood Mackenzie & Co, dir NatWest Securities Ltd; MSI; *Recreations* skiing, sailing; *Clubs* City of London, Household Division Yacht, Bembridge Sailing; *Style*— Simon P Meredith Hardy, Esq; ✉ Natwest Securities Ltd 135 Bishopsgate, London EC2M 3UR (☎ 0171 375 5000)

MEREDITH-WINDLE, Glynis Margaret; da of Donald Charles Frank Windle (d 1978), of London, and Gwynneth Maud, *née* Meredith (d 1988); *b* 14 Aug 1951; *Educ* Parliament Hill Sch for Girls (hockey blue, hockey capt), Hendon Gp of Hosps Sch of Nursing (SRN), Central Sch of Counselling and Therapy (Cert in Counselling 1991); *Career* qualified SRN 1973, med ward sister (then yst in UK) 1974, sister various med and coronary care units NHS hosps 1974–80; Llewelyn-Davies Weeks: joined as nurse planning conslt 1980, pioneer of patient-focused healthcare in UK (in association with Booz Allen and Hamilton) 1989, assoc LDW 1992–95; independent conslt to Dept of Health and others as Meredith-Windle Associates Health Planning Consultancy 1996–; fundraiser Sir Robert Mond Meml Tst for research into mental illness; ARCN 1970, MIHSM 1989, MInstD 1996; *Recreations* golf, cycling, badminton, reading, theatre, opera, Cajun dancing; *Clubs* Champneys, Aldwickbury Golf; *Style*— Ms Glynis M Meredith-Windle; ✉ Meredith-Windle Associates, 8 Dell Close, Harpenden, Herts AL5 4HP (☎ 01582 621539)

MERIFIELD, Anthony James; CB (1994); s of Francis Bertram Merifield (d 1964), of Chesterfield; *b* 5 March 1934; *Educ* Chesterfield Sch, Shrewsbury Sch, Wadham Coll Oxford (MA); *m* 6 Sept 1980, Pamela, da of Frederick Joseph Pratt (d 1982), of Manchester; *Career* Nat Serv 1952–54, 2 Lt 2 Royal Tank Regt; HM Overseas Civil Serv Kenya 1958–65; DHSS: princ 1965–71, asst sec 1971–77, under sec Industs and Exports Div 1978–79, under sec and dir of establishments HQ (DHSS) 1979–82; asst under sec of state NI Office 1982–86, under sec Dept of Health 1986–91 (memb NHS Mgmnt Bd and dir of Health Authy liaison 1986–88, dir of regional liaison 1989–91), under sec and head Senior and Public Appointments Gp Cabinet Office 1991–94, ceremonial offr Cabinet Office 1994–; memb RSA; *Clubs* Royal Cwlth Soc, Dulwich and Sydenham Hill Golf; *Style*— Anthony Merifield, Esq, CB; ✉ Cabinet Office, 53 Parliament Street, London SW1A 2NG (☎ 0171 210 5058)

MERLYN-REES, Baron (Life Peer UK 1992), of Morley and South Leeds in the County of West Yorkshire and of Cilfynydd in the County of Mid Glamorgan; Merlyn Merlyn-Rees; PC (1974); s of Levi Daniel Rees, of Cilfynydd, S Wales; assumed the surname of Merlyn-Rees by Deed Poll 1992; *b* 18 Dec 1920; *Educ* Harrow Weald GS, Goldsmiths' Coll London, LSE, Univ of London Inst of Educn; *m* 1949, Colleen Faith, da of Henry F Cleveley, of Kenton, Middx; 3 s (Hon Patrick Merlyn b 1954, Hon Gareth David b 1956, Hon Glyn Robert b 1960); *Career* served WWII RAF; schoolmaster (economics and history) 1949–60, economics lectr 1962–63; Parly candidate (Lab) Harrow E 1955, 1959 (twice, general election and by-election); MP (Lab): S Leeds 1963–83, Leeds S and Morley 1983–92; PPS to Chllr of the Exchequer 1964, Parly under sec at the MOD for the Army 1965–66 and RAF 1966–68, under sec of state Home Office 1968–70, oppn spokesman on NI and memb Shadow Cabinet 1972–74, NI sec 1974–76, home sec 1976–79, shadow home sec 1979–81, oppn front bench spokesman on energy 1981–83; memb: Franks Ctee on Official Secrets Act 1972, Franks Ctee on Falklands 1982; chm S Leeds Groundwork Tst; tstee, Groundwork Tst, Apex Tst; memb bd Municipal Mutual Insurance; pres Video Standards Cncl; chllr Univ of Glamorgan; Hon DLL Univ of Wales, Hon LLD Leeds 1992; *Books* Northern Ireland, A Personal Perspective (1985); *Style*— The Rt Hon Lord Merlyn-Rees, PC; ✉ c/o House of Lords, London SW1A 0PW

MERRICK, (Denise) Holly; da of Max Richardson, of London, and Daphne May, *née* Taylor; *b* 6 Feb 1946; *Educ* Hitchin GS for Girls, Univ of Reading, Univ of Sydney; *m* 1967 (m dis 1986), Colin Merrick; 1 s (Simon-Peter b 1968), 2 da (Kate b 1971, Sophy b (twin) 1971); m 2, 1995, Christopher Borkowski; *Career* product mangr General Foods International 1980–81 (asst product mangr 1979–80), consumer mktg mangr Cross Paperware (Bowater) 1981–84, mktg dir Sheaffer Pen Textron 1984–86, divnl gen mangr Thornton (confectioners) 1986–87, managing conslt and head of retail & mktg Binder-Hamlyn/BDO Consulting 1987–88, md Marketing Solutions Ltd 1990–94 (managing conslt and dir 1988–90), mktg dir Thermos Ltd 1994–95; dir/tstee Music in Oxford Ltd; memb: Mktg Soc 1986, IGD 1987; *Style*— Ms Holly Merrick

MERRICK, District Judge John Sebastian; *b* 13 June 1942; *Educ* Rose Hill Prep Sch Tunbridge Wells, St Albans Cathedral Sch, Law Soc Coll of Law; *Career* articled slr London 1959, admitted 1964; ptnr Berry and Berry Slrs 1970–92 (asst slr 1965–70), district judge (SE Circuit) 1992– (dep district judge 1981–92); memb: Law Soc, Int Bar Assoc, Assoc of Hungarian Lawyers; assoc Chartered Inst of Arbitrators; scout ldr 1965–85 (Wood badge, Long Serv Award, Chief Scouts Commendation); *Recreations* hillwalking (Mountain Leadership Cert, instructor ten yrs), travel, theatre, art, cooking, literature, fitness training, music, mediation, after dinner speaking, Nat Tst, William Morris Soc; *Clubs* Rotary; *Style*— District Judge J S Merrick; ✉ The Law Courts, William Street, Brighton, East Sussex BN2 2LG (☎ 01273 674421)

MERRICKS, Walter Hugh; s of Dick Merricks, of Icklesham, Rye, E Sussex, and Phoebe, *née* Woffenden (d 1985); *b* 4 June 1945; *Educ* Bradfield Coll Berks, Trinity Coll Oxford (MA); *m* 27 Nov 1982, Olivia, da of late Dr Elio Montuschi; 1 s (William b 1983), 1 da (Susannah b 1986), 1 step s (Daniel b 1971); *Career* admitted slr 1970, Hubbard travelling scholar 1971, dir Camden Community Law Centre 1972–76, lectr in law Brunel Univ 1976–81, legal affrs writer New Law Jl 1982–85, dir of professional and legal policy Law Soc 1995–96 (head of communications 1985–95), Insurance Ombudsman

1996–; memb: Royal Cmmn on Criminal Procedure 1978–81, Ctee on Fraud Trials 1984–86, Cncl King Alfred Sch; memb Law Soc 1970; *Style*— Walter Merricks, Esq; ✉ Insurance Ombudsman Bureau, City Gate One, 135 Park Street, London SE1 9EA (☎ 0171 928 4488, fax 0171 401 8700)

MERRIDALE, Philip David; CBE (1988); s of Ernest David Merridale (d 1970), of St Albans, Herts, and Ruby Edith, *née* Paull (d 1965); *b* 2 May 1927; *Educ* St Albans Sch; *m* 10 Sept 1955, (Judith) Anne Bonynge, da of Ernest James Parry (d 1972), of Romsey, Hants; 1 s (David b 1956), 2 da (Catherine b 1959, Alison b 1962); *Career* RA 1945, Intelligence Corps 1946–48; commercial supervisor Marconi Instruments Ltd, antiques and fine arts dealer 1958–88, licensed lay reader Diocese of Winchester 1968–88, memb Hants CC 1973–88; chm: Ramsey and Stockbridge Dist Cncl 1968–67, Hants Educn Authy 1974–88, Nat Cncl of Local Educn Authys 1983, Educn Ctee of Assoc of CCs 1983–85, Teaching as a Career for Sec of State DES 1990–, Corp of Rutland Coll 1994–; ldr Employers Panel for Teachers Pay Negotiations 1983–85, govr Portsmouth Poly 1974–88, memb Midlands Industl Tbnl 1988–; FRSA 1985; *Recreations* walking in the countryside; *Style*— Philip Merridale, Esq, CBE; ✉ April Cottage, Pilton, Rutland LE15 9PA (☎ 01780 720092)

MERRIFIELD, Air Cdre Anthony John; s of Rev Sidney Merrifield (d 1980), of Brooke, Norfolk, and Elizabeth Sarah Ann (d 1979); *b* 4 Aug 1926; *Educ* King's Sch Ely Cambs, KCH London (MB BS); *m* 2 Dec 1950, (Gwynedd Frances) Poppy, da of James Parker (d 1967), of Gosport, Hants; 2 s (Charles Matthew b 1952, Robin St Clair b 1954); *Career* RAF Med Branch 1951–87: conslt anaesthetist 1962, dir of anaesthetics 1973, Whittingham prof of aviation med 1985–87, QHP 1985–87; Joseph Clover lectr and Medal 1986, Pask Cert of Hon Assoc of Anaesthetists 1987; memb Bd Govrs King's Sch Ely; numerous contribs to med jls; memb: RSM, BMA, Assoc of Anaesthetics; MRCS 1950, FFARCS 1956, MIBiol 1973; *Recreations* boating, photography, music, reading; *Clubs* RAF; *Style*— Air Cdre Anthony Merrifield; ✉ 2 Barton Square, Ely, Cambs CB7 4DF (☎ 01353 664850)

MERRILLS, Austin; OBE (1981); s of Austin Merrills; *b* 15 April 1928; *Educ* King Edward VII Sch Sheffield, Univ of Sheffield; *m* 1953, Daphne Olivia, *née* Coates; 1 s, 2 da; *Career* chm Ireland Alloys (Holdings) Ltd; vice chm Bd of Govrs Glasgow Sch of Art; FRSA; *Recreations* skiing, biking, walking, rugby (spectator), travel, paintings and sculpture, food and wine, gardens; *Clubs* Caledonian; *Style*— Austin Merrills, Esq, OBE; ✉ The East Wing, Tyninghame House, Dunbar, East Lothian EH42 1XW (☎ 01620 860834, fax 01620 860669; office ☎ 01698 822461, fax 01698 825167)

MERRIMAN, District Judge Richard John; *b* 30 April 1947; *Educ* Oakham Sch, Univ of Liverpool (LLB); *m* 21 Aug 1971, Sheila Hepburn, da of Barclay Hepburn Reid; 1 da (Alexandra Jane b 17 June 1975), 1 s (Daniel George b 30 Nov 1977); *Career* admitted slr 1971, dep registrar Midland & Oxford Circuit 1986–92, district judge Leicester 1992–; memb Law Soc; *Recreations* squash, swimming, walking; *Style*— District Judge Merriman; ✉ Leicester County Court, 90 Wellington Street, Leicester

MERRISON, Lady; Maureen Michèle; da of John Michael Barry (d 1944), and Winifred Alice, *née* Raymond; *b* 29 Oct 1938; *Educ* Royal Masonic Sch for Girls, Bedford Coll Univ of London (BA); *m* 23 May 1970, as his 2 w, Sir Alexander (Alec) Walter Merrison, DL, FRS (d 1989), s of Henry Walter Merrison (d 1965); 1 s (Benedict b 1974), 1 da (Andria b 1972); *Career* lectr in history Univ of Bristol 1964–90; dir: HTV Group plc 1982–, Bristol and West Building Society 1990–, Western Provident Assoc 1990–, Greater Bristol Tst 1987–96; memb Bristol Devpt Corp 1993–96; vice pres Bishop Bristol's Urban Fund 1989–90, chm of Govrs Colston's Girls Sch 1992–96, chm Advsy Ctee on Historic Wreck Sites 1996–; govr Millfield Sch; FRSA 1993; *Style*— Lady Merrison; ✉ The Manor, Hinton Blewett, Bristol BS18 5AN (☎ 01761 452259); HTV Group plc, The Television Centre, Culverhouse Cross, Cardiff CF5 6XJ (☎ 0117 977 83660/0222 590590, fax 01222 59613, telex 497703)

MERRITT, Prof John Edward; s of Leonard Merritt (d 1942), and Janet Merritt (d 1960); *b* 13 June 1926; *Educ* Gosforth Modern Sch, Univ of Durham (BA), UCL (DipEdPsychol); *m* 12 June 1948, Denise, da of John George Redvers Edmundson (d 1965); 2 s (Austen David, John Quentin); *Career* RAF 1944–45, Green Howards 1945, Sandhurst RMA 1945–46, Lt Border Regt 1946–48; educnl psychologist Lancs LEA 1957–59, sr educnl psychologist Hull LEA 1960–64, lectr Univ of Durham 1964–70, prof of teacher educn Open Univ; chm Fifth World Congress on Reading Vienna 1974; memb Nat Cmmn of Inquiry into Uses of English 1973–75; Int Merit Award Int Reading Assoc 1977; Hon FCP 1994; *Books* Reading and the Curriculum (1971), The Reading Curriculum (1972), Reading: Today and Tomorrow (1972), What Shall We Teach? (1974); *Recreations* fell walking, climbing, running, theatre; *Clubs* Ambleside Amateur Athletics; *Style*— Prof John Merritt; ✉ Wetherlam, Fisherbeck Park, Ambleside, Cumbria LA22 OAJ (☎ 015394 32259)

MERRITT, Prof Neil; s of Leslie Alfred Merritt (d 1976), of Essex, and Gladys Irene Merritt; *b* 3 March 1939; *Educ* County HS Ilford Essex, Univ of Hull (LLB); *m* 5 Aug 1961, Jean, da of Geoffrey and Kay Fisher; 1 s (Giles Dominic b 25 Aug 1968), 1 da (Hannah Lucy Victoria b 28 Feb 1972); *Career* various teaching posts in law 1962–74, dep dir Chelmer Inst of Higher Educn (now Anglia Poly Univ) 1973–76, dir Ealing Coll of Higher Educn (became Poly of W London, now Thames Valley Univ) 1977–91 (prof ad hominem), vice-chllr Univ of Portsmouth 1992–94 (pres Portsmouth Poly 1991–92); visiting prof of law Indiana Univ Bloomington USA 1974 and 1976; chm/sec Assoc of Law Teachers 1965–72, sec/chm Standing Conf of Princs of Colls 1977–91, tstee/vice-chm Central Bureau for Educnl Visits and Exchanges 1980–86, vice-chm/chm Univs and Colls Employers Forum 1988–92, pres Euro Assoc of Higher Educn 1990–92 (hon pres 1993), chm Hillingdon Hosp Tst W London 1990–95, UK delegate Cncl of Europe Standing Conf on Univ Problems 1990–94; memb Nat Advsy Bd for Public Sector Higher Educn 1982–88; FRSA; *Books* Business Law (with E G Clayton, 1966); author of various newspaper and jl articles (esp Journal of Business Law, Management Decision and Festchriften); *Recreations* writing, sailing, opera, music; *Style*— Prof Neil Merritt

MERRIVALE, 3 Baron (UK 1925); Jack Henry Edmond Duke; s of 2 Baron, OBE (d 1951); *b* 27 Jan 1917; *Educ* Dulwich, private tuition SW France, Ecole des Sciences Politiques Paris; *m* 1, 30 Sept 1939 (m dis 1974), Colette, da of John Douglas Wise; 1 s, 1 da; m 2, 1975, Betty, widow of Paul Baron; *Heir* s, Hon Derek John Philip Duke; *Career* joined RAF 1940, Flt Lt 1944 (despatches); formerly chm Scotia Investments Ltd, past pres Anglo-Malagasy Soc; past pres: Inst of Traffic Admin, Railway Devpt Assoc; formerly chm Br Ctee for the Furthering of Rels with French-Speaking Africa; chm: Grecian Investments (Gibraltar) Ltd 1990–, GB-Senegal Friendship Assoc 1991; Chev Nat Order of Malagasy 1968, Cdr Nat Order of the Lion (Senegal) 1992; fndr memb Club of Dakar 1974; Freeman City of London 1979; FRSA 1964; *Style*— The Rt Hon the Lord Merrivale; ✉ 16 Brompton Lodge, 9–11 Cromwell Rd, London SW7 2JA (☎ 0171 581 5678)

MERRY, Gp Capt Robert Thomas George; s of Cyril Arthur Merry (d 1964), and Clara Catherine, *née* Stollmeyer (d 1988); *b* 25 Oct 1937; *Educ* Rossall, St Bartholomew's Hosp Med Coll London (MB BS); *m* 17 Aug 1963, Gillian Irene Kathleen, da of Francis Xavier Perkins (d 1944); 1 s (Charles b 1970), 2 da (Victoria b 1965, Alexandra b 1969); *Career* conslt neurologist to Defence Secdy Care Agency, conslt advsr in neurology to the RAF, conslt neurologist CAA; OStJ; MRCPsych, FRCP; *Recreations* gardening, cricket, golf; *Clubs* MCC, RAF; *Style*— Gp Capt Robert T G Merry; ✉ Central Medical Establishment, Kelvin House, 32 Cleveland Street, London W1P 5FB

MERRYLEES, Andrew; s of Andrew Merrylees (d 1984), and Mary McGowan, *née* Craig; *b* 13 Oct 1933; *Educ* Wishaw HS, Univ of Strathclyde (sr design prize, life drawing prize, BArch, Dip in Town Planning); *m* Mary Anne, da of James Dewar Crawford; 1 da (Fiona Jean b 28 June 1961), 2 s (Andrew Gary b 5 June 1963, James Scott b 30 Jan 1968); *Career* architect; Sir Basil Spence, Glover & Ferguson: joined as trainee 1957, assoc 1968, ptnr 1972–85; estab own practice Andrew Merrylees Associates 1985; conslt architect Standing Conf of Nat and Univ Libraries; external examiner: Duncan of Jordanstone Coll of Art, Dundee Sch of Architecture, Sch of Architecture Univ of Strathclyde; memb: Advsy Cncl for the Arts in Scotland, Edinburgh Festival Soc, Cockburn Assoc (memb Cncl 1987–89), Cncl RIAS; RIBA 1958, FRIAS 1977, FCSD 1978, RSA 1991 (ARSA 1984), FRSA 1993 *Major Projects* incl: Univ buildings at Edinburgh, Heriot-Watt, Dublin, Liverpool and Aston, Scottish Headquarters AA, Post Office sorting office, Housing Devpt Oban, National Library of Scotland, British Golf Museum; *Awards* RIBA Bronze Medal, Saltire Award, Civic Trust Award, Art in Architecture Award, RSA Gold Medal, Concrete Award, SCONUL Design Award; *Recreations* painting, cooking, walking; *Clubs* Scottish Arts'; *Style*— Andrew Merryless, Esq, RSA; ✉ 204 Bonkle Road, Newmains, Lanarkshire ML2 9AA (☎ 01698 384914); Quadrant, 17 Bernard Street, Edinburgh EH6 6PW (☎ 0131 555 0688, fax 0131 554 1850)

MERSEY, 4 Viscount (UK 1916); Richard Maurice Clive Bigham; also 13 Lord Nairne (S 1681), and Baron Mersey (UK 1910); s of 3 Viscount Mersey (d 1979), and Lady Katherine Evelyn Constance Petty-Fitzmaurice (Lady Nairne in her own right; d 1995), da of 6 Marquess of Lansdowne; *b* 8 July 1934; *Educ* Eton, Balliol Coll Oxford; *m* 6 May 1961, Joanna Dorothy Corsica Grey, er da of John Arnaud Robin Grey Murray, CBE (d 1993); 1 s (and 1 s decd); *Heir* s, Hon Edward John Hallam Bigham, Master of Nairne b 23 May 1966; *Career* served Irish Gds Germany and Egypt 1952–54, Lt; film dir and prodr (documentary); pres: Soc of Industl Emergency Servs Offrs (SIESO) 1987–91, Combined Heat and Power Assoc 1989–92; vice pres Parly Alternative Energy Gp 1992–; Hon FRAM 1995; *Books* The Hills of Cork and Kerry (1987); *Recreations* mountaineering, music; *Style*— The Rt Hon the Viscount Mersey; ✉ Bignor Park, Pulborough, West Sussex (☎ 01798 896214)

MERSON, Paul; *b* 20 March 1968; *Career* professional footballer (midfielder/forward); with Arsenal FC 1985–; league debut 1986; honours with Arsenal: League Championship 1989 and 1991, League Cup and FA Cup double 1993, Euro Cup Winners' Cup 1994; England: 14 full caps and 1 goal (as at Jan 1997); PFA Young Player of the Year 1989; *Style*— Paul Merson; ✉ Arsenal Football Club, Arsenal Stadium, Avenell Road, Highbury, London N5 1BU

MERTHYR, Barony of *see:* Lewis, Trevor

MERTON, John Ralph; MBE Mil (1942); s of Sir Thomas Ralph Merton, KBE (d 1969), and Violet Margery, da of Lt-Col William Harcourt Sawyer; *b* 7 May 1913; *Educ* Eton, Balliol Coll Oxford; *m* 1938, Viola Penelope, da of Adolf von Bernd (d 1975); 3 da (1 decd); *Career* served WWII Air Photo Reconnaissance Res, Lt-Col 1944, Legion of Merit USA; painter of portraits and other subjects; pictures at Windsor Castle (The Queen), Cardiff City Hall (The Princess of Wales), Nat Portrait Gall (two pictures), Christ's Coll Cambridge, Lincoln Coll Oxford, Inverary Castle, Eton Coll, Johns Hopkins Univ Baltimore and in private collections; exhibited at RA every year 1948–: first painting Daphne Wall saved from rejection by Sir Alfred Munnings PRA, Sarah and the Cat sent on tour by Arts Cncl 1950, Jane, Countess of Dalkeith (at Drumlanrig) given A Award by RA Selection Ctee 1958 (first time award given since 1918); 20 pictures exhibited at Colnaghi Bond St 1938, exhbn at Christopher Wood Gall London 1995; *Recreations* music, making things, underwater photography; *Style*— John Merton, Esq; ✉ Pound House, Oare, Nr Marlborough, Wilts SN8 4JA (☎ 01672 563539)

MERTON, Viscount; Simon John Horatio Nelson; s and h of 9 Earl Nelson; *b* 21 Sept 1971; *m* 17 July 1993, Ikuko, da of Hideo Umekage; *Style*— Viscount Merton

MERTON, William Ralph; s of Sir Thomas Ralph Merton, KBE, FRS (d 1969), of Berks, and Violet Marjory Sawyer (d 1976); *b* 25 Nov 1917; *Educ* Eton, Balliol Coll Oxford (MA); *m* 1, 6 July 1950, Anthea Caroline (d 1976), da of Henry F Lascelles (d 1936); 3 s (Michael b 1951, Rupert b 1953, Jeremy b 1961); m 2, 30 April 1977, Judy, da of Col Alexander John Buckley Rutherford, CVO, CBE (d 1979), of Henley-on-Thames; *Career* WWII served: Operational Res Unit HQ Coastal Cmd RAF 1941–43, sci asst to Lord Cherwell War Cabinet 1943–45; called to the Bar Inner Temple; merchant banker; dir: Fulmer Res Inst 1946–80 (chm 1958–74), Erlangers Ltd 1950–60; chm Alginate Industries Ltd 1952–79, dir Robert Fleming and Co Ltd 1963–80; chm: Robert Fleming Holdings Ltd 1974–80, Technology Investments Trust Ltd, Sterling Trust Ltd US & General Trust Corporation Ltd; FInstP; *Recreations* gardening, woodworking, tennis; *Style*— William Merton, Esq; ✉ Kingsbrook House, Headley, Thatcham, Berkshire RG19 8AW (☎ 01635 268458)

MERTTENS, Peter Mervyn; s of Victor H Merttens, CBE (d 1994), of Berkhamstead, and Evelyn, *née* Udall (d 1977); *b* 8 April 1930; *Educ* Malvern, St Catharine's Coll Cambridge (MA); *m* 6 July 1957, Mimi Cynthia, da of Stanley A Child, MBE (d 1990), of Catfield, Norfolk; 2 s (Robin, Brian); *Career* slr; Hamilton Harrison Matthews 1955–57, E African Power & Lighting Co Ltd 1957–62; slr and dir Colmans of Norwich 1962–84 (formerly J J Colman Ltd), slr and ptnr Eversheds (formerly Daynes Hill & Perks) 1984–92; chm Bd of Govrs Norwich City Coll of Further and Higher Educn, memb Cncl UEA, pres Norwich S Rotary Club, memb Cncl Norwich & Norfolk C of C; memb Law Soc; *Recreations* decoy duck carving, travel, golf; *Clubs* Royal Cromer; *Style*— Peter Merttens, Esq; ✉ Chestnuts, Catfield, Norfolk NR29 5DF (☎ and fax 01692 580458)

MESSER, Cholmeley Joseph; s of Col Arthur Albert Messer, DSO, CBE (d 1934), of Woking, Surrey, and Lilian Hope, *née* Dowling; *b* 20 March 1929; *Educ* Wellington Coll; *m* 1956, Ann Mary, da of Eliot Kingsmill Power (d 1969), of Pirbright, Surrey; 2 da; *Career* 2 Lt, KRRC, ME; slr, ptnr Lawrance Messer and Co slrs 1957–67; dir Save and Prosper Group Ltd 1968–89 (chm 1981–89); chm: Code of Advtg Practice Ctee 1976–78, Unit Tst Assoc 1979–81, London Pensions Fund Authy 1992–, Hamilton Life Assurance Co Ltd 1994–; dir: HFC Bank plc, Hamilton Insurance Co Ltd, Royal London Soc for Blind, First Step Housing Co Ltd; Liveryman Worshipful Co of Glass Sellers; *Recreations* golf, gardening, armchair sport, history; *Clubs* City of London, Woking Golf; *Style*— Cholmeley Messer, Esq; ✉ The Manor House, Normandy, Guildford, Surrey GU3 2AP (☎ 01483 810910)

MESSERVY-WHITING, Brig Graham G; MBE (1980); *b* 20 Oct 1946; *Educ* Lycée Français de Londres, Army Staff Coll, RAF Staff Coll, JSDC, RCDS; *m* 1 Feb 1969, Shirley, *née* Hitchinson; 1 s (Charles b 8 Sep 1972); *Career* cmmnd Intelligence Corps 1967; regtl duty incl: 1 KOSB and service in Germany, Libya, Cyprus and Hong Kong, cmd Intelligence and Security Gp Germany 1986–88; staff duty incl: plans offr N Ireland 1978–80, Secretariat of Chiefs of Staff MOD 1984–86, briefing offr to NATO Supreme Allied Cmd Europe 1988–91; mil advsr to Lord Owen as co-chm Int Conf on Former Yugoslavia 1992–93, promoted Brig 1993, res fell Centre for Def Studies King's Coll London 1993, Dir Def Commitments Overseas (Far E and W Hemisphere) MOD 1994–95, Dep Dir and COS Western European Union PC 1995–; memb: National Tst, Game Conservancy; MIL, FIMgt, fell RUSI; *Recreations* working gundogs, bridge; *Clubs* Army and Navy; *Style*— Brig G G Messervy-Whiting, MBE; ✉ Western European Union, 4 rue de la Regence, 1000 Bruxelles, Belgique

MESTEL, Prof Leon; s of Rabbi Solomon Mestel (d 1966), of London, and Rachel, *née* Brodetsky (d 1974); *b* 5 Aug 1927; *Educ* West Ham Secdy Sch London, Trinity Coll Cambridge (BA, PhD); *m* 15 Nov 1951, Sylvia Louise, da of Lt-Col Stanley James Cole, CMG, OBE (d 1949), of Cambridge; 2 s (Andrew Jonathan b 1957, Benjamin David b 1960), 2 da (Anne Leonora b 1953, Rosemary Judith b 1959); *Career* ICI res fell Univ of Leeds 1951–54, Cwlth Fund fell Princeton Univ Observatory 1954–55, fell St John's Coll Cambridge 1957–66, lectr in maths Univ of Cambridge 1958–66 (asst lectr 1955–58), visiting memb Inst of Advanced Studies Princeton 1961–62, JFK fell Weizmann Inst for Sci Israel 1966–67, prof of applied maths Univ of Manchester 1967–73, prof of astronomy Univ of Sussex 1973–92 (emeritus prof 1992); Eddington Medal Royal Astronomical Soc 1993; FRAS 1952, FRS 1977; *Books* Magnetohydrodynamics (jtly, 1974); *Recreations* reading, music; *Style—* Prof Leon Mestel, FRS; ✉ 13 Prince Edward's Road, Lewes, E Sussex BN7 1BJ (☎ 01273 472731); Division of Physics and Astronomy, University of Sussex, Falmer, Brighton BN1 9QH (☎ 01273 678088, fax 01273 678097, telex 877159, BHVTXS G)

MESTON, 3 Baron (UK 1919); James; QC (1996); s of 2 Baron Meston (d 1984), and Diana, Baroness Meston; *b* 10 Feb 1950; *Educ* Wellington, St Catharine's Coll Cambridge, Univ of Leicester; *m* 1974, Jean Rebecca Anne, yr da of John Carder, of Chalvington, Sussex; 1 s (Thomas), 2 da (Laura b 1980, Elspeth b 1988); *Heir* s, Hon Thomas James Dougall Meston b 21 Oct 1977; *Career* called to the Bar Middle Temple 1973; jr counsel to the Queen's Proctor 1992; *Clubs* Hawks; *Style—* The Rt Hon the Lord Meston, QC; ✉ Queen Elizabeth Building, Temple, London EC4Y 9BS

MESTON, Prof Michael Charles; s of Alexander Morrison Meston (d 1980), of Aberdeen, and Isabel Helen, *née* Robertson (d 1968); *b* 13 Dec 1932; *Educ* Robert Gordon's Coll Aberdeen, Univ of Aberdeen (MA, LLB), Univ of Chicago (JD); *m* 5 Sept 1958, Dorothea, da of James Munro (d 1947), of Montrose; 2 s (Donald b 1960, John b 1963); *Career* lectr in private law Univ of Glasgow 1959–64; Univ of Aberdeen: sr lectr 1964–68, prof of jurisprudence 1968–71, prof of Scots law 1971–96, prof emeritus 1996–, vice princ 1979–82, dean 1988–91; hon sheriff Grampian Highlands and Islands 1972–, temporary sheriff 1993–; govr Robert Gordon's Coll, tstee Nat Museum of Antiquities of Scotland 1982–85, dir Aberdeen Royal Hosps NHS Tst 1992–; memb Law Soc of Scotland 1957; *Books* The Succession (Scotland) Act 1964 (1964), The Matrimonial Homes (Family Protection) (Scotland) Act 1981 (1981), The Scottish Legal Tradition (1991); *Recreations* golf, clock repairing; *Clubs* Royal Northern and Univ, Royal Aberdeen Golf; *Style—* Prof Michael Meston; ✉ 4 Hamilton Place, Aberdeen AB15 4BH (☎ 01224 641554); Faculty of Law, University of Aberdeen, Old Aberdeen AB24 3UB (☎ 01224 272440, telex 73458 UNIABN G, fax 01224 272442)

METCALF, Prof David; s of Geoffrey Metcalf (d 1983), and Dorothy Rosa, *née* Vecchia; *b* 15 May 1942; *Educ* Univ of Manchester (MA), Univ of London (PhD); *m* 20 July 1968, Helen, da of Percival Harnett; 1 s (Thomas b 25 Nov 1980); *Career* special advsr to Min for Social Security 1976–79; prof of economics Univ of Kent 1977–85, prof of industl relations LSE 1985–95, dep dir Centre for Economic Performance LSE 1995–; memb: Royal Econ Soc, Br Univs' Industl Relations Assoc; *Books* Minimum Wage Policy in Great Britain (1981), New Perspectives on Industrial Disputes (1993); *Recreations* watching Tottenham Hotspur FC, horseracing; *Clubs* MCC; *Style—* Prof David Metcalf; ✉ London School of Economics, Houghton St, London WC2 (☎ 0171 955 7027, telex 24655 LSELON G, fax 0171 955 7424)

METCALF, Prof (David) Michael; s of Rev Thomas Metcalf, and Gladys Metcalf; *b* 8 May 1933; *Educ* St John's Coll Cambridge (MA, DPhil, DLitt); *m* 1958, Dorothy Evelyn, *née* Uren; 2 s, 1 da; *Career* keeper Heberden Coin Room Ashmolean Museum Oxford 1982– (asst keeper 1963–82); Univ of Oxford: fell Wolfson Coll 1982–, prof of numismatics 1996–; Royal Numismatic Soc: sec 1974–84, ed Numismatic Chronicle 1974–84, pres 1994–; pres UK Numismatic Tst 1994–; FSA; *Books* Coinage in South-Eastern Europe 820–1396 (1979), Coinage of the Crusades and the Latin East (1983, revised 1995), Sceattas in England and on the Continent (1984), Coinage in Ninth-century Northumbria (1987), Thrymsas and Sceattas in the Ashmolean Museum Oxford 3 Vols (1993–94), The Silver Coinage of Cyprus, 1285–1382 (1996); *Style—* Prof Michael Metcalf, FSA; ✉ Ashmolean Museum, Oxford OX1 2PH (☎ 01865 278062, fax 01865 278057)

METCALF, Ven Robert Laurence (Bob); s of Victor Noel Metcalf (d 1989), of Wallasey, Cheshire, and Phyllis Maud, *née* Dunwell (d 1995); *b* 18 Nov 1935; *Educ* Oldershaw GS Wallasey, St John's Coll Durham (BA, Rowing colours), Cranmer Hall Durham (DipTh); *m* 1964, Rachel Margaret, da of Rev William Herring; 2 s (Timothy Paul b 22 July 1967, Jonathan Mark b 22 May 1973), 3 da (Ruth Elizabeth (Mrs Andrew Pryce) b 21 Jan 1965, Angela Andrea b 13 March 1968, Sarah Emma Rebecca b 28 June 1980); *Career* Nat Serv REME 1955–57; ordained deacon 1962, priested 1963; curate: Christ Church Bootle 1962–65, i/c St John's Widnes 1965–67; vicar St Catharine Wigan 1967–75, dir Wigan Samaritans 1970–75, Diocesan Mothers' Union chaplain 1974–80, rector Holy Trinity Wavertree 1975–93, Diocesan dir of ordinands 1980–94 (asst diocesan dir of ordinands 1975–80), hon canon Liverpool Cathedral 1988–, archdeacon of Liverpool 1994–; chaplain Liverpool Blue Coat Sch 1975–94; memb: Round Table 1967–74, Rotary Club Toxteth 1990– (pres 1995–96); *Books* Celebration of Creation (1992), Prayers for Today's Church (contrib), Prayers for Today's World (contrib), For all the Family (contrib); *Recreations* walking, rowing, local radio (BBC Radio Merseyside) broadcasting, novel reading (political intrigue); *Style—* The Ven the Archdeacon of Liverpool; ✉ 38 Menlove Avenue, Allerton, Liverpool L18 2EF (☎ 0151 724 3956, fax 0151 729 0587); Church House, 1 Hanover Street, Liverpool L1 3DW (☎ 0151 709 9722)

METCALFE, Charles; s of Charles Metcalfe (d 1959), of Bentham, nr Lancaster, and Agnes, *née* Alderson (d 1973); *b* 27 Feb 1931; *Educ* Cheltenham, Liverpool Coll of Art and Design (NDD); *m* 15 March 1957, Mary Bell, da of Capt Charles Fancourt Harrison, MC; 1 s (Charles Harrison b 17 Nov 1958); *Career* Nat Serv Intelligence Corps 1951–53; worked in Fabric Dept Dickins and Jones London 1953–55, sales rep Ascher (Fabrics) Ltd London 1955–59; Liverpool Poly (formerly Liverpool Coll of Art): lectr in fashion and textiles 1959–64, sr lectr in charge of fashion 1964–67, head of Dept of Fashion and Textiles 1967–88, dep dir Sch of Art and Design 1988–89; advsy ed Allen & Unwin 1980–84, public lectr 1982–, dir Polycas Ltd 1983–90; fashion and textile conslt and designer of ceremonial robes 1989–, robemaker to John Moores Univ Liverpool 1989–95; external assessor: Poly of Wales 1977–78, Bradford Coll 1978–79, Bolton Tech Coll 1979, Manchester Poly 1986–88, N Staffords Poly 1987–90, Bristol Poly 1988–91; Poly Ctee memb: Academic Bd 1970–84 (rep on Poly Govrs Bd 1984), Art and Design Faculty Bd (chm 1971–73), Sci Faculty Bd 1973–75, Humanities and Business Studies Faculty Bd 1985–88; memb: Nat Cncl for Diplomas in Art and Design Fashion and Textile Subject Panel 1972–74, CNAA Fashion and Textile Subject Panel 1978–82, Professional and Educnl Affairs Ctee Textile Inst 1982–84, Cncl Textile Inst 1993– (Service medal 1993); chm: Design and Product Mktg Gp Textile Inst 1988–94 (memb 1984–), Design and Product Mktg Div 1994–96; dir Bluecoat Arts Centre Ltd 1988–, chm Bluecoat Gallery Liverpool 1988–93, chm Bluecoat Soc of Arts 1992–93 (memb 1988–93, vice chm 1989–92), memb Co Bluecoat Display Centre Ltd 1996–; memb European Textile Network 1995–; *Recreations* watching excellent television, attending European art exhibitions and festivals, opera and ballet; *Clubs* Cheshire and N Wales Orchid Soc; *Style—* Charles Metcalfe, Esq; ✉ 5 Mount Olive, Oxton, Birkenhead, Merseyside L43 5TT (☎ and fax 0151 652 4898)

METCALFE, George Ralph Anthony; s of Sir Ralph Ismay Metcalfe (d 1977), and Betty Penhorwood, *née* Pelling (d 1976); *b* 18 March 1936; *Educ* Lancing, Univ of Durham (BSc, BSc); *m* 11 Aug 1962, (Anne) Barbara, da of Anthony Watson, of Cumbria; 2 da (Elizabeth Anne (Mrs Smedley), Sarah Rosalind (Mrs Faulkner)); *Career* asst to MD Marine Div Richardsons Westgarth 1954–63, head of planning Polaris Project Vickers Armstrongs Engineers 1963–70, md Initial Services (chm and dir various subsids of BET and Initial Services) 1970–78, md Bath & Portland Group 1978–83, chm UMECO plc 1983–; former memb: Smaller Firms Cncl CBI, Economic Affrs Ctee CBI, Greebury Ctee CBI; memb Corp Govrs Ctee City Gp for Smaller Cos (CISCO); chm Berks Business Gp; Freeman City of London, Liveryman Worshipful Co of Shipwrights; FRSA; *Recreations* sailing, music, gardening; *Clubs* Travellers'; *Style—* George Metcalfe, Esq; ✉ 4 Tower Street, Cirencester, Glos GL7 1EF (☎ 01285 885303)

METCALFE, Hugh; OBE (1969); s of late Clifford Metcalfe, CBE, and late Florence Ellen Metcalfe; *b* 26 June 1928; *Educ* Harrow County GS, Imperial Coll London; *m* 19 April 1952, Pearl Allison; 3 s (Christopher b 1954, Andrew b 1956, Ian b 1960); *Career* air radar mechanic 1946–48; Bristol Aeroplane Company: joined 1951, design depts and project management in guided missiles and space, md Bristol (Naval) Div 1980–81, md Hatfield (Air Weapons) Div until 1982; chief exec Dynamics Gp British Aerospace plc 1982 (main bd dir 1982, dep chief exec 1984–88), dep chm Ricardo International plc 1989–96; memb: CBI Fin & Econ Ctee 1984–88, Engineering Industries Trg Bd 1985–88; govr: Univ of Herts 1988–93, St Mary Redcliffe Sch 1990–; Hon DSc Hatfield Poly, Hon DEng Univ of Bristol 1992; FRAeS 1968, FEng 1983; *Recreations* Opera London, London Philharmonic Choir; *Clubs* Athenaeum, Leander, Royal Society of Arts, Savages (Bristol); *Style—* Hugh Metcalfe, Esq, OBE, FEng; ✉ 28 Druid Stoke Avenue, Stoke Bishop, Bristol BS9 1DD (☎ 0117 908 0255)

METCALFE, Peter; s of Arthur Metcalfe, of Hawkshaw, Tottington, Bury, Lancs, and Marjorie, *née* Smith; *b* 1 Oct 1944; *Educ* Bury GS; *m* 26 July 1969, Patricia Jean, da of Frank Noel Brierley; 1 s (Nicholas Philip b 18 Jan 1975), 1 da (Jane Helen b 11 July 1976); *Career* Peat Marwick Mitchell 1961–70 (Manchester 1961–69, Leeds 1969–70); ptnr: J A Crawshaw & Co Bury 1970–87, KPMG Peat Marwick (following merger) 1987–92, Mitchell Charlesworth CAs 1993–; FCA 1975 (ACA 1969); *Recreations* table tennis, soccer, scouts (asst ldr); *Style—* Peter Metcalfe, Esq; ✉ Mitchell Charlesworth Chartered Accountants, Fountain Court, 68 Fountain Street, Manchester M2 2FB (☎ 0161 228 7883, fax 0161 236 3268)

METCALFE, Stanley Gordon; s of Stanley Hudson Metcalfe, and Jane Metcalfe (d 1975); *b* 20 June 1932; *Educ* Leeds GS, Pembroke Coll Oxford (MA); *m* 1968, Sarah, da of John F A Harter; 2 da; *Career* chm Ranks Hovis McDougall plc 1989–93 (dep chm 1987–89), chm Queens Moat Houses plc 1993–; *Recreations* golf, cricket; *Clubs* MCC, I Zingari; *Style—* Stanley Metcalfe, Esq; ✉ The Oast House, Lower Froyle, Alton, Hants GU34 4LX (☎ 01420 22310)

METGE, Dame (Alice) Joan; DBE (1987); da of Cedric Leslie Metge (d 1985), and Alice Mary, *née* Rigg (d 1980); *b* 21 Feb 1930; *Educ* Matamata Dist HS, Epsom Girls GS, Auckland Univ Coll (BA, MA), LSE (PhD, Hutchinson medal); *Career* research anthropologist and writer; lectr univ extension Univ of Auckland 1961–64 (jr lectr in geography 1952); Victoria Univ of Wellington: sr lectr in anthropology and Maori studies 1965–67, assoc prof of anthropology 1968–88, Capt James Cook res fell 1981–83; memb: Bd of Christian Educn Auckland Church of the Province of NZ 1963–64 (Wellington 1965–68), Prov Cncl for Christian Educn 1964–66, Prov Cmmn on Work Among the Maori People 1966–67, Prov Cmmn on the Ordination of Women 1969–71, Bd of Health Ctee on Drug Dependency and Drug Abuse 1968–73, Sci and Technol Advsy Ctee 1987–89, Waitangi Nat Tst Bd 1995–; hon fell: RAI 1989 (memb 1955), NZ Assoc of Social Anthropologists 1989 (memb 1976, chair 1979–80 and 1986–88); memb: Assoc of Social Anthropologists of the Cwlth 1958, Polynesian Soc 1951 (Elsdon Best Meml Medal 1987), NZ Fedn of Univ Women 1951, NZ Assoc for Women in Sci 1988; *Books* A New Maori Migration (1964), The Maoris of New Zealand (1967, revised 1976), Talking Past Each Other (with Patricia Kinloch, 1978), In and Out of Touch (1986), Te Kohao o Te Ngira (1990), New Growth From Old (1995); *Recreations* theatre, music, reading, gardening; *Style—* Dame Joan Metge, DBE; ✉ 3 Mariri Road, Onehunga, Auckland 1006, New Zealand

METHERELL, Ian Patrick; s of Clarence George Metherell, and Ethel Muriel, *née* Dyer; *b* 19 Sept 1943; *Educ* Bideford GS, Univ of Southampton (BA); *m* 7 April 1968, Louise Whitefield, da of James Edward Westwood (d 1986); 2 s (Andrew b 1977, Nicholas b 1981); *Career* PR conslt; chief exec MPR Leedex Group Ltd 1987–89, chm Proclaim Network Ltd 1991–; dir: EuroPR Ltd 1992–, AS2 Ltd 1994–; non-exec dir Mosaic Management Consulting Group 1984–88; treas PR Conslts Assoc 1987–89; FIPR 1988; *Style—* Ian Metherell, Esq; ✉ 2 Forge Close, Marsh Gibbon, nr Bicester, Oxfordshire OX6 OHZ (☎ 01869 277620, fax 01869 277003)

METHLEY, Peter Charles; s of Charles Harry Methley (d 1995), of Surrey, and Alice Elizabeth, *née* Stimpson (d 1984); *b* 2 April 1938; *Educ* King's Coll Sch; *m* 15 July 1961, Marianne, *née* Evans; 1 s (Michael Peter b 1965), 2 da (Lisette b 1963, Annette b 1970); *Career* insur broker Lloyd's; chm: Stewart and Wrightson International Group 1969–79, Leslie and Godwin Ltd 1979–85; chief exec C E Heath plc until 1986, chm and chief exec H J Symons Group of Cos 1987–93, currently conslt Stirling Cooke Insurance Brokers Ltd; played hockey for Guildford and Surrey 1956–70; Freeman City of London; Freeman: Worshipful Co of Insurers (fndr memb), Worshipful Co of Paviors; *Recreations* golf, tennis; *Clubs* Sunningdale Golf, Royal and Ancient Golf of St Andrews, City of London; *Style—* Peter Methley, Esq; ✉ Longreach, Links Road, Bramley, Surrey GU5 0AL (☎ 01483 893037, fax 01483 898231); business: 65 Leadenhall Street, London EC3A 2AD (☎ 0171 702 2062, fax 0171 454 0250)

METHUEN, Very Rev John Alan Robert; s of Rev Alan Robert Methuen (d 1992), of Stonesfield, Oxon, and Ruth Josephine Tyrrell, *née* Baker (d 1992); *b* 14 Aug 1947; *Educ* Eton Coll Choir Sch, St John's Coll Leatherhead, BNC Oxford (Coquitt exhibitioner, BA, MA), Cuddesdon Coll Oxford; *m* 1970, Bridget Mary, da of Rev Dr Wilfrid Seymour Andrews; 2 da (Judith Helen b 1972, Caroline Deborah b 1974); *Career* asst curate Fenny Stratford and Water Eaton Team Miny Milton Keynes 1971–74, priest i/c Dorney St James and asst chaplain Eton Coll warden Dorney Parish Eton Coll Project Conf Centre 1974–77, vicar of Reading St Mark 1977–83, rector of Hulme The Ascension Manchester 1983–95, dean of Ripon 1995–; memb (Manchester Diocese): Bishop's Cncl 1991–95, Decade of Evangelism Ctee 1992–95, Policy Ctee (Priorities Advsy Gp) 1993–95, Way Forward Monitoring Gp 1995; chaplain Reading YMCA Hostel 1977–83, pres Hulme and Moss Side Christian Fellowship 1984–85 and 1988–89, vice chm and exec dir Churches Work Scheme Ltd 1985–90; dir: Firmstart Manchester Ltd 1988–96, New City Furniture Ltd 1992–; memb: Open Door Mgmnt Ctee 1987–95, Manchester Interfaith Ctee 1988–95, Gtr Manchester Ecumenical Cncl 1992–95; Eton Coll: A-Level and Gen Divinity master 1974–77, visiting lectr 1977–; vice chm of govrs Birley Co HS Hulme 1984–89; chm of govrs: Royce Co Primary Sch Hulme 1984–95, St Philip's C of E Primary Sch Hulme 1985–95; chaplain: Cornbrook Centre Central Manchester Coll 1983–90, Trinity C of E HS Hulme 1984–85; Anglican chaplain Loreto RC Sixth Form Coll Hulme 1983–95, govr, chm Curriculum Ctee and memb Standing Ctee Trinity C of E HS Hulme 1984–95; dir Milton Keynes Community Drama Project 1972–74, asst dir

Bletchley Festival 1973–74, organiser and chm W Reading Festival 1979–83, chm Hulme Project Steering Ctee 1985–86, memb Bishop's Representative Exec Ctee Manchester Cncl for Community Rels 1984–95; memb Mgmnt Ctee: Drugs Advice and Support in Hulme 1989–95, Community Computing Ltd 1990–95; memb Standing Ctee Moss Side and Hulme Community Forum 1990–95; hon pres Manchester Anti-Racist Alliance 1991–95; chm: Social Issues Ctee Hulme City Challenge 1992–95, Hulme Educn Forum 1992–95; dir Hulme Regeneration Ltd 1993–95; Ripon Diocese: chm Ripon Diocesan Music Ctee 1995–, pres Ripon Cathedral Concert Soc 1995–, chm Friends of Ripon Cathedral 1995–, memb Bishops Cncl 1995–, govr Ripon Cathedral Primary Sch 1995–, chm Govrs Ripon Cathedral Choir Sch 1995–, patron Corrymeela Link NI 1996–; various radio, TV and press interviews, news items and documentaries on spiritual, moral and social issues; writer and dir The Christian Life series of Christian educn videos 1990–93; *Recreations* history and archaeology (Gerald Avery Near Eastern Archaeological Prize 1965); *Clubs* Manchester Luncheon, Claret and Chips Luncheon, Egypt Exploration Soc; *Style—* The Very Rev John Methuen; ✉ The Minster House, Ripon, North Yorks HG4 1PE (☎ 01765 603615)

METHUEN, 7 Baron (UK 1838); Robert Alexander Holt Methuen; s of 5 Baron Methuen (d 1975), and Grace Durning, *née* Holt (d 1972); suc his bro, 6 Baron 1994; *b* 22 July 1931; *Educ* Shrewsbury, Trinity Coll Cambridge; *m* 1, 1958 (m dis 1993), Mary Catherine Jane, da of Ven Charles German Hooper, Archdeacon of Ipswich; 2 da (Hon Charlotte Mary b 1964, Hon Henrietta Christian (Hon Mrs Methuen-Jones) b 1965); m 2, 1994, Margrit Andrea, da of Friedrich Karl Ernst Hadwiger, of Vienna; *Heir* cousin, Christopher Paul Mansel Campbell Methuen-Campbell b 1928; *Style—* The Lord Methuen; ✉ Caradice House, Fulbrook, Burford, Oxon

METLISS, Jonathan Alexander; s of Cyril Metliss, and Anita, *née* Lander; *b* 12 June 1949; *Educ* Haberdashers' Aske's Elstree, Univ of Southampton (LLB); *m* 15 Dec 1974, Vivienne Hilary, da of Samuel Woolf; 1 s (Joshua b 25 Nov 1980), 2 da (Miriam b 4 Nov 1983, Elizabeth b 4 July 1988); *Career* slr; asst slr Nabarro Nathanson 1973–76, merchant banker Capel Court Corp Sydney Aust 1976–78, asst slr Berwin Leighton 1978–82, sr corp fin ptnr and fndr memb S J Berwin 1982–; dir: Hamlet Group PLC (vice chm), Atapco (UK) Ltd, English National Investment Company plc, Lindow Investment Company Ltd, Pownall Investment Company Ltd, Interlaw Ltd 1993–, The Weizmann Inst Fndn; chm British Friends of Haifa Univ, vice chm Friends of the Weizmann Inst (UK); memb Exec: The Weizmann Inst Fndn, British-Israel Chamber of Commerce, Cwlth Jewish Cncl; jt sec and exec memb Inter-Parly Cncl Against Anti-Semitism; memb: Bd of Govrs Haifa Univ, Ctee on S African Trade (COSAT, a Br overseas trade bd business advsy advsy gp), Law Soc, Holborn Law Soc; *Recreations* squash, cricket, travel, work and S Africa; *Clubs* MCC, Middx CCC, Sussex CCC, RAC, Rugby; *Style—* Jonathan Metliss, Esq; ✉ S J Berwin & Co, 222 Gray's Inn Rd, London WC1X 8HB (☎ 0171 533 2222, fax 0171 533 2000)

METTER, Veronica Ann; da of Louis William Metter, of South Africa, and Valerie Phyllis, *née* Harris; *b* 9 Jan 1954; *Educ* Univ of the Witwatersrand (BA), Univ of London (BA); *Career* slr; ptnr Berwin Leighton 1987–; memb Law Soc; *Recreations* theatre, tennis; *Style—* Miss Veronica Metter; ✉ Berwin Leighton, Adelaide House, London Bridge, London EC4R 9HA (☎ 0171 623 3144, telex 886420, fax 0171 623 4416)

METZ, Jean Christian; s of Georges Jacques Metz, and Germaine Anne Marcy; *b* 25 Dec 1949; *Educ* École Polytechnique Paris, École Nationale d'Administration Paris; *m* 4 Dec 1976, Verena Maria, da of Kurt Engelbert Schneider, of Vienna; 2 s (Matthieu Georges Harald b 23 Oct 1980, Martin François Xavier b 22 Oct 1984), 2 da (Aglaé Martine b 25 May 1983, Clémence Eveline b 16 June 1988); *Career* various positions rising to under sec for monetary and budgetary affrs Treasy Dept French Miny of Economy and Finance 1975–86; Crédit Commercial de France: first sr vice pres 1986–93, head of fixed income trading 1986–90, head of int activities 1991–93; dir Charterhouse Bank Ltd and md Charterhouse plc i/c treasy and trading 1993–; *Style—* J C Metz, Esq; ✉ Charterhouse plc, 1 Paternoster Row, St Paul's, London EC4M 7DH (☎ 0171 522 3793, fax 0171 334 3636)

MEXBOROUGH, 8 Earl of (I 1766); John Christopher George Savile; also Baron Pollington (I 1753) and Viscount Pollington (I 1766); s of 7 Earl (d 1980; himself gs of the 4 Earl who, as Lord Gaverstock, featured in a minor role in Disraeli's Coningsby, and who, for the last seven and a half months of his life, enjoyed the distinction of being the last living ex-member of the unreformed House of Commons), and Josephine Bertha Emily, *née* Fletcher (d 1992); *b* 16 May 1931; *Educ* Eton, Worcester Coll Oxford; *m* 1, 1958 (m dis 1972), Lady Elisabeth Hariot Grimston, da of 6 Earl of Verulam; 1 s, 1 da; m 2, 1972, Catherine Joyce, da of James Kenneth Hope, CBE, DL, and formerly wife of Brig the Rt Hon Nicholas Crespigny Laurence Vivian, *qv*; 1 s (Hon James b 1976), 1 da (Lady Lucinda b 1973); *Heir* s, Viscount Pollington, *qv*; *Career* late 2 Lt Grenadier Gds; memb Inst of the Motor Indust; *Recreations* travel, motor cars, American music; *Clubs* All England Lawn Tennis, Air Sqdn, Mill Reef Antigua; *Style—* The Rt Hon the Earl of Mexborough; ✉ Arden Hall, Hawnby, York (☎ 01439 798348, fax 01439 798336); 14 Lennox Garden Mews, London SW1 (☎ 0171 589 3669, fax 0171 584 2836)

MEYER, Sir Anthony John Charles; 3 Bt (UK 1910), of Shortgrove, Newport, Essex; s of Sir Frank Cecil Meyer, 2 Bt, MP (d 1935), of Ayot House, Ayot St Lawrence, Herts, and Georgina, *née* Seeley (d 1962); *b* 27 Oct 1920; *Educ* Eton, New Coll Oxford; *m* 30 Oct 1941, Barbadee Violet, o da of A Charles Knight, JP, FSA (d 1958), of Herne Place, Sunningdale; 1 s ((Anthony) Ashley Frank b 1944), 3 da (Carolyn-Clare Barbadee (Mrs Sands) b 1943, Tessa Violet (Dr Tessa Murdoch, FSA) b 1955, Sally Minette (Mrs Marcus Vergette) b 1961); *Heir* s, (Anthony) Ashley Frank Meyer b 23 Aug 1944; *Career* Lt Scots Gds WWII; Foreign Serv: entered 1947, first sec Paris 1951–56, first sec Moscow 1956–58, FO 1958–62; MP (C): Eton and Slough 1964–66, Flint West 1970–83, Clwyd NW 1983–92; PPS to Rt Hon Maurice Macmillan as: Chief Sec Treasy 1970–72, Sec of State for Employment 1972–74; chm Franco-Br Parly Rels Ctee 1979–92; vice chm: Cons European Affairs Ctee 1979–83, Franco-Br Cncl (dep chm) 1986–; memb Speaker Panel of Chairmen 1985–92, fndr and dir Solon politcial jl 1969, policy dir European Movement (UK); Liveryman Worshipful Co of Clothworkers; Officier Légion d'Honneur (France) 1983; FRSA 1992; *Publications* A Federal Europe: Why Not ? (1992), Stand Up and Be Counted (1990); *Recreations* music, opera, travel, skiing, cooking; *Clubs* Beefsteak; *Style—* Sir Anthony Meyer, Bt; ✉ 9 Cottage Place, Brompton Square, London SW3 2BE (☎ 0171 589 7416, fax 0171 581 8510)

MEYER, Barrie John; s of Walter Bertram Meyer (d 1978), of Bournemouth, and Alice Emily Violet, *née* Elgar; *b* 21 Aug 1932; *Educ* Boscombe Secdy Sch Bournemouth; *m* 4 Sept 1965, Gillian, *née* Hubbard; 3 s (Stephen Barrie b 16 Jan 1967, Christopher John b 25 Sept 1968, Adrian Michael b 22 Sept 1970); *Career* cricket umpire; former professional football and cricket player; footballer: 139 appearances and 60 goals Bristol Rovers 1949–58, 10 appearances and 8 goals Plymouth Argyle 1958–59, 78 appearances and 31 goals Newport County 1959–61, 11 appearances and 8 goals Bristol City 1961–63, England Boys' Clubs cap 1946; cricketer Gloucestershire CCC 1957–72 (awarded county cap 1958); record with Gloucestershire: 405 matches, 5,368 runs, 826 dismissals as wicket-keeper; first class cricket umpire: appointed 1973, 26 test matches (debut 1978), 23 one day ints, 2 World Cup Finals, 10 domestic finals; *Recreations* golf, reading, music; *Style—* Barrie Meyer, Esq; ✉ c/o Test and County Cricket Board, Lord's Cricket Ground, St John's Wood Rd, London NW8 8QN (☎ 0171 286 4405)

MEYER, HE Christopher John Rome; CMG (1988); s of Flt Lt Reginald Henry Rome Meyer (ka 1944), and Evelyn, *née* Campani (now Mrs Sandy Landells); *b* 22 Feb 1944; *Educ* Lancing, Peterhouse Cambridge (MA), Sch of Advanced Int Studies Bologna; *m* 11 Dec 1976, Francoise Elizabeth, da of Air Cdre Sir Archie Winskill, KCVO, CBE, DFC, AE, *qv*; 2 s (James b 21 March 1978, William b 20 June 1984), 1 step s (Thomas (Hedges) b 28 Aug 1972); *Career* Dip Serv: third sec West and Central African Dept FO 1966–67, trg Russian language 1967–68, third (later second) sec Br Embassy Moscow 1968–70, second (later first) sec Madrid 1970–73, first sec E Euro and Soviet Dept FCO 1973–76, first sec planning staff 1976–78, first sec UK rep to Euro Community Brussels 1978–82, cnsllr and head of chancery Moscow 1982–84, head news dept and chief FCO spokesman 1984–88; visiting fell Centre for Int Affrs Harvard Univ 1988–89; min (commercial) Washington 1989–92, min and dep head of Mission Washington 1992–94, chief press sec to the PM 1994–96, HM ambass Germany 1997–; *Recreations* squash, reading, jazz; *Style—* HE Mr Christopher Meyer, CMG; ✉ c/o Foreign and Commonwealth Office (Bonn), King Charles Street, London SW1A 2AH

MEYER, Rev Conrad John Eustace; s of late William Eustace Meyer; *b* 2 July 1922; *Educ* Clifton, Pembroke Coll Cambridge, Westcott House; *m* 1960, Mary, da of late Alec John Wiltshire; *Career* Lt (S) RNVR and later chaplain RNVR; vicar Devoran Truro 1954–64; diocesan: youth chaplain 1956–60, sec for educn 1960–69; hon canon of Truro 1960–79, archdeacon of Bodmin 1969–79, examining chaplain to Bishop of Truro 1973–79, area bishop of Dorchester 1979–87, hon asst bishop Truro Dio 1990–94, provost of Western Div of the Woodard Schs 1970–92; ordained Roman Catholic priest 1995; vice pres SPCK 1990– (vice chm 1989–90, chm Appeal Ctee until 1990); chm Cornwall Civil Aid and co cmmr 1993–96; hon fell Woodard Corporation (Western Div) 1993–94, fell (hc) Inst of Civil Defence and Disaster Studies; *Recreations* civil defence, archaeology, swimming, walking; *Clubs* Royal Cwlth Tst; *Style—* The Rev Conrad Meyer; ✉ Hawk's Cliff, 38 Praze Rd, Newquay, Cornwall TR7 3AF (☎ 01637 873003)

MEYER, Michael Leverson; s of Percy Barrington Meyer (d 1955), of London, and Eleanor Rachel, *née* Benjamin (d 1929); *b* 11 June 1921; *Educ* Wellington Coll, Christ Church Oxford (MA); 1 da (Nora b 1968); *Career* Operational Res Section Bomber Cmd HQ 1942–45; lectr in Eng lit Uppsala Univ Sweden 1947–50; visiting prof of drama: Dartmouth Coll USA 1978, Univ of Colorado 1986, The Colorado Coll 1988, Hofstra Univ 1989, UCLA 1991; memb: Editorial Advsy Bd Good Food Guide 1958–72; author; FRSL 1971, govr LAMDA 1962–; Gold medal of the Swedish Acad 1964; Knight Cdr of the Order of the Polar Star first class Sweden 1977, Royal Norwegian Order of Merit 1995; *Books* Eight Oxford Poets (ed with Sidney Keyes and contrib, 1941), Collected Poems of Sidney Keyes (ed 1945), The Minos of Crete (by Sidney Keyes, ed, 1948), The End of the Corridor (novel, 1951), Henrik Ibsen: The Making of a Dramatist (1967), Henrik Ibsen: The Farewell to Poetry (1971), Henrik Ibsen: The Top of a Cold Mountain (1971, Whitbread biography prize), Summer Days (ed 1981), Ibsen on File (1985), Strindberg: a biography (1985), File on Strindberg (1986), Not Prince Hamlet (memoirs, 1989, published as Words Through a Windowpane USA); translated: The Long Ships (by Frans G Bengtsson, 1954) Ibsen Brand (1960), The Lady from the Sea (1960), John Gabriel Borkman (1960), When We Dead Awaken (1960), The Master Builder (1960), Little Eyolf (1961), Ghosts (1962), The Wild Duck (1962), Hedda Gabler (1962), Peer Gynt (1963), An Enemy of the People (1960), The Pillars of Society (1963), The Pretenders (1964), A Doll's House (1965), Rosmersholm (1966), Emperor and Galilean (1986), Strindberg: The Father (1964), Miss Julie (1964), Creditors (1964), The Stronger (1964), Playing with Fire (1964), Erik the Fourteenth (1964), Storm (1964), The Ghost Sonata (1964), A Dream Play (1973), To Damascus (1975), Easter (1975), The Dance of Death (1975), The Virgin Bride (1975), Fragments of a Life (by Hedi Fried, 1990), Strindberg's Master Olof (1991); *Plays* The Ortolan (1967), Lunatic and Lover (1981), The Odd Women (staged Royal Exchange Theatre Manchester, 1992), A Meeting in Rome (staged Edinburgh Festival, 1994); *Recreations* real tennis, eating, sleeping; *Clubs* Garrick, Savile, MCC; *Style—* Michael Meyer, Esq; ✉ 4 Montagu Square, London W1H 1RA

MEYER, Shelagh (aka Shelagh Macdonald); da of late Frank Brookesmith, of Broadstairs, Kent, and Marjory, *née* Beale; *b* 20 Dec 1937; *Educ* Brockenhurst High Sch Hants, Northfields-Kimbolton Girls' Sch, Blandford GS Dorset; *m* 1, 1968, late Gilbert H Macdonald; m 2, 1984, Philip Meyer, s of late Isaac Meyer; 1 step s (James Meyer b 1955), 1 step da (Margaret (Mrs Bimbane) b 1951); *Career* advertising copywriter 1956–60, head Copy Gp and assoc dir in various agencies 1960–69, creative dir and company ptnr 1976–84, freelance creative conslt 1984–; memb PEN 1983; *Books* novels (as Shelagh Macdonald): A Circle of Stones (1973), Five From Me, Five From You (1974), No End To Yesterday (Whitbread Prize, 1977); plays (as Shelagh Meyer): A Small Disturbance (1987), Q (1990); *Recreations* arts, theatre, books, bird and wildlife, food, people, learning demotic Greek and traditional Greek dancing, walking, swimming; *Style—* Shelagh Meyer; ✉ c/o Mark Lucas, Peters Fraser & Dunlop, 5th Floor, The Chambers, Chelsea Harbour, Lots Rd, London SW10 OXF (☎ 0171 376 7676, fax 0171 352 7356)

MEYERS, Dr Jeffrey; s of Rubin and Judith Meyers, of NYC; *b* 1939; *Educ* Univ of Michigan (BA, jr yr at Univ of Edinburgh), Univ of Calif Berkeley (MA, PhD); *Career* asst prof UCLA 1963–65, lectr Far East Div Univ of Maryland 1965–66, asst prof Tufts Univ Boston 1967–71, professional writer in London and Málaga 1971–75, assoc prof Univ of Colorado 1975–78, prof Univ of Colorado 1978–92, Jemison prof Univ of Alabama 1992, professional writer 1992–; visiting prof: Univ of Kent Canterbury 1979–80, Univ of Massachusetts Amherst 1982–83; visiting scholar Univ of Calif Berkeley 1986–87 and 1992–94, Univ of Colorado research lectr 1988; FRSL 1983; *Biographies* A Fever at the Core: The Idealist in Politics (1976), Married to Genius (1977), Katherine Mansfield: A Biography (1978), The Enemy: A Biography of Wyndham Lewis (1980), Hemingway: A Biography (1985), Manic Power: Robert Lowell and His Circle (1987), D H Lawrence: A Biography (1990), Joseph Conrad: A Biography (1991), Edgar Allan Poe: His Life and Legacy (1992), Scott Fitzgerald: A Biography (1994), Edmund Wilson: A Biography (1995), Robert Frost: A Biography (1996), Bogart: A Life in Hollywood (1997); *Literary Criticism* Fiction and the Colonial Experience (1973), The Wounded Spirit: A Study of 'Seven Pillars of Wisdom' (1973), A Reader's Guide to George Orwell (1975), Painting and the Novel (1975), Homosexuality and Literature 1890–1930 (1977), D H Lawrence and the Experience of Italy (1982), Disease and the Novel 1860–1960 (1985), The Spirit of Biography (1989); *Bibliographies* T E Lawrence: A Bibliography (1974), Catalogue of the Library of the Late Siegfried Sassoon (1975), George Orwell: An Annotated Bibliography of Criticism (1977); *Collections edited* George Orwell: The Critical Heritage (1975), Ernest Hemingway: The Critical Heritage (1982), Robert Lowell: Interviews and Memoirs (1988); *Original essays edited* Wyndham Lewis: A Revaluation (1980), Wyndham Lewis by Roy Campbell (1985), D H Lawrence and Tradition (1985), The Craft of Literary Biography (1985), The Legacy of D H Lawrence (1987), The Biographer's Art (1989), T E Lawrence: Soldier, Writer, Legend (1989), Graham Greene: A Revaluation (1990); *Recreations* tennis, travel; *Style—* Dr Jeffrey Meyers; ✉ 84 Stratford Road, Kensington, California 94707, USA

MEYJES, Sir Richard Anthony; kt (1972), DL (Surrey 1983); s of late Anthony Charles Dorian Meyjes; *b* 30 June 1918; *Educ* Univ Coll Sch Hampstead; *m* 1939, Margaret Doreen Morris; 3 s; *Career* served WWII; admitted slr 1946; Shell International Petroleum Company: London 1946–58, Manila 1958–64, mktg coordinator London 1964–70, dir and personnel coordinator London 1972–76; head Business Team Civil Serv 1970–72; dir: Coates Bros plc 1976–84 (chm 1977–84), Foseco 1976–89 (dep chm 1986–89), Portals Holdings 1976–88; chm Cncl Univ of Surrey 1980–85, pres Assoc of Optometrists 1995– (vice pres 1988–95), vice pres Fedn of Ophthalmic and Dispensing Opticians 1995–; tstee Vision Aid Overseas 1991–93 and 1994–; High Sheriff Surrey 1984–85; Master Worshipful Co of Spectacle Makers 1985–87; Hon DUniv Surrey 1988; CIMgt, FRSA, FInstD, FBCO; *Style—* Sir Richard Meyjes, DL; ✉ Long Hill House, The Sands, nr Farnham, Surrey GU10 1NQ (☎ and fax 01252 782601)

MEYNELL, Dame Alix Hester Marie (Lady Meynell); DBE (1949); da of late Surgn Cdr L Kilroy, RN, and late Hester Kilroy; *b* 2 Feb 1903; *Educ* Malvern Girls' Coll, Somerville Coll Oxford; *m* 1946, Sir Francis Meynell, RDI (d 1975); *Career* joined Civil Serv Bd of Trade 1925, seconded as sec Monopolies and Restrictive Practices Cmmn 1949–53, under sec Bd of Trade 1946–55, resigned Civil Serv 1955; called to the Bar 1956; md Nonesuch Press Ltd 1976–86; memb: SE Gas Board 1956–69 (chm Cons Cncl 1956–63), Harlow New Town Corpn 1956–65, ctees of investigation for England, Scotland and GB under Agric Mktg Acts 1956–65, Monopolies Cmmn 1965–68; *Books* Public Servant, Private Woman; *Style—* Dame Alix Meynell, DBE; ✉ Lion House, High Street, Lavenham, Suffolk CO10 9PR (☎ 01787 247526)

MEYNELL, Godfrey; MBE (1963); s of Capt Godfrey Meynell, VC, MC, QVO Corps of Guides (ka 1935), and Sophia Patricia, *née* Lowis; Derbyshire landowners since 12th century; *b* 20 July 1934; *Educ* Eton, Magdalene Coll Cambridge; *m* 11 June 1960, The Rev Honor Mary Meynell, da of Maj J H A Davis (d 1961); 1 s (Godfrey b 1964), 2 da (Diana Violet b 1962, Katharine Jill b 1966); *Career* formerly asst advsr W Aden Protectorate HM Overseas Civil Serv, Home Civil Serv 1968–94, regnl controller (Housing) DOE E Midlands Region, ret; High Sheriff of Derbyshire 1982–83; *Recreations* forestry, conservation; *Style—* Godfrey Meynell, Esq, MBE; ✉ Meynell Langley, Kirk Langley, Derby DE6 4NT (☎ 01332 824207)

MEYNELL, Hugh Bernard; s of Cuthbert Charles Meynell (d 1973), and Irene Mary, *née* Hickman; *b* 7 Jan 1931; *Educ* Ampleforth, Columbia Univ NY; *m* 23 June 1956, Paula Faine, da of Paul Ellis Gibbons (d 1972); 1 s (Edward James b 15 Dec 1959), 1 da (Rosemary Jane (Mrs Macmillan-Douglas) b 11 Oct 1957); *Career* Nat Serv 2 Lt RA 1949–51; chm Meynell Valves Ltd Wolverhampton 1978–88, dir S Staffs Water Co 1982–, chm Dynafluid 1988–; chm: Shropshire Rural Devpt Cmmn 1991, St Johns Ambulance Shropshire, tstees County Air Ambulance 1994; pres Boys Bde Wolverhampton; Freeman: City of London 1985, Worshipful Co of Plumbers 1985; MInstM 1976, memb Inst Sales Mgmnt 1979; *Recreations* shooting, cricket, tennis; *Clubs* MCC; *Style—* Hugh Meynell, Esq; ✉ Brockton Court, nr Shifnal, Shropshire TF11 9LZ (☎ 01952 730247); Dynafluid Ltd, Hortonwood 33, Telford TF1 4EX (fax 01952 677738)

MEYNELL, Hugo Ivo; s of Lt-Col Hugo Francis Meynell, OBE (d 1974), and Doris Isabel, *née* Morrison (d 1992); *b* 23 Nov 1931; *Educ* Stowe, RMA Sandhurst; *m* 1, 22 June 1961, Sarah Virginia, da of Gen Sir Richard McCreery, GCB, KBE, DSO, MC (d 1967); 2 s (Luke Hugo b 1964, Alexander Michael b 1966), 1 da (Lucia Anna b 1968); m 2, 30 April 1985, Audrey Tennant, da of George Henderson (d 1968), and widow of Peter Forsyth-Forrest; *Career* joined 12 Royal Lancers (POW) 1952, Malaya 1952–54, Capt 1955, Suez Landing 1956 (despatches 1957), WO 1960–62; The Economist Newspaper 1963 (dep md 1973, dir 1978), md The Economist Publications 1984–90; memb Cncl Buckingham Univ 1980; *Recreations* country pursuits; *Clubs* Cavalry and Guards; *Style—* Hugo I Meynell, Esq; ✉ 38 Halsey St, London SW3 (☎ 0171 589 5014); The Old Manor House, Whichford, Shipston on Stour, Warwickshire (☎ 0160 884 293)

MEYRIC HUGHES, Henry Andrew Carne; s of Reginald Richard Meyric Hughes (d 1961), and Jean Mary Carne Brooke, *née* Pratt; *b* 1 April 1942; *Educ* Shrewsbury Sch, Univ of Rennes, Univ of Munich, Univ Coll Oxford (BA), Univ of Sussex (MA); *m* 3 Aug 1968, Alison Hamilton, da of David Bruce Faulds (d 1976), of Chester; 1 s (Sam b 1975), 1 da (Henrietta b 1971); *Career* Br Cncl: asst regnl dir W Berlin 1968–71, asst rep (arts) France 1971–73, asst dir and curator of permanent collection Fine Arts Dept 1977–79, regnl dir N Italy Milan 1979–83, dir Visiting Arts Office GB and NI 1984–86, head of visual arts (formerly styled dir Fine Arts Dept) 1986–92; dir (i/c nat touring exhibitions and Arts Cncl Collection) Hayward Gallery London 1992–96 (curator/advsr 1996–); dir Riverside Tst 1986–, memb Ct RCA 1986–, hon memb Sr Common Room RCA 1988–, vice pres Br Section Int Assoc of Art Critics 1991– (pres 1988–91); memb Bd: Watermans Arts Centre Brentford 1991–93, Academy Forum 1992–, Inst for New Int Visual Arts 1993–; memb: Slade Ctee Univ of London 1988–, Faculty of Fine Arts The Br Sch at Rome 1988–92, Advsy Gp Hayward Gallery London 1986–92, CIMAM (UNESCO), Internationale Kunstausstellungsleitertagung eV (IKT, memb Int Bd 1992–), Mgmnt Ctee Matts Gallery London 1993–, Int Advsy Bd MANIFESTA Rotterdam 1993–, Göteborg Kunsthallen 1995–; observer: Art Panel Scottish Arts Cncl, Visual Arts Panel Arts Cncl of GB 1986–92; adjudicator Claremorris Open Ireland 1987; jury memb: Turner Prize 1988, European Painting Prize Oostende 1990; chm of jury Contemporary View competition RCA 1990, chm Selection Ctee for Eighty (touring exhibition) Strasbourg 1988, co-selector and catalogue contrib The Vigorous Imagination Edinburgh Festival 1987, cmmr Venice Biennale 1986–92 (Auerbach 1986, Cragg 1988, Kapoor 1990, Contemporary British Architecture 1991, Hamilton 1993); numerous contributions to exhibition catalogues, translator of historical and art historical publications from French and German, author of articles on cultural policy and contemporary art; Silver medal Czechoslovak Soc for Int Cultural Relations 1986; Officier de l'Ordre des Arts et des Lettres (France); FRSA 1988; *Recreations* music; *Style—* Henry Meyric Hughes, Esq; ✉ 13 Ashchurch Grove, London W12 (☎ 0181 749 4098); Director of Exhibitions, The Hayward Gallery, SBC, Royal Festival Hall, Belvedere Road, London SE1 8XX (☎ 0171 921 0600)

MEYRICK, *see:* Tapps-Gervis-Meyrick

MEYRICK, Sir David John Charlton; 4 Bt (UK 1880), of Bush, Pembrokeshire; s of Col Sir Thomas Frederick Meyrick, 3 Bt, TD, DL (d 1983), and his 1 w, Ivy Frances, *née* Pilkington (d 1947); *b* 2 Dec 1926; *Educ* Eton, Trinity Hall Cambridge (MA); *m* 29 Sept 1962, Penelope Anne, da of Cdr John Bertram Aubrey Marsden-Smedley, RN (d 1959); 3 s (Timothy Thomas Charlton b 1963, Simon Edward b 1965, Christopher John b 1967); *Heir* s, Timothy Thomas Charlton Meyrick b 5 Nov 1963; *Career* former chartered surveyor and land agent; *Recreations* riding, sailing; *Style—* Sir David Meyrick, Bt; ✉ Bush House, Gumfreston, Tenby, Dyfed SA70 8RA (☎ 01834 842974)

MEYRICK, Dr Roger Llewellyn; JP (1971); s of Thidal Francis Meyrick (d 1965), of Swansea, and Helen Viviene, *née* Jones (d 1979); *b* 31 March 1930; *Educ* Dulwich Coll, King's Coll London, King's Coll Hosp Univ of London (MB BS); *m* 6 March 1954, Barbara Treseder, da of Reginald George Coombs (d 1974), of Stroud, Gloucs; 1 s (Huw b 1 Jan 1966), 3 da (Olivia b 1 March 1955, Daryl b 28 April 1956, Clare b 16 Dec 1958); *Career* princ in gen med practice Lewisham London 1954–90, hosp practitioner in dermatology Lewisham Hosp 1972–90, facilitator in gen practice Lewisham and N Southwark 1988–90; RCGP: chm S London Faculty 1969–72, provost S London Faculty 1977–80; pres W Kent Medicochirurgical Soc 1972–73; chm Magistrates Assoc SE London 1987–90, Plymouth City Bench 1993–; Freeman City of London 1970, Liveryman Worshipful Soc of Apothecaries 1970; MRCS, LRCP, FRCGP, FRSM 1967, memb BMA 1954; *Books* Understanding Cancer (ed jtly, 1977), Principles of Practice Management (contrib, 1984), Patient Health Education; Historical Account of St Peter's Church, Peter Tavy, Devon (1992), Early Medical Practice in Lewisham, London (1993); *Recreations* local medical history, gardening; *Clubs* Royal Cwlth Soc; *Style—* Dr Roger Meyrick, JP; ✉ Boulters Tor, Smeardon Down, Peter Tavy, nr Tavistock, Devon PL19 9NX (☎ 01822 810525)

MEYRICK, Timothy Thomas Charlton; s and h of Sir David John Charlton Meyrick, 4 Bt, *qv*; *b* 5 Nov 1963; *Educ* Eton, Bristol Univ; *Style—* Timothy Meyrick, Esq; ✉ c/o Bush House, Gumfreston, Tenby, Dyfed

MEYSEY-THOMPSON, Sir (Humphrey) Simon; 4 Bt (UK 1874), of Kirby Hall, Yorkshire; s of Guy Herbert Meysey-Thompson (d 1961), and kinsman of Sir Algar de Clifford Charles Meysey-Thompson, 3 Bt (d 1967); *b* 31 March 1935; *Style—* Sir Simon Meysey-Thompson, Bt; ✉ 10 Church St, Woodbridge, Suffolk IP12 1DH (☎ 01394 382144)

MEZENTSEVA, Galina; *b* 8 Nov 1952; *Educ* Vaganova Ballet Acad St Petersburg; *Career* prima ballerina Kirov Ballet 1971–91 (joined as princ straight from Vaganova Sch), sometime princ dancer Scottish Ballet; has danced premières of ballets in venues incl Paris Opera, La Scala Milan, Royal Opera House Covent Garden, Lincoln Center NY; memb Scottish Ballet tour of Russia 1992 (incl return to Maryinsky Theatre St Petersburg, home of the former Kirov Ballet); *Roles* has danced entire Kirov repertoire, best known for classical roles incl Giselle, Odette/Odile and The Dying Swan; other major roles incl: Princess Aurora in The Sleeping Beauty, Kitri in Don Quixote, Nikia in La Bayadere, Zarema in The Fountain of Bakhchisarai, La Sylphide, Mekhmeneh Bahnu in Legend of Love, Esmerelda in Notre Dame de Paris, Nestan-Daredzhan in The Night in a Tiger's Skin, Balanchine's Who Cares?, Swanilda in Coppèlia; *Awards* numerous incl: first prize 3rd World Ballet Competition 1980, Laureate Award Moscow Int Ballet Competition, Gold Medal Japan Int Ballet Competition, Honoured Artist and People's Artist of the Soviet Union (highest award of former USSR); *Recreations* philosophy, history, music; *Style—* Ms Galina Mezentseva; ✉ c/o Irena Mitze, 99 Iverna Court, London W8 6TX (☎ 0171 937 9118)

MIALL, (Rowland) Leonard; OBE (1961); s of Rowland Miall (d 1955), of Lastingham, Yorks, and Sara Grace, *née* Dixon (d 1975); *b* 6 Nov 1914; *Educ* Bootham Sch York, Freiburg Univ, St John's Coll Cambridge; *m* 1, 18 Jan 1941, Lorna Barbara (d 1974), da of George Rackham (d 1974), of Bucks; 3 s (Roger b 1944, Tristram b 1947, St John b 1952), 1 da (Virginia b 1949); m 2, 10 Oct 1975, Sally Greenaway Bicknell, da of Gordon Leith, MC (d 1965), of Johannesburg; *Career* pres Cambridge Union 1936, ed Cambridge Review 1936, lectured in USA 1937, sec Br-American Assoc 1937–39, joined BBC, inaugurated talks broadcast to Europe 1939, German talks and features ed 1940–42, memb Br Political Warfare Mission to US 1942–44 (dir of news San Francisco 1943, head NY Office 1944), personal asst to Dep DG Political Warfare Exec 1944, attached to Psychological Warfare Div of SHAEF 1945; BBC: special corr Czechoslovakia 1945, actg dip corr 1945, chief corr in US 1945–53, head of TV Talks 1954, asst controller of Current Affrs and Talks TV 1961, special asst to dir of TV planning start of BBC2 1962, asst controller of Programme Servs TV 1963–66, rep in USA 1966–71, controller of Overseas and Foreign Rels 1971–74; res historian 1975–84, bdcasting historian 1985–; inaugurated BBC lunchtime lectures 1962, advsr Ctee on Broadcasting New Delhi 1965, fndr Cwlth Bdcasting Assoc 1975, dir Visnews Ltd 1976–93 (dep chm 1984–85), dir Reuters TV Ltd 1993–94; overseas dir BAFTA 1974–, memb Cncl Royal TV Soc 1984–91; Certificate of Appreciation NYC 1970; FRTS 1985, FRSA; *Publications* Richard Dimbleby, Broadcaster (ed, 1966), Inside the BBC: British Broadcasting Characters (1994); contrib to DNB and The Independent; *Recreations* travel, writing; *Clubs* Garrick, Union (Cambridge), Phyllis Court (Henley); *Style—* Leonard Miall, Esq, OBE; ✉ Maryfield Cottage, High St, Taplow Village, Maidenhead SL6 0EX (☎ 01628 604195, fax 01628 663621)

MICHAEL, Alun; JP (Cardiff 1972), MP (Lab) Cardiff South and Penarth (majority 10,425); *b* 22 Aug 1943; *Educ* Colwyn Bay GS, Univ of Keele; *m* 23 July 1966; 2 s, 3 da; *Career* journalist 1966–71, youth and community worker 1971–87, magistrate 1972– (chm Cardiff Juvenile Bench until 1986), memb Cardiff City Cncl 1973–89 (sometime chm Planning Ctee and Fin and Econ Devpt Ctee); MP (Lab) Cardiff S and Penarth 1987–, oppn whip 1987–88, shadow min for Welsh affrs 1988–92, shadow min for home affrs and for voluntary sector 1992–; chm Co-op Parly Gp 1990–92, currently chm All-Pty Gp on Somalia, sec All-Pty Gp for Colleges and vice-chm British-German Parly Gp; former chm All-Pty Gp on Alcohol Misuse and sec All-Pty Gp on Personal Social Services; chm Parly Friends of the Welsh National Opera, dep chm Cardiff Bay Opera House, vice-pres YHA, former vice-pres Building Societies Assoc; *Recreations* long-distance running, hill-walking, opera, music and reading; *Style—* Alun Michael, Esq, JP, MP; ✉ House of Commons, London SW1A 0AA (☎ 0171 219 3441); constituency office (☎ 01222 223533)

MICHAEL, Anthony Colin; s of Edwin George Michael (d 1993), and Maureen Ellen, *née* McCabe; *b* 18 Oct 1958; *Educ* Erith GS Kent, St Martin's Sch of Art (BA); *partner* Stephanie Joy Nash, *qv*; 1 s (Montgomery Louis Spencer b 6 May 1996); *Career* former gardener; self employed ptnr Michael Nash Associates 1984–; initially designers of record sleeves for artists incl Neneh Cherry, Fluke, Etienne Daho and Seal, subsequently cmmns for fashion designers Jasper Conran, Issey Miyake, Jil Sander and Philip Treacy, etc, graphic designers for Harvey Nichols own brand food products 1992–, packaging designers for Egg (fashion retail outlet) 1994; *Awards* (for Harvey Nichols food packaging) Gold Award D&AD for the Most Outstanding Packaging Range 1993, Silver Award D&AD for the Most Oustanding Packaging - Individual Pack 1994, Art Dirs' Club of Europe Award 1994, CSD Minerva Award for Graphic Design 1994 and NY Festivals Gold Medal and Grand Award 1994, Silver Award D&AD for Compact Disk Packaging for Massive Attack 1995, various others from music indust; *Style—* Anthony Michael, Esq; ✉ Michael Nash Associates, 44 Newman Street, London W1P 3PA (☎ 0171 631 3370, fax 0171 637 9629)

MICHAEL, Christine Helen; da of John Terence Hennessey, of Oldham, Lancs, and Helen, *née* Stringer; *b* 31 May 1954; *Educ* Notre Dame HS Manchester, Leeds Poly (BA), Leicester Poly (MBA); *m* 21 Oct 1994, Kelvin Michael, s of Alan Michael; 1 s (Louis John b 12 June 1996); *Career* account dir i/c business devpt and mktg strategy PD Design Consultancy 1984–88 (clients incl Sainsbury's, Argos, Post Office and Black & Decker), account dir i/c Euro business devpt Fords Design Group 1990–93 (clients incl Air France, Specsavers and Parker Pens), proprietor Michael Management Services 1993–; Int Gold Popai Award (for Parker Pens) 1992; CIM: memb 1978–, branch chm 1982–, memb Nat Cncl 1985–, Pres's Award 1990; memb: Ladies' Circle, PCC; *Recreations* classical music, tennis, aerobics, design and architecture; *Style—* Mrs Christine Michael; ✉ Michael Management Services, 22 Main Street, Marston Trussell, Market Harborough, Leics LE16 9TY (☎ 01858 461191, fax 01858 462347)

MICHAEL, Prof Christopher; s of David Parry Martin Michael, CBE (d 1986), of Newport, and Mary Horner, *née* Hayward; *b* 29 May 1942; *Educ* Jesus Coll Oxford (MA, DPhil); *m* 1964, Marilyn; 2 s (Nicholas b 1964, David b 1967); *Career* staff memb Theory Div CERN Geneva 1969–74, prof of theoretical physics Univ of Liverpool 1974–; FInstP 1976; *Publications* numerous res articles on theoretical high energy physics; *Recreations* underwater hockey, sub aqua diving; *Style—* Prof Christopher Michael; ✉ Division of Theoretical Physics, University of Liverpool, Liverpool L69 3BX (☎ 0151 794 3771, fax 0151 794 3784, telex 627095 UNILPL G)

MICHAEL, George, *né* Georgios Panayiotou; *b* 25 June 1963; *Educ* Bushey Meads Sch; *Career* singer and songwriter; formed Wham! 1981; released first single Wham Rap!

(Enjoy What You Do?) 1982; albums with Wham!: Fantastic (1983, reached UK no 1), Make It Big (1984, UK no 1), The Final (compilation, 1986, UK no 2); breakup of Wham! 1986; first solo single Careless Whisper (1984, UK no 1); solo albums: Faith (1987, UK no 1), Listen Without Prejudice, Vol 1 (1990, UK no 1), Older (1996, first album since legal dispute with Sony Music); singles: Jesus to a Child 1995, Fastlove (1996, UK no 1); has worked with: Smokey Robinson, Stevie Wonder, Elton John, *qv*, Aretha Franklin and others; awards incl: Songwriter of the Year Ivor Novello Awards 1985 and 1990, outstanding contrib to British Music BRIT Award 1986, Best British Male Artist BRIT Award 1988, R&B Grammy Award 1988, Album of the Year (for Faith) 1989, two American Music Awards 1989, Video Vanguard Award MTV 1989, Best British Album of the Year Award BRIT Award 1991, Best Male Singer Rolling Stone Readers' Awards 1991; organised and headlined HRH The Princess of Wales's Concert of Hope 1993; *Books* Bare (autobiography, 1990); *Style*— George Michael, Esq

MICHAEL, (Elizabeth) Rosemary; da of The Rev Ernest Stanley Rees Mackay Michael (d 1984), and Elizabeth Felicia, *née* Powell (d 1993); *b* 1 Aug 1939; *Educ* King Alfred Sch; *Career* PA to Dir of Educn Advertising Assoc 1965–68, promotions and events organiser The Sunday Times 1968–74, exec asst to md Thomson Organisation 1974–76, dir of courses and seminars CAM 1976–86 then Advertising Assoc 1986– (CAM courses and seminars transferred to Advertising Assoc 1986); advertising woman of the year (Adwoman Assoc) 1982; fell CAM Fndn; *Style*— Miss Rosemary Michael; ✉ Advertising Association, Abford House, 15 Wilton Road, London SW1V 1NJ (☎ 0171 828 2771, fax 0171 931 0376)

MICHAEL, Simon Laurence; s of Anthony Denis Michael, of London, and Regina, *née* Milstone; *b* 4 Jan 1955; *Educ* King's Coll London (LLB); *m* 7 Sept 1987, Elaine Laura, da of Cameron Hudson Duncan (d 1983); 1 s (Alastair b 1990), 1 da (Kay b 1988); *Career* called to the Bar Middle Temple 1978; memb: Assoc of Personal Injury Lawyers, Personal Injury Bar Assoc, Professional Negligence Bar Assoc; *Books* The Usurper (jtly, 1988), The Cut Throat (1989), The Long Lie (1991); *Style*— Simon Michael, Esq; ✉ Bedford Chambers (dx 36901 AMPTHILL, e-mail SLMichael@msn.com)

MICHAEL, Dr William Francis; s of Dr Stephen Ernest Michael (d 1971), of Croydon, and Dr Janet Michael, *née* Young; *b* 22 June 1936; *Educ* Winchester, New Coll Oxford (MA, DM); *m* 27 May 1972, Mary Ann, da of Bernard Sadler (d 1982), of Reading; 2 da (Victoria b 1974, Juliet b 1977); *Career* Nat Serv, 2 Lt RA 1955–56; jr med appts: St Thomas's Hosp, National Hosp 1967–70, Bart's 1970–74; conslt neurologist SE Thames Regnl Neurological Unit 1974–95, Neuroscience Centre King's Coll Hosp 1995–; memb: Assoc of Br Neurologists 1974, RSM; FRCP 1981; *Recreations* music, books, gardening, skiing; *Style*— Dr William Michael; ✉ 19 Durham Avenue, Bromley, Kent (☎ 0181 464 7685)

MICHAELS, Robert Stewart John; s of Alexander Michaels, of Stanmore, and Evelyn, *née* Susman; *b* 20 Dec 1941; *Educ* Ravensfield Coll Orange Hill, St Martin's Sch of Art, Université d'Aix En Provence; *m* 19 June 1966, Marilyn, da of Edward Lee; 2 s (Mark John Louis b 4 Oct 1972, Daniel David b 19 Sept 1977); *Career* chm and md Robert Michaels Holdings plc 1974–; dir: Mardan Properties Ltd, John Crowther plc 1987, Robert Mark Ltd, Marongate plc, Twenty One Clothing Company Ltd; tstee Bryanston Tst, memb Permanent Panel Nat Econ Devpt Office; cncllr (Cons) Knightsbridge Ward Westminster City Cncl 1990–94 (chm Investments Ctee, vice chm Financial Mgmnt and Personnel Ctee, whip 1991), dir Westminster Enterprise Agency 1990–, vice pres and memb Policy Gp Small Business Bureau 1991–, memb House of Lords Rural Economy Gp 1991; chm Bd of Govrs Sussex House Sch; Freeman City of London 1979, life memb Guild of Freemen City of London; Liveryman Worshipful Companies of: Horners, Farriers, Pattenmakers; FInstD 1980; *Recreations* family, reading, tennis, skiing, cricket, racing cars; *Clubs* Carlton, Royal Automobile, Ferrari Owners'; *Style*— Robert Michaels, Esq; ✉ Robert Michaels Holdings plc, 12 Great Portland St, London W1N 6JQ (☎ 0171 580 1656, fax 0171 706 4690)

MICHAELS-MOORE, Anthony; s of John Moore, of Grays, Essex, and Isabel, *née* Shephard; *b* 8 April 1957; *Educ* Gravesend Sch for Boys, Univ of Newcastle upon Tyne, St Mary's Teacher Trg Coll, RSAMD; *m* 16 Feb 1980, Ewa Bozena Maria, da of Stanislaw Migocki; 1 da (Kathryn Ashley Maria b 7 Feb 1987); *Career* baritone; teacher St John's CE Sch Crowborough 1979–84, opera course RSAMD 1984–85, professional debut Opera-go-Round Scottish Opera 1985; first Br winner Luciano Pavarotti/Opera Co of Philadelphia competition 1986; sung with orchs incl: Toronto Symphony, Scot Nat, The Philharmonia, Royal Philharmonic, LSO, CBSO, Vienna Philharmonic; *Roles* incl: Marcello in La Bohème (Opera North, Royal Opera House Covent Garden, ENO), Belcore in L'Elisir d'Amore, Dr Malatesta in Don Pasquale, (Royal Opera House), Ping in Turandot (Covent Garden), Forester in The Cunning Little Vixen (Covent Garden), Zurga in the Pearl Fishers (ENO debut 1987), Count Almaviva in The Marriage of Figaro (ENO, Bavarian State Opera), Figaro in The Barber of Seville (WNO debut 1990, Barcelona 1991, Royal Opera House 1993, Vienna 1995), Guglielmo in Cosi fan Tutte (USA debut Philadelphia 1988, Canadian Debut Canadian Opera Co 1991), Giorgio Germont in La Traviata (Opera North 1991), Marquis of Posa in Don Carlos (Opera North 1993 and Pittsburgh 1997), Licinius in La Vestale (La Scala Milan debut 1993), Lescaut in Manon Lescaut (Vienna Staatsoper debut 1994, Naples debut 1994), Sharpless in Madama Butterfly (Opèra Bastille debut 1994), Don Giovanni (Tel Aviv 1994), Hamlet Opera North 1995, Orestes in Iphigene en Tauride (Opera Bastille) 1995, Onegin in Eugene Onegin (Opera Bastille) 1995, Baron Scarpia in Tosca (Royal Opera House) 1996, Marcello in La Boheme and Silvio in Pagliacci (Met NY debut, 1996), Gerard in Andrea Chenier (Teatro Colon Buenos Aires debut, 1996), title role in Macbeth (Royal Opera House 1997); *Recordings* La Vestale (with La Scala under Riccardo Muti), The Fairy Queen (under Harnoncourt), Mendelssohn Die Erste Walpurgisnacht (with The Philharmonia), Orff Carmina Burana (with Vienna Philharmonic under Andre Previn), Gilbert & Sullivan Yeomen of the Guard, Szymanowski Stabat Mater (with The Philharmonia under Claus Peter Flor), Mercadante Orazi i Curiazi (Opera Rara recording), Opera Spectacular (with the Royal Philharmonic Orch), Die Fledermaus (video, with Royal Opera Co), Puccini Favourites (with Royal Opera Co), Lucia di Lammermoor (under Charles Mackerras); *Recreations* football, cricket, swimming, Indian food; *Style*— Anthony Michaels-Moore, Esq; ✉ c/o John Coast, Harold Holt Ltd, 31 Sinclair Road, London W14 0NS (☎ 0171 603 4600, fax 0171 603 0019)

MICHEL, Keith; s of Capt George Richard Michel, of E Horsley, Surrey, and Winifred Eve Michel (d 1972); *b* 19 May 1948; *Educ* Bradfield Coll, Fitzwilliam Coll Cambridge (MA, football blue 1968–70, Oxbridge rep team Japan 1969, Univ Crusaders CC); *m* 16 Dec 1972, Rosemary Suzannah, da of Stanley Joseph Simons, of Southgate, London; 1 s (Edward b 30 April 1980); *Career* slr; articled clerk Coward Chance (now Clifford Chance) 1971–73, asst slr Clyde & Co 1973–75, ptnr Holman Fenwick & Willan 1975– (former asst slr); author of various pubns incl: Lloyd's List, Lloyd's Maritime Commercial Law Quarterly, Law Society's Gazette; memb: Grasshoppers CC, Free Foresters CC, Old Bradfieldion FC, Cncl AFA; tstee Univ of Cambridge FC, clerk Bd of Govrs Bradfield Coll 1991–93; memb: Law Soc 1973, City of London Solicitors Co 1990; *Books* Contraband (1988), Countdown (1991), Caracara (1995); *Recreations* family life, football, cricket, windsurfing, history, archaeology, wildlife conservation; *Clubs* Hawks; *Style*— Keith Michel, Esq; ✉ Marlow House, Lloyds Ave, London EC3N 3AL (☎ 0171 488 2300, fax 0171 481 0316, telex 8812247 HFW LON)

MICHELL, Keith Joseph; s of Joseph Michell (d 1957), and Alice Maude Alsat (d 1957); *b* 1 Dec 1928; *Educ* Warnertown Sch, Port Pirie HS, SA Sch of Arts and Crafts, Adelaide Teachers Coll, Adelaide Univ, Old Vic Theatre Sch; *m* 1957, Jeannette Laura, da of Frank Sterk (d 1985); 1 s (Paul b 1960), 1 da (Helena b 1961); *Career* artist and actor; memb original Young Vic Theatre Co, first appearance And so to Bed (London) 1951; leading actor Shakespeare Meml Theatre Co 1952–56, joined Old Vic Co 1956, artistic dir Chichester Festival Theatre 1974–77; *Theatre* with Shakespeare Meml Theatre Co: Orsino in Twelfth Night, Macduff in Macbeth, Hotspur in Henry IV, Orlando in As you like it, Petuchio in The Taming of the Shrew, Theseus in A Midsummer Night's Dream, Archilles in Troilus and Cressida, Master Ford in The Merry Wives of Windsor, Parolles in All's Well That Ends Well (Parolles); with Old Vic Co: Benedick in Two Gentlemen of Verona, Antony in Antony & Cleopatra, Aaron in Titus Andronicus; other London roles incl: Oscar/Nector in Irma la Douce (also NY) 1958–61, lead role in Robert and Elizabeth 1964, The King's Mare 1966, Don Quixote in Man of La Mancha (also NY) 1968–70, Abelard in Abelard & Heloise (also NY) 1971, title role in Hamlet (Bankside) 1972, Robert Browning in Dear Love 1973; other credits incl:, The Director in Tonight We Improvise, Oedipus in Oedipus Tyrannus, Iago in Othello 1974, Cyrano in Cyrano De Bergerac 1975 (Othello and Cyrano presented at Hong Kong Arts Festival), Twelfth Night (dir and designer) 1976, Major Matthew in Monsieur Perrichons Travels 1976, In Order of Appearance (dir and designer) 1977, Magnus in The Apple Cart (toured Luxembourg, London, Brussels and Aust) 1977, Othello (tour to Aust), Sherlock Holmes in The Crucifer of Blood (London) 1979, Oscar in On the 20th Century (London) 1980, lead in Pete McGynty and the Dream Time (Melbourne Theatre Co) 1981, Captain Beaky Christmas Show London 1981–82, Sir Arthur in On the Rocks 1982, Prospero in The Tempest (Brisbane) 1982, One Man Show Port Pirie (Aust) 1982, Salieri in Amadeus 1983, La Cage aux Folles (San Francisco, NY, Sydney and Melbourne) 1985–86, Rochester in Jane Eyre (Chichester) 1986, Augustus John in Portraits (Malvern Festival and London) 1987, Gordon-Cumming in The Royal Baccarat Scandal (Chichester and London) 1988–89, Henry VIII 1991, George in Aspects of Love (Toronto 1991–92 and Chicago 1992), Scrooge Melbourne 1993–94, Caesar in Caesar and Cleopatra (Edmonton Canada) 1994, Brazilian Blue (Aust) 1995, Monsieur Amilear (Chichester) 1995; *Television* in UK incl: Pygmalion, Act of Violence, Mayerling Affair, Wuthering Heights, The Bergonzi Hand, Ring Round the Moon, Spread of the Eagle (series of Roman plays), An Ideal Husband, The Shifting Heart, Loyalties, Kain, The Six Wives of Henry VIII, Keith Michell Special, Keith Michell Christmas Show, Keith Michell at the Shows, Dear Love, Keith Michell in Concert at Chichester, Captain Beaky and his Band, Captain Beaky (Vol II); US TV incl: The Story of the Marlboroughs, Jacob and Joseph, The Story of David, The Tenth Month, The Day Christ Died, The Miracle, Murder She Wrote (series of 6); videos: Pirates of Penzance (Maj-Gen), The Gondoliers (Grand Inquisitor), Ruddigore (Robin Oakapple); *Films* appearances incl: Dangerous Exile, The Hell Fire Club, Seven Seas to Calais, The Executioner, House of Cards, Prudence and the Pill, Henry VIII and his Six Wives, Moments, The Deceivers; *Recordings* Ancient and Modern, At the Shows, Words Words Words, The Sonnet and the Prophet, Captain Beaky and his Band, Captain Beaky Vol II, Guys and Dolls (CD) 1995; *Exhibitions* one man painting shows: Jamaica 1960, New York 1962, Portugal 1963, Outback in Australia 1965, Don Quixote 1969, Abelard and Heloise 1972, Hamlet 1972, Self Portrait Henry VIII (screen print) 1972, Piktors Metamorphosis (lithograph) 1972, Shakespeare Sonnets (lithographs) 1974, Capt Beaky 1982, Alice In Wonderland 1982, Vincent Gall Adelaide 1989, Majorcan Paintings The Century Galleries 1991; *Awards* London Critics' Best Actor in a Musical (Man of La Mancha) 1968, Best Actor (Soc of Film and TV Arts) 1970, Show Business Personality of the Year (Grand Order of Water Rats) 1971, Top Actor (Sun TV Award) 1971, Special Award (Royal Variety Club of GB) 1971, Outstanding single performance by an actor (Royal Acad of TV Arts) 1971, British Film Award (Evening News) 1973, Logie Award (Aust) 1974; *Publications* illustrator Captain Beaky books of poems, author of Practically Macrobiotic Cook Book (1987); *Recreations* gardening, reading; *Style*— Keith Michell, Esq; ✉ c/o London Management, 2–4 Noel Street, London W1V 3RB (☎ 0171 287 9000, fax 0171 287 3036)

MICHELL, Prof (Alastair) Robert; s of Dr Charles Francis Michell (d 1960), of London, and Eva, *née* Freyhan; *b* 28 Dec 1940; *Educ* Dulwich, RVC London (BSc, BVetMed, PhD, DSc, MRCVS, pres RVC Students' Union); *m* 1963, Pauline, da of Frederick Arthur Mountford Selley; 1 da (Tania Claire b 1968); *Career* Harkness fell (Cwlth Fund of NY) Rockefeller Univ, Nat Inst of Health and UCLA (Cedars Sinai Hosp) USA 1969–71, Beit meml research fell in med 1971–73, MRC research fell Nephrology Section Univ of Chicago Med Sch 1974–76; RVC London: lectr in physiology 1976–83, reader in med 1983–93, prof of applied physiology and comparative med 1993–; chm RCVS/BVA Jt Ctee on Continuing Professional Devpt 1988–92; pres: Euro Soc for Vet Nephrology 1985–88, Vet Research Club 1988–89, RVC Alumnus Assoc 1989–91, Assoc of Vet Teachers and Research Workers 1994–95; memb Cncl: BVA 1983–85, 1988–92 and 1995–, RVC 1986–94 and 1995–, RCVS 1992–96 (elected memb), Comparative Med Section RSM (vice pres 1992–94); runner-up first Perspectives in Biology and Medicine writing award for young scientists 1975, Blaine award (Br Small Animal Vet Assoc) for outstanding contribs to the advancement of small animal med 1990, Weipers commemorative lectr (Central Vet Soc) 1991, George Fleming prize (Br Vet Jl) 1992; memb numerous professional bodies incl: Physiological Soc, Nutrition Soc, Assoc for Vet Clinical Pharmacology and Therapeutics, London Hypertension Soc, Renal Assoc; FRSM, FRSA; *Books* Renal Disease in Dogs and Cats: Comparative and Clinical Aspects (ed, 1988), An Introduction to Veterinary Anatomy and Physiology (jtly, 1989), Veterinary Fluid Therapy (jtly, 1989), The Advancement of Veterinary Science (ed, 4 vols, 1992), Clinical Biology of Sodium (1995); *Recreations* music, theatre, tennis, travel, writing; *Style*— Prof Robert Michell; ✉ Royal Veterinary College, Hawkshead Lane, North Mymms, Hatfield, Herts AL9 7TA (☎ 01707 666270, fax 01707 660671)

MICHELL, Prof Robert Hall (Bob); s of Rowland Charles Michell, and Elsie Lorna, *née* Hall; *b* 16 April 1941; *Educ* Crewkerne Sch Somerset, Univ of Birmingham (BSc, PhD, DSc); *m* 13 Jan 1967 (m dis 1971), June Mary, *née* Evans; m 2, 28 July 1992, Esther Margaret Oppenheim; 2 s (Jo b 1974, Ben b 1991), 1 da (Naomi b 1986); *Career* Harvard Med Sch 1966–68; Univ of Birmingham: res fell 1965–66 and 1968–70, lectr 1970–81, sr lectr 1981–84, reader in biochemistry 1984–86, prof 1986–87, Royal Soc res prof 1987–; memb Editorial Bd: Journal of Neurochemistry 1974–78, Cell Calcium 1979–89, Biochemical Journal 1982–88 (ed Advsy Panel 1981–82), Current Opinion in Cell Biology 1988–, Biological Sciences Review 1988–, Proceedings of The Royal Society of London 1989–, Journal of Molecular Endocrinology 1991–, Molecular Membrane Biology 1994–; fndn lectr RCPath 1989, Bertram Lewis Abrahams lectr RCP 1990, Wellcome visiting prof Univ of Vermont 1987, Royal Soc UK-Canada Rutherford lectr 1994; memb: Biochemical Soc (CIBA medal 1988), Br Nat Ctee for Pharmacology 1982–87, Br Nat Ctee for Biochemistry 1988–89, Physiological Systems and Disorders Res Bd MRC 1985–90, Brain Res Assoc, Br Soc for Cell Biology, Br Assoc for the Advancement of Sci, Royal Soc Int Rels Ctee 1991–94, Med and Scientific Advsy Panel Leukaemia Res Fund 1989–92, Advsy Bd Beit Meml Tst 1993–, Biochemistry Panel for 1996 Research Assessment Execise HEFC; chm Systems Bd Grants Ctee MRC 1988–90; memb Euro Molecular Biology Orgn (EMBO) 1991; govr Cadbury Sixth Form Coll 1991–; FRS 1986 (memb Cncl 1996–97); *Books* Membranes And Their Cellular Functions (with J B Finean and R Coleman, 1974, 3 edn 1984), New Comprehensive Biochemistry (contrib ed with

J B Finean, 1981), Cell Calcium (contrib ed, 1982), Inositol Lipids in Cellular Signalling (ed with J W Putney, 1987), Inositol Lipids and Transmembrane Signalling (ed with M J Berridge, 1988), Inositol Lipids and Cellular Signalling (ed with A H Drummond and C P Downes, 1989); *Style*— Prof Robert Michell; ✉ Centre for Clinical Research in Immunology and Signalling, The Medical School, University of Birmingham, Birmingham B15 2TT (☎ 0121 414 5413, fax 0121 414 6840, e-mail r.h.michell@bham.ac.uk)

MICHELL, Roger; s of H D Michell, and J Michell, *née* Green; *b* 5 June 1956; *Educ* Clifton Coll, Queens' Coll Cambridge (exhibitioner, BA); *m* Kate Buffery; 2 c (Harry b 6 Dec 1991, Rosie b 17 Mar 1996); *Career* director; Brighton Actors Workshop 1977, Thames TV training bursary Royal Ct 1978–80, RSC 1984–90, Drama Director's Course BBC TV 1990; Judith E Wilson sr fell Trinity Coll Cambridge 1989; *Theatre* for RSC incl: Temptation, The Dead Monkey, Restoration, Some Americans Abroad, Two Shakespearean Actors, The Constant Couple, Hamlet, Merchant of Venice; others incl: The Catch (Royal Court), The Coup (RNT), The Key Tag (Royal Court), Private Dick (Edinburgh Festival, Lyric), Marya (Old Vic), Under Milk Wood (RNT), My Night with Reg (Royal Court and West End), Some Sunny Day (Hampstead); *Films* Down Town Lagos 1991, Buddha of Suburbia 1993, Ready When You Are Mr Patel 1995, Persuasion 1995, My Night with Reg 1996; *Awards* Buzz Goodbody award RSC 1977, Edinburgh Fringe First award 1977, Drama Desk nomination NY 1990, BAFTA nomination for Buddha of Suburbia; for Persuasion incl: BAFTA, RTS nomination, Critics' Circle; *Style*— Roger Michell

MICHELMORE, Clifford Arthur (Cliff); CBE (1969); s of (Albert) Herbert Michelmore (d 1921), of Cowes, IOW, and Ellen, *née* Alford (d 1947); *b* 11 Dec 1919; *Educ* Cowes HS, RAF Coll, Leicester Coll of Technol; *m* 4 March 1950, Jean, da of Guy Vivian Metcalfe (d 1962), of Reigate, Surrey; 1 s (Guy Alford Michelmore, *qv* b 1957), 1 da (Jenny Gwen b 1959); *Career* RAF 1935–47; Br Forces Network 1947; joined BBC 1950; presenter: Tonight, 24 Hours, Holiday, Home on Sunday 1984–, Coastline (Radio 4) 1991–, Cliff's Countryside 1991–, BBC TV Lifeline; md: RMEMI 1970–80, Michelmore Enterprises 1967–, CP Video 1987–93; FRSA 1970; *Books* Businessman's Book of Golf (1981), Holidays in Britain (1986), Two-Way Story (with Jean Metcalfe, 1987); *Recreations* golf; *Clubs* RAF; *Style*— Cliff Michelmore, Esq, CBE; ✉ Northend Barn, South Harting, West Sussex GU31 5NR (☎ 01732 825665); Brookfield, Bembridge, IOW PO3 5XW (☎ 019837 2480)

MICHELMORE, Guy Alford; s of Cliff Michelmore, CBE, of Reigate, Surrey, and Jean Metcalfe; *b* 27 Aug 1957; *Educ* St John's Sch Leatherhead, Pembroke Coll Oxford (MA); *m* 12 March 1988, Agnieszka, da of Eugeniusz Piotrowski, of Sopot, Poland; 1 s (Leo Arthur b 26 Dec 1990); *Career* reporter Anglia TV 1981–83, presenter London Plus 1984–85, reporter and presenter BBC Breakfast Time 1985–87 (reporter 1983–84), reporter A Fair Cop (series of police complaints documentaries) 1987–88, presenter Weekend 1988, reporter Friday Report (documentary) 1988–89, main presenter Newsroom South East 1989–93, presenter The Hotseat BBC Radio 5; composer and music publisher, md Music for Television Ltd; section offr Surrey Special Constabulary 1976–88; memb Assoc of Professional Composers; *Recreations* watching birds; *Style*— Guy Michelmore, Esq; ✉ c/o Arlington Enterprises, 1–3 Charlotte Street, London W1 (☎ 0171 580 0702, fax 0171 580 4994)

MICHELS, David Michael Charles; *b* 8 Dec 1946; *m* 15 Sept 1970, Michelle Ann; *Career* various sales and mktg positions rising to worldwide mktg dir Grand Metropolitan 1966–81; Ladbroke Group plc: sales and mktg dir hotels 1981–83, md Leisure Div 1983–85, md Ladbroke Hotels 1985–87; sr vice pres sales and mktg Hilton International 1987–89, dep chm Hilton UK and exec vice pres Hilton Worldwide 1989–91, chief exec Stakis plc 1991–; Hon DLitt Glasgow Caledonian Univ; FHCIMA; *Recreations* tennis, reading; *Clubs* Vanderbilt; *Style*— David Michels, Esq; ✉ Stakis plc, 3 Atlantic Quay, York Street, Glasgow G2 8JH (☎ 0141 204 4321, fax 0141 204 3366)

MICHIE, Alastair John; s of John Michie (d 1965), of Alyth, Perthshire, and Margaret, *née* Heggie; *b* 21 March 1948; *Educ* Blairgowrie HS Perthshire; *m* 28 July 1971, Dawn Elizabeth, da of James Edward Thomson Wittet, of Alyth, Perthshire; 1 s (Graham James b 1980), 1 da (Caroline Jane b 1975); *Career* Clydesdale Bank plc 1964–74; co sec: Lloyds Bank International Ltd 1981–85 (asst sec 1978–80), Lloyds TSB Group plc (formerly Lloyds Bank plc) 1985–; memb CIB (Scotland) 1969; ACIS 1973, FCIS 1981; *Recreations* golf, squash, swimming; *Style*— Alastair Michie, Esq; ✉ 14 Marlyns Close, Burpham, Guildford, Surrey GU4 7LR (☎ 01483 826688); Lloyds TSB Group plc, 71 Lombard St, London EC3P 3BS (☎ 0171 626 1500, fax 0171 929 2901)

MICHIE, Prof David Alan Redpath; OBE (1997); s of James Beattie Michie (d 1960), and Anne Redpath, OBE (d 1965); *b* 30 Nov 1928; *Educ* Hawick HS, Edinburgh Coll of Art (DA); *m* 27 March 1951, Eileen Anderson, James Temple Michie (d 1931); 2 da (Alison Jane b 1953, Lindsey Elizabeth b 1955); *Career* Nat Serv RA 1947–49; lectr in drawing and painting Grays Sch of Art Aberdeen 1957–61; Edinburgh Coll of Art: lectr 1961–74, vice-princ 1974–77, head Sch of Drawing and Painting 1982–90; emeritus prof of painting Heriot-Watt Univ 1991– (prof 1988–91); memb: Gen Teaching Cncl for Scotland 1975–80, Edinburgh Festival Soc 1977–, Convocation and Ct Heriot-Watt Univ 1979–82, Cncl Br Sch in Rome 1980–85, Museums and Galleries Cmmn 1991–96; memb SSA 1955, RSA 1972 (ARSA 1964), RGI 1983, FRSA 1990, RWA 1991; *Solo Exhibitions* Mercury Gallery London 1966, 1969, 1971, 1974, 1980, 1983, 1992 and 1996, Mercury Gallery Edinburgh 1986, Lothian Region Chambers Edinburgh 1977, Scottish Gallery Edinburgh 1980 and 1994, The Loomshop Gallery Lower Largo 1981 and 1987, Kasteel De Hooge Vuursche Baarn and Mia Joosten Gallery Amsterdam 1991; *Group Exhibitions* incl: Fourteen Scottish Painters (Cwlth Inst London) 1963, Contemporary Scottish Painting (The Alamo Gallery London) 1978, Contemporary Art from Scotland (touring) 1981–82, Works on Paper (Faculty of Fine Art Gallery Belgrade) 1986, Artists' Self Portraits (Tate Gallery London) 1989, Sea and Shore (Scottish Gallery) 1989, Artist Families (Fine Art Soc Edinburgh) 1989, Guthrie Award Prize Winners Exhibition (Fine Art Soc Edinburgh and Glasgow) 1990, Art Studio Faculty Exhibition Univ of California Santa Barbara 1991, Scottish Art in the 20th Century (Royal W of Eng Acad Bristol) 1991, The Scottish Gallery - The First 150 Years (Edinburgh) 1992, The Edinburgh School (The Scottish Gallery) 1993, Contemporary Scottish Painting Hong Kong 1994 and 1996; *Collections* incl: HM The Queen, Allied Lyons, James Capel, Edinburgh Educn Authy, Robert Fleming Holdings, Kirkcaldy Art Gallery, Glasgow Art Gallery and Museum, Kleinwort, Heriot-Watt Univ, Liverpool Univ, Nuffield Fndn, Queen Elizabeth Coll London, NM Rothschild, RAC, Royal Scottish Acad, Royal W of Eng Acad, Scottish Life Assurance Co, Scottish Nat Gallery of Modern Art, Tate Gallery Archive; *Awards* Guthrie Award RSA 1964, David Cargill Prize RGI 1977, Lothian Region Award RSA 1977, Sir William Gillies scholarship RSA 1980, RGI Prize 1990, Cornelissen Prize RWA 1992; *Recreations* music, gardening; *Style*— Prof David Michie, OBE

MICHIE, Prof Donald; s of James Kilgour Michie (d 1967), and Marjorie Crain, *née* Pfeiffer (d 1986); *b* 11 Nov 1923; *Educ* Rugby, Balliol Coll Oxford (scholar, MA, DPhil, DSc); *m* 1, 1949 (m dis 1951), Zena Margaret, *née* Davies; 1 s (Christopher b 1950); m 2, 1952 (m dis 1958), Hon Anne Laura Dorinthea, *née* McLaren, da of 2 Baron Aberconway, CBE (d 1953); 1 s (Jonathan Mark b 1957), 2 da (Susan Fiona Dorinthea (Mrs Andrew Drummond-Murray) b 1955, Caroline Ruth b 1959); m 3, 1971, Jean Elizabeth *née* Crouch; *Career* FO Bletchley 1942–45; res assoc Univ of London 1952–58; Univ of Edinburgh: sr lectr in surgical sci 1958–62, reader 1962–65, dir experimental programming unit 1963–73, personal chair of machine intelligence 1967–84, head of machine intelligence res unit 1974–84, prof emeritus 1985–; chief scientist Turing Inst 1986–92 (dir of res 1984–86); ed-in-chief Machine Intelligence 1967–; assoc memb Josef Stefan Inst Slovenia 1995; Pioneer award (jtly with Dr Anne McLaren) of Int Embryo Transfer Soc 1988, Achievement Award of IEE 1995, Feigenbaum Medal Int Cong Exp Sys 1996; Hon DSc: CNAA 1991, Salford Univ 1992, Univ of Stirling 1993; FZS 1953, FRSE 1969, FBCS 1971; *Books* Machine Intelligence and Related Topics (1982), The Creative Computer (with Rory Johnston, 1984), On Machine Intelligence (2 edn, 1986); *Recreations* chess; *Clubs* New (Edinburgh); *Style*— Prof Donald Michie, FRSE; ✉ 6 Inveralmond Grove, Cramond, Edinburgh EH4 6RA (☎ 0131 336 3826, fax 0131 336 4603, e-mail D.Michie@ed.ac.uk)

MICHIE, Hon Mrs ((Janet) Ray); *née* Bannerman; MP (Lib Dem) Argyll and Bute (majority 2,622); er da of Baron Bannerman of Kildonan, OBE (Life Peer; d 1969), and Ray, *née* Mundell; *b* 4 Feb 1934; *Educ* Aberdeen HS for Girls, Lansdowne House Sch Edinburgh, Edinburgh Sch of Speech Therapy; *m* 1957, Lt-Col Iain Michie; 3 da; *Career* former area speech therapist Argyll & Clyde Health Bd; MP (Lib Dem) Argyll and Bute 1987–, Lib spokesman on tport and rural devpt 1987–88; Lib Dem (formerly SLD) spokeswoman: on Scotland 1988–, on Women's Issues 1988–94; chair Scottish Lib Dem Pty 1992–93; vice pres Coll of Speech and Language Therapists 1989–; MCST; *Style*— The Hon Mrs Michie, MP; ✉ House of Commons, London SW1A 0AA

MICHIE, William (Bill); MP (Lab) Sheffield Heeley (majority 14,954); s of Arthur Michie, and Violet Michie; *b* 24 Nov 1935; *Educ* Secdy Mod Sch; *m* 1987, Judith Ann; 2 s, 1 step s, 1 step da; *Career* electrician 1952–61, lab technician 1961–81, unemployed 1981–83, AEU (now AEEU) shop steward; cncllr: Sheffield City Cncl 1970–84 (chm Planning Ctee 1974–81, chm Employment Ctee 1981–83), S Yorks County Cncl 1974–86; MP (Lab) Sheffield Heeley 1983–; memb: Co-operative Pty, Select Ctee on Members' Interests 1992–96, Ctee of Privileges 1994–96; *Recreations* darts, soccer; *Clubs* WMC Affiliated; *Style*— Bill Michie, Esq, MP; ✉ House of Commons, London SW1A 0AA

MICKLEM, Prof Henry Spedding; s of Rev Edward Romilly Micklem (d 1960), of Oxford, and Phyllis Winifred, *née* Benham (d 1985); *b* 11 Oct 1933; *Educ* Rugby, Oriel Coll Oxford (MA, DPhil); *m* 1, 21 June 1958, Lisel Ruth (d 1990), da of William Edgar Wenallt Thomas, MBE (d 1963), of Stroud; 3 s (Thomas b 1963, James b 1965, David b 1967), 1 da (Naomi b 1961); m 2, 28 Dec 1994, Damaris Catherine Manson, da of Leslie Barratt (d 1991), of London; *Career* memb scientific staff MRC 1957–66; Univ of Edinburgh: lectr 1966–72, reader 1972–88, prof of immunobiology 1988–92, hon fell 1992–95, emeritus 1992–; visiting fell: Pasteur Inst Paris 1963–64, NY Univ Med Center 1988; visiting prof Stanford Univ 1978–79; author of papers in various scientific jls; memb Scientific Advsy Ctee The Melville Tst 1987–92, chm Meadows Chamber Orchestra 1993–; *Books* Tissue Grafting and Radiation (with J F Loutit, 1966); *Recreations* music; *Style*— Prof Henry Micklem; ✉ 1 Dryden Place, Edinburgh EH9 1RP (☎ 0131 667 5618, fax 0131 668 4825); Division of Biological Sciences, University of Edinburgh, Edinburgh EH9 3JT (☎ 0131 650 5496)

MICKLETHWAIT, (Richard) John; s of Richard Miles Micklethwait, and Jane Evelyn, *née* Codrington; *b* 11 Aug 1962; *Educ* Ampleforth, Magdalen Coll Oxford; *m* 1992, Fevronia Read; *Career* The Economist: finance writer 1987–89, media corr 1989–90, Los Angeles corr 1990–93, business ed 1993–; *Style*— John Micklethwait, Esq; ✉ The Economist, 25 St James' Street, London SW1A 1HG (☎ 0171 830 7000)

MICOU, Paul; *b* 22 April 1959; *Educ* Harvard (BA); *m* 6 Oct 1990, Anna Ulrika, *née* Nilsson; *Career* novelist; *Books* The Music Programme (Black Swan), The Cover Artist (Black Swan), The Death of David Debrizzi (Black Swan, 1991), Rotten Times (Black Swan, 1993), The Last Word (Black Swan, 1994), Adam's Wish (Bantam Press, 1994); *Style*— Paul Micou, Esq; ✉ c/o Bantam Press, Transworld Publishers Ltd, 61–63 Uxbridge Road, Ealing, London W5 5SA (☎ 0181 579 2652)

MIDDLEMAS, Prof (Robert) Keith; s of Robert James Middlemas (d 1994), of Northumberland, and Eleanor Mary, *née* Crane; *b* 26 May 1935; *Educ* Stowe, Pembroke Coll Cambridge (MA, DPhil, DLitt); *m* 30 Aug 1958, Susan Mary, da of Laurence Edward Paul Tremlett (d 1956); 1 s (Hugo b 1969), 3 da (Sophie b 1961, Lucy b 1964, Annabel b 1965); *Career* Mil Serv Kenya 1953–55; clerk in House of Commons 1958–67; Univ of Sussex: lectr in history 1967–76, reader in history 1976–86, prof of contemporary history 1986–; *Books* The Master Builders (1963), The Clydesiders (1965), Baldwin (with A J L Barnes, 1969), Diplomacy of Illusion (1972), Whitehall Diary by Thomas Jones (3 vols, ed 1969–71), Engineering and Politics in Southern Africa (1975), Politics in Industrial Society (1978), Power and the Party - Changing Faces of Communism in Western Europe (1979), Industry, Unions and Government - Twenty-One Years of NEDC (1984), Power, Competition and The State, Vol I - Britain in Search of Balance 1940–61 (1986), Vol II - Threats to The Post-War Settlement 1961–74 (1990), Vol III - The End of the Post-War Era (1991), Orchestrating Europe: Informal Politics of the European Community (1995); *Recreations* worldwide travel, landscape gardening, sailing; *Clubs* Flyfishers', North London Rifle; *Style*— Prof Keith Middlemas; ✉ West Burton House, West Burton, Pulborough, West Sussex (☎ 01798 831516); University of Sussex, Brighton, Sussex (☎ 01273 606755)

MIDDLESEX, Archdeacon of; *see:* Raphael, Ven Timothy John

MIDDLETON, Edward Bernard; s of Bernard Middleton (d 1987), and Bettie Mabel, *née* Knight; *b* 5 July 1948; *Educ* Aldenham; *m* 22 May 1971, Rosemary Spence, da of Maj Denis Frederick Spence Brown, MC, TD (d 1995), of Lincoln; 3 s (Nicholas b 1976, Simon b 1978, Hugo b 1982); *Career* sr Pannell Fitzpatrick & Co London 1971–73, mangr Pannell Bellhouse Mwangi & Co Nairobi 1973–75, ptnr Pannell Kerr Forster London 1979– (mangr 1975–79), dir Pannell Kerr Forster Associates 1996–; seconded to DTI as dir/under-sec in the Industl Devpt Unit; hon treas Hotel and Catering Benevolent Assoc 1992–; FCA 1972; *Recreations* sailing, photography; *Clubs* Salcombe Yacht; *Style*— Edward Middleton, Esq; ✉ Barrans, Bury Green, Little Hadham, Ware, Herts (☎ 01279 658684); Pannell Kerr Forster, New Garden House, 78 Hatton Garden, London EC1N 8JA (☎ 0171 831 7383, fax 0171 405 6736)

MIDDLETON, (John) Grant; s of Edward Francis Beresford Middleton, MBE, of Low Fell, and Veronica Mary, *née* Seed; *b* 8 March 1934; *Educ* Ushaw Coll Durham, Univ of Durham (LLB); *m* 30 Sept 1961, Pamela, da of Canon David Jones (d 1942); 1 s (James b 1964), 2 da (Catherine b 1966, Jessica b 1974); *Career* Royal Northumberland Fus: 2 Lt 1956–58, Lt 1958–59; Capt Army Legal Serv 1959; admitted slr 1955; sr ptnr Stoneham Langton & Passmore 1986–95 (ptnr 1961–95), conslt Bircham & Co 1995–; memb: Barnes and Sheen CAB, City of Westminster Law Soc (pres 1989–90), Law Soc 1956; *Recreations* Bach choir, chess, bridge, golf, motorcycling; *Clubs* Naval & Military; *Style*— Grant Middleton, Esq; ✉ 2 Kitson Road, Barnes, London SW13 9HJ (☎ 0181 748 5773); Bircham & Co, 1 Dean Farrar Street, London SW1H 0DY (☎ 0171 222 8044, fax 0171 222 3480)

MIDDLETON, Sir Lawrence Monck; 10 Bt (E 1662), of Belsay Castle, Northumberland; s of Lt Hugh Jeffery Middleton, RN (d 1914; 3 s of 7 Bt), suc bro, Sir Stephen Hugh Middleton, 9 Bt (d 1993); *b* 23 Oct 1912; *Educ* Eton, Univ of Edinburgh (BSc); *m* 1984, Mrs Primrose Westcombe, da of Lawrence Haynes Adams, of Shrubland House, Soham, Cambs; *Heir* kinsman, Henry Lambert Middleton b 1923; *Style*— Sir Lawrence Middleton, Bt; ✉ Estate Office, Belsay Castle, Newcastle upon Tyne NE20 0DY

MIDDLETON, 12 Baron (GB 1711); Sir (Digby) Michael Godfrey John Willoughby; 13 Bt (E 1677), MC (1945), DL (N Yorks); s of 11 Baron Middleton, KG (d 1970); *b* 1 May 1921; *Educ* Eton, Trinity Coll Cambridge; *m* 14 Oct 1947, Janet Marshall-Cornwall, JP (fndr chm Lloyd's External Names Assoc), da of Gen Sir James Handyside Marshall-Cornwall, KCB, CBE, DSO, MC; 3 s; *Heir* s, Hon Michael Charles James Willoughby; *Career* 2 Lt Coldstream Gds 1940, Temp Maj served in NW Europe 1944–45 (despatches and Croix de Guerre); land agent 1951; JP E Riding Yorks 1958; cncllr: E Riding 1964–74, N Yorks 1974–77; memb Yorks and Humberside Econ Planning Cncl 1968–79; pres: Yorks Agric Soc 1976, CLA 1981–83; Hon Col 2 Bn Yorks (TAVR) Volunteers 1976–88; memb: Nature Conservancy Cncl 1986–89, House of Lords Select Ctee on Euro Community; chm Food and Agriculture Sub-Ctee 1989–96; *Clubs* Boodle's; *Style*— The Rt Hon the Lord Middleton, MC, DL; ✉ Birdsall House, Birdsall, Malton, N Yorks YO17 9NR (☎ 01944 768202)

MIDDLETON, Michael Humfrey; CBE (1975); s of Humfrey Middleton (d 1976), and Lilian Irene, *née* Tillard (d 1939); *b* 1 Dec 1917; *Educ* King's Sch Canterbury; *m* 10 April 1954, Julie Margaret, da of Guy James Kay Harrison (d 1980), of Cark-in-Cartmel, Cumbria; 1 s (Hugo b 1955), 2 da (Kate b 1958, Rose b 1961); *Career* art critic The Spectator 1946–56, asst ed Picture Post 1948–52, ed House and Garden 1955–57, dir Civic Tst 1969–86, sec gen UK Campaign for Euro Architectural Year 1972–76, sec Architectural Heritage Fund 1976–86; conf papers, lectures, consultancy work in Europe, N America, Australia and SE Asia and SA; Pro Merito Medal of Cncl of Europe 1976; *Books* Group Practice in Design (1967), Man Made the Town (1987), Cities in Transition (1991); *Recreations* travel, the arts; *Style*— Michael Middleton, Esq, CBE; ✉ 84 Sirdar Rd, London W11 4EG

MIDDLETON, Ven Michael John; s of Bernard Middleton, and Gladys, *née* Thorpe; *b* 21 July 1940; *Educ* Weymouth GS, St Cuthbert's Soc Univ of Durham (BSc), Fitzwilliam Coll Cambridge (MA), Westcott House Cambridge; *m* 1965, Anne Elisabeth, da of Dr T H L Parker; 2 s (John Benedict b 1970, Matthew Thomas b 1971), 1 da (Susannah Naomi b 1976); *Career* curate St George's Jesmond Newcastle upon Tyne 1966–69; chaplain: St George's GS Cape Town 1969–72, The Kings Sch Tynemouth 1972–77; vicar St George's Jesmond 1977–85, rector of Hexham Northumberland 1985–92, proctor in convocation 1980–92, archdeacon of Swindon 1992–; *Recreations* walking, Westerns; *Style*— The Ven the Archdeacon of Swindon; ✉ 2 Louviers Way, Swindon, Wilts SN1 4DU (☎ 01793 644556, fax 01793 495352)

MIDDLETON, (David) Miles; CBE (1992); s of Harry Middleton (d 1990), of Corbridge, Northumberland, and Dorothy Hannah, *née* Nisbet; *b* 15 June 1938; *Educ* Sedbergh; *m* 1, 1962 (m dis 1979), Mary Elizabeth Gale; 1 s (Nicholas Miles Heathcliffe b 9 March 1966), 1 da (Georgina Claire b 9 Sept 1964); m 2, 1980, Elizabeth Mary (Bobbie) Lancaster; 2 step s (Charles Antony Lancaster, Benjamin Michael Lancaster), 2 step da (Victoria Mary Lancaster (Mrs Darrall), Katherine Elizabeth Lancaster (Mrs Oliver)); *Career* CA; articled Strachan & Co Newcastle-upon-Tyne 1956–61, qualified 1962, audit sr Coopers Brothers & Co Sheffield 1962–64; Coopers & Lybrand: mangr Zurich 1964–68, Newcastle-upon-Tyne 1968–71, opened office Middlesbrough 1971, ptnr 1974, ptnr in charge Middlesbrough until 1986, ptnr in charge Newcastle-upon-Tyne 1986–90, sr ptnr NE practice Coopers & Lybrand 1990–93; in practice Middleton Associates 1993–; Northern Soc of CAs: joined Teesside Ctee 1974, chm Teesside Branch 1982–83, pres Main Ctee 1986–87 (vice pres 1984, dep pres 1985–86); chm Northern Enterprise Limited; Teesside C of C: former memb Taxation Rating and Law Ctee, vice pres 1982, pres 1984–85; memb Econ and Industl Ctee Assoc of Br C of C, pres Assoc of Br C of C 1990–92 (dep chm 1988–90), memb Devpt Cncl Durham Univ, cmmr Rural Devpt Cmmn 1993–, dir North West Chambers of Commerce Assoc 1994–; FRSA, FCA 1972 (ACA 1962); *Recreations* sailing, golf, beekeeping, opera, ballet; *Clubs* Northern Counties (Newcastle-upon-Tyne), Royal Over-Seas League, Hexham Golf, Bassenthwaite Sailing; *Style*— Miles Middleton, Esq, CBE; ✉ Ingleboro, St Helen's Lane, Lorbridge, Northumberland NE45 5JD (☎ 01434 633546, fax 01434 632330)

MIDDLETON, Rear Adm (John) Patrick Windsor; CB (1992); s of Cdr John Henry Dudley Middleton (d 1989), of Wimbledon, and Norna Mary Tessimond, *née* Hitchings (d 1996); *b* 15 March 1938; *Educ* Cheltenham Coll, RNC Dartmouth, RN Engrg Coll Manadon Plymouth; *m* 31 March 1962, Jane Rodwell, da of Leslie Stephen Gibbs (d 1978), of Letchmore Heath, Radlett, Herts; 1 s (Toby b 1963), 1 da (Isobel b 1965); *Career* entered RN 1954; served HMS: Lion 1962, Ambush 1965, Warspite 1969; Cdr 1973, NDC 1976, HMS Blake 1977, Capt 1981; CSO(E): FOSM 1981, Falklands 1983; Capt naval drafting 1984, dir in serv submarines 1987, Rear Adm 1989, CSO(E) Fleet 1989, CSO (Support) Fleet 1991, ret 1992; chm Conservation Direct 1993–94, sec Royal Cmmn for the Exhibition of 1851 1995–; govr Care for the Mentally Handicapped 1993–; Liveryman Worshipful Co of Armourers and Brasiers 1971 (memb Ct of Assts 1995); MIMechE 1965, MIMarE 1965, FIMgt 1989; *Style*— Rear Adm Patrick Middleton, CB; ✉ Manora, Chilmark, Wiltshire SP3 5AH (☎ 01722 716231)

MIDDLETON, Sir Peter Edward; GCB (1989, KCB 1984); *b* 2 April 1934; *Educ* Sheffield City GS, Univ of Sheffield (BA), Univ of Bristol; *m* 1, 1964, Valerie Ann, *née* Lindup (d 1987); 1 s (Tom b 1965, d 1991), 1 da (Emma); m 2, 20 Jan 1990, Constance Jean Owen, *née* Close; 2 step s, 1 step da; *Career* served RAPC 1958–60; HM Treasy: sr info offr 1962, princ 1964, asst dir Centre for Admin Studies 1967–69, private sec to Chllr of the Exchequer 1969–72, press sec 1972–75, head Monetary Policy Div 1975, under sec 1976–80, dep sec 1980–83, perm sec 1983–91; chm Barclays de Zoete Wedd 1991–, dep chm Barclays Bank 1991–; non-exec dir: Bass PLC 1992–, General Accident PLC 1992–, United Utilities plc (formerly North West Water Group plc) 1994–; visiting fell Nuffield Coll Oxford 1981–89; dir English Chamber Orch and Music Soc 1992–, chm Inst of Contemporary British History 1992–; govr: London Business Sch 1984–90, Ditchley Fndn 1985, NIESR 1991–; memb: Cncl Manchester Business Sch 1985–92, Cncl Sheffield Univ 1991–, Exec Ctee Centre for Economic Policy Res 1991–, UK Advsy Bd Nat Economic Res Assoc 1991–; Cdre Civil Serv Sailing Assoc 1984–91; *Recreations* walking, opera, outdoor sports; *Clubs* Reform; *Style*— Sir Peter Middleton, GCB; ✉ Barclays Bank plc, 54 Lombard Street, London EC3P 3AH (☎ 0171 626 1567)

MIDDLETON, Stanley; s of Thomas Middleton (d 1936), of Bulwell, Nottingham, and Elizabeth Ann, *née* Burdett; *b* 1 Aug 1919; *Educ* Bulwell St Mary's, Highbury Sch Bulwell, High Pavement Sch Nottingham, Univ of London (BA), Univ of Nottingham (MEd); *m* 22 Dec 1951, Margaret Shirley Charnley, da of Herbert Welch (d 1971), and Winifred Vera, *née* Loop, of Ewell Surrey; 2 da (Penelope b 1956, Sarah b 1958); *Career* WWII RA and RAEC; head of English High Pavement Coll Nottingham 1958–81, Judith E Wilson visiting fell Emmanuel Coll Cambridge 1982–83; jt winner The Booker Prize for fiction (Holiday) 1974; Hon MA Univ of Nottingham 1975, Hon M Univ Open Univ; fell PEN; *Books* A Short Answer (1958), Harris's Requiem (1960), A Serious Woman (1961), The Just Exchange (1962), Two's Company (1963), Him They Compelled (1964), Terms of Reference (1966), The Golden Evening (1968), Wages of Virtue (1969), Apple of The Eye (1970), Brazen Prison (1971), Cold Gradations (1972), A Man Made of Smoke (1973), Holiday (1974), Distractions (1975), Still Waters (1976), Ends and Means (1977), Two Brothers (1978), In A Strange Land (1979), The Other Side (1980), Blind Understanding (1982), Entry into Jerusalem (1983), The Daysman (1984), Valley of Decision (1985), An After Dinner's Sleep (1986), After A Fashion (1987), Recovery (1988), Vacant Places (1989), Changes and Chances (1990), Beginning to End (1991), A Place to Stand (1992), Married Past Redemption (1993), Catalysts (1994), Toward the Sea (1995), Live and Learn (1996); *Recreations* music, walking, listening, painting; *Style*— Stanley Middleton, Esq; ✉ 42 Caledon Rd, Sherwood, Nottingham NG5 2NG; (☎ 0115 962 3085)

MIDDLETON, Bishop of 1994–; Rt Rev Stephen Squires Venner; s of Thomas Edward Venner (d 1980), and Hilda Lester, *née* Boon, of Weymouth, Dorset; *b* 19 June 1944; *Educ* Hardyes Sch Dorchester, Univ of Birmingham (BA), Linacre Coll Oxford (MA), London Inst of Educn (Postgrad CertEd); *m* 29 July 1972, Judith, da of Arthur Sivewright Johnstone; 2 s (Edward Stephen Squires b 24 April 1974, Thomas William Johnstone b 9 Jan 1980), 1 da (Alice Victoria b 15 Dec 1976); *Career* curate St Peter's Streatham 1968–71; hon curate: St Margaret Streatham Hill 1971–72, Ascension Balham 1972–74; head of RE St Paul's Girls' Sch Hammersmith 1972–74, vicar St Peter's Clapham 1974–76, Bishop of Southwark's chaplain to overseas students 1974–76; vicar: St John's Trowbridge 1976–82, Holy Trinity Weymouth 1982–94; rural dean of Weymouth 1988–93, canon and preb of Salisbury Cathedral 1989–94; chm: Salisbury Diocesan Bd of Educn 1989–94, Salisbury Diocesan House of Clergy 1992–94; memb: C of E Gen Synod 1985–95, Gen Synod Bd of Educn 1985–; vice-pres Woodard Corp 1995–; *Books* All God's Children? (chm of Working Pty, 1991); *Recreations* reprographics, water sports, walking, the family; *Style*— The Rt Rev the Bishop of Middleton; ✉ The Hollies, Manchester Road, Rochdale OL11 3QY (☎ 01706 358550, fax 01706 354851)

MIDDLETON, Tony Charles; s of Peter John Middleton, of Winchester, Hampshire, and Molly Caroline, *née* Carver; *b* 1 Feb 1964; *Educ* Montgomery of Alamein Winchester, Peter Symonds Sixth Form Coll Winchester; *m* 23 Sept 1989, Sherralyn Tessa, da of Phillip Paul Clarke; *Career* professional cricketer; Hampshire CCC 1983–95: first class debut 1984, awarded county cap 1990, over 105 first class appearances; cricket devpt offr Hampshire CCC 1995–; represented England A tour to Australia 1993; *Recreations* squash, badminton, gardening, real ale pubs; *Style*— Tony Middleton, Esq; ✉ Hampshire CCC, Northlands Rd, Southampton (☎ 01703 333788)

MIDGLEY, (David) William (Bill); s of Norman Midgley (d 1995), of Huddersfield, and Margaret, *née* Alderson (d 1986); *b* 1 Feb 1942; *Educ* Huddersfield Coll; *m* 1, 19 Dec 1964, Anne Christine (d 1976), da of Charles Foreman, of Huddersfield; 1 s (Edward William b 1967), 1 da (Rachel Sarah b 1969); m 2, 10 June 1977, Ada Margaret, da of John Banks; 1 da (Louise Isobel b 1980); *Career* chief exec Newcastle Building Society 1986–; chm: Newcastle Bank (Gibraltar) Ltd, NBS Financial Services Ltd, Newcastle Estate Agents Ltd, Strachans (Newcastle) Ltd, Adamscastle Ltd, Newcastle Developments Ltd, Newcastle Mortgage Corporation Ltd, The Newcastle Initiative, Newcastle Safer Cities, Partners in Racial Equality, Newcastle Concert Series, Newcastle City Centre Mgmnt Cmmn; pres Durham CCC; vice pres: Marie Curie Cancer Care, NE C of C; FCIB, FRSA; *Recreations* golf; *Clubs* Northern Counties; *Style*— Bill Midgley, Esq; ✉ 17 Beaumont Drive, Whitley Bay, Tyne and Wear NE25 9UT (☎ 0191 297 0401, fax 0191 251 1525); Newcastle Building Society, Portland House, New Bridge Street, Newcastle upon Tyne NE1 8AL (☎ 0191 244 2000, fax 0191 244 2203, car 0831 152794)

MIDLETON, 12 Viscount (I 1717); Alan Henry Brodrick; also Baron Brodrick of Midleton (I 1715) and Baron Brodrick of Peper Harow (GB 1796); the full designation of the Viscountcy is Midleton of Midleton; s of Alan Rupert Brodrick (d 1972), and Alice Elizabeth, *née* Roberts; suc uncle 11 Viscount 1988; *b* 4 Aug 1949; *Educ* St Edmund's Canterbury; *m* 1978, Julia Helen, da of Michael Pitt, of Lias Cottage, Compton Dundon, Somerton, Somerset; 2 s (Hon Ashley Rupert, Hon William Michael b 1982), 1 da (Hon Charlotte Helen b 1983); *Heir* s, Hon Ashley Rupert Brodrick b 25 Nov 1980; *Career* horologist; Keeper of Horology Gershom Parkington Collection Bury St Edmunds 1986–; memb Cncl and chm Br Horological Inst Museum Tst 1993–; FBHI; *Recreations* conservation of turret clocks, bicycling, walking; *Clubs* Athenaeum; *Style*— The Rt Hon the Viscount Midleton; ✉ 2 Burrells Orchard, Westley, Bury St Edmunds, Suffolk IP33 3TH

MIDWINTER, Prof Eric Clare; OBE (1992); *b* 11 Feb 1932; *Educ* St Catharine's Coll Cambridge (BA, MA), Univ of Liverpool (MEd), Univ of York (DPhil); *Career* academic appts 1955–68, dir of priority educnl project Liverpool 1968–75, head of Public Affrs Unit Nat Consumer Cncl London 1975–80, dir Centre for Policy on Ageing London 1980–91; chm: Advsy Centre for Educn 1976–80, London Regnl Passenger Ctee 1977–96, Health and Social Welfare Bd Open Univ 1983–90, Nat Community Educn Devpt Centre 1994–; memb: Prince of Wales' Advsy Ctee on Disability 1990–95, Advsy Ctee on Telecommunications for Disabled and Elderly People (DIEL) 1990–96; visiting prof of educn Univ of Exeter 1992; Hon Dr Open Univ 1989; *Books* Victorian Social Reform (1968), Social Administration in Lancashire (1969), Old Liverpool (1971), Nineteenth Century Education (1970), Teaching in the Urban Community School (ed, 1972), Education for sale (1977), Make 'em Laugh: Famous Comedians and Their World (1979), W G Grace: His Life and Times (1981), The Wage of Retirement: the Case for a New Pensions Policy (1985), Caring for Cash: the Issue of Private Domiciliary Care (1986), Fair Game: Myth and Reality in Sport (1986), The Lost Seasons: Cricket in Wartime (1987), New Design for Old (1988), Red Roses Crest the Caps (1989), Creating Chances (1990), The Old Order (1990), Out of Focus (1991), Brylcreem Summer: the 1947 Cricket Season (1991), The British Gas Report on Attitudes to Ageing (1991), The Illustrated History of County Cricket (1992), Lifelines (1993), The History of Social Welfare in Britain (1994), First Knock; Cricket's Opening Pairs (1994), Surrey CCC: 150 Years - A Celebration (1995), Darling Old Oval: Surrey Cricket at the Oval (1995), State Educator: The Life and Enduring Influence of W E Forster (1995); *Recreations* writing, sport, theatre; *Clubs* MCC, Lancashire CCC, Savage; *Style*— Prof Eric Midwinter, OBE; ✉ Savage Club, 1 Whitehall Place, London SW14 2HD (☎ 0171 930 8118)

MIDWINTER, Prof John Edwin; OBE (1984); s of Henry Clements Midwinter (d 1970), of Newbury, Berks, and Vera Joyce, *née* Rawlinson; *b* 8 March 1938; *Educ* St Bartholomew's GS Newbury, King's Coll London (BSc), External Dept Univ of London (PhD); *m* 15 July 1961, Maureen Ann, da of Charles Richard Holt of Wickham Market, Suffolk; 2 s (Timothy b 15 June 1963, Piers b 23 July 1968), 2 da (Philippa b 16 Sept 1964, Kim b 19 March 1966); *Career* Nat Serv RAF airborne radar instr Yatesbury Wiltshire 1956–58; sr scientific offr MOD RSRE Malvern Worcs 1961–67; sr res physicist: Perkin Elmer Corporation USA 1968–70, Allied Chemical Corporation USA 1970–71; head Optical Communications Div BT Res 1977–84 (head of section 1971–77), Pender prof and head of Electrical and Engrg Dept UCL 1984–, vice provost UCL 1994–; vice pres IEE 1994–; FInstP 1975, FIEE 1980, FIEEE 1983, FEng 1984, FRS 1985; *Books* Applied Non-Linear Optics (with F Zernike, 1973), Optical Fibres for Transmission (1979), Optical Fibre Communications (contrib, 1979), Fibre and Integrated Optics (contrib, 1979), New Directions in Guided Waves and Coherent Optics (contrib, 1983), Neural Computing Architectures (contrib, 1989), Optical Technology and Wideband Local Networks (ed with others, 1989), Photonic Switching (ed with H S Hinton, 1989); *Style*— Prof John Midwinter, OBE, FRS, FEng; ✉ Department of Electrical and Electronic Engineering, University College London, Torrington Place, London WC1E 7JE (☎ 0171 388 0427, fax 0171 388 9307, e-mail j.midwinter@ucl.ac.uk)

MIERS, Sir (Henry) David Alastair Capel; KBE (1985), CMG (1979); s of Col R D M C Miers, DSO (d 1974), and Honor Miers (d 1994); *b* 10 Jan 1937; *Educ* Winchester, Univ Coll Oxford; *m* 1966, Imelda Maria Emilia, *née* Wouters; 2 s, 1 da; *Career* Dip Serv; head ME Dept FCO 1980–83 (private sec to Min of State FO 1968, Paris 1972, cnsllr Tehran 1977–80), ambass Lebanon 1983–85, asst under sec FCO 1986–88, ambass:

Greece 1989–93, Netherlands 1993–Nov 1996; ret; Liveryman Worshipful Co of Tin Plate Workers; *Style*— Sir David Miers, KBE, CMG; ✉ c/o Foreign and Cwlth Office, King Charles St, London SW1A 2AH

MIERS, Richenda Francis Capel; da of Rear Adm Peter Douglas Herbert Raymond Pelly, CB, DSO (d 1980), of Alderney, CI, and Gwenllian Violet, *née* Edwardes (d 1987); *b* 27 Jan 1939; *Educ* Ipswich HS, Loreto Convent Gibraltar, Ipswich Tech Coll; *m* 3 April 1959, Col Douglas Alexander Nigel Capel Miers, s of Col Ronald Douglas Martin Capel Miers, DSO (d 1974), of Ross-Shire, Scotland; 1 s (Lucian b 1962), 3 da (Mary b 1961, Victoria b 1964, Henrietta b 1966); *Career* author; *Books* Told From An Island (as Richenda Francis, 1979); as Frances Ramsay: Carve It In Doves (1984), Mine Is The Heart (1984), No Other Desire (1984); Cumbria (as Richenda Miers, 1986), Cadogan Guide To Scotland (1987, 1989, 1991 and 1994), Cadogan Guide To Thailand, Burma (contrib as Francis Capel, 1988), The Blood Is Strong (as Richenda Francis, 1989), Cadogan Guide to Scotland's Highlands and Islands (as Richenda Miers, 1994); *Recreations* reading, writing, sailing, walking, gardening; *Style*— Mrs Douglas Miers; ✉ East Farmhouse, Wylye, Warminster, Wilts BA12 ORQ (☎ 01985 248219); Boisdale House, South Lochboisdale, Isle of South Uist, Scotland PA81 5UB

MIFLIN, Prof Benjamin John (Ben); s of Stanley Benjamin Miflin (d 1971), of Lower Slaughter, Glos, and Kathleen Noel, *née* Davies; *b* 7 Jan 1939; *Educ* Univ of Nottingham (BSc), Univ of Illinois (MS), Univ of London (PhD); *m* 3 Oct 1964, Hilary Frances, da of Wilfred Edward Newman; 3 da (Gail Kathryn b 12 Feb 1967, Clare Josephine b 2 Aug 1968, Johanna Frances b 8 May 1971); *Career* lectr in plant sciences Univ of Newcastle 1965–73, head Molecular Sciences Div Rothamsted Experimental Station 1983–85 (head Biochemistry Dept 1973–85), head of res devpt Ciba-Geigy Seeds 1985–93, dir Inst of Arable Crops Research 1994–; visiting prof of plant sciences Univ of Nottingham 1981–85 and 1994–; corresponding memb American Soc of Plant Physiologists; ed of several scientific books and author of over 100 scientific papers; *Recreations* tennis, theatre, gardening; *Style*— Prof Ben Miflin; ✉ 73 Theberton Street, London N1 0QY (☎ 0171 359 5738); Institute of Arable Crop Research, Rothamsted, Harpenden, Herts AL5 2JQ (☎ 01582 763133, fax 01582 461366)

MIFSUD, Jean-Pierre; s of Ernest Xavier Mifsud (d 1954), of Port Fouad, Egypt, and Eugenie, *née* Grima; *b* 26 Feb 1944; *Educ* College des Frères St-Marie, Ealing GS; *m* 1, 1966, Carole, *née* Fearnhead (decd); 1 da (Amelia b 1 July 1974), 1 s (Dominic Xavier b 17 June 1977); m 2, 1983, Janet Elizabeth, da of Ernest Aubrey Dedman; 1 step da (Sarah Kathleen b 3 Jan 1970), 1 step s (Ross James b 21 Aug 1975); *Career* hotelier; hotel and restaurant inspr AA until 1983 (joined 1970), proprietor: The Lake Country House Llangammarch Wells Powys 1983–, Dinham Hall Hotel Ludlow 1994–; Johansen's Restaurant of the Year 1991–92, AA 3 Red Stars and 2 rosettes for food 1995, RAC Blue Ribbon, Good Hotel Guide Welsh Country House of the Year (Cesar Award for Lake Country House Hotel) 1993, Pride of Britain Hotel; memb: Advsy Ctee Br Tourist Authy 1988–92, Accommodation Advsy Ctee Welsh Tourist Bd, Hotel Ctee Br Hospitality Assoc 1993–; *Recreations* antique collecting, architectural renovation; *Style*— Jean-Pierre Mifsud, Esq; ✉ Lake Country House Hotel, Llangammarch Wells, Powys LD4 4BS (☎ 01591 620202, fax 01591 620457)

MIGDAL, Clive Stephen; s of Jack Migdal (d 1977), of East London, SA, and Anne, *née* Cohen; *b* 19 Feb 1948; *Educ* Selborne Coll East London SA, Univ of Cape Town and Groote Schuur Hosp Cape Town SA (MB ChB, MD, DO); *Career* registrar in pathology Groote Schuur Hosp 1973 (house physician then house surgn 1972), SHO in ophthalmology Bart's 1974, registrar in ophthalmology Groote Schuur Hosp 1975–77, resident surgical offr (registrar and sr registrar) Moorfield Eye Hosp London 1977–80, sr registrar in ophthalmology Bart's 1980–89, clincial research fell Moorfields Eye Hosp 1981–94, conslt ophthalmic surgn The Western Eye Hosp and St Mary's Hosps 1989– (clinical dir of ophthalmology St Mary's and The Western Eye Hosps); memb Ophthalmic Servs Ctee BMA, vice chm Educn and Research Ctee Euro Glaucoma Soc; Gold Medal for Best Scientific Paper Int Congress of Ophthalmology Singapore 1990, Lewis Rudin Prize for Glaucoma Research 1995; memb: American Acad of Ophthalmology 1986, Euro Glaucoma Soc 1986, Assoc of Research and Vision in Ophthalmology 1992; BMA 1992; FRCS 1979, FRCOphth 1989 (memb Cncl); *Books* Duane's Clinical Ophthalmology (contrib chapter, 1992); *Recreations* swimming, schooling polo ponies, classical music; *Style*— Clive Migdal, Esq; ✉ The Western Eye Hospital, Marylebone Road, London NW1 5YE (☎ 0171 402 4211 ext 464, fax 0171 723 3621); 149 Harley Street, London W1N 2DE (☎ 0171 935 4444, fax 0171 486 3782)

MILBANK, Sir Anthony Frederick; 5 Bt (UK 1882), of Well, Co York, and of Hart, Co Durham; s of Maj Sir Mark Vane Milbank, 4 Bt, KCVO, MC (d 1984), and his 2 w, Hon Verena Aileen Maxwell (d 1995), da of 11 Baron Farnham; *b* 16 Aug 1939; *Educ* Eton; *m* 1970, Belinda Beatrice, yr da of Brig Adrian Clements Gore, DSO, of Horton Priory, Sellinge, Ashford, Kent; 2 s (Edward Mark Somerset b 1973, Toby Adrian Jameson b 1977), 1 da (Alexina Victoria b 1971); *Heir* s, Edward Mark Somerset Milbank b 9 April 1973; *Career* farmer and landowner; chm Moorland Assoc; RSPB Cncl memb; former: dir M & G Securities, memb CLA Executive Ctee, memb Nature Conservancy Cncl Ctee for England; *Recreations* all sports: field, individual and winter; *Style*— Sir Anthony Milbank, Bt; ✉ Barningham Park, Richmond, North Yorkshire DL11 7DW (☎ 01833 21202, fax 01833 21298)

MILBORNE-SWINNERTON-PILKINGTON, Richard Arthur; s and h of Sir Thomas Henry Milborne-Swinnerton-Pilkington, 14 Bt; *b* 4 Sept 1964; *Educ* Eton, RAC Cirencester; *m* 3 Feb 1994, Katya, da of Terence Clemence; 1 da (Elizabeth Rose b 30 Nov 1994); *Career* insur broker Willis Faber; *Recreations* racing, shooting; *Style*— Richard Milborne-Swinnerton-Pilkington, Esq

MILBORNE-SWINNERTON-PILKINGTON, Sir Thomas Henry; 14 Bt (NS 1635); o s of Sir Arthur William Milborne-Swinnerton-Pilkington, 13 Bt (d 1952), and Elizabeth Mary, er da of late Col John Fenwick Harrison, JP, DL, of King's Walden Bury, Hitchin; *b* 10 March 1934; *Educ* Eton; *m* 1961, Susan, eld da of Norman Stewart Rushton Adamson, of Durban, S Africa; 1 s, 2 da (Sarah b 1962, Joanna b 1967); *Heir* s Richard Arthur Milborne-Swinnerton-Pilkington b 4 Sept 1964; *Career* chm: Charente Steamship Co Ltd 1977–, Thomas & James Harrison Ltd 1980–; *Clubs* White's, City of London; *Style*— Sir Thomas Milborne-Swinnerton-Pilkington, Bt; ✉ King's Walden Bury, Hitchin, Herts

MILBORROW, Ruan Leslie; s of Robert Leslie Milborrow (d 1986), of Wanstead, London, and Elizabeth Edith, *née* Cook; *b* 11 July 1958; *Educ* Forest Sch Snaresbrook, RAC Cirencester (MRAC, DipFM); *Career* sr art dir Yellowhammer Advertising Ltd 1984–91, creative dir Harari Page Ltd 1993–; Freeman City of London 1984; MIPA 1989; *Recreations* music, literature, theatre; *Clubs* Cirencester Park Polo; *Style*— Ruan Milborrow, Esq; ✉ 10 Edwards College, South Cerney, Gloucestershire GL7 5TR (☎ 01285 862091); Harari Page Ltd, 42–46 Weymouth Street, London W1N 3LQ (☎ 0171 224 1980, fax 0171 224 1981)

MILBURN, Alan; MP (Lab) Darlington (majority 2,798); s of Evelyn Metcalfe; *b* 27 Jan 1958; *Educ* John Marlay Sch, Stokesley Comp Sch, Univ of Lancaster (BA), Univ of Newcastle upon Tyne; *partner* Ruth Briel; 1 s; *Career* co-ordinator Trade Union Studies Information Unit Newcastle 1984–90, sr business devpt offr N Tyneside Cncl 1990–92, MP (Lab) Darlington 1992–; chm PLP Treasy Dept Ctee 1992–95; shadow health spokesman 1995–96, shadow treasy spokesman 1996–; co-ordinator Sunderland Shipyards Campaign 1988–89, chm Newcastle Central Constituency Lab Pty 1988–90, pres NE Regn Mfrg Sci and Fin Union 1990–92; memb: Exec Northern Region Lab Party 1990–92, Public Accounts Ctee 1994–95; *Books* Jobs and Industry - The North Can Make It (1986), Plan for the North (1987), The Case for Regional Government (1989); *Recreations* cricket, football, music, cinema; *Style*— Alan Milburn, Esq, MP; ✉ House of Commons, London SW1A 0AA

MILBURN, Anthony; s of Lawrence Anderson Milburn (d 1958), of Halifax, and Constance, *née* Laskey (d 1985); *Educ* Rastrick GS, Univ of Bradford (BTech), Univ of Birmingham (MSc); *m* 4 June 1983, Julia Margaret, da of Maj Charles Pierson Weeden (d 1996); 1 s (Richard b 1988), 1 da (Catherine b 1986); *Career* trg mangr National Water Cncl 1972–80, exec dir Int Assoc on Water Quality 1981–; dir Walton Cycles Ltd; govr World Water Council, memb Collaborative Council on Water Supply and Sanitation; memb: American Soc of Assoc Execs, Union of Int Assocs, Water Environment Fedn, Assoc of Chief Executives of Voluntary Orgns; Freeman City of London, asst to Co of Water Conservators; MICE 1971, FCIWEM 1972, MInstD (Dip in Co Direction); *Books* Water Pollution Research and Control (ed, 1985, 1987, 1989, 1991), Water Quality Management (jt ed, 1993 and 1995); *Recreations* sailing, philosophy, modern jazz; *Style*— Anthony Milburn, Esq; ✉ International Association on Water Quality, Duchess House, 20 Masons Yard, Duke Street, St James's, London SW1Y 6BU (☎ 0171 839 8390, fax 0171 839 8299)

MILBURN, Sir Anthony Rupert; 5 Bt (UK 1905), of Guyzance, Parish of Acklington, Northumberland; s of Maj Rupert Leonard Eversley Milburn (d 1974, yr s of 3 Bt), and Anne Mary, *née* Scott-Murray (d 1991); suc unc, Sir John Nigel Milburn, 4 Bt (d 1985); *b* 17 April 1947; *Educ* Eton, RAC Cirencester; *m* 1977, Olivia Shirley, yst da of Capt Thomas Noel Catlow, CBE, DL, RN (ret), of Tunstall, Lancs; 2 s (Patrick Thomas b 1980, Edward Jake b 1987), 1 da (Lucy Camilla Anna b 1982); *Heir* s, Patrick Thomas Milburn b 4 Dec 1980; *Career* landowner and company dir; ARICS, MRAC; *Clubs* New (Edinburgh); *Style*— Sir Anthony Milburn, Bt; ✉ Guyzance Hall, Acklington, Morpeth, Northumberland NE65 9AG (☎ 01665 513047, fax 01665 513042)

MILBURN, Chris; *Educ* BSc (Chemical Engrg); *Career* Cadbury Schweppes plc: various appts incl prodn mgmnt, prodn control, materials mgmnt, fin and info systems mgmnt until 1988, i/c investor rels 1988–90, dir of corp communications 1990–96; dir of corp affrs BTR plc 1996–; *Recreations* walking, music, swimming; *Style*— Chris Milburn, Esq; ✉ BTR plc, Silvertown House, Vincent Square, London SW1P 2PL (☎ 0171 834 3848, fax 0171 821 3709)

MILBURN, Peter; s of Edward Franklin Milburn, of Bradford, W Yorks, and Joyce, *née* Ostler; *b* 28 Oct 1952; *Educ* Hanson GS Bradford; *m* 9 July 1977 (m dis 1988), Elizabeth Anne, da of David John Terence Cowsill, of Lower Swell, Gloucestershire; 1 s (Benjamin b 1981); *Career* prog controller Pennine Radio 1979–81; Red Dragon Radio: prog controller 1987–90, prog dir 1990–91, md 1991–96; md Lite AM 1996–; chm Variety Club of GB (Wales) 1994–96; *Recreations* travel, reading; *Style*— Peter Milburn, Esq; ✉ Lite AM, Quay West, Trafford Wharf Road, Trafford Park, Manchester M17 1FL (☎ 0161 872 1458)

MILDRED, Mark; s of John Mildred (d 1996), of Usk, Gwent, and Eileen Smith (d 1969); *b* 16 Sept 1948; *Educ* Lancing, Clare Coll Cambridge (exhibitioner, BA); *m* 19 Oct 1974, Sarah Ruth, da of Harold Christopher Rackham; 2 s (Joe b 13 July 1976, Tom b 16 May 1979); *Career* articled clerk B M Birnberg & Co 1973–75; ptnr: Messrs Mildred and Beaumont 1978–86, Pannone & Partners and Pannone Napier 1986–93, Evans Butler Wade 1993–95; prof of litigation Nottingham Law Sch 1995–, conslt in complex litigation matters 1995–; memb: Law Soc 1975, Soc of Labour Lawyers 1975, Assoc of Personal Injury Lawyers 1990 (coordinator Multi-Party Actions Special Interest Gp), Law Soc Consumer and Commercial Law Ctee, Legal Advsy Panel Nat Consumer Cncl; *Books* 1989 Group Actions - Learning From Opren (Nat Consumer Cncl, 1989), Butterworths Product Liability and Safety Encyclopaedia (1992), Butterworths Medical Negligence (contrib chapter on Class Actions, 1994), Product Liability: Law and Insurance (gen ed, 1994); *Recreations* singing, cooking, walking, racquet games; *Clubs* Scorpions, Battersea Labour; *Style*— Mark Mildred, Esq; ✉ 67 Sisters Avenue, London SW11 5SW (☎ and fax 0171 228 1321)

MILES, Adrian Spencer; s of Herbert Beal Miles (d 1952), of London, and Marjorie Phyllis, *née* Harris; *b* 16 Nov 1947; *Educ* Rutlish Sch, QMC London (LLB); *m* 28 June 1975, Hilary, da of William Nelson (d 1980); 1 s (Jonathan Francis b 20 May 1968), 2 da (Julie Clare b 11 Oct 1978, Anna Kirsty b 7 July 1980); *Career* admitted slr 1972, Boodle Hatfield 1972–74, Norton Rose 1974–76, ptnr Wilde Sapte 1976– (head Banking Dept); memb Law Soc; *Recreations* chess, tennis, music; *Style*— Adrian Miles, Esq; ✉ Wilde Sapte, 1 Fleet Place, London EC4M 7WS (☎ 0171 246 7018, fax 0171 246 7777)

MILES, Alastair Paul; s of John Charles Miles, of Harpenden, Herts, and Judith, *née* Baker; *b* 11 July 1961; *Educ* St Marylebone GS London, Guildhall Sch of Music and Drama (Performer's Dip in Flute Playing), Nat Opera Studio; *m* Alison Jane, *née* Parry; 2 s (Jonathan Henry Alastair b 31 Oct 1991, Gregory Charles Frederick b 27 July 1995); *Career* bass; given concert performances with numerous major orchs incl: LSO, London Philharmonic, Philharmonia, BBC Symphony, BBC Scottish, RPO, CBSO, Bournemouth Symphony and Bournemouth Sinfonietta, Ensemble d'Orchestre de Paris, Baltimore Symphony, NY Philharmonic, Atlanta Symphony, English Baroque Soloists, Concentus Musicus, London Classical Players, English Concert, Israel Philharmonic, Royal Scottish Nat Orch, Vienna Philharmonic, Boston Symphony; over thirty recordings for numerous labels; *Performances* operatic roles incl: debut as Truelove in The Rake's Progress (with Opera 80) 1985, Pietro in Simon Boccanegra (Glyndebourne Touring Opera) 1986–87, Colline in La Bohème (Vancouver Opera 1986–87, WNO 1988, ENO 1989, Opera de Lyon 1991), Knight of the Grail in Parsifal (Royal Opera House Covent Garden) 1988, Ferrando in Il Trovatore (Dublin Grand Opera) 1988, Poacher in The Cunning Little Vixen (ENO) 1988, Dikoy in Katya Kabanova (Glyndebourne Touring) 1988, Spirit Messenger in Die Frau ohne Schatten (WNO) 1988, Lamoral in Arabella and Madhouse Keeper in The Rake's Progress (Glyndebourne Festival) 1989, Raimondo in Lucia di Lammermoor (WNO) 1989, Don Basilio in The Barber of Seville and Speaker of the Temple in Die Zauberflöte (Glyndebourne Festival and Touring) 1990, Giorgio in I Puritani (Deutsche Oper Berlin) 1991, Sparafucile in Rigoletto (WNO) 1991, Da Silva in Ernani (WNO) 1992, Lord Sydney in Viaggio a Rheims (Covent Garden) 1992, Lorenzo in Montecchi (Covent Garden) 1992, Don Fernando in Fidelio (Covent Garden) 1992, Giorgio in I Puritani (San Francisco) 1993, Figaro in Lenozze di Figaro (Netherlands Opera) 1993, Sparafucile in Rigoletto (Covent Garden) 1994, Alidoro in La Cenerentola (Covent Garden), Colline in La Bohème (Covent Garden) 1995, Fiesco in Simon Boccanegra (Verdi Festival Covent Garden) 1995, Giorgio in I Puritani (Vienna State Opera) 1995, Zaccaria in Nabucco (WNO), Mephistopheles in Faust (WNO) 1995–96; *Awards* Decca/Kathleen Ferrier Prize 1986, Esso/Glyndebourne Touring Opera Award 1986, John Christie Award 1987; *Recreations* golf, cooking, flute playing, reading, decorative painting; *Clubs* Harpenden Golf, Old Philologians; *Style*— Alastair Miles, Esq; ✉ c/o IMG Artist Europe, Media House, 3 Burlington Lane, Chiswick, London W4 2TH (☎ 0181 747 9977, fax 0181 747 9131)

MILES, Anthony John; s of Paul Miles (d 1946), and Mollie, *née* Leitch; *b* 18 July 1930; *Educ* Royal GS High Wycombe; *m* 1 May 1975, Anne Elizabeth, da of William Sidney Bishop (d 1992), of New Ash Green, Kent; *Career* Daily Mirror: feature writer 1954–66, asst ed 1967–68, assoc ed 1968–71, ed 1971–74; chm Mirror Group Newspapers 1980–84 (editorial dir 1975–79), dir Reuters Ltd 1978–84, exec publisher Globe Communications

Corporation Florida USA 1985–90; memb: Press Cncl 1975–78, Br Exec Ctee Int Press Inst 1976–84; vice pres Newspaper Press Fund; *Recreations* bridge; *Clubs* Reform; *Style*— Anthony Miles, Esq; ✉ 197 Friern Barnet Lane, London N20 0NN

MILES, Brian; CBE (1994), RD; s of Terence Clifford Miles (d 1945), and Muriel Irene, *née* Terry (d 1992); *b* 23 Feb 1937; *Educ* Reeds Sch, HMS Conway Cadet Sch; *m* 10 Oct 1964, (Elizabeth) Anne, *née* Scott; 1 s (Martin b 30 Aug 1966), 2 da (Amanda b 29 May 1968, Sara b 10 April 1970); *Career* P & O Shipping Co: cadet 1954–57, deck offr 1958–64, master mariner (FG) 1964; RNLI: inspr of lifeboats 1964–73, staff appts 1974–81, dep dir 1982–87, dir 1988–; hon memb Parkstone Rotary Club; chm: Poole Arts Tst, Dolphin Tst; Freeman City of London 1993, Yr Bro Trinity House 1994, memb Hon Co of Master Mariners 1994; FNI, CIMgt 1994; *Recreations* country pursuits, walking, reading, music, theatre; *Style*— Brian Miles, Esq, CBE, RD; ✉ 8 Longfield Drive, West Parley, Ferndown, Dorset BH22 8TY (☎ 01202 571739); RNLI, West Quay Rd, Poole, Dorset BH15 1HZ (☎ 01202 663149, fax 01202 663167, telex 41328)

MILES, Prof Christopher John; s of Capt John Miles, MC (d 1979), and Clarice Baskerville, *née* Remnant (d 1986); *b* 19 April 1939; *Educ* Winchester, Institut des Hautes Études Cinématographiques; *m* 10 Nov 1967, Susan Helen Howard, da of John Anderson Armstrong, CB, OBE, TD (d 1990), of Cumbria; 1 da (Sophie b 30 Dec 1970); *Career* film director and producer; offr cadet Intelligence Corps 1959–60; bd memb Br Lion Films and Milesian Films 1963; prodns incl: Six Sided Triangle (Hollywood Oscar nomination) 1963, The Virgin and The Gypsy (voted best film in UK and USA by critics) 1969, The Maids (winner Les Yeux Fertiles Cannes Festival) 1974, Alternative Three (nominated TV Drama Awards) 1976, Priest of Love 1981, Lord Elgin and Some Stones of No Value 1985, Love in the Ancient World (TV series, also book, written with John Julius Norwich); work for theatre incl Skin of our Teeth Chicago (dir) 1973; lectr for Br Cncl during Br Film Year India 1985, lectr and film for Br Cncl Mauritius 1994; prof of film and TV RCA 1989–; fell RCA 1990; *Books* Alternative Three (1977); *Recreations* painting, long walks in Arcadia; *Clubs* Garrick; *Style*— Prof Christopher Miles; ✉ Calstone House, Calstone Wellington, Calne, Wiltshire SN11 8PY; Aghios Leos, Methoni, Peloponnese, Greece

MILES, Dillwyn; s of Joshua Miles (d 1932), of Newport, Pembrokeshire, and Anne Mariah, *née* Lewis (d 1946); *b* 25 May 1916; *Educ* Fishguard HS, UC of Wales Aberystwyth; *m* 2 Feb 1944, Joyce Eileen (d 1976), da of Lewis Craven Ord (d 1952), of Montreal and London; 1 s (Anthony b 1945), 1 da (Marilyn b 1946); *Career* ME (Army Capt) 1939–45, nat organiser Palestine House London 1945–48; community centres offr Wales 1948–54; dir: Pembrokeshire Community Cncl 1954–75, Dyfed Rural Cncl 1975–81; chm Nat Assoc of Local Cncls 1975–87 (vice pres 1987–); The Herald Bard 1967–; pres Pembrokeshire Historical Soc 1994–, vice pres Dyfed Wildlife Tst 1976–; memb: Pembrokeshire CC 1947–63, Cemaes RDC 1947–52, Pembrokeshire Coast Nat Park Ctee 1952–75, Haverfordwest Borough Cncl 1957–63, Soc for Promotion of Nature Reserves 1961–73, Nature Conservancy Cncl for Wales 1966–73, Sports Cncl for Wales 1969–70, Prince of Wales Ctee 1971–80; Mayor of Newport Pembrokeshire 1950, 1966, 1967 and 1979 (Alderman 1951–); Mayor of Haverfordwest 1961, Sheriff 1963; Burgess of the Ancient Borough of Newport 1935, Burgess of the Borough of Haverfordwest 1974; FRGS 1945; *Books* Sheriffs of the County of Pembroke (1974), The Royal National Eisteddfod of Wales (1978), A Pembrokeshire Anthology (1983), Portrait of Pembrokeshire (1984), Pembrokeshire Coast National Park (1987), The Secret of the Bards of the Isle of Britain (1992), The Description of Pembrokeshire (ed, 1994), The Ancient Borough of Newport in Pembrokeshire (1995); *Recreations* reading, writing, local history; *Clubs* Savile, Wig and Pen; *Style*— Dillwyn Miles, Esq; ✉ 9 St Anthony's Way, Haverfordwest, Pembrokeshire, Dyfed SA61 1EL (☎ 01437 765275)

MILES, Hamish Alexander Drummond; OBE (1987); s of James Edward (Hamish) Miles (d 1937), and Sheila Barbara, *née* Robertson (d 1954); *b* 19 Nov 1925; *Educ* Douai Sch, Univ of Edinburgh, Univ of Oxford; *m* 31 Aug 1957, Jean Marie, da of late Theodore Richard Smits, of New York; 2 s (Alexander, James), 2 da (Rachel, Helen); *Career* served 1944–47: Black Watch, 6 Br Independent Parachute Bde; asst curator Glasgow Art Gallery 1953–54, lectr in history of art (formerly asst lectr) Univ of Glasgow 1954–66, visiting lectr Smith Coll Mass 1960–61, prof of history of art Univ of Leicester 1966–70, Barber prof of fine arts and dir Barber Inst of Fine Arts 1970–90, dir emeritus Barber Inst of Fine Arts and prof at large Univ of Birmingham 1990–91 (prof emeritus 1992); tstee: Nat Galleries of Scotland 1967–87, Public Art Cmmns Agency 1987–94; memb Museums and Galleries Cmmn 1983–87; *Style*— Hamish Miles, Esq; ✉ 31 Drummond Place, Edinburgh EH3 6PW; Burnside, Kirkmichael, by Blairgowrie, Perthshire PH10 7NA

MILES, James Archibald Robertson; s of Hamish Alexander Drummond Miles, of Edinburgh, and Jean Marie, *née* Smits; *b* 8 Sept 1961; *Educ* King Edward's Sch Birmingham, New Coll Oxford (BA Chinese); *m* 1 Aug 1992, Catherine Ruth, da of Trenwith John Wallis Sampson; 1 s (Alistair John Robertson b 10 June 1996); *Career* business reporter South China Morning Post Hong Kong 1984; United Press International (UPI): Hong Kong reporter 1984–85, S Asia corr 1985–86, Beijing corr 1986–87; Beijing corr BBC Radio and Television 1987–94, Burton R Benjamin fell in bdcast journalism Michigan Univ 1994–95, Hong Kong corr BBC World Service 1995–; Reporter of the Year Sony Radio Awards 1990, One World Bdcasting Award 1990; *Publications* The Legacy of Tiananmen, China in Disarray (Univ of Michigan Press, 1996); *Recreations* shooting, walking; *Style*— James Miles, Esq; ✉ c/o Newsgathering Room 3108, BBC Broadcasting House, London W1A 1AA (☎ 0171 765 5284, fax 0171 636 9515)

MILES, Prof John Richard; s of Thomas William Miles (d 1988), and Hilda Mary, *née* Davis (d 1994); *b* 22 June 1944; *m* (m dis); *Career* designer and tutor; colourist designer and consit Fidelis Furnishing Fabrics (later amalgamated with Tootals) 1969–74, work shown in prototype Exhibition at Design Council 1970; designer of fashion furnishings and household textiles for worldwide market 1969–; clients incl: Courtaulds, Heal's, Liberty's, Christian Dior, Yves Saint Laurant; set up own studio: Calver & Pound Designs 1973–77, Peppermint Prints 1977–81; design dir of home furnishings and apparel fabrics Courtaulds Plc 1986–87 (design dir of home furnishings 1985–86); Next Interior: design mangr 1987, design and buying mangr 1987, gen mangr 1987–88; set up own studio Miles Whiston & Wright 1989–96, fndr John Miles Partnership 1996–; CNAA: chm Fashion and Textile Panel 1984–87 (memb 1978–81), memb Ctee for Art and Design 1984–87 and 1988–, specialist advsr to Ctee for Art and Design 1987; memb: Textile Ctee Design Centre Selection 1985–88 (memb Knitwear Ctee 1984–86), Selection Panel for Young Designers into Industry RSA 1987–89, Advsy Panel BFC 1994–; sr lectr i/c of textiles St Martin's Sch of Art 1974–75, head of Fashion Dept and Textiles Course leader Brighton Polytechnic 1979–85 prof of textiles and fashion Royal Coll of Art 1989–; fndr studio Miles Whiston and Wright 1988–, co-fndr and consit studio Claire and Lyn 1992; memb Industl Lead Body for Art and Design 1990–96, memb Res Assessment Panel Univ Funding Cncl 1992–; pt/t and visiting lectr; memb numerous academic ctees Brighton Polytechnic and Royal Coll of Art; internal and external assessor; memb Assoc of Heads of Degree Courses for Fashion and Textiles 1979–85; *Recreations* gardening, cooking, theatre, films, reading, music; *Style*— Prof John Miles; ✉ Royal College of Art, Kensington Gore, London SW7 2EU (☎ 0171 590 4361)

MILES, John Seeley; s of Thomas Miles (d 1965), and Winifred, *née* Seeley (d 1981); *b* 11 Feb 1931; *Educ* Beckenham GS, Beckenham Art Sch; *m* 1955, Louise Rachel, da of George Rowland Wilson (d 1983); 1 s (Jonathan b 1964), 2 da (Catherine b 1958, Sophia b 1960); *Career* asst to Hans Schmoller Penguin Books 1955–58, fndr ptnr Banks & Miles 1958–; conslt: Zoological Soc, Regents Park, Whipsnade 1958–62, Expanded Metal Co 1960–83, Consumers' Assoc 1964–84, PO 1972–83, Br Cncl 1968–83, Curwen Press 1970–73, E Midlands Arts Assoc 1974–79, Enschede en Zn Netherlands 1980–95, BT 1980, Br Airports Authy, Univ of Lancaster 1989, UN Univ Tokyo 1990, CUP 1991, UNHCR 1995–, Microscoft Corporation 1995–; design advsr: Monotype Corporation 1985–91, UEA 1990–, University of the West of England at Bristol 1992; typographic advsr HMSO 1985–; chm Arbitration Ctee Assoc Typographique Int 1984–94; Green Award for environmental design (with Colin Banks) 1989; govr Central Sch of Arts and Craft 1978–85; memb CGLI 1986; *Books* Design for Desktop Publishing (1987); *Recreations* gardening, painting; *Clubs* Double Crown; *Style*— John Miles, Esq; ✉ The Studio, Pit Cottage, The Dell, Tunstall Common, Suffolk IP12 2JR (☎ 01728 688889)

MILES, Keith Charles; s of Leslie Maurice Miles, of Reading, Berks, and Doris Ellen Wyard Miles; *b* 28 Nov 1941; *Educ* Owens Sch; *m* 20 Dec 1969, Slava, da of Jože Blenkuš (d 1977); 1 s (Andrew Karel Scott b 1973), 1 da (Jane Helena Louise b 1977); *Career* CA; dir of fin and ops Cable Authy 1985–88, dir of fin and admin Inst of Econ Affrs 1988–90, special advsr Putnam Hayes & Barlett 1989–90, co sec and gp fin dir Etam plc 1990–95; dir: Multiple Listing Services Ltd 1996–, Slovenia Trade and Investment Corporation Ltd 1996–; only English memb Economic Advsy Cncl of the Cabinet of Republic of Slovenia, hon sec-gen UK Representative Office Repub of Slovenia 1991–92, rep of Bank of Slovenia to Bank of England 1992–, rep Ljubljana Stock Exchange in UK 1995–; chm British-Slovene Soc 1993–; memb Review Body for Nursing Staff, Midwives, Health Visitors and Professions Allied to Nursing 1996–; Liveryman: Worshipful Co of Glass Sellers, Worshipful Co of CAs; FRSA; *Publications* various articles on accountancy, free market economics and Central & Eastern Europe; *Recreations* skiing, reading, swimming; *Style*— Keith Miles, Esq; ✉ 19 Elmtree Green, Gt Missenden, Bucks HP16 9AF (☎ 01494 863128)

MILES, Malcolm John; s of John Frederick Miles, MBE, of Kingston-upon-Thames, Surrey, and Phyllis Maud, *née* Umpelby (d 1991); *b* 5 March 1945; *Educ* London Coll For Distributive Trades (Dip Bus Studies), Univ of Chicago; *m* 22 Nov 1969, Ann Therisa, da of Roy Augustine O'Dwyer, of Dorking, Surrey; 1 s (Alexander Malcolm (Bertie) b 1978); *Career* 225 water sports Binibeca Minorca 1971; assoc dir Ted Bates advertising London 1975–76; McCann-Erickson Advertising London: account dir 1971–74, assoc dir 1977, bd dir 1980, dir account mgmnt, dep md 1984, md 1985–88, dir McCann Erickson Kenya, chm McCann UK Ltd, regnl mangr Africa and Middle East 1991–95, sr vice pres Europe 1991–93, exec vice pres Europe 1993–, area mangr Middle East and Central and Eastern Europe 1995–, memb Worldwide Mgmnt Bd 1995; memb: Tobacco Ctee EAAA Brussels 1980–84, Marketing Ctee CBI 1986–88, Cncl CBI 1987, Cncl IPA 1989; MCAM (1973), MAA (1969), FIPA 1990 (MIPA 1980); *Recreations* shooting, gardening, boats, family; *Clubs* RAC; *Style*— M J Miles, Esq; ✉ McCann-Erickson House, 36 Howland St, London W1A 1AT (☎ 0171 580 6690, fax 0171 915 2132, mobile 0385 277587, telex 28231)

MILES, (Henry) Michael Pearson; OBE (1989); s of Brig H G P Miles (d 1966), of London, and Margaret, *née* Mounsey (d 1974); *b* 19 April 1936; *Educ* Wellington; *m* 25 Oct 1967, Carol Jane, da of Harold Berg (d 1955); 2 s (Henry James Pearson b 1969, Mark Edward Pearson b 1975), 1 da (Sasha Jane Pearson b 1971); *Career* Nat Serv cmmnd Duke of Wellington's Regt 1955–57; md John Swire and Sons (Japan) Ltd 1973–76; dir: Hongkong & Shanghai Banking Corporation 1984–88, John Swire & Sons Ltd 1988–; former chm: John Swire & Sons (HK) Ltd, Cathay Pacific Airways Ltd, Hong Kong Tourist Assoc; dep chm Barings plc; also dir: BP plc 1994–, Fraser Insurance Services, Johnson Matthey plc, Portals plc, Thomas Cook Group, Fleming Far Eastern Investmt Tst, Sedgwick Lloyd's Underwriting Agents, BICC 1996–; memb: Bd Navy Army and Air Force Inst, Int Advsy Bd Creditanstalt Vienna, Anglo-Taiwan Trade Ctee, China-Britain Trade Group; govr Wellington Coll; *Recreations* golf, tennis, shooting; *Clubs* Royal & Ancient Golf, Berkshire Golf, Queen's; *Style*— Michael Miles, Esq, OBE; ✉ John Swire & Sons Ltd, Swire House, 59 Buckingham Gate, London SW1E 6AJ (☎ 0171 834 7717, fax 0171 630 0353, telex 888800)

MILES, Nicholas Charles James; s of Kenneth Norman Miles, of Crowborough, E Sussex, and Audrey Mary, *née* Rhodes; *b* 23 Oct 1958; *Educ* Tonbridge, Corpus Christi Coll Cambridge (BA); *m* 12 May 1990, Suzanne Katharine, *née* Chauveau; 3 da (Lucy Florence b 1 Sept 1991, Katharine Rose b 8 April 1993, Sophy Arabella b 26 March 1996); *Career* dir: BMP Business Ltd 1985–87, Lowe Bell Financial Ltd 1987–92; chief exec Financial Dynamics Ltd 1992–; performed in Death in the Aisles, Nightcap Cambridge Footlights Revues 1979; *Recreations* tennis, golf, shooting; *Clubs* Annabel's, Hurlingham, Bachelors; *Style*— Nicholas Miles, Esq; ✉ Financial Dynamics Ltd, 30 Furnival Street, London EC4 (☎ 0171 831 3113)

MILES, (Richard) Oliver; CMG (1984); *b* 1936; *Educ* Ampleforth, Merton Coll Oxford (MA); *m* 1968, Julia, *née* Weiner; 3 s (b 1972, 1973 and 1977), 1 da (b 1979); *Career* Nat Serv RN 1954–56; HM Dip Serv: joined FO 1960, MECAS 1960–61, actg political offr Abu Dhabi 1961–62, FO 1962–64, second sec Amman 1964–66, first sec Mukalla 1966–67, first sec and head of Chancery Aden 1967–68, head of Chancery Nicosia 1970–73, first sec FCO 1973–75, cnsllr Jedda 1975–77, cnsllr and consul-gen Athens 1977–80, head of NE and N African Dept FCO 1980–84, ambass Tripoli 1984, ambass and consul-gen Luxembourg 1985–88, on loan to Home Civil Serv 1988–90, asst under sec for economic affrs FCO 1990–91, first DG FCO/Dept of Trade and Indust Jt Directorate for Overseas Trade Servs 1991–93, ambass Athens 1993–March 1996, ret; non-exec dir Vickers Defence Systems 1991–93; sr conslt: MEC, mi2gi; *Style*— Oliver Miles, Esq, CMG; ✉ c/o Foreign and Commonwealth Office, King Charles Street, London SW1A 2AH

MILES, Peter Thomas; s of Thomas Harry Miles (d 1968); *b* 1 Aug 1939; *Educ* Bromsgrove Sch; *m* 18 June 1971, Gail, da of Trevor Davies; 2 c (Juliet Elizabeth b 24 Sept 1972, Edward Thomas b 10 Feb 1975); *Career* chartered accountant; ptnr: Russell Durie Kerr Watson & Co 1968, Spicer & Pegler (following merger), Touche Ross 1990–96 (following merger, now Deloitte & Touche); dir: T Westley Engineering Group plc, Certes Group plc, Corner Coventry Ltd; FCA; *Recreations* fly-fishing, tennis, gardening; *Style*— Peter T Miles, Esq; ✉ Mintz Cottage, Cakebole, Chaddesley Corbett, Worcestershire DY10 4RE (☎ and fax 01562 777179)

MILES, Sir Peter Tremayne; KCVO (1986); s of Lt-Col E W T Miles, MC (d 1943), of Kington Langley, Chippenham, Wilts, and Mary Albinia, *née* Gibbs (d 1979); *b* 26 June 1924; *Educ* Eton, RMA Sandhurst; *m* 25 July 1956, Philippa Helen, da of E M B (Jack) Tremlett (d 1977), of Chiddingfold, Surrey; 2 s (Napier b 1 Aug 1958, Patrick b 1 June 1960), 1 da (Davina b 8 Jan 1964, m 1989 Paul Morgan-Witts, s of Max Morgan Witts); *Career* 1 Royal Dragoons 1944–49; J F Thomasson and Co 1949–59, md Gerrard and National Discount Co Ltd 1964–80 (joined 1959); dir: P Murray Jones Ltd 1966–75, Astley and Pearce Hldgs 1975–80 (chm 1978–80); Keeper of the Privy Purse and Treas to HM The Queen 1981–87, Receiver Gen to Duchy of Lancaster 1981–87, memb Prince of Wales' Cncl 1981–87; dir British and Commonwealth Holdings plc 1988–90; *Clubs* White's, Pratt's, Cavalry and Guards', Swinley Forest Golf; *Style*— Sir Peter Miles, KCVO; ✉ Mill House, Southrop, Lechlade, Glos GL7 3NU

MILES, Philip John; s and h of Sir William Napier Maurice Miles, 6 Bt, *qv*; *b* 10 Aug 1953; *Style*— Philip Miles Esq

MILES, Roger Tremayne; s of Lt Cdr Peter Tremayne Miles, RN (d 1995), of Maidenhead, Berks, and Christine Valerie Walby, *née* Perks; *b* 9 March 1962; *Educ* Tonbridge, Trinity Coll Oxford (exhibitioner, MA); *m* 28 May 1990, Deirdra Mary, da of Patrick Gregory Moynihan, of Sidcup, Kent; 2 da (Ellen Frances Caitlin b 11 June 1993, Katherine (Kitty) May Dorothy b 2 Feb 1996); *Career* bd dir OTG (Oxford Theatre Group) Productions Ltd 1981–83, articled Price Waterhouse 1983–85, bd dir Charles Barker Ltd 1990–92, bd dir Georgeson and Company Ltd 1992–95, head of communications British Bankers' Assoc 1996–; MIPR 1991, MInstD 1994; *Recreations* fatherhood, music making, novels, new technologies; *Style*— Roger Miles, Esq; ✉ British Bankers' Association, Pinners Hall, 105–108 Old Broad Street, London EC2N 1EX (☎ 0171 216 8809)

MILES, Roy Edward Brian; s of Elsa, *née* McKinly, father decd; *b* 9 Feb 1935; *Educ* Bembridge Sch IOW, Sorbonne Paris; *m* 1971, Christine, da of Frank Rhodes, of Thorpe Underwood Hall, Yorks; *Career* art dealer; proprietor Roy Miles Gallery London; has sold to major museums worldwide incl Tate Gallery, V & A and Nat Portrait Gallery, first dealer to take major collection to Middle East, sold Canaletto's The Banqueting Hall for St James to Paul Mellon Collection, first Western dealer to buy major 1920's-1980's Russian paintings 1985–, gallery carries largest collection of Russian oil paintings in the West, sole agent for Sergei Chepik (Russia's leading contemporary artist); numerous radio and TV appearances; *Recreations* reading, classical music; *Clubs* Arts; *Style*— Roy Miles, Esq; ✉ Roy Miles Gallery, 29 Bruton Street, London W1X 7DB (☎ 0171 495 4747, fax 0171 495 6232)

MILES, Stephen Antony David; s of late Antony Richard Miles, of Chorleywood, Herts, and Marjorie, *née* Allwork; *b* 21 June 1947; *Educ* Marist Brothers Coll Inanda Johannesburg SA, Univ of the Witwatersrand Johannesburg (MB BCh); *Career* various trg posts in Johannesburg; sr registrar accident and emergency Bart's and UCH 1979–82, conslt Bart's and Homerton Hosp 1982–95, conslt Royal London and Homerton Hosps 1995–; immediate past pres Accident and Emergency Section RSM; med advsr to Bd London Ambulance Serv 1990–, hon sec Br Assoc for Accident and Emergency Med 1990–96; currently memb Bd Intercollegiate Faculty of Accident and Emergency Med; Freeman City of London 1984; FRCSEd 1975; memb: BMA 1980, RSM 1987; *Recreations* music, ballet, theatre; *Style*— Stephen Miles, Esq; ✉ Accident And Emergency Department, The Royal London Hospital, Whitechapel Road, London E1 1BB (☎ 0171 377 7000 ext 3008, fax 0171 377 7014)

MILES, Sir William Napier Maurice; 6 Bt (UK 1859), of Leigh Court, Somersetshire; s of Lt-Col Sir Charles William Miles, 5 Bt, OBE (d 1966); *b* 19 Oct 1913; *Educ* Stowe, Jesus Coll Cambridge; *m* 1946, Pamela, da of late Capt Michael Dillon; 1 s (Philip John b 1953), 2 da (Catherine Anne Elizabeth (Mrs Peter C Beloe) b 1947, Lorraine (Mrs Martin H Sessions-Hodge) b 1950); *Heir* s, Philip John Miles b 10 Aug 1953; *Career* chartered architect (ret); ARIBA; *Style*— Sir William Miles, Bt; ✉ Old Rectory House, Walton-in-Gordano, nr Clevedon BS21 7AW (☎ 01275 873365)

MILFORD, 3 Baron (UK 1939); Sir Hugo John Laurence Philipps; 3 Bt (UK 1919); s of 2 Baron Milford (d 1993), and his 1 w, Rosamond Nina, CBE (d 1990), da of Rudolph Chambers Lehmann; *b* 27 Aug 1929; *Educ* Eton, King's Coll Cambridge; *m* 1, 1951 (m dis 1958), Margaret, da of Capt Ralph Heathcote, DSO, RN; 1 da (Hon Anna Margaret (Hon Mrs Woodhouse) b 1954); m 2, 1959 (m dis 1984), Hon Mary Makins, eldest da of 1 Baron Sherfield, GCB, GCMG; 3 s (Hon Guy Wogan b 1961, Hon Roland Alexander b 1962, Hon Ivo Laurence b 1967), 1 da (Hon Katherine Nina b 1964); m 3, 26 Jan 1989, Mrs Felicity Leach; *Heir* s, Hon Guy Wogan Philipps b 25 July 1961; *Career* farmer; *Clubs* Boodle's, Pratt's; *Style*— The Rt Hon the Lord Milford; ✉ Llanstephan House, Llanstephan, Brecon, Powys LD3 0YR (☎ 01982 560693)

MILFORD, John Tillman; QC (1989); s of Dr Roy Douglas Milford (d 1982), of Grianachan, Strathtay, Perthshire, and Essie, *née* Rhind (d 1972); *b* 4 Feb 1946; *Educ* Hurstpierpoint, Univ of Exeter (LLB); *m* 1975, Mary Alice, da of Dr Edmund Anthony Spriggs (d 1989), of River House, Wylam, Northumberland; 3 da (Alice b 1977, Sarah b 1979, Emily b 1981); *Career* called to the Bar Inner Temple 1969; practising Newcastle upon Tyne 1970–, recorder of the Crown Court 1985–, head of Trinity Chambers Newcastle upon Tyne 1986–; *Recreations* fishing, shooting, beagling, gardening; *Clubs* Northern Counties (Newcastle upon Tyne), Durham County; *Style*— John Milford, Esq, QC; ✉ Hill House, Haydon Bridge, Hexham, Northumberland; Dalcharn, Tongue, Sutherland; 12 Trinity Chare, Quayside, Newcastle-upon-Tyne NE1 3DF (☎ 0191 232 1927)

MILFORD HAVEN, 4 Marquess of (UK 1917); George Ivar Louis Mountbatten; also Earl of Medina and Viscount Alderney (both UK 1917); s of 3 Marquess of Milford Haven, OBE, DSC (d 1970, himself gs of HSH Prince Louis of Battenberg, who relinquished, at the King's request, the style and title of Serene Highness and Prince of Battenberg, instead assuming the surname of Mountbatten by Royal Licence 1917); gn of late Earl Mountbatten of Burma and, through his paternal grandmother (Nada), ggggs of Emperor Nicholas I of Russia; *b* 6 June 1961; *Educ* Gordonstoun; *m* 8 March 1989 (m dis 1996), Sarah Georgina, er da of George Alfred Walker, fndr and former chief exec Brent Walker Group plc, and former w of Andreas L Antoniou; 1 s (Harry David Louis, Earl of Medina b 19 Oct 1991), 1 da (Lady Tatiana Helen Georgia b 16 April 1990); *Heir* s, Harry David Louis, Earl of Medina b 19 Oct 1991; *Style*— The Most Hon the Marquess of Milford Haven; ✉ 14 West Halkin Street, London SW1

MILFORD HAVEN, Janet, Marchioness of; Janet Mercedes Mountbatten; *née* Bryce; JP (Inner London 1979); o da of late Maj Francis Bryce, OBE, KRRC, and Gladys Jean, *née* Mosley; *b* 29 Sept 1937, Bermuda; *Educ* Trafalgar Sch for Girls Montreal Canada; *m* 17 Nov 1960, as his 2 w, 3 Marquess of Milford Haven, OBE, DSC (d 1970); 2 s (George, 4 Marquess of Milford Haven b 1961, Lord Ivar Mountbatten b 1963, *qqv*); *Career* Freeman City of London 1991; *Style*— The Most Hon Janet, Marchioness of Milford Haven, JP

MILKINA, Nina; da of Jacques Milkine, and Sophie Milkine; *b* 27 Jan 1919; *Educ* privately; *m* 1943, Alastair Robert Masson Sedgwick; 1 s (Alexander Paul b 1958), 1 da (Katrina b 1960); *Career* concert pianist noted for performances of Mozart's piano works; studied: Paris with Leon Conus of Moscow Conservatoire, composition with Sabaniev and Glazunov, in England with Harold Craxton and Tobias Matthay; first public performance with Lamoreux Orchestra in Paris aged 11, first composition published by Boosey and Hawkes aged 11; BBC cmmn to broadcast all Mozart's piano sonatas, gave Mozart Bicentenary Recital Edinburgh Int Festival; recorded for: Westminster Record Co, Pye, ASV; adjudicator at major music competitions; Hon RAM; *Recreations* chess, swimming; *Style*— Miss Nina Milkina; ✉ 17 Montagu Square, London W1H 1RD (☎ 0171 487 4588); Casa delle Colonne, S Pietro, Sardinia

MILL, Ian Alexander; s of Ronald MacLauchlan Mill (d 1984), and Thelma Anita, *née* Boliston; *b* 9 April 1958; *Educ* Epsom Coll, Univ of Cambridge (MA); *m* 13 June 1987, (Mary) Emma, da of Roger and Marian Clayden, of Los Gatos, California, USA; *Career* called to the Bar Middle Temple 1981; commercial barr specialising in entertainment law 1982–; *Recreations* cricket, golf, good food and wine, travel; *Clubs* MCC; *Style*— Ian Mill, Esq; ✉ 49 Moreton Pl, London SW1V 2NL (☎ and fax 0171 834 5804); 2 Hare Ct, Temple, London EC4Y 7BH (☎ 0171 583 1770, fax 0171 583 9269, telex 27139 LINLAW)

MILL, Peter Stuart; s of Donald Norman Mill (d 1981), of Downshire Hill, London, and Heather Mary, *née* Lavelle; *b* 21 June 1957; *Educ* Claremont High Kenton Middx, Watford Coll of Technol (DipAD); *m* 4 Oct 1987, Susan Ann, da of Dennis Austin Goode; 3 da (Helen Michelle b 23 Aug 1985, Hannah Catherine b 28 Dec 1988, Katie Heather b 15 June 1995); *Career* jr copywriter BBDO Advertising London 1975–76; copywriter: Fletcher Shelton Delaney 1976–78, Hall Advertising 1978–84; fndr ptnr and exec creative dir The Leith Agency 1984–, sr ptnr new business 1995–; recipient: Silver Campaign Press Award, Campaign Poster Award, EPICA Award, Cannes Advtg Film Festival Silver Lion, Br TV Advtg Silver Award, Scottish Advtg Awards annually 1988–93, Roses Awards annually 1988–94; memb D&AD 1983, MInstD 1985; *Style*— Peter Mill, Esq; ✉ 7 Burnside Road, Eddleston, Peebles EH45 8RH; The Leith Agency, The Canon Mill, Canon Street, Edinburgh EH3 5HE (☎ 0131 557 5840, fax 0131 557 5837, e-mail p.mill@silvermills.co.uk)

MILLA, Dr Peter John; s of John Milla (d 1961), of 32 Station Ave, Sandown, IOW, and Betty Violet, *née* Barton; *b* 4 Aug 1941; *Educ* Whitgift Sch, St Bartholomew's Hosp Med Coll (MB BS), Chelsea Coll Univ of London (MSc); *m* Sept 1969, (Pamela) Jane, da of John Davis, of 33 Almond Close, Bedhampton, Havant, Hants; 1 s (Richard b 1972), 1 da (Elizabeth b 1974); *Career* reader in paediatric gastroenterology Inst of Child Health Univ of London 1994– (sr lectr 1983–94); memb Ed Bd: Gut, Archives of Disease of Childhood, Journal of Paediatric Gastroenterology and Nutrition, Journal of Gastrointestinal Motility; advsr Wellcome Tst; sec Euro Soc of Paediatric Gastroenterology and Nutrition; memb Cncl United European Gastroenterology Fedn; memb: Br Paediatric Assoc, Br Soc of Gastroenterology, American Gastroenterology Assoc, Br Soc of Paediatric Gastroenterology and Nutrition; FRCP 1985; *Books* Harries' Paediatric Gastroenterology (ed with D R P Muller, 1988), Disorders of Gastrointestinal Motility (1988); *Recreations* sailing, motoring, gardening, model engineering; *Style*— Dr Peter J Milla; ✉ Gastroenterology Unit, Institute of Child Health, University of London, 30 Guilford St, London WC1N 1EH (☎ 0171 242 9789, fax 0171 404 6181)

MILLAN, Rt Hon Bruce; PC (1975); s of David Millan; *b* 5 Oct 1927; *Educ* Harris Acad Dundee; *m* 1953, Gwendoline May Fairey; 1 s, 1 da; *Career* MP (Lab): Glasgow Craigton 1959–83, Glasgow Govan 1983–88; Parly under sec: Def (RAF) 1964–66, Scotland 1966–70; oppn front bench spokesman on civil aviation then Scottish affairs 1970–74, min of state Scottish Office 1974–76, sec of state Scotland 1976–79, oppn front bench spokesman Scotland 1979–83, Euro cmmr 1989–Jan 1995; *Style*— The Rt Hon Bruce Millan; ✉ 1 Torridon Avenue, Glasgow G41 5LA (☎ 0141 427 6483)

MILLAR, *see:* Hoyer Millar

MILLAR, Anthony Bruce (Tony); s of James Desmond Millar (d 1965), and Josephine Georgina, *née* Brice; *b* 5 Oct 1941; *Educ* Haileybury Imperial Serv Coll; *m* 3 July 1964, Judith Anne, da of Capt John Edward Jester (d 1984), of Drayton, Hants; 2 da (Cassilda Anne b 1966, Katrina Mary b 1967); *Career* asst to gp mgmnt accountant and gp treas Viyella International Federation Ltd 1964–67; United Tport Overseas Ltd Nairobi 1967–70: chief accountant to subsidiary, gp internal auditor for E Africa, PA to chief agent, dep gp fin controller London 1970–72; conslt Fairfield Property Co 1975–77 (fin dir 1972–75), md Provincial Laundries Ltd 1977–81, dep chm Hawley Group Ltd 1981, hon pres The Albert Fisher Group PLC 1992– (chm 1982–92), chm San Andreas Resources Corporation 1994–; Freeman City of London, Liveryman Worshipful Company of Fruiterers; FCA 1974 (ACA 1964), CIMgt 1986; *Recreations* scuba diving, walking, bridge; *Clubs* Mark's; *Style*— Tony Millar, Esq; ✉ Frensham Vale House, Lower Bourne, Farnham, Surrey GU10 3JB

MILLAR, David William; s of Brig William Semple Millar, of Camberley, Surrey, and Maureen Heather, *née* Jones; *b* 30 Jan 1951; *Educ* Morrison's Academy, Univ of Edinburgh (BSc); *m* 3 Sept 1977, Daniele Yolande Germaine, da of Maurice Robert Ferreyrol; 1 s (Hamish Robert b 10 June 1983), 1 da (Pascaline Myrto b 10 Aug 1988); *Career* joined J Walter Thompson 1973, dir J Walter Thompson 1985–94, md JWT Direct 1990–94, head of communications strategy British Gas PLC 1995–; MIPA 1982; *Recreations* golf; *Clubs* Caledonian, Home Park Golf; *Style*— David Millar, Esq; ✉ British Gas PLC, Heron House, 322 High Holborn, London WC1V 7PW (☎ 0171 269 4313)

MILLAR, Douglas George; s of George Sydie Gray Millar (d 1982), and Doris Mary, *née* Morris; *b* 15 Feb 1946; *Educ* City of Norwich Sch, Univ of Bristol (BA), Univ of Reading (MA); *m* 1, 26 Aug 1967 (m dis 1986), Susan Mary, *née* Farrow; 1 da (Victoria Mary b 8 March 1972), 1 s (Timothy George b 8 Oct 1974); m 2, 23 May 1987, Jane Victoria, da of John Edgar Howard Smith; 1 s (George Oliver Howard b 20 April 1989), 1 da (Fleur Elizabeth b 26 July 1990); *Career* House of Commons: asst clerk 1968–73, sr clerk 1973–81, dep princ clerk 1981–89, clerk Def Ctee 1979–83, clerk i/c Private Membs Bills 1983–87, clerk Home Affairs Ctee 1987–89, concurrently princ clerk, clerk Fin Ctees, clerk Treasy and Civil Serv Ctee and sec Public Accounts Cmmn 1989–91, second clerk of Select Ctees 1991–94, clerk of Select Ctees and departmental fin offr 1994–; jt sec Assoc of Secs Gen of Parls 1971–77, memb Study of Parl Gp (jt sec 1980–83); chm Teddington Soc 1976–78 and 1982–83; contrib to Parly jls; *Recreations* family, watching football (Norwich City), golf; *Clubs* Roehampton, Parl Golfing Soc (hon sec 1995–); *Style*— Douglas Millar, Esq; ✉ Clerk of Select Committees, Committee Office, House of Commons, London SW1A 0AA

MILLAR, Sir Oliver Nicholas; GCVO (1988, KCVO 1973, CVO 1963, MVO 1953); s of Gerald Arthur Millar, MC (d 1975); *b* 26 April 1923; *Educ* Rugby, Courtauld Inst of Art; *m* 1954, Delia Mary, CVO (1996), da of Lt-Col Cuthbert Dawnay, MC (d 1964); 1 s, (Charles James), 3 da (Cynthia Mary, Lucy Anne, Beatrix Jane); *Career* dir The Royal Collection 1987–88; surveyor emeritus of pictures to HM The Queen 1988– (asst surveyor 1947, dep surveyor 1949–72, surveyor 1972–88); author of books and catalogues relating chiefly to the history of The Royal Collection and the arts in Stuart England; tstee Nat Portrait Gallery 1972–95; memb: Cncl of Friends of the Tate Gallery, Reviewing Ctee on Export of Works of Art 1975–87, Exec Ctee Nat Arts Collection Fund 1987–; tstee Nat Heritage Meml Fund 1988–92, chm Patrons of Br Art 1990–; FBA; *Recreations* grandchildren, drawing, gardening, listening to music, reading; *Clubs* Brooks's, MCC; *Style*— Sir Oliver Millar, GCVO, FBA; ✉ The Cottage, Rays Lane, Penn, Bucks (☎ 01494 812124)

MILLAR, Peter John; s of Norman Millar, of Ashby, Lincs, and Maureen Nelson, *née* McMaster; *b* 22 Feb 1955; *Educ* Bangor GS Co Down NI, Magdalen Coll Oxford (MA); *m* 1981, Jacqueline Carol, *née* Freeman; 2 s (Patrick James Arthur b 1984, Oscar Alexander b 1987); *Career* Reuters corr: Brussels 1978–79, E Berlin 1981–83, Moscow 1983–85; journalist Daily Telegraph 1985–86, Euro corr Sunday Telegraph 1986–89, central Euro corr Sunday Times 1989–90, dep ed The European 1990–91; freelance columnist, bdcaster and writer 1991–, contrib to Sunday Times, The Times, The European, Evening Standard, Granada TV and Sky TV; popular fiction critic The Times 1994–; beer columnist Sainsbury's Magazine 1994–; Foreign Corr of the Year Granada TV What the Papers Say awards 1989, commended in int reporter category Br press awards 1989–; *Books* Tomorrow Belongs To Me (1991); *Recreations* cooking, skiing, painting; *Clubs* 2 Brydges Place; *Style*— Peter Millar, Esq; ✉ 48 Brandram Road, London SE13 5RT (☎ 0181 318 2413); c/o The Times, 1 Pennington Street, London E1 9XN (☎ 0171 782 5000, fax 0171 488 3242)

MILLAR, (John) Richard; s of William Hugh Millar (d 1967), and Eileen Phyllis May Millar (d 1996); *b* 16 Feb 1940; *Educ* Wellington; *m* 2 Dec 1978, Rosemary Margaret, da of Alfred Thomas Hanson, of 3 Riverside, Gargrave, N Yorks; *Career* admitted slr 1963, sr ptnr Bischoff & Co 1990–93 (ptnr 1968–93), jt chm Frere Cholmeley Bischoff 1993–; hon slr: Br Uruguayan Soc, West London Ctee for the Protection of Children; memb

Law Soc Company Law Ctee (chm Collective Investment Scheme Sub-ctee), memb Law Soc 1963; Freeman City of London, Liveryman City of London Solicitors' Co; *Recreations* sailing, gardening; *Clubs* City of London, Offshore Yachts Class Owners Assoc, Little Ship; *Style*— Richard Millar, Esq; ✉ Frere Cholmeley Bischoff, 4 John Carpenter Street, London EC4Y 0NH (☎ 0171 615 8000, fax 0171 615 8080)

MILLAR, Sir Ronald Graeme; kt (1980); s of Ronald Hugh Millar, and Dorothy Ethel Dacre, *née* Hill; *b* 12 Nov 1919; *Educ* Charterhouse, King's Coll Cambridge; *Career* served WWII Sub Lt RNVR; playwright and political writer; speech writer to: Edward Heath 1970–74, Margaret Thatcher 1975–90, John Major 1991–; dep chm Theatre Royal Haymarket 1977–; former actor with appearances in Mr Bolfry, The Sacred Flame, Murder on the Nile, Jenny Jones, Zero Hour (own play); screenwriter in London and Hollywood where films worked on incl: Frieda, The Miniver Story, Scaramouche, Rose Marie, Betrayed, The Unknown Man, Never Let Me Go; plays produced in London incl: Frieda, Waiting for Gillian, The Bride and the Bachelor, The Bride Comes Back, Robert and Elizabeth (book and lyrics), Number 10, Abelard and Heloise; adaptations for the theatre of works by CP Snow incl: The Affair, The New Men, The Masters, The Case in Question, A Coat of Varnish; *Books* A View from the Wings (autobiography, 1993); *Recreations* music; *Clubs* Brooks's, Dramatists'; *Style*— Sir Ronald Millar; ✉ 7 Sheffield Terrace, London W8 (☎ 0171 727 8361)

MILLARD, Dennis Henry; s of Henry Edward Millard, of Durban, S Africa, and Edna Elizabeth, *née* Battale; *b* 28 Feb 1949; *Educ* Marist Brothers Coll, Univ of Natal (capt Natal under-20 rugby XV), Univ of Cape Town (MBA, Gold Medal); *m* 22 March 1972, Paula Teresa Felicity, da of late William Coulter; 1 da (Lisa Catherine b 1973), 2 s (Sean Patrick b 1976, James Henry b 1988); *Career* audit clerk then audit sr H E Mattinson & Partners CAs Durban 1967–73, mgmnt accountant then fin dir Hultrans Ltd Durban 1973–77, MBA 1978, gp mangr corp planning Huletts Corporation Durban 1979–80, gp mangr corp planning then fin dir Plate Glass Group Johannesburg 1980–93, fin dir Medeva plc London 1994–96, fin dir Cookson Group plc 1996–; memb S African Soc of CAs 1973, MInstD 1991; *Recreations* golf, tennis, jogging; *Clubs* Wisley Golf; *Style*— Dennis Millard, Esq; ✉ Cookson Group plc, 130 Wood Street, London EC2V 6EQ (☎ 0171 606 4400, fax 0171 606 2851)

MILLARD, Sir Guy Elwin; KCMG (1972, CMG 1957), CVO (1961); s of Col Baldwin Salter Millard, and Phyllis Mary Tetley; *b* 22 Jan 1917; *Educ* Charterhouse, Pembroke Coll Cambridge; *m* 1, 1946 (m dis 1963), Anne, da of Gordon Mackenzie, of Toronto; 1 s, 1 da; *m* 2, 1964, Mary Judy, da of James Dugdale by his 1 w Pamela, *née* Coventry; 2 s; *Career* served RN WWII; Foreign Serv 1939–76; min UK Delgn to NATO 1964–67, ambass Hungary 1967–69, min Washington 1970–71; ambass to: Sweden 1971–74, Italy 1974–76; chm Br-Italian Soc 1977–83; Grand Offr Order of Merit Italy; *Style*— Sir Guy Millard, KCMG, CVO; ✉ Fyfield Manor, Southrop, Glos GL7 3NZ (☎ 01367 850234)

MILLARD, Prof Peter Henry; s of Edward Joseph Millard (d 1968), and Thelma Fanny, *née* Burrows; *b* 18 July 1937; *Educ* MB BS, MD, MRCP, PhD 1993; *m* 27 Jan 1962, Alys Gillian, da of Hubert Morley Thomas, of Swansea, S Wales; 3 s (Paul William b 1963, Stephen b 1964, David b 1969); *Career* conslt in geriatric med St George's Hosp 1968–79, Eleanor Peel prof of geriatric med St George's Hosp Med Sch Univ of London 1979–; author of articles on mathematical modelling, ageing, dementia and social policy; memb: Guild of Catholic Doctors, Br Geriatric Soc (pres), Br Soc for Res on Ageing; FRCP 1978, FRIPH 1983; *Books* The Dwarfs and Their King; *Recreations* walking, reading obscure books; *Style*— Prof Peter Millard; ✉ Division of Geriatric Medicine, St George's Hospital Medical Sch, Cranmer Terrace, Tooting, London SW17 0QR (☎ 0181 725 5327, fax 0181 682 0962, telex 945291 SAGEMS G)

MILLEN, Brig Anthony Tristram Patrick; s of Maj Charles Reginald Millen, MC (d 1959), and Annie Mary, *née* Martin (d 1979); *b* 15 Dec 1928; *Educ* Mount St Mary's Coll, Staff Coll Camberley, Joint Servs Staff Coll; *m* 24 Nov 1954, Mary Alice Featherston, da of Maj Robin Quentin Featherston Johnston (ka 1941); 3 s (Robin b 1956, d 1990, Nicholas b 1958, Patrick b 1964, d 1964), 2 da (Alice b 1961, Philippa b 1966); *Career* 5 Royal Inniskilling Dragoon Gds 1948, CO Royal Hong Kong Regt (The Volunteers) 1969–71, def advsr Br High Cmmn Ottawa 1980–83, ret 1983; *Recreations* sailing; *Style*— Brig Anthony Millen; ✉ The Manor House, Hutton Sessay, Thirsk, North Yorkshire YO7 3BA (☎ 01845 501 444)

MILLEN, Roger James; s of George James Millen (d 1980), of Hampshire, and Maria Mia, *née* Richards (d 1954); *b* 23 April 1942; *Educ* St Paul's; *m* 30 July 1966, Katharine Mary, da of Edgar Charles Sawkins; 2 s (James Jonathan b 3 Dec 1969, Andrew Charles (twin) b 3 Dec 1969), 1 da (Katharine Clare b 14 Sept 1971); *Career* articled clerk Annan Dexter & Co; Dearden Lord Annan Morrish (became Dearden Farrow 1979): mangr 1972–75, ptnr 1975–82, managing ptnr Yorkshire Region 1982–87; ptnr BDO Binder Hamlyn 1987–94, ptnr Binder Hamlyn 1994–; pres W Yorkshire Soc of Chartered Accountants 1988–89; FCA 1979 (ACA 1969); *Recreations* golf, walking; *Clubs* Leeds; *Style*— Roger Millen, Esq; ✉ Binder Hamlyn, St Paul's House, Park Square, Leeds LS1 2PJ (☎ 0113 297 7432, fax 0113 242 5938)

MILLER, Ambrose Michael; s of Ambrose Miller, of Beer, Devon, and Margaret Dorothy, *née* Dennett; *b* 15 April 1950; *Educ* Radley, Magdalene Coll Cambridge, King's Coll London (BMus); *m* 4 April 1981, Celia Frances Sophia, da of Sir Desmond Arthur Pond (d 1986); *Career* mangr Royal Ballet Orchestra 1974–81, gen mangr Scottish Baroque Ensemble 1981–83, fndr and artistic dir European Union Chamber Orchestra 1983; Freeman City of London, Liveryman Worshipful Co of Musicians; *Recreations* cooking, reading; *Style*— Ambrose Miller, Esq; ✉ Fermain House, Dolphin Street, Colyton, Devon EX13 6LU (☎ 01297 552272, fax 01297 553744)

MILLER, Prof Andrew; s of William Hamilton Miller (d 1956), and Susan, *née* Auld (d 1978); *b* 15 Feb 1936; *Educ* Beath HS, Univ of Edinburgh (BSc, PhD), Univ of Oxford (MA); *m* 19 June 1962, Rosemary Singleton Hannah, da of Thomas Carlyle Fyvie (d 1962); 1 s (Stephen Andrew Fyvie b 23 Oct 1968), 1 da (Lisa Rosemary b 7 Aug 1966); *Career* res fell CSIRO Div of Protein Chemistry Melbourne Aust 1962–65, staff MRC Laboratory for Molecular Biology Cambridge 1965–66; Univ of Oxford: lectr in molecular biophysics 1966–83, fell Wolfson Coll 1967–83, hon fell Wolfson Coll 1995–; head of Euro Molecular Biology Laboratory Grenoble France 1975–80; Univ of Edinburgh: asst lectr in chemistry 1960–62, prof of biochemistry 1984–94, vice-dean of medicine 1991–93, vice-provost of med and veterinary med 1992–93, vice-princ 1993–94; princ and vice-chllr Univ of Stirling 1994–; dir of res Europe Synchrotron Radiation Facility Grenoble France 1986–91, memb Scientific Cncl Univ of Grenoble France 1990–91; memb: Ct of Univ of Edinburgh 1991–92, various ctees of Sci and Engrg Res Cncl 1970–86, Univ Grants Ctee 1985–88, Biological Sciences Advsy Gp Univ Funding Cncl 1989–; FRSE 1986; *Books* Minerals in Biology (co-ed, 1984); *Recreations* reading, music, walking; *Style*— Prof Andrew Miller, FRSE; ✉ Principal's Office, University of Stirling, Stirling FK9 4LA (☎ 01786 467011)

MILLER, Andrew; MP (Lab) Ellesmere Port and Neston (majority 1,989); s of Ernest Miller, and Daphne Miller; *b* 23 March 1949; *Educ* Hayling Island Secdy Sch, Highbury Tech Coll, LSE; *m*; 2 s, 1 da; *Career* technician Geology Dept Portsmouth Poly, student LSE 1976–77, regnl offr MSF 1977–92, MP (Lab) Ellesmere Port and Neston 1992–; *Style*— Andrew Miller, Esq, MP; ✉ House of Commons, London SW1A 0AA (☎ 0171 219 3580, 0151 357 3019, fax 0151 356 8226, e-mail Andrew.Miller@GEO2.poptel.org.uk)

MILLER, Barry; s of Maj Howard Alan Miller (d 1988), and Margaret Yvonne, *née* Richardson; *b* 11 May 1942; *Educ* Lancaster Royal GS; *m* 7 Sept 1968, Katrina Elizabeth, da of Maj Bernard Chandler (d 1979); 1 s (Andrew Geoffrey b 1975), 1 da (Caroline Jane b 1974); *Career* exec offr RAE Farnborough 1961–65; asst princ MOD London 1965–69; princ: Def Policy Staff 1969, Naval Personnel Div 1969–72, Equipment Secretariat Army 1972–73, Def Secretariat 1973–75, Civil Serv Dept 1975–77; asst sec: Civilian Mgmnt 1977–80, Def Secretariat 1980–83, Mgmnt Servs Orgn 1985–86; with RCDS 1984; DG: Def Quality Assurance 1986–92, Test and Evaluation 1992–94, Fin MOD 1994–; memb Bd: RN Film Corp 1969–72, BSI 1986–89; hon dep sec First Div Assoc 1969–73, chm Civil Serv Club 1990–94; *Recreations* military uniforms; *Style*— Barry Miller, Esq; ✉ Ministry of Defence, Main Building, Whitehall, London SW1A 2HB (☎ 0171 218 6384)

MILLER, Sir (Oswald) Bernard; kt (1967); s of Arthur Miller; *b* 25 March 1904; *Educ* Sloane Sch, Jesus Coll Oxford; *m* 1931, Jessica Marie Ffoulkes; 3 s; *Career* John Lewis Partnership: joined 1927, dir 1935, chm 1955–72; former memb: Monopolies Cmmn, Cncl for Industl Design, Econ Devpt Ctee for Distributive Trades (and chm Retail Distributors Assoc 1953); chm South Regnl RSA 1974–80 and memb Cncl RSA 1977–83; Univ of Southampton: chm Cncl 1982–88, treas 1974–82, pro chllr 1983–91, Hon LLD 1981; hon fell Jesus Coll Oxford 1968; *Books* Biography of Robert Harley, Earl of Oxford (1927); *Style*— Sir Bernard Miller; ✉ 3 Sutton Manor Mews, Sutton Scotney, Winchester, Hants (☎ 01962 760997)

MILLER, Bill; MEP (Lab) Glasgow (majority 43,158); s of George Miller, of Kilmarnock, and Janet, *née* MacDonald; *b* 22 July 1954; *Educ* Paisley Tech Coll, Kingston Poly (BSc, DipTP); *partner* Elizabeth Potter; 1 da (Kerry b 23 Dec 1988), 1 s (Keir b 11 Nov 1992); *Career* cnclr Strathclyde Regnl Cncl 1986–94; MEP (Lab) Glasgow 1994–; ARICS 1979; *Recreations* ties, record collecting, Kilmarnock FC; *Clubs* Castlemilk Labour; *Style*— Bill Miller, MEP; ✉ office: 9 Chisholm Street, Trongate, Glasgow G1 5HA (☎ 0141 552 2234, fax 0141 552 0297)

MILLER, Sheriff Colin Brown; s of James Miller (d 1980), of Paisley, and Isabella Millar Nicol Brown (d 1995); *b* 4 Oct 1946; *Educ* Paisley GS, Univ of Glasgow (LLB); *m* 28 Jan 1972, Joan Elizabeth, da of Robert Marshall Blyth; 3 s (James Douglas b 24 May 1973, Alasdair Robert b 7 July 1975, Euan Colin b 19 Jan 1977); *Career* legal apprentice Mitchells Johnston & Co Glasgow 1967–69, asst slr D S & W Semple Paisley 1969–70 (ptnr 1971), ptnr McFadyen & Semple Paisley 1971–91 (sr ptnr 1987–91), sheriff of S Strathclyde Dumfries & Galloway at Hamilton 1991–95 (at Ayr 1995–); legal advsr Waverley Steam Navigation Co Ltd and assoc cos 1976–91; dean Faculty of Procurators Paisley 1991; Law Soc of Scot: memb Cncl 1983–91, convener Conveyancing Ctee 1986–89, convener Judicial Procedure Ctee 1989–91, convener Rights of Audience in Supreme Courts Working Party 1990–91; SSC, NP; *Recreations* travel in Scandinavia, Clyde steamers, railways, motor vehicles and photography; *Style*— Sheriff Colin Miller; ✉ Sheriffs' Chambers, Sheriff Court, Wellington Square, Ayr KA7 1DR (☎ 01292 268474, fax 01292 282442)

MILLER, (James) David Frederick; CBE (1997); s of Sir John Wilson Edington Miller, KBE, CMG (d 1957), and Jessie Kathleen, *née* Reed (d 1966); *b* 5 Jan 1935; *Educ* Edinburgh Acad, Emmanuel Coll Cambridge (MA), LSE (Dip IPM); *m* 27 Feb 1965, Saffrey Blackett, da of Fred Oxley (d 1963); 3 s (Andrew b 21 Dec 1965, Simon b 13 Sept 1967, Matthew b 10 Aug 1970, d 1991), 1 da (Katherine b 28 June 1973); *Career* dir: J & P Coats Ltd 1972–92, Coats Patons plc 1977–92, Coats Viyella plc 1986–92, The Wolverhampton & Dudley Breweries plc 1984– (chm 1992–), Royal Scottish Orchestra Soc Ltd 1984, Outward Bound Tst Ltd 1985, The Edinburgh Acad 1985; govr Scottish Coll of Textiles; chm Scottish Vocational Educn Cncl 1992–, cmmr Queen Victoria School; chm Ct Univ of Stirling 1992–, dir Edinburgh Military Tattoo 1990–; Freeman: City of London, Worshipful Co of Needlemakers 1983; DUniv of Stirling 1984; FIPM, CIMgt; *Recreations* tennis, golf, gardening; *Style*— David Miller, Esq, CBE; ✉ 6 Belford Terrace, Edinburgh EH4 3DQ (☎ 0131 315 2882, fax 0131 315 2635)

MILLER, David James; s of James Samuel Miller, of Lymington, Hants, and Beryl Mary, *née* Jones; *b* 28 Feb 1952; *Educ* Stockport GS, Emmanuel Coll Cambridge (MA); *m* 17 Sept 1988, Sophie Kay Voss, da of Flemming Christian Rathsach, of Pindon Manor, Bucks; *Career* called to the Bar Middle Temple, dep chief exec Life Assurance & Unit Tst Regulatory Orgn 1986–89, gp sec Royal & Sun Alliance Insurance Group plc 1989– (legal advsr and unit tst business mangr 1977–86); *Recreations* travel, history of art; *Clubs* United Oxford and Cambridge Univ; *Style*— David Miller, Esq; ✉ 100 Rosebery Avenue, London EC1R 4TL (☎ 0171 833 3963); Royal & Sun Alliance Insurance Group plc, 1 Bartholomew Lane, London EC2N 2AB (☎ 0171 588 2345, fax 0171 588 1159)

MILLER, David John; OBE; s of Air Cdre John Douglas Miller, CBE, of Guildford, Surrey, and Sybil Francis, *née* Powell; *b* 7 March 1947; *Educ* Dragon Sch Oxford, St Edward's Sch Oxford, Jesus Coll Cambridge (MA); *m* 24 Jan 1976, Maryrose, da of John Edgar Dulley; 3 s (Fergie b 8 June 1979, Bertie b 26 March 1981, Gregory b 28 Nov 1984); *Career* Joseph Sebag stockbrokers 1969–72; Robert Fleming Group: joined 1972, special advsr to Govt of Abu Dhabi 1975–78, Jardine Fleming Hong Kong 1979–81, Jardine Fleming Tokyo 1981–88, dir Robert Fleming Holdings until 1992; md State Street Global Advisors 1992–94, chief exec Wheelock NatWest Ltd Hong Kong 1994–; *Recreations* golf, tennis, children; *Style*— David Miller, Esq, OBE; ✉ Wheelock Natwest Ltd, 43/F Natwest Tower, Times Square, Causeway Bay, Hong Kong (☎ 00 852 2966 2298, fax 00 852 2506 9546)

MILLER, Dr David Shaw; s of Bertram Miller (d 1966), and Renée Gertrude Anne, *née* Vieilleville; *b* 11 Aug 1937; *Educ* Beulah Hill, Univ of London (MSc, MB, MRCP); *m* 16 Sept 1967, Margaret Rosamund, da of Alan Hall, of Whitney, Oxon; 1 s (William James Shaw b 17 March 1973), 1 da (Katherine Elizabeth Shaw b 10 Oct 1970); *Career* registrar KCH 1965–67, Br Cncl travelling scholar 1967–69, lectr Nottingham Med Sch 1970–75, WHO travelling fell 1976, sr registrar Radcliffe Infirmary Oxford 1978–82, conslt Royal Devon and Exeter Hosp 1982–; pubns in scientific jls based on original res in GB, USA, Africa and India; Personal Grants Med Res Cncl 1972–76; Hon MA (Oxon) 1980; Freedom City of London 1991; *Recreations* riding, lawn tennis, walking; *Style*— Dr David Miller; ✉ Royal Devon & Exeter Hospital, Exeter, Devon (☎ 01392 405204)

MILLER, Sir Donald John; kt (1990); s of late John Miller, and late Maud, *née* White; *b* 8 Feb 1927; *Educ* Banchory Acad, Univ of Aberdeen (BSc); *m* 1973, Fay Glendinning Herriot; 1 s (Alasdair b 1 March 1979), 2 da (Nicola b 30 June 1974, Jane b 11 May 1976); *Career* engr Metropolitan Vickers 1947–53, engr Br Electricity Authy 1953–55, engr and mangr Preece Cardew & Rider (consulting engrs) 1955–66, chief engr N of Scotland Hydro-Electric Board 1966–74; S of Scotland Electricity Board: dir of engrg 1974–77, dep chm and gen mangr 1977–82, chm 1982–90; chm Scottish Power plc 1990–92; chm Power Div IEE 1977–78; Power Div Award and Williams Premium IEE; Hon DUniv Strathclyde 1992; hon memb BNES, FEng 1981, FIMechE, FIEE, FRSE 1987; *Recreations* sailing, gardening, hill walking; *Style*— Sir Donald Miller, FEng, FRSE; ✉ Puldohran, Gryffe Road, Kilmacolm, Renfrewshire PA13 4BA

MILLER, Francis Edward; s of Alfred Lewis Miller (d 1971), and Emily Johannah, *née* Lark (d 1993); *b* 20 Jan 1940; *Educ* Brixton Sch of Building, Univ of Westminster; *m* 28 Nov 1964 (m dis 1987), Valerie, da of Sydney Victor Read (d 1985); 2 s (Richard Lewis b 7 Nov 1970, John Francis b 24 May 1976); *Career* jr quantity surveyor 1956, subsequently surveyor and mangr of bldg and civil engrg projects, commenced practice 1972 (specializing in resolution of disputes in bldg, civil engrg and process industs as conslt, conciliator and arbitrator); ed Arbitration - News and Views (CIArb) 1991–93; memb Arbitration Panel: RICS 1975–94, CIArb; memb Worshipful Co of Arbitrators

1981; FRICS 1975–94, FCIArb 1975, assoc Inst of Patentees and Inventors 1975, FInstD 1979–91; *Books* Arbitration - Recommendations and Survey (1988), Building and Civil Engineering - Cost Value Comparison (1991), Arbitration - The Arbitrator and the Parties (1994), Civil Justice - Another Chance to Get it Right (1995), Disputes - The Avoidance and Resolution of Disputes; *Recreations* watercolour painting, writing, walking, talking; *Style*— Francis Miller, Esq; ✉ Candida, Harlequin Lane, Crowborough, East Sussex TN6 1HU (☎ 01892 662957)

MILLER, Harry; s of Sir Ernest Henry John Miller, 10 Bt (d 1960); h to Btcy of bro, Sir John Holmes Miller, 11 Bt, *qv*; *b* 15 Jan 1927; *m* 1954, Gwynedd Margaret, da of R P Sherriff, of Paraparaumu, New Zealand; 1 s (Anthony Thomas b 1955), 2 da (Sara Margaret (Mrs Laing) b 1957, Judith Christine b 1960); *Style*— Harry Miller, Esq; ✉ 53 Koha Road, Taupo, NZ

MILLER, Sir Hilary Duppa (Hal); kt (1988); s of Lt Cdr John Duppa-Miller (d 1994), GC, of Somerset West, SA, and Hon Barbara (d 1966), yr da of 1 Viscount Buckmaster; *b* 6 March 1929; *Educ* Eton, Merton Coll Oxford, Univ of London; *m* 1, 1956, Fiona McDermid; 2 s, 2 da; m 2, 1976, Jacqueline Roe, yr da of late Thomas Chambers Windsor Roe, of Brighton and Lady Londesborough; 1 s, 1 da; *Career* colonial serv Hong Kong 1955–68; MP (C): Bromsgrove and Redditch 1974–83, Bromsgrove 1983–92; PPS to: Sec of State for Defence 1979–81, Chllr of the Duchy of Lancaster 1981 (resigned), Leader of the House of Commons and Chm of Cons Party 1984; vice chm Cons Party 1984–87; chm Cosmopolitan Holdings Ltd; fell of Econ Devpt Inst of World Bank (Washington), chief exec Soc of Motor Mfrs and Traders 1991–93; Liveryman Worshipful Co of Coachmakers & Coach Harness Makers; FIMI; *Clubs* Vincent's (Oxford), Utd Oxford and Cambridge, Blackheath FC; *Style*— Sir Hal Miller; ✉ Moorcroft Farm, Sinton Green, Worcester WR2 6NW (☎ 01905 640309); Cosmopolitan Textile Co, Road Five, Industrial Estate, Winsford, Cheshire CW7 3QU (☎ 01606 551151)

MILLER, Hugh; s of James Weir Miller (d 1991), of Wishaw, Scotland, and Alice, *née* Waddell (d 1990); *b* 27 April 1937; *Educ* Wishaw Acad, Wishaw HS, Stow Coll, Univ of Glasgow; *m* 18 May 1981, Annette Elizabeth, da of Albert John Slater; 3 c (by previous marriages) (Lesley b 1960, James b 1967, Rachel b 1972); *Career* author; asst to Dr John Grierson 1959, princ photographer Scottish TV 1961–62, co-owner Unique Magic Co London 1963–70; memb: Magic Circle 1965, Mark Twain Soc USA 1976; *Books* The Open City (1973), Ambulance (1975), The Dissector (1976), The Saviour (1977), Casualty (1981), Silent Witnesses (1984), An Echo of Justice (1990), Skin Deep (1991), Indelible Evidence (1991), Scotland Yard (co-author, 1993), Seaforth (1994), Unquiet Minds (1994), Proclaimed in Blood (1995), Prime Target (1996); *Recreations* travel, walking, reading; *Style*— Hugh Miller, Esq; ✉ 40 St John's Court, Warwick, Warwickshire CV34 4NL (☎ 01926 491809, fax 01926 495407, e-mail hugh.miller@netclub-lon.com); c/o Lucas Alexander Whitley Ltd, 47 Emperor's Gate, London SW7 4HJ (☎ 0171 373 9258, fax 0171 373 4374)

MILLER, Dr Hugh Craig; s of James Miller, and Helen Elizabeth, *née* Craig; *b* 7 April 1942; *Educ* George Watson's Coll Edinburgh, Univ of Edinburgh (BSc, MB ChB); *m* 14 Sept 1968, Isobel Margaret, da of Robert Paterson; 1 s (James (Jamie) b 1972), 1 da (Catherine Jane b 1976); *Career* Royal Infirmary Edinburgh: house physician and surgn 1966–67, sr house offr 1967–68, registrar of cardiology 1970–72, conslt cardiologist 1975–; MRC res fell 1968–70, sr registrar Brompton Hosp London 1972–75, res fell Duke Univ Durham USA; memb: Br Cardiac Soc, BMA, Assoc of Physicians of GB and Ireland; FRCPE 1979; *Recreations* skiing, squash, sailing; *Style*— Dr Hugh Miller; ✉ 12 Dick Place, Edinburgh EH9 2JL (☎ 0131 667 4235); Cardiology Dept, Royal Infirmary, Edinburgh (☎ 0131 536 2002)

MILLER, Prof Hugh Graham; OBE (1996); s of Robert Graham Miller, of Auckland, NZ, and Anne Farmer *née* Fleming (d 1968); *b* 22 Nov 1939; *Educ* Strathallan Sch, Univ of Aberdeen (BSc, PhD, DSc); *m* 1, 4 July 1966 (m dis 1993), Thelma; 1 s (Ewen b 1969), 1 da (Andrea b 1971); m 2, 27 July 1994, June; *Career* princ scientific offr Macaulay Inst for Soil Res 1976 (scientific offr 1963, sr scientific offr 1970), prof and head Dept of Forestry Univ of Aberdeen 1984–; memb: Forestry Res Coordination Ctee, Scot Forestry Tst, Res Advsy Ctee Forestry Cmmn; pres Inst of Chartered Foresters 1994–96, chm FAO Forestry Educn Ctee; FICFor 1979, FRSE 1985, FRSA 1986, FIBiol 1988; *Recreations* the outdoors; *Clubs* Royal Northern and Univ; *Style*— Prof Hugh Miller, OBE, FRSE; ✉ 102 Osborne Place, Aberdeen AB25 2DU (☎ 01224 639872); Dept of Forestry, Univ of Aberdeen, Aberdeen AB24 5UA (☎ 01224 272666, telex 73458 UNIABN G, fax 01224 272685)

MILLER, Jack Michael; s of Col Harry Raymond (Pat) Miller, RAMC (decd), and Eileen Mary, *née* Whiteing, of Teddington; *b* 10 Jan 1946; *Educ* Cranleigh Sch; *m* 2 June 1972, Elizabeth Alison, da of late Lt-Col Ronald Francis Boyd Campbell and Pamela Muriel Desiree Campbell; 1 da (Caroline b 29 Dec 1977); *Career* gunner HAC; slr; articled Rider Heaton Meredith & Mills 1964–70; Midland Bank plc: Legal Dept 1970–93, sr legal advsr UK Banking 1988–93; sr legal advsr HSBC Holdings plc 1993–; memb Bedford Park Soc; Freeman of the City of London, Liveryman of the Worshipful Co of Haberdashers; *Recreations* cricket, sport generally, trivia; *Clubs* MCC, RAC, Oriental Cannons, The Cricket Soc, Law Society CC, Richmond CC; *Style*— Jack Miller, Esq; ✉ c/o HSBC Holdings plc, 10 Lower Thames Street, London EC3R 6AE (☎ 0171 260 3460, fax 0171 260 3446)

MILLER, James; CBE (1986); s of Sir James Miller, GBE (d 1977), of Belmont, Edinburgh, and Lady Ella Jane, *née* Stewart (d 1993); *b* 1 Sept 1934; *Educ* Edinburgh Acad, Harrow, Balliol Coll Oxford (MA); *m* 1, 27 July 1959, Kathleen (d 1966), da of James Dewar (d 1969), of Edinburgh; 1 s (James b 1962), 2 da (Susan b 1960, Gail b 1962); m 2, 11 Jan 1969, Iris, da of Thomas James Lloyd-Webb (d 1959), of Southampton; 1 da (Heather b 1970); *Career* RE 1956–58, cmmnd 2 Lt 1957; James Miller & Ptnrs (The Miller Gp Ltd 1986): joined 1958, dir 1960, md 1970–91, chm 1970–; non-exec dir: Bank of Scotland, British Linen Bank Group Ltd; Fedn of Civil Engrg Contractors: chm Scottish Section 1981–83, chm 1985, pres 1990–93; pres Edinburgh C of C 1981–83, Master Merchant Co of Edinburgh 1992–94 (ct asst 1982–85, treas 1990–92), chm Ct of Heriot-Watt Univ Edinburgh 1990–96; chm Scottish Branch Chartered Inst of Arbitrators 1985–87; Freeman: City of London 1956, Worshipful Co of Horners 1956; Hon DUniv Heriot-Watt 1996; FCIOB 1974, FCIArb 1976, CIMgt 1983; *Recreations* shooting; *Clubs* City Livery; *Style*— James Miller, Esq, CBE; ✉ Belmont, Ellersly Rd, Edinburgh EH12 6JA (☎ 0131 337 6595); The Miller Group Ltd, Miller House, 18 South Groathill Ave, Edinburgh EH4 2LW (☎ 0131 315 6107, fax 0131 315 6110)

MILLER, James Lawson; s of David Wardrop Miller (d 1966), and Helen Frew, *née* Baxter (d 1952); *b* 26 Jan 1931; *Educ* The John Lyon Sch Harrow, St John's Coll Cambridge (MA); *m* 29 June 1957, Margaret Ann, da of Beverley Robinson (d 1984); 2 s (David b 1958, Jeremy b 1959), 1 da (Jane b 1962); *Career* chartered builder, construction co chief exec; chm and dir: James Lawson Holdings Ltd, James Lawson Property Ltd 1965–; chm R Harding (Cookham) Ltd 1985–, dir Saxon Developments Ltd 1994–, dir The Shell Bay Holding Company Ltd 1996–; pres The Builders' Conference 1985; fell Chartered Inst of Building; *Books* Computer Aided Estimating (1977); *Recreations* duplicate bridge, Church of England activities; *Clubs* Leander; *Style*—James L Miller, Esq; ✉ Clavering, North Park, Gerrards Cross, Bucks SL9 8JP

MILLER, James Young; s of James Young Miller (d 1960), and Alison Lyons, *née* Brown; *b* 23 Jan 1942; *Educ* Glasgow HS; *m* 3 April 1970, Gillian Mhairi, da of Alan G Millar; 2 da (Susan b 19 June 1972, Fiona b 5 July 1974), 1 s (Donald b 29 Sept 1976); *Career* KPMG (formerly KPMG Peat Marwick): trainee Glasgow 1959–65, qualified CA 1965, mangr 1969–74 (asst mangr 1966–69), specialist forensic accounting ptnr 1974–, head of audit Scotland 1992– (Glasgow 1980–), memb UK Accounting and Audit Practice Ctees; MICAS 1965; *Recreations* golf, choral singing, music, reading; *Clubs* RSAC, Western, Glasgow Art; *Style*— James Miller, Esq; ✉ KPMG, 24 Blythswood Square, Glasgow G2 4QS (☎ 0141 226 5511, fax 0141 204 1584)

MILLER, Jeremy; *b* 26 March 1945; *Educ* Brighton Coll, RMA Sandhurst, St John's Coll Cambridge (MA), Universita per Stranieri Perugia Italy, City Univ London (post grad dip); *m*; 1 s, 1 da; *Career* served Royal Corps of Signals 1965–74, Capt; head of PR Mermaid Theatre 1975–76, bd dir and gp account dir Interco Business Consultants 1977–80, Hill and Knowlton (UK) Limited 1980–87 (head Technol Div 1981, dir 1984–87); Valin Pollen: memb Bd 1987–90, int dir 1989, asst md 1990; asst md Gavin Anderson & Company 1990–95, dir of marketing and external affrs Engineering Employers' Fedn 1996–; *Recreations* travel, theatre, contemporary cinema, 19th century European history, Italian art, cricket, bridge; *Style*— Jeremy Miller, Esq; ✉ 3 Melody Rd, Wandsworth, London SW18 2QW (☎ 0181 874 3650, fax 0181 871 2857); Engineering Employer's Federation, Tothill Street, London SW1H 9NQ (☎ 0171 222 7777, fax 0171 222 0792)

MILLER, Air Cdre John; CBE (1966), DFC (1945), AFC (1953); s of John William Miller, of Sprotborough, Yorks; *b* 3 Dec 1921; *Educ* Wath upon Dearne GS; *m* 1947, Joan Macgregor (decd); 1 s, 2 da; m 2, 1988, Philippa Anne, da of Maj I S Tailyour; *Career* Air Cdre RAF (ret); dir: UBM Group Ltd 1970–82, A J Gooding Group 1982–89; Liveryman Worshipful Co of Builders Merchants; FCA; *Clubs* RAF; *Style*— Air Cdre John Miller, CBE, DFC, AFC; ✉ Orchard Close, Pitchcombe, nr Stroud, Glos (☎ 01452 813477, fax 01452 813042)

MILLER, Prof (Christopher) John; s of Stanley Miller, of Henley on Thames, Oxon, and Joan Beryl Gill; *b* 4 Nov 1941; *Educ* Bishop Veseys GS Sutton Coldfield, Univ of Nottingham (BA, LLM); *m* 4 Sept 1964, Michèle Marie Juliette, da of Raymond Michel Guérault, of Paris; 1 s (Mark), 1 da (Anne Marie); *Career* barr; lectr in law Univ of Durham 1966–70, reader in common law Univ of Leeds (lectr in law 1970–77), prof of law Univ of Warwick 1980–89 (reader 1979); Univ of Birmingham: prof of English law 1989–, dean Faculty of Law 1994–; pt/t chm Social Security Appeals Tbnls and Disability Appeals Tbnls 1986–95; *Books* Product Liability (jtly, 1977), Product Liability and Safety Encyclopaedia (1979–96), Consumer and Trading Law: Cases and Materials (jtly, 1985), Comparative Product Liability (ed, 1986), Contempt of Court (1989), Business Law (jtly, 1991), Benjamin's Sale of Goods (jt ed, 1992); *Recreations* classical music, gardening, walking, sport; *Style*— Prof John Miller; ✉ Faculty of Law, Chancellor's Court, University of Birmingham, PO Box 363, Birmingham B15 2TT (☎ 0121 414 3172)

MILLER, John Albert Peter; s of Albert Ernest Miller (d 1966), and Irene Gertrude Ann, *née* Viellville (d 1989); *b* 30 July 1931; *Educ* St Joseph's Coll Beulah Hill, Croydon Art Sch; *Career* Nat Serv Lt RASC 1949–51; painter; memb Newlyn Soc of Artists (former chm), tstee Passmore Edwards Art Gallery Newlyn 1985–; vice pres: Three Spires Festival Truro 1990–, Truro Cathedral Music Fndn Appeal 1990–92; memb Truro Cathedral Fabric Advsy Ctee 1991–, hon lay canon Truro Cathedral 1993–; memb Cncl Sch of St Claire Penzance Woodard Schs 1990–95, patron The Tregellas Fndn 1995–; FRSA 1964; *Exhibitions* UK and abroad incl: annually with sole agent David Messum (8 Cork St London) 1981–, Images of Paradise (Christie's and Harewood House) 1989, Artists and Gardens (Nat Tst) 1991, The Englishman Abroad (Salisbury Festival) 1992, Contemporary Icons (Royal Albert Meml Museum Exeter) 1992, The Penwith Art Experience (Cuxhaven Germany) 1992, Showcase (Royal Cornwall Museum) 1994; *Commissions* incl: Nat Tst and Lord St Levan 10 historical paintings of St Michael's Mount 1979, Dean and Chapter Truro Cathedral Cornubia-Land of Saints 1980 (unveiled by HRH Prince of Wales), Exeter and Dist Hospice; *Public Collections* V & A, Cornwall CC, Avon CC, Royal Devon and Exeter Hosp; *Private and Corporate Collections* HRH The Prince of Wales, TRH The Prince and Princess Michael of Kent, BUPA Roding Hosp, Sony Europe, Cunard, John Lewis Partnership, Discipline Global Mobile; *Books* Cooking With Vegetables (with late Marika Hanbury Tenison, 1980), Leave Tomorrow Behind (1989), Sketchbook of Cornwall (1991), Seaside Sketchbook (1993); *Recreations* painting, pleasure and friends; *Style*— John Miller, Esq; ✉ The Old Cottage, Church Road, Lelant, St Ives, Cornwall TR26 3LD

MILLER, John Harmsworth; s of Charles Henry Miller (d 1984), and Brenda Ellen, *née* Borrett; *b* 18 Aug 1930; *Educ* Charterhouse, Architectural Assoc (DipAA, AA Tropical Dip); *m* 20 Feb 1957 (m dis 1975); 2 da; m 2, 15 Feb 1985, Susan Jane, da of Marcus Brumwell, CBE (d 1983); *Career* Nat Serv 13/18 Huzzars RAC 1948–50; architect; with Lyons Israel & Ellis London 1956–59, asst to Sir Leslie Martin 1959–61, ptnr Colquhoun & Miller 1961–90, ptnr John Miller & Partners 1990–; tutor 1961–73: Interior & Environmental Design Sch RCA, Architectural Assoc; visiting critic Cornell Univ Sch of Architecture NY 1966, 1968 and 1971, tutor Cambridge Univ Sch of Architecture 1969–70; visiting critic: Princeton Univ Sch of Architecture NJ 1979, Dublin Univ Sch of Architecture 1972–73; prof Sch of Environmental Design RCA 1975–85, chm Academic Policy Ctee RCA 1983–84; visiting prof: Dublin Univ Sch of Architecture 1985–86, Univ of Manchester Sch of Architecture 1986–87; external examiner: Architectural Assoc 1975, Poly of Central London 1976–80, Thames Poly Sch of Architecture 1981–85, Bath Univ Sch of Architecture 1982–85, Univ of London Bartlett Sch of Architecture 1986–88, Poly of South Bank Sch of Architecture 1986–89, Canterbury Sch of Architecture 1988–92; exhibitions of own work incl: Royal Coll of Art and Univ of Palermo 1974, Collegio Arquitectos Santiago Chile Biennale 1981, Paris Biennale 1983, Royal Academy Summer Exhbn 1984, National Gallery entries exhibition 9H Gallery 1986, Royal Academy Summer Exhibition 1988, 1989 and 1991, Univ of Valencia 1990, Stevens Building RCA 1992, Royal West of England Acad 1994, City of Valencia 1994, Frankfurt 1995, Barcelona 1995, Vienna 1995; guest ed Architectural Review 1964; assessor Civic Tst Awards 1978–86; memb: Cncl Architectural Assoc 1966, Awards Ctee Royal Inst of Architects 1967–68 and 1970, Cncl RCA 1980–83; ARIBA 1959, FRCA 1976, FRSA 1984; *Recreations* sailing; *Style*— John Miller, Esq; ✉ The Elephant House Brewery, 35 Hawley Crescent, London NW1 (☎ 0171 482 4686, fax 0171 267 9907)

MILLER, Sir John Holmes; 11 Bt (E 1705), of Chichester, Sussex; s of Sir Ernest Henry John Miller, 10 Bt (d 1960); *b* 1925; *m* 1950, Jocelyn Edwards; 2 da (Roslyn Mary b 1955, Diana Jocelyn b 1958); *Heir* bro, Harry Holmes Miller; *Style*— Sir John Miller, Bt; ✉ 1417 Mere Road, Taupo, New Zealand

MILLER, Air Vice-Marshal John Joseph; CB (1981); s of Frederick George Miller (d 1985), and Freda Ruth, *née* Haskins (d 1985); *b* 27 April 1928; *Educ* Portsmouth GS; *m* 10 Nov 1950, Adele Mary, da of Hubert Colleypriest (d 1957); 1 s (Michael b 1960), 2 da (Penelope b 1953, Robin Jennifer b 1958); *Career* RAF 1946–83; dir Personnel Mgmnt (RAF), MOD 1975–78, asst chief Def Staff (Personnel and Logistics) 1978–81, dir gen Personal Services (RAF) 1982–83; called to the Bar Gray's Inn 1958; dir Inst of Personnel Mgmnt 1983–89, pres Euro Assoc for Personnel Mgmnt 1987–89, dir of studies St George's House Windsor Castle 1989–94; *Recreations* theatre, music, book collecting; *Clubs* RAF; *Style*— Air Vice-Marshal John Miller, CB; ✉ 24 Floral Farm, Canford Magna, Wimborne, Dorset BH21 3AU

MILLER, Lt-Col Sir John Mansel; GCVO 1987 (KCVO 1974, CVO 1966), DSO (1944), MC (1944); 3 s of Brig-Gen Alfred Douglas Miller, CBE, DSO, JP, DL (d 1933), and Ella Geraldine, *née* Fletcher (d 1935); *b* 4 Feb 1919; *Educ* Eton, RMA Sandhurst; *Career* 2 Lt

Welsh Gds 1939, served WWII, ADC to Field Marshal Lord Wilson Washington DC 1945–47, cmd 1 Bn Welsh Gds 1958–61; Crown Equerry 1961–87; Extra Equerry to HM The Queen 1987–; pres: Coaching Club 1975–82, Hackney Horse Soc 1978–80 and 1994, Nat Light Horse Breeding Soc 1981–82, Br Driving Soc 1982–, Royal Windsor Horse Show Club 1985–90, Br Show Jumping Assoc 1989–93, Br Horse Soc 1992–94, Wheatley Scouts and RNLI, Rare Breeds Survival Tst 1995–; patron: Side-Saddle Assoc 1982–, Coloured Horse and Pony Soc 1988–93; hon dir Carriage Assoc of America 1989–; Liveryman Worshipful Co of: Loriners, Coachmakers & Coach Harness Makers; Yeoman Worshipful Co of Saddlers; *Recreations* hunting, shooting, polo, driving; *Clubs* Pratt's, White's, Windsor Constitutional; *Style—* Lt-Col Sir John Miller, GCVO, DSO, MC; ✉ Shotover House, Wheatley, Oxford OX9 1QS (☎ 01865 872450)

MILLER, Dr Jonathan Wolfe; CBE (1983); s of Emanuel Miller, DPM, FRCP; *b* 21 July 1934; *Educ* St Paul's, St John's Coll Cambridge (MB BCh); *m* 1956, Helen Rachel Collet; 2 s, 1 da; *Career* television, theatre and opera director; stage dir London and NY 1965–67, res fell in history of med UCL 1970–73, assoc dir Nat Theatre 1973–75, visiting prof in drama Westfield Coll London 1977–, assoc prodr ENO 1980–, artistic dir Old Vic 1988–90, res fell in neuro-psychology Univ of Sussex; memb Arts Cncl 1975–76, Silver medal Royal TV Soc 1981, Albert medal RSA 1990; From the Look of Things (lectures) 1995; fell UCL 1981, hon fell St John's Coll Cambridge 1982, hon fell RA 1991; Hon DLitt Univ of Leicester 1981; *Stage* Nottingham Playhouse: School for Scandal 1968, The Seagull 1969, The Malcontent 1973; Old Vic: King Lear 1970, The Merchant of Venice 1970, Andromache 1988, One Way Pendulum 1988, Bussy D'Ambois 1988, The Tempest 1988, Candide 1988, King Lear 1989, The Liar 1989; The Tempest (Mermaid) 1970, Hamlet (Arts Theatre Cambridge) 1970; NT: Danton's Death 1971, School for Scandal 1972, Measure for Measure 1974, Marriage of Figaro 1974, The Freeway 1974; Chichester: The Taming of the Shrew 1972, The Seagull 1973; Greenwich: Family Romances 1974, The Importance of Being Earnest 1975, All's Well 1975, She Would If She Could 1979; Long Day's Journey Into Night (Haymarket) 1986; The Taming of the Shrew: (RSC Stratford) 1987, (Barbican) 1988; jtly adapted and directed The Emperor (Royal Court, televised 1988) 1987; *Television* ed BBC Monitor 1965, directed films for BBC TV 1966, The Body in Question (BBC series) 1978, exec prodr BBC Shakespeare series 1979–81, presenter Madness series (ITV) 1991 and Born Talking; *Film* Take A Girl Like You 1970; *Opera* Arden Must Die (Sadler's Wells Theatre) 1974, The Cunning Little Vixen (Glyndebourne) 1975 and 1977; ENO: The Marriage of Figaro 1978 (directorial debut), The Turn of the Screw 1979, Arabella 1989, Otello 1981, Rigoletto 1982 and 1985, Don Giovanni 1985, The Magic Flute 1986, Tosca 1986 (transferred from Maggio Musicale Florence, subsequently revived Houston Grand Opera), The Mikado 1986, 1988 and 1993, The Barber of Seville 1987, The Turn of the Screw 1993, Rigoletto 1993, Rosenkavalier 1994, Carmen 1995; Kent Opera: Cosi Fan Tutte 1975, Rigoletto 1975, Orfeo 1976, Eugene Onegin 1977, La Traviata 1979, Falstaff 1980 and 1981, Fidelio 1982, 1983 and 1988; other prodns incl: Don Giovanni, Cosi Fan Tutte and The Marriage of Figaro (Maggio Musicale Florence) 1990–92, Fanciulla del West (La Scala), Katya Kabanova (Metropolitan Opera NY), Figaro (Vienna State Opera), The Magic Flute (Israel Philharmonic prodn) and Roberto Devereux (Monte Carlo Opera) 1990–92, Manon Lescaut (La Scala) 1992, Die Gezeichneten (Zurich Opera) 1992, Maria Stuarda (Monte Carlo Opera), Capriccio (Deutsche Staatsoper Berlin) 1993, Bach's St Matthew Passion (Holy Trinity London) 1993, Anna Bolena (Monte Carlo Opera) 1994, Falstaff (Zurich Opera) 1993, Fedora (Bregenz Festival) 1993, L'incoronazione di Poppea (Glimmerglass Opera) 1994, Cosi fan Tutte (Royal Opera House, debut) 1995, Pelléas and Mélisande (Metropolitan Opera NY) 1995; *Books* McLuhan (1971), Freud: The Man, His World, His Influence (ed, 1972), The Body in Question (1978), Subsequent Performances (1986), The Don Giovanni Book: Myths of Seduction and Betrayal (1990); *Style—* Dr Jonathan Miller, CBE; ✉ c/o IMG Artists Europe, Media House, 3 Burlington Lane, Chiswick, London W4 2TH (☎ 0181 747 9977, fax 0181 747 9131)

MILLER, Joseph Edward (Jem); s of Frederick Miller (d 1949), of India, and Jane Wanley, *née* Hall (d 1960); *b* 27 Dec 1934; *Educ* St Paul's Sch Darjeeling India, Brighton Coll Sussex; *m* 1, Sylvia June; 1 s (Christopher Keith b 3 Feb 1963), 1 da (Jane Marion b 23 Nov 1960); m 2, Margaret, da of Ralph Percival Jonas; *Career* PR exec; journalist in southern Africa 1953–63, joined PR Dept Anglo American Corporation 1963–71, sr dir Streets Financial 1972–82, formed own PR co 1982–84, md Burson-Marsteller Financial 1984–87, dep chm Lowe Bell Financial 1988–; vice chm PRCA (chm Professional Practices Ctee 1989–); Keeper of the Quaich 1989; MIPR 1972–89, MInstD 1975–89; *Recreations* cooking, photography; *Style—* Jem Miller, Esq; ✉ Lowe Bell Financial Ltd, 20 Red Lion Court, London EC4A 3HE (☎ 0171 353 9203, fax 0171 353 7980)

MILLER, Prof Keith John; s of George Miller (d 1955), of Blackburn, Lancashire, and Nora, *née* Curry (d 1980); *b* 12 Jan 1932; *Educ* Blackburn GS, Blackburn Tech Coll, Harris Inst Preston, Imperial Coll London (BSc), Queen Mary Coll London (PhD), Univ of Cambridge (MA, ScD); *m* 1, 3 Sept 1955 (m dis), Barbara, *née* Tomlinson; 3 da (Lynne b 28 Jan 1956, Denise b 1 Aug 1958, Janet Elizabeth 31 July 1959); m 2, 22 April 1982, Catherine Olive, da of Kenneth Alexander Corbett (d 1993); *Career* Leyland Motors: trade apprenticeship 1948–50, student apprenticeship 1950–52; res engr English Electric Rugby 1956–58, lectr in mechanical engrg Rugby Coll of Technology 1958–59, acting head Mechanical Engrg Dept Ahmadu Bello Univ Nigeria 1961–63 (sr lectr 1959–61), lectr in mechanical engrg QMC London 1963–66, lectr Dept of Materials QMC 1966–68, lectr in engrg Univ of Cambridge 1968–77; Univ of Sheffield: prof of mechanical engrg 1977–, head Dept of Mechanical Engrg 1982–87, dean Faculty of Engrg 1987–89, dir Structural Integrity Res Inst 1988–; fell Trinity Coll Cambridge 1970–; Fndrs' Gold Medal RGS 1981, Mungo Park Silver Medal Royal Scottish Geographical Soc 1981, Mechanics & Materials Award Japanese Soc of Mechanical Engrs (JSME) 1995; foreign memb Nat Acad of Scis Ukraine 1994, hon memb Deutscher Verband für Materialforschung und Prufung, hon life pres Int Conference Mechanical Behaviour of Materials (ICM) 1995; ldr int Karakoram (Himalayan) expdn (RGS 150th anniversary expdn) 1980, ldr of other expdns to Karakoram, Iceland, Greenland and Africa; FEng 1993; FRGS 1957, FIMechE 1983, FIM 1983, FRSA 1984, FIEE 1987, FCGI 1989; *Books* Continents in Collision; *Recreations* mountaineering, exploration, tennis; *Clubs* Alpine, Rugby Mountaineering, Climbers'; *Style—* Prof Keith Miller, FEng; ✉ 40 Stumperlowe Park Road, Fulwood, Sheffield, S10 3QP; Structural Integrity Research Institute, University of Sheffield, Faculty of Engineering, Mappin Street, Sheffield S1 3JD (☎ 0114 282 5239, fax 0114 275 3671)

MILLER, Dr Kenneth Allan Glen; CBE (1988); s of Dr Allan Frederick Miller (d 1967), of Edinburgh, and Margaret Hutchinson, *née* Glen (d 1971); *b* 27 July 1926; *Educ* Upper Canada Coll Toronto, Trinity Hall Cambridge (BA, MA), UCW Aberystwyth (PhD); *m* 24 April 1954, Dorothy Elaine, da of Dr Derek G Brown (d 1967), of W Kilbride; 3 s (Andrew b 1955, Ian b 1957, Allan b 1961); *Career* res asst to Prof of Physics Aberystwyth 1946–49; ICI: various posts on prodn and design Billingham 1949–59, seconded to Br Tport Cmmn 1959–60, asst tech mangr Heavy Organic Chemicals Div 1960–63, engrg mangr 1963–65, engrg dir 1965–71, engrg advsr to Main Bd 1971–74; md: APV Ltd 1974–77, APV plc 1977–82; dir gen Engrg Cncl 1982–88; dep chm ECCTIS 2000 Ltd 1990–96, chm Pollution Control and Measurement (Europe) Ltd (PCME Ltd) 1993–; dep chm Standing Conf on Schs' Sci and Technol 1990–96; memb: Ctee for Indust Technol 1972–76, Univ Grants Ctee 1981–83, Cncl Careers Res Advsy Centre 1988–96; chm Steering Ctee for Mfrg Advsy Serv 1977–81, hon fell Trinity Hall Cambridge 1992; FIMechE 1965, FEng 1981, CIMgt 1985; *Recreations* gardening, photography; *Clubs* Leander; *Style—* Dr Kenneth Miller, CBE, FEng; ✉ 4 Montrose Gdns, Oxshott, Leatherhead, Surrey KT22 OUU (☎ 01372 842093)

MILLER, Lisa; da of Glyn Beynon Davies (d 1979), and Dorothy, *née* Grant; *b* 9 Nov 1939; *Educ* King Edward VI HS for Girls, Lady Margaret Hall Oxford (MA); *m* 12 Sept 1965, Timothy Peter Francis Miller, *qv*, s of Col J F Miller, of Camberley; 2 s (Charles b 1977, Alexander b 1983), 2 da (Lucasta b 1966, Cressida b 1968); *Career* child psychotherapist Tavistock Clinic, ed Jl of Child Psychotherapy 1982–85, chm Assoc of Child Psychotherapists 1986–89; *Books* Closely Observed Infants (ed jtly, 1989), Understanding Your Baby (1991), Understanding Your 4 Year Old (1992), Understanding Your 8 Year Old (1993); *Style—* Mrs Lisa Miller; ✉ 9 Bartholomew Villas, London NW5 (☎ 0171 485 7294); The Tavistock Clinic, Belsize Lane, London NW3 (☎ 0171 435 7111)

MILLER, Michael; RD (1966), QC (1974); s of Lt-Cdr John Brian Peter Duppa-Miller, GC (d 1994), and The Hon Barbara, *née* Buckmaster (d 1966); *b* 28 June 1933; *Educ* Westminster, ChCh Oxford (BA, MA); *m* 1, 18 Oct 1958 (m dis 1991), Mary Elizabeth, da of late Donald Spiers Monteagle Barlow, of Harpenden, Herts; 2 s (George b 1962, Edward b 1970), 2 da (Charlotte b 1959, Alexandra b 1967); m 2, 1 May 1991, Barbara Lepine, prof of political philosophy Brunel Univ and da of late Thomas Goodwin, of Reydon, Suffolk; *Career* Ordinary Seaman RNVR 1950, Nat Serv 1955–57, cmmnd Sub-Lt RNVR 1956, Lt-Cdr RNR 1973, qualified Submarines; called to the Bar Lincoln's Inn 1958, practising at Chancery Bar and Int Bar 1959–, bencher 1984, memb Bar Cncl 1988–92, assoc memb Hong Kong Bar Assoc 1976–; memb Lab Pty 1964; *Style—* Michael Miller, Esq, RD, QC; ✉ 8 Stone Buildings, Lincoln's Inn, London WC2 3TA (☎ 0171 242 5002, fax 0171 831 9188)

MILLER, Michael Dawson; s of Cyril Gibson Risch Miller, CBE (d 1976), and Dorothy Alice, *née* North-Lewis; *b* 12 March 1928; *m* 17 July 1954, Gillian Margaret, da of Dr Eric Gordon-Fleming (d 1948); 3 da (Caroline b 1957, Clare b 1961, Jane b 1961); *Career* Parachute Regt Regs 1946–48 (TA 1949), HAC 1957–63; articled clerk 1949, in practice as slr 1954–55, ptnr Thos R Miller & Son 1962–90 (exec 1955–62, ptnr Bermuda 1969–90); dir: Shipowners Assurance Management Montreal 1973–84, AB Indemnitas Stockholm 1983–90, Thos Miller War Risks Services 1985–90; conslt Planning Bd for Ocean Shipping 1970–; Liveryman: Worshipful Co of Shipwrights 1977, Worshipful Co of Solicitors 1986; memb: Law Soc 1954, London Maritime Arbitrators' Assoc 1963; Silver medal Hellenic Merchant Marine Greece 1983; *Books* Marine War Risks (1 and 2 edns, winner Br Insur Law Assoc prize 1991); *Recreations* going to sea on small ships, opera, history, reaching remote places, ancient civilisations, targeting intellectuals; *Clubs* Royal Ocean Racing, Royal Bermuda Yacht, Royal Thames Yacht, City, Hurlingham; *Style—* Michael Miller, Esq; ✉ 52 Scarsdale Villas, London W8 6PP (☎ 0171 937 9935); Dairy Cottage, Donhead, St Andrews, Wilts; Thos R Miller & Son, International House, 26 Creechurch Lane, London EC3A 5BA (☎ 0171 283 4646, fax 0171 283 5614, telex 885271)

MILLER, Dr (John) Paul; s of John Frederick William Miller (d 1961), and Edith Mary Miller; *b* 10 July 1940; *Educ* Repton, Keble Coll Oxford (MA, DPhil, BM BCh), Univ of London (MSc), Guy's; *m* 19 Aug 1978, (Constance) Mary, da of Kenneth Anderson, of Farnham; 1 s (Christopher John Kenneth b 1984), 1 da (Claire b 1981), 1 adopted s (Nicholas Francis Haynes b 1977), 1 adopted da (Jackie Marie Haynes b 1979); *Career* house physician Guy's 1968, house surgn Addenbrooke's Hosp Cambridge 1969, team leader Save the Children Fund Nigerian Civil War, sr house offr and registrar Hammersmith Hosp 1970–72, hon sr registrar St James's Hosp Leeds 1972–75, lectr med Univ of Leeds 1972–75, sr lectr med Univ of Manchester 1975–81, hon conslt physician Univ Hosp of S Manchester 1975–81, visiting prof med Baylor Coll Houston (MRC travelling fell) 1978–79, conslt gastroenterologist Univ Hosp of S Manchester 1981– (clinical sub dean 1982–88); author of sci papers and reviews on: respiratory physiology, gastroenterology (especially peptic ulceration), disorders of lipoprotein metabolism; formerly: treas Br Hyperlipidaemia Assoc, regnl advsr N W Reg RCP; chm Cncl Ctee Med Protection Soc; memb Manchester Literary and Philosophical Soc; memb: Br Soc Gastroenterology, Assoc Physicians GB and Ireland; fell American Heart Assoc (memb Cncl Arteriosclerosis), FRCP 1982; *Recreations* running, walking, golf; *Style—* Dr Paul Miller; ✉ Department of Medicine, University Hospital of South Manchester, Manchester M20 2LR (☎ 0161 219 3823, fax 0161 434 5194)

MILLER, Peter Francis Nigel; s of Francis Gerald Miller (author, pen name Ambrose Heath, d 1969), of Bristol, and Dorothy Emily, *née* Leftwich (d 1973); *b* 8 May 1924; *Educ* King's Sch Canterbury, Sch of Architecture Canterbury; *m* 20 July 1950 (m dis 1984), Sheila Gillian Branthwayt, RI, painter, da of George Frederic Storrs Stratton (d 1937), of Newport, IOW; 1 s (Robert James Stratton b 1962), 2 da (Charlotte Mary Leftwich (Mrs Robert Carter) b 1957, Caroline Elizabeth Bradshaw (Mrs John Davies) b 1959); *Career* Army 1942–47, Lt, served NI, NW Europe, Austria, Italy and India, cmmnd Duke of Cornwall's LI 1943, attached Glasgow Highlanders (HLI) 1944; chartered architect, chartered designer, surveyor, stone conslt, surveyor to the Fabric Emeritus to Ely Cathedral and historic buildings conslt; asst to: Mrs Gaby Schreiber 1950, Sir Hugh Casson 1952; commenced practice: Peter Miller and Sheila Stratton 1954, Miller and Tritton 1956; Purcell Miller and Tritton: co-fndr 1965, sr ptnr 1973–88, consIt Norwich, Barnes, Winchester, Colchester, Sevenoaks, Canterbury, Ely, Dublin, Strelsund Germany, and 7 sub-offices 1988–94; surveyor to the fabric of Ely Cathedral 1974–94; FRIBA 1968 (ARIBA 1952), FSIA 1968 (MSIA 1956), FCSD; *Recreations* salmon and trout fishing; *Clubs* Norfolk; *Style—* Peter Miller, Esq; ✉ The Old Foundry House, Letheringsett, Holt, Norfolk NR25 7JL (☎ 01263 712329); The Studio, Thornage Watermill, Holt, Norfolk NR25 7QN (☎ 01263 711339)

MILLER, Sir Peter North; kt (1988); s of Cyril Thomas Gibson Risch Miller, CBE (d 1976), and Dorothy Alice North Miller, JP; *b* 28 Sept 1930; *Educ* Rugby, Lincoln Coll Oxford (MA), City Univ (DSc); *m* 4 Feb 1991, Jane Suzanne; 1 s (2 s, 1 da by previous m); *Career* Nat Serv Intelligence Corps 1949–50; joined Lloyd's 1953, called to the Bar 1954; Thomas R Miller & Son (Insurance): joined 1953, ptnr 1959, sr ptnr 1971; chm Thomas R Miller & Son (Holdings) Ltd 1971–83 and 1988–96 (name changed to The Miller Insurance Group Ltd 1991); Lloyd's Insur Brokers' Assoc Ctee: memb 1973–77, dep chm 1974–75, chm 1976–77; memb: Ctee on Invisible Exports 1975–77, Insurance Brokers' Registration Cncl 1977–81, Ctee of Lloyd's 1977–80 and 1982–89; chm: Lloyd's 1984–87, Br Ctee of Bureau Veritas 1980–; memb HM Commission of Lieutenancy for the City of London 1987–; Freeman City of London 1986; Liveryman: Worshipful Co of Insurers 1987, Worshipful Co of Shipwrights 1987; Hon DSc City Univ 1987, hon fell Lincoln Coll Oxford 1992; FRSA 1986; Commendatore Ordine al Merito della Repubblica Italiana 1989; *Recreations* all sport, incl tennis, running and sailing (except cricket), wine, music, gardening, old churches; *Clubs* City of London, Brooks's, Vincent's, Thames Hare and Hounds; *Style—* Sir Peter Miller; ✉ The Miller Insurance Group, Dawson House, 5 Jewry St, London EC3N 2EX (☎ 0171 488 2345, fax 0171 265 1423, telex 888905)

MILLER, Richard Hugh; QC (1995); s of Sir Stephen James Hamilton Miller, KCVO (d 1996), and Lady Heather Miller; *b* 1 Feb 1953; *Educ* Charterhouse, Univ of Sussex (BSc); *Career* called to the Bar Middle Temple 1976 (specialising in patent matters); *Books* Terrell on the Law of Patents (jt ed, 14 edn); *Recreations* travel, films; *Style—* Richard

Miller, Esq, QC; ✉ 3 New Square, Lincoln's Inn, London WC2A 3RS (☎ 0171 405 1111, fax 0171 405 7800)

MILLER, Richard Morgan; *Educ* Vanderbilt Univ Nashville (BA), Wharton Sch Univ of Pennsylvania; *m* Betty Ruth, *née* Randolph; 1 s (Richard), 2 da (Ellen, Claire); *Career* 1 Lt US Marine Corps 1953–55; salesman Dominion Insurance Agency 1955–58, fndr and pres Richard M Miller & Company 1958–70 (merged with Synecon Corporation 1970), fndr, dir, pres and chief exec Synercon Corporation and pres and chief exec Richard M Miller & Company 1970–76 (Synercon Corporation merged with Corroon & Black Corporation 1976); Corroon & Black Corporation: exec vice pres and chief operating offr 1976–78, pres and chief operating offr 1978–88, chief exec and pres 1988–89, chm and chief exec 1990 (merged with Willis Faber plc 1990); chief exec emeritus Willis Corroon Group plc 1995 (chief exec 1990–94), ret; dir: Meridian Insurance Company Bermuda, Consumer Benefit Life Insurance Company, Third National Bank, Third National Corporation; life assoc Vanderbilt University's Owen Graduate Sch of Mgmnt; memb: Nat Assoc of Casualty and Surety Agents, Nat Assoc of Insurance Brokers, Nat Assoc of Surety Bond Producers; tstee and memb Exec Ctee Insurance Inst of America; *Recreations* golf; *Clubs* New York Athletic (NYC), Belle Meade Country (TN), The City Midday (NYC), Mid Ocean (Bermuda), John's Island (FLA), The Golf Club of Tennessee, Phi Delta Theta Fraternity; *Style—* Richard Miller, Esq; ✉ c/o Willis Corroon Group plc, Ten Trinity Square, London EC3P 3AX

MILLER, Robin Anthony; s of William Ernest Alexander Miller, CBE, BEM (d 1970), of Plymouth, Devon, and Winifred Albreta, *née* Tavener; *b* 15 Sept 1937; *Educ* Devonport HS, Wadham Coll Oxford (MA); *m* 25 Aug 1962, Irene Joanna, da of Alistair James Kennedy, MRCVS (d 1977), of Thornhill, Dumfriesshire, Scotland; 2 s (Iain Douglas b 27 Nov 1969, Richard Scott b 23 Nov 1971), 1 da (Helen Lordella b 8 March 1976); *Career* called to the Bar Middle Temple 1960; recorder Crown Court 1978–; *Style—* Robin A Miller, Esq; ✉ St Michael's Lodge, 192 Devonport Rd, Plymouth PL1 5RD (☎ 01752 564943); 2 King's Bench Walk Temple London EC4Y 7DE

MILLER, (James Adrian) Rodney; s of Walter Miller, of Belfast, and Elizabeth Munnis; *b* 22 Jan 1949; *Educ* Dr Renshaw's Tutorial Coll Belfast, Univ of Ulster Coll of Art & Design (BA); *m* 25 Sept 1975, Patricia Woodburn, da of Frederick Wilmot, of Perth, Western Aust; 1 s (Jonathan Anthony Walter b 1977), 2 da (Victoria Beatrice b 1979, Emma Elizabeth b 1989); *Career* graphic designer: AFA Belfast 1972–73, N Ireland Housing Exec 1973–75; head Design Dept NIHE 1977–79 (sr graphic designer 1975–77), fndr Rodney Miller Associates 1979–; maj design projects: N Ireland Tourist Bd pubns, Zimbabwe Tourist Bd pubns, various public sector design projects; winner: Kodak award for Excellence (Br Business Calendar Awards) 1989, Three ICAD Bells Dublin 1994; past memb Nat Cncl CSD (chm NI Region 1990–92), design course advsr Univ of Ulster, memb HND Industl Liaison Panel Univ of Ulster; memb Design Forum, assoc memb D&AD, MCSD 1977; *Recreations* bird watching, fishing, family; *Style—* Rodney Miller, Esq; ✉ 16 Circular Road, West, Cultra, Holywood, Co Down BT18 0AT (☎ 01232 425468); Rodney Miller Associates, 21 Ormeau Avenue, Belfast, Northern Ireland BT2 8HD (☎ 01232 240785, fax 01232 232901)

MILLER, Ronald Alan; s of Eric Norman Miller (d 1978), of London, and Rosemary, *née* Winter; *b* 10 March 1951; *Educ* Westminster, St Bartholomew's Hosp Med Sch London (MB BS, MS); *m* 1, 1975 (m dis 1995), Sarah Jane, da of Richard Griffiths Lumley, of Ross on Wye, Glos; 1 s (Mark Rudolph b 1979), 1 da (Rosalind Margaret Louise b 1982); m 2, March 1996, Linda Katheryn, da of Michael James Stanley Berriman, of Petersfield, Hants; *Career* Hunterian prof of surgery RCS 1985, Simpson Smith lectr Charing Cross Hosp 1986; currently: dir Dept of Urology and Minimally Invasive Surgery Whittington, hon conslt Hosp of St John and Elizabeth; former postgrad dean Royal Northern Hosp, hon sr lectr Inst of Urology; author of 200 papers on urological subjects; Cutler Prize RCS 1984; sec N E Thames Advsy Ctee on Urology; memb: Cncl Biological Engrg Soc, Instrument Ctee Br Assoc Urological Surgns, Steering Ctee Soc of Minimally Invasive Therapy (hon treas), Cncl Urological Section RSM; consulting ed: Endourology, Urology, Jl of Minimally Invasive Surgery, Jl of Day Surgery, Jl of Ambulatory Surgery; memb: BMA, RSM, Br Assoc Urological Surgns, American Urological Assoc, Endo Urology Soc, Minimally Invasive Soc; Order of Lenin; FRGS, MB BS 1974, MRCS LRCP 1974, FRCSEng 1978, MS Lond 1986; *Books* Percutaneous Renal Surgery (1983), Endoscopic Surgery (1986), Second Generation Lithotripsy (1987); *Recreations* riding, climbing, shooting, reading, military history; *Style—* Ronald Miller, Esq; ✉ 39 Shepherds Hill, London N6 5QJ (☎ 0181 341 3422, fax 0181 340 1376)

MILLER, Sir Ronald Andrew Baird; kt (1993), CBE (1985); *Educ* Daniel Stewarts Coll Edinburgh, Univ of Edinburgh (BSc); *Career* chm Dawson International PLC until 1995, dep chm Scottish Amicable Life Assurance Society; non-exec dir: Christian Salvesen PLC, Securities Trust of Scotland plc; chm Br Knitting and Clothing Export Cncl, dir Scottish Textile Assoc; memb Ct Napier Univ; Freeman: City of London, Worshipful Co of Woolmen; Hon DSc Heriot Watt Univ 1992; MICAS; *Recreations* golf, skiing, travel, gardening, art, music; *Style—* Sir Ronald Miller, CBE; ✉ 7 Doune Terrace, Edinburgh EH3 6DY

MILLER, Ronald Kinsman; CB (1989); s of William Miller (d 1986), of Kelvedon, Essex, and Elsie May, *née* Kinsman (d 1956); *b* 12 Nov 1929; *Educ* Colchester Royal GS; *m* 1952, Doris Alice, da of Patrick Dew (d 1984), of Greenwich; 1 s (Timothy John b 1960), 1 da (Felicity Jane b 1958); *Career* Nat Serv RN 1948–50; called to the Bar Gray's Inn 1953; Inland Revenue: joined Slr's Office 1965, Law Offrs' Dept 1977–79, Solicitor of Inland Revenue 1986–90 (princ asst slr 1981); pt/t chm VAT Tbnls 1991–; *Recreations* music, reading, gardening; *Clubs* Athenaeum; *Style—* Ronald Miller, Esq, CB; ✉ 4 Liskeard Close, Chislehurst, Kent BR7 6RT (☎ 0181 467 8041)

MILLER, Dr Roy Frank; s of Thomas Richard Miller (d 1978), and Margaret Ann, *née* Tattum; *b* 20 Sept 1935; *Educ* Wembley Co GS, Univ of Exeter (BSc), Univ of London (PhD); *m* 18 March 1961, Ruth Naomi, da of William Kenchington (d 1956); 1 s (Stephen b 1965); *Career* Royal Holloway Coll London: lectr in physics 1960, sr lectr 1972–81, vice princ 1978, princ 1981–85; vice princ Royal Holloway and Bedford New Coll London 1985–; res assoc Case Western Res Univ Cleveland Ohio 1968–69; chm Inst of Classical Studies and Canterbury Hall Univ of London; tstee and govr Strode's Coll Egham; FInstP 1978, FRSA 1983, CPhys 1986; *Recreations* music, climbing; *Clubs* Athenaeum; *Style—* Dr Roy Miller; ✉ Celyn, 3 Parsonage Rd, Englefield Green, Egham, Surrey; Royal Holloway and Bedford New College, Egham, Surrey TW20 0EX (☎ 01784 434455, fax 01784 437520)

MILLER, Sidney James; s of Sidney Tomsett Miller (d 1967), of Cambridge, and Mary Ada, *née* Marshall (d 1980); *b* 25 Jan 1943; *Educ* Clifton, Jesus Coll Cambridge (MA); *m* 17 July 1971, Judith Branney, da of Lt-Col Bernard Passingham, OBE, TD; 3 s (Paul b 1973, John b 1976, Mark b 1979), 1 da (Clare b 1984); *Career* Knox fell Harvard 1964–65, VI Form classical master and asst housemaster Clifton 1965–68, head Classical Dept Eton 1971–73 (asst master and classical tutor 1968–73), dep headmaster Bridgewater Hall Comprehensive Sch Milton Keynes 1974–77; headmaster: Kingston GS 1977–86, Bedford Sch 1986–88; professional offr Sch Examinations and Assessment Cncl London 1988–89, higher exec offr DFE London 1989–; pres Kingston Rotary Club 1982–83 (memb 1978–86); area chm Int Ctee of Rotary 1983–86 (district chm designate 1986); chm: ISIS London and SE Region Ctee 1981–84 (memb 1978–84), Kingston Boys' Club 1985–86 (vice chm 1986); vice chm Mgmnt Ctee Kingston YMCA 1986 (memb 1984–86); memb: Bedford Rotary Club 1986–88, Bd of Visitors Latchmere House Remand Centre 1979–86 (and Local Review Ctee (Parole)), Bd of Visitors Bedford Prison 1987–88, Parochial Church Cncl (Castlethorpe Bucks 1974–77, Claygate Surrey 1979–82, Christ Church Bedford 1989–), Claygate Men's Fellowship Ctee 1983–86, Headmasters' Conference (HMC) Politics and PR Sub-Ctee 1980–84 and 1987–88, Kingston NAHT Ctee 1982–84, Ctee Jesus Coll Cambridge Soc 1982–85, Cncl ISCO 1984–87; HMC rep on SHA Liaison Ctee 1984–87, tstee Kingston YMCA 1985–86, advsr Bedford CAB 1995–; govr: Denmead Prep Sch Hampton 1979–86, Aldwickbury Sch Harpenden, Beechwood Park Sch Markyate, Kingshott Sch Hitchin and Rushmoor Sch Bedford 1987–88; memb Gen Synod 1994–95; *Recreations* watching all sports (especially athletics, cricket and rugby), acting, reading, theatre, cinema, classical music, choral singing; *Clubs* MCC, Achilles; *Style—* Sidney Miller, Esq; ✉ 43 Waterloo Rd, Bedford MK40 3PG

MILLER, Stewart Crichton; CBE (1990); s of William Young Crichton Miller (d 1964), of Kirkcaldy, Fife, and Grace Margaret, *née* Finlay; *b* 2 July 1934; *Educ* Kirkcaldy HS, Univ of Edinburgh (BSc); *m* 25 June 1960, Catherine Proudfoot, da of Alexander McCourtie (d 1957); 2 s (David b 1963, Gordon b 1965), 2 da (Sarah b 1970, Lucy b 1971); *Career* Rolls Royce: joined 1954, held various appts in technology design and devpt, chief engr RB211–535 1977–84, dir of advanced engrg 1984–85, bd memb 1985–, dir of engrg 1985–90, md Aerospace Gp 1991–92, dir of engrg and technol 1993–; chm Cncl Loughborough Univ of Technol; Hon DTech Loughborough 1992; FEng 1987, FRAeS 1986, FIMechE 1987, FRS 1996, FRSE 1996; *Recreations* music, walking; *Style—* Stewart Miller, Esq, CBE, FRS, FRSE, FEng; ✉ Rolls Royce plc, 65 Buckingham Gate, London SW1E 6AT (☎ 0171 222 9020, telex 918 091)

MILLER, Tammy Kelly; da of Peter James Miller, of Kampala, Uganda, and Mary Kathleen, *née* McDonnell; *b* 21 June 1967; *Educ* The Red Maids' Sch Bristol, Univ of Exeter (BSc); *Career* int hockey player; memb Clifton Ladies' Hockey Club 1985–; England: under 18 and under 21 caps, 77 full caps, debut v Spain 1988, fourth place World Cup Sydney 1990, Gold medal Euro Cup Brussels 1991, played World Cup Dublin 1994, fourth place Euro Cup Amsterdam 1995, AEWHA Cup Final with Clifton 1996; 70 GB caps since 1991, Bronze medal Olympic Games Barcelona 1992, fourth place Olympic Games Atlanta 1996; UK Hockey Player of the Year 1996; trainee actuary Sun Life Assurance Society Bristol; *Recreations* squash, badminton, travel; *Style—* Miss Tammy Miller; ✉ c/o All England Women's Hockey Association, 51 High St, Shrewsbury SY1 1ST

MILLER, Timothy Peter Francis (Tim); s of Col John Francis Miller, of Camberley, Surrey, and Barbara Mary, *née* Cooke; *b* 9 Nov 1940; *Educ* Douai Sch, Magdalen Coll Oxford (MA); *m* 12 Nov 1965, Lisa Miller, *qv*, da of Glyn Beynon Davies (d 1979); 2 s (Charles b 1977, Alexander b 1983), 2 da (Lucasta b 1966, Cressida b 1968); *Career* advtg exec 1962–79, md Framlington Group plc 1983–88 (dir 1979–88), dir M & G Group plc 1988–92, md Portfolio Fund Management Ltd 1994–; dir LAUTRO 1986–92; chm Charter 88 Exec Ctee 1990–94, govr Univ of E London 1994–, memb Ctee London Library 1995–; Parly candidate (C) Hackney North and Stoke Newington 1979; *Recreations* pictures, books, music, motor sport; *Clubs* Beefsteak, City of London, MCC; *Style—* Tim Miller; ✉ 9 Bartholomew Villas, London NW5 2LJ (☎ 0171 485 7294); Portfolio Fund Management Ltd, 64 London Wall, London EC2M 5TP (☎ 0171 638 0808, fax 0171 638 0050)

MILLER, Prof William Lockley; s of William Lockley Miller, of Hamilton, and Florence, *née* Ratcliffe (d 1986); *b* 12 Aug 1943; *Educ* Univ of Edinburgh (MA), Univ of Newcastle (PhD); *m* 19 July 1967, Dr Nancy Fiona Miller, da of David Thomson, of Newport-on-Tay, Fife; 2 s (Iain b 3 July 1971, Andrew b 15 June 1977), 1 da (Shona b 9 Nov 1974); *Career* prof of politics Univ of Strathclyde 1985 (lectr 1968–83, sr lectr 1983–85), Edward Caird prof of politics Univ of Glasgow 1985–; FBA 1994; *Books* Electoral Dynamics (1977), The End of British Politics? (1981), The Survey Method (1983), Elections and Voters (1987), Irrelevant Elections? (1988), How Voters Change (1990), Media and Voters (1991), Alternatives to Freedom (1995), Political Culture in Contemporary Britain (1996); *Style—* Prof William Miller, FBA; ✉ Department of Politics, Adam Smith Building, The University, Glasgow G12 8RT (☎ 0141 339 8855, fax 0141 330 5071, telex 777070 UNIGLA)

MILLER OF GLENLEE, Sir Stephen William Macdonald; 8 Bt (GB 1788), of Glenlee, Kirkcudbrightshire; s of Sir (Frederick William) Macdonald Miller of Glenlee, 7 Bt (d 1991), and (Marion Jane) Audrey, *née* Pettit; *b* 20 June 1953; *Educ* Rugby, St Bartholomew's Hosp (MB BS); *m* 1, 1978, Mary Carolyn (d 1989), o da of G B Owens, of Huddersfield; 1 s (James Stephen Macdonald b 1981), 1 da (Katherine Helen b 1983); m 2, 1990, Caroline Mary, da of Leslie A E Chasemore, of Shebbear, Devon, and widow of Harold Frederick Clark; *Heir* s, James Stephen Macdonald Miller of Glenlee b 25 July 1981; *Career* GP Shebbear; FRCS, FRCGP; *Style—* Sir Stephen Miller of Glenlee, Bt; ✉ The Lawn, Shebbear, Beaworthy, Devon EX21 5RU

MILLER OF HENDON, Baroness (Life Peer UK 1993), of Gore, in the London Borough of Barnet; Doreen Miller; MBE (1989), JP (Brent 1970); da of Bernard Henry Feldman; *b* 13 June 1933; *Educ* LSE; *m* 1955, Henry Lewis Miller, s of Ben Miller; 3 s (Hon Michael Steven b 1956, Hon Paul Howard b 1959, Hon David Philip b 1962); *Career* co dir; chm: Barnet Family Health Services Authority 1990–, Crown Agents 1990–; memb Monopolies & Mergers Cmmn 1992–93; chm Greater London Area Conservative Assocs 1993– (treas 1990–93); *Clubs* St Stephen's Constitutional, Reform, Carlton; *Style—* The Rt Hon Baroness Miller of Hendon, MBE, JP; ✉ c/o House of Lords, London SW1A 0PW

MILLER SMITH, Charles; *b* 1939; *Career* Unilever PLC: joined 1963, dir 1989–95, fin dir 1989–92, head of food operations Southern Europe 1993–95; Imperial Chemical Industries PLC: non-exec dir 1993–94, exec dir 1994–95, chief exec 1995–; non-exec dir: Midland Bank plc 1994–96, HSBC Holdings plc 1996–; FCA; *Clubs* National; *Style—* Charles Miller Smith, Esq; ✉ Imperial Chemical Industries PLC, Group Headquarters, 9 Millbank, London SW1P 3JF (☎ 0171 834 4444)

MILLETT, Anthea Christine; da of Rupert Millett, of Salisbury, Wilts, and Lucy, *née* Sutton; *b* 2 Nov 1941; *Educ* Erdington GS for Girls, Univ of London (BA); *Career* asst teacher: Channing Sch Highgate, Bournville Grammar-Tech Sch; head of dept Solihull HS, dep head Tile Hill Wood Sch Coventry; DFE 1978–92: successively HM inspr, staff inspr and chief inspr; dir of inspection OFSTED 1992–94, chief exec Teacher Training Agency 1995–; memb Taylor Ctee on the Management and Governance of Schools; *Style—* Ms Anthea Millett; ✉ Teacher Training Agency, Portland House, Stag Place, London SW1E 5TT

MILLETT, Rt Hon Lord Justice; Rt Hon Sir Peter Julian; kt (1986), PC (1994); s of Denis Millett (d 1965), of London, and Adele Millett, *née* Weinberg; *b* 23 June 1932; *Educ* Harrow, Trinity Hall Cambridge (MA); *m* 1959, Ann Mireille, da of David Harris (d 1980), of London; 3 s (Richard, Andrew, Robert d 1965); *Career* standing jr counsel to BOT and DTI 1967–73, QC 1973, bencher Lincoln's Inn 1980; memb Insolvency Law Review Ctee 1977–82, judge of the High Court of Justice (Chancery Div) 1986–94, a Lord Justice of Appeal 1994–; hon fell Trinity Hall Cambridge 1994; *Style—* Rt Hon Lord Justice Millett; ✉ 18 Portman Close, London W1H 9HJ (☎ 0171 935 1152); 38 Kewhurst Ave, Cooden, Sussex (☎ 014243 2970)

MILLETT, Timothy Patrick; *b* 6 Jan 1951; *Educ* St Benedict's Sch Ealing London, Wadham Coll Oxford (MA); *Career* called to the Bar Gray's Inn 1975; official of Court of Justice of the EC 1976; legal sec to advocate general: Sir Gordon Slynn 1984–88, Francis Jacobs 1988–89; currently legal advsr for admin affrs Court of Justice of the

EC; *Books* The Court of First Instance of the European Communities (1990); *Style—* Timothy Millett, Esq; ✉ Court of Justice of the European Communities, Luxembourg L-2925 (☎ 00 352 43031, fax 00 352 4303 2600, telex 2771 CJINFO LU)

MILLHAM, David Harry; s of Harry Sidney Millham (d 1982), and Emily Harriet Millham, *née* Edwards; *b* 20 June 1938; *Educ* William Morris Country Tech Coll Walthamstow, IMEDE Lausanne Switzerland; *m* 27 March 1965, Frances, da of Francis William DuBarry; 1 s (Alexander Gareth David b 20 March 1970), 1 da (Lisa Jane b 14 March 1967); *Career* Financial Times 1959–69 (new issues ed, gen fin news writer), The Times 1969–71 (new issues ed, contrib Fin Ed's Column), PR conslt ICFC 1971–74, dir Shandwick PR Company 1974–79; Shandwick Consultants: dep chm 1979–91, md Fin PR Div 1990–91; exec dep chm Streets International Ltd 1992, chm Millham Communications Ltd 1992–; Freeman City of London 1988; MInstD; *Recreations* watching football, gardening, reading, music; *Style—* David Millham, Esq; ✉ Millham Communications, 4 City Road, London EC1Y 2AA (☎ 0171 256 5756, fax 0171 638 7370)

MILLICHIP, Sir Frederick Albert (Bert); kt (1991); s of Hugh Bowater Millichip (d 1975), of West Bromwich, West Midlands, and Lily, *née* Pester (d 1940); *b* 5 Aug 1914; *Educ* Solihull Sch; *m* 1950, Joan Barbara, *née* Brown; 1 s (Peter b 1952), 1 da (Sally-Ann b 1953); *Career* Capt RA 1940–46; former sporting career: amateur footballer West Bromwich Albion 1934–35, cricketer West Bromwich Dartmouth CC 1932–39 and 1946–59 (capt 1954–59), memb Br Empire team 1941–42; qualified slr 1950, currently conslt Edge & Ellison Slrs; pres West Bromwich Albion FC 1983– (dir 1964–84, chm 1976–84), chm The Football Assoc 1981–96 (memb Cncl 1970, life vice pres 1970–); memb: Exec Ctee UEFA 1976–, UEFA Organising Ctee for Euro Championships 1981–, Organising Ctee FIFA 1982–, Referee's Ctee UEFA 1992–; chm of Govrs FA Nat Sch 1983–; DLitt Loughborough Univ of Technol 1995; *Recreations* golf, all sports, operatic music; *Style—* Sir Bert Millichip; ✉ c/o The Football Association, 16 Lancaster Gate, London W2 3LW (☎ 0171 262 4542)

MILLIGAN, Rt Hon Eric; *b* 27 Jan 1951; *Educ* Tynecastle HS, Napier Coll Edinburgh; *m* Janis; *Career* former printer; memb Edinburgh DC 1974–78, memb Lothian Regnl Cncl 1978–96 (chm Fin Ctee 1980–82 and 1986–90); convenor: Lothian Regnl Cncl 1990–96, City of Edinburgh Cncl 1995–96; Lord Provost and Lord Lt of the City of Edinburgh 1996–; cncllr Stenhouse Div West Edinburgh; dir: Edinburgh Festival Soc (also chm), Edinburgh Military Tattoo Ltd, Edinburgh Military Tattoo (Charity) Ltd; memb: Local Govt Mgmnt Bd, Local Govt Steering Ctee on Superannuation, Convention of Scottish Local Authorities 1980–82 and 1986–; pres COSLA 1988–90; memb Lab Party; *Recreations* football, rugby, music, gardening; *Style—* The Rt Hon Eric Milligan, JP; ✉ 22 Hailes Grove, Edinburgh EH13 0NE (☎ 0131 441 1528); The City of Edinburgh Council, City Chambers, High Street, Edinburgh EH1 1YJ (☎ 0131 200 2000)

MILLIGAN, Dr George William Elliott; s of George Burn Milligan (d 1985), of Tullochard, Kingussie, and Kathleen Dorothea Milligan; *b* 2 April 1945; *Educ* Trinity Coll Glenalmond, Univ Coll Oxford (BA), Univ of Glasgow (MEng), Univ of Cambridge (PhD); *m* 18 July 1966 (m dis 1992), Baroness Barbara Wanda Borowska, da of Baron Tadeusz Borowski, and Countess Janina, step da of Herbert Charles Story, of Tunbridge Wells; 2 s (Robert George b 1968, Jan Charles b 1970); *Career* chartered civil engnr; lectr Univ of Oxford and tutor and fell of Magdalen Coll Oxford 1979–96, dir Geotechnical Consulting Group 1996–; author of tech papers on soil mechanics and co-author of book on basic soil mechanics; *Recreations* golf, walking, fishing, music; *Style—* Dr George W E Milligan; ✉ 9 Lathbury Road, Oxford OX2 7AT (☎ and fax 01865 516407); Geotechnical Consulting Group, 1A Queensberry Place, London SW7 2DL (☎ 0171 581 8348, fax 0171 584 0157)

MILLIGAN, Iain Anstruther; QC (1991); s of Maj Wyndham MacBeth Moir Milligan, MBE, TD, of Church Hill House, Stalbridge, Dorset, and Helen Penelope Eirene, *née* Cassavetti; *b* 21 April 1950; *Educ* Eton, Magdalene Coll Cambridge (exhibitioner in engrg, scholar honoris causa in law, MA, Gymnastics half blue); *m* 19 May 1979, Zara Ann Louise, da of Sir Alexander Cadwallader Mainwaring Spearman (d 1982); 1 s (Ivar Francis b 1984), 2 da (Diana Rose b 1981, Evelyn Louise b 1983); *Career* called to the Bar Inner Temple 1973; *Recreations* forestry, walking; *Style—* Iain Milligan, Esq, QC; ✉ 38 Linden Gardens, London W2 4ER (☎ 0171 229 3083); Dunesslin, Dunscore, Dumfries DG2 0UR (01387 820345); 20 Essex Street, London WC2R 3AL (☎ 0171 583 9294, fax 0171 583 1341, telex 893468)

MILLIGAN, Terence Alan (Spike); Hon CBE (1992); s of Capt Leo Alphonso Milligan MSM, RA (d 1969), and Florence Winifred, *née* Kettleband; 4 generations RA Indian Army including Indian Mutiny; *b* 16 April 1918; *Educ* Convent of Jesus and Mary Poona, St Paul's Christian Brothers de la Salle Rangoon, SE London Poly; *m* 1, 1952, June Angela, da of Richard Marlowe; 1 s (Séan b 1954), 2 da (Laura b 1952, Silé b 1957); m 2, 1962, Patricia (d 1978), da of Capt William Ridgway; 1 da (Jane b 1966); m 3, 1983, Shelagh, da of Col Gordon Sinclair; *Career* WWII RA N Africa and Italy; actor and author; former factory worker, van boy, stockroom asst, asst stationery salesman and semi professional musician; *Stage* The Bed-Sitting Room, Son of Oblomov, Ben Gunn in Treasure Island (Mermaid) 1973 and 1974, one man show 1979 and 1980, writer Ubu Roi 1980, Spike Milligan and Friends (Lyric) 1982; *Radio* The Goon Show (incl special performance 1972 to mark 50th anniversary of BBC, Best British Radio Features Script, 1972), The Milligan Papers 1987; *TV* Show called Fred (ITV), World of Beachcomber (BBC), Q5 (BBC), Oh in Colour (BBC), A Milligan for All Seasons (BBC) 1972–73, Marty Feldman's Comedy Machine (ITV, writing and appearing - winner Golden Rose and special comedy award Montreux, 1972), The Melting Pot (BBC) 1975, Q7 (BBC series) 1977, Q8 1978, Q9 1979, winner TV Writer of the Year Award 1956; *Films* The Magic Christian 1971, The Devils 1971, The Cherry Picker 1972, Digby the Biggest Dog in the World 1972, Alice's Adventures in Wonderland 1972, The Three Musketeers 1973, The Great McGonagall 1975, The Last Remake of Beau Geste 1977, The Hound of the Baskervilles 1978, Monty Python's Life of Brian 1978, History of the World Part 1 1980, Yellowbeard 1983; winner British Comedy Awards Lifetime Achievement Award 1994; *Publications* Silly Verse for Kids (1959), Dustbin of Milligan (1961), Puckoon (1963), The Little Pot Boiler (1965), A Book of Bits (1965), Milliganimals (1968), The Bedside Milligan (1968), The Bed-Sitting Room (1969), The Bald Twit Lion (1970), Adolf Hitler, My Part in his Downfall (1971, filmed 1973, on record 1980), Milligan's Ark (1971), Small Dreams of a Scorpion (1972), The Goon Show Scripts (1972), Rommel: Gunner Who? (1973), Badjelly the Witch (for children, 1973), The Great McGonagall Scrapbook (with J Hobbs, 1975), The Milligan Book of Records, Games, Cartoons and Commercials (1975), Dip the Puppy (1975), Transports of Delight (1975), William McGonagall, the truth at last (1976), Monty, His Part in my Victory (1976), Goblins (illustrated by Heath Robinson, 1978), Mussolini, His Part in my Downfall (1978), Open Heart University (1978), Spike Milligan's Q Annual (1980), Unspun Socks for a Children's Laundry (1981), Indefinite Articles and Scunthorpe (1981), The 101 Best and Only Limericks of Spike Milligan (1982), Sir Nobonk and the Terrible, Awful, Dreadful, Naughty, Nasty Dragon (for children, illustrated by Carol Baker, 1982), The Goon Cartoons (1982), More Goon Cartoons (1983), There's A Lot Of It About (1983), The Melting Pot (1983), Spike Milligan's Further Transports of Delight (1985), Where have all the Bullets Gone? (autobiography, 1985), Floored Masterpieces with Worse Verse (illustrated by Tracey Boyd, 1985), Goodbye Soldier (1986), The Looney: an Irish fantasy (1987), The Mirror Running (poetry, 1987), Startling Verse for all the Family (children's poetry, 1987), The Lost Goon Shows (1987), Milligan's War (1988), McGonagall Meets George Gershwin (1988), It Ends with Magic (1990), William McGonagall Free Fall (1992), Peace Work: Peace/War (Michael Joseph, autobiography, vol 7, 1992), Hidden Words (poetry anthology, 1993), Depression And How To Survive It (1993), The Bible According to Spike Milligan (1993), Lady Chatterley's Lover According to Spike Milligan (1994), Wuthering Heights According to Spike Milligan (1994), Spike Milligan: A Celebration (1995); *Recreations* reading war histories, biographies, dining and wining, squash; *Clubs* Ronnie Scott's (life memb); *Style—* Spike Milligan, Esq, CBE; ✉ 9 Orme Court, Bayswater, London W2

MILLIGAN, His Hon Judge; Timothy James; s of late Dr Peter James Wyatt Milligan, and Rosemary Elizabeth Ann, *née* Dutton; *b* 16 March 1940; *Educ* Winchester, Grenoble Univ; *m* 31 Aug 1976, Sally Marcella, da of late Brig Robert T Priest, OBE, RA, and Lady Marcella Florence Slessor; 2 step s (Jonathan Ivor Robert Price b 2 Feb 1969, Alexander David William Price b 20 March 1971); *Career* solicitor; articled clerk Taylor & Humbert 1960–64, asst slr Leeds Smith 1967–69, asst slr then ptnr Triggs Turner & Co Guildford 1969–74, ptnr Warner & Richardson Winchester 1974–91, dep registrar 1976–86, asst recorder 1986–89, recorder 1989–91, HM coroner Central Hampshire 1982–91, circuit judge (Western Circuit) 1991–; memb: Law Soc 1967 (now hon), Coroners' Soc of GB 1982 (now hon); *Recreations* cricket, football, rackets, music, reading, theatre, cinema; *Clubs* Hampshire, Tennis & Rackets Assoc, Jesters, Hampshire CCC, MCC; *Style—* His Hon Judge Milligan

MILLIN, Peter Jack; s of Henry Millin (d 1977), of London, and Lily Millin, of USA; *b* 28 Dec 1930; *Educ* Farnham GS, Sch of Econ Science Univ of Liverpool, Adleman Soc (Psychology & Hypnotherapy); *m* 1969 (m dis); 1 s (David b 1960); *Career* psychologist, counsellor and hypnotherapist 1960–; princ Frendship/Marriage Bureau 1950–60, pres Professional Hypnotherapist Centre, princ Acad of Hypnotherapy, lectr various orgns and contrib to various jls; winner of various medals for ballroom dancing; memb Complementary Medicine Soc; *Recreations* philosophy, theatre, classical music, travel; *Clubs* Unique Social (fndr), Kaleidescape; *Style—* Peter Millin, Esq; ✉ 28 Lakeside Crescent, East Barnet, Hertfordshire EN4 8QJ (☎ 0181 441 9685); Academy of Hypnotherapy, 10 Harley Street, London W1 (☎ 0181 441 9685)

MILLINGTON, Caroline Sarah; da of Ernest Rogers Millington, of Couze, France, and Gwen, *née* Pickard (d 1979); *b* 4 Aug 1949; *Educ* Greycoat Hosp Sch Westminster, Univ of York (BA); *Career* trainee journalist BBC 1970–72; prodr: The World Tonight and Newsdesk (BBC Radio 4) 1973–77, Nationwide (BBC1) 1978–79, The Week in Westminster, Talking Politics, In Business and documentaries (BBC Radio 4) 1980–84, Brass Tacks (BBC2) 1986; special asst to BBC's Asst DG 1985; BBC Radio: asst head of current affrs magazine progs 1987, head of magazine progs 1988–93, controller of production 1993–96, controller of multimedia devpt 1996–; jt fndr, first chair and fell The Radio Academy; memb: NUJ, RTS; *Recreations* sketching and painting, walking, music; *Style—* Ms Caroline Millington; ✉ BBC Radio, Broadcasting House, London W1A 1AA (☎ 0171 765 4693, fax 0171 765 2903)

MILLINGTON, Gordon Stopford; OBE (1996); s of Percival Richard Millington (d 1981), of Killinchy, and Irene Ellen, *née* Forster; *b* 29 June 1935; *Educ* Campbell Coll, Queen's Univ of Belfast (BSc); *m* 30 April 1960, Margaret Jean, da of Leslie Pegler (d 1964), of Croydon; 2 s (Mark Stopford b 28 Feb 1962, Gavin Paul b 11 Dec 1965), 1 da (Kathryn Margaret b 26 Feb 1964); *Career* asst engr Sir William Halcrow & Partners 1957–59, ptnr Kirk McClure & Morton 1966–87 (engr 1959–66), sr ptnr Kirk McClure Morton 1988–; chm: Amelwood Ltd, Stanwood Estates Ltd; chm NI Assoc ICE 1979–80, pres Belfast Rotary Club 1980–81; chm: Bd of Govrs Grosvenor HS 1983–90, NI Branch IHT 1989–90, Structures and Building Bd Instn of Civil Engrs 1992–94, NI 2000 1992–; external examiner Cork Regnl Tech Coll; memb Exec Inst of Engrs of Ireland 1994–; FICE (vice pres 1994–96), FIStructE, FIEI (vice pres 1995–), FIHT, MASCE, MConsE; *Recreations* yachting; *Clubs* Killyleagh Yacht; *Style—* Gordon Millington, Esq, OBE; ✉ 27 Greystown Park, Belfast BT9 6UP (☎ 01232 611303); Kirk McClure Morton, Elmwood House, 74 Boucher Road, Belfast BT9 6BA (☎ 01232 667914, fax 01232 668286)

MILLMAN, Stewart Ian; s of Sidney Woolf Millman (d 1984), of London, and Doris, *née* Gerstein; *b* 21 Nov 1948; *Educ* City of London Sch, New Coll Oxford (BA, MA); *Career* Lazard Securities Ltd 1971–81 (dir 1979–81), de Zoete & Bevan 1981 (ptnr 1984), dir Barclays de Zoete Wedd Securities Ltd 1986–93, jt md de Zoete & Bevan Ltd 1988–9; NatWest Markets: dep chm Equity Primary Markets 1993–95, md Euro Investment Banking 1995–; memb Cncl Soc of Investmt Analysts 1979–89; tstee: New Coll Oxford Devpt Fund 1992–, Int Investmt Banking NatWest Markets 1995–; AIIMR; *Recreations* playing cricket, watching football, travel; *Style—* Stewart Millman, Esq; ✉ 27 Hyde Park Gardens Mews, London W2 2NX (☎ 0171 402 0608, fax 0171 402 1193); NatWest Markets, 135 Bishopsgate, London EC2M 3XT (☎ 0171 648 3026, fax 0171 375 5733)

MILLNER, Brian David; s of Edwin Millner (d 1932); *b* 7 Oct 1930; *Educ* Scarborough HS, Cambridge Univ (MA); *m* 1956, Adina Josephine, *née* Tonn; 1 s, 1 da; *Career* sundry Pilkington Gp Appointments 1954–73, marketing mangr Chance Pilkington 1973–79, dir 1979–80; dir: Chance (Optical) Ltd 1976–80, Chance Pilkington KK (Japan) 1977–80; gp public affairs advsr Pilkington plc 1980–93, public affairs conslt 1993–; *Recreations* motoring, gardening, reading, travel; *Style—* Brian Millner, Esq; ✉ 3 Church Walk, Tarleton, Lancs PR4 6TY (☎ 01772 814811)

MILLS, Angela Margaret; da of Dr Ronald Hubert Bonfield Mills (d 1989), and Audrey Vera, *née* Mountjoy; *b* 24 Jan 1948; *Educ* Vaynor and Penderyn Sch, Somerville Coll Oxford (BM BCh, MA), St Thomas' Hosp Med Sch; *Career* nat MO Family Planning Assoc 1983–88, hon lectr Dept of Obstetrics and Gynaecology Univ Coll Hosps London 1983–, currently conslt gynaecologist United Elizabeth Garrett Anderson Hosp and Hosp for Women Soho; author of various pubns in jls; chm London Soc Family Planning Doctors 1985–88, vice chm Nat Assoc of Family Planning Doctors 1989–93; memb: Sub Ctee RCOG on problems associated with AIDS in relation to obstetrics and gynaecology, Bd Faculty of Community Health 1991–94, Continuing Educn Sub Ctee of Faculty of Community Health 1990–94, Bd Faculty of Family Planning and Reproductive Health Care 1994–96 (chm Clinical and Scientific Ctee 1994–); memb: Cncl Nat Assoc of Family Planning Doctors 1993–94, American Soc of Fertility and Sterility, Soc of Advancement of Contraception, Br Soc of Clinical Colposcopists, BMA; FRCOG 1993, MFPHM 1996; *Recreations* travelling, music, gardening; *Clubs* Network, RSM, Club 2000; *Style—* Miss Angela Mills; ✉ 80 Harley St, London W1N 1AE (☎ 0171 637 0584, fax 0171 637 0242)

MILLS, Dame Barbara Jean Lyon; DBE (1997), QC (1986, NI 1991); da of John Lyon Warnock, and Nora Kitty Warnock; *b* 10 Aug 1940; *Educ* St Helen's Sch Northwood Middx, Lady Margaret Hall Oxford (Gibbs scholar, MA); *m* 1962, John Angus Donald Mills, s of Kenneth McKenzie Mills; 3 da (Sarah b 1963, Caroline b 1965, Lizzie b 1969), 1 s (Peter b 1971); *Career* called to the Bar Middle Temple 1963, recorder of the Crown Ct 1982–92, bencher 1990–; jr Treasury counsel Central Criminal Court 1981–86, legal assessor to GMC and GDC 1988–90, dir The Serious Fraud Office 1990–92, Dir of Public Prosecutions 1992–; memb: Criminal Injuries Compensation Bd 1988–90, Parole Bd 1990, Gen Advsy Cncl BBC 1991–92; Hon LLD: Univ of Hull 1993, Nottingham Trent Univ 1993, Guildhall Univ 1994; hon fell Lady Margaret Hall Oxford 1991; CIMgt 1993; *Style—* Dame Barbara Mills, DBE, QC; ✉ Crown Prosecution Service, 50 Ludgate Hill, London EC4M 7EX (☎ 0171 273 8098, fax 0171 329 8366, dx 300850 Ludgate EC4)

MILLS, Maj Bernard Herbert Gordon; CBE (1989); s of James Gordon Coleman Mills (d 1959), and Ellen, *née* Goodson (d 1974); *b* 21 Feb 1932; *Educ* St John's Sch Leatherhead,

RMA Sandhurst, Queens' Coll Cambridge (MA); *Career* enlisted RAC 1950, cmmnd Suffolk Regt 1952; served: Trieste, Germany, Cyprus; 22 SAS Regt 1955–57 Malaya, HQ 4 Div Germany 1959–60, 1 Royal Anglian Regt 1960–62 Berlin and UK, Muscat Regt Sultan of Oman's Armed Forces 1962–64, ret 1964; political advsr: Govt Kingdom of Yemen 1964–67, Govt Kingdom of Saudi Arabia 1967–69; field dir Nigeria Save the Children Fund 1969–70, del (later chief del) Int Union for Child Welfare in Nigeria, E Pakistan and Bangladesh 1970–74, dir Duranton Ltd (Antony Gibbs Gp) 1975–79; UN Relief and Works Agency: offr i/c Central Lebanon Area 1982–83, asst dir i/c operation S Lebanon 1983–85, dep dir Jordan 1985–86, dir of ops Gaza and rep Egypt 1986–88, chm European Co-Ordinating Ctee of NGO's on Palestine 1991–93, vice chm Cncl for the Advancement of Arab-British Understanding (CAABU) 1995– (dir 1991–94, memb Exec Ctee 1994–95); dir Bernard Mills Consultants Ltd; *Recreations* walking, conversation; *Clubs* Special Forces; *Style*— Maj Bernard Mills, CBE; ✉ 2 The Maltings, Walsham-le-Willows, Suffolk IP31 3BD (☎ 01359 258830)

MILLS, Vice Adm Sir Charles Piercy; KCB (1968, CB 1964), CBE (1957), DSC (1953); s of Capt Thomas Piercy Mills (d 1944), of Woking, and Eleanor May Mills (d 1978); *b* 4 Oct 1914; *Educ* RNC Dartmouth; *m* 1944, Anne, da of Cecil Francis Cumberlege (d 1975); 2 da; *Career* joined RN 1928, served WWII (despatches), Korea 1950–52, Capt 1953, Suez Operations 1956, Rear Adm 1963, Vice Adm 1966, Flag Offr 2 i/c Far East Fleet 1966–67, C-in-C Plymouth 1967–69, Lt-Govr and C-in-C Guernsey 1969–74; KStJ 1969; *Recreations* golf, yachting; *Style*— Vice Adm Sir Charles Mills, KCB, CBE, DSC; ✉ Aldewaye, Aldeburgh, Suffolk IP15 5ER (☎ 01728 452115)

MILLS, Christopher David; s of Fred Mills (d 1992), of Sheffield, and Grace Amy, *née* Milner (d 1976); *b* 15 April 1949; *Educ* Abbeydale Boys' GS, Univ of London (LLB); *m* 24 Oct 1984, (Diane) Elizabeth, da of Eric Skuse; 2 da (Harriet Elisheba Christy, Leonie Elisheba Christy); *Career* called to the Bar Inner Temple 1972; memb: RSPB, Sorby Nat History Soc; *Recreations* walking, birdwatching, badminton; *Style*— Christopher D Mills, Esq; ✉ Little Ranah Farm, Whams Road, Hazlehead, Sheffield S30 5HJ; 19 Figtree Lane, Sheffield S1 2DJ (☎ 0114 275 9708, fax 0114 272 4915)

MILLS, 3 Viscount (UK 1962); Sir Christopher Philip Roger Mills; 3 Bt (UK 1953); also Baron Mills (UK 1957); o s of 2 Viscount Mills (d 1988); *b* 20 May 1956; *m* 29 March 1980, Lesley Alison, er da of Alan Bailey, of Lichfield, Staffs; *Career* area mangr fisheries, recreation and ecology NRA NW Region 1991–95, area mangr Thames Region NE Area Environment Agency 1995–; memb Cncl: Inst of Fisheries Mgmnt, RSPB; memb All Pty Cons Gp of both Houses of Parliament and the Parly Environment Gp; *Style*— The Rt Hon Viscount Mills

MILLS, Colin James Edmund; s of James Oliver Mills (d 1986), of Holcot, Northamptonshire, and Ada, *née* Cox; *b* 28 Nov 1937; *Educ* Northampton GS, Leicester Sch of Architecture (Dip Arch); *m* 2 Sept 1961, Eileen Patricia, da of Charles Frederick Swain (d 1986); 1 s (James b 1965), 3 da (Kathryn b 1967, Rosalind b 1969, Clare b 1982); *Career* chartered architect; ptnr Morrison & Partners 1970–77, dir Morrison Design Partnership 1977–86, princ Colin J E Mills 1986–; *Recreations* painting, ornithology, reading; *Style*— Colin Mills, Esq; ✉ Roadend, Shiskine, Isle of Arran KA27 8EW (☎ 01770 860448)

MILLS, David John; s of Terence John Mills, and Geraldine Patricia, *née* Edwards; *b* 4 Jan 1963; *Educ* Wolverhampton GS, Gonville & Caius Coll Cambridge; *m* 27 July 1990, Janet Elizabeth, *née* Lazarus; 2 s (Frederick Lazarus b 26 April 1994, Albert Norman b 18 Nov 1995); *Career* ed The Artist's and Illustrator's Magazine 1986–89, md Arts and Leisure The Sunday Times 1996– (dep arts ed 1989–90, arts ed 1990–96); *Recreations* cricket, music; *Clubs* Groucho, Fleet Street Strollers Cricket; *Style*— David Mills, Esq; ✉ The Sunday Times, 1 Pennington Street, London E1 9XW (☎ 0171 782 5000)

MILLS, Edward David William; CBE (1959); s of late Edward Ernest Mills; *b* 19 March 1915; *Educ* Regent St Poly Sch of Architecture; *m* 1939, Elsie May, da of late W Bryant; 1 s, 1 da; *Career* chartered architect and design conslt; sr ptnr Edward D Mills and Ptnrs; patron Soc of Architectural Illustrators 1986–; author of books on bldg and architecture; RIBA: Alfred Bossom res fell, Churchill fell 1969; Hon DLitt Univ of Greenwich 1993; FRIBA, FCSD, FRSA; *Recreations* photography, writing, travel; *Style*— Edward D Mills, Esq, CBE; ✉ The Studio, Gate House Farm, Newchapel, Lingfield, Surrey RH7 6LF (☎ 01342 832241)

MILLS, Sir Frank; KCVO (1983), CMG (1971); s of Joseph Francis Mills; *b* 1923; *Educ* King Edward VI Sch Nuneaton, Emmanuel Coll Cambridge; *m* 1953, Trilby Foster; 1 s, 2 da; *Career* HM Dip Serv; high cmmr Ghana 1975–78, dir of communications 1978–81, high cmmr Bangladesh 1981–83; chm: Camberwell Health Authy 1984–89, Royal Cwlth Soc for the Blind 1985–92, Chichester Community Health Cncl 1993–95; *Style*— Sir Frank Mills, KCVO, CMG; ✉ 14 Sherborne Road, Chichester, Sussex PO19 3AA

MILLS, Geoffrey Thomas; s of Thomas Henry Mills (d 1975), and Margaret Jane, *née* Lewington (d 1936); *b* 13 Nov 1935; *Educ* Enfield GS, Clare Coll Cambridge (golf blue 1958); *m* Anne, da of Hugh Augustine Williams, and Sinah Williams, *née* Richards; 1 s (Patrick Hugh b 1973), 3 da (Rosie Grace b 1975, Annabel Sinah b 1976, Lucy Margaret Elizabeth b 1980); *Career* Nat Serv Corpl Clerk RASC 1954–56; foreign language asst Lyon France 1960–61, teacher French and Spanish Guthlaxton GS Leics, head of Spanish Sweyne Grammar Tech Sch Rayleigh Essex 1962–65; head of modern languages: Coborn Sch for Girls Bow 1965–69, Woodhouse GS Finchley 1969–73; dir of studies Longdean Sch Hemel Hempstead 1973–78, headmaster Manhood HS and Community Centre Selsey W Sussex 1978–83, headmaster Latymer Sch Edmonton 1983–; memb: SHA, NAHT; *Recreations* golf (Middx amateur golf champion 1958), bridge, reading; *Clubs* Mid Herts Golf; *Style*— Geoffrey Mills, Esq; ✉ The Latymer School, Haselbury Road, Edmonton, London N9 9TN (☎ 0181 807 2470, fax 0181 807 4125)

MILLS, Harold Hernshaw; CB (1995); s of Harold George Mills (d 1988), and Margaret Elliot Mills; *b* 2 March 1938; *Educ* Greenock HS, Univ of Glasgow (BSc, PhD); *m* 1 Aug 1973, Marion Elizabeth, da of John Beattie, of Poulton-Le- Fylde, Lancashire; *Career* cancer res scientist Roswell Park Meml Inst Buffalo NY USA 1962–64; lectr Univ of Glasgow 1964–69; princ Scot Home and Health Dept 1970–76, asst sec Scot Office 1976–81, Privy Cncl Office 1981–83, under sec Scot Devpt Dept 1984–88 (asst sec 1983–84), princ fin offr Scot Office 1988–92, sec Environment Dept Scot Office 1992–95, sec and head Devpt Dept Scot Office 1995–; *Style*— Harold Mills, Esq, CB; ✉ Scottish Office Development Department, Victoria Quay, Edinburgh (☎ 0131 244 0759)

MILLS, Hayley Catherine Rose Vivien; da of Sir John Mills, CBE, *qv*, and Mary Hayley-Bell, JP (author and playwright); *b* 18 April 1946; *Educ* Elmhurst Ballet Sch, Institute Alpine Videmanette Switzerland; *m* 20 June 1971 (m dis 1977), Roy Boulting, *qv*; 1 s (Crispian Boulting Mills b 18 Jan 1973); has issue by Leigh Lawson; 1 s (Jason (Ace) Lawson b 30 July 1976); *Career* actress; pres St John Ambulance W London Dist; patron: Mountview Theatre Sch, Mobility Tst, Peace Fndn, Jan de Vries Benevolent Tst, Teddington Theatre; fndr memb Ark and VIVA; *Theatre* incl: Peter Pan 1969, The Wild Duck 1970, Trelawney of the Wells 1972, The Three Sisters 1973, A Touch of Spring 1975, Rebecca 1977, My Fat Friend 1978, Hush of Hide 1979, The Importance of Being Earnest 1979, The Summer Party 1980, Tallys Folly 1982, The Secretary Bird 1983, Dial M for Murder 1984, Toys in the Attic 1986, The Kidnap Game 1991, The King and I (Gordon Frost Prodns Australia) 1991–92, Fallen Angels 1993, The Card 1994, Dead Guilty 1995–96, Brief Encounter 1996; *Television* incl: Deadly Strangers 1974, Only a Scream Away 1974, two Loveboat Specials 1978, The Flame Trees of Thika 1980, Illusion of Life 1981, Amazing Stories 1986, Murder She Wrote 1986, Tales of the Unexpected 1987, Good Morning Miss Bliss 1988, Back Home 1989, Walk of Life 1990, US Variety TV, The Danny Kaye Show, The Andy Williams Show; *Films* incl: Tiger Bay 1959, Pollyanna 1960, Parent Trap 1961, The Castaways 1962, Whistle Down the Wind 1962, Summer Magic 1963, The Moonspinners 1964, The Chalk Garden 1964, That Darn Cat 1965, Sky West & Crooked 1965, The Truth About Spring 1965, The Family Way 1966, The Trouble with Angels 1966, Pretty Polly 1967, Twisted Nerve 1968, Take A Girl Like You 1970, Endless Night 1972, Mr Forbush and the Penquins 1972, What Changed Charlie Farthing 1975, The Diamond Hunters 1975, Parent Trap II 1986, Parent Trap III 1989, Parent Trap IV 1989, Appointment with Death 1988; *Books* My God (1988); *Recreations* reading, travel, walking; *Clubs* St James's, Soho House; *Style*— Miss Hayley Mills; ✉ c/o Chatto & Linnit, Prince of Wales Theatre, Coventry Street, London W1V 7FE (☎ 0171 930 6677, fax 0171 930 0091)

MILLS, Iain Campbell; MP (C) Meriden (majority 14,699); s of John Steel Mills, and Margaret Leitch; *b* 21 April 1940; *Educ* Prince Edward Sch Salisbury, Rhodesia; *m* 1971, Gaynor Lynne Jeffries; *Career* with Dunlop Rhodesia 1961–64, mktg planning mangr Dunlop UK Ltd 1964–79 (responsible for all Dunlop racing tyre devpt 1966–70); MP (C) Meriden 1979–, sec to Cons Tport Ctee 1979–81; PPS to: Min of State for Indust 1981–82, Sec of State for Employment 1982–85, Sec of State for Trade and Indust 1983–85, Chm Cons Party 1985–87; memb Select Ctee on Employment 1987–, jt chm All Pty Car Indust Gp 1992–; *Clubs* Carlton, House of Commons Yacht; *Style*— Iain Mills, Esq, MP; ✉ House of Commons, London SW1A 0AA

MILLS, (George) Ian; s of George Haxton Mills, and Evelyn Mary, *née* Owen; *b* 19 Nov 1935; *Educ* Taunton's GS Southampton; *m* 1968, Margaret Elizabeth Dunstan; 1 s, 1 da (and 1 s decd); *Career* articled clerk Beal Young & Booth CAs Southampton 1954–60; Price Waterhouse: joined London Office 1960, seconded to World Bank team assisting Govt of Pakistan Treasy 1962–63; chief accountant Univ of Ibadan Nigeria 1965–68; Price Waterhouse: rejoined London Office 1968–70, mangr i/c Northern and Scot Mgmnt Consultancy Ops Newcastle upon Tyne 1970–73, ptnr i/c Africa Mgmnt Consultancy Ops London 1974–78, ptnr i/c UK Mktg 1978–82, nat dir of Central Govt servs 1983–85; Mgmnt Bd NHS: dir of fin mgmnt 1985–88, dir of resource mgmnt 1988–89; Price Waterhouse 1989–92: rejoined as sr ptnr i/c Business Devpt Europe, memb Euro Mgmnt Bd and World Mgmnt Ctee; dir and chm IHSM Consultants 1992–96; chm Lewisham and North Southwark Health Authy 1991–93, memb Ed Advsy Bd Health Serv Jl 1992–95, chm SE London Health Authy 1991–96, chm SE London Health Cmmn (later Authy) 1993–96, chm N Thames NHS 1996–; dir Blackheath Preservation Tst 1990–, memb Cncl of Mgmnt St Christopher's Hospice 1993–, tstee SE London Community Fndn 1995–; FCA 1960, FIMC 1964, MHSM 1985; *Clubs* Royal Commonwealth, Royal Soc of Arts; *Style*— Ian Mills, Esq; ✉ 60 Belmont Hill, London SE13 5DN (☎ 0181 852 2457); North Thames NHS Executive, Department of Health, 40 Eastbourne Terrace, London W2 3QR (☎ 0171 725 5300, fax 0171 258 0530)

MILLS, Prof Ian Mark; s of John Mills (d 1972), of Streatley, Berks, and Marguerita Alice Gertrude, *née* Gooding (d 1977); *b* 9 June 1930; *Educ* Leighton Park Sch Reading, Univ of Reading, Univ of Oxford; *m* 23 Aug 1957, Margaret Mary, da of Prof Julian Lewis Maynard (d 1954), of Univ of Minnesota; 1 s (William b 1960), 1 da (Jane b 1962); *Career* res fell: Univ of Minnesota 1954–56, Corpus Christi Coll Cambridge 1956–57; lectr, reader then prof Univ of Reading 1957–; memb Faraday Div Royal Soc of Chem, FRS 1996; *Books* Quantities, Units & Symbols in Physical Chemistry (1988 and 1993); *Recreations* walking, sailing; *Style*— Prof Ian Mills, FRS; ✉ Department of Chemistry, University of Reading, Berks RG6 2AD (☎ 0118 931 8456, fax 0118 931 1610, telex 847813)

MILLS, John Frederick; s of Henry Alfred Mills (d 1973), and Jean Margaret Aitchison; *b* 6 Sept 1950; *Educ* Highgate Sch, The Queen's Coll Oxford, Merton Coll Oxford (Domus sr scholar, BLitt, MA); *m* 1974, Jean Marie, da of Aloysius Theodore Correia; 1 s (Theodore b 1978), 3 da (Julia b 1980, Cecily b 1983, Claudia b 1983); *Career* DTI 1974–: private sec to Min of State for Indust 1976–78, princ 1978–81, seconded as princ asst sec Govt of Hong Kong 1981–85, asst sec and head of Int Telecommunications Policy Branch 1986–89, memb PM's Policy Unit 1989–92, under sec and dir of Consumer Affairs Office of Fair Trading 1992–95; chief exec Cornwall CC 1995–; govr Highgate Sch 1993–; *Style*— John Mills, Esq; ✉ Cornwall County Council, County Hall, Truro TR1 3AY (☎ 01872 322100, fax 01872 323836)

MILLS, John Glenton; JP (Liverpool 1976); s of Gwilym Eiriol Mills (d 1971), and Adelaide, *née* Glenton (d 1954); *b* 7 Oct 1925; *Educ* Windermere GS, RAF Tech Coll, Coll of the Fylde; *m* 6 Sept 1952, Beryl Edith, da of Edward Pope; 3 da (Judith b 1954, Sally b 1956, Jennifer b 1958), 1 s (Andrew b 1960); *Career* serv RAF 1943–47, student art coll 1948–50, head John Mills Photography 1955– (joined family business 1950); BIPP: memb 1949, assoc 1952, elected to Cncl 1960, pres 1966, hon fell 1993; chm Liverpool Round Table 1967, chm Birkenhead Abbey Field Soc (care for the elderly) 1984–; *Recreations* carpentry, photography, sailing; *Clubs* Athenaeum (Liverpool), A1, Trearddur Bay Sailing (flagstaff offr 1984–96); *Style*— John G Mills, Esq, JP, Hon FBIPP; ✉ John Mills Photography Ltd, 11 Hope Street, Liverpool, Merseyside L1 9BJ (☎ 0151 709 9822, fax 0151 709 6585)

MILLS, Sir John Lewis Ernest Watts; kt (1976), CBE (1960); *b* 22 Feb 1908; *Educ* Norwich; *m* 1941, Mary Hayley Bell, playwright; 1 s, 2 da; *Career* actor (won Academy Award Oscar 1971 as best supporting actor, for his part in Ryan's Daughter), prodr, dir; recent work incl: Harnessing Peacocks (ITV) 1993; memb Cncl of RADA 1965–, chm of the Stars Organisation for Spastics for 3 yrs, pres Mountview Theatre Sch; *Books* Up in the Clouds, Gentlemen Please (autobiography); *Recreations* golf, painting; *Clubs* Garrick, St James's (chm); *Style*— Sir John Mills, CBE; ✉ c/o ICM Ltd, Oxford House, 76 Oxford Street, London W1N 0AX (☎ 0171 636 6565, fax 0171 323 0101)

MILLS, John Micklethwait; OBE (1989), TD, DL (Hants 1970); s of Col Sir John Digby Mills, TD (d 1972), and Carola Marshall, *née* Tuck; *b* 29 Nov 1919; *Educ* Eton, Ch Ch Oxford (MA); *m* 2 Nov 1960, Mrs Prudence Mercy Emmeline Cooper-Key, da of Sir Ronald Wilfred Matthews (d 1959); 1 s (John b 1961); *Career* WWII 2 Lt Hampshire Regt 1939, 7 Commando Bardia and Crete (wounded), Warwicks Yeo ME and Italy, Capt 1943, Maj 1945; dep chm Bournemouth and West Hants Water Co (formerly W Hants and Bournemouth Water Cos, dir 1948–), appointed by Miny of Agric to Avon and Dorset River Bd 1959–63, dep chm Avon and Dorset River Authy 1963–74; Wessex Water Authy: chm Quality Advsy Panel 1974–83, chm Regnl Fishery Ctee 1974–89, Pollution Control Ctee 1988–89; Nat Rivers Authy (Wessex) 1989–90; High Sheriff Hants 1958, memb Ringwood RDC 1968–74, JP 1948–88 (chm Ringwood Bench 1979–84); Verderer of the New Forest 1960–64, pres Hampshire Branch CLA 1982–87 (chm 1967–70), fndr memb Timber Growers Orgn 1960 (chm Southern Region 1960–65); ARICS 1948; *Recreations* shooting, fishing; *Clubs* White's, MCC; *Style*— John Mills, Esq, OBE, TD, DL; ✉ Bisterne Manor, nr Ringwood, Hampshire BH24 3BN (☎ 01425 474246); 69 Porchester Terr, London W2

MILLS, Leif Anthony; CBE (1995); s of Victor William Mills (d 1967), and Bergliot, *née* Ström-Olsen (d 1989); *b* 25 March 1936; *Educ* Kingston GS, Balliol Coll Oxford (MA); *m* 2 Aug 1958, Gillian Margaret, da of William Henry Smith (d 1966); 2 s (Adam, Nathanial), 2 da (Susannah, Harriet); *Career* 2 Lt RMP 1957–59; Nat Union of Bank Employees (now Banking Insur and Fin Union) 1960–96: res offr 1960–62, asst gen sec 1962–68, dep gen sec 1968–72, gen sec 1972–96; Parly candidate (Lab): Salisbury gen election 1964, Salisbury by-election 1965; TUC: memb Non Manual Workers Advsy Ctee

1967–72, memb Gen Cncl 1983–, chm Fin Servs Ctee 1983, chm Educn and Trg Ctee 1989–, pres TUC 1994–95; memb: Manpower Econs Advsy Ctee on Equal Pay 1971, Ctee to Review the Functioning of Fin Instns (Wilson Ctee) 1977–80, Civil Serv Pay Res Unit Bd 1978–81, BBC Consultative Gp on Social Effects of TV 1978–80, Armed Forces Pay Review Body 1980–87, Monopolies and Mergers Cmmn 1982–91, Ctees TUC, Int Ctees FIET, Fin Reporting Cncl 1990–96, Nat Cncl for Vocational Qualifications 1992–96, Investors in People UK 1993–96, PIA Ombudsman Cncl 1994–, Cncl Consumers Assoc 1996–; tstee Civic Tst 1989–96, govr London Business Sch 1989–92, hon sec St John the Baptist PCC West Byfleet 1990–94; *Recreations* rowing, chess; *Clubs* United Oxford and Cambridge Univ, Weybridge Rowing; *Style*— Leif Mills, Esq, CBE; ✉ 31 Station Rd, West Byfleet, Surrey (☎ 019323 42829)

MILLS, Dr (John Owen) Manton; s of Rev Minnis Mills (d 1982), of Belfast, and Gladys Nora, *née* Streeter; *b* 17 May 1940; *Educ* The Methodist Coll Belfast, Queen's Univ Belfast (MB BCH, BAO); *m* 1, 16 Aug 1966 (m dis 1978), Elizabeth, da of Thomas Richardson (d 1965), of Belfast; 3 da (Catherine b 29 Aug 1967, Jennifer b 20 June 1969, Victoria b 28 June 1970); m 2, 5 March 1982, Anna, da of Dennis John McCormack, of London; 2 s (Christopher b 14 June 1983, David b 12 Dec 1985); *Career* conslt radiologist 1973–; dir Dept of Radiological Sciences Royal Brisbane Hosp Australia 1978–79, hon sec Royal Victoria Hosp Med Staff Ctee 1988–90, clinical dir of radiology Royal Gp of Hosps Belfast 1989–92; pres Ulster Radiological Soc 1986–87, memb Queensland Med Soc Aust and NI Medico-Legal Soc, hon fell Nova Scotia Assoc of Radiologists 1987; DRCOG 1966, DMRD 1971, FFR 1973, FRCR 1975; *Books* Accident and Emergency Medicine (1980, 2nd edn 1989), Trauma Care (contrib, 1981), Surgery of the Gut and Pancreas (contrib, 1985), Textbook of Radiological Diagnosis (contrib, 1988); *Recreations* gardening, reading; *Style*— Dr Manton Mills; ✉ Royal Victoria Hospital, Grosvenor Rd, Belfast (☎ 01232 240503)

MILLS, Michael Victor Leighton; s and h of Sir Peter Frederick Leighton Mills, 3 Bt; *b* 30 Aug 1957; *m* 29 Aug 1981, Susan; *Style*— Michael Mills, Esq

MILLS, Neil McLay; s of Leslie Hugh Mills (d 1980), and Gwladys Mills (d 1982); *b* 29 July 1923; *Educ* Epsom Coll, Univ Coll London; *m* 1950, Rosamond Mary, da of the late Col and Hon Mrs A C W Kimpton, of Pythouse, Tisbury, Wilts; 2 s, 2 da; *Career* served WWII Lt RNVR (despatches 1944); underwriting memb of Lloyd's 1955–91; chm: Bland Welch & Co 1965–74, Bland Payne Holdings 1974–79, Sedgwick Forbes Bland Payne 1979–80, Sedgwick Group plc 1980–84; dir: Midland Bank Ltd 1974–79, Wadlowgrosvenor International Ltd 1984–88, Thread-Needle Publishing Group plc 1986–94; memb Cncl Oak Hill Theological Coll 1958–62, vice pres Insur Inst of London 1971–84, tstee and govr Lord Mayor Treloar Tst 1975–81; *Recreations* farming, cooking, mowing; *Clubs* Pilgrims; *Style*— Neil McLay Mills, Esq; ✉ The Dower House, Upton Grey, nr Basingstoke, Hants (☎ 01256 862435, fax 01256 862642); 23 Bury Walk, London SW3 (☎ 0171 823 9636)

MILLS, Nigel Gordon; *b* 14 April 1955; *Career* ABN AMRO Hoare Govett (formerly Hoare Govett Ltd): joined as food mfrg sector investmt analyst 1978, dir 1985–, joined Corp Fin Dept 1986, md ABN AMRO Hoare Govett Corporate Finance 1994–; *Style*— Nigel Mills, Esq; ✉ ABN AMRO Hoare Govett, 4 Broadgate, London EC2M 7LE (☎ 0171 601 0101)

MILLS, Richard Michael; s of Richard Henry Mills (d 1979), of Surbiton, Surrey, and Catherine, *née* Keeley; *b* 26 June 1931; *m* 1, Feb 1960 (m dis 1967), Lynda, da of Charles Taylor; 1 da (Janey b 1960); m 2, 8 Aug 1983, Sheila Susan, da of James White (d 1986); 2 s (Matthew b 1986, Christopher b 1988); *Career* theatrical producer and manager; Nat Serv RAF 1949–51; asst stage mangr 1948: worked in every capacity in the theatre, incl acting and stage mgmnt; Bernard Delfont Ltd: joined 1962, dir 1967–, dep chm and chief exec 1970–, chm and chief exec 1979; md: Prince of Wales Theatre 1970–, Prince Edward Theatre 1978–; chm and chief exec Bernard Delfont Theatres Ltd (now Delfont Mackintosh Theatres Ltd) 1991–; exec dir First Leisure Corporation PLC 1982–94; memb: NT Bd 1976–91 (memb Finance and Gen Purposes Ctee 1976–91), Drama Panel Arts Cncl 1976–77, English Tourist Bd 1982–85; *Productions* over 100 West End shows worked on 1948–72; thereafter co-presented with Lord Delfont: The Good Old Bad Old Days, Mardi Gras, Brief Lives, Queen Daniella, Cinderella, Henry IV, Harvey, Sammy Cahn's Songbook, A Streetcar Named Desire, Good Companions, It's All Right If I Do It, Charley's Aunt, An Evening with Tommy Steele, Gomes, The Wolf, Danny La Rue Show, Beyond the Rainbow, Dad's Army, Plumber's Progress, Paul Daniels Magic Show, Underneath the Arches, Little Me, over 100 pantomimes and summer seasons; *Recreations* golf, poker; *Clubs* RAC, Coombe Hill Golf, Royal Mid-Surrey Golf; *Style*— Richard M Mills, Esq; ✉ Delfont Mackintosh Theatres Ltd, Prince of Wales Theatre, Coventry St, London W1V 8AS (☎ 0171 930 9901, fax 0171 930 8970)

MILLS, Robert Ferris (Roy); s of Robert Mills (d 1963), of Belfast, and Rachel Annie, *née* Ballantine (d 1993); *b* 21 Sept 1939; *Educ* Sullivan Upper Sch Holywood Co Down, The Queen's Univ Belfast (BA); *m* 1, 1968 (m dis 1978), Irene Sandra, *née* Miskelly; 1 s (Christopher Sinclair b 5 April 1970), 1 da (Carolyn Lesley b 27 April 1972); m 2, 29 Sept 1984, (Frances) Elizabeth, *née* Moore; 2 step da (Deborah, Vanessa); *Career* trainee tax inspr Inland Revenue London 1961–64, asst princ Miny of Commerce NI 1964–67 (incl 18 months as private sec to Min of Commerce, Rt Hon Brian Faulkner, DL, MP), dep princ (Housing) Miny of Devpt NI 1967–70, princ (Transportation) DOE NI 1970–74, asst sec (Policy & Planning) Dept of Health & Social Servs NI 1975–83, under sec (Social Security) Dept of Health & Social Servs NI 1983–90, under sec (Public Expenditure) Dept of Fin & Personnel 1990–96 (ret); *Recreations* golf, tennis, travel, television, gardening; *Clubs* Helen's Bay Golf, Hawarden Tennis; *Style*— Roy Mills; ✉ Linden, 103 Circular Road, Belfast, Northern Ireland BT4 2GD (☎ 01232 768221)

MILLS, Russell Thomas; s of Sqdn Ldr Harry Wyndham Mills, DFM, RAF, ret, of Bowir Farm, Llantwit Major, S Glamorgan, and Mary, *née* Jeyes; *b* 22 Nov 1952; *Educ* Royal Alexandra & Albert Sch Reigate, Canterbury Coll of Art, Maidstone Coll of Art (BA), Royal Coll of Art (MA, travelling scholarship Berlin, Berger award); *m* 17 Aug 1974, Ann Elizabeth, *née* Symes; 1 s (Samuel Asher b 4 Aug 1992); *Career* artist; individual exhibitions: Fine Lines (The Thumb Gallery) 1980, ...returns an echo (Curwen Gallery and tour) 1983, Ciphers (Curwen Gallery and Metropole Arts Centre Folkestone) 1986, Enter the Silences (Parco Space 5 Tokyo) 1987, Silent Systems (Curwen Gallery) 1989, Planet and Glow-Worm (Visual Arts Museum NY) 1989, Sixteen Shimmers (Parco Space 5 Tokyo and Kirin Plaza Osaka) 1990, Within Without (Huntington Gallery Boston) 1991, The Possible Slow Fuse (Pentagram Gallery London) 1995, RSC Works (RSC Stratford-upon-Avon and Barbican) 1995; two-person exhibitions: Ember Glance (with David Sylvian, Tokyo) 1990, Earth Murmurs (with Ian Walton, Curwen Gallery) 1992, Ember Glance (installation with Ian Walton & David Sylvian, Architectural Assoc London) 1993, Between Two Lights (installation with Ian Walton, Charlotte Mason Coll Ambleside Cumbria as pt of Ambleside Mountain Festival) 1994, MW Undark (exhbn with Ian Walton, Zeffirellis Ambleside Cumbria) 1994, Soundings: Sub Rosa (installation with Ian Walton and Hywel Davies Green Park Station Bath as pt of Bath Festival) 1995, Measured in Shadows (installation with Ian Walton, Tullic House Museum and AA Gallery Carlisle 1996 and Guinness Hopstone Dublin 1997), Looming (with Ian Walton, Eagle Gallery London) 1996; group exhibitions incl: Cyprus Summer School 1972, Geek Work (Air Gallery and Greenwich Theatre Art Gallery) 1977, Contemporary British Illustrators (Belgrave Gallery) 1978, Shoes (Neal St Gallery) 1979, Five English Artists (Galerie Mokum Amsterdam) 1979, Summer Reflections (Thumb Gallery) 1981, Hayward Annual (Hayward Gallery) 1982, Images for Today (Graves Art Gallery Sheffield) 1982, Britain Salutes New York (Brooklyn Museum of Modern Art NY) 1983, Out of Line (ICA) 1985, Ambit (Royal Festival Hall) 1985, Interaction (Camden Arts Centre) 1986, Critical Lines (Talbot Rice Gallery Edinburgh and Watershed Bristol) 1986, Art Meets Science (Smith's Gallery) 1986, Faber Artists (Cartoon Gallery) 1986, New British Design (Japan) 1987, Sydney Biennale (Art Gallery of NSW and Nat Gallery of Victoria) 1987 and 1988, Doobraak (Berlage Amsterdam) 1989, Pictures of Rock (Euro tour) 1990–91, The Art of Selling Songs (V & A) 1991, Art and Science (Plymouth City Museum and Art Gallery) 1991, Shelf Life (The Eagle Gallery London) 1994, Little Pieces from Big Stars (Flowers East Gallery London) 1994, Fuse (RCA) 1994, The Artists Bookfair Royal Festival Hall (with The Eagle Gallery London) 1995; numerous RCA and Curwen Gallery exhibitions; work in collections of: Br Cncl, Br Museum, Kent CC, Reuters, V & A, Tate Gallery; numerous cmmns from co's incl: Chatto & Windus Publishers, Decca Records, Polydor Records, Virgin Records, The Face, Harpers & Queen, The Sunday Times, Telegraph Magazine, Vogue; TV and Radio appearances incl: London Weekend Show (ITV) 1977, Arena - Double Vision (BBC2) 1980, People's Radio (Washington USA) 1986, Spanish Nat TV 1989, Fuji TV (Tokyo Japan) and Japanese Nat TV 1990; lectr at numerous colls, polys and schs of art throughout Britain and USA; International Editorial Design Three Award of Excellence 1983, D&AD Silver award 1984, Diamond Record Cover award (with Dave Coppenhall) Diamond Awards Festival Antwerp Belgium 1989; *Recreations* music, reading, contemplating natural phenomena; *Clubs* Bull Terrier; *Style*— Russell Mills; ✉ Loughrigg Holme, Under Loughrigg, Ambleside, Cumbria LA22 9LN (☎ and fax 015394 31278)

MILLS, (William) Stratton; s of John Victor Stratton Mills, CBE (d 1964), of Belfast, and Margaret Florence, *née* Byford (d 1992); *b* 1 July 1932; *Educ* Campbell Coll Belfast, Queen's Univ Belfast (LLB); *m* 7 Aug 1959, Merriel Eleanor Ria, da of Robert James Whitla (d 1981), of Belfast; 3 s (Jeremy Victor b 3 Aug 1966, Rupert James b 5 March 1968, Angus William b 23 Nov 1971); *Career* admitted slr NI 1958, ptnr Mills Selig Solicitors Belfast 1959–, chm Hampden Group plc 1992–, dir various private companies; MP (Unionist & Cons) Belfast North 1959–74 (ret), PPS to Parly Sec Miny of Tport 1961–64, chm Cons Pty Broadleaf Ctee 1970–73; memb: Estimates Ctee 1964–70, Exec Ctee 1922 Ctee of Cons Pty 1967–70 and 1973, One Nation Gp 1972–73; chm Ulster Orchestra Soc Ltd 1980–90; winner Arnold Goodman award (for encouragement of business sponsorship in the Arts) 1990; memb Cncl Winston Churchill Meml Tst 1990–95; *Recreations* golf, gardening; *Clubs* Carlton, Reform (Belfast); *Style*— Stratton Mills, Esq; ✉ 20 Callender St, Belfast (☎ 01232 243878, fax 01232 231956)

MILLS, William; s of William Frederick Mills (d 1963), of Blackheath, London, and Ada Maud, *née* East (d 1984); *b* 7 July 1938; *Educ* Sutton Valence; *m* 27 Feb 1965, Pamela Anne, da of Stanley Gilbert Dean; 1 s (James William b 11 July 1974), 2 da (Melissa Jane b 17 May 1970, Kate Emma b 24 Jan 1972); *Career* RE 1957–59; Prudential Assurance: taxation mangr 1977–80, controller 1980–84, chief accountant 1984–85, gp chief accountant Prudential Corporation 1985–89; md: Prudential Mortgage Co 1989–92, Mills Jones Consultants 1993–; memb Cncl ACCA 1991; Freeman: City of London, Worshipful Co of Painters and Stainers (treas); FCCA 1973; *Recreations* travel, opera, modern first editions; *Style*— William Mills, Esq; ✉ Sunbury, Foxhole Lane, Matfield, Tonbridge, Kent (☎ 01892 723464)

MILLWARD, Edwina Carole (Mrs David Bicker); da of Eric Millward, and Frances Morris, *née* Norton; *b* 20 Sept 1943; *Educ* Thornes House Sch Wakefield, Ilkley Coll of Housecraft, Univ of London (LLB); *m* 11 Nov 1972, David Charles Bicker, s of Arthur Charles Bicker; *Career* teacher 1965–67; admitted slr 1972; appointed by Lord Chllr to sit as dist judge in Co Court and Dist Registry High Court 1995; nat pres UK Fedn of Business and Professional Women 1985–87, pres Kent Law Soc 1994–95 (memb 1968–); FRSA; *Recreations* acting, swimming, needlework; *Style*— District Judge Edwina Millward; ✉ Bromley County Court, College Road, Bromley, BR1 3PX

MILLWARD, Dr Neil; s of Haydn Millward (d 1988), of Abergavenny, and Lilian Audrey, *née* Powley (d 1994); *b* 14 March 1942; *Educ* Queen Elizabeth's Sch Crediton Devon, Univ of Bristol (BSc), Univ of Manchester (PhD); *m* 28 Oct 1972, Pamela Hilary Marion, da of Maj Gilbert Hanley Thorp (d 1984), of Coates, W Sussex; 2 s (Piers b 1975, Christian b 1977); *Career* engr GEC Ltd 1964–66, res fell Univ of Manchester 1966–68, visiting scholar Harvard Business Sch 1968–69, res fell Manchester Business Sch 1969–73, industl rels offr Pay Bd 1973–74, princ res offr Dept of Employment 1974–89, sr fell Policy Studies Inst 1989–; *Books* Workplace Industrial Relations in Britain (with W W Daniel, 1983), British Workplace Industrial Relations 1980–1984 (with M Stevens, 1986), Workplace Industrial Relations in Transition (with M Stevens, D Smart and W R Hawes, 1992), The New Industrial Relations? (1994); *Recreations* sailing, crafts, music; *Clubs* Royal Ocean Racing; *Style*— Dr Neil Millward; ✉ 13 Mercers Rd, London N19 4PH (☎ 0171 281 2674); Policy Studies Inst, 100 Park Village East, London NW1 3SR (☎ 0171 468 2228)

MILLWATER, Dennis Curtis; s of William Milson Millwater (d 1974), of Rogerstone, Gwent, and Kathleen Irene Millwater (d 1969); *b* 31 March 1934; *Educ* Bassaleg GS Gwent, Univ of Bristol; *m* 5 Aug 1957, Marlene Beatrice, da of Kenneth Collins, of Cliffs End, Ramsgate; 3 s (Christopher b 26 April 1961, Grahame b 28 April 1963, Jonathan b 23 Aug 1967, d 1989), 1 da (Sara b 20 July 1977); *Career* pensions supt Northern Assurance Co Ltd 1957–68, pensions controller Commercial Union Group 1968–69, dir De Falbe Halsey Ltd 1969–71; gp dir: H Clarkson (Insurance Holdings) Ltd 1971–81, Clarkson Puckle Group Ltd 1981–87, Bain Clarkson Ltd 1987–94; chm Bain Clarkson (Financial Services) Ltd 1987–94; *Recreations* golf, music, cycling; *Style*— Dennis Millwater, Esq; ✉ Hall Barn, Preston St Mary, Nr Lavenham, Sudbury, Suffolk CO10 9NQ (☎ 01787 248215)

MILMAN, David Patrick; er s and h of Lt-Col Sir Derek Milman, 9 Bt, MC, *qv*; *b* 24 Aug 1945; *Educ* Univ of London (BEd, MA); *m* 1969, Christina, da of John William Hunt; 1 s (Thomas Hart b 1976), 1 da (Katharine Jane b 1975); *Career* headteacher 1981, asst dir Sch Mgmnt South 1989, sr area advsr NW Kent 1993 (area advsr 1991); *Books* Take a Look (1974/75), What Do You Think (1977), Senior Managers Personal Profile: Management Portfolio (jtly, 1991); *Style*— David Milman, Esq; ✉ 71 Camden Rd, Sevenoaks, Kent

MILMAN, Lt-Col Sir Derek; 9 Bt (GB 1800), of Levaton-in-Woodland, Devonshire; MC; 3 and yst s of Brig-Gen Sir Lionel Charles Patrick Milman, 7 Bt, CMG (d 1962), and Marjorie Aletta, *née* Clark-Kennedy (d 1980); suc his bro, Sir Dermot Lionel Kennedy Milman, 8 Bt (d 1990); *b* 23 June 1918; *Educ* Bedford Sch; *m* 1942, Christine, da of Alfred Whitehouse, of Sutton Coldfield; 2 s (David Patrick b 1945, Terence Martin b 1947); *Heir* s, David Patrick Milman (*qv*); *Career* Lt-Col (ret) 3 E Anglian Regt, formerly Pakistan Army and GSO Lahore Divn, served WWII with 5 Indian Divn in Middle East; *Style*— Lt-Col Sir Derek Milman, Bt, MC; ✉ Forge Cottage, Wilby Rd, Stradbroke, Suffolk IP21 5JN

MILMO, John Boyle; QC (1984); s of Dermod Hubert Francis Milmo (d 1973), and Eileen Clare, *née* White (d 1994); *b* 19 Jan 1943; *Educ* Downside Sch, Univ of Dublin (MA, LLB); *Career* called to the Bar Lincoln's Inn 1966, bencher 1992, recorder of the Crown Ct 1982–, head of chambers; memb Gen Cncl of the Bar 1992–; *Clubs* Utd Services (Nottingham); *Style*— John Milmo, Esq, QC; ✉ No 1 High Pavement, Nottingham NG1 1HF (☎ 0115 941 8218, fax 0115 941 8240)

MILNE, Alasdair David Gordon; s of Charles Milne, surgeon, by his w Edith; *b* 8 Oct 1930, in Cawnpore; *Educ* Winchester, New Coll Oxford; *m* 1954, Sheila Kirsten Graucob (d 1992); 2 s (Ruairidh, Seumas), 1 da (Kirsty); *Career* served in Gordon Highlanders; joined BBC as gen trainee 1954, with BBC TV Current Affairs 1955–57, dep ed Tonight 1957–61, ed 1961–62, head Tonight Productions 1963–65; left BBC to become ptnr Jay Baverstock Milne & Co (freelance TV film producers) 1965–67 and ran This Week for Rediffusion TV; controller BBC Scotland 1968–72, dir of programmes BBC TV 1973–77, md BBC TV 1977–82, dep dir-gen BBC 1980–82, dir-gen BBC 1982–87; Hon DUniv Stirling 1983, hon fell New Coll Oxford; *Style*— Alasdair Milne, Esq; ✉ 30 Holland Park Ave, London W11 3QU

MILNE, David Alistair; s of Peter Barry Milne, of Edinburgh, and Una Mary, *née* Horton; *b* 29 Aug 1952; *Educ* Malvern, Pembroke Coll Oxford (MA); *m* 30 Aug 1975, Clare Eveline Agatha, da of Maj Peter Howard Crassweller, of Edinburgh; 1 s (Andrew b 11 March 1983), 1 da (Nicola b 26 July 1979); *Career* Nippon Credit Bank 1974–77, dir Guinness Mahon and Co Ltd 1977–87, dir and head of capital markets British and Commonwealth Merchant Bank 1987–91, md Structured Finance Baltic plc 1992–93, dir MTM Partnership 1993–94, md Cedef Structured Finance Ltd 1994–; MCIB; *Recreations* tennis, bridge, theatre, ballet; *Clubs* Roehampton; *Style*— David Milne, Esq; ✉ 35 York Ave, London SW14 7LQ; Cedef Structured Finance Ltd, 100 Piccadilly, London W1V 9FN (☎ 0171 629 1944)

MILNE, David Calder; QC (1987); s of Ernest Ferguson Milne, OBE (d 1995), of Walton Heath, Surrey, and Helena Mary, *née* Harkness; *b* 22 Sept 1945; *Educ* Harrow, Univ of Oxford (MA); *m* 26 May 1978, Rosemary Ann, da of Frederick Bond (d 1979); 1 da (Bryony b 1980); *Career* CA 1969; articled to Whinney Murray & Co CAs 1966–69, called to the Bar Lincoln's Inn 1970, recorder 1994–; FCA (1974); *Recreations* natural history, music, golf, rugby football; *Clubs* Garrick, Hurlingham, Gnomes, Walton Heath Golf; *Style*— David Milne, Esq, QC; ✉ Pump Court Tax Chambers, 16 Bedford Row, London WC1R 4EB (☎ 0171 414 8080, fax 0171 414 8099)

MILNE, David Lee; *b* 10 Sept 1936; *Educ* Bedford Sch; *m*; 1 s (b 1962), 1 da (b 1966); *Career* trainee accountant Mann Judd & Co London 1954–60, Nat Serv as 2 Lt 29 Commando Regt RA 1960–62, asst accountant London Merchant Securities Ltd 1963–64, chief accountant Lynton Holdings Ltd 1964–66, internal conslt STC Ltd 1966–67, md Masoneilan Ltd (subsid of Studebaker-Worthington Group Inc) 1969–73 (fin dir 1968–69), gp fin dir Wilmot Breeden (Holdings) Ltd (automotive products and electronics mfrs) 1975–79 (md subsid Truflo Ltd 1973–75), gp fin dir Glynwed International plc 1979–96; MICAS 1960; *Style*— David Milne, Esq

MILNE, Hon George Alexander; s and h of 2 Baron Milne, *qv*; *b* 1 April 1941; *Educ* Winchester; *Career* Liveryman Worshipful Co of Grocers; *Style*— The Hon George Milne; ✉ 188 Broom Rd, Teddington, Middx (☎ 0181 977 9761)

MILNE, 2 Baron (UK 1933); George Douglass Milne; TD; s of Field Marshal 1 Baron Milne, GCB, GCMG, DSO (d 1948); *b* 10 Feb 1909; *Educ* Winchester, New Coll Oxford; *m* 2 April 1940, Cicely, 3 da of Ronald Leslie; 2 s, 1 da; *Heir* s, Hon George Alexander Milne, *qv*; *Career* Maj (TA) 1940; WWII 1939–45, NWEF, MEF, POW; CA; ptnr Arthur Young McClelland Moores 1954–73, dep chm London & Northern Gp 1973–87; Master Worshipful Co of Grocers 1961–62 (sr memb 1984–90); MICAS; *Style*— The Rt Hon the Lord Milne; ✉ 33 Lonsdale Rd, Barnes, London SW13 9JP (☎ 0181 748 6421)

MILNE, Prof Gordon Stewart; s of Arthur Milne, OBE (d 1984), of Edinburgh, and Thomasina, *née* Gilroy; *b* 1 Oct 1936; *Educ* Royal HS of Edinburgh, Leith Nautical Coll, Heriot-Watt Coll Edinburgh, Coll of Estate Mgmnt London; *m* 15 Oct 1961, Kathleen Mary; 2 s (Rhoderic Michael Stuart b 12 Feb 1965, Hector Arthur Stuart b 12 July 1966); *Career* local dir Guardian Royal Exchange Assurance 1979–92, md Scottish Metropolitan Property plc 1986–92 (dir 1969–92); memb Clyde Port Authy 1989–93; currently hon prof in land economy Univ of Aberdeen (visiting prof of land economy 1992–95); vice pres Edinburgh Jr C of C 1968–69, DG Euro Conf of Jr C of C 1972; non-exec dir J F European Utilities Trust PLC; memb NEDC Scot Strategy Planning Ctee 1974–76, former memb Exec Scot Devpt and Indust; chm: The European Urban Inst, Local Govt Property Cmmn (Scotland) 1995–; dep chm Sec of State for Scot Valuation and Rating Cncl 1996–; memb: Livingston Devpt Corp, Capital Advsy Ctee Scottish Higher Educn Funding Cncl 1993–95, Faculty of Advocates Disciplinary Tbnl, Gen Convocation Heriot-Watt Univ; conslt: Royal Incorporation of Architects in Scot, Napier Univ, Br Exec Serv Overseas; FRICS 1964; *Recreations* ornithology, hill walking, swimming, music; *Clubs* New (Edinburgh); *Style*— Prof Gordon S Milne; ✉ 5 Woodhall Rd, Colinton, Edinburgh EH13 0DQ (☎ and fax 0131 441 4814)

MILNE, Sir John Drummond; kt (1986); s of Frederick John Milne and Minnie Elizabeth Milne; *b* 13 Aug 1924; *Educ* Stowe, Trinity Coll Cambridge, RMC Sandhurst; *m* 1948, Joan Akroyd; 2 s, 2 da; *Career* served Coldstream Gds 1943–47; chm: Blue Circle Industries plc until 1990, DRG plc until 1989, Alfred McAlpine plc 1992–96; dir: Royal Insurance plc until 1995, Avon Rubber plc until 1995, Witan Investment Co plc until 1996, Solvay SA until 1996; *Recreations* golf, shooting; *Clubs* Boodle's, MCC, Berkshire Golf; *Style*— Sir John Milne; ✉ 84 Eccleston Sq, London SW1V 1PX (☎ 0171 828 3456, telex 927757 BC LDN G)

MILNE, John Duff; s of Alexander Keen Milne, of Dundee, and Margaret Harrow, *née* Duff; *b* 13 May 1942; *Educ* Harris Acad Dundee; *m* 29 March 1967, Jennifer Frances, da of Robert Lewis Brown (d 1989), of Dundee; 2 s (Grigor b 1970, Jonathan b 1973); *Career* newspaper sub ed D C Thomson Dundee 1959–63, newspaper sub ed and feature writer The Scotsman Edinburgh 1963–67, news ed Swiss Broadcasting Corp Bern 1967–71, presenter and reporter BBC Scotland 1971–; *Recreations* sport, music; *Style*— John Milne, Esq; ✉ BBC Broadcasting House, Queen Margaret Drive, Glasgow G12 8DG (☎ 0141 338 2676)

MILNE, John Frederick; s of Alexander Milne, of Essex, and Sheila, *née* Levett; *b* 20 Sept 1952; *Educ* St Joseph's Acad Blackheath, Chelsea Sch of Art, Ravensbourne Coll of Art (BA); *m* 1983, Sarah Letitia Beresford, da of Gp Capt H B Verity, DSO, DFC; 2 s (Alexander b 1983, Hugh b 1985); *Career* novelist; *Awards* John Llewelyn Rhys Prize 1985, Writers' Guild Award for Best Drama Serial 1992; *Books* incl: Tyro 1982, London Fields 1983, Out of The Blue 1985 (John Llewelyn Rhys Prize 1986), Wet Wickets and Dusty Balls 1986, Dead Birds 1986, Shadow Play 1987, Daddy's Girl 1988; *Television* scriptwriter on series incl: The Bill, Bergerac, Boon, Perfect Scoundrels, Eastenders, Taggart, Sam Saturday, Crime Story, Lovejoy, Pie in the Sky, Silent Witness; *Recreations* bricolage; *Style*— John Milne, Esq; ✉ c/o The Agency, 24 Pottery Lane, London W11 4LZ (☎ 0171 727 1346, fax 0171 727 9037)

MILNE, Dr Kenneth; OBE (1975); s of Samuel Baxter Milne (d 1978), and Sarah Elizabeth, *née* Birkett (d 1969); *b* 16 Nov 1925; *Educ* Royal GS Newcastle upon Tyne, Rugby Coll Technol & Arts, Univ of London (external, BScEng, PhD); *m* 1949, Audrey Isobel, da of Charles Edward Theodore Nelsey; *Career* BTH Co Ltd Rugby: engrg apprentice 1941–46, engr 1946–50, radar system designer 1950–60; Plessey Radar Ltd Cowes: radar system designer 1960–70, engrg mangr 1970–72, dir res 1972–78; ind electronic systems design conslt 1978–, visiting prof UCL 1978–; memb: MOD Def Sci Advsy Cncl 1967–73 and 1986–88, MOD (PE) Electronics Res Cncl 1963–80, NATO Industl Advsy Gp 1970–73, Ctee IEE 1957–79; organiser various confs IEE; Lord Brabazon Prize (Br IRE, 1965), Oliver Lodge Premium (IEE, 1988); FIEE 1969, FEng 1983; *Books* The Handbook of Antenna Design (jt ed, 1983); *Recreations* music; *Style*— Dr Kenneth Milne, OBE, FEng; ✉ 53 Bullimore Grove, Kenilworth, Warwickshire CV8 2QF (☎ 01926 512803)

MILNE, Kenneth Stewart (Kenny); s of Kenneth Grant Sim Milne, of Edinburgh, and Mary Gordon Milne (d 1974); *b* 1 Dec 1961; *Educ* George Heriots Sch, Stevenson Coll, Edinburgh; *m* 4 July 1987, Eleanor Jane, da of Alan Williamson; 1 s (Stuart Alan Kenneth b 28 Nov 1990), 1 da (Jenny Mary b 30 March 1992); *Career* rugby union hooker; clubs: Heriots FP RFC (capt) 1982–, Edinburgh U21, Barbarians RFC; rep: Edinburgh, Scotland B, Scotland A; Scotland: debut v Wales 1989, memb Grand Slam winning team 1990, tour NZ 1990, memb World Cup team 1991 and 1995, 39 caps; memb British Lions' team touring NZ 1993; sales rep Barr Printers Leith; *Recreations* fishing, golf; *Style*— Kenny Milne, Esq

MILNE, Lisa; *Educ* Royal Scottish Acad of Music & Drama; *Career* soprano; contract princ Scottish Opera; roles incl: Coryphée in Alceste, Dew Fairy in Hansel and Gretel, Zerlina in Don Giovanni, Susanna in Le Nozze di Figaro, Giannetta in L'Elisir d'Amore, Ilia in Idomeneo and Adele in Die Fledermaus; *Awards* Scottish Opera John Noble Bursary 1992, Maggie Teyte Prize 1993; *Style*— Ms Lisa Milne; ✉ c/o Lies Askonas Ltd, 6 Henrietta Street, London WC2E 8LA (☎ 0171 379 7700, fax 0171 242 1831)

MILNE, Neil Morrison; s of Brig John Brebner Morrison Milne, OBE, and Marjory, *née* Duncan; *b* 24 June 1951; *Educ* Royal HS Edinburgh, Univ of Edinburgh (MA) Univ of Nottingham (MA); *Career* Butler Till Ltd 1975–78, Standard Life Assurance Co 1978–81, sr mangr Euro Banking Co Ltd, exec dir York Trust Group plc 1984–90, md York Trust Ltd 1990–, md Copernicus Ventures Ltd 1994–; *Recreations* tennis, skiing, reading; *Clubs* RAC; *Style*— Neil M Milne, Esq; ✉ York Trust Ltd, St Paul's House, Park Square, Leeds LS1 2PJ (☎ 0113 246 0132, fax 0113 244 1425)

MILNE, Peter Alexander; s of late Alexander Ogston Milne, and Lilian Winifred, *née* Murray; *b* 23 April 1935; *Educ* Tynemouth Sch, Harwell Reactor Sch, Univ of Durham (BSc), Univ of Newcastle (PhD); *m* 1961, Beatrice Taylor Reid; 2 da; *Career* res asst Univ of Newcastle 1957–60, jr engr Union Castle Steamship 1960–61, tech mangr Wallsend Slipway and Engineering 1961–67 (student apprentice 1951–57), md Swan Hunter Shipbuilders 1974–78 (tech dir 1967–74); British Shipbuilders: md Shipbuilding Ops 1978–81, dir Engrg 1981–84, dir Merchant Shipbuilding and Composite Div 1984–87, dir Ship and Engine Building Div 1987–90; md BMT Cortec Ltd 1990–93, dir Alliance of Maritime Regional Interests in Europe (AMRIE) 1993–96; conslt 1996–; former memb: Cncl Inst of Marine Engrs, Advsy Ctee Sch of Marine Technol Univ of Newcastle; vice pres Ctee EEC Shipbuilders' Assoc 1987–89 (memb 1984–89), past pres and memb Cncl NE Coast Inst of Engrs and Shipbuilders; memb: Bd Lloyd's Register of Shipping 1984–91, Northern Regnl Cncl CBI 1985–, Northern Engrg Centre 1989–94 (chm 1990–94); tstee and memb Devpt Tst Univ of Newcastle upon Tyne 1981; numerous pubns in learned jls; Liveryman Worshipful Co of Shipwrights 1984; CEng, Eur Ing, FIMarE, FIMechE; *Recreations* squash, cricket; *Style*— Peter Milne, Esq; ✉ 14 Woodland Close, Earsdon Village, Whitley Bay, Tyne & Wear NE25 9LL (☎ 0191 252 2708); AMRIE, Northumbria House, Wallsend Research Station, Wallsend, Tyne & Wear NE28 6UY

MILNE ATKINSON, Patricia Wilda (Pat); da of Capt Philip Dennis Fernandes Ferreira (d 1979), and Margaret Cicely, *née* Leman (d 1983); *b* 6 May 1924; *Educ* Overstone Pneu Sch, Midland Agric Coll (now part of Univ of Nottingham) (Dip in Horticulture); *m* 29 July 1950, John Harald Milne Atkinson, s of Capt Harald Milne Atkinson (d 1964); 1 s (Charles John b 7 May 1961), 1 da (Annabelle Jane Milne (Mrs Holland) b 17 March 1955); *Career* landscape architect, principal in own private practice 1954–; specialist areas incl: hosp devpts, industl business parks, redesign of estates, sports centres; memb Cncl Landscape Inst 1984–86, fndr memb E Mids Landscape Chapter, memb Cncl Arboricultural Assoc 1983–; fell Landscape Inst 1958 (assoc 1948), assoc Arboricultural Soc 1982; *Recreations* vintage cars, fishing, gardening; *Style*— Mrs Pat Milne Atkinson; ✉ Hemington House, Hemington, Derby DE74 2RB (☎ 01332 810295)

MILNE-WATSON, Andrew Michael; s and h of Sir Michael Milne-Watson, 3 Bt, CBE; *b* 10 Nov 1944; *Educ* Eton; *m* 1, 1970, Beverley Jane Gabrielle, er da of late Philip Cotton, of Majorca; 1 s (David b 1971), 1 da (Emma b 1974); m 2, 1983, Mrs Gisella Stafford, da of Hans Tisdall, of Cheyne Walk, London; 1 s (Oliver b 1985); *Career* chm: Lewis Broadbent Advertising 1986–88, Minerva Publications Ltd 1988–90, GMW Fabrics 1989–; publishing dir ADR Associates Ltd 1993–; Liveryman Worshipful Co of Grocers; *Style*— Andrew Milne-Watson, Esq; ✉ 22 Musgrave Crescent, London SW6 4QE

MILNE-WATSON, Sir Michael; 3 Bt (UK 1937), of Ashley, Longbredy, Co Dorset, kt (1969), CBE (1953); yr s of Sir David Milne-Watson, 1 Bt, DL, sometime Chief of the Scottish Clans Assoc of London and md and govr of the Gas Light & Coke Co (d 1945); suc bro, Sir Ronald Milne-Watson, 2 Bt, 1982; *b* 16 Feb 1910; *Educ* Eton, Balliol Coll Oxford; *m* 1940, Mary Lisette, da of Harold Carleton Bagnall (d 1993), of Auckland, NZ; 1 s; *Heir* s, Andrew Michael Milne-Watson, *qv*; *Career* Sub-Lt RNVR served 1943–45; Gas Light & Coke Co: joined 1933, md 1945, govr 1946–49; chm N Thames Gas Bd 1949–64; Liveryman Grocers' Co 1947; dir Industrial & Commercial Financial Corp Ltd 1963–80, chm Richard Thomas & Baldwins Ltd 1964–67, dep chm Br Steel Corp 1967–69; dir: Northern Assurance Co Ltd 1960–65, Northern & Employers Assurance Co Ltd 1961–68, Commercial Union Assurance Co 1968–81; chm The William Press Group of Cos 1969–74, pres Cncl of Univ of Reading 1975–80, dir Fin Corp for Industry Ltd 1974–80; govr Br Utd Provident Assoc Ltd 1975 (chm 1976–81); pres: Soc of Br Gas Indust 1970–71, Pipeline Indust Guild 1971–72; govr Nuffield Nursing Homes Tst, chm BUPA 1976–81; Liveryman Worshipful Co of Grocers; *Recreations* fishing, walking; *Clubs* MCC, Leander, Athenaeum; *Style*— Sir Michael Milne-Watson, Bt, CBE; ✉ 39 Cadogan Place, London SW1X 9RX; The Stables, Oakfield, Mortimer, Berks (☎ 0118 983 2200)

MILNER, Prof (Arthur) David; s of Arthur Milner (d 1984), and Sarah-Ellen, *née* Gaunt (d 1965); *b* 16 July 1943; *Educ* Bradford GS, Lincoln Coll Oxford (Open scholar, MA), Inst of Psychiatry (Dip in Psychology, PhD); *m* 24 July 1965, Christine, *née* Armitage; 2 s (Benedict Jon b 28 July 1966, Edward b 5 Oct 1969); *Career* res asst Univ of London 1966–70; Univ of St Andrews: lectr in psychology 1970–82, sr lectr 1982–85, chm Dept of Psychology 1983–88, reader 1985–90, prof 1990–, dean Faculty of Science 1992–94, head Sch of Psychology 1994–; memb: Int Neuropsychological Symposium 1971, Experimental Psychology Soc 1972; FRSE 1992; *Books* The Neuropsychology of Consciousness (with Rugg, 1992), The Visual Brain in Action (with Goodale, 1995); *Recreations* walking, reading, films, jazz; *Style*— Prof A D Milner, FRSE; ✉ School of Psychology, University of St Andrews, St Andrews, Fife KY16 9AJ (☎ 01334 462065, fax 01334 463042)

MILNER, George; *b* 22 Aug 1931; *Educ* St Edmunds Coll, Univ Coll Dublin (MB BCh, BAO, DPM, FRCPsych); *m* 24 Oct 1959, Sheila Mary, *née* Wynne; 2 s (Paul b 2 Aug 1961, Andrew b 3 Dec 1963), 2 da (Gabrielle b 22 March 1960, Caroline b 4 Dec 1962); *Career* sr registrar Manchester Regnl Hosp Bd 1962–66, conslt psychiatrist Worcester Health Dist 1966–96, hon sr lectr Univ of Birmingham 1988–94 (clinical tutor 1979–94), examiner RCPsych and Univ of Birmingham; pt/t locum conslt in substance misuse Worcester Health Dist until 1996; memb: BMA, World Psychiatric Assoc 1988–, Mind, Turningpoint; FRCPsych (fndr memb RCPsych 1972); *Publications* subjects incl: substance misuse, Mental Health Act, Worcester devpt project, general psychiatry;

Recreations golf, music, arts; *Style*— George Milner, Esq; ✉ Acrefield, Norton Close, Worcester WR5 3EY (☎ 01905 353552)

MILNER, Prof John; s of James William Milner, of Derby, and Iris May, *née* Young; *b* 11 June 1946; *Educ* Bemrose GS Derby, Courtauld Inst of Art Univ of London (BA, PhD); *m* 1970, Lesley, da of late Denis Hill Marlow; 3 s (Henry George Marlow b 18 Mar 1971, Edward John b 16 July 1975, Michael James Denis b 21 April 1980); *Career* lectr Bournemouth and Poole Coll of Art and Hornsey Coll of Art London 1968–69; Dept of Fine Art Univ of Newcastle upon Tyne: lectr 1969, sr lectr 1979, reader 1985, head of Dept 1985–91, prof of art history 1992–; dir Hatton Gallery Univ of Newcastle upon Tyne until 1991; memb Assoc of Art Historians; *Awards* Leverhulme fellowship 1985 and 1993; *Books* Symbolists and Decadents (1971), Russian Revolutionary Art (1979), Vladimir Tatlin and the Russian Avant-Garde (1983), The Studios of Paris, the Captial of Art in the Late Nineteenth Century (1988), Mondrian (1992), Dictionary of Russian Artists (1994), Kazimir Malevich and the Art of Geometry (1996); *Recreations* painting; *Style*— Prof John Milner; ✉ Department of Fine Art, University of Newcastle upon Tyne NE1 7RU (☎ 0191 222 7377)

MILNER, Hon Richard James; s and h of 2 Baron Milner of Leeds; *b* 16 May 1959; *Educ* Charterhouse, Univ of Surrey (BSc); *m* 25 June 1988, Margaret Christine, yst da of Gerald Francis Voisin, of Jersey, CI; 2 da (Charlotte Emma b 8 May 1990, Nicola Louise Christine b 3 Feb 1992); *Career* Freeman City of London, Liveryman Worshipful Co of Clothworkers 1988; *Style*— The Hon Richard Milner

MILNER, Prof (Arthur John) Robin Gorell; s of Lt-Col John Theodore Milner, OBE (d 1957), of Tisbury, Wilts, and Muriel Emily, *née* Barnes-Gorell (d 1971); *b* 13 Jan 1934; *Educ* Eton, King's Coll Cambridge (Major scholar, BA); *m* 16 Nov 1963, Lucy Petronella, da of Frewen Moor (d 1984), of East Meon, Hants; 2 s (Gabriel John b 1965, Barnabas Mark b 1966), 1 da (Chloë June b 1968); *Career* Nat Serv 2 Lt RE 1952–54; mathematics teacher Marylebone GS 1959–60, computer programmer Ferranti Ltd 1960–63, mathematics lectr The City Univ London 1963–68; res assoc: in computing theory Univ Coll Swansea 1968–70, in artificial intelligence Stanford Univ Calif 1970–72; Univ of Edinburgh: lectr in computer science 1973–78, reader 1978–84, prof 1984–95; prof Computer Laboratory Univ of Cambridge 1995–; fndr memb Academia Europaea 1988; winner A M Turing Award (ACM) 1991; Hon DSc Chalmers Univ of Technol 1988; FRS, FBCS 1989, FRSE 1993; *Books* Edinburgh LCF (1978), A Calculus A Communicating Systems (1980), Communication and Concurrency (1989), Definition of Standard ML (1990), Commentary on Standard ML (1990); *Recreations* music, carpentry, walking; *Style*— Prof Robin Milner, FRS, FRSE; ✉ 24 Lyndewode Road, Cambridge CB1 2HN (☎ 01223 503159); University of Cambridge, The Computer Laboratory, New Museums Site, Cambridge CB2 3QG (☎ 01223 334718)

MILNER, Sir Timothy William Lycett; 10 Bt (GB 1717), of Nun Appleton Hall, Yorkshire; s of Sir (George Edward) Mordaunt Milner, 9 Bt (d 1995), and his 1 w Barbara Audrey, *née* Belsham (d 1951); *b* 11 Oct 1936; *Heir* bro, Charles Mordaunt Milner b 18 May 1944; *Style*— Sir Timothy Milner, Bt; ✉ c/o Oude Natte Valleij, Box 4, Klapmuts 7625, Cape, South Africa

MILNER OF LEEDS, 2 Baron (UK 1951); Arthur James Michael Milner; AE (1952); s of 1 Baron Milner of Leeds, PC, MC (d 1967); *b* 12 Sept 1923; *Educ* Oundle, Trinity Hall Cambridge (MA); *m* 1951, Sheila Margaret, da of late Gerald Hartley, of North Hill Ct, Leeds; 1 s, 1 da (and 1 da decd); *Heir* s, Hon Richard James Milner; *Career* sits as Labour Peer in House of Lords; joined RAFVR 1942, served 1942–46, cmmnd 1943; served with RAuxAF 609 (W Riding) Sqdn 1947–52, Flt Lt; slr 1951; conslt Gregory, Rowcliffe & Milners; oppn whip House of Lords 1971–74; Liveryman Worshipful Co of Clothworkers; *Clubs* RAF; *Style*— The Lord Milner of Leeds, AE; ✉ 2 The Inner Ct, Old Church St, London SW3 5BY (☎ 0171 352 7588); Gregory, Rowcliffe & Milners, 1 Bedford Row, London WC1R 4BZ (☎ 0171 242 0631)

MILNER WILLIAMS, Margaret Joyce; *née* Bowerman; da of Jack Bowerman, of Luton, Beds, and Anne Lilian, *née* James; *b* 28 Dec 1941; *Educ* Burlington Sch London, Goldsmiths' Coll London (CertEd); *m* 10 Sept 1966, Charles William Michael Milner-Williams, s of John William Milner-Williams, OBE (d 1985), of Wimbledon, and Nairobi, Kenya; 1 da (Victoria Margaret Anne b 1971); *Career* asst mistress Hugh Christie Sch Tonbridge 1963–64, Central Office organiser Greater London Young Cons 1964–66, Cons Pty agent West Lewisham constituency 1966–67, princ Hazelhurst Sch Wimbledon (accredited to BS 5750 1993) 1970– (asst mistress 1967–70), chm Hazelhurst (Wimbledon) Ltd; chm Independent Schs Assoc Inc and memb Jt Cncl 1982–85; memb: Ctee of Independent Schs Info Serv 1985–95, ISIS Assoc Ctee 1988–94, delegacy Goldsmiths' Coll 1976–82; Page scholar ESU 1988; MInstD 1993; *Recreations* music, reading, public speaking, travel; *Style*— Mrs Margaret Milner Williams; ✉ 10 Aston Court, Lansdowne Road, Wimbledon, London SW20 8AW; Manapouri, Allington, Wilts SP4 0BU; Parque Santiago, Playa de Las Americas, Tenerife, Canary Islands; Hazelhurst School, 17 The Downs, Wimbledon, London SW20 8HF (☎ 081 946 1704, fax 081 944 7050)

MILNES COATES, Prof Sir Anthony Robert; 4 Bt (UK 1911), of Helperby Hall, Helperby, North Riding of Yorkshire; only s of Lt-Col Sir Robert Edward James Clive Milnes-Coates, 3 Bt, DSO, JP (d 1982), and Lady (Ethel) Patricia Hare, da of 4 Earl of Listowel; *b* 8 Dec 1948; *Educ* Eton, St Thomas's Hosp (BSc, MB BS); *m* 1978, Harriet Ann, yr da of Raymond Burton, of The Old Rectory, Slingsby, York; 1 s (Thomas b 1986), 2 da (Sara b 1981, Sophie b 1984); *Heir* s, Thomas Milnes Coates b 19 Nov 1986; *Career* MRCP, MD; prof and chm Dept of Medical Microbiology St George's Hosp Med Sch London; *Style*— Prof Sir Anthony Milnes Coates, Bt; ✉ Hereford Cottage, 135 Gloucester Rd, London SW7 4TH; Helperby Hall, Helperby, York YO6 2PS

MILOW, Keith Arnold; s of Geoffrey Keith Milow, of Majorca, Spain, and Joan Ada, *née* Gear (d 1990); *b* 29 Dec 1945; *Educ* Baldock Secdy Modern Sch, Camberwell Sch of Art (DipAD), RCA; *Career* artist; *Solo Exhibitions* incl: Nigel Greenwood Inc 1970, 1973, 1974 and 1976, Gregory Fellows Exhibition (Leeds City Art Gallery) 1971, J Duffy & Sons NY 1973, Hester Van Royen Gallery London 1975, Kettles Yard Gallery Cambridge 1976, Gallerie Albert Baronian Belgium 1977, Park Square Gallery Leeds 1977, Just Crosses (Roundhouse Gallery) 1978, Galerie Loyse Openheim Geneva 1979, Annina Nosei Gallery NY 1981 and 1982, Nigel Greenwood Gallery 1986, Gouaches (Alexander Wood Gallery NY) 1987, John Davis Gallery NY 1988, 100 Drawings (Nigel Greenwood Gallery) 1989, 25 Drawings (Gallery 630B New Orleans and Nohra Haime Gallery NY) 1990; *Group exhibitions* incl: Young Contemporaries (Tate Gallery London) 1967, Mostra Mercato d'Arte Contemporan (Florence Italy) 1968, Six at the Haywood (Haywood Gallery) 1969, Works on Paper (Museum of Modern Art NY) 1970, The Road Show (Sao Paulo Biennale & S American tour) 1971, The New Art (Hayward Gallery) 1972, Homers (The Museum of Modern Art) 1973, Xieme Biennale of Art (Menton France) 1974, The British Exhibiton (Basel Art Fair) 1975, 25 Years of British Painting (RCA) 1976, Recent British Art (Br Cncl tour) 1977–78, The British Art Show (Sheffield) 1979, British Art Now (Solomon R Guggenheim Museum NY) 1980, Aspects of British Art Today (Tokyo Metropolitan Museum of Art) 1982, Pintura Britanica Contemporania (Museo Municipal Madrid) 1983, Chill Out (Kenkeleba Gallery NY) 1983, The Show Room (Michael Katz Gallery NY) 1985, Modern British Sculpture (Whitechapel Art Gallery) 1986, Emerging Artists 1978–1988: Selections from the Exxon Series (Solomon R Guggenheim Museum NY) 1987, Modern British Sculpture (The Tate Gallery Liverpool) 1988, Works on Lead (Nohra Haime Gallery NY) 1989, Sixth Sense (Pence Gallery Santa Monica) 1990, Personal Portraits (Annina Nosel Gallery NY) 1991; *Public collections* works in numerous incl: Imperial War Museum, Museum of Modern Art NY, Tate Gallery London, V & A Museum London, Nat Gallery of Australia; *Awards* Gregory Fellowship Univ of Leeds 1970–72, Harkness fellowship to USA 1972–74, Calouste Gulbenkian Fndn Visual Arts award 1976, major award Arts Cncl of GB 1979, first prize Tolly Cobbold/Eastern Arts Second Nat Exhibition 1979, Edward Albee Fndn award 1983; *Style*— Keith Milow, Esq; ✉ 32 W 20th St, New York, NY 1001, USA (☎ 00 1 212 929 0124)

MILROY, Very Rev Dominic Liston; OSB; s of Adam Milroy, by his w Clarita; *b* 18 April 1932; *Educ* Ampleforth, St Benet's Hall Oxford; *Career* prior Int Benedictine Coll of St Anselmo Rome 1974–79, headmaster Ampleforth 1980–92 (housemaster 1964–74, head modern languages 1963–74); chm Headmasters' Conf 1992; *Style*— The Very Rev Dom Dominic Milroy, OSB; ✉ Ampleforth Abbey, York YO6 4EN

MILSOM, Gerald Martin William; OBE (1987); s of Arthur Milsom (d 1983), of Dedham, Essex, and Dorothy Eileen, *née* Chambers (d 1990); *b* 28 Aug 1930; *Educ* Epsom Coll; *m* 1, 1957 (m dis), June Watson; 2 s (David b 1 Oct 1958, Paul b 6 Feb 1964), 1 da (Nicola b 9 Dec 1960); m 2, 1978, Diana Joy, da of Frank Pinhey, of Colchester; *Career* Nat Serv Lt Army Catering Corps 1949–51; hotelier, chm Milsom Hotels Dedham Ltd; fndr Pride of Britain Consortium of Country House Hotels 1983, chm BHRCA Bd Mgmnt 1989–91 (vice chm 1987–89); memb Essex CC 1963–73 (Alderman 1971), chm East Anglia Tourist Bd 1971–82 (currently vice pres), chm Bd of Tstees Dine-A-Mite Tst; Freeman City of London 1973, Liveryman Worshipful Co of Distillers 1973 (memb Ct of Assts); FHCIMA 1971, Master Innholder 1979; *Recreations* cricket, walking; *Clubs* MCC, Durban; *Style*— Gerald Milsom, Esq, OBE; ✉ Le Talbooth, Dedham, Colchester, Essex CO7 6HP (☎ 01206 323150, fax 01206 322309); PO Box 182, Southbroom 4277, Natal, South Africa

MILSOM, Prof Stroud Francis Charles (Toby); QC (1985); s of Harry Lincoln Milsom (d 1970), of Rock, Cornwall, and Isobel Vida, *née* Collins (d 1979); *b* 2 May 1923; *Educ* Charterhouse, Trinity Coll Cambridge (MA), Univ of Pennsylvania Law Sch; *m* 11 Aug 1955, Irène, da of Witold Szereszewski (d 1940), of Wola Krysztoporska, Poland; *Career* Admty 1944–45; lectr and fell Trinity Coll Cambridge 1948–55, fell tutor and dean New Coll Oxford 1956–64, prof of legal history Univ of London 1964–76, Maitland Meml lectr Cambridge 1972, prof of law Univ of Cambridge 1976–90 (fell St John's Coll 1976–), Ford's lectr in English history Oxford 1985–86, Carpentier lectr Columbia 1995; visiting prof: New York Univ Law School 1958–70, Yale Law Sch 1968–, Harvard Law Sch and Dept of History 1973, Colorado Law Sch 1977, Monash Law Sch 1981; pres Selden Soc 1985–88 (literary dir 1964–80); memb: Royal Cmmn on Historical Manuscripts 1975–, American Philosophical Soc 1984; hon bencher Lincoln's Inn 1970; Hon LLD Glasgow 1981, Hon LLD Chicago 1985; FBA 1967; *Books* Novae Narrationes (introduction, translation notes, 1963), Pollock & Maitland History of English Law (introduction to re-issue 1968), Historical Foundations of the Common Law (1968, 2 edn 1981), The Legal Framework of English Feudalism (1976), Studies in the History of the Common Law (1985), Sources of English Legal History (with J H Baker, 1986); *Clubs* Athenaeum; *Style*— Prof S F C Milsom, QC; ✉ 113 Grantchester Meadows, Cambridge CB3 9JN (☎ 01223 354100); St John's College, Cambridge CB2 1TP (☎ 01223 338600)

MILSTEIN, Dr César; CH (1995); *b* 8 Oct 1927; *Educ* Colegio Nacional Bahia Blanca, Universidad de Buenos Aires Facultad de Ciencias, Univ of Cambridge (PhD); *m* 1953, Celia Prilleltensky; *Career* Universidad de Buenos Aires 1952–57 (Instituto de Quimica Biologia, Facultad de Ciencias Medicas), Staff of Instituto Nacional de Microbiologia Buenos Aires 1957–58 and 1961–63, British Cncl fellowship 1958–60, Dept of Biochemistry Univ of Cambridge 1958–61, scientific staff Med Res Cncl Laboratory of Molecular Biology Cambridge 1963–95 (head Protein Chemistry Subdivision 1969–80, head of Protein and Nucleic Acid Chemistry Div 1981–93, memb Governing Bd 1975–79, dep dir 1988–95); emeritus fell Darwin Coll 1995– (fell 1981–95); memb: Euro Molecular Biology Orgn 1974, Deutsche Akademie der Naturforscher Leopolding 1984; hon memb: Scandanavian Immunological Socs 1970, American Inst of Immunologists 1979, La Sociedad de Medicina Interna de Bahia Blanca 1985, British Soc for Immunology 1985, Assoc Argentina de Alergia e Immunologia 1985, Sociedad Scientifica Argentina 1988; foreign assoc Nat Acad of Sci USA 1981, foreign hon memb American Acad of Arts and Sciences 1983, founding fell Third World Acad of Sciences 1983; Royal Soc: Wellcome Fndn Prize 1980, Royal Medal 1982, Copley Medal 1989; Nobel Prize in Physiology of Medicine 1985, RCS Walker Prize 1986; hon fell: Fitzwilliam Coll 1982, Int Soc of Haematology 1986, Nat Acad of Sciences of Argentina 1988, RSM 1992; Hon FRCP 1983, Hon FRCPath 1987, FRS 1975; *Publications* author of various papers and review articles on structure, evolution and genetics of antibodies; *Recreations* cooking, open air activities Sefe (Cambridge); *Style*— Dr César Milstein, CH, FRS; ✉ Medical Research Council Centre, Laboratory of Molecular Biology, Hills Rd, Cambridge CB2 2QH (☎ 01223 402248, fax 01223 412178)

MILTON, Alan James; MBE (1983); s of John Phillips Milton (d 1968), and Alice Bowen, *née* Jones (d 1977); *b* 23 June 1935; *Educ* Emanuel Sch London; *m* 25 March 1972, Heather Valerie, da of Douglas Roy Salt, OBE, of 1 The Ridings, Leavenheath, Suffolk; 2 s (Jason James b 1973, Damian John b 1976); *Career* trainee Glyn Mills and Co 1951–53; Nat Serv RAF 1953–55; Standard Chartered Bank Gp: official Bank of Br W Africa Ltd 1955, mangr Bank of W Africa Ltd 1958, mangr Standard Bank of W Africa Ltd 1966, mangr Standard Bank Nigeria Ltd 1969; mangr and asst gen mangr mktg First Bank of Nigeria Ltd 1984, dep regnl mangr The Chartered Bank Bombay 1984 (mangr W India 1986), mangr ops First Bank of Nigeria Ltd London 1988–89 (mangr mktg 1987), md and chief exec Merchant Bank Lagos Nigeria 1991–93, md and chief exec Societe Generale Bank (Nigeria) Ltd 1994–95, currently independent telecommunications conslt with Connaught Communications; former dir Standard Chartered Insurance Brokers Lagos; former tstee: St Saviours Sch Educn Tst Lagos, Corona Schs Lagos, Breach Candy Hosp Tst Bombay; formerly pres UK Citizens Assoc W India; *Recreations* golf, philately, table tennis, walking, reading, boating, classical music; *Clubs* Royal Over-Seas League, Lagos Yacht, Ikoyi (Lagos), Metropolitan (Lagos), Willingdon (Bombay), Lagos Motor Boat; *Style*— Alan J Milton, Esq, MBE; ✉ 24 Kings Walk, Shoreham-by-Sea, West Sussex BN43 5LG (☎ 01273 453931, fax 01273 441893); Vermont House, Vermont Way, East Preston, West Sussex BN16 1JX (☎ 01903 859100, fax 01903 771058)

MILTON, Prof Anthony Stuart; s of Ernest Thomas Milton (d 1964), of Beckenham, Kent, and Gladys Ethel Milton (d 1989); *b* 15 April 1934; *Educ* Cranleigh Sch, St Catherine's Coll Oxford (MA, DPhil, DSc); *m* 16 June 1962, Elizabeth Amaret, da of Russell Freeman, of Richmond, Virginia; 1 s (Nathaniel Gavin Nicolas b 6 Oct 1964), 2 da (Imogen Hillary b 7 Oct 1967, Kirstin Abigail b 8 Dec 1969); *Career* lectr Dartmouth Med Sch New Hampshire USA 1959–60, res fell Stanford Univ California USA 1960–61, res fell and hon lectr Univ of Edinburgh 1961–63, sr lectr Sch of Pharmacy Univ of London 1967–73 (lectr 1966–67); Univ of Aberdeen: prof of pharmacology 1973–94, prof of immunopharmacology 1994–; Dept of Pharmacology Univ of Cambridge 1996– (three year sabbatical from Aberdeen); md Univ of Aberdeen Trading Co (U-Travel) 1986–93; community cnclr 1982–85, tstee Aberdeen Int Youth Festival of Music and Arts 1985–91; memb: Physiological Soc, Br Pharmacological Soc; FRSA; *Books* Pyretics and Antipyretics (1982); *Recreations* collecting the stamps of Newfoundland, breeding Border Terriers; *Style*— Prof Anthony Milton; ✉ Chestnut Tree Farm, Whaddon, nr Royston, Cambs SG8 5RS (☎ 01223 207105); Department of Pharmacology, University of

Cambridge, Tennis Court Road, Cambridge CB2 1QJ (☎ 01223 334012, e-mail asm27@cam.ac.uk)

MILTON, Derek Francis; CMG (1990); s of Francis Henry Milton (d 1970), and Florence Elizabeth Maud, *née* Kirby (d 1950); *b* 11 Nov 1935; *Educ* Preston Manor County GS, Univ of Manchester (BA), Univ of Glasgow (Civil Serv res fellowship); *m* 1, 1960, Helge Kahle; 2 s (Mark Timothy, Robin Kai); m 2, 1977, Catherine Walmsley; *Career* Nat Serv RAF 1954–56; Colonial Office (E African, Int Relations and W Indies Depts) 1959–62, asst private sec to Cwlth and Colonial Sec 1962–64, CRO 1964–67, Cwlth PMs' Meeting Secretariat 1964; FCO: UK Mission to UN (NY) 1967–71, Br Embassy Rome 1972–75, Hong Kong Dept 1975–77, Br Embassy Caracas 1978–79, Dept of Trade 1980–82, Overseas Inspectorate 1982–84, Br Embassy Mexico 1984–87, RCDS 1988, high cmmr Kingston Jamaica 1989–95, non-res ambass Haiti 1989–95, ret, re-employed as dir of research for the Americas 1995–; *Recreations* Poland, travel, tennis, Queens Park Rangers FC, languages; *Style*— Derek Milton, Esq, CMG; ✉ c/o Foreign & Commonwealth Office, Old Admiralty Building, London SW1A 2AF

MILTON, Frank William; s of Capt Cyril Frank, of Worthing, Sussex, and Mabel Laura, *née* Neal; *b* 29 Nov 1949; *Educ* Hove Co GS, Univ Coll Oxford (BA); *m* 29 Sept 1973, Lesley Pamela, da of Capt Dennis Arthur Jack Adams, RE, of Glossop, Derbys; 2 s (Andrew Paul Frank, Graham Alexander Neil); *Career* trainee Turner & Newall 1972–73, sales asst Shell Chemicals UK Ltd 1973–75 (sales rep 1975–78), planning mangr Shell International Chemical Co Ltd 1978–80, ptnr Coopers & Lybrand Management Consultants 1984 (joined 1980); CDipAF, MInstM; *Recreations* hill walking, windsurfing, sailing, listening to jazz, running; *Style*— Frank Milton, Esq; ✉ Alligin, Norrels Drive, E Horsley, Surrey KT24 5DL (☎ 01483 283832); Coopers & Lybrand, 1 Embankment Place, London WC2N 6NN (☎ 0171 213 1515, fax 0171 213 2410)

MILTON-THOMPSON, Surgn Vice Adm Sir Godfrey James; KBE (1988); s of Rev James Milton-Thompson (d 1968), of Pool Hall, Menheniot, Cornwall, and May Le Mare, *née* Hoare (d 1982); *b* 25 April 1930; *Educ* Eastbourne Coll, Queens' Coll Cambridge (MA, MB BChir), St Thomas's Hosp; *m* 1952, Noreen Helena Frances, da of late Lt-Col Sir Desmond Fitzmaurice, of Boars Hill, Oxford; 3 da (Helena (Mrs Prichard), Richenda (Mrs Dixon), Louisa (Mrs Malone)); *Career* hon physician to HM The Queen 1982–90; Med DG (Naval) 1984–90, surgn gen Def Med Servs 1988–90; Hon Col 211 Wessex Field Hosp RAMC (V) 1990–95, chm Cornwall Community Health Tst 1990–93; Hospitaller OStJ 1991–95, Warden St Katharine's House Wantage 1993–, govr St Mary's Sch Wantage 1995–; KStJ (1990, CStJ 1985), memb Chapter Gen Order of St John 1988–; FRCP, DCH; *Recreations* fishing, literature, heraldry, collecting English paintings; *Clubs* Naval & Military; *Style*— Surgn Vice Adm Sir Godfrey Milton-Thompson, KBE; ✉ c/o Barclays Bank, The Parade, Liskeard, Cornwall PL14 6AR

MILVERTON, 2 Baron (UK 1947); Rev Fraser Arthur Richard Richards; s of 1 Baron Milverton, GCMG (d 1978), and Noelle Benda, da of Charles Basil Whitehead, of Torquay; *b* 21 July 1930; *Educ* Ridley Coll, Ontario, Clifton, Egerton Agricultural Coll Njoro Kenya, Bishop's Coll Cheshunt Herts; *m* 1957, Mary Dorothy, da of Leslie Aubrey Fly (d 1983; a composer of music, teacher and civil servant), of Bath; 2 da (Susan (Hon Mrs Cross) b 1962, Juliet (Hon Mrs Steuart-Corry) b 1964); *Heir* bro, Hon Michael Hugh Richards; *Career* sits as Cons peer in House of Lords; Royal Signals 1949–50, Kenya Police 1952–53; deacon 1957, ordained priest 1958; curate: St George's Beckenham Kent, St John the Baptist Sevenoaks Kent, St Nicholas Great Bookham Surrey; vicar Okewood Hill with Forest Green Surrey, rector Christian Malford with Sutton Benger and Tytherton Kellaways (Wilts) 1967–93, chaplain Wilts ACF until 1981; *Recreations* family, current affairs, reading, int rugby, cricket, tennis, swimming, music, theatre, Jamaica; *Style*— The Rev the Rt Hon the Lord Milverton; ✉ House of Lords, London SW1A 0PW

MILWARD, Prof Alan Steele; s of Joseph Thomas Milward (d 1965), and Dorothy, *née* Steele (d 1985); *b* 19 Jan 1935; *Educ* UCL (BA), LSE (PhD); *m* 23 Nov 1963 (sep 1986, m dis 1994), Claudine Jeanne Amelie, *née* Lemaitre; 1 da (Colette Victoire Zoe b 22 Feb 1977); has further da (Laura Katherine Milward-Lynch b 21 April 1992); *Career* lectr in econ history Univ of Edinburgh 1960–65, lectr Sch of Social Studies Univ of East Anglia 1965–68, assoc prof of economics Stanford Univ 1969–71, prof of Euro studies UMIST 1971–83, prof of contemporary history Euro Univ Inst 1983–86 and 1996–, prof of econ history LSE 1986–96; official historian Cabinet Office 1993–; visiting prof: Stanford Univ, Univ of Illinois, Ecole des Hautes Etudes en Sciences Sociales, Univ of Siegen, Univ of Oslo, Univ of Aarhus, Univ of Trondheim; memb: Econ History Soc, The Econ History Assoc, The German History Soc; Hon MA Univ of Manchester 1976; FBA 1987, fell Norwegian Acad of Arts and Scis 1994; *Books* The German Economy at War (1965), The New Order and The French Economy (1970), War, Economy and Society, 1939–45 (1979), The Reconstruction of Western Europe, 1945–51 (1984), The European Rescue of the Nation-State (1993); *Recreations* theatre; *Style*— Prof Alan Milward, FBA; ✉ Department of History, European University Institute, Villa Schifanoia, Via Boccaccio 121, Florence, Italy 50133; Cabinet Office Historical Records Section, Hepburn House, Marsham Street, London SW1P 4HW

MILWARD, Timothy Michael; s of Francis John Milward, and Rosemary Gwendoline, *née* Smedley-Aston; *b* 24 March 1937; *Educ* Rugby, Clare Coll Cambridge (MA, MB BCh); *m* 17 Jan 1970, Susan Isobel, da of Maj Glover Iggulden (d 1983), of Herne Bay, Kent; 4 da (Jessica b 24 Dec 1971, Caroline b 15 June 1973, Eleanor b 21 Aug 1978, Camilla (twin) b 21 Aug 1978); *Career* Nat Serv, midshipman RNR 1955–63, Lt in RNR; med trg St Thomas's Hosp London 1960–63, registrar in plastic surgery Canniesburn Hosp Glasgow 1971–72, sr registrar in plastic surgery QMH London 1972–76, Hand Surgery fell Louisville Kentucky USA 1975; conslt plastic surgn Leicester Royal Infirmary, Pilgrim Hosp Boston and Lincoln County Hosp 1976–; county med offr Leicestershire Branch Br Red Cross; memb Cncl Br Soc for Surgery of the Hand 1982–83; pres: Br Assoc of Aesthetic Plastic Surgns 1987–89, Br Assoc of Plastic Surgns 1996; FRCS 1966; *Recreations* squash, walking; *Style*— Timothy Milward, Esq; ✉ Leicester Royal Infirmary, Leicester LE1 5WW (☎ 0116 258 5286, fax 0116 272 0666)

MIMPRISS, Peter Hugh Trevor; yr s of Hugh Trevor Baber Mimpriss (d 1990), and Gwyneth Mary, *née* Bartley (d 1982); *b* 22 Aug 1943; *Educ* Sherborne; *m* 1, 1971 (m dis 1992), Hilary Ann Reed; 2 da (Isobel b 19 Oct 1973, Victoria b 22 Feb 1979); m 2, 1992, Elizabeth Lesley Molle; *Career* admitted slr 1967; ptnr Allen and Overy 1972–; chm Chariguard Group of Common Investment Funds 1994–; univ slr Univ of London 1995–; dir: Leeds Castle Fndn 1980–, Weston Park Fndn 1986–, Chatham Historic Dockyard Tst 1988–; chm Charity Law Assoc 1992–; tstee Edwina Mountbatten Tst; *Recreations* maritime history, vintage cars, collecting books; *Clubs* Athenaeum, Garrick; *Style*— Peter Mimpriss, Esq; ✉ Allen & Overy, One New Change, London EC4M 9QQ (☎ 0171 330 3000, fax 0171 330 9999)

MINALE, Marcello; s of Mario Minale (d 1988), of Naples, and Ida, *née* Cardani; *b* 15 Dec 1938; *Educ* Tech Sch Naples, Indust Design Sch Coll of Helsinki; *m* 1, 1965 (m dis 1974), Ebba, *née* Ocjemark; 1 s (Marcello Mario b 15 Feb 1966); m 2, 3 Nov 1975, Roberta, da of George Broadbridge, of Gillingham, Kent; 2 s (Manlio b 3 Nov 1976, Massimo b 15 Nov 1979); *Career* designer; chm Minale Tattersfield & Partners 1978–; pres: D & AD Assoc of London 1982, Awards for Outstanding Contrib to Br Design 1987; chm Tideway Sculler Sch; FCSD 1978; *Books* Design á la Minale Tattersfield (1976), Design: The World of Minale Tattersfield (1990), How to Run a Successful Multidisciplinary Design Company (1991), The Leader of the Pack (1993), The Image Maker (1995); *Recreations* rowing; *Clubs* Tideway Sculling Sch; *Style*— Marcello Minale, Esq; ✉ Minale, Tattersfield & Partners, The Courtyard, 37 Sheen Road, Richmond, Surrey TW9 1AJ (☎ 0181 948 7999, fax 0181 948 2435)

MINCHIN, Peter David; s of Maj Cecil Redvers Minchin (d 1953), of Ryde, IOW, and Ena Mary, *née* Flux (d 1974); *b* 5 March 1932; *Educ* Ryde Sch IOW, Allhallows Rousdon Devon; *m* 2 April 1960, Angela, da of Maj Henry Hugh Petley (d 1976), of Old Heathfield, Sussex; 2 s (David b 25 Dec 1963, Jeremy b 3 Sept 1965), 1 da (Alexandra b 2 Aug 1968); *Career* RN 1950–57: Lt (Observer) Fleet Air Arm 1955, ret 1957; Kitcat & Aitken 1958–63, ptnr Pidgeon de Smitt (and predecessor firms) 1963–81; gen mangr Securities Gp of Kuwait 1982–85, ptnr and dir Scrimgeour Vickers Ltd 1985–86, chm Chambers & Remington Ltd 1988–93, dir Lloyds Bank Stockbrokers Ltd 1986– (md 1986–90, chm 1990–93), chm Lloyds Investment Managers 1990–93; chm: Lloyds Merchant Bank Ltd 1992–93 (dir 1986–89, dep chm 1990–92), Central and Eastern European Fund 1992–, German Smaller Companies Investment Trust plc 1994–, Lloyds Smaller Companies Investment Trust plc 1995–; dir Stock Exchange 1991–94 (memb 1963, memb Cncl 1976–82 and 1988–91), dep chm Securities and Futures Authy 1994– (memb Bd 1988); memb Shoreham Port Authy 1995–; MSI; *Recreations* golf, bridge, reading; *Style*— Peter Minchin, Esq; ✉ 83 Defoe House, Barbican, London EC2Y 8DN (☎ 0171 588 5748); Wessons, Buckhurst Lane, Wadhurst, E Sussex TN5 6JU (☎ and fax 01892 782778)

MINDHAM, Prof Richard Hugh Shiels; s of Thomas Raper Mindham (d 1964), and Winifred Gertrude, *née* Shiels; *b* 25 March 1935; *Educ* King James's GS Knaresborough, Guy's Hosp Med Sch London (MB BS), The Inst of Psychiatry London (MD 1974); *m* 1971, Barbara Harris, da of James Reid; 1 da (Jane Louise b 1972), 1 s (Andrew Thomas James b 1976); *Career* asst surgn P & O Strathmore 1961–62, posts in med and neurology, surgery and obstetrics and gynaecology 1959–64, sr house offr York Clinic Guy's Hosp 1964, registrar in psychiatry Bethlem Royal and Maudsley Hosps 1965–68, res worker and lectr Inst of Psychiatry London 1968–72, reader in psychiatry Nottingham Univ Med Sch 1976–77 (sr lectr 1972–76); Univ of Leeds: Nuffield prof of psychiatry 1977–, dean of postgraduate studies 1994–94, dean Faculty of Med, Dentistry and Health 1996–; chief examiner Royal Coll of Psychiatrists 1995–; visiting prof John Hopkins Univ Baltimore 1982; FRCPsych 1977 (MRCPsych 1971), FRCPE 1978 (memb 1964); *Recreations* architecture, music; *Clubs* RSM; *Style*— Prof Richard Mindham; ✉ Division of Psychiatry and Behavioural Sciences, School of Medicine, University of Leeds, 15 Hyde Terrace, Leeds LS2 9LT (☎ 0113 233 2723, fax 0113 243 3719)

MINFORD, Prof (Anthony) Patrick Leslie; CBE (1996); s of Leslie Mackay Minford (d 1970), and Patricia Mary, *née* Sale; *b* 17 May 1943; *m* 10 Feb 1970, Rosemary Irene, da of Gordon Hedley Allcorn; 2 s (Paul, David), 1 da (Lucy); *Career* econ asst UK Miny of Overseas Devpt 1965–67, econ advsr Malawi Miny of Fin 1967–69, asst on econ matters of fin dir Courtauld Co 1970–71, econ advsr Balance of Payments Div UK Treasy 1971–73 (delgn to Br Embassy Washington 1973–74), Hallsworth res fell Univ of Manchester 1974–75, ed NIESR Economic Review 1975–76, Edward Gonner prof of applied economics Univ of Liverpool 1976–, visiting prof Cardiff Business Sch 1993–; memb: Monopolies and Mergers Cmmn 1990–96, HM Treasy independent panel of economic forecasting advisers 1992–96; *Books* Substitution Effects, Speculation and Exchange Rate Stability (1978), Unemployment: Cause and Cure (with D H Davies, M J Peel and A Sprague, 1983, 2 edn also with P Ashton, 1985), Rational Expectations and the New Macroeconomics (with D A Peel, 1983, 2 edn, sole author, as Rational Expectations Macroeconomics, 1992), The Housing Morass (with M J Peel and P Ashton, 1987), The Supply Side Revolution in Britain (1991), The Cost of Europe (ed/contrib, 1992); *Style*— Prof Patrick Minford, CBE; ✉ Department of Economics & Accounting, University of Liverpool, Eleanor Rathbone Building, Myrtle Street, Liverpool L69 3BX (☎ 0151 794 3031, fax 0151 794 3028, telex 627095 UNILPLG)

MINGAY, (Frederick) Ray; CMG (1992); s of Cecil Stanley Mingay (d 1985), and Madge Elizabeth Robinson (d 1976); *b* 7 July 1938; *Educ* Tottenham GS, St Catharine's Coll Cambridge (BA, MA exhibitioner), Univ of London; *m* 7 Aug 1963, Joan Heather, da of Rev David Archibald Ryce-Roberts (d 1976); 3 s (Benjamin b 1965, Rupert b 1966, George b 1976), 1 da (Julia b 1979); *Career* Nat Serv Army 1959–61; Miny of Tport 1962–64, Bd of Trade 1964–68, Rootes and Chrysler Motors 1968–70, consul Milan 1970–73, asst sec Dept of Trade 1973–78, cnsllr Br Embassy Washington 1978–83, under sec DTI 1983–88, consul gen Chicago 1988–92, head of Overseas Trade Div 3 DTI 1992–93, DG Export Promotion and head of DTI/FCO Jt Export Promotion Directorate 1993–96, dep sec DTI 1996–; FIMgt, FRSA; *Clubs* Reform; *Style*— Ray Mingay, Esq, CMG; ✉ Department of Trade and Industry, Kingsgate House, 66–74 Victoria Street, London SW1E 6SW (☎ 0171 215 4779, fax 0171 215 8237)

MINGOS, Prof (David) Michael Patrick; s of Vasso Mingos (d 1962), of Athens, and Rose Enid Billie, *née* Griffiths; *b* 6 Aug 1944; *Educ* Harvey GS Folkestone, King Edward VII Sch Lytham, UMIST (Dept of Chemistry prize, BSc), Univ of Sussex (DPhil); *m* 18 March 1967, Stacey Mary, da of Richard Joseph Fayrer Hosken; 1 da (Zoë Sarah b 14 Dec 1971), 1 s (Adam Toby Vasso b 2 Oct 1973); *Career* Fulbright fell Northwestern Univ Evanston Ill 1968–70, ICI fell Univ of Sussex 1970–71, lectr QMC London 1971–76; Univ of Oxford: lectr in chemistry 1976–90, reader 1990–92, fell Keble Coll 1976–92, lectr Pembroke Coll 1977–92, univ assessor 1991–92; Sir Edward Frankland BP prof of inorganic chemistry Imperial Coll London 1992–, dean Royal Coll of Science 1996–; memb 1989–: SERC, AFRC, ACOST, HEFCE, European Science Fndn Ctees; memb Editorial Bd: Transition Metal Chemistry, Structure and Bonding, Advances in Inorganic Chemistry, Chemistry Soc Reviews, New Jl of Chemistry, regnl ed Jl of Organometallic Chemistry; vice-pres Dalton Div RSC 1993–96; Corday Morgan Medal RSC 1980, Chemistries of Noble Metals Prize RSC 1983, Tilden lectr and Medal RSC 1988, Wilhelm Manchott Prize 1995, Michael Collins Award 1996; fell by special election Keble Coll Oxford 1993, distinguished prof Xi'an Petroleum Univ 1994; govr Harrow Sch; memb American Chemical Soc 1988; CChem, FRSC 1984, FRS 1992; *Books* Introduction to Cluster Chemistry (1990), Essentials of Inorganic Chemistry I (1995); *Recreations* tennis, cricket, walking, travelling; *Style*— Prof Michael Mingos, FRS; ✉ Chemistry Department, Imperial College of Science, Technology and Medicine, South Kensington, London SW7 2AY (☎ 0171 594 5753, fax 0171 594 5804)

MINOGUE, Prof Kenneth Robert; s of Denis Francis Minogue (d 1988), and Eunice Pearl, *née* Porter (d 1949); *b* 11 Sept 1930; *Educ* Sydney Boys' HS, Univ of Sydney (BA), LSE (BScEcon); *m* 16 June 1954, Valerie Pearson, da of Frederick George Hallett (d 1974); 1 s (Nicholas Robert b 1955), 1 da (Eunice Karen Hallett b 1957); *Career* asst lectr Univ of Exeter 1955–56; LSE: asst lectr 1956, sr lectr 1964, reader 1971, prof of political science 1984–95; dir Govt and Opposition Centre for Policy Studies, chm Bruges Groups 1991–93; *Books* The Liberal Mind (1963), Nationalism (1967), The Concept of a University (1974), Alien Powers: The Pure Theory of Ideology (1985), Politics: A Very Short Introduction (1995), Conservative Realism: New Essays in Conservatism (ed, 1996); *Recreations* wine, women and song; *Clubs* Garrick; *Style*— Prof Kenneth Minogue; ✉ 43 Perrymead St, London SW6 (☎ 0171 736 2380, fax 0171 371 9135); Dept of Government, London School of Economics and Political Science, Houghton St, London WC2A 2AE (☎ 0171 955 7188, fax 0171 831 1707, telex 24655 BLPES G)

MINOGUE, Martin Michael; s of Martin Bernard Minogue (d 1996), and Josephine Minogue (d 1985); *b* 23 Dec 1937; *Educ* King James's GS Knaresborough, Gonville & Caius Coll Cambridge (BA, MA); *m* 17 Aug 1968 (m dis 1985), Elizabeth, da of Harold Worthy Wray, of Darley, N Yorks; 2 s (Nicholas b 7 March 1974, Ben b 6 Nov 1975);

Career Nat Serv RAF 1957–59; second sec HM Diplomatic Serv (formerly third sec) 1962–66, asst princ BOT 1965–66, lectr in social sci Univ of Kent 1966–69; Univ of Manchester: lectr (later sr lectr) 1969–84, dir Int Devpt Centre 1984–96, currently sr research assoc Inst of Devpt Policy and Mgmnt; conslt UN Devpt Prog 1990–; *Books* African Aims and Attitudes (ed with J Molloy 1974), Documents on Contemporary British Government (ed 1977), A Consumers Guide to Local Government (ed 1977 and 1980), Perspectives on Development (ed with P Leeson, 1988); *Recreations* reading, cricket, tennis, golf; *Style—* Martin Minogue, Esq; ✉ 8 Bamford Rd, Didsbury, Manchester M20 8GW (☎ 0161 445 4669); Institute of Development Policy and Management, University of Manchester, Manchester M9 0FL (☎ 0161 275 2800, fax 0161 273 8829)

MINOPRIO, (Frank) Charles; 2 s of late (Charles) Anthony Minoprio, of Campden Hill, Kensington; *b* 9 Aug 1939; *Educ* Harrow, Grenoble Univ; *m* Patricia Mary (d 1995), er da of late Brian W Dixon, of Godstone; 1 s (George b 1969), 2 da (Victoria b 1966, Charlotte b 1972); *Career* served as Lt RA in Germany; wine conslt; dir: Haulfryn Est Co Ltd, Inst of Masters of Wine; chm Champagne Acad 1986; Master of the Worshipful Co of Distillers 1987 (memb Ct of Assts); *Recreations* tennis, squash, golf, gardening; *Style—* Charles Minoprio, Esq; ✉ The Manor House, Milton Ernest, Bedford (☎ 01234 822237, ☎ and fax 01234 822739)

MINTER, Jonathan Charles; s of John Minter, CBE, DL, of Essex, and Barbara Geraldine MacDonald, *née* Stanford; *b* 22 July 1949; *Educ* Repton, Univ of Birmingham (BA); *m* 9 July 1983, Diana Claire, da of Austin Brown, of Sussex; 1 s (Benjamin b 1986), 1 da (Isabel b 1988); *Career* md: Julius Baer Investment Management Inc, Julius Baer Investments Ltd, dir Julius Baer International Ltd; sr vice pres Bank Julius Baer & Co Ltd; Liveryman Worshipful Co of Skinners; *Recreations* shooting, sailing; *Clubs* Royal Ocean Racing, MCC; *Style—* Jonathan C Minter, Esq; ✉ Hill Farm House, Langham, nr Colchester, Essex CO4 5NX; Bank Julius Baer & Co Ltd, Bevis Marks House, Bevis Marks, London EC3A 7NE

MINTO, 6 Earl of (UK 1813); Gilbert Edward George Lariston Elliot-Murray-Kynynmound; 9 Bt (S 1700), MBE (Mil 1955), OBE (1986), JP (Roxburghshire 1961), DL (Borders Region 1983); also Baron Minto (GB 1797) and Viscount Melgund (UK 1813); s of 5 Earl of Minto (d 1975, s of 4 Earl, who was govr gen of Canada 1898–1904 and viceroy of India 1905–10), and Marion, OBE, da of George William Cook, of Montreal; *b* 19 June 1928; *Educ* Eton, RMA Sandhurst; *m* 1, 1952 (m dis 1965), Lady Caroline Child-Villiers, da of 9 Earl of Jersey; 1 s, 1 da; m 2, 1965, Mary Elizabeth (d 1983), da of late Peter Ballantine, of Gladstone, New Jersey, USA; m 3, 1991, Caroline Jane, da of Stanley Godfrey, of Ruislip, and formerly w of Christopher Larlham; *Heir* s, Viscount Melgund, *qv*; *Career* 2 Lt Scots Gds 1948, served in Malaya 1949–51; ADC to: C-in-C Far East Land Force 1951, CIGS 1953–55, Govr and C-in-C of Cyprus 1955, RARO 1956, ret as Capt; Brig Queen's Bodyguard for Scotland (Royal Co of Archers); chm Scottish Cncl on Alcoholism 1973–87 (pres 1987–), memb Borders Regnl Cncl 1974–80 and 1986–, convener 1990–, dep traffic cmmr Scotland 1975–81, exec vice pres S Scotland C of C 1978–80 (pres 1980–82), memb Exec Ctee COSLA 1990–; dir Noel Penny Turbines Ltd 1972–92; Vice Lord-Lt Borders Region (Roxburgh, Ettrick and Lauderdale) 1992–; *Clubs* Puffin's; *Style—* The Rt Hon the Earl of Minto, OBE, JP, DL; ✉ Minto, Hawick, Roxburghshire (☎ 0145 087 321)

MINTO, Graeme Sutherland; MBE (1984), JP; s of Dr Kenneth Ross Minto (d 1981), and Mona Isobel, *née* Claxon (d 1994); *b* 18 April 1943; *Educ* Oundle, Christ's Coll Cambridge (MA); *m* 3 Sept 1966, Mary Carolyn, da of John Priest; 1 s (Robert b 1975), 2 da (Lucy b 1968, Catherine b 1969); *Career* Domino Printing Sciences plc: fndr md 1978–84, chm 1978–88; former dir: Elmjet Ltd, Cantabrian Sports Ltd; dir: The Cambridge Building Society, Sports Aid Foundation-Eastern Ltd, W Eaden Lilley & Co Ltd; DMS, CIMgt, MIMechE, MIEE, CEng; *Publications* author and lectr on numerous occasions on ink jet printing and growth of high tech businesses; *Recreations* skiing, golf, Rotarian; *Style—* Graeme Minto, Esq, MBE, JP; ✉ 10 Chaucer Road, Cambridge CB2 2EB

MINTON, Michael James; s of Christmas Evans Minton (d 1959), of Oxford, and Sarah Ann, *née* Baker (d 1990); *b* 12 Dec 1935; *Educ* City of Oxford Sch, Oriel Coll Oxford (MA, DipM, Crawford Cup, premier prize CIM); *m* Barbara June, da of Eric Walter Walton; 2 da (Deborah Claire b 1960, Penelope Jayne b 1962); *Career* 2 Lt RAEC 1958–59; British Gas SE Region: mgmnt trainee 1960–61, dist mgmnt 1962–68, regnl sales mgmnt 1968–71, regnl mktg mgmnt 1972–75; British Gas S Region: regnl mktg mangr 1975–79, regnl serv mangr 1979–81, regnl dir of serv 1981–90; ops dir British Gas Wales 1990–94; devpt: Superwarmth Central Heating Systems 1970–71, Leisure Markets for Gas 1971–73, Servicecare for Gas Service 1981–84; CIM: pres Wessex Branch 1986–91 (chm 1979–81), nat cncllr 1989–91, memb Nat Exec 1990–95; FCIM, MCAM, professional assoc Inst of Gas Engrs; *Recreations* solo, opera and choral singing; *Style—* Michael Minton, Esq; ✉ Daneside, 20 Kivernell Road, Milford-on-Sea, Lymington, Hants SO41 0PQ (☎ 01590 643729)

MINTON, Yvonne Fay; da of Robert Thomas Minton (d 1974), of Sydney, Aust, and Alice, *née* Dean; *b* 4 Dec 1938; *Educ* Sydney Conservatorium of Music; *m* 21 Aug 1965, William Barclay, s of William Barclay (d 1964), of Scotland; 1 s (Malcolm Alexander b 1971), 1 da (Alison Elizabeth b 1973); *Career* mezzo-soprano; memb Royal Opera Covent Garden 1964–, guest memb Cologne Opera 1969–; guest singer: Aust Opera, Met Opera NY, Lyric Opera Chicago, San Francisco, Paris, Vienna, Bayreuth, Salzburg; Hon RAM; *Recordings* incl: Der Rosenkavalier, Marriage of Figaro, Parsifal, Tristan and Isolde, various song cycles; *Recreations* reading, gardening; *Style—* Ms Yvonne Minton, CBE; ✉ c/o Ingpen & Williams Ltd, 14 Kensington Court, London W8 5DN

MINTON-TAYLOR, Robert; s of late Richard Harold Minton-Taylor, MBE, of East Hagbourne, Oxfordshire, and Joan, *née* Bennett; *b* 25 Feb 1948; *Educ* Clayesmore Sch, Iwerne Minster Dorset, Wallingford GS Oxfordshire, Bournemouth Poly (now Bournemouth Univ); *m* 13 Sept 1986, Caroline, da of late dr Peter Deller, OBE; 2 s (Jasper, Fabian); *Career* journalist Link House Publications Croydon 1967–71, sr press offr Townsend Thoresen Car Ferries 1973–77, head of promotions European Ferries Group 1977–79; Burson-Marsteller 1979–94: main bd dir 1987–94, dir leisure travel and transport 1988–94, sr PR cncllr 1989–94, dir media servs 1990–94; md Charles Walls Public Relations 1994–95, tutor and lectr Leeds Metropolitan Univ 1995–, managing ptnr The Public Relations Practice 1997–; PR Week awards: nominated Best Design for Public Relations (for Atlantic Container Line) 1987, Best International Campaign (for Galileo) 1988, Best Non-Commercial Campaign (for Prince's Youth Business Tst) 1989; Inst of Public Relations Sword of Excellence Awards: Community Relations (for Business in the Community) 1990, Special Projects (for Seville World Expo '92) 1993; memb: Chartered Inst of Journalists 1971 (memb Cncl and Exec 1992–, pres 1992–93, chm Press and PR Div 1993–, exec memb Yorkshire regn), Seahorse Club 1982 (chm 1990), Travel Indust Mktg Gp 1988, Hotel Indust Mktg Gp 1990, Tourism Soc 1990, Media Soc (memb Cncl 1992–, dir 1995–); assoc memb Foreign Press Assoc 1992; MIPR 1980 (memb Cncl 1990–91 and 1993–96, chm Professional Practices Ctee 1995, vice chm 1996), fell Inst of Travel and Tourism 1986 (memb 1981, chm London and SE England Region 1986–90), MInstD 1991; *Recreations* journalism, family life, reading, Celtic, rock and blues music, theatre, French films, good food and wine, Yorkshire Dales, European travel, merchant ships; *Style—* Robert Minton-Taylor, Esq; ✉ The Coach House, Meadow Lane, Cononley, nr Skipton, N Yorks BD20 8NA (☎ 01535 630483, fax 01535 634773)

MIQUEL, Raymond Clive; CBE (1981); *b* 28 May 1931; married with children; *Career* Arthur Bell & Sons: joined 1956, md 1968–85, chm 1973–85; chm Wellington Importers Ltd USA 1984–85, Gleneagles Hotels plc 1984–85, chm and chief exec Belhaven plc 1986–88, dir Golf Fund plc 1989–94; chm and chief exec: Lees Group Ltd 1992–, Lees of Scotland Ltd 1993–; visiting prof of business devpt Univ of Glasgow 1984–, chm Scottish Sports Cncl 1987–91, govr Sports Aid Fndn; memb: Central Cncl of Physical Recreation, Sports Cncl 1988–91; CIMgt; *Style—* Raymond Miquel, Esq, CBE; ✉ Whitedene, Caledonian Crescent, Gleneagles, Perthshire (☎ 01764 662642)

MIRIC, Robin; s of Milorad Miric, of London, and Sonia Patricia, *née* Forbes; *b* 21 May 1955; *Educ* Highgate Sch London, City of London Poly (LLB); *Career* called to the Bar Gray's Inn 1978, admitted ad eundem memb Lincoln's Inn 1981; practice in criminal law, currently in chambers of Ronald Thwaites, QC; sec Surrey and S London Bar Mess 1990–93, memb South Eastern Circuit Liaison Ctee 1991–93, memb Circuit Ctee SE Circuit 1993–; *Recreations* opera; *Clubs* National Liberal; *Style—* Robin Miric, Esq; ✉ 10 King's Bench Walk, Temple, London EC4Y 7EB (☎ 0171 353 2501, fax 0171 353 0658)

MIRREN, Helen; *b* 26 July 1946; *Career* actress; *Theatre* RSC 1970–72 incl: Cressida in Troilus and Cressida, Julia in Two Gentlemen of Verona, Ophelia in Hamlet, Miss Julie, Man of Mode; other credits incl: International Centre of Theatre Research (with Peter Brook, Paris, Africa/America tour) 1972–73, Lady Macbeth in Macbeth (RSC) 1974, Teeth 'n' Smiles (Royal Court/Wyndhams) 1974, Nina in The Seagull (Lindsay Anderson Co) 1976, Ella in The Bed Before Yesterday (Lyric) 1976, Margaret in Henry VI parts 1, 2 and 3 (RSC) 1977–78, Isabella in Measure For Measure (Riverside) 1979, Duchess of Malfi (Royal Exchange Manchester 1980, Roundhouse 1981), Faith Healer (Royal Court) 1981, Cleopatra in Antony and Cleopatra (RSC) 1982–83, Moll in Roaring Girl (RSC) 1983, Extremities 1984, Madame Bovary (Watford Palace) 1987, Angela in Two Way Mirror (Young Vic) 1988, Sex Please, We're Italian (Young Vic) 1991, The Writing Game (New Haven, Conn) 1993, A Month in the Country (Albery 1994 and Roundabout NY 1995, nominated for Best Actress Tony Award); *Television* for BBC incl: Cousin Bette (series) 1971, Miss Julie 1972, Jackanory 1973, Little Minister 1973, The Changeling (with Stanley Baker) 1974, The Apple Cart 1974, The Philanthropist 1975, Mussolini and Claretta Petacci 1975, The Country Wife 1976, Rosalind in As You Like It 1978, Blue Remembered Hills 1978, Oresteia in The Serpent Son 1978, A Midsummer Night's Dream 1981, Mrs Reinhart (with WNET/USA) 1981, After the Party 1982, Imogen in Cymbeline 1982; for ATV incl: Behind the Scenes 1971, Coffin for the Bride 1973, Quiz Kids 1978; other credits incl: Bellamira (Thames) 1974, Coming Through (with Kenneth Branagh, Central) 1985, Alma Rattenbury in Cause Celebre (Anglia) 1987, Red King, White King (HBO) 1988; for Granada The Collection 1976, DCI Jane Tennison in Prime Suspect I, II, III and IV 1990–96; *Films* Age of Consent (co-starred with James Mason) 1969, Savage Messiah 1971, O Lucky Man 1972, Caligula 1976, Hussy 1979, The Long Good Friday (with Bob Hoskins) 1979, Fu Man Chu (co-starred with Peter Sellers) 1980, Excalibur 1981, Cal 1983 (Best Actress Award Cannes Film Festival 1984), 2010 1984, White Knights 1984, Heavenly Pursuits (with Tom Conti) 1985, Mosquito Coast (with Harrison Ford) 1986, Pascali's Island (with Ben Kingsley and Charles Dance) 1987, When the Whales Came (with Paul Schofield) 1988, Bethune, Making of a Hero 1988, The Cook, The Thief, His Wife and Her Lover (with Michael Gambon) 1989, The Comfort of Strangers 1989, Where Angels Fear to Tread, The Gift 1991, The Hawk 1992, Prince of Jutland 1993, Queen Charlotte in The Madness of King George 1994, Some Mothers Son 1995; *Awards* for Prime Suspect: Granada TV, BAFTA and BPG TV & Radio Best Actress Awards 1992, Emmy Award for Best Mini Series and BAFTA Best TV Actress Award 1993, BAFTA Best TV Actress Award 1994, Emmy Award for Best Actress 1996; *Style—* Ms Helen Mirren; ✉ c/o Ken McReddie Ltd, 91 Regent Street, London W1 7TB (☎ 0171 439 1456, fax 0171 734 6530)

MIRRLEES, Prof James Alexander; s of late Prof George B M Mirrlees; *b* 5 July 1936; *Educ* Trinity Coll Cambridge (BA, PhD), Univ of Edinburgh (MA); *m* 1961, Gillian Marjorie (d 1993); 2 da (Catriona, Fiona); *Career* advsr MIT Center for Int Studies India Project New Delhi 1962–63, asst lectr rising to lectr in economics Univ of Cambridge 1963–68 (fell Trinity Coll Cambridge), advsr Pakistan Inst of Devpt Economics Karachi 1966–68, Edgeworth prof Univ of Oxford 1968–95 (fell Nuffield Coll Oxford), visiting prof Dept of Economics MIT 1968, 1970–71, 1976 and 1987; prof of political economy Univ of Cambridge 1995– (fell Trinity Coll); Ford visiting prof Dept of Economics Univ of Calif Berkeley 1986, visiting prof Dept of Economics Yale Univ 1989, asst editor Review of Econ Studies 1969–74 (memb Bd 1963–); Econometric Soc: fell 1970–, memb Cncl 1970–74 and 1976–, vice pres 1980–82, pres 1983–84; memb Treasy Ctee on Policy Optimization 1976–78, co-editor Econometrica 1980–84; foreign hon memb: American Acad of Arts and Scis 1981, American Econ Assoc 1982; memb Cncl Royal Econ Soc 1982–, chm Assoc of Univ Teachers of Economics 1983–87, vice pres Atlantic Econ Soc 1986–, pres Royal Econ Soc 1989–92; Nobel Prize for Economics (jtly) 1996; Hon DLitt Univ of Warwick; FBA; *Publications* Manual of Industrial Project Analysis in Developing Countries Vol II (with I M D Little, 1969), An Exploration in the Theory of Income Taxation (Review of Eocnomic Studies, 1971), Optimal Taxation and Public Production (with P A Diamond, American Economic Review, 1971), On Producer Taxation (Review & Economics Studies, 1972), Notes on Welfare Economics, Information and Uncertainty (Essays in Equilibrium Behaviour under Uncertainty 1974), Arguments for Public Expenditure (Contemporary Economic Analysis 1979), The Economic Uses of Utilitarianism (Utilitarianism and Beyond 1982); *Recreations* reading detective stories, mathematics, playing the piano, travelling; *Style—* Prof James Mirrlees, FBA; ✉ Trinity College, Cambridge CB2 1TQ (☎ 01223 339516)

MIRVISH, David; CM; s of Edwin Mirvish, CBE, of Toronto, Ontario, Canada, and Anne, *née* Macklin; *b* 29 Aug 1944; *Career* theatrical prodr and owner The Old Vic Theatre London, The Princess of Wales and The Royal Alexandra Theatres Toronto; prodns and co-prodns: Candide (Olivier award winner, London), Too Clever by Half (Olivier award winner, London), Into the Woods (Evening Standard award winner, London), Les Misérables (Canada), The Good Times are Killing Me (New York), Crazy For You and Miss Saigon (Canada); dir: National Gallery of Canada, The Williamstown Theatre Festival (USA) until 1992, Toronto French Sch 1984–92, The National Theatre Sch of Canada 1989–91; memb: Canadian Cultural Property Export Review Bd 1983–86, Bd of Tstees Nat Gallery Ottawa; Rayne Award from Royal Nat Theatre, Toronto Theatre Alliance (DORA) Humanitarian Award 1992, Toronto Arts Award (Visual Art) 1994; *Style—* David Mirvish, Esq, CM; ✉ The Old Vic, Waterloo Rd, London SE1 8NB (☎ 0171 928 2651, fax 0171 261 9161); Mirvish Productions, 266 King St, W Toronto, Canada (☎ 00 1 416 593 0351, fax 00 1 416 593 9221)

MIRZOEFF, Edward; CVO (1993); s of late Eliachar Mirzoeff, of Edgware, Middx, and Penina, *née* Asherov; *b* 11 April 1936; *Educ* Hasmonean GS, Queen's Coll Oxford (BA, MA); *m* 4 June 1961, Judith, da of Harry Topper, of Finchley; 3 s (Nicholas b 1962, Daniel b 1965, Sacha b 1969); *Career* market researcher Social Surveys (Gallup Poll) Ltd 1959–60, asst ed Shoppers' Guide Magazine 1962–63; BBC TV 1963–; prodr and dir of many documentaries incl: Elizabeth R, Metro-land, A Passion for Churches, The Queen's Realm, The Front Garden, The Englishwoman and the Horse, Police - Harrow Road, The Regiment, Target Tirpitz, The Ritz, Torvill and Dean: Facing the Music, Treasures in Trust; series prodr: Choice, Bird's-Eye View, Year of the French, In at the

Deep End, Just Another Day, The Richard Dimbleby Lecture, A J P Taylor Lectures; ed 40 Minutes 1985–89; exec prodr of documentary series since 1982 incl most recently: Fire in the Blood, Pandora's Box, The Ark, Jancis Robinson's Wine Course, True Brits, Situation Vacant, The Living Dead, The House, Redcaps, A Woman Called Smith; awards: BAFTA award for best documentary 1982, BAFTA awards for best factual series 1986 and 1989, BFI TV award 1988, Samuelson award Birmingham Festival 1988, BAFTA Alan Clarke Award for outstanding contribution to television 1994; BAFTA: memb Cncl 1988–, vice chm TV 1991–94, chm 1995–97; FRSA; *Style*— Edward Mirzoeff, Esq, CVO; ✉ BBC Television, White City, 201 Wood Lane, London W12 7TS (☎ 0181 752 6242, fax 0181 752 6773)

MISCAMPBELL, Gillian Margaret Mary; *née* Gibb; OBE (1982), DL (Bucks 1993); da of Brig Francis William Gibb (d 1969), of Rosemount, Blairgowrie, Perthshire, and Agnes Winifred Gibb; *b* 31 Dec 1935; *Educ* St Leonard's Sch; *m* 5 April 1958, Alexander Malcolm Miscampbell, s of Alexander Miscampbell (d 1965), of Hoylake, Cheshire; 3 s (Andrew Ian Farquharson b 18 June 1959, Ian Alexander Francis b 27 Feb 1962, Alexander James b 19 Aug 1964); *Career* vice chm Nat Women's Advsy Ctee Cons Pty 1979–80; chm: Aylesbury Cons Assoc 1975–78, Aylesbury Vale Health Authy 1981–93, Bucks CC 1989–93 (memb 1977–93, chm Educ Ctee 1985–89); Univ of Buckingham: memb Cncl 1985–, chm Fin and Gen Purposes Ctee 1993–, vice chm Cncl 1994–; memb: Area Manpower Bd 1985–88, Bd Milton Keynes Devpt Corp 1990–92, Bucks Health Authy 1993–95; chm Stoke Mandeville NHS Tst 1995–; *Style*— Mrs Alec Miscampbell, OBE, DL; ✉ Rosemount, Upper Street, Quainton, Bucks HP22 4AY (☎ and fax 01296 655318)

MISCAMPBELL, Norman Alexander; QC (1974); s of Alexander Miscampbell (d 1965); *b* 20 Feb 1925; *Educ* St Edward's Sch, Trinity Coll Oxford; *m* 1961, Margaret, da of Berenger Kendall; 2 s, 2 da; *Career* called to the Bar Inner Temple 1952; Parly candidate (C) Newton-le-Willows (Lancs) 1955 and 1959, MP (C) Blackpool N 1962–92; PPS to Attorney-Gen 1972–74; *Style*— Norman Miscampbell, Esq, QC; ✉ 1 Temple Gardens, London EC4Y 9BB (☎ 0171 583 1315, fax 0171 583 0579)

MISHCON, Hon Miss Jane Malca (The Hon Mrs Landau); *née* Mishcon; da of Baron Mishcon (Life Baron); *b* 1950; *Educ* Univ of Oxford (MA); *m* 1, 1971 (m dis), Anthony Jay; 1 s (Adam), 1 da (Lucy); m 2, 30 Oct 1990, Edward Landau; *Career* called to the Bar Gray's Inn 1979, practising barr; *Style*— Miss Jane Mishcon; ✉ 4 Paper Buildings, Temple, London EC4Y 7EX (☎ 0171 353 3366)

MISHCON, (Hon) Peter Arnold; er s of Baron Mishcon (Life Peer), *qv*; *b* 1946; *Educ* City of London Sch, Birmingham Coll of Art, Poly of Central London (DipArch); *m* 1967, Penny Green; 1 s (Oliver b 1968), 3 da (Anna b 1972, Kate b 1973, Eliza b 1977); *Career* chartered architect and designer; princ Mishcon Associates 1976–; Housing Centre Trust Jubilee Award for Outstanding Achievement in Housing, Royal Borough of Kensington and Chelsea Environment Award, Times/RICS Conservation Award, Arango Design Fndn (USA) Award; chm: Unipass Transport Systems Ltd 1993–, Keniston Housing Association Ltd 1984–; RIBA; *Recreations* Nelson boats, breakfast, fixing things; *Style*— Peter Mishcon; ✉ Pembridge Studios, 27A Pembridge Villas, London W11 3EP (☎ 0171 229 9103, fax 0171 229 6744)

MISHCON, Hon Russell Orde; yr s of Baron Mishcon (Life Peer), *qv*; *b* 9 July 1948; *Educ* City of London Sch; *m* 6 Nov 1975, Marcia Regina Leigh; 1 s (Joel b 1977), 2 da (Portia b 1979, Honor b 1991); *Career* slr 1971; sr ptnr: Blatchfords 1974–80, Russell Mishcon & Co 1980–87; ptnr S J Berwin & Co 1987–92, chm European Development Corporation plc 1993–; *Recreations* polo; *Clubs* Guards' Polo; *Style*— The Hon Russell Mishcon

MISHCON, Baron (Life Peer UK 1978), of Lambeth, Greater London; Victor Mishcon; DL (Gtr London); s of Rabbi Arnold Mishcon, and Queenie Mishcon; *b* 14 Aug 1915; *Educ* City of London Sch; *m* 1976, Joan Estelle, da of Bernard Monty; 2 s and 1 da (by former marriage); *Career* sits as Labour Peer in House of Lords; slr 1937, conslt Mishcon De Reya; memb: Royal Nat Theatre Bd 1965–90, South Bank Theatre Bd 1977–82; former chm LCC and various ctees; former memb: GLC (chm Gen Purposes Ctee), ILEA, Lambeth Borough Cncl (chm Fin Ctee); contested (Lab): NW Leeds 1950, Bath 1951, Gravesend 1955 and 1959; chief oppn spokesman: Home Affrs 1983–90, Legal Affairs 1990–93; vice chm All Pty Solicitors Parly Gp; former memb various governmental ctees; Hon LLD Univ of Birmingham; hon QC 1992; hon Fell UCL; *Style*— The Rt Hon the Lord Mishcon, QC, DL; ✉ 21 Southampton Row, Holborn, London WC1 (☎ 0171 405 3711); House of Lords, London SW1A 0AA

MISIEWICZ, Dr J J; *b* 28 March 1930, Lwow, Poland; *Educ* Lord Weymouth's GS, Univ of London (BSc, MB BS); *m* Marjorie Alice; *Career* conslt physician and hon jt dir Dept of Gastroenterology and Nutrition Central Middx Hosp London; pres Br Soc of Gastroenterology 1987–88; ed: Gut 1980–87, Euro Jl of Gastroenterology and Hepatology 1989–; hon conslt gastroenterologist: British Airways, Royal Navy; FRCP, FRCPE; *Books* Diseases of the Gut and Pancreas (jt ed); also author of papers on peptic ulcer, Helicobacter pylori, irritable bowel syndrome and ulcerative colitis; *Recreations* friends, the arts, country, food; *Style*— Dr J J Misiewicz; ✉ Consulting Rooms, Princess Grace Hospital, 42–52 Nottingham Place, London W1M 3FD (☎ 0171 486 1234, fax 0171 487 4476); Department of Gastroenterology and Nutrition, Central Middlesex Hospital, London NW10 7NS (☎ 0181 453 2202, fax 0181 961 1317)

MISRA, Dr Prem Chandra; JP (Glasgow 1985); s of Dr Man Mohan Lal Misra (d 1980), of Hardoi India, and Bindeshawri (d 1970); *b* 24 July 1941; *Educ* KK Degree College Lucknow India (BSc), King George's Med Coll Lucknow India (MB BS), Royal Coll of Surgeons and Physicians Glasgow & Edinburgh (DPM); *m* 24 Jan 1970, Sandhya, da of Mr Manohar Lal Khanna, of Bombay, India; 1 s (Vivek b 1975), 2 da (Deepali b 1970, Nisha b 1980); *Career* demonstrator Dept of Human Physiology King George's Med Coll Lucknow India 1967, resident house surgn in gen surgery Royal Infirmary Wigan 1968–69, resident house physician in gen med Whelley Hosp Wigan 1969–70; Bolton Dist Gen Hosp Farnworth: resident sr house offr of gen psychiatry 1970–71, resident registrar of gen psychiatry 1971–73; Hollymoor Hosp Birmingham: sr psychiatric registrar 1973–76, conslt psychiatrist and sr clinical lectr Dept of Psychological Med Univ of Glasgow 1976–; memb Exec Ctee Strathclyde Community Relations Cncl 1981–87, pres Indian Assoc of Strathclyde, memb Bd of Dirs Scottish Refugee Cncl 1995–, fell American Gerontological Soc, memb affiliate Royal Coll of Psychiatrists; fell: Indian Psychiatric Soc 1980–, RSM; memb American Psychiatric Assoc 1974–, pres Br Soc of Med and Dental Hypnosis Scotland 1987–89 (hon sec Div of Psychiatry 1980–95, chm Academic Ctee 1993–), memb Ethical Ctee (Eastern Dist Glasgow) 1980–93, life memb Scottish Assoc for Mental Health, fndr Glasgow Assoc for Mental Health; memb: Exec Ctee European Soc of Hypnosis, Int Soc of Hypnosis, Int Sci Ctee of Sexuality and Handicap in Paris, Exec Ctee Br Soc of Res on Sex Educn; *Books* Modern Trends in Hypnosis (ed, with Waxman et al, 1985), author of 20 res papers on hypnosis and sexual disorders in med jls; *Recreations* classical music, walking in Scottish highlands, travelling to various countries in the world; *Style*— Dr Prem Misra; ✉ Consultant Psychiatrist and Senior Clinical Lecturer, Parkhead Hospital, Glasgow G31 5BA (☎ 0141 211 8300, fax 0141 211 8380)

MISTRY, Dhruva; s of Pramodray M Mistry, and Kantaben Mistry; *b* 1 Jan 1957; *Educ* MS Univ of Baroda Fine Arts Faculty (MA), RCA London (MA); *Career* artist in residence and fell Churchill Coll Cambridge and Kettle's Yard Cambridge 1984–85; work in public collections incl: Tate Gallery London, Arts Cncl, Br Cncl, Nat Museum of Wales Cardiff, Walker Art Gallery Liverpool, Contemporary Art Soc London, Hakone Open Air Museum Japan; RA 1991; *Exhibitions* solo incl: Arnolfini Bristol, Walker Art Gallery Liverpool 1986, Nigel Greenwood Gallery London 1987 and 1990, Collins Gallery Glasgow 1988, Laing Art Gallery Newcastle upon Tyne, Asian Artist Today 1994, Fukuoka Annual VII Fukuoka Art Museum Japan 1994; *Recreations* photography, reading, walking; *Style*— Dhruva Mistry, Esq, RA; ✉ c/o The Royal Academy, Burlington House, Piccadilly, London W1V 0DS (☎ 0171 439 7438, fax 0171 434 0837)

MITCHARD, Anthony Keith; s of Albert Ernest James Mitchard, and Florence, *née* West; *b* 26 Dec 1934; *Educ* King Edward's Sch Bath; *m* 31 March 1956, Kathleen Margaret, da of Albert Henry Smith; 2 s (Michael David b 25 Oct 1963, John Robert b 27 June 1967), 3 da (Andrea Marie b 27 Feb 1958, Susan Elizabeth b 16 Aug 1959, Alison Judith b 16 Aug 1971); *Career* dir Avon Rubber Co Ltd 1974, chief exec Avon Rubber plc 1986–94, ret; chm UK Safety plc; dir: Slatebond Ltd, Automotive Precision Holdings Ltd, Wellington Holdings plc, Morgan Grenfell Equity Income Trust plc; chm Community Cncl for Wiltshire; memb Cncl Univ of Bath; tstee Burnbake Tst; FPRI; *Recreations* golf, cricket, reading; *Style*— Anthony Mitchard, Esq; ✉ UK Safety plc, Lodge Road, Kingswood, Bristol BS15 1JB (☎ 0117 935 3336, fax 0117 935 3337)

MITCHARD, (Gerald Steven) Paul; s of Gerald Albert Mitchard, of Charlton, nr Malmesbury, Wilts, and Janet Margaret, *née* Gregory; *b* 2 Jan 1952; *Educ* Taunton Sch, Univ of Oxford (MA); *m* 1, 28 June 1980 (m dis 1985), Shirley Anne Mitchard, *qv*, da of Dennis Robert Wilkins Chappell; m 2, 2 May 1987, Dorothy Neleitha, da of Leslie Grant, of Hornsey, London; 2 s (David Max Gregory b 10 Feb 1988, George Henry Steven b 2 Dec 1990); *Career* asst slr Slaughter and May 1977–84; Simmons & Simmons: asst slr 1984–85, ptnr 1985–, currently head of litigation; qualified slr Hong Kong 1984; CEDR accredited mediator 1993; Liveryman City of London Solicitors' Co; memb: Law Soc 1977, American Bar Assoc, Int Bar Assoc, CPR's Panel of Distinguished Neutrals 1994; FCIArb 1993; *Recreations* squash, golf, reading, walking; *Style*— Paul Mitchard, Esq; ✉ Simmons & Simmons, 21 Wilson Street, London EC2M 2TX (☎ 0171 628 2020)

MITCHARD, Shirley Anne; da of Dennis Robert Wilkins Chappell, and Joan Gladys, *née* Woolcott; *b* 15 Feb 1953; *Educ* Weirfield Sch Taunton, Portsmouth Univ (BA); *m* 28 June 1980 (m dis 1985), (Gerald Steven) Paul Mitchard, *qv*; *Career* KPMG Peat Marwick 1975–81 (Tax Dept 1979–81), Tax Div Arthur Andersen & Co 1981–84 (sr mangr 1983), corp tax ptnr Clark Whitehill 1987– (joined 1985); ACA 1978, MInstD; *Recreations* interior decoration, gardening, working out, tennis; *Clubs* Barbican Health & Fitness; *Style*— Ms Shirley Mitchard; ✉ 27 Ashcombe Street, London SW6 3AW (☎ 0171 371 0609); Clark Whitehill, 25 New Street Sq, London EC4A 3LN (☎ 0171 353 1577)

MITCHELL, Adrian; *b* 24 Oct 1932; *Career* journalist and writer; Nat Serv RAF 1951–52; reporter 1955–63 (Oxford Mail, Evening Standard); freelance journalist: Daily Mail, The Sun, Sunday Times; Granada fell in the arts Univ of Lancaster 1967–69, fell Centre for the Humanities Wesleyan Univ USA 1972; resident writer: Sherman Theatre Cardiff 1974–75, Unicorn Theatre 1982–83; visiting fell Billericay Comp Sch 1978–80, Judith E Wilson fell Univ of Cambridge 1980–81, poetry ed New Statesman and Society 1994–96, Dylan Thomas fell UK Year of Lit Festival Swansea 1995–96; *Theatre* plays for the theatre: Tyger (NT), Man Friday (7:48 Theatre Co), Mind Your Head (Liverpool Everyman), A Seventh Man (Hampstead), White Suit Blues (Nottingham Playhouse), Uppendown Mooney (Welfare State International), The White Deer (Unicorn Theatre for Children), Hoagy Bix and Wolfgang Beethoven Bunkhaus (Tricycle Theatre), Mowgli's Jungle (Contact Theatre), C'mon Everybody (Tricycle Theatre), Satie Day/Night (Lyric Studio Hammersmith), Anna on Anna (Theatre Workshop Edinburgh), The Siege (Schs Nat Playwright Commissioning Gp); stage adaptations for NT: Animal Farm (lyrics), The Mayor of Zalamea, Fuente Ovejuna, The Government Inspector; stage adaptations for RSC: Marat/Sade, Life's a Dream (with John Barton); other stage adaptations: The Great Theatre of the World (Medieval Players), Peer Gynt (Oxford Playhouse), Mirandolina (Bristol Old Vic), Lost in a Mirror (Southwark Theatre); other stage shows: The Wild Animal Song Contest (Unicorn Theatre), In the Unlikely Event of an Emergency (South West Music Theatre), King Real (Ongar Youth Theatre), The Last Wild Wood in Sector 88 (Derby Music Theatre), The Pied Piper (NT), The Blue (Walk the Plank), Unicorn Island (Dartington), The Snow Queen (ESIPA, Albany USA), A New World and The Tears of the Indians (Southampton Nuffield Theatre), Sir Fool's Quest (Puppetcraft), Tom Kitten and His Friends (Unicorn Theatre), Tyger Two (Emmanuel Univ Boston); *Television Plays* Daft as a Brush, Silver Giant, Wooden Dwarf, The Fine Art of Bubble Blowing, Something Down There is Crying (BBC), You Must Believe All This, Glad Day (Thames TV); *Opera* Houdini (with Peter Schat); *Films* Man Friday (1975), King Real and the Hoodlums (1985); *Novels* If You See Me Comin' (1962), The Bodyguard (1970), Wartime (1973); *Poetry* Poems (1964), Out Loud (1968), Ride the Nightmare (1971), The Apeman Cometh (1975), For Beauty Douglas (collected poems 1953–79) (1982), On the Beach at Cambridge (1984), Nothingmas Day (1984), All My Own Stuff (1991), Adrian Mitchell's Greatest Hits - the Top Forty (1992), Blue Coffee (1996); *Children's Books incl* The Baron Rides Out (1985), The Baron on the Island of Cheese (1986), Our Mammoth (1986), The Baron all at Sea (1987), Our Mammoth goes to School (1987), Our Mammoth in the Snow (1989), All My Own Stuff (1992), The Orchard Book of Poems (1993), The Thirteen Secrets of Poetry (1993), Maudie and the Green Children (1996), Gynormous! (1996); *Style*— Adrian Mitchell, Esq; ✉ c/o Peters, Fraser and Dunlop, 5th Floor, The Chambers, Chelsea Harbour, Lots Rd, London SW10 0XF (☎ 0171 376 7676)

MITCHELL, Alison; da of Lancelot Mitchell, of Edinburgh, and Dorothy, *née* Watson; *b* 25 Dec 1952; *Educ* James Gillespie's HS for Girls, Univ of Edinburgh (BA); *m* 4 June 1983, Ronald William Pullen; 1 da (Laura Dorothy b 3 Jan 1985), 1 s (James Oliver b 2 May 1987); *Career* formerly fin journalist: The Press and Journal, The Times, The Sunday Express; indust reporter Central TV; fin specialist: Breakfast Time (BBC), Bazaar (BBC), Woman's Hour; presenter Money Spinner (C4); currently: presenter Money Box (Radio 4), fin expert Jimmy Young Prog and Good Morning with Ann and Nick (BBC 1); *Books* The Penguin Personal Finance Guide (1988), Your Money - Straight and Simple (1990), The Penguin Financial Guide to a Successful Retirement (1993); *Recreations* hill walking; *Style*— Ms Alison Mitchell; ✉ c/o BBC Radio 4, Broadcasting House, London W1A 1AA (☎ 0171 580 4468)

MITCHELL, Andrew John Bower; MP (C) Gedling (majority 10,637); s of Sir David Bower Mitchell, MP, *qv*, and Pamela Elaine, *née* Haward; *b* 23 March 1956; *Educ* Rugby, Jesus Coll Cambridge (MA); *m* 27 July 1985, Sharon Denise, da of David Benedict Bennett; 2 da (Hannah Katherine b 1987, Rosie Olivia Louise b 1990); *Career* 1 RTR (SSLC) 1975; pres Cambridge Union 1978, chm Cambridge Univ Cons Assoc 1977, chm The Coningsby Club (Cons Graduates) 1983–84; int and corp business Lazard Bros & Co Ltd 1979–87 (conslt 1987–92); Parly candidate (C) Sunderland S 1983, MP (C) Gedling 1987–; PPS to: Rt Hon William Waldegrave, as Min of State FCO 1988–90, Rt Hon John Wakeham as Sec of State for Energy 1990–92; sec One Nation Gp of Cons MPs 1989–92, a vice chm Cons Pty 1992–93, asst Govt whip 1992–94, lord cmmr and Govt whip 1994–95, Parly under-sec of state DSS 1995–; Liveryman Worshipful Co of Vintners; *Recreations* skiing, sailing, reading; *Clubs* Carlton and District Constitutional, Cambridge Union Soc, Carlton; *Style*— Andrew Mitchell, Esq, MP; ✉ 30 Gibson Square, Islington, London N1 (☎ 0171 226 5519); Dovecote Farmhouse, Tithby, Nottinghamshire (☎ 01949 839587); House of Commons, London SW1 (☎ 0171 219 4494)

MITCHELL, Andrew Robert; s of Malcolm Mitchell, of Highgate, London, and Edna Audrey Cherry, of Boca Raton, Florida; *b* 6 Aug 1954; *Educ* Haberdashers Askes Elstree, Cncl of Legal Educn; *m* 1, 1982 (m dis 1990), Patricia Anne, *née* Fairburn; m 2, Carolyn Anne Blore; 1 s (Harry Aubrey b 8 March 1993), 1 da (Tiffany Rose b 26 Aug 1994); *Career* called to the Bar Gray's Inn 1976, memb Irish Bar, head of chambers 32 Furnival St 1991–, asst recorder of the Crown Ct 1995–; memb: Criminal Bar Assoc, Justice; memb Cncl London Borough of Haringey 1984–94 (ldr oppn 1990 and 1991), Parly candidate (Cons) Islington S and Finsbury 1987; *Books* Confiscation (1992, Sweet & Maxwell); *Recreations* playing tennis, watching football and cricket; *Clubs* RAC, MCC; *Style—* Andrew Mitchell, Esq; ✉ Chambers of Andrew Mitchell, Furnival Chambers, 32 Furnival Street, London EC4A 1JQ (☎ 0171 405 3232, fax 0171 405 3322, mobile 0850 696520)

MITCHELL, Dr (John) Angus Macbeth; CB (1979), CVO (1961), MC (1946); s of John Fowler Mitchell, CIE (d 1984), of Bath, and Sheila Macbeth Mitchell, MBE (d 1994); both parents were joint authors of Monumental Inscriptions in 8 Scot counties; *b* 25 Aug 1924; *Educ* Marlborough, Brasenose Coll Oxford (BA); *m* 1948, Ann Katharine, da of Herbert Stansfield Williamson (d 1955), of Oxford; 2 s (Jonathan b 1951, Andrew b 1958), 2 da (Charlotte b 1953, Catherine b 1956); *Career* served WWII RAC, Capt NW Europe 1943–46; civil servant Scot Office 1949–84, sec Scot Educn Dept 1976–84; chm Ct Univ of Stirling 1984–92, memb Cmmn on Local Authy Accounts in Scotland 1985–89, chm Scot Action on Dementia 1985–94, vice-convener Scot Cncl of Voluntary Orgns 1986–91, memb Historic Bldgs Cncl for Scot 1988–94, sec Greyfriars Kirkyard Trust 1994–; Hon LLD Dundee 1983, Hon DUniv Stirling 1992; Kt Order of Orange-Nassau (Netherlands) 1946; *Books* Procedures for the Reorganisation of Schools in England (1987); *Recreations* old Penguins, genealogy, gravestones; *Clubs* New (Edinburgh); *Style—* Dr Angus Mitchell, CB, CVO, MC; ✉ 20 Regent Terrace, Edinburgh EH7 5BS (☎ 0131 556 7671)

MITCHELL, Austin Vernon; MP (Lab) Great Grimsby (majority 7,504); s of Richard Mitchell; *b* 19 Sept 1934; *Educ* Woodbottom Cncl Sch, Bingley GS, Manchester Univ, Nuffield Coll Oxford (DPhil); *m* 1 (m dis), Patricia Jackson; 2 da (Kiri, Susan); m 2, Linda McDougall; 1 s (Jonathan), 1 da (Hannah); *Career* former univ lectr in history and politics, journalist with Yorkshire TV 1969–71 and 1973–77, presenter BBC Current Affrs 1972–73, presenter and interviewer Sky Television 1989–· MP (Lab): Grimsby 1977–83, Great Grimsby 1983–; PPS to min of state for prices and consumer protection 1977–79, oppn whip, opposition front bench spokesman on trade and industry 1988–89; memb Treasy and Civil Service Select Ctee, former chm PLP Treasy Gp; fell of the Indust and Parly Tst, memb Exec Fabian Soc; *Books* incl: Westminster Man: A Tribal Anthology of the Commons People (1982), The Case for Labour (1983), Whigs in Opposition 1815–30, Politics and People in New Zealand, Half Gallon Quarter Acre Pavlova, Yorkshire Jokes, Teach Thissen Tyke, Can Labour Win Again?, Britain: Beyond the Blue Horizon, Competitive Socialism, Election 45; *Recreations* photography, comtemplating exercise; *Style—* Austin Mitchell, Esq, MP; ✉ House of Commons, London, SW1 (☎ 0171 219 4559)

MITCHELL, Dr Brian Redman; s of Irvin Mitchell (d 1969), of Marsh House, Oxenhope, Yorks, and Dora Eleanor, *née* Redman (d 1981); *b* 20 Sept 1929; *Educ* Sedbergh, Univ of Aberdeen (MA), Peterhouse Cambridge (PhD); *m* 1, 25 Aug 1952, Barbara, da of Douglas Gordon Hay (d 1946); m 2, 11 Sept 1968, Ann Leslie, da of David Leslie Birney (d 1942); 2 s (David b 1969, Peter b 1972); *Career* Flt Lt RAF, ret 1958; Univ of Cambridge: res offr Dept of Applied Econs 1958–67, univ lectr 1967–91, fell Trinity College 1967–; *Recreations* watching cricket and rugby football, gardening; *Clubs* Hawks, MCC; *Style—* Dr Brian Mitchell; ✉ 20 High Street, Toft, Cambridge CB3 7RL (☎ 01223 262516); Trinity College, Cambridge (☎ 01223 338502)

MITCHELL, Dr Charles James; s of Col P C Mitchell, MC, FRCPE, of Insch, Aberdeenshire, and Josephine Selina, *née* White; *b* 11 Nov 1946; *Educ* Trinity Coll Glenalmond, Univ of Edinburgh (BSc, MB ChB); *m* 21 Oct 1972, Elisabeth Bullen, da of Frank George Meakin, of Southfleet, Kent; 1 s (Alexander b 1977), 1 da (Alice b 1975); *Career* house physician Royal Infirmary Edinburgh 1971, SHO and registrar King's Coll Hosp London 1972–74, registrar Academic Dept of Med Royal Free Hosp London 1974–76, conslt physician Scarborough Health Authy 1981–, hon conslt physician St James's Univ Hosp Leeds 1981–92 (lectr in med 1976–81); pres Pancreatic Soc of GB and Ireland 1992 (memb Ctee 1981–84); memb: Br Soc of Gastroenterology (memb Ctee 1987–90), Euro Pancreatic Club; regnl advsr Royal Coll of Physicians 1994–; FRCPE 1987, FRCP 1988; *Books* Pancreatic Disease in Clinical Practice (ed jtly and contrib, 1981), Textbook of Gastroenterology (contrib, 1992); *Recreations* field sports, piping, gardening; *Clubs* Royal Scot Pipers Soc; *Style—* Dr Charles Mitchell; ✉ The Old Rectory, Ebberston, Scarborough, North Yorkshire; Leafield, Dalton, Dumfriesshire; Department of Gastroenterology, Scarborough Hospital, Scarborough (☎ 0723 368111)

MITCHELL, Christopher Meredyth; s of Francis John Lindley Mitchell (d 1958), of Old Heathfield, Sussex, and Irene Springett, *née* Butt (d 1949); *b* 16 Nov 1925; *Educ* Rossall Sch, Sidney Sussex Coll Cambridge (MA); *m* 13 Sept 1958, Hilary Margaret, da of John Howard Gaunt, of Manchester; 2 s (David b 1960, Steven b 1969), 1 da (Sarah b 1963); *Career* ptnr Kennedy & Donkin 1958, (jt sr pntr 1976–86), dir Kennedy & Donkin Group 1987–90; chm: Assoc of Consltg Engrs 1977–78, Br Conslts Bureau 1988–89; pres Br Section Societé des Ingénieurs et Scientifiques de France 1988–89; pres Woking Mind; memb: Woking UDC 1968–74, Woking Borough Cncl 1974–82; Mayor of Woking 1974–75; Freeman City of London, Liveryman Worshipful Co of Engrs 1988; FIEE; *Recreations* astronomy, ornithology, music, European languages; *Style—* Christopher Mitchell, Esq; ✉ Two Roods, 20 Warren Rd, Guildford, Surrey GU1 2HB (☎ and fax 01483 504407)

MITCHELL, Sir David Bower; kt (1988), DL (Hampshire 1995), MP (C) Hampshire North West (majority 17,848); s of James Mitchell (d 1959), and Mona Elizabeth Blackett, *née* Bower (d 1956); gs of Sir Alfred L Bower, 1 Bt, and Mona, *née* Blackett (*see* Burke's LG 18th edn vol II 1969, Blackett of Wylam); *b* 20 June 1928; *Educ* Aldenham; *m* 1954 (sep 1989), Pamela Elaine, da of Dr Clifford Haward; 2 s (Andrew John Bower Mitchell, MP, *qv*, Graham), 1 da (Suki); *Career* wine shipper; currently chm El Vino Co Ltd; memb St Pancras Cncl 1956–59; MP (C): Basingstoke 1964–83, Hants NW 1983–; oppn whip 1965–67, PPS to Social Servs Sec 1970–74, chm Cons Smaller Business Ctee 1974–79; Parly under sec of state for: indust 1979–81, NI 1981–83, tport 1983–86; min of state for tport 1986–88; memb Ct of Assts Worshipful Co of Vintners (Swan Warden 1989, Master 1992); *Clubs* Carlton; *Style—* Sir David Mitchell, DL, MP; ✉ 1 Hare Place, London EC4Y 1BJ (fax 0171 936 2367)

MITCHELL, David Smith; TD (1972 and 2 Bars); s of Edward Mitchell (d 1975), and Kathleen Mitchell (d 1990); *b* 5 Aug 1937; *Educ* Chesterfield Sch, Pembroke Coll Oxford (MA); *m* 14 Sept 1963, Karin, da of William Embleton Hall (d 1978); 1 s (Edward b 1972), 1 da (Anna-Marie b 1969); *Career* served RAF 1956–58, TA; co sec: various cos within J Lyons & Co Ltd 1961–72, J Lyons & Co Ltd 1983–87 (asst sec 1972–83), Allied-Lyons plc 1987–94, Allied Domecq plc (following name change) 1994–; FCIS; *Recreations* territorial army; *Clubs* RAF; *Style—* David Mitchell, Esq, TD; ✉ Allied Domecq plc, 24 Portland Place, London W1N 4BB (☎ 0171 323 9000, fax 0171 323 1744)

MITCHELL, David William; CBE (1983); s of William Baxter Mitchell (d 1983), and Betty Steel, *née* Allan (d 1959); *b* 4 Jan 1933; *Educ* Merchiston Castle Sch Edinburgh; *m* 1965, Lynda Katherine Marion, da of Herbert John Laurie Guy (d 1975); 1 da (Louisa-Jayne b 1972); *Career* cmmnd (NS) RSF 1950; memb Bd Western Regional Hosp 1965–72, pres Timber Trades Benevolent Soc of UK 1974, Scot Cncl CBI 1979–85, dir Mallinson-Denny (Scotland) 1977–90, Hunter Timber Scotland 1990–92, jt md M & N Norman (Timber) Ltd 1992–96 (non-exec 1996–); pres: Scot Timber Trade Assoc 1980–82, Scot Cons and Unionist Assoc 1981–83; memb: Scot Cncl (Devpt and Indust) 1984–, Bd Cumbernauld New Town 1985 (chm 1987–), Bd of Mgmnt Craighalbert Centre for Children with Motor Impairment 1992–96; treas Scot Cons Pty 1990–93; *Recreations* fishing, shooting, golf; *Clubs* Western (Glasgow), Prestwick, Royal and Ancient (St Andrews); *Style—* David W Mitchell, Esq, CBE; ✉ Dunmullin House, Blanefield, Stirlingshire G63 9AJ; Linwood Industrial Estate, Linwood, Renfrewshire PA3 3BD (☎ 01505 329124, fax 01505 328147)

MITCHELL, Air Cdre Sir (Arthur) Dennis; KBE (1977), CVO (1961), DFC (1944 and bar 1945), AFC (1943); s of late Col A Mitchell, DSO, RA; gggs of Col Hugh Henry Mitchell (who cmd 4 Bde at Battle of Waterloo and who was only Bde Cdr below the rank of Gen to be mentioned in Duke of Wellington's despatches), and Lady Harriet Somerset, da of 5 Duke of Beaufort; *b* 26 May 1918; *Educ* Nautical Coll Pangbourne, RAF Coll Cranwell; *m* 1949, Mireille Caroline, da of Comte Henri Cornet de Ways Ruart; 1 s (Michael); *Career* joined RAF 1936, served WWII, Dep Capt The Queen's Flight 1956–59, Capt 1962–64; ADC to HM The Queen 1958–62, extra equerry 1962–; md Aero Systems SA; fndr: Brussels Airways SA, Aero Distributors SA; *Recreations* golf; *Clubs* Naval and Military, RAF; *Style—* Air Cdre Sir Dennis Mitchell, KBE, CVO, DFC, AFC; ✉ 10 Chemin des Chasseurs, 1380 Ohain, Belgium (☎ 00 32 2 653 13 01, fax 00 32 2 653 15 17, office ☎ 00 32 2 652 22 22)

MITCHELL, Sir Derek Jack; KCB (1974, CB 1967), CVO (1966); s of late Sidney Mitchell, of Rottingdean, Sussex; *b* 5 March 1922; *Educ* St Paul's, Christ Church Oxford; *m* 1944, Miriam (d 1993), da of E F Jackson; 1 s (Anthony), 2 da (Sarah, Julia); *Career* served WWII RAC; joined HM Treasy 1947, private sec to Econ Sec 1948–49, private sec to Perm Sec and Official Head of Civil Serv (Sir Edward Bridges) 1954–56; princ private sec to: Chllr of Exchequer (Reginald Maudling) 1962–63, PM (Sir Alec Douglas-Home then Harold Wilson) 1964–66; dep under sec Dept of Economic Affrs 1966–67, dep sec MAFF 1967–69, econ min and head of UK Treasy and Supply Delgn Washington (also UK exec dir for IMF and IBRD) 1969–72, second perm sec (overseas fin) Treasy 1973–77; dir: Guinness Mahon & Co 1977–78, Bowater Corp 1979–84, Bowater Industries 1984–89, Bowater Inc 1984–93, Standard Chartered 1979–89; ind dir The Observer Ltd 1981–93, sr advsr Shearson Lehman Brothers Int 1979–88, chm Jocelyn Burton Silversmith and Goldsmith Ltd 1991–; memb: Royal Nat Theatre Bd 1977–95, Cncl UCL 1978–82, PLA 1979–82; chm Royal Nat Theatre Fndn 1989–, tstee Royal Nat Theatre Endowment Fund 1990–, governing tstee Nuffield Prov Hosps Tst 1978–; *Clubs* Garrick; *Style—* Sir Derek Mitchell, KCB, CVO; ✉ 9 Holmbush Rd, Putney, London SW15 3LE

MITCHELL, His Hon Judge Fergus Irvine; s of Sir George Mitchell, CB, QC (d 1978), and Elizabeth, *née* Leigh Pemberton (d 1989); *b* 30 March 1947; *Educ* Tiffin Boys' Sch Kingston; *m* 1 July 1972, Sally, yr da of late Sir Derrick Capper, QPM; 1 da (Rebecca Elizabeth b 22 March 1977), 1 s (Ewen George William b 15 Feb 1980); *Career* called to the Bar Gray's Inn 1971, head of chambers 1994–96, circuit judge (SE Circuit) 1996–; memb Gen Cncl of the Bar 1993–96 (memb Professional Conduct and Race Rels Ctees); *Recreations* farm in Aveyron (France), opera, military history; *Style—* His Hon Judge Fergus Mitchell; ✉ Snaresbrook Crown Court, Hollybush Hill, Snaresbrook, London E11 1QW (☎ 0181 982 5500)

MITCHELL, Geoffrey Bentley; s of Arthur Hale Mitchell (d 1990), and Eunice Bentley, *née* Wood (d 1989); *b* 20 June 1944; *Educ* Univ of Adelaide (BEcon); *m* 26 Jan 1967, Diedre Maria, *née* McKenna; 2 s (Mark James b 19 Oct 1971, Matthew Paul b 13 Oct 1973), 1 da (Melissa Kate b 22 Sept 1977); *Career* articled clerk Thomas Sara Macklin & Co Adelaide S Aust, lectr then sr lectr Univ of Adelaide 1966–77, reader The Flinders Univ S Aust 1977–81, sec gen International Accounting Standards Ctee 1981–85, tech dir ICAEW 1985–90; Barclays Bank plc: sr mangr 1991–93, head of accounting policies 1993–94, gp fin servs dir Chief Accountants Dept 1994–96, chief accountant 1996–; Freeman City of London 1995; memb Inst of CA in Aust 1967, FCA 1982; *Books* Principles of Accounting (Prentice Hall of Aust, 1981); *Recreations* tennis; *Clubs* Garrick, Naval and Military; *Style—* Geoffrey Mitchell, Esq; ✉ Scriventon Oast, Stockland Green, Speldhurst, Tunbridge Wells TN3 0TU (☎ 01892 863223); Barclays Bank plc, 54 Lombard Street, London EC3P 3AH (☎ 0171 699 3108, fax 0171 699 3300)

MITCHELL, Geoffrey Roger; s of Horace Stanley Mitchell (d 1974), of Fordingbridge, and Madge Amy, *née* Rogers (d 1984); *b* 6 June 1936; *Educ* Exeter Cathedral Choristers' Sch, Brentwood Sch; *Career* Nat Serv leading cadet educnl RN 1954–56; counter-tenor lay-clerk: Ely Cathedral 1957–60, Westminster Cathedral 1960–61; counter-tenor vicar-choral St Paul's Cathedral 1961–66, gen mangr John Alldis Choir 1966–, prof RAM and conductor Chamber Choir 1972–, conductor New London Singers 1972–87, dir Geoffrey Mitchell Choir 1975–, choral mangr BBC 1977–92; conductor Trinity Coll Music vocal ensemble 1977–89, guest conductor Camerata Antiqua Curitiba Brazil 1989–; chm Nat Fedn Cathedral Old Chorister Assocs 1992– (vice chm 1987–92); Hon ARAM 1981, Hon FTCL 1989; *Recreations* food, collecting antiques and prints, swimming; *Style—* Geoffrey Mitchell, Esq; ✉ 49 Chelmsford Rd, Woodford, London E18 2PW (☎ 0181 491 0962, fax 0181 491 0956)

MITCHELL, (George) Grant; s of Prof George Archibald Grant Mitchell, OBE, TD, (d 1993), and Mary *née* Cumming (d 1977); *b* 22 Sept 1939; *Educ* William Hulme's GS Manchester, Univ of Manchester Med Sch (MB ChB); *m* 14 July 1962, Sandra Joan; 1 s (Andrew b 1975), 2 da (Caroline b 1963, Victoria b 1965); *Career* house surgn and physician 1962–64: Manchester Royal Infirmary, Oldham Royal Infirmary, St Mary's Hosp; Geigy res fell Manchester Royal Infirmary 1964–65; princ in gen practice Altrincham Cheshire 1965–68; sr house offr and registrar 1968–73: Withington Hosp, St Mary's Hosp, Crumpsall Hosp; sr registrar in obstetrics Withington and Oldham Hosps 1973–76, conslt obstetrician and gynaecologist Hope Hosp Salford 1976–, hon lectr in obstetrics and gynaecology Univ of Manchester 1976–, clinical dir Dept of Obstetrics and Gynaecology and Cromwell IVF Unit Hope Hosp Salford 1994–; memb North of England Obsetrical and Gynaecological Soc 1973–; FRCSEd 1974, FRCOG 1984 (MRCOG 1971); *Recreations* travel, music, photography; *Style—* Grant Mitchell, Esq; ✉ 16 St John St, Manchester M3 4EA (☎ 0161 834 4282); Hope Hospital, Salford M6 8HD (☎ 0161 787 5259)

MITCHELL, Iain Grant; QC (1992); s of John Grant Mitchell (d 1990), of Perth, and Isabelle, *née* Gilhespie; *b* 15 Nov 1951; *Educ* Perth Acad, Univ of Edinburgh (LLB Hons); *Career* apprentice Steedman Ramage & Co WS 1973–75, admitted Faculty of Advocates 1976, pt/t tutor in mercantile law Univ of Edinburgh 1975–80, temporary sheriff 1992–; dir Sinfonia of Scotland Ltd 1990–93; local govt candidate (Cons) 1973–82; parly candidate (Cons): Falkirk West 1983, Kirkcaldy 1987, Cumbernauld and Kilsyth 1992; prospective parly candidate Dunfermline East; hon sec Scottish Cons and Unionist Assoc 1993–, vice chm Edinburgh Central Conservative Assoc 1994–; memb: Scottish Ctee Royal Inst of Int Affairs 1985–, Exec Ctee Scottish Cncl Euro Movement 1992–, Ctee Scottish Lawyers' Euro Gp 1993–, Scottish Ctee Soc for Computers and Law 1993–; chm Tst for Int Opera Theatre for Scotland 1984–, vice chm Scottish Baroque Ensemble Ltd 1988–; FSA Scot 1974, FRSA 1988; *Recreations* music and the arts, photography, cinema, walking, travel, finding enough hours in the day; *Clubs* Univ of Edinburgh Staff; *Style—*

Iain G Mitchell, Esq, QC; ✉ c/o Advocates' Library, Parliament House, High Street, Edinburgh EH1 1RF (☎ 0131 226 5071, fax 0131 225 3642, mobile 0836 700556)

MITCHELL, James; s of James William Mitchell (d 1951), and Wilhelmina Mitchell (d 1963); *b* 12 March 1926; *Educ* South Shields GS, St Edmund Hall Oxford (MA); *m* 1955 (m dis 1966), Norma (decd), da of late John Halliday; 2 s (Simon b 1957, Peter b 1959); m 2, 1967, Delia Lock (decd), *née* McCoy; *Career* writer; early work experience: actor, lectr, travel agent, barman; author of over 100 television scripts and various screenplays; Crime Writers' Assoc Award (for A Way Back) 1960, Screenwriters' Guild Award (for Callan) 1969, BAFTA Award (for Callan) 1970, Radio Industries and Sun Awards (for When the Boat Comes In) 1976; memb: Screenwriters' Guild 1966, Soc of Authors 1986; *Books* A Way Back (1959), Among Arabian Sands (1963), The Innocent Bystanders (1969), Callan (1969), When the Boat Comes In (1976), A Woman To Be Loved (1990), An Impossible Woman (1992), Leading Lady, So Far From Home (1995); *Recreations* travel, Aristology, military history; *Clubs* Lansdowne; *Style—* James Mitchell, Esq; ✉ c/o Blake Friedmann Agency, 37–41 Gower Street, London WC1E 6HH (☎ 0171 631 4331, fax 0171 323 1274)

MITCHELL, James Bryan; s of Lt Norman Keith Mitchell (d 1995), of Southampton, and Lt Daphne Jean Mitchell, *née* Howie; *b* 9 April 1951; *Educ* St Joseph's Coll Beulah Hill, Imperial Coll Univ of London (BSc), LSE (LLB); *m* 19 May 1979 (m dis 1996), Elaine Louise, da of Herbert Francis Jones (d 1973); 1 s (James Robert Seymour b 26 May 1989), 1 da (Alexandra Frances Diana-Rose b 4 April 1986); *Career* admitted slr 1980; ptnr: Barlow Lyde & Gilbert 1984–95, Stevens & Bolton 1995–; memb Law Soc; ARCS 1973, FSS 1974; *Clubs* RAC; *Style—* James Mitchell, Esq; ✉ Stevens & Bolton Solicitors, 1 The Billings, Walnut Place Close, Guildford, Surrey GU1 4TD (☎ 01483 734232, fax 01483 302254)

MITCHELL, Jeremy George Swale Hamilton; s of (George) Oswald Mitchell (d 1969), of Manchester and Bradford, and Josephine Garner (d 1962); *b* 25 May 1929; *Educ* Ampleforth, Brasenose and Nuffield Colls Oxford (MA); *m* 1, 28 July 1956 (m dis 1988), Margaret Mary, *née* Ayres; 3 s ((Paul) Laurence Damian b 1957, d 1986, Dominic Francis John b 1959, Alcuin Richard b 1964), 1 da ((Catherine) Veronica Mary b 1958); m 2, 16 March 1989, Janet Rosemary Powney, *née* Blower; *Career* Mil Serv 2 Lt RA 1948–49; dep res dir and dir of info Consumers' Assoc 1958–65, asst sec Nat Econ Devpt Office 1965–66, scientific sec then sec Social Sci Res Cncl 1966–74, dir of consumer affrs Office of Fair Trading 1974–77, dir Nat Consumer Cncl 1977–86, consumer policy advsr 1986–; vice chm Nat Cncl on Gambling; memb: Ind Ctee for the Supervision of Telephone Info Servs, Personal Investment Authy Bd, Scottish Consumer Cncl; visiting fell Euro Inst for the Media Düsseldorf; FSA; *Books* Social Science Research and Industry (jt ed 1971), Betting (1972), Marketing and the Consumer Movement (ed 1978), Electronic Banking and the Consumer (1988), Money and the Consumer (ed 1988), The Consumer and Financial Services (ed 1990), The Single European Market for Financial Services (1991), Television and the Viewer Interest (jt ed, 1994); *Style—* Jeremy Mitchell, Esq; ✉ 19 Eglinton Crescent, Edinburgh EH12 5BY (☎ 0131 346 2643, fax 0131 337 2092)

MITCHELL, John David; s of Charles Mitchell (d 1955), of Warrington, and Ruth, *née* Tilston; *b* 7 March 1942; *Educ* The Craig Windermere, Sedbergh; *m* 7 July 1970, Sarah; 1 s (Mark b 15 Feb 1974); *Career* mgmnt trainee Thames Board Mills 1959, trainee Henry Cooke 1960; Tilney & Co asset mangrs: joined 1962, ptnr 1977, md 1986– (following takeover by Charterhouse plc), chief exec 1993– (following MBO); dir various other cos; dir SFA 1995– (memb Stock Exchange 1977); *Recreations* golf, walking, gardening, travel, eating and drinking; *Clubs* Warrington Golf; *Style—* John Mitchell, Esq; ✉ Ashfield Cottages, Dark Lane, Higher Whitley, Warrington, Cheshire WA4 4QG (☎ 01925 730605); Tilney & Co, Royal Liver Buildings, Pier Head, Liverpool L3 1NY (☎ 0151 236 6000, fax 0151 236 1252)

MITCHELL, John Logan; QC (Scot 1987); s of Robert Mitchell (d 1988), and Dorothy, *née* Logan; *b* 23 June 1947; *Educ* Royal HS Edinburgh, Univ of Edinburgh (LLB); *m* 9 June 1973, Christine Browlee, da of Dr Robert Thomson (d 1996); 1 s (Stuart Logan b 4 Jan 1979), 1 da (Caroline Thomson b 10 Oct 1976); *Career* called to the Bar 1974; standing jr counsel to Dept of Agriculture and Fisheries and Forestry Cmmn 1979–81, advocate depute 1981–85; *Recreations* golf, hill walking, running; *Clubs* Mortonhall Golf; *Style—* John Mitchell, Esq, QC; ✉ 17 Braid Farm Road, Edinburgh EH10 6LE (☎ 0131 447 8099); Advocates' Library, Parliament House, Edinburgh (☎ 0131 226 5071)

MITCHELL, John Mackenzie; s of James Lindsay Mitchell (d 1942), and Dorothy Frances, *née* Clinch (d 1989); *b* 2 March 1924; *Educ* Erith GS, Erith & Dartford Tech Coll, Univ of London (BSc), City & Guilds Coll (DIC); *m* 19 March 1949, Barbara Ogilvie, da of Arthur Paul Miller; 1 s (Paul Lindsay b 25 July 1951), 1 da (Rosemary Christine 7 March 1954); *Career* General Electric Co Ltd Erith Kent: apprentice engr 1940–45, turbine design engr 1946–55, mangr and chief engr Power Plant Division 1963–65 (chief eng 1955–63); dir and chief mechanical engr C A Parsons & Co Ltd Newcastle upon Tyne 1971–74 (chief turbine engr 1965–71), engr devpt dir NEI Parsons Ltd Newcastle upon Tyne 1984–87 (engrg dir 1974–84); engrg conslt: Rolls Royce plc Derby 1989–91, NEI Parsons Ltd 1987–93, Parsons Power Generation Systems 1993–; chm Tech Ctee No5 (Steam Turbines) Int Electrotechnical Cmmn 1976–86, Parsons Memorial lecture 1980; FIMechE (MIMechE 1948), FEng 1981; *Books* author of numerous technical papers; *Recreations* travel, industrial archaeology, literature, music; *Style—* John Mitchell, Esq, FEng; ✉ 8 Linden Way, Ponteland, Newcastle upon Tyne NE20 9DP (☎ 01661 823824)

MITCHELL, Dr John Matthew; CBE (1975); s of Clifford George Arthur Mitchell (d 1933), and Grace Maud, *née* Jameson (d 1976); *b* 22 March 1925; *Educ* Ilford Co HS, Worcester Coll Oxford, Queens' Coll Cambridge (MA), Vienna Univ (PhD); *m* 5 April 1952, Eva, da of Dr Friedrich V Rupprecht (d 1964); 3 s (Oliver James Clifford b 1952, Gregory Charles Matthew b 1954, Dominic John Frederick b 1965), 1 da (Clarissa Maria b 1956); *Career* WWII Naval Intelligence 1943–46; Br Cncl: Austria, Egypt, Yugoslavia, E Pakistan, W Germany, Britain (controller Educn Sci and Med Div), asst DG, ret; fell Wolfson Coll Cambridge 1972–73, currently translator from French and German on art history and conslt on int cultural affrs; chm Cncl Inst of Linguists; FIL, memb Assoc of Art Historians; *Books* International Cultural Relations (1986); *Recreations* golf, theatre, chess, bridge; *Clubs* National Liberal, Tandridge GC; *Style—* Dr John Mitchell, CBE; ✉ The Cottage, Pains Hill Corner, Limpsfield, Surrey RH8 0RB (☎ 01883 723354)

MITCHELL, Jonathan James; QC (Scot 1992); s of John Angus Macbeth Mitchell, of Edinburgh, and Ann Katharine, *née* Williamson; *b* 9 Aug 1951; *Educ* Edinburgh Acad, Marlborough, New Coll Oxford (BA), Univ of Edinburgh (LLB); *m* 28 Aug 1987, Melinda Jane, da of Michael McGarry; 1 da (Hannah Catriona McGarry b 1 March 1988), 1 s (Ewan Patrick Macbeth b 28 December 1992); *Career* apprentice Simpson & Marwick 1976–77, legal offr Citizens' Rights Office 1977, asst to Allan Macdougall 1977–78, admitted to Faculty of Advocates 1979, temp sheriff 1988, dep social security cmmr 1994; *Books* Eviction and Rent Arrears (1994); *Recreations* children, walking; *Clubs* Scotch Malt Whisky Soc; *Style—* Jonathan Mitchell, Esq, QC; ✉ 30 Warriston Crescent, Edinburgh EH3 5LB (☎ 0131 557 0854); c/o Advocates' Library, Parliament House, Edinburgh EH1 1RF

MITCHELL, Jonathan Stuart; s of Rev Ronald Frank Mitchell, and Margery Mabel, *née* Callaghan; *b* 29 Jan 1947; *Educ* Mill Hill Sch, Trinity Coll Dublin (BA, MA); 1 s (Christian Stuart b 21 Nov 1980), 1 da (Emily Katharina b 4 April 1982); *Career* called to the Middle Temple, in practice SE Circuit 1974–; Mktg Div Courtaulds Textiles 1969–72, PR John Laing 1972–73; memb: Exec Ctee SDP Southwark 1981–87; local govt candidate: SDP Dulwich 1982, 1984 and 1986, Lib Dems Dulwich 1994; memb Herne Hill Baptist Church; *Recreations* gardening, swimming, rowing, sailing; *Style—* Jonathan Mitchell, Esq; ✉ 35 Pickwick Rd, Dulwich, London SE21 7JN; 3 Gray's Inn Square, Gray's Inn, London WC1R 5AH (☎ 0171 831 2311)

MITCHELL, Julian; s of late William Moncur Mitchell, and Christine Mary, *née* Browne (d 1994); *b* 1 May 1935; *Educ* Winchester, Wadham Coll Oxford (BA), St Antony's Coll Oxford; *Career* Nat Serv Sub Lt RNVR 1953–55; Harkness fell USA 1959–61, freelance writer 1962–, regular critic on BBC arts progs; formerly: govr Chelsea Sch of Art, memb Lit Ctee English Arts Cncl, chm Drama Ctee Welsh Arts Cncl; *Awards* incl John Llewellyn Rhys prize 1965, Somerset Maugham award 1966; *Books* Introduction (stories, 1960); novels: Imaginary Toys (1961), A Disturbing Influence (1962), As Far As You Can Go (1963), The White Father (1964), A Circle of Friends (1966), The Undiscovered Country (1968); Jennie, Lady Randolph Churchill (biography, with Peregrine Churchill, 1974); contrib: The Welsh History Review, The Monmouthshire Antiquary; *Stage Plays* incl: A Heritage and its History (1965), A Family and a Fortune (1975), Half-Life (1977), Another Country (1981, Play of the Year), Francis (1983), After Aida (1986), Falling Over England (1994); trans Pirandello's Henry IV (John Florio prize 1980), devised and narrated Adelina Patti - Queen of Song (1987), August (version of Chekhov's Uncle Vanya, 1994); *Films* Arabesque (dir Stanley Donen, 1965), Another Country (dir Marek Kanievska, 1984), Vincent and Theo (dir Robert Altman, 1990), August (dir Anthony Hopkins, 1995); *TV Work* incl: Elizabeth R (Emmy award 1971), A Question of Degree, Rust, Jennie, Lady Randolph Churchill (series), Abide With Me (Int Critics prize Monte Carlo and US Humanities award 1977), The Mysterious Stranger (Golden Eagle award 1983), Inspector Morse (RTS and Writers' Guild awards 1991), Survival of the Fittest, All the Waters of Wye (documentary); adaptations of books for screen incl: Persuasion, Staying On, The Good Soldier; author of numerous reviews for magazines and newspapers; *Style—* Julian Mitchell, Esq

MITCHELL, Katie Jane; da of Michael J Mitchell, of Marlborough, Wilts, and Sally, *née* Powell; *b* 23 Sept 1964; *Educ* Godolphn Sch Salisbury, Oakham Sch Rutland, Magdalen Coll Oxford; *Career* theatre director; began career as prodn asst Kings Head Theatre Club 1986–87; asst dir: Paines Plough 1987, The Writer's Company 1988, RSC 1988–89; fndr own co Classic on a Shoestring (COAS) 1990; assoc dir RSC 1996; *Theatre* Gate Theatre London/COAS prodns incl: Vassa Zheleznova 1990, Women of Troy 1991, The House of Bernarda Alba 1992; RSC prodns incl: Dybbuk 1992, Ghosts 1993, Henry IV (part III) 1994, Easter 1995, The Phoenician Women 1995; RNT prodns incl: Rutherford and Son 1994, Machine Wreckers 1995; other prodns incl: Arden of Faversham (COAS/Old Red Lion) 1990, Diarmuid and Graine (tour Poland) 1991, Live Like Pigs (COAS/Royal Court) 1993, The Last Ones (Abbey Theatre Dublin) 1993, Widowing of Mrs Holroyd (BBC 2) 1995, Don Giovanni (Welsh Nat Opera) 1996; *Awards* Winston Churchill Memorial Tst Travel Fellowship 1989, Time Out Theatre Award (for Arden of Faversham, Women of Troy and Vassa Zheleznova) 1991, Prudential/Arts Cncl of GB Award for contribution to Theatre 1995, Olivier Award nomination for Best Dir 1995, Evening Standard Award for Best Director (for The Phoenician Women) 1996; *Recreations* travel, reading, penny whistle; *Style—* Ms Katie Mitchell; ✉ c/o Sebastian Born, The Agency, 24 Pottery Lane, Holland Park, London W11 4LZ (☎ 0171 727 1346, fax 0171 727 9037)

MITCHELL, Keith Kirkman; OBE (1979); s of John Stanley Mitchell, and Annie Mitchell; *b* 25 May 1927; *Educ* Loughborough Coll; *m* 1950, Hannah Forrest; 2 s; *Career* teacher physical educn Wisbech GS 1950–52, dir of physical educn Manchester YMCA 1952–55, lectr in physical educn Univ of Leeds 1955–91; CCPR: chm Exec Ctee 1981–87 (memb 1971–), chm Games & Sports Div 1976–81, vice pres 1989–; memb: Sports Cncl 1975–87 (Policy & Resources Ctee 1985–87), Nat Olympic Ctee 1987–; Federation Internationale de Basketball: qualified as referee 1956, cmmr 1969–, memb Euro Tech Cmmn 1969–, memb World Tech Cmmn 1969–79, tech delegate to Olympic Games 1972–84, vice pres World Tech Cmmn 1976–84 (ex officio memb 1984–), memb Euro Exec Cmmn 1984–, memb Central Bd 1984–94, conf lectr; vice pres Euro Basketball Fedn 1994–; hon gen sec English Basketball Assoc 1953–84, mangr GB Olympic Team 1960–68; chm: Leeds Amateur Sports Cncl 1965–80, Yorkshire Basketball League 1965–91, Sports Devpt Ctee Yorkshire and Humberside Regnl Cncl of Sport and Recreation, British & Irish Basketball Fedn 1973–75, 1979–81 and 1987–; chm of govrs Leeds Athletics Inst 1977–80; vice pres: Univs Athletic Union 1960–, English Mini Basketball Assoc; pres: Leeds City Sports Fedn 1976–, Yorkshire and Humberside Sports Fedn 1980– (chm 1968–80), Cwlth Basketball Fedn 1980–, English Basketball Assoc 1985–; *Recreations* fishing, golf, cutting the lawn and sitting on it, food and wine; *Style—* Keith Mitchell, Esq, OBE; ✉ 7 Park Crescent, Guiseley, Leeds

MITCHELL, Dr Leslie Arthur; s of John Thomas Cornes Mitchell (d 1994), of Malpas, Cheshire, and Hilda May, *née* Lievesley; *b* 29 Feb 1940; *Educ* Sir John Talbots GS, Univ of Liverpool (BEng, PhD); *m* 16 March 1963, Janet Elsie, da of Charles William Bate (d 1973); 1 da (Kerry Janet b 9 June 1964), 2 s (Roderick Leslie b 5 Aug 1967, Alexander Leslie b 10 Dec 1977); *Career* CEGB: head of surface physics Berkeley Nuclear Laboratories 1971–76 (res offr 1964–71), laboratory mangr Marchwood Engrg Laboratories 1981–85 (branch mangr structural engrg 1976–81), dir of laboratories Technol Planning and Research 1987–89 (dir PWR 1985–87); head of business planning National Power 1989–90, dir of technol Nuclear Electric plc 1991–96 (head of business review and internal audit 1990–91), dir of technol and central engrg Magnox Electric plc 1996–; memb Radioactive Waste Mgmnt Advsy Ctee (RWMAC) DOE 1991–; chm Cncl TWI 1996–; memb Cncl ERA 1991–; FEng 1994, FIMechE 1992; *Recreations* Cotswold stone building renovation, gardening, reading, occasional golf; *Style—* Dr Leslie Mitchell, FEng; ✉ Magnox Electric plc, Berkeley Centre, Berkeley, Glos GL13 9PB (☎ 01453 812168, fax 01453 812121)

MITCHELL, Marilyn Margaret; da of David Glyndwr Walters, of Ottawa, Canada, and Ada Cecelia, *née* Wilson; *b* 11 July 1944; *Educ* St Augustine's Convent Ealing, Charing Cross Hosp Med Sch (MB BS, DCH); *m* 1, 1976 (m dis 1979); m 2, 11 Feb 1981, Ian Mitchell, s of Albert Mitchell, of Sheringham, Norfolk; 1 step s (Joel b 1973), 1 s (Janna b 1983), 2 da (Rachel Clare b 1977, Beth b 1985); *Career* house surgn Charing Cross Hosp 1970–71, SHO med and paediatrics Whittington Hosp 1971–72, SHO Bart's and Hackney 1973, registrar psychiatry N Middx Hosp 1974, GP 1975, SHO registrar and sr registrar W Suffolk Hosp and Cambridge 1976, assoc specialist child and family psychiatry Royal Ottawa Hosp 1980; locum conslt: Child and Family Guidance Clinic Esher 1931, conslt psychiatrist in adult psychiatry Cornwall 1982–95, currently conslt psychiatrist and lead clinician on continuing care and rehabilitation Cornwall Healthcare Tst St Austell; RCPsych: memb Exec Ctee, memb SW Region Exec Ctee, memb Social Rehabilitation Community Advice Gp; lead clinician Rehabilitation for Cornwall, chm Care Planning Gp for Mentally Ill in Cornwall, memb Liaison Working Gp for Implementation of Community Care Programme, med advsr Mental Health Forum, memb Cornwall Cncl for Sanelink; BMA award for res in mental health 1989; MRCPsych, memb Med Defence Union; *Recreations* rambling, opera, housecrafts and culinery skills; *Style—* Mrs Marilyn Mitchell; ✉ South Point, Beach Road, Carlyon Bay, Cornwall PL25 3PJ (☎ 01726 815624); Cornwall Healthcare Trust, 5 King's Avenue, St Austell, Cornwall PL25 4TT (☎ 01726 291213)

MITCHELL, Sheriff (James Lachlan) Martin; RD (1969); s of Lachlan Martin Victor Mitchell, OBE, MB ChB (d 1956), and Harriet Doris, *née* Riggall (d 1980); *b* 13 June 1929;

Educ Cargilfield, Sedbergh, Univ of Edinburgh (MA, LLB); *m* 16 April 1993, Jane Anne, da of Patrick Clement Cox (d 1982); *Career* Nat Serv RN 1954–56, Temp Actg Sub Lt RNVR(S) 1954 (perm 1956), Cdr RNR(S), ret 1974; advocate 1957–74, standing jr counsel in Scotland to Admty Bd 1963–74; Sheriff Lothians and Peebles (now Lothian and Borders) 1974–95, Floating Sheriff 1974–78, Sheriff at Edinburgh 1978–95 (Hon Sheriff Inverness 1983), a temp Sheriff 1971–74 and 1995–; govr Cargilfield Sch 1966–91; *Recreations* fishing, photography, the gramophone; *Clubs* New (Edinburgh), Highland (Inverness); *Style*— Sheriff Martin Mitchell, RD; ✉ 3 Great Stuart St, Edinburgh EH3 6AP (☎ 0131 225 3384)

MITCHELL, Dame Mona Ann; DCVO (1992, CVO 1985, LVO 1976); da of Maj-Gen Francis Neville Mitchell, CB, CBE, DSO (d 1954), and Ann Christian, *née* Livingstone-Learmonth (d 1988); *b* 20 Feb 1938; *Educ* North Foreland Lodge; *Career* sec: to late Mr Fulke Walwyn, CVO, racehorse trainer 1958–62, to Mr E Hardy Amies (now Sir Hardy Amies, KCVO), couturier 1963–68; private sec to HRH Princess Alexandra 1974–91 (sec 1968–74), extra lady-in-waiting 1968–; *Recreations* gardening and music; *Clubs* Army and Navy; *Style*— Dame Mona Mitchell, DCVO; ✉ Valley Farm, Blackford, Yeovil, Somerset BA22 7EF (☎ 01963 440304)

MITCHELL, Neil; *b* 8 June 1967; *Career* keyboardist with Wet Wet Wet; 14 top twenty singles incl 3 no 1's (With A Little Help From My Friends 1988 (raised over £600,000 for Childline), Goodnight Girl 1992, Love Is All Around 1994); albums with Wet Wet Wet: Popped In Souled Out (1987, UK no 1), The Memphis Sessions (1988, UK no 3), Holding Back The River (1989, UK no 2), High On The Happy Side (1992, UK no 1), End Of Part One (compilation, 1994, UK no 1), Picture This (1995); participated in: Prince's Trust Rock Gala 1988, 1989 and 1990, concert for Nelson Mandela's 70th birthday 1988, John Lennon Tribute concert 1990; *Style*— Neil Mitchell, Esq; ✉ c/o Wet TM Ltd, 14/16 Speirs Wharf, Port Dundas, Glasgow G4 9TB (☎ 0141 353 1515, fax 0141 353 3852)

MITCHELL, Patricia Anne; da of Derek Fairburn (d 1984), and Margaret Crossley, *née* Greenwood (d 1987); *b* 19 Feb 1957; *Educ* Sheffield HS (GPDST), Univ of Durham (BA); *m* 26 June 1982 (m dis 1992), Andrew Robert Mitchell, s of Malcolm Mitchell, of London; *Career* admitted slr 1981; ptnr Warner Cranston 1990–; memb Law Soc, memb RILA; *Style*— Patricia Mitchell; ✉ Warner Cranston, Pickfords Wharf, Clink Street, London SE1 9DG (☎ 0171 403 2900, fax 0171 403 4221, telex 9312133051 WNG)

MITCHELL, The Very Rev Patrick Reynolds; s of Lt-Col Percy Reynolds Mitchell, DSO (d 1954), of Whitestaunton Manor, Chard, Somerset, and Constance Margaret, *née* Kerby (d 1955); *b* 17 March 1930; *Educ* Eton, Merton Coll Oxford (MA), Wells Theological Coll; *m* 1, 1959, Mary Evelyn (d 1986), da of John Savile Phillips (d 1960); 3 s (Andrew Patrick b 1964, Julian Mark b 1968, Nicholas David b 1970), 1 da (Sarah Jane b 1962); m 2, 1988, Mrs Pamela Douglas-Pennant, da of late A G Le Marchant, of Wolford Lodge, Honiton, Devon, wid of Henry Douglas-Pennant (d 1986); *Career* Nat Serv Welsh Gds 1948–49; curate St Mark's Mansfield 1954–57, priest vicar Wells Cathedral, chaplain Wells Theological Coll 1957–61, vicar St James' Milton Portsmouth 1961–67, vicar Frome Selwood Somerset 1967–73, dean of Wells 1973–89, dean of Windsor and register of the Most Noble Order of the Garter 1989–; sr domestic chaplain to HM The Queen 1989–; res fell Merton Coll Oxford 1984, chm Deans and Provosts' Conf 1988–92; Hon Freeman City of Wells 1986; FSA; *Recreations* family, music, gardening, historical research; *Style*— The Very Rev Patrick Mitchell, FSA; ✉ The Deanery, Windsor Castle, Berks SL4 1NJ (☎ 01753 865561, fax 01753 819002)

MITCHELL, Paul England; s of Ronald England Mitchell, of Alderholt, Fordingbridge, Hants, and Katia Patricia, *née* Hannay; *b* 2 Nov 1951; *Educ* Canford, Univ of Bristol (LLB); *m* 18 Aug 1984, Catherine Anne; 1 da (Charlotte Daniele b 24 Sept 1986), 1 s (Mark England b 11 May 1989); *Career* articled clerk Joynson-Hicks 1974–76, ptnr Joynson-Hicks (now Taylor Joynson Garrett) 1978–; memb Advsy Bd Roald Dahl Fndn, memb Editorial Bd International Media Law; Freeman City of London, memb Worshipful Co of Fishmongers; memb Law Soc; *Recreations* family, sailing, food and wine; *Clubs* Wig & Pen; *Style*— Paul Mitchell, Esq; ✉ Taylor Joynson Garrett, Carmelite, 50 Victoria Embankment, London EC4Y 0DX (☎ 0171 353 1234, fax 0171 936 2666, mobile 0802 702864)

MITCHELL, Peter Stuart; s of William Edmund Chaloner Mitchell (d 1978), and Mabel, *née* Hodson (d 1974); *b* 5 Oct 1935; *Educ* St Andrew's Church Sch Preston, King Edward VII Sch Lytham St Anne's; *m* 1, 23 Dec 1957 (m dis 1974), Lillah; m 2, 19 July 1974, Barbara, da of James Haynes (d 1974); *Career* apprentice in engrg English Electric Preston Lancs 1952–60, trg in photography John Maltby Hendon 1960–61; photographer: Rolls Royce Spadeadam Cumberland 1961–66, Graphic Group Leeds 1966–69; industl photographer and head of dept Hepworth 4 Grandage (part of AE Group) 1970–78, industl photographer generating own business Foster 4 Skeffington 1979–80, in own business 1981–; pt/t tutor Herefordshire Coll of Art & Design 1984–; memb Admissions and Qualifications Panel for Industl and Architectural Photography BIPP; Inst of Incorporated Photographers: licentiate 1968, assoc 1972, fell 1976; FBIPP 1976 (memb 1968–), assoc memb Master Photographers' Assoc; *Recreations* photography, reading, classical music; *Style*— Peter Mitchell, Esq; ✉ 3 Acacia Close, Hereford HR2 6BP (☎ 01432 270859)

MITCHELL, Robert Henry (Robin); s of Henry Gordon Mitchell, of East Bergholt, Colchester, and Elizabeth Margaret Katherine, *née* Richards; *b* 17 Aug 1955; *Educ* Stowe, Peterhouse Cambridge (MA); *m* 16 June 1979, Helen Miranda, da of John Victor Akerman, of Brockenhurst, Hants; 1 s (Jonathan b 1988), 2 da (Philippa 1984, Claire b 1986); *Career* admitted slr 1980, ptnr Norton Rose 1986–; *Recreations* hockey, skiing, tennis, swimming; *Style*— Robin Mitchell, Esq; ✉ Norton Rose, Kempson House, Camomile Street, London EC3A 7AN (☎ 0171 283 6000, fax 0171 283 6500)

MITCHELL, Robin Paul; s of late Frederick James Mitchell, of Enfield, Middx, and Maud Patricia, *née* Pawson; *b* 15 Feb 1955; *Educ* Latymer Sch; *m* Maria Ann, da of Sean Joseph Kealy, of Enfield, Middx; 2 s (John Paul b 26 April 1979, David Frederick b 2 Feb 1981), 1 da (Lucy Elizabeth b 9 April 1986); *Career* Charles Stanley & Co: unauthorised clerk 1973–75, authorised clerk 1975–81, sr dealer 1981–85, head dealer 1985–; MSI; *Recreations* football, cricket, tennis, golf; *Clubs* Stock Exchange Veterans, Bush Hill Park Golf; *Style*— Robin Mitchell, Esq; ✉ Charles Stanley & Co, Garden House, 18 Finsbury Circus, London EC2M 7BL

MITCHELL, Stephen Graham; s of Derek Mitchell, of Loughborough, and Margaret, *née* Rigden; *b* 14 July 1949; *Educ* Loughborough GS, Univ of Manchester; *m* 27 Sept 1977, Barbara Vina, da of Robert Henry Gilder; 1 da (Francesca b 6 Oct 1988), 1 s (Struan b 15 Aug 1990); *Career* with Thomson Regional Newspapers until 1974; BBC Radio: journalist 1974–91, managing ed BBC Radio News 1991–93, ed radio news progs 1993–; *Recreations* spending time with my family; *Style*— Stephen Mitchell, Esq; ✉ BBC News & Current Affairs, Radio, Broadcasting House, Portland Place, London W1A 1AA (☎ 0171 765 5918, fax 0171 765 5818)

MITCHELL, Terence Croft; s of Arthur Croft Mitchell (d 1956), and Evelyn Violet, *née* Ware (d 1986); *b* 17 June 1929; *Educ* Holderness Sch New Hampshire USA, Bradfield Coll, St Catharine's Coll Cambridge (MA); *Career* craftsman REME 1947–49; asst master St Catherine's Sch Almondsbury 1954–56; resident study Tyndale House Cambridge 1956–58; Euro rep Aust Inst of Archaeology 1958–59; Dept of Western Asiatic Antiquities British Museum: asst keeper 1959–74, dep keeper 1974–83, keeper 1983–89; memb Ctee Palestine Exploration Fund, ed Monograph Series, chm Victoria Inst; *Books* Music and Civilisation (ed, Br Museum Yearbook 4 1980), The Bible in the British Museum Interpreting the Evidence (1988 and 1996), The Oxus Treasure (1989), Cambridge Ancient History III.1 & 2 (contrib 1982 and 1991); *Recreations* music, reading, landscape gardening; *Clubs* Athenaeum; *Style*— T C Mitchell, Esq

MITCHELL, Terence Leonard; s of Leonard Alfred James Mitchell, and Sarah Anne Mitchell; *b* 19 July 1934; *Educ* Worthing Boys HS, Univ of Auckland NZ (Dip Arch); *m* 1, 1961 (m dis); 1 s, 2 da; m 2, 1989, Antonina Knight, da of late Constantine Popoff; *Career* violinist and music teacher until age 26, played under the batons of Sir Adrian Boult, Sir Malcolm Sargeant and John Hopkins; since qualifying in 1964 practised as architect; notable works incl: award winning Cathedral Sq (Christchurch NZ) 1974, award winning Norman Kirk Courts (Christchurch NZ) 1978, holiday complex for Sudeley Castle 1985, The Hayes Retirement Village (Prestbury, Glos) 1987; now specialising in the restoration of historic buildings; ARIBA; *Recreations* English history and architecture, music, artist; *Style*— Terence Mitchell, Esq; ✉ 9 Kenelm Rise, Winchcombe, Cheltenham, Glos GW4 5JU (☎ 01242 603966 and 01242 603490)

MITCHELL, Valerie Joy; da of Henry Frederick Twidale, of Sao Paulo, Brazil, and Dorothy Mary, *née* Pierce, MBE; *b* 2 March 1941; *Educ* St Paul's Sch Sao Paulo Brazil, Beaufront Sch Surrey, McGill Univ Montreal Canada (BA); *m* 1, 15 Aug 1962 (m dis 1970), Henri Pierre, s of Frederic Henri Eschauzier; 2 s (Marc William Frederick b 30 Aug 1965, James Henri b 2 Jan 1967); m 2, 1 Sept 1972, Graham Rangeley, s of Arthur Mitchell; 1 da (Samantha Anna b 13 Jan 1974); *Career* lectr in opera, PR conslt to Mayer-Lismann Opera Workshop and PA to asst Dean of Arts and Science McGill Univ Montreal 1962–80; English-Speaking Union of the Commonwealth: asst Educn Dept 1980–83, dir of Branches and Cultural Affairs 1983–94, dep DG 1989–94, DG and sec-gen International Cncl 1994–; FRSA 1987; *Recreations* music, theatre, tennis, walking; *Style*— Mrs Valerie Mitchell; ✉ The English-Speaking Union, Dartmouth House, 37 Charles Street, London W1X 8AB (☎ 0171 493 3328, fax 0171 495 6108)

MITCHELL, William; s of William Mitchell (d 1959), and Eileen, *née* King; *b* 8 Aug 1944; *Educ* Campbell Coll Belfast, Oriel Coll Oxford (MA, dip in social studies); *m* 1, 1969, Pratima, *née* Bhatia; 1 da (Priya b 21 Feb 1971); m 2, 1993, Natalina, *née* Bertoli; 1 s (Luca b 4 May 1994); *Career* dir of int divs and gp bd dir Oxford University Press UK 1970–85, exec ed Reference Publishing Oxford University Press USA 1985–88, exec dir Children's Publishing Reed Publishing Group UK 1988–89, md Children's Publishing Div and md Reference Div HarperCollins Publishers UK 1990–92, md JM Dent Ltd and dep gp md Orion Publishing Group Ltd 1992–93, md Bertoli Mitchell Intellectual Property Brokers 1993–; *Recreations* normal; *Clubs* Groucho; *Style*— William Mitchell, Esq; ✉ 6A Park Walk, London SW10 0AD (☎ 0171 351 3594)

MITCHELL, Sir (Edgar) William John; kt (1990), CBE (1976); s of Edgar Mitchell (d 1964), of Kingsbridge, Devon, and Caroline Lauretta (d 1954), *née* Stoneman; *b* 25 Sept 1925; *Educ* Kingsbridge GS, Univ of Sheffield (BSc, MSc), Univ of Bristol (PhD), Univ of Oxford (MA); *m* 1, 1948; 1 s (Jonathan b 1963); m 2, 25 Jan 1985, Margaret Constance Davies, da of Capt Harry Brown (d 1925), of Kirkby Lonsdale, Cumbria; 1 step s (Martin b 1949), 1 step da (Philippa b 1953); *Career* res physicist Metropolitan Vickers Manchester 1946–51, seconded to Univ of Bristol 1948–50; Univ of Reading: fell 1951–52, lectr 1952, reader 1958, prof 1961, dean 1965–68, dep vice chllr 1976–78; Univ of Oxford: Dr Lees prof of experimental philosophy 1978–88, fell Wadham Coll 1978–, prof of physics 1988–90; author of numerous scientific papers on condensed matter physics; SERC: memb 1970–74 and 1982–85, chm Physics Ctee 1967–70 (memb 1965–70), chm Neutron Beam Res Ctee 1966–74, memb Nuclear Physics Bd 1980–85, chm of Cncl 1985–90; Institut Laue-Lengevin Grenoble: acting jt dir Inst Laue-Lengevin Grenoble 1973, memb Sci Cncl 1973–80; chm SE Region Computing Ctee 1974–76, memb Comité de Direction Solid State Physics Laboratory Ecole Normale and Univ of Paris 1975–79, memb Exec Ctee Univ Cncl for Non-Academic Staff 1979–82, memb Science Planning Gp for Spallation Neutron Source 1980–85, memb UGC Physical Sci Ctee 1982–85, memb Cncl Inst of Physics 1982–86, memb Mgmnt Bd Br Nat Space Centre 1986–90, memb Scientific Advsy Ctee for Nat Gallery 1987–, vice pres Euro Science Fndn 1990–92, pres Cncl CERN Geneva 1991–93, memb Ctee for Devpt of Euro Sci and Technol (CODEST) 1991–94, memb Euro Sciences and Technol Assembly (successor to CODEST) 1994–; Glazebrook Medal and Prize (sr medal) Inst of Physics 1996; Hon DSc: Univ of Reading 1987, Univ of Kent 1988, Univ of Budapest 1988, Univ of Birmingham 1990; FInstP, FRS 1986; Officer's Cross Order of Merit Germany 1991; *Recreations* opera, food, motoring, walking; *Clubs* Oxford and Cambridge; *Style*— Sir William Mitchell, CBE, FRS; ✉ Foxfield, Potkiln Lane, Goring Heath, Oxon RG8 7SR

MITCHELL, Rt Rev Mgr William Joseph; s of William Ernest Mitchell, of Bristol, and Katherine, *née* O'Donnell; *b* 4 Jan 1936; *Educ* St Brendan's Coll Bristol, Corpus Christi Coll Oxford (MA), Seminaire St Sulpice Paris, Pontifical Gregorian Univ Rome (LCL); *Career* ordained priest 1961, curate Pro-Cathedral Clifton Bristol 1963–64, sec to Bishop of Clifton 1964–75, parish priest St Bernadette Bristol 1975–78, rector Pontifical Beda Coll Rome 1978–87, appointed prelate of honour (monsignor) 1978, vicar gen Clifton and canon Clifton Diocesan Chapter 1987–; parish priest: St John's Bath 1988–90, St Antony's Bristol 1990–96, St Mary-on-the-Quay Bristol 1996–; *Style*— The Rt Rev Mgr William Mitchell; ✉ St Mary's Presbytery, 20 Colston Street, Bristol BS1 5AE (☎ 0117 926 4702)

MITCHELL-HEGGS, Dr Nita Ann; da of Maj (Dr) Lewis Posner (d 1975), and Olivia, *née* Jones; *b* 6 June 1942; *Educ* N London Collegiate Sch, London Hosp Med Coll (MB BS, FRCP, FFOM, DCH); *m* 26 July 1967, Dr Peter Francis Mitchell-Heggs, s of Maj Francis Sansome Mitchell-Heggs (d 1986); 2 da (Emily b 2 July 1974, Sophie b 23 March 1977); *Career* formerly held posts in paediatrics, psychiatry, occupational med, student health; currently conslt occupational physician St George's Health Care NHS Tst, sr lectr St George's Hosp Med Sch; affiliate RCPsych, memb SOM; *Publications* chapters and articles on student mental health, anxiety and depression; *Recreations* travel, skiing, theatre, opera; *Clubs* RAC; *Style*— Dr Nita Mitchell-Heggs; ✉ St George's Hospital, Blackshaw Rd, Tooting, London SW17 0QT (☎ 0181 725 1662, fax 0181 725 3087)

MITCHELL-INNES, Alistair Campbell; s of Peter Campbell Mitchell-Innes (d 1960); *b* 1 March 1934; *Educ* Charterhouse; *m* 1957, Penelope Ann, *née* Hill; 1 s, 2 da; *Career* Lt Queen's Own Royal W Kent Parachute Regt 1953–54; dir Macfisheries Ltd 1971–75, vice chm Walls Meat Co Ltd 1975–77, dir Brooke Bond Group plc 1979–85, chief exec Nabisco Group Ltd 1985–88; currently dep chm HP Bulmer (Holdings) plc; chm: Sidney C Banks plc 1994–, Anglo and Overseas Trust plc 1996–; dir: Next plc, Evans Halshaw plc; *Recreations* golf, gardening; *Clubs* Caledonian, MCC, The Berkshire Golf; *Style*— Alistair Mitchell-Innes, Esq; ✉ Langton Lodge, Station Road, Sunningdale, Berks SL5 0QR

MITCHINSON, David; s of Robert Stockdale Mitchinson (d 1988), of London, and Winifred May, *née* Earney (d 1975); *b* 8 Dec 1944; *Educ* Bath Academy of Art (Dip); *Career* designer; Kröller Müller Museum Otterlo 1967–68, Henry Moore 1968–77; The Henry Moore Foundation: joined 1977, keeper of graphics 1980–86, keeper of graphics and sculpture 1986–87, curator 1987– (organiser major exhbns 1982–95); dir: Raymond Spencer Co 1989–90, HMF Enterprises Ltd 1991–; tstee Hat Hill Sculpture Foundation Goodwood 1994–; *Publications* incl: Henry Moore Graphic Work 1973–86, Henry Moore: Unpublished Drawings 1972, With Henry Moore: The Artist at Work photographed by Gemma Levine 1978, Henry Moore Sculpture 1981, Life and Times, Henry Moore - A Short Biography 1984, Henry Moore: Life and Times 1995; *Style*— David Mitchinson,

Esq; ✉ The Henry Moore Foundation, Dane Tree House, Perry Green, Much Hadham, Herts SG10 6EE (☎ 01279 843333, fax 01279 843647)

MITCHISON, Prof Hon Denis Anthony; CMG (1984); s of Baron Mitchison, CBE (Life Peer, d 1970); *b* 6 Sept 1919; *Educ* Abbotsholme Sch, Trinity Coll Cambridge, Univ Coll Hosp London; *m* 1, 1940, Ruth Sylvia (d 1992), da of Hubert Gill; 2 s (Graeme, Terence), 2 da (Susan, Clare); m 2, 1993, Honora, da of Christopher Carlin; *Career* prof of Bacteriology Royal Postgraduate Med Sch 1971–84, ret; dir Med Res Cncl Unit for Laboratory Studies of Tuberculosis 1956–84, emeritus prof Univ of London, grant holder St George's Hosp Med Sch 1993–; *Style*— Prof the Hon Denis Mitchison, CMG; ✉ 14 Marlborough Rd, Richmond, Surrey (☎ and fax 0181 940 4751, work 0181 725 5704)

MITCHISON, Prof the Hon (John) Murdoch; 2 s of Baron Mitchison, CBE, QC (Life Peer, d 1970), and Naomi Mitchison, *née* Haldane, the writer; *b* 11 June 1922; *Educ* Winchester, Trinity Coll Cambridge; *m* 21 June 1947, Rosalind Mary, da of late Edward Murray Wrong, of Toronto, Canada; 1 s, 3 da; *Career* prof of zoology Univ of Edinburgh 1963–88; memb Sci Bd SRC 1976–79; memb Royal Cmmn on Environmental Pollution 1974–79; author; FRS, FRSE 1966; *Style*— Prof the Hon Murdoch Mitchison, FRS, FRSE; ✉ Great Yew, Ormiston, E Lothian EH35 5NJ (☎ 01875 340530, work 0131 650 5488)

MITCHISON, Baroness; Naomi Margaret; *née* Haldane; CBE (1985); da of late John Scott Haldane, CH; *b* 1 Nov 1897; *Educ* Dragon; *m* 1916, Baron Mitchison, CBE, QC (Life Peer, d 1970); 3 s, 2 da; *Career* author; hon fell Wolfson Coll Oxford 1983; Hon DLitt: Univ of Strathclyde, Univ of Stirling, Univ of Dundee, Heriot-Watt Univ; *Style*— The Rt Hon the Lady Mitchison, CBE; ✉ Carradale House, Carradale, Campbeltown, Scotland

MITSON, (Sydney) Allen; s of Sydney Mitson (d 1991), of Snaresbrook and St Margaret's Bay, Kent, and Catherine, *née* Gooding; *b* 24 May 1933; *Educ* Exeter Sch, Forest Sch, BA; *m* 1, 1959 (m dis 1971), Elizabeth Angela, da of R Garner (d 1966), of Buckhurst Hill, Essex; 2 s (Andrew b 1963, Michael b 1966); m 2, 1973, Valerie Angela, da of J Sherratt (d 1988), of Waltham Abbey, Essex; 1 step s (John b 1967); *Career* Nat Serv Royal Signals; sales promotion mangr Rotaflex 1960–65, fndr Emess Lighting 1966 (became public co 1980), md Emess Lighting (UK) Ltd 1980–89, chm Inlite Group 1989–91, business conslt 1992–; underwriting memb Lloyd's 1977–; Freeman City of London 1983, Liveryman Worshipful Co of Gold and Silver Wyre Drawers 1983–95; *Recreations* walking, swimming; *Style*— Allen Mitson, Esq; ✉ Seaways, Bay Hill, St Margaret's Bay, nr Dover, Kent CT15 6DU (☎ 01304 853418, fax 01304 853313)

MITTLER, Prof Peter Joseph; CBE (1981); s of Dr Gustav Mittler (d 1962), of Leeds, and Gertrude Mittler (d 1987); *b* 2 April 1930; *Educ* Merchant Taylors' Crosby, Pembroke Coll Cambridge (MA, PhD); *m* 2 April 1955, Helle, da of Dr Ernest Katscher (d 1980), of Vienna; 3 s (Paul b 1955, Stephen b 1959, Martin b 1964); *Career* Nat Serv Ordnance Corps 1949–50, RAMC 1950– (Capt Res); clinical psychologist 1954–63, lectr in psychology Birkbeck Coll London 1963–68, prof of special educn and dir Hester Adrian Res Centre 1968–82, emeritus prof of special educn 1995, dir Sch of Educn and dean Faculty of Educn Univ of Manchester 1991–94; former memb: Sch Examination and Assessment Cncl 1988–90, Prince of Wales Advsy Gp on Disability 1984–90; pres Int League of Socs for Persons with Mental Handicap 1982–86; hon fell Manchester Poly 1985; FBPsS 1966, Chartered Psychologist 1989; *Books* Psychological Assessment (1970), Study of Twins (1971), Advances in Mental Handicap Research (2 vols 1981, 1983), Parents, Professionals and Mentally Handicapped People (1983), Staff Training (1987), Training and Special Educational Needs (1988), Teacher Training for Special Needs in Europe (1995), Changing Policy and Practice for People with Learning Disabilities (1995); *Recreations* travel, listening to music; *Style*— Prof Peter Mittler, CBE; ✉ School of Education, The University, Manchester M13 9PL (☎ 0161 275 3498; home ☎/fax 0161 434 5625)

MITTWOCH, Prof Ursula; da of Prof Eugen Mittwoch (d 1942), and Dr Anna Hermine Mittwoch, *née* Lipmann (d 1968); *b* 21 March 1924; *Educ* Henrietta Barnett Sch, Univ of London (BSc, PhD, DSc); *m* 21 Dec 1954, Bernard Victor Springer; 1 da (Caroline b 1960); *Career* external sci staff MRC 1958–62, prof of genetics UCL 1985–89 (lectr 1963–80, reader 1980–85), hon visiting prof London Hosp Med Coll 1989–90, visiting prof Queen Mary & Westfield Coll 1990–, hon res fell UCL 1992–; FIBiol 1973; *Books* Sex Chromosomes (1967), Genetics of Sex Differentiation (1973); *Recreations* buying books; *Style*— Prof Ursula Mittwoch; ✉ 73 Leverton Street, London NW5 2NX (☎ 0171 267 1560, e-mail u.mittwoch@qmw.ac.uk)

MNGOMEZULU, HE Rev Percy Sipho; *b* 6 May 1938, Lubuli, Swaziland; *Educ* Mount Hargreaves Secdy Sch Matatiele Cape Province, Univ of Fort Hare Cape Province (Bachelor of Arts in Law), Univ of South Africa (Bachelor of Law); *m*; 2 s, 1 da; *Career* Swazi diplomat; temp clerk Mofolo Municipal Offices Johannesburg 1960–63, univ student 1964–67, clerk rising to instr in banking Barclays Bank Ltd 1968–73; Swazi Govt: asst sec 1974–77, princ sec Miny of Commerce 1981–87, princ sec Miny of Justice 1988–92, princ sec PM's Office 1992–94; ambass to Ct of St James's 1994–; *Style*— HE Rev Percy Mngomezulu; ✉ High Commission of the Kingdom of Swaziland, 20 Buckingham Gate, London SW1E 6LB (☎ 0171 630 6611)

MO, Timothy Peter; s of Peter Mo Wan Lung, and Barbara Helena, *née* Falkingham; *b* 30 Dec 1950; *Educ* Mill Hill Sch, St John's Coll Oxford (BA); *Career* novelist; *Books* The Monkey King (1978), Sour Sweet (1982), An Insular Possession (1986), The Redundancy of Courage (1991), Brownout on Breadfruit Boulevard (1995); *Recreations* diving; *Style*— Timothy Mo, Esq

MOAT, Frank Robert; s of Frank Robert Moat (d 1976), of Tynemouth, and Grace, *née* Hibbert (d 1989); *b* 10 Aug 1948; *Educ* Giggleswick, The Coll of Law (LLB); *Career* called to the Bar Lincoln's Inn 1970; memb Western Circuit, in practice in London and on the Western Circuit, recorder 1995–; rep on the Bar Cncl Western Circuit 1989 and 1990; memb Wine Ctee of the Western Circuit 1988–92 and 1994–, fndr memb Ctee Kensington and Chelsea Nat Tst Asso; FCIArb; *Recreations* theatre, music, antiques, architecture; *Clubs* Garrick; *Style*— Frank Moat, Esq; ✉ 3 Pump Court, Temple, London EC4Y 7AJ (☎ 0171 353 0711, fax 0171 353 3319)

MOATE, Sir Roger Denis; kt (1993), MP (C) Faversham (majority 16,351); s of late Harold Stanley Moate, of Chiswick, and Elizabeth Freestone; *b* 12 May 1938; *Educ* Latymer Upper Sch; *m* 1 (m dis), Hazel Joy, OBE, da of late F J Skinner, of Somerset; 1 s, 1 da; m 2, Auriol, da of late W B G Cran, of Huddersfield; 1 da; *Career* registered insur broker, past chm Lloyd's Brokers Frank Bradford & Co Ltd, past chm Theatre Prodns plc; dir: Robinco Group plc, Euro Mktg Info Ltd; MP (C) Faversham 1970– (also contested 1966), memb Select Ctee on Agriculture 1995–; hon sec Br American Parly Gp 1974–81, chm Br Norwegian Parly Gp 1988–, memb Ct of Referees; pres Marden Fruit Show; *Recreations* skiing, tennis; *Style*— Sir Roger Moate, MP; ✉ House of Commons, London SW1A 0AA

MOBBS, Sir (Gerald) Nigel; kt (1986); s of Lt-Col Gerald Aubrey Mobbs (d 1976), of Gt Missenden, and Elizabeth, *née* Lanchester; *b* 22 Sept 1937; *Educ* Marlborough, Christ Church Oxford; *m* 14 Sept 1961, Hon (Pamela) Jane Marguerite Berry, da of 2 Viscount Kemsley; 1 s (Christopher William b 1965), 2 da (Virginia Elizabeth (Mrs Simon Astill) b 1968, Penelope Helen b (twin) 1968); *Career* Slough Estates plc: joined 1960, dir 1963, md 1971, chm and chief exec 1976–; non-exec chm: Kingfisher plc 1995–96 (dir 1983–96), Bovis Homes 1997–; dir: Charterhouse Group 1974–83 (chm 1977–83), Barclays Bank plc 1979–, Cookson Holdings 1985–93, Charterhouse Group International (USA) 1985–, Howard de Walden Estates 1989–; hon treas Conservative Party 1993–; chm: Property Servs Agency Advsy Bd 1980–86, Aims of Industry 1985–, Cncl Univ of Buckingham 1987–, DTI Advsy Panel on Deregulation 1988–94, Groundwork Fndn 1990–94, Reading Construction Forum 1995–; pres: Br Property Fedn 1979–81, British Cncl for Offices 1990–91; vice pres Assoc of Br Cs of C 1976– (chm 1974–76), memb Cncl Univ of Reading 1987–90, memb Cwlth War Graves Cmmn 1988–; High Sheriff of Bucks 1982–83; Lord Lt of Bucks 1997– (DL 1985–96); Master Worshipful Co of Spectacle Makers 1989–90; Hon DSc City Univ 1988, Hon DUniv Buckingham 1993; hon fell Coll of Estate Mgmnt, hon memb RICS 1990; OStJ 1987; *Recreations* riding, hunting, skiing, golf; *Clubs* Brooks's, Toronto; *Style*— Sir Nigel Mobbs; ✉ Widmer Lodge, Princes Risborough Bucks HP27 0RJ (☎ 01494 488 265); Slough Estates plc, 234 Bath Road, Slough, Bucks SL1 4EE (☎ 01753 537171)

MOBERLY, Sir John Campbell; KBE (1984), CMG (1976); 2 s of Sir Walter Hamilton Moberly, GBE, KCB, DSO (d 1973), and Gwendolen, *née* Gardner (d 1975); *b* 27 May 1925; *Educ* Winchester, Magdalen Coll Oxford (BA); *m* 18 April 1959, Patience, yst da of Sir Richard George Proby, 1 Bt, MC (d 1979), of Elton Hall, Peterborough; 2 s (Richard b 1962, Nicholas b 1963), 1 da (Clare b 1967); *Career* serv WWII RN 1943–47, Lt RNVR (despatches); HM Foreign (later Dip) Serv: entered 1950, served London, Lebanon, Bahrain, Kuwait, Qatar and Greece, USA 1950–73, dir MECAS 1973–75, ambass to Jordan 1975–79, asst under sec FCO 1979–82, ambass to Iraq 1982–85, ret; conslt to Middle East Prog RIIA; *Clubs* RAC, Leander (Henley-on-Thames); *Style*— Sir John Moberly, KBE, CMG; ✉ 35 Pymers Mead, Croxted Rd, W Dulwich, London SE21 8NH (☎ 0181 670 2680); The Cedars, Temple Sowerby, Penrith, Cumbria CA10 1RZ (☎ 017683 61437)

MOBERLY, Sir Patrick Hamilton; KCMG (1986, CMG 1978); yr s of George Hamilton Moberly, MC (d 1972), and Alice Violet, *née* Cooke-Hurle (d 1954); ggs of George Moberly, headmaster of Winchester and Bishop of Salisbury; *b* 2 Sept 1928; *Educ* Winchester, Trinity Coll Oxford; *m* 5 May 1955, Mary Frances, da of Capt Hugh de L Penfold (d 1979), of Guernsey, CI; 2 s (Andrew b 1960, James b 1962), 1 da (Jennifer b 1958); *Career* HM Dip Serv 1951–88, with postings in Iraq, Czechoslovakia, Senegal, London, Canada and Israel 1953–74, asst under sec of state 1976–81; ambass: Israel 1981–84, S Africa 1984–87; *Recreations* tennis, opera, canal boating; *Clubs* Utd Oxford & Cambridge Univ; *Style*— Sir Patrick Moberly, KCMG; ✉ 38 Lingfield Rd, London SW19 4PZ

MOBERLY, Robert William Gardner; s of Sir Walter Hamilton Moberly, GBE, KCB, DSO (d 1973), and Gwendolen, *née* Gardner (d 1975); *Educ* Winchester, Lincoln Coll Oxford (BA, Capt of Boats, Desborough Medal); *m* 7 Jan 1992, (Patricia) Mary Lewis, *qv*, da of late Donald Cornes; 1 da (Scarlett Rose b 28 May 1992); *Career* 2 Lt Oxford and Bucks LI 1951–53, seconded to Northern Rhodesia Regt 1952, ADC to GOC E Africa (Sir Alexander Cameron) 1953; Beecham Foods Ltd 1960–63, Foote Cone & Belding Ltd (advertising) 1964–83 (dir 1979–83), fndr ptnr and md Lewis Moberly Ltd (design conslts) 1983–; fndr memb DBA, memb Mktg Soc 1966, FRSA 1996; *Recreations* golf; *Clubs* Leander; *Style*— Robert Moberly, Esq; ✉ 10 Furlong Road, London N7 8LS (☎ 0171 607 4553, fax 0171 607 6909); Whalleybourne Farm, Wrentnall, nr Pulverbatch, Shropshire SY5 8EB (☎ 01743 792878); Lewis Moberly Ltd, 33 Gresse Street, London W1P 2LP (☎ 0171 580 9252, fax 0171 255 1971)

MOBERLY, William James Dorward; s of Brig James Vincent Charles Moberly, DSO, OBE (d 1982), and Brida Helen Mary, *née* Espeut (d 1980); *b* 4 Sept 1938; *Educ* Blundell's (scholar), Sidney Sussex Coll Cambridge (scholar, MA); *m* 17 Oct 1970, Angela, da of Thomas Eric Douglas Mason (d 1990); 2 s (Nicholas James, Mark Thomas); *Career* CA; articled clerk Ball Baker Deed & Co 1960–63, asst Thomson McLintock & Co 1963–66; ptnr Pannell Kerr Forster (and predecessor firms Ball Baker Deed & Co and Ball Baker Carnaby Deed) 1966–96; fin conslt Bilton plc 1996–; treas Friends of Cobham Cottage Hosp; Liveryman Worshipful Co of Curriers; *Books* Partnership Management; *Recreations* golf, gardening, bridge; *Clubs* St George's Hill Golf, Rye Golf, Royal North Devon Golf; *Style*— William Moberly, Esq; ✉ 125 Fairmile Lane, Cobham, Surrey KT11 2BU (☎ 01932 864698); Bilton plc, Bilton House, 54/58 Uxbridge Road, Ealing, London W5 2TL (☎ 0181 567 7777, fax 0181 840 0249)

MODAHL, Diane Dolores; da of Mr and Mrs Edwards; *b* 17 June 1966; *Educ* Univ of Manchester (BA); *Career* athlete; memb Sale Harriers Manchester Athletics Club, jr UK int 1984, full UK int 1985–; achievements at 800m: English Schs champion 1984, WAAA champion 1986 and 1987, UK Champion 1987, Silver medal Cwlth Games 1986, finallist Olympic Games Seoul 1988, finallist Euro Championships Split Yugoslavia 1990, Gold medal Cwlth Games Auckland NZ 1990, semi-finallist Olympic Games Barcelona 1992, 4th place World Championships 1993; record holder Br 600m 1988 (1 minute 26.1 seconds); ranked No 1 800m UK 1987–90 and 1992–94; *Style*— Mrs Diane Modahl; ✉ British Athletic Federation, 225a Bristol Road, Edgbaston, Birmingham B5 7UB

MODGILL, Vijay Kumar; s of Sansari Lal Modgill, of NZ, and Dwarka, *née* Devi (d 1978); *b* 1 Sept 1942; *Educ* Eastleigh Sch Nairobi, Leeds Univ Med Sch (MB ChB); *m* 14 Sept 1974, (Elizabeth) Margaret, da of John Harrop Lawton, CBE (d 1987), of Wakefield, Yorks; 1 s (Alexander b 1979), 2 da (Victoria b 1977, Elizabeth b 1985); *Career* house physician Leeds Univ Med Sch 1967–68, registrar St James's Hosp Leeds 1968–70 (house surgn 1968), sr registrar Leeds and Bradford Hosps 1972, conslt in vascular and gen surgery Halifax Gen Hosp 1975– (clinical tutor 1975–83); chm of Med Staff Ctee 1986–89, currently chm of Med Ctee of Elland BUPA Hosp; memb Vascular Soc of GB; memb Assoc of Surgns of GB, FRCS 1972, FRCSEd 1972; *Publications* Renal Transplants; *Recreations* golf, cricket; *Clubs* Lightcliffe Golf (Halifax), Fixby Golf (Huddersfield), member of XL; *Style*— Vijay Modgill, Esq; ✉ Linden Lea, Cecil Avenue, Lightcliffe, Halifax, West Yorkshire (☎ 01422 202182); Halifax General Hospital, Salterhebble, Halifax (☎ 01422 357171); Elland BUPA Hospital, Elland Lane, Elland, Halifax (☎ 01422 375577)

MOFFAT, Alexander; s of John Moffat (d 1956), of Cowdenbeath, Fife, and Agnes Hunter, *née* Lawson (d 1995); *b* 23 March 1943; *Educ* Daniel Stewart's Coll Edinburgh, Edinburgh Coll of Art (Andrew Grant scholar, Dip in Art); *m* 1968 (m dis 1983), Susan Potten; 1 s (Colin b 1969); *Career* artist; photographer Scottish Central Library 1966–74, dir New 57 Gallery Edinburgh 1968–78; visiting lectr: Winchester Sch of Art 1973–74, Croydon Sch of Art 1974–75, RCA 1986–88; Glasgow Sch of Art: lectr in painting studios 1979–88, sr lectr in painting studios Glasgow Sch of Art 1988–92, head of painting 1992–; external examiner: Canterbury Coll of Art (Kent Inst) 1988–91, N Staffordshire Poly Stoke 1989–92; external expert Univ of London 1993–; Scottish Arts Cncl 1982–84 (memb Cncl, memb Art Ctee, chm Awards Panel), memb Bd Fruitmarket Gallery Edinburgh 1986–92, chm Bd ALBA magazine 1988–92; writer of numerous catalogue texts; memb Edinburgh Festival Soc; *Solo Exhibitions* incl: A View of the Portrait (Scottish National Portrait Gallery) 1973, Gallery of the Press Club Warsaw 1975, Seven Poets (Third Eye Centre Glasgow and tour) 1981–83, Portrait Drawings (N E of Scotland Library and Museums Service) 1984, Portraits of Painters (Scottish Nat Gallery of Modern Art) 1988, Glasgow Art Gallery & Museum 1990, Pittencrieff House Museum Dunfermline 1991; *Group Exhibitions* incl: Scottish Realism (Scottish Arts Cncl tour) 1971, The Human Clay (Hayward Gallery London and Scottish Nat Gallery of Modern Art) 1976, Three Painters (Midland Gp Gallery, Nottingham) 1978, Narrative Paintings (Arnolfini Bristol and ICA London) 1979, Private Views (Arts Cncl of GB and tour) 1982, In Their Circumstances (Lincoln Usher Gallery) 1985–86, Picturing People: Figurative Painting from Britain 1945–89 (Far East tour) 1989, Scottish Art since 1990

(Scottish Nat Gall of Modern Art) 1989–90, Turning the Century (Raab Gallery London & Berlin) 1990, The Discerning Eye (Mall Galleries London) 1990, The Line of Tradition (National Galleries of Scotland) 1993, The Scottish Renaissance (Hong Kong Land Co Hong Kong) 1996; *Work in public collections of* Scottish Nat Portrait Gallery, Scottish Nat Gallery of Modern Art, Arts Cncl of GB, Yale Centre for British Art; *Clubs* The Glasgow Art; *Style—* Alexander Moffat, Esq; ✉ 20 Haddington Place, Edinburgh, Scotland EH7 4AF (☎ 0131 556 2731); Glasgow School of Art, 167 Renfrew St, Glasgow G3 6RQ (☎ 0141 353 4566)

MOFFAT, Alistair Murray; *b* 16 June 1950; *Educ* Kelso HS, Univ of St Andrews (MA), Univ of Edinburgh (CertEd), Univ of London (MPhil); *m* Lindsay, *née* Thomas; 1 s, 2 da; *Career* organiser Edinburgh Festival Fringe 1976–81; Scottish Television: arts correspondent, prodr then controller of features 1981–90, dir of progs 1990–93, chief exec Scottish Television Enterprises 1993–; *Books* The Edinburgh Fringe (1978), Kelsae - A History of Kelso from Earliest Times (1985), Remembering Charles Rennie Mackintosh (1989); *Recreations* sleeping, supporting Kelso RFC; *Style—* Alistair Moffat; ✉ Scottish Television plc, Cowcaddens, Glasgow G2 3PR

MOFFAT, Lt-Gen Sir (William) Cameron; KBE (1985, OBE 1975); s of William Weir Moffat (d 1958), and Margaret Robertson, *née* Garrett (d 1973); *b* 8 Sept 1929; *Educ* Kings Park Sch Glasgow, Rothesay Acad, Univ of Glasgow (MB ChB, Rowing colours), RCS (Hallett prize); *m* 29 Sept 1953, Audrey Acquroff, da of Robert Watson (d 1969); 1 s (Christopher John Cameron b 24 March 1961); *Career* RAMC 1954–88: conslt surgn 1964, prof of mil surgery RAMC Coll and RCS (Eng) 1970–75, CO BMH Rinteln 1978–80, cmd med HQ1 (Br) Corps 1980–83, PMO UKLF 1983–85, Surgn Gen and DGAMS 1985–88, ret; chief med advsr Br Red Cross Soc 1988–94, ret; Hon Freeman Worshipful Co of Barbers; Hon DSc Glasgow 1991; FRCS 1963; CStJ 1985; *Style—* Lt-Gen Sir Cameron Moffat, KBE; ✉ Kippax, Pound Green, Freshwater, Isle of Wight PO40 9HH

MOFFAT, David A; s of James Graham Moffat, of Cambridge, and Myra Constance, *née* Paul; *b* 27 June 1947; *Educ* St Nicholas' Sch Northwood, Univ of London (BSc, MB BS, LRCP, MRCS, FRCS, MA 1985); *m* 5 Dec 1970, Jane Elizabeth, da of Flt Lt David Dougherty Warwick, DFC, of Northwood Middx; 2 s (Simon b 11 May 1976, Mark b 10 Oct 1979), 1 da (Claire b 29 Oct 1974); *Career* sr registrar The London Hosp 1977–79, fell in otoneurosurgery Stanford Univ California 1979–80, conslt ENT surgn Westminster Hosp London 1980, conslt ENT surgn Addenbrooke's Hosp Cambridge and assoc lectr Univ of Cambridge 1981–, estab E Anglian and Supra Regnl Otoneurosurgical Serv base in Cambridge; author of papers and chapters on: otological surgery, otology, otoneurosurgery, skull base surgery, audiology, evoked response audiometry; vice pres and treas Otology Section RSM; memb: Med Defence Union, Politzer Soc, Intercollegiate Faculty Bd; Br rep IFOS; *Recreations* theatre, golf; *Clubs* Gog Magog; *Style—* David Moffat, Esq; ✉ Department of Otolaryngological and Skull Base Surgery, Addenbrooke's Hospital, Hills Rd, Cambridge CB2 2QQ (☎ 01223 217578, fax 01223 217559)

MOFFAT, Gwen Mary; *b* 3 July 1924; *Educ* Hove County GS; *Career* author; memb: Soc of Authors, Crime Writers' Assoc, Mystery Writers of America; *Books* novels: Lady with a Cool Eye (1973), Deviant Death (1973), The Corpse Road (1974), Miss Pink at the Edge of the World (1975), Hard Option (1975), Over the Sea to Death (1976), A Short Time to Live (1976), Persons Unknown (1978), Die Like a Dog (1982), The Buckskin Girl (1982), Last Chance Country (1983), Grizzly Trail (1984), Snare (1987), The Stone Hawk (1989), Rage (1990), The Raptor Zone (1990), Pit Bull (1991), Veronica's Sisters (1992), The Outside Edge (1993), Cue the Battered Wife (1994); non-fiction: Space Below My Feet (1961), Two Star Red (1964), On My Home Ground (1968), Survival Count (1972), Hard Road West (1981), The Storm Seekers (1989); *Recreations* mountaineering; *Clubs* Pinnacle, Alpine, Sierra; *Style—* Miss Gwen Moffat; ✉ c/o Laurence Pollinger Ltd, 18 Maddox Street, Mayfair, London W1R 0EU (☎ 0171 629 9761, fax 0171 629 9765)

MOFFAT, Dr Robin John Russell; s of A C Russell Moffat (d 1969), of London, and Gladys Leonora, *née* Taperell (d 1959); *b* 18 Oct 1927; *Educ* Whitgift, Guy's Hosp Med Sch, Univ of London (DObstRCOG); *m* 1; 2 s (Jeremy Guy b 7 Dec 1954, Dr Timothy Julian b 3 Nov 1960), 1 da (Pamela Jane (Mrs Peter Blake) b 25 Aug 1951); m 2, 18 Nov 1980, Beryl Gwendoline Longmoor, *née* Wild; *Career* Nat Serv RN 1946–48, ORA (SBA Branch) RN Hosp Haslar; house surgn Guy's Hosp 1954–55, house physician Croydon Hosp 1957, resident obstetrician Mayday Hosp 1957–58, in gen med practice Croydon 1958–88, met police surgn 1959–88, sr forensic med examiner 1988–; hon sec RSM, MO Whitgift Fndn 1960–90, hon lectr St George's Hosp London; tstee Sussex Beacon; memb (former pres) Croydon Med Soc, fndr memb Croydon Medico-Legal Soc, chm Met Gp Assoc of Police Surgns; fell/tstee: MOs of Schs Assoc (former pres), Br Acad of Forensic Sciences, Cons Med Soc, BMA; Liveryman Worshipful Soc of Apothecaries; FRSM (former pres Section of Clinical Forensic Med), LRCP, MRCS 1954, FRCGP 1991 (MRCGP 1962); *Recreations* theatre, book collection; *Clubs* RSM, Carlton; *Style—* Dr Robin Moffat; ✉ 8 Arundel Terrace, Kemp Town, Brighton, E Sussex BN2 1GA (☎ 01273 674552, fax 01273 693871); 10 Harley St, London WIN 1AA (☎ 0171 580 4280, fax 0171 637 5227, mobile 0378 901935)

MOFFAT, Sheilagh; da of Alexander Findlay (d 1968), and Daphne Mary, *née* Ireland (d 1990); *b* 24 Nov 1948; *Educ* Bishops Coll Columbo Sri Lanka, Albyn Sch for Girls Aberdeen; *m* 11 Sept 1971, David Cunningham Moffat, s of James Cunningham Moffat; 1 da (Caroline Alexandra b 12 Jan 1981); *Career* chartered accountant; articled clerk Deloitte Plender Griffiths & Co London 1966–70, fndr own practice 1973; dir Mutual Accountants Professional Indemnity Co 1988–; memb Cncl ICAEW 1994–; pres Warwicks Soc of CAs 1990–91, hon sec Birmingham & District Soc of CAs Ctee (GP bd rep 1992), hon treas Warwicks Co Branch Br Red Cross Soc 1975–95; FCA 1979 (ACA 1970), MinstD; *Recreations* teenage daughter, antiques, films, reading; *Style—* Mrs Sheilagh Moffat; ✉ Moffat & Co, 5 Clarendon Place, Leamington Spa, Warwicks CV32 5QL (☎ 01926 334373, fax 01926 881464)

MOFFATT, Clive; s of Harold and Olive Moffatt; *b* 27 Dec 1948; *Educ* Thornes House Sch, LSE (BSc); *m* 1977, Kathleen, da of Robert Maguire; 1 s, 1 da; *Career* res economist to New Zealand Treasury 1972–75; conslt economist and writer Economist Intelligence Unit Ltd London 1975–76, chief sub-ed (fin unit and CEEFAX) BBC 1976–78, business ed Investors Chronicle 1978–79, corporate affrs conslt Guinness Peat Group plc 1979–81, chief exec Blackrod Ltd 1981–88, fndr and md Moffatt Associates (mktg consultancy) 1988–; *Recreations* rugby, tennis, art, music; *Style—* Clive Moffatt, Esq; ✉ 3 Waldeck Road, London W13 8LY (☎ 0181 997 2128)

MOFFATT, Prof (Henry) Keith; s of Frederick Henry Moffatt (d 1974), and Emmeline Marchant, *née* Fleming; *b* 12 April 1935; *Educ* George Watson's Coll Edinburgh, Univ of Edinburgh (BSc), Trinity Coll Cambridge (scholar, Ferguson scholar, BA, PhD, ScD, Smith's prize); *m* 17 Dec 1960, Katherine (Linty), da of Rev David Syme Stiven, MC, DD (d 1986); 2 s (Fergus b 1961 d 1987, Peter b 1962), 2 da (Hester b 1966, Penelope b 1967); *Career* Dept of Applied Mathematics and Theoretical Physics Univ of Cambridge: asst lectr 1961–64, lectr 1964–76, head of dept 1983–91; Trinity Coll Cambridge: fell lectr and dir Studies in Mathematics 1961–76, tutor 1970–74, sr tutor 1975, professorial fell 1980–; prof of applied mathematics Univ of Bristol 1977–80, prof of mathematical physics Univ of Cambridge 1980–, professeur (temps partiel) en Mécanique Ecole Polytechnique Palaiseau 1992–, dir Isaac Newton Inst Univ of Cambridge 1996–; Royal Society rep on Br Nat Ctee on Theoretical and Applied Mechanics 1976–89, sec IUTAM Congress Ctee 1984–92 (memb 1980–), memb Gen Assembly of IUTAM 1980–, memb Bureau of IUTAM 1992–; Docteur (hc) Inst Nat Poly Grenoble 1987, Hon DSc State Univ of NY 1990; foreign memb Royal Netherlands Acad of Arts and Sciences 1991, Academia Europaea 1994; FRS 1986, FRSE 1988; *Books* Magnetic Field Generation in Electrically Conducting Fluids (1978), Topological Fluid Mechanics (ed, 1990), Topological Aspects of the Dynamics of Fluids and Plasmas (ed, 1992); *Style—* Prof Keith Moffatt, FRS, FRSE; ✉ 6 Banhams Close, Cambridge CB4 1HX (☎ 01223 363338); Trinity College, Cambridge; Isaac Newton Institute for Mathematical Sciences, Clarkson Road, Cambridge CB3 0EH (☎ 01223 335980, fax 01223 330508)

MOFFATT, Nigel; *b* 22 May 1954; *Career* playwright, singer/songwriter and poet; recorded Peace, Love and Harmony for Respond Records 1984, performed African Crisis and Poetry for Here and Now (Central TV) 1984, founded Writers' Gp Walsall 1984; writer in residence: Nat Theatre Studio 1985, Haymarket Theatre Leicester 1988, Shrewsbury Prison 1996–; Winston Churchill travel fellowship 1989; advsr to W Midlands Arts; plays: Rhapsody in Black 'n' White (Nat Theatre Studio) 1985, Tony (Nat Theatre Studio 1985, Oval House 1987), Mamma Decemba (Temba Theatre Co and Birmingham Reperatory Co) 1987, Keeping Walsall Boxed In (W Midlands Arts Cncl) 1987, Opportunity (cmmnd by Br Film Inst) 1987, Prime Time (Haymarket Leicester) 1989, Beau Monde (Br Film Inst) 1990, Stop the Carnival (Cannon Hill Puppet Theatre) 1991; radio plays: Lifetime (BBC) 1988, Lame Ducks (BBC) 1989, Selling Out (BBC) 1989, Wishful Thinking (BBC) 1990, Mamma Decemba (BBC) 1994; TV: When Love Dies (Channel 4) 1989, Opportunity (BBC) 1992, Strange Fruit (BBC) 1993; awards: Samuel Beckett Award for Mamma Decemba 1987, Giles Cooper Award for Lifetime 1987; *Style—* Nigel Moffatt, Esq

MOFFATT, Dr William Henry; OBE (1987), JP (1977); s of John Harry Moffatt, MPSI (d 1967), of Belfast, and Edith Margaret, *née* Reid (d 1961); *b* 11 April 1926; *Educ* Methodist Coll Belfast, Queen's Univ Belfast (MB BCh, BAO); *m* 12 June 1959, Elsie Mary, da of Samuel Bullock, of Enniskillen, Co Fermanagh (decd); 1 s (John Samuel William b 1964), 2 da (Emily Ann b 1961, Christine Mary b 1968); *Career* Nat Serv Capt RAMC Suez Canal Zone 1951–53; conslt physician in Geriatric Medicine Newtownabbey Hosp Gp 1965–88, dir NI Hosp Advsy Serv 1984–91; memb: tstees Leopardstown Park Hosp Tst, Dublin (disabled Irish ex-servicemen of WWs I&II), War Pensions Ctee for NI, Research Ethical Ctee Univ of Ulster, Ctee Belfast Charitable Soc; FRCPI; *Recreations* gardening, fishing, reading; *Style—* Dr William H Moffatt, OBE, JP; ✉ 7 School Lane, Greenisland, Carrickfergus, NI BT38 8RF (☎ 01232 863253)

MOGER, Christopher Richard Derwent; QC (1992); s of Richard Vernon Derwent Moger, of Dartmouth, S Devon, and late Cecile Eva Rosales, *née* Power; *b* 28 July 1949; *Educ* Sherborne, Univ of Bristol (LLB); *m* 1, 1974 (m dis 1991), Victoria, da of Arthur George Cecil Trollope, of Overton, Hants; 3 s (Robin b 1979, Sholto b 1981, Dominic b 1985); m 2, 30 Oct 1991, Prudence, da of Francis Anthony Leopold da Cunha, of Bowden, Cheshire; *Career* called to the Bar Inner Temple 1972, recorder of the Crown Ct 1993–; *Recreations* fishing, tennis, chess; *Clubs* Garrick; *Style—* Christopher Moger, Esq, QC; ✉ 4 Pump Court, Temple, London EC4Y 7AN (☎ 0171 353 2656, fax 0171 583 2036, telex 8813250 Reflex G)

MOGFORD, Clive Hale; s of Gordon Sydney Holmes Mogford (d 1971), and Alice Binnie, *née* Hale; *b* 28 Nov 1942; *Educ* Doncaster GS, Pembroke Coll Oxford (Ashmore Open scholar, MA), Univ of Sussex (PGCE); *m* Arpita, da of M M Roy; 1 da (Maddie); *Career* British Council: trainee 1966–67, asst rep Belgium and Luxembourg 1967–70, trg in educn devpt Univ of Sussex 1970–71, asst dir staff recruitment 1971–72, asst rep India 1972–77, asst dir educn contracts 1977, staff inspr 1977–79, rep UAE 1979–82, rep Cameroon 1982–86, dir Cyprus 1986–92, dir Saudi Arabia 1992–95; sr educn advsr Egyptian Embassy London 1996–; *Books* From Realism to Surrealism (trans, 1972); *Recreations* music, Flemish art, science fiction, golf, wines of Burgundy; *Clubs* Commonwealth Tst, Royal Over-Seas League, Oxford Soc; *Style—* Clive Mogford, Esq; ✉ 1 Grosvenor Court, 99 Sloane Street, London SW1X 9PF (☎ and fax 0171 235 6175)

MOGG, Gen Sir John; GCB (1972, KCB 1966, CB 1964), CBE (1960), DSO (1944 and Bar 1944), DL (Oxford 1979); s of Capt H B Mogg, MC, by his w Alice, *née* Ballard; *b* 17 Feb 1913; *Educ* Malvern, RMC Sandhurst (Sword of Honour); *m* 1939, Cecilia Margaret, yr da of Rev John Molesworth (himself 5 in descent from 1 Viscount Molesworth); 3 s (Brig Nigel (Royal Green Jackets) b 1940, m Tessa Wright, 2 s; Patrick b 1942; Rev Timothy, who has assumed the name Rawdon-Mogg, b 1945, m Rachel Eastman; 2 s, 1 da); *Career* served Coldstream Gds 1935–37, Oxford & Bucks LI 1937, served WWII (despatches), joined Durham LI & served NW Europe 1944–45; instr Staff Coll 1948–50, Cdr 10 Para Bn 1950–52, chief instr Warminster Inf Sch 1952–54, GSO 1 IDC 1954–56, Cdr Cwlth Bde Gp Malaya 1958–60, War Office 1961–62, Cmdt RMA Sandhurst 1963–66; Col Cmdt: The Army Air Corps 1964–74, The Royal Green Jackets 1965–75; Cdr 1 Corps 1966–68, GOC-in-C S Cmd 1968, Army Strategic Cmd 1968–70, Adj-Gen 1970–73, Dep Supreme Allied Cdr Europe 1973–76, Hon Col 10 Parachute Bn 1973–78; ADC Gen to HM 1971–74; pres: Army Cricket Assoc, Br Horse Soc 1972, Int Horse Show 1978–80, Ex-Services Mental Welfare Soc 1976–80, Army Benevolent Fund 1980– (chm 1976); chm Operation Drake for Young Explorers 1978–81; helicopter pilot; dir Lloyds Bank (S Midland Regional Bd) 1976–80; Vice Lord-Lt Oxon 1979–88; govr: Malvern Coll, Bradfield Coll; patron Lady Grove's Hosp Fund for Offrs 1993–; Hon Liveryman Worshipful Co of Fruiterers; Meritorious Medal (Malaya); *Recreations* cricket and most field sports; *Clubs* Army and Navy, Cavalry, MCC, I Zingari, Pitt; *Style—* Gen Sir John Mogg, GCB, CBE, DSO, DL; ✉ Church Close, Watlington, Oxon (☎ 0149 161 2247)

MOGG, John Frederick; s of Thomas W Mogg, and Cora M Mogg; *b* 5 Oct 1943; *Educ* Bishop Vesey's GS, Univ of Birmingham (BA); *m* 1967, Anne, *née* Smith; 1 da, 1 s; *Career* Rediffusion Ltd 1965–74; princ: Office of Fair Trading 1974–76, Dept of Trade 1976–79; first sec UK Permanent Rep 1979–82; DTI: asst sec Minerals and Metals Div 1982–85, princ private sec to Sec of State 1985–86, under sec Euro Policy Div 1986–87, under sec Industl Materials Market Div 1987–89; dep head Euro Secretariat Cabinet Office 1989–90; Euro Cmmn: dep DG Industry and Internal Market (DG III) 1990–93, DG Internal Market and Fin Servs (DG XV) 1993–; *Style—* John F Mogg, Esq; ✉ Commission of the European Communities DG XV, Rue de la Loi 200, Brussels, B-1049 Brussels (☎ 00 32 2 299 11 11, fax 00 32 2 295 65 00)

MOGGACH, Deborah; da of Richard Alexander Hough, and Helen Charlotte, *née* Woodyatt; *b* 28 June 1948; *Educ* Camden Sch for Girls London, Queen's Coll London, Univ of Bristol (BA), Univ of London; *m* 1971 (m dis), Anthony Austin Moggach; 1 s (Alexander b 1 Sept 1975), 1 da (Charlotte Flora b 9 May 1977); *Career* OUP 1970–72, journalist and teacher Pakistan 1972–74, full-time writer (for newspapers, magazines and tv) and novelist 1975–; Young Journalist of the Year 1975; winner Best Adapted TV Series Award Writer's Guild 1993; *Novels* incl: You Must Be Sisters (1978), Close to Home (1979), A Quiet Drink (1980), Hot Water Man (1982), Porky (1983), To Have and To Hold (1986), Smile and Other Stories (1988), Driving in the Dark (1989), Stolen (1990), The Stand-In (1991), The Ex-Wives (1993), Changing Babies and Other Stories (1995), Seesaw (1996), Close Relations (1997); *Short stories* in various anthologies incl: Best Short Stories 1986, Best Short Stories 1988, The Best of Fiction Magazine (1986), The Woman's Hour Book of Short Stories (1990), Best Short Stories 1991; *Plays* Double-Take (produced 1990 and 1992); *Television* series: To Have and To Hold, Stolen, Goggle-Eyes (adaptation); *Recreations* riding, gardening, walking through cities at dusk looking into people's windows; *Style—* Ms Deborah Moggach; ✉ c/o Curtis Brown

Group Ltd, 28–29 Haymarket, London SW1Y 4SP (☎ 0171 396 6600, fax 0171 396 0110); c/o Rochelle Stevens & Co Ltd, 2 Terrett's Place, Upper Street, London N1 1QZ (☎ 0171 359 3500, fax 0171 354 5729)

MOGGRIDGE, Harry Traherne (Hal); OBE; s of Lt-Col Harry Weston Moggridge, CMG, Chevalier de la Legion d'Honneur (d 1961), of Tonbridge, Kent, and Helen Mary Ferrier Taylor (artist, d 1989); *b* 2 Feb 1936; *Educ* Tonbridge, AA (Leverhulme scholar, AADipl); *m* 1 Dec 1962, Catherine (Cass) Grevile Herbert; 2 s (Geoffrey b 8 Sept 1967, Lawrence b 19 Feb 1970), 1 da (Harriet b 23 Sept 1965); *Career* Nottinghamshire CC 1960, asst to Sir Geoffrey Jellicoe 1961–63, site architect Sir William Halcrow & Partners Tema Harbour Ghana 1964–65, landscape asst GLC 1966–67, own landscape design practice, ptnr Colvin and Moggridge Landscape Consultants 1969– (ptnr with late Brenda Colvin, CBE, continuing today with Christopher Carter and David McQuitty), prof of landscape architecture Univ of Sheffield 1984–86; memb Cncl Landscape Inst 1970–83 and 1987–93 (hon sec, vice pres and pres 1979–81, chm Int Ctee and del to Int Fedn of Landscape Architects 1987–93), chm The Landscape Foundation 1995–; memb: Bd Landscape Res Gp 1983–88, Royal Fine Art Cmmn 1988–, Nat Tst Architectural Panel 1990–; PPLI, FIHort, RIBA, FRSA; *Publications* author of numerous articles and chapters of books describing works or technical subjects; *Recreations* looking at pictures, gardens, buildings, towns, landscapes and people in these places, walking, theatre; *Clubs* Royal Soc of Arts, Farmers'; *Style*— Hal Moggridge, Esq, OBE; ✉ Colvin and Moggridge, Filkins, Lechlade, Glos GL7 3JQ (☎ 01367 860225, fax 01367 860564)

MOHR, Dr Peter Dean; s of Dean Mohr, of Toledo, Ohio, USA, and Lucy, *née* Smith; *b* 25 Jan 1945; *Educ* St Joseph's Coll Blackpool, Univ of Manchester (BSc, MB ChB, MSc, PhD); *m* Julie; 2 s (Neil b 1973, Nicholas b 1975), 1 da (Jaqueline b 1970); *Career* conslt neurologist Salford Royal Hosp and Hope Hosp Salford 1977–; FRCP 1990; *Recreations* history of medicine; *Style*— Dr Peter Mohr; ✉ Department of Neurology, Hope Hospital, Eccles Old Road, Salford M6 8HD (☎ 0161 789 7373)

MOHYEDDIN, Zia; *b* 20 June 1931; *Educ* Punjab Univ (BA), RADA; *m* 1974, (m dis) Nahid Siddiqui; 3 s; m 2 1994 Azya Zaidi; *Career* actor, producer and director; leading roles in principal theatres: Pakistan 1956–57, UK 1959–71; dir gen Pakistan Nat Performing Ensemble 1971–77, presenter and prodr Here and Now Central TV 1980–; lectr on cultural topics, ctee memb Arts Cncl; *Theatre* incl: A Passage to India 1960, The Alchemist 1964, The Merchant of Venice 1966, Volpone 1967, The Guide 1968, On The Rocks 1969, Measure for Measure 1981, Film Film Film 1986; *Television* incl: The Hidden Truth 1964, Gangsters 1979, The Jewel in the Crown 1983, King of the Ghetto 1986, Mountbatten Last Viceroy 1988, Shalom Salaam 1989, Immaculate Conception 1990–91, Family Pride 1991–92; *Film* incl: Lawrence of Arabia 1961, Sammy Going South 1963, The Sailor from Gibraltar 1965, Khartoum 1965, Ashanti 1982, Assam Garden 1985; *Recreations* reading, bridge; *Clubs* Savile; *Style*— Zia Mohyeddin, Esq; ✉ c/o Plunket Green Ltd, 21 Golden Green, London W1R 3PA (☎ 0171 434 3801, fax 0171 494 1547)

MOIR, Dr (Alexander Thomas) Boyd; s of Dr William Dugald McKinlay Moir (d 1990), and Margaret, *née* Shepley; *b* 1 Aug 1939; *Educ* George Heriot Sch Edinburgh, Univ of Edinburgh Med Sch (MB ChB, BSc, PhD); *m* 11 Aug 1962, Isabel May, da of Richard Greig Sheehan; 2 da (Alison May b 9 Dec 1964, Fiona Margaret b 23 April 1966), 1 s (William Greig b 6 March 1970); *Career* rotating internship New York 1964–65; Brain Metabolism Res Unit Univ of Edinburgh: joined Medical Res Cncl staff 1965–67, registrar and subsequently sr registrar Therapeutics and Clinical Toxicology 1967–72; SO Home and Health Dept: sr med offr 1972–77, princ med offr 1977–86, dir of Chief Scientific Office and dep chief scientist 1986–96, ret; hon staff of public health med Univ of Glasgow; numerous articles and papers on public health med; FRSS 1974, FRCP (Edin) 1979 (MRCP 1972), FIBiol 1979, MFOM 1985, FRCP (Glas) 1986, FIFST 1987, FRCPath 1988 (MRCPath 1976), FFPHM 1993; *Recreations* playing games, listening to music, reading, walking, folk history; *Style*— Dr Boyd Moir; ✉ 23 Murrayfield Gardens, Edinburgh EH12 6DG (☎ 0131 337 3937)

MOIR, Christopher Ernest; s and h of Sir Ernest Ian Royds Moir, 3 Bt, *qv*; *b* 22 May 1955; *Educ* King's Coll Sch Wimbledon; *m* 1983, Vanessa, yr da of Victor Alfred Crosby, of Merton Park, London, and former w of Joseph William Kirtikar; 2 s (Oliver Royds b 1984, Alexander Victor b (twin) 1984), 1 step da (Nina Louise b 1976); *Heir* Oliver Royds Moir; *Career* CA; *Style*— Christopher Moir, Esq; ✉ 77 Dora Rd, Wimbledon, London SW19 7JT

MOIR, Sir Ernest Ian Royds; 3 Bt (UK 1916), of Whitehanger, Fernhurst, Co Sussex; s of Sir Arrol Moir, 2 Bt (d 1957), and Dorothy Blanche, *née* Royds (d 1991); *b* 9 June 1925; *Educ* Rugby, Gonville and Caius Coll Cambridge (BA 1949); *m* 1954, Margaret Hanham, da of George Eric Carter, of Huddersfield, Yorks; 3 s (Christopher Ernest b 1955, Timothy James b 1959, Nicholas Ian b 1961); *Heir* s, Christopher Ernest Moir, *qv*; *Style*— Sir Ernest Moir, Bt; ✉ Three Gates, 174 Coombe Lane West, Kingston upon Thames, Surrey KT2 7DE (☎ 0181 942 7394)

MOIR, Lance Stuart; *b* 26 Jan 1957; *Career* account mangr Corp Banking Dept Grindlays Bank plc 1980–85, treas Br Home Stores plc 1985–86, head of corp fin and planning Storehouse plc 1988–90 (gp treas 1986–88), dir of corp fin Bass plc 1991–94, sr conslt MTM Partnership Ltd 1995–97, ind conslt 1995–97, fin dir First Choice Holidays plc Feb 1997–; lectr in treasy mgmnt Cranford Sch of Mgmnt; memb Examination Review Bd Assoc of Corp Treasurers; occasional contrib the Treasurer and Banking World; ACIB 1983, FCT 1990; *Books* Introduction to Corporate Finance (memb Ed Panel), The ACT Guide to Managing Liquidity, The Finance Management Manual; *Recreations* singing, opera; *Style*— Lance Moir; ✉ First Choice Holidays plc, First Choice House, London Road, West Sussex RH10 2GX (☎ 01293 560777)

MOISEIWITSCH, Prof Benjamin Lawrence (Benno); s of Jacob Moiseiwitsch (d 1957), and Chana, *née* Kotlerman (d 1984); *b* 6 Dec 1927; *Educ* Royal Liberty Sch Romford, UCL (BSc, PhD); *m* 20 June 1953, Sheelagh Mary, *née* McKeon; 2 s (Julian b 1962, Nicholas b 1968), 2 da (Tatiana b 1954, Lisa b 1957); *Career* Queen's Univ of Belfast: lectr in applied mathematics 1952–62, reader in applied mathematics 1962–68, prof of applied mathematics 1968–93 (prof emeritus 1993), dean of Faculty of Sci 1972–75, head Dept of Applied Mathematics and Theoretical Physics 1977–89; memb Royal Irish Acad Dublin, fell Former Physical Soc of London; *Books* Variational Principles (1966), Integral Equations (1977); *Recreations* music; *Style*— Prof Benno Moiseiwitsch; ✉ 21 Knocktern Gardens, Belfast, Northern Ireland BT4 3LZ (☎ 01232 658332); Department of Applied Mathematics and Theoretical Physics, The Queen's University of Belfast, Belfast BT7 1NN (☎ 01232 245133 ext 3158, fax 01232 247895, telex 74487)

MOKE, Johnny; s of James Charles Rowley (d 1974), and Lily May, *née* Skinner; *b* 2 Sept 1945; *Educ* McEntree Tech Sch London; *m* 11 April 1977, Hazel, da of Alberto Gregorio Gomes, of Salcette Goa, India; 2 da (Sunny Star b 4 Aug 1972, Soraya Sultana b 12 Jan 1988); *Career* shoe designer; collections for fashion shows of: Adeline André Paris 1985–88, Koji Tatsuno, Arabella Pollen, Georgina Godley, Vivienne Westwood, Moschino; exhibitions: Kunst Museum Vienna 1988, Institut Objekt Kultur Glassen Germany 1988, V & A 1990 and 1995; int coverage in fashion magazines; memb Select Ctee Design Cncl 1987; *Recreations* arts, travel; *Style*— Johnny Moke, Esq; ✉ 396 Kings Rd, London SW10 (☎ 0171 351 2232, fax 0171 351 2232)

MOLDEN, Dr Nigel Charles; JP (Burnham 1991); s of Percival Ernest Molden, of Headington, Oxford, and Daisy Mary, *née* Currill; *b* 17 Aug 1948; *Educ* City of Oxford HS, Univ of London (BSc), Brunel Univ (MSc), Fairfax Univ (PhD); *m* 14 Aug 1971, (Hilary) Julia, da of Frederick Withers Lichfield (d 1969); 3 s (Nicholas Stuart b 1974, Simon Charles b 1977, Alexander Giles b 1983); *Career* chm: Magnum Music Group Ltd 1985–, Magnum Industries Ltd, Magnum America Inc; Beaconsfield town cncllr 1989–91, Chiltern dist cncllr 1991–95; chm: Beaconsfield Town Cons Assoc 1991–93, Seer Green & Jordans Cons Assoc 1991–94; govr Royal GS High Wycombe 1989–93; Freeman City of London 1990, Liveryman Worshipful Co of Marketors 1989; FCIM 1988, FInstD 1982, FIMgt 1987, FRSA 1995; *Recreations* music, rugby football, motor sports; *Clubs* Carlton, Royal Over-Seas League; *Style*— Dr N C Molden, JP; ✉ Ashcombe House, Deanwood Rd, Jordans, Beaconsfield, Bucks HP9 2UU (☎ 01494 678177, fax 01494 673328); Apartment 11, 100 Piccadilly, London W1V 5FN; Stone Cottage, Cowl Lane, Winchcombe, Glos; Magnum House, High St, Lane End, Bucks HP14 3JG (☎ 01494 882858, fax 01494 882631)

MOLE, David Richard Penton; QC (1990); s of Rev Arthur Penton Mole, of Pershore, Worcs, and Margaret Isobel, *née* Heggie; *b* 1 April 1943; *Educ* Trinity Coll Dublin (MA), LSE (LLM); *m* 29 March 1969, Anu-Reet, da of Alfred Nigol; 3 s (Matthew David Penton b 20 Nov 1971, Joseph Tobias b 9 April 1974, Thomas Alfred William b 24 Aug 1978), 1 da (Susannah Juliet Martha b 5 July 1984); *Career* lectr City of London Poly 1967–74; called to the Bar Inner Temple 1970 (ad eundem Gray's Inn 1973), standing jr counsel to the Inland Revenue (Rating and Valuation) 1984–90, recorder of the Crown Court 1995–; *Recreations* sailing, skiing, walking, drawing and painting; *Style*— David Mole, Esq, QC; ✉ 4–5 Gray's Inn Square, Gray's Inn, London WC1R 5AY (☎ 0171 404 5252, fax 0171 242 7803)

MOLESWORTH, 11 Viscount (I 1716); Richard Gosset Molesworth; also Baron Philipstown (I 1716); s of 10 Viscount (d 1961); 3 Viscount (Richard, d 1758), was ADC to Duke of Marlborough, whose life he saved at Battle of Ramillies by giving his horse to the unhorsed Duke (he later became C-in-C of HM Forces in Ireland); *b* 31 Oct 1907; *Educ* Lancing; *m* 1958, Anne Florence (d 1983), da of John Mark Freeman Cohen; 2 s; *Heir* s, Hon Robert Bysse Kelham Molesworth; *Career* serv WWII, RAF (Middle E Forces); former farmer; Freeman City of London 1978; *Style*— The Rt Hon the Viscount Molesworth

MOLESWORTH, Hon Robert Bysse Kelham; s and h of 11 Viscount Molesworth, by his w, Anne, *née* Cohen (d 1983); *b* 4 June 1959; *Educ* Cheltenham, Univ of Sussex (BA); *Style*— The Hon Robert Molesworth; ✉ c/o Garden Flat, 2 Bishopswood Rd, Highgate, London N6 4PR

MOLESWORTH-ST AUBYN, Lt-Col Sir (John) Arscott; 15 Bt (E 1689), of Pencarrow, Cornwall; MBE (1963), JP (Devon 1971), DL (Cornwall 1971); s of Sir John Molesworth-St Aubyn, 14 Bt, CBE (d 1985), and Celia Marjorie (d 1965), da of Lt-Col Valentine Vivian, CMG, DSO, MVO; *b* 15 Dec 1926; *Educ* Eton; *m* 2 May 1957, Iona Audrey Armatrude, da of Adm Sir Francis Loftus Tottenham, KCB, CBE (d 1966); 2 s, 1 da; *Heir* s, William Molesworth-St Aubyn, b 23 Nov 1958; *Career* serv KRRC and Royal Green Jackets (in Libya, Egypt, Palestine, Malaya, Brunei, British Guiana and Borneo) 1945–69, Staff Coll 1959, Jt Servs Staff Coll 1964, Lt-Col 1967–69; High Sheriff Cornwall 1975; chm W Local Land Drainage Ctee SW Water Authy and W Local Flood Alleviation Ctee NRA 1974–92, memb Exec Cncl Historic Houses Assoc 1978–, vice chm SW Region Timber Growers UK 1978–94; memb and former chm Devon and Cornwall Branches CLA; *Recreations* shooting, ornithology; *Clubs* Army and Navy; *Style*— Lt-Col Sir Arscott Molesworth-St Aubyn, Bt, MBE, JP, DL; ✉ Pencarrow, Bodmin, Cornwall PL30 3AE

MOLL, (John Graeme) Francis; s of Frederick Charles Moll (d 1994), of Sheffield, S Yorks, and Anita Lilian, *née* Francis; *b* 15 Aug 1947; *Educ* Repton; *Career* Royal Free Hosp and Sch of Med London: radiographer 1969–74, scientific and med photographer 1974–, radiation protection supervisor 1987–; chm Braintree and Bocking Civic Soc 1988–, dir and tstee Braintree and Bocking Civic Society Ltd 1991–; memb: Anglian Water Customer Consultative Ctee (S Gp) 1984–89, The GB-China Centre, Royal Cwlth Soc; churchwarden SS Peter and Paul Black Notley 1985–87; Freeman City of London, Liveryman Worshipful Co of Apothecaries 1968; DSR 1969, AIMI 1986, ARPS 1986; *Recreations* health services research and economics, learning putonghua, Chinese cinema and theatre, music, community affairs, chess, studying and working; *Style*— Francis Moll, Esq; ✉ 10 Brook Close, Braintree, Essex CM7 2PY (☎ 01376 325974); Department of Histopathology, Royal Free Hospital School of Medicine, Rowland Hill Street, Hampstead, London NW3 2PF (☎ 0171 794 0500 ext 3544)

MOLLAN, Prof Raymond Alexander Boyce; s of Alexander Mollan, of Belfast, and Margaret Emma Boyce (d 1984); *b* 10 Aug 1943; *Educ* Belfast Royal Acad, Queen's Univ (MB BCh, BAO, HD); *m* 1 Sept 1969, Patricia Ann Fairbanks, da of Alexander Scott (d 1961); 3 s (Ian Alexander b 1972, Andrew John b 1973, David William b 1975), 1 da (Susan Patricia b 1977); *Career* RNR 1968–84; trg grades: med 1964–69, obstetrics 1970–72, surgery 1972–74, orthopaedic surgery 1974–79; conslt orthopaedic surgn Ulster Hosp 1979–80; Queen's Univ Belfast: sr lectr in orthopaedic surgery 1980–84, prof of orthopaedic surgery 1984–95; currently orthopaedic surgn Green Park Trust Belfast; Br Orthopaedic Assoc: past chm Educn Ctee, past memb Cncl, past chm Info Technol Ctee; fndr memb and treas Br Hip Soc; memb: Irish, Edinburgh and English Coll of Surgns, BMA, Irish Orthopaedic Assoc; *Recreations* sailing, skiing; *Clubs* The Naval, Royal Ulster Yacht; *Style*— Prof Raymond Mollan; ✉ 167 Bangor Rd, Holywood, Co Down BT18 0ET (☎ 01232 423529); Department Orthopaedic Surgery, Musgrave Park Hospital, Belfast BT18 01ET (☎ 01232 669501, fax 01232 661112, telex 74487)

MOLLISON, Prof Denis; s of Prof Patrick Loudon Mollison, and Margaret Doreen, *née* Peirce; *b* 28 June 1945; *Educ* Westminster, Trinity Coll Cambridge (ScD); *m* 1 June 1978, Jennifer, da of Dr John Hutton; 1 s (Charles b 1986), 3 da (Clare b 1979, Hazel b 1980, Daisy b 1982); *Career* res fell King's Coll Cambridge 1969–73; Heriot-Watt Univ: lectr 1973–79, reader 1979–86, prof of applied probability 1986–; SERC visiting fell Isaac Newton Inst and visiting fell commoner Trinity Coll Cambridge 1993; author of various res papers on epidemics, ecology and wave energy; chm Mountain Bothies Assoc 1978–94 (sec 1974–78); memb: Cncl Nat Tst Scotland 1979–84, Bernoulli Soc 1980; John Muir Tst: co-fndr 1983, tstee 1986–, convenor Property and Res Ctee 1988–92, convenor Fundraising Ctee 1992, convenor Policy Ctee 1993–96; FRSS 1977; *Recreations* hill walking and bothying, photography, music, squash; *Style*— Prof Denis Mollison; ✉ The Laigh House, Inveresk, Musselburgh, Scotland EH21 7TD (☎ 0131 665 2055); Department of Actuarial Maths & Statistics, Heriot-Watt University, Riccarton, Edinburgh EH14 4AS (☎ 0131 451 3200, fax 0131 451 3249, e-mail d.mollison@hw.ac.uk, internet http://www.ma.hw.ac.uk/-denis)

MOLLOY, Michael John; s of John George Molloy, of Ealing, London, and Margaret Ellen, *née* West; *b* 22 Dec 1940; *Educ* Ealing Sch of Art; *m* 13 June 1964, Sandra June, da of Hubert Edwin Foley (d 1988), of Suffolk; 3 da (Jane b 1965, Catherine b 1966, Alexandra b 1968); *Career* ed: Mirror Magazine 1969–70, Daily Mirror 1975–85; ed in chief Mirror Group Newspapers 1985–90 (dir Mirror Group Newspapers 1976); *Books* The Black Dwarf (1985), The Kid from Riga (1987), The Harlot of Jericho (1989), The Century (1990), The Gallery (1991), Sweet Sixteen (1992), Cat's Paw (1993); *Recreations* writing; *Clubs* Savile; *Style*— Michael Molloy, Esq; ✉ 62 Culmington Rd, Ealing, London W13 9NH

MOLLOY, Michael William; s of William Molloy (d 1982), of Sydney, Aust, and Alice, *née* McMahon (d 1975); *b* 5 Jan 1940; *Educ* Sydney Aust; *m* 10 Nov 1983 (m dis 1992),

Adrienne Esther, da of Charles Dolesch, of Phoenix, Arizona; *Career* director of photography; also camera operator for: Nick Roeg (Performance and Walkabout), Stanley Kubrick (Clockwork Orange), Barry Lyndon; memb Br Soc of Cinematographers; *Films* incl: Mad Dog, Summerfield, The Shout, The Kidnapping of the President, Shock Treatment, Dead Easy, The Return of Captain Invincible, Reflections, The Hit, Bethune (dir by Phillip Borson and starred Donald Sutherland on location in China), Scandal (dir by Michael Caton-Jones and starred John Hurt and Joanne Whalley); *Recreations* still photography, cooking, fishing; *Style*— Michael Molloy, Esq; ✉ c/o CCA Management, 4 Court Lodge, 48 Sloane Square, London SW14 8AT (☎ 0171 730 8857, fax 0171 730 6971)

MOLLOY, Baron (Life Peer 1981), of Ealing in Greater London; William John Molloy; s of William John Molloy; *b* 26 Oct 1918; *Educ* Elementary Sch Swansea, Univ of Wales, Univ Coll Swansea; *m* 1, 1946, Eva Lewis (d 1980); 1 da (Hon Marion Ann (Hon Mrs Motl) b 1947); m 2, 1981 (m dis 1987), Doris Paines; *Career* served: TA Field Co 1938, Field Cos RE 1939–46; memb: TGWU 1936–46, Civil Service Union 1946–52, Co-op and USDAW 1952; Parly advsr UNISON, ed Civil Service Review 1947–52, ldr Fulham Borough Cncl 1952–62, MP (Lab) Ealing N 1964–79, former vice chm Parly Lab Pty Gp for Common Market and Euro Affairs, chm PLP Social Services Gp 1974, Parly advsr London Trades Cncl Tport Ctee 1968–79; memb House of Commons Estimates Ctee 1968–70, PPS to PMG and Min of Posts and Telecommunications Assemblies Cncl of Europe and WEU 1969–73; memb: Parly and Scientific Ctee 1982–, EC, CAABU, Ct Univ of Reading 1968, Exec Cncl RGS 1976; Parly and Scientific Assoc political consIt Br Library Assoc 1984–, former advsr to Arab League; nat vice pres Royal British Legion, patron Metropolitan Area Royal Br Legion 1994, hon pres Univ of London Union and Debating Soc 1983–, hon pres Stirling Univ Debt Soc 1989, pres and tstee Health Visitors Assoc; hon fell Univ of Wales 1987, hon assoc Br Vetinary Assoc, fell World Assoc of Arts and Sciences; *Recreations* horse-riding, music, collecting dictionaries; *Style*— The Rt Hon Lord Molloy; ✉ 2a Uneeda Drive, Greenford, Middx UB6 8QB; House of Lords, Westminster, London SW1 (☎ 0171 219 6710)

MOLONY, (Sir) (Thomas) Desmond; 3 Bt (UK 1925), of the City of Dublin (but does not use title); s of Sir Hugh Francis Molony, 2 Bt (d 1976); *b* 13 March 1937; *Educ* Ampleforth, Trinity Coll Dublin; *m* 1962, Doris, da of late E W Foley, of Cork; 4 da (Jennifer Mary b 1963, Grace Ann b 1964, Daphne Julia Rose b 1965, Lynda Jacqueline Clare b 1967); *Heir* cousin, Peter John Molony, *qv*, b 17 Aug 1937; *Style*— Desmond Molony, Esq; ✉ 4/39 Gipps Street, Toowoomba, Queensland, Australia

MOLONY, Peter John; s of Sir Joseph Thomas Molony, KCVO, QC (d 1978), and Carmen Mary, *née* Dent (now Mrs Reginald Slay); hp to Btcy of kinsman (Sir) (Thomas) Desmond Molony (3 Bt, *qv*, who does not use title); *b* 17 Aug 1937; *Educ* Downside, Trinity Coll Cambridge (MA); *m* 1964, Elizabeth Mary, eldest da of Henry Clervaux Chaytor, of Cambridge; 4 s ((James) Sebastian b 1965, (John) Benjamin b 1966, (Simon) Benedict b 1972, (Thomas) Francis b 1975), 1 da ((Carmen) Jane b 1967); *Career* sr vice pres Sea Containers Inc 1968–73; dir: Post Office 1973–75, Scottish & Newcastle Breweries 1975–79, Rolls-Royce plc 1979–86; md: Chaytor King Ltd 1986–93, Addis Ltd 1993–94, Otford Group Ltd 1995–; dir Postern Executive Group Ltd 1992–; non-exec dir Allied Leisure plc 1994–; FCA; *Recreations* music, gardening; *Clubs* IOD; *Style*— Peter J Molony, Esq; ✉ Rock House, Great Elm, nr Frome, Somerset BA11 3NY (☎ 01373 812332); 1 Eaton Place, London SW1X 8BN (☎ 0171 235 2939, fax 0171 235 4342)

MOLYNEAUX, Rt Hon Sir James Henry; PC (1983), KBE (1996), MP (UU) Lagan Valley (majority 23,565); s of William Molyneaux (d 1953), of Seacash, Killead, Co Antrim; *b* 27 Aug 1920; *Educ* Aldergrove Sch Co Antrim; *Career* served RAF 1941–46; MP (UU): Antrim South 1970–83, Lagan Valley 1983–; vice pres UU Cncl 1974–79, ldr UU Parly Pty 1974–95, ldr UU Pty 1979–95; memb Antrim CC 1964–1973, vice chm Eastern Special Care Hosp Ctee 1966–73, chm Antrim Branch of NI Assoc for Mental Health 1967–1970; JP Co Antrim 1957–86; *Style*— The Rt Hon Sir James Molyneaux, KBE, MP; ✉ Aldergrove, Crumlin, Co Antrim, NI (☎ 01849 422545)

MOLYNEUX, Anne; da of late Robert Molyneux, and Audrey, *née* Young; *b* 12 Jan 1959; *Educ* Southport HS for Girls, Univ of Sheffield (LLB), Chester Coll of Law; *m* 30 May 1987, Joseph Jeremy Ogden, s of late Robert David Ogden; 1 da (Joanna Frances b 19 April 1988), 1 s (Henry Robert b 23 Dec 1989); *Career* articled clerk Jacobson Ridley 1981–84; assoc ptnr Lawrence Messer & Co 1984–87; Masons: joined 1987, ptnr 1989–, head of property litigation 1992–; speaker various confs incl Law Soc and Worshipful Co of Painter Stainers; memb Law Soc; *Recreations* family, literature; *Clubs* Ealing and Fulham Book; *Style*— Ms Anne Molyneux; ✉ Masons, 30 Aylesbury Street, London EC1R 0ER (☎ 0171 490 4000, fax 0171 490 2545)

MOLYNEUX, Prof David Hurst; s of Reginald Frank Molyneux (d 1974), of Northwich, and Monica Foden Stubbs; *b* 9 April 1943; *Educ* Denstone Coll Staffs, Emmanuel Coll Cambridge (MA, PhD), Univ of Salford (DSc); *m* 1969, Anita Elisabeth, da of George Edgar Bateson; 1 da (Elisabeth Camilla b 18 Dec 1974), 1 s (Oliver James b 7 Jan 1978); *Career* lectr in parasitology Liverpool Sch of Tropical Med 1968–77 (seconded to Nigeria 1970–72, seconded to Burkina Faso as project mangr UN Devpt Prog/WHO 1975–77); Univ of Salford: prof of biology 1977–91, dean Faculty of Sci 1984–88, chm Dept of Biological Scis 1988–91; dir Liverpool Sch of Tropical Med 1992–; Chalmers medal Royal Soc of Tropical Med 1986, Wright medal British Soc for Parasitology 1988; pres British Soc for Parasitology 1992–94, vice pres Royal Soc of Tropical Med and Hygiene 1995–97; FIBiol 1984; *Books* Biology of Trypanosoma and Leishmania (with R W Ashford, 1983); *Recreations* golf, antiques, African art; *Clubs* Delamere Forest Golf; *Style*— Prof David Molyneux; ✉ School of Tropical Medicine, Pembroke Place, Liverpool L3 5QA (☎ 0151 708 9393, fax 0151 707 0155)

MOLYNEUX-CHILD, Lt-Col John Walter; TD (1972); s of Lt-Col Thomas M Child (d 1991), TD, of Guildford, Surrey, and Agnes Eileen Molyneux (d 1984); *b* 5 Aug 1939; *Educ* Clifton, King's Coll Univ of London (BSc); *m* 14 Sept 1968 (m dis 1978), Sydney Pearl Ann Wilcox; 2 s (Patrick Gordon Osborne b 26 March 1971, Rory William Hugh Allingham b 12 Nov 1975); *Career* cmmnd REME(TA) 1959, Capt and Adj Surrey Yeo 1967–68, Maj 1975, Lt-Col 1984, RARO 1985; dir Surrey Printed Circuits Ltd 1967–, mktg dir Teknis Group Ltd 1968–69 (gp md 1969–75), gp chm Surrey Group 1978– (gp md 1975–78), dir Manorial Lordships Ltd 1991–; pres: Br Electro Static Manufacturers Assoc, The Ripley Soc; patron Soc of Manorial Lords; Lord of the Manors of Dedswell and Papworth; MCIM 1969; *Books* The Evolution of the English Manorial System (1987), RFI/EMI Shielding Materials - A Designer's Guide (1992), EMC Shielding Materials (1996); *Recreations* golf, countryside conservation, oil painting, local history, heraldry, resurrection of traditional Surrey countryside traditions such as blessing the fields and ale tasting ceremonies; *Clubs* Guildford Golf, Send United Football (patron); *Style*— Lt-Col John Molyneux-Child, TD; ✉ Croxteth Hall, Ripley, Surrey GU23 6EX (☎ 01483 225435); Surrey Group of Companies, Surrey House, London Rd, Staines, Middx TW18 4HR (☎ 01784 461393, fax 01784 469868)

MONBIOT, George; s of Raymond Monbiot, *qv*, of Henley-on-Thames, and Rosalie Vivien Gresham Cooke, OBE, da of late R G Cooke, CBE, MP; *b* 27 Jan 1963; *Educ* Stowe, Brasenose Coll Oxford (open scholar, BA); *Career* investigative journalist, author and broadcaster; prodr natural history and environment progs BBC Radio 4 1985–87, prodr current affrs BBC World Service 1987, researching and writing book Poisoned Arrows: An Investigative Journey Through Indonesia 1987–89, researching and writing book Amazon Watershed (also series on Radio 4) 1989–91, prodr and presenter Your Furniture, Their Lives (BBC 2) and fndr Forest Network (campaign to stop mahogany imports) 1989–91, researching and writing No Man's Land: An Investigative Journey Through Kenya and Tanzania (prodr and presenter No Man's Land series Radio 4) 1992–94, columnist The Guardian and presenter If I Were Prime Minister (Channel 4) 1996, presenter Going Back (Radio 4) 1996; visiting fell Green Coll Oxford 1993–95; fndr The Land is Ours Campaign 1995; lectr FCO; radio production award Sony Awards 1987, Lloyd's National Screenwriting Award (for The Norwegian) 1987, United Nations Global 500 Award for outstanding environmental achievement 1995, named by Evening Standard as one of 25 most influential people in Britain 1996; *Books* Poisoned Arrows: An Investigative Journey Through Indonesia (1989), Amazon Watershed (Sir Peter Kent Award, 1991), No Man's Land: An Investigative Journey Through Kenya and Tanzania (1994); *Recreations* natural history, palaeontology, playing soccer, ultimate frisbee, folk music, wood carving; *Style*— George Monbiot, Esq

MONBIOT, Raymond Geoffrey; CBE (1994, MBE 1981); s of Maurice Ferdinand Monbiot (d 1976), and Ruth Monbiot (d 1995); *b* 1 Sept 1937; *Educ* Westminster, London Business Sch; *m* 1961, Rosalie Vivien Gresham, OBE (1992), da of R G Cooke, CBE, MP (d 1970); 3 children; *Career* J Lyons & Co Ltd 1956–78, md Associated Biscuits Ltd 1978–82; chm: Campbell's UK Ltd 1982–88, Campbell's Soups Ltd 1983–88; pres Campbell's Frozen Foods Europe 1987–88; chm and md Rotherfield Management Ltd 1988–, vice chm R & B Provisions Ltd 1990–95; dir: Pets Choice Ltd 1991–, Paterson Bronte Ltd 1993–95, Arran Provisions Ltd 1993–95, Canadian Pizza plc 1996–; chm: BIM Westminster Branch 1978–82, Upper Thames Euro Constituency 1982–84, Oxon and Bucks Euro Constituency 1984–89, Cons Pty Nat Trade and Indust Forum 1988–96, Wessex Area Cons Pty 1995–; memb Cons Pty: NEC 1987–, Fin and Gen Purposes Ctee 1989–93 and 1995–; pres S Oxfordshire Cons Assoc 1980–92 (chm 1974–78); memb: Cncl BIM 1981–84, Business Liaison Ctee London Business Sch 1984–88; chm Duke of Edinburgh Award for Industl Projects Northants then Berks 1976–87; Prince Philip Cert of Recognition 1987; Freeman City of London 1990, Liveryman Worshipful Co of Butchers; *Books* How to Manage Your Boss (1980); *Recreations* writing, charity work, cooking; *Clubs* IOD, Leander; *Style*— Raymond Monbiot, Esq, CBE; ✉ Peppard House, Peppard Common, Henley-on-Thames, Oxon RG9 5JE (☎ 01491 628695, fax 01491 628293)

MONCADA, Dr Salvador Enrique; s of Salvador Moncada, of Tegucigalpa, Honduras, and Jenny Seidner (d 1985); *b* 3 Dec 1944; *Educ* Univ of El Salvador (MD), Univ of London (PhD); *children* 1 s (Salvador Ernesto b 6 May 1972, d 1982), 1 da (Claudia Regina b 15 Nov 1966); *Career* The Wellcome Res Laboratories: dir of Theraputic Res Div 1984–86, dir of res 1986–95; dir The Cruciform Project UCL 1995–; editorial work: ed Gen Pharmacology Section Prostaglandins 1975–80, consIt ed Prostaglandins 1980; memb Editorial Bd: British Journal of Pharmacology 1980–85, Atherosclerosis 1980, European Journal of Clinical Investigation 1986, Thrombosis Research 1989; scientific ed The British Medical Bulletin no 39 Part 3; recipient of numerous int med awards incl: Royal Medal, Prince of Asturias Prize, Amsterdam Prize; inventor of various patented pharmaceutical compositions; memb Br Pharmacological Soc 1974, hon memb Colombian Soc of Int Med 1982, hon memb Peruvian Pharmacological Soc 1983, FRS 1988, memb Nat Acad of Scis 1994, FRCP 1994; *Books* Prostacyclin in Pregnancy (ed jtly, 1983), Nitric Oxide from L-arginine: a bioregulatory system (1990), Clinical Relevance of Nitric Oxide in the Cardiovascular System (1991), The Biology of Nitric Oxide (Parts 1–5, 1992–96); *Recreations* music, theatre, literature; *Style*— Dr Salvador Moncada, FRS; ✉ Appartment 5 Clink Wharf, Clink Street, London SE1 9DG; The Cruciform Project, 140 Tottenham Court Road, London W1P 9LN

MONCK, Sir Nicholas Jeremy (Nick); KCB (1994, CB 1988); s of Bosworth Monck (d 1961), and Stella Mary, *née* Cock; *b* 9 March 1935; *Educ* Eton, King's Coll Cambridge, Univ of Pennsylvania, LSE; *m* 1960, Elizabeth Mary Kirwan; 3 s; *Career* asst princ MOP 1959–62, NEDO 1962–65, NBPI 1965–66, sr economist Miny of Agriculture Tanzania 1966–69; HM Treasy: joined 1969, asst sec 1971, princ private sec to Chllr of the Exchequer 1976–77, under sec 1977–84, dep sec 1984–90, second perm sec (public expenditure) 1990–92; perm sec Employment Dept Gp 1993–95, ret; chm British Dyslexia Assoc, memb Bd IMRO, consIt to Govts in Hungary, Mexico and S Africa; memb BSC 1978–80; *Style*— Sir Nick Monck, KCB

MONCKTON, Alan Stobart; DL (Staffs 1988); s of Maj R F P Monckton, TD, DL (d 1975); *b* 5 Sept 1934; *Educ* Eton; *m* 1961, Joanna Mary, *née* Bird; 2 s (Piers b 1962, Toby b 1970, and 1 s decd), 2 da (Davina b 1964, Sophie b 1967 (twin)); *Career* chartered surveyor, landowner, farmer, forester; dir: NFSO Ltd 1964–72, Halifax Building Soc 1973–90, Savills (Ag & Res) Ltd 1992–95 and various private cos; memb: CLA (chm Staffs branch 1979–81), Royal Forestry Soc Cncl 1973–83 and 1989–96, Cncl Timber Growers Orgn 1985–94; fell Woodard Corp 1979–93; High Sheriff of Staffs 1975–76; FRICS; *Recreations* bridge (Bridge Life Master 1971), shooting, philately; *Style*— Alan Monckton, Esq, DL; ✉ Stretton Hall, Stafford ST19 9LQ (☎ 01902 850214)

MONCKTON, Hon Anthony Leopold Colyer; yst s of 2 Viscount Monckton of Brenchley, CB, OBE, MC, DL; *b* 25 Sept 1960; *Educ* Harrow, Magdalene Coll Cambridge; *m* 1985, Philippa Susan, yr da of late Gervase Christopher Brinsmade Wingfield; 1 s (Edward Gervase Colyer b 1988), 1 da (Camilla Mary b 1989); *Career* cmmnd 9/12 Royal Lancers 1982, Capt 1984, ret 1987; second sec FCO 1987, UK Disarmament Delgn Geneva 1990–92, first sec 1991, first sec FCO 1992, first sec (pol) Zagreb 1996–; *Clubs* MCC, Cavalry and Guards'; *Style*— The Hon Anthony Monckton; ✉ c/o FCO, King Charles Street, London SW1A 2AH

MONCKTON, Hon Christopher Walter; kt SMO Malta (1973), DL (1987–96); s and h of 2 Viscount Monckton of Brenchley, CB, OBE, MC, DL, *qv*, by his w Marianna Laetitia, da of Cdr Robert Tatton Bower, RN; *b* 14 Feb 1952; *Educ* Harrow, Churchill Coll Cambridge (MA), Univ Coll Cardiff (Dip Journalism); *m* 19 May 1990, Juliet Mary Anne, da of Jørgen Malherbe Jensen, of London; *Career* ldr writer Yorkshire Post 1975–77 (reporter 1974–75), press offr Cons Central Office 1977–78, ed The Universe 1979–81, managing ed Telegraph Sunday Magazine 1981–82, ldr writer The Standard 1982, special advsr to PM's Policy Unit (Home Affrs) 1982–86, asst ed Today 1986–87, consltg ed and chief ldr writer Evening Standard 1987–92, dir Christopher Monckton Ltd public affrs consIts 1987–; memb St John Ambulance Bd Wetherby Div 1976–77, sec CPS Health, Employment and Policy Study Gps 1981–82, tstee Hales Trophy for the Blue Riband of the Atlantic 1990–, govr London Oratory Sch 1991–96; Liveryman Worshipful Co of Broderers; student memb Middle Temple 1979–, OStJ 1973; *Books* The Laker Story (with Ivan Fallon, 1982); *Recreations* clocks and sundials, computers, cycling, fell walking, inventions, motor-cycling, number theory, politics, public speaking, punting, recreational mathematics, science fiction, Scotland, Yorkshire; *Clubs* Beefsteak, Brooks's, Pratt's; *Style*— The Hon Christopher Monckton; ✉ Crimonmogate, Lonmay, Fraserburgh, Aberdeenshire AB43 8SE (☎ 01346 532401, fax 01346 532203)

MONCKTON, Joanna Mary; da of George Carlos Bird (d 1983), and Mary Elizabeth, *née* Norrington; *b* 31 May 1941; *Educ* Oxton House Sch Kenton Exeter; *m* 30 Sept 1961, Alan Stobart Monckton, s of Maj R F P Monckton (d 1975); 3 s (Piers Alastair Carlos b 1962, Simon b 1967 d 1969, Toby Philip Carlos b 1970), 2 da (Davina Claire (Mrs Gerard Downes) b 1964, Sophie Louise (twin) b 1967); *Career* lay memb Lichfield Dio Gen Synod C of E 1990–; High Sheriff of Staffs 1995–96; Staffs chm Cancer Relief Macmillan Fund, county ctee chm NSPCC; *Style*— Mrs Alan Monckton; ✉ Stretton Hall, Stafford ST19 9LQ

MONCKTON, Hon (John) Philip; s and h of 12 Viscount Galway, *qv*, and Fiona Margaret Monckton, *née* Taylor; *b* 8 April 1952; *Educ* Univ of W Ontario (MA); *m* 1980 (m dis 1992), Deborah Kathleen, da of A Bruce Holmes, of Ottawa, Canada; *Career* vice pres Steepe & Co Sales Promotion Agency, memb Canadian Olympic Rowing Team 1974–84, Gold Medal Pan-Am Games 1975, Silver Medal Pan-Am Games 1984, Bronze Medal Olympic Games 1984, BC Premiers Award, Sport Canada Certificate of Excellence, Cara pres Award 1984; *Recreations* rowing, squash; *Clubs* Vancouver Rowing, Burnaby Lake Rowing; *Style—* The Hon J Philip Monckton

MONCKTON OF BRENCHLEY, 2 Viscount (UK 1957); Maj-Gen Gilbert Walter Riversdale Monckton; CB (1966), OBE (1956), MC (1940), DL (Kent 1970); s of 1 Viscount Monckton of Brenchley, GCVO, KCMG, PC, MC, QC (d 1965), by his w Mary, da of Sir Thomas Colyer-Fergusson, 3rd Bt; *b* 3 Nov 1915; *Educ* Harrow, Trinity Coll Cambridge (MA); *m* 1950, Marianna Laetitia, OStJ, Dame of Honour & Devotion (Sovereign Mil Order Malta), pres St John's Ambulance Kent 1972–80, and High Sheriff Kent 1981–82, 3 da of Cdr Robert Tatton Bower, of Gatto-Murina Palace, Mdina, Malta, by his w Hon Henrietta, *née* Strickland, 4 da of 1 and last Baron Strickland; 4 s, 1 da (Hon Rosamond Mary Lawson, *qv*, who m Hon Dominic Ralph Campden Lawson, *qv*); *Heir* s, Hon Christopher Walter Monckton; *Career* serv WWII; dep dir Personnel Admin 1962, DPR War Office (Maj-Gen) 1963–65, COS HQ BAOR 1965–67; Liveryman Worshipful Co of Broderers 1962 (Master 1978); pres: Kent Assoc of Boys' Clubs 1965–78, Inst of Heraldic and Genealogical Studies 1965, Kent Archaeological Assoc 1968–75, Medway Productivity Assoc 1968–74, Maidstone and Dist Football League 1968, Br Archaeological Awards; vice-chm Scout Assoc Kent 1968–74; pres Anglo-Belgian Union 1974–80; chm Cncl of the OStJ for Kent 1969–74; memb Ct of Assts Worshipful Co of Broderers; Grand Offr Order of Leopold II (Belgium 1978), Cmdr Order of the Crown (Belgium) KStJ; Bailiff Grand Cross Obedience Sov Mil Order Malta, Grand Cross Merit 1980; FSA; *Clubs* Brooks's, MCC, Casino Maltese; *Style—* The Rt Hon the Viscount Monckton of Brenchley, CB, OBE, MC, DL, FSA; ✉ Runhams Farm, Runham Lane, Harrietsham, Maidstone, Kent ME17 1NJ (☎ 01622 850313)

MONCREIFF, 5 Baron (UK 1874); Lt-Col Sir Harry Robert Wellwood Moncreiff; 15 Bt (NS 1626), of Moncreiff and 5 Bt (UK 1873), of Tulliebole; s of 4 Baron (d 1942); *b* 4 Feb 1915; *Educ* Fettes; *m* 1952, Enid Marion Watson (d 1985), da of late Maj H W Locke, of Belmont, Dollar, Clackmannan; 1 s; *Heir* s, Hon Rhoderick Harry Wellwood Moncreiff, *qv*; *Career* 2 Lt RASC 1939, Maj 1943, ret 1958, Hon Lt-Col; *Style—* The Rt Hon the Lord Moncreiff; ✉ Tulliebole Castle, Fossoway, Kinross (☎ 01577 840236)

MONCREIFF, Hon Rhoderick Harry Wellwood; s and h of 5 Baron Moncreiff, *qv*; *b* 22 March 1954; *Educ* E of Scotland Coll of Agric (HND); *m* 1982, Alison Elizabeth Anne, o da of late James Duncan Alastair Ross, of West Mayfield, Dollar, Clackmannanshire: 2 s (Harry James Wellwood b 12 Aug 1986, James Gavin Francis b 29 July 1988); *Style—* The Hon Rhoderick Moncreiff

MONCREIFFE OF MONCREIFFE, (Katharine) Elisabeth; 24 Feudal Baroness of Moncreiffe; da of Cdr Sir Guy Moncreiffe of that Ilk, RN, 9 Bt, 22 Feudal Baron and sis of Capt Sir David Moncreiffe of that Ilk, MC, 10 Bt and 23 Feudal Baron; *b* 23 May 1920; *Educ* privately London, Paris, Munich, Florence; *Heir* Hon Peregrine Moncreiffe of Moncreiffe, *qv*; *Career* served WWII WRNS, special duties linguist; *Recreations* breeder and int championship judge of German Shepherd dogs; *Clubs* Kennel; *Style—* Miss Moncreiffe of Moncreiffe; ✉ Moncreiffe, Bridge of Earn, Perthshire PH2 8PZ

MONCREIFFE OF MONCREIFFE, Hon Peregrine David Euan Malcolm; Fiar of the Barony of Moncreiffe and Baron of Easter Moncreiffe (both Scottish territorial baronies); 2 s of late Countess of Erroll (d 1978), and Sir Iain Moncreiffe of that Ilk, 11 Bt (d 1985); *b* 16 Feb 1951; *Educ* Eton, Christ Church Oxford (MA); *m* 27 July 1988, Miranda Mary, da of Capt Mervyn Fox-Pitt, of Grange Scrymgeour, Cupar, Fife; 1 s (Ossian Peregrine T G b 3 Feb 1991), 3 da (Idina May b 3 Nov 1992, Elisabeth Miranda b 2 Feb 1995, another b 19 Nov 1996); *Career* Lt Atholl Highlanders; Slains Pursuivant 1970–78; investmt banker; Credit Suisse First Boston 1972–82, Lehman Bros Kuhn Loeb/Shearson Lehman 1982–86, E F Hutton & Co 1986–88, currently exec dir Buchanan Partners Ltd; Royal Commissioner on the Ancient and Historical Monuments of Scotland 1989–94; memb Royal Co of Archers (Queen's Body Gd for Scotland); Freeman City of London, memb Worshipful Co of Fishmongers 1987; *Recreations* running, rowing, rustic pursuits, dance; *Clubs* Turf, White's, Pratt's, Puffins (Edinburgh), New (Edinburgh), Leander, Brook (NY); *Style—* The Hon Peregrine Moncreiffe of Moncreiffe; ✉ Easter Moncreiffe, Perthshire PH2 8QA (☎ 01738 813833)

MONCREIFFE OF THAT ILK, Lady; Hermione Patricia; *née* Faulkner; o da of Lt-Col Walter Douglas Faulkner, MC (ka 1940), and Patricia Katharine (now Patricia, Countess of Dundee); *b* 14 Jan 1937; *m* 1 May 1966, Sir Rupert Iain Kay Moncreiffe of that Ilk, 11 Bt (d 1985); 2 step s (Earl of Erroll, Hon Peregrine Moncreiffe of that Ilk, *qqv*), 1 step da (Lady Alexandra Connell); *Style—* Lady Moncreiffe of that Ilk; ✉ 24 Gordon Place, London W8 4JE

MOND, Gary Stephen; s of Ferdinand Mond, of London, and Frances, *née* Henry; *b* 11 May 1959; *Educ* Univ Coll Sch Hampstead, Trinity Coll Cambridge (MA); *Career* CA 1981–84, Guinness Mahon & Co Ltd 1984–86, assoc dir Chancery Corporate Services Ltd 1986–89, Greig Middleton & Co Ltd 1989–91, fin business and trg conslt 1992–, conslt City Univ Business Sch 1992–; chm Gtr London Young Cons 1985–86, asst treas Chelsea Cons Assoc 1986–88, md Bow Publications Ltd 1987–88, Parly candidate (C) Hamilton Scot 1987, Parly candidate (C) Mansfield 1992, CPC chm Chelsea Cons Assoc 1995–, cncllr Royal Borough of Kensington and Chelsea 1996–; competitive butterfly swimmer, Nat Under 14 champion 1972, GB Int and Olympic trialist 1976, Cambridge blue, former World Record holder long distance butterfly (six and a quarter miles) 1980; FCA 1995 (ACA 1985); *Recreations* swimming, theatre, chess; *Clubs* Coningsby; *Style—* Gary Mond, Esq; ✉ 56 Coleherne Ct, Old Brompton Rd, London SW5 0EF (☎ 0171 244 7413, fax 0171 460 8765)

MONDAL, Dr Bijoy Krishna; s of Jagneswar Mondal (d 1974), of Pirojpur, Barisal, and Madhu Bala Mondal (d 1983); *b* 28 Sept 1940; *Educ* Dacca Univ (MB BS), Univ of Liverpool (DTM&H); *m* 12 March 1971, Dolly, da of Dr Jagadish Chandra Mandal, of Calcutta; 1 s (Krishnendu b 9 Oct 1981), 2 da (Bipasha b 16 April 1975, Bidisha b 21 April 1980); *Career* house offr in gen surgery Dacca Med Coll Hosp 1964–65, house offr in gen med St Tydfil 1965–66; sr house offr in gen med: Warrington Gen Hosp 1966–67, Ashton Gen Hosp 1967–68; med registrar: in gen med The Grange Hosp Northwich 1968–70, in gen med/chest Ladywell Hosp Salford 1970–74; sr registrar in geriatric med Dudley Rd Hosp Birmingham 1974–75, conslt physician in geriatric med Rotherham Health Authy 1975–, clinical dir Badsley Moor Lane/Wathwood Hosps Unit 1990– (unit gen mangr 1985–); numerous articles in professional jls on: haematology, endocrinology, rheumatology, neurology; exec memb BMA (chm Rotherham div 1990), past cncl memb Br Geriatric Soc, pres Rotherham Parkinson's Disease Soc, chm Rotherham Stroke Club, memb Overseas Doctors' Assoc; FRCPG 1984, FRCPE 1986, FRCP 1987 (MRCP 1973); *Recreations* gardening, photography, travel; *Style—* Dr Bijoy Mondal; ✉ Medicine for the Elderly Unit, Rotherham General Hospital NHS Trust, Moorgate Road, Rotherham, S Yorks S60 2UD (☎ 01709 820000)

MONDAY, Christopher Harry; s of Clifford Walter Monday (d 1992), and Isobel Phyllis Grace, *née* Lear (d 1992); *b* 1 June 1943; *Educ* Thornbury GS, Swansea Coll of Technol (Inst of Marine Engrs prize, OND), Riversdale Tech Coll, Bristol Coll of Technol (HNC in Mech Eng); *m* 21 Oct 1967, Heather, da of William Bengree Burgess; 1 s (Richard Paul b 13 Oct 1976); *Career* Shell Oil Co: apprentice 1959–64, fifth engr offr 1964–65; sub assembly supervisor Automatic Handling Ltd 1965–68, sr tech engr (tech engr 1968–70) Rolls Royce Aero Engines Ltd 1970–76; NNC Ltd: res engr 1976–77, site rep 1977–81, section head (Electronics) 1981–87, sr section head 1987–90, gp head 1990–92, tech sales exec 1992–94; head of tech servs CIC Ltd; dir of Community Integrated Care Ltd 1989–94, md CTSS Ltd 1990–, chm Inst of Tech Engrs 1983–85, memb Engrg Cncl 1988–; FIMechE (currently pres NW Region and hon treas) 1991; *Recreations* DIY (built my own house), travel, badminton, fanatic supporter of American football; *Style—* Christopher Monday, Esq; ✉ The Dairy, Bradley Hall, Bradley Lane, Frodsham, Cheshire WA6 7EP (☎ 01928 733221); CIC Ltd, Ashley House, Ashley Way West, Widnes, Cheshire WA8 7RD (☎ 0151 420 3637, fax 0151 495 3146)

MONE, Rt Rev John; *see:* Paisley, Bishop of (RC)

MONEY, Ernle David Drummond; CBE (1996); s of Lt-Col E F D Money, DSO (d 1970), of Cambridge, and Dorothy Blanche Sidney (d 1984), o da of David Anderson, of Forfar, Scotland; *b* 17 Feb 1931; *Educ* Marlborough, Oriel Coll Oxford (MA); *m* 1, 1960 (m dis), Susan Barbara, da of Lt-Col Dudley S Lister, MC, The Buffs, of Hurlingham; 2 s (Horry b 1963, Jolyon b 1964); 2 da (Sophie b 1961, Pandora b 1966); m 2, 1991, Bella (d 1993), da of Krishendat Maharaj, of Trinidad and Tobago; *Career* called to the Bar Lincoln's Inn 1958, memb Gen Cncl of Bar 1962–66, MP (C) Ipswich 1970–74, oppn shadow min for the Arts 1974, co-opted memb GLC Arts Bd 1973–74 and 1975–76; conslt to various art galleries and on Victorian pictures, fine arts corr The Contemporary Review 1968–; pres Ipswich Town FC Supporters 1974–80; ctee memb various heritage organisations; *Books* The Nasmyth Family of Painters (with Peter Johnson, 1975), Margaret Thatcher a biography (with Peter Johnson, 1976); *Recreations* football, opera, pictures, antiques; *Clubs* Carlton, Norfolk; *Style—* Ernle Money, Esq, CBE; ✉ 10 St John's Villas, London N19 (☎ 0171 272 6815)

MONEY, John Kyrle; s of Edward Douglas Money (d 1974), and Edith Lillian (d 1984); the Money family have been East India merchants since 1850; *b* 21 March 1927; *Educ* Stowe, Trinity Coll Cambridge; *m* 1, 1957 (m dis), Verena Mann, of Frankfurt; 2 da (Patricia b 1958, Joanna b 1961); m 2, 1983, Sally Elizabeth, da of Michael Staples (d 1990), of Tadworth, Surrey; 1 da (Kate b 1984), 1 s (Oliver b 1986); *Career* RN 1944–48; East India merchant and co dir 1951–79, chm Rubber Growers Association 1978, dir Peacock Estates Ltd; *Books* A Plantation Family (1979), Planting Tales of Joy and Sorrow (1989); *Clubs* Bunbury; *Style—* John K Money, Esq; ✉ 18 Pembroke Gardens Close, London W8 6HR (☎ and fax 0171 602 2211)

MONEY-COUTTS, Hon Mrs ((Penelope) Ann Clare); da of Thomas Addis Emmet (d 1934), and Baroness Emmet of Amberley (Life Peer); *b* 1932; *m* 1951 (m dis 1965), Hon Hugo Nevill Money-Coutts; 2 s, 1 da; *Career* govr Cobham Hall Kent 1962–86; EEC Brussels 1972–73, sec gen Euro Orgn for Res and Treatment of Cancer (EORTC) Fndn 1976–; *Style—* The Hon Mrs A Money-Coutts; ✉ Flat 4, 43 Onslow Square, London SW7 3LR; EORTC Foundation, Kemble House, Kemble St, London WC2B 4AJ

MONEY-COUTTS, Hon Crispin James Alan Nevill; eldest s and h of 8 Baron Latymer, *qv*; *b* 8 March 1955; *Educ* Eton, Keble Coll Oxford; *m* 1, 1978 (m dis 1995), Hon Lucy Rose Deedes, yst da of Baron Deedes (Life Peer); 1 s (Drummond William Thomas b 11 May 1986), 2 da (Sophia Patience b 1985, Evelyn Rose b 1988); m 2, 2 Aug 1995, Shaunagh Anne Henrietta, former w of Thomas Peter William Heneage, and da of (George Silver) Oliver Annesley Colthurst, *qv*; *Career* E F Hutton, Bankers Trust International and European Banking Co 1977–86, currently memb Coutts Gp Exec Coutts & Co (joined 1986); *Clubs* Marks, Knepp Castle Polo (chm); *Style—* The Hon Crispin Money-Coutts; ✉ c/o Coutts & Co, 440 Strand, London WC2R 0QS

MONEY-COUTTS, Sir David Burdett; KCVO (1991); s of Lt-Col the Hon Alexander Burdett Money-Coutts, OBE (d 1994; 2 s of 6 Baron Latymer), and Mary Elspeth (d 1990; er da of Sir Reginald Arthur Hobhouse, 5 Bt); *b* 19 July 1931; *Educ* Eton, New Coll Oxford (MA); *m* 17 May 1958, (Helen) Penelope June Utten, da of Cdr Killingworth Richard Utten Todd, RIN; 1 s (Benjamin b 1961), 2 da (Harriet b 1959 (who m 1985, Martin Pottinger, *qv*), Laura b 1965); *Career* served 1 Royal Dragoons 1950–51, Royal Glos Hussars (TA) 1951–67; Coutts & Co: joined 1954, dir 1958–96, md 1970–86, chm 1976–93; chm Coutts & Co International Holding AG 1991–93; dir: National Discount Co 1964–69, United States & General Trust Corporation 1964–73, Charities Investment Managers 1964– (chm 1984–), Gerrard & National Holdings plc 1969– (dep chm 1969–89), Dun & Bradstreet 1973–87, National Westminster Bank 1976–90 (dir SE Region 1969–88, chm SE Region 1986–88, chm S Advsy Bd 1988–92), Phoenix Assurance 1978–85, Sun Alliance and London Insurance 1984–90, M & G Group 1987–97 (chm 1990–97); hon treas Nat Assoc of Almshouses 1960–92; govr Middx Hosp 1962–74 (chm Med Sch 1974–88); memb: Cncl UCL 1987–, Health Educn Cncl 1973–76, Kensington Chelsea and Westminster AHA(T) 1974–82 (vice chm 1976–82), Bloomsbury Health Authy 1982–90 (vice chm 1982–88); chm Old Etonian Tst 1976– (hon fell Eton Coll 1996); tstee: Multiple Sclerosis Soc 1967–, Mansfield Coll Oxford 1988–95; FCIB; *Clubs* Leander; *Style—* Sir David Money-Coutts, KCVO; ✉ Magpie House, Peppard Common, Henley-on-Thames, Oxon RG9 5JG (☎ 01491 628497, ☎ and fax 01491 628005)

MONINS, Ian Richard; s of Capt John Eaton Monins, JP (d 1939), of Kent, and Margaret Louise, *née* Carter (d 1982); one of the oldest Kentish families dating back to 11 century; *b* 13 April 1930; *Educ* Groton USA, Eton; *m* 2 April 1954, Patricia Lillian, da of Percival Read (d 1967), of Kent; 2 s (Symond b 1958, Stephen b 1961), 2 da (Gay b 1955, Daryl b 1956); *Career* Nat Serv Lt The Buffs 1950–52; farmer; md Gaychild Ltd 1954–69; chm: Richmond Grange (St Martin) 1971–, St Louis Holdings and subsids 1974–, Jewel Holdings 1984–; coinage advsr to Jersey States Treasy 1980–86; vice pres: Société Jersiase 1981–83, 1985–87 and 1989–90, Jersey Heritage Tst 1986–87; FRNS; *Recreations* tennis, building follies, numismatics; *Style—* Ian R Monins, Esq; ✉ Homeland, St John, Jersey JE3 4AB (☎ 01534 861618, fax 01534 865339)

MONK, Prof Anthony John (Tony); s of John Andrew Monk, and Dorothy Marjorie, *née* Pettifer; *b* 11 Sept 1936; *Educ* Windsor County Boys' Sch, UCL (Dip Arch, Alfred Bossom Atelier Prize), Yale Univ (Henry Fund fellow, ESU scholar, MArch); *m* 1964, Ann Monk, JP; 1 s (Craig Antony b 1973), 1 da (Jane Elizabeth b 1977); *Career* jt winner Paisley Civic Centre architecture competition 1963; fndr ptnr Hutchison Locke & Monk (architects) 1964–88, fndr and non-exec dir Acton Housing Assoc 1969–74, md HLM Architects Ltd 1988–91, non-exec dir Building Centre London 1991–96, prof of architecture Univ of Luton 1994– (Pr lectr 1994), architectural advsr Lottery Awards Panel Sports Cncl 1995–; negotiator RIBA Part I exemption for BSc(Hons) Architecture 1993; author of numerous publications featuring architectural projects; RIBA 1961, ARIAS 1967, FFB 1968, MBAE 1994; *Awards* Paisley Civic Centre Tst Award 1968, Civic Tst Commendation Darville House Windsor 1983, Civic Tst Award and Brick Devpt Assoc Award Chariott House Windsor 1985, Building Magazine Premier Practice Award (nationwide competition) HLM Architects 1991, DOE Housing Project Design Award Cromwell House Mortlake 1992; *Recreations* cricket, golf; *Clubs* MCC; *Style—* Prof Tony Monk; ✉ Millrun, White Lilies Island, Mill Lane, Windsor, Berks SL4 5JH (☎ 01753 861917); Anthony Monk and Associates, 1 St Stephen's House, Arthur Road, Windsor, Berks SL4 5JH (☎ 01753 621940, fax 01732 842130)

MONK, Paul Nicholas; s of George Benbow Monk, of Godalming, Surrey, and Rosina Gwendoline, *née* Ross; *b* 3 Dec 1949; *Educ* Royal GS Guildford, Pembroke Coll Oxford (MA); *m* 14 Feb 1985, Roma Olivia Cannon, da of Hamilton Haigh; 2 da (Georgina,

Lucinda), 1 s (Charles); *Career* slr 1974; articled to Durrant Cooper & Hambling 1972–74, Allen & Overy 1975– (ptnr 1979–); memb Worshipful Co of Slrs; memb: Law Soc 1972, Int Bar Assoc; *Recreations* sailing, cross-country skiing; *Clubs* Hurlingham, Royal Southern Yacht; *Style—* Paul Monk, Esq; ✉ Allen & Overy, One New Change, London EC4M 9QQ (☎ 0171 330 3000, fax 0171 330 9999)

MONK, Ronald William (Ron); s of William George Monk (d 1979), of Guildford, Surrey, and Edith May, *née* Barnes (d 1985); *b* 8 Oct 1928; *Educ* Woking Co GS, Coll of Estate Mgmnt; *m* 7 July 1962, Jennifer Leach (Jennie), da of Capt Warren Leach Smith (d 1977), of Milford, Surrey; 1 s (Alastair b 15 July 1968); *Career* chartered surveyor, conslt quantity surveyor, registered arbitrator; Queen's Westminster's Rifles/Queen's Royal Rifles 1955–62; RICS: memb Gen Cncl 1973–90, memb Professional Practice Ctee 1973–90, chm Rules of Conduct Ctee 1983–88, chm Surrey Branch 1972–73, memb Official Referees Courts Users Ctee 1982–; construction indust arbitrator 1966–, ind surveyor; chm: Shalford Parish Cncl 1973–83, Surrey Co Assoc of Parish and Town Cncls 1975–78; Freeman City of London 1979; FRICS 1951, FCIArb 1968; *Recreations* walking, gardening, railways (including model railways); *Style—* R W Monk, Esq; ✉ Orchard House, 17 Denton Rd, Meads, Eastbourne, E Sussex BN20 7SS (☎ 01323 726249, fax 01323 649739)

MONK, Stephanie; *b* 9 Aug 1943; *m* 25 Oct 1986, Gernot Schwetz; *Career* personnel devpt mangr Tate & Lyle plc 1978–82 (joined 1965), gp personnel and communications dir London International Group plc 1982–90, gp personnel dir Granada Group plc 1990–; memb Cncl ACAS; *Style—* Miss Stephanie Monk; ✉ Granada Group plc, Stornoway House, 13 Cleveland Row, London SW1A 1GG (☎ 0171 451 3000)

MONK BRETTON, 3 Baron (UK 1884); John Charles Dodson; DL (E Sussex 1983); s of 2 Baron, CB, JP, DL (d 1933), by his w Ruth (herself da of Hon Charles Brand and gda of 1 Viscount Hampden and 23 Baron Dacre); *b* 17 July 1924; *Educ* Westminster, New Coll Oxford; *m* 1958, Zoë Diana, da of Ian Douglas Murray Scott (d 1974); 2 s; *Heir* s, Hon Christopher Mark Dodson; *Career* takes Cons whip in House of Lords; farmer; *Clubs* Brooks's; *Style—* The Rt Hon the Lord Monk Bretton, DL; ✉ Shelley's Folly, Cooksbridge, nr Lewes, E Sussex BN8 4SU (☎ 01273 400231)

MONKS, John; *Educ* Univ of Nottingham (BA); *Career* jr mangr Plessey Co Ltd 1967–69; gen sec TUC 1994– (joined 1969); *Style—* John Monks, Esq; ✉ Trades Union Congress, Congress House, Great Russell Street, London WC1B 3LS

MONKS, John Christopher; *Educ* Liverpool Poly, RCA (MA); *Career* artist; visiting artist Garner Tullis Workshop Santa Barbara California 1987, British Council artist in residence British Inst Madrid 1990; numerous solo exhibitions incl Evidence 1989 and New Work 1990 (both Paton Gallery London); work in group exhibitions incl: New Contemporaries (ICA London, prizewinner) 1976, Three College Show (RCA) 1979, Alternative Tate (Paton Gallery London) 1982, Artists for the 1990s (Paton Gallery) 1984, Monotypes (Paton Gallery) 1986, Birthday Offering (five years of Paton Gallery) 1986, Six Figurative Painters (Paton Gallery) 1987, 20 British Artists (London, Glasgow, NY) 1988, Metropolitan Museum of Art (NY) 1988, Recent Work (Paton Gallery) 1990, The New British Painting (Queen's Museum NY) 1990, Paton Gallery 1993, Beaux Arts London 1994, Artists of Fame and Promise (Beaux Arts) 1995; work in collections incl: Metropolitan Museum of Art (NY), Contemporary Art Society (London), Gulbenkian Foundation (Lisbon Portugal), Arts Council (GB), British Institute (Madrid), Manchester City Museum, Yale Center for British Art (Conn USA), Unilever plc, Ocean Trading and Transport plc; awarded British Council grant for working visit to NY 1990; guest lecture tour of American Art Centres Spring 1992, guest speaker Tate Gallery 1993; *Style—* John Monks, Esq; ✉ Beaux Arts, 22 Cork Street, London W1X 1HB (☎ 0171 437 5799, fax 0171 437 5798)

MONKS, Sandra Elizabeth; TD; da of George Jagger (d 1993), and Maisie Campbell, *née* Watson; *b* 27 March 1945; *Educ* Grove Acad Broughty Ferry, Santa Ana Jr Coll UCLA; *m* 1965 (m dis 1970), Terence John Monks; *Career* civil servant Dept of Educn 1962–66, insurance exec International Group Plans Inc Washington DC 1966–68; D C Thomson & Co Ltd 1970–: sub-ed Romeo magazine, sub-ed Jackie magazine, chief sub-ed Jackie, ed Jackie, ed Annabel magazine, ed My Weekly magazine, fiction and rights ed; Maj RCS (TA) 39th (City of London) (V) (SC), ret; *Recreations* Territorial Army, horse riding, swimming, sailing; *Style—* Ms Sandra Monks, TD; ✉ My Weekly Magazine, D C Thomson & Co Ltd, 80 Kingsway East, Dundee DD4 8SL (☎ 01382 23131, fax 01382 452491)

MONKSWELL, 5 Baron (UK 1885); Gerard Collier; s of William Adrian Larry Collier, MB (disclaimed Barony of Monkswell for life 1964; d 1984), and his 2 w, Helen, *née* Dunbar; *b* 28 Jan 1947; *Educ* George Heriot's Sch Edinburgh, Portsmouth Poly; *m* 1974, Ann Valerie, da of James Collins, of Liverpool; 2 s (James Adrian b 1977, William Robert Gerard b 1979); 1 da (Laura Jennifer b 1975); *Heir* s Hon James Adrian b 29 March 1977; *Career* memb Manchester City Cncl 1989–94; serv admin mangr MF Industl 1984–89, product quality engr Massey Ferguson Man Co Ltd 1972–84; *Recreations* swimming, watching films, reading; *Style—* The Rt Hon the Lord Monkswell; ✉ Arley House, 513 Barlow Moor Rd, Chorlton, Manchester M21 8AQ (☎ 0161 881 3887)

MONRO, Sir Hector Seymour Peter; kt (1981), PC (1995), AE (1953), JP (Dumfries 1963), DL (1973), MP (C) Dumfries (majority 6,415); s of late Capt Alastair Monro, Cameron Highlanders (s of Brig Gen Seymour Monro, CB, and Lady Ida, eldest da of 5 Earl of Lisburne), and Marion, da of Lt-Gen Sir John Ewart, KCB, JP; *b* 4 Oct 1922; *Educ* Canford, King's Coll Cambridge; *m* 1, 1949, Elizabeth Anne, da of Maj Harry Welch, of the Sherwood Foresters, formerly of Longstone Hall, Derbyshire; 2 s; m 2, 23 Dec 1994, Mrs Doris Kaestner, of Woodbrook, Baltimore, Maryland; *Career* served WWII as Flt-Lt RAF, RAuxAF 1946–53; MP (C) Dumfries 1964–, Scottish Cons whip 1967–70, Lord cmmr Treasy 1970–71, Parly under-sec Scottish Office 1971–74; oppn spokesman on: Scottish Affrs 1974–75, Sport 1974–79; Parly under-sec Environment 1979–81 (with special responsibility for sport); Parly under-sec of state Scottish Office 1992–95; chm Dumfriesshire Unionist Assoc 1958–63; memb: Royal Co of Archers (Queen's Body Guard for Scotland), Dumfries T&AFA 1959–67, NFU Scotland Area Exec Ctee; Hon Air Cdre 2622 (Highlands) RAuxAF Regt Sqdn 1982–, Hon Inspr Gen RAuxAF 1990–; pres: Scottish Rugby Union 1976–77, Auto Cycle Union 1983–90, Nat Small-Bore Rifle Assoc 1987–92; memb Nature Conservancy Cncl 1982–91; *Recreations* country sports, vintage cars, flying, golf; *Clubs* RAF, RSAC, MCC, R&A; *Style—* Rt Hon Sir Hector Monro, AE, JP, DL, MP; ✉ Williamwood, Kirtlebridge, Dumfries (☎ 014615 00213)

MONRO, (Andrew) Hugh; s of Andrew Killey Monro, MD, FRCS (d 1993), of Rye, Sussex, and Diana Louise, *née* Rhys; *b* 2 March 1950; *Educ* Rugby, Pembroke Coll Cambridge (MA, PGCE); *m* 27 July 1974, Elizabeth Clare, da of Lyndon Rust, of Mayhill, Glos; 1 s (James b 1983), 1 da (Lucy b 1980); *Career* production mangr Metal Box Co 1972–73; teacher Haileybury 1974–79 (Noble & Greenough Boston Mass 1977–78), head of history and housemaster Loretto Sch 1980–86; headmaster: Worksop Coll 1986–90, Clifton College 1990–; govr: Terrington Sch Yorks, Beaudesert Sch Minchinhampton, St John's-on-the-Hill Chepstow; *Recreations* golf, American politics; *Clubs* Hawks; *Style—* Hugh Monro, Esq; ✉ Headmaster's House, Clifton Coll, Clifton, Bristol BS8 2HR

MONRO, James Lawrence; s of John Kirkpatrick Monro, of Marlborough, Wiltshire, and Landon, *née* Reed; *b* 17 Nov 1939; *Educ* Sherborne, The London Hosp Med Coll (MB BS); *m* 29 Sept 1973, Caroline Jane, da of Robert Dunlop, MBE, of Aldingbourne, nr Chichester, W Sussex; 2 s (Charles b 13 Aug 1975, Andrew b 10 Aug 1981), 1 da (Rosanne b 21 Nov 1978); *Career* surgical registrar The London Hosp 1967–69, res surgical offr Brompton Hosp 1969–70; sr registrar Cardio Thoracic Unit: Green Lane Hosp Auckland NZ 1970–72, The London Hosp 1972–73; conslt cardiac surgn Dept Cardiac Surgery Gen Hosp Southampton 1973–; memb BMA 1964, FRCS 1969; memb: Soc of Cardiothoracic Surgeons of GB and I 1974, Euro Assoc for Cardio Thoracic Surgery 1987; *Books* A Colour Atlas of Cardiac Surgery- Acquired Heart Disease (1982), A Colour Atlas of Cardiac Surgery- Congenital Heart Disease (1984); *Recreations* skiing, riding, tennis; *Style—* James Monro, Esq; ✉ The Department of Cardiac Surgery, The General Hospital, Southhampton (☎ 01703 777222 ext 6241)

MONRO, Dr Jean Anne; *b* 31 May 1936; *Educ* St Helen's Sch Northwood Middx, London Hosp Med Coll (MB BS, Dip IBEM); *m* 1 (widowed); 2 s (Alister, Neil); m 2, 1993, Andrew Fountain; *Career* house offr London Hosp 1960; W Herts Hosp Gp: sr house offr geriatric medicine 1962 (paediatrics 1961), registrar 1963, med asst 1967–79; hon clinical asst Nat Hosp for Nervous Diseases London 1974–84, assoc physician Edgware Gen Hosp 1979–82, conslt clinical allergist Humana Hosp Wellington London 1982–84; med dir Depts of Allergy and Environmental Medicine: Nightingale Hosp London 1984–86, Allergy and Environmental Medicine Clinic Hemel Hempstead 1984–88, Lister Hosp London 1986–89, Breakspear Hosp for Allergy and Environmental Medicine Abbots Langley Herts 1988–93, Breakspear Hosp Hemel Hempstead 1993–, Hosp of St John and St Elizabeth London 1989, London Welbeck Hosp; conslt physician in environmental med Fachkrankenhaus Nordfriesland Schleswig-Holstein 1994–; med advsr to: Environmental Medicine Fndn, Sanity, Henry Doubleday Res Assoc, Coeliac Assoc; author of numerous pubns on allergy and nutrition related topics; formerly med journalist contributing to Hospital Doctor, Doctor and other jls; memb: RSM, Br Soc for Allergy and Environmental Medicine, Hunterian Soc, Br Soc of Immunology, Bd Inst of Functional Med 1994–; former memb Sub Ctee of Central Ctee for Hosp Med Servs; listed in UK Register of Expert Witnesses 1996–, registered as expert witness Action for the Victims of Med Accidents 1996–, environmental med advsr Soc for the Promotion of Nutritional Therapy 1996–, fell American Acad for Environmental Medicine; diplomate Int Bd of Environmental Med; memb: American Coll of Occupational and Environment Med, Soc of Occupational Med (GB); MRCS, LRCP, FAAEM; *Books* incl: Good Food Gluten Free (ed), Good Food to Fight Migraine (ed), Some Dietary Approaches to Disease Management (1974), Chemical Children (jtly, 1987), Handbook of Food Allergy (contrib, 1987), Food Allergy and Intolerance (contrib), Immunology of Myalgic Encephalomyelitis (contrib, 1988), Breakspear Guide to Allergies (contrib, 1991); *Style—* Dr Jean Monro; ✉ Consultant Physician, Breakspear Hospital for Allergy & Environmental Medicine, Belswains Lane, Hemel Hempstead, Herts HP3 9HP (☎ 01442 61333, fax 01422 66388)

MONROE, Alexander John (Alex); s of William Stuart Monroe, of Suffolk, and Peggy-Ann, *née* Parish; *b* 27 June 1963; *Educ* Ipswich Sch for Boys, Ipswich Art Sch, Sir John Cass Sch of Art (BA); *Career* jewellery designer/mfr (estab 1987); exhibitions incl: Jablonex Int Jewellery Fair Czechoslovakia 1987, Br Designer Show London 1987 and 1990, Pret à Porter NY 1988, Fish and Foul (Hibiscus Gallery) 1989, A Beast of an Exhibition (Hollyhouse Gallery) 1989, London Works 1991, Sundials in the Study London 1991, London Works (Smiths Gallery London) 1991, The Who's Who Exhibition London 1992, London Designer Show 1992, Crafts in Performance (Crafts Cncl) 1993, Premier Classe 1993; work cmmnd by: Br Museum, BBC, World Gold Cncl, Browns (London), Barneys (NYC); work in the collections of: Sedgwick collection, Sainsbury private collection; Prince's Tst bursary 1987, Design Centre selection 1988, Gtr London Arts bursary (to make sundials) 1991; pt/t tutor Camden and Central London Insts and lectr Croydon Coll, London Enterprise Agency and Battersea Adult Educn 1988; memb Br Sundial Soc 1992–; *Publications* A Guide to Sundials with Special Reference to Portable Dial and Navigational Equipment (1990); *Recreations* sailing; *Style—* Alex Monroe, Esq; ✉ 9a Iliffe Yard, London SE17 3QA (☎ 0171 703 8507)

MONSON, (John) Guy Elmhirst; s of Maj the Hon Jeremy Monson, and Hon Patricia Mary Monson; *b* 11 Sept 1962; *Educ* Eton, Univ of Oxford (BA); *m* 17 March 1995, Lady Rose Mildred FitzRoy, da of 11 Duke of Grafton, KG, *qv*; 1 da (Olivia Effie Fortune b 8 Dec 1995); *Career* Sarasin Investment Management Ltd: joined 1984, dir 1989–, chief investment offr 1993–; memb IMRO; *Recreations* flying, real tennis; *Clubs* White's, Pratt's; *Style—* Guy Monson, Esq; ✉ Sarasin Investment Management Ltd, 37–39 St Andrews Hill, London EC4V 5DD (☎ 0171 236 3366, fax 0171 248 0173)

MONSON, Maj Hon Jeremy David Alfonso John; 2 s of 10 Baron Monson (d 1958); *b* 29 Sept 1934; *Educ* Eton, RMA Sandhurst; *m* 4 Dec 1958, Patricia Mary, yr da of Maj George Barker, MFH (killed whilst hunting 1947), of Stanlake Park, Twyford, Berks; 1 s (John) Guy Elmhirst Monson, *qv*), 1 da (Antonia Debonnaire b 1959); *Career* 2 Lt Grenadier Gds 1954, served in UK, Malta, Cyprus, British Guiana, BAOR, Maj 1964, mil asst to Def Services Sec 1964–66, ret (invalided) 1967; memb: Berks CC 1981–93, Thames Valley Police Authy 1982–93; chm Cncl of the Order of St John for Royal Berkshire 1992–; High Sheriff for Royal Co of Berks 1994–95; OStJ; *Clubs* Cavalry and Guards', White's; *Style—* Major the Hon Jeremy Monson; ✉ Keepers Cottage, Scarletts Wood, Hare Hatch, nr Reading, Berks RG10 9TL

MONSON, 11 Baron (GB 1728); Sir John Monson; 15 Bt (E 1611); s of 10 Baron Monson (d 1958), and Bettie Northrup, da of late Lt-Col E Alexander Powell of Connecticut, USA (who m 2, 1962, Capt James Arnold Phillips d 1983); *b* 3 May 1932; *Educ* Eton, Trinity Coll Cambridge; *m* 1955, Emma, da of Anthony Devas (d 1958), and Mrs Rupert Shephard (d 1987); 3 s; *Heir* s, Hon Nicholas John Monson, *qv*; *Career* sits as Independent in House of Lords; pres Soc for Individual Freedom; *Style—* The Rt Hon the Lord Monson; ✉ The Manor House, South Carlton, Lincoln (☎ 01522 730263)

MONSON, Hon Nicholas John; s and h of 11 Baron Monson, *qv*; *b* 19 Oct 1955; *Educ* Eton; *m* 1981, Hilary, only da of Kenneth Martin, of Nairobi; 1 s (Alexander), 1 da (Isabella); *Career* PR and journalist; fndr and ed The Magazine 1982–84, dir Strategic Solutions (PR) 1985–87, md Grenfell Communications Ltd (PR) 1987–93; *Books* The Nouveaux Pauvres (1984); *Recreations* backgammon, chess, tennis; *Clubs* The Lincolnshire; *Style—* The Hon Nicholas Monson

MONTAGU, Nicholas Lionel John (Nick); CB (1993); s of John Eric Montagu (d 1990), and Barbara Joyce Montagu, OBE, *née* Gollin (d 1991); *b* 12 March 1944; *Educ* Rugby, New Coll Oxford (MA); *m* 8 Aug 1974, Jennian, da of Ford Irvine Geddes, MBE; 2 da (Clare Barbara b 1976, Johanna Kythé b 1980); *Career* lectr in philosophy Univ of Reading 1969–74 (asst lectr 1966–69); DHSS (DSS 1989–): princ 1974, seconded to Cabinet Office 1978–79, asst sec 1981, under sec 1986, dep sec 1990; Dept of Tport 1992–; FCIT; *Publications* Brought to Account (Report of Scrutiny on National Insurance Records) 1981; *Recreations* cooking, wild flowers; *Style—* Nick Montagu, Esq, CB; ✉ Department of Transport, Great Minster House 76 Marsham Street, London SW1P 4DR (☎ 0171 271 5690, fax 0171 271 5699)

MONTAGU DOUGLAS SCOTT, Lord (William Henry) John; 2 s of 9 and 11 Duke of Buccleuch and Queensberry, KT, VRD, JP; *b* 6 Aug 1957; *m* 11 Feb 1990, Mrs (Hafize) Berrin Torolsan, o da of Halil Torolsan, of Istanbul, Turkey; *Career* ed Cornucopia Magazine Istanbul 1992–; page of honour to HM The Queen; *Clubs* Travellers (London); *Style—* The Lord John Montagu Douglas Scott; ✉ Valikonagi Caddesi 62, Nisantasi, Istanbul, Turkey

MONTAGU OF BEAULIEU, 3 Baron (UK 1885); Edward John Barrington Douglas-Scott-Montagu; s of 2 Baron, KCIE, CSI, VD, JP, DL, pioneer motorist and sometime MP New Forest (d 1929, gs of 5 Duke of Buccleuch and Queensberry, KG, KT), by his 2 w, (Alice) Pearl, *née*Crake (d 1996, aged 101); *b* 20 Oct 1926; *Educ* St Peters Ct Broadstairs, Ridley Coll Ontario, Eton, New Coll Oxford; *m* 1, 1959 (m dis 1974), (Elizabeth) Belinda, o da of Capt Hon John de Bathe Crossley, JP (d 1935, yr bro of 2 Baron Somerleyton); 1 s, 1 da (Hon Mary Rachel b 1964); m 2, 1974, Fiona Margaret, da of R L D Herbert; 1 s (Hon Jonathan Deane b 1975); *Heir* s, Hon Ralph Douglas-Scott-Montagu b 13 March 1961; *Career* sits as Cons peer in House of Lords; proprietor of Beaulieu Estate and Abbey (originally a Cistercian fndn of 1204); served with Grenadier Gds 1945–48; fndr opened Montagu Motor Museum 1952 and Motor Cycle Museum 1956, fndr Nat Motor Museum at Beaulieu 1972; fndr and ed Veteran and Vintage Magazine 1956–79; pres: Historic Houses Assoc 1973–78, Union of European Historic Houses 1978–81, Fédération Internationale des Voitures Anciennes 1980–83, Museums Assoc 1982–84, Southern Tourist Bd, Assoc of Br Tport Museums, Tport Tst; memb Devpt Cmmn 1980–84, chm English Heritage (aka Historic Bldgs and Monuments Cmmn) 1983–92; pres: Fedn Br Historic Vehicle Clubs 1989–, UK Vineyards Assoc, Tourism Soc; chllr Wine Guild of the UK; author and lectr; hon memb RICS, FRSA, FIMI; *Publications* The Motoring Montagus (1959), Jaguar (1961), The Gordon Bennett Races (1963), Lost Causes of Motoring: Europe (Vol I and II, 1969 and 1971), Early Days on the Road (1976), Royalty on the Road (1980), Home James (1982), The British Motorist (1987), English Heritage (1987), Daimler Century (1995); *Recreations* shooting, water sports, sailing (yacht 'Cygnet of Beaulieu'), music, travel; *Clubs* House of Lords Yacht (Vice-Cdre), Beaulieu River Sailing (Cdre), Nelson Boat Owners' (Cdre), and many historic vehicle clubs; *Style*— The Rt Hon the Lord Montagu of Beaulieu; ✉ Palace House, Beaulieu, Brockenhurst, Hants SO42 7ZN (☎ 01590 612345, fax 01590 612623); Flat 11, Wyndham House, 24 Bryanston Sq, London W1H 7FJ (☎ 0171 262 2603, fax 0171 724 3262)

MONTAGU-POLLOCK, Sir Giles Hampden; 5 Bt (UK 1872), of the Khyber Pass; s of Sir George Seymour Montagu-Pollock, 4 Bt (d 1985), and Karen-Sofie (d 1991), da of Hans Ludvig Dedekam, of Oslo, Norway; *b* 19 Oct 1928; *Educ* Eton, de Havilland Aeronautical Technical Sch; *m* 1963, Caroline Veronica, yr da of late Richard Francis Russell, of Wimbledon, London SW19; 1 s, 1 da (Sophie Amelia b 1969); *Heir* s, Guy Maximilian Montagu-Pollock, *qv*; *Career* with Airspeed Ltd 1949–51, G P Eliot at Lloyd's 1951–52, de Havilland Engine Co Ltd 1952–56; advtg mangr: Bristol Aeroplane Co Ltd 1956–59, Bristol Siddeley Engines Ltd 1959–61; assoc dir J Walter Thompson Co Ltd 1961–69; dir: C Vernon & Sons Ltd 1969–71, Acumen Marketing Group 1971–74, 119 Pall Mall Ltd 1972–78; mgmnt conslt in mktg 1974–, assoc of John Stork & Partners Ltd 1980–88, Korn/Ferry, Carré/Orban International Ltd 1988–; MCIM, MInstD; *Recreations* water-skiing, sailing, photography; *Style*— Sir Giles Montagu-Pollock, Bt; ✉ The White House, 7 Washington Rd, London SW13 9BG (☎ 0181 748 8491)

MONTAGU-POLLOCK, Guy Maximilian; s and h of Sir Giles Hampden Montagu-Pollock, 5 Bt, *qv*, and Caroline Veronica, da of Richard F Russell; *b* 27 Aug 1966; *Educ* Eton, Hatfield Poly; *Recreations* photography, computer graphics, motor-racing and classic car collecting, 18th century music, jazz and Linn hi-fi; *Clubs* Matra Enthusiasts, BMW Drivers; *Style*— Guy Montagu-Pollock, Esq; ✉ c/o The White House, 7 Washington Rd, Barnes, London SW13 9BG

MONTAGUE, Adrian Alastair; s of Charles Edward Montague (d 1985), of Godden Green, Sevenoaks, Kent, and Olive, *née* Jones (d 1956); *b* 28 Feb 1948; *Educ* Mill Hill Sch, Trinity Hall Cambridge (MA); *m* 1, May 1970 (m dis 1982), Pamela Joyce; 1 s (Edward b 1977), 2 da (Emma b 1974, Olivia b 1980); m 2, 8 Nov 1986, Penelope Jane Webb; 1 s (William b 1988); *Career* Linklaters & Paines: asst slr 1973–74, asst slr Paris 1974–77, asst slr London 1977–79, ptnr 1979–94; dir and head of project fin Kleinwort Benson Ltd 1994–; Int Bar Assoc section on business law ctee: vice chm 1982–86, chm 1987, sub ctee chm 1988–89; memb Law Soc; *Books* Joint Ventures (ed with C G E Nightingale, 1989); *Style*— Adrian Montague, Esq; ✉ Kleinwort Benson Ltd, PO Box 560, 20 Fenchurch Street, London EC3P 3DB (☎ 0171 623 8000, fax 0171 956 6144)

MONTAGUE, Michael Jacob; CBE (1970); s of late David Elias Montague and Ethel Montague; *b* 10 March 1932; *Educ* High Wycombe Boys' GS, Magdalen Coll Sch Oxford; *Career* fndr Gatehill Beco Ltd 1959, co sold to Valor 1962 (joined as dep md), chm Valor 1965, fndr Hospitality Hotels Ltd (operating hotels in Cyprus, Italy and Turkey) 1970; non-exec dir: President Entertainments 1985–87, Pleasurama plc 1987–89; created Yale & Valor plc 1987–92, pres Hana Maui Deluxe Hotel and Ranch Hawaii 1990–93, non-exec dir Jarvis Hotels Ltd (41 hotels in UK) 1990–, non-exec dir and non-exec chm American interests Williams Holdings plc (following merger with Yale & Valor plc) 1991–93, fndr Montague Multinational Ltd 1991; chm Cyprus Tourism Advsy Ctee 1969–74, chm Enquiry into Overseas Trade Organisation 1974 (chm Enquiry into Indust, Investment and Fin 1976), chm English Tourist Bd 1979–84, memb Ordnance Survey Advsy Bd 1983–85, pres British Assoc of Industl Eds 1983–85, chm Nat Consumer Cncl 1985–87, vice pres Cncl Royal Albert Hall 1985–94, pres Oxford Brookes Univ Assoc 1990, chm Bd Henley Festival Ltd 1991–94 (ctee memb Friends of Henley Festival 1991), govr Oxford Brookes Univ 1991–, memb Select Fundraising Ctee Entertainment Artistes' Benevolent Fund 1991–95, dir Greater London Enterprise Ltd 1991–92; memb Millenium Cmmn; *Recreations* poetry, dogs, travel; *Clubs* Oriental; *Style*— Michael Montague, Esq, CBE; ✉ 5 Clareville Grove, London SW7 5AU

MONTAGUE, Air Cdre Ruth Mary Bryceson; da of Griffith John Griffiths (d 1991), and Nancy Bryceson Wrigley (d 1987); *b* 1 June 1939; *Educ* Cavendish GS for Girls Buxton, Bedford Coll London (BSc); *m* 12 Feb 1966, Roland Arthur Montague, s of Reginald George Montague (d 1950); *Career* cmmnd RAF 1962, UK and Far E 1962–66, UK 1966–80, HQ Strike Cmd 1980–83, RAF Staff Coll 1983–86, dir Women's RAF 1989–94 (dep dir 1986–89); ADC to HM The Queen 1989–94; chm Ctee on Women in the NATO Forces 1992–93; memb: Cncl and Fin and Gen Purposes Ctee RAF Benevolent Fund 1994–, Cncl Royal Holloway Univ of London 1994–; FRSA 1993; *Recreations* cookery, tapestry, gardening, swimming, world travel; *Clubs* RAF; *Style*— Air Cdre Ruth Montague; ✉ c/o National Westminster Bank plc, PO Box 873, 7 High Street, Marlow, Bucks SL7 1BZ

MONTAGUE BROWNE, Anthony Arthur Duncan; CBE (1965, OBE 1955), DFC (1945); s of Lt-Col Andrew Duncan Montague Browne, DSO, OBE (d 1969), of Ross-on-Wye, and Violet Evelyn (d 1969), da of late Sir Arthur Downes, of Milford, Salop; *b* 8 May 1923; *Educ* Stowe, Magdalen Coll Oxford (scholar), abroad; *m* 1, 1950 (m dis 1970), Noel Evelyn, da of Frank Arnold-Wallinger; 1 da (Jane Evelyn b 1953); m 2, 1970, Mrs Shelagh Margery Macklin, da of Col Hugh Waddell Mulligan, CMG (d 1982), of Cheshire; *Career* served WWII as Pilot RAF; entered HM Dip Serv 1946, FO 1946–49, Br Embassy Paris 1949–52, private sec to Prime Minister (Sir Winston Churchill) 1952–55, seconded as private sec to Sir Winston Churchill 1956–65, seconded to Royal Household 1965–67, resigned as cncllr 1967; md Gerrard & National plc 1967–83; dir: Columbia Pictures Production (UK) Ltd 1967–72, International Life Insurance Ltd 1967–70; chm Land Leisure plc 1987–88, dep chm Highland Participants plc 1987–89, dir Security Pacific Trust (Bahamas) Ltd 1986–89; author of various articles in nat press; tstee Winston Churchill Memorial Trust, vice pres Univs' Fedn for Animal Welfare; Hon DL Westminster Coll Fulton USA (1988); Freeman City of London 1988; *Books* Long Sunset; *Recreations* wildlife, reading; *Clubs* Boodle's, Pratt's; *Style*— Anthony Montague Browne, Esq, CBE, DFC; ✉ Hawkridge Cottages, Bucklebury, nr Reading, Berks RG7 6EG (☎ 0118 971 2578); 99A Prince of Wales Mansions, Prince of Wales Drive, Battersea, London SW11 (☎ 0171 720 4210)

MONTAGUE-JOHNSTONE, Roland Richard; s of Maj Roy Henry Montague-Johnstone, MBE, of 16 Leonard Court, London W8, and Barbara Marjorie, *née* Warre (d 1990); *b* 22 Jan 1941; *Educ* Eton; *m* 24 Feb 1968, Sara Outram Boileau, da of Lt-Col John Garway Outram Whitehead, MC and Bar (d 1983), of 10 Blackfriars St, Canterbury; 2 s (Andrew, William); *Career* KRRC served NI and Berlin 1958–62; admitted slr 1967; ptnr Slaughter and May 1973–91 (articled clerk 1962–67, asst slr 1967–73); Warden St Mary the Virgin Powerstock 1994–; memb: Law Soc, CLA; *Recreations* reading, walking, gardening; *Clubs* Celer Et Audax, Royal Green Jackets, English Speaking Union, Royal Over-Seas League; *Style*— Roland Montague-Johnstone, Esq; ✉ Poorton Hill, Powerstock, Bridport, Dorset DT6 3TJ

MONTAGUE-MASON, Perry; s of Arthur John Mason (d 1991), of Brighton, and Lily Beulah, *née* Montague; *b* 12 Nov 1956; *Educ* St Marylebone GS, Royal Acad of Music; *m* June 1979 (m dis 1981), Elizabeth, *née* Staples; *partner* since 1985, (Elisabeth) Anne Collis; 1 step da (Sally Elisabeth Sophia Lawrence-Archer b 1979); *Career* memb BBC Concert Orch 1976–80, guest princ London Philharmonic Orch; guest ldr: BBC Concert Orch, Ulster Orch, New Symphony Orch, New Sadler's Wells Opera Orch; co-ldr London Chamber Orch; ldr Mantovani Orch 1983–91, ldr and artistic dir Nat Symphony Orch 1992– (chm 1984–); many major West End musicals incl Phantom of the Opera; numerous performances on radio and TV; memb: Perry Montague-Mason Trio, Lochrian String Quartet, Quartet Caravaggio; memb Ctee Central London Branch Musicians' Union 1990–93; ARAM, MInstD; *Recreations* ornithology, walking, riding, reading; *Style*— Perry Montague-Mason, Esq; ✉ c/o National Symphony Orchestra, Jumps Road, Churt, Farnham, Surrey GU10 2JY (☎ 01252 792315, fax 01252 795120)

MONTEAGLE OF BRANDON, 6 Baron (UK 1839); Gerald Spring Rice; s of 5 Baron (d 1946), and Emilie de Kosenko (d 1981), da of late Mrs Edward Brooks, of NY; *b* 5 July 1926; *Educ* Harrow; *m* 1949, Anne, da of Col Guy James Brownlow, DSO, DL (d 1960); 1 s, 3 da; *Heir* s, Hon Charles James Spring Rice; *Career* Capt Irish Gds, ret 1955; memb: London Stock Exchange 1958–76, Lloyd's 1978–, HM Body Guard of Hon Corps of Gentlemen-at-Arms 1978–96; *Clubs* Cavalry and Guards', Pratt's, Kildare St and University (Dublin); *Style*— The Rt Hon the Lord Monteagle of Brandon; ✉ 242A Fulham Rd, London SW10 9NA (☎ 0171 351 3455)

MONTEFIORE, Rt Rev Hugh William; s of late Charles Sebag-Montefiore, OBE (whose f, Arthur, was paternal gs of Sarah, sis of Sir Moses Montefiore, 1 Bt, and a philanthropist); *b* 12 May 1920; *Educ* Rugby, St John's Coll Oxford (MA), Cambridge (BD); *m* 1 Jan 1945, Elisabeth Mary Macdonald, da of late Rev William Paton, DD; 3 da; *Career* ordained priest 1950; former examining chaplain of Bishops of: Newcastle, Worcester, Coventry, Blackburn; dean and fell Gonville and Caius Coll Cambridge 1953–63, canon theologian of Coventry 1959–69, vicar Great St Mary's Cambridge 1963–70, hon canon of Ely Cath 1969–70, bishop suffragan of Kingston-upon-Thames 1970–78, bishop of Birmingham 1978–87; chm C of E Gen Synod's Board of Social Responsibility 1983–87; author; chm: Transport 2000 1987–93, Nat Tst for the Homeless 1987–96, Friends of the Earth Tst 1991–96, Transport 2000 Tst 1993–96; hon fell St John's Coll Oxford 1981; Hon DD: Aberdeen 1976, Birmingham 1984; *Recreations* walking, watercolour painting; *Clubs* Beefsteak, Royal Cwlth Soc; *Style*— The Rt Rev Hugh Montefiore; ✉ 23 Bellevue Rd, Wandsworth Common, London SW17 7EB (☎ 0181 672 669)

MONTERO, Fernan Gonzalo; s of Adolfo Montero (d 1987), of Argentina, and Donne Strang Montero, of Chicago, Illinois, USA; *b* 22 May 1948; *Educ* Univ of Wisconsin USA (Bachelor of Business Admin/Int Business), Northwestern Univ USA (Master of Journalism/Advertising); *m* Cheryl Bowman; *Career* Young & Rubicam Advertising: joined 1972, chief exec offr Argentina 1982–84, dep area mangr Latin America 1985–87, corp dir i/c business devpt 1987–90, memb Bd of Dirs Y&R 1991–, chm and chief exec offr Latin America 1991–93, memb Corp Exec Ctee Y&R 1992–, chm and chief exec offr Europe 1993–; *Clubs* Bath & Raquet, Harry's, Mark's, Annabel's; *Style*— Fernan Montero, Esq; ✉ Young & Rubicam Europe, Greater London House, Hampstead Road, London NW1 7QP (☎ 0171 611 6301)

MONTGOMERIE, Colin; s of James Montgomerie, sec of Royal Troon Golf Club; *b* 23 June 1963; *m* June 1990, Eimear, *née* Wilson; 1 da (Olivia Rose b March 1993); *Career* professional golfer; amateur victories: Scottish Amateur Stroke-play Championship 1985, Scottish Amateur Championship 1987; tournament victories since turning professional 1987: Portuguese Open 1989, Scandinavian Masters 1991, Dutch Open 1993, Vovlo Masters 1993, Spanish Open 1994, Murphy's English Open 1994, Volvo German Open 1994 and 1995, Trophee Lancome 1995, Dubai Classic 1996, Irish Open 1996, Sun City Million Dollar Challenge 1996; US Open: 1993 (third), 1994 (second); US PGA 1995 (second); team memb: Eisenhower Trophy (amateur) 1984 and 1986, Walker Cup (amateur) 1985 and 1987, Ryder Cup 1991, 1993 and 1995 (winners), Alfred Dunhill Cup 1988, 1991, 1992, 1993, 1994 and 1995 (winners), World Cup 1988, 1991, 1992, and 1993; Henry Cotton Rookie of the Year 1988, winner European Order of Merit 1993, 1994 and 1995; *Recreations* motor cars, music; *Style*— Colin Montgomerie, Esq; ✉ c/o International Management Group, Pier House, Strand on the Green, London W4 3NN

MONTGOMERIE, Lord; Hugh Archibald William Montgomerie; s and h of 18 Earl of Eglinton and Winton; *b* 24 July 1966; *m* 19 Dec 1991, S Alexandra, eldest da of Niel Redpath, of London, SW6; *Career* Sub Lt RN 1988–93; operations mangr Gander & White Shipping Ltd 1996–; *Style*— Lord Montgomerie; ✉ 17 Ormiston Grove, London W12 0JR

MONTGOMERIE, Lorna Burnett (Mrs John Anderson); da of (James) Fraser Montgomerie, of Helensburgh, Dunbartonshire, and Jane Burnett Sangster (Jean), *née* McCulloch; *b* 23 Oct 1953; *Educ* St George's Sch Montreal, North London Collegiate Sch Edgware, Churchill Coll Cambridge (MA), Coll of Law Lancaster Gate; *m* 8 July 1983, John Venner Anderson, s of Prof John Anderson, of Park Langley, Beckenham, Kent; 1 s, 1 da (twins b 15 July 1992); *Career* admitted slr 1978, asst slr Biddle & Co 1978–80, annotator Halsbury's Statutes 1981, ed Encyclopaedia of Forms and Precedents (4 edn) 1981–85; Butterworths Ltd: R & D mangr 1985–89, editorial systems mangr 1989–93, ed Statutory Materials 1993–; articles written for: Dance 1986–87, The New Law Journal 1987–88, Holborn Report and Articles in Holborn (for Holborn Law Soc) 1989–92; memb: Ctee of Holborn Law Soc 1983–, London Legal Educn Ctee (as rep for Holborn Law Soc) 1988–89, Law Soc Panel monitoring articles in Holborn Area 1987–; memb Law Soc 1978; *Recreations* reading, DIY, house renovation, sailing; *Style*— Ms Lorna Montgomerie; ✉ Butterworths Ltd, Halsbury House, 35 Chancery Lane, London WC2A 1EL (☎ 0171 400 2500, fax 0171 400 2842)

MONTGOMERY, HE Dr Alan Everard; CMG (1993); s of Philip Napier Montgomery (d 1967), and Honor Violet Coleman, *née* Price; *b* 11 March 1938; *Educ* Royal GS Guildford, County of Stafford Trg Coll (CertEd, colours Rugby), Birkbeck Coll Univ of London (BA, PhD); *m* 16 July 1960, Janet Barton (d 1994); 1 s (Magnus b 1971), 1 da (Justine b 1976); *Career* Nat Serv Corpl Middlesex Regt 1957–59; teacher: Staffordshire Educn Authy 1961–62, ILEA 1962–65; lectr Univ of Birmingham 1969–72; HM Dip Serv: joined FCO 1972, first sec FCO 1972–75, Dhaka 1975–77, Ottawa 1977–80, FCO 1980–83, cnsllr GATT and UNCTAD UK mission Geneva 1983–87, cnsllr consul gen and head of Chancery Jakarta 1987–89, head Migration and Visa Dept FCO 1989–92, HM ambass to the Philippines 1992–95, high cmmr to Tanzania 1995–; *publications*

Lloyd George: 12 essays (contrib, 1971), Cambridge Hist Jl (contrib); *Recreations* theatre, jazz, writing pantomimes, gardening; *Style—* HE Dr Alan Montgomery, CMG; ✉ c/o Foreign & Commonwealth Office, (Dar es Salaam), King Charles Street, London SW1A 2AH

MONTGOMERY, Alexander Jamieson (Alex); s of Walter Montgomery, of Eastbourne, and Helen, *née* Jamieson; *b* 12 Aug 1943; *Educ* Hyndland Sr Sch Glasgow, Skerry's Coll Glasgow; *m* 9 June 1970, Anne, da of James Robertson; 2 da (Helen Robertson b 16 June 1972, Katie Elizabeth b 24 Jan 1974); *Career* sports writer; various jobs Glasgow 1959–61, football reporter Sunday Post and Weekly News Glasgow/Newcastle/Manchester 1963–68, news ed Illustrated Carpenter and Builder 1968, news reporter Sunday Express 1968, sub-ed Goal! magazine 1968 (for one week), sports reporter Hayter's Sports Agency 1968–70, sports reporter Daily Mail 1970–71; The Sun: football reporter 1971–83, chief football writer 1983–92, football feature writer 1992–93; chief football news reporter Today 1993–95, chief football reporter News of the World 1996–; chm Football Writers' Assoc 1994–95 (vice chm 1993); *Recreations* any sport, music; *Clubs* Wig and Pen; *Style—* Mr Alex Montgomery; ✉ 36 Downside Close, Eastbourne, E Sussex BN20 8EL (☎ 01323 736176, mobile 0385 728909)

MONTGOMERY, (Hugh) Bryan Greville; s of Hugh Roger Greville Montgomery, MC, and Molly Audrey Montgomery, OBE, *née* Neele; *b* 26 March 1929; *Educ* Repton, Lincoln Coll Oxford (MA, Fleming fell 1996); *Career* fndr memb Oxford Univ Wine and Food Soc, conslt and advsr on trade fairs and developing countries for UN, conslt Int Garden Festival Liverpool 1984, chm Andry Montgomery gp of cos (organisers, mangrs and conslts in exhibitions) until 1994; chm: Br Assoc of Exhibition Organisers 1970, Int Ctee American Nat Assoc of Exposition Mangrs 1980–82 and 1990–92, Br Exhibition Promotion Cncl 1981–83; pres Union des Foires Int 1994– (vice pres 1987–93); memb: Cncl Design and Industs Assoc 1983–85, Advsy Bd Inst of Hotel Mgmnt Montreux 1986–, London Regnl Ctee CBI 1987–89, Br Overseas Trade Bd 1990–93, Bd World Trade Centres Assoc 1996–; chm: Interbuild Fund 1972–, Tstees Supply of Equipment to Charity Hosps Overseas (ECHO) 1978–89, The Building Museum 1988–, Br Architectural Library Tst 1989–; vice chm Bldg Conservation Tst 1979–94; tstee: The Cubitt Tst 1982–, Music for the World 1990–92; hon treas Contemporary Art Soc 1980–82, cncllr Acad of St Martin-in-the-Fields Concert Soc; memb Exec Ctee: Nat Fund for Res into Crippling Diseases 1970–91, CGLI 1974–; chm The Montgomery Network; Liveryman Worshipful Co of Tylers and Bricklayers 1952 (Master 1980–81, tstee Charitable and Pension Tsts 1981–), Master Co of World Traders 1995; voted Siberian Foreign Businessman in Novosibirsk 1993; Silver Jubilee medal 1977, Pro Arte Hungaria medal 1991, Brooch of the City of Utrecht 1992; *Books* Industrial Fairs and Developing Countries (UNIDO, 1975), Going into Trade Fairs (UNCTAD/GATT, 1982), Exhibition Planning and Design (1989); also contrib to int Trade Forum; *Recreations* travelling in Siberia and China, wine tasting, collecting contemporary sculpture; *Clubs* United Oxford and Cambridge Univ, City Livery; *Style—* Bryan Montgomery, Esq; ✉ 11 Manchester Square, London W1M 5AB (☎ 0171 486 1951); Snells Farm, Amersham Common, Bucks HP7 9QN

MONTGOMERY, Clare Patricia; QC (1996); da of Dr Stephen Ross Montgomery, of Haslemere, Surrey, and Ann Margaret, *née* Barlow; *b* 29 April 1958; *Educ* Millfield, UCL (LLB); *m* 14 Dec 1991, Victor Stefan Melleney; 1 da (Natasha b 27 Dec 1994); *Career* called to the Bar Gray's Inn 1980; capt Br Women's Foil Team 1992–; *Style—* Miss Clare Montgomery, QC; ✉ 3 Raymond Buildings, Gray's Inn, London WC1R 5BH (☎ 0171 831 3833, fax 0171 242 4221)

MONTGOMERY, David; CMG (1984), OBE (1972); s of late David Montgomery, and Mary, *née* Walker Cunningham; *b* 29 July 1927; *m* 1955, Margaret Newman; 1 s, 1 da; *Career* RN 1945–48; HM Dip Serv: FO 1949–52, Bucharest 1952–53, FO 1953–55, Bonn 1955–58, Düsseldorf 1958–61, Rangoon 1961–63, Ottawa 1963–64, Regina Saskatchewan 1964–65, FCO 1966–68, Bangkok 1968–72, Zagreb 1973–76, FCO 1976–79, British dep high cmmr to Barbados 1980–84 and (non-resident) to Antigua and Barbuda, Dominica, Grenada, St Kitts and Nevis, St Lucia, St Vincent and the Grenadines; ret 1984; FCO 1987–91; *Clubs* Royal Overseas; *Style—* David Montgomery, Esq, CMG, OBE; ✉ 8 Ross Court, Putney Hill, London SW15 3NY

MONTGOMERY, Sir (Basil Henry) David; 9 Bt (UK 1801), of Stanhope, Peeblesshire, JP (Kinross-shire 1966), DL (Kinross 1960 and Perth 1975); s of Lt-Col Henry Keith Purvis-Russell Montgomery, OBE (d 1954), suc uncle, Sir Basil Russell Purvis-Russell-Hamilton-Montgomery, 8 Bt (d 1964); *b* 20 March 1931; *Educ* Eton; *m* 1956, Delia, da of Adm Sir (John) Peter Lorne Reid, GCB, CVO; 2 s (1 decd), 4 da (Caroline Jean (Mrs Nicholas J K Liddle) b 1959, Davina Lucy (Mrs Humphrey M Butler) b 1961, Iona Margaret b 1972, Laura Elizabeth b 1974); *Heir* s, James David Keith Montgomery (b 13 June 1957); *Career* Tayside Regnl Cncl 1974–79, vice pres Convention of Scottish Local Authorities (COSLA) 1978–79, Nature Conservancy Cncl 1974–79, chm Forestry Commission 1979–89, Lord Lieut of Perth and Kinross 1995; Hon LLD Dundee 1977; *Style—* Sir David Montgomery, Bt, JP; ✉ Home Farm, Kinross KY13 7EU

MONTGOMERY, David; *b* 8 Feb 1937, Brooklyn, NYC; *Educ* Midwood HS, Juillard Sch of Music; *m* 1 (m dis); 2 da; m 2, 1982, Martine King; 1 s, 1 da; *Career* former musician; professional photographer 1964–; worked for: Jocelyn Stevens at Queen Magazine, The Sunday Times Magazine, Vogue, Tatler, Harpers & Queen, Rolling Stone, New York Times; has photographed: HM Queen Elizabeth II, HM Queen Elizabeth The Queen Mother, Lord Home, Lord Callaghan, Sir Edward Heath, Lady Thatcher, King Hussein of Jordan, The Duke and Duchess of York plus innumerable personalities; winner many int awards; *Recreations* gardening, photography, contemporary guitar; *Style—* David Montgomery, Esq; ✉ c/o M & M Management, Studio B, 11 Edith Grove, London SW10 (☎ 0171 352 6667, fax 0171 351 3714)

MONTGOMERY, David John; s of William John Montgomery, and Margaret Jean, *née* Flaherty; *b* 6 Nov 1948; *Educ* Bangor GS, Queen's Univ Belfast (BA); *m* 1, 12 April 1971 (m dis 1987), Susan Frances Buchanan, da of James Francis Buchanan Russell, QC; m 2, 6 May 1989, Heidi, da of Dr Edward Kingstone, of McMaster, Ontario; *Career* asst chief sub ed Daily Mirror 1978–80 (sub ed 1973–78), chief sub ed The Sun 1980–82, asst ed Sunday People 1982–84, ed News of the World 1985–87, ed and md Today 1987–91 (Newspaper of the Year 1988); md News UK 1987–91; chief exec Mirror Group Newspapers 1992–; dir: News Group Newspapers 1986–91, Satellite TV plc 1986–91, London Live Television 1991–, Caledonian Newspaper Publishing Ltd 1992, Newspaper Publishing 1994–, Donohue 1992–95, Scottish Television 1995–, Press Assoc 1996–; *Style—* David Montgomery, Esq; ✉ Mirror Group Newspapers PLC, One Canada Square, Canary Wharf, London E14 5AP (☎ 0171 510 3000, fax 0171 510 3405)

MONTGOMERY, Sir (William) Fergus; kt (1985), MP (C) Altrincham and Sale (majority 16,791); s of William and Winifred Montgomery of Hebburn; *b* 25 Nov 1927; *Educ* Jarrow GS, Bede Coll Durham; *m* Joyce, da of George Riddle, of Jarrow; *Career* RN 1946–48; memb Hebburn Cncl 1950–58; Young Cons Orgn: nat vice chm 1954–57, nat chm 1957–58; Parly candidate (C) Consett 1955; MP (C): Newcastle upon Tyne E 1959–64, Brierley Hill (Staffs) 1967–Feb 1974, Altrincham and Sale Oct 1974–; PPS to: Sec of State for Educn and Science 1973–74, Ldr of the Oppn 1975–76; chm House of Commons Ctee of Selection 1992–; *Style—* Sir Fergus Montgomery, MP; ✉ 181 Ashley Gdns, Emery Hill St, London SW1 (☎ 0171 834 7905); 6 Groby Place, Altrincham, Cheshire (☎ 0161 928 1983)

MONTGOMERY, James David Keith; s and h of Sir (Basil Henry) David Montgomery, 9 Bt, and Delia, *née* Reid; *b* 13 June 1957; *Educ* Eton, Univ of Exeter; *m* 24 Sept 1983, Elizabeth Lynette, eldest da of Lyndon Evans, of Tyla Morris, Pentyrch, Glamorgan; 1 s (Edward Henry James b 1986), 1 da (Iona Rosanna b 1988); *Career* Capt Black Watch 1976–85; N M Rothschild 1985–89, Adam & Co plc Edinburgh 1989–91, Hambros Bank PLC 1991–94, Hill Samuel Asset Management Edinburgh 1994–; *Recreations* golf, cricket, sailing, photography; *Style—* James Montgomery, Esq

MONTGOMERY, John Duncan; JP (1985); s of Lionel Eric Montgomery (d 1975), of Wimbledon, and Katherine Mary, *née* Ambler (d 1977); *b* 12 Nov 1928; *Educ* King's Coll Sch Wimbledon, LSE (LLB, LLM); *m* 31 March 1956, Pauline Mary, da of Douglas Gordon Sutherland (d 1973), of Croydon; 2 da (Susan (Mrs Thomas) b 1959, Jennifer (Mrs Strudwick) b 1962); *Career* admitted slr 1951; Treasy Slr's Dept 1960–68, legal advsr Beecham Products 1974–75, co sec Shell UK Ltd 1979–88 (head of Legal Div 1975–88), memb Monopolies and Mergers Cmmn 1989–95; former chm Merton Youth Orgns; Freeman City of London 1987, Liveryman Worshipful Co of Loriners 1988; FRSA 1981; *Recreations* dinghy sailing, photography; *Clubs* MCC, City Livery; *Style—* John Montgomery, Esq, JP; ✉ 6 White Lodge Close, Sutton, Surrey SM2 5TQ

MONTGOMERY, Ken Johnston; s of John Montgomery (d 1991), of Kilmarnock, and Catherine Gillespie, *née* Johnston; *b* 15 June 1941; *Educ* Bentink Sch Kilmarnock, Kilmarnock Acad; *m* May 1969, Pat, da of Douglas Matthews; 1 s (Nial b July 1971), 1 da (Leanne b May 1975); *Career* journalist; Kilmarnock Standard (jr reporter, feature writer, sportswriter/film critic) 1956–61, football writer then sports ed Yorkshire Evening Post 1961–65, freelance East Mid News Service Doncaster then South Yorkshire News Service Sheffield 1965–66; Sunday Mirror: football writer 1966–86, chief football writer 1986–96, tennis corr 1967–96; former memb Ctee London Press Club; memb: Football Writers' Assoc 1967 (current memb and former chm Ctee), Sports Writers' Assoc 1967, Lawn Tennis Writers' Assoc 1967; *Books* London Football Annual, Yorkshire Football Annual; *Recreations* watching horse-racing, cards (solo and cribbage), poster designing; *Clubs* Barkingside Royal British Legion (former memb branch and club ctees); *Style—* Ken Montgomery, Esq; ✉ 6 Chase Lane, Barkingside, Essex (☎ 0181 554 2455)

MONTGOMERY, Richard John; s of Basil Richard Montgomery, of Tonbridge, Kent, and Mary Elizabeth, *née* Goddard; *b* 5 May 1955; *Educ* Tonbridge, Univ of Newcastle upon Tyne (MB BS); *m* 3 July 1982, Angela, da of John Todd, of Newcastle upon Tyne; 1 s (Duncan Richard b 16 Nov 1991), 3 da (Clare Louise b 20 Sept 1987, Esme Helen b 16 Feb 1993, Eleanor Frances b 29 Nov 1995); *Career* demonstrator in anatomy Univ of Newcastle Med Sch 1979–80; post grad trg Northern Region: surgery 1980–83, orthopaedic surgery 1983–88; orthopaedic res fell Mayo Clinic Rochester Minnesota USA 1986–87, conslt in traumatic and orthopaedic surgery N and S Tees Health Dist 1989–91, conslt in traumatic and orthopaedic surgery S Tees Health Dist 1991–; hon clinical lectr Faculty of Med Univ of Newcastle upon Tyne 1996–, hon lectr Sch of Human Studies Univ of Teeside 1996–; memb: Br Soc for Childrens Orthopaedic Surgery, Br Orthopaedic Assoc, BMA; FRCSEd 1983; *Recreations* aviation (holder of PPL); *Style—* Richard Montgomery, Esq; ✉ Middlesbrough General Hospital, Ayresome Green Lane, Middlesbrough, Cleveland TS5 5AZ (☎ 01642 854215)

MONTGOMERY, Dr Stephen Ross; s of Sir Frank Percival Montgomery (d 1972), of Belfast, and Joan, *née* Christopherson (d 1990); *b* 15 Jan 1931; *Educ* Trinity Coll Glenalmond, Clare Coll Cambridge (MA), MIT (SM, ScD); *m* 15 June 1955, Ann, da of Stewart Irlam Barlow (d 1942), of Northumberland; 1 s (Bruce b 1956), 3 da (Clare b 1958, Joy b 1961, Jane b 1963); *Career* chartered mechanical engr; UCL 1958–96: formerly lectr and sr lectr in mechanical engrg, mangr London Centre for Marine Technol, dir of external relations; CEng, FIMechE; *Recreations* converting houses; *Style—* Dr Stephen R Montgomery; ✉ Telegraph Cottage, Blackdown, Haslemere, Surrey GU27 3BS (☎ 01428 654297)

MONTGOMERY CUNINGHAME, Sir John Christopher Foggo; 12 Bt (NS 1672), of Corsehill, Ayrshire; s of Col Sir Thomas Andrew Alexander Montgomery Cuninghame, 10 Bt, DSO, JP (d 1945) and his 2 w, Nancy Macaulay, *née* Foggo; suc bro Sir William Andrew Malcolm Martin Oliphant Montgomery Cuninghame, 11 Bt (d 1959); *b* 24 July 1935; *Educ* Fettes, Worcester Coll Oxford; *m* 9 Sept 1964, Laura Violet, 2 da of Sir Godfrey Nicholson, 1 Bt (d 1991); 3 da (Christian Elizabeth b 1967, Georgiana Rose b 1969, Elizabeth Clara b 1971); *Heir* none; *Career* Nat Serv 2 Lt Rifle Bde; dir: Purolite International Ltd, Bedford Capital Finance Corp, Alloy Technology International Inc; *Clubs* Boodle's, Pratt's; *Style—* Sir John Montgomery Cuninghame, Bt; ✉ The Old Rectory, Brightwalton, Newbury, Berks RG16 0BL

MONTGOMERY OF ALAMEIN, 2 Viscount (UK 1946); David Bernard Montgomery; CBE (1975); o s of 1 Viscount Montgomery of Alamein, KG, GCB, DSO (d 1976), and Elizabeth, *née* Hobart (d 1937); *b* 18 Aug 1928; *Educ* Winchester, Trinity Coll Cambridge; *m* 1, 27 Feb 1953 (m dis 1967), Mary Raymond, yr da of Sir Charles Connell (d 1973); 1 s, 1 da; m 2, 30 Jan 1970, Tessa, da of Lt-Gen Sir Frederick A M Browning, GCVO, KBE, CB, DSO (d 1965), and Lady Browning, DBE (Daphne du Maurier, the writer, d 1989), and former w of Maj Peter de Zulueta; *Heir* s, Hon Henry David Montgomery; *Career* sits as Cons peer in House of Lords; dir Yardley International 1963–74, md Terimar Services Ltd (overseas trade consultancy) 1974–, chm Baring Puma Fund 1991–; memb Editorial Advsy Bd Vision Interamericana 1974–94; cncllr Royal Borough of Kensington and Chelsea 1974–78; chm: Hispanic and Luso Brasilian Cncl Canning House 1978–80 (pres 1987–94), Antofagasta (Chile) and Bolivia Railway Co and subsids 1980–82; vice pres Brazilian C of C GB 1983– (chm 1980–82), chm European Atlantic Group 1992–94 (pres 1994–); non-exec dir: Korn/Ferry Int 1977–93, Northern Engrg Industs 1980–87; patron D-Day and Normandy Fellowship 1980–94, Eighth Army Veterans Assoc 1984–; pres: Restaurateurs Assoc of GB 1982–90 (patron 1990), Centre for International Briefing Farnham Castle 1983–, Anglo-Argentine Soc 1976–87, Redgrave Theatre Farnham 1978–90, Anglo-Belgian Soc 1994–; Liveryman Worshipful Co of Mercers; *Books* The Lonely Leader - Monty 1944–45 (with Alistair Horne, 1994); *Clubs* Garrick, Royal Fowey Yacht, Canning; *Style—* The Rt Hon Viscount Montgomery of Alamein, CBE; ✉ 54 Cadogan Square, London SW1X OJW (☎ 0171 589 8747, fax 0171 589 5020)

MONTLAKE, Henry Joseph; s of Alfred Montlake, and Hetty Montlake; *b* 22 Aug 1930; *Educ* Ludlow GS, Univ of London (LLB); *m* 14 Sept 1952, Ruth Rochelle, *née* Allen; 4 s (Jonathan b 18 Oct 1956, Andrew b 2 July 1958, Nicholas b 30 Dec 1959, Charles b 13 Jan 1962); *Career* cmmnd RASC 1954; admitted slr 1952; cmmr for Oaths 1955, sr ptnr H Montlake & Co 1954–, dep registrar of Co Cts 1970–78, dep circuit judge and asst recorder 1978–83, recorder Crown Ct 1983–; chm Ilford Round Table 1962–63, capt Abridge Golf Club 1965 (chm 1964); pres: W Essex Law Soc 1977–78, Assoc of Jewish Golf Clubs and Socs 1983–94 (sec 1977–83); ctee memb Ethics Ctee of IVF Unit of BUPA Roding Hosp 1991–; govr Redbridge Coll of FE 1991–; memb Law Soc; *Recreations* golf, The Times crossword, people, travel; *Clubs* Wig and Pen, Dyrham Park Golf, Abridge Golf and Country; *Style—* Henry Montlake, Esq; ✉ Chelston, 5 St Mary's Avenue, Wanstead, London E11 2NR (☎ 0181 989 7228); 197 High Road, Ilford, Essex IG1 1LX (☎ 0181 553 1311, fax 0181 553 3066)

MONTMORENCY, *see:* de Montmorency

MONTROSE, 8 Duke of (S 1707); Sir James Graham; 11 Bt (S 1625), of Braco; also Lord Graham (S 1445), Earl of Montrose (S 1505), Marquess of Montrose (S 1644, new charter granted 1706), Marquess of Graham and Buchanan, Earl of Kincardine, Viscount Dundaff, Lord Aberuthven, Mugdock and Fintrie (all S 1707), Earl Graham and Baron Graham (GB 1722); also Hereditary Sheriff of Dunbartonshire; s of 7 Duke of Montrose (d 1992), and his 1 w, Isobel Veronica, *née* Sellar (d 1990); *b* 6 April 1935; *Educ* Loretto; *m* 1970, Catherine Elizabeth MacDonnell, yst da of Capt Norman Andrew Thompson Young (d 1942), Queen's Own Cameron Highlanders of Canada; 2 s (Marquess of Graham b 1973, Lord Ronald John Christopher b 1975), 1 da (Lady Hermione Elizabeth b 1971); *Heir* s, Marquess of Graham b 16 Aug 1973; *Career* Brig Royal Co of Archers (Queen's Body Guard for Scotland) 1976–; memb Cncl Scottish Nat Farmers' Union 1981–86 and 1987–90; OStJ 1978; *Clubs* Royal Scottish Pipers' Soc, Royal Highland Agric Soc; *Style*— His Grace the Duke of Montrose; ✉ Auchmar, Drymen, Glasgow (☎ 01360 60307)

MONTROSE, Kenneth; s of Harry Montrose (d 1955), of London, and Sophie, *née* Davis (d 1976); *b* 13 Jan 1928; *Educ* Glendale Coll Southend-on-Sea, Westfield Modern Sch Hinckley Leics; *m* 12 March 1949, Mary (d 1984), da of William Joseph Moreton (d 1972), of Hinckley, Leics; 1 s (Michael b 27 Sept 1949), 1 da (Gillian Mary b 29 Nov 1953); *Career* enlisted boys serv RN 1945, serv air mechanic 1 class Far East, demobbed 1947, seaman (sr position) Merchant Marines 1947–48; tech author Leyland Motors Gp 1950–54 (publicity mangr 1954–63), started own bldg and investmt co 1963, chm Broadgate Printing Group 1963–; contrib to various tech manuals; *Recreations* cars, gardening, walking; *Clubs* Wellington, Wig & Pen, Chestnuts, Tudor; *Style*— Kenneth Montrose, Esq; ✉ Broadgate Printing Group, Crondal Rd, Exhall, Coventry (☎ 01203 361800)

MOODIE, David Garrioch; s of late Peter Alexander Moodie; *b* 19 May 1926; *m* 1952, Mary Smith Hunter, *née* Williamson; 1 s, 1 da; *Career* CA; md Black & Edgington plc 1973–84, chm Andrew Mitchell Group plc 1984–96, ret; MICAS; *Recreations* golf, skiing, sailing; *Clubs* Caledonian; *Style*— David Moodie, Esq

MOODY, (David) Barry Drury; s of Thomas Drury Moody (d 1988), of Melton Mowbray, and Edna Mary, *née* Jackson (d 1995); *b* 23 April 1949; *Educ* Uppingham, Univ of Nottingham (LLB); *Career* admitted slr 1973; ptnr Lovell White Durrant (formerly Lovell White & King) 1978–; Freeman City of London Slrs' Co 1974; memb Law Soc 1973; *Recreations* golf, travel, music; *Style*— Barry Moody, Esq; ✉ Lovell White Durrant, 65 Holborn Viaduct, London EC1A 2DY (☎ 0171 236 0066, fax 0171 248 0084, telex 887122 LWD G)

MOODY, Prof (Anthony) David; s of Edward Tabrum Moody, of Lower Hutt, New Zealand, and Nora, *née* Gordon; *b* 21 Jan 1932; *Educ* St Patrick's Coll Wellington NZ, Canterbury Coll Univ of NZ (MA), Univ of Oxford (BA, MA); *Career* Shirtcliffe fell Univ of NZ 1953–55, asst info offr UNHCR Geneva 1957–58, sr lectr Univ of Melbourne 1958–64, Nuffield Fndn travelling fell 1965, memb Dept of English and related lit Univ of York 1966–; *Books* Virginia Woolf (1963), Shakespeare: "The Merchant of Venice" (1964), "The Waste Land" In Different Voices (ed, 1972), Thomas Stearns Eliot: Poet (1979 and 1994), At the Antipodes: Homage to Paul Valèry (1982), News Odes: The El Salvador Sequence (1984), The Cambridge Companion to T S Eliot (ed, 1994), Tracing T.S. Eliot's Spirit: essays (1996); *Recreations* Bedlam Press, music, hill walking, tennis, travel; *Style*— Prof A David Moody; ✉ Church Green House, Old Church Lane, Pateley Bridge, N Yorks HG3 5LZ; Department of English & Related Literature, University of York, York YO1 5DD (☎ 01904 433353)

MOODY, (David) John; s of Norman Day Moody (d 1970), and Catherine Isabel Moody, of Lytham St Annes, Lancashire; *b* 19 Feb 1950; *Educ* Nottingham HS, Jesus Coll Cambridge (MA, golf blue 1971 and 1972); *m* Eileen Jean Nelson, *née* Smith; 1 s (James Day b 28 Jan 1979), 1 da (Helen Isabel b 18 April 1980); *Career* Ingham Clegg & Crowther (Preston): articled clerk 1972–75, admitted slr 1975, slr 1975–80, ptnr 1980–89; ptnr Yates Barnes (Chorley) 1989–90, managing ptnr Eversheds (Manchester) 1993– (ptnr and head Property Dept 1990–93); memb Law Soc; *Recreations* golf (memb Oxford and Cambridge Golf Soc), overseas travel, mowing the lawn and terrorising the cat; *Clubs* Hawks (Cambridge), Portal Golf; *Style*— John Moody, Esq; ✉ The Close, Catherine Road, Bowdon, Cheshire WA14 2TD (☎ 0161 941 3998); Eversheds, London Scottish House, 24 Mount Street, Manchester M2 3DB (☎ 0161 832 6666, fax 0161 832 5337)

MOODY, Philip Edward; s of Frederick Osborne Moody, and Hilda Laura, *née* Frost; *b* 28 July 1954; *Educ* Bentley GS Calne Wilts; *Career* CA; articled clerk Monahan & Co Chippenham 1972–82, fndr ptnr Solomon Hare Chippenham 1983–88, sr ptnr and lead corporate fin ptnr Solomon Hare Bristol 1989–, fndr chm Gimlet Group 1989–; FCA 1990 (ACA 1980), ATII 1982; *Recreations* walking, photography, theatre, snooker, cricket; *Style*— Philip Moody, Esq; ✉ Clevelands, Lansdown Road, Bath, Somerset BA1 5TD (☎ 01225 480046); Solomon Hare, Oakfield House, Oakfield Grove, Clifton, Bristol BS8 2BN (☎ 0117 923 8555, fax 0117 923 8666, mobile 0836 360084, e-mail 101326.1015@compuserve.com)

MOODY, Ronald (Ron); s of Bernard Moody (d 1964), of London, and Kate, *née* Ogus (d 1980); *b* 8 Jan 1924; *Educ* LSE (BSc); *m* 14 Dec 1987, Therese, da of Michael John Blackburn, of Penzance, Cornwall; 5 s (Daniel Maximilian, Matthew Alexander, Michael Orlando, Jonathan Barnaby, Conrad Augustus), 1 da (Catherine Laura); *Career* actor and writer; Sgt Educn Section RAF 1943–48; pres Clowns Int; Freeman City of London 1987; memb: Variety Club of GB, Br Actors' Equity (also USA and Canada), American Acad of Motion Picture Arts and Scis, Screen Actors' Guild; *Theatre* incl: For Amusement Only 1955, Candide 1959, Oliver! 1960, Clandestine Marriage, Peter Pan, Richard III, HMS Pinafore, Sherlock Holmes, Move Along Sideways (one-man show) 1991, The Streets of Dublin 1992, The Animals of Farthing Wood 1993, Bertie 1993, Peter Pan (musical) 1994; dir Kafka in Love (King's Head) 1991; *Musicals* written: Joey Joey 1966, Saturnalia 1971, Move Along Sideways 1976, The Showman 1977, Nine Lives 1991; *Television* various appearances UK and USA; *Films* incl: Oliver! 1967, Twelve Chairs 1970, Flight of the Doves, Dogpound Shuffle, Ghost in Monte Carlo, Kid in King Arthur's Court 1995, Take Pity 1995; *Awards* Oscar nominee 1969, Golden Globe 1969, Variety Club Film 1969, Moscow Golden Bear 1970, Antoinette Perry nominee 1984, Theatre World 1984; *Books* My LSE (1979), The Devil You Don't (1980), Very Very Slightly Imperfect (1983), Off the Cuff (1987), The Amazon Box (1994); *Recreations* tennis, oil painting, cartoons, driving; *Style*— Ron Moody, Esq; ✉ c/o Eric Glass Ltd, 28 Berkeley Square, London W1X 6HD (☎ 0171 629 7162)

MOODY, Susan Elizabeth; da of Frederick Chesney Horwood (d 1990), and Ursula Margaret (Kym), *née* Wheeler Robinson (d 1989); *Educ* Oxford HS for Girls, Open Univ (BA); *m* 1, 1961, Dr Walter F Bertsch (d 1984), s of Bernard J Bertsch, of San Diego, California; 2 s (Jonathon Andrew Richard b 1962, Timothy David b 1963); m 2, 1972, John Edward James Moody; 1 s (Benedick Adam John b 1973); *Career* author; memb: Soc of Authors, Crime Writers' Assoc (chm 1989–90), Exec Ctee of Int Assoc of Crime Writers, Detection Club 1988, Romantic Novelists' Assoc; *Books* Penny Black (1984), Penny Dreadful (1984), Penny Post (1985), Penny Royal (1986), Penny Wise (1988), Penny Pinching (1989), Penny Saving (1991), Playing with Fire (1990), Hush-a-Bye (1991), House of Moons (1993), Takeout Double (1993), Love Over Gold (1993), Grand Slam (1994), The Italian Garden (1994), King of Hearts (1994), Misselthwaite (1995), Doubled in Spades (1996); *Style*— Susan Moody; ✉ c/o Peters Fraser & Dunlop Ltd, 503 The Chambers, Chelsea Harbour, Lots Road, London SW10 0XF (☎ 0171 376 7676, fax 0171 352 7356)

MOODY-STUART, Dr Mark; *b* 15 Sept 1940, Antigua; *Educ* Univ of Cambridge (BA, PhD); *m*; 4 c; *Career* Royal Dutch/Shell Group: joined Shell Internationale Petroleum Maatschappij BV as geologist 1966, worked as geologist in Spain, Oman and Brunei 1966–72, chief geologist Australia 1972–76, i/c North Sea oil exploration teams 1976–78, servs mangr Brunei 1978–79, mangr Western Div Shell Petroleum Development Co of Nigeria 1979–82, gen mangr Shell Group of Cos Turkey 1982–86, chm and chief exec Shell Cos in Malaysia 1986–90, gp exploration and prodn coordinator 1990–94, dir Shell International Petroleum Co 1991–, a gp md 1991–, an md Shell Transport and Trading Co plc 1991–; *Recreations* sailing, travel; *Style*— Dr Mark Moody-Stuart; ✉ The Shell Transport & Trading Co plc, Shell Centre, London SE1 7NA (☎ 0171 934 1234)

MOOLGAOKER, Arvind Sumant; s of Sumant Moolgaoker (d 1989), of Bombay, India, and Leela, *née* Welingkar; *b* 15 March 1934; *Educ* St Joseph's Northpoint Darjeeling India, Cathedral and John Connon Boys' HS Bombay, Grant Med Coll Bombay (MB BS, MD); *m* 1, 1964, Jill, *née* Canning (d 1973); 1 s (Anil b 14 Dec 1970), 2 da (Nikki b 9 Sept 1966, Nina b 7 March 1968); m 2, 19 Jan 1975, Jean, da of David Fielding, of Rossendale Lancs; *Career* lectr and sr registrar Nuffield Dept of Obstetrics and Gynaecology 1966–71, conslt obstetrician and gynaecologist Basingstoke and Dist Hosps 1971–; invented Moolgaokers Obstetric Forceps 1957; FRSM 1964, FRCOG 1979; *Recreations* fishing, fly-dressing, shooting, photography; *Style*— Arvind Moolgaoker, Esq; ✉ Kymore, 128 Cliddesden Rd, Basingstoke, Hants RG21 3HH (☎ 01256 55677)

MOOLLAN, Sir Cassam Ismael; kt (1982), QC (Mauritius 1969); s of Ismael Mahomed Moollan (d 1972), and Fatimah, *née* Nazroo (d 1962); *b* 26 Feb 1927; *Educ* Royal Coll Port Louis, LSE, Univ of London (LLB); *m* 1954, Rassool Bibie Adam, da of Adam Sulliman Moollan (d 1964); 1 s (Oomar), 2 da (Aisha, Naseem); *Career* called to the Bar Lincoln's Inn; private practice Mauritius 1951–55, dist magistrate 1955–58, crown counsel 1958–64, sr crown counsel 1964–66, solicitor-gen 1966–70, puisne judge Supreme Court Mauritius 1970–78, sr puisne judge 1978, chief justice Mauritius 1982–88; actg govr-gen on several occasions between 1984–88; legal conslt; dir: S E Asia Bank Ltd Mauritius, Provident Real Estate Fund Ltd Mauritius; Chevalier de la Legion d'Honneur France 1986; *Recreations* bridge, Indian classical and semi-classical music; *Style*— Sir Cassam Moollan, QC; ✉ 22 Hitchcock Ave, Quatre Bornes, Mauritius (☎ 00 230 454 6949); 43 Sir William Newton St, Port Louis, Mauritius (☎ 00 230 212 0794 and 00 230 208 3881, fax 00 230 208 8351)

MOON, *see:* Graham-Moon

MOON, Michael (Mick); s of Donald Charles Moon, and Marjorie, *née* Metcalfe; *b* 9 Nov 1937; *Educ* Shoreham GS, Chelsea Sch of Art, RCA; *m* Anjum, da of Abdul Khalid Khan; 2 s (Timur b 26 Aug 1977, Adam Khalid b 9 Feb 1982); *Career* artist; sr lectr in painting Slade Sch of Art 1973–90; *Solo Exhibitions* Waddington Galleries 1969, 1970, 1972, 1978, 1984, 1986 and 1992, Tate Gallery 1976, Dolan Maxwell Philadelphia 1986, Pace Prints NY 1987, Kass Meridien Gallery Chicago 1992; *Group Exhibitions* Young Contemporaries Exhbn 1963, Caulfield Hodgkin Moon (Paris) 1972, La Peinture Anglaise d'Aujord'hui (Musée d'Art Paris) 1973, British Painting (Hayward Gallery) 1974, Recent Purchases of the Arts Cncl (Serpentine Gallery) 1983, Perspecta Survey of Work in Australia 1983, American and European Monoprints (Pace Gallery NYC) 1987; major Arts Cncl award 1980, first prize John Moores Exhbn 1984, Gulbenkian Print Award; *Work in Public Collections* Art Gallery of NSW Sydney, Arts Cncl Collection, Scottish Nat Gallery, Tate Gallery, Univ Coll Gallery, V & A; RA 1994; *Style*— Mick Moon, Esq, RA; ✉ Waddington Galleries Ltd, 11 Cork St, London W1X 1PD (☎ 0171 439 1866, fax 0171 734 1549)

MOON, Peter Geoffrey; s of Roland Charles Moon, of Vereley, and Bernice Moon; *b* 4 Nov 1949; *Educ* Brockenhurst GS, UCL (BSc (Econ)); *m* 31 May 1975, Susan Elizabeth Williams; 3 c (Richard David b 5 Aug 1978, Katherine Helen (twin) b 1978, Simon Edward b 26 Aug 1980); *Career* Central Bd of Fin Church of England 1972–75, Slater Walker Securities 1975–78, National Provident Institution 1978–85, British Airways Pensions 1985–92, Universities Superannuation Scheme 1992–; advsr: Teeside Superannuation Fund, Lincoln Superannuation Fund; chm Thackeray's House Restaurant Ltd; AIIMR; *Style*— Peter Moon, Esq; ✉ The Universities Superannuation Scheme Ltd, 11th Floor, 1 Angel Court, London EC2R 7HJ (☎ 0171 972 0300, fax 0171 600 4815)

MOON, Sir Roger; 6 Bt (UK 1887), of Copsewood, Stoke, Co Warwick; s of Jasper Moon, OBE (d 1975, gs of 1 Bt); suc bro, Sir Edward Moon, MC, 5 Bt, 1988; *b* 17 Nov 1914; *Educ* Sedbergh; *m* 16 Dec 1950, Meg, da of late Col Arthur Mainwaring Maxwell, DSO, MC; 3 da (Sarah Corinna b 1951, Gillian Adèle (Mrs Johnston) b 1954, Patricia Isolda (Mrs Hogg) b 1955); *Heir* bro, Humphrey Moon b 9 Oct 1920; *Recreations* golf, gardening; *Style*— Sir Roger Moon, Bt; ✉ The Barn House, Wykey, Ruyton-XI-Towns, Shropshire SY4 1JA (☎ 01939 260354)

MOON, Rupert Henry St John Barker; s of Henry John Moon, and Audrey Colleen, *née* Barker; *b* 1 Feb 1968; *Educ* Wolverhampton GS, Queen Mary's GS Walsall, Univ of Glamorgan (BA); *Career* Rugby Union scrum-half; clubs: Walsall RFC, Abertillery RFC, Neath RFC, currently Llanelli RFC (capt); Wales: debut v France 1993, 19 full caps; 4 times Welsh Cup winners, 2 Man of the Match awards; TV and radio presenter, researcher and prodn mangr; *Style*— Rupert Moon, Esq; ✉ 21 Alpha Place, Trallwn, Pontypridd, Mid Glamorgan CF37 4RT (☎ 01554 774060, mobile 0374 604802, fax 01554 778385)

MOONEY, Bel; da of Edward Mooney, and Gladys, *née* Norbury; *b* 8 Oct 1946; *Educ* Aigburth Vale Girls' HS Liverpool, Trowbridge Girls' HS Wiltshire, UCL (BA); *m* 1968, Jonathan Dimbleby, *qv*, s of Richard Dimbleby, CBE (d 1965); 1 s (Daniel Richard b 1974), 1 da (Katharine Rose b 1980); *Career* asst to the ed then contributing ed Nova magazine 1971–75, freelance contrib (Guardian, Times, Observer, New Statesman, Sunday Times, Daily Express amongst others) 1972–81; columnist: Cosmopolitan, Daily Mirror, Sunday Times, The Listener; TV presenter 1980–86 (Mothers By Daughters (C4), Fathers by Sons (C4), Dora Russell (BBC2), Ellen Wilkinson (BBC2)), presenter Radio 4 1985–95 (Women: Equal Sex?, American Authors, Turning Points, A Perspective For Living, Devout Sceptics); dir Friends of Great Ormond Street 1993–; fell UCL 1994; *Non-Fiction Books* The Year of the Child (1979), Differences of Opinion (1984), Bel Mooney's Somerset (1989), Perspectives for Living (1992); *Novels* The Windsurf Boy (1983), The Anderson Question (1985), The Fourth of July (1988), Lost Footsteps (1993); *Children's Books* Liza's Yellow boat (also illustrated by the author, 1980), I Don't Want To! (1985), The Stove Haunting (1986), I Can't Find It! (1988), It's Not Fair (1989), A Flower of Jet (1990), But You Promised! (1990), Why Not? (1990), I Know! (1991), I'm Scared (1994), The Voices of Silence (1994), I Wish! (1995), Why me? (1996), I'm Bored (1997), Joining the Rainbow (1997); *Satire* Father Kissmass and Mother Claws (with Gerald Scarfe, 1985); *Anthology* From This Day Forward (1989); *Recreations* literature, art, music, friends, churches; *Clubs* The Groucho; *Style*— Miss Bel Mooney; ✉ c/o David Higham Associates, 5 Lower John Street, London W1 (☎ 0171 437 7888)

MOONIE, Dr Lewis George; MP (Lab) Kirkcaldy (majority 9,126); *b* 25 Feb 1947; *Educ* Grove Acad Dundee, Univ of St Andrews (MB ChB), Univ of Edinburgh (MSc); *m*; 2 c; *Career* jr med posts 1970–75, DPM 1975, sr med advsr and clinical pharmacologist in the pharmaceutical indust in Holland, Switzerland and Edinburgh 1976–80, conslt in public health Fife Health Bd 1984–87 (trainee in community med 1980–84), MP (Lab) Kirkcaldy 1987–; memb Treasy Select Ctee 1988–89; oppn spokesman: trade and industry 1989–92, science and technol 1992–94, industry 1994–95, nat heritage 1995–;

MFCM 1984, MRCPsych 1979; *Style*— Dr Lewis Moonie, MP; ✉ 25 High Street, Kirkcaldy, Fife KY1 1LQ; House of Commons, London SW1A 0AA (☎ 0171 219 3000)

MOONMAN, Prof Eric; OBE (1991); s of Borach Moonman (d 1953), and Leah, *née* Bernstein (d 1959); *b* 29 April 1929; *Educ* Christ Church Southport, Univ of Manchester (MSc), Univ of Liverpool (Dip Social Sci); *m* 9 Sept 1962 (m dis 1991), Jane, da of Edward Dillon, of Lancs; 2 s (Daniel b 10 July 1966, Joshua b 27 Jan 1972), 1 da (Natasha b 19 April 1968); *Career* Nat Serv Kings Liverpool Regt 1951–53; human rels advsr Br Inst Mgmnt 1956–62, leader of Stepney Cncl 1958–62, memb Tower Hamlets Cncl 1963–67; MP: Basildon 1966–70, Billericay 1974–79; govr Br Film Inst 1978–83, dir Gp Rels Educn Tst 1979–88, chm Islington Health Authy 1980–90, memb Bloomsbury and Islington DHA 1990–93; HM treas Toynbee Hall 1979–93, sr vice pres Bd of Deps of Br Jews 1986–91 and 1994–, visiting prof of health mgmnt City Univ 1990–, dir Natural History Museum Tst 1990–92, chm Essex Radio 1991–; conslt Int Red Cross Namibia and Zimbabwe 1992–95, chair Continuing Care Appeals Panel City of Liverpool 1996–; FIMgt 1959; *Books* The Manager and the Organisation (1961), Communications in an Expanding Organisation (1970), Relevant Partnership (1971), Alternative Environment (1984), Violent Society (1987); *Recreations* cinema, theatre, football (watching), tennis (playing); *Style*— Prof Eric Moonman, OBE; ✉ 1 Beacon Hill, London N7 9LY (☎ 01702 333711)

MOOR, Philip Drury; s of Rev David Moor, and Evangeline, *née* White; *b* 15 July 1959; *Educ* Canford, Pembroke Coll Oxford; *m* 18 July 1987, Gillian Elizabeth, *née* Stark; 2 da (Alice Elizabeth b 24 May 1992, Emily Ruth b 9 Sept 1995); *Career* called to the Bar Inner Temple 1982; memb: Gen Cncl of the Bar 1987–89, Family Law Bar Assoc Ctee 1987–, Cncl of Legal Educn 1988–91, Bd of Examiners 1989–92, Phillips Ctee on Financing Pupillage 1989; *Books* contrib (with N Mostyn) to Family Law; *Recreations* cricket, association football; *Style*— Philip Moor, Esq; ✉ 1 Mitre Court Buildings, Temple, London EC4Y 7BS (☎ 0171 797 7070, fax 0171 797 7435)

MOORCOCK, Michael John; s of Arthur Edward Moorcock, of Worthing, W Sussex, and June, *née* Taylor; *b* 18 Dec 1939; *Educ* Michael Hall Sussex, Pitman's Coll Croydon Surrey; *m* 1, 25 Oct 1962 (m dis 1978), Hilary Denham Bailey; 1 s (Max Edward b 24 Feb 1971), 2 da (Sophie Elizabeth b 3 Sept 1963, Katherine Helen b 5 Sept 1964); m 2, 7 May 1978 (m dis 1983), Jill Riches; m 3, 23 Sept 1983, Linda Mullens Steele; *Career* author 1956–; ed: Tarzan Adventures 1957–, Fleetway Publications 1959–, Liberal Party 1961–, New Worlds 1964; awards incl: August Derleth Award (four times, 1971–75), Nebula Award 1968, World Fantasy Award 1979, Guardian Fiction Prize 1977; memb: Liberty, NSPCC, Amnesty Int, Southern Poverty Law Center, Charter 88, Authors' Guild, Soc of Authors; *Books* over 100 books incl: Byzantium Endures (1981), The Laughter of Carthage (1984), Mother London (1988), Jerusalem Commands (1992), Blood (1994), Fabulous Harbours (1995), The War Amongst the Angels (1996); omnibus novels reissued by Orion 1992 and 1993: Von Bek, The Eternal Champion, Corum, Sailing to Utopia, The Nomad of the Time Streams, The Dancers at the End of Time, Elric of Melniboné, The New Nature of the Catastrophe, The Prince with the Silver Hand, Legends from the End of Time, Stormbringer, Earl Aubec, Count Brass, Gloriana, The Brothel in Rosenstrasse, Behold the Man, Breakfast in the Ruins, Jerry Cornelius Quartet, A Cornelius Calendar; ed of numerous anthologies, collections and short stories; *Recreations* camel racing, mountaineering; *Style*— Michael Moorcock, Esq; ✉ c/o Giles Gordon, Curtis Brown Group Ltd, 28–29 Haymarket, London SW1Y 4SP (☎ 0171 396 6600); USA (☎ and fax 00 1 512 321 5000)

MOORCROFT, David Robert; MBE (1983); s of Robert Moorcroft, of Coventry, and Mildred, *née* Hardy; *b* 10 April 1953; *Educ* Woodlands Comp Sch, Tile Hill Coll of Further Educn, Loughborough Univ (BEd); *m* Linda Ann, da of John Ward; 1 s (Paul David b 4 May 1981), 1 da (Lucy Ann b 19 April 1985); *Career* former int athlete; sr GB debut 1973, AAA 1500m champion 1978, UK 1500m and 5000m champion 1980; achievements incl: seventh 1500m Olympic Games Montreal 1976, Gold medal 1500m Cwlth Games Edmonton 1978, Bronze medal 1500m Euro Championships Prague 1978, semi-finalist 5000m Olympic Games Moscow 1980, Gold medal 5000m Europa Cup Zagreb 1981, Gold medal 5000m Cwlth Games Brisbane 1982, Bronze medal Euro Championships Athens 1982, finalist 5000m Olympic Games LA 1984; records: world 5000m 13:00:41 Oslo 1982, Euro 3000m 7:32:79 Crystal Palace 1982; school teacher 1976–81, dir charitable tst 1981–, memb commentary teams BBC TV and Radio 1983–; *Style*— David Moorcroft, Esq, MBE

MOORE, Alan Edward; CBE (1980); s of Charles Edward Moore (d 1986), of Hemel Hempstead, Herts, and Ethel, *née* Middleton (d 1989); *b* 5 June 1936; *Educ* Berkhamsted Sch; *m* 2 Sept 1961, Margaret Patricia, *née* Beckley; 1 s (Andrew b 9 May 1968), 1 da (Kathryn Moore b 9 May 1963); *Career* RAF; joined Glyn Mills & Co 1953, dep dir Williams & Glyn Bank 1971–74, dir gen Bahrain Monetary Agency Bahrain 1974–79, dir Lloyds Bank Int 1980–84; Lloyds Bank Plc: treas 1986–88, dir of corp banking and treasy 1988–94, bd dir 1989–95, dep chief exec and treas 1994–95; dep chief exec and treas Lloyds TSB Group plc (following merger) 1995–; AIB 1958, ACIS 1963, FACT 1985; *Recreations* photography, railway history, travel; *Style*— Alan Moore, Esq, CBE; ✉ Lloyds TSB Group plc, 71 Lombard Street, London EC3P 3BS (☎ 0171 626 1500)

MOORE, Brian; s of James Bernard Moore, and Eileen, *née* McFadden; *b* 25 Aug 1921; *m* Oct 1967, Jean Denney; *Career* novelist; recipient Que Lit Prize 1958, Guggenheim fell 1959, US Nat Arts and Letters award 1961, Canadian Cncl sr fell 1962 and 1976, Govr-Gen of Canada's Fiction award 1961 and 1975, recipient W H Smith award 1975, James Tait Black Meml award 1975, Scottish Arts Cncl int fell 1983, Heinemann award Royal Soc of Lit 1986, Sunday Express Book of the Year award 1988; Hon DLitt: The Queen's Univ of Belfast 1987, The Nat Univ of Ireland (UCD) 1991; FRCS, FRSL 1968; *Books* The Lonely Passion of Judith Hearne (1955), The Feast of Lupercal (1957), The Luck of Ginger Coffey (1960), An Answer from Limbo (1962), The Emperor of Ice-Cream (1965), I Am Mary Dunne (1968), Fergus (1970), The Revolution Script (1971), Catholics (1972), The Great Victorian Collection (1975), The Doctor's Wife (1976), The Mangan Inheritance (1979), The Temptation of Eileen Hughes (1981), Cold Heaven (1983), Black Robe (1985), The Color of Blood (1987), Lies of Silence (1990), No Other Life (1993), The Statement (1995); *Style*— Brian Moore; ✉ 33958 Pacific Coast Highway, Malibu, Calif 90265, USA; c/o Curtis Brown Ltd, 10 Astor Place, New York 10003, USA (fax 00 1 310 457 7940)

MOORE, Brian Baden; s of Baden Kimberley Moore (d 1969), of Benenden, Kent, and Elsie Norah, *née* Sharpe (d 1987); *b* 28 Feb 1932; *Educ* Cranbrook Sch Kent; *m* 19 March 1955, Eileen Betty, da of William Cole (d 1973), of Bromley, Kent; 2 s (Christopher b 1958, Simon b 1961); *Career* Nat Serv PO RAF 1950–52; sports reporter and sub ed: World Sports 1955, Exchange Telegraph 1957, The Times 1958; football commentator and presenter BBC Radio 1960–67, football commentator and sports presenter ITV 1967–, presenter of documentary series Brian Moore Meets...; dir Gillingham FC 1978–85; *Style*— Brian Moore, Esq; ✉ c/o Sommerfield Ltd, 35 Old Queen Street, London SW1H 9JD (☎ 0171 222 9070, fax 0171 222 5591)

MOORE, Prof Brian Cecil Joseph; *b* 10 Feb 1946; *Educ* Sir Walter St John's GS Battersea, St Catharine's Coll Cambridge (exhibitioner, MA), Univ of Cambridge (PhD); *Career* Aectr in psychology Univ of Reading 1971–73, Fulbright-Hays sr scholar and visiting prof Dept of Psychology Brooklyn Coll City Univ NY USA 1973–74, lectr in psychology Univ of Reading 1974–77; Univ of Cambridge: lectr in experimental psychology 1977–89, reader in auditory perception 1989–95, prof of auditory perception 1995–; fell Wolfson Coll Cambridge 1983–; Univ of California at Berkeley: visiting researcher 1985, visiting prof Dept of Psychology 1990; visiting conslt prof Dept of Bioengrg Univ of Ulster 1991–93; pres Assoc of Independent Hearing Healthcare Professionals; memb: Experimental Psychology Soc, Cambridge Philosophical Soc, Br Soc of Audiology, American Speech-Language-Hearing Assoc, Audio Engrg Soc, Acoustical Soc of Japan, American Auditory Soc; memb Editorial Bd: Br Jl of Audiology, Jl of Auditory Neuroscience, Jl Acoustical Soc of Japan, Jl Audiology and Neuro-otology; sometime memb various MRC ctees and advsy gps (incl MRC's Hearing Research Ctee 1986–94) 1979–95; memb Scientific Advsy Bd Resound Corp USA; T S Littler prize Br Soc of Audiology 1983; fell Acoustical Soc of America 1985, Van Houten fell Inst for Perception Research Eindhoven 1994; *Books* An Introduction to the Psychology of Hearing (1977, 2 edn 1982, 3 edn 1989, 4 edn 1997), Frequency Selectivity in Hearing (ed, 1986), Auditory Frequency Selectivity (ed with R D Patterson, 1986), Hearing (ed, 1995), Perceptual Consequences of Cochlear Damage (1995); also author of numerous book chapters, papers and articles in learned jls; *Style*— Prof Brian Moore; ✉ Department of Experimental Psychology, University of Cambridge, Downing Street, Cambridge CB2 3EB (☎ 01223 333574, fax 01223 333564, e-mail BCJM@CUS.CAM.AC.UK)

MOORE, Brian Christopher; *b* 11 Jan 1962; *Educ* Univ of Nottingham (LLB); *Career* rugby union hooker; clubs: Old Crossleylans RUFC, Nottingham RFC (capt), Harlequins FC 1990–95, ret; came out of retirement and joined Richmond FC 1996; England: B rep (capt) 1985, full debut v Scotland 1987, memb World Cup squad 1987 (3 appearances), tour Aust and Fiji 1988 (3 test appearances), tour Romania 1989, tour Argentina 1990, memb Grand Slam winning team 1991 and 1992, memb runners-up team World Cup 1991, 4th place World Cup S Africa 1995, 64 caps, ret from int rugby 1995 (following World Cup); memb Br Lions tour Aust 1989 (3 test appearances) and NZ 1993 (2 test appearances), tour to S Africa 1994 (2 test appearances); Whitbread/Rugby World Player of the Year 1990; commercial insur litigation ptnr Edward Lewis Slrs, wine columnist Today, dir Playervision Ltd (England players' co); pres READY charity; memb: Law Soc, Securities Assoc; *Recreations* opera, ballet; *Style*— Brian Moore, Esq; ✉ Edward Lewis Solicitors, Verulam Gardens, 70 Gray's Inn Road, London WC1X 8NF (☎ 0171 404 5566, fax 0171 404 2244)

MOORE, Charles Hilary; s of Richard Gillachrist Moore, of Brussels, and Ann Hilary, *née* Miles; *b* 31 Oct 1956; *Educ* Eton, Trinity Coll Cambridge (BA); *m* 1981, Caroline Mary (fell Peterhouse Cambridge), da of Ralph Lambert Baxter, of Brasted Chart, Kent; 1 s (William b 1 April 1990), 1 da (Katharine, twin); *Career* editorial staff Daily Telegraph 1979, ldr writer Daily Telegraph 1981–83, asst ed and political columnist The Spectator 1983–84, ed The Spectator 1984–90, weekly columnist The Daily Express 1987–90, fortnightly column Another Voice The Spectator 1990–95, dep ed The Daily Telegraph 1990–92, ed The Sunday Telegraph 1992–95, ed The Daily Telegraph 1995–; memb Cncl The Anglo-Hong Kong Tst, tstee T E Utley Meml Fund; *Publications* 1936 (ed with C Hawtree, 1986), The Church in Crisis (with A N Wilson & Gavin Stamp, 1986), A Tory Seer - The Selected Journalism of T E Utley (ed with Simon Heffer, 1989); *Clubs* Beefsteak; *Style*— Charles Moore, Esq; ✉ The Daily Telegraph, 1 Canada Square, Canary Wharf, London E14 5DT

MOORE, Christopher M; o s of Sir Harry Moore, CBE, *qv*; *b* 1 Dec 1944; *Educ* Winchester, Pembroke Coll Cambridge (MA); *m* 2 Sept 1972, Charlotte C, da of J Glessing, of Montague, Hankham, E Sussex; 3 s (Tercel R, Wilaf M, Frederic C); *Career* investment banking/businessman; dir: Jardine Fleming and Co Ltd 1973–76, Robert Fleming and Co Ltd 1977–95, Robert Fleming Holdings Ltd 1988–95, Stop Loss Mutual Insurance Association Ltd 1992–; chm: Fleming Ventures Ltd 1992–, Moore Corporation 1995–, Calderburn PLC 1996–; sr advsr to Chm of Lloyd's 1996–; FCA; *Recreations* country sports, flying, tennis, music, books; *Clubs* White's, Pratt's, Leander; *Style*— Christopher Moore, Esq; ✉ Thornborough Grounds, Buckingham MK18 2NB (☎ 01280 812170); 28 Dover Street, London W1X 4AE (☎ 0171 491 0491, fax 0171 493 6763)

MOORE, David John; s of Rev Stanley Moore (d 1977), and Gladys Alice Jane, *née* Cory (d 1992); *b* 8 June 1943; *Educ* Ipswich Sch Suffolk; *Career* Barton Mayhew & Co London 1962–69, Barton Mayhew/Peat Marwick Mitchell Barcelona Spain 1969–72; Grant Thornton (formerly Thornton Baker)1972–95: ptnr London Office 1977–86, managing ptnr E Anglia 1986–95; memb Cncl and chm Iberian Ctee London C of C 1985–88, memb E Region Cncl and chm Suffolk County Ctee CBI 1988–91, govr Ipswich Sch 1989–, pres Old Ipswichian Club 1994; FCA (ACA 1968); *Recreations* cricket, travel, golf; *Clubs* MCC, Lord's Taverners, Hintlesham Hall Golf; *Style*— David Moore, Esq; ✉ 24 Maitland Court, Lancaster Terrace, London W2 3PA (☎ 0171 262 1189)

MOORE, Prof David Moresby; s of Moresby George Moore (d 1979), of Barnard Castle, Co Durham, and Elizabeth, *née* Grange (d 1994); *b* 26 July 1933; *Educ* Barnard Castle Sch, Univ Coll Durham (BSc, PhD, DSc); *m* 26 July 1957, Ida Elizabeth, da of Herbert Shaw (d 1956), of Carlisle, Cumberland; 2 s (Wayne Peter b July 1961, Lloyd Randal b Sept 1969); *Career* res offr CSIRO Canberra Aust 1957–59, res botanist Univ of California at Los Angeles 1959–61, lectr in botany Univ of Leicester 1961–68, prof of botany Univ of Reading 1976–94 (reader in plant taxonomy 1968–76, prof emeritus 1994–); pres Systematics Assoc 1979–82, sec gen Flora Europaea 1985–89, ed Flora de Chile 1987–; memb: Soc Botany Argentina, Botanical Soc of Br; chm Ed Ctee Lichen Flora of GB and I; FLS; Claudio Gay medal Univ Concepción Chile 1987; *Books* Flora Europea (1963–93), Vascular Flora of Falkland Islands (1968), Plant Cytogenetics (1977), Green Planet (1982), Flora of Tierra del Fuego (1983), Flora Europea Checklist and Chromosome Index (1983), Current Concepts in Plant Taxonomy (1984), La Transecta Botánica de Patagonia Austral (1984), Flora of the British Isles (3 edn 1987, revised 1990), Garden Earth (1991); *Recreations* walking, reading; *Style*— Prof David Moore; ✉ 26 Eric Avenue, Emmer Green, Reading, Berks RG4 8QX (☎ 0118 947 2132); Department of Botany, Plant Science Laboratories, University of Reading, Whiteknights, PO Box 221, Reading RG6 2AS (☎ 0118 931 8165, fax 0118 975 3676, telex 847813 RULIB G)

MOORE, Debbie; *children* 1 da (Lara b 1973); *Career* former fashion model; fndr chm md and fashion designer Pineapple Dance Studios (which joined unlisted securities market 1982) 1979, 1 Pineapple centre opened in Covent Garden, London, licensing of Pineapple name on range of footwear and hosiery; various Pineapple Fashion Stores plus nationwide concessions; Business Woman of the Year 1984; *Books* Pineapple Dance Book (1983, paperback 1985), When A Woman Means Business (1989); *Style*— Ms Debbie Moore; ✉ Debbie Moore Enterprises Ltd, 6a Langley Street, London WC2H 9JA (☎ 0171 379 8090, fax 0171 836 0803)

MOORE, Prof Derek William; s of William McPherson Moore (d 1979), and Elsie Marjorie, *née* Patterson (d 1969); *b* 19 April 1931; *Educ* S Shields Boy's HS, Univ of Cambridge (MA, PhD); *Career* lectr in maths Univ of Bristol 1960, sr fell Nat Acad of Sciences 1964; Imperial Coll: sr lectr 1967, reader in theoretical fluid mechanics 1968, prof of applied mathematics Imperial Coll 1973–96, sr research fell 1996–; Sherman Fairchild Distinguished Scholar Calif Inst of Technol 1986–87; hon memb American Acad of Arts and Sciences 1985; FRS 1990; *Recreations* jazz saxophone; *Style*— Prof Derek Moore; ✉ Dept of Maths, Imperial College, Prince Consort Road, London SW7 (☎ 0171 594 8501)

MOORE, Dudley Stuart John; s of John Moore (d 1971), of Dagenham, Essex, and Ada Frances, *née* Hughes (d 1981); *b* 19 April 1935; *Educ* Co HS Dagenham, Guildhall

Sch of Music, Magdalen Coll Oxford (BA, BMus); *m* 1, 1966 (m dis 1971), Suzy Kendall; m 2, 1975 (m dis 1977), Tuesday Weld; 1 s (Patrick b 1976); m 3, 1988 (m dis 1992), Brogan Lane; m 4, 1994, Nicole Rothschild; *Career* actor and musician; *Television* debut 1959; appearances incl: Beyond the Fringe, Sunday Night at the London Palladium, Love Story, Royal Command Performance, Wayne and Shuster, Eamonn Andrews Show, Music International, Late Night Line Up, Not Only But Also (3 series), Billy Cotton Band Show, Juke Box Jury, Now, Ready Steady Go, The Whole Scene Going, Prince of Wales Show, Top of the Pops, Bruce Forsyth Show, Dusty Springfield Show, Cilla Black, Dudley, Orchestra! (TV with Sir Georg Solti), Concerto! (TV with Michael Tilson Thomas), Parallel Lives (Showtime Cable Channel) 1994, Daddy's Girls (CBS) 1994; *Films* incl: The Wrong Box, 30 is a Dangerous Age Cynthia, Alice in Wonderland, Those Daring Young Men in Their Jaunty Jalopies, Bedazzled, The Bed Sitting Room, Hound of the Baskervilles, Foul Play, 10, Wholly Moses, Arthur (Oscar nomination 1983, Golden Globe Award 1983), Six Weeks, Romantic Comedy, Lovesick, Unfaithfully Yours, Best Defense, Micki and Maude (Golden Globe Award 1985), Santa Claus - the Movie, Like Father Like Son, Arthur II - On the Rocks, Crazy People, Blame It On The Bellboy; *Awards* winner of 2 Tony and 1 Grammy Awards; *Albums* Beyond The Fringe and All That Jazz, The Other Side of Dudley Moore, Derek and Clive - Live, Derek and Clive - Ad Nauseam, and Derek and Clive-Come Again, 30 Is a Dangerous Age Cynthia, Bedazzled, Dudley Moore Trio - Down Under, Dudley Moore and Cleo Laine - Smilin' Through, The Music of Dudley Moore - Double Album, Songs Without Words (released in USA); *Clubs* St James's, Annabel's, Harry's Bar, Tramp; *Style*— Dudley Moore, Esq; ✉ 73 Market St, Venice, California 90291 USA (fax 001 310 450 4988)

MOORE, Fionna Patricia; da of Maj Samuel James Moore, and Margaret Patricia Moore, *née* Boyd; *b* 18 May 1950; *Educ* Croydon HS for Girls (GPDST), UCL (BSc), UCH Med Sch (MB BS); *m* 12 April 1980, Richard Philip Ward; 2 s (Jonathan b 1982, Patrick b 1988), 2 da (Victoria b 1975, Jennifer b 1985); *Career* registrar in gen surgery St James and St George's Hosps 1980–81, Bayer res fell UCH 1981–83 (registrar in surgery 1978–80), sr registrar in accident and emergency med Ealing Central Middx and Hammersmith Hosps 1983–85; conslt in accident and emergency med: UCH and Middx Hosp 1985–, John Radcliffe Coll Oxford; memb RSM, FRCS, FRCSE; *Recreations* reading, music, walking; *Style*— Miss Fionna Moore; ✉ Accident and Emergency Dept, John Radcliffe Hospitals Trust, Headley Way, Headington, Oxford OX3 9DU (☎ 01865 741166)

MOORE, Sir Henry Roderick (Harry); kt (1978), CBE (1971); er s of Roderick Edward Moore (d 1946); *b* 19 Aug 1915; *Educ* Malvern, Pembroke Coll Cambridge; *m* 1944, Beatrice Margaret, da of Maj J W Seigne (d 1955); 1 s (Christopher M Moore, *qv*), 1 da; *Career* Lt to Lt-Col 1939–46, served N Africa, Italy and N Europe; chartered accountant 1939, dir Hill Samuel Gp 1949–79; chm: Associated Engineering 1955–75, Staveley Industries 1970–79, Molins plc 1978–85; chm: Bd of Govrs The London Hosp 1960–74, NE Thames RHA 1974–84; High Sheriff Bucks 1966; *Recreations* shooting, racing; *Clubs* White's, Pratt's, Leander, Rand (Johannesburg); *Style*— Sir Harry Moore, CBE; ✉ 15 Chesterfield House, Chesterfield Gardens, London W1Y 5TD (☎ 0171 491 0666)

MOORE, Jane; da of Prof John Moore, of Oxford, and Patricia, *née* Richardson; *b* 17 May 1962; *Educ* Worcester Girls' GS, South Glamorgan Inst of Higher Educn Cardiff (Dip); *Career* journalist; trainee reporter Solihull W Midlands 1981–83, news reporter Birmingham Post and Mail 1983–86, freelance reporter The People 1986–, pop columnist The Sun 1986–87, freelance researcher Thames News 1987–88; Today: feature writer 1988, Royal corr 1989, dep news ed 1989, feature ed 1990; features ed Daily Mirror 1993–; *Recreations* canoeing, rock climbing, photography; *Style*— Miss Jane Moore; ✉ Daily Mirror, 1 Canada Square, Canary Wharf, London E14 (☎ 0171 293 3313, fax 0171 293 3834)

MOORE, Maj-Gen Sir (John) Jeremy; KCB (1982, CB 1982), OBE (Mil 1973), MC (1952, and Bar 1962); s of Lt-Col Charles Percival Moore, MC (d 1959), and (Alice Hylda) Mary, *née* Bibby (d 1994); *b* 5 July 1928; *Educ* Cheltenham; *m* 1966, Veryan Julia Margaret Acworth; 1 s (Andrew b 1971), 2 da (Helen b 1967, Sarah b 1969); *Career* joined RM 1947, CO 42 Commando RM 1972–73, Cmdt RM Sch of Music 1973–75, Royal Coll of Defence Studies 1976, Cdr 3 Commando Bde RM 1977–79, Maj-Gen Commando Forces RM 1979–82, Cdr Land Forces Falkland Islands during campaign of 1982, on staff CDS 1982, ret 1983; dir gen Food and Drink Fedn 1984–85, defence conslt 1985–; pres RM Assoc 1990–93, Hon Col Cmdt RM 1991–93, Hon Col Wilts ACF 1991–93; former memb Cncl Cheltenham Coll, former govr Knighton House Sch, tstee Suzy Lamplugh Tst 1989–; *Recreations* music, painting, sailing, hillwalking; *Style*— Maj-Gen Sir Jeremy Moore, KCB, OBE, MC

MOORE, John Edward; s of late Sqdn Ldr Joseph Enos Moore, of Marlow, Bucks, and Audrey Sheila, *née* Matthews; *b* 15 Nov 1947; *Educ* Royal GS High Wycombe, Univ of London (LLB); *m* 12 April 1971, Diana, da of John Horend Dixon, MBE, of Ealing; 3 s (James b 1974, Alexander b 1976, Thomas b 1988); *Career* civilian gliding instr RAF(VR)T 1967–77; admitted slr 1973; Macfarlanes: joined 1979, head property dept 1986–94, currently ptnr in charge healthcare; lectr and author of articles on agric law, public and private sector ptnrships, commercial property and VAT; memb: Party Sub-Ctee Agric Law Assoc, Agric Law Assoc, City of London Slrs Co, Law Soc; *Recreations* flying; *Style*— John Moore, Esq; ✉ Messrs Macfarlanes, 10 Norwich St, London EC4A 1BD (☎ 0171 831 9222, fax 0171 831 9607, telex 296381)

MOORE, Capt John Evelyn; s of Maj William John Moore (d 1958), of Melbourn, Cambridge, and Evelyn Elizabeth, *née* Hooper (d 1935); *b* 1 Nov 1921; *Educ* Sherborne, RN Staff Coll; *m* 8 Jan 1945 (m dis 1967), Joan, da of Capt Frank Pardoe (d 1962), of S Africa; 1 s (Peter b 8 Jan 1958), 2 da (Lavinia b 19 Jan 1947, Fay b 4 Sept 1950); m 2, Barbara, *née* Kerry; *Career* special entry cadet RN 1939; served (1939–49) HM Ships Rodney, Impulsive, Nigeria and Challenger and HM Subs Truant, Rover, Trident, Vigorous and Tradewind; in cmd HM Sub Totem 1949–50, RN Staff Coll 1950–51, Staff 2 S/M Sqdn 1951–52, serv HM Ships Dainty and Diamond 1952–54; in cmd: HM Sub Alaric 1954–55, HM Subs Tactician and Telemachus 1955–57; Cdr NATO SO Plans NE Med 1957, Admty (Plans Div) 1960–63, Cdr Sub HMS Dolphin 1963–65, in cmd 7 Sub Sqdn Singapore 1965–67, Capt COS Naval Home Cmd 1967–69, Def Intelligence Staff i/c Soviet Naval Intelligence 1969–72, ret 1972; ed Jane's Fighting Ships 1972–87; prof of international relations: Univ of Aberdeen 1987–90, Univ of St Andrews 1990–92; FRGS 1942; *Books* Seapower and Politics, The Soviet Navy Today, Submarine Development, Warships of Royal Navy, Warships of Soviet Navy, Submarine Warfare Today and Tomorrow (jtly); *Recreations* gardening, swimming, archaeology; *Style*— Capt John Moore, RN; ✉ Elmhurst, Rickney, Hailsham, E Sussex BN27 1SF (☎ 01323 765862/763294)

MOORE, Sir John Michael; KCVO (1983), CB (1974), DSC (1944); s of Algernon William Moore (d 1970), and Amy Elizabeth, *née* Jeffreys (d 1940); *b* 2 April 1921; *Educ* Whitgift Middle Sch Croydon, Selwyn Coll Cambridge; *m* 1, 1947 (m dis 1963), Kathleen, da of Capt C C Pawley (d 1982); 1 s, 1 da; m 2, 1963 (m dis 1985), Margaret, da of J Ward (d 1935); m 3, 1986, Jacqueline Cingel, MBE; *Career* Lt RNVR 1940–46, with Miny of Transport and DOE 1946–72, dep sec (personnel mgmnt) CSD 1972–78, second Crown Estate cmmr 1978–83, chm Lymington Harbour Cmmn 1993– (dep chm 1990–93); Humane Soc Bronze medal 1942; *Recreations* sailing, mountain walking; *Clubs* Royal Lymington Yacht; *Style*— Sir John Moore, KCVO, CB, DSC; ✉ 38 Daniells Walk, Lymington, Hampshire SO41 3PN (☎ 01590 679963)

MOORE, Dr John Michael; JP (S Worcester, 1986); s of Roy Moore, CBE (d 1992), and Muriel Edith, *née* Shill (d 1959); *b* 12 Dec 1935; *Educ* Rugby, Clare Coll Cambridge (MA, PhD); *m* 9 July 1960, Jill Mary (d 1995), da of Alan Lawson Maycock (d 1967); 1 s (Nicholas b 1962); *Career* asst master: Winchester Coll 1960–64, Radley Coll 1964–83, headmaster The King's Sch Worcester 1983–; chm Choir Schools Assoc 1991–93; fell Center for Hellenic Studies Washington DC 1970–71, hon fell Inst for Advanced Res in Humanities Univ of Birmingham 1986–95; *Books* The Manuscript Tradition of Polybius (1965), Res Gestae Divi Augusti (jt ed with P A Brunt, 1967, 2 edn 1973), Variorum (jt ed with J J Evans, 1969), Timecharts (1969), Aristotle and Xenophon on Democracy and Oligarchy (1975, 2 edn 1983), various articles; *Recreations* painting, travel, gardening; *Style*— Dr John Moore, JP; ✉ The King's School, Worcester WR1 2LH (☎ 01905 23016, fax 01905 25511)

MOORE, Dr Kevin Charles; s of Dr Donald Charles Moore (d 1989), and Nellie Partington (d 1985); *b* 25 Jan 1941; *Educ* Giggleswick Sch, Univ of Manchester Med Sch (MB ChB); *m* 23 Feb 1972, Jillian Margaret, da of Frank Bromley (d 1984); 1 da (Alison b 1972); *Career* conslt anaesthetist Oldham 1973–, chm Med Staff Ctee Oldham 1981–85, chm Rochdale Private Surgical Unit 1983–88, treas Br Med Laser Assoc 1987–, treas World Assoc of Laser Therapy 1994–, vice pres Int Laser Therapy Assoc 1988–94, dir Highfield Private Hosp Rochdale 1988–91; memb Oldham Health Authy 1987–90; chm: Governing Cncl Dr Kershaw's Hospice Oldham 1992– (memb 1982–92, med dir 1994–), Med Advsy Ctee BMI Highfield Hosp 1991–, Highfield M R Scanning plc 1992–; FFARCS 1972; *Recreations* horse riding, carriage driving; *Style*— Dr Kevin Moore; ✉ Hutch Royd Farm, Parrock Nook, Rishworth, Sowerby Bridge, W Yorks HX6 4RF (☎ 01422 823498); Department of Anaesthesia, The Royal Oldham Hospital, Rochdale Rd, Oldham, Lancs OL1 2JH (☎ 0161 627 8828, fax 01422 824556)

MOORE, Michael; s of Gerald Edward Moore (d 1975), of Rangoon, Burma, and Shwe Mu Tha Soe; *Educ* Methodist Eng HS Rangoon, Hackney Downs Sch London, Univ of Leicester (BSc), Univ of Aberdeen (MLitt), Nat Coll for Hypnosis & Psychotherapy, UK Training Centre for Neuro-Linguistic Programming; *Career* pilot RAFVR; memb Contact Counselling Servs: Univ of Aberdeen 1978–79, Univ of Keele 1979–81; res and admin asst Cmmn for Int Justice and Peace 1981–82; psychologist and specialist in human performance ('Helping People Achieve') and conflict resolution 1982–; assoc Powerfax Learning Systems Ltd; memb: Br Psychological Soc 1987, Assoc of Neuro-Linguistic Programming 1987; *Recreations* philosophy, comparative religion, languages, TA, flying; *Style*— Michael Moore, Esq; ✉ 130 Harley St, London W1N 1AH (☎ 0171 935 6558)

MOORE, Vice Adm Sir Michael Anthony Claes; KBE (1997), LVO (1982); s of Lt A D W Moore, RN (d 1942), and Ebba Agneta, *née* Wachtmeister; *b* 6 Jan 1942; *Educ* Wellington Coll, RNC Dartmouth; *m* Penelope Moore, JP, *née* Lawson; 1 s, 3 da; *Career* Royal Navy: Midshipman 1960–75, Cdr 1975–80, Capt 1980–90, Rear Adm 1990–94, Vice Adm 1994–; CO: HMS Beachampton, HMS Tartar, HMS Andromeda and 8 Frigate Sqdn; COS COMNAVSOUTH Naples; memb Royal Swedish Military Sciences, yr bro Trinity House, MInstD; *Style*— Vice Adm Sir Michael Moore, KBE, LVO; ✉ c/o Naval Secretary, HM Naval Base, Portsmouth, Hants

MOORE, Michael Rodney Newton; CBE (1996); *b* 15 March 1936; *Educ* Magdalen Coll Oxford, Harvard Business Sch (MBA); *Career* called to the Bar 1961; chm: Linx Printing Technologies plc 1993– (dir 1992–), Quicks Group plc 1993– (dir 1992–), London International Group plc 1994– (dir 1994–); jt dep chm Clerical Medical and General Life Assurance Society 1996– (dir 1993–); dir: Which? Ltd 1993–, Finsbury Smaller Companies Tst 1996–, Brixton Estate 1996–; tstee Public Concern at Work 1996–; *Style*— Michael Moore, Esq, CBE; ✉ London International Group plc, 35 New Bridge Street, London EC4V 6BJ (☎ 0171 489 1977)

MOORE, Mike; s of Jack Francis Moore, BEM, of Epsom, Surrey, and Joan Florence, *née* Walker; *b* 6 Jan 1954; *Educ* Bideford Sch of Art and Design, Reading Sch of Art and Design; *m* Helen; 1 s (Harry b 13 July 1990), 1 da (Sophie b 28 June 1992); *Career* photographer: Thomson Regnl Newspapers 1976–79, London Evening Standard 1980–85, The Today Newspaper 1986–93, Daily Mirror 1993–; *Awards* Midland Bank Press Awards commendation 1977 and 1978, World Press Photo Fndn Gold medal 1978, Br Press Awards commendations 1981 and 1991, Ilford Press Awards commendation 1984 and 1991, Royal Photographer of the Year 1987, Press Photographer of the Year 1987, Kodak Press Awards commendation (two) 1991, Nikon Press Awards commendation 1991, News Photographer of the Year 1991, Gulf War medal 1991; *Books* Desert War (1991); *Style*— Mike Moore, Esq; ✉ Daily Mirror Picture Desk, 1 Canada Square Canary Wharf, London E14 5AP (☎ 0171 293 3851, mobile 0831 385778)

MOORE, Nigel Sandford Johnson; s of Raymond Johnson Moore (d 1977), and Lucy Mary, *née* Kirby; *b* 12 April 1944; *Educ* Radley; *m* 16 Aug 1969, Elizabeth Ann, da of Joseph Henry Bowker (d 1986); 1 s (Peter b 9 Jan 1983), 2 da (Louise b 20 Feb 1974, Rachel b 1 March 1977); *Career* Buckley Hall Devin & Co 1962–68; Ernst and Young 1968–: Sydney Aust 1969–71, ptnr UK 1973–, human resources ptnr 1973–81, Mktg Dept 1983–86, managing ptnr London Office 1986–88, dir of client servs Europe 1988–90, regnl managing ptnr Eastern Europe 1990–96, dir Int Lending Orgns 1994–96, dir Energy Servs Gp 1996–; FCA 1977; *Recreations* theatre, golf, tennis; *Clubs* City of London, IOD, The Pilgrims, Wildernesse; *Style*— Nigel Moore, Esq; ✉ Vinesgate, Chart Lane, Brasted Chart, Westerham, Kent TN16 1LR (☎ 01959 564510); Ernst and Young, Becket House, 1 Lambeth Palace Rd, London SE1 7EU (☎ 0171 931 3444, fax 0171 931 4541, telex 885234)

MOORE, (Sir) Dr Norman Winfrid; 3 Bt (UK 1919), of Hancox, Whatlington, Sussex (has established his claim but does not use title); s of Sir Alan Hilary Moore, 2 Bt, MB (d 1959); *b* 24 Feb 1923; *Educ* Eton, Trinity Coll Cambridge (BA 1943); *m* 14 July 1950, Janet, PhD, o da of Paul Singer; 1 s (Peter Alan Cutlack b 1951), 2 da (Caroline Mary Phyllis (Mrs Richard A Cohen) b 1953, Helena Meriel (Mrs David Alexander) b 1957); *Heir* s, Peter Alan Cutlack Moore b 21 Sept 1951; *Career* Lt RA, served 1942–45 War; principal scientific offr Nature Conservancy Cncl 1958–65, sr principal scientific offr 1965–83, ret; visiting prof Wye Coll Univ of London 1979–83; *Books* Dragonflies (with Philip S Corbet and Cynthia Longfield, 1960), Hedges (with E Pollard and M D Hooper, 1974), The Bird of Time: The Science and Politics of Nature Conservation (1987); *Style*— Dr Norman Moore; ✉ The Farm House, 117 Boxworth End, Swavesey, Cambridge CB4 5RA

MOORE, Dr Patrick (CALDWELL-); CBE (1989, OBE 1968); s of Capt Charles Caldwell-Moore, MC (d 1947), and Gertrude Lilian, *née* White (d 1981); *b* 4 March 1923; *Educ* privately; *Career* served WWII RAF 1940–45, Flt Lt, navigator with Bomber Cmd; dir Armagh Planetarium 1965–68; author, broadcaster, astronomer; vice pres Br Astronomical Assoc (pres 1982–84); Hon DSc: Univ of Lancaster 1979, Hatfield Poly 1989, Univ of Birmingham 1990, Univ of Keele 1994, Univ of Leicester 1996; FRAS 1945, FRSA 1949; hon memb various foreign scientific socs; *Books* over 150 books, mainly astronomical; *Recreations* cricket, chess, tennis, music (xylophone player); *Clubs* Athenaeum, Sussex CCC, Lord's Taverners; *Style*— Dr Patrick Moore, CBE; ✉ Farthings, West St, Selsey, West Sussex PO20 9AD (☎ 01243 603668)

MOORE, Peter David; s of Frederick Cecil Moore, and Joan Lambert *née* Wickham; *b* 5 June 1945; *Educ* King George V GS Southport Lancs; *m* 28 April 1973, Susan Janet, da of Duncan Ferguson Ure; 1 s (Stephen David b 5 May 1978), 1 da (Philippa Jane b 1 Jan 1976); *Career* Arthur Andersen 1969–71, Sterling Treasury Dealer Bankers Trust

Co 1971–72; fin dir Trio Holdings plc (holding co of Martin Bierbaum Group plc) 1979– (co sec 1972–79); FCA 1969; *Recreations* sporting; *Clubs* Richmond RFC, Dorking RFC; *Style—* Peter Moore, Esq; ✉ c/o Martin Bierbaum Group plc, 4 Deans Court, London EC4V 5AA

MOORE, Prof Peter Gerald; TD (1963); s of Leonard Jiggens Moore, of Wimbledon, and Ruby Silvester, *née* Wilburn (d 1978); *b* 5 April 1928; *Educ* King's Coll Sch Wimbledon, UCL (BSc, PhD), Princeton USA; *m* 27 Sept 1958, Sonja Enevoldson, da of William Ivor Thomas, of Cooden (d 1973); 2 s (Richard b 1963, Charles b 1967), 1 da (Penelope (Mrs Lawrenson) b 1960); *Career* 2 Lt 3 Regt RHA 1949–51, 2 Lt (later Lt then Capt) 290 Field Regt (City of London) RA TA 1951–61, Capt (later Maj) 254 Field Regt RA TA 1961–65; lectr UCL 1951–56, asst econ advsr NCB 1956–59, head statistical servs Reed Paper Group 1959–65; London Business Sch: prof of statistics 1965–, dep princ 1972–84, princ 1984–89, hon fell 1993; pt/t ptnr Duncan C Fraser 1974–77; pt/t dir: Copeman Paterson Ltd 1984–89, Elf Petroleum UK plc 1989–94; memb: Drs and Dentists Renumeration Body 1971–89, Ctee on 1971 Census Security 1971–73, UGC 1978–84 (vice chm 1980–83); conslt: Wilson Ctee on Financial Institutions 1977–80, Pugh-Roberts Associates Cambridge Mass 1989–95; memb Cncl: Univ of Sci and Technol Hong Kong 1986–92, UCL 1989–; fell UCL 1988, Gresham prof of rhetoric Gresham Coll 1992–; Liveryman Worshipful Co of Tallow Chandlers (memb Ct 1987–, Master 1994–95, Dep Master 1996); Hon DSc Heriot Watt Univ 1985; FRSS (Guy medallist 1970, Chambers medallist 1995, pres 1989–91), FIA 1956 (pres 1984–86), CIMgt 1985; *Books* include: Anatomy of Decisions (1976), Reason By Numbers (1980), The Business of Risk (1983), Basic Operational Research (1986); *Recreations* golf, walking, travelling; *Clubs* Athenaeum, Knole Park Golf; *Style—* Prof Peter Moore, TD; ✉ 3 Chartway, The Vine, Sevenoaks, Kent TN13 3RU (☎ 01732 451 936); London Business School, Sussex Place, Regent's Park, London NW1 4SA (☎ 0171 262 5050, fax 0171 724 7875)

MOORE, Philip John; s of Cecil Moore, of Stamford Bridge, York, and Marjorie, *née* Brewer; *b* 30 Sept 1943; *Educ* Maidstone GS, RCM; *m* 1, 9 Nov 1968 (m dis 1979); 1 s (Thomas), 2 da (Sophia, Bianca); *Career* asst music master Eton 1965–68, asst organist Canterbury Cathedral 1968–74, organist and master of the choristers Guildford Cathedral 1974–82, organist and master of the music York Minster 1983–; memb: RCM Union 1962, Composers' Guild of GB 1987, Performing Rights Soc 1988; Hon BMus Dunelm; FRCO 1962, GRSM, ARCM; *Recreations* collecting Imari and old fountain pens, flying kites, motor cars; *Style—* Philip Moore, Esq; ✉ 1 Minster Court, York YO1 2JJ (☎ 01904 642526, fax 01904 654604)

MOORE, Richard Hobart John deCourcy; s of Hobart Harold deCourcy Moore (d 1981), and Elizabeth Helen, *née* Tod; *b* 31 Aug 1949; *Educ* Stowe Sch; *m* 30 April 1977, Lucy Annabelle, da of Victor Sefton-Smith, and Barbette, *née* Salt (now Lady Millais); 1 s (Francis Richard Hobart deCourcy b 25 June 1985), 1 da (Natasha Elizabeth Victoria b 1 Nov 1993); *Career* Moore Stephens: articled clerk 1968–72, CA 1972, ptnr 1975–, sr ptnr 1989–; Freeman City of London 1974, Liveryman Worshipful Co of Vintners, Liveryman Worshipful Co of Shipwrights (memb Ct of Assts); FCA 1979 (ACA 1972); *Recreations* real tennis, cricket; *Clubs* MCC, Boodle's; *Style—* Richard Moore, Esq; ✉ 11 Chelsea Park Gardens, London SW3 6AF (☎ 0171 352 7594); Moore Stephens, St Paul's House, Warwick Lane, London EC4P 4BN (☎ 0171 248 4499)

MOORE, Prof Robert Samuel; s of Douglas Kenneth Moore, of Rhos-on-Sea, and Kathleen Phyllis Moore; *b* 3 June 1936; *Educ* Beckenham and Penge County GS, RNC Dartmouth, Univ of Hull (BA), Univ of Durham (PhD); *m* 16 Aug 1969, Lindy Ruth, da of late Sir Alan Parker, of Shenstone, Sutton-cum-Beckingham; 1 s (David Kenneth b 1974), 1 da (Heloise Kathryn b 1976); *Career* RN 1952–61; sociology lectr Univ of Durham 1965–69, sr lectr in sociology Univ of Aberdeen 1970–75, reader in sociology 1975–77, prof of sociology 1977–89, Eleanor Rathbone prof of sociology Univ of Liverpool 1989–; vice pres Aberdeen City Anti Apartheid, chm Grampian Community Relations Cncl until 1989; memb: Assoc Univ Teachers, Lab Party, CND, Scientists Against Nuclear Arms, Br Sociological Assoc 1964–, Br Assoc 1965–; FRSA; *Books* Race, Community and Conflict (with John Rex, 1967), Pitmen, Preachers and Politics (1970), Slamming the Door (with Tina Wallace, 1975), Racism and Black Resistance in Britain (1975), The Social Impact of Oil (1982), Women in the North Sea Oil Industry (with Peter Wybrow, 1985), Ethnic Statistics and the 1991 Census (1995); *Recreations* gardening, photography; *Style—* Prof Robert Moore; ✉ The University of Liverpool, PO Box 147, Liverpool L69 3BX (☎ 0151 794 2985, fax 0151 794 2997, telex 627095 UNILPL G, e-mail rsmoore@liverpool.ac.uk)

MOORE, Roger; *b* 14 Oct 1927; *Educ* Battersea GS, RADA; *m* 1 (m dis 1953), Doorn van Steyn; m 2, 1953 (m dis 1969), Dorothy Squires; m 3, Luisa Mattioli; 2 s, 1 da; *Career* actor; chm Stars Organisation for Spastics 1973–76, UNICEF special ambass 1991–; *Television* Ivanhoe 1958, The Alaskans 1959, Maverick 1960, The Saint 1962–68, The Persuaders 1972–73, The Muppet Show 1980, The Wedding of Prince Andrew and Sarah Ferguson (ABC-TV) 1986, Happy Anniversary 007 (ABC-TV) 1987, The Dame Edna Experience Christmas Show (LWT) 1987, James Bond - 30th Anniversary (LWT) 1992, The Man Who Wouldn't Die (Universal) 1992; *Film* extra in Caesar and Cleopatra 1945, Trottie True 1949, The Last Time I Saw Paris 1954, Interrupted Melody 1955, The King's Thief 1955, Diane 1956, The Miracle 1959, Gold of the Seven Saints 1961, Rachel Cade 1961, Rape of the Sabines 1961, No Man's Land 1961, Crossplot 1969, The Man Who Haunted Himself 1970, Gold 1974, That Lucky Touch (Who Needs Friends?) 1975, Shout at the Devil 1975, Street People (Sicilian Cross) 1975, Sherlock Holmes in New York 1976, Wild Geese 1977, Escape to Athena 1978, North Sea Hi-jack 1979, The Sea Wolves 1979/80, Sunday Lovers 1980, The Cannonball Run 1980, Curse of the Pink Panther 1982, The Naked Face 1983, Bed & Breakfast 1989, Bullseye 1989, Fire, Ice and Dynamite 1990, The Quest 1995; as Cdr James Bond: Live and Let Die 1973, The Man with the Golden Gun 1974, The Spy Who Loved Me 1976, Moonraker 1978, For Your Eyes Only 1980/81, Octopussy 1982, A View to a Kill 1984; *Awards* nominated: Golden Globe World Film Favourite Award (USA) 1980, Man of the Year Award (Friars Club of NY) 1986, Bambi Lifetime Achievement Award (Germany) 1990; *Publications* James Bond Diary (1973); *Style—* Roger Moore, Esq; ✉ c/o Denis Selinger, ICM Ltd, Oxford House, 76 Oxford Street, London W1N 0AX (☎ 0171 636 6565, fax 0171 323 0101)

MOORE, Stephen; s of Stanley Moore (d 1992), of Highgate, London, and Mary Elisabeth, *née* Bruce-Anderson (d 1978); *b* 11 Dec 1937; *Educ* Archbishop Tenison's GS London, Central Sch of Speech and Drama (winner The Lawrence Olivier Award); *m* 1, Barbara Mognaz; 3 c (Robyn, Guy, Hedda); m 2, Celestine Randall; 1 c (Charlotte); m 3, Beth morris; m 4, Noelyn George; 1 c (Sophie Martha George-Moore); *Career* actor; prof stage debut 1959 as 1st Immigration Officer in A View from the Bridge (Theatre Royal Windsor), London stage debut 1959 as William in As You Like It (Old Vic Theatre Co); many radio plays, dramas and short stories incl The Hitch Hikers Guide to the Galaxy; *Theatre* numerous appearances; Old Vic Theatre Co 1959–61 incl: A Midsummer Night's Dream, Dr Faustus, Twelfth Night, The White Devil, Saint Joan, Romeo and Juliet, Mourning Becomes Electra; Theatre Royal Windsor 1959–1968 incl: Pride and Prejudice, Present Laughter, An Ideal Husband, The Importance of Being Ernest; Mermaid Theatre 1962–67 incl: The Plough and the Stars, The Good Soldier Schweyk, The Trojan Wars; Royal Court 1963–72 incl: Julius Caeser, Ojections to Sex and Violence, Treats; Colchester Rep Co 1967–68 incl: A Day In The Life of Joe Egg, Spring and Port Wine (also dir), Forget-Me-Not Lane; Bristol Old Vic 1969–71 incl: Major Barbara, Macbeth, A Streetcar Named Desire, Woyzeck, The Iceman Cometh, Who's Afraid of Virginia Woolf; RSC 1973–86 incl: Section Nine, Peter Pan, Henry VIII, Twelfth Night, All's Well That Ends Well, Poppy, Mother Courage, A Penny for a Song; RNT 1977–1990 incl: Bedroom Farce, State of Revolution, Plenty, The Romans in Britain, The Life of Galileo, Love for Love, The Threepenny Opera, Dalliance, The Shaughraun, Peer Gynt, Piano; West End appearances incl: Hughie and Others (Duchess) 1963, It's a Two Foot Six Inches Above The Ground World (Wyndam's) 1970, Treats (Mayfair) 1976, New Found Land (Arts Theatre) 1977, Bedroom Farce (Prince of Wales, also Broadway) 1978, The Hardshoulder (Aldwych) 1983, Paris Match (Garrick) 1989, Reflected Glory (Vaudeville) 1992; *Television* debut in 1962 as Georges in Dinner With the Family (BBC); since then over 200 appearance incl: Three Men in a Boat, Brideshead Revisited, The Secret Diary - The Growing Pains of Adrian Mole, Rock Follies, Middlemarch, Solo, Just Between Ourselves, Small World, Soldiers Talking Cleanly, Love on A Gunboat, Just William, The Last Place on Earth, Love on a Branchline, The Beat Goes On, The Queen's Nose, The Missing Postman; guest appearances with Fry & Laurie, Dawn French, Emma Thompson, Rowan Atkinson, Lenny Henry, Alexei Sayle and Harry Enfield; *Films* roles incl: Young Man in The White Bus, Major Steele in A Bridge Too Far, Michael in White Bird, Guy in Diversion, Howard in Pilkington's Pluck, Mr Jolly in Clockwise, Roscoe in Under Suspicion, MacKenzie in Brassed Off; *Awards* winner of SWET Award for Best Actor in a Revival for A Doll's House (RSC prodn) 1982; 1983 SWET Award nominations incl: Best Actor in a Musical, Best Supporting Actor, Best Actor in a Revival; Tony Award nomination for Broadway prodn of All's Well That Ends Well 1983; *Recreations* supporter Chelsea FC, motor cycling, music, computing; *Style—* Stephen Moore, Esq; ✉ c/o Markham & Froggatt Ltd, Julian House, 4 Windmill Street, London W1P 1HF (☎ 0171 636 4412, fax 0171 637 5233)

MOORE, Stuart Alfred; s of Alfred Moore (d 1995), and Kathleen, *née* Dodd (d 1986); *b* 9 Oct 1939; *Educ* Stockport Sch, Univ of Manchester (BA, MA(Econ), Cobden Prize); *m* 1966, Diana Mary, da of Laurence Thomas Michael Connery, of Ashton-under-Lyne; 2 s (Christopher John b 1967, Michael Stuart b 1970), 1 da (Lucy Jane b 1968); *Career* Univ of Manchester: computer offr 1960–64, res associate 1964–66, lectr 1966–74, dir Res Support Unit Faculty of Econ and Social Studies 1970–80, sr lectr 1974–92, dean Faculty of Econ and Social Studies 1980–83, pro vice-chllr 1985–90, dep vice chllr 1990– (actg vice-chllr 1990–92), Robert Ottley prof of quantitative studies 1992–; chm Central Manchester Healthcare NHS Tst 1991–; memb: Royal Statistical Soc, Royal Economic Soc, Econometric Soc, American Statistical Assoc; author of various academic pubns; *Recreations* music, gardening, photography, travel, detective stories; *Style—* Prof S A Moore; ✉ Vice Chancellor's Office, The University, Manchester M13 9PL (☎ 0161 275 7400, fax 0161 272 6313); Central Manchester Healthcare NHS Trust, Cobbett House, Manchester Royal Infirmary, Oxford Road, Manchester M13 9WL (☎ 0161 276 4181, fax 0161 273 6211)

MOORE, Terence (Terry); CBE (1993); s of Arthur Doncaster Moore, and Dorothy Irene Gladys, *née* Godwin; *b* 24 Dec 1931; *Educ* Strand Sch Univ of London (BScEcon), Harvard Business Sch; *m* 17 Sept 1955, Tessa Catherine, da of Ernest Walter Wynne; 2 s (Simon Jeremy b 1961, Adam Gavin b 1965), 1 da (Anna Louise b 1968); *Career* Nat Serv Army; mktg, fin and economics appts Shell International 1948–64, economist Locana Corp 1964–65; Conoco Ltd: economist, mangr econ planning, gen mangr and dir 1965–74, dep md Mktg Ops 1974–79, md Supply and Trading 1979–86, gp md/chief exec offr 1986–95, conslt 1995–; pres Oil Industs Club 1989–90; govr Greenwich Theatre 1992–; ACII, AICS, FRSA, FInstPet 1996 (hon sec 1995); *Recreations* jogging, badminton, reading, music; *Style—* Terry Moore, Esq, CBE; ✉ 5 Gun Wharf, 130 Wapping High St, London E1 9NH (☎ and fax 0171 481 0853); Conoco, Park House, 116 Park Street, London W1Y 4NN (☎ 0171 408 6434, fax 0171 408 6989)

MOORE, Sir William Roger Clotworthy; 3 Bt (UK 1932), of Moore Lodge, Co Antrim; TD (1963), DL (Co Antrim 1990); s of Sir William Samson Moore, DL, JP, 2 Bt (d 1978), and Ethel Coburn Gordon (d 1973); *b* 17 May 1927; *Educ* Marlborough, RMC Sandhurst; *m* May 1954, Gillian, da of John Brown, of Co Antrim; 1 s (Richard William b 1955), 1 da (Belinda Jane (Mrs Timothy B Duncan) b 1956); *Heir* s, Richard William Moore b 8 May 1955; *Career* Lt Royal Inniskilling Fusiliers 1945, Maj North Irish Horse 1958; Grand Juror Co Antrim 1952–68, High Sheriff Co Antrim 1964; prison visitor 1965–71, chm Bd of Visitors HM Prison Castledillon Co Armagh 1971–72, memb Parole Bd for Scotland 1981–83 BBC broadcaster 1964–66; *Recreations* shooting, country pursuits, travel; *Clubs* Army and Navy; *Style—* Sir William Moore, Bt, TD, DL; ✉ Moore Lodge, Ballymoney, Co Antrim, NI

MOORE-BICK, Hon Mr Justice; Hon Sir Martin James; kt (1995); s of John Ninian Moore-Bick, and Kathleen Margaret, *née* Beall; *b* 6 Dec 1946; *Educ* Skinners Sch Tunbridge Wells, Christ's Coll Cambridge (MA); *m* 3 Aug 1974, Tessa Penelope, da of George Michael Gee; 2 s (Christopher b 1980, Matthew b 1983), 2 da (Catherine b 1977, Elizabeth b 1977); *Career* called to the Bar Inner Temple 1969 (bencher 1992), recorder of the Crown Court 1990–95, judge of the High Court of Justice (Queen's Bench Div) 1995–; churchwarden St Peter's Stonegate; *Recreations* music, literature, gardening; *Style—* The Hon Mr Justice Moore-Bick; ✉ Royal Courts of Justice, Strand, London WC2A 2LL

MOORE-GILLON, Dr John Christopher; *b* 2 Jan 1953; *Educ* Tiffin Sch, St Catharine's Coll Cambridge (MA), St Thomas's Hosp Med Sch (MD), FRCP; *m* 1980, Victoria, *née* Kirby; 1 s (Edwin b 1984), 2 da (Olivia b 1986, Claudia b 1994); *Career* chm Br Lung Fndn 1994–, conslt physician Dept of Respiratory Med St Bartholomew's Hosp 1988–; hon sec Br Thoracic Soc 1992–94; Liveryman Worshipful Soc of Apothecaries; *Style—* Dr John Moore-Gillon; ✉ Department of Respiratory Medicine, St Bartholomew's Hospital, West Smithfield, London EC1A 7BE

MOORE OF LOWER MARSH, Baron (Life Peer UK 1992), of Lower Marsh in the London Borough of Lambeth; John Edward Michael Moore; PC (1986); s of Edward O Moore, of Brighton; *b* 26 Nov 1937; *Educ* Licensed Victuallers' Sch Slough, LSE (BSc); *m* 1962, Sheila Sarah, da of Richard Tillotson, of Illinois, USA; 2 s (Hon Martin b 1970, Hon Richard b 1972), 1 da (Hon Stephanie b 1968); *Career* Nat Serv Royal Sussex Regt Korea 1955–57; LSE: chm Cons Assoc 1958–59, pres Students' Union 1959–60, memb Ct of Govrs 1977–; worked in banking and stockbroking and took part in Democratic politics in Chicago 1961–65; MP (C) Croydon Central Feb 1974–92; vice chm Cons Pty 1975–79, Parly under sec Energy 1979–83, (min of state) econ sec Treasy June-Oct 1983, fin sec Treasy (responsibilities incl taxation and privatisation) 1983–86; sec of state for: Tport 1986–87, Health and Social Servs, Social Security 1987–July 1989; chm: Dean Witter International Ltd 1975–79 (dir 1968–79), Monitor Europe 1991–, Credit Suisse Asset Management Ltd UK 1992– (dir 1991–), Credit Suisse Investment Management Australia 1995– (dir 1995–), Credit Suisse Investment Management Ltd 1996– (dir 1996–), Credit Suisse Investment Management Group Ltd 1996– (dir 1995–); pres Energy Saving Trust Ltd 1995– (dir and chm 1992–95); dir: Gartmore Investment Management Group Ltd 1990–91, Monitor Company Inc USA 1991–, Swiss American Corporation 1992–96, GTECH Corporation 1992–, Blue Circle Industries plc 1993–, Camelot Holdings Ltd 1993–94, Camelot Group Plc 1994–, Rolls-Royce plc 1994– (dep chm 1996–), The Central European Growth Fund Plc 1995–, BEA Associates 1996–; memb: Advsy Bd Marvin & Palmer Associates Inc USA 1989– (dir 1994–), Supervisory Bd ITT Automotive Europe GmbH 1994–, Cncl IOD; *Recreations* sport; *Clubs* Carlton, RAC; *Style—* The Rt Hon Lord Moore of Lower Marsh,

PC; ✉ Credit Suisse Asset Management Ltd, Beaufort House, 15 St Botolph Street, London EC3A 7JJ (☎ 0171 426 2626, fax 0171 247 4509)

MOORE OF WOLVERCOTE, Baron (Life Peer UK 1986), of Wolvercote in the City of Oxford; Philip Brian Cecil Moore; GCB (1985, KCB 1980, CB 1973), GCVO (1983, KCVO 1976), CMG (1966), QSO (1986), PC (1977); s of Cecil Moore, ICS (d 1950), and Alice Mona, *née* Bath (d 1967); *b* 6 April 1921; *Educ* Dragon Sch Oxford, Cheltenham, BNC Oxford; *m* 28 Aug 1945, Joanna Ursula, da of Capt M E Greenop, DCLI (d 1972); 2 da (Hon Sally Jane (Hon Mrs Leachman) b 9 June 1949, Hon Jill Georgina (Hon Mrs Gabriel) b 2 Dec 1951); *Career* served WW II RAF Bomber Cmd, and POW; PPS to First Lord of the Admty 1957–58 (asst private sec 1950–51), dep high cmmr Singapore 1963–65 (dep UK cmmr 1961–63), chief of PR MOD 1965–66, private sec to HM The Queen and keeper of the Queen's Archives 1977–86 (dep private sec 1972–77, asst private sec 1966–72); chm Tstees King George VI and Queen Elizabeth Fndn of St Catharines, vice-pres Soc for Promoting Christian Knowledge; hon fell Brasenose Coll Oxford 1981; *Recreations* golf, shooting, fishing; *Clubs* Athenaeum, MCC; *Style*— The Rt Hon Lord Moore of Wolvercote, PC, GCB, GCVO, CMG, QSO; ✉ Apartment 64, Hampton Court Palace, Surrey KT8 9AU (☎ 0181 943 4695)

MOORE-SMITH, Dr Bryan; s of Dr Cyril Moore-Smith (d 1937), and Kathleen Frances, *née* O'Donoghue (d 1982); *b* 6 Nov 1930; *Educ* Ampleforth, Oriel Coll Oxford (MA, BM BCh), St Thomas's Hosp; *m* 26 May 1962, Elizabeth Jean, da of Leonard George Dale (d 1964); 1 s (James Patrick b 1965), 1 da (Caroline Frances b 1963); *Career* conslt in geriatric med 1968–95, ret, clinical dir Directorate of Health Care of Elderly Ipswich Hosp 1990–95; memb Cncl and treas Br Geriatric Soc 1969–75, memb and sec Geriatrics Ctee RCP 1971–90, dir Ipswich Abbeyfields Soc 1973–, dir Orwell Abbeyfields Soc 1990–, chm Ipswich Hosp Med Staff Ctee 1976–77, conslt memb Ipswich Dist Mgmnt Team 1977–79, secondments to Health Advsy Serv 1976–91, advsr Overseas Div Help the Aged 1983–; Dip in Geriatric Med RCP: fndr memb Examiners Bd 1983–, host examiner 1986–96, chm 1990–96; memb: Occupational Therapist Bd Cncl for Professions Supplementary to Med 1986–, Jt Validation Bd Coll of Occupational Therapy CPSM 1989–92 and 1995–, Shadow Art Therapists Bd 1994–, Professional and Linguistics Assessment Bd GMC 1996–; conslt memb E Suffolk Health Authy 1987–90; contrib to med pubns 1970–; chm Parents Ctee and Bd of Govrs Convent of Jesus and Mary Ipswich 1973–82, memb Geriatrics Soc 1965–; *Recreations* gardening, travel, music, art; *Style*— Dr Bryan Moore-Smith; ✉ Wolmers, Stonham Aspal, Stowmarket, Suffolk IP14 6AS (☎ 01449 711261)

MOOREHEAD, Caroline; *b* 28 Oct 1944; *Educ* French Lycées London and Rome, Sorbonne, Univ of London (BA); *m*; 2 c; *Career* child psychologist Rome 1967–68, reporter Time Magazine Rome 1968–69, feature writer Daily Telegraph Magazine 1969–70, features ed Times Educational Supplement 1970–73, specialist in human rights and feature writer The Times 1973–88, human rights corr and feature contrib The Independent 1988–93; contribs and reviews for TES, TLS, London Review of Books, Spectator, New Statesman, New Society, Listener, Literary Review, Sunday Telegraph, Harpers, Departures, Traveler (US); memb: Wolfenden Ctee on Voluntary Work 1977, London Library Ctee 1990–, Human Rights Mission Eminent Persons to Moscow 1990, Exec Ctee PEN 1993– (memb Writers in Prison Ctee 1989–), Cncl RSL, Ctee Redress Tst; cncl memb and tstee Index on Censorship 1990–, tstee Br Inst of Human Rights, conslt various refugee ctees, judge various literary and human rights prizes; memb Soc of Authors 1990, FRSL; *Television* script writer: Forty Minutes Troublesome People (also presenter, BBC) 1987, Prisoners of Conscience (also assoc prodr, two 10–part series BBC) 1988–91, Children and Human Rights (UN film), Human Rights, Human Wrongs (also assoc prodr, BBC series); *Books* trans of novel and 3 art books from French and Italian 1967–70, Fortune's Hostages (1980), Sidney Bernstein: A Biography (1983), Freya Stark: A Biography (1985), Troublesome People (1987), Beyond the Rim of the World: The Letters of Freya Stark (ed, 1988), Betrayed: Children in Today's World (1989), Bertrand Russell: A Life (1993), The Lost Treasures of Troy (1994), The International Committee of the Red Cross: Profile and History (1996); *Pamphlets* incl: Working Children (Anti-slavery Soc, 1987), Children of Namibia (Oxfam, 1988), A Guide to Human Rights (BBC, 1992); *Style*— Ms Caroline Moorehead, FRSL; ✉ 36 Fitzroy Road, London NW1 8TY; c/o Anthony Sheil, Sheil Land Associates, 43 Doughty Street, London WC1N 2LF

MOORES, Peter; CBE (1991), DL (Lancashire 1992); s of Sir John Moores, CBE (d 1993), and late Ruby, *née* Knowles; *b* 9 April 1932; *Educ* Eton, ChCh Oxford; *m* 1960 (m dis), Luciana (d 1994), da of Salvatore Pinto, of Naples; 1 s (Alexis), 1 da (Donatella); *Career* dir Singer and Friedlander 1972–92, chm The Littlewoods Organisation 1977–80 (dir 1965–93); tstee Tate Gallery 1978–85, govr BBC 1981–83; fndr patron Peter Moores Fndn 1964, fndr Compton Verney House Tst 1993; Hon MA ChCh Oxford, Gold Medal of the Italian Republic 1974; Hon RNCM 1985; *Recreations* opera, fishing, shooting; *Style*— Peter Moores, Esq, CBE, DL; ✉ Parbold Hall, Wigan, Lancashire WN8 1TG

MOORES, Yvonne; da of Tom Abraham Quick, of Netley, Hampshire, and Phyllis, *née* Jeremiah (d 1988); *b* 14 June 1941; *Educ* Itchen GS Southampton, Southampton Sch of Nursing; *m* 1, 1969 (m dis 1973), Bruce Holmes Ramsden; m 2, 8 Nov 1975, Brian Moores, s of Edward Moores (d 1949); *Career* princ nursing offr: North London HMC 1971–72, West Manchester HMC 1973–74; district nursing offr North District Manchester AHA 1974–76, area nursing offr Manchester AHA 1977–81; chief nursing offr: The Welsh Office 1982–88, The Scottish Office Home and Health Dept 1988–92, Dept of Health (and dir of Nursing NHS Exec) 1992–; memb: Dept of Health Policy Bd, NHS Exec, RCN, Cncl Univ of Southampton; Hon DSc Univ of Portsmouth, Hon DCL Northumbria Univ, Hon MA De Montfort Univ Leicester; hon fell Univ of Wales; Hon FFPHM, Hon FRCP; CIMgt; *Books* contrib author: NHS Management Perspectives for Doctors, International Administration of Nursing Services; *Recreations* golf; *Style*— Mrs Yvonne Moores; ✉ Simm Carr Farm, Simm Carr Lane, Shibden Dale, Halifax, W Yorks HX3 7UL (☎ 01422 321628); Department of Health, Richmond House, Whitehall, London (☎ 0171 210 5597)

MOORHEAD, Prof John; s of Patrick Moorhead (d 1960), and Mary, *née* Ashurst; *b* 1 Dec 1932; *Educ* St Edward's Coll Liverpool, Univ of Liverpool Med Sch (MB ChB, FRCP 1973), Georgetown Univ Hosp Washington DC; *m* 20 June 1967, Anna; 1 da (Alison b 25 Sept 1973); *Career* asst prof Georgetown Univ Hosp Washington DC 1964–67, conslt nephrologist Royal Free Hosp 1967–, sec gen Int Soc of Nephrology 1975–82, prof of renal med Royal Free Hosp Sch of Med and UCL 1993–, med dir Royal Free Hosp 1993–; princ tstee J F Moorhead Research Trust, special tstee Royal Free Hosp, tstee Peter Samuel Research Tst; FRCP; *Publications* author of 1 book and over 300 papers on subjects incl: progressive kidney disease, especially as influence by lipids and lipoproteins, molecular cell biology of progressive renal disease, organisational evolution; *Recreations* music, piano; *Style*— Prof John Moorhead; ✉ The Royal Free Hospital, Department of Nephrology and Transplantation, Pond Street, London NW3 2QG (☎ 0171 830 2930, fax 0171 830 2125)

MOORHOUSE, Adrian David; MBE (1987); s of Clifford Moorhouse, of Bingley, W Yorks, and Kathleen, *née* Thompson; *b* 24 May 1964; *Educ* Bradford GS; *Career* breaststroke swimmer; Olympic Games 1988 Gold 100m (fourth place 1984, eigth place 1992); Cwlth Games: 1982 Gold 100m (Silver 4x100m medley relay, Bronze 200m), 1986 Gold 200m (Silver 100m, Silver 4x100m medley relay), 1990 Gold 100m (Silver 4x100m medley relay); Euro Championships: 1983 Gold 200m (Silver 100m), 1985 Gold 100m, 1987 Gold 100m (Bronze 200m, Silver 4x100m medley relay), 1989 Gold 100m, 1991 Silver 100m; Silver 100m World Championships 1991; former holder: world record 100m breaststroke short course, world record 100m breaststroke long course (until 1991), Euro and Cwlth record 100m breaststroke long course; youth devpt offr Amateur Swimming Assoc 1993–95; competitors' rep Nat Olympic Ctee 1994–; vice patron Nat Playing Fields Assoc, patron SPARKS charity, vice patron Br Sports Assoc for the Disabled; dir: Manchester 2002 Ltd, Manchester Commonwealth Games Ltd, Lane 4 Ltd; memb Nat Lottery Sports Panel 1994–; Hon MA Univ of Bradford; *Recreations* music, films, literature; *Style*— Adrian Moorhouse, Esq, MBE; ✉ St Heliers, Cottingley Bar, Bingley, West Yorkshire (☎ 01274 562624)

MOORHOUSE, Geoffrey; s of William Heald (d 1971), and Gladys, *née* Hoyle; stepson of Richard Moorhouse; *b* 29 Nov 1931; *Educ* Bury GS; *m* 1, May 1956 (m dis 1974), Janet Marion, da of Alec Murray (d 1978), of Christchurch, NZ; 2 s (Andrew b 1961, Michael b 1966), 2 da (Jane b 1960, Brigid b 1965, d 1981); m 2, Sept 1974 (m dis 1978), Barbara Jane, *née* Woodward; m 3, June 1983, Marilyn Isobel, *née* Edwards; *Career* coder RN 1950–52; journalist 1952–70 (chief features writer Manchester Guardian 1963–70), author; FRGS 1972–95, FRSL 1982; *Books* The Other England (1964), Against All Reason (1969), Calcutta (1971), The Missionaries (1973), The Fearful Void (1974), The Diplomats (1977), The Boat and The Town (1979), The Best-Loved Game (1979, Cricket Soc award), India Britannica (1983), Lord's (1983), To the Frontier (1984, Thomas Cook award), Imperial City (1988), At the George (1989), Apples in the Snow (1990), Hell's Foundations - A Town, its Myths and Gallipoli (1992), OM: an Indian Pilgrimage (1993), A People's Game: the Centenary History of Rugby League 1895–1995 (1995), Sun Dancing: a Medieval Vision (1997); *Recreations* listening to music, gardening, hill walking, looking at buildings, watching cricket and both forms of rugby; *Clubs* Lancashire CC; *Style*— Geoffrey Moorhouse, FRSL; ✉ Park House, Gayle, nr Hawes, N Yorks DL8 3RT (☎ 01969 667456)

MOORHOUSE, (Cecil) James Olaf; MEP (EPP) London S and Surrey E (majority 8,739); s of late Capt Sidney James Moorhouse; *b* 1 Jan 1924; *Educ* St Paul's, King's Coll London (BSci Eng), Imperial Coll London (DIC); *m* 1958 (m dis 1995), Elizabeth, da of late Dr Charles Huxtable, MC; 1 s (Olaf), 1 da (Phoebe); *Career* MEP: London S (EDG 1979–84), London S and Surrey E (EDG 1984–92, EPP 1992–); project engr BOAC 1948–53, tech advsr Shell International Petroleum Co and Shell Operating Cos 1953–72; environmental conservation advsr Shell UK Ltd 1972–73; gp environmental affairs advsr RTZ 1973–80 (conslt 1981–84); EDG tport spokesman 1979–84, vice chm and EPP dep coordinator on Euro Parl's External Econ Rels 1989–94; vice chm delgn Euro Parl's EFTA Parliamentarians 1984–86 (EDG Tport spokesman 1979–84 and 1987–89), chm delgn to Northern Europe 1979–84, human rights co-ordinator EPP 1994–, co-pres Inter-Parly Gp on Tibet; Parly rapporteur 1984–94 on: trade and econ rels between Euro Community and Japan, trade and econ rels between the EC and the countries of the Pacific Basin, econ significance of Antarctica; currently Parly rapporteur on trade and econ rels between EU and: Japan, Pakistan, Gulf States, Australia; *Clubs* RAC, Carlton, Surrey CCC; *Style*— James Moorhouse, Esq, MEP; ✉ 1 Dean Farrar Street, Westminster, London SW1H 0DY (☎ 0171 416 01093/94, fax 0171 416 0095)

MOORHOUSE, Peter William; s of Francis Moorhouse, and Dorothy Moorhouse; *b* 25 Dec 1938; *Educ* Stonyhurst Coll; *m* Jane, *née* Catton; 2 s, 1 da; *Career* divnl dir Schweppes Group 1980–87 (joined 1961); chm Police Complaints Authority 1996– (appointed 1988, dep chm 1991–96); memb Local Review Ctee Parole Bd 1973–88 (chm 1977–79 and 1986–88); *Recreations* art, opera, inland boating, walking; *Style*— Peter W Moorhouse, Esq; ✉ Police Complaints Authority, 10 Great George Street, London SW1P 3AE (☎ 0171 273 6450)

MOORIN, Eur Ing Raymond Leslie; s of Joseph Wilson Moorin (d 1957), and Edith, *née* Waterston (d 1985); *b* 1 March 1939; *Educ* Emanuel Sch, Wandsworth Tech Coll, Borough Poly; *m* 14 Aug 1965, (Victoria) Wendy, da of Edwin McCleod Miller, of Merseyside; 3 s (Robert b 1966, Patrick b 1969, Matthew b 1971); *Career* bldg servs engr Slough Borough Cncl 1964–70, mechanical and electrical engr Dept of Educn & Sci 1970–72, assoc HL Dawson and Assocs 1972–73, sr ptnr Multi Building Services Design Partnership 1973–; CEng, MInstE 1968, MIMechE 1969, MInstR 1972, FCIBSE 1975, MConsE 1976, FRSA 1988; *Recreations* golf, squash, tennis; *Clubs* Burnham Beeches GC; *Style*— Eur Ing Raymond Moorin; ✉ Lyndale, 21 Coates Lane, High Wycombe, Bucks HP13 5EY (☎ 01494 533147); 3 Easton Street, High Wycombe, Bucks HP11 1NJ (☎ 01494 474712, fax 01494 474738)

MOORSOM, Patrick William Pierre; s of Frederick William Moorsom (d 1971), of Dinas Powys, Glamorgan, and Jeanne Juliette, *née* Phelippon; *b* 30 Oct 1942; *Educ* Downside, Jesus Coll Cambridge (BA, Squash blue); *m* 14 Sept 1965, Dominique Ann, da of Andre Leroy; 1 s (Pierre Frederick Andre), 3 da (Natasha Juliet, Sophie Ann, Stephanie Helene); *Career* CA Arthur Andersen & Co 1965–69; dir: Rothschild Intercontinental Bank 1969–78, Barclays Merchant Bank 1978–81; md Cayzer Ltd 1981–87, vice chm Guinness Mahon & Co Ltd 1987–91, sr mangr Midland Private Banking 1991–94, md Brown, Shipley & Co Ltd 1996–; chm Regent Inns plc 1989–95; FCA 1971; *Style*— Patrick Moorsom, Esq; ✉ 9 Holland Park Court, Holland Park Gardens, London W14 8DN (☎ 0171 602 9437)

MOOS, Khursheed Francis; OBE (1995); s of Jehangir Dhanjishah Moos (d 1973), and Maria Gerritje, *née* Tulp; *b* 1 Nov 1934; *Educ* Dulwich, Univ of London (BDS, MB BS), Guy's Hosp, Westminster Hosp; *m* 23 June 1962, Katharine, da of George Stewart Addison (d 1952); 2 s (Christopher b 1964, John b 1968), 1 da (Hilary b 1966); *Career* Nat Serv RADC 1959–61, Lt 1959, Capt 1960; registrar in oral surgery Mount Vernon Hosp Middx 1966–67, sr registrar in oral surgery Univ of Wales Cardiff Dental Sch 1967–69; conslt oral surgn: South Warwicks, Coventry, E Birmingham Hosps 1969–74; conslt oral and maxillofacial surgn Plastic and Maxillofacial Unit Canniesburn Hosp Glasgow 1974–, civilian conslt oral surgn to RN 1976–, hon prof of oral and maxillofacial surgery Univ of Glasgow 1992–; visiting prof Univ of Otago NZ 1988; fellowship examiner: RCSEd, RCPSGlas, RCSI; pres: BAOMS 1991–92, Craniofacial Soc of GB 1994–95; dean Dental Faculty RCPSGlas 1992–95; chm: Special Advsy Ctee in Oral Surgery and Oral Med 1985–89, Intercollegiate Speciality Advsy Bd in Oral and Maxillofacial Surgery 1995–; memb: BAOMS 1964, BDA 1958, BMA 1964, RSM 1965, Euro Assoc Cranio Maxillofacial Surgery, Int Assoc Oral Maxillofacial Surgery; *Books* Surgery of the Mouth and Jaws (contrib, 1985), Companion to Dental Studies (contrib, 1986), Plastic Surgery in Infancy and Childhood (contrib, 1988); *Recreations* music, natural history, philately, eastern philosophy, gardening; *Style*— Khursheed F Moos, Esq, OBE; ✉ Dept of Oral and Maxillofacial Surgery, Regional Plastic and Maxillofacial Unit, Canniesburn Hospital, Bearsden, Glasgow G61 1QL (☎ 0141 211 5757, fax 0141 211 5652)

MORAHAN, Christopher Thomas; s of Thomas Hugo Morahan (d 1969), and Nancy Charlotte, *née* Baker (d 1977); *b* 9 July 1929; *Educ* Highgate, Old Vic Theatre Sch; *m* 1, 1954, Joan, *née* Murray (d 1973); 2 s (Ben, Andrew), 1 da (Lucy d 1990); m 2, 1974, Anna (actress as Anna Carteret), da of late Col Peter Wilkinson, of Pulborough, W Sussex; 2 da (Rebecca, Harriet); *Career* television, theatre and film director; Nat Serv RA 1947–49, 2 Lt; dir Greenpoint films, head of plays BBC TV 1972–76; assoc Nat Theatre 1977–88; *Theatre* prodns incl: Little Murders (RSC), This Story of Yours, Flint, State of Revolution (NT), Man and Superman (NT), Wild Honey (NT), Melon, Major Barbara, The Devil's Disciple (RNT), The Handyman; *Television* prodns incl: Talking to a Stranger 1966, The Gorge 1967, The Jewel in the Crown 1984 (Int Emmy 1984), In the Secret State 1985, After Pilkington 1987 (Prix Italia 1987), Troubles 1988, The Heat of The Day 1989, Old Flames 1990, Can You Hear Me Thinking? 1990, The Common Pursuit 1991, Ashenden, Unnatural Pursuits 1992 (Int Emmy 1993), The Bullion Boys (Int Emmy 1994) 1993, Summerdays Dream 1994, It Might be You 1995, The Peacock Spring 1996, Element of Doubt 1997; *Films* incl: Clockwise 1986, Paper Mask 1990; *Awards* for theatre: Olivier, Plays and Players Drama, London Standard Awards (for Wild Honey); for TV: SFTA Best Play Dir 1969, BAFTA Best Series Dir 1985, Desmond Davis Award for Outstanding Creative Achievement in TV 1985, Broadcasting Press Guild Award 1984, Primetime Emmy Award 1985; *Recreations* photography, birdwatching,; *Clubs* Garrick; *Style*— Christopher Morahan, Esq; ✉ c/o Michael Whitehall Ltd, 125 Gloucester Road, London SW7 4TE (☎ 0171 244 8466, fax 0171 244 9060)

MORALES-LANDIVAR, HE Carlos E; s of Armando Morales-Gozmáu (d 1990), and Malena Landivar Navarrè (d 1994); *b* 30 Sept 1943, La Paz, Bolivia; *Educ* German Sch of La Paz, Univ of Buenos Aires (graduate in civil engrg), Harvard Univ (MPA); *m* Norga, *née* Pardo-Valle; 2 da (Adriana, Natalia), 1 s (Carlos E); *Career* Bolivian diplomat; min of Energy and Hydrocarbons (Paz Estenssoro admin) 1985–87, sec of Indust and Commerce (cabinet of Pres Gonzalo Sánchez de Lozada) 1993–95, ambass to the Ct of St James's (concurrently ambass to The Netherlands, Finland, Sweden and Norway) 1995–; former pres: Nat Exports Cncl (CONEX), Nat Inst for Exports Promotion (INPEX), Tech Assistance Serv for the Small Enterprise (SAT); former dir Andean Development Corp-CAF; former govt rep: Andean Pact Cmmn, 'Bolivia Exporta' fndn; variously dir, chief exec offr and pres several banking, mfrg and construction companies; pres/vice pres: Bolivian Chamber of Construction 1972–81, Bolivian Confedn of Private Enterprises 1972–91, Bolivian Roads Assoc 1980–93, American C of C of Bolivia 1992–93; memb: Interamerican Construction Fedn, Bolivian Soc of Engrs (former chm), Bolivian Cncl of Engrs, Argentinian Cncl of Engrs; former prof Bolivian Catholic Univ, assoc prof Bolivian Inst for Business Studies; active memb various social, cultural and professional assocs in Bolivia and Latin America; fndr Harvard Club in Bolivia 1993; *Recreations* tennis, golf, swimming; *Style*— HE Señor Carlos E Morales-Landivar; ✉ Embassy of Bolivia, 106 Eaton Square, London SW1W 9AD (☎ 0171 235 4248, fax 0171 235 1286)

MORAN, Andrew Gerard; QC (1994); s of Francis Michael Moran (d 1979), of Widnes, and Winifrede, *née* Plant (d 1971); *b* 19 Oct 1953; *Educ* West Park GS St Helens, BRNC Dartmouth, Balliol Coll Oxford (BA); *m* 17 Feb 1977, Carole Jane, da of James Sullivan; 5 s (Michael b 1978, James b 1980, Peter b 1984, Kevin b 1987, John b 1989), 1 da (Claire Louise b 1982); *Career* univ cadetship RN 1972; called to the Bar Gray's Inn 1976; memb Commercial Bar Assoc; *Recreations* travel, sport, walking; *Style*— Andrew Moran, Esq, QC; ✉ Byrom Chambers, 25 Byrom Street, Manchester M3 4PF (☎ 0161 834 5238, fax 0161 834 0394); Byrom Chambers, 61 Fleet Street, London EC4Y 1JU (☎ 0171 353 4363, fax 0171 583 1491)

MORAN, Dr John Denton; RD (1977); s of Paul Francis Moran (d 1989), of Marine Gate, Brighton, and Mary, *née* Denton; *b* 3 Nov 1940; *Educ* Downside, Univ of London, St George's Hosp London (MB BS), Guy's Hosp London (LDS, RCS, Cert FPA, Dip Psycho-Sexual Counselling); *m* 16 June 1973, Jane, da of Gen Sir Malcolm Cartwright-Taylor, KCB (d 1969); 1 s (Paul b 29 Jan 1976), 2 da (Iona b 16 Sept 1973, Louise b 18 March 1975); *Career* RNR: Surgn Sub Lt (dental) 1962, Surgn Lt (dental) 1964, Surgn Lt Cdr (dental) 1969, dental offr HMS Centaur RN 1965, med and dental offr White City and Jamaica Rd RMR, resigned 1979; dental house surgn Bart's 1964, med house surgn ENT Dept St George's Hosp Tooting 1970, med house physician Christchurch and Boscombe Hosps Bournemouth 1971, GP Brandon Manitoba Canada 1972, private dental practice Harley St 1973–; MO: Margaret Pyke Centre 1974, Marie Stopes 1978–, Menopause Clinic 1979–; Freeman City of London 1979, Liveryman Worshipful Co of Barber Surgns 1980; assoc memb Zoological Soc, memb BMA, FRSM; *Recreations* golf, shooting, skiing, walking, bridge; *Clubs* RAC, Royal Ashdown, Sloop; *Style*— Dr John Moran, RD; ✉ Belvedere Farm, Cinder Hill Lane, Horsted Keynes, W Sussex (☎ 01825 790246); 92 Harley St, London W12 (☎ 0171 935 2182)

MORAN, 2 Baron (UK 1943); (Richard) John McMoran Wilson; KCMG (1981, CMG 1970); s of 1 Baron, MC (d 1977), formerly Dr (then Sir) Charles McMoran Wilson, and Dorothy, *née* Dufton (d 1983); *b* 22 Sept 1924; *Educ* Eton, King's Coll Cambridge; *m* 29 Dec 1948, Shirley Rowntree, eldest da of late George James Harris, MC, of Bossall Hall, York; 2 s, 1 da; *Heir* s, Hon James Wilson; *Career* served WWII RNVR, HMS Belfast, motor torpedo boats and HM destroyer Oribi; entered Foreign Service 1945, served in Ankara, Tel-Aviv, Rio de Janeiro, Washington and S Africa, head of W African Dept Foreign Office 1968–73, concurrently non-resident ambass Chad 1970–73; ambass: Hungary 1973–76, Portugal 1976–81; high cmmr Canada 1981–84; sits as cross-bencher in House of Lords; chm All-Party Conservation Gp of both Houses of Parliament; Euro Communities Ctee House of Lords: memb Indust Sub-ctee 1984–86, memb Environment Sub-ctee 1986–91, memb Agric Sub-ctee 1991–95; other House of Lords ctees: memb Sub-ctee of the Sci and Technol Ctee on the Scientific Base of the Nature Conservancy Cncl 1990–, memb Sub-ctee of the Sci and Technol Ctee on Fish Stocks 1995–, Sub-ctee on the 1996 Inter-Governmental Conf 1995–; pres: Welsh Salmon and Trout Anglers Assoc 1988–95, Radnorshire Wildlife Tst 1994–; vice pres RSPB (memb Cncl 1989–94); chm: Wildlife and Countryside Link 1990–95, Regnl Fisheries Advsy Ctee, Welsh Region Nat Rivers Authy 1989–94; vice chm Atlantic Salmon Tst; Grand Cross Order of the Infante Portugal 1978; *Books* CB: A Life of Sir Henry Campbell-Bannerman (Whitbread award for biography 1973), Fairfax (1985); *Recreations* fishing, fly-tying, bird watching; *Clubs* Flyfishers' (pres 1987–88); *Style*— The Rt Hon Lord Moran, KCMG; ✉ c/o House of Lords, Westminster, London SW1

MORAN, Air Vice-Marshal Manus Francis; s of John Moran (d 1952), of Rathgar, Dublin, and Kathleen, *née* Coyle (d 1965); *b* 18 April 1927; *Educ* Mount St Joseph Abbey Roscrea Ireland, Univ Coll Dublin (MB BCh, BAO, MCh), DLO RCP and RCS; *m* 26 July 1954, Maureen Elizabeth Martin, da of Martin Dilks (d 1950), of Kirby Muxloe, Leicester; 2 s (John b 1956 d 1986, David b 1963), 3 da (Frances b 1955, Anne b 1958, Jane b 1960); *Career* joined RAF 1954, Air Vice-Marshal 1988, ret; house surgeon and house physician St Vincent's Hosp Dublin 1952, trainee in gen practice Lutterworth nr Rugby 1953, sr house offr Marston Green Hosp Birmingham and Hosp for Sick Children Park St Hull 1954; RAF: assigned to Central Med Estab London 1954, trainee in otorhinolaryngology (ORL) Wroughton 1955–57, offr-in-charge ORL Dept (Weeton 1957–59, Akrotiri Cyprus 1959–62, Halton 1964–66), conslt in ORL (Changi Singapore 1965–68, Nocton Hall 1968–76, Wegberg Germany 1976–78, Princess Alexandra Hosp Wroughton 1979–83), conslt advsr in ORL to RAF 1983–88 (memb RAF Ethical Sub-ctee), lectr in otolaryngology Inst of Aviation Med Farnborough 1983–88, dean of Air Force Med 1988, sr conslt to the RAF 1990–91; civilian ENT surgn Princess Alexandra's Hosp RAF Wroughton Swindon 1991–95, visiting conslt Leicester Nuffield Hosp 1993–, conslt to Metropolitan Police 1994–; QHP 1988–91; memb: Sections of Laryngology/Otology Royal Soc of Med (pres Section of Laryngology 1991–92), Cncl Br Assoc of Otorhinolaryngologists 1980–86, Environmental Noise Advsy Ctee 1980–86, ORL Advsy Ctee Wessex Region NHS 1986–91, Bd Co-operation North 1992–, Editorial Bd American ENT Jl 1994–; special tstee Royal Nat Throat, Nose and Ear Hosp London 1992–; memb Gen Ctee 6th Br Academic Conf in ORL 1980–83, hon sec Gen Ctee 7th Br Academic Conf in ORL 1984–87, chm Gen Ctee 8th Br Academic Conf 1989–91, memb Holding Ctee Br Academic Conf 1991–96; chm Marston Meysey Parish Room Ctee (Registered Charity) 1988–91; Freeman City of London, chm Livery Ctee Worshipful Soc of Apothecaries 1994–96; Medical Soc (UCD) Gold Medal 1951, RCS Lady Cade Medal for contrib to ORL 1980; CStJ 1990; fndr memb The Joseph Soc; memb: Irish Otological Soc, Portmann Fndn, American Acad of Facial, Plastic and Reconstructive Surgns; MRAeS 1984, FRACS 1996; hon fell Euro Acad of Facial Surgery, Hon FRCSI 1991; *Publications* Upper Respiratory Problems in the Yellow Nail Syndrome (jtly); contribs to jls on ORL; *Recreations* walking, poetry, theology; *Clubs* RAF; *Style*— Air Vice-Marshal Manus Moran, RAF (ret)

MORAN, Michael Edward (Mike); s of Edward Moran, of Barkingside, Ilford, Essex, and Iris Jean, *née* Munn; *b* 16 Feb 1960; *Educ* Buckhurst Hill Co HS, Ealing Coll of HE (BA Business Studies, Dip MRS); *m* 8 Dec 1984, Sonya Caroline; 1 s (Oliver Eduard b 1 Jan 1989), 2 da (Rebecca b 15 April 1991, Gabriella b 27 Sept 1992); *Career* Ford Motor Company Ltd 1982–96: sales and after sales experience Ford of Britain 1982–89, mangr of trg Ford of Europe Brussels 1989–90, fleet sales/mktg Ford of Britain 1990–93, dir of sales and mktg Ford of Spain Madrid 1994–96; mktg dir Toyota (GB) Ltd 1996–; memb MRS 1982; *Recreations* golf, skiing, motor sports; *Clubs* Reigate Hill Golf; *Style*— Mike Moran, Esq; ✉ Toyota (GB) Ltd, The Quadrangle, Station Road, Redhill, Surrey RH1 1PX (☎ 01737 785048, fax 01737 768237)

MORAY, 20 Earl of (S 1562); Douglas John Moray Stuart; also Lord Abernethy and Strathearn (S 1562), Lord Doune (S 1581), Lord St Colme (S 1611), and Baron Stuart of Castle Stuart (GB 1796); s of 19 Earl of Moray (d 1974; himself 11 in descent from 1 Earl, an illegitimate s of James V of Scotland, Regent of Scotland from 1567 until his murder in 1570 by Hamilton of Bothwellhaugh), and Mabel Helen Maud (May) (d 1968), only child of late Benjamin 'Matabele' Wilson, of Battlefields, S Rhodesia; *b* 13 Feb 1928; *Educ* Trinity Coll Cambridge (BA), Hilton Coll Natal; *m* 27 Jan 1964, Lady Malvina Dorothea Murray, er da of 7 Earl of Mansfield (d 1971); 1 s, 1 da (Lady Louisa); *Heir* s, John Douglas Stuart, Lord Doune b 29 Aug 1966; *Career* JP (Perthshire 1968–96); FRICS; *Clubs* New (Edinburgh); *Style*— The Rt Hon the Earl of Moray; ✉ Doune Park, Doune, Perthshire (☎ 01786 841333); Darnaway Castle, Forres, Moray (☎ 01309 672101)

MORAY, ROSS AND CAITHNESS, Bishop of 1994–; Rt Rev Gregor Macgregor; s of Gregor Macgregor (d 1952), of Glasgow, and Jean, *née* Baird (d 1973); *b* 17 Nov 1933; *Educ* Hutchesons' Boys' GS Glasgow, Univ of St Andrews (MA, BD); *m* 8 June 1956, Elizabeth Jean, da of Albert E Harris; 3 da (Elizabeth Ann Macgregor, *qv* b 26 April 1958, Lorna Margery b 3 Aug 1961, Mary Jean b 26 Oct 1966), 1 s (Andrew b 21 May 1964); *Career* Nat Serv Sub Lt (S) RN 1952–54; shipping mangr Morphy Richards (Astral) Ltd Dundee 1954–61, student Univ of St Andrews 1961–67, min Church of Scotland Stromness Orkney 1967–73, student Aberdeen Coll of Educn 1973–74, head of religious educn Glenrothes HS Fife 1974–81, rector St Luke's Glenrothes 1981–85, vice provost Cathedral of the Isles Cumbrae 1985, rector St James' Dollor 1986–90, mission priest St Luke's Western Hailes Edinburgh 1991–94; *Recreations* walking, Rugby Union, reading; *Style*— The Rt Rev the Bishop of Moray, Ross and Caithness; ✉ 34 Rangemore Road, Inverness IV3 5AE (☎ 01463 231059)

MORCOM, (John) Brian; s of Albert John Morcom (d 1975), of Carmarthen, and Alice Maud, *née* Jones (d 1981); *b* 31 May 1925; *Educ* Queen Elizabeth GS Carmarthen, Balliol Coll Oxford (state scholar, MA); *Children* by 2 marriages (twice widowed), 1 s (Huw Charles b 13 May 1960), 1 da (Sian Mary (Mrs Wilson) b 5 June 1968); *Career* called to the Bar Inner Temple 1951 (ad eundem Lincoln's Inn 1954), in practice Wales and Chester Circuit 1954–81, social security cmmr 1981–, child support cmmr 1993–; memb Bd Examiners' Council of Legal Education 1955–81; *Books* Estate Duty Savings (5 edns 1959–72), Capital Transfer Tax (1976, 2 edn 1978); *Recreations* Welsh genealogy, forestry; *Clubs* Royal Commonwealth Society, London Welsh Association; *Style*— Brian Morcom, Esq; ✉ Social Security Commission, Harp House, 83–86 Farringdon Street, London EC4A 4DH

MORCOM, Christopher; QC (1991); s of (Alfred) Rupert Morcom (d 1996), of Ombersley, Worcs, and Mary, *née* Carslake (d 1994); *b* 4 Feb 1939; *Educ* Sherborne (music exhibitioner), Trinity Coll Cambridge (exhibitioner, MA); *m* 3 Sept 1966, Diane, da of late Jose A Toledo; 1 s (Darrell Kenneth b 15 Feb 1969), 2 da (Charmian b 19 Jan 1968, Melanie Carmen b 3 March 1972); *Career* called to the Bar Middle Temple 1963 (Harmsworth entrance exhibitioner, Astbury scholar, bencher 1996), head of chambers; chm Competition Law Assoc 1985–, pres Ligue Internationale du Droit de la Concurrence (LIDC) 1996– (vice pres 1994–96); *Books* Service Marks - A Guide to the New Law (1987), A Guide to the Trade Marks Act 1994 (1994); *Recreations* music, walking; *Clubs* Athenaeum; *Style*— Christopher Morcom, Esq, QC; ✉ 1 Essex Court, Temple, London EC4Y 9AR (☎ 0171 936 3030, fax 0171 583 1606)

MORCOS, Dr Sameh Kamel; *b* 19 April 1949; *Educ* Maronite Sch Cairo Egypt, Univ of Cairo (MB BCh); *Career* radiologist; pre-regisration house jobs Cairo Univ Teaching Hosps 1971–72, resident in gen surgery and orthopaedics Benha Gen Hosp Egypt 1972–73; sr house offr: in orthopaedics and casualty Bedford Gen Hosp England 1973, in casualty Noble's Hosp IOM 1973–74, in orthopaedics Queen Mary's Hosp for Children Carshalton Surrey 1974–75, in orthopaedics Rowley Bristow Orthopaedic Hosp Pyrford Surrey and St Peter's Hosp Chertsey Surrey 1975–76, in surgical rotation Taunton and Somerset Hosps 1976–78; sr registrar in radiodiagnosis Sheffield Teaching Hosps 1981–83 (registrar 1978–81), conslt radiologist Northern Gen Hosp Sheffield UK 1983–; recipient: Graham-Hodgson scholarship RCR 1987, Flude Meml prize BIR 1993, Nuclear Electric Research travel bursary 1994; author of numerous articles in learned jls; ECF MG (USA) 1974, FRCS (Glasgow) 1978, DMRD (London) 1981, fell Faculty of Radiologists RCS (Dublin) 1982, FRCR (London) 1982, memb Chest Radiologists Assoc; memb: BRS, Int Congress of Bronchology, Euro Soc of Thoracic Imaging, BMA (chm Sheffield Div 1991–92); hon fell Overseas Doctors Assoc 1988 (memb Nat Exec Ctee 1982–93, chm Sheffield Dist Div of Radiology 1992–95); *Style*— Dr Sameh Morcos; ✉ Northern General Hospital, Herries Rd, Sheffield S5 7AU (☎ 0114 271 4339, fax 0114 261 1791)

MORDAUNT, Gerald Charles; s of Eustace John Mordaunt (d 1988), and Anne Francis, *née* Gilmour (d 1976); *b* 16 July 1939; *Educ* Wellington Coll; *m* Sept 1965 (m dis 1981), Carol, da of Brig R M Villiers, DSO (d 1973), of Scotland; 2 s (James b 1967, Christopher b 1969), 2 da (Tanya b 1974, Harriet b 1980); *Career* chm Credit Lyonnais Laing (formerly Laing and Cruickshank) 1987– (joined 1959); MSI; *Recreations* tennis, shooting, wine; *Style*— Gerald C Mordaunt, Esq; ✉ Hovells Farm, Coggeshall, Colchester, Essex (☎ 013765 61700); Credit Lyonnais Laing, Broadwalk House, 5 Appold Street, London EC2A 2DA (☎ 0171 588 4000, fax 0171 588 0290)

MORDAUNT, Sir Richard Nigel Charles; 14 Bt (E 1611), of Massingham Parva, Norfolk; s of Lt-Col Sir Nigel John Mordaunt, 13 Bt, MBE (d 1979); *b* 12 May 1940; *Educ* Wellington Coll; *m* 1964, Myriam Atchia; 1 s, 1 da (Michele b 1965); *Heir* s, Kim John Mordaunt b 1966; *Style*— Sir Richard Mordaunt, Bt; ✉ 1/11 Motherwell Street, South Yarra, Melbourne, Victoria 3141, Australia

MORDUE, Richard Eric; s of Ralph Yielder Mordue (d 1980), of Hexham, and Helen Mary, *née* Downie; *b* 14 June 1941; *Educ* Royal GS Newcastle upon Tyne, King's Coll Durham (BSc), Michigan State Univ (MS); *m* 30 June 1979, Christine, da of Dr Jack Phillips; 1 s (John b 13 May 1980), 1 da (Heather b 15 March 1982); *Career* dir of

Economics and Statistics MAFF 1989–96 (economist 1964–82, head of Horticulture Div 1982–88), ret; *Recreations* golf, bridge; *Clubs* Civil Service; *Style*— Richard Mordue, Esq

MORE-MOLYNEUX, Maj James Robert; OBE (1983), DL; s of Brig-Gen Francis More-Molyneux Longbourne, CMG, DSO, and Gwendoline, da of Adm Sir Robert More-Molyneux, GCB; *b* 17 June 1920; *Educ* Eton, Univ of Cambridge; *m* 1948, Susan, da of Capt Frederick Bellinger; 1 s (Michael George); *Career* WWII, Italy; landowner; fndr: Loseley Dairy Products Ltd, Guildway Ltd, Loseley Christian Tst; High Sheriff of Surrey 1974, Vice Lord-Lt Surrey 1982–96; Bledisloe Gold medal for Landowners 1984; *Books* The Loseley Challenge (1995); *Clubs* Farmers'; *Style*— Maj James More-Molyneux, OBE, DL; ✉ Loseley Park, Guildford, Surrey GU3 1HS (☎ 01483 66090); estate office (☎ 01483 304440, fax 01483 302036)

MORE NISBETT, Patrea Evelyn; da of David Agar MacDonald (d 1967), of Dorset, and Elisabeth May, *née* Ferguson; *b* 2 March 1944; *Educ* Cranborne Chase, Sorbonne, House of Citizenship Bucks; *m* 2 March 1968, George Alan More Nisbett, s of Surgn Cdr John Graham More Nisbett (d 1991), of Mid Lothian; 3 s (William David Hamilton b 1979, Alexander Talbot John b 1982, Charles Neilson George b 1984); *Career* Harpers and Queen Magazine, contrib Sloane Ranger Handbook; writer and broadcaster, The Good Schools Guide, Gap and Univeristy Guides, advsr to travel indust; *Style*— Mrs Patrea Evelyn More Nisbett; ✉ 43 Godfrey St, London SW3 3SX (☎ 0171 352 3259, fax 0171 351 1300, mobile 0385 396946); The Drum, Gilmerton, Edinburgh EH17 8RX (☎ 0131 664 7215, fax 0131 658 1944)

MOREAU, David Merlin; s of Capt Reginald Ernest Moreau (d 1970), of Sutton St Nicholas, Herefordshire, and Winifred Mary Moreau (d 1982); *b* 9 Oct 1927; *Educ* King's Sch Canterbury, Jesus Coll Cambridge (BA, MA); *m* 22 Dec 1956, Elizabeth Mary, da of John Walter Rees; 1 s (Alexander Piers Merlin b 5 Aug 1966), 1 da (Sally P J b 20 Nov 1964 d 1988); *Career* Nat Serv radar specialist and head Educn Centre RAF Gibraltar 1946–48; export mangr John Wyeth & Brothers 1952–56, Euro market controller Beecham Overseas 1956–64, fndr and md Syntex Pharmaceuticals Maidenhead 1965–70, chm Weddel Pharmaceuticals 1970–80, md Elga Products Ltd Lane End Bucks 1972–80, dir Dewplan Group 1980–84 (conslt 1984–), md Chiltern Water Treatment 1980–83, dir DNAX California 1980–83, dir International Family Health (charity) 1994–; author of numerous articles in pubns incl: Sunday Times, New Scientist, Financial Times, Chemical Engineer, Defence Journal, Guardian, Director, Chief Executive; own series BBC Radio 4 1984–; chm Local Cons Pty; former memb Cncl: Assoc of Br Pharmaceutical Indust, SIMA; memb Soc of Authors 1963; Freeman City of London 1989, Liveryman Guild of Air Pilots and Air Navigators 1989; FZS 1968, FRSM 1972, CIMgt 1979; *Books* The Simple Life (1963), That Built-In Urge (1965), Summers End (1966), Look Behind You (1973), More Wrestling than Dancing (1990); *Recreations* piloting own plane, radio broadcasting, languages, skiing, collecting Ferraris, guitar, photography; *Clubs* RSM; *Style*— David Moreau, Esq; ✉ Rowley Cottage, Langley Park, Bucks SL3 6DT (☎ 01753 663201, fax 01753 664218); c/o Dewplan Ltd, Beechwood Hall, Kingsmead Rd, High Wycombe, Bucks HP11 1LA (☎ 01494 557334, fax 01494 465489)

MORELAND, Robert John; s of Samuel John Moreland, MC, TD, of Gloucester, and Norah Molly, *née* Haines (d 1980); *b* 21 Aug 1941; *Educ* Glasgow Acad, Dean Close Sch Cheltenham, Univ of Nottingham (BA), Univ of Warwick; *Career* civil servant Canada 1966–72, mgmnt conslt Touche Ross & Co 1974–; MEP (EDG) Staffs 1979–84; Westminster City Cncl: cncllr Knightsbridge Ward 1990–, dep chief whip 1991–93, chief whip 1993–94, chm of the environment 1994–95, chm of planning and the environment 1995–; memb Econ and Social Ctee of Euro Community 1986– (chm Section on Regnl Policy and Town Planning 1990–); *Books* Transport for Europe (jtly 1983); *Recreations* swimming, skiing, golf, watching cricket; *Clubs* Carlton, RAC; *Style*— Robert Moreland, Esq; ✉ 3 The Firs, Heathville Rd, Gloucester GL1 3EW (☎ 01452 22612); 7 Vauxhall Walk, London SE11 5JT; Economic and Social Committee, rue Ravenstein 2, B-1000 Brussels, Belgium (☎ 00 322 519 9011, fax 00 322 513 4893); c/o Prima Europe, 14 Soho Square, London W1V 5FB (☎ 0171 287 6676, fax 0171 287 8139)

MORETON, Anthony John; s of William Herbert Moreton (d 1969), of Cardiff, and Margaret Clara, *née* Jenkins (d 1978); *b* 8 July 1930; *Educ* Penarth County Sch, Cardiff Tech Coll (BSc Econ), Ruskin Coll Oxford, Exeter Coll Oxford (MA); *m* 27 May 1967, Ena, da of Thomas Kendall (d 1955), of Merthyr Tydfil; *Career* Nat Serv cmmnd Flying Offr RAF 1954–56; ldr writer and sub ed Western Mail 1956–58, features sub ed News Chronicle 1958–60, Daily Telegraph 1960–63; Financial Times: joined 1963, regnl affrs ed 1977–87, Welsh corr 1987–92; cncllr: London Borough of Wandsworth 1962–65 (chm Libraries Ctee), London Borough of Lambeth 1965–68 (chm Fin and Gen Purposes Ctee); chm Bd Welsh Economic Review 1991–93, memb BBC Bdcasting Cncl for Wales 1993–; dir Merthyr Tydfil Heritage Tst 1994–; dep chm North Glamorgan NHS Trust 1996–; treas Holy Trinity Clapham 1962–74, chm Lambeth Arts and Recreations Assoc 1966–72, churchwarden St Gwynno's Vaynor Merthyr Tydfil 1985–89 and 1996–; Liveryman Worshipful Co of Glovers 1985, memb Welsh Livery Guild 1993; *Recreations* golf, gardening, walking; *Clubs* Cardiff and County, Aberdare Golf; *Style*— Anthony Moreton, Esq; ✉ Pandy Farm, Merthyr Tydfil, Glamorgan CF47 8PA (☎ 01685 723003, fax 01685 389885)

MORETON, Sir John Oscar; KCMG (1977, CMG 1966), KCVO (1976), MC (1944); s of Rev Charles Oscar Moreton, of Chipping Norton, Oxon; *b* 28 Dec 1917; *Educ* St Edward's Sch Oxford, Trinity Coll Oxford; *m* 1945, Margaret Katherine, da of Sir John Claud Fortescue Fryer, KBE, FRS (d 1948); 3 da; *Career* served WWII RA, Maj 1945; asst master Uppingham 1946–48; HM Dip Serv: joined Colonial Office 1948, Kenya 1953–55, private sec to Sec of State 1955–59, CRO 1960, Nigeria 1961–64, IDC 1965, asst under sec Cwlth Office 1965–68, asst under sec FCO 1968–69, ambass Vietnam 1969–71, high cmmr Malta 1972–74, dep perm rep (status of ambass) UK Mission to UN 1974–75, min Br Embassy Washington 1975–77; dir Wates Fndn 1978–87, chm Surrey Branch Oxford Soc 1979–88; Gentleman Usher of the Blue Rod Order of St Michael and St George 1979–92; *Clubs* Army and Navy; *Style*— Sir John Moreton, KCMG, KCVO, MC; ✉ Woodside House, Woodside Rd, Cobham, Surrey KT11 2QR

MORETON, (Cecil) Peter; s of Cecil Roland Moreton, of Wellingborough, Northants, and Jessie Maud Moreton, of Northants; *b* 25 July 1927; *Educ* Wellingborough Sch, Univ of London, Coll of Estate Mgmnt; *m* 6 April 1953, Eileen, da of Walter Harry Frost (d 1962), of Barton Seagrave, Kettering, Northants; 1 s (Nicolas b 1961), 1 da (Penny b 1958); *Career* articled clerk W & H Peacock Bedford 1944–52, asst H P Barnsley Hereford 1952–53, asst Stimpson Lock & Vince Watford 1953–59, regnl surveyor Northampton Town & Co Building Soc 1959–70, chief surveyor Anglia Building Soc 1977–87 (dep chief surveyor 1970–77), regular appearances on nat and local TV and radio as spokesman on housing and valuation matters, regular writer in UK and int magazines, ed Surveyors Insurance News Serv, exec ed The Surveyors Factbook, freelance weekly broadcaster for BBC 1982–, conslt surveyor to RICS Insurance Services Ltd London 1987–96, regular lectr on surveying matters, external examiner for the Coll of Estate Mgmnt 1993–96; dir: Northants Tenancies Ltd 1991–95, Nene Valley Tenancies Ltd 1991–95, Winsford Tenancies Ltd 1992–96; past pres Round Table Watford and Northampton (past chm and sec), past chm RICS branches Beds, Herts, Leics, Northants (sec), past pres Nene Valley Rotary Club (sec), dist govr Rotary Dist 1070 1991–92, chm RIBI PR Ctee 1992–94, past appeals organiser OPWA, past chm Happy Feet Appeal; past chm: ARC Ctee, Deaf Appeal, Northants 47 Surveyors, CBSI Branch, 41 Club; memb: Derngate Soc, The Charter Soc, RICS Energy Efficiency Ctee, Surveyors Panel to the BSA 1977–87; Paul Harris Fell Rotary Int 1985; govr Weston Favell Upper Sch 1992–; FRICS 1965, FCBSI 1985, FSVA 1988, FCIB 1993; *Recreations* sport, golf, cricket, gardening, music; *Clubs* Rotary; *Style*— Peter Moreton, Esq; ✉ 86 Church Way, Weston Favell, Northampton NN3 3BY (☎ 01604 406371)

MOREY, Anthony Bernard Nicholas (Tony); CBE (1993); s of Bernard Rowland Morey (d 1976), of Christchurch, Dorset, and Madeleine Mary Rose, *née* Dowling (d 1995); *b* 6 Dec 1936; *Educ* Wimbledon Coll; *m* 3 Feb 1961, Agni Campbell, da of late William Lavery Kerr, of Epsom, Surrey; 2 s (Paul David b 1965, John Michael Anthony b 1970), 1 da (Nicola Anne b 1962); *Career* HM Dip Serv 1957–96, ret; postings incl: Kuwait, Madras, Tehran, Kabul, Washington, Zagreb, Lagos; consul gen Moscow 1985–88, dep high cmmr Madras 1989–91, ambass Mongolia 1991–93, dep high cmmr Calcutta 1993–96; *Recreations* gardening, music, viticulture, golf, cats; *Clubs* Royal Cwlth, Oriental, Royal Calcutta Turf; *Style*— Tony Morey, Esq, CBE; ✉ Smugglers Cottage, Seaway Lane, Abbotsbury, Dorset

MORGAN, *see:* Hughes-Morgan

MORGAN, Alan William; s of Alfred Charles Morgan, ISO, of Stoke Bishop, Bristol, and Eliza Dora, *née* Sproul-Cran; *b* 4 Oct 1951; *Educ* Clifton, Trinity Coll Oxford (MA), Harvard Business Sch (MBA); *m* 17 Oct 1981, Janet Cullis, da of Rainier Campbell Connolly, FRCS, of London; 2 s (Campbell b 1983, Edward b 1986), 1 da (Georgina b 1988); *Career* called to the Bar Middle Temple 1974, Brandts 1974–76, Harvard Business Sch 1976–78, currently dir McKinsey & Co (joined 1978); *Recreations* horse racing, theatre, books, walking; *Clubs* RAC, Hurlingham, Glos CCC; *Style*— Alan Morgan, Esq; ✉ McKinsey & Co, 1 Jermyn Street, London SW1Y 4UH (☎ 0171 839 8040, fax 0171 873 5686)

MORGAN, The Rt Rev Alan Wyndham; *see:* Sherwood, Bishop of

MORGAN, Andrew Vladimir Rhydwen; s of His Hon Judge Peter Hopkin Morgan, and Josephine Mouncey, *née* Travers; *b* 20 Oct 1942; *Educ* Abermâd Sch Aberystwyth, Harrow, RADA; *m* 21 Jan 1967, Jacqueline, da of Dennis Webb, of Knaresborough, Yorks; 1 s (Nicholas Simon Hopkin b 9 June 1968), 1 da (Zöe Olivia Lucy b 28 Dec 1972); *Career* freelance film and television director; work incl: Swallows and Amazons for Ever (Int Emmy), Dr Who, Casualty, Little Sir Nicholas, Little Lord Fauntleroy, The Prince and the Pauper; Freeman City of London 1965, Liveryman Worshipful Co Fishmongers 1965; *Recreations* inland waterways; *Style*— Andrew Morgan, Esq; ✉ 28 Wyndham Street, London W1H 1DD (☎ 0171 723 4507, fax 0171 723 5238)

MORGAN, Arthur William Crawford (Tony); s of late Arthur James Morgan, and late Violet Morgan; *b* 24 Aug 1931; *Educ* Hereford HS, Westcliff HS, Inst of Business Mgmnt; *m* 18 June 1955, Valerie Anne, da of late Arthur J Williams; 3 s (Simon Anthony Crawford b 31 July 1957, Christopher James Crawford b 25 Oct 1958, Timothy John Crawford b 24 April 1961); *Career* Nat Serv RAF Mountbatten; Silver medallist sailing Flying Dutchman Tokyo Olympics 1964, chm and chief exec Purle Bros 1964–71, dir Redland 1971–73, govr of The BBC 1971–76, fndr and ptnr Morgan Hemmingway Investment Bank 1973–77, dep chm Wimpey Waste Management 1978–81, chm Wistech plc 1984–90; non-exec dir Alexander Corporation; fndr and chm Nat Assoc of Waste Disposal Contractors 1968–73; fndr: Campaign for Social Democracy 1973, Nat Ctee for Electoral Reform; exec tstee Youth At Risk; jt Yachtsman of the Year 1965; memb: Br Olympic Yachting Appeal 1970, Cncl Royal Yachting Assoc 1968–72; chm The Hunger Project Tst 1984–89; currently chief exec The Industrial Soc; FRSA; *Publications* author of various technical papers; *Recreations* running, skiing, squash, windsurfing, sailing (yacht 'More Opposition' in Admiral's Cup); *Clubs* Royal Thames; *Style*— Tony Morgan, Esq; ✉ Bovingdon, Marlow Common, Buckinghamshire SL7 2QR (☎ 01628 890654, fax 01628 890628); The Industrial Society, Robert Hyde House, 48 Bryanston Square, London W1H 7LN (☎ 0171 262 2401, fax 0171 706 1240)

MORGAN, Rt Rev Dr Barry Cennydd; *see:* Bangor, Bishop of

MORGAN, Brian David Gwynne; *b* 2 March 1935; *Educ* Univ of London (MB BS, MRCS LRCP); *m*; 3 c; *Career* house physician UCH London 1960 (house surgn 1959), hon prosector RCS 1960, casualty surgical offr UCH 1961, surgical registrar St Richard's Hosp Chichester 1962, sr registrar in gen surgery UCH 1966–67 (surgical registrar 1963–66), sr registrar in plastic surgery Mount Vernon Hosp Dec 1967–70 (registrar May-Dec 1967), conslt plastic surgn Shotley Bridge Gen Hosp, Sunderland Gen, S Shields and Children's Hosp Newcastle 1970–72; conslt plastic surgn: Bedford Gen Hosp 1972–81, The Lister Hosp Stevenage 1972–88; sr conslt plastic surgn: UCH 1972–, Regnl Plastic Surgery Unit Mount Vernon Hosp Northwood 1972–; currently hon conslt King Edward VII Hosp for Officers and St Luke's Hosp for the Clergy; Emlyn Lewis Meml lecture 1994; pres Plastic Surgery Section RSM 1984, sec Br Assoc of Plastic Surgns 1984–86, treas Br Assoc of Aesthetic Plastic Surgns 1985–87; memb Cncl: RCS 1991– (chm Ct of Examiners 1988–), Euro Assoc of Plastic Surgns 1989–91; memb: Br Burns Soc, Br Craniofacial Soc, Br Assoc of Plastic Surgns, Br Assoc of Aesthetic Plastic Surgns, Br Hand Soc, German Plastic Surgery Assoc, Royal Instn; FRCS 1962, fell UC London 1992, FRCOphth 1995; *Books* Essentials of Plastic and Reconstructive Surgery (1986, trans into Serbo-Croat 1991); author of chapters in various text-books; *Recreations* painting in watercolours and oils, sailing, windsurfing, scuba diving, formerly hang gliding; *Style*— B D G Morgan, Esq; ✉ Private Consulting Rooms, University College Hospital, London WC1E 6AU (☎ 0171 383 7395, fax 0171 380 9816)

MORGAN, Christopher; s of Geoffrey Morgan (d 1991), of Ashtead, Surrey, and Bertha Florence, *née* Jaffe (d 1948); *b* 6 Oct 1937; *Educ* Oundle, St John's Coll Cambridge (MA), Univ of Heidelberg; *m* 18 Sept 1971, Pamela Rosamund, da of John Kellock Laurence, of Ham Common, Richmond, Surrey; 1 s (James Edward Laurence b 1977), 2 da (Juliette Rachel b 1973, Claudia Lucy b 1974); *Career* Coopers & Lybrand: articled 1959, ptnr 1973–92; non-exec dir: Windsor Life Assurance Co Ltd 1992–94, Inst for the Study of Drug Dependence 1992–, Stalwart Group Ltd 1994–, Rayner and Keeler Ltd 1996–; FCA 1972 (ACA 1962); *Books* A Brief Guide to the Sandilands Report (1975), The Securities Association's Capital Adequacy Requirements (1988), Auditing Investment Businesses (1989); *Recreations* piano, walking, rowing; *Clubs* Barnes & Castlenau Music Soc, Dacre Boat; *Style*— Christopher Morgan, Esq; ✉ 13 Laurel Road, London SW13 0EE (☎ and fax 0181 878 4620)

MORGAN, Vice Adm Sir (Charles) Christopher; KBE (1996); s of Capt Horace Leslie Morgan, CMG, DSO, RN (d 1973), and Kathleen Hilda, *née* Bellhouse (d 1972); *b* 11 March 1939; *Educ* Clifton Coll; *m* 14 Feb 1970, Susan Caroline, da of William Sturge Goodbody (d 1962); 3 da (Kirsty Joanna b 26 Aug 1970, Victoria Kate b 26 Nov 1972, Juliet Anne b 5 Dec 1978); *Career* initial trg BRNC Dartmouth 1957–59, served HMS Paladin first Cod War Iceland 1959–60, Amphibious Warfare Sqn Persian Gulf 1960–62 (incl Kuwait crisis 1961), 2 i/c HMS Woolaston 1962–64 (incl Brunei rebellion and Indonesia confrontation), Flag Lt to C-in-C Home Fleet 1964–66, i/c HMS Greatford 1966 (active serv Singapore), Specialist Navigation Course HMS Dryad 1966–67, exchange serv Royal Australian Navy 1967–69, Sqn Navigation Offr to Capt F4 HMS Juno 1970–72, Advanced Navigation Course 1973, Flag Navigating Offr to FOF1/FOF2 HMS Tiger and Blake 1973–76, Cdr i/c HMS Eskimo 1976–78, attended Nat Def Coll 1978–79, Cdr Sea Trg Portland 1979–81, Capt Operational Requirements Div MOD 1981–83, RCDS 1984, Capt 5 Destroyer Sqn (i/c HMS Southampton) 1986–87, on staff of JSDC 1987–89, Rear Adm Naval Sec 1990–92, Vice Adm 1992, Flag Offr Scotland, Northern England and NI (FOSNNI) 1992–96, ret; govr Clifton Coll 1993–; pres RN Lawn Tennis Assoc 1990–, vice pres RN Rugby Union 1993–, ctee memb Navy Club 1990–, tstee The

Royal Navy Benevolent Society for Officers 1996–; Yr Bro Trinity House 1977; FIMgt 1980, FRIN 1996 (MRIN 1990); *Recreations* golf, tennis, skiing, wine, gardening, reading; *Clubs* Army and Navy, Royal N Devon Golf, Sherborne Golf; *Style—* Vice Adm Sir Christopher Morgan, KBE

MORGAN, Clifford Isaac (Cliff); CVO (1986), OBE (1977); *b* 7 April 1930; *Educ* Tonyrefail GS South Wales; *m* 1955, Nuala Martin; 2 c; *Career* former Rugby Union Player for Wales, Brit Lions and Barbarians 1951–1959; broadcasting 1958–; BBC: sports organiser Wales 1959, ed Sportsview and Grandstand 1961–64, ed Sport Radio 1972–74, head Radio Sport and Outside Broadcasts 1974–75; ed This Week (ITV) 1964–66, freelance 1966–72; recent freelance tv/radio progs: Sport on Four, Down the River, My Heroes, Rugby Special (commentator); appeared with Henry Cooper in A Question of Sport (first series), subject of This is Your Life 1988; pres: Cystic Fibrosis Tst in Wales, Assoc for Disabled in Wales; vice pres: Nat Children's Home, London Welsh Tst; Hon MA Univ of Wales 1988, HonD Univ of Keele 1989, Hon LLD Univ of Bristol 1996; *Books* Beyond the Fields of Play (autobiography); *Style—* Cliff Morgan, Esq, CVO, OBE; ✉ c/o API Personality Management Ltd, 141–143 Drury Lane, London WC2B 5TB (☎ 0171 379 4625, fax 0171 836 1735)

MORGAN, Darren Thomas; s of Morgan Morgan, of Gwent, and Cynthia Rosina, *née* Snell; *b* 3 May 1966; *Educ* Pontllanfraith Comp Sch; *Career* professional snooker player 1988–; achievements: Welsh amateur 1987, Welsh Masters 1987, world amateur champion 1987, winner Pontin's Professional 1988, One Frame Int champion 1990, winner Senator Welsh Professional champion 1990 and 1991, winner Regal Welsh Professional 1991, semi-finalist Mita Masters 1991, Regal Welsh finalist 1992, Asian finalist 1993, semi-finalist UK Championship 1994 (quarter-finalist 1993), semi-finalist World Championship 1994 (quarter-finalist 1990), winner Irish Benson and Hedges Masters 1995; *Recreations* fishing, playing golf, tennis, watching films, listening to music, keeping tropical fish; *Style—* Darren Morgan, Esq; ✉ Glendale Farm, Fleur de Lys, Blackwood, Gwent NP2 1UP (☎ 01495 200736); Red Triangle Snooker Club, High Street, Pontywain, Crosskeys, Gwent (☎ 01495 271991)

MORGAN, David George; RD; s of Frederick David Morgan (d 1981), and Betty Suzanne, *née* Henderson; *b* 21 Sept 1946; *Educ* Forres Acad, Univ of St Andrews (BSc); *m* 1, 17 May 1969, Helen, *née* Campell; 1 s (Hamish Robert David b 1 Feb 1971), 1 da (Fiona Helen Ruby b 22 Oct 1974); m 2, 21 July 1989, Ruth Mary Morgan, JP, da of John Culpan, of Harrogate; *Career* Pilot Offr RAFVR 1964–68; Lt Cdr RNR 1975–89; Cooperative Insurance Society 1968–71, Royal Liver Friendly Society 1974–78, asst gen mangr Ideal Insurance Company Ltd 1978–84, pensions mangr AE Pensions 1984–85, pensions mangr Nestlé Rowntree Pensions 1985–93, head of gp pensions Nestlé UK 1993–; pres Birmingham Actuarial Soc 1982–83, memb Cncl Nat Assoc of Pension Funds 1990–, chm Yorkshire Gp Nat Assoc of Pension Funds 1991–93, vice chm Nat Assoc of Pension Funds 1995–96; FIA 1970; *Recreations* reading, walking; *Style—* David Morgan, Esq, RD; ✉ 16 Upfield, Croydon, Surrey CR0 5DQ (☎ 0181 654 3242); Nestlé Pensions, St George's House, Croydon, Surrey CR9 1NR (☎ 0181 667 5967, fax 0181 781 0526)

MORGAN, David Graham; s of Edward Aneurin Morgan (d 1985), and Ceridwen Isabel, *née* Davies; *b* 18 May 1943; *Educ* Sexey's Sch Bruton Somerset, Univ of Wales (BSc); *m* 1 Jan 1966, Gloria Patricia, da of John Simon Cartlidge, of Swansea; 1 s (Stephen James b 1972), 1 da (Anna Louise b 1976); *Career* planning asst Kent CC 1966–69, sr planner Glamorgan CC 1969–71, princ planner Cardiff City Cncl 1971–73, dir W S Atkins Consultants 1984– (princ planner 1973–79, assoc planner 1979–84); chm Planning and Devpt Ctee British Consultants Bureau; memb Land Use Panel CBI, treas Assoc of Conslt Planners; MRTPI 1970; *Recreations* athletics, tennis, gardening; *Style—* David Morgan, Esq; ✉ Glendale, Deepdene Park Rd, Dorking, Surrey RH5 4AW (☎ 01306 883105); W S Atkins Planning Consultants, Woodcote Grove, Ashley Rd, Epsom, Surrey KT18 5BW (☎ 01372 726140, fax 01372 740055, telex 266701)

MORGAN, David Llewellyn; eld s of David Bernard Morgan, JP (d 1955), of Cardiff, and Eleanor Mary, *née* Walker; *b* 5 Oct 1932; *Educ* Charterhouse, Trinity Coll Cambridge (MA); *Career* admitted slr 1959; asst slr Herbert Smith 1963–65, conslt Richards Butler 1993– (asst slr 1959–63, ptnr 1965–93); non-exec dir Deymel Investmts Ltd (holding co of David Morgan Ltd Cardiff) 1966– (chm 1977–); Liveryman: Worshipful Co of Clockmakers 1963, City of London Slrs Co; memb: Law Soc 1959, City of London Law Soc (Co Law Sub Ctee); *Clubs* Travellers', White's, City Univ, Cardiff and County; *Style—* D Ll Morgan, Esq; ✉ Flat 15, 52 Pont St, London SW1X 0AE (☎ 0171 589 3538); Richards Butler, Beaufort House, 15 St Botolph St, London EC3A 7EE (☎ 0171 247 6555, fax 0171 247 5091, telex 949494 RBLAW G)

MORGAN, Prof David Rhys; s of Philip Haydn Percival Morgan (d 1974), and Annie Irene, *née* Rees (d 1981); *b* 22 May 1937; *Educ* Queen Elizabeth GS Carmarthen, Jesus Coll Oxford (MA), Emmanuel Coll Cambridge (PhD); *m* 27 July 1963, Sally Lewis, da of Colton Theodore Lewis (d 1984), of Binghamton, NY, USA; 2 s (Christopher b 18 July 1968, Timothy b 18 Sept 1970), 1 da (Siân b 28 June 1973); *Career* Nat Serv RAF 1955–57; Univ of Liverpool: lectr 1965, sr lectr 1973, reader 1987, prof 1989–, head Sch of Politics and Communication Studies 1995–96; visiting prof: State Univ of NY Albany USA 1974–75, George Washington Univ Washington DC 1981–82, Rhodes Coll Memphis Tennessee USA 1986; guest scholar Brookings Inst Washington DC 1978 and 1979; memb: Cncl of American Political Sci Assoc 1986–88, Exec Ctee Political Studies Assoc UK 1988–96; FRHistSoc 1981; *Books* Suffragists and Democrats (1972), Suffragists and Liberals (1975), City Politics and the Press (with Harvey Cox, 1973), The Capitol Press Corps (1978), The Flacks of Washington (1986); *Recreations* walking, travel; *Style—* Prof David Morgan; ✉ Roxby Building, The University, PO Box 147, Liverpool L69 3BX (☎ 0151 794 2890, fax 0151 708 6502, telex 627095 UNILPI G)

MORGAN, David Rhys; s of Emrys John Morgan, of Marhamchurch, Bude, Cornwall, and Effie Corinna Margaret, *née* Robinson; *b* 15 June 1949; *Educ* Bude GS, Bournemouth Tech Coll (HND), Watford Tech Coll (Dip in Advtg and Mktg); *Career* J Walter Thompson London 1971–72, Ogilvy Benson & Mather 1973–76, Interlink Advertising 1976–79, account dir Geers Gross Advertising 1980–86, bd dir Clark & Taylor Advertising (formerly (In The) Marketplace London Ltd) 1988–96 (account dir 1987), ptnr Hardy Birkinshaw Advertising 1996–; *Recreations* skiing, motor sport, squash, travel; *Style—* David Morgan, Esq; ✉ Hardy Birkinshaw Advertising, 24 Store Street, London WC1E 7BA (☎ 0171 436 5990, fax 0171 436 6012)

MORGAN, Col David Richard; OBE (1971), TD (1963), DL (Merseyside 1976); s of Samuel Morgan, DCM (d 1966), and Elizabeth, *née* Roberts (d 1956); *b* 27 Aug 1921; *Educ* Neath, St Luke's Coll Univ of Exeter (Dip Physical Educn); *m* 1955, Sarah Gaynor (d 1991), da of David Charles Roberts (d 1968), of Liverpool; 2 s (Huw, John), 1 da (Siân); *Career* served Palestine and Cyprus, Lt-Col, CO Univ of Liverpool OTC 1963–72, Hon Col Merseyside ACF; schoolmaster (ret); chm: ACF Sports & PA Ctee NW England 1983–90, Army Benevolent Fund Merseyside Appeal, Haigh Homes Merseyside Appeal; memb: Cncl The King's Regt, Mil Educn Ctee Univ of Liverpool; hon life pres Deeside and Merseyside Assoc Royal Regt of Wales; High Sheriff of Merseyside 1989–90; pres: Liverpool Artists' Club 1993, Merchant Taylors' Sch (Crosby) Old Boys' Assoc 1992; *Recreations* supporting rugby (former player Glamorgan, Devon, Lancashire (Capt)), music, tree husbandry; *Clubs* Waterloo (pres 1997–98), Liverpool Artists', Hillside Golf; *Style—* Col David Morgan, OBE, TD, DL; ✉ 28 Hastings Rd, Birkdale, Southport, Merseyside PR8 2LW (☎ 01704 564298)

MORGAN, David Thomas; s of Noel David Morgan, of Stevenage, Herts, and Janet Catherine, *née* McSorley; *b* 22 Jan 1946; *Educ* Neath GS, Alleyne's GS Stevenage, Univ of Newcastle upon Tyne (BA); *m* 1968, Quita, da of Herbert Sidney Valentine; 2 da (Aimee b 10 Dec 1968, Candy 10 Aug 1970); *Career* planning asst Somerset CC 1968–70, Worcester CC (Droitwich development) 1970–71, Peterborough Development Corporation 1971–81, dir of planning servs London Docklands Development Corporation 1985–87 (housing devpt mangr 1981–85), chief exec Black Country Development Corporation 1987–; MRTPI 1971; *Recreations* amateur dramatics, fishing, horse racing, cribbage; *Style—* David T Morgan, Esq; ✉ 3 Riverside Court, Caunsall, Nr Kidderminster, Worcs DY11 5YW (☎ 01562 851688); Chief Executive, Black Country Development Corporation, Black Country House, Rounds Green Road, Oldbury, West Midlands B69 2DG (☎ 0121 511 2000)

MORGAN, David Treharne; TD (1983); s of Maj Hugh Treharne Morgan, OBE, TD, of Alchornes, Lordswell Lane, Crowborough, Sussex, and Betty Gladys Boys, *née* Schreiber; *b* 21 Oct 1941; *Educ* Dragon Sch, Winchester, Innsbruck Univ; *m* 7 July 1973, Heather, da of William Thomson (d 1953), of Steilston House, Dumfries; 1 da (Claire b 2 Aug 1979); *Career* TA; joined HAC 1964, cmmnd 2 Lt 1975, transferred RCT 1977, Lt movement control offr 1977, Capt 2 i/c 282 MC Sqdn 1979, Maj Cmdg 281 MC Sqdn 1984, Lt Col Liaison offr to MOD (Netherlands) 1988, Lt Col Liaison offr All Arms Liaison Unit RLC until 1996, ret; admitted slr 1970; ptnr: R A Roberts 1973–83, Wright Son & Pepper 1987–; vice pres Holborn Law Soc; memb Fedn of Euro Bars Cmmn on Multidisciplinary partnerships; chm: North Norfolk Railway plc 1973–92 (dir 1973–), Association of Railway Preservation Societies Ltd, The South Yorkshire Railway Ltd, Heritage Afloat; dir: West Somerset Railway plc 1982–, Swindon Historic Castings Ltd, The Association of Independent Railways and Preservtion Socs Ltd, The Solent Steam Packet Ltd, Great Central Railway plc, Maritime Tst, Cutty Sark Ltd; pres Fedecrail (European Fedn of Museum and Tourist Railways) 1992, dep pres Transport Tst (former chm), vice pres Severn Valley Railway, memb Railway Heritage Ctee; treas The Trauma Fndn; Freeman City of London 1982, Liveryman Worshipful Co of Glaziers; memb Law Soc 1970, FInstD, MCIT; *Recreations* skiing, sailing, preserved railways; *Clubs* Norfolk; *Style—* David Morgan, Esq, TD; ✉ 7 Cheyne Place, London SW3 4HH (☎ 0171 352 6077); Wright Son & Pepper, 9 Gray's Inn Square, London WC1R 5JF (☎ 0171 242 5473, fax 0171 831 7454)

MORGAN, Prof Derec Llwyd; s of Ewart Lloyd Morgan (d 1970), and Margaret, *née* Jones (d 1984); *b* 15 Nov 1943; *Educ* Amman Valley GS, Univ Coll of N Wales Bangor (BA), Jesus Coll Oxford (DPhil); *m* 1965, Jane, da of Richard Edwards; 1 da (Elin b 17 Dec 1966); *Career* research fell Univ of Wales 1967–69, lectr UCW Aberystwyth 1969–74; UCNW Bangor: subsequently lectr, sr lectr then reader 1975–89, dir Research Centre Wales 1985–89; UCW Aberystwyth: prof of Welsh 1989–95, vice-princ 1994–95, vice-chllr and princ 1995–; non-exec dir Royal Mail for Wales and the Marches 1996–; memb: Gen Advsy Cncl BBC 1984–90, Broadcasting Cncl for Wales 1990–95, Bd of Celtic Studies Univ of Wales 1990–, Ct and Cncl Nat Library of Wales 1995–, Governing Body Inst of Grassland and Environmental Research 1995–; Royal Nat Eisteddfod of Wales: chm Cncl 1979–82 and 1985–86, pres Ct 1989–93; chm Exec Ctee Nat Eisteddfod Ynys Môn 1983; Welsh Arts Cncl Literature Prize 1971, Ellis Jones Griffith Prize 1982; hon fell Univ of Wales Bangor 1996; *Publications* Y Tân Melys (1966), Pryderi (1970), Barddoniaeth Thomas Gwynn Jones: Astudiaeth (1972), Kate Roberts (1974, 2 edn 1991), Cerddi '75 (ed, 1975), Iliad Homer (1976), Adnabod Deg (ed, 1977), Gwna yn Llawen, Wr Ieuanc (1987), Y Diwygiad Mawr (1981, trans, The Great Awakening in Wales, 1988), Williams Pantycelyn (1983), Pobl Pantycelyn (1986), Glas y Nef: Cerddi ac Emynau John Roberts Llanfwrog (ed, 1987), Cefn y Byd (1987), Emynau Williams Pantycelyn (ed, 1991), Meddwl a Dychymyg Williams Pantycelyn (ed, 1991), Charles Edwards (1994); *Recreations* cricket, Swansea City FC, reading; *Clubs* Premier, Glamorgan CCC; *Style—* Prof Derec Llwyd Morgan; ✉ Old College, King Street, Aberystwyth, Ceredigion, Dyfed SY23 2AX (☎ 01970 622002, fax 01970 611446, e-mail cat@abcr.ac.uk)

MORGAN, Derek William Charles; OBE (1997), DL; s of Thomas Brinley Morgan (d 1978), of Neath, and Brenda Vanessa, *née* Megraw (d 1992); *b* 28 Nov 1934; *Educ* Neath GS, Univ of Nottingham (BA); *m* 17 Aug 1963, Anne Yvette, da of Evan Morgan Davies (d 1977), of Bridgend; 2 da (Siân, Louise); *Career* Nat Serv RE 1956–58; mangr Littlewoods Ltd 1958–61, plant mangr Ilford Ltd 1961–67, dir PA Consulting Group 1967–90, dir Business Action Team (Birmingham) Ltd 1988–90, chm Abtrust Preferred Income Trust plc 1991–, dir Moulded Foams (Wales) Ltd 1991–; non-exec dir: Morganite Electrical Carbon Ltd 1982–, Corgi Toys Ltd 1987–89; memb: Neath Devpt Partnership 1981–88, Welsh Health Common Servs Authy 1982–90, Mid Glamorgan Health Authy 1987–92, Wales Regnl Cncl CBI 1987–, Birmingham Chamber of Indust and Commerce 1987–90, BT Advsy Forum for Wales 1991–; chm: Ogwr Partnership Tst 1988–95, Artificial Limb and Appliance Serv Ctee for Wales 1988–90, PA Pension Scheme 1988–, Mid Glamorgan Educn Business Partnership 1989–95, Welsh Wildlife Appeal 1989–93, Bridgend & Dist NHS Tst 1992–95, Prince's Youth Business Tst S Wales 1993–, Univ Hosp of Wales Healthcare NHS Tst 1995–; govr Univ Coll Swansea 1982–, pres Cardiff C of C and Industry 1990–91, chm St David's Hall and New Theatre Trust 1990–; High Sheriff Mid Glamorgan 1988–89; Freeman City of London 1986, Liveryman Worshipful Co of Tin Plate (Wire) Workers 1986; hon doctorate Univ of Glamorgan 1995; FIMC 1976, FIMgt 1979; *Recreations* walking, wine, reading, cricket; *Clubs* Cardiff and Co (Cardiff); *Style—* Derek Morgan, Esq, OBE, DL; ✉ Erw Graig, Merthyr Mawr, Bridgend CF32 0NU

MORGAN, Domini Margaret; da of The Hon Alfred Clive Lawrence, CBE (d 1926), of Middleton House, Middleton Cheney, Banbury, Oxon, and Mildred Margaret Dew (d 1964); *b* 8 May 1925; *Educ* St Giles Sch Blandford; *m* 14 June 1979, Arnold Frank Morgan, s of Frank Augustus Morgan (d 1982); *Career* horsewoman, judge, breeder and coach; formerly translator and sec FO; show jumping winner Area Int Trials; dressage competitions: Pris St George's Rotterdam 1967, England and Int Grand Prix successes on San Fernando (11 place Olympics Mexico 1968), Dressage Horse of the Year 1969–73, winner Hamburg Dressage Derby 1971 (3 place 1970); breeder of nat champion showjumpers; awarded Churchill Fellowship for Dressage 1973; Br Dressage Ctee: memb, memb Trg Ctee 1970–90, selector 1975–, memb Young Rider Ctee 1981–90, FEI int judge 1980, official int judge 1989; initiated Talent Spotting Scheme; coached winning W Aust Pony Club team 1981–88; *Recreations* skiing, travelling, European languages, clay modelling of horses and dogs, husband's farm; *Style—* Mrs Domini Morgan; ✉ Teddards, Filching, Jevington, Polegate, E Sussex BN26 5QA (☎ 01323 484816)

MORGAN, (Mair) Eluned; MEP (Lab) Wales Mid and W (majority 29,234); da of Canon Bob Morgan, and Elaine, *née* Evans; *b* 16 Feb 1967; *Educ* Ysgol Gyfun Gymraeg Glantaf, United World Coll of the Atlantic (scholar), Univ of Strasbourg, Complutense Univ Madrid, Univ of Hull (BA); *Career* stagiaire Euro Parl 1990, S4C 1991, Agenda TV 1992, TV documentary researcher BBC Wales 1993, MEP (Lab) Wales Mid and W 1994–; *Style—* Ms Eluned Morgan, MEP; ✉ 2 Queen Street, Carmarthen, Dyfed, SA31 1JR (☎ 01267 222205, fax 01267 223343)

MORGAN, Fay (Mrs Roger Oates); da of Philip Hugh Morgan, of Goodwick, Dyfed, and Iris Friend, *née* John; *b* 18 Dec 1946; *Educ* Bishopswood Secdy Sch, Hornsey Coll of Art (DipAD), RCA (MDes); *m* 31 July 1976, Roger Kendrew Oates, *qv*, s of William Oates; 1 s (Daniel Morgan Oates b 25 Jan 1979); *Career* textile designer; set up own studio London 1970–75, dir Weavers Workshop Edinburgh 1973–75, pt/t lectr Goldsmiths' Coll London 1975–79, memb Governing Body Herefordshire Coll of Art & Design 1989–95; Morgan Oates Partnership at the House in the Yard Ledbury 1975–86, Morgan & Oates Ltd 1986– (designing for own label and clients incl Ralph Lauren, Christian Dior, Sonia Rykiel, Donna Karan and Laura Asley), sr ptnr Roger Oates Design Associates partnership 1987–; work in exhibitions incl: The Craftsman's Art (V & A Museum) 1973, The House in the Yard Textiles from the Workshop of Fay Morgan and Roger Oates (Welsh Arts Cncl Cardiff and tour) 1978, Tufted Rugs (Environment London) 1980, Texstyles (Crafts Cncl London and tour) 1984–85, Design Awards (Lloyd's Building London) 1988; awarded: USA ROSCOE award 1984, British Design award 1988, Duke of Edinburgh's certificate for services to design; contrib various TV prodns; *Books* Clothes Without Patterns (1977); *Style—* Ms Fay Morgan; ✉ Roger Oates Design Associates, The Long Barn, Eastnor, Ledbury, Herefordshire HR8 1EL (☎ 01531 632718, fax 01531 631361)

MORGAN, Fidelis; da of Peter N Horswill, of Colchester, and Fidelis, *née* Morgan; *b* 8 Aug 1952; *Educ* Farnborough Hill Convent, Upper Chine Sch, Univ of Birmingham (BA); *Career* actress and writer; *Theatre* incl: Clara Hibbert in The Vortex (Garrick and Glasgow Citizens), Angustias in The House of Bernarda Alba (Nottingham Playhouse), Crawshaw in Savages (W Yorkshire Playhouse), title role in Arturo Ui (Liverpool Everyman), Ruth Fischer in Berlin Days/Hollywood Nights (The Place and tour); Glasgow Citizens Theatre: Queen Elizabeth in Mary Stuart, Ruth in Blithe Spirit, Anna in Anna Karenina, title role in The Mother, Kath in Entertaining Mr Sloane, Andree in A Waste of Time, Putana in 'Tis a Pity She's a Whore, Duchess of Berwick in Lady Windemere's Fan, Metella in French Knickers, Hippolyta in The Custom of the Country, Lucrezia in the Impressario of Smyrna, Mrs Peachum in Threepenny Opera, Brigida in Country Life; *Television* appearances incl: Jeeves and Wooster, Mr Majeika, The Bill, Lizzies Pictures; *Books* incl: The Female Wits (1981), A Woman of No Character (1986), Bluff Your Way in Theatre (1986), The Well Known Trouble-Maker (1988), A Misogynist's Source Book (1989), The Female Tatler (1991), The Years Between (1994), My Dark Rosaleen (1994), Wicked (1995); *Plays* Pamela (with Giles Havergal, 1985), Hangover Square (1990); *Awards* nominated Most Promising Playwright in Plays & Players 1986, LIPA'96 (co-winner); *Recreations* music, cooking, reading; *Style—* Fidelis Morgan; ✉ c/o ICM Ltd, Oxford House, 76 Oxford Street, London W1N 0AX (☎ 0171 636 6565, fax 0171 323 0101)

MORGAN, Frederick William; s of Frederick William Morgan (d 1986), and Esther Ellen, *née* Mackay (d 1967); *b* 23 Dec 1927; *Educ* Bartley Green Secdy Modern Sch Birmingham, Ruskin Coll Oxford (Robert Addy Hopkinson scholar), Pembroke Coll Oxford (mature state scholar, MA); *m* 2 Sept 1976, Selvamalar Kanagasabai, da of Kanagasabai, of Jaffna, Sri Lanka; *Career* apprentice electrician Harborne Electrics Birmingham 1941–44, lab technician Univ of Birmingham 1944–48, trainee mangr WH Smiths Bookshop Redruth 1948–53, events mangr responsible for Observer Mace Debating Tournaments, Sunday Times Drama Festival, etc for Nat Union of Students 1959–64, DG WI Youth Tst Fund Port of Spain Trinidad 1964–66, dir Hereward Phillips Ltd London 1966–69, assoc dir Planned Public Relations Ltd London 1969–72 (seconded to OUP), sr conslt Max Redlich Ltd London 1972–76, md Progress Information Services 1976–85, jt md PR & CI Political Communications (later Countrywide Political Communications) 1985–91, ind conslt 1991–; Parly candidate (Lab): Honiton Devon 1959, S Dorset 1964; exec memb Lab Movement in Europe 1989–; memb NUJ 1964; FIPR 1989 (MIPR 1966); *Recreations* reading, sailing, politics; *Clubs* United Oxford & Cambridge University; *Style—* Frederick Morgan, Esq; ✉ Public Affairs Consultant, 25 Lucien Road, Wimbledon Park, London SW19 8EL (☎ 0181 947 0270)

MORGAN, Geoffrey Thomas; CB (1991); s of Thomas Evan Morgan (d 1979), of Wargrave, Berkshire, and Nora, *née* Flynn (d 1984); *b* 12 April 1931; *Educ* Roundhay Sch Leeds; *m* 2 April 1960, Heather Maureen, da of Capt William Henry Trick (d 1984), of Neath, Glamorgan; 2 da (Siân b 1964, Emma b 1967); *Career* Nat Serv RCS 1950–52; civil servant; Ministries of Supply and Aviation 1952–65, HM Treasy 1965–68 and 1981–83, CSD 1968–81, seconded to Arthur Guinness Son & Co 1970–72, Cabinet Office 1983–91 (under sec 1985), dir Public Appointments Unit 1985–91; advsr: World Bank (Washington) 1977–78, UN (NY) 1987–88, Southern Africa Devpt Unit Civil Serv Coll 1991–, Coopers and Lybrand Mgmnt Conslts 1991–; memb overseas missions to: China 1988 and 1991, Hungary 1990 and 1995, Jamaica 1991, Namibia 1994, South Africa 1992 and 1995; chm Public Admin Ctee Western European Union 1990–91; FRSA 1996; *Style—* Geoffrey Morgan, Esq, CB; ✉ Coopers & Lybrand, EP7–141, 1 Embankment Place, London WC2N 6NN (☎ 0171 213 2963)

MORGAN, His Hon Judge (David) Glyn; s of Dr Richard Glyn Morgan, MC (d 1972), and Nancy, *née* Griffiths (d 1984); *b* 31 March 1933; *Educ* Newport HS, Mill Hill Sch (Buckland exhibitioner), Merton Coll Oxford (MA); *m* 1959, Ailsa Murray, da of Archibald McPherson Strang; 3 da (Sian Louise, Catherine Mary (Mrs Phillip Mould), Sara Elen); *Career* Nat Serv cmmnd Queen's Bays (2 Dragoon Gds) 1955 (served Jordan and Libya), Capt AER, Dep Col 1 Queen's Dragoon Gds 1976; mgmnt trainee General Motors (GB) Ltd 1956; called to the Bar Middle Temple 1958, recorder of the Crown Court 1974–84 (asst recorder Cardiff 1971), asst cmmr Local Govt Boundary Cmmn for Wales 1976–83, asst cmmr Parly Boundary Cmmn for Wales (Gwent & Powys) and for Review of Euro Assembly Constituencies 1983–84, circuit judge (Wales & Chester Circuit) 1984–; hon pres Royal Nat Eisteddfod (Newport) 1988, memb Hon Soc of Cymmrodorion; *Recreations* fishing, country pursuits, opera; *Clubs* Cavalry & Guards, Cardiff & County; *Style—* His Hon Judge Glyn Morgan; ✉ Newport County Court, Olympia House (3rd Floor), Upper Dock Street, Newport, Gwent NP9 1PQ (☎ 01633 255267)

MORGAN, (John) Gwynfryn (Gwyn); s of Arthur Glyndwr Morgan (d 1964), Mary, *née* Walters (d 1963); *b* 16 Feb 1934; *Educ* Aberdare GS, UCW Aberystwyth (BA, MA, DipEd); *m* 1, 27 Aug 1960 (m dis 1975), (Joan) Margaret, *née* Taylor; 1 da (Sian b 2 Jan 1964); m 2, 6 April 1979 (m dis 1989) Colette Ann, *née* Rumball; 2 s (Gregory b 24 Dec 1974, Eliot b 22 Sept 1979), 1 da (Joanna b 23 Aug 1977); m 3, 9 Feb 1990, Margery Sue, *née* Greenfeld; *Career* pres NUS 1960–62, sec gen Int Student Conferences 1962–65, dep gen sec Br Lab Pty 1968–72 (int sec 1965–68); chef de cabinet Rt Hon George Thomson EC Cmmn 1973–75, head EC office Wales 1975–79, head press and info EC delgn Canada 1979–83, head EC representation Turkey 1983–87, head EC delgn Israel 1987–93, head EC delgn Thailand (covering Thailand, Cambodia, Malaysia, Myanmar (Burma), Laos and Vietnam) 1993–95, head SE Asia Div EC Brussels 1995–; author of numerous articles in political jls; assoc prof Univ of Guelph Canada, vice pres London Welsh Rugby Club, fell Royal Cwlth Soc; commandeur d'honneur Chaine des Rotisseurs; *Recreations* rugby, cricket, crosswords, wine tasting; *Clubs* Reform, Cardiff and Co, MCC; *Style—* Gwyn Morgan, Esq; ✉ Head of South-East Asia Division, Commission of the European Communities, Rue de la Loi 200, B-1049 Brussels, Belgium (☎ 00 32 2 299 11 11, fax 00 32 2 299 10 61)

MORGAN, Helen (Mrs Grandon); *b* 20 July 1966; *Educ* Porthcawl Comp Sch; *m* 17 June 1995, Michael Grandon (former Welsh athlete); 1 s (Matthew Richard Grandon b 19 June 1996); *Career* int hockey player (goalkeeper); memb Swansea Ladies Hockey Club; 30 Wales caps, 17 GB caps 1990–; memb GB squad Olympic Games Barcelona 1992 (Bronze medal); former capt Welsh Women's Football Team (centre half); jewellry maker; *Recreations* pop music, crosswords; *Style—* Miss Helen Morgan; ✉ 93 West Park Drive, Porthcawl, Mid-Glamorgan, S Wales CF36 3RN (☎ 01656 772046); c/o Welsh Hockey Association, 1 White Hart Lane, Caerleon, Monmouthshire NP6 1AB

MORGAN, Howard James; s of Thomas James Morgan, of N Wales, and Olive Victoria, *née* Oldnall; *b* 21 April 1949; *Educ* Fairfax HS Sutton Coldfield, Univ of Newcastle upon Tyne (MA); *m* 27 Aug 1977, Susan Ann, da of Alexander Sandilands; 2 s (Alexander James b 26 May 1985, Rupert Thomas Oldnall b 23 March 1991), 1 da (Romilly Grace Victoria b 27 March 1989); *Career* artist; numerous Royal and private cmmns incl: HM The Queen, HM The Queen of the Netherlands (Unilever Tricentennial celebrations), HRH Prince Michael of Kent (for Mark Masons), TRH The Prince and Princess of Hanover, Aintoinette Sibley NPG, Mr and Mrs Neil McConnell (USA) 1992, Chelsea Arts Club (for Absolut Vodka) 1994, Lady Bell, Mr & Mrs Nick Mason (1996); permanent display of work Nat Portrait Gallery; *Subject Work* incl: Shanty Pictures (In Plymouth Towne, A Drop of Nelson's Blood... and Mingulay) 1990–91, Golden Gate Quartet 1994, Monticello watercolours of Jefferson's House (for Civilization magazine) 1994; *Exhibitions* incl: Anthony Mould 1983, Richmond Gallery 1986–87, 1988, 1989 and 1990 (Difficult Red, Le Soirée du Comte Frederique de la Chasseur, Dinner Party-Tiananmen Square, etc), Cadogan Contemporary Watercolours 1988, 1989, 1990 and 1991, Claridges 1989, Thomas Agnew 1989 and 1996, Park Walk Gallery (lithography) 1990, Leighton House Exhibition 1993; RP 1986; *Recreations* riding, 1938 Citroën, books; *Clubs* Chelsea Arts, Beefsteak; *Style—* Howard Morgan, Esq, RP; ✉ studio 401, 1–2 Wandsworth Rd, Battersea, London SW8 (☎ 0171 720 1181); 12 Rectory Grove, Clapham Old Town, London SW4 0EA

MORGAN, His Hon Judge Hugh Marsden; s of Hugh Thomas Morgan (d 1986), of Cyncoed, Cardiff, and Irene, *née* Rees (d 1969); *b* 17 March 1940; *Educ* Cardiff HS, Magdalen Coll Oxford (open scholar, BCL, MA); *m* 18 March 1967, Amanda Jane, da of John Hubert Morton Tapley (d 1987), of Temple Cloud, Bath, Somerset; 2 s (Richard b 1972, Charles b 1978), 1 da (Zoë b 1975); *Career* called to the Bar Gray's Inn 1964, in practice on SE Circuit, recorder of the Crown Court 1987–95, circuit judge (SE Circuit) 1995–; memb: Lord Chllr's Matrimonial Causes Rule Ctee 1989–91, Family Proceedings Rule Ctee 1991–93, Fees and Legal Aid Ctee Senate and Bar Cncl 1976–82, Ctee of Family Law Bar Assoc 1976–89, Wine Ctee SE Circuit 1986–88; *Recreations* gardening, reading, listening; *Style—* His Hon Judge Hugh Morgan; ✉ Kingston upon Thames County Court, St James Road, Kingston upon Thames, Surrey (☎ 0181 546 8843)

MORGAN, James Rees; s of Dr Richard Glyn Morgan, MC (d 1972), of Newport, Gwent, and Nancy, *née* Griffiths (d 1984); *b* 14 Aug 1936; *Educ* Mill Hill Sch, Magdalene Coll Cambridge (MA), Univ of Birmingham (MSc); *m* 5 Nov 1960, Jane, da of David Murray MacFarlane (d 1988), of Newport, Gwent; 1 s (Charles James Glyn b 1962), 1 da (Amelia Kate b 1963); *Career* Nat Serv RAF 1954–56, pilot 1955 ('wings' 1956), PO Royal AAF, 614 Sqdn 1956; Massey Ferguson 1959–62, gp planning engr Automotive Products 1963–64, mgmnt conslt Arthur Young & Co 1964–66, operational res scientist Inst for Operational Res 1966–73; Arthur Young: mgmnt conslt 1973–90, dir 1978, ptnr 1981; fndr: James Morgan Associates 1990, Morgan Harris Burrows 1991; memb: Stratford upon Avon RDC 1969–74, Stratford DC 1973–76; business efficiency advsr to HM's Chief Inspr of Constabulary 1990, chm Home Office Working Group on Partnership in Crime Prevention 1990; *Recreations* gardening, skiing, watching rugby football, theatre; *Clubs* Royal Air Force Club, The Birmingham; *Style—* James Morgan, Esq; ✉ Kineton, Warwicks (☎ 01926 640459)

MORGAN, Dr Janet; *see:* Balfour of Burleigh, Lady

MORGAN, Joan; da of Sidney Arthur Morgan (d 1947), film director and screenwriter, and Evelyn, *née* Wood (d 1958); *b* 1 Feb 1905; *Educ* Ellerker Coll Richmond and privately; *Career* former child actress, later novelist and playwright; resident star Shoreham Beach Studios 1919–21, Hollywood contract offer declined by father 1920, retired from acting 1931; WWII Miny of Supply; involved in conversion of old buildings into houses 1958–77 (incl a school, a church, Huntercombe Golf Clubhouse and 1770 James Wyatt Palladian toll house in Henley); memb: Henley Soc (former ctee memb, former hon sec), Cncl for the Protection of Rural England; memb: Henley Film Soc, Soc of Authors; *Films* first film role aged 8 as Little Lord Fauntleroy (unreleased), first film released The Cup Final Mystery 1914 (in which dragged from Crystal Palace lake in a sack); leading roles in numerous other films incl: The World's Desire (with Dame Lilian Braithwaite) 1915, Light (with Arthur Wontner) 1915, Her Greatest Performance (with Dame Ellen Terry) 1916, Little Dorrit (with Lady Tree, directed by father) 1920, Two Little Wooden Shoes, The Road to London (with Bryant Washburn), Swallow (South Africa) 1921, Lilac Sunbonnet, Lowland Cinderella, A Window in Piccadilly, last film Her Reputation (directed by father) 1931; *Theatre* incl A Pierrot's Christmas (Apollo Shaftesbury Avenue, for impressario Andre Charlot) 1917, The Fool (with Sara Sothern, mother of Elizabeth Taylor, Apollo Shaftesbury Avenue) 1924, Padre (Lyceum) 1926; *Plays* ten performed incl: This was a Woman (Comedy Theatre London then Paris 1944, filmed later televised), Shadow on the Sun (1951), The Valley and the Peak (1952, televised), Doctor Jo (Aldwych Theatre London 1955, televised), Square Dance (Vienna 1957, televised), The Hours of Darkness (1960); *Novels* incl: Citizen of Westminster (1939), Camera! (1940), The Toad Beneath the Harrow (1942), The Hanging Wood (1950, adapted for television as A Question of Guilt 1977), Gentleman's Relish (1962), Seven Springs to Gravesend (1972); *Non-fiction* Backwater (1942), The Casebook of Capability Morgan (1965); *Screenplays* incl The Alley Cat (Berlin) 1928, The Flag Lieutenant (with Anne Neagle) 1932, The Minstrel Boy (with Chili Bouchier) 1937; *Style—* Miss Joan Morgan; ✉ c/o The Toll House, Marlow Road, Henley-on-Thames, Oxon RG9 2JA

MORGAN, (Ivor) John; s of Capt Alfred Morgan (d 1961), of London, and Dorothy, *née* Barnet; *b* 25 April 1931; *Educ* Taunton Sch Somerset; *m* 9 June 1956, Shirley, da of Henry Morison Bullen (d 1987), of Staindrop, Co Durham; 2 da (Penelope b 1957, Jane b 1960); *Career* Lt RA 1953–56; Higgs & Hill plc 1948–60; md: Builders Amalgamated Ltd 1960–66, Higgs & Hill Property Holdings 1966–74; pres/dir gen Golf St Cyprien SA France 1975–79, md British Urban Development 1989–92, sr ptnr John Morgan Associates 1975–92, proprietor George House Gallery 1992–; fndr memb Mary Rose Tst; vice chm of Govrs Wispers Sch Haslemere 1970–75, hon librarian to Flyfishers' Club 1990–; Diplome de Prestige De Tourisme France 1977; Freeman City of London 1955, Liveryman Worshipful Co of Paviors 1974; FCIOB, MCIM; *Recreations* fly-fishing, sailing, vintage sports cars; *Clubs* Flyfishers', Piscatorial Soc, Royal Artillery Yacht, Vintage Sports Car; *Style—* John Morgan, Esq; ✉ George House, Petworth, Sussex GU28 0AB (☎ and fax 01798 342312); Le PetitMas, Golf St Cyprien, St Cyprien, France

MORGAN, Sir John Albert Leigh; KCMG (1989, CMG 1982); s of John Edward Rowland Morgan, and Ivy Ann Ashton; *b* 21 June 1929; *Educ* LSE (BSc Econ); *m* 1, 26 July 1961 (m dis 1976), Hon Fionn Frances Bride O'Neill, da of 3 Baron O'Neill (d 1944); 1 s, 2 da; m 2, 1976, Angela Mary Eleanor, da of Patrick Warre Rathbone; 1 s, 1 da; *Career* served Army 1947–49, cmmnd 1948; HM Dip Serv 1951–89: served in Moscow (twice), Peking and Rio de Janeiro, head Far Eastern Dept FCO 1970–72, head Cultural Relations Dept FCO 1972–80, ambass Korea 1980–83, ambass Poland 1983–86, ambass Mexico 1986–89, ret; md (int relations) Maxwell Communications Corp 1989–90, dir Christie's 1993–95; chm: INVESCO (formerly Drayton) Korea Trust plc 1993– (dir 1991–), East European Development Trust 1994–; dir: INVESCO Europe Ltd 1994–, INVESCO Japan Discovery Trust 1994–; chm ALEA (Bermuda) 1996–, pres Actions Asia Emergent (Paris) 1996–; chm Anglo Korean Soc 1990–95, pres Int Fedn of the Phonographic Indust 1990–93; tstee: Br Museum 1991–, Br Museum Devpt Tst 1991–;

dir Royal Philharmonic Orch 1992–Dec 1995 (chm RPO Devpt Tst 1993–95), memb Int Ctee ESU 1992–, chm LSE Fndn 1994–, dir South Bank Foundation Ltd 1995–; Hon LLD Mexican Inst of Int Law, Hon DSc (Politics) Univ of Korea; Order of the Aztec Eagle (Mexico) 1994; hon fell LSE, FRSA, FRAS; *Clubs* Travellers'; *Style*— Sir John Morgan, KCMG; ✉ 41 Hugh Street, London SW1V 1QJ (☎ 0171 921 1037); Beaumont Cottage, South Brewham, Somerset BA10 0JZ (☎ 01749 850606)

MORGAN, His Hon Judge John Ambrose; s of Joseph Michael Morgan (d 1973), of Liverpool, and Monica Mary, *née* Horan (d 1994); *b* 22 Sept 1934; *Educ* St Edward's Coll Liverpool, Univ of Liverpool (Emmott meml scholar, Alsopp prizewinner, LLB); *m* 19 Dec 1970, Rosalie Mary, da of Harold Edward Tyson (d 1995), and Jane Tyson, *née* Railston (d 1977); 2 s (Matthew Jardine b 24 Nov 1972, Benedict Edward b 20 June 1974); *Career* Nat Serv RAF 1958–60; articled to Town Clerk Bootle, asst slr Preston Corp 1960–62, asst slr Liverpool Corp 1962–64, slr with J Frodsham & Sons Prescot, St Helens and Widnes 1964–70, called to the Bar Grays Inn 1970, practiced at the Bar Northern Circuit 1970–90, dep stipendiary magistrate 1982–90, recorder 1988–90 (asst recorder 1983–88), circuit judge (Northern Circuit) 1990–; chm Govrs St Edward's Coll 1986–95; pres Liverpool RFC 1980–82 (former player 1st XV); *Recreations* golf, amateur operatics, rugby football (writing and broadcasting); *Clubs* Athenaeum (Liverpool), Woolton Golf, Liverpool St Helens Rugby, Sefton CC, Liverpool Bar CC (pres 1993–); *Style*— His Hon Judge John Morgan; ✉ Queen Elizabeth II Law Courts, Derby Square, Liverpool L2 1XA (☎ 0151 473 7373)

MORGAN, John Christopher; s of Ieuan Gwyn Jones Morgan, of Winchester, and Gwen, *née* Littlechild; *b* 31 Dec 1955; *Educ* Peter Symonds Winchester, Univ of Reading (BSc), Open Univ (MBA); *m* 1 Sept 1984, Rosalind Jane, da of John Kendrew; 2 s (James b 1986, Charles b 1988), 1 da (Anna b 1989); *Career* chief exec: Morgan Sindall plc 1977–, Overbury Group plc 1985–; ISVA; *Recreations* sailing; *Clubs* Mudeford Sailing; *Style*— John Morgan, Esq; ✉ Morgan Sindall plc, 16 Noel Street, London W1V 4DA (☎ 0171 292 5300)

MORGAN, John Mansel; s of Jestyn Mansel Morgan, of Los Angeles, USA, and Sally Morgan (d 1979); *b* 18 May 1939; *Educ* Dynevor GS, Univ Coll Swansea (BSc); *m* 24 Aug 1963, Janice Dennis, da of Daniel Jones (d 1975); 2 da (Justine Fay b 19 Sept 1969, Julia Sian b 21 Nov 1971); *Career* Laporte Titanium Ltd 1961–65, Porvair Ltd 1965–71, Flotex Ltd 1971–76, Orr & Boss & Partners 1976–79, chm and chief exec Porvair plc 1979–; chm Roydon Parish Cncl; CEng, FIChemE; *Recreations* cricket, skiing, golf; *Style*— John M Morgan, Esq; ✉ Porvair plc, Estuary Road, Riverside Industrial Estate, King's Lynn, Norfolk PE30 2HS (☎ 01553 761111, fax 01553 764637, telex 817115)

MORGAN, John White; s of John White Morgan (d 1973), of Bridge of Allan, and Catherine, *née* Halliday; *b* 11 March 1946; *Educ* Greenock Acad; *m* Morag Nicol, da of William McFarlane; 2 da (Megan Sarah b 14 Sept 1973, Erika Catherine b 11 Jan 1977); *Career* md: Simpson & Gemmell 1972–78, Woolward Royds 1978–80, Morgan Associates 1980–89; chm and md The Morgan Partnership 1993– (md 1990–93); dir: Forth Valley Enterprise, Bridge of Allan Highland Games; memb Incorporation of Maltmen; MInstM 1980; *Recreations* art gallery and gift shop, Highland Games, Robert Burns, Town of Stirling, football, public speaking; *Clubs* Old Manor Burns (chm); *Style*— John W Morgan, Esq; ✉ The Morgan Partnership, The Wheatsheaf Building, Speirs Wharf, Port Dundas, Glasgow G4 9TB (☎ 0141 332 1234, fax 0141 332 5032, mobile 0836 790035)

MORGAN, John William Harold (Bill); s of John Henry Morgan (d 1973), and Florence Ada, *née* Dorricott (d 1989); *b* 13 Dec 1927; *Educ* Wednesbury Boys' HS, Univ of Birmingham (BSc); *m* 1952, Barbara, da of Wilfred Harrison; 2 da (Elaine, Jane); *Career* Nat Serv Flying Offr RAF 1949–51; various sr mgmnt roles in English Electric Co 1951–69, md English Electric-AEI Machines Gp (following merger with GEC) 1969–73; asst md and main board dir: GEC plc 1973–83, Hill Samuel & Co 1983–89, Simon Engineering plc 1983–88; dep chm Petbow Holdings plc 1983–86; chm: AMEC plc 1984–88 (dir 1983), Staffs Cable Ltd 1989–93, Trafford Park Development Corporation 1990–; dir: AMEC plc 1988–91, Pitney Bowes plc 1989–92, Tekdata Ltd 1989–, UMIST Ventures Ltd 1989–; additional memb Monopolies and Mergers Cmmn 1991–; Royal Soc S G Brown award and medal (for outstanding contrib to the promotion and devpt of mechanical inventions) 1968; memb Cncl Fellowship of Engrg 1987–90; FEng 1978, FIMechE, MIEE, FRSA; *Style*— J W H Morgan, Esq, FEng; ✉ Mullion, Whitmore Heath, Newcastle-under-Lyme, Staffs (☎ 01782 680462); Trafford Park Development Corporation, Trafford Wharf Rd, Trafford Park, Manchester M17 1EX (☎ 0161 848 8000)

MORGAN, Prof Keith John; s of Conway Frederick John Morgan (d 1940), and Winifred, *née* Allen; *b* 14 Dec 1929; *Educ* Manchester GS, Brasenose Coll Oxford (Brackenbury scholar, jr and sr Hulme scholar, BA, BSc, MA, DPhil); *m* 23 March 1957, Hilary Adeline, da of Irby Chapman; 1 da (Susan Jane b 18 March 1963); *Career* sr res fell Miny of Supply 1955–57, res fell ICI 1957–58, lectr Univ of Birmingham 1958–64, AEC fell Purdue Univ USA 1960–61; Dept of Chemistry Univ of Lancaster: lectr 1964–65, sr lectr 1965–68, prof 1968–86; sr pro-vice chllr Univ of Lancaster 1978–86 (pro-vice chllr 1973–78), vice chllr Univ of Newcastle NSW Australia 1987–93 (prof emeritus 1993–), prof Univ of Electro-Communications Tokyo 1993–95; visiting prof Hiroshima Univ 1995–; chm: ISCOL Ltd 1978–86, LANCORD Ltd 1978–86, Uldeco Ltd 1978–86; dir TUNRA Ltd 1987–93; dep chm Hunter Technol Devpt Centre 1987–93, dir Newcastle C of C 1988–93, memb Hunter Econ Devpt Cncl 1989–93; chm: Australian Inst of Management (NSW) 1989–92, Inst for Industl Econs 1990–93, AVCC Copyright Ctee 1990–92, Newcastle GS 1991–93 (currently dir); memb NSW Environmental Res Tst 1990–93; Lancashire County Council: vice-chm Dist Liaison Ctee for Educn 1983–86 (memb 1977–86), memb Storey Inst Management Ctee 1982–86, memb Adult Educn Co-ordinating Ctee 1983–86; memb Cncl Lancashire Polytechnic 1985–87, chm Bentham GS 1982–86 (govr 1974–86); author of numerous contribs to learned jls; Hon DSc Univ of Newcastle NSW 1993; FRSC, FRACI, FAIM; *Recreations* cricket, mountains, Mozart; *Clubs* Royal Cwlth Soc, Newcastle NSW; *Style*— Prof Keith Morgan; ✉ 1421–1 Taguchi, Saijo, Higashi-Hiroshima, Japan (☎ 00 81 824 854777); Hiroshima University, Research Institute for Higher Education, Higashi-Hiroshima, 739 Japan (☎ 00 81 824 246233, fax 00 81 824 227104)

MORGAN, Kenneth; OBE (1978); s of Albert Edward Morgan (d 1975), of Downend, Bristol, and Lily Maud, *née* Stafford (d 1995); *b* 3 Nov 1928; *Educ* Stockport GS; *m* 1950, Margaret Cynthia, da of Roland Ellis Wilson (d 1981), of Stockport; 3 da (Helen Frances (Mrs J E Brown), Sarah Caroline (Mrs N J Martin), Jane Charlotte (Jenny)); *Career* Lt RAOC 1946–49 (Egypt and Palestine); successivley journalist with Stockport Express, Kemsley Newspapers and Exchange Telegraph Co until 1962; NUJ: Central London sec 1962–66, nat organiser 1966–70, gen sec 1970–77; Press Cncl: consultative memb 1970–77, jt sec 1977–78, dep dir and conciliator 1978–79, dir 1980–90; conslt on press freedom and press ethics 1992–; cnsllr Bureau Int Fedn of Journalists Brussels 1970–78; memb: Exec Ctee Nat Fedn of Professional Workers 1970–77, Jt Standing Ctee Nat Newspaper Indust 1976–77, Pro Tem Ctee World Assoc of Press Cncls 1989–92; dir: Press Complaints Cmmn 1991–, Journalists in Europe Ltd, Reuters Founders Share Co; tstee: Reuters 1984–, Journalists' Copyright Fund 1995– (chm of tstees 1996–); conslt Nat Media Cmmn Ghana 1995–; govr ESU 1992–, hon sec ESU of the Cwlth 1993–; assoc Int Press Inst 1980, FRSA; *Publications* Press Conduct in the Sutcliffe Case (1983), New Connexions: The Power to Inform (with D Christie, 1989); contrib: El Poder Judicial en le Conjunto de los Poderes del Estado y de la Sociedad, Media Freedom and Accountability (1989), The Independence of the Journalist, Is de Klant of de Kraut Koning (1990), Beyond the Courtroom: Alternatives for Resolving Press Disputes (1991), Allmänhetens Pressombudsman Årsberattelser (1992); *Recreations* theatre, history, inland waterways, travel; *Style*— Kenneth Morgan Esq, OBE; ✉ 151 Overhill Rd, Dulwich, London SE22 0PT (☎ 0181 693 6585)

MORGAN, Kenneth; s of Edward John Morgan (d 1981), of East Acton, London, and Kate, *née* Reed; *b* 8 July 1946; *Educ* St Clement Danes GS; *m* 28 June 1969, Jean Margaret, da of Edward Albert Woods, of Dagenham, Essex; 4 da (Sarah b and d 1972, Alexandra Jane b 1973, Joanna Louise b 1976, d 1978, Elizabeth Susan b 1979); *Career* CA 1968; sr ptnr Summers Morgan & Co 1977– (jr ptnr 1970); FCA; *Recreations* St Andrew's Church Chorleywood; *Style*— Kenneth Morgan, Esq; ✉ Old Berkeley, Homefield Rd, Chorleywood, Herts WD3 5QJ (☎ 01923 284459); Summers Morgan & Co, 1st Floor, Sheraton House, Lower Rd, Chorleywood, Herts WD3 5LH (☎ 01923 284212, fax 01923 284056)

MORGAN, Prof Kenneth Owen; s of David James Morgan (d 1978), of Aberystwyth, and Margaret, *née* Owen; *b* 16 May 1934; *Educ* Univ Coll Sch, Oriel Coll Oxford (BA, MA, DPhil, DLitt); *m* 4 Jan 1973, Jane (d 1992), da of Gunther Keeler (d 1949), of W Germany; 1 s (David b 4 July 1974), 1 da (Katherine Louise b 22 Sept 1977); *Career* lectr in history Univ Coll Swansea 1958–66 (sr lectr 1965–66), visiting fell American Cncl of Learned Socs Univ of Columbia NY 1962–63, fell and praelector in modern history and politics The Queen's Coll Oxford 1966–89, lectr Univ of Oxford 1967–89 and 1995–; vice chllr Univ of Wales Aberystwyth 1989–95, sr vice chllr Univ of Wales 1993–95, research prof Univ of Wales Aberystwyth 1995–; BBC political commentator on elections, radio and TV 1964–79; ed Welsh History Review 1965–; memb: Bd Celtic Studies 1972–, Welsh Political Archive 1985–, Cncl Nat Library of Wales 1989–95; trustee St Deiniol's Library; hon fell Univ Coll Swansea 1985, supernumerary fell Jesus Coll Oxford 1991–92, hon fell The Queens' Coll Oxford 1992; FRHistS 1964, FBA 1983; *Books* Wales in British Politics 1868–1922 (1963, 3 edn 1980), David Lloyd George - Welsh Radical as World Statesman (2 edn 1964), Freedom or Sacrilege? (1966), Keir Hardie (1967), Lloyd George - Family Letters 1885–1936 (1973), Lloyd George (1974), Keir Hardie - Radical and Socialist (1975), Consensus and Disunity - the Lloyd George Coalition Government 1918–1922 (1979), Portrait of a Progressive - the Political Career of Christopher, Viscount Addison (1980), Rebirth of a Nation - Wales 1880–1980 (1981), David Lloyd George 1863–1945 (1981), The Age of Lloyd George (3 edn, 1983), Welsh Society and Nationhood - Historical Essays (1984), The Oxford Illustrated History of Britain (1984, many edns), Labour People - Leaders and Lieutenants, Hardie to Kinnock (1987), The Oxford History of Britain (1988), The Red Dragon and the Red Flag - The Cases of James Griffiths and Aneurin Bevan (1989), The People's Peace - British History 1945–1990 (2 edn, 1992), Modern Wales, Politics, Places and People (1995); official biographer of Lord Callaghan of Cardiff; *Recreations* architecture, music, sport, travel (especially France and Italy); *Clubs* Athenaeum; *Style*— Prof Kenneth Morgan, FBA; ✉ The Croft, 63 Millwood End, Long Hanborough, Witney, Oxon OX8 8BP (☎ 01993 881341)

MORGAN, (Frank) Leslie; CBE (1988, MBE 1973); s of Edward Arthur Morgan (d 1959), of Llanfair-Caereinion, Powys, and Beatrice, *née* Jones (d 1930); *b* 7 Nov 1926; *Educ* Llanfair GS, Univ Coll of Wales (BA); *m* 16 June 1962, Victoria Stoker, da of Harold Jeffery (d 1972), of Wollaston, Worcs; 1 s (Christopher b 1969), 2 da (Amanda b 1964, Penelope b 1966); *Career* Capt RAOC 1945–48 (reserve 1950–59); chm: Morgan Bros (Mid Wales) Ltd 1959–, Mid Wales Devpt (devpt bd for rural Wales) 1981–89; memb: Welsh Cncl 1970–79, Welsh Devpt Agency 1981–89, Welsh Tourist Bd 1982–89, Br Tourist Authy Devpt Ctee 1982–89; dir: Abbey National Building Society 1981–90, Devpt Corp of Wales 1981–83; chm and pres Montgomeryshire Cons Assoc 1964–81; pres: Montgomeryshire Agric Soc 1986, Montgomeryshire Cons Assoc 1989–92; chm Policy Ctee Save Montgomeryshire Campaign 1993; *Recreations* reading, travel, jogging, swimming, cycling; *Style*— Leslie Morgan, Esq, CBE; ✉ Wentworth House, Llangyniew, Welshpool, Powys, UK (☎ 01938 810462)

MORGAN, Marilynne Ann; CB (1996); da of J Emlyn Williams (d 1984), and Roma Elizabeth, *née* Ellis (d 1992); *b* 22 June 1946; *Educ* Gads Hill Place Sch, Bedford Coll (BA); *m* 26 Sept 1970, Nicholas Alan Morgan, eld s of Rear Adm Sir Patrick Morgan, KCVO, CB, DSC (d 1989); *Career* called to the Bar Middle Temple 1972; DHSS: legal asst 1973, sr legal asst 1978, asst slr 1982, princ asst slr (grade 3) 1985–91; DOE: dep slr 1991–92, slr and legal advsr (grade 2) 1992–, sr dir Legal and Corp Servs Gp 1996–; contrib articles to learned jls; chm: Legal Section First Div Assoc 1984–86 (vice-chm 1983–84), Departmental Talk Force 1994–95; memb Gen Cncl of the Bar 1986–92; *Books* Halsbury's Laws of England (contrib 4 edn), Vaughan's Law of the European Communities (contrib, 1990); *Recreations* homely pursuits; *Clubs* Univ Women's; *Style*— Mrs Marilynne A Morgan, CB; ✉ Department of the Environment, Eland House, Stag Place, London SW1E 5DU

MORGAN, Michael Albert Joseph; *b* 22 April 1943; *Educ* Dyffryn GS, Univ Coll of Wales Aberystwyth (BSc); *m* 26 July 1969, Beryl, da of Harry Culpan (d 1972); 1 s (Owen b 1972), 1 da (Katie b 1975); *Career* conslt English Electric Leo Marconi Computers 1965, personnel dir Northern Dairies 1978–84 (joined as personnel offr 1967), personnel dir Northern Foods plc 1984–; vice chm Northern and Yorkshire RHA, tstee Employment Policy Inst; FIPD; *Recreations* classical music, food, books, Hull Football Club; *Style*— Michael Morgan, Esq; ✉ Northern Foods plc, Beverley House, St Stephen's Square, Hull HU1 3XG (☎ 01482 325432, fax 01482 326009, telex 597149 NFOODS G)

MORGAN, Paul Hyacinth; QC (1992); s of Daniel Morgan (d 1977), of Londonderry, and Veronica Mary, *née* Elder; *b* 17 Aug 1952; *Educ* St Columbs Coll Londonderry, Peterhouse Cambridge (scholar), Lincoln's Inn (Hardwicke scholar, Droop scholar); *m* 19 April 1980, Sheila Ruth, da of Arthur Reginald Harvey; 3 s (Daniel Arthur b 17 Oct 1982, Edwin Hugh Rory b 22 Oct 1985, Leo Robert b 26 Sept 1987); *Career* called to the Bar 1975, joined chambers of Ronald Bernstein QC at 11 King's Bench Walk Temple which removed to Falcon Chambers; *Publications* incl: Megarry on Rent Acts (jt ed, 1988, 11th edn), Woodfall on Landlord and Tenant (jt ed, 1994, 28th edn), Gale on Casements (jt ed, 1996, 16th edn); *Style*— Paul Morgan, Esq, QC; ✉ Falcon Chambers, Falcon Court, London EC4Y 1AA (☎ 0171 353 2484, fax 0171 353 1261)

MORGAN, Paul William David; s of Evan John Morgan (d 1987), and Sonia Myfanwy Morgan, of Blackwood, Gwent, S Wales; *b* 12 Nov 1948; *Educ* Pengam GS, Ealing Sch of Business (BA); *m* 29 Dec 1988, Linda Anne, *née* Jenner; 2 s (Matthew John b 9 Feb 1989, Alexander David b 25 July 1994); *Career* brand mangr: Res Projects Smiths Industries 1971–72 (mktg trainee Clock and Watch Div 1967–71), Snacks Div United Biscuits 1972–74; RHM Foods: brand mangr 1975–77, sr brand mangr 1977–79, mktg mangr 1979–81, sr mktg mangr 1981–84; The Brand Development Company: mktg dir 1984–86, jt managing ptnr 1986–89, md 1989–; memb: Mktg Soc 1987, Market Research Society 1995; *Recreations* sport, reading, music; *Clubs* Brentham Lawn Tennis, Ealing RFC, Beaconsfield Tennis; *Style*— Paul Morgan, Esq; ✉ 7 Shrimpton Close, Knotty Green, Beaconsfield, Bucks (☎ 01494 673630); The Brand Development Company, 50 Longacre, London WC2E 9JR (☎ 0171 497 9727, fax 0171 497 3581)

MORGAN, Peter William Lloyd; s of Matthew Morgan (d 1974), of Sketty, Swansea, and Margaret Gwynneth Morgan; *b* 9 May 1936; *Educ* Llandovery Coll, Trinity Hall Cambridge (MA); *m* 18 April 1964, Elisabeth Susanne, da of William Edward Davis; 3

da (Justine Elisabeth b 9 Aug 1965, Penelope Susanne b 4 March 1967, Gabrielle Margaret b 11 Sept 1969); *Career* IBM: joined 1959, sales dir London 1971, gp dir mktg IBM Europe, Middle East and Africa (Paris based) 1975, dir IBM UK 1983–87, dir IBM UK Holdings 1987–89; DG Institute of Directors 1989–94 (dir Director Publications Ltd 1989–93, chm 1993–94); chm: South Wales Electricity plc (Swalec) 1996– (non-exec dir 1989–95), NPI (formerly National Provident Institution) 1996– (non-exec dir 1990–95, dep chm 1995), Pace Micro Technology plc 1996–; non-exec dir: Nat Computing Centre 1981–89, Firth (Holdings) plc, Zergo Holdings plc; memb Economic and Social Ctee Euro Community 1994–; memb Lloyd's 1987, Freeman City of London, Liveryman Worshipful Co of Information Technologists 1992, FInstD; *Recreations* gardening, skiing, history, dog walking; *Clubs* United Oxford and Cambridge Univ; *Style*— Peter Morgan, Esq; ✉ 40 Catherine Place, London SW1E 6HL (☎ 0171 829 9989)

MORGAN, Piers; s of Anthony Glynne Pughe-Morgan, and Gabrielle Georgina Sybille, *née* Oliver; *b* 30 March 1965; *Educ* Chailey Sch E Sussex, Lewes Priory 6th Form Coll E Sussex, Harlow Journalism Coll; *m* 13 July 1991, Marion Elizabeth, da of Niall Shalloe; 1 s (Spencer William b 26 July 1993); *Career* reporter Surrey and S London Newspapers 1987–89, showbiz ed The Sun 1989–94; ed: News of the World 1994–95, Daily Mirror 1995–; National Newspaper Editor of the Year 1994 (Newspaper Focus Awards) 1995; *Books* Private Lives of the Stars (1990), Secret Lives of the Stars (1991), Phillip Schofield - To Dream a Dream (1992), Take That - Our Story (1993), Take That - On The Road (1994); *Recreations* cricket, Arsenal FC; *Clubs* Tramp, Newick Cricket; *Style*— Piers Morgan, Esq; ✉ Editor, Daily Mirror, 1 Canada Square, Canary Wharf, London E14 5AP (☎ 0171 293 3000)

MORGAN, (Hywel) Rhodri; MP (Lab) Cardiff W (majority 9,291); s of T J Morgan (d 1986), of Bishopston, nr Swansea, and Huana, *née* Rees; *b* 29 Sept 1939; *Educ* Whitchurch GS Cardiff, St John's Coll Oxford (open exhibition, BA), Harvard Univ (Williams scholar, MA); *m* 1967, Julie, da of Jack Edwards; 1 s (Stuart), 2 da (Mari, Siani); *Career* tutor-organiser WEA SE Wales region 1963–65; res offr: Cardiff City Planning Dept 1965–66, Planning Div Welsh Office 1966–68 and 1970–72, DoE 1968–70; econ advsr DTI 1972–74, industl devpt offr S Glamorgan CC 1974–80, head EEC Office for Wales 1980–87; MP (Lab) Cardiff W 1987–; front bench spokesman on: Energy 1988–92, Welsh Affrs 1992–; memb Dept of Energy Severn Barrage Ctee 1978–81; *Books* Cardiff: Half and Half a Capital (1994); *Recreations* tennis, dolphin watching, wood-carving, barbecue cooking; *Clubs* Canton Labour, Canton Rugby, Fairwater Rugby; *Style*— Rhodri Morgan, MP; ✉ Lower House, Michaelston-le-Pit, Dinas Powys, Glamorgan CF64 4HE (☎ 01222 514262); 4th Floor, Transport House, 1 Cathedral Road, Cardiff CF1 9SD (☎ 01222 223207, fax 01222 230422)

MORGAN, Richard Martin; s of His Hon Judge H Trevor Morgan, QC, DL (d 1976), of Swansea, W Glamorgan, and Leslie Martin, *née* Phillips (d 1982); *b* 25 June 1940; *Educ* Sherborne, Univ of Cambridge (MA, DipEd), Univ of York; *m* 20 July 1968, Margaret Kathryn, step da of The Rt Rev Bishop Launcelot Fleming, KCVO (d 1990); 3 da (Pippa b 1969, Victoria b 1971, Rachel b 1975); *Career* housemaster Radley Coll 1969 (asst master 1963), headmaster Cheltenham Coll 1978–90, warden Radley Coll 1991–; *Recreations* watercolours, walking, rackets; *Clubs* Free Foresters, Jesters; *Style*— Richard Morgan, Esq; ✉ Radley College, Abingdon, Oxon OX14 2HR (☎ 01235 543127)

MORGAN, Robert; s of James Morgan, of Llantwit Major, S Glamorgan, and Edith, *née* Templeman; *b* 27 March 1967; *Educ* Llaniltud Fawr Comp Sch; *Career* international diver; clubs: Cardiff 1979–82, Highgate 1982–89 and 1990–, Barnet Copthal 1989–90, Sheffield 1992–; achievements incl: Amateur Swimming Assoc under 14 springboard champion 1980, Br highboard champion 1984–, Br springboard champion 1985, 1989, 1990, 1991, 1992 and 1993, Gold Medal highboard Cwlth Games 1990 (Bronze 1986, Silver 1994), sixth place highboard World Championships 1991 and 1994, Bronze Medal highboard Euro Championships 1991, Silver Medal highboard Euro Championships 1993; also competed: Olympic Games 1984, 1988, 1992 and 1996 (highboard 5th place), World Cup 1989 and 1991 (6th place), Goodwill Games 1990; records: Br highboard 1989, Cwlth Games highboard 1990; *Recreations* sport, golf; *Style*— Robert Morgan, Esq; ✉ 13 Windmill Close, Llantwit Major, South Glamorgan CF61 2SW (☎ 01446 794203)

MORGAN, Robert John; s of late Ioan Brynfab Morgan, of Woodford Green, Essex, and late Doris Eileen Morgan; *b* 19 Feb 1941; *Educ* Forest Sch Snaresbrook, St Peter's Coll Oxford, Guy's Hosp London (Golding-Bird scholar); *m* 29 Jan 1977, Anita Joan, da of John Richardson; 2 s (William Ioan James, Henry Christopher George), 1 da (Jessica Rhiannon); *Career* various jr appointments Guy's Hosp, Guildford Hosps and The London Hosp 1967–75, sr registrar in urology St Peter's Hosps 1975–78, sr lectr in urology Inst of Urology London and hon conslt urologist St Peter's Hosps 1978–81, conslt urological surgn Whittington and Royal Free Hosps 1981–88, hon sr lectr in surgery UCH Med Sch 1982–88; currently: conslt urological surgn Royal Free Hosp, lectr in surgery Univ of London, hon sr lectr in surgery Royal Free Hosp Sch of Med, hon conslt urological surgn St Luke's Hosp for the Clergy, King Edward VII Hosp for Officers and the Hosp of St John and St Elizabeth London; Liveryman Worshipful Soc of Apothecaries 1978, Freeman City of London; hon memb SE Section American Urological Assoc; memb various med socs incl Br Assoc of Urological Surgns (hon sec and memb Cncl 1989–93); *Recreations* reading, fishing; *Clubs* Travellers; *Style*— Robert J Morgan, Esq; ✉ Royal Free Hospital, Pond Street, London NW3 2QG; 147 Harley Street, London W1N 1DL (☎ 0171 486 3345, fax 0171 486 3782)

MORGAN, Robert St Clair (Rob); s of Ioan St Clair Morgan (d 1985), and Pamela Joyce, *née* Robinson; *b* 29 Dec 1957; *Educ* The Judd Sch Tonbridge, Univ of Manchester (BA); *m* Amanda Jane, da of Eddis Charman Box; 2 s (Thomas St Clair b 4 May 1984, Charles St Clair b 25 Dec 1990), 1 da (Jennifer Rose b 20 Oct 1987); *Career* Cadbury Schweppes 1980–85: grad trainee, asst product mangr, product mangr; sr product mangr rising to product gp mangr General Foods 1985–87; Kelloggs 1987–95: mktg devpt mangr UK, mktg devpt mangr Europe, latterly mktg dir UK and Repub of Ireland; md Turtle Wax Manufacturing 1996–97, strategic mktg dir Boots Healthcare International 1997–; *Recreations* sport; *Style*— Rob Morgan, Esq; ✉ Boots Healthcare, 1 Thane Road, Nottingham NG2 3AA (☎ 0115 955 4400)

MORGAN, Robin Richard; s of Raymond Morgan, and Jean Edith Bennett; *b* 16 Sept 1953; *Educ* King Edward VI GS Stourbridge; *m* 31 July 1977, Ruth Winefride Mary; 2 s, 1 da; *Career* journalist and author; County Express Stourbridge 1971–73, Evening Echo Hemel Hempstead 1973–78; Sunday Times: reporter 1979–83, dep news ed 1983–85, ed Insight 1985–87, features ed 1987–89; ed Sunday Express 1989–91, asst ed Sunday Times 1991–92, ed Sunday Times Magazine 1992–93, editorial dir designate Reader's Digest 1993–94, consulting ed Sunday Times 1994–95, ed Sunday Times Magazine 1995–; Campaigning Journalist of the Year 1983 (commended 1982); *Books* The Falklands War (co-author, 1982), Rainbow Warrior (co-author, 1986), Bullion (co-author, 1988), Manpower (ed, 1988), Ambush (co-author, 1989); *Recreations* reading, travel; *Style*— Robin Morgan, Esq; ✉ Sunday Times, 1 Pennington Street, Wapping, London E1 (☎ 0171 782 7850)

MORGAN, Prof Rodney Emrys; s of William Emrys Morgan (d 1976), of Ystalfera, Glamorgan, and Jesmine Lilian, *née* Reed; *b* 16 Feb 1942; *Educ* Haberdashers' Aske's, Paston GS, Univ of Southampton (BSc, Dip Soc Studies); *m* 19 August 1966, Karin Birgitta, da of Folke Mortimer Lang, of Växjö, Sweden; 3 s (Magnus Rodney b 4 Oct 1968, Tobias Mortimer b 26 Feb 1970, Benjamin Emrys Folke b 20 July 1972); *Career* sr lectr in criminology Univ of Bath 1981–89 (lectr 1972–81); Univ of Bristol: reader in criminology 1989–90, prof of criminal justice 1990–, dean Faculty of Law 1992–95; visiting fell Univ of Oxford 1985–87, visiting prof Univ of W Australia 1991; currently chm London Prisons Community Links and Criminal Justice Ctee Bristol Racial Equality Cncl; assessor to Lord Justice Woolf's inquiry into prison riots 1990–91; expert advsr to: Amnesty Int on custodial conditions 1986–, Cncl of Europe on custodial conditions 1989–; JP City of Bath 1974–95; memb: independent inquiry into role and responsibilities of the police 1993–95, Br Soc of Criminology, numerous ctees concerned with criminal justice policy; *Books* A Taste of Prison (1976), The Future of the Prison System (1980), Prisons and Accountability (1985), Coming to Terms with Policing (1989), The Oxford Handbook of Criminology (1994), The Politics of Sentencing Reform (1995); memb editorial ctees of various learned jls incuding: British Journal of Criminology, Howard Journal, Policing and Society; *Recreations* sailing, theatre, gardening; *Style*— Prof Rodney Morgan; ✉ Beech House, Lansdown Road, Bath BA1 5EG (☎ 01225 316676); Faculty of Law, University of Bristol, Wills Memorial Building, Queens Road, Bristol BS8 1RT (☎ 0117 928 7442, fax 0117 925 1870)

MORGAN, (Evan) Roger; s of Evan Morgan, of Carshalton Beeches, Surrey, and Stella, *née* Gough; *b* 18 April 1945; *Educ* Whitgift Sch S Croydon, Battersea Coll of Advanced Technol; *m* 1967 (m dis 1995), Elizabeth, da of Clive Lewis; 1 s (Christopher b 1972), 1 da (Ellen b 1976); *Career* civil servant; Dept of Educn and Sci: joined 1964, entry to fast-stream 1972, princ 1976, asst sec Schs Funding and Governance Div 1981–86, Higher Educn Policy and Univ Funding Div 1986–92, under sec Further Educn 1992–94, Int Relations & Youth 1994–95; asst dir Int Dept for Educn and Employment (following merger in 1995) 1995–; contrib official educn pubns; *Recreations* making music, cycling, gadgets; *Style*— Roger Morgan, Esq; ✉ Department for Education and Employment, Caxton House, 6–12 Tothill Street, London SW1H 9NF (☎ 0171 273 5815, fax 0171 273 5890, e-mail ERMorgan@dfee.gov.uk)

MORGAN, Roger Hugh Vaughan Charles; CBE (1991); o s of Charles Langbridge Morgan, FRSL, membre de l'Institut de France (d 1958), and Hilda Campbell Vaughan, FRSL (d 1985); bro of Marchioness of Anglesey, DBE, *qv*; *b* 8 July 1926; *Educ* Phillips Acad Andover Mass, Eton, BNC Oxford (MA); *m* 1, 15 Sept 1951 (m dis 1965), (Catherine Lucie) Harriet, da of Gordon Waterfield, of Hythe, Kent; 2 s (Piers b 1952 (decd), James b 1955), 1 da (Lucie (Mrs Jean-Noel Bert) b 1959); m 2, 26 Feb 1965, Susan, da of Hugo Vogel (d 1966), of Milwaukee, USA; 1 s (Tobias b 1968); *Career* Gren Guards 1944–47 (Capt); House of Commons Library 1951–63, House of Lords Library 1963–91 (librarian 1977–91); *Recreations* photography, painting; *Clubs* Garrick, Beefsteak, Saintsbury; *Style*— Roger Morgan, Esq, CBE; ✉ 30 St Peter's Square, London W6 9UH (☎ 0181 563 7881, fax 0181 563 7881); Cliff Cottage, Laugharne, Carmarthenshire SA33 4SD (☎ 01994 427398)

MORGAN, Terry Keith; s of Keith Morgan (d 1985), of Cwmbran, Gwent, and Ivy Margaret, *née* Went; *b* 28 Dec 1948; *Educ* Croesyceiliog Secdy Modern, Newport & Monmouth Tech Coll (HND), Univ of Birmingham (MSc); *m* 22 Aug 1970, Ann Elizabeth, da of Kingsley Jones; 1 da (Rebecca Elizabeth b 24 April 1978), 1 s (Rhys Keith b 16 June 1980); *Career* Lucas Girling: craft apprentice 1965–68, student apprentice 1968–72, prodn engr 1972–78, prod engr 1978–80; res mangr Leyland Vehicles 1980–83, mfrg mangr Leyland Bus 1983–85; Land Rover Ltd: prodn dir Range Rover 1985–87, prodn ops dir 1987–89; Rover Group: ops dir 1989–90, md Land Rover Vehicles 1991–94; md Royal Ordnance Div British Aerospace Defence Ltd 1994–96, dir of personnel British Aerospace PLC 1997–; chm: Central England Training & Enterprise Cncl, Solihull Chamber of Commerce and Industry; memb: Bd Investors in People UK, Solihull Health Authy, Exec Industrial Soc; MIMfgE 1975, FIEE 1994, FEng 1995; *Awards* Silver Medal Inst of Mgmnt; *Recreations* golf, rugby; *Clubs* Copt Heath Golf; *Style*— Terry Morgan, Esq, FEng; ✉ 51 Lady Byron Lane, Knowle, Solihull, W Midlands B93 9AX (☎ 01564 777560); British Aerospace PLC, Warwick House, PO Box 87, Farnborough Aerospace Centre, Farnborough, Hants GU14 6YU

MORGAN, Dr Thomas Clifford Naunton; s of Sir Clifford Naunton Morgan (d 1986), of Berks, and Ena Muriel, *née* Evans (d 1993); *b* 9 March 1948; *Educ* Harrow, Univ of London St Bartholomew's Hosp (MRCS, LRCP, MB BS); *m* 16 June 1974, Dr Rosemary Naunton Morgan, da of Maj Arthur William Hayward Bradstreet (d 1987), of Buxted, Sussex; 3 da (Nicola Anne b 3 Dec 1977, Katherine Lucy b 24 Aug 1981, Louise Polly b 8 Oct 1985); *Career* house surgn 1974; conslt radiologist: West Middlesex Univ Hosp 1988–; Liveryman Worshipful Co of Barbers 1974, Freeman City of London 1974; memb: BMA, MDU; FRCS 1978, FRCR 1987; *Recreations* shooting, tennis, windsurfing; *Clubs* Roehampton; *Style*— Dr Thomas Naunton Morgan; ✉ 3 Campion Rd, Putney, London SW15 6NN (☎ 0181 789 5211); West Middlesex University Hospital NHS Trust, Isleworth TW7 6AF (☎ 0181 565 5865/6/7); New Victoria Hospital, 184 Coombe Lane West, Kingston-upon-Thames, Surrey KT2 7EG (☎ 0181 949 9030, fax 0181 949 9032); X-Ray Department, West Middlesex University Hospital (fax 0181 565 5251); Knightsbridge Diagnostic Ultrasound, 53 Sloane Street, London SW1X 9SW (☎ and fax 0171 245 1278)

MORGAN, Prof (David) Vernon; s of David Vernon Grenville Morgan (d 1941), and Isobel Lovinia, *née* Emanuell (d 1996); *b* 13 July 1941; *Educ* Llanelli Boys' GS, Univ of Wales Aberystwyth (BSc), Gonville and Caius Coll Cambridge (PhD), Univ of Leeds (DSc); *m* 31 July 1965, Jean, da of Francis Anderson (d 1979); 1 s (Dyfrig b 3 Sept 1973), 1 da (Suzanne b 22 Jan 1969); *Career* Cavendish Laboratory Cambridge: Univ of Wales fell 1966–68, Harwell fell 1968–70; Univ of Leeds: lectr 1970–77, sr lectr 1977–80, reader 1980–85; Univ of Wales Cardiff: prof of microelectronics 1985–, head Sch of Electrical & Systems Engrg 1992–94, head Cardiff Sch of Engrg 1995–; visiting prof Cornell Univ 1978 and 1979; vice pres IOP 1992–96; IEE: memb Divnl Bd on Electronics, chm Books Publication Ctee, memb Accreditation Ctee; memb MOD Electronic Materials and Devices Ctee; FIEE, FInstP, sr memb IEEE of USA, FEng 1996; *Books* Introduction to Semiconductor Microtechnology (1983), Gallium Arsenide for Device and Integrated Circuits (1986); *Recreations* golf, hill walking; *Style*— Prof Vernon Morgan, FEng; ✉ Cardiff School of Engineering, Queen's Building, PO Box 917, University of Wales, Cardiff, Wales (☎ 01222 874424, fax 01222 874420)

MORGAN, Vernon Alick; s of Lionel Haydn Morgan, of Dorchester, Dorset, and Anne, *née* Coombe; *b* 15 June 1960; *Educ* Dorchester Secdy Modern, Bournemouth Coll of Art, Salisbury Coll of Art (scholarship, professional qualifying exam); *m* 4 May 1985, Nicola Anne, da of Thomas Francis (Tom) Sutton; 1 s (Charlie Thomas Dorset b 24 May 1988), 1 da (Jessie Anne b 14 Aug 1985); *Career* pt/t apprentice G Woollat 1972–74, photographer Roles & Parker Advertising 1979–80, studio mangr and photographer Charles Barker and Rapier Arts 1980–82, freelance Charles Barker 1982–83; proprietor: Vernon Morgan Studios specialising in photographing food for editorial and advtg clients 1983–, The Prop Store props hire business 1991–; inclusion in AFEAP awards 1986–87, Deloitte Bookseller award for best book jacket 1988; memb Assoc of Photographers 1981–91 (treas 1983–85); *Recreations* travel in Europe especially France, eating, fine wines, ornithology; *Style*— Vernon Morgan, Esq; ✉ 6 Wyneham Rd, London SE24 9NT (☎ 0171 326 0210); Vernon Morgan Studios, 16A Crane Grove, Highbury, London N7 8LE (☎ 0171 607 5837, 0171 607 5803, fax 0171 607 0640)

MORGAN, Prof Walter Thomas James; CBE (1959); s of Walter Morgan (d 1917), and Annie Morgan (d 1991); *b* 5 Oct 1900; *Educ* Raines Fndn, Univ of London (PhD, DSc), ETH Zurich Switzerland (DrScTech); *Career* Beit Memorial med res fell 1927–28, first asst and biochemist Serum Dept Lister Inst 1928–37, Rockfeller res fell ETH Zurich 1936; Lister Inst: reader 1938–51, prof of biochemistry 1951–68 (now prof emeritus), dep dir 1952–68, dir 1972–75; memb Sci Advsy Cncl 1956; hon memb: Biochemical Soc 1968, Br and Int Soc of Blood Transfusion 1980, Int Endotoxin Soc 1988; Croonian Lecture Royal Soc 1959; winner: Conway Evans prize 1964, Karl Landsteiner award USA 1967, Royal medal Royal Soc 1968, Paul Ehrlich prize Germany 1968, Philip Levine award in Clinical Pathology USA 1990; Hon MD Univ of Basle 1964, Hon DSc Univ of Michigan USA 1969; FRS 1949 (vice pres 1961–63), Hon FRCP 1982; *Clubs* Athenaeum; *Style*— Prof Walter Morgan, CBE, FRS; ✉ 57 Woodbury Drive, Sutton, Surrey SM2 5RA (☎ 0181 642 2319)

MORGAN-GILES, Rear Adm Sir Morgan Charles; kt (1985), DSO (1944), OBE (1943, MBE 1942), GM (1942), DL (Hants 1983); s of F C Morgan-Giles, OBE (Naval Architect, d 1964), of Teignmouth, Devon, and Ivy Carus-Wilson (d 1936); *b* 19 June 1914; *Educ* Clifton; *m* 1, 11 May 1946, Pamela (d 1966), da of Philip Bushell, of Sydney, Australia; 2 s (Philip b 1949, Rodney (m Sarah, da of Sir Hereward Wake, Bt, *qv*) b 1955), 4 da (Penelope (Mrs Cartwright) b 1947, Melita (m Hon Victor Lampson, now Lord Killearn) b 1951, Camilla (m John, er s of Sir Eric Drake, CBE, DL (d 1996)) b 1953 d 1988, Alexandra (m Lt Col Edward Bolitho) b 1958); m 2, 1968, Mrs Marigold Steel (d 1995), da of late Percy Lowe; *Career* Cadet RN 1932, China Station 1933–35, HMS Echo 1936, torpedo specialist 1938; WWII: Atlantic convoys, Norway, Med, West Desert and Tobruk Garrison 1941, attached RAF 1942, sr naval offr Vis (Dalmatia) and liaison with Commandos and Marshal Tito's Partisan Forces 1943–44, RN Staff Coll 1945, Force W Bangkok and Far East 1945, HMS Norfolk 1946; Trieste 1948–49, i/c HMS Chieftain 1950–51, Admty 1953–54, Capt Chief of Intelligence Staff Far East 1953–54, Capt (D) Dartmouth Trg Sqdn 1957–58, Capt HMS Vernon 1959–60, i/c HMS Belfast Far East Station 1961–62, Adm Pres RN Coll Greenwich 1962, ret at own request 1964; MP (C) Winchester 1964–79; vice chm Cons Def Ctee 1965–75, chm HMS Belfast Tst 1971–78, life vice pres RNLI 1989– (memb Mgmnt Ctee 1971–); Prime Warden Worshipful Co of Shipwrights 1987–88 (Freeman 1965–); Partisan Star Yugoslavia 1953; *Recreations* sailing, country pursuits; *Clubs* Royal Yacht Sqdn; *Style*— Rear Adm Sir Morgan Morgan-Giles, DSO, OBE, GM, DL; ✉ The Anchor Flat, Stansted Park, Rowlands Castle, Hampshire PO9 6DX (☎ 01705 413068)

MORGAN-OWEN, John Gethin; CB (1984), MBE (1945), QC (1981); s of Maj-Gen Llewellyn Isaac Gethin Morgan-Owen, CB, CMG, CBE, DSO (d 1960), of Alton, Hants, and Ethel Berry, *née* Walford (d 1950); family descends from Sir John Owen, Royalist Sgt-Maj-Gen in N Wales during Civil War; *b* 22 Aug 1914; *Educ* Shrewsbury, Trinity Coll Oxford (BA); *m* 1950, Mary, da of Capt Frederick James Rimington, MBE, (d 1941); 2 s (Gethin, Huw), 1 da (Margaret); *Career* served WWII, 2 Lt Supplementary Res S Wales Borderers 1939, 2 Bn S Wales Borderers 1939–44, N Norway 1940, D Day landing 1944, DAA & QMG 146 Inf Bde 1944–45; called to the Bar Inner Temple, Wales and Chester Circuit, practised at Cardiff, dep judge advocate 1952, asst judge advocate gen 1966, dep judge advocate gen Germany 1970–72, vice judge advocate gen 1972–79, judge advocate gen of the Forces 1979–84, jt chm Disciplinary Appeals Ctee ICAEW 1985–87; *Recreations* beagling, inland waterways, travel, croquet; *Clubs* Army and Navy; *Style*— John Morgan-Owen, Esq, CB, MBE, QC; ✉ St Nicholas House, Kingsley Bordon, Hants GU35 9NW

MORGAN-OWEN, John Maddox; DL (Derby 1986); s of Lt-Col Morgan Maddox Morgan-Owen, DSO, TD, JP (d 1950), of Willington Hall, Derbys, and Doris Marjorie, *née* Turner (d 1957); *b* 26 June 1931; *Educ* Shrewsbury; *m* 4 Oct 1958, Elsa Courtenay (Jill), da of Cdr Ronald Arthur Orlando Bridgeman, RD, RNR (d 1962), of Rockliffe Hall, Flintshire; 1 s (Timothy Maddox b 1961); *Career* Derbyshire Yeo 1949–52, 24 Regt of Foot S Wales Borderers 1952–55; insurance conslt; gen cmmr of Income Tax 1972–, chm E Mids Museum Serv 1988–; memb: Derbyshire CC 1967– (dep ldr Cons Gp 1977–92, ldr 1992–95 and 1996–), S Derbyshire Dist Cncl 1973–79, Derbyshire Ctee TAVR 1974–, COSIRA Derbyshire Ctee 1972–88; vice chm Derbyshire Historic Bldgs Tst 1984–; govr Repton Sch 1972–81; High Sheriff for Co of Derbyshire 1995; *Recreations* shooting, music; *Clubs* MCC; *Style*— John Morgan-Owen, Esq, DL; ✉ Pennfield House, Melbourne, Derby DE73 1EQ (☎ and fax 01332 862774)

MORGAN-WITTS, Maxwell; s of George Frederick Vincent Lionel Morgan-Witts (d 1944); *b* 27 Sept 1931; *Educ* Mount Royal Coll Calgary, Acad of TV and Film Arts Toronto; *m* 1958, Pauline Ann Lynette, da of Alan Lawson (d 1982); 1 s, 1 da; *Career* CBC TV actor/presenter 1952; radio prodr/writer India, Sri Lanka, Aust and Canada 1953–55; exec prodr Granada TV 1956–64; exec ed documentary film series BBC TV 1964–72; author, independent prodr of TV films and corporate videos 1972–; chm MMW Productions Ltd; *Books* (written jtly) incl: The San Francisco Earthquake, Voyage of the Damned, The Day Guernica Died, The Day The World Ended, The Day The Bubble Burst, Pontiff, Enola Gay; *Recreations* sailing, swimming, skiing, theatre, travel; *Style*— Maxwell Morgan-Witts, Esq; ✉ 26 Woodsford Square, London W14 8DP; 3 Place du Lac, Le Village, Les Hauts de Vaugrenier, 06270 Villeneuve-Loubet, France

MORGANS, (John) Barrie; *b* 9 Nov 1941; *Educ* Dyffryn GS Port Talbot, Swansea Tech Coll; *m*; 1 s, 2 da; *Career* fin mangr British Steel until 1964 (joined 1957), fin mangr British Rail 1965–67; IBM: cost accountant then pricing mangr Havant Hants 1967–61, fin mangr Southern Area IBM Europe Paris 1971–73, controller IBM UK Ltd 1975–78, dir of fin 1978–86, dir of fin and planning 1986–92, dir of quality and mgmnt servs 1992–95, chm and chief exec IBM UK Ltd 1996– (chief exec 1995–), dir IBM United Kingdom Holdings Ltd; non-exec chm Plasmon plc, non-exec dir Checkout Holdings Ltd, memb Investmt Ctee New Court Ventures and Old Court Ventures; govr Chichester Coll of Technol, memb Target Team Business in the Environment; FCCA, FRSA; *Recreations* good wine, food, skiing, travel; *Style*— J Barrie Morgans, Esq; ✉ IBM United Kingdom Ltd, PO Box 41, North Harbour, Portsmouth, Hants PO6 3AU (☎ 01705 564404, fax 01705 389543, Internet uk_ceo@uk.ibm.com)

MORGANS, Ronald Leslie (Ron); s of late Oliver Leslie Morgans, of Maidstone, and Dorothy, *née* Dean; *b* 21 Nov 1942; *Educ* Samuel Pepys Sch; *m* 18 Sept 1967 (m dis 1988), Janet Lillian, da of Sydney Cutbill (d 1972); 2 da (Samantha b 11 Nov 1969, Catherine b 1 Nov 1972); *Career* journalist: Sunday Express 1959–63, Daily Herald and Sun 1963–67; picture ed: Daily Express 1969–72, Daily Mail 1976–79; exec picture ed Sun 1980–82, assoc picture ed Daily Mirror 1982–85; launch picture ed Today 1985–89, asst ed Today 1989–93, asst ed (Pictures) Daily Mirror 1993–; past chm Picture Eds' Ctee Newspaper Proprietors' Assoc; friend: Royal Acad, Fedn of Br Artists; *Books* Great Pictures of the Year (1969); *Style*— Ron Morgans; ✉ Daily Mirror Newspaper, 1 Canada Square, Canary Wharf, London E14 5AP (☎ 0171 293 3851, fax 0171 293 3983)

MORGENSTERN, Philip Louis; s of Maurice Joseph Morgenstern (d 1966), and Celia, *née* Hausmann; *b* 15 Jan 1932; *Educ* St Paul's, Univ of London (BA); *m* 1961, Estelle Pamela, da of Jakoba Erenberg; 2 s (Neil Hardy Iain b 31 March 1965, Matthew Joseph b 6 Jan 1968), 2 da (Ava Miriam b 18 Oct 1963, Deborah Sarah b 15 April 1972); *Career* Nicholson Graham & Jones: articled clerk 1954, ptnr 1962, sr ptnr 1981–95; sec GB-Sasakawa Foundation 1986; tstee: Inst of Jewish Studies 1989, Jewish Law Publication Fund, Kessler Fndn; Freeman City of London; memb: Law Soc, Worshipful Co of Slrs; *Recreations* hermeneutic and rhetorical exegesis of ancient texts, music, art history; *Style*— Philip Morgenstern, Esq; ✉ c/o Nicholson Graham & Jones Slrs, 110 Cannon Street, London EC4N 6AR (☎ 0171 648 9000, fax 0171 648 9001)

MORIARTY, Gerald Evelyn; QC (1974); s of Lt Col Gerald Ruadh Moriarty (d 1981), and Eileen, *née* Moloney (d 1978); *b* 23 Aug 1928; *Educ* Downside, St John's Coll Oxford (MA); *m* 17 June 1961, Judith Mary, da of Hon William Robert Atkin (d 1984); 4 s (Michael b 25 Aug 1962, Matthew b 12 Aug 1963, Thomas b 20 Jan 1966, John b 12 Jan 1973); *Career* called to the Bar Lincoln's Inn 1951, recorder 1976, chm exam in public Bedfordshire Structure Plan 1978, bencher 1983, memb Gen Cncl of the Bar 1986–90; *Recreations* golf, reading; *Clubs* Reform; *Style*— Gerald Moriarty, Esq, QC; ✉ 15 Campden Street, London W8 7EP; 2 Mitre Court Buildings, Temple, London EC4Y 7BX (☎ 0171 583 1380)

MORIARTY, Michael John; CB (1988); s of Edward William Patrick Moriarty, OBE (d 1993), and May Lilian, *née* Bostock (d 1987); *b* 3 July 1930; *Educ* Reading Sch, St John's Coll Oxford (Sir Thomas White scholar, MA); *m* 1960, Rachel Milward, da of John Thompson (d 1991); 1 s (Patrick b 1966), 2 da (Joanna b 1961, Clare b 1963); *Career* Home Office: asst princ 1954, private sec to Parly Under Secs of State 1957–59, princ 1959, Civil Serv Selection Bd 1962–63, Cabinet Office 1965–67, asst sec 1967, private sec to Home Sec 1968, asst under sec of state 1975–84, head Criminal Policy Dept 1975–79, seconded to NI office 1979–81, head Broadcasting Dept 1981–84, deputy under sec of state and princ estab offr 1984–90; chm Cncl of Euro Ctee on Crime Problems 1978–79 (UK rep 1976–79), dep chm Radio Authy 1994– (memb 1991–), sub treasurer Chichester Cathedral 1991–, church cmmr 1996–; *Style*— Michael Moriarty, Esq, CB; ✉ 22 Westgate, Chichester, West Sussex PO19 3EU (☎ 01243 789985)

MORICE, Prof Peter Beaumont; s of Charles Henry Morice, of Southampton, and Mabel Stephanie, *née* Horspool (d 1978); *b* 15 May 1926; *Educ* Farnham GS, Univ of Bristol (BSc), Univ of London (PhD, DSc); *m* 1, 23 May 1952 (m dis 1986), Margaret, *née* Ransom; 1 s (Simon b 1953), 2 da (Verity (Mrs Laing) b 1955, Katherine (Mrs Daley) b 1961); m 2, 15 Oct 1986, Rita Corless, *née* Dunk; *Career* asst engr Surrey CC 1947–48, research engr and head of structures research Cement and Concrete Assoc 1948–57, prof of civil engrg Univ of Southampton 1958–91 (now emeritus prof), visiting prof Ecole Nationale des Ponts et Chaussées 1986–; FEng 1989, FICE, FIStructE; Order of Sultan Qaboos Oman 1986; *Books* Prestressed Concrete (1956), Linear Structural Analysis; *Recreations* painting, pottery, sailing, gardening; *Clubs* Island Sailing; *Style*— Prof Peter Morice, FEng; ✉ 12 Abbotts Way, Highfield, Southampton SO17 1QT (☎ 01703 557641); 47 Sun Hill, Cowes, IOW; Le Coure, La Sauvetat, 32500 Fleurance, France (☎ 00 33 05 62 65 21 75); Department of Civil £ngineering, The University, Southampton SO17 1BJ (☎ 01703 592692, fax 01703 594986)

MORISON, Hugh; s of Archibald Ian Morison, of Felpham, Sussex, and Enid Rose, *née* Mawer; *b* 22 Nov 1943; *Educ* Chichester HS for Boys, St Catherine's Coll Oxford (MA); *m* 1, 1971 (m dis 1993), Marion, da of Fred Aubrey Smithers, of Lincoln; 2 da (Emma b 1972, Lucy b 1975); m 2, 1993, Ilona, da of Sandor Roth, of Budapest; *Career* Civil Serv SO 1966–93: under sec Scottish Home and Health Dept 1984–88, Indust Dept for Scotland 1988–93; DG Scotch Whisky Assoc 1994–; memb: Health Appointments Advsy Ctee (Scotland) 1994–, Exec Ctee Barony Housing Assoc Ltd 1996–; FRSA; *Recreations* hill walking, literature, archaeology; *Clubs* New (Edinburgh), Royal Commonwealth Soc; *Style*— Hugh Morison, Esq; ✉ Scotch Whisky Association, 20 Atholl Crescent, Edinburgh EH3 8HF (☎ 0131 229 4383, fax 0131 229 3051)

MORISON, The Hon Lord; (Alastair) Malcolm Morison; QC (1965); s of Sir Ronald Peter Morison, QC (d 1976), of Iden, Sussex, and Frances Isabelle, *née* Salvesen; *b* 12 Feb 1931; *Educ* Winchester, Edinburgh Univ (MA, LLB); *m* 1, 1957 (m dis 1975), Lindsay Oatts; 1 s (Simon), 1 da (Joanna); m 2, 2 Feb 1980, Birgitte, da of Axel Hendil, of Copenhagen, Denmark; *Career* senator Coll of Justice in Scotland 1985; *Recreations* fishing; *Clubs* New (Edinburgh); *Style*— The Hon Lord Morison, QC; ✉ Parliament House, Edinburgh EH1 1RF (☎ 0131 226 5071)

MORISON, Hon Mr Justice; Sir Thomas Richard Atkin; kt (1993); s of late Harold Thomas Brash Morison, of Ensor Mews, London, and Hon Nancy Morison, *née* Atkin (d 1978); gs of Lord Atkin (Baron Atkin of Aberdovey) and Lord Morison; *b* 15 Jan 1939; *Educ* Winchester, Univ of Oxford; *m* 1963 (m dis 1993), Judith Rachel Walton, da of Rev R J W Morris, OBE, of Shaftesbury; 1 s (Ben b 1969), 1 da (Lucy b 1967); *Career* called to the Bar Gray's Inn 1960, QC 1979, judge of the High Court of Justice (Queen's Bench Div) 1993–, judge Employment Appeal Tbnl 1994–; Liveryman Worshipful Co of Grocers; *Recreations* sailing; *Clubs* Oriental; *Style*— The Hon Mr Justice Morison; ✉ Royal Courts of Justice, Strand, London WC2A 2LL

MORLAND, Brig Anthony Douglas; MBE (1974); s of Philip Maynard Morland (d 1967), of Borth, and Kathleen, *née* Douglas (d 1986); *b* 27 Jan 1935; *Educ* Mount House, Allhallows, Staff Coll, NDC; *m* 30 June 1962, Jenefer, da of Lt-Col R A Sawers (d 1978), of Rustington; 2 s (Giles Philip Maxwell b 1964, Charles Peregrine b 1967), 1 da (Jane b 1963); *Career* cmmnd RA RMA Sandhurst 1955, Battery Cdr G Para Battery RHA 1972–75, CO 49 Field Regt 1977–80, Cdr Corps Air Def/Dep Cdr Artillery Div 1980–83, dep nat rep SHAPE 1983–86, def and mil attaché Madrid 1986–89; chief exec The Anthony Nolan Bone Marrow Tst 1989–; md Anthony Nolan Marketing; memb: Euro Gp for Bone Marrow Transplantation, World Marrow Donor Prog; Economienda de Orden Civil (Spain) 1988; *Recreations* golf, gardening, Liverpool FC, antiques, St Bernard dogs, philately; *Style*— Brig Anthony Morland, MBE; ✉ The Anthony Nolan Bone Marrow Trust, Royal Free Hospital, London NW3 2QG (☎ 0171 284 1234, fax 0171 284 8202)

MORLAND, Martin Robert; CMG (1985); eldest s of Sir Oscar Charles Morland, GBE, KCMG (d 1980), and Alice Elizabeth (d 1995), da of Rt Hon Sir Francis Oswald Lindley, GCMG, CB, CBE (d 1950); *b* 23 Sept 1933; *m* 6 June 1964, Jennifer Avril Mary, o da of Ninian John Frederick Hanbury-Tracy (d 1971); 2 s (William b 1965, Anthony b 1967), 1 da (Catherine b 1966); *Career* Nat Serv Grenadier Gds 1954–56; HM Dip Serv: Br Embassy Rangoon 1957–60, News Dept FO 1961, UK Delgn Geneva 1965–67, private sec to Lord Chalfont 1967–68, Euro Integration Dept FCO 1965–73, cnsllr Rome 1973–77, seconded to Cabinet Office as head of EEC Referendum Unit 1975, head of Maritime Aviation and Environment Dept FCO 1977–79, cnsllr and head of Chancery Washington 1979–82, seconded to Hardcastle & Co Ltd 1982–84, under-sec Cabinet Office 1984–86, ambass to Burma 1986–90, permanent rep to UN and other orgns Geneva 1990–93; chm GATT Working Party for admission of Chinese Taipeh 1993–; dir of public affairs BNFL PLC 1994–96; *Clubs* Garrick; *Style*— Martin R Morland, Esq, CMG; ✉ 50 Britannia Road, London SW6 2JP (☎ 0171 731 1686, fax 0171 731 4141)

MORLAND, Miles Quintin; s of Cdr Henry Morland, RN, and Vivienne Yzabel Suzanne Nicholson Walters, *née* Hogg; *b* 18 Dec 1943; *Educ* Radley, Lincoln Coll Oxford; *m* 10 March 1972, Guislaine, da of Guy Vincent Chastenet de la Maisoneuve; 2 da (Katherine Natasha b 29 Aug 1973, Georgia Susanna b 18 Dec 1976); *Career* md The First Boston Corp 1983–89, chm Blakeney Management Ltd 1989–; dir: Foreign & Colonial Emerging Markets Trust, East Europe Development Fund, Oryx JIA, India Liberalisation Fund, Turkish Growth Fund, Alliance Middle East Fund, Asian Technololgy Fund, Blakeney Investors; *Publications* The Man Who Broke out of the Bank (1992); *Recreations* visiting insanitary countries; *Clubs* Travellers' (Paris), Boodle's; *Style*— Miles Morland, Esq; ✉ The Rudyard Kipling, 106 Cheyne Walk, London SW10 0DG

MORLEY, Alastair Robert; s of Charles Geoffrey Morley, of Chigwell, Essex, and Elizabeth Jay Mackison; *b* 21 Nov 1950; *Educ* Felsted Sch, Pembroke Coll Oxford (MA); *m* 6 Aug 1977, Pamela Margaret, da of Ralph Lusty; 1 s (William b 8 March 1984), 2 da (Susannah b 23 Oct 1979, Emma b 21 May 1981); *Career* admitted slr 1977; ptnr

Herbert Smith 1986 (joined 1975); admitted avocat au barreau de Paris 1993; memb Law Soc; ACIArb; *Style—* Alastair Morley, Esq; ✉ Herbert Smith, Exchange House, Primrose Street, London EC2A 2HS (☎ 0171 374 8000, telex 886633, fax 0171 496 0043); 41 Avenue George V, Paris 75008 (☎ 00 33 1 4723 9124, fax 00 33 1 4720 9213)

MORLEY, Dr Colin John; s of Cedric Morley, of Cambridge, and Hilda Catherine; *b* 19 April 1943; *Educ* Eltham Coll, Univ of Cambridge (MA, MB BChir, DCH, MD); *m* Ruth, da of Henry Doling, of Cambridge; 2 s (Malcolm b 1970, Simon b 1972); *Career* hon conslt paediatrician Addenbrooke's Hosp 1979–, lectr Univ of Cambridge 1979–; FRCP; *Style—* Dr Colin Morley; ✉ Department of Paediatrics, Addenbrookes Hospital, Cambridge CB2 2QQ (☎ 01223 336886)

MORLEY, David Howard; s of Glyn Morley, of Bromsgrove, Worcs, and Yvonne, *née* Auvache; *b* 21 Sept 1956; *Educ* Queens Park HS Chester, St John's Coll Cambridge; *m* 4 Sept 1982, Susan Diana, da of Denis C Radcliffe, of Huxley, nr Chester, Cheshire; 2 s (William b 27 Jan 1987, Thomas b 13 April 1989), 2 da (Emma b 20 May 1985, Rachael b 11 Jan 1992); *Career* admitted slr 1982, ptnr Allen & Overy 1988–; memb Law Soc; *Style—* David Morley, Esq; ✉ Allen & Overy, One New Change, London EC4M 9QQ (☎ 0171 330 3000, fax 0171 330 9999)

MORLEY, Elliot Anthony; MP (Lab) Glanford and Scunthorpe (majority 8,412); s of Anthony Morley, of Ormskirk, and Margaret, *née* Walsh (d 1985); *b* 6 July 1952; *Educ* St Margaret's HS Liverpool, Hull Coll of Educn (CertEd, BEd); *m* 20 Oct 1975, Patricia Winnifrid Broderick, da of Chief Supt Matthew Hunt, QPM, of Yarm; 1 s (Jonathan b 1985), 1 da (Kathryn b 1981); *Career* teacher 1975–87, head of special needs Greatfield Senior HS; cncllr Hull City Cncl 1979–86 (chm Tport Ctee 1981–85); MP (Lab) Glanford and Scunthorpe 1987–, oppn spokesman on food agric and rural affairs with responsibility for fisheries and animal welfare 1989–; vice pres Wildlife Link, tstee Birds of The Humber Tst, pres Humber and North Lincs RSPCA; memb Cncl: RSPB, Br Tst for Ornithology; *Recreations* ornithology, travel, conservation; *Clubs* Kinsley Labour; *Style—* Elliot Morley, Esq, MP; ✉ House of Commons, London SW1A 0AA (☎ 0171 219 3000, Parly office 01724 842000)

MORLEY, Eric Douglas; s of William Joseph Morley (d 1921), of London, and Bertha Louise, *née* Menzies (d 1929); *b* 26 Sept 1918; *Educ* St Martin's in the Fields, Whitstable GS, Army Sch of Educn; *m* 13 Aug 1960, Julia Evelyn, da of William Pritchard; 4 s (Julian b 1958, Michael b 1961, Stephen b 1963, John b 1964), 1 da (Kathryn b 1968 d 1985); *Career* band boy Royal Fusiliers 1934, Sgt Inf 1939, cmmnd Lt 1943, later Capt RASC, demobilised 1946; Mecca Dancing: publicity sales mangr, dir 1951, asst md 1953, jt md 1959, md 1964; dir Grand Metropolitan Ltd 1969–79, chm Mecca Ltd 1971–79, jt chm Belhaven Brewery 1979; originator BBC TV's Come Dancing (world's longest running TV series); introduced first Miss World competition 1951 and first Mr World competition 1996, exec chm Miss World Group; former pres Variety Clubs Int, pres Outward Bound Tst; Parly candidate (Cons) Dulwich 1979; Liveryman Worshipful Co of Marketors 1984 (Freeman 1980); French Dunkirk Medal; *Books* Miss World Story (1967); *Recreations* music, the French horn, all sports incl marathon; *Clubs* MCC; *Style—* Eric Morley; ✉ Miss World Group, 21 Golden Square, London W1R 3PA (☎ 0171 734 9211, fax 0171 439 1218)

MORLEY, John; s of William John Morley, of Beckenham, and Annie Daisy, *née* Miller; *b* 12 Sept 1942; *Educ* Ravensbourne Coll of Art, Royal Acad Schools; *m* 22 Dec 1972, Diana Rosemary Morley; 1 da (Tess b 12 June 1973); *Career* artist; one-man expos: Charleston Festival Sussex 1974, Royal Acad of Art London 1975, Festival Gallery Bath 1977, Piccadilly Gallery 1982, 1985 and 1987; gp expos incl: Royal Acad Summer Expos 1962–89, Eggs Langton Gallery London 1977, Nat Arts Collections Fund Toubridge 1980, The Garden Expo Ellingham Mill Art Soc 1982, The Glory of the Garden Sotheby & Co in conjunction with Royal Horticultural Soc 1987, The Garden Show Gainsborough's Home Sudbury; A Week in the Country (BBC TV film) 1982, The Long Perspective (cmmnd by Nat Tst's Fndn of Art) 1987, Artists in National Parks (V & A, Stafford Art Gallery, Berwick Borough Museum, Hexham Abbey, York City Art Gallery, Birmingham Museum and Art Gallery) 1988, Kings Lynn Festival Contemporary Paintings a Personal Choice by Brinsley Ford (Fermoy Gallery) 1988; awarded Herbert Baker scholarship by PRA 1985; *Books* illustrated: Nine Poems (Even Machin, 1987), The Secret Garden (1989), Great Tew (Simon Rae, 1989), Laelia Anceps (Orchid) The Plantsman Vol II (1989); *Recreations* gardening, music; *Style—* John Morley, Esq; ✉ North Green Only, Stoven, Beccles, Suffolk

MORLEY, John Harwood; s of George Frederick Morley (d 1990), and Doris, *née* Simpson Rushton (d 1987); *b* 5 Dec 1933; *Educ* Henry Mellish GS, Exeter Coll Oxford (MA); *m* 2 Jan 1960, Jacqueline, da of Kenneth Edward Morgan (d 1988); 3 da (Harriet b 2 Oct 1960, Emily b 12 Nov 1963, Alice b 24 May 1966); *Career* archivist Ipswich Corporation 1958–59, art asst Herbert Art Gall Coventry 1959–61, keeper of art Leicester Museums 1961–65; dir: Bradford City Museums 1965–68, Royal Pavilion Arts Gall & Museums Brighton 1968–85; keeper Dept of Furniture and Interior Design V & A 1985–89; sec and fndr memb Friends of the Royal Pavilion 1972–85, chm and fndr memb The Brighton Soc 1973–75, chm Decorative Arts Soc 1975–85 (pres 1986), patron The Thirties Soc 1985; memb Cncl: Nat Tst 1985–89, Attingham Summer Sch Tst 1983–88; tstee: The Edward James Fndn 1976–82, The Geffrye Museum 1990–94; FMA 1967; *Books* Death, Heaven and the Victorians (1971), Designs and Drawings - The Making of the Royal Pavilion (1984), Regency Design 1790–1840 (1993); *Recreations* music, gardening, reading, museums & houses; *Style—* John Morley, Esq; ✉ 11 Vine Place, Brighton, East Sussex

MORLEY, 6 Earl of (UK 1815); Lt-Col John St Aubyn (Parker); JP (Plymouth 1972); Viscount Boringdon (UK 1815), Baron Boringdon (GB 1784); s of Hon John Holford Parker (d 1955); suc unc, 5 Earl, 1962; *b* 29 May 1923; *Educ* Eton; *m* 1955, Johanna Katherine, da of Sir John Molesworth-St Aubyn, 14 Bt, CBE; 1 s, 1 da; *Heir* s, Viscount Boringdon; *Career* 2 Lt KRRC 1942, transferred to Royal Fus 1947; served: NW Europe 1944–45, Palestine and Egypt 1945–48, Korea 1952–53, ME 1953–55 and 1956; Staff Coll Camberley 1957, cmd 1 Bn Royal Fus 1965–67, Lt-Col, ret 1970; pres: Plymouth Inc Chamber of Trade and Commerce 1970–, W Country Tourist Bd 1971–89, Fedn of C of C and Traders Assocs of Co of Cornwall 1972–79; chm Farm Indust Ltd Truro 1970–86; regnl dir Devon and Cornwall Regnl Bd Lloyds Bank 1971–91; dir: Lloyds Bank Ltd 1974–78, Lloyds Bank UK Management Ltd 1978–85; chm Plymouth Sound Ltd 1974–94; govr: Seale-Hayne Agric Coll 1973–92, Plymouth Poly 1975–82 (chm 1977–82); memb Devon and Cornwall Regnl Ctee Nat Tst 1969–84; Lord-Lt Devon 1982– (DL 1973, Vice Lord-Lt 1978–82); KStJ; pres: Cncl of Order of St John for Devon 1979, Devon Co FA 1979–87; Hon Col: Devon ACF 1978–87, 4 Bn Devonshire and Dorset Regt 1987–92; *Style—* The Rt Hon the Earl of Morley, JP; ✉ Pound House, Buckland Monachorum, Yelverton, S Devon PL20 7LJ (☎ 01822 853162)

MORLEY, Kevin Thomas; s of Vincent Aloysius Morley (d 1975), of Liverpool, and Sarah Margaret, *née* Day; *b* 5 May 1950; *Educ* Univ of Surrey (BSc), Aston Univ Sch of Mgmnt (MSc, MBA); *m* 27 Sept 1980, Kathleen Elizabeth, da of Henry Joseph Coburn; 1 s (Stephen James b 21 July 1983), 1 da (Helen Sarah b 9 July 1987); *Career* Interpet 1970–72 (sales rep, sales mangr, mktg mangr); gen mangr: PAS Limited 1972–73, WCS Limited 1973–77; Ford Motor Co: zone mangr 1978–79, mangr Fleet Sales 1979–80, mangr Truck Sales 1980–81, dist mangr of Trucks Scot 1981–82, dist mangr of Cars and Trucks 1982–84, mktg mangr Cars 1984, mktg mangr Cars and Trucks 1984–86; The Rover Group (formerly Austin Rover): dir mktg 1986–87, dir mktg and UK sales 1987, commercial dir 1987–88, memb Bd 1988, md Rover Cars 1991–92; fndr chm Kevin Morley Group (incorporating Kevin Morley Marketing, Kudos Marketing and Kevin Morley Europe Holdings) 1992–; non-exec chm Birkdale Group 1995–; currently non-exec dir DFS Furniture; Freeman City of London 1988, Liveryman Worshipful Co of Coachmakers & Coach Harness Makers; memb: Inst of the Motor Industry, Soc of Motor Manufacturers and Traders; MCIM; *Recreations* rallying, scuba diving, tennis, squash, reading, music; *Style—* Kevin Morley, Esq

MORLEY, Michael Harlow Fenton; s of Very Rev Dean Fenton Morley of Bath (d 1995), and Marjorie Rosa, *née* Robinson; *b* 18 June 1940; *Educ* Radley, Univ of Cambridge (MA), Univ of Harvard (MBA); *m* 1963, Delia Elizabeth, da of Charles J Robertson, of Combe Hay Manor, Bath (d 1983); 1 s (Oliver b 1971), 2 da (Candida b 1965, Octavia b 1968); *Career* Samuel Montagu & Co 1968–72, chm London & Western Trust Ltd 1972–74, chief exec C Tennant Sons & Co Ltd 1974–81, md Charterhouse Group plc 1981–84, chm Paragon Group Ltd 1984–88, dep chm and formerly chief exec Portals Group plc 1988–95, chm Close Brothers Group plc 1995– (non-exec dir 1985–); non-exec dir: Globe Investment Trust plc 1989–90, Foreign & Colonial PEP Investment Trust plc 1993–, Private Equity Trust plc 1994–; chm Monteverdi Tst 1985–89; *Recreations* tennis, shooting, piano; *Clubs* Brooks's, Leander; *Style—* Michael Morley, Esq; ✉ The Manor House, Priston, Bath BA2 9EH

MORLEY, Dr (William) Neil; RD (1969, clasp 1979); s of Eric Morley, JP (d 1964), of 22 North Park Rd, Bradford, West Yorks, and Barbara, *née* Mitchell (d 1986); *b* 16 Feb 1930; *Educ* Merchiston Castle Sch Edinburgh, Univ of Edinburgh (MB ChB); *m* 13 March 1958, Patricia, da of Walter McDonald; 3 s (David b 1963, Alistair b 1964, Christopher b 1966), 1 da (Carolyn b 1961); *Career* Surgn Lt HMS Falcon 1955–57, served Malta, Surgn Lt Cdr RNR 1959–84; conslt dermatologist Gtr Glasgow Health Bd 1963–95, civil conslt to RN in Scotland 1979–95, conslt dermatologist Health Care International 1995–; memb Med Appeal Tbnl DSS 1979–; FRCP Edinburgh 1970, FRCP Glasgow 1977, memb Incorporation of Barbers of Glasgow 1987, FRSM; *Books* Colour Atlas of Paediatric Dermatology; *Recreations* golf, fishing; *Clubs* Glasgow GC; *Style—* Dr Neil Morley, RD; ✉ Parkhall, Balfron, Glasgow G63 OLQ (☎ 01360 440124)

MORLEY, Sheridan Robert; s of Robert Morley, CBE (d 1992), the actor, playwright and author, and Joan, *née* Buckmaster; *b* 5 Dec 1941; *Educ* Sizewell Hall Suffolk, Merton Coll Oxford (MA); *m* 1, 1965 (m dis 1991), Margaret Gudejko; 1 s, 2 da; m 2, 7 June 1995, Ruth, da of Samuel Leon, of Regents Park, London and East Grinstead, W Sussex; *Career* writer and broadcaster; newscaster, reporter and scriptwriter ITN 1964–67, interviewer Late Night Line Up (BBC2) 1967–71, presenter Film Night (BBC2) 1972, dep features ed The Times 1973–75, drama critic Punch 1975–89 (arts ed 1975–88), arts diarist and TV critic The Times 1989–90, London Drama critic International Herald Tribune 1976–, The Spectator 1992–, columnist Variety 1992–94; Arts Journalist of the Year (BP Awards 1990); regular presenter: Kaleidoscope (Radio 4), Meridian (BBC World Service), Arts Programme (Radio 2) 1990–; frequent radio and tv broadcasts on the performing arts; contrib to: The Times, The Evening Standard, The Radio Times, The Mail on Sunday, The Sunday Telegraph, Playbill (NY), High Life, The Field, The Australian, Illustrated London News, Boz, The Resident, London Magazine, Epicurean, Theatreprint; memb Drama Panel Br Cncl 1982–; narrator: Side by Side by Sondheim 1981–82, Noël and Gertie (also author, Coward anthology) 1983–86, Spread a Little Happiness 1992; solo show My Life and Other Disasters; also cabaret: Fancy Our Meeting and A Talent to Amuse (London and NY); *Books* A Talent to Amuse: the life of Noël Coward (1969), Review Copies (1975), Oscar Wilde (1976), Sybil Thorndike (1977), Marlene Dietrich (1977), Gladys Cooper (1979), Noël Coward and his Friends (with Cole Lesley and Graham Payn, 1979), The Stephen Sondheim Songbook (1979), Gertrude Lawrence (1981), The Noël Coward Diaries (ed, with Graham Payn, 1982), Tales from the Hollywood Raj (1983), Shooting Stars (1983), The Theatregoers' Quiz Book (1983), Katherine Hepburn (1984), The Other Side of The Moon (the biography of David Niven, 1985), Ingrid Bergman (1985), The Great Stars (1986), Spread A Little Happiness (1986), Elizabeth Taylor (1988), Out in the Midday Sun (1988), Odd Man Out - The Life of James Mason (1989), Our Theatres in the 80s (1990), The Methuen Book of Theatrical Short Stories (1992), Robert My Father (1993), Audrey Hepburn (1993), The Methuen Book of Movie Stories (1994), Shall We Dance - the life of Ginger Rogers (1995), Rank Outsider, The Career of Dirk Bogarde (1996), Gene Kelly (with Ruth Leon, 1996); editor of theatre annuals and film and theatre studies incl Punch at the Theatre (1980); *Recreations* talking, swimming, eating, narrating Side by Side by Sondheim and Noël and Gertie; *Clubs* Garrick; *Style—* Sheridan Morley, Esq; ✉ 5 Admiral Square, Chelsea Harbour, London SW10 0UU

MORPETH, Sir Douglas Spottiswoode; kt (1981), TD; s of late Robert Spottiswoode Morpeth, and late Louisa Rankine Dobson; *b* 6 June 1924; *Educ* George Watson's Coll Edinburgh, Univ of Edinburgh (BCom); *m* 1951, Anne Rutherford, da of late Ian Cardean Bell, OBE, MC; 2 s, 2 da; *Career* formerly: sr ptnr Touche Ross & Co CAs, chm Clerical Medical & General Life Assurance Society (ret 1994), dep chm Brixton Estate plc (ret 1994); first chm of tstees Br Telecom Staff Superannuation Scheme 1982–92, dir Allied Irish Bank 1985–91; chm British Borneo Petroleum Syndicate 1986–95; hon treas RCM 1984–96; Cmd 1st Regt HAC (RHA) 1964–66, vice pres HAC 1986–88; pres ICAEW 1972–73, Master Worshipful Co of CAs 1977; FCA, FRCM; *Recreations* golf, gardening; *Clubs* Athenaeum, Caledonian; *Style—* Sir Douglas Morpeth, TD

MORPETH, Iain Cardean Spottiswoode; TD (1991); s of Sir Douglas Spottiswoode Morpeth, TD, of Winterden House, Shamley Green, Guildford, Surrey, and Anne Rutherford, *née* Bell; *b* 28 Dec 1953; *Educ* Fettes, Univ of Bristol (LLB); *m* 30 June 1979, Angela Susan, da of Sir Thomas Gordon Devitt, 2 Bt (d 1995), of Colchester, Essex; 3 s (Richard Douglas Gordon b 18 Nov 1985, Duncan Hugh Sinclair b 1 Dec 1987, James Rutherford Thomas b 17 Oct 1992), 1 da (Catherine Louise Nicholl b 10 Feb 1990); *Career* admitted slr 1978, ptnr Clifford Chance 1988–; Liveryman Worshipful Co of Slrs 1993; memb Law Soc; *Publications* Joint Ventures in Property, Structures and Precedent (contrib); *Recreations* fishing, hill walking; *Style—* Iain Morpeth, Esq; ✉ Clifford Chance, 200 Aldersgate Street, London EC1A 4JJ (☎ 0171 600 1000, fax 0171 600 5555)

MORPHET, David Ian; s of Albert Morphet (d 1960), and Sarah Elizabeth, *née* Marsden; *b* 24 Jan 1940; *Educ* St John's Coll, Cambridge; *m* 2 March 1968, Sarah Gillian, da of Maj Michael Francis Sedgwick; 2 s (William b 1971, Matthew b 1973), 1 da (Jessica b 1970); *Career* HM Dip Serv 1961–74; asst private sec to Foreign Sec 1966–68, first sec Br Embassy Madrid 1969–72; Dept of Energy 1975–78; Midlands Electicity Bd: dep chm 1978–79, under sec Electricity, Energy Policy and Atomic Energy Divs 1980–89; dir BICC Cables Ltd 1981–89, dir of planning and devpt Balfour Beatty Ltd 1989–91, dir of Govt affrs BICC plc 1991–95; UK govr IAEA 1985–89, chm CBI Export Fin Ctee 1992–96; chm National Schizophrenia Fellowship 1977–83, memb Bd Barking Power Ltd 1993–; *Clubs* Athenaeum; *Style—* David Morphet, Esq; ✉ 11 Daisy Lane, London SW6 3DD (☎ 0171 736 2659)

MORPHET, Richard Edward; s of Horace Morphet (d 1987), and Eleanor, *née* Shaw; *b* 2 Oct 1938; *Educ* Bootham Sch York, LSE (BA); *m* 1965, Sally, *née* Richmond; 2 da (Selina b 1967, Thea b 1969); *Career* Fine Arts Dept British Council 1963–66; Tate Gallery: asst keeper 1966–73, dep keeper 1973–86, keeper of the Modern Collection 1986–96, keeper emeritus of the Modern Collection 1996–; author of various exhibition catalogues and magazine articles; *Style—* Richard Morphet; ✉ Tate Gallery, Millbank, London SW1P 4RG (☎ 0171 887 8852, fax 0171 887 8859)

MORPURGO, Prof Jack Eric; s of Mark Morpurgo (d 1953), of Islington, London, and Nancy, *née* Cook (d 1934); *b* 26 April 1918; *Educ* Christ's Hosp, Univ of New Brunswick Canada, Coll of William and Mary Virginia (BA), Univ of Durham, Univ of London; *m* 16 July 1947, Catherine Noel Kippe (d 1993), da of Prof Emile Cammaerts, CBE (d 1955), of Radlett, Herts; 3 s (Pieter b 1941, Michael b 1943, Mark b 1948), 1 da (Katharine b 1953); *Career* RA: enlisted 1939, cmmnd 1940, served in India, Eritrea, Middle East, Greece and Italy, Capt 1942, Maj 1944, sr ops SO Allied Forces Piraeus 1944, Lt-Col 1945, GSO I PR WO 1945, demobilised 1946; Penguin Books Ltd: PR offr 1945–46, ed and hist advsr 1946–69; asst dir Nuffield Fndn 1951–54; Nat Book League: DG 1955–70, dep chm 1969–71, vice pres 1971–85; conslt to UNESCO; dir of Asian seminars on reading materials: Rangoon 1957, Madras 1959; prof: American Studies Univ of Geneva 1968–70, American Lit Univ of Leeds 1970–83; visiting professorships have included Rockefeller Res Center; dir: Sexton Agency & Press Ltd 1983–, md P & M Youngman Carter Ltd 1984–; chm Nuffield Working Party on Medical and Nursing Libraries, govr Abbotsholme Sch 1953–56; Christ's Hosp: donations govr 1968, almoner 1972–89, dep chm 1984–85; chm Pestalozzi Village 1969–74, govr British and Foreign Schs Soc 1970–75, reg broadcaster on radio and TV; hon fell: Coll of William and Mary, Australian Nat Univ; Hon DLitt Univ of Maine 1961, Hon LitD Elmira 1965, Hon DHL William and Mary Coll 1971, Hon DH Idaho 1983, Hon DA Billings Montana 1995; Phi Beta Kappa 1947; Yorkshire Post Special Literary Award 1980; *Books* American Excursion (1949), Charles Lamb and Elia (1949, revised ed 1993), Poems of John Keats (ed, 1953), History of the United States (with Russel B Nye, 1955), The Road to Athens (1963), Venice (with Martin Hurlimann, 1964), Cooper The Spy (ed, 1968), Barnes Wallis (1972), Treason at West Point (1975), Their Majesties' Royall Colledge (1976), Allen Lane - King Penguin (1979), Verses Humorous and Post-humorous (1981), Cobbett in America (ed, 1984), The Return of Mr Campion (ed, 1989), Christ's Hospital (with G A T Allan, 1984), Master of None - An Autobiography (1990), Christ's Hospital - An Introductory History (1991); *Recreations* watching rugby football, listening to music; *Clubs* Army and Navy, Christ's Hospital, Pilgrims; *Style*— Prof Jack Morpurgo; ✉ 12 Laurence Mews, Askew Road, London W12 9AT (☎ 0181 740 0012); Sexton Agency and Press Ltd, 12 Laurence Mews, Askew Rd, London W12 9AT (☎ 0181 743 5676)

MORPURGO DAVIES, Prof Anna Elbina Laura Margherita; da of Augusto Morpurgo (d 1939), and Maria, *née* Castelnuovo (d 1991), of Rome; *b* 21 June 1937; *Educ* Liceo-Ginnasio Giulio Cesare Rome, Univ of Rome (MA); *m* 8 Sept 1962 (m dis 1978), John Kenyon Davies, s of Harold Davies; *Career* assistente in classical philology Univ of Rome 1959–61, jr fell Center for Hellenic Studies Washington DC 1961–62, lectr in classical philology Univ of Oxford 1964–71, fell St Hilda's Coll Oxford 1966–71, prof of comparative philology Univ of Oxford 1971–, fell Somerville Coll Oxford 1971–; visiting prof: Univ of Pennsylvania 1971, Yale Univ 1977; Collitz prof Linguistic Soc of America 1975, Semple lectr Univ of Cincinnati 1983, TBL Webster prof Stanford Univ 1988, Jackson lectr Harvard Univ 1990; delegate OUP 1992; pres Br Philological Soc 1976–80 (hon vice pres 1980–); foreign hon memb American Acad of Arts & Sciences 1986, corresponding memb Oesterreichische Akademie der Wissenschaften (Wien) 1988, hon memb Linguistic Soc of America 1993, memb Academia Europaea 1989, foreign memb American Philosophical Soc 1991, corresponding memb Académie des inscriptions et belles-lettres Institut de France 1992, Premio Pinceo per la Linguistica Accademia dei Lincei 1996; hon fell St Hilda's Coll Oxford 1972; Hon DLitt Univ of St Andrews 1981; FSA 1974, FBA 1985; *Books* Mycenaeae Graecitatis Lexicon (1963), Linear B/A 1984 Survey (ed with Y Duhoux, 1985), La Linguistica dell' Ottocento (1996); numerous articles in Br and foreign periodicals; *Style*— Prof Anna Morpurgo Davies, FSA, FBA; ✉ Somerville College, Oxford OX2 6HD (☎ 01865 270 600, fax 01865 270616)

MORRELL, David William James; s of Rev William Wilson Morrell, MBE, TD (d 1958), and Grace, *née* Reid (d 1991); *b* 26 July 1933; *Educ* George Watson's Coll Edinburgh, Univ of Edinburgh (MA, LLB); *m* 19 Sept 1960, Margaret Rosemary, da of Walter Lewis; 1 da (Fiona Margaret), 2 s (Ewan William, Malcolm David); *Career* apprentice slr Shepherd & Wedderburn WS 1954–57, admin asst King's Coll Newcastle 1957–60, asst registrar and careers advsr Univ of Exeter 1960–64, sr asst registrar Univ of Essex 1964–66, registrar and sec Univ of Strathclyde 1973–89 (academic registrar 1966–73), conslt to Institutional Mgmnt in Higher Educn Prog of OECD Paris 1989–90, Scottish Legal Servs ombudsman 1991–94, vice chm Lomond Healthcare NHS Trust 1996– (chm 1995–96); vice chm of Ct Univ of Paisley 1993– (govr Paisley Coll of Technol 1990–93), govr Scottish Centre for Motor Impaired Children Craighalbert 1994–; pt/t lay observer for Scotland 1989–91, elder Church of Scotland; FRSA 1992; *Recreations* history, environment, hill-walking, angling; *Style*— David Morrell, Esq; ✉ 29 Barclay Drive, Helensburgh G84 9RA (☎ 01436 674875)

MORRELL, Frances Maine; da of Frank Galleway, and Beatrice Galleway; *b* 28 Dec 1937; *Educ* Queen Anne Sch York; *m* 1964, Brian Morrell; 1 da; *Career* policy advsr to: Sec of State for Indust, Sec of State for Energy 1974–79; leader ILEA 1983–87, memb GLC Islington S and Finsbury 1981–86; sec Speaker's Cmmn on Citizenship 1988–91, sr research fell Queen Mary and Westfield Coll 1991–92, exec dir Inst for Citizenship Studies 1992–; *Books* From the Electors of Bristol: a study of constituents' grievances, A Ten Year Industrial Strategy for Britain (with Benn and Cripps), A Planned Energy Policy for Britain (with Benn and Cripps), Manifesto: A radical strategy for Britain's future (jtly), Children of the Future: The Battle For Britain's Schools (1989); *Style*— Mrs Frances Morrell

MORRELL, Leslie James; OBE (1986), JP (1962); s of James Morrell, DL, and Eileen, *née* Browne; *b* 26 Dec 1931; *Educ* Portora Royal Sch Enniskillen, Queen's Univ Belfast (BAgric); *m* 1958, Anne, da of Robert W Wallace, OBE (d 1973), of Belfast; 2 s (Richard, Jonathan), 1 da (Clare); *Career* Londonderry CC 1968–73, NI Assembly 1973–75, Miny of Agric NI Exec 1973–74, fndr chm James Butcher Housing Association Ltd 1976–82 (sec 1982–92); fndr sec Oaklee Housing Association Ltd 1992–; chm: Virus Tested Seed Potato Growers' Assoc 1978–88, NI Water Cncl 1982–93, NI Agric Advsy Ctee of BBC 1986–90, Gen Advsy Ctee of BBC 1980–86; fndr memb: NI Fedn Housing Assoc (chm 1978–80), NI Inst of Agric Science 1960–; memb: Coleraine Borough Cncl 1973–77, Royal Ulster Agric Soc; *Style*— Leslie J Morrell, Esq, OBE, JP; ✉ Dunboe House, Castlerock, Coleraine, BT51 4UB (☎ 01265 848352)

MORRELL, Peter John; s of Arthur Markham Morrell (d 1984), of Oxford, and Geraldine Doris, *née* Harvey (d 1992), of Devon; *b* 28 Feb 1931; *Educ* numerous schs (latterly Worthing HS), Kingston upon Thames Coll of Art (NDD), RCA (life drawing and life painting prizes, ARCA); *m* 1, 1958, Yvonne Nichol; m 2, 1964, Margaret Froud; 1 s (Steven b 1967), 1 da (Nicola b 1971); m 3, 1981, Helene Halstuch, of New York; *Career* artist; pt/t lectr in fine art painting: Maidstone Coll of Art 1961–62, Sir John Cass Sch of Art 1962–65, Hornsey Coll of Art 1962–70, St Martin's Coll of Art 1969–70, Central Sch of Art and Design 1970–92; instigated summer schs at Central Sch of Art and Design 1986 (now lectr) and Sol del Rey 1992–; numerous solo and gp exhbns, work in numerous private and public collections; memb London Gp 1990–; RWS 1983; *Awards* Br Cncl Prize 1955, Arts Cncl Prize 1959, Prix de Rome in Painting 1959; *Recreations* gardening; *Style*— Peter Morrell, Esq; ✉ Sol del Rey, Carnac-Rouffiac, 46140 Luzech, France (☎ 00 33 65 36 96 84)

MORRELL, His Hon Judge; Peter Richard; s of Frank Richard Morrell (d 1974), of Whitehill House, Dane End, Hertfordshire, and Florence Ethel, *née* Gleave (d 1992); *b* 25 May 1944; *Educ* Westminster, Univ Coll Oxford (MA); *m* 6 June 1970, (Helen) Mary Vint, da of Capt William Norman Collins, of Peterborough; 2 da (Helen b 1971, Harriet b 1976); *Career* admitted slr 1970; called to the Bar Gray's Inn 1974; recorder Crown Ct 1990–92, circuit judge (Midland and Oxford Circuit) 1992–; Parly candidate Ilkeston Derbys 1974; *Recreations* shooting, fishing, photography; *Style*— His Hon Judge Morrell; ✉ Crown Building, Rivergate, Peterborough PE1 1EJ (☎ 01733 346342)

MORRICE, Philip; s of William Hunter Morrice (d 1967), of Aberdeen, and Catherine Jane, *née* Cowie (d 1988); *b* 31 Dec 1943; *Educ* Robert Gordon's Coll Aberdeen; *m* 1 April 1989, (Margaret) Clare, da of Dr John Bower, of Guildford, Surrey; 1 s (Nicholas), 1 da (Rachael); *Career* HM Dip Serv: Br High Cmmn Kuala Lumpur 1964–67, FCO 1967–69, Br Embassy Caracas 1969–72, UK Delegation to OECD Paris 1973–75, UK permanent rep to EC Brussels 1975–78, FCO 1978–81, Br Embassy Rome 1981–85, economic and commercial cnsllr Br High Cmmn Lagos 1986–88, minister-cnsllr, consul-gen and dir of trade promotion Br Embassy Brasilia 1988–92, seconded as dir British Trade and Cultural Office Taipei 1992–95, consul-gen Sydney and dir-gen of trade and investment promotion Aust 1995; *Books* The Schweppes Guide to Scotch (1983), The Whisky Distilleries of Scotland and Ireland (1987); *Recreations* tennis, golf, travel, writing; *Clubs* RAC, Royal Over-Seas League, Union (Sydney), Tattersalls (Sydney), Pioneers (Sydney), Royal Sydney Golf; *Style*— Philip Morrice, Esq; ✉ c/o Foreign & Commonwealth Office (Sydney), King Charles St, London SW1A 2AH; British Consulate-General, Sydney, Australia (☎ 00 61 2 247 3617, fax 00 61 2 233 1826)

MORRIS, *see also:* Temple-Morris

MORRIS, Albert (Bert); *b* 21 Oct 1934; *Educ* Skerrys Coll Liverpool, MIT; *m* Patricia, *née* Lane; 1 s (Jonathan), 1 da (Ailsa); *Career* National Westminster Bank plc: head of money transmission 1979–83, gen mangr Mgmnt Servs (former dep gen mangr 1983–85) 1985–88, dir 1989–94, chief exec Support Servs 1989–92, dep gp chief exec 1992–94, ret; dir: Westments Ltd 1985–94, Eftpos UK Ltd 1987–94, APACS (Admin) Ltd, National Westminster Life Assurance Ltd 1992–94; sr advsr IBOS (international electronic bank payment system) 1995–96; non-exec dir Regent Associates Ltd; chm: BACS Ltd 1985–94, Centre-file Ltd, Office of the Banking Ombudsman 1985–87; sometime memb Cncl Chartered Inst of Bankers, non-exec memb Bd DSS 1993; Liveryman Worshipful Co of Info Technologists; FCIB, FRSA; *Recreations* golf, politics; *Style*— Bert Morris, Esq

MORRIS, Sir (Arnold) Alec; KBE (1981), CB (1979); s of Harry Morris (d 1973), and Ivy, *née* Marshall (d 1987); *b* 11 March 1926; *Educ* King Edward Sch East Retford, King's Coll London, Univ of Southampton; *m* 8 June 1946, Moyna Patricia, da of Norman Boyle (d 1950); 1 s (Piers Hamilton b 1954), 1 da (Susan Catriona (twin) b 22 Oct 1954); *Career* cmmnd RAF 1945, SASO HQ No 90 Gp 1972, RCDS 1974, dir Signals 1975–76, DG strategic electronic systems MOD 1976–79, AO i/c Engrg HQ Strike Cmd 1979–81, Chief Engr RAF 1981–83, ret as Air Marshal; exec British Aerospace 1984–91; tstee Young Electronic Designer Awards 1987–; pres: Herts Sci and Technol Regnl Orgn 1984–91, Soc of Electronic and Radio Technicians 1975–89; FEng 1989, FIEE 1971, FRAeS 1973; *Recreations* tennis, gardens; *Clubs* RAF; *Style*— Sir Alec Morris, KBE, CB, FEng; ✉ Graham House, The Avenue, Combe Down, Bath, Somerset BA2 5EH

MORRIS, Rt Hon Alfred; PC (1979), AO (1991), QSO (1989), MP (Lab & Co-op) Manchester Wythenshawe (majority 11,996); s of George Henry Morris, and Jessie, *née* Murphy; *b* 23 March 1928; *Educ* Ruskin Coll Oxford, St Catherine's Coll Oxford; *m* 1950, Irene Jones; 2 s, 2 da; *Career* former schoolmaster; Parly candidate (Lab & Co-op) Liverpool Garston 1951, MP (Lab & Co-op) Manchester Wythenshawe 1964–; PPS to: Min of Agric Fisheries and Food 1964–67, Lord Pres of the Cncl and ldr of House of Commons 1968–70; memb Gen Advsy Cncl BBC 1968–74 and 1983–; chm PLP Food and Agric Gp 1971–74 (vice chm 1970–71), Britain's first min for the disabled 1974–79; chm World Planning Gp appointed to draft Charter for the 1980s for disabled people worldwide 1979–80; oppn front bench spokesman: on social servs 1979–81 (and 1970–74), for the disabled 1981–92; chm: Co-op Parly Gp 1982–84, Anzac Gp of MPs and Peers 1982–; jt treas Br-American Parly Gp 1983–; piloted Chronically Sick and Disabled Persons Act 1970 through Parl as a private memb, also the Food and Drugs (Milk) Act 1970 and the Police Act 1972; first recipient of Field Marshal Lord Harding award for distinguished serv to the disabled 1971; Louis Braille Meml award for outstanding servs to the blind 1972; tstee of Crisis at Christmas and Earl Snowdon's Fund for Handicapped Students; chm Managing Tstees of Parly Contributory Pension Scheme and of House of Commons Members' Fund; chm Parly and Sci Ctee 1988–91, appointed to Select Ctee of Privileges 1994, pres Co-op Congress 1995; hon fell Manchester Metropolitan Univ 1990; hon assoc BVA 1982; *Books* Human Relations in Industry (1960), VAT: A Tax on the Consumer (1970), Parliamentary Scrutiny by Committee (1971); author of numerous publications on the problems and needs of disabled people; *Recreations* gardening, tennis, snooker and chess; *Style*— The Rt Hon Alfred Morris, AO, QSO, MP; ✉ House of Commons, London SW1A 0AA; 20 Hitherwood Drive, London SE19 1XB

MORRIS, Alfred Cosier; s of Stanley Bernard Morris (d 1970), of Anlaby, E Yorks, and Jennie, *née* Fletcher (d 1994); *b* 12 Nov 1941; *Educ* Hymers Coll Hull, Univ of Lancaster (MA); *m* 26 Sept 1970, Annette, da of Eamonn Donovan, of Cork, Ireland; 1 da (Jessica b 24 April 1980); *Career* articled clerk Oliver Mackrill 1958–63, co sec fin controller and dir various cos 1963–71, sr Leverhulme res fell in univ planning and orgn Univ of Sussex 1971–74, visiting lectr in fin mgmnt Univ of Warwick 1973, gp mgmnt accountant Arthur Guinness Ltd 1974–76, mgmnt conslt Deloitte Haskins & Sells 1976–77, fin advsr subsids of Arthur Guinness 1977–80, acting dir South Bank Poly 1985–86 (dep dir 1980–85), dir Bristol Poly 1986–92, vice chllr Univ of the W of England at Bristol 1992–; dir Bristol and West Building Society 1992–; chm: Bristol Old Vic 1992–94, Patrons of the Bristol Old Vic Ltd 1992–; advsr House of Commons Select Ctee on Educn Sci and Arts 1980–83, memb Higher Educn Quality Cncl 1992–94, memb Higher Educn Funding Cncl for Wales 1992–; tstee Bristol Cathedral; fell Humberside Coll; Hon DL Univ of Bristol; FCA 1963, FSS, FRSA; *Books* Resources and Higher Education (jt ed and contrib, 1982); *Recreations* windsurfing, sailing; *Style*— Alfred Morris, Esq; ✉ Park Court, Sodbury Common, Old Sodbury BS17 6PX (☎ 01454 319900); University of the West of England, Frenchay Coldharbour Lane Campus, Bristol BS16 1QY (☎ 0117 976 3994, fax 0117 976 3972)

MORRIS, Prof Alun Owen; s of Arthur Morris (d 1969), of Ruthin, and Jennie, *née* Owen; *b* 17 Aug 1935; *Educ* Brynhyfryd Sch Ruthin, Univ Coll of North Wales Bangor (BSc, PhD); *m* 1, 16 April 1960, Margaret Erina (d 1987), da of Rev William Jones, of Caernarfon; 1 s (Iwan b 1964), 2 da (Lowri b 1962, Angharad b 1971); m 2, 11 April 1992, Mary, da of Moses Jones, of Aberystwyth; *Career* prof UCW Aberystwyth 1969– (asst lectr 1959–61, lectr 1961–66, sr lectr 1966–69, vice princ 1986–90); London Mathematical Soc: memb Cncl 1974–78, jt ed 1983–88, vice pres 1993–94, treas 1994–; chm Higher Educn Section Jt Mathematical Cncl 1993–95, memb Mathematics Ctee UGC 1986–89, advsr to Univ Funding Cncl 1989–93; memb: London Mathematical Soc 1960, American Mathematical Soc 1962; *Books* Linear Algebra - An Introduction (1978, 2 edn 1982); *Style*— Prof Alun Morris; ✉ Hiraethog, Cae Melyn, Aberystwyth, Dyfed SY23 2HA (☎ 01970 623464); Department of Mathematics, University of Wales, Aberystwyth, Dyfed SY23 3BZ (☎ and fax 01970 622752)

MORRIS, Andrew Bernard; s of Samuel Cyril Morris, and Golda, *née* Berkowitz; *b* 16 Oct 1952; *Educ* Christ's Coll GS, Coll for the Distributive Trades (HND Business Studies); *m* 29 June 1976, Jennifer Amanda, da of late Arthur Leslie Maizner; 2 da (Amy Louise b 10 June 1979, Sophie Victoria b 5 Oct 1981), 1 s (Ben Oliver b 24 Sept 1987); *Career* apprentice rising to sales role City Industrial Ltd (family shopfitting co) 1973–76, jt md Jontique (City Industrial subsid) 1976–80, sales and mktg dir City Industrial Ltd 1981–85, md Business Design Centre 1989– (bd dir 1986–89); *Recreations* family, contemporary art, running, cycling, tennis, film, theatre, food and drink; *Style*— Andrew Morris, Esq; ✉ Business Design Centre Ltd, 52 Upper Street, London N1 0QH (☎ 0171 359 3535, fax 0171 226 0590)

MORRIS, HE Andrew James; s of John Albert Morris (d 1989), and Clara Gladys, *née* James; *b* 22 March 1939; *Educ* English Sch Nicosia Cyprus; *m* 9 Sept 1961, Ann Christine, da of Henry Healy; 2 s (Stephen Henry b b 5 May 1964, Graham Andrew b 26 Oct 1971); *Career* trainee Barclays Bank 1958–60, Royal Artillery 1960–64; HM Dip Serv: FO 1964–65, British Embassy Kuwait 1965–69, Mission in Salisbury 1969, British Embassy Sofia 1969–71, FCO 1971–73, British Embassy Muscat 1973–76, British Consulate-General San Francisco 1976–78, consul British Consulate-General Los Angeles 1978–82, FCO 1982–86, first sec/dep high cmmr Kabuna 1986–89, dep high cmmr Port Moresby 1989–93, high cmmr to Tonga 1994–; *Recreations* swimming, fishing, hiking; *Style*— HE Mr Andrew Morris; ✉ The Residency, British High Commission, PO Box 56, Nuku'alofa, Kingdom of Tonga; c/o Foreign and Commonwealth Office (Nuku'alofa), King Charles Street, London SW1A 2AH

MORRIS, Anthony; s of Francis Victor Morris (d 1964), and Winifred Morris, *née* Cooper (d 1978); *b* 2 Aug 1938; *Educ* Oxford Sch of Art (Dip in Design), Royal Acad Schs (David Murray scholar, Leverhulme scholar, RAS Cert); *m* 1970, Aileen Sybil, *née* Griffiths; *Career* portraitist; one man exhbn Medici Gall London 1981; RP 1971, NEAC 1994; *Commissions* Prof Myers in Bodelian Library 1964, Lord Perry of Walton 1970, The Hon Thomas Iremonger, MP 1973, Prof K P Liddelow 1986, Sir Sacheverll Sitwell, Bt, CBE, The Rt Rev David Halsey, Bishop of Carlisle 1989, Rev Kenneth Loveless, MBE, RNR 1993; *Recreations* painting and sculpture, classical music and opera, wildlife and conservation; *Style*— Anthony Morris, Esq, RP; ✉ Church House, Clodock, Longtown, Herefordshire HR2 0NY (☎ 01873 860267); c/o The Royal Society of Portrait Painters, 17 Carlton House Terrace, London SW1Y 5BD (☎ 0171 930 6844, fax 0171 839 7830)

MORRIS, Dr Anthony Isaac; s of Moshe Morris (d 1991), of Manchester, and Betty, *née* Harris (d 1977); *b* 18 Aug 1946; *Educ* Salford GS, Univ of Manchester (BSc, MSc, MB ChB, MD); *m* 16 Sept 1972, (Joan) Sheila, da of Eric Broadhurst (d 1970); 2 s (Daniel b 19 Feb 1976, David b 2 Aug 1978); *Career* sr house offr Manchester Royal Infirmary 1971–72 (house offr 1970–71), med registrar Whittington and UCH London 1972–74, lectr in med Univ of Manchester 1974–79, res fell in hepatology Univ of Pittsburgh USA 1978–79, sr lectr in med Univ of Liverpool 1979–85, conslt physician and gastroenterologist 1985–; chm: Henry Cohen House, Merseyside and Lancs Cncl on Alcoholism; vice pres Endoscopy Ctee Br Soc of Gastroenterology (educn offr Endoscopy Ctee); FRCP 1985 (MRCP 1972); *Books* ECG'S for Examinations (1975), Illustrated Case Histories in Gastroenterology (1994), Clinician's Manual on Gastro-Oesaphageal Reflux Disease (1994); *Recreations* sailing, music; *Style*— Dr Anthony Morris; ✉ 7 Cromptons Lane, Calderstones, Liverpool L18 3EU; 52 Link Unit, Royal Liverpool University Hospital, Prescot St, Liverpool L7 8XP (☎ 0151 706 3554)

MORRIS, Anthony Paul; QC (1991); s of Isaac Morris Morris (d 1966), and Margaret Miriam, *née* Hassan; *b* 6 March 1948; *Educ* Manchester GS, Keble Coll Oxford (MA); *m* 26 Sept 1985, Jennifer Morys (Jennie), da of Maurice George Foley (d 1962); 2 s (Guy b 1977, Charles b 1980); *Career* called to the Bar Gray's Inn 1970, recorder of the Crown Ct 1988; *Recreations* standing on the touch-line, making stripes; *Style*— Anthony Morris, Esq, QC; ✉ Peel Court Chambers, 45 Hardman Street, Manchester M3 3HA (☎ 0161 832 3791, fax 0161 835 3054)

MORRIS, Brian Robert; s of Robert Oliver Morris (d 1981), of Oswestry, Salop, and Phyllis Marian, *née* Larkin (d 1985); *b* 11 June 1941; *Educ* Haberdashers' Aske's, University of Aston (MSc); *m* 16 August 1968, Jane Anne, da of George Frederick Green; 2 s (Christopher Edward, Julian Alexander); *Career* gp personnel advsr Guest Keen and Nettlefolds Limited 1972–73, Cabinet Office HM Treasy 1974–82, dep head PM's Efficiency Unit 10 Downing St 1982–84, NZ State Servs Cmmn 1984–85, head of Superannuation Div HM Treasy 1985–86, chm W F Corroon Ltd (UK) 1994– (chief exec 1989–93), chief exec W F Corroon International 1993–; *Books* The European Community - A Guide for Business and Government (3 edn 1990); *Style*— Brian Morris, Esq; ✉ W F Corroon Ltd, Ten Trinity Square, London EC3P 3AX (☎ 0171 975 2810, 0171 975 2888)

MORRIS, Charles Evan Henry (Harry); CBE (1990); s of Thomas Silvan Morris (d 1981), of Swansea, West Glamorgan, and Mary Isobel, *née* Williamson (d 1992); *b* 7 May 1926; *Educ* Rugby, Clare Coll Cambridge (BA); *m* 1955, Mansil, da of Iorri Owen Martin; 2 s (Martyn b 1956, Stephen b 1959); *Career* RN 1947–49; The Steel Company of Wales: trainee and shift foreman 1949–52, asst to chief engr 1952–54, works engr 1954–56, chief devpt engr 1956–59, dep chief engr Steel Div 1959–62, gen mangr Iron and Steel Div 1964–66 (asst gen mangr 1962–64), dir ops 1966–67; tech md British Steel Corporation 1970–77 (dir-in-charge SCW Div 1967–70), pres and chief exec Ferrco Engineering Ltd (subsid of Co-Steel International) 1977–83, tech vice pres Co-Steel International Ltd 1983–85, chief exec Sheerness Steel Company plc 1985–91; chm: Kent Enterprise Agencies Ltd 1991–95, FEFC SE Region 1993–96; chm Ctee on Technol IISI 1975–77; memb: Cncl Nat Acad Awards, Gen Advsy Cncl BBC, Cncl IMechE, Cncl CBI; former pres: The Inst of Metals 1988–89, Br Ind Steel Prodrs' Assoc 1988; memb Cncl and vice pres: Iron and Steel Inst (until 1974), Metals Soc (until 1977); chm SE Region CBI, dep chm Kent TEC Limited until 1991; Liveryman Worshipful Co of Engrs 1990, Freeman City of London; Bessemer Gold Medal Inst of Metals 1992; FIM 1984, FEng 1988, FIMechE; *Recreations* golf, bridge, sailing, photography; *Clubs* Royal Over-Seas League; *Style*— Harry Morris, Esq, CBE, FEng; ✉ Old Forge House, Boughton Aluph, Ashford, Kent TN25 4JB (☎ 01233 643301, fax 01233 633390)

MORRIS, Rt Hon Charles Richard; PC (1978), DL (Gtr Manchester 1984); s of George Morris; *b* 14 Dec 1926; *Educ* Brookdale Park Sch Manchester; *m* 1950, Pauline, da of Albert Dunn, of Manchester; 2 da; *Career* served RE 1945–48; pres Clayton Lab Pty 1950–52, memb Manchester Corp 1954–64 (chm Tport Ctee 1959–62, dep chm Estab Ctee 1963–64), memb PO Workers Union (memb Nat Exec Cncl 1959–63); Parly candidate (Lab) Cheadle Div Cheshire 1959, MP (Lab) Manchester Openshaw Dec 1963–83; PPS to Postmaster-Gen 1964, asst Govt whip 1966–67, vice chamberlain HM Household 1967–69, treas HM Household (dep chief whip) 1969–70, PPS to Rt Hon Harold Wilson (when Ldr of the Oppn) 1970–74; min of state: DOE 1974, CSD 1974–79; oppn front bench spokesman and dep shadow ldr of the House 1981–83; chm Oldham and Rochdale Groundwork Tst 1983–, dep chm Ponti's Group Ltd 1987–, chm Covent Garden London GRE Tenants' Gp; *Style*— The Rt Hon Charles Morris, DL; ✉ 24 Buxton Rd West, Disley, Stockport, Cheshire (☎ 0166 376 2450)

MORRIS, Prof Christopher David; s of David Richard Christopher Morris, of Doncaster, and Ethel Margaret, *née* Back; *b* 14 April 1946; *Educ* Queen Elizabeth's GS Blackburn, Grey Coll Univ of Durham (BA), Worcester Coll Oxford (DipEd); *m* 21 July 1981, Colleen Elizabeth, da of William Batey; *Career* asst lectr in history and archaeology Hockerill Coll of Educn Bishops Stortford Herts 1968–72; Univ of Durham: lectr in archaeology Dept of Archaeology 1972–81, sr lectr 1981–88, reader in viking archaeology 1988–90; prof of archaeology Univ of Glasgow 1990–; memb Inst of Field Archaeologists 1984; FSAScot 1974, FSA 1981, FRHistS 1996, FRSE 1996; *publications incl* The Birsay Bay Project (Vol 1 1989, Vol 2 1996), Norse and Later Subsistence and Settlement in the North Atlantic (ed, 1992), The Viking Age in Caithness, Orkney and the North Atlantic (ed, 1993), Freswick Links. A Norse Settlement in Caithness (1995); *Recreations* opera, music, walking, skiing; *Style*— Prof Christopher Morris, FSA, FRSE; ✉ Department of Archaeology, University of Glasgow, 10 Professors' Square, Glasgow G12 8QQ (☎ 0141 330 4422, fax 0141 307 8044, e-mail CDM@ARCHAEOLOGY.GLA.AC.UK)

MORRIS, Rev David; MEP (Lab) South Wales West (majority 84,970); *Career* MEP (Lab): Mid and West Wales 1984–94, South Wales West 1994–; *Style*— Rev David Morris, MEP; ✉ 39 St James Crescent, Swansea SA1 6DR

MORRIS, David Edward Alban; s of Clifford Morris (d 1981), and Florence Irene, *née* Thomas; *b* 24 Aug 1935; *Educ* Shrewsbury, Univ Coll Oxford (MA); *m* 23 Sept 1972, Moira Louise, da of Dr Alfred William Callaghan; 2 s (William b 11 Sept 1974, Richard b 16 June 1977); *Career* ptnr KPMG Peat Marwick 1974–92, dir The Peninsular and Oriental Steam Navigation Co 1992–; FCA, FCT; *Clubs* United Oxford and Cambridge Univ, Hurlingham; *Style*— David Morris, Esq; ✉ 3 Spencer Hill, London SW19 4PA; P&O, Peninsular House, 79 Pall Mall, London SW1Y 5EJ (☎ 0171 930 4343)

MORRIS, His Hon Judge David Griffiths; s of Capt Thomas Griffiths Morris, and Margaret Eileen, *née* Osborne; *b* 10 March 1940; *Educ* Abingdon Sch, Kings Coll London (LLB); *m* May 1971, Carolyn Mary, *née* Miller; 1 s (Owen Thomas b January 1977), 1 da (Hannah Bethan b April 1975); *Career* called to the Bar Lincoln's Inn 1965, asst recorder 1979–84, head chambers Cardiff 1984–94 (local jr 1981–87, recorder 1984–94), circuit judge (Wales & Chester Circuit) 1994–; fndr memb: Llanmaes Community Cncl 1982–84, Llantwit Major Round Table, Llantwit Major 41 Club, Llantwit Major Rotary Club (pres 1984–85); sr vice pres Pontypool RFC 1993–; *Recreations* rugby union football, cricket, swimming, theatre, reading, gardening; *Clubs* Cardiff and County, United Services Mess Cardiff; *Style*— His Hon Judge David Morris; ✉ Bryn Hafren, Newport Rd, Castleton, Nr Cardiff, S Glamorgan CF3 8UN; 30 Park Place, Cardiff, S Glam CF1 3BA (☎ 01222 398421, fax 01222 3987245)

MORRIS, Prof David Lawson; s of John Lawson Morris, of Herefordshire, and Mary J E, *née* Lewis; *b* 28 May 1952; *Educ* Univ of Birmingham (MB ChB, MD), Univ of Nottingham (PhD); *m* 11 May 1974, Milja Katrina, da of Osmo Taito Vuori (d 1985), of Mantsala, Finland; 1 s (Christopher Lawson b 1979), 2 da (Maija Bronwen b 1975, Katherine Saija b 1976); *Career* res fell to prof M R B Keighly The Gen Hosp Birmingham 1980–83; Univ Hosp Nottingham: lectr 1983–86, sr lectr 1986–89, reader in surgery 1989; currently prof Dept of Surgery St George's Hosp Sydney; author of pubns on upper gastro-intestinal bleeding, chemotherapy of hydatid disease, hormonal control of gastro-intestinal cancer and treatment of liver metastases; memb Br Soc Gastroenterology, fell Surgical Res Soc, FRSTM&H; *Style*— Prof David Morris; ✉ Department of Surgery, St George Hospital, Kogarah, Sydney, New South Wales 2217, Australia

MORRIS, David Richard; s of Frederick George Morris, and Marjorie Amy, *née* Brown; *b* 25 July 1934; *Educ* John Lyon Sch, Imperial Coll London (BSc(Eng), ACGI); *m* 1961, Ann Carole, *née* Birch; 2 s, 1 da; *Career* graduate engrg apprentice D Napier & Son rising to divnl chief devpt engr and divnl gen mangr English Electric 1956–69, divnl gen mangr and div dir General Electric Co 1969–75, md subsid of Sears Holdings Plc 1975–80, dir Delta Group Plc 1984–88 (divnl md 1980–88), chm Northern Electric Plc 1989–; FIMechE, CEng, FRSA; *Recreations* sailing, golf, tennis; *Clubs* Northern Counties, Carlton; *Style*— David Morris, Esq

MORRIS, David Scott; s of John Hilary Morris (d 1994), of Bow Brickhill, Bucks, and Frances Deans, *née* Cooper (d 1995); *b* 20 Dec 1940; *Educ* Westmont Sch IOW, Royal Liberty GS Essex; *m* 23 Oct 1965, Jennifer Lois, da of Alan George Skinner (d 1986), of Pymble, Sydney, Australia; 1 da (Catriona Lucy Scott b 1967); *Career* admitted slr 1965; HM coroner: for Huntingdon 1987, for Bedfordshire 1992; pres: Milton Keynes and Dist Law Soc 1985–86, Beds Law Soc 1987–88; legal memb Mental Health Review Tbnl 1989; memb Law Soc, MInstD; *Recreations* travel, gardening, cycling, walking; *Clubs* Carlton; *Style*— David S Morris, Esq; ✉ The Old Vicarage, Granborough, Bucks (☎ 01296 670217); Ashton House, 495 Silbury Boulevard, Central Milton Keynes MK9 2AH (☎ 01908 662277, fax 01908 675667)

MORRIS, Dr Derek James; s of Denis William Morris, and Olive Margaret, *née* Collison; *b* 23 Dec 1945; *Educ* Harrow County GS, St Edmund Hall Oxford (MA), Nuffield Coll Oxford (DPhil); *m* 4 Oct 1975, Susan Mary, da of Walter Whittles; 2 s (Alastair Henry Whittles b 14 Nov 1981, Roderick William Tudor b 6 July 1984); *Career* research fell Centre for Business and Industl Studies Univ of Warwick 1969–70; Univ of Oxford: fell and tutor Oriel Coll and CUF lectr in economics 1970–, Sir John Hicks research fell 1991–92, reader in economics 1996–; economic dir NEDO 1981–84, dir and chm Oxford Economic Forecasting Ltd 1984–, dep chm Monopolies and Mergers Cmmn 1995– (memb 1991); visiting prof Univ of California Irvine 1986–87; memb Royal Economic Soc 1985; *Books* The Economic System in the UK (ed, 1977, 3 edn 1985), Industrial Economics: Theory and Evidence (1979), Unquoted Companies (1984), Strategic Behaviour and Industrial Competition (ed), Industrial Economics and Organisation (1991), State Owned Enterprises and Economic Reform in China 1979–87; also author numerous articles; *Recreations* skiing, badminton, watching rugby; *Clubs* Reform; *Style*— Dr Derek Morris; ✉ Oriel College, Oxford OX1 4EW (☎ 01865 276555)

MORRIS, Dr Desmond John; s of Capt Harry Howe Morris (d 1942), and Dorothy Marjorie Fuller, *née* Hunt (d 1996); *b* 24 Jan 1928; *Educ* Dauntsey's Sch Wiltshire, Univ of Birmingham (BSc), Univ of Oxford (DPhil); *m* 1952, Ramona Joy, da of Windsor Baulch, of Marlborough, Wiltshire; 1 s (Jason b 1968); *Career* zoological res worker Univ of Oxford 1954–56, head of Granada TV and Film Unit at Zoological Soc of London 1956–59, curator of mammals at Zoological Soc of London 1959–67, dir Inst of Contemporary Arts 1967–68, res fell Wolfson Coll Oxford 1973–81; TV series: Zootime (weekly, 1956–67), Life (fortnightly, 1965–67), The Human Race (1982), The Animals Roadshow (1987–89), The Animal Contract (1989), Animal Country (1991–96), The Human Animal (1994); one man (paintings) shows: London Gallery 1950, Ashmolean Museum Oxford 1952, Stooshnoff Fine Art London 1974, Quadrangle Gallery Oxford 1976, Lasson Gallery London 1976, Public Art Gallery Swindon 1977, Galerie d'Eendt Amsterdam 1978, Mayor Gallery London 1987, Shippee Gallery New York 1988, Keats Gallery Knokke 1988, Mayor Gallery London 1989 and 1991, Galerie Michele Heyraud Paris 1991, Public Art Gallery Swindon 1993, Mayor Gallery 1994, Public Art Galleries Stoke and Nottingham 1996; *Books* The Reproductive Behaviour of the Ten-spined Stickleback (1958), The Story of Congo (1958), Curious Creatures (1961), The Biology of Art (1962), Apes and Monkeys (1964), The Big Cats (1965), The Mammals, a Guide to the Living Species (1965), Men and Snakes (with Ramona Morris, 1965), Men and Apes (with Ramona Morris, 1966), Men and Pandas (with Ramona Morris, 1966), Zootime (1966), Primate Ethology (ed, 1967), The Naked Ape (1967), The Human Zoo (1969), Patterns of Reproductive Behaviour (1970), Intimate Behaviour (1971), Manwatching, a Field-guide to Human Behaviour (1977), Gestures, their Origins and Distribution (jtly, 1979), Animal Days (autobiography, 1979), The Soccer Tribe (1981), Inrock (fiction, 1983), The Book of Ages (1983), The Art of Ancient Cyprus (1985), Bodywatching, a Field-guide to the Human Species (1985), The Illustrated Naked Ape (1986), Catwatching (1986), Dogwatching (1986), The Secret Surrealist (1987), Catlore (1987), The Animals Roadshow (1988), Horsewatching (1988), The Animal Contract (1990), Animalwatching (1990), Babywatching (1991), Christmas Watching (1992), The World of Animals (1993),

The Naked Ape Triology (1994), The Human Animal (1994), The Illustrated Catwatching (1994), Bodytalk: a World Guide to Gestures (1994), Illustrated Babywatching (1995), Illustrated Dogwatching (1996), Catworld, a Feline Encyclopedia (1996); *Recreations* painting, archaeology; *Style*— Dr Desmond Morris; ✉ c/o Jonathan Cape, 25 Vauxhall Bridge Rd, London SW1V 2SA

MORRIS, Ernest John (Johnny); OBE (1984); s of Ernest Edward Morris (d 1951), and Fanny Collorick (d 1933); *b* 20 June 1916; *m* 1951, Sybil Eileen (d 1989), da of Charles Minett (d 1951); *Career* broadcaster; radio: Johnny's Jaunts, Around the World in 25 Years; TV: The Hot Chestnut Man, Animal Magic (ran for 21 yrs); concert performances incl several one-man operas (words by Johnny Morris, music by David Haslam, Douglas Coombes and Sidney Sager); *Recreations* singing, gardening, watching wildlife; *Style*— Johnny Morris, Esq, OBE; ✉ Hopgrass Barn, Bath Road, Hungerford, Berks RG17 0SL

MORRIS, (George) Eryl; *b* 16 Aug 1943; *Educ* LSE (BSc (1st Class) Economics), Harvard Business Sch (MBA); *m*; 1 da; *Career* Courtaulds plc: joined 1970, md International Red Hand Marine Coatings 1973–74 (commercial dir 1971, gen mangr 1972), chm and chief exec International Paint Bd 1984–87 (joined bd 1974–76, dep gp md 1976–78, gp md 1978–84), main bd exec dir 1981–, responsible for Films and Packaging 1987–92, responsible for devpt of Courtaulds in the Far East 1992–, memb Gp Exec 1986–, dep chief exec (Devpt) Courtaulds plc 1994–; non-exec dir: Manweb plc 1990–95, Courtaulds Textiles plc 1995–; FCA 1968; *Style*— Eryl Morris, Esq; ✉ Courtaulds plc, 50 George Street, London W1A 2BB (☎ 0171 612 1000, fax 0171 612 1500)

MORRIS, Estelle; MP (Lab) Birmingham Yardley (majority 162); da of Charles Morris, former MP, and Pauline Morris; *b* 17 June 1952; *Educ* Whalley Range HS, Coventry Coll of Educn; *Career* teacher Sidney Stringer Sch and Community Coll 1974–92, MP (Lab) Birmingham Yardley 1992–, oppn whip 1994–, oppn spokesperson on educn 1995–; cncllr Warwick DC 1979–91 (ldr Lab Gp 1982–89); *Style*— Ms Estelle Morris, MP; ✉ House of Commons, London SW1A 0AA (☎ 0171 219 3000, fax 0171 219 2170)

MORRIS, Frank; s of Michael Joseph Morris (d 1981), of Uttoxeter, Staffs, and Mary Agnes, *née* Lavin; *b* 13 July 1948; *Educ* St Joseph's Coll Stoke-on-Trent, Imperial Coll London (BSc, full colours, Union Gen Award for social activities); *m* 6 Sept 1969, Ann Jeanette, da of Robert McIlquham; 1 s (David John b 21 Jan 1972); *Career* asst exec engr PO Research Station Dollis Hill London 1967–74, exec engr PO Engineering 1974–79, design and devpt dir Kent Process Control Luton 1983–89 (design mangr 1979–83), associate director and manager of consulting practice Cambridge Consultants Ltd 1995– (divnl mangr 1989–94); govr The Highfield Sch Letchworth 1986– (chm of govrs 1988–95); assoc City and Guilds of London Inst, chartered electrical engr, MIEE, sr memb Instrument Soc of America; *Style*— Frank Morris, Esq; ✉ Cambridge Consultants Ltd, Science Park, Milton Road, Cambridge CB4 4DW (☎ 01223 420024, fax 01223 423373, car 0385 242257)

MORRIS, Gareth Charles Walter; s of Walter Henry Morris (d 1938), and Enid, *née* Payne (d 1981); *b* 13 May 1920; *Educ* Bristol Cathedral Sch, Royal Acad of Music; *m* 1, 1954 (m dis 1974); 1 da (Emily b 14 June 1955); m 2, 18 Dec 1975, Patricia Mary, da of Neil Murray (d 1990), of Romsey, Hampshire, and Sheila Murray; 1 s (Thomas Neil Gareth b 12 Oct 1976), 2 da (Mary Eleanor b 24 July 1978, Catharine Margaret b 13 Oct 1981); *Career* RAF 1939–45; prof RAM 1945–85; flautist; princ flautist Philharmonia Orch 1948–72, adjudicator GB and abroad, played at Coronation Westminster Abbey 1953; gave first British performances of works by Alwyn, Bowen, Gerhard, Ghedini, Honegger, Ibert, Jacob, Koechlin, Martin, Martinu, Piston, Poulenc, Prokofiev, Rawsthorne, Reizenstein, Roussel, Seiber and Wellesz; memb Cncl and chm Music Ctee RSA; govr RSM, tstee Loan Fund for Musical Instruments; memb RSM, FRAM 1950 (ARAM 1945), FRSA 1967; *Books* Flute Technique (OUP, 1991); *Recreations* antiquarian horology, books; *Clubs* Royal Over-Seas League; *Style*— Gareth Morris, Esq; ✉ 4 West Mall, Clifton, Bristol BS8 4BH (☎ 0117 973 4966)

MORRIS, Harvey James; s of Kenneth Montague Morris (d 1969), and Mary, *née* Hutchison (d 1992); *b* 3 April 1946; *Educ* Wilson's GS Camberwell, Queens' Coll Cambridge (BA, MA); *m* 1976 (sep 1991), Sarah Margaret Perry; 2 s (Jack b and d 1981, Joseph b 1983), 1 da (Rose b 1986); *Career* gen reporter: Walthamstow Guardian 1969–71, East Anglian Daily Times Ipswich 1971–72; sub ed Associated Press London 1972–73; Reuters 1973–86: news ed Latin America 1976–79, chief corr Teheran 1979–80, actg chief corr Beirut 1980, dip corr 1981–83, energy corr 1984, political corr 1984–86; The Independent 1986–: asst foreign ed 1986–88, Middle East ed 1988–90, dep foreign ed 1990–92, foreign ed 1992–94; ed Geneva Post Switzerland 1994–; *Style*— Harvey Morris, Esq

MORRIS, Hugh; s of Roger Morris, of Cowbridge, S Glamorgan, and Anne Morris; *b* 5 Oct 1963; *Educ* Blundell's, S Glamorgan Inst of Higher Educn; *Career* professional cricketer; Glamorgan CCC: debut v Leics 1981, awarded county cap 1986, capt 1986–89 and 1993–95, 250 first class appearances; England: 9 sch int matches, 5 Young England tests, 3 test matches (v W Indies Edgbaston/Oval and Sri Lanka Lord's 1991); rugby: formerly memb Aberavon RFC, Welsh Students cap v France 1984; off-season employment: coaching, journalism; *Recreations* music, travelling, golf, rugby; *Style*— Hugh Morris, Esq; ✉ Glamorgan CCC, Sophia Gardens, Cardiff CF1 9XR (☎ 01222 343478, fax 01222 377044)

MORRIS, Ingrid Mary; da of Robert W Morris, and Edith, *née* Bundy; *b* 10 Oct 1945; *Educ* Nat Cathedral Sch for Girls Washington DC, Herts and Essex HS Bishop's Stortford, Architectural Assoc Sch of Architecture (AADipl, SADG); *m* 1 s (Vasiles b 1981); *Career* architect; estab Bone and Morris private practice with Jeanne Bone 1976 (formerly with McNab and Jamieson 1968–69, Piano and Rogers 1972–74); former memb Co of Women in Architecture 1974–76; visiting lectr: Royal Univ of Malta 1974–77, Univ of Queensland 1982; hon librarian and memb Cncl Architectural Assoc 1985–97, RIBA rep on ARCUK Educn Ctee 1987, RIBA assessor RIBA Housing Awards Northern Region 1988, external examiner Architectural and Engrg degree course Univ of Westminster 1993–95; memb AA, RIBA; *Recreations* swimming, skiing, painting; *Clubs* Arts, Architecture, Chelsea Arts; *Style*— Miss Ingrid Morris; ✉ 37 Mossop St, London SW3 2NB (☎ 0171 589 8535); Bone and Morris, 66 Ravenscourt Road, London W6 0UG (☎ 0181 741 9926, fax 0181 563 0015)

MORRIS, Jack Anthony; s of Samuel Cyril Morris, of London, and Golda, *née* Berkovitch, of London; *b* 23 June 1956; *Educ* Christ's Coll GS; *m* 1 Nov 1983, Susan Anne, da of Harry Lee, of London; 1 da (Emily Kate b 14 May 1985), 2 s (Robert Edward b 27 May 1987, Harry Samuel b 18 March 1993); *Career* chm: The Business Design Centre London 1992– (dep chm 1985–91), City Industrial Ltd 1992– (dep chm 1985–91), North London Area CBI 1994– (memb London Region Cncl 1993–); tstee: The Morris Charitable Tst 1989–, Islington Building Preservation Tst 1996–; special advsr to Bd City and Inner London North TEC 1993–95, govr North London Coll 1992–94, chm City & Islington Coll 1996– (vice chm 1994–96); FInstD 1988; *Recreations* cycling, classical cinema and film music, piano, charity work; *Style*— Jack Morris, Esq; ✉ The Business Design Centre, Upper St, Islington Green, London N1 0QH (☎ 0171 359 3535, fax 0171 226 0590)

MORRIS, Dr Jackie Evelyn; da of Prof Norman Morris, *qv*, and Lucy, *née* Rivlin; *b* 26 June 1948; *Educ* Camden Sch for Girls London, St Mary's Hosp Med Sch Univ of London (MB BS, MRCP); *m* 1974, Dr Martin Howard Seifert, *qv*; 1 da (Victoria b 1975), 1 s (Benjamin b 1978); *Career* house appts St Mary's Hosp and Hillingdon Hosp Uxbridge, subsequently SHO (rotation med) Central Middx Hosp 1972–74, med registrar St Mary's Hosp Paddington 1974–75, pt/t sr registrar in geriatric med UCH London 1975–79; conslt physician: St Mary's Hosp Med Sch 1979–85, Royal Free Hosp Med Sch 1985– (seconded Dept of Health 1992–94); Frohlich visiting prof UCLA 1987; hon dep sec and sec Br Geriatric Soc 1984–89, hon sec Geriatrics and Gerontology Section RSM 1991–94 (pres 1996–), pres Central London Branch Parkinson's Disease Soc 1991–, chm Age Concern London 1994–; memb Editorial Bd: Br Jl of Hosp Med 1984–90, RSM Jl 1992–; examiner RCP Dip in Geriatric Med 1996–; memb: Disability Living Allowance Bd 1994–95, Arthritis Care Services Ctee 1994–95; FRCP 1990; articles on community problems of elderly people; *Recreations* reading, friends, music, children, husband; *Style*— Dr Jackie Morris; ✉ 45 Whitehall Park, London N19 3TW (☎ 0171 281 0400); Royal Free Hospital, Pond Street, London NW3 (☎ 0171 794 0500)

MORRIS, James Shepherd; s of Thomas Shepherd Morris (d 1985), and Johanna Sime, *née* Malcolm (d 1985); *b* 22 Aug 1931; *Educ* Daniel Stewart's Coll Edinburgh, Edinburgh Sch of Architecture (DipArch), Univ of Pennsylvania (MLA); *m* 27 June 1959, Eleanor Kenner, da of Lawrence Meredith Clemson Smith, OBE; 2 s (Malcolm b 2 Aug 1962, Houston b 7 March 1966), 1 da (Alexandra b 28 Aug 1969); *Career* Nat Serv 2 Lt RE 1957–59; ptnr Morris and Steedman Architects Edinburgh; clients incl: Univ of Edinburgh, Univ of Strathclyde, Princess Margaret Rose Hosp, Countryside Cmmn for Scotland; watercolour artist (exhibited RSA); chm Fellowship Ctee RIAS 1985–87; memb Cncl: RIAS, Edinburgh AA 1969–71, Royal Scottish Academy 1990 (hon treas 1991–); memb Br Arts Cncl London 1973–80, tstee Nat Museum of Antiquities 1980–86, vice chm Scottish Arts Cncl 1970–80 (chm Art Ctee 1976–80); British Steel award 1971, RIBA award 1974, Euro Architectural Heritage award 1975, Euro Heritage Business and Indust award 1975, 9 Civic Tst awards 1962–90; RSA 1989, ARSA 1975, FRIAS, ALI, ARIBA; *Publications* author of various articles in RIBA Jls; *Recreations* golf, tennis, skiing, painting, hillwalking; *Clubs* New (Edinburgh), Philadelphia Cricket (Philadelphia), Valderrama (Spain); *Style*— James Morris, Esq; ✉ Morris and Steedman, 38 Young Street Lane North, Edinburgh EH2 4JD (☎ 0131 226 6563, fax 0131 220 0224)

MORRIS, (Catharine) Jan; *b* 2 Oct 1926; *Educ* Univ of Oxford (MA); *Career* author; memb Gorsedd of Bards Nat Eisteddfod of Wales; Hon DLitt: Univ of Wales, Univ of Glamorgan; hon fell Univ Coll of Wales Aberystwyth; FRSL; *Books* Venice (1960), Spain (1964), Oxford (1965), The Pax Britannica Trilogy (1973–78), Conundrum (1974), The Venetian Empire (1980), The Matter of Wales (1984), Last Letters from Hav (1985), Among the Cities (1985), Manhattan '45 (1987), Hong Kong (1988), Pleasures of a Tangled Life (1989), Sydney (1992), O Canada! (1992), A Machynlleth Triad (1993), Fisher's Face (1995); The Oxford Book of Oxford (ed, 1978), Travels with Virginia Woolf (ed, 1993); 6 books of collected travel essays; *Style*— Ms Jan Morris, FRSL; ✉ Trefan Morys, Llanystumdwy, Gwynedd, Wales (☎ 01766 522222, fax 01766 522426)

MORRIS, Dr Jean Daveena Ogilvy; CBE (1989, MBE 1973); da of the Rev David Porter Howie (d 1973), of Kilmarnock, and Veena, *née* Christie (d 1955); *b* 28 Jan 1929; *Educ* Kilmarnock Acad, Univ of St Andrews (MA, MEd); *m* 3 Sept 1952, William James, s of William John Morris (d 1958), of Cardiff; 1 s (David b 1960); *Career* clinical psychologist: Royal Hosp for Sick Children Edinburgh 1950–52, St David's Hosp Cardiff 1952–53; conslt clinical psychologist Quarrier's Homes Bridge of Weir Renfrewshire 1971–87; cncllr and bailie Peterhead Town Cncl 1959–67, cncllr Aberdeen CC 1962–67; memb Abbeyfield Society Scotland Ltd 1967–89, chm BBC and ITV Appeals Ctee for Scot 1967–73, chm Parole Bd for Scot 1980–92 (memb 1974–92), vice chm TSB Scot Fndn 1986–94, chm Scotia House Development Co Glasgow 1986–, memb Scot Advsy Bd Abbey National plc 1986–92, chm Abbeyfield Glasgow Society Ltd 1992–; memb: Ct Univ of St Andrews 1994– (vice pres 1995–), Scot Criminal Justice Forum 1996–; Parly cmmr 1985–; Hon LLD: Dundee 1993, St Andrews 1994; OStJ 1989; *Recreations* swimming; *Clubs* New (Edinburgh), Royal Scottish Automobile (Glasgow); *Style*— Dr Jean Morris, CBE; ✉ 94 St Andrews Drive, Glasgow G41 4RX (☎ 0141 427 2757); Scotia House Ltd, 15a Woodside Crescent, Glasgow G3 7UL (☎ 0141 332 5792)

MORRIS, Jennifer Ann; *Educ* Univ of Wales Cardiff (BA); *Career* teaching 1962–, head of dept 1964, head of faculty 1966, dep head Fareham Sch Rugby, dep head Ashlawn Sch Rugby 1985, headteacher Southfield Sch Kettering 1988–; co-operated devpt of student-teacher assessment with educn dept Univ of Warwick 1977, memb Steering Ctee for devpt of INSET LEA 1979, liaised with LEA offrs to develop numerous educnl programmes; author of numerous articles on educn; memb Standing Advsy Ctee for Grant Maintained Schs 1991–94, chair Personnel Sub-Ctee Standing Advsy Ctee 1992–94, pres Northants Assoc of Heads of Grant Maintained Schs 1993–; *Style*— Mrs Jennifer Morris; ✉ Fox Hollow, Eaglesfield, Norton, Northants NN11 5XN; Southfield School for Girls, Lewis Road, Kettering NN15 6HE

MORRIS, Rt Hon John; PC (1970), QC (1973), MP (Lab) Aberavon (majority 21,310); s of D W Morris, of Talybont, Cardiganshire; *b* 1931; *Educ* Ardwyn Aberystwyth, Univ Coll of Wales Aberystwyth, Gonville and Caius Cambridge, Acad of Int Law The Hague; *m* 1959, Margaret, da of Edward Lewis, OBE, JP, of Llandysul; 3 da; *Career* served Royal Welch Fusiliers and Welch Regt; called to the Bar Gray's Inn 1954, legal advsr Farmers' Union of Wales, recorder of the Crown Court SE Circuit 1982–; MP (Lab) Aberavon 1959–, Parly sec Miny of Power 1964–66, jt Parly sec for tport 1966–68, min for defence (equipment) 1968–70, sec of state for Wales 1974–79, oppn spokesman on legal affrs and shadow attorney-gen 1979–81 and 1983–; memb: UK Delgn Consultative Assembly Cncl of Europe and WEU 1963–64, N Atlantic Assembly 1970–74; Hon LLD Univ of Wales 1983; *Style*— The Rt Hon John Morris, QC, MP; ✉ House of Commons, London SW1A 0AA

MORRIS, John Edward; s of George Edward Morris, and Jean, *née* Pennance; *b* 1 April 1964; *Educ* Shavington Comp Sch Cheshire, Dane Bank Coll of Further Education; *m* 30 Sept 1990, Sally Ann, da of Patrick Walter Fish; 1 s (Thomas Edward b 27 June 1991); *Career* professional cricketer; Derbyshire CCC 1982–94 (awarded county cap 1986), joined Durham CCC 1994–; Griqualand West SA off-season 1988–89 and 1993–94; England: Test match debut v India Lord's 1990, played in all 3 Tests v India 1990, memb tour Aust and NZ 1990–91, played eight one day internationals; Refuge Assurance League winners Derbyshire 1990, winner Benson and Hedges Cup 1993; youngest player ever to score 100 in the history of Sunday League Cricket; *Recreations* fly fishing, golf, avid sports watcher; *Style*— John Morris, Esq; ✉ c/o Durham CCC, County Ground, Riverside, Chester-le-Street, Co Durham DH3 3QR

MORRIS, Prof John Llewelyn; s of John Noel Morris, of Tonyrefail, and Myfanwy Jones, *née* Moss Davies; *b* 19 Sept 1943; *Educ* Tywyn Secdy Sch, Univ of Leicester (BSc), Univ of St Andrews (PhD); *m* 11 Sept 1965, Sylvia Eileen, da of William Lloyd Williams (d 1961), and Rachel, *née* Jones (d 1966); 2 s (Jamie b 15 June 1966, Jules b 13 Nov 1970), 1 da (Rachel b 28 March 1969); *Career* Univ of Dundee: NCR post-doctoral fell 1967–69, lectr in computer sci 1969–75, prof 1986–; Waterloo Univ: visiting assoc prof 1973–74, assoc prof 1975–83, prof 1983–86; FIMA 1972, CMath; *Books* Computers and Computing (with J R Rushforth, 1973), Computational Methods in Elementary Numerical Analysis (1983); *Recreations* squash, hill walking, music, reading; *Style*— Prof John Morris; ✉ Mathematics & Computer Science Department, University of Dundee, Dundee, Scotland (☎ 01382 223181, fax 01382 201604, telex 76293)

MORRIS, John Michael Douglas; s of Charles Edward Douglas Morris (d 1988), of Northampton, and Mary Kathleen, *née* Murphy (d 1986); *b* 10 Aug 1935; *Educ* Dulwich, John Fisher Sch; *m* 5 June 1958, Jill Margaret, da of Wilfred John Walker (d 1962), of

Northampton; 2 s (Matthew b 1964, Robert b 1968), 2 da (Nicola (Mrs Kilpin) b 1959, Joanne (Mrs Gooding) b 1961); *Career* Nat Serv discharged due to injury 1957; reporter Northampton Chronicle and Echo 1953–60; sports sub ed Evening Standard 1960–67, gp sports ed Utd Newpapers 1967–77, freelance writer and publican 1977–79, ran sports freelance agency Northampton 1979–86, gen sec Br Boxing Bd of Control 1986– (admin steward 1981–86); former chm and hon sec Br Boxing Writers Club, memb Bd of Govrs World Boxing Cncl 1986–; co sec European Boxing Union Ltd 1992–; *Books* Sports biographies: Come in No 3 (1977), Box On (1984); Play Better Tennis; *Recreations* amateur acting, reading; *Style*— John Morris, Esq; ✉ 1 Parkside, 14 Court Downs Road, Beckenham, Kent BR3 6TN; British Boxing Board of Control, Jack Petersen House, 52a Borough High Street, London SE1 1XW (☎ 0171 403 5879, fax 0171 378 6670)

MORRIS, Judith Anne; da of Harold Morris (d 1986), of London, and Eve, *née* Sutton; *b* 23 Aug 1948; *Educ* Buckingham Gate Sch, Camden HS for Girls, City Univ London (BSc, MSc); *Career* sr sessional optometrist Contact Lens Dept Moorfields Eye Hosp London 1971–94, dir Inst of Optometry London 1991– (sr lectr 1983–91); pres Br Contact Lens Assoc 1983–84 (ed jl of Br Contact Lens Assoc 1984–89), memb Lambeth Southwark and Lewisham FPC 1988–90, pres Br Coll of Optometrists 1989–90 (cncl memb and examiner 1980–); Freeman City of London 1972, Liveryman Worshipful Co of Spectacle Makers 1992; fell Br Coll of Optometrists 1971; *Recreations* theatre, ballet, bridge; *Style*— Miss Judith Morris; ✉ 9 Cosway St, London NW1 5NR (☎ 0171 724 1176); The Institute of Optometry, 56 Newington Causeway, London SE1 (☎ 0171 407 4183)

MORRIS, (Robert) Leslie; s of Lt-Col John Douglas Leslie Morris, OBE (d 1994), of Melton Constable, Norfolk, and Doris Mabel, *née* Young; *b* 16 Sept 1939; *Educ* Felsted; *m* 10 Aug 1963, Maureen Iris, da of Edward Day; 1 s (David Leslie b 1967), 1 da (Lynda Leslie b 1965); *Career* CA 1963, articled clerk Grant Thornton (formerly Thornton Baker), asst accountant Williams Harvey Ltd 1965–67, chief accountant A King & Sons Ltd 1967–70, Glaciator Ltd 1970–74, co sec Cresswell & Williamson Ltd 1974–83, self-employed CA 1983–88, ptnr Harris Kafton 1988–; FCA 1963, ATII 1963; *Recreations* sea and freshwater angling, backstage local operatic soc; *Clubs* Fakenham Angling, Fakenham Operatic; *Style*— R Leslie Morris, Esq; ✉ Old White Horse, Briningham, Melton Constable, Norfolk NR24 2PY (☎ 01263 860 514); Harris Kafton, 1 Royal Oak Chambers, Fakenham, Norfolk NR21 9DY (☎ 01328 851306)

MORRIS, Mali; *b* 5 Feb 1945; *Educ* Sir Hugh Owen GS Caernarfon, John Bright GS Llandudno, Univ of Newcastle upon Tyne (Hatton scholarship in painting, BA), Univ of Reading (MFA); *Career* artist; sr lectr Chelsea Sch of Art, fifteen solo shows since 1979; gp exhibitions incl: Summer Show 3 (Serpentine Gallery) 1977, Whitechapel Open 1983, 1985, 1986, 1988, 1992 and 1994, Athena Awards (Barbican) 1988, John Moores (Walker Art Gallery Liverpool) 1980 and 1989, Colour in Modern Painting (Stoke-on-Trent) 1990, Contemporary British Painting (BC Canada) 1991, British Abstraction (Flowers East) London 1994 and 1996; int shows: France, Luxembourg, Netherlands, Cyprus, USA, Eastern Europe, Canada, Brazil, Botswana; public collections incl: Arts Cncl of GB, Br Cncl, Contemporary Art Soc, Northern Arts, Welsh Arts Cncl, The Whitworth Art Gallery Manchester, Lloyd's of London, Nat Museum Gaborone; *Awards* Arts Cncl Award 1976, GLAA Major Award 1979, Elephant Tst Award, Univ of Reading Res Award 1983, Lorne Award 1994–95; *Style*— Mali Morris; ✉ c/o Francis Graham-Dixon Gallery, 17–18 Great Sutton St, London EC1V ODN (☎ 0171 250 1962, fax 0171 490 1069)

MORRIS, Margaret Faith; da of Claud Morris, of Penzance, Cornwall, and Patricia Morris; *b* 4 Nov 1955; *Educ* Laban Centre for Movement & Dance (BA), Principia Coll USA, Queens Coll London; *Career* dancer/performer Murray Louis Dance Co 1976–90; dance teacher 1978–96: Laban Centre, London Contemporary Dance Sch, Coker Colls USA, Transitions Dance Co, Diversions Dance Co, Phoenix Dance Co; choreographer/dir 1980–96: Institute Theatre Co 1980, Transitions Dance Co 1985, various films and theatre; mgmnt conslt 1989–90: Alta Associates, Shapiro & Smith Dance NY, Nikolais and Louis Dance; writer various jls 1986–96; artistic dir Phoenix Dance Company 1991–; dir Bonnie Bird Choreography Fund, govr Northern Sch of Contemporary Dance, artistic advsr Transitions Dance Co; memb: Accreditation Team Cncl for Dance Educn and Trg, Equity (USA), American Guild of Musical Artists (AGMA), Dance Critics Assoc; *Awards* New Choreographers Award, Gulbenkian Rockefeller Fndn Award; *Recreations* singing, scuba-diving; *Style*— Ms Margaret Morris; ✉ Phoenix Dance Company, 3 St Peter's Buildings, St Peter's Square, Leeds LS9 8AH (☎ 0113 242 3486, fax 0113 244 4736)

MORRIS, Michael Charles; OBE (1992); s of Charles Edward Morris (d 1975), and Elspeth Mary, *née* Wright; *b* 21 Sept 1934; *Educ* Neston County Secdy Sch, Birkenhead Tech Coll (ONC, HNC); *m* 22 Feb 1958, Ann Rosina, da of late John Arthur Jones; 2 s (David Philip b 1959, Richard John b 1960), 2 da (Leslie Jayne b 1962, Kathryn Ann b 1973); *Career* Nat Serv RAF 1957–59; mgmnt trainee Morgan Refractories Ltd 1959–60 (apprentice 1950–57), project engr Nuclear Physics Res Laboratory Univ of Liverpool 1960–64, engr Nat Inst for Res in Nuclear Sci (NIRNS) Daresbury Laboratory 1964–82 (NIRNS became part of SERC 1965), project mangr and dep dir Royal Greenwich Observatory SERC 1982–90, assoc dir technology and chief engr Rutherford Appleton Laboratory SERC 1990–94 (became EPSRC April 1994); memb Engrg Res Cmmn SERC 1991–94; ret; FIMechE 1978 (MIMechE 1961), FRSA 1989, FEng 1994; *Recreations* yachts and yachting; *Style*— Michael Morris, Esq, OBE, FEng; ✉ Badgers, Selmeston, Polegate, East Sussex BN26 6UA (☎ 01323 811562)

MORRIS, 3 Baron (UK 1918); Michael David Morris; er twin s of 2 Baron Morris (d 1975), and Jean Beatrice, *née* Maitland-Makgill-Crichton (d 1989, having m 2, Baron Salmon (Life Peer)); *b* 9 Dec 1937; *Educ* Downside; *m* 1, 1959 (m dis 1962), Denise Eleanor, da of Morley Richards; m 2, 1962 (m dis 1969), Jennifer, da of Tristram Gilbert; 2 da; m 3, 1980, Juliet Susan, twin da of Anthony Buckingham; 2 s, 1 da (Hon Lucy Juliet b 18 June 1981); *Heir* s, Hon Thomas Anthony Salmon Morris b 2 July 1982; *Career* sits as Conservative in House of Lords; FICA; *Style*— The Rt Hon Lord Morris; ✉ 8 Carlos Place, London W1 (☎ 0171 499 2807)

MORRIS, Rt Hon Michael Wolfgang Laurence; PC (1994), MP (C) Northampton South (majority 16,973); s of late Cyril Laurence Morris; *b* 25 Nov 1936; *Educ* Bedford Sch, St Catharine's Coll Cambridge (MA); *m* 1960, Ann Phyllis, da of Percy Appleby (d 1973); 2 s (Julian b 1961, Jocelyn b 1972), 1 da (Susannah b 1965); *Career* Nat Serv pilot offr RAF and NATO Wings; dir Benton & Bowles (advertising agency) 1971–81, fndr AM Int Public Affrs Conslts 1976–92; Parly candidate (C) Islington N 1966, MP (C) Northampton S Feb 1974–; PPS to Min of State NI Office 1979–81, memb Public Accounts Ctee 1979–92; former chm: Br-Sri Lanka Parly Gp, Br Singapore Parly Gp, Br Malaysia Gp, Br Burma Gp; vice chm Br-Indonsia Gp; treas: Br-Thailand Gp, Br-Asian Gp; memb: Cncl of Europe and Western Euro Union 1983–91, Speaker's Panel of Chairmen 1984–92; chm Ways and Means Ctee and dep speaker 1992–; chm Bedford Sch 1989– (govr 1982–); *Recreations* field sports, cricket, golf (former capt Parly Golf Soc), shooting, tennis, heritage, forestry, budgerigars; *Clubs* Carlton, George Row (Northampton), John O'Gaunt Golf, Port Stanley Golf, MCC, All England Lawn Tennis, Royal St George's Golf; *Style*— The Rt Hon Michael Morris, MP; ✉ Caesar's Camp, Sandy, Beds (☎ 01767 680388)

MORRIS, Nicholas Guy Ussher; s of Cdr Guy Philip Ussher Morris, DSC (d 1941), and Sybil Ernestine, *née* Lee; *b* 15 April 1940; *Educ* Charterhouse, Christ Church Oxford (MA); *m* 27 July 1963, (Charlotte) Susan Margaret, da of T L Wilkinson; 1 s (Richard b 1968), 2 da (Elizabeth b 1966, Katherine b 1971); *Career* Vickers da Costa 1962–65, Beecham Gp Ltd 1965–69, group sec H P Bulmer (Holdings) Ltd 1969–78, corp sec Br Shipbuilders 1978–82, gp sec Unigate PLC 1982–92, gp sec Glaxo Wellcome plc (formerly Glaxo Holdings plc) 1992–96, ret; chm Cncl Malvern Coll 1994–; *Recreations* family; *Style*— Nicholas Morris, Esq; ✉ Woodfield House, Oxford Road, Clifton Hampden, Oxon OX14 3EW (☎ 01865 407149)

MORRIS, Norma Frances; da of Henry Albert Bevis (d 1984), of Chadwell Heath, Essex, and Lilian Eliza, *née* Flexon (d 1993); *b* 17 April 1935; *Educ* Ilford Co HS, UCL (BA, MA, George Smith prize); *m* 14 July 1960, Samuel Francis Morris, s of Samuel Morris (d 1969), of Linden Gardens, London; 1 s (John Stephen b 1967), 2 da (Jane Albertine b 1965, Anne Caroline b 1970); *Career* TEFL Paris 1956–57, asst lectr Univ of Hull 1959–60; MRC: various admin appts 1960–76, estab offr 1976–78, head of accommodation and industl liaison 1978–84, head of fin 1984–89, admin sec 1989–95; visiting fell UCL 1995–; memb and dep chm Nat Biological Standards Bd; FRSA; *Recreations* canoeing, opera, edible fungi; *Style*— Ms Norma Morris; ✉ Department of Science and Technology Studies, University College London, Gower Street, London WC1E 6BT (☎ 0171 391 1328, fax 0171 916 2425, e-mail norma.morris@ucl.ac.uk)

MORRIS, Prof Norman Frederick; s of Frederick William Morris (d 1974), of Luton, Beds, and Evelyn, *née* Biggs (d 1971); *b* 26 Feb 1920; *Educ* Dunstable Sch, St Mary's Hosp Med Sch Univ of London (MB BS); *m* 2 June 1944, Lucia Xenia (Lucy), da of Dr Benjamin Rivlin (d 1964), of Stratford, London; 2 s (David, Nicholas), 2 da (Dr Jackie Morris, *qv*, Vanessa); *Career* Sqdn Ldr RAFVR (Med Section) 1946–48; res surgical offr East Ham Meml Hosp 1945–46 (dep res 1944–45), sr registrar Dept of Obstetrics & Gynaecology Royal Postgrad Med Sch 1950–53 (departmental reader 1956–58), sr lectr Dept of Obstetrics & Gynaecology Univ Coll Hosp 1953–56, prof of obstetrics and gynaecology Charing Cross Hosp Med Sch 1958–85, med dir IVF Unit Cromwell Hosp 1986–; dean Faculty of Med Univ of London 1971–76 (dep vice chllr 1974–80), dep chm NW Thames Health Authy 1976–80; sec gen Cwlth Health Fndn 1994; fndr and pres Int Soc of Psychosomatic Obstetrics and Gynaecology 1972–80; chm Br Soc of Psychosomatic Obstetrics and Gynaecology and Andrology 1988–94 (hon pres 1994–), Advsy Ctee to Cwlth Secretariat Health Devpt Programme 1990–; tstee and chm Scientific Ctee Little Fndn 1992–; hon memb: Societas Gynaecologa et Obstetrica Italica 1979, Aust Soc of Psychosomatic Obstetrics and Gynaecology 1981; fell RSM (pres Section of Obstetrics and Gynaecology 1979), FRCOG; govr St Paul's Sch for Boys and Girls 1975–90, treas Int Soc for the Investigation of Stress 1990–; *Books* The Baby Book (1953–90), Sterilisation of Men and Women (1976); *Recreations* travelling (preferably in the East), music, reading; *Clubs* Athenaeum; *Style*— Prof Norman Morris; ✉ Flat 3, The Etons, Eton Avenue, London NW3 3EL; Cromwell Hosp, Cromwell Rd, SW5 (☎ 0171 431 4626)

MORRIS, Paul Christopher Early; s of Christopher John Morris, of Kensington, and Alice Ruth, *née* Early; *b* 21 Sept 1950; *Educ* Westminster Abbey Choir Sch, Westminster, UCNW Bangor (BA); *m* 1991, Rosemary Kinross; 2 s (Nicholas Paul Makumbi b 16 Oct 1992, Benedict Patrick Mulira b 31 Oct 1994); *Career* organist and choirmaster Christ Church Llanfairfechan N Wales 1970–73; admitted slr 1978, ptnr Winckworth & Pemberton 1981– (asst slr 1978–81); slr: Southwark Diocesan Bd of Fin, London Diocesan Fund; registrar Diocese of Southwark, jt registrar Diocese of Leicester, chapter clerk Southwark Cathedral; hon slr St Luke's Hosp for the Clergy; Freeman City of London 1984; Liveryman: Worshipful Co of Wheelwrights 1984, Worshipful Co of Weavers 1993; *Recreations* music; *Clubs* Oriental; *Style*— Paul Morris, Esq; ✉ Winckworth & Pemberton, 35 Great Peter St, Westminster SW1P 3LR (☎ 0171 593 5000, fax 0171 593 5099)

MORRIS, Paul William; s of William Henry Morris (d 1987), of Bexhill-on-Sea, and late Norah, *née* Abbott; *b* 20 May 1942; *Educ* Downsmeade Sch Eastbourne; *m* 30 Jan 1965, Carole, da of William Joseph Cornelius Owden, of Tunbridge Wells; 2 s (Nicholas b 1967, Dominic b 1972), 2 da (Karen b 1969, Elizabeth b 1979); *Career* articled clerk HS Humphrey and Co Eastbourne, sr tax ptnr Binder Hamlyn (now part of Arthur Andersen Worldwide Orgn) 1983–96 (joined 1972), ret; Freeman City of London, Liveryman Worshipful Co of Painter Stainers; FCA (ACA 1966); *Recreations* cricket, tennis, walking, painting, art, theatre; *Style*— Paul Morris, Esq; ✉ c/o Binder Hamlyn, 20 Old Bailey, London EC4M 7BH

MORRIS, Prof Peter Edwin; s of Stewart Silvester Morris, and Doris Maud, *née* Wilson; *b* 13 Nov 1947; *Educ* Weston-super-Mare GS, Univ of Exeter (BA, PhD); *m* 17 Sept 1976, Priscilla Jane, da of Ronald Kelley, of Costa Di Vaghia, 20122 Quenza, Corse Du Sud, France; 2 da (Lucy b 1979, Susan b 1988); *Career* lectr in psychology Open Univ 1972–74, prof of psychology and personal chair Univ of Lancaster 1989– (lectr 1974–84, sr lectr 1984–89, head of Psychology Dept 1987–93); memb Exec Ctee Save Br Sci 1986–88; Br Psychological Soc: hon gen sec 1983–86, chm Scientific Affrs Bd 1988–89, pres elect 1989–90, pres 1990–91, vice pres 1991–92, chm Jt Ctee for Funding in Higher Educn 1991–; memb Experimental Psychology Soc, FBPsS, CPsychol, FRSA; *Books* Visual Imagery and Consciousness (jtly, 1983), Cognition in Action (1987, 2 edn 1994); ed: Aspects of Memory (1978), Practical Aspects of Memory (1978), Applied Problems in Memory (1979), Everyday Memory, Actions and Absentmindedness (1984), Modelling Cognition (1987), Practical Aspects of Memory: Current Research and Issues (2 vols, 1988), Aspects of Memory: The Practical Aspects (1992), The Psychology of Memory (3 vols, 1993), Theoretical Aspects of Memory (1994); *Recreations* fell walking, local history, bird watching, gardening; *Style*— Prof Peter Morris; ✉ Psychology Dept, Lancaster University, Lancaster LA1 4YF (☎ 01524 593885, telex 65111 Lancuf G, fax 01524 841710)

MORRIS, Hon (George) Redmond Fitzpatrick; s and h of 3 Baron Killanin, MBE, TD; *b* 26 Jan 1947; *Educ* Gonzaga Coll Dublin, Ampleforth, Trinity Coll Dublin; *m* 1972, Pauline, da of Geoffrey Horton, of The Lawns, Cabinteely, Co Dublin; 1 s (Luke), 1 da (Olivia); *Career* film prodr; *Style*— The Hon Redmond Morris; ✉ Doughty Cottage, Richmond Hill, Richmond, Surrey TW10 6RN

MORRIS, (Thomas) Richard; s of Capt Thomas Griffiths Morris, and Margaret Eileen, *née* Osborne; *b* 29 Oct 1945; *Educ* Abingdon Sch, Univ of Birmingham (LLB); *m* 18 Oct 1975, Vanessa Jane; 1 s (Nicholas b 30 April 1979), 1 da (Miriam b 12 Feb 1978); *Career* Lt 6 QEO Gurkha Rifles 1969–71, served Malaysia, Hong Kong, Nepal, India, Capt 6 Queens Regt (Vol) 1971–75; articled clerk Norton Rose Botterell & Roche London 1971–73, admitted slr 1974, ptnr D J Freeman & Co London 1987–91, estab T R Morris slrs 1991–; occasional contribs Estates Times Magazine, Architects Journal; ward clerk Ward of Bishopsgate London 1986–; Freeman City of London 1981, Liveryman Worshipful Co of Slrs 1981; memb Law Soc, memb Inst of Export; *Recreations* hockey, swimming, gardening; *Clubs* City Livery, Anglo-Portuguese Soc; *Style*— Richard Morris, Esq; ✉ Swn Aderyn, Sandisplatt Road, Maidenhead, Berks SL6 4NB (☎ and fax 01628 789827)

MORRIS, Richard Francis Maxwell; s of Maxwell Morris (d 1996), of Pulborough, W Sussex, and Freda, *née* Abelson (d 1981); *b* 11 Sept 1944; *Educ* Eton, New Coll Oxford (MA), Coll of Law London; *m* 1, 1974 (m dis 1978), Sarah Quill; m 2, 1983, Marian Sperling; 2 da (Harriet b 1984, Jessica b 1986); *Career* slr Farrer & Co 1967–71, dep head Sterling Banking Dept Grindlay Brandts Ltd 1971–75, gen mangr Corp Fin S G Warburg & Co Ltd 1975–79; Hodder & Stoughton Holdings Ltd: fin dir then md Educational & Academic Publishing 1979–89, jt md 1989–91; chief exec Associated

Board of the Royal Schools of Music 1993–; dir: Southern Radio plc (formerly Invicta Sound plc) 1984–92, The Lancet Ltd 1986–91; md Edward Arnold (Publishers) Ltd 1987–91; memb: Governing Body Kent Opera 1985–90, Exec Ctee Music Educn Cncl 1995–; fndr Almaviva Opera 1989; hon RCM; *Recreations* singing, golf, tennis; *Clubs* Athenaeum; *Style*— Richard Morris, Esq; ✉ Associated Board of the Royal Schools of Music, 14 Bedford Square, London WC1B 3JG (☎ 0171 636 5400, fax 0171 436 4520)

MORRIS, Prof Richard Graham Michael; s of Robert Walter Morris, of Old Harlow, Essex, and Edith Mary, *née* Bundy (d 1996); *b* 27 June 1948; *Educ* St Alban's Sch Washington DC, Marlborough, Univ of Cambridge (BA), Univ of Sussex (DPhil); *m* 18 May 1985, Hilary Ann, da of Ian D Lewis; 2 da (Louise Edith b 4 June 1988, Josephine Claire b 26 March 1991); *Career* Addison-Wheeler res fell Univ of Durham 1973–75, sr scientific offr British Museum 1975–77, res Science and Features Dept BBC TV 1977, lectr Univ of St Andrews 1977–86, prof of neuroscience and dir Centre for Neuroscience Univ of Edinburgh 1993– (reader 1988–93); MRC res fell 1983–86, visiting prof MIT 1991, Segerfalk lectr Univ of Lund 1991; memb: MRC Neurosciences Grants Ctee 1981–85, MRC Neurosciences Bd 1993–, Editorial Advsy Bd Trends in Neurosciences, Editorial Bd Learning and Memory, Experimental Psychology Soc (hon sec 1985–89), Brain Res Assoc (chm 1990–94), Euro Neuroscience Assoc, Euro Brain and Behaviour Soc; FRSE 1994; *Books* Parallel Distributed Processing: Implications for Psychology and Neurobiology (ed, 1990); *Recreations* sailing; *Clubs* Royal Yachting Assoc, Port Edgar Sailing; *Style*— Prof Richard Morris, FRSE; ✉ Centre for Neuroscience, University of Edinburgh, Crichton Street, Edinburgh EH8 9LE (☎ 0131 650 3518/4562, fax 0131 650 4579, e-mail r.g.m.morris@ed.ac.uk)

MORRIS, Richard Keith; s of John Richard Morris, and Elsie Myra, *née* Wearne; *b* 8 Oct 1947; *Educ* Denstone Coll Staffs, Pembroke Coll Oxford (MA, pres Univ Opera Club), Univ of York (BPhil music); *m* 1971, Jane Hilda, da of David Holmes Whiteley; 2 s (David Edward b 27 Feb 1972, Henry John b 23 July 1982), 1 da (Eva Judith Ann b 21 July 1974); *Career* res asst York Minster excavations 1971–74, res offr Cncl for British Archaeology 1978–88 (churches offr 1975–78), lectr Univ of York 1988–91, dir Cncl for British Archaeology 1991–, hon visiting prof Dept of Archaeology Univ of York 1995–; runner up Yorkshire Post Best First Book Award 1979, Educnl Film/Video for Archaeology Channel 4 Award 1988, Frend Medallist Soc of Antiquaries 1992; FSA 1982, MIFA 1986; *Books* Cathedrals and Abbeys of England and Wales (1979), The Church in British Archaeology (1983), Churches in the Landscape (1989), Guy Gibson (1994); *Recreations* writing, music, opera, aviation history; *Style*— Richard Morris, Esq; ✉ Council for British Archaeology, Bowes Morrell House, 111 Walmgate, York YO1 2UA (☎ 01904 671417, fax 01904 671384)

MORRIS, Sir (James) Richard Samuel; kt (1992), CBE (1986); s of James John Morris (d 1976), and Kathleen Mary, *née* McNaughton (d 1976); *b* 20 Nov 1925; *Educ* Ardingly Coll, Univ of Birmingham (BSc ChemEng); *m* 1958, Marion Reid, da of Dr James Sinclair; 2 s (Simon b 1960, Andrew b 1962), 2 da (Jane b 1963, Katherine b 1965); *Career* mil serv 1944–48, Capt Welsh Gds; Courtaulds Ltd 1950–78 (dir 1967–78), dir BNFL 1971–85, visiting prof of chem engrg Univ of Strathclyde 1979–87, chm and md Brown and Root (UK) Ltd 1980–92, chm UK Nirex Ltd 1989–; industl advsr Barclays Bank 1980–85; chm of cncl and pro-chllr Univ of Loughborough 1982–95; FEng 1977; *Recreations* gardening, farming, shooting; *Clubs* Athenaeum; *Style*— Sir Richard Morris, CBE, FEng; ✉ Breadsall Manor, Breadsall Village, Derby DE21 5LL (☎ 01332 831368)

MORRIS, Sir Robert Byng; 10 Bt (UK 1806), of Clasemont, Glamorganshire; s of late Percy Byng Morris, himself gs of Sir John Morris, 2 Bt (whose wife was Hon Lucy Juliana Byng, 7 and yst da of 5 Viscount Torrington); suc second cousin, Sir Cedric Lockwood Morris, 9 Bt, 1982; *b* 25 Feb 1913; *m* 1947, Christine Kathleen, da of Archibald Field, of Toddington, Glos; 1 s (Allan Lindsay), 3 da (Geraldine Ann (Mrs Thomas Millard) b 1948, Gillian (Mrs Jamieson) b 1950, Roberta Crystal b 1965); *Heir* s, Allan Lindsay Morris, b 27 Nov 1961, m 1986, Cheronne Denise, eldest da of Dale Whitford, of Goonhavern, Cornwall; 1 s (Sennen John b 5 June 1995), 1 da (Chelsea Alana b 29 Aug 1992); *Style*— Sir Robert Morris, Bt

MORRIS, Prof Robert John (Bob); *b* 12 Oct 1943; *Educ* Acklam Hall GS Middlesbrough, Keble Coll Oxford (BA), Nuffield Coll Oxford (DPhil); *m* Barbara Anne; 1 s (George b 1969), 1 da (Helen b 1971); *Career* Univ of Edinburgh: lectr in economic history 1968–80, sr lectr 1980–91, prof of economic and social history 1991–; FRHistS 1990; *Books* Cholera (1974), Class and Class Consciousness in the Industrial Revolution (1976), Class, Sect and Party 1820–1850 (1988), various other publications; *Recreations* growing vegetables; *Style*— Prof Bob Morris; ✉ Department of Economic and Social History, University of Edinburgh, William Robertson Building, George Square, Edinburgh EH8 9JY (☎ 0131 650 3834, fax 0131 650 3843)

MORRIS, Prof Robert Lyle; s of Robert Neil Morris, of Flagler Beach, Florida, and Lyal, *née* Bish; *b* 9 July 1942; *Educ* Crafton HS, Univ of Pittsburgh (BS), Duke Univ (PhD); *m* Joanna, da of John Du Barry (d 1984); 2 da (Lila b 1977, Vanessa b 1977); *Career* postdoctoral fell Center for the Study of Ageing and Human Devpt Duke Univ 1969–71, res co-ordinator Psychical Res Fndn 1971–74, lectr tutorial prog Univ of California at Santa Barbara 1974–80, lectr Sch of Social Sciences Univ of California at Irvine 1978–80, sr res scientist Sch of Computer and Info Sci Syracuse Univ 1980–85, Koestler prof of parapsychology Dept of Psychology Univ of Edinburgh 1985–; memb: Parapsychological Assoc 1967–, Soc for Scientific Exploration 1982–, Bd of Tstees Soc for Psychical Res 1985–92; *Books* Foundations of Parapsychology (jtly, 1986), Guidelines for Testing Psychic Claimants (jtly, 1995); *Style*— Prof Robert Morris; ✉ Psychology Department, University of Edinburgh, 7 George Square, Edinburgh EH8 9JZ (☎ 0131 650 3343, fax 0131 650 3461)

MORRIS, Robert Vernon; s of Harold Vernon Morris, MRCVS (d 1986), of Hereford, and Dorothy Agnes, *née* Foulkes (d 1994); *b* 27 May 1932; *Educ* St Mary's Coll Bitterne Park Southampton, LSE (LLB); *m* 19 Sept 1959, Patricia Margaret, da of Thomas Norman Trevor (d 1968), of Gloucester; 3 s (Nicholas b 1960, Timothy b 1963, James b 1965), 1 da (Sally b 1970); *Career* Nat Serv 1956–58, Intelligence Corps GCHQ Cheltenham; slr Supreme Ct 1957, sr ptnr Rowberry Morris Glos (and assoc offices); chm: Glos Legal Assoc 1985–88, Social Security Appeal Tbnl (Wales and SW) 1980–, Child Support Appeal Tbnls (Wales and SW) 1993–; pres Glos Rotary Club 1981–82, chm Glos Civic Tst 1983–, sec Glos Historic Bldgs 1980–; cdr St John Ambulance Glos 1988–94; chm Cncl Order of St John Glos 1994–, memb Chapter Gen Order of St John 1996–; KJStJ 1996 (OStJ 1986, CStJ 1991); memb Law Soc 1957; *Recreations* jogging, inner city conservation; *Clubs* St John House, LSE; *Style*— Robert Morris, Esq; ✉ The Hill House, Hartpury, Glos GL19 3DB (☎ 01452 700235); Morroway House, Station Rd, Glos GL1 1DW (☎ 01452 301903, fax 01452 411115, DX 7500 Gloucester)

MORRIS, Rear Adm Roger Oliver; CB (1990); s of Dr Oliver Nixon Morris (d 1983), of Plymouth, and Sybil Helga (Mollie), *née* Hudson (d 1973); *b* 1 Sept 1932; *Educ* Mount House Sch Tavistock, RNC Dartmouth; *Career* Cmd HM Ships: Medusa 1964–65, Beagle 1968–70, Fawn 1972, Hecla 1975–78, Hydra 1970–71 and 1979–80; RCDS 1978; dir of hydrographic plans and surveys in Hydrographic Dept Taunton 1980–82, asst hydrographer 1982–84, hydrographer of the Navy 1985–90; chm Cncl Soc for Nautical Res 1989–94; FRGS, FRIN; *Books* Charts and Surveys in Peace and War (1995); *Recreations* heraldry, opera, ornithology; *Clubs* Royal Cwlth Soc; *Style*— Rear Adm R O Morris, CB; ✉ Orchard House, Quantock View, Bishops Lydeard, Somerset TA4 3AW

MORRIS, Simon James; s of Kenneth Stapleton Morris, of Cape Town, and Grace, *née* Skitmore; *b* 24 Jan 1958; *Educ* Whitgift Sch, Gonville and Caius Coll Cambridge (MA); *Career* admitted slr 1982; ptnr Cameron Markby Hewitt 1988– (currently head of Fin Servs Dept); chm Cambridge Univ Cons Assoc 1979, memb Cncl London Topographical Soc 1983–; *Books* Financial Services: Regulating Investment Business (1989, 2 edn 1995); *Recreations* history of London; *Style*— Simon Morris, Esq; ✉ Cameron Markby Hewitt, 40 Tower Hill, London EC3N 4BB (☎ 0171 702 2345, fax 0171 702 2302)

MORRIS, Very Rev Timothy David; s of Joseph Ernest Morris (d 1991), of Galashiels, and Mabel Elizabeth Morris; *b* 17 Aug 1948; *Educ* King Edward VI Prep and Grammar Sch Bath, Coll of Estate Mgmnt Univ of London (BSc), Trinity Coll Bristol (CertTheol), DipTh (Bristol); *m* 1, 18 March 1972 (m dis 1987); 1 da (Fiona Ann b 15 Sept 1976); m 2, Irene Elizabeth, *née* Lyness; *Career* asst estate surveyor Miny of Public Bldg and Works Edinburgh 1972–75; ordained deacon 1975, priested 1976; curate St Thomas's Corstorphine Edinburgh 1975–77; rector: St James' Leith Edinburgh 1977–83, St Ninian's Troon 1983–85, St Peter's Galashiels 1985–; rural dean of Borders 1992–, dean of Edinburgh 1992–; assoc memb RICS 1974; *Recreations* rugby, cricket, gardening, travel; *Style*— The Very Rev the Dean of Edinburgh; ✉ The Rectory, Parsonage Road, Galashiels, Selkirkshire TD1 3HS (☎ and fax 01896 753118); The Diocesan Centre, Diocese of Edinburgh, 21 Grosvenor Crescent, Edinburgh EH12 5EE (☎ 0131 538 7033, fax 0131 538 7088)

MORRIS, Sir Trefor Alfred; kt (1996), CBE (1992), QPM (1985); s of Kenneth Alfred Morris (d 1984), and Amy Ursula (d 1992); *b* 22 Dec 1934; *Educ* Manchester Tech HS, Univ of Manchester (Dip in Criminology), Nat Exec Inst USA (Dip); *m* 22 March 1958, Martha Margaret, 2 da (Hazel Anne, Catherine Lindsay); *Career* served Army 1953–55; Manchester City Police then Manchester and Salford Police 1955–75; Gtr Manchester Police: Constable to Chief Supt, asst Chief Constable 1976–79; Chief Constable Herts Constabulary 1984–90 (dep Chief Constable 1979–84), HM Chief Inspr of Constabulary 1993–96 (Inspr Cambridge 1990–93); chm Police Information Technology Orgn 1996–; OStJ 1984, CIMgt 1986 (MIMgt 1974), FRSA 1993; *Recreations* golf, walking, music, gardening, wine; *Clubs* Royal Overseas, Welwyn Garden City Golf; *Style*— Sir Trefor Morris, CBE, QPM; ✉ Home Office, Horseferry House, Dean Ryle Street, London SW1P 2AW (☎ 0171 217 8925, fax 0171 217 8602)

MORRIS, Trevor John; s of Peter Morris, of E Grinsted, and Dorothy, *née* Haines; *b* 13 July 1955; *Educ* Drayton Manor GS, Univ of Exeter (BA); *m* 21 May 1982, Claire, *née* Laven; 2 da (Olivia b 27 Oct 1988, Flora b 22 August 1991); *Career* asst to mktg dir Fenwick of Bond Street 1977–79, mktg servs mangr OEM plc 1979–81; The Quentin Bell Organisation: campaign dir 1982–84, md 1984–; memb Mktg Soc; MIPR; *Recreations* reading, theatre, football; *Clubs* 2 Brydges Place, Peg's; *Style*— Trevor Morris, Esq; ✉ The Quentin Bell Organisation, 22 Endell Street, Covent Garden, London WC2H 9AD (☎ 0171 379 0304, fax 0171 379 5483)

MORRIS, Prof Trevor Raymond; s of Ivor Raymond Morris, CBE (d 1971), and Dorothy May, *née* Parker (d 1976); *b* 11 April 1930; *Educ* Rendcomb Coll, Univ of Reading (BSc, PhD, DSc); *m* 1, 17 April 1954, (Elisabeth) Jean, *née* Warren (d 1992); 3 s (Stephen b 1956, Jonathan b 1959, Andrew b 1962), 2 da (Wendy b 1957, Virginia b 1964); m 2, 4 March 1994, Mary, *née* Gillett; *Career* Nat Serv RASC 1954–56; prof Univ of Reading 1981– (lectr 1957–69, reader 1969–81); FIBiol 1974; *Style*— Prof Trevor Morris; ✉ Middle Nesley, 36 Shinfield Road, Reading RG2 7BW (☎ 0118 987 2529); University of Reading, Whiteknights, Reading RG6 2AT (☎ 0118 931 8470)

MORRIS, William (Bill); *b* 19 Oct 1938, Jamaica; *Educ* Handsworth Tech Coll; *m* Minetta (d 1990); 2 s (Garry, Clyde); *Career* TGWU: joined 1958, shop steward Hardy Spicers 1963–73, Nottingham/Derby dist organiser 1973–76, Northampton dist sec 1976–79, nat sec Passenger Servs Trade Gp 1979–86, dep sec 1986–92, gen sec 1992–; memb Gen Cncl and Exec Ctee TUC 1988– (chm Task Gp on Representation at Work, TUC Youth Ctee and TUC Regional Cncls Consultative Ctee), memb Exec Bd Int Transport Workers' Fedn 1994–, memb Cncl ACAS 1995–; past chm Conf Arrangements Ctee Lab Pty; memb: Cmmn for Racial Equality 1977–87, Prince of Wales Youth Business Tst 1987–90, Employment Appeals Tbnl 1988–, Economic and Social Affrs Ctee EC 1990–95; memb Gen Advsy Bd: IBA 1981–86, BBC 1987–88; memb governing cncls: Nene Coll, Luton Univ, Atlantic Coll; hon degrees: Southbank Univ, Open Univ, Leeds Metropolitan Univ; FRSA, FCGI; *Recreations* family life, walking, gardening, music; *Style*— Mr Bill Morris; ✉ Transport and General Workers' Union, Transport House, 16 Palace Street, Victoria, London SW1E 5JD (☎ 0171 828 7788, fax 0171 931 7258)

MORRIS, Very Rev William James; KCVO (1995), JP (Glasgow 1971); o s of William John Morris, and Eliza Cecilia Cameron Johnson; *b* 22 Aug 1925; *Educ* Cardiff HS, Univ of Wales (BA, BD), Univ of Edinburgh (PhD); *m* 1952, Jean Daveena Ogilvy, CBE, o da of Rev David Porter Howie, of Kilmarnock, Ayrshire; 1 s; *Career* ordained 1951; minister: St David's Buckhaven 1953–57, Peterhead Old Parish 1957–67; chaplain HM Prison Peterhead 1963–67; memb Convocation of Univ of Strathclyde, chm Cncl Soc of Friends of Glasgow Cathedral, minister of Glasgow Cathedral 1967–; chaplain: to HM The Queen in Scotland 1969–96 (extra chaplain 1996–), to the Lord High Cmmr to Gen Assembly of Church of Scotland 1975–76, to the Queen's Body Guard for Scotland (Royal Co of Archers); Dean of the Chapel Royal in Scotland 1991–96; memb: IBA Scotland 1979–84, Bd of Govrs Jordanhill Coll of Educn 1983–91; hon pres City of Glasgow Soc of Social Serv; hon memb: Rotary Clubs of Dennistoun and Glasgow, Royal Scottish Automobile Club, RNVR Club; chaplain Strathclyde Police; hon vice pres Glasgow Bn The Boys' Bde; pres Saint Andrew Soc (Glasgow); ChStJ; Hon LLD Strathclyde 1974, Hon DD Glasgow 1979, Hon FRCPS Glasgow; *Books* A Walk Through Glasgow Cathedral (1986); *Recreations* being a paternalistic do-gooder, gardening, sunbathing in SW France; *Clubs* New (Edinburgh); *Style*— The Very Rev William Morris, KCVO, JP; ✉ 94 St Andrews Drive, Glasgow G41 4RX (☎ 0141 427 2757, fax 0141 427 5253)

MORRIS-MARSHAM, Jack Richard; s of Richard Henry Anstruther Morris-Marsham (d 1975), of Spilfeathers, Ingatestone, Essex, and Iris Rose Sophia Blackburn, *née* Larking (d 1992); *b* 27 Nov 1936; *Educ* Eton; *m* 1, 7 Sept 1963 (m dis 1978), Agnes Margaret (Molly), da of Maj-Gen Walter Rutherfoord Goodman, CB, DSO, MC (d 1976), of Woodbridge, Suffolk; 2 s (James Jonathan b 1964, Dominic Rutherfoord b 1967), 1 da (Tiffany Jane b 1969); m 2, 30 June 1978, Ann Christine (d 1980), da of Howard Sarjent Backhouse (d 1990), of Storrington, Sussex; m 3, 28 May 1983, Serena Sybil, da of Gp Capt Geoffrey K Fairtlough (d 1992), of Ballybrittas, Co Leix; *Career* Lt Cdr RNR 1954–73; mktg dir BMW Concessionaires 1970–74; The Colt Car Co Ltd: mktg dir 1974–81, md 1981–82, vice chm 1982–94; dir Julius Rutherfoord & Co Ltd 1995–; *Recreations* bridge, shooting, snorkelling, gardening; *Clubs* Naval; *Style*— Jack Morris-Marsham, Esq; ✉ Brookside, Ewen, Cirencester, Glos GL7 6BU (☎ 01285 770555, fax 01285 770656)

MORRIS OF BALGONIE AND EDDERGOLL, Yr, Stuart Gordon Cathal; s of Raymond Stanley Morris of Balgonie and Eddergoll, and Margaret Newton Morris, *née* Stuart; matriculated arms (Morris of Balgonie & Eddergoll quartered with Stuart) Court of the Lord Lyon Edinburgh 1987; *b* 17 April 1965; *Educ* Bell-Baxter HS, Elmwood Coll, Univ of Birmingham; *Career* historian, armorist, author; fndr memb Scottish Castles Assoc, fndr memb Heraldry Soc of Scotland; Lt Col and ADC to HE the Govr of the State of Georgia; Liveryman Worshipful Co of Meadmakers 1982; FSA (Scot) 1983, FRSA 1990 (assoc 1986); Cdr Order of Polonia Restituta 1990; *Recreations* archery, heraldry, genealogy, mead making, historical researching, painting; *Style*— The Younger of Balgonie and Eddergoll; ✉ Balgonie Castle, by Markinch, Fife KY7 6HQ (☎ 01592 750119, fax 01592 753103)

MORRIS OF CASTLE MORRIS, Baron (Life Peer UK 1990), of St Dogmaels in the County of Dyfed; Brian Robert Morris; s of Capt William Robert Morris, RN (d 1964), of Cardiff, and Ellen Elizabeth, *née* Shelley (d 1977); *b* 4 Dec 1930; *Educ* Cardiff HS, Worcester Coll Oxford (MA, DPhil); *m* 18 Aug 1955, Sandra Mary, da of Percival Samuel James (d 1967); 1 s (Hon Christopher Justin Robert b 1959), 1 da (Hon Lindsay Alison Mary (Hon Mrs Boxall) b 1957); *Career* Nat Serv with 1 Bn Welch Regt 1949–51, 4 Bn Welch Regt (TA) 1951–56; fell Shakespeare Inst Univ of Birmingham 1956–58; lectr Univ of Reading 1960–65 (asst lectr 1958–60), sr lectr Univ of York 1967–71 (lectr 1965–67); prof of Eng lit Univ of Sheffield (becoming dep dean and public orator) 1971–80; princ St David's Univ Coll Lampeter 1980–91; chm: Lit Panel Yorks Arts Assoc 1973–77, UGC/NAB Working Pty on Librarianship and Info Sci 1986–87, Museums and Galleries Cmmn 1985–90 (memb 1975–), Cncl Prince of Wales's Inst of Architecture 1993–; vice pres: Welsh Advsy Ctee Br Cncl 1983–91, Cncl for Nat Parks 1985–, Museums Assoc 1985–87, Anthony Panizzi Fndn 1987–91, Prayer Book Soc 1990–, Arkwright Soc 1992–; pres: Welsh Historic Gardens Tst 1988–, W Wales Arts Assoc 1990–93, Brontë Soc 1996–; memb: Yr Academi Gymreig 1979–, Archbishops' Cncl on Evangelism 1971–75, Cncl Poetry Soc 1980–85, Nat Library of Wales 1981–91, Br Library Bd 1980–91, Welsh Arts Cncl 1983–86 (memb Lit Ctee 1978–86); tstee: Nat Portrait Gallery 1977– (vice chm 1993–), Nat Heritage Meml Fund 1980–91, Museum of Empire and Commonwealth 1991–, Campaign for the Protection of Rural Wales 1991–; dir Middleton Botanic Garden 1994–; gen ed: New Mermaid Dramatists 1964–82, New Arden Shakespeare 1974–82; Hon DLitt Univ of Sheffield 1991, Hon LLD Univ of Wales 1992; sits as Lab peer in House of Lords, oppn dep chief whip 1992– (oppn whip 1990–92), princ oppn spokesman on educn 1994–; *Books* The Poems of John Cleveland (with Eleanor Withington, 1967), John Cleveland: a Bibliography of his Poems (1967), New Mermaid Critical Commentaries 1 to 3 (1969–72), Mary Quant's London (1973), Ritual Murder (ed, 1980), Harri Webb (Writers of Wales series, 1993); *Edited Plays* Ford's The Broken Heart (1965), 'Tis Pity She's A Whore (1968), Tourneur's The Atheist's Tragedy (with Roma Gill, 1976), Shakespeare's The Taming of the Shrew (1981); *Poetry* Tide Race (1976), Stones in the Brook (1978), Dear Tokens (1987); *Recreations* music, mountains, museums; *Clubs* Athenaeum; *Style*— The Rt Hon Lord Morris of Castle Morris; ✉ The Old Hall, Foolow, Eyam, Via Sheffield, Derbyshire S30 1QR (☎ 01433 631186)

MORRIS OF KENWOOD, 2 Baron (UK 1950); Philip Geoffrey Morris; JP (Inner London 1967); s of 1 Baron (d 1954); *b* 18 June 1928; *Educ* Loughborough Coll Sch, Loughborough Coll; *m* 1958, Hon Ruth Joan Gertrude Rahle, da of Baron Janner (Life Peer); 1 s, 3 da; *Heir* s, Hon Jonathan David Morris; *Career* RAF: served 1946–49, rejoined 1951–55, flying offr 1953; *Style*— The Rt Hon the Lord Morris of Kenwood, JP; ✉ Lawn Cottage, Orchard Rise, Kingston, Surrey KT2 7EY (☎ 0181 942 6321)

MORRISH, Peter Jeffery; s of Charles Reginald Morrish, DSC, KPM, (d 1950), and Florence May, *née* Jeffery (d 1972); *b* 16 April 1927; *Educ* Peter Symonds' Sch Winchester, Univ of Edinburgh; *m* 12 April 1951, Norah Annette, da of Michael Devaney; 3 s (Peter Michael Jeffery b 2 April 1952, Philip Reginald Devaney Jeffery b 5 Oct 1956, Richard Mark b 16 May 1958); *Career* RN 1945–47, Met Police 1948–49, asst supt Northern Rhodesia Police 1950–61, flying offr RAF 1961–63; dep clerk Bow St Magistrates' Ct 1964, clerk of the Cts Co of London QS 1965, a clerk of the peace Lancs QS 1966–68, dep clerk of the peace Mddx QS 1968–70, dep clerk of the Central Criminal Ct under the City Corp of the City of London 1970–74, asst registrar Criminal Appeals Office Royal Cts of Justice 1974–78; called to the Bar Grays Inn 1962; head of chambers: 1 Hare Ct Temple 1985, Goldsmith Chambers Temple 1986–; Freeman City of London 1994; memb SE Circuit 1978, assoc memb Magistrates' Assoc 1966, memb Criminal Bar Assoc 1978; *Publications* Criminal Law Vol Halsbury's Laws of England (contrib, 4th edn), The Crown Court Index (with His Hon Judge Ian McLean, 16 edns 1972–92), The Magistrates' Court Index (11 edns 1976–92), The Trial of Breathalyser Offences (3 edns 1976–90), Forms of Indictment (with His Hon Judge Katkhuda, 1990); *Recreations* writing, drawing, walking and looking after three grandchildren from time to time; *Clubs* Norfolk, Wig & Pen; *Style*— Peter J Morrish, Esq; ✉ Goldsmith Chambers, Goldsmith Building, Temple, London EC4Y 7BL (☎ 0171 353 6802, fax 0171 583 5255)

MORRISON, His Hon Judge; Alexander John Henderson; s of Dr Alexander Morrison (d 1978), and Jean Walker Murdoch (d 1961); *b* 16 Nov 1927; *Educ* Derby Sch, Emmanuel Coll Cambridge (MA, LLB); *m* 1978, Hon Philippa Ann, da of 1 Baron Hives (d 1965); *Career* called to the Bar Gray's Inn 1951, dep chm Derbyshire QS 1964–71, recorder of the Crown Ct 1971–80, circuit judge (Midland and Oxford Circuit) 1980–, currently resident judge Derby; regnl chm of Industl Tbnls 1971–80, pres Mental Health Review Tbnls 1983; *Recreations* golf (pres Derbyshire Union of Golf Clubs 1979–81); *Style*— His Hon Judge Morrison; ✉ Derby Combined Court Centre, Morledge, Derby (☎ 01332 622600, fax 01332 622543)

MORRISON, Alistair Neil; s of Jamie Ian Morrison, of Bermuda, and Aileen Rose, *née* Wingate; *b* 4 Nov 1956; *Educ* Ardingly, Harrow Coll (BA); *m* 25 July 1980, Janis Anne, da of James Cecil Edwards, OBE, JP (d 1964); 1 s (Nicholas James b 14 Nov 1981), 1 da (Olivia Rose b 24 Dec 1985); *Career* freelance photographer 1982–; clients incl: Observer Magazine, Sunday Times Magazine, Sunday Telegraph Magazine, You Magazine, Illustrated London News, The Field, Country Homes and Interiors, Riva, Mirabella, Harpers and Queen, Amica, Interview; work in collections incl Nat Portrait Gallery; *Exhibitions* incl: NT 1982, Faces of Our Time (NT) 1985, Stars of the British Screen (Nat Portrait Gallery) 1985–86, Twenty For Today (Nat Portrait Gallery) 1986, Olivier 80th Birthday Tribute (Nat Portrait Gallery and Hamiltons Gallery) 1989; *Recreations* swimming, travelling; *Style*— Alistair Morrison, Esq; ✉ 1 Archer Court, 75 Kennel Ride, North Ascot, Berks SL5 7NU (☎ 01344 886145)

MORRISON, Hon Antoinette Sara Frances Sibell; *née* Long; da of 2 Viscount Long (ka 1944), and Frances Laura, *née* Charteris (d 1990); *b* 9 Aug 1934; *Educ* England, France; *m* 1954 (m dis), Hon Charles Andrew Morrison, *qv*; 1 s, 1 da; *Career* dir General Electric Co 1975–; non-exec dir: Abbey National Building Society (now Abbey National plc) 1979–95, Carlton Television Ltd 1991–, The Fourth Channel Television Co 1980–85, Imperial Group 1982–86; chm Nat Cncl for Voluntary Organisations 1977–81 (vice chm 1970–77); hon fell Imperial Coll 1993 (govr 1986–); memb: Cncl of Policy Studies Inst 1983–93, UK Round Table for Sustainable Devpt 1995; former memb: Nat Consumer Cncl, The Volunteer Centre, Wilts CC (until 1970); dir Nat Radiological Protection Bd 1989–; Hon DBA Univ of Coventry 1994; *Style*— The Hon Sara Morrison; ✉ 16 Groom Place, London SW1X 7BA; Wyndham's Farm, Wedhampton, Devizes, Wilts SN10 3QE

MORRISON, Dr (Philip) Blake; s of Arthur Blakemore Morrison (d 1991), of Skipton, Yorks, and Agnes, *née* O'Shea; *b* 8 Oct 1950; *Educ* Ermysteds GS Skipton, Univ of Nottingham (BA), McMaster Univ Ontario (MA), Univ Coll London (PhD); *m* 1976, Katherine Ann, da of Robert C Drake; 2 s (Seth Nicholas b 1981, Gabriel Eli b 1989), 1 da (Aphra Grace b 1984); *Career* various pt/t teaching posts 1976–81 (Open Univ, Goldsmiths' Coll, Furzedown Coll), poetry and fiction ed TLS 1978–81, dep literary ed Observer 1981–86 (literary ed 1986–89); Independent on Sunday: literary ed 1990–94, staff writer 1994–95; poet; *Awards* Eric Gregory Award, Somerset Maugham Award, Dylan Thomas Meml Prize, EM Forster Award, Volvo/Waterstone's Award for Non-Fiction 1993; memb Mgmnt Bd Poetry Soc 1980–83, chm Poetry Book Soc 1984–87; FRSL 1990; *Books* Movement (1980), Dark Glasses (1984), The Ballad of the Yorkshire Ripper (1987), The Yellow House (Children's Book, 1987), And When Did You Last See Your Father? (Memoir, 1993), As If (non-fiction, 1997); *Recreations* tennis, football; *Style*— Dr Blake Morrison; ✉ Peters Fraser & Dunlop Ltd, 503 The Chambers, Chelsea Harbour, Lots Road, London SW10 0XF (☎ 0171 352 4446, fax 0171 352 7356)

MORRISON, Hon Sir Charles Andrew; kt (1988), DL (Hereford and Worcester 1995); 2 s of 1 Baron Margadale, TD, JP (d 1996); bro of Maj 2 Baron Margadale, *qv*, Hon Mary Anne Morrison, DCVO, *qv*, and Rt Hon Sir Peter Morrison (d 1995); gs of 2 Viscount Hambleden; *b* 25 June 1932; *Educ* Eton; *m* 1, 28 Oct 1954, Hon (Antoinette) Sara Frances Sibell, *qv*, da of 2 Viscount Long; 1 s, 1 da; m 2, 1984, Rosalind Elizabeth, da of late Hon Richard Edward Lygon (d 1970), and formerly w of Gerald John Ward; *Career* 2 Lt Life Gds 1951–52, Capt Royal Wilts Yeo 1952–66; MP (C) Devizes 1964–92, vice chm 1922 Ctee 1974–83, chm Nat Ctee for Electoral Reform 1985–92; dir: Sothebys 1989–95, Bankers Insurance Co Ltd 1989–93; chm: The Game Conservancy 1987–94, Br Tst for Conservation Volunteers 1972–78 (pres 1978–82), Allerton Research and Educn Tst 1994–, Population Concern 1995–; pres Nat Anglers Cncl 1986–91, Nat Light Horse Breeding Soc 1995–96; memb: Cncl Salmon & Trout Assoc 1966–, Bd of Dirs of Global Ctee of Parliamentarians on Population and Devpt 1984–91; memb Ct of Assts Worshipful Co of Fishmongers (prime warden 1986–87); *Recreations* shooting, gardening, fishing; *Clubs* White's, Pratt's; *Style*— The Hon Sir Charles Morrison; ✉ Madresfield Court, Madresfield, Malvern, Worcs WR13 5AU (☎ 01684 573024)

MORRISON, Colin; s of Percy Morrison (d 1986), of London, and Elfrieda Edith, *née* Swann; *b* 15 Oct 1951; *Educ* Royal Wanstead Sch, Stanford Univ Calif (1986); *m* 1985, Mary Louise, da of Henry Ratcliffe; 2 da (Emily Louise b 12 Nov 1986, Kate Elizabeth 15 Dec 1989); *Career* trainee BBC World Serv/TV 1969–71, sub-ed and reporter Lloyd's List, showbusiness columnist Sunday Press (Dublin) and freelance journalist 1971–74, journalist, ed, then gp ed IPC Marine Publications 1974–78, US ed Vokos Publications USA 1978–79, md IPC Consumer Press 1983–85 (publisher/dir 1979–83); Reed Publishing Group: dir 1985–91, md/chm various consumer and business magazines, direct mktg and newstrade distribution cos 1985–88, dep chief exec 1989–91; chm Emap Business Communications (and its UK, French and German subsids) 1991–95, dir Emap plc 1991–95; md Australian Consolidated Press (and various Australian/Asian subsids of Publishing and Broadcasting Ltd) 1996–, dir Presse Publishing (UK) Ltd 1996–; dir Periodical Publishers' Assoc 1989–96, chm Magazine Publishers of Australia 1996–; govr Royal Wanstead Sch Fndn; *Books* Nowhere Else (1993); *Recreations* tennis, magazines, movies, music; *Clubs* Groucho, Publicity Club of London, RAC; *Style*— Colin Morrison, Esq; ✉ 22 Cowdroy Avenue, Cammeray, NSW 2062, Australia (☎ 00 612 9953 9404, office 00 612 9282 8098)

MORRISON, 2 Baron (UK 1945); Dennis Glossop Morrison; s of 1 Baron, PC (d 1953); *b* 21 June 1914; *Educ* Tottenham County Sch; *m* 1, 1940 (m dis 1958), Florence, da of Augustus Hennes, of Tottenham; m 2, 1959, (m dis 1975), Joan, da of Willam Meech, of Acton; *Heir* none; *Career* formerly with Metal Box Co; Lord-Lt's rep for Tottenham 1955–, vice pres Acton C of C until 1987; *Style*— The Rt Hon the Lord Morrison; ✉ 7 Ullswater Avenue, Felixstowe, Suffolk (☎ 0139 42 77405)

MORRISON, Dennis John; s of Leonard Tait Morrison, of Sale, Cheshire, and Alice, *née* Hutson; *b* 20 May 1942; *Educ* Ashton upon Mersey Boys Sch, Lymm GS, Univ of Manchester (BA, Dip Town and Country Planning); *m* 18 March 1967, Frances Joan (Polly), da of Frank Pollard, of Roundhay, Leeds; 1 s (Duncan John b 1971), 1 da (Rosalyn Jane b 1973); *Career* planning offr Lancashire CC 1966–70, sr planning offr Welsh Office Cardiff 1970–75, reg superintending planner DOE Manchester 1975–81, head NW Enterprise Unit DOE Manchester 1981–84, regnl controller Merseyside Task Force Liverpool 1984–89, regnl dir E Midlands Region DOE and Tport Nottingham 1989–94, dir Environment and Tport Govt Office for the E Midlands 1994–97, regional dir Govt Office for Merseyside 1997–; memb Exec Ctee Liverpool Anglican Cathedral; Freeman Burgess of the Altrincham Court LEET; MRTPI, FRGS; *Recreations* antiquarian horologist, collector of antiquarian books, gardening, hill walking; *Clubs* Altrincham 41; *Style*— Dennis Morrison, Esq; ✉ Government Office for Merseyside, Cunard Building, Pier Head, Liverpool L3 1QB (☎ 0151 224 6300, fax 0151 224 6474)

MORRISON, Frances Margaret (Fran); da of Lt Cdr William Morrison, OBE, RNVR, of Cove, Scotland, and Hilary Mary, *née* Wootton; *Educ* Queen's Park Sch Glasgow, St Andrew's Univ (MA); *m* 1984 (m dis), Trevor Deaves, s of Alan Deaves, of Cranleigh, Surrey; 2 s (Adam b 1984, Dominic b 1986); *Career* broadcaster and media conslt, oil indust public affairs mangr; news and current affrs reporter/presenter BBC Radio and TV, sole female memb presenting team of BBC TV's Newsnight at its launch 1979; reporter/presenter BBC TV: Nationwide 1981–83, 60 Minutes 1983–84; reporter BBC TV Watchdog 1984–85, reporter various documentary progs BBC TV 1978–86, presenter various arts and music progs BBC TV 1978–86; reporter/presenter Thames TV, Channel 4, Sky TV and BBC Radio Womans Hour 1986–91; media conslt 1986–91, freelance journalist 1978–91, head of media rels and communications Shell UK Ltd 1991–; memb Scottish Cncl Devpt and Indust; MInstPet 1992, FRSA 1992; *Recreations* travel, theatre, visual arts; *Clubs* RTS, Network; *Style*— Ms Fran Morrison; ✉ c/o Shell UK Ltd, Shell-Mex House, Strand, London WC2R 0DX (☎ 0171 257 3000)

MORRISON, Eur Ing (Alexander) Fraser; CBE (1993); s of Alexander Ferrier Sharp Morrison, and Catherine Colina, *née* Fraser; *b* 20 March 1948; *Educ* Tain Royal Acad, Univ of Edinburgh (BSc); *m* 23 Sept 1972, Patricia Janice, da of late Peter David Murphy; 1 s (Alexander Peter b 13 Jan 1974), 2 da (Claire Catherine b 6 June 1975, Sarah-Jane b 21 Aug 1977); *Career* md Morrison Construction Group 1976–84 (dir 1970–76), chm and md Morrison Construction Gp Ltd 1984–96, exec chm Morrison Construction Gp plc 1996–; dir Shand Ltd 1978–89, Alexander Shand Holdings Ltd 1982–86; non-exec dir Clydesdale Bank plc 1994–; FCEC: chm Scotland 1991–92, chm 1993–94, vice pres 1994–; chm Highlands and Islands Enterprise 1992– (dir 1991–92); Hon DTech 1995; CEng, MIHT, FRSA 1990, FICE 1993, FScotvec 1994, FCIOB 1995; *Recreations* golf, skiing, shooting, opera, art; *Style*— Eur Ing Fraser Morrison, CBE; ✉ Highlands and Islands Enterprise, Bridge House, 20 Bridge Street, Inverness IV1 1QR; Morrison Construction Group Ltd, Morrison House, 12 Atholl Crescent, Edinburgh, Scotland EH3 8HA (☎ 0131 228 4188, fax 0131 337 1880)

MORRISON, (William) Garth; CBE (1994), DL (1984); s of Walter Courtenay Morrison (d 1993), of Dale Court, Gullane, East Lothian, and Audrey Elizabeth, *née* Gilbert; *b* 8 April 1943; *Educ* Pembroke Coll Cambridge, Pangbourne Coll (Queen's Gold medal), RNC Dartmouth (Queen's Telescope), RNEC Manadon (Queen's Sword), RNC Greenwich; *m* 25 July 1970, Gillian, da of Stanley Cheetham, of Oldham, Lancs; 2 s (Alastair b 22 Nov 1972, Christopher b 15 May 1974), 1 da (Clare (twin) b 15 May 1974); *Career* served RN 1961–73 (ret Lt); farmer in family partnership 1973–, dir Top Hat Holdings (formerly Scotfresh Ltd) 1975–; The Scout Assoc: area cmmr E Lothian 1973–81, chief cmmr Scotland 1981–88, chief scout UK and dependent territories 1988–96; memb World Scout Ctee 1991–; chm East and Midlothian NHS Tst 1993–; memb: Lothian and Borders Ctee of Royal Jubilee and Prince's Tsts 1979–86, Scot Community Educn Cncl 1988–95 (hon fell 1995), Nat Lottery Charities Bd 1995–; tstee Lamp of Lothian Collegiate Tst 1978–; MIEE 1973; *Books* chapter in The Scottish Juvenile Justice System (ed Martin and Murray, 1982); *Recreations* golf, sailing, scouting; *Clubs* Naval, New (Edinburgh); *Style*—

W Garth Morrison, Esq, CBE, DL; ✉ West Fenton, North Berwick, East Lothian EH39 5AL (☎ 01620 842154); W Courtenay Morrison & Co, West Fenton, North Berwick, East Lothian EH39 5AL (☎ 01620 842154, fax 01620 842052)

MORRISON, Prof George Chalmers; s of Donald Crerar Morrison (d 1956), of Bearsden, Glasgow, and Annie Sibbald, *née* Johnston (d 1984); *b* 14 May 1930; *Educ* Bearsden Acad, Univ of Glasgow (BSc, PhD); *m* 7 Oct 1961, Prudence, da of Albert Donald Valentine Knowers (d 1975), of Lymington, Hants; 3 da (Leslie b 25 Aug 1962, Vanessa b 10 Jan 1965, Nicola b 24 Dec 1965); *Career* res assoc Univ of Chicago 1957–60, princ scientific offr AERE Harwell 1961–65 (res fell 1954–57), scientist Argonne Nat Laboratory Illinois 1965–73; Univ of Birmingham: prof 1973– (chair of nuclear structure), dep dean Faculty of Sci 1985–88, dean Faculty of Sci 1988–91, head Sch of Physics and Space Res 1990–; author of numerous papers in int scientific jls and contributor to scientific pubns; SERC: memb Nuclear Structure Ctee 1974–78, 1982–86 and 1991–94, chm 1992–94, memb Nuclear Physics Bd 1984–87 and 1992–94, memb Physics Ctee 1984–87, chm Nuclear Physics Ctee 1994; memb: Working Gp on Nuclear Physics Euro Sci Fndn 1981–84, Bd Nuclear Physics Div Euro Physical Soc 1984–92, Nuclear Physics Euro Co-ord Ctee 1993–, Exec Ctee Euro Physical Soc Cncl 1993– (Cncl del 1991–); FInstP, FAPS; *Recreations* golf, walking, philately; *Clubs* Harborne Golf; *Style*— Prof George Morrison; ✉ 184 Lordswood Rd, Harborne, Birmingham, West Midlands B17 8QH (☎ 0121 427 3248); School of Physics and Space Research, The University of Birmingham, Edgbaston, Birmingham B15 2TT (☎ 0121 414 4565, fax 0121 414 4577, telex 333762 UOBHAM G)

MORRISON, James Fyffe Thomson; s of John Morrison (d 1952), and Margaret Morrison (d 1984); *b* 11 April 1932; *Educ* Hillhead HS Glasgow, Glasgow Sch of Art (scholar, DA), Jordanhill Coll of Educn; *m* 12 April 1955, Dorothy Jean Allison, da of James Barclay McCormack; 1 s (John Coull b 25 Aug 1959), 1 da (Judith Kate b 10 Aug 1961); *Career* oil and watercolour painter; visiting artist Hospitalfield House 1962 and 1963, head of dept Duncan of Jordanstone Coll of Art 1978–87 (lectr 1965–78); *Solo Exhibitions* McClure Gall 1959, Scottish Gall 1959, 1989 and 1992, Reid Gall 1962, Vaughan Coll Leicester 1968, Richard Demarco Gall 1968, Compass Gall 1970, Galleria Vaccarino 1971, Steiger Gall 1973, Düsseldorf Kunstmesse 1974, Edinburgh Festival Exhbn (Scottish Gall) 1978, Thackery Gall 1979, Fine Art Soc 1986, Waddington and Sheill Gall 1987, Perth Festival Exhbn (Perth Museum and Art Gall) 1988, Macaulay Gall 1989, William Hardie Gall 1990, Riverside Gall 1991; *Work in Various Collections* incl: Scottish Arts Cncl, Aberdeen Art Gall, Dundee Museum and Art Gall, Kelvingrove Art Gall and Museum, Perth Museum and Art Gall, Bank of Scotland, Univ of Edinburgh, Tayside Educn Ctee, British Linen Bank, Grampian Television, Clydesdale Bank, Univ of Glasgow, BBC, Low and Bonar plc; numerous works in private collections in USA, Britain, Canada and Europe; presenter Scope (BBC) 1976–, writer and presenter A Scottish Picture Show (STV) 1988; memb: Soc of Scottish Artists 1963 (Cncl 1964–67), Bd of Govrs Duncan Jordanstone Coll of Art 1988–; Torrance Award RGI 1958, Arts Cncl Travelling Award 1968; Hon DUniv Stirling 1986; RSW 1968, RSA 1992 (ARSA 1973); *Publications* Aff the Squerr (2 edn 1990), Paris in Winter (1992); *Recreations* playing the recorder in a chamber group; *Clubs* Rotary, Montrose, Edzell Golf; *Style*— James Morrison, RSA; ✉ Craigview House, Usan, Montrose, Angus, Tayside DD10 9SD (☎ 01674 672639); The Scottish Gallery, 16 Dundas Street, Edinburgh

MORRISON, John; s of Thomas Patrick Morrison, and Marie, *née* Boylan; *b* 6 March 1949; *Educ* St Edward's Coll Liverpool, St Catherine's Coll Oxford (BA); *m* 29 Feb 1980, Judith, da of Ronald Lee, of Bury, Lancashire; 1 s (Nicholas b 1981), 1 da (Joanna b 1984); *Career* news trainee BBC 1971, scriptwriter ITN 1973, prog ed Channel 4 News 1982, features ed The Independent 1986, ed Newsnight BBC 1987, ed Assignment BBC 1990, ed Six O'Clock News BBC 1993–95, managing ed BBC News 1995–; *Style*— John Morrison, Esq; ✉ Rm 6239, BBC Television Centre, London W12 (☎ 0181 743 8000)

MORRISON, Ven John Anthony; s of Leslie Claude Morrison (d 1967), of Hastings, Sussex, and Mary Sharland, da of Sir Frank Newson-Smith, 1 Bt (d 1971); *b* 11 March 1938; *Educ* Haileybury, Jesus Coll Cambridge (BA, MA), Lincoln Coll Oxford (MA), Chichester Theol Coll; *m* 20 July 1968, Angela, da of Jonathan Eric Bush (d 1978), of Leatherhead; 2 s (Dominic b 19 June 1970, Nicholas b 11 May 1974), 1 da (Philippa b 26 March 1972); *Career* ordained deacon Birmingham 1964, priest 1965; curate: St Peter Birmingham 1964–68, St Michael-at-the-North Gate Oxford 1968–74; chaplain Lincoln Coll Oxford 1968–74, vicar Basildon Berks 1974–82, rural dean Bradfield 1978–82, vicar Aylesbury Bucks 1982–90, rural dean Aylesbury 1985–89, archdeacon of Buckingham 1990–; memb Gen Synod 1980–90; Freeman City of London 1961, memb Ct Worshipful Co of Spectaclemakers 1994 (Liveryman 1962); *Recreations* coaching rowing; *Clubs* Leander, Vincent's; *Style*— The Ven the Archdeacon of Buckingham; ✉ 60 Wendover Rd, Aylesbury, Bucks HP21 9LW (☎ 01296 23269)

MORRISON, Hon (Dame) Mary Anne; DCVO (1982, CVO 1970); does not use style of Dame; da of 1 Baron Margadale (d 1996), sis of 2 Baron Margadale, *qv*, Hon Sir Charles Morrison, *qv*, and Rt Hon Sir Peter Morrison (d 1995); *b* 17 May 1937; *Educ* Heathfield Sch Ascot, abroad; *Career* woman of the bedchamber to HM The Queen 1960–; *Style*— The Hon Mary Morrison, DCVO; (☎ 01747 870366)

MORRISON, Michael John; s of John Percy Morrison, JP, and Kathleen Morrison; *b* 31 March 1939; *Educ* Fettes, St Catharine's Coll Cambridge (MA, LLB); *m* 11 Sept 1965, June; 1 s (Nicholas James b 21 Dec 1967), 1 da (Louise Charlotte b 23 June 1971); *Career* admitted slr 1965; ptnr Parker Garrett 1969–82; sr ptnr: Taylor Garrett 1988 (ptnr 1982–88), Taylor Joynson Garrett 1989–; chm: Yuills Ltd 1975–, Rye Machinery Ltd 1989–; dir: Leif Hoegh UK Ltd 1978–, Norwegian American Cruises UK Ltd 1980–87; memb Law Soc; *Recreations* golf, squash; *Clubs* RAC, Moor Park Golf; *Style*— Michael Morrison, Esq; ✉ Taylor Joynson Garrett, Carmelite, 50 Victoria Embankment, London EC4Y 0DX (☎ 0171 353 1234, fax 0171 936 2666)

MORRISON, (Andrew) Neil; QFSM (1989); s of Andrew Steel Morrison (d 1993), and Margueritta Wilkin, *née* Caird (d 1985); *b* 8 Sept 1937; *Educ* Arbroath HS, Dundee Coll of Technol (Dip in Educnl Technol); *m* 9 March 1963, Kathleen Alexander, da of Robert Walker Rutherford (d 1969); 1 s (Andrew Robert b 30 June 1964); *Career* armourer REME, 1 Bn King's Own Scottish Borderers Malaya and Singapore, Int Guard Berlin; Angus Fire Brigade: fireman 1962–70, leading fireman 1970–71, sub-offr 1971–74, station offr 1974–75; Tayside Fire Brigade: station offr 1975–76, divnl offr grade I 1979–80 (grade III 1976–79); firemaster Grampian Fire Brigade 1985–93 (dep firemaster 1980–85); HM chief inspr of Fire Services for Scotland 1994–; dir Chief and Assistant Chief Fire Officers' Assoc (CACFOA) Research Ltd 1985–91; Inst of Fire Engineers: Scottish regnl rep 1985–93, memb Int Cncl 1985–93, Pubns Ctee 1985–93; memb: Scottish Central Fire Brigades Advsy Cncl Scottish Office, Fire Protection Assoc, BSI Ctee, Euro CEN Ctee, Civil Service Selection Bd for Brigade Command Fire Service Coll; pres: Phoenix Club for disabled young people 1983–93, CACFOA (UK) 1991–92; vice-pres Fire Service Nat Benevolent Fund, sec to District No 7 (Scotland) 1986–92; Hon DTech Robert Gordon Univ 1994; General Service medal and clasp (Malaya) 1956, Fire Service Long Service and Good Conduct medal 1992; FIFireE (MIFireE 1970); *Recreations* curling, golfing, hill walking and swimming; *Style*— Neil Morrison, Esq, QFSM; ✉ Mill of Cranhill, Banchory Devenick, Aberdeen AB1 5YR (☎ 01224 869800); The Scottish Office, Home and Health Department, St Andrew's House, Edinburgh EH1 3DG (☎ 0131 244 2342, fax 0131 244 2683)

MORRISON, Sheriff Nigel Murray Paton; QC (Scot 1988); s of David Paton Morrison (d 1968), of Edinburgh, and Dilys Trenholm Pritchard or Morrison (d 1995); *b* 18 March 1948; *Educ* Rannoch Sch; *Career* called to the Bar Inner Temple 1972, admitted to Scot Bar 1975; asst ed Session Cases 1976–82, asst clerk to Rules Cncl 1978–84, clerk of faculty Faculty of Advocates 1979–86, standing jr counsel to Scot Devpt Dept (planning) 1982–86, temp sheriff 1982–96, Sheriff of Lothian and Borders 1996–; chm Social Security Appeal Tbnl 1982–91, counsel to Sec of State under the Private Legislation Procedure (Scot) Act (1936) 1986–96, first counsel to Lord Pres of Ct of Session 1989–96 (jr and second counsel 1984–89), chm Med Appeal Tbnl 1991–96; contrib to Stair Memorial Encyclopaedia of the Laws of Scotland, princ author Green's Annotated Rules of the Court of Session; tstee Nat Library of Scot 1989–; memb Faculty of Advocates; *Recreations* being taken for walks by my black labrador dog, music, riding, Scottish country dancing; *Clubs* New (Edinburgh); *Style*— Sheriff Nigel Morrison, QC; ✉ 9 India St, Edinburgh EH3 6HA (☎ 0181 225 2807, fax 0131 225 5688); Sheriff's Chambers, Sheriff Court House, 27 Chambers Street, Edinburgh EH1 1LB (☎ 0131 225 2525, fax 0131 225 4422)

MORRISON, Richard Duncan; s of Donald Melville Morrison, and Winifred Mary, *née* Stocks; *b* 24 July 1954; *Educ* Univ Coll Sch, Magdalene Coll Cambridge (MA); *m* 1977, Marian, da of Joseph Plant; 2 s (Philip b 1984, Edmund b 1988), 1 da (Katharine b 1985); *Career* asst ed Classical Music Magazine 1977–84, dep ed Early Music Magazine 1985–89; The Times: music critic 1984–89, dep arts ed 1989–90, arts ed 1990–; FRSA 1995; *Recreations* walking, playing the organ; *Style*— Richard Morrison, Esq; ✉ 11 Sunningfields Crescent, London NW4 4RD (☎ 0181 202 8028); The Times, 1 Pennington Street, London E1 9XN (☎ 0171 782 5167, fax 0171 782 5748)

MORRISON, Robert Charles (Bob); Dr Robert Bruce Morrison, of Bucklebury, Reading, and Christine Davidson, *née* Henry; *b* 22 June 1961; *Educ* St Edward's Sch Tilehurst Reading, Abingdon Sch Oxon; *m* 20 July 1985, Hazel Ann, da of (William) John Rudd; 1 s (Simon b 1995); *Career* Radio 210: music presenter 1979–80, trainee journalist 1980–82, journalist 1982–85, sports ed 1985–90, head of news and sport 1990–96; owner First Eleven Sport (sports publicity and promotion co) 1996–; *Recreations* reading, computer programming, transport, photography; *Style*— Bob Morrison, Esq; ✉ First Eleven Sport, PO Box 11, Reading, Berks RG6 3DT (☎ 0118 931 1244, fax 0118 975 7764, e-mail FIRST11@aol.com)

MORRISON, Prof Ronald; s of David Morrison, of Airdrie, and Catherine, *née* Turner (d 1958); *b* 15 April 1946; *Educ* Eastbank Acad, Univ of Strathclyde (BSc), Univ of Glasgow (MSc), Univ of St Andrews (PhD); *m* 17 Oct 1975, Ann Margaret, da of Alistair MacDonald, of Edinburgh; 1 s (David b 1979), 1 da (Catriona b 1981); *Career* prof of software engrg Univ of St Andrews 1985– (sr res fell 1971–72, lectr 1972–84, reader 1984–85); pres Scottish Cross Country Union 1986–87, vice pres Scottish Athletics Fedn 1995–; *Books* Davie & Morrison Recursive Descent Compiling (jtly, 1981), Cole & Morrison Introduction to S-Algol Programming (jtly, 1982), Sommerville & Morrison Software Development with Ada (jtly, 1987), Atkinson, Burneman & Morrison Data Types and Persistence (1988), Hull, Morrison, Stemple Database Programming Languages (1989); *Recreations* golf, athletics, cross-country running; *Clubs* St Andrews Golf, Fife Athletic; *Style*— Prof Ronald Morrison; ✉ School of Mathematical and Computational Science, University of St Andrews, North Haugh, St Andrews, Fife KY16 9SS (☎ 01334 476161, fax 01334 476068, e-mail ron@dcs.st_and.ac.uk)

MORRISON, Stephen Roger (Steve); s of Hyman Michael Morrison, and Rebecca, *née* Zolkwer; *b* 3 March 1947; *Educ* Univ of Edinburgh, Nat Film Sch; *m* 1979, Gayle Valerie, *née* Broughall; *Career* Granada Television: joined to set up Northern Documentary Unit 1974, subsquently prodr/dir World in Action, head of regnl progs then head of features and documentaries until 1987, dir of progs 1987–92, md 1993–94; md: Granada Broadcasting 1992, LWT 1994–96; dep chief exec TV Div Granada Group plc 1995, chief operating offr Granada Media Group 1996–; chm: Laser 1995–, ITV Marketing Gp 1995–96, Granada Sky Broadcasting 1996–; also currently chief exec Granada Film (fndr mid 1980's); Granada network credits incl: The Spanish Civil War, Disappearing World, China, Scully (comedy-drama), The Road to 1984, 28–Up (fourth Seven-Up series); Granada film credits incl: prodr The Magic Toyshop and The Fruit Machine, exec prodr My Left Foot, The Field and Jack & Sarah; memb Bd: British Screen Advsy Cncl, BFI, Edinburgh Int Film Festival; dir British Screen Finance; *Recreations* tennis, reading, films and theatre, talking and dining, touring delicatessens; *Clubs* Garrick; *Style*— Steve Morrison, Esq; ✉ Granada Media Group Ltd, The London Television Centre, Upper Ground, London SE1 9LT (☎ 0171 261 3037, fax 0171 620 1405)

MORRISON-BELL, Sir William Hollin Dayrell; 4 Bt (UK 1905), of Otterburn Hall, Elsdon, Northumberland; s of Capt Sir Charles Reginald Francis Morrison-Bell, 3 Bt (d 1967), and Prudence Caroline, *née* Davies; *b* 21 June 1956; *Educ* Eton, St Edmund Hall Oxford; *m* 6 Oct 1984, Cynthia Hélène Marie, yr da of Teddy White, of Apt A6, Résidence Alexandra, 1837 Châeau d'Oeux, Switzerland; 1 s (Thomas Charles Edward b 1985); *Heir* s, Thomas Charles Edward Morrison-Bell b 13 Feb 1985; *Career* solicitor; legal advsr for Air Products plc; *Style*— Sir William Morrison-Bell, Bt; ✉ 106 Bishop's Rd, London SW6 7AR (☎ 0171 736 4940); Highgreen, Tarset, Hexham, Northumberland (☎ 01434 240223); Air Products plc, Hersham Place, Molesey Road, Walton on Thames, Surrey KT12 4RZ

MORRISON-LOW, Eur Ing Sir James Richard; 3 Bt (UK 1908), of Kilmaron, Co Fife, DL (Fife 1978); s of Sir Walter John Morrison-Low, 2 Bt, JP (d 1955; assumed by deed poll the additional surname of Morrison 1924), and Dorothy Ruth, *née* de Quincey (d 1946); Sir James Low, 1 Bt, was Lord Provost of Dundee 1893–96; *b* 3 Aug 1925; *Educ* Harrow, Merchiston, Faraday House (Dip); *m* 1953, Ann Rawson, da of Air Cdre Robert Gordon, CB, CMG, DSO (d 1954); 1 s (Richard Walter b 1959), 3 da (Alison Dorothy b 1955, Jean Elspeth (Mrs Larry Keim) b 1957, Susan Elizabeth (Mrs Graham Latham) b 1963); *Heir* s, Richard Walter Morrison-Low b 4 Aug 1959; *Career* serv 1943–47, Royal Corps of Signals, Capt; electrical engineer Osborne & Hunter Ltd Glasgow 1952, dir 1956–89; ptnr Kilmaron Electrical Co 1982–; trustee Cupar TSB 1958–78, tstee Fife Area Bd TSB 1978–82; chm Scottish Traction Engine Soc 1961–63; dir Nat Inspection Cncl for Electrical Installation Contracting 1982–88, pres Electrical Contractors Assoc of Scotland 1982–84; memb: Technical Ctee Assoc Internationale des Entreprises d'Equipement Electrique 1981–95, Wiring Regulations Ctee Inst of Electrical Engrs 1982–95; chm Fife Area Scout Cncl 1966–84; Hon Pipe Maj of Royal Scottish Pipers' Soc 1981–83; landowner (80 acres); CEng, MIEE, FInstD 1982, Eur Ing 1990; *Recreations* piping, shooting, fishing, steam rollers & traction engines; *Clubs* New (Edinburgh); *Style*— Eur Ing Sir James Morrison-Low, Bt, DL; ✉ Kilmaron Castle, nr Cupar, Fife KY15 4NE (☎ 01334 652248)

MORRISON-LOW, Richard Walter; s and h of Sir James Richard Morrison-Low, 3 Bt, *qv*; *b* 4 Aug 1959; *Style*— Richard Morrison-Low, Esq

MORRISS, Nicholas Anson; s of Kenneth Cherry Morriss, MBE, of Haslemere, Surrey, and Diana Mary, *née* Gunning; *b* 17 Sept 1950; *Educ* Radley, Univ of York (BA); *m* 29 June 1974, Suzette Anne, da of late Richard Tilney, of Orford, Suffolk; 1 s (Alexander b 11 Feb 1984), 1 da (Fenella b 27 June 1987); *Career* CA; Price Waterhouse: London 1972–76, Cape Town 1976–78, mangr London 1978–79; asst dir Barclays de Zoete Wedd (formerly Barclays Merchant Bank) 1979–86, ptnr corp fin Coopers & Lybrand (formerly Deloitte Haskins & Sells) 1986–; FCA 1975; *Recreations* squash, golf, skiing, tennis;

Style— Nicholas Morriss, Esq; ✉ Coopers & Lybrand, 1800 M Street NW, Washington DC 20036 (☎ 001 202 822 5557, fax 001 202 457 0983)

MORRISS, Peter Warren; s of George Edward Morriss, of Bognor Regis, Sussex, and Esther Christina Frances, *née* Moodie; *b* 14 Feb 1942; *Educ* Bancroft's Sch; *m* 1968, Heather Eva Morton; 2 s (Christopher Warren b 1974, Stephen James b 1980); *Career* Thomson McLintock & Co (now KPMG): apprentice, qualified ICAS 1968, ptnr 1977–; sr visiting fell lectr City Univ Business Sch 1974–; memb EDP Ctee ICAS 1977–80, vice chm IT Faculty Ctee ICAEW; ACA 1977 (CA 1968), FBCS 1981 (MBCS 1975), FIIA; *Recreations* golf, music, sailing; *Clubs* Scribes, Chigwell Golf; *Style*— Peter W Morriss, Esq; ✉ KPMG, 8 Salisbury Square, London EC4Y 8BB (☎ 0171 311 1000)

MORRISSEY, Caroline Susan; da of Philip John Stanley, of Woking, Surrey, and Rita Dagmar, *née* Hillwood (d 1992); *b* 29 Jan 1955; *Educ* Woking Co GS for Girls, W London Coll, Univ of Lancaster (BEd); *partner* Franz Andres; 3 da (Corrina Marie b 19 Oct 1980, Astrid Zoe b 1 Dec 1983, Frances Amy b 30 April 1987), 1 s (Andri Niculin b 25 July 1995); *Career* teacher: Brown Rigg Sch 1979–80, Inlingua Sch Switzerland 1981–83; British Council: educnl and cultural asst Berne 1984–91, dir Switzerland 1995– (mangr 1991–95); *Recreations* photography; *Style*— Ms Caroline Morrissey; ✉ The British Council, British Embassy, Thunstrasse 50, 3000 Berne 15, Switzerland

MORRISSEY, Charles Anthony Filose; s of Peter Anthony Filose Morrissey, of Little Bridges, Langshott Wood, nr Horley, Surrey, and Sheila Margaret, *née* Berrett (d 1984); *b* 10 Aug 1953; *Educ* North Sch Turners Hill Crawley Sussex; *m* 14 Sept 1985, Lucy Caroline, da of Robert Piper; 1 s (Henry Peter Filose b 14 Aug 1990); *Career* trainee journalist rising to news ed Commercial Motor (IPC Business Press) 1973–77, sr reporter New Civil Engineer 1977–79, chief reporter Crawley Observer (Westminster Press) 1979–83, reporter Evening Argus Brighton 1983–84, head of news Radio Mercury 1984–86, prodr later ed AM Programme London Broadcasting Co 1986–89; ITN: joined as news ed 1989, head of radio and ed Independent Radio News & prodr ITN World News until 1995; head of broadcasting The Press Assoc 1995–; Gold Medal (for documentary on Braer Oil Tanker disaster) Int Radio Awards/New York Festival 1993; *Recreations* golf, cricket, walking, photography; *Clubs* MCC (assoc); *Style*— Charles Morrissey, Esq; ✉ The Press Association, 85 Fleet Street, London EC4P 4BE (☎ 0171 353 7440)

MORRISSEY, Michael Peter; s of Peter Anthony Morrissey, of Langshott Wood, Surrey, and Sheila Margaret, *née* Berrett (d 1984); *b* 15 Aug 1959; *Educ* Worth Sch Sussex, RMA Sandhurst; *m* 30 May 1987, Sally-Anne, da of Derek Harris, of St Buryan, Cornwall; 1 s (Hugo William b 18 March 1993), 2 da (Rosie Henrietta b 16 Aug 1990, Olivia Mary b 27 March 1996); *Career* enlisted 1977; Irish Guards: cmmnd 2 Lt 1978, Lt 1980, Capt 1983, Maj 1988, Company Cmd 1 Irish Guards; serv: Cyprus, Kenya, NI, Belize, Canada, Germany; Thornton Management Ltd London 1989–91, Mercury Asset Management Group plc 1991– (dir Mercury Investment Services 1994–); *Recreations* shooting, riding, rugby, cricket; *Clubs* Cavalry and Guards; *Style*— Michael Morrissey, Esq; ✉ Home Farm, Kineton, Guiting Power, Glos GL54 5UG; Mercury Asset Management Group plc, 33 King William Street, London EC4R 9AS (☎ 0171 280 2503, fax 0171 280 2820)

MORROCCO, Alberto; OBE (1993); s of Domenico Antonio Morrocco (d 1935), and Celesta, *née* Crolla (d 1956); *b* 14 Dec 1917; *Educ* Sunnybank Sch Aberdeen, Gray's Sch of Art Aberdeen (DA, Carnegie Travelling scholar, Guthrie award); *m* 15 Jan 1941, Vera Cockburn, da of Laurence Mercer, MM (d 1963); 2 s (Leon Francesco b 1942, Laurence John Nicholas b 1947), 1 da (Annalisa Celesta Camilla Madhuri Simonetta b 1962); *Career* RAMC 1940–46; head Sch of Painting Duncan of Jordanstone Coll of Art 1950–82; recent exhbns incl Aberdeen Art Gallery 1993; memb: Scot Fine Arts Cncl, Saltire Soc Arts Panel; hon memb: RSE 1995, Saltire Soc 1995, RIAS 1995; Hon LLD Univ of Dundee, Hon DUniv Stirling; RSA 1962 (ARSA 1951), memb RSW 1965, RP 1975, memb RGI 1977; *Clubs* Scottish Arts; *Style*— Alberto Morrocco, Esq, OBE; ✉ Binrock House, 456 Perth Road, Dundee, Scotland (☎ 01382 69319)

MORROW, Anne Margaretta; da of Reginald Andrew MacKenzie Morrow (d 1960), and Winifred Maude Biddulph Townsend; *Educ* Cheshunt County GS, Hornsey Coll of Art (NDD), Royal Coll of Art (MA RCA); *m* (m dis), John Michael Edwards, s of Benjamin Edwards (d 1946); 1 da (Astrid Charlotte); *Career* illustrator; advertising 1976–85: Habitat, Yorkshire Bank, The Post Office; media 1976–89: Sunday Times, The Observer, The Independent; in house illustrator Financial Times 1985–88, illustration ed The Guardian 1994– (joined 1988); publishing 1976–85: BBC Pubns, Penguin Books, Oxford University Press, Marshall Cavendish, Octopus Books; television 1976–85: TVS (Land of Green Ginger), BBC TV (Jackanory, Mata Hari), Thames TV (Rainbow); exhibitions: RCA, Assoc Illustrators 1980, European Illustration 1981 and 1983, Henry Moore Gallery RCA 1988; fndr memb and hon treas RCA Soc 1981–89; memb: Assoc Illustrators Gallery Ctee 1982–85, Editorial Ctee Best of British Illustration Awards 1994; appointed ex student to RCA Coll Court 1982–86 and 1988–91; *Recreations* painting, theatre, music, travel; *Style*— Miss Anne Morrow; ✉ 15 The Terrace, Barnes, London SW13 0NP (☎ 0181 876 5599); The Guardian, 119 Farringdon Rd, London EC1 (☎ 0171 239 9939)

MORROW, Graham Eric; QC (1996); s of George Eric Morrow, of Liverpool, and Freda, *née* Duckett; *b* 14 June 1951; *Educ* Liverpool Coll, Univ of Newcastle-upon-Tyne (LLB); *m* 31 Jan 1987, Rosalind Nola, da of Samuel Ellis; 1 s (Philip Ellis b 24 July 1987), 2 step da (Erika Suzanne Patrick b 11 May 1971, Lisa Danielle Patrick 6 Oct 1973); *Career* called to the Bar Lincoln's Inn 1974, asst recorder 1990–; *Recreations* skiing, cricket, hockey; *Style*— Graham Morrow, Esq, QC; ✉ Exchange Chambers, Pearl Assurance House, Derby Square, Liverpool L2 9XX (☎ 0151 236 7747, fax 0151 236 3433)

MORROW, Sir Ian Thomas; kt (1973); s of Thomas George Morrow (d 1973), and Jamesina, *née* Hunter (d 1919); *b* 8 June 1912; *Educ* Dollar Acad; *m* 1, 1940 (m dis 1967), Elizabeth Mary Thackeray (decd); 1 s, 1 da; m 2, 1967, Sylvia Jane, da of Arthur Taylor; 1 da; *Career* asst accountant Brocklehurst Whiston Amalgamated Ltd 1937–40, jt sr ptnr Robson Morrow & Co 1942–51, md Brush Group 1953–58; chm: Kenwood Manufacturing Co 1961–68, Associated Fire Alarms 1965–72, MAI plc 1974–93 (dir 1993–94), UK Optical & Industrial Holdings 1979–86 (dep chm and md 1958–86), Strong and Fisher (Holdings) plc 1981–90, Additional Underwriting Agencies (No 3) Ltd 1985–, Scotia Holdings plc (formerly Efamol Holdings plc) 1986–95, Beale Dobie & Co Ltd 1989–, Walbrook Insurance Co Ltd 1990–92, Thurne Group Ltd 1993–; dep chm: Siebe Gorman Holdings 1970–82, Rolls Royce Ltd 1970–71, Rolls Royce (1971) Ltd (md 1971–72) 1971–73; dir: Hambros plc 1972–90 (dep chm 1983–86), Laird Group 1973–92 (chm 1975–87), International Harvester Co of GB Ltd 1974–85, Psion plc 1987–, C E Heath plc 1988–; memb: Cncl Inst of Cost and Works Accountants (now CIMA) 1952–70 (pres 1956–57, Gold medallist 1961), Cncl Inst of CAs of Scotland 1968–72 and 1979–82 (vice pres 1970–72, 1979–80 and 1980–81, pres 1981–82), Press Cncl 1974–80; Liveryman: Worshipful Co of Chartered Accountants, Worshipful Co of Spectacle Makers; ACA, FCMA, JDipMA, FIMgt, CIEE; *Recreations* reading, music, golf, skiing; *Clubs* Nat Lib, RAC, Royal and Ancient (St Andrews); *Style*— Sir Ian Morrow; ✉ 2 Albert Terrace Mews, London NW1 7TA (☎ 0171 722 7110); Hambros Bank Ltd, 41 Tower Hill, London EC3N 4HA (☎ 0171 702 3524, fax 0171 481 1048)

MORSE, Christopher George John (Robin); s of John Morse, of Swansea, and Margaret, *née* Maliphant; *b* 28 June 1947; *Educ* Malvern, Wadham Coll Oxford (MA, BCL); *m* 26 March 1983, Louise Angela, da of Ronald Stott (d 1974), of Mirfield, W Yorks; 1 s (Richard b 24 May 1985); *Career* called to the Bar 1971; visiting prof: John Marshall Law Sch Chicago 1979–80, Leuven Univ Belgium 1982; King's Coll London: lectr in law 1971–88, reader in law 1988–92, prof of law 1992–, dean and head of Sch of Law 1992–93; *Books* Torts in Private International Law (1978), The Conflict of Laws (ed, 11 edn 1987, 12 edn 1993), Benjamin's Sale of Goods (ed, 3 edn 1987, 4 edn 1992), Public Policy in Transnational Relationships (1991), Chitty on Contracts (ed, 27 edn 1994); *Recreations* travel, Swansea City AFC; *Style*— Prof Robin Morse; ✉ School of Law, King's College, London WC2R 2LS (☎ 0171 836 5454, fax 0171 873 2465)

MORSE, David Thomas; s of Thomas Walter Morse (d 1984), of London, and Emily Annie, *née* Garrett; *b* 10 Nov 1943; *Educ* Royal Ballet School (White Lodge); *m* 9 Oct 1971, Marion, da of Charles Arnold Browell Tait, OBE; *Career* ballet dancer; with the Royal Ballet 1961–65; princ character artist Birmingham Royal Ballet (formerly Sadler's Wells Royal Ballet) 1989–; roles with co incl: the Rake in The Rake's Progress, Jaspar in Pineapple Poll, Hilarion in Giselle, Polichinelle in Meadow of Proverbs, Punch in Punch and the Street Party, The Dago and Popular Song in Facade, Bootface in The Lady and the Fool, Widow Simone in La Fille Mal Gardée, Carabosse in The Sleeping Beauty, Henry Hobson in Hobson's Choice, Lord Capulet in Romeo and Juliet; choreography incl the works Pandora and Birdscape for Sadler's Wells; awarded Polish ballet's bicentenial medal of honour; *Recreations* photography, reading, music; *Style*— David Morse, Esq; ✉ Birmingham Royal Ballet, Birmingham Hippodrome Theatre, Thorp St, Birmingham B5 4AU (☎ 0121 622 2555)

MORSE, Sir (Christopher) Jeremy; KCMG (1975); s of late Francis John Morse, and Kinbarra, *née* Armfield-Marrow; *b* 10 Dec 1928; *Educ* Winchester, New Coll Oxford; *m* 1955, Belinda Marianne, da of Lt-Col R B Y Mills; 3 s, 1 da; *Career* Nat Serv Lt KRRC 1948–49; exec dir Bank of England 1965–72, chm Lloyds Bank 1977–93 (dep chm 1975–77); non-exec dir: ICI 1981–93, Zeneca Group plc 1993–; chm: Ctee of London Clearing Bankers 1980–82, Deputies Ctee of Twenty IMF 1972–74; pres: Br Bankers Assoc 1984–90, Euro Banking Fedn 1988–90, Chartered Inst of Bankers 1992–93; memb: Cncl Lloyd's 1987–, NEDC 1977–81, Ct Bank of England 1993–; former chm City Arts Tst, FIDE judge for Chess Compositions 1975–, former pres Br Chess Problem Soc; warden Winchester Coll 1987–, chllr Univ of Bristol 1988–; *Recreations* poetry, problems and puzzles, coarse gardening, golf; *Clubs* Athenaeum; *Style*— Sir Jeremy Morse, KCMG; ✉ 102a Drayton Gdns, London SW10 9RJ (☎ 0171 370 2265)

MORSE, Rodney John; s of James Morse (d 1986), and Elsie, *née* Cripps; *b* 26 Jan 1944; *m* 25 May 1968, (Maureen) Ann, da of John Kenny Woodward (d 1990), of Leighton Buzzard, Beds; 1 da (Carrie Alisa b 25 Aug 1971); *Career* aviation underwriter Lloyd's 1986–94; dir: Wellington Underwriting Agencies Ltd 1986–94, Lloyd's Aviation Claims Centre Ltd 1986–93; underwriter Westminster Aviation Insurance Group 1995–; ACII; *Clubs* RAC; *Style*— Rodney Morse, Esq; ✉ Linwood, Sevenoaks Rd, Ightham, Sevenoaks, Kent (☎ 01732 882537); Westminster Aviation Insurance Group, 2 White Lion Court, Cornhill, London EC3V 3NP (☎ 0171 283 6600, fax 0171 626 1437)

MORTENSEN, Juliet Lilias; da of Rear Adm Rupert St Vincent Sherbrooke, VC, CB, DSO (d 1972), of Oxton, Notts, and Rosemary Neville, *née* Buckley; *b* 27 Feb 1931; *Educ* Toorak Coll Frankston Victoria Aust, Hatherop Castle; *m* 15 Oct 1955, Cdr Axel Mortensen, DL, RN (d 1983), s of Andreas Mortensen, of Yorks; 3 da (Andrea (Mrs O'Donnell) b 1957, Olivia (Mrs Trelawny Williams) b 1960, Emily (Mrs Christopher Eadie) b 1963); *Career* chm Notts Branch of CLA 1990–92; High Sheriff of Nottinghamshire 1993–94; *Style*— Mrs Axel Mortensen; (☎ 0115 965 2085, fax 0115 965 2961)

MORTENSEN, Neil James McCready; s of Peter John McCready Mortensen, of Laleham, Middx, and Rhoda, *née* Bamber; *b* 16 Oct 1949; *Educ* Hampton Sch, Univ of Birmingham (MB ChB), Univ of Bristol (MD); *m* 16 June 1973, Jane Alison, da of Lt-Col Paul Baker, of Shortlands, Kent; 1 s (James b 1979), 2 da (Gemma b 1977, Chloe b 1981); *Career* conslt sr lectr Univ of Bristol and Dept of Surgery Bristol Royal Infirmary 1983–86, conslt surgn John Radcliffe Hosp Oxford 1986–, hon reader in surgery Univ of Oxford 1986–; memb: Ctee Surgical Section Br Soc of Gastroenterology 1987–, Cncl Br Soc of Gastroenterology 1992–, Cncl Assoc of Coloproctology Great Britain and Ireland, Br Jl of Surgery Soc Ltd, Editorial Ctee Br Jl of Surgery; co-ed Int Jl Colo Rectal Disease 1985–; hon sec Cncl Coloproctology Section RSM; memb Green Coll Oxford 1987–, hon treas Surgical Res Soc 1988; FRCS 1980; *Books* Colo Rectal Cancer (1989), An Atlas of Rectal Ultrasound (1991), Restorative Proctocolectomy (1993); *Recreations* tennis, farming; *Style*— Neil Mortensen, Esq; ✉ Department of Colorectal Surgery, John Radcliffe Hospital, Oxford OX3 9DU (☎ 01865 220926)

MORTIMER, Prof Ann Margaret; da of Harry Mortimer, of Gomersal, W Yorks, and Muriel, *née* Wood; *b* 11 May 1957; *Educ* Heckmondwike GS, Univ of Leicester (MB ChB, BSc), Univ of Leeds (MMedSc); *m* 5 Jan 1985, (Edward) John Turner; *Career* lectr in psychiatry Univ of Leeds 1986–88, conslt psychiatrist St Luke's Hosp Huddersfield 1988, sr lectr in psychiatry Charing Cross and Westminster Med Sch (Univ of London) 1991–95, foundation chair of psychiatry Postgraduate Med Sch Univ of Hull 1995–; MRCPsych 1985; *Books* numerous pubns on schizophrenia; *Recreations* skiing, piano playing, gardening; *Clubs* The Vibram Mountaineering; *Style*— Prof Ann Mortimer; ✉ The Postgraduate Medical School, University of Hull, Kingston-upon-Hull, Hull HU6 7RX (☎ 01482 346311)

MORTIMER, Anthony; *Career* singer/songwriter; fndr memb East 17 with Brian Harvey, *qv*, John Hendy, *qv* and Terry Coldwell, *qv*; 14 top twenty singles; singles incl: House Of Love 1992, Slow It Down, Gold, Deep 1993, West End Girls 1993, It's Alright 1993, Around the World 1994, Steam (UK no 4) 1994, Stay Another Day (UK no 1) 1994, Let It Rain 1995, Hold My Body Tight 1995, Thunder 1995, Do U Still 1996, Someone to Love 1996, Hey Child 1997; albums: Walthamstow (UK no 1, platinum disc, 1992), Steam (UK no 4, 1994), Up All Night (UK no 7, 1995); winner Ivor Novello Award (for Stay Another Day); *Style*— Anthony Mortimer, Esq; ✉ c/o London Records 90 Ltd, PO Box 1422, Chancellor's House, Chancellor's Road, London W6 9RS (☎ 0181 910 5111, fax 0181 741 2600)

MORTIMER, Edward James; s of Rt Rev Robert Cecil Mortimer, DD, Bishop of Exeter 1949–73 (d 1976), and Mary Hope, *née* Walker (d 1992); *b* 22 Dec 1943; *Educ* Summer Fields Oxford, Eton, Balliol Coll Oxford; *m* 1968, Elizabeth Anne, da of John Zanetti; 2 s (Horatio b 1970, Matthew b 1973), 2 da (Frances b 1978, Phoebe b 1980); *Career* asst d'Anglais Lycée Faidherbe St Louis-du-Sénégal 1962, fell All Souls Coll Oxford 1965–72 and 1984–86, foreign specialist and leader writer The Times 1973–85 (asst Paris corr 1967–70), sr assoc Carnegie Endowment (NY) 1980–81, series conslt Roosevelt's Children (Channel 4) 1985–87, foreign affairs ed Financial Times 1987–; res assoc IISS 1990–91, hon prof Dept of Govt and Int Rels Univ of Warwick 1993–; awards: winner first David Watt Meml prize 1988, European Press Prize 1993 (jtly); *Books* France and the Africans (1969), Eurocommunism, Myth or Reality (1979), Faith and Power, The Politics of Islam (1982), Rise of the French Communist Party (1984), Roosevelt's Children (1987), European Security After the Cold War (IISS Adelphi paper, 1992); *Recreations* conversation, travel, family life; *Clubs* Beefsteak, Groucho; *Style*— Edward Mortimer, Esq; ✉ Financial Times, 1 Southwark Bridge, London SE1 9HL (☎ 0171 873 4855, fax 0171 873 3193)

MORTIMER, James E (Jamie); s of James Edward Mortimer, and Renee Mabel, *née* Horton; *b* 9 Nov 1947; *Educ* Latymer Upper Sch, Wadham Coll Oxford (MA, BPhil); *m* 6 Sept 1969, Lesley Patricia, *née* Young; *Career* HM Treasy: econ asst 1971–72, sr econ asst 1972–74, econ advsr 1974–80 (macro-econ policy 1974–77, taxation 1977–80), princ (industl policy) 1980–83, grade 5 1983–91 (European Community budget 1983–89, public expenditure 1989–91), grade 3 Aid and Export Fin Gp (hd UK Delgn to the Paris Club) 1991–95, Treasy Offr of Accounts and dep dir Fin Mgmnt Audit and Reporting Directorate 1995–; *Recreations* soccer, cricket, golf, bird-spotting, cinema; *Clubs* RAC, Old Latymerians, Sunbury Golf; *Style—* Jamie Mortimer, Esq; ✉ Treasury Officer of Accounts, HM Treasury, Parliament Street, London SW1P 3AG (☎ 0171 270 4479, fax 0171 270 4311)

MORTIMER, John Clifford; CBE (1986), QC (1966); s of Clifford Mortimer, and Kathleen May, *née* Smith; *b* 21 April 1923; *Educ* Harrow, Brasenose Coll Oxford; *m* 1, 1949 (m dis 1972), Penelope Ruth Mortimer, *qv*, *née* Fletcher; 1 s (Jeremy), 1 da (Sally); m 2, Penelope, *née* Gollop; 2 da; *Career* barrister, playwright and author; called to the Bar 1948, master of the bench Inner Temple 1975; plays incl: The Dock Brief (1958), What Shall We Tell Caroline (1958), The Wrong Side of the Park (1960), Two Stars for Comfort (1962), The Judge (1967), Voyage Round My Father (1970, filmed 1982), I Claudius (1972, adapted from Robert Graves), Collaborators (1973), The Bells of Hell (1977); film script John Mary (1970); television scripts incl: Brideshead Revisited (1981), Edwin (1984), Under the Hammer (1993); works of fiction incl: Charade (1947), Three Winters (1956), Will Shakespeare and Entertainment (1977), Rumpole of the Bailey (1978, BAFTA Writer of the Year Award), The Trials of Rumpole (1979), Rumpole's Return (1980, televised), Regina vs Rumpole (1981), Rumpole for the Defence (1982), Rumpole and the Golden Thread (1983, televised), Paradise Postponed (1985, televised 1986), Rumpole's Last Case (1987), Summers Lease (1988, televised 1989), Rumpole and the Age of Miracles (1989), Titmuss Regained (1990, televised 1991), Rumpole À La Carte (1990), Dunster (1992), Rumpole on Trial (1992), Rumpole and the Angel of Death (1995); trans incl: A Flea in Her Ear (1965), The Lady From Maxim's (1977), A Little Hotel on the Side (for Nat Theatre) 1984, Die Fledermaus (for Covent Garden Opera) 1988; interviews incl: In Character (1983), Character Parts (1986); autobiog: Clinging to the Wreckage (1982, Yorkshire Post Book of the Year), Murderers and other Friends (1994); Christmas Carol (dramatised) RSC 1994; ed The Oxford Book of Villains (1992); pres Berks Bucks & Oxon Naturalists Tst 1984–90, memb Nat Theatre Bd 1968–89; chm: RSL 1990–, Royal Ct Theatre 1990–; pres Howard League of Penal Reform 1992–; writers award BAFTA; Hon DLitt Susquehanna Univ 1985, Hon LLD Exeter 1986, Hon DLitt St Andrews 1987, Hon DLitt Nottingham 1988, Hon DUniv Brunel 1990; Italia Prize 1958; FRSL; *Recreations* working, gardening, opera; *Clubs* Garrick; *Style—* John Mortimer, Esq, CBE, QC; ✉ c/o Peters Fraser & Dunlop Ltd, 503 The Chambers, Chelsea Harbour, Lots Road, London SW10 0XF (☎ 0171 352 4446, fax 0171 352 7356)

MORTIMER, Katharine Mary Hope; da of Rt Rev Robert Cecil Mortimer, DD, Bishop of Exeter 1949–73 (d 1976), and Mary Hope, *née* Walker (d 1992); *b* 28 May 1946; *Educ* St Mary and St Anne Abbots Bromley, Somerville Coll Oxford (BA, BPhil); *m* 1, 7 July 1973 (m dis 1986), John Noel Nicholson, s of Rev John Malcolm Nicholson (d 1982); 1 s (Andrew Robert b 1982); m 2, 19 May 1990, Robert Michael Dean, s of Daniel Dean; *Career* dir: National Bus Company (non-exec) 1979–91, N M Rothschild & Sons Ltd 1985–89 (non-exec 1988–89), Centre for Econ Policy Res (non-exec) 1986–91, N M Rothschild Asset Management (Holdings) 1987–89 (non-exec 1988–89); seconded as dir of policy Securities and Investments Bd 1985–87, chief exec Walker Books Ltd 1988–89, ind conslt 1989–, fin sector advsr to the UK Know How Fund 1989–; govr Imperial Coll of Sci and Technol 1987–91, tstee Inst for Public Policy Res 1989–92; memb: Cncl ESRC 1984–86, governing body Inst of Devpt Studies Sussex 1983–95, BBC General Advsy Cncl 1987–91, Royal Cmmn for the Exhibition of 1851 1987–, Bd of the Crown Agents 1990–, Bd British Nuclear Fuels plc 1992–, Monopolies and Mergers Cmmn 1995–; *Style—* Miss Katharine Mortimer; ✉ Lower Corscombe, Okehampton, Devon EX20 1SD (☎ 01837 840431)

MORTIMER, Penelope Ruth; da of Rev Arthur Forbes Gerard Fletcher (d 1959), and Caroline Amy, *née* Maggs (d 1973); *b* 19 Sept 1918; *Educ* Croydon HS, New Sch Streatham, Blencathra Rhyl, Garden Sch Lane End, St Elphin's Sch for Daughters of the Clergy, Univ Coll London; *m* 1, 1937 (m dis 1949), Charles Francis Dimont, 4 da (Madelon, Caroline, Julia, Deborah); m 2, 1949 (m dis 1972), John Clifford Mortimer, QC, *qv*; 1 s (Jeremy), 1 da (Sally); *Career* writer; FRSL; *Books* Johanna (as Penelope Dimont, 1947), A Villa in Summer (1954), The Bright Prison (1956), With Love & Lizards (with John Mortimer, 1957), Daddy's Gone A-Hunting (1958), Saturday Lunch with The Brownings (1960), The Pumpkin Eater (1962), My Friend Says It's Bulletproof (1967), The Home (1971), Long Distance (1974), About Time (autobiog, 1979, Whitbread prize), The Handyman (1983), Queen Elizabeth: A Life of the Queen Mother (1986), Portrait of a Marriage (screenplay, 1990), About Time Too (autobiog, 1993); *Style—* Penelope Mortimer, FRSL; ✉ 19 St Gabriel's Road, London NW2 4DS (☎ 0181 452 8551, fax 0181 208 1946)

MORTIMER, Robert (Bob); *b* 23 May 1959; *Career* comedian, part of comedy duo with Vic Reeves, *qv*; *Television* Vic Reeves Big Night Out 1990 and 1991, Weekenders (both Channel 4) 1992, The Smell of Reeves and Mortimer (2 series, BBC) 1993 and 1995, A Night in with Vic and Bob (Boxing Day Special) 1993, Shooting Stars 1995 and 1996, A Nose Through Nature 1995; *Tours* Vic Reeves Big Night Out 1990 and 1991, The Smell of Reeves and Mortimer 1994, The Smell of Reeves and Moritmer: The Weathercock Tour 1495 1995; *Awards* BAFTA Award for Originality 1991, Best Live Performance British Comedy Awards 1992, Best Comedy Series British Comedy Awards 1993; *Recordings* Dizzy (single, UK no 1), I Will Cure You (album), I'm A Believer; *Books* Big Night In (1991), Smell of Reeves and Mortimer (1993); *Style—* Bob Mortimer; ✉ c/o PBJ Management Ltd, 5 Soho Square, London W1V 5DE (☎ 0171 287 1112, fax 0171 287 1448)

MORTIMORE, Prof Peter John; OBE (1993); s of Claude Mortimore (d 1982), of Richmond, Surrey, and Rose, *née* Townsend; *b* 17 Jan 1942; *Educ* Chiswick GS, Univ of London (BSc, MSc, PhD); *m* 19 April 1965, Jo Marie, da of Michael Hargaden (d 1986), of Monmouth, Gwent; 3 da (Joanna b 1966, Rebecca b 1967, Claudia b 1968); *Career* teacher secdy sch 1965–73; res offr Inst of Psychiatry 1975–78, memb HMI 1978, dir of res and statistics ILEA 1979–85, asst educn offr (sec) ILEA 1985–88, prof and dir Sch of Educn Lancaster Univ 1988–90; Univ of London: prof of educn 1990–, dir Inst of Educn 1994– (dep dir 1990–94); memb: Br Psychological Soc, Assoc for Child Psychology and Psychiatry, Br Educnl Res Assoc, American Educnl Res Assoc; FBPsS 1988, FRSA 1990, FCP 1994; *Books* Fifteen Thousand Hours (co-author, 1979), Behaviour Problems in Schools (1984), Helpful Servant not Dominating Master (1986), School Matters (1988), The Primary Head (1991), The Secondary Head (1991), Managing Associate Staff (1993), Planning Matters (1995); *Recreations* music, theatre, walking; *Style—* Prof Peter Mortimore, OBE; ✉ Institute of Education, University of London, 20 Bedford Way, London WC1H 0AL (☎ 0171 612 6004, fax 0171 612 6089)

MORTIMORE, Simon Anthony; QC (1991); s of Robert Anthony Mortimore (d 1995), and Katharine Elizabeth, *née* Mackenzie Caine (d 1986); *b* 12 April 1950; *Educ* Westminster, Univ of Exeter (LLB); *m* 26 March 1983, Fiona Elizabeth, da of Bernard Maurice Jacobson (d 1988); 1 s (Edward Robert b 20 Jan 1988), 1 da (Laura Alexandra b 21 Feb 1985); *Career* called to the Bar Inner Temple 1972, dep bankruptcy registrar High Ct 1987–; *Books* Bullen Leake & Jacobs Precedents of Pleading (contrib 13 edn, 1990); *Recreations* golf; *Clubs* Hurlingham, Royal Mid Surrey Golf, Royal St George's Golf; *Style—* Simon Mortimore, Esq, QC; ✉ 3/4 South Square, Gray's Inn, London WC1R 5HP (☎ 0171 696 9900, fax 0171 696 9911, telex 920757 COSOL G)

MORTON, Alan James; s of Walter Morton (d 1974), and Agnes, *née* Watson; *b* 7 May 1944; *Educ* Roundhay GS; *m* 8 Aug 1970, Celia Joan, da of Dixon Charles Merry-Howe, 2 s (Iain James b 10 Feb 1974, Andrew Charles b 19 Jan 1977); *Career* CA 1969; ptnr i/c Leeds Office Armitage & Norton 1985–87 (formerly articled clerk, ptnr 1974, memb Nat Exec 1985–87); KPMG: ptnr 1987–, regnl business servs co-ordinator NE Region 1987–91, memb Nat Business Servs Ctee 1987–91, Business Unit managing ptnr Huddersfield 1990–; *Recreations* golf, walking, watching rugby union; *Clubs* Moortown Golf, Roundhegians; *Style—* Alan Morton, Esq; ✉ 9 Gateland Drive, Shadwell, Leeds LS17 8HU (☎ 0113 273 7292); KPMG, Station St Buildings, Huddersfield HD1 1LZ (☎ 01484 421433, fax 01484 518447, car 0860 670624)

MORTON, (John) Andrew; s of John Douglas Morton (d 1975), of Nutfield, Surrey, and Anne Marjorie, *née* Gray; *b* 5 July 1943; *Educ* Charterhouse, Merton College Oxford (BA); *m* 6 Dec 1975, Angela Fern Gage, da of Cdr Leonard Gage Wheeler, RN, of Alresford, Hants; 1 da (Fiona Anne b 1978); *Career* Univ of Oxford Air Sqdn RAFVR 1963–65; admitted slr 1968; ptnr Allen & Overy 1973– (asst slr 1968–73); dir Avenor Services Ltd; *Recreations* sailing, golf, skiing; *Clubs* Offshore Cruising, Royal Wimbledon Golf; *Style—* Andrew Morton, Esq; ✉ Allen & Overy, One New Change, London EC4M 9QQ (☎ 0171 330 3000, fax 0171 330 9999); Allen & Overy Legal Services, Dimitrovsky Pereulok 9, 103031, Moscow, Russian Federation (☎ 00 7501 258 3111, fax 00 7501 258 3113)

MORTON, Adm Sir Anthony Storrs; GBE (1982), KCB (1978), DL (1989); s of Dr Harold Morton, of Bridlington; *b* 6 Nov 1923; *Educ* St Anselm's Bakewell, Loretto; *Career* joined RN 1941, Cdr 1956, Capt 1964, Sr Naval Offr NI 1968–70, Rear Adm 1971, naval memb Sr DSD RCDS 1971–72, ACDS (Policy) 1973, Vice Adm 1975, flag offr First Flotilla 1975–77, Vice CDS 1977–78, vice chief Naval Staff 1978–80, Adm 1979, UK mil rep NATO 1980–83, ret RN 1984; King of Arms of Order of British Empire 1983–, Rear Adm of UK 1988–90, Vice Adm of UK 1990–93; OStJ 1990; *Recreations* sailing, fishing, shooting; *Clubs* RYS, RCC, ICC; *Style—* Adm Sir Anthony Morton, GBE, KCB, DL; ✉ c/o Barclays Bank Plc, 50 Jewry St, Winchester SO23 8RG

MORTON, His Hon Judge; (David) Christopher; s of Rev Alexander Francis Morton (d 1991), and Esther Ann, *née* Williams; *b* 1 Dec 1943; *Educ* Worksop Coll Notts, Fitzwilliam Coll Cambridge (BA, LLB); *m* Aug 1970, Sandra Jo, da of Alvin Kobes, of Nebraska; 1 da (Sarah Ceinwen b 8 April 1973), 3 s (Geraint Deiniol James b 28 April 1976, Emlyn David Gruffydd b 22 April 1980, Rhys Benjamin Hywel b 13 June 1982); *Career* called to the Bar Inner Temple 1968, recorder of the Crown Court 1988–92, circuit judge (Wales and Chester Circuit) 1992–; *Recreations* family, railways; *Clubs* Royal Over-Seas League; *Style—* His Hon Judge Morton; ✉ 80 Eaton Crescent, Swansea SA1 4QN

MORTON, 21 Earl of (S 1458); John Charles Sholto Douglas; also Lord Aberdour (no actual cr, but designation of the eld s & h, incorporated with the Earldom in a charter of 1638, where the Earls of Morton are described as *domini Abirdour*); head of the male line of the Douglas family worldwide; s of Hon Charles William Sholto Douglas (d 1960, 2 s of 19 Earl of Morton); suc cous, 20 Earl 1976; *b* 19 March 1927; *m* 1949, Mary Sheila, da of late Rev Canon John Stanley Gibbs, MC, of Didmarton House, Badminton, Glos; 2 s, 1 da; *Heir* s, Lord Aberdour, *qv*; *Career* ptnr Dalmahoy Farms, chm Edinburgh Polo Club; Lord Lt West Lothian (DL 1982); *Clubs* Edinburgh Polo, Dalmahoy Country; *Style—* The Rt Hon the Earl of Morton; ✉ Dalmahoy, Kirknewton, Midlothian (☎ 0131 333 1331)

MORTON, Dr Paul Greville; s of John Morton (d 1974), of Wolverhampton, and Ethel Harvey (d 1974); *b* 7 Aug 1922; *Educ* Wolverhampton Secdy Sch, Univ of London (BSc, DSc); *m* 18 April 1943, Florence Beatrice, da of Benjamin Hughes; 2 s (Raymond Paul b 23 July 1944, John Graham b 15 Aug 1949), 1 da (Maxine Susan b 31 March 1959); *Career* Boulton Paul Aircraft Wolverhampton: aircraft apprentice 1938–43, aircraft designer 1944–50, project engr 1951–59; supt Nelson Engineering Laboratories English Electric Company 1960–72, head Mechanical Div Stafford Laboratory GEC 1973–77, mangr Mechanical Laboratory GEC Research Ltd 1978–87; visiting prof: Univ of Strathclyde 1982–88, Univ of Bath 1989–92, Cranfield Univ 1992–; Nelson Gold medal awarded by GEC 1985; FIMechE 1967, FEng 1985, FRSA 1987; *Recreations* music; *Style—* Dr Paul Morton, FEng; ✉ 15 Firsway, Wolverhampton WV6 8BJ (☎ 01902 762770)

MORTON, Ralph Nicholas; s of John Frank Morton, and Nancy Margaret, *née* White; *b* 19 Sept 1958; *Educ* Alleyn's Sch Dulwich, Westfield Coll London (BA); *m* 26 May 1984, Alison Ellenor, da of Robert George Sharpe (d 1987); 1 s (Matthew James b 25 May 1992), 1 da (Sarah-Ellen b 25 Feb 1996); *Career* ed asst Philatelic Monthly 1981–82, prodn ed Autosport 1984–86 (ed asst 1982–84); What Car?: prodn ed 1986–88, dep ed 1988–89, assoc ed 1989–92, ed 1992–94, exec ed 1994–; ed-in-chief Haymarket motoring magazines 1994–; memb ctee Guild of Motoring Writers 1993–; *Recreations* swimming, hockey, cycling, reading; *Clubs* Edward Alleyn Hockey (sec 1990–92); *Style—* Ralph Morton, Esq; ✉ Haymarket Motoring Publications Ltd, 38–42 Hampton Road, Teddington, Middlesex TW11 0JE (☎ 0181 943 5917, fax 0181 943 5933)

MORTON, Reginald John (Reg); s of Maj John Henry Morton (d 1987), of Manchester, and Alice Blanche Gladys, *née* Chappelier (d 1990); *b* 17 Sept 1951; *Educ* Manchester GS, Univ of Birmingham (LLB); *m* 6 Oct 1979, Jennifer Mary, da of Reginald Carr, of Small Dole, W Sussex; 2 s (Jonathan b 1985, Thomas b 1988), 1 da (Katherine b 1992); *Career* slr Clifford Chance (formerly Clifford-Turner) 1975–85; Titmuss Sainer Dechert: joined 1985, partner 1987–, currently head Financial Services; memb Law Soc 1975; *Recreations* snooker, golf; *Style—* Reg Morton, Esq; ✉ Titmuss Sainer Dechert, 2 Serjeants' Inn, London EC4Y 1LT (☎ 0171 583 5353, fax 0171 353 3683, car 08367 45939, telex 23823 ADVICE G)

MORTON, Dr Richard Emile; s of Donald Morton, and Mary, *née* Wilkinson; *b* 10 Nov 1949; *Educ* Bexley GS, St John's Coll Oxford (BA, BM BCh), UCH; *m* 1 May 1976, April Joy Georgina, da of William Milne (d 1979); 1 s (Robert William), 2 da (Alice Elizabeth, Lucy Jenniffer); *Career* registrar in paediatrics Hosp for Sick Children Gt Ormond St, sr registrar in paediatrics London Hosp and Queen Elizabeth Hosp for Children Hackney, conslt paediatrician Derbyshire Childrens Hosp; chm Umbrella, sec BPA Child Disability and Devpt Gp; FRCP; *Recreations* family, music, running; *Style—* Dr Richard Morton; ✉ Derbyshire Children's Hospital, North St, Derby (☎ 01332 340131)

MORTON, Robert Edward; s of Charles Morton, and Yvonne, *née* Galea; *b* 20 May 1956; *Educ* Canford Sch Wimborne Dorset, Oriel Coll Oxford (MA); *m* 12 Dec 1981; 2 da (Caroline b 13 Aug 1983, Georgina b 21 Jan 1985); *Career* res analyst: Simon & Coates 1978–83, de Zoete & Bevan 1983–86 (ptnr 1986); dir and head Conglomerates and Business Servs Res Teams: Barclays de Zoete Wedd 1986–92, Charterhouse Tilney 1992–; MSI; *Recreations* squash, music, sailing; *Clubs* RAC; *Style—* Robert Morton, Esq; ✉ 28 Cambridge St, Pimlico, London SW1V 4QH (☎ 0171 828 7955)

MORTON-FLAGGE, Alastair Hamilton Arnold; s of late Lt-Col C P E Morton-Flagge, of Kirkcudbrightshire, and Flora May, *née* Hamilton; *b* 2 Dec 1938; *m* 1962 (m dis 1980), Nathalie, *née* Lefèvre; 2 da (Sophie Annabel b 1964, Valentine Nathalie b 1967); *Career* professional photographer; Nat Serv 2 Lt RCS; staff photographer Press Association (London, Washington, Middle East) 1962–66, freelance for Glasgow Herald and other Scottish newspapers 1966–75, ptnr PPM Bureau London (specialising in editorial and advertising photography) 1975–82, freelance editorial and advertising photographer 1982–; memb Int Inst of Advertising Photographers; *Style—* Alastair H Morton-Flagge, Esq; ✉ Kambia, Western Road, Andover, Hants SP10 2JQ

MORTON JACK, His Hon Judge David; s of Col William Andrew Morton Jack, OBE (d 1950), of Lemonfield Co, Galway, and Margery Elizabeth Happell (d 1978); *b* 5 Nov 1936; *Educ* Stowe, Trinity Coll Oxford (MA); *m* 1972, Elvira Rosemary, da of Francis Gallo Rentoul, of 1 Chara Place, London; 4 s (Edward b 1975, Richard b 1977, Henry b 1979, George b 1981); *Career* 2 Lt Royal Irish Fusiliers 1955–57 (Lt AER 1957–60); called to the Bar Lincoln's Inn, in practice SE Circuit 1962–86, recorder of the Crown Ct 1979–86, circuit judge (SE Circuit) 1986–; *Recreations* fishing, shooting, reading, music; *Style—* His Hon Judge David Morton Jack; ✉ 1 Harcourt Buildings, Temple, London EC4Y 9DA

MOSCO, Maisie; *b* Manchester; *Educ* state sch; *m* Gerald Mosco (d 1993); 2 s (Maurice, Stephen), 2 da (Marilyn, Carole); *Career* formerly journalist, fiction writer since 1960s; early work for theatre, author of 14 radio plays and 12 novels; *Books* incl: Almonds and Raisins trilogy; *Style—* Ms Maisie Mosco; ✉ c/o Harper Collins Publishers, 77–85 Fulham Palace Road, Hammersmith, London W6 8JB

MOSCOW, Dr David; s of Emanuel Moscow (d 1981), and Rachel, *née* Davidovitch; *b* 3 May 1937; *Educ* Parmiter's GS London, Univ of London (BSc), Univ of Leicester, Univ of Leeds (PhD); *m* 1, 1960 (m dis 1972), Jennifer Dianne, da of William Thomas Redgate (d 1986); 4 da (Sarah b 1964, Susan b 1967, Emma b 1968, Linda b 1969); m 2, 1975, Patricia Ann, da of Frank Edward Gostling, OBE, of Oxshott, Surrey; *Career* personnel offr BAC 1960–63, lectr Univ of Leeds 1963–67, res assoc Netherlands Inst for Preventive Med 1967–70, jt md Sheppard Moscow and Associates Ltd 1984–86 (chm 1970–84); conslt to: ICI, Shell, other multi-national orgns, NHS, Bank of England; FInstD 1977, FIMgt 1983, FIMC 1986; *Recreations* golf, sculpture; *Style—* Dr David Moscow; ✉ Rochester House, Parkfield, Sevenoaks, Kent TN15 (☎ 01732 761007)

MOSELEY, Sir George Walker; KCB (1982, CB 1978); s of William Moseley, MBE, and Bella Moseley; *b* 7 Feb 1925; *Educ* Glasgow HS, St Bees Sch Cumberland, Wadham Coll Oxford (MA); *m* 1, 1950, Anne Mercer (d 1989); m 2, 1990, Madge James; 1 s, 1 da; *Career* serv RAF and RAF Levies Iraq 1943–48; Miny Housing and Local Govt: asst private sec to Min 1951–52, private sec to Parly Sec 1952–54, princ private sec to Min 1963–65, asst sec 1965–70, under sec 1970–76; dep sec DOE 1976–78, dep sec CSD 1978–80, second perm sec DOE 1980–81, perm sec DOE 1981–85; cmmr Historic Bldgs and Monuments Cmmn 1986–91; chm: Br Cement Assoc 1987–96, Civic Tst 1990–; memb Advsy Cncl on Public Records 1989–92; *Style—* Sir George Moseley, KCB; ✉ Churchmead, Church Lane, Widdington, Saffron Walden, Essex CB11 3SF

MOSELEY, His Hon Judge; (Thomas) Hywel; QC (1985); s of Rev Luther Moseley (d 1994), and Megan Eiluned, *née* Howells (d 1977); *b* 27 Sept 1936; *Educ* Caterham Sch Surrey, Queens' Coll Cambridge (MA, LLM); *m* 25 June 1960, Monique Germaine Thérèse, da of Edmond Gaston Drufin (d 1977); 3 da (Catrin b 1961, Eirian (twin) b 1961, Gwenda b 1969); *Career* called to the Bar Gray's Inn 1964, in practice Wales and Chester Circuit 1964, recorder 1981, circuit judge (Wales and Chester Circuit) 1989–; prof of law Univ Coll of Wales Aberystwyth 1970–83; memb Insolvency Rules Ctee 1993–; *Recreations* beekeeping; *Style—* His Hon Judge Moseley, QC; ✉ Nantceiro, Llanbadarn Fawr, Aberystwyth, Dyfed SY23 3HW (☎ and fax 01970 623532); 6 Belgrave Court, 25 Cowbridge Road East, Cardiff CF1 9BJ (☎ and fax 01222 237769)

MOSELEY, Dr Ivan Frederick; s of Frederick Clarence Moseley (d 1994), and Edith Sophia, *née* Smith (d 1987); *b* 29 May 1940; *Educ* Latymer Upper Sch, St Mary's Hosp Med Sch Univ of London (BSc, MB BS, DMRD, MD, MRCP), Centre for the Study of Philosophy and Health Care Univ Coll Swansea (PhD); *m* 22 April 1967, Mary Cheyne Thomson, da of George Malcolm, of Royston, Cambs (d 1991); 1 s (James b 1978), 1 da (Hannah b 1968); *Career* house offr: St Mary's Hosp Paddington 1965–66, Whittington Hosp 1967; sr house offr: Royal Marsden Hosp 1967–68, London Chest Hosp 1968; sr registrar in radiology Bart's 1970–72 (registrar 1968–70), clinical assoc fell Mount Zion Hosp and postdoctoral scholar Univ of California San Francisco 1972–73; consultant radiologist: National Hosp Queen Sq London 1975– (sr registrar 1973–75, dir of radiology 1994–), Wellington Hosp London 1975–87, Moorfields Eye Hosp London 1984– (dir of radiology 1987–), hon conslt Royal Surrey County Hosp Guildford 1988–92; Br Cncl visiting prof Université de Nancy 1978; visiting prof: Univ of California San Francisco 1982, Univ of Hong Kong 1988, Univ of Auckland 1988; Br rep Euro Union of Med Specialists 1988–; Wellcome Tst scholar Univ of West Indies Jamaica 1964, CIBA/INSERM scholar Hôpital Lariboisière Paris 1974, Euro Soc of Neuroradiology prize 1976; ed Neuroradiology 1993; memb: Br Soc of Neuroradiologists 1975 (sec 1986–90), Euro Soc of Neuroradiology 1976, BIR 1978, European Soc for Philosophy of Med and Health Care 1992; assoc memb Société Française de Neuroradiologie 1974; FFR 1972, FRCR 1975, FRSM 1980, FRCP 1985; *Books* Computer Tomographie des Kopfes (contrib, 1978), Computerized Tomography in Neuro-Ophthalmology (contrib, 1982), Diagnostic Imaging in Neurological Disease (1986), Magnetic Resonance Imaging in Diseases of the Nervous System (1988); *Recreations* music, wine, bullfighting, graphic arts; *Clubs* Arts, Spanish, Club Taurino of London (sec gen 1985–90, pres 1990–); *Style—* Dr Ivan Moseley; ✉ National Hospital for Neurology & Neurosurgery, Queen Square, London WC1N 3BG (☎ 0171 837 7660, fax 0171 278 5122)

MOSELEY, Peter Charles; s of Charles Henry Moseley (d 1982), and Edna Mary, *née* Hill, of Fakenham, Norfolk; *Educ* Selwyn Coll Cambridge (MA), dip in mgmnt studies; *m* 25 March 1967, Joy, da of Lewis Pincombe (d 1983); 2 s (Nicholas Peter b 29 Sept 1970, John Paul b 4 Aug 1972); *Career* grad trainee Morganite Carbon Ltd 1965–66, Quaker Oats Ltd 1966–78; sales and mktg dir: C Shippam Ltd 1978–85, HP Foods Ltd 1985–89; sr conslt Bergenroth & Co Ltd 1989–92, bd sales and mktg dir John Lusty Group plc and md The Foodfinders Ltd 1992–93, md Garma Gourmet (UK) Ltd 1994–; Mktg Soc: memb Mgmnt Ctee 1985–95, chm 1992–93, fell 1993; memb Mktg Gp of GB; *Recreations* squash, reading (novels), western movies, theatre; *Clubs* Old Dunstonians, Old Selwynians; *Style—* Peter C Moseley, Esq; ✉ Garma Gourmet (UK) Ltd, 7 Britannia Court, The Green, West Drayton, Middlesex UB7 7PN (☎ 01895 432800, fax 01895 432703, car 0468 618184)

MOSER, Sir Claus Adolf; KCB (1973), CBE (1965); s of Dr Ernest Moser, and Lotte Moser; *b* 24 Nov 1922; *Educ* Frensham Heights Sch, LSE; *m* 1949, Mary Oxlin; 1 s, 2 da; *Career* LSE: asst lectr 1946–49, lectr 1949–55, reader 1955–61, prof of social statistics 1961–70, visiting prof 1970–75; statistical advsr Ctee for Higher Educn 1961–64, dir Central Statistical Office and head Govt Statistical Serv 1967–78, visiting fell Nuffield Coll Oxford 1972–80, pres Royal Statistical Soc 1978–80; memb: Governing Body RAM 1967–79, BBC Music Advsy Ctee 1971–; chm Bd of Dirs Royal Opera House Covent Garden 1974–87, vice chm NM Rothschild & Sons 1978–84 (dir 1984–90); dir: Economist Intelligence Unit 1979–83, The Economist 1979–, Equity and Law Life Assurance Society 1980–87, Octopus Publishing Group 1982–88, chm Harold Holt Ltd 1990–; warden Wadham Coll Oxford 1984–, chllr Univ of Keele 1986–; tstee: Pilgrim Tst 1982–, Br Museum 1988–, London Philharmonic Orch 1988–; pres Br Assoc for the Advancement of Sci 1989–90; FBA 1969; Hon FRAM, hon fell LSE; Hon DSc: Univ of Southampton, Univ of Leeds, City Univ London, Univ of Sussex, Univ of Wales, Liverpool; Hon DUniv: Keele, Surrey, York, Edinburgh, Open Univ; Hon DTech Brunel Univ; Cdr de l'Ordre National du Mérite (France); *Style—* Sir Claus Moser, KCB, CBE; ✉ 3 Regent's Park Terrace, London NW1 7EE (☎ 0171 485 1619)

MOSER, Robin Allan Shedden; s of Allan Hugh Shedden Moser (d 1970), of Betchworth, Surrey, and Mary Dorothy Chatfeild-Clarke, *née* Shanks; *b* 3 June 1947; *Educ* Radley; *m* 17 Feb 1973, Sally, da of Walter Douglas Knowles (d 1985), of Beckenham, Kent; 3 s (Robert David b 1975, Patrick Allan b 1978, Edward Alexander b 1983); *Career* CA and banker; md and chief exec Alexanders Discount plc 1984–, dir Credit Lyonnais Capital Markets PLC 1986–; chm London Discount Market Assoc 1992–94; FCA; *Recreations* golf, sailing; *Clubs* Saffron Walden Golf; *Style—* Robin Moser, Esq; ✉ Mallows Green Farm, Manuden, Bishop's Stortford, Herts CM23 1BS; Alexanders Discount plc, Broadwalk House, 5 Appold St, London EC2A 2DA (☎ 0171 588 1234)

MOSES, Colin John; *b* 13 Sept 1962; *Educ* Woodhouse Grove Sch Bradford, Univ of Sheffield (BArch, DipArch); *Career* currently design dir RMJM Ltd; *Style—* Colin Moses, Esq; ✉ RMJM Ltd, 83 Paul Street, London EC2A 4NQ (☎ 0171 251 5588, fax 0171 250 3131)

MOSES, Geoffrey Haydn; s of Canon Haydn Moses (d 1983), of Llanelli Vicarage, Dyfed, and Beryl Mary, *née* Lloyd); *b* 24 Sept 1952; *Educ* Ystalyfera GS, Emmanuel Coll Cambridge (BA, Cricket blue), King's Coll London (PGCE); *m* 24 July 1981, Anne Elizabeth, da of Harry Mason; *Career* bass; princ singer WNO 1978–82; *Performances* Barber of Seville (WNO 1978, Scottish Opera 1984, Hamburg State Opera 1984), Tales of Hoffman (Royal Opera House Covent Garden) 1981, Don Giovanni (Glyndebourne Touring Opera 1982, Kent Opera 1983), Madame Butterfly (Opera North) 1983, Arabella (Glyndebourne Festival Opera) 1983, Simon Boccanegra (Belgian Opera) 1983, Salome (Netherlands Opera) 1988, Falstaff (WNO 1988–92, touring NY, Paris, Milan and Tokyo), La Favorita, Tristan & Isolde, Eugene Onegin and Lucia di Lammermoor (all WNO 1993), Peter Grimes (Glyndebourne Festival) 1994; concerts and recitals at: Gothenberg, Frankfurt Alte Oper, Royal Festival Hall, Royal Albert Hall; dubut Deutche Opera Berlin (I Puritani) 1991, dubut Opera de Nancy (Somnambula) 1991, Hong Kong Festival (Marriage of Figaro) 1991; *Recreations* walking, cricket, reading, wine; *Style—* Geoffrey Moses, Esq; ✉ IMG Artists Europe, Media House, 3 Burlington Lane, London W4 2TH (☎ 0181 747 9977, fax 0181 747 9131)

MOSES, Very Rev Dr John Henry; s of Henry William Moses (d 1975), of London, and Ada Elizabeth Moses; *b* 12 Jan 1938; *Educ* Ealing GS, Univ of Nottingham, Trinity Hall Cambridge, Lincoln Theol Coll (BA, PhD, Gladstone Meml prize); *m* 25 July 1964, Susan Elizabeth, da of James Wainwright (d 1980), of London; 1 s (Richard), 2 da (Rachel, Catherine); *Career* asst curate St Andrew's Bedford 1964–70, rector Coventry East Team Ministry 1970–77, examining chaplain to Bishop of Coventry 1972–77, rural dean Coventry East 1973–77, archdeacon of Southend 1977–82, provost of Chelmsford 1982–96, dean of St Paul's 1996–; church cmmr 1988–; *Clubs* Athenaeum; *Style—* The Very Rev the Dean of St Paul's; ✉ The Deanery, 9 Amen Court, London EC4M 7BU (☎ 0171 236 2827)

MOSESSON, John Gunnar; s of Torsten Johannes Mosesson (d 1974); *b* 9 July 1938; *Educ* Frensham Heights Sch, Univ of Keele (BA), Royal Coll of Music (ARCM); *m* 1, 1968 (m dis 1980), Jennifer Davies; 2 s (Dargan b 1972, Truan b 1976), 1 da (Gaël b 1970); m 2, 1985 (m dis 1990), Ruth Marland; m 3, 1990, Baroness Anne, da of Baron Jack Anstruther Carl Knutson Bonde; 1 da (Cecilia b 1991); *Career* staff memb: John Laing Res and Devpt 1959–61, Univ of Keele 1961–65; md T F Sampson Ltd 1965; chm: T F Sampson Ltd 1974–, Stramit International 1982– (md 1974–82); vice pres Friends Aldeburgh Fndn 1985–; memb Cncl: Historic Houses Assoc 1987–, E Anglian Tourist Bd 1990–, Suffolk Gdns Tst 1995–; *Recreations* music, tennis, golf, heritage issues; *Clubs* Chelsea Arts; *Style—* John Mosesson, Esq; ✉ Otley Hall, Otley, Suffolk IP6 9PA (☎ 01473 890264, fax 01473 890803); Stramit International Ltd, Creeting Road, Stowmarket, Suffolk IP14 5BA (☎ 01449 613564, fax 01449 678381)

MOSEY, Roger; s of late Geoffrey Swain Mosey, of Washingborough, Lincoln, and Marie, *née* Pilkington; *b* 4 Jan 1958; *Educ* Bradford GS, Wadham Coll Oxford (MA); *Career* with Pennine Radio Ltd Bradford 1979–80; BBC: reporter BBC Radio Lincolnshire 1980–82, prodr BBC Radio Northampton 1982–83, prodr The Week in Westminster BBC Radio 4 1983–84, prodr Today 1984–86, prodr BBC New York Bureau 1986–87, ed PM 1987–89, ed The World at One 1989–93, ed The Today Programme 1993–96, exec ed Radio 4 current affairs progs 1996, controller Radio 5 Live 1996–; One World Bdcasting Tst Award 1990, Br Environment and Media Award 1990, 1991 and 1995, Sony Gold Award 1994, Bdcasting Press Guild Radio Prog of the Year 1995, Best Speech-Based Breakfast Show Sony Radio Awards 1995, Voice of the Listener & Viewer Award for Outstanding Radio Prog 1996; *Recreations* travel, cinema, computers, reading political biographies and thrillers; *Style—* Roger Mosey, Esq; ✉ BBC, Broadcasting House, London W1A 1AA (☎ 0171 580 4468)

MOSHINSKY, Elijah; s of Abraham Moshinsky, and Eva, *née* Krasavitsky; *b* 8 Jan 1946; *Educ* Camberwell, Melbourne Univ (BA), St Antony's Coll Oxford (DPhil); *m* 5 June 1970, Ruth, da of Oscar Dyttman, of Melbourne, Aust; 2 s (Benjamin b 6 Dec 1980, Jonathan b 5 May 1983); *Career* producer; *Theatre* for NT: Troilus and Cressida 1976, The Force of Habit 1976; for West End: Three Sisters (Albery) 1987, Light Up the Sky (Globe) 1987, Another Time (Wyndham's) 1990, Shadowlands (Queen's) 1990, Becket 1991, Reflected Glory (Vaudeville) 1992, Cyrano de Bergerac (Haymarket) 1992; *Opera* princ guest prodr Royal Opera House 1975–88; prodns at Royal Opera House: Peter Grimes 1974, Lohengrin 1979, The Rakes Progress 1980, Macbeth 1981, Samson and Delilah 1981, Handel's Samson 1985, Otello 1986, Die Entführung aus dem Serail 1987, Attila 1990, Simon Boccanegra 1991; for ENO: Le Grand Macabre 1980, The Mastersingers of Nuremberg 1984; *Television* BBC incl: All's Well that Ends Well 1980, A Midsummer Night's Dream 1981, Cymbeline 1982, Coriolanus 1983, Love's Labours Lost 1984, Ghosts 1986; *Film* The Green Man (Kingsley Amis) 1990; *Recreations* reading, music; *Clubs* Garrick; *Style—* Elijah Moshinsky, Esq; ✉ c/o William Morris Agency (UK) Ltd, 31/32 Soho Square, London W1V 6DG (☎ 0171 434 2191, fax 0171 437 0238)

MOSIMANN, Anton; s of Otto Albert Mosimann, and Olga, *née* Von Burg (d 1966); *b* 23 Feb 1947; *m* 13 April 1973, Kathrin, da of Jakob Roth; 2 s (Philipp Anton b 1975, Mark Andreas b 1977); *Career* apprentice Hotel Baeren Twann Switzerland 1962–64, commis entremetier Palace Hotel Villars 1964–65, commis gardemanger Cavalieri Hilton Rome 1965, chef tournant and sous chef Queen Elizabeth Hotel Montreal 1966–69; chef tournant: Palace Hotel Montreux 1969, Palace Hotel St Moritz 1969–70; exec chef Swiss Pavilion Expo 70 Osaka Japan 1970, chef entremetier Palace Hotel Lausanne 1970; sous chef: Palace Hotel Lucerne summer seasons 1971–73, Kulm Hotel St Moritz winter seasons 1972–73 and 1973–74 (chef restaurateur 1971–72); commis pâtissier Palace Hotel Gstaad 1974–75, dir of cuisine Dorchester London 1986–88 (maître chef des cuisines 1975), chef patron Mosimann's London 1988–; frequent TV and radio appearances incl: Mosimann Naturally (C4) 1991 and 1994, and as co-presenter My Favourite Nosh (BBC) 1996; winner of numerous Gold medals and awards worldwide; Hon Dr Culinary Arts Johnson and Wales Univ South Carolina; La Croix de Chevalier du Mérite Agricole, Swiss Ambassador of the Year 1995; *Books* Cuisine à la Carte (1981), The Great Seafood Book (1985), Cuisine Naturelle (1985), Anton Mosimann's Fish Cuisine (1988), The Art of Anton Mosimann (1989), Cooking with Mosimann (1989), Mosimann Naturally (1991), The Essential Mosimann (1993), Mosimann's World (1996); *Recreations* jogging, squash, vintage cars, collecting antique cookery books; *Style—* Anton Mosimann, Esq; ✉ Mosimann's, 11B West Halkin St, Belgrave Square, London SW1X 8JL (☎ 0171 235 9625, fax 0171 245 6354)

MOSLEY, Prof Derek John; s of Frederick Mosley (d 1981), of Potters Bar, and Louise Ellen, *née* Wallis; *b* 11 Nov 1934; *Educ* Watford Boys' GS, Univ of Durham (BA), Univ of Cambridge (MA, PhD); *m* 29 Dec 1962, Margot, da of Harry Firth (d 1946), of Lytham St Annes; 2 da (Karen Angela b 9 June 1967, Nicole Andrea b 22 June 1969); *Career* Univ of Sheffield: asst lectr in classics and ancient history 1959–62, lectr 1962–68, sr lectr 1968–75, reader 1975, prof of ancient history and classical archaeology 1975–88, dean of arts 1987–88; prof of classics and ancient history Univ of Warwick 1988–94; visiting lectr in history Univ of Michigan 1965–66; memb AUT (pres Sheffield Local Assoc 1982–84); *Books* Envoys and Diplomacy in Ancient Greece (1973), Ancient Greek Diplomacy (with FE Adcock, 1975), Antike Diplomatie (jtly, 1980); *Recreations* music, walking, philately, travel; *Style*— Prof Derek Mosley; ✉ Department of Classics and Ancient History, University of Warwick, Coventry CV4 7AL (☎ 01203 523523)

MOSLEY, Max Rufus; 4 s (but only 2 by his 2 w, Diana, *see* Hon Lady Mosley) of Sir Oswald Mosley, 6 Bt; *b* 13 April 1940; *Educ* ChCh Oxford (sec Union Soc 1960); *m* 1960, Jean Marjorie, er da of James Taylor; 2 s (Alexander b 1970, Patrick b 1972); *Career* called to the Bar Gray's Inn 1964, fndr dir March Cars Ltd, legal advsr to Formula One Constructors Assoc; pres Fedn Internationale du Sport Automobile, pres Fedn Internationale de l'Automobile; *Recreations* snowboarding, walking; *Style*— Max Mosley, Esq; ✉ 8 Place de la Concorde, 75008 Paris, France (☎ 00 331 43 12 44 55)

MOSLEY, Nicholas; *see:* Ravensdale, 3 Baron

MOSLEY, Hon Shaun Nicholas; s and h of 3 Baron Ravensdale, MC, *qv*; *b* 5 Aug 1949; *Educ* Bryanston Sch, Hertford Coll Oxford; *m* 3 Feb 1979, Teresa Frances, da of Daniel Clifford; 5 s (Daniel Nicholas b 1982, Matthew b 1985, Francis b 1988, Aidan b 1991, Thomas b 199–); *Style*— The Hon Shaun Mosley

MOSLEY, Simon James; yr s of John Arthur Noel Mosley (3 s of Sir Oswald Mosley, 5 Bt, and his 1 w, Katharine, da of Capt Justinian Edwards-Heathcote), and his 1 w, Caroline Edith Sutton, *née* Timmis; *b* 8 April 1927; *Educ* Eton, Christ Church Oxford; *m* 15 Dec 1957, Maria, o da of Iraklis Zeris (d 1980); 1 s (George b 1959), 1 da (Claire b 1964); *Career* slr 1956–93, pres Holborn Law Soc 1967–68, memb Cncl Law Soc 1969–81; govr The Coll of Law 1973–91; chm: Octavian Group Ltd 1984–86, Trinity International Holdings plc Group 1985–94; *Clubs* Cavalry and Guards'; *Style*— Simon Mosley, Esq; ✉ 59 Onslow Gardens, London SW7 3QF

MOSS, Anthony David; s of David Samuel Moss (d 1970), of Eltham Coll, London, and Phyllis Holland, *née* Newton (d 1973); *b* 24 Jan 1932; *Educ* Cranbrook, Jesus Coll Cambridge (MA); *m* 25 Aug 1956, Jennifer Ann, JP, da of Prof William Hume-Rothery, OBE, FRS (d 1968), of Oxford; 1 s (Nicholas Hume b 1962), 2 da (Philippa Jane b 1960, Charlotte Katharine b 1966); *Career* Nat Serv cmmnd Libya 1951–52; Metal Box Co Ltd 1956–64; admitted slr 1968; ptnr Hyde Mahon Bridges (formerly Hyde Mahon & Pascall) 1969–91; Freeman City of London 1964, Liveryman and memb Ct Worshipful Co of Ironmongers (Master 1987–88), memb Ct of Common Cncl Corp of London (Tower Ward) 1989–, Sheriff City of London 1992–93; govr: Christ's Hosp 1981–, Museum of London 1992–, Bridwell Royal Hosp 1993–; tstee Geffrye Museum 1990–95, vice chm and hon treas Metropolitan Public Gardens Assoc 1993–; memb Order of the Crown of Brunei 1992, Cdr Order of Infante dom Henrique (Portugal) 1993; memb: Georgian Gp, London Topographical Soc, Law Soc; *Recreations* historic buildings, London history, walking; *Clubs* United Wards, City Livery; *Style*— Anthony Moss, Esq; ✉ The Bury Farm, Chesham, Bucks HP5 2JU (☎ 01494 775878)

MOSS, Christopher John; QC (1994); s of John Gordon (Jack) Moss (d 1984), of Kingston-upon-Thames, and Joyce Mirren (Joy), *née* Stephany; *b* 4 Aug 1948; *Educ* Bryanston, Univ Coll London (LLB); *m* 1, 11 Dec 1971 (m dis 1987), Gail Susan, da of late Frederick Pearson; 2 da (Melanie Jane b 17 Feb 1975, Rebecca Caroline b 1 Sept 1980), 1 s (Nicholas John b 17 Sept 1977); *m* 2, 31 March 1988 (sep 1994), Tracy Louise, da of Geoffrey Levy; 1 s (Aaron Geoffrey b 2 Oct 1989), 1 da (Liberty Michele b 10 April 1992); *Career* called to the Bar Gray's Inn 1972, recorder of the Crown Court 1993–; memb Criminal Bar Assoc 1980–; *Recreations* playing the piano and piano accordion; *Style*— Christopher Moss, Esq, QC; ✉ 5 Essex Court, 1st Floor, Temple, London EC4Y 9AH (☎ 0171 583 2825, fax 0171 583 1723)

MOSS, David Christopher; s of Charles Clifford Moss, and Marjorie Sylvia, *née* Hutchings; *b* 17 April 1946; *Educ* King's Sch Chester, Magdalene Coll Cambridge (BA); *m* 13 Aug 1971, Angela Mary, da of John Valentine Wood; 1 s (James Henry b 1976); *Career* Civil Serv: MPBW 1968–70, DOE 1970–77, Dept of Tport 1977–79, HM Treasy 1979–80, Dept of Tport 1980–81, DOE 1981–83, Dept of Tport 1983–94 (under sec Int Aviation), Euro Civil Aviation Conf 1988–93 (chm Econ Ctee II 1988–90, pres 1990–93); Railtrack plc: commercial dir 1994–95, Euro affrs dir 1995–; *Recreations* opera, wine, ecclesiastical architecture; *Clubs* United Oxford & Cambridge University; *Style*— David Moss, Esq; ✉ European Affairs Director, Railtrack plc, 40 Bernard Street, London WC1N 1BY (☎ 0171 344 7384); rue Ducale 85/87, 1000 Brussels, Belgium (☎ 00 32 2 551 0980)

MOSS, David John; s of John Henry Moss, and Doris Fenna; *b* 23 May 1947; *Educ* Sevenoaks Sch, St John's Coll Cambridge (MA), Central London Poly (DMS); *m* 24 May 1975, Susan Elizabeth, da of Reginald Victor Runnalls (d 1982); 3 s (Oliver Richard b 21 April 1976, Benjamin Roland (twin), Jonathan Edward b 1 Dec 1980); *Career* mgmnt accountant Philips 1970–73 (mgmnt trainee 1968–70), asst fin offr St Thomas' Hosp 1973–74; dist fin offr: Enfield 1974–79, East Dorset 1979–85; unit gen mangr: Poole Gen Hosp 1985–88, Southampton Gen Hosp 1988–90; gen mangr Southampton Univ Hosps 1990–93, chief exec Southampton Univ Hosps NHS Tst 1993–; memb CIPFA 1979, FCMA 1981, FIMgt 1984, memb Inst of Health Servs Mgmnt 1979; FRSA 1994; *Books* Managing Nursing (co-author, 1984); *Recreations* history, golf, badminton, opera, tennis, cricket; *Style*— David Moss, Esq; ✉ Southampton University Hospitals Tst, Southampton General Hospital, Tremona Rd, Southampton, Hants (☎ 01703 796172)

MOSS, David Joseph; CMG (1989); s of Herbert Joseph Moss (d 1961), and Irene Gertrude Moss; *b* 6 Nov 1938; *Educ* Hampton GS; *m* 3 June 1961, Joan Lillian, da of Alfred Herbert Tyler (d 1987); 1 s (James b 1970, d 1991), 1 da (Catherine b 1971); *Career* FO 1957, Nat Serv RAF 1957–59, FO 1959–62, 3 sec Bangkok 1962–65, FO 1966–69, 1 sec La Paz 1969–70, FCO 1970–73, 1 sec and head of Chancery The Hague 1974–77, 1 sec FCO 1978–79, cnsllr 1979–83, cnsllr, head of Chancery and dep perm rep UK Mission Geneva 1983–87, asst under sec of state FCO 1987–90, Br high cmmr NZ and non-resident high cmmr Western Samoa/non-resident govr Pitcairn, Henderson, Dulcie and Oeno Islands 1990–94, high cmmr Malaysia 1994–; *Recreations* reading, walking; *Style*— HE Mr David Moss, CMG; ✉ c/o Foreign and Commonwealth Office (Kuala Lumpur), King Charles Street, London SW1A 2AH

MOSS, David Reginald; s of Frank Moss, and Iris, *née* Thornton; *b* 11 March 1949; *Educ* Stockport Sch, Faculty of Art and Design Liverpool Poly (DipAD, RSA bursary); *m* 10 Aug 1971, Pauline Althea, da of Edward Scott Jones; 3 s (Robin James b 10 Nov 1973, Andrew Thornton b 20 Sept 1978, Laurence Scott (twin) b 20 Sept 1978); *Career* visualiser Clough Howard & Richards 1971–73; Brunning Advertising Liverpool: sr visualiser 1973–74, art dir 1974–75, creative controller 1975–76, creative dir 1977; exec prodr Five Cities Films 1977–79, bd account dir Michael Bungey DFS Liverpool 1979–85, account dir Brunning Advertising Yorkshire 1985–86, fndr md Quadrant Advertising and Marketing 1986–; memb Manchester Publicity Assoc; MIPA 1991; *Recreations* tennis, golf; *Style*— David Moss, Esq; ✉ Quadrant Advertising & Marketing Ltd, Central House, Central Way, Winwick Street, Warrington, Cheshire WA2 7TT (☎ 01925 411217, fax 01925 572971)

MOSS, Dr Edward; s of George Moss (d 1962), of Shipley, W Yorks, and Elizabeth Mary, *née* Dunn; *b* 10 Sept 1948; *Educ* Bradford GS, Univ of Edinburgh (MB ChB, MD); *m* 10 July 1972, Elizabeth Marie, da of the late William Arthur Tonkin, of Douglas, IOM; 2 s (Nicholas William George, Christopher Edward Stuart); *Career* house offr in gen surgery Bradford Royal Infirmary 1973 (house offr in med 1972), sr house offr in anaesthetics United Leeds Hosps 1973, registrar anaesthetics The Gen Infirmary at Leeds 1974, lectr in anaesthesia Univ of Leeds 1976, sr registrar in anaesthetics Yorks RHA 1977, conslt anaesthetist United Leeds Teaching Hosps NHS Tst 1979, sr clinical lectr Univ of Leeds 1989 (clinical lectr in anaesthesia 1979), examiner Royal Coll of Anaesthetists 1990; memb: Yorks Soc of Anaesthetists, The Neuroanaesthesia Soc of GB and Ireland, BMA, Assoc of Anaesthetists of GB and Ireland, Royal Soc of Med; FRCA; *Books* Aspects of Recovery from Anaesthesia (ed with I Hindmarch, J G Jones, 1987); *Recreations* golf; *Style*— Dr Edward Moss; ✉ 10 Dunstarn Lane, Adel, Leeds LS16 8EL (☎ 0113 267 9635); Dept of Anaesthetics, The General Infirmary at Leeds, Great George St, Leeds, W Yorkshire LS1 3EX (☎ 0113 292 6672)

MOSS, Gabriel Stephen; QC (1989); *b* 8 Sept 1949; *Educ* Univ of Oxford (Eldon scholar, BA, BCL, MA); *m* 1979, Judith; 1 da; *Career* called to the Bar Lincoln's Inn 1974 (Hardwicke and Cassel scholarships), in practice specialising in business and fin law; fndr memb Bd Insolvency Res Unit King's Coll London 1991–; memb: Editorial Bd Insolvency Intelligence 1991– (chm 1994–), Insolvency Law Sub-Ctee of the Consumer and Commercial Law Ctee Law Soc 1991–; formerly: lectr Univ of Connecticut Law Sch, pt/t lectr/tutor Univ of Oxford, LSE and Cncl of Legal Educn; *Books* Rowlatt on Principal and Surety (ed jtly, 4 edn 1982), Law of Receivers of Companies (jtly, 1986, 2 edn 1994), Ryde on Rating (contrib, 1990); *Recreations* chess, gardening, foreign travel, tennis; *Style*— Gabriel Moss, Esq, QC; ✉ 3/4 South Square, Gray's Inn, London WC1 (☎ 0171 696 9900, fax 0171 696 9911)

MOSS, Kate; da of Peter Edward Moss, and Linda Rosina, *née* Shephard; *b* 16 Jan 1974; *Educ* Riddlesdown HS Croydon Surrey; *Career* fashion model; various worldwide campaigns 1991 (Dolce & Gabana, Katherine Hamnett, Versace and Versace Versus, Yves Saint Laurent Rive Gauche, Pret a Porter and Opium fragrance), US campaign for Banana Republic 1991; exclusive worldwide contract with Calvin Klein 1992–; campaigns incl: Calvin Klein Obsession fragrance 1993, CK One fragrance 1994; appeared in the film Unzipped 1996; Fashion Personality of the Year British Fashion Awards 1995; *Books* Kate (1995); *Style*— Miss Kate Moss; ✉ c/o Storm Model Management, 5 Jubilee Place, London SW3 3TD (☎ 0171 376 7764)

MOSS, Ven Leonard Godfrey (Len); s of Clarence Walter Moss (d 1969), of Morden, Surrey, and Frances Lilian Vera, *née* Stanbridge; *b* 11 July 1932; *Educ* Sutton Co GS, The Poly Regent Street, King's Coll London and Warminster (BD, AKC); *m* 27 March 1954, Everell Annette, da of Albert Sydney Reed; 2 s (Paul b 27 Aug 1962 d 1996, Andrew b 5 May 1964), 1 da (Caroline Jane b 27 July b 1966); *Career* quantity surveyor's asst L A Francis & Sons 1948–54, Nat Serv RE 1954–56; curate: St Margaret's Putney 1960–63, Cheam (i/c St Alban's) 1963–67; vicar Much Dewchurch with Llanwarne and Llandinabo 1967–72, ecumenical offr Hereford Dio 1969–83, vicar Marden with Amberley and Wisteston 1972–84, preb Hereford Cathedral 1979–, Bishop of Hereford's offr for social responsibility 1983–91, canon non-residentiary Hereford Cathedral 1984–91, archdeacon of Hereford and canon residentiary Hereford Cathedral 1991–; memb Gen Synod 1970–; *Books* The People, the Land and The Church (contrib, 1987); *Recreations* reading, walking, listening to music, folk-dancing; *Style*— The Ven the Archdeacon of Hereford; ✉ The Archdeacon's House, The Close, Hereford HR1 2NG (☎ 01432 272873)

MOSS, Lewis David; CBE (1985), DL (Berks 1984); s of Samuel Algernon Montague Moss (d 1948), and Lily, *née* Goodman (d 1959); *b* 15 Feb 1922; *Educ* Univ Coll Sch, City of London Coll; *m* 1, 17 April 1947, Elizabeth Joy (d 1982), da of Sydney Flatau (d 1953); 2 s (Roger b 1950, Stephen b 1952), 1 da (Mrs Virginia Campus b 1956); *m* 2, 24 Oct 1987, Vivien Lowenstein, *née* Lissauer; *Career* Capt RA 1941–46, served N Africa, Italy, Greece and Austria; sr ptnr Moss & Ptnrs; chm: Grosvenor Securities Gp of Companies, Terminus Securities Ltd; London Docklands Devpt Corpn: memb Bd 1981–91, memb Exec Ctee 1985–91, chm Skillnet 1988–91, memb Bd Docklands Light Railway 1988–91, chm Docklands Enterprise Centre 1989–91; memb: London City Airport Consultative Ctee 1988–91, Tower Hamlets Health Authy 1989–93 (vice chm); tstee Bacon's City Technol Coll 1991–92; ACC: memb Exec Cncl 1977–89, ldr and chm Policy Ctee 1983–86 (vice chm 1985–86), memb Liaison Body with Audit Cmmn 1983–86, memb Local Authys Conditions of Service Advsy Bd 1983–86, memb Consultative Cncl on Local Govt Fin 1983–89, memb Cmmn for Local Admin in England 1983–89, memb Standing Conf of Local and Regnl Authys of Europe 1983–89; co cncllr Wokingham 1971–89; Berks CC: chm Policy Ctee and ldr 1977–79, vice chm 1979–80, chm 1980–82, chm Cons Gp 1983–86; memb Thames Valley Police Authy 1977–89, tstee Wokingham Cons Assoc 1978–; memb: Exec Ctee Nat Union Cons and Unionist Assocs 1983–89 and 1995–, Nat Local Govt Advsy Ctee 1983–89, Cons Bd of Fin 1993–; chm Cons Nat Property Advsy Ctee 1993– (memb 1989–, chm Southern Region 1989–); memb Cncl Order of St John Berks, Assoc Offr (Brother) Order of St John; patron Coll of Estate Mgmnt Univ of Reading, memb Corpn Univ Coll Sch, memb County Bd Young Enterprise 1992–96; High Sheriff of Berkshire 1991–92; Freeman City of London, Liveryman Worshipful Co of Glovers 1965; memb Inc Soc of Valuers and Auctioneers (nat pres 1969–70), memb Int Real Estate Fedn, FSVA; *Recreations* travel, art collection; *Clubs* Carlton, United & Cecil (vice chm 1992), Guards' Polo, RAC; *Style*— Lewis Moss, Esq, CBE, DL; ✉ Tilney House, 5 Tilney St, London W1X 6JL (☎ 0171 629 9933, fax 0171 493 5561)

MOSS, Malcolm Douglas; MP (C) Cambridgeshire North East (majority 15,093); s of Norman Moss (d 1976), and Annie, *née* Gay; *b* 6 March 1943; *Educ* Audenshaw GS, St John's Coll Cambridge (MA, CertEd); *m* 28 Dec 1965, Vivien Lorraine, da of Albert Peake (d 1964); 2 da (Alison Claire b 1969, Sarah Nicole b 1972); *Career* asst master then head of Geography and Economics Dept Blundell's Sch Tiverton 1966–70, gen mangr Barwick Assocs 1972–74 (insurance conslt 1971–72), co-fndr and dir Mandrake (Insurance and Finance Brokers) Ltd 1974–94 (chm 1986–92, changed name to Mandrake Associates Ltd 1988), chm Mandrake Gp plc 1986–88; chm Fens Business Enterprise Tst Ltd 1983–87; dir: Mandrake (Insurance Services) Ltd 1976–81, Mandrake Collinge Ltd 1977–86, Mandrake (Insurance Advisory Service) Ltd 1978, Mandrake (Financial Managment) Ltd 1985–87, Fens Business Enterprises Trust Ltd 1983–94; MP (C) Cambs NE 1987–, vice chm Cons Backbench Energy Ctee 1989–92 (jt sec 1987–89), memb Select Ctee on Energy 1988–91, PPS to Tristan Garel-Jones as Min of State FCO 1991–93, PPS to Sir Patrick Mayhew as Sec of State for NI 1993–94, Parly under-sec of state Northern Ireland Office 1994–; cncllr: Wisbech Town Cncl 1979–87, Fenland DC 1983–87, Cambs CC 1985–87; *Recreations* amateur dramatics, tennis, skiing; *Clubs* Lords and Commons Tennis and Ski; *Style*— Malcolm Moss, Esq, MP; ✉ House of Commons (☎ 0171 219 6933, secretary 0171 219 6365); business address: 111 High Street, March, Cambs PE15 (☎ 01354 56541)

MOSS, Martin Grenville; CBE (1975); s of Horace Grenville Moss (d 1975), and Gladys Ethel, *née* Wootton (d 1981); *b* 17 July 1923; *Educ* Lancing; *m* 2 Feb 1953, Jane Hope Bown; 2 s (Matthew b 4 June 1955, Hugo b 24 Feb 1962), 1 da (Louisa b 25 Oct 1958); *Career* pilot, Sqdn Ldr RAF 1942–46; sr welfare offr Iraq and Persia 1945–46; md:

Woollands Knightsbridge 1953–66, Debenham and Freebody 1964–66, Simpson Piccadilly 1966–73 and 1980–85; chm and chief exec offr May Department Stores International USA 1974–80, dir Nat Tst Enterprises 1985–88; dep chm Design Cncl 1971–75 (memb 1964–75); chm Cncl RSA 1983–85 (memb Cncl 1977–93); memb: Cncl RCA 1953–58, Royal Fine Art Cmmn 1982–84; Order of the Lion of Finland 1970; *Recreations* gardening, painting, classic cars; *Clubs* RAF; *Style*— Martin Moss, Esq, CBE; ✉ Parsonage Farm, Bentworth, Alton, Hants GU34 5RB

MOSS, (John) Michael; CB (1996); s of Ernest Moss, of Accrington, Lancs (d 1989), and Mary, *née* Greenwood; *b* 21 April 1936; *Educ* Accrington GS, King's Coll Cambridge (foundation scholar, MA); *Career* Air Miny: asst princ 1960–63, private sec to Air Memb for Supply and Orgn 1962–63, princ 1963–64; MOD: integrated 1964, private sec to Parly Under Sec of State for Def for the RAF 1969–70, asst sec 1971–72; Cabinet Office: estab offr 1972–75, sec Radcliffe Ctee of PCs on Ministerial Memoirs 1975; MOD: asst sec 1976–83, RCDS 1983, asst under sec of state (Air) procurement exec 1984–88, fell Center for Int Affairs Harvard Univ 1988–89, asst under sec of state (Naval Personnel) 1989–96, cmd sec to Second Sea Lord and C-in-C Naval Home Cmd 1994–96, ret; *Recreations* travel, photography, choral singing; *Clubs* United Oxford and Cambridge Univ, RAF; *Style*— Michael Moss, Esq, CB; ✉ c/o Royal Bank of Scotland, 119 Blackburn Road, Accrington, Lancs BB5 0AA

MOSS, Montague George; s of Harry Neville Moss (d 1982), and Ida Sophia, *née* Woolf (d 1971); *b* 21 April 1924; *Educ* Harrow, New Coll Oxford; *m* 28 Sept 1955, Jane, da of David Levi (d 1994); 2 s (Andrew b 7 Feb 1958, David b 15 Sept 1959), 1 da (Joanna b 15 Aug 1956); *Career* served Army 1943–47, cmmnd KRRC 1944, demobbed as Capt; Moss Bros Ltd: dir 1953–87, chm 1981–87, pres 1987–; pres: Fedn of Merchant Tailors of GB 1965–66 and 1985–86, Tailors Benevolent Inst 1980–; Freeman City of London 1948, Liveryman Worshipful Co of Carmen 1949; *Recreations* public speaking, music; *Clubs* Jesters, MCC, Old Harrovian Eton Fives; *Style*— Montague Moss, Esq; ✉ 4 Melina Place, London NW8 9SA (☎ 0171 286 0114); Moss Bros, Covent Garden, London WC2E 8JD (☎ 0171 240 4062, fax 0171 379 5652)

MOSS, (Michael Eric) Peter; s of (Kenneth) Vivian Moss, of Stockport, and Eileen Nora, *née* Ward; *b* 11 May 1941; *Educ* Loughborough GS; *m* 14 Sept 1963, Christina Mary, da of John Joseph Williams; 3 s (Kevin Michael b 12 Aug 1965, Mark Vivian b 8 Nov 1966, Paul William Peter b 9 Sept 1969); *Career* AXA Equity & Law Life Assurance Society plc: joined Equity & Law 1958, qualified as actuary 1968, various mgmnt appts in claims and customer servicing depts 1969–83, personnel mangr 1983–91, gen mangr i/c personnel 1991–93, main bd dir and gen mangr i/c customer servs, office servs and legal servs 1993–, also dir AXA Finance Ltd and AXA Equity & Law Trustees Ltd 1993–; FIA 1968; *Recreations* music, theatre, reading, sport of most kind (watching 1st class rugby, playing golf and squash), keeping fit; *Style*— Peter Moss, Esq; ✉ AXA Equity & Law Life Assurance Society plc, Amersham Road, High Wycombe, Bucks HP13 5AL (☎ 01494 466006, fax 01494 466746)

MOSS, Peter Jonathan; s of Capt John Cottam Moss, of Sutton Green, nr Guildford, and Joyce Alison, *née* Blunn (d 1977); *b* 29 March 1951; *Educ* Charterhouse; *m* Rosanne Marilyn, da of late Alexander James Houston, of Emsworth, nr Chichester; 3 s (Alexander b 28 Oct 1981, Benjamin b 14 Nov 1983, Patrick b 22 April 1987); *Career* called to the Bar Lincoln's Inn 1976; memb Mental Health Review Tbnl 1994; Freeman City of London 1985, Liveryman Worshipful Co of Clockmakers 1987; *Recreations* golf, windsurfing, skiing, cricket; *Clubs* New Zealand Golf, MCC; *Style*— Peter Moss, Esq; ✉ 9–12 Bell Yard, London WC2A 2LF (☎ 0171 400 1800, fax 0171 404 1405)

MOSS, His Hon Judge Ronald Trevor; s of Maurice Moss, and Sarah, *née* Camlett; *b* 1 Oct 1942; *Educ* Univ of Nottingham (BA); *m* 28 March 1971, Cindy, da of Archie Fiddleman; 1 s (Andrew b 18 Dec 1972), 1 da (Clare b 14 Nov 1974); *Career* admitted slr 1968, ptnr Moss Beachley slrs 1972–84, metropolitan stipendiary magistrate 1984–93, chm Youth Ct 1986–93, chm Family Ct 1991–93, memb Inner London Probation ctee 1991–93, circuit judge (SE Circuit) 1993–; *Recreations* golf, scrabble, watching association football (Watford FC); *Clubs* Moor Park Golf; *Style*— His Hon Judge Moss; ✉ Luton Crown Court, 7 George Street, Luton, Beds LU1 2AA

MOSS, Stephen Raymond; s of Raymond Moss, and Catherine, *née* Croome; *b* 30 July 1957; *Educ* Hartridge HS Newport Gwent, Balliol Coll Oxford (BA), Univ of London (MA); *m* 1984, Helen Mary Bonnich; 1 s (Timothy b 1986); *Career* worked previously in magazine and book publishing; The Guardian: sometime dep arts ed and dep features ed 1989–95, literary ed 1995–; *Recreations* cricket, chess, riding; *Style*— Stephen Moss, Esq; ✉ The Guardian, 119 Farringdon Road, London EC1R 3ER (☎ 0171 278 2332, fax 0171 713 4366)

MOSS, Stirling; OBE (1957); s of Alfred Moss, and Aileen Moss; *b* 17 Sept 1929; *Educ* Haileybury, Imperial Service Coll; *m* 1, 1957 (m dis 1960), Kathleen, da of F Stuart Molson, of Canada; m 2, 1964 (m dis 1968), Elaine, da of A Barbarino, of New York; 1 da; m 3, 1980, Susan, da of Stuart Paine of London; 1 s; *Career* racing driver 1947–62; learnt to drive aged 6, built own Cooper-Alta 1953, Br Nat Champion 1950–52, 1954–59 and 1961; winner: Tourist Trophy 1950–51, 1955 and 1958–61, Coupe des Alpes 1952–54, Alpine Gold Cup 1954, Italian Mille Miglia 1955 (only Englishman to win); competed in 494 races, rallies, sprints, land speed records and endurance runs, completed 366 and won 222; Grand Prix & successes incl: Targa Florio 1955, Br 1955 and 1957, Italian 1956–57 and 1959, NZ 1956 and 1959, Monaco 1956 and 1960–61, Leguna Seca 1960–61, US 1959–60, Aust 1956, Bari 1956, Pesara 1957, Swedish 1957, Dutch 1958, Argentinian 1958, Moroccan 1958, Buenos Aires 1958, Melbourne 1958, Villareal 1958, Caen 1958, Portuguese 1959, S African 1960, Cuban 1960, Austrian 1960, Cape Town 1960, Watkins Glen 1960, German 1961, Modena 1961; Driver of the Year 1954 and 1961, holder of 1500cc World speed record driving MG EX181 at 240mph; md Stirling Moss Ltd; dir: Designs Unlimited Ltd, SM Design & Interior Decorating Co, Hankoe Stove Enamelling Ltd; former dir of racing Johnson's Wax; judge: Miss World (4 times), Miss Universe 1974; former demonstrator Dunlop Rubber Co (travelled across India and Malaysia); conslt incl work for: Ferodo Opel Germany and Chrysler Aust; has given numerous lecture tours across US and in UK, NZ, Aust and Hong Kong; *Books* Stirling Moss's Book of Motor Sport (1955), In the Track of Speed (1957), Stirling Moss's Second Book of Motor Sport (1958), Le Mans (1959), My Favourite Car Stories (1960), A Turn at the Wheel (1961), All But My Life (1963), Design and Behaviour of the Racing Car (1964), How to Watch Motor Racing (1975), Motor Racing and All That (1980), My Cars, My Career (1987), Fangio, A Pirelli Album (1991), Great Drives in the Lakes (1993), Motor Racing Masterpieces (1994); *Recreations* snow skiing, water skiing, dancing, spear-fishing, model making, theatre, designing; *Clubs* Br Racing Drivers', Br Automobile Racing, Br Racing and Sports Car, Road Racing Drivers of America, 200mph, Lord's Taverners, RAC, International des Anciens Pilotes des Grand Prix; chm or pres of 36 motoring clubs; *Style*— Stirling Moss, Esq, OBE; ✉ 46 Shepherd St, London W1Y 8JN (☎ 0171 499 7967, 0171 499 3727, fax 0171 499 4104)

MOSS, Stuart; s of Morris Moss (d 1976), of London, and Bertha Moss; *b* 31 Dec 1944; *Educ* Grocers' Co Sch, Regent St Poly (DipArch); *m* 1, 24 June 1973 (m dis 1985), Layn Sandra, da of Ronald Feldman, of London; 2 s (Lucas Ryan b 1974, Daniel Miles b 1979), 1 da (Zoë Anastasis b 1982); m 2, 1993, Lesley Ben Evan; 1 s (Jacob Jeffrey b 7 Aug 1993); *Career* qualified as chartered architect 1972; assoc with Robert Turner Architects 1973–75, formed partnership with John Bennett 1975–84, formed Moss & Co Architects 1985–; author of various articles written for architectural magazines; RIBA, ARCUK; *Recreations* films and the visual arts, reading, travel; *Style*— Stuart Moss, Esq; ✉ Moss & Co Architects, 165 Brecknock Rd, London N19 5AD (☎ 0171 485 0770, fax 0171 485 1005)

MOSS, Timothy Campbell; s of William Denniss Moss (d 1991), and Phyllis May *née* Charnock (d 1971); *b* 31 Jan 1937; *Educ* Wintringham GS; *m* 13 Sept 1969, Sheila Elizabeth, da of Samuel Dunwoody (d 1983); 2 da (Claire b 1971, Rachel b 1973); *Career* Nat Serv RAEC 1959–61, Sgt; articled clerk Forrester Boyd & Co 1953–58, Coopers & Lybrand 1961– (ptnr 1974–); FCA 1959; *Recreations* golf, bridge; *Clubs* Croham Hurst Golf; *Style*— Timothy C Moss, Esq; ✉ Coopers & Lybrand, Plumtree Court, London EC4A 4HT (☎ 0171 213 1007, fax 0171 213 1330)

MOSSE, Katharine Louise (Kate); da of Richard Hugh Mosse, of Chichester, and Barbara Mary, *née* Towlson; *b* 20 Oct 1961; *Educ* Chichester HS for Girls, New Coll Oxford (BA, MA); *Partner* Greg Charles Mosse, *né* Dunk; 1 da (Martha b 25 Feb 1990), 1 s (Felix b 8 Oct 1992); *Career* various positions rising to ed dir Random House (UK) 1985–92, author/broadcaster 1992–; co-fndr/admin Orange Prize for Fiction (chair Judging Panel 1996); memb Labour Party; former memb: Women in Publishing, Women in Management in Publishing, NUJ; *Books* Becoming a Mother (Virago, 1993 and 1997), The House: A Year in the Life of the Royal Opera House Covent Garden (BBC Books, 1996), Eskimo Kissing (Hodder & Stoughton, 1996), The Cinnamon Dock (Hodder & Stoughton, 1997); *Recreations* classical music, swimming, politics, walking; *Style*— Ms Kate Mosse; ✉ c/o Mark Lucas, Lucas Alexander Whitley Ltd, Elsinore House, 77 Fulham Palace Road, London W6 8JA

MOSSELMANS, Carel Maurits; TD; s of Adriaan Willem Mosselmans (d 1956), of The Hague, Holland, and Jonkvrouwe Nancy Henriette van der Wyck (d 1963); *b* 9 March 1929; *Educ* Stowe, Trinity Coll Cambridge (MA); *m* 4 Jan 1962, Hon Prudence Fiona, da of Baron McCorquodale of Newton, KCVO, PC (d 1971); 2 s (Michael b 1962, Frederick b 1964); *Career* Lt Queen's Bays 2 Dragoon Gds 1947–49, City of London Yeo (Rough Riders) TA 1949, Inns of Ct and City Yeo 1961 (Lt-Col cmdg Regt 1963); dir: Sedgwick Collins and Co Ltd 1963 (joined 1952), Sedgwick Collins (Underwriting) Ltd 1971 (md 1972), Sedgwick Forbes Holdings Ltd 1978; chm: Sedgwick Lloyd's Underwriting Agents Ltd 1974–89, Sedgwick Forbes Marine Ltd 1974–78, Sedgwick Forbes Services Ltd 1978–81, Sedgwick Ltd 1981–84, Sedgwick Group plc 1984–89 (dep chm 1982–84), The Sumitomo Marine & Fire Insurance Co (Europe) Ltd 1981–90 (dir 1975–81); non-exec dir: Coutts & Co 1981–95, Rothschild Asset Management Ltd 1989– (chm 1990–93); chm: Rothschild International Asset Management Ltd 1989–96, Rothschild Fund Management Ltd 1990–96; dir Rothschilds Continuation Ltd 1990–; chm: Exco plc 1991–96, Janson Green Holdings Ltd 1993–, Janson Green Ltd 1993–; *Recreations* shooting, music, fishing, golf; *Clubs* White's, Cavalry & Guards'; *Style*— Carel Mosselmans, Esq, TD; ✉ 15 Chelsea Square, London SW3 6LF (☎ 0171 352 0621); Rothschild Asset Management Limited, Five Arrows House, St Swithin's Lane, London EC4N 8NR (☎ 0171 634 2804)

MOSSOP, James; s of James Mossop (d 1943), and Emma, *née* Wilson (d 1965); *b* 2 Aug 1936; *Educ* Barrow-in-Furness GS; *m* 1958 (m dis 1975), June, *née* Large; 1 s (John James b 1960), 1 da (Judith Lyn b 1959); *Career* sports writer; North Western Evening Mail Barrow-in-Furness 1954–61 (jr reporter, sr reporter, sub-ed, dep sports ed), sports sub-ed Daily Mail Manchester 1961–63, sports writer Sunday Express (Manchester) 1963–74, chief sports writer Sunday Express 1974–96, sports feature writer Sunday Telegraph 1996–; major assignments incl: Olympic Games 1976, 1980, 1984, 1988, 1992 and 1996, football World Cup 1970, 1978, 1982, 1986, 1990 and 1994, numerous golf, boxing, motor racing, athletics and cricket events; commended Br Press Awards 1980 and 1982, winner Minet Olympic Sports Writer of the Year (Br Sports Journalism Awards) 1993; memb: Sports Writers' Assoc, Assoc of Golf Writers, Boxing Writers' Club, Football Writers' Assoc; *Recreations* golf; *Clubs* Scribes, Hendon Golf, Ashton-on-Mersey Golf, European Golf (Wicklow Ireland); *Style*— James Mossop, Esq; ✉ 11 Greville House, Lower Road, Harrow-on-the-Hill, Middx HA2 0HB (☎ and fax 0181 422 5131, mobile 0410 908362)

MOSTYN, Gen Sir (Joseph) David Frederick; KCB (1984), CBE (1974, MBE 1962); s of J P Mostyn (d 1929), and M C Keenan, *née* Moss (d 1995); *b* 28 Nov 1928; *Educ* Downside, RMA Sandhurst; *m* 1952, Diana Patricia, da of Col Sheridan, MC (d 1950); 4 s (Philip, Mark, Rupert, Matthew), 2 da (Celia, Kate); *Career* cmmnd Oxford and Bucks LI 1948, Canadian Staff Coll 1958, 1 Royal Green Jackets Malaya, Borneo 1962–63 (despatches 1963), instr Staff Coll Camberley 1963–66, MOD 1967–68, cmd 2 Royal Green Jackets 1969–71, Cmdt Tactics Wing Sch of Infantry 1971–72, cmd 8 Inf Bde 1972–74, dep dir Army Trg 1974–75, RCDS 1976, BGS Rhine Army 1977, dir Personal Servs 1978–80, GOC Berlin 1980–83, mil sec 1983–86, Adj-Gen 1986–88; Col Cmdt: Light Div 1983–86, Army Legal Corps 1983–88, ADC (Gen) 1986–89; Kt SMO Malta 1974; 43rd and 52nd Regtl Ctee, special cmmr Duke of York's Royal Mil Sch 1989–96; chm: Lyme Regis Hosp Tst 1990–96, Cncl of Mgmnt Joseph Weld Hospice Tst 1990–, Fin Ctee Lyme Regis RC Parish 1989–94; pres: Royal Br Legion Devonshire 1992–, Uplyme and Lym Valley Soc 1989–; landowner (220 acres); *Recreations* all field sports; *Clubs* Army and Navy; *Style*— Gen Sir David Mostyn, KCB, CBE; ✉ c/o Lloyds Bank, 54 Broad St, Lyme Regis, Dorset

MOSTYN, Hon Llewellyn Roger Lloyd; s and h of 5 Baron Mostyn, MC, by his 1 w Yvonne (*see* Maj Sir William Wrixon-Becher, Bt, MC); *b* 26 Sept 1948; *Educ* Eton, The Inns of Ct Sch of Law; *m* 1974, Denise Suzanne, da of Roger Duvanel, an artist, of France; 1 s (Gregory Philip Roger Lloyd b 1984), 1 da (Alexandra Stephanie b 1975); *Career* late Capt Army Legal Servs; called to the Bar Middle Temple 1973 (practising Criminal Bar), pt/t teacher at Bromley Coll of Technol; *Recreations* literature, history, classical music, tennis, sport, rugger; *Style*— The Hon Llewellyn Mostyn; ✉ 9 Anderson Street, London SW3 (☎ 0171 584 3059); c/o 4 Paper Buildings, London EC4

MOSTYN, 5 Baron (UK 1831); Capt Sir Roger Edward Lloyd Lloyd-Mostyn; 6 Bt (GB 1778), MC (1942); s of 4 Baron (d 1965); *b* 17 April 1920; *Educ* Eton, RMC Sandhurst; *m* 1, 1943, Yvonne Margaret, da of A Stuart Johnson, of Henshall Hall, Congleton, Cheshire; 1 s, 1 da; m 2, Mrs Sheila Edmondson Shaw, OBE, DL, da of Maj Reginald Fairweather; *Heir* s, Hon Llewellyn Roger Lloyd Lloyd-Mostyn; *Career* 2 Lt 9 Lancers 1939 (despatches 1940), temp Maj 1945; *Style*— The Rt Hon the Lord Mostyn, MC; ✉ Mostyn Hall, Mostyn, Clwyd, N Wales CH8 9AN (☎ 01745 560222)

MOSTYN, (Sir) William Basil John; *de jure* 15 Bt (E 1670), of Talacre, Flintshire, but claim has not yet been submitted for entry on the Official Roll of the Baronetage; o s of Sir Jeremy John Anthony Mostyn, 14 Bt (d 1988), and Cristina Beatrice Maria, o da of Marchese Pier-Paolo Vladimiro Orengo; sr male rep of Tudor Trevor, Lord of Hereford (10 cent); *b* 15 Oct 1975; *Heir* unc, Trevor Alexander Richard Mostyn b 23 May 1946; *Style*— William Mostyn, Esq; ✉ The Coach House, Lower Heyford, Oxon

MOTH, Peter; *b* 1936; *Educ* St John's Coll Oxford, Mansfield Coll Oxford; *m* Ruth; 1 s, 1 da; *Career* Tyne Tees Television Ltd: successively head of news, head of documentaries and current affrs, dep controller of progs, dir of public affrs 1986–93, dir of bdcasting 1993–96, ret; chm: Arts Marketing Co, Advsy Bd Newcastle Salvation Army; bd memb: Beamish Devpt Tst, Jarrow 700; govr: Univ of Sunderland, RGS Newcastle; tstee Newcastle Cathedral Tst; min St Andrews United Reformed Church; FRTS 1996; *Recreations* swimming, reading; *Style*— Peter Moth, Esq

MOTHERWELL, Bishop of (RC) 1983–; Rt Rev Joseph Devine; s of Joseph Devine (d 1989), and Christina, *née* Murphy (d 1981); *b* 7 Aug 1937; *Educ* Blairs Coll Aberdeen, St Peter's Coll Dumbarton, Pontificial Scots Coll Rome, Gregorian Univ Rome

(PhD); *Career* personal sec to Archbishop of Glasgow 1964–66, lectr in philosophy St Peter's Coll Dumbarton 1966–74, chaplain Glasgow Univ 1974–77, auxiliary bishop Glasgow 1977–83; Papal Bene Merenti 1962; *Recreations* reading, music, soccer; *Style*— The Rt Rev the Bishop of Motherwell; ✉ Bishop's House, 17 Viewpark Rd, Motherwell ML1 3ER (☎ 01698 63715)

MOTION, Andrew; s of Lt-Col A R Motion, of Braintree, Essex, and C G Motion (d 1982); *b* 26 Oct 1952; *Educ* Radley, Univ Coll Oxford; *m* 1985, Jan, da of C M Dalley, of Maldon, Essex; 2 s (Andrew Jesse b 26 July 1986, Lucas Edward b 19 May 1988), 1 da (Sidonie Gillian Elizabeth (twin) b 19 May 1988); *Career* freelance writer; prizes incl: Avon Observer prize 1982, John Llewelyn Rhys prize 1984, Somerset Maugham award 1987, Dylan Thomas prize 1988, Whitbread award for biography 1993; *Books* Dangerous Play, The Lamberts, Natural Causes, The Pale Companion, Love in a Life, Famous for the Creatures, Philip Larkin: A Writer's Life (biography, 1993), The Price of Everything (1994); *Style*— Andrew Motion, Esq; ✉ c/o Faber & Faber Ltd, 3 Queen Square, London WC1N 3AU (☎ 0171 465 0045, fax 0171 465 0034)

MOTSON, John; s of Rev William Motson (d 1992), of Worthing, W Sussex, and Gwendoline Mary Motson (d 1991); *b* 10 July 1945; *Educ* Culford Sch Bury St Edmunds, Nat Cncl for Trg of Journalists (Cert); *m* 1976, (Jennifer) Anne, da of Cyril Jobling (d 1991), and Marion Jobling; 1 s (Frederick James b 4 Feb 1986); *Career* football commentator and reporter; news and sports reporter Barnet Press 1963–67, sports writer and sub ed Morning Telegraph Sheffield 1967–68, freelance BBC Radio Sheffield 1968, presenter, reporter and commentator (football, boxing, tennis) BBC Network Radio Sports Dept 1968–71, football commentator and reporter BBC TV (incl Match of the Day, Sportsnight, Grandstand and other outside bdcasts) 1971–; major events as commentator: all World Cups 1974– (incl finals 1982–), all Euro Championships 1976– (incl finals 1980–), FA Cup Final annually 1977–; writer and narrator over 20 football videos for BBC Enterprises 1987–, also numerous club histories and Match of the Day compilations; *Books* Second to None: Great Teams of Post-War Soccer (1972), The History of the European Cup (with John Rowlinson, 1980), Match of the Day: the Complete Record (1992, reprinted 1994), Motty's Diary (1996); *Recreations* running (half marathons and 10km races), reading novels, theatre, cinema, watching sport; *Clubs* Rugby, Scribes West International; *Style*— John Motson, Esq; ✉ c/o Match of the Day, BBC Television, Television Centre, London W12 7RJ

MOTT, Dr David Hugh; s and h of Sir John Harmar Mott, 3 Bt, *qv*; *b* 1 May 1952; *Educ* Shrewsbury, Univ of Sussex (BSc), Birkbeck Coll London (MSc), QMC London (PhD); *m* 1980, Amanda Jane, o da of Lt Cdr D W P Fryer, RN (ret); 2 s (Matthew David b 1982, Jonathan William b 1984); *Career* princ conslt Data Sciences 1986–; memb BCS; CEng; *Recreations* music; *Style*— Dr David Mott

MOTT, John Charles Spencer; *b* 18 Dec 1926; *Educ* Brixton Sch of Building, Battersea Poly, Rutherford Coll of Technol Newcastle upon Tyne; *m* 1953, Patricia Mary; 2 s; *Career* serv Lt RM 1943–46; chm and chief exec French Kier Holdings plc 1974–86 (dir 1963–); chm: May Gurney Holdings Ltd (construction gp) 1986–89, William Sindall plc (construction gp) 1990–94; dir RMC Group plc, ret; FEng 1982, FICE, FIStructE, CIMgt; *Recreations* golf; *Clubs* Danish; *Style*— John Mott, Esq, FEng; ✉ 91 Long Road, Cambridge CB2 2HE (☎ 01223 841320)

MOTT, Sir John Harmar; 3 Bt (UK 1930), of Ditchling, Co Sussex; s of Sir Adrian Spear Mott, 2 Bt (d 1964), and Mary Katherine, *née* Stanton (d 1972); *b* 21 July 1922; *Educ* Radley, New Coll Oxford (MA, BM BCh), Middx Hosp; *m* 1950, Elizabeth, da of Hugh Carson, FRCS (d 1981), of Selly Oak, Birmingham; 1 s (David Hugh b 1952), 2 da (Jennifer (Mrs Robert A Buckey) b 1954, Alison Mary b 1958); *Heir* s, David Hugh Mott b 1 May 1952; *Career* served 1939–45 RAF, Flying Offr 1943–46, Far East; qualified med practitioner 1951; regnl med offr DHSS 1969–84, ret; MRCGP; *Recreations* photography, classical archaeology and history; *Style*— Sir John Mott, Bt; ✉ Staniford, Brookside, Kingsley, Cheshire WA6 8BG (☎ 01928 788123)

MOTT, His Hon Judge; Michael Duncan; s of Francis John Mott (d 1979), and Gwendolen, *née* Mayhew; *b* 8 Dec 1940; *Educ* Rugby, Gonville and Caius Coll Cambridge (MA); *m* 19 Dec 1970, Phyllis Ann, da of V James Gavin, of Dubuque, Iowa, USA; 2 s (Timothy b 1972, Jonathan b 1975); *Career* called to the Bar Inner Temple 1963, in chambers Birmingham 1964–69, resident magistrate Kenya 1969–71, in practice Midland and Oxford circuit 1972–85, dep circuit judge 1976–80, recorder 1980–85, circuit judge (Midland and Oxford Circuit) 1985–; parish cncllr 1982–86, parish organist 1984–; memb Hon Soc of Inner Temple; *Recreations* music, travel, skiing, tennis; *Clubs* Cambridge Union, Union and County (Worcs); *Style*— His Hon Judge Mott; ✉ c/o Midland and Oxford Circuit Office, The Priory Courts, 33 Bull Street, Birmingham B4 6DW (☎ 0121 627 1700)

MOTT, Philip Charles; QC (1991); s of Charles Kynaston Mott (d 1981), of Taunton, Somerset, and Elsa, *née* Smith; *b* 20 April 1948; *Educ* King's Coll Taunton, Worcester Coll Oxford (BA, MA); *m* 19 Nov 1977, Penelope Ann, da of Edward Caffery; 2 da (Sarah b 1981, Catherine b 1983); *Career* called to Bar Inner Temple 1970, practising Western Circuit 1970–, recorder of the Crown Ct 1987–; *Recreations* the countryside, sailing; *Clubs* Bar Yacht; *Style*— Philip Mott, Esq, QC; ✉ 35 Essex Street, Temple, London WC2R 3AR (☎ 0171 353 6381, fax 0171 583 1786)

MOTTERSHEAD, Derek Stuart; s of Alan Mottershead (d 1954), of Blackpool, and Irene, *née* Huyton; *b* 2 Sept 1947; *Educ* Royal Masonic Sch Bushey Herts, Univ of Manchester (BSc); *m* 1 Sept 1969 (m dis 1988), Jean, da of James Arthur Wright, of Nelson, Lancs; 3 da (Sarah b 11 April 1972, Lucy b 17 Feb 1982, Gillian (adopted) b 30 May 1964); *Career* mktg dir Pretty Polly Ltd (winner Br Mktg awards 3 consecutive years) 1976–80, Euro mktg dir Lee Apparel UK Ltd (subsid Vanity Fair Corp America) 1980–82, mktg dir Lee Cooper Ltd 1982–84, md All-time Sportswear UK Ltd 1984–87, md Prontaprint plc 1987–92 (chm Prontaprint Communications Ltd, md Prontaprint International Ltd, jt gp md Continuous Stationery plc), jt md Prontaprint Group Plc 1992–93, chm and md Prontaprint Ltd, chm and md The Franchise Option 1993–, md Bang and Olufsen UK Ltd 1994–; chm Br Franchise Assoc 1992–93, vice pres Br Small Business Bureau; memb: Br Inst of Mktg, IOD; *Recreations* private aviation, shooting; *Clubs* Teeside Flying; *Style*— Derek Mottershead, Esq; ✉ Bang and Olufsen UK Ltd, Unit 630, Wharfedale Road, Winnersh, Wokingham, Berks (☎ 0118 969 2288, fax 0118 969 3388)

MOTTISTONE, 4 Baron (UK 1933); David Peter Seely; CBE (1984); 4 s of 1 Baron Mottistone, CB, CMG, DSO, TD, PC (d 1947; himself 4 s of Sir Charles Seely, 1 Bt), by his 2 w, Hon Evelyn Izmé Murray, JP, da of 10 Lord and 1 Viscount Elibank and widow of George Nicholson (s of Sir Charles Nicholson, 1 Bt) - by whom she was mother of Sir John Nicholson, 2 Bt; Lord Mottistone succeeded his half-bro, 3 Baron, 1966; *b* 16 Dec 1920, (HRH The Duke of Windsor stood sponsor); *Educ* RN Coll Dartmouth; *m* 1944, Anthea Christine, da of Victor McMullan, of Co Down; 2 s, 3 da (1 decd); *Heir* s, Hon Peter John Philip Seely; *Career* sits as Cons in House of Lords; Cdr RN 1955, Capt RN 1960 (D) 24 Escort Sqdn 1963–65; ret at own request 1967; dir personnel trg Radio Rentals Ltd 1967–69, dir Distributive Indust Trg Bd 1969–75; dir Cake & Biscuit Alliance 1975–81, parly advsr Biscuit, Cake, Chocolate & Confectionary Alliance 1981– (export sec 1981–83); Dep Lord-Lt IOW 1981, Lord-Lt IOW 1986–95, Govr IOW 1992–95; KStJ 1989; pres East Wessex TAVRA 1990–93; Hon DLitt Bournemouth Univ 1993; FIEE, FIPM, FIMgt; *Clubs* Royal Yacht Sqdn, Royal Cruising, Royal Naval Sailing Assoc, Island Sailing, Royal Cwlth Soc; *Style*— The Rt Hon the Lord Mottistone, CBE; ✉ Old Parsonage, Mottistone, IOW PO30 4EE (☎ 01983 740264)

MOTTRAM, Maj-Gen John Frederick; CB (1982), MVO (1976), OBE (1969); s of F W Mottram (d 1972), and Margaret Mottram (d 1984); *b* 9 June 1930; *m* 1956, Jennifer, da of M J Thomas (d 1971); 1 s, 1 da; *Career* RM 1948, jt warfare attaché Br Embassy Washington 1974–77, Col Gen Staff Dept of Cmdt Gen RM and ADC to HM The Queen 1978–80, Maj-Gen Trg and Res Forces RM 1980–83; dir gen Fertiliser Mfrs Assoc 1983–86; chief exec Gen Cncl of Bar 1987–94; *Recreations* fishing, water colour painting; *Clubs* Army and Navy; *Style*— Maj-Gen John Mottram, CB, MVO, OBE; ✉ c/o Army and Navy Club, Pall Mall, London SW1

MOTTRAM, Richard Clive; s of John Mottram (d 1991), of Chislehurst, Kent, and Florence Bertha, *née* Yates; *b* 23 April 1946; *Educ* King Edward VI Camp Hill Sch Birmingham, Univ of Keele (BA); *m* 24 July 1971, Dr Fiona Margaret Mottram, da of Keith David Erskine (d 1974); 3 s (Keith b 1974, David b 1981, Thomas b 1985), 1 da (Ruth b 1977); *Career* Home Civil Serv, assigned MOD 1968, Cabinet Office 1975–77, private sec to Perm Under Sec of State MOD 1979–81, private sec to Sec of State for Def 1982–86, asst under sec MOD 1986–89, dep under sec (policy) MOD 1989–92; perm sec: Office of Public Service and Science 1992–95, MOD 1995–; memb Bd of Dirs Cwlth Assoc for Public Admin and Mgmnt 1994–; Hon DLitt Univ of Keele 1996; *Recreations* theatre, cinema, tennis; *Style*— Richard Mottram, Esq; ✉ Ministry of Defence, Main Building, Whitehall, London SW1 (☎ 0171 218 2193)

MOUATT, (Richard) Brian; CBE (1997); s of Laurance Rayson Mouatt (d 1991), and Grace Marion Campbell, *née* Davison (d 1974); *b* 4 Sept 1936; *Educ* Blundell's, Univ of Edinburgh (BDS); *m* 1962, Ursula, da of Hans Wälti; 1 s (Steven Richard b 1 Jan 1963), 1 da (Susannah Helen Nicole b 22 Sept 1966); *Career* Sqdn Ldr Dental Branch RAF 1960–65; dental offr Dept of Public Health Bournemouth 1965–68, chief dental offr Govt of Repub of Zambia 1968–72, princ in gen dental practice Dorset 1972–84; dental offr then sr dental offr DHSS 1984–90, chief dental offr Dept of Health 1990–96, ret; hon sr res fell Eastman Dental Inst Univ of London; memb: BDA, Faculty of Gen Dental Practice; MGDS RCS; *Recreations* travel, watercolour painting; *Clubs* Athenaeum; *Style*— Mr R B Mouatt, CBE; ✉ c/o Department of Health, Richmond House, 79 Whitehall, London SW1A 2NS

MOUGHTIN, Prof (James) Clifford; s of James Henry Moughtin (d 1979), and Mary Eleonor, *née* Brown (d 1984); *b* 14 May 1932; *Educ* Mold Alun GS, Bootle GS, Univ of Liverpool (BArch, MCD, MA), Queen's Univ of Belfast (PhD); *m* 1, 1956 (m dis 1980), Maureen Philomena; 3 s (Mark James b 1957, Nicholas Paul b 1959, Timothy John b 1964); m 2, 21 Sept 1981, Catherine, da of John McMahon (d 1971); *Career* architect; Singapore Improvement Tst 1957–60, Univ of Kwame Nkrumah Ghana 1960–61, Univ of Ahmadu Bello Nigeria 1961–63, Univ of Liverpool 1963–64, lectr and prof Queen's Univ of Belfast 1964–74, prof Univ of Nottingham 1974–95; currently princ CITYFORM 21; RIBA; memb: RTPI, RAI; *Books* Hausa Architecture (1985), Nigerian Traditional Architecture (1987), Who Needs Development? (1990), Urban Design - Street and Square (1992), Urban Design - Ornament and Decoration (1995), Urban Design: Green Dimensions (1996); *Recreations* watercolour painting and travel; *Style*— Prof Clifford Moughtin; ✉ 1 Yeomans Court, The Park, Nottingham (☎ 0115 947 2933); Casa McMahon-Moughtin, Valley of Indolence, Eira Da Palma, Apt 297, 8800 Tavira, Portugal

MOULAND, Mark Gary; s of Sidney Mouland, of The Old Deer Park, Stoneleigh, Warwicks, and Shirley Anne Easby; *b* 23 April 1961; *Educ* Westbourne House Penarth, Millfield; *m* 4 Dec 1985, Marianne, da of Richard Essam; 2 da (Stephanie Louise b 24 Oct 1987, Kimberley Jane b 11 March 1989); *Career* golfer; amateur: Br Boy Champion 1976, BBC Wales Jr Sportsman of the Year 1976, Welsh Boy Int 1976–78 (capt 1978), Br Boy Int (v Continent of Europe) 1977 and 1978, Welsh Int 1978 and 1979; professional 1981–: winner Care Plan Int 1986, winner KLM Dutch Open 1986, participant Dunhill Cup 1986, 1988, 1989, 1990, 1993, and 1995, World Cup 1988, 1989, 1990, 1992, 1993, and 1995, Kirin Cup 1988; *Recreations* snooker, travel, tv, shooting, fishing; *Style*— Mark Mouland, Esq; ✉ c/o Stoneleigh Deer Park Golf Ltd, The Clubhouse, The Old Deer Park, Coventry Road, Stoneleigh, Warwickshire CB8 3DR (☎ 01203 639991, fax 01203 692471)

MOULD, Christopher Peter; s of Peter Sidney Mould, of Pembrokeshire, and Phyllida Charlotte Elaine, *née* Ormond; *b* 30 Nov 1958; *Educ* Royal GS High Wycombe, Magdalen Coll Oxford (BA), LSE (MSc); *m* 18 Aug 1979, Angela Geraldine, da of Roger Ellis Druce; 4 da (Hannah Elizabeth b 26 Dec 1984, Verity Ruth b 20 June 1986, Alicia Ellen Joy b 27 April 1990, Madeleine Grace b 4 June 1993); *Career* fund raiser LEPRA 1982, planning asst NE Thames RHA 1982–83, planning mangr Southend Health Authy 1983–86, hosp mangr Southend Hosp 1986–88, gen mangr Community and Mental Health Servs S Beds Health Authy 1989–91 (gen mangr Mental Health 1988–89), chief exec (designate) S Beds Community Health Care NHS Tst 1991–92, dist gen mangr Salisbury Health Authy and chief exec Salisbury Health Care 1992–94, chief exec Salisbury Health Care NHS Tst 1994–; currently chm Health Care Forum of the Care Sector Consortium; S and W Region rep Human Resources Standing Ctee NHS Tst Federation; appraisal fellowship Nuffield Prov Hosps Tst, 4th prize RIPA/Hay Award for Managerial Innovation 1989; MHSM, DipHSM; *Recreations* jazz guitar, squash, Christian preaching; *Style*— Christopher Mould, Esq; ✉ Salisbury District Hospital, Salisbury, Wiltshire SP2 8BJ (☎ 01722 336262 ext 2753)

MOULTON, Dr Alexander Eric; CBE (1976); s of John Coney Moulton, and Beryl Latimer, *née* Greene; *b* 9 April 1920; *Educ* Marlborough, Kings Coll Cambridge (MA); *Career* innovating engr, inventor of the Moulton Bicycle, Hydrolastic and Hydragas car suspension, the Moulton Coach and others; fndr: Moulton Development Ltd 1956, Moulton Bicycles 1962; chm Ctee on Engrg Design Educn Design Cncl 1975–76 (producing Moulton Report); RDI (Master of Faculty 1981–83); Hon Doctorate Royal Coll of Art 1967, Hon DSc Univ of Bath 1971; MIMechE 1979, FEng 1980 (vice pres 1986–89); *Awards* incl: Design Centre Award 1964, Gold Medal Triennale Milan 1964, Bid Lake Memb Plaque for Encouragement to Cycling 1964, Queen's Award for Indust 1967, Design Medal Soc of Industl Artists and Designers 1976, James Clayton Prize, Crompton-Lanchester Medal, Thomas Hawksley Gold Medal; *Publications* numerous on engrg and educn; *Recreations* cycling, canoeing, shooting; *Clubs* Brooks's; *Style*— Dr Alexander Moulton, CBE, FEng; ✉ The Hall, Bradford-on-Avon, Wilts BA15 1AH (☎ 01225 865895, fax 01225 864742)

MOULTON, Jonathan Paul (Jon); s of Douglas Cecil Moulton (d 1992), of Stoke-on-Trent, and Elsie Turner Moulton (d 1984); *b* 15 Oct 1950; *Educ* Hanley HS, Univ of Lancaster (BA); *m* 13 Aug 1973, Pauline Marie, da of Stanley Dunn, of Stoke-on-Trent; 1 s (Spencer Jonathan b 1980), 1 da (Rebecca Clare b 1978); *Career* mangr Coopers & Lybrand 1972–80; Citicorp Venture Capital: dir NY 1980–81, gen mangr London 1981–85, managing ptnr Schroder Ventures 1985–94; dep chm Parker Pen Ltd 1986–93; non-exec dir: Haden MacLellan Holdings plc 1987–, Appledore Holdings Ltd 1990–93, Ushers Holdings plc 1991–, R J B Mining Plc 1992–94, Unicorn Abrasives Plc 1995–, Prestige Holdings Ltd 1995–, United Texon Plc 1995–, Brands Hatch Leisure Holdings PLC 1995–; dir Apax & Co 1994–97, managing ptnr Alchemy Partners 1997–; chm British Allergy Fndn 1996–; FCA 1983, FIMgt; *Recreations* chess, fishing; *Style*— Jon Moulton, Esq; ✉ 57 Kippington Rd, Sevenoaks, Kent TN13 2LL (☎ 01732 450025, fax 01732 742436)

MOULTRIE, John Farbon (Jack); CBE (1980); s of John Felix Hawksford Moultrie (d 1961), and Elsie May, *née* Wass; *b* 26 June 1914; *Educ* Loxford Secdy Modern Ilford, Coll of Estate Mgmnt; *m* 2 Sept 1939, Irene Hazel (d 1982), da of Thomas James Cast (d 1945); 3 da (Margaret b 1942, Vivian b 1944, Katherine b 1946); *Career* Capt HG 1940–44; chartered surveyor; articled 1930, sr ptnr 1956–86; cncllr: Dagenham Borough Cncl 1950–60, Hornchurch UDC 1960–65; London Borough Cncl of Havering 1965–86: cncllr 1965–86, ldr 1968–71, 1974–77, 1979–82 and 1982–84, ldr of oppn 1971–74, Mayor 1977–78; chm: Rush Green Hosp League of Friends (fndr and pres), Oldchurch Hosp Scanner Appeal, LAMIT; Gen Cmmr of Taxes (Barking); pres: Upminster Cons Assoc, Rotary Club Dagenham 1962–63; served on LBA and AMA; JP 1954–86 (chm Barking Bench NE London); Liveryman Worshipful Co of Bakers 1964; Freeman: City of London 1964, London Borough of Havering 1986; FRICS; *Recreations* bowls, gardening, local politics; *Clubs* Carlton; *Style—* Jack Moultrie, Esq, CBE; ✉ 8 Castle Hill Court, Huntingdon, Cambs PE18 6TJ (☎ 01480 414801); 1 High Road, Chadwell Heath, Romford, Essex RM6 6PX (☎ 0181 590 1219)

MOUNFIELD, Dr Peter Reginald; s of Reginald Howard Mounfield (d 1969), of Benllech, Anglesey, Gwynedd, and Irene, *née* Williams (d 1992); *b* 15 Feb 1935; *Educ* Canon Slade GS Bolton, Univ of Nottingham (BA, PhD); *m* 12 Sept 1959, Patricia, da of Ernest John Jarrett (d 1991); 2 s (John, David); *Career* asst lectr then lectr Dept of Geography and Anthropology Univ Coll of Wales Aberystwyth 1958–68, head Dept of Geography Univ of Leicester 1988–91 (lectr then sr lectr 1968–); visiting assoc prof Dept of Geography and Regnl Planning Univ of Cincinnati Ohio USA 1966–67, sr Fulbright scholar 1966–67, sr visiting res fell Jesus Coll Oxford 1988; *Books* World Nuclear Power (1991); *Recreations* playing tennis, walking, watching cricket; *Clubs* RGS; *Style—* Dr Peter Mounfield; ✉ Department of Geography, University of Leicester, University Rd, Leicester LE1 7RH (☎ 0116 252 3840, fax 0116 252 3854, telex 347250 LEICUN G)

MOUNSEY, Joseph Backhouse; s of Colin Anthony Mounsey, of Surrey, and Helen, *née* Roake; *b* 27 March 1949; *Educ* Leighton Park Sch Reading, New Coll Oxford (MA); *m* 1; 1 da (Elizabeth Helen b 1979); m 2, Josephne Jennifer, da of Albert Edward Hance; *Career* The Manufacturers Life Insurance Co: vice pres int investmts 1980–86, gen mangr 1986–88, sr vice pres 1988, exec vice pres insur operations 1988, sr vice pres int investmts 1991, sr vice pres Toronto 1994–; chm Manulife International Investment Management Ltd; dir: Manufacturers Life Insurance Company (USA), Elliot & Page, Seamark Asset Management, PT Dharmala Manulife, OUB Manulife Pte; *Clubs* Reform; *Style—* Joseph Mounsey, Esq; ✉ Manulife, 200 Bloor Street East, Toronto, Ontario, Canada, M4W 1E5

MOUNSEY-HEYSHAM, Giles Gubbins; s of Maj Richard Herchard Gubbins Mounsey-Heysham (d 1960), of Castletown, Rockcliffe, Carlisle, and Mrs Isobel Margaret Rowcliffe; *b* 15 Aug 1948; *Educ* Gordonstoun, Royal Agric Coll Cirencester; *m* 24 April 1982, Penelope Auriol, da of William Anthony Twiston-Davies (see Debrett's Peerage and Baronetage, Archdale, Bt); 3 s (Toby b 23 Jan 1984, Benjamin b 3 March 1986, Rory b 2 Feb 1989), 1 da (Anna b 29 May 1991); *Career* chartered surveyor; Smiths Gore 1970–72, Cluttons 1973– (ptnr 1976); memb Ct of Assts Worshipful Co of Grocers; FRICS 1982 (memb 1972); *Recreations* music, skiing, walking, travelling, shooting; *Clubs* Boodle's, Pratt's; *Style—* Giles Mounsey-Heysham, Esq; ✉ Castletown, Rockcliffe, Carlisle CA6 4BN (☎ 01228 74792); Cluttons, Castletown, Rockcliffe, Carlisle (☎ 01228 74792, fax 01228 74464)

MOUNT, (Sir) (William Robert) Ferdinand; 3 Bt (UK 1921), of Wasing Place, Reading, Berks, but does not use his title; s of Robert Francis Mount (d 1969, 2 s of Sir William Arthur Mount, 1 Bt, CBE), and his 1 w, Lady Julia Agnes Cynthia Pakenham (d 1956), da of 5 Earl of Longford; suc unc, Sir William Malcolm Mount, 2 Bt (d 1993); *b* 2 July 1939; *Educ* Eton, Vienna Univ, Ch Ch Oxford; *m* 1968, Julia Margaret, twin da of Archibald Julian Lucas; 2 s (and 1 s decd), 1 da; *Heir* s, William Robert Horatio Mount b 1969; *Career* former CRD desk offr (home affrs and health and social security); former chief ldr writer Daily Mail, columnist The Standard 1980–82, political correspondent The Spectator to 1982; head PM's Policy Unit 1982–84, literary ed The Spectator 1984–85, columnist Daily Telegraph 1985–90, ed Times Literary Supplement 1991–; *Books* The Theatre of Politics (1972), The Man Who Rode Ampersand (1975), The Clique (1978), The Subversive Family (1982), The Selkirk Strip (1987), Of Love And Asthma (1991, Hawthornden Prize 1992), The British Constitution Now (1992), Umbrella (1994), The Liquidator (1995); *Style—* Ferdinand Mount, Esq; ✉ 17 Ripplevale Grove, London N1 1HS (☎ 0171 607 5398); Times Literary Supplement, Admiral House, 66–68 East Smithfield, London E1 9XY (☎ 0171 782 3000)

MOUNT, Margaret Rose (Peggy); OBE (1996); da of Alfred Mount (d 1928), of Leigh-on-Sea, and Rose Mount; *Career* actress; early years spent in repertory; first major performance in Sailor Beware (Strand Theatre) 1955; *Theatre* incl: Farewell, Farewell Eugene, All Things Bright and Beautiful, Romeo and Juliet, Mrs Hardcastle in She Stoops to Conquer, Oh Clarence, The Bandwagon, When We Are Married, Mrs Malaprop in The Rivals, Lady Catherine in The Circle, Signed and Sealed, Il Campielo (NT), Plunder (NT), Larkrise to Candleford (NT), Blithe Spirit and My Giddy Aunt (toured Middle East), Jubilee and Rookery Nook (Birmingham Rep, transferred to Shaftesbury Theatre), Mrs Tucker's Pageant (Theatre Royal Stratford), Sister George in The Killing of Sister George (Watermill Theatre Newbury), Fiddlers Three (tour), The Confederacy (tour), The Mating Game (tour); with The RSC at Stratford 1983–85 appearing in: The Dillon, Measure for Measure, Mary, After The Queen, The Happiest Days of Your Life; recent theatre work: Ursula The Pig Woman in Bartholomew Fair (Open Theatre Regent's Park), Miss Hannigan in Annie, Madame Arcati in Blithe Spirit, Olive Harriet Smythe in Move Over Mrs Markham, Nan in A Breath of Spring, Marina in Uncle Vanya; *Television* incl: The Larkins, George and the Dragon, Lollipop Loves Mr Mole, You're Only Young Twice, The Wonderful TV Times, Spice Island Farewell, Looks Familiar, Just Like Mum, The End of the Pier Show, Alice Jolie in The Trial of Klaus Barbie, The Judge in Punishment Without Crime (with Donald Pleasance), Child's Play (with Frankie Howerd), Casualty, Virtual Murder; *Films* incl: The Naked Truth (with Peter Sellers), Hotel Paradiso (with Alec Guinness), Oliver, Inn for Trouble, One Way Pendulum, Ladies Who Do; *Style—* Ms Peggy Mount, OBE; ✉ c/o Paul du Fer (☎ 0181 992 3336, 0171 497 5111)

MOUNT, Paul Morrow; s of Ernest Edward Mount, and Elsie Gertrude, *née* Morrow; *b* 8 June 1922; *Educ* Newton Abbot GS, Paignton Sch of Art, RCA; *m* 1, 1947 (m dis), Jeanne Rosemary Martin; 1 s (Martin b 1950), 1 da (Margaret b 1956); m 2, 11 Oct 1978, June Sylvia, da of Lt Col William George Hilary Miles, RM; *Career* served WWII with Friends' Ambulance Unit, attached to 13 Bn Med, 2 Div Blindee (Free French); initiated and ran Art Dept Yaba Nigeria 1955–61, freelance sculptor 1962–; cmmns incl: Br Steel Corp, Fibreglass Ltd St Helens, York House Bristol, CRS and Leo supermarkets, Swiss Embassy Tafawa Balewa Square, Chase Manhattan Bank Lagos, Bauchi Meml Nigeria, cabinet offices Accra; exhbn en Permanence New Art Centre Roche Court and Beaux Arts W1; ARCA 1948, RWA, memb Penwith Soc; *Recreations* music; *Style—* Paul Mount, Esq; ✉ Nancherrow Studio, St Just, Penzance, Cornwall TR19 7LA (☎ 01736 788 552)

MOUNT CHARLES, Earl of; Henry Vivian Pierpoint Conyngham; s and h of 7 Marquess Conyngham, *qv*, by his 1 w, Eileen Wren, *née* Newsam; *b* 23 May 1951; *Educ* Harrow, Harvard Univ; *m* 1, 1971 (m dis 1985), Juliet Ann, da of Robert R B Kitson, of Churchtown, Morval, Cornwall; 1 s (Alexander Burton, Viscount Slane b 1975), 1 da (Lady Henrietta Tamara Juliet b 1976); m 2, 1985, Lady Iona Charlotte Grimston, yst da of 6 Earl of Verulam (d 1973); 1 da (Lady Tamara Jane b 17 April 1991); *Heir* s, Alexander Burton, Viscount Slane b 30 Jan 1975; *Career* Irish Rep Sothebys 1976–78; consultant Sothebys 1978–84; chm: Slane Castle Ltd, Slane Castle Productions; tstee Irish Youth Foundation; dir Grapevine Arts Centre, Dublin; landowner (1450 acres); *Clubs* Kildare St & University, Dublin (Dublin); *Style—* Earl of Mount Charles; ✉ Beauparc House, Beauparc, Navan, Co Meath

MOUNT EDGCUMBE, 8 Earl of (GB 1789); Robert Charles Edgcumbe; also Viscount Mount Edgcumbe and Valletort (GB 1781) and Baron Edgcumbe of Mount Edgcumbe (GB 1742); s of George Aubrey Valletort Edgcumbe (d 1977, bro of 7 Earl, who d 1982) and his 1 w, Meta, da of late Charles Robert Lhoyer, of Nancy, France; descended from Sir Richard Edgcombe (d 1489), a supporter of Henry Tudor, Earl of Richmond (later Henry VII), who was knighted on the field of Bosworth, and later became a PC and comptroller of the Household; *b* 1 June 1939; *m* 1960 (m dis 1988), Joan Ivy, da of Ernest Wall, of Otorohanga, NZ; 5 da; *Heir* half-bro, Piers Edgcumbe, *qv*; *Career* farmer; ex mangr Lands and Survey Dept NZ; landowner (2200 acres); *Style—* The Rt Hon The Earl of Mount Edgcumbe; ✉ Empacombe House, Mount Edgcumbe, Cornwall PL10 1HZ

MOUNTAIN, Sir Denis Mortimer; 3 Bt (UK 1922), of Oare Manor, Co Somerset, and Brendon, Co Devon; s of Lt-Col Sir Brian Edward Stanley Mountain, 2 Bt (d 1977), and Doris Elsie, *née* Lamb; *b* 2 June 1929; *Educ* Eton; *m* 18 Feb 1958, (Hélène) Fleur Mary, da of John William Kirwan-Taylor (d 1994), of Switzerland; 2 s (Edward Brian Stanford b 1961, William Denis Charles b 1966), 1 da (Georgina Lily Fleur (Mrs Nigel C B Macpherson) b 1959); *Heir* s, Edward Brian Stanford Mountain b 19 March 1961; *Career* Lt Royal Horse Guards; chm and md Eagle Star Insur Co Ltd 1974–85 (dir 1959), pres Eagle Star Hldgs plc 1985–93; dir: Philip Hill Investmt Tst plc 1967–86, Rank Orgn plc 1968–94, Bank of Nova Scotia (Canada) 1978–, Allied London Properties plc 1986–; *Recreations* fishing, shooting; *Clubs* Nat Sporting, Blues and Royals; *Style—* Sir Denis Mountain, Bt; ✉ 12 Queens Elm Square, Old Church St, London SW3 6ED (☎ 0171 352 4331); The Manor, Morestead, nr Winchester, Hants SO21 1LZ (☎ 01962 777237)

MOUNTAIN, Edward Brian Stanford; s and h of Sir Denis Mortimer Mountain, 3 Bt, *qv*; *b* 19 March 1961; *Educ* Univ of Manchester (BSc, Dip fm Man); *m* 24 Oct 1987, Charlotte Sarah Jesson, da of His Honour Judge Henry Pownall, QC, of London; 2 s (Thomas Denis Edward b 14 Aug 1989, Harry Brian Pownall b 21 June 1991), 1 da (Camilla Margaret b 1 April 1993); *Career* Maj The Blues and Royals, ret 1992; land agency; *Recreations* shooting, fishing, skiing; *Clubs* Cavalry and Guards'; *Style—* Edward Mountain, Esq

MOUNTBATTEN, Lord Ivar Alexander Michael; yr s of 3 Marquess of Milford Haven, OBE, DSC (d 1970), and Janet, Marchioness of Milford Haven, *qv*; *b* 9 March 1963; *Educ* Gordonstoun, Middlebury Coll Vermont USA (BA Geology); *m* 23 April 1994, Penelope Ann Vere, da of Colin Thompson, of Warminster, Wilts; 1 da (Ella Louise Georgina b 20 March 1996); *Career* Monarch Resources Venezuela 1987–88; dir: Delta Minerals Corp Bermuda 1988–, AEI Redifusion 1995–; tstee Regain, The Tst for Sporting Tetraplegics 1994–; *Recreations* skiing, windsurfing, flying, shooting; *Clubs* Buck's; *Style—* The Lord Ivar Mountbatten; ✉ Moyns Park, Birdbrook, Essex CO9 4BP (☎ 01440 730073, fax 01440 730060)

MOUNTBATTEN OF BURMA, Countess (UK 1947); Patricia Edwina Victoria Knatchbull; CBE (1991), CD (1976), JP (Kent 1971), DL (Kent 1973); also Viscountess Mountbatten of Burma (UK 1946), Baroness Romsey (UK 1947); da of Adm of the Fleet 1 Earl Mountbatten of Burma, KG, GCB, OM, GCSI, GCIE, GCVO, DSO, PC, FRS (assas 1979), and Hon Edwina Ashley, CI, GBE, DCVO (d 1960, da of 1 and last Baron Mount Temple, himself gs of 7 Earl of Shaftesbury, the philanthropist); Edwina's mother was Maud, da of Sir Ernest Cassel, the banker and friend of Edward VII; sister of Lady Pamela Hicks, *qv*; *b* 14 Feb 1924; *Educ* Malta, England, NYC; *m* 26 Oct 1946, 7 Baron Brabourne, CBE, *qv*; 4 s (and 1 twin s k 1979, with his gf), 2 da; *Heir* s, Lord Romsey, *qv*; *Career* served 1943–46 WRNS; Col-in-Chief Princess Patricia's Canadian Light Inf 1974; Vice Lord Lieutenant Kent 1984; vice-pres: BRCS, NSPCC, Kent Rural Community Cncl, SSAFA, FPA, Nat Childbirth Tst, Royal Life Saving Soc, Shaftesbury Soc, Royal Coll of Nursing, Nat Soc for Cancer Relief, Royal Nat Coll for the Blind; pres: SOS Children's Villages, Shaftesbury Homes and Arethusa, Kent Branch Save the Children, Kent Branch Relate, Friends of Cassel Hosp and of William Harvey Hosp; hon vice pres: British Maritime Charitable Fndn, Soc for Nautical Research; vice patron Burma Star Assoc; chm: Sir Ernest Cassel Educn Tst, Edwina Mountbatten Tst; patron: Legion of Frontiersmen of the Commonwealth, Commando Assoc, VAD (RN) Assoc, Nurses' Welfare Tst, Compassionate Friends, HMS Kelly Reunion Assoc, East Kent Hospice, Kent Cncl on Drug Addiction, Kent Chest Heart and Stroke Assoc, Mote House Cheshire Home, Kent Handicapped Orphans' Caring Assoc, Kent Childrens' Houses Society, Chatham Dockyard Hist Soc, Ashford Samaritans, Ashford Umbrella Club, T S Churchill Sea Cadets Ashford; govr Ashford Sch, tstee The Kent Community Housing Tst; DStJ 1981; *Style—* The Rt Hon the Countess Mountbatten of Burma, CBE, CD, JP, DL; ✉ Newhouse, Mersham, Ashford, Kent TN25 6NQ (☎ 01233 503636, fax 01233 503636); 41 Montpelier Walk, London SW7 1JH (☎ 0171 589 8829, fax 0171 584 0024)

MOUNTEVANS, 3 Baron (UK 1945); (Edward Patrick) Broke Andvord Evans; s of 2 Baron Mountevans (d 1974); *b* 1 Feb 1943; *Educ* Rugby, Trinity Coll Oxford; *m* 1974, Johanna, da of Antonius Keyzer, of The Hague; *Heir* bro, Hon Jeffrey Richard Evans, *qv*; *Career* Lt ret 74 MC regt RCT, AER 1966; joined management of Consolidated Gold Fields Ltd 1966; joined British Tourist Authority 1972, mangr Sweden and Finland 1973, mangr Promotion Services 1976, asst marketing mangr 1982–; *Recreations* reading, travel; *Style—* The Rt Hon the Lord Mountevans; ✉ c/o The House of Lords, London SW1

MOUNTEVANS, Deirdre, Baroness; Deirdre Grace; da of John O'Connell, of Buxton House, Co Cork; *m* 1940, 2 Baron Mountevans (d 1974); *Career* memb: British Red Cross, Governing Body Age Concern; hon pres Kensington and Chelsea Age Concern (chm Appeals Ctee), hon vice pres Elderly Accomodation Council, house chm DGHH Vicarage Nursing Home, tstee Nicholas Freeman Meml Tst; *Style—* The Rt Hon Deirdre, Lady Mountevans; ✉ Lady Mountevans, 2 Durwood House, Kensington Court, London W8 5BH

MOUNTFIELD, Peter; s of Alexander Stuart Mountfield (d 1984), of Lanthwaite, Hightown, Liverpool, and Agnes Elizabeth, *née* Gurney (d 1987); *b* 2 April 1935; *Educ* Merchant Taylors' Crosby, Trinity Coll Cambridge (BA), Harvard Univ; *m* 1958, Evelyn Margaret, da of Walter Frederick Smithies (d 1963), of Liverpool; 3 s (Andrew b 1962, Benjamin b 1964, Christopher b 1968); *Career* civil serv HM Treasy 1958–91 (under sec 1977–91), exec sec to the Jt IMF/IBRD Devpt Ctee 1991–; *Recreations* walking, reading, looking at buildings; *Style—* Peter Mountfield, Esq; ✉ Development Ctee, 1818 H Street NW, Washington DC 20433, USA

MOUNTFORD, Margaret Rose; *née* Gamble; da of James Ross Gamble, of Bangor, NI, and Kathleen Margaret, *née* Stevenson; *b* 24 Nov 1951; *Educ* Strathearn Sch Belfast, Girton Coll Cambridge (MA); *Career* admitted slr 1976, ptnr Herbert Smith 1983–; Liveryman Worshipful Co of Solicitors; memb Law Soc; *Recreations* travel, opera, wine; *Style—* Ms Margaret Mountford; ✉ Herbert Smith, Exchange House, Primrose Street, London EC2A 2HS (☎ 0171 374 8000, fax 0171 496 0043)

MOUNTFORD, Roger Philip; s of Stanley W A Mountford, of Leatherhead, Surrey (d 1984), and Evelyn Mary Richardson (d 1979); *b* 5 June 1948; *Educ* Kingston GS, LSE (BSc), Stanford Graduate Sch of Business (Sloan fell, MS); *m* 24 July 1981, Jane Rosemary, da of The Rev Canon Eric Edwin Stanton, hon Canon of Canterbury (d 1984); 3 da (Laura Jane b 1983, Annabel Louise b 1985, Nicola Mary b 1989); *Career* PA to Rt Hon Edward Heath 1969–70 and during 1970 and 1974 gen elections, nat chm Fedn of Cons Students 1970–71, memb Carlton Club Political Ctee 1990–; merchant banker; md Hambro Pacific Ltd Hong Kong 1983–89, Hambros Bank Ltd 1971– (dir 1984–); non-exec dir Quadrilion Publishing Limited 1995–; Freeman of the City of London 1974, Liveryman Worshipful Co of Stationers and Newspaper Makers 1992; *Recreations* riding, opera; *Clubs* Carlton, Hong Kong, Royal Hong Kong Jockey, London Capital (hon bd of advsrs); *Style—* Roger Mountford, Esq; ✉ Hambros Bank Ltd, 41 Tower Hill, London EC3N 4HA (☎ 0171 480 5000)

MOUNTFORD, (John) Toby; s of John Dennis Mountford, of Mead House, 3 Station Rd, Thames Ditton, Surrey, and Wendy, *née* Gowlland; *b* 4 Nov 1954; *Educ* Wellington, Univ of Durham (BSc Econ); *Career* articled clerk then CA Price Waterhouse London 1976–80, mgmnt accountant Int Div Beecham Pharmaceuticals 1980–81, fin PR dir Streets Financial Ltd 1981–87, dir Citigate Communications Ltd 1987–; tstee The Holy Trinity Malshanger Tst, memb Holy Trinity Church PCC Brompton; ACA 1980; *Books* Practice Development - A Guide to Marketing Techniques for Accountants (1985); *Recreations* skiing, walking, swimming, theatre; *Clubs* Holmes Place, Barbican; *Style—* Toby Mountford, Esq; ✉ Citigate Communications Limited, 26 Finsbury Square, London EC2A 1DS (☎ 0171 282 8000, fax 0171 282 8010)

MOUNTGARRET, 17 Viscount (I 1550); Richard Henry Piers Butler; also Baron Mountgarret (UK 1911, which sits as in House of Lords); s of 16 Viscount Mountgarret (d 1966); hp to Earldoms of Ossory and Ormonde, also to Chief Butlership of Ireland; *b* 8 Nov 1936; *Educ* Eton, Sandhurst; *m* 1, 1960 (m dis 1969), Gillian, da of Cyril Buckley, of Chelsea; 2 s, 1 da; m 2, 1970, Mrs Jennifer Fattorini, da of Capt D Wills, of Wrington, Somerset; m 3, 1983, Mrs Angela Ruth Waddington, da of Thomas Porter, of Tadcaster; *Heir* s, Hon Piers James Richard Butler; *Career* formerly Capt Irish Gds; pres Yorkshire County Cricket Club 1984–90; *Recreations* shooting, stalking, cricket; *Clubs* White's, Pratt's; *Style—* The Rt Hon the Viscount Mountgarret; ✉ Stainley House, South Stainley, Harrogate, Yorks (☎ 01423 770087, fax 01423 770193); 42 Ebury Bridge Road, London SW1 (☎ 0171 823 6145)

MOURBY, Adrian Roy Bradshaw; s of Roy Mourby, of Welshpool, Montgomeryshire, and Peggy, *née* Bradshaw; *Educ* King Edward VI Camp Hill Sch Birmingham, Univ of Wales (BA), Univ of Bristol Film Sch (postgrad); *m* 19 July 1980, Katharine Mary, da of John Richard Trevena Nicholas (d 1971), of West Penwith, Cornwall; 1 da (Miranda Jane b 1987), 1 s (John James b 1990); *Career* BBC TV and Radio 1979–91; currently writer, broadcaster, independent prodr and journalist; Smith-Kline Award for Radio Journalism 1983, commendation Sony Radio Awards 1985, BAFTA/Cymru Best English Drama Award 1991, Celtic Film Festival Best Short Drama Award 1994, Sony Silver Award for Radio Writing 1995; others from Francisco Film Festival 1993 and NY Int Radio Festival 1994; writer of 8 broadcast plays, numerous radio talks, two Radio 4 comedy series Whatever Happened to...? and Silkies, writer, prodr and presenter of independent documentary Nimrod, contrib entertainments to Last Night of the Proms 1994 and 1995 and Christmas on Radio 4 1993 and 1995; *Books* We Think the World of Him (novel, 1996), The Four of Us (novel, 1997); *Recreations* eating, drinking and talking, architecture and a few good films; *Clubs* Royal Over-Seas; *Style—* Adrian Mourby; ✉ c/o Lutyens & Rubinstein, 231 Westbourne Park Road, London W11 1EB (☎ 0171 792 4855, fax 0171 792 4833)

MOURGUE, Harold George; s of Alfred George Mourgue (d 1972), and Maria May, *née* Hunter (d 1969); *b* 7 Sept 1927; *Educ* Colfes GS, Ilfracombe GS; *m* 3 April 1949, Joan Elsa Stella, da of John William Simms (d 1974); 1 s (Anthony John b 1950), 1 da (Jacqueline Susan b 1953); *Career* RN 1945–47; Harker Holloway & Co CAs 1948–53, CA 1953; mgmnt accountant and mangr Unilever 1953–60, fin controller and dir and gen mangr Ultra Radio & TV Ltd 1961–63, chief accountant Thorn Electrical Industries 1962–68; Thorn EMI plc: co sec 1967–72, fin dir 1970–85, vice chm 1985–87; non-exec dir: T & N plc (formerly Turner & Newall plc) 1983–95, Rolls-Royce plc 1985–, Thames Television plc 1985–92, N M Rothschild Asset Management Ltd 1989–93, Nuswift plc 1989–91; chm: Inmos plc 1985–87, Kenwood Appliances plc 1989–96, Thorn EMI Pension Fund, Rolls Royce Pension Fund, T & N Pension Fund 1988–95; tstee Laporte plc Pension Fund; memb Industl Devpt Advsy Bd 1985–92; FCA, CIMgt; *Recreations* music, theatre, gardening, literature; *Style—* Harold Mourgue, Esq; ✉ Eastbourne (fax 01323 639547)

MOUSSA, Pierre Louis; *b* 5 March 1922; *Educ* Lycée Ampère and Lycée du Parc Lyon France, École Normale Supérieure (Lettres) Paris, Agrégé des Lettres 1943; *m* 14 August 1957, Anne-Marie, *née* Trousseau; *Career* various assignments with French Admin 1949–62: tech advsr to the Sec for Fin and Econ Affrs 1949–51, dir of Cabinet Min for French Overseas Territories 1954, under-sec for econ affrs and planification for French overseas territories 1954–59, dir of civil aviation 1959–62; dir Dept of Ops Africa World Bank 1962–64, chm Fedn of French Insur Co 1965–69; Paribas Group 1969–81: sr exec vice pres, dep chm, chm and chief exec offr; fndr Finance and Development Inc 1982 (chm 1982–87), fndr Pallas Holdings (Luxembourg) 1984 (chm 1984–92), fndr and dir Pallas Invest (Luxembourg) 1989 (chm 1989–90); chm: Sud et Progrès (France), Strand Associates Ltd (Guernsey); dir: Compagnie Industrielle Pallas-Comipar (France), Delta Management (Guernsey) Ltd, CERUS (France); former prof: Inst for Political Studies (IEP) Paris, Nat Sch of Administration (ENA) Paris; Officier de la Légion d'Honneur (France 1976), Officier de l'Ordre National du Mérite (France 1966), Médaille Aéronautique (France 1962), Commandeur de l'Ordre National Mauritanien (1965), Commandeur de l'Ordre National de l'Etoile Equatoriale (Gabon 1972), Commandeur de l'Ordre National du Lion (Senegal 1975), Officier de l'Ordre National de Boyaca (Colombia 1954), Officier du Ouissam Alaouite, Officier de l'Ordre de la République Tunisienne (1972), Officier du Nicham el Anouar, Chevalier de l'Etoile Noire du Bénin; *Publications* Les Chances Économiques de la Communauté Franco-Africaine (1958), Les Nations Prolétaires (1959), L'Économie de la Zone Franc (1960), Les Etats-Unis et les Nations Prolétaires (1965), La Roue de la Fortune, Souvenirs d'un Financier (1989), Caliban Naufragé (1994); *Clubs* RAC, Automobile Club de France (Paris); *Style—* Pierre Moussa, Esq; ✉ c/o Strand Partners Ltd, 110 Park Street, London W1Y 3RB (☎ 0171 409 3494, fax 0171 409 1761); Sud et Progrès, 20 Rue Quentin-Bauchart, 75008 Paris, France (☎ 00 33 1 40 70 75 38, fax 00 33 1 40 70 78 51)

MOUTAFIAN, Princess Helena; MBE (1976); da of Prince Alexei Gagarin (d 1938), and Countess Ana Phillipovitz (d 1944); *b* 2 May 1930; *m* 14 Jan 1955, Artin Moutafian (d 1992), s of Nikogos Moutafian (d Armenia 1914); 2 s (Nicholas b 6 Nov 1958, Mark b 21 Dec 1960); *Career* vice pres Help the Aged (pres Ladies' Ctee), fndr pres Anglo-Russian Children Appeal, vice pres Ladies' Ctee European-Atlantic Gp, hon vice pres Women's Cncl, life patron NSPCC, patron Cwlth Countries' League; memb: Br Assoc of Women Entrepreneurs, Int PEN, Inst of Journalists; fell Soil Assoc; FRGS, FRZS; DStJ 1990; Croix de Chevalier (Ordre de la Courtoisie Française) 1976, Etoile Civique (Grande Médaille de Vermeil de la Ville de Paris) 1977; Freedom City of Paris 1977; awarded Silver Medal of Grollo d'Ore for paintings of Venice; *Recreations* painting, writing; *Clubs* English-Speaking Union; *Style—* Princess Helena Moutafian, MBE; ✉ 12 Greenaway Gardens, Hampstead, London NW3 7DH

MOWAT, David McIvor; JP (Edinburgh 1968); s of Ian McIvor Mowat (d 1985), and Mary Isabelle Simpson, *née* Steel; *b* 12 March 1939; *Educ* Edinburgh Acad, Univ of Edinburgh (MA), Open Univ (BA); *m* 20 June 1964, (Elinor) Anne, da of Eric Edward Birtwistle (d 1974); 3 da (Sarah Jane b 4 Sept 1965, Anna Katherine (Kate) b 25 April 1967, Julia Claire b 9 Jan 1969); *Career* journalist, broadcaster, conslt; chief exec: Edinburgh Chamber of Commerce and Manufactures 1968–90, Chamber Developments Ltd 1974, Edinburghs Capital Ltd, Who's Who in Business In Scotland Ltd; dir and chief exec Iatros Ltd; dir: St Andrews Golf Club (Manufacturing) Ltd, Counselling InterExec Edinburgh Ltd; former pres Br Chamber of Commerce Execs 1987–89; FRSA 1986; *Style—* David Mowat, Esq, JP; ✉ 37 Orchard Rd South, Edinburgh EH4 3JA (☎ 0131 332 6865); Iatros Limited, Dundee (fax 01382 561590)

MOWAT, Magnus Charles; s of John F M Mowat, MBE (d 1988), of Ellesmere, Shropshire and Elizabeth Rebecca, *née* Murray (d 1977); *b* 5 April 1940; *Educ* Haileybury; *m* 27 April 1968, Mary Lynette St Lo, da of Alan D Stoddart (d 1994), of Crowcombe, Taunton, Somerset; 3 s (Charles b 15 April 1969, Alexander b 27 June 1970, Hugh b 7 June 1973); *Career* CA; Peat Marwick Mitchell & Co 1959–67, Hill Samuel & Co Ltd 1968–70, ptnr Illingworth & Henriques Stockbrokers 1970–84, dir Barclays de Zoete Wedd Ltd 1984–90; non-exec dir: Allen plc, AF plc, EFT plc, Ryalux Carpets Ltd; chm: Booths Charities Manchester, Manchester YMCA, Manchester Branch IOD; FCA 1964; *Recreations* shooting, gardening, music; *Clubs* Boodle's, St James' (Manchester); *Style—* Magnus Mowat, Esq; ✉ New Park House, Whitegate, Northwich, Cheshire (☎ 01606 889 659, mobile 0836 519329)

MOWAT, Her Hon Judge; Mary Jane Stormont; da of late Duncan McKay Stormont Mowat, and Jane Archibald Mowat, *née* Milne; *b* 7 July 1948; *Educ* Sherborne Sch for Girls, Lady Margaret Hall Oxford (MA), Inns of Court Sch of Law; *m* Dr Nicholas Michael John Woodhouse, s of The Hon C M Woodhouse; 1 s (Thomas Duncan b 4 Feb 1987); *Career* called to the Bar Inner Temple 1973, circuit judge (SE Circuit) 1996–; *Recreations* music, walking, reading; *Style—* Her Hon Judge Mowat; ✉ St Albans Crown Court, 4 Bricket Road, St Albans, Herts AL1 3HY

MOWBRAY, Sir John Robert; 6 Bt (UK 1880), of Warennes Wood, Berkshire; JP (W Suffolk 1972), DL (Suffolk 1993); s of Sir George Robert Mowbray, 5 Bt, KBE (d 1969), and Diana Margaret, *née* Hughes (d 1996); *b* 1 March 1932; *Educ* Eton, New Coll Oxford; *m* 1957, Lavinia Mary, da of Lt-Col Francis Edgar Hugonin, OBE, JP, RA; 3 da (Mary Clare (Mrs James D Delevingne) b 1959, Teresa Jane b 1961, Katherine Diana (Mrs David Chastel de Boinville) b 1965); *Heir* none; *Style—* Sir John Mowbray, Bt, JP, DL; ✉ The Hill House, Duffs Hill, Glemsford, Suffolk CO10 7PP (☎ 01787 281930)

MOWBRAY, SEGRAVE AND STOURTON, 26, 27 and 23 Baron (E 1283, 1295 and 1448 respectively); Charles Edward Stourton; CBE (1982); s of 25 Baron Mowbray, (26) Segrave and (22) Stourton, MC, JP (d 1965; himself gs of 23, 24 and 20 Baron, who had inherited the Barony of Stourton from his f, and had abeyance of Baronies of Mowbray and Segrave terminated in his favour 1878) and of Sheila, da of Hon Edward W K Gully, CB (d 1931; 2 s of 1 Viscount Selby); *b* 11 March 1923; *Educ* Ampleforth, Ch Ch Oxford; *m* 1952, Hon Jane Faith de Yarburgh-Bateson, da of 5 Baron Deramore (d 1964), by his w Nina Macpherson-Grant; 2 s; *Heir* s, Hon Edward William Stephen Stourton; *Career* sits as Conservative in House of Lords; Lt Grenadier Gds 1943; memb of Lloyd's 1952; dir Securicor (Southern) Ltd 1965–66, Securicor (Scotland) 1966–70; Cons whip in House of Lords and front bench spokesman 1967–70 and 1974–78; lord in waiting 1970–74 and 1979–80; dep chief oppn whip House of Lords 1978–79; chllr of the Primrose League 1974–79; chm: Ghadeco (UK) Ltd 1986–, Teaco Ltd 1993; hon pres Safety Glazing Assoc 1975–78; Kt of Honour and Devotion SMO Malta, Bailiff Grand Cross and pres Br Assoc of the Constantinian Order of St George; *Style—* The Rt Hon the Lord Mowbray, Segrave and Stourton, CBE; ✉ Marcus, by Forfar, Angus DD8 3QU (☎ 01307 850219); 23 Warwick Square, London SW1V 2AB

MOWL, Colin John; s of Arthur Sidney Mowl (d 1993), and Ada, *née* Bartlett (d 1993); *b* 19 Oct 1947; *Educ* Lawrence Sheriff Sch Rugby, LSE (MSc); *m* 27 June 1980, Kathleen Patricia, da of Michael Joseph Gallagher; 1 s (Thomas b 24 Oct 1983), 1 da (Sophie b 27 June 1985); *Career* econ asst Miny of Tport 1970–72; HM Treasy: sr econ asst 1972–74, econ advsr 1974–83, seconded as res mangr Forex Research Ltd 1983, sr econ advsr 1983–90, head Macro Economic Analysis and Forecast Gp 1990–94, dep dir Macroeconomic Policy and Prospects 1995, dep dir Budget and Public Finances 1995–; *Recreations* most sport (now only as a spectator), family; *Style—* Colin Mowl, Esq; ✉ HM Treasury, Parliament Street, London SW1P 3AG (☎ 0171 270 4419, fax 0171 270 4827)

MOWLAM, Dr Marjorie; MP (Lab) Redcar (majority 11,577); da of Frank William Mowlam (d 1980), and Bettina Mary, *née* Rogers; *b* 18 Sept 1949; *Educ* Coundon Court Comp Sch, Univ of Durham (BA), Univ of Iowa (MA, PhD); *Career* res asst to: Tony Benn MP 1971–72, Alvin Toffler 1972–73; lectr: Univ of Wisconsin 1976–77, Florida State Univ 1977–78, Univ of Newcastle upon Tyne 1979–83; sr admin Northern Coll Barnsley 1984–87; joined Lab Pty 1969, MP (Lab) Redcar 1987–, oppn front bench spokesperson on NI 1988–89, spokesperson for City and corporate affrs in Lab Pty Trade and Industry Team 1989–92, memb Shadow Cabinet 1992–; chief oppn spokesperson on: Citizen's Charter and women's issues 1992–93, national heritage 1993–94, Northern Ireland 1994–; currently shadow sec of state for Northern Ireland; memb TGWU; *Books* Debate on Disarmament (jt ed, 1982); *Recreations* jigsaws, swimming; *Style—* Dr Marjorie Mowlam, MP; ✉ PO Box 77, Redcar, Cleveland TS10 1YE (☎ 01642 490404, fax 01642 489260); House of Commons, Westminster, London SW1A 0AA (☎ 0171 219 5066, fax 0171 219 2466)

MOWLL, Christopher Martyn; s of Christopher Kilvinton Mowll (d 1940), and Doris Ellen, *née* Hutchinson (d 1986); *b* 14 Aug 1932; *Educ* Epsom Coll, Gonville and Caius Coll Cambridge (MA); *m* 4 Oct 1958, Margaret Frances, da of John Maclelland Laird (d 1988); 4 s (Gordon Howard Martyn b 1959, Ian Robert b 1961, David Christopher b 1961, Richard Laird b 1965); *Career* admitted slr 1956; slr and clerk to Worshipful Co of Clothworkers and sec to Clothworker's Fndn 1978–92; memb: Cncl Nat Library for the Blind 1964–79, Cncl Metropolitan Soc for the Blind 1964– (treas 1965–79, vice chm 1971–79, chm 1979–), Exec Cncl RNIB 1982–, Br-Australia Bicentennial Ctee 1984–88, Exec Ctee Assoc of Charitable Fndns 1989–92, Cncl The Shaftesbury Soc 1993–; Hon LLD Univ of Leeds 1992; Freeman City of London 1979, Warden Worshipful Co of Clothworkers 1994–96 (Liveryman 1979, Asst 1992); memb Law Soc 1956–92; *Style—* Christopher Mowll, Esq; ✉ 15 West Hill, Sanderstead, South Croydon, Surrey CR2 0SB (☎ 0181 657 1207)

MOWSCHENSON, Terence Rennie; QC (1995); s of Henry Mowschenson (d 1994), and Hanny Mowschenson (d 1992); *b* 7 June 1953; *Educ* Peterhouse, Queen Mary Coll London (LLB), Exeter Coll Oxford (BCL); *m* 10 Oct 1992, Judith Angela, da of Christopher Strang; *Career* called to the Bar Middle Temple 1977, in practice Chambers of P G Whiteman, QC 1978–90, Chambers of Sam Stamler, QC 1990–95; memb: Chancery & Commercial Bar Assocs, Insolvency Lawyers' Assoc; FCIArb 1991; *Recreations* opera; *Clubs* RAC; *Style—* Terence Mowschenson, Esq, QC; ✉ 1 Essex Court, Ground Floor, Temple, London EC4Y 9AR (☎ 0171 583 2000, fax 0171 583 0118)

MOXLEY, Raymond James (Ray); s of Rev Henry Roberts Moxley (d 1953), of Oxford, and Ruby Alice, *née* Gems (d 1972); *b* 28 July 1923; *Educ* Caterham, Oxford Sch of Architecture; *m* 12 Oct 1949 (m dis 1972), Jacqueline Marjorie, da of Orlando Beater (d 1954), of Standlake, Oxon; 1 s (Mike b 1950), 2 da (Caroline b 1956, Alison b 1959); *Career* trooper RHG 1942; RE: joined 1943, cmmnd 1944, Capt 1945, demobbed 1946; architect; fndr own practice 1953–65, dir and chm Moxley Jenner & Partners (London) Ltd 1986– (fndr ptnr 1965); visiting lectr 1953–: Univ of Bristol Sch of Architecture, Univ of Reading, Univ of Manchester; lectr: W of Eng Coll of Art 1965–69, Bristol Poly 1969–71; RIBA: assessor regnl awards 1968, rep Ct of Univ of Bath 1968–69, memb Cncl 1972–78, first hon librarian 1975–77, vice pres 1973–75; DOE Housing Awards: assessor E Midlands Region 1977, chm SE Region 1979, chm London Region 1980; chm: Bristol Bldg and Design Centre 1965–70, Assoc of Conslt Architects 1974–77, Soc for Advanced Methods of Mgmnt 1978, London Assoc of Conslt Architects 1984–86; pres Bristol and Somerset Soc of Architects 1968–69, vice pres Design and Industs Assoc 1989; hon fell Univ of West of England Bristol 1989; Freeman City of London 1975; Liveryman: Worshipful Co of Basketmakers, Worshipful Co of Chartered Architects; FRIBA, FRSA, RWA; *Books* Building Construction Vol 1 (23 edn); ed: Build International (1973–74), ACA Illustrated Directory of Architects (1983 and 1984), The Architects Guide to Fee Negotiation (1983), Architects Eye, Building Management by Professionals; *Recreations* sailing; *Clubs* Royal Western Yacht, RAC; *Style*— Ray Moxley, Esq; ✉ Moxley Jenner & Partners (London) Ltd, 10 The Belvedere, Chelsea Harbour, London SW10 0XA (☎ 0171 352 2813, fax 0171 627 2533)

MOXON, Martyn Douglas; s of Derek Moxon (d 1984), of Barnsley, South Yorks, and Audrey, *née* Scarborough; *b* 4 May 1960; *Educ* Holgate GS Barnsley; *m* Susan, da of late (Edgar) Duncan Slack; 1 da (Charlotte Louise b 13 March 1990), 1 s (Jonathon James b 6 May 1993); *Career* professional cricketer; capt N of England under 15 and under 19 teams; Yorkshire CCC: scored 116 on debut v Essex 1981, awarded county cap 1984, Capt 1990–; England: 10 Test matches (debut v NZ Lords 1986), 8 one day Ints (debut v India Nagpur 1985), tours to India/Australia 1984–85 and NZ/Aust 1988, B tour to Sri Lanka 1986, capt A team tour Bermuda/W Indies 1992 and A team tour to Aust 1993; trainee Barclays Bank 1978–80; *Recreations* supporting Barnsley FC and Everton FC; *Style*— Martyn Moxon, Esq; ✉ Yorkshire CCC, Headingley Cricket Ground, Leeds LS6 3BU (☎ 0113 278 7394, fax 0113 278 4099)

MOXON, Rev Canon Michael Anthony; s of Rev Canon Charles Moxon (Canon Residentiary and Precentor of Salisbury Cathedral, d 1985), of Salisbury, Wilts, and Phyllis Mary, *née* Carter; *b* 23 Jan 1942; *Educ* Merchant Taylors', Univ of Durham, Univ of London (BD, MA), Salisbury Theol Coll; *m* 9 Jan 1969, Sarah Jane, da of Francis Kynaston Needham Cresswell (d 1982), of Littlehampton; 2 s (Nicholas b 21 Nov 1969, Benjamin (twin) b 21 Nov 1969), 1 da (Emma-Jane b 1 Aug 1971); *Career* ordained: deacon 1970, priest 1971; asst priest Lowestoft Gp Ministry 1970–74, minor canon St Paul's Cathedral 1974–81 (jr cardinal 1974–78, sr cardinal 1978–79), warden Coll of Minor Canons 1979–81, sacrist St Paul's Cathedral 1977–81, vicar Tewkesbury with Walton Cardiff 1981–90, canon of Windsor and chaplain in the Great Park 1990–; proctor in convocation (memb Gen Synod) 1985–90, chaplain to HM The Queen 1986–; memb Cncl for the Care of Churches 1985–91; *Recreations* reading, music, cricket; *Style*— The Rev Canon Michael Moxon; ✉ The Chaplain's Lodge, The Great Park, Windsor, Berks SL4 2HP (☎ 01784 432434)

MOXON, Prof (Edward) Richard; s of Gerald Richard Moxon, CBE (d 1980), and Margaret, *née* Forster Mohun; *b* 16 July 1941; *Educ* Shrewsbury Sch, St John's Coll Cambridge (BA, MA, BChir); *m* 20 Oct 1973, Marianne, da of Prof George Graham; 2 s (Christopher Alan b 1978, Timothy Stewart b 1987), 1 da (Sarah Graham b 1981); *Career* sr house offr Hosp for Sick Children 1969, res fell Children's Hosp Med Centre Boston USA 1971–74 (asst resident paediatric 1970), asst prof of paediatrics Johns Hopkins Univ Hosp Baltimore USA 1974–78 (assoc prof and Eudowood chief of paediatric infectious diseases 1978–84), prof of paediatrics Univ of Oxford 1984–; *Recreations* sport, music, literature; *Style*— Prof Richard Moxon; ✉ Dept of Paediatrics, John Radcliffe Hospital, Headington OX3 9DU

MOXON BROWNE, Robert William; QC (1990); s of Kendall Edward Moxon-Browne, and Sheila Heron, *née* Weatherbe; *b* 26 June 1946; *Educ* Gordonstoun, Univ Coll Oxford (BA); *m* 26 June 1968, Kerstin Elizabet, da of Oscar Warne; 1 s (James Weatherbe b 7 April 1977), 1 da (Emily Kendall b 20 Oct 1973); *Career* called to Bar Gray's Inn 1969, recorder 1991–, dep official referee 1992–; *Recreations* theatre, gardening, cooking; *Style*— Robert Moxon Browne, Esq, QC; ✉ 37 Mowbray Road, London NW6 7QS

MOYES, James Christopher (Jim); *b* 29 April 1943; *Educ* Maidstone Coll of Art, Univ of Kent (BA); *m* 1, 1969 (m dis 1981), Elizabeth McKee; 1 da (Sara Jo b 1969); m 2, 1987, Joanna Margaret, da of Col David E G Price; 2 da (Beatrice Oliphant b 1987, Clementine b 1990); *Career* laboratory asst and quality control technician Watneys Laboratories 1959–64, merchant marine 1964–66, artist and gallery asst 1971–, fndr Momart plc (int fine art serv co, Royal Warrant holder), estab Momart fellowship (artist in residence Tate Gallery Liverpool); lectr in art handling techniques; memb: Assoc of American Museums Registrars' Ctee, Ctee Contemporary Art Soc, Museums Assoc; *Recreations* art exhibitions and other arts related activities; *Style*— Jim Moyes, Esq; ✉ Momart plc, 199–205 Richmond Road, London E8 3NJ (☎ 0181 986 3624, fax 0181 533 0122)

MOYLE, Rt Hon Roland Dunstan; PC (1978); s of Baron Moyle, CBE, JP, sometime MP Stourbridge & PPS to Clement Attlee (Life Peer d 1974), and his 1 w, Elizabeth; *b* 12 March 1928; *Educ* Bexleyheath and Llanidloes County Sch Powys, Univ Coll of Wales (Aberystwyth), Trinity Hall Cambridge; *m* 1956, Shelagh Patricia Hogan; 1 s, 1 da; *Career* served Royal Welch Fusiliers 1949–51; called to the Bar Gray's Inn; served various industrial relations posts in Wales Gas Bd, Gas Cncl, Electricity Cncl; MP (Lab): Lewisham N 1966–74, Lewisham East 1974–83; PPS to: Chief Sec Treasury 1966–69, Home Sec 1969–70; oppn spokesman: Army 1971, Higher Education and Science 1972–74; parly sec Miny Agric Fisheries and Food 1974; min of state: NI 1974–76, State Health 1976–79; front bench oppn spokesman: Health 1979–81, Foreign and Cwlth Affrs 1981–83, Defence and Disarmament 1983; dep chm Police Complaints Authy 1985–91, exec memb Nat Health Serv Support Fedn 1991–; former memb Race Relations and Immigration Select Ctee, vice-chm PLP Def Gp, sec and exec cncl memb British American Parly Gp 1968–83; *Style*— The Rt Hon Roland Moyle; ✉ 19 Montpelier Row, Blackheath, London SE3 0RL

MOYNE, 3 Baron (UK 1932); Jonathan Bryan Guinness; s of 2 Baron Moyne (d 1992), and his 1 w, Hon Diana, *née* Freeman Mitford (da of 2 Baron Redesdale and who subsequently m Sir Oswald Mosley, 6 Bt, *see* Mosley, Hon Lady); *b* 16 March 1930; *Educ* Eton (King's Scholar), Trinity Coll Oxford (MA); *m* 1, 1951 (m dis 1963), Ingrid Olivia Georgia, da of late Maj Guy Richard Charles Wyndham, MC (ggs of 1 Baron Leconfield); 2 s (Hon Jasper Jonathan Richard b 1954, Hon Valentine Guy Bryan b 1959), 1 da (Hon Catherine Ingrid (Hon Mrs Fleetwood Hesketh) b 1952); m 2, 1964, Mrs Suzanne Phillips, da of Harold William Denis Lisney, of Gerona, Spain, and formerly w of Timothy Phillips; 1 s (Hon Sebastian Walter Denis b 1964), 1 da (Hon Daphne Suzannah Diana Joan (Hon Mrs Niarchos) b 1967); further children by Susan Mary Taylor; 1 s (Thomas Julian Guinness-Taylor b 1986), 2 da (Diana Rose Guinness-Taylor b 1981, Aster Mary Guinness-Taylor b 1984); *Heir* s, Hon Jasper Jonathan Richard Guinness b 1954; *Career* dir: A Guinness Son & Co 1961–88, Leopold Joseph & Sons 1963–91; former Reuters journalist, chm Monday Club 1970–72; *Clubs* Beefsteak; *Style*— The Rt Hon Lord Moyne; ✉ House of Lords, London SW1A 0PW

MOYNIHAN, Hon Colin Berkeley; s of 2 Baron Moynihan, OBE, TD (d 1965), and June Elizabeth, *née* Hopkins; *b* 13 Sept 1955; *Educ* Monmouth Sch, Univ Coll Oxford (MA, Rowing and Boxing double blue); *m* 7 March 1992, Gaynor-Louise, only da of Paul G Metcalf, of Healing, S Humberside; 2 s (Nicholas Ewan Berkeley b 31 March 1994, George Edward Berkeley b 4 June 1995); *Career* pres Oxford Union Soc 1976; personal asst to chm Tate & Lyle Ltd 1978–80, mangr Tate & Lyle Agribusiness 1980–82, chief exec Ridgways Tea and Coffee Merchants 1980–83; MP (C) Lewisham East 1983–92; political asst to Foreign Sec 1983, PPS to Rt Hon Kenneth Clarke as Min of Health and PMG 1986–87, Parly under-sec of state: DOE and min for Sport 1987–90, Dept of Energy 1990–92; memb: Bow Gp 1978 (chm Bow Gp Industry Ctee 1985–87), Paddington Cons Mgmnt Ctee 1980–81; sec: Cons Foreign and Cwlth Affairs Ctee 1985, Major Spectator Sports Ctee CCPR 1979–87, CCPR Enquiry into Sponsorship of Sport 1982–83; memb Sports Cncl 1982–85, steward British Boxing Bd of Control 1979–87; tstee: Oxford Univ Boat Club 1980–83, Sports Aid Tst 1983–87; govr Sports Aid Fndn (London and SE) 1980–82, chm All Party Gp on Afghanistan 1984, vice chm Cons Backbenchers Sports Ctee; chm: Govt Inner City Working Gp on Sport and Recreation 1988, Govt Review Gp on Sport for the Disabled 1989, Govt Renewable Energy Advsy Gp 1991–; fndr memb Worldwatch Inst Europe 1991; Freeman City of London 1978, Liveryman Worshipful Co of Haberdashers; Olympic Silver medal Rowing 1980; Int Rowing Fedn: World Gold medal Lightweight Rowing 1978, World Silver medal Rowing 1981; *Recreations* collecting Nonsuch books, music, sport; *Clubs* Brooks's, Royal Commonwealth Soc, Vincent's (Oxford); *Style*— The Hon Colin Moynihan

MOYOLA, Baron (Life Peer UK 1971), of Castledawson, Co Londonderry; James Dawson Chichester-Clark; PC (NI 1966), DL (Co Derry 1954); s of Capt James L C Chichester-Clark, DSO and bar (d 1933), and Mrs C E Brackenbury, of Moyola Park, Castle Dawson, Co Derry, N Ireland; bro of Sir Robin Chichester-Clark, *qv*; *b* 12 Feb 1923; *Educ* Eton; *m* 1959, Moyra Maud, da of Brig Arthur de Burgh Morris, CBE, DSO, and wid of Capt T G Haughton; 1 step s, 2 da (Hon Fiona (Hon Mrs Fisher) b 1960, Hon Tara Olivia (Hon Mrs Whitley) b 1962); *Career* sits as Cons Peer in House of Lords; memb N Ireland Parliament 1960–71: chief whip 1963–67, ldr of the House and chief whip 1966–67, min of Agric 1967–69; prime minister 1969–71; *Recreations* shooting, fishing, gardening; *Style*— The Rt Hon the Lord Moyola, PC, DL; ✉ Moyola Park, Castledawson, Co Derry, N Ireland

MSIMANG, HE Mendi Meinrad Themba Boy; *b* 1928, Johannesburg; *Educ* Marianhill, Univ Coll of Roma Lesotho (BA); *m* Dr Mantombazana Tshabalala; 4 c from prev m; *Career* South African diplomat; early career experience: Rand Steam Laundries (co-fndr Laundry Workers' Union), asbestos assayer Costa Rican Consulate; African Nat Congress: personal sec to Sec-Gen, subsequently articled clerk in SA's first black law practice (estab by Nelson Mandela and Oliver Thambo), rep ANC Mission to UK and Ireland 1960, co-fndr first ANC newsletter 'South Africa in Fact', second ed successor jl 'Spotlight on South Africa' E Africa, admin sec first ANC Nat Exec Ctee in Exile E Africa, chm Regional Political Ctee, educn offr liaising with UNESCO and other educnl instns, memb Educn Cncl, admin sec Office of the Treas-Gen Zambia, chief rep of the ANC to India 1969, chief rep to the UK and Ireland 1988 (ANC rep at various int confs and meetings incl UN in NY and Switzerland, Orgn of African Unity, Non-Aligned Movement, Southern Africa Devpt Conf and Eastern and Southern African Preferential Assoc), memb ANC Nat Exec Ctee 1990–91, organiser first maj ANC Int Solidarity Conf SA 1993, elected to Nat Assembly of Republic of SA 1994, subsequently memb Constitutional Assembly, Select Ctee on Trade and Indust, Select Ctee on Foreign Affrs and Foreign Rels Ctee, temp chm Nat Assembly and chm ANC Parly Caucus; South African high cmmr to the Ct of St James's 1995–; chairperson Nelson Mandela Children's Fund, fell Rotarian Rotary Club of London, vice pres Royal Over-Seas League; *Recreations* football, golf, music, reading, theatre; *Style*— HE Mr Mendi Msimang; ✉ South African High Commission, South Africa House, Trafalgar Square, London WC2N 5DP (☎ 0171 451 7299, fax 0171 451 7283)

MTESA, HE Love; s of William Mutesa (d 1988), and Olive, *née* Lupunga; *b* 9 July 1942; *Educ* Macy Coll NYC (BSc 1992–94), Univ of Westminster (MA 1993), Int Inst of Public Admin Paris (Dip in Int Relations), UN Languages Center NYC (Dip in French); *m* 27 March 1967, Marie Madeleine, *née* Lumbwe; 5 c (Anne b 26 Jan 1968, Sylvia b 23 March 1970, Chilao b 3 Sept 1974, Mwelwa b Jan 1976, Bwanga b 25 Oct 1977); *Career* Zambian diplomat; primary sch teacher Ndola Zambia 1962–64, second sec Zambian Embassy Kinshasa Zaire 1966–69, first sec Zambian Embassy Addis Ababa Ethiopia 1970–73, cnsllr Zambian Embassy Kinshasa 1974–75, dir of Africa and ME Dept Miny of Foreign Affairs Lusaka 1975–80, dep high cmmr Harare Zimbabwe 1980–82, dep perm rep of Zambia to the UN NYC 1982–85, chm Movement for Multi-Party Democracy Lusaka Dist 1990–92, high cmmr of Zambia to the Ct of St James's and ambass extraordinary and plenipotentiary of Zambia to Ireland and to The Holy See 1992–; *Style*— HE Mr Love Mtesa; ✉ Zambia High Commission, No 2 Palace Gate, London W8 5LS (☎ 0171 589 6655, fax 0171 581 1353)

MUCKLE, David Sutherland; s of John Leslie Muckle, and Ruth, *née* Sutherland; *b* 30 Aug 1939; *Educ* Univ of Durham (MB BS), Univs of Oxford and Newcastle (MS MD); *m* Christine; 2 da (Carolyn Jane b 22 July 1964, Deborah Christine b 17 July 1966); *Career* res assoc Univ of Durham 1963; orthopaedic surgn: Radcliffe Infirmary Oxford, Oxford United FC and Oxford Univ 1970–77, Cleveland AHA 1977–; held various visiting professorships in Japan, Caribbean and USA 1977–82, visiting prof Univ of Teesside 1994–; examiner Royal Coll of Surgns of Edinburgh 1989–; med advsr to the Football Assoc, UEFA and FIFA; med offr: UEFA Nations Cup Final Gotenburg 1992, Euro 96 Final Wembley 1996; winner President's Prize in Orthopaedic Res 1973–74; author of various articles on biochemistry of soft tissue injuries, femoral neck fractures and cancer oncology; memb: Br Orthopaedic Res Soc 1973, Br Orthopaedic Assoc 1974, Royal Geographical Soc 1984; FRCS, FRCSE; *Books* A Doctor's Look at Life and History (1970), Sports Injuries (1971), Femoral Neck Fractures (1977), Injuries in Sport (1977), An Outline of Orthopaedic Practice (1985), An Outline of Fractures and Dislocations (1985); *Recreations* natural history, classical English literature, sport in general; *Style*— David S Muckle, Esq; ✉ Redcroft, 72 The Grove, Marton-in-Cleveland, Middlesbrough TS7 8AJ (☎ 01642 317382); Department of Orthopaedics, South Tees NHS Trust, Cleveland TS5 5AZ (☎ 01642 850850)

MUCKLOW, Dr Edward Stuart; s of Dr Stuart Leslie Mucklow (d 1976), and Dr Alexandra Winifred, *née* Groves (d 1981); *b* 24 Jan 1932; *Educ* Radley, Exeter Coll Oxford (BA 1954, MA, BM BCh 1957), UCH Med Sch London (DObstRCOG 1960, DCH Eng 1963), Univ of Edinburgh, FRSM 1963, FRCPEd 1986 (MRCPEd 1966), FRCP 1989, DTM RCP&SI 1995; *m* 2 April 1966, Dr Mary Lynn Cashel, da of Maurice Cashel; 2 s (Stuart b 1968, Gordon b 1975), 2 da (Clare b 1970, Celia b 1972); *Career* Nat Serv Capt RAMC 1960–62; ships surgn Messrs Submarine Cables Ltd Brazil 1959, house offr obstetrics Royal Postgrad Med Sch London 1959, sr house offr Hosp for Sick Children Gt Ormond St 1962–63, jr lectr in paediatrics UCH Med Sch 1963–64 (house physician and surgn 1958–59), lectr in child health Univ of Oxford 1966–68, seconded as chief of paediatrics Abdulla Fouad Hosp Dammam Saudi Arabia 1979–80; conslt paediatrician: IOW 1968–97, Portsmouth Health Dist 1968–92; hon clinical lectr in child health Univ of Southampton Med Sch 1973–97; author of various articles on: the newborn, tuberculosis, diabetes, genetics, pancreatitis in children, chemistry set poisoning, rheumatic fever incl leader article in The Lancet 1985; former pres and chm IOW Hockey Club, life memb

Ryeworth CC, memb Oxford Univ Occasionals Hockey Club, participant in Veteran World Hockey Cup 1986; chm Whitecroft Sports Ground Tst 1993–; memb: Cncl Paediatric Section Royal Soc of Med 1983–86, Editorial Bd Practical Diabetes (dep ed 1984–89), BPA, BMA Neonatal Soc; *Recreations* learning Arabic and Modern Greek, hockey, cricket, gardening, Islamic art and Arab history; *Style*— Dr Edward Mucklow; ✉ Keep Cottage, 5 Castle Lane, Carisbrooke, Isle of Wight PO30 1PH (☎ 01983 522096); Paediatric Department, St Mary's Hospital, Newport, Isle of Wight PO30 5TG (☎ 01983 524081, ext 4280, fax 01983 822569, telex 869466 Taravs G)

MUDDIMAN, Noel; CBE (1992, OBE 1985), GSM (Bar 1979 and 1991); step s of Arthur George Muddiman (d 1976), and s of Flora May, *née* Holdsworth; *b* 17 Dec 1943; *Educ* Borden GS, RMA Sandhurst; *m* 25 Oct 1969, Patricia Anne, *née* Sevage; 2 s (Andrew Robert b 1 April 1973, Matthew b 21 July 1980); *Career* served Army until 1995 (joined 1965); Army Staff Coll Camberley 1975, Nat Def Coll 1980, head of Personnel and Logistics Falkland Is 1985–86, princ logistic planner Br Forces Germany 1987–90, cdr Tport and Movements BAOR 1990–92, cdr Logistic Support Gp (Middle East) March-Aug 1991, planned and executed operation to remove Br Army from Kuwait and Saudi Arabia 1991, RCDS 1992, cmdt Army Sch of Mechanical Tport 1992–95, ret Army (with rank of Brig) 1995; dir Motability (charity) 1995– (sec 10th Anniversary Tst Fund 1995); tstee Museum of Army Tport 1992–95, memb Humberside TEC 1995; Freeman of Oerlinghausen (Germany) 1984, awarded Gulf War Medal (Norway) 1992; FILog 1992, FCIT 1995, FIMI 1996; *Books* Blackadder's War (jtly, 1995); *Recreations* hashing, gardening, photography; *Clubs* RASC/RCT Officers', Movement Control Officers'; *Style*— Noel Muddiman, Esq, CBE; ✉ Motability, Goodman House, Station Approach, Harlow, Essex CM20 2ET (☎ 01279 632010, fax 01279 632002, mobile 0860 648271)

MUDDIMER, Robert Michael (Bob); *b* 30 Jan 1933; *Educ* Kibworth Beauchamp GS, Univ of Nottingham (BSc(MechEng)); *m* 1959, Marguerite Mary, da of late Thomas Henry Conroy; 2 s (James Robert b 1 May 1961, Richard John b 21 Dec 1964), 1 da (Catherine Elizabeth b 15 Oct 1963); *Career* in materials mgmnt Lansing Bagnall Ltd 1965–68, dir BTR Industries Ltd 1969–80, dir Molins Tobacco Industries Ltd 1981–86, dir Tomkins plc 1986– (jt md 1995–), chm RHM Ltd 1993–96 (following acquisition by Tomkins), chm The Gates Corporation Denver Colorado 1996–; FIMfgE, CIMgt; *Recreations* golf, sailing, wood clockmaking; *Clubs* Leicestershire Golf, Dayton Racquet; *Style*— Bob Muddimer, Esq; ✉ Tomkins plc, East Putney House, 84 Upper Richmond Road, London SW15 2ST (☎ 0181 871 4544, fax 0181 877 9700)

MUDIE, Colin Crichton; *b* Edinburgh; *Educ* Scotland and England; *m* Rosemary Horder; *Career* naval architect and yacht designer; design apprentice: British Power Co Hythe Southampton, Laurent Giles & Partners yacht designers Lymington; fndr independent design firm (partnerd by w): Westminster London 1958–68, Lymington 1968–; designs incl sail trg vessels, special reproduction, expedition and exploration boats, power boats, sailing yachts, motor cruisers, motor sailers, workboats, pilot boats and dinghies; design work incl: TS Royalist (23 metre brigantine for Sea Cadet Corps) 1971, STS Lord Nelson (43 metre barque for the Jubilee Sailing Tst) 1986, STS Young Endeavour (35 metre brigantine - official gift of the British nation to Australia to mark the 1988 Bicentennial) 1987, HMRB Zinat al Bihaar (50 metre dhow (Baghla)) 1988, KLD Tunas Samudera (35 metre brigantine for the Royal Malaysian Navy) 1989, Aileach (12 metre birlinn which re-enacted Lord of the Isles voyages 1991 and 1992) 1991, Matthew (reconstruction of vessel to retrace John Cabot's 1497 historic voyage from Bristol to Newfoundland and back 1997) 1995, INV Tarangini (43 barque for Indian Navy) 1995; for Tim Severin: Brendan (11 metre curragh) 1975, sohar (20 metre dhow) 1980, Argo (16.5 metre galley) 1984; Winston Churchill fell 1968, Lloyd's Award (for best design and construction for the sail trg brig Royalist) 1971, RINA Small Craft Medal (for outstanding contribs to the Small Craft Indust) 1984, Br Design Cncl Award (for sail trg barque Lord Nelson) 1993; past memb: Hovercraft Ctee CAA Air Requirements Bd, Marine Technol Ctee and Mech and Electrical Engrg Requirements Bd Dept of Indust, Mary Rose Structure Advsy Panel, Steering Ctee Yacht and Boat Design Course Southampton Inst of HE; a vice pres and memb Ctee of Mgmnt RNLI; CEng, FRINA (memb Cncl), FRIN, FCSD, RDI 1995; *Books* Motor Boats and Boating, Power Boats, Sopranino (with Patrick Ellam), The Story of the Sailing Ship (with Rosemary Mudie), Power Yachts (with Rosemary Mudie), The Sailing Ship (with Rosemary Mudie); also author of various conf papers and pubns; *Recreations* sailing, model boats, books; *Clubs* Royal Lymington Yacht, Royal Ocean Racing, Ocean Cruising, Square Rigger; *Style*— Colin Mudie, Esq; ✉ Bywater Lodge, Pierside, Lymington, Hants SO41 5SB

MUELLER, Dame Anne Elisabeth; DCB (1988, CB 1980); da of Herbert Constantin Mueller (d 1952), and Phoebe Ann, *née* Beevers (d 1973); *b* 15 Oct 1930; *Educ* Wakefield Girls HS, Somerville Coll Oxford (MA); *m* 1958 (m dis 1978), James Hugh Robertson, s of Sir James Robertson, KT, GCMG, GCVO (d 1983); *Career* dep sec Dept of Trade and Indust 1977–84, dir European Investment Bank 1978–84; second perm sec: Cabinet Office (head of Mgmnt and Personnel Office) 1984–87, HM Treasy 1987–90; dir: British Sky Broadcasting 1991–, Sedgwick Lloyd's Underwriting Agents 1992–95; first chllr De Montfort Univ (formerly Leicester Poly) 1991–95 (now govr); cmmr Rural Devpt Cmmn 1990–, vice pres Care International 1992–; hon fell Somerville Coll 1980; *Clubs* United Oxford & Cambridge University; *Style*— Dame Anne Mueller, DCB; ✉ 46 Kensington Heights, Campden Hill Rd, London W8 7BD (☎ 0171 727 4780, fax 0171 792 8490)

MUELLER, Rudolf G; *b* 28 May 1934; *Educ* primary and secdy schs St Gallen Switzerland, Swiss Federal Commercial Dip, Int Mgmnt Inst Geneva (Dip Univ of Geneva); *m* Christiane, *née* Béroud; 2 s (b 1962 and 1965); *Career* with Adolph Saurer AG Arbon Switzerland 1954–56, various appts United Trading Co Basle and Nigeria 1956–68, studying at Int Mgmnt Inst Geneva 1968–69, i/c Euro Office James Capel & Co Geneva and md James Capel Far East 1969–77; Union Bank of Switzerland: joined Zurich 1977, opened Singapore Branch 1978 (mangr 1978–82), first vice pres 1981–83, head of securities sales and trading worldwide Zurich 1982–87, sr vice pres 1983, regnl mangr London and exec vice pres (UK) 1987–91, chm and chief exec UBS Phillips & Drew Ltd 1989–94, exec vice pres Europe 1991–96, chm UBS UK Ltd 1994–; chm SOFFEX Zurich 1986–88; non-exec dir: London Stock Exchange 1991–95 (memb 1988), TI Group plc 1996–, Lend Lease Corporation Ltd 1996–; memb Chm's Ctee London Investment Banking Assoc (formerly Br Merchant Banking Assoc) 1992–, dir IMI Kiev 1993–; dir Royal Opera House 1996– (tstee 1992–); *Recreations* glf, skiing, hiking, oenology; *Style*— Mr Rudolf G Mueller; ✉ UBS UK Ltd, 100 Liverpool Street, London EC2M 2RH (☎ 0171 901 3333)

MUGURIAN, Gordon Haig; s of Murgadich Mugurian (d 1942), of Hampstead, London, and Hilda Louise, *née* Hammond (d 1957); *b* 29 Dec 1926; *Educ* Eaglehurst Coll Northampton, Northampton Polytechnic London; *m* 9 Oct 1965, Jan Olive, da of Hugh Caley Parker, of Thorpe St Andrew, Norwich; 1 s (Robert b 1968), 1 da (Helen b 1971); *Career* three year articled pupillage to County Engr and Surveyor Middlesex 1944–47, site engr agent and construction mangr John Mowlem and Co 1947–56, agent and construction mangr Tarmac Civil Engineering Ltd 1969–73, project engr ET Leach and Ptnrs Whitchurch 1973–77, fndr G H Mugurian and Partners 1977–; arbitrator 1988–; Inst of Civil Engrg Surveyors: memb Mgmnt Cncl 1977–93, chm Cncl 1979–85, life vice pres 1986, pres 1992–93; memb Cncl Chartered Inst of Arbitrators 1990–92 (chm NW Branch Ctee 1990–91); Freeman City of London 1982, Liveryman Worshipful Co of Arbitrators 1984 (Freeman 1981); FInstCES 1972, memb Soc of Construction Law 1983, FCIArb 1984 (ACIArb 1980); *Recreations* sail cruising, gardening, painting; *Clubs* Royal Welsh Yacht; *Style*— Gordon H Mugurian, Esq; ✉ G H Mugurian and Partners, Brookdale House, High Street, Tattenhall, Chester CH3 9PX (☎ 01829 70740, fax 01829 71075)

MUIR, Prof Alexander Laird; s of Andrew Muir (d 1982), of Crieff, and Helena, *née* Bauld; *b* 12 April 1937; *Educ* Morrisons Acad Crieff, Fettes Coll Edinburgh, Univ of Edinburgh (MB ChB, MD, MRCP(Edin)); *m* Berenice, da of Edward Snelgrove; 1 da (Alicia b 19 Nov 1972), 1 s (Andrew b 18 Sept 1974); *Career* house surgn Leeds Gen Infirmary and house physician Edinburgh Royal Infirmary 1961–62, sr house offr Leeds General Infirmary 1962–63, British Antarctic Survey 1963–65, asst lectr rising to lectr Dept of Med Univ of Edinburgh 1965–70, MRC travelling fell McGill Univ Montreal 1970–71, lectr Dept of Med Univ of Edinburgh 1971–73, conslt physician Manchester Royal Infirmary 1973–74, sr lectr rising to reader Dept of Med Univ of Edinburgh 1974–89, postgrad dean of med Univ of Edinburgh 1990–; physician to HM the Queen in Scotland 1985–96, hon physician to the Army in Scotland 1986–; FRCPE 1976, FRCR 1986, FRCSE 1994; *Recreations* reading, golf, sailing, skiing; *Style*— Prof Alexander Muir; ✉ University of Edinburgh, Old College, South Bridge, Edinburgh EH8 9YL

MUIR, Elizabeth Jean; da of Capt Kenneth Edward Muir, MBE, of Bridgend, S Wales, and Elsie, *née* Harris; *b* 20 Aug 1947; *Educ* Cowbridge Girls HS, Homerton Coll Cambridge, Cardiff Coll of Educn (DipEd), Univ of Wales Cardiff (MScEcon), Univ of Bristol (currently researching Euro Women Entrepreneurs for doctoral thesis); *Career* mktg conslt, freelance writer, trainer and guest speaker; maths and physics teacher Cardiff Secdy Schs 1967–73, creative exec Parke-Davis Pharmaceuticals 1973–76, prod gp mangr Warner Lambert Animal Health 1976–78, sales and mktg controller Memory Lane Cakes (Dalgety Spillers Co) 1978–82, fndr and md The Alternative Marketing Department Ltd 1982– (currently a Euro women's educn and trg orgn and specialist Euro mktg co particularly in Greece), conslt to the EC 1992–94; dir Women in Enterprise 1996–; first woman memb Welsh Regnl Cncl CBI 1985–91; memb: Women's Forum Wales 1994–, Syllabus Advsy Gp Community Nursing and Health Visiting 1993–, Br Hellenic C of C 1988–; memb Bd: Welsh Water Authy 1986–89, Health Promotion Authy for Wales 1987–91, SHAW Homes 1988–, S Glam Family Health Serv Authy 1990–96; MCIM, MInstSM; memb: Br Sociological Assoc, Women's Studies Network (UK) Assoc; *Books* Marketing - A Way Forward for Community Nursing Services (jtly, 1993), 'The Highest Honour' in Our Sisters Land - The Changing Identities of Women in Wales (contrib, 1994), Enterprising Women of Europe - Training, Education, Personal and Business Support (EC pubn, 1994); *Recreations* public speaking, dinner parties with friends, travel in Greece; *Style*— Miss Elizabeth J Muir; ✉ Sunningdale House, 13 Tydraw Rd, Roath Pk, Cardiff CF2 5HA (☎ and fax 01222 499214)

MUIR, Frank; CBE (1980); s of Charles James Muir, and Margaret, *née* Harding; *b* 5 Feb 1920; *Educ* Chatham House Ramsgate, Leyton County HS; *m* 16 July 1949, Polly, *née* McIrvine; 1 s (Jamie), 1 da (Sally); *Career* served RAF 1940–46; writer and broadcaster with Denis Norden, *qv*, (writing comedy scripts) 1947–64, resident in TV and radio panel games, asst head of BBC Light Entertainment Gp 1964–67, head of entertainment London Weekend TV 1968–69, resumed TV Series Call My Bluff 1970; Lord Rector St Andrews Univ 1977–79; Hon LLD Univ of St Andrews 1978, Hon DLitt Univ of Kent 1982; *Books* The Frank Muir Book: An Irreverent Companion to Social History, A Book at Bathtime, What-a-Mess children's stories, The Oxford Book of Humorous Prose, The Walpole Orange; *Recreations* not working; *Clubs* Garrick; *Style*— Frank Muir, Esq, CBE; ✉ Anners, Thorpe, Egham, Surrey (☎ 01932 562759); A Torra, Monticello, Corsica

MUIR, Prof (Isabella) Helen Mary; CBE (1981); da of George Basil Fairlie Muir, ICS (d 1959), and Gwladys Helen Muir (d 1969); *b* 20 Aug 1920; *Educ* Downe House, Somerville Coll Oxford (MA, DPhil, DSc); *Career* res fell Sir William Dunn Sch of Pathology Oxford Univ 1947–48, scientific staff Nat Inst for Medical Research Biochemistry Div (London) 1948–54, Empire rheumatism res fell St Mary's Hosp Medical Unit 1954–58, Pearl res fell and hon lectr St Mary's Hosp Med Sch 1959–66, head Biochemistry Div Kennedy Inst of Rheumatology 1966–86 (dir 1977–90), hon prof Charing Cross Hospital Medical Sch 1979–95; visiting prof Dept of Biochemistry and Genetics Univ of Newcastle Med Sch 1995, hon visiting prof in biochemistry Sch of Biological Scis Univ of Manchester 1996–; memb Bd and Cncl MRC 1973–77, tstee Wellcome Tst 1982–90; memb: Cncl Royal Soc 1982–83, Cncl Chelsea Coll London 1982–85, Governing Bd Strangeways Res Lab Cambridge 1978–90; memb Advsy or Editorial Bds/Ctees: Biochem Jl 1964–70, Annals Rheumatic Diseases 1973–79, Nuffield Fndn 1981–83, Jl of Orthopaedic Res 1982–90, RCP William Gibson Res Scholarships 1984–90, Glycoconjugate Jl 1984–90, Max-Planck Gesellschaft (Rhematology) 1989–93, Int Inst of Cell and Molecular Pathology Brussels 1989–90, Res in Ageing 1987–; Hon DSc: Edinburgh 1982, Strathclyde 1983, Brunel 1990; Heberden orator London 1976, Feldberg Fndn Award 1977, Bunim Medal of American Arthritis Assoc 1978, pres Heberden Soc 1980, Volvo Int Prize 1980, Neil Hamilton Fairley Medal of the Royal College of Physicians for an Outstanding Contribution to Medicine 1981, Ciba Medal of the Biochemical Society 1981, Steindler Award Orthopaedic Soc of USA 1982, Ciba Int Award for Lifetime Achievements in Inflammation Res 1993; hon memb American Soc of Biological Chemists 1982, foreign memb Royal Swedish Acad of Sci 1989, FRS 1977; *Recreations* music, gardening, equestrian sports, natural history; *Style*— Prof Helen Muir, CBE, FRS; ✉ School of Biological Sciences, University of Manchester, Oxford Road, Manchester M13 9PL

MUIR, Jim; s of John Muir-Long Muir (d 1963), and Constance Jeannie, *née* Gilmour; *b* 3 June 1948; *Educ* Sedbergh, Univ of Cambridge (BA in Arabic, Wright Prize); *m* 1, 1968, Carleen, *née* Batstone; 2 s (Judd b 1970, Joseph b 1972); m 2, 1986, Joumana, *née* Sayegh; 2 da (Shona b 1987, Diyala b 1992); *Career* ed Frank Cass & Co publishers 1970–74, Beirut corr Inter Press Service (IPS) 1975–78, freelance corr in Beirut for BBC and others 1978–80, freelance corr in Cyprus for BBC, Sunday Times, Daily Telegraph, Christian Science Monitor, National Public Radio (US) and Middle East International 1980–95 (covering Lebanon and Middle E, also covering Afghanistan and Bosnia 1993–94), BBC Middle East corr based Cairo 1995–; *Recreations* ornithology, squash, travel, hill walking; *Style*— Jim Muir, Esq; ✉ c/o Room 3084, BBC Radio News and Current Affairs, Broadcasting House, London W1A 1AA

MUIR, Dr Richard Ernest; s of Kenneth Richard Muir, of Birstwith, Harrogate, and Edna Violet, *née* Huggall; *b* 18 June 1943; *Educ* Univ of Aberdeen (MA, PhD); *m* 13 Oct 1978, Nina Bina-Kumari, da of Indrajit Rajpal; *Career* lectr in geography Trinity Coll Dublin 1970–71, lectr and sr lectr in geography Cambridge Coll of Art and Technol 1971–80, freelance author and photographer 1981–94, sr lectr in geography Univ Coll of Ripon and York St John 1994–; ed: Nat Tst Histories, Countryside Cmmn Nat Parks; Yorks Arts Literary Award 1982–83; various articles in Observer, Sunday Times, Geographical Magazine, NY Times; memb: FOE, CPRE, Yorks Dales Soc; *Books* Modern Political Geography (1975), Geography Politics and Behaviour (1980), The English Village (1980), Riddles in The British Landscape (1981), The Shell Guide to Reading The Landscape (1981), The Lost Villages of Britain (1982), History From The Air (1983), Visions of The Past (with C Taylor, 1983), The National Trust Guide to Prehistoric and Roman Britain (with H Welfare, 1983), A Traveller's History of Britain and Ireland (1984), The Shell Countryside Book (with E Duffey, 1984), The National Trust Guide to Dark Age and Medieval Britain (1985), The National Trust Guide to Rivers of Britain (with N Muir, 1986), Landscape and Nature Photography (1986), Old Yorkshire (1987), Hedgerows (with N Muir, 1988), The Countryside Encyclopaedia (1988), Fields (with N

Muir, 1989), Portraits of the Past (1989), Barleybridge (1990), Castles and Strongholds (1990), The Dales of Yorkshire (1991), The Villages of England (1992), Coastlines (1993), Political Geography: A New Introduction (1997), Yorkshire Landscapes (1997); *Recreations* historical and environmental issues relating to British landscape, landscape photography; *Style—* Dr Richard Muir; ✉ Waterfall Close, Station Rd, Birstwith, Harrogate HG3 3AG (☎ 01423 771644)

MUIR, (Sir) Richard James Kay; 4 Bt (UK 1892), of Deanston, Perthshire (does not use title); s of Sir John Harling Muir, 3 Bt, TD (d 1994), and Elizabeth Mary, *née* Dundas; *b* 25 May 1939; *m* 1, 1965 (m dis 1974), Susan Elizabeth, da of George Albert Gardener, of Calcutta and Leamington Spa; 2 da (Louisa Jane b 1967, Catherine Elizabeth b 1968); m 2, 1975, Lady Linda Mary Cole, da of 6 Earl of Enniskillen (d 1989); 2 da (Daisy Mary b 1977, Anna Charlotte b 1979); *Heir* bro, Ian Charles Muir b 16 Sept 1940; *Style—* Richard Muir, Esq; ✉ Park House, Blair Drummond, by Stirling, Perthshire

MUIR, HE Richard John Sutherland; CMG (1994); s of John William Muir (d 1989), and Edna Joan, *née* Hodges (d 1982); *b* 25 Aug 1942; *Educ* Stationers' Co Sch, Univ of Reading (BA); *m* 1965, Caroline, da of Thomas Simpson; 1 da (Catherine Emma Louise b 1970), 1 s (Alistair Richard Charles b 1972); *Career* HM Dip Serv: third sec and desk offr Guidance and Information Policy Dept FCO 1964–65, student MECAS 1965–67, second sec (Commercial) British Embassy Jeddah 1967–70, second sec British Embassy Tunis 1970–72, first sec and section head Latin American Dept then Near E Africa Dept 1973–75, first sec Chancery British Embassy Washington 1975–79, seconded to Int Div Dept of Energy 1979–81, cnsllr and DG British Embassy Liaison Office Riyadh 1981–85, dep head Overseas Estates Dept 1985–87, head of Information Dept 1987–90, Cabinet Office Top Mgmnt Prog 1991, Prime Minister's Efficiency Unit 1991, princ fin offr and chief inspr 1991–94, ambass Sultanate of Oman 1994–; *Recreations* hill walking, theatre, opera; *Style—* HE Mr Richard Muir, CMG; ✉ c/o Foreign and Commonwealth Office (Muscat), King Charles Street, London SW1A 2AH

MUIR, Robert Charles Malcolm; s of Maj Charles Malcolm Muir, RM (d 1987), and Marjorie Anne Muir; *b* 9 Jan 1939; *Educ* Chichester HS for Boys; *m* 23 Sept 1961, Doreen Mary, s of Alfred Clarke; 1 da (Deborah Anne James b 5 Oct 1962), 1 s (Nigel Charles Muir b 30 July 1965); *Career* mgmnt trainee Littlewoods 1960–62, supermarket mangr Tesco 1962–63, successivley area mangr, gen mangr then regnl dir ABF (Finfare & Alliance Cash & Carry) 1963–70, md Budgetts Cash & Carry 1970–73, operations dir International Stores and md Superstores Div 1973–83, md Booker Wholesale Foods and md Booker Cash & Carry 1983–89, chm chief exec Booker Cash & Carry 1990–92; Booker Belmont Wholesale Ltd: chief exec 1992–93, chm (non-exec) 1993–; dir of business devpt Booker PLC 1993–; *Recreations* cricket, fishing; *Style—* Robert Muir, Esq; ✉ Booker PLC, Portland House, Stag Place, London SW1E 5AY (☎ 0171 411 5500, fax 0171 630 8029)

MUIR, Tom; *b* 15 Feb 1936; *Educ* Univ of Leeds (BA); *m*; 2 c; *Career* commercial trainee then buyer GEC Gp 1953–59; DTI: asst princ 1962–65, princ 1965–68, seconded as first sec UK Permanent Delgn to OECD 1968–71, asst sec 1973–75, seconded as head Indust and Energy Section UK Permanent Representation to EC Brussels 1975–79, under sec 1982, head Insurance Div 1982–87, head Overseas Trade Div 1987–89, head Int Trade Policy Div 1989–92, head Textiles and Retailing Div 1992–94, ret 1994; dir British Retail Consortium 1994–; FRSA, FCIS 1994; *Recreations* walking, swimming, reading, looking at pictures and buildings, travel; *Style—* Tom Muir, Esq; ✉ British Retail Consortium, Bedford House, 69/79 Fulham High Street, London SW6 3JW

MUIR MACKENZIE, Sir Alexander Alwyne Brinton; 7 Bt (UK 1805), of Delvine, Perthshire; s of Sir Robert Henry Muir Mackenzie, 6 Bt (d 1970), and Charmian Cecil de Vere, *née* Brinton (d 1962); *b* 8 Dec 1955; *Educ* Eton, Trinity Coll Cambridge; *m* 1984, Susan Carolyn, yst da of John David Henzell Hayter, of Dolivers, Holwell, nr Sherborne, Dorset; 1 s (Archie Robert David b 17 Feb 1989), 1 da (Georgina Mary b 1987); *Heir* s, Archie Robert David Muir Mackenzie b 17 Feb 1989; *Style—* Sir Alexander Muir Mackenzie, Bt; ✉ Buckshaw House, Holwell, nr Sherborne, Dorset DT9 5LD

MUIR WOOD, Sir Alan Marshall; kt (1981); s of Edward Stephen Wood, and Dorothy, *née* Webb; *b* 8 Aug 1921; *Educ* Abbotsholme Sch, Peterhouse Cambridge; *m* 1943, Winifred Leyton Lanagan (Dr W L Wood, mathematician); 3 s; *Career* served WWII, engr offr RN; former asst engr BR (Southern Region) and res asst Docks and Inland Waterways Exec; sr ptnr Sir William Halcrow & Partners 1979–84 (ptnr 1964–84, formerly asst then sr engr, now conslt); dir: Halcrow Fox & Associates 1977–84, Orange Fish Consultants; first (and hon life) pres Int Tunnelling Assoc; studies for Channel Tunnel intermittently since 1958; fell Imperial Coll 1981; hon fell: Peterhouse 1982, Portsmouth Poly 1984; Hon LLD Univ of Dundee 1985; Hon DSc: City Univ 1978, Univ of Southampton 1986; Hon DEng Univ of Bristol 1991; Telford medal 1976, James Alfred Ewing medal 1984; FEng 1977, FICE (pres 1977–78), FRS; *Books* Coastal Hydraulics (1969, 2 edn with C A Fleming 1981); *Clubs* Athenaeum; *Style—* Sir Alan Muir Wood, FEng, FRS; ✉ Franklands, Pangbourne, Berks RG8 8JY (☎ 0118 984 2833)

MUIRHEAD, Alastair William; s of William Calliope Muirhead, OBE (d 1983), and Joan Andrade, *née* Sutherland; *b* 12 Sept 1953; *Educ* Tonbridge, St John's Coll Oxford (BA); *m* 19 April 1980, Linda Anne, da of Robert Johnson, of Wakefield; 3 da (Joanna b 19 Feb 1983, Nicola b 12 March 1985, Catriona b 16 Aug 1989); *Career* Price Waterhouse 1976–80, Saudi International Bank 1980–84, md Charterhouse Bank Ltd 1984–96, ptnr The Phoenix Partnership 1996–; Hon MA Oxon; ACA; *Recreations* fly-fishing, gardening, hill walking; *Style—* Alastair W Muirhead, Esq; ✉ The Phoenix Partnership, One Laurence Pountney Hill, London EC4R 0EU (☎ 0171 638 3818, fax 0171 638 3487)

MUIRHEAD, Sir David Francis; KCMG (1976, CMG 1964), CVO (1957); s of late David Muirhead; *b* 30 Dec 1918; *Educ* Cranbrook Sch; *m* 1942, Hon Elspeth, *née* Hope-Morley (d 1989); 2 s, 1 da; *Career* served WWII; FO: joined 1947, cnsllr 1960–65, under sec 1966–67; ambass: Peru 1967–70, Portugal 1970–74, Belgium 1974–78; Grand Cross Mil Order of Christ (Portugal) 1973, Grand Cross Order of Distinguished Serv (Peru) 1985; *Clubs* Travellers'; *Style—* Sir David Muirhead, KCMG, CVO; ✉ 16 Pitt Street, London W8 4NY (☎ 0171 937 2443)

MUIRHEAD-ALLWOOD, Sarah Kathryn (formerly Muirhead-Allwood, William Forster Gillespie); name changed by statutory declaration 1996; c of Maj W R Muirhead (d 1946), and Joyce, *née* Forster; *b* 4 Jan 1947; *Educ* Wellington, St Thomas Hosp Med Sch (BSc, MB BS, MRCS, LRCP); *m* 1983; 2 s (William Ritchie b 12 Sept 1984, James Miles b 3 July 1986); *Career* St Thomas' Hosp: house surgn 1971–72, sr house offr 1972–73, anatomy demonstrator 1973; sr house offr Stoke Mandeville Hosp 1973–74; registrar: UCH 1974–77, Charing Cross Hosp 1977–78; sr registrar 1978–84 (Queen Mary's Hospital Roehampton, Westminster Hosp, Royal Nat Orthopaedic Hosp, UCH); conslt orthopaedic surgn: Whittington Hosp 1984, Royal Nat Orthopaedic Hosp 1991, King Edward VII's Hosp for Offrs; hon sr clinical lectr UCL 1984; hon conslt: St Lukes Hosp for the Clergy 1984, Hosp of St John and St Elizabeth; memb: Br Orthopaedic Assoc 1980, BMA 1983, Br Hip Soc 1989; FRCS; *Books* contrib: Joint Replacement - State of the Art (1990), Recent Advances in Orthopaedic Surgery (1991), Grays Anatomy (1995); *Recreations* sailing; *Style—* Miss Sarah Muirhead-Allwood; ✉ 19 Wimpole St, London W1M 7AD (☎ 0171 935 8488, fax 0171 636 5758)

MUKHAMEDOV, Irek; s of Djardat Rasulievich Mukhamedov, of Kazan, USSR, and Rashida Nizamovna, *née* Fatkulina; *b* 8 March 1960; *Educ* Moscow Ballet School; *m* 23 March 1990, Maria, da of Leonid Kovbas; 1 da (Alexandra Cholpon b 22 Aug 1990); *Career* ballet dancer; soloist Moscow Classical Ballet 1978–81, former princ dancer Bolshoi Ballet, currently princ dancer Royal Ballet; *Performances* with Bolshoi incl: Spartakus, Don Quixote, Ivan the Terrible, Golden Age, Romeo and Juliet, Raymonda, Giselle, Nutcracker, Swan Lake; with Royal Ballet incl: La Bayadere, Manon (2 roles), Nutcracker, Raymonda, Winter Dreams, The Judas Tree; other performances incl: Roland Petit's Cyrano de Bergerac, Nureyev's Sleeping Beauty (Grand Opera Paris and Vienna Opera), Nureyev's Don Quixote (Flanders Ballet), Balanchine's Apollo (Vienna); *Awards* incl: Grand Prix Moscow IV competition, Gandersen Best Dancer in the World, Laurence Olivier Best Acting Prize, Evening Standard Ballet Award 1993; *Recreations* dedication to art of ballet, family; *Style—* Irek Mukhamedov, Esq; ✉ The Royal Ballet, Royal Opera House, Covent Garden, London WC2E 9DD (☎ 0171 240 1200)

MUKHERJEE, Tara Kumar; s of Sushil Chandra Mukherjee (d 1976), of Calcutta, India, and Sova Moyee, *née* Banerjee; *b* 20 Dec 1923; *Educ* Scottish Church Collegiate Sch Calcutta India, Univ of Calcutta; *m* 15 May 1951, Betty Patricia, da of David Derby (d 1982), of Leicester; 1 s (Karl b 1956), 1 da (Jasmin b 1952); *Career* shop mangr Bata Shoe Co Ltd India 1941–44, buyer Brevitt Shoes Leicester 1951–56, sundries buyer British Shoe Corporation 1956–66, prodn admin Priestley Footwear Ltd Gt Harwood 1966–68, head store mangr British Shoe Corporation 1968–70, branch mangr Save and Prosper Group 1978–84 (dist mangr 1970–78), area mangr Guardian Royal Exchange 1985–88, md Owl Financial Services Ltd 1988; pres: Confedn of Indian Orgns UK 1975–, Migrants Forum of the Euro Union 1990, Indian Film Soc Leicester; chm Gtr London Translation Unit 1993; memb: Br Euro Movement, Cncl of Mgmnt Coronary Prevention Gp 1985–; tstee: Haymarket Theatre Leicester, Asian Community Resources Tst London; currently chm Charter 90 for Asians; played for Bihar Ranji Cricket trophy 1941; FLIA, FRSA; *Recreations* first class cricket; *Clubs* Leicestershire CC, Indian Nat (Leicester); *Style—* Tara Mukherjee, Esq; ✉ Tallah, 1 Park Avenue, Hutton, Brentwood, Essex CM13 2QL (☎ 01277 215438); UE Migrants' Forum, 51 Viking Way, Brentwood, Essex CM15 9HY (☎ 01227 263207, fax 01227 260300)

MULCAHY, Sir Geoffrey John; kt (1993); s of late Maurice Frederick Mulcahy; *b* 7 Feb 1942; *Educ* King's Sch Worcester, Univ of Manchester, Harvard Univ (MBA); *m* 1964, Valerie Elizabeth, *née* Ison; 1 s, 1 da; *Career* labour relations, mktg and planning Esso Corporation, fin dir British Sugar Corporation Ltd 1977–82; Kingfisher plc (formerly Woolworth Holdings plc): dir 1983–, gp md 1984–86, chief exec 1986–93 and 1995–, chm 1990–95, exec chm 1993–95; non-exec dir: Bass plc 1989–, BNP UK Holdings Ltd 1994–; formerly non-exec dir: BT plc, Eurotunnel until 1995; *Recreations* squash, sailing; *Clubs* RAC, Lansdowne, Carlton; *Style—* Sir Geoffrey Mulcahy; ✉ Kingfisher plc, North West House, 119 Marylebone Road, London NW1 5PX (☎ 0171 724 7749)

MULCAHY, Russell Ian; s of Edward Joseph Mulcahy (d 1988), and Joan, *née* Sydney; *b* 23 June 1953; *Educ* Corrimal HS NSW Aust; *Career* film ed Channel 7 Sydney Aust, winner Sydney Film Fest with 2 short films 1976 and 1977, moved to England 1978; filmed numerous pop videos and video albums since 1980 incl: Derek and Clive Get the Horn (for Peter Cook and Dudley Moore), Duran Duran The Video Album, The Tubes Completion Backwards Principle, Elton John The Fox; feature films incl: Razorback 1984, Arena An Absurd Notion (with Duran Duran) 1985, Highlander (with Christopher Lambert and Sean Connery) 1986, Highlander II 1990, Ricochet (with Denzel Washington and John Lithgow) 1991; awards incl: BAFTA Special Craft Award 1982, American Videos Award best dir 1982, Int Film and TV Festival silver and bronze awards 1983, two Grammy Awards best long and short videos 1983, D & AD Awards best dir and best music video 1983, Br Phonographic Indust Award video of the year 1984, three American video Awards 1984, Golden Rose of Montreux best story-line (music section) 1986, (USA) Clio Award for best corporate TV commercial 1989 BP The Mission; memb Directors Guild of America; *Recreations* scuba diving, writing, cinema, theatre; *Clubs* Brown's; *Style—* Russell Mulcahy, Esq; ✉ c/o Ray Rathbone Films, 8 Portland Mews, London W1V 3FJ (☎ 0171 439 3666)

MULDOON, Prof Paul Benedict; s of Patrick Muldoon (d 1985), and Brigid, *née* Regan (d 1974); *b* 20 June 1951; *Educ* St Patrick's Coll Armagh, Queen's Univ Belfast (BA); *Career* prodr Arts Progs (Radio) BBC Northern Ireland (sr prodr 1978–85), TV prodr BBC Northern Ireland 1985–86, Judith E Wilson visiting fell Univ of Cambridge 1986–87, creative writing fell UEA 1987, pt/t teacher Writing Div Sch of the Arts Colombia Univ 1987–88, pt/t teacher Creative Writing Prog Princeton Univ 1987–88, writer-in-residence 92nd Street 'Y' New York 1988, Roberta Holloway lectr Univ of California at Berkeley 1989, visiting prof Univ of Massachusetts Amherst 1989–90; Princeton Univ: lectr 1990–95, dir Creative Writing Prog 1993–, prof 1995–; memb Aosdana (Irish Acad of Artists); FRSL 1981, *Awards* Eric Gregory Award 1972, Sir Geoffrey Faber Meml Award 1980 and 1991, John Simon Guggenheim Meml Fellowship 1990, shortlisted Aristeion Euro Translation Prize 1994, shortlisted Forward Poetry Prize 1994, T S Eliot Prize 1994, American Acad of Arts and Letters Award for Literature 1996; *Poetry* Knowing My Place (1971), New Weather (1973), Spirit of Dawn (1975), Mules (1977), Names and Addresses (1978), Immram (1980), Why Brownlee Left (1980), Out of Siberia (1982), Quoof (1983), The Wishbone (1984), Selected Poems 1968–83 (1986), Meeting the British (1987), Madoc: A Mystery (1990), Selected Poems 1968–86 (1987 and 1993), Incantata (1994), The Prince of the Quotidian (1994), The Annals of Chile (1994), New Selected Poems 1968–94 (1996), Kerry Slides (1996); *Drama* Monkeys (TV play, BBC 1989), Shining Brow (opera, 1993), Six Honest Serving Men (play, 1995); *Children* The Last Thesaurus (1995), The O-O's Party (1981 and 1997); *Edited* The Scrake of Dawn (1979), The Faber Book of Contemporary Irish Poetry (1986), The Essential Byron (1989), The Faber Book of Beasts (1997); *Other Work* numerous recordings and readings, anthologies and translations and interviews and criticisms; *Style—* Prof Paul Muldoon, FRSL; ✉ c/o Faber and Faber, 3 Queen Square, London WC1N 3AU

MULDOON, Sara Penn; da of Henry Norman Sellers (d 1976), and Elisabeth Merial Penn *née* Hardinge Tyler; *b* 15 May 1948; *Educ* Macclesfield HS for Girls, Univ of Sheffield (BA), Univ of Leicester (Cert in Museum Studies); *m* 1976 (sep), Michael Christopher Muldoon; 1 s (Matthew Christopher b 12 July 1981); *Career* keeper of social history Coventry Museums 1974–83, dir Norton Priory Museum Cheshire 1983–86, curator Ipswich Museums & Galleries 1987–; AMA 1973; *Recreations* the arts, walking, food; *Style—* Mrs Sara Muldoon; ✉ Ipswich Borough Council Museums & Galleries, High Street, Ipswich, Suffolk IP1 3QH (☎ 01473 213761/263550, fax 01473 281274)

MULFORD, Dr David Campbell; s of Robert Lewis Mulford (d 1950), of Rockford, Illinois, and Theodora Moellenhauer Mulford Countryman (d 1988); *b* 27 June 1937; *Educ* Lawrence Univ Wisconsin (BA Econ cum laude), Univ of Cape Town (Rotary Fndn Int Fellowship), Boston Univ (Woodrow Wilson Fellowship, MA), St Antony's Coll Oxford (Technical Co-operation Grant, Ford Fndn Fellowship, DPhil); *m* 19 Oct 1985, Jeannie, *née* Simmons; 2 s (Ian Edward); *Career* special asst to sec and under sec Treasy White House 1965–66, md and head Int Fin White Weld & Co Inc 1966–84 (seconded to Saudi Arabian Monetary Agency 1974–84); under sec and asst sec Treasy for Int Affairs USA 1984–92; major appts 1984–92 incl: sr int econ policy official Treasy, US dep for co-ordination of econ policies with other G-7 nations, head admin Yen/Dollar negotiations with Japan, sr advsr on fin assistance to Russia, ldr int debt strategy, devpt and implementation of Baker/Brady Plans and Pres Bush's Enterprise Initiative for Americas, ldr US Delegation estab of EBRD; vice-chm CS First Boston Inc 1992–, chm CS First Boston Ltd 1993–; Hon PhD Law Lawrence Univ 1984, Legion d'Honneur 1990, distinguished Alumni Award Boston Univ 1992, Alexander Hamilton Award US Treasy

1992, Order of May for Merit Argentina 1993, Officer's Cross Medal of Merit Poland 1995; memb: Cncl on Foreign Rels, Centre for Strategic and Int Studies Washington DC, White House Fellows Assoc, RIIA; *Books* Northern Rhodesia General Election (1962), Zambia - The Politics of Independence (1967); *Recreations* golf, running; *Clubs* Metropolitan (Washington DC); *Style*— Dr David C Mulford; ✉ CS First Boston Ltd, One Cabot Square, London E14 4QJ (☎ 0171 516 3574, fax 0171 516 3501)

MULGAN, Dr Geoffrey J (Geoff); *b* 28 Aug 1961; *Educ* Univ of Oxford (BA), PCL (PhD); *Career* investmt exec Greater London Enterprise Bd 1984–86, Harkness fell MIT 1986–88, lectr Poly of Central London and memb Comedia consulting gp 1988–90, policy advsr to Gordon Brown MP as shadow chllr 1990–92, fell Br Film Inst 1992–93, fndr and dir Demos (independent think-tank) 1993–; visiting prof UCL; dir/tstee: Photographers Gallery, Crime Concern, Political Quarterly; contrib numerous articles to pubns incl The Times, Financial Times, Guardian, Independent, New Statesman; *Books* Saturday Night or Sunday Morning (with Ken Worpole, 1987), The Question of Quality (ed, 1990), Communication and Control (1991), The Hollywood of Europe (ed BBC monograph series, 1993), Reconnecting Taxation (with Robin Murray, 1993), Politics in an Antipolitical Age (1994); *Style*— Dr Geoff Mulgan; ✉ Demos, 9 Bridewell Place, London EC4V 6AP (☎ 0171 353 4479, fax 0171 353 4481, e-mail demos.demon.co.uk)

MULHOLLAND, Hon Brian Henry; o s and h of 5 Baron Dunleath, *qv*, and his 2 w, Elizabeth M, *née* Hyde (d 1989); *b* 25 Sept 1950; *Educ* Eton; *m* 1976, Mary Joanna, yst da of Maj Robert John Fuller Whistler, of Achaeon, Camberley, Surrey; 2 s (Andrew Henry b 15 Dec 1981, William Alexander b 15 Feb 1986), 1 da (Tara Miranda b 15 April 1980); *Career* landowner and co dir; brands mangr Matthew Clark Gp plc with responsibility for Irish Distillers 1982–85, dir Lanyon Developments Ltd 1985–91, admin Belle Isle Estate 1991–94, dir Dunleath Estates Ltd 1994–; *Recreations* shooting, fishing, gardening; *Clubs* MCC, Kildare Street and University (Dublin); *Style*— The Hon Brian Mulholland; ✉ Caroline Cottage, Clandeboye Estate, Bangor, Northern Ireland BT19 1RN (☎ 01247 853394, fax 01247 852451); Dunleath Estates Ltd, Ballywalter Park Farm, Newtownards, Northern Ireland BT22 2PA (☎ 01247 758264, fax 01247 758818)

MULHOLLAND, Clare; da of James Mulholland (d 1969), of Glasgow, and Elizabeth, *née* Lochrin; *b* 17 June 1939; *Educ* Notre Dame HS Glasgow, Univ of Glasgow (MA); *Career* with ICI 1961–64, Granada Television 1964–65, TWW Ltd 1965–68, HTV Ltd 1968–71; Independent Television Cmmn (Independent Bdcasting Authy until 1990): regnl exec Bristol 1971–78, regnl offr Midlands 1978–82, dep dir of TV 1983–90, dir of progs 1991–96, dep chief exec 1996–; tstee Scottish Film Prodn Fund 1984–90, memb Arts Cncl of GB (and chm of its Film Video and Bdcasting Panel) 1986–94; FRTS 1988; *Recreations* theatre, cinema, travel; *Style*— Miss Clare Mulholland; ✉ The Independent Television Commission, 33 Foley Street, London W1P 7LB (☎ 0171 306 7775, fax 0171 306 7772)

MULHOLLAND, Dr (Hugh) Connor; s of William Hugh Mulholland (d 1987), of Belfast, and Agnes, *née* Connor; *b* 10 Sept 1938; *Educ* Campbell Coll Belfast, Queen's Univ Belfast (BSc, MB BCh, BAO); *m* 18 Dec 1968, (Hannah Eileen) Sandra, da of Frederick William Hedgecock (d 1984), of Belfast; 2 s (Michael b 1969, Gareth b 1975), 1 da (Shona 1972); *Career* asst prof Dept of Med Christian Med Coll Univ of Punjab 1969–71; res fellowship: NI Hosp Authy 1972–74, Ontario Heart Fndn 1974–76; conslt paediatric cardiologist Royal Belfast Hosp for Sick Children 1976–; Royal Gp of Hosps: co chm Regnl Med Cardiology Centre 1983–93, clinical dir cardiology and cardiothoracic surgn 1990–, clinical dir paediatrics 1995–; memb: NY Acad of Scis, Br Cardiac Soc, Irish Cardiac Soc, Assoc of Euro Paediatric Cardiologists, Ulster Paediatric Assoc (pres 1991–92), BMA, Belfast City YMCA; FRCPE 1979; *Recreations* hill walking, reading, photography; *Style*— Dr Connor Mulholland; ✉ Regional Medical Cardiology Centre, Royal Victoria Hospital, Belfast B12 6BA (☎ 01232 240503, fax 01232 240899)

MULHOLLAND, John Peter Patrick; s of John Llewellyn Mulholland (d 1989, eld s of Hon Alfred John Mulholland, himself s of 1 Baron Dunleath), and Helen, *née* Moss (d 1993); *b* 2 Sept 1929; *Educ* Berkhamsted Sch, Sch of Slavonic Studies London (BA), Trinity Coll Dublin (BL), Royal Agric Coll (Dip Advanced Farm Mgmnt); *m* 15 Dec 1973, Rosemary Kathleen Vaughan, da of Charles Hawkins, MC, of Cirencester; 2 s (John Charles b 1975, James Patrick b 1977); *Career* freelance journalist 1955–: Latin American corr News Chronicle 1959–61, prog organiser BBC External Serv 1963–69, numerous articles on fin and tax; called to the Bar: Middle Temple 1969, King's Inns Dublin 1975; in practice: Southampton and London 1969–, Repub of Ireland 1975–; sr lectr in law Royal Agric Coll 1980–88; memb: Chancery Bar Assoc 1970, Lincoln's Inn 1971; MRAC 1980, ACIArb 1992; *Books* Practical Puppetry (1961), Brazil 1968 (1968), Ploughing of Rights of Way (jtly, 1988); *Recreations* hunting, shooting, equestrian sports; *Style*— John Mulholland, Esq; ✉ New Cottage, Painswick, Glos GL6 6UA (☎ 01452 812960); 17 Old Buildings, Lincoln's Inn, London WC2A 3UP (☎ 0171 405 9653)

MULHOLLAND, Prof Robert Charles; s of Philip Mulholland (d 1965), and Eileen, *née* Dwyer; *b* 4 Dec 1934; *Educ* Prior Park Coll Bath, London Hosp Med Sch; *m* 5 June 1965, Elizabeth, da of George Kennedy (d 1960); 2 s (Andrew b 19 Dec 1967, Seamus b 9 April 1969), 1 da (Sarah (twin) b 9 April 1969); *Career* Aust Navy 1959–61; sr house offr Royal Nat Orthopaedic Hosp 1965, registrar Bart's 1965–67, registrar and sr registrar Robert Jones and Agnes Hunt Orthopaedic Hosp 1967–72, instr and on faculty Univ of Washington Seattle 1969–71, conslt orthopaedic surgn Harlow Wood Orthopaedic Hosp and Nottingham Univ Hosp 1972–, special prof in orthopaedic and accident surgery Univ of Nottingham; pres: Soc of Back Pain Res 1981–84, Int Soc for Study of the Lumbar Spine 1990–91; author pubns on aspects of low back pain and problems of the lumbar spine; memb: RSM, Br Orthopaedic Assoc; FRCS; *Books* Back Pain Methods of Clinical Investigation and Assessment (ed with D Hukins, 1986); *Recreations* sailing; *Style*— Prof Robert Mulholland

MULKERN, John; CBE (1987), JP (Surrey 1988); s of Thomas Mulkern (d 1973), of Stretford, Manchester, and Annie Proctor, *née* Tennant (d 1984); *b* 15 Jan 1931; *Educ* Stretford GS, Harvard Business Sch; *m* 5 June 1954, May Egerton, da of Arthur Peters (d 1987), of Leatherhead, Surrey; 1 s (Neil b 1959), 3 da (Susan b 1957, Gaynor b 1962, Rosalind b 1967); *Career* various posts rising to princ Minys of Supply and Aviation 1949–65; Br Airports Authy 1965–87: head of fin, dep dir admin and personnel, dep gen mangr Heathrow, dir Gatwick, md 1977–87, chm British Airports International Ltd 1978–82; int aviation conslt 1987–; chm: Manchester Handling Ltd 1988–93, Granik Ltd 1990–91; dir: London Luton Airport Ltd 1991–, Reliance Aviation Security Ltd 1992–94; pres: Western Euro Airports Assoc 1981–83, Int Civil Airports Assoc (Europe) 1986–87; chm Airports Assocs Coordinating Cncl 1982, memb Bd Airport Operators Cncl Int 1978–81; Ordre Du Zaire 1975 (Chevalier Zaire Nouveau Civil), Malaysian Distinguished Order of Chivalry Class Five 1974, Cavalheiro Order of Rio Branco Class Five Brazil 1976, Chevalier de L'Ordre National Du Mérite France 1976; FCIT 1973 (memb Cncl 1979–82), CIMgt 1981, FInstD 1982; *Recreations* travel, music, theatre; *Style*— John Mulkern, Esq, CBE, JP

MULLALY, Terence Frederick Stanley; s of Col Brian Reginald Mullaly (d 1965), and Eileen Dorothy Stanley (d 1973); gf Maj Gen Sir Herbert Mullaly, KCMG, CB, CSI, Cdr East Coast Defences during 1914–18 War; *b* 14 Nov 1927; *Educ* India, England, Japan, Canada, Downing Coll Cambridge (MA); *m* 1949, Elizabeth Helen, da of Frank Burkitt, of Bournemouth; *Career* art historian and art critic The Daily Telegraph 1958–86; visiting prof Finch Coll NY 1967–72; pres Br Section Int Assoc of Art Critics 1967–73, vice chm Br Art Medal Soc 1982–87 (pres 1988–); memb: Advsy Ctee Cracow Art Festival 1974, Palermo Art Festival 1976, Cncl Attingham Summer Sch Tst 1985–90, Cncl Derby Porcelain Int Soc 1985–88, Cncl Royal Numismatic Soc 1993–95, Cncl Friends of Univ of Cyprus 1995–; artistic advsr of Grand Tours 1975–89, dir Specialtours 1986, UK del Conference on Security and Co-operation in Europe (CSCE) Cultural Forum Budapest 1985; British-Italian Soc: memb Exec Ctee 1996–, ed Soc Jl 1996–; Premio Pietro Torta per il Restauro di Venezia 1983, Socio Straniero, Ateneo Veneto, Commendatore Ordine Al Merito della Repubblica Italiana 1974, l'Ordre du Mérite Culturel Poland 1974, OM Poland (Silver medal) 1977, SM Ordine Constantiniano di S Giorgio (Silver medal) 1982; FSA, FSA (Scot), FRNS, FRSA; *Books* Ruskin a Verona (1966), catalogue of the exhibition Disegni veronesi del Cinquecento (1971), Cinquant' Anni di Pittura veronese 1580–1630 (contrib, 1974), catalogue of the exhibition Modern Hungarian Medals (ed and contrib, 1984), Affreschi del Rinascimento a Verona (jtly, 1987), Caterina Cornaro - Queen of Cyprus (jtly, 1989), catalogue of the exhibition Zofia Demkowska, Wrocklaw (contrib, 1997), Anne Redpath (1995); author of articles in numerous learned jls and magazines; *Style*— Terence Mullaly, Esq, FSA; ✉ Waterside House, Lower St, Pulborough, W Sussex RH20 2BH (☎ 01798 872104, fax 01798 874422)

MULLAN, Lt Cdr Charles Heron; CBE (1979), VRD (1949), DL (Co Down 1974); s of Frederick Heron Mullan, DL (d 1972), of Cairn Hill, Newry, and Minnie, *née* Broackes (d 1948); *b* 17 Feb 1912; *Educ* Castle Park Dalkey, Rossall, Clare Coll Cambridge (BA, MA); *m* 6 Sept 1940, Marcella Elizabeth Sharpe, da of James Alexander McCullagh (d 1954), of Ballycastle, Co Antrim; 1 s (Christopher Desmond Heron b 5 Sept 1947); *Career* joined RNVR 1936, Lt 1940, Lt Cdr 1948; served 1939–45 with RN: Channel, N Sea, N Atlantic; slr 1948; MP (UU) Imperial Parliament Co Down 1946–50; memb Ulster Unionist Cncl 1946–60; resident magistrate N Ireland 1960–82, stipendiary magistrate Belfast 1964–79; King Haakon VII War Decoration (Norway) 1944; *Recreations* ornithology, walking; *Style*— Lt Cdr Charles Mullan, CBE, VRD, DL; ✉ Casanbarra, Carrickmore Road, Ballycastle, Co Antrim BT54 6QS, Northern Ireland (☎ 012657 62323)

MULLARKEY, David Charles; s of Daniel Francis Mullarkey, of Finchley, London, and Alice Cecelia, *née* Dillon; *b* 4 Feb 1956; *Educ* Finchley Catholic GS, Univ of Nottingham (LLB); *m* Aug 1984, Beverley Ann, da of Anthony George Carter, of Beckenham, Kent; 1 s (Daniel Nicholas b 14 Aug 1989), 1 da (Laura Ann b 10 June 1987); *Career* admitted slr 1982, Hong Kong 1986; ptnr Linklaters & Paines 1988– (Tax Dept 1982–84 and 1988–94, Hong Kong Office 1984–86 and 1994–); memb: Law Soc, Int Bar Assoc; *Style*— David Mullarkey, Esq; ✉ Linklaters & Paines, 14F Alexandra House, Chater Road, Hong Kong

MULLEN, Larry, Jr; s of Larry Mullen, of Dublin, and Maureen Mullen; *b* 31 Oct 1961; *Educ* Mount Temple Sch; *partner* Ann Acheson; *Career* drummer and fndr memb U2 1978– (with Bono, *qv*, The Edge, *qv*, and Adam Clayton, *qv*); first U2 release U23 (EP) 1979; *Albums* Boy 1980, October 1981, War 1983 (entered UK chart at no 1), Under A Blood Red Sky (live album) 1983, The Unforgettable Fire 1984 (entered UK charts at no 1), The Joshua Tree 1987 (entered UK charts at no 1, fastest selling album ever in UK), Rattle & Hum 1988 (entered UK charts at No 1), Achtung Baby 1991, Zooropa 1993 (No 1 in 18 countries); *Singles* incl: Fire 1981, New Year's Day (first UK Top Ten hit) 1983, Pride (In the Name of Love) 1984, Unforgettable Fire 1985, With or Without You 1987, I Still Haven't Found What I'm Looking For 1987, Where The Streets Have No Name 1987, Desire (first UK no 1 single) 1988, Angel of Harlem 1988, When Love Comes to Town 1989, All I Want Is You 1989, Night & Day (for AIDS benefit LP Red Hot & Blue) 1990, The Fly (entered UK charts at no 1) 1991, Stay 1993; *Film* Rattle & Hum 1988; *Tours* incl: UK, US, Belgium and Holland 1980, UK, US, Ireland and Europe 1981–83, Aust, NZ and Europe 1984, A Conspiracy of Hope (Amnesty International Tour) 1986, world Joshua Tree tour 1987, Rattle & Hum tour 1988, Zoo TV world tour (played to 5m people) 1992–93; also appeared at: Live Aid 1985 (Best Live Aid Performance Rolling Stone Readers' Poll 1986), Self Aid Dublin, Smile Jamaica (Dominion Theatre, in aid of hurricane disaster relief) 1988, New Year's Eve concert Dublin (broadcast live to Europe and USSR) 1989; performed at venues incl: Wembley Stadium, Madison Square Garden NY, Longest Day Festival Milton Keynes Bowl, Croke Park Dublin, Sun Devil Stadium Arizona; *Awards* Grammy awards: Album of the Year (The Joshua Tree) 1987, Best Rock Performance (Joshua Tree tour) 1987, Best Rock Performance (Desire) 1989, Best Video (Where The Streets Have No Name) 1989, Best Alternative Album (Zooropa) 1993; others incl: Best Band Rolling Stone Readers' Poll 1986 (also jt winner Critics' Poll), Band of the Year Rolling Stone Writers' Poll 1984, Best International Act BPI Awards 1989 and 1990, Best Live Act BPI Awards 1993; *Style*— Larry Mullen, Jr; ✉ c/o Regine Moylett Publicity, First Floor, 145a Ladbroke Grove, London W10 6HJ (☎ 0171 221 0554, fax 0171 221 8532)

MULLEN, Dr Richard; s of Dr Richard W Mullen, of Paterson, NJ, USA, and Eleanor Wild Mullen; *b* 25 May 1945; *Educ* Seton Hall Univ (BA), Fordham Univ (MA), St Edmund Hall Oxford (DPhil); *Career* tutor in history and politics Univ of Oxford and London 1969–78, literary ed Christian World 1978–79, historical advsr CBS TV 1981, author numerous historical and literary features for BBC Radio 1981–, ed Contemporary Review 1991–; edited: The Pamphleteer 1813–28 (29 vols, 1978), Frances Trollope Domestic Manners of the Americans (1984), Malachi's Cove and Other Stories and Essays by Anthony Trollope (1985); BBC documentaries and features incl progs on Queen Victoria, Anthony Trollope, Charles Lamb, John Galsworthy, William Pitt, Lord Palmerston, Scott Fitzgerald, Edward Fitzgerald; Weaver fellowship 1972; *Books* Victoria: Portrait of a Queen (with James Munson, 1987), Anthony Trollope: A Victorian in His World (1990, winner Yorkshire Post Book of the Year award 1991), The Sayings of Anthony Trollope (1992), Anthony Trollope: A Pocket Anthology, Birds of Passage: Five Englishwomen in Search of America, The Penguin Companion to Trollope (with James Munson); *Recreations* music, walking, reading; *Style*— Dr Richard Mullen; ✉ 27 Middle Way, Oxford OX2 7LG (☎ 01865 557831)

MULLENS, Lt-Gen Sir Anthony Richard Guy; KCB (1989), OBE (1978, MBE 1974); s of Brig Guy John de Wette Mullens, OBE (d 1981), and Gwendoline Joan, *née* Maclean (d 1996); *b* 10 May 1936; *Educ* Eton, RMA Sandhurst; *m* 31 Oct 1964, Dawn Elizabeth Hermione, da of Lt-Col John Walter Pease (d 1983); *Career* cmmnd 4th/7th Royal Dragoon Gds 1956, ADC to Cdr 1st Br Corps 1958–60, Adj 1963, Staff Coll Camberley 1967–68, MOD 1968–70, regtl duty 1970–72, Bde Maj 1972, dir of staff Staff Coll 1973–76, CO 4th/7th Royal Dragoon Gds 1976–78, HQ BAOR 1978–80, Cdr 7th Armd Brigade 1980–82, Mil Sec Dept MOD 1982–85, GOC 1st Armd Div 1985–87, Asst Chief of Def Staff Operational Requirements (Land Systems) MOD 1987–89, Dep Chief of Def Staff (Systems) MOD 1989–92; Hon Col Royal Dragoon Guards 1994–; conslt to British Rail on personnel and equipment 1992–95, assoc Varley Walker (Human Resource Consultants) 1994–; Liveryman Worshipful Co of Coachmakers & Coach Harness Makers 1977, Renter Warden Worshipful Co of Armourers and Brasiers 1996 (Liveryman 1974, memb Ct of Assts 1993); Niedersachsen Verdienstkreuz (am Bande 1982, First Class 1987); *Recreations* travel, riding, skiing; *Clubs* Cavalry and Guards'; *Style*— Lt-Gen Sir Anthony Mullens, KCB, OBE; ✉ c/o Lloyds Private Banking Ltd, 50 Grosvenor Street, London W1X 9FH

MULLER, Franz Joseph; QC (1978); s of Wilhelm Muller (d 1982), and Anne Maria Muller, *née* Ravens (d 1989); *b* 19 Nov 1938; *Educ* Mount St Mary's Coll, Univ of Sheffield (LLB); *m* 1985, Helena, da of Mieczyslaw Bartosz; 2 s (Julian b 1986, Henry b 1988); *Career* called to the Bar Gray's Inn 1961, called to the NI Bar 1982; graduate apprentice

United Steel Cos 1960–61, commercial assoc Workington Iron & Steel Co Ltd 1961–63; commenced practice at the Bar 1964, recorder Crown Ct 1977–, head of chambers; non-exec dir: Richards of Sheffield (Holdings) plc 1969–77, Satinsteel Ltd 1970–77, Rodgers Wostenholm Ltd 1975–77; memb Sr Common Room Univ Coll Durham 1981, govr Mount St Mary's Coll 1984–86; *Recreations* fell walking, listening to music, skiing; *Style*— Franz Muller, Esq, QC; ✉ 11 King's Bench Walk, Temple, London EC4Y 7EQ (☎ 0171 353 3337, fax 0171 353 3337); Goodbard House, 3rd Floor, Infirmary Street, Leeds LS1 2JS (☎ 0113 245 1156, fax 0113 244 5564)

MULLER, Leticia; da of Heinz Müller, of Pretoria, S Africa, and Mee-Fong, *née* Son; *b* 16 Aug 1970; *Educ* Hamburg State Theatre Ballet Sch, Art Sch Pretoria S Africa; *Career* ballet dancer; Pact Ballet S Africa: joined 1988, soloist 1992–94, princ 1994–95; princ Birmingham Royal Ballet 1995–; *Roles* with Pact Ballet incl: Giselle, Anna Karenina, Papillon, Katherina in Taming of the Shrew, Swanilda, Natasha in War and Peace, Aegina in Spartacus, Who Cares?, Still Life at the Penguin Cafe; with Birmingham Royal Ballet: Maggie Hobson in Hobson's Choice, leading role in Carmina Burana, The Nutcracker, The Cage, cr role of Bathsheba Everdeene in Far From the Madding Crowd; *Awards* Friends of the Pact Ballet Award for Most Promising Newcomer 1989, Nederburg Ballet Award for Best Female Dancer 1991, Lilian Solomon Award for Best Female Dancer 1992, Vita Award for most outstanding performance by female dancer 1993, 1994, 1995; *Recreations* travelling, reading, music; *Style*— Ms Leticia Muller; ✉ The Birmingham Royal Ballet, Birmingham Hippodrome, Thorp Street, Birmingham B5 4AU (☎ 0121 622 2555, fax 0121 622 5038)

MULLER, Dr Ralph Louis Junius; s of Carl Muller (d 1937), and Sarah Muller (d 1982); *b* 30 June 1933; *Educ* Summerhill Sch Suffolk, Univ of London (BSc, PhD, DSc); *m* 1, 1958 (m dis), Gretta, da of Vernon Shearer; 1 da (Karen b 16 Oct 1959), 1 s (Julian b 7 Aug 1961); m 2, 1979, Annie, da of Rafael Badilla; 1 da (Harriet b 2 Oct 1981), 1 s (Barnaby b 29 March 1985); *Career* scientific offr ODM 1959–61, lectr in parasitology Univ of Ibadan 1962–66, sr lectr LSHTM 1966–80, dir Int Inst of Parasitology 1981–93; hon sec Br Soc for Parasitology 1995–; pres Euro Fedn of Parasitologists 1988–92, sec Int Filariasis Assoc 1978–; ed: Jl of Helminthology, Advances in Parasitology; FRSTM & H 1968, FIBiol 1974; *Books* Worms and Disease (1975), Bibliography of Onchocerciasis (1987), Medical Parasitology (1990); *Recreations* tennis, beekeeping, photography, pen collecting; *Style*— Dr Ralph Muller; ✉ 22 Cranbrook Drive, St Albans, Herts AL4 0SS (☎ 01727 852605, fax 01727 856871); International Institute of Parasitology, 395A Hatfield Road, St Albans, Herts AL4 0XU

MULLETT, (Aidan) Anthony; CBE (1993), QPM (1982); s of Bartholomew Joseph Mullett (d 1976), and Mary Kate, *née* Sheehan (d 1980); *b* 24 May 1933; *Educ* Moat Boys' Sch Leicester; *m* 7 Sept 1957, Monica Elizabeth, da of Paul Gerald Coney (d 1968); 1 s (Philip b 1963), 1 da (Beverley b 1958); *Career* RAF 1950–56; Leicester City Police 1957, Leicestershire and Rutland Constabulary 1966, asst chief constable West Mercia Constabulary 1975, dep chief constable Dyfed Powys Police 1982, chief constable West Mercia Constabulary 1985, DG National Criminal Intelligence Serv 1991–93, ret 1993; *Recreations* golf; *Clubs* Droitwich Golf and Country; *Style*— Anthony Mullett, Esq, CBE, QPM; ✉ 23 Dugard Way, Droitwich Spa, Worcs WR9 8UX

MULLIGAN, Tracy Dima; da of Frederick George Mulligan (d 1994), of Esher, Surrey, and Gladys, *née* Egerton; *b* 6 May 1962; *Educ* Kingston Poly, Chelsea Sch of Art (BTec dip), St Martin's Sch of Art (BA); *Career* fashion designer; early career experience as hair stylist with The Ginger Group and Sanrizz London 1978–83, subesquent experience as sales asst with fashion retailers Jospeh and Browns; gp finalist Jigsaw Womenswear Competition 1988, finalist Garroulds Corp Clothing Competition 1989, finalist Imperial Cancer Res Fund Design Competition and Charity Fashion Show 1989, asst womenswear designer Daniel Hechter Paris 1991, fndr ptnr Sonnentag Mulligan 1992–96, freelance consultancy for Design Intelligence and French Connection 1996–; freelance teaching Central st Martin's 1995–; selected to show during London Fashion Week (Harvey Nichols) and sponsored by BFC to exhibit at British Fashion Week (Ritz Hotel) 1993, sponsored by Harvey Nichols/Perrier for catwalk show 1994, sponsored by Stirling Group plc for catwalk show 1994, sponsored by DTI for catwalk show in Osaka and to exhibit in Tokyo 1994, sponsored by Marks and Spencer for catwalk show and stand Oct 1995; nominated: British Design/New Generation Lloyds Bank British Fashion Awards 1992, 1993 and 1994; speaker Addressing Dressing (with Sally Brampton and Betty Jackson) ICA Fashion Talks 1993; *Recreations* meditation, travel, swimming; *Style*— Ms Tracy Mulligan; ✉ Top Floor, 35 Redcliffe Gardens, London SW10 9BH (☎ and fax 0171 352 1129)

MULLIN, Christopher John (Chris); MP (Lab) Sunderland South (majority 14,501); s of Leslie Mullin, and Theresa, *née* Foley; *b* 12 Dec 1947; *Educ* St Joseph's (De La Salle) Birkfield, Univ of Hull (LLB); *m* 1987, Nguyen Thi Ngoc, da of Nguyen Tang Minh, of Kontum, Vietnam; 1 da (Sarah b 2 Nov 1989); *Career* trainee scheme Mirror Group Newspapers 1969–71, freelance journalist 1972–74, BBC World Service 1974–78, freelance 1978–82, ed Tribune 1982–84, author 1984–87; Parly candidate (Lab): North Devon 1970, Kingston upon Thames 1974; MP (Lab) Sunderland S 1987–; memb Home Affairs Select Ctee 1992–; *Publications* The Tibetans (1981), How to Select or Reselect your MP (1981), A Very British Coup (1982), The Last Man Out of Saigon (1986), Error of Judgement - The Truth about the Birmingham Pub Bombings (1986), The Year of the Fire Monkey (1991); *Recreations* walking, talking, travelling; *Style*— Chris Mullin, Esq, MP; ✉ House of Commons, London SW1A 0AA (☎ 0171 219 3000)

MULLIN, Geoffrey Kenneth (Geoff); s of Kenneth Mullin (d 1986), of Garstang, Lancs, and Lily, *née* Butcher (d 1976); *b* 11 Sept 1942; *Educ* Burnage GS for Boys Manchester, Royal Victoria Coll of Music (Dip); *m* 5 Dec 1970 (m dis 1989), Caroline Moira, da of William Frederick Irving Stephenson (d 1988), of Henley, Oxon; 1 da (Crystal b 1973); *Career* schoolteacher 1960–61, civil servant 1962–64, professional musician, singer, songwriter with recordings for DECCA and CBS 1964–68; advertising mangr and journalist 1968–70: Record Mirror, Music Week, Billboard; freelance prodr with BBC 1970–73, record prodr for various artists incl Marmalade and the Troggs 1970–73; prodr BBC Radio Two 1973–94: Simon Bates 1973–74, Jack Jackson, Terry Wogan 1975–79, David Hamilton 1979–80, Kenny Everett 1980–82, Sounds of the Sixties (Keith Fordyce) 1983–84, Ken Bruce 1985–86, Your Hundred Best Tunes (Alan Keith) 1987, Anne Robinson, Michael Aspel, The Earl Spencer, Wally Whyton, Maureen Lipman, Sue Cook, Brian Blessed and Anna Raeburn 1988–90, Jimmy Young, Terry Wogan and Glen Campbell's A to Z of Country Music 1991, Brian Hayes Breakfast Show 1992, Country Music Assoc Awards Show 1992, Radio 2 Country Season 1992, Buddy Concert for Nat Music Day 1992, Michael Aspel Xmas Special 1992, Wake Up to Wogan 1993, Elizabeth Power 1993, Beatles Day with George Martin 1993, Sarah Kennedy 1993, Country Style (BBC World Serv) 1993, Michael Aspel Sunday Show 1994 (Gold Sony Radio Award, Best Breakfast Show for Non-Contemporary Music 1994); head of music Melody FM (formerly Melody Radio) 1994–: VJ Day Music Thames Relay 1995, Ella Fitzgerald Special Tribute (with David Jacobs, CBE); judge Sony Awards 1995, memb Ctee Music and Radio Conf 1995; *Recreations* squash, skiing, reading, travel, music, films, theatre; *Style*— Geoffrey Mullin, Esq; ✉ 11 Lancaster Road, St Albans, Herts AL1 4EP (☎ 01727 848222); Melody FM, 180 Brompton Road, London SW3 1HF (☎ 0171 581 1054, 0171 581 7000)

MULLIN, Prof John William; s of Frederick Mullin (d 1972), of Queen's Ferry, Chester, and Kathleen Nellie, *née* Oppy (d 1988); *b* 22 Aug 1925; *Educ* Hawarden Co Sch, Univ Coll Cardiff (BSc, DSc), UCL (PhD); *m* 22 Aug 1952, Averil Margaret, da of William Davies (d 1971), of Cwmgwili, Carmarthen; 1 s (Jonathan b 1957), 1 da (Susan b 1960); *Career* RAF 1945–48; UCL: lectr chemical engrg 1956–61, reader 1961–69, prof 1969–85, Ramsay meml prof and head of dept 1985–90, dean of engrg 1975–77, vice provost 1980–86, Crabtree orator 1993; dean of engrg Univ of London 1980–85; memb: Ct of Govrs Univ Coll Cardiff 1982–, Cncl Sch of Pharmacy 1983– (vice chm 1988–), Parly Gp for Engrg Devpt 1994–; winner of Moulton medal Inst of Chem Engrs 1970, Kurnakov meml medal USSR Acad of Scis 1991; Dr (honoris causa) Institut National Polytechnique de Toulouse 1989; Freeman City of London 1984, memb Worshipful Co of Engrs 1984; memb Hon Soc Cymmrodorion 1983; fell: Univ Coll Cardiff 1981, UCL 1981; FRSC (1958), FIChemE 1959, FEng 1983; *Books* Industrial Crystallization (ed, 1976), Crystallization (3 edn, 1993); *Recreations* gardening; *Clubs* Athenaeum; *Style*— Prof John Mullin, FEng; ✉ 4 Milton Rd, Ickenham, Uxbridge, Middx UB10 8NQ; Department of Chemical Engineering, UCL, Torrington Place, London WC1E 7JE (☎ 0171 387 7050)

MULLINER, Stephen Nigel; s of Dr Gerald Norman Mulliner, of Osmington, Weymouth, Dorset, and Kathleen Wilma, *née* Ritchie; *b* 4 Sept 1953; *Educ* Downside, Emmanuel Coll Cambridge (MA, LLB), Inns of Court Sch of Law; *m* 18 Aug 1979, Sarah Lucinda, da of Lt-Col John Arthur Speirs, of Coombe Bissett, Salisbury, Wilts; 2 s (Andrew b 1983, Jonathan b 1985), 2 da (Lucy b 1983, Charlotte b 1989); *Career* called to the Bar 1978; assoc dir Swiss Bank Corporation Investment Banking Ltd 1987–89, gen mangr Tokai International Ltd 1989–91, gen mangr Arbitrage and Derivatives Dept Tokai Capital Markets Ltd 1991–, exec dir Tokai Derivative Products Ltd 1995–; non-exec chm James Smith Estates plc 1989– (non-exec dir 1988–); Br Open Croquet champion 1988 and 1990, President's Cup winner 1981, 1983, 1986, 1987 and 1992, Men's champion 1985 and 1986, World Invitation Singles champion 1986 1987 and 1988, Br Open Doubles champion 1980, 1981, 1984, 1986, 1988 and 1994, Euro Open champion 1993, 1994 and 1995; chm Croquet Assoc 1990–92; *Books* The World of Croquet (1987), Play The Game - Croquet (1989); *Recreations* croquet, golf, tennis, real tennis, running; *Style*— Stephen Mulliner, Esq; ✉ c/o Tokai Capital Markets Ltd, 1 Exchange Square, London EC2A 2JL (☎ 0171 638 6030, fax 0171 588 5875)

MULLINS, Anthony Roy (Tony); s of Royston George Mullins (d 1985), and Evelyn Hilda Mullins; *b* 20 Sept 1939; *Educ* Loughton Sch, SW Essex Tech Coll, London Sch of Printing; *m* 1, 1964 (m dis 1995), Patricia Janet Stone; 2 s (John b 1969, Benjamin b 1973), 1 da (Nicola b 1971); m 2, Julie Elizabeth, da of Dr and Mrs Peter Hacking; *Career* art asst: BDMW Design Group 1960–61, Sunday Times Magazine 1962–64; art ed The Observer Magazine 1967–76, art dir The Observer Newspaper 1976–95, conslt art dir Graphic News 1995–; winner of various D&AD awards for magazine work and overall winner Focus Newspaper of the Year Design Award 1995 (jtly); FSTD; *Recreations* theatre, tennis; *Style*— Tony Mullins; ✉ 50 St Peter's Close, Wandsworth Common, London SW17 7UH (☎ 0181 672 6466); Graphic News, Unit 7 Utopia Village, Chalcot Road, London NW1 8LH (☎ 0171 722 4673, fax 0171 586 3567)

MULLINS, Rt Rev Daniel Joseph; *see:* Menevia, Bishop of (RC)

MULLINS, Edwin Brandt; s of Claud William Mullins (d 1968), and Elizabeth Gwendolen, *née* Brandt; *b* 14 Sept 1933; *Educ* Midhurst GS, Merton Coll Oxford (BA, MA); *m* 1, 1960, Gillian (d 1982); 1 s (Jason), 2 da (Frances, Selina); m 2, 1984, Anne; *Career* author, TV and radio scriptwriter; TV series incl: 100 Great Paintings, The Great Art Collection, A Love Affair with Nature, Masterworks, Paradise on Earth, Montparnasse Revisited; *Books* Alfred Wallis (1967 and 1994), Braque (1968), The Pilgrimage to Santiago (1974), Great Paintings (1981), Sirens (1983), The Painted Witch (1985), The Arts of Britian (1983), The Golden Bird (1987), The Lands of the Sea (1988), The Royal Collection (1992), The Devil's Work (1996), others under a pseudonym; *Recreations* art galleries, reading, walking, natural history, watching cricket; *Style*— Edwin Mullins, Esq; ✉ c/o Curtis Brown Ltd, 4th Floor, Haymarket House, 28–29 Haymarket, London SW1Y 4SP

MULLINS, Brig Keith Alexander; s of Reginald Mullins (d 1983), of Yeovil, Somerset, and Mabel Phylis, *née* Rochester (d 1989); *b* 9 March 1937; *Educ* Porchester Sch Bournemouth, Univ of Exeter (BA, CBiol); *m* 1, 16 Dec 1961 (m dis 1985), Janet; 1 s (Stephen John b 16 Oct 1964), 1 da (Vanessa Louise b 22 June 1967); m 2, 8 Jan 1986, Carolyn Margaret, da of George William Charlton Thompson, of Newcastle-upon-Tyne; *Career* RAF (Suez Campaign 1956) 1955–58, Army 1963–93 (Lt 1963); schoolmaster 1961–63, Nat Def Coll 1979 (NDC), CO 1 Ord Bn 1981–83 (Lt Col) 1 Armd Div, DCOS Falklands 1983–84 (Col) HQ BFI, DA Jakarta 1985–87 (Col) British Embassy, ACOS Cyprus 1987–89 (Col) HQ BF Cyprus, dir (Brig) DSCS Bicester 1989–90, dir (Brig) D Log IS (Army) 1991; project mangr GEC Marconi Projects Malaysia 1991–95; self-employed mgmnt conslt and stockbreeder 1995–; memb Nat Computing Centre (NCC); FIMgt 1985, MIBiol 1984, MBCS 1989; *Recreations* reading, farming, tennis, war games; *Clubs* The Naval Club; *Style*— Brig Keith Mullins; ✉ Alexander Associates and Rochester Poll Herefords, Rochester House, Lower Easthams, Crewkerne, Somerset TA18 7NU (☎ 01460 78450, fax 01460 78844)

MUMFORD, Lady Mary Katharine; *née* Fitzalan Howard; DCVO (1995, CVO 1982, LVO 1974); da of 16 Duke of Norfolk, KG, GCVO, GBE, TD, PC (d 1975); hp to Lordship of Herries of Terregles; *b* 14 Aug 1940; *m* 1986, Gp Capt Anthony Mumford, CVO, OBE; *Career* lady-in-waiting to HRH Princess Alexandra, the Hon Lady Ogilvy, GCVO 1964–; *Style*— The Lady Mary Mumford, DCVO; ✉ North Stoke Cottage, North Stoke, Arundel, W Sussex; Lantonside, Glencaple, Dumfries

MUMMERY, *see also:* Lockhart-Mummery

MUMMERY, Rt Hon Lord Justice; Rt Hon Sir John Frank; kt (1989), PC (1996); s of Frank Stanley Mummery, of Bridge, Kent, and Ruth, *née* Coleman; *b* 5 Sept 1938; *Educ* Oakleigh House, Dover Co GS, Pembroke Coll Oxford (MA, BCL); *m* 11 March 1967, Elizabeth Anne Lamond, da of Dr Glyn Lackie (d 1985), of Edinburgh; 1 s (David b 1974), 1 da (Joanna b 1968); *Career* Nat Serv Border Regt RAEC 1957–59; called to the Bar Gray's Inn 1964, counsel attorney gen in charity matters 1977–81, jr treasy counsel Chancery 1981–89, bencher Gray's Inn 1985, recorder 1989, judge of the High Ct of Justice (Chancery Div) 1989–96, a Lord Justice of Appeal 1996–; pres Employment Appeal Tbnl 1993–96; memb Legal Advsy Cmmn of Gen Synod of C of E 1988–; hon fell Pembroke Coll Oxford 1989, govr Inns of Ct Sch of Law 1996–; *Books* Copinger and Skone on Copyright (jt ed 13 edn, 1991); *Recreations* long walks with family, friends and alone; *Style*— The Rt Hon Sir John Mummery; ✉ c/o Royal Courts of Justice, Strand, London WC2A 2LL

MUNASINGHE, (Leelananda) Sepala; s of Lairis Appu Munasinghe (d 1992), of Kurunegala, Sri Lanka, and Joslyn, *née* Samarasinghe (d 1990); *b* 2 Jan 1937; *Educ* Trinity Coll Kandy Sri Lanka; *m* 21 May 1964, Dorothea Brunhildis, da of Wilhelm Karger (d 1968), of Ostbevern, Germany; 2 da (Karin b 1965, Gitanjali b 1968); *Career* called to the Bar Lincoln's Inn 1963; advocate Surpreme Court of Ceylon 1964, attorney at law Supreme Court of Sri Lanka 1972; chm: Social Security Appeals Tbnl 1986–, Disability Appeals Tbnl 1991– (both UK); asst cmmr Parly Boundary Cmmn for England 1992–95, special adjudicator Immigration Appeals Authy 1995–; govr Waldegrave Sch for Girls 1980–83, memb Birmingham City Cncl Public Inquiry into Handsworth Riots 1986; *Recreations* cooking, reading, travelling; *Clubs* Capri (Colombo); *Style*— Sepala Munasinghe, Esq; ✉ 235 London Rd, Twickenham, Middx TW1 1ES (☎ and fax 0181 892 5947)

MUNDAY, John; s of Rodney H J Munday (d 1967), and Ethel Emma, *née* Cutting (d 1965); *b* 10 Aug 1924; *Educ* Portsmouth N GS, King's Coll Durham (BA, MA); *m* 4 Sept 1953, Brenda, da of Norman C Warden (d 1962); 2 s (Oliver John b 1957, Hugo Timothy b 1960); *Career* asst Portsmouth Public Libraries and Museums Dept 1940–42; served RN 1942–46, Sub Lt RNVR 1944–46; National Maritime Museum: asst keeper 1951, dep keeper 1969, keeper Dept of Weapons and Antiquities 1976–84, curator emeritus 1984–; memb: Devpt Ctee SS Great Britain Project Bristol 1980–, Advsy Tech Ctee HMS Victory 1985–; hon vice pres Soc for Nautical Res; FSA 1972; *Books* incl: Oar Maces of Admiralty (1966), Dress of the British Sailor (1977), Naval Cannon (1987), E W Cooke RA FRS, A Man of his Time (1996); author of numerous specialist articles; *Recreations* painting, collecting; *Style*— John Munday, Esq, FSA; ✉ Fourteen The Beach, Walmer, Kent CT14 7HE (☎ 01304 374493)

MUNDAY, Peter James; s of Frederick Lewis James Munday (d 1987), of Esher, Surrey, and Lily Charlotte Rebecca, *née* Fowler; *b* 31 Oct 1938; *m* 1 (m dis 1984), Inger Kristina Fageresjo; 1 da (Lisa Kristina b 1975); m 2, 22 Dec 1984, Linda Ann (Lin), da of Leslie Breckon, of Cardiff; 2 da (Emma Sophie b 1986, Zara Jane b 1989); *Career* Nat Serv RCS 1957–59; admitted slr 1968, NP 1975; sr ptnr Mundays 1976– (ptnr 1968–); tstee: Princess Alice Hospice Esher, Esher War Meml Property Fund, Friends of St George's Church Esher, Hospice Educn Centre Tst; Freeman City of London, Liveryman Worshipful Co of Bakers; memb: Law Soc 1968, Notaries Soc 1975; *Recreations* hockey, squash, cricket; *Clubs* MCC; *Style*— Peter Munday, Esq; ✉ Pinewood Lodge, Warren Lane, Oxshott, Surrey (☎ 01372 467272); Mundays, Crown House, Church Rd, Claygate, Esher, Surrey (☎ 01372 467272, fax 01372 463782)

MUNDAY, Eur Ing Raymond Geoffrey Todd; s of John Dale Munday (d 1925), of Lancs, and Florence Adelaide, *née* Worthington (d 1980); *b* 15 March 1922; *Educ* King George V Sch Southport (BSc), RCS London; *m* 14 Sept 1946, Angela Catherine, da of Horace Clive Burdett (d 1964), and Elizabeth Agnes, *née* Frost (d 1984); 1 s (David b 1947), 2 da (Catherine b 1954, Rosemary b 1958); *Career* aerospace engr Bristol Aeroplane Co 1949; Br Aerospace: dir of electronic and space systems (Bristol) 1978, dir and gen mangr Space and Communications Div Stevenage 1981, ret 1984; UK rep Arianespace 1984–93, currently space conslt; chm UK Industl Space Ctee 1982–84; chartered engr 1968, Eur Ing 1988, ARCS, FRAeS; *Clubs* Naval; *Style*— Eur Ing Raymond G T Munday; ✉ 53 High St, Ashwell, Herts SG7 5NP (☎ 01462 742760)

MUNDAY-CHANIN, Christopher John; *Educ* East Ham GS, Polytechnic of the South Bank (BA, RIBA Graduate Dip Part 1), Polytechnic of North London, Open Univ; *Career* engrg asst Haden Young (H & V Consultants) 1963–65; architectural asst: GMW Partnership (Architects) 1965–67, Charringtons Architects Dept 1967–68; John Lewis Partnership Architects Dept 1968–69, estates mangr and architectural asst Caters Estate Department 1969–74, project controller Fitch & Co 1974–79, sr designer Stewart McColl Design Associates 1979, project architect GMW Partnership 1979–80, sr designer and assoc AID (AIDCOM PLC) Design Consultants 1980–82; assoc dir: Conran Associates 1982–83, Fitch & Co 1983–87 (and divnl dir); McColl Ltd: divnl dir 1987–91, gp dir of interiors 1988–91, md of interiors (London) 1988–91, dir S & P McColl 1989–91, dir Walker Group McColl 1990–91; jt fndr, princ and design dir Chanin Hartland & Ullathorne (with Neil Hartland and Peter Ullathorne) 1991–; external examiner for BA (Hons) three dimensional design course Univ of Central England in Birmingham 1993–96; memb Westminster C of C, assoc Chartered Inst of Building; MCSD, FIMgt, FRSA; *Recreations* flying, clay pigeon and target shooting, walking, theatre, mountain biking, philosophy, classic cars, material arts, art and architecture - particularly historic buildings; *Clubs* RAC, Stapleford Flying; *Style*— Christopher Munday-Chanin, Esq; ✉ Chanin Hartland Ullathorne Ltd, 57 Cambridge Street, London SW1V 4PS (☎ 0171 932 0696, fax 0171 932 0675)

MUNDEN, Michael Ronald; s of Alfred Gilburt Munden, of Bridport, Dorset, and Sheila Munden; *b* 8 Jan 1946; *Educ* Hardyes Sch, Univ of Aix Marseille, Univ of Southampton (LLB); *m* 30 Oct 1971, Sally Léontine, step da of Dr Peter McGregor; 2 s (Thomas b 27 May 1978, Marc b 19 June 1980); *Career* ptnr Herbert Smith (joined 1970); Freeman City of London Slrs' Co; memb Law Soc 1970; *Recreations* riding, tennis, amateur farming; *Style*— Michael Munden, Esq; ✉ Herbert Smith, Exchange House, Primrose Street, London EC2A 2HS (☎ 0171 374 8000, fax 0171 496 0043)

MUNDY, Anthony Richard; s of Peter Gordon Mundy, of Bedford Ave, London, and Betty, *née* Hall; *b* 25 April 1948; *Educ* Mill Hill Sch, Univ of London (MB BS, MS); *m* 20 Sept 1975 (m dis 1992), Marilyn June, da of Edward Ashton, of South Ockendon, Essex; 1 s (Harry b 1986), 1 da (Emily b 1977); *partner* Debra Ann, da of late Owen Hendley; 1 da (Katie b 1995); *Career* trg in gen surgery and urology Guys Hosp London, CO and conslt surgn Force Base Hosp Muscat Oman 1977–78, conslt urological surgn Lewisham Hosp 1981–86, sr lectr in urology Inst of Urology and UMDS 1981–91; prof of urology Univ of London at Guy's Hosp and Inst of Urology 1991–; dir Inst of Urology and Nephrology, clinical dir of urology ane nephrology UCL Hosps; conslt urological surgn: Guy's Hosp 1981–, St Peter's Hosps 1986–; visiting conslt urologist St Luke's Hosp Malta 1984–; hon conslt urological surgeon Nat Hosp for Neurology and Neurosurgery; chm Specialist Advsy Ctee in Urology; memb Ctee Br Assoc of Urological Surgns, memb Exec Ctee Euro Assoc of Urology, memb Exec Ctee Br Jl of Urology Urological Res, memb Jt Ctee on Higher Surgical Trg, memb Bd Euro Urological Scholarship Fndn, memb Scientific Ctee Br Urological Fndn, fndn memb Soc of Genito-Urinary Reconstructive Surgeons, examiner and memb Intercollegiate Bd FRCS (Urology); convener and fndr memb Urological Research Soc; hon memb Urological Soc of Australia, Malaysia and Singapore; MRCP 1974, FRCS 1975; *Books* Urodynamics - Principles Practice and Application (1984, 2 edn 1994), Scientific Basis of Urology (1986), Current Operative Surgery-Urology (1988), The Neuropathic Bladder in Childhood (1990), Urodynamic and Reconstructive Surgery of the Lower Urinary tract (1992); author of various papers, chapters and articles on the treatment of incontinece and reconstructive urology; *Style*— Anthony Mundy, Esq; ✉ Emblem House, Tooley Street, London SE1 2PR (☎ 0171 403 1221, fax 0171 403 1667, e-mail MUNDYUROL@aol.com)

MUNFORD, Dr William Arthur; MBE (1946); s of Ernest Charles Munford (d 1948), of London, and Florence Margaret, *née* Dinneen (d 1959); *b* 27 April 1911; *Educ* Hornsey Co Sch, LSE (BSc, PhD); *m* 25 Aug 1934, Hazel Despard, da of Frank Arthur Wilmer (d 1956), of London; 2 s ((Arthur) Michael b 1935, Jeremy b 1940), 1 da ((Linda) Alison Cynthia b 1945); *Career* borough librarian Dover 1934–45, food exec offr and emergency feeding organiser Dover 1939–45, city librarian Cambridge 1945–53, dir gen and librarian Nat Library for the Blind 1954–82 (librarian emeritus 1982–); tstee Ulverscroft Fndn 1973–93, memb Soc of Bookmen; Hon FLA 1977 (FLA 1933); *Books* Books for Basic Stock (1939), Penny Rate (1951), William Ewart MP (1960), Edward Edwards (1963), Louis Stanley Jast (with W G Fry, 1966), James Duff Brown (1968), A History of the Library Association 1877–1977 (1976), The Incomparable Mac: Sir J Y W Macalister (with S Godbolt, 1983), Who Was Who in British Librarianship 1800–1985 (1987); *Recreations* reading, writing, rough gardening, wood sawing, cycling, serendipity; *Clubs* National Liberal; *Style*— Dr William Munford, MBE; ✉ 11 Manor Court, Pinehurst, Grange Rd, Cambridge CB3 9BE (☎ 01223 362962)

MUNIR, Dr (Ashley) Edward; s of Hon Sir Mehmed Munir, CBE (d 1957), and Lady Vessime Munir, *née* Ziai (d 1979); *b* 14 Feb 1934; *Educ* Brentwood, St John's Coll Cambridge (MA), King's Coll London (MPhil, PhD); *m* 6 June 1960, Sureyya, da of Shukri Dormen, of Istanbul, Turkey; 1 s (Simon b 24 Oct 1964); *Career* called to the Bar Gray's Inn 1956, crown counsel 1960–64, legal asst Govt Legal Serv 1964, under sec MAFF 1982, resumed practice at the Bar 1993; *Books* Perinatal Rights (1983), Fisheries after Factortame (1991), Mentally Disordered Offenders (1993); *Recreations* walking, playing the double-bass, listening to music; *Style*— Dr Edward Munir; ✉ 1 Harcourt Buildings, Temple, London EC4Y 9DA (☎ 0171 353 0375, fax 0171 353 4170, DX 1051 ChanceryLane)

MUNKENBECK, Alfred Hedges III; s of Alfred Hedges Munkenbeck Jr, of Old Greenwich, Connecticut, USA, and Adelaide Celina, *née* Rickert; *b* 26 March 1947; *Educ* Le Rosey Rolle Switzerland, The Canterbury Sch USA, Dartmouth Coll USA (BA), Harvard (MArch); *m* 1992, Paula Reed; 1 da (Chloe Adelaide b June 1993), 1 s (Alfred Hedges IV b Oct 1995); *Career* architect; worked with James Stirling Architects on Stuttgart Contemporary Art Museum 1977–80, urban design conslt for Yanbu and MOIT new towns, Umm al Qura Univ and Royal palaces Saudi Arabia 1980–85; sr ptnr Munkenbeck & Marshall 1985–; projects incl: Raymond Revuebar, Yohji Yamamoto shop Sloane St, office buildings at Jessica Sq, Wandsworth and 87 Lancaster Rd, Notting Hill, Orsino Restaurant Holland Park, golf resort Bahrain, Metro Photographic Clerkenwell, private houses for Charles Saatchi, Norman Parkinson and Tricia Guild in London, apartment buildings at 9–11 New Wharf Rd, Kings Cross and Alaska 800, Southwark; lectr in architectural design: Univs of Cambridge and Kingston, The AA; assessor Civic Trust Awards; author of articles on Munkenbeck & Marshall in relevant pubns; RIBA 1980; *Awards* RFAC Building of the Year commendation 1992, Kensington and Chelsea Environmental Award 1992, Civic Trust commendation 1996; *Recreations* skiing, sailing, sandcastles; *Clubs* Groucho, Guilda's, The Architecture; *Style*— Alfred Munkenbeck, Esq; ✉ Munkenbeck & Marshall, 3 Pine Street, London EC1R 0JH

MUNN, Dr Charles William; s of David Shearer Munn (d 1968), of Glasgow, and Elizabeth McCowan, *née* Renfrew; *b* 26 May 1948; *Educ* Queens Park Secdy Sch Glasgow, Univ of Strathclyde (BA), Univ of Glasgow (PhD), Jordanhill Coll of Educn (CertEd); *m* 1 Sept 1973, Andrea, da of David Cuthbertson and Violet Cuthbertson; 1 s (David Stuart b 19 Aug 1977, Kirsten Elizabeth b 8 April 1981); *Career* clerk and teller various Glasgow branches British Linen Bank 1964–67, student 1967–75, lectr Dept of Finance and Accountancy Glasgow Coll of Technol (now Glasgow Caledonian Univ) 1975–78, lectr then sr lectr Dept of Econ History Univ of Glasgow 1978–88, chief exec Chartered Inst of Bankers in Scotland 1988–; FCIBS 1993, FRSA 1993; *Books* The Scottish Provincial Banking Companies 1747–1864 (1981), Banking in Scotland (1982), The Clydesdale Bank: The First 150 Years (1988); *Recreations* reading, writing, golf; *Clubs* New (Edinburgh), College (Glasgow), Aberdour Golf; *Style*— Dr Charles W Munn; ✉ 1 Ross Avenue, Dalgety Bay, Fife KY11 5YN (☎ 01383 824567); The Chartered Institute of Bankers in Scotland, 19 Rutland Square, Edinburgh EH1 2DE (☎ 0131 229 9869, fax 0131 229 1852)

MUNN, Sir James; OBE (1976); s of Douglas Herbert Hamilton Munn (d 1973), and Margaret Graham, *née* Dunn (d 1965); *b* 27 July 1920; *Educ* Stirling HS, Univ of Glasgow (MA); *m* 1946, Muriel Jean Millar, da of Norman MacLeod Moles (d 1964); 1 da (Elizabeth d 1996); *Career* Indian Civil Serv 1941–48, dep sec Supply Dept Govt of Bihar; teacher 1948–83; rector: Rutherglen Acad 1966–70, Cathkin HS 1970–83; chm Consultative Ctee on the Curriculum 1980–87, Manpower Servs Ctee for Scotland 1984–88, Manpower Servs Cmmn 1987–88, Univ cmmr 1988–95; Officier d' Académie (1967); *Style*— Sir James Munn, OBE; ✉ 4 Kincath Avenue, Rutherglen, Glasgow G73 4RP (☎ 0141 634 4654)

MUNN, Prof Robert William; s of William Anderson Munn (d 1989), and Kathleen Maud, *née* Bishop (d 1981); *b* 16 Jan 1945; *Educ* Huish's GS Taunton, Univ of Bristol (BSc, PhD), Univ of Manchester (DSc); *m* 24 June 1967, Patricia Lorna, da of Robert William Moyle (d 1965); 1 s (Nicholas b 1971), 1 da (Philippa b 1974); *Career* postdoctorate fell Nat Res Cncl of Canada 1968–70, ICI Postdoctoral fell Univ of Edinburgh 1970–71, visiting fell Aust Nat Univ 1982; UMIST: lectr 1971–80, reader 1980–84, prof of chemical physics 1984–, vice princ 1987–90, dean 1994–; coordinating ed Jl of Molecular Electronics 1985–91, assoc ed Advanced Materials for Optics and Electronics 1992–, numerous pubns in scientific jls; FRSC, CChem 1987, FInstP, CPhys 1987; *Books* Molecular Electromagnetism (with A Hinchliffe), Magnetism and Optics of Molecular Crystals (with J W Rohleder); *Recreations* guitar, linguistics; *Style*— Prof Robert Munn; ✉ Dept of Chemistry, UMIST, PO Box 88, Manchester M60 1QD (☎ 0161 200 4534, fax 0161 200 4584, telex 666094 UMIST G)

MUNRO, *see:* Gun-Munro

MUNRO, Sir Alan Gordon; KCMG (1990, CMG 1984); s of Sir Gordon Munro, KCMG, MC, and Lilian Muriel, *née* Beit; *b* 17 Aug 1935; *Educ* Wellington, Clare Coll Cambridge (MA); *m* 1962, Rosemary Grania, da of Cdr N A Bacon; 2 s (twins), 2 da; *Career* HM Dip Serv: consul gen Rio de Janeiro 1974–77, head of East African Dept FCO 1977–78, head of Middle East Dept 1979, head of Personnel Operations Dept 1979–81, dir of ME Def Sales MOD 1981–83, HM ambass Algiers 1984–87, dep under sec of state FCO 1987–89, HM ambass Riyadh 1989–93; vice-chm cncl of British Red Cross 1994–; advsr: General Electric Co, Tate & Lyle plc, Nissho Iwai Europe PLC, Sir Alexander Gibb and Partners; non-exec dir Schroder Asseily Ltd; chm Beit Tst for Central Africa, pres Soc for Algerian Studies, dir Arab-Br C of C; memb: Cncl ME Assoc, Governing Cncl Imperial Coll of Science; *Books* An Arabian Affair: Politics and Diplomacy Behind the Gulf War (1996); *Recreations* Middle East travel, conservation, history, gardens; *Clubs* Travellers'; *Style*— Sir Alan Munro, KCMG; ✉ 41 Upper Grosvenor Street, London W1X 9AG

MUNRO, Alan Keith; s of Angus Alexanda Munro, of Scotland, and Brenda Margaret Martin; *b* 14 Jan 1967; *Educ* Barnwell Sch Stevenage; *Career* professional jockey; apprentice to: B Hills 1983–86, M Brittain 1986–89; retained by W O'Gorman as first jockey 1990–, second retainer Mrs L Ramsden 1990–, full jockey March 1990–, personal jockey to HRH Prince Fahd Salman 1991–, club jockey Royal Hong Kong Jockey Club 1993–96, first foreign jockey granted contract to ride in Japan (three-month contract 1994 and 1995); first ride Newbury 1984 (Papperetto), first win Yarmouth 1985 (Sentimental Roses), rode in Italy close season 1986, rode in USA close season 1987, 1988 and 1989; major wins: Spanish Derby 1990 (Akalarre), Spanish Grand Prix 1990 (Akalarre), Heinz 57 Group 1 1990 (Mac's Imp), Epsom Derby 1991 (Generous), Irish Derby 1991 (Generous), King George VI & Queen Elizabeth Diamond Stakes 1991 (Generous), Coventry Stakes 1991 (Dilum); rode Timeless Times to record-equalling 16 wins for a two-year old in one season 1990, rode five winners in a day Aug 23 1990, placed eighth in Flat Jockeys' Table 1990, completed over 100 winners for first time 1991; *Style*— Alan Munro, Esq; (☎ 01763 289370, fax 01763 289568)

MUNRO, Alexander; s of William Munro (d 1985), and Jane Munro; *b* 5 June 1943; *Educ* Acad Fortrose, Univ of Aberdeen (MB ChB, ChM); *m* 17 July 1970, Maureen; 2 s (Niall b 1971, Calum b 1982), 1 da (Kirsty b 1973); *Career* sr surgical registrar Aberdeen Royal Infirmary 1975–78, res surgical offr St Mark's Hosp 1977, conslt gen surgn Raigmore Hosp 1978–, hon sr lectr Univ of Aberdeen 1978; author of papers on gastrointestinal surgery and surgical trg, prodr of video films on surgical procedures; current res interest use of simulators in surgical trg; pres Highland Div Ileostomy Assoc GB, memb Cncl Assoc of Surgns of GB and I; FRCSEd 1972, FRCSGlas 1993; *Recreations* gardening, church activities, outdoor sports; *Style*— Alexander Munro, Esq; ✉ 23 Eriskay Rd, Inverness IV2 3LX (☎ 01463 223804); Dept of Surgery, Raigmore Hospital, Inverness IV2 3UJ

MUNRO, Dame Alison; DBE (1985, CBE 1964); da of Dr John Donald (d 1927), of Paisley, and Helen Barrow Wilson (d 1927); *b* 12 Feb 1914, Liskeard, Cornwall; *Educ* Queens Coll Harley St, Girls' HS Wynberg SA, St Paul's Girls' Sch London, St Hilda's Coll Oxford (MA); *m* 3 Sept 1939, Alan Lamont Munro (ka 1941), s of Prof J W Munro, CBE (d 1968), of Sunningdale, Berks; 1 s (Alan b 1941); *Career* PA to Sir Robert Watson-Watt, Miny of Aircraft Prodn 1942–45, princ Miny of Civil Aviation 1945, asst sec Miny of Tport and Civil Aviation 1949, under sec Miny of Aviation 1958, high mistress St Paul's Girls' Sch 1964–74; chm: Training Cncl for the Teachers of the Mentally Handicapped 1966–69, Merton Sutton and Wandsworth AHA 1974–82, Chichester Health Authy 1982–88; memb: Bd British European Airways 1966–73, Br Library 1973–79, Br Tourist Authy 1973–81; chm: Central Tport Consultative Ctee 1980–85, DHSS Maternity Servs Advsy Ctee 1980–85, Code Monitoring Ctee on Baby Milk 1985–89, Equipment Appeal St Richard's Hospital 1995–; cdre W Wittering Sailing Club 1986–88, govr Chichester HS for Girls 1990–94, pres Chichester and Dist Caledonian Soc 1992–; Woman of the Year 1958; *Recreations* Scottish country dancing, sailing, garden, bridge; *Clubs* Civil Service, Goodwood Country; *Style*— Dame Alison Munro, DBE; ✉ Harbour Way, Ellanore Lane, W Wittering, W Sussex PO20 8AN (☎ and fax 01243 513274)

MUNRO, Alison Lorne; da of Neil Munro (d 1986), of Hordle, near Lymington, Hants, and Anne Monteith, *née* Blyth (d 1989); *b* 19 April 1943; *Educ* Fernhill Manor Sch for Girls' New Milton; *m* 30 July 1966, Peter James Hamilton, s of Keith Hamilton Wadley; 1 s (James Rufus Hamilton b 22 June 1973), 1 da (Katie Amber b 26 March 1971); *Career* asst feature writer Woman magazine 1964–65 (fashion asst 1962–64), jr fashion ed Sunday Times 1965–66, proprietor children's clothes shop Cambridge 1966–67, Lesley Lake Public Relations 1967–71 (account exec, account mangr, dir); md: Munro Deighton Public Relations Limited 1971–84, Munro & Forster Communications Ltd 1985–; memb PRCA; *Recreations* work, family, skiing, cooking; *Style*— Miss Alison Munro; ✉ Munro & Forster Communications Ltd, 37 Soho Square, London W1V 5DG (☎ 0171 439 7177, fax 0171 437 0553)

MUNRO, Allan; s of Allan Pollock Munro, and Margaret McKinnon, *née* Summers; *b* 20 Sept 1947; *Educ* Broughton Secdy Sch; *m* 22 March 1969, Elizabeth Pragnell, da of John Munro Brand; 2 s (Jamie b 26 Oct 1974, Richard b 24 Feb 1977); *Career* Ivory & Sime plc: joined 1964, head of dealing room 1972–87, responsible for fixed interest portfolios 1976–91, dir 1984–, chm Mgmnt Ctee 1990–92; *Recreations* all sports; *Clubs* Edinburgh Sports, Bruntsfield Links Golfing Assoc; *Style*— Allan Munro, Esq; ✉ Ivory & Sime plc, One Charlotte Square, Edinburgh EH2 4DZ (☎ 0131 225 1357, fax 0131 225 2375, telex 727242 IVORYS G)

MUNRO, Christopher Iain Craddock; s of W H Munro (d 1970), and Mary Ross, *née* Craddock; *b* 5 March 1949; *Educ* Trinity Coll Glenalmond, Univ of Edinburgh (LLB); *m* 1973, Hon Diana Mary Munro, *née* Colville, da of 2 Baron Clydesmuir (d 1996); 1 s (Andrew James William b 26 Dec 1979), 1 da (Fiona Mary b 11 June 1976); *Career* Watson Galbraith & Co chartered accountants 1972–75, qualified CA 1975; Robert Fleming & Co: joined 1976, dir Jardine Fleming Holdings and Jardine Fleming Securities HK 1984–86, dir Robert Fleming Securities 1986, dir Robert Fleming Holdings 1988–94; chief exec River and Mercantile Investment Management Ltd 1994–96, business conslt 1997–: NCL Investments Ltd, Beckwith Asset Management Ltd; *Recreations* shooting, golf, theatre; *Clubs* White's, Royal and Ancient, Muirfield; *Style*— Christopher Munro, Esq; ✉ 26 Pembrokes Square, London W8 6PB

MUNRO, Colin Andrew; s of Capt Frederick Bertram Munro (d 1963), and Jane Eliza, *née* Taylor; *b* 24 Oct 1946; *Educ* George Watson's Coll Edinburgh, Univ of Edinburgh (MA); *m* 1967, Ehrengard Maria, da of Rudolf Heinrich (d 1981); 2 s (Peter b 25 Dec 1967, Richard b 27 Jan 1978); *Career* asst princ Bd of Inland Revenue 1968–69, third sec FCO 1969–71, third then second sec Bonn 1971–73, second then first sec Kuala Lumpur 1973–77, FCO 1977, private sec to Min of State 1979–80, head of chancery Bucharest 1981–82, FCO 1983, dep head Western Euro Dept 1985, dep head of mission E Berlin 1987–90, HM consul-gen Frankfurt 1990, head OSCE Cncl of Europe Dept 1993–; *Publications* contribs to journals of Prince Albert Society, Coburg; *Recreations* history, sports especially hockey, cricket, skiing; *Clubs* Royal Selangor Kuala Lumpur, Reform; *Style*— Colin A Munro, Esq

MUNRO, Prof Colin Roy; s of James Smith Munro (d 1970), and Isabel, *née* Thomson (d 1993); *b* 17 May 1949; *Educ* Aberdeen GS, Univ of Aberdeen (LLB), Open Univ (BA); *m* 10 April 1976, Ruth Elizabeth, da of Dr Thomas Leonard Cheesbrough Pratt; 1 s (Philip Edward b 12 Dec 1980), 1 da (Sally Joanna b 22 Sept 1982); *Career* lectr in law: Univ of Birmingham 1971–72, Univ of Durham 1972–80; reader in law and dean Sch of Law Univ of Essex 1984–85 (sr lectr 1980–84), prof of law Univ of Manchester 1985–90 (dean Faculty of Law 1986–88), prof of constitutional law Univ of Edinburgh 1990– (dean Faculty of Law 1992–94); memb Soc of Public Teachers of Law 1971–; *Books* Thalidomide: The Legal Aftermath (with H Teff, 1976), Television, Censorship and the Law (1979), Studies in Constitutional Law (1987), Sentencing, Judicial Discretion and Training (with M Wasik, 1992); *Recreations* sport, film and theatre, beer and skittles; *Clubs* Univ of Edinburgh Staff; *Style*— Prof Colin Munro; ✉ University of Edinburgh, Old College, South Bridge, Edinburgh EH8 9YL (☎ 0131 650 2056, fax 0131 662 0724)

MUNRO, Dr Dowling Donald; s of John Munro (d 1980), of Gt Missenden, Bucks, and Etta Mansfield, *née* Cottrell (d 1992); *b* 29 May 1931; *Educ* Merchant Taylor's Sch Crosby, Univ of London, Royal Free Hosp Sch of Med (MD); *m* 1, 7 Sept 1962, Pamela Grace (d 1977); 2 da (Fiona b 1964, Janet b 1966); m 2, 22 March 1980, Isabella Sinclair, da of Alexander Baillie Macdonald (d 1954), of Lanarkshire, Scot; 2 step da (Jane Tillotson b 1964, Helen Robinson b 1967); *Career* Capt RAMC Cyprus; US public health res fell in dermatology Western Reserve Univ of Cleveland Ohio 1964; conslt dermatologist: Bart's 1968–93, Harley Street 1968–; civilian conslt dermatologist RN 1981–; pubns in med jls incl British Journal of Dermatology; *Books* Steroids and the Skin (ed, 1976); *Recreations* apiculture, horticulture, ornithology; *Clubs* RSM; *Style*— Dr Dowling D Munro; ✉ Old Ley, Burtons Lane, Chalfont St Giles, Bucks HP8 4BQ (☎ 01494 762189); 99 Harley St, London W1N 1DF (☎ 0171 486 2554, fax 0171 224 2736)

MUNRO, Graeme Neil; s of Daniel Munro (d 1985), and Nancy Kirkwood, *née* Smith; *b* 28 Aug 1944; *Educ* Daniel Stewart's Coll Edinburgh, Univ of St Andrews (Ramsay Residential scholar, MA); *m* 1972, Nicola Susan, *qv*, da of late Ernest Derek Wells; 1 da (Rachel Helen Nicola b 1976), 1 s (Keith Alexander b 1981); *Career* Scottish Devpt Dept SO: asst princ 1968–70, seconded to Falkirk Town Cncl 1970–71, private sec to Sec 1971–72, princ 1972–79, asst sec 1979–90, dir Historic Buildings and Monuments 1990–91, dir and chief exec Historic Scotland 1991–; FSA (Scot) 1990; *Recreations* walking, gardening, travel, local history; *Style*— Graeme Munro, Esq; ✉ Historic Scotland, Longmore House, Salisbury Place, Edinburgh EH9 1SH (☎ 0131 668 8696, fax 0131 668 8699)

MUNRO, Hugh Murray; s of Hugh Munro (d 1992), of Aberdeen, and Alice Wilson, *née* Murray (d 1985); *b* 30 Dec 1946; *Educ* Aberdeen GS, Univ of Strathclyde (BA), Univ of Glasgow (MEng); *m* 9 Aug 1974, Valerie Morag, da of Stuart Ingram (d 1984), of Glasgow; 1 s (Craig), 1 da (Lorna); *Career* ptnr Arthur Andersen and Co Glasgow 1981–87 (joined 1968); office managing ptnr: Arthur Young Aberdeen 1987–89, Ernst & Young Aberdeen 1989–; MICAS; *Recreations* skiing, curling, gardening; *Clubs* Aberdeen Petroleum, FP, Aberdeen Rotary; *Style*— Hugh Munro, Esq; ✉ Ernst & Young, 50 Huntly St, Aberdeen (☎ 01224 640033, fax 01224 630753)

MUNRO, Dr Ian Arthur Hoyle; s of Gordon Alexander Munro (d 1934), of Bradford, Yorks, and Muriel Rebecca, *née* Hoyle (d 1938); *b* 5 Nov 1923; *Educ* Huddersfield Coll, Lancaster Royal GS, Paston Sch North Walsham, Royal Liberty Sch Romford, Univ of London Guy's Hosp Med Sch (MB BS); *m* 4 Aug 1948, Dr Olive Isabel, da of Ernest John Jackson (d 1946); 3 s (Andrew b 1950, Robert b 1960, John b 1965), 2 da (Jane b 1952, Deborah b 1956); *Career* RAMC 1947–50, radiologist Br Mil Hosp Klagenfurt BTA; editorial staff The Lancet 1951–88 (ed 1976–88); chm Assoc for the Promotion of Health Care in the Former Soviet Union 1988–93, vice pres Medical Action for Global Security 1988–, pres Physicians for Human Rights (UK) 1991–; FRCP 1984; *Recreations* cricket, crosswords; *Clubs* Athenaeum, Yorks CCC; *Style*— Dr Ian Munro; ✉ Oakwood, Bayley's Hill, Sevenoaks, Kent TN14 6HS (☎ 01732 454993)

MUNRO, Dr John Forbes; OBE; s of John Bennet Lorimer Munro, CBE, CMG (d 1993), and Gladys Maie Forbes, *née* Simmons (d 1965); *b* 25 June 1933; *Educ* Univ of Edinburgh (MB ChB(Hons)); *m* Elizabeth Jean Durell, da of Dr James Colin Caird, OBE (d 1990); 3 da (Patricia Jane Mary b 1960, Elizabeth Ann Caird b 1962, Jennifer Kathleen Margaret b 1965); *Career* conslt physician Eastern Gen Hosp 1968–92, pt/t sr lectr Dept of Med Western Gen Hosp Univ of Edinburgh 1971–92, hon fell Univ of Edinburgh 1992–, registrar RCPEd 1993–; Cullen prize RCPEd 1994; fell Coll of Physicians and Surgns Bangladesh 1995, FRCPE; *Books* Macleod's Clinical Examination (co-ed, 9 edn 1995); *Recreations* contemporary art, gardening; *Style*— Dr John Munro, OBE; ✉ Backhill, Carberry, nr Musselburgh, E Lothian EH21 8QD (☎ 0131 663 4935)

MUNRO, Jonathan Charles; *b* 8 July 1966; *Educ* Doncaster GS, Univ of Nottingham (BA); *Career* ITN Ltd: joined as editorial trainee 1987, prodr Ireland (based Belfast) 1989–90, prodr Gulf War coverage (based Saudi Arabia then Kuwait City) 1990–91, N of England corr 1992–94, Europe corr (based Brussels) 1994–; *Style*— Jonathan Munro, Esq; ✉ c/o Independent Television News, 200 Gray's Inn Road, London WC1X 8XZ

MUNRO, (David) Michael; s of Charles Rowcliffe Munro, of Edinburgh, and Moira Rennie, *née* Ainslie; *b* 3 Nov 1944; *Educ* Trinity Coll Glenalmond; *m* 22 Sept 1973, Jeanine (Tina) Beverley, da of Lt-Col James Lindsay-Stewart, of Prov Alicante, Spain; 3 da (Alexandra b 22 Dec 1977, Antonia b 22 May 1982, Annabel b 31 Jan 1987); *Career* CA 1968; investment analyst Kleinwort Benson 1968–70, ptnr Chiene & Tait CA 1970–83; exec dir: Quayle Munro Ltd 1983–96, Guinness Mahon & Co Ltd 1996–; chm Pittencrieff Resources plc; dir Fife Indmar Plc; *Recreations* fishing, shooting; *Clubs* New (Edinburgh); *Style*— Michael Munro, Esq; ✉ Cockairnie House, Aberdour, Fife KY3 0RZ (☎ 01383 860363); Guinness Mahon & Co Ltd, 1 St Colme Street, Edinburgh EH3 6AA (☎ 0131 220 8266, fax 0131 220 8332)

MUNRO, Nicola Susan; da of Ernest Derek Wells (d 1972), and Barbara Gurney Wells; *b* 11 Jan 1948; *Educ* Harrogate GS, Univ of Warwick (BA); *m* 1972, Graeme Neil Munro, *qv*, s of Daniel Munro; 1 da (Rachel Helen Nicola b 7 Sept 1976), 1 s (Keith Alexander b 30 Sept 1981); *Career* Scottish Office: various posts in health, educn, criminal justice, civil law and personnel 1970–86, head Hosp Specialist Services Div Dept of Health 1986–89, head Urban and Local Econ Policy Div Devpt Dept 1989–92, head 5–14 Curriculum and Careers Div Educn and Industry Dept 1992–95, under sec for public health policy Dept of Health 1995–; memb: Action Aid, Oldhamstocks Flower Show; FRSA 1995; *Recreations* family, travel, gardening, theatre, natural and built heritage; *Style*— Mrs Nicola Munro; ✉ Scottish Office, Room 166, St Andrew's House, Edinburgh EH1 3DG (☎ 0131 244 2133, fax 0131 244 2835)

MUNRO, Robert Malcolm; s of late Malcolm William Munro, of Chelmsford, and Sheila Mary, *née* Lamont (d 1983); *b* 16 May 1937; *Educ* Trinity, Mid-Essex Tech Coll, Manchester Business Sch; *m* 25 March 1961, Irene Mavis, da of late William David Percy, of Chelmsford; 2 s (Nigel Robert b 1964, Philip Spencer b 1966); *Career* branch mangr Lloyds & Scottish Finance Ltd 1958–68, asst gen mangr ELCO (Hambros Bank) 1968–72, md Williams & Glyns Leasing Co Ltd 1972–80, dir Nordic Bank Ltd 1980–83, exec dir The Union Discount Company of London plc 1983–90, banking and leasing conslt Munro Associates 1990–; chm Int Ctee ELA 1976–81; memb: Mgmnt Ctee ELA 1973–90, Cncl LEASEUROPE 1976–81; dep chm Mid Essex Hosp Servs NHS Tst 1992–, chm VRL Publishing Ltd; *Books* The Leasing Handbook (with D R Soper, 1992); *Recreations* tennis, golf, music, theatre; *Style*— Robert Munro, Esq; ✉ Munro Associates, 115 Queens Quay, 58 Upper Thames Street, London EC4V 3EH

MUNRO-FERGUSON OF RAITH AND NOVAR, Arthur Brocklehurst Luttrell; assumed name Munro-Ferguson and recognised by the Lord Lyon in the designation 'Munro-Ferguson of Raith and Novar' 1951; s of Ralph Paganel Luttrell (d 1978), and Alice, *née* Brocklehurst (d 1958); his father's mother was sis of 1 and last Viscount Novar of Raith (d 1934); *b* 10 Nov 1921; *Educ* Stowe, Trinity Coll Cambridge (BA), Univ of Edinburgh, Univ of Aberdeen (BSc); *m* 1, 1952 (m dis 1980), Jane Euphemia Beatrice, da of Lewis Reynolds (d 1940), of Natal; 2 s, 2 da; m 2, Mary Griselda, da of William Robertson (d 1935), and formerly w of John Chubb; *Career* served WWII in Far East, Royal Corps of Signals, Capt; chm Scottish Woodland Owners and Timber Growers 1977–80; *Clubs* Army and Navy; *Style*— Arthur Munro-Ferguson of Raith and Novar; ✉ Fyrish House, Evanton, Ross-shire IV16 9XL (☎ 01349 830284); Novar Estates Office, Evanton IV16 9XL (☎ 01349 830208, fax 01349 830546)

MUNRO OF LINDERTIS, Sir Alasdair Thomas Ian; 6 Bt (UK 1825), of Lindertis, Forfarshire; s of Sir (Thomas) Torquil Alphonso Munro of Lindertis, 5 Bt, JP (d 1985), and his 1 w, Beatrice Maude (d 1974), da of Robert Sanderson Whitaker, of Villa Sofia, Palermo; *b* 6 July 1927; *Educ* Landon Sch USA, Georgetown Univ Washington DC, Univ of Pennsylvania, IMEDE Lausanne Switzerland; *m* 1954, Marguerite Lillian, da of late Franklin R Loy, of Dayton, Ohio, USA; 1 s (Keith Gordon b 1959), 1 da (Karen Fiona (Mrs Robert D Macmichael, Jr) b 1956); *Heir* s, Keith Gordon Munro b 3 May 1959; *Career* importer of Scottish Antiques; dir St Andrew's Soc of Vermont; *Style*— Sir Alasdair Munro of Lindertis, Bt; ✉ River Ridge, Box 940, Waitsfield, Vermont 05673, USA

MUNSTER, 7 Earl of (UK 1831); Anthony Charles FitzClarence; also Viscount FitzClarence and Baron Tewkesbury (both UK 1831); s of 6 Earl of Munster (d 1983), and his 1 w, Monica Sheila Grayson (d 1958, having obtained a divorce 1930), da of Lt-Col Sir Mulleneux Grayson, KBE, 1 Bt; gggs of King William IV and Mrs Jordan, the actress, by whom he had ten children; *b* 21 March 1926; *Educ* St Edward's Sch Oxford; *m* 1, 1949 (m dis 1966), Louise Marguerite Diane, da of Louis Delvigne, of Liège, Belgium; 2 da (Lady Tara Frances (Lady Tara Heffler) b 1952, Lady Finola Dominique (Lady Finola Poynton) b 1953); m 2, 1966 (m dis 1979), Mrs Pamela Margaret Hyde, da of Arthur Spooner; 1 da (Lady Georgina b 1966); m 3, 1979, (Dorothy) Alexa (d 1995), yst da of Lt-Col Edward Boyd Maxwell, OBE, MC (d 1973); *Heir* none; *Career* served RN 1942–47; graphic designer 1950–79, Daily Mirror Newspapers 1957–66, IPC Newspaper Div (Sun) 1966–69, freelance 1971–79; stained glass conservator for: the Burrell Museum 1979–83, the Chapel (stained glass) Studio Herts 1983–89; FRSA 1987; *Style*— The Rt Hon the Earl of Munster; ✉ The House of Lords, London SW1

MUNTON, Timothy Alan (Tim); s of Alan Munton, of Chadwell, Melton Mowbray, Leicestershire, and Brenda Mary, *née* Cox; *b* 30 July 1965; *Educ* King Edward VIII Upper Sch Melton Mowbray Leics; *m* 20 Sept 1986, Helen Lesley, da of Paul Phillip Jones; 1 da (Camilla Dallas b 13 Aug 1988), 1 s (Harrison George Samuel b 17 Feb 1992); *Career* professional cricketer; played for: Leicestershire 2nd XI 1982–84, Nat Cricket Assoc Tour to Holland 1983, England Schools v Young Australia 1983; Warwickshire CCC: joined 1985, County Championship debut 1986, memb NatWest Trophy winning side 1989, awarded county cap 1989, Player of the Year 1990, 1991 and 1994, vice capt 1993–96, capt 1997–, winners Benson & Hedges Cup 1994, runners-up NatWest Trophy 1994, winners Britannic Assurance County Championships 1994, winners Axa Equity & Law Sunday League 1994; England: rep under 25 v India 1990, memb A tours to Pakistan 1991 and W Indies 1992, test debut v Pakistan Old Trafford 1992; brewery salesman Bass Mitchells and Butlers Sales off-seasons 1988–, sales mangr Mktg Dept Warwickshire CCC winter 1994; *Style—* Tim Munton, Esq; ✉ Warwickshire County Cricket Club, The County Ground, Edgbaston, Birmingham B5 (☎ 0121 446 4422)

MURAKAMI, Takashi; *b* 28 March 1937; *Educ* Keio Univ Tokyo (BA), Univ of California Berkeley (MBA); *m* 26 June 1965, Masako; 1 s (Gen b 1971), 2 da (Junko b 1966, Akiko b 1968); *Career* Nikko Securities Co Ltd 1960–86, md Nikko Capital Management UK Ltd 1987–; *Recreations* golf, baseball; *Style—* Takashi Murakami, Esq; ✉ Nikko Capital Management (UK) Ltd, 17 Godliman St, London EC4V 5BD (☎ 0171 246 9201, fax 0171 236 8034, telex 885879 NICAM G)

MURANKA, Tony; s of Albert Muranka, of Clayton, Bradford, West Yorkshire, and Freda Joyce, *née* Fieldhouse; *b* 21 May 1952; *Educ* Grange GS, Bradford Coll of Art (DA); *Career* advertising art dir and creative dir; Designers and Art Directors Assoc Silver award: 1978, 1984, 1987; Campaign Press Silver award 1986, Campaign Poster Silver award 1981; Creative Circle Honours Gold awards: 1984, 1985 (twice), 1986 (twice), 1987, 1988 (twice), 1989; Br TV Silver award 1985; *Recreations* Enduro competitor, playing blues guitar, canoeing, sleeping; *Style—* Tony Muranka, Esq; ✉ 23 Clarence Rd, Kew, Richmond, Surrey TW9 3NL (☎ 0181 948 7443)

MURCH, Fiona Margaret; da of John Edward King, of Llandaff, Cardiff, and Mary Margaret, *née* Beaton; *b* 14 Aug 1957; *Educ* Godolphin and Latymer Girls Sch, Howells Sch Llandaff, SOAS (Rhuvon Guest prize, BA); *m* 1980, Simon Harry, s of Henry Osborne Murch; 1 da (Rosalind Lesley Margaret b 27 Oct 1993); *Career* prodr Hausa/African section BBC World Service 1978–81, trainee BBC News 1981, prodr Newsnight 1985–86 (asst prodr 1981–85); sr prodr: BBC Breakfast Time 1986–87, Newsnight 1987–88, The Late Show 1988–89; political corr and news presenter C4 News/ITN 1992–94 (arts corr and news presenter 1989–92), dep ed Assignment BBC TV 1994–; memb NUJ 1978–; *Recreations* reading, tennis; *Style—* Ms Fiona Murch; ✉ BBC Television, White City, Wood Lane, London W12 (☎ 0181 752 7503)

MURCHISON, Prof Duncan George; s of John Kenneth Murchison (d 1934), and Maude Gertrude Mitchell Murchison, *née* Tordoff (d 1964); *b* 13 Jan 1928; *Educ* Glasgow HS, Morrisons Acad Crieff, Univ of Durham (BSc, PhD); *m* 1, 23 July 1953 (m dis 1981), Dorothy Jean, da of Edward Charlton (d 1961); 2 s (Roderick b 28 June 1957, Torquil b 22 Sept 1959), 2 da (Kate b 10 March 1962, Rona b 10 March 1962 (d 1962)); m 2, 27 July 1982 (m dis 1993), Gail Adrienne, da of Robert Hermon (d 1960); 1 s (Peter b 23 Feb 1984), 2 da (Hanna b 28 Oct 1981, Rosie b 26 July 1988); *Career* lectr Univ of Durham 1960–64; Univ of Newcastle: lectr 1964–68, sr lectr 1968–71, reader in geochemistry 1971–76, personal prof 1976–93 (now emeritus), dean Faculty of Sci 1980–83, head Dept of Geology 1982–86, pro vice chllr 1986–93; author of numerous publications in fields of reflected light microscopy, organic petrology and geochemistry; pres: Royal Microscopial Soc 1976–78, Int Cmmn on Coal Petrology 1979–83; vice pres Geological Soc 1995–97; Hon FRMS, FGS, FRSE 1973; *Recreations* fishing, philately; *Style—* Prof Duncan Murchison, FRSE; ✉ Fossil Fuels and Environmental Geochemistry, Drummond Building, University of Newcastle upon Tyne, 6 Kensington Terrace, Newcastle upon Tyne NE1 7RU (☎ 0191 222 6605)

MURCHISON, Lilian Elizabeth; da of John Alexander Murchison (d 1958), of Alness, Ross and Cromarty, Scotland, and Mary Nicholson, *née* MacIver; *b* 29 April 1936; *Educ* Invergordon Acad, Univ of Edinburgh (MB ChB), Univ of Glasgow (PhD); *Career* memb scientific staff MRC Atheroma Res Unit Glasgow 1963–68, sr tutor Royal Victoria Hosp Belfast 1969–71, lectr Dept of Therapeutics and Clinical Pharmacology Univ of Aberdeen 1971–76, conslt physician and hon clinical sr lectr Aberdeen Royal Infirmary 1976–; regnl sec Grampian and Highlands and Islands Christian Medical Fellowship, fell RSPB, fndr Friends of Scottish Monuments, memb Nat Tst (Scotland); MRCP(UK) 1970, FRCP Edinburgh 1981, FRCP London 1987; *Recreations* overseas travel, hill walking; *Style—* Miss Lilian Murchison; ✉ 9 Highgate Gardens, Aberdeen, Scotland AB11 7TZ (☎ 01224 588532); Wards 27/28, Aberdeen Royal Infirmary, Foresterhill, Aberdeen AB25 2ZN (☎ 01224 681818 ext 52258)

MURDIN, Dr Paul Geoffrey; OBE (1988); s of Robert Samuel Frederick Rodham Murdin, and Ethel, *née* Chubb; *b* 5 Jan 1942; *Educ* Trinity Sch of John Whitgift, Wadham Coll Oxford (BA), Univ of Rochester NY (PhD); *m* 8 Aug 1964, Lesley Carol, da of Frederick Milburn; 2 s (Benedict Neil b 1966, Alexander Nicholas b 1970), 1 da (Louisa Jane b 1974); *Career* princ scientific offr Royal Greenwich Observatory 1974–75 (sr res fell 1971–74), princ res scientist Anglo-Australian Observatory 1975–78; Royal Greenwich Observatory: princ scientific offr 1978–81, sr princ scientific offr and head La Palma Ops Dept 1981–87, head Astronomy Dept 1987–91, dep dir 1990–91 and 1993–94; dir and head Royal Observatory Edinburgh 1991–93; head of Astronomy Div Particle Physics and Astronomy Res Cncl 1994–, dir Sci and Microgravity Br Nat Space Centre 1994–; memb Bd of Tstees Nat Maritime Museum, pres Euro Astronomical Soc, memb Int Astronomical Union; FRAS, FInstP; *Books* Astronomers Telescope (1962), Radio Waves From Space (1964), New Astronomy (1978), Catalogue of the Universe (1979), Colours of the Stars (1984), End in Fire (1990); *Style—* Dr Paul Murdin, OBE; ✉ Particle Physics & Astronomy Research Council, Polaris House, North Star Avenue, Swindon SN2 1ET (☎ 01793 442075, fax 01793 442003)

MURDOCH, Andrew James; s of James Clive Leonard Murdoch (d 1981), and Adela Marjorie, *née* Gepp; *b* 16 Nov 1949; *Educ* Charterhouse, Pembroke Coll Cambridge (MA); *m* 1972, Lynn Hilary, da of Vernon Cecil Thompson; 1 s (Simon Scott b 16 April 1976), 1 da (Hilary Caroline Noel b 17 Dec 1979); *Career* architect; HKPA 1973–78, Eric Lyons Cunningham Partnership 1978–79, Cambridge Design 1979–80, John S Bonnington Partnership 1980–84, Fitzroy Robinson Ltd (formerly The Fitzroy Robinson Partnership) 1984– (currently chm); RIBA; *Recreations* painting, golf; *Clubs* Royal Ashdown Forest Golf; *Style—* Andrew Murdoch, Esq; ✉ Fitzroy Robinson Ltd, 77 Portland Place, London W1N 4EP (☎ 0171 636 8033)

MURDOCH, Dame Elisabeth Joy; AC (1989), DBE (1963, CBE 1961); da of Rupert Greene and Marie, *née* de Lancey Forth; *b* 1909; *m* 1928, Sir Keith Arthur Murdoch (d 1952, chm and md The Herald and Weekly Times, dir and fndr Aust Newsprint Mills Pty Ltd, dir-gen of Information for Cwlth of Australia); 1 s (Rupert Murdoch, *qv*), 3 da; *Career* pres Royal Children's Hosp Melbourne 1954–65, tstee Nat Gallery Vic 1968–76; chm: Ctee of Mgmnt Victorian Tapestry Workshops 1986–88, tstess McClelland Gallery; Hon LLD Melbourne 1982; *Style—* Dame Elisabeth Murdoch, AC, DBE; ✉ Cruden Farm, Langwarrin, Vic 3910, Australia

MURDOCH, Gordon Stuart; QC (1995); s of Ian William Murdoch (d 1978), and Margaret Henderson McLaren, *née* Scott (d 1974); *b* 7 June 1947; *Educ* Falkirk HS, Sidney Sussex Coll Cambridge (MA, LLB); *m* 27 Dec 1976, Sally Kay, da of Henry Cummings, of Ludlow, Shropshire; 2 s (Thomas b 1979, Alexander b 1982); *Career* called to the Bar Inner Temple 1970, recorder of the Crown Court 1995– (asst recorder 1991–95); memb: Family Law Bar Assoc (memb Ctee 1992–94 and 1995–), London Common Law and Commercial Bar Assoc; *Recreations* music, walking; *Style—* Gordon Murdoch, Esq, QC; ✉ 4 Paper Buildings, Temple, London EC4Y 7EX (☎ 0171 583 0816, fax 0171 353 4979)

MURDOCH, Dame Iris; DBE (1987, CBE 1976); da of Wills John Hughes Murdoch, and Irene Alice Richardson; *b* 15 July 1919; *Educ* Froebel Educnl Inst London, Badminton Sch Bristol, Somerville Coll Oxford (hon fell 1977); *m* 1956, Prof John Oliver Bayley, Warton prof of English Lit and fell St Catherine's Coll Oxford; *Career* author and philosopher; asst princ HM Treasury 1942–45, admin offr UNRRA 1945–46, Studentship Newnham Coll Cambridge 1947–48, fell and tutor St Anne's Coll Oxford 1948–63 (hon fell 1963–), lectr Royal Coll of Art 1964–67, Hon DLitt Oxon 1987, Hon LittD Cantab 1993; CLit 1987; *Books* Sartre - Romantic Rationalist (1953), Under the Net (1954), The Flight from the Enchanter (1955), The Sandcastle (1957), The Bell (1958), A Severed Head (1961, play 1963, with J B Priestley), An Unofficial Rose (1962), The Unicorn (1963), The Italian Girl (1964, play 1967, with James Saunders), The Red and the Green (1965), The Time of the Angels (1966), The Nice and The Good (1968), Bruno's Dream (1969), A Fairly Honourable Defeat (1970), The Sovereignty of Good (1970), An Accidental Man (1971), The Black Prince (1973, James Tait Black Memorial Prize, play 1989), A Word Child (1975), Henry and Cato (1976), The Fire and the Sun (1977), The Sea, the Sea (1978, Booker Prize 1978), Nuns and Soldiers (1980), Metaphysics as a Guide to Morals (1992); *Plays* The Servants and the Snow (1970), The Three Arrows (1972), Art and Eros (1980); *Poems* A Year of Birds (1978), The Philospher's Pupil (1983), The Good Apprentice (1985), Acastos (1985), The Book and the Brotherhood (1987), The Message to the Planet (1989), The Green Knight (1993), Jackson's Dilemma (1995); *Style—* Dame Iris Murdoch, DBE

MURDOCH, John; s of James Duncan Murdoch, OBE (d 1979), and Elsie Elisabeth, *née* Hardman (d 1989); *b* 1 April 1945; *Educ* Shrewsbury, Magdalen Coll Oxford (BA), King's Coll London (MPhil); *m* 1, 9 Sept 1967 (m dis 1986), Prudence Helen, da of Brig WR Smith-Windham, CBE, DSO, of Pitney, Somerset; 1 s (Thomas Duncan b 1970), 2 da (Clarissa Helen b 1972, Rosamond Elsie b 1977); m 2, 9 Nov 1990, Susan Barbara, da of late Alan Lambert, of Little Bookham, Surrey; *Career* asst keeper Dept of Art City Museum and Art Gallery Birmingham 1969–73; V&A: dep keeper Dept of Paintings 1977–85 (asst keeper 1973–77), keeper dept of prints drawings photographs and paintings 1986–89, asst dir in charge of collections 1989–93; dir Courtauld Inst Galleries 1993–; tstee: Wordsworth Library and Museum Dove Cottage, The William Morris Gallery Walthamstow; memb Cncl Walpole Soc; *Books* David Cox (1970), Byron (1974), Forty-Two English Watercolours (1977), The English Miniature (1981), Discovery of the Lake District (1984), Painters and The Derby China Works (1987); *Style—* John Murdoch, Esq; ✉ Brick Hill, Burghclere, nr Newbury, Berks (☎ 01635 278295); Courtauld Institute Galleries, Somerset House, London WC2 0RN

MURDOCH, Dr Peter Stevenson; s of John Duncan Murdoch, TD (d 1988), and Zoe Mann, *née* Hannay (d 1987); *b* 16 Oct 1950; *Educ* Haileybury, Guy's Hosp Med Sch (MB BS); *m* 28 Dec 1974, Sarah, da of Tor Ingemar Lundegard; 2 s (Neil b 1976, John b 1979); *Career* med supt Presbyterian Jt Hosp Uburu Nigeria 1975–81, sr registrar in geriatric med Royal Victoria Hosp Edinburgh 1981–82, conslt physician in geriatric med Falkirk and Dist Royal Infirmary 1983–; memb Policy Ctee Br Geriatrics Soc; tstee and vice chm Dementia Servs Devpt Tst; FRCPEd 1987, FRCPGlas 1993; *Style—* Dr Peter Murdoch; ✉ 4 Abercromby Place, Stirling, Falkirk FK8 2QP (☎ 01786 473087); Falkirk and District Royal Infirmary, Falkirk FK1 5QE (☎ 01324 624000)

MURDOCH, Robert Clive; s of Lt-Col Clive Murdoch, DSO (d 1944), and Janet Homewood, *née* Motion (d 1963); *b* 7 March 1922; *Educ* Wellington; *m* 1, 1951 (m dis 1976), Mary Anne, da of late Capt A K MacEwan; 3 da (Miranda Jane b 1954, Serena Janet b 1957, Camilla Anne b 1958); m 2, 1978, Susan Mary, da of late Eric Graham Mattingley; *Career* WWII Capt Grenadier Gds, served N Africa, Italy 1942–46; farmer 1947–; dir Hops Mktg Bd 1955–82, Checkers and Checkers Growers Ltd 1957–88; *Recreations* farming, all country pursuits; *Clubs* Farmers'; *Style—* Robert C Murdoch, Esq; ✉ Wester Hill, Linton, Maidstone, Kent ME17 4BT (☎ 01622 745277)

MURDOCH, (Keith) Rupert; AC (1984); only s of Sir Keith Murdoch, sometime chm & md The Herald & Weekly Times Ltd, Melbourne Herald, Sun-News Pictorial, Weekly Times (d 1952), by his w Dame Elisabeth Murdoch, AC, DBE, *qv*; *b* 11 March 1931; *Educ* Geelong GS, Worcester Coll Oxford (MA); *m* 1, 1956 (m dis); 1 da (Pru); m 2, 1967, Anna Maria, da of J Torv, of Scotland; 2 s (Lachlan, James), 1 da (Elisabeth m Elkin Kwesi Pianim); *Career* publisher; chm and chief exec The News Corporation Ltd, chm and pres News America Publishing Inc, jt chm Ansett Transport Industries 1982–92 (jt chief exec and md 1979–82), chm and chief exec offr 20th Century Fox until 1996 (currently dir); dir: News International, dir Harper Collins Publishers Ltd 1989–, British Sky Broadcasting plc 1990–; UK newspapers owned incl The Sun and The Times; hon fell Worcester Coll Oxford 1982–; *Style—* Rupert Murdoch, Esq, AC; ✉ 2 Holt St, Sydney, NSW 2000, Australia; c/o News America Inc, 1211 Avenue of the Americas, New York 10036, USA; Times Newspapers Limited, PO Box 495, Virginia St, London E1 9XY; 20th Century Fox, 10201, W Pico Blvd, Los Angeles 90035, USA

MURDOCK, Christopher; s of Dr Charles Rutherford Murdock (d 1968), and Eirene Nolan, *née* Baird; *b* 15 Aug 1946; *Educ* Brackenber House Belfast, Portora Royal Sch Enniskillen; *m* 31 Jan 1970, Dorothy Rosemary Richardson; 2 s (Christopher Jeremy b 1973, Antony John b 1975), 1 da (Rosemary Sarah Alexandra b 1980); *Career* joined NHS 1965, asst dist admin offr Armagh and Dungannon Dist 1974–75, dist personnel offr S Belfast Dist 1975–76, asst dist admin offr E Belfast and Castlereagh Dist 1976–84; gp admin Purdysburn Unit of Mgmnt 1984–89, sr mangr Eastern Health and Social Services Bd 1989–, currently on attachment to DHSS Mgmnt Exec as sr project mangr; MHSM, DipHSM, MIMgt; *Recreations* photography, supporting children's equestrian interests, Donegal (Inishowen), wines; *Clubs* IEC Wine Society; *Style—* Christopher Murdock, Esq; ✉ c/o Integration of Nursing and Midwifery Education with Higher Educaton Project Board for Northern Ireland, Eastern Area College of Nursing (Northside), The Ulster Hospital, Dundonald, Belfast BT16 0RH (☎ 01232 550411); Ballyhomra House, Comber Road, Hillsborough, Co Down BT26 6NA; Ballybrack Lodge, Moville, Co Donegal, Ireland

MURE, Kenneth Nisbet; QC (Scot 1989); s of late Robert Mure, and Katherine Mure; *b* 11 April 1947; *Educ* Glasgow HS, Univ of Glasgow (MA, LLB); *Career* admitted to the Scots Bar 1975, called to the English Bar Gray's Inn 1990; lectr in Law Faculty Univ of Glasgow 1971–83; temp sheriff Scotland 1982–; FTII 1971; *Style—* Kenneth Mure, Esq, QC; ✉ Advocates' Library, Edinburgh EH1 1RF (☎ 0131 226 5071)

MURFIN, Dr David Edward; s of Leslie Walter Murfin (d 1989), and Elizabeth Ann, *née* Jones (d 1984); *b* 15 June 1946; *Educ* Gowerton Boys' GS Swansea, King's Coll London (MB BS, DRCOG, MRCGP), St George's Hosp London; *m* 1972, Ann Margaret, da of Mervyn Henry Lewis; 1 da (Rhian Nicola b 5 Dec 1973), 1 s (Owen David b 16 April 1976); *Career* house surgn St George's Hosp London 1970–71, house physician Peterborough Dist Hosp 1971; SHO: in obstetrics St Paul's Hosp Cheltenham 1971–72, in paediatrics Oldchurch Hosp Romford 1972, in paediatrics and casualty Queen Elizabeth Hosp Barbados 1972–73, in psychiatry Swansea 1974; princ in gen practice 1974–; RCGP: memb SW Wales Faculty 1976–, faculty sec 1981–86, faculty chm 1987–90, faculty rep on Cncl 1984–90 and 1993–, chm Servs to Membs and Faculties Div 1987–90, memb Editorial Bd 1988–, hon ed Connection 1993–, vice chm Cncl 1994–; gen practice trainer 1980–, gen practice advsr to Assoc of the Br Pharmaceutical Indust 1991–; author of various pubns in learned jls; FRCGP 1985; *Recreations* reading, walking, cycling; *Style*— Dr David Murfin; ✉ Brynteg Surgery, Brynmawr Avenue, Ammanford, Dyfed SA18 2DA (☎ 01269 592058, fax 01269 595845)

MURFITT, Catriona Anne Campbell; da of Dr Alfred Ian Campbell Murfitt (d 1983), and Anne, *née* Ritchie; *b* 16 Jan 1958; *Educ* St Mary's Convent Sch Ascot, Leicester Poly Sch of Law (BA); *Career* called to the Bar Gray's Inn 1981; in practice SE Circuit 1982–; memb Family Law Bar Assoc; FRSA; *Recreations* skiing, gardening, art, sacred choral music; *Style*— Miss Catriona Murfitt; ✉ 1 Mitre Court Buildings, Temple, London EC4 (☎ 0171 797 7070)

MURIE, John Andrew; s of John Andrew Murie, of Airdrie, and Jessie, *née* Sutherland; *b* 7 Aug 1949; *Educ* Univ of Glasgow (BSc, MB ChB, MD), Univ of Minnesota Minneapolis USA, Univ of Oxford (MA); *m* 7 Sept 1977, Edythe, da of James Munn, of Glasgow; 1 da (Emma Jane b 1986); *Career* clinical reader in surgery Univ of Oxford 1984–89, conslt surgn John Radcliffe Hosp Oxford 1984–89, fell Green Coll Oxford 1984–89, clinical dir of surgery and conslt surgn The Royal Infirmary of Edinburgh 1989–, hon sr lectr in surgery Univ of Edinburgh 1989–, jt sr ed The British Journal of Surgery 1996– (review ed 1989–96); hon editorial sec Assoc of Surgeons of GB and Ireland 1996–; FRCPS 1979, FRCSEd 1993; *Recreations* golf, swimming, food and wine; *Style*— John Murie, Esq; ✉ 105 Caiyside, Edinburgh EH10 7HR (☎ 0131 445 3334); Dept of Surgery, The Royal Infirmary, 1 Lauriston Place, Edinburgh EH3 9YW (☎ 0131 536 1613, fax 0131 536 3927); BUPA, Murrayfield Hospital, 122 Corstorphine Rd, Edinburgh EH12 6UD (☎ 0131 334 0363, fax 0131 334 7338, telex 727442 UNIVED G)

MURISON, Robert Fraser; OBE (1978), QPM (1971), DL (Fife 1975); s of William Murison (d 1937); *b* 15 Feb 1919; *Educ* Dunfermline HS, Univ of Glasgow; *m* 1948, Isobel Stirrat, *née* Tennent; 2 da; *Career* serv WWII Black Watch and 8 Gurkha Rifles 1942–46, Capt India and Sumatra; police offr Lanarkshire Constabulary 1937–42 and 1946–63, dep cmdt Scottish Police Coll 1963–65, chief constable Fife 1965–84, N Zone Home Def Police Cdr Designate 1974–84; vice-pres Fife Girl Guides, memb Fife Ctee British Red Cross; *Recreations* gardening, amateur radio; *Style*— Robert F Murison, Esq, OBE, QPM, DL; ✉ 2 Abbots Walk, Kirkcaldy, Fife KY2 5NL (☎ 01592 262436)

MURLEY, Sir Reginald Sydney; KBE (1979), TD (1948); s of Sydney Herbert Murley (d 1968), of New York, and Beatrice Maud, *née* Baylis (d 1951); *b* 2 Aug 1916; *Educ* Dulwich, St Bartholomew's Hosp Univ of London (MB BS, MS); *m* 1 Feb 1947, Daphne, da of Ralph Eddowes Garrod (d 1964); 3 s (David Peter b 1949, Gavin Michael b 1951, Anthony Jonathan b 1957), 3 da (Susan Elizabeth Butler (step da) b 1942, Jennifer Jane b 1948, Hilary Daphne b 1953); *Career* served WWII RAMC, Field Units, Surgn to No 1 and 2 Maxillofacial Surgical Units; No 53 Field Surgical Unit, Maj 1939–45, TA Middle E, E Africa, Italy, NW Europe; anatomy demonstrator 1946, surgical chief asst Bart's 1946–49; conslt surgeon: St Albans Hosp 1947–80, Royal Northern Hosp 1952–80; hon conslt surgn Bart's 1979–; Mackenzie Mackinnon res fell RCP and RCS, Cattlin res fell Bart's 1950–51; pres: RCS 1977–80, Hunterian Soc 1970, Med Soc London 1982, Harveian Soc 1983, John Charnley Tst 1983–; Hunterian Soc orator 1978; hon fell: RACS 1979, Coll of Surgns SA 1979, RCS in Ireland 1980; hon memb: Italian Surgical Soc 1979, Polish Surgical Soc 1983, Br Assoc of Plastic Surgns 1983, Br Assoc of Clinical Anatomists 1983, Reading Pathological Soc 1985, Int Soc of Surgery 1991, Independent Doctors' Forum 1995; Hon Freeman Worshipful Co of Barbers; Hon FDS RCS 1980; vice-pres Int Soc of Surgery 1985–86; RCS: Hunterian prof 1950, orator 1981, Bradshaw lectr 1981; Pybus lecture and medal N of Eng Surgical Soc 1975, Syme orator RACS 1979, Sir Thomas and Lady Edith Williams lecture and medal Belfast 1979, Mitchener lectr Royal Army Med Coll 1980 and 1993; pres Fellowship for Freedom in Med 1972–86, memb Cncl Freedom Assoc 1982–, patron Jagiellonian Tst, memb Cncl Health and Welfare Unit Inst of Economic Affairs 1986–, memb Cncl Social Affairs Unit 1986–; tstee Migraine Tst 1995–, patron of Youth and Family Concern 1984–; Liveryman Worshipful Soc of Apothecaries; *Publications* Surgical Roots and Branches (autobiography, 1990), The Case Books of John Honter, FRS (co-ed, 1993); author of various med and surgical papers on thyroid, breast, vascular, and salivary diseases; contribs to: surgical textbooks, papers on medical economics and surgery; MRCS 1939, LRCP 1939, FRCS 1946, MS 1948; *Recreations* reading, history & economics, gardening, music; *Clubs* Royal Automobile; *Style*— Sir Reginald Murley, KBE, TD; ✉ Cobden Hill House, 63 Cobden Hill, Radlett, Herts WD7 7JN; Consulting Suite, Wellington Hospital, Wellington Place NW8 9LE

MURNAGHAN, Dermot John; s of Vincent Patrick George Murnaghan, of Wisbech, and Wendy, *née* Bush; *b* 26 Dec 1957; *Educ* Sullivan Upper Sch Holywood Co Down, Univ of Sussex (BA, MA), City Univ (Postgrad Dip in Journalism); *m* Maria, da of Patrick Keegan; 1 da (Kitty Niamh b 13 March 1992); *Career* reporter: Coventry Evening Telegraph 1984–85, The Business Programme (Channel 4) 1985–88; corr/presenter Euro Business Channel 1988–89, presenter Channel 4 Daily 1989–90, newscaster ITN 1990–, presenter The Big Story (ITV) 1993–; *Documentaries* A Whale of a Mess (Channel 4) Against the Odds (Channel 4); *Recreations* racing, tennis, running, theatre; *Style*— Dermot Murnaghan, Esq; ✉ ITN, 200 Gray's Inn Road, London WC1 8XZ (☎ 0171 833 3000)

MUROFUSHI, Minoru; *b* 22 Sept 1931; *m*; 1 da; *Career* ITOCHU Corporation Japan (formerly known as C Itoh & Co Ltd): joined 1956, various positions rising to vice pres US ops New York 1963–72, returned Tokyo 1972, gen mangr Overseas Admin and Corp Project Planning and Devpt Depts 1977–84, main bd dir 1985–, chief exec offr C Itoh & Co (America) NY 1986–89, returned Tokyo 1989, sr md 1989–90, pres and chief exec offr 1990–; non-exec dir HSBC Holdings plc 1992–; chm: Int Affrs Ctee Tokyo C of C and Industry, Ctee on Corp Laws and Regulations Keizai Doyukai (Japan Assoc of Corporate Execs), Japan-N America Ctee Keidanren (Japan Fedn of Economic Orgns); vice chm The Japan Foreign Trade Cncl; memb Exec Ctee Trilateral Cmmn; *Recreations* golf; *Clubs* Tokyo Golf, Three Hundred (Tokyo); *Style*— M Murofushi, Esq; ✉ Itochu Corporation, 5–1 Kita Aoyama 2–chome, Minato-ku, Tokyo 107, Japan (☎ 00 81 3 3497 2020)

MURPHY, Alan Denis; s of James Denis Murphy (d 1984), of Norwich, and Ruby Lilian, *née* Aaron (d 1995); *b* 13 March 1939; *Educ* St Joseph's Coll Beulah Hill, Rugby Coll of Engrg (Dip in Electrical Engrg); *m* 23 Feb 1963, Kay Anita, da of Cecil Wakelin; 1 s (Neil Andrew b 27 June 1965), 1 da (Nicola Joanne b 29 June 1969); *Career* commercial engr AEI (Rugby) Ltd steelworks automation Port Talbot 1961–62, devpt engrg GEC (Telecoms) Ltd Coventry 1962–66, project engr Elliott Process Automation Leicester 1966–69, gen mangr Leicester Automation Centre Leicester Poly (now de Montfort Univ) 1969–73, conslt PA Management Birmingham 1973–75, gp mangr PA Technology Cambridge 1976–78; Cambridge Consultants Ltd advanced mfrg technol: gp mangr 1978–81, mktg mangr 1981–83, bd/mktg dir 1983–; FIEE 1984, FIMC 1986; *Publications* Packaging for the Environment (co-author, 1991); *Recreations* music, golf, building and restoring classic cars; *Clubs* Brampton Park Golf; *Style*— Alan Murphy, Esq; ✉ Cambridge Consultants, Science Park, Milton Road, Cambridge CB4 4DW (☎ 01223 420024, fax 01223 423373, mobile 0385 351452)

MURPHY, Sheriff Andrew John; s of Robert James Murphy, of Glasgow, and Robina, *née* Scott; *b* 16 Jan 1946; *Educ* Allan Glen's Sch Glasgow, Univ of Edinburgh (MA, LLB); *m* 20 Nov 1980, Susan Margaret, da of Dr Peter Dewar Thomson, OBE, of Dingwall; 2 s (Patrick Andrew Sean b 1983, Simon Peter Scott b 1987), 2 da (Lucy Jane Robina b 1978, Sarah Belle Margaret b 1979); *Career* 2 Lt RA (TA) 1971–73, Flt Lt RAF 1973–75; admitted Faculty of Advocates and called to the Bar Scotland 1970, called to the Bar Middle Temple 1990; crown counsel Hong Kong 1975–79, standing jr counsel to Registrar Gen for Scotland 1982–85, temp Sheriff 1983–85; Sheriff: of Grampian Highlands and Islands at Peterhead and Banff 1985–91, of Tayside Central and Fife 1991–; ordained deacon (NSM), hon curate St Margaret of Scotland Aberdeen 1995–; *Style*— Sheriff Andrew Murphy; ✉ Sheriff's Chambers, Sheriff Court House, Main Street, Camelon, Falkirk FK1 4AR

MURPHY, Prof Brian; s of James Murphy (d 1987), of Huddersfield, and Winifred Helen, *née* Ellis (d 1990); *b* 20 May 1940; *Educ* Rotherham GS, Univ of Lancaster (MSc), Open Univ (BA); *m* 18 Dec 1982, Vivienne; *Career* rating and auditing asst Rotherham County Borough 1956–61, accountancy and auditing asst Castleford Borough Council 1961–63, head of Accountancy Section West Riding County Council 1963–64, sr accountant Oxford County Borough Council 1964–66, lectr in management accountancy Worcester Tech Coll 1966–69; Univ of Huddersfield (formerly Huddersfield Poly): sr lectr in management accountancy 1969–70, princ lectr 1970–71, head of Accountancy Div 1971–72, head of Dept of Accountancy and Fin 1972–87, prof (for life) 1987–; md BWD Rensburg Unit Trust Managers Limited 1988–; former dir Clifton Language Services Ltd; former dir and co sec: Double M Construction Ltd, Daleside Developments Ltd; memb: Inst of Public Finance and Accountancy 1963, Chartered Inst of Cost and Management Accountants 1971; fell Assoc of Certified Accountants 1982; memb The Securities Inst 1992; *Books* Management Accounting (3 edn, 1986); *Recreations* golf, classic cars, cycling; *Style*— Prof Brian Murphy

MURPHY, Brian Arthur; s of Arthur Albert Murphy (d 1982), and Constance Margaret, *née* Young; *b* 3 May 1951; *Educ* Emanuel Sch London, Keble Coll Oxford (BA); *m* 30 April 1977, Jane, da of John Champion Stevenson, of Atherstone, Warks; 1 s (Giles b 10 March 1980), 1 da (Leila b 14 June 1982); *Career* slr, dep head legal servs Allied Lyons plc 1982, sr assoc Ashurst Morris Crisp 1989; Freeman City of London, Liveryman Worshipful Co of Founders; memb Law Soc 1976; *Clubs* Ski Club of GB; *Style*— Brian Murphy, Esq; ✉ The Old Rectory, Little Brickhill, Bucks MK17 9NA (☎ 0171 638 1111, fax 0171 972 7990)

MURPHY, Brian Gordon; s of Albert Gordon Murphy, and Doris Edna Murphy; *b* 18 Oct 1940; *Educ* Mill Hill Sch; *m* 3 Nov 1973, Judith Ann, da of Frederick Robert Parkinson; *Career* admitted slr 1966, ptnr Knapp Fishers Westminster 1968–87, ptnr Farrer and Co Lincoln's Inn Fields 1987–92, building societies ombudsman 1992–; memb Cncl Law Soc 1982–93, pres City of Westminster Law Soc 1983–84, chm Employment Law Ctee Law Soc 1987–90, pt/t industl tribunal chm 1991–92, cncl memb Incorporated Cncl of Law Reporting for England and Wales 1992–96; *Recreations* golf, theatre, photography, travel; *Clubs* Phyllis Court (Henley); *Style*— Brian Murphy, Esq; ✉ Building Societies Ombudsman, Millbank Tower, Millbank, London SW1P 4XS (☎ 0171 931 0044, fax 0171 931 8485)

MURPHY, Hon Christopher Philip Yorke; s of Philip John Murphy, and Dorothy Betty Murphy; *b* 20 April 1947; *Educ* Devonport HS, Queen's Coll Oxford (MA); *m* 1969, Sandra Gillian, da of William John Ashton; *Career* former assoc dir D'Arcy MacManus & Masius; pres Oxford Univ Cons Assoc 1967, held various Cons Party offices 1968–72, parish cncllr Windlesham Surrey 1972–76, Parly candidate (C) Bethnal Green and Bow Feb and Oct 1974, MP (C) Welwyn Hatfield 1979–87, memb Select Ctee on Statutory Instruments 1980–87 (and its representative on Cwlth Delegated Legislation Ctee 1980–87); vice chm: Cons Parly Urban and New Town Affairs Ctee 1980–87, Cons Parly Arts and Heritage Ctee 1981–86; UK delegate to Cncl of Europe/WEU 1983–87; vice pres: C of E Artistic Heritage Cmmn 1984–87, C of E Youth and Drugs Cmmn 1986–87; memb Chief Pleas of Sark 1989–90, vice pres Int Ctee of Chief Pleas 1989–90; hon sec La Société Serequiaise 1988–90; memb: Cncl La Société Guernesiaise 1988–90, Arts Cncl of Bailiwick of Guernsey 1988–90; sec Sodor and Man Diocesan Synod and Bishop's advsr 1991–, chapter clerk St German's Cathedral 1992–, diocesan sec 1993–; memb: Nat Ctee for 900 Anniversary of Domesday Book 1986; life memb Cwlth Parly Assoc; Freeman City of London, Hon Citizen of Cork; FRSA; *Recreations* arts, heritage, travel, conservation, politics, walking, horticulture; *Clubs* Oxford Union; *Style*— Hon Christopher Murphy; ✉ Cooil Voorath, The Cronk, Ballaugh, Isle of Man

MURPHY, Prof Elaine; da of Roger Lawson (d 1978), of Nottingham, and Nell, *née* Allitt; *b* 16 Jan 1947; *Educ* West Bridgford GS Nottingham, Univ of Manchester Med Sch (MB ChB, MD, research prize RCPsych); *m* 1969, John Matthew Murphy, *qv*, s of Daniel Murphy (d 1975), of Ilford, Essex; *Career* psychiatric trg London Teaching Hosps, subsequently research registrar Bedford Coll London, conslt psychiatrist NE Thames RHA 1981–83, prof of old age psychiatry Univ of London 1983–; vice chm Mental Health Act Cmmn 1987–94, chm City and Hackney Community Servs NHS Tst 1995–; Dr (hc) Univ of Stirling 1993; FRCPsych; *Books* After the Asylums (1991), Dementia and Mental Illness in Older People (2 edn 1993), The Falling Shadow (with Blom-Cooper and Hally, 1995); *Recreations* Italy, opera, furniture (medieval to 17th century); *Style*— Prof Elaine Murphy; ✉ City and Hackney Community Services NHS Trust, St Leonard's Primary Care Centre, Nuttall Street, London N1 (☎ 0171 601 7755)

MURPHY, Elizabeth (Liz); da of James Murphy (d 1981), and Elizabeth, *née* Mair; *b* 14 Nov 1959; *Educ* Sacred Heart HS Paisley, St Margaret's Secdy Sch Paisley, Napier Coll of Commerce (NCTJ Proficiency Cert, ESSO Student Journalist of the Year Special Prize, NCTJ Year Prize); *m* 19 Sept 1992, Steven Le Comber, s of Peter Le Comber; *Career* reporter and features writer Paisley Daily Express 1978–83; features writer: Evening Express Aberdeen 1983–85, Woman's Own London 1985–87; features ed Best 1988–90 (dep features ed 1987–88), assoc ed Me March-Nov 1990, dep ed Best 1990–92, freelance writer (incl actg practicals co-ordinator Woman Jan-June 1993, actg dep ed TV Times 1993–94), ed TV Times 1994–; Young Journalist of the Year for 1984 Scottish Press Awards 1985; memb Br Soc of Magazine Eds 1994; *Recreations* watching TV (especially soaps), swimming, skiing; *Style*— Ms Liz Murphy; ✉ TV Times, King's Reach Tower, Stamford Street, London SE1 9LS (☎ 0171 261 7814, fax 0171 261 7777)

MURPHY, Gerald James; JP; s of James Murphy (d 1956), and Agnes Murphy, *née* Youles; *Educ* Finchley GS, The Architectural Association Sch of Architecture (AADipl); *Career* fndr ptnr architectural practice Gerald Murphy & Ptnrs 1962, after amalgamation sr ptnr Gerald Murphy Burles Newton & Ptnrs; works of note incl: Brentwood Cathedral, New Docklands Church, conversion of Wembley Stadium for Pope's visit; non-exec dir of Enfield & Haringey Health Authy 1993–; Cons Pty candidate 1973–78, chm London N Euro Constituency Cncl 1978–84, former int pres Serra Int, vice chm Issues Ctee Catholic Union of GB; Freeman City of London; KCSG, kt Grand Cross of the Religious Order of the Holy Sepulchre of Jerusalem; ARIBA, ACIArb; *Recreations* filming, painting; *Style*— Gerald J Murphy, JP; ✉ 8 Highgate High St, London N6 5JL (☎ 0181 341 1277)

MURPHY, Gerard; *Career* actor; assoc dir Independent Radio Drama Co; *Theatre* incl: title role in Pericles (Theatre Royal Stratford East), Brachiano in The White Devil (Greenwich), Goetz in The Devil and the Good Lord (Lyric Hammersmith), Theseus in Phaedra (Old Vic and West End), Athdark in The Saxon Shore (Almeida), Elis in Easter (Haymarket Leicester), Jesus in Broken Nails (St Peter's Cathedral Belfast); as assoc artist of RSC: Johnny Boyle in Juno and the Paycock, Frank in The Witch of Edmonton, Prince Hal in Henry IV Parts I and II, Sam Mowbray in Country Dancing, Oberon in A Midsummer Night's Dream, Palamon in Two Noble Kinsmen, Roger in The Balcony, Solange in The Maids, Green Eyes in Deathwatch, Graham Cutter in Speculators, title role in Doctor Faustus, Petruchio in The Taming of the Shrew, Oedipus in The Theban

Plays; as director work incl: Deathwatch (co-dir, RSC Barbican), The Maids (co-dir, RSC Barbican), Edward II (RSC Swan Theatre Stratford-upon-Avon and Barbican London); most recently The Atheists Tragedy (Birmingham Rep) 1995; *Television* incl: Roy in Catchpenny Twist (BBC), George in The Best of Friends (BBC), Jack Clitheroe in The Plough and the Stars (BBC), Rory in My Son, My Son (BBC series), Gilberto in Facing The Sun (Thames), title role in Keats (2 plays, BBC), Inspector Snow in Charteris and Caldicott (BBC series), Richard in Silver Nemesis (Dr Who 25th anniversary series); most recently McCallum (STV) 1995, Taggart (STV) 1995; narration on Nicaragua South Bank Show (LWT); *Films* incl: Father Larkin in Sacred Hearts (Channel 4), Girl In A Swing (Minedream Ltd); most recently Waterworld (Universal) 1995, Commission (Academy Films) 1995; *Radio* incl: In The Jungle of the Cities (BBC Radio 3 drama), The Narrator in The Lord of the Rings (BBC Radio 4 drama), title role in The Elephant Man (BBC Radio 4 drama), Hugo Ball in Dada and Co (BBC Radio 4), Giving In (BBC Radio short story reading), Goetz in The Devil and the God Almighty (BBC Radio 4), Danton in Danton's Death (BBC Radio 4), The Drunkard (BBC Radio morning story), Monday, Tuesday (BBC Radio morning story), Ball The Wall (BBC Radio short story reading), Woman in Blue (BBC Radio 4), Mark Antony in Julius Caesar (BBC Radio 3 drama), John Clare in The Fool (BBC Radio 3 Drama), Prometheus in Seize The Fire (BBC Radio drama), Jack in The Belle of Belfast City (BBC Radio 4 drama), Charlie Marlow in Heart of Darkness, Douglas in Valley of Fear (both Ind Radio drama), Auden - Lyric and Form (poetry readings, BBC Radio 3), Shelley (BBC Radio 3), title role in The Real Don Juan (BBC Radio 3), Atahuallpa in Royal Hunt of the Sun (World Service), narrator of Children of the Dead End (BBC Radio 4), Blue Glass and the Sun God (BBC Radio 3), Prisoners of Honour (BBC Radio 4 series), Rev Sam Hawthorne in Balleylenon (BBC Radio 4 Drama), title role in Barry Lyndon (BBC Radio 4 Drama), Something Misunderstood (Unique Broadcasting for Radio 4), The Nuremberg Trials (BBC Radio 4); *Style*— Gerard Murphy, Esq; ✉ c/o Mayer & Eden Ltd, 34 Kingly Court, London W1R 5LE (☎ 0171 434 1242, fax 0171 287 5834)

MURPHY, Ian Patrick; QC (1992); s of Patrick Murphy, of Cardiff, and Irene Grace, *née* Hooper; *b* 1 July 1949; *Educ* St Illtyd's Coll Cardiff, LSE (LLB); *m* 31 Aug 1974, Penelope Gay, da of Gerald Hugh-Smith (d 1965), of Hove, Sussex; 2 da (Anna b 1982, Charlotte b 1984); *Career* chartering clerk Baltic Exchange 1970–71, called to the Bar 1972, recorder of the Crown Ct 1990– (asst recorder 1986–90), asst cmmr to the Parly Boundary Cmmr for Wales 1996–; *Recreations* golf, skiing, rugby and cricket; *Clubs* Royal Porthcawl GC, Cardiff County; *Style*— Ian Murphy, Esq, QC; ✉ Chambers, 9 Park Place, Cardiff CF1 3DP (☎ 01222 382731, fax 01222 222542)

MURPHY, Rev Canon John Gervase Maurice Walker (Gerry); LVO (1987); s of Capt William Stafford Murphy, MC (d 1951), of Bangor, NI, and Yvonne Iris, *née* Wilson (d 1971); *b* 20 Aug 1926; *Educ* Methodist Coll Belfast, Univ of Dublin (BA, MA); *m* 1957, Joy Hilda Miriam, da of Canon T L Livermore, MA, of Heacham; 5 da (Maryan (Mrs Laurence Piano), Desiree (Mrs James Pennington), Nicola (Mrs Gary Templeton), Geraldine (Mrs Stephen Kadera), Felicity); *Career* ordained Church of Ireland 1952, curate Lurgan 1952–55; Royal Army Chaplains Dept 1955–77; sr chaplain: Br Cwlth Bde 1964–67, RMA Sandhurst 1971–73; asst chaplain gen Germany: BAOR 1973–75, SEAT Dist 1975–77; bishop's chaplain to holidaymakers Norfolk Broads; rural dean: Blofield 1978–79, Heacham and Rising 1985–87; rector of the Falkland Is and Christ Church Cathedral Stanley 1987–91, hon canon Norwich 1987– (canon emeritus 1987); rector of Sandringham Gp of Parishes and domestic chaplain to HM The Queen 1979–87, chaplain to HM The Queen 1987–96 (extra chaplain to HM The Queen 1996–), chaplain of the Chapels Royal of St Peter ad Vincula and St John the Evangelist within HM Tower of London 1991–96; chaplain to Lord Mayor of London 1993–94, hon fell and vice pres Br Assoc for Physical Trg; *Recreations* sports (played int rugby for Ireland 1952/54/58, Barbarians 1957); *Clubs* London Irish RFC, Public Sch Wanderers RFC, East India (hon chaplain); *Style*— The Rev Canon Gerry Murphy, LVO; ✉ Saffron Close, Ringstead Road, Heacham, Norfolk PE31 7JA (☎ 01485 572351)

MURPHY, John Matthew; s of Daniel Murphy (d 1975), of Ilford, Essex, and Kathleen, *née* O'Carroll; *b* 20 Feb 1944; *Educ* St Ignatius Coll, Univ of Manchester (BA), Brunel Univ (MTech Business Admin); *m* 1969, Prof Elaine Murphy, *qv*, da of Roger Lawson (d 1978), of Nottingham; *Career* mgmnt trainee rising to corp planner Leesona Ltd Heywood Lancs and Leesona Corporation Warwick Rhode Island USA 1965–70, corp planner Dunlop Ltd London 1970–74, fndr chm Interbrand Group plc London (also NY, Chicago, San Francisco, Sydney, Tokyo, Seoul, Singapore, Hamburg, Milan and Johannesburg) 1974–96 (conslt 1996–); visiting prof of mktg Open Univ 1993–; Freeman City of Cincinnati USA; *Books* Branding - a Key Marketing Tool (ed, 1985), How to Design Trade Marks and Logos (with M Rowe, 1988), Brand Valuation (ed, 1989), Brand Strategy (1990); *Recreations* antiques, gardening, travel; *Style*— John Murphy, Esq; ✉ The Grange, Brockdish, Diss, Norfolk IP21 4JE (☎ 01379 668238); Interbrand Group plc, 40 Long Acre, Covent Garden, London WC2E 9JT (☎ 0171 240 4040, fax 0171 836 0516)

MURPHY, John Michael Murphy; *b* 7 Sept 1945; *Career* artist; *Solo Exhibitions* Serpentine Gallery London 1971, Museum of Modern Art Oxford 1972, Jack Wendler Gallery London 1973, Selected Works (Museum of Modern Art Oxford) 1975, Nature Morte - Collected Works (The New Gallery Inst of Contemporary Art London) 1976, An Art of Exhchange - Featuring The Picture Frame or Egg Note (Barry Barker Gallery London 1976, The Work of Art Is...AJ JM (Barry Barker Gallery London) 1977, Galerie Arno Kohnen Dusseldorf 1978, Desire Not Geometry (Barry Barker Gallery London) 1979, Lesson on Money (Art Projects Melbourne) 1980, Objects of Desire (Piwna Warsaw) 1980, John Murphy (Arts Cncl of NI Gallery Belfast) 1981, (D) (E) (L) (T) (A) (The Orchard Gallery Dery NI) 1982, The Nocturnal Inscription Represents...(Vereniging voor het Museum van Hedendaagse Kunst Gent) 1983, Beyond the Fixing of Appearances (Serpentine Gallery London) 1984, Stuck in the Milky Way (Lisson Gallery London) 1985, Whitechapel Art Gallery London 1987–88, Arnolfini Gallery Bristol 1988, Instruments of Attack (Galerie Yvon Lambert Paris) 1988, Galeria Marga Paz Madrid 1988, Phoenix - Sagitta - Horologium - Reticulum - Libra - Ursa Major (Asher/Faure Gallery Los Angeles) 1989, Silent Vertigo (Lisson Gallery London) 1990, John Weber Gallery NY 1991, Christine Burgin Gallery NY 1991, Remains to be Seen (John Weber Gallery NYC) 1992, No Representation, No Intention, No Trace Yvon Lambert Paris) 1992, The Sense of Resemblance (Lisson Gallery) 1992, The Tone that Calls the Song (Galerie Bruges la Morte Bruges) 1992, Lisson Gallery London 1996, A Portrait of the Artist as a Deaf Man Douglas Hyde Gallery Dublin 1996, Galerie de Luxembourg 1996; *Gp Exhibitions* incl: London Now in Berlin (Akademie der Kunste Berlin) 1971, Drawing (Museum of Modern Art Oxford) 1972, Contemporary Art Society Recent Acquisitions (Gulbenkian Hall RCA Gallery London) 1975, Eight British Artists (C A Y C Buenos Aires) 1976, Art - Museum des Geldes (Stadliche Kunsthalle Dusseldorf) 1978, Europa '79 (Kunst der 80er Jahre Stuttgart) 1979, Lang'uages (Third Eye Centre Glasgow) 1979, British Art 1940–80 (Hayward Gallery London) 1980, Through the Summer (Lisson Gallery London) 1981, Collazione Inglese (Scuola di San Pasquale Venice) 1982, Who's Afraid of Red Yellow and Blue (Arnolofini Gallery Bristol) 1985, L'Indifferent (Jon Hansard Gallery Southampton) 1985, Falls the Shadow Recent British and European Art (Hayward Gallery London) 1986, Aperto '86 XLII Biennale di Venezia 1986, Made in London (Jack Shainman Gallery Washington DC and NY) 1987–88, British Art - the Literate Link (Asher/Faure Gallery Los Angeles) 1988, Blasphemies Ecstasies Cries (Serpentine Gallery London) 1989, Now for the Future - Purchases for the Arts Council Collection since 1984 (Hayward Gallery London) 1990, De Pictura (Galerie Bruges la morte Brugge) 1990, John Weber Gallery NY 1991, Les Couleurs de l'argent (Musée de la Poste Paris) 1991, Out of Sight, Out of Mind (Lisson Gallery London) 1993, The Sublime Void (or the Memory of the Imagination) (Koninklijk Museum voor Schone Kunsten Antwerpen) 1993, Paula Rego John Murphy and Avis Newman (Saatchi Gallery London) 1996, Das Abenteuer Der Malerei (Kunstverein für die Rheinlande, Westfalen, Dusseldorf and Stuttgart) 1996; work represented in: numerous articles and reviews for both nat and trade magazines, exhibition catalogues and books incl New British Art in the Saatchi Collection (Allistair Hicks, 1989); *Style*— John Murphy, Esq; ✉ Lisson Gallery, 67 Lisson St, London NW1 5DA (☎ 0171 724 2739, fax 0171 724 7124)

MURPHY, John Terence; s of Francis Joseph Murphy, of Blandford St Mary, Dorset, and Barbara Pauline, *née* Daft; *b* 16 Jan 1948; *Educ* Downside, Magdalen Coll Oxford (MA); *m* 11 Sept 1981, Jocelyn, da of Joseph Wang (d 1986), of Honiara, Guadalcanal, Solomon Islands; 1 da (Georgia Elizabeth b 1988); *Career* admitted slr 1971; ptnr: Crawley & de Reya 1976–78, Bartletts de Reya 1978–88, Theodore Goddard 1988–92; chm The International Business Library Ltd 1993–; memb: Law Soc Working Pty on Central and E Europe, Int Cncl for New Initiatives in East/West Cooperation, DTI Soviet Working Pty on Consortia Jt Ventures, Int C of C Ctee on E Euro Rels; vice chm Br-Polish Legal Assoc, sec Br-Hungarian Legal Assoc, memb Br Advsy Bd to Know How Funds; *Books* Joint Ventures in Poland (1987), Joint Ventures in the Soviet Union (1988), Joint Ventures in Poland: The New Legislation (1990), Joint Ventures in Hungary (1990), Investment in CIS (1991), International Business Glossary (1994); *Recreations* sailing, swimming, music, reading; *Clubs* RNVR Yacht, Law Soc Yacht, Cruising Association, E Europe Business; *Style*— John Murphy, Esq; ✉ 94 Bromfelde Rd, London SW4 6PS (☎ 0171 622 0229, fax 0171 498 5155)

MURPHY, Sir Leslie Frederick; kt (1978); s of Frederick Charles Murphy; *b* 17 Nov 1915; *Educ* Southall GS, Birkbeck Coll London; *m* 1, 1940, Marjorie Iris Cowell (d 1991); 1 s (Vernon Leslie, *qv*), 1 da; *m* 2, 1993, Dorothy Anne Murray; *Career* chm: NEB 1977–79 (dep chm 1975–77); dir: Petroleum Economics 1980–94, Unigate 1968–75, Schroders 1979–89 (dep chm 1973–75), Simon Engrg 1980–85; memb NEDC 1977–79; memb Bd Church Army 1964–94 (vice pres 1994–), chm Church Army Housing 1973–82; *Recreations* golf, music; *Clubs* Oriental; *Style*— Sir Leslie Murphy; ✉ Hedgerley, Barton Common Road, Barton-on-Sea, Hants BH25 5PR

MURPHY, Michael; s of Francis Murphy (d 1989), and Dorothy Byrne, *née* Kenny; *b* 12 Feb 1954; *Educ* Lourdes Secdy Sch Glasgow, Napier Coll Edinburgh; *m* 29 May 1982, Carolynne Dawn, da of Derrick Thomas Evans; 1 s ((Michael) Stuart b 1984), 1 da (Kimberly Jane b 1987); *Career* journalist Johnston Newspaper Group 1972–76, press offr Greater Glasgow Passenger Transport Group 1976–78, PRO Ind Coope Scotland 1978–79, md PR Consultants Scotland 1979–91; chm: Quorum Graphic Design 1988–91, The PR Centre Ltd 1988–91, Causeway Communications Ltd 1991–, PR Consultants Scotland 1993–94; chief exec offr Shandwick Hong Kong Ltd 1994–; memb Scottish Young Business Gp Inst of Public Relations; FSA (Scot); *Recreations* keeping fit, reading; *Style*— Michael Murphy, Esq; ✉ Shandwick Hong Kong Ltd, 18–F Dina House, Ruttonjee Centre, 11 Duddell Street, Central, Hong Kong (☎ 00 852 2845 1008, fax 00 852 2868 0224)

MURPHY, Dr Michael Furber; s of Arthur Furber Murphy (d 1989), and Dr Jean Marjorie Frazer; *b* 2 May 1951; *Educ* Malvern, St Bartholomew's Hosp (MB BS, MD); *m* 1 Sept 1984, Dr (Elizabeth) Sarah Green, da of Prof L L Green, of Wirral, Merseyside; 1 s (James Nicholas Furber b 16 March 1993), 1 da (Anna Cordelia Furber b 16 May 1995); *Career* St Bartholomew's Hosp: house physician 1974, registrar in haematology 1978–79, sr registrar 1979–84, sr lectr and hon conslt 1985–; sr house offr in med: St Leonard's Hosp, Brompton Hosp and Nat Heart Hosp 1975–78; sec Br Ctee for Standards in Haematology 1992–95; Kenneth Goldsmith award Br Blood Transfusion Soc 1994; FRCP 1993 (MRCP 1976), FRCPath 1994 (MRCPath 1982); *Recreations* theatre, golf, wine tasting; *Style*— Dr Michael Murphy; ✉ Church Farm, Upper Lambourn, nr Hungerford, Berkshire (☎ 01488 72770); Department of Haematology, St Bartholomew's Hospital, London EC1A 7BE (☎ 0171 601 8214, fax 0171 601 8215)

MURPHY, Patrick Wallace; s of Lawrence Vincent Murphy (d 1989), and Agnes Elsie Ethel, *née* Dunn (d 1964); *b* 16 Aug 1944; *Educ* St Chad's Coll Wolverhampton, Trinity Hall Cambridge (BA); *m* 1972, Denise Lillieth, *née* Fullarton-Fullarton; 2 s (Patrick Vincent b 1976, Matthew John b 1979); *Career* MAFF: asst princ 1966–71, princ 1971–74, first sec (Agric and Commercial) British Embassy Washington 1974–78, asst sec and controller of Plant Variety Rights 1978–82, asst sec and head of Land Use and Tenure Div 1982–86, under sec and head of Milk and Potatoes Gp 1986–89, under sec and head of Pesticides, Veterinary Medicines and Emergencies Gp 1989–93, grade 3 and head of European Community Gp 1993–94, grade 3 and head of Countryside Gp 1994–96; conslt 1996–; *Recreations* cricket, gardening, tennis, travel; *Style*— Patrick Murphy, Esq; ✉ home: (☎ and fax 01252 703151)

MURPHY, Paul Peter; MP (Lab) Torfaen (majority 20,754); s of Ronald Murphy, and Marjorie Murphy (d 1984); *b* 25 Nov 1948; *Educ* St Francis RC Sch Abersychan, W Monmouth Sch Pontypool, Oriel Coll Oxford (MA); *Career* lectr in history and politics Ebbw Vale Coll of Further Educn 1971–87; memb Torfaen Borough 1973–87, MP (Lab) Torfaen 1987–; oppn front bench spokesman on: Welsh affrs 1988–, defence 1995–; oppn spokesman on: N Ireland 1994–95, foreign affairs 1995–; *Recreations* music; *Style*— Paul Murphy, Esq, MP; ✉ House of Commons, Westminster, London SW1A 0AA

MURPHY, Penelope Gay; da of Gerald Hugh-Smith (d 1965), of Hove, Sussex, and Pamela Daphne, *née* Miller; *b* 28 Oct 1949; *Educ* Brighton & Hove HS, LSE (LLB); *m* 31 Aug 1974, Ian Patrick, QC, s of Patrick Murphy, of Cardiff, South Glamorgan; 2 da (Anna b 1982, Charlotte b 1984); *Career* ct clerk Dir of Public Prosecutions Old Bailey 1971–73, admitted slr 1976, ptnr Edwards Geldard of Cardiff 1977–; treas S Wales Branch Assoc of Women Slrs 1984–; memb Law Soc 1976–; *Recreations* family life, theatre, skiing, tennis; *Style*— Mrs Penelope Murphy; ✉ 3 Llandaff Chase, Llandaff, Cardiff, South Glamorgan CF5 2NA (☎ 01222 238239); Edwards Geldard, Dumfries House, Dumfries Place, Cardiff CF1 4YF (☎ 01222 238239, fax 01222 237268)

MURPHY, Dr Simon Francis; MEP (Lab) Midlands W (majority 54,823); s of Patrick Joseph Murphy, and Mary Frances, *née* Phillips; *b* 24 Feb 1962; *Educ* Sacred Heart Coll Droitwich Worcs, North Worcs Coll of Further and Higher Educn Bromsgrove Worcs, Univ Coll of Wales Aberystwyth (BSc(Econ), PhD); *m* 2 May 1992, Bridget Lee, da of Dennis George Brickley; *Career* tutor Dept of Political Sci UCW Aberystwyth 1984–86, PA to Leader of Lab Gp Wolverhampton MBC 1986–89, research and press offr to John Bird, MEP 1989–94, MEP (Lab) Midlands W 1994–; contested Wolverhampton S W gen election 1992; sec British Beer Club in Europe; *Books* Contemporary Minority Nationalisms (contrib chapter, 1988); *Recreations* running, reading, cooking, popular music; *Style*— Dr Simon Murphy, MEP; ✉ Rooms 2/3, Gresham Chambers, 14 Lichfield Street, Wolverhampton WV1 1DP (☎ 01902 831777, fax 01902 831888, e-mail (GeoNet) Geo2: simon.murphy)

MURPHY, Stuart John; s of John William Murphy, OBE (d 1978), of Salisbury, Wilts, and Kathleen Beryl, *née* Lait; *b* 7 Feb 1933; *Educ* City of London Sch, Poly of Central London (DipArch, DipTP); *m* 2 Dec 1966, Jane Elizabeth, da of George Tinkler (d 1963), of London; 1 s (Giles b 1969), 1 da (Sara b 1972); *Career* London Div RNVR 1950–63, Nat Serv 1958–59, Sub Lt RNR 1959, serv 1 Lt Vernon Sqdn; ret 1963; architect;

Architect's Dept London CC 1956–63, sr architect Llewellyn Davies & Weeks 1963–65, gp architect City of Westminster Dept of Architecture and Planning 1965–68, controller of architecture (borough architect) London Borough of Harrow 1971–76 (dep borough architect and planner 1968–71), city architect and planning offr Corp of City of London 1979–86 (dep city architect and planning offr 1976–79), conslt chartered architect town-planner and urban design conslt to Govt depts and private clients 1987–; vice pres and hon treas RIBA 1991–93 (chm Public Sector Gp 1987–89, chm Disciplinary Ctee 1989–91), former pres Cities of London and Westminster Soc of Architects 1984–86, sr vice pres Soc of Chief Architects of Local Authys, memb various socs involved with civic amenity and urban design; parish clerk St Lawrence Jewry Next Guildhall Church 1978–; chm of govrs The Lady Eleanor Holles Sch Hampton 1996–, tstee The Suzy Lamplugh Tst 1994–; Freeman City of London 1954, Liveryman Worshipful Co of Merchant Taylors 1968, memb Ct Worshipful Co of Parish Clerks 1995, fndr memb Worshipful Co of Chartered Architects 1984 (chm Organising Ctee 1984–85, Master 1992–93); FRIBA 1970, FRTPI 1973, FRSA 1977, FIMgt 1978, MAE 1988; *Recreations* theatre and music hall history, gardening; *Clubs* Athenaeum, Players' Theatre; *Style—* Stuart J Murphy, Esq; ✉ Coval Lodge, 6 Coval Lane, London SW14 7DS (fax 0181 876 6050)

MURPHY, Thomas James; s of James Murphy, and Beatrice Mary, *née* Strand; *b* 26 June 1956; *Educ* Salesian Sch Chertsey, Univ of Sussex (BA), Univ of Warwick (MBA); *m* 18 Dec 1976, Janet Anne, da of James Sallis (d 1990); 4 s (Thomas b 1980, Michael b 1983, David b 1985, Simon b 1989); *Career* journalist; kitchen porter 1977, trainee journalist Slough Observer 1978–81, sports ed Bucks Advertiser 1981–82, ed Staines Informer 1982–84, ed East Grinstead Courier 1984–86, journalist The Independent 1986–87, dep chief sub-ed London Evening News 1987, ed The Universe 1988–90 (columnist 1988–92), journalist The Times 1990–; *Recreations* singing at karaoke nights; *Style—* Thomas Murphy, Esq; ✉ The Times, 1 Pennington St, London E1 9XN (☎ 0171 782 5000, fax 0171 782 5136, telex 262141)

MURPHY, Vernon Leslie; s of Sir Leslie Murphy, *qv*, of Barton-on-Sea, Hants, and Marjorie Iris Murphy (d 1991); *b* 28 July 1944; *Educ* Westminster, Gonville and Caius Coll Cambridge (MA); *m* Sept 1974, Joan Bridget Mary, da of Thomas Anthony Leonard; 2 da (Olivia Bridget b 26 Jan 1978, Juliet Rosemary b 19 March 1982); *Career* British Airports Authority: joined as graduate trainee 1966, asst to Chief Exec 1969–71, successively dep mangr Terminal 2 Heathrow, sales mangr Heathrow Airport then gen mangr Terminal 1 Heathrow until 1980, gen mangr Aberdeen Airport 1980–84, dep md Gatwick Airport Ltd 1984–88, md Glasgow Airport Ltd 1988–92, md Scottish Airports Ltd 1988– (also currently chm); dep chm Renfrewshire Enterprise Co 1991–; keeper of the Quaife 1992; FCIT 1984, FRSA 1995; *Recreations* cricket, music, steam trains; *Clubs* RAC; *Style—* Vernon Murphy, Esq; ✉ Scottish Airports Ltd, Saint Andrews Drive, Glasgow Airport, Paisley, Renfrewshire PA3 2SW (☎ 0141 848 4583, fax 0141 848 4444)

MURPHY-O'CONNOR, Rt Rev Cormac; *see:* Arundel and Brighton, Bishop of

MURRAY, Alan Adams; s of William Murray (d 1973), and Christina Margaret, *née* Adam; *b* 16 Dec 1948; *Educ* Perth Acad, Heriot-Watt Univ Edinburgh (Dip in Banking and Fin Studies); *m* 1970, Margaret Lucretia, *née* McBeth; 1 s (Steven Alan b 1975), 1 da (Lynne Louise b 1977); *Career* Bank of Scotland 1965–75; British Linen Bank Ltd: asst loans controller 1975–77, loans controller 1977–79, exec asst 1979, asst mangr 1980–82, mangr 1982–83, asst dir 1983–84, divnl dir 1984–87, dir 1987–, head of banking 1989–; dir British Linen Bank Group Ltd 1991–; FCIBS 1994 (MCIBS 1972); *Recreations* tennis, badminton, golf; *Style—* Alan Murray, Esq; ✉ The British Linen Bank Ltd, PO Box 49, 4 Melville St, Edinburgh EH3 7NZ (☎ 0131 243 8341, fax 0131 243 8310)

MURRAY, Sir (John) Antony Jerningham; kt (1987), CBE (1980); s of Capt John Challenger Murray (d 1939), of Oaksey Manor, Malmesbury, Wilts, and Cecilia Annette, *née* Jerningham; *b* 21 Jan 1921; *Educ* Eton, New Coll Oxford; *m* 23 July 1943, Hon Winifred Mary Hardinge, da of 2 Baron Hardinge of Penshurst, GCB, GCVO, MC, PC (d 1960); 1 s ((George) Alexander John b 8 Dec 1947); *Career* 2 Lt Grenadier Guards 1941, Capt 1945, Maj 1946, ret; dir Christmas Island Phosphate Co Ltd 1947–51, dep chm W India Ctee 1961–63 (chm 1963–65, vice-pres 1966–), hon advsr to Govt of Barbados in UK 1961–; tstee Sir Frank Worrell UK Meml Fund; *Recreations* salmon fishing; *Clubs* Boodle's, White's, RAC; *Style—* Sir Antony Murray, CBE; ✉ Woodmancote Manor Cottage, Cirencester, Glos GL7 7ED (☎ 01285 831226)

MURRAY, Colin Keith; s of Brig George Murray, CBE, DSO, MC (d 1983), and Betty, *née* Wheeler (d 1982); *b* 18 June 1932; *Educ* Wellington; *m* 1 Feb 1964, Precelly, da of Col David Davies-Scourfield, MC, of Eversley Cross House, Eversley Cross, Hants; 1 s, 2 da; *Career* Seaforth Highlanders and 1 Bn King's African Rifles 1950–51, TA 1952–64; CT Bowring & Co Ltd 1953–63, R J Kiln & Co Ltd 1963–95 (chm 1985–95); memb Cncl Lloyd's 1983–86 and 1989–92 (dep chm 1989–90); dir Kiln Capital plc 1994, tstee Equitas Holdings Ltd 1996–; dir St Joseph's Soc 1985–, chm Tst in Childrens 1994–, pres Youth Clubs Hants and IOW 1996–; Lt City of London 1993; Liveryman Worshipful Co of Insurers; *Recreations* music, bridge, gardening, country sports; *Clubs* Boodle's, Flyfishers', The City; *Style—* Colin Murray, Esq; ✉ The Long House, Hurstbourne Priors, nr Whitchurch, Hampshire RG28 7SB (☎ 01256 892606, fax 01256 893969)

MURRAY, David Edward; s of David Ian Murray (d 1975), and Roma Murray; *b* 14 Oct 1951; *Educ* Fettes, Broughton HS; *m* 22 July 1972, Louise Violet (decd); 2 s (David Douglas b 1973, Keith Andrew b 1975); *Career* fndr and chm Murray International Holdings and subsidiaries 1976–, chm Glasgow Rangers Football Club plc 1988–; chm UK 2000 Scotland 1987–88, govr Clifton Hall Sch 1987–89; Hon Dr of Business Heriot-Watt Univ 1986; *Recreations* collecting wine, watching sport; *Style—* David Murray, Esq; ✉ Murray House, 4 Redheughs Rigg, South Gyle, Edinburgh EH12 9DQ (☎ 0131 317 7000, fax 0131 317 7111)

MURRAY, Denis James; s of Dr James Murray (d 1956), of Evesham, Worcs, and Helen, *née* McKeever (d 1977); *b* 7 May 1951; *Educ* St Malachy's Coll Belfast, Trinity Coll Dublin (BA); *m* 22 April 1978, Joyce, *née* Linehan; 2 da (Claire b 26 Oct 1981, Sophie b 17 Dec 1986), 2 s (Gavin b 6 June 1984, James b 19 Aug 1989); *Career* reporter Belfast Telegraph 1974–77 (graduate trainee 1974), reporter RTE 1977–82; BBC: Dublin corr 1982–84, Northern Ireland political corr 1984–88, Ireland corr 1988–; *Recreations* playing and watching sport, books, music; *Style—* Denis Murray, Esq; ✉ c/o BBC Broadcasting House, Ormeau Avenue, Belfast BT2 8HQ (☎ 01232 338000, fax 01232 338806, mobile 0831 877000)

MURRAY, Rt Hon Sir Donald Bruce; PC (1989); s of Charles Benjamin Murray (d 1977), and Agnes Mary, *née* Patterson (d 1955); *b* 24 Jan 1923; *Educ* Belfast Royal Acad, Queen's Univ Belfast (LLB), Trinity Coll Dublin (BA); *m* 21 Aug 1953, Rhoda Margaret, da of Thomas Parke (d 1973); 3 s (Adrian Timothy Lawrence b 30 Oct 1954, Paul Ralph Stephen b 27 April 1961), 1 da (Rosalind Louise b 9 May 1958); *Career* called to the Bar Gray's Inn 1945, asst Parly draftsman to NI Govt 1945–51, asst lectr Faculty of Law Queen's Univ Belfast 1951–53, called to the NI Bar 1953, QC NI 1964, chm Gen Cncl of Bar of NI 1972–75, judge High Ct (Chancery Div) NI 1975–89, judge Restrictive Practices Ct 1987–93, Lord Justice of Appeal Supreme Ct of NI 1989–93; dep chm Boundary Cmmn for NI 1976–84; chm Incorporated Cncl of Law Reporting for NI 1974–87 (memb 1971), chm Bd SLS Legal Publications (NI) 1988–94; memb: Jt Standing Ctee of Bars of UK and Bar of Ireland 1972–75, Departmental Ctee on Registration of Title to Land in NI, Legal Advsy Ctee of Standing Ctee of Gen Synod Church of Ireland; govr Belfast Royal Acad 1972–95, memb bd Cathedral of St Anne Belfast 1945–95; memb Hon Soc of Inn of Ct NI (Bencher 1971), memb Hon Soc of Gray's Inn (Hon Bencher 1987); Hon LLD Queen's Univ Belfast 1996; *Recreations* playing the piano, DX-ing, snooker; *Clubs* Royal Belfast Golf; *Style—* The Rt Hon Sir Donald Murray; ✉ Hightrees, Ballylesson, Belfast BT8 8JT (☎ 01232 826687)

MURRAY, Sir Donald Frederick; KCVO (1983), CMG (1973), DL (Kent 1992); s of Archibald Thomas Murray (d 1960), and Freda May, *née* Byfield (d 1964); *b* 14 June 1924; *Educ* Colfes GS, King's Sch Canterbury, Worcester Coll Oxford; *m* 17 Dec 1949, Marjorie, da of Charles Culverwell (d 1977); 3 s (Ian b 1951, Neil b 1958, Alexander b 1960), 1 da (Gillian b 1953); *Career* RM (41 Commando) 1943–46; Foreign Serv: entered FO 1948, third sec Warsaw 1948, FO 1951, second sec Vienna 1953, first sec political office ME Forces 1956, FO 1957, first sec commerce Stockholm 1958, first sec and head of Chancery Saigon 1962, FO 1964, cnsllr 1965, head of SE Asia Dept 1966, cnsllr Tehran 1969, RCDS 1973, HM ambass Tripoli 1974, asst under sec of state FCO 1977, HM ambass Stockholm 1980, ret 1984; assessor chm Civil Serv Selection Bd 1984–86, complaints cmmr Channel Tunnel 1987–95; dir: Goodlass Wall & Co Ltd 1985–90, ColArt Fine Art and Graphics Ltd (Winsor and Newton) 1991–96; tstee World Resource Fndn 1986–96, vice pres Kent Co SSAFA 1991–96 (chm 1985–90); Grand Cross Order of North Star (Sweden) 1983; *Style—* Sir Donald Murray, KCVO, CMG, DL; ✉ Oxney House, Wittersham, Kent TN30 7ED

MURRAY, Edward Davidson; s of Thomas Loch Murray, of Ayrshire, and May Fox, *née* Davidson; *b* 10 Nov 1951; *Educ* George Watson's Coll (rowing colours), Univ of St Andrews (MA), Heriot Watt Univ (Dip Accountancy); *m* 1976, Jean Elizabeth, eld da of Dr James Innes; 3 s (Gavin James b 15 Aug 1980, Nigel Edward b 22 June 1983, Simon Innes b 6 June 1987); *Career* with Arthur Young (now Ernst & Young) Edinburgh until 1982, corp fin dir Br Linen Bank Edinburgh 1991– (joined 1982); MICAS 1979; *Recreations* hill walking, squash, tennis, cycling, classic cars, theatre, food, wine; *Clubs* Watsonian, Colinton Lawn Tennis, Edinburgh Sports; *Style—* Edward Murray, Esq; ✉ Copinsay, 27 Barnshot Road, Edinburgh EH13 0DJ (☎ 0131 441 4774); British Linen Bank Ltd, PO Box 49, 4 Melville Street, Edinburgh EH3 7NZ (☎ 0131 243 8329, fax 0131 243 8324)

MURRAY, Ewan Skinner; OBE (1984); s of Alexander Murray (d 1959), of Glasgow, and Sophia, *née* Smith (d 1984); *b* 18 Sept 1931; *Educ* Hyndland Sr Secdy Sch Glasgow; *m* 24 Jan 1992, Margaret Ann, da of William Wisdom (d 1991); *Career* Nat Serv RAF Tenga, Singapore 1950–51; insur official Iron Trades Insurance Group 1960–91; memb Garscube Harriers 1947– (hon sec 1952–62), ctee memb Scottish Cross Country Union 1956– (hon gen sec 1963–71, pres 1972, life vice pres 1979–), ctee memb Scottish Amateur Athletic Assoc 1960– (hon treas 1970–71, hon gen sec 1971–83, life vice pres 1981–); Br Olympic Assoc: athletics admin offr Moscow 1980, cncl memb 1984–89, dir 1987–91; Cwlth Games Cncl for Scotland: cncl memb 1973–83, athletics team mangr Brisbane 1982, vice chm 1983–87, chm 1987–90; Br Amateur Athletic Bd: cncl memb 1972–84, selection ctee memb 1972–84, team admin offr 1978–80, chm 1984–89, hon life vice pres 1987–91; cncl memb Euro Athletic Assoc 1987–91; life memb British Athletics Fedn 1991; OStJ 1987, FSA(Scot); *Recreations* athletics; *Clubs* Western (Glasgow); *Style—* Ewan Murray, Esq, OBE; ✉ 25 Bearsden Road, Glasgow G13 1YL (☎ 0141 959 4436)

MURRAY, Gordon; CB (1994); s of James Murray (d 1965), of Aberdeen, and Annie Hardie Center (d 1970); *b* 25 Aug 1935; *Educ* Kirkcaldy HS, Univ of Edinburgh (BSc, PhD); *m* 28 March 1964, Janet, da of George Yerrington (d 1961), of Wolverhampton; 2 s (Andrew, Peter), 1 da (Helen); *Career* res fell: Atomic Energy of Canada 1960–62, UKEAE Harwell 1962–65; lectr Univ of Manchester 1965–69, princ Scottish Home and Health Dept 1970–77, asst sec Scot Educn Dept 1977–79, Central Servs Scot Office 1979–86, dir Scot Cts Admin 1986–95; ordained Methodist min 1993; *Recreations* reading, hill walking, gardening; *Style—* Gordon Murray, Esq, CB; ✉ The Manse, 25 Sherford Close, Wareham, Dorset BH20 4JL (☎ 01929 551930)

MURRAY, (Ian) Gordon; s of William Gordon Murray (d 1984), and Rosemary Morrison, *née* Irvine; *b* 18 June 1946; *Educ* Glenwood HS Durban, Natal Tech Coll (Dip Mech Engrg, Arthur May prize); *m* 4 June 1970, Stella Lynne, da of Victor Gane; 1 s (Christopher Dylan b 23 Jan 1978); *Career* motorsport designer; design draughtsman SA 1964–69, moved to England 1969; Brabham: design draughtsman 1970–73, chief designer 1973–74, tech dir 1974–86; tech dir: McLaren International 1986–90, McLaren Cars Ltd 1990–; dir TAG McLaren Group 1990–; achievements as designer: 51 grand prix wins, 4 World Drivers' Formula One Championships, 2 World Constructors' Formula One Championships, McLaren F1 (fastest road car in the world), McLaren F1 GTR (winner Le Mans 1995, Global Endurance GT series, European Endurance GT series); winner various awards for motorsport design; memb: S African Inst of Mech Engrs, Inst of Engrg Designers; *Recreations* motor sport, music, art; *Style—* Gordon Murray, Esq; ✉ McLaren Cars Motorsport, Unit 14, Woking Business Park, Albert Drive, Woking, Surrey GU21 5JY (☎ 01483 730206, fax 01483 730208)

MURRAY, (James) Iain; s of James Ian Murray (d 1977), and Jean Parker, *née* McLeod Baxter (d 1984); *b* 12 Nov 1932; *Educ* Rugby, Corpus Christi Coll Cambridge (BA, MA); *m* 21 March 1969, Ursula Jane, da of Eric Sayle, MD (d 1985); 1 s (Alexander b 9 Nov 1972), 2 da (Katharine (Mrs N J C Williams) b 13 July 1970, Fiona b 10 Aug 1979); *Career* Nat Serv 1951, Sgt RCS; articled clerk Freshfields 1956–59, admitted slr 1959, Robert Fleming & Co Ltd 1960–62 (seconded for 9 months on Wall St to G H Walker Investmt Bankers), slr Linklaters & Paines 1963–92 (ptnr 1967–92); Co Law Ctee: City of London Slrs Co 1967–77, Law Soc 1968–78, CBI Co Ctee 1987–93; memb of the Incorporation of Maltmen in Glasgow 1954, Liveryman City of London Slrs Co, memb Law Soc 1959; *Recreations* walking; *Clubs* The City of London, Travellers', New (Edinburgh); *Style—* Iain Murray, Esq

MURRAY, Sir James; KCMG (1978, CMG 1966); s of James Hamilton Murray (d 1938), of King's Cross, Isle of Arran, by his w Hester Macneill Buie; *b* 3 Aug 1919; *Educ* Bellahouston Acad, Univ of Glasgow; *m* 1982, Mrs Jill Charmian Chapuisat, *née* Gordon-Hall; 2 step da; *Career* serv WWII RA India, Burma, Malaya rising to GSO 2 WO; with FO (later FCO) 1947–80: ambass to Rwanda and Burundi 1962–63, dep head UK Delgn to EEC 1963–65, cnsllr Djakarta 1967, head Far East Dept FO 1967–70, consul-gen San Francisco 1970–73, asst under-sec FCO 1973–74, dep perm rep to UN in NY 1974–78 with rank of ambass 1976, ambass and perm rep to UN at Geneva 1978–79; Hanson Industs NY 1983–92, Withrow prof of govt Deep Springs Coll Ca 1990; *Clubs* Brook (NY), Brooks's, Beefsteak, Pratt's; *Style—* Sir James Murray, KCMG; ✉ 220 Columbia Heights, Brooklyn Heights, New York, NY 11201, USA (☎ 718 852 3320)

MURRAY, Prof James Dickson; s of Peter Murray, and Sarah Murray; *b* 2 Jan 1931; *Educ* Dumfries Acad, Univ of St Andrews (BSc, PhD), Univ of Oxford (MA, DSc); *m* 1959, Sheila Todd Murray; 1 s, 1 da; *Career* lectr: Univ of Durham 1955–56, Harvard (Gordon MacKay lectr and res fell) 1956–59, UCL 1959–61; fell and maths tutor Hertford Coll Oxford 1961–63, res assoc Harvard 1963–64, prof of engrg mechanics Univ of Michigan 1964–67, visiting fell St Catherine's Coll Oxford 1967, prof of maths Univ of NY 1967–70, Guggenheim fell Pasteur Inst Paris 1968; Univ of Oxford: reader 1972–86, dir Centre for Mathematical Biology 1983–92, sr res fell CCC 1985–86 (fell and tutor 1970–85), prof of mathematical biology 1986–92 (now emeritus), professorial fell CCC 1986–92; visiting prof: Nat Tsing Hua Univ 1975, Univ of Florence 1976, MIT 1979, Univ of Iowa 1979, Univ of Utah 1979 and 1985, Univ of Guelph 1980, Univ of Heidelberg 1980, CIT 1983, Southern Methodist Univ Dallas 1984, Univ of Calif 1985, Univ of Angers 1993, Univ of Paris 1994 and 1995; Robert F Philip prof Univ of

Washington 1988–94 (prof of applied maths, adjunct prof of zoology); pres Euro Soc for Mathematical and Theoretical Biology 1992–94; memb Editorial Bd: Jl of Theoretical Biol, Jl of Mathematical Biol, Jl of Maths Applied in Med and Biol, Bulletin of Mathematical Biology, Jl of Nonlinear Sci, Chaos and Bifurcation, Lecture Notes in Biomaths, Biomaths series; author of numerous articles in learned jls; Hon DSc St Andrews; FRS 1985, FRSE 1979; *Books* Asymptotic Analysis (1974, 2 edn 1984), Nonlinear Differential Equation Models in Biology (1977), Theories of Biological Pattern Formation (co-ed S Brenner, L Wolpert 1981), Modelling Patterns of Space and Time (co-ed W Jäger 1984), Mathematical Biology (1989, 2 corrected edn, 1993), Experimental and Theoretical Advances in Biological Pattern Formation (co-ed H G Othmer, P K Maini, 1993); *Style—* Prof J D Murray, FRS, FRSE; ✉ La Combe, St Laurent des Batons, 24510 Ste Alvere, France

MURRAY, Jennifer Susan (Jenni); da of Alvin Bailey, of Barnsley, Yorks, and Winifred, *née* Jones; *b* 12 May 1950; *Educ* Barnsley Girls' HS, Univ of Hull (BA); *m* 1 (m dis), Brian Murray; 2 s (Edward Louis b 1983, Charles Edgar b 1987); *Career* prodr and presenter BBC Radio Bristol 1973–76, presenter reporter BBC TV South 1977–82; presenter: Newsnight (BBC TV Lime Grove) 1983–85, Today (BBC Radio 4) 1986–87, Woman's Hour (BBC Radio 4) 1987–, This Sunday (Granada TV); documentary films for TV incl: The Duchy of Cornwall, Everyman, Stand by Your Man, Breaking the Chain, Here's Looking At You; vice pres FPA; Hon DLitt Univ of Bradford; *Books* The Woman's Hour; *Recreations* horses, books, swimming, the children; *Style—* Ms Jenni Murray; ✉ Woman's Hour, BBC Broadcasting House, London W1A 1AA (☎ 0171 580 4468); agent Speakeasy (☎ 0116 240 4101), literary agent Barbara Levy (☎ 0171 435 9046)

MURRAY, John Joseph; s of Kevin Thomas Murray, of Bridge of Weir, Renfrewshire, and Mary, *née* Leahy (d 1973); *b* 10 May 1953; *Educ* Fort Augustus Abbey Sch, Caledonian Univ, Univ of Leeds (LLB); *Career* admitted slr 1979; articled clerk Smallpeice & Merriman 1977–79, ptnr Nabarro Nathanson 1986– (asst slr 1979); chm Tax and Legislation Sub-Ctee, memb Ctee Assoc of Pensioneer Trustees; memb: Law Soc, Assoc of Pension Lawyers, Int Pension and Employee Benefits Lawyers Assoc; *Recreations* reading, travel, music, cinema, sport, video; *Style—* John Murray, Esq; ✉ Nabarro Nathanson, 50 Stratton Street, London W1X 6NX (☎ 0171 493 9933, fax 0171 629 7900, telex 8813144 NABAROG)

MURRAY, Prof John Joseph; CBE (1997); s of John Gerald Murray (d 1980), of Bradford, W Yorks, and Margaret Sheila, *née* Parle (d 1979); *b* 28 Dec 1941; *Educ* St Bedes GS Bradford, Univ of Leeds (BDS, MDS, PhD); *m* 28 March 1967, Valerie, da of Harry Allen (d 1969), of Heanor, Derbys; 2 s (Mark b 14 March 1975, Christopher b 3 Nov 1976); *Career* res fell in children's dentistry Univ of Leeds 1966–70, reader Inst of Dental Surgery Univ of London 1975–77 (sr lectr in children's dentistry 1970–75); Univ of Newcastle upon Tyne: prof of child dental health 1977–92, dental postgrad sub dean 1982–92, dean of dentistry 1992–; asst scientific ed British Dental Journal 1985–92, pres Br Paedodontic Soc 1985 (conslt advsr to chief med offr 1982–92); Dept of Health: memb Standing Dental Advsy Ctee 1980– (chm 1992–), memb Ctee on Continuing Educn Trg 1985–; memb BDA, FDS RCS 1973, MCCD RCS 1989; *Books* The Acid Etch Technique in Paedodontics and Orthodontics (jtly), Fluorides in Caries Prevention (1 edn 1976, 2 and 3 edns jtly 1982 and 1991), Prevention of Oral Disease (ed, 1983, 3 edn 1996); *Recreations* golf, bridge, photography; *Clubs* Ponteland Golf; *Style—* Prof John Murray, CBE; ✉ Dean of Dentistry, Dental School, Framlington Place, University of Newcastle upon Tyne, Newcastle upon Tyne NE2 4BW (☎ 0191 222 8340, fax 0191 222 6137)

MURRAY, Kenneth Alexander George; CB (1977); s of late George Dickie, and Isobella Murray; *b* 17 June 1916; *Educ* Skene St and Central Schs Aberdeen, Univ of Aberdeen (MA, BEd); *m* 1942, Elizabeth Ward, da of late Arthur Simpson; 1 da (Alison); *Career* dir Civil Serv Selection Bd and cmmr Civil Serv 1964–77, special advsr to the Home Office on Police Serv, Prison Serv and Fire Serv Selection 1977–; dir Home Office Unit 1977–80; selection advsr to Church of Scotland and C of E; formerly selection advsr to Govts of Nigeria, Pakistan and India; FBPsS; *Recreations* reading, theatre, bridge, cricket; *Clubs* MCC, Royal Cwlth Soc; *Style—* Kenneth Murray, Esq, CB; ✉ 15 Melvinshaw, Leatherhead, Surrey (☎ 01372 372995)

MURRAY, Martin Charles; s of Brian Murray, of Crosby, and Muriel Gertrude, *née* Spense; *b* 13 April 1955; *Educ* Merchant Taylors', Emmanuel Coll Cambridge (MA, LLB), Harvard Univ (LLM); *Career* admitted slr 1981, Clifford Chance 1979–83, Berisford plc 1983–86, Hanson PLC 1986–97, company sec and legal dir The Energy Group PLC 1997–; memb Law Soc; *Recreations* wine, food, music, opera, travel; *Style—* Martin Murray, Esq; ✉ 21 The Crescent, Barnes, London SW13 0NN (☎ 0181 878 7627); The Energy Group PLC, 117 Piccadilly, London W1R 9FJ (☎ 0171 647 3200, fax 0171 647 3201)

MURRAY, Prof Maxwell; s of Maxwell Murray (d 1981), and Martha Letham, *née* Davidson; *b* 3 May 1939; *Educ* Shawlands Acad, Univ of Glasgow (BVMS, PhD, DVM); *m* 8 Sept 1976, Christine Madelaine, da of Maj Ronald Lewis Allen, of 117 Titwood Rd, Glasgow; 1 s (Maxwell b 1979), 2 da (Katie b 1978, Kirsty b 1983); *Career* lectr in vet pathology Univ of Nairobi 1963–65, sr scientist Int Laboratory for Res on Animal Diseases Nairobi 1975–85; Univ of Glasgow: lectr in vet pathology 1965–74, sr lectr 1974–75, prof of vet med 1985–, currently head of Dept; FRCPath 1984, FRSE 1984; *Books* Current Trends in Immunology and Genetics and their Implications for Parasitic Diseases (1978), Livestock Productivity and Trypanotolerance: Network Training Manual (1983); *Recreations* family, football, philosophy; *Style—* Prof Maxwell Murray, FRSE; ✉ 21 Ledcameroch Rd, Bearsden, Glasgow G61 4AE (☎ 0141 942 6476); Dept of Veterinary Medicine, University of Glasgow Veterinary School, Bearsden Rd, Bearsden, Glasgow G61 1QH (☎ 0141 339 8855, fax 0141 942 7215, telex 777070 UNIGLA)

MURRAY, Neil Alastair Charles; s of Alastair Richardson Murray, of Wimbledon, and Patricia Stella Ray, *née* Jones; *b* 25 Feb 1954; *Educ* King George V Sch Hong Kong, Univ of Southampton (LLB), City Univ (MA); *m* 1 Sept 1984, Patricia Susan, da of John Herbert Mulholland, of Connecticut, USA; 1 s (James b 4 July 1987), 1 da (Stephanie b 18 June 1989); *Career* admitted slr 1980; Boodle Hatfield & Co London 1978–80, Legal Dept ICI 1980, Norton Rose 1980–85, ptnr Travers Smith Braithwaite 1987– (joined 1985); Freeman Worshipful Co of Slrs; memb Law Soc; *Recreations* music, golf, skiing, fitness; *Clubs* Wig and Pen; *Style—* Neil Murray, Esq; ✉ Travers Smith Braithwaite, 10 Snow Hill, London EC1A 2AL (☎ 0171 248 9133, fax 0171 236 3728)

MURRAY, Nicholas Julyan Edward; s of Sir (Francis) Ralph Hay Murray, KCMG, CB (d 1986), of Whaddon Hall Mews, Whaddon, Bucks, and Mauricette, *née* Countess von Kuenburg (d 1996); *b* 7 March 1939; *Educ* Bedford Sch, English Sch Cairo, Univ of St Andrews (MA); *m* 14 July 1973, Caroline Anne, da of Capt A McClintock, of Glenbower, Coolbawn, Nenagh, Co Tipperary, Ireland; 1 da (Anstice Aileen Thérèse b 22 Jan 1981); *Career* S H Benson Ltd 1962–71 (dir 1968), dir Ogilvy Benson & Mather Ltd 1971–72, md Murray Parry & Ptnrs 1972–81, dir Woodyer Hutson Chapman 1981–86, md Conzept Int Mgmnt Business Devpt Conslts 1986–; memb and professional advsr Bd of Trade (missions Tokyo 1968, San Francisco 1969); chm Friends of the Vale of Aylesbury 1987–92 (memb ctee 1975–, vice-chm 1985); FInstD; *Books* Chronicle of the Villages of the Vale of Aylesbury (1986); *Recreations* sailing; *Clubs* Sussex Yacht, Lough Derg Yacht; *Style—* Nicholas Murray, Esq; ✉ 38 Perrers Rd, London W6; CIA-Conzept Int, 1 Paris Garden, London SWE1 0NV (☎ 0171 633 0008)

MURRAY, Master; Nigel; s of Dr Ronald Ormiston Murray, MBE (Mil) (d 1995), and Catherine Joan Suzette, *née* Gauvain (d 1980); *b* 22 Jan 1944; *Educ* Stowe; *m* 1970, Shirley, da of Cdr Bernard Kieran Charles Arbuthnot, DSC, RN (d 1975), of Youghal, Co Cork; 1 da (Iona b 1972), 1 s (Simon b 1974); *Career* called to the Bar Inner Temple 1965, in practice Western Circuit 1966–90 (save when a judge High Ct of Botswana 1984–87), Master of the Supreme Ct (Queen's Bench Div) 1991–, recorder 1994– (asst recorder 1982); an ed Supreme Court Practice 1991–; *Recreations* golf; *Clubs* Garrick, Berkshire Golf, Rye Golf; *Style—* Master Murray; ✉ c/o Royal Courts of Justice, Strand, London WC2A 2LL

MURRAY, Prof Noreen Elizabeth; da of John and Lilian Grace Parker; *b* 26 Feb 1935; *Educ* King's Coll London (BSc), Univ of Birmingham (PhD); *m* 1958, Kenneth Murray; *Career* res assoc: Stanford Univ 1960–64, Univ of Cambridge 1964–67, Molecular Genetics Unit MRC Edinburgh 1968–74; Dept of Molecular Biology Univ of Edinburgh: successively lectr, sr lectr, reader 1974–88, prof of molecular genetics 1988–; scientist Euro Molecular Biology Laboratory Heidelberg 1980–82; memb: EMBO, Genetics Soc USA; pres Genetical Soc 1987–90; author of original res papers and reviews of genetics and molecular biology; FRS 1982, FRSE 1989; *Recreations* gardening; *Style—* Prof Noreen Murray, FRS, FRSE; ✉ Institute of Cell and Molecular Biology, University of Edinburgh, Mayfield Road, Edinburgh EH9 3JR (☎ 0131 650 5374)

MURRAY, Norman Loch; s of Thomas Loch Murray, of Cumnock, Ayrshire, and May Fox, *née* Davidson; *b* 17 March 1948; *Educ* George Watson's Coll Edinburgh, Heriot Watt Univ Edinburgh (BA), Harvard Grad Sch of Business Admin Cambridge Mass USA (PMD); *m* 17 March 1973, Pamela Anne, da of George Low; 2 s (Niall, Andrew); *Career* Scottish and Newcastle Breweries plc Edinburgh 1971–73, Arthur Young & Co Edinburgh 1973–77, Peat Marwick Mitchell & Co Hong Kong 1977–80, The Royal Bank of Scotland plc Edinburgh 1980–85; dir: Charterhouse Development Capital Ltd 1985–89, Morgan Grenfell & Co Ltd 1989–, Morgan Grenfell Development Capital France SA 1995–; chief exec and head Private Equity Business Morgan Grenfell Development Capital Ltd 1996– (dep chief exec 1989–96); non-exec dir: Burn Stewart Distillers plc 1988–90, Taunton Cider plc 1991–92, Bristow Helicopter Group Ltd 1991–, EuroDollar (Holdings) plc 1993–94, Beni Food Group Ltd 1994–; vice chm Br Venture Capital Assoc (memb Cncl and chm Legal and Tech Ctee), memb Cncl Inst of CAs of Scotland (memb Fin and General Purposes Ctee); memb Co of Merchants of City of Edinburgh; FRSA; *Books* Making Corporate Reports Valuable (jtly, 1988); *Recreations* squash, golf, climbing; *Clubs* Royal Scottish Automobile, Luffness New Golf, Watsonian, Harvard Business School, Royal Hong Kong Yacht; *Style—* Norman Murray, Esq; ✉ Morgan Grenfell Development Capital Ltd, 35 St Andrew Square, Edinburgh EH2 2AD (☎ 0131 557 8600, fax 0131 557 8306)

MURRAY, Pete; OBE; s of Harry James (d 1937), of IOW, and Violet Caroline, *née* Reece; *b* 19 Sept 1925; *Educ* St Pauls Hammersmith, RADA; *m* 1, 23 Feb 1952 (m dis 1963), Germaine Graff; m 2, 22 May 1973, Patricia Alice, da of Harry Victor Crabb, of London; 1 s (Michael Murray b 1952 d 1981); *Career* served RAF 1943–45; Arts Repertory Theatre Cambridge, played Cliff in Power Without Glory (Booth Theatre NY) 1948, Last Enemy TV and nominated Actor of the Year 1956, Six Five Special rock and jazz show (BBC TV) 1957, Open House (BBC Radio 2) 1969–80, LBC Radio 1984–94; memb: Stars Orgn for Spastics, Lord's Taverners, Grand Order of Water Rats; *Books* One Day I'll Forget My Trousers (1975); *Recreations* tennis, golf, theatre; *Clubs* Roehampton; *Style—* Pete Murray, Esq, OBE; ✉ c/o Tony Lewis Entertainments Ltd, Regent House, 235–241 Regent Street, London W1 (☎ 0171 734 2285)

MURRAY, Peter; OBE (1996); *b* 1941, Middlesbrough; *Educ* Teeside Coll of Art, Univ of Leeds; *Career* teacher and curator; exhibited extensively until 1975 (paintings, drawings and prints in several public and private collections); taught in general, further and higher educn, lectr/visiting tutor to colls, polys and univs throughout Britain and abroad, formerly princ lectr responsible for postgrad studies Bretton Hall Coll W Yorks; fndr and exec dir Yorkshire Sculpture Park (pioneering the siting and exhibiting of sculpture in the open air) 1977–; organised maj open air exhibitions incl: Henry Moore and Landscape (largest ever open Henry Moore exhibition), Scultura - Carving from Carrara, Massa and Pietrasanta 1988, Emile Antoine Bourdelle - Pioneer of the Future 1989, Contemporary Stone Carving from Zimbabwe, Lynn Chadwick 1991–92, Phillip King, Barry Flanagan 1992, Jorgen Haugen Sorenson Retrospective and Fritz Wotruba 1993, Elizabeth Frink Meml 1994, Ed Paolozzi 70th Birthday Exhbn 1994, Kan Yasuda 1994; organiser and dir first Open Air Sculpture Symposium in Britain 1983, made presentations at Int Sculpture Confs USA 1982, Japan 1984 and San Francisco 1994; sponsored by: French Govt to visit Paris and northern France 1984, Canadian Govt to visit Canada 1981 and 1986, Br Cncl to visit India 1988, Zimbabwe 1990, Thailand 1991, N America 1992, 1993 and 1994, Germany 1993 and Austria 1993; estab: Artist Residences, Public Sculpture Workshops, Educn and Outreach Prog, Access Sculpture Trail at Yorks Sculpture Park; author of reviews for arts jls, contrib to several Radio and TV progs incl Review of Jacob Epstein exhibition BBC Radio 4 Kaleidoscope 1987, contrib to catalogues for exhibitions for other galleries and organisations nationally and internationally; hon fell RCA 1989; *Publications* incl: Sculpture Parks in Britain (Studio International, 1983), Sculpture Parks - Origins & Aims (Arts Review Yearbook, 1983), Zimbabwe Carving (Arts Review Yearbook, 1990); *Style—* Peter Murray, Esq, OBE; ✉ Yorkshire Sculpture Park, Bretton Hall Coll, West Bretton, Wakefield, West Yorkshire WF4 4LG (☎ 01924 830579)

MURRAY, Prof Robin MacGregor; s of James Alistair Campbell Murray (d 1979), of Glasgow, and Helen, *née* MacGregor (d 1992); *b* 31 Jan 1944; *Educ* Royal HS Edinburgh, Univ of Glasgow (MB ChB, MD), Univ of London (MPhil, DSc); *m* Shelagh, da of Frank Harris; 1 s (Graham Keith b 8 Feb 1972), 1 da (Claire Alison b 22 May 1978); *Career* SHO and registrar: Dept of Med Univ of Glasgow 1969–72, Maudsley Hosp 1972–76; Inst of Psychiatry: sr lectr 1978, dean 1982, prof of psychological med 1989–; visiting fell Nat Inst of Mental Health Washington 1976, pres Assoc of European Psychiatrists 1995–96; *Style—* Prof Robin Murray; ✉ Department of Psychological Medicine, Institute of Psychiatry, DeCrespigny Park, London SE5 8AF (☎ 0171 703 6091)

MURRAY, Rt Hon Lord; Ronald King; PC (1974); s of James King Murray; *b* 15 June 1922; *Educ* George Watson's Coll Edinburgh, Univ of Edinburgh, Jesus Coll Oxford; *m* 1950, Sheila Winifred Gamlin; 1 s, 1 da; *Career* served WWII REME India and SEAC; called to Scottish Bar 1953, standing jr counsel to BOT in Scotland 1961–64, QC Scotland 1967, sr advocate-dep 1967–70 (advocate-dep 1964–67), Lord Advocate 1974–79, Lord of Session 1979–95; MP (Lab) Leith 1970–79; *Recreations* sailing, astronomy; *Style—* The Rt Hon Lord Murray; ✉ 1 Inverleith Grove, Edinburgh EH3 5PB (☎ 0131 551 5330)

MURRAY, Dame (Alice) Rosemary; DBE (1977), JP (Cambridge 1953), DL (Cambs 1982); da of Adm Arthur John Layard Murray, CB, DSO, OBE (d 1959), and Ellen Maxwell, *née* Spooner (d 1976); *b* 28 July 1913; *Educ* Lady Margaret Hall Oxford (MA, DPhil); *Career* lectr in chemistry: Royal Holloway Coll London 1937–40, Univ of Sheffield 1941–43; served WWII chief offr WRNS 1942–46; Univ of Cambridge: lectr in chemistry Girton Coll 1946–54, demonstrator in chemistry 1947–52, tutor in charge New Hall 1954–64, pres New Hall 1964–82, vice chllr 1975–77; memb: Wages Cncl 1968–93, Cncl GPSDT 1969–92, Armed Forces Pay Review Body 1973–83; dir Midland Bank 1978–84, ind dir The Observer 1981–93; former chm Keswick Hall Coll of Educn and Cambridge Inst of Educn, past pres Nat Assoc for Adult Educn; hon fell: New Hall, Girton Coll and Robinson Coll Univ of Cambridge, Lady Margaret Hall Univ of Oxford;

Hon DSc: New Univ Ulster, Univ of Leeds, Univ of Pennsylvania, Wellesley Coll; Hon DCL Univ of Oxford; Hon DL Univ of S California; Hon LLD: Univ of Sheffield, Univ of Cambridge; Liveryman Goldsmiths' Co 1978; *Style—* Dame Rosemary Murray, DBE, JP, DL; ✉ 3 Oxford Road, Old Marston, Oxford OX3 0PQ

MURRAY, Sir Rowland William; 15 Bt (NS 1630), of Dunerne, Fifeshire; s of Sir Rowland William Patrick Murray, 14 Bt (d 1994), and his 1 w Josephine Margaret, *née* Murphy (d 1989); *b* 22 Sept 1947; *Educ* Georgia State Univ; *m* 1970, Nancy Diane, da of George C Newberry, of New Smyrna Beach, Florida; 1 s (Rowland William b 1979), 1 da (Ryan McCabe b 10 Feb 1974); *Heir* s, Rowland William Murray b 31 July 1979; *Career* memb Bd of Tstees Marist Sch Atlanta Georgia; *Clubs* Brookwood Midtown Atlanta Rotary, Ansley Golf; *Style—* Sir Rowland Murray, Bt; ✉ 4364 E Brookhaven Drive, Atlanta, Georgia 30319, USA

MURRAY, Yvonne Carole Grace; MBE (1991); *b* 4 Oct 1964; *Career* athlete; memb Lucozade Motherwell Dist Athletics Club, jr UK int 1981–82, full UK int 1983–; achievements at 3000m: Scot champion 1982, WAAA champion 1988, UK champion 1985 and 1987, Bronze medal Euro Championships 1986, Bronze medal Cwlth Games 1986, Silver medal Euro Cup 1987 and 1989, Gold medal Euro Indoor Championships 1987 (Bronze 1984, Silver 1985), Bronze medal Olympic Games 1988, Gold medal World Cup 1989, Silver medal Cwlth Games 1990, Euro champion 1990, Gold medal World Indoor Championships 1993 Silver medal Euro Championships 1994, Gold medal World Cup 1994; Bronze medal 1500m Euro Cup 1993, UK 5000m champion 1983, Scot 800m champion 1983, winner Gaymers' road race series 1985, Gold medal 10000m Cwlth Games 1994; holder various Scot and UK records; Female Athlete of the Year Br Athletics Writers' Assoc 1989 and 1990; BBC Scotland Sports Personality of the Year 1994; Hon MA Univ of Strathclyde 1995; *Style—* Miss Yvonne Murray, MBE; ✉ c/o British Athletic Federation, 225a Bristol Road, Edgbaston, Bristol B5 7UB (☎ 0121 440 5000, fax 0121 440 0555)

MURRAY-LEACH, Roger; s of Robert Murray-Leach, of Newport, Shropshire (d 1949), and Mary Barbara, *née* Caisley (d 1986); *b* 25 June 1943; *Educ* Aldenham, Architectural Assoc Sch; *m* 1, 1 June 1968 (m dis), Sandra Elizabeth, da of John Tallent, of Herefordshire; 1 s (Robert b 17 Feb 1978), 1 da (Tamsin b 13 April 1972), 1 s adopted (Jon James (JJ) b 20 April 1974); m 2, 2 Sept 1995, Dale Mackenzie, da of Tom Tillotson, of Oxfordshire; *Career* prodn designer; films incl: Local Hero 1983, Defence of the Realm 1986, A Fish Called Wanda 1988, Fierce Creatures 1996; Freeman: Worshipful Co of Haberdashers 1970, City of London 1969; *Recreations* riding, skiing; *Style—* Roger Murray-Leach, Esq; ✉ Nettleton Mill, Castle Combe, nr Chippenham, Wilts SN14 7NJ

MURRAY-LESLIE, Dr Christian Francis Victor; s of Francis Murray-Leslie, of Boxnoor, Herts, and Nancy Joan, *née* Brenthall (d 1947); *b* 12 July 1944; *Educ* Hemel Hempstead GS, Middlesex Hosp Med Sch (MB BS); *m* 7 June 1972, Margaret Ann, da of Arthur Charles Harmer, of Hartshorne, Derbyshire; 2 s (Nicholas John b 1972, Robin Charles b 1974), 1 da (Catherine Arbella b 1980); *Career* registrar in med 1971–72, registrar in med and cardiology 1972–73, lectr and res asst 1973–74, sr registrar in rheumatology and rehabilitation Univ of Leeds 1974–77, conslt in rheumatology and rehabilitation med Derbyshire Royal Infirmary 1977, conslt i/c Nat Demonstration Centre in Rehabilitation Derby 1980, clinical dir Orthotics and Disability Res Centre Derby 1980, visiting prof Univ of Loughborough 1988; dir Derby Disabled Driving Centre, past chm Assoc of Driver Educn of People With Disabilities; memb: BMA, Br Soc Rehabilitation Med (hon sec), Soc for Res in Rehabilitation; *Books* Recent Advances in Rheumatology (contrib); author of papers on driving for disabled people; *Recreations* walking, birdwatching, gardening, music; *Style—* Dr Christian Murray-Leslie; ✉ Derbyshire Royal Infirmary, London Rd, Derby DE1 2QY (☎ 01332 347141)

MURRAY-LYON, Dr Iain Malcolm; s of Ranald Malcolm Murray-Lyon (d 1970), of Edinburgh, and Jennipher, *née* Dryburgh; *b* 28 Aug 1940; *Educ* Loretto, Univ of Edinburgh (BSc, MB ChB, MD); *m* 7 Nov 1981, Teresa Elvira, da of Antonio Gonzalez Montero, of Buenos Aires; 1 s (Andrew Malcolm b 1984), 1 da (Caroline Claire b 1982); *Career* hon sr lectr Liver Unit KCH 1972–74; conslt physician and gastroenterologist: Charing Cross Hosp 1974–, Chelsea Westminster Hosp 1993–; hon conslt physician: Hosp of St John & St Elizabeth 1976–, King Edward VII Hosp for Offrs 1990–; author of over 150 pubns in the areas of liver disease and gastroenterology; former: censor Royal Coll of Physicians, chm Liver Section Br Soc of Gastroenterology, sec Br Assoc for Study of the Liver (memb); Liveryman Worshipful Soc of Apothecaries; FRCP 1980, FRCPE 1980; *Recreations* golf, skiing, tennis; *Clubs* Brooks's, Hurlingham; *Style—* Dr Iain Murray-Lyon; ✉ 12 St James's Gardens, London W11 4RD (☎ 0171 602 1806); 149 Harley Street, London W1N 2DE (☎ 0171 935 6747/4444); Charing Cross Hospital, London W6 8RF

MURRAY OF BLACKBARONY, Sir Nigel Andrew Digby; 15 Bt (NS 1628), of Blackbarony, Peeblesshire; s of Sir Alan John Digby Murray of Blackbarony, 14 Bt (d 1978), and Mabel Elisabeth, *née* Schiele; *b* 15 Aug 1944; *Educ* St Paul's Sch Argentina, Salesian Agric Tech Sch, RAC Cirencester; *m* 1980, Diana Margaret, da of Robert Campbell Bray; 1 s (Alexander Nigel Robert b 1981), 2 da (Rachel Elisabeth Vanda Digby b 1982, Evelyn Caroline Digby b 1987); *Heir* s, Alexander Nigel Robert Murray b 1 July 1981; *Career* farms own land (crops, dairy, bees); private pilot's licence from Midland Sch of Flying at Castle Donnington; landowner; *Recreations* tennis, golf, rowing, camping, mountain walking, fishing; *Style—* Sir Nigel Murray of Blackbarony, Bt; ✉ Establecimiento Tinamú, CC 115, 2624 Arias, Provincia de Córdoba, Argentina (☎ 00 54 0468 40031)

MURRAY OF EPPING FOREST, Baron (Life Peer UK 1985), of Telford, Co Shropshire; Lionel (Len) Murray; OBE (1966), PC (1976); *b* 2 Aug 1922; *Educ* Wellington GS Salop, London Univ, NCLC, New Coll Oxford; *m* 1945, Heather Woolf; 2 s (Hon Stephen William b 1959, Hon David Paul b 1960), 2 da (Hon Nicola Ruth b 1954, Hon Sarah Isobel b 1959); *Career* gen sec TUC 1973–84 (joined 1947, head econ dept 1954–69, asst gen sec 1969–73); memb NEDC 1973–; memb Anglo-German Fndn for Study of Industl Soc Bd Tstees 1977–; hon fell: Sheffield City Poly, New Coll Oxford; Hon DSc: Aston, Salford; Hon LLD St Andrews; *Style—* The Rt Hon the Lord Murray of Epping Forest, OBE, PC; ✉ 29 The Crescent, Laughton, Essex

MURRAY OF GRAVESEND, Baroness; Margaret Anne; *née* Wakeford; JP (1971); da of Frederick Charles Wakeford, of Crayford; *b* 6 Dec 1928; *m* 1960, Baron Murray of Gravesend (Life Peer) (d 1980); 1 s, 1 da; *Career* mangr Gravesend Churches Housing Assoc 1972–93; memb: Lambeth Cncl 1958–65, Dartford and Gravesend Dist Health Authy 1982–89, Co-Operative Party, Fabian Soc, Soroptimists, Labour Party, Gravesham Borough Cncl 1992– (Dep Mayor 1994, Mayor 1995–96), Mgmnt Bd (Kent) Cooperative Wholesale Soc SE Regnl Gp 1991–94, SE Co-op Regnl Political Ctee 1994–; pres: N Kent Sunday Football League 1980–, Gravesend Branch Nat Assoc of Widows 1981–, Gravesend Branch NSPCC 1985–; vice pres Gravesend Cncl for Racial Equality 1989–92; memb Dartford and Gravesham Community Health Cncl 1995; chair: Soroptimist Housing Assoc 1994–, Co-operative Friends of Jamaica 1995–; vice chair: House of Mercy 1993–, Community Services Ctee Gravesham BC 1996–; tstee: Elizabeth Huggins Tst 1994–, yhenry Pinnock Tst 1994–; govr: St John's RC Sch, Westcourt CP Sch; hon clerk to Knights Almshouse Tst Northfleet; *Style—* The Rt Hon Lady Murray of Gravesend, JP; ✉ 13 Parrock Rd, Gravesend, Kent (☎ 01474 365958)

MURRAY OF OCHTERTYRE, Sir Patrick Ian Keith; 12 Bt (NS 1673), of Ochtertyre, Perthshire; s of Sir William Patrick Keith Murray of Ochtertyre, 11 Bt (d 1977), and Susan Elizabeth Hudson, *née* Jones; *b* 22 March 1965; *Educ* Christ Coll Brecon Powys, London Acad of Music & Dramatic Art; *Heir* kinsman, Maj Peter Keith-Murray b 12 July 1935; *Style—* Sir Patrick Murray of Ochtertyre, Bt; ✉ Sheep House, Hay-on-Wye, Hereford

MURRAY-PHILIPSON, Robin Hylton; DL (Leics 1994); s of Hylton Ralph Murray-Philipson, MP (d 1934), and Monica Lloyd, *née* Beasley-Robinson (d 1994); *b* 5 June 1927; *Educ* Eton; *m* Oct 1954, Catherine Cornelia (Nini), da of late Brig Robert Tilney, CBE, DSO, TD, DL; 1 s (Hylton b 1959), 3 da (Cornelia b 1955, Suzie b 1961, Kate b 1963); *Career* Lt Grenadier Guards 1945–48; owner: Executive Travel Ltd 1957–75, Executive Helicopters Ltd 1960–64; dir: Helicopter Sales Ltd 1960–70, Trans World Helicopters Ltd 1967–72; md Serenissima Travel Ltd 1973–86, pt/t Marie Curie Cancer Care 1986–94 (patron Marie Curie Cancer Care Leics 1994–); jt rep National Art Collections Fund (Leics and Rutland) 1986–, fndr Leicestershire Crimebeat; High Sheriff for Co of Leics 1993–94; *Recreations* shooting, skiing, tennis, travel; *Clubs* White's; *Style—* Robin Murray-Philipson, Esq, DL; ✉ Blaston, Market Harborough, Leics LE16 8DE (☎ 01858 555233); 31 Astell Street, London SW3 3RT (☎ 0171 352 1250)

MURRELL, David Brian; s of William Percy John Murrell (d 1988), of Minehead, Somerset, and Muriel Mary Elizabeth, *née* Stevens (d 1988); *b* 7 Feb 1946; *Educ* Taunton Sch; *m* 29 Nov 1969, Sheila Mary, da of Lt Alured Francis Fairlie-Clarke (d 1984), of Norton Fitzwarren, Somerset; 1 s (Alan b 1970), 2 da (Deborah b 1972, Julia b 1974); *Career* qualified as CA with Amherst and Shapland of Minehead 1967; KPMG: joined 1968, ptnr 1981–, head of UK media and entertainment indust practice 1984–, chm UK and Euro info communications and entertainment practice 1994–, chm UK and int marketing 1996–; accounting tax and consulting servs provided to: The Observer, BBC, Virgin, PolyGram, LWT, Cordiant, Rank Orgn, Chrysalis, Classic FM, Teletext UK, UK Gold, NBC, Ticketmaster, Moving Pictures Int, Radio Acad, Mechanical Copyright Protection Soc, Producers Alliance for Cinema and TV, Inst of Contemporary Arts, Cinema and TV Benevolent Fund, Pink Floyd, Amnesty and Rolling Stones pop tours; jt sponsor: Publisher of the Year Award, Br TV Advertising Awards, Nat Newspaper Advtg Awards, Campaign Press Awards, Ind Radio Advertising Awards, IPA Effectiveness Awards Jazz FM Film Preview of Week and Classic FM at the Movies; treas Comic Relief, fin tutor Nat Film and TV Sch, barker Variety Club; memb: BAFTA, RTS, Marketing Soc; FCA 1978 (ACA 1968); *Publications* author of numerous articles on finance and tax in leading media & entertainment indust trade magazines; *Recreations* golf, photography, motor cycling, club car trials; *Clubs* West Hill Golf, Old Tauntonians London Golfing Soc (former capt), Wooden Spoon Soc; *Style—* David Murrell, Esq; ✉ KPMG, 1 Puddle Dock, Blackfriars, London EC4V 3PD (☎ 0171 311 1000, fax 0171 311 3311)

MURRELL, Geoffrey David George; CMG (1993), OBE (1987); s of Stanley Hector Murrell (d 1976), and Kathleen Margaret, *née* Martin (d 1980); *b* 19 Dec 1934; *Educ* Minchenden GS Southgate, Lincoln Coll Oxford (MA); *m* 26 Nov 1962, Kathleen Ruth, *née* Berton; 1 s (Timothy John b 1967), 3 da (Sarah Louise b 1964, Kate Elizabeth b 1970, Alice Margaret b 1978); *Career* Br Embassy Moscow: third sec 1961–64, second sec 1968–70; princ res offr FCO 1970–75, first sec Belgrade 1975–78, reg dir Res Dept FCO 1978–83, cnsllr Moscow 1983–87, res cnsllr for Soviet Affairs FCO 1988–91, min-cnsllr Moscow 1991–94; *Books* Russia's Transition to Democracy, An Internal Political History 1989–1996 (1996); *Recreations* tennis, guitar; *Clubs* United Oxford and Cambridge Univ; *Style—* Geoffrey Murrell, Esq, CMG, OBE; ✉ c/o Foreign & Commonwealth Office, King Charles St, London SW1A 2AH

MURSELL, Sir Peter; kt (1969), MBE (1941), DL (W Sussex 1962); s of T A Mursell, of Kettering; *b* 20 Jan 1913; *Educ* Bedales Sch, Downing Coll Cambridge; *m* 1938, Cicely, da of M F North, of Weybridge; 2 s, 2 da; *Career* Serv WWII Sr Cdr ATA; former memb: Ctee Mgmt in Local Govt, Royal Cmmn on Local Govt in England, Water Space Amenity Cmmn, Inland Waterways Amenity Advsy Cncl; chm W Sussex CC 1962–67 and 1969–74 (memb 1947–74), Vice Lord Lt W Sussex 1974–90; *Clubs* Farmers'; *Style—* Sir Peter Mursell, MBE, DL; ✉ Taints Orchard, The Street, Washington, W Sussex RH20 4AS (☎ 01903 893062)

MURTA, Prof Kenneth Hall; s of John Henry Murta (d 1976), of Sunderland, Co Durham, and Florence, *née* Hall (d 1977); *b* 24 Sept 1929; *Educ* Bede GS Sunderland, Univ of Durham, Univ of Sheffield (DipArch, BArch); *m* 1 April 1955, Joan, da of Joseph Wilson; 2 s (Andrew John b 1956, Eden Wilson b 1966), 2 da (Catherine Anne b 1958, Patricia Zaria b 1960); *Career* Nat Serv RAF 1947–49; asst architect S W Milburn & Partners Sunderland 1954–56, princ architect Newcastle City 1956–59, sr lectr Ahmadu Bello Univ Nigeria 1959–62; Univ of Sheffield: lectr then sr lectr 1962–74, prof of architecture 1975–94 (prof emeritus 1994), dean Faculty Of Architectural Studies 1974–77 and 1984–88; significant designs incl: Anglican Cathedral Kaduna Northern Nigeria, alterations to PM's House Kaduna, St John Park Sheffield, St Luke Lodgemoor Sheffield, All Saints Church Dewsbury, St Laurence Church Heanor, Christ Church Pitsmoor Sheffield, All Saints Church Denaby Main, Christ Church Stannington Sheffield, St Lawrence Frodingham Scunthorpe, All Saints Totley Sheffield, St Laurence Thrybergh, Pilgrims Club Fordcombe Kent; chm: Yorks Region RIBA 1985, Bd of Architectural Educn ARCUK 1991–96 (vice chm 1990–91, chm 1991–97), Fabric Advsy Ctee Sheffield Cathedral 1992–97; dir Sheffield Regeneration Ltd 1990–97 (chm 1996–97); hon sec The Ecclesiological Soc 1992–97; FRIBA 1968 (ARIBA 1954), FRSA 1981; *Recreations* cricket, soccer, travel, church visiting, walking in cities on Sundays; *Clubs* Royal Over-Seas League; *Style—* Prof Kenneth Murta; ✉ Underedge, Back Lane, Hathersage, Derbyshire (☎ 01433 650833)

MURTON OF LINDISFARNE, Baron (Life Peer UK 1979), of Hexham, Co Northumberland; (Henry) Oscar Murton; OBE (1946), TD (1947, clasp 1951), PC (1976), JP (Poole 1963); o s of late Henry Edgar Crossley Murton, of Hexham, Northumberland; *b* 8 May 1914; *Educ* Uppingham; *m* 1, 1939, Constance (d 1977), da of late Fergus O'Loughlin Connell, of Low Fell, Co Durham; 1 s (Hon (Henry) Peter John Connell b 1941), 1 da (Hon Melanie Frances Isobel Connell (Hon Mrs Vickery) b 1946 d 1986); m 2, 1979, Pauline Teresa, yst da of late Thomas Keenan, of Johannesburg; *Career* serv Royal Northumberland Fus (TA) 1934–39, Staff Coll Camberley 1939, Lt-Col Gen Staff 1942–46; md Dept Stores NE England 1949–57; MP (C) Poole 1964–79, asst govt whip 1971–72, lord cmmr Treasy 1972–73, dep chm Ways and Means 1973–76 (chm and dep speaker 1976–79), dep chm of Ctees House of Lords 1981–, dep speaker 1983–; *Recreations* sailing, painting; *Style—* The Rt Hon the Lord Murton of Lindisfarne, OBE, TD, PC; ✉ 49 Carlisle Mansions, Carlisle Place, London SW1P 1HY (☎ 0171 834 8226)

MUSGRAVE, Christopher John Shane; s and h of Sir Richard James Musgrave, 7 Bt, *qv*; *b* 23 Oct 1959; *Style—* Christopher Musgrave, Esq

MUSGRAVE, Sir Christopher Patrick Charles; 15 Bt (E 1611), of Hartley Castle, Westmorland; s of Sir Charles Musgrave, 14 Bt (d 1970), and Olive Louise Avril, *née* Cringle; *b* 14 April 1949; *m* 1, 1978 (m dis 1992), Megan, da of Walter Inman, of Hull; 2 da (Helena b 1981, Antonia b 1987); m 2, 1995, Carol, da of Geoffrey Lawson, of Chandler's Ford, Hants; *Heir* bro, Julian Nigel Chardin Musgrave b 8 Dec 1951; *Recreations* sailing; *Style—* Sir Christopher Musgrave, Bt; ✉ c/o National Westminster Bank, West Street, Fareham, Hants

MUSGRAVE, Julian Nigel Chardin; s of Sir Charles Musgrave, 14 Bt (d 1970); h to Btcy of bro, Sir Christopher Patrick Charles Musgrave, 15 Bt, *qv*; *b* 8 Dec 1951; *Educ* S Wymondham Coll, QMC London (BSc); *m* 1975, Gulshanbanu Buddrudin; 2 da (Anar b

1980, Ruth b 1983); *Career* currently md Games World Ltd; mktg conslt; MInstM; *Recreations* music; *Style*— Julian Musgrave, Esq

MUSGRAVE, Mark Jonathan; s of Sir (Frank) Cyril Musgrave, KCB (d 1986), of Cornerfield, Flixton, nr Bungay, Suffolk, and Jean Elsie, *née* Soulsby (d 1993); *b* 6 Oct 1952; *Educ* Haileybury; *m* 1 Sept 1979, Belinda Joan, da of John Hugh Clerk (d 1976), of Kingston, Jamaica; 2 s (William b 1984, George b 1988), 1 da (Chloe b 1987); *Career* admitted slr 1977; Speechly Bircham: ptnr 1981–, personnel ptnr 1988–91, dep managing ptnr 1989–90, fin ptnr 1992–95, managing ptnr 1995–; memb: Justinians 1989, Law Soc 1977, New England Co 1993; *Recreations* tennis, gardening, travel; *Style*— Mark Musgrave, Esq; ✉ Pitchards House, Halstead, Essex CO9 1JH (☎ 01787 472393); Speechly Bircham, Bouverie House, 154 Fleet St, London EC4A 2HX (☎ 0171 353 3290)

MUSGRAVE, Sir Richard James; 7 Bt (I 1782), of Tourin, Waterford; s of Sir Christopher Norman Musgrave, 6 Bt, OBE (d 1956); *b* 10 Feb 1922; *Educ* Stowe; *m* 1958, Maria, da of late Col Mario Cambanis, of Athens; 2 s (Christopher John Shane b 1959, Michael Shane b 1968), 4 da (Olivia Mirabel b 1958, Anastasia Maria (Mrs Robert M Wilson-Wright) b 1961, Charlotte Elizabeth (Mrs James Hanly) b 1963, Alexandra Victoria b 1965); *Heir* s, Christopher John Shane Musgrave b 23 Oct 1959; *Career* 2 Lt 1940, serv 1940–45 India, Middle E, Capt Poona Horse, 17 Queen Victoria's Own Cavalry; *Recreations* shooting, bridge; *Clubs* Kildare Street (Dublin); *Style*— Sir Richard Musgrave, Bt; ✉ Komito, Syros, Greece (fax 00 30 281 23508)

MUSGRAVE, Rosanne Kimble; da of Gp Capt John Raymond Musgrave, DSO, TD, of Burnham Thorpe, Norfolk, and Joanne, *née* Folwell; *b* 31 Jan 1952; *Educ* Cheltenham Ladies' Coll, St Anne's Coll Oxford (MA), Univ of Reading (MA), Inst of Educn Univ of London (PGCE); *Career* asst teacher of Eng: Latymer GS 1976–79, Camden Sch for Girls (ILEA) 1979–82; head of Eng: Channing Sch Highgate 1982–84, Haberdashers' Aske's Sch for Girls Elstree 1984–89; headmistress Blackheath HS (GPDST) London 1989–; *Recreations* letterpress printing, DIY; *Style*— Miss Rosanne Musgrave; ✉ Blackheath High School (GPDST), Vanbrugh Park, London SE3 7AG (☎ 0181 853 2929, fax 0181 853 3663)

MUSGRAVE, Thea (Mrs Peter Mark); da of James P Musgrave (d 1971), of Edinburgh, and Joan, *née* Hacking; *b* 27 May 1928; *Educ* Moreton Hall Oswestry, Univ of Edinburgh (MusB), private study in Paris with Nadia Boulanger; *m* 2 Oct 1971, Peter Mark, s of Irving Mark (d 1987), of Sarasota, Florida; *Career* composer; active as conductor of own work; performances at festivals: Edinburgh, Warsaw, Aldeburgh, Cheltenham, Zagreb, Florence Maggio Musicale, Venice Biennale; numerous broadcastings and recordings; distinguished prof Queen's Coll City Univ NY; hon fell New Hall Cambridge 1973; Hon Doctorates: Cncl Nat Academic Awards 1976, Smith Coll USA 1979, Old Dominion Univ Norfolk Virginia 1980, Univ of Glasgow 1995; *Orchestral works* incl: Beauty and the Beast (ballet) 1968–69, Concerto for Clarinet and Orchestra (cmmnd Royal Philharmonic Soc in assoc with Calouste Gulbenkian Fndn) 1968, Horn Concerto 1971, Viola Concerto (cmmnd BBC) 1973, Peripeteia (cmmnd RPO) 1981, The Seasons (cmmnd Acad of St Martin's in the Fields) 1988, Song of the Enchanter (cmmnd Helsinki Philharmonic) 1990, Autumn Sonata (cmmnd Victoria Soames) 1993, Journey Through a Japanese Landscape (cmmnd Br Assoc of Symphonic Bands and Wind Ensembles and Consortium of Music Colleges) 1993–94, Helios (cmmnd St Magnus Festival) 1994; *Chamber and instrumental works* incl: Chamber Concerto No 1 1962, Chamber Concerto No 2 1966, Chamber Concerto No 3 1966, Space Play (cmmnd Serge Koussevitzky Music Fndn) 1974, Pierrot 1985, Wind Quintet (cmmnd Barlow Endowment for music composition) 1992, Postcards from Spain (cmmd Sam Dorsey & Tidewater Classical Guitar Soc) 1995; *Vocal and choral music* incl: Rorate Coeli 1973, For the Time Being: Advent 1986, Midnight (cmmnd Laura Lane & Nova Singers) 1992, Wild Winter (cmmnd Lichfield Festival) 1993, On the Underground Set No 1: On Gratitude, Love & Madness (cmmnd Canzonetta) 1994, On the Underground Set No 2: The Strange and the Exotic (cmmnd Ithaca Coll) 1994, On the Underground Set No 3: A Medieval Summer (cmmnd Ionian Singers) 1995; *Operas* incl: The Voice of Ariadne (cmmnd Royal Opera House) 1973, Mary Queen of Scots (cmmnd Scottish Opera) 1975–77, A Christmas Carol (cmmnd Virginia Opera Assoc) 1978–79, Harriet, An Occurrence at Owl Creek Bridge (cmmnd BBC) 1981, The Woman Called Moses (cmmnd jtly Royal Opera House and Virginia Opera Assoc) 1984, Simon Bolivar (cmmnd Los Angeles Music Center and Scottish Opera) 1989–92; *Style*— Miss Thea Musgrave; ✉ c/o Novello & Co Ltd, 8–9 Frith Street, London W1V 5TZ (☎ 0171 434 0066, fax 0171 287 6329)

MUSGROVE, Harold John; s of Harold John Musgrove (d 1984), and Francis, *née* Clements (d 1983); *b* 19 Nov 1930; *Educ* King Edward GS Birmingham, Birmingham Tech Coll; *m* 1959, Jacqueline; 2 s (Michael b 1963, James b 1972), 2 da (Sarah b 1969, Laura b 1970); *Career* cmmnd navigator RAF 1945; various positions Austin Motor Co 1945–63, memb sr mgmnt Truck and Bus Gp Leyland Motor Corp 1963–78; Austin Morris Ltd: dir of mfrg 1978–79, md 1979–80, chm and md 1980–81, chm Light Medium Cars Gp 1981–82; chm and chief exec Austin Rover Group 1982–86, chm Power Supplies and Lighting Gp Chloride plc 1991–92 (chm Industl Battery Sector 1988–91); dir: Chloride plc 1989–92, Metalrax Group 1987–; chm W Midland Ambulance Trust 1992–94, chm Birmingham Heartlands & Solihull Hosp NHS Tst 1994–; pres Birmingham C of C 1987–88, pres Aston Villa FC 1986–96; Midlander of the Year award 1980, Instn of Prodn Engrs Int award 1981, The Soc of Engrs Churchill Medal 1982; FIMI 1985; *Recreations* golf, soccer; *Style*— Harold John Musgrove, Esq; ✉ The Lodge, Laverton, Broadway, Worcs WR12 7NA

MUSHIN, Alan Spencer; s of Dr Louis Mushin (d 1984); *b* 31 Jan 1938; *Educ* Haberdashers' Aske's, London Hosp Med Coll (MB BS); *m* 27 Feb 1972, Joan Carolyn, da of Dr Simon Behrman, of Harley St, London; 1 s (James b 1976), 1 da (Rosalind b 1974); *Career* conslt: ophthalmic surgn Moorfield Eye Hosp London, Royal London Hosp, Queen Elizabeth Hosp for Children; memb Br Paediatric Assoc; fell Royal Coll of Ophthalmologists; BMA, FRSM, FRCS; *Books* papers on paediatric ophthalmology; *Recreations* photography, philately, gardening; *Clubs* Savage; *Style*— Alan S Mushin, Esq; ✉ 935 Finchley Rd, London NW11 7PE (☎ 0181 455 7212); 82 Harley Street, London W1N 1AE (☎ 0171 580 3116); The Dower House, Oxney, St Margarets-at-Cliffe, Kent

MUSKERRY, 9 Baron (I 1781); Sir Robert Fitzmaurice Deane; 14 Bt (I 1710); s of 8 Baron Muskerry (d 14 Oct 1988), and Betty Fairbridge, *née* Palmer (d 20 Aug 1988); *b* 26 March 1948; *Educ* Sandford Park Sch Dublin, Trinity Coll Dublin (BA, BAI); *m* 1975, Rita Brink, of Pietermaritzburg, S Africa; 1 s (Hon Jonathan Fitzmaurice b 1986), 2 da (Hon Nicola b 1976, Hon Catherine b 1978); *Heir* s, Hon Jonathan Fitzmaurice Deane b 7 June 1986; *Career* shipyard mangr Dorbyl Marine, dir Dorbyl Marine Ltd; md: Stride Ltd, Bridco Ltd, Elgin Brown and Hamer (Pty) Ltd; *Style*— The Rt Hon Lord Muskerry; ✉ 725 Ridge Road, Berea, Durban 4001, S Africa

MUSSELLWHITE, Philip; *b* 6 Nov 1938; *Educ* Langley Sch Loddon Norfolk; *m* 1962; 2 c; *Career* Pauls plc group: mangr Tower Mills Ltd (subsid of Pauls Foods Ltd) 1964–71, sales mangr E Anglia Pauls & Whites Foods Ltd 1971–74, area gen mangr Pauls & Whites Foods Ltd 1974–77 (bd dir 1976), asst md Pauls Agriculture Ltd 1977–81, Pauls & Whites International Ltd 1981–84, md Pauls Flavours & Fragrances Ltd and main bd dir Pauls plc 1984–87; md Hubbard Commercial Products Ltd 1987–89, gp co sec Serif Cowells plc 1989–92; chm Ipswich Hospital NHS Tst 1992–; vice pres Suffolk Agricultural Assoc 1996, memb Exec Ctee UK Agric Supply Assoc 1974–77, exec memb Br Essence Mfrs Assoc 1984–87, memb Cncl Suffolk c of C 1994–, sec Suffolk Branch IOD 1992–96; sec Int Flying Fifteen Assoc 1971–74, memb Ipswich Dock Users' Ctee 1974–77, treas and exec memb Ipswich and Suffolk Marriage Guidance Cncl (now Relate) 1978–84; FIMgt 1984; *Recreations* sailing (cruising), music, theatre, reading, gardening, the countryside; *Clubs* Farmers'; *Style*— Philip Mussellwhite, Esq; ✉ Low Farm, Eyke, Woodbridge, Suffolk IP12 2QF; Ipswich Hospital NHS Trust, Heath Road Wing, Ipswich, Suffolk IP4 5PD

MUSSELWHITE, Nigel; CBE (1994), QFSM (1984); *b* 29 Nov 1939; *Educ* Bromley County GS; *Career* fireman; divnl offr London 1959–74; City of London Police 1960–61, London Fire Bde 1961–76 (1959–60), divnl offr and sr instr Fire Servs Coll 1974–76; Somerset Fire Bde: dep chief offr 1976–78, chief fire offr 1978–89; Her Majesty's Inspr of Fire Servs 1989; awarded Fire Serv Medal for long serv and good conduct 1981; OStJ; AIFireE, MISM; Merité Fédéral France 1981; *Recreations* motor racing, golf, sailing, model making; *Clubs* St Johns; *Style*— Nigel Musselwhite, Esq, CBE, QFSM; ✉ Rhodes Cottage, Banklands, North Newton, Taunton, Somerset TA7 0DQ; Home Office Fire Service Inspectorate, Wiltshire Court, Farnsby Street, Swindon, Wiltshire SN1 5AN (☎ 01793 616480)

MUSSON, Gen Sir Geoffrey Randolph Dixon; GCB (1970), CBE (1945), DSO (1944); s of Robert Dixon Musson (d 1957); *b* 9 June 1910; *Educ* Shrewsbury, Trinity Hall Cambridge; *m* 1939, Hon Elspeth Lorraine; 1 s, 1 da (decd); *Career* 2 Lt KSLI 1930, Brig 1944, cmd Cwlth Forces in Korea 1954–55, Maj-Gen 1958, Maj-Gen cmd 7 Armd Div 1958 and 5 Div 1958–59, COS MELF 1959–62, Col KSLI 1963–68, Lt-Gen GOC Northern Cmd 1964–67, Adj Gen MOD 1967–70, Gen 1968, Col LI 1968–72; vice chm Nat Savings Ctee, chm HM Forces Savings Ctee 1970–78, vice pres Royal Patriotic Fund Corpn 1974–83, pres Victory (Servs) Club 1970–80; *Clubs* Army and Navy; *Style*— Gen Sir Geoffrey Musson, GCB, CBE, DSO; ✉ Barn Cottage, Hurstbourne Tarrant, Andover, Hants SP11 0BD (☎ 0126 473 6354)

MUSTILL, Baron (Life Peer UK 1992), of Pateley Bridge in the County of North Yorkshire; Sir Michael John Mustill; kt (1978), PC (1985); s of Clement William Mustill; *b* 10 May 1931; *Educ* Oundle, St John's Coll Cambridge; *m* 1, 1960 (m dis 1983), Beryl Reid Davies; 2 c; m 2, Caroline Phillips; 1 step da; *Career* barr Gray's Inn 1955, QC 1968, recorder of the Crown Ct 1972–78, judge High Ct of Justice (Queen's Bench Div) 1978–85, a Lord Justice of Appeal 1985–91, a Lord of Appeal in Ordinary 1991–; chm Civil Serv Appeal Tbnl 1971–78; Liveryman Worshipful Co of Grocers; FBA 1996; *Style*— The Rt Hon Lord Mustill, FBA; ✉ c/o House of Lords, London SW1A 0PW

MUSTOE, Nicholas (Nick); s of Raymond Mustoe, of Claygate, Surrey, and Maureen, *née* Pringle; *b* 7 July 1961; *Educ* Wimbledon Coll, Esher Coll, Coll of Distributive Trades; *Career* account mangr Foote Cone & Belding advtg agency 1981–84, account mangr rising to asst md/client servs dir Lowe Howard-Spink 1984–93, fndr chief exec Mustoe Merriman Herring Levy Ltd 1993–; *Recreations* golf, squash, relaxing, work; *Style*— Nick Mustoe, Esq; ✉ Mustoe Merriman Herring Levy, 133 Long Acre, Covent Garden, London WC2E 9AG (☎ 0171 379 9999, fax 0171 379 8487)

MUSTON, (Frederick Charles) Lee; s of Howard Alfred Paul Muston, and Rose Amelia Muston, of Chaddesden, Derby; *b* 13 Sept 1943; *Educ* Bemrose GS, Bishop Lonsdale Coll, Open Univ (BA, CertEd); *m* 20 Aug 1966, Irene Mary, *née* Barker; 1 s (Nicholas John b 17 Oct 1971), 1 da (Jena Victoria b 20 Dec 1973); *Career* asst teacher Darwin Co Secdy Sch Breadsall Derby 1965–67, head Liberal Studies Dept Spondon House Sch Derby 1967–70, head Humanities Dept Cranbourne Sch Basingstoke 1970–74, dep headmaster Larkmead Sch Abingdon 1974–80, headteacher Middleton Park HS Leeds 1980–84, headteacher Fakenham HS 1984–; *Recreations* rugby, cricket, poetry, cooking; *Style*— Lee Muston, Esq; ✉ Fakenham High School, Wells Road, Fakenham, Norfolk NR21 7HP (☎ 01328 862238, 01328 862545, fax 01328 855337)

MUSTOW, Stuart Norman; CBE (1995); s of Norman Eric Mustow (d 1976), of Birmingham, and Mabel Florence, *née* Purcell (d 1972); *b* 26 Nov 1928; *Educ* King Edward VI GS Birmingham, Coll of Advanced Tech Birmingham (now Univ of Aston) (BSc); *m* 8 Aug 1964, Sigrid Hertha, da of Georg Wendt, of Germany; 2 s (Stephen Eric b 16 March 1966, Paul Stuart b 19 Sept 1969), 1 da (Ruth Eleanor b 11 Oct 1967); *Career* various appointments in local govt, dep borough engr and surveyor Wolverhampton 1966–69, city engr and surveyor Stoke-on-Trent 1969–74, county surveyor West Midlands CC 1974–86, consulting engr 1986–, dir WS Atkins conslts 1986–94; chm Streetworks Advsy Ctee to Sec of State for Tport 1987–95; pres: Inst Municipal Engineers 1980, ICE 1993–94; vice pres Royal Acad of Engrg 1995–, memb Cncl (now Senate) Engrg Cncl 1995–; visiting prof Univ of Ulster 1993–; chm Birmingham Standing Conf for the Single Homeless 1988–95; Viva Award Worshipful Co of Carmen (jtly with West Mids CC) 1984, Parkman medal ICE (with P B Ronan) 1989; Hon DSc Aston 1994; FICE 1969, FIHT 1970, FEng 1982, FRSA; *Recreations* mountain walking, swimming, church, social work; *Style*— Stuart Mustow, Esq, CBE, FEng; ✉ c/o Royal Academy of Engineering, 29 Great Peter Street, London SW1P 3LW

MYDDELTON, Prof David Roderic; s of Dr Geoffrey Cheadle Myddelton, of Glutieres-sur-Ollon, Switzerland, and Jacqueline Esther, *née* Nathan; *b* 11 April 1940; *Educ* Eton, Harvard Business Sch (MBA); *m* 28 April 1986, Hatherley Angela d'Abo; 1 step s (Charles b 1975), 1 step da (Louisa b 1974); *Career* CA 1961; lectr fin and accounting Cranfield 1965–69, lectr accounting London Business Sch 1969–72, prof of fin and accounting Cranfield 1972–; chm Academic Advsy Cncl Univ of Buckingham, a managing tstee Inst of Economic Affairs; ACIS 1966, FCA 1971; *Books* The Power to Destroy (1969, 2 edn 1994), The Meaning of Company Accounts (1971, 6 edn 1996), On A Cloth Untrue (1984), The Economy And Business Decisions (1984), Essential Management Accounting (1987, 2 edn 1992), Accounting and Financial Decisions (1991), The Essence of Financial Management (1994); *Recreations* crossword puzzles, jigsaw puzzles; *Style*— Prof D R Myddelton; ✉ Cranfield Sch of Management, Cranfield, Bedford MK43 OAL (☎ 01234 754404)

MYDDELTON, Roger Hugh; *Educ* Univ of Cambridge; *Career* admitted slr 1966, with Rank Xerox Ltd 1968–78; Courtaulds plc: joined 1978, gp legal advsr 1979–88, also dir of corp affrs 1986–88; Grand Metropolitan plc: gp legal dir and co sec 1988–, also i/c risk mgmnt and insurance; dir: Centre for Alternative Dispute Resolution (CEDR), ProShare; *Style*— Roger Myddelton, Esq; ✉ Grand Metropolitan plc, 8 Henrietta Place, London W1M 9AG (☎ 0171 518 5277, fax 0171 518 4637)

MYERS, Allan James; QC (1988); *b* 14 Oct 1947; *Educ* Monivae Coll Hamilton Victoria, Univ of Melbourne (BA, LLB), Univ of Oxford (BCL); *Career* barr and slr Supreme Court of Victoria 1971, asst prof of law Osgood Hall Law Sch Yorke Univ Toronto 1972–73, visiting fell Wadham Coll Oxford 1973, assoc Corr & Corr slrs 1974–75, ind lectr in law Univ of Melbourne 1974–88, signed Roll of Counsel Victoria 1975; barr and slr: Supreme Court of Aust Capital Territory 1977, Supreme Court of Western Aust 1978, Supreme Court Tasmania 1986, Supreme Court of S Aust 1986; barr: NSW 1984, Queensland 1990, Northern Territory 1990; appointed QC: Victoria 1986, Tasmania 1987, S Aust 1987, Western Aust 1987, Aust Capital Territory 1987, NSW 1987, Queensland 1990, Northern Territory 1990; called to the English Bar Lincoln's Inn 1988; former memb Cncl Taxation Inst of Australia; regular presenter of papers at legal conventions; *Publications* Australian Taxation Review (ed 1975–93), author of numerous articles on revenue law; *Style*— Allan Myers, Esq, QC; ✉ c/o Chambers Administrator, 4 Field Court, Gray's Inn, London WC1R 5EA (☎ 0171 440 6900, fax 0171 242 0197)

MYERS, Bernard Ian; s of Edward Nathan Myers (d 1986), and Isabel Violet, *née* Viner; *b* 2 April 1944; *Educ* Hendon Co GS, LSE (BSc Econ); *m* 17 Sept 1967, Sandra Hannah, da of Samuel Barc (d 1980); 1 s (Andrew b 1972), 2 da (Lara b 1969, Lyndsey b 1974); *Career* accountant 1962–72, merchant banker 1972–; dir many cos incl: Shield Tst Ltd 1976–, Spiremore Ltd 1986–, N M R Int NV 1983, Rothschilds Continuation Holdings AG 1983–, Rothschilds Continuation Ltd 1984–, Rothschild Inc 1984–, Smith New Ct plc 1985–95, md (gp fin and overseas) N M Rothschild & Sons Ltd 1988–, (dir 1976); FCA; *Recreations* opera, golf, theatre; *Style—* Bernard I Myers, Esq; ✉ N M Rothschild & Sons Ltd, New Ct, St Swithin's Lane, London EC4P 4DU (☎ 0171 280 5000, fax 0171 929 1643)

MYERS, Dr Edward David; s of Barnet Myers (d 1965), of Harare, Zimbabwe, and Annie Hilda, *née* Rubinstein (d 1978); *b* 15 July 1925; *Educ* Prince Edward Sch Harare Zimbabwe, Capetown Univ (MB ChB, DTM&H, DPM); *m* 14 Jan 1966, Sybil Brearley, da of John Chatfield (d 1981), of Stoke-on-Trent, Staffs; 2 s (Benjamin John b 19 March 1967, David Edward b 4 Jan 1969); *Career* res med offr Gen Hosp Salisbury S Rhodesia 1949; house physician: High Wycombe War Meml Hosp Bucks, St Andrew's Hosp London, Whittington Hosp London, Neuro-Surgical Unit Oldchurch Hosp Romford Essex 1950–52; med registrar Royal Infirmary Preston 1952–54, psychiatric registrar Banstead, Surrey and Charing Cross Hosps 1956–59, conslt psychiatrist in private practice and sessional conslt in psychiatry Harare Central Hosp Salisbury S Rhodesia 1960–62, sr psychiatric registrar St Edward's Hosp Cheddleton and City Gen Hosp Stoke-on-Trent 1963–66, conslt psychiatrist N Staffs Health Dist 1966–91 (ret), sr res fell in psychiatry Dept of Postgrad Med Univ of Keele 1980–90, hon res fell in psychiatry Sch of Postgrad Med and Biological Sciences Univ of Keele 1991–; author of several papers on compliance with treatment, attempted suicide and psychoendocrinology; memb: Br Assoc of Psychopharmacology, Hosp Conslts and Specialists Assoc; Osler Club of London; FRCP(Ed), FRCPsych; *Recreations* fly-fishing, bowls, theatre-going, medical history; *Style—* Dr Edward Myers; ✉ St David's, 96 Lancaster Rd, Newcastle-under-Lyme, Staffordshire ST5 1DS

MYERS, (Harry) Eric; QC (1967); s of Harry Moss Myers, and Alice Muriel, *née* Serjeant; *b* 10 Jan 1914; *Educ* Bedford Sch; *m* 1951, Lorna Babette Kitson, *née* Blackburn; *Career* joined HAC City of London 1931; admitted slr 1936, called to the Bar Middle Temple 1945, prosecuting counsel to Bd of Inland Revenue 1965; QC Gibraltar 1977; *Style—* Eric Myers, Esq, QC; ✉ 10 King's Bench Walk, Temple, London EC4Y 7EB

MYERS, Gordon Elliot; CMG (1979); s of William Lionel Myers (d 1984), and Yvonne, *née* Arthur (d 1938); *b* 4 July 1929; *Educ* Kilburn GS, Univ Coll Oxford (MA); *m* 23 April 1963, Wendy Jane, da of Charles Thomas Lambert (d 1971), of London; 2 s (Andrew James b 1964, Malcolm John b 1965), 1 da (Lucinda Joy Lambert b 1968); *Career* formerly under sec of Arable Crops, Pigs and Poultry MAFF, min (Agric) Office of UK Permanent Representative to Euro Communities 1975–79, ret 1989; memb Euro Cmmn Working Gp on Simplification of Common Agric Policy 1990–94, currently Euro rep Caribbean Banana Exporters' Assoc; *Recreations* music, theatre, gardening, tennis; *Clubs* Utd Oxford and Cambridge; *Style—* Gordon Myers, Esq, CMG; ✉ Woodlands, Nugents Park, Hatch End, Middx HA5 4RA

MYERS, Ian David; s of Stuart Charles Myers, of Oxshott, Surrey, and Enid, *née* Alexander; *b* 3 Aug 1954; *Educ* Latymer Upper Sch London, Pembroke Coll Oxford (MA); *m* 1976, Helen Rosemary, *née* Bennett; 2 s (Nikolai James Elliot b 23 April 1982, Anatoly Cornelius Constantine Wreyland b 18 Dec 1987), 1 da (Anastasia Tiffany b 2 July 1979); *Career* White Weld & Co London 1977–78 (NY office 1976–77), chm PaineWebber International (UK) Ltd 1990– (joined 1978, dir 1987), dir PaineWebber Inc 1989–; *Style—* Ian Myers, Esq; ✉ PaineWebber International (UK) Ltd, 1 Finsbury Ave, London EC2M 2PA (☎ 0171 422 2000)

MYERS, John David; s of Frank Myers (d 1949), and Monica, *née* Paden (d 1973); *b* 30 Oct 1937; *Educ* Marist Coll Hull, St Mary's Coll Strawberry Hill Middx, Loughborough Coll of Physical Educn, Univ of Hull; *m* 17 April 1974, Anne McGeough, wid, da of Michael Purcell (d 1985); 1 s (Ian James b 1972); *Career* sch master 1958–64, called to the Bar Gray's Inn 1968, Hull practice 1969–82, chm Industl Tbnls 1982–; *Recreations* music, wine, golf, bridge, cooking; *Style—* John Myers, Esq; ✉ Regional Office of Industrial Tribunals, Quayside House, 110 Quayside, Newcastle upon Tyne NE1 3DX

MYERS, Prof Norman; s of John Myers (d 1963), of Whitehall, nr Slaidburn, Yorks, and Gladys, *née* Haworth (d 1994); *b* 24 Aug 1934; *Educ* Clitheroe Royal GS, Keble Coll Oxford (MA), Univ of California Berkeley (PhD); *m* 11 Dec 1965, Dorothy Mary, da of Frank Halliman (d 1966), of Nairobi, Kenya; 2 da (Malindi b 3 Oct 1970, Mara b 13 Aug 1973); *Career* Nat Serv RA 1952–53 (invalided out); dist offr Overseas Admin Kenya 1958–60, teacher Delamere Boys' Sch Nairobi 1961–64, professional wildlife photographer and TV film-maker E Africa 1965–68, conslt in environment and devpt 1972–; res and projects in over 80 countries incl assignments for: The World Bank, UN agencies, Nat Acads of US, OECD, EEC, World Cmmn Environment and Devpt; foreign assoc US Nat Acad of Scis, Pew scholar in conservation and environment, fell Green Coll Univ of Oxford, chm and visiting prof of int environment Univ of Utrecht Netherlands; visiting prof: Univ of Kent, Univ of Texas and Cornell Univ, Univ of Cape Town; Regents lectr Univ of California, res assoc Oxford Forestry Inst and Int Devpt Centre Univ of Oxford, sr fell World Wildlife Fund US; memb: Int Platform Assoc, Global Cncl World Resources Inst, bd of dirs of 16 orgns; fell: World Acad Arts and Sci 1988, American Assoc for the Advancement of Science 1990; FRSA 1993, FLS 1993; *Awards* Gold medal and Order of Golden Ark World Wildlife Fund International, Gold medal of New York Zoological Soc, Global 500 Roll of Honour UN Environment Programme, Special Achievement award International Environment Protection Sierra Club US, Distinguished Achievement award Soc for Conservation Biology, Gold medal San Diego Zoological Soc, jt recipient Volvo Environment Prize 1992, UN Sasakawa Environment Prize 1995; *Books* The Long African Day (1972), The Sinking Ark (1979), Conversion of Tropical Moist Forests (1980), A Wealth of Wild Species (1983), The Primary Source: Tropical Forests and Our Future (1984 and 1992), The Gaia Atlas of Planet Management (1986), Future Worlds (1990), Tropical Forests and Climate (1991), Ultimate Security: The Environmental Basis of Political Stability (1993), Scarcity or Abundance: A Debate on the Environment (1994); author over 200 papers in professional jls; *Recreations* marathon running, photography, mountaineering; *Clubs* Achilles; *Style—* Prof Norman Myers; ✉ Upper Meadow, Old Road, Headington, Oxford OX3 8SZ (☎ 01865 750387, fax 01865 741538, e-mail normanmyers@gn.apc.org)

MYERS, Sir Philip Alan; kt (1985), OBE (1977), QPM (1972), DL (Clwyd 1983); *b* 7 Feb 1931; *m* 1951, Hazel; 2 s; *Career* Shrops Constabulary 1950–67, W Mercia Police 1967–68, dep chief constable Gwynedd Constabulary 1968–70, chief constable N Wales Police 1970–81, one of HM's Insprs of Constabulary 1982–93; *Style—* Sir Philip Myers, OBE, QPM, DL

MYERS, Richard Scales; s of Harry Myers (d 1978), of Mirfield, and Bertha, *née* Morgan (d 1986); *b* 13 July 1954; *Educ* Bolton Sch Lancs; *m* 1983, Jacky; 2 da (Georgina Foy, Olivia Jane); *Career* reporter and sub ed Farnworth Journal 1972–74, reporter Bolton Evening News 1974–76, duty ed BRMB Radio 1976–79, sr sub ed and reporter RTE Dublin 1979–81, chief writer Early Evening News and News at Ten ITN 1981–83, prodr RTE Dublin 1985–86, ed and head of news TSW Plymouth 1986–89, prodr and ed London News LWT 1989–91; Westcountry Television Ltd: controller of news and current affairs 1991–95, dir of news and sport 1995–; *Recreations* cookery, wines, music, travel; *Style—* Richard Myers, Esq; ✉ Westcountry Television Ltd, Western Wood Way, Langage Science Park, Plymouth, Devon PL7 5BG (☎ 01752 333330, fax 01752 333444)

MYERS, Simon Nicholas; s of Brian Edward Myers (d 1992), and Avery Long, *née* Stephens; *b* 25 Oct 1963; *Educ* Marple Ridge HS, Coventry Poly (BSc); *m* 6 July 1990, Karen Marie, da of John Hamilton Schouw; 2 da (Sophie Elizabeth, Olivia Grace); *Career* advtg exec; Gold Greenlees Trott: account mangr 1986–89, account dir 1989–91, assoc dir 1990–91; independent world travel 1991–92; account dir Simons Palmer Denton Clemmow and Johnson 1992–94, jt dep md Collett Dickenson Pearce and Partners 1996– (dir-in-charge/head of account mgmnt 1994–96); *Style—* Simon Myers, Esq; ✉ Collett Dickenson Pearce & Partners, 33–34 Soho Square, London W1V 6DP (☎ 0171 292 4099, fax 0171 292 4012)

MYERSCOUGH, Ishbel; da of Henry Ferdinand Myerscough, of London, and Elizabeth Cricthton Fraser; *b* 5 Nov 1968; *Educ* Highbury Hill HS, City of London Sch for Girls, Glasgow Sch of Art (BA), Slade Sch of Art (postgrad with distinction); *Career* artist; *Exhibitions* incl: Van Gough Self-Portrait Exhbn (Burrell Collection Glasgow) 1990–91, RSA Student Exhbns Edinburgh 1990 and 1991, Nat Portrait Gallery Portrait Competition Exhbn 1990, 1991 and 1992, one man show Turtle Quay Art Centre London 1992, RGI 131st Annual Exhbn McLellan Gallery Glasgow 1992, ROI annual show Mall Gallery London 1994, Treasures of the Nat Portrait Gallery (touring show Japan) 1995–96, Group Realist Show Berlin 1995; *Awards* incl: John & Mabel Craig Bequest 1990 and 1991, Elizabeth Greenshields Fndn award 1991 and 1993, first prize in gp Hunting/Observer plc Prize for Art 1992, Nat Portrait Gallery BP Portrait Awards 1st prize 1995 (commended 1991 and 1993, 3rd prize 1992), National Westminster Bank prize for Art 3rd prize; *Style—* Miss Ishbel Myerscough; ✉ Anthony Mould Ltd, 173 New Bond Street, London W1Y 9PF (☎ 0171 491 4627, fax 0171 355 3865)

MYERSCOUGH-JONES, (Arthur) David; s of Frederick Cecil Sidney Jones, and Lilian Dorothy Jones; *b* 15 Sept 1934; *Educ* Bickerton House Sch Southport, Southport Sch of Art, Central Sch of Art (DA); *m* 23 Feb 1963, (Ursula Theodora Joy) Pelo, da of Charles Graham Cumpston (d 1968), of Barton Hall, Pooley Bridge, Cumbria; 1 s (Richard b 23 June 1969), 3 da (Frances b 21 Feb 1966, Ellen b 21 July 1971, Madeleine b 15 Sept 1974); *Career* theatre designer; Citizens Theatre Glasgow 1958–60, res designer Mermaid Theatre London 1961–65; TV designer: Peter Grimes 1969, Winterreise 1970, Owen Wingrave B Britten (world premiere) 1971, The Flying Dutchman (Royal TV Soc Award) 1976, Therese Raquin (BAFTA Design Award, D&AD Gold and Silver awards) 1983, Orde Wingate Trilogy, The Beggars Opera, Cosi Fan Tutte and The Theban Plays (ACE Nomination for Art Direction Los Angeles) 1988 and 1989; recent prodns for BBC TV incl: How Many Miles to Babylon, A Midsummer Night's Dream, Virtuoso, The Master Builder, Metamorphosis, Bomber Harris, Circles of Deceit; adapted Trevor Nunn's RSC prodn of Othello for television 1989, freelance prodn designer 1990–; recent prodns: Stagelands 1992, You Never Can Tell 1995 and Cold Comfort Farm 1996 (all Michael Friend Theatre Prodns), La Bohème (Bath City Opera) 1992, The Hawk (feature film, Initial/BBC), Il Trovatore and Il Barbiere di Siviglia (Festival Opera Walnut Creek Calif) 1993, La Traviata and The Turn of the Screw (Bath and Wessex Opera) 1993, The Rime of the Ancient Mariner (BBC) 1994, Young Jung (BBC) 1994, Don Giovanni and Rigoletto (Bath and Wessex Opera and Opera Northern Ireland) 1994; FCSD 1985; *Recreations* music, opera and painting; *Style—* David Myerscough-Jones; ✉ 6 The Vineyards, Bath BA1 5NA (☎ and fax 01225 319479)

MYERSON, His Hon Judge Arthur Levey; QC (1974); s of Barnett Myerson, of Leeds, and Eda Jane, *née* Lewene; *b* 25 July 1928; *Educ* Blackpool GS, Queens' Coll Cambridge (BA, LLB), Open Univ (BA); *m* 1960, Elaine Shirley, da of Sam Harris, of Leeds; 2 s (Simon, Nicholas); *Career* RAF 1946–48 AC1; called to the Bar 1952, circuit judge (NE Circuit) 1978–, pres Cncl of Circuit Judges 1991–92 (memb Ctee 1985–92); *Recreations* reading, walking, sailing; *Clubs* Cwlth Tst, Moor Allerton Golf; *Style—* His Hon Judge Arthur Myerson, QC; ✉ Courthouse, Oxford Place, Leeds LS7

MYERSON, Jonathan Scott; JP (1993); s of Aubrey Selwyn Myerson, QC (d 1986), and Helen Margaret, *née* Lavis; *b* 12 Jan 1960; *Educ* Westminster, Lincoln Coll Oxford (MA, ed Isis, vice pres OUDS); *m* Julie Susan Myerson; 2 s (Jacob Aubrey b 31 Jan 1989, Raphael Benjamin b 16 April 1992), 1 da (Chloë Emilia b 1 Jan 1991); *Career* director and playwright; awarded Regional Theatre Trainee Directors Bursary 1983; memb Cncl Directors' Guild of GB 1986 and 1988–89 (vice chm 1990), memb Writers' Guild of GB (Radio Ctee 1994–, exec cncl 1996); *Theatre* resident dir Harrogate Theatre 1983–85 prodns incl: Ubu (writer-dir), Jane Eyre and The Woman In White (writer); staff dir Nat Theatre 1986–87 incl: Sung and Unsung, Wiener Schnitzler (also writer), Diary of a Somebody (also writer); as freelance dir: Diary of a Somebody (King's Head and Boulevard), Every Good Boy Deserves Favour (RPO at Queen Elizabeth Hall), Tartuffe Today (Lyric Theatre Belfast); as writer: Iliad (London and Edinburgh) 1982, Tantalus (Edinburgh) 1983, Odyssey (Edinburgh) 1983, Making a Difference (Oxford Playhouse Co) 1981, Candide (Oxford Playhouse) 1981, Wiener Schnitzler (NT) 1987; *Radio* plays incl: Candide (BBC World Serv) 1986, One of Our Aircraft Is Missing (Radio 4) 1987, God's Scapegoat (Radio 3) 1988, In Spite or Because (Radio 4) 1990, Hereafter (Radio 4) 1992, Not Just for Christmas (Radio 4) 1993, You Choose (Radio 4, writer-dir) 1993, Angel Standing (Radio 4) 1994, Inherit the Kingdom (trilogy of plays: A Great Gulf Fixed, My Bed in the Darkness, Get Wisdom Get Understanding, Radio 4) 1995, That Silent Sea (Radio 4) 1996; episodes of Citizens (Radio 4) 1989, The Verdict (Radio 4) 1993; *Televison* incl: episodes of The Bill, EastEnders, Medics, Jupiter Moon; *Film* animations: David and Saul, Daniel, The Canterbury Tales; *Recreations* cricket (playing but better at watching), buying books, cooking for others, and silence; *Style—* Jonathan Myerson, Esq, JP; ✉ c/o Valerie Hoskins Associates, 20 Charlotte Street, London W1P 1HJ (☎ 0171 637 4490, fax 0171 637 4493)

MYERSON, Julie Susan; da of Geoffrey Pike (d 1991), and Maritza Simpson, *née* Jackson; *b* 2 June 1960; *Educ* Nottingham HS for Girls, Univ of Bristol (BA); *Partner* Jonathan Myerson; 2 s (Jacob b 1989, Raphael b 1992), 1 da (Chloë b 1991); *Career* writer; sometime memb Press Office Nat Theatre, Press Office Walker Books, weekly columnist Independent 1995–96; vol telephone counsellor Childline; *Novels* Sleepwalking (1994, shortlisted John Llewellyn Rhys Prize 1995), The Touch (1996); *Style—* Ms Julie Myerson; ✉ c/o Gill Coleridge, Rogers, Coleridge & White, 20 Powis Mews, London W11 1JN (☎ 0171 221 3717)

MYHILL, Stephen Richard; s of Frederick James Myhill, and Sybil Eileen Myhill (d 1976); *b* 17 June 1945; *Educ* Hatfield Sch; *m* 1, 24 Sept 1966 (m dis 1980), Anne Beatrice, da of Eric William Hyatt (d 1990), of Birch Green, Hertford; 2 s (Carl b 23 July 1968, Douglas b 12 Nov 1970); m 2, 26 Jan 1985, Susan Ann, da of Peter Cresswell, of Kensington; 1 s (Edward b 16 May 1990), 2 da (Kirsty b 29 Oct 1985, Sophie b 18 Aug 1987); *Career* Midland Bank 1962–71, Access Credit Card 1972–79, gen mangr Diners Club Saudi Arabia 1979–80, vice pres Citibank (UK) 1981–87, dir personal banking Girobank 1987–91, commercial dir Birmingham Midshires Building Soc 1992–, md Birmingham Midshires Mortgage Services Ltd 1996–; chm Birmingham Midshires (Guernsey) Ltd 1994–; ACIB 1967; *Recreations* golf, tennis, travel; *Style—* Stephen Myhill, Esq; ✉ 33 Marshal's Drive, St Albans, Herts AL1 4RB (☎ 01727 760657)

MYLAND, (Howard) David; CB (1988); s of John Tarrant Myland (d 1957), and Frances Grace, *née* Hopgood (d 1978); *b* 23 June 1929; *Educ* Queen Mary's Basingstoke; *m* 18 Aug 1951, Barbara Pearl, da of Sydney Walter Mills (d 1982); 2 s (Richard b 1955,

Anthony b 1960), 1 da (Sarah b 1957); *Career* Intelligence Corps 1948–50; Exchequer and Audit Dept (became Nat Audit Office 1984) 1948–89: dep dir 1972, dir 1977, dep sec 1979, asst auditor gen 1982, dep comptroller and auditor gen 1984–89; memb Inst of Public Fin and Accountancy 1981; *Recreations* travel, contract bridge; *Style*— David Myland, Esq, CB

MYLES, David Fairlie; CBE (1988); s of Robert Cownie Myles (d 1973), of Dalbog, Edzell, Brechin, Scotland, and Mary Ann Sidey, *née* Fairlie (d 1963); *b* 30 May 1925; *Educ* Brechin HS; *m* 7 Feb 1951, Janet Isabella, da of David Gall, of Glenskenno, Montrose; 2 s (Robert Gall, Peter David), 2 da (Catherine MacDonald (now Mrs Booth), Lorna Isobel (now Mrs Sinclair)); *Career* RM 1943–46; tenant hill farmer 1958–; dir Kincardineshire Auction Mart Ltd 1963–81; memb: Tport Users Consultative Ctee Scotland 1973–79, Meat Promotion Exec MLC 1975–79, N of Scotland Hydro-Electric Bd 1985–89, Dairy Produce Quota Tbnl for Scotland 1985–; govt appointee Potato Mktg Bd 1988–; MP (Cons) Banff 1979–83, Cons candidate Orkney and Shetland election 1983, dist cncllr Angus 1984–96; NFU Scotland: exec chm Angus area, memb Cncl 1970–79, convenor Orgn and Publicity Ctee 1976–79; pres N Angus and Mearns Cons Pty 1974–78 (chm 1971–74), memb: Angus Tourist Bd 1984–92, Guildry of Brechin (fiscal 1991–92, dean 1993 and 1994); Lord Pres Court of the Deans of Scotland 1995–96; session clerk Edzell/Lethendy Parish Church; *Recreations* curling, traditional Scots fiddle music; *Clubs* Brechin Rotary, London Farmers; *Style*— David Myles, Esq, CBE; ✉ The Gorse, Dunlappie Road Edzell, Angus DD9 7UB (☎ 01356 648207); Dalbog, Edzell, Brechin, Angus DD9 7UU (☎ 01356 648265)

MYLES, Lynda Robbie; da of Alexander Watt Myles (d 1967), and Kathleen Kilgour, *née* Polson (d 1994); *b* 2 May 1947; *Educ* Univ of Edinburgh (MA); *m* 1972 (m dis 1978), Dr David John Will; *Career* dir Edinburgh International Film Festival 1973–80, curator of film Pacific Film Archive Univ of California Berkeley 1980–82, film conslt Channel Four Television 1982–83, prodr Enigma Films 1983–86 (work incl Defence of the Realm 1986), sr vice pres Columbia Pictures 1986–88, commissioning ed Independent Drama Gp BBC Television 1989–91, co-prodr Alan Parker's film The Commitments 1991; independent film prodr 1992–: prodr Stephen Frears' film The Snapper 1993 and The Van 1996; bd memb Br Film and TV Prodrs' Assoc 1986–88, chair Women in Film 1990–91, exec dir East-West Prodrs' Seminar 1991–94, govr BFI 1993–96; *Awards* BFI Award for services to Br film culture 1982, BAFTA Best Film Award (with Alan Parker and Roger Randall-Cutler) for The Commitments 1992, Br Film Critics' Best Br Prodr Award (with Roger Randall-Cutler) 1992, RTS Award for Best Single Drama 1994 and Banff TV Festival Award for Best Single Film 1994 and Prix Italia 1994 and Premio Goya 1995 for The Snapper; *Books* The Movie Brats (with Michael Pye, 1979); *Clubs* Groucho; *Style*— Ms Lynda Myles; ✉ Pandora Productions Ltd, 83 Highbury Hill, London N5 1SX (☎ 0171 354 3384, fax 0171 354 4892)

MYLNE, Nigel James; QC (1984); s of Maj Harold James Mylne (10 Royal Hussars, d 1942), and Dorothy Evelyn Hogg, *née* Safford (d 1985); *b* 11 June 1939; *Educ* Eton; *m* 1, 4 April 1967 (m dis 1978), Julie Felicity Selena, da of Cdr Christopher Phillpotts, RN (d 1982); 2 s (Jonathan b 1970, Dominic b 1972), 1 da (Jessica b 1969); m 2, 18 Jan 1980, Mrs Judy Camilla Wilson, da of Maj Francis Gawain Hamilton Monteith (d 1975); 1 s (James b 1981); *Career* Nat Serv 2 Lt 10 Royal Hussars; called to the Bar Middle Temple 1963, recorder of the Crown Ct 1983–, bencher 1995; Liveryman Worshipful Co of Haberdashers; *Recreations* beekeeping; *Clubs* White's, Garrick, Pratt's; *Style*— Nigel Mylne, Esq, QC; ✉ 67 Thurleigh Road, London SW12 8TZ (☎ 0181 673 2200); 2 Harcourt Buildings, Temple, London EC4 (☎ 0171 353 2112)

MYLVAHAN, Dr Natarajan; s of Nurani Natarajan, and Saraswathy; *b* 29 June 1948; *Educ* Sri Lanka (MB BS, MD, DCH, FRCP, MRCS, LRCP); *m* 4 July 1976, Kalpana, da of K Ranganathan; 1 s (Kailash Natarajan Mylvahan); *Career* registrar in med Mansfield Dist and Gen Hosp Notts 1979–80, sr registrar in geriatrics St Mary's Gp Paddington London 1980–82, conslt physician for elderly Derby City General Hosp Tst 1982–; *Style*— Dr Natarajan Mylvahan; ✉ Hawksworth, 54 Ford Lane, Allestree, Derby DE3 2EW (☎ 01332 553370); Derby City General Hospital Trust, London Road, Derby (☎ 01332 340131)

MYNERS, Paul; *b* 1 April 1948; *m* 3 Oct 1995, Alison A I Macleod; 1 s (Bartholomew Piers Trevelyan b 28 Feb 1996); *Career* chm and chief exec Gartmore Investment Management plc, chm Gartmore plc; non-exec dir: PowerGen plc (chm Audit Ctee) until 1996, English & Scottish Investors Ltd; chm Assoc of Investmt Cos; memb: Panel on Takeovrs and Mergers, Fin Reporting Cncl; memb Advsy Bd: London Symphony Orch, Royal Academy Tst; *Style*— Paul Myners, Esq; ✉ Gartmore Investment Management plc, Gartmore House, 16–18 Monument Street, London EC3R 8AJ (☎ 0171 782 2000, fax 0171 782 2075)

MYNORS, Peter Thomas Baskerville; s of Thomas Halliday Baskerville Mynors, of Wadhurst, E Sussex, and Dagmar, *née* Sjögren; *b* 2 Jan 1943; *Educ* Marlborough, Oriel Coll Oxford; *m* 5 Sept 1970, Rosemary Ann, da of late Col Oscar Leslie Boord, MC; 1 s (Robert Thomas Baskerville b 5 Aug 1976), 1 da (Camilla Greta Baskerville b 2 Aug 1974); *Career* CA; with British Council Libya 1964–65; Coopers & Lybrand: joined 1965, Tehran 1970, New York 1971–72, chm Insur Indust Gp; memb: Walker Ctee on Lloyd's 1992, Insurance Ctee ICAEW 1993; regular speaker at insur seminars, memb ICAEW 1968; *Books* Starting a UK Insurance Company (1986); *Recreations* sailing, gardening, castles, opera; *Style*— Peter Mynors, Esq; ✉ Coopers & Lybrand, 1 Embankment Place, London WC2N 6NN (☎ 0171 583 5000, fax 0171 822 4652)

MYNORS, Sir Richard Baskerville; 2 Bt (UK 1964), of Treago, Co Hereford; s of Sir Humphrey Charles Baskerville Mynors, 1 Bt (d 1989); *b* 5 May 1947; *Educ* Marlborough, Corpus Christi Coll Cambridge; *m* 1970, Fiona Bridget, da of late Rt Rev George Edmund Reindorp; 3 da (Alexandra Fiona b 1975, Frances Veronica b 1978, Victoria Jane b 1983); *Heir* none; *Career* schoolmaster and asst dir of music King's Sch Macclesfield 1970–73; dir of music: Wolverhampton G S 1973–81, Merchant Taylors' Sch Crosby 1981–88, Belmont Abbey Sch Hereford 1988–90; landowner and freelance musician 1990–; *Recreations* gardening, DIY, organ building, viticulture; *Style*— Sir Richard Mynors, Bt; ✉ Treago, St Weonards, Hereford HR2 8QB (☎ 01981 580208)

MYRES, Rear Adm John Antony Lovell; CB (1993); yr s of Dr (John) Nowell Linton Myres, CBE, FSA (d 1989), of The Manor House, Kennington, Oxford, and Joan Mary Lovell, *née* Stevens; *b* 11 April 1936; *Educ* Winchester; *m* 21 Aug 1965, Alison Anne, da of Lt David Lawrence Carr, RN (ka 1941); 3 s (David Miles b 1966, Peter John Lukis b 1967, Charles Christopher Linton b 1969); *Career* RN; joined 1954, specialized hydrographic surveyor 1959; commands: HMS Woodlark 1969–71, HMS Fox 1972–73, HMS Hecla 1974 (also 1977–78 and 1981–82); Hydrographer Royal Australian Navy 1982–85; RN: Dir Hydrographic Plans and Surveys 1986–87, Capt Hydrographic Surveying Flotilla 1988–89, Hydrographer of the Navy 1990–94, Chief Exec Hydrographic Office Defence Support Agency 1990–94, ret 1994; Freeman City of London 1990, Liveryman Worshipful Co of Chartered Surveyors 1990, Younger Brother of Trinity House 1990, Guild Burgess of Preston 1952; FRICS 1974–95, FRIN 1994 (MRIN 1989), FRGS 1993; memb: Orders and Medals Res Soc 1984, Hydrographic Soc 1985; *Recreations* naval history, medallic history; *Style*— Rear Adm J A L Myres, CB

MYRTLE, Brig Andrew Dewe; CB (1988), CBE (1979, MBE 1967); s of Lt-Col J Y E Myrtle, DSO (ka N Africa 1941), and Doreen May, *née* Lake (who m 2, Brig T E M Battersby and d 1996); *b* 17 Dec 1932; *Educ* Winchester, RMA Sandhurst; *m* 19 Oct 1973, Mary-Rose, da of Neville Montague Ford, of Bembridge, IOW and Patricia, *née* Smiles (who m 2, Sir Nigel Fisher, MC); 2 da (Lucy Jane b 10 June 1975, Emma May b 30 March 1977); *Career* 1 KOSB: NI 1953–55, Malaysia and Singapore 1956–58, Berlin 1959–60; Sch of Inf 1960–62, Army Staff Coll 1962; 1 KOSB Radfan 1963, Bde Maj 24 Inf Bde Aden 1964–66; 1 KOSB: BAOR 1967–69, CO BAOR and Belfast 1969–71; mil asst to Adj Gen 1971–74, cmdt Jr Div Staff Coll 1974–77, Bde Cdr NI 1977–79, RCDS 1979, DDMO MOD 1980–83, asst cmdt RMAS 1983–85, cdr Land Forces Cyprus 1986–88; ADC to HM the Queen 1985–88; chief exec and sec Tennis and Rackets Assoc 1989–; *Recreations* golf, tennis, real tennis, fly fishing; *Clubs* Army and Navy, MCC, Queen's, Huntercombe; *Style*— Brig Andrew Myrtle, CB, CBE; ✉ c/o The Tennis and Rackets Association, The Queen's Club, Palliser Rd, West Kensington, London W14 9EQ (☎ 0171 386 3447/8, fax 0171 385 7424)

N

NAAS, Lord; Charles Diarmuidh John Bourke; s and h of 10 Earl of Mayo, *qv*; *b* 11 June 1953; *Educ* St Aubyn's Rottingdean, Portora Royal Sch Enniskillen, Queen's Univ Belfast, Bolton St Coll of Technol Dublin; *m* 1, 1975 (m dis 1979), Marie Antoinette Cronnelly; 1 da (Hon Corinne Mary Jane b 1975); m 2, 1985, Marie Veronica, da of Francis Mannion, of Clifden, Co Galway; 2 s (Hon Richard Thomas b 1985, Hon Eoin Patrick b 1989); *Style*— Lord Naas; ✉ Derryinver, Beach Rd, Clifden, Co Galway, Eire

NABARRO, Sir John David Nunes; kt (1982); s of Dr David Nunes Nabarro (d 1958); *b* 21 Dec 1915; *Educ* Oundle, UCL (MD); *m* 1948, Joan Margaret, da of William Gladstone Cockrell (d 1946); 2 s, 2 da; *Career* actg Lt-Col RAMC TA; physician; emeritus conslt physician Middx Hosp, hon conslt physician Royal Prince Alfred Hosp Sydney; dir: Cobbold Laboratories, Middx Hosp Med Sch 1970–81; fell UCL, chm Jt Conslts Ctee 1979–84; *Recreations* gardening; *Style*— Sir John Nabarro; ✉ 33 Woodside Ave, London N12 8AT (☎ 0181 445 7925)

NAGANO, Kent; *Career* conductor; studied with Seiji Ozawa, Pierre Boulez, Leonard Bernstein; music dir Opera de Lyon 1989, assoc princ guest conductor LSO 1990, music dir Hallé Orch 1992–, music dir Berkeley Symphony Orch California; premieres incl: Messiaen The Transfiguration (USA), St Francois d'Assise (Paris Opera), John Adams The Death of Klinghoffer (Brussels) 1991; other performances incl: Mahler Symphony No 9 (Boston Symphony Orch) 1984, Berg Wozzec, Strauss Salome (with Paris Opera), Strauss Elektra (La Scala), John Adams Nixon in China, Weill Mahagonny (Los Angeles Opera), Milhaud Christopher Columbus (San Francisco Opera), Poulenc Dialogues des Carmelites (debut with Metropolitan Opera New York) 1994, Stravinsky Oedipus Rex and Symphony of Psalms (Salzburg Festival) 1994; winner first Seaver National Endowment for the Arts Award 1984; *Recordings* incl: Prokofiev Love for Three Oranges (Gramophone Magazine Record of the Year 1990, Best Opera Recording Award 1990, nominated Grammy Award 1990), Poulenc Dialogues des Carmelites (winner Gramophone Opera Award 1993), John Adams The Death of Klinghoffer (nominated Grammy Award 1993), Busoni Turandot (nominated Grammy Award 1995), Floyd Susannah (winner Grammy Award 1995), Stravinsky The Rake's Progress (with Lyon Opera, 1996); *Style*— Kent Nagano, Esq; ✉ c/o Van Walsum Management, 25 Wadham Road, London SW15 2LR (☎ 0181 874 6344, fax 0181 877 0077)

NAGGAR, Guy Anthony; s of Albert Naggar, of Italy, and Marjorie, *née* Smouha; *b* 14 Oct 1940; *Educ* Ecole Centrale des Arts et Manufactures Paris; *m* 6 Dec 1964, Hon Marion, da of Baron Samuel of Wych Cross (Life Baron, d 1987); 2 s (Albert b 15 July 1967, Jonathan b 24 Jan 1971), 1 da (Diane b 11 May 1969); *Career* dir: Banque Financière de la Cité Geneva 1970–88, Charterhouse Group Ltd 1980–81; chm Dawnay Day & Co Ltd 1981–; *Style*— Guy Naggar, Esq; ✉ 15 Grosvenor Gardens, London SW1W 0BD (☎ 0171 834 8060)

NAGLER, Neville Anthony; s of Gerald Joseph Nagler, of London, and Sylvia, *née* Vernon; *b* 2 Jan 1945; *Educ* St George's Sch Mill Hill, Christ's Coll Finchley, Jesus Coll Cambridge (scholar, MA, history prizes); *m* 28 Feb 1971, Judy Maxine, da of Jack Leon Mordant; 1 da (Danielle b 25 June 1973), 1 s (Tristan b 11 March 1976); *Career* HM Treasy: joined 1967, private sec to Chllr of Exchequer 1970–71, princ 1972–75; Home Office: princ (firearms and contingency planning) Police Dept 1975–77, princ (police powers and procedures) Police Dept 1977–80, asst sec (race rels policy) Community Rels Dept 1980–83, head of Drugs and Extradition Policy Dept (concurrently UK rep to UN Cmmn on Narcotic Drugs, chm Cncl of Europe Drug Co-operation Gp) 1983–88, head of Fin Div (responsible for local govt servs) 1988–91; chief exec Bd of Deps of British Jews 1991–; Haldane Essay Prize 1979, Cert of Appreciation UN Drug Enforcement Admin 1988; *Recreations* music appreciation, wine making, DIY/home improvements; *Style*— Neville Nagler, Esq; ✉ Board of Deputies of British Jews, Commonwealth House, 1–19 New Oxford Street, London WC1A 1NF (☎ 0171 543 5400, fax 0171 543 0010)

NAHUM, Peter John; s of Denis E Nahum, of Colombia, and Allison Faith, *née* Cooke; *b* 19 Jan 1947; *Educ* Sherborne; *m* 29 Aug 1987, Renate Angelika, da of Herr Ewald Meiser, of Germany; *Career* dir Peter Wilson's Sotheby's 1966–84; regular contrib as painting expert Antiques Roadshow 1980– (discovered lost Richard Dadd painting 1986, subsequently sold to Br Museum); currently art dealer and publisher; *Books* Prices of Victorian Painting Drawings and Watercolours (1976), Monograms of Victorian and Edwardian Artists (1976), Cross Section, British Art in the 20th Century (1988), British Art From the 20th Century (1989), Burne-Jones, The Pre-Raphaelites & Their Century (1989), Burne-Jones: A Quest for Love (1993); *Recreations* gardening, sailing, photography, theatre, travel, walking; *Clubs* Reform; *Style*— Peter Nahum, Esq; ✉ 5 Ryder St, London SW1Y 6PY (☎ 0171 930 6059, fax 0171 930 4678)

NAIPAUL, Sir Vidiadhar Surajprasad (Vidia); kt (1990); *b* 1932; *Educ* Univ Coll Oxford (BA); *m* 1955, Patricia Ann Hale (d 1996); *Career* author; recent awards incl David Cohen British Literature Prize 1993; Hon DLitt: Cambridge 1983, London 1988, Oxford 1992; CLit 1994; *Books* The Mystic Masseur (winner of John Llewelyn Rhys Memorial prize, 1958), A House for Mr Biswas (1961), In A Free State (winner of Booker prize, 1971), A Bend in the River (1979), The Return of Eva Peron (1980), Among the Believers (1981), The Enigma of Arrival (1987), A Turn in the South (1989), India: A Million Mutinies Now (1990), A Way in the World (1994); *Style*— Sir Vidia Naipaul; ✉ c/o Aitken & Stone Ltd, 29 Fernshaw Road, London SW10 0TG (☎ 0171 351 7561, fax 0171 376 3594)

NAIRN, Andrew; s of Capt Andrew Nairn, MC (d 1971), of Glasgow, and Margaret Cornfoot, *née* Turner (d 1972); *b* 31 July 1944; *Educ* Strathallan Sch; *m* 1, 25 April 1970 (m dis 1983), Susan Anne, da of Richard Alphonse Napier; 1 s (Jonathan Richard b 1981), 1 da (Penelope Margaret b 1976); m 2, 1983, Glynis Vivienne, *née* Sweet; 1 step s (Barnaby Craggs b 1971), 1 step da (Charlotte Craggs b 1974); *Career* trainee CA Thomson Jackson Gourlay and Taylor 1962–67; Kidsons Impey (formerly Hodgson Impey): joined 1967, ptnr 1970–, London region managing ptnr 1990–93; England and Wales area sec and treas ICAS; dep chm Dulwich Cons Assoc 1978; MICAS; *Recreations* fly fishing, golf; *Clubs* Savile; *Style*— Andrew Nairn, Esq; ✉ 52 Redhill Wood, New Ash Green, Kent DA3 8QP (☎ 01474 873 724); Kidsons Impey, 20–26 Cursitor St, London EC4A 1HY (☎ 0171 405 2088, fax 0171 831 2206)

NAIRN, Nicholas (Nick); s of James and Irene Nairn, of Lochend House, Port of Mentieth, Stirling; *b* 12 Jan 1959; *Educ* McLaren HS, Glasgow Nautical Coll; *m* 30 Jan 1986, Fiona, da of Hector Macdonald; *Career* served Merchant Navy 1976–83 (third navigating offr 1980–83); chef/patron Braeval restaurant by Aberfoyle Stirling 1986– (renovation 1984–86); presenter: Ready Steady Cook (BBC 2) 1995–, Wild Harvest with Nick Nairn (BBC 2) 1996, Who'll do the Pudding? (BBC 1) 1996, Wild Harvest 2 with Nick Nairn (BBC 2) 1997; *Awards* Scottish Field/Bollinger Newcomer of the Yr 1987, Acorn award Caterer and Hotelkeeper Magazine 1988, Scottish Field/Carlton Best Restaurant in Category 1988, Michelin Red M award 1990, Scottish Field/Charles Heidsieck Scottish Restaurant of the Yr 1990, Good Food Guide County Restaurant of the Yr 1991, Michelin Star 1991–, 3 AA Rosettes 1991–, Macallan/Decanter Scottish Restaurant of the Yr 1992, Scottish Field/Bowmore Restaurant of the Yr 1992, 4/5 Good Food Guide 1996; fndr memb: Scottish Chefs' Assoc 1993 (memb Advsy Bd), Scottish Martell Cordon Bleu Assoc 1994; memb Masterchefs of GB 1992; *Recreations* cycling (VC Olympia Cycling Club), windsurfing, wine, eating out, travel, Scottish art, theatre; *Style*— Nick Nairn, Esq; ✉ Braeval Old Mill, By Aberfoyle, Stirling FK8 3UY (☎ 01877 382711, fax 01877 382400)

NAIRNE, Alexander Robert (Sandy); s of Rt Hon Sir Patrick Dalmahoy Nairne, KCB, MC, *qv*, of Yew Tree, Chilson, nr Charlbury, Oxon, and Penelope Chauncy, *née* Bridges; *b* 8 June 1953; *Educ* Radley, Univ Coll Oxford (MA, memb Isis Boat Crew); *partner* Prof Sylvia Elizabeth Tickner (Lisa); 1 s (Kit b 1984), 1 da (Eleanor b 1987); *Career* asst dir: Museum of Modern Art Oxford 1974–76, Modern Collection Tate Gallery London 1976–79; dir of exhibitions ICA London 1980–84, freelance curator and writer 1984–87, dir of visual arts Arts Cncl of GB London 1987–92, sr res fell Getty Grant Prog 1992–93, dir of public and regnl servs Tate Gallery London 1994–; memb: Exec Ctee Art Galleries Assoc 1976–81, Exec Ctee Gtr London Arts 1983–86, Art and Architecture Advsy Panel RSA 1990–; advsr Works of Art Ctee Br Library 1989–91; *Books* British Sculpture in the Twentieth Century (jt ed, 1981), Picturing the System (jt ed, 1981), State of the Art (1987); *Recreations* punting; *Clubs* Chelsea Arts; *Style*— Sandy Nairne, Esq; ✉ c/o Tate Gallery, Millbank, London SW1P 4RG

NAIRNE, Rt Hon Sir Patrick Dalmahoy; GCB (1981, KCB 1975, CB 1971), MC (1943), PC (1982); s of Lt-Col Charles Silvester Nairne (d 1966), of Plover Hill, Compton, Winchester, and Edith Dalmahoy, *née* Kemp (d 1975); *b* 15 Aug 1921; *Educ* Radley, Univ of Oxford (MA); *m* 1948, Penelope Chauncy, er da of Lt-Col Robert Francis Bridges, RAMC, by his w Charlotte, da of Edward Luard (seventh in descent from Abraham Luard, who settled in England 1685 as a result of the Revocation of the Edict of Nantes); 3 s (Alexander b 1953, James b 1960, Andrew (twin) b 1960), 3 da (Katharine b 1949, Fiona b 1951, Margaret b 1961); *Career* formerly with Admty (joined 1947); perm sec DHSS 1975–81, second perm sec Cabinet Office 1973–75, dep under sec MOD 1970–73 (asst under sec logistics 1967–70, private sec to Def Sec 1965–67); master St Catherine's Coll Oxford 1981–88 (hon fell 1988), chllr Univ of Essex 1983–; tstee: Nat Maritime Museum 1981–91, Joseph Rowntree Fndn 1982–96, Nat Aids Tst 1987–95; vice pres Soc of Italic Handwriting 1987, chm W Midlands Bd and memb Gp Bd Central Ind TV 1990–92, Advsy Bd Oxford Museum of Modern Art; chm: Nuffield Cncl on Bioethics 1991–96, Cmmn on Conduct of Referendums 1996–, Irene Wellington Educn Tst; memb: Cncl Radley Coll 1975–, Cncl Ditchley Fndn, Falkland Island Review Ctee 1982, Cncl Oxford Soc 1994; church cmmr 1993; govt monitor Hong Kong 1984; pres: Seamen's Hosp Soc, Oxfordshire Craft Guild; hon fell University Coll Oxford 1981; Hon LLD: Univ of Leicester 1980, Univ of St Andrews 1984; Hon DUniv Essex 1983; FRSA; *Recreations* water colour painting; *Clubs* United Oxford and Cambridge Universities; *Style*— The Rt Hon Sir Patrick Nairne, GCB, MC; ✉ Yew Tree, Chilson, Chipping Norton, Oxon OX7 3HU

NAISH, John Alexander; s of William Henry Naish (d 1987), and Elizabeth Lyon, *née* Pirie (d 1993); *b* 12 April 1948; *Educ* Queen Elizabeth's Hosp Bristol, Dr Challoner's GS Amersham, City of London Coll (BA); *m* 18 Sept 1982, Bonnie Kam Pik, da of Pham Tak, of Hong Kong; 2 s (William b 3 April 1987, Henry b 3 Aug 1989); *Career* dir Hill Samuel Bank Ltd 1985–93, former dir of corp fin NatWest Markets Tokyo, currently dir of investment banking Asia Pacific NatWest Markets London; FCIB 1983; *Recreations* golf, astronomy, music; *Clubs* Oriental, Royal Over-Seas League, Tokyo; *Style*— John Naish, Esq; ✉ 12 Waldegrave Gardens, Strawberry Hill, Twickenham, Middx TW1 4PG (☎ 0181 892 7953)

NAISMITH, Robert James; s of Robert James Sinclair Naismith (d 1967), and Ann, *née* Smith (d 1970); *b* 4 March 1916; *Educ* Heriot-Watt Coll, Edinburgh Coll of Art (Dip Art in Architecutre, DipTP); *Career* architect; engaged in post-war plans for Greenock after blitz and future plans coalfields in Lothians, jt sr ptnr Sir Frank Mears and Ptnrs 1952–85 (ptnr 1950); burgh architect: Penicuik 1945–75, Dalkeith 1950–75; planning conslt Perth 1950–75; sometime conslt to: Edinburgh, Inverness, Lanark, Hawick, Tranent, Inverkeithing; Civic Tst Award for rebuilding in town centre Selkirk, Civic Tst Commendation for Conservation in High St Dalkeith; dir survey of bldgs in Scot countryside 1983–85; restoration work: Darnley House, Glengarry Lodge, Spittals House; exhibited architectural watercolours in: Royal Acad, Royal Scot Acad, RHA, Glasgow; various pubns in jls; former memb: Nat Ctee Scot Heritage Soc, RIAS Cncl, Ctee RIBA, Ctee ARCUK; former vice chm Edinburgh Architectural Assoc; FRIBA, FSA Scot, FRIAS, FRTPI (ret); *Books* Buildings of the Scottish Countryside (1985), The Story of Scotland's Towns (1989); *Recreations* travel, painting and drawing, photography; *Clubs* Scottish Arts; *Style*— Robert Naismith, Esq; ✉ 14 Ramsay Garden, Royal Mile, Edinburgh EH1 2NA (☎ 0131 225 2273)

NALDER, Hon Sir Crawford David; kt (1974); s of H A Nalder; *b* 14 Feb 1910; *Educ* State Sch Wagin, Wesley Coll Perth; *m* 1, 1934, Olive M (d 1973); 1 s, 2 da; m 2, 1974, Brenda Wade (d 1988); *Career* MLA WA (Country Pty): for Wagin 1947–50, for Katanning 1950–74; min: for War Serv Land Settlement 1959–66, for Agric 1959–71, for Electricity 1962–71; ldr Country Pty 1962–73, dep premier WA 1962–71; farmer; *Style*— The Hon Sir Crawford Nalder; ✉ 7 Morriett Street, Attadale, WA 6156, Australia

NALECZ, Halima; da of Antoni Krzywicz-Nowohonski (d 1921), of Dukszty, Poland, and Maria Larysa, *née* Domanska (d 1940); *b* 2 Feb 1917; *Educ* Lycee Filomatow Wilno, Univ of Stefan Batory London; *m* Zygmunt Nalecz (d 1985); *Career* artist; co-fndr New Vision Centre Gallery 1956, fndr The Drian Galleries 1957; promoter of numerous artists incl: John Ballany, William Crozier, Joseph Lacass, Bazil Alkazzi, Leon Zack; formerly designer of decor for ballet, opera and film; works in numerous private collections in

England, France, Italy, Canada, USA, Germany, Spain, Sweden and Israel; Bronze medal European Prize for Painting Kursaal Ostend Belgium 1969 and 1971; fell Free Painters and Sculptors 1954; memb: Hampstead Arts Cncl 1955, Artists International Assoc 1956, Women's Int Art Club 1959; Golden Orders of Merit for Polish Culture and for Polish Communities in GB; Freeman City of Gdansk; *Solo Exhibitions* Walker Galleries London 1956, New Vision Centre London 1957 and 1959, Country Town Gallery Lewes E Sussex 1967, Ewan Phillips Gallery London 1967, Drian Galleries 1968, 1969, 1971, 1973, 1975, 1983, 1990 and 1992, Kunsverein Freiburg Germany 1970, Kungsgaten Göteborg Sweden 1970, Royal Free Hosp London 1976, Hayes Gallery Sheffield 1976, Nat Museum Warsaw 1978, Nat Museum Gdansk 1984, Zacheta Warsaw 1987, Polish Cultural Inst 1993; *Gp Exhibitions* incl: La Mostra Interplanteria (Rome) 1953, Salon des Realities Nouvelles Paris 1958, Galerie von Reutlingen Germany 1958, Galerie Muller Stuttgart 1958, Salons des Comparisons Paris 1959, WIAC New Gallery Belfast 1965, RA Summer Exhbn 1966, 1967 and 1968, Ben-Uri Gallery London 1967, and 1968 and 1976, Free Painters and Sculptors (Goethe Inst Bergen Norway) 1968, Lorensberg Art Gallery Göteborg Sweden 1968, European Prize Ostend Belgium 1971, Centaur Gallery London 1976, RCA London 1978, Nat Gallery Warsaw 1978, Mall Gallery London 1980, Loggia Gallery London 1992; life and work documented in two films: Halima in Wonderland, Halima in Fairyland; *Style*— Mrs Halima Nalecz; ✉ Flat 3, 84 Marine Parade, Brighton, E Sussex BN2 1AY (☎ 01273 696890); c/o Drian Galleries, 7 Porchester Place, London W2 (☎ 0171 723 9473 or 0171 723 8289)

NALL, Sir Michael Joseph; 2 Bt (UK 1954), of Hoveringham, Co Nottingham, DL (Notts 1970); s of Col Sir Joseph Nall, 1 Bt, DSO, TD, DL (d 1958); *b* 6 Oct 1921; *Educ* Wellington; *m* 1951, Angela Loveday Hanbury, da of Air Chief Marshal Sir (William) Alec Coryton, KCB, KBE, MVO, DFC; 2 s (Edward William Joseph b 1952, Alexander Michael b 1956); *Heir* s, Edward William Joseph Nall b 24 Oct 1952; *Career* joined RN 1939, serv at sea 1939–45, qualified in gunnery 1946–47, psc(m) 1949, Lt Cdr 1950, ret 1961; gen mangr Guide Dogs for the Blind Assoc 1961–64, High Sheriff Notts 1971, Vice Lord-Lt of Notts 1989–91; pres Nottingham Chamber of Commerce & Industry 1972–74; banker, ret; chm: Southwell Diocesan Pastoral Ctee 1968–86, Nottinghamshire Scout Cncl and Assoc 1968–88, Robin Hood Charity Tst 1974–88, Papplewick Pumping Station Tst 1974–; pres: Nottinghamshire Rural Community Cncl 1976–, Nottingham Mechanics Inst 1976–89; *Recreations* field sports; *Clubs* Army & Navy, United Services, Nottingham; *Style*— Sir Michael Nall, Bt, DL; ✉ Hoveringham Hall, Nottingham NG14 7JR (☎ 0115 966 3634)

NALLY, Margaret Alice; da of Percy Sidney Hutley (d 1952), of Braintree, Essex, and Madge, *née* Neale (d 1960); *b* 12 Aug 1922; *Educ* Braintree Co HS, DipPR (CAM); *m* Bertram Francis Nally; 2 da (Sonya Frances b 14 April 1945, Denise Margaret b 7 July 1946), 1 s (Patrick James b 16 Aug 1947); *Career* WWII Serv: social serv and sec 1940–42, radio mechanic WRNS Fleet Air Arm 1942–45; retail mgmnt and journalism 1945–55, head PR depts of three advtg agencies 1955–65, ind PR conslt and writer 1965–; IPR: assoc 1957, memb 1961, fell 1972, first woman pres 1976, Sir Stephen Tallents medal 1987, hon fell 1995; hon fell Euro Confedn of PR (CERP) 1994 (hon memb 1989); *Books* Selling Consumer Goods to West Germany (1970), Selling Consumer Goods to France (1971), International Public Relations in Practice (ed, 1991); *Style*— Mrs Margaret Nally; ✉ 6 Rosebery Road, London SW2 4DE (☎ 0181 678 1922, fax 0181 674 3067)

NANDY, Hon Mrs (Ann Luise); *née* Byers; da of Baron Byers, OBE, PC, DL (Life Baron, d 1984), and Baroness Byers; *b* 30 April 1946; *Educ* Sherborne, Univ of York (BA), Univ of Bradford (MA); *m* 1, 1972 (m dis 1987), Dipak Nandy; 2 da (Francesca b 1977, Lisa b 1979); m 2, 1994, Ray Fitzwalter, *qv*; *Career* library clerk House of Commons Library 1968–71, asst ed Where magazine 1971–73, head family servs dept London Cncl of Social Serv 1973–77, res student Univ of Bradford 1977–82, res with Granada TV 1982–84, prodr and ed Current Affrs Granada TV 1984–93, ind prodr and co-dir Ray Fitzwalter Assocs 1993–; *Style*— The Hon Mrs Nandy; ✉ Ray Fitzwalter Associates, 22 Lloyd Street, Manchester M2 5WA (☎ 0161 832 3337, fax 0161 832 5535)

NANNE, Edmundo; s of Edmundo Nanne Mata (d 1960), and Josefina, *née* Zirion (d 1983); *b* 15 Sept 1924; *Educ* Colegio de Infantes, Universidad de san Carlos de Guatemala; *m* 30 April 1949, Ella Villagran Kramer, da of Francisco Villagran de Leon; 1 da (Guisela b 19 Nov 1950), 3 s (Edgar b 21 Nov 1952, Estuardo b 1 Feb 1954, Mauricio b 8 Sept 1958); *Career* Guatemalan diplomat; dir Instituto de Fomento de la Produccion 1954–55, mangr Distribuidora de Fabricas SA 1963–91, dir and pres Camara de Comercio 1968–76, fndr dir Instituto Tecnico de Capacitaction y Productividad (INTECAP) 1972–76, tstee Universidad Francisco Marroquin 1972–, dir and pres Federacion de Camaras de Comercio de Centro-America y Panama 1973–74, fndr dir Corporacion Financiera Nacional Corfina 1974–75, memb Counsel of State Consejo de Estado 1974–78, dir Empresa Electrica de Guatemala SA 1976–78, dir and pres Federacion de Entidades Privadas de Centro-America (FEDEPRICA) 1976–80, Central American rep/memb Bd of Dirs Consejo Interamericano de Comercio y Produccion (CICYP) 1976–82, admin Sucesion de Enrique Salazar Liekens 1977–92, memb Bd of Dirs Junta Monetaria (Central Bank) 1978–82, dir and pres Asociacion de Amigos del Pais 1980–84, vice pres Fundacion Tecnologica 1985–92, mangr Representaciones Tamub 1986–89, Guatemalan ambass to the Ct of St James's 1992–96; *Recreations* sailing, hiking; *Clubs* Rotary, Tennis Club of Guatemala, University; *Style*— Mr Edmundo Nanne

NAPIER, Sir Charles Joseph; 6 Bt (UK 1867), of Merrion Square, Dublin; o s of Sir Robert (Robin) Surtees Napier, 5 Bt (d 1994), and Jennifer Beryl, *née* Daw; *b* 15 April 1973; *Educ* Eton, Univ of Edinburgh (MA); *Heir* unc, John Lennox Napier b 1934; *Career* Scottish European Aid 1995–96, Royal National Theatre 1996–; *Recreations* fencing, fishing, many others; *Style*— Sir Charles Napier, Bt; ✉ Woodlands, Martyr Worthy, Winchester, Hants SO21 1AT

NAPIER, Christopher Lennox; s of Capt Lennox William Napier, DSO, DSC, RN, and Elizabeth Eve, *née* Lindsay (d 1996); *b* 5 Dec 1944; *Educ* Sherborne, Britannia RNC Dartmouth; *m* 1971, Susan Margaret, da of Ian McLauchlan (d 1985); 1 s (James b 1972), 1 da (Georgina b 1976); *Career* joined BRNC Dartmouth 1962, qualified submarines 1966, ret as Lt Cdr 1976; Clifford Turner: articled clerk 1976–78, admitted slr 1979, slr 1979–83, ptnr 1983–87; ptnr Clifford Chance 1987–; pres Petersfield Soc; Freeman City of London 1987; memb: Law Soc 1979, UKELA 1989–, Nautical Inst; MRIN 1975; *Recreations* walking, reading, skiing, sailing; *Style*— Christopher Napier, Esq; ✉ Clifford Chance, 200 Aldersgate Street, London EC4A 4JJ (☎ 0171 600 1000, fax 0171 600 5555)

NAPIER, Master of; Hon Francis David Charles Napier; s and h of 14 Lord Napier and (5) Ettrick; *b* 3 Nov 1962; *Educ* Stanbridge Earl Sch, S Thames Coll (Computer Dip); *m* 8 May 1993, Zara Jane, o da of Hugh Dermot McCalmont, *qv*; 1 s (William Alexander Hugh b 10 June 1996); *Career* R F Kershaw Ltd (Lloyd's Member Agency) 1982–92, dir Heath Bloodstock Ltd; *Recreations* flat racing, skiing, hill-walking; *Clubs* Turf, Pratt's; *Style*— The Master of Napier; ✉ 23 Poyntz Road, London SW11 5BH

NAPIER, John; s of James Edward Thomas Napier, and Florence Emma, *née* Godbold; *b* 1 March 1944; *Educ* Hornsey Coll of Art, Central Sch of Art & Crafts; *m* 1 (m dis 1985), Andreane Neofitou; 1 s (Julian b 1965), 1 da (Elise b 1968); m 2 (m dis 1995), Donna King; 1 s (James b 1984), 1 da (Jessica b 1988); *Career* set designer; Royal Designer for Industry (RDI) 1996; assoc designer Royal Shakespeare Co; *Theatre and Film* 150 film, musical and theatrical prodns incl: The Ruling Class 1968, The Fun War 1968, Muzeeka 1968, George Frederick 1968, Turista 1968, Cancer 1969, Isabel's a Jezebel 1969, Mister 1970, The Foursome 1970, The Lovers of Viorne 1970, Lear 1970, Jump 1971, Sam Sam 1971, Big Wolf 1971, The Devils (ENO) 1972, Equus (NT) 1972, The Party 1972, Knuckle 1973, Kings & Clowns 1974, The Travelling Music Show 1974, Hedda Gabler (RSC) 1974, Much Ado About Nothing 1975, The Comedy of Errors (RSC) 1975, King Lear (RSC) 1975, Macbeth (RSC) 1975, A Midsummer Night's Dream 1976, As You Like It 1976, The Merry Wives of Windsor 1977, Twelfth Night 1977, Three Sisters 1977, Once in a Lifetime 1977, Lohengrin (Royal Opera House, SWET Award), The Greeks (RSC) 1979, Nicholas Nickleby (RSC, SWET and Tony Awards) 1979, Cats (Tony Award) 1980, Henry IV Parts I & II 1981, Peter Pan (RSC) 1981, Idomeneo (Glyndebourne) 1982, Macbeth (Royal Opera House) 1983, Starlight Express (Tony Award 1987) 1984, Les Misérables (Tony Award 1987) 1985, Time (Dominion) 1986, Captain EO (Disney film starring Michael Jackson) 1987, Miss Saigon 1989, Siegfried and Roy (The Mirage Las Vegas) 1989, Children of Eden 1990, Hook (Steven Spielberg film) 1991, Trelawny of the Wells (RNT) 1993, Sunset Boulevard 1993 (Tony Award 1995), Burning Blue (Haymarket (Olivier Award for Best Set Design 1996)) 1995, The Tower (Almeida) 1995, Who's Afraid of Virginia Woolf? (Almeida and Aldwych) 1996, Jane Eyre (Toronto) 1996, Jesus Christ Superstar (Lyceum) 1996; *Recreations* photography; *Style*— John Napier, Esq; ✉ c/o MLR, 200 Fulham Road, London SW10 (☎ 0171 351 5442, fax 0171 351 4560)

NAPIER, John Alan; s of William Arthur Napier, of Sudbury, and Barbara Eileen, *née* Chatten (d 1962); *b* 22 Aug 1942; *Educ* Colchester Royal GS, N E Essex Tech Coll, Emmanuel Coll Cambridge (BA); *m* 1, 24 June 1961 (m dis), Gillian Joyce, *née* Reed; 2 s (Stephen Paul b 1 Dec 1961, Russell John b 15 Sept 1965), 1 da (Karen Clare b 3 Oct 1963); m 2, 12 March 1992, Caroline Mary Elizabeth, da of Charles Jarvis; 1 da (Amelia Caroline b 17 Sept 1992); *Career* trainee prodn staff offr QB Newspapers Colchester 1960–63, works mangr International Printers 1963–66; md: Index Printers Dunstable 1969–72, QB Newspapers 1972–74; exec dir James Hardie Industries Aust 1976–87; md: AGB Plc UK 1987–91, Hays plc 1991–; *Recreations* golf, sailing, family; *Style*— John Napier, Esq; ✉ Hays plc, Hays House, Millmead, Guildford, Surrey GU2 5HJ (☎ 01483 302203, fax 01483 300388)

NAPIER, Maj-Gen Lennox Alexander Hawkins; CB (1983), OBE (1970), MC (1957), DL (1984); s of Maj Charles McNaughton Napier; *b* 28 June 1928; *Educ* Radley, RMA Sandhurst; *m* 1959, Jennifer Wilson; 1 s, 2 da; *Career* cmmnd S Wales Borderers 1948, cmd 1 Bn S Wales Borderers and 1 Bn Royal Regt of Wales 1967–70, instr Jt Services Staff Coll 1970–72, MOD 1972–74, Bde Cdr Berlin Inf Bde 1974–76, Div Brig Prince of Wales's Div 1976–80, GOC Wales 1980–83, ret; Col Cmdt Prince of Wales's Div 1980–83, Col Royal Regt of Wales (24/41 Foot) 1983–89; inspr Public Inquiries 1983–, chm Central Rail Users Consultative Ctee 1985–95; vice Lord Lieut for Gwent 1995; OstJ 1969; *Books* Armed Services Careers Year Book 1987–88; *Recreations* riding, shooting, bees; *Clubs* Landsdowne; *Style*— Maj-Gen Lennox Napier, CB, OBE, MC, DL; ✉ Osbaston Farm, Monmouth, Monmouthshire NP5 4BW

NAPIER, (Thomas) Michael; s of Montague Keith Napier (d 1975), and Mary, *née* Mather (d 1954); *b* 11 June 1946; *Educ* Loughborough GS, Hulme Hall Univ of Manchester (Open Exhibition, First XV Rugby); *m* 27 Dec 1969, Denise Christine; 1 s (Frederick John b 31 Oct 1980), 2 da (Holly Danielle b 26 June 1973, Amy Abigail b 9 June 1975); *Career* articled clerk Malcolm H Moss Moss Toone & Deane Loughborough 1968–70, asst slr W H Thompson Manchester 1970–72, sr ptnr Irwin Mitchell Sheffield, Leeds, Birmingham and London 1983– (ptnr Sheffield 1973), jt sr ptnr Pannone Napier 1985–94; visiting prof of gp litigation and disaster law Nottingham Law Sch 1992–, chm Centre of Advanced Litigation 1992–; editorial conslt: Personal & Medical Injuries Law Letter, Medical Law Review; Mental Health Act Cmmn: cmmr 1983–92, jt vice chm 1985–88, chm NE region 1985–89; former pres S Yorks Medico-Legal Soc, memb Governing Bd Assoc of Trial Lawyers of America, pres Assoc of Personal Injury Lawyers 1994–96; chm Hosp Advsy Ctee Rampton Hosp 1992–96, memb Cncl JUSTICE 1995–; Freeman Co of Cutlers in Hallamshire 1992; memb Law Soc 1970 (memb Cncl 1993–, chm Civil Litigation Ctee 1996–); *Recreations* mountain biking in Norfolk; *Clubs* Athenaeum; *Style*— Michael Napier, Esq; ✉ Bridge House, Ford, Ridgeway, Sheffield S12 3YD (☎ 01246 433221); The Manor House, Great Walsingham, Norfolk (☎ 01328 820213); Irwin Mitchell, St Peter's House, Hartshead, Sheffield S1 2EL (☎ 0114 276 7777, fax 0114 275 3306, mobile 0860 268553)

NAPIER, (Trevylyan) Miles Wentworth; s of Cdr Trevylyan Michael Napier, DSC, RN (d 1940), of Stokehill Wood, Buckland Monachorum, S Devon (*see* Burke's Landed Gentry, 1965), and Priscilla, *née* Hayter (da of Sir William Goodenough Hayter, KBE, KCMG); *b* 12 Oct 1934; *Educ* Wellington, Millfield; *m* 20 April 1971, Mary Philomena Ann, da of Edward Bourke, of Rathfarnham, Co Dublin; 1 s (Lennox b 20 May 1975); *Career* Rifle Bde and 60 Rifles 1952–54, offr cadet Leics and Derbys Yeo 1967–68; handicapper to Jockey Club and Nat Hunt Ctee 1964–67, conslt to Bloodstock and Racing Data (Prestel) 1981–89; memb: Racing Press 1973–, Br Sporting Art Tst, Friends of Pavilion Opera; lectr on racing and bloodstock breeding (incl Nat Stud); author; *Books* Thoroughbred Pedigrees Simplified (1973), Breeding a Racehorse (1975), Blood Will Tell (1978), The Racing Men of TV (1979), Keylocks Dams or Winners of All Flat Races in Great Britain and Ireland (co-compiler 1967–68 and 1979–84), Treasures of the Bloodstock Breeders Review (compiled with Leon Rasmussen), The Racing Business (compiled with Warwickshire Coll); *Recreations* riding, sporting art, history, opera; *Style*— Miles Napier, Esq; ✉ Banbury House, Gt Easton, Market Harborough, Leicestershire (☎ 01536 770449)

NAPIER, Sir Oliver John; kt (1985); s of James Joseph Napier (d 1975), of Belfast, and Sarah Frances Napier, *née* Bready; *b* 11 July 1935; *Educ* St Malachys Coll Belfast, Queen's Univ Belfast (LLB); *m* 1961, Kathleen Brigid, of Belfast; 3 s (James, John, Kevin), 5 da (Brigid, Veronica, Nuala, Emma, Mary-Jo); *Career* slr, memb Bd of Examiners Law Soc of NI 1964–68, min of Law Reform NI Exec 1973–74; memb: Belfast City Cncl 1977–89, NI Assembly 1973–74 and 1982–86, NI Constitutional Convention 1975–76; ldr Alliance Pty of N Ireland 1973–84, chm Standing Advsy Cmmn on Human Rights 1988–92; *Recreations* gardening; *Clubs* Northern Law; *Style*— Sir Oliver Napier; ✉ Glenlyon, Victoria Rd, Holywood, Co Down, NI (☎ 012317 5986); Napier & Sons Solicitors, 1/9 Castle Arcade, High St, Belfast (☎ 01232 244602)

NAPIER, Robert Stewart; s of Andrew Napier (d 1967), and Lilian V, *née* Ritchie; *b* 21 July 1947; *Educ* Sedbergh, Sidney Sussex Coll Cambridge (BA, MA), Harvard Business Sch (AMP); *m* 17 Dec 1977, Patricia Gray Stewart; 1 da (Catriona Rose Stewart b 1984); *Career* Rio Tinto Zinc Corp 1969–73, Brandts Ltd 1973–75, Fisons Ltd 1975–81; Redland plc: fin dir 1981–87, gp md 1987–, chief exec 1991–; non-exec dir: United Biscuits (Holdings) plc 1992–, Rentokil Group plc 1996–; pres Nat Cncl of Building Materials Producers 1996; *Style*— Robert Napier, Esq; ✉ Redland plc, Redland House, Reigate, Surrey RH2 0SJ (☎ 01737 242488, fax 01737 221938, telex 28626)

NAPIER AND ETTRICK, 14 Lord (Napier S 1627) and 5 Baron (Ettrick UK 1872); Chief of the name of Napier, and 23 of Merchistoun; Sir Francis Nigel Napier; 11 Bt (Nova Scotia 1666), of Thirlestane, KCVO (1992, CVO 1985, LVO 1980), DL (Selkirkshire 1974, Ettrick and Lauderdale 1975); eld s of 13 Lord Napier and Ettrick, TD, JP, DL (d 1954, twelfth in descent from first Lord, himself s of John Napier of Merchistoun, the inventor of logarithms), and Violet Muir, *née* Newson (d 1992); the Napiers of Merchistoun are co-heirs general of the ancient Celtic Earls of Lennox; *b* 5

Dec 1930; *Educ* Eton, RMA Sandhurst; *m* 1958, Delia Mary, da of Maj Archibald D B Pearson; 2 s (Master of Napier b 1962, Hon Nicholas b 1971), 2 da (Hon Louisa (Hon Mrs Morrison) b 1961, Hon Georgina (Hon Mrs Walker) b 1969); *Heir* s, Master of Napier; *Career* Maj Scots Gds (R of O), Malaya 1950–51 (invalided); Adjt 1 Bn Scots Gds 1955–57; Equerry to HRH the late Duke of Gloucester 1958–60 (ret 1960), sits as Ind Peer in House in Lords, in the City 1960–62, Dep Ceremonial and Protocol Sec Cwlth Rels Office 1962–68; Cons Whip House of Lords 1970–71, Private Sec, Comptroller and Equerry to HRH The Princess Margaret, Countess of Snowdon 1974– (Comptroller and Equerry 1973); pres St John Ambulance Assoc and Bde London 1975–83; memb Queen's Body Guard for Scotland (The Royal Co of Archers) 1953–, on behalf of The Queen handed over the Instruments of Independence to Tuvalu (Ellice Islands) 1979; Hon DLitt Napier Univ 1993; KStJ 1991 (CStJ 1988, OStJ 1982); Liveryman Worshipful Co of Grocers 1963; memb: Standing Cncl of Scottish Chiefs, Exec Ctee Standing Cncl of the Baronetage; *Clubs* White's, Pratt's, Pitt, Royal Caledonian Hunt; *Style*— Major the Lord Napier and Ettrick, KCVO, DL; ✉ Thirlestane, Ettrick, Selkirkshire; Nottingham Cottage, Kensington Palace, London W8 4PU

NAPIER OF MAGDALA, 6 Baron (UK 1868), in Abyssinia and of Caryngton, Co Chester; Robert Alan Napier; eld s of 5 Baron Napier of Magdala, OBE (d 1987), and Elizabeth Marian, *née* Hunt; *b* 6 Sept 1940; *Educ* Winchester, St John's Coll Cambridge (MA); *m* 4 Jan 1964, Frances Clare, er da of late Alan Frank Skinner, OBE, of Monks Close, Woolpit, Suffolk; 1 s (Hon James Robert b 29 Jan 1966), 1 da (Hon Frances Catherine b 2 July 1964); *Heir* s, Hon James Robert Napier; *Career* conslt port management and operations; *Recreations* sailing, playing the 'cello, trout fishing; *Clubs* Leander; *Style*— The Rt Hon Lord Napier of Magdala; ✉ The Coach House, Kingsbury Street, Marlborough, Wilts SN8 1HU (☎ and fax 01672 512333)

NAPIER OF MERCHISTOUN, Sir John Archibald Lennox; 14 Bt (NS 1627), of Merchistoun; s of Sir William Archibald Napier, of Merchistoun, 13 Bt (d 1990), and Kathleen Mabel, *née* Greaves; descended from John Napier, inventor of logarithms; *b* 6 Dec 1946; *Educ* St Stithians, Univ of Witwatersrand Johannesburg (BSc, MSc, PhD); *m* 9 Dec 1969, Erica Susan, da of late Kurt Kingsfield, of Johannesburg; 1 s (Hugh Robert Lennox b 1977), 1 da (Natalie Ann b 1973); *Heir* s, Hugh Robert Lennox Napier b 1 Aug 1977; *Career* res engr; fell SA Inst of Mining and Metallurgy; *Clubs* Johannesburg Country; *Style*— Sir John Napier of Merchistoun, Bt; ✉ Merchistoun, PO Box 65177, Benmore 2010, Transvaal, S Africa (☎ 00 27 11 783 2611)

NAPPER, John Pelham; s of John Mortimer Napper (artist, d 1951), and Dorothy Charlotte, *née* Hill (Dorothy Ilma, actress and singer, d 1976); *b* 17 Sept 1916; *Educ* Frensham Heights, private tutors, Dundee Sch of Art, Royal Acad Schs of Art; *m* 1, 8 June 1935 (m dis 1945), Hedwig Sophie Armour (d 1996); m 2, 20 Nov 1945, Pauline, da of Col Paul Victor Davidson, DSO, Royal Warwicks Regt (d 1946); *Career* served WWII, cmmnd RA 1941, War Artist to Ceylon Cmd 1943, seconded to RNVR 1944, demobbed 1946; painter; teacher life painting St Martin's Sch of Art 1949–57, lived and worked in France 1957–68, visiting prof Fine Arts Univ of Southern Illinois Carbondale USA 1968–69; *Solo Exhibitions* The Leicester Galleries London 1949, 1961 and 1962, The Adams Gallery London 1957 and 1959, The Walker Art Gallery Liverpool (Retrospective) 1959, La Maison de la Pensée Francaise Paris 1960, Galerie Lahumière Paris 1963 and 1965, Galerie Hervé Paris 1965, Larcada Gallery NY 1967, 1970, 1972, 1975 and 1977, Browse & Darby Ltd London 1978 and 1980, Oldham Art Gallery (Retrospective) 1984, Thos Agnew and Sons Ltd London 1986, Albemarle Gallery London 1988, 1990 and 1991, Gillian Jason Gallery London 1993, Ludlow Festival 1994, Colnaghi Gallery London 1996; *Awards* Medaille d'Argent Salon des Artistes Françaises (Paris) 1947, Int Exhibition of Fine Arts (Moscow) 1957, The Critics' Prize (awarded by the Int Assoc of Art Critics) 1961; AAUP 1968; *Books* Life Drawing (with Nicholas Mosley, 1954); *Recreations* cookery, gardening, book collecting; *Style*— John Napper, Esq; ✉ Steadvallets Farm, Bromfield, nr Ludlow, Shropshire SY8 2LB (☎ 01584 856247)

NAQVI, Syed (Zakir Husain) Haider; s of Syed Ather Husain Naqvi (d 1954), and Saghir Fatima, *née* Rizvi; *b* 14 Oct 1949; *Educ* Karachi Univ (BCom, MA Econ); *m* Marja-Liisa, da of Paavo Ilmari Nyyssönen, of Sorsakoski, Finland; 2 da (Chantal Samreen b 1980, Sabrina Yasmeen b 1986); *Career* CA; internal auditor Philip Industries (UK) Ltd 1975–77, gp fin controller London Export Corporation (Holdings) Ltd 1977–78, ptnr Haider Naqvi & Co CAs 1978–; FCA 1973, assoc Inst of Chartered Secs and Admins 1974; *Recreations* poetry, snooker, chess; *Style*— Syed Haider Naqvi, Esq; ✉ Concept House, 225 Hale Lane, Edgware, Middx HA8 9QF (☎ 0181 958 8015, fax 0181 958 8535)

NARBETT, Roger David; s of (William) John Narbett, of Queens Hotel Belbroughton, and Sheila Mary, *née* Hudson; *b* 4 May 1960; *Educ* Smethwick Hall Boys Sch, Halesowen Coll (City & Guilds); *m* 1 Oct 1988, Joanne, da of Thomas Marshall; 1 s (Oliver Daniel b 5 March 1989), 1 da (Simone Victoria b 15 Aug 1991); *Career* chef; Savoy Hotel London 1979–81, The Waterside Inn Bray Berks 1981–82, Le Gavroche London 1982–83, Les Freres Troisgros Roanne France May-July 1983; chef/ptnr (with father): The Bell Inn Belbroughton Worcs 1983–88, Sloans Restaurant Edgbaston 1986–92; exec sous chef Dorchester Hotel London 1992–94, exec chef The Lygon Arms Broadway Worcs 1994–; chef England Football Team 1989–; chm Regnl Finals Nestle Toque D'Or Student Competition 1989–; memb Restaurateurs Assoc of GB, memb Food and Cookery Assoc, master chef Craft Guild of Chefs, memb Academie Culinaire de France; *Awards* winner Taste of England Competition 1979, finalist Commis Chef of the Year Academie Culinaire de France 1983, Young Chef of the Year Restaurateurs Assoc of GB 1985, winner 30 under 30 Acorn Awards 1987, Chef of the Year Craft Guild of Chefs 1990 (runner up 1988), Meilleur Ouvrier de Grande Bretagne 1991, UK finalist Pierre Taittinger Int Culinary Prize 1992, finalist Wedgewood Chef and Potter Competition 1996; *Recreations* health and fitness, music, fine wines, agriculture; *Style*— Roger Narbett, Esq; ✉ The Lygon Arms, High Street, Broadway, Worcestershire WR12 7DU (☎ 01386 854420, fax 01386 858611)

NASH, Prof Andrew Samuel; s of Rev Samuel George Hall Nash (d 1993), of Cambridge, and Kathleen Grace, *née* Wells; *b* 1 Aug 1944; *Educ* The Judd Sch Tonbridge Kent, Southend on Sea Municipal Coll, Univ of Glasgow (BVMS, Silver medal for clinical med, PhD); *m* 1 Nov 1968, Rosemary Truscott, da of Rev John Harris Hamilton; 1 da (Heather Jane b 14 Oct 1971), 1 s (Graham Paul b 26 June 1975); *Career* veterinary asst in gen practice Ilfracombe N Devon 1967–72; Univ of Glasgow Veterinary Sch: house physician 1973–75, lectr 1975–85, sr lectr 1985–92, titular prof Dept of Veterinary Med 1992–95, dir of the Veterinary Hosp 1993–96, prof of small animal med 1995–, vice dean for student affairs 1995–; recognised specialist in small animal internal diseases (RCVS) 1993–; dir Glasgow Dog & Cat Home 1982–95, memb Bd and convenor Animal Welfare Centres Ctee Scottish Soc for the Prevention of Cruelty to Animals (SSPCA) 1995–, hon memb Soft-Coated Wheaten Terrier Club of GB 1988–, hon pres The Scottish Cat Club 1990–, pres Euro Soc for Veterinary Nephrology and Urology 1992–94; organist Sandyford-Henderson Meml Church of Scot 1994–; MRCVS 1967; memb: BVA (W of Scot) 1973–, Assoc of Veterinary Teachers and Res Workers 1974–, Br Small Animal Veterinary Assoc 1993–; Dip Euro Coll of Veterinary Internal Med 1995; CBiol 1993, FIBiol 1993; *Publications* author of numerous book chapters and papers published in veterinary jls; *Style*— Prof Andrew Nash; ✉ Division of Small Animal Clinical Studies, Department of Veterinary Clinical Studies, University of Glasgow Veterinary School, Bearsden Road, Glasgow G61 1QH (☎ 0141 330 5700 ext 5743, fax 0141 942 7215, e-mail gvma19@udcf.gla.ac.uk)

NASH, Prof Anthony Aubrey; s of Alfred Nash (d 1967), of Coalville, Leics, and Mabel Evelyn, *née* Garrett; *b* 6 March 1949; *Educ* Newbridge Secdy Mod Coalville, Loughborough Coll, Queen Elizabeth Coll London (BSc), Univ of Birmingham (MSc, PhD); *m* 1979, Marion Eileen, da of Eric James Bazeley; 4 da (Laura Amy b 25 Feb 1980, Ruth Ellen b 23 Jan 1983, Esther Jane b 29 April 1985, Hannah Bethan b 24 Feb 1990); *Career* lectr Dept of Pathology Univ of Cambridge 1989–94 (research assoc 1977–84), prof and head Dept of Vet Pathology Univ of Edinburgh 1994–; Eleanor Roosevelt fell 1989–90; memb: Soc for Gen Microbiology, Br Soc of Immunology; *Books* Mims Pathogenesis of Infectious Disease (1995); *Style*— Prof Anthony Nash; ✉ Department of Veterinary Pathology, University of Edinburgh, Summerhall, Edinburgh EH9 1QH (☎ 0130 650 6164, fax 0130 650 6511)

NASH, David Harwood; s of Victor Nash, of Welwyn, Herts, and Anne, *née* Richardson; *Educ* St Albans Sch; *m* 1, 20 June 1963, Susan Margaret (d 1991), da of John Charlesworth Haldane; 1 s (James Harwood), 2 da (Charlotte Louise Harwood, Annabel Haldane); m 2, Rosemary Janet Wiggin, da of David Orr; *Career* ptnr: Binder Hamlyn 1966–76, Pannell Kerr Forster (and predecessor firms) 1977–91, Riches and Company 1991–; dir Pelham Investment Property plc 1984–; memb Brompton Soc; FCA; *Recreations* skiing, sailing, tennis; *Clubs* Royal Thames Yacht, MCC, Harlequin Football; *Style*— David Nash, Esq; ✉ 10 Pelham Street, London SW7 2NG (☎ 0171 225 0702); Riches & Co, 43 Dover Street, London W1X 3RE (☎ 0171 408 2440)

NASH, David John; s of Herbert John Nash, of Swanage, Dorset, and Daphne Diana, *née* Wedekind; *b* 12 May 1942; *Educ* Ashdown House, Marlborough, Université de Neuchatel Switzerland; *m* 1, 1966, Judith, *née* Small; 1 da (Sarah b 30 Jan 1970); m 2, 1986, Lucy Mitchell-Innes, 2 da (Josephine Clare b 14 Nov 1987, Isobel Daphne 16 April 1990); *Career* Sotheby's: London 1961–63, asst rep NY 1963–66 dir 1966–78, dir Painting Dept Sotheby's USA 1978–89, sr vice-pres and worldwide dir of Impressionist and Modern Painting Dept 1989–96; dir Mitchell-Innes & Nash Fine Art Consultants and Dealers 1996–; memb Art Advsy Panel US Internal Revenue Serv 1984–; *Style*— David Nash, Esq; ✉ 1060 Fifth Avenue, New York City, New York 10021, USA; Mitchell-Innes & Nash, 1018 Madison Avenue, New York City, New York 10021, USA (☎ 00 1 212 744 7400)

NASH, David P; *Career* formerly with ICI plc and Cadbury Schweppes plc; Grand Metropolitan plc: main bd dir 1989–96, gp fin dir 1989–93, chm and chief exec Food Sector 1993–96; chm Amicus Healthcare Group; non-exec chm Kenwood Appliances 1996–; non-exec dir: Investmt Mgmnt Regulatory Orgn (IMRO), Sun Life and Provincial Holdings, Cable and Wireless; hon treas: NABC, Prince of Wales' Business Leaders' Forum; *Style*— David Nash, Esq

NASH, His Hon Judge (Timothy Michael) Ellison; s of Denis Frederick Ellison Nash, of Bickley, Kent, and Joan Mary, *née* Andrew; *b* 10 Dec 1939; *Educ* Dulwich Coll; *m* 1965, Gael, da of Dr A M Roy; 2 s (Matthew b 14 July 1967, Oliver b 15 Feb 1971), 1 da (Charlotte b 12 June 1973); *Career* called to the Bar Gray's Inn 1964; standing counsel: DHSS 1974–79, DTI 1976–90; recorder 1990–94 (asst recorder 1987–89), circuit judge 1994–; chm Home Office Police Appeals Tbnl 1988–94, legal assessor to GMC 1989–94, examiner Dio of Canterbury 1990–94; special constable Met Police 1961–79; *Recreations* walking round in ever decreasing circles; *Style*— His Hon Judge Ellison Nash; ✉ c/o Canterbury Combined Court Centre, The Law Courts, Chaucer Road, Canterbury, Kent CT1 1ZA (☎ 01227 819200)

NASH, Eric Stanley; s of Stanley Noah Nash (d 1975), of Paulton, Somerset, and Ina Louisa Nash (d 1978); *b* 17 May 1944; *Educ* Midsomer Norton GS, Univ of Bristol (BDS), Univ of Wales (MSc); *m* 14 June 1969, Enid Dorothy, da of Walter Perry, of Farrington Gurney, Avon; 2 s (Richard John b 10 Oct 1981, Michael James b 8 June 1983); *Career* jr posts: Bristol Hosps 1967–68, United Cardiff Hosps 1968–72; lectr Univ of Wales Coll of Med 1973–79, conslt oral and maxillofacial surgn Mid Glamorgan Health Authy; lectr and author of articles in Br Jl of Oral Surgery; memb: Welsh Dental Ctee, Welsh Postgrad Cncl; Welsh postgrad advsr Royal Coll, dir Dental Postgrad Educn for Wales 1991–, memb Welsh Standing Ctee for Postgraduate Pharmaceutical Educn 1995–; FDS RCS, fell Assoc of Oral and Maxillofacial Surgery 1979; *Recreations* church organisation, playing the organ, music; *Style*— Eric Nash, Esq; ✉ Mendip House, 43 Penlline Road, Whitchurch, Cardiff, South Glamorgan CF4 2AB (☎ 01222 627548); Oral Surgery Department, Prince Charles Hospital, Merthyr Tydfil, Mid Glamorgan; Room 155, Dental School, University of Wales College of Medicine, Heath Park, Cardiff

NASH, John Alfred Stoddard; s of Lewis John Alfred Maurice Nash, and Josephine Karen, *née* Stoddard (d 1962); *b* 22 March 1949; *Educ* Milton Abbey Sch, CCC Oxford (MA); *m* 6 Aug 1983, Caroline Jennifer, da of Geoffrey Hamilton Paul (d 1985); 1 s (Charles b 1985), 1 da (Josephine b 1984); *Career* asst dir Lazard Brothers and Co Ltd 1975–83, md Advent Ltd 1986 (joined 1983), chm British Venture Capital Association 1988–89, chm Nash, Sells & Partners Ltd 1989–; *Recreations* golf, tennis, skiing; *Clubs* Turf; *Style*— John Nash, Esq; ✉ Nash, Sells & Partners Ltd, 25 Buckingham Gate, London SW1E 6LD (☎ 0171 828 6944)

NASH, John Edward; s of Joseph Ronald Nash (d 1977); *b* 25 June 1925; *Educ* Univ of Sydney (BEcon), Balliol Coll Oxford (BPhil); *m* 1947, Ralda Everard Tyndall, *née* Herring; 2 s (Antony James, Jeremy Robert), 2 da (Regina Jane, Camilla Kate); *Career* dir: Samuel Montagu & Co Ltd 1956–73, Monetary Affrs EEC Cmmn 1973–77, Reckitt & Colman Ltd 1977–87 (1966–73), SG Warburg & Co Ltd London 1977–87; chm Mercury Money Market Trust 1978–86, memb Advsy Bd SG Warburg Bank AG Zurich 1987–94 (chm 1977–87), memb Supervisory Bd Bank Winter AG Vienna 1996–; res fell Nuffield Coll Oxford 1966–69; hon treas and memb Bd of Tstees World Wide Fund for Nature 1985–93; *Recreations* golf, skiing, horse racing, music; *Clubs* Turf, MCC; *Style*— John Nash, Esq; ✉ Chalet Gstelli, CH-3781 Gsteig-bei-Gstaad, Switzerland (☎ 00 41 30 51162)

NASH, Brig (Llewellyn James) Richard; s of Brig Llewellyn Charles Montgomery Nash, OBE, DL (d 1979), and Janet Catherine, *née* Adam (d 1988); *b* 1 Nov 1940; *Educ* Wellington, RMA Sandhurst, Staff Coll Camberley; *m* 8 May 1971, Rosamond Diana, da of Montague George de Courcy-Ireland (d 1987); 3 da (Emma b 1974, Louise b 1976, Juliet b 1981); *Career* cmmnd 12 Lancers 1960, 9/12 Lancers 1960, helicopter pilot, instr Aust Staff Coll 1980–81, Cmd 9/12 Royal Lancers (Prince of Wales) 1982–84, Chief of Personal Staff to Dep Cdr in Chief AFHQ Central Europe 1985, Cdr 143 Inf Bde 1988–92, HQ AFCENT 1992–94, Asst Cmdt RMA Sandhurst 1994–95; dir of training Racing and Thoroughbred Breeding Trg Bd; *Recreations* hunting, fishing, skiing, tennis; *Clubs* Cavalry & Guards; *Style*— Brig Richard Nash

NASH, Stephanie Joy; da of Alfred Raymond Nash (d 1973), and Mary, *née* Spencer; *b* 20 March 1959; *Educ* Oldfields Hall Sch for Girls Uttoxeter, Sch of St Mary & St Anne Abbots Bromley (Duke of Edinburgh Gold award), St Martin's Sch of Art (BA); *partner* Anthony Colin Michael, *qv*; 1 s (Montgomery Louis Spencer b 6 May 1996); *Career* Island Records: graphic designer 1981–86, art dir 1986–88; full-time ptnr Michael Nash Associates 1988– (fndr ptnr 1984); initially designers of record sleeves for artists incl Neneh Cherry, Fluke, Etienne Daho and Seal, subsequently cmmns for fashion designers Jasper Conran, Issey Miyake, Jil Sander and Philip Treacy, etc, graphic designers for Harvey Nichols own brand food products 1992–, packaging designers for Egg (fashion retail outlet) 1994; *Awards* (for Harvey Nichols food packaging) Gold Award D&AD for the Most Outstanding Packing Range 1993, Silver Award D&AD for the Most

Outstanding Packaging - Individual Pack 1994, Art Dirs' Club of Europe Award 1994, CSD Minerva Award for Graphic Design 1994 and NY Festivals Gold Medal and Grand Award 1994, Silver Award D&AD for Compact Disk Packaging for Massive Attack 1995, various others from music indust; *Style—* Miss Stephanie Nash; ✉ Michael Nash Associates, 42–44 Newman Street, London W1P 3PA (☎ 0171 631 3370, fax 0171 637 9629)

NASH, HE Stephen Thomas; s of Thomas Gerald Elwin Nash (d 1963), of Canford Magna, Dorset, and Gwendolen Selina, *née* Osmaston (d 1989); *b* 22 March 1942; *Educ* Cheltenham Coll, Pembroke Coll Cambridge (MA Economics and History), SOAS London (Arabic studies), Queen's Coll Oxford (MA Ethnology); *m* 1, 1967, Rose-Marie, *née* Bornstrand; 1 s (b 1971); m 2, 1977, Boonying, *née* Permkasikam; 2 da (b 1977 and 1985); *Career* asst dir Br Cncl Baghdad 1965–67; HM Dip Serv 1967–: third sec Caracas 1968–69, third then second sec Bogotá 1970–72, SE Asia Treaty Orgn Bangkok 1975–77, dep head of mission Guatemala City 1979–81, dep high cmmr Belmopan (Belize) 1981–82, head of Indo-China Section FCO 1984–86, chargé d'affaires Managua (Nicaragua) 1986–88, on secondment to British Aerospace 1989–91, EC Monitor Mission to Former Yugoslavia Zagreb 1991, chargé d'affaires Tirana (Albania) 1993–95, HM ambass Tbilisi (Georgia) 1995–; *Recreations* skiing, rowing, languages, viola-playing; *Style—* HE Mr Stephen Nash; ✉ c/o Foreign & Commonwealth Office (Tbilisi), King Charles Street, London SW1A 2AH (☎ 00 995 32 955497, 00 995 32 001065)

NASH, Dr Timothy Paul (Tim); s of Flt Lt Laurence Nash (d 1970), and Margaret Ellen, *née* Davis (d 1985); *b* 13 Aug 1946; *Educ* Changi GS, Andover GS, Univ Coll Hosp Med Sch London Univ (MB BS); *m* 18 Oct 1969, Bridget Eleanor, da of William Albert Harrison, of Tonbridge; 1 s (Matthew b 2 Dec 1981), 3 da (Deborah b 23 Feb 1972, Rebecca b 24 April 1974, Juliette b 3 April 1980); *Career* conslt in anaesthetics and pain mgmnt Basingstoke and N Hants Health Authy 1976–94, conslt in pain mgmnt The Walton Centre for Pain Relief Liverpool 1995–, hon clinical lectr Univ of Liverpool 1995–; ed Frontiers of Pain 1988–92, asst ed The Pain Clinic 1989–95; pres The Pain Soc 1994–96 (fndr ed IPS Forum 1982–85, sec 1985–88); chm: Pain Speciality Working Gp NHS Clinical Terms Project 1992–, Task Force on Educnl Standards (memb Cncl), Euro Fedn of Chapters, Int Assoc for the Study of Pain 1995– (also memb task forces on taxonomy and data retrieval); memb: BMA, RSM, Assoc of Anaesthetists, Cncl Nat Back Pain Assoc; FFARCS 1974; *Publications* contrib to: Pain (1985, 1986), Chronic Non-Cancer Pain (1987), The Pain Clinic (1987, 1990 and 1992), British Medical Journal (1988), British Journal of Hospital Medicine (1991), Medicine International (1991 and 1995), International Journal of Pain Therapy (1993), Read Codes (3 version, 1994), Anaesthesia Review 12 (1995); *Recreations* music, reading, hiking, badminton, cricket; *Style—* Dr Tim Nash; ✉ The Walton Centre for Pain Relief, Rice Lane, Liverpool L9 1AE (☎ 0151 525 4593, fax 0151 529 4458)

NASH, Ven Trevor Gifford; s of Frederick Walter Gifford Nash (d 1963), of Bedford, and Elsie Violet Louise Nash, JP, *née* Martin (d 1984); *b* 3 May 1930; *Educ* Haileybury, Clare Coll Cambridge (MA), Cuddesdon Coll Oxford; *m* 28 Oct 1957, Wanda Elizabeth, da of Sir Leslie Brian Freeston, KCMG, OBE (d 1958), of Kent; 4 da (Lois b 1958, Penelope b 1960, Phoebe b 1964, Joanna b 1968); *Career* Nat Serv Greece 1948–50; ordained 1955, chaplain TA 1956–61; curate: Cheshunt, Kingston upon Thames 1955–61; priest-in-charge Stevenage 1961–63, vicar of Leagrave Luton 1963–67, sr chaplain St George's Hosp London 1967–73, vicar St Lawrence and St Swithin Winchester 1973–82, Bishop's advsr for Miny of Healing 1973–, priest-in-charge Holy Trinity Winchester 1977–82, rural dean of Winchester 1977–82, hon canon of Winchester 1980–, archdeacon of Basingstoke 1982–90 (archdeacon emeritus 1990–), warden Guild of St Raphael 1995–; memb Gen Synod 1983–90, exec co-ordinator Acorn Tst for Advsrs (ecumenical) for Miny of Health and Healing England, pres Guild of Health 1990–, memb Exec Ctee Churches Cncl for Health and Healing 1993–; dir Luton Samaritans 1966–67; *Recreations* music, sport, reading, oil painting; *Style—* The Ven Trevor Nash; ✉ The Corner Stone, 50b Hyde Street, Winchester, Hants SO23 7DY (☎ 01962 861759)

NASH, Prof William Frederick; CBE (1987); s of William Henry Nash (d 1960), and Doris, *née* Jenkins; *b* 28 Jan 1925; *Educ* Amman Valley GS, Univ Coll of Wales Swansea (BSc, MSc), Univ of Manchester (PhD); *m* 18 Aug 1951, (Gladys) Christabel, da of Stephen Williams (d 1942); 1 s (Dylan Llywellyn b 16 April 1962), 1 da (Sîan Christabel (Mrs Crosby) b 16 May 1959); *Career* res physicist Metropolitan Vickers Manchester 1945–48, head Dept of Physics Univ of Nottingham 1981–84 (asst lectr, lectr, sr lectr 1950–64, reader in physics 1964–74, prof of physics 1974–90, pro vice chllr 1974–80, prof emeritus 1991), author of over 100 articles on cosmic rays and astrophysics; chm Home Defence Scientific Advsy Ctee 1973–95, chief regnl sci advsr Number 3 Regn Home Defence 1964–95, chm E Midlands Univs Military Educn Ctee 1973–90, memb Astronomy and Space Res Bd SERC 1980–84; Queen's Silver Jubilee Medal 1977; CPhys, FInstP, FRAS, FRSA; *Recreations* rugby (played when young), operatic singing, walking, travel; *Style—* Prof William Nash, CBE; ✉ 6 Spean Drive, Aspley Hall, Nottingham NG8 3NQ (☎ 0115 929 6607); Department of Physics, The University, Nottingham NG7 2RD (☎ 0115 951 5169, fax 0115 951 5180, telex 37346 UNINOTG)

NASON, Col Ian Geoffrey; s of Lt Col C F Nason, OBE (d 1988), of Guernsey, and Eleanor Ethel May, *née* Carey; *b* 11 Nov 1936; *Educ* Wellington; *m* 31 Dec 1960, Anne Mary, da of Lt-Col J W McKergow (d 1961), of NZ; 2 s (Andrew John Fortescue b 18 Oct 1965, James Henry Fortescue b 18 Nov 1970), 2 da (Julia Anne b 24 Aug 1962, Sara Anne Catherine b 24 July 1964); *Career* cmmnd Seaforth Highlanders 1956, Staff Coll Canada 1967, Nat Def Coll 1977, cmd 1 Bn Queen's Own Highlanders 1977–79, instr Nigerian Staff Coll 1979–81, COS HQ Br Forces Falkland Islands 1983, Col Cdr RMA Sandhurst 1984–86, DA Br High Cmmn 1987–91; civil servant HQ Land Cmd 1992–; chm Army Ornithological Soc 1994–; Chief Aku-Tubo of Bakana Island Rivers State Nigeria; *Books* Enjoy Nigeria (1991, 2nd edn 1993); *Recreations* bird photography, golf, travel; *Style—* Col Ian Nason; ✉ Mount Sorrel Farm, Broad Chalke, Salisbury, Wiltshire SP5 5HQ (☎ 01722 780296)

NATHAN, Dr Anthony Wayne; s of Murray Nathan, of London, and Pamela Simone, *née* Spack; *b* 10 Sept 1952; *Educ* Haberdashers' Aske's, Middx Hosp Med Sch (MB BS, MD); *m* 11 July 1975, Alison Jane, da of John Dick Campbell; 1 s (Mark Richard b 9 Feb 1981), 1 da (Emma Michelle b 4 March 1979); *Career* house physician Middx Hosp London 1975–76, house surgn in neurosurgery The Royal Infirmary Sheffield Feb-July 1976, sr house offr in gen med and clinical pharmacology Hammersmith Hosp London 1976–77, sr house offr in cardiology Brompton Hosp London Feb-July 1977, sr house offr in renal and transplant med Guy's Hosp London 1977–78, registrar in gen med Royal Free Hosp London March 1978–79; Bart's London: registrar in cardiology 1979–81, hon sr registrar in cardiology 1981–87, conslt cardiologist 1987–; hon conslt in cardiology Hosp for Sick Children London 1989–; sec Br Pacing and Electrophysiology Group, former sr ed Jl of Electrophysiology; currently contrib papers to various other learned jls; Int Cardiac Pacing Soc Award for Scientific Excellence 1983; memb: Br Cardiac Soc, Br Cardiovascular Interventional Soc, Br Med Laser Assoc, Br Pacing and Electrophysiology Gp (memb Cncl), Euro Laser Assoc, Int Soc for Heart Transplantation, N American Soc of Pacing and Electrophysiology (memb Advsy Cncl), MRS, RSM; hon memb Spanish Soc of Cardiology, fndr fell Euro Soc of Cardiology, Fell American Coll of Cardiology, FRCP 1992; *Recreations* tennis, golf, theatre, contemporary British art; *Style—* Dr Anthony W Nathan; ✉ Department of Cardiology, St Bartholomew's Hospital, West Smithfield, London EC1A 7BE (☎ 0171 601 8708, fax 0171 601 7170); BUPA Hospital Bushey, Heathbourne Road, Bushey, Herts WD2 1RD (☎ 0181 420 4471, fax 0181 420 4472); 62 Wimpole St, London W1M 7DE (☎ 0171 487 3887)

NATHAN, Clemens Neumann; s of Kurt Arthur Nathan (d 1958), of London, and Dr Else Nathan, *née* Kanin; *b* 24 Aug 1933; *Educ* Berkhampsted Sch, Scottish Coll of Textiles, Univ of Leeds; *m* 4 June 1963, (Barbara) Rachel, da of Geoffrey H Whitehill (d 1971), of London; 1 s (Richard Abraham b 15 Oct 1965), 2 da (Jennifer Ruth b 13 May 1964, Elizabeth Rebecca b 18 Oct 1970); *Career* chm Cunart Co Ltd 1958–, conslt textile technologist on bd of various textile orgns, govt advsr; vice pres Anglo Jewish Assoc (pres 1983–89), jt chm CCJO (UN NGO); presidential advsr Alliance Israelite Universelle; former vice pres Textile Inst, memb Int Cncl; author on mktg and textiles; Textile Inst Medal (for servs to textile indust and Inst) 1987; hon fell Shenkar Coll of Technol Israel 1994, visiting fell Sch of Slavonic and East Euro Studies Univ of London; Freeman City of London, Liveryman Worshipful Co of Glovers; CTex, FTI, FRAI, FRSA; Cavaliere Al Merito Della Republica Italiana, Israel Econ Cncl Medal, Grosse Ehrenzeichen Austria; *Recreations* swimming, mountaineering, art, history, music; *Clubs* Athenaeum; *Style—* Clemens Nathan, Esq; ✉ 2 Ellerdale Close, London NW3 6BE; Cunart Co Ltd, 231 Oxford St, London W1R 2HA (☎ 0171 437 1355, fax 0171 439 6721, telex 25362)

NATHAN, David; s of Joseph Nathan (d 1978), and Doris, *née* Ingleby (d 1994); *b* 9 Dec 1926; *Educ* elementary and rudimentary schs in Manchester; *m* 31 March 1957, Norma Rebecca, da of James and Stella Ellis; 2 s (Paul Daniel b 28 Nov 1961, John Steven b 2 March 1964); *Career* writer; RN 1944–47; copy boy and copy taker News Chronicle 1942–44, reporter St Helens Reporter 1947–49, reporter, theatre critic and London ed Nottingham Guardian and Evening Post 1949–52, syndication news ed Daily Mail 1952–54, re-write ed Associated Press 1954–55, reporter, feature writer, theatre critic, and chief entertainment writer Daily Herald (became The Sun) 1955–69, sub-ed The Observer 1971–78; Jewish Chronicle: theatre critic 1971–, dep ed 1978–91; contrib to numerous newspapers and magazines incl: The Times, Independent, Observer, Daily and Sunday Telegraph, Mail on Sunday, Plays and Players, Plays International; tstee The Critics Circle (pres 1986–88); runner up Critic of the Yr Nat Newspaper Awards 1978; *Fiction* The Freeloader, The Story So Far; *Non-Fiction* Hancock (biog with Freddie Hancock), Glenda Jackson, John Hurt - An Actor's Progress, Shaw and Politics (contrib); *Plays* A Good Human Story (Granada TV, RTS highly commended award), The Belman of London (Radio 3), The Bohemians (Radio 4); *Scriptwriting* That Was the Week That Was (with Dennis Potter), Not So Much a Programme, More a Way of Life (Radio 3), The Eleventh Hour; *Recreations* fishing, boats; *Style—* David Nathan; ✉ 16 Augustus Close, Brentford Dock, Brentford, Middx TW8 8QE (☎ 0181 568 8987); c/o Giles Gordon, Curtis Brown Group Ltd, 28–29 Haymarket, London SW1Y 4SP (☎ 0171 396 6600, fax 0171 396 0110)

NATHAN, Janet; *b* 31 March 1938, London; *Educ* St Martin's Sch of Art London; *Career* Artist; *Solo Exhibitions* Newcastle Poly Art Gallery 1979, Air Gallery London 1981, Ikon Gallery Birmingham 1982, Ferens Art Gallery Hull 1982, Riverside Studios London 1983, Howard Gardens Gallery Cardiff 1983, Mappin Art Gallery Sheffield 1984, Windsor Old Ct Windsor 1986, Warwick Arts Tst London 1988, Hampstead Theatre 1991, The Gallery at John Jones 1992, Chelsea Arts Club London 1993, Reed's Wharf Gallery London 1995; *Group Exhibitions* incl: The British Art Show (Arts Cncl touring, Arnolfini Bristol, Newcastle upon Tyne and Mappin Art Gallery Sheffield), Royal Acad Summer Exhbn 1980–83 and 1987–, Painted Constructions (ICA London) 1980, Art and the Sea (Third Eye Centre Glasgow 1981 and ICA London 1982), Coloured Constructions (Ikon Gallery Birmingham and touring), Whitechapel Open Exhbn 1983 and 1984, Leicestershire Exhbn (annually) 1983–93, 10 London Artists (Scandinavian tour) 1983, TWSA Touring Exhbn 1984, The London Group (Morley Coll and RCA) 1984, Crawford Centre for the Arts (Univ of St Andrews) 1985, Scarborough Festival 1985, Art on a Plate (Serpentine Gallery London) 1987, John Moores 15 Exhbn 1987, London Group Members Exhbn 1981–93, London Group (RCA) 1990, Riverside One London 1990, The Discerning Eye (invited by Sir Roger de Gray, PRA) Exhbn London 1990, Redfern Gallery London 1992, Leicestershire Exhbn 1993, London Group (London Inst and Barbican) 1993, Bruton Street Gallery 1993, RGI Glasgow 1993, Summer Exhbn (William Jackson Gallery) 1994, London Group (London Inst Chelsea Arts Club) 1994, Contemporary British Artists (Smiths Galleries London and Business Design Centre London) 1995, John Moores 19 Exhbn 1995, London Group 1995 and 1996, Cross Currents (Reeds Wharf and Barbican) 1996; *Work in Collections* Walker Art Gallery Liverpool, ICI HQ Millbank, Exchange House Broadgate, Leics Educn Authy, HRH The Princess Margaret, Lord Snowdon, Lonhro Group, Smiths Industries, Unilever House, Pentland Industries, Coopers & Lybrand, Chelsea and Westminster Hosp, private collections in Britain, Ametrica and Europe; *Style—* Ms Janet Nathan; ✉ 19 Belsize Square, London NW3 4HT (☎ 0171 431 1188)

NATHAN, Michael Ronald; s of Maj Cyril H Nathan (d 1977), of Prestwick, Chiddingfold, Surrey, and Violet, *née* Simon (d 1974); *b* 20 July 1927; *Educ* St Cyprian's Sch, Charterhouse; *m* 21 Oct 1984, Jennifer Madelin, da of Mr Eric Abrahams; *Career* articled clerk Whinney Smith & Whinney 1948–51, conslt Baker Tilly (and predecessor firms) 1990– (ptnr 1953–90); pres Stepney Jewish (B'nai B'rith) Clubs & Settlement 1978–95 (hon treas 1954–95), memb Cncl Guild of Glass Engravers 1981– (chm 1982–85 and 1993–94, pres 1994–), hon treas Assoc for Jewish Youth 1954–95, hon treas Jewish Welfare Bd 1959–69, memb Advsy Cncl Jewish Youth Fund 1955–95, chm United Charities Fund Liberal Jewish Synagogue 1962–; Master Worshipful Co of Glass Sellers 1973–74 (tstee Charity Fund 1974–); FCA 1958 (ACA 1951); *Recreations* art, glass (especially modern glass engraving), music, reading, gardening, cricket, entertaining family and friends; *Clubs* The Samuel Pepys; *Style—* Michael Nathan, Esq; ✉ c/o Baker Tilly, 2 Bloomsbury St, London WC1B 3ST (☎ 0171 413 5100)

NATHAN, Peter Geoffrey; DL (Greater London 1991); s of Maj Cyril H Nathan, FCA (d 1977), of Prestwick, Chiddingfold, Surrey, and Violet, *née* Simon (d 1974); *b* 27 July 1929; *Educ* Summer Fields, Charterhouse, Oriel Coll Oxford (MA), Univ of Paris (Dip in Etudes de Civilisation Française); *m* 14 May 1970, Caroline Monica, da of Lt Cdr Anthony C Mullen, RINVR (d 1991); 2 s (Hugo b 1975, Anthony b 1981), 2 da (Arabella b 1972, Venetia b 1973); *Career* writer RN 1948–49; admitted slr 1958; Herbert Oppenheimer Nathan & Vandyk 1954–88 (ptnr 1959–88); conslt: Boodle Hatfield 1988–92, Wood Awdry Wansbroughs 1992–; chm London Playing Fields Soc 1984– (dep chm Peter May Meml Appeal 1995–), Nat Heritage Sec's ministerial nominee London Cncl for Sport and Recreation 1992–95, memb Cncl London Sport 1996–; tstee Oriel Coll Devpt Tst until 1996 (patron 1996–), chm Oriel Law Soc until 1996, chm Oriel Law Fellowship Appeal until 1996; chm Chiddingfold Branch of Farnham Cons Assoc 1965–70; memb: Community Health Cncl for Kensington, Chelsea and Westminster representing Royal Borough of Kensington and Chelsea 1974–78, Cncl British Heart Fndn 1976–93, Ct City Univ 1989–93, Livery Consultative Ctee Corp of London, Cncl Anglo-Swiss Soc; successively memb Post Office User Area Cncls for City of London and London W2–W14 1988–93; chm Butterflies CC 1986–93 (hon treas 1961–86); recipient Nat Playing Fields Assoc Pres's Cert for servs to the playing fields movement 1992; Freeman City of London 1961, Master Worshipful Co of Gold and Silver Wyre Drawers 1989 (memb Ct of Assts, chm Tercentenary 1993 Exhbn Ctee); hon memb Geographical Assoc; memb Law Soc; *Recreations* cricket, golf, tennis, riding, reading, wine, opera, gardening; *Clubs* MCC, Vincent's, Oriental, City Univ; *Style—* P G Nathan,

Esq, DL; ✉ Hollybrook House, Broughton Gifford, Wiltshire SN12 8PH; 28 Abingdon Mansions, London W8 6AB; Wood Awdry Wansbroughs, 3 St Mary Street, Chippenham, Wiltshire SN15 3JL (☎ 01249 444422, fax 01249 443666)

NATHAN, Philip Charles; s of Denis William Nathan, of S Woodham Ferrers, Essex, and Grace Pauline, *née* Brennan; *b* 11 May 1951; *Educ* Alexandra Park Sch; *Career* stockbroker; head of dealing Charles Stanley & Co Ltd; Lions Clubs Int: former pres Rayleigh, S Woodham Ferrers Essex, multiple dist offr GB & Ireland 1991–94, dist govr E Anglia 1995–96, chm Cncl of Govrs Br Isles and Ireland 1996–97; memb: Stock Exchange Veterans' Club Ctee (charity steward), Stock Exchange Benevolent Fund Ctee, Lime Street Ward Club; Freeman City of London; MSI; *Style—* Philip Nathan, Esq; ✉ Charles Stanley & Co Ltd, 25 Luke St, London EC2A 4AR (☎ 0171 729 5484, fax 0171 739 1738, telex 8952218, mobile 0385 380069)

NATHAN, 2 Baron (UK 1940); Capt Roger Carol Michael Nathan; s of 1 Baron, PC (d 1963); bro of Hon Lady Waley-Cohen; *b* 5 Dec 1922; *Educ* Stowe, New Coll Oxford; *m* 1950, Philippa, da of Maj Joseph Bernard Solomon, MC, of Sutton End, Pulborough, Sussex; 1 s, 2 da; *Heir* s, Hon Rupert Harry Bernard Nathan; *Career* served WWII, Capt 17/21 Lancers (despatches, wounded twice); slr; sr ptnr Herbert Oppenheimer Nathan & Vandyk until 1986, conslt Denton Hall Burgin and Warrens to 1992; hon assoc memb Bar Assoc of City of NY, pres Jewish Welfare Bd 1967–71, hon pres Central Br Fund for Jewish Relief and Rehabilitation 1977– (chm 1971–77), vice pres RSA 1977– (chm 1975–77); vice chm Cancer Res Campaign 1987– (chm Exec Ctee 1970–75, treas 1979–87); memb: Royal Cmmn on Environmental Pollution 1979–89, House of Lords Select Ctee on Euro Communities 1983–88 and 1990–93; chm (House of Lords): Environment Sub Ctee 1983–87 and 1990–92, Select Ctee on Murder and Life Imprisonment 1988–89, Animal Procedures Ctee 1990–93; pres: UK Environmental Law Assoc 1987–92, Nat Soc for Clean Air 1987–89, Soc of Sussex Downsmen 1987–93, Weald and Downland Open Air Museum 1994–; chm: Inst of Environment Assessment 1990–91, Ct of Discipline Univ of Cambridge 1989–92, S Downs Conservation Bd 1992–; memb Cncl Univ of Sussex; Master Worshipful Co of Gardeners 1963; Hon LLD Sussex; FSA, FRSA, FRGS; *Clubs* Athenaeum, Cavalry and Guards'; *Style—* The Rt Hon the Lord Nathan; ✉ Collyers Farm, Lickfold, Petworth, W Sussex GU18 9DU (☎ 0179 85 284, fax 0179 85 619)

NATHAN, Hon Rupert Harry Bernard; s and h of 2 Baron Nathan, *qv*; *b* 26 May 1957; *Educ* Charterhouse, Univ of Durham (BA); *m* 17 Oct 1987, Ann, da of A S Hewitt, of Aldingbourne, Chichester, Sussex; *Career* dir Export Intercontinental Ltd; Liveryman Worshipful Co of Gardeners; *Recreations* motor cycles, golf, travel; *Style—* The Hon Rupert Nathan

NATHAN, Sara Catherine; da of Derek Maurice Nathan, of New Malden, Surrey, and Mary Catherine, *née* Lavine; *Educ* Wimbledon HS, New Hall Cambridge (BA, vice pres Cambridge Union), Stanford Univ California (Harkness fell); *m* 15 July 1984, Malcolm John Singer, s of Gerald Singer, of Finchley; 1 da (Rachel Fonya b 23 Jan 1989), 1 s (Jonathan Joseph b 5 June 1991); *Career* BBC: news trainee 1980–82, prodr/sr prodr BBC News and Current Affrs (on News, Newsnight, Breakfast Time and The Money Programme) 1982–87, output ed Breakfast News and Newsnight 1989–92, results ed Gen Election 1992, asst to Jenny Abramsky as ed News & Current Affrs Radio/controller Radio 5 Live 1992–93, ed The Magazine (Radio 5 Live) 1994–95; ed Channel Four News ITN 1995–; *Awards* Sony Radio Awards: Gold for Best Response to a News Event 1995, Silver for Best Topical Phone-in 1995; *Recreations* feeling guilty about my children; *Style—* Ms Sara Nathan; ✉ Independent Television News Ltd, 200 Gray's Inn Road, London WC1X 8XZ (☎ 0171 430 4508, fax 0171 430 4607)

NATKIEL, Rod; s of Daniel Natkiel (d 1986), and Marjorie Jessie, *née* Pinkham (d 1988); *b* 30 Jan 1952; *Educ* Kingston GS, Univ of Bristol (BA); *m* 6 Nov 1976, Janet Ruth; 2 s (Rory b 29 Aug 1978, Alastair b 6 March 1981); *Career* Arts Cncl Bursary trainee dir 1976, assoc dir and resident musical dir Contact Theatre Manchester 1975–78, dir/prodr BBC TV Light Entertainment Dept Scotland 1978–84; freelance exec prodr/dir in entertainment, drama, current affairs and news and md RVN Productions Ltd 1984–92 (progs incl The Ward, Young Krypton, Dramarama (BAFTA nominee), News at One, Channel 4 News, The Parliament Programme, Way Ahead (BAFTA Award 1987), A Week In Politics, Highway, The Krypton Factor (Premios Ondas award Festival of Euro Bdcasting Madrid 1987), and various foreign progs); head of network television BBC Midlands and East (Pebble Mill) 1992–; conslt prodn exec Birmingham Media Devpt Agency 1992–93; visiting prof of television studies Univ of Central England 1993–; *Recreations* squash, cricket, DIY; *Style—* Rod Natkiel, Esq; ✉ BBC Television, Pebble Mill Road, Birmingham B5 7QQ (☎ 0121 414 8027, fax 0121 414 8295)

NAUGHTON, Philip Anthony; QC (1988); s of Francis Naughton, of Littlehampton, Sussex, and Madeleine, *née* Wales; *b* 18 May 1943; *Educ* Wimbledon Coll, Univ of Nottingham (LLB); *m* 6 July 1968, Barbara Jane, da of Prof F E Bruce, of Esher, Surrey; 2 s (Sebastian b 18 March 1974, Felix b 24 April 1978), 1 da (Charlotte b 8 Sept 1972); *Career* in indust 1964–71, called to the Bar Gray's Inn 1970, bencher 1997; *Recreations* walking, fishing, sailing, theatre, music; *Style—* Philip Naughton, Esq, QC; ✉ 3 Serjeants' Inn, London EC4Y 1BQ (☎ 0171 353 5537, fax 0171 353 0425)

NAWRAT, Christopher John (Chris); s of Stanislaw Jerzy Nawrat (d 1976), of London, and Margaret Jane Patricia, *née* Maguire; *b* 6 Feb 1949; *Educ* Salesian Coll London, Univ of Edinburgh, Univ of Essex (BA); *m* 26 July 1975, Christine Patricia (d 1996), da of Daniel Patrick Boyle; *Career* sports journalist Morning Star 1979–81, ed National Student 1981–83; The Sunday Times: columnist (Inside Track) 1983–85, dep sports ed 1986–88, sports ed 1988–94; internet sports ed Channel 4 1996–; Pools Forecaster of the Year 1979–80, Sports Reporter of the Year (special joint award with Nick Pitt) 1984–85, Sports Pages Design Award Nat Sunday Newspapers 1987, 1988 and 1990; memb: NUJ, Sports Writers' Assoc; *Books* The Sunday Times Chronicle of Twentieth Century Sport (with Steve Hutchings and Greg Struthers, 1992, 3 edn 1996), The Traveller's Food and Wine Guide to Spain and Portugal (with Christine Boyle, 1994), The Sunday Times Illustrated History of Football (with Steve Hutchings, 1994, 3 edn 1996); *Recreations* reading, cinema, theatre, cooking, television, Spain; *Clubs* Reform; *Style—* Chris Nawrat, Esq; ✉ 4 Hawksmoor Mews, 200 Cable Street, London E1 ODG (☎ 0171 791 2507, e-mail 101455.1043@compuserve.com)

NAYLER, Georgina Ruth; da of Dennis Victor Nayler, of Chitterne, Wiltshire, and Yvonne Dorothy, *née* Loader; *b* 16 March 1959; *Educ* Brentwood Co HS, Univ of Warwick (BA); *Career* Nat Heritage Memorial Fund: joined 1982, asst dir 1986, dep dir 1988, dir 1989–95; dir The Pilgrim Trust 1996–; memb Historic Buildings Cncl for Scotland 1990–96; *Recreations* gardening; *Style—* Miss Georgina Nayler; ✉ The Pilgrim Trust, Fielden House, Little College Street, London SW1P 3SH

NAYLOR, Albert Edward (Eddy); s of Albert Victor Naylor (d 1989), and Mary, *née* Roberts (d 1987); *b* 12 Oct 1925; *Educ* Alsop HS Liverpool, Univ of Liverpool (BEng, MEng, DipTP); *m* 10 Sept 1949, Mildred, da of Archibald Milton Gillies; 1 s (Mervyn Edward b 4 July 1956), 3 da (Susan Mildred (Mrs Wood) b 20 Dec 1951, Janet Averil (Mrs Relfe) b 10 Sept 1953, Fiona Mary (Mrs Ollier) b 6 May 1962); *Career* graduate under agreement to Sir James Drake Co Surveyor of Lancashire 1946, civil engr to City of Liverpool 1949, sr engr to Co Borough of Birkenhead 1952, asst borough engr to Co Borough of Bootle 1956, dep borough engr to Co Borough of Luton 1964, city engr to City of Leeds and engr to Leeds and Bradford Airport 1970, exec dir of transportation and traffic W Yorks Met Co and engr to Leeds and Bradford Airpot 1974, co engr to Gtr Manchester Met Co and engr to Manchester Int Airport 1979–86; md: Waste Treatment Ltd 1979–86, Man-Oil Ltd 1983–88; ret local govt 1986; consulting engr and transportation advsr 1986– (advsr to Dept of Tport); past chm Assoc of Municipal Engrs, vice pres ICE; FIHT 1964, FICE 1976, FEng 1982, FRSA 1982; *Recreations* reading, family historical society; *Clubs* Rotary; *Style—* Eddy Naylor, Esq, FEng; ✉ Greenhill, Greenhill Common, Lower Whitley, Warrington, Cheshire WA4 4JD (☎ 01925 730396)

NAYLOR, Allan Peter; s of Geoffrey Alan Naylor, of West Kirby, Wirral, and Joyce Ethel, *née* Chappell; *b* 21 Dec 1952; *Educ* Calday Grange GS; *m* 18 Oct 1975, (Margaret) Joan, da of Thomas Stanley Wilson (d 1980); 1 s (Stephen John b 12 Nov 1981), 1 da (Rachel Anne b 10 Sept 1985); *Career* articled clerk Stacey Williams CAs Liverpool 1971–75, mangr Pannell Kerr Forster (after merger) 1975–80, fin controller then fin dir Outlook (Glass & Aluminum) Ltd 1980–84, ptnr Leonard Batty & Son Halifax 1985–89 (PA to Sr Ptnr 1984–85), ptnr i/c Halifax Office Revell Ward (following merger) 1989–93, in sole practice 1993–; tstee Rowntree Mackintosh Fund for Calderdale, non-exec dir Calderdale Family Health Serv Authy, local advsr Prince of Wales Tst; pres Calderdale Soc 1991–92, memb Cncl ICAEW 1992–93; FCA (ACA 1975); *Recreations* golf, rugby; *Style—* Allan P Naylor, Esq; ✉ 10 Bolehill Park, Hove Edge, Brighouse, W Yorks HD6 2RS (☎ 01484 721286); 46B Bradford Road, Brighouse, W Yorks HD6 1RY (☎ 01484 722222, fax 01484 712868)

NAYLOR, David Malcolm Broadley; s of Frank Broadley Naylor (d 1968), of Guiseley, nr Leeds, and Joyce, *née* Clarke (d 1990); *b* 2 July 1944; *Educ* Rossall Sch Fleetwood Blackpool Lancs; *m* 1 (m dis); 2 s (James b 7 June 1971, Robert b 28 April 1973); m 2, Valerie Ann, *née* Sutcliffe; 2 step c (Craig b 29 June 1969, Sonia b 7 March 1973); *Career* articled clerk Smithson Blackburn & Co Leeds 1961–66, qualified chartered accountant 1966; Grant Thornton (formerly Thornton Baker): joined 1966, ptnr 1976–, managing ptnr Leeds office 1981–90, memb Policy Bd 1987–90, managing ptnr NE Region 1990–94, sr ptnr NE Region 1994–; memb Cncl and treas Leeds C of C 1994– (memb Cncl 1978–90); CA (ACA 1966); *Recreations* collection and restoration of vintage MG sports cars, model railways, DIY; *Clubs* Leeds, MG Car, Naylor Car; *Style—* David Naylor, Esq; ✉ High Field, Hall Drive, Sand Hutton, York YO4 1LA (☎ 01904 468594); Grant Thornton, St John's Centre, 110 Albion Street, Leeds LS2 8LA (☎ 0113 245 5514)

NAYLOR, Douglas Rodger (Doug); s of Leslie Naylor, of Manchester, and Isabella Graham Barclay, *née* McLachlan; *b* 31 Dec 1955; *Educ* Chethams Hosp Sch of Music Manchester, Univ of Liverpool; *m* 7 June 1986, Linda Jane, da of Dr Richard Arthur de Keler Glover; 2 s (Richard Duncan Glover b 20 Nov 1986, Matthew Lawrence b 9 Jan 1990); *Career* screenwriter, producer and director; writer for series incl: Son of Cliche (BBC Radio 4, Sony Award for Best Comedy, Ondas Award), Carrott's Lib (BBC TV, BAFTA Award), Three of a Kind (BBC TV, BAFTA Award), Spitting Image (a head writer and prodr, ITV, Montreux Rose and International Emmy awards); co-creator, prodr and writer (with Rob Grant): Red Dwarf (6 series, BBC2, various awards incl International Emmy for Best Popular Arts Prog 1994), Red Dwarf VII (writer and exec prodr), The 10%ers (2 series Carlton TV/ITV Network, Silver Medal NY Festival 1994) 1993–; co-fndr Grant Naylor Productions Ltd; memb: Performing Rights Soc, BAFTA; *Books* Red Dwarf: Infinity Welcomes Careful Drivers (with Rob Grant, 1989), Red Dwarf: Better than Life (with Rob Grant, 1990), Red Dwarf: Last Human (1995); *Recreations* film and theatre, reading, shouting abuse at Merchant Ivory movies; *Style—* Doug Naylor, Esq; ✉ Grant Naylor Productions Ltd, Suite 950–951, The David Lean Building, Shepperton Studios, Studios Road, Shepperton, Middx TW17 0QD (☎ 01932 572552, fax 01932 572484)

NAYLOR, Edward Michael; s of Frederick Naylor (d 1988), and Margaret Mary, *née* Corfield (d 1984); *b* 27 Aug 1936; *Educ* St Marys Coll Crosby, Univ of Liverpool (LLB); *m* 6 Aug 1964, Anne Veronica, da of Alan Yates; 2 s (Gregory Michael b 11 Jan 1967, Matthew John b 28 May 1973), 3 da (Sarah Jane b 29 May 1965, Lucy Marguerite b 17 April 1970, Emily Marcella b 29 Aug 1974); *Career* slr; Herbert Green & Co: articled 1956–60, asst slr 1961–63, ptnr 1963–86 (merged Rutherfords 1986); ptnr: Rutherfords 1986–88 (merger 1988), Weightman Rutherfords 1988– (now Weightmans); sch govr, life govr Imperial Cancer Res Fund, memb Liverpool Law Soc 1961–; memb Law Soc 1961; *Recreations* squash, tennis, sailing, golf; *Clubs* Racquet (Liverpool), Aughton Lawn Tennis, Mussock Hall Golf; *Style—* Edward Naylor, Esq; ✉ Weightmans, Richmond House, 1 Rumford Place, Liverpool L3 9QW (☎ 0151 227 2601, fax 0151 227 3223)

NAYLOR, Prof Ernest; s of Joseph Naylor (d 1961), and Evelyn Keeton (d 1981); *b* 19 May 1931; *Educ* Swanwick Hall, Univ of Sheffield (BSc), Univ of Liverpool (PhD, DSc); *m* 7 Sept 1956, (Carol) Gillian, da of Harold Denovan Bruce (d 1970); 2 da (Elizabeth, Helen); *Career* cmmnd RAF Educn Branch 1954–56; reader in zoology Univ Coll Swansea 1968 (asst lectr 1956, lectr 1959, lectr 1963), prof of marine biology Univ of Liverpool 1971–82, dir Port Erin Marine Laboratory IOM 1971–82; Univ Coll of N Wales: Lloyd Roberts prof of zoology 1982–88, head of Sch of Animal Biology 1983–88, Lloyd Roberts prof of marine zoology Sch of Ocean Sci 1988–96, dean of sci 1989–91, head Sch of Ocean Sci 1992–96, prof emeritus 1996–; cncl memb NERC 1976–82, specialist advsr to House of Lords Select Ctee on Marine Sci and Technol 1985; memb: Coordinating Ctee on Marine Sci and Technol 1988–91, Inter Agency Ctee on Marine Sci and Technol 1992–; FIBiol 1972; *Books* British Marine Isopods (1972), Cyclical Phenomena in Marine Plants and Animals (jt ed with R G Hartnoll 1979); *Recreations* gardening; *Style—* Prof Ernest Naylor; ✉ School of Ocean Sciences, University of Wales Bangor, Marine Science Laboratories, Menai Bridge, Anglesey, Gwynedd LL59 5EY (☎ 01248 351151, fax 01248 382612)

NAYLOR, (Charles) John; OBE (1993); s of late Arthur Edgar Naylor, MBE, and Elizabeth Mary Naylor (d 1991); *b* 17 Aug 1943; *Educ* Royal GS Newcastle upon Tyne, Haberdashers' Aske's, Clare Coll Cambridge (MA); *m* 1968, Margery; 2 s; *Career* jr and sr exec posts in indust 1965–75, dir YMCA Nat Centre Lakeside Cumbria 1975–80, dep nat sec Nat Cncl of YMCA's 1980–82, nat sec Nat Cncl of YMCA's 1982–93, sec and treas Carnegie UK Tst 1993–, chm Assoc of Heads of Outdoor Centres 1979–80, vice chm Nat Cncl for Vol Youth Servs 1985–88, memb Nat Advsy Cncl for the Youth Serv 1985–88, chm of tstees Brathay Exploration Group 1995–; FRSA, CIMgt; *Recreations* running, the outdoors (particularly mountains), theatre, church, golf; *Style—* C John Naylor, Esq, OBE; ✉ Carnegie UK Trust, Comely Park House, Dunfermline, Fife KY12 7EJ (☎ 01383 721445, fax 01383 620682)

NAYLOR, Prof Malcolm Neville; RD (1967), DL (1992); s of Roland B Naylor, MBE (d 1969), of Walsall, Staffs, and Mabel Louisa, *née* Neville (d 1976); *b* 30 Jan 1926; *Educ* Queen Mary's Sch Walsall, Univ of Glasgow, Univ of Birmingham (BSc, BDS), Univ of London (PhD); *m* 10 Jan 1956, (Doreen) Mary, da of Horace E Jackson, CBE (d 1966), of Gerrard Cross, Bucks; 1 s (Andrew b 1960); *Career* RNVR and RNR 1943–77: Seaman Offr 1943–47, served HMS Suffolk, dental offr 1954–77, ret as Surgn Capt (D) and princ dental surgn RNR; civil conslt dental surgn RN 1969–91, jr hosp appts Birmingham and Dundee 1954–59; Guy's Hosp and Univ of London: res fell Dental Sch 1959–62, sr lectr in preventive dentistry Dental Sch 1962–66, reader 1966–70, hon conslt 1966–91, prof of preventive dentistry 1970–91, head of Dept of Periodontology and Preventive Dentistry 1980–91; hon sr res fell Inst of Dental Surgery 1991–; res hon affiliate Forsyth Dental Center Boston Mass 1975–; chm: Cncl Mil Educn Ctees of Univs of UK 1982–89, Mil Educn Ctee Univ of London 1979–91, Bd of Studies in Dentistry 1989–91 (dep chm 1986–89); memb Bd of Govrs UMDS 1987–91; memb Sea Cadet Assoc Cncl 1976–94, chm Sea Cadet Sport cncl 1975–, vice chm Bacons Sch 1978–90, chm of govrs St Saviours and St Olaves Sch 1987–; govr: Whitelands Coll 1972–96, Roehampton Inst for Higher Educn 1976–96, Wye Coll Univ of London 1991–; lay reader C of E 1974–; Queen's hon dental surgn 1976; Hon Col Univ of London OTC 1979–94; rep DL Borough of Lambeth 1994–; Hon Liveryman Worshipful Co of Bakers 1981, Freeman City of London 1981; memb: BDA 1955 (Tomes medal 1987), IADR Br Div 1959 (treas Br Div 1974–90, pres 1990–92), FRSM 1959 (pres Odontology Section 1984–85); FDSRCS (Eng) 1958, Hon FDS RCPS (Glas) 1992; *Recreations* sailing (cruising off-shore), home and family; *Clubs* Royal Yacht Assoc, RN Sailing Assoc; *Style—* Prof Malcolm N Naylor, RD, DL; ✉ Carrick Lodge, Roehampton, London SW15 5BN (☎ 0181 788 5045); Institute of Dental Surgery, Eastman Dental Hospital, 256 Gray's Inn Rd, London WC1X 8LD (☎ 0171 915 1193, fax 0171 915 2012)

NAYLOR, Martin James; s of James Naylor (d 1989), of Morley, Yorks, and Lilian Farrar (d 1990); *b* 11 Oct 1944; *Educ* Dewsbury and Batley Tech and Art Sch, Leeds Art Coll, RCA (MA); *m* 17 Sept 1996, Dr Liliana Maler; *Career* artist; living and working in Argentina 1993–; art advsr Psychology Dept Univ of Leeds 1966–67; lectr: Lancaster Poly 1970–71, RCA 1972–78, Hornsey Coll of Art 1972–73, Wimbledon Art Sch 1972–73; visiting prof: Ecole Nationale des Arts Decoratifs Nice 1972–73, Ecole Nationale des Beaux Arts Bourges 1976; tutor RCA 1974–75 and 1977–84, assoc visiting lectr Chelsea Sch of Art 1974–75, head Sculpture Dept Hornsey Coll of Art 1977–84 (pt/t lectr 1974–75), artist in residence Cité Internationale des Arts Paris 1982, artist in residence Altos de Chavon La Romana Dominican Repub 1985, artist in residence/sr visiting fell Br Sch at Rome 1987, artist in residence MOMO Buenos Aires 1993, visiting artist The New York Studio Sch NYC 1993; work in numerous public collections; Freedom of the City of La Plata Buenos Aires 1993; FRSA 1989; *Solo Exhibitions* incl: Lane Gallery Bradford 1966, Serpentine Gallery London 1972, Arnolfini Gallery Bristol 1973, Rowan Gallery London 1974, 1975, 1977 and 1980, Sculpture and Drawings 1973–76 (Sunderland Arts Centre and MOMA Oxford) 1976, XIV Saô Paulo Biennal 1977, A View Beyond the City (Rowan Gallery London) 1978, Installation Corroboree Gallery (Univ of Iowa) 1979, Works on Paper - Paris 1982 (Juda Rowan Gallery) 1983, Newcastle Poly Art Gallery 1983, Between Discipline and Desire (Galerie Artem Quimper France) 1985, Galeria Principal (Altos de Chavon La Romana Dominican Repub) 1985, La Galeria Santo Domingo 1986, Serpentine Gallery London 1986, Leeds Art Gallery 1986, Walker Art Gallery Liverpool 1987, Galerie Leger Malmö Sweden 1988, Between Discipline and Desire (Centro Cuidad de Buenos Aires Argentina, Museo Nacional de Artes Plasticas Uruguay, Museo de Arte Moderna Rio de Janeiro Brazil) 1990, Museo de Arte São Paulo Brazil, Yale Center for Br Art 1992, Sonoma Museum of Fine Art Calif, Museum of Modern Art Buenos Aires 1993, Estudio Lisenbeg Buenos Aires 1993, Palacio Municipal La Plata Buenos Aires 1993, Museo de Arte Moderno Mendoza 1994, Museum of Contemporary Art Cordoba Argentina 1994, Charles Cowles Gallery NY 1995, AAA Gallery NY 1995, Fundation Perez Celis Buenos Aires, Important Mischief (Centro Cultural Borges Buenos Aires) 1996; *Group Exhibitions* incl: Young Contemporaries (FBA Galleries London) 1969, Three Sculptors from the RCA (Eton) 1970, Drawings (MOMA Oxford) 1972, British Sculptors '72 (Royal Acad/Redfern Gallery London), Art into Landscape (Serpentine Gallery) 1974, Contemporary British Drawings (XIII Bienal de Saô Paolo) 1975, Gallery Artists (Rowan Gallery) 1976, Royal Acad Summer Exhibition 1977, 1978, 1985, 1987, 1990, 1991 and 1992, Artists Market (Covent Garden) 1978, Sculptors Drawings (Minories Gallery Colchester) 1979, Growing Up with Art (Leicestershire collection Whitechapel Gallery) 1980, Hayward Annual 1982: British Drawing (Hayward Gallery London and Fruitmarket Gallery Edinburgh) 1982, John Moores Liverpool Exhibition 15 (Walker Art Gallery Liverpool) 1987, Athena Award (Barbican Centre London) 1987, Homage to the Square (Flaxman Gallery London) 1988, Group Show - Selected Works by Gallery Artists and Summer Exhibition (Mayor Rowan Gallery London) 1990, Whitechapel Open (invited) 1992, Royal Acad (invited) 1992; *Awards* Peter Stuyvesant Fndn prize 1969, Arts Cncl award 1971, Gregory fell in sculpture Univ of Leeds 1973, jt first prize Art into Landscape Serpentine Gallery 1974, Gulbenkian Fndn Visual Arts award 1975, prizewinner John Moores Liverpool Exhibition 11 1978, Arts Cncl of GB award 1979, Lorne Bequest Univ of London 1984, purchase grant Elephant Tst 1984, Henry Moore Fndn award 1985, Henry Moore Tst award 1992, Br Cncl award 1992; *Recreations* polo, horseriding; *Clubs* Chelsea Arts; *Style—* Martin Naylor, Esq; ✉ Studio, 1 Cahill Street, London EC1Y 8PH; Arroyo 845 p9q, Buenos Aires 1007, Argentina; Lyrical Valhalla, Boca de Chavon, The Dominican Republic

NAYLOR, Maj-Gen (David) Murray; CB (1992), MBE (1972), DL; s of Thomas Humphrey Naylor (d 1966), of Ashton, Chester, and Dorothy Isobel Durning, *née* Holt (d 1986); *b* 5 March 1938; *Educ* Eton; *m* 31 July 1965, Rosemary Gillian, da of Major WW Hicks Beach, TD, DL (d 1974), of Witcombe Park, Gloucester; 3 s (Nicholas John b 13 March 1967, Duncan Hugh b 17 Oct 1968, Christopher William b 29 May 1972); *Career* Nat Serv enlisted 1956, cmmnd 1957, Cdr 2 Bn Scots Gds Munster and Londonderry 1976–79, GSO 1 Dir Staff at Staff Coll Camberley 1979–80, asst dir Def Policy Staff MOD 1980–81, Cdr 22 Armoured Bde Hohne W Germany 1982–84, dep mil sec MOD 1985–87, Cdr NE Dist 1987–89 (also Cdr 2 Infantry Div), dir TA and Orgn in Army Dept MOD 1989–92, ret; appt chm N Yorkshire Ambulance Service NHS Tst 1992–; vice chm St Peter's Sch York 1991–; currently chm Ryedale Cons Assoc; *Recreations* tennis, shooting, stalking, walking, travel; *Clubs* Cavalry and Guards; *Style—* Maj-Gen Murray Naylor, CB, MBE, DL; ✉ Minster Hill, Huttons Ambo, York YO6 7HJ (☎ 01653 695008, fax 01653 698474)

NAYLOR, Robert Antony; s of Francis Thomas Naylor, of Reading, and Kathleen Mary, *née* Donellan; *b* 13 Nov 1949; *Educ* Salesian Coll Oxford, Presentation Coll Reading, Univ of London (BSc); *m* 9 Nov 1974, Jane Karen, da of Charles Evans; 1 s (James Richard), 1 da (Victoria Jane); *Career* graduate mgmnt trainee NW Thames RHA 1972–74, hosp sec Nat Hosp for Nervous Diseases London 1974–77, sector admin Kent AHA 1977–79, dist admin Enfield DHA 1979–84, gen mangr E Birmingham Hosp 1986–90, chief exec Birmingham Heartlands Hosp NHS Tst 1991–; proprietor Henley Hotel Henley-in-Arden Warwickshire 1988–; AHSM; *Recreations* golf, squash; *Style—* Robert Naylor, Esq; ✉ Darley Mill, Darley Green, Knowle, Warwickshire B93 8PU; Birmingham Heartlands Hospital Trust, 45 Bordesley Green East, Birmingham B9 5ST (☎ 0121 766 6611)

NAYLOR-LEYLAND, Sir Philip Vyvian; 4 Bt (UK 1895), of Hyde Park House, Albert Gate, Co London; s of Sir Vivyan Edward Naylor-Leyland, 3 Bt (d 1987), and Hon Elizabeth Anne Marie Gabrielle Fitzalan Howard, da of 2 Viscount Fitzalan of Derwent; *b* 9 Aug 1953; *Educ* Eton, Sandhurst, Univ of New York, RAC Cirencester; *m* 1980, Lady Isabella Lambton, 5 and yst da of Antony Claud Frederick Lambton, *qv* (6 Earl of Durham, who disclaimed his peerage 1970); 3 s (Thomas Philip b 1982, George Antony b 1989, Edward Claud b 1993), 1 da (Violet Mary b 1983); *Heir* s, Thomas Philip Naylor-Leyland b 22 Jan 1982; *Career* Lt LG (ret); pres National Coursing Club 1988–, chm Peterborough Royal Foxhound Show Soc 1995– (vice chm 1989–95); dir: Milton (Peterborough) Estates Co, Nantclwyd Farms Ltd; *Recreations* hunting, coursing, shooting; *Clubs* Whites; *Style—* Sir Philip Naylor-Leyland, Bt; ✉ Nantclwyd Hall, Ruthin, N Wales; The Ferry House, Milton Park, Peterborough, Cambs

NAYLOR-SMITH, Ruth Elizabeth; da of Wilfred Naylor of Retford, Notts, and Phyllis Mary, *née* Hague; *b* 15 June 1951; *Educ* Chislehurst and Sidcup Girls' GS, Poly of Central London (Dip for Sec Linguists), Univ of Barcelona (Dip Ed); *Career* teacher La Casa Inglesa Madrid 1972–74, organised and ran holiday courses for foreign students Regent School of English London 1974–77, Linguaphone Institute Ltd 1977–81 (sales exec, sales mangr), md Mardev Ltd (now pt of Reed Business Publishing) 1981–92, mktg dir Economist Intelligence Unit 1992–94, md Uni-Marketing 1994–; vice chm Br List Brokers Assoc 1987–89, memb Advertising Assoc Data Protection Ctee 1987–89, chm Br Direct Marketing Assoc 1989–94; memb: Bd Direct Mail Servs Standards Bd 1990, Int Advsy Bd American Direct Marketing Assoc 1990–92, Inst of Direct Mktg 1994; *Publications* BDMA Direct Marketing Handbook (contrib, 1991); *Recreations* golf, reading, swimming, embroidery; *Style—* Ms Ruth Naylor-Smith; ✉ Managing Director, Uni-Marketing, Swan Centre, Fishers Lane, London W4 1RX (☎ 0181 995 1919, fax 0181 742 7245)

NAZEMI, Shayesteh; da of Kazem Nazemi (d 1987), of Yazd, Iran, and Mahsumeh Knokhodchian; *Educ* Charters Towers Sch for Ladies, Brighton Coll of Art, St Martin's Sch of Art (BA); *m* 1969; 1 da (Shahpari b 1970), 1 s (Shahriar b 1972); *Career* fashion designer (producing couture cashmere and silk knit designs); commenced career designing couture evening wear (sold exclusively to Harrods, Harvey Nichols and Fortnum and Masons) 1965, subsequent experience designing for the Empress of Iran during 1970s (concurrently designing costumes for film (a few of which starred in) and cmmnd to design the Persian Women's Army uniform during Shah's reign), currently md Shi Cashmere (estab 1980, shops and showrooms opened London and Japan, first British co to be invited to show at the IGEDO catwalk show Dusseldorf 1991, work exhibited in V&A); *Recreations* painting, dancing ballet, yoga, riding, water-skiing, tennis; *Style—* Ms Shayesteh Nazemi; ✉ Shi Cashmere, 30 Lowndes Street, Belgravia, London SW1X 9JQ (☎ 0171 235 3829, fax 0171 245 0944)

NAZIR-ALI, Rt Rev Dr Michael James; *see:* Rochester, Bishop of

NEAGU, Paul; s of Tudor Neagu, and Rozalia, *née* Florian (d 1988); *b* 1938, Bucharest; *Educ* Lyceum Simion Barnutiu Timisoara, Inst of Beaux Arts N Grigorescu Bucharest Romania; *Career* artist, sculptor and painter; moved to UK 1969; fine art lectr: Hornsey Sch of Art 1972–79, Royal College of Art 1976–78, Chelsea Sch of Art 1976–80, Slade Sch of Art 1985–90; external assessor CNNA; Sargant fell British Sch at Rome 1991–92; work incl: Palpable and Tactile Objects (early combinations of materials) 1968–72, Human Figure (drawing for rites) 1972–74, Anthropocosmos (organicity and cosmos) 1969–95, Performance (four rituals) 1970–77, Generative Art Gp (amalgamated works by five fictional artists) 1974–76, Hyphen (first analogical catalytic sculpture) 1975–95, Modern Energy Painting (oils on plywood, canvas) 1977–91, Architecture (imaginary architecture) 1977–92, Drawings on Photographs (projected context) 1975–90, Nine Catalytic Stations (polyphonic gp of catalytic sculpture) 1975–87, Public Monuments (real site) 1969–93, Tossing Fish Over Gate (a visual hermeneutics) 1981–92, Unnamed (infinite self) 1983–94, Newhyphen (paintings) 1992–94, Poems (working poems) 1969–93, The Ceremony of Contradictions (installations) 1993–94, Epagage (sculpture) 1992–93, Sacramentalia 1995, Ten Right Angels 1995, Unanimity 1995, Reorganising of Nothing 1996; co-dir Generative Art Tst 1995–; *Recreations* philosophy, cycling; *Style—* Paul Neagu, Esq; ✉ c/o 31c Jackson Road, London N7 6ES (☎ 0171 607 7858)

NEAL, Prof Alan Christopher; s of Harold Joseph Neal, of Bath, and Gladys May, *née* Lovelock; *b* 9 Jan 1950; *Educ* City of Bath Boys' Sch, Univ of Warwick (LLB), LSE (LLM), Univ of Stockholm Sweden (DGLS); *m* 30 July 1981, Alessandra, da of Dr Alessandro Tadini (d 1974), of Lucca, Italy; 1 s (James Alexander b 1984), 1 da (Francesca Jane b 1986); *Career* called to the Bar Gray's Inn 1975, in practice Midland and Oxford Circuit; pt/t chm Industl Tbnls 1995–; ed in chief The International Journal of Comparative Labour Law and Industrial Relations 1984–95, prof of law Univ of Leicester 1988– (lectr 1976–86, sr lectr 1986–88); visiting prof: Salford Univ 1992, Univ of Paris I (Sorbonne) 1993–; *Books* A Perspective on Labour Law (1982), Law and the Weaker Party (ed, 5 vols 1981–92), Collective Agreements and Collective Bargaining (1984), European Communities Health and Safety Legislation (1992), Developing the Social Dimension in an Enlarged European Union (1995); *Recreations* hockey (formerly Somerset and Warwickshire), skiing, music; *Style—* Prof Alan Neal; ✉ High Trees House, Hall Wood, Hallaton, Leicestershire LE16 8UH (☎ 01858 555465, fax 01858 555397, car 0802 577953); Faculty of Law, The University, Leicester LE1 7RH (☎ 0116 252 2368/70, telex 347250 LEICUN G, fax 0116 252 2699); Barristers' Chambers, 2 New Street, Leicester LE1 5NA (☎ 0116 262 5906, fax 0116 251 2023)

NEAL, Sir Eric James; AC (1988), kt (1982), CVO (1992); s of James Charles Neal (d 1971), and May Neal (d 1981); *b* 3 June 1924; *Educ* SA Sch of Mines; *m* 4 March 1950, (Thelma) Joan, da of Richard Edwin Bowden; 2 s; *Career* dir: Boral Ltd 1972–92 (chief exec 1973–87, md 1982–87), Wormald Int Ltd 1978–85, Oil Co of Aust 1982–87, John Fairfax Ltd 1986–87, Coca-Cola Amatil Ltd 1987–96, BHP Ltd 1988–94, AMP Society 1992; chm: Westpac Banking Corpn 1989–92 (dep chm 1987–88), Atlas Copco Australia Pty Ltd 1989–96, Metal Manufacturers Ltd 1990–96 (dir 1987–96); Govr of the State of South Aust 1996–; nat pres Australian Inst of Co Dirs 1990–92; memb: Def Review Ctee 1981–82, Australian Opera Cncl 1983–96, General Motors Australia Advsy Cncl 1987–94, Bank of Montreal Int Advsy Cncl 1986–88, Defence Industry Ctee 1988–90; nat chm Duke of Edinburgh's Award Scheme 1984–91, chair HRH The Duke of Edinburgh's Sixth Cwlth Study Conf 1986; DEng (hc), DUniv (UNISA); fell Aust Acad of Technological Sciences and Engrg, fell Inst of Engrs (Aust); CEng; *Recreations* reading, sailing, naval history; *Clubs* ustralasian Pioneers, Union, Melbourne; *Style—* Sir Eric Neal, AC, CVO; ✉ c/o Government House, Adelaide, PO Box 2373, Adelaide SA 5001, Australia (☎ 00 61 8 8223 6166, fax 00 61 8 8223 6049)

NEAL, Frederick Albert; CMG (1990); s of Frederick William George Neal (d 1971), and Fanny Elizabeth Neal (d 1979); *b* 22 Dec 1932; *Educ* Univ of Cambridge, Univ of London (BA); *m* 1958, Gloria Maria, da of Alfred Moirano, of London; *Career* Govt Serv, econ cnsllr Br High Cmmn Ottawa 1975–80, Dept of Trade 1980–83, UK permanent rep to Int Civil Aviation Orgn 1983–93; Aviation Conslt 1993–; Liveryman Worshipful Co of Fletchers; *Recreations* golf; *Clubs* Royal Over-Seas League, South Herts Golf, Hadley Wood Golf; *Style—* Frederick Neal, Esq, CMG; ✉ Flat 2, Hambledon Court, 19B Crescent East, Hadley Wood, Herts EN4 01EY

NEAL, Gub Matthew Michael; s of Michael David Neal, and Barbara Lisette, *née* Carter; *b* 24 Jan 1959; *Educ* Eton, Univ of Exeter (BA), Univ of California Berkeley (postgrad directing course, exchange scholarship); *m* 1991, Anna, da of Glynne Price; 1 s (William b 8 Nov 1993); *Career* prodr London Int Festival of Theatre 1981–84, floor mangr BBC TV 1985–87, script ed BBC TV 1987–89, television drama prodr 1989–; fndr Gub Neal Productions Ltd 1995, controller of drama Granada TV 1995–; prodr films and series incl: Medics (Granada TV) 1990, The Cloning of Joanna May (Granada) 1991, Angels (Granada) 1991, The Humming Bird Tree (BBC Films) 1992, Cracker (Granada) 1993, Bad Boys (BBC Films) 1994; exec prodr Hillsborough (Granada) 1996; memb: BAFTA, Equity; *Awards* Best Film Award (for The Humming Bird Tree) Rheims TV Festival 1993; for Cracker: RTS Award for Best Series 1994, American Cable Ace Award 1995, BAFTA Best Series nomination 1994, Prix Italia nomination 1995; *Recreations* walking, motorbiking, skiing, cycling, art history, photography; *Clubs* Pegs; *Style—* Gub Neal, Esq; ✉ Drama Department, Granada Television Ltd, The London Television Centre, Upper Ground, London SE1 9LT (☎ 0171 620 1620)

NEAL, Harry Morton; CBE (1991); s of Godfrey French Neal (d 1985), and Janet Bryce Morton (d 1960); *b* 21 Nov 1931; *Educ* Uppingham, Univ of London (BSc), City and Guilds Coll (FCGI); *m* 1954, Cecilia Elizabeth, da of Col Mervyn Crawford, DSO (d 1977);

1 s (Michael b 1956), 3 da (Camilla b 1960, Janet b 1961, Alexandra (Mrs Rupert Asquith) b 1967); *Career* Flying Offr RAF 1953; Harry Neal Ltd (bldg and civil engrg contractors): md 1963–86, chm 1985–90; dir: Connaught Hotel Ltd 1966– (chm 1980–94), Savoy Hotel 1982–93; chm: St Anselm Development Co Ltd 1985–, Harry Neal (City) Ltd 1990–; memb Lloyd's; memb: Technician Educn Cncl 1982–83, Business and Technology Educn Cncl 1983–94; chm City and Guilds of London Inst 1979–91; memb: Ct of City Univ 1982–91, Mgmnt Ctee Courtauld Inst of Art 1983–; memb Bd of Govrs: Willesden Tech Coll 1983–86, Imperial Coll Univ of London 1988–, Francis Holland Sch 1988– (vice chm 1996–); pres Middx W Co Scout Cncl 1983–, memb Delegacy St Mary's Hosp Med Sch 1993–; tstee: Buckminster Estate 1969–, Samuel Courtauld Tst 1989–, HRH Prince of Wales Inst of Architecture 1991– (memb Bd of Advsrs 1993–); Liveryman Worshipful Co of Carpenters (Middle Warden 1995, Sr Warden 1996); Chev de Tastevin 1981; FIC, FCIOB, FRSA; *Recreations* gardening, shooting; *Style*— Harry Neal, Esq, CBE; ✉ Great Sarratt Hall, Sarratt, Rickmansworth, Herts WD3 4PD

NEAL, Sir Leonard Francis; kt (1974), CBE (1971); s of Arthur Henry Neal (d 1939), and Emma Mary Neal (d 1947); *b* 27 Aug 1913; *Educ* LSE, Trinity Coll Cambridge (MA); *m* 1939, Mary Lillian Puttock; 1 s (Geoffrey), 1 da (Susan); *Career* industl rels conslt; memb Br Railways Bd 1967–71; chm: Cmmn on Industl Rels 1971–74, MAT Tport Int Gp 1974–83; non-exec dir Pilkington Bros 1976–83; chm: Employment Conditions Abroad Ltd 1976–84, Trade Union Reform Ctee, Centre for Policy Studies 1978–86; sometime visiting prof of industl rels Univ of Manchester, broadcaster and lectr; *Books* The Managers Guide to Industrial Relations; *Recreations* gardening, reading; *Style*— Sir Leonard Neal, CBE; ✉ Towcester, Northants NN12 7UY

NEAL, Nicholas Geoffrey; s of Francis Richard Neal, and Sheila Rosemary, *née* Bennett; *b* 6 June 1949; *Educ* Cardiff HS, Univ of Wales (LLB), Bristol Law Sch; *Career* asst clerk to the Justices Cardiff 1971–74, admitted as slr 1973; S Glamorgan CC: asst slr 1974–80, asst county slr 1980–87, chief slr 1987–92; dep chief exec and legal advsr Land Authy for Wales 1992–; hon slr: S Glamorgan Community Foundation, Cardiff Action for Single Homeless, Norwegian Church Preservation Tst; memb Bd of Visitors Cardiff Prison 1984–92, memb Law Soc 1975–, memb Soc of Cty Secs 1980–92; *Recreations* badminton, opera, reading; *Style*— Nicholas Neal, Esq; ✉ Land Authority for Wales, The Custom House, Custom House Street, Cardiff CF1 5AP (☎ 01222 223444, fax 01222 223334)

NEALE, Frank Leslie George; s of Hugh Neale, and Mona, *née* Clarkson; *b* 25 Aug 1950; *Educ* King Henry VIII Sch Coventry, St John's Coll Cambridge (MA), Manchester Business Sch (MBA); *m* 16 June 1976, Helen, da of Ronald Carter; 3 s (Michael James b 29 May 1979, Jeremy John Simon b 20 Jan 1985, Rory William b 1 Jan 1989); *Career* Econ Intelligence Unit 1973–77, PA Mgmnt Conslts 1977–83, Citicorp Venture Capital 1983–88, ptnr Phildrew Ventures; dir: Arncliffe Homes, Iona Software, Locum Group, Prime Time Recruitment; former vice chm Cncl Br Venture Capital Assoc; MIMC, FRSA; *Recreations* ballet, swimming, reading; *Clubs* Watford FC Supporters'; *Style*— Frank Neale, Esq; ✉ c/o Phildrew Ventures, Triton Court, 14 Finsbury Square, London EC2 1PD (☎ 0171 628 6366, fax 0171 638 6217)

NEALE, Sir Gerrard Anthony; kt (1990); s of Charles Woodhouse Neale (d 1985), of Painswick, Glos, and Phyllis Muriel, *née* Harrison; *b* 25 June 1941; *Educ* Bedford Sch; *m* 29 Dec 1965, Deirdre Elizabeth, da of late Charles Howard McCann (Lt Cdr RN), of Cornwall; 1 s (Alexander Charles b 7 June 1973), 2 da (Belinda Clare b 23 July 1967, Tania Katharine (Mrs Luke Hallam) b 7 Jan 1970); *Career* admitted slr 1966; head govt and public affairs Radcliffe & Co Westminster Solicitors; MP (C) Cornwall N 1979–92 (also contested 1974); *Recreations* sailing, golf; *Style*— Sir Gerrard Neale

NEALE, Prof John William; s of John William Neale (d 1975), of Bewdley, Worcs, and Elsie Mabel, *née* Preston (d 1982); *b* 19 Nov 1926; *Educ* King Charles I Sch Kidderminster, Univ of Manchester (BSc, DSc), Univ of Hull (PhD); *m* 30 July 1952, Patti Myrena, da of Frank Cyril Hullah (d 1973), of Derby; 2 s (John Anthony George b 1957, William Lawrence b 1966), 1 da (Elizabeth Myrena b 1955); *Career* RNVR, demobbed 1947; visiting prof: Univ of Kansas USA 1964–65, Univ of Rio Grande Do Sol Brazil 1971, Univ of Waterloo Canada 1975; prof of micropalaeontology Univ of Hull 1979–90 (asst lectr 1949, lectr, sr lectr, reader), visiting prof Univ of Shizuoka Japan 1985; author of over 100 scientific pubns, world authority on ostracod crustacea, ed Stero-Atlas of Ostracod Shells 1975–88; field work worldwide incl: Aust, China, Russian Caucasus, Tibet; has 12 species and 4 genera named after him, awarded John Philips medal for contrib to palaeontology and stratigraphy in the N of E 1986; pres: Br Micropalaeontological Soc 1978–80, Yorks Geological Soc 1980–82; currently memb Int Geological Cmmn Working Gp on Jurassic Cretaceous Boundary and Non-Marine Cretaceous Correlation; fndr memb Br Micropalaeontological Soc, memb Yorkshire Geological Soc 1949, hon life memb Hull Geological Soc; *Books* Grundzüge der Zoologichen Micropaläontologië (ed and part trans 2 vols 1963 and 1965), The Taxonomy, Morphology and Ecology of Recent Ostracoda (1969), The Ostracod Fauna from the Santonian Chalk of Gingin W Aust (1975); *Recreations* gardening, music, singing in local operatic societies, travel; *Style*— Prof John Neale; ✉ Etherington House, 640 Beverley High Road, Hull HU6 7JH (☎ 01482 445873)

NEALE, Michael Cooper; CB (1987); s of Frank Neale (d 1966), of Findon, Sussex and Nottingham, and Edith Kathleen, *née* Penney (d 1993); *b* 2 Dec 1929; *Educ* W Bridgford GS Nottingham, QMC London (BSc, MSc); *m* 13 Oct 1956, Thelma, da of Charles Weare (d 1971), of Worthing, Sussex; 1 s (Nicholas b 1961), 2 da (Judith b 1959, Elizabeth b 1962); *Career* engr offr RAF 1953–56, served Aden; Scientific Civil Serv 1956–87, dep dir (R&D) Nat Gas Turbine Estab 1973–80, DG engines MOD 1980–87; sec Royal Cmmn for the Exhibition of 1851 1987–94, non-exec co dir 1988–93, currently industl conslt; Royal Aeronautical Soc Silver medallist 1987; *Recreations* following cricket, railway history; *Clubs* Athenaeum, Royal Over-Seas League; *Style*— Michael Neale, Esq, CB; ✉ Quill Cottage, 32 Hound Street, Sherborne, Dorset DT9 3AA (☎ 01935 814332)

NEALE, Michael John; OBE (1984); s of Harold Arthur Neale (d 1940), of Surbiton, and Patricia Kathleen, *née* MacMahon (d 1985); *b* 14 Dec 1926; *Educ* St Edwards Oxford, Imperial Coll London (Whitworth scholar, BSc (Eng), DIC); *Career* apprentice Rolls Royce Derby 1944–49, res assoc Imperial Coll London 1950–55; Glacier Metal Co Ltd: engrg research mangr 1956–58, mangr design and technol 1958–62; int consltg engr 1962–, chm Neale Consulting Engineers Ltd 1975– (md 1965–75); FEng 1981, FIMechE 1965 (pres IMechE 1990–91); *Books* The Tribology Handbook (1973, 2 edn 1995), Couplings and Shaft Alignment (1991); *Recreations* restoring antique furniture, buildings and machinery; *Clubs* Athenaeum; *Style*— Michael Neale, Esq, OBE, FEng; ✉ Chalkdell, Herriard, Hants RG25 2PR (☎ 01256 381380, fax 01256 381802); Neale Consulting Engineers Ltd, 43 Downing St, Farnham, Surrey GU9 7PH (☎ 01252 722255, fax 01252 737106)

NEALE, Phillip Anthony (Phil); s of Geoffrey Baker Neale, and Elsie May, *née* Waby; *b* 5 June 1954; *Educ* Frederick Gough GS Scunthorpe, John Leggot Sixth Form Coll Scunthorpe, Univ of Leeds (BA); *m* 26 Sept 1976, Christine Mary Barton; 1 s (Craig Andrew b 11 Feb 1982), 1 da (Kelly Joanne b 9 Nov 1979); *Career* professional cricketer; Worcestershire CCC: 1975–92, awarded county cap 1978, capt 1982–91, benefit 1988; represented England B 1982; honours as capt Worcestershire CCC: County Championship 1988 and 1989, Refuge Assurance League 1987 and 1988 (runners up 1989), Benson & Hedges Cup 1991, Refuge Assurance Cup 1991; record for ten seasons as capt Worcestershire 1991, Player of the Year Britannic Assurance Championship 1989; professional footballer Lincoln City off-seasons 1974–85 (over 350 appearances), teacher Royal GS Worcester 1986–89, England A team cricket mangr for 1993 winter tour to S Africa and 1994–95 winter tour to India and Bangladesh, England U19 tour mangr for winter tour to Pakistan 1996–97; dir of cricket Northamptonshire CCC until 1995, dir of coaching Warwickshire CCC 1995–; ptnr Phil Neale Enterprises mktg and promotion 1993–; *Books* A Double Life (autobiography, 1990); *Recreations* reading, golf, spending time with my family; *Style*— Phil Neale, Esq; ✉ Director of Coaching, Warwickshire CCC, County Ground, Edgbaston, Birmingham B5 7QU (☎ 0121 446 4422)

NEAMAN, Prof Yfrah; OBE (1983); *b* 13 Feb 1923; *Educ* Premier Prix Conservatoire National Supérieur de Musique Paris, studies with Carl Flesch, Jacques Thibaud and Max Rostal; *m* 16 March 1963, Gillian Mary, da of Maurice E Shaw (d 1977), of London; 1 s (Samuel Lister b 1964), 1 da (Rachel Cecilia b 1965); *Career* Guildhall Sch of Music & Drama: prof of violin, head of Strings Dept 1962–78, head of Dept of Advanced Solo Studies 1974–; recitals, concerts with orchestras, radio and TV appearances, public masterclasses in Europe, N and S America, China, Japan, Korea, Africa and Asia; artistic dir London Int String Quartet Competition, artistic advsr Wells Cathedral Sch England; recordings made for Argo, Lyrita and Yugoton records; ed several works by various composers; Freeman City of London, Liveryman Worshipful Co of Musicians; FGSM; *Style*— Prof Yfrah Neaman, OBE; ✉ 11 Chadwell St, London EC1R 1XD (☎ 0171 837 4455); Guildhall School of Music & Drama, Barbican, London EC2Y 8DT (☎ 0171 628 2571)

NEAME, Christopher Elwin; s of Ronald Neame, CBE, and Beryl Yolanda Heanly; *b* 24 Dec 1942; *Educ* King's Sch Canterbury; *m* April 1966 (m dis 1972), Heather Marilyn, da of Dick Wade (d 1972); 1 s (Gareth Elwin b 8 March 1967), 2 da (Shuna b 16 July 1968, Emma b 28 May 1970); *Career* prodr tv series The Flame Trees of Thika 1980, wrote stage play of Monsignor Quixote 1988 (prodr and wrote screenplay which won Christopher Award NY 1987), prodr Bye Bye Baby (Prix Europa winner) 1991, Feast of July (prodr and writer) 1994; memb: BAFTA, The Writers' Guild of GB, Producers' Guild of America; Indust memb Brit Film Cmmn; *Recreations* photography; *Style*— Christopher Neame, Esq; ✉ Upper Ensign House, Selling Road, Old Wives Lees, nr Canterbury, Kent CT4 8BB (☎ 01227 752 791/2, fax 01227 752 793, mobile 0973 111360)

NEAME, Robert Harry Beale; DL (Kent 1992); s of Jasper Beale Neame (d 1961), and Violet Evelyn, *née* Cobb (d 1976); The Neame family have been resident in E Kent and can be traced back 500 years; *b* 25 Feb 1934; *Educ* Harrow; *m* 1, 1961, Sally Elizabeth, *née* Corben; 1 s (Jonathan), 2 da (Charlotte, Sarah); m 2, 1974, Yvonne Mary, *née* Mackenzie; 1 da (Moray); *Career* cmmnd 17/21 Lancers 1953–55 (army Racquets champion 1954); chm Shepherd Neame Ltd 1971– (joined 1956, dir 1957, mktg dir 1961), former dir and chm Faversham Laundry Co, regnl dir National Westminster Bank plc 1982–92; dir: Kent Econ Devpt Bd 1984–89, Folkestone Racecourse 1984– (chm 1989); local dir Royal Insurance (UK) Ltd 1971–; memb Faversham CC 1965–89, ldr Kent CC 1982–84; chm: SE Eng Tourist Bd 1979–90, Int Union of Local Authys 1986–89; memb Assoc of Brewing; *Recreations* shooting, riding, cricket, golf, squash, racquets; *Clubs* MCC, I Zingari, Butterflies, Escorts, Jesters, Band of Brothers, Press, Royal St George's, Free Forresters; *Style*— Robert Neame, Esq, DL; ✉ Dane Court Farmhouse, Kits Hill, Selling, Faversham, Kent (☎ 01227 752284); c/o Shepherd Neame Ltd, 17 Court St, Faversham, Kent ME13 7AX (☎ 01795 532206)

NEARN, Graham Bradshaw; s of Henry John Nearn (d 1986), and Eva Charlotte, *née* Sayers (d 1992); *b* 29 Sept 1933; *Educ* Purley County GS, City of London Coll; *m* 5 March 1966, (Margaret) Jane, da of Dr John Stewart Norwell (d 1984); 2 s (Robert Bradshaw b 24 April 1967, Simon John 27 March 1969), 2 da (Eliza Alexandra Jane b 2 Nov 1972, Janina Charlotte b 5 May 1977); *Career* md Caterham Cars Ltd (mfr Caterham Super Seven sports car, formerly Lotus Seven) 1970– (dir 1959–), chm London Property Conversions Ltd 1972–; chm Specialist Car Mfrs Gp SMMT; *Books* The Caterham & Lotus Sevens (1986), Caterham Sevens (1996); *Recreations* golf, sailing, motor sport; *Clubs* Holtye Golf, Whitstable Yacht, Aston Martin Owners, Lotus 7; *Style*— Graham Nearn, Esq; ✉ Winburne, Ashurst, Kent TN3 9TB (☎ 01892 740341); 34 Island Wall, Whitstable, Kent; Caterham Cars Ltd, Seven House, Townend, Caterham, Surrey CR3 5UG (☎ 01883 346666, fax 01883 349086, car tel 0836 340683)

NEARS, Colin Gray; s of William Charles Nears (d 1974), of Ipswich, and Winifred Mildred, *née* Gray (d 1983); *b* 19 March 1933; *Educ* Ipswich Sch, King's Coll Cambridge (MA); *Career* freelance TV dir; prodr music and arts BBC TV 1967–87, author and dir of progs (on literature, the Visual Arts, music and dance); ed Review 1971–72; memb Cncl and chm Advsy Panel on Dance Arts Cncl of GB 1982–90, dep chm Ballet Bd Royal Opera House 1992– (memb 1990–), chm Bd Birmingham Royal Ballet 1993–; govr Royal Ballet 1995–, memb Bd of Dirs Royal Opera House 1995–; BAFTA Award for Best Specialised Programme 1973, Prix Italia Music Prize 1982; *Recreations* reading, gardening, painting, swimming; *Style*— Colin Nears, Esq; ✉ 16 Ashchurch Terrace, London W12 9SL (☎ 0181 749 3615)

NEARY, Martin Gerard James; s of Leonard Walter Neary (d 1996), of Walton-on-Thames, and Jeanne Marguerite, *née* Thébault; *b* 28 March 1940; *Educ* City of London Sch, Chapel Royal Choir, Gonville and Caius Coll Cambridge (organ scholar, MA); *m* 22 April 1967, Penelope Jane, da of Sir Brian Warren (d 1996), of London, and Dame Josephine Barnes, DBE, *qv*; 1 s (Thomas b 1974), 2 da (Nicola b 1969, Alice b 1972); *Career* prof of organ Trinity Coll London 1963–72, organist and master of music St Margaret's Westminster 1965–71; conductor: Twickenham Musical Soc 1966–72, St Margaret's Westminster Singers 1967–71, Waynflete Singers 1972–87; organist and master of the music Winchester Cathedral 1972–87, organist and master of the choristers Westminster Abbey 1988–, lectr in church music Royal Acad of Music 1989–; guest conductor: Academy of Ancient Music, Bournemouth Symphony Orchestra, English Chamber Orchestra, London Symphony Orchestra, Winchester Baroque Ensemble 1982–87, Westminster Baroque Ensemble 1988, Brandenburg Orchestra 1991; 12 foreign tours with Winchester Cathedral Choir 1978–87, toured America (thrice), France (twice), Germany, Hungary, Switzerland, Russia and Ukraine with Westminster Abbey Choir 1988–94; dir Southern Cathedrals Festival 1972, 1975, 1978, 1981, 1984 and 1987; many organ recitals and broadcasts in UK, Europe, America, Aust, NZ, Korea and India, has conducted premières of music by many Br composers, numerous recordings incl Purcell Music for Queen Mary; pres: Cathedral Organists' Assoc 1985–88, Royal Coll of Organists 1988–90 and 1996–, Organists' Benevolent League 1988–; chm Herbert Howells Soc 1993–; hon citizen Texas 1971; Grammy Award nomination 1996; Hon FTCL 1969, Hon RAM 1988; FRCO; *Books* Early French Organ Music (ed 2 vols, 1975); *Recreations* watching cricket, visiting Test Match grounds throughout the world; *Clubs* Athenaeum, Middx CCC; *Style*— Martin Neary, Esq; ✉ 2 Little Cloister, Westminster Abbey, London SW1P 3PL (☎ 0171 222 6923, fax 0171 222 1025); Chapter Office, 20 Dean's Yard, London SW1P 3PA (☎ 0171 222 5152)

NEASOM, Norman; s of Arthur Neasom, of Redditch, Worcs, and Ethel, *née* Palmer, of Droitwich, Worcs; *b* 7 Nov 1915; *Educ* Redditch Secdy Sch, Birmingham Central Coll of Art and Crafts; *m* 8 Aug 1949, Jessie Mary (d 1994), da of John Davis; 2 da (Helen Mary, Jean Catherine); *Career* artist; lectr: Sch of Painting Birmingham Coll of Art 1946–54, Redditch Sch of Art 1954–80, ret; exhibited at RA, RWS, Royal Birmingham Soc of Artists; work in W Midlands Arts permanent collection, numerous private collections; memb Royal Birmingham Soc of Artists 1947, RWS 1978; *Recreations* formerly sailing; *Clubs* Redditch Sailing (fndr memb, life memb and tstee); *Style*—

Norman Neasom, Esq; ✉ 95 Bromfield Road, Redditch, Worcs B97 4PN (☎ 01527 544601)

NEATE, Francis Webb; s of Francis Webb Neate (d 1982), of Kew, Richmond, Surrey, and Fiona L M, *née* O'Brien; *b* 13 May 1940; *Educ* St Wilfrid's Sch Seaford Sussex, St Paul's, Brasenose Coll Oxford (BA), Univ of Chicago Law Sch (JD); *m* 25 Aug 1962, Patricia Ann, da of Anthony Vincent Hugh Mulligan (d 1984), of Putney, London; 2 s (Vincent b 1968, Patrick b 1970), 2 da (Polly b 1966, Emily b 1973); *Career* assoc Davis Polk & Wardwell NY 1963; admitted slr 1966; Slaughter and May: articled clerk 1964–66, asst slr 1966–71, ptnr 1972–; chm treas Int Bar Assoc; memb: Law Soc, City of London Slrs' Co; *Recreations* cricket, reading, family; *Clubs* MCC, Berkshire CCC, Richmond CC, Falkland CC; *Style—* Francis Neate, Esq; ✉ Slaughter and May, 35 Basinghall St, London EC2V 5DB (☎ 0171 600 1200)

NEAVE, Prof Guy Richard Irvine; s of Lt Cdr Arundel Richard York Neave, DSC (d 1977), and Barbara Marie, *née* Liardet (d 1979); *b* 27 Dec 1941; *Educ* Kings Sch Worcester, Univ of London (BA, PhD); *m* 6 Dec 1986, Martine Gabriele Thérèse, da of Claude Herlant, of Woluwe Saint Pierre, Belgium; 1 s (Joel b 3 Aug 1988), 1 da (Magali, twin); *Career* lectr in history Wales 1967–69, res fell Univ of Edinburgh 1969–75, prof of comparative and gen educn Amsterdam Netherlands 1978–80, directeur de recherche Paris 1981–85 (maitre de recherche 1975–78), prof of comparative educn Univ of London 1986–90; memb Soc Res in Higher Educn; ed: Higher Education Policy, European Jl of Education (jt) 1980–91; fell Cwlth of Aust Fellowship 1993; FRSA 1987; *Books* How They Fared (1975), An Improper Sixth Year (jtly, 1976), Modèles D'Egalité (1976), The EEC And Education (1985), La Communidad Europea Y La Educactión (1987), Prometheus Bound (jtly, 1991), The Teaching Nation (1992), Encyclopedia of Higher Education (jt ed in chief, 4 vols, 1992), Government and higher education relationships across three continents: the Winds of Change (jtly, 1994); *Recreations* jogging, bricolage; *Clubs* Anglo-Belgian; *Style—* Prof Guy Neave; ✉ 31 Square Saint Germain, F78100 Saint Germain En Laye, France; International Association of Universities, 1 rue Miollis, F75732 Paris Cedex 15, France (☎ 00 331 45 68 2545, fax 00 331 47 34 76 05)

NEAVE, Julius Arthur Sheffield; CBE (1978, MBE 1944), JP (Brentwood), DL (Essex 1983); s of late Col Richard Neave, and Helen Mary Elizabeth, *née* Miller; *b* 17 July 1919; *Educ* Sherborne; *m* 1951, Helen Margery, da of the late Col P M Acton-Adams, DSO; 3 da; *Career* served in 13/18 Royal Hussars; Mercantile & General Reinsurance Company Ltd: joined 1938, gen mangr 1966–80, md 1980–82; dir Prudential Corporation plc 1982–92; first chm Reinsurance Offices Assoc; received Founders' Award Gold Medal of Int Seminars 1977; pres: Insurance Inst London 1976–77, Geneva Assoc 1983–86, Chartered Insurance Inst 1983–84; Master Worshipful Co of Insurers 1984; High Sheriff of Essex 1987–88; *Recreations* golf, shooting, fishing, tennis, needlework; *Clubs* Cavalry & Guards'; *Style—* Julius Neave, Esq, CBE, JP, DL; ✉ Mill Green Park, Ingatestone, Essex CM4 0JB (☎ 01277 353036, fax 01277 355885)

NEAVE, Sir Paul Arundell; 7 Bt (GB 1795), of Dagnam Park, Essex; s of Sir Arundell Thomas Clifton Neave, 6 Bt (d 1992), and Richenda Alice Ione (d 1994), da of Sir Robert Joshua Paul, 5 Bt (d 1955); *b* 13 Dec 1948; *Educ* Eton; *m* 1976, Coralie Jane Louise, da of Sir Robert George Caldwell Kinahan, ERD, of Castle Upton, Templepatrick, Co Antrim; 2 s (Frederick Paul Kinahan b 25 Jan 1981, Julian Robin Kinahan b 1983); *Heir* s, Frederick Paul Kinahan Neave b 25 Jan 1981; *Career* stockbroker; dir Henderson Crosthwaite Ltd; MSI (memb Stock Exchange 1980); *Recreations* gardening; *Clubs* Boodle's; *Style—* Sir Paul Neave, Bt; ✉ Queen's House, Monk Sherborne, Hants RG26 5HH

NEBHRAJANI, Vir Tirathdas; s of Tirathdas Totaldas Nebhrajani (d 1975), and Dharmi, *née* Sirwani; *b* 9 Aug 1930; *Educ* Premier HS Karachi, Univ of Bombay, Assam Med Coll (Indian Central Govt scholar), Gauhati Univ Assam (MB BS), DLO (RCS), FRCSEd (1969); *m* 1 Sept 1961, Jayantee, da of Arun Kumar Chanda; 2 da (Sharmila (Mrs Peter Charles Wallace) b 30 March 1966, Malini (Mrs Stephen Peter Richards) b 22 Jan 1969); *Career* res offr ENT and gen surgery Assam Medical Coll 1958–60, various appts 1960–72 (Dudley Road Hosp Birmingham, Whipps Cross Hosp London, Western Infirmary Glasgow); present appts: conslt otologist John Scott Audiology Clinic CELFAC, conslt ENT surgn Manor House Hosp London and BUPA Roding Hosp Redbridge; exec and fndr memb Doctors Assoc for Medical Aid (working primarily in India); memb: Rotary Club Redbridge Essex, Sindhi Assoc UK; former chm and memb Anandam UK, patron Bengali Cultural Assoc UK; memb BMA 1960; *Recreations* cultural activites, fund raising for charities, photography, reading, travelling; *Style—* Vir Nebhrajani, Esq; ✉ 22 Harley St, Suite 5, London W1N 1AA (☎ 0171 637 0491)

NEEDELL, Timothy Richard (Tiff); s of Anthony Fairey Needell (d 1994), and Diana May, *née* Pelly (d 1988); *b* 29 Oct 1951; *Educ* Ottershaw Boarding Sch, City Univ London (BSc); *m* 17 Dec 1988, Patricia Louise (Patsy), da of Leslie Arthur Rowles; 2 s (Jack Michael b 23 Jan 1992, Harry Alexander b 25 Feb 1996); *Career* racing driver, TV presenter and writer; formerly structural design engr George Wimpey & Co Ltd; racing driver: Formula Ford 1600 1971–76 (Townsend Thoresen champion 1975), Formula Ford 2000 1975–76, Formula 3 1976–78, Formula 2 and Formula Atlantic 1977–84, Br Formula 1 1979, Grand Prix with Team Ensign 1980, World Endurance Sportscars 1981–92 (third Le Mans 24–hr race 1990), British Touring Cars 1993–94, Global GT Championship 1995–; joined BBC TV motor racing commentary team 1981, contrib Top Gear (BBC TV) 1987–, columnist and feature writer Top Gear magazine; *Recreations* golf; *Clubs* British Racing Drivers; *Style—* Tiff Needell, Esq; ✉ c/o Blackburn Sachs Associates, Eastgate House, 16–19 Eastcastle Street, London W1N 7PA (☎ 0171 636 7744, fax 0171 636 5757)

NEEDHAM, Gp Capt David Arthur (Dan); s of Arthur Needham (ka 1941), and Kathleen Elizabeth, *née* Mathews; *b* 27 Sept 1941; *Educ* King Edward VI GS East Retford Notts, RAF Coll Cranwell, Open Univ (BA); *m* 1 Aug 1964, Margaret, da of Albert Clayton (d 1963); 2 s (Paul b 23 July 1970, James b 16 May 1973), 1 da (Marianne b 11 Dec 1979); *Career* cmmnd RAF 1963, 101 Sqdn 1964–68, 12 Sqdn 1971–73, Sqdn Ldr 1971, Wing Cdr 1981, Gp Capt 1990, Stn Cdr RAF Turnhouse Edinburgh 1991–93, ret 1994; dir (Scotland) RAF Benevolent Fund 1994–, vice chm Lowland TAVRA 1995; FIMgt 1994; *Recreations* family, golf, skiing; *Clubs* RAF; *Style—* Gp Capt D A Needham; ✉ RAF Benevolent Fund, 20 Queen Street, Edinburgh EH2 1JX (☎ 0131 225 6421)

NEEDHAM, Peter Southwood; s of William Needham, of Hobart, Tasmania; *b* 9 Jan 1924; *Educ* Hobart HS; *m* 1, 1945, Anne Louise; 2 da (Elizabeth Anne (Mrs McCormick), Rosemary Jane (Mrs McCrary)); m 2, 1971, Susan Augusta, da of Philip H Band, of Westhampton Beach, NY; 3 step children; *Career* formerly with: Commonwealth Bank of Australia, RAAF, GKN, Fisons, Venesta, Wilkins & Mitchell; currently: md GHN Limited (career mgmnt conslts), chief exec Penna plc; ABIA, FIMgt, FInstD, FRSA; *Clubs* Hurlingham, RAF, RSM; *Style—* Peter Needham, Esq; ✉ c/o GHN Ltd, 16 Hanover Square, London W1R 9AJ (☎ 0171 493 5239, fax 0171 629 9245)

NEEDHAM, Phillip; s of Ephraim Needham, of Dunstable, and Mabel Jessie, *née* Foskett; *b* 21 April 1940; *Educ* Ashton GS Dunstable, Univ of Birmingham (BSc), Imperial Coll London (MSc); *m* 24 March 1962, Patricia Ann, da of Henry Farr, of Leighton Buzzard; 2 s (Paul b 1963, David b 1964), 2 da (Jennifer b 1967, Claire b 1974); *Career* Agric Devpt and Advsy Servs MAFF: head of soil sci 1982–85, sr agric scientist 1985–87, dep dir R & D 1987–88, dir farm and countryside serv and commercial dir 1988–91, dir of ops 1991–95, chief exec 1995–; *Style—* Phillip Needham, Esq; ✉ ADAS, Oxford Spires Business Park, The Boulevard, Kidlington, Oxon OX5 1NZ (☎ 01865 845002)

NEEDHAM, Rt Hon Richard Francis; PC (1994), MP (C) Wiltshire North (majority 16,388); 6 Earl of Kilmorey (I 1822), also Hereditary Abbot of the Exempt Jurisdiction of Newry and Mourne, Viscount Kilmorey (I 1625) and Viscount Newry and Morne (I 1822), but does not use titles; s of 5 Earl of Kilmorey (d 1977), and Helen, da of Sir Lionel Faudel-Phillips, 3 and last Bt; *b* 29 Jan 1942; *Educ* Eton; *m* 1965, Sigrid Juliane, da of late Ernst Thiessen, and Mrs John Gairdner; 2 s (Viscount Newry and Morne b 1966, Hon Andrew b 1969), 1 da (Lady Christina b 1977); *Heir* s, Viscount Newry and Morne; *Career* PA to Rt Hon James Prior MP (oppn spokesman on employment) 1974–79; MP (C): Chippenham 1979–83, Wilts N 1983–; sec Cons Employment Ctee 1979–81 (vice-chm 1981–83), chm All Parly Productivity Ctee 1982–83, memb Public Accounts Ctee 1982–83; PPS to: Rt Hon James Prior as sec of state for NI 1983–84, Rt Hon Patrick Jenkins as sec of state for environment 1984–85; min of health for NI 1985–89, min of environment for NI 1985–92, min for the economy for NI 1989–92, min of trade DTI 1992–94; exec dir GEC plc; non-exec dir: Mivan Holdings Ltd, Dyson Appliances Ltd; underwriting memb Lloyd's, chm: RGM Print Holdings Ltd 1970–85, Gleneagles Hospital UK Ltd; govr Br Inst of Florence 1983–85; fndr memb: Anglo-Japanese 2000 Gp, Anglo-Korean Forum for the Future 1993; formerly cncllr (C) Somerset CC; *Publications* The Honourable Member (1983); *Clubs* Pratt's, Beefsteak; *Style—* The Rt Hon Richard Needham, MP; ✉ House of Commons, London SW1A 0AA (☎ 0171 219 3000)

NEEDHAM, Richard Joseph; s of Douglas Martyn William Needham, of Timber Edge, Heath End, Wigginton, nr Tring, Herts, and Vera Gwenllian, *née* Bowen; *b* 2 July 1946; *Educ* Berkhamsted Sch Herts, Poly of North London (BSc, DipArch); *m* 11 Dec 1976, Rosalyn Jill, da of Leslie James Attryde, of Crestwood, Hill Green Lane, Wigginton, Herts; 2 s (Robert b 29 Nov 1981, Edward b 16 Nov 1985); *Career* with John Penton Chartered Architect St Albans (specialising in design for disabled) 1974–77, ptnr Melvin Lansley & Mark Chartered Architects 1988–90 (joined 1977, assoc 1981), conslt Hurd Rolland Partnership (incorporating Melvin Lansley & Mark) 1990– (specialising in construction technol, bldg litigation, conservation and failure investigation); memb Cons Pty; ARCUK 1975, RIBA 1981, MBAE 1989; *Recreations* photography, walking, cycling, reading, gardening; *Style—* Richard Needham, Esq; ✉ Hurd Rolland Partnership, 32 Fitzroy Square, London W1P 5HH (☎ 0171 387 9595)

NEEDHAM, Sheila June; da of Steven Ellis Needham (d 1981), and Grace Kathleen, *née* Tarrant (d 1987); *b* 22 June 1937; *Educ* Sutton HS; *Career* held several secretarial positions in London and USA 1955–71; dir Scribe-Ex Ltd 1965–74, fndr and md Needham Printers Ltd 1974–92, md Needham's Design & Print Ltd 1993–; govr Haberdashers' Aske's Hatcham Coll; vice pres City of London Branch Inst of Mgmnt (formerly BIM) 1995– (chm 1993–95); pres: NE Dist London Printing Assoc 1981, Farringdon Ward Club 1984–85; memb Br Assoc of Women Entrepreneurs; Freeman City of London, Liveryman Worshipful Co of Stationers and Newspaper Makers; FIMgt, FRSA; *Recreations* travel, theatre, walking, gardening, sunshine; *Clubs* City Livery, IOD, Forum UK; *Style—* Miss Sheila J Needham; ✉ Needhams Design & Print Ltd, 60 Rivington Street, London EC2A 3AY (☎ 0171 613 1116, fax 0171 613 1016)

NEEDLE, Clive; MEP (Lab) Norfolk (majority 26,287); *b* 22 Sept 1956; *Educ* Southend HS, Aston Univ; *m* 1979, Roslyn; 2 da (Heather b 1983, Sorrel b 1989); *Career* Norfolk Lab Pty: variously press offr, constituency sec and memb district and regnl exec ctees 1984–86, gen election agent Mid Norfolk 1987, professional organiser S Norfolk 1987, elected sec Norfolk County 1990–94, Parly candidate S Norfolk 1992, MEP (Lab) Norfolk 1994–; community cncllr 1984–86; memb: regnl health bd 1984–86, GMB, S Norfolk Environment Forum, CAB and Youth and Community Management Ctees; govr of two schs 1984–94; *Recreations* most sports, reading, art, cooking; *Style—* Clive Needle, MEP; ✉ 59 Bethel Street, Norwich, Norfolk NR2 1NL (☎ 01603 631802, fax 01603 618376); European Parliament, 93–113 Rue Belliard, 1040 Brussels, Belgium

NEELY, William Robert Nicholas (Bill); s of William John Neely (d 1960), and Lucy Patricia, *née* Larney; *b* 21 May 1959; *Educ* St Malachy's Coll Belfast, Queen's Univ Belfast (BA); *m* 5 June 1988, Marion, da of John Kerr; 1 da (Sarah Caroline Kerr b 20 June 1989); *Career* reporter News & Current Affairs Dept BBC: NI 1981–87, London 1987–88; reporter/presenter Sky News Sky TV 1989, Washington corr ITN 1991–96 (reporter 1989–90), Europe corr 1997–; *Recreations* reading, soccer, swimming; *Style—* Bill Neely, Esq; ✉ Independent Television News, 200 Gray's Inn Road, London WC1 8XZ (☎ 0171 833 3000)

NEESON, David Ivor; s of (Horace) Ivor Charles Neeson, of Belchamp St Paul, Essex, and Jean Gibson, *née* Wade; *b* 19 Oct 1946; *Educ* Beal GS Ilford Essex; *m* 28 Dec 1972, Christine Pearl, da of Frank Hunt (d 1980), of Romford, Essex; 1 s (Rory), 1 da (Eloisa); *Career* investmt asst Corp of Lloyd's 1965–67, stockjobber and ptnr Bisgood Bishop and Co 1967–76, vice pres Merrill Lynch International 1976–82; Morgan Stanley International: joined 1982, vice pres 1984, exec dir 1985, md 1986–92; dir: J L Investment Management 1993–, Saffron Consultancy 1993–; govr: Plaxtol Primary Sch 1996–, Ightham Primary Sch 1996–; MSI; *Recreations* golf, tennis, shooting, hiking, fly fishing; *Clubs* Royal Cinque Ports Golf, Wildernesse Golf (Seal), London Golf, Loch Lomond Golf; *Style—* David Neeson, Esq; ✉ c/o J L Investment Management, 1 Epsom Square, Trowbridge, Wiltshire BA14 0XG

NEGUS, Her Hon Judge; Norma Florence (Mrs David Turner-Samuels); *née* Miss Norma Shellabear; da of George David Shellabear, and Kate Laura, *née* Calvert; *b* 31 July 1932; *Educ* Malvern Girls' Coll; *m* 1, 1956 (m dis 1960), Richard Negus; m 2, 1976, David Jessel Turner-Samuels, QC, *qv*; *Career* fashion promotion in UK Canada and USA 1950–61, merchandise ed Harper's Bazaar 1962–63, asst promotion mangr Vogue and House and Garden 1963–65, unit mangr Merchandising and Fashion Promotion Unit Trends 1965–67, export mktg mangr Glenoit UK 1967–68; called to the Bar Gray's Inn 1970; met stipendiary magistrate 1984–90, asst recorder 1985–89, recorder 1989–90, circuit judge (SE Circuit) 1990–; *Recreations* writing, swimming, travel; *Style—* Her Hon Judge Norma Negus; ✉ The Crown Court, 1 English Grounds, Southwark, London SE1 2HU (☎ 0171 522 7200)

NEGUS, Richard Charles; s of Bertie Arthur Charles Negus (d 1967), of Quendon, Essex, and Kate, *née* Brassington (d 1947); *b* 29 Aug 1927; *Educ* Battersea GS, Camberwell Sch of Arts & Crafts; *m* 20 Sept 1949, Pamela Denise; 2 s (Dominic Charles b 1952, Toby Wheatcroft b 1953), 1 da (Kate Georgina b 1955); *Career* conslt designer; staff Festival of Britain 1948–51; fndr ptnr: Negus Sharland 1951, Negus & Negus 1970–87; private practice 1987–; conslt to: Cotton Bd 1960–67, BNEC 1969–75, Lloyds Bank 1972–75, British Airways 1972–85 and 1990–, City of Westminster 1973–75, Pakistan Airlines 1975–90, Rank Organisation 1979–82, Vickers plc and Rolls Royce plc 1980–82, SDP 1981–87, N Dairies 1985–87, Royal Armouries 1984–, Nat Maritime Museum 1984–86, Science Museum 1987–89, John Lewis 1987–89, English Heritage 1983–, Emirates Airline 1985–, Royal Parks & Palace DOE, NT 1989–91, Dubai Port Authy 1990–, Royal Coll of Music 1994–; memb: Designers and Art Dirs Assoc, Post Office Stamps Advsy Ctee, Design Cncl 1981–87; assessor Schs of Art: Birmingham, Bradford, Norwich, Kent Inst of Art; memb Ct RCA; former govr Schs of Art: Camberwell, Chelsea; lectr various Colls of Art; memb: CNAA, BTEC; memb Tylers & Bricklayers Co; FCSD (former pres), FSTD, FRSA, Hon FRCM; *Books* Designing for Export, Airline Liveries, Writing on the Wall; contrib to: The Designer, Design

Magazine, Graphics, Gebrauchgraphick, Architectural Review, Architect's Journal, Rolls Royce Magazine; *Recreations* gardening, yachting; *Style—* Richard Negus, Esq; ✉ Little Gravenhurst, Stairbridge Lane, Bolney, W Sussex (☎ 01444 881841)

NEIDPATH, Lord; James Donald Charteris; full title Lord Douglas of Neidpath, Lyne and Munard; s and h of 12 Earl of Wemyss and (8 of) March, KT, JP, *qv*; *b* 22 June 1948; *Educ* Eton, Univ Coll Oxford, St Antony's Oxford, RAC Cirencester (BA, DPhil, Dip Rural Estate Mgmnt); *m* 1, 1983 (m dis 1988), Catherine Ingrid, da of Hon Jonathan Bryan Guinness, later 3 Baron Moyne; 1 s (Hon (Francis) Richard b 1984), 1 da (Hon Mary Olivia b 1987); m 2, 29 Dec 1995, Amanda Claire Marion, yst da of Basil Percy Terence Feilding (d 1986); *Heir* s, Hon Francis Richard Charteris, b 15 Sept 1984; *Career* page of honour to HM Queen Elizabeth The Queen Mother 1962–64, memb Royal Co of Archers (Queen's Body Guard for Scotland); land agent, ARICS; *Books* The Singapore Naval Base and the Defence of Britain's Eastern Empire 1919–41 (1981); historial reviews in The Spectator, Literary Review and Field; *Recreations* history; *Clubs* Brooks's, Pratt's, Puffins, Ognisko Polskie; *Style—* Lord Neidpath; ✉ Stanway, Cheltenham, Glos (☎ 01386 584469)

NEIL, Andrew Ferguson; s of Maj James Neil (d 1987), and Mary, *née* Ferguson (d 1993); *b* 21 May 1949; *Educ* Paisley GS, Univ of Glasgow (MA); *Career* Cons Res Dept 1971–72, UK ed The Economist 1982–83 (joined staff 1973), ed The Sunday Times 1983–94, exec chm Sky TV 1988–90, exec ed Fox News (New York) June-Dec 1994; freelance bdcaster, writer and media conslt 1994–, co-presenter The Midnight Hour (BBC 2) 1994–, columnist The Sunday Times and Daily Mail 1994–96, contrib ed Vanity Fair 1994, presenter The Andrew Neil Show (BBC 2) 1995–, ed-in-chief European Press Holdings Ltd (The Scotsman, Scotland on Sunday, Edinburgh Evening News and The European) 1996–; co-proprietor The Country Gentleman's Assoc; *Books* The Cable Revolution (1982), Full Disclosure (autobiography, 1996); *Recreations* skiing, dining out in London, New York, Aspen and Côte d'Azur; *Clubs* RAC, Tramp; *Style—* Andrew Neil, Esq; ✉ The Scotsman, 20 North Bridge, Edinburgh EH1 1YT (☎ 0131 225 2468, fax 0131 226 7420); Glenburn Enterprises, PO Box 584, London SW7 3QY (☎ and fax 0171 577 4666)

NEIL, Arthur; s of James McDavid Neil (d 1987), of Falkirk, Stirlingshire, and Catherine, *née* Dunn (1978); *b* 2 Nov 1929; *Educ* Falkirk HS, Scottish Hotel Sch; *m* 1, 3 March 1958 (m dis 1990), Rosemary Georgina, da of George Paterson Gibson; 1 s (James Gibson b 8 Dec 1958), 2 da (Jennifer Marguerite b 8 June 1960, Victoria Catherine b 4 Oct 1962); m 2, 5 May 1992, Gabrielle Jane (Mrs Rutherford); *Career* apprentice cook Glasgow Central Hotel 1946–47, messing offr Army Catering Corps 1949–51, asst mangr Goring Hotel London 1951–52, stagiaire Bellevue Palace Hotel Berne 1952–53, mangr rising to dir Open Arms Hotel 1954–95, md Grange Inn St Andrews 1965–75, dir Shieldness Produce Ltd 1950–86, md Howard Hotel Edinburgh 1970–89; Scot mangr Hotel and Catering Industry Trg Bd 1967–70, govr Queen Margaret Coll Edinburgh 1974–80, chm Master Innholder 1982 (memb 1978), memb Bd Scotvec 1986–88; Freeman City of London 1979, FHCIMA; *Recreations* golf, shooting, travel, reading; *Clubs* New (Edinburgh), Hon Co of Edinburgh Golfers (Muirfield); *Style—* Arthur Neil, Esq; ✉ Whin Cottage, Nisbet Road, Gullane, East Lothian EH31 2BQ (☎ and fax 01620 842258)

NEIL, Ronald; *b* 16 June 1942, Glasgow; *Educ* Glasgow HS; *Career* BBC: regnl radio and TV reporter BBC Scotland Aberdeen 1966, film dir and prodr Current Affrs Dept London (working on Nationwide, Tonight and 24 Hours) 1970, dep ed Tonight and Newsnight, ed That's Life, ed Newsnight 1980, founding ed Breakfast Time and Six O'Clock News 1983–85, overall ed BBC Television News 1985–87, dir BBC News and Current Affrs 1988–89 (dep dir 1987–88), md BBC Regnl Bdcasting 1989–96, also head of BBC Annual Performance Review 1993–96, chief exec BBC Prodn 1996–; memb Ctee of Mgmnt RNLI; *Style—* Ronald Neil, Esq; ✉ Chief Executive BBC Production, Broadcasting House, London W1A 1AA (☎ 0171 580 4468)

NEILAN, Sarah; *Educ* Univ of Oxford (MA); *m*; 4 children; *Career* author and journalist; formerly book ed; author of numerous book reviews, educnl articles, serials, newspaper articles and short stories; memb Soc of Authors, memb PEN; Mary Elgin Award 1976; *Books* The Braganza Pursuit (1976), An Air of Glory (1977), Paradise (1982), The Old Enchantment (1990), The Kennedys Abroad (ed series children's books); *Recreations* travel, tapestry, looking at pictures; *Style—* Ms Sarah Neilan; ✉ c/o Peters Fraser & Dunlop Ltd, 503 The Chambers, Chelsea Harbour, Lots Road, London SW10 0XF (☎ 0171 352 4446, fax 0171 352 7356)

NEILAND, Prof Brendan Robert; s of Arthur Neiland (d 1990), and Joan Agnes Bessie, *née* Whiley; *b* 23 Oct 1941; *Educ* Lowestoft Co GS Birmingham, St Philips GS Birmingham, St Augustine's Seminary Co Cavan Eire, Birmingham Coll of Art (dip), RCA (MA); *m* 1970, Hilary Vivienne, da of late Morris Salter; 2 da (Naomi b 23 Aug 1974, Lucy 17 Feb 1977); *Career* artist; gallery artist: Angela Flowers Gallery 1970–78, Fischer Fine Art 1978–92, Redfern Gallery 1992–; pt/t teaching: Manchester Art Coll 1969–73, Brighton Art Coll 1983–; prof Univ of Brighton 1996; *Solo Exhibitions* Flowers Gallery 1971–72 and 1974–76, Fischer Fine Art 1979–84 and 1987–91, Tate Gallery 1988, RIBA Galleries 1989, Redfern Gallery London 1993, Reading Coll Reading 1993; touring show 1992–: Gardner Art Centre Brighton, Milton Keynes Exhbn Gallery, N Centre for Contemporary Art Sunderland, Stafford Art Gallery, Grundy Art Gallery Blackpool; *Gp Exhibitions* Bradford Int Print Biennale 1970, 1972, 1974, 1976, 1982 and 1986, From Britain '75 Helsinki Finland 1975, Arts Cncl Coll Hayward 1976, Eight British Realists Meisel Gallery NYC 1983, Pintura Britanica Municipal Museum Madrid 1983, Images et Imaginaires d'Architecture Centre Georges Pompidou Paris 1984, Artists in National Parts V & A and touring UK and USA 1988, Printmaking from Britain Moscow 1989, The New Patrons NACF Christie's London 1992, RA Summer Exhbn 1979–81 and 1986–92, five paintings for InterCity 225 (later used for posters) 1990–91 and others; awards: CAS Purchase Prize Northern Young Contemporaries 1968, Arthur Tooth's Prize Young Contemporaries 1969, Silver Medal RCA 1969, Minton Scholarship 1969, Arts Cncl Minor Award 1972, John Moores XI Prizewinner 1978, scholar Crabtree Fndn 1982, Daler Rowney Award RA Summer Exhbn 1989; co-operated in making of video Commissioned Art and Professional Practice (dir Gavin Nettleton 1991); lectr Buildings Within Buildings, Reflections on Paintings RIBA 1989; fell Royal Soc of Painters and Etchers 1988–93; RA 1992, FRSA 1996; *Recreations* listening to the Radio 3 cricket commentary, drinking fine wines; *Clubs* Chelsea Arts; *Style—* Prof Brendan Neiland, RA; ✉ 24 The Chase, Clapham, London SW4 0NH (☎ 0171 720 3393); Crepe, La Greve sur le Mignon, 17170 Courçon, France (☎ 4601 6297); c/o Redfern Gallery, 20 Cork Street, London W1X 2HL (☎ 0171 734 1732/0578, fax 0171 494 2908)

NEILL, Rt Hon Sir Brian Thomas; kt (1978), PC (1985); s of Sir Thomas Neill, JP (d 1937); bro of Sir Patrick Neill, QC, *qv*; *b* 2 Aug 1923; *Educ* Highgate, CCC Oxford (MA); *m* 1956, Sally Margaret Backus; 3 s; *Career* served WWII Rifle Bde; called to the Bar Inner Temple 1949, QC 1968, recorder of the Crown Ct 1972–78, judge of the High Ct of Justice (Queen's Bench Div) 1978–84, a Lord Justice of Appeal 1985–96, ret; chm Ctee on Rhodesia Travel Restrictions 1973–78; memb Ct of Assts Worshipful Co of Turners (Master 1980–81); *Style—* The Rt Hon Sir Brian Neill; ✉ c/o Royal Courts of Justice, Strand, London WC2A 2LL

NEILL, Rev Bruce Ferguson; s of Thomas Ferguson Neill (d 1996), of Haddington, East Lothian, and Jane, *née* Bruce (d 1996); *b* 9 Jan 1941; *Educ* Hamilton Acad, Univ of Glasgow (MA), Trinity Coll Glasgow (BD); *m* 22 June 1966, Ishbel, da of Iain Macdonald; 1 da (Catriona Jane b 24 May 1967), 2 s (Calum Bruce Macdonald b 25 Aug 1968, Fergus Samuel b 13 Feb 1982); *Career* asst min Drumchapel Parish Church Glasgow 1964–66, min Townhill Parish Church Dunfermline 1966–71, chaplain Royal Navy 1971–96, princ chaplain Church of Scotland and Free Churches (Naval) 1991–96, QHC 1991–96, min Maxton and Mertoun with St Boswells 1996–; *Recreations* woodwork, model making, sailing, reading; *Style—* The Rev Bruce F Neill; ✉ The Manse, Main Street, St Boswells, Roxburghshire TD6 0BB (☎ 01835 822255)

NEILL, Lt-Col Sir (James) Hugh; KCVO (1996), CBE (1969), TD (1950), JP (S Yorks 1985); s of Col Sir Frederick Neill, CBE, DSO, TD (d 1967); *b* 29 March 1921; *Educ* Rugby; *m* 1, 1943, Jane Margaret (d 1980), *née* Shuttleworth; 2 da (and 1 decd); m 2, 1982, Catherine Anne Maria, *née* O'Leary; 1 s; *Career* Lt-Col RE WWII, served Norway, India, Burma and Germany; Hon Col 4 Bn Yorks Volunteers 1988–93; pres James Neill Holdings Ltd (chm 1963–89); pres Sheffield C of C 1984–85; Master Cutler Hallamshire 1958–59, High Sheriff Hallamshire 1971–72, Lord Lt S Yorks 1985–96 (DL 1974); *Recreations* golf, racing, horse trials, shooting; *Clubs* R & A, Hon Co of Edinburgh Golfers, Lindrick Golf (Sheffield), East India; *Style—* Lt-Col Sir Hugh Neill, KCVO, CBE, TD; ✉ Barn Cottage, Lindrick Common, nr Worksop, Notts S81 8BA (☎ 01909 562806)

NEILL, Rt Hon Sir Ivan; kt (1973), PC (NI 1950); *b* 1 July 1906; *Educ* Ravenscroft Nat Sch, Shaftesbury House Tutorial Coll Belfast, Queen's Univ Belfast (BSc); *m* 1928, Margaret Helena Allen; *Career* WWII Maj RE; memb NI Parliament 1949–73; min of: Lab and Nat Insur 1950–62, Home Affrs 1952, Educn 1962–64; min of Fin and ldr House of Commons 1964, resigned from govt 1965, min of Devpt 1968–69, speaker House of Commons 1969–73; FRGS; *Publications* Church and State (1995), A Chorus of Cameos (1995); *Style—* The Rt Hon Sir Ivan Neill; ✉ Cranagh Cottage, Warren Road, Donaghadee, Co Down BT21 0PQ, Northern Ireland

NEILL, John Mitchell; CBE (1994); s of Justin Bernard Neill, and Johanna Elisabeth, *née* Bastiaans; *b* 21 July 1947; *Educ* George Heriott Sch Edinburgh, Univ of Strathclyde (BA, MBA, DBA); *m* 24 May 1975, Jacqueline Anne, da of Phillip Brown (d 1985); 2 s (Richard John b 19 July 1979, Alexander James b 4 Nov 1982); *Career* mktg mangr Europe AC Delco 1972–73 (planning mangr 1969–71), sales and mktg dir British Leyland Parts & KD Div 1976 (merchandising mangr 1974–75); md: Leyland Car Parts Div 1977–78, BL Components 1979–80, Unipart Group 1981–82, gp md Unipart Group Ltd 1983–86, gp chief exec Unipart Group of Cos 1987–; non-exec dir: Bank of England 1996–, Charter PLC; SMMT: vice pres, memb Cncl, memb Exec Ctee; vice pres: C & G, Inst of Motor Indust, BEN; memb: Cncl Business in the Community Bd, Cncl IOD, Alumni Bd Univ of Strathclyde; tstee Nat Motor Museum; FInstM; *Recreations* tennis, skiing; *Style—* John M Neill, Esq, CBE; ✉ UGC Ltd, Unipart House, Cowley, Oxford OX4 2PG (☎ 01865 778966, fax 01865 713790, telex 83331)

NEILL, Rt Rev John Robert Winder; *see:* Tuam, Killala and Achonry, Bishop of

NEILL, Sir (Francis) Patrick; kt (1983), QC (1966); s of Sir Thomas Neill, JP (d 1937); bro of Rt Hon Sir Brian Neill, *qv*; *b* 8 Aug 1926; *Educ* Highgate Sch, Magdalen Coll Oxford; *m* 1954, Caroline Susan, da of Sir Piers Debenham, 2 Bt (d 1964); 4 s, 2 da; *Career* served Rifle Bde 1944–47; called to the Bar Gray's Inn 1951, bencher 1971, treas 1990, jt head of chambers; judge of Cts of Appeal of Jersey and Guernsey 1977–94; chm Press Cncl 1978–83, first chm Cncl for Securities Industry 1978–85, chm DTI Ctee of Inquiry into Regulatory Arrangements at Lloyd's 1986–87; warden All Souls Coll Oxford 1977–95 (fell 1950–77), vice chllr Univ of Oxford 1985–89; *Style—* Sir Patrick Neill, QC; ✉ 1 Hare Court, First Floor, Temple, London EC4Y 7BE (☎ 0171 353 3171, fax 0171 583 9127)

NEILL, Robert James MacGillivray; s of John MacGillivray Neill, of Ilford, Essex, and Elsie May, *née* Chaston; *b* 24 June 1952; *Educ* Abbs Cross Sch Hornchurch Essex, LSE (LLB); *Career* called to the Bar: Middle Temple 1975, King's Inns Dublin 1992; former dir: NE Thames Business Advsy Centre, Energy Concern Ltd; memb: Havering London Borough Cncl 1974–90 (chief whip), GLC for Romford (C) 1985–86; first ldr London Fire & Civil Defence Authy 1985–87, oppn spokesman Fire and Public Protection Ctee Assoc of Met Authorities; Parly candidate (C) Dagenham 1983 and 1987; chm Gtr London Conservative Political Centre 1990–93, chm Gtr London Area Nat Union of Cons Assoc 1996- (dep chm 1993–96), memb Nat Union Exec 1992–; author of various articles and pamphlets on civil defence, legal affairs, small businesses, etc; *Recreations* sailing, travel, opera; *Clubs* Athenaeum, Carlton, St Stephen's Constitutional, Bar Yacht; *Style—* Robert Neill, Esq; ✉ 3 Hare Court, Temple, London, EC4Y 7BJ (☎ 0171 353 7561, fax 0171 353 7741)

NEILL, Robert Moore; s of Charles Neill (d 1991), of Donaghadee, NI, and Elizabeth Ida, *née* Moore; *b* 16 Sept 1950; *Educ* Campbell Coll Belfast, Queen's Univ Belfast (LLB), Coll of Law Guildford; *Career* admitted slr: England and Wales 1976, Hong Kong 1987; Herbert Smith: articled clerk 1974–76, ptnr 1984–, sr litigation ptnr Hong Kong Office 1987–90; memb: Law Soc, City of London Slrs' Company; *Recreations* sailing, tennis, theatre, travel; *Clubs* RAC, Royal Hong Kong Yacht, Campden Hill Lawn Tennis; *Style—* Robert Neill, Esq; ✉ 109 Abbotsbury Road, Holland Park, London W14 8EP (☎ 0171 603 9145); Herbert Smith, Exchange House, Primrose Street, London EC2A 2HS (☎ 0171 374 8000, fax 0171 496 0043)

NEILL, Rose Mary Margaret; da of Roger Henry James Neill (d 1979), and Doreen Elizabeth, *née* Morrice; *b* 29 Nov 1958; *Educ* Mount Sch York, City and E London Coll; *m* 22 Feb 1985, (Robert) John Magill, s of Thomas Stewart Magill (d 1987); 2 s (Roger Thomas b 23 June 1986, Henry Harley Peter b 11 Sept 1988); *Career* newscaster, sports presenter and gen prog presenter; Ulster TV Ltd 1978–86; BBC Belfast 1986–: co presenter main evening news prog, newscaster and writer for other daily bulletins; regular broadcaster Pick of the Week radio prog, host of hour long chat show BBC Radio, writer and presenter various TV documentaries; involved in annual Children in Need TV presentation and Royal Dublin Horse Show; memb Ctee NI Mother and Baby appeal, hon patron Ulster Cancer Res Campaign; *Recreations* hunting, skiing (water and snow), sailing, travelling, tennis; *Clubs* Royal Ulster Yacht, Strangford Lough Yacht, E Down Fox Hounds, Windsor Lawn Tennis; *Style—* Miss Rose Neill; ✉ BBC, Broadcasting House, Ormeau Avenue, Belfast BT2 8HQ (☎ 01232 338000)

NEILL, (James) Ruary Drummond; s of Thomas Neill (d 1969), and Elsie Margaret Wilson, *née* Sharp; *b* 9 Jan 1959; *Educ* Glebe House Sch Norfolk, Gresham's Norfolk, Univ of London (BA); *m* 5 Sept 1987, Hilary Jane Vipan, da of Peter Harvey Bourne; 1 s (Tom Callum Ruary b 21 Jan 1993), 1 da (Georgina Kim Jane b 13 Feb 1990); *Career* Chartered Bank Abu Dhabi UAE 1981–83, Chartered Bank Hong Kong 1983–85, Rowe & Pitman then Warburg Securities London 1985–88; Schroder Securities Ltd: joined 1988, dir 1990–94, head of int sales Asian Div 1993–94; md Schroder Securities (Hong Kong) Ltd 1990–93; dir of Asian Div SBC Warburg 1994–; *Recreations* shooting, farming, reading; *Clubs* Travellers; *Style—* Ruary Neill, Esq; ✉ Patmore Lodge, Albury, nr Ware, Herts SG11 2LT (☎ 01279 771323); SBC Warburg, 1 Finsbury Avenue, London EC2A 2PA (☎ 0171 606 1066)

NEILL, Sam; OBE; s of Dermot Neill (d 1992), of NZ, and Priscilla, *née* Ingham; *b* 14 Sept 1947; *Educ* Christ's Coll NZ, Canterbury Univ NZ; *m* 1990, Noriku Watanabe; 1 s (Tim b 1983), 1 da (Elena b 1991); *Career* actor; *Television* incl: Reilly Ace of Spies, Family Pictures; *Films* appeared in over 30 features incl: Evil Angels, Jungle Book, Victory, Restoration, Dead Calm, Death in Brunswick, My Brilliant Career, Jurassic Park, The Piano, Restoration; *Recreations* gardening, skiing, fly fishing; *Style—* Sam Neill,

Esq, OBE; ✉ c/o ICM Ltd, Oxford House, 76 Oxford Street, London W1N 0AX (☎ 0171 636 6565, fax 0171 323 0101)

NEILLY, Gordon Joseph; *b* 2 July 1960; *Educ* Univ of Edinburgh (BComm); *m* (Elizabeth) Ruth Neilly; *Career* CA; Peat Marwick McLintock 1981–84, business devpt dir Ivory & Sime PLC 1990– (accountant 1984–90); *Recreations* football, rugby, water skiing, driving; *Style*— Gordon Neilly, Esq; ✉ Ivory & Sime PLC, One Charlotte Square, Edinburgh EH2 4DZ (☎ 0131 225 1357, fax 0131 225 2375)

NEILSON, Lt-Col Ian Godfrey; DFC (1944), TD (1951); er s of James Wilson Neilson (d 1927), of Glasgow, and Marion Beatrice, *née* Saunders (d 1976); *b* 4 Dec 1918; *Educ* Glasgow Acad, Univ of Glasgow (BL); *m* 2 June 1945 (Dorothy) Alison St Clair, da of Robert Alexander Aytoun (d 1920), of Birmingham; 1 s (Hamish Rollo Aytoun b 1949), 1 da (Catherine Alison St Clair Kellett b 1951); *Career* RA: cmmnd 2 Lt RA TA 1939, Field Artillery 1940, flying trg No 8 EFTS RAF 1940, Capt (RA) 651 Air Observation Post Sqdn RAF 1941, later 652 Sqdn, served Normandy 1944; GSO2 (Maj): RA Branch HQ 21 Army Gp 1944, Royal Signals Branch HQ BAOR 1945; cmd War Crimes Investigation Unit 1945 as Lt-Col, demobilised 1946; formed and cmd 666 (Scottish) Air Observation Post Sqdn RAuxAF as Maj RA (TA) 1948 (relinquished cmd 1953); legal apprentice Wright Johnson & Mackenzie 1936, admitted slr 1946; RICS: Scottish sec 1946, asst sec London 1953, under-sec HQ 1961; bde sec Boys' Bde 1966, clerk to govrs Cripplegate Fndn and Cripplegate Educn Fndn 1974, ret 1981; BIM City of London Branch: hon sec 1976–79, chm 1979–81, vice pres 1981–87; sr instr RYA 1977–87, pres London Section Glasgow Academical Club 1977–79; chm: Epsom Choral Soc 1977–81, Bd of Tstees The Chapel of St George Heathrow Airport 1983– (memb 1978–), Queenhithe Ward Club London 1977–78; dir and jt sec Utd Reformed Church Tst 1982–95, church elder St Andrews URC Cheam 1972–83, vice pres Air Observation Post Offrs' Assoc 1978– (chm 1995–96), hon vice pres The Boys' Bde 1972–, cncl memb Christchurch Marlborough 1984–90 and 1992–; tstee: St Peter's Tst Marlborough 1985–, Douglas Haig Meml Homes Assoc 1979–96; Freeman: City of London 1975, Liveryman Guild of Air Pilots and Air Navigators 1978 (Freeman 1976–78); FIMgt 1980; *Books* Tower and Town - Marlborough (hon ed, 1984–95); *Recreations* golf, music, gardening, sailing; *Clubs* Athenaeum, Marlborough Golf, Chartered Surveyors' Golfing; *Style*— Lt-Col Ian Neilson, DFC, TD; ✉ The Paddock, Kingsbury St, Marlborough, Wiltshire SN8 1HZ (☎ 01672 515114)

NEILSON, Maj Nigel Fraser; MC; s of Lt-Col William Neilson, DSO (d 1960), of Hawkes Bay, NZ, and Maud Frances Alice, *née* Anson (d 1967); *b* 12 Dec 1919; *Educ* Wellington House Westgate-on-Sea, Hereworth NZ, Christ's Coll NZ, RADA; *m* 22 Oct 1949, Pamela Catherine Georgina (d 1989), da of Capt Samuel Marshal Philpot Sheppard (d 1945), of Coulsden, Surrey; 1 s (Peter Nigel b 1958), 1 da (Susan Catherine Hiraani b 1952); *Career* Staffs Yeo, served 1 Cavalry Div Palestine, transferred to Trans-Jordanian Frontier Force Cavalry Regt (took part in the last cavalry charge in history against French Spahis), returned Staffs Yeo (tanks) El Alamein Western Desert, GSO3 7 Armd Div, Anzio landing Italy, Allied force HQ Algiers, psc, joined SAS HQ, transferred 2 Liaison French SAS served Holland and France, served COS Bergen Norway; returned to theatre 1946, played and sang in many shows and concerts in London and USA, had own BBC programme Beginners Please, 2 i/c PR Dept J Walter Thompson, left to become personal conslt to A S Onassis (introduced by Sir Winston Churchill), opened own int PR Co representing major int cos: London, NZ, Malaysia, Singapore, US, Australia; helped produce HRH Prince Charles's first int Broadcast, represented Queen's Silver Jubilee Appeal, former pres and memb Ctee NZ Soc, currently independent int PR conslt; Legion D'Honneur, Croix de Guerre Avec Palme; *Recreations* shooting; *Clubs* Buck's, Annabel's, Special Forces; *Style*— Maj Nigel Neilson, MC; ✉ Battenhurst Farm, Battenhurst Road, Stonegate, Wadhurst TN5 7DU; c/o Coutts & Co, 1 Old Park Lane, London W1Y 4AL

NEILSON, Richard Alvin; CMG (1987), LVO (1968); s of Robert Neilson (d 1974), and Ethel, *née* Duke; *b* 9 July 1937; *Educ* Burnley GS, Univ of Leeds (BA, MA), Univ of Wisconsin; *m* 21 Aug 1961, Olive, da of Herbert Stanley Tyler, of Leighton Buzzard, Beds; 1 s (Paul b 8 Jan 1963); *Career* asst lectr Univ of Edinburgh 1960–61; joined FO 1961; second sec Leopoldville (Kinshasa) 1963–65, treas Centre for Admin Studies 1965, first sec Santiago 1966–69, first sec Canberra 1969–73, FCO 1973–77, cnsllr 1977, seconded to NI office as head of political affrs Belfast 1977–79, dep high cmmr Lusaka 1979–80, chargé 1979–80, dep govr and political advsr Gibraltar 1981–84, head SED FCO 1984–86; HM ambassador: Bogota 1987–90, Santiago 1990–93; high cmmr Trinidad and Tobago 1994–96, ret; FRGS 1964, FIMgt 1982; *Recreations* chess, cricket, sailing; *Clubs* Royal Cwlth, Queen's Park Cricket (Trinidad); *Style*— Richard Neilson, Esq, CMG, LVO; ✉ Maynes Hill Farm, Hoggeston, Bucks MK18 3LG (☎ 01296 714837)

NELDER, Prof John Ashworth; s of Reginald Charles Nelder (d 1979), and Edith May Ashworth Briggs (d 1954); *b* 8 Oct 1924; *Educ* Blundell's, Sidney Sussex Coll Cambridge, Univ of Birmingham (DSc); *m* 13 Jan 1954, Mary, da of Reginald Hawkes (d 1969); 1 s (Jan b 1956), 1 da (Rosalind b 1958); *Career* WWII RAF 1943–46; head Statistics Dept: Nat Vegetable Res Station 1950–68, Rothamsted Experimental Station 1968–84; visiting prof Imperial Coll London 1972–; pres: Int Biometric Soc 1978–79, Royal Statistical Soc 1985–86; Hon DSc Université Paul Sabatier Toulouse 1981; FRS 1981, Fell Int Statistical Inst; *Books* Generalized Linear Models (with P McCullagh); *Recreations* music (especially piano playing), natural history; *Style*— Prof John Nelder, FRS; ✉ Cumberland Cottage, Crown St, Redbourn, St Albans AL3 7JX (☎ 0158 279 2907); Imperial College, Mathematics Dept, 180 Queen's Gate, London SW7 2BZ (☎ 0171 594 8526)

NELIGAN, His Hon Judge John Oliver; s of Desmond Neligan (d 1993), of NZ, and Penelope Anne, *née* Mason (d 1996); *b* 21 June 1944; *Educ* Brickwall Sch Northiam Sussex; *m* May 1971, Mary Brigid, *née* Daniel; 2 da (Fiona Claire b Oct 1974, Caroline Mary b Jan 1977), 1 s (Andrew James b Jan 1978); *Career* admitted slr 1969, called to the Bar Middle Temple 1975, in practice Western Circuit 1975–96, recorder 1994–96, circuit judge (Western Circuit) 1996–; *Recreations* walking, gardening, painting; *Style*— His Hon Judge John Neligan; ✉ c/o Western Circuit Office, Bridge House, Sion Place, Clifton, Bristol BS8 4BN

NELIGAN, His Hon Judge; Michael Hugh Desmond; s of Desmond West Edmund Neligan, OBE (d 1993), of Storrington, W Sussex, and his 1 w, Penelope Anne, *née* Mason (d 1996); *b* 2 Dec 1936; *Educ* Bradfield, Jesus Coll Cambridge; *m* 4 Sept 1965, Lynn, da of late Keith Taylor Maidment; 3 da (Sophie Leonora b 27 Feb 1967, Francesca Beth b 8 Feb 1969, Alexandra Louise b 30 Aug 1975); *Career* Nat Serv cmmnd 2 Lt Royal Sussex Regt 1955–57 (seconded to King's African Rifles serving with 23, 2/3 and 4 Bns Kenya and Uganda); called to the Bar Middle Temple 1962, prosecuting counsel to The Crown Central Criminal Court 1972–87 (to Inland Revenue 1970–72), stipendiary magistrate 1987–90, circuit judge (SE Circuit) 1990–; *Style*— His Hon Judge Neligan; ✉ The Crown Court, Barker Rd, Maidstone, Kent ME16 8EQ (☎ 01622 754966)

NELIGAN, Timothy Patrick Moore; s of Moore Dermot Neligan (d 1977), of Worthing, and Margaret Joan, *née* Cockell (d 1975); *b* 16 June 1934; *Educ* Tonbridge; *m* 30 Nov 1957, Felicity Caroline, da of Norman Rycroft, of Thornton Hough, Cheshire; 2 s (Patrick b 1963, Timothy b 1963), 2 da (Henrietta b 1958, Kate b 1959); *Career* pupil Capt H Ryan Price racehorse trainer 1953–55, exec Agric Div ICI 1955–57, brewer and mangr Arthur Guinness (Park Royal) Ltd 1957–73, dir Goodwood Racecourse Ltd 1973–77, md United Racecourses Ltd 1977–94; Freeman City of London 1980, Liveryman Worshipful Co of Farriers (Master 1990–91, memb Ct of Assts); MInstM 1973, MCIM 1989, FRSA 1991; OStJ 1990; *Books* The Epsom Derby (with Roger Mortimer, 1984), The Derby (with Alistair Burnet, 1993); *Recreations* fishing, travel; *Style*— Timothy Neligan, Esq; ✉ Toll House, Sandown Park, Esher, Surrey KT10 9AJ (☎ 01372 467839)

NELMES, Dianne Gwenllian; da of late James Allen Nelmes, and Celandine, *née* Kimber; *b* 6 March 1951; *Educ* The Holt Girls' GS Wokingham, Univ of Newcastle upon Tyne (BA); *m* 17 May 1986, Ian McBride, s of Robert McBride; *Career* pres Newcastle Univ Students' Union 1973–74, graduate trainee Thomson Newspapers 1974–78 (variously sr news reporter, municipal corr and property reporter The Journal Newcastle), regional journalist and on-screen reporter/presenter BBC TV North East 1978–83; Granada Television: dep news ed Granada News 1983, researcher World in Action 1984; prodr/dir Brass Tacks BBC News & Current Affrs 1987–88; rejoined Granada Television as launch ed This Morning 1988, exec prodr Entertainment Dept 1989–92 (series launched incl You've Been Framed, Stars in their Eyes, In Suspicious Circumstances); dir of news and current affrs Meridian Broadcasting (from start of franchise) 1992; Granada Television: rejoined Granada as exec prodr World in Action 1992, head of factual progs 1993–94, controller of factual progs 1994–95, dir of programming Granada Satellite Television 1995–; memb: BAFTA, Chiswick Refuge; FRTS; *Recreations* canal boating; *Style*— Ms Dianne Nelmes; ✉ Granada Television Ltd, Quay Street, Manchester M60 9EA (☎ 0161 832 7211 extn 2836)

NELSON, Alan David; s of W S A Nelson, of Harrowlands Park, Surrey, and Olive Violet, *née* Hillman; *b* 6 June 1954; *Educ* Sir Bernard Lovell Boys' Sch, Prince of Wales Coll Dover Kent; *m* 13 Sept 1985, Margaret Pauline, da of William Kennefick (d 1991), of Co Cork, Ireland; 2 da (Diana Alice b 1992, Corinna b 1995); *Career* art dealer Lane Fine Art 1974–; memb: BADA, LAPADA; *Recreations* yachting, golf; *Clubs* East Cork Golf; *Style*— Alan Nelson, Esq; ✉ 1 Badgers Walk, Ferndown, Dorset; Loughane, County Cork, Rep of Ireland; Lane Fine Art, 123 New Bond St, London W1 (☎ 0171 499 5020, fax 0171 495 2496)

NELSON, (Richard) Anthony; MP (C) Chichester (majority 20,887); s of late Gp Capt R Gordon Nelson, and Mrs J M Nelson; *b* 11 June 1948; *Educ* Harrow, Christ's Coll Cambridge (MA); *m* 1974, Caroline Victoria, da of B A Butler; 1 s (Carlton b 1981), 1 da (Charlotte-Anne b 1979); *Career* Parly candidate (C) Leeds E Feb 1974, MP (C) Chichester Oct 1974–; memb Select Ctees on: Sci and Technol 1975–79, Televising Proceedings of the House 1988–91; PPS to: Min for Housing and Construction 1979–83, Min for Armed Forces 1983–92; economic sec to the Treasy 1992–94, min of state at the Treasy 1994–95, min of state DTI 1995–; dir Chichester Festival Theatre 1982–92, pres Sussex Training and Downs Enterprise Agency Ltd 1985–92; FRSA; *Recreations* music, rugby; *Style*— Anthony Nelson, Esq, MP; ✉ House of Commons, London SW1A 0AA

NELSON, (Gerald) Brian; CBE (1994); s of Robert Nelson (d 1982), and Helen, *née* Lessels (d 1960); *b* 31 May 1930; *Educ* Porth GS, Kings Coll Cambridge (BA, MA); *m* 1, 1955, Evelyn Rose (d 1993), da of James Evans; 2 s (Matthew Patrick b 1963, Edward Joseph b 1965), 1 da (Penelope Margaret b 1968); m 2, 1993, Margaret Bertha Crane, da of Edmund Roser Quick; *Career* Nat Serv RAF 1948–50; H P Bulmer Holdings PLC: research chemist 1954–60, chief chemist 1960–65, technical dir 1965–67, prodn dir 1967–69, md Cider Div 1969–75, gp md and chief exec 1975–89, dep chm 1989–90 (ret); non-exec dir: Wales and the Marches Bd BT 1979–84, Viking Packaging Gp 1987–89, Herefordshire Health Authy 1990–93, Citrus Colloids Ltd 1993–; chm: Home-Grown Cereals Authy 1989–, Hereford Hosps NHS Tst 1993–; memb: West Midlands Regnl Cncl CBI 1989–90, Cncl Food From Britain 1989–, Cncl Three Counties Agric Soc 1992–; govr: Univ of Bristol Research Station Long Ashton 1970–82, Herefordshire Tech Coll 1975–80, Hereford Cathedral Sch 1980– (dir Hereford Cathedral Sch Ltd 1987–); tstee Hereford Cider Museum Tst 1993–; *Recreations* hill walking, bird watching, music; *Clubs* United Oxford & Cambridge Univ; *Style*— Brian Nelson, Esq, CBE; ✉ Pentwyn, Poston, Vowchurch, Herefordshire HR2 0RJ; Home Grown Cereals Authority, Hamlyn House, Highgate Hill, London N19 5PR (☎ 0171 263 3391, fax 0171 561 6218)

NELSON, David Brian; s of Victor Harry Nelson (d 1987), of Leicester, and Edna Mary, *née* Elliot (d 1987); *b* 15 April 1951; *Educ* Longslade Sch Birstall Leics, Loughbrough Coll of Art, Hornsey Coll of Art (DipAD), Royal Coll of Art (MA, travelling scholar Northern Italy); *m* 13 Aug 1977, Caroline Georgette, da of John Weston Evans; 2 da (Aimee Jacqueline b 17 Oct 1979, Bibiana Christina b 9 Nov 1983); *Career* architect; dir Foster & Partners (formerly Sir Norman Foster & Partners) 1984– (joined 1976); former projects incl: Hong Kong and Shanghai Bank 1979–85 (latterly project ldr), dir i/c Televisa HQ Mexico City, American Airforce Museum Duxford Cambridge, Century Tower Tokyo, Millennium Tower (and numerous other projects Japan), Bilbao Metro System Northern Spain and Duisburg Micro Electronic Centre Germany; currently ptnr i/c Canary Wharf Station (Jubilee Line), New German Parliament Berlin (Reichstag) and Ju-shi HQ Shanghai; *Style*— David Nelson, Esq; ✉ Foster & Partners, Riverside Three, 22 Hester Road, London SW11 4AN (☎ 0171 738 0455, fax 0171 738 1107/1108)

NELSON, Dr Elizabeth Hawkins; da of Harry Dadmun Nelson (d 1965), of Summit, New Jersey, and Gretchen, *née* Hawkins (d 1984); *b* 27 Jan 1931; *Educ* Hanover HS Hanover New Hampshire, Middlebury Coll Vermont (BA), Inst of Psychiatry Univ of London (PhD); *m* 1, 1960 (m dis 1972), Ivan Piercy; 2 s (Christopher b 5 March 1963, Nicholas b 3 Aug 1965), 1 da (Catherine b 15 Sept 1961); m 2, 26 July 1975, Claude Jacob Esterson, s of Elias Esterson; *Career* res psychologist Mars Ltd 1953–55, dir and md Res Unit Benton and Bowles Ltd 1957–64 (market res exec 1955–57), fndr dir and chm Taylor Nelson Group 1965–92; chm Addison Consultancy Group plc 1989–91, chm Taylor Nelson AGB 1992, chief exec Princess Royal Tst for Carers 1992–96; chm UK Ecolabelling Bd 1992–, memb Pay Review Body Doctors and Dentists 1992–; non-exec dir The Royal Bank of Scotland plc 1987–; past pres World Assoc of Public Opinion Res, memb Cncl Open Univ 1992–; memb Forum (UK); FRSA; *Recreations* bridge, choral singing, opera; *Style*— Dr Elizabeth Nelson; ✉ 57 Home Park Road, Wimbledon, London SW19 (☎ 0181 946 2317, car 0860 223690, e-mail liznlson53@aol.com)

NELSON, Hon James Jonathan; yr s of 2 Baron Nelson of Stafford (d 1995); *b* 17 June 1947; *Educ* Ampleforth, McGill Univ Canada (BCom); *m* 18 Nov 1977, Lucilla Mary, da of Roger Gopsill Brown, of Albrighton, Shropshire; 3 da (Camilla Amy b 1982, Lara Kitty b 1986, Eloise Violet b 1988); *Career* commercial banking offr Morgan Guaranty Tst Co of New York 1969–73, dir Foreign & Colonial Management Ltd 1974–, md Foreign & Colonial Ventures Ltd 1985–; Freeman City of London 1986, Liveryman Worshipful Co of Goldsmiths 1989; *Recreations* golf, tennis, skiing, shooting, fishing; *Clubs* Queen's, Hurlingham, New Zealand; *Style*— The Hon James Nelson; ✉ 82 Tachbrook Street, London SW1V 2NB; Foreign & Colonial Ventures Ltd, 8th Floor, Exchange House, Primrose Street, London EC2A 2NY (☎ 0171 782 9829, fax 0171 782 9834)

NELSON, Sir Jamie Charles Vernon Hope; 4 Bt (UK 1912), of Acton Park, Acton, of Denbigh; eldest s of Sir William Vernon Hope Nelson, 3 Bt, OBE (d 1991), and Hon Elizabeth-Ann Bevil Cary, da of 14 Viscount Falkland; *b* 23 Oct 1949; *Educ* Redrice; *m* 25 June 1983, Maralynn Pyatt, da of late Albert Pyatt Hedge, of Audenshaw, Lincs; 1 s (Liam Chester b 1982); *Heir* bro, Dominic William Michael Nelson b 13 March 1957; *Career* forester, teacher; *Style*— Sir Jamie Nelson, Bt; ✉ 39 Montacute Road, Tintinhull, Yeovil, Somerset BA22 8QD

NELSON, Prof Janet Laughland; da of William Wilson Muir (d 1965), and Elizabeth Barnes, *née* Laughland (d 1991); *b* 28 March 1942; *Educ* Keswick Sch Cumbria, Newnham Coll Cambridge (BA, PhD); *m* 1965, Howard George Horatio Nelson; 1 da

(Elizabeth Muir b 1972), 1 s (William Horatio b 1974); *Career* King's Coll London: lectr 1970–87, reader 1987–92, prof 1992–, dir Centre for Late Antique and Medieval Studies 1994–; pres Ecclesiastical History Society 1993–94 (memb 1969–); memb and Dept rep AUT 1970–; memb: Lab Pty 1961–, Confraternity of St James 1990–; FRHistS 1981, FBA 1996; *Books* Politics and Ritual in the Early Middle Ages (1986), The Annals of St Bertin (1991), Charles the Bald (1992), The Frankish World (1996); *Recreations* music, walking; *Style*— Prof Janet L Nelson, FBA; ✉ 71 Oglander Road, London, SE15 4DD; Department of History, King's College London, Strand, London WC2R 2LS (☎ 0171 836 5454 ext 1086, fax 0171 873 2052)

NELSON, John Frederick; *b* 26 July 1947; *Educ* Marlborough; *m*; 3 c; *Career* Kleinwort Benson: joined (corp fin) 1971, a vice pres Kleinwort Benson Inc NY 1973–75, dir Kleinwort Benson Ltd 1980–86; Lazard Brothers & Co Ltd: md 1986–, vice chm 1990–; FCA (ACA 1970); *Style*— John Nelson, Esq; ✉ Lazard Brothers & Co Ltd, 21 Moorfields, London EC2P 2HT (☎ 0171 588 2721, fax 0171 628 7747)

NELSON, John Graeme; s of Charles Nelson (d 1985), and Jean, *née* Blackstock; *b* 19 June 1947; *Educ* Aylesbury GS, Slough GS, Univ of Manchester (BA); *m* 19 June 1971, Pauline Viola, da of Stanley Arthur Dickinson, of Hayes, Bromley, Kent; 2 s (Andrew b 1973, Ian b 1976), 1 da (Clare b 1979); *Career* BR: management trainee Western Region 1968–71, asst station mangr Liverpool St 1971–73, area passenger mangr Shenfield 1973–77, passenger sales offr Leeds 1977–79, passenger mangr Sheffield Div 1979–81, PA to Chief Exec BRB 1981–82, parcels mangr Southern Region 1982–84, nat business mangr Red Star Parcels 1984–87, gen mangr Eastern Region 1987–92, dir InterCity E Coast Main Line 1991–92, md Network SouthEast 1992–94, md British Rail South and East 1994–; memb: London Regnl Cncl CBI, Cncl London C of C, Br Tport Police Ctee; *Recreations* piano, football, badminton, rugby league; *Style*— John Nelson, Esq; ✉ British Railways, Euston House, 24 Eversholt Street, London NW1 1DN (☎ 0171 320 0254, fax 0171 320 0981)

NELSON, Judith Manes; da of Virgil D Manes (d 1967), of Elmhurst, Illinois, and Genevieve Ingels Manes; *b* 10 Sept 1939; *Educ* York Community HS Elmhurst, St Olaf Coll Northfield Minnesota (BA); *m* 1961, Alan H Nelson, s of Arthur F Nelson; 1 s (Christopher b Dec 1965), 1 da (Jennifer b March 1968); *Career* soprano; Euro debut Graz Austria 1972; appeared with orchs incl: Acad of Ancient Music, Eng Concert, Monteverdi Baroque Soloists, BBC Symphony Orch, Boston Early Music Festival Orch, Handel and Haydn Soc Orch, Philharmonia Baroque Orch, Tafelmusik, American Bach Soloists, Atlanta, Baltimore, San Francisco and St Louis Symphony Orchs, Los Angeles Philharmonic, Washington Nat Orch, Manila Symphony Orch; awarded Alfred Hertz Meml scholarship from Univ of Calif Berkeley; Hon Dr of Fine Arts St Olaf Coll Northfield Minnesota 1989; *Performances* operatic roles incl: Roberto in La Griselda (Berkeley Calfornia) 1972, Drusilla in L'Incoronazione di Poppea (Theatre de la Monnaie Brussels 1978, Landestheater Innsbruck 1979), title role in Il Sant'Alessio (Teatro Valle Rome 1981, Landestheater Innsbruck 1983, Nakamichi Festival UCLA 1988), Marzia in Il Tito (Landestheater Innsbruck, Teatro Malibran Rome) 1982, Falsirena in La Catena d'Adone (Malmö Sweden) 1984, Amastre in Xerse (Innsbruck, Utrecht) 1985, Aricie in Hippolyte and Aricie (San Francisco Concert Opera) 1987, Clorinda in Il Combattimento di Tancredi e Clorinda (Santa Fe Chamber Music Festival) 1989, Serpina in La Serva Padrona (Santa Fe Chamber Music Festival) 1990, Belinda in Dido & Aeneas (Folger Shakespeare Lib Washington DC) 1995, Tamiri in Il Rè Pastore (San Francisco) 1996, Cleeone in Télémaque (San Francisco) 1996; *Recordings* incl: Bach's Magnificat in E flat major (with the Acad of Ancient Music) and Wedding Cantata and Mass in B minor (with the Bach Ensemble), Handel's Apollo e Dafne (with the Philharmonic Baroque Orch), Duetti e Cantate da Camera (with Concerto Vocale) and Messiah (with the Acad of Ancient Music), Haydn's Great Organ Mass, St Nicholas Mass, Missa Brevis and Mass for England (all with the Acad of Ancient Music), Monteverdi's L'Incoronazione di Poppea (with the Berkeley Collegium Musicum) and Madrigali Erotici (with the Consort of Musicke), Locke's Music from the Tempest (with the Acad of Ancient Music), Purcell's Dido and Aeneas (with the Taverner Consort and Players), Don Quixote (with the Acad of Ancient Music), The Fairy Queen (with the Eng Baroque Ensemble) and eight vols of theatre music with the Acad of Ancient Music, Scarlatti's La Griselda (with the Univ of Calif Orch), Vivaldi's Gloria in D major (with the Acad of Ancient Music), works by Amy, Campra, Cavalli, Charpentier, Cesti, Couperin, Dufay, Durante, Frescobaldi, D'India, Ives, Mondonville, Monteclair, Rossi, Schubert, Steffani, Stradella and Strozzi, various anthologies; *Recreations* taking long walks, learning about history, art, architecture; *Style*— Ms Judith Nelson; ✉ 2600 Buena Vista Way, Berkeley, CA 94708, California, USA (☎ 001 510 848 1992)

NELSON, Nigel David; s of David Gordon Nelson (d 1978), and Iris May, *née* Phillips; *b* 16 April 1954; *Educ* Sutton Valence Sch Kent; *children* 2 s (Marcus, Dominic), 2 da (Nicolette, Cordelia); *Career* reporter: Kent Evening Post 1972–75 (crime reporter 1973–75), Daily Mail 1975–79 (royal reporter 1978, New York corr 1978–79); freelance US corr 1979–82, feature writer Sunday Mirror 1982–86, political ed The People 1986–; memb NUJ; *Books* The Porton Phial (1991); *Recreations* eating, drinking and being merry; *Clubs* Parliamentary Sports; *Style*— Nigel Nelson, Esq; ✉ The People, 1 Canada Square, Canary Wharf, London E14 5AP (☎ 0171 293 3059, fax 0171 293 3517)

NELSON, Paul Maurice; s of Aubrey Nelson, of Putney, London, and Myrtle, *née* Herman; *b* 22 Aug 1956; *Educ* Latymer Upper Sch, CCC Cambridge (BA, MA); *m* 1 May 1983, Dora Jennifer Lawson; *Career* ptnr Linklaters & Paines 1987– (articled clerk 1979–81, asst slr 1981–87); memb Law Soc 1981 (memb Co Law Ctee); *Style*— Paul Nelson, Esq; ✉ Linklaters & Paines, 59–67 Gresham Street, London EC2V 7LP (☎ 0171 606 7080, fax 0171 606 5113)

NELSON, 9 Earl (UK 1805); Peter John Horatio Nelson; also Baron Nelson of the Nile and of Hilborough (UK 1801) and Viscount Merton of Trafalgar and of Merton (UK 1805); s of Capt Hon John Nelson, RA (5 s of 5 Earl and yr bro of 6, 7 and 8 Earls); Lord Nelson (suc uncle, 8 Earl, Sept 1981) is fifth in descent from the 2 Earl; the 2 Earl's mother Susannah was sister to the 1 Earl and his yr bro, the celebrated naval hero; Horatio Nelson's Barony of Nelson (GB) and Viscountcy of Nelson (UK) were extinguished with him, but his Barony of Nelson of the Nile & of Hilborough have descended to the present Peer along with his er bro's Earldom and Viscountcy (the two last titles being created, like the aforesaid Barony, with special remainder to ensure the survival of dignities honouring one of Britain's greatest sons); the Admiral's Dukedom of Brontë, however, passed, through the marriage of the 1 Earl's da Charlotte with the 2 Baron Bridport, to the Viscounts Bridport; *b* 9 Oct 1941; *Educ* St Joseph's Coll Ipswich, Nat Inst of Agric Lincs; *m* 1, 1969, Maureen Diana, da of Edward Patrick Quinn, of Kilkenny; 1 s (and 1 s, Peter Francis Horatio, b and d 1970), 1 da (Lady Deborah Jane Mary b 1974); m 2, Sept 1992, Tracy Cowie; 1 s (Edward James Horatio b 1994); *Heir* s, Viscount Merton, *qv*; *Career* pres: Royal Naval Commando Assoc, Nelson Soc; vice-pres Jubilee Sailing Tst; hon life memb: Royal Naval Assoc, Royal Naval Museum; pres Int Fingerprint Soc; *Clubs* St James's; *Style*— The Rt Hon the Earl Nelson; ✉ House of Lords, London SW1A 0PW

NELSON, Air Marshal Sir (Sidney) Richard Carlyle; KCB (1963, CB 1962), OBE (1949); s of M O Nelson, of Smithville, Ontario, Canada, and Jane Amelia, *née* Cartwright (d 1970); *b* 14 Nov 1907; *Educ* Univ of Alberta Canada (MD), Graduate RAF Staff Coll; *m* 1939, Christina Elizabeth, da of W S Powell, of London; 2 s (Richard, Peter); *Career* joined RAF 1935, served WWII, Gp Capt 1953, Air Cdre 1957, PMO Tech Trg Cmd 1957–59, Air Vice-Marshal 1959, PMO Bomber Cmd 1959–62, QHP 1961–67, Air Marshal 1962, dir-gen RAF Med Servs 1962–67, ret; dir of res and med servs Aspro-Nicholas 1967–72; Liveryman Worshipful Soc of Apothecaries; *Recreations* fishing, golf; *Clubs* RAF; *Style*— Air Marshal Sir Richard Nelson, KCB, OBE; ✉ Caffyn's Copse, Shappen Hill Lane, Burley, Ringwood, Hants BH24 4EP

NELSON, Hon Mr Justice; Hon Sir Robert Franklyn; kt (1996); s of Clarence William Nelson, of North Rigton, Harrogate, Yorks, and Lucie Margaret, *née* Kirkby; *b* 19 Sept 1942; *Educ* Repton, St John's Coll Cambridge (MA); *m* 14 Sept 1968, Anne-Marie Sabina, da of Francis William George Hall, of Hook Green, Wilmington, Kent; 2 s (Joshua b 1970, Bartholomew b 1973); *Career* called to the Bar Middle Temple 1965, QC 1985, recorder 1986–96, bencher 1993, a judge of the High Court of Justice (Queen's Bench Div) 1996–; *Recreations* opera, cricket, golf; *Style*— The Hon Mr Justice Nelson; ✉ Royal Courts of Justice, Strand, London WC2

NELSON-JONES, John Austen; s of late Dr Archibald Nelson-Jones, of Putney, and Constance Vera, *née* Riley (d 1996); *b* 26 July 1934; *Educ* Repton, Trinity Coll Oxford; *m* 31 Aug 1963, Helene, da of John George William Wood (d 1976); 2 s (Michael, Martin); *Career* Nat Serv 2 Lt 1 Regt RHA 1954–55; admitted slr 1963, ptnr Field Fisher and Martineau 1968–89, currently managing ptnr Field Fisher Waterhouse; memb Cncl: Nat Consumer Cncl 1987–92 (chm Legal Advsy Panel), City Technol Tst 1987–; memb Bd Job Ownership Ltd 1986–95, res sec Bow Group 1968 and 1969, taxation ed Law Soc Gazette 1972–80; memb: Law Soc 1963, Int Bar Assoc 1982 (chm Travel and Tourism Law Ctee 1987–91); FRSA 1991; *Books* Nelson-Jones Practical Tax Saving (3 edn, 1976), Employee Ownership (1987), Package Holiday Law and Contracts (3 edn, 1993); contrib numerous articles to professional jls; *Recreations* walking, music, reading, supporting Wimbledon FC; *Clubs* Hurlingham; *Style*— John Nelson-Jones, Esq; ✉ Field Fisher Waterhouse, 41 Vine St, London EC3N 2AA (☎ 0171 481 4841, fax 0171 488 0084, telex 262613 ADIDEM G)

NELSON-JONES, Rodney Michael; s of late Dr Archibald Nelson-Jones, of Putney, London, and Constance Vera, *née* Riley (d 1996); *b* 11 Feb 1947; *Educ* Repton, Hertford Coll Oxford (MA); *m* 21 Sept 1988, Kusum, da of Babulal Keshavji, of Derby; 1 s; *Career* admitted slr 1975; Prothero & Prothero 1973–77, L Bingham & Co 1977–83, ptnr i/c Personal Injury Litigation Dept Field Fisher Waterhouse 1983–; memb M1 Air Crash Steering Ctee 1989–93; *Books* co-author: Product Liability - The New Law Under The Consumer Protection Act 1987 (2 edn 1988), Personal Injury Limitation Law (1994), Medical Negligence Case Law (2 edn 1995); conbrib: Butterworths Personal Injury Litigation Service (1988), Structured Settlements - A Practical Guide (1993); *Periodicals* Personal Injury Interest Calculation (annually, 1980–), Nelson-Jones and Nuttall's Tax and Interest Tables (5 edn 1992), FFW Personal Injury News (quarterly, 1992–), Special Damages Statistics (annually, 1994–); *Recreations* cinema, music, tennis, travel; *Style*— Rodney Nelson-Jones, Esq; ✉ 69 Warrington Crescent, London W9 1EH; Field Fisher Waterhouse, 41 Vine St, London EC3N 2AA (☎ 0171 481 4841)

NELSON OF STAFFORD, 3 Baron (UK 1960); Sir Henry Roy George Nelson; 3 Bt (UK 1955), of Hilcote Hall, Co Stafford; s of 2 Baron Nelson of Stafford (d 1995), and Pamela Roy, *née* Bird; *b* 26 Oct 1943; *Educ* Ampleforth, King's Coll Cambridge (MA); *m* 8 June 1968, Dorothy, yr da of Leslie Caley, of Tibthorpe Manor, Driffield, E Yorks; 1 s (Alistair William Henry b 1973), 1 da (Sarah Jane b 1981); *Heir* s, Hon Alistair William Henry Nelson b 1973; *Career* joined RHP Bearings 1970; gen mangr: transmission bearings 1973–78, automotive bearings 1978–81; mfrg dir industl bearings 1981–83; md: Hopkinsons Ltd 1983–85, Industl and Distribution Divs Pegler-Hattersley plc 1985–86, GSPK Ltd group 1986–90, Power Transmission Div Fenner plc 1991–92, ops dir TIB plc 1993–; memb Govt Ctee of Enquiry into Engrg Profession 1978–80; FIMechE, MIEE, CEng; *Style*— The Rt Hon Lord Nelson of Stafford; ✉ Eastlands, Tibthorpe, Driffield, E Yorks YO25 9LD (☎ 01377 229244)

NELSON-SMITH, David Austin; s of Adrian Nelson-Smith (d 1978); *b* 6 April 1936; *Educ* Brighton Coll, CCC Cambridge; *m* 1965, Joyce Yvonne, *née* Naef; 1 s (Mark b 1966), 1 da (Nicola b 1968); *Career* chm and md Tradax England Ltd 1978–83, chm Sun Valley Poultry 1987–96, dir Cargill UK Ltd 1983–90, dir Cargill plc 1990–96, vice pres Cargill Europe 1993–96; pres Grain and Feedstuffs Trade Assoc 1985–86, pres Comité du Commerce des Cereales et des Aliments du Betail de la CEE 1987–88; *Style*— David Nelson-Smith, Esq; ✉ Cargill plc, Knowle Hill Park, Cobham, Surrey KT11 2PD

NEOPTOLEMOS, Prof John Phitoyiannis; *b* 30 June 1951; *Educ* Owen's GS N London, Churchill Coll Cambridge, Guy's Hosp London (MA, MB BChir), Univ of Leicester (MD); *m* 2 Feb 1974, Linda Joan, da of Richard Blaylock, of Kenton, Newcastle-upon-Tyne; 1 s (Ptolemy b 11 Aug 1978), 1 da (Eleni b 12 May 1981); *Career* Guy's Hosp London 1976–77, Leicester Royal Infirmary 1978–84 and 1986–87, UCSD San Diego California 1984–85, reader Univ Dept of Surgery Birmingham and conslt surgn City Hosp 1987–94, prof of surgery Queen Elizabeth Hosp Birmingham 1994–96, prof of surgery and head of dept Royal Liverpool Univ Hosp 1996–; Hunterian prof of surgery RCS 1987–88; Rodney Smith prize 1987, Moynihan travelling fell Assoc of Surgns of GB and I 1988, RSM travelling prof (USA) 1989, Eybers visiting prof S Africa 1994; scientific contribs to aetiology, diagnosis and treatment of gastrointestinal disease especially relating to the pancreas, bilary tree and liver; pres Pancreatic Soc of GB and I 1994–95 (memb Ctee 1987–90); memb World Cncl Int Hepato-Pancreato-Bilary Assoc 1995–98; memb Ctee Surgical Research Soc 1994–, memb Cncl Euro Pancreatic Club 1995–, memb World Cncl Int Assoc on Pancreatology 1996–; chm Euro Study Gp for Pancreatic Cancer 1991–; FRCS; *Recreations* squash; *Style*— Prof John P Neoptolemos; ✉ Department of Surgery, Royal Liverpool University Hospital, 5th Floor, UCD Building, Daulby Street, Liverpool L69 3GA (☎ 0151 706 4175, fax 0151 706 5798)

NEPEAN, Lt-Col Sir Evan Yorke; 6 Bt (UK 1802), of Bothenhampton, Dorsetshire; s of Maj Sir Charles Evan Molyneux Yorke Nepean, 5 Bt (d 1953); *b* 23 Nov 1909; *Educ* Winchester, Downing Coll Cambridge (BA 1931, MA 1947); *m* 1940, (Georgiana) Cicely, da of late Maj N E G Willoughby, Middx Regt; 3 da (Susan Cicely (Mrs Martin Aylmer-Hall) b 1941, Judith Sarah (Mrs Noel Goldthorp) b 1946, Gillian Helen (Mrs Paul Stevens) b 1950); *Heir* none; *Career* served 1932–57 with Royal Corps of Signals, UK, India, Middle East, Far East and BAOR, Lt-Col 1943, ret 1957; MIEE, CEng; *Recreations* bell ringing, amateur radio; *Style*— Lt-Col Sir Evan Nepean, Bt; ✉ Allwyns, 43 Queens Road, Devizes, Wilts SN10 5HW

NERURKAR, Richard David; s of David Janardan Nerurkar, and Iris Elizabeth, *née* Griffiths; *b* 6 Jan 1964; *Educ* Bradford GS, University Coll Oxford (BA), Harvard Univ (Harkness fell, MA); *m* 14 Sept 1996, Gail Jewell Grose Davey; *Career* teacher Marlborough Coll 1989–91, asst sec Church Missionary Soc 1992–95; int athlete 1989–; 18th place World Cross-Country Championships 1990; 5th place: 10,000m European Athletic Championships 1990, 10,000m World Athletic Championships 1991, Olympic Games Marathon 1996; 17th place 10,000m Olympic Games 1992, World Cup marathon champion 1993, 4th place Euro Championships Marathon 1994, 7th place World Championships marathon 1995; *Style*— Richard Nerurkar, Esq; ✉ 21 Springfield Road, Teddington, Middx TW11 9AP (☎ 0181 943 5310)

NESBITT, Garry; s of Harry Nesbitt (d 1968), and May Nesbitt; *b* 6 Dec 1942; *Educ* Aida Foster Stage Sch; *m* 28 Aug 1971, Penny, da of E S A Baker; 2 s (Tristan b 1974, Julian b 1989), 2 da (Tania b 1978, Carola b 1981); *Career* fndr Our Price Music Retail Chain 1971 (business floated 1984 and acquired by WH Smith 1986); chm: Crockfords Casino (floated 1993), Ragdale Hall Health Hydro Leics; *Recreations* keeping fit, tennis, water skiing, fine wine collecting; *Style*— Garry Nesbitt, Esq; ✉ Crockfords Casino, 30 Curzon Street, London W1Y 7AE (☎ 0171 493 7771)

NESBITT, Prof Robert William; s of Thomas Dodgson Nesbitt (d 1977), of Blyth, Northumberland, and Mary Florence Nesbitt (d 1983); *b* 26 Sept 1936; *Educ* Blyth GS, Univ of Durham (BSc, PhD); *m* 24 Oct 1959, Catherine, da of Peter Robertson (d 1976), of Blyth, Northumberland; 3 da (Carolyn Anne b 1960, Joanne Louise b 1964, Jacqueline Clare b 1969); *Career* geologist Greenland Geological Survey 1958–59; Univ of Adelaide Aust: lectr 1962–68, sr lectr 1968–72, reader 1972–80; visiting res fell Univ of Yale 1968, visiting prof Université de Rennes 1979–92, dean of sci Univ of Southampton 1987–90 (prof of geology 1980–); subject advsr Univ Funding Cncl 1985–93; hon corr Geological Soc of Australia, chm Ctee of Heads of Geoscience Dept 1992, memb Cncl Geological Soc London 1994–; FGSA 1976, FGS 1980; *Recreations* golf, scuba diving; *Style*— Prof Robert Nesbitt; ✉ Department of Geology, University of Southampton, Southampton, Hants SO9 5NH (☎ 01703 592037, fax 01703 593052)

NESTOR, Capt Martin John Ralph; OBE (1985), ADC (1993); s of John Martin Nestor (d 1985), of Huddersfield, Yorks, and Gladys, *née* Earnshaw (d 1985); *b* 29 Jan 1940; *Educ* Royds Hall GS Huddersfield; *m* 28 Dec 1963, Jacqueline, *née* Collier; 3 da (Clare b 19 Aug 1966, Julia b 30 March 1968, Sarah b 27 Feb 1974); *Career* joined RN 1967: nuclear trg and submarine serv 1967–70, HMS Norfolk 1971–73, RN Air Station Yeovilton 1973–75, exchange offr USN 1976–78, HMS Hermes 1978–80, RN Staff Coll 1980, Cdr 1980, HMS Collingwood 1980–81, special appt MOD London (Falklands War) 1982, HMS Invincible 1982–84, MOD London 1984–88, Capt 1986, NATO Def Coll Rome 1988–89, Int Military Staff NATO HQ 1989–93, MOD London 1993; NCB 1958–59, ICI 1963–67; memb (later treas) North Curry PCC 1985–88; ARIC 1965; *Recreations* tennis, gardening; *Clubs* Army and Navy; *Style*— Capt Martin J R Nestor, OBE, ADC, RN

NETHERCOT, Prof David Arthur; s of Arthur Owen Martin Nethercot (d 1980), and Dorothy May, *née* Bearman (d 1996); *b* 26 April 1946; *Educ* Minchenden GS London, Univ of Wales (Page prize and medal, BSc, DSc, PhD); *m* 3 Aug 1968, Hedd Dwynwen, da of John Byron Evans; 2 da (Susanna Kate b 29 Dec 1971, Emily Victoria b 4 March 1975); *Career* ICI fell Univ of Wales 1970–71, lectr and reader Univ of Sheffield 1971–89; Univ of Nottingham: prof of civil engrg 1989–, head of dept 1994–; visiting prof: Japan Soc for Promotion of Science Univ of Nagoya 1980, Swiss Federal Inst of Technology Lausanne 1990; ctee memb and chm: BSI, EPSRC; memb Cncl Steel Construction Inst 1992–, chm Jt Bd of Moderators 1996–; FIStructE 1989 (memb 1976, memb Cncl 1986–89 and 1991–95, hon sec 1995–96); FEng 1993, FICE 1995; *Awards* ICE: Miller Prize 1971, Telford Premium 1991; IStructE: Oscar Faber bronze medal 1989, Murray Buxton prize 1992, Henry Adams dip 1994; *Books* Design for Structural Stability (1985), Limit States Design of Structural Steelwork (1991); author of over 200 papers on structural engineering; *Recreations* sport; *Style*— Prof D A Nethercot, FEng; ✉ Department of Civil Engineering, University of Nottingham, University Park, Nottingham NG7 2RD (☎ 0115 951 3904, fax 0115 951 3898)

NETHERCOTT, Stuart; *b* 21 March 1973; *Career* professional footballer (defender); joined Tottenham Hotspur 1991, on loan to Maidstone (league debut 1991) and Barnet 1991–92; memb England under 21 team; *Style*— Stuart Nethercott, Esq; ✉ c/o Tottenham Hotspur FC, 748 High Road, Tottenham, London N17 0AP (☎ 0181 808 6666)

NETHERTHORPE, 3 Baron (UK 1959); James Frederick Turner; s of 2 Baron Netherthorpe (d 1982); *b* 7 Jan 1964; *Educ* Harrow; *m* 10 Dec 1989, (Elizabeth) Curran, da of Edward William Fahan, of Redding, Connecticut, USA; 1 s (Hon Andrew James Edward b 24 March 1993), 1 da (Hon Megan Anna Curran b 19 Nov 1994); *Heir* s, Hon Andrew James Edward Turner b 24 March 1993; *Style*— The Rt Hon the Lord Netherthorpe; ✉ Boothby Hall, Boothby Pagnell, Grantham, Lincs (☎ 01476 585374)

NETHERTON, Derek Nigel Donald; s of John Gordon Netherton, of London, and Beryl Agnes, *née* Freeman; *b* 4 Jan 1945; *Educ* Charterhouse, King's Coll Cambridge (MA); *m* 8 May 1976, Pamela Jane, da of Col W Rollo Corkill, of Banstead, Surrey; 4 s (Charles b 1981, George b 1984, Patrick b 1987, David (twin) b 1987); *Career* dir J Henry Schroder Wagg 1981–96, non-exec dir: St James's Place Capital 1996–, J Rothschild Assurance Holdings 1996–; FIA; *Style*— Derek Netherton, Esq; ✉ c/o Schroder Properties Ltd, Level 4, Senator House, 85 Queen Victoria Street, London EC4V 4EJ (☎ 0171 382 6357)

NETTLE, David Richard; s of Gerald Nettle, of Redruth, and Viola, *née* Tregenza; *b* 10 June 1956; *Educ* Redruth GS, RCM London; *Career* concert pianist; worldwide appearances with Richard Markham, *qv*, as Nettle-Markham Piano Duo: North American debut 1979, London debut (Wigmore Hall) 1982, Far East tour 1983, Middle East tours 1983 and 1985, African and Aust tours 1992/93, regular US tours, frequent performances at princ Euro festivals incl BBC Proms; *Recordings* incl: The Rite of Spring and Petrushka (1984), The Planets (1985), Dyson's The Blacksmiths (1987), Delius and Grainger Folksongs (1988), Rossini's Petite Messe Solennelle (1990), Carnival of the Animals (1991), Nettle & Markham in England (1993), Arnold-Piano Duet Concerto (1993), Nettle & Markham in America (1994), Arnold-2 Piano Concerto (1994), Nettle & Markham in France (1996); *Awards* Norris prize 1977, Music Retailers' Assoc Award Award for best chamber music record 1985; *Recreations* travel, cooking, wining and dining, tennis, chess, photography, languages, writing, naturism; *Style*— David Nettle, Esq; ✉ The Old Power House, Atherton St, London SW11 2JE (☎ 0171 738 9427, fax 0171 738 2765)

NETTLES, John; *Career* actor; early stage work incl plays at Royal Court, Traverse Theatre Edinburgh and Theatre 69; *Repertory* Northcott Theatre Exeter: Jimmy Porter in Look Back in Anger, Feste in Twelfth Night, Vladimir in Waiting For Godot, Mompesson in Roses of Eyam, Tranio in Taming of the Shrew; Bristol Old Vic: Thersites in Troillus and Cressida, Sganarelle in Don Juan, Harold in The Philanthropist, Joey in Butley, Alwa in Lulu, Ed in Entertaining Mr Sloane; Crucible Theatre Sheffield: Charles Surface in School for Scandal; Derby Playhouse: Leonard in Time and Time Again, Brian in A Day in the Death of Joe Egg; RSC: Florizel in A Winter's Tale, Thersites in Troilus and Cressida, Maxwell in Destiny, Godber in That Good Between Us, Kung Tu in The Bundle, Von Lieres in A Miserable Death, Detective in The Factory Birds, Priest in Frozen Assets, Bassanio in The Merchant of Venice, Lucio in Measure For Measure, Thompson in The Churchill Play, Harry Thunder in Wild Oats, Alexei Tourbin in The White Guard, Ernest in Once in a Lifetime, La Ronde, The Hollow Crown (USA tour) 1981; most recent RSC 1992–: Leontes in The Winter's Tale, Page in The Merry Wives of Windsor, Caesar in Antony and Cleopatra, Merecraft in The Devil is an Ass 1995, Julius Caesar; *Other Theatre* incl: Lord Foppington in The Relapse (Old Vic) 1981, title role in Butley (Fortune Theatre); *Pantomine* Abanazar in Aladdin (Theatre Royal Bath), Sheriff of Nottingham in Babes in the Wood (Palace Theatre Manchester), Bluebeard the Pirate in Robinson Crusoe (Theatre Royal Plymouth and New Theatre Cardiff), King Rat in Dick Whittington (Palace Theatre Manchester 1990–91 and Wimbledon/Leeds 1991–92); *Television* LWT incl: Black Beauty, Holding On; BBC incl: The Liver Birds, The Merchant of Venice, Bergerac 1981–90, Bergerac Special 1991, Hands Across the Sea 1991; Submarine (narrator, series); title role in Robin Hood (Radio); other credits incl: A Family at War (Granada), Dickens of London (Yorkshire), Boon (Central, guest lead role); *Books* Nudity in a Public Place (semi-autobiographical, 1991); *Style*— John Nettles, Esq; ✉ c/o Saraband Associates, 265 Liverpool Rd, London N1 1LX (☎ 0171 609 5313, fax 0171 609 2370)

NEUBERG, Roger Wolfe; s of Klaus Neuberg, of London, and Herta, *née* Hausler (d 1986); *b* 24 May 1941; *Educ* Hendon Co GS, Middx Hosp Med Sch (MB BS); *m* 16 Aug 1964, Ruth Denise, da of Manning Ephron (d 1984), of Bournemouth; 2 s (Guy b 1966, Kim b 1967); *Career* conslt obstetrician and gynaecologist; registrar Middlesex Hosp and Hosp for Women; sr registrar: John Radcliffe Hosp, Oxford and Royal Berkshire Hosp; conslt and dir of infertility servs Leicester Royal Infirmary; memb: Br Fertility Soc, Assoc of Broadcasting Doctors; LRCP 1965, MRCS 1965, FRCOG 1983; *Books* So You Want to Have a Baby (1985, 4 edn 1996), Infertility (1991, 2 edn 1994), Obstetrics: A Practical Manual (1995); *Recreations* aikido, old time music hall, gardening; *Style*— Roger Neuberg, Esq; ✉ 9 Barrington Rd, Stoneygate, Leicester LE2 2RA (☎ 0116 255 3933); Maternity Dept, Leicester Royal Infirmary, Leicester (☎ 0116 258 6426)

NEUBERGER, Hon Mr Justice; Hon Sir David Edmond; kt (1996); s of Prof Albert Neuberger, CBE, FRS (d 1996), and Lilian Ida, *née* Dreyfus; *b* 10 Jan 1948; *Educ* Westminster, Christ Church Oxford; *m* Angela, da of Brig Peter Holdsworth; 2 s (Nicholas b 1979, Max b 1981), 1 da (Jessica b 1977); *Career* N M Rothschild & Sons 1970–73, called to the Bar Lincoln's Inn 1974 (bencher 1993), QC 1987, recorder 1990–96, former jt head of Falcon chambers, judge of the High Court of Justice (Chancery Div) 1996–; *Style*— The Hon Mr Justice Neuberger; ✉ Royal Courts of Justice, Strand, London WC2A 2LL (☎ 0171 936 7280)

NEUBERGER, Dr James Max; s of Prof Albert Neuberger, CBE (d 1996), of London, and Lilian Ida, *née* Dreyfus; *b* 4 Nov 1949; *Educ* Westminster, ChCh Oxford (MA, BM BCh, DM); *m* 14 Sept 1979, Belinda Patricia, da of Patrick Joseph Keogh, of Manchester; 2 s (Oliver b 1980, Edmund b 1984), 2 da (Francesca b 1982, Octavia b 1988); *Career* sr lectr in med King's Coll Hosp London 1980–86, conslt physician Queen Elizabeth Hosp Birmingham 1986–; MRCP 1977, FRCP 1991; *Books* Liver Annual (1988), Immunology of Liver Transplantation (1993), Liver Transplantation (1994); *Recreations* fishing, gardening, reading; *Style*— Dr James Neuberger; ✉ The Moat House, Radford Rd, Alvechurch, Worcs B48 7ST (☎ 0121 445 1773); Queen Elizabeth Hospital, Edgbaston, Birmingham B15 2TH (☎ 0121 472 1311)

NEUBERGER, Rabbi Julia Babette Sarah; da of Walter Manfred Schwab (d 1996), of London, and Alice, *née* Rosenthal; *b* 27 Feb 1950; *Educ* S Hampstead HS for Girls, Newnham Coll Cambridge, Leo Baeck Coll London; *m* 17 Sept 1973, Anthony John Neuberger, s of Prof Albert Neuberger, CBE (d 1996), of London; 1 s (Matthew b 2 July 1981), 1 da (Harriet b 16 June 1979); *Career* rabbi S London Liberal Synagogue 1977–89, visiting fell King's Fund Inst 1989–91, visiting and Harkness fell Harvard Med Sch 1991–92, fell King's Fund Coll London 1992–, chllr Univ of Ulster 1994–; chair Camden and Islington Community Health Servs NHS Tst 1992–; memb: Human Fertilisation and Embryology Authy 1990–95, Ethics Ctee BMA 1992–94, Gen Med Cncl 1993–, Med Research Cncl 1995–, Library Cmmn 1995–; memb Cncl: Save the Children Fund 1994–, UCL 1993–; tstee Runnymede Tst, vice pres Patients' Assoc; regular broadcaster; Hon Doctorates: Univ of Humberside, Univ of Ulster, Univ of Stirling, City Univ, Oxford Brookes Univ, Univ of Teesside, Univ of Nottingham; *Books* The Story of Judaism (for children, 1986), Caring for Dying People of Different Faiths (1987, 2nd edn 1994), Days of Decision (ed, 1987), Whatever's Happening to Women (1991), A Necessary End (ed with John White, 1991), The Things That Matter (ed, 1993), Ethics and Healthcare: Research Ethics Ctees in the UK (1992), On Being Jewish (1995); *Clubs* Groucho; *Style*— Rabbi Julia Neuberger; ✉ 36 Orlando Rd, London SW4 0LF

NEUBERGER, Dr Michael Samuel; s of Prof Albert Neuberger, CBE, FRS (d 1996), of London, and Lilian Ida, *née* Dreyfus; *b* 2 Nov 1953; *Educ* Westminster, Trinity Coll Cambridge (scholar, MA), Imperial Coll Univ of London (PhD); *m* 6 Sept 1991, Dr Gillian Anne Pyman; 2 da (Anna Saskia b 5 Sept 1992, Lydia b 18 May 1994); *Career* SRC postdoctoral fell Univ of London 1977–79, EMBO fell Inst of Genetics Univ of Cologne 1979–80; Univ of Cambridge: res fell Trinity Coll 1977–81, memb of staff MRC Laboratory of Molecular Biology 1980–, fell and dir of studies in cell biology and biochemistry Trinity Coll 1985–; int res scholar Howard Hughes Med Inst 1992; memb EMBO 1989; FRS 1993; *Style*— Dr Michael Neuberger, FRS; ✉ MRC Laboratory of Molecular Biology, Hills Road, Cambridge CB2 2QH (☎ 01223 402245, fax 01223 412178)

NEUBERT, Sir Michael Jon; kt (1990), MP (C) Romford (majority 11,420); s of Frederick Neubert; *b* 3 Sept 1933; *Educ* Queen Elizabeth's Sch Barnet, Bromley GS, RCM, Downing Coll Cambridge; *m* 1959, Sally Felicity Bilger; 1 s; *Career* industl and travel conslt; ldr Bromley Cncl 1967–70, Mayor 1972–73, chm Bromley Cons Assoc 1968–69; Parly candidate (C): Hammersmith N 1966, Romford 1970; MP (C): Havering Romford Feb 1974–83, Romford 1983–; PPS to: Min for Social Security and the Disabled 1980, Mins of State NI Office 1981, Min of State for Employment 1981–82, Lord Cockfield as Trade Sec 1982–83; asst Govt whip 1983–86, a Lord Cmmr of the Treasy (Govt whip) 1986–88; vice chamberlain of the Royal Household 1988; under sec of state: for the Armed Forces 1988–89, for defence procurement 1989–90; chm Cons Backbench Employment Ctee 1992–; memb Exec 1922 Ctee 1992–; *Books* Running your own Society (1967); *Recreations* music, theatre, cinema, literature, scriptwriting, countryside; *Clubs* Romford Cons and Constitutional; *Style*— Sir Michael Neubert, MP; ✉ House of Commons, London SW1A 0AA

NEUMANN, Jan; CBE (1984); s of Frantisek Neumann (d 1940); *b* 26 June 1924; *Educ* Friends' Sch Gt Ayton, Univ of London (BSc); *m* 1, 1947, Barbara Joyce (d 1992), da of Ernest Gove (d 1938); 2 s; m 2, 1993, Irene McCusker, da of Harry Wragg (d 1976); *Career* Flt Sgt RAF, Flt Engr Coastal Cmd; CEng; dir: YARD Ltd 1969–1988, Yarrow & Co Ltd 1978–87, Scottish Nuclear Ltd 1989–93 (non-exec); memb Bd S of Scotland Electricity Bd 1986–88, pres Inst of Engineers and Shipbuilders in Scotland 1993–95; FEng 1981; *Recreations* swimming, bowling; *Style*— Jan Neumann, Esq, CBE, FEng; ✉ 38 Norwood Park, Bearsden, Glasgow G61 2RZ (☎ 0141 942 5371)

NEVILE, Christopher William Kenneth; s of Kenneth Nevile (d 1960), of Swinderby, Lincoln, and Elizabeth Mary, *née* Brown; *b* 27 April 1957; *Educ* St Hugh's Wood Hall SPA, Rugby, Exeter Univ (LLB); *m* Sept 1993, Charlotte Brodie (Charlie), da of Dr Jeremy Lee-Potter, of Ker House Stoborough, Dorset, and Lynda Lee-Potter; 1 s (Kit Brodie Kenneth b 9 Oct 1995); *Career* stockbroker; assoc dir Scrimgeour Vickers until 1987; dir Adams & Nevile Ltd 1987–95, md Granville Investment Management Ltd 1995–; *Recreations* fishing, cricket; *Clubs* Barbican Health Centre; *Style*— Christopher W K Nevile, Esq; ✉ 45A Moreton Street, London SW1 (☎ 0171 931 8120); Granville Investment Management Ltd, Mint House, 77 Mansell Street, London E1 8AF (☎ 0171 488 1212)

NEVILL, Amanda Elizabeth; da of John Henry Howard King, of Bardsey, Yorkshire, and Jill, *née* Livett; *b* 21 March 1957; *Educ* Bar Convent York, British Inst France; *m* 3 May 1980 (m dis 1986), Dominic John Nevill, s of John Nevill, of Folkstone, Kent; 2 da (Abigail b 15 July 1982, Cordelia b 19 Oct 1984); *Career* Rowan Gallery London 1978–79, Francis Kyle Gallery London 1979–80, Bath Int Festival Contemporary Art Fair 1980–84, sec The Royal Photographic Soc Bath 1990–94 (admin 1985), head National Museum of Photography, Film & Television 1994–; *Recreations* art, literature, music; *Style*— Mrs Amanda Nevill; ✉ National Museum of Photography, Film & Television, Pictureville, Bradford BD1 1NQ (☎ 01274 727488)

NEVILL, Prof Bernard Richard; s of R G Nevill (d 1941); *b* 24 Sept 1934; *Educ* St Martin's Sch of Art, RCA; *Career* lectr: Shoreditch Coll 1954–56, Central Sch Art and Design 1957–60, St Martin's Sch of Art and RCA 1959–74; freelance illustrator 1956–60 (incl Good Housekeeping, Woman's Journal, Vogue, Harpers Bazaar), freelance journalist

1956–60 (incl Vogue, Sketch), designer then design dir Liberty Prints 1961–71, memb Advsy Panel Nat Dip Design 1964–66, art critic Vogue 1965–66, govr Croydon Coll Art 1966–67, designer and design dir Ten Cate Holland 1969–71, design conslt Cantoni Italy 1971–84, prof of textile design RCA 1984–89 (fell 1985); commissions and collections incl: Cotton Board Manchester 1950, For Liberty 1961–71, Verve 1960, Cravate, Islamic 1963, Jazz 1964, Tango 1966, Renaissance 1967, Chameleon 1969, Cantoni Casa 1977, Int Wool Secretariat 1975–77, English Country House Collection for Sekers Int 1981–82, Romanex de Boussac France 1982–87, Unitika Co Ltd Japan 1990–, Pierre Frey France 1991–, collection of furnishing textiles for Château de Bagnols France 1991–, collections of dress and furnishing textiles designed for DMC Texunion France 1992–, KBC Germany; designed costumes for: films (Genevieve 1953, Next to No Time 1955, The Admirable Crichton 1957), musicals (Marigold 1958), opera (Cosi fan Tutte Glyndebourne 1960); redesigned Long Gallery, British Embassy Washington 1982; cmmnd to restore interiors of Eastnor Castle Herefordshire 1990–, presently rebuilding the remaining wing and restoring the landscape of Fonthill Abbey; memb: Victorian Soc, Chelsea Soc; FRSA 1966–77, FSIA 1970–87, FCSD 1987; *Recreations* admiring well-built walls and buildings, passionate conservationist and environmentalist, tree worshipper; *Style*— Prof Bernard Nevill; ✉ West House, Glebe Place, London SW3 5JP; Fonthill Abbey, nr Salisbury, Wiltshire

NEVILL, Lady Rupert; Lady (Anne) Camilla Eveline; *née* Wallop; da of 9 Earl of Portsmouth (d 1984); *b* 12 July 1925; *Educ* Longstowe Hall; *m* 1944, Lord Rupert Nevill, CVO, JP, DL (d 1982), yr s of 4 Marquess of Abergavenny, sometime private sec to HRH The Duke of Edinburgh; 2 s (Guy b 1945, d 1993; Christopher b 1955), 2 da (Angela b 1948, Henrietta b 1964); *Career* served with WREN in London; pres: Regnl Arts Bd for Kent Surrey and Sussex (chm 1972–89), E Sussex and W Kent branch of NSPCC; dir Southern Television, former tstee Charities Aid Fndn, memb Reviewing Ctee on Export of Works of Art 1982–86, tstee Glyndebourne Arts Tst, chm Regnl Ctee Kent and E Sussex Nat Tst, vice pres Brighton Festival, tstee Royal Pavilion Brighton; *Style*— The Lady Rupert Nevill; ✉ 35 Upper Addison Gardens, London W14 (☎ 0171 603 4919/603 4957); Old House Farm, Glynde, Lewes, Sussex (☎ 01273 813706)

NEVILL, Maj-Gen Cosmo Alexander Richard; CB (1958), CBE (1954, OBE (Mil) 1943), DSO (1944); s of Maj Charles Nevill, DSO, OBE (d 1940), of Eccleston, Leamington Spa, and ggs of Charles Nevill, of Nevill Holt, Leics who married Lady Georgina Bingham sis of F M 3 Earl of Lucan; *b* 14 July 1907; *Educ* Harrow, Sandhurst; *m* 1934, Grania, da of Maj Guy Goodliffe, MC, of Birdstown, Co Donegal, and gda of Col Sir Frederick Shaw, 5 Bt, of Bushy Park, Co Dublin; 1 s (Capt Richard Nevill, m 1961 Caroline, da of Adm Sir Guy Grantham, GCB, CBE, DSO), 1 da (Charmian, m 1965 Capt David Gwynne-James); *Career* 2 Lt Royal Fusiliers 1927; served WWII 1941–43 on Gen Wavell's Staff Delhi and cmd 2 Bn Devonshire Regt D-Day Normandy 1944; on Mil Staff Ctee UN New York 1946–48; cmd 1 Bn Royal Fus 1950–51, cmdt Sch of Inf 1954–56, GOC 2 Inf Div 1956–58, Maj-Gen 1957, ret 1960; Col Royal Fusiliers (City of London Regt) 1959–63; memb W Suffolk CC 1962–67; hon lay canon St Edmundsbury Cathedral 1979–85; Freeman City of London 1962; *Recreations* painting; *Clubs* Army and Navy, I Zingari; *Style*— Maj-Gen Cosmo Nevill, CB, CBE, DSO; ✉ Holt, Edwardstone, Sudbury, Suffolk CO10 5PJ (☎ 01787 210428)

NEVILL, John Robert Ralph Austin; s of Frederick Reginald Nevill (d 1949), of Rosecroft, Newbury, Berks, and Jeanne, *née* Fageol (d 1975); *b* 15 Feb 1928; *Educ* Ampleforth; *m* 30 July 1955, Ann Margaret Mary, da of Archibald Corble (d 1944), of Cookham, Berks; 4 s (Dominic b 1957, Ralph b 1959, Christopher b 1962, Anthony b 1966), 2 da (Cecilia b 1956, Caroline b 1960); *Career* Lt DCLI 1947–48; dir: Nevill Developments 1956–, The Nevill Gallery; formerly: dir Family Housing Assoc Folkestone Area, chm and vice pres Canterbury and E Kent Branch English Speaking Union, chm and pres SE Region English Speaking Union, memb Ctee SE Arts Assoc; memb Ctee Canterbury Arts Cncl; hon memb Rutherford Coll Univ of Kent at Canterbury; Freeman City of London, Liveryman and memb Ct Worshipful Co of Gardeners; memb Hon Soc of Gray's Inn 1951; Knight of Honour and Devotion Br Assoc Sovereign Mil Order of Malta; *Recreations* travelling, fishing, photography, painting; *Clubs* Athenaeum, The English Speaking Union; *Style*— John Nevill, Esq; ✉ 5 Tite St, London SW3 4JU; 8 Radnor Cliff, Folkestone, Kent CT20 2JN (☎ 0171 352 7368/01303 248403); Nevill Gallery, 43 St Peter's St, Canterbury, Kent CT1 2BG (☎ 01227 765291)

NEVILLE, Dr Adam Matthew; CBE (1994), TD (1963); *b* 5 Feb 1923; *Educ* Univ of London (BSc, MSc, PhD, DSc), Univ of Leeds (DSc); *m* 29 March 1952, Mary Hallam, *née* Cousins; 1 s (Adam Andrew b 11 May 1955), 1 da (Elizabeth Louise b 5 Feb 1953); *Career* War Serv Middle East and Italy, Maj RETA; practising and academic engr 1950–, prof of civil engrg Univ of Leeds 1968–78, princ and vice chllr Univ of Dundee 1978–87, conslt and arbitrator 1987–, ptnr A & M Neville Engineering 1987–; pres Concrete Soc 1974–75, chm Ctee of Princs of Scottish Univs 1984–86, pres Cncl of Europe Ctee on Univs 1984–86; memb Advsy Cncl Br Library 1989–94, memb Nat Academics Policy Advsy Gp 1992–97, vice pres Royal Acad of Engineering (formerly Fellowship of Engineering) 1992–95; Freeman City of London 1977; memb: Worshipful Co of Fan Makers 1978, Bonnetmaker Craft of Dundee 1979; Hon LLD St Andrews 1987, hon memb American Concrete Inst 1986; OStJ 1983; FICE, FIStructE, FRSE 1979, FEng 1986; *Books* Properties of Concrete (1963, 1995), Basic Statistical Methods (with J B Kennedy, 1964, 1986), Creep of Concrete: Plain, Reinforced and Prestressed (1970), Structural Analysis: A Unified Classical and Matrix Approach (with A Ghali, 1977, 1996), Hardened Concrete: Physical and Mechanical Aspects (1971), High Alumina Cement Concrete (1975), Creep of Plain and Structural Concrete (with W H Dilger and J J Brooks, 1983), Concrete Technology (with J J Brooks, 1987); *Recreations* skiing, travel; *Clubs* Athenaeum, New (Edinburgh), Travelers' Century (Los Angeles); *Style*— Dr Adam Neville, CBE, TD, FRSE, FEng; ✉ 24 Gun Wharf, 130 Wapping High St, London E1 9NH (☎ 0171 265 1087)

NEVILLE, Dr Elizabeth Louise; da of Dr Adam Neville, CBE, of London, and Dr Mary Hallam, *née* Cousins; *b* 5 Feb 1953; *Educ* Univ of Oxford (MA), Univ of London (PhD); *children* 1 s (Matthew Edward Burbeck b 1983), 1 da (Katherine Mary Burbeck b 1985); *Career* joined Metropolitan Police 1973, transferred Thames Valley Police 1986, Asst Chief Constable Sussex Police 1991–94, Dep Chief Constable Northants Police 1994–; FRSA; *Recreations* skiing, cycling, riding, walking, sailing, opera; *Clubs* Reform; *Style*— Dr Elizabeth Neville; ✉ Northamptonshire Police, Constabulary Headquarters, Wootton Hall, Northampton (☎ 01604 700700)

NEVILLE, Gary; *b* 18 Feb 1975; *Educ* Elton HS Bury; *Career* professional footballer; Manchester United: Sch of Excellence 1986, signed schoolboy forms 1989, trainee 1991, first team debut Euro Cup v Torpedo Moscow 1992, League debut v Coventry May 1994, Premier League champions 1996, winners FA Cup 1996 (runners up 1995), winners Charity Shield 1996; England: debut v Japan June 1995, 16 caps (as at Jan 1997); *Recreations* golf; *Style*— Gary Neville; ✉ c/o Manchester United FC, Old Trafford, Manchester M16 0RA

NEVILLE, His Hon Judge (Eric) Graham; *b* 12 Nov 1933; *Educ* Kelly Coll Tavistock, Sidney Sussex Coll Cambridge; *m* 20 August 1966, Jacqueline Catherine; *Career* RAF Gen Duty Flying Offr 1952–54; recorder of Crown Ct 1975–80, circuit judge (Western Circuit) 1980–; Hon Air Cdre 3 (Co of Devon) Maritime HQ Unit RAuxAF 1995; *Recreations* yachting; *Clubs* Royal Western Yacht, Royal Fowey Yacht; *Style*— His Hon Judge Graham Neville; ✉ Exeter Crown Court, The Castle, Exeter

NEVILLE, Prof (Alexander) Munro; s of Alexander Munro Neville (d 1983), of Troon, Ayrshire, and Georgina Stewart, *née* Gerrard (d 1989); *b* 24 March 1935; *Educ* Univ of Glasgow (MB ChB, PhD, MD), Harvard Univ Boston, Univ of London (DSc), RCPath; *m* 5 Sept 1961, Anne Margaret Stroyan, da of Dr Hugh Black (d 1975), of Paisley; 1 s (Munro b 26 Nov 1964), 1 da (Judeth b 25 Nov 1963); *Career* sr lectr in pathology Univ of Glasgow 1967–70, res fell Inst of Cancer Res MRC London 1970–73, prof of pathology Univ of London 1973–85; Ludwig Inst for Cancer Res: dir 1975–85, dir Zurich and London 1985–92, sci sec and assoc dir 1992–; currently treas Royal Coll of Pathologists; FRCPath 1979 (MRCPath 1969); *Recreations* golf, gardening, history; *Clubs* Athenaeum, Banstead Downs; *Style*— Prof Munro Neville; ✉ 6 Woodlands Park, Boxhill, Tadworth, Surrey KT20 7JL (☎ 01737 844113, fax 01737 844287); Ludwig Institute for Cancer Research, 6th Floor, Glen House, Stag Place, London SW1E 5AG (☎ 0171 828 0202, fax 0171 828 5427)

NEVILLE, Philip (Phil); *b* 21 Jan 1977; *Educ* Elton HS Bury; *Career* professional footballer; Manchester Utd: Sch of Excellence 1988, signed schoolboy forms 1990, trainee 1993, first team debut FA Cup 3rd round v Wrexham 1995, Premier League debut v Manchester City Jan 1995, Premier League champions 1996, winners FA Cup 1996; England: Under 21 debut Toulon Tournament 1995 (6 caps), full debut v China May 1996; *Recreations* golf, cricket; *Style*— Phil Neville; ✉ c/o Manchester United FC, Old Trafford, Manchester M16 0RA

NEVILLE-JONES, Dame (Lilian) Pauline; DCMG (1996, CMG 1987); da of Roland Neville-Jones, RAMC (ka 1941), and Cecilia Emily Millicent Winn, *née* Rath, step da of Dr John Michael Winn; *b* 2 Nov 1939; *Educ* Leeds Girls' HS, Lady Margaret Hall Oxford (BA); *Career* HM Dip Serv 1963–96: joined FCO 1963, third sec Salisbury Rhodesia 1964–65, third sec (later second sec) Singapore 1965–68, FCO 1968–71 (dealing with Med), first sec Washington 1971–75, dep chef de cabinet (later chef de cabinet) to Christopher Tugendhat, Cmmn of Euro Communities Brussels 1977–82, sabbatical Royal Inst of Int Affrs London and Institut Francais des Relations Internationales Paris 1982–83, head of policy planning staff FCO 1983–87, min (econ) Bonn Embassy 1987–91 (min 1988–91), dep under sec for overseas and defence Cabinet Office 1991–94 (chm Jt Intelligence Ctee 1993–94), political dir FCO 1994–96; sr advsr to Carl Bildt, High Rep for the Civilian Peace Implementation for Bosnia Feb-July 1996; head of global business strategy NatWest Markets 1996–, chm NatWest Markets France 1996–; *Recreations* cooking, gardening, antiques; *Style*— Dame Pauline Neville-Jones, DCMG; ✉ NatWest Markets, 135 Bishopsgate, London EC2M 3UR (☎ 0171 648 3028)

NEVILLE-ROLFE, Lucy Jeanne; da of Edmund Neville-Rolfe, and Margaret Elizabeth, *née* Evans; sis of Marianne Neville-Rolfe, *qv*; *b* 2 Jan 1953; *Educ* St Mary's Shaftesbury and Cambridge, Somerville Coll Oxford (MA); *m* Richard John Packer; 4 s (Thomas Edmund b 21 June 1981, William Henry b 17 Aug 1984, Harold Charles b 24 Nov 1988, Samuel Inigo b 19 August 1994); *Career* MAFF 1973–92: private sec to Rt Hon John Silkin MP 1977–79, Euro Community policy on Sheepmeat and Milk 1979–86, head of Land Use and Tenure Div 1986–89, Food Safety Act Div 1989–90, head of Personnel 1990–92; memb Prime Minister's Policy Unit 1992–94, head Deregulation Unit Cabinet Office (formerly DTI) 1995–; non-exec dir: John Laing Construction 1991–92, Holloway White Allom 1991–92; *Recreations* cricket, racing, gardening, art, architecture, theatre; *Style*— Miss Lucy Neville-Rolfe; ✉ Deregulation Unit, Cabinet Office, Horse Guards Road, London SW1P 3AL (☎ 0171 270 3000)

NEVILLE-ROLFE, Marianne Teresa; da of Edmund Neville-Rolfe, of Ark Farm, Tisbury, Wiltshire, and Margaret Elizabeth, *née* Evans; sis of Lucy Neville-Rolfe, *qv*; *b* 9 Oct 1944; *Educ* St Mary's Convent Shaftesbury, Lady Margaret Hall Oxford (BA); *m* 16 Sept 1972 (m dis 1992), David William John Blake, *qv*; *Career* with CBI 1965–73 (head Brussels Office 1971–72); DTI: princ 1973, asst sec 1982, grade 3 under sec 1987; chief exec Civil Service Coll 1990–94, also prog dir Top Mgmnt Prog until 1994, regnl dir Govt Office for NW 1994–; FRSA; *Style*— Ms Marianne Neville-Rolfe; ✉ Government Office NW, Sunley Tower, Piccadilly Plaza, Manchester M1 4BA

NEVIN, Charles William; s of John Francis Nevin (d 1991), of St Helens, Lancs, and Jean Emmie, *née* Davey; *b* 27 March 1951; *Educ* Mount St Mary's Coll Derbys, Univ Coll Oxford; *m* 1988, Liv Barbara, da of William Bernard O'Hanlon; 2 s; *Career* Granada Television 1974–75, Liverpool Daily Post and Echo 1975–79, Daily and Sunday Telegraph 1979–88; freelance writer 1988–; diary ed Independent on Sunday 1993–; *Recreations* watching Rugby League and learning Spanish; *Clubs* Berkshire Press; *Style*— Charles Nevin, Esq; ✉ 10 St Stephen's Terrace, London SW8 1DH (☎ 0171 582 9932)

NEVIN, His Hon (Thomas) Richard; TD (1949 and Bar), JP (1965); s of late Thomas Nevin, JP, of Mirfield, Yorks; *b* 9 Dec 1916; *Educ* Bilton Grange, Shrewsbury Sch, Leeds Univ (LLB); *m* 1955 (m dis 1979), Brenda Micaela, da of of Dr B C Andrade-Thompson, MC; 1 s (and 1 decd); *Career* Lt-Col RA TA, London Bombardment, India and Burma; barr NE Circuit, asst recorder of Leeds 1961–64, recorder of Doncaster 1964–67, dep chm Yorks W Riding QS 1965–71 and E Riding 1968–71, chm Northern Agric Land Tbnl 1963–67 (dep chm 1961–63), a circuit judge (formerly judge of County Cts) 1967–84, a dep high court judge 1974–84; appointed by Min of Tport to conduct enquiries under Merchant Shipping Acts 1986–89; hon life memb Cncl of HM Circuit Judges; Freeman City of London; *Recreations* numismatics and our past; *Style*— His Hon Richard Nevin, TD, JP

NEVITT, Dr Peter John; s of Albert Nevitt, of Deganwy, N Wales, and Honoria Nevitt; *b* 20 Dec 1932; *Educ* Univ of Manchester (BSc), Univ of London (MSc); *m* 1959, Janet Willsher; 2 s (Gareth Alastair b 1961, David Richard b 1962), 1 da (Julia Mary b 1964); *Career* formerly dir Truck Ops Ford of Europe and vice chm Iveco Ford Truck Ltd; exec chm Cosworth Engineering (div of Vickers Group plc) until 1993 (ret), engineering conslt 1993–; currently dir Yearco Ltd; non-exec dir Motor Indust Research Assoc; visiting prof in engrg design Loughborough Univ (Hon DTech); memb Cncl Royal Acad of Engrg 1993– (chm Programmes Ctee 1993–95), memb Cncl Bureau and Tech Ctee FISITA, former memb Cncl IMechE; MRAeS, FIMechE, FEng 1986; *Clubs* golf, gardening; *Style*— Dr Peter Nevitt, FEng; ✉ Plas Eithin, Llys Helig Drive, Llandudno, Gwynedd LL30 2XB

NEW, Maj-Gen Sir Laurence Anthony Wallis; kt (1990), CB (1986), CBE (1980); s of Lt-Col Stanley William New, MBE (d 1956), and Constance Mary, *née* Marhsall (d 1970); *b* 25 Feb 1932; *Educ* King William's Coll Isle of Man, RMA Sandhurst; *m* 11 Aug 1956, Anna Doreen, da of Gp Capt Conrad Edward Howe Verity, OBE (d 1984); 2 s (Richard b 1961, Robert b 1969), 2 da (Amanda b 1958, Deborah Ann b 1966); *Career* cmmnd RTR 1952; served in Hong Kong, Germany, Malaya and Borneo, CO 4 RTR 1971–73, Bde Maj 20 Armd Bde 1971, def and mil attaché Tel Aviv 1974–77, Col GS MOD 1977–79, Brig GS MOD 1980–82, ACGS (Op Reqs) 1983–84, ACDS (Land Systems) MOD 1984–85; Lt Govr and Capt Gen of the Isle of Man and Pres of Tynwald 1985–90; Col Cmdt RTR 1986–93, vice pres TA & VRA 1985–90, county pres St John Ambulance 1985–90; chm: Prince's Tst IOM 1985–90, Bishop Barrow Tstees 1985–90; churchwarden St Peter upon Cornhill London 1987–95; pres: Soldiers' and Airmen's Scripture Readers Assoc 1986–, Manannan Festival of Music and the Arts 1987–, Assoc of Mil Christian Fellowships 1991–, Friends of Gaiety Theatre 1996–, Normand Veterans Assoc (IOM) 1996–, Mannin Art Gp 1996–; vice pres Offrs' Christian Union 1989–93; gen sec Offrs' Pensions Soc Ltd 1990–95, dir: OPS Investment Co Ltd 1990–, Victory Widows' Campaign 1994–95; patron Burma Star Assoc (IOM) 1995–; Freeman City of London

1985, Liveryman Worshipful Co of Glass Sellers 1985–91; CIMgt 1986 (FIMgt 1979); KStJ 1985; *Recreations* water colour painting, cello, gardening; *Clubs* Army and Navy; *Style*— Maj-Gen Sir Laurence New, CB, CBE; ✉ Ballaquark, Laxey, Isle of Man IM4 7PH (fax 01624 861933, e-mail generalnew@enterprise.net)

NEWALL, Christopher Stirling; s of Peter Stirling Newall, and Rosemary, *née* Marriage; *b* 8 April 1951; *Educ* The Downs Sch, Abbotsholme Sch, Courtauld Inst London (BA); *m* 10 Oct 1985, Jenifer Hylda, da of the late Sir Derek Ryan, 3 Bt; 2 s (Alfred Stirling b 8 Feb 1987, George Stirling b 20 Jan 1990); *Career* writer and art historian; conslt Dept of Victorian Paintings Sotheby's 1994–; research fell Univ of Northumbria 1996; Companion of Guild of St George 1995; *Books* Victorian Watercolours (1987), George Price Boyce (catalogue Tate Gall exhbn, 1987), The Art of Lord Leighton (1990), Victorian Landscape Watercolors (with Scott Wilcox, catalogue Yale Center for British Art, 1992), Victorian Painting (with Robin Hamlyn and Julian Treuherz, catalogue of exhbn at Neue Pinakothek Munich and Prado Madrid, 1993), John William Inchbold (catalogue Leeds City Art Gallery, 1993), The Grosvenor Gallery Exhibitions (1995), Frederic Leighton (contrib, catalogue Royal Acad of Arts, 1996); *Style*— Christopher Newall, Esq; ✉ 17 Lonsdale Square, London N1 1EN (☎ 0171 607 4360, fax 0171 607 5806)

NEWALL, 2 Baron (UK 1946); Francis Storer Eaton Newall; DL (London); s of Marshal of the RAF 1 Baron Newall, GCB, OM, GCMG, CBE, AM (d 1963, Chief of Air Staff during Battle of Britain); *b* 23 June 1930; *Educ* Eton, Sandhurst; *m* 1956, Pamela, da of Hugh Rowcliffe, TD, of Pinkney Park, Malmesbury (d 1978), by his 1 w, Margaret (da of Sir Henry Farrington, 6 Bt); 2 s, 1 da; *Heir* s, Hon Richard Newall; *Career* takes Cons whip in Lords; Capt 11 Hussars, served Germany, Malaya, Singapore, NI; adj Royal Glos Hussars; conslt and company dir; Cons whip and oppn front bench spokesman Lords 1976–79, fndr memb House of Lords All Pty Def Study Gp, del W Euro Union and Cncl of Europe 1983–, responsible for Farriers Registration Acts and Betting and Gaming Amendment (Greyhound Racing) Acts; led Parly visits to Cyprus, Oman, Bahrain, Qatar, Morocco; chm Br Greyhound Racing Bd, pres SPANA (Soc for Protection of Animals Abroad); friend of Romania; memb Ct of Assts Worshipful Co of Merchant Taylors, Liveryman Worshipful Co of Farriers; *Recreations* shooting, tennis, travel; *Clubs* Cavalry and Guards'; *Style*— The Rt Hon the Lord Newall, DL; ✉ Wotton Underwood, Aylesbury, Bucks (☎ 01844 238376); 18 Lennox Gdns, London SW1 (☎ 0171 589 9370, fax 0171 219 5979)

NEWALL, Sir Paul Henry; kt (1994), TD (1967), JP (City of London 1981), DL (Greater London 1977); s of Leopold Newall (d 1956), and Frances Evelyn, *née* Bean (d 1981); *b* 17 Sept 1934; *Educ* Harrow, Magdalene Coll Cambridge (MA); *m* 1 March 1969, Penelope Moyra, da of Sir Julian Ridsdale, CBE, *qv*; 2 s (Rupert b 1971, Jamie b 1973); *Career* Nat Serv 1953–55: cmmnd Royal Fusiliers, served Egypt and Sudan; TA 1955–70: Maj 1961, cmd City of London Co 5 Bn RRF 1967–70; chm City of London TA & VRA 1986–89, vice chm TAVRA for Gtr London 1989–95, Hon Col The London Regt 1995–; ptnr Loeb Rhoades & Co 1971–77; overseas dir: Shearson Loeb Rhoades (UK) 1979–81, Shearson American Express (UK) 1981–84; dir Shearson Lehman International Ltd 1985–93; exec dir: Shearson Lehman Hutton Securities 1988–90, Lehman Bros Securities 1990–92; sr advsr Lehman Bros 1992–; non-exec dir Guardian Royal Exchange plc 1995–; vice pres Inst of Export 1995–; tstee: Temple Bar Tst, City of London Endowment Tst for St Paul's Cathedral, Morden Coll; govr Mencap City Fndn, patron Samaritans Nat Appeal, vice pres City of London Br Red Cross 1986–, churchwarden St Stephen Walbrook; memb: Friends of St Paul's Cathedral, City Heritage Soc, Samuel Pepys Soc, Cncl City Univ; hon visiting magistrate HM Tower of London 1988–; City of London: one of HM's Lts 1975–, elected Ct of Common Cncl 1980–81, Alderman (Walbrook Ward) 1981–, Sheriff 1989–90, Lord Mayor of London 1993–94; Liveryman Worshipful Co of Gold and Silver Wyre Drawers 1980–, memb Guild of Freemen of the City of London 1988– (memb Ct 1988–91), memb Hon Co of Freeman of the City of London of N America; Hon Freeman Worshipful Co of Fuellers, Hon Freeman and Liveryman Worshipful Co of Marketors; Master Worshipful Co of Bakers 1990–91, pres Assoc of Livery Masters 1993/94–; hon memb Incorporation of Bakers of Glasgow and Burgess of the City of Glasgow 1995–; hon rep for City of Seoul, memb Partnership Korea Advsy Gp; Hon DLitt City Univ 1993; KStJ; *Books* Japan and the City of London (1996); *Recreations* fencing, fly fishing, water skiing, tennis, trees; *Clubs* City Livery, Walbrook Ward (pres), United Wards, East India, MCC; *Style*— Sir Paul Newall, TD, DL; ✉ c/o Guildhall, London EC2P 2EJ

NEWALL, Hon Richard Hugh Eaton; s and h of 2 Baron Newall, *qv*; *b* 19 Feb 1961; *m* 24 Aug 1996, Keira N, 2 da of Robert Glen, of Forest Hill, Oxford; *Style*— The Hon Richard Newall

NEWARK, Archdeacon of; *see:* Hawtin, Ven David Christopher

NEWARK, Quentin; s of Derek Newark, and Jean, *née* Thornhill; *b* 24 Sept 1961; *Educ* Purley HS for Boys, Kingston Poly (fndn course), Brighton Poly (BA); *Career* book designer: Mitchell Beazley Publishers 1985, Faber and Faber Publishers 1985–86; Pentagram Design: sr designer 1986–91, clients incl Faber and Faber, Santa Barbara Museum of Art, Washington Museum of Art, Asea Brown Boveri, V&A Museum (identity and signage); Atelier Design (ptnrship with John Powner): formed 1991, projects incl Br Rail exhibition on the environment, The Encylopedia of the 21st Century for Mitchell Beazley, work for Philips, Wiggins Teape and Arthur Anderson; memb 02 int environmental design gp; memb Sign Design Inst; lectured at Pembroke Coll Oxford and Epsom Sch of Art and Design; *Style*— Quentin Newark, Esq; ✉ 37 Kenilworth Rd, London E3 5RH (☎ 0181 981 6612); Atelier, 14 The Dove Centre, 109 Bartholomew Road, London NW5 2BJ (☎ 0171 284 2215)

NEWBERRY, Raymond Scudamore (Ray); OBE (1989); s of James Henry Newberry, of Westbury on Trym, Bristol, and Doris Ada, *née* Scudamore (d 1989); *b* 8 Feb 1935; *Educ* Bristol GS, Selwyn Coll Cambridge (BA), Univ of Leeds (DipTEFL), Univ of Bristol (DipEd); *m* 26 Aug 1967, Angelina, da of Odell Nance (d 1948), of South Carolina, USA; 1 s (Conrad b 1972), 1 da (Clare b 1969); *Career* Nat Serv Intelligence Corps 1953–55; lectr in English Univ of Baghdad 1959–62; Br Cncl: joined 1962, lectr Tehran 1963–64, educn offr Eastern India 1964–66, head Dept of English Advanced Teacher Trg Coll Winneba Ghana 1966–70, advsr Miny of Educn Singapore 1970–74, rep Colombia 1975–80, dir North and Latin America Dept 1980–82, dir America and Pacific Dept 1982–84, rep Australia 1984–89, dir Brazil 1990–94, ret; conslt London Film Cmmn 1996–; *Books* Between You and Me (with Alan Maley, 1970); *Recreations* bookbinding, golf; *Style*— Ray Newberry, Esq, OBE; ✉ Silverwood, 8 Wildwood Close, Woking, Surrey GU22 8PL

NEWBERY, Prof David Michael; s of Alan Newbery, of Gosport, Hants, and Betty, *née* Roche; *b* 1 June 1943; *Educ* Portsmouth GS, Trinity Coll Cambridge (scholar, MA, PhD); *m* 1975, Dr Terri Apter, da of Dr Nathaniel Apter; 2 da (Miranda b 1979, Julia b 1983); *Career* economist Treasy Tanzanian Govt 1965–66; Univ of Cambridge: asst lectr 1966–71, lectr 1971–86, reader in economics 1986–88, prof of applied economics and dir Dept of Applied Economics 1988–, professorial fell Churchill Coll 1988– (teaching fell 1965–88); div chief Public Economics Div World Bank 1981–83; res assoc Cowles Fndn Yale Univ 1969, assoc prof Stanford Univ 1976–77, visiting prof Princeton Univ 1985, visiting scholar IMF 1987, Ford visiting prof Univ of California Berkeley 1987–88, sr res fell Inst for Policy Reform 1990–; memb Environmental Economics Academic Panel DOE 1992–, pres Euro Economic Assoc 1996; Frisch medal Econometric Soc 1990, Harry Johnson prize Canadian Economics Assoc 1993; fell: Centre for Economic Policy Res 1984, Econometric Soc 1989; FBA 1991; *Books* Project Appraisal in Practice (jtly, 1976), The Theory of Commodity Price Stabilization: a study in the economics of risk (with J E Stiglitz, 1981), The Theory of Taxation for Developing Countries (ed, 1987), Hungary, An Economy in Transition (ed, 1993); *Recreations* squash, skiing; *Style*— Prof David Newbery, FBA; ✉ Department of Applied Economics, University of Cambridge, Sidgwick Avenue, Cambridge CB3 9DE (☎ 01223 335247, fax 01223 335299)

NEWBERY, Dr John; s of late Vickery John Newbery, and Grace Dorothy, *née* Smithson; *b* 8 April 1927; *Educ* Tiffin Sch, UCL (BSc, PhD); *m* 1, 1956 (m dis 1989), Wayne Poynton Kitching; 2 s (Michael, Christopher); m 2, 1991, Pamela Ann Church; *Career* engrg geologist Snowy Mountains Authy Aust 1952–56, chief geologist Binnie & Partners 1958–67, ptnr Howard Humphreys & Partners; consltg engrg geologist/dam panellist 1967–72 and 1980–; Cdr Order of Crown of Thailand 1980; FEng 1990, FICE, FASCE, FIWEM, FGS (vice pres 1982–84); *Clubs* RAC; *Style*— Dr John Newbery, FEng; ✉ Montrose, 19 Broomfield Ride, Oxshott, Leatherhead, Surrey KT22 0LP (☎ 01372 842266, fax 01372 844060)

NEWBIGGING, David Kennedy; OBE (1982), DL (Wilts 1993); s of David Locke Newbigging, CBE, MC (d 1948), and Lucy Margaret Newbigging (d 1970); *b* 19 Jan 1934; *Educ* Oundle; *m* 1968, Carolyn Susan, da of Geoffrey Band (d 1974); 1 s, 2 da; *Career* 2 Lt Nat Serv KOSB; Jardine Matheson & Co Ltd: joined 1954, dir 1967, md 1970, chm and sr md 1975–83; chm: Hongkong & Kowloon Wharf & Godown Co Ltd 1970–80, Hong Kong Land 1975–83 (also md), Hongkong Electric Holdings Ltd 1982–83 (dir 1975–83), Jardine Fleming Holdings Ltd 1975–83, Hong Kong Tourist Assoc 1977–82, Hong Kong General Chamber of Commerce 1980–82, Rentokil Group plc 1987–94 (dir 1986–94), Redfearn plc 1988, NM UK Limited 1990–93, Ivory and Sime plc 1992–95 (dir 1987–91), Maritime Transport Services Ltd 1993–95, Faupel Trading Group plc 1994– (dir 1989–93), Equitas Holdings Limited 1995–, Equitas Management Services Limited 1995–, Equitas Reinsurance Limited 1995–, Equitas Limited 1996–; dep chm: Provincial Group plc 1985–91 (dir 1984–91), Friends' Provident Life Office 1996– (dir 1993); dir: Hongkong & Shanghai Banking Corp 1975–83, Hongkong Telephone Co Ltd 1975–83, Rennies Consolidated Holdings Ltd 1975–83, Provincial Insurance plc 1984–86, Provincial Life Assurance Co Ltd 1984–86, The British Coal Corporation (formerly the National Coal Bd) 1984–87, CIN Management Ltd 1985–87, United Meridian Corporation (USA) 1987–, Wah Kwong Shipping Holdings Ltd (Hong Kong) 1992–, Market Bd Corporation of Lloyd's 1993–95; memb: Int Cncl Morgan Guaranty Tst Co of NY 1977–85, Hongkong Legislative Cncl 1978–82, Hongkong Exec Cncl 1980–84; tstee King Mahendra UK Tst for Nature Conservation 1988–; chm: Wilts Community Fndn 1991–, Cncl The Missions to Seamen 1993– (vice chm Cncl and chm Exec Ctee 1986–93); Liveryman Worshipful Co of Grocers; *Recreations* Chinese art, most outdoor sports; *Clubs* Boodle's, Hongkong (Hong Kong), The Royal Hong Kong Jockey; *Style*— David Newbigging, Esq, OBE, DL; ✉ Wah Kwong House, 9th Floor, 10 Albert Embankment, London SE1 7SP (☎ 0171 582 1234, fax 0171 582 5522)

NEWBOLD, Yve Monica; da of Thomas Peter Radcliffe (d 1963), and Anne Gertrude, *née* Flynn; *b* 6 July 1940; *Educ* Blessed Sacrament Convent Hove Sussex, Univ of London (LLB), Coll of Law; *m* 1958, Anthony Newbold; 3 s (Timothy b 1960, Jonathan b 1964, Toby b 1965), 1 da (Lorraine b 1959); *Career* admitted slr 1970, staff lawyer IBM (UK) 1968–71, chief staff counsel Rank Xerox 1972–79, int counsel Xerox Corporation USA 1979–82, euro counsel Walt Disney Productions Ltd 1982–86, co sec Hanson plc 1986–95, chief exec Pro Ned Ltd 1995–; non-exec dir British Telecommunications plc 1991–; govr London Business Sch 1990; memb: Sr Salary Review Body, Demos; *Style*— Mrs Yve Newbold; ✉ Pro Ned Ltd, Devonshire House, Mayfair Place, London W1X 5FH (☎ 0171 493 4567, fax 0171 493 4177)

NEWBON, Gary; s of Jack Newbon (d 1982), and Preeva, *née* Cooklin; *b* 15 March 1945; *Educ* Culford Sch Bury-St-Edmunds Suffolk; *m* 26 Oct 1973, Katharine Janet, da of Bernard While (d 1982), of Birmingham; 2 s (Laurence Jon b 16 Aug 1977, Neil Christie (twin) b 16 Aug 1977), 1 da (Claire Rosalie b 5 June 1975); *Career* journalist Jeacock's News Agency Cambridge 1964–67; sports writer: Hayter's Sports Agency, Westward TV Plymouth 1970–71 (sports presenter 1968–70); ATV Network Ltd: sports presenter 1971–74, sports presenter and ed 1974–77, sports writer 1977–81; controller of sport Central TV 1987– (head of sport 1982–87); ITV reporter: Olympic Games 1972, 1980 and 1988, World Cup Soccer 1974, 1982, 1986, 1990 and 1994; memb: Lord's Taverners, Variety Club of GB, SOS; *Books* Over the Sticks and Under Starters Orders (with late Michael Ayres, 1970 and 1971); *Recreations* jazz, blues, rock and roll, drinking champagne; *Style*— Gary Newbon, Esq; ✉ Central Independent Television plc, Broad St, Birmingham B1 2JP (☎ 0121 643 9898, fax 0121 616 1699, telex 338966)

NEWBOROUGH, 7 Baron (I 1776); Robert Charles Michael Vaughan Wynn; 9 Bt (GB 1742), DSC (1942); s of 6 Baron Newborough, OBE, JP, DL (d 1965); *b* 24 April 1917; *Educ* Oundle; *m* 1, 1945 (m dis 1971), Rosamund, da of Maj Robert Barbour, of Bolesworth Castle, Tattenhall, Cheshire; 1 s, 2 da; m 2, 1971, Jennifer, yst da of late Capt Cecil Allen, RN, and Lady (Eirene) Morgan; *Heir* s, Hon Robert Wynn; *Career* served 2 Lt 9 Lancers, 5 Inniskilling Dragoon Gds and Lt 16/5 Lancers 1935–39, invalided 1940, took part in Dunkirk evacuation as civilian, cmmnd RNVR, served in command MTB 74 St Nazaire raid 1942 (despatches and DSC, wounded, POW Colditz, escaped); farmer; High Sheriff Merioneth 1963; *Recreations* fishing, yachting; *Clubs* Naval & Military, Goat and Bembridge Sailing; *Style*— The Rt Hon the Lord Newborough, DSC; ✉ Rûg, Corwen, Clwyd, N Wales LL21 0EH (☎ 01490 412510; Estate Office: 01490 412153)

NEWBOUND, Maurice Ernest; s of Ernest Henry Newbound (d 1959), and Violet Lily, *née* Roberts (d 1969); *b* 13 April 1925; *m* 1, 22 March 1945 (m dis 1973), Ivy Christine, da of Charles Young; 1 s (David b 1952); m 2, 12 April 1975, Shirley Jean Nena, da of Arthur Ratcliffe; *Career* RAF 1943–45; md and chm: Westbourne International Holdings Ltd 1957–83, Westbourne Group Pty Ltd 1969–73, G S Estates Ltd 1974–; chm Swan House Special Events Ltd 1988–92; launched: Britain's first shopfitting magazine 1954, several pubns and exhibitions at home and abroad, still a conslt on several; pres: Advsy Cncl of IDD 1965–94, Natural Health Network 1982–; chm: Somerset Centre IOD 1979–81, Holistic Health Contact Gp 1984–, Advsy Cncl for UK Natural Health Week 1988–; memb: Parly Gp for Alternative and Complementary Med, Br Export Gp 1958–64, Ctee Somerset Rural Devpt Cmmn 1981–, Core Gp Whole Health Inst, Bristol Cancer Help Centre Cncl; vice pres Nat Consultative Cncl (now Br Complementary Medicine Assoc) 1991–; memb: Guild of Food Writers, Guild of Health Writers; FInstM 1977; *Books* Catering for Health and Special Diets; *Recreations* swimming, gardening; *Clubs* Victory; *Style*— Maurice Newbound, Esq; ✉ Chardstock House, Chard, Somerset TA20 2TL (☎ 01460 63229, fax 01460 63809)

NEWBURGH, 12 Earl of (S 1660); Filippo Giambattista Camillo Francesco Aldo Maria Rospigliosi; also Viscount Kynnaird and Lord Levingston (S 1660), Prince Rospigliosi (HRE 1668 by Emperor Leopold I and Papal 1854 by Pope Pius IX), 14 Prince of Castiglione (by the Sicilian cr of 1602, and a further cr of the kingdom of Italy 1897), 11 Duke of Zagarolo (Papal 1668), Marquis of Giuliana (Sicily 1543, It 1897), Count of Chiusa (Sic 1535, It 1897), Baron di Valcorrente e della Miraglia (Sic 1780, It 1897), Lord (Signore) of Aidone, Burgio, Contessa, and Trappeto (1854), conscribed Roman Noble (1854), and Patrician of Venice (1667), Genoa (1786) and Pistoia; s of 11 Earl of Newburgh (d 1986), and Donna Giulia, da of Don Guido Carlo dei Duchi Visconti di Modrone, Count of Lonate Pozzolo; *b* 4 July 1942; *m* 1972, Baronessa Donna Luisa, da of Count Annibale Caccia Dominioni; 1 da (Princess Benedetta Francesca Maria b 1974); *Heir* da, Mistress of Newburgh, b 4 June 1974; *Style—* Prince Rospigliosi; ✉ Piazza St Ambrogio 16, 20123 Milan, Italy

NEWBURY, Anthony Charles; s of Charles Renton Newbury (d 1986), of Aust, and Isabella Dawson, *née* Davie; *b* 19 Jan 1940; *Educ* Melbourne C of E GS, Univ of Melbourne (BDSc, LDS, MDSc, John Tomes medal in oral surgery, prize in orthodontics), DGDP RCS (Eng); *m* 1, 16 May 1964, Delia Kate Frances, da of Frank Kelynge Miles; 1 s (Andrew Charles b 9 May 1967), 1 da (Kim Frances b 9 Dec 1965); m 2, 4 Oct 1986, Brigitte, da of Hans Eigenberger (d 1990); *Career* pt/t sr lectr Dept of Anatomy and sr clinical demonstrator Dept of Restorative Dentistry Univ of Melbourne 1964–69, gen dental practice Melbourne 1963–64, specialist orthodontic practice Melbourne 1965–70, private practice Harley St London 1972–; fndr memb: The Oral Hygiene Centre 1977, Dental Diners Study Club 1968, Euro Dental Soc 1983; fndr and chm Br Dental Soc for Clinical Nutrition 1985; pres Int Acad of Oral Med and Toxicology; memb: Fedn Dentaire Internationale 1964–, Myofunctional Therapy Assoc of America, Soc of Orthobionomy, Br Soc for the Study of Orthodontics 1971–, Euro Orthodontic Soc 1970–; fndr tstee Oral Hygiene Fndn Charity 1978, fell Int Coll of Dentists 1980, invited memb Pierre Fauchard Acad 1987, assoc memb American Dental Assoc; Aust Dental Assoc: sec Dental Health Ctee 1966–69, memb Organising Ctee Nat Congress 1968; Br Dental Assoc: memb organising Ctee (World Congress 1974, Centenary Congress 1978), pres Metropolitan Branch 1982–83 (hon sec 1976–82); memb Cncl Odontological Section of Royal Soc of Medicine 1987–89, past cncllr Br Dental Health Fndn, past memb Chicago Dental Soc; *Books* contrib to Mercury and Other Toxic Metals in Humans (1989); *Recreations* tennis, golf, reading, art; *Clubs* Royal Soc of Med, Graduate Union, Hurlingham, Queens, Peninsula Country Golf, Cwlth Golf; *Style—* Anthony Newbury, Esq; ✉ 72 Harley St, London W1N 1AE (☎ 0171 580 3168, fax 0171 436 0959)

NEWBY, (George) Eric; CBE (1994), MC; s of George Arthur Newby, and Hilda, *née* Pomroy; *b* 6 Dec 1919; *Educ* St Paul's; *m* 1946, Wanda, da of Viktor Skof; 1 s, 1 da; *Career* author; Dorland advertising agency 1936–38, apprentice and ordinary seaman 4 masted Finnish barque Moshulu 1938–39, served Black Watch and Special Boat Section 1939–45 (POW 1942–45), women's fashion business 1946–56 (with Worth Paquin 1955–56), Secker & Warburg 1956–59, central buyer of model dresses John Lewis Partnership 1959–63, travel ed The Observer and gen ed Time Off Books 1964–73; travels and explorations: explored in Nuristan and made an unsuccessful attempt to climb Mir Samir in Afghan Hindu Kush 1956, descended Ganges with wife 1963; memb Assoc of Cape Horners; Hon LLD Bournemouth Univ 1994, hon doctorate Open Univ 1996; FRSL, FRGS; *Books* The Last Grain Race (1956), A Short Walk in the Hindu Kush (1958), Something Wholesale (1962), Slowly Down the Ganges (1966), Time Off in Southern Italy (1966), Grain Race: Pictures of Life Before the Mast in a Windjammer 1968, The Wonders of Britain (jt author, 1968), The Wonders of Ireland (jt author, 1969), Love and War in the Apennines (1971), The World of Evelyn Waugh (jt author, 1973), Ganga (with photographs by Raghubir Singh, 1973), World Atlas of Exploration (1975), Great Ascents (1977), The Big Red Train Ride (1978), A Traveller's Life (1982), On the Shores of the Mediterranean (1984), A Book of Travellers' Tales (1985), Round Ireland in Low Gear (1987), What the Traveller Saw (1989), A Small Place in Italy (1994), A Merry Dance Around the World (1995); *Recreations* walking, cycling; *Clubs* Garrick; *Style—* Eric Newby, Esq, CBE, MC, FRSL; ✉ Pine View House, 4 Pine View Close, Chilworth, Surrey GU4 8RS (☎ 01483 571430)

NEWBY, (Percy) Howard; CBE (1972); s of Percy Newby (d 1961), of Wendover, Bucks, and Isobel Clutsam, *née* Bryant (d 1980); *b* 25 June 1918; *Educ* Hanley Castle GS Worcester, St Paul's Coll Cheltenham; *m* 12 July 1945, Joan, da of Harry Charles Thompson (d 1965), of Wendover, Bucks; 2 da (Sarah (Mrs Schenk) b 1947, Katharine (Mrs Sinclair) b 1963); *Career* RAMC 1939–42; lectr Cairo Univ 1942–46; BBC Radio 3 (formerly the Third Programme) 1958–78: joined as controller 1958, dir of programmes 1971–75, md 1975–78; chm English Stage Company 1978–85; Atlantic Award for Literature 1946, Somerset Maugham Prize 1948, Yorkshire Post Fiction Award 1968, Booker Prize 1969; memb Soc of Authors 1947; *Books* A Journey to the Interior (1945), The Picnic of Sakkara (1955), Something to Answer For (1968), Saladin in his Time (1983), Coming In With The Tide (1991), Something About Women (1995); *Style—* Howard Newby, Esq, CBE; ✉ Garsington House, Garsington, Oxford OX44 9AB (☎ 01865 361420)

NEWBY, Prof Howard Joseph; CBE (1995); s of Alfred Joseph Newby, and Constance Annie, *née* Potts; *b* 10 Dec 1947; *Educ* John Port GS Etwall Derbyshire, Atlantic Coll Glamorgan, Univ of Essex (BA, PhD); *m* 4 July 1970, Janet Elizabeth; 2 s (Stephen b 1980, Jake b 1983); *Career* Univ of Essex: lectr in sociology 1972–75, sr lectr 1975–79, reader 1979–83, prof of sociology 1983–88; dir ESRC Data Archive 1983–88, prof of sociology and rural sociology Univ of Wisconsin Madison USA 1980–83; visiting appts: Univ of NSW Sydney 1976, Univ of Newcastle upon Tyne 1983–84; chm ESRC 1988–94, vice chllr Univ of Southampton 1994–; memb Rural Devpt Cmmn, chm Centre for Exploitation of Science and Technol 1995–; *Books* incl: The Deferential Worker (1977), Green and Pleasant Land? (2 edn, 1985), Country Life (1987), The Countryside in Question (1988); jtly: Community Studies (1971), Property Paternalism and Power (1978), The Problem of Sociology (1983), Social Class in Modern Britain (1988); *Recreations* family life, gardening, Derby county, railways; *Clubs* Athenaeum; *Style—* Prof Howard Newby, CBE; ✉ Birchwood, Heatherlands Road, Chilworth, Southampton, Hants SO16 7JD; University of Southampton, Highfield, Southampton SO17 1BJ (☎ 01703 592801)

NEWBY, John; s of Harry Newby, of Garforth, Leeds, and Ann Newby; *b* 17 Dec 1939; *Educ* St Anne's Sch Leeds, City HS Leeds; *m* 28 Sept 1963, Margaret Ann, da of Andy Wilson, of Scarborough; 2 da (Helen b 31 Aug 1966, Carmel b 28 July 1968); *Career* dir Wiggins Plant Ltd 1983–; chm and md: Wiggin Gee Group Ltd 1996– (md 1988–), Wiggin Gee Construction 1996– (md 1991–); FCIOB; *Recreations* golf, philately, gardening; *Clubs* London Rugby, Chelsea; *Style—* John Newby, Esq; ✉ Wiggins Gee Group, 10 and 11 Argent Court, Sylvan Way, Southfields Business Park, Basildon, Essex SS15 6TG (☎ 01268 541654)

NEWCASTLE, 10 Bishop of (1882) 1981–; Rt Rev Andrew Alexander Kenny Graham; patron of the Archdeaconries of Northumberland and Lindisfarne, four residentiary Canonries, the Hon Canonries, and seventy-five livings; the see of Newcastle was founded in May 1882; s of Andrew Harrison Graham (d 1954), and Magdalene Graham (d 1955); *b* 7 Aug 1929; *Educ* Tonbridge, St John's Coll Oxford; *Career* chaplain and lectr Worcester Coll Oxford 1958–70 (fell and tutor 1960–70), warden Lincoln Theol Coll 1970–77, bishop suffragan of Bedford 1977–81; chm: Advsy Cncl for Church's Ministry 1983–87, Doctrine Cmmn 1987–95; hon fell: St John's Coll Oxford, Worcester Coll Oxford; DD (Lambeth); *Recreations* hill walking; *Clubs* Utd Oxford and Cambridge; *Style—* The Rt Rev the Lord Bishop of Newcastle; ✉ Bishop's House, 29 Moor Road South, Gosforth, Newcastle upon Tyne NE3 1PA (☎ 0191 285 2220)

NEWCOMBE, Barry; s of Ronald William Newcombe (d 1991), of Northampton, and Doris May, *née* Underwood (d 1991); *b* 21 Dec 1939; *Educ* Northampton GS; *m* 30 Dec 1967, Maureen, da of Douglas Brooks; 1 s (Andrew James b 1 Nov 1970), 1 da (Kerry Margaret b 18 June 1968); *Career* sports writer; trainee journalist then rugby corr Chronicle and Echo Northampton 1957–64, staff writer Hayter's Agency 1964–65; rugby and tennis corr: Evening Standard 1965–84, Sunday Express 1984–; former: chm Rugby Writers' Club, press offr Teddington Soc; treas Lawn Tennis Writers' Assoc (former chm); *Books* Carling's England (1991), Upfront with Jeff Probyn (1993); *Recreations* woodland studies; *Clubs* Northampton FC (vice pres), Harlequin FC, Rugby Writers', Lawn Tennis Writers' Assoc, Boxing Writers'; *Style—* Barry Newcombe, Esq; ✉ Sunday Express, Ludgate House, 245 Blackfriars Rd, London SE1 9UX (☎ 0171 922 7305, fax 0171 922 7964, car 0836 728510)

NEWCOMBE, John Fernley; s of Arthur Fernley Newcombe (d 1978), of Worksop, Notts, and Norah Kathleen Newcombe; *b* 12 May 1928; *Educ* King Edward VI Sch Retford, Trinity Coll Cambridge (MA), Bart's London (MB MChir); *m* 4 July 1953, Barbara Joan, da of Charles Arnold Brittain (d 1979), of Dore, Sheffield; 1 s (Guy Charles Fernley b 1962), 1 da (Alyson Clare b 1960); *Career* conslt surgn Central Middx Hosp London 1965–93 (ret), sub dean Middx Hosp Med Sch 1970–76; pres Med Soc of London 1986–87; FRCS (past memb Ct of Examiners); *Recreations* golf, gliding, painting; *Style—* John Newcombe, Esq; ✉ 36 Sandy Lodge Rd, Rickmansworth, Herts WD3 1LJ (☎ 01923 822370)

NEWELL, Prof Alan Francis; *b* 1 March 1941; *Educ* St Philip's GS, Univ of Birmingham; *m* 31 July 1965, Margaret Eleanor, *née* Morgan; 1 s (David b 1976), 2 da (Anna b 1968, Catherine b 1969); *Career* res engr Standard Telecommunication Laboratories 1965–69, lectr in electronics Univ of Southampton 1969–80; Univ of Dundee: NCR prof of electronics and microcomputer systems and dir Microcomputer Centre 1980–, dep princ 1993–95, head of Applied Computer Studies Div Dept of Mathematics and Computer Science 1995–; memb Advsy Bd Coll of Occupational Therapy; hon fell Coll of Speech and Language Therapists; FIEE, FBCS, FRSE 1992; *Recreations* family life, sailing; *Clubs* Wormit Boating; *Style—* Prof Alan Newell, FRSE; ✉ Applied Computer Studies Division, Microcentre, Department of Mathematics and Computer Science, The University, Dundee DD1 4HN, Scotland (☎ 01382 344145, fax 01382 345509, e-mail afn@mcs.dundee.ac.uk)

NEWELL, Christopher William Paul; s of Lt-Col Nicolas Gambier Newell (d 1980), and Edith Alice, *née* Edgill (d 1984); *b* 30 Nov 1950; *Educ* Wellington, Univ of Southampton (LLB); *Career* called to the Bar Middle Temple 1973, in private practice 1973–75; sr legal asst: Dept of Dir of Public Prosecutions 1978–79 and 1983–86 (legal asst 1975–78), Law Offr's Dept 1979–83; asst DPP 1986, branch crown prosecutor Crown Prosecution Serv 1986–87, asst legal sec Law Offr's Dept 1987–89, dir of headquarters casework Crown Prosecution Serv 1989–93, dir of casework Crown Prosecution Serv 1993–96, dir of casework evaluation Crown Prosecution Serv 1996–; *Recreations* sport, travel; *Clubs* RAC; *Style—* Christopher Newell, Esq; ✉ Crown Prosecution Service, 50 Ludgate Hill, London EC4M 7EX (☎ 0171 273 1226, fax 0171 329 8167)

NEWELL, Frances; *m* John Sorrell, *qv*; 3 c; *Career* fndr and co chm Newell and Sorrell Ltd (identity and design conslts) 1976–; judge: BBC Design Awards, D&AD Awards; chair City & Guilds Nat Advsy Ctee for Craft Design and Art 1994–96; memb: City & Guilds Sr Awards Ctee, Bd Royal Acad Enterprises, Exec Ctee Mencap Blue Sky Appeal, Colour Gp; FRSA, FCSD; *Awards* seven D&AD Design Effectiveness Awards, five Silver D&AD Awards, five Clios, five Gold Awards NY Festival, one Silver Award NY Festival, Eurobest Award, two Art Director's Club of Euro Awards, two Br Environment and Media Awards, two Mktg Design Awards; *Style—* Frances Newell; ✉ Newell & Sorrell Ltd, 4 Utopia Village, Chalcot Road, London NW1 8LH (☎ 0171 722 1113, fax 0171 722 0259)

NEWELL, Rosemary Anne (Romy); da of John Eric Crewe (d 1990), of Orton House, Lower Penn, Wolverhampton, and Rachael, *née* Kemp; *b* 18 May 1951; *Educ* Headington Sch Oxford, Wolverhampton Business Coll (Dip Business Studies), Welsh Sch of Occupational Therapy (Dip Coll of Occupational Therapists), Univ of Southampton (Chest Heart and Stroke Assoc scholar, Postgrad Dip); *m* 1 June 1991, Paul Newell; 1 s (Ashley Fala Christian b 15 May 1992); *Career* basic grade occupational therapist New Cross Hosp Wolverhampton 1972–73, sr II occupational therapist Rivermead Rehabilitation Centre Oxford 1975–76 (basic grade 1973–75), project worker Equipment for the Disabled Oxford RHA Feb-May 1976, head IV occupational therapist Mary Marlborough Lodge Oxford 1978–80 (sr II 1976–78), research fell Univ of Southampton 1980–81, freelance seating conslt 1981–83; sr I occupational therapist: Westerlea Sch for Spastics Edinburgh Jan-Sept 1982, St Columba's Hospice Edinburgh 1982–83; head III occupational therapist City Hosp Edinburgh 1984–86 (locum sr I occupational therapist 1983–84), head II occupational therapist Stoke Mandeville Hosp Aylesbury 1986–90, proprietor Tyneholm House Nursing Home East Lothian 1986–, freelance rehabilitation conslt and personal injury claims cost assessor 1990–; fndr memb Soc for Tissue Viability 1981–; former memb: DHSS Wheelchair Review Ctee, Coll of Occupational Therapists Specialisation Ctee, HCC/40 (Wheelchairs) BSI; former treas Oxford Regnl Gp of Occupational Therapists; former chm: Oxford Area Gp of Occupational Therapists, Scottish Res Special Interest Gp; former advsr West German Govt Wheelchair Technol Gp; clinical reviewer: Br Jl Occupational Therapy, Gerontology Jl; professional advsr McColl Ctee; memb Biological Engineering Soc 1982, Postgrad Dip in Rehabilitation Studies (Univ of Southampton), memb Coll of Occupational Therapist (DipCOT) 1972, State Registered occupational therapist 1972; pioneer and developer of methods and equipment to improve comfort of the wheelchair bound and to prevent sitting induced pressure sores; *Books* The Hospital Wheelchair (1981), Pressure Sores: Prevention and Treatment (contrib 1983), Wheelchairs - A Guide to Clinical Prescripton (with E Williams, H Hill & G Cochrane, 1982), author of numerous articles in various learned jls; *Recreations* boating, gardening, travelling; *Clubs* Ski Club of GB; *Style—* Mrs Romy Newell; ✉ Rathburne House, Longformacus, Duns, Berwickshire TD11 3PG (☎ 01361 890291, fax 01361 890605); Tyneholm House Nursing Home, Pencaitland, East Lothian EH34 5DJ (☎ 01875 340708, fax 01875 341240)

NEWENS, (Arthur) Stanley; MEP (Lab) London Central (majority 25,059); s of Arthur Ernest Newens (d 1977), of Loughton, Essex, and Celia Jenny, *née* Furssedonn (d 1966); *b* 4 Feb 1930; *Educ* Buckhurst Hill Co HS, UCL (BA); *m* 1, 1954, Ann (d 1962), da of John Barlow Sherratt (d 1966), of Stoke-on-Trent; 2 da; m 2, 1966, Sandra Christina, da of John Arthur McMullen Frith, of Chingford; 1 s, 2 da; *Career* miner (coalface worker) 1952–56, teacher 1956–64 and 1970–74; MP: Epping (Lab) 1964–70, Harlow (Lab and Co-op) 1974–83; chm Liberation (formerly Movement for Colonial Freedom) 1967–92 (now pres); former memb Central Exec Ctee Co-op Union and Exec Ctee Co-op Pty, pres London Co-op Soc 1977–81 (dir 1971–77); MEP (Lab) London Central 1984–; chm: PLP Foreign Affrs Ctee 1982–83, Tribune Gp of Lab MPs 1982–83, Br Labour Gp in Euro Parl 1985–87; pres Euro Parly Delgn to Central America and Mexico 1995–96; organising sec Harlow Cncl for Vol Servs 1983–84; author of several books and pamphlets on politics and local history; *Recreations* family, reading, historical research, gardening; *Style—* Stanley Newens, Esq, MEP; ✉ The Leys, 18 Park Hill, Harlow, Essex (☎ 01279 420108)

NEWEY, Adrian Martin; s of Richard Martin Newey, of Stratford-on-Avon, and Joan Edwina, *née* Calvert; *b* 26 Dec 1958; *Educ* Repton Sch, Leamington Coll of Further Educn (OND), Univ of Southampton (BSc); *m* 1, 13 Aug 1983 (m dis 1991), Amanda, *née* Hitchens; 2 da (Charlotte Katie b 28 Aug 1986, Hannah Louise b 3 Feb 1989); m 2, 1 Aug 1992, Marigold Phillippa, da of Peter Proudfoot; 1 da (Imogen Victoria b 30 Aug 1993); *Career* race car designer; aerodynamicist Formula 1 project Fittipaldi 1980–82; March Engineering: race engr Formula 2 1982, designer American series sports racing car 1982–84 (won championship 1983 and 1984), designer and race engr Indycars USA

1984–87 (won Indianapolis 500 each year); tech dir Formula 1 March Racing 1987–90, chief designer Formula 1 Williams Grand Prix Engineering 1990– (won Drivers' Championship 1992 and 1993, Constructors' Championship 1992, 1993 and 1994); *Recreations* motorcycling, tennis; *Clubs* Jaguar Drivers, Bimota Owners; *Style*— Adrian Newey, Esq; ✉ Williams Grand Prix Engineering Ltd, Grove, Wantage, Oxfordshire (☎ 01235 777700)

NEWHOUSE, Archie Henry; MBE (1995); s of George Newhouse (d 1982), of Walthamstow, London, and Mildred Louise, *née* Goltenboth (d 1988); *b* 4 March 1933; *Educ* Leyton County HS; *m* 11 Nov 1953, Vera May, da of William Blow (d 1944), of Tottenham, London; 3 s (Colin b 1946 (by adoption), Douglas b 1955, David b 1956), 1 da (Vivienne b 1947 (by adoption)); *Career* cricket corr Sports Weekly 1950–53, sports editor West Herts Post 1953–55; causal sub-ed 1953–65: Reynolds News, Daily Express, News of the World; Greyhound Express: chief sub ed 1956–60, ed 1960–65; greyhound ed Sporting Life 1965–84; National Greyhound Racing Club Ltd: dep sec to sec 1985–87, chief exec 1987–95; chief exec British Greyhound Racing Bd 1987–95, dir British Greyhound Racing Fund 1992–95, memb Cncl World Greyhound Racing Fedn 1988–96 (sec gen 1990–93), sec to tstees Retired Greyhound Tst 1987–95; memb NUJ 1950– (elected life memb 1996); *Recreations* French provincial life, writing, travel, photography; *Style*— Archie Newhouse, Esq, MBE; ✉ Bezut, 30700 Baron, France (☎ 00 33 66 22 41 82)

NEWHOUSE, Ernest George; s of Herbert Henry Newhouse (d 1970), and Ilse Therese, *née* Frank; *b* 16 Dec 1937; *Educ* Merchant Taylors' Northwood, St John's Coll Oxford (scholar, MA, MSc); *m* 26 July 1969, Jean, da of Graham William Gready (d 1984); 1 s (Richard b 1970), 1 da (Caroline b 1973); *Career* Unilever 1961–68, fin analyst W R Grace Ltd 1969–73, fin mangr Wallington Weston & Co (Marley Tile Gp) 1973–78, head of fin BBC Bristol 1978–82, chief accountant BBC World Serv 1982–93, fin controller BBC World Service 1993–94, fin dir Barbican Centre 1996–; dir and sec People's Voices (charitable co) 1995–, memb Chesham Bois PC 1995–; *Recreations* travel, piano, astronomy; *Clubs* Amersham and Wells Lions; *Style*— Ernest Newhouse, Esq; ✉ Capesthorne, 80 Bois Lane, Chesham Bois, Amersham, Bucks HP6 6BZ (☎ 01494 726915)

NEWING, Chief Constable John Frederick; QPM (1988); *b* 1 March 1940; *Educ* Kettering GS, Univ of Leeds (BA); *m* 28 Sept 1963, Margaret Newing; 2 s (Stephen b 1966, Matthew b 1970), 1 da (Jacqueline b 1975); *Career* Barclays Bank 1958–62; Metropolitan Police: Constable Limehouse 1963, Constable Wallington 1963–67, Sergeant Wandsworth Common 1967 and 1968, Special Course Staff Coll 1967–68, Station Sergeant Battersea 1968–69, Inspr Kingston 1969, Bramshill scholarship to Univ of Leeds 1969–72, Inspr Holborn 1972–74, Chief Inspr Community Relations Branch 1974–77, Supt Staff Offr to the Cmmr 1977–80, Chief Supt Marylebone 1980–81, Sr Cmd Course Staff Coll 1981, Cmdt Recruit Trg Sch 1981–82, Cdr Community Relations Branch 1982–84, Cdr Public Order Branch 1984–85, Dep Asst Cmmr No 2 Area 1985, Dep Asst Cmmr No 6 Area 1985–87, ldr of team for devpt of user requirement for nat police computer Police Nat Computer Orgn 1987–90, Chief Constable Derbyshire Constabulary 1990–; *Style*— Chief Constable John Newing, QPM; ✉ Derbyshire Constabulary HQ, Butterley Hall, Ripley, Derbyshire DE5 3RS (☎ 01773 570100)

NEWINGTON, Sir Michael John; KCMG (1993, CMG 1982); s of John Tompsett Newington, of Spalding, Lincs, and Grace, *née* Lumley (d 1990); *b* 10 July 1932; *Educ* Stamford Sch, St John's Coll Oxford (MA, Swimming half blue); *m* 29 Dec 1956, Nina, da of Richard Gordon-Jones (d 1940); 1 s (Nicholas Gordon Tompsett b 1962), 1 da (Nina Michelle b 1958); *Career* Nat Serv Pilot Offr RAF 1951–52; HM Dip Serv: joined 1955, Economic Survey Section Hong Kong 1957–58, resigned 1959; Metals Div ICI 1959–60; rejoined HM Dip Serv 1960, second then first sec (economic) British Embassy Bonn 1961–65, first sec British High Cmmn Lagos 1965–68, asst head Sci & Technol Dept FCO 1968–72, cnsllr (sci & technol) Bonn 1972–75, cnsllr and consul gen Tel Aviv 1975–78, head Rep of Ireland Dept FCO 1978–81, HM consul gen Düsseldorf 1981–85; HM ambassador: Caracas and Santo Domingo 1985–87, Brasilia 1987–92; ret 1992; *Recreations* golf, gardening; *Style*— Sir Michael Newington, KCMG; ✉ Inces, Scaynes Hill, West Sussex RH17 7NG (☎ 01444 831348, fax 01444 831449)

NEWIS, Kenneth; CB (1967), CVO (1970, MVO 1958); s of Herbert Thomas Newis (d 1943), of Manchester, and Gladys, *née* Lindop (d 1961); *b* 9 Nov 1916; *Educ* Manchester GS, St John's Coll Cambridge (MA); *m* 1943, Kathleen, da of John Barrow (d 1977), of Davenport, Cheshire; 2 da (Gillian, Margaret); *Career* former civil servant: HM Office of Works etc 1938–70, sec Scot Devpt Dept Scot Office 1973–76, ret 1976; pres Queen's Hall (Edinburgh) Ltd 1992– (fndr chm 1977); vice chm Cockburn Assoc (Civic Tst Edinburgh) until 1994; FRSAMD 1995; *Recreations* music; *Clubs* New (Edinburgh); *Style*— Kenneth Newis, Esq, CB, CVO; ✉ 10/9 St Margaret's Place, Thirlestane Road, Edinburgh EH9 1AY (☎ 0131 447 4138)

NEWLAND, Prof David Edward; s of Robert William Newland (d 1979), of Knebworth, Herts, and Marion Amelia, *née* Dearman (d 1993); *b* 8 May 1936; *Educ* Alleyne's Sch Stevenage, Selwyn Coll Cambridge (MA, ScD), MIT (ScD); *m* 18 July 1959, Patricia Frances, da of Philip Mayne, of Marton, N Yorkshire; 2 s (Andrew David William b 1961, Richard David Philip b 1963); *Career* English Electric Co London 1957–61, instr and asst prof MIT 1961–64, lectr (later sr lectr) Imperial Coll London 1964–67, prof of mechanical engrg Univ of Sheffield 1967–76; Univ of Cambridge: prof of engrg (1875) 1976–, fell Selwyn Coll 1976–, currently head Dept of Engrg; memb Royal Cmmn on Environmental Pollution 1984–89, visitor Tport and Road Res Laboratory 1990–92, memb Engrg Cncl Working Party on Engrs and Risk Issues 1991–94, cncl memb Royal Acad of Engrg 1985–88, govr St Paul's Schs 1978–93, churchwarden Ickleton 1979–87; FEng 1982, FIMechE, FIEE; *Books* An Introduction to Random Vibrations, Spectral and Wavelet Analysis (3 edn, 1993), Mechanical Vibration Analysis and Computation (1989); *Recreations* music, jogging (London marathon etc), golf; *Clubs* Athenaeum; *Style*— Prof David Newland, FEng; ✉ Cambridge University Engineering Department, Trumpington St, Cambridge CB2 1PZ (☎ 01223 332670, fax 01223 359153)

NEWLAND, Peter John; s of Alec John Newland, of Stratford-upon-Avon, and Mary Monica, *née* Leahy (d 1995); *b* 30 March 1943; *Educ* Douai Sch; *m* 29 June 1969, Philippa Ernestine Marshall, da of Philip Marshall Healey; 3 da (Isabel Louise Cave b 12 June 1971, Joanna Lucy b 20 July 1974, Susannah Elizabeth b 29 March 1981); *Career* articled clerk Clement Keys & Son Birmingham 1960–66, qualified chartered accountant 1966, Peat Marwick Mitchell & Co Birmingham 1966–68, fin planner Unbrako Limited Coventry 1968–70, mangr Arthur Young McClelland Moores & Co Birmingham 1970–75, ptnr Ernst & Young Bristol 1975–93, finance admin mangr John Cabot CTC 1993–; *Recreations* golf, tennis, bridge; *Style*— Peter Newland, Esq; ✉ The Cottage, Northfields, Lansdown, Bath BA1 5TN (☎ 01225 315143)

NEWLANDS, David Baxter; s of George Frederick Newlands (d 1981), and Helen Fredericka Newlands; *b* 13 Sept 1946; *Educ* Edinburgh Acad; *m* 31 March 1973, Susan Helena, da of Ernest Ferguson Milne, OBE, of Walton on the Hill, Surrey; 2 s (Edward b 27 June 1981, Andrew b 27 Sept 1983), 2 da (Katharine b 11 Jan 1977, Jennifer b 17 Nov 1978); *Career* ptnr Touche Ross and Co 1977–86 (joined 1963), fin dir Saatchi and Saatchi plc 1986–89, fin dir GEC plc 1989–; FCA 1969; *Recreations* golf, bridge; *Clubs* RAC, Walton Heath Golf, Sutton and Epsom RFC; *Style*— David Newlands, Esq; ✉ The General Electric Company plc, 1 Stanhope Gate, London W1A 1EH (☎ 0171 493 8484)

NEWLANDS, Prof Edward Stewart; s of Harold James Newlands (d 1977), of Burghfield Common, nr Reading and Jersey, and Janet Paul, *née* Stewart (d 1992); *b* 10 June 1942; *Educ* King's Sch Bruton Somerset, Exeter Coll Oxford (open scholar, BA), Middx Hosp Med Sch (univ scholar, BM BCh), PhD (London); *m* 1965, Elizabeth Ann, da of E Ronald Raworth; *Career* house physician Middx Hosp then house surgn St Charles' Hosp London 1967, SHO Royal Northern Hosp London 1968, house physician Brompton Hosp London and locum registrar Royal Marsden Hosp 1969, research asst Dept of Immunology Middx Hosp 1970–73, lectr in clinical oncology and hon sr registrar Westminster Hosp 1973–74; Charing Cross Hosp: reader in med oncology and hon conslt physician Dept of Med Oncology 1988–90 (lectr and hon sr registrar 1974–76, sr lectr and hon consit physician 1977–88), dir Dept of Health Trophoblastic Disease Unit 1990–, dir Supraregional Tumour Marker Assay Laboratory 1990–; prof of cancer med Charing Cross and Wesminster Med Sch 1991–; industl collaboration with Schering-Plough Corporation for the development of the anti-cancer drug temozolomide; tstee: Gunnar Nilsson Cancer Research Tst Fund, Cancer Treatment and Research Tst; memb: RSM, American Assoc for Cancer Research, American Soc for Clinical Oncology, Euro Soc for Med Oncology, Euro Assoc for Cancer Research, Br Assoc for Cancer Research; FRCP 1983; *Books* Carcinoma in Situ and Carcinoma of the Testis: Biology and Treatment (contrib, 1987), Textbook of Gynaecological Oncology (contrib, 1991), Triazenes, Chemical, Biological and Clinical Aspects (contrib, 1991), Bailliere's Clinical Obstetrics and Gynaecology (Vol 6 no 3, 1992), Obstetrics and Gynaecology: A Critical Approach to the Clinical Problems (contrib, 1992), Gestational Trophoblastic Disease (jt ed, 1997); *Recreations* classical music, art, travel, wine; *Style*— Prof Edward Newlands; ✉ Department of Medical Oncology, Charing Cross Hospital, Fulham Palace Road, London W6 8RF (☎ 0181 846 1419, fax 0181 846 1443)

NEWLANDS, Prof George McLeod; s of George Newlands (d 1973), of Perth, and Mary Newlands; *b* 12 July 1941; *Educ* Perth Acad, Univ of Edinburgh (MA, BD, PhD), Univ of Heidelberg, Churchill Coll Cambridge (MA); *m* 1 Sept 1967, (Mary) Elizabeth, da of Rev Prof Ronald S Wallace, of Edinburgh; 3 s (Stewart b 1971, Murray b 1974, Craig b 1977); *Career* minister Church of Scotland, priest C of E; lectr in divinity Univ of Glasgow 1969–73, univ lectr in divinity Univ of Cambridge 1973–86, fell Wolfson Coll Cambridge 1975–82, fell and dean Trinity Hall Cambridge 1982–86, prof of divinity Univ of Glasgow 1986– (dean Faculty of Divinity 1988–90), princ Trinity Coll 1991–; *Books* Hilary of Poitiers (1978), Theology of the Love of God (1980), The Church of God (1984), Making Christian Decisions (1985), God in Christian Perspective (1994); *Recreations* walking, music; *Clubs* New (Edinburgh); *Style*— Prof George Newlands; ✉ 24 Queen's Crescent, Edinburgh EH9 2BB (☎ 0131 667 1472); Faculty of Divinity, The University, Glasgow G12 8QQ (☎ 0141 339 8855)

NEWLANDS OF LAURISTON, William Alexander; s of Frank Newlands (d 1971), of Balnamuir, Ballinluig, Perthshire, and Annie Shand-Henderson (d 1986); the family is descended from Jasper Newlands of that Ilk (in record 1469) of Nithsdale and from the barony of Newlands in the Sheriffdom of Kincardine; Laird of Lauriston (Castle founded 1243, Glenfiddich award 1992); granted the arms of Newlands by Lyon Court 1987; *b* 5 Nov 1934; *Educ* Dollar Acad, Robert Gordon's Coll Aberdeen, Churchill fell 1968; *m* 1, 1960, Kathleen Cook (m dis 1976); 1 s (Hamish Newlands of Lauriston Yr b 1965); 2 da (Fiona b 1960, Riona b 1962); m 2, 1985, Dorothy Straton, da of late John Walker, of Montrose, and 20th in direct descent from Sir Alexander Straton of Lauriston, who signed the Declaration of Arbroath (1320); *Career* Far East Air Force 1953–55; Game Conservancy, Int Union for Conservation of Nature (Morges, Switzerland); (as Willy Newlands) travel ed Daily Mail 1982–92; Scots Away (TV series) 1993; London ed Alliance Press Features 1994–, ed/prodr Travel Eye (America Online) 1996; Travel Writer of the Year 1983–84 and 1987–88; *Style*— William Newlands of Lauriston; ✉ 26 Old Church St, Chelsea, London SW3 5BY; Lauriston Castle, St Cyrus, Kincardineshire (☎ 01674 850488)

NEWMAN, Andrea; *b* 1938; *Educ* Univ of London (BA, MA); *m* 1959 (m dis 1973); *Career* writer; teacher 1961–64; memb Writers' Guild of GB; *Fiction* A Share of the World (1964), Mirage (1965), The Cage (1966), Three Into Two Won't Go (1967), Alexa (1968), A Bouquet of Barbed Wire (1969), An Evil Streak (1977), Mackenzie (1980), A Sense of Guilt (1988), A Gift of Poison (1991), Triangles (short stories, 1990); author of over 45 TV scripts, incl: Bouquet of Barbed Wire, Alexa, Mackenzie and A Sense of Guilt; *Recreations* listening to classical music, swimming, driving; *Style*— Ms Andrea Newman; ✉ c/o A P Watt, 20 John Street, London WC1

NEWMAN, Catherine Mary; QC (1995); da of Dr Ernest Newman (d 1971), of London, and Josephine, *née* McLaughlin (d 1991); *b* 7 Feb 1954; *Educ* Convent of The Sacred Heart HS, UCL (LLB 1st class); *m* 1982, Ian Gouldsbrough; 1 s (Charles b 1987), 1 da (Mary Hope b 1991); *Career* called to the Bar Middle Temple (Harmsworth scholar) 1979, dep registrar in bankruptcy; memb Bar Cncl 1987–90, hon sec Chancery Bar Assoc 1989–94; *Style*— Miss Catherine Newman, QC; ✉ 13 Old Square, Ground Floor, Lincoln's Inn, London WC2A 3UA (☎ 0171 404 4800, fax 0171 405 4267)

NEWMAN, His Hon Judge Cyril Wilfred Francis; QC (1982); s of Wilfred James Newman (d 1970), and Cecilia Beatrice Lily Newman (d 1977); *b* 2 July 1937; *Educ* Sacred Heart Coll Droitwich, Lewes Co GS, Merton Coll Oxford (MA); *m* 1966, Winifred, da of Theodore de Kok (d 1993), of Zürich, Switzerland; 2 s, 1 da; *Career* barr 1960; asst cmmr Parly Boundary Cmmn for Eng 1976, recorder (SE Circuit) 1982–, memb Criminal Injuries Compensation Bd 1985–86, circuit judge (SE Circuit) 1986–, official referee High Ct of Justice 1994–; pres: Oxford Univ Law Soc 1959, OU Middle Temple Soc 1959; *Recreations* sailing, country sports, skiing, swimming, memb Ashford Choral Soc, music; *Clubs* Bar Yacht (hon treas 1973–88, rear cdre 1985); *Style*— His Hon Judge Cyril Newman, QC; ✉ Orlestone Grange, Orlestone, nr Ashford, Kent TN26 2EB (☎ 01233 732306)

NEWMAN, Derek Anthony; s of Maurice John Newman, of Ashtead, Surrey, and Christine Newman, *née* Grieve; *b* 7 April 1944; *Educ* Chorlton GS Manchester, City Univ (MBA); *m* 1968, Patricia Ann Wynne; 3 c (Michelle b 15 March 1972, David b 14 Jan 1975, Lisa b 3 Nov 1977); *Career* audit mangr Touche Ross 1968–73 (articled clerk 1965–68), fin controller First National Finance Ltd 1973–75; Chemical Bank: fin controller 1975–76, vice pres fin 1976–78, vice pres and head of corp fin NY 1978–81, vice pres fin insts 1981–85; Canadian Imperial Bank of Commerce: gen mangr UK and Ireland 1985–86, sr vice pres Europe, Africa and ME 1987–90 (vice pres 1986–87), head of Europe 1990–91, chief executive CIBC/Wood Gundy Group Europe 1990–91; chief operating offr Summit Group plc 1991–94, chief fin offr Nomura Securities plc 1994–; FCA; *Recreations* windsurfing, golf, swimming; *Clubs* RAC; *Style*— Derek Newman, Esq; ✉ Nomura Securities plc, 1 St Martins Le Grand, London EC1A 4NT (☎ 0171 320 2556)

NEWMAN, Sir Francis Hugh Cecil; 4 Bt (UK 1912), of Cecil Lodge, Newmarket, Co Cambridge; s of Sir Gerard Robert Henry Sigismund Newman, 3 Bt (d 1987), and Caroline Philippa, *née* Neville (now Mrs Andrew Crawshaw); *b* 12 June 1963; *Educ* Eton, Univ of Pennsylvania USA; *m* 18 Dec 1990, Katharine M, yr da of (Cecil Ralph) Timothy Edwards (d 1996), of Grendon Court, Upton Bishop, Ross-on-Wye, Herefordshire; 2 s (Thomas Ralph Gerard b 7 Jan 1993, Arthur Guy Hugh b 28 April 1996), 1 da (Lily May Violet b 22 May 1994); *Heir* s, Thomas Ralph Gerard Newman b 7 Jan 1993; *Career* N M Rothschild Asset Mgmnt Ltd, vice chm Galloway Group Ltd, dir Cadweb Ltd;

Recreations shooting, family, farming; *Clubs* Eton Vikings; *Style—* Sir Francis Newman, Bt; ✉ Burloes Hall, Royston, Herts SG8 9NE (☎ 01763 242150, fax 01763 249629)

NEWMAN, Sir Geoffrey Robert; 6 Bt (UK 1836), of Mamhead, Devonshire; s of Sir Ralph Alured Newman, 5 Bt (d 1968), and Hon Ann Rosemary Hope Newman, *née* Hope-Morley; *b* 2 June 1947; *Educ* Heatherdown Sch, Kelly Coll; *m* 1980, Mary Elizabeth, yr da of Col Sir Martin St John Valentine Gibbs, KCVO, CB, DSO, TD (d 1992); 1 s (Robert Melvil b 1985), 3 da (Frances Joyce b 1983, Elsie Laura b 1987, Louisa Bridget b 1990); *Heir* s, Robert Melvil Newman b 4 Oct 1985; *Career* 1 Bn Grenadier Gds 1967–70, Lt T&AVR until 1979; Daniel Greenaway & Sons Ltd 1973–75; memb Transglobe Expedition 1977–79; dir Blackpool Sands (Devon) Utilities Co Ltd 1970–; Wadlow Grosvenor Internat 1980–90; corporate film and video prodn, walk leader and guide for The Wayfarers 1990–; dir Dartmouth & District Tourism Services Ltd 1992–; memb S Devon Assoc of Tourist Attractions 1995–; FRGS; *Style—* Sir Geoffrey Newman, Bt; ✉ Sanders, Stoke Fleming, Dartmouth, South Devon TQ6 0PY

NEWMAN, Hon Mr Justice; Hon Sir George Michael; kt (1995); s of Wilfred James Newman (d 1970), of Seaford, Sussex, and Celia Beatrice Lily, *née* Browne (d 1977); *b* 4 July 1941; *Educ* Lewes Co GS, St Catharine's Coll Cambridge; *m* 1966, Hilary Alice Gibbs, da of late Robert Gibbs Chandler, of Battle, Sussex; 2 s (Benedict b 1968, Matthew b 1970), 1 da (Clarissa b 1971); *Career* called to the Bar Middle Temple 1965, recorder of the Crown Court 1985–95, bencher Middle Temple 1989, a judge of the High Court of Justice (Queen's Bench Div) 1995–; FRSA 1991; *Recreations* tennis, skiing, walking; *Style—* The Hon Mr Justice Newman; ✉ The Royal Courts of Justice, Strand, London WC2A 2LL

NEWMAN, (Paul) John; s of Wilfred James Newman (d 1970), and Cecilia, *née* Browne (d 1977); *b* 22 Nov 1931; *Educ* Sacred Heart Coll Droitwich Worcs; *m* 4 April 1961, Heulwen, da of Capt Edgar Vittle; 2 s (Duncan Paul b 26 May 1963, Richard Adrian b 1 Jan 1966); *Career* purser Peninsular and Oriental Steam Navigation Co 1954–61; Merchant Navy and Airline Offrs' Assoc: various appts 1961–84 incl admin offr, national sec, chief negotiator and asst gen sec; gen sec NUMAST 1989–93 (dep gen sec 1985–88), chm Merchant Navy Offrs Pension Fund 1993–; memb Gen Cncl of TUC 1990–92; *Recreations* golf, gardening; *Style—* John Newman, Esq; ✉ 57 Park Road, Brentwood, Essex CM14 4TX (☎ 01277 215796)

NEWMAN, John Arthur; s of C Gordon Newman, of West Clandon, and Ruth, *née* Seabrook; *b* 12 Dec 1946; *Educ* St Albans Sch Herts, St John's Coll Cambridge; *m* 1, (m dis), Freya Darvall; 2 s (Alexander John b 18 May 1971, Michael Christopher b 22 Dec 1973); *Career* articled clerk Cooper Bros and Co 1967, mangr Tax Dept Arthur Andersen & Co 1971, sr international tax mangr Touche Ross & Co 1973, estab own practice 1976, merged with Chantrey Vellacott (ptnr until 1994) 1986, ptnr Smith & Williamson 1994–; memb main ctee LSCA 1979–87 and 1993–; memb Cncl ICAEW 1987–93 and 1995–; Assoc of Accounting Technicians: memb Cncl 1989–, vice pres 1995–96, pres 1996–; FCA; *Publications* UK/US Double Tax Agreement (1980), Controlled Foreign Corporations (1985); *Recreations* hellenophile; *Style—* John A Newman, Esq; ✉ 1 Ritherdon Road, London SW17 8QE; Smith & Williamson, 1 Riding House Street, London W1A 3AS (☎ 0171 612 8896, fax 0171 631 0586)

NEWMAN, John Francis; s of Sir Cecil Gustavus Newman, 2 Bt (d 1955), and Joan Newman, CBE (d 1969), da of Canon Hon Robert Grimston (s of 2 Earl of Verulam); *b* 25 Jan 1930; *Educ* Eton, Sandhurst; *m* 1963, Caroline, da of Lt-Col Angus Rose, of Perthshire (d 1981); 1 s (Anthony J C b 27 June 1966), 2 da (Henrietta C M A (Countess of Caledon) b 23 Jan 1964, Sarahjane C b 20 April 1968); *Career* former Lt RHG; past chm: Rom River Co, Hoogovens UK Ltd; currently chm Galloway Group Ltd, non-exec dir Blick plc, Avocet Mining PLC and other cos; *Recreations* shooting, farming, golf; *Clubs* White's, Pratt's, MCC; *Style—* John Newman, Esq; ✉ 7 Gertrude Street, London SW10 0JN (☎ 0171 352 7808); Compton Park, Compton Chamberlayne, Salisbury, Wilts (☎ 01722 714294, fax 01722 714813)

NEWMAN, Dr John Howard; s of Edward Howard Newman (d 1975), of Sevenoaks, Kent, and Mary Newman (d 1993); *b* 14 June 1943; *Educ* Clare Coll Cambridge (MA), Guys Hosp (MB BChir); *m* 31 July 1971, (Elizabeth) Anne, da of David Reynolds Cox (d 1994), of Torquay; 2 s (Bruce b 1973, Ian b 1979), 1 da (Rachel b 1975); *Career* conslt orthopaedic surgn Bristol Royal Infirmary 1978–; former memb: Specialist Advsy Ctee in Orthopaedics, Overseas Doctors' Trg Ctee; memb: RCS, BOA 1971, BASK 1984, BMA, Cncl BOA 1992; FRCS 1971; *Recreations* rackets, golf, watersports; *Clubs* Boasters; *Style—* Dr John Newman; ✉ 2 Clifton Park, Bristol (☎ 0117 973 4262)

NEWMAN, Karl Max; CB (1979); s of Dr Karl Neumann (d 1978), and Alice, *née* Gruenebaum (d 1958); *b* 26 March 1919; *Educ* Ottershaw Coll, ChCh Oxford (MA); *m* 1952, Annette Muriel, da of Ronald Cross Sheen (d 1973); 1 s, 1 da; *Career* Army 1940–42; called to the Bar Gray's Inn 1946, barr 1946–49; Lord Chllr's Office: legal asst 1949–56, sr legal asst 1956–62, asst slr 1962–72, under sec 1972–82; legal advsr Euro Unit Cabinet Office 1972–82, counsel to Chm of Ctees House of Lords 1982–87, bencher Gray's Inn 1987; hon fell Br Inst of Int and Comparative Law 1990; *Recreations* travelling, philately, visiting picture galleries; *Clubs* Utd Oxford and Cambridge Univ; *Style—* Karl Newman, Esq, CB; ✉ 17 Marryat Rd, Wimbledon, London SW19 5BB (☎ and fax 0181 946 3430)

NEWMAN, Sir Kenneth Leslie; GBE (1987), kt (1978), QPM (1982); s of John William Newman, and Florence Newman; *b* 15 Aug 1926; *Educ* Univ of London (LLB); *m* 1949, Eileen Lilian; 1 s, 1 da; *Career* WWII RAF; Palestine Police 1946–48, Met Police 1948–73, Cdr New Scotland Yard 1972, Chief Constable RUC 1976–79 (Sr Dep Chief Constable 1973), Cmdt Bramshill Police Coll and HM Inspr Constabulary 1980–82, Met Police Cmmr 1982–87; vice pres Def Manufacturers' Assoc; tstee: Police Fndn, Community Action Tst, World Humanity Action Tst 1993–; memb Mgmnt Ctee Automobile Assoc 1987–96, registrar Imperial Soc of Knights Bachelor, pres Assoc of Police and Public Security Suppliers 1993–; non-exec dir various cos; visiting prof of law Univ of Bristol 1987–88; Grand Offr of the Order of Orange Nassau (Netherlands) 1982, Commandeur de l'Ordre National de la Legion d'Honneur (France) 1984, Encomienda de Numero del Order del Merito Civil (Spain) 1986, Knight Commander of the Order of Merit (W Germany) 1986, Grand Offr of the Order of the Lion of Malawi 1985, Nat Order of the Aztec Eagle (Class II, Mexico) 1985, Medal of Merit (Class I, Quatar) 1985, Order of King Abdul Aziz (Class I, Saudi Arabia) 1987, Grand Officer du Wissam Alouite (Morocco) 1987, Order of Bahrein (Class II, Bahrein) 1984; CIMgt, KStJ 1987; *Style—* Sir Kenneth Newman, GBE, QPM; ✉ c/o New Scotland Yard, Broadway, London SW1

NEWMAN, Kevin; *b* 1957; *Educ* Univ of Keele (BA), Univ of Essex (MA); *m* Cathy; 2 s (Benjamin b 1989, Joshua b 1991), 1 da (Naomi b 1996); *Career* trainee programmer rising to sr project mangr Mars Group Services 1981–85; Woolworths plc: joined as info centre mangr 1985, then business systems mangr, dir of Mgmnt Info Systems (i/c all gp IT) until 1989; First Direct: i/c systems devpt prior to launch 1989, ops dir 1990–91, chief exec 1991–; *Recreations* squash, golf, running, gym workout, skiing, American football; *Style—* Kevin Newman, Esq; ✉ First Direct, Millshaw Park Lane, Leeds LS98 1FD (☎ 0113 276 6100)

NEWMAN, Dr Lotte Therese (Mrs N E Aronsohn); OBE (1991); da of Dr George Newman (d 1976), of London, and Dr Tilly Meyer (d 1966); *b* 22 Jan 1929; *Educ* N London Collegiate Sch, Univ of Birmingham (BSc), KCL and Westminster Hosp Med Schs (MB BS, LRCP, MRCS); *m* 1959, Norman Edward Aronsohn, s of Solomon Aronsohn; 1 da (Simone b 9 April 1960), 3 s (Simon b 22 May 1961, David b 29 Aug 1963, Alex b 14 Oct 1965); *Career* successively: casualty offr Westminster Hosp, paediatric house offr Westminster Children's Hosp, sr house offr St Stephen's Hosp, sr house offr in obstetrics and gynaecology Hillingdon Hosp, GP locum Edgware and Queensway; in gen practice 1960–, pres RCGP 1994; Purkinje medal Czechoslovak Soc of Gen Practice 1987, Sir David Bruce lecture and medal (first female lectr) RAMC 1989, Mackenzie lecture and medal RCGP 1991, Baron der Heyden de Lancey meml award 1992; Freeman City of London 1987, memb Worshipful Soc of Apothecaries 1987; MRCGP 1967; memb: GMC 1984, BMA 1985; FRCGP 1977, FRSM 1977; *Recreations* spending time with family, listening, music, boating; *Clubs* RAC; *Style—* Dr Lotte Newman, OBE; ✉ The White House, 1 Ardwick Road, London NW2 2BX (☎ 0171 435 6630, fax 0171 435 6672)

NEWMAN, Michael Henry; s of Henry Ernest Newman, of E Croydon, Surrey, and Rhoda May, *née* Symonds (d 1986); *b* 19 Oct 1945; *Educ* Whitgift Sch; *m* 15 Jan 1977, Jennifer Mary, da of Matthew McCargo Roger (d 1977), of Glasgow; *Career* CA 1968; chief exec Britannia Arrow Holdings plc 1979–86 (dir from 1977), dep chm National Employers Life Assurance Co Ltd 1983–86, dir Singer & Friedlander 1984–86, chief exec Prudential Corporation Asia Ltd 1989–90, sr mgmnt Prudential Corporation plc 1990–92, conslt Prudential Assurance Co Ltd 1993–; *Recreations* travel, gardening; *Clubs* Singapore Town; *Style—* Michael Newman, Esq; ✉ 37 Wool Road, Wimbledon, London SW20 0HN (☎ 0181 947 9756); Prudential Assurance Co, 250 Euston Road, London NW1 2PQ (☎ 0171 334 6681, fax 0171 334 6331)

NEWMAN, Nanette (Mrs Bryan Forbes); da of Sidney Newman, and Ruby Newman; *b* 29 May 1934; *Educ* Sternhold Coll London, Italia Conti Stage Sch, RADA; *m* 1955, Bryan Forbes, *qv*; 2 da (Emma Forbes, *qv*, Sarah, m John Standing, *qv*); *Career* actress and writer; *Television* appearances incl: Call my Bluff, What's My Line, The Fun Food Factory (series), London Scene, Stay With Me 'Till Morning, title role in Jessie, Let There be Love, Late Expectations, The Endless Game; *Films* incl: The L-Shaped Room 1962, The Wrong Arm of the Law 1962, Seance on a Wet Afternoon 1963, The Wrong Box 1965, The Whisperers 1966, Deadfall 1967, The Madwoman of Chaillot 1968, The Raging Moon 1971 (Variety Club Best Film Actress Award), The Stepford Wives 1974, International Velvet 1978 (Evening News Best Film Actress Award); *Books* God Bless Love (1972), Lots of Love (1973), Vote for Love (1976), The Root Children (1978), The Pig Who Never Was (1979), The Dog Lovers Coffee Table Book (1982), The Cat Lovers Coffee Table Book (1983), My Granny was a Frightful Bore (1983), A Cat and Mouse Love Story (1984), Christmas Cookbook (1984), Pigalev (1985), Archie (1986), Summer Cookbook (1986), Small Beginnings (1987), Entertaining with Nanette Newman (1988), Bad Baby (1988), Charlie the Noisy Caterpillar (1989), Sharing (1989), ABC (1990), 123 (1991), Cooking for Friends (1991), Spider the Horrible Cat (1992), There's A Bear in the Bath (1993), There's A Bear in the Classroom (1996), Take 3 Cooks (1996); *Recreations* needlepoint; *Style—* Miss Nanette Newman; ✉ c/o Chatto & Linnit, Prince of Wales Theatre, Coventry Street, London W1V 7FE (☎ 0171 930 6677, fax 0171 930 0091)

NEWMAN, Peter John; s of Peter Laurence Newman, TD, FIEE (d 1994), of Collingtree, Northants, and Susan Newman; *b* 5 July 1938; *Educ* St John's Johannesburg, St John's Coll Cambridge; *m* 1963, Patricia Anne, *née* Wright; 3 s; *Career* Davy Corp cos 1960–91: gen mangr Loewy Robertson Engrg Co 1979 (Queen's award for Export 1980), md Davy McKee (Sheffield) 1984–87, chief exec Metals Div 1988–90, main bd dir Human Resources Davy Corporation 1990–91, vice chm ANI Aurora plc 1994–; pres Dorset C of C 1983, chm Bd of Govrs Sheffield Hallam Univ (formerly Sheffield City Poly) 1988–93, memb of bd Sheffield Devpt Corp 1988–; FIMechE; *Recreations* sailing, skiing, gardening; *Style—* Peter Newman, Esq; ✉ White Edge, Froggatt Edge, Calver, nr Sheffield (☎ 01433 630314)

NEWMAN, Prof Ronald Charles (Ron); s of Charles Henry Newman (d 1983), and Margaret Victoria May, *née* Cooper (d 1985); *b* 10 Dec 1931; *Educ* Tottenham GS, Imperial Coll London (BSc, DIC, PhD); *m* 7 April 1956, Jill Laura, da of Robert Charles Weeks (d 1949); 2 da (Susan Laura (Mrs Lee) b 1959, Vivienne Heather (Mrs Cadman) b 1962); *Career* res scientist AEI Central Res Laboratory Aldermaston Court Aldermaston Berks 1955–63, sr res scientist AEI Res Laboratory Rugby Warwickshire 1964; Univ of Reading: lectr J J Thomson Physical Laboratory 1964–69, reader 1969–75, prof 1975–88, visiting prof 1989; prof and assoc dir IRC semi-conductor materials Imperial Coll 1989–; memb EPSRC Coll Functional Materials, vice chm MPI Fachbeirat Halle; memb: Br Assoc for Crystal Growth, Material Res Soc USA; ARCS, FInstP; *Books* Infrared Studies of Crystal Defects (1973); *Recreations* music, photography, foreign travel; *Style—* Prof Ron Newman; ✉ Maiden Oak, 23 Betchworth Ave, Earley, Reading, Berks RG6 7RH (☎ 0118 966 3816); Interdisciplinary Research Centre for Semiconductor Materials, The Blackett Laboratory, Imperial College of Science Technology and Medicine, Prince Consort Rd, London SW7 2BZ (☎ 0171 594 6666, fax 0171 581 3817, telex 929484, e-mail r.newman@ic.ac.uk)

NEWMAN, Vice Adm Sir Roy Thomas; KCB (1992, CB 1991); *Educ* Queen Elizabeth's GS Barnet; *m*; 4 s; *Career* joined RN 1954, specialised in anti-submarine warfare (ASW) 1963, instr HMS Dolphin Submarine Sch, served ASW frigate HMS Hardy, joined Submarine Serv 1966, served HMS Otus and Warspite, instr Jt ASW Sch Londonderry, cmd submarine HMS Onyx; Cdr 1971, 2 i/c HMS London, Nat Defence Coll course 1972, various appts on staff of Flag Offr Submarines and MOD, cmd ASW frigate HMS Naiad; Capt 1979, Operational Requirements Dept MOD Central Staff Directorate, cmd HMS Dolphin, 1st Submarine Squadron and Submarine Sch 1981, involved in evacuation of UK troops from Lebanon 1984, Capt 7th Frigate Sqdn and cmd HMS Cleopatra, Dir Naval Warfare MOD 1986–88; Rear Adm 1988, Flag Offr Sea Trg 1988–90, Dep Cdr Fleet and COS to C-in-C Fleet 1990–92, Naval Dep to Jt Cdr Operation Granby RAF High Wycombe 1991; Vice Adm 1991, Flag Offr Plymouth and Cdr Central Sub Area Eastern Atlantic 1992–96; responsible for 50th anniversary commemoration of the Battle of the Atlantic May 1993; *Style—* Vice Adm Sir Roy Newman, KCB; ✉ Foxdenton, 16 Links Lane, Rowlands Castle, Hants PO9 6AE

NEWMAN, Sydney; OC (1981); *b* 1 April 1917; *Educ* Central Sch Toronto; *m* 1944, Margaret Elizabeth, *née* McRae (d 1981); 3 da (Deirdre, Jennifer, Gillian); *Career* formerly painter; industl, theatre and interior designer, still and cinema photographer; Nat Film Bd of Canada: splicer boy 1941, ed and dir Armed Forces trg films and war info shorts 1942, prodr Canada Carries On 1945–52, exec prodr i/c of all films for cinema incl short films, newsreels, films for children and travel films 1947–52, prodr of over 300 documentaries incl UN Suffer Little Children It's Fun to Sing (Venice award), Ski Skill, After Prison, What? (Canada award), assigned to NBC NY to report on TV techniques 1949–50, govt film cmmr and chief exec 1970–75; CBC TV 1952–58: dir of features and outside broadcasts, supervisor of drama, prodr of General Motors Theatre, On Camera, Ford Theatre and Graphic 1954, prodr of first plays by Arthur Hailey, Mordecai Richler etc; ABC TV England 1958–63: prodr Armchair Theatre, supervisor of drama (cmmnd first on-air plays of Alun Owen, Harold Pinter, Angus Wilson, Robert Muller, Hugh Leonard and Peter Luke), created The Avengers; BBC TV 1963–68: head of Drama and Opera Gp, created Dr Who; prodr: Stephen D (by Hugh Leonard, Tea Party (by Harold Pinter), The Rise and Fall of the City of Mahogany (opera by Kurt Weill and Berthold Brecht); responsible for the Wednesday Play, The Forsyth Saga etc; exec prodr of feature films Associated Picture Corporation 1969, dir of progs CRTC Ottawa 1970; Canadian Govt Film Cmmr and chief exec Nat Film Bd of Canada 1970–75; dir: Canadian Film Development Corporation 1970–75, CBC 1972–75; tstee Nat Arts Centre 1970–75, special advsr on film to Sec of State 1975–77, govr Canadian Conf to the Arts 1978–82; awards from: Soc of Film and TV Arts, Writers' Guild of GB; special recognition award from Soc of Motion Pictures and TV Engrs (US) 1975; memb: New Western Film and TV Fedn 1978–84, BAFTA, RTS; Kt of Mark Twain (US), hon life memb Dirs' Guild of Canada, memb BAFTA, FRSA (UK) 1967, FRTS 1990; *Recreations* sculpture, painting; *Style*— Sydney Newman, Esq, OC; ✉ 3 Nesbitt Drive, Toronto, Ontario M4W 2GZ, Canada

NEWMAN, Tony William; s of William Newman (d 1973), of London, and Annie Newman; *b* 3 Sept 1947; *Educ* St Bernard's Sch; *Career* BBC TV 1971–91: dir and prodr of shows incl Top of the Pops, Wogan, Two Ronnies; *Recreations* golf; *Clubs* Sundridge Park Golf; *Style*— Tony Newman, Esq; ✉ 32 Honor Oak Rise, Honor Oak, Forest Hill, London SE23 (☎ 0181 291 3365)

NEWMAN, Warren J; *b* 20 July 1947; *Educ* LCP (DipCAM (PR), MAIE(Dip)); *m* Avril; 1 s, 1 da; *Career* asst to Gen Ed John Lewis Partnership 1963–68, gp ed South Londoner Newspapers 1968–72, sr info offr London Borough of Newham 1972–74, chief public relations offr London Borough of Hounslow 1974–78, head of public relations London Borough of Southwark 1978–84, dir of public relations NFU 1984–89, dir of communications AEA Technology (UK Atomic Energy Authority) 1989–91, head of UK corp relations Générale des Eaux Group 1991–94, chief exec BACTA 1995–; memb IPR Govt Affairs Gp; FIPR; *Books* The Practice of PR (contrib); *Style*— Warren Newman, Esq; ✉ 8 Thalia Close, Greenwich, London SE10 9NA (☎ and fax 0181 858 4918, e-mail 100651.3651@compuserve.com)

NEWMAN TURNER, Roger Geoffrey; s of Frank Newman Turner (d 1964), of Letchworth, Herts, of Lorna Mary, *née* Clarke (d 1976); *b* 29 April 1940; *Educ* Sidcot Sch, Br Coll of Naturopathy and Osteopathy (Naturopathic Dip, Dip in Osteopathy), Br Coll of Acupuncture (Licentiate Dip in Acupuncture, BAc); *m* 1966, Birgid, da of Carl Rath, of Stuttgart; 1 da (Nicole b 1966), 1 s (Julian b 1968); *Career* naturopath, osteopath and acupuncturist in private practice 1963–; sec Res Soc for Natural Therapeutics 1966–75, ed Br Jl of Acupuncture 1982–93, pres Br Acupuncture Assoc 1990–92, chm Res Cncl for Complementary Med 1993– (tstee 1983–); memb: Register of Naturopaths, Register of Osteopaths; fell Br Acupuncture Cncl; *Books* incl: First Aid Nature's Way (1969), Diets to Help Hay Fever and Asthma (1970), Diets to Help Heart Disorders (1971), Diets to Help Control Cholesterol (1978), Naturopathic Medicine (1984), Self Help for Angina (1987), Hay Fever Handbook (1988), Banish Back Pain (1989); *Recreations* acting, singing, theatre, opera, cricket; *Style*— Roger Newman Turner, Esq; ✉ 1 Harley Street, London W1N 1DA (☎ 0171 436 1446)

NEWMARCH, Michael George (Mick); s of George Langdon Newmarch, and Phyllis Georgina, *née* Crandon; *b* 19 May 1938; *Educ* Tottenham Co GS, Univ of London (BSc external); *m* 10 Oct 1959, Audrey Ann, da of Cecil Clark; 1 s (Timothy b 1963), 2 da (Kate b 1966, Joanne b 1971); *Career* The Prudential Corporation: joined Economic Intelligence Dept Prudential Assurance Co Ltd 1955, sr asst investmt mangr 1976–78, dep investmt mangr 1979–80, investmt mangr and chief exec offr Prudential Portfolio Managers Ltd 1981–89, chief exec Prudential Corporation 1990–95, chm Prudential Assurance Company 1990–95, chm Prudential Portfolio Managers 1990–95; non-exec dir Celltech plc 1996–; vice chm Princess Royal Tst for Carers 1995–, tstee Berks Community Tst 1996–; memb Advsy Cncl Orch of the Age of Enlightenment 1995–; AIIMR; *Recreations* salmon-fishing, fly-tying, music, opera, cinema, bridge; *Clubs* Flyfishers; *Style*— Mick Newmarch, Esq

NEWNS, Sir (Alfred) Foley (Francis Polden); KCMG (1963, CMG 1957), CVO (1961); s of Rev Alfred Newns (d 1930); *b* 30 Jan 1909; *Educ* Christ's Hosp, St Catharine's Coll Cambridge; *m* 1, 1936, Emma Jean (d 1984), da of Ambrose Bateman (d 1950); 1 s, 1 da; m 2, 9 April 1988, Mrs Beryl Wattles; *Career* colonial admin serv Nigeria 1932, sec to Cncl of Ministers 1951–54, sec to Govr Gen and Cncl of Ministers 1955–59, dep govr Sierra Leone 1960, actg govr 1960, advsr to Govt 1961–63, sec to Cabinet Govt of Bahamas 1964–71; FRSA; *Recreations* nature study, music, art, African affairs; *Style*— Sir Foley Newns, KCMG, CVO; ✉ 47 Barrow Rd, Cambridge CB2 2AR (☎ 01223 356903)

NEWPORT, Philip John (Phil); s of John Newport, and Sheila Diana Newport; *b* 11 Oct 1962; *Educ* Royal GS High Wycombe, Portsmouth Poly (BA); *m* 26 Oct 1985, Christine; 1 s (Nathan b 10 May 1989); *Career* professional cricketer; minor counties Buckinghamshire CCC 1981–82; Worcestershire CCC: debut 1982, capped 1986, co champions 1988 and 1989, Sunday League champions 1987 and 1988, Benson & Hedges Cup winners 1991, winners NatWest Trophy 1994; Boland SA off-season 1987–88, N Transvaal SA off season 1992–93; England: 3 test matches 1988–91, memb A tour to Pakistan 1990–91; *Recreations* cinema, eating out, soccer, golf; *Style*— Phil Newport, Esq; ✉ Worcestershire CCC, County Ground, New Rd, Worcester WR2 4QQ (☎ 01905 422694)

NEWRY AND MORNE, Viscount; Robert Francis John; s and h of Richard Needham, 6 Earl of Kilmorey (who does not use the title); *b* 30 May 1966; *Educ* Eton, Lady Margaret Hall Oxford, Imperial Coll London (MBA); *m* 13 April 1991, Laura Mary, o da of Michael Tregaskis, of Cosham, Hants; *Career* business devpt mangr Inchcape Pacific Hong Kong; *Clubs* Pratt's; *Style*— Viscount Newry and Morne; ✉ 2901 Bamboo Grove, Kennedy Road, Wanchai, Hong Kong (☎ 00 852 233 1126, fax 00 852 530 1041)

NEWSAM, Sir Peter Anthony; kt (1987); s of William Oswald Newsam (d 1974), of Maidenhead; *b* 2 Nov 1928; *Educ* Clifton, Queen's Coll Oxford; *m* 1, 1953 (m dis), Elizabeth Joy Greg; 4 s, 1 da; m 2, 1988, Sue Addinell; 1 da; *Career* former civil servant BOT (asst princ); schoolmaster 1956–63, asst educn offr Yorks N Riding 1963–66, asst dir of educn Cumberland 1966–70, dep educn offr Yorks W Riding 1970–72, educn offr ILEA 1977–82 (dep educn offr 1972–76), chm Cmmn for Racial Equality 1982–87, sec Assoc of CCs 1987–89; Univ of London: dir Inst of Educn 1989–94, dep vice-chllr 1992–94; *Style*— Sir Peter Newsam; ✉ 44 Lady Somerset Road, London NW5 1TU

NEWSOME, Dr David Hay; s of Capt Charles Todd Newsome, OBE (d 1970), of Gannaway Farm, Norton Lindsey, Warwickshire, and Elsie Mary, *née* Hay (d 1960); *b* 15 June 1929; *Educ* Rossall, Emmanuel Coll Cambridge (MA, LittD); *m* 12 April 1955, Joan Florence, da of Lt-Col Leslie Hamilton Trist, DSO, MC (d 1979), of Coldwaltham, Sussex; 4 da (Clare Elizabeth b 25 May 1956, Janet Mary b 22 Sept 1958, (Anne) Louise b 25 Jan 1960, Cordelia Jane b 22 Jan 1961); *Career* Nat Serv 1948–50, Capt RAEC (substantive Lt); asst master Wellington Coll 1954–59, fell Emmanuel Coll Cambridge 1959–70 (sr tutor 1965–70), univ lectr in ecclesiastical history Cambridge 1961–70, headmaster Christ's Hospital Horsham 1970–79, master of Wellington Coll 1980–89; memb Governing Bodies: Westcott House Cambridge 1960–65, Ardingly Coll 1965–69, Eastbourne Coll 1965–69, Epsom Coll 1965–69; FRHistS 1970, FRSL 1980; *Books* A History of Wellington College 1859–1959 (1959), Godliness and Good Learning (1961), The Parting of Friends (1966), Two Classes of Men (1974), On the Edge of Paradise: A C Benson the Diarist (1980, Whitbread prize for biography of the year), Edwardian Excursions (1981), The Convert Cardinals: Newman and Manning (1993); *Recreations* music, opera, fell-walking; *Clubs* East India, Devonshire, Sports and Public Schools; *Style*— Dr David Newsome; ✉ The Retreat, Thornthwaite, Keswick, Cumbria (☎ 01768 778372)

NEWSOME, Roy; s of Norman Newsome (d 1959), of Elland, and Minnie, *née* Crompton (d 1971); *b* 17 July 1930; *Educ* Elland C of E Sch, Halifax Tech Coll, BMus (Durham); *m* 18 Dec 1954, Muriel, da of William Wilson; 2 s (Neil Michael b 21 July 1960, Martin John b 14 July 1963); *Career* brass band personality, conductor, adjudicator, composer; conducting appts incl: Black Dyke Mills Band 1966–77, Besses o' th' Barn 1978–85, Fairey Engineering Band 1986–89, Sun Life Band 1989–96; music dir Nat Youth Brass Band of GB 1984–, presenter of Listen To The Band (BBC Radio 2) 1986–94, head of band studies and band musicianship UC Salford 1976–89 (awarded Hon Grad Dip in Band Musicianship in recognition of outstanding contrib to band music throughout the world 1989); guest conductor: Tomra Brass Norway, Breeze Brass Band Japan; pres Nat Assoc of Brass Band Conductors 1992–; has circa 100 published compositions and arrangements incl Concerto for Piano and Brass Band first performed at the Royal Albert Hall; adjudicated major brass band contests and nat championships in: UK, Switzerland, Holland, Belgium, Norway, USA, Aust, NZ; author of books on band history; Silver medal The Worshipful Co of Musicians for services to brass bands 1976; FRCO, ARCM; *Recreations* motoring, reading, good food and wine; *Style*— Roy Newsome, Esq; ✉ 17 Belmont Drive, Seddons Farm, Bury, Lancashire BL8 2HU (☎ and fax 0161 764 2009)

NEWSOME, Victor George; s of George Newsome (d 1991), of Leeds, and Margaret Westmoreland (d 1968); *b* 16 June 1935; *Educ* Leeds Coll of Art (Rome scholar in painting); *m* thrice; 1 s (Joseph), 1 da (Susanna); *Career* Nat Serv 1955–57; painter and sculptor; teaching appts at: Leicester Sch of Art 1962–63, Nottingham Sch of Art 1963–64, Hull Coll of Art 1964–70; teaching appts between 1970–77: Camberwell Sch of Art and Crafts, Goldsmiths' Coll Univ of London, Faculty of Art and Design Brighton Poly, Canterbury Coll of Art, Wimbledon Sch of Art and Chelsea Sch of Art; currently teaches drawing at the RCA; work in several private and public collections incl Arts Cncl of GB, V & A Museum and British Museum; *Solo Exhibitions* incl: Grabowski Gallery London 1966, Anthony d'Offay Gallery London 1976, Hester van Royen Gallery London 1979, Ikon Gallery Birmingham 1979, Anne Berthoud Gallery London 1981, Marlborough Fine Art London 1987, Stoppenbach & Delestre London 1992; *Group Exhibitions* The Visual Adventure (Drian Gallery London) 1962, London Group (Camden Art Centre London) 1963, The Inner Image (Grabowski Gallery London) 1964, The New Generation (Whitechapel Gallery London) 1966, Edinburgh Open 100 (Univ of Edinburgh) 1967, Interim (Whitechapel Gallery London) 1968, Six at the Hayward Gallery 1969, Play Orbit (ICA Gallery London) 1969, British Painting '74 (Hayward Gallery London) 1974, Artists' Market (Warehouse Gallery London) 1973, 1976 and 1978, The British Art Show (Arts Cncl touring exhibition) 1979–80, Peter Moores Show (Walker Art Gallery Liverpool) 1981, Recent Work by Gallery Artists (Marlborough Fine Art London) 1983, 1984, 1988, 1989, and 1990, British Artists in Italy 1920–80 (Canterbury Coll of Art touring exhibition) 1985, The Foundation Veranneman invites Marlborough (Kruishoutern Belgium) 1986–87, Royal Acad Summer Exhibition 1991, The Primacy of Drawing (Arts Cncl touring exhibition) 1991, The Large Print Show (Jill George Gallery London) 1991–92, The Primacy of Drawing (touring) 1992, Royal Academy Summer Exhibition 1992, ISIS Gallery Leigh-on-Sea 1992, Gillian Jason Gallery London 1993, The Hunting Art Prize Exhibition (Royal Coll of Art London and Glasgow Art Gallery and Museum) 1994, The Discerning Eye Exhibition (Mall Galleries London) 1996, Artspace Gallery London 1996; *Awards* Prix de Rome 1960, Peter Stuyvesant travel bursary to America 1966, prizewinner Structure' 66, jt first prizewinner Edinburgh Open 100 1967, The Millichope Fndn Award for Drawing 1992; *Recreations* being sociable; *Style*— Victor Newsome, Esq; ✉ Independent Studio, 4 Elizabeth Mews, London NW3 4TL (☎ 0171 722 0514)

NEWSON-SMITH, Sir John Kenneth; 2 Bt (UK 1944), of Totteridge, Co Hertford, DL (City of London 1947); s of Sir Frank Newson-Smith, 1 Bt (d 1971); *b* 9 Jan 1911; *Educ* Dover Coll, Jesus Coll Cambridge (MA); *m* 1, 1945 (m dis 1971), Vera Margaret, da of late Dr Wilfred Greenhouse Allt, CVO, CBE; 1 s, 2 da; m 2, 1972, Anne (d 1987), da of late Harold Burns; m 3, 1988, Mrs Sarah Lucretia Wimberley Ramsay, da of Robert Bicknell; *Heir* s, Peter Frank Graham Newson Smith b 8 May 1947; *Career* joined HAC 1933, RN 1939, Lt RNVR 1941, served Free French Navy 1941–42; memb Stock Exchange 1938–78 (ptnr Fielding Newson-Smith & Co); memb: Ct of Common Cncl 1945–76, (dep 1961–76), HM Cmmn of Lieutenancy for City of London 1947–76; Liveryman: Worshipful Co of Merchant Taylors, Worshipful Co of Spectaclemakers, Worshipful Co fo Turners (Master 1969); *Clubs* City Livery, Army and Navy; *Style*— Sir John Newson-Smith, Bt

NEWSON-SMITH, Peter Frank Graham; s and h of Sir John Kenneth Newson-Smith, 2 Bt, *qv*, and his 1 w, Vera Margaret Greenhouse Allt; paternal gf was Lord Mayor of London; maternal gf was Dr Greenhouse Allt, CVO, CBE, princ of Trinity Coll of Music London; *b* 8 May 1947; *Educ* Dover Coll, Trinity Coll of Music; *m* 1974, Mary-Ann, da of Cyril C Collins, of Old Woodstock, Oxon, and formerly w of Anthony Owens; 1 s (Oliver Nicholas Peter b 1975), 1 da (Emma, b 1977); *Career* dir of music Clayesmore Preparatory Sch; Freeman City of London 1969, Liveryman Worshipful Co of Musicians 1971; *Recreations* gardening, sailing; *Style*— Peter Newson-Smith, Esq; ✉ Lovells Court, Burton Street, Marnhull, Sturminster Newton, Dorset DT10 1JJ (☎ 01258 820652, fax 01258 820487); Clayesmore Preparatory School, Iwerne Minster, Blandford Forum, Dorset DT11 8PH

NEWTH, Jonathan Gildon; s of Terence Conrad Newth (d 1994), of Appledore, Devon, and Winifred Gertrude Mary, *née* Lack (d 1991); *b* 6 March 1939; *Educ* Aldenham Sch, Central Sch of Speech and Drama; *m* 1, 1964 (m dis 1978), Joanna, da of Dr S V Brookes; 2 s (Benjamin b 1965, Daniel b 1968); m 2, 1979, Gay, da of R A Wilde; 3 da (Rosalind b 1980, Eliza b 1982, Charlotte b 1988), 1 s (George b 1985); *Career* actor; *Theatre* Open Air Theatre Regents Park: Lysander in A Midsummer Night's Dream 1966, Camillo in A Winters Tale 1988, Quince in A Midsummer Night's Dream 1988; RSC: Bonaventure in 'Tis Pity She's A Whore 1991–92, Capulet in Romeo and Juliet 1991–92, Player King in Hamlet 1992–93; other roles incl: The School for Scandal (Theatre Royal Haymarket and USA) 1962–63, The Creeper (St Martins) 1965, Robert in Meeting At Night (Duke of Yorks) 1972, Richard in Rents (Lyric Hammersmith) 1982, Col Tallboys in Too True to be Good 1986, Fred in The Viewing (Greenwich) 1987, Bill Coles in Other Peoples Money (Lyric) 1990, Leonato in Much Ado About Nothing (Queens) 1993, Mr Bennet in Pride and Prejudice (nat tour) 1995; *Television* incl: Lord Rochford in The Six Wives of Henry VIII 1968, Capt Blamey in Poldark 1972, Brig Jefferson in Tenko 1984, Josh in Fainthearted Feminist 1984, Boustead in Voyage Around My Father 1984, Russell in After Henry 1987–92, Matthew Pocket in Great Expectations 1988, Dr Eliot in Casualty 1996; *Radio* incl: Green Mansions and The Siege of Krishnapur (Book At Bedtime); *Films* incl: Far from the Madding Crowd, Yellow Dog, Pope John Paul II, North Sea Hi-Jack, Accounts, Judge in Incognito 1996; *Style*— Jonathan Newth, Esq; ✉ c/o Caroline Dawson Associates, Apartment 9, 47 Courtfield Road, London SW7 4DB (☎ 0171 370 0708, fax 0171 835 1403)

NEWTON, Rt Hon Antony Harold (Tony); PC (1988), OBE (1972), MP (C) Braintree (majority 17,494); s of Harold Newton, of Dovercourt, Harwich; *b* 29 Aug 1937; *Educ* Friends' Sch Saffron Walden, Trinity Coll Oxford; *m* 1, 1962 (m dis 1986), Janet Dianne, er da of Phillip Huxley, of Sidcup; 2 da; m 2, 1986, Mrs Patricia Gilthorpe; 1 step s, 2 step da; *Career* pres Oxford Univ Cons Assoc 1958, pres Oxford Union 1959, sometime vice chm Fedn of Univ Cons and Unionist Assocs; economist, former sec and res sec Bow Gp, asst dir CRD 1970–74 (head Econ Section 1965–70); Parly candidate (C) Sheffield Brightside 1970, MP (C) Braintree Feb 1974–, asst govt whip 1979–81, a Lord Cmmr of the Treasy (govt whip) 1981–82, Parly under sec DHSS 1982, min for the disabled 1983–84, min for social security and the disabled 1984–86, min for health

1986–88, Chllr of the Duchy of Lancaster and min for trade and indust 1988–89, sec of state for social security DSS 1989–92, Lord Pres of the Cncl and Ldr of the House of Commons 1992–; *Style*— The Rt Hon Tony Newton, OBE, MP; ✉ House of Commons, London SW1A 0AA (☎ 0171 219 3000)

NEWTON, Air Vice-Marshal Barry Hamilton; CB (1988), OBE (1975); s of Bernard Hamilton Newton, FCA (d 1932), of Southgate, Middx, and Dorothy Mary Newton, *née* Thomas (d 1979); *b* 1 April 1932; *Educ* Highgate Sch, RAF Coll Cranwell; *m* 1959, Lavinia, da of Col John James Aitken, CMG, DSO, OBE (d 1947), of Taunton, Somerset; 1 s (Charles), 1 da (Melanie); *Career* cmmnd RAF 1953, Personal Staff Offr to Cdr Second Allied Tactical Air Force and CINC RAF Germany 1967, OC Ops Wing RAF Cottesmore 1969, asst dir Def Policy 1978, Cabinet Office 1979–81, Air Cdre Flying Trg HQ RAF Support Cmd 1982, sr dir Staff (Air) RCDS 1984, Cmdt Jt Serv Def Coll Greenwich 1986, ADC to HM The Queen 1983; a gentleman usher to HM The Queen 1989–, memb Cncl TA&VR Assoc 1989–; *Recreations* shooting, music, reading; *Clubs* RAF; *Style*— Air Vice-Marshal Barry Newton, CB, OBE; ✉ c/o National Westminster Bank plc, 48 Blue Boar Row, Salisbury, Wilts SP1 1DF

NEWTON, Dr Charmian Rosemary; da of Frederick Cleland Newton, of Weybridge, Surrey, and Mildred Edith, *née* Owen; *b* 3 April 1943; *Educ* St Maur's Convent Weybridge, King's Coll London, Westminster Med Sch (MB BS, DObstRCOG); *m* 30 Jan 1971, Timothy Richard Hornsby, s of Harker William Hornsby (d 1974); 1 s (Adrian b 1977), 1 da (Gabrielle b 1975); *Career* house offr Westminster Hosp and Queen Mary's Hosp Roehampton 1965–66, sr house offr in med Whittington Hosp 1967–68, med registrar St Mary's Hosp Paddington 1968–69, res registrar St Mark's Hosp London 1969–72, med registrar St George's Hosp London 1972–73; sr med registrar: Central Middx Hosp 1973–75, Middx Hosp 1975–77; conslt physician: S London Hosp for Women 1978–84, St James's Hosp 1978–88, St George's Hosp 1988–; memb: BSG 1973, BMA 1965; MRCP 1967 (collegiate memb 1979), FRSM 1970, memb BDA 1981; FRCP 1993; *Recreations* opera, ballet, skiing; *Clubs* RSM, SCGB; *Style*— Dr Charmian Newton; ✉ Norman Tanner Unit, St George's Hospital, Blackshaw Rd, London SW17 0QT (☎ 0181 725 3032)

NEWTON, Christopher John; s of Henry Newton (d 1975), of Leicester and London, and Florence Alice, *née* Wilton (d 1978); *b* 24 June 1936; *Educ* Market Bosworth GS, Royal Ballet Sch Sadler's Wells; *Career* joined Royal Ballet Co Corps de Ballet 1954–1970 (soloist 1958–70), joined Faculty of US Int Univ San Diego California to teach dance notation and repertoire 1970–73; Royal Ballet: re-joined as dance notator and repetiteur 1973–80, ballet master 1980–88, artistic co-ordinator 1988; has re-produced ballets of Frederick Ashton, Antony Tudor, Rudolph Nureyev and Roland Petit 1970–88 for American Ballet Theatre, Joffrey Ballet, SF Ballet, Paris Opera Ballet and Deutsch Oper Ballet of Berlin, also staged own production of Swan Lake - Act III for Pennsylvania Ballet; re-produced and staged Frederick Ashton's 3 act ballet Ondine from incomplete film records 1988 (created in 1958 and last performed in 1966); MRAD, AIChor; *Recreations* textile crafts; *Style*— Christopher Newton, Esq; ✉ Royal Ballet Company, Royal Opera House, Covent Garden, London WC2E 9DD (☎ 0171 240 1200, telex 27988)

NEWTON, David Alexander; s of Alexander Newton, of Eye, Suffolk, and Hazel, *née* Little; *b* 6 Oct 1942; *Educ* Morecambe GS; *m* 6 March 1965, Kathleen Mary, da of George Ernest Moore; 1 da (Rebecca b 8 Dec 1965), 1 s (Stewart Alexander b 25 Sept 1967); *Career* trainee Provincial Insurance Co 1958–61, mgmnt trainee J Bibby & Sons 1961–66, area mangr Cobb Breeding Co 1966–68, gen mangr Anglian Hatcheries 1968–71, agric dir Sovereign Group 1971–81; Hillsdown Group: md Ross Poultry 1981–82, chm Ross Group 1982–85, chm and chief exec offr Buxted Ltd 1983–87, dep chm Maple Leaf Foods Canada 1992–95 (pres and chief exec offr 1987–92), chief exec offr Hillsdown Group 1993–96 (chief operating offr 1992–93); dir: Carrs Milling PLC, Bodfari Ltd, Bernard Matthews PLC; ptnr K&D Partnership; dir various gp cos 1982–92; FInstD, CIM, FRSA; *Recreations* golf, watching sports, music; *Clubs* Diss Golf (Norfolk); *Style*— David Newton, Esq; ✉ Falcon House, Mellis, Eye, Suffolk IP23 8DS (☎ 01379 783561, fax 01379 788327)

NEWTON, David Robert; s of Harry King Newton (d 1967), of Hampstead, and Hilda Elizabeth Constance, *née* Humber (d 1991); *b* 19 March 1932; *Educ* Borden GS Sittingbourne Kent, Medway Coll of Art Rochester Kent (NDD); *m* 1, 25 Oct 1958 (d 1973), Pauline Marion, da of late Desmond Mars White; 2 s (Simon b 12 June 1959, Joseph b 19 Oct 1964); m 2, 15 March 1975, Benedicte Anne-Marie, da of late Michel Paitard; 2 da (Elodie Sarah b 4 Oct 1975, Charlotte Amelie b 28 Feb 1979); *Career* served British South Africa Police Zimbabwe 1953–55; Barker McCormac Advertising Zimbabwe 1955–59; art dir: Young & Rubicam London 1959–64, Davidson Pearce (now BMP Needham) 1964–69; ptnr Lippa Newton Ltd advtg consultancy 1969–90, sr writer Abbott Mead Vickers BBDO Ltd London 1990–; numerous D&AD awards incl: Silver (for best b&w advertisement in a consumer magazine) 1967, Silver (for the outstanding trade b&w advertisement) 1976; work published in 100 Great Advertisements (Times Newspapers/Mirror Group Newspapers); Poster of the Month Award (Creative Review in conjunction with Arthur Maiden) 1993; memb: D&AD 1963, ICA London 1991; *Books* The World of Small Ads (1978), The Gobbledegook and Other Strange Creatures (1979); *Recreations* drawing and painting, geneology; *Style*— David Newton, Esq; ✉ Abbott Mead Vickers BBDO Ltd, 191 Old Marylebone Road, London NW1 5DW (☎ 0171 402 4100)

NEWTON, Derek Henry; s of Sidney Wellington Newton (d 1976), of Worthing, Sussex, and Sylvia May, *née* West (d 1959); *b* 14 March 1933; *Educ* Emanuel Sch; *m* 18 May 1957, Judith Ann (d 1995), da of Rowland Hart (d 1973); 2 da (Katherine Jane (Mrs Smith) b 3 Sept 1960, Amanda Jean (Mrs Roberts) b 4 Nov 1962); *Career* Nat Serv Lt RA 1952–54; insur broker; chm C E Heath plc 1983–87; dir: Glaxo Insurance (Bermuda) Ltd 1980–93, Glaxo Trustees Ltd 1980–92, Glaxo Pharmaceuticals Trustees Ltd 1980–92, Clarges Pharmaceuticals Trustees Ltd 1985–92; govr BUPA Medical Research & Development Ltd 1981–95; cncllr for Oxshott and Stoke D'Abernon Esher UDC 1968–71; Liveryman Worshipful Co of Insurers; FCII 1957; *Recreations* cricket, golf; *Clubs* Surrey CCC (chm 1979–94), MCC; *Style*— Derek Newton, Esq; ✉ Pantiles, Meadway, Oxshott, Surrey KT22 OLZ (☎ 01372 842273, fax 01372 843913)

NEWTON, Rev George Peter Howgill; s and h of Sir (Harry) Michael Rex Newton, 3 Bt, *qv*; *b* 26 March 1962; *Educ* Sherborne, Pembroke Coll Cambridge (MA); *m* 30 Jan 1988, Jane L, twin da of late John Rymer; 2 da (Sarah Rebecca b 4 Jan 1991, Kate Evangeline b 11 Nov 1992); *Career* assoc vicar St Thomas' Blackpool 1993–; Liveryman Worshipful Co of Girdlers; *Style*— The Rev George Newton; (☎ 01253 302679)

NEWTON, Sir (Leslie) Gordon; kt (1966); s of John Newton; *b* 1907; *Educ* Blundell's, Sidney Sussex Coll Cambridge; *m* 1935, Peggy Ellen Warren (d 1995); 1 s (decd); *Career* ed The Financial Times 1950–72 (dir 1967–72); chm LBC 1974–77; dir: Trust House Forte 1973–80, Mills & Allen (International); *Style*— Sir Gordon Newton

NEWTON, (Robert Edward) Ian; s of John Newton, of Digswell, Welwyn, Herts, and Ethel, *née* Albiston (d 1967); *b* 4 Aug 1946; *Educ* Dulwich Coll (princ bassoon London Schs' Symphony Orch), Oriel Coll Oxford (MA, capt coll cross-country team), Inst of Educn Univ of London (PGCE); *m* 1969, Fiona Olive, da of Norman Sidney Pallant, of Loughton, Essex; 1 da (Meg Fiona b 1973), 1 s (Alastair Norman John b 1977); *Career* Rugby Sch: physics teacher 1968–92, sixth form girls' housemaster 1976–92, head of physics 1991–92; headmaster Bedales Sch 1992–94, OFSTED inspr and conslt in educn 1995–; MInstP, CPhys, FRSA; *Books* Wave Physics (1990); *Recreations* sailing, playing the bassoon, walking; *Clubs* Royal Naval Sailing Assoc; *Style*— Ian Newton, Esq; ✉ 22 Hillmorton Road, Rugby, Warwickshire CV22 5AA (☎ 01788 561393)

NEWTON, Prof Ian; s of Haydn Edwin Newton (d 1980), of Chesterfield, Derbyshire, and Nellie, *née* Stubbs (d 1986); *b* 17 Jan 1940; *Educ* Chesterfield Boys' GS, Univ of Bristol (BSc), Univ of Oxford (DPhil, DSc); *m* 21 July 1962, Halina Teresa, da of Edward Bialkowski; 2 s (Michael Peter b 1965, Robert Edward b 1967), 1 da (Diana Catherine b 1969); *Career* post-doctoral research Univ of Oxford 1964–67; Nature Conservancy Edinburgh: research on waterfowl populations 1967–71, research on birds of prey 1971–79; Inst of Terrestrial Ecology: head of Pollution Research Unit 1979–84, special merit post grade 5 1992– (grade 6 1984–92); visiting prof in ornithology Univ of Oxford 1994–; Union Medal Br Ornithologists Union 1988, Gold Medal Br Ecological Soc 1989, medal RSPB 1991, President's Award Raptor Research Fndn 1993, Marsh Award in Conservational Biology Zoological Soc 1995, Elliott Cowes Award American Ornithologists Union 1995; memb: Br Ecological Soc (pres 1994–95), Br Ornithologists Union (vice-pres 1989–93); hon memb American Ornithologists Union; FRS 1993, FRSE 1994; *Books* Finches (1972), Population Ecology of Raptors (1979), The Sparrowhawk (1986), Lifetime Reproduction in Birds (ed, 1989); *Recreations* walking, travel, fruit growing; *Style*— Prof Ian Newton, FRS, FRSE; ✉ Institute of Terrestrial Ecology, Monks Wood, Abbots Ripton, Huntingdon, Cambs PE17 2LS (☎ 01487 773381, fax 01487 773467)

NEWTON, Ian Stenhouse; s of Peter Stenhouse Newton (d 1982), of Cardiff, and Esmé, *née* Jones (d 1994); *b* 6 Sept 1951; *Educ* Cardiff HS, New Coll Oxford (MA); *children* 2 da (Kate b 1979, Ailsa b 1983); *Career* articled clerk and slr Biddle & Co 1974–77; Percy Partnership: legal advsr 1978–81, admin and fin ptnr 1982–92; dir and sec Insight Computer Systems Ltd 1981–92, ptnr and sec PTP Landscape 1985–92, dir Wren Insurance Association Ltd 1987–92, ptnr and sec PTP Design Group 1990–92, dir and sec PTP Seward Ltd 1991–92, mgmnt conslt Stenhouse Consultancy 1992–; qualified neuro-linguistic programmer and Time Line therapy practitioner 1992; past memb Partnership Secs Panel ICSA 1985–89, past chm Cardiff and SE Wales Branch ICSA 1986, hon sec Chartered Secs Golf Soc 1989–94; certified NLP trainer 1993; FCIS 1981, FIMgt 1985; *Recreations* golf, Eastern philosophy; *Clubs* Cardiff and County, Royal Porthcawl Golf, Llanishen Golf, Wig and Pen; *Style*— Ian Newton, Esq; ✉ 36 Plasturton Gardens, Pontcanna, Cardiff, South Glamorgan CF1 9HF (☎ 01222 377723)

NEWTON, Rev Dr John Anthony; s of Charles Victor Newton (d 1963), and Kathleen, *née* Marchant (d 1990); *b* 28 Sept 1930; *Educ* Boston GS, Univ Coll Hull (BA), Inst of Historical Res Univ of London (PhD), Fitzwilliam Coll Cambridge (MA); *m* 28 Dec 1963, Rachel, da of Maurice Horne Giddings (d 1968), of Louth, Lincs; 4 s (Mark b 5 Nov 1964, Christopher b 27 Sept 1966, David b 31 Dec 1970, William b 24 March 1976); *Career* chaplain Kent Coll Canterbury 1955, asst tutor Richmond Coll 1958, min Louth Lincs 1961; tutor in church history: Didsbury Coll Bristol 1965, St Paul's Coll Limuru Kenya 1972; princ Wesley Coll Bristol 1973, supt W London Mission 1978, pres Methodist Conf 1981–82, chm Liverpool Dist of Methodist Church 1986–95, Free Church moderator for Merseyside and jt pres Merseyside Churches Ecumenical Assembly 1987–95, hon canon Lincoln Cathedral 1988; pres The Chesterton Soc 1991–, jt pres Churches Together in England 1990–94, warden John Wesley's Chapel Bristol 1995–; Hon DLitt Hull 1982, hon fell Liverpool John Moores Univ 1993; DD (Lambeth) 1995; *Books* Susanna Wesley and the Puritan Tradition in Methodism (1969), The Palestine Problem (1971), Search for a Saint: Edward King (1977), Marcus Ward (1984), Heart Speaks To Heart (1994); *Recreations* walking, reading, book collecting; *Clubs* Penn; *Style*— The Rev Dr John Newton; ✉ 3 College Road, Westbury-on-Trym, Bristol BS9 3EJ (☎ 0117 959 3225)

NEWTON, John Garnar; s and h of Sir Kenneth Garnar Newton, 3 Bt, OBE, TD, *qv*; *b* 10 July 1945; *Educ* Reed's Sch Cobham; *m* 27 May 1972, Jacynth Anne Kay, *née* Miller; 3 s (Timothy Garnar b 1973, Alistair Blair b (twin) 1973, Andrew Robert b 1975); *Style*— John Newton, Esq; ✉ North House, Wyboston, Beds

NEWTON, Dr John Henry; s of Dr J E Newton (d 1979), and Jessie Elizabeth, *née* Sherwood (d 1985); *b* 8 Oct 1939; *Educ* Blundell's, Charing Cross Hosp Univ of London (MB BS, DMRD); *m* 24 Aug 1968, Valerie Faith, da of Frederick Arthur Mullineux (d 1977); 1 s (Simon James b 1970), 2 da (Antoinette Sophie b 1969, Lucinda Helen b 1972); *Career* registrar Bristol United Hospital 1967–69, sr registrar Charing Cross Hospital 1970–72, conslt radiologist Bedford Hospital 1972–, chm Radiodiagnostic Sub-ctee NW Thames RHA 1989–92; FFR 1971, FRCR 1975; *Recreations* travel, opera, photography; *Style*— Dr John Newton; ✉ 8 Days Lane, Biddenham, Bedford MK40 4AD (☎ 01234 363828); Bedford Hospital, Kempston Rd, Bedford MK42 9DJ (☎ 01234 355122)

NEWTON, Prof John Richard; s of Geoffrey Tayler Newton, of Woking, Surrey, and Nora, *née* Waddington (d 1986); *b* 14 April 1938; *Educ* Uppingham, Bart's Med Sch (MB BS, MD), LLM 1994; *m* 1 July 1967, Mary Patricia, da of Henry Percy Burdis (d 1986); 1 s (Simon Geoffrey Waddington b 4 July 1969 d 1975), 2 da (Rebecca Sophie Patersson b 26 Sept 1971, Shelley Marianne b 19 May 1975); *Career* postgrad med trg: Bart's, Queen Charlotte's Hosp for Women, Royal Sussex County Hosp, KCH, London, Univ Hosp Uppsala Sweden, Health Sci Centre San Antonio Texas USA; sr lectr and hon conslt KCH 1972–79, Lawson Tait prof of obstetrics and gynaecology Univ of Birmingham 1979–; author of numerous pubns on human reproduction and contraception; memb GMC; chm: FPA Med Advsy Ctee 1980–, WHO task force on long acting methods of contraception 1987–93; memb: Euro Soc of Gynaecological Endoscopy, Fndn Bd Faculty of Family Planning and Reproductive Med, Med Advsy Bd IPPF 1994–96; sec Br Fertility Soc 1988–93 (fndr memb); vice pres: Br Soc of Gynaecological Endoscopy, Birmingham and Midland Obstetrics and Gynaecology Soc; memb Soc for the Advancement of Contraception; MRCOG 1987, FRCOG 1982, MFFP 1993; *Books* Pocket Obstetrics & Gynaecology (edns 9, 10, 11, 12, 13); *Recreations* sailing, skiing; *Style*— Prof John Newton; ✉ Department of Obstetrics and Gynaecology, Birmingham University Medical School, Queen Elizabeth Medical Centre, Edgbaston, Birmingham B15 2TG (☎ 0121 627 2695, fax 0121 414 1576)

NEWTON, Sir Kenneth Garnar; 3 Bt (UK 1924), of Beckenham, Co Kent; OBE (1969, MBE 1944), TD; s of Sir Edgar Henry Newton, 2 Bt (d 1971); *b* 4 June 1918; *Educ* Wellington; *m* 1944, Margaret Isabel (d 1979), da of Rev Dr George Blair, of Dundee; 2 s (John Garnar b 1945, Peter Blair b 1950); *Heir* s, John Garnar Newton b 10 July 1945; *Career* served WWII, Lt-Col 1944; gen cmmr for Income Tax 1961–93; md Garnar Booth plc 1961–83 (chm 1972–87); pres: Br Leather Fedn 1968–69, Int Cncl of Tanners 1972–78; Master: Worshipful Co of Leathersellers 1977–78, Worshipful Co of Feltmakers 1983–84; chm Bd of Govrs Colfe's Sch 1982–93; *Style*— Sir Kenneth Newton, Bt, OBE, TD; ✉ Oaklands, Harborough Gorse, West Chiltington, West Sussex RH20 2RU

NEWTON, Mark Robert; s of Robert William Banner Newton (d 1982), and Cicely Kathleen, *née* Radmall (d 1989); *b* 2 June 1954; *Educ* Eton, RAC Cirencester; *m* 12 May 1979, Diana Sarah, da of Maj Sir Robert David Black, 3 Bt, of Goring-on-Thames, Oxon; 2 s (William David Rupert b 7 Dec 1989, James Robert George b 3 Nov 1993); *Career* chartered surveyor; ptnr Fisher Hoggarth 1985–; chm: Leics Branch Game Conservancy Tst 1995–, Midlands Branch Royal Forestry Soc 1994–95; district cnllr Langtons Ward Harborough District Cncl 1995–; memb: Game Conservancy, Royal Forestry Soc; FRICS 1986; *Recreations* fishing, shooting; *Style*— Mark Newton, Esq; ✉ The Old Rectory, Church Langton, Leics LE16 7SX (☎ 01858 545600); Fisher Hoggarth, 40 High St,

Market Harborough, Leics LE16 7NX (☎ 01858 410200, fax 01858 410207, car 0860 514474)

NEWTON, Sir (Harry) Michael Rex; 3 Bt (UK 1900), of The Wood, Sydenham Hill, Lewisham, Kent, and Kottingham House, Burton-on-Trent, Co Stafford; s of Sir Harry Kottingham Newton, 2 Bt, OBE (d 1951), and Myrtle Irene, *née* Grantham (d 1977); *b* 7 Feb 1923; *Educ* Eastbourne Coll; *m* 1958, Pauline Jane, o da of Richard John Frederick Howgill, CBE, of Branscombe, Sullington Warren, Storrington, Sussex; 1 s, 3 (adopted) da (Lucinda Jane b 1964, (Julia) Kate (Mrs Daryn Hufton-Rees) b 1967, Jennifer Anne b (twin) 1967); *Heir* s, Rev George Peter Howgill Newton, *qv*; *Career* served 1941–46 with KRRC; dir Thomas Parsons & Sons Ltd; memb Ct of Assts Worshipful Co of Girdlers (past Master); Freeman City of London; winner of 1953 Fastnet Race; *Clubs* Royal Ocean Racing; *Style*— Sir Michael Newton, Bt; ✉ Cliff House, Old Lyme Road, Charmouth, Dorset DT6 6BW (☎ 01297 60704)

NEWTON, Dr Ray William; *b* 8 Dec 1944; *Educ* Univ of Edinburgh (MB, MRCP); *Career* formerly med registrar Royal Infirmary Edinburgh, conslt physician Ninwells Hosp and Med Sch 1977– (hon sr lectr Dept of Med and Dept of Clinical Pharmacology and clinical dir Directorate of Gen Med); external examiner (MB ChB and MSc in Endocrinology) Univ of Glasgow; conslt i/c Dundee Diabetic Serv; NHS: memb Nat Med Advsy Ctee 1992– (chm Div of Med 1989–92), clinical dir of med 1994–; RCPEd: Tayside regnl advsr 1983–, memb Educn Ctee 1990–, memb Overseas Ctee 1990–, memb Cncl 1992–; visiting clinical tutor Queen Elizabeth Hosp Hong Kong 1988; chm: Jt Royal Colls Working Gp on SHO Trg 1993, Jt Colls Review on Doctors in Basic Med Trg 1995; Br Diabetic Soc: chm Scottish Ctee 1989–92, memb Exec Cncl 1989–92, memb Med and Scientific Ctee 1990–92; chm: Scottish Study Gp for the Care of the Young Diabetic 1989–91, Scottish Implementation Task Force on Care in Childhood and Adolescence 1994; FRCPEd 1981, FRCPGlas 1995; *Books* Endocrinology - The New Medicine (jt ed, 1983), Diabetes in Childhood and Adolescence (jtly, 1995); author of numour book chapters and pubns on diabetes and endocrinology; *Style*— Dr Ray Newton; ✉ Department of Medicine, Ninewells Hospital, Dundee DD2 1UB (☎ 01382 60111)

NEWTON, 5 Baron (UK 1892); Richard Thomas Legh; s of 4 Baron Newton (d 1992), and Priscilla, *née* Egerton-Warburton (now Mrs Frederick Fryer); *b* 11 Jan 1950; *Educ* Eton, ChCh Oxford; *m* 1978, Rosemary Whitfoot, da of Herbert Whitfoot Clarke, of Eastbourne; 1 s (Piers Richard b 25 Oct 1979), 1 da (Alessandra Mary b 24 Aug 1978); *Heir* s, Hon Piers Richard Legh b 25 Oct 1979; *Career* slr, gen cmmr of Income Tax 1983–; cncllr Wealden DC 1987–; memb Sussex Downs Cons Bd 1992–95; *Style*— The Rt Hon the Lord Newton; ✉ Laughton Park Farm, Laughton, Lewes, E Sussex BN8 6BU (☎ 01825 840627, fax 01825 841048)

NEWTON, Rodney Stephen; s of Amos Bernard Newton (d 1981), of Birmingham, and Winifred Nellie, *née* York; *b* 31 July 1945; *Educ* King's Heath HS Birmingham, Lordwood Boys' Sch Birmingham, Birmingham Sch of Music; *m* 19 Sept 1970, Jennifer Kathleen, da of Denis Williams, of Halesowen, Worcs; 2 s (Matthew b 15 Sept 1977, Christopher b 24 April 1980); *Career* orchestral timpanist percussionist, composer and lectr 1967–; BBC trg orchestra 1967–70, ENO orchestra 1974–85, promotion mangr United Music Publishers 1979–82, music conslt London Int Film Sch 1988–, lectr in composition and orchestration London Coll of Music 1995–, visiting lectr in film music RAM 1995–; compositions in: 9 symphonies, 5 string quartets, flute concerto, music for brass band, chamber and vocal works; film and TV scores incl: The Pyrates, The Watch House (BBC TV), Lucinda Lambton's A-Z of Britain (BBC TV), Theatre of Paint (BEU Prodns), Change at Clapham Junction (Thames TV); commercial recordings incl Variations for Percussion, Four Spanish Impressions (Chandos Records), Capriccio (Doyen Records), Heroes and Warriors (Marcophone Records), Seascapes (EMU Prodn Music Library); memb: Composers Guild of GB, Assoc of Professional Composers, Advsy Cncl to Br Music Information Centre; *Recreations* reading, cinema, eating out; *Style*— Rodney Newton, Esq; ✉ c/o London International Film School, 24 Shelton St, London WC2H 9HP (☎ 0171 240 0168, fax 0171 497 3718)

NEWTON, Roger Surtees; s of Percival Newton (d 1953), and Constance Mabel, *née* Shutter (d 1991); *b* 7 Aug 1928; *Educ* Glyn GS Epsom; *m* 1, 1950 (m dis 1979), Patricia Dudley, *née* Cox; 1 s (Mark Surtees b 1953), 1 da (Sally Patricia (Mrs Mackey) b 1956); m 2, 1980, Else Grete, da of Peder S Skov, of Herning, Denmark; *Career* Navigating Offr British Merchant Navy 1944–48, Second Offr 1948–50; trainee S H Benson advtg agency 1950–51, publicity asst ICI Pharmaceuticals 1951–53, successively publicity mangr, promotions mangr then dep mktg dir Ciba-Geigy Manchester 1953–63, gen advtg mangr Glaxo Laboratories 1963–68, mktg dir Parke-Davis & Co 1968–74, md Warner Lambert Scandinavia 1974–77, vice pres Warner Lambert UK 1978–83, md Newton Communications Ltd 1983–; co-ordinator Wessex Pharmaceutical Group 1983–; non-exec chm: Pharmaceutical Proteins Ltd 1987–96 (non-exec dir 1996–), The Leith Advertising Agency 1987–95 (non-exec dir 1995–), Silvermills Group Ltd (parent co) 1993–, One-to-One Direct 1992–, EH6 Ltd 1992–, Department S Ltd 1992–; chm Gwent Health Authority 1990–94 (memb 1986–, vice chm 1988–89); MCIM 1962, FInstD 1983; *Style*— Roger S Newton, Esq; ✉ Forester's Lodge, Itton, Chepstow, Gwent NP6 6BZ (☎ 01291 641344, fax 01291 641822); Newton Communications Ltd, 35 Moor Street, Chepstow, Gwent NP6 5DE (☎ 01291 627733, fax 01291 627133)

NEWTON, Stewart Worth; *b* 31 Oct 1941; *m* Jannion; 3 da (Catherine, Antonia, Lucy); *Career* investment mgmnt; formerly with: Touche Ross CAs, W Greenwell stockbrokers, Ivory & Sime plc; currently chm Newton Investment Management; FCA; *Style*— Stewart Newton, Esq; ✉ Newton Investment Management, 71 Queen Victoria Street, London EC4V 4DR (☎ 0171 332 9000)

NEWTON, Sir (Charles) Wilfrid; kt (1993), CBE (1988); s of Gore Mansfield Newton (d 1966), of Durban, SA, and Catherine, *née* Knox Darcus (d 1972); *b* 11 Dec 1928; *Educ* Highlands N HS Johannesburg SA, Univ of Witwatersrand (cert in theory of accountancy); *m* 6 Feb 1954, Felicity Mary Lynn, da of John Lynn Thomas (d 1973), of Johannesburg, SA; 2 s (Gavin b 1957, Thomas b 1964), 2 da (Tessa (Mrs Purvis) b 1958, Glynis (Mrs Murphy) b 1960); *Career* Samuel Thomson & Young CAs SA 1947–55; Mobil Oil Corporation: territory accounting and fin mangr SA 1955–62, controller Mobil Sekiyu KK Tokyo 1962–63, fin mangr and dep gen mangr E Africa Nairobi 1963–65, fin dir Mobil Sekiyu KK Tokyo and chief fin offr Mobil interests Japan 1965–68; Turner and Newall: fin dir 1968, md of fin and planning 1974, md of plastics chemicals and mining 1976, gp md 1979, chief exec 1982–83; chm: Mass Transit Railway Corporation Hong Kong 1983–89, London Regional Transport 1989–94, London Underground Ltd 1989–94, Raglan Properties plc 1993–, Jacobs Holdings PLC 1994–; non-exec dir: Hongkong Bank 1986–92, HSBC Holdings plc 1990–, Midland Bank plc 1992–, Sketchley plc 1991–; memb Pres's Ctee CBI 1990–94; memb Worshipful Co of Horners, Freeman City of London; memb Transvaal Soc of Accountants 1956, fndr memb Inst of CA's of SA 1979, CIMgt 1974, fell Hong Kong Mgmnt Assoc 1987, hon fell Hong Kong Inst of Engrs 1994, FCIT 1989, FRSA 1990, Hon FEng 1993; *Recreations* sailing, reading, current affairs, economics; *Clubs* Wanderers' (Johannesburg), Carlton, Hong Kong, Royal Hong Kong Yacht, Aberdeen Boat, Royal Lymington Yacht, Little Ship; *Style*— Sir Wilfrid Newton, CBE, Hon FEng; ✉ Newtons Gate, 12 Ramley Road, Pennington, Lymington, Hants S041 8GQ (☎ 01590 679750, fax 01590 677990); 7a Balmoral House, Windsor Way, Brook Green, London W14 0UF; 24 Berkeley Square, London W1X 5HB (☎ 0171 629 1339, fax 0171 629 0728)

NEWTON DUNN, William Francis (Bill); s of Lt-Col Owen Frank Newton Dunn, OBE (d 1995), and Barbara Mary, *née* Brooke (d 1995); *b* 3 Oct 1941; *Educ* Marlborough, Gonville and Caius Cambridge (MA), INSEAD Business Sch Fontainebleau (MBA); *m* 17 Oct 1970, Anna Terez Arki; 1 s (Thomas b 1973), 1 da (Daisy b 1976); *Career* MEP (Cons) Lincolnshire 1979–94, chm Cons MEPs 1993–94 (dep ldr 1991–93); formerly with Fisons Fertilisers, currently dir and share-holder Neil Lasher Silverware Ltd; Liveryman Worshipful Co of Haberdashers; *Books* Greater in Europe (1986), Big Wing 1992; *Style*— Bill Newton Dunn, Esq; ✉ 27 Sterndale Road, London W14 0HT (☎ 0171 602 6187); Neil Lasher Silverware Ltd (☎ 0171 613 2113)

NG, Dr Weng Cheong; s of Kam Sooi Ng, and Ng-Sung Ngan-Lui; *b* 18 Sept 1943; *Educ* Methodist Boys' Sch Penang, Univ of Singapore (MB BS), Royal Coll of Physicians and Surgeons (DPath), Univ of London (DCP), Univ of Mahidol (DTM&H); *m* 25 Sept 1971, Chew Pek Choo, da of Chew Poh Leang; 1 s (Paul b 4 Jan 1979); *Career* MO: Rural Health Trg Sch Jitra Malaysia 1970–71, Inst of Med Res Kuala Lumpur Malaysia 1971–75; registrar Gen Infirmary Salisbury 1978; sr registrar: Southampton and Poole Gen Hosps 1978–80, Pathology Dept Singapore 1981–83; conslt histopathologist Princess Margaret Hosp Swindon 1983–; memb: Assoc of Clinical Pathologists, Br Soc of Clinical Cytology, BMA; MRCPath 1979, FCAP 1982, FRCPath 1991; *Recreations* chess, music, swimming; *Style*— Dr Weng Cheong Ng; ✉ Pathology Department, Princess Margaret Hospital, Okus Road, Swindon, Wiltshire SN1 4JU (☎ 01793 536231 ext 6336)

NGALI, HE Mwanyengela; s of Ngali Maganga Mwarori (d 1947), of Taita-Taveta District, Kenya, and Ruth Mkandoo Mdawida; *b* 1 Jan 1947; *Educ* Alliance HS Kikuyu Kenya, Univ of Nairobi (BCom Mktg); *m* 15 Aug 1970, Elizabeth Wuganga Mwawaya; *Career* Kenyan diplomat; sales exec Kenya Broadcasting Corporation 1971–72, sales rep Esso Standard Kenya Ltd 1972–73; commercial attaché: Kenya Embassy Washington DC 1974–81, Kenya High Cmmn London 1981–82; first sec Kenya High Cmmn Kampala 1983–84, cnsllr Kenya Embassy Riyadh Saudi Arabia 1984–87, under sec Miny of Commerce Nairobi 1987–92, dir of political affrs Miny of Foreign Affrs Nairobi April-Aug 1992, actg high cmmr to the Ct of St James's 1992–93, high cmmr Kenya High Cmmn Ottawa 1993–95, high cmmr to the Ct of St James's (concurrently ambass to Switzerland and Ireland) 1996–; memb: Kenya Harambee Movement, Royal Cwlth Soc, Kenya Soc; *Publications* Mwana Taabu Na Michezo Mingine Ya Kuigiza (1970); *Recreations* walking, cycling, tennis, reading; *Style*— HE Mr Mwanyengela Ngali; ✉ Kenya High Commission, 45 Portland Place, London W1N 4AS (☎ 0171 636 2371, fax 0171 323 6717)

NICE, Geoffrey; QC (1990); s of William Charles Nice (d 1992), and Mahala Anne, *née* Tarryer (d 1982); *b* 21 Oct 1945; *Educ* St Dunstan's Coll Catford, Keble Coll Oxford; *m* 1974, Philippa, da of Kemlo Abbot Cronin Gross, OBE; 3 da (Amelia b 1975, Taffa b 1976, Mahalah b 1980); *Career* barr, recorder Crown Court 1987–; memb Criminal Injuries Compensation Bd 1995–; bencher Inner Temple 1996; Parly candidate (SDP/Lib Alliance) Dover 1983 and 1987; *Style*— Geoffrey Nice, Esq, QC; ✉ Farrars Building, Temple, London EC4 (☎ 0171 583 9241)

NICHOL, David Brett; s of Philip George Nichol (d 1974), of Gullane, E Lothian, and Kathleen, *née* Brett; *b* 20 April 1945; *Educ* Sedbergh; *m* 22 July 1977, Judith Mary, da of Godfrey Arthur Parker (d 1966), of Godalming, Surrey; 4 da (Alexandra b 1979, Tessa b 1981, Leonie b 1982, Flora b 1986); *Career* CA; Deloitte & Co 1962–68, County Bank London 1968–70, Martin Corpn Australia 1970–71, W I Carr Hong Kong 1971–72, dir Ivory & Sime plc 1972–92, md Ivory & Sime Asia Ltd 1989–91, managing ptnr Rossie House Investment Management 1992–; non-exec dir: Pacific Assets Trust plc 1985–, Nippon Assets Investments SA 1993–; tstee Royal Botanic Gdns Edinburgh 1986–89; FCA; *Recreations* shooting, skiing, golf; *Clubs* New (Edinburgh), R & A, Hon Co of Edinburgh Golfers, Shek-o (Hong Kong); *Style*— David B Nichol, Esq; ✉ Rossie, Forgandenny, Perthshire PH2 9EH; Rossie House Investment Management, Forgandenny, Perth PH2 9EH (☎ 01738 813223, fax 01738 813256)

NICHOL, Sir Duncan Kirkbride; kt (1993), CBE (1989); s of James Nichol (d 1989), and Mabel Nichol (d 1984); *b* 30 May 1941; *Educ* Bradford GS, Univ of St Andrews (MA); *m* 18 March 1972, Elizabeth Elliott Mitchell, da of Herbert Wilkinson (d 1967), of Blackpool; 1 s (Andrew b 1973), 1 da (Rachael b 1977); *Career* hosp sec Manchester Royal Infirmary 1969–73, dep gp sec and acting gp sec Univ Hosp Mgmnt Ctee of S Manchester 1973–74, dist admin S Manchester Dist 1974–77, area admin Salford DHA 1977–81, regnl gen mangr Mersey RHA 1984–89 (regnl admin 1981–84), chief exec offr NHS Mgmnt Exec 1989–94; prof i/c Centre for Int Healthcare Mgmnt and dir Health Servs Mgmnt Unit Univ of Manchester 1994–; non-exec dir: Prison Service 1994–, BUPA 1994–; memb Central Health Servs Cncl 1980–81, pres IMSM 1984–85 (memb Cncl 1976–), chm Kings Fund Educn Ctee 1991–94, govr Henley Mgmnt Coll 1993–; Hon DLitt Univ of Salford 1991; CIMgt 1988, FHSM 1990; *Recreations* golf, walking; *Style*— Sir Duncan Nichol, CBE; ✉ 1 Pipers Close, Heswell, Wirral, Merseyside L60 9LJ (☎ 0151 342 2699)

NICHOL, John Connell; s of James Nichol (d 1953), of Walker, Newcastle-upon-Tyne, and Sarah, *née* Connell; *b* 21 March 1945; *Educ* Wallsend GS, Heaton GS, Sunderland Tech Coll (ONC, HNC); *m* 1 (m dis), Sylvia, *née* Trench; 1 da (Joanne b 27 Sept 1969), 1 s (John Christopher b 16 Oct 1972); m 2, Michaela Anne Bates; 2 da (Sara Anne Muriel b 10 Oct 1984, Lucy Jane b 14 April 1987); *Career* NCB Physics Research Labs 1961–63, Grubb Parsons Thiw Film Research Labs 1963–64, Torbay Electro-Research Labs 1964–66; Tyne Tees Television (now Yorkshire-Tyne Tees TV): joined 1966, engrg mangr 1977–80, dep tech controller 1980–88, tech controller 1988–93, gp head of engrg 1993–; memb RTS 1977; rep Northumberland at chess, former amateur football player; *Recreations* golf, gardening, reading, DIY, sport; *Clubs* Alnmouth Golf; *Style*— John Nichol, Esq; ✉ Yorkshire Tyne Tees Television, The Television Centre, Kirkstall Road, Leeds LS3 1JS (☎ 0113 243 8283, fax 0113 242 9521)

NICHOLAS, Sir David; kt (1989), CBE (1982); *b* 25 Jan 1930; *Educ* Neath GS, Univ Coll of Wales Aberystwyth (BA); *m* 1952, Juliet Powell Davies; 1 s (James), 1 da (Helen); *Career* Nat Serv Army 1951–53; journalist: Wakefield Express, Yorkshire Post, Daily Telegraph, Observer; ITN: joined 1960, dep ed 1963, ed and chief exec 1977–89, chm and chief exec 1989–90, chm 1990–92; dir Channel Four Corporation 1992–, consulting ed Channel 1 London (cable TV), chm Circle Communications Ltd, chm Spritz News Television; visiting ed: Graduate Sch of Journalism Berkeley (Univ of California) 1993, Sch of Journalism Univ of Colorado Boulder 1994, Sch of Journalism Univ of N Carolina Chapel Hill; fellow UCW Aberystwyth; Hon LLD Univ of Wales; FRTS; *Recreations* sailing, walking, riding; *Clubs* Reform; *Style*— Sir David Nicholas, CBE; ✉ Lodge Stables, 2f Kidbrooke Park Rd, London SE3 0LW (☎ 0181 319 2823, fax 0181 319 2417)

NICHOLAS, Prof Herbert George; s of Rev William Daniel Nicholas, of Treharris, and Mary Elizabeth Nicholas; *b* 8 June 1911; *Educ* Mill Hill, New Coll Oxford (MA), Yale Univ; *Career* American Div MOI 1941–45, first sec Br Embassy Washington 1945–46, fell and tutor Exeter Coll Oxford 1944–51 (lectr 1938–44), lectr in modern history and politics Univ of Oxford 1948–56, Faculty fell Nuffield Coll Oxford 1948–57, fell New Coll Oxford 1951–78 (hon fell 1980–), Nuffield reader in comparative study of insts 1956–69, Rhodes prof of American history and instns 1969–78; dir New Coll Devpt Fund 1989–93; chm Br Assoc for American Studies 1960–62; Hon DUniv of Pittsburgh 1968; FBA 1969 (vice pres 1975–76); *Books* The American Union (1948), The British General Election of 1950 (1951), To the Hustings (1956), The United Nations as a Political Institution (1952, 5 edn 1975), Britain and the United States (1963), The Nature of

American Politics (1980), Washington Despatches 1941–45 (ed, 1981); *Recreations* gardening, listening to music; *Clubs* Athenaeum; *Style—* Prof Herbert Nicholas, FBA; ✉ New College, Oxford OX1 3BN (☎ 01865 279555)

NICHOLAS, Sir Herbert Richard (Harry); kt (1970), OBE (1949); s of Richard Henry Nicholas; *b* 13 March 1905; *Educ* Elementary Sch Bristol, evening classes, correspondence courses; *m* 1932, Rosina Grace Brown; *Career* asst-gen sec Tport and Gen Workers' Union 1956–68 (actg gen sec 1964–66); TUC Gen Cncl 1964–67, memb Nat Exec Ctee Labour Party 1956–64 and 1967–68, treas Labour Party 1960–64, gen sec Labour Party 1968–72; *Style—* Sir Harry Nicholas, OBE; ✉ 33 Madeira Rd, Streatham, London SW16 2DG (☎ 0181 769 7989)

NICHOLAS, Mark Charles Jefford; s of Peter Jefford Nicholas (d 1968), and Anne Evelyn (stage name Loxley, m Brian Widlake, TV and radio presenter incl Money Programme and World at One); *b* 29 Sept 1959; *Educ* Bradfield; *Career* professional cricketer Hampshire CCC 1977–95: debut 1978, awarded county cap 1982, capt 1984–95; honours: winner John Player Sunday League 1986, winner Benson & Hedges Cup 1988 and 1992, winner NatWest Trophy 1992; capt: 4 unofficial Test matches v Sri Lanka 1986, 3 unofficial Test matches v Zimbabwe 1990, 10 unofficial one day Ints, England under 25 v NZ 1986, England Counties tour Zimbabwe 1985, MCC v Aust 1985 (scored 115 not out); Advtg Dept The Observer 1980, PR conslt Hill & Knowlton (UK) Ltd 1987–88, publisher various cricket magazines, TV and radio commentator, journalist Daily Telegraph, presenter and commentator Sky TV; *Recreations* music, theatre, golf (golf handicap 8, caddie Euro tour 1992), food and wine; *Style—* Mark Nicholas, Esq; ✉ c/o The Daily Telegraph, 1 Canada Square, Canary Wharf, London E14 5DT

NICHOLAS, Dr Michael Bernard; s of Bernard Victor Herbert Nicholas (d 1975), and Dorothy, *née* Gilfillan; *b* 31 Aug 1938; *Educ* City of London Sch, Trinity Coll of Music (jr exhibitioner), Jesus Coll Oxford (organ scholar, BA, MA); *m* 1975, Heather Grant, *née* Rowdon; 2 s (Mark Alexander b 1976, Benjamin William (twin)); *Career* organist and choirmaster Louth Parish Church Lincs 1960–64, organist and choirmaster St Matthew's Church Northampton 1965–71, organist and master of the choristers Norwich Cathedral 1971–94, chief exec Royal Coll of Organists 1994–; dir of music King Edward VI GS Lincs 1960–64, dir of music Northampton GS 1965–71, pt/t lectr in music Univ of E Anglia 1971–94, currently organist and dir of music All Saints' Church Blackheath; conductor: Louth Choral and Orchestral Soc 1960–64, Northampton Bach Choir and Orch 1965–71, St Matthew's Singers 1965–71, Norwich Philharmonic Chorus 1972–94, Allegri Singers 1994–; memb: Exec Ctee Church Music Soc, Exec Ctee Guild of Church Musicians, Exec Ctee Organists' Benevolent League, Bd St Albans Int Organ Festival; Hon DMus Univ of E Anglia 1995; FRCO 1958 (chm 1964), FRSA 1987; *Music Pubns* Sightsinging (RSCM, 1966), From the Rising of the Sun (Elkin 1979), Versicles and Responses (Novello, 1988), various choral pieces and arrangements; *Recreations* walking in E Suffolk, reading, real ale; *Style—* Dr Michael Nicholas; ✉ Royal College of Organists, 7 St Andrews Street, Holborn, London EC4A 3LQ (☎ 0171 936 3606, fax 0171 353 8244)

NICHOLAS, Trevor Ian; s of Harold Lionel Nicholas (d 1990), of Twickenham, Middx, and Gwendoline Doris, *née* Blyth; *b* 14 Sept 1936; *Educ* Hampton GS, Harvard Business Sch; *m* 17 Oct 1959, Ruth, da of Gottlieb Joswig (d 1954); 2 da (Kim b 1 April 1961, Katja b 12 Sept 1963); *Career* Barclays Bank plc: mangr business advsy serv 1974–75, gen mangr asst 1977, asst gen mangr software devpt 1978–79, divnl gen mangr Barclaycard 1980–82, divnl gen mangr mgmnt servs 1982–84, gen mangr resources 1985–87, dir info systems and resources 1988–89, chief info offr 1989–90; princ I/T conslt Business-Technology Interface 1990–; memb: Nat Tst, RSPB, Ramblers' Assoc, RHS, Royal Nat Rose Soc, Wildfowl Tst, Royal Forestry Soc; Liveryman Worshipful Co of Information Technologists; FCIB; *Recreations* music, reading, photography, natural history, conservation; *Style—* Trevor Nicholas, Esq; ✉ Wellwood, 24 Meadway, Berkhamsted, Herts HP4 2PN (☎ 01442 866921, fax 01442 874398)

NICHOLL, His Hon Judge Anthony John David; s of Brig David William Dillwyn Nicholl (d 1972), and Mrs D W D Nicholl (d 1975); *b* 3 May 1935; *Educ* Eton, Pembroke Coll Oxford; *m* 1961, Hermione Mary, da of William Harcourt Palmer Landon (d 1978); 1 s (William b 19 May 1962), 2 da (Charlotte b 30 Oct 1963, Lucy b 4 June 1967); *Career* called to the Bar Lincoln's Inn 1958, in practice London 1958–61 and Birmingham 1961–88, head of Chambers 1976–87, recorder Crown Ct 1978–88, chm Fountain Ct Chambers Birmingham 1984–88, circuit judge (Midland and Oxford Circuit) 1988–; *Recreations* history, walking, listening to music, motoring; *Clubs* VSCC; *Style—* His Hon Judge Anthony Nicholl; ✉ c/o Birmingham Crown Court, Newton Street, Birmingham B4 6NE

NICHOLLS, *see:* Harmar-Nicholls

NICHOLLS, Brian; s of Ralph Nicholls (d 1994), of Crieff, Scotland, and Kathleen, *née* Bulled (d 1966); *b* 21 Sept 1928; *Educ* Haberdashers' Aske's, Regent St Poly (BSc), Harvard Business Sch; *m* 1961, Mary Elizabeth, da of Alexander Harley, of Milnathort, Scotland; 1 s (Simon b 1964), 2 da (Jane b 1966, Anne b 1968); *Career* dir: CJB Projects Ltd 1972–75, CJB Pipelines Ltd 1974–75; dep chm CJB - Mohandessi Iran 1975; dir: John Brown Engrg 1978–91, JBE Inc (USA) 1982–90; vice pres: John Brown Power Ltd 1987–90, Rugby Power Co 1989–91; industl advsr Dept of Trade 1975–78, business conslt Scottish Enterprise 1991–, chm Scottish Cos Exporting to the ME 1992–93, dir Scottish Opera 1993–; memb Cncl: Br Chemical Engrg Contractors Assoc 1973–75, Br Overseas Trade Bd 1978; vice pres Scottish Cncl for Devpt and Indust 1984–; memb: Incorporation of Coopers of Glasgow 1991, Merchants' House of Glasgow 1990; *Recreations* hill walking, sailing, music, writing; *Clubs* Royal Northern and Clyde Yacht, Western (Glasgow); *Style—* Brian Nicholls, Esq; ✉ Croy, Shandon, by Helensburgh, Dunbartonshire Scotland G84 8NN

NICHOLLS, Dr Christine Stephanie; da of Christopher James Metcalfe (d 1986), of Mombasa, Kenya, and Olive, *née* Kennedy (d 1982); *b* 23 Jan 1943; *Educ* Kenya HS, Lady Margaret Hall Oxford (BA, MA), St Antony's Coll Oxford (DPhil); *m* 12 March 1966, Anthony James Nicholls, s of Ernest Alfred Nicholls (d 1981), of Carshalton, Surrey; 1 s (Alexander b 1970), 2 da (Caroline b 1972, Isabel b 1974); *Career* Henry Charles Chapman res fell Inst of Cwlth Studies Univ of London 1968–69, freelance writer BBC 1970–74; *Books* The Swahili Coast (1971), Cataract (with Philip Awdry, 1985), Dictionary of National Biography (jt ed 1971, ed twentieth century supplements 1989–95), Power - A Political History of the Twentieth Century (1990), Missing Persons (1993), Hutchinson Encyclopaedia of Biography (ed, 1996); *Recreations* reading novels, playing the flute; *Style—* Dr Christine Nicholls; ✉ 27 Davenant Rd, Oxford OX2 8BU (☎ 01865 511320, e-mail christine.nicholls@sant.ox.ac.uk)

NICHOLLS, Clive Victor; QC (1982); s of Alfred Charles Victor Nicholls, and Lilian Mary, *née* May; *b* 29 Aug 1932; *Educ* Brighton Coll, Trinity Coll Dublin (MA, LLB), Sidney Sussex Coll Cambridge (BA, LLM); *m* 23 July 1960, Alison Virginia, da of late Leonard Arthur Oliver; 3 s (Jeremy Oliver b 1962, James Colin Oliver b 1967, John Patrick Oliver b 1969), 3 da (Jacqueline Alison b 1963, Judie Victoria b 1965, Jill Caroline b 1965); *Career* called to the Bar Gray's Inn 1957, recorder of Crown Court 1984–, head of chambers, master of the Bench 1989, barr Supreme Ct of the Australian Capital Territory 1991; tstee and former chm Bob Champion Cancer Tst; patron Multiple Birth Assoc; *Recreations* sailing, fly-fishing; *Style—* Clive Nicholls, Esq, QC; ✉ 3 Raymond Buildings, Gray's Inn, London WC1R 5BH (☎ 0171 831 3833, fax 0171 242 4221)

NICHOLLS, Colin Alfred Arthur; QC (1981); s of Alfred Charles Victor Nicholls (d 1987), and Lilian Mary, *née* May (d 1990); *b* 29 Aug 1932; *Educ* Brighton Coll, Univ of Dublin (MA, LLB); *m* 23 Oct 1976, Clarissa Allison Spenlove, da of Clive Dixon (d 1976); 2 s (Benjamin Clive b 30 Aug 1977, Jonathan Charles b 6 Jan 1979); *Career* called to the Bar Gray's Inn (Albion Richardson Award) 1957 (bencher 1989); recorder of the Crown Ct 1983–; vice pres Cwlth Lawyers' Assoc, patron Multiple Births Fndn; hon memb Historical Soc TCD 1958– (auditor 1956); *Recreations* painting (exhibitor RHA); *Clubs* Garrick; *Style—* Colin Nicholls, Esq, QC; ✉ 3 Raymond Buildings, Gray's Inn, London WC1R 5BH (☎ 0171 831 3833, fax 0171 242 4221, car 0836 717 941)

NICHOLLS, David Alan; CB (1989), CMG (1984); s of Thomas Edward Nicholls (d 1971), and Beatrice Winifred Nicholls (d 1992); *Educ* Cheshunt GS, St John's Coll Cambridge (MA); *m* 1955, Margaret; 2 da (Amanda, Camilla); *Career* entered Home Civil Serv 1954; asst sec MOD 1969–75, Cabinet Office 1975–77, under sec MOD 1977–80, asst sec-gen NATO 1980–84, dep under sec MOD 1984–90; defence conslt; visiting fell Magdalene Coll Cambridge 1989–90, sr Pol-Mil assoc Inst for Foreign Policy Analysis 1990–; memb Visiting Ctee Royal Coll of Art 1991–93; hon sr lectr Univ of Birmingham 1992–; assoc fell RIIA 1990–92, dir Public Administration International 1995–; chm Soc for Italic Handwriting 1995–96; *Recreations* sketching, printmaking; *Clubs* Nat Lib; *Style—* David Nicholls, Esq, CB, CMG; ✉ c/o Midland Bank, Church Stretton, Shropshire SY6 6BT

NICHOLLS, David Andrew; s of Gordon Robert Nicholls (d 1973), of Deal, Kent, and Maureen Rachel, *née* Waddon; *b* 15 Jan 1957; *Educ* Walmer Secdy Sch Deal Kent, Thanet Tech Coll Broadstairs Kent, Westminster Coll London (City and Guilds); *m* March 1984, Carolyn Ann, da of Charles Milner Jacobs; 2 s (Daniel Gordon Charles b March 1985, Dean Stephen Robert b Oct 1989); *Career* chef de partie Waldorf Hotel London 1975–76, successively chef tournant, saucier then gardemanger Dorchester Hotel London 1976–79, chef saucier then sous chef Hotel Intercontinental London 1979–81, chef/dir The Old Lodge Restaurant Limpsfield Surrey 1981–83, head chef Waltons Restaurant London 1983–86; exec chef: Britannia Intercontinental Hotel London 1986–89, Royal Garden Hotel London 1989–92; exec head chef Ritz Hotel London 1992–; memb: British Div Toques Blance, Guild de Fromagers France; hon memb Chain de Rotisseurs, chm Academie Culinaire de France Grande Bretagne (Affiliates); *Recreations* golf, squash, gardening; *Style—* David Nicholls, Esq; ✉ Executive Chef, The Ritz, 150 Piccadilly, London W1 (☎ 0171 493 8181)

NICHOLLS, (Ralph) John; s of Clifton Wilson Nicholls (d 1991), and Muriel Morten, *née* Heathcote; *b* 20 May 1943, Wilby, Northants; *Educ* Felsted Sch Essex, Gonville and Caius Coll Cambridge (BA), London Hosp Med Sch (entrance scholar, George Riddock prize in neurology, T A M Ross prize in clinical med, H L B Haking prize in gynaecology), Univ of Cambridge (MB BChir, MChir (distinction in med), FRCS (Eng) (Halett prize)); *m* 1966, Stella Mary; 4 c (b 1967, 1969, 1972 and 1977); *Career* house physician Med Unit then house surgn Surgical Unit The London Hosp 1967–68, demonstrator in anatomy London Hosp Med Coll 1968–69, casualty offr Lewisham Hosp 1969–70, clinical asst St Mark's Hosp for Diseases of The Rectum and Colon London 1971–73; The London Hosp: jr lectr Surgical Unit 1970–71, registrar 1971, lectr in surgery Surgical Unit 1972, registrar 1972–73, sr registrar 1974–76; clinical asst Chirurgische Universitatsklinik Heidelberg (Alexander von Humboldt fell) 1976–77, registrar the London Hosp 1978, resident surgical offr St Mark's Hosp 1978, conslt surgn St Mark's Hosp and sr lectr (ICRF) St Bartholomew's Hosp 1978–, conslt surgn St Thomas's Hosp 1982–93; currently: hon sr lectr in surgery Imperial Coll London and dean St Mark's Academic Inst, conslt surgn St Mark's Hosp; memb Cncl: Assoc of Coloproctology of GB and I (chm Educn sub-ctee); sec Section of Coloproctology RSM 1992–93, memb Specialist Advsy Ctee in Gen Surgery; memb: Br Soc of Gastroenterology, Swiss Soc for Gastroenterology; hon memb French Soc of Proctology, membre d'Honneur Assoc Française de Chirurgie, hon fell Brasilian Coll of Surgns, Hon FRCSGlas; ed Int Jl of Colorectal Disease, memb Editorial Bd Italian Jl of Gastroenterology; *Books* Colorectal Disease: An Introduction for Surgeons and Physicians (jt ed, 1981), Coloproctology: Diagnosis and Outpatient Management (with R E Glass, 1985), Restorative Proctocolectomy (ed with N J McC Mortensen and D C C Bartolo, 1993), Colon and Rectal Surgery (ed with R R Dozois, 1997); contrib various book chapters and author of numerous pubns in learned jls; *Clubs* Athenaeum, St Alban's, Royal Blackheath Golf, Royal Fowey Yacht; *Style—* John Nicholls, Esq; ✉ St Mark's Hospital, Watford Road, Harrow HA1 3UJ (☎ 0171 935 4444)

NICHOLLS, Prof John Graham; s of late Dr Nicolai Nicholls, and Charlotte, *née* Kaphan (d 1994); *b* 19 Dec 1929; *Educ* Berkhamsted Sch, King's Coll London (BSc), UCL (PhD), Charing Cross Hosp (MB BS); *m* 22 Oct 1988, Nancy Venable; 2 s (Julian b 11 May 1964, Stephen b 7 June 1966); *Career* house offr Casualty and Radiotherapy Charing Cross Hosp 1956–57, Beit meml fell UCL 1957–60, departmental demonstrator Dept of Physiology Oxford 1960–62, assoc prof of physiology Yale Med Sch 1965–68, assoc prof of neurobiology Harvard Med Sch 1968–73 (res assoc 1962–65), prof of neurobiology Stanford Med Sch 1973–83, prof of pharmacology Biocenter 1983–; FRS 1988; *Books* The Search for Connexions (1987), From Neuron to Brain (3 edn with A R Martin and B G Wallace, 1992); *Recreations* music, literature, S American history; *Clubs* Athenaeum; *Style—* Prof John Nicholls, FRS; ✉ Turkheimerstrasse 74, Basel 4055, Switzerland (☎ 00 41 61 3829654); Department of Pharmacology, Biocenter, Klingelbergstrasse 70, Basel 4056, Switzerland (☎ 00 41 61 2672230, fax 00 41 61 2672208)

NICHOLLS, Rt Rev John (Jack); *see:* Lancaster, Bishop of

NICHOLLS, Jonathan Clive; s of David and Jill Nicholls; *b* 27 Oct 1957; *Educ* Uppingham, Univ of Manchester (BA Economics and Accountancy), Harvard Business Sch (PMD); *m* 11 Sept 1982, Julie; *Career* auditor Peat Marwick Mitchell & Co 1979–83, chief accountant P S Refson & Co (merchant bank) 1983–85; Abbey National Building Society: mangr Fin Servs 1985–86, commercial mangr Business Devpt 1987–88; dir Corp Fin and Capital Markets Abbey National Treasury Services plc 1988–94, dir and dep chief exec Abbey National Treasury Services plc and dep treas Abbey National plc 1994–96, treas Hanson plc 1996–; ACA 1982, FCT 1989; *Recreations* sailing, skiing, cycling, travel, food and wine, opera; *Style—* Jonathan Nicholls, Esq; ✉ Hanson plc, 1 Grosvenor Place, London SW1X 7JH (direct ☎ 0171 235 8835, fax 0171 259 5336)

NICHOLLS, Nigel Hamilton; CBE (1982); s of Bernard Cecil Hamilton Nicholls, of Dorking, Surrey (d 1969), and Enid Kathleen Nicholls, *née* Gwynne (d 1989); *b* 19 Feb 1938; *Educ* King's Sch Canterbury, St John's Oxford (MA); *m* 14 Oct 1967, Isobel Judith, da of Rev Canon Maurice Dean, of Malvern, Worcs; 2 s (Jonathan b 1969, Christopher b 1972); *Career* asst princ Admty 1962, MOD 1964, asst private sec Min for RN 1965–66, princ 1966, directing staff RCDS 1971–73, asst private sec to Sec of State for Def 1973–74, asst sec 1974, def cnsllr UK Delgn to MBFR Talks Vienna 1977–80 (dep head of delgn 1978–80), asst under sec of state 1984, Cabinet Office 1986–89, clerk of the Privy Council 1992–; *Recreations* choral singing, genealogy, mountain walking; *Clubs* United Oxford and Cambridge Univ; *Style—* Nigel Nicholls, Esq, CBE; ✉ Privy Council Office, Whitehall, London SW1A 2AT

NICHOLLS, Patrick Charles Martyn; MP (C) Teignbridge (majority 8,856); s of Douglas Charles Martyn Nicholls (d 1950), and Margaret Josephine Nicholls (d 1982); *b* 14 Nov 1948; *Educ* St Peter's Harefield, Redrice Coll; *m* 1976, Bridget Elizabeth Fergus, da of Edward Alan Owens, of Otterton, Devon; 1 s, 2 da; *Career* admitted slr 1974; MP (C) Teignbridge 1983–; memb: Standing Ctee on Police and Criminal Evidence Bill,

Standing Ctee on Video Recordings Bill, Select Ctee on Social Security 1990–; PPS to Rt Hon John Gummer as Min of State MAFF July 1986–May 1987; Parly under sec of state: Dept of Employment 1987–90, DOE July-Nov 1990; Cons majority ldr Social Security Select Ctee 1990–93, bd memb Westminster Fndn for Democracy 1992–94, memb N Atlantic Assembly Delgn 1992–, chm All Pty Anglo-Indonesia Parly Gp 1992–; co-opted memb Soc of Cons Lawyers 1983– (vice chm Ctee 1985–87); vice chm: Cons Backbench Legal Ctee 1992– (jt sec 1983–92), Cons Party 1993–94; steward Br Boxing Bd 1985–87; Freeman City of London; *Recreations* skiing, opera, theatre and historical research; *Style*— Patrick Nicholls, Esq, MP; ✉ c/o House of Commons, London SW1A 0AA (☎ 0171 219 4095)

NICHOLLS, Dr (David) Paul; s of Albert Edward Nicholls (d 1991), of Much Hoole, Preston, Lancs, and Alice, *née* Thomson (d 1967); *b* 10 Sept 1946; *Educ* Hutton GS Preston, Univ of Manchester (MB ChB, MD); *m* 1, Mary Nash (d 1977); m 2, 18 July 1981, Esme Mary, da of Norman Whitehead, of 4 Killowen Crescent, Lisburn; 1 s (Stephen b 1989), 2 da (Riona b 1985, Ciara b 1986); *Career* tutor in med Hope Hosp Salford, sr registrar in med Belfast City Hosp, currently conslt physician Royal Victoria Hosp Belfast; FRCP 1991 (MRCP 1974), FECS 1989; *Recreations* music, sailing, golf, photography, old cars; *Clubs* Royal Portrush Golf, Carrickfergus Sailing; *Style*— Dr Paul Nicholls; ✉ 2 Printshop Road, Templepatrick, Co Antrim BT39 0HZ (☎ 01849 433351); Royal Victoria Hospital, Belfast BT12 6BA (☎ 01232 240503)

NICHOLLS, Robert Michael (Bob); CBE (1995); s of Herbert Edgar Nicholls (d 1977), and Bennetta L'Estrange, *née* Burges; *b* 28 July 1939; *Educ* Hampton Sch, UCW (BA, treas Students' Union, dep ldr expedition to Kurdistan), Univ of Manchester (DSA); *m* 9 Dec 1961, Dr Deirin Deirdre O'Sullivan, da of Dr Frank O'Sullivan (d 1955); 4 s (Kevin Paul b 1965, Clive Ranulf John b 1967, Liam Dougal b 1969, Alec Eoin b 1971); *Career* house govr St Stephen's Hosp Chelsea 1966–68, asst clerk of the govrs St Thomas's Hosp 1968–72, dep gp sec Southampton Univ Hosp Mgmnt Ctee 1972–74, dist admin Southampton and S West Hampshire Health Dist 1974–77, area admin Newcastle Area Health Authy 1977–81, regnl admin S Western Regnl Health Authy 1981–85, dist gen mangr Southmead Health Dist 1985–88, chief exec Oxford Regnl Health Authy 1988–93, seconded as exec dir London Implementation Gp NHS Mgmnt Exec 1993–96, health mgmnt conslt 1996–; memb: Inst of Health Serv Mangrs (former memb Cncl, nat pres 1983–84), King's Fund Educn Ctee 1974–79, Health Educn Cncl 1984–87, Calman Ctee on Med Trg 1993, GMC 1996–; memb Green Coll Oxford, assoc fell Templeton Coll 1996–; FHSM 1993 (AHSM 1965); *Books* Resources in Medicine (contrib, 1970), Working with People (contrib, 1983), Rationing of Health Care in Medicine (contrib, 1993); *Recreations* cricket, golf, walking, birdwatching, opera, jazz; *Clubs* Lensbury, Ronnie Scott's; *Style*— Bob Nicholls, Esq, CBE; ✉ Templeton College, Kennington, Oxford OX1 5NY (☎ 01865 735422, fax 01865 736374)

NICHOLLS, Susan Frances (Sue) (Hon Susan Harmar-Nicholls); da of Baron Harmar-Nicholls, JP (Life Peer and 1 Bt), *qv*; *b* 23 Nov 1943; *m* 6 July, 1993, Mark Eden, the actor; *Career* actress; trained RADA; early theatre work nationwide, appeared in London Assurance (RSC); numerous TV roles incl: Crossroads, The Fall and Rise of Reginald Perrin, Rent-a-Ghost, Up the Elephant and Round the Castle, Audrey Roberts in Coronation Street 1979–; *Style*— Sue Nicholls

NICHOLLS OF BIRKENHEAD, Baron (Life Peer UK 1994), of Stoke D'Abernon in the County of Surrey; Sir Donald James Nicholls; kt (1983), PC (1986); yr s of late William Greenhow Nicholls and late Eleanor Jane Nicholls; *b* 25 Jan 1933; *Educ* Birkenhead Sch, Liverpool Univ (LLB), Trinity Hall, Camb (MA, LLB); *m* 1960, Jennifer Mary, yr da of late W E C Thomas, MB, BCh, MRCOG, JP; 2 s, 1 da; *Career* called to the Bar Middle Temple 1958, QC 1974, Bencher 1981, judge of the High Court of Justice (Chancery Div) 1983–86; Lord Justice of Appeal 1986–91; vice-chllr of the Supreme Court 1991–94; Lord of Appeal in Ordinary 1994–; *Style*— The Rt Hon the Lord Nicholls of Birkenhead, PC; ✉ House of Lords, London SW1A 0PW

NICHOLS, Rev Barry Edward; s of Albert Owen Nichols (d 1986), and Gwendoline Cicely, *née* Rumbold (d 1981); *b* 23 Jan 1940; *Educ* Epsom Coll, Southwark Ordination Course; *m* 28 Feb 1970, Anne, da of Frederick Albert Hastings, BEM, of Surbiton, Surrey; 1 s (Stephen b 1977), 2 da (Sarah b 1972, Rebecca b 1977); *Career* Arthur Young: joined 1957, ptnr 1970–89, managing ptnr 1983–85; ptnr Ernst & Young (following merger) 1989–; ordained priest C of E 1970, hon curate St Andrew's and St Mark's Surbiton Surrey 1969–92, hon canon Southwark Cathedral 1990–92; dean for Ministers in Secular Employment Kingston Episcopal Area 1990–92, govr Anglican Centre Rome 1990–, chm N Surrey Gp Scope 1993–; FCA; *Recreations* reading, swimming, walking, cycling; *Style*— The Rev Barry Nichols; ✉ 19 Arterberry Road, Wimbledon, London SW20 8AF (☎ 0181 944 1452, fax 0181 879 0154); Ernst & Young, Becket House, 1 Lambeth Palace Rd, London SE1 7EU (☎ 0171 928 2000, fax 0171 928 1345, direct line 0171 931 3644)

NICHOLS, Prof David; s of Arnold William Nichols (d 1972), of Broadmayne, Dorset, and Kathleen Jessie, *née* Harries (d 1975); *b* 21 June 1930; *Educ* Hardye's Sch Dorchester, Univ of Oxford (BA, MA, DPhil); *m* 6 Aug 1955, Anne, da of Frank Dutton Rowland (d 1983), of Weymouth, Dorset; 1 s (John b 17 April 1964), 3 da (Jocelyn b 8 June 1958, Jennifer b 4 Sept 1959, Jane b 26 Dec 1962); *Career* Nat Serv RAF 1949–51, Flying Offr 1951; lectr in zoology Univ of Oxford 1957–69, fell of St Peter's Coll Oxford 1964–69; Univ of Exeter: prof of biological scis 1969–95 (prof emeritus 1995), dean of sci 1984–87, dep vice chllr 1987–91; memb: Cncl Marine Biological Assoc of UK 1970–73, 1977–80 and 1983–86, Ctee NERC 1980–83, Advsy Ctee on Sci for The Nature Conservancy Cncl 1982–85, Cncl Nat Conf of Univ Professors 1989–93 (vice chm 1991–93), Maritime Project Bd English Nature 1994–; FIBiol, CBiol; *Books* Echinoderms (4 edn, 1969), The Oxford Book of Invertebrates (2 edn, 1971); *Recreations* walking, photography; *Style*— Prof David Nichols; ✉ Department of Biological Sciences, Hatherly Laboratories, Prince of Wales Rd, Exeter, Devon EX4 4PS (☎ 01392 263777, fax 01392 263700, telex 42894 EXUNIV G, e-mail d.nichols@exeter.ac.uk)

NICHOLS, Dinah Alison; CB (1995); da of Sydney Hirst Nichols (d 1982), and Elsie Freda, *née* Pratt; *b* 28 Sept 1943; *Educ* Wyggeston GS for Girls Leicester, Bedford Coll London (Reid arts scholar, BA); *Career* Miny of Tport: asst princ 1965–69, Winston Churchill Meml fellowship to study tport in Japan 1969, asst private sec to the Min of Tport 1969–70, princ Railways Policy 1970–74; princ Cabinet Office 1974–77, asst sec (Radioactive Waste) DOE 1977–80, asst sec (Ports) Dept of Tport 1980–81, asst sec (Inner Cities) DOE 1981–83, princ private sec to the Sec of State for Tport 1983–85; DOE: dir Admin Resources 1985–88, under sec (Water) 1988–91, dep sec (Property and Construction) 1991–93, dep sec (Housing and Construction) 1994–96, DG Environmental Protection 1996–; memb Commonwealth War Graves Cmmn 1993–; non-exec dir: John Laing ETE 1987–90, Anglian Water plc 1992–95; dir: Cities in Schools 1995–, Toynbee Housing Assoc 1996–; FRSA; *Recreations* mountain and fell walking, choral singing, music, theatre, travel; *Clubs* Swiss Alpine; *Style*— Ms Dinah Nichols, CB; ✉ Director General, Environmental Protection, Department of the Environment, 2 Marsham Street, London SW1P 3EB (☎ 0171 276 3570)

NICHOLS, Jeremy Gareth Lane; *b* 20 May 1943; *Educ* Lancing, Fitzwilliam Coll Cambridge (MA, Athletics half blue), Univ of Perugia (Dip of Teaching); *m* ; 1 s (Rupert), 3 da (Lucy, Victoria, Emma); *Career* house tutor Rugby Sch 1966–67; Eton Coll: asst Eng master 1967–89, house master 1980–89, master i/c of soccer and first XI coach 1969–79, second cricket XI coach and master 1974–79, Exchange Scheme Gilman Sch Baltimore Maryland 1979–80 (elected to Cum Laude Soc); headmaster Stowe Sch 1990–; Villiers Park Educnl Tst 1989; govr: Aysgarth Sch Yorks, Beachborough Sch Northants, Davenies Berks, Lockers Park Herts, Papplewick Berks, Swanbourne House Bucks, Wellesley House Kent; memb Ctee Friends of Lancing Chapel; *Clubs* Free Foresters CC, I Zingari CC, Corinthian Casuals AFC; *Style*— Jeremy Nichols, Esq; ✉ Stowe School, Kinloss, Stowe, Bucks MK18 5EH (☎ 01280 813164, fax 01280 822769)

NICHOLS, (Peter) John; s of Peter Nichols, of Bowdon, Cheshire, and Edith Nan, *née* Rhodes; *b* 24 Dec 1949; *Educ* Shrewsbury, Univ of Leicester (BSc); *m* 15 Sep 1973, Elaine Mary, da of late William H W Chadwick; 2 s (James b 1979, Matthew b 1982), 1 da (Katharine b 1986); *Career* J N Nichols (Vimto) plc: joined 1970–, dir 1978–86, md 1986–; *Recreations* golf, sailing, skiing; *Clubs* Ringway Golf, Nefyn Golf, South Caernarvonshire Yacht, Bowden Lawn Tennis; *Style*— John Nichols, Esq; ✉ Hatton Cottage, Hatton, Cheshire WA4 5NY; J N Nichols (Vimto) plc, Ledson Road, Wythenshawe, Manchester M23 9NL (☎ 0161 998 8801, fax 0161 998 9446, car 0374 163888)

NICHOLS, Peter Richard; s of Richard George (d 1965), of Bristol, and Violet Annie Ladysmith Poole (d 1992); *b* 31 July 1927; *Educ* Bristol GS, Bristol Old Vic Theatre Sch; *m* 1960, Thelma, da of George Reginald Reed, of Bristol; 1 s (Daniel), 3 da (Abigail d 1971, Louise, Catherine); *Career* actor, teacher, journalist, playwright and director; visiting writer Nat Inst of Educn Singapore 1994; FRSL; *Screen and stage* plays incl: The Gorge (TV), A Day in the Death of Joe Egg (stage and screen), Forget-me-not Lane (stage), Privates on Parade (stage and screen), Passion Play (stage), Poppy (stage musical), Blue Murder (written and dir, Show of Strength Co Bristol) 1995; *Awards* 4 Evening Standard Drama, 2 Oliviers, Critics' Circle, Tony; *Books* Feeling You're Behind (autobiography, 1984); *Recreations* reading his own diary, complaining about cars and muzak; *Style*— Peter Nichols, Esq, FRSL; ✉ c/o Rochelle Stevens & Co Ltd, 2 Terrett's Place, Upper Street, London N1 1QZ (☎ 0171 359 3900, fax 0171 354 5729)

NICHOLS, Robin Anthony; s of Thomas George Nichols (d 1981), of Eastcote, Middx, and Irene Joan Buck; gs of Thomas George Nichols, OBE (despatches thrice, 1935); *b* 28 April 1944; *Educ* Pinner Co GS, City of London Coll for Chartered Bldg Soc Exams; *m* 5 March 1967, Paula Theresa, da of Joseph Severin Spiegelhalter (d 1984), of Wembley, Middx; 1 s (Grant Anthony b 1970), 1 da (Sarah Kate b 1973); *Career* md Greenwich Building Society 1981–, dir Building Society Ombudsman Co Ltd 1987; memb Cncl: Bldg Socs Assoc 1983–, Bldg Soc ombudsman 1987–; govr Blackheath HS 1987–91; FCIB; *Recreations* sport, music, theatre, MENSA; *Style*— Robin Nichols, Esq; ✉ 15 Highfield Drive, Shortlands, Bromley, Kent BR2 0RX (☎ 0181 460 3369); 279 Greenwich High Rd, London SE10 8NL (☎ 0181 858 8212)

NICHOLS, Roger David Edward; s of Edward Compton Lowther Nichols (d 1945), and Dorothy Norah, *née* West (d 1994); *b* 6 April 1939; *Educ* Harrow, Worcester Coll Oxford (BA, open exhibitioner); *m* 11 April 1964, Sarah, eld da of Antony Bydder Edwards; 2 s (Thomas Edward b 7 March 1965, Jeremy Owen b 22 Aug 1966), 1 da (Olwen Beatrice b 5 May 1969); *Career* asst master St Michael's Coll Tenbury 1966–73, lectr Open Univ 1974–80, lectr Univ of Birmingham 1974–80; freelance writer and broadcaster 1980–; FRCO 1964; *Books* Debussy (1972), Messiaen (1975), Ravel (1977), Debussy Letters (ed and trans, 1987), Ravel Remembered (1987), Pelléas et Mélisande (with R Langham Smith, 1989), Debussy Remembered (1992); *Recreations* playing chamber music, walking the Welsh hills; *Style*— Roger Nichols, Esq; ✉ The School House, The Square, Kington, Herefordshire HR5 3BA (☎ 01544 231742)

NICHOLS, Prof Roy Woodward; s of late Ernest Nichols, of Rawdon, Yorkshire, and late Sarah Jane, *née* Woodward; *b* 9 June 1923; *Educ* Loughborough Coll, Univ of Sheffield (BMet, DMet, Mappin Nesthill and Ledbury medals and prizes); *m* 30 Aug 1948, Jacqueline, da of late Valentine Woods, of Barrow-on-Soar; 2 s (Mark Andrew, Paul Stewart), 1 da (Claire Angele); *Career* Lt (AE)(A) RNVR 1942–46; design apprentice Kirkstall Forge Ltd 1939–42, scientific and sr scientific offr Miny of Supply Woolwich Armament Res & Devpt Estab 1949–56, princ scientific offr and res mangr Materials Res Laboratory UKAEA Culcheth 1956–71, head Engrg and Materials Laboratories UKAEA Risley 1976–85 (dep head 1971–76); visiting prof: Paisley Coll Scot 1980–, Imperial Coll London 1985–94; private conslt 1985–, chm Management Bd Prog for Inspection of Steel Components OECD/CEC 1980–; pres Int Cncl on Pressure Vessel Technol, chm UK Govt Enquiry on Pressure Vessels 1969; former pres: Inst of Metallurgists, Int Congress on Fracture; former chm The Welding Inst Cncl; FIM 1950, FEng 1979; hon fell: The Welding Inst, BINDT, Int Congress on Fracture, Canadian Fracture Fndn; FIMechE; *Books* International Journal of Pressure Vessels and Piping (ed, 1971–), Pressure Vessel Engineering Technology (ed, 1971), Developments in PV Engineering Technology (Vol 1 1979, Vol 5 1987), Non-Destructive Testing (1989); *Recreations* music, gardening, bridge, walking; *Style*— Prof Roy Nichols, FEng; ✉ Nichols Consultancies, Squirrels, 35 Cockney Hill, Tilehurst, Reading RG30 4HF (☎ 0118 941 7892)

NICHOLS, Steven Leslie (Steve); s of Ralph William Nichols, and Josephine Mary, *née* Beaumont; *b* 7 March 1958; *Educ* Lowestoft GS, Univ of Surrey (BSc), Coll of Acupuncture Leamington Spa, Univ of Stirling (MSc); *m* Christine Anne, *née* Davies (d 1988); *Career* games consultant; fndr Aztral Games 1982–; publisher and ed Games Monthly 1988–89, sales and tech dir Quorum Game Development Ltd 1990; inventor and publisher/mfr over 50 board games; fndr Post-Human Movement, assoc memb Inst of Reprographic Technol 1986, memb British Psychological Soc 1993–; *Books* The Primal Eye - A Crash Course in the Evolution of Intelligence (1987); *Recreations* shogi, tennis, computing, chess; *Style*— Steve Nichols, Esq; ✉ 54 Wykebeck Mount, Leeds LS9 0HW (☎ 0113 225 0635)

NICHOLS, Rt Rev Vincent Gerard; s of Henry Joseph Nichols, and Mary Nichols, *née* Russell; *b* 8 Nov 1945; *Educ* St Mary's Coll Crosby, Gregorian Univ Rome (STL, PhL), Univ of Manchester (MA), Loyola Univ Chicago (MEd); *Career* chaplain St John Rigby VI Form Coll Wigan 1972–77, priest in the inner city of Liverpool 1978–81, dir of Upholland Northern Inst Lancs (with responsibility for the in-service training of clergy and for adult Christian educn 1981–84); advsr Cardinal Hume and Archbishop Worlock at the Int Synods of Bishops 1980, 1983, 1987 and 1991, gen sec Bishops' Conf of England and Wales 1984–92, Catholic bishop in North London 1992–; del Synod of Bishops 1994; *Style*— The Rt Rev Vincent Nichols; ✉ Catholic Bishop in North London, Westminster House, Watford Way, Hendon, London NW4 4TY

NICHOLSON, Sir Bryan Hubert; kt (1987); s of Reginald Hubert Nicholson (d 1977); *b* 6 June 1932; *Educ* Palmers Sch Grays, Oriel Coll Oxford; *m* 1956, Mary Elizabeth, da of Albert Cyril Harrison; 2 children; *Career* Nat Serv Lt; dir Sperry Rand (Australia) Pty Ltd 1966–69, dir Sperry Rand Ltd UK 1969–72; chm: Rank Xerox (UK) Ltd 1980–84 (dir 1972–84, dir Rank Xerox Ltd 1977–87), Manpower Services Cmmn 1984–87, The Post Office (also chief exec) 1987–92, BUPA 1992–, Varity Europe Ltd 1993–96, Financial Reporting Cncl 1993– (dep chm 1993–96); CBI: chm Educn and Trg Affrs Ctee 1990–93, dep pres 1993–94, pres 1994–96; chm: Nationalised Industs' Chairmen's Gp 1988–90, CNAA 1988–91, Nat Cncl for Vocational Qualifications 1990–93, The Industrial Soc 1990–93; non-exec dir: Evode Group plc 1981–84, Baker Perkins Holdings plc 1982–84, GKN plc 1991–, LucasVarity 1996–; pro chllr and chm Cncl Open Univ 1996–; memb NEDC 1985–92; chllr Sheffield Hallam Univ 1992–; *Recreations* tennis, bridge; *Clubs* United Oxford and Cambridge Univ (chm 1995–); *Style*— Sir Bryan Nicholson; ✉ Point Piper, Lilley Drive, Kingswood, Surrey KT20 6JA

NICHOLSON, Sir Charles Christian; 3 Bt (UK 1912), of Harrington Gdns, Royal Borough of Kensington; s of Sir John Norris Nicholson, 2 Bt, KBE, CIE (d 1993), and

(Vittoria) Vivien, *née* Trewhella (d 1991); *b* 15 Dec 1941; *Educ* Ampleforth, Magdalen Coll Oxford; *m* 1975, Martha Rodman, da of Col Stuart Warren Don, and wid of Niall Hamilton Anstruther-Gough-Calthorpe; *Heir* bro, James Richard Nicholson b 27 Oct 1947; *Style*— Sir Charles Nicholson, Bt; ✉ Turners Green Farm, Elvetham, Hook, Hants RG27 8BE

NICHOLSON, Clive Anthony Holme; s of Dennis Thomas Holme Nicholson, MBE, of Barnet, Herts, and Eileen Blanche, *née* Fitkin; *b* 24 Feb 1947; *Educ* Merchant Taylors'; *m* 12 Dec 1970, Patricia Mary, da of Ernest Johnson (d 1979), of Lancaster; 3 da (Amanda b 5 Dec 1972, Zoe b 27 May 1975, Gemma b 8 Aug 1981); *Career* CA; Deloitte & Co Lusaka Zambia 1970–72; Saffery Champness (formerly Safferys) 1972– (ptnr 1975–, managing ptnr 1990–); Liveryman Worshipful Co of Merchant Taylors 1974; FCA 1979, FHKSA 1985; *Style*— Clive A H Nicholson, Esq; ✉ Squirrel Lodge, Longworth House Estate, Longworth, Abingdon OX13 5HH (☎ 01865 820276); Saffery Champness, Fairfax House, Fulwood Place, Gray's Inn, London WC1V 6UB (☎ 0171 405 2828, fax 0171 405 7887)

NICHOLSON, David; s of Herbert Charles Denton (Frenchie) Nicholson (d 1987), of Prestbury, Cheltenham, Glos, and Diana, *née* Holman; *b* 19 March 1939; *Educ* Haileybury and ISC; *m* 31 May 1962, Dinah Caroline, da of John Geoffrey Pugh; 2 s (Philip b 1963, John Charles b 1965); *Career* jockey 1951–74, racehorse trainer 1968–; first winner at 16 in first ride over hurdles, third place in Nat Hunt table with 63 winners 1960–61; major wins incl: Imperial Cup on Farmer's Boy 1960, 3 successive Welsh Grand Nationals on Limonali (twice) and Clover Bud 1959–61, Schweppes Gold Trophy on Elan 1965, Whitbread Gold Cup on Mill House 1967, County Hurdle Cheltenham 1973; ret after a winning ride on What A Buck at Hereford 1974 bringing his career total to 594; took out trainer's licence 1968; big race wins incl: SGB Chase Ascot with What A Buck 1974, Grand Military Gold Cup Sandown (twice) with Burnt Oak 1985 and 1987, Mackeson Gold Cup Cheltenham Embassy Chase Final Ascot and Black & White Gold Cup Chase Leopardstown with Very Promising 1985, Mackeson Gold Cup with Another Coral 1991, Daily Express Triumph Hurdle Cheltenham with Solar Cloud 1986 and Mysilv 1994, Tote Gold Cup Cheltenham with Charter Party 1988, Arkle Trophy Cheltenham 1989 and Castleford Chase Wetherby 1990 and 1991 with Waterloo Boy, Arlington Chase Final Cheltenham with Al Hashimi 1990, King George VI Chase with Barton Bank 1993, Queen Mother Champion Chase with Viking Flagship 1994 and 1995, Scottish Grand National with Moorcroft Boy 1996; one of only six Nat Hunt trainers to train 100 winners in a season (1992–93 season); ran Nat Hunt Cricket XI for 20 years; champion Nat Hunt trainer 1993–94 and 1994–95; *Recreations* cricket, spectator all sports; *Style*— David Nicholson, Esq; ✉ Jackdaws' Castle, Temple Guiting, nr Cheltenham, Glos GL54 5XU (☎ 01386 584209, fax 01386 584218)

NICHOLSON, David John; MP (C) Taunton (majority 3,336); s of late John Francis Nicholson, and Lucy, *née* Battrum; *b* 17 Aug 1944; *Educ* Queen Elizabeth GS Blackburn, Christ Church Oxford (MA); *m* 23 May 1981, Frances Mary, da of late Brig T E H Helby (d 1984), of Aveton Gifford, nr Kingsbridge, S Devon; 2 s (Julian b 1984, Alexander b 1990), 1 da (Eleanor b 1986); *Career* head of Political Section Cons Res Dept 1974–82, dep dir-gen Assoc of Br C of C 1986–87 (dir 1982–86), MP (C) Taunton 1987–, sec Cons Backbench Social Security Ctee 1988–90, PPS to Rt Hon Lynda Chalker as min for overseas devpt 1990–92, sec All-Party Parly Gp on Population and Development 1990–94, chm Cons South West Membs Ctee 1994–95 (vice chm 1992–93), sec Cons Backbench Agric Ctee 1995–; memb Commons Select Ctee: on Public Accounts 1992–94, on the Parly Cmmr for Admin (the Ombudsman) 1992–, on Employment 1994–96, Educn and Employment 1996–; *Books* co-ed: The Leo Amery Diaries (Vol I 1980), The Empire at Bay (Vol II 1988); *Recreations* travel, gardening, music, the country; *Clubs* Taunton Cons, Wellington Cons; *Style*— David Nicholson, Esq, MP; ✉ Allshire, nr Brushford, Somerset EX16 9JG; House of Commons, London (☎ 0171 219 3000)

NICHOLSON, Emma Harriet; MP (C until Dec 1995 whereafter Lib Dem) Devon West and Torridge (majority 3,614); 3 da of Sir Godfrey Nicholson, 1 and last Bt (d 1991), and Lady Katharine Constance, *née* Lindsay (d 1972), da of 27 Earl of Crawford and Balcarres; *b* 16 Oct 1941; *Educ* Portsdown Lodge Sch Sussex, St Mary's Sch Wantage, RAM (LRAM, ARCM); *m* 9 May 1987, Sir Michael Harris Caine, *qv*, s of Sir Sydney Caine, KCMG; 2 step c, 1 ward; *Career* computer software programmer and engr ITC (now ICL) 1962–66, computer conslt John Tyzack & Ptnrs 1967–69, computer and gen mgmnt conslt McLintock Mann and Whinney Murray 1969–73; dir of fundraising The Save the Children Fund 1977–85 (joined 1974), fndr and bd memb Stichting Redt de Kinderen (Netherlands) 1982–88, fndr and memb Comité d'Honneur Sauvez Les Enfants (France) 1983; conslt 1985–87: World Assoc of Girl Guides and Girl Scouts, The Duke of Edinburgh's Award Scheme, Foster Parents Plan UK, Westminster Children's Hosp; Parly candidate (C) Blythe Valley 1979, MP (C until Dec 1995, whereafter Lib Dem) Devon W and Torridge 1987–; vice chm Cons Party (with special responsibility for women) 1983–87, PPS to Michael Jack as min of state 1992–95 (successively at Home Office, MAFF and HM Treasy); visiting fell St Anthony's Coll Oxford 1995–96; All Party Parly Gps: chm Br Iraq Gp, chm Oman Gp, chm Kuwait Gp, co-chm UNA Advsy Gp, co-dep chm Br Iranian Gp, treas Saudi Arabia Gp, treas Romanian Children Gp, treas Positive European Gp, treas Br Caribbean Gp, sec Syrian Gp, sec Human Rights Gp, fndr and former chm Euro Information Market Gp; cncl memb: UNICEF, Howard League for Penal Reform, Media Soc, Industry Churches Forum, Africa 95; memb: Euro Standing Ctee A, Standing Ctee on Statutory Instruments, Select Ctee on Employment 1990–91; dir: Cities in Schs, Nicholson Productions Ltd; chm: AMAR Appeal, Iraqi Humanitarian Relief Ctee until 1996 (also vice patron until 1996), Access for Disabled People to Arts Premises Today (ADAPT) until 1996 (also patron until 1996), Blind in Business 1993–95, Emily Trust Appeal Ctee, UNA Advsy Gp UNESCO (co-chm), Int Year of the Disabled UNESCO; vice chm: European Movement, Relatives' Assoc; pres numerous charitable orgns in Devon; vice pres: Assoc of Dist Cncls, Br Tinnitus Assoc, Nat Assoc for Maternal and Child Welfare, Small Farmers' Assoc, Br Leprosy Relief Assoc (LEPRA); patron numerous charitable and other orgns incl: Int Ctee for a Free Iraq, Ecaterina Iliescu Meml Lecture, Orphan Aid to Romania, Br Deaf Accord, Nat Deaf Blind and Rubella Assoc, AMANA (soc to promote understanding of Islam), Soc for the Freedom of the City of London Municipality, Freedom Cncl, Berith Fndn, Appeal Ctee Methodist Church Home Mission Div, Reading Industl Therapy Orgn, Women into IT Fndn, Women's Engrg Soc, Women's Business Assoc, Federal Tst for Educn and Res, Devon Daycare Tst, Sense South West, Opera South West, PHAB South West, Deaf Educn through Listening and Talking (DELTA), Nat Music and Disability Information Service; tstee: Covent Garden Cancer Res Tst, Motor Neurone Disease Assoc, World Meml Fund for Disaster Relief; memb: Mgmnt Bd European Movement, Guild of Mgmnt Conslts, Forum UK, RIIA, Centre for Policy Studies, Inst of Economic Affrs, Cncl for Arab-Br Understanding, Prince of Wales Advsy Tst on Disability, Advsy Cncl Justis Legal Databases, Exeter Univ Devpt Ctee, Br Romanian Assoc, West Regnl Assoc for the Deaf, Editorial Panel 300 Group, Advsy Bd Women of Tomorrow Awards, London Business Women's Network, Appeal Ctee Royal Acad of Music, Advsy Cncl Utd World Fndn, Advsy Cncl Centre for Adoptive Identity Studies Univ of E London; Freeman Worshipful Co of Info Technologists; fell Indust and Parliament Tst, FRSA 1990; *Books* Why Does the West Forget? (1993); author of various articles and pamphlets; *Recreations* music (organ, piano, cello and singing), chess, walking, reading; *Clubs* Reform; *Style*— Ms Emma Nicholson, MP; ✉ House of Commons, London SW1A 0AA (☎ 0171 219 3000)

NICHOLSON, Rev Prof Ernest Wilson; s of Ernest Tedford Nicholson (d 1977), Veronica Muriel, *née* Wilson (d 1963); *b* 26 Sept 1938; *Educ* Portadown Coll, Trinity Coll Dublin (BA, MA), Univ of Glasgow (PhD), Univ of Cambridge (BD, DD), Univ of Oxford (DD by incorporation); *m* 5 April 1962, Hazel, da of Samuel John Jackson; 1 s (Peter), 3 da (Rosalind, Kathryn, Jane); *Career* lectr in Hebrew and Semitic languages Trinity Coll Dublin 1962–72; Univ of Cambridge: lectr in divinity 1967–79, fell Wolfson Coll 1967–69, fell and chaplain Pembroke Coll 1969–79, dean 1973–79; Univ of Oxford: Oriel prof of the interpretation of Holy Scripture and fell Oriel Coll 1979–90, provost Oriel Coll 1990–, pro-vice-chllr Univ of Oxford 1993–; chm Jardine Fndn 1993–; Cdr of the Order of Merit of the Italian Republic; hon fell: Trinity Coll Dublin, Wolfson Coll Cambridge, St Peter's Coll Oxford; FBA 1987; *Recreations* music, walking; *Style*— The Rev Prof Ernest Nicholson, FBA; ✉ Provost's Lodgings, Oriel College, Oxford OX1 4EW (☎ 01865 276533)

NICHOLSON, Frank; s of Douglas Nicholson (d 1984), of Durham, and Pauline Nicholson; *b* 11 Feb 1954; *Educ* Harrow, Magdalene Coll Cambridge (MA); *m* 12 April 1986, Lavinia, *née* Stourton; 3 s (Simon b 1989, Hugo b 1991, Edward b 1994); *Career* Debenham Tewson & Chinnocks 1976–81, md Vaux Breweries Ltd 1984–; chm City of Sunderland Partnership; hon fell and dep chm Univ of Sunderland; winner Prince of Wales' Ambassador's Award 1995; FRICS 1977; *Recreations* countryside pursuits; *Clubs* RAC, Northern Counties; *Style*— Frank Nicholson, Esq; ✉ Vaux Group plc, The Brewery, Sunderland, Tyne & Wear SU1 3AN (☎ 0191 567 6277, fax 0191 565 7822)

NICHOLSON, George Howard Joseph; er s of Roydon Joseph Nicholson, and Evelyn Sophia Carlton, *née* Reader; *b* 4 April 1936; *Educ* Wellington Coll; *m* 13 Aug 1974, Adèle Janet, er da of late Richard Barbour, of Bolesworth Castle, Tattenhall, Chester; 2 s (Joseph William b 1975, Oliver Christian b 1977); *Career* Nat Serv King's Dragoon Gds, Lt Inns of Ct Regt (TA); cub reporter Vancouver Sun 1956, advertising and fundraising exec; appeal sec: Br Olympic Assoc 1978–, Commonwealth Games Cncl for England 1978–90; memb Ctee Incorporated Church Bldg Soc 1966–78, former gp chm Westminster Christian Cncl, former chm Human Rights Soc, govr Bacon Sch Bermondsey 1965–75, tstee City & Metropolitan Welfare Charity; former borough cncllr RBK and C, Parly candidate (C) Bermondsey and Rotherhithe 1970; Liveryman Worshipful Co of Leathersellers (memb Ct of Assts 1990); *Recreations* visiting historic churches; *Clubs* Brooks's; *Style*— George Nicholson, Esq; ✉ 16 Chelsea Embankment, London SW3 4LA (☎ 0171 352 9202); Coomb Dale Lodge, Bickerton, Malpas, Cheshire (☎ 01829 782425); British Olympic Association, 1 Wandsworth Plain, London SW18 1EH (☎ 0181 871 2677, fax 0181 871 9104)

NICHOLSON, Sheriff Principal (Charles) Gordon Brown; QC (Scot 1982); s of William Addison Nicholson, OBE (d 1987), of Edinburgh, and Jean Brown (d 1967); *b* 11 Sept 1935; *Educ* George Watson's Coll Edinburgh, Univ of Edinburgh (MA, LLB); *m* 1963, Hazel Mary, da of Robert Riddle Nixon (d 1976); 2 s (David, Robin); *Career* called to the Bar Scotland 1961, advocate depute 1968–70; Sheriff of Dumfries and Galloway at Dumfries 1970–76, Sheriff of Lothian and Borders 1976–82, cmmr Scot Law Cmmn 1982–90, Sheriff Princ of Lothian and Borders and Sheriff of Chancery 1990–; *Books* The Law and Practice of Sentencing in Scotland 1981 (supplement, 1985, 2 edn 1992); *Recreations* golf, music; *Clubs* New (Edinburgh), Honourable Co of Edinburgh Golfers; *Style*— Sheriff Principal Gordon Nicholson, QC; ✉ Back O'Redfern, 24C Colinton Road, Edinburgh EH10 5DX (☎ 0131 447 4300, fax 0131 447 3274); Sheriff Court House, Chambers St, Edinburgh (☎ 0131 225 2525)

NICHOLSON, Graham Beattie; s of John Arthur Nicholson (d 1975), and Ena Patricia Nicholson; *b* 22 Feb 1949; *Educ* Bloxham Sch, Trinity Hall Cambridge; *m* 30 Oct 1982, Pamela Soei Luang, *née* Tan; 1 da (Vanessa b 1978); *Career* slr; Freshfields: NY office 1979–80, ptnr 1980–, Singapore office 1980–83, managing ptnr Co Dept 1986–90, managing ptnr 1990–93; memb City of London Slrs' Co 1983; memb Law Soc; *Recreations* music, sailing, racquet sports; *Style*— Graham Nicholson, Esq; ✉ Whitefriars, 65 Fleet St, London EC4Y 1HS (☎ 0171 936 4000)

NICHOLSON, James Frederick (Jim); MEP (UUP) N Ireland (UUP votes 133,459); s of Thomas Richard Nicholson, of Ballyards, Armagh (d 1987), and Matilda, *née* Morrow (d 1984); *b* 29 Jan 1945; *m* 30 Nov 1968, Elizabeth, *née* Gibson; 6 s, 1 da; *Career* elected: Armagh Dist Cncl 1975–, NI Assembly 1982–86; MP 1983–85; MEP (UUP) N Ireland 1989–; farmer; *Recreations* walking, football; *Style*— Jim Nicholson, Esq, MEP; ✉ 3 Glengall Street, Belfast BT12 5AE (☎ 01232 439431, fax 01232 246738)

NICHOLSON, Jeremy Dawson; s of Maj Rodney Scholfield Nicholson, of Birdham, and Leta, *née* Dawson; *b* 14 March 1945; *Educ* Wellington; *m* 15 June 1968, Sarah Helen, da of Michael Richards; 2 s (Anthony Charles b 31 May 1969, Michael Dawson b 21 May 1973), 1 da (Charlotte Helen b 23 March 1971); *Career* Josolyne Layton-Bennett (formerly Layton-Bennett Billingham & Co): articled clerk 1964–68, mangr 1971–75, ptnr 1975–81; ptnr: Arthur Young 1981–89, Ernst & Young 1989–; FCA 1979 (ACA 1968); *Recreations* golf, theatre, music; *Clubs* MCC, Caledonian Club; *Style*— Jeremy Nicholson, Esq; ✉ Ernst & Young, Apex Plaza, Forbury Rd, Reading, Berkshire RG1 1YE (☎ 0118 950 0611)

NICHOLSON, Dr John William; s of Leslie Vaughan Nicholson, of Twickenham, and Barbara Ada Elizabeth, *née* Taylor; *b* 9 Feb 1955; *Educ* Thames Valley GS Twickenham, Kingston Poly (BSc), South Bank Poly (PhD); *m* 1977, Suzette Blygh, da of David Leonard Shopland; 2 s (Andrew Vaughan b 22 Nov 1982, Peter John b 22 July 1993), 2 da (Bethany Jane b 2 July 1985, Rafaelle Mary b 13 May 1988); *Career* SERC post-doctoral research fell South Bank Poly 1981–83; Lab of the Govt Chemist: higher scientific offr 1983–86, sr scientific offr 1986–89, princ scientific offr 1989–92, sr lectr Dental Biomaterials Unit King's Coll Sch of Med and Dentistry London 1992–; nationally elected memb Cncl Royal Soc of Chemistry 1992–95; CChem 1980, FRSC 1991, Eur Chem 1993; *Books* The Chemistry of Polymers (1991), Acid-Base Cements (with A D Wilson, 1993); also author of over 75 scholarly papers published in peer-refereed jls; *Recreations* watching cricket, history and philosophy of science; *Style*— Dr John Nicholson; ✉ 52 Buckingham Road, Hampton, Middx TW12 3JG (☎ 0181 979 8379); The Dental School, King's College School of Medicine and Dentistry, Caldecot Road, London SE5 9RW (☎ 0171 346 3520)

NICHOLSON, Malcolm G C; *b* 4 March 1949; *Educ* Haileybury, Univ of Cambridge (BA, LLB), Brussels (Dip en Droit Européen); *m* Diana Fay Nicholson; 2 s (James, Peter), 4 da (Claire, Laura, Briony, Emily); *Career* ptnr Slaughter and May 1981– (specialising in European, Regulatory and Commercial Law); *Style*— Malcolm Nicholson, Esq; ✉ Slaughter & May, 35 Basinghall Street, London EC2V 5DB (☎ 0171 600 1200)

NICHOLSON, Mavis; da of Richard John Mainwaring, and Olive Irene Mainwaring; *b* 19 Oct 1930; *Educ* Neath Co Sch for Girls, Univ of Swansea; *m* 16 Aug 1952, Geoffrey George Nicholson, s of George Llewelyn Nicholson; 3 s (Steve b 24 July 1958, Lewis b 13 May 1960, Harry b 10 Feb 1963); *Career* advertising copywriter; Hulton scholarship Mather and Crowther; employed by: LPE, Greenleys, Clifford Bloxhams; freelance writer, from home the home ed Nova; writer: Observer, Sunday Times, Evening Standard, personal column Family Circle; columnist South Wales Echo, agony aunt Oldie Magazine; TV presenter 1971–, progs incl: Good Afternoon, Afternoon, Afternoon Plus, A+, Mavis Meets, Mavis Wanting to Know, BBC Open Air, Mavis of 4, Mavis Catches up With, BBC Garden Party, Relative Values, Third Wave, In With Mavis, Local Hero,

Moments of Crisis, Faces of the Family (C4), Oldie TV; presenter prog in Wales (Radio 2 Arts); hon fell Univ of Swansea; pres Montgomery Wild-life Tst; memb Amnesty Int and Labour Pty; *Books* Help Yourself (1974), Martha, Jane and Me: A Girlhood in Wales (1991), What Did You Do in the War Mummy?; *Recreations* my three grandchildren Ben, Tess and Sam, table tennis, photography, reading, gardening; *Style*— Mrs Mavis Nicholson; ✉ c/o Jon Thurley (Agent), 213 Linen Hall, 156 Regent St, London W1R 5TA (☎ 0171 437 9545)

NICHOLSON, (Edward) Max; CB (1948), CVO (1971); s of Edward Prichard Nicholson (d 1945), of Hangersley, Ringwood, Hants, and Constance Caroline, *née* Oldmeadow (d 1945); *b* 12 July 1904; *Educ* Sedbergh, Hertford Coll Oxford; *m* 1, 6 Aug 1932 (m dis 1964), Eleanor Mary Lloyd, da of George Edward Crawford, of Putney, London; 2 s (Piers b 1934, Thomas Gavin b 1938 d 1995); m 2, 1965, Marie Antoinette Mauerhofer; 1 s (David Ian b 1965); *Career* asst ed The Week-End Review London 1930–33, gen sec PEP 1933–39, controller of lit Miny of Info 1939, head Econ and Int Allied Branch Miny of Shipping (became Miny of War Tport 1940), head Allocation of Tonnage Div and Miny rep on Anglo-US Combined Shipping Adjustment Bd Miny of War Tport 1941–45, chm Anglo-Soviet Shipping Ctee (attended Quebec, Cairo, Yalta and Potsdam Confs) 1941–45, head office of Lord Pres of the Cncl 1945–52, DG Nature Conservancy 1952–65, chm Land Use Conslts 1965–89; chm: Br Tst for Ornithology 1947–49 (first hon sec 1933–39), Official Ctee Festival of Br 1951, London Looks Forward Conf 1977, Environmental Ctee of London Celebrations for the Queen's Jubilee 1977; tstee Earthwatch Europe 1989–93 (chm 1989–90); memb: Advsy Cncl on Scientific Policy 1948–64, Cwlth Scientific Ctee 1948–64, Special Ctee of Int Cncl of Scientific Unions for Int Biological Programme (convener conservation section) 1963–74; tstee The Observer 1952–65, pres RSPB 1980–85; vice pres: Wildfowl Tst (now Wildfowl and Wetlands Trust) 1978–, WWF/UK 1983–; hon memb: Br Ecological Soc, Royal Town Planning Inst; hon fell: American Ornithologists' Union, RIBA, Hertford Coll Oxford 1993; Europa Preis für Landespflege 1972, Commandeur Order of the Golden Ark Netherlands 1973, Fndrs Medal British Tst for Ornithology 1991; Hon LLD Aberdeen 1964, Hon Dr London Royal Coll of Art 1978, Hon DL Birmingham 1983; MBOU, FRSA (vice pres 1978–82), FRGS; *Books* incl: Birds in England (1926), How Birds Live (1927), Birds and Men (1951), Oxford Birds of the Western Palearctic (ed 9 vols, 1977–94), The System (1967), The Environmental Revolution (1970), The New Environmental Age (1987), Bird-Watching in London (1995); *Clubs* Athenaeum; *Style*— Max Nicholson, Esq, CB, CVO; ✉ 13 Upper Cheyne Row, London SW3 5JW

NICHOLSON, The Rt Hon Lord Justice; Rt Hon Sir (James) Michael Anthony; kt (1988), PC (1995); s of Cyril Anthony de Lacy Nicholson, QC, DL (d 1963), of Beech Hill, Ardmore, Co Londonderry, and Eleanor Gerad, *née* Caffrey (d 1972); *b* 4 Feb 1933; *Educ* Downside, Trinity Coll Cambridge (MA); *m* 7 July 1973, Augusta Mary Ada, da of Thomas F Doyle (d 1979), and Elizabeth Doyle (d 1994), of Ardmanagh, Passage West, Co Cork; 1 s (Thomas b 7 May 1977), 2 da (Emma b 10 Jan 1975, Tessa b 26 July 1978); *Career* called to the Bar: NI 1956, Gray's Inn 1962, Ireland 1975; QC 1971, bencher Inn of Ct of NI 1978– (treas 1990), hon bencher Gray's Inn 1994–; sr crown counsel: Co Fermanagh 1971–73, Co Tyrone 1973–77, Co Londonderry 1977–81; chm Bar Cncl 1983–85; judge High Court of Justice NI 1986–95; Lord Justice of Appeal NI 1995–; chm Mental Health Review Tbnl 1973–76; memb Standing Advsy Cmmn on Human Rights in NI 1976–78; High Sheriff Co Londonderry 1972; *Recreations* cricket, chess; *Clubs* MCC; *Style*— The Rt Hon Lord Justice Nicholson; ✉ Royal Courts of Justice, Chichester St, Belfast, Northern Ireland BT1 3JF (☎ 01232 235111)

NICHOLSON, Michael Thomas; OBE (1991); s of Alan Alfred Nicholson (d 1956), of Romford, and Doris Alice, *née* Reid (d 1963); *b* 9 Jan 1937; *Educ* Prince Rupert Wilhemshaven Germany, Univ of Leicester (BA); *m* Diana; 2 s (Tom b 17 Jan 1972, William b 19 May 1973), 1 adopted da (Natasha b 7 Oct 1982); *Career* served RAF 1955–57; political writer DC Thompson 1962–63; ITN: foreign corr 1963–82 and 1985–, bureau corr Southern Africa 1976–81, newscaster 1982–85, Washington corr Channel 4 1989, currently sr foreign corr; wars covered incl: Nigeria/Biafra 1968–69, Ulster 1968–75, Vietnam 1969–75, Cambodia (incl invasion of Laos) 1972–75, Jordan (incl Dawson's Field and Black September) 1970, Indo-Pakistan War 1971, Yom Kippur War 1973, Rhodesian War 1973–80, invasion of Cyprus 1974, Beirut Lebanon 1975, Angolan Civil War 1975–78, Falklands War (awarded Falklands medal) 1982, Gulf War (awarded Gulf medal) 1991; *Awards* American Emmy nomination 1969, British Broadcasting Guild award 1974, RTS award 1974, Silver Nymph award (for Vietnam report) Monte Carlo Film Festival 1975, RTS Reporter of the Year (for Angola 1979, for Falklands 1983, for Yugoslavia 1992), BAFTA Richard Dimbleby award 1983, VALA award 1983, RTS Journalist of the Year 1991; FRGS 1983, fell Royal Cwlth Soc 1983; *Books* Partridge Kite (1978), Red Joker (1979), December Ultimatum (1981), Across The Limpopo (1985), Pilgrims Rest (1987), A Measure of Danger (1991), Natasha's Story (1993); *Recreations* tennis, sailing; *Clubs* Groucho; *Style*— Michael Nicholson, Esq, OBE; ✉ Independent Television News, 200 Gray's Inn Rd, London WC1X 8XZ (☎ 0171 833 3000)

NICHOLSON, Sir Paul Douglas; kt (1993); eld s of Frank Douglas Nicholson, TD, DL (d 1984), and Pauline, yr da of Maj Sir Thomas Lawson-Tancred, 9 Bt; *b* 7 March 1938; *Educ* Harrow, Clare Coll Cambridge; *m* 1970, Sarah, 4 and yst da of Sir Edmund Bacon, 13 and 14 Bt, KG, KBE, TD (d 1982), of Raveningham Hall, Norfolk; 1 da; *Career* Lt Coldstream Guards 1956–58; CA Price Waterhouse 1964; Vaux Group plc: exec 1965, dir 1967, chm 1976–; non-exec dir: Northern Electric plc, Yorkshire-Tyne Tees Television Holdings plc, Northern Development Company 1987–; chm: Northern Region CBI 1977–79, Northern Bd Nat Enterprise Bd 1979–84, Northern Investors Ltd 1984–89, Tyne & Wear Devpt Corp 1987–, Brewers and Licensed Retailers' Assoc 1994–96, Co Durham Fndn 1995–; pres North East C of C 1995–96; High Sheriff of Co Durham 1980–81, Lord-Lt Co Durham 1997– (DL 1980–97); Liveryman: Worshipful Co of Grocers, Worshipful Co of Brewers; *Recreations* shooting, deerstalking, driving horses (pres Coaching Club 1990–); *Clubs* Boodle's, Northern Counties; *Style*— Sir Paul Nicholson; ✉ Quarry Hill, Brancepeth, Durham DH7 8DW (☎ 0191 3780275, fax 0191 378 3015); Vaux Group plc, The Brewery, Sunderland, Tyne and Wear SR1 3AN (☎ 0191 567 6277, fax 0191 510 3479)

NICHOLSON, Peter C; *Career* dir Crest Nicholson plc 1972– (exec 1972–88, non-exec 1988–), non-exec dir Lloyds Bank plc 1990–, non-exec dir MIF Limited 1993–; chm: Camper & Nicholsons Ltd 1968–78, South West Property One Ltd 1988–, South West Waterside Property One plc 1990–, South East Waterside Property One plc 1990–, Carisbrooke Shipping plc 1990–, Leeds Permanent Building Society Flexible Options 1–10 plc 1993–, Caledonian Property One Ltd 1994–, Central London Property One Ltd 1994–, Countrywide Property One Ltd 1994–, Income Property One Ltd 1994–, Midland Property One and Two Ltd 1994–, Northern Property One and Two Ltd 1994–, Sheltered Property Rental Ltd 1994–, South East Property One Ltd 1994–; *Style*— Peter Nicholson, Esq; ✉ Mere House, Hamble, Southampton SO31 4JB (☎ 01703 455019, fax 01703 455834)

NICHOLSON, Richard Arthur; *b* 14 May 1935; *Educ* Stowe, Guy's Hosp Med Sch (LRCP); *m* 18 Jan 1964, Diana Mary, da of Lt-Col Arthur Robinson (d 1985), of Hedon, nr Hull; 2 s (Mark b 1 March 1965, Philip b 31 July 1968), 1 da (Sally b 30 Sept 1966); *Career* Nat Serv Lt (former sub Lt) RNVR 1953–55; conslt orthopaedic and accident surgn and med dir Pontefract Hosps Tst; memb: BMA, Br Orthopaedic Assoc; MRCS, FRCS Glasgow; *Books* papers: Blunt Abdominal Trauma in Head Injuries (1966), Peptic Ulceration in Myocardial Infarction (1967), 20 Years of Bone and Joint Tuberculosis (1975); *Recreations* hunting, shooting, listening to music, silversmith with own mark registered at Goldsmith Hall; *Style*— Richard Nicholson, Esq; ✉ Thorpe Grange Farm, Thorpe Audlin, nr Pontefract, W Yorkshire WF8 3HG (☎ 01977 620629); The Orthopaedic Department, Pontefract General Infirmary, Southgate, Pontefract (☎ 01977 600600); Methley Park Private Hospital, Metley Lane, Methley, nr Leeds (☎ 01977 518518)

NICHOLSON, Robin Alaster; s of Gerald Hugh Nicholson (d 1970), of Bayford, and Margaret Evelyn, *née* Hanbury; *b* 27 July 1944; *Educ* Eton, Magdalene Coll Cambridge (MA), UCL (MSc), RIBA Sch Design Prize 1969; *m* 18 Dec 1969, Fiona Mary, da of Brig Garth Bird; 3 s (Zachary Luke b 7 March 1971, Solomon Rufus Seb b 13 Sept 1974, Caspian Ned b 5 June 1978); *Career* architect; Yorke Rosenberg Mardall London 1966–67, Evan Walker Associates Toronto 1967, James Stirling Chartered Architects London 1969–73, Boza Lührs and Muzard Santiago Chile 1973, UCL 1974–76, Poly of N London 1976–79, Edward Cullinan Architects 1979–; visiting fell Univ of Wales 1984; memb Cncl: RIBA 1991– (vice pres 1992–94), ARCUK 1994–; vice chm Construction Indust Cncl 1995–; memb Architects and Engrs for Social Responsibility, RIBA; *Recreations* gardening; *Style*— Robin Nicholson, Esq; ✉ Edward Cullinan Architects, 1 Baldwin Terrace, London N1 7RU (☎ 0171 704 1975, fax 0171 354 2739)

NICHOLSON, Sir Robin Buchanan; kt (1985); s of late Carroll Nicholson and Nancy Esther Nicholson (d 1993); *b* 12 Aug 1934; *Educ* Oundle, St Catharine's Coll Cambridge (PhD); *m* 1958, Elizabeth Mary (d 1988), da of Sir Sydney Caffyn; 1 s, 2 da; *Career* Univ of Cambridge: demonstrator in metallurgy 1960, lectr in metallurgy 1964, fell Christ's Coll 1962–66 (hon fell 1984); prof of metallurgy Univ of Manchester 1966; md Inco Europe 1976–81 (dir 1975–81), chief sci advsr Cabinet Office 1981–85; exec dir Pilkington plc 1986–96; non-exec dir: Rolls Royce plc 1986–, BP plc 1987–; memb SRC 1978–81; Liveryman Worshipful Co of Goldsmiths; FRS 1978, FEng 1980, FIM, MInstP; *Clubs* MCC; *Style*— Sir Robin Nicholson, FEng, FRS; ✉ Penson Farm, Diptford, Totnes, Devon TQ9 7NN

NICHOLSON, Roy Knollys Ellard; s of Basil Ellard Nicholson (d 1985), and Gilda Gwendolyn, *née* Maurice-Green; *b* 4 Dec 1946; *Educ* Oundle, Bachschule Schloss Rettershof Königstein im Taunus Germany; *m* 1976, Bridget Mary, da of Paul Patterson Davis; 2 s (Tim Paul b 1978, Andrew Charles b 1980); *Career* KPMG (formerly Peat Marwick Mitchell & Co): qualified 1971, mangr 1975, sr mangr 1980, ptnr 1984–, currently corp fin ptnr and head of valuations; MSI, FCA; *Recreations* golf, tennis, watching rugby, Norfolk; *Clubs* Walton Heath Golf, Royal West Norfolk Golf; *Style*— Roy Nicholson, Esq; ✉ KPMG Corporate Finance, 8 Salisbury Square, London EC4Y 8BB (☎ 0171 311 1000, fax 0171 311 8276)

NICKELL, Prof Stephen John; s of John Edward Hilary Nickell (d 1962) and Phyllis, *née* Vicary (d 1975); *b* 25 April 1944; *Educ* Merchant Taylors', Pembroke Coll Cambridge (scholarship, BA), LSE (MSc, Ely Devons prize); *m* 25 June 1976, Susan Elizabeth, da of Peter Nicholas Pegden, of Bridlington, Yorks; 1 da (Katherine Jane b 30 Sept 1979), 1 s (William Thomas b 16 Oct 1981); *Career* mathematics teacher Hendon Co Sch 1965–68; prof of economics: LSE 1979–84 (lectr 1970–77, reader 1977–79), (and dir) Inst of Economics and Statistics Univ of Oxford 1984–; professorial fell Nuffield Coll Oxford 1984–; chm Research Grants Bd ESRC 1990–94 (also memb); memb Cncl Royal Economic Soc 1984–94, fell Econometric Soc 1980 (memb Cncl 1987–93); Fell Br Acad 1993; *Books* The Investment Decisions of Firms (1978), The Rise in Unemployment (ed, 1987), Unemployment (1991), The Unemployment Crisis (1994), The Performance of Companies (1995); *Recreations* reading, riding; *Style*— Prof Stephen Nickell, FBA; ✉ The Old Bakehouse, Horn Hill, Barford St Michael, Banbury, Oxon OX15 0RQ (☎ 01869 338486); Institute of Economics and Statistics, St Cross Building, Manor Rd, Oxford OX1 3UL (☎ 01865 271087, fax 01865 271094)

NICKLEN, Steve; *b* 2 May 1953; *Educ* Univ of Leeds (BSc); *m* 13 Oct 1983, Mary Jean Madden Budd; 1 da (Julia Victoria Maiel b 28 Sept 1987), 1 s (Peter George Thomas b 18 April 1989); *Career* research scientist Addenbrooke's Hosp and Pembroke Coll Cambridge 1974–78, private sec to four Secretaries of State DTI 1979–85, conslt Hay Management Consultants 1985–87, dir Kinsley Lord Management Consultants 1987–94, dir of audit support Audit Cmmn 1994– (responsibilities incl pubn of Citizens Charter PIS for local govt); MInstD 1996; *Recreations* classical music, swimming, walking, 19th century novels, political history, food and drink; *Style*— Steve Nicklen, Esq; ✉ 48 Rosendale Road, West Dulwich, London SE21; Post Office Cottage, Sedlescombe, Battle, East Sussex; Director of Audit Support, The Audit Commisson, 1 Vincent Square, London SW1P 2PN (☎ 0171 828 1212, fax 0171 976 6187)

NICKLESS, Christopher John; yr s of Rev Canon Victor George Nickless, of Ford Place, Ford Lane, Wrotham Heath, Kent, and Grace Kathleen, *née* Hepburn-Whyte; *b* 17 Sept 1947; *Educ* The King's Sch Rochester, Univ of Birmingham (BA); *m* 11 April 1987, Mairi, da of Lt-Col Robert Andrew Garden, of Sandwich, Kent; *Career* asst master The King's Sch Rochester 1968–82; Jr Sch King's Sch Rochester: dep master 1982–87, dep headmaster 1987–90; King's Sch Rochester: headmaster pre prep sch 1988–90, headmaster prep sch 1991–; memb: CSA, IAPS, NAHT; ind memb St Margaret's Ward Rochester City Cncl 1972; elected: Medway DC 1973, Medway Borough Cncl 1976 and 1979, Rochester upon Medway City Cncl 1983 and 1987; life memb: Nat Tst for Scotland, English Heritage; steward Cathedral Church of Christ and the Blessed Virgin Mary Rochester, life govr RNLI, pres Borstal CC 1986–93, memb Kent Archaeological Soc, life fell RSPB, assoc Iona Community; *Recreations* cricket, music, gardening, walking; *Clubs* Kent CCC (life memb), Warwicks CCC; *Style*— Christopher Nickless, Esq; ✉ The Hawthorns, 121 Maidstone Road, Chatham, Kent ME4 6JA (☎ 01634 841037); The Preparatory School, King Edward Rd, Rochester, Kent ME1 1UB (☎ 01634 843657, fax 01634 840569)

NICKLIN, Keith Richard; s of James Edward Nicklin (d 1979), of London, and May Marjorie; *b* 12 Dec 1935; *m* 12 Aug 1983, Judith Louise, da of Leslie Eric Whiting (d 1983); 2 da (Amy b 1983, Sophie b 1986); *Career* chm: Leopard Ltd, Nicklin Advertising Ltd, KRT Ltd; FIPA; *Recreations* horse racing, fishing; *Clubs* Les Ambassadeurs; *Style*— Keith Nicklin, Esq; ✉ Chairman, Leopard Ltd, 40 Marsh Wall, London Docklands, London E14 9TP (☎ 0171 512 1000, fax 0171 512 1999)

NICKLIN, Stephen Richard; s of Richard Patrick Nicklin (d 1982), of Rugby, Warwicks, and Elsie Joan, *née* Crisp; *b* 20 April 1952; *Educ* Sloane GS; *m* 3 March 1979, (Mary) Theresa, da of Vincent O'Shea (d 1995), Collooney, Co Sligo, Eire; 3 s (Edward b 1981, Anthony b 1988, Luke (twin) b 1988), 1 da (Emily b 1985); *Career* BBC 1970; unit mangr: Newsnight BBC 1984–87, American Elections BBC 1984, Election 87 BBC 1985–87, Channel 4 News ITN 1987–89; ITN: editorial mangr 1989–91, home news mangr 1991–93, input mangr 1993–94, gen mangr ITV Dept 1994–95, resource mangr 1996–; memb RTS; *Style*— Stephen Nicklin, Esq; ✉ ITN Ltd, 200 Gray's Inn Rd, London WC1X 8XZ (☎ 0171 833 3000, fax 0171 430 4644, e-mail steve.nicklin@ITN.co.uk)

NICKOLLS, Malcolm Charles; s of Capt Charles Nickolls (d 1985), and Lillian Rose, *née* Taylor; *b* 20 March 1944; *Educ* Rickmansworth GS, Univ of London (LLB), Brighton Coll of Art (DipArch), Thames Poly (Dip Landscape Arch); *m* 26 Aug 1967, Mary Delia Margaret, da of Ronald Edward Groves, CBE; 2 da (Joanna Helen b 8 Nov 1973, Deborah Sally b 31 Aug 1976); *Career* architect and landscape architect; private practice under style of NKD Architects 1975–; princ building J Paul Getty Jr Conservation Centre (Nat

Film Archive); ARCUK: memb Cncl 1979–, hon offr 1982–, chair Professional Purposes 1982–92, vice chair Cncl 1992–94, chair Cncl 1994–; RIBA: memb Cncl 1989–96, chair Discipline Ctee 1992–94; memb Landscape Inst 1977; MCIArb 1976, FRSA 1989; *Recreations* cycling, computers, technology, science, invention; *Style*— Malcolm Nickolls, Esq; ✉ NKD, 27 Rickfords Hill, Aylesbury, Buckinghamshire (☎ 01296 397272, fax 01296 436330)

NICKSON, Baron (Life Peer UK 1994), of Renagour in the District of Stirling; Sir David Wigley Nickson; KBE (1987, CBE 1981), DL (Stirling and Falkirk 1982); s of Geoffrey Wigley Nickson (d 1983), and Janet Mary, *née* Dobie (d 1994); *b* 27 Nov 1929; *Educ* Eton, RMA Sandhurst; *m* 18 Oct 1952, (Helen) Louise, da of late Lt-Col Louis Latrobe Cockcraft, DSO, MVO; 3 da (Hon Felicity (Hon Mrs (James) Lewis) b 3 Nov 1955, Hon Lucy (Hon Mrs (Melfort) Campbell) b 8 July 1959, Hon Rosemary (Hon Mrs (Alastair) Campbell) b 11 Feb 1963); *Career* regular cmmn Coldstream Gds 1949–54; William Collins plc: joined 1954, dir 1959–76, vice chm and gp md 1976–83; dir Radio Clyde Ltd 1981–85; Scottish & Newcastle plc: dir 1981–95, dep chm 1982, chm 1983–89; chm Clydesdale Bank plc 1991– (dir 1981–, dep chm 1990–91), dep chm General Accident plc 1993– (dir 1971–); dir: Edinburgh Investment Trust plc 1981–94, Hambros plc, National Australia Bank 1991–96; pres CBI 1986–88 (chm for Scot 1979–81); chm: Countryside Cmmn for Scot 1983–85, Senior Salaries Review Body 1989–95, Scottish Devpt Agency 1989–91, Scottish Enterprise 1990–93; memb: Scottish Ind Devpt Advsy Bd 1974–79, Scottish Econ Cncl 1979–, NEDC 1985–88; chm Atlantic Salmon Tst 1988–95; chllr Glasgow Caledonian Univ 1993–; Brig Queen's Body Guard for Scotland (Royal Co of Archers); Hon Doctorate: Univ of Stirling, Napier Univ, Paisley Univ, Glasgow Caledonian Univ; FRSE 1987; *Recreations* fishing, shooting, stalking, birdwatching, countryside; *Clubs* Boodle's, Flyfishers', MCC, Western (Glasgow); *Style*— The Rt Hon Lord Nickson, KBE, DL, FRSE; ✉ Renagour House, Aberfoyle, Stirling FK8 3TF (☎ 01877 382275); Clydesdale Bank PLC, 30 St Vincent Place, Glasgow G1 2HL (☎ 0141 223 2002)

NICOL, Alexander David (Sandy); *b* 11 July 1938; *Career* md NEI Peebles 1976–83, dep chief exec British Linen Bank Ltd 1989– (dir 1983–); CA; *Recreations* golf; *Style*— Sandy Nicol, Esq; ✉ The British Linen Bank Ltd, 4 Melville St, Edinburgh EH3 7NZ (direct ☎ 0131 243 8304, fax 0131 243 8310)

NICOL, Andrew George Lindsay; QC (1995); s of Duncan Rennie Nicol (d 1991), and Margaret, *née* Mason (d 1967); *b* 9 May 1951; *Educ* City of London Freemen's Sch, Selwyn Coll Cambridge (BA, LLB), Harvard Law Sch (LLM); *children* 2 s; *Career* special asst to dir Housing and Community Dept State of California 1975–76, asst Allen Allen & Hemsley Slrs Sydney 1976–77, lectr in law LSE 1977–87; called to the Bar Middle Temple 1978; *Books* Subjects, Citizens, Aliens and Others (with Ann Dummett, 1990), Media Law (with G Robertson QC, 1992); *Recreations* family, walking; *Style*— Andrew Nicol, Esq, QC; ✉ Doughty Street Chambers, 11 Doughty Street, London WC1N 2PG (☎ 0171 404 1313, fax 0171 404 2283)

NICOL, Angus Sebastian Torquil Eyers; s of Henry James Nicol (d 1977), and Phyllis Mary, *née* Eyers; *b* 11 April 1933; *Educ* RNC Dartmouth; *m* 20 April 1968, Eleanor Denise, da of Lt Cdr William Lefevre Brodrick (ka 1943); 2 da (Catharine Sophia b 1968, Augusta Devorgilla Margaret b 1972); *Career* RN (ret as Sub-Lt 1956), served HMS Euryalus, HM MMS 1630, HMS Brocklesby, and HMS Coquette; literary ed Cassell & Co 1956–61; called to the Bar Middle Temple 1963, recorder 1982–; author of poems and short stories in Gaelic; fndr memb and first vice chm The Monday Club 1961, dir The Highland Soc of London 1981– (sec 1982–), sr steward The Argyllshire Gathering 1983, lectr in Gaelic Central London Adult Educn Inst 1982–, conductor London Gaelic Choir 1985–90, tstee of Urras Clann Mhic Neacail 1987–; chm: Disciplinary Ctee Potato Mktg Bd 1988–, VAT Tribunal 1988–, SE Area Legal Aid Ctee 1991; cmmr Clan MacNicol for all the Territories of GB S of the River Tweed and for Europe; memb Gaelic Soc of Inverness; FSA (Scot); *Recreations* shooting, fishing, sailing, music, gastronomy, Gaelic literature; *Clubs* Flyfishers', Royal Highland Yacht; *Style*— Angus Nicol, Esq; ✉ 5 Paper Buildings, Temple, London EC4Y 7HB (☎ 0171 353 8494)

NICOL, Prof Donald MacGillivray; s of Rev George Manson Nicol (d 1957), and Mary Patterson, *née* MacGillivray; *b* 4 Feb 1923; *Educ* King Edward VII Sch Sheffield, St Paul's London, Pembroke Coll Cambridge (MA, PhD), Br Sch of Archaeology Athens; *m* 15 July 1950, Joan Mary, da of Lt-Col Sir Walter Campbell, KCIE (d 1974); 3 s (Christopher, Stephen, Theodore); *Career* Friends' Ambulance Unit 1942–46; lectr in classics Univ Coll Dublin 1952–64, visiting fell Dumbarton Oaks Washington DC 1964–65, visiting prof Byzantine history Univ of Indiana 1965–66, sr lectr and reader in Byzantine history Univ of Edinburgh 1966–70; King's Coll London: Koraes prof of modern Greek and Byzantine history language and literature 1970–88, asst princ and vice princ 1977–81; prof emeritus Univ of London 1988; dir The Gennadius Library Athens 1989–92; FBA, MRIA, FRHistS, FKC; *Books* The Despotate of Epiros 1204–1267 (1957), The Byzantine Family of Kantakouzenos (1968), The Last Centuries of Byzantium 1261–1453 (1972, 2 edn 1993), Byzantium - Its Ecclesiastical History and Relations with the Western World (1972), Meteora - The Rock Monasteries of Thessaly (2 edn, 1975), Church and Society in the Last Centuries of Byzantium (1979), The End of the Byzantine Empire (1979), The Despotate of Epiros 1267–1479 - A Contribution to the History of Greece in the Middle Ages (1984), Studies in Late Byzantine History and Prosopography (1986), Byzantium and Venice - A Study in Diplomatic and Cultural Relations (1988), A Biographical Dictionary of the Byzantine Empire (1991), The Immortal Emperor. The Life and Legend of Constantine Palaiologos, Last Emperor of the Romans (1992), The Byzantine Lady. Ten Portraits, 1250–1500 (1994), The Reluctant Emperor. A Biography of John Cantacuzene, Byzantine emperor and monk, c 1295–1383 (1996); *Recreations* book-binding; *Style*— Prof Donald Nicol, FBA; ✉ 16 Courtyards, Little Shelford, Cambridge CB2 5ER (☎ 01223 843 406)

NICOL, Michael George (Mike); s of Desmond James Nicol, of Cape Town, South Africa, and June Florence, *née* Westbrook; *b* 17 Nov 1951; *Educ* Univ of South Africa (BA Hons); *partner* Jill Gallimore; *Career* writer; journalist and book page ed To The Point Magazine 1974–76, journalist The Star Johannesburg 1976–79, ed African Wildlife Magazine 1979–81, freelance journalist 1981–85, assoc ed Leadership Magazine 1986–89, writer 1989–; Ingrid Jonker Award for Poetry 1980; *Books* Among the Souvenirs (poetry, 1978), The Powers That Be (fiction, 1989), A Good-Looking Corpse (history, 1991), This Day and Age (fiction, 1992), This Sad Place (poetry, 1993), Horseman (fiction, 1994), The Waiting Country (memoir, 1995); *Style*— Mike Nicol, Esq; ✉ A P Watt Ltd, 20 John Street, London WC1N 2DR (☎ 0171 405 6774, fax 0171 831 2154)

NICOL, Michael John; s of John Chalfont Nicol, of Barnet, Herts, and Jean Etta, *née* Crawley; *b* 8 May 1940; *Educ* Queen Elizabeth's Barnet, Univ of London (LLB); *m* (m dis 1985), Carol Ann, *née* Howie; 3 da (Kate b 1969, Amanda b 1971, Lucy b 1975); *Career* admitted slr 1963; currently ptnr Wedlake Bell; memb Law Soc 1963; *Recreations* bridge, badminton, croquet; *Clubs* MCC, British Sportman's; *Style*— Michael Nicol, Esq; ✉ Wedlake Bell, 16 Bedford Street, Covent Garden, London WC2E 9HE (☎ 0171 379 7266, fax 0171 836 6117)

NICOL, Stephen (Steve); s of James Caldwell Nicol (d 1986), of Troon, Ayshire, and Helen, *née* Murchie; *b* 11 Dec 1961; *Educ* Marr Coll; *m* 9 June 1982, Eleanor, da of James McMath; 1 s (Michael Stephen b 1984), 1 da (Katy Caldwell b 1986); *Career* professional footballer; Ayr Utd 1979–81 (89 appearances); Liverpool 1981: joined for a fee of £300,000, full debut Aug 1982, over 300 appearances; with Sheffield Wednesday 1995–; Scotland: 13 under 21 caps, 23 full caps, appeared in World Cup 1986 in Mexico; represented Ayrshire at rugby and athletics; 4 League Championship medals, 3 FA Cup Winners' medals (and 1 Losers'), 1 Milk Cup Winners' medal, 1 European Cup Winners' medal (and 1 Losers'); Football Writers' Assoc Player of the Year 1989; *Recreations* pool, golf, tennis, squash, snooker, playing with the kids; *Style*— Steve Nicol, Esq; ✉ Sheffield Wednesday Football Club, Hillsborough, Sheffield S6 1SW

NICOL, Baroness (Life Peer UK 1982), of Newnham, Co Cambridge; (Olive Mary) Wendy Nicol; JP (1972); da of James Rowe-Hunter (d 1962), and Harriet Hannah (d 1932); *b* 21 March 1923; *Educ* Cahir Sch Ireland; *m* 1947, Dr Alexander Douglas Ian Nicol, CBE, s of Alexander Nicol (d 1962); 2 s (Hon Adrian Timothy b 1949, Hon Colin Douglas b 1950), 1 da (Hon Jane Lesley (Hon Mrs John) b 1954); *Career* Civil Serv 1943–48; cncllr Cambridge City Cncl 1972–82 (chm Environment Ctee 1978–82), Cambridge City Bench 1972–86; memb: Supplementary Benefits Tbnl 1976–78, Careers Serv Consultative Panel 1978–81; oppn whip 1983–87 (oppn dep chief whip 1987–89); spokesman on natural environment 1983–92; memb Select Ctee: on Euro Communities 1986–91, on Sci and Technol 1990–93, on Europe (memb Environment and Social Affairs sub Ctee) 1993–96, on Sustainable Devpt 1994–95; dep speaker House of Lords 1995–; memb Ecclesiastical Ctee 1990–96; public serv in many and varied areas; FRGS 1990; *Recreations* reading, walking, gardening; *Style*— The Rt Hon the Lady Nicol, JP; ✉ 39 Grantchester Rd, Newnham, Cambridge CB3 9ED (☎ 01223 323 733)

NICOLAIDES, Prof Kypros Herodotou; s of Dr Herodotos Nicolaides, of Paphos, Cyprus, and Antigoni, *née* Theodotos; *b* 9 April 1953; *Educ* The English School Nicosia, KCL (BSc), King's Coll Hosp Med Sch (MB BS); *Career* house offr in gen surgery Eastbourne Gen Hosp 1979, house offr in obstetrics and gynaecology KCH 1980 (house offr in gen med 1979–80), med offr Cyprus Nat Gd 1980; SHO in obstetrics and gynaecology: City Hosp Nottingham 1981–82, Queen's Univ Hosp Nottingham 1982; prof of fetal med (personal chair) and conslt in obstetrics KCH Sch of Med 1992– (res fell and hon registrar 1982–83, lectr and hon registrar 1983–86, sr lectr and hon sr registrar 1986–89, sr lectr and conslt 1989–92), dir Harris Birthright Res Centre for Fetal Med KCH Sch of Med 1989– (dep dir 1986–89); RCOG rep Working Pty on the Recognition and Mgmnt of Fetal Abnormalities 1988; memb: SE Thames Regnl Specialist Subctee in Genetics 1989–92, Euro Ctee on Doppler Technol in Perinatal Med 1989, Med Advsy Bd of the Toxoplasmosis Tst 1989–, Advsy Bd for Support After Termination for Abnormality 1991–, Euro Inst of Prenatal Diagnosis Dexeus Univ Inst 1991, Jt WHO and World Fedn of Haemophilia Study Gp on the Control of Haemophilia 1992, SELCA Diabetes Forum Gp 1992; memb Editorial Bds: Fetal Diagnosis and Therapy, Ultrasound in Obstetrics and Gynaecology, Israeli Jl of Obstetrics and Gynaecology, Turkish Jl of Obstetrics and Gynaecology, Progresos en Diagnostico Prenatal, Jl of Maternal-Fetal Med, References en Gynecologie Obstetrique, Ultrasound; pres Cyprus Assoc of Perinatology 1990; memb: Int Fetoscopy Gp 1982, Int Fetal Surgery and Med Soc 1984, Panhellenic Soc of Perinatology 1985, The Neonatal Soc 1988, Asociacion Espanola de Diagnostico Prenatal 1989, Indian Soc for Prenatal Diagnosis and Therapy 1989, Soc for Research into Hydrocephalus and Spina Bifida 1989, Euro Soc of Paediatric Urology 1990, Int Soc of the Fetus as a Patient 1991, Devptl Pathology Soc 1992; MRCOG 1984; *Publications* author of invited papers and review articles, and ed of various chapters in med reference books; *Style*— Prof Kyprianos Nicolaides, Esq; ✉ Harris Birthright Research Centre, Department of Fetal Medicine, King's College Hospital Medical School, London SE5 8RX (☎ 0171 924 0894/0714, fax 0171 738 3740)

NICOLI, Eric Luciano; s of Virgilio Nicoli (d 1978), and Ida, *née* Zanga (d 1990); *b* 5 Aug 1950; *Educ* Diss GS Norfolk, King's Coll London (BSc); *m* 1977, Rosalind Mary, da of Cyril Edward West; 1 da (Kate b 29 Feb 1984), 1 s (Tom b 9 May 1986); *Career* various market res then mktg posts Rowntree 1972–80; United Biscuits: various mktg posts 1980–84, UK business planning dir 1984, md UB Frozen Foods Jan-Dec 1985, md UB Brands 1986–89, dir United Biscuits (Holdings) plc 1989–, chief exec Euro Ops 1989–90, gp chief exec 1991–; non-exec dir EMI Group plc (formerly THORN EMI plc) 1993–; dep chm: Business in the Community 1991–, Per Cent Club 1993–; memb: Cncl ISBA 1987–92, Exec Ctee FDF 1990–, Advsy Ctee on Advtg COI 1990–95, Policy Issues Cncl Inst of Grocery Distribution 1990–; *Recreations* sport, music, food; *Style*— Eric Nicoli, Esq; ✉ United Biscuits (Holdings) plc, Church Road, West Drayton, Middx UB7 7PR (☎ 01895 432100, fax 01895 432131)

NICOLL, Sir William; KCMG (1992, CMG 1974); s of Ralph Nicoll (d 1947), of Dundee, and Christina Mowbray, *née* Melville (d 1959); *b* 28 June 1927; *Educ* Morgan Acad Dundee, Univ of St Andrews (MA), Univ of Dundee (LLD); *m* 1954, Helen Morison, da of William Morison Martin, MM (d 1970), of Pitlochry; 2 da (Sheila, Barbara); *Career* dep UK perm rep to the EEC 1977–82, dir gen Cncl of Euro Communities 1982–91, Fulbright EC fell George Mason Univ Virginia USA 1991–92, ed Euro Business Jl 1993–; advsr HOL EC Ctee 1995–; *Books* Understanding the New European Community (with Prof T C Salmon, 1993), The State of the EC (contrib, 1993), Margaret Thatcher, Prime Minister Indomitable (contrib, 1994), Beyond Maastricht (contrib, 1994), Perspectives in European Business (co-ed, 1995), Government and Industry (contrib, 1995), Building the European Union (with Prof T C Salmon, 1997); *Clubs* Royal Over-Seas League; *Style*— Sir William Nicoll, KCMG; ✉ Outback, Nackington Road, Canterbury, Kent CT4 7AX (☎ 01227 456495)

NICOLLE, Frederick Villeneuve; s of Arthur Villeneuve Nicolle (d 1971), of St Peters House, Jersey, and Alice, *née* Cobbold (d 1981); *b* 11 March 1931; *Educ* Eton, Univ of Cambridge (BA, MB BChir, MChir); *m* 1957, Helia Immaculata Stuart-Walker, da of Edward Alan Walker; 2 da (Miranda b 1958, Edwina b 1961), 1 s (Hugo b 1963); *Career* McLoughlan fell 1964, conslt plastic surgn Montreal Gen Hosp and Montreal Children's Hosp and lectr Faculty of Med McGill Univ Montreal 1964–69, conslt plastic surgn Hammersmith Hosp London and sr lectr in surgery Univ of London and the Royal Postgrad Med Sch London 1970–81, in full time private practice in aesthetic and reconstructive plastic surgery 1982–; pres Br Assoc of Aesthetic Plastic Surgery 1984–86, pres Chelsea Clinical Soc 1986, treas Int Soc of Aesthetic Plastic Surgery 1986–92, pres Int Alpine Surgical Soc; memb: Br Assoc of Plastic Surgery, Br Assoc of Aesthetic Plastic Surgery, Int Soc of Aesthetic Surgery, American Soc of Aesthetic Plastic Surgery; FRCS 1963; *Books* The Care of the Rheumatoid Hand (1975), Surgery of the Rheumatoid Hand (1979), Breast Augmentation (1977), Some Methods of Improving Results of Reduction Mammoplasty and Mastopexy (1983), The Hand (1985), Aesthetic Rhinoplasty (1994); *Recreations* painting, skiing, shooting, fishing, tennis; *Clubs* White's; *Style*— F V Nicolle, Esq; ✉ Flat 3/4, 56 Eaton Place, London SW1X 8AT (fax 0171 235 0575)

NICOLLE, Robert Arthur Bethune (Bobby); s of Arthur Villeneuve Nicolle (d 1970), of Jersey, and Alice Margarite, *née* Cobbold (d 1980); *b* 24 Sept 1934; *Educ* Eton, Trinity Coll Cambridge (MA); *m* 21 Jan 1963, Anne Carolyn, da of Sir Anthony Kershaw, MC, MP, of Badminton, Glos; 2 s (Darcy b 1965, Harry b 1971), 1 da (Fiona (Mrs Jonathan Norbury) b 1967); *Career* Lt Grenadier Gds active serv Cyprus 1957–58; joined Kleinwort Sons & Co merchant bankers 1958; formerly dir Kleinwort Benson Ltd, dir Matheson Investment Management Ltd 1989–; treas IRIS Fund 1973, dir Colonial Mutual Life Insur of Aust 1987–; special tstee: St Thomas' Hosp 1981–, Guy's Hosp 1996–; advsr Worldwide Fund for Nature in Switzerland (formerly World Wildlife Fund) 1988–92, treas HOST (Hosting for Overseas Students) 1992; *Recreations* skiing, shooting, fox hunting; *Clubs* Buck's, White's; *Style*— R A B Nicolle, Esq; ✉ 45 Gloucester St, London SW1; The Tithe Barn, Didmarton, Badminton GL9 1DT; Matheson Investment Management Ltd, Jardine House, 6 Crutched Friars, London EC3N 2HT (☎ 0171 528 4000)

NICOLSON, Allan Thomas McLean; s of John Nicolson (d 1969), and Elizabeth Helen Allan, *née* Thomson; *b* 25 April 1949; *Educ* Hamilton Acad, Univ of Glasgow (LLB); *m* 10 Aug 1974, Allison Stoddart, da of Douglas Lawson Fullarton (d 1986); 2 s (John Douglas b 1979, Richard Thomas b 1985), 1 da (Claire Elizabeth b 1977); *Career* ptnr McGrigor Donald 1975– (currently head Taxation Dept), called to the Scottish Bar 1982, dir Legal Resources Ltd 1989–91; hon sec to St Mungo prize 1979–92; memb Law Soc of Scotland; *Recreations* rugby, cricket, opera, family life; *Clubs* Western Glasgow; *Style*— Allan Nicolson, Esq; ✉ McGrigor Donald, Pacific House, 70 Wellington St, Glasgow G2 6SB (☎ 0141 248 6677, fax 0141 204 1351, telex 778744 M)

NICOLSON, Fiona; da of Edward James Hart, of Helensburgh, and Margaret McLean, *née* Wilson; *b* 22 June 1954; *Educ* Glasgow HS for Girls, Jordanhill Coll of Educn Univ of Glasgow (MA, LLB, DipLP, teaching cert); *m* 2, 10 April 1996, Francis Hugh Binnie, s of late Dr H Binnie; 2 c from prev m (Alexander David Nicolson b 28 Sept 1976, Anna Fiona Jane Nicolson b 17 April 1978); *Career* ptnr and head Intellectual Property Gp Bird Semple Fyfe Ireland 1991–93 (slr and assoc 1986–91), ptnr and head Intellectual Property Dept Maclay Murray & Spens 1994–; non-exec dir St Andrews Clinics for Children, memb Bd Anniesland Coll Glasgow, chm Scottish Branch and memb Cncl Licensing Execs Soc UK; memb Law Soc of Scotland 1986; *Publications* A Directory of Technology Transfer Services in Scotland (co-ed, 1992); *Recreations* swimming, tennis, travel; *Clubs* Royal Scottish Automobile; *Style*— Ms Fiona Nicolson; ✉ Maclay Murray & Spens, 151 St Vincent Street, Glasgow G2 5NJ (☎ 0141 248 5011, fax 0141 248 5819, e-mail fmmn@maclaymurrayspens.uk)

NICOLSON, Hon Mrs (Katharine Ingrid Mary Isabel); *née* Ramsay of Mar; da and heiress of Lady Saltoun, *qv*, by her husb Capt Alexander Ramsay of Mar, Grenadier Gds; assumed surname and arms of Fraser by Warrant of Lord Lyon Kings of Arms 1973; through her f's mother (late Lady Patricia Ramsay, da of HRH The Duke of Connaught, 3 s of Queen Victoria), Mrs Nicolson is 3 cous of HM The Queen; *b* 11 Oct 1957; *m* 3 May 1980, Capt Mark Malise Nicolson, Irish Gds, o s of Maj Malise Allen Nicolson, MC (d 1995), of Frog Hall, Tilston, Malpas, Cheshire; 1 s (Alexander William Malise Fraser b 5 July 1990), 2 da (Louise Alexandra Patricia b 2 Sept 1984, Juliet Victoria Katharine b 3 March 1988); *Style*— The Hon Mrs Nicolson; ✉ 41 Napier Ave, London SW6 3PS

NICOLSON, Nigel; MBE (1945); s of Hon Sir Harold Nicolson, KCVO, CMG, sometime MP Leics W (d 1968, the biographer, critic and broadcaster, 3 s of 1 Baron Carnock), and Hon Vita (Victoria) Sackville-West, CH, JP (also a writer, author of The Edwardians), only child of 3 Baron Sackville; bro of late Benedict Nicolson, the art historian; hp to 1 cousin, 4 Baron Carnock; *b* 19 Jan 1917; *Educ* Eton, Balliol Coll Oxford; *m* 1953, Philippa, da of Sir Gervais Tennyson d'Eyncourt, 2 Bt; 1 s (Adam b 1957), 2 da (Juliet (Mrs James Macmillan Scott) b 9 June 1954, Rebecca (Mrs Guy Philipps) b 1963); *Career* dir Weidenfeld and Nicolson 1946–92; MP (C) Bournemouth and Christchurch 1952–59; FRSL; author; *Books* incl: Lord of the Isles (1960), Great Houses of Britain (1965), Harold Nicolson: Diaries and Letters 1930–39 (1966), 1939–45 (1967), 1945–62 (ed of 3 vols, 1968), Portrait of a Marriage (1973), Alex (Field Marshal Alexander of Tunis) (1973), Letters of Virginia Woolf (editor 6 vols, 1975–1980), Mary Curzon (1977, Whitbread Prize), Kent (1988), Jane Austen's Houses (1991); *Recreations* archaeology; *Clubs* Beefsteak; *Style*— Nigel Nicolson, Esq, MBE; ✉ Sissinghurst Castle, Cranbrook, Kent TN17 2AB (☎ 01580 714239)

NICOLSON, Sanders Nairn; s of William Holmes Nicolson (d 1966), of Glasgow, and Eleanor Mary, *née* Dunlop; *b* 23 July 1944; *Educ* Glasgow HS for Boys, Gordonstoun, Regent St Poly London; *children* 1 s (Jamie Nairn Nicolson-Gray b 13 May 1986), 1 da (Rosanna Cailin Nicolson-Gray b 14 Dec 1988); *Career* starving artist, gardener and dish washer 1966–68, self-taught fashion photographer Foto Partners 1968–71, freelance photographer 1971–; solo exhibitions: Waves (Pentax Gallery London 1979), Maske (The Association Gallery London 1989); judge Assoc of Photographers Awards 1996; recipient Assoc of Photographers (formerly AFAEP) awards: Gold 1984, Silver 1986 and 1989, Merit 1989 and 1993; *Recreations* fly-fishing, gardening, music, food and wine, painting, photography; *Style*— Sanders Nicolson, Esq; ✉ Charity House, 14/15 Perseverance Works, 38 Kingsland Road, London E2 8DD (☎ 0171 739 6987, fax 0171 729 4056)

NIDDRIE, Robert Charles (Bob); s of Robert Hutchin Niddrie (d 1975), of Morestead, Winchester, and Gladys Ellen, *née* Vaudin; *b* 29 Jan 1935; *Educ* Brockenhurst GS; *m* 11 Sept 1965, Maureen Joy, da of Leonard Willis (d 1976), of Morestead, Winchester; 1 s (Alastair b 13 Sept 1967), 2 da (Alison b 15 Dec 1969, Rachel b 30 Dec 1971); *Career* RMR 1957–59 (MNE) and 1962–72 (Capt), Nat Serv RM and 2 Lt Queen's Own Nigeria Regt 1959–61; Whittaker Bailey & Co chartered accountants 1952–59 and 1962–75 (ptnr 1963–75, amalgamated with Price Waterhouse 1975), ptnr Price Waterhouse 1975–92 (sr ptnr i/c Southampton Office); local non-exec dir Coutts & Co Winchester 1992–; non-exec chm Southampton Cargo Handling plc 1993–; non-exec dir: Sovereign Employee Benefits Ltd 1993–95, Hotel Du Vin Ltd 1994–, Bournemouth Orchestras 1986–96, Meridian Charitable Bdcasting Tst 1993–; Round Table: chm Southampton No 4 1971–72 (pres 1978–79), chm Area 1 1973–74; fndr chm IOD Hants and IOW Branch 1980–86 (memb Ctee 1980–89, memb Cncl 1980–86); memb: Winchester Cathedral Guild of Vol Guides, 41 Club Southampton; tstee: Duphar Pension Scheme, TVS Telethon Tst 1988–93, Mayflower Theatre Tst, The Royal Marines Museum; vice patron Rose Road Assoc; govr King Edward VI Sch Southampton; FCA 1958, ATII 1964; Independence medal (Nigeria) 1960, Congo medal (UN) 1961; *Recreations* gardening, books, travel, music, theatre, wine; *Style*— Bob Niddrie, Esq; ✉ Morestead House, Morestead, Winchester, Hants SO21 1LZ (☎ 01962 777397)

NIEDUSZYŃSKI, Anthony John; s of Tadeusz Adolf Antoni Nieduszyński (d 1971), and Madaleine Gladys Lilian, *née* Huggler (d 1981); *b* 7 Jan 1939; *Educ* St Paul's Sch, Merton Coll Oxford (MA); *m* 14 June 1980, Frances, da of Wing Cdr Max Oxford, OBE (d 1980), of Topsham; 1 da (Alida Maria b 1982); *Career* princ BOT 1968–72 (asst princ 1964–67, private sec to Pres 1967–68); princ private sec to: Minister for Trade and Consumer Affrs 1972–74, Sec of State for Trade 1974; asst sec: Dept of Prices and Consumer Protection 1974–77, Dept of Indust 1977–82, Home Office 1982–83, DTI 1983–84; under sec DTI 1985–93, sec Monopolies and Mergers Cmmn 1993–96; *Recreations* gardening, riding, skating, linguistics, opera, ballet; *Clubs* Polish Hearth; *Style*— Anthony Nieduszyński, Esq; ✉ 8 Walpole Gardens, Twickenham, Middlesex TW2 5SJ (☎ 0181 894 3738)

NIENOW, Prof Alvin William; s of Alvin William Nienow (d 1969), and Mary May, *née* Hawthorn (d 1968); *b* 19 June 1937; *Educ* St Clement Dane's GS, UCL (BSc, PhD, DSc); *m* 29 Aug 1959, Helen Mary; 2 s (Gary John b 1963, Peter William b 1965), 1 da (Fiona Mary b 1961); *Career* chem engr various industs 1958–63, hon res fell UCL 1980– (lectr and sr lectr 1963–80), prof of biochem engrg Univ of Birmingham 1989– (prof of chm engrg 1980–89); memb Rhône Poulenc Conseil Technologique 1988–; Moulton medallist Inst of Chem Engrs 1984, sr visiting fellowship Japanese Soc for Promotion of Sci 1986, Jan E Purkyne medal Czech Acad of Science 1993; author and co-author of over 200 papers in chem and biochem engrg jls and conf proceedings; SERC: chm Chem Engrg Sub Ctee 1981–83, memb Biotechnology Directorate Ctee 1990–93, memb Engrg Bd 1991–94; Inst of Chem Engrs: memb Cncl and hon librarian 1984–88, rep on Euro Fedn of Chem Engrs Sci Advsy Ctee 1987–94, memb Euro Fedn Biotechnology Bioreactor Performance Working Party 1988–; AFRC: memb Cncl, memb Food Res Ctee and chm Engrg Advsy Gp 1987–89, Food Res Grants Bd 1988–91; BBSRC: Planning and Resource Ctee, Engrg and Physical Sciences Ctee 1994–96; memb Advsy Ctee Czech Triennial Int Chem Engrg Congress 1986–, memb DTI Mgmnt Gp LINK in Biochem Engrg 1988–, memb Standing Ctee for Engrg Royal Acad of Engrg 1996–, memb Governing Body Silsoe Research Inst 1996–; MIChemE 1964, FIChemE 1980, FEng 1985; *Books* Mixing in the Process Industries (1985, 2nd edn 1993); *Recreations* sport, travel, dancing; *Clubs* MCC, Athenaeum, Edgbaston Priory; *Style*— Prof Alvin W Nienow, FEng; ✉ School of Chemical Engineering, University of Birmingham, Birmingham B15 2TT (☎ 0121 414 5325, fax 0121 141 5324, e-mail A.W.Nienow@bhm.ac.uk)

NIGHTINGALE, Sir Charles Manners Gamaliel; 17 Bt (E 1628), of Newport Pond, Essex; s of Sir Charles Athelstan Nightingale, 16 Bt (d 1977), and (Evelyn) Nadine Frances, *née* Diggens (d 1995); *b* 21 Feb 1947; *Educ* St Paul's, Open Univ (BA 1990); *Heir* 2 cous, Edward Lacy George Nightingale b 11 May 1938; *Career* Grade 7 Dept of Health 1996–; *Style*— Sir Charles Nightingale, Bt; ✉ 16 Unity Grove, Harrogate, N Yorks HG1 2AQ

NIGHTINGALE, Edward Lacy George; s of late Manners Percy Nightingale, MRCS, LRCP; hp of 2 cous Sir Charles Manners Gamaliel Nightingale, 17 Bt; *b* 11 May 1938; *Educ* Exeter Sch; *Career* Master Mariner 1966, left Merchant Navy 1974; sub-postmaster Lynmouth 1975–92, ret; cncllr: Devon CC 1981–85, N Devon DC 1987– (ldr independent gp); vice chm Exmoor Nat Park Ctee 1982–85; *Recreations* all types of sport; *Style*— Edward Nightingale, Esq; ✉ Kneesworth, Lynton, N Devon EX35 6HQ (☎ 01598 752204)

NIGHTINGALE, Sir John Cyprian; kt (1975), CBE (1970), BEM (1941), QPM (1965), DL (Essex 1975); s of Herbert Paul Nightingale (d 1965), of Sydenham, London; *b* 16 Sept 1913; *Educ* Cardinal Vaughan Sch, UCL; *m* 1947, Patricia Mary, da of Dr Norman Maclaren, of West Kilbride, Ayrshire; *Career* serv RNVR 1943–45; joined Metropolitan Police 1935; chief constable Essex 1962 and 1975–78 (asst chief constable 1958–62), chief constable of Essex and Southend on Sea 1969–75, chm Police Cncl 1976–78, memb Parole Bd 1978–82; *Style*— Sir John Nightingale, CBE, BEM, QPM, DL; ✉ Great Whitman's Farm, Purleigh, Essex CM3 6RW

NIGHTINGALE, Nicholas John; s of Christopher (Toby) Nightingale (d 1970); *b* 29 Aug 1942; *Educ* Brighton, Hove and Sussex GS, Trinity Coll Dublin, Harvard Business Sch; *Career* slr Slaughter & May 1970–74, ptnr Patterson Glenton & Stracey 1974, slr and co sec Rowntree Mackintosh 1975–85, exec dir Rowntree plc 1985–89; dir: Tom Smith Crackers Ltd 1983–85, Original Cookie Co Ltd 1985–89, Cookie Jar Ltd 1989–, Ellis Patents Ltd 1990–; co sec Tate & Lyle plc 1989–93; nat sec YMCA England 1994–; chm Service 9 Bristol 1966–70; vice chm Yorkshire Rural Community Cncl 1985–89, treas YMCA Met Region 1992–93; memb Law Soc; *Recreations* growing trees (especially apple), croquet; *Style*— Nicholas Nightingale, Esq; ✉ National Secretary, National Council of YMCAs, 3–9 Southampton Row, London WC2 5AH (☎ 0171 242 2451)

NIGHTINGALE, Richard Mervyn; s of Edward Humphrey Nightingale, CMG (d 1996), of Nunjoro Farm, Naivasha, Kenya, E Africa, and Evelyn Mary, *née* Ray; *b* 9 July 1954; *Educ* Rugby, Emmanuel Coll Cambridge (MA, DipArch); *Career* architect; with practices in Nairobi, London and Hong Kong 1977–81, Colin St John Wilson and Partners 1981–85, estab partnership with Hugh Cullum as Hugh Cullum and Richard Nightingale Architects 1985; articles published in: Architects Journal, Building Design, International Architect, Interni, Baumeister, Building Magazine; work exhibited at: Royal Acad, RIBA, Fitzwilliam Museum Cambridge, Building Centre London, Br Cncl Nairobi; tstee Southwark Festival 1996; memb RIBA; *Building work published* House in Hampstead (1988), New British High Commission Nairobi (1989), New Teaching Space North Westminster Sch (1991), Embassy Theatre Extension Central Sch of Speech and Drama; *Style*— Richard Nightingale, Esq; ✉ 30A Parkhill Road, London NW3 (☎ 0171 482 1213); 61 Judd Street, London WC1H 9QT (☎ 0171 383 4466, fax 0171 383 4465)

NIGHTINGALE OF CROMARTY, Yr, John Bartholomew Wakelyn; er s and h of Michael David Nightingale of Cromarty, OBE, *qv*; *b* 7 Sept 1960; *Educ* Winchester, Magdalen Coll Oxford (MA, DPhil); *Career* Harmsworth sr res scholar Merton Coll Oxford 1984–86; fell Magdalen Coll Oxford 1986–; chm Black Isle Civic Tst 1993–; tstee: Cromarty Harbour, Cromarty Arts Tst; author of articles on medieval history; *Recreations* woodland management, restoration of old buildings; *Clubs* Athenaeum; *Style*— John Nightingale, Esq; ✉ Cromarty House, Ross and Cromarty IVII 8XS (☎ 01381 600265); 21 Dartmouth Row, Greenwich, London SE10 8AW (☎ 0181 692 6033)

NIGHTINGALE OF CROMARTY, Michael David; OBE (1960); Baron of Cromarty (feudal); s of Victor Russell John Nightingale (d 1951), of Wormshill, Kent, and Bathsheba, *née* Buhay (d 1942); *b* 6 Dec 1927; *Educ* Winchester, Wye Coll London (BSc), Magdalen Coll Oxford (BLitt); *m* 1, 21 July 1951 (m dis), Antonia, da of Stephen Coleby Morland, of Glastonbury; m 2, 28 April 1956, Hilary Marion Olwen, da of John Eric Jones (d 1933), of Swansea; 2 s (John b 1960, Alexander b 1964), 3 da (Emma b 1957, Rebecca b 1958, Rachel b 1966); *Career* asst to investmt mangr Anglo-Iranian Oil Co 1951–53, investmt advsr Univ of London 1954–66, advsr Kuwait Investment Bd 1961–62, dir Charterhouse Japhet Ltd 1965–70; chm: Anglo-Indonesian Corporation plc 1971–96, The Chillington Corporation plc 1986–89, Anglo-Eastern Plantations plc 1985–90; memb Bd Cwlth Devpt Corp 1985–92; sec: Museums Assoc and ed Museums Journal 1954–60, Museum Ctee Carnegie UK Tst 1954–60; memb: Advsy Cncl for Export of Works of Art 1954–60, Br Ctee Int Cncl of Museums 1956–60, Canterbury Diocesan Advsy Ctee 1964–79, Kent CC 1973–77, Maidstone Borough Cncl 1973– (chm Planning Ctee 1973–77, ldr 1976–77, Mayor 1984–85), Exec Ctee SE Arts Assoc 1974–77, Area Archaeological Advsy Ctee SE England 1974–79, Panel of Chairmen Gen Synod C of E 1984–85 (memb 1979–85); chm: Churches Ctee Kent Archaeological Soc 1973–, North Downs Soc 1983–, Cromarty Arts Tst 1987–; Esquire Bedell Univ of London 1953–94, dep steward Royal Manor of Wye 1954–, warden Rochester Bridge 1989–92 (memb 1985–), pres Cobham New Coll 1989–92; Lord of the Manor of Wormshill and a Lord of the Level of Romney Marsh; Freeman City of London; FSA 1956; *Recreations* antiquarian, musical; *Style*— Michael Nightingale of Cromarty, OBE, FSA; ✉ Cromarty House, Ross and Cromarty IV11 8XS (☎ 01381 600265); Wormshill Ct, Sittingbourne, Kent ME9 0TS (☎ 01622 884235)

NIKOVSKI, HE Risto; s of Kiro Nikovski, of Skopje, Republic of Macedonia, and Elisaveta, *née* Gutesha (d 1974); *b* 13 May 1942; *Educ* Faculty of Economics Univ of Zagreb Croatia; *m* 2 Sept 1967, Suzanna; 1 s (Aleksandar b 2 March 1968), 1 da (Ana b 23 March 1970); *Career* Macedonian diplomat; head Dept of Mktg and PR OHIS Chemical Indust Gp Skopje Macedonia 1967–71; Ex-Yougoslav Federal Miny of Foreign Affrs 1971–83: diplomat Peking 1972–76, diplomat Havana 1977–81; under sec Miny of Info Govt of the Republic of Macedonia 1983–85; Ex-Yougoslav Federal Miny of Foreign Affrs 1986–92: diplomat Jakarta 1986–88, diplomat Kuala Lumpur 1986–90, special advsr 1990–92; under sec Miny of Foreign Rels Republic of Macedonia 1992–93, Govt rep in GB 1993–94, ambass to the Ct of St James's (concurrently accredited to Republic of Ireland and to Iceland) 1994–; participant in numerous multilateral confs in NY, Vienna, Havana, Nairobi and Bali, variously delgn head to various countries; *Recreations* moutaineering, chess; *Style*— HE Mr Risto Nikovski; ✉ Embassy of the Republic of Macedonia, 10 Harcourt House, 19a Cavendish Square, London W1M 9AD (☎ 0171 499 5152, fax 0171 499 2864)

NILSSON, HE Lars-Åke; s of Hans and Olga Nilsson; *b* 23 April 1943; *Educ* Univ of Lund Sweden (MBA); *m* 1974, Charlotte, *née* Arnell; *Career* Swedish diplomat; joined Swedish Diplomatic Serv 1968, attaché Paris 1969–70, attaché and second sec Tokyo 1970–73, second sec Washington 1973–76, first sec Stockholm 1976–79, dep asst under-sec Stockholm 1979–80, cnsllr London 1980–84, min Moscow 1984–88, ambass Prague 1988–91, perm under-sec Stockholm 1991–95, ambass to the Ct of St James's 1995–; author of various articles and booklets; *Recreations* reading, talking, spectator sports, especially cricket and football; *Clubs* Travellers, Savile, Sällskapet (Stockholm), Swedish Jockey; *Style*— HE Mr Lars-Åke Nilsson; ✉ Embassy of Sweden, 11 Montagu Place, London W1H 2AL (☎ 0171 724 2101, fax 0171 724 4174)

NIMMO, Derek Robert; s of Harry Nimmo (d 1959), and Marjorie Sudbury, *née* Hardy (d 1988); *b* 19 Sept 1930; *Educ* Quarry Sch Liverpool; *m* 9 April 1955, Patricia Sybil Anne, da of Alfred John Brown (d 1955), of Santiago, Chile; 2 s (Timothy St John b 1956, Piers James Alexander b 1967, m, 1995, Marina Flowers), 1 da (Amanda Kate Victoria b 1959, m 1, 1983 (m dis 1990) Hon Nicholas Howard, m 2, 1991, William Christie); *Career* actor, author and producer; Freeman City of London; Hon MA Univ of Leicester; first appearance Bolton Hippodrome as Ensign Blades in Quality St; *Theatre* incl: Waltz of The Toreadors (Criterion) 1957, Duel of Angels (Apollo) 1958, How Say You? (Aldwych) 1959, The Amorous Prawn (Savill) 1959, The Irregular Verb To Love (Criterion) 1961, See How They Run (Vaudeville) 1964, Charlie Girl (Adelphi 1965–71 and overseas 1972), Why Not Stay for Breakfast? (Apollo 1973–75, and overseas 1975), Same Time Next Year (Prince of Wales) 1978, See How They Run, A Friend Indeed (Shaftesbury) 1984, The Cabinet Minister (Albery) 1991–92; *Television* series incl: All Gas and Gaiters, Oh Brother, Oh Father, Sorry I'm Single, The Bed Sit Girl, My Honourable Mrs, The World of Wooster, Blandings Castle, Life Begins at Forty, Third Time Lucky, Hell's Bells, If It's Saturday it must be Nimmo, Just a Nimmo; *Radio* Just a Minute 1967–, produced and appeared in numerous prodns which toured world-wide for Intercontinental Entertainment 1975–; *Films* incl: Casino Royale, The Amorous Prawn, The Bargee, Joey Boy, A Talent for Loving, The Liquidator, Tamahine, One of our Dinosaurs is Missing; *Books* Derek Nimmo's Drinking Companion (1979), Shaken & Stirred (1984), Oh Come On All Ye Faithful! (1986), Not In Front Of The Servants (1987), Up Mount Everest Without A Paddle (1988), As the Actress Said to the Bishop (1989), Wonderful Window Boxes (1990), Derek Nimmo's Table Talk (1990), Memorable Dinners (ed, 1991); *Recreations* travel, collecting 17th and 18th century English walnut furniture, horse racing; *Clubs* Garrick, Beefsteak, Lord's Taverners; *Style*— Derek Nimmo, Esq; ✉ c/o Barry Burnett Organisation Ltd, Suite 42–43, Grafton House, 2–3 Golden Square, London W1R 3AD (☎ 0171 437 7048/9, fax 0171 734 6118)

NIMMO, Ian Alister; *b* 14 Oct 1934; *Educ* Royal Sch of Dunkeld, Breadalbane Acad; *m* 11 July 1959, Grace Paul; 2 s (Alasdair b 1962, Struan b 1973), 1 da (Wendy b 1960); *Career* Nat Serv 2 Lt RSF 1955–57; ed: The Weekly Scotsman 1963–66, Teesside Evening Gazette 1970–76, Edinburgh Evening News 1976–89, editorial conslt and author 1989–; vice pres Newspaper Press Fund; *Books* Robert Burns (1965), Portrait of Edinburgh (1968), The Bold Adventure (1969), Scotland at War (1989), The Commonwealth Games (1989), Edinburgh: The New Town (1991), Edinburgh's Green Heritage (1996); *Recreations* the outdoors, fly fishing, painting, writing; *Clubs* Scottish Arts; *Style*— Ian Nimmo, Esq; ✉ The Yett, Lamancha, by West Linton, Peeblesshire EH46 7BD (☎ 01968 675457)

NIMMO, Dr Walter Sneddon; *b* 2 April 1947; *Educ* Bathgate Acad, Univ of Edinburgh (BSc, MB ChB, MD, MRCP); *m* 24 March 1972, Moyra Elizabeth, *née* Cavin; 1 s (Thomas William John b 21 Aug 1976), 1 da (Kathryn Margaret b 7 Nov 1980); *Career* Sir Stanley Davidson lectr in clinical pharmacology Univ of Edinburgh 1973–76, lectr in anaesthesia Univ of Edinburgh 1977–79, sr lectr in anaesthesia Univ of Glasgow 1979–84, prof of anaesthesia Univ of Sheffield 1984–88, chm and chief exec Inveresk Clinical Research 1988–96, chief exec Inveresk Research 1996–; FRCA 1977, FRCP 1984, FANZCA 1988, FRCPEd 1988 (memb Cncl), FRCPGlas 1988, FFPM 1993; *Books* editor of 11 textbooks in anaesthesia, clinical measurement and drug absorption, author of over 100 papers in academic jls; *Style*— Dr Walter Nimmo; ✉ 86 Ravelston Dykes, Edinburgh EH12 6HE (☎ 0131 313 3188); Inveresk Research, Tranent EH33 3NE (☎ 01875 614545, fax 01875 614555)

NIMMO SMITH, Hon Lord; William Austin; s of Dr Robert Herman Nimmo Smith (d 1991), and Ann, *née* Wood; *b* 6 Nov 1942; *Educ* Eton, Balliol Coll Oxford (BA), Univ of Edinburgh (LLB); *m* 1968, Dr Jennifer, da of Rev David Main; 1 da (Harriet b 1972), 1 s (Alexander b 1974); *Career* admitted to Faculty of Advocates 1969, standing jr counsel to Dept of Employment 1977–82, QC (Scot) 1982, advocate depute 1983–86, chm Med Appeal Tbnls 1986–91, temp judge Court of Session 1995–96, Senator Coll of Justice in Scotland (Lord of Session) 1996–; pt/t memb Scot Law Cmmn 1988–96; *Recreations* mountaineering, music; *Clubs* New (Edinburgh); *Style*— The Hon Lord Nimmo Smith; ✉ Court of Session, Parliament House, Edinburgh EH1 1RQ (☎ 0131 225 2595)

NIND, Philip Frederick; OBE (1979), TD (1946); s of William Walker Nind, CIE (d 1964), of Oxford, and Lilian Marie Feodore, *née* Scott (d 1968); *b* 2 Jan 1918; *Educ* Blundell's, Balliol Coll Oxford (MA); *m* 28 Aug 1944, Fay Allardice (d 1991), da of Capt John Roland Forbes Errington (d 1945); 2 da (Nicola b 1945, Charlotte b 1949); *Career* WWII Royal Fusiliers 1939–46, SOE Greece and Albania 1943–44, Mil Govt Berlin 1945–46, ret Maj; Shell Group of Companies 1939–68 (Venezuela, Cyprus, Lebanon, Jordan, London); dir Fndn for Mgmnt Educn 1968–83, sec Cncl of Indust for Mgmnt Educn 1969–83, vice pres Euro Fndn for Mgmnt Devpt Brussels 1978–83; served on various ctees of: CBI, CNAA, UGC, NEDO; memb Exec Ctee Royal Acad of Dancing 1970–88, chm Abinger Common Cons Assoc 1977–79 (pres 1992–); hon fell London Business Sch; CIMgt 1968–83, FRSA 1983; Chevalier Order of Cedars of Lebanon 1959, Grand Cross Orders of St Mark and Holy Sepulchre Greek Orthodox Church 1959; *Books* A Firm Foundation (1985), Never a Dull Moment (1991); *Clubs* Special Forces; *Style*— Philip Nind, Esq, OBE, TD

NINIS, Ven Richard Betts; s of Capt George Woodward Ninis, and Mary Gertrude, *née* Betts; *b* 25 Oct 1931; *Educ* Sherborne, Lincoln Coll Oxford (MA), Bishop's Hostel Lincoln Theological Coll; *m* 29 May 1967, (Penelope) Jane, da of Sir Edmund George Harwood, CB, KBE (d 1964), of Alfriston, Sussex; 2 s (Robert George, James Andrew Meredith), 1 da (Rachel Hilary); *Career* curate Poplar All Saints London 1955–62, vicar Hereford St Martin 1962–71, diocesan missioner 1969–74, prebendary of Hereford Cathedral 1970–74, Telford planning offr 1970–74, canon residentiary and treas Lichfield Cathedral 1974–; archdeacon: of Stafford 1974–80, of Lichfield 1980–; chm United Soc for Propagation of the Gospel 1988–91, govr Univ of Derby; *Recreations* gardening; *Style*— The Ven The Archdeacon of Lichfield; ✉ 24 The Close, Lichfield, Staffordshire WS13 7LD (☎ 01543 258813, fax 01543 419478)

NISBET, Prof Hugh Barr; s of Thomas Nisbet (d 1977), of Edinburgh, and Lucy Mary, *née* Hainsworth; *b* 24 Aug 1940; *Educ* Dollar Acad, Univ of Edinburgh (MA, PhD); *m* 1, 26 Dec 1962 (m dis 1981), Monika Luise Ingeborg, da of Wilhelm Otto Uecker, of Guben, Germany; 2 s (Arnold b 1966, Marcus b 1968); m 2, 24 Nov 1995, Angela Maureen Parker, da of Cecil Chapman, of Great Yarmouth; *Career* reader Univ of Bristol 1972–73 (asst lectr 1965–67, lectr 1967–72), prof of German Univ of St Andrews 1974–81, prof of modern languages (German) and fell Sidney Sussex Coll Cambridge 1982–; memb: Ctee Modern Humanities Res Assoc 1972–84, Gen Teaching Cncl Scotland 1978–81, Bd Govrs Dollar Acad 1978–81, Cncl English Goethe Soc 1978–, Ctee Goethe-Gesellschaft 1991–95, Nat Cncl for Modern Languages 1983–90; pres Br Soc Eighteenth Century Studies 1986–88 (vice pres 1984–86), tstee Kurt Hahn Tst 1988–95; *Books* Herder and the Philosophy and History of Science (1970), Goethe and the Scientific Tradition (1972); *Recreations* music, art history, cycling; *Style*— Prof H B Nisbet; ✉ Sidney Sussex Coll, Cambridge CB2 3HU (☎ 01223 338877)

NISBET, Prof Robin George Murdoch; s of Robert George Nisbet (d 1955), of Glasgow, and Agnes Thomson, *née* Husband (d 1973); *b* 21 May 1925; *Educ* Glasgow Acad, Univ of Glasgow (MA), Balliol Coll Oxford (MA); *m* 16 April 1969, (Evelyn Pamela) Anne, da of Dr John Alfred Wood (d 1953); *Career* tutor in classics CCC Oxford 1952–70, prof of Latin Univ of Oxford 1970–92; hon fell: Balliol Coll Oxford 1989, CCC Oxford 1992; FBA 1967; *Books* commentary on Cicero in Pisonem (1961); commentary on Horace: Odes I (1970), Odes II (1978), Collected Papers on Latin Literature (1995); *Style*— Prof Robin Nisbet, FBA; ✉ 80 Abingdon Road, Cumnor, Oxford OX2 9QW (☎ 01865 862482)

NISBET-SMITH, Dugal; CBE (1996); s of David Nisbet-Smith, and Margaret Nisbet-Smith, of Invercargill, NZ; *b* 6 March 1935; *Educ* Southland Boys' HS NZ; *m* 1959, Dr Ann Patricia Nisbet-Smith, da of John Taylor, of Gt Harwood, Lancs; 1 s, 2 da; *Career* Scottish Daily Record and Sunday Mail: devpt mangr 1969–71, prodn dir 1971–73, md 1974–78; dir Mirror Group Newspapers 1976–78, dir and gen mangr Times Newspapers Ltd 1978–80, md Times Newspapers 1980–81, int publishing advsr to HH The Aga Khan 1981–83; dir The Newspaper Soc 1983–; *Recreations* travel, sculpture, painting; *Style*— Dugal Nisbet-Smith, Esq, CBE; ✉ The Butterfly, Borough Lane, Great Finborough, Stowmarket, Suffolk IP14 3AS

NISH, Prof Ian Hill; CBE (1990); s of David C Nish (d 1961), of Edinburgh, and Marion, *née* Hill; *b* 3 June 1926; *Educ* George Watson's Coll Edinburgh, Univ of Edinburgh (MA), Univ of London (MA, PhD); *m* 29 Dec 1965, Rona Margaret, da of Harold Thomas Speirs, CBE (d 1982), of Hampton Court, Middx; 2 da (Fiona Rosalind b 1967, Alison Margaret b 1969); *Career* served Army 1944–48, demobbed as Capt; Univ of Sydney NSW 1957–62, prof of int history LSE 1980–91 (joined 1962, emeritus prof 1991), dean Faculty of Economics and Political Sci Univ of London 1986–90; pres: Br Assoc for Japanese Studies 1979–80, Euro Assoc for Japanese Studies 1985–88; chm Japan Fndn Endowment Ctee 1981–90; Order of the Rising Sun Japan (Gold Rays with neck ribbon) 1991; Japan Fndn award 1991; *Books* Anglo-Japanese Alliance (1964), Story of Japan (1968), Alliance in Decline (1972), Anglo-Japanese Alienation (1978), Origins of Russo-Japanese War (1984), European Studies on Japan (1987), Japan's Struggle with Internationalism, 1931–1933 (1993); *Recreations* golf, music, tennis; *Style*— Prof Ian Nish, CBE; ✉ Oakdene, 33 Charlwood Drive, Oxshott, Surrey KT22 0HB (☎ 01372 842975)

NISSEN, David Edgar Joseph; s of Tunnnock Edgar Nissen, of Hove, and Elsie, *née* Thorne; *b* 27 Nov 1942; *Educ* King's Sch Chester, UCL (LLB); *m* 1 Nov 1969, Pauline Jennifer, da of Harry George Spencer Meaden, of Bexhill-on-Sea; 2 da (Rachel Jane b 1973, Sarah Elizabeth b 1976); *Career* prosecuting slr Sussex Police Authy 1970–73; HM Customs and Excise: joined 1973, asst slr 1983–87, princ asst slr 1987–90, slr 1992–95 (legal advsr to Dept of Energy 1990–92), legal advsr to Home Office 1995–; memb Law Soc 1969; *Recreations* photography, opera, walking; *Style*— David Nissen, Esq; ✉ Home Office, 50 Queen Anne's Gate, London SW1H 9AT

NISSEN, George Maitland; CBE (1987); s of Col Peter Norman Nissen (d 1930), and Lauretta, *née* Maitland (d 1954); *b* 29 March 1930; *Educ* Eton, Trinity Coll Cambridge; *m* 1956, Jane Edmunds, *née* Bird; 2 s, 2 da; *Career* KRRC 2/Lt, Royal Greenjackets TA Capt; memb Stock Exchange 1956–, memb Cncl of Int Stock Exchange 1973–91, dep chm of the Stock Exchange 1978–81, sr ptnr Pember & Boyle 1982–86, dir Morgan Grenfell Gp 1985–87, chm Foreign & Colonial Emerging Mkts Tst 1987–, chm Investmt Mgmnt Regulatory Orgn 1989–92; chm The Book Guild 1993–; *Recreations* music, railways, walking; *Style*— George Nissen, Esq, CBE; ✉ Swan House, Chiswick Mall, London W4 (☎ 0181 994 8203, fax 0181 742 8198)

NIVEN, Dr Alastair Neil Robertson; s of Harold Robertson Niven, and Elizabeth Isobel Robertson, *née* Mair (d 1993); *b* 25 Feb 1944; *Educ* Dulwich, Univ of Cambridge (MA), Univ of Ghana (MA), Univ of Leeds (PhD); *m* 22 Aug 1970, Helen Margaret, da of Claude William Trow (d 1983); 1 s (Alexander b 1985), 1 da (Isabella b 1981); *Career* lectr: Univ of Ghana 1968–69, Univ of Leeds 1969–70, Univ of Stirling 1970–78; dir gen Africa Centre London 1978–84, Chapman fell Inst of Cwlth Studies Univ of London 1984–85, special asst to Sec Gen Assoc of Cwlth Univs 1985–87, dir of literature Arts Cncl of GB 1987– (Arts Cncl of England since 1994); chm: Public Schs Debating Assoc England and Wales 1961–62, UK Cncl for Overseas Student Affrs 1987–92, Literature Panel Gtr London Arts Assoc 1981–84; judge of the Booker Prize 1994; *Books* D H Lawrence: The Novels (1978), The Yoke of Pity: The Fictional Writings of Mulk Raj Anand (1978), D H Lawrence (1980), The Commonwealth of Univs (with Sir Hugh W Springer, 1987), Under Another Sky: The Commonwealth Poetry Prize Anthology (ed, 1987); *Recreations* theatre, travel; *Clubs* Royal Cwlth Soc; *Style*— Dr Alastair Niven; ✉ Eden House, 28 Weathercock Lane, Woburn Sands, Bucks MK17 8NT (☎ 01908 582310); Arts Council, 14 Gt Peter St, London SW1P 3NQ (☎ 0171 333 0100)

NIVEN, Dr Colin Harold Robertson; s of Harold Robertson Niven, of Woburn, Beds, and Elizabeth Isobel Robertson, *née* Mair; *b* 29 Sept 1941; *Educ* Dulwich, Gonville and Caius Coll Cambridge (MA), Brasenose Coll Oxford (DipEd), Nancy (L ès L), Lille (Dr de l'Université); *Career* teacher and housemaster Fettes 1965–73, head of modern languages Sherborne 1973–83, princ Island Sch Hong Kong 1983–87, princ St George's English Sch Rome Italy 1987–91; visiting fell Westminster Coll Oxford 1991–92, headmaster Alleyn's Sch Dulwich 1992–; FRSA; *Books* studies of: Voltaire's Candide (1980), Thomas Mann's Tonio Kröger (1982); critical edn of Vailland's Un Jeune Homme Seul (1983); *Recreations* travel, opera, sport; *Clubs* Royal Over-Seas League, Royal Cwlth Soc; *Style*— Dr Colin Niven; ✉ 8 Dulwich Village, Dulwich, London SE21 7AL

NIVEN, Peter David; s of William Robert Niven, and Joan Arnott, *née* Batchelor; *b* 7 Aug 1964; *Educ* Strathallan Sch; *m* 10 June 1992, Ruth Marguerita, da of Richard Fredrick Ullyott; 1 s (William Mark b 16 Oct 1993), 1 da (Mary Victoria b 28 June 1995); *Career* Nat Hunt jockey; major races won: Bula Hurdle 1986, William Hill Golden Spurs 1992 and 1994, Mum Melling Novice Chase 1993 and 1994, Sun Alliance Chase 1994, Eider Chase 1995; *Recreations* golf, any sport; *Style*— Peter Niven, Esq

NIX, Prof John Sydney; s of John William Nix (d 1968), of SE London, and Eleanor Elizabeth, *née* Stears (d 1978); *b* 27 July 1927; *Educ* Brockley Co Sch, Univ Coll of the South West (BSc Econ), Cambridge (MA); *m* 7 Oct 1950, Mavis Marian, da of George Cooper, of Teignmouth; 1 s (Robert David John b 10 Jan 1955), 2 da (Alison Mary b 23 July 1952, Jennifer Ann b 7 May 1959); *Career* Instr Lt RN 1948–51; sr res offr Farm Econs Branch Univ of Cambridge 1957–61 (1951–61); Wye Coll London: farm mgmnt liaison offr and lectr 1961–70, sr tutor 1970–72, sr lectr 1972–75, head Farm Business Unit 1974–89, reader 1975–82, prof of farm business mgmnt (personal chair) 1982–89, emeritus prof 1989–, fell 1995; fndr memb Farm Mgmnt Assoc 1965, prog advsr Southern TV 1966–81; chm: Editorial Ctee of Farm Management (CMA) 1971–95, Bd of Farm Mgmnt (BIM) 1979–81; pres: Agric Economics Soc 1990–91, Kingshay Farming Tst 1991–, Assoc of Ind Crop Conslts 1993–; Nat Award for Outstanding Contrib to

Advancement of Mgmnt in Agric IBIM (now Inst of Mgmnt) 1982; author of numerous articles for jls, memb various nat study gps and advsy ctees; CIMgt 1983, FRSA 1984, FRAgS 1985, FIAgrM 1993; *Books* Farm Planning and Control (with C S Barnard, 2 edn, 1979), Farm Mechanisation For Profit (with W Butterworth, 1983), Land and Estate Management (2 edn 1989), Farm Management Pocketbook (27 edn 1996); *Recreations* theatre, cinema, travel, rugby, cricket; *Clubs* Farmers'; *Style*— Prof John Nix; ✉ Wye Coll, Wye, Ashford, Kent TN25 5AH (☎ 01233 812401, fax 01233 813498, telex 96118)

NIXON, Sir Edwin Ronald; kt (1984), CBE (1974), DL (Hampshire 1987); s of William Archdale Nixon, and Ethel, *née* Corrigan; *b* 21 June 1925; *Educ* Alderman Newton's Sch Leicester, Selwyn Coll Cambridge (MA); *m* 1952, Joan Lilian, *née* Hill (d 1995); 1 s (Christopher), 1 da (Carol); *Career* IBM UK Holdings Ltd: chief exec 1965–85, chm and chief exec 1979–86, chm 1979–90; dep chm NatWest Bank plc 1987–96 (dir 1975–96), chm NatWest Gp Pensions Tst 1992– chm Amersham International plc 1988–96 (dir 1987–96), dir Royal Insurance plc 1980–88; chm Cncl Leicester Univ 1992–; vice pres Chartered Inst of Mktg; Liveryman Worshipful Co of Marketors; *Recreations* music, golf; *Clubs* Athenaeum; *Style*— Sir Edwin Nixon, CBE, DL; ✉ Starkes Heath, Rogate, Petersfield, Hants GU31 5EJ; NatWest Group, 41 Lothbury, London EC2P 2BP (☎ 0171 726 1000)

NIXON, (Philip) Graham; s of Horace Stanley Nixon of Burbage, Leicestershire, and Dorothy Mary, *née* Collidge; *b* 12 June 1942; *Educ* Hinckley GS, Leicester Coll of Art; *m* 3 July 1965, Maureen, da of Edward Wilford, of Sunways, Doctors Fields, Earl Shilton, Leics; 2 s (Mark b 1967 (decd), Paul b 1969); *Career* chm: Ferry Pickering Group plc; dir: Ferry Pickering Sales Ltd, Ferry Pickering Boxes Ltd, Ferry Pickering Publishing Ltd, Ferry Pickering Plastics Ltd, Ferry Pickering Mouldings Ltd, Ferry Pickering Toolmakers Ltd; *Recreations* shooting and sports in general; *Style*— Graham Nixon, Esq; ✉ Ferry Pickering Group plc, The Groom's Cottage, Misterton, Lutterworth, Leics LE17 4JP (direct ☎ 01455 558890)

NIXON, James Robert; s of Dr Robert Samuel Nixon, of Bangor, Co Down, and Veda, *née* McKee; *b* 2 Sept 1943; *Educ* Bangor GS Co Down, Trinity Coll Dublin (MB BCh, BAO, MA), Univ of Liverpool (MChOrth); *m* 23 June 1967, Katherine, da of Ronald Stoddart Nesbitt, of Dublin; 1 s (Alexander b 1972), 1 da (Holly b 1968); *Career* former conslt orthopaedic surgn Belfast City Hosp, currently conslt orthopaedic surgn Musgrave Park Hosp, med dir Green Park Healthcare Tst Belfast, clinical lectr in orthopaedics Queen's Univ Belfast, examiner RCS Ireland; sec Irish Orthopaedic Assoc, chm RYA NI 1983–86; FRCS Ireland 1971, FRCS England 1972; *Recreations* sailing, fishing; *Clubs* Royal North of Ireland Yachting, Royal Ulster Yacht, Irish Cruising; *Style*— James Nixon, Esq; ✉ 7 Mount Pleasant, Belfast BT9 5DS NI (☎ 01232 666508); Withers Orthopaedic Centre, Musgrave Park Hosp, Belfast 9, NI (☎ 01232 669501)

NIXON, John Edwin; s of Edwin Nixon, and Dorothy, *née* Hall; *b* 5 Dec 1948; *Educ* Univ of Edinburgh Med Sch (MB ChB, ChM), Univ of Oxford (MA), FRCS; *m* Bridget Anne, da of late Dr S John Coulson, of Stratton-on-the-Fosse, nr Bath, Somerset; 1 s (David John b 1976), 2 da (Susannah Jane b 1980, Natasha Elizabeth b 1985); *Career* clinical reader in orthopaedic surgery Univ of Oxford, former conslt orthopaedic surgn King's Coll Hosp, currently conslt orthopaedic surgn Charing Cross and Hammersmith Hosp, sr examiner Univ of London; memb sr common room Oriel Coll Oxford; ed and pt author int reference work on Spinal Stenosis, also publications on joint replacement, arthroscopy, trauma, foot surgery and spinal surgery and spinal biomechanics; memb BMA, FRSM; fell: Girdlestone Orthopaedic Soc, Br Orthopaedic Assoc, Br Orthopaedic Spinal Soc, Chelsea Clinical Soc; *Recreations* family, travel, sailing, skiing, golf; *Style*— John E Nixon, Esq; ✉ 148 Harley St, London W1N 1AH (☎ 0171 935 1207); Charing Cross Hospital, Fulham Palace Road, London W6 (☎ 0171 487 5020, car 0860 267861)

NIXON, Prof John Forster; s of Edward Forster Nixon, MBE (d 1989), and Mary, *née* Lytton (d 1993); *b* 27 Jan 1937; *Educ* Whitehaven GS, Univ of Manchester (BSc, PhD, DSc), Univ of Cambridge, Univ of Southern California; *m* 19 Nov 1960, Kim, da of John Thomas Smith (d 1987); 1 s (Jonathan Forster b 23 March 1966), 1 da ((Susan) Joanna Forster b 16 July 1964); *Career* ICI res fell Cambridge 1962–64, lectr in chemistry Univ of St Andrews 1964–66; dean Sch of Chemistry Univ of Sussex 1989–92 (lectr in chemistry 1966, reader 1975, prof 1986–); Royal Soc Leverhulme Sr res fell 1993–94; visiting prof: Victoria Univ Canada 1971, Simon Fraser Univ Canada 1976; titular memb Inorganic Nomenclature Cmmn IUPAC 1986–88, memb: Inorganic Chemistry Panel SERC 1986–89, Editorial Bd Phosphorus, Sulphur, Silicon Journal 1989–, Dalton Cncl 1994–; *Awards* Royal Soc of Chemistry: Corday-Morgan medal and prize 1973, Main Gp Element prize and medal 1985, Tilden lectureship and prize 1992; FRS 1994; *Publications* over 300 contribs to a variety of chemistry jls; *Recreations* playing tennis, badminton, squash, walking, theatre, watching cricket; *Style*— Prof John Nixon, FRS; ✉ School of Chemistry, Physics and Environmental Science, University of Sussex, Brighton, Sussex BN1 9QJ (☎ 01273 678536, fax 01273 677196); Juggs Barn, The Street, Kingston, Lewes, E Sussex (☎ 01273 483993)

NIXON, Rev Sir Kenneth Michael John Basil; 4 Bt (UK 1906), of Roebuck Grove, Milltown, Co Dublin, and Merrion Square, City of Dublin, SJ; s of Maj Sir Christopher William Nixon, 2 Bt, DSO, suc bro Maj Sir Christopher John Louis Joseph Nixon, MC, 3 Bt 1978; *b* 22 Feb 1919; *Educ* Beaumont Coll, Heythrop Coll Oxon; *Heir* bro, Maj Cecil Dominic Henry Joseph Nixon, MC b 5 Feb 1920; *Career* RC priest; ordained 1952; teaching memb of the Jesuit Community at St George's Coll Salisbury 1954–93 (hon chaplain 1993–), tutor and chaplain LCBL Convent Borrowdale, asst priest St Gerard's Parish Borrowdale; memb Harare Diocesan Marriage Tbnl; fell: Zimbabwe Schs Cricket Assoc, Mashonaland Cricket Umpires Assoc (hon life memb), Mashonaland Rugby Assoc, Old Georgian Assoc (hon life memb); *Style*— The Rev Sir Kenneth Nixon, Bt, SJ; ✉ St George's Coll, PB 7727, Causeway, Zimbabwe (☎ 00 263 722 724650, fax 00 263 4 723832)

NIXON, HE Patrick Michael; CMG (1989), OBE (1984); s of John Moylett Gerard Nixon, of Chilmark, Wilts, and late Hilary Mary, *née* Paterson (d 1956); *b* 1 Aug 1944; *Educ* Downside, Magdalene Coll Cambridge (MA); *m* 26 Oct 1968, Elizabeth Rose, da of Edward Carlton, of Southampton, and late Dora Carlton; 4 s (Simon b 1970, Paul b 1971, Christopher b 1975, Damian b 1978); *Career* Dip Serv 1965, MECAS Lebanon 1966–68, third sec (later second sec) Br Embassy Cairo 1968–70, second sec (commercial) Br Embassy Lima 1970–73, first sec FCO 1973–77, first sec and head of Chancery Br Embassy Tripoli 1977–80, dir Br Info Servs NY 1980–83, asst (later head) NE and N Africa dept FCO 1983–87, ambass State of Qatar at Doha 1987–90, cnsllr FCO 1990–93, high cmmr Zambia 1994–; Offr Brazil Order of the Southern Cross 1976; *Style*— HE Mr Patrick Nixon, CMG, OBE; ✉ c/o Foreign & Commonwealth Office, (Zambia), King Charles Street, London SW1

NIXON, Rev Rosemary Ann; da of Edwin Nixon, of City of Durham, and Dorothy, *née* Hall; *b* 25 May 1945; *Educ* Bishop Grosseteste Coll of Educn Lincoln (CertEd), Trinity Theol Coll Bristol (BD), Univ of Durham (MA), Univ of Edinburgh (MTh); *Career* sch teacher Russell Scott Primary Sch Denton Manchester 1966–69, lay worker St Luke's W Hampstead London 1973–75, tutor in Old Testament studies Cranmer Hall St John's Coll Durham 1975–89, dir St John's Coll Extension Prog 1983–89, team deacon and dir St John's Coll Urban Studies Unit Parish of Gateshead 1990–92, dir of studies Coates Hall Theol Coll Edinburgh 1992–95, princ Theol Inst of the Scottish Episcopal Church 1995–; *Books* Who's The Greatest? (Nat Soc (C of E) for Promoting Religious Educn, 1985); *Recreations* walking, music, friends; *Style*— The Rev Rosemary Nixon; ✉ Theological Institute of the Scottish Episcopal Church, 21 Inverleith Terrace, Edinburgh EH3 5NS (☎ 0131 343 2038, fax 0131 315 3754)

NIXON, Dr William Charles; s of Charles Marlborough Nixon (d 1951), and Winifred Westcott (d 1975); *b* 28 Nov 1926; *Educ* Humberside Collegiate Inst, Toronto, Queen's Univ Kingston Ontario (BA, MA, skiing champion and capt of ski team 1946–47), Univ of Cambridge (PhD, ScD); *m* 1, 3 June 1948, Joyce (d 1986), da of Arthur Angus Fraser; 1 s (Douglas Fraser b 12 June 1960), 1 da (Andrea Carol b 14 June 1958); m 2, 22 July 1989, Glenys Baker, da of Wilfred Hutchinson; *Career* Royal Navy Fleet Air Arm Pilot Cadet 1944–45; industl res asst General Electric Company USA 1952–53, nat sci fndn fell Stanford and Redlands Univs Calif 1956; Univ of Cambridge: academic researcher (physics) 1953–55, assoc electrical industs fell in physics 1956–59, asst dir of res Engrg Dept 1959–62, lectr Engrg Dept 1962–89, fell of Peterhouse 1962–94 (emeritus fell 1994–), proctor Univ of Cambridge 1991–94, coll ed Peterhouse 1994–; fndr ed and ed in chief Microelectronic Engineering Journal 1981–; shared award Electrochemical Soc of America 1982; chm: Electron Microscopy Gp Inst of Physics 1970–72 (former memb Ctee), Cambridge Area Ctee IEE 1985–86, E Anglian Centre Ctee 1990–91; memb: Professional Gp E5 IEE 1976–82, Mgmnt and Design M1 Ctee IEE 1984–87, Sci Educn and Technol Divnl Bd IEE 1987–90, Centres Bd IEE 1989–91, Cncl IEE 1989–92, Royal Inst; vice pres and memb Cncl Soc for the Application Res Cambridge, FInstP 1969, CPhys, FIEE 1981, CEng 1981, FEng 1986; *Books* X-Ray Microscopy (with VE Cosslett, 1960), Electron Microscopy and Analysis (ed, 1971), Scanning Electron Microscopy: Systems and Applications (ed, 1973), Microcircuit Engineering (ed with H Ahmed, 1980); *Recreations* travel; *Style*— Dr William Nixon, FEng; ✉ Peterhouse, University of Cambridge, Cambridge CB2 1RD (☎ 01223 338200, fax 01223 337578)

NOAH, Prof Norman David; s of Jack David Noah, of Wallington, Surrey, and Jane Rachel, *née* Samuel (d 1961); *b* 7 July 1939; *Educ* India and London, St Thomas's Hosp Med Sch London (MB BS, MRCP, MFCM); *m* 7 March 1971, Veronica Hilary, da of Bruno Kiwi; 2 s (Benedict Joel David b 16 April 1974, Joshua Luke Alexander b 2 July 1975), 1 da (Olivia Rachel Emma b 16 Feb 1979); *Career* house surgn Worthing Hosp 1964; St Thomas's Hosp: house physician 1964–65, SHO 1965–66, registrar 1966; SHO West End Hosp for Neurology and Neurosurgery 1967–68, research asst Dept of Experimental Pathology Cardiothoracic Inst The Brompton Hosp and registrar Paddington and Kensington Chest Clinic and St Charles' Hosp London 1968–70, sr epidemiologist Epidemiological Research Lab Central Public Health Lab London 1971–76, hon community physician Brent and Harrow AHA 1977–78, conslt epidemiologist Communicable Disease Surveillance Centre 1977–89, hon sr lectr Dept of Clinical Epidemiology and Social Med Royal Free Hosp Sch of Med 1979–89, hon conslt in control of infection Shenley Hosp 1983–89, prof and head Dept of Public Health and Epidemiology King's Coll Hosp Sch of Med and Dentistry 1989–, dir of public health King's Healthcare 1989–; distinguished visitor Dept of Public Health and Primary Care Royal Free Hosp Sch of Med 1989–94, conslt in communicable disease Thames Regn NRA 1989–, conslt Acupuncture Cncl of GB 1990–, hon conslt Communicable Disease Surveillance Centre 1993–; jt conslt to WHO/Int Epidemiological Assoc on epidemiology 1987, advsr to Aust Nat Univ Canberra on formation of CDSC/CDC type centre for surveillance of infectious diseases 1989, chm WHO meeting on acute respiratory infections Geneva 1990, advsr to WHO and Govt of China on the surveillance and control of infectious diseases March 1995; sec and memb Exec Cncl Int Epidemiological Assoc 1993–96; memb: MRC Sub-ctee on Respiratory Syncytial Virus 1980–94, RCP Working Pty on Prevention 1988–91, Specialist Advsy Ctee and Educn Ctee FPHM 1993–96, Med Advsy Ctee British Liver Tst 1994–; author of various book chapters and numerous original and leading articles in learned jls; editorial rep Section of Epidemiology and Community Med and memb Cncl RSM 1981–96; FFPHM, FRCP; *Recreations* cricket, music, food and wine, travel, hoarding (magpie syndrome) and oniomania; *Clubs* MCC; *Style*— Prof Norman Noah; ✉ Orley Rise, Orley Farm Road, Harrow-on-the Hill, Middx HA1 3PE (☎ 0181 422 2649); Department of Epidemiology and Public Health, King's College School of Medicine and Dentistry, Bessemer Road, London SE5 9PJ (☎ 0171 346 3170, fax 0171 737 3556)

NOAKES, Rt Rev George; s of David John Noakes (d 1948), of Bwlchllan, Lampeter, Dyfed, and Elizabeth Mary Noakes (d 1987); *b* 13 Sept 1924; *Educ* Tregaron Co Sch, Univ Coll of Wales Aberystwyth (BA), Wycliffe Hall Oxford; *m* 23 April 1957, Jean Margaretta, da of Samuel Richard Davies (d 1933); *Career* ordained: deacon 1950, priest 1952; curate of Lampeter 1950–56; vicar: Eglwyswrw with Meline 1956–59, Tregaron 1959–67, Eglwys Dewi Sant Cardiff 1967–76; rector Aberystwyth 1976–80, canon St Davids Cathedral 1977–79, archdeacon of Cardigan 1979–82, vicar Llanychearn with Llanddeiniol 1980–82, bishop of St Davids 1982–91, archbishop of Wales 1987–91; Hon DD Univ of Wales 1990; *Recreations* angling; *Style*— The Rt Rev George Noakes; ✉ Hafod Lon, Rhydargaeau, Carmarthen, Dyfed SA32 7DT (☎ 01267 253302)

NOAKES, Michael; s of Basil Henry Noakes (d 1969), of Horley and then Reigate, Surrey, and Mary Josephine, *née* Gerard (d 1989); *b* 28 Oct 1933; *Educ* Downside, Reigate Sch of Art, RA Schs London; *m* 9 July 1960, Vivien Noakes, FRSL, *qv*, the writer, da of Marcus Langley (d 1977), of Reigate, Surrey; 2 s (Jonathan b 1963, Benedict b 1965), 1 da (Anya b 1961); *Career* Nat Serv 1954–56, Subaltern; portrait and landscape painter; numerous TV and radio appearances on art subjects; subject of: Portrait BBC 2 (with Eric Morley, 1977 and 1978), Changing Places BBC1 (with Jak, 1989); art corr Town & Around BBC 1964–68; ROI: elected memb 1964, vice pres 1968–72, pres 1972–78, hon cncl memb 1978–; RP: elected memb 1967, memb Cncl 1969–72, 1972–74, 1978–80 and 1993–95; dir Fedn of Br Artists 1981–83 (govr 1972–81); hon memb: Nat Soc, United Soc; former chm Contemporary Portrait Soc, former pres Soc of Catholic Artists, former FRSA; platinum disc award (for record sleeve Portrait of Sinatra, 1977); Freeman City of London; *Exhibitions* RA, ROI, RBA, RSMA, RP, Nat Soc, Young Contemporaries, Contemporary Portrait Soc, Grosvenor and Upper Grosvenor Galleries, Grafton Galleries (also New Grafton, Upper Grafton), Woodstock Galleries, RGI; *Represented in Collections of* HM The Queen, Prince of Wales, Br Museum, Nat Portrait Gallery Perm Collection, numerous univs, House of Commons, Frank Sinatra, Guildhall London; *Portraits* incl: The Queen (cmmnd for centenary of Manchester Town Hall in the Queen's Silver Jubliee Year, and also as Col-in-Chief, the Queen's Lancs Regt), Queen Elizabeth The Queen Mother (as Chllr of Univ of London, and also as Patron Royal Assoc for Disability and Rehabilitation), The Princess Royal (for Saddlers' Co, and also as The Princess Royal (as Col-in-Chief Royal Signals), The Prince of Wales (as Col-in-Chief 2 KEO Gurkhas, and also as Patron of RCPsych), The Duke and Duchess of York (for City of York), The Duchess of Kent (for Clothworkers' Co), Margaret Thatcher when PM (for Grocers' Co), President Clinton (for Rhodes House Oxford), Princess Ashraf of Iran, Sir Timothy Bevan (as chm Barclays), Sir John Chalstrey (as Lord Mayor of London), Lord Denning (as Master of the Rolls), Sir Alec Guinness, Most Rev David Hope (Archbishop of York and when Bishop of London), Cardinal Hume, Robert Hardy, Sir Andrew Huxley (as pres Royal Soc), Lord Justice of Appeal Sir Donald Nicholls (now Lord Nicholls), Airey Neave, JB Priestley, Sir Ralph Richardson, Archbishop Runcie of Canterbury, Lord Selwyn-Lloyd (as speaker House of Commons), Lord Wolfenden (as dir Br Museum); *Group Portraits* incl: Queen Elizabeth The Queen Mother opening Overlord Embroidery to public view (with The Duke of Norfolk, Princess Alice Countess of Athlone, Earl Mountbatten, and others), The Princess Royal being admitted to Livery of Worshipful Co of Woolmen, The Five Lords of Appeal in Ordinary for the Middle Temple (Lord

Cross, Lord Diplock, Lord Salmon, Lord Wilberforce, Lord Simon), a commission for the Corporation of London to mark the Royal Silver Wedding featuring all senior members of the Royal Family at that time; *Books* A Professional Approach to Oil Painting (1968), contrib to various journals and books on art subjects; *Recreations* idling; *Clubs* Garrick; *Style*— Michael Noakes; ✉ 146 Hamilton Terrace, St John's Wood, London NW8 9UX (☎ 0171 328 6754, fax and answerphone 0171 625 1220)

NOAKES, Vivien; da of Marcus Langley (d 1977), and Helen, *née* Oldfield Box (d 1983); *b* 16 Feb 1937; *Educ* Manchester Coll Oxford, Somerville Coll Oxford (sr scholar); *m* 9 July 1960, Michael Noakes, *qv*, s of Basil Noakes (d 1969); 1 da (Anya b 19 June 1961), 2 s (Jonathan b 15 May 1963, Benedict b 9 Feb 1965); *Career* writer; lectr Somerville Coll Oxford, guest curator of the maj exhibition Edward Lear at the Royal Acad of Arts and Nat Academy of Design NY 1985; Philip and Frances Hofer lectr Harvard Univ 1988; FRSL; *Books* Edward Lear: The Life of a Wanderer (1968, 2 edn 1979, 3 edn 1985), For Lovers of Edward Lear (1978), Scenes from Victorian Life (1979), Edward Lear 1812–1888: the catalogue of the Royal Academy Exhibition (1985), Selected Letters of Edward Lear (1988), The Painter Edward Lear (1991); *Recreations* friends, reading, cooking; *Style*— Vivien Noakes, FRSL; ✉ 146 Hamilton Terrace, London NW8 9UX (☎ 0171 328 6754, fax and answerphone 0171 625 1220)

NOBBS, David Gordon; s of (Cyril) Gordon Nobbs (d 1968), and Gwendoline, *née* Williams (d 1995); *b* 13 March 1935; *Educ* Marlborough, St John's Coll Cambridge (BA); *m* 1968 (sep 1992), Mary Jane, da of Daniel Alfred Emmanuel Blatchford (d 1980); 2 step s (David b 1953, Christopher b 1955), 1 step da (Kim b 1957); *Career* writer 1960–; reporter Sheffield Star 1958–60; Br Comedy Award for Top Br TV Comedy Screenwriter 1990; *Television* series incl: The Fall and Rise of Reginald Perrin (three series) 1976–78, Fairly Secret Army (Channel 4), A Bit of a Do 1989, Rich Tea and Sympathy 1991, The Life and Times of Henry Pratt (adapted from Second From Last in the Sack Race) 1992, Love on a Branch Line 1994, The Legacy of Reginald Perrin 1996; TV films incl Stalag Luft 1993; contrib to: That Was the Week the Was, The Two Ronnies, The Frost Report, Sez Les, and others; *Plays* incl: Our Young Mr Wignall 1976, Cupid's Darts 1981, Dogfood Dan and the Carmarthen Cowboy 1982; *Books* The Itinerant Lodger (1965), Ostrich Country (1968), A Piece of the Sky is Missing (1969), The Death of Reginald Perrin (1975, later retitled The Fall and Rise of Reginald Perrin), The Return of Reginald Perrin (1977), The Better World of Reginald Perrin (1978), Second From Last in the Sack Race (1983), A Bit of a Do (1986), Pratt of the Argus (1988), Fair Do's (1990), The Cucumber Man (1994), The Legacy of Reginald Perrin (1995); *Recreations* the arts, eating, drinking, travel, bridge, cricket and soccer; *Style*— David Nobbs, Esq; ✉ c/o Jonathan Clowes Ltd, Iron Bridge House, Bridge Approach, London NW1 8BD (☎ 0171 722 7674, fax 0171 722 7677)

NOBES, Prof Christopher William; s of Harold Alfred Nobes, and Beryl Muriel, *née* Ramsay; *b* 20 March 1950; *Educ* Portsmouth GS, Univ of Exeter (BA, PhD); *m* 27 March 1982 (m dis 1988); *Career* head internal audit Hambro Life Assur 1973–75, lectr Univ of Exeter 1975–82; prof of economics: Univ of Strathclyde 1982–86, Univ of Reading 1987–; memb Accounting Standards Ctee UK and Ireland 1987–90, vice chm Accounting Ctee Fédération Des Experts Comptables Européens, UK rep on Bd of Int Accounting Standards Ctee 1993–; FCCA 1973; *Books* incl: Comparative International Accounting (1981, 1985, 1991 and 1995), Accountants' Liability in the 1980's (with E P Minnis 1985), Pocket Accountant (1986), Issues in Multinational Accounting (with R H Parker 1988), Interpreting European Financial Statements (1994); contribs incl: Some Topics in International Accounting (1978), The Fourth Directive and the United Kingdom (1984), Imputation Systems of Corporation Tax within the EEC (1984, 1985); *Style*— Prof Christopher Nobes; ✉ University of Reading, Department of Economics, PO Box 218 Reading, Berks RG6 6AA (☎ 0118 931 8228, fax 0118 975 0236)

NOBLE, Adrian Keith; s of William John Noble (d 1987), of Chichester, Sussex, and Violet Ena, *née* Wells; *b* 19 July 1950; *Educ* Chichester HS, Univ of Bristol (BA), Drama Centre London; *m* June 1991, Joanne, *née* Pearce; 1 s, 1 da; *Career* assoc dir Bristol Old Vic Co 1976–80; RSC Co: assoc dir 1981–89, artistic dir elect 1990, artistic dir 1991–; guest dir Manchester Royal Exchange Theatre Co; recent prodns Stratford incl: King Lear, 1993, A Midsummer Night's Dream 1994, Romeo and Juliet 1995, The Cherry Orchard 1995; film A Midsummer Night's Dream 1996; Hon DLitt: Univ of Birmingham 1994, Univ of Bristol 1996; *Style*— Adrian Noble, Esq; ✉ c/o Barbican Theatre, Silk Street, London EC2Y 8BQ (☎ 0171 628 3351)

NOBLE, Andrew Stephen; JP; s of Sir Peter Scott Noble, and Mary, *née* Stephen; *b* 14 Feb 1934; *Educ* Aberdeen GS, Univ of St Andrews (MA), St John's Coll Cambridge (MA), Univ of Aberdeen (LLD); *m* 7 Aug 1959, Margaret Birrell, *née* Rayne; 2 s (Michael James b 28 May 1963, Peter Stephen b 12 Sept 1966), 1 da (Alison Mary b 29 March 1961); *Career* ICI plc: asst mangr admin servs Billingham Agric Div 1963–65 (tech offr 1959–63), gp operational/res mangr Gp Mgmnt Servs Dept 1965–69, tech sec to Main Bd Policy Gp Head Office 1969–73; Debenhams plc (Head Office): corp planning mangr 1973–76, main bd dir of devpt and planning 1976–79, md Admin Servs and Devpt 1979–81, md Store Ops and Servs 1981–86; chm: Specialeyes plc 1986–92, G & F Retail Ltd 1988–91, Liverpool Victoria Friendly Soc 1993– (non-exec dir 1992); non-exec dir Bentalls plc 1987–96; chm: Assoc of Retail Distributors 1981–82, Oxford St Assoc 1984–85; vice pres: Br Retailers Assoc 1988–91 (chm 1984–86), Br Retail Consortium 1992– (dep chm 1988–91); memb Cncl: ESRC 1984–90, Manchester Business Sch 1985–92; memb Ealing Health Authy 1990–91, chm Ealing Hosp NHS Tst 1991–94, ind dir Wandsworth Community NHS Tst 1996–; FCMA, FIMA, FInstD, FRSA 1994; *Recreations* golf, theatre, opera, reading; *Clubs* Oriental, Royal Scottish Automobile, Wimbledon Park Golf, Royal Wimbledon Golf; *Style*— Andrew S Noble, Esq, JP; ✉ Liverpool Victoria Friendly Society, Victoria House, Southampton Row, London WC1B 4DB (☎ 0171 405 4377, fax 0171 404 0390)

NOBLE, Barrie Paul; s of Major Frederic Arthur Noble (d 1978), of South Leigh Manor, Oxon, and Henrietta, *née* Evans (d 1992); *b* 17 Oct 1938; *Educ* Hele's Sch Exeter, New Coll Oxford (BA), Univ of Dakar Senegal; *m* 17 July 1965, Alexandra (Sandra) Helene, da of Robert Frederick Truman Giddings (d 1989), of Cap Del Prat Gran, Encamp, Andorra; 1 s (Timothy b 1966); *Career* HM Dip Serv; FO 1962, third later second sec Br Embassy Leopoldville (Kinshasa) 1965, second sec (commercial) Br Dep High Cmmr Kaduna 1967, first sec FCO 1969, Br Embassy Warsaw 1972, FCO 1975, cnsllr UK Mission to the UN Geneva 1980, cnsllr FCO 1984–89, cnsllr Br Embassy Paris 1989–93; chm Civil Serv Selection Bd 1993–; *Recreations* skiing, bridge, ancient cars, grass cutting; *Clubs* RAF, Ski of GB, Rolls Royce Enthusiasts; *Style*— Barrie Noble, Esq; ✉ c/o Coutts & Co, 440 Strand, London WC2

NOBLE, Sheriff David; JP (1970); s of Donald Noble (d 1942), slr, of Inverness, and Helen Kirk Lynn, *née* Melville (d 1971); *b* 11 Feb 1923; *Educ* Inverness Royal Acad, Univ of Edinburgh (MA, LLB, summa cum laude); *m* 1947, Marjorie Scott, da of James Scott Smith (d 1971), of Bramhall, Cheshire; 2 s (Andrew, David), 1 da (Jill); *Career* served RAF Bomber Cmd Europe 1942–46, Flt Lt; slr; WS Edinburgh 1949–83; Sheriff at Oban and Fort William 1983–95; *Recreations* sailing, photography; *Style*— Sheriff David Noble, WS; ✉ Woodhouselee, North Connel, Oban, Argyll PA37 1QZ (☎ 01631 710678)

NOBLE, Sir David Brunel; 6 Bt (UK 1902), of Ardmore and Ardardan Noble, Cardross, Co Dumbarton; er s of Sir Marc Brunel Noble, 5 Bt, CBE (d 1991), and Jennifer Lorna (Jane), *née* Mein-Austin; *b* 25 Dec 1961; *Educ* Eton; *m* 1, 26 Sept 1987 (m dis 1993), Virginia Ann, yr da of late Roderick Lancaster Wetherall, MBE, of St Mary's Platt, Kent; 2 s (Roderick Lancaster Brunel b 8 Dec 1988, Alexander David b 28 Feb 1990); m 2, 29 Oct 1993, Stephanie, da of Daniel Digby, of Rainham, Kent; 2 s (Connor Daniel b 2 Jan 1993, Drew Marc b (twin) 2 Jan 1993, d 10 Jan 1993), 1 da (Megan Lorna Annette b 2 June 1995); *Heir* s, Roderick Lancaster Brunel Noble b 8 Dec 1988; *Style*— Sir David Noble, Bt; ✉ Deerleap House, Knockholt, Sevenoaks, Kent TN14 7NP

NOBLE, Prof Denis; s of George Noble (Flt Lt RFC, d 1957), and Ethel, *née* Rutherford; *b* 16 Nov 1936; *Educ* Emanuel Sch London, UCL (BSc, PhD); *m* Jan 1965, Susan Jennifer, da of Flt Lt Leslie H Barfield; 1 da (Penelope Jean b 27 Aug 1967), 1 adopted s (Julian Aidan b 29 Aug 1970); *Career* asst lectr physiology UCL 1961–64, tutorial fell Balliol Coll Oxford 1963–84, praefectus of Holywell Manor 1971–89, Burdon Sanderson prof of cardiovascular physiology Univ of Oxford 1984–; fndr dir: Oxsoft Ltd 1984–, Takhus Inc 1994–; has made numerous appearances on radio and TV, and writer of various articles published in nat press; fell UCL 1986, foreign sec The Physiological Soc 1986–92 (hon sec 1974–80), chm Int Congress of Physiological Sciences 1993, sec gen Int Union of Physiological Sciences 1994, memb Founding Gp Save Br Sci; Hon FRCP 1988; FRS 1979; correspondant étranger de l'Académie Royale de Medecine de Belgique, Gold medal Br Heart Fndn 1985, Pierre Rijlant prize Royal Acad of Med Belgium 1992; *Books* The Initiation of the Heart Beat (1975), Electric Current Flow in Excitable Cells (1975), Goals, No Goals and Own Goals (1989), Sodium-Calcium Exchange (1989), The Logic of Life (1993); *Recreations* foreign languages, guitar; *Style*— Prof Denis Noble; ✉ University Laboratory of Physiology, Parks Road, Oxford OX1 3PT (☎ 01865 272533, fax 01865 272554)

NOBLE, Sir (Thomas Alexander) Fraser; kt (1971), MBE (1947); s of Simon Noble, of Cromdale, Morayshire (d 1926); *b* 29 April 1918; *Educ* Nairn Acad, Univ of Aberdeen; *m* 1945, Barbara Anne Mabel, da of John Sinclair, of Nairn; 1 s, 1 da; *Career* mil serv 1939–40; entered ICS 1940, serv NWFP 1941–47; lectr in political economy Univ of Aberdeen 1948–57, sec Carnegie Tst for Scottish Univs 1957–62, vice chllr Univ of Leicester 1962–76, memb and chm various govt advsy ctees; chm: Advsy Cncl on Probation and After Care 1965–70, UK Ctee of Vice Chllrs and Princs 1970–72; vice chllr and princ Univ of Aberdeen 1976–81; Hon LLD: Aberdeen 1968, Leicester 1976, Glasgow 1981, Washington Coll Maryland USA 1981; FRSE 1977; *Recreations* golf; *Style*— Sir Fraser Noble, MBE, FRSE; ✉ Hedgerley, Victoria St, Nairn (☎ 01667 453151)

NOBLE, Gillian (Gill); da of John Noble, of Aberdeen, and Jessie Mae, *née* Bonnington; *b* 18 Nov 1947; *Educ* Univ of Aberdeen (MA), UCL (MSc); *Career* economic asst DOE 1969–76; HM Treasury: various positions in planning and control of public expenditure, local govt fin, inner city policy and the water indust 1976–84, pensions and social security 1984–87, asst sec 1986, head Banking Div 1987–92, head Educn, Science and Nat Heritage Div 1992–93, under sec 1993, head ST Group 1993–95, dep dir of local govt, health, law and order 1995–; *Recreations* listening to music, visiting heritage properties; *Style*— Miss Gill Noble; ✉ HM Treasury, Parliament Street, London SW1P 3AG (☎ 0171 270 4500)

NOBLE, Sir Iain Andrew; 3 Bt (UK 1923), OBE, of Ardkinglas and Eilean Iarmain, Co Inverness; er s of Sir Andrew Napier Noble, 2 Bt, KCMG (d 1987), and Sigrid, *née* Michelet; *b* 8 Sept 1935; *Educ* Shanghai, Buenos Aires, Eton, Univ Coll Oxford (MA); *m* 27 Oct 1990, Lucilla Charlotte James, da of Col Hector Andrew Courtney Mackenzie of Dalmore, OBE, MC, TD, JP, DL (d 1988), of The House of Rosskeen, Invergordon, Ross-shire; *Heir* bro, Timothy Peter Noble, *qv*; *Career* Nat Serv 1954–56, 2 Lt Intelligence Corps 1956–59, 2 Lt Argyll and Sutherland Highlanders (TA); exec Scottish Cncl (Devpt and Indust) Edinburgh 1964–69, jt fndr and md Noble Grossart Ltd (merchant bankers) Edinburgh 1969–72, co fndr and chm Seaforth Maritime Ltd Aberdeen (offshore oil servs) 1972–77; chm: Lennox Oil Co plc Edinburgh 1980–84, Noble Group Ltd Edinburgh (merchant bankers and investment managers) 1980–, Skye Bridge Ltd 1994–; co fndr and dir Adam & Co plc 1983–93; dir: Darnaway Venture Capital plc 1984–, Independent Insurance Group plc 1985–, Premium Trust plc 1993–; proprietor: Pràban na Linne Ltd ('The Gaelic Whiskies') 1976–, Fearann Eilean Iairmain estate in Skye 1972–96; dep chm Traversee Theatre Co 1966–69, memb Ct Univ of Edinburgh 1970–72, co-fndr and tstee Sabhal Mor Ostaig (Gaelic Business Coll) 1975–85; tstee: Nat Museums of Scotland 1987–91, Nat Museum of Scotland Charitable Tst 1989–; memb The Securities Assoc (now SFA) 1988–; pres The Saltire Soc 1992–96; chm: Scot-Aust Bicentenial Cairn Ctee 1987–88, Scots Australian Cncl and Tst 1990–; Scotsman of the Year (Knights Templar Award) 1982; *Clubs* New (Edinburgh); *Style*— Sir Iain Noble of Ardkinglas and Eilean Iarmain; ✉ An Lamraig, Eilean Iarmain, An T-Eilean Sgitheanach IV43 8QR; offices: An Oifig, Eilean Iarmain, Isle of Skye IV43 8QR (☎ 01471 833266, fax 01471 833260); Noble & Co Ltd, 76 George Street, Edinburgh EH2 (☎ 0131 225 9677, fax 0131 225 5479)

NOBLE, James Douglas Campbell; s of Capt Frederick Burnaby Noble, RN (d 1946), and Elsie Mackintosh, *née* Mackintosh (d 1962); *b* 20 April 1921; *Educ* Bradfield Coll, Canford; *m* 1, 25 Aug 1956, Patricia Jean, da of Harold Strange Taylor-Young, FRCS; 1 s (Robert b 1965), 3 da (Sarah b 1957, Charlotte b 1960, Diana b 1961); m 2, 15 April 1978, Teresa Jane, da of Lt-Col Douglas Forster, DSO (d 1983) 11th Hussars (Prince Albert's Own), and Joan Forster (d 1992); *Career* The Royal Sussex Regt 1940, cmmnd The Argyll & Sutherland Highlanders 1940, 2 Bn A&SH Singapore 1941, POW Thailand 1942–45, ret 1946; Investmt Dept Kleinwort Sons & Co 1946–52, memb Stock Exchange London 1953–82; ptnr: Fielding Newson & Smith & Co 1953–62, Colegrave & Co 1962–73, Kitcat & Aitken 1973–81; H M Tennent Ltd: fin dir 1958–73, chm 1973–77; investment advsr to King George V's Pension Fund for Actors and Actresses (1911) 1960–82; memb: Bd of Visitors and Local Review Bd HM Prison Chelmsford 1972–87, Ctee Stars Orgn for Spastics 1974–76, Investmt Ctee Peterhouse Cambridge 1983–85; tstee: Royal Ballet Benevolent Fund 1978–84, Cambridge Health Authy Tst Fndn 1986–88; official speaker for The Far East POWs Assoc (E Anglia) 1984–, lectr to 22 Special Air Services Regt Courses Stirling Lines Hereford 1985–91, lectr to Staff Coll Camberley Realities of War Conf 1989–92, official speaker for the Burma Star Herts Cambs and Essex Borders Branch; fndr memb A Company of Speakers (Christian charitable tst) 1989; received the UK Templeton Individual award for pioneering in religion 1992; *Recreations* walking, reading, writing, correspondence, conversation, travel, preaching, lecturing; *Clubs* The Free Foresters, The Arabs CC; *Style*— James Noble, Esq; ✉ 25 Portugal Place, Cambridge CB5 8AF (☎ 01223 312277)

NOBLE, Prof Mark Ian Munro; s of Leslie Ewart Noble (d 1985), of Sunbury, Surrey, and Jessie Munro, *née* Wilson (d 1993); *b* 6 Sept 1935; *Educ* Hampton GS, Bart's Med Coll London (DSc, PhD, MD); *m* 1985, Dr A J Drake-Holland; 3 c; *Career* sr fell Cardiovascular Research Inst San Francisco 1966–68, sr lectr and conslt physician Charing Cross Hosp Med Sch London 1971–73 (lectr Dept of Med 1968–71), sr investigator Midhurst Med Research Inst Midhurst W Sussex 1973–83, Boerhaave prof of med Univ of Leiden 1982, prof of cardiovascular med Charing Cross and Westminster Med Sch 1989–, hon conslt physician Hammersmith Hosps NHS Tst (research dir for cardiology) and Chelsea and Westminster Hosp 1989–, visiting prof Nat Heart and Lung Inst London 1989–; FRCP, FESC; *Books* The Cardiac Cycle (1979), Cardiac Metabolism (jtly, 1983), Starling's Law of the Heart Revisited (jtly, 1988), The Interval-Force Relationship of the Heart: Bowditch Revisited (jtly, 1992); numerous book chapters and full original papers; *Recreations* opera, gardening, classical music; *Clubs* RSM; *Style*—

Prof Mark Noble; ✉ Academic Unit of Cardiovascular Medicine, Charing Cross and Westminster Medical School, Fulham Palace Road, London W6 8RF (☎ 0181 846 1032, fax 0181 846 7678)

NOBLE, Peter Saxton Fitzjames; CBE (1977); 2 s of Sir Humphrey Noble, 4 Bt, MBE, MC (d 1968), of Walwick Hall, Humshaugh, Hexham, Northumberland, former High Sheriff of Northumberland (d 1968), and Celia Stewart Weigall (d 1982); bro of Sir Marc Noble, 5 Bt (d 1991), and descendant of Sir Andrew Noble, 1 Bt, famous physicist and expert on explosives; *b* 22 May 1929; *Educ* Eton, Magdalene Coll Cambridge; *m* 1, 1954 (m dis 1966), Elizabeth Emmeline, da of Launcelot William Gregory Eccles, CMG, MC; 1 s (Simon Peter Saxton Fanshaw b 1958); m 2, 1966 (m dis 1980), Helena Margaret, da of Thomas Essery Rose-Richards and formerly w of David Anthony Harries; 1 s (James Essery Brunel b 1968); m 3, 1980, Penelope Margaret, da of late Leslie Landeau; *Career* int wine conslt; former chm: UK Wine and Spirit Assoc, Wine Devpt Bd; dir: International Wine & Spirit Competition Ltd, The Grape Connection Ltd; president d'honneur EEC Wine and Spirit Gp, pres UK Wine and Spirit Assoc 1991–92; *Style*— Peter Noble, Esq, CBE; ✉ Flax Cottage, 17 Ham Common, Richmond, Surrey TW10 7JB (☎ 0181 940 7576)

NOBLE, Timothy Peter; yr s of Sir Andrew Napier Noble, 2 Bt, KCMG (d 1987); hp of bro Sir Iain Andrew Noble, 3 Bt, *qv*; *b* 21 Dec 1943; *Educ* Eton, Univ Coll Oxford (MA), INSEAD Fontainebleau (MBA); *m* 1976, Elizabeth Mary, da of late Alexander Wallace Aitken; 2 s (Lorne Andrew Wallace b 1980, Andrew Iain Brunel b 1984), 1 da (Sasha Heidi Elizabeth b 1978); *Career* called to the Bar Gray's Inn 1969; exec dir Lyle Shipping plc Glasgow 1976–84, chief exec Noble Group Ltd Edinburgh 1984–; dir: Premium Underwriting plc, Waverley Mining Finance plc; chm: Hardy Underwriting plc, Royal Scottish Nat Orchestra Tst; dir The British Ski Fedn; *Clubs* New (Edinburgh); *Style*— Timothy Noble, Esq; ✉ Ardnahane, Barnton Ave, Edinburgh EH4 6JJ; Noble Group Ltd, 5 Darnaway Street, Edinburgh EH3 6DW (☎ 0131 225 9677, fax 0131 225 5479)

NOEL, Lady Celestria; *see:* Hales, Lady Celestria Magdalen Mary

NOEL, Hon Gerard Eyre; s of 4 Earl of Gainsborough, OBE (d 1927); *b* 1926; *Educ* Georgetown USA, Exeter Coll Oxford; *m* 1958, Adele Julie Patricia, da of late Maj V N B Were and Mrs M J Were, OBE; 2 s, 1 da; *Career* barr Inner Temple 1952; author, publisher, journalist and lectr; dir Search Press 1972–; Catholic Herald: ed 1971–83, editorial dir 1983–; contested (L) Argyll 1959; hon treas Cncl of Christians and Jews 1974–79; sr research fell St Anne's Coll Oxford 1993–; Liveryman Worshipful Co of Stationers and Newspapermakers; Freeman City of London; *Books* Paul VI, The Path from Rome, Goldwater, Harold Wilson, Princess Alice, The Great Lock-Out of 1926, The Anatomy of the Catholic Church, Ena, Spain's English Queen; also various translations; *Clubs* Athenaeum, Garrick, White's; *Style*— The Hon Gerard Noel; ✉ Westington Mill, Chipping Campden, Glos GL55 6EB

NOEL, Hon Thomas; s of 5 Earl of Gainsborough; *b* 9 March 1958; *Educ* Ampleforth, RAC Cirencester (MRAC 1980); *Career* Savills 1981–83, Humberts 1983–84; dir: Bride Hall plc 1987– (joined 1984), Barnsdale Lodge Ltd 1989–; chm and chief exec Metropolitan Realty Tst (UK) Ltd 1984–; memb: CLA, Royal Forestry Soc; FRICS 1982; *Recreations* shooting, skiing, flying fixed and rotary aircraft (vintage and modern); *Clubs* Pratt's, The Air Squadron; *Style*— The Hon Thomas Noel; ✉ Bride Hall plc, 19 Queen Street, London W1 (☎ 0171 493 3996, fax 0171 499 4388, car 0836 261647)

NOEL-BAKER, Hon Francis Edward; s of late Baron Noel-Baker, PC (Life Peer UK 1977, d 1982), and Irene (d 1956); *b* 7 Jan 1920; *Educ* Westminster, Gordonstoun, King's Coll Cambridge; *m* 1957, Barbara Christina, yr da of late Engineer Josef Sonander (d 1936), of Norrköping, Sweden; 4 s (1 decd), 1 da; *Career* joined Royal Tank Regt 1940, transferred Intelligence Corps 1941 (despatches), Capt 1942, Maj 1943; MP (Lab) Brentford and Chiswick 1945–50; BBC Euro Service 1950–53, ed World Horizon Magazine 1951–54; MP (Lab) Swindon 1955–69, resigned from Lab Pty 1969 and joined SDP 1981, left and joined Cons Pty 1984; chm: Br Greek Parly Gp 1958–69, PLP Overseas Devpt Ctee 1964–68, UN Parly Ctee 1966–69; fndr pres Euro Cncl for the Village and Small Town (ECOVAST), hon pres Union of Forest Owners of Greece 1968–, govr Campion Sch Athens 1974–78; dir: North Euboean Enterprises Ltd 1973–, Fini Fisheries Cyprus 1976–90; memb Ecology Party 1978–, Soil Assoc 1979–; Cometable de Guyene 1988–; *Books* Greece the Whole Story (1945), Spanish Summary (1946), The Spy Web (1954), The Land & People of Greece (1957), Looking at Greece (1968), My Cyprus File (1986), Book Eight (1987), Three Saints and Poseidon (1988); *Recreations* gardening, writing; *Clubs* Special Forces (London), Athens Club, Travellers (London); *Style*— The Hon Francis Noel-Baker; ✉ Greece (☎ 00 30 227 41204, fax 00 30 227 41190); office: 74 Westbourne Terrace, London W2 6QR (☎ 0171 262 8400, fax 0171 402 4278)

NOEL-BUXTON, 3 Baron (UK 1930); Martin Connal Noel-Buxton; s of 2 Baron Noel-Buxton (d 1980), by his 1 w, Nancy, *née* Connal; *b* 8 Dec 1940; *Educ* Bryanston, Balliol Coll Oxford; *m* 1, 1964 (m dis 1968), Miranda Mary (d 1979), da of Maj Hugo Atherton Chisenhale-Marsh (d 1996), of Gaynes Park, Epping, Essex; m 2, 1972 (m dis 1982), Sarah Margaret Surridge (who m, 1982, Peter E W Adam), da of Neil Charles Wolseley Barrett TD, of Twickenham Rd, Teddington; 1 s, 1 da (Hon Lucy Margaret b 1977); m 3, 18 Dec 1986, Mrs Abigail Marie Granger, da of Eric Philip Richard Clent; 1 da (Hon Antonia Helen Isabella b 11 Dec 1989); *Heir* s, Hon Charles Connal Noel-Buxton b 17 April 1975; *Career* slr 1966; *Style*— The Rt Hon the Lord Noel-Buxton; ✉ House of Lords, London SW1A 0PW

NOEL-PATON, Hon (Frederick) Ranald; o s of Baron Ferrier, ED, DL (Life Peer, d 1992), and Joane Mary, *née* Wiles (d 1984); *b* 7 Nov 1938; *Educ* Rugby, Haverford Coll Pennsylvania, McGill Univ Montreal (BA), Napier Univ (DBA); *m* 1973, Patricia, da of late Gen Sir William Gurdon Stirling, GCB, CBE, DSO; 4 da; *Career* Br Utd Airways Ltd 1965–70, Br Caledonian Airways Ltd 1970–86; gen mangr: W Africa 1975–79, Far E 1980–86; dir Caledonian Far E Airways 1984–86; gp md John Menzies plc; dir: Pacific Assets Trust plc, General Accident plc; *Recreations* gardening, golf, fishing, ornithology, the arts; *Clubs* New (Edinburgh), Hong Kong, Shek O Country; *Style*— The Hon Ranald Noel-Paton; ✉ Easter Dunbarnie, Bridge of Earn, Perth PH2 9ED; John Menzies plc, 108 Princes Street, Edinburgh EH2 3AA (☎ 0131 225 8555, fax 0131 459 1150)

NOEST, Peter J; s of Maj A J F Noest, of Dulwich, and Maria Gerbrands-Noest; *b* 12 June 1948; *Educ* St George's Coll, Weybridge, The RAC Cirencester; *m* 1, (m dis 1993), Lisabeth Penelope Moody; 1 s (Timothy Peter b 1974), 1 da (Lisa Jane b 1976); m 2, 1993, Jocelyn Claire, yr da of Alan Douglas Spencer; *Career* chartered surveyor (land agency and general practice); Knight Frank & Rutley: ptnr Amsterdam 1972–77, ptnr London 1977–81, full equity ptnr 1981, resigned 1983; Hampton & Sons: conslt, sr commercial ptnr 1984; dir of Capital Consultancy Group; md P H Gillingham (Investments) Ltd; FRICS; *Books* contributor to Office Development, Estates Gazette (1985); *Recreations* shooting, hunting, tennis, farming, conservation, forestry, travel, wine; *Clubs* Turf; *Style*— Peter Noest, Esq; ✉ Dolmans Cottage, Hankerton, nr Malmesbury, Wilts SN16 9LH (☎ 01666 577018)

NOKES, Barbara Ann; da of Harry Smith, of Exeter, Devon, and late Beatrice Maud, *née* Kirk; *b* 29 April 1942; *Educ* Clapham Co GS, Friern Rd Secdy Sch; *m* 1, 29 Feb 1962 (m dis 1970), Stewart Charteris; m 2, 28 June 1974 (m dis 1994), Roger Nokes, s of Charles Nokes (decd), and Margaret Nokes, of Frinton-on-Sea, Essex; 1 s (Luke Charles Edward b 6 July 1984), 1 da (Daisy Lysistrata b 27 Oct 1978); *Career* copywriter: various advtg agencies 1962–68, Doyle Dane Bernbach Ltd 1969–75 and 1976–80 (dep creative dir and bd memb), Collett Dickenson Pearce 1975–76, Boase Massimi Pollitt 1981–82; fndr ptnr, dep creative dir and bd memb Bartle Bogle Hegarty Ltd 1982–92, exec creative dir KHBB Ltd (formerly CME-KHBB Ltd) 1993–95, a creative dir and memb Bd Grey Advertising Ltd 1996–; winner of numerous Gold and Silver D & AD awards, Campaign Press and Poster, Cannes TV, BTAA Epica and Eurobest awards for clients incl: Volkswagen, Creda, Robertson's, Levi's, Dr White's, Audi, Pernod; memb: D & AD Assoc, Creative Circle; MIPA; *Recreations* restoring antiques, travelling, my children; *Clubs* Groucho's, Women's Advertising Club of London, Soho House; *Style*— Ms Barbara Nokes; ✉ Grey Advertising Ltd, 215–227 Great Portland Street, London W1N 5HD (☎ 0171 413 2528, fax 0171 413 2218)

NOKES, David Leonard; s of Anthony John Nokes, and Ethel Murray, *née* Smith; *b* 11 March 1948; *Educ* King's Coll Sch Wimbledon, Christ's Coll Cambridge (open scholar, BA, PhD); *Career* Adelaide Stoll res scholar Christ's Coll Cambridge 1969, reader in Eng lit King's Coll London 1988– (lectr Eng 1973–); regular reviewer for TLS, The Spectator, BBC Radio, The Sunday Times; memb Br Soc for Eighteenth-Century Studies (treas 1982–83); FRSL 1994; *Books* Jonathan Swift, A Hypocrite Reversed (1985, James Tait Black Meml Prize for biography), Raillery and Rage, A Study of 18th Century Satire (1987), Joseph Andrews, A Master Study (1987), John Gay, A Profession of Friendship (1995); *Television* No Country for Old Men: The Long Exile of Jonathan Swift (BBC Omnibus film) 1981, co-writer Clarissa (BBC serial adapted from Richardson's novel) 1991, The Count of Solar (BBC Screen Two) 1992, The Tenant of Wildfell Hall (BBC serial adapted from Anne Bronte's novel) 1996; *Recreations* reading, writing; *Clubs* The Johnson; *Style*— David Nokes, Esq, FRSL; ✉ Department of English, King's College, University of London, Strand, London WC2R 2LS (☎ 0171 836 5454)

NOLAN, Benjamin; QC (1992); s of Benjamin Nolan (d 1951), and Jenifer, *née*, Mercer; *b* 19 July 1948; *Educ* St Joseph's Coll Blackpool, Newcastle upon Tyne Poly, Univ of London (LLB); *m* 24 Aug 1973, Noreen Frances, da of Dr John Kelly; 2 da (Georgina b 19 Aug 1978, Katharine b 29 Nov 1980); *Career* called to the Bar 1971, in practice in the Chambers of John M Collins 9 Woodhouse Sq Leeds 1971–, recorder 1989–; *Recreations* cooking, swimming, walking, gardening, music; *Style*— Benjamin Nolan, Esq, QC; ✉ 9 Woodhouse Square, Leeds LS3 1AD (☎ 0113 245 1986, fax 0113 244 8623)

NOLAN, Dr Daniel Joseph; s of Peter Nolan (d 1972), of Vevay Rd, Bray, Co Wicklow, Ireland, and Norah Josephine, *née* Hegarty (d 1990); *b* 17 Aug 1937; *Educ* Presentation Coll Bray Co Wicklow, Univ Coll Dublin (MD); *m* 29 March 1967, (Brighid) Rosarie, da of Martin Commins (d 1969); 2 s (Donal b 1970, Edward b 1973), 1 da (Winifred b 1968); *Career* house physician Mater Misericordiae Hosp Dublin 1965–66, house offr Rotunda Hosp Dublin 1966–67, sr house offr Chase Farm Hosp Enfield 1967–68, registrar and sr registrar radiology Utd Bristol Hosps 1968–74, conslt radiologist Oxford Radcliffe Tst 1974–, clinical lectr Univ of Oxford 1974–; MRCP, FRCR; *Books* Radiological Atlas of Biliary and Pancreatic Disease (jtly 1978), The Double Contrast Barium Meal - A Radiological Atlas (1980), Radiological Atlas of Gastrointestinal Disease (1983), Imaging of Small Intestinal Tumours (jtly, 1997); *Recreations* sailing, cycling; *Clubs* RSM, Royal Southern Yacht; *Style*— Dr Daniel J Nolan; ✉ Department of Radiology, John Radcliffe Hospital, Oxford OX3 9DU (☎ 01865 220813/8, fax 01865 220801)

NOLAN, David John; s of late David Nolan, of Liverpool, and late Constance Cordelia, *née* O'Donaghue; *b* 8 May 1949; *Educ* St Edward's Coll Liverpool, Royal Manchester Coll of Music; *children* 1 s (Jonathan David b 1978); *Career* princ violin LSO 1974–76, ldr London Philharmonic Orchestra 1976–92, ldr Philharmonia Orchestra 1992–94; frequent soloist with major Br orchs and conductors, wide concerto repertoire ranging from Bach to Berg; ARMCM; *Recreations* jogging, curries; *Style*— David Nolan, Esq; ✉ 126 Turney Road, Dulwich, London SE21 7JJ (☎ 0171 733 1653)

NOLAN, Deidre Patricia (Dee); (Mrs John Southgate); da of Raphael Harvey Nolan, of Naracoorte, S Aust, and Zita Anne, *née* McVeigh; *b* 2 April 1953; *Educ* Loreto Convent Adelaide S Aust, St Catherine's Ontario Canada; *m* 1, 1976 (m dis), Michael Gough, s of Roy Gough; m 2, 1988, John Reginald Southgate, s of Reginald Samuel Southgate; *Career* journalist; staff reporter The Herald Melbourne Aust 1971–76, The Australian Women's Weekly 1976–79 (feature writer, dep bureau chief), dep features ed Woman's Own 1980–81, Women 1981–84 (features ed, asst ed), Daily Express 1984–85 (dep women's ed, dep features ed), features ed Daily Mirror 1985–86; ed: Sunday Express Magazine 1986–89, Metropolitan Home 1989–91; asst ed Daily Mail 1992, ed YOU magazine 1992–; chm Br Soc of Magazine Eds 1988; *Recreations* golf, food and wine, opera; *Style*— Ms Dee Nolan; ✉ YOU Magazine, Northcliffe House, 2 Derry Street, London W8 5TT (☎ 0171 938 6000, fax 0171 938 4609)

NOLAN, Julia Mary; da of William Roy Lewis, of Hampshire, and Margaret, *née* Fay; *b* 10 Feb 1958; *Educ* Wolverhampton Girls' HS, The Mountbatten Sch, Barton Peveril Coll; *m* Oct 1984, Paul Joseph Nolan; 2 s (Benjamin b May 1987, Alexander b June 1989), 1 da (Rhiannon b Dec 1991); *Career* Reader's Digest publishers 1977–79, Franklin Watts publishers 1979–80, Marshall Editions publishers 1980, Allen Brady & Marsh advtg 1981–85, Publicis advtg 1985, The Boots Co plc 1986–89, advtg mangr Nat Dairy Cncl 1989–93, mktg communications mangr W H Smith Retail 1993–; memb Mktg Soc 1990; *Recreations* reading, gardening; *Style*— Mrs Julia Nolan; ✉ Pollards Farmhouse, Clanville, Hants SP11 9JE

NOLAN, Hon Michael Alfred Anthony; s of Baron Nolan (Life Peer), and Margaret, *née* Noyes; *b* 17 June 1955; *Educ* Ampleforth, St Benet's Hall Oxford (MA), City Univ (Dip Law); *m* 26 May 1984, Adeline Mei Choo, da of Henry S H Oh, of Singapore; 2 s (Hugh b 1986, Felix b 1992), 1 da (Sophia b 1989); *Career* called to the Bar Middle Temple 1981; contrib to Atkins Court Forms (Arbitration, Carriers, Commercial Court, Insurance); memb: Commercial Bar Assoc, London Common Law and Commercial Bar Assoc; *Recreations* swimming, tennis, skiing, books, plays, films, opera; *Clubs* Oxford Union, RAC, Millennium, Hurlingham; *Style*— The Hon Michael Nolan; ✉ Chambers of David Steel QC, 4 Essex Court, Temple EC4Y 9AJ (☎ 0171 797 7970, fax 0171 353 0998)

NOLAN, Baron (UK 1994), of Brasted, Co Kent; Sir Michael Patrick Nolan; kt (1982), PC (1991); yr s of James Thomas Nolan, and Jane, *née* Walsh; *b* 10 Sept 1928; *Educ* Ampleforth, Wadham Coll Oxford; *m* 1953, Margaret, yr da of Alfred Noyes, CBE, the poet, by his w Mary, da of Capt Jasper Graham Mayne, CBE, of Gidleigh Park, Chagford, Devon; 1 s (Hon Michael, *qv*), 4 da; *Career* served RA 1947–49 and TA 1949–55; High Court Judge (Queen's Bench) 1982–91; presiding judge Western Circuit 1985–88; recorder Crown Ct 1975–82, QC 1968, QC (NI) 1974, called to the Bar NI 1974, called to the Bar Middle Temple 1953, memb Bar Cncl 1973–74, memb Senate Inns of Ct and Bar 1974–81, treas 1977–79, Lord Justice of Appeal 1991–93, Lord of Appeal in Ordinary 1994–; chm Ctee on Standards in Public Life 1994–; hon fell Wadham Coll Oxford 1992; memb: Sandilands Ctee on Inflation Accounting 1973–75, Governing Body Convent of Sacred Heart Woldingham 1973–82; govr Combe Bank Sch 1974–82; *Clubs* Army and Navy, Boodle's, MCC; *Style*— The Rt Hon Lord Nolan, PC; ✉ House of Lords, London SW1A 0PW

NOLDER, Terence Robert; s of Walter George Nolder (d 1978), and Lily, *née* Walker; *b* 12 May 1946; *Educ* Ealing Mead Co Sch, Chelsea Sch of Art, Harrow Sch of Art (DipAD, first prize BA Concorde Uniform/Nat Bridal, Nat Menswear and Knitwear Competitions); *m* 29 April 1972, Helene Janine Lavernia, da of Placido Antonio Jaime Lavernia; 1 da (Elise Grace b 8 June 1983); *Career* fashion designer; head evening designer Quorum 1977–81, Terence Nolder London 1981–92, Terence Nolder Ltd 1992–; British Designer of the Year 1981; dir Fashion Acts (initiative to raise money to help people with HIV infection); *Recreations* antiques, music, interest in interiors, charity work for children; *Style*— Terence Nolder, Esq; ✉ Terence Nolder Ltd, 40 Margaret Street, London W1N 7FB (☎ 0171 491 8161, fax 0171 491 8160)

NOON, Anthony John; s of John Michael Noon (d 1967), of Sutton, Surrey, and Amelia Lucy, *née* Newman (d 1958); *b* 20 Dec 1932; *Educ* Boys HS Sutton, Epsom Coll (LLB); *m* 30 March 1964, Cecilia Mary, da of William Cecil Graham, of Epsom, Surrey; 2 da (Jennifer Caroline b 1965, Jacqueline Anne b 1975); *Career* RAF Pilot Officer 1956; slr 1955, asst slr Wanstead and Woodford Borough Cncl 1958–60, slr Babcock & Wilcox Ltd 1960–63, dir legal and contract servs The Plessey Co plc 1976– (dep legal advsr 1963–71, legal advsr 1971–76); memb Law Soc 1955; *Recreations* reading, walking, windsurfing; *Style*— Anthony Noon, Esq; ✉ 13 Dover Road, Branksome Park, Poole, Dorset BH13 6DZ (☎ 01202 751643); The Plessey Company Ltd, Vicarage Lane, Ilford, Essex IG1 4AQ (direct ☎ 0181 553 8055, fax 0181 553 8279, telex 897971)

NOONEY, David Matthew; s of Matthew Patrick Nooney, of Mottingham, SE London, and May Margaret, *née* King; *b* 2 Aug 1945; *Educ* St Joseph's Acad Blackheath; *m* 1973, Maureen Georgina, da of Patrick George Revell; 1 adopted da (Clara Jane b 12 Aug 1980); *Career* HM Treasy 1965–86; Lord Chancellor's Dept: mgmnt accounting advsr 1986–88, head Resources Div 1988–91, head Civil Business Div 1991–93, head Legal Servs and Agencies Div 1993; dir of corp servs Crown Prosecution Service 1993–; FICMA; *Recreations* sport, theatre, crosswords, poetry; *Style*— David Nooney, Esq; ✉ Crown Prosecution Service, 50 Ludgate Hill, London EC4M 7EX (☎ 0171 273 8114, fax 0171 329 8168)

NORBURN, Prof David; s of Rev Canon Richard Greville Norburn (d 1978), and Constance Elizabeth, *née* Flint; *b* 18 Feb 1941; *Educ* Bolton Sch, LSE (BEcon), City Univ (PhD); *m* 1, 1962 (m dis 1975), Veronica, *née* Ellis; 1 s (Joel b 5 Nov 1969), 1 da (Sophie b 15 April 1967); m 2, 6 June 1975, Prof Sue Birley; *Career* sr res fell in business policy City Univ London 1970–72, sr lectr in business policy London Business Sch 1972–82, Franklin D Schurz prof in strategic mgmnt (inaugural chair) Univ of Notre Dame USA 1982–85, chair of strategic mgmnt Cranfield Sch of Mgmnt 1986–87, inaugural chair of mgmnt Univ of London 1987–; dir: The Mgmnt Sch Imperial Coll of Sci Technol and Med 1987, Main Bd Newchurch & Co 1985, Whurr Publishing Ltd; ed Euro Business Jl 1987, fndr memb and dir Strategic Mgmnt Soc; numerous articles in scholastic jls; FRSA 1988, CIMgt 1989; *Books* British Business Policy (with D Channon and J Stopford, 1975); *Recreations* antiquarian horology, competitive tennis, carpentry; *Clubs* Athenaeum; *Style*— Prof David Norburn; ✉ The Management School, Imperial College of Science, Technology & Medicine, 53 Prince's Gate, Exhibition Rd, London SW7 2PG (☎ 0171 589 5111, fax 0171 823 7685, telex 261503)

NORBURY, John Karel; s of Frederick Thomas Henry Norbury (d 1985), of Morville, Shropshire, and Magdalena, *née* Potmesilova; *b* 16 May 1940; *Educ* The Latymer Sch, Univ Coll of Wales Aberystwyth (BSc), Univ of Wolverhampton (BA); *m* 1964, Rachel Elizabeth, da of Dr John Richard Timmis Turner; 2 s (Nicholas John b 4 Sept 1968, Giles Richard b 2 April 1970); *Career* articled clerk CF Middleton & Co 1963–67, co accountant Sun Valley Poultry Ltd 1967–69, audit mangr and then ptnr Spicer Oppenheim Birmingham 1974–90 (memb Nat Partnership Bd 1988–90), ptnr Touche Ross & Co Birmingham (following merger) 1990–92, J K Norbury & Co 1992–; pres: Birmingham & West Midlands Soc of CAs 1987–88, Birmingham Book Club 1989–91; memb Hereford Diocesan Bd of Finance; FCA (ACA 1968); *Recreations* fly-fishing, shooting, walking; *Clubs* The Fly-fishers', The Birmingham; *Style*— John Norbury, Esq; ✉ Morville Hall, nr Bridgnorth, Shropshire WV16 5NB (☎ 01746 714224)

NORBURY, 6 Earl of (I 1827); Noel Terence Graham-Toler; also Baron Norwood (I 1797), Baron Norbury (I 1800), and Viscount Glandine (I 1827); s of 5 Earl (d 1955); *b* 1 Jan 1939; *m* 1965, (Rosamund Margaret) Anne, da of late Francis Mathew; 1 s, 1 da (Lady Patricia Margaret b 1970); *Heir* s, Richard James, Viscount Glandine b 5 March 1967; *Clubs* RAC; *Style*— The Earl of Norbury

NORCLIFFE, (Thomas) Anthony Firth; s of Thomas Stainthorpe Norcliffe (d 1990), of Liphook, Hants, and Doris Margaret, *née* Firth; *b* 21 Jan 1941; *Educ* Felsted, Royal Free Hosp Med Sch, Royal Dental Hosp, Univ of the Pacific Dental Sch (Saunders scholar, BDS, LDS RCS, Gold medal); *m* 1, 1 April 1966 (m dis 1994), Susan Howard, da of Michael Howard Rawlings (d 1943); 1 s (Thomas b 1977), 2 da (Sarah b 1967, Belinda b 1970); m 2, 1995, Vicki, da of Martin Elliston; *Career* dental surgn Harley St London 1964– (currently sr ptnr Norcliffe Invest Jacobs & Ward); fell: Int Coll of Dentists 1984, Piere Fauchard Acad 1987; Dip in Gen Dental Practice 1992; Freeman City of London 1978, Jr Warden Worshipful Co of Curriers (Liveryman 1978); memb: BDA, FDI; *Recreations* English watercolours, music, golf, wine; *Clubs* RSM, Royal Worlington Golf; *Style*— Anthony Norcliffe, Esq; ✉ 90 Harley St, London W1 (☎ 0171 935 2249)

NORCROSS, Lawrence John Charles; OBE (1986); s of Frederick Marshall Norcross (d 1934), and Florence Kate, *née* Hedges (d 1979); *b* 14 April 1927; *Educ* Moor Lane Sch Chessington Surrey, Ruskin Coll Oxford, Univ of Leeds (BA); *m* 17 Aug 1958, (Janet) Margaret, da of John William Wallace; 3 s (Matthew b 25 May 1959, Alastair b 22 Sept 1960, Daniel b 14 April 1969), 1 da (Joanna b 27 Aug 1962); *Career* served RN 1942–49 (E Indies Fleet 1944–45, HMS Nigeria); asst master: Singlegate Sch 1957–61, Abbey Wood Sch 1961–63; housemaster Battersea Co Sch 1963–74, headmaster Highbury Grove Sch 1975–87 (dep head 1974–75); memb: Exec Ctee Nat Cncl for Educnl Standards 1977–89 (tstee 1982–89), Educn Study Gp Centre for Policy Studies 1980–, Univ Entrance and Schools Examination Cncl Univ of London 1979–84, Hillgate Gp, HMC 1985–87; dir and tstee: Grant Maintained Schools Fndn, Ind Primary and Secdy Educn Tst (IPSET) 1988–93, Educn Res Tst 1985–; dir Choice in Educn; *Books* The ILEA, A Case for Reform (with F Naylor, 1981), The ILEA after the Abolition of the GLC (with F Naylor and J McIntosh, 1985), The Wayward Curriculum (contrib, 1986), GCSE: The Egalitarian Fallacy (1990); *Recreations* watching cricket, wining and dining, listening to music, solving crosswords; *Clubs* St Stephen's Constitutional, Surrey CCC; *Style*— Lawrence Norcross, Esq, OBE; ✉ Crockwell Cottage, Crockwell Street, Long Compton, Shipston-on-Stour, Warwickshire CV36 5JN (☎ 01608 684662); 3 St Nicholas Mansions, 6–8 Trinity Crescent, London SW17 7AF (☎ 0181 767 4299)

NORDEN, Denis; CBE (1980); s of George Norden (d 1977), and Jenny Norden (d 1979); *b* 6 Feb 1922; *Educ* City of London Sch; *m* 1943, Avril Rosen; 1 s (Nicolas), 1 da (Maggie); *Career* writer and broadcaster; collaborated with Frank Muir, *qv*, 1947–64, solo TV and film writer 1964–; co-author (with Frank Muir): Take It From Here (radio series), Whacko! (TV series); panellist: My Word! (radio series) 1956–93, My Music (TV and radio series) 1967–92; author of film screenplays incl Buona Sera Mrs Campbell; writer and presenter: Looks Familiar (Thames TV) 1973–86, It'll be Alright on the Night (LWT) 1977–97, Denis Norden's Laughter File, Denis Norden's Trailer Cinema, Laughter by Royal Command, 40 Years of ITV Laughter (Parts 1, 2 and 3) 1995; *Books* My Word (series with Frank Muir), The Utterly Ultimate My Word Collection, Coming To You Live (with Sybil Harper and Norma Gilbert); *Recreations* loitering; *Clubs* Odeon Saturday Morning; *Style*— Denis Norden, Esq, CBE; ✉ c/o April Young, 11 Woodlands Road, Barnes, London SW13 0JZ (☎ 0181 876 7030)

NORDMANN, HE François; *b* 1942, Fribourg; *Educ* Fribourg and Geneva (LLB); *m*; *Career* Swiss diplomat; joined Federal Dept of Foreign Affrs 1971, subsequently completed trg Berne and London until 1973, staff Political Secretariat Berne 1973–75, diplomatic sec to Head of Dept (Foreign Min) 1975–80, cnsllr (political) Swiss Perm Mission to UN 1980–84, ambass to Guatemala (concurrently to Costa Rica, Honduras, Nicaragua, El Salvador and Panama) 1984–87, ambass and head Swiss Perm Delgn to UNESCO Paris 1987–92, ambass/dir Directorate of Int Orgns Berne 1992–94, ambass to the Ct of St James's Dec 1994–; *Style*— HE Monsieur François Nordmann; ✉ Embassy of Switzerland, 16/18 Montagu Place, London W1H 2BQ (☎ 0171 616 6000)

NORELL, Dr Jacob Solomon (Jack); s of Henry Norell (d 1981), and Moulouk, *née* Nehorai (d 1988); *b* 3 March 1927; *Educ* Guy's Hosp Med Sch (MB BS, MRCS, LRCP, LMSSA); *m* Aug 1948 (m dis 1971), Brenda; 3 s (Paul b 1952, David b 1953, Michael b 1954); *Career* princ GP 1956–90; memb and ldr Balint Gps 1957–; postgrad and med trainer 1966–89, dean of studies RCGP 1974–81, exec offr JCPTGP 1976–81; ed The Practitioner 1982–83; pres: Balint Soc UK 1984–87, RSM Section of General Practice 1989–90; special ambass for Eastern Europe Int Balint Fedn 1993 (pres 1989–93); memb: Med Soc of London, Balint Soc, RSM, RAM; FRCGP 1972; *Books* Six Minutes for the Patient (1973), Training for General Practice (1981), What Sort of Doctor? (1985), What Balint Means to Me (1989); *Style*— Dr Jack Norell; ✉ 50 Nottingham Terrace, York Gate, Regent's Park, London NW1 4QD (☎ 0171 486 2979)

NORFOLK, Jeremy Paul; s of David Ernest Norfolk, and Olive, *née* Bellerby; *b* 7 March 1948; *Educ* Kingswood Sch Bath, The King's Sch Canterbury, Univ of Aberdeen (MA); *m* 20 July 1972, Rosemary Frances, da of George Austen Raffan (d 1980); 1 s (Guy b 15 July 1974), 1 da (Claire b 3 Nov 1976); *Career* Citibank NA 1975–83, md Adam & Co plc 1988–91 (joined 1983), Investicni Banka Prague 1992–93, md Cater Allen Holdings (Jersey) Ltd 1993–; *Recreations* golf, tennis, gardening; *Style*— Jeremy Norfolk, Esq; ✉ Cater Allen Holdings (Jersey) Ltd, Cater Allen House, Commercial Street, St Helier, Jersey (☎ 01534 878898)

NORFOLK, Lawrence; s of Michael Norfolk, of Christchurch, and Shirley Kathleen, *née* Blake; *b* 1 Oct 1963; *Educ* King Edward VI Sch Bath, King's Coll London (BA, AKC); *Career* writer; memb: British Parachute Assoc 1992–, Soc of Authors 1992–; *Books* Lemprière's Dictionary (1991, Somerset Maugham Award for Fiction 1992), The Pope's Rhinoceros (1996); *Recreations* sky-diving; *Style*— Lawrence Norfolk, Esq; ✉ c/o Blake Friedmann Literary Agency, 37–41 Gower Street, London WC1E 6HH

NORFOLK, 17 Duke of (Premier E Dukedom 1483 with precedence 1397); Miles Francis Fitzalan Howard; KG (1983), GCVO (1986), kt SMO Malta, CB (1966), CBE (1960), MC (1944), DL (W Sussex 1977); also Earl of Arundel (E 1139 if the claim by tenure, which was admitted by the Crown in 1433, is recognised; otherwise 1292; either way, the Premier E Earldom), Baron Beaumont (E 1309), Baron Maltravers (E 1330), Earl of Surrey (E 1483), Baron FitzAlan, Baron Clun, Baron Oswaldestre (all E 1627), Earl of Norfolk (E 1644), and Baron Howard of Glossop (UK 1869); Earl Marshal and Hereditary Marshal of England (1672) and Chief Butler of England; s of 3 Baron Howard of Glossop, MBE (d 1972) and Baroness Beaumont, OBE (d 1971); suc 2 cous once removed (16 Duke) 1975; *b* 21 July 1915; *Educ* Ampleforth, Ch Ch Oxford (MA, hon student 1983); *m* 1949, Anne Mary Teresa, CBE (1992), jt chm Help The Hospices, da of Wing Cdr Gerald Constable-Maxwell, MC, DFC, AFC, through whom she enjoys the same degree of kinship with the 16 Duke as her husb; 2 s, 3 da; *Heir* s, Earl of Arundel; *Career* sits as Cons in House of Lords; served WWII France, N Africa, Sicily, Italy (despatches, MC) and NW Europe; head of Br Mil Mission to Russian Forces in Germany 1957–59, cmd 70 Bde KAR 1961–63, GOC 1 Div 1963–65; dir: Mgmnt and Support Intelligence MOD 1965–66, Serv Intelligence MOD 1966–67, ret Maj-Gen Grenadier Gds; chm Arundel Castle Tstees Ltd, pres Building Socs Assoc 1982–86; hon fell St Edmund's Coll Cambridge 1983, Grand Cross of the Order of Pius IX 1977; hon bencher Inner Temple 1984–; memb Ct of Assts Worshipful Co of Fishmongers; *Style*— Maj-Gen His Grace The Duke of Norfolk, KG, GCVO, CB, CBE, MC, DL; ✉ Carlton Towers, Goole, Humberside DN14 9LZ (☎ 01405 860243); Bacres House, Hambleden, Henley-on-Thames, Oxon RG9 6RY (☎ 01491 571350); Arundel Castle, Sussex BN18 9AB (☎ 01903 882173); 61 Clabon Mews, London SW1X OEQ (☎ 0171 584 3430)

NORLAND, Christopher Charles; s of Richard Felix Norland (d 1962), and Mary Wanklyn, *née* Black (d 1980); *b* 26 May 1937; *Educ* Leighton Park Sch; *m* 15 Dec 1962, Patricia Ann Noel, da of Richard Noel Jones; 1 s (David Richard Christopher b 26 March 1966), 2 da (Annelies b 2 May 1964, Gabrielle Clare b 24 Aug 1973); *Career* Nat Serv RAF 1955–57; CA; articled clerk rising to sr ptnr elect Finnie & Co Chartered Accountants and predecessor firms 1958–82, md IFICO plc 1982–89, dir of corp fin Rea Brothers Ltd 1990–96; non-exec dir: Reliance Security Group plc 1980–, Trumpf Ltd 1984–, Exmoor Dual Investment Trust plc 1988–, FISCL Capital Partners Ltd 1990–; non-exec chm: Frank Usher Holdings plc 1986–, Silk Industries plc 1989–, Cloroquay Ltd 1990–, Richoux Ltd 1995–, De Baer Corporate Clothing PlC 1996–; Freeman City of London; FCA 1972 (ACA 1963), FRSA 1996; *Recreations* tennis, skiing, walking, opera; *Style*— Christopher Norland, Esq; ✉ Winters Farm, Witherenden, Mayfield, East Sussex TN20 6RP (☎ 01435 873988, fax 01435 873942)

NORMAN, Andrew; s of Russell Norman, of Ipswich, and Nora Norman; *b* 21 Sept 1943; *Educ* Tower Ramparts Secdy Sch Ipswich; *m* (m dis); 1 s (Steven b 9 Oct 1970), 1 da (Kirsti b 24 Sept 1972); *Career* sports mktg; promotions offr Br Athletic Fedn Ltd (BAF) 1987–94; memb: Grand Prix Cmmns IAAF, Euro Athletics Fedn Mktg Cmmn, Working Pty on Amateurism in Sport CCPR 1988; *Recreations* sport, theatre; *Style*— Andrew Norman, Esq

NORMAN, Rear Adm Anthony Mansfeldt; CB (1989); s of Cecil Mansfeldt Norman (d 1963), and Jean Seymour, *née* Vale (d 1963); *b* 16 Dec 1934; *Educ* RNC Dartmouth; *m* 26 March 1962, Judith, da of Raymond Pye (d 1984); 1 s (Christopher b 31 Oct 1964), 1 da (Caroline Louise b 26 Dec 1962); *Career* RN; various appts at sea and ashore 1948–65, exchange with USN San Diego California 1965–67, staff ops offr 2 Frigate Sqdn 1967–69, staff ops offr Flag Offr Aircraft Carriers 1969–72, Admty Underwater Estab 1972–73, Nat Def Coll 1974, CO HMS Mohawk 1975, CO HMS Argonaut 1976, Fleet anti-submarine warfare offr 1976–78, CO HMS Broadsword 1978–81, dep dir Naval Plans 1981–83, Capt 2 Frigate Sqdn and CO HMS Broadsword 1983–85, Capt Sch of Maritime Ops 1983–85, DG Naval Personnel Servs 1986–89; bursar St Catharine's Coll Cambridge 1989; MA (Cantab) 1992; FIPM; *Recreations* tennis, squash, hill walking, bridge, music appreciation; *Clubs* Army and Navy, Veterans of Great Britain LTC; *Style*— Rear Adm Anthony Norman, CB; ✉ Bursar, St Catharine's College, Cambridge CB2 1RL

NORMAN, Archibald John (Archie); *b* 1 May 1954; *Career* formerly: with Citibank NA, ptnr McKinsey & Co Ltd (joined 1979); fin dir Kingfisher plc 1986–91, chm Chartwell Land plc until 1991, chief exec Asda plc 1991–96 (chm 1997–); non-exec dir British Rail (now Railtrack) 1992–; prospective Party candidate (Cons) Tunbridge Wells 1997; *Style*— Archie Norman, Esq; ✉ Asda Group plc, Asda House, Southbank, Great Wilson Street, Leeds LS11 5AD (☎ 0113 243 5435)

NORMAN, Barry Leslie; s of Leslie Norman (d 1993; film prodr (Mandy, The Cruel Sea) and dir (Dunkirk, The Long and the Short and the Tall)), and Elizabeth, *née* Crafford; *b* 21 Aug 1933; *Educ* Highgate; *m* 1957, Mary Diana, da of late Arthur Narracott; 2 da (Samantha, Emma); *Career* author and broadcaster; dir Film Finance Corp 1980–85; writer and presenter BBC TV: Film '73–'81 and '83–'97, The Hollywood Greats 1977–79 and 1984–85, Talking Pictures 1988; presenter BBC Radio 4: Today 1974–76, Going Places 1977–81, Breakaway 1979–80, The Chip Shop 1984, How Far Can You Go 1990; winner: Richard Dimbleby award BAFTA 1980, Publishing Magazine award for Columnist of the Year Radio Times 1990, special award London Film Critics Circle 1995, Special Achievement award Guild of Provincial Film Writers 1995; Hon DLitt Univ of E Anglia 1991; *Books* fiction: The Matter of Mandrake, The Hounds of Sparta, End Product, To Nick A Good Body, A Series of Defeats, Have A Nice Day, Sticky Wicket, The Birdog Tape (Chapmans, 1992); non-fiction: Tales of the Redundance Kid, The Hollywood Greats, Film Greats, The Movie Greats, Talking Pictures, 100 Best Films of the Century (1992), The Mickey Mouse Affair (1995); *Recreations* cricket; *Clubs* Groucho, Lord's Taverners; *Style*— Barry Norman, Esq; ✉ c/o Curtis Brown, 4th Floor, Haymarket House, 28–29 Haymarket, London SW1Y 4SP (☎ 0171 396 6600)

NORMAN, David Mark; s of Lt-Col Mark Richard Norman, CBE (d 1994), of Much Hadham, Herts, and Helen, *née* Bryan; *b* 30 Jan 1941; *Educ* Eton, McGill Univ (BA), Harvard Business Sch (MBA); *m* 9 July 1966, Diana Anne, da of John Vincent Sheffield, CBE, of Whitchurch, Hampshire; 1 s (Jonathan b 1972), 3 da (Anna b 1967, Isabella b 1971, Davina b 1981); *Career* Norcros Ltd 1967–77 (dir of ops and main bd dir 1975–77), chief exec Norcros Printing & Packaging 1971–75, md Russell Reynolds Associates Inc 1978–82 (exec dir 1977–78); chm: Norman Resources Ltd 1982–83, Norman Broadbent International Ltd 1983–, BNB Resources plc 1987–; non-exec dir Alex Brown & Sons Inc Baltimore 1992–96; govr Royal Ballet Sch, chm Tennis and Rackets Assoc; *Recreations* golf, tennis, rackets, classical music, opera, ballet; *Clubs* Boodle's, All England Lawn Tennis and Croquet, Queen's, RAC; *Style*— David Norman, Esq; ✉ Burkham House, Alton, Hants GU34 5RS (☎ 01256 381211); BNB Resources PLC, 30 Farringdon Street, London EC4A 4EA (☎ 0171 634 1075, fax 0171 489 9330)

NORMAN, Rev Dr Edward Robert; *b* 22 Nov 1938; *Educ* Sir George Monoux Sch Walthamstow, Selwyn Coll Cambridge (MA, PhD, DD), Lincoln Theol Coll; *Career* Univ of Cambridge: fell Selwyn Coll 1962–64, fell and tutor Jesus Coll 1964–71, univ lectr in history 1966–88, dean of Peterhouse 1971–88, emeritus fell Peterhouse; ordained 1965, asst chaplain Addenbrooke's Hosp 1972–82, dean and chaplain Peterhouse 1971–88, six preacher of Canterbury Cathedral 1984–90, chaplain of Christ Church Coll Canterbury 1988–95, canon treas of York Minster 1995–; hon visiting prof Univ of York 1996–; memb Archbishops' Cmmn on the Cathedrals 1992; NATO res fell 1966–67, BBC Reith lectr 1978, Birkbeck lectr 1979, Prideaux lectr Univ of Exeter 1980, Hannepin lectr Hamline Univ St Paul Minnesota 1981, Ross McWhirter Meml lectr 1982, Wilkinson prof of church history Wycliffe Coll Univ of Toronto 1982–83, Haberdashers' Golden lectr 1984, Suntory-Toyota lectr LSE 1983–84, associated scholar Ethics & Public Policy Center Washington 1986–; sec Cambridge Faculty Bd of History 1969–71; memb: Cncl of the Senate Univ of Cambridge 1978–82, Advsy Bd Centre for the Study of Economics and Religion The Fraser Inst Vancouver 1980–; Swan-Hellenic lectr 1979–, weekly columnist Daily Telegraph 1992–; *Awards* Thirlwall prize Cambridge 1967, Sandford St Martin prize for Religious Bdcasting 1990; FRSA, FRHistS; *Books* contrib: The Catholic Church and Ireland 1859–1873 (1965), The Catholic Church and Irish Politics in the Eighteen-Sixties (1966), Anti-Catholicism in Victorian England (1968), The Conscience of the State in North America (1968), The Early Development of Irish Society (1969), History of Modern Ireland (1971), Church and Society in Modern England (1976), Christianity and the World Order (BBC Reith lectures, 1979), Christianity in the Southern Hemisphere (Birkbeck lectures, 1981), The English Catholic Church in the Nineteenth Century (1984), Roman Catholicism in England from the Elizabethan Settlement to the Second Vatican Council (1985), The Victorian Christian Socialists (1987), The House of God: A History of Churches (1990), Entering the Darkness (1991); *Style*— The Rev Dr Edward Norman; ✉ 3 Minster Court, York YO1 2JJ (☎ 01904 625599)

NORMAN, Ven Garth; s of Harry Norman (d 1963), and Freda Norman (d 1992); *b* 26 Nov 1938; *Educ* Henry Mellish GS Nottingham, Univ of Durham (BA DipTh, MA), Univ of Cambridge (PGCE), Univ of E Anglia (MEd); *m* Jacqueline Elisabeth, da of late John Yunge-Bateman; 1 s (Mark b 2 April 1980); *Career* curate St Anne's Wandsworth 1963–66, team rector Trunch Norfolk 1971–83 (team vicar 1966–71), rural dean of Repps 1975–83, princ Chiltern Christian Trg Scheme (Oxford Dio) 1983–88, Rochester diocesan dir of trg 1988–94, archdeacon of Bromley 1994–; *Recreations* music, walking; *Style*— The Ven the Archdeacon of Bromley; ✉ 6 Horton Way, Farningham, Kent DA4 0DQ (☎ 01322 864522)

NORMAN, Geoffrey; OBE (1995); s of William Frederick Trafalgar Norman (d 1972), and Vera May, *née* Goodfellow (d 1988); *b* 25 March 1935; *Educ* Harrow Co Sch, Brasenose Coll Oxford (MA); *m* 1958, Dorothy Frances (d 1978), da of Donald Thomas Henry King, of Devon (d 1989); 2 s (Neil, Mark), 2 da (Helen, Clare); *Career* admitted slr 1959, clerk to the Justices N Hertfordshire 1966–77, sec Magistrates' Assoc 1978–86, memb Magistrates' Courts Rules Ctee 1989–92; memb Legal Aid Duty Slr Ctee 1983–85, dep sec of Cmmns 1986–95; JP Inner London 1982–91; Freeman: City of London, Worshipful Co of Curriers; *Recreations* painting, badminton; *Style*— Geoffrey Norman, Esq, OBE; ✉ Easter Cottage, Gosmore, Hitchin, Herts SG4 7QH

NORMAN, Jeremy Gordon; yr s of Roland Frank Holdway Norman (d 1958), of London, and Muriel (Peggy) Harvard, *née* Johnson (now Mrs Sim); *b* 18 May 1947; *Educ* St Andrew's Eastbourne, Harrow, Univ of Cambridge (MA); *partner* since 1978, Derek Norton Frost, *qv*; *Career* chm and md Burke's Peerage Ltd 1974–83; started and owned night clubs: Embassy 1978–80, Heaven 1979–83, eMbargo 1989–91; chm and md Soho Athletic Club 1994–; dir: Derek Frost Associates Ltd (design), Blakenhall & Co Ltd (property), Citychance Ltd (property), Ovalhouse Ltd; formerly dir: Pasta Pasta, La Reserve Wines; fndr tstee Nat Aids Tst (resigned 1989), fndr chm CRUSAID (resigned 1987); *Recreations* boats, archaeology, weight training, natural history; *Clubs* Mark's; *Style*— Jeremy Norman, Esq; ✉ Moreton Yard, London SW1V 2NT; 2 Needsore, Warren Lane, Beaulieu, Hants; Firm 4 Ltd, The Furniture Cave, 533 King's Rd, London SW10 0TZ (☎ 0171 828 1776, fax 0171 976 5059)

NORMAN, Prof John; s of Sydney Norman (d 1973), of Knaresborough, Yorkshire, and Annie, *née* Wilkinson; *b* 22 Feb 1935; *Educ* King James' GS Knaresborough, Univ of Leeds (MB ChB, PhD); *m* 10 Jan 1962, Rowena Mary, da of William Walker Lister, of Otley, Yorkshire; 2 s (Andrew, Alistair); *Career* sr lectr in anaesthetics Royal Postgrad Med Sch and hon conslt anaesthetist Hammersmith Hosp London 1967–75, fndn prof of anaesthetics Univ of Southampton 1975–; memb Cncl Royal Coll Anaesthetists; FRCA, FANZCA; *Recreations* music, walking; *Style*— Prof John Norman; ✉ 2 Russell Place, Highfield, Southampton, Hants SO17 1NU (☎ 01703 555177); Shackleton Department of Anaesthetics, Southampton General Hospital, Tremona Rd, Southampton SO16 6YD (☎ 01703 796137, fax 01703 794348)

NORMAN, (Herbert) John La French; s of Herbert La French Norman, of London, and Hilda Caroline, *née* West (d 1993); *b* 15 Jan 1932; *Educ* King Edward VI Sch Norwich, Imperial Coll London (BSc); *m* 11 Aug 1956, Jill Frances, da of Bernard Thomas Sharp (d 1953); 1 s (Bernard b 1965), 2 da (Elizabeth b 1961, Sarah b 1962); *Career* Wm Hill & Son and Norman & Beard Ltd (organ builders by appt to HM The Queen): dir 1960–70, md 1970–74; responsible for work on organs in cathedrals incl: Gloucester, Norwich, Lichfield, Chelmsford, Brisbane; other work incl organs in: Bath Abbey, Southwell Minster, concert hall of Royal Coll of Organists; organ conslt since 1974 at: Lancing Coll, Sedbergh Sch, Mill Hill Sch, Pershore Abbey, Gibraltar Cathedral, St Mary's Pro-Cathedral Dublin, Stratford upon Avon Parish Church, Oakham Parish Church, Liberal Jewish Synagogue St John's Wood, St Margaret's Westminster, the Handel organ at St Lawrence Little Stanmore, St Helen's Bishopsgate, Palace of Westminster, Chapel of St Mary Undercroft; memb: Cathedrals Fabric Cmmn for England 1991–, Organs Ctee Cncl for Care of Churches 1987–, London Diocesan Advsy Ctee 1989–, Music Instrument Advsy Bd London Guildhall Univ; ed: Musical Instrument Technology 1969–, The Organbuilder 1983–, IN SIGHT 1991–95; churchwarden Holy Trinity Lyonsdown New Barnet 1986–, memb Synod Diocese of St Albans 1980–86; Freeman City of London, Liveryman Worshipful Co of Musicians 1972; ARCS, FIMIT, fell Inc Soc of Organ Builders; *Books* The Organ Today (1966, revised edn 1980), The Organs of Britain (1984); *Recreations* writing, music, architecture; *Style*— John Norman, Esq; ✉ 15 Baxendale, London N20 0EG (☎ 0181 445 0801)

NORMAN, Sir Mark Annesley; 3 Bt (UK 1915), of Honeyhanger, Parish of Shottermill, Co Surrey; s of Air Cdre Sir (Henry) Nigel St Valery Norman, 2 Bt, CBE (d 1943), and Lady Perkins (d 1986); *b* 8 Feb 1927; *Educ* Winchester, RMC; *m* 1953, Joanna Camilla, da of Lt-Col Ian James Kilgour and Aura (ggda of Gen Sir George Walker, 1 Bt, GCB, KCTS); 2 s (Nigel James b 5 Feb 1956, Antony Rory b 9 Sept 1963), 1 da (Lucinda Fay b 7 Dec 1965); *Heir* s, Nigel James Norman b 5 Feb 1956; *Career* late Lt Coldstream Gds and Flying Offr 601 (Co of London) Sqdn RAuxAF, dir aviation and shipping companies 1948–88; High Sheriff Oxfordshire 1983/84, Air Cdre RAuxAF 1983, Hon Air Cdre 4624 (Co of Oxford) Movements Sqdn RAuxAF 1984–; Dep Lt Oxfordshire 1985–; chm St Luke's Oxford 1986–88; patron and churchwarden St Peter's Church Wilcote; *Recreations* gardening, workshop, offshore motor cruising; *Clubs* White's, Pratt's, RAF, RSN Yacht, MCC; *Style*— Sir Mark Norman, Bt; ✉ Wilcote Manor, Wilcote, Chipping Norton, Oxfordshire OX7 3EB (☎ 01993 868357, fax 01993 868032)

NORMAN, Nigel James; s and h of Sir Mark Annesley Norman, 3 Bt, DL, *qv*; *b* 5 Feb 1956; *m* 1, 1985 (m dis 1989), Joanna Rosemary Jane, da of Michael Montagu George Naylor-Leyland, MC, of Church Farm, Coates, Cirencester, Glos; m 2, 1994, Juliet Clare Louise, da of Richard Lloyd Baxendale, of Aston Park House, Aston Rowant, Oxfordshire; 2 s (Antony b 10 March 1995, Mark b 26 May 1996); *Career* 13/18 Royal Hussars (QMO), (dispatches 1979), Sultan of Oman's Armoured Regt, ret Maj 1983; Morgan Grenfell Asset Management Ltd, dir Morgan Grenfell International Funds Management Ltd 1990–; *Clubs* White's, Annabel's; *Style*— Nigel Norman, Esq; ✉ Wilcote Manor, Charlbury, Oxon OX7 3EB

NORMAN, Dr Remington Harvard; s of Wing Cdr Roland Frank Holdway (d 1957), of London, and Prof Muriel Harvard Sim, *née* Johnson; *b* 3 Dec 1944; *Educ* Harrow, Hertford Coll Oxford (MA, DPhil), Inst of Masters of Wine (MW); *m* 1 (m dis); m 2, 23 Sept 1984, Geraldine Marie Claire Norman; *Career* chm Holdway Group of Companies 1972–88; memb Academie Internationale du Vin; *Books* incl: The Great Domaines of Burgundy, Rhône Renaissance (Drink Book of the Yr Glenfiddich Awards 1996, Andre Simon Prize 1996, Prix du Champaine Lanson 1996); *Recreations* qualified ski instr, opera (esp Wagner), organ music; *Clubs* Garrick; *Style*— Dr Remington Norman

NORMAN, Robert David (Rob); s of Malcolm Norman (d 1971), of London, and Angela Frances, *née* Cymbalist; *b* 30 March 1960; *Educ* UCS, Pinner VI Form Coll, Trent Poly (BA); *m* 1,11986; m 2, 11 Feb 1996, Katherine Jane Helen, da of Stanley Marber; *Career* mgmnt trainee Texaco UK 1978–79, software mktg mangr Data Communications Corp 1983–84, media planner/buyer Colman RSCG 1985–86 (media trainee 1984), account dir CIA Group plc 1987 (sr media planner 1986), exec media dir WM Media Ltd (jt venture between CIA Group plc and Woollams Moira Gaskin O'Malley Ltd) 1990–94 (dir 1988–89), head of Euro Interactive Media Div CIA Group plc 1994–97 (conslt 1997–), sr vice pres Prisma Sports and Media 1997–; chm Sutton Jones Multimedia; MInstD 1989; *Recreations* bobsleighing (completed Cresta Run), collecting antiquarian cookery books, pop art, supporting Tottenham Hotspur FC, opera; *Style*— Rob Norman, Esq; ✉ c/o CIA Group plc, 1 Paris Garden, London SE1 8NU (☎ 0171 633 9999)

NORMAN, Sir Ronald; kt (1995), OBE (1986), DL; s of Leonard William Norman (d 1970), of Hendon, London, and Elsie Louise, *née* Cooke (d 1978); *b* 29 April 1937; *Educ* Dulwich, King's Coll London (BSc); *m* 1, 15 July 1961 (m dis 1973), Jennifer Mary, da of Edward Lionel Mansfield (d 1984), of Troutbeck, Cumbria; 2 s (Guy b 1962, Richard b 1964), 1 da (Sally-Ann b 1968); m 2, 1973, Joyce, da of George William Lyon (d 1971), of Hartlepool; *Career* 2 Lt RE; C M Yuill Hartlepool Developers: md 1966–76, chm and md 1976–85; chm R Norman Durham Developers 1985–93, dir Quality Care Homes plc 1994–, chm Student Loans Co 1996–; chm Teeside Devpt Corpn 1987–, pres Cleveland Community Fndn 1996–; Hon Col 34 Sig Regt (V) 1996–; MICE; *Recreations* walking, photography, book-collecting; *Style*— Sir Ronald Norman, OBE, DL; ✉ Hart-on-the-Hill, Dalton Piercy, Hartlepool, Cleveland TS27 3HY

NORMAN, Prof (Kenneth) Roy; s of Clement Norman (d 1978), and Peggy, *née* Nichols (d 1980); *b* 21 July 1925; *Educ* Taunton Sch Somerset, Downing Coll Cambridge (BA, MA); *m* 12 Aug 1953, Pamela Norman, da of George Raymont; 1 s (Timothy), 1 da (Felicity); *Career* WWII Lt RA, served Br and Indian Armies; fell and tutor Downing Coll Cambridge 1952–64; Univ of Cambridge: lectr 1955–78, reader 1978–90, prof of Indian studies 1990–92, prof emeritus of Indian Studies 1992–; foreign memb Royal Danish Acad 1983; FBA 1985; *Books* Elders Verses I (1969), Elders Verses II (1971), Pali Literature (1983), The Group of Discourses (1984), Collected Papers I (1990), Collected Papers II (1991), Collected Papers III (1992), The Group of Discourses II (1992), Collected Papers IV (1993), Collected Papers V (1994), Collected Papers VI (1996); *Recreations* walking and reading; *Style*— Prof K R Norman, FBA; ✉ 6 Huttles Green, Shepreth, Royston, Herts SG8 6PR (☎ 01763 260541)

NORMAN, Shane Henry; s of late Peter Alfred Norman, of Aldbourne, Wilts, and late Patricia Mary, *née* Wilders; *b* 12 Sept 1946; *Educ* Ampleforth, Lincoln Coll Oxford (MA); *m* 29 Aug 1981, Claudia Maria Leonor, da of Dr Jorge Antonio Villabona Abril, of Bucaramanga, Colombia; 1 s (Alexander b 22 July 1985); *Career* account exec James Capel & Co London 1968–78, assoc dir James Capel (Far East) Ltd Hong Kong 1978–80, int investment mangr Nat Employers Mutual Gen Insurance Assoc London 1980–82, investment dir NM Rothschild & Sons (Hong Kong) Ltd 1982–88, md and gen mangr Pierson Heldring and Pierson NV Hong Kong 1988–92; ind conslt on mergers and acquisitions 1992–; Hong Kong ptnr RCP & Partners Geneva 1993–, md RCP & Partners (Asia) Ltd 1995–, md RCP & Partners (Hong Kong) Ltd 1996–; dir Coleridge Cole & Robertson (HK) Ltd 1993–; memb: Ctee on Unit Tsts of the Securities and Futures Cmmn Hong Kong 1987–92, Exec Ctee Deposit-taking Companies Assoc (HK) 1985–92, Hong Kong Inst of Investment Analysts, Tech Analysts' Soc of HK, Financial Execs Inst (HK); *Recreations* sailing, motoring, music, photography; *Clubs* Royal Hong Kong Yacht (HK), Ocean Cruising (UK); *Style*— Shane Norman, Esq; ✉ 602 Chinachem Hollywood Centre, 1–13 Hollywood Road, Central, Hong Kong (☎ 00 852 2526 7811, fax 00 852 2526 7290, e-mail rep@hk.linage.net)

NORMANBY, 5 Marquess of (UK 1838); Constantine Edmund Walter Phipps; also Baron Mulgrave (I 1767), Baron Mulgrave (GB 1794), Earl of Mulgrave and Viscount Normanby (UK 1812); s of 4 Marquess of Normanby, KG, CBE (d 1994), and Hon Grania Maeve Rosaura Guinness, da of 1 Baron Moyne, DSO, TD, PC; *b* 24 Feb 1954; *Educ* Eton, Worcester Coll Oxford; *m* 1990, Mrs Nicola St Aubyn, da of Milton Shulman, *qv*; 1 s (John Samuel Constantine, Earl of Mulgrave b 26 Nov 1994), 1 da (Lady Sibylla Victoria Evelyn b 6 Aug 1992); *Heir* s, John Samuel Constantine, Earl of Mulgrave b 26 Nov 1994; *Career* writer, co dir; *Publications*(as Constantine Phipps) Careful with the Sharks (1985), Among the Thin Ghosts (1989); *Clubs* Travellers'; *Style*— The Most Hon the Marquess of Normanby; ✉ Mulgrave Castle, Whitby, N Yorks; More House, 52 Tite Street, London SW3 4JA; (☎ office 0171 352 3174, fax 0171 376 8921)

NORMAND, Prof (Ian) Colin Stuart; s of Sir Charles William Blyth Normand, CIE (d 1982), of Winchester, and Alison, *née* Maclennan (d 1953); *b* 18 Feb 1928; *Educ* Winchester Coll, Balliol Coll Oxford (MA, DM), St Marys Hosp Med Sch; *m* 30 June 1961, Dr Jean McIldowie, da of Dr John McIldowie Hope Smellie (d 1959), of Liverpool; 1 s (Christopher b 1963), 2 da (Alison b 1962, Caroline b 1966); *Career* Capt RAMC 1954–58, service in UK and Malaya; resident posts and military serv 1953–59; sr paediatric registrar UCH 1960–64, res fell Johns Hopkins Hosp 1964–65, sr lectr paediatrics UCH Med Sch 1966–71; Univ of Southampton: prof of child health 1971–93, dean Faculty of Med Univ of Southampton 1990–93, prof emeritus 1993–; non-exec dir Southampton Univ Hosps NHS Tst 1993–; tstee Lord Mayor Treloar Coll Alton 1993– (govr 1986–); FRCP 1971 (MRCP 1956); *Recreations* golf, skiing, gardening; *Style—* Prof Colin Normand; ✉ 23 St Thomas Street, Winchester, Hants SO23 9HJ (☎ 01962 852550)

NORMANTON, 6 Earl of (I 1806); Shaun James Christian Wellbore Ellis Agar; also Baron Mendip (GB 1794), Baron Somerton (I 1795 & UK 1873, which sits as), and Viscount Somerton (I 1800); s of 5 Earl of Normanton (d 1967), and his 2 w, Lady Fiona Pratt, da of 4 Marquess Camden; *b* 21 Aug 1945; *Educ* Eton; *m* 29 April 1970, Victoria Susan, da of Jack Beard (d 1989), of Ringwood, Hants; 1 s, 2 da (Lady Portia b 1976, Lady Marisa b 1979); *Heir* s, Viscount Somerton b 1982; *Career* Capt Blues & Royals until 1972; farmer (7,000 acres in Hants); *Recreations* shooting, skiing; *Clubs* White's, Royal Yacht Sqdn; *Style—* The Rt Hon the Earl of Normanton; ✉ Somerley, Ringwood, Hants (☎ 01425 473253; office: 01425 473621)

NORMANTON, Sir Tom; kt (1987), TD; s of late Tom O Normanton; *b* 12 March 1917; *Educ* Manchester GS, Univ of Manchester (BA); *m* 1942, Annabel Bettine, da of late Dr Fred Yates; 2 s, 1 da; *Career* WWII 1939–46 (Europe and N Africa despatches), Maj; Parly candidate (C) Rochdale 1959 and 1964, MP (C) Cheadle 1970–87, UK memb Euro Parl Strasbourg 1973–79, oppn energy spokesman 1975–79, MEP (EDG) Cheshire E 1979–89, Hon MEP 1989; MInstD 1947–, vice-chm Manchester Branch IOD 1969–71, pres Br Textile Employers Assoc 1970–71; memb Cncl: Br Employers Confederation 1949–56, (founder) CBI 1956–76; dir: Manchester C of C 1970–89, Industrial Training Services Ltd 1972–95, N Regnl Bd Commercial Union Assurance PLC 1974–86; conslt on Europe to Midland Bank Group 1980–91; pres Int Fedn of Cotton and Allied Textiles Industs 1976–78, chm Euro All Pty Gp of Friends with Israel 1979–89; memb: Supervisory Bd Euro Inst for Security 1986–90, Bd Paneuropean Union Int 1989–; pres New Forest branch Normandy Veterans Assoc 1990–, chm Hampshire Remembers D-Day Ltd 1993–95; *Clubs* Beefsteak, RYS, Royal Lymington YC; *Style—* Sir Tom Normanton, TD; ✉ Nelson House, Nelson Place, Lymington, Hants SO41 3RT (☎ and fax 01590 675095)

NORMINGTON, David John; s of Ronald Normington (d 1976), and Kathleen, *née* Towler; *b* 18 Oct 1951; *Educ* Bradford GS, Corpus Christi Coll Oxford (MA); *m* 30 March 1985, Winifred Anne Charlotte, *née* Harris; *Career* Dept for Educn and Employment (formerly Dept of Employment): joined 1973, princ private sec to Sec of State for Employment 1983–84, regnl dir employment service (London and S East) 1987–89, dir of strategy and employment policy 1989–92, dir personnel and development 1992–95, dir Personnel and Support Servs 1995–; *Recreations* cricket, tennis, watching ballet, gardening; *Style—* David J Normington, Esq; ✉ Director of Personnel and Support Services, Department for Education and Employment, Great Smith Street, London SW1P 3BT (☎ 0171 925 6512)

NORREYS, Lord; Henry Mark Willoughby Bertie; er s and h of 14 Earl of Lindsey and (9 of) Abingdon, *qv*; *b* 6 June 1958; *Educ* Eton, Univ of Edinburgh; *m* 8 Dec 1989, Lucinda Sol, 2 da of Christopher Stewart Moorsom of Chelsea, and Mrs Bayard Osborn, of Andalusia, Spain; 1 s (b 15 Jan 1996); *Heir* s, b 15 Jan 1996; *Career* kt SMOM; *Clubs* Pratt's, Puffin's (Edinburgh); *Style—* Lord Norreys; ✉ Alameda de la Alcaldesa 1, Urb La Virginia, 29600 Marbella (Malaga), Spain

NORRIE, 2 Baron (UK 1957); George Willoughby Moke; s of 1 Baron Norrie, GCMG, GCVO, CB, DSO, MC (d 1977), and Jocelyn Helen (d 1938), da of Richard Henry Gosling, of Hawthorn Hill; *b* 27 April 1936; *Educ* Eton, RMA Sandhurst; *m* 1964, Celia Marguerite, JP, da of Major John Pelham Mann, MC, of New York, USA; 1 s, 2 da (Hon Clare b 1966, Hon Julia b 1968); *Heir* s, Mark Willoughby John Norrie b 31 March 1972; *Career* cmmnd 11 Hussars (PAO) 1956, ADC to C in C M East Cmd 1960–61, GSO3 (int) 4 Gds Bde 1967–69, ret 1970; dir: Fairfield Nurseries (Hermitage) Ltd 1976–89, Int Garden Centre (Br Gp) Ltd 1984–86, Hilliers (Fairfield) Ltd 1989; vice pres and memb Tree Cncl 1991; pres Br Tst for Conservation Volunteers 1989–; dir Conservation Practice Ltd 1988–91; House of Lords Euro Communities Ctee (Environment) 1988–92; cncl memb Winston Churchill Meml Tst 1993–; pres Nat Kidney Fedn 1994–, vice pres Cncl for Nat Parks 1991–, UK patron Royal Life Saving Soc; *Clubs* MCC, Whites, Cavalry and Guards'; *Style—* The Rt Hon the Lord Norrie; ✉ House of Lords, London SW1A 0PW

NORRIE, Hon Guy Bainbridge; s of 1 Baron Norrie, GCMG, GCVO, CB, DSO, MC (d 1977), and his 2 w, Patricia Merryweather, da of late Emerson Muschamp Bainbridge, MP; *b* 3 May 1940; *Educ* Eton; *m* 1968, Sarah Georgina, o da of Maj George Rudolph Hanbury Fielding, DSO, of Grévire d'Amont, Château d'Oex, Vaud, Switzerland; 2 s (Andrew b 1970, James b 1973); *Career* Lt-Col (ret) Royal Hussars; GSO3 HQ 1 Br Corps 1966–67, GS03 HQ Defense Intelligence Staff (Far East) 1969–71, RN Staff Coll 1972, GSO2 MOD Directorate of Army Trg 1973–74, GSO1 Directing Staff, Staff Coll Camberley 1977–78; appointed one of HM Body Guard of the Hon Corps of Gentlemen at Arms 1990; Lloyd's underwriting agent; dir: Willis Faber & Dumas (Agencies) Ltd 1980–83, Beaumont Underwriting Agencies Ltd 1981–85, Wellington Underwriting Agencies Ltd 1986–91, Wellington Members Agency Ltd 1990–96, Stace Barr Wellington Ltd 1996–; *Recreations* fishing, shooting, skiing; *Clubs* White's, City of London, Cavalry and Guards'; *Style—* The Hon Guy Norrie; ✉ Old Church Farm, Broughton, nr Stockbridge, Hants SO20 8AA (☎ 01794 301758, fax 01794 301157); Stace Barr Wellington Ltd, 2 Minster Court, Mincing Lane, London EC3R 7FB (☎ 0171 929 2811, fax 0171 220 7234)

NORRINGTON, Humphrey Thomas; s of late Sir Arthur Norrington, and late Edith Joyce, *née* Carver; *b* 8 May 1936; *Educ* Dragon Sch Oxford, Winchester, Worcester Coll Oxford; *m* 14 Sept 1963, Frances Guenn, da of late Charles John Percy Bateson; 2 s, 2 da; *Career* Barclays Bank plc: joined 1960, dir 1985–93, vice chm 1991–93, ret; tstee Opportunity Tst; chm World Vision UK; dir Mildmay Mission Hosp; memb: Cncl RCM, Cncl RSPB; Freeman City of London, Liveryman Worshipful Co of Skinners; FCIB; *Recreations* music, countryside; *Clubs* Utd Oxford & Cambridge Univ; *Style—* Humphrey Norrington, Esq; ✉ Hill House, Frithsden Copse, Berkhamsted, Herts HP2 4RQ (☎ 01442 871855)

NORRINGTON, Ian Arthur; s of Charles Arthur Norrington, of Peterborough, Victoria, Aust, and Georgina Marina, *née* Beardmore (d 1974); *b* 1 Oct 1936; *Educ* Downside; *m* 21 Sept 1968, Brigitte Maria, *née* Albrecht; 1 s (Christopher Charles b 1972), 1 da (Antonia Jane b 1974); *Career* Midshipman RNVR served Home and Med Fleets 1955–57, Sub Lt RNVR 1957, Lt RNR 1958; De Beers Consolidated Mines Ltd (The Diamond Trading Co Ltd) 1957–71: ptnr W I Carr Sons and Co 1971–79, ptnr Grieveson Grant and Co 1979–86, dir Kleinwort Benson Securities Ltd 1986–90, conslt Fiduciary Trust International Ltd 1990–91, assoc Durlacher & Co plc 1991–93, assoc Walker Crips Weddle Beck plc 1993–; pres St Gregory's Soc (Downside Old Boys) 1993–96; Liveryman Worshipful Co of Goldsmiths; memb Int Stock Exchange 1974–92, MSI (Dip); *Recreations* fishing, shooting, tennis, jewellery design and manufacture; *Clubs* Stephen Green (Dublin), Flyfishers'; *Style—* Ian Norrington, Esq; ✉ Burrows Close, Lawbrook Lane, Shere, Surrey GU5 9QN

NORRINGTON, Roger Arthur Carver; CBE (1990, OBE 1980); s of late Sir Arthur Norrington, and late Edith Joyce, *née* Carver; *b* 16 March 1934; *Educ* Dragon Sch Oxford, Westminster, Clare Coll Cambridge (BA); *m* 1, 1964 (m dis 1982), Susan Elizabeth McLean, *née* May; 1 s, 1 da; m 2, 1986, Karalyn Mary, *née* Lawrence; 1 s (b 14 April 1993); *Career* conductor music dir Schütz Choir of London 1962–, freelance singer 1962–72, princ conductor Kent Opera 1966–84, currently assoc princ guest conductor LPO; musical dir: London Classical players 1978–, Orchestra of St Lukes NY 1990–94; co-dir Early Opera Project 1984–, princ conductor Bournemouth Sinfonietta 1985–89, co-dir Historic Arts 1986–; débuts: Br 1962, BBC radio 1964, TV 1967, Germany Austria Denmark and Finland 1966, Portugal 1970, Italy 1971, France and Belgium 1972, USA 1974, Holland 1975, Switzerland 1976; guest conductor for many Br and Foreign Orchs appearing at: Covent Garden, The Coliseum, The Proms, NY, Boston, San Francisco, Paris, Vienna and elsewhere; regular broadcasts at home and abroad, numerous recordings, occasional contrib to various musical jls; Hon DUniv York 1991, Hon DMus Univ of Kent 1994, hon fell Clare Coll Cambridge 1991; Cavaliere Order al Merita della Repubblica Italiana 1981; FRCM, Hon RAM; *Style—* Roger Norrington, Esq, CBE

NORRIS, *see:* Foxley-Norris

NORRIS, Alan John; s of Jesse Oliver Norris (d 1980), of Newport, Gwent, and Queenie Iris Norris; *b* 7 June 1942; *Educ* St Julians Newport Gwent, Newport and Monmouthshire Coll of Advanced Technol (HNC, Dip); *m* 1, 31 July 1965 (m dis 1969), Jane Margot Inkin, da of Vernon Dixon; m 2, 14 June 1975, Penelope Catherine, da of Lt-Col (William) Edwin Daniel (d 1974), of Leigh, Surrey; 1 s (Oliver William Edwin b 28 June 1982); *Career* graduate trainee to orgn & method offr Alcan 1960–66, princ orgn & method offr Osram (GEC) 1966–67, latterly systems and programming mangr United Glass (formerly sr systems analyst, computer ops mangr) 1967–76, London branch mangr Computer People 1976–79, chm and chief exec Gatton Consltg Gp (formerly Computastaff Gp) 1979–; past chm Computing Sec FRES; Freeman City of London, Liveryman Worshipful Co of Information Technologists; MInstM 1968; *Recreations* skiing, swimming, golf, travel, wine, meteorology; *Clubs* RAC; *Style—* Alan Norris, Esq; ✉ Lovelands Mead, Lovelands Lane, Kingswood, Tadworth, Surrey KT20 6XG (☎ 01737 248151); Gatton Place, St Matthews Rd, Redhill, Surrey RH1 1TA (☎ 01737 774100, fax 01737 772949)

NORRIS, Prof Christopher Charles; s of Charles Frederick Norris (d 1979), of Leigh-on-Sea, Essex, and Edith Eliza, *née* Ward; *b* 6 Nov 1947; *Educ* East Ham GS, Univ of London (BA, PhD); *m* 17 April 1971, Alison, da of Thomas W Newton and Kathleen, *née* Davidson, of Fakenham, Norfolk; 2 da (Clare Tamasin b 1978, Jennifer Mary b 1983); *Career* lectr Univ of Duisburg W Germany 1974–76, asst ed Books and Bookmen 1976–77; Univ of Wales: lectr 1978–85, reader 1985–87, personal chair 1987–; visiting prof: Univ of Calif Berkeley 1986, City Univ of NY 1988, Tulane Univ 1992, Dartmouth Coll New Hampshire 1994; assoc fell Dept of Philosophy Univ of Warwick 1990–; vice-pres British Soc of Aesthetics 1993–; *Books* incl: William Empson and the Philosophy of Literary Criticism (1978), Deconstruction: Theory and Practice (1982), Shostakovich: the man and his music (ed, 1982), The Deconstructive Turn: Essays in the Rhetoric of Philosophy (1983), Inside the Myth: George Orwell - views from the left (ed, 1984), The Contest of Faculties: Philosophy and Theory after Deconstruction (1985), Derrida (1987), Post-Structuralist Readings of English Poetry (ed, 1987), Paul de Man: Deconstruction and the Critique of Aesthetic Ideology (1988), What Is Deconstruction? (jtly, 1988), Deconstruction and the Interests of Theory (1989), Music and the Politics of Culture (ed, 1989), What's Wrong with Postmodernism (1990), Spinoza and the Origins of Modern Critical Theory (1991), Uncritical Theory: Postmodernism, Intellectuals and the Gulf War (1992), The Truth About Postmodernism (1993), William Empson: the critical achievement (ed, 1993), Truth and the Ethics of Criticism (1994), Reclaiming Truth: contribution to a critique of cultural relativism (1996), Resources of Realism: prospects for post analytic philosophy (1996); Critics of the Twentieth Century (gen ed); *Recreations* music (memb Côr Cochion, Cardiff), travel, model aircraft; *Style—* Prof Christopher Norris; ✉ 14 Belle Vue Terrace, Penarth, South Glamorgan, Wales CF64 1DB (☎ 01222 708165); Department of Philosophy, University of Wales, PO Box 94, Cardiff CF1 3XB (☎ 01222 874822, telex 498635, fax 01222 371921)

NORRIS, David Owen; s of Albert Norris, of Long Buckby, Northants, and Margaret Amy, *née* Owen; *b* 16 June 1953; *Educ* Daventry GS, RAM, Keble Coll Oxford (BA, MA); *children* 2 s (Barnaby William b 1987, Josiah George b 1989); *Career* pianist; prof: RAM 1978–89, Trinity Coll of Music 1996–; dir: Petworth Festival 1986–92, Cardiff Festival 1992–95; chm Steans Inst Chicago 1991–, Gresham prof of music 1993–; radio presenter (progs incl The Works series); first Gilmore Artist 1991; FRAM, FRCO; *Recreations* wine and rock concerts; *Style—* David Owen Norris, Esq; ✉ 60 Old Oak Lane, London NW10 6UB (☎ 0181 961 4830)

NORRIS, Sir Eric George; KCMG (1969, CMG 1963); s of Henry Frederick Norris, of Bengeo, Hertford (d 1944); *b* 14 March 1918; *Educ* Hertford GS, St Catharine's Coll Cambridge; *m* 1941, Pamela, da of Cyril Crane, of Southsea, Hants; 3 da; *Career* Nat Serv Maj RCS 1940–46; joined Dominions Office 1946, Br Embassy Dublin 1948–50, UK High Cmmn Pakistan 1952–55, UK High Cmmn Delhi 1956–57, dep high cmmr Bombay 1957–60, IDC 1961, dep Br high cmmr Calcutta 1962–65, Cwlth Office 1965–68, Br high cmmr Kenya 1968–72, dep under sec of State FCO 1972–73, Br high cmmr Malaysia 1974–77 (ret); dir: Gray Mackenzie Ltd 1978–88, London Sumatra Plantations Ltd 1978–88; chm Royal Cwlth Soc 1980–84, dep chm Inchcape and Co 1981–86 (dir 1977–88); *Clubs* E India; *Style—* Sir Eric Norris, KCMG; ✉ Tilings, Goring Road, Steyning, West Sussex BN44 3GF (☎ 01903 879064)

NORRIS, Brig His Hon Judge; (Alaric) Philip; OBE (1981); s of Charles Henry Norris (d 1951), and Maud Frances, *née* Neild; *b* 20 Sept 1942; *Educ* Sir William Turner's Sch Coatham Redcar, Queens' Coll Cambridge (MA); *m* 1 April 1967, Pamela Margaret, *née* Parker; 3 s (Adam Charles Philip b 19 Sept 1969, Benjamin Edward b 21 Jan 1972, Toby Alexander b 10 Feb 1975); *Career* admitted slr 1968, cmmnd Army Legal Servs 1970, served BAOR, NEARELF, Berlin, MOD, SHAPE, NI, UKLF, USA, Geneva, ret Army (with rank of Brig) 1995; circuit judge (SE Circuit) 1995–; *Recreations* a bit of all sorts, but not golf; *Style—* Brig His Hon Judge Norris, OBE; ✉ c/o Woolwich Crown Court, 2 Belmarsh Road, London SE28 0EY

NORRIS, Steven John; MP (C) Epping Forest (majority 20,188); s of John Francis Birkett Norris, and Eileen Winifred, *née* Walsh; *b* 24 May 1945; *Educ* Liverpool Inst HS, Worcester Coll Oxford (MA); *m* 23 Aug 1969 (sep), Peta Veronica, da of Rear Adm Peter Cecil-Gibson, CB; 2 s; *Career* MP (C): Oxford E 1983–87, Epping Forest 1988–; memb Select Ctee on Social Servs 1985, PPS to Home Sec 1990–92, Parly under-sec of state Dept of Transport (min for transport London local transport and road safety) 1992–96; cncllr Berks CC 1977–85, memb Berks Area Health Authy 1979–82, vice chm W Berks DHA 1982–85; former govr Mary Hare GS for the Deaf, fndr Alcohol and Drug Addiction Prevention and Treatment Tst; fndr and former chm: The Crime Concern Trust Ltd, The Grant Maintained Schs Tst; Freeman City of London, Liveryman Worshipful Co of Coachmakers and Coach Harness Makers; Companion Inst of Civil Engrs; *Recreations* reading; *Clubs* Brooks's; *Style—* Steven Norris, Esq, MP; ✉ House of Commons, London SW1A 0AA (☎ 0171 219 3000)

NORRIS, Sydney George; CB; s of George Samuel Norris (d 1980), of Liverpool, and Agnes Rosa, *née* George (d 1993); *b* 22 Aug 1937; *Educ* Liverpool Inst HS for Boys, Univ Coll Oxford (MA), Univ of Cambridge (Dip in Criminology), Univ of California (MCrim); *m* 1965, Brigid Molyneux, da of Geoffrey Molyneux FitzGibbon (d 1990), of Wotton under Edge; 2 s (Simon b 1969, Daniel b 1971), 1 da (Sarah b 1967); *Career* 2 Lt Intelligence Corps 1956–58; Harkness fell 1968–70, princ Home Office 1967–74 (asst princ 1963–67), sec Advsy Cncl on Penal System 1970–73, princ private sec Home Office 1973–74; asst sec: Prison Dept 1974–79, Treasy 1979–81, Home Office Estab Dept 1981–82; princ estab and fin offr NI Office 1982–85, dir Operational Policy Prison Serv 1985–88, asst under sec Police Home Office 1988–90, princ fin offr Home Office 1990–; *Recreations* running, fell walking, gardening, piano; *Style*— Sydney G Norris, Esq, CB; ✉ Director of Planning and Finance, Home Office, 50 Queen Anne's Gate, London SW1H 9AT

NORRIS, Prof (William) Tobias; s of Eric Tobias Norris (d 1979), and Calah Mary, *née* Bullard (d 1995); *b* 18 April 1937; *Educ* Manchester GS, Pembroke Coll Cambridge (MA), MIT (ScD); *m* 26 Aug 1978, Joan, da of Clifford Robert Rivers (d 1984); 1 s (Robert b 1982), 2 da (Calah b 1979, Emily b 1985); *Career* res offr Central Electricity Res Laboratories 1962, res mangr CEGB NW 1971, head Electrical Engrg Div CERL Leatherhead 1973, Nat Grid prof of power engrg Aston Univ 1985–94; chm Br Orienteering Fedn 1979–82; FIEE, FIMechE, FCSD; *Recreations* orienteering, watercolouring; *Style*— Prof Tobias Norris; ✉ Department of Mechanical and Electrical Engineering, University of Aston, Birmingham B4 7ET (☎ 0121 359 3611, fax 0121 333 5809, telex 336997 UNIAST G, e-mail w.t.norris@aston.ac.uk)

NORRIS, William John; s of John Phillips Norris, QGM, of Salisbury, Wilts, and Joan Hattersley, *née* Barnes; *b* 3 Oct 1951; *Educ* Sherborne, New Coll Oxford (MA); *m* 3 Oct 1987, Lesley Jacqueline, da of Douglas Osborne, of Hythe, Kent; 2 da (Charlotte Louise b 15 Oct 1988, Emily Clare b 6 Oct 1990); *Career* called to the Bar Middle Temple 1974; former amateur jockey; *Books* The Collected Letters of C W Catte (ed); *Recreations* racing, sailing, cricket; *Clubs* Royal Cruising, Lobsters; *Style*— William Norris, Esq; ✉ Lobster Cottage, Lower Daggons, Fordingbridge, Hants (☎ 01725 517375); Farrar's Building, Temple, London EC4 (☎ 0171 583 9241)

NORRIS, William Vernon Wentworth; s of William Henry Norris, of Shepperton-on-Thames, Middx, and Eileen Louise, *née* Willmott; *b* 11 May 1937; *Educ* Bedford Sch; *m* 1, 10 Oct 1960 (m dis 1982), Penelope Anne, da of Herbert James Dimmock (d 1987), of Brookwood, Surrey; 1 s (Richard b 1965), 1 da (Sally b 1962); m 2, 5 May 1982, Catherine, da of Bernard James Knowles; 1 da (Katie b 1982); *Career* admitted slr 1959; lectr Gibson & Weldon 1959–61, Allen & Overy 1961– (ptnr 1964); past chm Law Soc Revenue Law Ctee, govr Christ's Hosp, memb Addington Soc; memb Law Soc 1959; FTII 1994; *Recreations* poetry; *Style*— William Norris, Esq; ✉ Allen & Overy, One New Change, London EC4M 9QQ (☎ 0171 330 3000, fax 0171 330 9999, telex 8812801)

NORSTER, Robert Leonard; s of Leonard George Norster, of Blaina, Gwent, and Evelyn Marian, *née* King; *b* 23 June 1957; *Educ* Hafod-y-Ddol GS, Nantyglo Comp, Gwent Coll of HE, Univ of Cardiff (BA, PGTC); *m* 10 Sept 1986, Catherine Halina, da of Ronald Delwyn James Price; *Career* team manager Welsh RU 1991–95, chm Rugby Union Players Assoc (RUPA) 1996–; former rugby union lock forward; clubs: Abertillery RFC 1975–76, Cardiff RFC 1977 (capt 1987, 1988); Wales: debut v Romania 1979, Five Nations debut v Scotland 1982, 34 caps; British Lions: tour NZ (2 test appearances) 1983, tour Australia (1 test appearance) 1989; memb World XV v S Africa 1989, many appearances for Barbarians; Rank Xerox (UK) Ltd 1982–89, mktg mangr Standard Chartered Group 1990–; Rugby Writers' Player of the Year 1986; *Recreations* golf, country life; *Style*— Robert Norster, Esq; ✉ c/o Welsh Rugby Union, Cardiff Arms Park, PO Box 22, Cardiff CF1 1JL (☎ 01222 390111)

NORTH, Jeremy William Francis; s and h of Sir (William) Jonathan Frederick North, 2 Bt, *qv*; *b* 5 May 1960; *Educ* Marlborough; *m* 1986, Lucy, da of G A van der Meulen; 2 s (Jocelyn Montagu Dudley b 23 March 1989, Francis Augustus Roderick b 9 June 1990), 2 da (Polly Antonia b 17 Sept 1992, Lydia Calypso Helena b 2 Nov 1995); *Style*— Jeremy North, Esq; ✉ Standerwick Court, Frome, Somerset BA11 2PP

NORTH, Prof John David; s of John Ernest North (d 1988), of Cheltenham, Glos, and Gertrude Anne North (d 1989); *b* 19 May 1934; *Educ* Batley GS, Merton Coll Oxford (MA, DPhil, DLitt), Univ of London (BSc); *m* 6 April 1957, Marion Jean Pizzey, da of J H Pizzey, of Bournemouth; 1 s (Richard b 1961), 2 da (Julian b 1962, Rachel b 1966); *Career* Univ of Oxford: Nuffield res fell in history and philosophy of science 1963–68, Museum of History of Science 1968–77; prof of history of philosophy and the exact sciences Univ of Groningen The Netherlands 1977–; memb Royal Dutch Acad, foreign memb Royal Danish Acad, memb Academia Leopoldina (Halle, Germany), corresponding FBA; Acad Int d'Hist des Sciences: secrétaire perpétuel honoraire, Médaille Alexandre Koyré 1989; *Books* The Measure of the Universe (1965, 1967 and 1990), Richard of Wallingford (1976), Horoscopes and History (1986), Chaucer's Universe (1988 and 1990), The Universal Frame (1989), Stars, Minds and Fate (1989), The Fontana History of Astronomy and Cosmology (1994), Stonehenge: Neolithic Man and the Cosmos (1996); *Style*— Prof John North, FBA; ✉ Kamperfoelieweg 25, 9765 HJ Paterswolde, The Netherlands (☎ 00 31 5907 91846 (NL)); Filosofisch Instituut, A-Weg 30, 9718 CW Groningen, The Netherlands (☎ 00 31 50 636153, fax 00 31 50 636160); 28 Chalfont Road, Oxford OX2 6TH (☎ 01865 558458)

NORTH, John Joseph; s of Lt-Col Frederick James North, MC (d 1948), of Halifax, Nova Scotia, Canada, and Annie Elizabeth, *née* Matthews (d 1977); *b* 7 Nov 1926; *Educ* Rendcomb Coll, Univ of Reading (BSc), Univ of California (MS); *m* 3 May 1958, Sheila Barbara, da of Frederick George Mercer (d 1959), of Walton on the Hill, Stafford; 2 s (Christopher Frederick John b 29 Oct 1960, David Charles b 16 May 1963); *Career* RN 1945–48; agric offr Nat Agric Advsy Serv 1951–54, Kellog fellowship Univ of California 1954–56; MAFF: regnl agronomist 1956–71, regnl agric offr 1971–73, sr agric offr 1973–79, chief agric offr 1979–85; assoc Univ of Cambridge 1987– (sr visiting fell 1985), memb Cncl Royal Agric Soc England, chm Br Crop Protection Cncl 1990–94; FBiol 1974; *Recreations* golf, gardening; *Style*— John North, Esq; ✉ Summerfield, 28 Hauxton Road, Little Shelford, Cambridge CB2 5HJ (☎ 01223 843369); University of Cambridge, Department of Land Economy, 19 Silver Street, Cambridge CB3 9EP (☎ 01223 337147)

NORTH, Sir (William) Jonathan Frederick; 2 Bt (UK 1920), of Southwell, Co Nottingham; s of Hon John Montagu William North (d 1987, s of 8 Earl of Guilford), and late 1 w, Muriel Norton, *née* Hicking; suc (under special remainder) his maternal gf, Sir William Norton Hicking, 1 Bt, 1947; *b* 6 Feb 1931; *Educ* Marlborough; *m* 1956, Sara Virginia, da of late Air Chief Marshal Sir (James) Donald Innes Hardman, GBE, KCB, DFC; 1 s (Jeremy William Francis b 1960, *qv*), 2 da (Charlotte Amelia (Mrs Mathew Tester) b 1958, Harriet Cordelia Henrietta (Mrs Thomas Thistlethwayte) b 1963); *Heir* s, Jeremy William Francis North b 5 May 1960; *Style*— Sir Jonathan North, Bt; ✉ Frogmore, Weston-under-Penyard, Herefordshire HR9 5TQ

NORTH, Dr Peter Machin; CBE (1989), Hon QC (1993); s of Geoffrey Machin North (d 1974), and Freda Brunt, *née* Smith (d 1991); *b* 30 Aug 1936; *Educ* Oakham Sch, Keble Coll Oxford; *m* 1960, Stephanie Mary, eld da of Thomas L Chadwick (d 1963); 2 s (Nicholas Machin b 1964, James William Thomas b 1971), 1 da (Jane Amanda b 1962); *Career* Lt Royal Leics Regt Cyprus 1955–56; teaching asst Northwestern Univ Sch of Law Chicago 1960–61; lectr: Univ Coll of Wales Aberystwyth 1961–63, Univ of Nottingham 1963–65; tutor in law Keble Coll Oxford 1965–76 (fell 1965–84), law cmmr for Eng and Wales 1976–84, princ Jesus Coll Oxford 1984–, vice chllr Univ of Oxford 1993–; chm: Road Traffic Law Review 1985–88, Ind Review of Parades and Marches in NI 1996–; hon fell: Keble Coll Oxford 1984, Univ Coll of N Wales, Trinity Coll Carmarthen, Univ of Wales Aberystwyth; hon bencher Inner Temple; FBA; *Recreations* locking; *Style*— Dr Peter North, CBE, QC, FBA; ✉ Jesus College, Oxford OX1 3DW (☎ 01865 279701, fax 01865 279687)

NORTH, Lord; Piers Edward Brownlow; s and h of 9 Earl of Guilford, DL; *b* 9 March 1971; *m* 26 March 1994, Michèle C, da of late Gilbert Desvaux de Marigny, of Curepipe, Mauritius, and Mrs Eric Story, of Durban, S Africa; *Style*— Lord North; ✉ Waldershare Park, Dover, Kent

NORTHAMPTON, Archdeacon of; *see:* Chapman, Ven Michael Robin

NORTHAMPTON, 7 Marquess of (UK 1812); Spencer Douglas David Compton; DL (Northants 1979); also Earl of Northampton (UK 1618), Earl Compton, and Baron Wilmington (both UK 1812); patron of 9 livings; s of 6 Marquess of Northampton, DSO (d 1978), and his 2 w, Virginia, yst da of David Rimington Heaton, DSO, of Brookfield, Crownhill, S Devon; *b* 2 April 1946; *Educ* Eton; *m* 1, 13 June 1967 (m dis 1973), Henriette Luisa Maria, o da of late Baron Adolph William Carel Bentinck, sometime Netherlands ambass to France; 1 s, 1 da; m 2, 1974 (m dis 1977), Annette Marie, da of Charles Anthony Russell Smallwood; m 3, 1977 (m dis 1983), Rosemary Ashley Morritt, o da of P G M Hancock, of Truro, and formerly w of Hon Charles Dawson-Damer (bro of 7 Earl of Portarlington); 1 da; m 4, 1985 (m dis 1989), Hannelore Ellen (Fritzi), da of late Hermann Erhardt, of Landsberg-am-Lech, and formerly w of Hon Michael Pearson (now 4 Viscount Cowdray); 1 da; m 5, 10 Dec 1990, Mrs Pamela Kyprios; *Heir* s, Earl Compton; *Career* landowner and proprietor of Castle Ashby (constructed 1574, with an Inigo Jones frontage of 1635) and Compton Wynyates (built 1480–1520); asst Grand Master United Grand Lodge of England 1995–; *Recreations* Freemasonry; *Clubs* Turf; *Style*— The Most Hon the Marquess of Northampton, DL; ✉ Compton Wynyates, Tysoe, Warwick (☎ 01295 680629); Castle Ashby, Northampton (☎ 01604 696696)

NORTHARD, Eur Ing John Henry; CBE (1986, OBE 1979); s of William Henry Northard (d 1979), and Nellie, *née* Ingham (d 1989); *b* 23 Dec 1926; *Educ* St Bede's GS Bradford Yorks, Barnsley Mining and Tech Coll; *m* 11 Oct 1952, Marian Josephine, da of George Frederick Lay (d 1938); 2 s (Richard b 1953, Martin b 1955), 2 da (Barbara b 1957, Victoria b 1970); *Career* colliery mangr Yorks 1955–57, gp mangr Leics Collieries 1963–65 (colliery mangr 1957–63), dep chief mining engr Staffs Collieries 1965–70; NCB: area dir N Derby area 1973–81 (area dep dir (mining) 1970–73), area dir Western Area 1981–85, dir corp ops 1985; dep chm British Coal Corporation 1988 (memb Bd 1986), chm British Coal Enterprise Ltd 1991–93, ret; pres Inst of Mining Engrs 1982, vice pres Coal Trades Benevolent Assoc (nat chm 1986), first vice chm Organising Ctee World Mining Congress, memb Industl Tbnls 1992–; SBStJ 1981; CEng, FEng 1984, Hon FIMinE, CIMgt; *Style*— Eur Ing John Northard, CBE, FEng; ✉ Rydal, 196 Ashgate Road, Chesterfield, Derbyshire S40 4AL (☎ 01246 232260)

NORTHBOURNE, 5 Baron (UK 1884); Sir Christopher George Walter James; 6 Bt (GB 1791); only s of 4 Baron Northbourne (d 1982), of Northbourne Court, Kent, and Katharine Louise (d 1980), yr da of late George Nickerson, of Boston, Mass, and his w Ellen (d 1950), who m as her 2 husb Rear Adm Hon Sir Horace Hood, KCB, MVO, DSO (ka Jutland 1916), and was by him mother of 6 and 7 Viscounts Hood; *b* 18 Feb 1926; *Educ* Eton, Magdalen Coll Oxford (MA); *m* 29 July 1959, Marie-Sygne (Lady Northbourne, *qv*), da of Henri Louis Claudel and gda of Paul Claudel, poet and diplomat; 3 s (Hon Charles Walter Henri b 14 June 1960, Hon Anthony Christopher Walter Paul b 14 Jan 1963, Hon Sebastian Richard Edward Cuthbert b 7 March 1966), 1 da (Hon Ophelia Mary Katherine Christine Aliki b 23 Aug 1969); *Heir* eldest s, Hon Charles b 14 June 1960; *Career* farmer; chm: Betteshanger Farms Ltd 1975–, Kent Salads Ltd 1987–92; dir: Anglo Indonesian Corp 1971–96, Chillington Corp PLC 1986–96, Center Parcs Ltd 1987–96, Center Parcs PLC 1988–96; regnl dir Lloyds Bank plc 1986–90; sits as Ind in House of Lords (special interests agric, educ, children's affairs); FRICS; *Clubs* Brooks's, Royal Yacht Squadron; *Style*— The Rt Hon the Lord Northbourne; ✉ Coldharbour, Northbourne, Kent CT14 0NT (☎ 01304 611277, fax 01304 611128); 11 Eaton Place, London SW1X 8BN (☎ 0171 235 6790, fax 0171 235 6224)

NORTHBOURNE, Baroness; Marie-Sygne; da of Henri Louis Claudel, of France, and Christine, *née* Diplarakos; *b* 13 Feb 1937; *Educ* Lycée Français de Bruxelles, Sorbonne; *m* 29 July 1959, 5 Baron Northbourne, *qv*; 3 s, 1 da; *Career* chm Bd of Govrs Northbourne Park Sch 1979, memb Cncl Univ of Kent at Canterbury 1984, tstee Kent Fndn 1987, chm Kent Community Housing Tst 1990, dir Kent Training and Enterprise Cncl 1993; *Style*— The Rt Hon Lady Northbourne; ✉ Coldharbour, Northbourne, Deal, Kent CT14 0NT(☎ 01304 611 277); 11 Eaton Place, London SW1X 8BN (☎ 0171 235 6790)

NORTHBROOK, 6 Baron (UK 1866), of Stratton, Co Hants; Sir Francis Thomas Baring; 8 Bt (GB 1793); o s of 5 Baron Northbrook (d 1990), and Rowena Margaret, da of Brig-Gen Sir William Henry Manning, GCMG, KBE, CB (d 1932); *b* 21 Feb 1954; *Educ* Winchester, Univ of Bristol; *m* 27 June 1987, Amelia Sarah Elizabeth, er da of Dr Reginald David Taylor, of Hursley, Hants; 3 da (Hon Arabella Constance Elizabeth b 1989, Hon Venetia Harriet Anne b 1991, Hon Cosima Evelyn Maud b 1994); *Heir* (to Baronetcy only) kinsman, Peter Baring b 1939; *Career* trainee accountant Dixon Wilson Ltd 1976–80, Baring Brothers & Co Ltd 1981–89, sr investment mangr Taylor Young Investment Management Ltd 1990–93, investment fund mangr Smith & Williamson 1993–95, chm Northbrook Farms Ltd 1996–; tstee Winchester Med Tst 1990–; *Recreations* cricket, skiing, shooting; *Clubs* City University, White's; *Style*— The Rt Hon Lord Northbrook; ✉ c/o House of Lords, London SW1

NORTHCOTE, Donald Henry; s of Frederick Northcote (d 1983); *b* 27 Dec 1921; *Educ* George Monoux GS, Univ of London, Univ of Cambridge (BSc, MA, PhD, ScD); *m* 1948, Eva Marjorie, *née* Mayo; 2 da; *Career* prof of plant biochemistry Univ of Cambridge 1972–89, Master Sidney Sussex Coll Cambridge 1976–92 (now fell); hon fell Downing Coll Cambridge 1977–; FRS 1968; *Recreations* sailing (yacht 'Sprite'); *Clubs* United Oxford and Cambridge; *Style*— Donald Northcote, Esq, FRS; ✉ 100 North Street, Burwell, Cambridge CB5 0BB (☎ 01638 743924)

NORTHCOTE, His Hon Peter Colston; s of William George Northcote (d 1936), and Edith Mary, *née* Watkins (d 1943); *b* 23 Oct 1920; *Educ* Ellesmere Coll, Univ of Bristol; *m* 1947, Patricia Elizabeth, da of James Roger Bickley (d 1983); 2 s (Robin, Michael (both decd)); *Career* WWII Maj Rajput Regt Far E 1939–46; called to the Bar Inner Temple 1948, circuit judge 1973–89; chm: Nat Insur Tbnl, W Midland Rent Tbnl, Agric Lands Tbnl; *Recreations* travel, music, winter sports; *Clubs* Army and Navy; *Style*— His Hon Peter Northcote; ✉ Wroxeter Grange, Shrewsbury, Salop (☎ 01743 761279)

NORTHCOTT, Montague Walter Desmond; s of Cdr W C Northcott, JP, DL, RNR (d 1965), of Hampstead, and Irene Violet, *née* Lay (d 1972); *b* 25 April 1931; *Educ* Harrow; *m* 24 Aug 1966, Annie Margaret Durrance; 1 s (Richard Walter Montague b 1967), 1 da (Joanna Rosemary Marion b 1969); *Career* Royal Navy 1949–51; Cunard Steamship Co 1951–67, Hogg Robinson Travel 1968–96; underwriting member of Lloyd's 1977–95, tstee Northcott Fndn; govr: Haberdashers' Aske's Schs 1972–82, Jones GS Fndn 1985–88; chm St Andrews Church Little Berkhampsted Restoration Appeal 1987–91; Master: Worshipful Co of Haberdashers 1985, Worshipful Co of Painter-Stainers 1989;

Liveryman Worshipful Co of Loriners; FITT; *Recreations* tennis, golf, swimming, gardening; *Clubs* RAC, City Livery; *Style*— Montague Northcott, Esq; ✉ Pedders Barn, Berden, nr Bishops Stortford, Hertfordshire CM23 1AY

NORTHESK, 14 Earl of (S 1647); David John MacRae Carnegie; also Lord Rosehill and Inglismaldie (S precedence 1639); s of 13 Earl of Northesk (d 1994), and his 1 w, Jean Margaret, *née* MacRae (d 1989); *b* 3 Nov 1954; *Educ* Eton, Univ Coll London; *m* 1979, Jacqueline, da of David Reid, of Sintra, Portugal; 1 s (Alexander Robert MacRae, Lord Rosehill b 16 Nov 1980), 3 da (Lady Sarah Louise Mary b 29 Oct 1982, Lady Fiona Jean Elizabeth b 24 March 1987, Lady Sophie Margaret Jean b 9 Jan 1990); *Heir* s, Lord Rosehill b 16 Nov 1980; *Career* farmer and company dir; *Recreations* gardening, shooting; *Clubs* Kennel Club; *Style*— The Rt Hon the Earl of Northesk; ✉ House of Lords, Westminster, SW1A 0PW

NORTHFIELD, Baron (Life Peer UK 1975), of Telford, Co Shropshire; (William) Donald Chapman; s of William Henry Chapman, of Barnsley, Yorks; *b* 25 Nov 1923; *Educ* Barnsley GS, Emmanuel Coll Cambridge (MA); *Career* sits as Lab peer in House of Lords; formerly memb Cambridge Borough Cncl, gen sec Fabian Soc 1949–53, MP (Lab) Birmingham (Northfield) 1951–70; res fell Nuffield Coll Oxford 1971–73, visiting fell Centre for Contemporary European Studies Univ of Sussex 1973; chm: HM Devpt Cmmrs 1974–80, Telford New Town Devpt Corpn 1975–87, Consortium Devpts Ltd 1985–91; co dir; economist, writer; *Style*— The Rt Hon the Lord Northfield; ✉ House of Lords, London SW1A 0PW

NORTHLAND, Viscount; Edward John Knox; er s and h of 7 Earl of Ranfurly, *qv*; *b* 21 May 1957; *Educ* Leys Sch, Loughborough Univ (BSc); *m* 1, 1980 (m dis 1984), Rachel Sarah, da of Frank Hilton Lee; m 2, 1994, Johannah Humphrey, da of late Sqdn Ldr Harry Richard Walton, MBE; 1 s (Hon Adam Harry b 7 Dec 1994), 1 da (Hon Helen Catherine b 16 Aug 1996); *Style*— Viscount Northland; ✉ 62 Crooms Hill, London SE10 8HG

NORTHMORE-BALL, Martin Dacre; s of Dr Godfrey Dacre Jennings Ball, of Warminster, Wilts, and Judith Marion, *née* Northmore (d 1979); *b* 14 Feb 1943; *Educ* Clifton, King's Coll Cambridge (MA), St Thomas's Hosp Med Sch (MB BChir); *m* 26 July 1969, Averina Constance Frances, da of Prof Sir Francis Gerald William Knowles, 6 Bt (d 1974), of Avebury Manor, Wilts; 2 s (Dacre b 1970 d 1975, Lawrence b 1986), 1 da (Laetitia b 1976); *Career* registrar Charing Cross and King's Coll Hosps 1973–76, sr registrar Addenbrooke's Hosp Cambridge 1979–81 (registrar 1975–78), clinical fell Univ of Toronto 1978–79; currently: conslt orthopaedic surgn and dir Unit for Jt Reconstruction Robert Jones and Agnes Hunt Orthopaedic Hosp Oswestry, sr clinical lectr Univ of Keele; co-ed Hip International; memb: BMA, Euro Hip Soc; fndr memb Br Hip Soc, fell Br Orthopaedic Assoc, FRCS 1973, CIMechE; *Recreations* study of antiquities, books, travel; *Style*— Martin Northmore-Ball, Esq; ✉ Higher Grange, Ellesmere, Shropshire SY12 9DH (☎ 01691 623737); The Robert Jones and Agnes Hunt Orthopaedic Hospital, Oswestry, Shropshire SY10 7AG (☎ 01691 404557, fax 01691 404067)

NORTHOLT, Archdeacon of; *see:* Broadbent, Ven Peter Alan

NORTHOVER, James Walter Edward; s of Maurice Alexander Northover (d 1975), and Gladys Mary, *née* Frost (d 1981); *b* 19 Nov 1946; *Educ* Ardingly, Kingston Coll of Art, London Coll of Printing (DipAD, BA); *m* 1975, Gillian Mary Denise, da of John Thomas Kinsman; 1 s (Maxim b 1984), 2 da (Sophie b 1979, Romy b 1982); *Career* sr designer Conran Design Group 1970–72, assoc dir Fitch & Co 1972–75, md Lloyd Northover (graphic design, corp identity and design mgmnt conslts) 1975–93, vice chm Lloyd Northover Citigate 1993–; current and former clients incl: BAA, Barclays de Zoete Wedd, BRS, BUPA, Courtaulds, HMSO, Hong Kong Mass Transit Railway Corporation, John Lewis Partnership, Land Transport Authority of Singapore, Tesco; Design Effectiveness Awards 1989 (Grand Prix) and 1992; lectr at business and design confs, author of various articles for business and design media; memb: D & AD Assoc, Design Mgmnt Inst; FCSD, FRSA; *Style*— James Northover, Esq; ✉ Lloyd Northover Citigate Ltd, 8 Smarts Place, London WC2B 5LW (☎ 0171 430 1100, fax 0171 430 1490)

NORTHRIDGE, Nigel; *b* 31 Jan 1956; *Educ* Sullivan Upper Sch, NI Poly; *m* Linda Elizabeth; 1 s (Richard b 3 March 1984), 2 da (Kate b 30 May 1986, Emma b 31 Aug 1991); *Career* Gallaher Ltd: joined as trainee mangr 1976, asst brand mangr 1981–84, mktg mangr 1984–86, divnl dir Iberia 1986–89, gen mangr Europe 1989–90, bd dir Gallaher International Ltd 1989–90, md Gallaher (Dublin) Ltd 1990–94, sales and mktg dir/bd dir Gallaher Tobacco Ltd 1994–; *Style*— Nigel Northridge, Esq; ✉ Gallaher Tobacco Ltd, Members Hill, Brooklands Road, Weybridge, Surrey KT13 0QU (☎ 01932 859777)

NORTHROP, Antony Patrick Clinton; *Educ* King's Canterbury, Univ of Oxford; *m* Hilary; 2 s (Augustus, Joshua), 1 da (Electra); *Career* currently md Touchstone Securities Ltd; *Style*— Antony Northrop, Esq; ✉ Touchstone Securities Limited, 63 Curzon Street, London W1Y 7PE (☎ 0171 491 0302, fax 0171 491 0416)

NORTHUMBERLAND, Archdeacon of; *see:* Elliott, Ven Peter

NORTHUMBERLAND, Duchess of; Elizabeth Diana; er da of 8 Duke of Buccleuch, KT, GCVO, TD, PC (d 1973); *b* 20 Jan 1922; *m* 12 June 1946, 10 Duke of Northumberland, KG, GCVO, TD, PC, JP (d 1988); 3 s (11 Duke (d 1995), 12 Duke, Lord James b 1965), 3 da (Lady Caroline de Cabarrús, Lady Victoria Cuthbert, Lady Julia Harvey) (and 1 da decd); *Career* served WWII 1942–46 in the WRNS; *Style*— Her Grace Elizabeth, Duchess of Northumberland; ✉ Friars Well, Alnwick, Northumberland NE66 2LJ; Clive Lodge, Albury, Guildford, Surrey GU5 9AF

NORTHUMBERLAND, 12 Duke of; Sir Ralph George Algernon Percy; 15 Bt (E 1660); also Baron Percy (GB 1723), Earl of Northumberland and Baron Warkworth (GB 1749), Earl Percy (GB 1776), Earl of Beverly (GB 1790), and Lord Lovaine, Baron of Alnwick (GB 1784); 2 s of 10 Duke of Northumberland, KG, GCVO, TD, PC (d 1988); suc bro 11 Duke of Northumberland (d 1995); *b* 16 Nov 1956; *Educ* Eton, Christ Church Oxford; *m* 1979, (Isobel) Jane Miller, da of John Walter Maxwell Miller Richard, of Edinburgh; 2 s (George Dominic, Earl Percy b 1984, Lord Max Ralph b 1990), 2 da (Lady Catherine Sarah b 1982, Lady Melissa Jane b 1987); *Heir* s, Earl Percy b 4 May 1984; *Career* chartered surveyor, publisher, landowner; ARICS; *Recreations* shooting, fishing, painting, skiing, tennis, snooker; *Style*— His Grace the Duke of Northumberland; ✉ Alnwick Castle, Northumberland NE66 1NG; Syon House, Brentford, Middx TW8 8JF

NORTON, Cyril Arthur John; CBE (1980); yr s of John Henry Norton (d 1939), of Hayes, Kent, and Louisa Alice, *née* Block (d 1970); *b* 13 Oct 1916; *Educ* Haberdashers' Aske's; *m* 8 Dec 1945, Jacqueline Yvonne Monica, da of Frank Richmond-Coggan (d 1958), of Hayes, Kent; 1 s (Anthony b 1951 d 1980), 1 step s (Peter Thompson b 1944 d 1968); *Career* WWII cmmnd Queen's Royal Regt 1940, Maj 1943, serv NW Europe 1944–45; Cons agent: E Woolwich 1948–50, Battersea 1950–56; Cons Central Office agent Northern Counties 1956–61, sec Gtr London Planning Ctee 1961–63, chief Central Office agent Gtr London Area 1963–73; dir The Russell Partnership Ltd (public and Parly affrs advsrs) 1974–; chm Political Ctee Junior Carlton Club 1975–77 (vice chm 1973–75); Freeman: City of London 1937, Worshipful Co of Shipwrights 1937; Polonia Restituta (offr) awarded by Polish Govt in exile 1971; *Recreations* theatre, travel, watching cricket; *Clubs* Carlton, Army and Navy, MCC; *Style*— Cyril Norton, Esq, CBE; ✉ Flat 2, 7 Third Ave, Hove, Sussex BN3 2PB (☎ 01273 739823); The Russell Partnership Ltd, 16 Great College St, London SW1P 3RX (☎ 0171 222 2096, fax 0171 222 8550)

NORTON, Col (Ian) Geoffrey; TD (1963), JP (1973), DL (S Yorks 1979); s of Cyril Needham Norton, MBE (d 1979), of Sheffield, and Winifred Mary, *née* Creswick (d 1973); *b* 8 June 1931; *Educ* Stowe; *m* 4 April 1961, Eileen, da of Ernest Hughes (d 1996); *Career* Nat Serv 1949–51, cmmnd RASC 1950, TA 1951–76, Hallamshire Bn York and Lancaster Regt 1951–67, Yorks Volunteers 1967–72, cmd 1 Bn Yorks Volunteers 1970–72, Dep Cdr (TAVR) NE Dist 1973–76, Regtl Col Yorkshire Volunteers, ADC to HM The Queen 1973–78; Hon Col: 1 Bn Yorkshire Vols 1989–93, Univ of Sheffield OTC 1990–, 4th/5th Bn The Green Howards 1993–94; vice pres York and Lancaster Regt 1993–; chm: John Norton and Son (Sheffield) Ltd 1976– (md 1965–76), Shirley Aldred and Co Ltd 1976–94 (dir 1959–76); treas SSAFA Sheffield 1993–; chm: Yorks and Humberside TAVR Assoc 1985–91, Friends of Sheffield Children's Hosp 1979–85, St George's Chapel Sheffield Cathedral 1982–, Sheffield Def Studies Dining Club 1992–; *Recreations* pottering in the garden, music, reading; *Style*— Col Geoffrey Norton, TD, JP, DL; ✉ 22 Cortworth Rd, Sheffield S11 9LP (☎ 0114 236 6304)

NORTON, Hilary Sharon Braverman (known professionally as Hilary Blume); da of Henry Braverman (d 1986), of London, and Muriel, *née* Millin; *b* 9 Jan 1945; *Educ* LSE, Univ of Sussex; *m* 1, 5 Sept 1965 (m dis 1977), Prof Stuart Blume; 2 s (Toby b 22 Aug 1972, Joby b 12 July 1975); m 2, 25 July 1977, Michael Aslan Norton, s of Richard Michael Norton (d 1985); 1 da (Poppy b 15 June 1978); *Career* dir Charities Advsy Tst 1982–, dir Greenway Hotels India; tstee Finnart House Tst; *Books* Fund-raising: A Comprehensive Handbook, The Charity Trading Handbook, The Museum Trading Handbook, Charity Christmas Cards, Charity Shop Handbook; *Style*— Mrs Michael Norton; ✉ Charities Advisory Trust, Radius Works, Back Lane, London NW3 1HL (☎ 0171 794 9835, fax 0171 431 3739)

NORTON, James; s of Norton May; *b* 12 July 1931; *Educ* West Hill Boys' Sch Stalybridge; *m* 18 August 1956, Dora, da of Edward Ashworth; 1 s (James Edward b 1970); *Career* worked for Stalybridge, Hyde, Mossley and Dukinfield Transport Bds 1945–61 (left as internal auditor), RAF 1961–80 (left with rank of Wing Cdr), chief exec Arthritis and Rheumatism Cncl for Research 1980–; ACIS 1956, MIMgt 1972; *Recreations* walking, cricket and Manchester United; *Clubs* RAF; *Style*— James Norton, Esq; ✉ Arthritis & Rheumatism Council for Research, Copeman House, St Mary's Court, Chesterfield S41 7TD (☎ 01246 558033, fax 01246 558007)

NORTON, (Michael) James; s of Christopher Stephen Norton, of Birchington, Kent, and Lilian Ivy, *née* Buckley; *b* 15 Dec 1952; *Educ* Roan Sch for Boys Blackheath (exhibitioner), Univ of Sheffield (BEng, Mappin medal); *m* 29 May 1976, Barbara, da of Joseph Leslie Foster; 1 s (Stephen b 26 July 1979); *Career* Exec engr Computer Systems Div Post Office (Telecoms) 1974–81; British Telecom: head of gp Systems Evolution and Standards Dept 1981–83, seconded to IT Standards Unit DTI 1983, head of section SESD 1983–84, sr mangr Advanced Networks Mktg BT National Networks 1984–86, sr mangr Int Business Devpt BT International 1986–87; dir Vendor Consultancy Practice Butler Cox PLC 1987–90, dir of mktg Cable & Wireless Europe 1990–93; chief exec Radiocommunications Agency DTI 1993–; AMIEE 1974, FRSA 1993; *Recreations* reading, music, amateur radio; *Style*— James Norton, Esq; ✉ Radiocommunications Agency, New King's Beam House, 22 Upper Ground, London SE1 9SA (☎ 0171 211 0570, fax 0171 211 0571)

NORTON, 8 Baron (UK 1878); James Nigel Arden Adderley; er s of 7 Baron Norton, OBE (d 1993), and Betty Margaret, *née* Hannah; *b* 2 June 1947; *Educ* Downside; *m* 1971 (m dis 1989), Jacqueline Julie, eldest da of Guy W Willett; 1 s (Hon Edward James Arden b 1982), 1 da (Hon Olivia Fleur Elizabeth b 1979); *Heir* s, Hon Edward James Arden Adderley b 19 Oct 1982; *Career* FCA 1970; *Recreations* flying, skiing, music; *Style*— The Rt Hon the Lord Norton; ✉ 11 Picaterre, Alderney, CI

NORTON, John Charles; *b* 22 April 1937; *Educ* Dulwich Coll, Univ Coll Oxford (MA); *m* 1962, Dianne, *née* Lloyd; 2 s (James b 1963, Adam b 1968), 1 da (Emma b 1966); *Career* ptnr Arthur Andersen 1971–95 (joined 1961), dir and hon treas Arab-Br C of C 1995–; memb Oil Indust Accounting Ctee; FCA 1974 (ACA 1964), FInstPet 1975; *Recreations* opera, rugby, travel; *Clubs* Brooks's, Vincent's; *Style*— John Norton, Esq; ✉ 6 Parkside Gardens, London SW19 5EY (☎ 0181 944 6856, fax 0181 944 9316)

NORTON, John Lindsey; s of Frederick Raymond Norton (d 1981), and Doris Ann, *née* Jobson (d 1988); *b* 21 May 1935; *Educ* Winchester, Univ of Cambridge (MA); *m* 10 Oct 1959, Judith Ann, da of Brig Arthur Bird; 3 da (Bridget Ann b 6 Dec 1960, Claire Elizabeth b 25 May 1963, Sophie b 6 April 1965); *Career* Binder Hamlyn: joined 1963, ptnr (specialist in taxation, fin advice) 1966, nat managing ptnr 1981–87, chm BDO Binder (int firm) 1987–91, sr ptnr Binder Hamlyn 1992–96; chm Barking Power Ltd 1995–, dir Thames Valley Power Ltd 1995–; memb Disciplinary Appeals Ctee ICAEW 1989; chm NSPCC 1995– (treas 1991–95); FCA; *Recreations* gardening, walking; *Style*— John Norton, Esq; ✉ c/o NSPCC, National Centre, 42 Curtain Road, London EC2A 3NH (☎ 0171 825 2500, fax 0171 825 2525)

NORTON, Prof Philip; s of George Ernest Norton (d 1987), and Ena Dawson, *née* Ingham; *b* 5 March 1951; *Educ* Univ of Sheffield (BA, PhD), Univ of Pennsylvania (MA); *Career* Univ of Hull: lectr in politics 1977–82, sr lectr in politics 1982–84, reader in politics 1984–86, prof of govt 1986– (youngest prof of politics in UK), dir Centre for Legislative Studies 1992–; memb Exec Ctee: Study of Parl Gp 1981–93, Br Politics Gp in USA 1983–95 (pres 1988–90), Political Studies Assoc of UK 1983–89, Res Ctee of Legislative Specialists Int Political Sci Assoc 1991– (co-chair 1994–); pres Politics Assoc 1993–; assoc ed Political Studies 1987–93, ed Jl of Legislative Studies 1995–; FRSA 1995; *Books* incl: The Commons in Perspective (1981), Conservatives and Conservatism (jtly, 1981), The Constitution in Flux (1982), The British Polity (1984, 3 edn 1993), Legislatures (ed, 1990), Back from Westminster (jtly, 1993), Does Parliament Matter? (1993), The Conservative Party (ed, 1996); *Recreations* table-tennis, walking; *Clubs* Royal Cwlth Soc, Royal Over-Seas League; *Style*— Prof Philip Norton; ✉ 30 Mizzen Road, Hull, East Yorkshire HU6 7AG (☎ 01482 807538, fax 01482 854168); Department of Politics, University of Hull, Hull HU6 7RX (☎ 01482 465863, fax 01482 466208)

NORTON, Richard William Fisher; s of Richard Glover Norton, and Phillipa Margaret, *née* Fisher; *b* 4 Oct 1959; *Educ* Summer Fields, Radley; *m* 1987, Caroline Nicola Amy, da of Col Charles Taylor, MC, and Diana Elizabeth, *née* Gott; 2 da (Victoria b 1992, Lucinda b 1994); *Career* slr Linklaters & Paines 1983–87, slr and ptnr Charles Russell 1987–; *Recreations* golf, shooting and dogs; *Clubs* MCC, Annabel's; *Style*— Richard Norton, Esq; ✉ Pell Mell, Redmarley D'Abitot, Glos and Killowen House, Bayshill Road, Cheltenham, Glos

NORTON, Robert; s of Ernest Robert Norton (d 1981), and Elsie Margaret, *née* Nix (d 1981); *b* 6 Jan 1941; *Educ* Downing Coll Cambridge, St Thomas's Hosp Med Sch (MA, MB BChir); *m* 29 July 1967, Ann Venetta Anderson, da of Romeo Alfredo Pazzi (d 1967); 2 s (Andrew b 20 Nov 1968, Christopher b 26 July 1970), 1 da (Colette b 23 Nov 1972); *Career* sr registrar in cardiothoracic surgery Edinburgh Royal Infirmary and City Hosps 1976–80; conslt cardiothoracic surgn West Midlands Regnl Health Authy 1980–; memb: Soc of Cardiothoracic Surgns, Br Cardiac Soc, Euro Soc of Cardiothoracic Surgns; Intercollegiate Bd examiner 1992–; FRCS 1972; *Style*— Robert Norton, Esq; ✉ Northfield, 6 Amherst Rd, Kenilworth, Warwickshire CV8 1AH (☎ 01926 57870); Walsgrave Hospital, Coventry CV2 2DX (☎ 01203 602020); Priory Hospital, Edgbaston, Birmingham B5 7UG (☎ 0121 440 2323)

NORTON, Prof Trevor Alan; s of Alan Norton, and Agnes, *née* Walsh; *b* 28 July 1940; *Educ* Blyth GS, Univ of Liverpool (BSc, PhD); *m* 26 July 1968, Win Marian; 1 s (Paul

Martin b 1974), 1 da (Rachel Jane b 1971); *Career* Regius prof of marine biology Bergen Norway 1981, titular prof of botany Univ of Glasgow 1982–83, prof of marine biology Univ of Liverpool 1983–, dir of Port Erin Marine Laboratory 1983–; author of 150 res pubns; pres Br Phycological Soc 1989–91, pres Int Phycological Soc 1991–93; chm Aquatic Life Sciences Natural Environmental Res Cncl 1988–90; cncl memb: Marine Biological Assoc UK, Int Phycological Soc; FRSE 1985, FIBiol 1987; *Books* The Zonation of Rocky Shores (in The Ecology of Rocky Coasts, 1985), An Atlas of the Seaweeds of Britain and Ireland (1986), Marine Ecology in Biology of the Red Algae (1990), The Exploitable Living Resources of the Irish Sea (1990); *Recreations* writing, gardening, watching movies; *Style*— Prof Trevor Norton, FRSE; ✉ Whindyke, Bradda West, Port Erin, Isle of Man IM9 6PN (☎ 01624 832027, fax 01624 835788)

NORTON-GRIFFITHS, Sir John; 3 Bt (UK 1922), of Wonham, Betchworth, Co Surrey; s of Maj Sir Peter Norton-Griffiths, 2 Bt (d 1983), and Kathryn, *née* Schrafft (d 1980); *b* 4 Oct 1938; *Educ* Eton; *m* 1964, Marilyn Margaret, da of Norman Grimley, of S Blundellsands, Liverpool; *Heir* bro, Dr Michael Norton-Griffiths b 11 Jan 1941; *Career* Sub-Lt RN; chartered accountant, pres Main Street Computers Inc 1980–; FCA; *Style*— Sir John Norton-Griffiths, Bt; ✉ 17 Royal Drive, Bricktown, NJ 08723, USA

NORTON-GRIFFITHS, Dr Michael; yr s of Sir Peter Norton-Griffiths, 2 Bt (d 1983); hp of bro, Sir John Norton-Griffiths, 3 Bt, *qv*; *b* 11 Jan 1941; *Educ* Eton, Keble Coll Oxford (BA, DPhil); *m* 9 Jan 1965, Ann, o da of late Gp Capt Blair Alexander Fraser, RAF, of Bath (whose mother was Joan, da of Blair Cochrane, OBE, JP, ggs of 9 Earl of Dundonald); 1 s (Alastair b 23 Feb 1976); *Career* dir Serengeti Ecological Monitoring Programme Tanzania 1969–73; ind environmental conslt Kenya 1974–76; md EcoSystems Ltd environmental conslts Kenya 1977–87; Sahel programme coordinator, International Union for the Conservation of Nature and Natural Resources (IUCN), East African regnl office Kenya 1987–88, coordinator Pan African environment monitoring network UN Environment Prog (UNEP) Nairobi 1989–90, coordinator UNEP/UNITAR (UN Inst for Trg and Res) African Programme Nairobi 1990–; *Books* Counting Animals (2nd edn, 1978), Serengeti: Dynamics of an Ecosystem (1979), The IUCN Sahel Studies 1989 (1989); *Recreations* flying, ballooning, deep sea fishing, snakes; *Clubs* Muthaiga Country; *Style*— Dr Michael Norton-Griffiths; ✉ Box 24532, Nairobi, Kenya

NORTON-TAYLOR, Richard Seymour; *b* 6 June 1944; *Educ* King's Sch Canterbury, Hertford Coll Oxford (BA), Coll of Europe Bruges; *Career* freelance journalist; positions 1969–73 incl: EEC corr Washington Post, writer The Economist, writer Financial Times, broadcaster BBC Brussels; The Guardian: corr Brussels 1973–75, corr Whitehall 1975–85, security and intelligence corr 1985–; contrib to various radio and TV progs on the intelligence services; Freedom of Information Campaign Journalist of the Year 1986, Freedom of Information Campaign Special Award 1995; *Books* Whose Land Is It Anyway (1981), The Ponting Affair (1985), Blacklist (1988), In Defence Of The Realm? (1990), GCHQ: A Conflict of Loyalties 1984–1991, Truth is a Difficult Concept: Inside the Scott Inquiry (1995), Knee Deep in Dishonour: The Scott Report and its Aftermath (1996); *Plays* Half The Picture (1994, (based on Scott arms to Iraq inquiry)), Nuremberg (1996); *Clubs* Travellers'; *Style*— Richard Norton-Taylor, Esq; ✉ The Guardian, 119 Farringdon Rd, London EC1R 3ER (☎ 0171 278 2332, fax 0171 239 9787)

NORWICH, Archdeacon of; *see:* Offer, Ven Clifford

NORWICH, Dean of; *see:* Platten, Very Rev Stephen

NORWICH, 2 Viscount (UK 1952); John Julius Cooper; CVO (1993); s of 1 Viscount Norwich, GCMG, DSO, PC (Duff Cooper), sec of State for War 1935–37, First Lord of Admiralty 1937–38, min of Info 1940–41, and ambass to France 1944–47, and Lady Diana Cooper, *née* Manners (d 1986); *b* 15 Sept 1929; *Educ* Upper Canada Coll Toronto, Eton, Univ of Strasbourg, New Coll Oxford; *m* 1, 1952 (m dis 1985), Anne Frances May, da of Hon Sir Bede Clifford, GCMG, CB, MVO (yst s of 10 Baron Clifford of Chudleigh), and Alice, *née* Gundry, of Cleveland, Ohio; 1 s, 1 da; m 2, 1989, Mary (Mollie), da of 1 Baron Sherfield, GCB, GCMG, and former w of Hon Hugo John Laurence Philipps (now 3 Baron Milford); *Heir* s, Hon Jason Cooper; *Career* author, broadcaster (as 'John Julius Norwich'); with FO 1952–64; chm Colnaghi Ltd, Venice in Peril Fund, World Monuments Fund; maker of some thirty programmes (historical or art-historical) for television; FRSL, FRGS, FRSA; Ordine al Merito della Repubblica Italiana; *Books* two-volume history of Norman Sicily: The Normans in the South, The Kingdom in the Sun (published in one volume as The Normans in Sicily, 1992); two-volume history of Venice: The Rise to Empire, The Greatness and the Fall; Mount Athos, Sahara, The Architecture of Southern England, Christmas Crackers, Fifty Years of Glyndebourne; three-volume History of Byzantium: The Early Centuries, The Apogee, The Decline and Fall; More Christmas Crackers; *Recreations* Venice, commonplace books, playing the piano; *Clubs* Beefsteak; *Style*— The Rt Hon the Viscount Norwich, CVO; ✉ 24 Blomfield Rd, London W9 1AD (☎ 0171 286 5050, fax 0171 266 2561)

NORWICH, 70 Bishop of (cr 1091) 1985–; Rt Rev Peter John Nott; s of Cecil Frederick Wilder Nott (d 1956), and Rosina Mabel, *née* Bailey; *b* 30 Dec 1933; *Educ* Bristol GS, Dulwich Coll, RMA Sandhurst, Fitzwilliam Coll Cambridge (MA), Westcott House Cambridge; *m* 1961, Elizabeth May, da of Herman Philip Maingot (d 1942); 1 s (Andrew), 3 da (Joanna (Mrs Simon Pullen), Victoria (Mrs Angus Saer), Lucy (Mrs Peter Stone)); *Career* Regular Army 1951–55, Lt RA; deacon 1961, priest 1962; curate of Harpenden 1961–64, chaplain and fell Fitzwilliam Coll Cambridge 1964–69, chaplain New Hall Cambridge 1966–69, rector of Beaconsfield 1969–77, bishop of Taunton 1977–85; hon fell Fitzwilliam Coll Cambridge 1993; *Recreations* gardening, sketching, fishing; *Clubs* Norfolk (Norwich); *Style*— The Rt Rev the Lord Bishop of Norwich; ✉ Bishop's House, Norwich NR3 1SB (☎ 01603 629001)

NORWOOD, Graham Michael Mark; *b* 24 Oct 1956; *Educ* St Boniface's Coll Plymouth (head pupil), S Glamorgan Inst Cardiff (NCTJ Cert), Univ Coll Swansea; *m*; *Career* joined BBC as news trainee 1979, sub-ed BBC Radio News 1980–81, sub-ed BBC TV News 1981; BBC Ceefax: sub-ed 1981–83, chief sub-ed 1983–87, duty ed 1987–90, ed 1990–; ed BBC Travel Information 1994, special asst to head BBC Newsgathering 1995–; secondments to develop teletext services for: RTE Dublin 1983, KTTV Los Angeles 1984, Hungarian Teletext 1989, Singapore Broadcasting Corp 1992; also seconded to relaunch of BBC Breakfast News 1989; BBC rep on Teletext Working Gp European Bdcasting Union; *Recreations* the media, motor sport, cinema, theatre, writing; *Style*— Graham Norwood; ✉ Room 5200, BBC Television Centre, Wood Lane, London W12 7RJ (☎ 0181 576 4620, fax 0181 749 4848)

NOSS, John Bramble; s of John Noss (d 1956), of Portsmouth, and Vera Ethel, *née* Mattingly; *b* 20 Dec 1935; *Educ* Portsmouth GS; *m* 6 July 1957, Shirley May, da of Harry Cyril Andrews (d 1986), of Portsmouth; 2 s (Steven John b 1961, Robin Philip b 1966), 1 da (Kim Caroline Graham b 1959); *Career* served RAF 1955–57; HM Dip Serv: Beirut 1957–59, Copenhagen 1960–63, FO 1964, Russian language trg 1964–65, third then second sec (commercial) Moscow 1965–68, second sec (commercial) Santiago 1968–70, FCO 1970–73, first sec (econ) Pretoria 1974–77, first sec (commercial) Moscow 1977–78, FCO 1978–81, consul (inward investmt) Br Consulate-Gen NY 1981–85, Br high cmmr Honiara Solomon Islands 1986–88, dep head of mission and cnsllr (commercial and econ) Helsinki 1988–91, consul-gen Perth 1991–93; International Primary Aluminium Inst 1994– (dep sec gen 1995–); *Recreations* reading, photography, golf; *Style*— John Noss, Esq; ✉ 8 Hither Chantlers, Langton Green, Tunbridge Wells, Kent TN3 0BJ; International Primary Aluminium Institute, New Zealand House, Haymarket, London SW1Y 4TE (☎ 0171 930 0528, fax 0171 321 0183)

NOSSAL, Sir Gustav Joseph Victor; AC (1989), kt (1977), CBE (1970); s of Rudolf Immanuel Nossal (d 1962), and Irene Maria Nossal; *b* 4 June 1931; *Educ* Sydney Univ (MB, BS), Melbourne Univ (PhD); *m* 1955, Lyn Beatrix, da of Mark Ernest Dunnicliff; 2 s, 2 da; *Career* res fell Walter and Eliza Hall Inst of Med Res 1957–59, asst prof Stanford Univ Sch of Med California USA 1959–61, dir Walter and Eliza Hall Inst of Med Res 1965– (dep dir 1961–65); non-exec dir: CRA Ltd 1977–, RTZ Corporation plc 1995– (following unification with CRA); pres Aust Acad of Sci; FRS 1982; *Style*— Sir Gustav Nossal, AC, CBE, FRS; ✉ The Walter & Eliza Hall Institute of Medical Research, Post Office, Royal Melbourne Hospital, Victoria 3050, Australia

NOSSITER, Prof Thomas Johnson; s of Alfred Nossiter (d 1989), of Stockton-on-Tees, and Margaret, *née* Hume; *b* 24 Dec 1937; *Educ* Stockton GS, Exeter Coll Oxford (BA), Nuffield Coll Oxford (DPhil); *m* Jean Mary, da of Irvin Clay, of Marsden, W Yorks; 2 s (Thomas b 1976, William b 1978); *Career* Nat Serv Royal Signals 1956–58; LSE: lectr 1973, sr lectr 1977, chm Bd of Examiners BSc External 1980–, reader 1983, chm Working Party on Revision of BSc External 1983, chm Bd of Studies in Economics 1984–85, dean Graduate Sch 1986–89, academic govr 1988–92, professorship in govt 1989–94, prof emeritus 1996–; visiting professorship Univ of Leeds 1994–; state guest Kerala, India 1977, visiting prof of politics Kerala, India 1973 1977 and 1983, state guest W Bengal 1983, visiting res fell and acting dir Centre for TV Res Univ of Leeds (lectr in social studies 1964), cmmnd evidence to Peacock Ctee 1986; dir Sangam Books London; conslt to UN Office on Somalia 1996; co-fndr Newlay Conservation Soc Leeds; memb: Political Studies Assoc RIIA, BASAS; hon citizen Tralee 1991; *Books* ed: Imagination and Precision in the Social Sciences (1971), Influence, Opinion and Political Idioms in Reformed England (1975), Communism in Kerala (1982), Research on Range and Quality of Broadcasting Services (1986), Marxist State Goverments in India (1988), Broadcasting Finance in Transition (with J G Blumler, 1991), Local quasi national administrative structures in Somaliland (1996); *Recreations* gardening, walking; *Style*— Prof Tom Nossiter; ✉ University of Leeds, Leeds LS2 9JT (☎ and fax 0113 258 2126); London School of Economics, Houghton Street, London WC2A 2AE

NOTLEY, Somerled MacDonald; s of Lt Col George Harry Norman Notley, of Kirkcaldy, Fife, and Catherine, *née* MacDonald; *b* 30 March 1954; *Educ* George Watson's Coll Edinburgh, Univ of Edinburgh (LLB); *Career* apprentice Menzies Dougal & Milligan 1977–79; slr: Church of Scotland 1979–80, Standard Life Assurance Co 1980–81; Brodies: legal asst 1981–87, assoc 1987–89, ptnr 1989–, currently dir Rural Property Dept; memb: Law Soc, Soc of Writers to HM Signet 1993; *Recreations* angling, skiing, music, reading, antiques; *Style*— Somerled Notley, Esq; ✉ Brodies WS, 15 Atholl Crescent, Edinburgh EH3 8HA (☎ 0131 228 3777)

NOTMAN, Gaynor; da of Sydney Moore, of Hatfield, Herts, and Mavis Irene, *née* Edden; *b* 9 Sept 1954; *Educ* St Audrey's Secdy Modern Sch, Watford Coll of Art and Design (DipAD); *m* 27 May 1988, Thomas Samuel Notman, s of James Michael Forest Notman; *Career* sr designer (gp print design) Nesbit Phipps & Froome 1979–81 (jr designer 1976–79), art dir BSB Dorland Advertising 1981–91, ptnr Notman Parminter advtg 1991–; recipient: numerous D&AD and Clio Awards, Bronze and Silver Awards (Creative Circle), Gold Award (NY Film Festival), Campaign Poster Award; memb D&AD; *Recreations* cinema, writing, entertaining, family, antiques, art; *Style*— Mrs Gaynor Notman; ✉ The Basement, 31 Canfield Gardens, London NW6 3JP (☎ 0171 625 5502)

NOTT, Rt Hon Sir John William Frederic; KCB (1983), PC (1979); s of Richard W K Nott (d 1993), of Bideford, Devon, and Phyllis Mary, *née* Francis; *b* 1 Feb 1932; *Educ* Bradfield, Trinity Coll Cambridge (pres of the Union 1959); *m* 1959, Miloska Sekol; 2 s, 1 da; *Career* served 2 Gurkha Rifles 1952–56, barr 1959, gen mangr S G Warburg 1960–66; MP (C) Cornwall St Ives 1966–83, min of state Treasy 1972–74; oppn spokesman: Trade 1976–79, Treasy and Econ Affrs 1975–76; trade sec 1979–81, def sec 1981–83; exec chm Lazard Bros 1985–90 (exec dir 1983); chm Hillsdown Holdings plc 1993– (non-exec dir 1991–93); dir: Royal Insurance plc 1986–91, AMEC plc 1991–93; advsr Apax Partners; *Style*— The Rt Hon Sir John Nott, KCB; ✉ Hillsdown House, 32 Hampstead High Street, London NW3 1QD (☎ 0171 794 0677)

NOTT, Kathleen Cecilia; da of Philip A Nott (d 1932), and Ellen Cecilia Nott (d 1972); *Educ* Mary Datchelor Sch, King's Coll London, Somerville Coll Oxford (Open exhibitioner); *m* 1929 (m dis), Christopher Edmund Gervase Bailey; *Career* WWII ARP; poet, novelist, critic, philosopher; regular contrib The Observer ca 1955–80, contrib to numerous English and American jls; vice pres PEN English Centre (pres 1974–75), pres Progressive League 1960–62, ed PEN International 1960–88; FRSL; *Poetry* Landscapes and Departures (1947), Poems from the North (1956), Creatures and Emblems (1960), Elegies and Other Poems (1981); *Novels* Mile End (1938), The Dry Deluge (1947), Private Fires (1960), An Elderly Retired Man (1963); *Philosophy and Criticism* The Emperor's Clothes (1953), Philosophy and Human Nature (1962), A Soul in the Quad (1969), The Good Want Power (1977); *General* A Clean Well-Lighted Place - A Private View of Sweden (1961); *Recreations* playing the piano, gardening; *Clubs* University Women's, Society of Authors, PEN; *Style*— Ms Kathleen Nott, FRSL; ✉ Wemyss Lodge, Ermin Street, Stratton St Margaret, Swindon, Wilts

NOTT, Rt Rev Peter John; *see:* Norwich, Bishop of

NOTT, Richard; *Career* fndr ptnr Workers For Freedom (with Graham Fraser, *qv*); formerly fashion asst to Valentino Rome, subsquently lectr in fashion Kingston Poly, opened own menswear shop Soho 1985, expanded to womenswear exporting to NY, LA, Tokyo, Paris and Milan, first collection shown London 1987, currently shows regularly in London and Paris; BFC Designer of the Year Award 1989; *Style*— Richard Nott, Esq; ✉ Workers for Freedom Ltd, 6 Spice Court, London SW11 3UE

NOTTINGHAM, Bishop of (RC) 1974–; Rt Rev James Joseph McGuinness; s of Michael McGuinness, and Margaret, *née* McClean; *b* 2 Oct 1925; *Educ* St Columb's Coll Derry, St Patrick's Coll Carlow, Oscott Coll Birmingham; *Career* ordained 1950, curate St Mary's Derby 1950–53, sec to Bishop Ellis 1953–56, parish priest Corpus Christi Parish Clifton Nottingham 1956–72, vicar gen Nottingham Diocese 1969, coadjutor Bishop of Nottingham and titular Bishop of St German 1972; *Recreations* gardening; *Style*— The Rt Rev the Bishop of Nottingham; ✉ Bishop's House, 27 Cavendish Rd East, The Park, Nottingham NG7 1BB (☎ 0115 947 4786, fax 0115 947 5235)

NOULTON, John David; s of John Noulton (d 1993), of London, and Kathleen, *née* Sheehan; *b* 5 Jan 1939; *Educ* Clapham Coll; *m* 7 Oct 1961, Anne Elizabeth, da of Edward Byrne (d 1985); 3 s (Mark John b 1963, Stephen Anthony b 1965, Simon Anthony b 1966), 1 da (Jane Antonina b 1968); *Career* asst princ Dept of Tport 1970–72, princ DOE 1972–76, private sec to Min of State Rt Hon Denis Howell, MP 1976–78, sec Property Servs Agency 1978–81, under sec Dept of Tport 1985–89 (asst sec 1981–85); dir British Channel Tunnel Co plc 1982–89, chm Channel Tunnel Intergovernmental Cmmn 1989, dir Marine and Ports 1989, admin dir Transmanche Link 1989–92, dir public affairs Eurotunnel PLC 1992–; friend of Richmond Park, memb Kingston Soc; MCIT 1986, FRSA 1992, companion memb ICE 1994; *Recreations* walking, riding, boating, writing, music; *Style*— John Noulton, Esq; ✉ 12 Ladderstile Ride, Kingston Hill, Coombe, Surrey KT2 7LP (☎ 0181 546 3855); Eurotunnel PLC, One Canada Square, Canary Wharf, London E14 5DU (☎ 0171 715 6641)

NOURSE, Christopher Stuart; s of Rev John Nourse (sometime succentor of St George's Chapel Windsor Castle and precentor of Canterbury Cathedral), of Devon, and

Helen Jane Macdonald, *née* Allison (d 1992); *b* 13 Aug 1946; *Educ* Hurstpierpoint Coll, Univ of Edinburgh (LLB), Middle Temple; *Career* legal exec Life Offices Assoc 1970–72; various managerial positions: Royal Opera House, English Opera Gp, Royal Ballet New Group 1972–76; gen mangr and admin Sadler's Wells Royal Ballet 1976–90, admin dir The Birmingham Royal Ballet 1990–91, asst to Gen Dir Royal Opera House 1991–96, admin dir and co sec Royal Opera House Tst 1996–; *Recreations* the performing and visual arts, eating out, the Orient, the countryside; *Style*— Christopher Nourse, Esq; ✉ Royal Opera House, Covent Garden, London WC2E 9DD (☎ 0171 240 1200, fax 0171 379 7057)

NOURSE, Rt Hon Lord Justice; Rt Hon Sir Martin Charles; kt (1980), PC (1985); s of late Henry Edward Nourse, MD, MRCP, of Cambridge, and Ethel Millicent, da of Rt Hon Sir Charles Henry Sargant, Lord Justice of Appeal; *b* 3 April 1932; *Educ* Winchester, Corpus Christi Coll Cambridge; *m* 1972, Lavinia, da of late Cdr David Malim; 1 s (Harry b 1977), 1 da (Charlotte b 1975); *Career* 2 Lt (Nat Service) Rifle Bde 1951–52, London Rifle Bde Rangers (TA) 1952–55, Lt 1953; called to the Bar Lincoln's Inn 1956, bencher 1978, memb Gen Cncl of the Bar 1964–68, jr counsel to Bd of Trade in Chancery Matters 1967–70, QC 1970, attorney-gen Duchy of Lancaster 1976–80, judge of the Courts of Appeal of Jersey and Guernsey 1977–80, judge of the High Court of Justice (Chancery Div) 1980–85, a Lord Justice of Appeal 1985–, pres Cncl of Inns of Ct 1992–95; hon fell Christi Coll Cambridge 1988, fell Winchester 1993; *Style*— The Rt Hon Lord Justice Nourse; ✉ Royal Courts of Justice, Strand, London WC2A 2LL

NOVE, Charles; s of Prof Alec Nove (d 1994), of Glasgow, and Irene, *née* MacPherson; *b* 29 June 1960; *Educ* Kelvinside Acad Glasgow; *m* 1983, Anne Elizabeth, *née* McDougall; 2 s (Jamie b 12 Dec 1988, Andrew b 2 July 1992); *Career* presenter BBC Radio Scotland 1978–81; BBC Radio 2: announcer 1981–89, presenter Night-time 1982–, presenter Cinema Two 1988–91; freelance broadcaster (also voice over work for radio and TV commercials) 1989–; commentator/presenter Come Dancing (BBC TV) 1984–95, commentator UK Dance Championships (BBC TV) 1988–94; commentaries and voice overs on BBC TV progs incl: World Circus Championships, Moscow State Circus, Variety Club Awards, Sci-Tech Awards, Matchpoint, Points of View, presenter Variety Club Tribute to Shirley Maclaine 1990; presenter Lord Mayor's Show 1991; *Recreations* photography, aviation, music, Scottish highlands and islands; *Style*— Charles Nove, Esq; ✉ c/o Bryan Drew Ltd, Mezzanine, Quadrant House, 80–82 Regent St, London W1R 6AU (☎ 0171 437 2293, fax 0171 437 0561)

NOWAK, Krysia Danuta Michna; da of Sqdn Ldr Wladyslaw Jan Nowak (d 1982), and Henrietta Nowak (d 1994); *b* 18 March 1948; *Educ* Notre Dame GS Sheffield, Henry Hartland GS Workshop, Ealing Coll London (BA), Garnett Coll Univ of London (PGCE); *Career* artist; Br Cncl lectr Poznan Univ Poland 1977 and 1978, lectr American Inst of Foreign Study in Paris, Florence, Rome, Amsterdam and Munich 1979–82; held pt/t positions at: The Drian Galleries London 1973, The Grabowski Gallery London 1973, Inst of Contemporary Art London 1973, 359 Gallery Nottingham 1974 (asst), Sheffield City Art Galleries 1975–87 (art educn offr); freelance interior designer for hospitals and clinics 1991–; arts advsr Northern Gen Hosp 1992–; Sheffield City Cncl: memb Cleansing Dept Keep Br Tidy 1985–87, Dept of Land and Planning A City Centre for People 1985–87, arts designer and advsr Arundel Gate Scheme 1985–87, public subway mural Hollywood Parade Sheffield; voluntary work: League of Friends N Gen Hosp 1979–82, sec Polish Med Aid Appeal Sheffield 1981, organiser charity fashion show for Ethiopia Graves Art Gallery Sheffield 1985, organiser designer fashion show Wentworth House 1987; pres Worksop Soc of Artists 1976, tstee York Arts Space Assoc 1986–87, fndr memb Anglo-Polish Soc Sheffield 1986–87, memb Open Learning Ctee BBC Radio Sheffield 1986–87, memb Assoc of Polish Artists 1996; numerous paintings in public and private collections; *Solo Exhibitions* Drian Galleries, Waterloo Gallery, Stoke on Trent, Nottingham Playhouse, Crucible Theatre Sheffield, Philip Francis Gallery Sheffield, Worksop Library, Univ of Sheffield; *Awards* shortlisted for Woman of the Midlands 1987, winner Dulux 2nd Nat Prize for Community Arts Project 1987; *Books* Poland (contrib), The Planet of the Towers (illustrator, 1982); *Recreations* painting, cooking, travelling, design (interior design and graphics), mural painting; *Style*— Miss Krysia D Michna Nowak; ✉ 7 Graham Road, London NW4 3DH

NOWELL, Peter Jack; s of Roger Nowell (d 1991), of Reading, and Suzanne Elisabeth Nowell (d 1995); *b* 13 Oct 1948; *Educ* Reading Sch, LSE (MSc); *m* 1 May 1976, Wendy Margaret, da of Raymond Bonfield (d 1986); 2 da (Lucy b 1977, Emma b 1980); *Career* equity fund mangr Prudential Assurance Co Ltd 1971–81, fixed income dir Prudential Portfolio Managers 1982–87, chief exec Prudential Corporate Pensions 1988–90, gp chief actuary Prudential Corporation plc 1991–; FIA 1974; *Recreations* skiing; *Style*— Peter Nowell, Esq; ✉ Prudential Corporation, 142 Holborn Bars, London EC1N 2NH (☎ 0171 548 3152, fax 0171 548 3620)

NUGEE, Edward George; TD (1964), QC (1977); s of Brig George Travers Nugee, CBE, DSO, MC (d 1977), and Violet Mary Brooks, *née* Richards, of Henley-on-Thames, Oxon; *b* 9 Aug 1928; *Educ* Radley, Worcester Coll Oxford (BA, MA), Eldon Law Scholarship 1953; *m* 1 Dec 1955, Rachel Elizabeth Nugee, JP, da of Lt-Col John Moritz Makower, MBE, MC (d 1989), of Henley-on-Thames, Oxon; 4 s (John b 1956, Christopher b 1959, Andrew b 1961, Richard b 1963); *Career* Nat Serv RA 1947–49 (office of COS Far East Land Forces, Singapore 1948–49), TA serv Intelligence Corps 100 APIU 1950–64, ret Capt 1964; called to the Bar Inner Temple 1955 (bencher 1976, treas 1996) ad eundem Lincoln's Inn 1968, head of chambers; poor man's lawyer Lewisham CAB 1954–72, dep High Ct judge 1982–; memb: Bar Cncl 1961–65, CAB Advsy Ctee Family Welfare Assoc 1969–72, Ctee Gtr London CAB 1972–74, Mgmnt Ctee Forest Hill Advice Centre 1972–76, Cncl Legal Educn 1967–90 (chm bd of studies 1976–82), Common Professional Examination Bd 1976–89 (chm 1981–87), Advsy Ctee on Legal Educn 1971–90, Inst of Conveyancers 1971– (pres 1986–87); jr counsel to Land Cmmn 1967–71, counsel for litigation under Commons' Registration Act (1965) 1968–77; conveyancing counsel 1972–77 to: Treasy, WO, MAFF, Forestry Cmmn, MOD, DOE; Lord Chllr's Law Reform Ctee 1973–; conveyancing counsel of the Ct 1976–77; chm Ctee of Inquiry into Mgmnt of Privately Owned Blocks of Flats 1984–85; chm govrs Brambletye Sch 1972–77, memb Cncl Radley Coll 1975–95, churchwarden Hampstead Parish Church 1979–83, church cmmr 1990– (memb Bd of Govrs 1993–); *Books* Nathan on the Charities Act 1960 (jtly, 1962), Halsbury's Laws of England (3 edn Landlord and Tenant, jt ed 1958; Real Property, jt ed 1960; 4 edn Real Property, jt ed 1982); *Recreations* travel, history, church and family life; *Style*— Edward Nugee, Esq, TD, QC; ✉ 10 Heath Hurst Rd, Hampstead, London NW3 2RX (☎ 0171 435 9204); Wilberforce Chambers, 8 New Square, Lincoln's Inn, London WC2A 3QP (☎ 0171 306 0102, fax 0171 306 0095)

NUGENT, Christopher George Ridley; s and h of Sir Robin George Colborne Nugent, 5 Bt, *qv*; *b* 5 Oct 1949; *Educ* Eton, Univ of E Anglia; *m* 1985, Jacqueline, *née* Vagba; 3 s; *Style*— Christopher Nugent, Esq

NUGENT, Sir John Edwin Lavallin; 7 Bt (I 1795), of Ballinlough, Westmeath; 4 Count Nugent (Austrian Empire); er s of Sir Hugh Charles Nugent, 6 Bt (d 1983), and Margaret Mary Lavallin, *née* Puxley; *b* 16 March 1933; *Educ* Eton; *m* 1959, Penelope Anne, er da of Brig Richard Nigel Hanbury, CBE, TD, DL (d 1972); 1 s, 1 da (Grania Clare b 1969); *Heir* s, Nicholas Myles John Nugent b 17 Feb 1967; *Career* Lt Irish Gds; formerly JP Berks, High Sheriff of Berks 1981; *Recreations* gardening, shooting, fishing; *Clubs* Kildare and University (Dublin); *Style*— Sir John Nugent, Bt; ✉ Ballinlough Castle, Clonmellon, Navan, Co Meath, Ireland (☎ 00 353 46 33135)

NUGENT, John Michael; s of late James Patrick Nugent, and Beatrice May, *née* Peart; *b* 26 Jan 1942; *Educ* Stretford GS, Univ of Manchester (BA (Econ)); *m* 1967, Kay, da of late Thomas Thompson, of Barton Moss, Manchester; *Career* WCB Containers Ltd: sales dir 1971–72, md 1972–79, chm 1979–82; dir White Child & Beney Ltd 1973–80, chm White Child & Beney Group Ltd 1980–82; chm 1982–: The Stamford Group Ltd, Opto International Ltd, Opto International Inc, Mailbox International Ltd, Mailbox Mouldings Ltd, Micropol Ltd; *Recreations* golf, cricket, supporting Manchester United, travel; *Clubs* Mellor and Townscliffe Golf; *Style*— John M Nugent, Esq; ✉ 38 Fernwood, Marple Bridge, Cheshire SX6 5BE (☎ 0161 449 8567); The Stamford Group Ltd, Bayley St, Stalybridge, Cheshire SK15 1QQ (☎ 0161 330 6511)

NUGENT, Sir Peter Walter James; 5 Bt (UK 1831), of Donore, Westmeath; s of Sir Walter Richard Nugent, 4 Bt (d 1955); *b* 26 Jan 1920; *Educ* Downside; *m* 1947, Anne Judith, da of Maj Robert Smyth, of Gaybrook, Mullingar, Co Westmeath; 2 s ((Walter) Richard Middleton b 1947, Andrew Robert b 1951), 2 da (Fiona Georgina (Mrs John S Bellingham) b 1949, Laura Anne b 1954); *Heir* s, (Walter) Richard Middleton Nugent, *qv*; *Career* 2 Lt Hampshire Regt 1941 (and with 10 Baluch Regt in India), Maj 1945; Tattersall's Irish agent 1973–83; dir Tattersall's Newmarket and Tattersall's (Ireland); ret 1989; *Style*— Sir Peter Nugent, Bt; ✉ Baybush, Straffan, Co Kildare (☎ 01 6288541)

NUGENT, (Walter) Richard Middleton; s and heir of Sir Peter Walter James Nugent, 5 Bt, *qv*; *b* 15 Nov 1947; *Educ* Downside; *m* 1985, Okabe Kayoko; *Career* fin dir (Keiri Torishimariyaku) IMS Japan Kabushiki Kaisha; FCA 1970; *Recreations* gardening, piano; *Style*— Richard Nugent, Esq; ✉ 61–66 Yaguchi-dai, Naka-ku, Yokohama, 231, Japan

NUGENT, Sir Robin George Colborne; 5 Bt (UK 1806), of Waddesdon, Berkshire; s of Capt Sir (George) Guy Bulwer Nugent, 4 Bt (d 1970), and Maisie Esther, *née* Bigsby (d 1992); *b* 11 July 1925; *Educ* Eton, RWA Sch of Architecture; *m* 1, 1947 (m dis 1967), Ursula Mary, da of Lt-Gen Sir Herbert Fothergill Cooke, KCB, KBE, CSI, DSO (d 1936); 2 s (Christopher George Ridley b 1949, Patrick Guy b 1959), 1 da (Philippa Mary b 1951); m 2, 1967, Victoria Anna Irmgard, da of Dr Peter Cartellieri; *Heir* s, Christopher George Ridley Nugent, *qv*; *Career* Lt Grenadier Gds 1944–48; ARIBA; *Style*— Sir Robin Nugent, Bt

NUGENT, Sean Charles Weston; *b* 16 Feb 1965; *see:* Delvin, Sean Charles Weston Nugent

NUNAN, Manus; QC (1962); s of Manus Timothy Nunan, (d 1979); *b* 26 March 1926; *Educ* St Mary's Coll Dublin, Trinity Coll Dublin; *m* 1, 1960 (m dis), Anne Monique, da of Jean Fradin (d 1978); 1 da (Nathalie b 1961); m 2, 1971 (m dis), Anne, *née* Harrison; 1 s (Manus b 1972); m 3, 1987, Valerie, *née* Robinson; *Career* called to the Bar King's Inns 1950, ad eundem Gray's Inn 1956; Colonial Legal Servs 1953–64: crown counsel Nigeria 1953–62, slr gen Northern Nigeria 1962–64, min of Govt and memb Exec Cncl of Northern Nigeria 1962; recorder Crown Ct 1978–84; lectr since 1986 on: Life and Trials of Oscar Wilde, Dr Samuel Johnson and his circle, Talleyrand, Bernard Shaw, Oliver Gogarty, Never Listen to an Irishman (autobiographical lecture); Evelyn Wrench lectr English Speaking Union of US 1988, visiting lectr Broward Community Coll Florida US 1989; lectr: American Irish Historical Soc NY 1990, Nat Portrait Gallery 1991, Shaw Soc 1992; festival lectr: Bournemouth Int Festival 1992, Shirley Soc Cambridge 1993, Centre Cult Irlandais Paris 1994; *Clubs* Kildare St and Univ (Dublin); *Style*— Manus Nunan, Esq, QC; ✉ La Calmeraie, Route de l'Aude, 09110 Aix les Thermes, France (☎ 00 33 5 61 64 24 93)

NUNBURNHOLME, 4 Baron (UK 1906); Ben Charles Wilson; s of 3 Baron Nunburnholme (d 1974), and Lady Mary Thynne (d 1974), da of 5 Marquess of Bath; *b* 16 July 1928; *Educ* Eton; *m* 1958 (m dis), Ines Dolores Jean, da of HE Gerard Walravens, of Brussels; 4 da; *Heir* bro, Hon Charles Thomas Wilson; *Career* Capt RHG 1953, Maj 1962, resigned 1969; *Style*— The Rt Hon the Lord Nunburnholme; ✉ c/o House of Lords, London SW1

NUNDY, Julian William; s of George William Nundy, of Fairlight, East Sussex, and Lilian, *née* Eckersley; *b* 3 March 1947; *Educ* Archbishop Tenison's GS, Univ of Nottingham (BA), Kiev Univ USSR; *m* 26 Nov 1976, Fabienne Sylvie Marie Christine, da of Joseph Moullot (d 1983), 1 da (Sophie Marie Chloë b 23 May 1985); *Career* Reuters: joined 1970, corr Moscow 1971–74, corr Paris 1975–80, chief corr Brussels 1980–81; bureau chief Cairo Newsweek 1981–83 (Beirut 1981), International Herald Tribune 1983–89 (news ed, copy ed, corr), asst foreign ed Independent on Sunday 1989–91, corr Paris The Independent 1991–94; pres Anglo-American Press Assoc of Paris 1993–94; winner Mary Hemingway award The Overseas Press Club of America for the best magazine coverage from abroad (Israeli invasion of Lebanon); *Style*— Julian Nundy, Esq; ✉ 5 Passage d'Enfer, 75014 Paris (☎ 00 331 43 21 39 05, fax 00 331 43 21 39 51)

NUNN, Christopher Leslie; s of Walter Leslie Nunn (d 1990), and Beatrice Rose, *née* Jones (d 1989); *b* 14 March 1943; *Educ* Highgate Sch, LSE (BScEcon); *m* 15 Nov 1969, Lynne Margaret Rochelle, da of Cdr Richard Hosking Hughes (d 1994); 2 s (Richard b 1974, Peter b 1978); *Career* Arthur Andersen: joined 1965, qualified CA 1968, London office 1965–76, ptnr 1976, head of audit div Birmingham 1976–80, head of audit gp London 1980–90, i/c UK tech gp and risk mgmnt and compliance 1990–; memb urgent issues task force Accounting Standards Bd 1994–; FCA (memb Auditing Ctee 1994–); *Style*— Christopher Nunn, Esq; ✉ Arthur Andersen, 1 Surrey Street, London WC2R 2PS (☎ 0171 438 3570, fax 0171 831 1133)

NUNN, Rear Adm John Richard Danford; CB (1980); s of Surgn Capt Gerald Nunn, OBE (d 1967), and Edith Florence, *née* Brown; *b* 12 April 1925; *Educ* Epsom Coll, RN Engrg Coll (BSc), RN Coll Greenwich (MSc), Downing Coll Cambridge (MPhil); *m* 1951, Katharine Mary, da of Leonard Paris (d 1970); 3 da; *Career* RN, served: Home Fleet and British Pacific Fleet 1945 (HMS Devonshire, HMS Vengeance 1947), Korean and Malaysian Emergency 1950 (HMS Amethyst), Mediterranean 1957 (HMS Tiger), Home Fleet and Far East 1967 (HMS Glamorgan); chief engr Sea Dart 1968–70, Cabinet Office 1970–73, NATO Defence Coll 1974–75, SACLANT 1975–78, Port Admiral Rosyth 1978–80; fell commoner Downing Coll Cambridge 1980, ed The Naval Review 1980–83, bursar and official fell Exeter Coll Oxford 1981–88; vice chm of govrs Peter Symond's Coll Winchester 1992–; *Recreations* sailing (yacht 'Solenteer'), tennis, gliding, travel; *Clubs* Naval, Royal Naval Sailing Assoc; *Style*— Rear Adm John Nunn, CB; ✉ Warner's Cottage, Keepers Hill, Corhampton, Southampton, Hants SO32 3LL (☎ 01489 877287); 2 Sadler Walk, St Ebbe's, Oxford OX1 1DP (☎ 01865 244681)

NUNN, Trevor Robert; CBE (1978); s of Robert Alexander Nunn, and Dorothy May, *née* Piper; *b* 14 Jan 1940; *Educ* Northgate GS Ipswich, Downing Coll Cambridge (BA), Univ of Newcastle upon Tyne (MA); *m* 1, 1969 (m dis 1986), Janet Suzman, *qv*; 1 s (Joshua b 1980); m 2, 1986 (m dis 1991), Sharon Lee, *née* Hill; 2 da (Laurie b 1986, Amy b 1989); m 3, 1994, Imogen Stubbs, *qv*; 1 da (Ellie b 1991), 1 s (Jesse b 1996); *Career* theatre and film director; Belgrade Theatre Coventry: The Caucasian Chalk Circle, Peer Gynt, Around the World in Eighty Days (musical); Royal Shakespeare Co (assoc dir 1964–68, chief exec and artistic dir 1968–78, chief exec and jt artistic dir 1978–86); dir for RSC: The Revenger's Tragedy, The Relapse, The Alchemist, Henry V, The Taming of the Shrew, King Lear, Much Ado About Nothing, The Winter's Tale, Henry VIII, Hamlet, Antony and Cleopatra (also for ATV, BAFTA Award for Best Single Play Prodn), Hedda Gabler (also as a film), Macbeth (also for Thames TV), Coriolanus, Julius Caesar, Titus Andronicus, Romeo and Juliet, The Comedy of Errors (also for ATV, musical version - Ivor Novello Award for Best British Musical, SWET Award for Best

Musical), The Alchemist, As You Like It, Once in a Life-time (Plays and Players London Theatre Critics' Award - Best Production, New Standard Drama Awards - Sydney Edwards Award for Best Director), Three Sisters, Nicholas Nickleby (New Standard Drama Awards - Sydney Edwards for Best Director, SWET Award for Best Director, Drama Review London Theatre Critics' Award - Best Production, Tony Award - Best Director, special citation as Outstanding Broadway Production in All Categories, Emmy Award - Best Best TV Serial; shown on TV in London and NY, with John Caird), Juno and the Paycock (Drama Review London Theatre Critics' Award - Best Revival), Henry IV Parts I and II, All's Well That Ends Well, Peter Pan (with John Caird), Les Miserables (London and Worldwide, with John Caird), Fair Maid of the West, Othello (also for BBC TV), The Blue Angel (Stratford 1991, Globe 1992), Measure for Measure (Stratford) 1991 (Young Vic) 1992; freelance dir: Cats (worldwide, Tony Award - Best Director of a Musical) 1981, Idomeneo (Glyndebourne Opera) 1982, Starlight Express (London and NY) 1984, Lady Jane (film) 1985, Chess (London and NY) 1986, Porgy and Bess (Glyndebourne Opera 1986, Royal Opera House 1992), Aspects of Love (London and NY) 1989, The Baker's Wife 1989, Timon of Athens (Young Vic Theatre, Evening Standard Award for Best Dir) 1991, Cosi Fan Tutte (Glyndebourne Opera) 1991, Heartbreak House (Yvonne Arnaud Guildford and Haymarket) 1992, Arcadia (RNT 1993, Haymarket 1994, NY 1995), Sunset Boulevard (London and Los Angeles 1993, NY 1994), Twelfth Night (film) 1996; memb Arts Council 1994–96; artistic dir RNT 1997–; *Books* A; *Style*— Trevor Nunn, Esq, CBE; ✉ Homevale Ltd, Third Floor, 140a Gloucester Mansions, Cambridge Circus, London WC2H 8HD (☎ 0171 240 5435, fax 0171 240 1945)

NUNNELEY, Charles Kenneth Roylance; s of Robin Michael Charles Nunneley, of Holt, Norfolk, and Patricia Mary, *née* Roylance, of Pluckley, Kent; *b* 3 April 1936; *Educ* Eton; *m* 1961, Catherine Elizabeth Armstrong, da of Sir Denys Burton Buckley, of London; 1 s (Luke b 1963), 3 da (Alice b 1964, Clare b 1967, Frances b 1969); *Career* 2 Lt Scots Gds, served chiefly BAOR; merchant banker; Robert Fleming Holdings: dir 1968–96, dep chm 1986–96, former chm or dir of various other Fleming Gp cos; chm: Save & Prosper Group (Fleming subsid) 1989–96, Fleming Income & Capital Investment Trust 1993–, Nationwide Building Society 1996– (dir 1994–), Monks Investment Trust 1996– (dir 1977–); dep chm Clerical Medical & General Life Assurance Society 1978–96 (dir 1974–96); dir: Macmillan Ltd 1982–95, HM Publishers Holdings 1995–96; chm: Institutional Fund Mangrs' Assoc 1989–92, Investmt Mgmnt Regulatory Orgn (IMRO) 1992– (dir 1986–); memb Panel on Takeovers and Mergers; govr Oundle Sch 1975–; Nat Tst: chm 1996–, chm Fin Ctee 1991–96, memb Exec Ctee 1992–, memb Cncl 1992–; memb Court of Assts Worshipful Co of Grocers 1975– (Master 1982–83); CA 1961; *Recreations* walking, shooting, photography; *Style*— C K R Nunneley, Esq; ✉ Nationwide Building Society, Hogarth House, 136 High Holborn, London WC1V 6PW (☎ 0171 826 2121)

NUNNERLEY, Dr Heather Bell; *Educ* Calder High Sch, Univ of Liverpool (state scholar, MB ChB DObst RCOG, DMRD, MRCP); *Career* house physician then house surgn Royal Southern Hosp Liverpool 1956–57; SHO: in child health Alder Hey Children's Hosp Liverpool 1957–58, in obstetrics Mill Road Maternity Hosp Liverpool 1958–59; in gen practice Stafford 1959–65 (princ 1960–65); King's Coll Hosp: trainee registrar in radiology 1965–67, sr registrar in radiology 1967–74 (Br Inst of Radiology scholarship to Stockholm 1972), gp conslt in radiology 1974–86, dir Dept of Diagnostic Radiology 1986–96, care gp dir of diagnostic radiology and nuclear med 1987–96; dir SE London Breast Screening Serv 1987–; Royal Coll of Radiologists: memb Faculty Bd of Radiodiagnosis 1984–86, memb Cncl 1986–89, past vice pres Mammography Gp, chm Clinical Dirs' Gp 1992–96; chm: Regional Higher Awards Ctee SE Thames 1991–94, Conslts' Ctee King's Healthcare 1993–95, S Thames (E) Regional Radiology Speciality Ctee; formerly pres Radiology Section RSM, memb Advsy Gp in Radiology to Dept of Health 1988–92; recognised teacher Univ of London, former examiner for final fellowship Royal Coll of Radiologists in London and overseas; author of various articles in learned jls; FRCR; *Style*— Dr Heather B Nunnerley; ✉ Diagnostic Radiology Department, King's College Hospital, Denmark Hill, London SE5 9RS (☎ 0171 737 4000, fax 0171 346 3445)

NURSAW, Sir James; KCB (1992, CB 1983), QC (1988); s of William George Nursaw, FCIS, ACII (d 1994), and Lilian May, *née* Howell; *b* 18 Oct 1932; *Educ* Bancroft's Sch, Christ's Coll Cambridge (MA, LLB); *m* 29 Aug 1959, Eira, da of E W Caryl-Thomas (d 1968); 2 da (Margaret (Mrs Hallybone), Catherine); *Career* Nat Serv Flying Offr RAF; called to the Bar Middle Temple 1955; sr res offr Univ of Cambridge Dept of Criminal Sci 1958, joined Home Office 1959, legal sec Law Officers Dept 1980–83, legal advsr Home Office and NI Office 1983–88, HM Procurator Gen and Treasy slr 1988–92, bencher Middle Temple 1989, counsel to Chm of Ctees House of Lords 1992–; Liveryman Worshipful Co of Loriners; *Clubs* United Oxford and Cambridge Univ, MCC; *Style*— Sir James Nursaw, KCB, QC

NURSE, Dr Paul Maxime; *b* 25 Jan 1949; *Educ* Harrow County GS, Univ of Birmingham (BSc, John Humphrey's meml prize), UEA (PhD); *m* 2 da; *Career* res asst Microbiology Dept Twyford Laboratories 1967, Royal Soc res fell Inst of Microbiology Univ of Bern Switzerland 1973, SERC res fell Dept of Zoology Univ of Edinburgh 1974–78 (advanced res fell 1978–80), MRC sr res fell Sch of Biology Univ of Sussex 1980–84, head of Cell Cycle Control Laboratory Imperial Cancer Res Fund London 1984–87, Iveagh prof of microbiology Univ of Oxford 1987–91, Napier res prof of the Royal Soc at Univ of Oxford 1991–, DG Imperial Cancer Research Fund Sept 1996– (previously dir of res Laboratories); visiting prof Univ of Copenhagen 1981; author of over 100 pubns in learned jls; speaker at over 200 seminars in res insts worldwide, speaker chm and organiser at over 30 int meetings and confs dealing with yeast molecular biology and genetics and cell cycle and growth control; memb: EMBO 1987, Ctee UK Genetical Soc 1987 (pres 1990–94), EMBL Scientific Advsy Ctee 1989; FRS 1989; *Awards* Fleming lectr Soc of Gen Microbiology 1985, Florey lectr Royal Soc 1990, Marjory Stephenson lectr Soc of Gen Microbiology 1990, CIBA Medal UK Biochemical Soc 1991, Louis Jeantet Prize for Medicine Switzerland 1992, Gairdner Fndn Int Award 1992, Royal Soc Wellcome Medal 1993, Jimenez Diaz Meml Award Spain 1993, Rosenstiel Award and Medal USA 1993, Dunham lectr Harvard 1994, Purkyne Medal Czech Republic 1994, Pezcoller Award for Oncology Research Italy 1995, Bradshaw lectr RCP London 1995, Royal Soc Royal Medal 1995, Dr Josef Steiner Prize Switzerland 1996, Dr H P Heineken Prize for Biochemistry and Biophysics The Netherlands 1996; *Style*— Dr Paul Nurse, FRS; ✉ Director General, Imperial Cancer Research Fund, PO Box 123, Lincoln's Inn Fields, London WC2A 3PX (☎ 0171 269 3436, fax 0171 269 3610)

NURSTEN, Prof Harry Erwin; s of Sergius Nursten (d 1950), of Ilkley, and Helene, *née* Breslauer (d 1971); *Educ* Ilkley GS, Univ of Leeds (BSc, PhD, DSc); *m* 23 Dec 1950, Jean Patricia, da of Arnold Frobisher (d 1972), of Leeds, and Hilda, *née* Wood (d 1991); *Career* Bradford Dyers' Assoc res fell Dept of Colour Chemistry Univ of Leeds 1949–52, lectr in dyeing and textile chemistry Nottingham and Dist Tech Coll 1952–54; Univ of Leeds: lectr Dept of Leather Industs 1955–65, assoc lectr Dept of Organic Chemistry 1962–65, sr lectr Procter Dept 1965–70, reader Procter Dept 1970–76; Univ of Reading: prof of food sci 1976–92, head of dept 1976–86, head Dept of Food Sci and Technol 1986–89, head Sub-Dept of Food Sci 1989–91, prof emeritus 1992–; MIT: res assoc Dept of Nutrition, Food Sci and Technol 1961–62, fell Sch for Advanced Study 1962; visiting prof: Dept of Food Sci and Technol Univ of Calif Davis 1966, Inst of Food, Nutrition and Family Science Univ of Zimbabwe 1994; memb ARC/MRC Ctee on Food and Nutrition Res Working Pty on Non-Nutritive Constituents of Foods 1971–73; Bill Littlejohn Meml Medallion lectr Br Soc of Flavourists 1974; pres Soc of Leather Technologists and Chemists 1974–76, chief examiner Inst of Food Sci and Technol 1982–90 (examiner 1978–81); Br Cncl assignments to: Malaysia 1982 and 1988, Portugal 1988 and 1990, Cyprus 1990, Zimbabwe 1991; memb: Soc of Dyers and Colourists 1945, Soc of Chemical Indust 1951, Chemical Soc 1951, Sigma Xi 1962, FRIC 1957, FIFST 1972, inaugural fell Soc of Leather Technologists and Chemists 1986 (memb 1955); *Books* Azo and Diazo Chemistry (trans, 1961), Progress in Flavour Research (ed jtly, 1979), Key Mechanistic Problems Posed by the Maillard Reaction incl: The Maillard Reaction in Food Processing, Human Nutrition and Physiology (1990), Analytical Aspects of Thearubigins incl: Recent Advances in the Chemistry and Biochemistry of Tea (1994); numerous scientific papers; *Style*— Prof Harry Nursten; ✉ Department of Food Science and Technology, University of Reading, Whiteknights, PO Box 226, Reading RG6 6AP (☎ 0118 931 6725, fax 0118 931 0080)

NURTON, Brig (John) Michael Anthony; OBE, MC; s of Francis John Nurton (d 1989), and Rhoda Winifred, *née* Morgan (d 1983); *b* 22 Jan 1940; *Educ* Wellington Coll, Trinity Coll Cambridge; *m* 28 Oct 1972, (Elizabeth Ann) Annabel, da of J R Catchpole and Mrs T R Bland; 1 s (George b 22 Mar 1976), 1 da (Katherine b 9 June 1974); *Career* cmmnd Scots Gds 1961, 1 Bn Scots Gds in Far East and UK 1961–69, Staff Coll Camberley 1973, Cmd 9 Bn UDR 1981–83, MA to Dep Chief of Def Staff 1983–86, Cmd 56 London Bde 1988–91, Dir IT Strategy MOD 1991, Dir Logistic IT Systems 1991–95, ret; defence conslt 1995–; *Recreations* sailing, real tennis, skiing; *Clubs* Royal Yacht Squadron, Cavalry and Guards'; *Style*— Brig Michael Nurton, OBE, MC

NUSSEY, Dr Ian David; OBE (1988); s of Dr Adolph Marcus Nussey (d 1993), and Susannah Rayner Nussey (d 1981); *b* 4 April 1936; *Educ* Bromsgrove Sch, Downing Coll Cambridge (MA, Engrg Assoc prize), Univ of Birmingham (PhD); *m* 1976, Gillian Patricia, da of Dr Thomas Russell and Enid Stanley Stevens; 2 da (Emma Frances Guest b 1966 (step da), Jessica Clare b 1977); *Career* Lucas Industries 1958–62, IBM United Kingdom Ltd 1963– (mangr Warwick Devpt Gp); contrib to various jls associated with mfrg and info technol; various public service appts; visiting prof: Univ of Loughborough 1973–76, Univ of Newcastle 1976–, Univ of Salford 1983–94, Univ of Wales 1986–; memb Cncl Univ of Warwick 1989–; vice pres: Inst of Mfrg Engrs 1990–91, IEE 1995– (chm Mfrg Div 1991–92); memb Senate Engrg Cncl; winner Sargent award Soc of Mfrg Engrs USA 1988; Freeman City of London, Liveryman Worshipful Co of Engrs 1983; FEng 1985, FIEE, FIMechE, FBCS, FRSA; *Recreations* gardening, theatre going, canal restoration, skiing, golf; *Clubs* Athenaeum; *Style*— Dr Ian Nussey, OBE, FEng; ✉ Cidermill Farm House, Ardens Grafton, nr Alcester, Warwickshire B49 6DS (☎ 01789 773356); IBM United Kingdom Ltd, PO Box 31, Warwick CV34 5JL (☎ 01926 464192, fax 01926 311345)

NUTE, (Patricia) Jill; da of Cyril John Tomkin, of Mawgan Porth, Cornwall, and Margaret Elizabeth, *née* Owens; *b* 26 Dec 1946; *Educ* Our Lady's Convent Sch Barrow-in-Furness, Ulverston GS, Univ of Liverpool (BVSc, MRCVS, rep England Br Univs Riding Clubs Assoc Int Championships 1968 and Euro Univ Riding Championships Munich 1970, full colours and Royal Blue); *m* 10 Oct 1970, Geoffrey Nute, s of Nehemiah Gordon Philip Nute (d 1986); 2 s (Rupert Geoffrey b 4 Nov 1978, Alistair Thomas b 30 Nov 1980), 1 da (Claire Louise (twin) b 30 Nov 1980); *Career* asst: Hargreaves Fox and Rushton mixed vet practice Lake District 1970, Moody and Beach Droitwich 1971–72, P W Laing Leominster 1972–76; in own practice (with husb) Wadebridge Cornwall 1976–; official vet surgn N Cornwall DC 1988–95, princ official vet surgn Meat Hygiene Serv MAFF 1995; memb Cncl: BVA 1976–92, RCVS 1993– (treas 1996–); pres Soc of Practising Vet Surgns 1991–92; *Books* First Aid and Care of Wildlife (jtly, 1984); *Recreations* reading, gardening, Pony Club, picking fleas off six cats who share the household; *Clubs* RSM; *Style*— Mrs Jill Nute; ✉ The Veterinary Surgery, Fair Park Road, Wadebridge, Cornwall PL27 7NT (☎ 01208 813258, fax 01208 815301)

NUTKINS, Terry; *Career* television personality specialising in marine and other animals; worked with elephants London Zoo aged 8, with otters for naturalist and author Gavin Maxwell aged 12; BBC: advsr on dolphin filming for Animal Magic 1977, presenter (with Johnny Morris) Animal Magic 1980–85, presenter Really Wild Show 1985– (winner BAFTA Award), Really Wild Roadshows 1990–, Animal Corner (BBC Radio 4) 1987–90, Growing Up Wild 1993, 1994 and 1995, own weekly prog Radio 5 1993, prodr and presenter commercial videos for Sea Life Centres Notts County Cncl 1994 and 1995, narrator Really Wild Animal Tape (audio cassette) 1995; numerous guest appearances on other TV and radio children's, entertainment and documentary progs, BBC live roadshows and exhibitions, pantomimes and stage presentations; author of various articles on natural history for Watch, BBC Wildlife, Countryside and other magazines; *Books* Nutkins on Pets (1989); *Style*— Terry Nutkins, Esq; ✉ c/o John Miles Organisation, Cadbury Camp Lane, Clapton-in-Gordano, Bristol BS20 9SB (☎ 01275 854675, fax 01275 810186)

NUTTALL, Prof Anthony David; s of Kenneth Nuttall (d 1975), of Worthing, Sussex, and Hilda Mary, *née* Addison; *b* 25 April 1937; *Educ* Hereford Cathedral Sch, Watford GS, Merton Coll Oxford (BA, BLitt); *m* 1960, Mary, da of Ernest Percy Donagh; 1 s (William James b 24 July 1965), 1 da (Mary Addison b 22 June 1967); *Career* Univ of Sussex: lectr 1962–1970, reader in English 1970–73, prof of English 1973–84, pro-vice-chllr 1978–81; Univ of Oxford: fell New Coll 1984, tutor for graduates New Coll 1985–89, reader in English 1990–92, prof of English 1992–; *Books* Two Concepts of Allegory (1967), A Common Sky: Philosophy and the Literary Imagination (1974), Dostoevsky's Crime and Punishment: Murder as Philosophical Experiment (1978), Overheard by God (1980, South East Arts literature prize), A New Mimesis (1983), Pope's Essay on Man (1984), Timon of Athens (1989), The Stoic in Love (1989), Openings (1992), Why Does Tragedy Give Pleasure (1996); *Recreations* walking, looking at architecture; *Style*— Prof A D Nuttall; ✉ New College, University of Oxford, Oxford OX1 3BN (☎ 01865 279555, fax 01865 279590)

NUTTALL, Christopher Guy; s of Derek Reginald Nuttall, of Northwich, Cheshire, and Doris Joan Bentley, *née* Johnson; *b* 16 Aug 1957; *Educ* Sir John Deane's GS Northwich Cheshire, UCL (BA); *m* 1993, Nishanthri Wickramasinghe, of Colombo, Sri Lanka; 1 da (Constance Geneva b 16 Oct 1995); *Career* journalist; Warrington Guardian Series newspapers 1978–81; BBC: journalist 1982–, foreign corr BBC World Serv 1988, Sri Lanka corr 1988–90, Washington corr BBC World Serv 1991–93, foreign affrs corr BBC World Serv 1994–95, Ankara corr BBC World Service 1995–; *Recreations* cycling, cinema, computers; *Style*— Christopher Nuttall, Esq; ✉ c/o BBC World Service News, Bush House, The Strand, London WC2B 4PH (☎ 0171 240 3456)

NUTTALL, Christopher Peter; *b* 20 April 1939; *Educ* Univ of Keele (BA), Univ of California (MA); *Career* Home Office: res offr 1963–66, sr res offr 1966–72, head res projects (criminal justice) 1972–74, on staff Crime Policy Planning Unit 1974–75, princ res offr 1971–75; Miny of the Solicitor General Canada: dir of Res Programmes 1975–79, dir of Res Div 1979–80, asst dep slr gen Programs Branch 1982–87, asst dep slr gen Corrections Branch 1987–89; asst under sec of state and dir of res and statistics Home Office 1989–; memb: Fed/Provincial Task Force on Nat Criminal Justice Statistics, Fed Deputy Mins Ctee on AIDS; co-chair: Fed/Provincial Working Gp on Justice for Victims of Crime, Miny of the Slr Gen/Voluntary Sector Co-ordinating Ctee; UK delegate to UN Congress on Crime 1990; fndr: Nat Crime Prevention Week (Canada) 1983,

Fed/Provincial Programme on Women In Conflict With The Law 1983–88; fell UN Human Rights Inst 1967–68; author of numerous articles in jls; *Style*— Christopher Nuttall, Esq; ✉ Home Office, 50 Queen Anne's Gate, London SW1H 9AT (☎ 0171 273 2616, fax 0171 273 3674)

NUTTALL, Rev Derek; MBE (1990); s of Charles William Nuttall (d 1956), of Codnor Park, Derbyshire, and Doris Nuttall (d 1976); *b* 23 Sept 1937; *Educ* Somercotes Secdy Sch Derbyshire, Overdale Theol Coll Selly Oak Birmingham; *m* 24 July 1965, Margaret Hathaway (d 1993), da of Rev Principal Arthur Lawson Brown (d 1984); 2 s (David b 2 May 1969, Andrew b 12 May 1971), 1 da (Alison b 30 March 1967); *Career* semi skilled industl work 1953–60, office clerk 1960–61, Theol Coll 1961–65, Ministry Falkirk 1965–67, ordained 1967, vice chm Central Scotland Branch The Samaritans, miny and community work Aberfan 1967–74, dir CRUSE Bereavement Care 1978–90 (nat organiser 1974–78), minister Windsor United Reformed Church 1990–; chaplain: Thames Valley Hospice Windsor 1993–, King Edward VII Hosp Windsor 1992–; gen sec: Community Assoc, Church and Community Ctees; memb Exec of Int Fedn of Widow/Widower Organisations 1980–89, sec Working Pty on Social and Psychological Aspects of Disasters 1989–91, chm Churches Together in Windsor 1992–95, convenor Pastoral Cmmn URC Reading and Oxford District 1995–; *Books* Early Days of Grieving (1991); *Recreations* golf, reading, music; *Style*— The Rev Derek Nuttall, MBE; ✉ 10 Clifton Rise, Windsor, Berkshire (☎ 01753 854558); Christ Church United Reformed Church, William St, Windsor, Berkshire

NUTTALL, Harry; s and h of Sir Nicholas Keith Lillington Nuttall, 3 Bt, *qv*; *b* 2 Jan 1963; *m* 27 April 1996, Kelly Marie, o da of Anthony E Allen, of Raleigh, N Carolina, and Mrs Susanne Allen Haley, of Orlando, Florida; *Career* racing driver; *Clubs* British Racing Drivers', White's; *Style*— Harry Nuttall, Esq; ✉ 5 Redcliffe Square, London SW10 9LA

NUTTALL, Sir Nicholas Keith Lillington; 3 Bt (UK 1922), of Chasefield, Parish of Bowdon, Co Chester; s of Lt-Col Sir (Edmund) Keith Nuttall, 2 Bt (d on active service 1941); *b* 21 Sept 1933; *Educ* Eton, RMA Sandhurst; *m* 1, 1960 (m dis 1971), Rosemary Caroline, da of Christopher York, DL, sometime MP for Ripon, of Long Marston Manor, Long Marston; 1 s (Harry b 1963), 1 da (Tamara b 1967); m 2, 1971 (m dis 1975), Julia Jill Beresford, da of Col Thomas Williamson, DSO (d 1987), and former w of Darel Sausmarez Carey; m 3, 1975 (m dis 1983), Miranda Elizabeth Louise, former w of late Peter Richard Henry Sellers, CBE, the actor, and da of Richard St John Quarry; 3 da (Gytha Miranda b 1975, Amber Louise b 1976, Olympia Jubilee b 1977); m 4, 1983, Eugenie Marie Alicia, eldest da of William Thomas McWeeney; 1 s (Nicholas Alexander David b 1985); *Heir* s, Harry Nuttall, *qv*; *Career* Maj RHG, ret 1968; *Clubs* White's; *Style*— Sir Nicholas Nuttall, Bt; ✉ PO Box N7776, Nassau, Bahamas (☎ 00 1 809 32 67938)

NUTTALL, (Benjamin William) Stuart; MBE (1990), JP (Chesterfield); s of William Nuttall (d 1972), and Eleanor, *née* Broomhead; *b* 14 Jan 1933; *Educ* Lady Manners GS Bakewell, Leicester Coll of Advanced Technol, Chesterfield Coll of Technol; *m* 19 Feb 1955, Eileen Margaret, da of Francis Joseph Eady (d 1977); 2 da (Jacqueline (Mrs Thornhill) b 24 April 1958, Caroline (Mrs Ludlam) b 8 Oct 1959); *Career* Nat Serv RAF 1951–53; mgmnt trainee to prodn mangr heavy tube div Tube Investmts Ltd 1953–66, prodn mangr Cable Div Aerialite Ltd 1966–68, plant mangr Corby Tube Works 1968–70, dep md USI Engrg 1970–72, md The Clay Cross Co 1972–; chm Biwater Industries Ltd until 1994, corporate dir Biwater Ltd until 1994; dir: N Derbys C of C and Indust, vice-pres Chesterfield and Dist Bowls Assoc; pres Clay Cross div St John Ambulance Bde until 1995, chm Leonard Cheshire Homes Alfreton Derbyshire 1996–; memb Worshipful Co of Founders, Freedom City of London 1988; CEng 1967, FIProdE 1960, FIBF 1977, FIQ 1982, FIIM 1979, FInstD 1985; *Recreations* motor sport, horse breeding, various sporting activities; *Clubs* Aston Martin Owners', RAC; *Style*— Stuart Nuttall, Esq, MBE, JP; ✉ The Spinney, Ashover Rd, Woolley Moor, Alfreton, Derbys DE55 6FF (☎ 01246 590266)

NUTTGENS, Patrick John; CBE (1982); s of Joseph Edward Nuttgens (d 1982), and Kathleen Mary, *née* Clarke (d 1937); *b* 2 March 1930; *Educ* Ratcliffe Coll Leicester, Univ of Edinburgh (MA, PhD), Edinburgh Coll of Art (DipArch); *m* 21 Aug 1954, Bridget Ann, da of Dr Alexander Guthrie Badenoch (d 1964), of Edinburgh; 6 s (Nicholas, James, Kurt, Giles, Alexander, Tom) 3 da (Lucy, Susan, Peggy); *Career* lectr Univ of Edinburgh 1957–62, prof Univ of York 1968–70 (reader 1962–68), dir Leeds Poly 1970–86; chm: York Georgian Soc 1970–93 (sec 1962–70), York Theatre Royal 1990–; Royal Cmmn on Historical Monuments for Scotland, Royal Fine Art Cmmn 1983–90; memb Building Review Team Leonard Cheshire Fndn 1993–; reg contrib A Word in Edgeways (radio), memb N of England team Round Britain Quiz (BBC Radio 4); DUniv: York 1985, Open Univ 1985; DLitt: Univ of Sheffield 1985, Heriot Watt Univ 1990; ARIBA, FRSA, ARIAS; *Books* Landscape of Ideas (1972), York the Continuing City (1974), Leeds (1979), Mitchell Beazley Pocket Guide to Architecture (1980), Story of Architecture (1983), Understanding Modern Architecture (1988), What Should We Teach And How Should We Teach It? (1988), The Home Front (1989); *Television* Sir Edwin Lutyens, Cuthbert Broderick, Aspects of Modern Architecture, Social Housing (new series); *Recreations* reading, writing, drawing, broadcasting; *Style*— Patrick Nuttgens, Esq, CBE; ✉ Roselea Cottage, Terrington, York, YO6 4PP (☎ 01653 84408)

NUTTING, Rt Hon Sir (Harold) Anthony; 3 Bt (UK 1902), of St Helens, Booterstown, Co Dublin, PC (1954); s of Lt-Col Sir Harold Stansmore Nutting, 2 Bt (d 1972); *b* 11 Jan 1920; *Educ* Eton, Trinity Coll Cambridge; *m* 1, 1941 (m dis 1959), Gillian Leonora, da of Edward Jolliffe Strutt; 2 s (John Grenfell, David Anthony, *qqv*), 1 da (Zara Nina b 1947); m 2, 1961, Anne Gunning (d 1990), da of Arnold Barthrop Parker, of Cuckfield, Sussex; m 3, 1991, Margarita, da of Carlos Sanchez; *Heir* s, John Grenfell Nutting b 28 Aug 1942; *Career* serv Leicestershire Yeo 1939–40, served France, Spain and Italy 1940–45; MP (C) Melton 1945–56, jt Parly under sec of state for Foreign Affairs 1951–54, min of state 1954–56, ldr UK Delegation to UN Assembly and to UN Disarmament Cmmn 1954–56; resigned 1956; chm: Young Conservative Movement 1946, Cons Nat Union 1950, Cons NEC 1951; special writer New York Herald Tribune 1957–59; author; *Books* Lawrence of Arabia (1961), The Arabs (1964), Gordon of Khartoum (1966), No End of a Lesson (1967), Scramble for Africa (1968), Nasser (1972); *Style*— The Rt Hon Sir Anthony Nutting, Bt; ✉ Achentoul, Kinbrace, Sutherland

NUTTING, David Anthony; DL (Essex 1988); yr s of Rt Hon Sir (Harold) Anthony Nutting, 3 Bt, *qv*; *b* 13 Sept 1944; *Educ* Eton, Trinity Coll Cambridge (MA); *m* 25 April 1974, Tessa Anne, o da of Sir Nigel John Mordaunt, 13 Bt, MBE (d 1979); 3 da (Belinda b 18 Aug 1975, Serena b 24 Nov 1977, Alexandra b 27 Dec 1978); *Career* chm: Strutt & Parker (Farms) Ltd 1987–, Select Sires Ltd 1982–89, Bridge Farm Dairies Ltd 1987–95; dir: Lavenham Investments Ltd, Lavenham Fen Farms Ltd; chm: Essex Agric Soc 1985–90, Br Cattle Breeders Club 1978–79; memb Advsy Bd Inst of Animal Physiology 1983–86; pres Holstein Friesian Soc 1990; tstee Cambridge Univ Veterinary Sch Tst 1994; Freeman Worshipful Co of Farmers 1975; *Recreations* fishing, shooting, racing; *Style*— David Nutting, Esq, DL; ✉ Whitelands, Hatfield Peverel, Chelmsford, Essex CM3 2AG (☎ 01245 382224, fax 01245 381942)

NUTTING, Prof Jack; s of Edgar Nutting (d 1973), of Mirfield, W Yorkshire, and Ethel, *née* France (d 1985); *b* 8 June 1924; *Educ* Univ of Leeds (BSc, PhD), Univ of Cambridge (MA, ScD); *m* 1, 4 Sept 1950, Thelma (d 1994), da of Thomas Kippax (d 1967), of Morecambe; 1 s (Peter Robert b 1961), 2 da (Alison Rosemary (Mrs Murray) b 1953, Jean Ruth (Mrs Tyson) b 1957); m 2, 1995, Diana Kathleen, wid of Cedric Walters; *Career* lectr Dept of Metallurgy Univ of Cambridge 1954–60 (demonstrator 1949–54); Univ of Leeds: prof of metallurgy and head of dept 1960–89, emeritus prof 1989; visiting prof of metallurgy Univ of Barcelona Spain 1991–; former pres: Inst of Metallurgists, The Metals Soc, Hist Metallurgy Soc; pres Richard Thorpe Soc Mirfield Free GS 1986–94; Beilby Medal and Prize 1964, Hatfield Medal and Prize 1967, Platinum Medal 1988; Hon DSc: Acad Mining and Metallurgy Krakow Poland 1969, Univ of Moratuwa Sri Lanka; FIM 1960, FEng 1981; *Books* The Microstructure of Metals (1965); *Recreations* walking, photography, cooking, gardening; *Style*— Prof Jack Nutting, FEng; ✉ 19 Cliveden Mead, Maidenhead, Berks SL6 8HE (☎ and fax 01628 770063)

NUTTING, John Grenfell; QC (1995); s and h of Rt Hon Sir (Harold) Anthony Nutting, 3 Bt, *qv*; *b* 28 Aug 1942; *Educ* Eton, McGill Univ Canada (BA); *m* 1973, Diane, da of Capt Duncan Kirk, and widow of 2 Earl Beatty; 1 s (James Edward Sebastian b 1977), 1 da (Victoria Emily b 1975), 1 step s, 1 step da; *Career* called to the Bar Middle Temple 1968, bencher 1991; first sr treasy counsel 1993–95 (jr treasy counsel 1981, first jr treasy counsel 1987–88, sr treasy counsel 1988–93), recorder of the Crown Court 1986–, judge of the Cts of Appeal of Jersey and Guernsey 1995–; memb Bar Cncl 1976–80 and 1986–87, chm Young Bar 1978–79, vice chm Criminal Bar Assoc 1995–; *Clubs* White's, Pratt's; *Style*— John Nutting, Esq, QC; ✉ 3 Raymond Buildings, Gray's Inn, London WC2; Chicheley Hall, Newport Pagnell, Bucks MK16 9JJ; K3, Albany, Piccadilly, London

NUTTING, Peter Robert; JP (Inner London 1978); s of Capt Arthur Ronald Stansmore Nutting, OBE, MC (d 1964), of N Breache Manor, Ewhurst, and Patricia Elizabeth, *née* Jameson; *b* 22 Oct 1935; *Educ* Cheam, Eton; *m* 1965, Cecilia Hester Marie-Louise, da of Cosmo Rea Russell, of Lenham, Kent; 2 s, 1 da; *Career* Lt Irish Gds, Suez Canal 1955–56; stockbroker; ptnr W I Carr & Sons Co 1963–67, last chm E & J Burke Ltd 1965–68 (gf, Sir John Nutting, 1 Bt, was first chm); chm: IGI Insurance Co Ltd, FMW International Insurance Brokers Ltd; conslt and dir of a number of public and private cos; former memb Cncl Lloyd's; Liveryman Worshipful Co of Gunmakers; landowner (350 acres); *Recreations* shooting, fishing, tennis, golf, sailing; *Clubs* Royal Yacht Squadron, Boodle's, Pratt's, MCC; *Style*— Peter Nutting, Esq, JP; ✉ North Breache Manor, Ewhurst, Surrey (☎ 01483 277328); 103 More Close, St Paul's Court, London W14 (☎ 0181 846 9734)

NYE, Prof John Frederick; s of Hadyn Percival Nye, MC (d 1977), of Hove and Old Marston, and Jessie Mary, *née* Hague (d 1950); *b* 26 Feb 1923; *Educ* Stowe, King's Coll Cambridge (MA, PhD); *m* 28 Dec 1953, Georgiana, da of Walter Ernest Wiebenson, of Bellingham, Washington, USA; 1 s (Stephen b 1960), 2 da (Hilary b 1957, Carolyn b 1963); *Career* univ demonstrator Dept of Mineralogy Univ of Cambridge 1949–51, memb Tech Staff Bell Telephone Labs N Jersey USA 1952–53; Univ of Bristol: lectr 1953–65, reader 1965–69, prof 1969–85, Melville Wills prof of physics 1985–88, emeritus prof 1988–; pres: Int Glaciological Soc 1966–69, Int Cmmn of Snow and Ice 1971–75; Antarctic Serv medal USA 1974; FRS 1976, foreign memb Royal Swedish Acad of Sci; *Books* Physical Properties of Crystals (2 edn, 1985); *Recreations* gardening; *Style*— Prof John Nye, FRS; ✉ 45 Canynge Rd, Bristol BS8 3LH (☎ 0117 973 3769); H H Wills Physics Laboratory, Tyndall Ave, Bristol BS8 1TL (☎ 0117 928 8727)

NYE, Robert Thomas; s of Oswald William Nye (d 1990), of Southend-on-Sea, Essex, and Frances Dorothy, *née* Weller; *b* 15 March 1939; *Educ* Southend HS; *m* 1, 1959 (m dis 1967), Judith Pratt; 3 s (Jack, Taliesin, Malory); m 2, 1968, Aileen, da of Robert Campbell (d 1972), of Whang House, Beith, Ayrshire; 1 da (Rebecca), 1 step s (Owen), 1 step da (Sharon); *Career* poet, novelist and critic; gen literary reviewer The Scotsman 1962–, reviewer of new fiction The Guardian 1966–92, poetry ed The Scotsman 1967–, poetry critic The Times 1971–96, gen literary reviewer The Times 1996–; FRSL 1977; *Awards* Eric Gregory award 1963, Scottish Arts Cncl bursary 1970 and 1973 and publication award 1970 and 1976, James Kennaway memorial award 1970, Guardian Fiction prize 1976, Hawthornden prize 1977, Soc of Authors' travelling scholarship 1991; *Poems* Juvenilia 1 (1961), Juvenilia 2 (1963), Darker Ends (1969), Agnus Dei (1973), Two Prayers (1974), Five Dreams (1974), Divisions on a Ground (1976), A Collection of Poems 1955–88 (1989), 14 Poèmes (1994), Henry James and other Poems (1995), Collected Poems (1995); *Novels* Doubtfire (1967), Falstaff (1976), Merlin (1978), Faust (1980), The Voyage of the Destiny (1982), The Memoirs of Lord Byron (1989), The Life and Death of My Lord Gilles de Rais (1990), Mrs Shakespeare: The Complete Works (1993); *Short Stories* Tales I Told My Mother (1969), The Facts of Life and Other Fictions (1983); *Editions* A Choice of Sir Walter Ralegh's Verse (1972), William Barnes of Dorset: A Selection of his Poems (1973), A Choice of Swinburne's Verse (1973), The Faber Book of Sonnets (1976), The English Sermon 1750–1850 (1976), PEN New Poetry (1986), First Awakenings: The Early Poems of Laura Riding (with Elizabeth Friedmann and Alan J Clark, 1992), A Selection of the Poems of Laura Riding (1994); *Plays* Sawney Bean (with William Watson, 1970), The Seven Deadly Sins: A Mask (1974), Penthesilea, Fugue and Sisters (1975); *Stories for Children* March Has Horse's Ears (1966), Taliesin (1966), Beowulf (1968), Wishing Gold (1970), Poor Pumpkin (1971), Once Upon Three Times (1978), Out of the World and Back Again (1977), The Bird of the Golden Land (1980), Harry Pay the Pirate (1981), Three Tales (1983), Lord Fox and Other Spine-Chilling Tales (1997); *Recreations* gambling; *Style*— Robert Nye, Esq; ✉ c/o Sheil Land Associates, 43 Doughty St, London WC1N 2LF (☎ 0171 405 9351)

NYMAN, Bernard Martin; s of Raymond Nyman, of Chigwell, Essex, and Jean, *née* Geffner (d 1984); *b* 27 Feb 1954; *Educ* Royal Liberty Sch Gidea Park Essex, Univ of Sheffield (BA Law); *m* July 1986, Carole Gloria, da of Harold Stern; 2 da (Jessica b 29 Nov 1988, Ella b 9 June 1993); *Career* articled clerk Wedlake Bell London 1977–79, admitted slr 1979, slr Rubinstein Callingham 1979–83, ptnr Rubinstein Callingham 1983–94 (merged with Manches & Co), ptnr Manches & Co 1994– (specialising in intellectual property law with particular reference to publishing industry); memb: Law Soc 1979, Int Assoc of Entertainment Lawyers 1993; *Publications* The Encyclopaedia of Forms and Precedents (Butterworths, contrib to Copyright section Vol 21, 1991, revision in progress), Adams: Character Merchandising (Butterworths, contrib 2 edn 1996); *Recreations* jazz, films, theatre, family; *Style*— Bernard Nyman, Esq; ✉ Manches & Co, Aldwych House, 81 Aldwych, London WC2B 4RB (☎ 0171 404 4433, fax 0171 430 1133)

NYMAN, Dr Cyril Richard; s of James Nyman (d 1955), and Rose Caroline, *née* James (d 1992); *b* 19 May 1943; *Educ* Malmesbury GS Wilts, Univ of London (MB BS, LRCP, MRCS); *m* 6 June 1970, Jill Elizabeth, da of Robert Charles Ricketts; 1 da (Sarah b 1976); *Career* HS Professorial Surgical Unit St Mary's Hosp London 1968, registrar gen and thoracic med St Thomas's Hosp London 1971–75, sr registrar cardiorespiratory med St Mary's Hosp 1975–79, conslt physician in cardiorespiratory med pilgrim Hosp Lincs 1979–; clinical tutor Univ of Leicester; chm Pilgrim Scanner Appeal; pres: Pilgrim Heart and Lung Fund, Boston Branch Br Heart Fndn, memb: Br Lung Fndn, Br Cardiac Soc, Br Thoracic Soc, Br Soc of Echocardiography; awarded Illuminated Scroll Boston for services to community 1992; DRCOG 1970, FRCP 1987 (MRCP 1971); *Books* Some Common Medical Disorders (1988), Heart and Lung Disease (1989); *Recreations* swimming, jogging, shooting, archery, music; *Clubs* Boston Swimming, Harlequin FC, Skegness RFC (vice pres), Spilsby Rotary; *Style*— Dr Cyril R Nyman; ✉ Stoke Lodge, 116 Tower Road, Boston, Lincs PE21 9AU (☎ 01205 351748), Pilgrim Hospital, Sibsey Road, Boston, Lincs PE21 9QS (☎ 01205 364801)

O

OAKELEY, Dr Henry Francis; s of Rowland Henry Oakeley, of Chipping Campden, Glos, and Diana Margaret, *née* Hayward; *b* 22 July 1941; *Educ* Clifton, St Thomas's Hosp Med Sch, Univ of London (MB BS); *m* 20 Jan 1968 (m dis 1988), Penelope Susan, da of late Dr Wilfred Barlow; 2 s (Matthew Thomas b 15 Dec 1968, Edward James b 29 March 1970), 1 da (Rachel Mary b 15 Jan 1973); *Career* house offr and sr house offr St Thomas' Hosp, Nat Hosp Queen Square and Frenchay Hosp 1965–69, registrar St Thomas' Hosp, Maudsley Hosp and St George's Hosp 1970–72, sr registrar Maudsley Hosp 1972–73, conslt psychiatrist St Thomas' Hosp 1973–96, ret; holder nat collection of Lycastes and Anguloas for which awarded RHS Gold medals Chelsea 1990, 1991, 1992, and Holford medal 1991 and 1992; RHS: memb Cncl, Orchid Ctee, Orchid Registration Advsy Ctee, Picture Ctee, Bursaries and Expeditions Ctee, chm Pubns Ctee, chm Shows Ctee; chm The Hort Club London, vice chm Orchid Soc of GB, pres S London Botanic Inst, sec Advsy Ctee Chelsea Physic Garden, res assoc Royal Botanic Gardens Kew; Liveryman Worshipful Soc of Apothecaries 1974, Freeman City of London 1980; MRCPsych 1972, FRCP 1989 (MRCP 1969), FLS 1993; *Publications* Richard Oakeley, Royalist and Country Gentleman 1580–1653 (1989), Lycaste Species, The Essential Guide (1993), many articles on lycastes and anguloas in American Orchid Soc Bulletin, Orchid Review, Die Orchideen, Orchid Digest, etc; *Recreations* orchids, gardening, history of medicine, genealogy; *Clubs* Horticultural; *Style*— Dr Henry Oakeley; ✉ 77 Copers Cope Road, Beckenham, Kent BR3 1NR (☎ 0181 658 0358, fax 0181 658 0359, e-mail 100552.416@COMPUSERVE.COM)

OAKELEY, Sir John Digby Atholl; 8 Bt (GB 1790), of Shrewsbury; s of Sir (Edward) Atholl Oakeley, 7 Bt (d 1987); *b* 27 Nov 1932; *Educ* by private tutor; *m* 1958, Maureen Frances, da of John Cox (d 1965), of Hamble, Hants; 1 s (Robert John Atholl b 13 Aug 1963), 1 da (Marina Anne (Mrs Robert Gordon) b 1961); *Heir* s, Robert John Atholl Oakeley b 13 Aug 1963; *Career* md Dehler Yachts UK; winner 20 Nat, 3 Euro and 2 World Championships in various sailing craft, rep GB in the Americas Cup and in Olympics (sailing); author; *Books* Winning, Downwind Sailing, Sailing Manual; *Recreations* sailing (yacht 'Daylight'); *Clubs* Warsash Sailing; *Style*— Sir John Oakeley, Bt; ✉ 10 Bursledon Heights, Long Lane, Bursledon, Hants (☎ 01703 560446); Dehler Yachts UK, Hamble Point, Hamble, Hants (☎ 01703 458260)

OAKES, Sir Christopher; 3 Bt (UK 1939), of Nassau, Bahama Islands; s of Sir Sydney Oakes, 2 Bt (d 1966); *b* 10 July 1949; *Educ* Bredon Tewkesbury, Georgia Military Acad USA; *m* 1978, Julie Dawn, da of Donovan Cowan, of Canada; 1 s (Victor b 1983), 1 da (Greta Anna Eunice b 1979); *Heir* s, Victor Oakes b 7 March 1983; *Style*— Sir Christopher Oakes, Bt; ✉ Site 15, Comp 18 RR7, Vernon, BC V1T 7Z3, Canada

OAKES, Christopher John; s of William Oakes (d 1970), and Kathleen Self; *b* 13 Aug 1955; *Educ* Butley Modern Sch Suffolk, Ipswich Civic Coll Suffolk, Colchester Tech Coll Essex; *m* 16 June 1984, Caroline, da of Nowell Dyrek Scott; *Career* apprentice (under Mr Malcolm Long) Seckford Hall Hotel Woodbridge Suffolk 1971–73, apprentice and commis Le Talbooth Restaurant Dedham Essex 1973–74, chef tournant Post Hotel Davos Switzerland 1974–75, sr chef de partie and sous chef (under Mr Sam Chalmers) Le Talbooth Restaurant Dedham Essex 1975–77, Gleneagles Hotel Scotland 1977, understudy to Mr Colin Cooper-English Plough Restaurant Clanfield Oxon 1977–78, sous chef (under Mr Chris Oakley) Pier at Harwich Essex 1978–80, head chef The Castle Hotel Taunton 1983–86 (sous chef under Mr John Hornsby 1980–83), chef/proprietor Oakes Restaurant Stroud Glos 1986–95, exec chef The Stafford St James's Place London 1995–; nominated in 10 Star Chefs of Tomorrow AA Guide 1984, rosette AA Guide 1984–86 and 1988–91 (3 rosettes 1992–95, 2 rosettes 1997), star in Michelin Guide 1984–87 and 1989–95, star in Egon Ronay Guide 1984–86 and 1988–95, entry in Good Food Guide 1985–86 and 1988–95, entry Good Hotel Guide 1984–85, entry Ackerman Guide 1987–88 and received White 4–leaf Clover award 1989–90, 1990–91, 1991–92, 1992–93, 1993–94 and 1994–95; Master Chef of GB 1986 (assoc memb Inst of Master Chefs of GB 1983–86); Grand Officier du Cordon Bleu Culinaire, Epicurien Prix d'Excellence Gastronomique de Circle Epicurien Mondial; *Recreations* reading and collecting cookery books, walking; *Style*— Christopher Oakes, Esq; ✉ c/o The Stafford, St James's Place, London SW1A 1NJ (☎ 0171 493 0111, fax 0171 493 7121)

OAKES, Rt Hon Gordon James; PC (1979), MP (Lab) Halton (majority 18,204); s of James Oakes (d 1957), of Widnes, and Florence, *née* Hewitt (d 1969); *b* 22 June 1931; *Educ* Wade Deacon Sch Widnes, Univ of Liverpool (BA); *m* 11 Sept 1952, Esther, da of Joseph O'Neill (d 1976), of Widnes; 3 s (Howard b 1956, Timothy b 1960, Julian b 1963); *Career* admitted slr 1956; Mayor Widnes 1964–65 (elected Borough Cncl 1952), chm Widnes Lab Pty 1953–58; Parly candidate (Lab): Bebington 1959, Moss Side Manchester (by-election) 1961; MP (Lab): Bolton W 1964–70, Widnes 1971–83, Halton 1983–; Parly under sec for: environment 1974–76, energy 1976; oppn front bench spokesman on environment (incl local govt) 1970–74 and 1979–83, min of state DES 1976–79; memb: Br delgn NATO Parliamentarians 1967–70, Race Rels Select Ctee 1969–70, NW Regnl Exec Lab Pty, Cwlth Parly Assoc Exec Ctee 1979–; vice-pres: Inst of Public Health Insprs ACC 1983–, Bldg Societies Assoc 1984–; *Recreations* caravanning, travel; *Style*— The Rt Hon Gordon Oakes, MP; ✉ House of Commons, London SW1A 0AA (☎ 0171 219 4139)

OAKES, Judith Miriam; MBE (1987); da of Geoffrey Redford Oakes, of 37 Copse Avenue, West Wickham, Kent, and Marjorie Olive Oakes; *b* 14 Feb 1958; *Educ* Bullers Wood Secdy Sch; *Career* athlete; memb Croydon Harriers 1971–, jr UK int 1974–76, 77 sr UK caps 1976–91 and 1994–; achievements at shot put: Gold medal Cwlth Games 1982 and 1994 (Silver 1986 and 1990, Bronze 1978), Bronze medal Euro Indoor Championships 1979, fourth place Olympic Games 1984, winner 37 Br titles; achievements at powerlifting: world champion 1981, 1982, 1988 (runner up 1983 and 1990), Euro champion 1983–90, Br champion 10 times; achievements at weightlifting: Bronze medal clean and jerk World Championships 1988, Bronze medal snatch and overall World Championships 1989, Gold medal snatch and overall Euro Championships 1989 (Silver clean and jerk), Gold medal clean and jerk and overall Euro Championships 1990 (Silver snatch), first all sections EEC Championships 1990; records: UK shot put, various UK powerlifting and weightlifting, most Br titles; bank clerk 1976–82, self-employed fitness coach Wimbledon FC 1982–85, lectr in fitness Raworth Centre Coll 1986–91; currently: admin CCAS (co involved in charitable donations), admin work Millwall FC, asst team mangr England Athletics Assoc (women) 1993; athletes' rep BAAB 1983–84, life memb Br Amateur Weightlifting Assoc; *Recreations* cooking Chinese food, science fiction books and films, memb WWF, conscious of environmental issues; *Style*— Miss Judith Oakes, MBE; ✉ ICAS Marketing, 2 Gipsy Hill, Crystal Palace, London SE19 1NL

OAKES, Richard; *Career* guitarist and pianist; joined Suede Sept 1994; UK no 21 single Together (double A-side with New Generation) 1995, Trash 1996; album: Coming Up (1996, UK no 1); *Style*— Richard Oakes, Esq; ✉ c/o Interceptor Enterprises, The Greenhouse, 34–38 Provost Street, London N1 7NG (☎ 0171 490 8460, fax 0171 490 8372)

OAKES, Robin Geoffrey; s of Geoffrey Albert Oakes, of Norwich, and Doris Florence, *née* Catton; *b* 18 Feb 1946; *Educ* City of Norwich Sch, Univ of Birmingham (BCom); *m* 16 Aug 1969, Lorna Hazel, da of Albert O'Neill; 3 da (Claire Lorna b 8 April 1972, Helen Esther b 1 July 1974, Juliet Elizabeth b 14 Aug 1980); *Career* articled clerk Coopers & Lybrand 1968–71 (later gp audit mangr); Neville Russell: joined as nat audit and accounts tech mangr 1981–83, sr mangr 1983–84, ptnr 1985– (managing ptnr London Office, memb firm's Nat Cncl); seminar speaker and author of various articles; FCA 1979 (ACA 1971); *Books* Business Briefing - Insurance Brokers (1985, latest edn 1996), An Industry and Accounting Guide: Insurance Brokers (1990, 2 edn 1994); *Recreations* church leadership, family, garden; *Clubs* Lloyds; *Style*— Robin Oakes, Esq; ✉ Neville Russell, 24 Bevis Marks, London EC3A 7NR (☎ 0171 377 1000, fax 0171 377 8931)

OAKES, William Lyness; OBE (1987); s of William Lyness Oakes (d 1964), and Hilda Mary, *née* Hardy (d 1970); *b* 20 Feb 1919; *Educ* Bedford Sch, Guy's Hosp (LDSRCS); *m* 1, 1 Oct 1942, Joan Anne (d 1972), da of late Maj T L Squires, OBE; 1 s (Robert b 1948), 2 da (Wendy b 1944, Susan b 1950); m 2, 2 Feb 1974, Helen Patricia, da of Howard Green, of Bussage, Stroud, Glos; *Career* dental surgn RN 1942–46; in private practice 1946–81; hon dental surgn: Gloucester Infirmary 1947–48, Horton Rd Hosp 1947–48; chm Glos Local Dental Ctee 1968–80, former memb SW Region Dental Advsy Ctee, chm Glos Family Practitioner Ctee 1977–90 (memb 1974–90), memb Glos CC 1981–89, chm Glos Tourist Jt Ctee 1986–89, vice pres Heart of Eng Tourist Bd 1989– (exec memb 1981–89, chm Devpt Ctee 1986–89); *Recreations* gardening, music, meeting people; *Style*— William Oakes, Esq, OBE; ✉ Birds Frith Farm, Far Oakridge, Stroud, Glos GL6 7PB (☎ 01285 760482)

OAKESHOTT, Matthew Alan; s of Keith Robertson Oakeshott, CMG, of Horsham, Sussex (d 1974), and Jill Oakeshott, *née* Clutterbuck; *b* 10 Jan 1947; *Educ* Charterhouse, Univ Coll and Nuffield Coll Oxford (scholar, MA); *m* 1976, Dr Philippa Poulton, da of Dr Christopher Poulton; 2 s (Joseph Andrew b 1979, Luke Christopher b 1985), 1 da (Rachel Jill b 1982); *Career* economist Kenya Miny of Fin and Econ Planning 1968–70, special advsr to Rt Hon Roy Jenkins, MP 1972–76, investmt mangr then dir Warburg Investment Management Ltd (now Mercury Asset Management) 1976–81, investmt mangr Courtaulds Pension Fund 1981–85, fndr and jt md OLIM Ltd 1986–; jt investmt dir: Value & Income Trust plc 1986–, OLIM Convertible Trust plc 1989–; investmt advsr GEC Pension Funds 1995–; city cncllr Oxford 1972–76; parly candidate: (Lab) Horsham and Crawley Oct 1974, (SDP/Lib Alliance) Cambridge 1983; memb SDP Nat Ctee 1981–82; *Books* By-Elections in British Politics (contrib, 1974); *Recreations* music, elections, supporting Arsenal; *Style*— Matthew Oakeshott, Esq; ✉ OLIM Limited, Pollen House, 10–12 Cork Street, London W1X 1PD (☎ 0171 439 4400)

OAKLEY, Prof Celia Mary; da of Arthur Howard Oakley (d 1963), of Guildford, Surrey, and Minnie Isabel, *née* Stevenson (d 1989); *b* 14 May 1931; *Educ* Berkhamsted Sch, Royal Free Hosp Sch of Med Univ of London (MRCS, LRCP, MB BS, MRCP, FRCP, MD, Winifred Ladds prize in physiology, Walter Culverwell prize in anatomy, Edward Hanson prize in physiology, AM Bird prize for pre-clinical studies, Proxime Accessit Univ Gold medal, Helen Prideaux prize for the pre-registration year); *m* 11 June 1960, Dr Ronald Blackwood Pridie, s of George Pridie; 1 s (Peter b 1968 (decd)), 2 da (Susan b 1961, Alison b 1965); *Career* house physician: Royal Free Hosp 1955 (house surgn 1954), Brompton Hosp 1955; res pathologist Royal Free Hosp 1956, house physician to the Cardiac Dept Brompton Hosp 1957, house physician and sr house offr Nat Hosp for Nervous Diseases 1957, registrar Dept of Med Hammersmith Hosp 1957–60, res fell Cardiopulmonary Laboratory Univ of Rochester and Strong Meml Hosp USA 1960–61; Hammersmith Hosp and The Royal Postgrad Med Sch: sr registrar Dept of Med (Cardiology) and tutor in med 1961–63, asst lectr in med 1963–64, lectr in med and hon conslt physician 1965–67, sr lectr in med (Cardiology) 1967–74, currently prof of cardiology; hon conslt cardiologist St Mary's Hosp London; examiner MRCP 1982–; Univ of London: recognised teacher 1969, examiner Dip in Cardiology 1984–; memb: Cncl Br Cardiac Soc 1977–80, Cncl RCP 1978–81 (censor 1988–90), Cncl Thoracic Soc 1978–81, Transplant Advsy Panel Dept of Health 1982–88, Ctee on Safety of Med 1992–95; author of numerous med articles in learned jls; memb Editorial Bd: Jl of Internal Medicine 1990–, Int Jl of Cardiology 1990–; memb: Assoc of Physicians of GB and I, Br Cardiac Soc, Euro Soc of Cardiology, American Coll of Cardiology, MRS, Int Med Soc, RSM (past vice pres Clinic Section), BMA, Int Soc and Fedn of Cardiology (past chm Cncl on Cardiomyopathies and memb Scientific Bd); hon memb Pakistan, Colombian, Venezuelan, Chilean, Peruvian and Hellenic Socs of Cardiology; *Recreations* country pursuits, travelling; *Clubs* RCP; *Style*— Prof Celia M Oakley; ✉ Long Crendon Manor, Long Crendon, Bucks HP18 9DZ (☎ 01844 208246); Hammersmith Hospital, Du Cane Road, London W12 0NN (☎ 0181 383 3141, fax 0181 740 8373)

OAKLEY, Christopher John; s of Ronald Oakley (d 1965), of Tunbridge Wells, Kent, and Joyce Barbara, *née* Tolhurst; *b* 11 Nov 1941; *Educ* The Skinners Sch Tunbridge Wells; *m* 8 Oct 1962 (m dis 1986), Linda Margaret, da of William John Edward Viney, of Tunbridge Wells; 1 s, 2 da; m 2, Moira Jean, da of H Martingale; 2 step da, 1 s; *Career* dep ed Yorkshire Post 1976–81, ed Lancashire Evening Post 1981–83; dir: Lancashire Evening Post Ltd 1982–83, Liverpool Daily Post and Echo Ltd 1983–89; ed in chief/md Birmingham Post and Mail Ltd 1989–91; pres Guild of British Newspaper Editors 1990–91, gp chief exec Midland Independent Newspapers Ltd 1991–; *Style*— Christopher Oakley, Esq; ✉ Midland Independent Newspapers plc, PO Box 18, 28 Colmore Circus, Queensway, Birmingham B4 6AX (☎ 0121 234 5611, fax 0121 233 0173)

OAKLEY, Dr (George) David Gastineau; s of Douglas Edward Oakley, and Barbara Mary, *née* Earle; *b* 26 April 1948; *Educ* Rugby, Cambridge Univ (MB BChir, MA), Westminster Med Sch; *m* 29 Sept 1979, Clare Elizabeth, da of Christopher Brent-Smith;

1 s (Sam b 1982), 1 da (Charlotte b 1988); *Career* former sr house offr and registrar City General Hosp Stoke-on-Trent, registrar cardiology Hammersmith Hosp 1977–79; Northern Gen Hosp Tst Sheffield: sr registrar 1979–84, currently conslt cardiologist N Trent Regnl Health Authy (hon appointment Univ of Sheffield); articles: ischaemic heart disease, pregnancy and heart disease, athletes hearts; memb: Br Cardiac Soc, Ctee Br Heart Fndn; FRCP 1988 (MRCP 1975); *Recreations* music, skiing; *Style*— Dr David Oakley; ✉ Cardiothoracic Unit, Northern General Hospital Trust, Sheffield S5 7AU (☎ 0114 243 4343 ext 4953)

OAKLEY, Geoffrey Michael Whittall; s of Harold Whittall Oakley, of St Martins, Guernsey, and Hazel Louise, *née* Peters; *b* 22 April 1953; *Educ* Oundle; *m* 3 April 1987, Joanna Helen, da of Fred Morgan Hodges, of Harborne, Birmingham; 1 s (Nicholas Frederick James b 1989), 2 da (Georgina Louise b 1987, Olivia Sarah Helen b 1990); *Career* ptnr Margetts & Addenbrooke 1977–86; non-exec dir: Aero Needles Group plc 1976–84, Margetts Financial Services Ltd 1985; dir: National Investment Group plc 1986–90, Capel-Cure Myers Capital Management 1990–, J A Main Ltd; MSI (memb Stock Exchange 1976), memb Int Stock Exchange 1976; *Recreations* theatre, local history, antiques; *Style*— Geoffrey Oakley, Esq; ✉ St Mary's Close, 10 St Mary's Rd, Harborne, Birmingham B17 OHA (☎ 0121 427 7150); Capel-Cure Myers Capital Management, York House, 38 Great Charles St, Birmingham B3 3JU (☎ 0121 200 2002)

OAKLEY, Margaret Mary; da of Roger Dickinson (d 1951), and Hilda, *née* Smart (d 1951); *b* 3 Sept 1928; *Educ* Notre Dame Leeds, Mount Pleasant Training Coll Liverpool; *m* Aug 1950, Kenneth Oakley; 2 s (Martin b Nov 1952, Christopher b Oct 1954); *Career* athletics administrator; involved in schools athletics 1948–, involved in club and county athletics admin 1954–, team official England and GB athletic teams 1965–86 (incl Olympic Games 1976 and 1980, Cwlth Games 1978, 1982 and 1986); chm Women's Amateur Athletic Assoc 1983–91 (hon sec Northern Counties WAAA 1965–91), memb Br Amateur Athletics Bd 1980–91, memb Cncl Br Athletic Fedn 1991–95, pres N of England Athletic Assoc 1993–94; life vice pres Athletic Assoc of England; primary sch teacher 1948–89 (headteacher for 16 years); *Style*— Mrs Margaret Oakley; ✉ 10 Byemoor Close, Great Ayton, North Yorks TS9 6LY (☎ 01642 723182)

OAKLEY, Michael Dudley; s of Lt Cdr (George) Eric Oakley, RN (d 1996), of Clifton on Teme, Worcester, and Dr Margaret Dorothy Dudley, *née* Brown (d 1993); *b* 5 Nov 1944; *Educ* Oundle, Coll of Law; *m* 7 Oct 1967, Jennifer Catherine, da of Richard Percy Lazenby (d 1987), of Bulmer, York; 1 s (William b 3 Oct 1973), 2 da (Catherine b 2 Nov 1969, Victoria b 6 Nov 1971); *Career* slr; former ptnr Oakleys, currently conslt Crombie Wilkinson & Oakley; HM coroner N Yorks 1979–, NP 1985–; lay memb Gen Synod C of E representing diocese of York 1980–95; memb: Working Party on Ordination of Women to the Priesthood, Cathedral Statutes Cmmn, various legislative revision ctees, panel of chm of Gen Synod; non-exec dir North Yorks Ambulance Tst; pt/t chm: CSA Tbnl, SSAT Tbnl; clerk and co sec Queen Margaret's Sch (York) Ltd; pres Yorkshire Law Soc 1991–92; *Recreations* tennis, swimming, fishing, shooting; *Clubs* Sloane; *Style*— Michael Oakley, Esq; ✉ Rose Cottage, Oswaldkirk, York YO6 5XT (☎ 01439 788339, fax 01439 788037); Crombie Wilkinson & Oakley, 4 Old Malton Gate, Malton, N Yorks YO17 0EQ (☎ 01653 600070, fax 01653 600049, car tel 0860 789957)

OAKLEY, Robin Francis Leigh; s of Joseph Henry Oakley, of East Molesey, Surrey, and Alice Barbara Oakley; *b* 20 Aug 1941; *Educ* Wellington Coll, BNC Oxford (MA); *m* 4 June 1966, Carolyn Susan Germaine, da of late Leonard Rumball; 1 s (Alexander Guy Leigh b 12 Aug 1973), 1 da (Annabel Louise Germaine b 19 July 1971); *Career* political corr Liverpool Daily Post 1967–70 (feature writer then sub ed 1964–67), Crossbencher columnist then asst ed Sunday Express 1970–79, political ed and asst ed Now! magazine 1979–81, asst ed Daily Mail 1981–86; political ed: The Times 1986–92, BBC 1992–; racing columnist The Spectator 1995–; presenter The Power of Patronage (BBC Radio series) 1991; author of school books on current affairs issues; *Recreations* theatre, horse racing, swimming, bird watching; *Clubs* RAC; *Style*— Robin Oakley, Esq; ✉ BBC, Press Gallery, House of Commons, Westminster, London SW1A 0AA (☎ 0171 973 6010)

OAKLEY, (Horace) Roy; CBE (1978); s of late Horace William Oakley, of Luton, Beds, and late Beatrice Anne, *née* Parker; *b* 26 Dec 1920; *Educ* Ashton GS Dunstable, UCL (BSc, MSc, Vernon Harcourt prize); *m* 1949, Evelyn Elsie, da of Joseph A Mariner, JP; 1 s (Richard b 1953), 3 da (Elizabeth b 1951, Susan b 1954, Katharine b 1957); *Career* graduate engr Mott Hay & Anderson 1941–42, served as Lt RE 1943–47 (despatches), lectr Dept of Civil Engrg UCL 1950–52; Watson Hawksley (formerly JD DM Watson): engr 1948–50, ptnr 1952–85, sr ptnr 1969–85, conslt 1985–93; memb Bd BSI 1979–82; memb Cncl: ICE 1968–74, UCL 1974–84, Br Hydro-Mechanics Res Assoc 1978–85, Fellowship of Engrg 1987–89; pres Inst of Water Pollution Control 1983–84, vice pres Construction Industs Res and Info Assoc 1986–89 (chm 1982–86), chm Br Water Industs Gp 1984–86; fell: Inst of Water Pollution Control (now IWEM) 1948, Inst of Civil Engrs 1949; FRSA 1968, FEng 1983; *Publications* numerous technical papers for professional instns and int confs; *Recreations* sport, walking, gardening, painting; *Style*— Roy Oakley, Esq, CBE, FEng; ✉ Thistledown, 53 The Park, St Albans, Herts AL1 4RX (☎ 01727 855928)

OAKS, Agnes; da of Juhan Oaks, of Estonia, and Valentina, *née* Troffimova; *b* 29 May 1970; *Educ* Tallin Ballet Sch, Vaganova Inst Moscow; *m* 1990, Thomas Edur, *qv*, s of Enn Edur; *Career* Estonia State Ballet School: Coppelia 1987, Paquita 1988; Estonia State Opera Ballet: Sleeping Beauty 1989, Swan Lake 1990, Romeo & Juliet 1990; princ rising to sr princ English National Ballet 1990–96, Birmingham Royal Ballet 1996–; roles incl: Hynd's Coppelia 1990, Ben Stevenson's The Nutcracker 1990, Les Sylphide 1990, 3 Preludes 1990, Our Waltzes 1990, Sanguine Fan 1990, Bianca in Taming of the Shrew, Olga in Eugene Onegin, Our Waltzes, Apollo, Cinderella, Etudes, Four Last Songs, Sphinx, Hynd's Sleeping Beauty (world premiere), Raissa Struchkova's Swan Lake (world premiere), Impromtu, Spectre de la Rose 1992, cr title role Derek Deane's Gisselle 1994, Paquita 1994, Romeo and Juliet 1995, Dream Alice in Alice in Wonderland 1995, Christopher Dean's Encounters 1996, Peter Wright's Swan Lake, Peter Wright's Nutcracker, David Bintley's Nutcracker Sweeties, Peter Wright's Sleeping Beauty; Best Couple with her ptnr Thomas Edur Int Ballet Competition Jackson Mississippi 1990; *Recreations* walking, travel; *Style*— Ms Agnes Oaks; ✉ English National Ballet, Markova House, 39 Jay Mews, London SW7 2ES (☎ 0171 581 1245, fax 0171 225 0827)

OAKSEY, 2 Baron (UK 1947), and 4 Baron Trevethin (UK 1921); John Geoffrey Tristram Lawrence; OBE, JP; known as Lord Oaksey; s of 3 and 1 Baron Trevethin and Oaksey, DSO, TD (d 1971); *b* 21 March 1929; *Educ* Eton, New Coll Oxford, Yale Law Sch; *m* 1, 1959 (m dis 1987), Victoria Mary, da of Maj John Dennistoun, MBE (d 1980); 1 s (Hon Patrick), 1 da (Hon Sara Victoria b 1961); m 2, 7 March 1988, Mrs Rachel Crocker; *Heir* s, Hon Patrick John Tristram Lawrence b 29 June 1960; *Career* Lt 9 Lancers and P/O RAFVR; racing corr to: Daily Telegraph (as 'Marlborough') 1957–94, Sunday Telegraph 1961–88, Horse and Hound (as 'Audax') 1959–88; columnist Racing Post 1988–90; TV racing commentator (World of Sport, Channel 4 Racing) 1969–; pres: Beverley Race Club, Cheltenham and Three Counties Race Club, Horses and Ponies Protection Assoc (HAPPA); dir HTV West; *Recreations* riding, skiing; *Clubs* Brooks's; *Style*— The Rt Hon the Lord Oaksey, OBE, JP; ✉ Hill Farm, Oaksey, Malmesbury, Wilts SN16 9HS (☎ 01666 577303, fax 01666 577962)

OAKSHOTT, Hon Sir Anthony Hendrie; 2 Bt (UK 1959), of Bebington, Co Palatine of Chester; s of Baron Oakshott, MBE (Life Peer and 1 Bt, d 1975); *b* 10 Oct 1929; *Educ* Rugby; *m* 1965 (m dis 1981), Valerie Anne Doreen (d 1988), formerly w of (1) Donald John Ross and (2) Michael de Pret-Roose, and da of Jack Vlasto, of Hurst, Berks; *Heir* bro, Hon Michael Arthur John Oakshott b 12 April 1932; *Clubs* White's; *Style*— The Hon Sir Anthony Oakshott, Bt; ✉ Farmcote, Bledington, Oxfordshire OX7 6UX

OAKSHOTT, Hon Michael Arthur John; s of Baron Oakshott, MBE (Life Peer and 1 Bt, d 1975); hp to Baronetcy of bro, Hon Sir Anthony Hendrie Oakshott, 2 Bt, *qv*; *b* 12 April 1932; *Educ* Rugby; *m* 1, 27 April 1957, Christina Rose Methuen (d 1985), da of late Thomas Banks, of Solai, Kenya; 3 s (Thomas Hendrie b 1959, Charles Michael b 1961, Angus Withington b 1965); m 2, 8 April 1988, Mrs Helen Clare Jones, da of late Edward Ravell, of Woodhall Spa, Lincs; *Style*— The Hon Michael Oakshott; ✉ Isle Tower, Holywood, Dumfries DG2 0RW (☎ 01387 720596, fax 01387 721234)

OATEN, Michael John; s of Frederick Atkins Oaten (d 1991), and Lilian May, *née* Lock; *b* 1 May 1943; *Educ* Egham Sch, LSE (BSc); *m* Susan Wendy, *née* Precious; 2 s (Simon b 18 April 1977, Marcus b 1 Nov 1983), 2 da (Nicola b 30 Sept 1978, Sarah b 30 Sept 1982); *Career* articled clerk Rooke Lane & Co CA's 1961–62; Arthur Andersen & Co: articled clerk 1965–67, sr clerk 1967–70, mangr Audit 1970–, ptnr 1976–, managing ptnr S E Asia Singapore 1980–84, dir of Educn Consulting and Change Mgmnt 1985–89, head of Corp Fin 1986–, global managing dir of Corp Fin 1992–; FCA 1967; *Books* Obtaining A Quotation For French Companies On The London Stock Exchange (1975), Banking In Singapore (1983); *Recreations* skiing, riding, tennis, travel, walking up mountains; *Clubs* Tanglin (Singapore); *Style*— Michael Oaten, Esq; ✉ Arthur Andersen & Co, 1 Surrey Street, London WC2R 2PS (☎ 0171 438 3118, fax 0171 438 5990)

OATES, Geoffrey Donald; s of Thomas Oates (d 1970), of Poole, Dorset, and Dorothy Verne, *née* Jones (d 1967); *b* 16 May 1929; *Educ* Wolsingham GS Co Durham, Univ of Birmingham (BSc, MB ChB), Univ of Illinois Chicago USA (MS); *m* 1, 23 June 1954, Molly Parfitt (d 1973), da of Thomas Edwards (d 1977), of Abercynon, Glamorgam; 1 s (John b 1955), 1 da (Susan b 1957); m 2, Elizabeth Anne, da of Archibald Ronald Wife (d 1975), of E Dereham, Norfolk; *Career* Capt RAMC 1955–57; Fulbright travel scholarship 1963–64, res fell and instr in surgery Univ of Illinois 1963–64, conslt surgn S Birmingham Health Authy (formerly United Birmingham Hosps) and sr clinical lectr Univ of Birmingham 1967–94, conslt surgn emeritus 1994–; memb: Colo-Rectal Sub-Ctee UK Co-ordinating Ctee for Cancer Res, Br Assoc of Endocrine Surgery, Int Assoc of Endocrine Surgns, Br Assoc of Surgical Oncology, Société Internationale de Chirurgie; RSM: pres Section of Oncology 1982–83, pres Section of Coloproctology 1989–90; pres: Assoc of Coloproctology of GB and Ireland 1990–91, W Midlands Surgical Soc 1991–92; scientific sec Working Pty on Colorectal Cancer MRC; hon memb Société Nationale Française de Colo-Proctologie 1990; fell Assoc of Surgns of GB and Ireland, FRCS 1959, FRSM 1967; *Books* contrib: The Pathological Basis of Medicine (1972), Clinical Trials (1977); Updates in Colo-Proctology (jt ed, 1992); *Recreations* salmon fishing, golf, skiing, photography; *Clubs* Army and Navy; *Style*— Geoffrey Oates, Esq; ✉ 14 Hintlesham Ave, Edgbaston, Birmingham, West Midlands B15 2PH (☎ and fax 0121 454 3257); Consulting Rooms, 81 Harborne Rd, Edgbaston, Birmingham B15 3HG (☎ 0121 455 9496, fax 0121 455 0288)

OATES, Rev Canon John; s of John Oates (d 1964), of Yorkshire, and Ethel, *née* McCann (d 1959); *b* 14 May 1930; *Educ* Queen Elizabeth Sch Wakefield, Soc of the Sacred Mission Kelham; *m* 16 Jan 1962, Sylvia Mary, da of Herbert Charles Harris (d 1977), of Rickmansworth, Herts; 3 s (Jeremy b 20 Aug 1963, Alistair b 19 May 1968, Jonathan b 28 Dec 1969), 1 da (Rebecca b 6 Feb 1966); *Career* curate Eton Coll Mission Hackney Wick 1957–60, devpt offr C of E Youth Cncl and memb staff Bd of Educn 1960–64, devpt sec C of E Cncl for Cwlth Settlement 1964–65 (gen sec 1965–70), sec C of E Ctee on Migration and Int Affairs 1969–71; vicar Richmond Surrey 1970–84, rural dean Richmond and Barnes 1979–84, rector St Bride's Fleet St 1984–, area dean City of London 1997–; memb Unilever Central Ethical Compliance Gp 1990–; commissary: to Archbishop of Perth W Aust and Bishop of N W Aust 1968–75, to Archbishop of Jerusalem 1969–75, to Bishop of Bunbury 1969–; hon canon Bunbury 1969–, chapter clerk City Deanery 1994–; pres Richmond and Barnes Mental Health Assoc 1972–74; Freeman City of London; chaplain: Press Club, Inst of Journalists, Inst of PR, Publicity Club of London 1984–, Worshipful Co of Marketors 1984–, Worshipful Co of Stationers and Newspaper Makers 1990–, Worshipful Co of Turners of London 1995–; *Recreations* walking, travel, squash, broadcasting; *Clubs* Athenaeum, London Press, Wig and Pen; *Style*— The Rev Canon John Oates; ✉ St Bride's Rectory, Fleet Street, London EC4Y 8AU (☎ 0171 583 0239, 0171 353 1301, fax 0171 583 4867)

OATES, (John) Keith; s of John Alfred Oates (d 1983), of Bispham, Blackpool, Lancs, and Katherine Mary, *née* Hole; *b* 3 July 1942; *Educ* King's Sch Chester, Arnold Sch Blackpool, LSE (BSc), UMIST (Dip Tech), Univ of Bristol (MSc); *m* 25 May 1968, Helen Mary, da of Donald Charles Matthew Blake (d 1985), of Sale, Cheshire; 1 s (Jake b 1976), 3 da (Cathee b 1970, Kirsten b 1971, Felicity b 1982); *Career* work study trainee Reed Paper Gp 1965–66, budgets and planning mangr IBM UK Ltd 1966–73, gp fin controller Rolls Royce Ltd 1973–74, controller Black & Decker Europe 1974–78, vice pres fin Thyssen Bornemisza 1978–84; Marks & Spencer plc: fin dir 1984–91, md international ops, expenditure/fin activities, estates and store devpt 1991–, dep chm 1994–; non-exec dir: John Laing Plc 1987–89, BT plc 1994–, Guinness plc 1995–; memb: Cncl CBI 1988–, Bd of Govrs BBC 1988–93, Bd London First 1993–, Sports Cncl of Great Britain 1993–; memb 100 Gp of Chartered Accountants 1985–94; memb Cncl (govr) Wycombe Abbey Sch 1995–, pres UMIST Assoc 1996–; FCT 1982, CIMgt 1992, FRSA; *Recreations* spectator sports (association football, athletics, boxing & cricket), skiing, tennis; *Clubs* Supporter de L'Association Sportive de Monaco, Tennis Club de Monaco; *Style*— Keith Oates, Esq; ✉ Marks and Spencer plc, Michael House, 37–67 Baker St, London W1A IDN (☎ 0171 268 6427, fax 0171 268 2713, telex 267141)

OATES, Laurence Campbell; s of Stanley Oates (d 1995), and Norah, *née* Meek (d 1984); *b* 14 May 1946; *Educ* Beckenham and Penge GS Kent, Univ of Bristol (LLB); *m* 26 Oct 1968, Brenda Lilian, da of John Trevor Hardwick, of Stourbridge, W Midlands; 1 s (Adrian Laurence b 1974), 1 da (Marianne Louise b 1972); *Career* called to the Bar Middle Temple 1968, in practice 1969–76; legal advsr Dept of Employment involved in industl relations law reform 1977–80, legal sec Law Offrs' Dept advising on civil and constitutional law 1981–84, asst treasy slr Dept of Transport advising on civil aviation law 1984–88, under sec and head Legal and Law Reform Gp Lord Chancellor's Dept 1989–92, circuit admin Midland and Oxford Circuit 1992–94, assoc head Policy Gp Lord Chllr's Dept 1995–96, dir Magistrates' Courts Gp Lord Chllr's Dept 1996–; *Recreations* music, golf; *Style*— Laurence Oates, Esq; ✉ Lord Chancellor's Department, Selborne House, 54–60 Victoria Street, London SW1 (☎ 0171 210 8809)

OATES, Roger Kendrew; s of William Oates (d 1987), and Mary Dorothy, *née* Mayne (d 1957); *b* 25 June 1946; *Educ* Thirsk Sch, York Sch of Art, Farnham Sch of Art (DipAD), Kidderminster Coll; *m* 31 July 1976, Fay Morgan, *qv*, da of Philip Hugh Morgan; 1 s (Daniel Morgan Oates b 25 Jan 1979); *Career* textile designer; set up own studio Ledbury Herefordshire 1971–75, dir and chm Craftsman's Mark Ltd 1971–75, lectr at numerous colls of art England and Aust 1971–75; Morgan Oates partnership at The House in the Yard Ledbury 1975–86, Morgan & Oates Ltd 1986– (designing for own label and clients incl Ralph Lauren, Christian Dior, Sonia Rykiel, Donna Karan and Laura Ashley); sr ptnr Roger Oates Design Associates partnership 1987–; work in exhibitions incl: The Craftsman's Art (V & A Museum) 1973, The House in the Yard - Textiles from the

Workshop of Fay Morgan & Roger Oates (Welsh Arts Council Cardiff and tour) 1978, Tufted Rugs (Environment London) 1980, Texstyles (Crafts Council London and tour) 1984–85, Design Awards (Lloyd's Building London) 1988; awarded: USA ROSCOE Award 1984, British Design Award 1988, Duke of Edinburgh's certificate for services to design; contrib various TV prodns; *Style*— Roger Oates, Esq; ✉ Roger Oates Design Associates, The Long Barn, Eastnor, Ledbury, Herefordshire HR8 1EL (☎ 01531 632718, fax 01531 631361)

OATES, Stephen Michael; s of Michael Robert Hulbert Oates, of Ryde, IOW, and Joan Audrey, *née* Langridge; *b* 20 Nov 1961; *Educ* Ryde Sch, Portsmouth Poly; *m* 2 Aug 1986 (m dis 1994), Sarah Dawn, da of John Ernest Blake; ptnr Marie Elizabeth Allen; *Career* Isle of Wight Radio Ltd and Isle of Wight Radio (Holdings) plc: fndr memb, jt md and co sec 1989–92; valuation surveyor Sir Francis Pittis & Son/Prudential Property Services 1987–89 (formerly asst property valuation surveyor), dir Isle of Wight Railway Co Ltd; md Wessex FM 1993–, fndr memb applicant gp and first md South West Sussex Radio Ltd; ASVA; *Recreations* Audio production, steam railways, hiking; *Style*— Stephen Oates, Esq; ✉ Wessex FM, Radio House, Trinity Street, Dorchester, Dorset DT1 1DJ (☎ 01305 250333, fax 01305 250052); South West Sussex Radio Ltd (☎ 01243 773600, fax 01243 5336060)

OATES, Sir Thomas; kt (1972), CMG (1962), OBE (1958, MBE 1946); er s of Thomas Oates, of Wadebridge, Cornwall; *b* 5 Nov 1917; *Educ* Callington GS Cornwall, Trinity Coll Cambridge (MA); *Career* Admty Scientific Staff 1940–46, temp Lt RNVR; entered Colonial Admin Serv Nigeria 1948, seconded to HM Treasy 1953, fin sec Br Honduras 1955, Aden 1959–63, dep high cmmr Aden and Protectorate of South Arabia 1963–67, perm sec Gibraltar 1968–69, dep govr Gibraltar 1969–71, govr and C-in-C St Helena 1971–76; *Recreations* photography; *Clubs* East India, Commonwealth Trust; *Style*— Sir Thomas Oates, CMG, OBE; ✉ Tristan, Trevone, Padstow, Cornwall PL28 8QX

OATLEY, Clive; s of James William Oatley, OBE, FRIBA (d 1987), and Christina Margaret, *née* Webb, of Burcote, Inglewood Park, St Lawrence, Isle of Wight; *b* 3 April 1938; *Educ* St Paul's, St Catharine's Coll Cambridge (MA); *m* 1, 1963; 1 s (Maxwell James b 1976); m 2, 1977, Brooke Randolph, da of Hon Joseph Simpson Farland, former US ambass to Panama, Pakistan and Iran, of Virginia USA; 1 da (Virginia Lawson b 1977); *Career* Lt 5 Royal Inniskilling Dragoon Gds 1956–58; PA to md rising to mangr of distribution econ Shellmex & BP Ltd 1961–66, mktg co-ordinator Marathon Oil Co Geneva 1966–69, dir crude oil trading Tampimex Gp Monte Carlo 1969–84 (chm 1975–84), chm Bridge Oil Group of Companies 1985–; *Recreations* golf, tennis; *Clubs* Hurlingham, Hawks, United Oxford & Cambridge Univ, Royal Wimbledon Golf, RAC, Monaco Yacht; *Style*— Clive Oatley, Esq; ✉ c/o Bridge Oil (UK) Ltd, 141 Kings Road, London SW3 4PW (☎ 0171 351 2221, fax 0171 351 4241)

OATLEY, Neil Vernon; s of Ronald Stanley Oatley, of Istead Rise, Kent, and Audrey Helen, *née* Munday; *b* 12 June 1954; *Educ* Gravesend GS, Loughborough Univ (BTech); *partner* Peta Geraldine Brown; *Career* race car designer (Formula 1); engr Williams Grand Prix Engineering 1977–84, designer Formula One Race Car Engineering 1984–86, chief designer McLaren International 1989– (designer 1986–); *Recreations* music (rock and classical), motorcycling, reading; *Style*— Neil Oatley, Esq; ✉ Culvers, Littleworth Road, The Sands, Seale, Farnham, Surrey GU10 1JN (☎ 01252 782210); McLaren International Ltd, Woking Business Park, Albert Drive, Woking, Surrey GU21 5JY (☎ 01483 728211, fax 01483 720097)

OBERTELLI, Ricci; *Educ* Hotel Mgmnt and Catering trg course Italy; *Career* hotelier; extensive experience in London including Claridge's, The Savoy and The Ritz, subsequently various mgmnt positions rising to sales and mktg dir Four Seasons Inn on the Park, mangr rising to dir and gen mangr The Dorchester 1986– (responsible for complete refurbishment 1988–90); dep nat delegate for GB Euro Hotel Mangrs Assoc; FHCIMA, Master Innholder; memb: Chaîne des Rotisseurs, Réunion des Gastronomes, Ordre des Côteaux de Champagne, Acad of Food and Wine Serv, Inst of Dirs; *Style*— Ricci Obertelli, Esq; ✉ Director and General Manager, The Dorchester, Park Lane, London W1A 2HJ (☎ 0171 629 8888, fax 0171 409 0114)

OBHOLZER, Dr Anton Meinhard; s of Anton Max Karl Obholzer (d 1985), of Cape Town, SA, and Eva Maria Clarissa, *née* von Hartungen (d 1985); *b* 16 Nov 1938; *Educ* Christian Brothers' Sch Kimberley SA, Univ of Stellenbosch SA (BSc), Univ of Cape Town SA (MB ChB, DPM); *m* 16 Feb 1963, Annabel Harriet Barbara, da of Dr Christopher Jarvis Molteno; 1 da (Clarissa Judith b 9 Dec 1966), 2 s (Anton Manfred b 29 June 1968, Rupert John b 27 March 1970); *Career* conslt child psychiatrist Child Guidance Trg Centre 1975–80; conslt psychiatrist Tavistock Clinic 1980– (chm 1985–93), chief exec Tavistock and Portman NHS Tst 1993–; assoc prof Dept of Sociology Brunel Univ 1989–; hon prof: Univ of Vienna 1994, Univ of Klagenfurth 1994, Univ of Innsbruck 1994; memb Br Psycho Analytical Soc, FRCPsych (memb Cncl 1991–); *Books* with M Baraister: Cape Country Furniture (1978), Town Furniture of the Cape (1985), The Cape House and its Interior (1987); The Unconscious at Work (ed jtly with Vega Roberts, 1994); *Style*— Dr Anton Obholzer; ✉ Tavistock and Portman NHS Trust, 120 Belsize Lane, London NW3 5BA (☎ 0171 435 7111, fax 0171 447 3709)

OBOLENSKY, Prof Sir Dimitri; kt (1984); s of Prince Dimitri Obolensky (d 1964), of Antibes, France, and Mary, *née* Countess Shuvalov; descended from Rurik, the Scandinavian fndr of the Russian state ca 862, whose dynasty ruled Russia until 1598; *b* 1 April 1918; *Educ* Lycée Pasteur Paris, Trinity Coll Cambridge (MA, PhD), Univ of Oxford (DLitt); *m* 1947 (m dis 1989), Elisabeth Lopukhin; *Career* lectr in Slavonic studies Univ of Cambridge 1946–48, prof of Russian and Balkan history Univ of Oxford 1961–85 (reader in Russian and Balkan medieval history 1949–61, student (fell) ChCh 1950–85); visiting prof in many foreign univs; fell Trinity Coll Cambridge 1942–48 (hon fell 1991), vice pres Br Acad 1983–85; Hon Dr: Sorbonne 1980, Sofia Univ of Bulgaria 1989; Hon DLitt Univ of Birmingham 1988; foreign memb: American Philosophical Soc, Serbian Acad of Arts and Sci, Russian Acad of Scis; corresponding memb Acad of Athens; FBA, FSA, FRHistS; *Clubs* Athenaeum; *Style*— Prof Sir Dimitri Obolensky, FBA; ✉ 29 Belsyre Court, Woodstock Road, Oxford OX2 6HU (☎ 01865 56496)

OBOLENSKY, Prince Nikolai; s of Prince Michael Obolensky (d 1995), of Madrid, Spain, and Anne, *née* Helbronner (d 1980); descends from Rurik who conquered Russia in 860s; *b* 7 June 1956; *Educ* Harrow, RMA Sandhurst, Univ of Durham (BA), IMEDE Lausanne (MBA); *m* 1987, Charlotte Isabella, *née* Sharpe; 1 s (Alexei b 24 Nov 1990), 2 da (Isabella b 28 Oct 1993, Larissa b 9 Sept 1995); *Career* Maj 17/21 Lancers 1986–(cmmnd 1976, Lt 1978, Capt 1981), ret 1988; Ernst & Young CAs: conslt 1989, sr conslt 1990, managing conslt 1991; Gateway Foodmarkets: exec co-ordinator of change prog 1991, launch dir of new fascias 1992, devpt dir 1993–; md Rurikof & Co 1993–; ptnr Harding & Yorke 1994–96; devpt dir The Centre for Tomorrow's Co 1995–; dir: Cape to Cape 2000 1996–, Leadership in Action 1996–; FRGS, FRSA, MInstD, MIMC; *Books* Practical Business Re-engineering: Tools and Techniques for Achieving Effective Change (1994), A Strategy for the Ecu (jtly 1990); *Recreations* mountaineering, flying, athletics; *Clubs* Lansdowne; *Style*— Prince Nikolai Obolensky; ✉ c/o National Westminster Bank, 92 High St, Harrow-on-the-Hill, Middx HA1 3LR (fax 0117 986 0216, e-mail 100322.1753@compuserve.com)

OBORNE, Brig John Douglas; OBE (1989); s of Lt-Col Tom D Oborne, DSO (d 1985), and Elsie Cottrill, *née* Booth (d 1992); *b* 29 Feb 1928; *Educ* Wellington, RMA Sandhurst; *m* 9 Oct 1954, Margaret Elizabeth, da of Cdr A R P Brown (d 1973); 3 s (Peter Alan b 1957, Nicholas David b 1961, James Richard b 1963); *Career* Br Army cmmnd into 4/7 Royal Dragoon Gds 1948; Staff Coll Camberley 1961, Jt Servs Staff Coll 1968, Br Liaison Offr US Army Armor Centre Fort Knox 1969–71, chief instr Junior Div Staff Coll 1971–73, cdr Br Army Trg Team in Sudan 1973–75, def advsr Br High Cmmn India 1977–80, vice pres Regular Cmmns Bd 1980–82; ADC to HM The Queen 1980–82; Def Attaché Br Embassy Dublin 1984–89, Br sec British-Irish Inter-Parly Body 1990–; *Recreations* golf, travel; *Clubs* Cavalry and Guards'; *Style*— Brig John Oborne, OBE

O'BOYLE, Patrick John; s of James O'Boyle, of Glasgow, Scotland, and Elizabeth, *née* Dunlop (d 1980); *b* 12 April 1941; *Educ* St Aloysius Coll Glasgow, Univ of Glasgow (MB ChB); *m* 4 Sept 1968, Emilia Maria, *née* Galli; 1 s (Stephen James b 26 Sept 1973), 1 da (Marie-Claire b 16 Aug 1971); *Career* lectr Univ of Leeds 1972–74, sr urological registrar Liverpool 1974–79, conslt urologist Somerset 1979– (chm SW Region Urological Ctee 1993–); pioneer of micro video endoscopic operating techniques and laser surgery, author of numerous pubns on devpts in technology applicable to surgery; ChM Univ of Liverpool; memb: RSM (memb Cncl), Br Assoc of Urological Surgns (memb Cncl); FRCSEd; *Recreations* golf, skiing, sailing; *Clubs* Taunton and Pickeridge; *Style*— Patrick O'Boyle, Esq; ✉ Wild Oak Cottage, Wild Oak Lane, Trull, Taunton TA3 7JS (☎ 01823 278057); Musgrove Park Hospital, Taunton, Somerset (☎ 01823 333444 ext 2103)

O'BRIEN, Barry John; s of John O'Brien, and Patricia, *née* Barry; *b* 27 Oct 1952; *Educ* St Illtyd's Coll Cardiff, UCL (LLB); *m* 29 Sept 1984, Susan Margaret; 2 s (William James, Thomas Barry), 1 da (Joanna Elizabeth); *Career* slr Slaughter and May 1978–83 (articled clerk 1976–78), ptnr Freshfields 1986– (slr 1983–86); Liveryman Worshipful Co Slrs; memb Law Soc; *Recreations* sport; *Style*— Barry J O'Brien, Esq; ✉ 9 Highbury Terrace, London N5 (☎ 0171 359 2354); Whitefriars, 65 Fleet St, London EC4 (☎ 0171 936 4000)

O'BRIEN, Conor Cruise; s of Francis Cruise O'Brien, and Katherine, *née* Sheehy; *b* 3 Nov 1917; *Educ* Sandford Park Sch Dublin, Trinity Coll Dublin (BA, PhD); *m* 1, 1939 (m dis 1962), Christine Foster; 1 s, 2 da; m 2, 1962, Máire Mac Entee; 1 adopted s, 1 adopted da; *Career* Dept of External Affrs Ireland: entered 1944, cnsllr Paris 1955–56, head of UN Section and memb Irish Delgn to UN 1956–60, asst sec 1960, rep of Sec Gen of UN in Katanga 1961; vice chllr Univ of Ghana 1962–65, Albert Schweitzer prof of humanities NY Univ 1965–69, TD (Lab) Dublin NE 1969–77 (min for posts and telegraphs 1973–77), memb Senate Republic of Ireland 1977–79, ed-in-chief The Observer 1979–81; contributing ed The Atlantic (Boston), contrib The Independent and The Irish Independent; pro-chllr Univ of Dublin 1973–, visiting fell Nuffield Coll Oxford 1973–75, fell St Catherine's Coll Oxford 1978–81, visiting prof and Montgomery fell Dartmouth Coll USA 1984–85, sr research fell Nat Centre for the Humanities Durham N Carolina 1993; memb: Royal Irish Acad, Royal Soc of Lit; Hon DLitt: Univ of Bradford 1971, Univ of Ghana 1974, Univ of Edinburgh 1976, Nice Univ 1978, Coleraine 1981, Queen's Univ Belfast 1984; Valiant for Truth Media award 1979; *Books* Maria Cross (under pseudonym Donat O'Donnell 1952, reprinted under own name 1963), Parnell and his Party (1957), The Shaping of Modern Ireland (ed, 1959), To Katanga and Back (1962), Conflicting Concepts of the UN (1964), Writers and Politics (1965), The UN: Sacred Drama (1967), Murderous Angels (1968), Power and Consciousness (ed, 1969), Conor Cruise O'Brien Introduces Ireland (1969), Edmund Burke: Reflections on the Revolution in France (ed, 1969), Camus (1969), A Concise History of Ireland (with Máire Cruise O'Brien, 1972, revd edn 1993), The Suspecting Glance (with Máire Cruise O'Brien, 1972), States of Ireland (1972), Herod (1978), Neighbours: the Ewart-Biggs memorial lectures 1978–79 (1980), The Siege: the Saga of Israel and Zionism (1986), Passion and Cunning (1988), God Land: Reflections on Religion and Nationalism (1988), The Great Melody: A Thematic Biography of Edmund Burke (1992), Ancestral Voices: Religion and Nationalism in Ireland (1994); *Recreations* travelling; *Clubs* Athenaeum; *Style*— Conor Cruise O'Brien, Esq; ✉ Whitewater, Howth Summit, Dublin, Ireland (☎ 00 353 1 8322474)

O'BRIEN, Prof Denis Patrick; s of Patrick Kevin O'Brien (d 1944), of Oaklands, Welwyn, Herts, and Dorothy Elizabeth, *née* Crisp (d 1985); *b* 24 May 1939; *Educ* Douai Sch, UCL (BSc Econ), Queen's Univ Belfast (PhD); *m* 5 Aug 1961, Eileen Patricia (d 1985), da of Martin O'Brien (d 1987), of Bognor Regis; 1 s (Martin Michael), 2 da (Ann Elizabeth, Alison Mary); m 2, 11 Sept 1993, Julia, da of John Brian Stapleton, of Gosport; 1 da (Juliet Florence); *Career* reader in econs Queen's Univ Belfast 1970–72 (asst lectr 1963–65, lectr 1965–70), prof of econs Univ of Durham 1972–; memb Cncl Royal Econ Soc 1978–83; FBA; *Books* J R McCulloch (1970), The Correspondence of Lord Overstone (3 vol, 1971), Competition in British Industry (jtly, 1974), The Classical Economists (1975), Competition Policy, Profitability and Growth (jtly, 1979), Pioneers of Modern Economics in Britain (jtly, 1981), Authorship Puzzles in The History of Economics: A Statistical Approach (jtly, 1982), Lionel Robbins (1988), Thomas Joplin and Classical Macroeconomics (1993), Methodology, Money and the Firm (2 vols, 1994); *Recreations* the violin; *Style*— Prof D P O'Brien, FBA; ✉ Department of Economics, University of Durham, 23–26 Old Elvet, Durham DH1 3HY (☎ 0191 374 7272)

O'BRIEN, Dermod Patrick; QC (1983); s of Lt Dermod Donatus O'Brien (d 1939), and Helen Doreen Lesley, *née* Scott O'Connor (d 1971); *b* 23 Nov 1939; *Educ* Ampleforth, St Catherine's Coll Oxford (MA); *m* 1974, Zoë Susan, da of Roderick Edward Norris, of Sussex; 2 s (Edward b 1977, Timothy b 1980); *Career* called to the Bar Inner Temple 1962; recorder of the Crown Court (Western Circuit) 1978–; bencher Inner Temple 1993; govr Milton Abbey Sch 1992–; landowner; *Recreations* fishing, shooting, skiing; *Style*— Dermod P O'Brien, Esq, QC; ✉ Little Daux Farm, Billingshurst, West Sussex RH14 9DB (☎ 01403 784800, fax 01403 785349); 2 Temple Gardens, Temple, London EC4Y 9AY (☎ 0171 583 6041, fax 0171 583 2094)

O'BRIEN, Chief Constable Desmond; OBE, QPM; s of Joseph O'Brien (d 1972), of Belfast, and Adelaide, *née* Cadden (d 1959); *b* 31 March 1934; *Educ* St Mary's Secdy Sch Belfast, Brunel Univ; *m* 1975, Susan, da of Albert Fradley; 1 da (Tamsin Lucinda b 28 Oct 1978); *Career* supt RUC 1953–73, chief supt Police Staff Coll Bramshill 1973–75, chief supt RUC 1975–78, asst chief constable Greater Manchester Police 1978–83, dep chief constable Kent Co Police 1983–89, chief constable British Transport Police 1989–; memb ACPO 1978; *Recreations* country activities, walking, fly fishing; *Style*— Chief Constable Desmond O'Brien, OBE, QPM; ✉ British Transport Police, PO Box 260, 15 Tavistock Place, London WC1H 9SJ (☎ 0171 388 7541, fax 0171 383 3023)

O'BRIEN, Sir Frederick William Fitzgerald; kt (1984), QC (Scot 1960); s of Dr Charles Henry Fitzgerald O'Brien, of Edinburgh (d 1968), and Helen Jane MacDonald (d 1962); *b* 19 July 1917; *Educ* Royal HS, Univ of Edinburgh (MA, LLB); *m* 1950, Audrey Muriel, da of Joseph Lloyd Owen, of Windsor, Ontario; 2 s (David b 1954, Neil b 1957), 1 da (Susan b 1952); *Career* admitted Faculty of Advocates 1947, cmmr Mental Welfare Cmmn of Scot 1962–65, home advocate depute 1964–65, sheriff princ of Caithness Sutherland Orkney and Shetland 1965–75, interim sheriff princ of Aberdeen Kincardine and Banff 1969–71 and S Strathclyde 1981, sheriff princ N Strathclyde 1975–78 and Lothian and Borders 1978–89, sheriff of Chancery in Scot 1978–89; chm: Sheriff Ct Rules Cncl 1975–81, Northern Lighthouse Bd 1983–84 and 1985–87, Med Appeal Tbnls 1990–92, Edinburgh Sir Walter Scott Club 1989–92; *Recreations* music, golf; *Clubs* New (Edinburgh), Scot Arts, Bruntsfield Golf; *Style*— Sir Frederick O'Brien, QC; ✉ 22 Arboretum Road, Edinburgh EH3 5PN (☎ 0131 552 1923)

O'BRIEN, James Patrick Arland; yr s of late John David O'Brien; hp of bro, Sir Timothy O'Brien, 7 Bt; *b* 22 Dec 1964; *Educ* Millfield; *m* Lianna, *née* Mace; 1 s (Silas); *Style*— James O'Brien, Esq

O'BRIEN, Most Rev Keith Michael Patrick; *see:* St Andrews and Edinburgh, Archbishop of (RC)

O'BRIEN, Rt Rev (Thomas) Kevin; s of Jack O'Brien (d 1944), and Mary O'Brien (d 1978); *b* 18 Feb 1923; *Educ* Christian Brothers Coll Cork, All Hallows Coll Dublin; *Career* superior Catholic Missionary Soc 1960–71, vicar gen Dio of Leeds 1971–81; parish priest: St Patrick's Huddersfield 1971–79, St Francis Bradford 1979–81; aux bishop of Middlesbrough (RC) and titular bishop of Ard Carna 1981–; *Recreations* walking, reading; *Style*— The Rt Rev Kevin O'Brien; ✉ St Charles' Rectory, Jarratt Street, Hull HU1 3HB (☎ 01482 329100)

O'BRIEN, (Charles) Michael; s of Richard Alfred O'Brien, CBE (d 1970), of Beckenham, Kent, later of Queensland, Aust, and Nora, *née* McKay (1956); *b* 17 Jan 1919; *Educ* Westminster, ChCh Oxford (MA); *m* 4 Nov 1950, Joyce, da of Rupert Henry Prebble (d 1956), of Beckenham, Kent; 2 s (Philip b 1952, Christopher b 1954); *Career* WWII, cmmnd 2 Lt RA 1940, Capt RA Burma (despatches), demobbed 1946; actuary; asst actuary Equitable Life Assurance Society 1952, gen mangr and actuary Royal National Pension Fund for Nurses 1955–84, dir M & G Life Assurance Co Ltd 1984–94; govr Westminster Sch 1972–95, chm Federated Pension Servs 1983–89; FIA 1949 (hon sec 1961–63, pres 1976–78), FPMI; *Recreations* shooting, training and working gundogs, golf; *Style*— Michael O'Brien, Esq; ✉ The Boundary, Goodley Stock, Crockham Hill, Edenbridge, Kent TN8 6TA (☎ 01732 866349)

O'BRIEN, Dr (John) Michael; s of Peter O'Brien (d 1977), of Melton Mowbray, Leics, and Nellie, *née* Harrap (d 1975); *b* 30 Dec 1935; *Educ* Stockport GS, Univ of Manchester Med Sch (MB ChB, pres Univ Boat Club, sec Univ Athletic Union), Univ of Liverpool (DPH, Trevor Lloyd Hughes gold medal and prize); *m* 1960, Constance Amy, da of Albert Edward Dalton (d 1955); 2 da (Sarah Jane b 1963, Rachel Elizabeth b 1964); *Career* house offr posts Manchester Royal Infirmary and St Mary's Hosp Manchester 1962, tutor in clinical surgery (hon registrar) Manchester Royal Infirmary 1963, princ in gen practice Kidsgrove Staffs 1964 and 1965, med inspr of aliens and Cwlth immigrants 1966–81, dep med offr of health and dep princ sch med offr Kingston-upon-Hull 1969 and 1970 (actg sr asst med offr 1968), dep port med offr Hull and Goole Port HA 1969–70, dep county med offr and dep princ sch med offr Durham CC 1970–74 (pt/t factory doctor 1971–73), area med offr Durham AHA 1974–81; Northern RHA: regional specialist in community med 1981–85, actg postgrad dean 1984–85; E Anglian RHA: regional dir of public health 1985–93, exec dir 1990–93; postgraduate advsr in public health med Northern and Yorkshire RHA 1994–, chm Standing Clinical Advsy Gp Newcastle and N Tyneside HA 1994–96, hon sr research assoc Dept of Med and memb Cncl Univ of Newcastle upon Tyne 1994–, chm Northumberland HA 1995–; pres: Faculty of Public Health 1992–95 (vice pres 1989–92), Soc of Public Health 1995–96; memb various working parties for Govt depts incl Working Pty on Health of the Nation and the Med Profession 1995; sr memb Hughes Hall Cambridge 1987–93, assoc lectr MB and DPH Courses Univ of Cambridge Clinical Sch 1989–93; chm: Bd of Mgmnt Inst of Public Health Cambridge 1991–93, Public Health Med Consultative Ctee 1992–94; vice chm Conf of Colls 1993–95; author of numerous pubns in professional and academic jls; QHP 1990–93, Hon FFOM 1993; FFPHM RCP 1980, FRCP 1990 (memb Cncl 1992–95), FRCPath 1992, FRCPE 1996; *Recreations* gardening; *Clubs* Sloane; *Style*— Dr Michael O'Brien; ✉ Low House, Ridsdale, Hexham, Northumberland NE48 2TF (☎ and fax 01434 270368); Northumberland Health Authority, East Cottingwood, Morpeth, Northumberland NE61 2PD (☎ 01670 514331, fax 01670 518873)

O'BRIEN, Michael Anthony; s of Dr Donal O'Brien, and Patricia Mary, *née* Dowdall (d 1990); *b* 7 Sept 1950; *Educ* The Oratory Sch Reading, Trinity Coll Dublin (BA, BAI); *m* 7 Sept 1971, Robin Patricia Antonia, da of Roger Greene (d 1954), of Wellington Quay, Dublin; 4 da (Louise b 1974, Pippa b 1976, Tara b 1977, Alice b 1987); *Career* qualified CA; asst dir C T Bowring & Co (Lloyd's brokers) 1975–78, gp fin controller Mining Investment Corporation Ltd 1978–79, chief exec Anglo International Mining Corporation Ltd 1979–82; chm and chief exec Loupiptar plc and subsids 1982–91, chief exec Healthcare Group Ltd and subsids; memb S of England Agric Soc; FCA; *Recreations* horses, ponies, swimming, tennis; *Style*— Michael O'Brien, Esq; ✉ Beresford House, Plumpton Green, Lewes, East Sussex BN8 4EN (☎ 01273 890009, fax 01273 890043)

O'BRIEN, Oswald; s of Thomas O'Brien, and Elizabeth O'Brien; *b* 6 April 1928; *Educ* St Mary's GS Darlington, Fircroft Coll Birmingham, Univ of Durham (BA); *m* 1950, Freda Rosina Pascoe; 1 s; *Career* RN 1945–48; Tutor WEA 1963–64, staff tutor Univ of Durham 1964–78, sr industl rels offr Cmmn on Industl Rels 1970–72 (secondment), dir of studies and vice princ Co-Op Coll 1978–83; Dept of Employment second ACAS arbitrator in shipbuilding 1968–78, chm Soc of Industl Tutors 1978–82, dir Workplace Advsy Service Alcohol Concern 1986–93 (dir Educn Div 1984–86); freelance lectr 1983–; former pres, sec and treas Darlington Lab Pty; MP (Lab) Darlington March-June 1983, contested (Lab) Darlington 1987; former memb Darlington County Borough and Dist Cncls, memb Durham CC 1990– (chm Performance Review Ctee), chm Darlington CAB 1989–94; FIMgt; *Books* Going Comprehensive (jtly 1970), Drink and Drugs at Work (jtly); *Recreations* singing, dancing, reading, conversation, opera; *Style*— Oswald O'Brien, Esq; ✉ 6 Hillclose Avenue, Darlington, Co Durham DL3 8BH (☎ 01325 351440)

O'BRIEN, Prof Patrick Karl; s of William Patrick O'Brien, of Coggeshall, Essex, and Elizabeth, *née* Stockhausen; *b* 12 Aug 1932; *m* 15 April 1959, Cassy, da of Charles Cobham; 1 s (Stephen b 23 March 1972), 2 da (Karen b 18 Nov 1964, Helen b 18 Nov 1966); *Career* Univ of London: res fell 1960–63, lectr 1963–70, reader in economics and econ history 1967–70, univ reader in econ history and professorial fell St Anthony's Coll Oxford 1984–90 (univ lectr in econ history and faculty fell 1970–84); memb Econ History Soc; FRHistS, FBA, FRSA; *Books* The Revolution in Egypt's Economic System (1966), The New Economic History of the Railways (1977), Economic Development in Britain and France 1780–1914: Two Paths to the Twentieth Century (jtly with C Keyder), Productivity in the Economics of Europe in the 19th and 20th Centuries (ed jtly, 1983), Railways and the Economic Development of Western Europe 1930–1914 (ed, 1983), International Productivity Comparisons 1750–1939 (ed, 1986), The Economic Effects of the Civil War (1988), contrib to numerous learned jls; *Recreations* tennis, squash, art history, walking; *Style*— Prof Patrick O'Brien, FBA; ✉ 33 Tavistock Square, London WC1; Institute of Historical Research, Senate House, London University, London WC1E 7HU (☎ 0171 636 0272, fax 0171 436 2183)

O'BRIEN, His Hon Judge; Patrick William; s of William Columba O'Brien, of Melksham, Wiltshire, and Ethel Minnie, *née* Austin; *b* 20 June 1945; *Educ* St Joseph's Acad Blackheath, Queens' Coll Cambridge (MA, LLM),; *m* 23 May 1970, Antoinette Magdeleine, da of Louis Wattebot; 1 s (Nicholas William Wattebot O'Brien b 11 Oct 1971), 2 da (Charlotte Clementine Wattebot O'Brien b 11 Aug 1973), Juliet Gisela Magdeleine Wattebot O'Brien b 11 April 1975); *Career* called to the Bar Lincoln's Inn 1968 (Mansfield scholar), in practice in chambers of Lord Havers 1970–91, recorder 1987–91 (asst recorder 1984–87), circuit judge (SE Circuit) 1991–; *Recreations* music, cricket; *Clubs* MCC, Highgate CC, Great Canfield CC; *Style*— His Hon Judge O'Brien; ✉ Crown Court, New Street, Chelmsford, Essex CM1 1EL (☎ 01245 603000)

O'BRIEN, Sir Richard; kt (1980), DSO (1944), MC (1942, and Bar 1944); s of Dr Charles O'Brien and Marjorie Maude O'Brien; *b* 15 Feb 1920; *Educ* Oundle, Clare Coll Cambridge (MA); *m* 1951, Elizabeth M D Craig; 2 s, 3 da; *Career* served WWII N Africa, ME, Italy and Greece with Sherwood Foresters and Leicester Regt, PA to C-in-C 21 Army Gp 1945–46; devpt offr Nat Assoc of Boys' Clubs 1946–48, various positions rising to prodn dir Richard Sutcliffe Ltd Wakefield 1948–58, dir and gen mangr Head Wrightson Mineral Engrg Ltd 1958–61, dir of industl rels British Motor Corp 1961–66, industl advsr (manpower) DEA 1966–68, dir of manpower and exec dir Delta Metal 1972–76 (joined 1968); chm: CBI Employment Policy Ctee 1971–76, Crown Appointments Cmmn 1979, Concordia (youth serv vols) 1981–87, Engrg Indust Trg Bd 1982–85, Archbishops' Cmmn on Urban Priority Areas 1983–85, Industl Participation Assoc 1983–86, Policy Studies Inst 1984–90 (memb 1978–), Employment Inst and Charter for Jobs 1985–87, Community Educn Devpt Centre 1989–94, Church Times 1990–, Chiswick House Friends 1996–; dep chm: Associated Marine and Related Charities (AMARC) 1988–91, Church Urban Fund 1988–94; memb: NEDC 1977–82, Engrg Cncl 1985–88; pres: British Inst of Industl Therapy 1982–87, Inst of Trg and Devpt 1983–84, Nat Assoc of Colls of Further and HE 1983–85, Campaign for Work 1988–90; memb Cncl: Industl Soc 1962–86, Univ of Birmingham 1969–88, Hymns Ancient & Modern 1984–; memb Ct of Governors Aministrative Staff Coll Henley 1977–83; JP Wakefield 1955–61; Hon DSc Aston Univ 1979; Hon LLD: Univ of Bath 1981, Univ of Liverpool 1981, Univ of Birmingham 1982; Hon DLitt: Univ of Warwick 1983, CNNA 1988; Hon DCL Lambeth 1987; hon fell Sheffield Hallam Univ (formerly Sheffield City Poly) 1980; *Books* contrib: Conflict at Work (BBC pubn, 1971), Montgomery at Close Quarters (1985), Seekers and Finders (1985); *Style*— Sir Richard O'Brien, DSO, MC; ✉ 53 Abingdon Villas, London W8 6XA (☎ 0171 937 8944)

O'BRIEN, Richard; s of Alec James Morley-Smith, of Tauranga, New Zealand, and Doreen Mary, *née* O'Brien; *m* 1, 1971 (m dis 1979), Kimi Wong; 1 s (Linus b 1 May 1972); m 2, 1982, Jane Elizabeth Moss; 1 s (Joshua b 22 June 1983), 1 da (Amelia b 9 Jan 1989); *Career* actor, presenter and writer 1967–; dir Druidcrest Music Publishing; memb: Equity, Publishing Rights Soc; *Theatre* early work incl: Robert and Elizabeth, Gulliver's Travels, Hair, Jesus Christ Superstar; four prodns at Royal Court Theatre (writer of two incl The Rocky Horror Show); *Television* A Hymn for Jim (writer, BBC), The Crystal Maze (presenter, Channel 4) 1987–93, The Ink Thief (actor, Tyne Tees for ITV) 1993; *Film* The Rocky Horror Picture Show; *Awards* for Rocky Horror Show: Evening Standard Award for Best Musical of 1973, Plays and Players Award for Best Musical of 1973, Golden Scroll Award from The Academy of Science Fiction, Fantasy and Horror Films; *Recreations* work; *Clubs* The Chelsea Arts, The Gothic Soc; *Style*— Richard O'Brien, Esq; ✉ c/o Jonathan Altaras Associates, 27 Floral Street, London WC2E 9DP (☎ 0171 836 8722, fax 0171 836 6066)

O'BRIEN, Air Vice-Marshal Robert Peter (Bob); OBE (1983); s of Maj Thomas Joseph O'Brien, and Doris Winifred O'Brien; *b* 1 Nov 1941; *Educ* Salesian Coll Farnborough, RAF Coll Cranwell (BA (external) London); *m* 11 April 1964, Carole Evelyn Anne, *née* Wallace; 2 s; *Career* joined RAF 1959, RAF Coll Cranwell 1959–92, cmmnd pilot 1962, first flying tour on photo reconnaissance Canberras No 31 Sqdn, subsequently flying instr RAF Valley, ground appointment as ADC, converted to Buccaneer RN then flt cdr No XV Sqdn RAF Laarbruch, Army Staff Coll 1974, Wing Cdr 1977, cmd Univ of London Air Sqdn 1977–80, first chief instr Tornado GR1 Tri-National Tornado Trg Estab 1980–83, cmd RAF Marham 1983–85, dep dir Air Offensive MOD 1985–88, AO cmdg Air HQ Br Forces Cyprus then dep cdr and COS 1988–91, dir of Infrastructure (RAF) MOD 1991, Air Vice-Marshal 1992, cmdt JSDC RNC Greenwich 1992–94, Air Sec 1994–; QCVSA 1996; *Recreations* sailing, hill walking; *Clubs* RAF; *Style*— Air Vice-Marshal Bob O'Brien, OBE; ✉ Air Secretary, RAF Personnel Management Centre, Headquarters Personnel and Training Command, Innsworth, Gloucester GL3 1EZ (☎ 01452 712612 ext 7849, fax 01452 510805)

O'BRIEN, Prof (Patrick Michael) Shaughn; s of Patrick Michael O'Brien (d 1978), and Joan, *née* Edelston; *b* 1 April 1948; *Educ* Pontypridd Boys' GS, Univ of Wales, Welsh Nat Sch of Med (MB BCh, MD); *m* 10 Aug 1985, Sandra Louise, da of Edward Arthur Norman (d 1979), of Henley-on-Thames; 1 s (James b 1986), 1 da (Louise b 1988); *Career* lectr and hon sr registrar Univ of Nottingham 1979–84, sr lectr and hon conslt in obstetrics and gynaecology Royal Free Hosp Sch of Med London 1984–89; Keele Univ: fndn prof of obstetrics and gynaecology 1989–, memb Cncl 1996–, memb Senate 1996–; conslt obstetrician and gynaecologist North Staffordshire Hosps 1989–; RCOG: publications offr 1996–, convenor of study groups 1996–; author of papers on premenstrual syndrome, menopause, fetal monitoring, pregnancy hypertension, labour, prostaglandins and menorrhagia; FRCOG 1991 (MRCOG 1979); *Books* Premenstrual Syndrome (1987); *Recreations* classical music, jazz, clarinet/saxophone, skiing, tennis; *Clubs* RSM, Ronnie Scott's; *Style*— Prof Shaughn O'Brien; ✉ Upper Farm House, Field Aston, Newport, Shropshire TF10 9LE (☎ 01952 811510); Keele Univsersity, Academic Department of Obstetrics & Gynaecology, School of Postgraduate Medicine, Thornburrow Drive, Hartshill, Stoke-on-Trent, Staffordshire ST4 7QB (☎ 01782 718472, fax 01782 747319)

O'BRIEN, (Robert) Stephen; CBE (1987); s of Robert Henry O'Brien (d 1969), and Clare Winifred, *née* Edwards (d 1975); *b* 14 Aug 1936; *Educ* Sherborne; *m* 1, 1958 (m dis 1989), Zoe O'Brien; 2 s (Dermot b 1962, Paul b 1969), 2 da (Rachel b 1965, Louise b 1966); m 2, 30 June 1989, Meriel, *née* Barclay; *Career* Charles Fulton and Co Ltd: joined 1956, dir 1964, chm 1970–82; chm Foreign Exchange & Currency Deposit Assoc 1968–72, vice chm Business in the Community 1992– (chief exec 1983–92); ordained deacon 1971, hon curate St Lawrence Jewry 1973–82; chm: Christian Action 1976–88, Fullemploy Gp 1973–91, UK 2000 1988–91; fell and memb Cncl RSA 1987–91, tstee Prince's Youth Business Tst 1987–, chief exec London First, tstee and vice chm Church Urban Fund 1994–, govr Univ of E London 1996–, dir Prince of Wales Business Leaders Forum; Hon LLD Liverpool 1994; *Recreations* gardening, cooking; *Style*— Stephen O'Brien, Esq, CBE; ✉ London First, Caxton House, 6 Tothill Street, London SW1H 9NA (☎ 0171 222 1445, fax 0171 222 1448)

O'BRIEN, Timothy Brian; s of Brian Palliser Tighe O'Brien (d 1966), and Elinor Laura, *née* Mackenzie; *b* 8 March 1929; *Educ* Wellington, CCC Cambridge (MA), Yale; *Career* designer: BBC Design Dept 1954, Assoc Rediffusion 1955–56; head of design ABC TV 1956–66, theatrical designer (in partnership with Tazeena Firth 1961–79); recent prodns incl Love's Labours Lost (RSC) 1990, War and Peace (Kirov St Petersburg) 1991, Eugene Onegin (Royal Opera House) 1993, The Merry Wives of Windsor (RNT) 1995, Outis (La Scala Milan) 1996; chm Soc of Br Theatre Designers 1984–91; Gold Medal for set design Prague Quadriennale 1975, jt winner Golden Triga for best national exhibit Prague Quadriennale 1991; RDI 1991; *Recreations* sailing (co owner 'Bathsheba Everdene'); *Style*— Timothy O'Brien, Esq; ✉ 33 Lansdowne Gardens, London SW8 2EQ (☎ 0171 622 5384, fax 0171 720 5348)

O'BRIEN, (Michael) Vincent; s of Daniel Patrick O'Brien (d 1943); *b* 9 April 1917; *Educ* Mungret Jesuit Coll Limerick; *m* 1951, Jacqueline, *née* Wittenoom; 2 s (David, Charles), 3 da (Elizabeth McClory, Susan Magnier, Jane Myerscough); *Career* former racehorse trainer (ret 1994); began training Co Cork 1944, moved to Co Tipperary 1951, won all major English and Irish steeplechases (3 consecutive Grand Nationals, Champion Hurdles and 4 Gold Cups); since 1959 concentrated on flat racing; trained winners of: 16 English classics (incl 6 Derbys) and 27 Irish classics (incl 6 Irish Derbys), French Derby, 3 Prix de l'Arc de Triomphe, Washington Int, Breeder's Cup Mile; trainer of Nijinsky (first triple crown winner since 1935); Hon LLD Nat Univ 1983, Hon DSc Univ of Ulster 1995; *Recreations* golf; *Style*— Dr M Vincent O'Brien; ✉ Ballydoyle House, Cashel, Co Tipperary, Ireland (☎ 00 353 62 61222, fax 00 353 62 61677)

O'BRIEN, William; JP, MP (Lab) Normanton (majority 8,950); *Educ* Univ of Leeds; *m* Jean; 3 da; *Career* MP (Lab) Normanton 1983–; oppn front bench spokesman: on Environment (covering housing, local govt fin and local govt) 1988–92, on NI 1992–; memb: Public Accounts Ctee 1983, Energy Select Ctee 1986, Standing Ctee to consider the 1995 Environment Agency Bill; memb Wakefield Dist Cncl 1973–83 (former dep ldr and chm Fin and Gen Purposes Ctee); special interests: waste mgmnt, roads, tport, air quality; memb Yorkshire Water Authy 1974–83; memb NUM 1945– (local branch official 1956–83); *Recreations* reading; *Style*— William O'Brien, Esq, JP, MP; ✉ House of Commons, London SW1A 0AA

O'BRIEN, Adm Sir William Donough; KCB (1969, CB 1966), DSC (1942); s of Maj William Donough O'Brien (d 1916); *b* 13 Nov 1916; *Educ* RNC Dartmouth; *m* 1943, Rita, da of Lt-Col Albert Micallef, ISO, of Malta; 1 s, 2 da; *Career* joined RN 1930, served WWII, Flag Offr Aircraft Carriers 1966–67, Cdr Far East Fleet 1967–69, Adm 1969, C-in-C Western Fleet 1970–71, ret; chm: King George's Fund for Sailors 1974–86, Kennet and Avon Canal Tst 1974–91; pres Assoc of RN Offrs 1974–88 (Rear Adm UK 1979–84, Vice Adm UK 1984–86); *Clubs* Army and Navy; *Style*— Adm Sir William O'Brien, KCB, DSC; ✉ The Black Barn, Steeple Ashton, Trowbridge, Wilts BA14 6EU (☎ 01380 870496)

O'BYRNE, Michael; QPM (1996); s of Michael O'Byrne, and Sarah, *née* MacLean (d 1995); *Educ* King's Coll London (LLB); *m* 21 Dec 1971, Carole, da of Samuel Leslie; 1 da (Kathryn b 14 May 1975); *Career* joined Royal Hong Kong Police 1966 (served Marine Police and in New Territories 1966–70); Met Police Serv: constable Notting Hill 1970, Special Course Police Staff Coll 1973–74, Sgt 1973, based Vine Street Police Station 1974–75, inspr Bow Street Police Station 1975, King's Coll London 1975–78, rejoined Met Police Tooting Div 1978–79, called to the Bar Middle Temple 1978, Policy and Analysis Unit Community Rels Branch New Scotland Yard 1979–82, chief inspr Chelsea Police Station 1982–83, memb Policy Ctee Support Gp New Scotland Yard; Surrey Constabulary: supt 1983 (i/c planning 1984–85), cmd Dorking Sub Div 1985–87, Sr Cmd Course Police Staff Coll 1987, chief supt i/c staff servs 1987–89; asst chief constable (ops) Thames Valley Police 1991 (asst chief constable (support) 1989–91); chief constable Bedfordshire Constabulary 1996– (dep chief constable 1991–96); *Recreations* football, squash, golf; *Style*— Chief Constable Michael O'Byrne, QPM; ✉ Bedfordshire Police HQ, Woburn Road, Kempston, Bedford MK43 9AX (☎ 01234 841212)

O'CALLAGHAN, Michael Henry Desmond; s of Gerald Robert Lambert O'Callaghan, of Sevenoaks, Kent, and Dorothy Betty, *née* Doggett (d 1991); *b* 15 July 1941; *Educ* Clare House Sch Beckenham, Bedford Sch; *m* 8 April 1972 (sep), Hilary Suzanne, da of late John Walter Smith; 1 s (Richard b 8 April 1976), 1 da (Clare b 19 March 1974); *Career* Spicer & Pegler CAs: articled clerk 1958–63, Tax Dept London 1964–74, Cambridge Office 1974, ptnr 1975–87; ptnr: Spicer & Oppenheim 1987–91, Touche Ross (following merger, now Deloitte & Touche) Cambridge 1991–; FTII 1964, FCA 1974 (ACA 1964); *Recreations* bell-ringing, classical music; *Style*— Michael O'Callaghan, Esq; ✉ Deloitte & Touche, Leda House, Station Road, Cambridge CB1 2RN (☎ 01223 460222, fax 01223 350839)

O'CATHAIN, Baroness (Life Peer UK 1991), of The Barbican in the City of London; Detta Bishop; OBE (1983); da of Caoimhghin O'Cathain (d 1986), of Dublin, and Margaret, *née* Prior (d 1977); *b* 3 Feb 1938; *Educ* Laurel Hill Limerick Ireland, Univ Coll Dublin (BA); *m* 4 June 1968, William Ernest John Bishop, s of William Bishop (d 1968), of Bristol; *Career* former md milk marketing Milk Marketing Board, md Barbican Centre 1990–95; dir Midland Bank plc 1984–93; non-exec dir: Tesco plc 1985–, Sears plc 1987–94, British Airways plc 1993–, BET plc 1994–96, BNP Holdings (UK) Ltd 1995–; vice pres Chartered Inst of Mktg 1996–; *Recreations* reading, walking, swimming, theatre, music; *Style*— The Baroness O'Cathain, OBE; ✉ Eglantine, Tower House Gardens, Arundel, W Sussex BN18 9RU (☎ and fax 01903 883775)

OCEAN, Humphrey; s of Capt Maurice Erdeswick Butler-Bowdon, OBE (1984), and Anne, *née* Darlington; *b* 22 June 1951; *Educ* Ampleforth, Canterbury Coll of Art (BA); *m* 3 March 1982, Miranda, da of Dr Michael Argyle, of Oxford; 2 da (Ruby b 1982, Beatrice b 1986); *Career* artist; winner of 1982 Imperial Tobacco Portait Award; *Work in Collections* Imperial War Museum, Scot Nat Portrait Gallery, Ferens Art Gallery, Southwark Collection, National Portrait Gallery London, Wolverhampton Art Gallery, QMC London, Hertford Coll Oxford, Nuffield Coll Oxford, Somerville Coll Oxford, Royal Library Windsor, Royal Opera House Covent Garden, Univ of E Anglia, Wolfson Coll Cambridge, Univ of Birmingham; *Commissions for Portraits* incl: Philip Larkin, Paul McCartney, A J Ayer, Graham Greene, Lord Callaghan, Lord Whitelaw, Tony Benn; *Solo Exhibitions* incl: Nat Portrait Gallery 1984, Ferens Art Gallery Hull and touring 1986–87, Double Portrait (Tate Gallery Liverpool and touring) 1991–92, Angela Flowers Gallery 1994; *Books* The Ocean View (1982), Big Mouth: The Amazon Speaks (1990); *Recreations* noticing birds, motorcycling; *Style*— Humphrey Ocean, Esq; ✉ 22 Marmora Rd, London SE22 0RX (☎ 0181 693 8387, studio ☎ and fax 0171 820 7764)

OCKRENT, Mike Robert; s of Charles Ockrent (d 1980), of London and Eve, *née* Edels; *b* 18 June 1946; *Educ* Highgate Sch, Univ of Edinburgh (BSc); *m* 1, (dis); 1 da (Natasha Mary b 1978), 1 s (Ben Charles b 1981); m 2, 31 Dec 1995, Susan Stromans; *Career* director; trainee dir (ITV scholar) Perth Theatre 1969–73 (later assoc dir to Joan Knight), artistic dir Traverse Theatre Edinburgh 1973–76, freelance dir 1976–; memb: Equity, Dirs' Guild of UK, SSDC (USA); *Stage Prodns incl* Union Jack and Bonzo (Hampstead), The Plumber's Progress (Prince of Wales), The Admirable Crichton (Greenwich), Once a Catholic (Royal Court, Wyndham & Helen Hayes Theatre), A Respectable Wedding (Open Space), And A Nightingale Sang (Queen's), Ducking Out (Duke of York), Short List (Hampstead), The Nerd (Aldwych), Who Plays Wins (Vaudeville), Look No Hans (Strand), Educating Rita (Piccadilly (West End Mangrs Award for Best Comedy)), Passion Play (Wyndham (Evening Standard Award for Best Play)), Look! Look! (Aldwych), Atkinson at the Atkinson, Zenobia (RSC Young Vic) 1995; NT prodns: Watch on the Rhine, Inner Voices, Laurence Olivier's 80th Birthday Celebrations, Int Workshops Santa Fe, New Mexico; *Musical Productions* Just So (Tricycle), Me And My Girl (Adelphi and Marquis Theatre NY (Olivier, Ivor Novello, Drama Magazine Awards for Best Musical, Drama Desk Award Best Dir, nominated for 13 Tony Awards)), Follies (Shaftesbury (Olivier, Evening Standard, Plays & Players and Drama Magazine Awards for Best Musical)), Crazy for You (Prince Edward and Broadway (Tony Award for Best Musical 1992, Olivier Award for Best Musical 1993)), A Christmas Carol (Madison Square Gardens NY) 1994, Big (Shubert Theatre NY) 1996 *Films* Dancin' Thru The Dark (BBC (Formost Pictures, British Screen, Popular Choice Venice Film Festival, Confederation International des Cinema d'Art et Essai Award La Baule Festival)) 1990, Money for Nothing (BBC Screen One) 1993; *Books* Running Down Broadway (1992); *Recreations* tennis, swimming; *Style*— Mike Ockrent, Esq; ✉ c/o Saraband Associates, 265 Liverpool Road, London N1 1LX (☎ 0171 609 5313, fax 0171 609 2370)

O'CONNELL, Bernard John; s of William O'Connell, and Dorothy, *née* Veale; *b* 22 Nov 1942; *Educ* St Brendan's Coll, Univ of Sheffield; *m* 12 Feb 1966, Mary Jacqueline, da of Capt Norman Clark (d 1959); 1 s (James b 1967), 1 da (Anna b 1971); *Career* consumer res mangr Cadbury's 1967–69, mktg mangr Imperial Tobacco 1969–72, chm and md Market Solutions 1973–78, md Noble Whelan O'Connell 1978–84, chm The O'Connell Partnership 1984–; mktg awards: Silver 1975, Gold 1975 and 1977, Grand Prix 1977; *Recreations* golf, skiing, guitar; *Clubs* Chartridge Park Golf, Launceston Golf; *Style*— Bernard O'Connell, Esq; ✉ Woodland Court, Long Park, Chesham Bois, Amersham, Bucks; 301 Brompton Road, London SW3

O'CONNELL, Dr David Henry Anthony; s of David Andrew O'Connell, and late Ellen Mary, *née* Paul; *b* 26 Feb 1955; *Educ* Presentation Brothers Coll Cork, Univ Coll Cork (MB BCh, BAO), DRCOG, MICGP; *Career* family doctor, house physician and house surgn Royal Hosp Wolverhampton 1978–79, GP registrar St Bartholomew's and Hackney Hosp Vocational Trg Scheme 1979–82, family doctor 1982–; chm and dist jr exec City and Hackney Health Dist 1980–81, med advsr and memb Mgmnt Ctee St Wilfrid's Residential Home Chelsea 1984–, dir of various med companies 1990–, memb Exec Ctee, sec Audit Sub-ctee and chm Insurance Sub-ctee Independent Doctors' Forum 1991–93, memb Cncl RSH 1994–; author of various contribs to popular med jls; Knight of Magistral Grace Sovereign Mil Order of Malta 1993, Cross of Merit 1987, Bronze medal 1994; Liveryman Worshipful Soc of Apothecaries 1995 (Yeoman 1985); memb BMA 1978, FRSM 1982; fell: Med Soc of London 1985, Chelsea Clinic Soc 1985; FRIPHH 1993, FRSH 1994; *Recreations* wine and travel; *Clubs* RAC, IOD, Sloane, Carlton; *Style*— Dr David H A O'Connell; ✉ 41 Elystan Place, Chelsea Green, London SW3 3JY (☎ 0171 584 9779, fax 0171 584 3779); 25 Sloane Court West, London SW3 4TD

O'CONNELL, Prof James Michael; s of James Patrick O'Connell (d 1942), and Agnes, *née* Harrington (d 1935); *b* 22 Oct 1925; *Educ* Nat Univ of Ireland (BA, MA), Univ of Louvain (PhD); *m* 21 March 1975, Rosemary, da of Albert Victor Harris, of Bangor, Co Down; 1 s (Patrick b 7 Oct 1980), 2 da (Sheila b 29 May 1976, Deirdre b 10 May 1978), 1 step da (Sanjida b 30 June 1970); *Career* lectr UCL 1958–67, prof of govt Ahmadu Bello Univ Nigeria 1967–75, dean of arts NI Poly 1976–78, prof of peace studies Univ of Bradford 1978–95 (pro vice chllr 1982–86); assoc Inst of Devpt Studies Univ of Sussex, chm Advsy Ctee CSISV Univ of Leicester, memb Race and Community Rels Ctee Bd for Social Responsibility C of E; *Books* Education and Nation Building in Africa (1965), Nigeria 1965: crisis and criticism (1966), Education and Power in Nigeria (1977), The Meaning of Irish Place Names (1980), The Meaning of English Place Names (1984), Peace With Work To Do (1985), Notes Towards a Theology of Peace (1989), Making The Future: thinking and acting about peace in Britain (1989); *Recreations* study of the meaning of place names, reading novels; *Style*— Prof James O'Connell; ✉ Dept of Peace Studies, University of Bradford, Richmond Rd, Bradford, West Yorkshire BD7 1DP (☎ 01274 733466, telex 51309 UNIBFD, fax 01274 305340)

O'CONNELL, Sir Maurice James Donagh MacCarthy; 7 Bt (UK 1869), of Lakeview, Killarney, Co Kerry, and of Ballybeggan, Tralee, Co Kerry; er s of Sir Morgan Donal Conail O'Connell, 6 Bt (d 1989), and Elizabeth, *née* MacCarthy-O'Leary; *b* 10 June 1958; *Educ* Ampleforth; *m* 11 Sept 1993, Francesca Susan, o da of Clive Raleigh, of Hong Kong; *Heir* bro, John Morgan Ross MacCarthy O'Connell b 17 April 1960; *Style*— Sir Maurice O'Connell, Bt; ✉ Lakeview House, Killarney, Co Kerry, Republic of Ireland

O'CONNOR, Prof Brian Thomas; s of Edward O'Connor (d 1934), of Brisbane, Aust, and Eileen Maloney (d 1975); *b* 27 Sept 1929; *Educ* St Joseph's Coll Brisbane Aust, Univ of Queensland (MB BS, MS), Univ of Liverpool (MChOrth); *m* 20 June 1959, Rae Lynette, da of Herbert Elder Hunter (d 1986), of Brisbane; 2 s (Sean b 21 Nov 1962, Brian b 27 June 1970), 2 da (Kerstin b 28 Dec 1960, Tamsin b 6 May 1966); *Career* first asst to Nuffield Prof of Orthopaedic Surgery Univ of Oxford 1965–67, dir The Robert Jones and Agnes Hunt Orthopaedic Hosp, Oswestry Shropshire 1967–68, Robert Jones Prof of Orthopaedics in Univ of Birmingham (at the Robert Jones Agnes Hunt Hosp) 1968–94, ret; fndr memb of Exec, Ctee of Mgmnt and Ed Bd of Injury Br Jl of Accident Surgery, memb Ed Bd of Archiv fur Orthopaedische und Unfall-Chirugie, memb ABC Travelling Fellows Club; memb: Girdlestone Soc, Naughton-Dunn Orthopaedic Club, W German Armed Forces Med Soc 1961, Old Oswestrians Soc; fell Br Orthopaedic Assoc, fell American Fracture Assoc 1971, fell Hungarian Orthopaedic Assoc 1979, fell Venezuelan Orthopaedic Assoc 1979, fell Greek Orthopaedic Assoc 1985, FRCS, FRACS; *Books* The Severely Injured Limb (1983), Bone Grafting and Bone Substitutes; *Recreations* reading, collecting militaria; *Style*— Prof Brian O'Connor; ✉ Pen-Isa'r Glyn Hall, Bronygarth, Oswestry, Shropshire (☎ 01691 773523); Coronet, 995 Brunswick St, New Farm, Brisbane, Australia; Institute of Orthopaedics, The Robert Jones and Agnes Hunt Orthopaedic Hospital, Oswestry, Shropshire (☎ 01691 655311, fax 01691 657968)

O'CONNOR, Christy, Jr; s of John O'Connor (d 1985), and Elizabeth, *née* Noon; *b* 19 Aug 1948; *Educ* Claddagh Nat Sch, St Endas Coll, Galway Tech Coll; *m* 26 Jan 1976, Ann, da of Danial O'Boyle; 1 da (Ann b 28 Oct 1976), 2 s (Nigel Christopher b 12 Dec 1978, Darren b 14 July 1981); *Career* golf professional 1966–; took up golf in Galway 1963; clubs: South Shields Co Durham 1966, Royal Dublin (with Christy O'Connor, Sr) 1967, taught youth team of Holland 1968, Carlow Ireland 1969–75, Shannon 1975–80, Galway Bay Golf & Country Club (pt owner) 1980–; titles won: Irish Match Play 1973, 1975 and 1977, Zambian Open 1974, Irish Open 1975, Martini Int 1975, Sumrie-Bournemouth Better-ball (with Eamonn Darcy) 1976 and 1978, Jersey Open 1989, Kenya Open 1990, Br Masters 1992; team events: Ryder Cup 1975 and 1989 (hit shot to retain Cup for Europe), World Cup, Dunhill Cup, Philip Morris Int, Hennessey Cup; course records: 62 Moor Park London 1976, 61 Grange Golf Club Dublin 1984, 64 Royal St Georges (incl 7 birdies in a row) 1985; first Irish professional to play in the US Masters (1977) and World Series of Golf (1992); awards: Harry Varden Gold medal (as leading Br or Irish in Open) 1976, 1983 and 1985, Texico Award twice, Irish Sportsman of the Year 1989; involved with charity work for mentally handicapped and hospice; *Recreations* shooting, fishing, having a few pints, working on the land, touring Ireland with my family; *Style*— Christy O'Connor, Jr

O'CONNOR, Rt Rev Cormac Murphy; *see:* Arundel and Brighton, Bishop of (RC)

O'CONNOR, Des; *b* 12 Jan 1932; *Career* entertainer and chat-show host; former Butlin's Red Coat; *Theatre* professional debut Palace Theatre Newcastle 1953, compere Sunday Night at the London Palladium, completed 1,000th performance at London Palladium in his own show, cabaret Talk of the Town London, one-man show UK, Canada and Australia since 1980, pantomime Cinderella (London Palladium 1985, Theatre Royal Plymouth 1990, Hippodrome Birmingham 1991, New Victoria Theatre Woking 1992), numerous Royal Show appearances and summer seasons; Canada & USA: headlined three seasons London Palladium Show in Toronto and Ottawa, seasons at The Royal York Hotel and Royal Alexandra Theatre, two all-star galas at The MGM Grand Hotel Las Vegas; Australia: theatre and cabaret performances over many years, broke all box-office records St George's League Club Sydney 1975, appeared at Sydney Opera House; *Television* host: Spot the Tune 1958, own series since 1963, two series screened US then worldwide 1975, Des O'Connor Tonight since 1977–, Des O'Connor Now 1985, TV Times Awards ceremony 1989–90 and 1990–91, Take Your Pick (three series) 1992 and 1994, Pot of Gold (series) 1993; *Recordings* first record Careless Hands reached number one in charts and sold over one million copies 1967, numerous singles and albums released since, album Des O'Connor sold over 250,000 copies 1984, released Sky Boat Song with Roger Whittaker entering Top Twenty charts 1986, album Portrait for Columbia (Gold on release) 1992; *Style*— Des O'Connor, Esq; ✉ c/o Lake-Smith Griffin Associates, 15 Maiden Lane, London WC2E 7NA (☎ 0171 836 1020, fax 0171 836 1040)

O'CONNOR, John Scorror; s of Vernon Feargus O'Connor (d 1946), of Leicester, and Anne, *née* Scorror (d 1963); *b* 11 Aug 1913; *Educ* Wyggeston Sch Leicester, Leicester Coll of Art, RCA (scholarship), Univ of London (postgrad year); *m* Jenny, da of Henry Tennant; 1 s (Michael Feargus b 21 June 1946); *Career* artist; teacher of illustration Birmingham Coll of Art then head of illustration and drawing W of England Coll of

Art Bristol until 1940, served RAF 1940–46, dep head Hastings Sch of Art 1946–48, head Colchester Sch of Art 1948–64; visiting lectr: St Martin's Coll of Art 1964–74, Glasgow Sch of Art 1974–82; work in numerous private and public collections; former memb Cncl Crafts Centre of GB; hon memb Soc of Wood Engravers, sr memb RWS; *Exhibitions* incl: Zwemmer Gallery, Royal Academy, New Grafton Gallery, St Paul's Gallery, Retrospective (painting and book illustration) Glasgow Sch of Art 19777, Goldmark Gallery Uppingham 1993, Rocket Gallery 1995; *Books* numerous written and illustrated incl: Canals, Barges and People (1950), A Pattern of People (1959), Landscape Painting (1964), Technique of Wood Engraving (1971), Introducing Relief Printing (1973), Landscape Drawing (1977), Duke's Village (1988), Wood Engravings of John O'Connor (1989), Twins (1991), Knipton (1996); illustrator of numerous other books; *Style*— John O'Connor, Esq; ✉ Craigmore, Parton, by Castle Douglas, Dumfries & Galloway DG7 3NL (☎ 01644 470239)

O'CONNOR, Joseph Victor; s of John Oliver Vincent O'Connor, of Dublin, and Joanna Marie, *née* O'Grady (d 1985); bro of Sinead O'Connor, *qv*; *b* 20 Sept 1963; *Educ* Blackrock Coll Dublin, Univ Coll Dublin (BA, MA); *Career* writer; *Awards* Hennessy First Fiction Award 1989, New Irish Writer of the Year 1989, Travel Writing Award Time Out Magazine 1990, Macaulay fell Irish Arts Cncl 1993, special Jury Prize (for A Stone of the Heart) Cork Int Film Festival 1992, shortlisted for the Whitbread Prize 1992; *Fiction* Cowboys and Indians (1991), True Believers (short stories, 1991), Desperadoes (1994); *Filmscripts* A Stone of the Heart (1992), The Long Way Home (1993), Ailsa (1993); *Other* Even the Olives Are Bleeding: the Life and Times of Charles Donnelly (1992); *Recreations* avarice, pride, envy, sloth, lust, gluttony, anger and aerobics; *Style*— Joseph O'Connor, Esq; ✉ c/o Blake Friedmann Literary Agency, 37–41 Gower Street, London WC1E 6HH (☎ 0171 631 4331, fax 0171 323 1274)

O'CONNOR, Air Vice-Marshal Patrick Joseph Gerard; CB (1975), OBE (1943); s of Charles Edward O'Connor (d 1942), of Boston House, Straffan, Co Kildare, Ireland, and Mary Josephine, *née* Doyle (d 1966); *b* 21 Aug 1914; *Educ* Mount St Joseph Coll Roscrea Co Tipperary, Nat Univ of Ireland; *m* 16 July 1946, Elsie Elizabeth, da of David Craven (d 1945), of Leeds, Yorks; 1 s (Charles b 1951), 3 da (Mary b 1947 d 1977, Anna b 1948, Geraldine b 1950); *Career* RAF Med Branch 1940–77, Air Vice-Marshal, conslt advsr neurology and psychiatry RAF, hon physician to HM The Queen; conslt neurology and psychiatry: CAA 1977–93, BA 1977, Harley St 1977–; memb: RSM 1950, Int Acad Aviation Med, ABN; FRCPsych, FRCP; *Books* International Civil Aviation Organization Manual, Standards for Neurology and Psychiatry (1970); *Recreations* gardening; *Clubs* RAF; *Style*— Air Vice-Marshal Patrick O'Connor, CB, OBE; ✉ St Benedicts, Bacombe Lane, Wendover, Bucks HP22 6EQ (☎ 01296 623329, fax 01296 696893); 10 Harley St, London W1N 1AA (☎ 0171 636 6504, fax 0171 637 5227)

O'CONNOR, Rt Hon Sir Patrick McCarthy; kt (1966), PC (1980); s of William Patrick O'Connor; *b* 28 Dec 1914; *Educ* Downside, Merton Coll Oxford (hon fell 1987); *m* 1938, Mary Garland (d 1984), da of William Griffin, KC, of Vancouver; 2 s, 2 da; *Career* called to the Bar Inner Temple 1940, jr counsel to PO 1954–60, QC 1960, recorder Kings Lynn 1959–61, recorder Southend 1961–66, High Ct judge (Queen's Bench Div) 1966–80, Lord Justice of Appeal 1980–89, ret 1989; govr Guy's Hosp 1956–60, dep chm IOW QS 1957–71, vice chm Parole Bd 1974–75; *Style*— The Rt Hon Sir Patrick O'Connor; ✉ 210 Rivermead Court, London SW6 3SG (☎ 0171 731 3563)

O'CONNOR, Patrick Michael Joseph; QC (1993); *b* 7 Aug 1949; *Educ* St Francis Xavier's Sch Liverpool, UCL (LLB); *m* 1986; 2 da; *Career* called to the Bar Inner Temple 1970; author of articles in Criminal Law Review and other journals; *Books* Justice in Error (contrib, 1993); *Style*— Patrick O'Connor, Esq, QC; ✉ 1 Crown Office Row, Temple, London EC4Y 7HH (☎ 0171 797 7111, fax 0171 797 7120, e-mail p.oconnor@dial.pipex.com)

O'CONNOR, Sinead; sis of Joseph Victor O'Connor, *qv*; *b* 12 Dec 1966; *Educ* Dublin Coll of Music; *Career* singer; former band memb Ton Ton Macoute 1985–87; solo career: 1 UK and US no 1 (Nothing Compares 2 U 1990, double platinum); solo albums incl: The Lion and the Cobra (1987), I Do Not Want What I Haven't Got (1990, UK no 1), Universal Mother (1994); Year of the Horse tour 1990; video The Value of Innocence; acting debut Hush-A-Bye-Baby 1990; *Awards* incl: Best International Solo Artist BRIT Awards 1991, 3 MTV Music Awards incl Best Video of the Year (for Nothing Compares 2 U) 1990; *Style*— Ms Sinead O'Connor; ✉ c/o Chrysalis Records, EMI House, 43 Brook Green, London W6 7EF (☎ 0171 605 5490)

O'CONNOR, Tom; s of Patrick O'Connor, and Theresa, *née* Stack (d 1982); *b* 31 Oct 1939; *Educ* St Mary's Coll GS Crosby, Simmaries Coll (DipEd); *m* Patricia; 1 s (Stephen), 3 da (Anne, Frances, Helen); *Career* entertainer and TV host; maths teacher St Joan of Arc Sch Bootle 1962–74, professional entertainer 1974–; TV debut on Opportunity Knocks (winning 3 shows) 1974; host TV shows: Wednesday at Eight, The Tom O'Connor Show, Night Out at the Casino, London Night Out, The Tom O'Connor Show; quiz and game show host: Name That Tune (Thames), Gambit (Anglia), Zodiac (Anglia), Password (C4), I've Got a Secret (BBC1), Cross Wits (Tyne Tees), A Question of Entertainment (BBC1); stage acting debut as Pike in The Perils of the Pond (Playhouse Weston-super-Mare) 1991, numerous cabaret tours, summer seasons and pantomimes; *Books* Tom O'Connor's Book of Liverpool Humour (1987), Tom O'Connor's Book of the World's Worst Jokes (1991), From the Wood to the Tees (1992), One Flew Over the Clubhouse (1993), Take a Funny Turn (1994), Follow Me, I'm Right Behind You! (1995); *Recreations* golf; *Style*— Tom O'Connor, Esq; ✉ c/o Positive Management, 1 The Stiles, Ormskirk, Lancs L39 3QG (☎ 01695 570258, fax 01695 578757)

O'CONOR CAMERON, Desmond Roderic; s and h of Denis Armar O'Conor, The O'Conor Don, and Elizabeth, *née* Marris (now Mrs Elizabeth Cameron); *b* 22 Sept 1938; *Educ* Sherborne; *m* 23 May 1964, Virginia Anne, da of late Sir Michael Sanigear Williams, KCMG, and Joy, *née* Hunt; 1 s (Philip Hugh O'Conor b 17 Feb 1967), 2 da (Emma Joy (Mrs Mark Leveson-Gower) b 17 April 1965, Denise Sarah b 8 Dec 1970); *Career* Bank of London and Montreal Ltd Guatemala and Honduras 1960–64, J Henry Schroder Wagg & Co Ltd London 1964–79, dir Schroders Int Ltd London 1977–79; currently dir: Kleinwort Benson Ltd London, Kleinwort Benson Argentina SA Buenos Aires, Kleinwort Benson Chile Ltd Santiago, Kleinwort Benson South Andes Ltd Santiago, Kleinwort Benson do Brasil S/C Ltd Rio de Janeiro, Kleinwort Benson España SA Madrid, Kleinwort Benson Iberfomento SA Madrid, Brazilian Smaller Companies Investment Trust plc 1993–; dir Latin American Trade Advisory Gp (LATAG) 1986–89 and 1995– (Bd of Trade sponsored organisation), chm Sailors and Soldiers Home Eastbourne; *Recreations* tennis, sailing; *Style*— Desmond O'Conor Cameron, Esq; ✉ Kleinwort Benson Ltd, 20 Fenchurch Street, London EC3 (☎ 0171 623 8000); Horsegrove House, Rotherfield, Sussex

O'CONOR DON, The; Denis Armar O'Conor; O Conchubhair Dun; s of Charles O'Conor (27 in descent from Conor, Concovar or Conchobhar, King of Connaught in tenth century and from whom the family name derives), and Evelyn, yst da of Adm the Hon Armar Lowry-Corry, himself 2 s of 3 Earl of Belmore; the present O'Conor Don's forbear 23 generations back was Turlough Mor O'Conor (d 1163), High King over all Ireland; suc his 2 cous (a Jesuit priest) Nov 1981; *b* 1912; *Educ* Downside; *m* 1, 1937 (m dis 1943), Elizabeth, da of Rev Stanley Punshon Marris; 1 s (Desmond Roderic Cameron b 1938); m 2, 1943, Rosemary June, da of Capt James Piers O'Connell-Hewett; 2 s (Kieran Denis b 1958, Rory Dominic b 1963); *Heir* s, Desmond Roderic Cameron O'Conor (b 1938, m 1964 Virginia, eldest da of Sir Michael Williams, KCMG (d 1984)); 1 s Philip b 1967, 2 da Emma b 1965, Denise b 1971); *Career* Grand Cordon St Stanislaus, Grand Cordon Polonia Restituta, Gran Cruz Rey Fernando Guanarteme; *Recreations* hound breeding and showing, beagling; *Style*— The O'Conor Don; ✉ Ashbourne, Corrig Rd, Dun Laoghaire, Co Dublin, Eire (☎ 00 353 1 280 2422)

ODAM, Prof George Neville; s of George Odam (d 1979), of Beccles, Suffolk, and Muriel, *née* Tawell (d 1964); *b* 30 Sept 1938; *Educ* Sir John Leman Sch, Univ of Manchester (BA Mus), Univ of London (Music Teachers' Cert), Univ of Southampton (BMus, MPhil); *m* 15 April 1963, Penelope Anne Lloyd, da of Oliver Lloyd Smith (d 1979), of Beccles, Suffolk; 1 s (Timothy b 1964), 1 da (Joanna b 1966); *Career* composer; Totton GS Hants 1961–65, Bath Coll of Higher Educn 1966– (prof of music educn 1993–); compositions: Cantata for Christmas 1967, Angry Arrow 1969, St George and the Dragon 1970, Tutankhamun 1971, Inca 1975, Robin Hood 1978, Peredur (opera) 1979, Concerto for piano and timpani 1980, Baba Yaga 1984; fndr and conductor Nat Scouts and Guides Symphony Orchestra, chm UK Cncl for Music Educn and Trg 1988–91, vice chm SEAC Music Ctee; memb: ISM (warden of MES 1986–87), SW Arts Bd 1994– (chm Educn Steering Gp Ctee 1988–94); chm Nat Music & Disability Info Serv 1991–84; Music Industries Assoc Award for Outstanding Servs to Music Educn 1994; *Books* Silver Burdett and Ginn Music Books 1–4 (1989), The Sounding Symbol (Stanley Thornes, 1995), The Sounds of Music Books 1–7 (Stanley Thornes, 1996); *Recreations* drawing and painting, computer graphics and DTP, poetry, travel; *Clubs* Combe Grove; *Style*— Prof George Odam, Esq; ✉ Bramble House, The Street, Farmborough, Bath, Somerset BA3 1AL (☎ 01761 470182); Bath College of Higher Education, Newton Park, Newton St Loe, Bath BA2 9BN (☎ 01225 873701 ext 340)

ODAM, Joseph; JP (1969), DL (Cambs 1989); s of Frank Moore Odam (d 1953), and Edna Jessie Maud Miller (d 1967); *b* 8 Dec 1925; *Educ* King's Sch Peterborough, Bedford Sch, Worcester Coll Oxford (Short Mil Course); *m* 21 April 1956, Jane Margaret, da of Harold Howarth (d 1956), of Burton in Kendal, Westmorland; 2 da (Stella Jane b 1957, Josephine Ann Lucinda b 1963); *Career* Reg Army Capt 1 Royal Tank Regt 1944–51; dir Sidney C Banks plc 1966–93, chm Peterborough Hosps NHS Tst 1993–; farmer; dep pres E of Eng Agric Soc 1980– (chm 1969–72, hon life vice pres 1976–); chm Peterborough Magistrates' Bench 1985–88; Liveryman of the City of London, Liveryman Worshipful Co of Farmers 1980; Jubilee Medal 1977; Shrieve of the Co of Cambridgeshire 1989–; *Recreations* tennis; *Clubs* Farmers'; *Style*— Joseph Odam, Esq, JP, DL; ✉ Haynes Farm, Thorney Rd, Eye, Peterborough, Cambs PE6 7UA (☎ 01733 222456)

O'DAY, Prudence Anne (Prue); da of Dr Kevin John O'Day (d 1961), of Melbourne, and Bernadette Anne Hay (d 1983), of London; *b* 12 June 1946; *Educ* Mandeville Hall Melbourne, UCL, Westminster Coll; *m* 16 Jan 1971, Donald William Sievwright Anderson; 1 s (William Sievwright b 23 April 1975), 1 da (Amelia (Amy) b 11 Feb 1977); *Career* managed London Graphic Arts Gallery 1966–68, work with Ira Gale (Rembrandt expert) 1968–69, volunteer ICA Galleries 1968–69, researcher and buyer London Arts Gallery 1969–71, fndr (with husband) Anderson O'Day (formerly 20th Century Prints) 1971 (dir 1986–) and Anderson O'Day Gallery 1986, art conslt 1971–; curator survey exhbn of British prints Brooklyn Museum NYC 1974; co-fndr and treas Portobello Galleries Assoc 1986–, co-fndr Portobello Contemporary Art Festival 1986, co-fndr and sec Portobello Arts trust 1988–, memb Steering Ctee Art Works for London Lighthouse 1993 1991, memb Selection Panel Cleveland Drawing Biennale 1991; *Books* Prints & Drawings Fifteenth to Twentieth Century (1969), Ian Jones - Exhibition Catalogue (1991); *Recreations* politics, theatre, dance, contemporary art, literature and music, cinema, gardening, birdwatching, swimming, tennis and most sports as a spectator; *Clubs* Chelsea Arts; *Style*— Ms Prue O'Day; ✉ Anderson O'Day Gallery, 5 St Quintin Avenue, London W10 6NX (☎ 0181 969 8085)

ODDIE, Bill; *b* 7 July 1941; *Educ* Halesowen GS, King Edward's Sch Birmingham, Pembroke Coll Cambridge; *m* 1, Jean Hart; 2 da (Kate b 1968, Bonnie b 1971); m 2, Laura Beaumont; 1 da (Rose b 1985); *Career* writer and performer; memb: cncl RSPB, Wildfowl and Wetland's Tst, The Worldwide Fund for Nature; pres Northumberland Wildlife Tst; rep: Birdlife Int, Friends of The Earth, Plantlife, RSNC; *Theatre* as writer/performer incl: Cambridge Circus (transfered from Cambridge Footlights to London, NZ, USA), TW3 (touring co); as performer incl: Cousin Kevin in Tommy, Koko in Mikado (ENO), Childrens Variety Show (London Palladium); one pantomime as performer, one as writer; *Television* as writer/performer incl: TW3 (first appearances), The Braden Beat, BBC3, Twice A Fortnight (first series, co-writer Graeme Garden, BBC), Then Broaden Your Mind (with Graeme Garden and Tim Brooke Taylor), The Goodies (co-writer Graeme Garden, eight series, 3 specials, twice winner Silver Rose of Montreux), From the Top (Central); with co-writer Laura Beaumont: The Bubblegum Brigade (HTV); as writer incl: scripts for That Was the Week That Was, numerous sketches for TW3, Ronnie Barker, Tommy Cooper etc; with Graeme Garden incl: Doctor In the House (50 episodes), At Large, The Astronauts (Central), Jim Henson's Animal Show (scripts and songs); as presenter incl: The Saturday Banana (Southern), Time for a Story (Granada), Fax (3 series, BBC), Ask Oddie (2 series, HTV), Festival (BBC); as narrator incl: Tubby the Tuba, The Snowman, Peter and the Wolf; numerous voice overs for commercials and animations; Wildlife progs incl: Oddie in Paradise (Papua New Guinea), The Great Bird Race, The Bird Business, For the Birds (USA cable), Bird in the Nest (BBC), Birding with Bill Oddie (own series, 1997); recent guest appearance The Detectives (with Jasper Carrott and Robert Powell); *Radio* I'm Sorry I'll Read That Again (co-writer Graeme Garden, over 100 shows, BBC); as presenter incl: Breakaway (BBC), numerous shows on Jazz FM and GLR; *Recordings* with The Goodies: 5 top ten singles incl The Funky Gibbon, The Inbetweenies (both silver), 3 albums (1 silver); From the Top; *Books* as writer, illustrator and photographer incl: Bill Oddie's Little Black Bird Book, Gone Birding, Follow that Bird, Bird Watching with Bill Oddie, Bird Watching for Under Tens, Bill Oddie's Colouring Guides; numeous articles for magazine and newspapers; numerous Goodies Books with Graeme Garden an Tim Brooke Taylor; with Laura Beaumont The Toilet Book (UK and worldwide); *Recreations* sports, drums, percussion, saxophone, music; *Style*— Bill Oddie; ✉ agents: London Management, 2–4 Noel Street, London W1V 3RB (☎ 0171 287 9000, fax 0171 287 3036); Roger Hancock Ltd, 4 Water Lane, London NW1 8NZ (☎ 0171 267 4418); voice overs c/o Yakkity Yak (☎ 0171 430 2600)

ODDIE, Christopher Peter; s of late Alfred Birtwistle Oddie, of N Lancs, and late Elsie Mary, *née* Bateman; *b* 26 Sept 1948; *Educ* King Edward VII Sch Lytham Lancs; *m* 12 June 1971, Gail, da of Maj Horace George Ablett; 2 s (Simon Christopher b 19 Sept 1975, Matthew David b 1 July 1979); *Career* CA 1978; articled clerk T & H P Bee Preston 1967–72; ptnr: Tyson Westall CAs Lancs 1973–76, Grant Thornton CAs (formerly Thornton Baker) 1976–86; sr ptnr Lonsdale and Partners CAs Lancaster and branches 1986–; FICA; *Recreations* sailing; *Clubs* Lancaster Loyne Rotary, S Caernarvonshire Yacht, Abersoch Golf; *Style*— Christopher Oddie, Esq; ✉ Springfields, Brettargh Drive, Lancaster LA1 5BN (☎ 01524 61858); Lonsdale & Partners, Priory Close, St Marys Gate, Lancaster LA1 1XB (☎ 01524 62801, fax 01524 37764)

ODDIE, Elaine Anne; da of Brian John Cory, of Hartley, Kent, and Molly, *née* Williams; *b* 11 Feb 1955; *Educ* Gravesend Girls' Sch, King's Coll Cambridge (MA); *m* 3 July 1976 (m dis), Alan James Oddie; *Career* articled clerk Brebner Allen & Trapp 1976–79, fin accountant Yardley International Ltd 1979–82; ptnr: Mason Charlesworth & Co 1982–89, Morison Stoneham 1989–; memb N Thames Gas Consumers' Cncl 1981–84, pres S Essex Soc of Chartered Accountants 1990–91, memb Cncl ICAEW, memb Exec Ctee Squash

Rackets Assoc 1994–; FCA 1989 (ACA 1979); *Recreations* squash, running, walking; *Style—* Ms Elaine Oddie; ✉ Morison Stoneham, Moriston House, 75 Springfield Rd, Chelmsford, Essex CM2 6JB (☎ 01245 492920, fax 01245 490841, e-mail 106104.3447@ compuserve.com); 7 Bellway Court, Grosvenor Road, Westcliff-on-Sea, Essex SS0 8EP

ODDY, Dr (William) Andrew; s of William Tingle Oddy (d 1985), and Hilda Florence, *née* Dalby; *b* 6 Jan 1942; *Educ* Bradford GS, New Coll Oxford (BA, BSc, MA, DSc); *m* 4 Aug 1965, Patricia Anne, da of Albert Edward Whitaker, of Upton upon Severn, Worcs; 1 s (Guy b 1968), 1 da (Frances b 1970); *Career* Br Museum: scientific offr 1966–69, sr scientific offr 1969–75, princ scientific offr 1975–81, head of conservation 1981–85, keeper of conservation 1985–; hon res fell UCL 1992–; author of over 200 papers, articles, notes and reviews in learned jls, ed and jt ed of the proceedings of 9 conferences; memb several learned socs and numerous ctees connected with the conservation of museum objects; Freeman: Worshipful Co of Goldsmiths 1986, City of London 1986; FSA 1973; *Books* Romanesque Metalwork: Copper Alloys and their Decoration (with Susan La Niece and Neil Stratford, 1986), The Art of the Conservator (ed and co-author, 1992); *Recreations* travel; *Style—* Dr Andrew Oddy, FSA; ✉ Department of Conservation, The British Museum, London WC1B 3DG (☎ 0171 323 8223, fax 0171 323 8636)

ODDY, Christine; MEP (Lab) Coventry and Warwickshire North (majority 43,901); da of Eric Lawson Oddy, and Audrey Mary, *née* Latham; *b* 20 Sept 1955; *Educ* UCL (LLB), Institut d'Études Européenes Brussels (licenciée spéciale en droit Européen, Belgian Govt scholar, Walter Page Hine travel scholar, Cncl of Europe travel scholar), Birkbeck Coll London (MScEcon); *Career* Stagiaire at European Commission Brussels 1979–80, articled clerk 1980–82, admitted slr 1982, charity worker 1982–83, law lectr City of London Poly 1984–89, assoc fell Dept of Sociology Univ of Warwick; MEP (Lab): Midlands Central 1989–94, Coventry and Warwicks N 1994–; memb Inst for Employment Rights; memb Editorial Bd Int Jl of Discrimination and the Law; memb: Bentham Soc, Haldane Soc, Industl Law Soc, Law Soc; hon fell Professional Business and Tech Mgmnt, MRIIA, FRSA; *Recreations* arts, cinema, theatre and wine; *Clubs* English Speaking Union; *Style—* Ms Christine Oddy, MEP; ✉ 3 Copthall House, Station Square, Coventry CV1 2FZ (☎ 01203 552328, fax 01203 551424)

O'DELL, June Patricia; OBE (1990); da of Lt Leonard Frederick Vickery (d 1940), and Myra Sarah, *née* Soden (d 1972); *b* 9 June 1929; *Educ* Edgehill Girls' Coll Bideford N Devon, Plymouth Tech Coll; *m* 9 Feb 1951 (m dis 1963), Ronald Desmond O'Dell; 1 s (Richard Patrick b 27 Feb 1952), 2 da (Caroline b 16 Nov 1955, Alison Julia b 27 July 1957); *Career* princ Chesneys Estate Agents 1965–88, nat pres UK Fedn of Business and Professional Women 1983–85, chair Int Fedn of Business and Professional Women Employment Ctee 1983–87, dep chair Equal Opportunities Cmmn 1986–90, memb Euro Advsy Ctee for Equal Treatment Between Women and Men 1986–90, dir Eachdale Devpts 1988–; non-exec dir Aylesbury Vale Community Care Health Tst 1992–; RSA: memb Women's Advsy Gp 1985–95, memb Cncl 1992–, chm Fellowship and Marketing Ctee 1994–, memb Women's Forum 1996–; memb: Women's Fin Panel National and Provincial Building Society 1988–95, Authorised Conveyancing Practitioners Bd 1991–94, Lord Chllr's Legal Aid Advsy Ctee 1992–94, Bd Probus Womens Housing Soc 1992–; vice chm Probus 1996–; tstee Women Returners Network 1994–96; FRSA 1987; *Recreations* opera, music, reading, theatre, the countryside, watching equestrian events; *Clubs* University Women's; *Style—* Mrs June O'Dell, OBE; ✉ Gable End, High Street, Great Missenden, Bucks HP16 9AA (☎ 01494 890185)

ODELL, Prof Peter Randon; s of Frank James Odell (d 1978), of Coalville, Leicester, and Grace Edna, *née* Randon (d 1954); *b* 1 July 1930; *Educ* King Edward VII GS Coalville Leicester, Univ of Birmingham (BA, PhD, W A Cadbury prize, Univ Graduate scholarship), Fletcher Sch of Law and Diplomacy, Tufts Univ Boston USA (AM); *m* 17 Aug 1957, Jean Mary, da of Ewan John McKintosh (d 1991), of Isle of Man; 2 s (Nigel Peter b 1958, Mark John b 1965), 2 da (Deborah Grace b 1960, Susannah Mary b 1967); *Career* RAF Educn Offr 1954–57, Flying Offr 1954–56, Flt Lt 1956–57; economist Shell International Petroleum Company Ltd 1958–61, sr lectr in econ geography LSE 1966–68 (lectr 1961–66); prof of econ geography Netherlands Sch of Economics 1968–73; Erasmus Univ Rotterdam: prof of econ geography 1973–81, prof of int energy studies 1982–91, prof emeritus 1992–; visiting prof: Coll of Europe Bruges 1984–90, LSE 1985–; Killam visiting fell Univ of Calgary Canada 1989, visiting scholar Univ of Cambridge 1996–; IAEE Prize for Outstanding Contrib to Energy Economics 1991, Royal Scottish Geographical Soc Centenary Medal 1993; Euro Parly candidate (SLD) Suffolk and S E Cambridgeshire 1989; memb: Int Assoc for Energy Economics, Royal Cwlth Tst, Chatham House, RIIA; FInstPet, FRSA, FRGS; *Books* An Economic Geography of Oil (1963), Natural Gas in Western Europe - A Case Study in the Economic Geography of Energy Resources (1969), Oil and World Power - A Geographical Interpretation (1970, 8 edn 1986), Economies and Societies in Latin America - A Geographical Interpretation (with D A Preston, 1973, 1978), The North Sea Oil Province: A Simulation of Development 1969–2029 (with K E Rosing, 1975), The West European Energy Economy - The Case for Self-Sufficiency (1976), The Pressures of Oil - A Strategy for Economic Revival (with L Vallenilla, 1978), The Future of Oil (with K E Rosing, 1980, 1983), The International Oil Industry (with J Rees, 1987), Global and Regional Energy Supplies (1991), The Evolution of the European Energy Economy 1945–1995 (1997); *Recreations* mountain walking, local history; *Clubs* Royal Commonwealth, Ipswich and Suffolk; *Style—* Prof Peter Odell; ✉ 7 Constitution Hill, Ipswich, Suffolk IP1 3RG (☎ 01473 253376, fax 01473 259125); Erasmus University, Postbus 1738, 3000 DR Rotterdam, Netherlands (☎ 00 31 10 408 1461, fax 00 31 10 452 7009)

ODELL, Sir Stanley John; kt (1986); s of George Frederick Odell (d 1990), and Florence May, *née* Roberts (d 1972); *b* 20 Nov 1929; *Educ* Bedford Modern Sch; *m* 4 Dec 1952, (Eileen) Grace, da of Reginald Edward Percival Stuart; 4 da (Sally (Mrs Strong) b 1954, Carol (Mrs Parry) b 1956, Julie (Mrs Warner) b 1958, Susan (Mrs Dann) b 1961); *Career* former chm Mid Bedfordshire Cons Assoc and Cons E Provincial Area; chm: Nat Union of Cons and Unionist Assocs, S Beds Community Health Care Tst; memb Ct Luton Univ, churchwarden All Saints Church Campton; *Recreations* politics, shooting; *Clubs* Farmers'; *Style—* Sir Stanley Odell; ✉ Woodhall Farm, Campton, Shefford, Beds SG17 5PB (☎ 01462 813 230)

ODGERS, Sir Graeme David William; kt (1997); s of William Arthur Odgers (d 1950), and Elizabeth Minty, *née* Rennie (d 1987); *b* 10 March 1934; *Educ* St John's Coll Johannesburg, Gonville and Caius Coll Cambridge, Harvard Business Sch (MBA); *m* 1957, Diana Patricia, *née* Berge; 1 s (John), 2 da (Mary, Juliet) and 1 da decd; *Career* dir Keith Shipton & Co Ltd 1965–72, chm Odgers & Co (mgmnt conslts) 1970–74, C T Bowring (Insurance) Holdings Ltd 1972–74, dir Indust Devpt Unit DOI 1974–77, assoc dir (fin) GEC 1977–78, gp md Tarmac plc 1983–86 (gp fin dir 1979–83); BT: pt/t memb Bd 1983–86, UK govt dir 1984–86, dep chm and chief fin offr 1986–87, gp md 1987–90; non-exec dir: Dalgety 1987–93, National and Provincial Building Society 1990–93; chief exec Alfred McAlpine plc 1990–93; chm Monopolies and Mergers Cmmn 1993–; *Recreations* golf; *Clubs* Wilderness; *Style—* Sir Graeme Odgers; ✉ Brome House, High St, W Malling, Kent ME19 6NE; Monopolies and Mergers Commission, 48 Carey Street, London WC2A 2HX (☎ 0171 324 1467)

ODLING-SMEE, John Charles; s of Rev Charles William Odling-Smee (d 1990), of Brearton, N Yorks, and Katharine Hamilton, *née* Aitchison; *b* 13 April 1943; *Educ* Durham Sch, St John's Coll Cambridge (MA); *m* 1996, Carmela Veneroso; *Career* res offr Inst of Econs and Statistics Univ of Oxford 1968–71 and 1972–73, fell in econs Oriel Coll 1966–70, econ res offr Govt of Ghana 1971–72, sr res offr Centre for Urban Econs LSE 1973–75, econ advsr Central Policy Review Staff 1975–77, sr econ advsr HM Treasy 1977–80, sr economist IMF 1981–82, dep chief econ advsr HM Treasy 1989–90 (under-sec in econs 1982–89), dept dir IMF 1992– (sr advsr 1990–91); author of articles in learned jls; *Books* British Economic Growth 1855–1973 (with R C O Matthews and C H Feinstein, 1982); *Style—* John Odling-Smee, Esq; ✉ 3506 Garfield Street NW, Washington DC 20007, USA (☎ 00 1 202 338 3471)

ODLING-SMEE, Peter Guy; s of Lt-Col Alfred John Odling-Smee, OBE (d 1987), of Newton Ferrers, nr Plymouth, Devon, and Dorothy Nancy, *née* Bowles (d 1982); *b* 30 June 1938; *Educ* Charterhouse, Britannia RNC Dartmouth; *m* 12 July 1968, Marianne, da of Grosser Helge Fischer (d 1972), of Korsor, Denmark; 2 s (Christopher b 19 Oct 1970, Michael Kristian b 22 Nov 1973); *Career* RN; Sub Lt 1959, trg HMS Victorious and minesweepers, joined RN Surveying Serv 1960, specialised in hydrographic surveying worldwide, i/c RN Antarctic Survey Pty 1967–68, sr instr RN Sch of Hydrographic Surveying HMS Drake Plymouth, ret Lt Cdr 1976; sr surveyor Kelvin Hughes Ltd (worked Saudi Arabia, Indonesia, Libya) 1976–79, princ Odling-Smee Oberman Assoc 1979–, sr lectr in marine sci Polytechnic South West 1982–89, currently hydrographic conslt; UK rep Advsy Bd on Standards of Competence for Hydrographic Surveyors, memb Training and Education Ctee RICS; FRICS; *Recreations* horse riding, foxhunting, Himalayan trekking, skiing, sailing; *Clubs* Royal Western Yacht; *Style—* Peter Odling-Smee, Esq; ✉ Hanger Farm, Cornwood, nr Ivybridge, Devon PL21 9HP (☎ 01752 837370)

ODLING-SMEE, (George) William; s of Rev Charles William Odling-Smee (d 1990), of Brearton, nr Harrogate, Yorkshire, and Katharine Hamilton, *née* Aitchison; *b* 21 April 1935; *Educ* Durham Sch, Kings Coll Newcastle upon Tyne, Univ of Durham; *m* 30 July 1959, Anne Marie, da of Walter Louis Thacker (ka 1944); 3 s (Patrick William b 1963, James Louis b 1965, Hugh Hamilton b 1973), 3 da (Margaret Emma b 1960, Katherine Anne b 1962, Elizabeth Mary b 1971, d 1974); *Career* med supt St Raphael's Hosp Giddalur South India 1961–64, dir Child Med Care Unit Enugu Nigeria 1969, sr tutor in surgery Queen's Univ of Belfast 1970–73, sr lectr in surgery and conslt surgn Royal Victoria Hosp Belfast 1973–; FRCS (England) 1968 (memb Ct), FRCS (Ireland) 1987 (memb Ct); *Books* Trauma Care (1981), Breast Cancer (1989); *Recreations* theology; *Style—* William Odling-Smee, Esq; ✉ 10 Deramore Park South, Belfast BT9 5JY, Northern Ireland; Royal Victoria Hospital, Grosvenor Rd, Belfast BT12 6BA (☎ 240503 ext 2658)

ODONE, Cristina; da of Augusto Odone, of Washington DC, and Ulla Sjöström Odone; *b* 11 Nov 1960; *Educ* Nat Cathedral Sch Washington, St Clare's Hall Oxford, Worcester Coll Oxford (BA); *Career* freelance journalist 1982–83 (articles published in Cosmopolitan, Harper's & Queen, TES, Daily Telegraph, Company, The Independent); journalist: The Catholic Herald 1983–85, The Times Diary 1986; conslt Odone Assocs Washington DC (lobbyists at World Bank on behalf of euro cos) 1987–92, ed The Catholic Herald 1992–96, TV critic The Daily Telegraph 1996–; *Books* The Shrine (novel, 1996); *Recreations* reading, walking, travelling, entertaining; *Style—* Miss Cristina Odone; ✉ c/o The Daily Telegraph, 1 Canada Square, Canary Wharf, London E14 5DT

ODONI, Prof Robert Winston Keith; s of (Anthony Vincent) Walter Odoni, of London, and Lois Marie, *née* Conner (d 1984); *b* 14 July 1947; *Educ* Queen Elizabeth's GS, Univ of Exeter (BSc), Downing Coll Cambridge (PhD); *m* 1 July 1972, Josephine Anne, da of Joseph Ding, of Cambridge; 2 s (Martin b 1975, Russell b 1984), 1 da (Theresa b 1973); *Career* temp lectr pure maths Liverpool Univ 1971–72, res fell pure maths Glasgow Univ 1972–73; Exeter Univ: lectr pure maths 1973–79, reader number theory 1979–85, prof number theory 1985–89; prof mathematics Glasgow Univ 1989–; memb: London Mathematical Soc 1973 (memb editorial bd 1987–), Cambridge Philosophical Soc 1973, American Mathematical Soc 1976, Société Mathématique de France 1981; FRSE 1996; *Books* author of numerous res articles in major mathematical jls; *Recreations* music, foreign languages, country walks, swimming, cricket; *Style—* Prof Robert Odoni, FRSE; ✉ Dept of Mathematics, Univ of Glasgow, Glasgow G12 8QW (☎ 0141 339 8855)

O'DONNELL, Augustine Thomas (Gus); CB (1994); s of James O'Donnell, and Helen, *née* McLean; *b* 1 Oct 1952; *Educ* Salesian Coll Battersea, Univ of Warwick (BA), Nuffield Coll Oxford (soccer blue, MPhil); *m* 1979, Melanie Joan Elizabeth, *née* Timmis; 1 da (Kirstin Elizabeth b 3 Nov 1990); *Career* lectr in political economy Univ of Glasgow 1975–79, economist HM Treasy 1979–85, first sec Br Embassy Washington DC 1985–88, sr econ advsr HM Treasy 1988–89, Treasy chief press sec 1989–90, Prime Minister's chief press sec 1990–94, head of monetary gp HM Treasy 1994–97, econ min Br Embassy Washington and UK exec dir IMF and IBRD 1997–; *Recreations* football, tennis, skiing; *Style—* Gus O'Donnell, Esq, CB; ✉ c/o The British Embassy, 3100 Massachusetts Avenue, NW, Washington DC, 20008, USA

O'DONNELL, Hugh; s of John O'Donnell of Ireland, and Jean O'Donnell; *Educ* Camberwell Coll of Art, Falmouth Coll of Art (BA), Birmingham Coll of Art (HDip AD, prize Sir Whitworth Wallace Tst), RCA; *m* Tina Eden; 1 da (Kristie b 1983); *Career* artist; *Solo Exhibitions* incl: Works on Paper (Nishimura Gallery Tokyo) 1976, Air Gallery London 1977, Paintings and Drawings (Ikon Gallery Birmingham) 1979, Rahr-West Museum Wisconsin 1983, Marlborough Gallery (London 1985, NY 1986 and 1987), Works on Paper and Monoprints (Marlborough Gallery NY) 1984, Works on Paper (Marlborough Graphics London) 1984, Paintings (Marlborough Gallery NY) 1987, Paintings (Eva Cohen Gallery Chicago 1990, Hokin Gallery Palm Beach Florida 1989), Paintings and Works on Paper (Eva Cohen Gallery Chicago) 1990, Paintings (Marlborough Gallery NY) 1991, The Lake Series (Denise Cade Gallery NY 1992, Jan Abrams Gallery LA 1994, Freedman Gallery Pennsylvania 1995, Art Museum Univ of Memphis 1995), The Body Echo Project (Freedman Gallery Pennsylvania 1995, Art Museum Univ of Memphis 1995); *Gp Exhibitions* incl: first exhibition 1972, Br Art Now (Guggenheim Museum NY) 1980, Decorative Arts Award 1988 (designs for jewels - collaboration with Ros Conway, Sotheby's London Museum of Modern Art), Kyoto Japan, Arte & Alchimia (XLII Venice Biennale) 1986, The Question of Drawing (South Campus Gallery Miami, travelled) 1989, Works on Paper: Amenoff, Barth, O'Donnell (Tomoko Liguori Gallery NY) 1990, Marlborough en Pelaires (Centre Cultural Contemporani Pelaires Palma de Mallorca) 1990, Drawings Only (Denise Cade Gallery NY) 1992, Innovations in Collaborative Print Making: Kenneth Tyler 1963–92 (Yokohama Museum of Art and tour of Japan) 1992–93, Drawing in Black and White: Selections from the Permanent Collection (Museum of Modern Art NY) 1993, First Thoughts: Working Drawings by Seven Artists (Bristol-Myers Squibb Co Princeton) 1993, Selection of Prints from Graphics Studio (Greenfield Gallery LA) 1993, Works on Paper (Margret Biederman Gallery Munich) 1994, The Computer in the Studio (DeCordova Museum and Sculpture Park Lincoln MA) 1994, Works Selected by Dore Ashton (Bill Maynes Gallery NY) 1994–95, An American Passion: The Kasen Summer Collection of Contemporary British Painting (McLellan Galleries Glasgow) 1994–95; selected public collections: Br Cncl UK, Solomon R Guggenheim Museum NY, London Contempory Arts Soc, Met Museum of Modern Art NY, Museum of Modern Art NY, V & A, Arts Cncl of GB, Virginia Museum of Fine Arts, Nat Gallery of Art Washington DC; Purchase award Arts Cncl of GB 1978 (Arts Cncl award 1978); set and costume designs for: Red Steps (London Contemporary Dance Theatre), Drawn Breath (Siobhan Davies Dance Company, 1989 Digit Dance award); numerous appearances on American television; *Style*— Hugh O'Donnell, Esq; ✉ 34 Shearer Road, Washington, CT 06793, USA (☎ 00 1 203 860 868 9770, fax 00 1 203 860 868 9717)

O'DONNELL, James Anthony; s of Dr James Joseph Gerard O'Donnell (d 1978), and Dr Gillian Anne O'Donnell, *née* Moody; *b* 15 Aug 1961; *Educ* Westcliff HS Essex, RCM, Jesus Coll Cambridge (organ scholar, open scholar in music, BA, MA); *Career* master of music Westminster Cathedral 1988– (asst master 1982–88), lectr in church music studies RAM 1990–; RCO Performer of the Year 1987; memb Cncl RCO 1989–; FRCO 1983; *Recreations* opera, food and wine, playing squash; *Style*— James O'Donnell, Esq; ✉ Westminster Cathedral Clergy House, 42 Francis Street, London SW1P 1QW (☎ 0171 798 9066/9057, fax 0171 798 9091)

O'DONNELL, Dr Michael; s of Dr James Michael O'Donnell (d 1957), and Nora, *née* O'Sullivan (d 1976); *b* 20 Oct 1928; *Educ* Stonyhurst, Trinity Hall Cambridge, St Thomas' Hosp; *m* 1952, Catherine, da of Frank Dorrington Ward (d 1972); 1 s (James), 2 da (Frances, Lucy); *Career* family doctor 1953–64; ed World Medicine 1966–81, contrib to Stop the Week (BBC) 1977–92, chm My Word (BBC) 1983–, writer and presenter Relative Values 1986–; written and presented TV documentaries in USA and UK incl: Inside Medicine (BBC) 1973, A Part of Life (YTV) 1977, Is Your Brain Really Necessary? (YTV) 1978, Medical Express (BBC) 1983, Plague of Hearts (BBC) 1983, O'Donnell Investigates (BBC) 1985, 1986 and 1988, Health, Wealth and Happiness (BBC) 1989; memb GMC 1971–; FRCGP; *Books* The Devil's Prison (1982), An Insider's Guide to the Games Doctors Play (1986), The Long Walk Home (1988), How to Succeed in Business without Sacrificing Your Health (1988), Serious Professional Misconduct (1993), The Bhamjee Beat (1995); contrib: The Times, The Guardian, Daily Mail, Daily Telegraph; *Recreations* walking, golf, music; *Clubs* Garrick; *Style*— Dr Michael O'Donnell; ✉ Handon Cottage, Markwick Lane, Loxhill, Godalming, Surrey GU8 4BD (☎ 01486 32295)

O'DONNELL, Ron; s of James Brogan O'Donnell (d 1989), and Susan McKee, *née* McCartney; *b* 28 Oct 1952; *Educ* Jacqueline, da of William John McDonald; 2 s (Robert b 12 March 1977, Ross b 14 Aug 1979), 1 da (Kim b 21 Feb 1974); *Career* trainee photographer Stirling Univ 1970–76; *Solo Exhibition* The Vigorous Imagination (Scottish Nat Gallery of Modern Art) 1987; *Group Exhibitions* incl: Cross References (Walker Art Centre Minneapolis), 1987, The Rampant Scots (Art Space San Francisco) 1988, Masters of Photography (V & A) 1986, Mysterious Coincidences (Photographers Gallery London) 1987, Sanders Gallery New York 1987, British Cncl Barcelona 1988, Scottish Art since 1900 (Nat Gall of Modern Art) 1989, Through the Looking Glass (Barbican) 1989, Raab Gallery Berlin 1989, The New North (Tate Gallery Liverpool and tour), Betzalel Hebrew Univ Jerusalem 1989, L'Invention d'un Art (Centre Georges Pompidou) 1989, California State Univ Los Angeles 1990, Images en Miettes (Centre Georges Pompidou) 1991, Rotterdam Biennale 1992, touring exhibition 1994; *Awards* Scottish Arts Cncl Award for Photography 1979, Fox Talbot Award for Photography 1987; *Style*— Ron O'Donnell, Esq

O'DONOGHUE, (James) Bernard; s of Bartholomew James O'Donoghue (d 1962), of Cullen, Co Cork, and Mary Josephine, *née* McNulty (d 1979); *b* 14 Dec 1945; *Educ* Coláiste Pádraig Millstreet Co Cork, St Bede's Coll Manchester, Lincoln Coll Oxford (BA, BPhil); *m* 23 July 1977, Heather O'Donoghue, Vigfusson-Rausing reader in old Icelandic Univ of Oxford and fell of Linacre Coll Oxford, da of Roderick MacKinnon, and Sheila MacKinnon; 2 da (Ellen Mary b 11 Sept 1978, Josephine Sheila b 26 Dec 1986), 1 s (Thomas Roderick b 4 Jan 1981); *Career* writer; trainee systems analyst IBM (UK) 1968–69, tutor in English language and Medieval literature Magdalen Coll Oxford 1971–95, fell in English Wadham Coll Oxford 1995–; memb AUT 1971–; *Books* The Courtly Love Tradition (1982); *Poetry* Razorblades and Pencils (1984), Poaching Rights (1987), The Absent Signifier (1990), The Weakness (1991, winner Southern Arts Award), Gunpowder (1995, winner Whitbread Poetry Prize); *Recreations* classical and Irish music, Manchester City FC; *Style*— Bernard O'Donoghue, Esq; ✉ 14 Hill Top Road, Oxford OX4 1PB (☎ 01865 243662); Wadham College, Oxford OX1 3PN

O'DONOGHUE, Daniel; s of Daniel O'Donoghue (d 1994), of Knockroe, Castlerea, Roscommon, Eire, and Sabina, *née* Carey (d 1976); *b* 27 March 1947; *Educ* St Bede's Coll Manchester, Univ of Sheffield (BEng); *m* 1 April 1972, Suzanne Lynne Andromeda, da of Harold Hamer Holman; 3 s (Timothy Peter Joseph b 4 Dec 1977, James Edward Michael b 27 Aug 1980, Alexander Daniel Hogarth b 13 Sept 1982), 1 da (Johanna Morgan Driella b 12 Jan 1985); *Career* advtg exec; trainee GUS 1968–69; market res mangr Europe Rowntree 1973–76 (market res offr 1969–73), marketing offr Shepherd Building 1976–77, account planner Ogilvy Benson Mather 1977–79; planning dir: CDP/Aspect 1979–82, McCormicks 1982–87, Publicis (formerly McCormicks) 1987–88; dep chm Publicis-FCB Group 1989–, jt chief exec Publicis 1991– (vice chm 1988–91); memb MRS 1973, FIPA (chm Bibliography Ctee 1989–90, memb Cncl 1989–93), memb Educn Cncl D&AD; *Recreations* fine art collecting, football; *Clubs* Soho House; *Style*— Daniel O'Donoghue, Esq; ✉ Woodcroft Castle, Marholm, Peterborough, Cambridgeshire PE6 7HW; Publicis Ltd, 82 Baker Street, London W1M 2AE (☎ 0171 935 4426, fax 0171 935 7251)

O'DONOGHUE, Denise; da of Micheal O'Donoghue (d 1991), and Margaret (Maura), *née* McMahon (d 1993); *Educ* St Dominic's Girls' Sch, Univ of York (BA Hons); *Career* administrator Independent Prodrs' Assoc then prodr Who Dares Wins (Channel Four) until 1986; md and co-owner: Hat Trick Productions Ltd 1986–, Hat Trick Films Ltd 1992–; Hat Trick programmes incl: Father Ted, Drop the Dead Donkey, Have I Got News for You, Clive Anderson All Talk, Game On, Whose Line is it Anyway?; *Awards* for A Very Open Prison: 1995 Writers' Guild Award for Best Television Play or Film; for Clive Anderson Talks Back: Clive Anderson ITV/Channel 4 TV Personality of the Year 1991, Brit Comedy Awards Winner, Top Entertainment Presenter Award, 1995 Tric Awards Winner; for Drop the Dead Donkey: 1995 Brit Comedy Awards Winner, Best Channel 4 Sitcom, Best Comedy Series; for Eleven Men Against Eleven: 1996 RTS Awards Winner, Best Single Drama); for Father Ted: 1996 BAFTA Winner, Best Comedy, 1995 Brit Comedy Awards Winner, Best New TV Comedy, 1995 Brit Comedy Awards, Ardal O'Hanlon Best TV Comedy Newcomer; for Have I Got News for You (1995 Tric Awards Winner, Angus Deayton BBC TV Personality of the Year, 1993 Independent Awards Winner, Top Comedy Programme; for Whose Line is it Anyway?: 1991, 1992, 1994 and 1995 Ace Awards Winner, Best Int Comedy Special or Series; other Hat Trick prodns Awards: Indie Pioneer Award 1995 and 1996, Independent on Sunday Top 100 Privately Owned Businesses 1991, 1992 and 1993, Broadcast Magazine Best Prodn Company Award 1992; *Style*— Ms Denise O'Donoghue; ✉ Hat Trick Productions, 10 Livonia Street, London W1V 3PH (☎ 0171 434 2451, fax 0171 287 9791/0171 437 0773)

O'DONOGHUE, Hughie Eugene; s of Daniel O'Donoghue (d 1994), and Sabina Carey (d 1976); *b* 5 July 1953; *Educ* St Augustine's RC GS Manchester, Trinity and All Saints' Colls Leeds, Goldsmiths' Coll Univ of London (MA, CertEd); *m* 18 May 1974, Clare, da of Thomas Patrick Reynolds (d 1987); 2 s (Matthew Thomas b 12 Nov 1974, Vincent John Domhnall b 26 July 1987), 1 da (Kathryn Sabina b 20 July 1985); *Career* artist; solo exhibitions incl: Air Gallery London 1984, Nat Gallery London 1985, Fabian Carlsson Gallery London 1986 and 1989, Galleria Carini Florence Italy 1987, Art Now Gallery Gothenburg Sweden 1987, Kilkenny Festival 1991, Gallery Helmut Pabst Frankfurt 1991, Thirteen Drawings from the Human Body (Jill George Gallery) 1993, A Painted Passion (Atlantis Upper Gallery) 1993; gp exhibitions incl: Whitechapel Open (Whitechapel Art Gallery London) 1982, 1983, 1986, 1988 and 1992, 10 Years at Air (Air Gallery London) 1984, Works on Paper (Anthony Reynolds Gallery London and Galleria Carini Florance Italy) 1986, New Year New Work (Fabian Carlsson Gallery London) 1987, Nuovi Territori dell Arte: Europa/America (Francavilla al Mare Italy) 1987, The Romantic Tradition in Contemporary British Painting (Sala de Exposiciones Murcia, Circulo de Bellas Artes Madrid, Ikon Gallery Birmingham) 1988, Landscape and Beyond (Cleveland Gallery Middlesbrough) 1988, Ways of Telling (Oriel Mostyn Llandudno Wales) 1989, Drawing '89 Cleveland (UK) 9th Int Drawing Biennale (prizewinner), School of London 1989, Works on Paper (Odette Gilbert Gallery London) 1989, Roads to Abstraction (Whitworth Art Gallery Manchester) 1990, The Forces of Nature - Landscape as Metaphor (Manchester City Art Galleries) 1990; work in several public collections; *Awards* Artist's awards Lincolnshire and Humberside Arts Assoc 1977 and 1978, 1979, Artist in Industry fellowship Yorkshire Arts Assoc 1983, artist in residence Nat Gallery London (Nat Gallery and Arts Cncl of GB) 1984; *PI* Hughie O'Donoghue Paintings and Drawings 1983–86 (1986), Hughie O'Donoghue Opera 1986–87 (1987), Crow Paintings Hughie O'Donoghue (1989), Fires (1989), Thirteen Drawings from the Human Body (1993); *Style*— Hughie O'Donoghue, Esq; ✉ Kilfane Glebe, Thomastown, Co Kilkenny, Ireland; Unit 7, Larnaca Works, Grange Walk, London SE1 (☎ 0171 231 8751); c/o Purdy Hicks Gallery, 65 Hopton Street, London SE1 9GZ (☎ 0171 237 6062)

O'DONOGHUE, His Hon Michael; s of Dr James O'Donoghue, MB (d 1948), of Boundary St, Liverpool, and Vera Maude, *née* Cox (d 1981); *b* 10 June 1929; *Educ* Rhyl County Sch, Univ of Liverpool (LLB); *Career* served RAF 1951–53, Flying Offr; called to the Bar Gray's Inn 1951, practised at the Chancery Bar 1954–82, circuit judge 1982–94; pt/t lectr in law Univ of Liverpool 1966–82, pt/t memb Lands Tbnl 1988–94; *Recreations* music, sailing (yacht 'Equity III'), photography, painting; *Clubs* Athenaeum (Liverpool), Royal Welsh Yacht (Cdre 1980–82, pres 1993–); *Style*— His Hon Michael O'Donoghue

O'DONOGHUE, Rt Rev Patrick Augustine; s of Daniel O'Donoghue (d 1970), of Mourne Abbey, Mallow, Cork, and Sheila, *née* Twomey (d 1985); *Educ* Patrician Acad Mallow Cork, Campion House Coll Osterley Isleworth, St Edmund's Coll Ware Herts; *Career* ordained RC priest 1967; Dio of Westminster: memb Diocesan Mission Team 1970–73, rector Allen Hall Diocesan Seminary Chelsea 1985–90, admin Westminster Cathedral 1990–93, aux bishop (with responsibility for Western area) 1993–; involvement with other orgns incl: The Passage Day Centre for the Poor, Cardinal Hume Centre for Young Homeless, The Lillie Road Centre for Children in Care, Acton Homeless Concern, St Pancras Housing Assoc, Christian Arts Tst; *Recreations* walking (in countryside), travel, theatre, football (spectator); *Style*— The Rt Rev Patrick O'Donoghue, Bishop in West London; ✉ Our Lady and St Bridget, 112 Twickenham Road, Isleworth, Middx TW7 6DL (☎ and fax 0181 568 7371)

O'DONOGHUE, Rodney Charles (Rod); s of George Albert O'Donoghue (d 1988), and Doris Ada, *née* Matthews; *b* 10 June 1938; *Educ* Merchant Taylors'; *m* 17 Oct 1964, Kay Patricia, da of Clifford Montague Lewis; 2 s (Mark Christopher b 20 Feb 1970, Richard James b 24 Sept 1977), 1 da (Kerry Frances b 26 July 1974); *Career* articled clerk Singleton Fabian & Co CAs 1956–61, audit staff Monkhouse Stoneham & Co 1961–63, fin dir Kimberly-Clark Ltd 1965–72 (asst fin mangr 1963–65), gp controller Rank Xerox Group 1972–83, gp fin dir Pritchard Services Group 1983–86; gp fin dir Inchcape plc 1986–; FCA (ACA 1961), FCT; *Recreations* history, genealogy (runs the worldwide O'Donoghue One Name Soc), writing O'Donoghue - People and Places and also The O'Donoghue Trail, nature, golf, walking; *Clubs* IOD; *Style*— Rod O'Donoghue, Esq; ✉ The Coach House, Little Gaddesden, Berkhamsted, Herts HP4 1PH (e-mail Rod@histgen.demon.co.uk); Inchcape plc, 33 Cavendish Square, London W1M 9HF (☎ 0171 546 0022, fax 0171 533 9116)

O'DONOGHUE OF THE GLENS, The; Geoffrey Paul Vincent O'Donoghue; *b* 19 July 1937; *m* 13 Feb 1963, Frances, da of James Kelly; 3 s, 4 da; *Heir* s, Conor, b Nov 1964; *Style*— The O'Donoghue of the Glens; ✉ Glas Choill, Screggan, Tullamore, Co Offaly; The Glens, Flesk, Co Kerry

O'DONOVAN, Prof Katherine; da of Prof John O'Donovan, TD (d 1982), of Dublin, and Kathleen, *née* Mahon (d 1991); *b* 7 Feb 1942; *Educ* Nat Univ of Ireland (BCL), Univ of Strasbourg (Diplôme de Droit Comparé), Harvard Law Sch (LLM), Univ of Kent (PhD); *m* 5 June 1971, Julian Davey, s of F V Davey, of Fernhurst, Sussex; 1 da (Julia b 4 Nov 1979); *Career* lectr in law: Queen's Univ Belfast 1965–69, Haile Sellassie I Univ Ethiopia 1969–72, Univ of Sussex 1972–73, Univ of Kent 1973–79, Univ of Malaya 1979–81, Univ of Kent 1981–85, Univ of Hong Kong 1985–88, Univ of Kent 1988–95; prof of law Queen Mary and Westfield Coll London 1995–; visiting prof Univ of Paris, Jean Monnet fell Euro Univ Inst Florence 1991–92; memb: Specialist Panel on Law CNAA, Cwlth Soc, Int Soc on Family Law, Cncl Soc of Public Teachers of Law, Nat Tst, RSPB; govr Canterbury Sch; *Books* Sexual Divisions in Law (1985), Equality and Sex Discrimination Law (1988), Family Law Matters (1993); *Clubs* Hong Kong, Cwlth Tst; *Style*— Prof Katherine O'Donovan; ✉ Faculty of Law, Queen Mary and Westfield College, Mile End Road, London E1 4NS (☎ 0171 755 3276)

O'DONOVAN, The; Morgan Gerald (Daniel) O'Donovan; s of Brig The O'Donovan, MC (Morgan (John) Winthrop, d 1969), of Hollybrook House, Skibbereen, Co Cork, and Cornelia, *née* Bagnell (d 1974); officially recognised Chief of the Name of one of the most ancient families of Ireland, traceable from Gaelic times; *b* 4 May 1931; *Educ* Stowe, Trinity Coll Cambridge (MA); *m* 19 Sept 1959, Frances Jane, da of Field Marshal Sir Gerald Walter Robert Templer, KG, GCB, GCMG, KBE, DSO (d 1979); 1 s (Morgan (Teige) Gerald b 1961), 2 da ((Katharine) Jane b 1962, Cecilia (Mary) Cornelia b 1966); *Heir* s, Morgan (Teige) Gerald O'Donovan; *Career* farmer; J & P Coats Ltd Glasgow 1954–63, mgmnt appts in Cuba, Colombia, Singapore, Australia, Revertex Ltd London 1963–70, md Wates & Co Ltd Dublin 1972–77 (joined 1970); memb Exec Ctee of Representative Body Church of Ireland, govr Midleton Coll Co Cork; *Recreations* shooting, fishing, bird watching, vintage cars; *Clubs* Kildare Street and University Dublin; *Style*— The O'Donovan; ✉ Hollybrook House, Skibbereen, Co Cork, Ireland (☎ 0128 21245)

O'DONOVAN, Rev Prof Oliver Michael Timothy; *b* 28 June 1945; *m* 1978, Joan Lockwood; 2 s (Matthew Augustine b 1981, Paul Jeremiah b 1986); *Career* ordained priest 1973 (deacon 1972), tutor Wycliffe Hall Oxford 1972–77, hon asst curate St Helen's Abingdon 1972–76, prof of systematic theology Wycliffe Coll Toronto Sch of Theology 1972–82 (asst 1977–81, assoc 1981–82), memb Church of England Bd for Social Responsibility 1976–77 & 1982–85, examining chaplain to Bishop of Toronto and memb Candidates Ctee of Diocese of Toronto 1978–82, regius prof of moral and pastoral theology Univ of Oxford and canon of Ch Ch Oxford 1982–; memb: Canadian Anglican-Roman Catholic Dialogue 1979–82, Jt Orthodox-Anglican Doctrinal Discussions 1982–85, Archbishop of Canterbury's Gp on the Law of Affinity 1982–84, Working Pty on Human Fertilization and Embryology of the Church of England Bd for Social Responsibility 1982–85, Mgmnt Ctee Ian Ramsey Centre St Cross Coll Oxford 1983–89, Anglican Roman Catholic Int Cmmn 1985–90, Cncl Wycliffe Hall Oxford 1985–95, House of Bishops' Working Gp on Marriage in Church after Divorce 1996–, Church of England Doctrine Cmmn 1996–; Chevasse Lectr Wycliffe Hall Oxford 1985, Church of Ireland Theological lectr Queen's Univ Belfast 1986, pastoral theology lectr Univ of Durham 1987, select preacher Univ of Oxford 1982, 1987, 1988 and 1993, Assize preacher Birmingham Cathedral 1988, Hulsean preacher Univ of Cambridge 1989, visiting lectr St Patrick's Coll Maynooth Ireland 1989, Payton lectr Fuller Theological

Seminary Passadena Calif 1989, Paddock lectr Gen Theological Seminary NY 1990–, Hulsean lectr Univ of Cambridge 1994, Hooker lectr McMaster Univ Ontario 1996; chm Bd of Faculty of Theology Univ of Oxford 1990–92; *Books* The Problem of Self-Love in Saint Augustine (1980), Begotten or Made? (1984), Resurrection and Moral Order (1986), On the Thirty Nine Articles: a Conversation with Tudor Christianity (1986), Peace and Certainty; a theological essay on deterrence (1989), The Desire of the Nations: rediscovering the roots of political theology (1996); *Style—* Rev Prof Oliver O'Donovan; ✉ Christ Church, Oxford OX1 1DP (☎ and fax 01865 276219)

O'DONOVAN, Timothy Charles Melville (Tim); s of John Conan Marshall Thornton O'Donovan (d 1964), of London, and Enid Muriel Liddell (d 1958); *b* 10 Feb 1932; *Educ* Marlborough; *m* 19 Sept 1958, Veronica Alacoque, da of Leslie White (d 1981), of Hawkley, Hants; 2 s (Michael b 1962, Richard b 1966); *Career* Nat Serv with Life Gds 1950–52; dir Common Cause Ltd 1964–95, chm Eckersley Hicks & Co Ltd Lloyd's Brokers 1979–84, dir of public affrs Bain Clarkson 1987–91; tstee Br Monarchy Museum Tst 1979–; chm: A Princess for Wales Exhibition 1981, Pollution Abatement Technol Award Scheme 1983–87, Better Environment Awards for Industry 1987–92; hon sec Soc of the Friends of St George's and Descendants of the Knights of the Garter 1992–; vice capt of lay stewards St George's Chapel Windsor Castle 1993– (steward 1978, dep vice capt 1983–93); tstee The Environment Fndn 1985–, div pres Maidenhead Div St John's Ambulance 1996–; memb The Queen's Birthday Ctee 1986; exhibitions organised: E-II-R - A Celebration 1986, Sixty Years a Queen (Windsor Castle) 1987, Ninety Memorable Years to Celebrate The Queen Mother's 90th birthday, The Queen is Crowned (Windsor Castle) 1993, Prince Philip His Life and Work; author of annual survey of Royal Family duties since 1979 in The Times and Illustrated London News; FRSA 1984; *Books* Above The Law?; *Recreations* watching cricket, photography, collecting royal memorabilia, reading the Court Circular; *Clubs* MCC; *Style—* Tim O'Donovan, Esq; ✉ Mariners, The Avenue, Datchet, Berks SL3 9DH; The Curfew Tower, Windsor Castle, Berks SL4 1NJ (☎ 01753 860629)

O'DOWD, David Joseph; CBE (1995), QPM (1988); s of Michael Joseph O'Dowd (d 1972), of Oadby, Leicestershire, and Helen, *née* Merrin; *b* 20 Feb 1942; *Educ* Gartree HS Oadby Leicester, Univ of Leicester (Dip Social Studies), Open Univ (BA), Univ of Aston (MSc), FBI Nat Acad USA; *m* 7 Sept 1963, Carole Ann, da of Charles Albert Watson, of Leicester; 1 s (Andrew David b 29 Jan 1967), 1 da (Sharon Marie b 3 Dec 1964); *Career* Sgt, Inspr and Chief Inspr CID Leicester City Police 1961, Supt W Midlands Police Coventry and Birmingham 1977; head of traffic policing, dir of complaints and discipline Investigation Bureau and head of strategic planning and policy Analysis Unit Metropolitan Police New Scotland Yard 1984; Chief Constable Northamptonshire Police 1986–93 (Asst Chief Constable head of operations 1982), HM Inspr of Constabulary 1993–96, HM Chief Inspr of Constabulary 1996–; Cabinet Office Top Mgmnt Prog 1986, rep Br Chief Constables Nat Exec Inst FBI Acad Washington 1988; visiting teaching fell Mgmnt Centre Univ of Aston Birmingham, fell Nene Coll Northampton; CIMgt 1988; *Recreations* golf, gardening, decorating; *Style—* David J O'Dowd, Esq, CBE, QPM; ✉ Her Majesty's Chief Inspector of Constabulary, Room 565, Home Office, 50 Queen Anne's Gate, London SW1H 9AT (☎ 0171 273 3084, fax 0171 273 4031)

O'DRISCOLL, Michael; s of Michael James O'Driscoll, of Hemingbrough, N Yorks, and Esther O'Driscoll; *b* 6 Aug 1939; *Educ* Archbishop Holgate's GS York, Univ of Leeds (MB, ChB), Univ of Bristol (MCh); *m* 28 Nov 1966, Susan Leah, da of Sam Lewis (d 1982), of Leeds; 2 s (Daniel b 1 July 1968, Gavin b 9 Aug 1969), 1 da (Philippa b 11 May 1972); *Career* offr's trg corps parachute section Univ of Leeds 1957–62; lectr orthopaedics Univ of Bristol 1969–77, visiting orthopaedic surgn Hebden Green Special Sch Winsford, currently conslt orthopaedic surgn Robert Jones and Agnes Hunt Orthopaedic Hosp Shropshire and Leighton Hosp Cheshire; memb: Fortress Study Gp, Back Pain Soc; patron Darren Kennerley Tst; FRCS 1967, memb SICOT 1983; *Recreations* fell walking, travelling, study of fortification, architecture, tanks and aircraft; *Clubs* Old Oswestrians; *Style—* Michael O'Driscoll; ✉ Leighton Hosp, Crewe, Cheshire; Robert Jones and Agnes Hunt Orthopaedic Hosp, Oswestry, Shropshire (☎ 01270 255141)

O'DRISCOLL, Suzanne Elizabeth; da of William George O'Driscoll, of Blackthorn, Bicester, Oxon, and Cynthia Anne, *née* Wright; *b* 7 June 1955; *Educ* St Joseph's Convent Reading, Berkshire Coll of Art, Central Sch of Art and Design London (BA), Slade Sch of Fine Art UCL (MND, Boise travelling scholarship to Mexico and Guatemala); *Career* artist; *Solo Exhibitions* incl: Air Gallery 1984, Anderson O'Day Gallery London 1987, 1989, South Hill Park Art Centre Bracknell Berkshire 1987, Solomon Gallery Dublin 1992, CCA Galleries Oxford 1993; *Group Exhibitions* incl: Three Decades of Artists from Inner London Art Schs 1953–83 RA London 1983, St John's Smith Square 1985, Space Artists B P London 1985, Air Gallery Picture Fair 1986, Anderson O'Day Gallery 1986, Open Studio Show Berry St London 1987, Heads Anderson O'Day 1987, Contemporary Arts Soc Market London annually 1987–, Oxford Gallery Oxford 1988, Drawing Show Thumb Gallery London 1988, Fish Exhibition South Hill Park, Bracknell 1988, Int Contemporary Art Fair London 1989 and 1990, Bath Contemporary Arts Fair 1989, Painting of the Week (Channel 4 TV) 1989, Works on Paper Thumb Gallery 1990, Encounters Oxford Gallery 1991, Art for a Fairer World OXFAM touring 1992, Archer Exhbn London 1992, Subtitles Mostra (Br Sch at Rome) 1994; *Commissions* for: Southampton Gen Hosp 1985, Harold Wood Gen Hosp Essex 1986, Radcliffe Infirmary Hosp Oxford 1986, RA Baileys Dublin 1994; work in various collections; artist in residence: Bracknell Sch Berkshire 1987, Rhos y Gwalian Wales 1987, Maidenhead Teachers Centre 1988; featured in Assessment and Evaluation in the Arts 1987; Edwin Austin Meml Rome scholarship 1993/94; *Style—* Ms Suzanne O'Driscoll; ✉ The Studio, Ash Barn House, Blackthorn, Bicester, Oxon OX6 0TG (☎ 01869 323992)

O'DWYER, Thomas Rankin (Thom); s of Bryan Keating O'Dwyer (d 1982), and Patricia Rang O'Dwyer (d 1993); *b* 30 April 1954; *Educ* George Washington HS Alexandria Virginia USA, Parsons Sch of Design NY USA (BA), St Martin's Sch of Art; *Career* fashion conslt Nigel French Enterprises Ltd 1971–79; fashion ed: Men's Wear Magazine 1980–86, Fashion Weekly 1986–88, Sunday Mirror Magazine 1988–90; ed-in-chief He Lines 1990–93, tutor Epsom Sch of Art and Design 1992–93, ed-in-chief in-house magazine and PR Planet-London model agency 1993–95, ed Prime 1995–96, features ed What Fashion 1996–; freelance work incl: Marie Claire, The Guardian (men's fashion corr 1984–88), DR - The Fashion Business, Living, Daily Express, DX Magazine, Daily Mirror, Clothes Show Magazine, Underlines, Unique, Ritz, Blitz, Evening Standard, Chat, Take a Break, New Woman, Ms London, For Women, Vada, Wales on Sunday, Daily Star, Boyz, Out!, The Hit, Sunday Mirror, Sunday Correspondent, You Magazine, Capital Expo City Passport magazine; TV appearances incl: Night Network (style presenter), South of Watford, Six O'Clock Show, Calendar Yorkshire TV (won documentary of the year award/BAFTA), After the News, James Whale Radio Show, Breakfast TV (BBC), Style Spot (BSB), The Big Breakfast, The James Whale Show; radio appearances incl: Loose Ends, (first all male) Woman's Hour, Radio One, LBC Radio; chm seminar on men's fashion at ICA; judge: Woman Magazine Designer of the Year competition, Courtelle Design Awards; guest lectr: London Coll of Fashion, RCA, St Martin's Sch of Art, Leicester Poly, Kingston Poly; memb NUJ; *Recreations* eclectic and catholic, incl touring picturesque East End pubs, greyhound racing, mud wrestling, Aquatonic floating, soul food cooking, reading (esp biographies, travel books, the Bible and Victor Lewis-Smith); *Style—* Thom O'Dwyer, Esq; ✉ 38 The Cloisters, 145 Commercial St, London E1 6EB (☎ 0171 377 6201)

ODY, Jonathan Wilmot; s of Robert Henry Morton Ody (d 1978), and Joan Elizabeth, *née* Hunter; *b* 24 Dec 1941; *Educ* Malvern; *m* 3 Sept 1967 (m dis 1973), Evelyn, *née* Porter; 2 s (Andrew, Ian); m 2, 28 Feb 1981, Noelle Maria Anne, *née* Bolton; 1 s (Robin), 1 step s (Benedict); *Career* admitted slr 1965; ptnr: Pattinson & Brewer 1968–69, Norton Rose 1973–; Liveryman Worshipful Co of Slrs 1973; memb Law Soc 1964; *Recreations* food and wine, France; *Clubs* MCC, Le Cercle de la Fraternité; *Style—* Jonathan Ody, Esq; ✉ Kempson House, Camomile Street, London EC3A 7AN (☎ 0171 283 6000, fax 0171 283 6500)

OEHLER, Justus Wilhelm; s of Hans-Albrecht Oehler, of Haigerloch, Germany, and Othilt, *née* Edelmann; *b* 22 Feb 1961; *Educ* Fachhochschule München Germany (Dip (FH) Kommunikations-Design), Central Sch of Art and Design London (MA Graphic Design); *Career* graphic designer; formerly with Büro Rolf Müller Germany, ptnr Pentagram Design Ltd 1995– (joined 1989); projects incl: corp identity for World Economic Forum, Nat Portrait Gallery, Forsyte Saunders Kerman slrs and Museum für Post und Kommunikation Germany, promotional lit for TSE Cashmere, signage project for Fleet Place office devpt City of London, brochure design for Spink and Son; *Style—* Justus Oehler, Esq; ✉ Pentagram Design Ltd, 11 Needham Road, London W11 2RP (☎ 0171 229 3477, fax 0171 727 9932)

OEHLERS, Maj-Gen Gordon Richard; CB (1987); s of Dr Roderick Clarke Oehlers (d 1950), and Hazel Ethne, *née* Van Geyzel; *b* 19 April 1933; *Educ* St Andrew's Sch, Singapore; *m* 27 Oct 1956, Rosie; 1 s (Michael b 1963), 1 da (Elizabeth b 1966); *Career* cmmnd RCS 1958, UK and ME 1958–64, Adj 4 Div Signals Regt 1964–66, CO 7 Signal Regt 1973–76, cdr 1 Br Corps RCS 1977–79, dir Ops Requirements 4 Army 1979–84; asst CDS (cmd, control, communications and info system) 1984–87, Col Cmdt RCS 1987–93; dir of Security and Investigation Br Telecom 1987–93; chm Royal Signals Inst 1990–93, dir The Corps of Commissionaires 1993–; memb: Govt Radio Spectrum Review Ctee 1990–91, Inspectorate of the Securities Industs Bd 1990–93; Hon Col 31 Signal Regt (Volunteers) 1988–93; pres Br Wireless Dinner Club 1986–87; FIEE, CEng; *Recreations* lawn tennis, golf, bridge; *Style—* Maj-Gen Gordon Oehlers, CB; ✉ c/o National Westminster Bank plc, Petersfield, Hants

OESTERHELT, HE Dr Jürgen; *b* 19 Aug 1935, Munich; *Educ* Univ of Munich (LLD), Columbia Univ NY (Master of Comparative Law); *m* 2 c; *Career* German diplomat; lawyer Paris office Sullivan and Cromwell NY 1963–64; joined Foreign Office Bonn 1964, Moscow 1965–66, Foreign Office Bonn 1966–67, memb Observer Mission to UN 1967–71, Trade Mission Sofia 1971–74, Foreign Office Bonn 1974–77, min Athens 1977–80; Foreign Office Bonn 1980–92: head of div Legal Dept 1980–85, dir Political Dept 1985–86, DG Legal Dept and legal advsr 1986–92; ambass: to Turkey 1992–95, to the Ct of St James's 1995–; *Style—* HE Dr Jürgen Oesterhelt; ✉ Embassy of the Federal Republic of Germany, 23 Belgrave Square, London SW1X 8PZ (☎ 0171 824 1301, fax 0171 824 1315)

OESTREICHER, Christine Marguerite Nunes; da of Bryan Harold Nunes Carvalho, and Margaret Elizabeth, *née* Guthrie; *b* 29 Oct 1940; *Educ* St Paul's Girls' Sch; *m* 1, 1958, Andrew Hall Montagu Best; 2 da (Francesca Jane b 1959, Katherine Elizabeth b 1961); m 2, 1963, Milton Daniel Oestreicher; 1 da (Lily Josephine b 1964); *Career* film producer; set up Flamingo Pictures (with James Scott) 1981; memb: PACT, Acad of Motion Picture Arts and Sciences; *Films* incl: Chance History Art (co-prodr with James Scott 1979, Silver Prize Melbourne Film Festival 1981), Couples and Robbers 1981 (Oscar nomination 1982), A Shocking Accident 1982 (Oscar winner 1983), Samson and Delilah 1983, Every Picture Tells A Story 1984, Loser Takes All 1989; *Style—* Christine Oestreicher

OF MAR, *see:* Mar

O'FAOLAIN, (Anna) Julia; da of Sean O'Faolain (d 1991), of Co Dublin, Ireland, and Eileen, *née* Gould (d 1989); *b* 6 June 1932; *Educ* Convent of The Sacred Heart Monkstown, Univ Coll Dublin (BA, MA), Università di Roma, Sorbonne Paris; *m* 1957, Lauro René Martines; 1 s (Lucien Christopher b 1959); *Career* writer; worked as translator and teacher; memb Soc of Authors; *Books* fiction: We Might See Sights! and other stories (1968), Godded and Codded (1970, published as Three Lovers 1971), Man in the Cellar (1974), Women in the Wall (1975), No Country for Young Men (1980), Daughters of Passion (1982), The Obedient Wife (1982), The Irish Signorina (1984), The Judas Cloth (1992); Not in God's Image - Women in History from the Greeks to the Victorians (co-ed, 1973); translator: Two Memoirs of Renaissance Florence: The Diaries of Buonaccorso Pitti and Gregorio Dati (1967), A Man of Parts (1968); *Recreations* karate, gardening; *Style—* Ms Julia O'Faolain; ✉ Rogers, Coleridge & White Ltd, 20 Powis Mews, London W11 1JN (☎ 0171 221 3717, fax 0171 229 9084)

O'FERRALL, Patrick Charles Kenneth; OBE (1989); s of Rev Kenneth John Spence O'Ferrall (d 1977), and Isoult May, *née* Bennett (d 1977); *b* 27 May 1934; *Educ* Winchester, New Coll Oxford (MA); *m* Mary Dorothea, da of Maj Cyril Edward Lugard (d 1970), and Katharine Isabel Beatrice, *née* Carroll (d 1981); 1 s (Mark Edward Cormac b 29 Feb 1964), 2 da (Nicola Maeve (Mrs Slynn) b 7 Dec 1961, Katharine Susannah b 16 Oct 1965); *Career* Nat Serv 2 Lt Royal Fusiliers 1952–54; various positions Iraq Petroleum Group (incl in Abu Dhabi, Qatar, Oman and Beirut) 1958–70, BP area coordinator for Abu Dhabi Marine Areas Ltd and BP Eastern Agencies 1971–73, Total CFP 1974–77; Total Oil Marine PLC: joined as commercial mangr 1970, dir Gas Gathering Pipeline (North Sea) Ltd 1977–78, dir TOMEC (responsible for co-ordination of Alwyn North project) 1983, projects co-ordination mangr 1985–90; chm Lloyd's Register of Shipping 1993– (dep chm 1991); memb Offshore Indust Advsy Bd 1991–94; lay reader C of E 1961–; chm City Branch Outward Bound Assoc; jr vice pres Aldgate Ward Club 1996; Master Worshipful Co of Coachmakers and Coach Harness Makers 1993–94, Liveryman Shipwrights' Co 1992, Hon Liveryman Master Mariners' Co 1993; FRSA 1993, CIMgt 1994; *Recreations* tennis, golf, crosswords, violin playing and singing, walking, wine; *Clubs* MCC, RSA; *Style—* Patrick O'Ferrall, Esq, OBE; ✉ Ashstead Farm House, Ashstead Lane, Godalming, Surrey GU7 1SU (☎ 01483 417601); Lloyd's Register of Shipping, 100 Leadenhall Street, London EC3A EBP (☎ 0171 423 2200, fax 0171 423 2037)

OFFEN, James Frank; s of Frank George Offen (d 1985), of Oxford, and Edna May, *née* Smith (d 1986); *b* 19 July 1935; *Educ* Sir William Borlase Sch Marlow, Coll of Estate Management; *m* 1, 14 Dec 1957, Dorinne Ellen Gardner; 3 s (Nicholas John b 19 June 1959, Simon Brian b 18 Oct 1962, Christopher James b 12 Nov 1967, d 1991); m 2, 6 Sept 1982, Susan Mary, *née* Burton; *Career* surveyor; estates surveyor Lagos Exec Devpt Bd Nigeria 1960–62, Buckell & Ballard chartered surveyors Oxford 1962–85, sr ptnr James Offen & Partners chartered surveyors and estate agents 1985–; hon treas RICS 1990–94 (memb Gen Cncl 1973–), chm Bd Coll of Estate Mgmnt 1985–90; fell and estates bursar Oriel Coll Oxford 1993–; Freeman City of London 1977, Liveryman Worshipful Co of Chartered Surveyors 1977; FRICS 1965; *Recreations* reading, travel, playing tennis, skiing, watching cricket; *Clubs* Athenaeum, MCC; *Style—* James Offen, Esq; ✉ Linden Cottage, Union Street, Woodstock, Oxford OX20 1JF (☎ 01993 813194, fax 01993 813242); James Offen & Partners, 25 Beaumont St, Oxford OX1 2NP (☎ 01865 512394, fax 01865 310237)

OFFEN, Nigel; *Educ* St Bartholomew's Hosp London; *Career* post-graduate trg in hosps in and around London incl Royal London Hosp, conslt gen surgn Whipps Cross Hosp 1976–90 (pt/t unit gen mangr 1988–90), subsequent appt as regional lead in clinical audit and quality improvement NE Thames RHA, chief exec Essex Rivers Healthcare NHS Tst 1993–; memb Clinical Outcomes Gp, dir Br Assoc of Med Mangrs; *Style*— Nigel Offen, Esq; ✉ Essex Rivers Healthcare NHS Trust, Trust HQ, Colchester General Hospital, Turner Road, Colchester CO4 5JL (☎ 01206 853535, fax 01206 854877)

OFFER, Ven Clifford; s of Rev Canon Clifford Jesse Offer (d 1964), of Ightham, Kent, and Jocelyn Mary, *née* Kerr; *b* 10 Aug 1943; *Educ* King's Sch Canterbury, Univ of Exeter (BA), Westcott House Theol Coll; *m* 1980, Dr Catherine Mary Lloyd, da of Dr George Marner Lloyd; 2 da (Isabel Mary b 28 Sept 1981, Rebecca Catherine b 11 Oct 1985); *Career* curate of Bromley Parish Church 1969–74, team vicar Parish of Southampton (City Centre) 1974–83, team rector of Hitchin 1983–93, archdeacon of Norwich and canon residentiary of Norwich Cathedral 1994–; *Books* King Offa in Hitchin (1992); *Recreations* model making, tennis, swimming, Mediaeval and Saxon history, collecting Merchant Navy Livery Company buttons; *Style*— The Ven the Archdeacon of Norwich; ✉ 26 The Close, Norwich, Norfolk NR1 4DZ (☎ 01603 620375)

OFFIAH, Martin; MBE (1997); s of G O Offiah, of Nigeria, and Regina, *née* Klenoh; *b* 29 Dec 1966; *Educ* Woolverstone Hall, Liverpool Poly; *Career* Rugby winger; clubs: Ipswich RUFC 1983–85, Roslyn Park RUFC 1985–87, Widnes RLFC 1987–91, Wigan RLFC 1991–96, London Broncos RLFC 1996–, Bedford RUFC 1996–; honours with Wigan: League Champions 1991–92, 1992–93, 1993–94 and 1995–96, winners Challenge Cup 1992, 1993, 1994 and 1995, World Club Champions 1994, winners Save & Prosper Sevens 1996; 29 Rugby League GB caps, subject of book Offiah: Blaze of Glory; *Recreations* music, acting, basketball; *Style*— Martin Offiah, Esq, MBE; ✉ c/o London Broncos, Crystal Palace National Sports Centre, Ledrington Road, Upper Norwood, London SE19 2BB (☎ 0181 776 6670)

OFFORD, Prof Robin Ewart; s of Frank Etchelles Offord (d 1994), and Eileen Elisabeth, *née* Plunkett, of Wissett, Suffolk; *b* 28 June 1940; *Educ* Owen's Sch, Peterhouse Cambridge (MA, PhD); *m* 3 July 1963, Valerie Edna, da of Ronald Wheatley (d 1971); 1 s (Alan b 1964), 2 da (Jane b 1967, Alice b 1973); *Career* fell Univ Coll Oxford 1968–73 (univ lectr in molecular biophysics 1972–80), fell and tutor in biochemistry Christ Church Oxford 1973–80, prof and dir Département de Biochimie Médicale Université de Genève 1980–, pres Sch of Basic Med Geneva 1994– (vice-pres 1992–94); ed Biochemical Journal 1972–79; memb: local ctees of Christian Aid 1970–80, editorial bds of various scientific jls 1972–, various ctees and bds of the UK Med Res Cncl and UK Miny of Health, Comité Scientifique de la Fondation Jeantet de Médecine 1985–88; jt sci fndr Gryphon Sciences Corporation S San Francisco 1994; *Books* A Guidebook to Biochemistry (with MD Yudkin, 1971, various new edns and foreign translations 1972–), Comprehensible Biochemistry (with MD Yudkin, 1973), Biochemistry (1975, Spanish translation 1976), Semisynthetic Peptides and Proteins (with C di Bello, 1977), Simple Macromolecules (1979), Macromolecular Complexes (1979), Semisynthetic Proteins (1980); *Recreations* comparative linguistics, scuba diving, windsurfing, cross-country skiing; *Style*— Prof Robin Offord; ✉ Bardonnex, Switzerland; Church Hanborough, Oxon; Département de Biochimie Médicale, Centre Médical Universitaire, 1211 Genève 4, Suisse (☎ 00 41 22 702 54 70, fax 00 41 22 346 87 58)

OGATA, Shijuro; s of Taketora Ogata (d 1956), of Tokyo, and Koto Ogata (d 1974); *b* 16 Nov 1927; *Educ* Univ of Tokyo, Fletcher Sch of Law and Diplomacy (MA); *m* 21 Jan 1961, Sadako, da of Toyoichi Nakamura; 1 s (Atsushi b 12 Jan 1962), 1 da (Akiko b 1 May 1967); *Career* Bank of Japan: joined 1950, various appts in Tokyo, London and New York, dep govr international relations 1984–86; dep govr Japan Development Bank 1986–91, non-exec dir Barclays plc 1991–95; memb: Trilateral Cmmn, Gp of Thirty; Japan Society of NY Award 1992; *Books* International Financial Integration - The Policy Challenges (with Richard N Cooper and Horst Schulmann, 1989); *Recreations* tennis, reading, writing; *Clubs* Foreign Correspondents' Club of Japan, Japan National Press, Tokyo Lawn Tennis; *Style*— Shijuro Ogata, Esq; ✉ 3-29-18 Denenchozu, Ota-ku, Tokyo 145, Japan

OGBORN, Anthony Douglas Ronald (Tony); s of Dr Ronald Sherrington Ogborn, of Sutton Coldfield, and Margery Mary, *née* Norris; *b* 22 Dec 1938; *Educ* King Edward's Sch Birmingham, Univ Coll Oxford (BA, MA, BM BCh); *m* 5 Aug 1967, Monica, da of Oswald Faithfull Shipton; 1 s (Ian b 1969); *Career* sr registrar in obstetrics and gynaecology Northampton and Hammersmith Hosps 1973–77, sr conslt obstetrician and gynaecologist NW Thames Region at Bedford Hosp 1977–; treas NW Thames Regnl Ctee Hosp Med Servs 1980–86; memb: N Beds Health Authy 1982–86, NW Thames Region Perinatal Working Pty 1982–89, N Beds Dist Advsy Bd 1988–90; MRCOG 1969, FRCOG 1982; *Recreations* gardening, photography, windsurfing; *Clubs* Priory Sailing (Bedford); *Style*— Tony Ogborn, Esq; ✉ Bedford Hospital, Kempston Rd, Bedford (☎ 01234 792067)

OGDEN, Alan; s of Graeme Ogden (d 1985), and Mary, *née* Howes; *b* 5 July 1948; *Educ* Eton, RMA Sandhurst; *m* Josephine, da of Sir Ian Hunter; 1 s (Richard b 1980); *Career* Grenadier Gds 1966–78; mangr Financial Times Ltd (SE Asia and Australasia) 1978–82, devpt dir St James Corporate Communications 1982–83, dep chief exec offr Charles Barker City 1983–88; Hill and Knowlton: md 1988–91, dep chm 1992–, dir Eastern Europe 1993–, dir European Financial PR 1994–; MIPR, FIMgt; *Recreations* mountaineering, travelling; *Style*— Alan Ogden, Esq; ✉ Hill and Knowlton, 5–11 Theobalds Rd, London WC1X 8SH (☎ 0171 413 3000, fax 0171 413 3118, e-mail aogden@hillandknowlton.com)

OGDEN, Sir (Edward) Michael; kt (1989), QC (1968); s of Edward Cannon Ogden (d 1933), of Hove, Sussex, and Daisy, *née* Paris; *b* 9 April 1926; *Educ* Downside, Jesus Coll Cambridge (MA); *m* 21 Dec 1951, Joan Kathleen, da of Pius Charles Brodrick, of Bolton; 2 s (Edward, Henry), 2 da (Celia (Comtesse de Borchgrave d'Altena), Lucy (Mrs Stuart Fox)); *Career* Royal Glos Hussars, Capt 16/5 Queen's Royal Lancers 1944–47, Capt Inns of Ct Regt TA 1950–56; called to the Bar Lincoln's Inn 1950, bencher 1977; recorder Hastings 1971, recorder Crown Ct 1972–, treas Bar Cncl 1972–75, ldr SE Circuit 1975–78; memb Cncl: Union Internationale Des Avocats 1962–83, Legal Educn 1969–74, Int Bar Assoc 1983–87; chm: Criminal Injuries Compensation Bd 1975–89 (memb 1968–89), Interprofessional Working Pty which produced actuarial tables for use in personal injury and fatal accident cases (enacted as The Ogden Tables Civil Edvidence Act 1995); the assessor of compensation for Home Office for miscarriages of justice 1977–89; pres Sea Fish Licence Tbnl 1993–94, chm ICAEW Disciplinary Appeal Ctee 1993–; FCIArb; *Clubs* Cavalry and Guards'; *Style*— Sir Michael Ogden, QC; ✉ 2 Crown Office Row, Temple, London EC4Y 7HJ (☎ 0171 797 8100, fax 0171 797 8101)

OGDEN, Dr Peter James; s of James Platt Ogden (d 1994), and Frances Ogden; *b* 26 May 1947; *Educ* Univ of Durham (BSc, PhD), Harvard Business Sch (MBA); *m* 22 Aug 1970, Catherine Rose, da of Harold Blincoe; 2 s (Cameron b 9 Oct 1977, Edward b 18 Aug 1981), 1 da (Tiffany b 1 Oct 1975); *Career* exec dir Merrill Lynch International Bank Ltd 1976–81; md: Merrill Lynch White Weld Capital Markets Group 1976–81, Morgan Stanley & Co 1981–87 (advsy dir 1987–); chm Computacenter Ltd 1987–; non-exec dir: Abbey National plc 1994–, Anglo & Overseas Trust plc; dir MC & Cie Ltd (investmt bank); *Style*— Dr Peter Ogden; ✉ Computacenter Ltd, 93–101 Blackfriars Rd, London SE1 8HW (☎ 0171 620 2222)

OGILVIE, Sir Alec Drummond; kt (1965); s of Sir George Drummond Ogilvie, KCIE, CSI (d 1966); *b* 17 May 1913; *Educ* Cheltenham Coll; *m* 1945, Lesley Constance Woollan; 2 s; *Career* served WWII Gurkha Rifles IA (POW); chm Andrew Yule & Co Calcutta 1962–65 (md 1956); pres Associated Chambers of Commerce and Industry India 1964–65; chm Powell Duffryn 1969–78 (dep chm 1967–69); dir: Westinghouse Brake & Signal Co Ltd 1966–79, Lindustries 1973–79, J Lyons & Co 1977–78; former memb Cncl King Edward VII's Hosp for Offrs 1967 (vice pres 1979), memb Cncl Cheltenham Coll 1973–85 (dep pres 1983–85); *Recreations* gardening, walking; *Clubs* Oriental, MCC; *Style*— Sir Alec Ogilvie

OGILVIE, Dame Bridget Margaret; DBE (1997); da of late John Mylne Ogilvie, and Margaret Beryl, *née* McRae; *b* 24 March 1938; *Educ* New England Girls' Sch, Univ of New England (BRurSc), Univ of Cambridge (PhD, ScD); *Career* worked in Parasitology Div National Inst for Medical Research 1963–81, Ian McMaster fell Animal Health Div CSIRO 1971–72; Wellcome Trust: co-ordinator Tropical Med Prog 1979–81, dep sec and asst dir 1981–84, dep dir Science 1984–89, dir Science Progs 1989–91, the dir 1991–98; non-exec dir Zeneca Group PLC 1997–; visiting prof Dept of Biology Imperial Coll London 1985–92; tstee Science Museum 1992–; Hon ScD: Univ of Nottingham 1994, Univ of Salford 1994, Univ of Westminster 1994, Univ of Glasgow 1995, Univ of Bristol 1995, Aust Nat Univ 1995, Univ of Buckingham 1996, Nat Univ of Ireland 1996, Oxford Brookes Univ 1996; Hon MD Univ of Newcastle 1996, Hon LLD Univ of Dublin 1996; Distinguished Alumni Award Univ of New England 1994, Lloyd of Kilgerran Prize 1994; hon memb: Br Soc for Parisitology 1990, American Soc of Parasitologists 1992; hon assoc RCVS 1993; hon fell: UCL 1993, Girton Coll Cambridge 1993; fndn hon fell RVC 1994, Hon FRCP 1996 (Hon MRCP 1992); FIBiol 1985, FRCPath 1992; contrib to numerous scientific papers and jls; *Style*— Dame Bridget Ogilvie, DBE; ✉ Director, The Wellcome Trust, 183 Euston Road, London NW1 2BE (☎ 0171 611 8888, fax 0171 611 8735)

OGILVIE, Kenneth David Buchanan (Ken); s of Edward Eugene Ogilvie, of Sheerness, Kent, and Betty Thompson, *née* Buchanan; *b* 8 April 1948; *Educ* Selhurst GS Croydon; *m* 30 June 1979, Lynda Anne, da of Brian Grosvenor Dowle, of Leatherhead, Surrey; 1 s (Robin b 1983), 2 da (Caroline b 1981, Susannah b 1986); *Career* CA; trained with G H Attenborough & Co London, qualified 1969; Deloitte Plender Griffiths & Co (now Coopers & Lybrand): joined 1970, seconded to Amsterdam office 1972, seconded to Johannesburg office 1972–77, ptnr SA 1977, transferred to Gaborone Botswana 1977, ptnr i/c of Botswana territory 1977–82, returned to UK 1983, ptnr Nottingham office 1983–92, ptnr i/c Corp Fin Midlands Region 1992–; FCA 1969, AIT 1970, assoc Inst of CAs in SA 1974; *Recreations* used to hold a pilot's licence, playing guitar, swimming, tropical fish keeping, photography, elderly motorcycle restoration; *Style*— Ken Ogilvie, Esq; ✉ Coopers & Lybrand, 35 Newhall Street, Birmingham B3 3DX (☎ 0121 200 4000, car 0850 616167)

OGILVIE-LAING OF KINKELL, Gerald; *b* 11 Feb 1936; *Educ* Berkhamsted Sch, RMA Sandhurst, St Martin's Sch of Art (NDD); *m* 1, 1962 (m dis 1967), Jennifer Anne Redway; 1 da (Yseult (Mrs Hughes) b 8 April 1962); m 2, 1969 (m dis 1985), Galina Vasilievna Golikova; 2 s (Farquhar Piotr b 12 March 1970, Alexander Gerald Vasilli b 2 Feb 1972); m 3, 1988, Adaline Havemeyer, *née* Frelinghuysen; 2 s (Titus Christian Havemeyer Oberon b 21 June 1991, Clovis Quintus Frelinghuysen Endymion b 1993); *Career* sculptor and artist; cmmnd 5 Fus (Royal Northumberland Fus) 1955–60; artist in residence Aspen Inst for Humanistic Studies Colorado 1966; visiting prof: Univ of New Mexico 1976–77, Univ of Columbia NY 1986–87; work in collections of: Tate Gallery, V & A Museum, Nat Portrait Gall, Museum of Modern Art NY, Whitney Museum, Museum of Modern Art NY, Whitney Museum NY; maj cmmns incl: Callanish Univ of Strathclyde, Wise and Foolish Virgins Edinburgh, Fountain of Sabrina Bristol, Conan Doyle Meml Edinburgh, Axis Mundi Edinburgh, Bank Station London (dragons), Twickenham Rugby Stadium (four sculptures); Civic Tst award 1971; memb: Ctee Scot Arts Cncl 1978–80, Royal Fine Art Cmmn for Scot 1987–95; FRBS; *Books* Kinkell: The Reconstruction of a Scottish Castle (1974, 2 edn 1984); *Clubs* Chelsea Arts; *Style*— Gerald Ogilvie-Laing of Kinkell; ✉ Kinkell Castle, Ross-shire, Scotland IV7 8AT (☎ 01349 861485); 901 Lexington Avenue, New York, NY 10021, USA (☎ 00 1 212 772 6268)

OGILVIE THOMPSON, Julian; s of late Hon N Ogilvie Thompson (chief justice SA to 1974), of Cape Province; *b* 27 Jan 1934; *Educ* Diocesan Coll Rondebosch Cape, Worcester Coll Oxford (Rhodes scholar); *m* 1956, Hon Tessa Brand (Hon Mrs Ogilvie Thompson); 2 s (Christopher William b 1958, Anthony Thomas b 1964), 2 da (Rachel Amanda (Mrs R M Keene) b 1960, Leila Katharine (Mrs H A Barnett) b 1965), all four of whom are in remainder to the Barony of Dacre; *Career* chm: Anglo American Corp SA, De Beers Consolidated Mines, Minorco SA, De Beers Centenary; Hon LLD Rhodes Univ; Cdr of the Order of the Crown (Belgium), Grand Official of the Order of Bernardo O'Higgins (Chile); *Recreations* shooting, fishing, golf; *Clubs* White's, Rand (Johannesburg), Kimberley, Brook (NY); *Style*— Julian Ogilvie Thompson, Esq; ✉ Froome, Froome St, Athol Ext 3, Johannesburg, S Africa (☎ 00 27 11 884 3925, office 00 27 11 638 2157)

OGILVY, Rt Hon Sir Angus James Bruce; KCVO (1989), PC (1997); s of 12 (de facto 9) Earl of Airlie, KT, GCVO, MC (d 1968), and Lady Mary Alexandra Marie Bridget Coke (d 1984), da of 3 Earl of Leicester, GCVO; *b* 14 Sept 1928; *Educ* Eton, Trinity Coll Oxford (MA); *m* 1963, HRH Princess Alexandra of Kent (*see* Royal Family section); 1 s (James Robert Bruce b 29 Feb 1964, *qv*), 1 da (Marina Victoria Alexandra b 31 July 1966); *Career* Scots Gds 1946–48; memb Queen's Body Guard for Scotland (The Royal Co of Archers); pres: The Imperial Cancer Res Fund 1964–94, Youth Clubs UK (formerly Nat Assoc of Youth Clubs) 1969–89 (chm 1964–69), The Carr-Gomm Soc 1983–; chm Advsy Cncl of the Prince's Youth Business Tst 1986– (also tstee); patron Arthritis Care (formerly The Br Rheumatism and Arthritis Soc) 1978– (chm 1963–69, pres 1969–78); patron The Scottish Wildlife Tst 1974–90 (pres 1969–74), patron Friends of Youth Clubs 1993–; vice-pres The Friends of the Elderly & Gentlefolk's Help 1969– (chm 1963–69, treas 1952–63); vice patron NCH Action for Children 1986–; tstee: The Leeds Castle Fndn 1975–, The Prince's Tst 1993–, King George's Jubilee Tst 1995–, The Queen's Silver Jubilee Tst 1995–; memb: Governing Cncl of Business in the Community 1984–, Governing Cncl of Soc for Promotion of Christian Knowledge 1984–94; Liveryman Worshipful Company of Goldsmiths, Worshipful Co of Tallow Chandlers; dir various public cos; *Recreations* architecture, reading, music; *Clubs* White's; *Style*— The Rt Hon Sir Angus Ogilvy, KCVO; ✉ Thatched House Lodge, Richmond Park, Surrey TW10 5HP (☎ 0181 546 8833)

OGILVY, Lord; David John Ogilvy; s and h of 13 Earl of Airlie, *qv*; *b* 9 March 1958; *m* 1, 1981 (m dis 1990), Hon Geraldine Theodora Mary Gabriel Harmsworth, da of 3 Viscount Rothermere, *qv*; 1 da (Hon Augusta b 1981); m 2, 1991, Tarka, da of John Kings, of Austin, Texas, USA; 2 s (David Huxley, Master of Ogilvy b 11 Dec 1991, Hon Joseph Skene b 19..); *Career* page of honour to HM The Queen 1971; md Richard L Feigen (UK) Ltd; musician; *Clubs* Pratt's; *Style*— Lord Ogilvy; ✉ Airlie Castle, Kirriemuir, Angus

OGILVY, Sir Francis Gilbert Arthur; 14 Bt (NS 1626), of Inverquharity, Forfarshire; o s of Sir David John Wilfrid Ogilvy, 13 Bt (d 1992), and Penelope Mary Ursula, *née* Hills; *b* 22 April 1969; *Educ* Edin Acad, Glenalmond, RAC Cirencester, Univ of Reading (BSc); *m* 12 Oct 1996, Dorothy Margaret, eldest da of Rev Jock and Rev Margaret Stein, of Carbery Tower, E Lothian; *Heir* kinsman, Andrew John Ogilvy b 23 April 1972; *Career* chartered surveyor; ARICS; *Style*— Sir Francis Ogilvy, Bt; ✉ Winton House, Pencaitland, East Lothian EH34 5AT (☎ 01875 341308/9)

OGILVY, Hon James Donald Diarmid; s of 12 Earl of Airlie, KT, GCVO, MC, and Lady Alexandra Coke, da of 3 Earl of Leicester; *b* 28 June 1934; *Educ* Eton; *m* 1, 1959,

(Magda) June, da of Robert Ducas, of New York; 2 s (Shamus Diarmid Ducas b 1966, Diarmid James Ducas b 1970), 2 da (Laura Jane b 1960, Emma Louise b 1962); m 2, 1980, Lady Caroline, *née* Child-Villiers, da of 9 Earl of Jersey and former w of (1) Viscount Melgund, MBE (now 6 Earl of Minto), and (2) Hon John Stuart (s of 1 Viscount Stuart of Findhorn); *Career* Lt Scots Gds 1952–54; page of honour to King George VI 1947–51; ptnr Rowe & Pitman 1962–86, chm Rowan Investment Managers 1972–86, chm Mercury Rowan Mullens 1986–88, vice chm Mercury Asset Management plc 1986–88, chief exec Foreign & Colonial Management Ltd 1988–; dir Foreign & Colonial Investment Trust plc 1990–; govr Queen Charlotte's and Chelsea Hosps 1966–76, chm Inst of Obstetrics and Gynaecology 1983–86; memb Royal Co of Archers (Queen's Body Guard for Scotland); *Clubs* White's; *Style*— The Hon James Ogilvy; ✉ Sedgebrook Manor, Sedgebrook, Grantham, Lincs (☎ 01949 842337); 51 Eaton Square, London SW1 (☎ 0171 235 7595); Foreign & Colonial Management Ltd, Exchange House, Primrose St, London EC2A 2NY (☎ 0171 628 8000, fax 0171 628 8188)

OGILVY, James Robert Bruce; o s of Rt Hon Sir Angus Ogilvy, KCVO, *qv*, and HRH Princess Alexandra, GCVO, o da of HRH 1 Duke of Kent; *b* 29 Feb 1964; *Educ* Eton; *m* 30 July 1988, Julia Caroline (b 28 Oct 1964), eldest da of Charles Frederick Melville Rawlinson, *qv*; 1s (Alexander Charles b 12 Nov 1996), 1 da (Flora Alexandra b 15 Dec 1994); *Style*— James Ogilvy, Esq

OGILVY-WEDDERBURN, Sir Andrew John Alexander; 7 Bt (UK 1803), of Balindean, Perthshire; descended from Sir Alexander Wedderburn, 4 Bt (S 1704), of Blackness, who served as a volunteer at the Battle of Culloden (1746) where he was taken prisoner and executed, and his estate forfeited. His descendants continued to assume the title until Sir David (7 Bt, but for the attainder) was cr Bt in the present UK creation, with special remainder to the heirs male of the 4 Bt of the original creation; s of Cdr Sir (John) Peter Ogilvy-Wedderburn, 6 Bt (d 1977), and Elizabeth Katharine, *née* Cox; *b* 4 Aug 1952; *Educ* Gordonstoun; *m* 1984, Gillian Meade, da of Richard Boyle Adderley, MBE, of Shepherds Hill, Pickering, N Yorks; 3 s (Peter Robert Alexander, Geordie Richard Andrew b (twin) 1987, Sam b 1990 d 1992), 1 da (Katherine b 1985); *Heir* s, Peter Robert Alexander Ogilvy-Wedderburn b 20 April 1987; *Career* Queen's Commendation for Valuable Serv 1996; *Recreations* bobsleighing (memb British Bobsleigh Team 1974–80, British Olympic Bobsleigh Team Innsbruck 1976 and Lake Placid 1980, British 2 man bobsleigh champion 1976–77 and 1978–79), skiing, shooting; *Style*— Sir Andrew Ogilvy-Wedderburn, Bt; ✉ Silvie, Alyth, Blairgowrie, Perthshire PH11 8NA (☎ 01828 633522)

OGLESBY, Peter Rogerson; CB (1982); s of Leonard William Oglesby (d 1975), and Jessie, *née* Rogerson (d 1980); *b* 15 July 1922; *Educ* Woodhouse Grove Sch Yorks; *m* 1947, Doreen Hilda, da of Douglas James Hudson (d 1963); 3 da (Susan b 1952, Jane b 1955, Mary b 1957); *Career* civil servant; princ private sec to: Douglas Houghton 1964–66, Michael Stewart 1966–68, Richard Crossman 1968; Cabinet Office 1968–70: sec of Occupational Pension Bd 1973–74, under sec and head of Social Security Fin Div 1976–79, dep sec of Social Security Policy 1979–82; *Recreations* gardening; *Style*— Peter Oglesby, Esq, CB; ✉ 41 Draycot Rd, Wanstead, London E11 2NX

OGMORE, 2 Baron (UK 1950); Gwilym Rees Rees-Williams; s of 1 Baron Ogmore (d 1976), and Constance, *née* Wills; *b* 5 May 1931; *Educ* Mill Hill; *m* 1967, Gillian, da of Maurice Slack, of Hindley, Lancs; 2 da (Christine b 1968, Jennet b 1970); *Heir* bro, Hon Morgan Rees-Williams; *Recreations* reading, driving, walking; *Style*— The Rt Hon Lord Ogmore; ✉ c/o House of Lords, London SW1A 0PW

OGNALL, Hon Mr Justice; Hon Sir Harry; kt (1986); s of late Leo Ognall, and Cecilia Ognall; *b* 9 Jan 1934; *Educ* Leeds GS, Lincoln Coll Oxford (MA), Univ of Virginia (LLM); *m* 1; 2 s, 1 da; m 2, 1977, Elizabeth Young; 2 step s; *Career* called to the Bar Gray's Inn 1958, QC 1973, bencher 1983, joined NE Circuit, recorder of the Crown Court 1972–86; judge of the High Court of Justice (Queen's Bench Div) 1986–, memb Criminal Injuries Compensation Bd 1976, arbitrator Motor Insurers' Bureau Agreement 1979–85, memb Senate of Inns of Ct 1980–83 (memb Planning Ctee and Professional Conduct Ctee), chm Criminal Ctee Judicial Studies Bd 1986–89, memb Parole Bd England & Wales 1989–91 (vice chm 1990–91); *Recreations* golf, travel, music; *Style*— The Hon Mr Justice Ognall; ✉ Royal Courts of Justice, Strand, London WC2A 2LL

OGORKIEWICZ, Prof Richard Marian; s of Col Marian Anthony Ogorkiewicz (d 1962), of Poland, and Waldyna, *née* Pryfer (d 1986); *b* 2 May 1926; *Educ* SRW Sch Warsaw, Lycée de C Norwid Paris, George Heriot's Sch Edinburgh, Imperial Coll London (BSc, MSc); *Career* devpt engr: Ford Motor Co 1952–55, Humber Ltd 1955–57; lectr in mech engrg Imperial Coll London 1957–85, conslt to various cos involved with armoured fighting vehicles 1972–; consulting ed Int Defense Review 1988–; visiting prof RMCS; memb various sci advsy ctees: Miny of Aviation 1964–70, Miny of Technol 1967–71, MOD 1972–; pres Friends of the Tank Museum Dorset 1987–93 (tstee 1993–); FIMechE 1970; *Books* Armour (1960), Design and Development of Fighting Vehicles (1968), Armoured Forces (1970), Technology of Tanks 2 vols (1991); *Recreations* gardening, walking; *Style*— Prof Richard Ogorkiewicz; ✉ 18 Temple Sheen, East Sheen, London SW14 7RP (☎ 0181 876 5149)

O'GORMAN, Dr Margaret Elizabeth Nelson; da of William James O'Gorman (d 1957), and Mary Ethel O'Gorman (d 1994); *b* 20 July 1938; *Educ* Ipswich HS, Univ of Glasgow (MB ChB, DipPsychMed), MRCPsych; *Career* former sr registrar Royal Hosp Sick Children Glasgow, conslt Child and Adolescent Psychiatry Forth Valley Health Bd Stirling Royal Infirmary 1971–96, ret; former hon visiting lectr Dept Sociology Univ of Stirling; *Recreations* gardening, windsurfing, quilting; *Style*— Dr Margaret O'Gorman; ✉ Westholm, Low Town, Thornhill, Stirlingshire FK8 3PX

O'GORMAN, William Andrew (Bill); s of William Gerard (Paddy) O'Gorman (d 1969), of Newmarket, and Marie Eaton, *née* MacLeod; *b* 22 March 1948; *Educ* Newmarket GS; *m* 1973, Elaine, da of James Cunningham; 3 c (Emma Samantha, William Evert (Joey), PJ); *Career* racehorse trainer 1969–, first flat trainer to hold jockey's licence 1973; twice trained horses equalling The Bards world record set in 1885 of 16 wins in juvenile season (Provideo 1984 and Timeless Times (USA) 1990); *Style*— Bill O'Gorman, Esq

O'GRADY, Prof Francis William; CBE (1984), TD (1970); s of Francis Joseph O'Grady (d 1961), and Lilian Maud Hitchock (d 1977); *b* 7 Nov 1925; *Educ* St Ignatius Coll, Archbishop Tenison's GS, Univ of London (MSc, MD); *m* 17 May 1951, Madeleine Marie-Therese, da of Julien Becquart (d 1950); 3 da (Siobhan b 1952, Catherine b 1955, Michele b 1959); *Career* Nat Serv sr specialist in pathology 1954–56, T&AVR 1956–73; asst pathologist Middx Hosp: 1952–54, 1956–58, 1961–62; asst prof of environmental med Johns Hopkins Univ 1959–60, reader and prof of bacteriology St Bartholomew's Hosp 1962–74, fndn prof of microbiology Univ of Nottingham 1974–88, chief scientist DHSS 1986–90; Ctee on Safety of Med 1971–75, Ctee on Review of Meds 1975–79; memb: Public Health Laboratory Serv Bd 1980–86 and 1993–96, MRC 1980–84 and 1986–90, Nat Biological Standards Bd 1983–86; FRCPath 1972, FRCP 1976, Hon FFPM 1989; *Books* Antibiotic and Chemotherapy (7 ed, 1997), Microbial Perturbation of Host Responses (1981); *Style*— Prof Francis O'Grady, CBE, TD; ✉ 32 Wollaton Hall Drive, Nottingham NG8 1AF (☎ 0115 978 3944)

OGSTON, Prof Derek; CBE (1995); s of Frederick John Ogston (d 1981), of Aberdeen, and Ellen Mary, *née* Duncan (d 1993); *b* 31 May 1932; *Educ* King's Coll Sch Wimbledon, Univ of Aberdeen (MA, MB ChB, PhD, MD, DSc); *m* 19 July 1963, (Cecilia) Marie, da of William Charles Clark (d 1975), of Aberdeen; 1 s (Keith b 1969), 2 da (Catriona b 1971, Nicola b 1973); *Career* Univ of Aberdeen: regius prof of physiology 1977–83, prof of med 1983–97, dean Faculty of Med 1984–87, vice princ 1987–Sept 1992 and Nov 1992–97, currently sr vice-princ; vice chm Grampian Health Bd 1993–97 (memb 1991–97); FRCPE 1973, FRCP 1977, FRSE 1982, FIBiol 1987; *Books* Physiology of Hemostasis (1983), Antifibrinolytic Drugs (1984), Venous Thrombosis: Causation and Prediction (1987); *Recreations* travel; *Style*— Prof Derek Ogston, CBE, FRSE; ✉ 64 Rubislaw Den South, Aberdeen, Grampian (☎ 01224 316587); Vice-Principal's Office, University of Aberdeen, Regent Walk, Aberdeen, Grampian (☎ 01224 272017)

OGUS, Prof Anthony Ian; s of Samuel Joseph Ogus (d 1981), of Blackheath, and Sadie Phyllis, *née* Green; *b* 30 Aug 1945; *Educ* St Dunstan's Coll, Magdalen Coll Oxford (BA, BCL, MA); *m* 26 July 1980, Catherine, da of Marc Klein (d 1975), of Strasbourg; *Career* asst lectr Univ of Leicester 1967–69, tutorial fell Mansfield Coll Oxford 1969–75, sr res fell Centre for Socio-Legal Studies Oxford; prof: Univ of Newcastle upon Tyne 1978–87, Faculty of Law Univ of Manchester 1987–; memb Social Security Advsy Ctee 1993–; *Books* Law of Damages (1973), Law of Social Security (with E M Barendt, 1978, 2 edn, 1982, 3 edn with N Wikeley, 1988, 4 edn, 1995), Policing Pollution (with G M Richardson and P Burrows, 1983), Readings in the Economics of Law and Regulation (with C Veljanouski, 1984), Report to the Lord Chancellor on the Costs and Effectiveness of Conciliation in England and Wales (with M Jones-Lee, J Walker and others, 1989), Regulation: Legal Form and Economic Theory (1994); *Recreations* theatre, music, reading, walking; *Clubs* Utd Oxford and Cambridge; *Style*— Prof Anthony Ogus; ✉ Faculty of Law, University of Manchester, Oxford Road, Manchester M13 9PL (☎ 0161 275 3572, fax 0161 275 3579)

OGUS, Hugh Joseph; s of Louis Ogus (d 1951), of London, and Anne, *née* Goldstein (d 1986); *b* 23 Jan 1934; *Educ* Central Fndn Sch London, Queen Mary Coll London (BA); *m* 14 Aug 1960, Mavis, da of Michael Mendel (d 1971), of London; 1 s (Simon b 1964), 1 da (Deborah b 1967); *Career* various jr mgmnt posts Philips Electrical Ltd 1957–67, commercial dir Salamandre Metalworks Ltd 1968–73, chm and md Poselco Ltd 1984–94 (md 1973–84), dir Cryselco Ltd 1992–93, chm Fusebox Ltd 1990–; memb Cncl: Light Indust Fedn 1977– (pres 1982–83), CIBSE 1986–89 and 1993–96 (chm Lighting Div 1993–94, vice pres 1994–96); fndr chm Lighting Educn Tst 1995; chm of Govrs: Mill Hill Oral Sch for Deaf Children 1987–89 (treas 1977–87), Mary Hare GS for the Deaf 1992– (vice chm of Govrs 1984–92, chm of fin 1980–94); vice chm of Govrs London Sch of Foreign Trade 1982–87; hon vice pres (former chm) 4th Hendon Scouts and Guides; Freeman City of London 1983, Liveryman Worshipful Co of Lightmongers (Master 1994–95); assoc CIBSE 1977; *Recreations* music, travel, swimming, horology; *Style*— Hugh J Ogus, Esq; ✉ Oakhills, 10 Spring Lake, Stanmore, Middx HA7 3BX (☎ and fax 0181 954 0657); Fusebox Ltd, 1 The Metropolitan Centre, Bristol Road, Greenford, Middlesex UB6 8UW (☎ 0181 813 0101, fax 0181 813 0099)

O'HAGAN, Antony Richard (Tony); TD (1976, 1 Clasp 1982, 2 Clasp 1988); s of Capt Desmond O'Hagan, CMG, of Kiambu, Kenya, and Pamela Jane, *née* Symes-Thompson; *b* 3 Oct 1942; *Educ* Wellington; *m* 6 Dec 1975, Caroline Jessica, da of Walter Herbert Franklin (d 1987), of Gt Rissington, Glos; 1 s (Richard Franklin b 19 Oct 1979), 1 da (Clare Pamela b 6 Sept 1976); *Career* HAC: non-cmmnd serv 1962–67, 2 Lt 1967, Capt 1975, Maj 1982; TA watch keeper 3 Armd Div HQRA 1984–90; mangr Coopers & Lybrand 1972–73, gp accountant Hays Wharf Group 1973–76, fin accountant Freemans Mail Order 1977–82, fin dir St Martin's Property Corporation Ltd 1986– (chief accountant 1982–85); vice pres HAC 1990–92 (treas 1987–90, memb Ct of Assts 1978–); tstee Chindits Old Comrades Assoc 1989–; Freeman City of London 1979, clerk Ward of Bridge and Bridge Without 1996; Liveryman Worshipful Co of Fanmakers 1980 (chm Livery Ctee 1989, memb Ct of Assts 1994); FCA 1978; *Recreations* tennis, swimming, skiing, fishing, gardening; *Clubs* Army and Navy; *Style*— A R O'Hagan, Esq, TD; ✉ 8 Anglefield Rd, Berkhamsted, Herts HP4 3JA (☎ 01442 875 682); St Martin's Property Corporation Ltd, Adelaide House, London Bridge EC4R 9DT (☎ 0171 626 3411, fax 0171 623 3382)

O'HAGAN, 4 Baron (UK 1870); Charles Towneley Strachey; s of Hon Anthony Strachey (d 1955), who assumed surname Strachey *vice* Towneley-O'Hagan 1938 and added forename Towneley; he was s of 3 Baron O'Hagan (d 1961) by his 1 w, Hon Frances Strachey (da of 1 Baron Strachie); *b* 6 Sept 1945; *Educ* Eton, New Coll Oxford; *m* 1, 1967 (m dis 1984), HSH Princess Tamara, former w of Lt Cdr Thomas Smith-Dorrien-Smith, of Tresco Abbey, Isles of Scilly, and er da of HSH Prince Michael Imeretinsky (of the Princely family of Bagration, sometime rulers of an independent Georgia), RAFVR, of Menton; 1 da (Hon Nino b 1968); m 2, 1985 (m dis 1995), Mrs Mary Claire Parsons, only da of Rev Leslie Roose-Francis, of Trencoth, Blisland, Bodmin, Cornwall; 1 da (Hon Antonia b 1986); m 3, 1995, Mrs Elizabeth Lesley Eve Macnamara, o da of late Hubert Smith, of Amara, Whipton Lane, Exeter; *Heir* bro, Hon Richard Strachey; *Career* page of honour to HM 1959–62; MEP (ind) 1973–75, MEP (Cons) Devon 1979–94; sits as Cons in House of Lords, cons whip and front bench spokesman in the House of Lords 1977–79; Liveryman Worshipful Co of Mercers; *Clubs* Pratt's, Turf; *Style*— The Rt Hon the Lord O'Hagan; ✉ The Old Rectory, Weare Giffard, Bideford, Devon EX39 4PQ

O'HAGAN, Simon Timothy Byard; s of Maj Alan Bernard O'Hagan, of Langley, Maidstone, Kent, and Heather Mary Byard, *née* White; *b* 25 Sept 1957; *Educ* King's Sch Rochester, Univ of Birmingham (BA); *m* 6 May 1989, Lindsay Carol, da of Laurence Frederick John Bray; 2 da (Isabel Clare b 23 Dec 1990, Eleanor Catherine b 8 Nov 1993); *Career* sports journalist: The Kent Messenger 1978–81, The Times 1982–89, The Independent/The Independent on Sunday 1990–; ed Talk (the magazine of the National Deaf Children's Soc) 1983–85; *Books* Touches of Class (contrib, 1990), Moments of Greatness (contrib, 1990), The Independent on Sunday Book of Sports Questions and Answers (co-ed, 1994), Not Just a Game (contrib, 1995); *Style*— Simon O'Hagan, Esq; ✉ Independent on Sunday, 1 Canada Square, Canary Wharf, London E14 5AP (☎ 0171 293 2000, fax 0171 293 2894)

O'HANLON, Redmond Douglas; s of Canon William Douglas O'Hanlon, of Swanage, Dorset, and Philippa Katherine O'Hanlon; *b* 5 June 1947; *Educ* Marlborough, Merton Coll Oxford (MA, MPhil, DPhil); *m* 6 April 1967, Belinda Margaret, da of Desmond Ingham Harty; 1 da (Puffin Annabelinda b 26 Feb 1985), 1 s (Galen Redmond b 2 Aug 1988); *Career* writer; St Antony's Coll Oxford: sr scholar 1971–72, Alistair Horne res fell 1972–73, sr visitor 1985–89, sr assoc memb 1989–95; ed natural history The Times Literary Supplement 1981–95; memb: Literature panel Arts Cncl 1971–74, Soc for the History of Natural History 1982, Br Ornithological Union 1986; Le Prix de L'Astrolabe 1989; FRGS 1984, FRSL 1993; *Books* Charles Darwin 1809–1882: A Centennial Commemorative (contrib 1982), Joseph Conrad and Charles Darwin: The Influence of Scientific Thought on Conrad's Fiction (1984), Into the Heart of Borneo (1984), In Trouble Again, A Journey between the Orinoco and the Amazon (1988), Congo Journey (1996); *Recreations* pond-watching by torchlight; *Clubs* Rainforest; *Style*— Redmond O'Hanlon, Esq, FRSL; ✉ c/o Peters, Fraser and Dunlop Ltd, The Chambers, Chelsea Harbour, Lots Road, London SW10 0XF (☎ 0171 344 1000, fax 0171 352 7356)

O'HARA, Edward; MP (Lab) Knowsley S (majority 22,011); s of Robert Edward O'Hara, and Clare, *née* Davies; *b* 1 Oct 1937; *Educ* Liverpool Collegiate Sch, Magdalen Coll Oxford (MA), Univ of London (DipEd (Adv), PGCE); *m* 1962, Lillian, da of Thomas Hopkins; 2 s, 1 da; *Career* asst teacher: Perse Sch Cambridge 1962–65, Birkenhead Sch 1966–70; lectr and princ lectr C F Mott Coll of Educn 1970–74, princ lectr, sr tutor and dean of postgrad studies City of Liverpool Coll of Higher Educn 1974–83, head of curriculum studies Sch of Educn and Community Studies Liverpool Poly 1983–90; MP (Lab) Knowsley S 1990–; memb Knowsley BC 1975–91 (memb all Standing Ctees, chm Libraries and Arts, Finance, Youth, Educn and Econ, Devpt and Planning Ctees), memb Educn and Planning and Econ Devpt Ctees AMA; memb: Bd of Management NFER 1986–90, Euro Assoc of Teachers, Socialist Educn Assoc; hon memb and Parly advsr Assoc of Chief Educn Social Workers; memb: Labour Movement in Europe, Communauté de Travail des Régions Européennes de Tradition Industrielle 1989–90, Perm Ctee Assembly of Euro Regions 1987–90; tstee Community Devpt Fndn, memb Fabian Soc, memb Bd of Mgmnt Royal Liverpool Philharmonic Soc 1987–90; corresponding memb Fndn for Hellenic Culture; *Recreations* music (classical/jazz/folk especially Rembetiko), reading, theatre, travel, Greek language and culture; *Clubs* Halewood Labour, Lyme Grove Labour (Knowsley); *Style*— Edward O'Hara, Esq, MP; ✉ House of Commons, London SW1A 0AA (☎ 0171 219 4538/5232, fax 0171 219 4952)

O'HARA, Dr Sydney; *b* 6 Jan 1935; *Educ* Univ of Glasgow (BSc, PhD); *m*; 2 s; *Career* engr; res gp ldr Westinghouse Research Laboratories 1959–64, res assoc and lectr Stanford Univ 1964–69; British Telecom plc (formerly PO): joined R & D Dept 1969, dep dir Transmission Dept 1980–81, dep dir Special Projects 1981–82, chief exec Special Servs 1982–85, dir Products and Servs 1985–87, md BT Special Businesses and chm Cellnet 1987–91; currently dir Gp Devpt Cable and Wireless plc; non-exec dir Tricom Communications; FEng 1984, FInstP, FIEE; *Publications* author of numerous articles in scientific jls; *Style*— Dr Sydney O'Hara, FEng; ✉ 12 Cenacle Close, Hampstead, London NW3 7UE (☎ 0171 435 8097, fax 0171 794 2813)

O'HARE, Kevin Patrick; s of Michael J O'Hare, and Anne Veronica, *née* O'Callaghan; bro of Michael O'Hare, *qv*; *Educ* White Lodge (Royal Ballet Lower Sch), The Royal Ballet Upper Sch, Royal Danish Ballet; *Career* ballet dancer; Sadler's Wells Royal Ballet (now Birmingham Royal Ballet): first soloist 1989, principal dancer 1990; roles incl: Prince Sigfried in Swan Lake, Albrecht in Giselle, The Poet in Les Syphides, Colas in La Fille Mal Gardée, The Prince in Sleeping Beauty, Oberon in A Midsummer Night's Dream, Man in Two Pigeons; dances principal roles in ballets by Ashton, Balanchine, Bintley and Macmillan, created roles in ballets by David Bintley, Graham Lustig and William Tukett, debut as Romeo in new prodn of Macmillan's Romeo and Juliet 1992, guest appearances with Royal Ballet Covent Garden 1992, and in Milan, Brussels, Hong Kong, China, Japan and Holland; *Style*— Kevin O'Hare, Esq; ✉ The Birmingham Royal Ballet, Birmingham Hippodrome, Thorpe Street, Birmingham B5 4AU (☎ 0121 622 2555)

O'HARE, Michael James; s of Michael Joseph O'Hare, and Anne Veronica, *née* O'Callaghan; bro of Kevin O'Hare, *qv*; *b* 7 Dec 1960; *Educ* Marist Coll Hull, The Royal Ballet Sch; *m* 1996, Julie Ann, *née* Francis; *Career* ballet dancer; The Birmingham Royal Ballet (formerly Sadler's Wells Royal Ballet): joined 1980, soloist 1984, princ 1987–; performed a wide range of princ roles within repertoire (character, demi-character and classical) in ballets by: Ashton, MacMillan, Balanchine, De Valois, Cranko and others; the first dancer to perform all three male roles (Alain, Colas and Widow Simone) in Ashton's La Fille Mal Gardée; has danced numerous seasons at Sadler's Wells, the Royal Opera House Covent Garden and The Birmingham Hippodrome and has toured extensively worldwide; has worked with numerous younger choreographers; created role of Will Mossop in Hobson's Choice with choreographer David Bintley (first performance Royal Opera House 1989 and shown on BBC 2 1990); most recent performances incl: Eros in Sylvia (David Bintley), Satan in Job (De Valois Ballet, at Coventry Cathedral), La Fille Mal Gardée (at Teatro Regio Torino), The Prodigal Son (Balanchine), The Prince in The Sleeping Beauty, Carmina Burana and the role of Gabriel Oak in Far From the Madding Crowd (both David Bintley) 1996; *Style*— Michael O'Hare, Esq; ✉ The Birmingham Royal Ballet, Birmingham Hippodrome, Thorp Street, Birmingham B5 4AU (☎ 0121 622 2555)

O'HIGGINS, Prof Paul; s of Richard Leo O'Higgins, MC, MRCVS (d 1973), of Uxbridge, Middx, and Elizabeth, *née* Deane (d 1984); *b* 5 Oct 1927; *Educ* St Columba's Coll Rathfarnham Co Dublin, Trinity Coll Dublin (MA, LLD), Clare Coll Cambridge (MA, PhD, LLD); *m* May 1951, Rachel Elizabeth, da of Prof Alan Dudley Bush, of Radlett, Herts; 1 s (Niall b 29 May 1961), 3 da (Maeve b 16 Feb 1953, Siobhan b 21 Sept 1956, Niav b 23 April 1964); *Career* Univ of Cambridge: fell Christ's Coll 1959– (vice-master 1992–95), univ lectr 1965–79, reader in labour law 1979–84; lectr in labour law Cncl of Legal Educn and Inns of Ct Sch of Law 1976–84, regius prof of laws Trinity Coll Dublin 1984–87, prof of law King's Coll London 1987–92 (emeritus prof 1992); hon prof of law Trinity Coll Dublin 1992–, visiting prof of law City Univ 1992–96; hon fell Trinity Coll Dublin 1996; author; Joseph L Andrews Bibliographical award of the American Assoc of Law Libraries 1987; memb Office of Manpower Economics Advsy Ctee on Equal Pay 1970–72; chm Cambridge branch: Nat Cncl for Civil Liberties 1970–78, Assoc of Univ Teachers 1971–75; memb: Bureau Euro Inst of Social Security 1970–95, Staff Side Panel Civil Serv Arbitration Tbnl 1972–84; patron Cambridge Univ Grad Soc 1972–84, tstee Cambridge Union Soc 1973–84; vice pres: Inst of Safety and Public Protection 1973–, Haldane Soc 1981–, Inst Employment Rights 1989–; govr Br Inst of Human Rights 1988–; MRIA 1986, memb Acad of Euro Private Lawyers 1994; *Books* Bibliography of Periodical Literature Relating to Irish Law (1966, supplements 1975 and 1983), Public Employee Trade Unionism in the UK - The Legal Framework (with Ann Arbor, 1971), Censorship in Britain (1972), A Bibliography of British & Irish Labour Law (1975), Workers' Rights (1976), Employment Law (4 edn 1981), Labour Law in Great Britain and Ireland to 1978 (1981), Discrimination in Employment in Northern Ireland (1984), A Bibliography of Irish Trials and other Legal Proceedings (1986), A Bibliography of the Literature on British & Irish Social Security Law (1986), The Common Law Tradition - Essays in Irish Legal History (1990), Lessons from Northern Ireland (1991), A Bibliography of British and Irish Labour Law 1979–90 (1995); *Recreations* travel, talk, wine; *Clubs* Royal Dublin Soc; *Style*— Prof Paul O'Higgins; ✉ Christ's Coll Cambridge CB2 3BU (☎ 01223 334900, fax 01223 334904)

OHLSON, Sir Brian Eric Christopher; 3 Bt (UK 1920), of Scarborough, North Riding of Co of Yorkshire; s of Sir Eric James Ohlson, 2 Bt (d 1983), and Marjorie Joan, *née* Roosmale-Cocq; *b* 27 July 1936; *Educ* Harrow, RMA Sandhurst; *Heir* bro, Peter Michael Ohlson b 18 May 1939; *Career* cmmnd Coldstream Gds 1956, Capt, ret 1961; money broker; *Recreations* safaris, racing, cricket, theatre, bridge; *Clubs* Hurlingham, MCC, Cavalry and Guards'; *Style*— Sir Brian Ohlson, Bt; ✉ 1 Courtfield Gdns, London SW5

OHLSON, Jonny; s of Kenneth Banks Ohlson, OBE, of Walton-on-the-Hill, Tadworth, Surrey, and Elizabeth Jill, *née* Thain; *b* 28 Sept 1962; *Educ* Eastbourne Coll, Cranbrook Michigan (ESU scholar), Oxford Poly; *Career* Haymarket Publishing Gp 1983–84, assoc dir Wagner Advertising 1985–86, bd dir Saatchi & Saatchi Advertising 1987–92, md Griffin Bacal Advertising 1993–96; chm IPA Soc 1992–94; MIPA; *Recreations* progressive music, bridge, sport, Chelsea FC; *Style*— Jonny Ohlson, Esq

OHLSON, Peter Michael; s of Sir Eric James Ohlson, 2 Bt (d 1983); hp of bro Sir Brian Eric Christopher Ohlson, 3 Bt, *qv*; *b* 18 May 1939; *Educ* Harrow, Trinity Coll Cambridge (BA); *m* 18 Oct 1968, Sarah, o da of Maj-Gen Thomas Brodie, CB, CBE, DSO; 2 da; *Career* md Express Dairy 1976–85, sr ptnr Tyzack & Partners 1995– (ptnr 1985–95); *Style*— Peter Ohlson, Esq; ✉ 33 The Avenue, Kew, Surrey

O'HORA, Ronan; s of Desmond O'Hora, and Gertrude, *née* Maguire; *b* 9 Jan 1964; *Educ* St Bede's Coll Manchester, RNCM; *m* 5 Jan 1991, Hannah Alice, *née* Bell; *Career* concert pianist; London concerto debut with Philharmonia Barbican Hall 1989, London recital debut Wigmore Hall 1989, US debut with Florida Philharmonic Orch Miami 1990; played with orchs incl: Royal Philharmonic, London Philharmonic, BBC Symphony and Philharmonic Orchs, Acad of St Martin-in-the-Field's, Hallé Orch, Royal Liverpool Philharmonic, Tonhalle Orch of Zurich, Indianapolis Symphony Orch; played concertos and recitals in numerous countries incl: Germany, France, Switzerland, Holland, Italy, Scandinavia, Belgium, Austria, Yugoslavia, Poland, Ireland, Portugal, Canada, Czechoslovakia; currently sr tutor RNCM; *Awards* Silver Medal Worshipful Co of Musicians 1984, Dayas Gold Medal 1984, Stefania Niekrasz Prize 1985; *Recordings* Britten Music for Two Pianos (with Stephen Hough), concertos by Grieg, Tchaikovsky and Mozart with the RPO, solo recordings of Chopin, Schubert and Debussy; numerous recordings for bdcasting cos incl: BBC TV and Radio, Netherlands TV and Radio, Polish TV, Czech TV; *Recreations* theatre; *Style*— Ronan O'Hora, Esq; ✉ 11 Daresbury Rd, Chorlton, Manchester M21 1NA (☎ 0161 881 3575, fax 0161 882 0313)

OJOMOH, Steve Oziegbe; *b* 25 May 1970; *Educ* West Buckland Sch N Devon, Univ of West of England Bristol; *Career* rugby union forward; clubs: Rosslyn Park RFC 1988–89, Bath RFC 1989– (over 90 appearances, incl 4 Cup Final victories 1992–96 and 4 League Championships); England: Schools toured Australia 1988, under 19's 1989–91, under 21's 1991–92, toured NZ 1992 and Canada 1993 A & B team, full debut v Ireland 1994, toured S Africa 1994, memb Grand Slam winning team 1995, memb World Cup squad (4 caps) 1995 (4th place), 11 full caps; memb England Seven's team Dubai Seven's (semi finalists) 1993; athletics: county champion long jump, triple jump and discus, Southwest decathlon champion; variously accounts clerk, sports promotional offr, broker; *Recreations* watching, films, golf, sport on TV; *Style*— Steve Ojomoh, Esq; ✉ c/o MP Associates, 156 Sutherland, London W9 1HP (☎ 0171 286 1793)

O'KANE, Maggie; s of Peter O'Kane, of Skerries, Co Dublin, and Maura, *née* McNeil; *Educ* Assumption Convent Ballynahinch Co Down, Loreto Convent Balbriggan Co Dublin, Coll of Commerce Dublin (journalism), Univ Coll Dublin; *Career* reporter Magill Magazine Ireland 1980–82, journalist Sunday Tribune Ireland 1982–84, TV reporter Irish television 1984–89, scholarship to Journalistes En Europe Fndn Paris 1989, covered E Europe for Irish Times and RTE 1989–90, Gulf War for The Irish Times, freelance 1991– (working for Mail on Sunday, Guardian, Economist and Sunday Times in Beirut, Kuwait, N Iraq, Croatia and Bosnia), currently staff corr Guardian (foreign corr covering Haiti and former Yugoslavia 1994); television progs incl: documentary on Haiti (BBC) 1995, documentary on anniversary of Gulf War (Channel 4) 1996; *Awards* Journalist of the Year What the Papers Say Awards 1992, Journalist of the Year and Foreign Corr (jt) British Press Awards 1992, Foreign Corr (jt) of the Year Amnesty Int 1993, Br TV Documentary Award (for Bloody Bosnia) Channel 4 1993, runner-up RTS Reporter of the Year 1993, James Cameron Award for int and domestic reporting 1996; *Style*— Ms Maggie O'Kane; ✉ The Guardian, 119 Farringdon Road London EC1R 3ER (☎ 0171 278 2332, fax 0171 239 9787)

O'KEEFFE, (Peter) Laurence; CMG (1983), CVO (1974); s of Richard O'Keeffe (d 1982), and Alice Gertrude Chase (d 1993); *b* 9 July 1931; *Educ* De la Salle Coll Toronto Canada, St Francis Xavier's Coll Liverpool, Univ of Oxford (BA); *m* 1954, Suzanne Marie, da of Francis Jousse, of Versailles, France; 3 da (Catherine, Isabel, Juliet); *Career* HM ambass Dakar Senegal (also accredited to Mali, Mauretania, Guinea, Guinea-Bissau, Cape Verde Islands) 1982–85; resident chm Civil Serv Selection Bd (Dip Serv) 1986, ambass/head of delgn to the Vienna CSCE conf 1986–89, ambass to Czechoslovakia 1989–91; *Books* as Laurence Halley: Simultaneous Equations (1975), Abiding City (1986), Ancient Affections (1985); *Recreations* gardening, playing the piano; *Clubs* Savile; *Style*— Laurence O'Keeffe, Esq, CMG, CVO; ✉ Wylye Cottage, Great Wishford, Salisbury, Wilts SP2 0PD (☎ 01722 790820)

OKEOVER, *see:* Walker-Okeover

OKRI, Ben; s of Silver Okri, and Grace Okri; *b* 15 March 1959; *Educ* Univ of Essex; *Career* author; broadcaster and presenter BBC 1983–85, poetry ed W Africa 1983–86, fell commoner Trinity Coll Cambridge 1991–93; one of 200 leaders of tomorrow World Economic Forum 1993; memb: Soc of Authors, PEN International; *Awards* Cwlth Prize for Africa 1987, Paris Review Prize for Fiction 1987, Booker Prize 1991, Premio Letterario Internazionale Chianti Ruffino-Antico Fattore 1993, Premio Grinzane Cavour 1994, Crystal Award 1995; *Books* Flowers and Shadows (novel, 1980), The Landscapes Within (novel, 1982), Incidents at the Shrine (stories, 1986), Stars of the New Curfew (stories, 1988), The Famished Road (novel, 1991), An African Elegy (poems, 1992), Songs of Enchantment (novel, 1993), Astonishing the Gods (novel, 1995), Birds of Heaven (essays, 1996), Dangerous Love (novel, 1996), A Way of Being Free (essays, 1997); *Recreations* music, art, theatre, martial arts, good conversation, dancing and silence; *Style*— Ben Okri, Esq; ✉ c/o Orion Publishing Group, Orion House, 5 Upper St Martin's Lane, London WC2H 9EA (☎ 0171 240 3444, fax 0171 240 4822)

OLDENBURG, HH Duke Friedrich August Nikolaus Udo Peter Philipp of; elder s of HH Duke Peter of Oldenburg (2 s of HRH Nikolaus, Hereditary Grand Duke of Oldenburg, descended from Egilmar I, Count of Aldenburg, who was living in 1108; Hereditary Grand Duke Nikolaus m HSH Princess Helene of Waldeck and Pyrmont, whose paternal grandmother was HSH Princess Helene of Nassau; Princess Helene of Nassau's paternal gf's mother was Princess Caroline of Orange, whose mother was Princess Anne (Princess Royal), eldest da of King George II of Great Britain), by his w HSH Princess Gertrud, 2 da of HSH Udo, 6 Prince zu Löwenstein-Wertheim-Freudenberg; *b* 26 Sept 1952; *m* 9 Jan 1982, Belinda, da of Maj (Alison) Digby Tatham Warter, DSO (d 1993), of Nanyuki, Kenya, and Jane, *née* Boyd (whose mother was Lady Mary Egerton, o da of 5 Earl of Wilton); 3 da (Anastasia (Daisy) b 10 Oct 1982, Alice b 15 April 1986, Cara b 14 June 1993); *Career* farmer; *Style*— His Highness Duke Friedrich August of Oldenburg; ✉ Anstey Hall, Anstey, Buntingford, Herts SG9 0BY

OLDERSHAW, Dr Paul John; s of Harold Oldershaw (d 1981), and Irene, *née* Summerlin; *b* 23 Sept 1947; *Educ* Henry Mellish GS Nottingham, Emmanuel Coll Cambridge (exhibitioner and scholar in natural scis, MB BChir, MA, MD, Colin McKenzie prize, Albert Hopkinson award, Peake prize), St Thomas' Hosp Med Sch; *Career* jr hosp appts St Thomas', St Peter's and Brompton Hosps 1973–75, rotating med registrar Worthing Gen Hosp (gen med) and St Thomas' Hosp (gen med and nephrology) 1975–77, Br Heart Fndn research fell St Thomas' Hosp Med Unit 1977–79, cardiac registrar Brompton Hosp 1979–81, sr registrar Cardiac Dept St George's Hosp 1981–82; Royal Brompton Nat Heart and Lung Hosp: conslt cardiologist 1982–, dir of cardiology 1992–; Br Cardiac Soc: memb Cncl 1986–90, sec 1988–92, chm Pubns Ctee 1990–93, memb Prog and Meetings Ctee 1991–95; Br Heart Fndn: memb Educn Ctee 1986–90, memb Factfile Ctee 1986–90; Euro Soc of Cardiology: memb Scientific Exec Ctee 1990–, memb Valvular Heart Disease Working Pty 1992–; memb Adult Congenital Heart Disease Working Pty Br Cardiac Soc 1993–; numerous post-graduate awards incl Br Heart Fndn Research Award (with Andrew Bishop) to study right ventricular function using impedance catheterisation 1993–; memb Editorial Bds: Br Heart Jl 1986–90, Int Jl of Cardiology 1986–92, Euro Heart Jl 1990–; referee: BMJ, Lancet; memb: Med Research Soc 1977, Br Cardiac Soc 1981; FRCP 1990 (MRCP 1975), FESC 1991 (MESC 1982), FACC 1991 (MACC 1982); *Books* A Practice of Cardiac Catheterisation (with D Mendel, 1986), Textbook of Adult and Paediatric Echocardiography and Doppler Echocardiography (with M St John Sutton, 1989), Cardiology Dictionary (with R A Anderson and J R Dawson, 1990), A Practical Guide to Congenital Heart Disease in Adults (with A Redington and D F Shore, 1994); author of numerous pubns in academic jls; *Recreations* opera, wine; *Style—* Dr Paul Oldershaw; ✉ 76 Carlton Hill, St John's Wood, London NW8 (☎ 0171 625 6829); Royal Brompton Hospital, Sydney Street, London SW3 6NP (☎ 0171 352 8121, fax 0171 351 8629)

OLDFIELD, Bruce; OBE (1990); *b* 14 July 1950; *Educ* Spennymoor GS Durham, Ripon GS, Sheffield Poly (DipEd), Ravensbourne Coll of Art, St Martin's Coll of Art; *Career* fashion designer; designed for Henri Bendel NY and other stores 1973–74, freelance cmmns incl film wardrobe for Charlotte Rampling 1974–75, first collection 1975, estab couture div 1978, opened London shop and redeveloped ready-to-wear collection with couture collection 1984–, Br rep Aust Bicentennial Wool Collection Fashion Show Sydney Opera House 1988; memb Panel Whitbread Literary Awards 1987, organised Bruce Oldfield for Barnardos Gala evenings attended by HRH The Princess of Wales 1985 and 1988; Northern Personality of the Year Variety Club 1985, subject of TV documentary A Journey into Fashion (Tyne Tees TV) 1990; hon fell: Sheffield City Poly 1987, Royal Coll of Art 1990, Hatfield Coll Univ of Durham 1991; *Books* Bruce Oldfield's Season (contrib, 1987); *Recreations* reading, music, films, driving; *Style—* Bruce Oldfield, Esq, OBE; ✉ c/o Bruce Oldfield Ltd, 27 Beauchamp Place, London SW3 1NJ (☎ 0171 584 1363)

OLDFIELD, John; JP (1979); *b* 19 March 1948; *Educ* Regional Coll of Art Batley; *m*; 2 da (Charlotte Jane b 1976, Georgina Elizabeth b 1978); *Career* pt/t asst lectr in graphic design 1967–68; The Charles Walls Group and associated cos: account exec 1969–70, account dir 1970–76, bd dir 1976–83, md and chief exec 1983–; chm Northern Branch IPA 1993–96, memb Cncl IPA 1996–; chm ANAA 1992–; govr and tstee Bradford Girls' GS 1983–96; Variety Club of GB: barker 1980–, chm Yorks regn 1987; FIPA 1993 (MIPA 1972); *Recreations* charity, classic cars, gardening; *Style—* John Oldfield, Esq, JP; ✉ Charles Walls Group Ltd, Town Gate, Calverley, Leeds LS28 5SS (☎ 0113 255 2171, fax 0113 255 1162)

OLDFIELD, Michael Gordon (Mike); s of Raymond Henry Oldfield, of Stuttgart, Germany, and Maureen Bernadine, *née* Liston (d 1976); *b* 15 May 1953; *Educ* Highlands Sch Reading, Hornchurch GS Essex, St Edward's Reading, Presentation Coll Reading; *ptnr* 1; 2 s (Dougal b 17 Sept 1981, Luke b 11 April 1986), 1 da (Molly b 30 Nov 1979); ptnr 2; 1 s (Noah b 8 March 1990), 1 da (Greta b 28 April 1988); *Career* musician; first recording with sister Sally Oldfield 1969, 3 recordings with Kevin Ayres 1970–72; solo albums 1973–: Tubular Bells, Hergest Ridge, Ommadawn, Incantations, Exposed, Platinum, QE2, Five Miles Out, Crises, The Killing Fields, Discovery, Islands, Earth Moving, Amarok, Heaven's Open, Tubular Bells II, The Songs of Distant Earth; various major tours incl two world tours; 50 Gold and 15 Platinum discs worldwide, Grammy award, Golden Globe, Ivor Novello and BAFTA nominations; Freeman City of London; involved with Blue Peter Cambodian Appeal and hostage release work; *Recreations* skiing, cycling, squash; *Style—* Mike Oldfield, Esq; ✉ c/o Clive Banks, 1 Glenthorne Mews, 115A Glenthorne Road, London W6 0LJ (☎ 0181 748 5036, fax 0181 748 3356)

OLDFIELD, Pamela; *Career* writer; worked as teacher for 11 yrs and sec for 5 yrs; *Books* incl: A Dutiful Wife (1989), Sweet Sally Lunn (1990), The Halliday Girls (1991), The Passionate Exile (1993), String of Blue Beads (1994); also author of numerous children's books; *Style—* Ms Pamela Oldfield; ✉ c/o Faber & Faber Ltd, 3 Queen Square, London WC1N 3AU

OLDHAM, Christopher David Fitzjohn; s of Cdr Frederick William Fitzjohn Oldham, OBE (d 1984), of Halstead, Essex, and Thereza Jessie, *née* Hawes; *b* 22 May 1934; *Educ* Harrow; *m* 21 Aug 1975, Susan Hilary, da of Hugh Arthur Heneage Fitzgerald Finch (d 1975), of Tunbridge Wells, Kent; 1 s (William b 1976); *Career* Nat Serv RN 1952–54; admitted slr 1960, sr ptnr Vizards London 1982–; former dep chm Lansdowne Club, former stewardship advsr Southwark Diocese, former churchwarden; memb Law Soc; *Recreations* freemasonry, local church affairs, gardening, stalking, railway modelling, historical reading; *Clubs* Lansdowne; *Style—* Christopher Oldham, Esq; ✉ 6 Parkfields, Putney, London SW15 6NH (☎ 0181 789 5765); Vizards, 42 Bedford Row, London WC1R 4JL (☎ 0171 405 6302, fax 0171 405 6248)

OLDHAM, Gavin David Redvers; s of David George Redvers Oldham, of Buckinghamshire, and Penelope Barbara, *née* Royle; *b* 5 May 1949; *Educ* Eton, Trinity Coll Cambridge (MA); *m* 17 May 1975, Virginia Russell, da of Rodney Fryer Russell, of Dorset; *Career* CSE Aircraft Services Ltd 1971–76, ptnr Wedd Durlacher Mordaunt & Co 1984–86 (joined 1976), secretariat Barclays de Zoete Wedd 1984–86, chm Barclayshare Ltd 1989–90 (chief exec 1986–89); chm and chief exec The Share Centre (Holdings) Ltd 1990–; memb: Cncl Economic Res 1989–, The Securities Inst, General Synod (House of Laity) for Diocese of Oxford; MInstD; *Clubs* Leander; *Style—* Gavin Oldham, Esq; ✉ PO Box 1000, Tring, Herts HP23 4JR (☎ 01442 890800, fax 01442 891191)

OLDING, Dr Simon; s of Roy Edward Olding, of Dawlish, Devon, and Rita Frances, *née* Heard; *b* 9 March 1954; *Educ* Hele's GS Exeter, Fitzwilliam Coll Cambridge (MA, Leathersellers scholar), Univ of Edinburgh (PhD); *m* July 1990, Isabel, da of Noel Hughes; *Career* asst keeper for ceramics Glasgow Museums and Art Galleries 1980–82 (graduate trainee 1979–80), asst curator of art Salisbury Museum 1982–85, London museums offr and asst dir for museum devpt Area Museums Serv for SE England 1985–89, head of arts and museums Bournemouth Borough Cncl 1989–; fndr memb Bd Southern Arts, chm Bd Salisbury Arts Centre, past memb Cncl Museum Assoc, past memb Nat Campaign for the Arts; FMA 1991 (AMA 1982, Trevor Walden prize), FRSA 1994; *Books* Michael Cullimore (1986), A Vision of Dartmoor (with C Jane Baker, 1990), Exploring Museums - London (1991), Marcus Tate Photographs (1993), Russell-Cotes Commissions (1994); *Recreations* the arts; *Style—* Dr Simon Olding; ✉ 13 Avenue Road, Winchester, Hampshire SO22 5AQ (☎ 01962 869821); Russell-Cotes Art Gallery and Museum, East Cliff, Bournemouth BH1 3AA (☎ 01202 451800, fax 01202 451851)

OLDRIDGE, John Norman Leslie; *b* 26 Jan 1947; *Educ* Oundle, Oxford Sch of Architecture (DipArch); *Career* ptnr Chapman Taylor Partners 1987– (joined 1973, assoc 1977); RIBA 1977, memb Ordre des Architectes 1990; *Recreations* offshore sailing, skiing; *Clubs* Royal Southampton Yacht; *Style—* John Oldridge, Esq; ✉ Chapman Taylor Partners, 364 Kensington High Street, London W14 8NS (☎ 0171 371 3000)

OLDROYD, Elizabeth Mary (Liddy); da of Frederick Oldroyd (d 1967), of Guildford, Surrey, and Elsie May, *née* Cooke; *b* 16 June 1955; *Educ* Guildford Co GS for Girls, Univ of York (BA); *m* Peter Howard Gwilliam, s of late Reginald Gwilliam; 1 da (Amy Elizabeth b 7 March 1986), 2 s (George Frederick b 22 Feb 1989, Harry Reginald b 31 March 1995); *Career* director; actress on fringe 1977–78, announcer/writer BBC World Service 1978–79, trainee dir LWT 1986 (prodn asst 1979–86); credits incl: Weekend World, Six O'Clock Show (LWT), various children's drama (TVS), Drop the Dead Donkey, Spitting Image, S&M, After Henry, Desmonds, Terry and Julian, Mad and Sandie, The Posse, Paul Merton - The Series, The Waltons (documentary), Paris (with Alexei Sayle), Ruby Wax (as creative advisor), Life After Birth, Hold (drama); commercials with Julie Walters and Paul Merton; *Awards* for Drop the Dead Donkey: Comedy Award 1990, 1991, 1993, 1995, Emmy Award USA 1991, 1993, Radio Times Award 1992, Indie Award 1993, BAFTA 1994, Royal Television Soc 1995; Women in Film Kodak Award for Creativity 1992, Montreux Award for S&M 1992; *Recreations* all forms of music, theatre, riding, swimming; *Style—* Miss Liddy Oldroyd; ✉ c/o Seifert-Dench Associates, 24 D'Arblay Street, London W1V 3FH (☎ 0171 437 4551, fax 0171 439 1355); c/o Seifert Dench, 24 D'Arblay Street, London W1V 3FH (☎ 0171 437 4551, fax 0171 439 1355)

OLDWORTH, Richard Anthony; s of Anthony Gilbert Frederick Oldworth, of Blackdown, Sussex, and Patricia, *née* Thompson; *b* 5 June 1957; *Educ* Radley, City of London Poly; *m*; 1 da; *Career* CA; Peat Marwick Mitchell 1976–80, corporate finance exec County Bank 1980–83, head of corporate finance Bisgood Bishop & Co 1983–84, chief exec Buchanan Communications 1984–; ACA 1980; *Recreations* flying, motorsport; *Clubs* City of London, Royal Solent Yacht; *Style—* Richard Oldworth, Esq; ✉ Buchanan Communications, 36 St Andrew's Hill, London EC4 5DE (☎ 0171 489 1441, fax 0171 489 1436)

O'LEARY, (Edmund) Eamon; OBE (1991); s of James O'Leary (d 1961), and Margaret Mary, *née* Cullinane; *b* 14 Aug 1933; *Educ* St Kieran's Coll Kilkenny, Univ Coll Cork (BE); *m* 9 June 1958, Denise, da of Dennis Coffey (d 1955); 2 da (Michele Ann b 26 Nov 1960, Clodagh Denise b 10 March 1964); *Career* res engr Waterford CC 1954–58, asst engr Rendel Palmer Tritton 1958–59, sr ptnr Veryard & Partners 1971–93 (ptnr 1959–71), chm Veryards Ltd 1993–; chm: S Wales Branch ICE 1978, S Wales Inst of Engrs 1988, Concrete Soc Wales 1970 and 1976 (pres 1989), Tenovus; hon res fell Univ of Wales Cardiff, assoc Poly of Wales 1991; FICE, FIStructE, MIHT, FRSA, MConsE; *Recreations* golf; *Clubs* Royal Porthcawl Golf; *Style—* Eamon O'Leary, Esq, OBE; ✉ 39 Heol Don, Whitchurch, Cardiff CF4 2AS (☎ 01222 626516); Veryards Ltd, Crwys House, Crwys Rd, Cardiff CF2 4NB (☎ 01222 222664, fax 01222 384520)

O'LEARY, Terence Daniel; CMG (1982); s of Daniel O'Leary (d 1948), and Mary, *née* Duggan (d 1979); *b* 18 Aug 1928; *Educ* Dulwich Coll, St John's Coll Cambridge (MA); *m* 1960, Janet Douglas, da of Dr Hugh Berney (d 1978), of Masterton, NZ; 2 s (John, Daniel (twins)), 1 da (Helen); *Career* served Queen's Royal Regt, Capt; HM Dip Serv 1953–88; served: NZ, India, Tanganyika, Australia, Cabinet Off, S Africa, NZ; sr civil dir Nat Def Coll 1978–81; Br high cmmr Sierra Leone 1981–84, Br high cmmr NZ and Western Samoa and govr of Pitcairn 1984–87; memb EC Monitoring Mission Jugoslavia (Zagreb) 1991–92; chm Petworth Preservation 1989–; cncllr Petworth 1994–; *Recreations* croquet and cutting grass; *Clubs* Travellers', Wellington (NZ); *Style—* T D O'Leary, Esq, CMG; ✉ The Old Rectory, Petworth, W Sussex (☎ 01798 343335)

OLINS, Wallace (Wally); s of Alfred Olins (d 1970), and Rachel, *née* Muscovitch (d 1961); *b* 19 Dec 1930; *Educ* Highgate Sch, St Peter's Coll Oxford (MA); *m* 1, 1957 (m dis 1989), Maria Renate Olga Laura Steinert; 2 s (Rufus Laurence b 1961, Benjamin Toby b 1967), 1 da ((Sarah) Edwina b 1959); m 2, 1990, Dornie; 1 da (Harriet Rachel Hildegard); *Career* Nat Serv 1950–51; SH Benson (now part of Ogilvy & Mather): joined 1954, in India latterly as md Bombay 1957–62; md Caps Design London 1962–64, jt fndr Greers Gross Olins 1964, chm Wolff Olins (jt fndr with Michael Wolff 1965); visiting lectr in design mgmnt London Business Sch 1984–89; visiting prof Mgmnt Sch: Imperial Coll 1987–91, Lancaster Univ 1991–, Duxx Mexico 1995–, Copenhagen Business Sch 1993–; vice pres CSD 1982–85, chm Design Dimension Educnl Tst 1987–94; dir Health Educn Authy 1996–; memb Cncl RSA 1989–95; FCSD; *Books* The Corporate Personality (1978), The Wolff Olins Guide to Corporate Identity (1983), The Wolff Olins Guide to Design Management (1985), Corporate Identity (1989), International Corporate Identity (1995), The New Guide to Identity (1996); *Recreations* looking at buildings, shopping for books, theatre, old cars; *Clubs* Groucho; *Style—* Wally Olins; ✉ The Wolff Olins Business Limited, 10 Regents Wharf, All Saints Street, London N1 9RL (☎ 0171 713 7733, fax 0171 713 0217, telex 261438, car 0850 346495)

OLIVEIRA, Prof David Benjamin Graeme; s of Anthony Benjamin Oliveira (d 1983), and Pamela Avril, *née* Maitland-Heriot; *b* 11 Sept 1955; *Educ* CCC Cambridge (Smyth scholar, MB BChir, MA), Westminster Hosp Med Sch London, PhD (London), FRCP; *m* 14 April 1984, Patricia Margaret, da of Gp Capt J E F Williams, CBE; 2 s (Benjamin b 30 April 1985, Samuel b 26 May 1987), 1 da (Amelia b 24 Nov 1988); *Career* house physician then house surgn Westminster Hosp London 1979–80; SHO: Hammersmith Hosp London 1980–81, Nat Hosp for Nervous Diseases Queen Square 1981, Brompton Hosp London 1981–82, Renal Unit Guy's Hosp London 1982; registrar rotation Ealing Hosp then Renal Unit Hammersmith Hosp 1982–84, MRC trg fell UCL 1984–87; Univ of Cambridge: Lister Inst research fell Sch of Clinical Med 1987–95, univ lectr 1995; Addenbrooke's Hosp Cambridge: sr registrar in nephrology 1990–91, hon conslt physician 1991–95; fndn prof of renal med St George's Hosp Med Sch 1995–; memb: Lister Inst of Preventive Med, Editorial Bd Clinical and Experiment Immunology; author of numerous articles in learned jls; *Recreations* bridge, natural history (especially insects), computers; *Style—* Prof David Oliveira; ✉ Division of Renal Medicine, St George's Hospital Medical School, Cranmer Terrace, Tooting, London SW17 0RE (☎ 0181 725 5038, e-mail doliveir@sghms.ac.uk)

OLIVER, Alexander Fraser; s of James Alexander Oliver (d 1976), of Bridge of Allan, and Helenor, *née* Bryce (d 1977); *b* 27 June 1944; *Educ* HS of Stirling, RSAMD, Vienna Acad of Music and Dramatic Art; *Career* tenor; international operatic debut Vienna Chamber Opera 1967, solo recital debut Purcell Rooms London 1969; appeared with numerous major opera cos incl: Glyndebourne Touring Opera, Glyndebourne Festival Opera, Royal Opera Co, ENO, WNO, Scottish Opera, Netherlands Opera, Zurich Opera, Brussels Opera, La Scala Milan, La Fenice Venice, Paris Opera; *Recordings* incl: L'Incoronazione di Poppea (under Harnoncourt, Teldek), Il Ritorno d'Ulisse in Patria (under Raymond Leppard, CBS), Les Contes d'Hoffman (under Sylvan Cambreling, EMI); *Recreations* living and staying alive, friendships, sleeping; *Style—* Alexander Oliver, Esq; ✉ c/o IMG Artists, Media House, Unit 2, 3 Burlington Lane, London W4 2TH (☎ 0181 747 9977, fax 0181 747 9131)

OLIVER, David James; s of Charles William Reginald James Oliver, of Gravesend, and Margaret Winifred, *née* Gay (d 1986); *b* 7 April 1952; *Educ* Gravesend Sch, Christ Church Oxford (scholar, MA); *m* 23 August 1975, Sarah Catherine, da of Charles Antony Penton (d 1992); 2 da (Katharine Elizabeth b 10 Aug 1980, Deborah Rosamund b 23 April 1982); *Career* worked in City Div Williams & Glyns Bank 1975–76; Arthur Andersen: joined 1976, ACA 1979, head E Anglian Tax Practice 1985–93, tax ptnr 1986–, London Office 1993–; memb Personal Tax Sub-Ctee ICAEW; co-fndr Emmaus UK; FCA 1989; *Recreations* cycling, birdwatching, languages, literature; *Style—* David Oliver, Esq; ✉ 3 Wingate Close, Trumpington, Cambridge CB2 2HW (☎ 01223 840910); 110 Thomas More House, Barbican, London (☎ 0171 638 2156); Arthur Andersen, 1 Surrey Street, London WC2R 2PS (☎ 0171 438 3329, fax 0171 438 2984, mobile 0860 901840)

OLIVER, Hon David Keightley Rideal; QC (1986); o s of Baron Oliver of Aylmerton, PC (Life Peer), *qv*, and his 1 w, Mary Chichester, *née* Rideal (d 1985); *b* 4 June 1949, ; *Educ* Westminster, Trinity Hall Cambridge (BA), Université Libre de Bruxelles (Lic Special en Droit Européen); *m* 1, 5 April 1972 (m dis 1987), Maria Luisa, da of Juan Mirasierras, of Avenida Reina Vitoria, Madrid, Spain; 2 s (Daniel b 1974, Thomas b 1976); m 2, 20 Feb 1988, Judith Britannia Caroline, da of David Henry John Griffiths Powell; 2 s (Rhodri b 1990, Alexander Rollo Tristram b 1993); *Career* called to the Bar Lincoln's Inn 1972, bencher Lincoln's Inn 1994; standing counsel to dir gen of Fair Trading 1980–86; *Recreations* gardening, bird watching, rough shooting, tennis; *Style—* The Hon David Oliver, QC; ✉ 13 Old Square, Lincoln's Inn, London WC2A 3UA (☎ 0171 404 4800, fax 0171 405 4267)

OLIVER, Prof Dawn; da of Ernest Gordon Borrett Taylor (d 1989), and Ann Zoë Mieke Taylor (d 1961); *b* 7 June 1942; *Educ* Notting Hill and Ealing HS, Newnham Coll Cambridge (BA, MA, PhD); *m* 6 Jan 1967, Stephen J L Oliver, s of Capt P D Oliver, RN (d 1979); 1 s (Adam b 1970), 2 da (Rebecca b 1969, Rosemary b 1972); *Career* called to the Bar Middle Temple 1965; in practice 1965–69, conslt Legal Action Gp 1973–76; Univ

Coll London: lectr in law 1976–88, sr lectr 1988–90, reader in public law 1990–93, prof of constitutional law, dean of the faculty and head of dept 1993–; memb: Inst of Public Policy Res working gp on a constitution for the UK 1990–91, Hansard Soc Cmmn on Election Campaigns 1990–91, Editorial Bd The Democratic Audit 1990–, Study of Parliament Gp 1992–, Justice Working Party on Interventions in Public Interest Cases 1994–95, Advsy Bd Constitution Unit 1995–; ed Public Law 1993–; assoc fell Newnham Coll Cambridge 1996–; *Books* The Changing Constitution (ed with J L Jowell, 1985, 2 edn 1989, 3 edn 1994), Cohabitation - The Legal Implications (1987), New Directions in Judicial Review (ed with J L Jowell, 1988), Economical with the Truth - The Law and the Media in a Democracy (ed with D Kingsford Smith, 1989), Government in the United Kingdom: The Search for Accountability, Effectiveness and Citizenship (1991), The Foundations of Citizenship (with D Heater, 1994), Public Service Reforms (with G Drewry, 1996), Halsbury's Laws of England Constitutional Law (5 edn, ed with Lord Lester of Herne Hill, QC, 1996); *Style*— Professor Dawn Oliver; ✉ University Coll London, Law Faculty, Bentham Hse, Endsleigh Gdns, London WC1H 0EG (☎ and fax 0171 391 1409, e-mail d.oliver@ucl.ac.uk)

OLIVER, Edward Morgan; s of Raife Morgan Oliver (d 1963), of Long Melford, Suffolk, and Nancy Evelyn, *née* Cutler (d 1985); *b* 22 April 1942; *Educ* Felsted; *m* 7 Aug 1965, (Carol) Louise, da of Edgar Cecil Watts (d 1975), of Ditchingham, Bungay, Suffolk; 1 s (Dr Raife Morgan Oliver b 1967), 1 da (Lynn Bridget b 1970); *Career* CA; ptnr: Peters Elworthy & Moore 1967–70, Shipleys 1971–; memb Herts CC 1972–80 (chm Highways Ctee 1977–80), Cons candidate NE Derbys 1979; sec King George's Pension Fund for Actors and Actresses 1971–; govr Bishop's Stortford Coll; Freeman City of London, Liveryman Worshipful Co of Vintners 1966; FCA 1965; *Recreations* field sports, amateur dramatics, gardening; *Clubs* Travellers'; *Style*— Edward Oliver, Esq; ✉ Maple Cottage, Arkesden Rd, Clavering, nr Saffron Waldon, Essex; Shipleys, 10 Orange Street, London WC2 7DQ (☎ 0171 312 0000, fax 0171 312 0022)

OLIVER, Chief Constable Ian Thomas; QPM (1984); s of Thomas Oliver, GM (d 1967), and Mary Elizabeth, *née* Burton; *b* 24 Jan 1940; *Educ* Hampton GS Middx, Univ of Nottingham (LLB, MPhil), Univ of Strathclyde (PhD); *m* 22 Feb 1964, Elsie, *née* Chalmers; 1 da (Stephanie Katherine b 20 Dec 1965), 2 s (Guy Thomas b 29 Sept 1967, Craig Stewart b 15 May 1969); *Career* constable rising to supt Metropolitan Police 1961–77, awarded Cwlth Fndn bursary to Kenya 1972, asst chief constable Mgmnt Servs Northumbria Police 1978–79 (chief supt 1977–78), chief constable Central Scotland Police 1979–90, chief constable Grampian Police 1990–; awarded Winston Churchill Travelling Fellowship to North America (drugs educn progs) 1986; memb: Editorial Bd Criminal Law Review 1989–, Home Sec's Firearms Consultative Ctee 1989, various ctees IACP 1982–; pres ACPO Scotland 1983–84 and 1993–94; memb: Int Criminal Justice Symposium State Univ of New York 1982, L'Ordre de Bon Temps Nova Scotia 1985; chm Nat Police Lifeboat Appeal Ctee 1990–92; FRSA 1993; *Books* The Metropolitan Police Approach to the Prosecution of Juvenile Offenders (1977), Police, Government and Accountability (1987, 2 edn 1996); *Clubs* Royal Air Force; *Style*— Chief Constable Ian Oliver, QPM; ✉ Grampian Police HQ, Queen Street, Aberdeen AB10 1ZA (☎ 01224 639111, fax 01224 640465)

OLIVER, Ven John Michael; s of Frederick Cecil Oliver (d 1941), and Mary, *née* Hobson (d 1985); *b* 7 Sept 1939; *Educ* Ripon GS, St David's UC Lampeter (BA), Ripon Hall Oxford; *m* Aug 1964, Anne Elizabeth, da of Arthur Barlow, of Oldham, Lancs; 3 da (Ruth Elizabeth (Mrs Paul Lawes) b 1966, Catherine Helen b 1968, Alison Mary b 1971); *Career* ordained: deacon 1964, priest 1965; asst curate: St Peter Harrogate 1964–67, St Peter Bramley Leeds 1967–72; vicar: St Mary Harrogate 1972–78, Beeston Leeds 1978–92; ecumenical offr for Leeds 1980–85, rural dean of Armley 1986–92, hon canon Ripon Cathedral 1987–, archdeacon of Leeds 1992–; *Recreations* watching and playing sport, theatre, reluctant gardening; *Style*— The Ven the Archdeacon of Leeds; ✉ Archdeacon's Lodge, 2 Halcyon Hill, Leeds LS7 3PU (☎ and fax 0113 269 0594)

OLIVER, Mark Leo; s of Rudolf Oliver, of London, and Anita, *née* Levinson; *b* 19 Sept 1963; *Educ* Orange Hill HS, Hertford Coll Oxford (BA); *m* Victoria Rosalind, *née* Pugh; *Career* econ analyst National Economic Research Associates 1985–87 (work incl conslt to Peacock Ctee on funding of the BBC), conslt and media gp mangr Deloitte Haskins & Sells Consultancy 1987–89; BBC Policy and Planning Unit: business analyst 1989–90, business policy advsr to BBC Bd of Mgmnt (on corp strategy and operational efficiency and effectiveness) 1990–93, chief advsr (corp strategy) 1993–95; md Oliver & Ohlbaum Associates Ltd 1995–; *Style*— Mark Oliver, Esq; ✉ Oliver & Ohlbaum Associates Ltd, 11 Barlby Road, London W10 6AN (☎ 0181 960 0120, fax 0181 960 5311)

OLIVER, Michael Edgar; s of Alan Oliver (d 1991), and Marguerite, *née* Moore (d 1986); *b* 20 July 1937; *Educ* St Clement Danes GS; *Career* presenter: Music Weekly BBC Radio 3 1975–90, Kaleidoscope BBC Radio 4 1975–87, Soundings BBC Radio 3 1990–92; reviewer Gramophone 1973–; memb: An Comunn Gaidhealach (The Highlands Assoc), Sabhal Mor Ostaig (Gaelic Coll), Nat Tst for Scotland; former chm English Song Award; formerly active in anti-nuclear movement; *Books* Igor Stravinsky (1995), Benjamin Britten (1996); contributor to: British Music Now (ed Foreman, 1975), End Games (ed Stewart, 1989), Song on Record (ed Blyth, 1988), Choral Music on Record (ed Blyth, 1991), International Encyclopedia of Dance (ed Dorris, 1993); *Recreations* travel, visual arts, food; *Style*— Michael Oliver, Esq; ✉ 129 Crouch Hill, London N8 9QH (☎ 0181 340 6668); via Castello 34, 06066 Oro, Piegaro (PG), Italy

OLIVER, Prof Michael Francis; CBE (1985); s of Capt Wilfrid Francis Lenn Oliver, MC (d 1940); *b* 3 July 1925; *Educ* Marlborough, Univ of Edinburgh (MD); *m* 1, 1948 (m dis 1979), Margaret Yool, da of Maj James Yool Abbey, DSO, MC (d 1932); 2 s (and 1 s decd), 1 da; m 2, 1985, Helen Louise, da of Cyril Cockrell; *Career* Univ of Edinburgh: personal prof of cardiology 1976–78, Duke of Edinburgh prof of Cardiology Univ of Edinburgh 1978–89, Wynn Inst for Metabolic Res London 1989–93, currently emeritus prof; hon prof Univ of London at Nat Heart and Lung Inst 1989–; UK rep Advsy Panel for Cardiovascular Diseases WHO 1972–; chm: BBC Med Advsy Gp Scotland 1975–80, DOT Advsy Panel on Cardiovascular Diseases 1983–90; pres: Br Cardiac Soc 1981–85, RCPEd 1985–88; examiner Univs of Cambridge, Wales, Leeds and Edinburgh; FRCP, FRCPE, FFPHM, FRACP; Hon MD Karolinska 1980, Hon MD Bologna 1985; Hon FACC, FRSE 1987; *Publications* 5 books and 350 papers on metabolic, clinical and epidemologic aspects of heart disease; *Recreations* the Italians; *Clubs* Athenaeum, New (Edinburgh); *Style*— Prof Michael Oliver, CBE, FRSE; ✉ 21 Keepier Wharf, Narrow Street, London E14 8DH; Apecolle, Loc Spedalicchio, 06019 Umbertide (PG), Italy

OLIVER, (James) Michael Yorrick; JP (1987); s of Sqdn Ldr George Leonard Jack Oliver (d 1984), of Mallorca, and Patricia Rosamund, *née* Douglas; *b* 13 July 1940; *Educ* Brunswick Sch, Wellington Coll; *m* 22 June 1963, Sally Elizabeth Honor, da of George Gerhard Exner (d 1965), of London W1; 2 da (Sophia Tugela Rosamund b 14 Oct 1969, Justine Umthandi Electra b 29 Dec 1971); *Career* asst mangr Rediffusion Ltd Leicester 1959–63, mangr Helios Ltd Johannesburg 1965–70; ptnr Kitcat & Aitken 1977–86 (joined 1970), dir Kitcat Aitken & Co 1986–90, md Carr Kitcat & Aitken 1990–93; dir Lloyds Investment Managers Ltd 1994–; dir: Oliver's Wharf Management Co 1970–, Gabhaig Hydro Power Co 1988–, Centrepoint Soho (charity for homelessness) 1992–, The First Spanish Investment Trust 1994–, German Investment Trust 1994–, The German Smaller Companies Investment Trust 1994–, Highland Light & Power 1994–, The Central & Eastern European Fund 1995–, The Euro-Spain Fund 1996–; tstee: UK Growth & Income Fund, The Income Plus Fund; alderman Ward of Bishopsgate 1987– (memb Ct of Common Cncl 1980–87); govr: Bishopsgate Fndn, King Edward's Sch Witley, Christ's Hosp 1979–; chm Steering Ctee The Port of London and Docklands Museum; memb: City of London Archaeological Tst, Museum of London Devpt Cncl 1990–, Ctee City of London Historical Soc; tstee The Geffrye Museum 1992–; memb Ct Worshipful Co of Ironmongers (Master 1991–92); MSI(dip), AIIMR; OStJ; FRGS; *Recreations* archaeology, travel; *Clubs* City Livery; *Style*— Michael Oliver, Esq, JP; ✉ Hill Samuel Asset Management Ltd, 10 Fleet Place, London EC4M 7RH (☎ 0171 203 3494, fax 0171 203 3412); Paradise House, Paradise Island, off Grantchester St, Cambridge CB3 9HY; 3A Oliver's Wharf, Wapping High Street, London E1 9PJ

OLIVER, Dr Ronald Martin; CB (1989), RD; s of Cuthbert Hanson Oliver (d 1972), of Strawberry Hill, and Cecilia *née* O'Dockery (d 1981); *b* 28 May 1929; *Educ* King's Coll Sch Wimbledon, King's Coll London, St George's Hosp London (MB BS, MRCS, LRCP, MD, MRCP, MFPHM, MFOM, DCH DIH, DPH); *m* 2 March 1957, Susanna (Sue) Treves, da of Dr Alfred Delatour Blackwell, of Taunton; 3 s (Richard b 1958, James b 1960, Philip b 1966), 1 da (Sarah b 1971); *Career* Surgn Lt RNVR 1953–55, Surgn Lt Cdr 1959; jr hosp appts St George's Hosp 1952–56, trainee asst GP 1956–57, asst county MO Surrey CC 1957–59; MO: London Tport Exec 1959–62, Treasy Med Serv 1962–64; physician Br Embassy Moscow 1964–66, MO then SMO Civil Serv Med Advsy Serv 1966–74, SMO then sr princ MO DHSS, dep CMO Dept of Health 1974–89; govr Manor House Sch Little Bookham (chm 1995–); memb BMA, FRSM; *Recreations* golf, gardening, sailing; *Style*— Dr Ronald Oliver, CB, RD; ✉ Greenhill House, Beech Ave, Effingham, Surrey KT24 5PH (☎ 01372 452887)

OLIVER, Rev Canon Stephen John; s of John Oliver, of Northampton, and Nora, *née* Greenalgh; *b* 7 Jan 1948; *Educ* Manchester GS, King's Coll London, St Augustine's Coll Canterbury; *m* 1969, Hilary Joan, da of the Rev Basil Barkham; 2 s (Simon Andrew b 1971, Adam David b 1973); *Career* curate Clifton Team Miny 1970–74, vicar Christ Church Newark Notts 1974–79, rector St Mary's Plumtree 1979–85, chief prodr Religious Progs BBC 1985–91, rector of Leeds 1991–97, canon residentiary St Paul's Cathedral London 1997–; hon canon Ripon Cathedral 1996, memb BBC Task Force 1991, memb Liturgical Cmmn C of E 1991–; chm: Govrs Leeds Girls High Sch 1993–96, Govrs Agnes Stewart High Sch 1994–96; *Style*— The Rev Canon Stephen Oliver; ✉ 3 Amen Court, London EC4

OLIVER, His Hon Stephen John Lindsay; QC; s of Phillip Daniel Oliver (Capt RN, d 1979),of Carlton, and Audrey Mary Taylor; *b* 14 Nov 1938; *Educ* Rugby Sch 1952–56, Oriel Coll Oxford 1959–62 (MA Jurisprudence); *m* 1967, Ann Dawn, da of Gordon Taylor (d 1989); 1 s (Adam b 1970), 2 da (Rebecca b 1969, Rosemary b 1972); *Career* RNVR (submariner) 1957–59; barr; bencher 1987, asst Parly boundary cmmr, recorder 1989–91, circuit judge SE Circuit 1991–92, presiding special cmmr 1992–, pres VAT Tbnls 1992–94, pres VAT and Duties Tbnls 1994–; chm Blackheath Concert Halls 1986–92, memb Cncl London Sinfonietta 1993–; *Recreations* music, sailing; *Clubs* Groucho; *Style*— His Hon Stephen Oliver, QC; ✉ 15 Bedford Avenue, London WC1B 3AS (☎ 0171 631 4242)

OLIVER, Vaughan William; s of Ernest Oliver, and Doreen, *née* Tindale; *b* 12 Sept 1957; *Educ* Ferryhill GS, Newcastle upon Tyne Poly (BA Hons); *Career* graphic designer, art dir; packaging designer: Benchmark 1980, Michael Peters Gp 1981; record cover designer (under name 23 Envelope, with Nigel Grierson), 4AD (record co) 1983–88, freelance (under name v23, with Chris Bigg) 1988–; record covers for gps incl: Cocteau Twins, Heidi Berry, His Name is Alive, Lush, Pixies, The Psychedelic Furs, This Mortal Coil, The Breeders, David Sylvian; gp exhibitions incl: British Design, New Traditions (Boymans Museum Rotterdam) 1989, Pictures of Rock (Denmark) 1990, British Design 1790–1990 (Calif) 1990, Best of British Design (Tokyo) 1990, The Art of Selling Songs 1690–1990 (V&A) 1991; solo exhibitions: Exhibition/Exposition (Nantes, St Brieuc 1990, Paris 1991), Expo 23 (Tokyo) 1991, Glove (Osaka) 1992 and (Tokyo) 1993, 13 Year Itch (ICA London) 1993, This Rimy River (LA and UK) 1994, Is Minty a Man? (Newcastle-upon-Tyne) 1996; other design work includes: book jackets (Serpents Tail, Picador), book design (Tokyo Salamander, Shinro Ohtake), freelance music projects (Virgin, RCA, East West), TV title sequences for BBC2 (Snub TV, Gimme 8)), conf publicity (Kingston Poly, V&A Museum), fashion catalogue (John Galliano), TV statio identity, design and direction (Documania, Canal Plus, Madrid), posters (Angeli Preljocaj, Paris and Young Vic London), TV advert (Microsoft); memb Assoc of Music Indust Designers (AMID); *Style*— Vaughan Oliver, Esq; ✉ v23, 15 Alma Road, London SW18 1AA (☎ 0181 870 9724, fax 0181 874 6600)

OLIVER-BELLASIS, Hugh Richard; s of Lt-Col John Oliver-Bellasis, DSO, JP, DL (d 1979), and Anne Mary, *née* Bates; *b* 11 April 1945; *Educ* Winchester, RMA Sandhurst; *m* 7 Aug 1971, Daphne Phoebe, da of Christopher Parsons, of Hatchwood House, Odiham; 2 da (Joanna b 8 April 1975, Nicola b 12 June 1978); *Career* 2 Lt Royal Fusiliers City of London Regt 1964, Welsh Gds 1970, Maj 1977 (ret); dir Manydown Co Ltd 1964–, farmer 1980–, chm Hants Farm Devpts 1985–; vice chm Parish Cncl 1980–; Hants Co rep Cncl NFU 1990; Game Conservancy Tst: chm Lowland Ecology Unit 1990–, chm of research planning 1994–; chm Br Deer Soc 1986–96, memb Cncl RASE, vice chm Parly Land Use and Environment Ctee NFU 1994–; Freeman City of London 1967; Liveryman: Worshipful Co of Merchant Taylors 1971, Worshipful Co of Gunmakers 1990; memb Grasshoppers' Assoc 1989, FRAgS 1992 (assoc 1990); *Recreations* field sports, wine, food, motor racing; *Clubs* Army and Navy, Boodle's, Farmers', MCC; *Style*— Hugh Oliver-Bellasis, Esq; ✉ Wootton House, Wootton St Lawrence, Basingstoke, Hants RG23 8PE; The Manydown Co, Upper Farm, Basingstoke, Hants RG23 8PE (☎ 01256 781145, fax 01256 782666)

OLIVER-JONES, Stephen; QC (1996); s of Arthur William Jones, of King's Stanley, Stroud, Glos, and Kathleen, *née* Woodcock (d 1993); *b* 6 July 1947; *Educ* Marling Sch Stroud, Univ Coll Durham (BA Law/Economics); *m* 16 Dec 1972, Margaret Anne, da of Ronald Thomas Richardson; 1 da (Clare Felicity b 21 March 1979), 1 s (Robin Stephen b 19 March 1982); *Career* lectr in law Durham Tech Coll 1968–70, called to the Bar Inner Temple 1970, recorder 1993 (asst recorder 1968); memb: Professional Negligence Bar Assoc 1993, Personal Injury Bar Assoc 1995, AVMA 1996; *Recreations* fly-fishing and philately; *Clubs* Royal Philatelic Society of London; *Style*— Stephen Oliver-Jones, Esq, QC; ✉ 5 Fountain Court, Steelhouse Lane, Birmingham B4 6DR (☎ 0121 606 0500, fax 0121 606 1501)

OLIVER OF AYLMERTON, Baron (Life Peer UK 1986), of Aylmerton, Co Norfolk; Peter Raymond Oliver; kt (1974), PC (1980); s of David Thomas Oliver (d 1947), and Alice Maud, da of George Kirby; *b* 7 March 1921; *Educ* The Leys Sch Cambridge, Trinity Hall Cambridge (hon fellow 1980); *m* 1, 1945, Mary Chichester (d 1985), da of Sir Eric Keightley Rideal, MBE, FRS; 1 s (Hon David Keightley Rideal, *qv*, b 1949), 1 da (Hon Sarah Chichester b 1951); m 2, 1987, Wendy Anne, widow of Ivon Lloyd Lewis Jones; *Career* barr Lincoln's Inn 1948; QC 1965; High Court Judge (Chancery) 1974–80; Lord Justice of Appeal 1980–86; memb Restrictive Practices Ct 1976–80; chm Review Body on High Ct Chancery Div 1979–81; memb Supreme Court Rule Ctee 1982–85; Lord of Appeal in Ordinary 1986–92; *Style*— The Rt Hon Lord Oliver of Aylmerton, PC; ✉ c/o House of Lords, London SW1A 0PW

OLIVEY, Alan Keith; s of Hugh Norman Olivey (d 1980), of Upper Norwood, London, and Kathleen, *née* Mills (d 1991); *b* 14 Oct 1947; *Educ* Heath Clark GS Croydon; *m* 11 Sept 1971, Janet Mary, da of Raymond Edgar Crewes Hutton, of Beckenham, Kent; 1 s (Richard b 1981), 1 da (Louise b 1977); *Career* CA; Sydenham Snowden Nicholson &

Co 1964–71, ptnr Ernst & Young 1980– (joined 1971); FCA 1970, ATII 1970; *Recreations* golf, gardening, philately, photography; *Style*— Alan Olivey, Esq; ✉ 75 Elwill Way, Beckenham, Kent BR3 2RY (☎ 0181 658 1519); Rolls House, 7 Rolls Buildings, Fetter Lane, London EC4A 1NH (☎ 0171 931 2376, fax 0171 353 8134, telex 885234 ERNSLO G)

OLIVIER, Joan Sheila Ross; *b* 30 April 1941; *Educ* Morrisons Acad Crieff Perthshire, Rosa Bassett Streatham, Queen Mary Coll London (BA), Hughes Hall Cambridge (PGCE); *m* 6 Aug 1966, John Eric Hordern Olivier; 1 s (James Maximilian Dering b 6 July 1978); *Career* Camden Sch for Girls: history teacher 1964–67, head History Dept 1967–73, schs examination supervisor 1970–73; Lady Margaret Sch London: dep head 1973–84, headmistress 1984–; Lady Margaret featured in The Independent's Good Sch Guide and Evening Standard's Best State Schs in London; *Recreations* bad bridge and even worse golf; *Style*— Mrs Joan Olivier; ✉ Lady Margaret School, Parson's Green, London SW6 4UN (☎ 0171 736 7138)

OLIVIER, Hon Richard; s of Baron Olivier (Life Peer, d 1989), and his 3 w, Joan Plowright, *qv*; *b* 1961; *Educ* UCLA; *m* 28 June 1987, Shelley Marie Dupuis, *née* Herrich; 1 s (Troilus (Troy) b 1988), 1 da ((Natalie) Alessandra b 1990), and 1 step da (Kaya Rose); *Career* theatre and film dir; *Style*— The Hon Richard Olivier

OLLERENSHAW, Dame Kathleen Mary; DBE (1971), DL (1987); da of Charles Timpson, JP (d 1967), and Mary Elizabeth, *née* Stops (d 1954); *b* 1 Oct 1912, Manchester; *Educ* Ladybarn House Sch Manchester, St Leonards Sch St Andrews, Somerville Coll Oxford (MA, DPhil); *m* 1939, Col Robert Ollerenshaw, ERD, TD, JP, DL (d 1986): 1 s, 1 da (decd); *Career* chm: Assoc of Governing Bodies of Girls' Public Schs 1963–69, Manchester Educn Ctee 1967–70, Manchester Poly 1968–72 (hon fell 1978), Ct of RNCM 1968–86 (companion 1978), Educn Ctee Assoc of Municipal Corporations 1968–71; author of numerous res papers in mathematical jls; Manchester CC 1956–80: Alderman 1970–74, Lord Mayor 1975–76, dep Lord Mayor 1976–77, ldr Cons opposition 1977–79, Hon Alderman 1980–; vice pres Br Assoc for Commercial and Industl Educn (memb delgn to USSR 1963); memb: Central Advsy Cncl on Educn in England 1960–63, CNAA 1964–74, SSRC 1971–75, Layfield Ctee of Enquiry into Local Govt Fin 1974–76; pres: St Leonards Sch St Andrews 1976–, Manchester Technol Assoc 1981 (hon memb 1976–), Manchester Statistical Soc 1983–85; hon fell: City and Guilds London Inst 1980 (memb Educn Ctee 1960–73), Inst of Mathematics and its Applications 1990 (fell 1964, memb Cncl 1972–, pres 1979–80), UMIST 1987 (vice pres 1977–86); hon memb Manchester Literary and Philosophical Soc 1981; dep pro chllr Univ of Lancaster 1978–91 (memb Ct 1991–), pro chllr Univ of Salford 1983–89; dir Manchester Independent Radio Ltd 1972–83; memb Manchester Astronomical Soc 1990– (vice pres 1994–); Hon Col Manchester and Salford Univ OTC 1977–81; DStJ 1983 (CStJ 1978), chm Cncl Order of St John Greater Manchester 1974–89, memb Chapter General Order of St John 1978–96; Mancunian of the Year Jr C of C 1977; hon fell Somerville Coll Oxford 1978; Freeman City of Manchester 1984; Hon DSc Salford 1975, Hon LLD Manchester 1976, Hon DSc CNAA 1976, Hon DSc Lancaster 1992, Hon LLD Liverpool 1994; Hon FIMA 1988, FCP FCGI; CMath; DStJ; *Books* Education of Girls (1958), The Girls' Schools (1967), Returning to Teaching (1974), The Lord Mayor's Party (1976), First Citizen (1977), Reversible Squares, A Combinatorial Problem (1997); *Recreations* astronomy; *Clubs* English-Speaking Union; *Style*— Dame Kathleen Ollerenshaw, DBE, DL; ✉ 2 Pine Rd, Didsbury, Manchester M20 6UY (☎ 0161 445 2948)

OLLEY, Martin Burgess; s of Robert William Olley (d 1969), of Sheringham, Norfolk, and Dorothy Lillian Alexander, *née* Burgess (d 1941); *b* 11 Aug 1932; *Educ* Gresham's Sch Holt Norfolk, Coll of Estate Mgmnt London; *m* 1 (m dis 1971), Averil Rosemary Phyllis, *née* Cann; 2 s (Clive Matthew Burgess b 1961, Edward Martin Burgess b 1967), 1 da (Lucy Ann Burgess b 1963); m 2, 14 June 1980, Moira Bernadette, da of Joseph Kelly (d 1968); *Career* RAF 1950–52; Norwich Union: London Estates mangr 1973–80, Norwich estates mangr 1980–82, chief estates mangr 1983–; memb Gen Cncl Br Property Fedn, former pres Norwich Wanderers CC; Freeman City of London 1974, Liveryman Worshipful Co of Woolmen 1978; FRICS; *Recreations* golf, boating, squash, tennis, walking; *Clubs* RAC, Norfolk Broads Yacht; *Style*— Martin Olley, Esq; ✉ 1 Marston Lane, Eaton, Norwich, Norfolk NR4 6LZ (☎ 01603 456495); 55 Netheravon Rd, Chiswick, London W1 (☎ 0181 994 1392); Norwich Union Real Estate Managers Ltd, Sentinel House, 37 Surrey St, Norwich NR1 3PW (☎ 01603 682256, fax 01603 683950, telex 97388)

OLLIFF, Barry Martin; s of Clarence Martin William Olliff, and Patricia Joan, *née* Greenley; *b* 31 Dec 1944; *Educ* Hinchley Wood County Secdy Sch; *m* Margaret Ann, da of Francis Samuel Thomas Cleave; 1 s (Andrew James), 1 da (Samantha Claire); *Career* various appts in investment depts of: Rowe Swann & Co Stockbrokers 1962–63, Denny Bros/Pinchin Denny Stockjobbers 1963–79, Laing & Cruickshank Stockbrokers 1979–86 (dir 1983–86); md Olliff & Partners plc 1987–, md City of London Unit Trust Managers 1991–; MSI; *Recreations* cricket, skiing; *Style*— Barry Olliff, Esq; ✉ Olliff & Partners PLC, 10 Eastcheap, London EC3M 1AJ (☎ 0171 374 0191, fax 0171 374 2063)

OLNER, William John (Bill); MP (Lab) Nuneaton (majority 1,631); s of late C William Olner, and Lillian Olner; *b* 9 May 1942; *Educ* Atherstone Secdy Modern Sch, N Warwicks Tech Coll; *m* 10 March 1962, Gillian, da of David Everitt; *Career* apprentice engr Armstrong Siddeley Motors, skilled machinist Rolls Royce Coventry until 1992, AEU branch sec 1972–92; MP (Lab, AEU sponsored) Nuneaton 1992–; memb Select Ctee for Environment 1995–; Nuneaton BC: cncllr 1971–93, chm Planning Ctee 1974–76, chm Policy and Resources Ctee 1982–86, chm Environmental Health Ctee 1990–92, dep ldr 1980–82, ldr 1982–86; *Recreations* working for local hospice, walking, current affairs, television; *Style*— Bill Olner, Esq, MP; ✉ House of Commons, London SW1A 0AA

OLNEY, Robert C; s of Herbert M Olney, of USA; *b* 19 Aug 1926; *Educ* Cornell (BA); *m* 1, 1948, Wanda, *née* Gasch (d 1988); 3 c; m 2, 14 March 1992, Ann W Bell; *Career* National Advertising Co Chicago: gen sales mangr 1959, mktg dir 1969, div dir 1973, vice pres gen mangr 1976–79; chm and md 3M UK plc 1979–88, chm Yale and Nutone Inc 1987–91, pres Tudor Holdings Inc; dir: Merton Assoc Ltd, Penna plc until 1995, Revere Holdings Inc NY 1995–; memb Ct of Assts Worshipful Co of Upholders; CIMgt; *Recreations* golf, skiing; *Clubs* Hinsdale Golf, RAC, Greenville Country; *Style*— Robert C Olney, Esq; ✉ 32 Lakeside Grange, Oatlands Park, Weybridge, Surrey KT13 9ZE (☎ 01932 821561, fax 01932 821472)

O'LOGHLEN, Sir Colman Michael; 6 Bt (UK 1838), of Drumconora, Ennis; s of Henry Ross O'Loghlen (d 1944), and Doris Irene, *née* Horne; suc uncle, Sir Charles Hugh Ross O'Loghlen, 5 Bt (d 1951); *b* 6 April 1916; *Educ* Xavier Coll Melbourne, Melbourne Univ (LLB); *m* 1939, Margaret, da of Francis O'Halloran, of Melbourne; 6 s (Michael b 1945, Bryan b 1946, Ross b 1948, Hugh b 1952, 2 others), 2 da (Margaret b 1940, Janet b 1942); *Heir* s, Michael O'Loghlen, *qv*; *Career* served 1942–45 with AIF New Guinea, Capt 1945; stipendiary magistrate Lae New Guinea, former actg judge of Supreme Ct of Territory of Papua and New Guinea; *Style*— Sir Colman O'Loghlen, Bt; ✉ Ellengrove, Queensland 4077, Australia

O'LOGHLEN, Michael; s and h of Sir Colman O'Loghlen, 6 Bt, *qv*; *b* 21 May 1945; *Style*— Michael O'Loghlen, Esq

OLSEN, Gary Kenneth (formerly Grant); s of Kenneth George Grant (d 1968), and Patricia, *née* Haste (d 1966); *b* 3 Nov 1957; *Educ* Archbishop Tenison GS; *m* 1991, Jane Elizabeth Anthony; 1 s (Jake Elwood Grant b 1993), 1 da (India Rose b 1996); *Career* actor; *Theatre* incl: Metamorphosis 1986, Up On The Roof 1987, Serious Money 1987–88, On The Ledge (RNT) 1993, April in Paris (Ambassadors) 1994, Macbeth (Liverpool Everyman) 1995; *Television* incl: The Bill 1984, Prospects 1985, Come Home Charlie and Face Them 1990, Two Point Four Children 1991–96, Health and Efficiency 1993; *Recreations* golf, snooker; *Clubs* Fred's, Warley Park Golf, Great Haddam Golf; *Style*— Gary Olsen, Esq; ✉ c/o Lou Coulson, 37 Berwick Street, London W1V 3RF (☎ 0171 734 9633, fax 0171 439 7569)

OLSEN, John Richard; s of (Lawrence) Nigel Guy Olsen, of Saffron Walden, Essex, and Rosemary Elizabeth, *née* Kies; *b* 7 Jan 1964; *Educ* Charterhouse, Univ of Durham (BA Archaeology); *m* 9 May 1992, Juliet Mary; 1 da (Lucy b 15 Dec 1993), 1 s (Jack b 30 Aug 1995); *Career* Broad Street Associates PR 1986–89, Shandwick Consultants 1990– (currently dir); *Recreations* family, sailing, golf; *Clubs* RAC; *Style*— John Olsen, Esq; ✉ St Breward, Rickford, Worplesdon, Surrey GU3 3PH (☎ 01483 235188); Shandwick Consultants Ltd, Aldermary House, 10–15 Queen Street, London EC4N 1TX (☎ 0171 329 0096, fax 0171 919 9886)

OLSEN, Roy; s of John Sigmund Olsen (d 1971), and Florence Mary, *née* Ashworth; *b* 20 April 1945; *Educ* Margaret's Anfield Liverpool, Art HS Liverpool, Coll of Bldg Liverpool; *m* 22 July 1972, Francesca Carey, da of Capt William Sidney Hall, MC, of Wales; 2 s (Luke Joen b 1975, Alexander Hall b 1976); *Career* architect; conslt in private practice Bigmore Olsen Bennett; architectural awards from Snowdonia Nat Park, Montgomery Design Award, Stone Fedn, RIBA; *Recreations* golf; *Clubs* Royal St David's Golf (capt 1995–96), Dolgellau Golf (capt 1984–85); *Style*— Roy Olsen, Esq; ✉ Trem Yr Eglwys, Dolgellau, Gwynedd (☎ 01341 423071); Bigmore Olsen Bennett, Arran Buildings, Dolgellau, Gwynedd (☎ 01341 422932, fax 01341 422044)

OLVER, Sir Stephen John Linley; KBE (1975, MBE 1947), CMG (1965); s of late Rev S E L Olver; *b* 16 June 1916; *Educ* Stowe; *m* 1953, Maria, da of Gino Morena, of Gubbio, Italy; 1 s; *Career* served Indian Political Service 1944–47, Br Diplomatic Service Karachi 1947–50, FO 1950–53, Berlin 1953–56, Bangkok 1956–58, FO 1958–61, cnsllr Washington 1961–64, FO 1965–66, The Hague 1967–69; high cmmr: Sierra Leone 1969–72, Cyprus 1973–75; *Style*— Sir Stephen Olver, KBE, CMG; ✉ 6 Saffrons Court, Compton Place Road, Eastbourne, Sussex BN21 1DX (☎ 01323 643462)

OLYMPITIS, Emmanuel John; s of John Emmanuel Olympitis, and Argyro, *née* Theodorou; *b* 19 Dec 1948; *Educ* King's Sch Canterbury, Univ Coll London (LLB); *m* 26 Oct 1979 (m dis 1983), Jan Cushing; 1 s (John Emmanuel b 1981); m 2, 1 Dec 1995, Clare, da of Michael John Benjamin Todhunter; *Career* dir Bankers Trust International Ltd 1976–80, vice pres Bankers Trust Co NY 1976– 80, pres Centaur Resources Inc NY 1980–84, ptnr America Acquisitions Co NY 1981–85; md Aitken Hume Group 1986–88, chief exec and dir Aitken Hume International plc 1988–89; dir: Aitken Hume Bank plc 1988–89, Sentinel Life plc 1988–89, National Securities & Research Corporation NY 1988–89; chm Johnson & Higgins Ltd 1993–96, gp md Johnson and Higgins Holdings Ltd 1992–96, dir Johnson & Higgins UK Ltd 1992–96; memb GB Int Fencing Squad 1966–70, memb Kent County Fencing Team 1966–70 (Foil and Epée champion 1966); *Books* By Victories Undone (1988); *Recreations* writing, sailing; *Clubs* Turf, Spouting Rock Beach Club (Rhode Island); *Style*— Emmanuel Olympitis, Esq; ✉ Cranley Lodge, 132B Fulham Road, London SW3 (☎ 0171 370 4009); Kalymnos, Dodecanese Islands, Greece

O'MALLEY, His Honour Judge; Stephen Keppel; *b* 21 July 1940; *Educ* Ampleforth Coll, Wadham Coll Oxford; *m* 1963, Frances Mary, da of Stewart Ryan; 4 s, 2 da; *Career* called to the Bar Inner Temple 1962, recorder 1978–89, circuit judge (Western Circuit) 1989–; wine treas of the Western Circuit 1986–89; co-fndr Bar European Gp 1977; *Books* European Civil Practice (1989); *Style*— His Honour Judge O'Malley; ✉ Taunton Crown Court, Taunton, Somerset

OMAN, Dr Julia Trevelyan (Lady Strong); CBE (1986); da of Charles Chichele Oman (d 1982), and Joan, *née* Trevelyan; *b* 11 July 1930; *Educ* Royal Coll of Art (Royal scholar, Silver medal); *m* 1971, Sir Roy Colin Strong, FSA, *qv*; *Career* designer; with BBC TV 1955–67 (prodns incl Alice in Wonderland 1966); Designer of the Year 1967, NCTA Best Art Dir award 1983; photographic contrib Architectural Review and Vogue, contrib drawings Country Life; Hon DLitt Univ of Bristol 1987; FCSD, RDI 1977; *Theatre* Brief Lives 1967 and 1974, Country Dance 1967, Forty Years On 1968, The Merchant of Venice 1970, Othello 1971, The Importance of Being Earnest (Vienna) 1976, Hay Fever and the Wild Duck (London) 1980, The Shoemaker's Holiday (National Theatre) 1981, Mr and Mrs Nobody (Garrick) 1986, A Man for All Seasons (Chichester and Savoy) 1987, The Best of Friends (Apollo) 1988, Beatrix (Chichester) 1996; *Ballet* Enigma Variations (Royal Ballet) 1968 and (BRB) 1984, A Month in the Country (Royal Ballet) 1976, Le Papillon (Sir Frederick Ashton Pas-de-Deux) 1977, Voices of Spring (Ashton Pas-de-Deux, Royal Ballet 1977, Het Nationale Ballet Amsterdam 1989), Sospiri (Ashton Pas-de-Deux) 1980, Swan Lake (Boston Ballet) 1981, Nutcracker (Royal Ballet) 1984, A Month in the Country (Nat Ballet of Canada) 1995; *Opera* Eugene Onegin (Royal Opera House Covent Garden) 1971, Un Ballo in Maschera (Hamburg) 1973, La Boheme (Covent Garden 1974), Die Fledermaus (Covent Garden) 1977, Die Csardasfürstin (Kassel) 1982, Otello (Stockholm) 1983, Arabella (Glyndebourne) 1984, The Consul (Connecticut Grand Opera) 1985; *Television* Hay Fever (Denmark) 1978, Separate Tables (HTV and HBO) 1982; *Films* Vote, Vote, Vote for Nigel Barton (Dennis Potter, BBC) 1965, Alice in Wonderland (BBC) 1966, The Charge of the Light Brigade (art dir) 1967, Laughter in the Dark (art dir) 1968, Julius Caesar (prodn designer) 1969, Straw Dogs (design conslt) 1971; *Exhibitions* Samuel Pepys (Nat Portrait Gallery) 1970, Mme Tussaud's Hall of Historical Tableaux; *Books* Street Children (photographs, with text by B S Johnson, 1964), Elizabeth R (with Roy Strong, 1971), Mary Queen of Scots (with Roy Strong, 1972), The English Year (with Roy Strong, 1982), A Celebration of Gardens (with Roy Strong, 1991), The Wonderful Art of Embroidery (text for Gianni Versace's Vanitas, 1992), A Country Life (with Roy Strong, 1994); *Style*— Dr Julia Trevelyan Oman, CBE; ✉ Oman Productions Ltd, The Laskett, Much Birch, Hereford HR2 8HZ

OMAND, David Bruce; s of James Bruce Omand (d 1980), and Esther, *née* Dewar; *b* 15 April 1947; *Educ* Glasgow Acad, Corpus Christi Coll Cambridge (fndn scholar, BA); *m* Feb 1971, Elizabeth Marjorie, da of Geoffrey Wales (d 1990); 1 s (Duncan b 1978), 1 da (Helen b 1975); *Career* joined GCHQ 1969; MOD: asst princ 1970, private sec to Chief Procurement Exec 1973, asst private sec to Sec of State for Def 1973–75 and 1979–80, princ 1975, asst sec 1981, private sec to Sec of State for Def 1981–82, seconded as def cnsllr to FCO Delgn to Nato Brussels 1985–88, under sec grade 3 1988, asst under sec of state (Mgmnt Strategy) 1988–91, asst under sec of state (Programmes) 1991–92, dep under-sec of state (Policy) 1992–96; head of GCHQ 1996–; *Recreations* hillwalking, opera; *Clubs* Reform; *Style*— David Omand, Esq; ✉ GCHQ, Priors Road, Oakley, Cheltenham, Gloucestershire

O'MARA, Kate; *b* 10 Aug 1939; *children* 1 s (Dickon b 3 Jan 1963); *Career* actress 1963–; founder and dir of The British Actors Theatre Co 1987–; patron: Thorndike Theatre Leatherhead, Theatre Royal Portsmouth, Guildford Sch of Acting; vice-pres The Royal Mail Charity - Mailshot; numerous TV and Film appearances; *Theatre* seasons incl: The Flora Robson Playhouse 1963–64, The Shakespeare for Schools Co 1964, The New Theatre Bromley 1965, The Ashcroft Theatre Croydon 1965; credits incl: Jessica in The Merchant of Venice (Stockton-On-Tees) 1963, Lydia Languish in The Rivals (Welsh National Theatre Co) 1965–66, The Italian Girl (Wyndhams) 1968, The Spoils of Poynton (Mayfair) 1970, Love for Love (Watford) 1971, An Ideal Husband (Watford) 1971, Of Mice and Men (New Theatre Bromley) 1972, Suddenly At Home (Fortune) 1972–73, Elvira in Blithe Spirit (Bristol Old Vic) 1974, Sherlock's Last Case (Open Space Theatre)

1974, Hedda Gabler (Harrogate) 1976, Louka in Arms and The Man (Hong Kong Festival) 1976–77, Kate in Taming of the Shrew (Ludlow Festival) 1978, Rosaline in Love's Labours Lost (Thorndike) 1978, Cyrenne in Rattle of A Simple Man (tour) 1978, Cleopatra in Antony and Cleopatra (Thorndike) 1979, Lena in Misalliance (Birmingham Rep) 1979, T S Eliot's The Elder Statesman (Birmingham Rep) 1979, The Crucifer of Blood (Haymarket London) 1979, Night and Day (post-London tour) 1980, Beatrice in Much Ado About Nothing (New Shakespeare Co) 1981, Kate in Taming of the Shrew (New Shakespeare Co) 1982, Titania/Hippolyta in A Midsummer Night's Dream (New Shakespeare Co) 1982, Cleopatra in Antony and Cleopatra (Nottingham Playhouse) 1982, Millamant in The Way of the World (Nottingham Playhouse) 1982, Duet for One (post-London tour and former Yugoslavia) 1982, Lady Macbeth in An Evening with the Macbeths (Mercury Colchester) 1983, The Merry Wives of Windsor (New Shakespeare Co) 1984, Light Up the Sky (Old Vic) 1985, Goneril in King Lear (Compass Theatre Co) 1987, Light Up the Sky (Globe) 1987, Kate in The Taming of the Shrew (Jerash Festival Jordan) 1988, Berinthia in The Relapse (tour and Mermaid Theatre London) 1988–89, The Last Englishman (Orange Tree Richmond) 1990, Martha in Who's Afraid of Virginia Woolf 1990, Lilli Vanessi in Kiss Me Kate (RSC Remount tour) 1991, Lady Fanciful in The Provoked Wife (Royal National Theatre Studio) 1992, Rosabel in Venus Oberved (Chichester Festival) 1992, Jacky Lane in King Lear In New York (Chichester Festival) 1992, Eve in Cain (Chichester Festival/Minerva Theatre) 1992, Mrs Cheveley in An Ideal Husband (Peter Hall Co) 1994, Kiss and Tell (author and actor, tour) 1994, Maria Wislake in On Approval (Peter Hall Co) 1994, premiere of Bernard Shaw's The Simpleton of The Unexpected Isles (Orange Tree Richmond) 1995, Rachel in My Cousin Rachel (tour and Vienna, nominated for Best Actress Manchester Evening News Awards) 1996; *British Actors Theatre Co* credits incl: Kate in Taming of the Shrew (tour) 1987, Rosalind in As You Like It (tour) 1989, Cleopatra in Antony and Cleopatra (tour) 1989, Olivia in Twelfth Night (also director) 1996; *Books* author of When She Was Bad (novel, 1992), Goodtime Girl (novel, 1993), A Woman's Survival Kit (lifestyle); *Recreations* walking, classical music, reading, home decorating; *Style*— Ms Kate O'Mara; ✉ c/o Michael Ladkin Personal Management, Suite One, Ground Floor, 1 Duchess Street, London W1N 3DE (☎ 0171 436 4626, fax 0171 436 4627)

O'MORCHOE, The; David Nial Creagh O'Morchoe; CB (1979), MBE (1966); formerly of Oulartleigh and Monamolin; s of Col Nial Creagh O'Morchoe (The O'Morchoe), d 1970, when suc by his s David as Chieftain; *b* 17 May 1928; *Educ* St Columba's Coll Dublin, RMA Sandhurst; *m* 1955, Margaret (*Style* Madam O'Morchoe), da of Frank Brewitt, of Cork; 2 s (Dermot b 1956, Kevin b 1958), 2 da (Deirdre b 1960 (decd), Maureen b 1964); *Career* served Royal Irish Fus from 1948 in M East, Med, NW Europe, Kenya, Oman, late Cdr of Sultan of Oman's Land Forces, ret 1979; memb: Church of Ireland General Synod 1993–, Rep Church Body C of E 1994; fell St Columba's Coll (chm of fellows 1988); chm Standing Cncl of Irish Chiefs and Chieftains 1994–, memb Cncl Concern Worldwide (sec 1989), chm SSAFA/Forces Help Soc (Irish Republic) 1986–; *Recreations* sailing; *Clubs* Friendly Brothers, Irish Cruising; *Style*— The O'Morchoe, CB, MBE; ✉ c/o Bank of Ireland, Gorey, Co Wexford, Ireland

ONDAATJE, (Philip) Michael; s of Philip Mervyn Ondaatje, of Sri Lanka, and Doris, *née* Gratiaen; *b* 12 Sept 1943; *Educ* St Thomas' Coll Sri Lanka, Dulwich Coll, Bishop's Univ Quebec, Univ of Toronto (BA), Queen's Univ Ontario (MA); *Career* prof English Dept Glendon Coll York Univ Toronto 1970–; ed Coach House Press 1970–94; Booker Prize for Fiction 1992; *Books* The Collected Works of Billy The Kid, Coming Through Slaughter, Running in the Family (memoir), In the Skin of a Lion, The Cinnamon Peeler (poetry), The English Patient; *Style*— Michael Ondaatje, Esq

O'NEIL, Roger; s of James William O'Neil (d 1980), and Claire Williams O'Neil (d 1981); *b* 22 Feb 1938; *Educ* Laurel Hill Acad USA, Univ of Notre Dame Indiana (BSc), Cornell Univ NY (MBA); *m* 30 Oct 1976, Joan, da of Mark Mathewson, of California; 1 da (Claire Kathyrn b 1980), 1 s (Mark Daniel b 1983); *Career* Mobil Oil Corporation 1961–92; former chm: Mobil Oil Cyprus Ltd, Mobil SE Asia, Mobil Oil Italiana SPA; chm and chief exec Mobil Oil Co Ltd 1987–91, dir/vice pres Mobil Europe Ltd 1991–92, exec vice pres Statoil Group 1992–; non-exec bd memb Borealis A/S Copenhagen; vice pres Inst of Petroleum; memb: President's Cncl Asia Soc NY, Advsy Bd Cornell Univ Johnson Sch of Business NY; FRSA 1988, FInstPet 1988; *Recreations* tennis, skiing, music, archaeology; *Clubs* RAC, Hurlingham; *Style*— Roger O'Neil, Esq; ✉ 3 Ormonde Gate, London SW3; Statoil, PO Box 300, N-4001 Stavanger, Norway (☎ 4751 805133, fax 4751 807042)

O'NEIL, William A; CM (1995); *Educ* Univ of Toronto; *m*; 3 c; *Career* various engrg positions Federal Dept of Tport 1949–55, successively div engr, regnl dir and dir of construction St Lawrence Seaway Authy 1955–71, cmmr Canadian Coast Guard and dep admin Canadian Marine Transportation Administration (CMTA) Federal Dept of Tport 1975–80 (dep admin Marine Servs CMTA 1971–75); St Lawrence Seaway Authy 1980–90: pres and chief exec offr, dir Canarctic Shipping Company, pres Seaway International Bridge Corporation, memb Bd Thousand Islands Bridge Authy; sec-gen International Maritime Organisation (IMO) 1990– (Canadian rep to Cncl 1972–90, chm Cncl 1980–90); Canadian del Permanent International Assoc of Navigation Congresses 1984–90, chm Canadian Ctee Lloyd's Register of Shipping 1987–88, memb Bd Int Maritime Bureau 1991–, chm Governing Body Int Maritime Law Inst 1991–; Nat Union of Marine Aviation and Shipping Tport Offrs (NUMAST): hon memb 1995, NUMAST Award 1995; hon memb: Canadian Maritime Law Assoc 1989, Hon Co of Master Mariners 1990, Int Maritime Pilots' Assoc 1991, Soc of Naval Architects and Marine Engrs Singapore 1992, Int Fedn of Shipmasters Assocs 1993, Int Assoc of Lighthouse Authys 1994, Soc of Naval Architects and Marine Engrs USA 1995; chllr World Maritime Univ 1991– (memb Bd of Govrs and Exec Ctee 1983–90); Hon Dip Canadian Coast Guard Coll 1990; Hon LLD: Univ of Malta 1993, Meml Univ of Newfoundland Canada 1996; Hon DSc Nottingham Trent Univ 1994; Distinguished Public Service Award US Govt 1980, Commander Ordre National des Cèdres Lebanon 1995, SEATRADE Personality of the Year Award 1995, Gold Medal Professional Engrs Ontario 1995, Admiral's Medal Canada 1995, memb Engrg Alumni Hall of Distinction Univ of Toronto 1996; memb: Assoc of Professional Engrs of Ontario (Engrg Medal for engrg achievement 1972), American Soc of Civil Engrs; FCIT, FRSA, FEng 1994; hon fell Nautical Inst UK 1996; *Style*— William A O'Neil, Esq, CM, FEng; ✉ 4 Albert Embankment, London SE1 7SR (☎ 0171 587 3100, fax 0171 587 3210)

O'NEILL, Dr Brendan Richard; s of Dr John C O'Neill, of St Helens, Lancs; *b* 6 Dec 1948; *Educ* West Park GS St Helen's, Churchill Coll Cambridge (MA), Univ of E Anglia (PhD); *m* 21 July 1979, Margaret; 2 da (Katherine b 15 May 1980, Elizabeth b 13 May 1982), 1 s (John b 10 Aug 1984); *Career* graduate trainee Ford Motor Co Brentwood 1973–75, various financial appts Leyland Vehicles Ltd 1975–81, gp audit mangr BICC Ltd 1981–83, gp financial controller Midland Bank plc 1986–87 (joined 1983); Guinness PLC: dir of financial control 1987, fin dir United Distillers 1987–91, regnl md Int Region (Central and S America, Middle E and Africa) United Distillers 1991–93, md Guinness Brewing Worldwide and main bd dir Guinness PLC 1993–, also chm GUD Pension Fund Trust Ltd; bd memb United Distillers PLC; non-exec dir: E-Map, Fin Ctee ICRF; FCMA (memb Cncl ICMA 1987–90); *Style*— Dr Brendan O'Neill; ✉ Guinness Brewing Worldwide, Park Royal Brewery, London NW10 7RR (☎ 0181 965 7700, fax 0181 963 5138)

O'NEILL, Denis Basil; s of Gilbert Joseph Lane O'Neill (d 1961), of Putney, London, and Winifred Mary, *née* Erskine-White (d 1980); *b* 23 July 1922; *Educ* Douai Sch, Imperial Coll London (BSc, ACGI); *m* 27 Feb 1954, Jacqueline Mary, da of Guy Holman Tatum (d 1968), of Kensington, London; 2 s (Duncan b 1957, Robin b 1960), 1 da (Susan (Mrs Paul Austen) b 1955); *Career* WWII Maj RE DAQMG HQ Central Cmd India 1942–47; consltg engr (vibration and noise) 1949–, chm Hawkes & Co Savile Row 1969–71, dir Civil Engineering Dynamics Ltd 1989–; memb: Drafting Ctee British Standard Code of Practice 2012, Ctee Soc for Earthquake and Civil Engrg Dynamics 1972–77, Steering Ctee CIRIA Piling Vibration Res Project 1982–; author First TRRL Report on Traffic Vibration and Heritage Bldgs 1988; MICE 1963; *Recreations* music, theatre, travel, video photography, grandchildren; *Clubs* Hurlingham; *Style*— Denis O'Neill, Esq; ✉ 58 Rivermead Court, Ranelagh Gardens, London SW6 3RY

O'NEILL, Dennis James; s of Dr William Patrick O'Neill (d 1986), of Adelaide House, Pontarddulais, S Wales, and Eva Ann, *née* Rees; *b* 25 Feb 1948; *Educ* Gowerton GS, studied singing privately with Frederick Cox in London and Campogalliani, Mantova, Ricci in Rome; *m* 1, 4 April 1970 (m dis 1987), Margaret Ruth, da of Rev Edward Collins, of Old Harlow, Essex; 1 s (Sean b 22 Dec 1979), 1 da (Clare b 21 July 1977); m 2, 11 Jan 1988, Ellen, da of Hans Einar Folkestad, of Tybakken, Norway; *Career* tenor and broadcaster; operatic debuts: Royal Opera House Covent Garden 1979 (annually thereafter), Metropolitan Opera NYC 1986, Vienna State Opera 1981, Hamburg State Opera 1981, San Francisco 1984, Chicago Lyric 1985, Paris Opera 1986, Deutche Oper Berlin 1989, Bayerische Staatsoper 1992 (annually thereafter); many recordings; presenter Dennis O'Neill BBC 2; pres Friends of WNO, fndr Dennis O'Neill Bursary; FTCL, ARCM, FWCMD; *Recreations* cookery; *Style*— Dennis O'Neill, Esq; ✉ c/o Ingpen & Williams, 14 Kensington Court, London W8 (☎ 0171 937 5158/9, fax 01222 340660)

O'NEILL, Derham Charles; s of Charles Daniel O'Neill (d 1984), and Phyllis, *née* Derham (d 1983); *b* 4 July 1943; *Educ* St Mary's Coll Crosby, Univ of Manchester (LLB), Manchester Business Sch (MBA); *m* 5 Aug 1967, Patricia, da of William Kay (d 1963); 1 s (Derham Aidan b 1977), 1 da (Katharine Alexandra b 1975); *Career* admitted slr 1968; md Brown Shipley Fund Mgmnt Ltd 1979–80, corp fin ptnr Clifford Turner (now Clifford Chance) 1981–; memb Alternative Investment Market Appeals Ctee London Stock Exchange; Freeman Worshipful Co of Slrs; memb Law Soc; *Books* Management Buyouts (contrib, 1988); *Recreations* windsurfing, skiing, swimming, poetry, moral philosophy; *Style*— Derham O'Neill, Esq; ✉ Clifford Chance, 200 Aldersgate Street, London EC1A 4JY (☎ 0171 600 1000, fax 0171 600 5555)

O'NEILL, Eamonn Patrick; s of Edward O'Neill, of Co Offaly, Ireland, and Bridget, *née* O'Reilly; *b* 25 March 1967; *Educ* St Aidan's HS Wishaw, Univ of Strathclyde (BA); *m* 21 Sept 1991, Sarah, da of Prof David Kellam Sterling; *Career* freelance journalist 1989–90; Scottish Television: researcher 1990–92, assoc prodr 1992–93, prodr and dir 1993–95; prodr network factual progs Scottish Television Enterprises 1995–; prodr various documentaries Channel 4; nominated BAFTA Documentary Award for The Truth of Christmas Island (Dispatches strand) 1991; memb NUJ; *Books* No Risk Involved (1991); *Recreations* reading, writing, wife, family; *Style*— Eamonn O'Neill Esq; ✉ Scottish Television plc, Cowcaddens, Glasgow G2 3PR (☎ 0141 332 9999, fax 0141 332 6982, mobile 0831 446061)

O'NEILL, Rev Prof John Cochrane; s of John Archibald O'Neill (d 1982), of Melbourne, Australia, and Beni Alberta, *née* Cochrane (d 1994); *b* 8 Dec 1930; *Educ* Melbourne C of E GS, Univ of Melbourne (BA), Ormond Coll Theol Hall (BD), Univ of Cambridge (PhD); *m* 17 April 1954, Judith Beatrice, da of John Ramsden Lyall (d 1981), of Melbourne, 3 da (Rachel b 1957, Catherine b 1959, Philippa b 1961); *Career* Dunn prof of New Testament language, lit and theol Westminster Coll Cambridge 1964–85, prof of New Testament language, lit and theol Univ of Edinburgh 1985–96; *Books* The Theology of Acts in its Historical Setting (2 edn, 1970), The Puzzle of 1 John (1966), The Recovery of Paul's Letter to the Galatians (1972), Paul's Letter to the Romans (1975), Messiah - Six Lectures on the Ministry of Jesus (2 edn, 1984), The Bible's Authority - A Portrait Gallery of Thinkers from Lessing to Bultmann (1991), Who Did Jesus Think He Was? (1995); *Recreations* swimming, camping, walking; *Style*— The Rev Prof John O'Neill; ✉ 9 Lonsdale Terrace, Edinburgh EH3 9HN (☎ 0131 229 6070)

O'NEILL, Martin John; MP (Lab) Clackmannan (majority 8,503); s of John O'Neill; *b* 6 Jan 1945; *Educ* Trinity Acad Edinburgh, Heriot Watt Univ, Moray House Educn Coll Edinburgh; *m* 1973, Elaine Samuel; 2 s; *Career* former insur clerk, asst examiner Scottish Estate Duty Office, secondary schoolteacher, tutor Open Univ; MP (Lab): Stirlingshire E and Clackmannan 1979–83, Clackmannan 1983–; memb Select Ctee Scottish Affrs 1979–80, oppn front bench spokesman on: Scottish Affrs 1980–84, defence and disarmament 1984–88; princ oppn spokesman on: defence 1988–92, energy 1992–95; chm Trade and Industry Select Ctee 1995–; *Style*— Martin O'Neill, Esq, MP; ✉ House of Commons, London SW1A 0AA (☎ 0171 219 4548); constituency office: 19 Mar Street, Alloa FK10 1HR (☎ 01259 721536)

O'NEILL, Michael; s of Byron Valentine O'Neill, of Ackworth, W Yorks, and Mildred, *née* Machin; *b* 2 Aug 1956; *Educ* King's GS Pontefract, Abraham Moss FE Coll Manchester, Univ of Hull (BA); *m* (m dis 1987); 1 s (Scott Nigel b 3 Jan 1975), 1 da (Rachel Katie b 15 Nov 1984); *partner* Helen Elizabeth Costello; *Career* trainee journalist Hull Daily Mail 1980–83; reporter: Viking Radio Manchester 1984–85, Piccadilly Radio Manchester 1985–87, Manchester Evening News 1987; Independent Radio News (IRN) 1987–: successively reporter, intake ed then int ed, ed IRN International 1992–; mktg exec ITN 1993–, proprietor of own mktg and sales business; memb Assoc of Br Eds 1993; *Books* The Ever Birds of Space (poetry, 1977); *Recreations* trying to tire out my daughter, films, travel, books, having fun; *Style*— Michael O'Neill, Esq; ✉ ITN, 200 Gray's Inn Road, London WC1X 8XZ (☎ 0171 430 4828, mobile 0374 103547)

O'NEILL, Dr Onora Sylvia; CBE (1995); da of Sir Con Douglas Walter O'Neill, KCMG (d 1988), and Rosemary Margaret, *née* Prichard, now Lady Garvey; *b* 23 Aug 1941; *Educ* St Paul's Girls' Sch, Somerville Coll Oxford (scholar, MA), Harvard Univ (PhD); *m* 1963 (m dis 1974), Edward John Nell, s of Edward John Nell; 2 s (Adam Edward O'Neill b 1967, Jacob Rowan b 1969); *Career* asst then assoc prof Barnard Coll Columbia Univ NYC 1970–77, lectr then prof of philosophy Univ of Essex 1978–92, princ Newnham Coll Cambridge 1992–; visiting appts: Australian Nat Univ 1984, Univ of Santa Clara Calif 1985, Wissenschaftskolleg Berlin 1989–90; pres Aristotelian Soc 1988–89; foreign hon memb American Acad of Arts & Sciences 1993; FBA 1993; *Books* Acting on Principle (1976), Faces of Hunger (1986), Constructions of Reason (1989); *Recreations* walking and talking; *Style*— Dr Onora O'Neill, CBE, FBA; ✉ Newnham College, Cambridge CB3 9DF (☎ 01223 335821, fax 01223 359155)

O'NEILL, 4 Baron (UK 1868); Raymond Arthur Clanaboy O'Neill; TD (1970); s of 3 Baron O'Neill (ka Italy 1944); the O'Neills stem from the oldest traceable family in Europe; *b* 1 Sept 1933; *Educ* Eton, RAC Cirencester; *m* 11 June 1963, Georgina Mary, da of Lord George Montagu Douglas Scott (3 s of 7 Duke of Buccleuch), of The Alms House, Weekley, Kettering, Northants; 3 s (Hon Shane b 25 July 1965, Hon Tyrone b 24 June 1966, Hon Rory b 20 Dec 1968); *Heir* s, Hon Shane O'Neill; *Career* short service cmmn 11 Hussars Prince Albert's Own 1952–53, joined NI Horse (TA) 1954; Maj cmdg D (N Irish Horse) Sqdn The Royal Yeomanry Regt 1967–69, cmdg N Irish Horse Cadres 1969–71, RARO 1971; Hon Col: D Sqdn (RYR) 1986–91, 69 (N Irish Horse) Signals Sqdn (V) 1988–93; dir: Shanes Developments Ltd, Shanes Castle Estates Co, Romney Hythe & Dymchurch Railway plc; chm: Ulster Countryside Ctee 1971–75, NI Tourist Bd 1975–80; tstee Ulster Folk and Tport Museum 1969–90 (vice chm 1987–90); pres: The Railway Preservation Soc of Ireland 1964–, NI Assoc of Youth Clubs (Youth Action)

1968–, The Royal Ulster Agric Soc 1984–86 (chm Fin Ctee 1974–83); memb: NT Ctee for NI 1980–91 (chm 1981–91), Cncl for Nature Conservation and Countryside 1989–92; cmmr Museums and Galleries Cmmn 1987–94; chm: NI Museums Advsy Ctee 1989–91, NI Museums Cncl 1993–; memb Bd Nat Gallery of Ireland 1993–; Lord-Lt Co Antrim 1994 (DL 1967); *Recreations* railways, vintage motoring, gardening, boats, shooting, walking, swimming; *Clubs* Turf; *Style*— The Rt Hon the Lord O'Neill, TD; ✉ Shanes Castle, Antrim, NI BT41 4NE (☎ 018494 63264, fax 01849 468457); Conigre House, Calne, Wilts (☎ 01249 812354)

O'NEILL, Robert James (Robin); CMG (1978); s of Robert Francis O'Neill (d 1975), of Chelmsford, Essex, and Dorothy May, *née* Golding (d 1983); *b* 17 June 1932; *Educ* King Edward VI Sch Chelmsford, Trinity Coll Cambridge (MA); *m* 1958, Helen Mary, da of Horace Wells Juniper; 1 s (Mark), 2 da (Celia, Miranda); *Career* HM Dip Serv (formerly HM Foreign Serv) 1955, served Ankara 1957–60, Dakar 1961–63, Bonn 1968–72, dep govr Gibraltar 1978–81, under-sec Cabinet Office 1981–84, asst under-sec of State Foreign and Cwlth Office 1984–86, ambass to Austria and concurrently head of UK delgn to negotiations on mutual reduction of forces and armaments and associated measures in Central Europe 1986–89, ambass to Belgium 1989–92, EC Presidency rep for Macedonia 1992, ret 1992; EU rep OSCE Bosnia Elections Task Force 1995; *Recreations* diplomatic history, hill walking; *Clubs* Travellers', Royal Anglo-Belgian; *Style*— Robin O'Neill, Esq, CMG; ✉ 4 Castle Street, Saffron Walden, Essex CB10 1BP (☎ 01799 520291)

O'NEILL, Prof Robert John; AO (1988); s of Joseph Henry O'Neill (d 1982), of Melbourne, Australia, and Janet Gibbon, *née* Grant; *b* 5 Nov 1936; *Educ* Scotch Coll Melbourne, Royal Mil Coll of Aust, Univ of Melbourne (B E Rankine prize in mgmnt), BNC Oxford (Rhodes scholar, MA, DPhil); *m* 23 Oct 1965, Sally Margaret, da of Donald Frank Burnard, of Adelaide, Aust; 2 da (Katherine Melinda b 1968, Jennifer Louisa b 1971); *Career* Aust Army 1955–68: staff cadet 1955–58, Lt 1958–62, Capt 1962–67 (active serv Vietnam 1966–67, despatches 1967), Maj 1967–68; lectr in mil history Royal Mil Coll of Aust 1967–69, sr fell Dept of Int Relations Res Sch of Pacific Studies Aust Nat Univ 1969 (professorial fell 1977–82), head Aust Nat Univ Strategic and Defence Studies Centre 1971–82, conslt to Aust Govt and expert witness before various Parly Ctee enquiries 1969–82, dir IISS London 1982–87 (memb Cncl 1977–82 and 1992–, vice chm 1994–96, chm 1996–), Chichele prof of the history of war Univ of Oxford and fell All Souls Coll 1987–, hon fell BNC Oxford 1990, co-dir All Souls Foreign Policy Studies Prog 1989–; chm Delegacy for Mil Instruction Univ of Oxford 1990–; dep chm Imperial War Museum 1996– (tstee 1990–), memb: Bd Int Peace Acad New York 1990–, Salzburg Seminar 1992–, Advsy Bd Investmt Co of America LA 1987–, Cwlth Sec Gen's Advsy Gp on Security of Small States 1984–85, The Rhodes Tst 1995–, Canberra Cmmn on the Elimination of Nuclear Weapons 1995–96; govr Ditchley Fndn 1989–, cmmr Cwlth War Graves Cmmn 1991–; Armed Servs ed Australian Dictionary of Biography 1971–; non-exec dir: The Shell Transport and Trading Company plc 1992–, Capital World Growth and Income Fund Inc LA 1992–, Capital Income Builder Inc LA 1992–; Hon Col 5 (Volunteer) Bn Royal Green Jackets 1993–; fell Acad of Social Sciences in Australia 1978, FIE (Aust) 1981–96, FRHistS 1989; *Books* The German Army and the Nazi Party 1933–39 (1966), Vietnam Task (1968), General Giap: Politician and Strategist (1969), The Strategic Nuclear Balance (ed, 1975), Insecurity: the Spread of Weapons in the Indian and Pacific Oceans (ed, 1978), New Directions in Strategic Thinking (ed with David Horner, 1981), Australia in the Korean War 1950–53 (Vol 1 1981, Vol 2 1985), Security in East Asia (ed, 1984), The Conduct of East-West Relations in the 1980s (ed, 1985), New Technology and Western Security Policy (ed, 1985), Doctrine, the Alliance and Arms Control (ed, 1986), East Asia, The West and International Security (ed, 1987), Hedley Bull on Arms Control (ed with David N Schwartz, 1987), Prospects for Security in the Mediterranean (ed, 1988), The West and the Third World (ed with John Vincent, 1990), Securing Peace in Europe 1945–62 (ed with Beatrice Heuser, 1992), War Strategy and International Politics (ed with Lawrence Freedman and Paul Hayes, 1992); *Recreations* walking, local history; *Style*— Prof Robert O'Neill, AO; ✉ All Souls College, Oxford OX1 4AL (☎ 01865 279379, fax 01865 279299)

O'NEILL, Hon Shane Sebastian Clanaboy; s and h of 4 Baron O'Neill, TD, DL; *b* 25 July 1965; *Educ* Eton, RAC Cirencester; *Style*— The Hon Shane O'Neill

O'NEILL, Shirley; da of Patrick O'Neill, of Atherstone, Warwicks, and Betty, *née* Ford; *b* 21 Aug 1947; *Educ* Nuneaton Sch of Art, Walthamstow Coll of Art, The Royal Academy Sch; *Career* artist; *Group Exhibitions* as a memb of The Wapping Studio Collective of Artists 1975–84, summer show at Serpentine Gallery 1982, Francis Graham Gallery 1988; first solo exhibition Francis Graham-Dixon Gallery 1989; *Recreations* travelling, photography; *Style*— Miss Shirley O'Neill; ✉ Studio 3, 98–100 Tottenham Road, London N1 4DP (☎ 0171 249 7292); Francis Graham-Dixon Gallery, 17–18 Great Sutton St, London EC1V ODN (☎ 0171 250 1962, fax 0171 490 1069)

O'NEILL, Terence Patrick (Terry); s of Leonard Victor O'Neill (d 1980), of Cork, Ireland, and Josephine Mary, *née* Gallagher (d 1978); *b* 30 July 1938; *Educ* Gunnersbury GS; *m* 1, Vera Day; 1 s (Keegan Alexander), 1 da (Sarah Jane); m 2, Faye Dunaway; 1 s (Liam Walker); *Career* professional jazz drummer since 1952 in leading London clubs incl The Flamingo, The Florida and The Mapleton; Nat Serv PT instr; professional photographer: took first published pictures of The Beatles and The Rolling Stones, photographic biographer of emerging 60s personalities incl Jean Shrimpton, Terence Stamp and Michael Caine, became int celebrity photographer to politicians, royalty and rock and pop stars, work published in 52 countries (average 500 front covers per annum); *Books* Legends; *Recreations* music, reading, cooking, all sport; *Style*— Terry O'Neill, Esq

ONG, Benny; *b* 1956, Singapore; *Educ* St Martin's Sch of Art; *Career* fashion designer; Benny Ong Designer Collection 1975–, Benny Ong diffusion label ONG 1989–, third label Bene 1992–; represented GB in Young Designer Show sponsored by Snia Viscosa Italy Milas 1979; private label designs for: Austin Reed London 1983, House of Fraser stores London 1988; opened 2 retail outlets Singapore 1992; major design projects incl for The Sch of Meditation London and corp uniforms for: BAA 1987–89, BT 1989, Raffles Hotel 1991; included in Vogue History of Twentieth Century Fashion (by Jane Mulvagh, 1988); *Recreations* swimming, tennis, philosophy; *Style*— Benny Ong, Esq; ✉ 3a Moreton Terrace, London SW1V 2NS (☎ 0171 834 9688, fax 0171 233 8920)

ONIANS, Richard Anderson; s of Frank Arnold Onians (d 1986), of Thetford, Norfolk, and Marie Elise, *née* Anderson (d 1957); *b* 21 April 1940; *Educ* Thetford GS, Stanford Exec Program; *m* 1961, Marianne Dorothy, da of Archibald Laidlaw (d 1978), and Evelyn, *née* Oliver (d 1989); 1 da (Sarah b 1963, m Jean Francois De Wael of Brussels), 1 s (Henry b 1965, m Julia Oliver of Savannah, Ga); *Career* Monsanto Co 1959–84: mktg and gen mgmnt positions in pharmaceuticals, consumer prods and organic chemicals (with assignments in USA, Europe, Far East and Latin America), dir corporate strategic planning 1978–81, vice pres electronics and venture capital 1981–84; managing ptnr Baring Private Equity Partners Ltd 1984–; dir: Anglia Region Br Rail 1990–93, fund mgmnt cos (in Belgium, Germany, Greece, Mexico, Singapore and Spain), Greater London Enterprise Ltd, York Ltd, ARCA Merchant Spa Milan, Procuritas AB Stockholm, BPB plc London, Sanctuary Screen Productions Ltd, Gemphus SCA Aix-en-Provence; fndr chm Euro Venture Capital Assoc 1985–86, dir SE England Industl Devpt Bd, dir Centre for Tomorrows Company, chm E Anglia Tourist Bd 1996–; FRSA 1986 (memb Cncl 1991–, treas 1994–96, dep chm 1996–); *Recreations* books, art history, visual arts; *Clubs* Savile; *Style*— Richard Onians, Esq; ✉ Baring Private Equity Partners, 33 Cavendish Square, London W1M 0BQ (☎ 0171 290 5000, fax 0171 290 5020)

ONIONS, Ronald Edward Derek; OBE (1984); s of Benjamin Edward Onions (d 1970), and Elizabeth Amelia, *née* Lewin (d 1973); *b* 27 Aug 1929; *Educ* Edmonton County GS; *m* 1951, Doris Margaret, da of Reginald Monro Moody (d 1987); 2 da (Sarah, Louise); *Career* journalist; newspaper journalist 1950–58, Southern TV news ed 1958–60, reporter prodr and newscaster BBC News and Current Affrs 1960–67, BBC news prodr NY and co-ordinator for EBU 1967–72, head of news Capital Radio 1973–74, ed IRN 1974–77, ed dir LBC/IRN 1977–83, managing ed Special Projects Visnews 1983–89, station dir Jazz FM 1989–91, broadcasting conslt 1991–; *Recreations* skiing, bird watching; *Style*— Ronald Onions, Esq, OBE; ✉ 53 Portsmouth Rd, Surbiton, Surrey (☎ 0181 390 0654); 41 Oaklands Ave, Saltdean, Sussex (☎ 01273 304077)

ONSLOW, Rt Hon Sir Cranley Gordon Douglas; KCMG (1993), PC (1988), MP (C) Woking (majority 19,842); s of Francis Robert Douglas Onslow (d 1938); *b* 8 June 1926; *Educ* Harrow, Oriel Coll Oxford, Univ of Geneva; *m* 1955, Lady June Onslow, *qv*; 1 s, 3 da; *Career* serv RAC 1944–48 and Co of London Yeo (TA) 1948–52; FO 1951–60 (serv Burma); MP (C) Woking 1964–; chm 1922 Ctee 1984–92 (exec memb 1968–72, 1981–82 and 1983–92); chm Cons Aviation Ctee 1970–72 and 1979–82, Parly under sec for aerospace and shipping DTI 1972–74; oppn spokesman: on health and social security 1974–75, on defence 1975–76; memb UK Delegation Cncl of Europe and WEU 1977–81, chm Select Ctee on Defence 1981–82, min of state FCO 1982–83; chm Redifon MEL Ltd; chm Nautical Museums Tst; memb Cncl: Anglers Conservation Assoc (vice chm), Atlantic Salmon Tst, Salmon and Trout Assoc, Nat Rifle Assoc; Liveryman Worshipful Co of Fishmongers; *Clubs* Travellers', Beefsteak; *Style*— The Rt Hon Sir Cranley Onslow, KCMG, MP; ✉ House of Commons, London SW1A 0AA (☎ 0171 219 3000)

ONSLOW, Sir John Roger Wilmot; 8 Bt (GB 1797), of Althain, Lancashire; s of Sir Richard Wilmot Onslow, 7 Bt, TD (d 1963); *b* 21 July 1932; *Educ* Cheltenham; *m* 1, 1955 (m dis 1973), Catherine Zoia, da of Henry Atherton Greenway, of The Manor, Compton Abdale, nr Cheltenham; 1 s (Richard Paul Atherton b 1958), 1 da (Joanna Elizabeth b 1956); m 2, 1976, Susan Fay, 2 da of E M Hughes, of Frankston, Vic, Aust; *Heir* s, Richard Paul Atherton Onslow, *qv*; *Style*— Sir John Onslow, Bt; ✉ c/o Barclays Bank Ltd, Fowey, Cornwall

ONSLOW, Lady June Ann; *née* Hay; da of 14 Earl of Kinnoull (d 1938), by his 2 w, Mary Ethel Isobel, *née* Meyrick (d 1938); *b* 1932; *m* 1955, Rt Hon Sir Cranley Gordon Douglas Onslow, KCMG, MP, *qv*; 1 s, 3 da; *Career* tstee: Leonard Cheshire Fndn 1973–86, Guide Dogs for the Blind 1984–88, Bristol Cancer Help Centre 1989–91; govr King Edward's Sch Witley Surrey 1986–, non-exec dir North Downs Community Health Unit 1993–; *Style*— The Lady June Onslow

ONSLOW, 7 Earl of (UK 1801); Sir Michael William Coplestone Dillon Onslow; 11 Bt (E 1674, of 2 cr, with precedency 1660); also Baron Onslow (GB 1716), Baron Cranley (GB 1776), and Viscount Cranley (UK 1801); high steward of Guildford; s of 6 Earl, KBE, MC, TD (d 1971), and Pamela, Countess of Onslow; bro-in-law of Auberon Waugh, *qv*; *b* 28 Feb 1938; *Educ* Eton, Sorbonne; *m* 1964, Robin, o da of Maj Robert Lee Bullard III, of Atlanta, Ga (Lady Onslow's mother subsequently m Lord Aberconway as his 2 w); 1 s, 2 da (Lady Arabella b 1970, Lady Charlotte b 1977); *Heir* s, Viscount Cranley, *qv*; *Career* sits as Conservative in House of Lords; Lloyd's underwriter, dir of various cos; farmer (800 acres in Surrey); served Life Gds M East; sometime govr Univ Coll Buckingham, govr Royal GS Guildford; *Style*— The Rt Hon the Earl of Onslow; ✉ Temple Court, Clandon Park, Guildford, Surrey (☎ 01483 222754)

ONSLOW, Richard; s of Rt Hon Sir Cranley Onslow, KCMG, MP, *qv*, of Fernhurst, W Sussex, and Lady June Hay; *b* 27 June 1956; *Educ* Harrow, Oxford Univ (MA), City Univ (DPL); *m* 27 July 1985, Phyllida, da of Michael Moore, OBE, of Lindsey, Ipswich, Suffolk; 1 s (Thomas), 1 da (Isabella); *Career* called to the Bar Inner Temple 1982; *Recreations* shooting, fishing, real tennis, cricket; *Clubs* MCC, Stragglers of Asia Cricket, Lords and Commons Cricket, Hampshire; *Style*— Richard Onslow, Esq; ✉ 2 King's Bench Walk, Temple, London EC4 (☎ 0171 353 1746)

ONSLOW, Richard Paul Atherton; s and h of Sir John Roger Wilmot Onslow, 8 Bt, *qv*; *b* 16 Sept 1958; *Style*— Richard Onslow Esq

ONWIN, Glen; *b* 1947; *Educ* Edinburgh Coll of Art (DA), Moray House Coll of Educn; *Career* artist; art teacher Edinburgh 1972–79; visiting lectr: Glasgow Sch of Art 1979, Duncan of Jordanstone Coll of Art 1980, Grays Sch of Art Aberdeen 1983, Edinburgh Coll of Art pt/t lectr 1979–87; Edinburgh Coll of Art Sch of Drawing and Painting: lectr 1987–94, dir of post grad studies 1992–, sr lectr 1994–; worked Scottish Arts Cncl Studio Amsterdam 1979; memb Bd New 57 Gall 1974–84; exhbn selector Scottish Art Now 1982; Scottish Arts Cncl 1972; *Solo Exhibitions* Scottish Arts Cncl Gallery 1975, Serpentine Gallery London 1975, Arnolfini Gallery Bristol 1978, ICA London 1978, Third Eye Glasgow 1979, Fruit Market Gallery Edinburgh 1979, AIR Gallery London 1982, Crawford Arts Centre St Andrews 1989, Space-Ex Exeter 1989, John Hansard Gallery Southampton 1991, As Above so Below (Square Chapel Halifax, an installation with The Henry Moore Sculpture Trust), Flammable Solid Flammable Liquid (Tramway Glasgow, site specific installation) 1994, and others; *Gp Exhibitions* Video Exhibition (Serpentine Gallery) 1975, Scottish Sculpture (Kelvingrove Museum Glasgow) 1975, Ulster Museum of Art Belfast 1976, Aspects of Landscape (British Cncl touring exhbn) 1976, Works on Paper (RA) 1977, Scottish Nat Gallery of Modern Art Edinburgh 1978, Invited Artists (RSA Festival Exhbn) 1979, Un Certain Art Anglais (ARC Musee d'Art Moderne Paris) 1979, JP2 Palais des Beaux Arts Brussels 1979, Demarcations (Demarco Gallery Edinburgh) 1984, City Arts Centre Edinburgh 1985, Sarajevo Winter Festival Sarajevo 1988, Scottish Art Since 1900 (Scottish Nat Gallery of Modern Art 1989 and Barbican 1990), Fruitmarket Open (Fruitmarket Gallery Edinburgh) 1990, From Art to Archaeology (S Bank Centre touring) 1991–92, and others; *Public Collections* British Cncl, Contemporary Arts Soc, Scottish Arts Cncl, Scottish Nat Gallery of Modern Art, Univ of Salford, Arts Cncl of GB, Kelvingrove Museum, City Art Centre Edinburgh, Whitworth Art Gallery Manchester; *Style*— Glen Onwin, Esq; ✉ 77 Duke Street, Leith, Edinburgh EH6 8HN

ONZIA, Koenraad Roger Mathilde (Koen); s of Hubert Onzia, and Paula, *née* Dils; *b* 3 March 1961; *Educ* Ballet Sch of Antwerp; *Career* princ ballet dancer; began performing career with Royal Ballet of Flanders; London Festival Ballet: joined 1982, soloist 1984 (rejoined Royal Ballet of Flanders until 1986), princ dancer 1986; princ dancer: Houston Ballet 1989, English National Ballet 1990–91, Rudra Béjart Lausanne 1992–; freelance 1991–92; guest artist performances with Paris Opera, the Deutsch Opera Berlin, Brussels Cirque Royale, Nat Ballet of Caracas in Madrid and Caracas, Inoue Ballet Fndn Tokyo; partners incl: Galina Panova, Trinidad Sevillano, Lynn Charles; repertoire incl: Don Quixote Pas de deux and Le Corsaire, George Balanchine's Allegro Brilliante and Apollo, Romeo in Rudolf Nureyev's Romeo and Juliet, the jester in Ben Stevenson's Cinderella, Ronald Hynd's The Seasons, Natalia Makarova's La Bayadère and the prince in Swan Lake, Romeo in Valery Panov's Romeo and Juliet, the prince in Cinderella, Prince Myshkin in The Idiot, Michael Jackson in Moves, the prince in Peter Schaufuss's The Nutcracker, Albrecht in Alicia Alonso and Mary Skeaping's Giselle, Lenski in John Cranko's Onegin, Chopin in Vincente Nebrada's George Sand, the young man in Masao Sugi's Snow Princess, Harold Lander's Etudes, the leading man in Maurice Bejart's Bolero, Frantz in Ronald Hynd's Coppelia, Siobban Davies' Dancing

Ledge; *Awards* Bronze medallist Varna Int Ballet competition, Gold medallist Lausanne and Jackson Mississippi, nominee SWET award for Outstanding Individual Performance of the Year (Ronald Hynd's The Seasons) 1983, nominee Lawrence Olivier awards (for Christopher Bruce's Cruel Garden and Swansong) 1988, winner Time Out award (for Swansong) 1991; *Recreations* landscape gardening, Bonsaï training; *Style*— Koen Onzia; (☎ 0181 968 8872, fax 0171 792 0924); Switzerland (☎ 00 41 21 624 06 43)

OPENSHAW, David Kay; s of Frank Kay Openshaw, of Nelson, Lancs, and Florence, *née* Haworth; *b* 31 Oct 1946; *Educ* Nelson GS, Wadham Coll Oxford, Univ of Bradford Mgmnt Centre; *m* Jacqueline; 1 da (Jane b 6 Nov 1980), 1 s (Tom b 9 Sept 1982); *Career* ops dir Volvo UK 1980–85, md Lex Specialist Car Group 1986–90, vice pres Lex Electronics USA 1990–91, md Motorway Tyres and Accessories Ltd 1992–; croquet player: memb Harrow Oak Croquet Club 1971– (capt 1976–), memb GB team 1979– (capt 1982–94); honours incl: Br Open champion 1979, 1981 and 1985, Br mens champion 1981, 1991 and 1995, US Open champion 1991, Canadian Open champion 1991, runner-up World Championship 1991; GB rep: v Aust and NZ 1979, 1982, 1986, 1990, and 1993, v USA 1985, 1987, 1988, 1989, 1990, 1991, 1992 and 1994; record for longest winning sequence of matches (39) May-Aug 1981; chess player: rep Lancs 1966–70, capt Oxford Univ 1968; *Style*— David Openshaw, Esq; ✉ 45 Baring Rd, Beaconsfield, Bucks HP9 2NF (☎ 01494 676387)

OPENSHAW, (Charles) Peter Lawford; QC (1991); s of His Hon Judge William Harrison Openshaw (d 1981), of Broughton, Preston, Lancs, and Elisabeth Joyce Emily, *née* Lawford; *b* 21 Dec 1947; *Educ* Harrow, St Catharine's Coll Cambridge (MA); *m* 15 Dec 1979, Caroline Jane, da of Vincent Seymour Swift, of Brookhouse, Lancs; 1 s (Henry b 1986), 1 da (Alexandra b 1984); *Career* called to the Bar 1970, practised on Northern circuit, junior 1973, asst recorder 1984–88, recorder 1988–; *Recreations* general country pursuits; *Clubs* United Oxford and Cambridge; *Style*— Peter Openshaw, Esq, QC; ✉ Peel Court Chambers, 45 Hardman Street, Manchester (☎ 0161 832 3791)

OPIE, Alan John; s of Jack Opie (d 1985), and Doris Winifred, *née* Bennetts; *b* 22 March 1945; *Educ* Truro Sch, Guildhall Sch of Music and Drama (AGSM), London Opera Centre (Cinzano scholar); *m* 18 April 1970, Kathleen Ann, da of Ernest Smales; 1 s (James Alexander b 1976), 1 da (Helen Louise b 1979); *Career* princ baritone ENO 1973–; performed with: Royal Opera, Glyndebourne Festival Opera, Scottish Opera, Opera North, Eng Opera Gp, Chicago Lyric Opera, Bayreuth Festival, Paris Opera, Netherlands Opera, Brussels Opera, Hong Kong Festival, Buxton Festival, Stadtsoper Berlin, Bavarian State Opera, Wexford Festival, New York Metropolitan Opera, BBC Symphony Chorus and Orch (BBC Proms 1996), La Scala Milan (1996); concerts in: UK, Europe, USA; recordings with: CBS, EMI, Decca, Hyperion, Chandos; *Recreations* golf; *Clubs* Leatherhead Golf; *Style*— Alan Opie, Esq

OPIE, Iona Margaret Balfour; da of Sir Robert George Archibald, CMG, DSO (d 1953), and Olive Chapman, *née* Cant (d 1982); *b* 13 Oct 1923; *Educ* Sandecotes Sch; *m* 2 Sept 1943, Peter Mason Opie (d 1982); 2 s (James b 13 Oct 1944, Robert b 5 April 1947), 1 da (Letitia b 25 Oct 1949); *Career* author; pubns with Peter Opie incl: The Oxford Dictionary of Nursery Rhymes (1951), The Lore and Language of Schoolchildren (1959), Children's Games in Street and Playground (1969), The Oxford Book of Children's Verse (1973), The Classic Fairy Tales (1974), The Singing Game (1985); The People in the Playground (sole author, 1993); Hon MA: Univ of Oxford 1962, Open Univ 1987; Hon DLitt: Univ of Southampton 1987, Univ of Nottingham 1991; *Recreations* eating picnics on hillsides; *Style*— Mrs Iona Opie; ✉ Westerfield House, West Liss, Hants GU33 6JQ (☎ 01730 893309)

OPIE, Lisa Jane; MBE (1995); da of Rex Opie, of St Martin's, Guernsey, CI, and Robina Mary, *née* Waller; *b* 15 Aug 1963; *Educ* Blanchelande Convent Sch (Guernsey); *Career* squash player; world jr champion Canada 1981; winner: British Nat Championship 1981, 1983, 1986 and 1987, Aust Open 1986 and 1987, Singapore Open 1988 and 1989, Malaysian Open 1988, Irish Open 1986 and 1988, British Open 1991 (first British ladies win for 30 years); runner up: British Open 1981, 1983, 1985 and 1986, World Open 1985 and 1987; memb England team 1981–93, winner World Teams Event 1985 and 1987 (capt), ret from professional squash due to back problem 1994; voted second Sports Writers Awards 1991; memb Women's Int Squash Players' Assoc; Freedom of Nottingham; *Recreations* travelling, listening to music, theatre, concerts, art, cooking; *Clubs* The Park Squash (Nottingham), King's Squash (Guernsey); *Style*— Miss Lisa Opie, MBE

OPPEN, Richard John Stuart; s of Arthur Harrie Oppen (d 1976), and Muriel Evelyn, *née* Dent (d 1984); *b* 29 Jan 1937; *Educ* Dulwich Prep, City of London Sch; *m* 1 June 1963, Wendy, da of Leslie William Day Suffield (d 1979); 1 s (James b 11 July 1969), 1 da (Lucy b 27 Jan 1972); *Career* Nat Serv 3 Carabiniers (3DG) 1955–57; dir Galbraiths Ltd 1984–88, md Berge Y Cia (UK) Ltd 1989–; Freeman City of London 1980, Liveryman Worshipful Co of Shipwrights 1982, Freeman Worshipful Co of Watermen and Lightermen 1995; *Recreations* country pursuits; *Clubs* Army & Navy, RSAC, Lloyds; *Style*— Richard Oppen, Esq; ✉ 7 Church Row, Plaxtol, Kent (☎ 01732 810311); Berge Y Cia (UK) Ltd, 47 Albemarle Street, London W1 (☎ 0171 499 3186, fax 0171 495 4808, telex 261675)

OPPENHEIM, (Tan Sri) Sir Alexander; kt (1961), OBE (1955); s of Rev Harris Jacob Oppenheim (d 1944); *b* 4 Feb 1903; *Educ* Manchester GS, Balliol Coll Oxford; *m* 1, 1930 (m dis 1977), Beatrice Templer *née* Nesbit (d 1982); 1 da; m 2, Margaret Ng; 2 s; *Career* tutor in mathematics Univ of Oxford 1924–27, lectr in mathematics Univ of Edinburgh 1930–31, prof of mathematics Raffles Coll 1931–48; Univ of Malaya: prof of mathematics 1949–57, dean of Faculty of Arts 1949–51 and 1954, acting vice chllr 1955, vice chllr 1957–65; ret 1965; visiting prof: Univ of Reading 1965–68, Univ of Ghana 1968–73, Univ of Benin Nigeria 1973–77; FRSE 1956; *Style*— Sir Alexander Oppenheim, OBE, FRSE; ✉ Matson House, Remenham, Henley-on-Thames, Oxon RG9 3HB (☎ 01491 572049)

OPPENHEIM, Sir Duncan Morris; kt (1960); s of late Watkin Oppenheim, TD, of St Helens, Lancs; *b* 6 Aug 1904; *Educ* Repton; *m* 1, 1932, Joyce Mary Mitcheson (d 1933); m 2, 1936, Susan May (d 1964), da of Brig-Gen Ernest Macnaghten, CMG, DSO (d 1948); 1 s, 1 da; *Career* admitted slr 1929; asst slr Linklaters & Paines 1929–34; British American Tobacco Co: slr 1934, dir 1943, chm 1953–66, pres 1966–72, advsr 1972–74; dir: Lloyds Bank 1956–74, Equity & Law Life Assurance Society 1966–75; chm: RCA 1956–72, Design Cncl (formerly Cncl of Industl Design) 1960–72, Br Nat Ctee of Int C of C 1963–64, Court of Govrs Admin Staff Coll Henley 1963–71, Royal Inst of Int Affrs 1966–71, Tobacco Securities Tst 1969–74, Overseas Devpt Ctee of CBI 1970–74, V&A Associates 1976–81 (memb Advsy Cncl V&A 1967–80), Cncl St John's Smith Square 1990– (tstee and memb Cncl 1972–94, chm Cncl 1989–94); dep chm Cwlth Devpt Fin Co 1968–74; dep chm Crafts Cncl (formerly Crafts Advsy Ctee) 1971–83; govr Repton Sch 1959–79; pt/t Civil Def City of Westminster 1938–45; pictures painted of air-raid incidents in Westminster in archives of Imperial War Museum; one-man exhbns: Upper Grosvenor Gallery 1971, Spinks 1980 and 1983, New Grafton Gallery 1985, 1988 and 1992; gp exhbns: London Group 1954, Royal Acad of Arts Summer Exhbns 1957 and 1962–82; Bicentenary Medal RSA 1969, Hon FCSD 1972, Hon Dr and Hon Fell RCA; *Clubs* Athenaeum, Royal Yacht Sqdn; *Style*— Sir Duncan Oppenheim; ✉ 43 Edwardes Square, Kensington, London W8 6HH (☎ 0171 603 7431)

OPPENHEIM, (James) Nicholas; *b* 15 June 1947; *Educ* Edinburgh Acad, Univ of Columbia; *Career* dir: Kellock plc 1976–86 and 1988–, Sterling Credit Group plc 1980–82, Argyle Trust plc 1982–91, The Smaller Companies International Trust plc 1982–89, Sterling Trust plc (formerly Dewey Warren Holdings Ltd) 1983–91, Courtwell Group plc 1986–90, Northern Leisure 1987–; *Style*— Nicholas Oppenheim, Esq; ✉ Northern Leisure plc 39 King Street, London EC2V 2DQ (☎ 0171 623 9021, fax 0171 606 3025)

OPPENHEIM, Hon Phillip Anthony Charles Lawrence; MP (C) Amber Valley (majority 712); o s of Henry M Oppenheim (d 1980), and Baroness Oppenheim-Barnes, PC (Life Peer), *qv*, *b* 20 March 1956; *Educ* Harrow, Oriel Coll Oxford (MA); *Career* former dir What to Buy plc (own co founded 1978, sold to Reed International 1989), publishing offices in London and New York; MP (C) Amber Valley 1983–, PPS to Rt Hon Kenneth Clarke 1988–94; Parly under-sec of state: Dept of Employment 1994–95, DTI 1995–96; Exchequer sec to the Treasy 1996–; landowner (270 acres); *Publications* The New Masters (1991), Trade Wars (1992), and 3 books on new technology; *Recreations* rugby, chess, travel, reading, tennis, skiing; *Clubs* Leabrooks Miners Welfare, Annabel's; *Style*— The Hon Phillip Oppenheim, MP; ✉ House of Commons, London SW1A 0AA (☎ 0171 219 4058)

OPPENHEIM-BARNES, Baroness (Life Peer UK 1989), of Gloucester in the Co of Gloucester; Sally Oppenheim-Barnes; PC (1979); da of late Mark and Jeanette Viner, of Sheffield; *b* 26 July 1930; *Educ* Sheffield HS, Lowther Coll N Wales; *m* 1, 1949, Henry M Oppenheim (d 1980); 1 s (Hon Phillip Oppenheim, *qv*), 2 da (Hon Carolyn (Hon Mrs Selman) b 1951, Hon Rose Anne (Hon Mrs Mattick) b 1955); m 2, 1984, John Barnes; *Career* MP (Cons) Gloucester 1970–87 (when her s Philip, *qv*, was elected MP 1983, it was the first time that both a mother and son sat in the same Parl); formerly social worker with ILEA; chm Cons Parly Prices and Consumer Protection Ctee 1973–74 (vice-chm 1971–73), front bench oppn spokesman (seat in Shadow Cabinet) Prices and Consumer Protection 1974–79, min state (consumer affrs) Dept of Trade 1979–82, chm Ctee of Enquiry into Pedestrian Safety at Public Road Level Crossings 1982–; non-exec dir: Boots Co Main Bd 1982–93, Fleming High Income Investment Tst 1989–, HFC Bank plc 1990–; memb House of Commons Ctee of Privileges, pres Br Red Cross Soc Glos Dist; chm Nat Consumer Cncl 1987–89; Nat Waterway Museum Tst until 1990; *Recreations* tennis, bridge; *Clubs* Glos Cons, Vanderbilt Racquet; *Style*— The Baroness Oppenheim-Barnes, PC; ✉ Quietways, The Highlands, Painswick, Gloucestershire

OPPENHEIMER, Lady (Laetitia) Helen; da of Sir Hugh Lucas-Tooth (later Sir Hugh Munro-Lucas-Tooth), 1 Bt (d 1985), of Fordingbridge, Hants, and Lady Lucas-Tooth (later Lady Munro-Lucas-Tooth), OBE, *née* Laetitia Florence Findlay (d 1978); *b* 30 Dec 1926; *Educ* Cheltenham Ladies' Coll, Lady Margaret Hall Oxford (BPhil, MA); *m* 12 July 1947, Sir Michael Bernard Grenville Oppenheimer, Bt, *qv*; 3 da (Henrietta Laetitia Grenville (Mrs Adam L Scott) b 1954, Matilda Magdalen Grenville (Mrs Neil G A King) b 1956, Xanthe Jennifer Grenville (Hon Mrs Ivo A R Mosley) b 1958); *Career* lectr in ethics Cuddesdon Theological Coll 1964–69; served on: Archbishop of Canterbury's Gp on the law of divorce (report, Putting Asunder 1966), C of E Marriage Cmmn (report, Marriage Divorce and the Church 1971), Working Party Advsy Cncl for the Church's Ministry (report, Teaching Christian Ethics 1974), C of E Working Party on Educn in Personal Relationships (chm), The Inter-Anglican Theological and Doctrinal Cmmn (report, For the Sake of the Kingdom 1986), Gen Synod Working Party on the Law of Marriage (report, An Honourable Estate 1988); pres: Lady Margaret Hall Assoc of Senior Members 1988–90, Soc for the Study of Christian Ethics 1989–91; DD (Lambeth) 1993; *Books* Law and Love (1962), The Character of Christian Morality (1965, 2 edn 1974), Incarnation and Immanence (1973), The Marriage Bond (1976), The Hope of Happiness (1983), Looking before and after: The Archbishop of Canterbury's Lent Book for 1988 (published in USA as The Hope of Heaven), Marriage (In series Ethics: our choices 1990), Finding and Following: talking with children about God (1994) (published in USA as Helping children find God: a book for parents, teachers and clergy, 1995); *Style*— Lady Oppenheimer; ✉ L'Aiguillon, Grouville, Jersey, Channel Islands JE3 9AP (☎ 01534 854466)

OPPENHEIMER, His Hon Judge Michael Anthony; s of Felix Oppenheimer (d 1962), of Highgate, and Ingeborg Hanna Oppenheimer; *b* 22 Sept 1946; *Educ* Westminster, LSE (LLB); *m* 14 April 1973, Nicola Anne Oppenheimer, *qv*, da of Basil Vincent Brotherton (d 1961), of Pinner; 1 da (Rebecca b 14 April 1978), 1 s (James Felix Vincent b 15 Oct 1980); *Career* called to the Bar Middle Temple 1970 (Blackstone exhibitioner); memb SE Circuit, asst recorder 1985, recorder 1989, circuit judge (SE Circuit) 1991–; *Recreations* cinema, theatre, books, wine and food, performing and listening to music; *Clubs* Athenaeum; *Style*— His Hon Judge Michael Oppenheimer; ✉ c/o The Athenaeum, 107 Pall Mall, London SW1Y 5ER

OPPENHEIMER, Sir Michael Bernard Grenville; 3 Bt (UK 1921), of Stoke Poges, Co Bucks; s of Sir Michael Oppenheimer, 2 Bt (d 1933 in a flying accident), and Caroline, da of Sir Robert Harvey, 2 and last Bt (d 1972); *b* 27 May 1924; *Educ* Charterhouse, ChCh Oxford (MA, BLitt); *m* 1947, (Laetitia) Helen, *qv*, er da of Sir Hugh Munro-Lucas-Tooth, 1 Bt; 3 da (Henrietta Laetitia Grenville (Mrs Adam L Scott) b 1954, Matilda Magdalen Grenville (Mrs Neil G A King) b 1956, Xanthe Jennifer Grenville (Hon Mrs Ivo A R Mosley) b 1958); *Heir* none; *Career* served WWII, Middle East and Italy, SA Artillery, Lt; university lecturer in politics: Lincoln Coll Oxford 1955–68, Magdalen Coll Oxford 1966–68; *Clubs* Kimberley (S Africa), Victoria (Jersey); *Style*— Sir Michael Oppenheimer, Bt; ✉ L'Aiguillon, Grouville, Jersey, Channel Islands JE3 9AP (☎ 01534 854466)

OPPENHEIMER, Nicola Anne; da of Basil Vincent Brotherton (d 1961), and Joan Pamela, *née* Green; *b* 30 Sept 1950; *Educ* St Margaret's Sch Bushey, Queen Mary Coll Univ of London (LLB); *m* 14 April 1973, His Hon Judge Michael Anthony Oppenheimer, *qv*; 1 da (Rebecca Anne Julia b 14 April 1978), 1 s (James Felix Vincent b 15 Oct 1980); *Career* called to the Bar Middle Temple 1972; Lord Chancellor's Department: legal asst Criminal Appeal Office 1973–77, sr legal asst 1978–85, Judicial Appointments Div 1985–87, head of Personnel Mgmnt Div 1987–91, head of Legal Servs and Agencies Div 1991–93, princ estab and fin offr 1993–; *Recreations* early music, theatre, skiing, walking; *Style*— Mrs Nicola Oppenheimer; ✉ Lord Chancellor's Department, Selborne House, 54–60 Victoria Street, London SW1E 6QW (☎ 0171 210 8519, fax 0171 210 8752)

OPPENHEIMER, Peter Morris; s of Friedrich Rudolf Oppenheimer (d 1994), of London, and Charlotte Oppenheimer (d 1996); *b* 16 April 1938; *Educ* Haberdashers' Aske's, Queen's Coll Oxford (MA); *m* 30 July 1964, Catherine Violet Rosalie Pasternak, da of Eliot Trevor Oakeshott Slater, CBE, MD (d 1983); 2 s (Daniel b 1967, Joseph b 1971), 1 da (Tamara b 1973); *Career* Nat Serv RN 1956–58, ret Lt Cdr RNR 1978; Bank for International Settlements 1961–64, res fell and actg investmt bursar Nuffield Coll Oxford 1964–67, fell in economics ChCh Oxford 1967–, visiting prof int fin London Graduate Sch of Business Studies 1977–78, chief economist Shell Int Petroleum Co 1985–86; Freeman Worshipful Co of Haberdashers 1987; *Recreations* swimming, skiing, theatre, opera, music; *Style*— Peter Oppenheimer, Esq; ✉ 6 Linton Rd, Oxford OX2 6UG (☎ 01865 58226); Christ Church, Oxford OX1 1DP (☎ 01865 276220, fax 01865 794199, car 0831 114616)

ORAM, Baron (Life Peer UK 1975), of Brighton, in the Co of E Sussex; Albert Edward Oram; s of Henry Oram (d 1963), and Ada Edith Oram; *b* 13 Aug 1913; *Educ* Burgess Hill Elementary Sch, Brighton GS, LSE; *m* 1956, (Frances) Joan, da of Arthur Charles Barber, of Lewes, Sussex; 2 s (Hon Mark b 1967, Hon Robin b 1968); *Career* served WWII 1942–45; sits as Labour peer in House of Lords; research offr Co-operative Party 1946–55; MP (Lab and Co-op) East Ham (South) 1955–74; Parly sec Miny of

Overseas Devpt 1964–69; a lord-in-waiting to HM The Queen (govt whip) 1976–78, Lords rep on Shadow Cabinet 1983–87; chm Co-Operative Development Agency 1978–81; *Books* Changes in China (with Nora Stettner); *Style*— The Rt Hon the Lord Oram; ✉ 19 Ridgeside Ave, Patcham, Brighton, E Sussex BN1 8WD (☎ 01273 505333)

ORAM, Douglas Richard; s of Alfred Richard Oram (d 1980), of London, and Gladys, *née* Lungley (d 1955); *b* 29 March 1942; *Educ* Licensed Victuallers' Sch, Southgate Co GS, Hendon Tech Coll; *m* 24 Sept 1966, Jannet Adyne, da of Ascensio Joseph Echevarria (d 1988), and Obdulia Ines, *née* Irureta (d 1992), of Villajoyosa, Alicante, Spain; 2 s (Somerset b 17 March 1981, Sebastian b 12 Nov 1982); *Career* purchasing mangr then dir Centre Hotels (Cranston) Ltd 1965–75, purchasing mangr The Dorchester 1975–78, purchasing dir Comfort Hotels Int 1978–85, gp purchasing mangr Metropole Hotels 1985–; former dir Telecommunications Numbering and Addressing Bd Ltd; former memb POUNC; former chm: Membership Servs Ctee BHRCA, Champagne Acad; memb: Advsy Ctee on Telecommunications for England, Bd of Mgmnt Hotel and Catering Benevolent Assoc, Old Metronians Assoc, Champagne Acad Old Boys' Assoc; former vice chm Child Growth Fndn; co-ordinator Bone Dysplasia Gp; chm PM Club London, 5th Hampstead Scout Gp, tstee Sheffield Children's Hospital Limb Inequality Service; former memb Camden Lay Visitors' Panel; Chevalier de l'Ordre des Coteaux de Champagne; FHCIMA 1984, MCIPS 1988; *Books* A Leg Lengthening Diary - One Family's Experiences (with Jannet Oram, 1994); *Clubs* Royal Over-Seas League; *Style*— Douglas Oram, Esq; ✉ Metropole Hotels (Holdings) Limited, PO Box 335, National Exhibition Centre, Birmingham B40 1PT (☎ 0121 780 4266, fax 0121 780 2116)

ORANGE, Charles William; s of Richard Brian Orange (d 1963), of Oxshott, Surrey, and Mary Alice Kekewich, *née* Harvey (d 1979); *b* 23 June 1942; *Educ* Winchester; *m* 14 July 1973, Jane (d 1990), da of (George) Peter Humphreys-Davies, CBE (d 1986), of Bucks Green, Sussex; 3 s (Richard b 1975, Hugh b 1978, George b 1980); m 2, 6 July 1996, Rosemary, da of Raymond Cory, CBE, of Llanblethian, S Glamorgan, and Vivienne, *née* Roberts (d 1988); *Career* asst mangr Peat Marwick Mitchell & Co 1968–71, gp fin controller UBM Group plc 1973–82; fin dir: AAH Holdings plc 1982–84, Associated British Ports 1985–, Associated British Ports Holdings plc 1987–; former memb Ctee West of Eng Soc of CAs; FCA; *Recreations* tennis, opera, sheep; *Style*— Charles Orange, Esq; ✉ Hascombe Place, Godalming, Surrey GU8 4JA; Associated British Ports Holdings plc, 150 Holborn, London EC1N 2LR (☎ 0171 430 1177, fax 0171 430 2692, telex 23913)

ORANMORE AND BROWNE, 4 Baron (I 1836); Dominick Geoffrey Edward Browne; also (sits as) 2 Baron Mereworth (UK 1926); s of 3 Baron, KP, PC (d 1927), and Lady Olwen Ponsonby, da of 8 Earl of Bessborough, KP; *b* 21 Oct 1901; *Educ* Eton, Ch Ch Oxford; *m* 1, 1925 (m dis 1936), Mildred Helen (d 1980), da of Hon Thomas Egerton (d 1953); 2 s, 1 da (and 2 da decd); m 2, 1936 (m dis 1950), Oonagh (d 1995), da of Hon Arthur Ernest Guinness (d 1949), gda of 1 Earl of Iveagh; 1 s (and 2 s decd); m 3, 1950, Constance Vera (the actress Sally Gray), da of Charles Stevens; *Heir* s, Hon Dominick Geoffrey Thomas Browne; *Style*— The Rt Hon the Lord Oranmore and Browne; ✉ 52 Eaton Place, London SW1

ORCHARD, John Charles Johnson; s of Ronald Stark Orchard, of London and Nancy Margaret, *née* Heywood (d 1986); *b* 9 March 1939; *Educ* Harrow Emmanuel Coll Cambridge (MA, LLB); *m* 12 Aug 1967, Cynthia Diana, da of Cdr Clifford Maddocks (d 1974); 1 s (Alaister b 1971), 1 da (Alexandra b 1969); *Career* Nat Serv Sub Lt RNR 1958–60; admitted slr 1967; Syndey Morse & Co London 1963–68, ptnr Pinsent & Co (merged with Simpson Curtis to form Pinsent Curtis, May 1995) Birmingham (joined 1968); *Recreations* Chinese porcelain, shooting, flyfishing, prawning, gardening, English period furniture, pre-Columbian pottery, rackets, tennis; *Style*— John Orchard, Esq; ✉ Pinsent Curtis, 3 Colmore Circus, Birmingham B4 6BH (☎ 0121 200 1050, fax 0121 626 1040, telex 335101 PINCO G)

ORCHARD, Dr Robin Theodore; s of George William Orchard (d 1991), of Bexley Heath, Kent, and Christobel Edith Orchard; *b* 4 Oct 1940; *Educ* Chislehurst and Sidcup GS, Charing Cross Hosp Med Sch Univ of London (MB BS); *m* 5 June 1965, Ann Seymour, da of Dr Thomas Seymour Jones (d 1986), of Wimborne, Dorset; 2 s (Timothy, Christopher), 2 da (Kathryn, Elizabeth); *Career* sr registrar Charing Cross Hosp WC2 and W6 1970–74, sr lectr in med Royal Dental Hosp 1976–82, post grad clinical tutor St Helier Hosp 1978–86; conslt physician 1974–: St Helier Hosp Carshalton, Sutton Hosp, St Anthony's Hosp N Cheam; hon sr lectr St George's Hosp Med Sch 1982–, Univ of London examiner in medicine and dental surgery 1982–; churchwarden St John's Selsdon Sy 1982–87, memb Addington Deanery Synod 1988–; Univ memb Croydon D H A 1987–90, med dir St Helier Hosp Tst 1991–, memb Cncl St George's Hosp Med Sch 1991–; FRCP 1982, FRSM, MRCS; *Recreations* cricket; *Style*— Dr Robin Orchard; ✉ Bowlers End, 67 Croham Rd, S Croydon, Surrey CR2 7HF (☎ 0181 680 0253); St Helier Hospital, Wrythe Lane, Carshalton (☎ 0181 644 4343)

ORCHARD, Stephen; s of Leslie Orchard, of Oldham, and Ellen, *née* Cassells; *b* 13 April 1958; *Educ* Chadderton GS, St Peter's Coll Oxford, Nat Broadcasting Sch (scholar); *Career* CQSW Barnet House Univ of Oxford 1980–82, social worker High Wycombe SSD 1982–85; GWR Radio: broadcaster 1985–92, prog controller 1988–92, station dir 1992–94, gp prog dir GWR Group plc 1994–; memb Equity 1986; *Recreations* soccer, half marathon running, period property renovation; *Style*— Stephen Orchard, Esq; ✉ GWR Group, PO Box 2345, Westlea, Swindon, Wilts

ORCHARD, Stephen Michael; s of Stephen Henry Orchard (d 1965), and Ellen Frances, *née* Marsh (d 1986); *b* 5 Aug 1944; *Educ* Swanage GS; *m* 6 Sept 1969, Pauline Martha, da of George Rossell; 1 s (Michael Henry b 3 Jan 1972), 1 da (Suzanne Ellen b 27 Nov 1974); *Career* Lord Chancellor's Dept 1961–88, chief exec Legal Aid Board 1989– (memb 1992–); *Recreations* bird watching, walking, cooking; *Style*— Stephen Orchard, Esq; ✉ Legal Aid Board, 85 Gray's Inn Road, London WC1X 8AA (☎ 0171 813 1000)

ORCHARD-LISLE, Mervyn Christopher; s of Ulric Lock Orchard-Lisle (d 1955), and Thelma Julie Spelman, *née* Burdett; *b* 6 June 1946; *Educ* Marlborough, Univ of Newcastle upon Tyne (BA, BArch); *m* 24 March 1979, Angela Jane, da of Edmund Louis Saunders (d 1996); 1 s (Alexander b 1985), 1 da (Lucy b 1983); *Career* chartered architect in private practice 1973–, sr ptnr Gotelee Orchard-Lisle; RIBA 1973; *Recreations* watercolours, books, motor cars, family life; *Style*— Mervyn Orchard-Lisle, Esq; ✉ Shepherd's Cottage, East Woodhay, Newbury, Berks (☎ 01635 254282); Gotelee Orchard-Lisle, 6 Cromwell Place, Northbrook Street, Newbury, Berks RG14 1AF (☎ 01635 36600, fax 01635 31421)

ORCHARD-LISLE, Paul David; CBE (1988), TD (1971), DL (1986); s of Mervyn George Orchard-Lisle, MBE, of Les Vergers, Tourrettes sur Loup, Vence, France, and Phyllis Yvonne, *née* Jones (d 1975); *b* 3 Aug 1938; *Educ* Marlborough, Trinity Hall Cambridge (MA); *Career* chartered surveyor, sr ptnr Healey & Baker 1988–; pres RICS 1985–86; dep chm Slough Estates plc 1992–; Brig (TA) UKLF 1985; govr: Harrow Sch 1987–, West Buckland Sch 1985–, Marlborough Coll 1990–; pres Cncl Univ of Reading; Liveryman Worshipful Co of Chartered Surveyors; FRICS, FRSA; *Recreations* golf; *Clubs* Athenaeum; *Style*— Paul Orchard-Lisle, Esq, CBE, TD, DL; ✉ Bedford House, Bidwell, Bedfordshire LU5 6JP (☎ 01582 867317); Healey & Baker, 29 St George St, Hanover Square, London W1A 3BG (☎ 0171 514 2000)

ORDE, *see:* Campbell-Orde

ORDE, His Hon Judge; Denis Alan; s of John Orde, CBE (d 1992), of Littlehoughton Hall, Northumberland, and Charlotte Lilian Orde (d 1975); *b* 28 Aug 1932; *Educ* Univ of Oxford (MA); *m* 1961, Jennifer Jane, da of Dr John Longworth (d 1982), of Mill Hill, Masham, Yorks; 2 da (Georgina Jane, Philippa Denise); *Career* served Army 1950–52, cmmnd 2 Lt 1951; RA (TA) 1952–64; called to the Bar Inner Temple 1956 (pupil studentship 1956, Profumo prize 1959), recorder Crown Ct 1972–79, circuit judge sitting in Crown Ct NE and London 1979–, liaison judge to Magistrates 1983–, resident (designated) judge of a Crown Court 1986–, chm Criminal Justice Liaison Ctee for Northumberland, Tyne & Wear and Durham 1995; memb Chollerton PCC 1980–91, vice pres Northumberland Lawn Tennis Assoc 1982–, memb Lord Chllr's Co Advsy Ctee 1986–, ex-officio govr Christ's Hosp Sherburn 1993–; pres OUCA 1954; *Recreations* family history, cricket, listening to music, biography, travel in France, writing; *Clubs* Northern Counties; *Style*— His Hon Judge Orde; ✉ c/o North Eastern Circuit Office, 17th Floor, West Riding House, Albion Street, Leeds LS1 5AA (☎ 0113 244 1841)

ORDE-POWLETT, Hon Harry Algar Nigel; s and h of 7 Baron Bolton and his 1 w, Hon Christine Helena, *née* Weld-Forester (now Hon Mrs Miles), da of 7 Baron Forester; *b* 14 Feb 1954; *Educ* Eton; *m* 1977, Philippa, da of Maj Peter Tapply; 3 s (Thomas Peter Algar b 16 July 1979, William Benjamin b 1981, Nicholas Mark b 1985); *Style*— The Hon Harry Orde-Powlett; ✉ Wensley Hall, Wensley, Leyburn, N Yorks DL8 4HN

O'REILLY, Francis Joseph; s of Lt-Col Charles Joseph O'Reilly, DSO, MC (d 1952), of Naas, Co Kildare, and Dorothy Mary Martin (d 1978); *b* 15 Nov 1922; *Educ* Ampleforth, Trinity Coll Dublin (BA, BAI, LLD); *m* 1950, Teresa Mary, da of Capt John Williams, MC (d 1965), of Co Offaly, Ireland; 3 s (Charles, Peter, Paul), 7 da (Mary, Jane, Olivia, Margaret, Rose, Louise, Julie); *Career* Lt RE 1943–46, 7 Indian Divnl Engrs SE Asia Cmd 1945–46; chm: John Power & Son Ltd 1955–66, Player and Wills (Ireland) Ltd 1964–81, Irish Distillers Group plc 1966–83, TI Irish Raleigh 1971–80, Ulster Bank Ltd 1982–90; dir: Ulster Bank Ltd 1961–74 (dep chm 1974–82), National Westminster Bank plc 1982–90, Irish Distillers Group plc 1983–88; pres: Royal Dublin Soc 1986–89 (chm Exec Ctee 1980–86), Equestrian Fedn of Ireland 1964–79, Mktg Inst of Ireland 1983–85, Inst of Bankers in Ireland 1985–86; chllr Trinity Coll Univ of Dublin 1985– (pro-chllr 1983–85); Irish rep Fedn Equestre Internationale 1964–79; memb and tstee: Turf Club 1967–, Irish Nat Hunt Steeplechase Ctee 1967–; chm Kildare Hunt Club 1968–93 (tstee 1993–); MMRIA 1987, FIMgt (Ireland) 1983, fell Inst of Engrs in Ireland 1987; *Recreations* fox-hunting, racing, gardening, reading; *Clubs* Kildare Street and Univ (Dublin), Turf (Ireland); *Style*— Francis O'Reilly, Esq; ✉ The Glebe, Rathmore, Naas, Co Kildare, Ireland (☎ 0145 62136)

O'REILLY, Prof John James; s of Patrick William O'Reilly (d 1969), of Bromsgrove, Worcs, and Dorothy Anne Lewis (d 1968); *b* 1 Dec 1946; *Educ* Sacred Heart Coll Droitwich, Brunel Univ (BTech, DSc), Univ of Essex (PhD); *m* 18 July 1968, Margaret, da of Lewis Brooke (d 1983), of Coven, Staffs; 1 s (Edward James b 1986), 1 da (Jenny Ann b 1978); *Career* Ultra Electonics Ltd 1969–72, sr lectr Univ of Essex 1972–85, researcher PO Res Centre 1978–79, prof of electronic engrg Univ of Wales at Bangor 1985–94, princ research fell BT Laboratories 1993–94, chair of telecommunications UCL 1994–; chief exec/dep chm IDB Ltd 1985–94; chm EPSRC Communications and Distributed Systems Ctee, memb EPSRC/DTI Info Technol Advsy Bd 1991–94; CEng, FIEE 1988 (MIEE 1983), FEng 1993; *Books* Telecommunication Principles (1984, 2 edn 1989), Optimisation Methods in Electronics and Communications (1984), Problems of Randomness in Communications Engineering (1984); *Recreations* family, music, theatre; *Clubs* Athenaeum; *Style*— Prof John O'Reilly, FEng; ✉ UCL, Torrington Place, London WC1E 7JE (☎ 0171 380 7300, fax 0171 388 9307, e-mail j.oreilly@eleceng.ucl.ac.uk)

O'REILLY, Wilfred John (Wilf); *b* 22 Aug 1964; *Career* speed skater; *Achievements* 500m: Gold medal Olympic Games 1988, Gold medal World Championships 1990 and 1991 (Bronze medal 1985 and 1988, Silver medal 1992); 1000m: Gold medal Olympic Games 1988, Gold medal World Championships 1991 (Silver medal 1989); Silver medal 1500m World Championships 1984, British champion 1982–89 and 1991 (second 1993), overall Euro champion 1983, 1986 and 1992; world record holder: 400m, 800m, 1500m; *Style*— Wilf O'Reilly, Esq; ✉ PO Box 174, Birmingham B5 7PJ (☎ 0121 440 1703)

ORFORD, Dr Philip; s of Basil Henry Orford (d 1984), of Hampton in Arden, and Jacqueline Mary, *née* Hesketh; *b* 27 Oct 1953; *Educ* Wellesbourne Sch, Greenmore Coll, Queen's Coll, Karlsruhe Univ, Kensington Univ, California State Univ (MSc, PhD); *m* 6 April 1985, Carole Anne; 1 s (Alexander Graham b 6 Oct 1988), 1 da (Heldi Louise b 24 Oct 1990); *Career* Greenmore Coll Offr Trg Unit 1967–72; subsequently: chm Wang Communications User Gp, reviewer Univ of California Riverside, memb Ctee Unix Interest Gp (Computing), Esprit-It specialist Brussels, systems devpt conslt incl implementation of large scale computer aided design systems, business systems and quality mgmnt systems, conslt engr, info technologist and tport specialist; conslt: British Rail Research 1976–89, Network North 1991–93, Transmark Ltd; major tport projects incl: Heathrow Alternative Link, jt venture with Deutsche Bahn 1994, jt venture with Polish State Railways and CIE 1995, project conslt for Thorburn Colquhoun Ltd 1994 (signalling, logistics, interfacing of road/rail systems), devpt of new rail detection device 1995; govr: Royal Agric Soc of England, Three Counties Agric Soc; memb: Assoc of Agric, NY Acad of Scis; MIEEE, MIDPM, MBCS, MInstD, FPWI; *Books* Analogue Design Concepts (1978), Design & Development of a 16 Channel Multi-Plexer (1982), Robotics & Artificial Intelligence (1985), Heathrow - An Alternative Link (1993), Peterborough - Sterling Way (1994), Joint Venture - Deutsche Bahn (1995); *Recreations* farming, electronics, country pursuits; *Clubs* Fentham, Sheraton Int, Directors, Carlton; *Style*— Dr Philip Orford; ✉ Hampton Associates, Meriden Road, Hampton in Arden, W Midlands B92 0BS (☎ and fax 01675 442600)

ORGA (D'ARCY-ORGA), (Hüsnü) Ateş; s of Capt Irfan Orga (d 1970), of Wadhurst, E Sussex, and Margaret Veronica, *née* D'Arcy-Wright (d 1974); *b* 6 Nov 1944; *Educ* Univ of Durham (BMus), Trinity Coll of Music (FTCL); *m* 1, 23 Nov 1974 (m dis 1991), Josephine, da of Walter Richard Sidney Prior, of Ticehurst, E Sussex; 1 s (Alexander b 1983), 1 da (Chloë b 1980); m 2, 8 May 1992 (m dis 1996), Ruth Frances, da of Harry Davis, of Hod Hasharon, Israel; 1 da (Francesca b 1993); *Career* prog annotator London Sinfonietta 1968–73, music info and presentation asst BBC Music Div London 1971–75, ind record, radio and video prodr 1972–, lectr in music and concert dir Univ of Surrey 1975–90, artistic dir Inst of Armenian Music London 1976–80, princ prog annotator LSO 1976–81, dir Ateş Orga Associates 1990–; examiner: Univ of Cambridge Local Examinations 1978–85, Assoc Bd Royal Schools of Music 1981–96, Univ of Malta 1993–95; artistic conslt Sutton Place Heritage Tst Guildford 1983–86, artistic advsr Acad of the London Mozarteum 1988–89, record prodr and conslt Collins Classics 1988–90, music dir V & A Club 1988, record prodr Hyperion 1990–95, Naxos/Marco Polo 1994–, music prodr Music and the Mind (C4) 1996; special projects conslt The Entertainment Corporation 1990, special projects dir Georgina Ivor Associates 1991–95; artistic dir: MusicArmenia 78 London 1978, Yvonne Arnaud Theatre Appeal Concerts 1985, Liszt and His Contemporaries, Beethoven Plus, The Gallic Muse, Mainly Schumann Festivals Guildford 1986–89, Guildford 91 Int Music Festival 1991, Piano Masterworks (Nikolai Demidenko) Belfast 1991–92 and Wigmore Hall London 1993, Virtuoso Romantics (Marc-André Hamelin) Wigmore Hall London 1994, Vienna Nights (Medici String Quartet) St John's Smith Square 1995; memb Jury: Br Liszt Piano Competition Guildford 1976, Alkan Centenary Piano Competition Croydon 1988, RPS Music Awards 1990–93; contrib: International Music Guide, The Listener, The Literary Review, Music and Musicians International, The Musical Times, Records and Recording, Hi Fi News, BBC Music Magazine, The Ultimate Encyclopedia of Classical Music (1995), The Ultimate

Encyclopedia of Musical Instruments (1996), BBC Music Magazine Top 1000 CD's Guide (1996); music panel chm SE Arts Regnl Arts Assoc 1985–88 (vice chm 1984), memb Univ of S California Sch of Performing Arts Int Advsy Cncl on Armenian Musical Studies 1980–81; Royal Philharmonic Soc Music Award (Best Concert Series) 1993; *Books* The Proms (1974), Chopin: His Life and Times (1976), Beethoven: His Life and Times (1978), Records and Recording Classical Guides (1977–78), Portrait of a Turkish Family (Afterword, 1988); music publications: Chopin Three Piano Pieces (1968), Beethoven Sonata in C WoO 51 (1978); *Recreations* music occidental and oriental, food, watching people, matters Eastern European; *Style*— Ateş Orga, Esq; ✉ 32 Norwich Road, Hethersett, Norfolk NR9 3DD (☎ and fax 01603 810085, e-mail orga.music@paston.co.uk)

ORGAN, (Harold) Bryan; s of Harold Victor and Helen Dorothy Organ; *b* 31 Aug 1935; *Educ* Loughborough Coll of Art, Royal Academy Schs London; *m* Sandra Mary Mills; *Career* artist; lectr in drawing and painting Loughborough 1959–65; *Solo Exhibitions* Leicester, London, New York, Baukunst Cologne, Turin; represented: Kunsthalle, Darmstadt, Mostra Mercatao d'Arte Contemporanea Florence, 3rd Int Exhibitions of Drawing Germany, Sao Paulo Museum of Art Brazil; works in private and public collections in England, France, Germany, Italy, Switzerland, USA, Canada, Brazil; portraits include: Sir Michael Tippett, David Hicks, Mary Quant, Princess Margaret, Elton John, Harold Macmillan, The Prince of Wales, The Princess of Wales, Lord Denning, James Callaghan, The Duke of Edinburgh 1983; Hon MA Loughborough, Hon DLitt Univ of Leicester; *Style*— Bryan Organ, Esq; ✉ The Stables, Marston Trussell, nr Market Harborough, Leics; c/o Redfern Gallery, 20 Cork St, London W1

O'RIORDAN, Brian Colman; s of Patrick Joseph O'Riordan (d 1974), and Bridget, *née* Madigan (d 1995); *b* 25 Oct 1935; *Educ* Blackrock Coll Dublin, Univ Coll Cork (BDSI); *m* 17 Aug 1963, Valerie Ann, da of Rev Richard Rogers; 2 s (Sean Peter b 12 March 1968, Kieran Paul b 5 Oct 1970), 2 da (Rebecca Jane b 3 July 1969, Susannah Niamh b 24 Oct 1971); *Career* conslt oral surgn: Mount Vernon Hosp 1970–94, St Albans City Hosp 1970–94, Royal Nat Orthopaedic Hosp 1970–94; conslt dental radiologist King's Coll Sch of Med and Dentistry London; pres Br Soc of Dental and Maxillo-Facial Radiology 1981–82, rep Bd of Br Dental Assoc 1984–, treas Br Soc of Oral and Maxillo-Facial Surgery 1986–89 (memb Cncl 1983–86); chm: Cncl Middx and Herts Branch BDA 1986–89, Steering Ctee to set up Euro Assoc for Dental and Maxillo-Facial Radiology; vice chm Regnl Dental Ctee NW Thames RHA; past chm: Regnl Ctee for Hosp Dental Services, Regnl Postgrad Ctee Br Postgrad Med Fedn; memb Examining Bd RCR; Hon Diploma in Dental Radiology 1984; memb: BDA, BAOMS, BSDMFR, IADMFR; FDI, FDSRCS (Eng); *Books* Forensic Dentistry (contrib, 1974), Self Assessment Manual RCS (contrib, 1991); *Recreations* photography, singing, archaeology, taking a sideways look; *Style*— Brian O'Riordan; ✉ 45 Wimpole Street, London W1M 7DG (☎ 0171 224 0996, fax 01923 211210)

O'RIORDAN, Prof Jeffrey Lima Hayes; s of Dr Michael Joseph O'Riordan (d 1975), of Newport, Monmouthshire; *b* 27 March 1931; *Educ* Newport HS for Boys, Pembroke Coll Oxford, Middx Hosp; *m* 6 July 1963, Sarah Julia, da of Lt-Col Robert Lesley Berridge, MC (d 1983), of Currabiny, Co Cork; 3 s (Dermot b 1964, Mark b 1965 d 1982, Dominic b 1968), 3 da (Shelagh b 1966, Kathleen b 1971, Philippa b 1978); *Career* Nat Serv 1959–61; current posts held at Middx Hosp London: prof in Metabolic Med (UCL), hon conslt physician (former registrar); former visiting assoc Nat Inst of Arthritis and Metabolic Disorders Bethesda, former examiner Med Conjoint Bd; author of numerous papers on molecular biology of calciotrophic hormones, hyperparathyroidism, metabolic bone disease, vitamin D deficiency and resistance; memb: Assoc of Physicians, American Endocrine Soc; FRCP 1971 (memb 1959); *Books* Essentials of Endocrinology; *Recreations* sailing; *Clubs* Royal Cruising; *Style*— Prof Jeffrey O'Riordan; ✉ The Middlesex Hospital, Mortimer St, London W1 (☎ 0171 380 9446, fax 0171 636 3151)

O'RIORDAN, Rear Adm John Patrick Bruce (Paddy); CBE (1982), JP (Northants 1991); s of Surgn Capt Timothy Joseph O'Riordan, RN (d 1966), of Bergh Apton, Norwich, and Bertha Carson, *née* Young (d 1983); *b* 15 Jan 1936; *Educ* Kelly Coll; *m* 15 Aug 1959, Jane, da of John Alexander Mitchell (d 1996), of Kirkcudbright, Scotland; 1 s (Tim b 1965), 2 da (Susie (Mrs Graham) b 1960, Katherine (Mrs Beattie) b 1966); *Career* Nat Serv, midshipman RNVR 1954, transferred RN, cmd HMS Porpoise 1968–69 and HMS Dreadnought 1972–74; cmd: Submarine Sea Trg Orgn 1976–78, RCDS 1979, guided missile destroyer HMS Glasgow 1980–81 (disaster relief ops St Lucia after Hurricane Allen 1980); asst COS policy to Supreme Allied Cdr Atlantic Virginia USA 1982–84, dir naval warfare MOD 1984–86 (ADC to HM the Queen 1985), Rear Adm mil dep cmdt NATO Def Coll Rome 1986–89; chief exec St Andrew's Hosp Northampton 1990–, dir Ind Healthcare Assoc 1993–, chm SSAFA Northants 1996–; FIMgt 1985; *Recreations* sailing, sketching, rugby football, country pursuits; *Clubs* The Royal Navy of 1765 and 1785, Army and Navy, Royal Yacht Sqdn, RNSA; *Style*— Rear Adm Paddy O'Riordan, CBE, JP; ✉ The Little Rectory, Whilton, nr Daventry, Northamptonshire NN11 5NN (☎ 01327 843274); Nether Crae, Mossdale, Kirkcudbrightshire DG7 2NL (☎ 01644 450644)

O'RIORDAN, Prof Timothy (Tim); s of Kevin Denis O'Riordan, and Norah Joyce, *née* Lucas (d 1996); *b* 21 Feb 1942; *Educ* George Heriot's Sch Edinburgh, Univ of Edinburgh (MA), Cornell Univ (MS), Univ of Cambridge (PhD); *m* 18 May 1968, Ann Morison, da of Elmsley Philip (d 1992); 2 da (Katharine Louise b 24 Jan 1977, Alice Janet b 31 May 1979); *Career* asst prof Dept of Geography Simon Fraser Univ Burnaby BC 1967–70 (assoc prof 1970–74), reader Sch of Environmental Scis UEA 1974–80 (prof 1980–); currently assoc dir Centre for Social and Economic Research on the Global Environment; memb: Broads Authy (chm Environment Ctee), Econ and Social Res Cncl (chm Environment Working Gp), Dow Chemical Corporate Environmental Advsy Ctee, Core Faculty HRH The Prince of Wales's Business and Environment Prog, Environmental Advsy Bd Eastern Gp plc; *Books* Progress in Resource Management (1971), Environmentalism (1976, 1981), Sizewell B: An Anatomy of the Inquiry (1988), The Greening of the Machinery of Government (1990), Interpreting the Precautionary Principle (1994), Environmental Science for Environmental Management (1994), Politics of Climate Change: A European Perspective (1996), EU Taxation (1996); *Recreations* classical music (double bass playing); *Style*— Prof Tim O'Riordan; ✉ Wheatlands, Hethersett Lane, Colney, Norwich NR4 7TT (☎ 01603 810534); School of Environmental Sciences, University of East Anglia, Norwich NR4 7TJ (☎ 01603 592840, fax 01603 250558)

ORKNEY, 8 Earl of (S 1696); Cecil O'Bryen Fitz-Maurice; also Viscount Kirkwall and Lord Dechmont (both S 1696); s of late Douglas Frederick Harold Fitz-Maurice (himself gs of Cdr Hon Frederick Fitz-Maurice, who was in turn 3 s of 5 Earl); suc kinsman, 7 Earl, 1951 (succession approved by Lyon Ct 1955); *b* 3 July 1919; *m* 1953, Rose Katherine Durk (d 1995), da of late J W D Silley; *Heir* kinsman, Oliver Peter St John; *Career* sits as Conservative peer in House of Lords; joined RASC 1939, served 1939–45 (N Africa, Italy, France, Germany and Holland) and 1950–51 (Korea); *Style*— The Rt Hon Earl of Orkney; ✉ 4 Summerland, Princes Rd, Ferndown, Dorset (☎ 01202 893178)

ORLEBAR, Christopher John Dugmore; s of Col John H R Orlebar (d 1989), OBE, of St Helens, IOW, and Louise, *née* Crowe; *b* 4 Feb 1945; *Educ* Rugby, Univ of Southampton, Coll of Air Trg Hamble; *m* 5 Feb 1972, Nicola Dorothy Mary, er da of Dr Leslie Ford (d 1987), of Sheringham, Norfolk; 1 s (Edward b 1977), 1 da (Caroline b 1979); *Career* Cadet Pilot Southampton Univ Air Sqdn 1964–66, trainee pilot Coll of Air Trg Hamble 1967–69, First Offr and Navigator VC10 (awarded basic Instrs Trg Course), CAA course Stansted for examiner/instr 1973, Sr First Offr Concorde 1976–86, appointed examiner/instr to Concorde Fleet, chartered 2 Concordes for celebration of 50 anniversary of Schneider Trophy 1981; organised BBC documentary on Concorde in QED series 1983, writer and presenter BBC TV series Jet Trail 1984, initiator and conslt Faster than a Speeding Bullet (C4 Equinox) 1989, tech conslt Ch4 documentary on Air Traffic Control in Equinox series 1993; Capt Boeing 737 with BA 1986–, trg capt 1994–; Freeman City of London 1975, Liveryman Guild of Air Pilots and Air Navigators; memb Royal Aeronautical Soc, MRAeS 1984; *Books* The Concorde Story (with BA and Air France, 1986), Tenth Impression (1996); *Recreations* family, photography, music, sailing, canoeing, tennis, gardening; *Clubs* Air League; *Style*— Christopher Orlebar, Esq; ✉ Holt Cottage, Fairoak Lane, Oxshott, Surrey KT22 0TW (☎ and fax 01372 842100); British Airways, London (Heathrow) Airport, PO Box 10, Hounslow, Middlesex TW6 2JA

ORMAN, Dr Stanley; s of Jack Orman (d 1974), and Ettie, *née* Steiner (d 1984); *b* 6 Feb 1935; *Educ* Hackney Downs GS, King's Coll London (BSc, PhD); *m* 1960, Helen, da of Joseph Hourman (d 1982); 1 s (David b 1961), 2 da (Ann b 1963, Lynn b 1969); *Career* Fullbright scholar, post doctoral res Brandeis Univ Waltham Mass USA, res in materials sci 1961–74, chief weapon system engr Chevaline 1981–82, min and cncllr Br Embassy Washington 1982–84, under sec MOD 1984, dir gen Strategic Def Initiative Participation Office 1986–90 (dep dir Awre Aldermaston 1984–86); chief exec GTS Inc Washington 1990–96, chief exec Orman Assoc Inc 1996–; Jelf Medalist Kings Coll 1957; *Publications* Faith in G.O.D.S - Stability in the Nuclear Age (1991); author of over 150 other pubns; *Recreations* sport, reading, designing bow ties; *Style*— Dr Stanley Orman; ✉ 17825 Stoneridge Drive, Gaithersburg, Maryland 20878, USA (☎ 00 1 301 670 0685)

ORME, Prof Michael Christopher L'Estrange; s of Christopher Robert L'Estrange Orme, TD (d 1979), of Poole, Dorset, and Muriel Evelyn Janet, *née* Thomson; *b* 13 June 1940; *Educ* Sherborne, Univ of Cambridge (MA, MB BChir, MD); *m* 15 April 1967, (Joan) Patricia, da of Stanley Abbott, OBE, of Coulsdon, Surrey; 1 s (Robert Martin b 10 July 1969); *Career* Univ of Liverpool: sr lectr clinical pharmacology 1975–81, reader 1981–84, prof pharmacology and therapeutics 1984–, dean of Faculty of Medicine 1991–96; dir of educn and trg N W Regnl Office NHS Exec 1996–; hon conslt physician Liverpool Health Authy; memb GMC 1994–96; sec: clinical pharmacology section Br Pharmacological Soc 1982–88, clinical section Int Union of Pharmacology 1987–92; hon sec Euro Assoc of Clinical Pharmacology and Therapeutics 1995–; govr Birkenhead School Ltd 1991–; FRCP 1980; *Books* Medicines - The Self Help Guide (1988), Human Lactation (1989), Therapeutic Drugs (1991); *Recreations* sailing, astronomy; *Clubs* Dee Sailing; *Style*— Prof Michael Orme; ✉ Wychwood, 80 Brimstage Rd, Heswall, Wirral, Merseyside L60 1XQ (☎ 0151 342 3269); Department of Pharmacology and Therapeutics, New Medical School, Ashton St, Liverpool L69 3BX (☎ 0151 706 4260, fax 0151 794 5540)

ORME, Prof Nicholas; s of Edward Howell Orme, and Kathleen, *née* Plowright (d 1971); *Educ* Bristol Cathedral Sch, Magdalen Coll Oxford (BA, MA, DPhil, DLitt); *m* 4 July 1981, Rona, da of James S Monro; 1 da (Verity b 1984); *Career* Univ of Exeter: lectr 1964–81, reader in history 1981–88, prof of history 1988–, Nuffield Fndn res fell 1991–92, Leverhulme Tst res fell 1993–94; chm Exeter Cathedral Fabric Advsy Ctee, pres Exeter Hist Assoc, ed Devon and Cornwall Record Soc; FSA 1985; FRHistS 1979; *Books* English Schools in the Middle Ages (1973), Education in the West of England (1976), The Minor Clergy of Exeter Cathedral (1980), Early British Swimming (1983), From Childhood to Chivalry (1984), Exeter Cathedral As It Was (1986), Education and Society in Medieval and Renaissance England (1989), John Lydgate, Table Manners for Children (ed, 1989), Unity and Variety: A History of the Church in Devon and Cornwall (ed, 1991), Nicholas Roscarrock's Lives of the Saints (ed, 1992), The First English Hospitals 1070–1570 (with Margaret Webster, 1995), White Bird Flying (1995), English Church Dedications (1996); *Clubs* Devon & Exeter Inst; *Style*— Prof Nicholas Orme; ✉ Dept of History and Archaeology, University of Exeter, Exeter EX4 4QH (☎ 01392 264340)

ORME, Rt Hon Stanley (Stan); PC (1974), MP (Lab) Salford East (majority 11,235); s of Sherwood Orme; *b* 5 April 1923; *Educ* tech sch (pt/t), Nat Cncl Labour Colls and WEA; *m* 1951, Irene Mary, da of Vernon Fletcher Harris; *Career* served RAF as Warrant Offr Air-Bomber Navigator (Bomber Cmd) 1942–47 in Europe & M East; Parly candidate (Lab) Stockport S 1959; MP (Lab): Salford W 1964–83, Salford E 1983–; min of state: NI Office 1974–76, DHSS 1976, for social security 1976–77; min for social security (with seat in Cabinet) 1977–79; chief oppn spokesman (and memb Shadow Cabinet): on indust Dec 1980–Nov 1983, on energy Nov 1983–87; chm Parly Lab Party 1987–92; memb Select Ctee: of Privileges 1994–95, on Standards in Public Life 1995–96; chm All Pty Parly Cricket Gp; memb AEEU; Hon DSc Univ of Salford 1985; *Recreations* walking, reading American literature, music (jazz and opera), supporting Manchester United, cricket; *Clubs* Lancs County Cricket; *Style*— The Rt Hon Stan Orme, MP; ✉ 8 Northwood Grove, Sale, Cheshire M33 3DZ (☎ 0161 973 5341); House of Commons, London SW1A 0AA (☎ 0171 219 3000)

ORMEROD, Ben; s of John Ormerod, of Suffolk, and Paula Taylor, of Mortlake; *b* 24 Oct 1958; *Educ* St Christopher's Sch Letchworth, Central Sch of Speech and Drama; *partner* since May 1990, Aïcha Kossoko; *Career* lighting designer; began career with Andrew Visnevski's Cherub Co; other cos incl: Kick Theatre, Buick of Signs, ATC, Cheek by Jowl, 7:84 Scotland, Théâtre de Complicité, Major Road; designed lighting for The Calico Museum Ahmedabad; *Theatre* for RNT incl: Bent, Accidental Death of an Anarchist, The Winter's Tale, Uncle Vanya; RSC incl: The Revenger's Tragedy; for Leicester Haymarket incl: Krapp's Last Tape (also Riverside Studios) 1990, Our Country's Good 1991; for West Yorkshire Playhouse incl: Life is a Dream 1992, Betrayal 1994; for English Touring Theatre incl: Hamlet (also Donmar Warehouse) 1993, No Man's Land 1994, The Doll's House 1994, Hedda Gabler (also Donmar Warehouse) 1996; other credits incl: Pal Joey (Bristol Old Vic) 1991, A View from the Bridge (Sheffield Crucible) 1991, Cyrano de Bergerac (Vembo Theatre, Athens) 1992, Coriolanus, Rennaissance (both Chichester Festival) 1992, Macbeth (Tzeni Karezi, Athens) 1994, The Winslow Boy (Plymouth Theatre Royal, tour, The Globe) 1994, Casement (Moving Theatre at Riverside Studios) 1995, A Crocodile Looking at Birds (Lyric Hammersmith) 1995, The Government Inspector (Tzeni Karezi Theatre, Athens) 1995, Hamlet (OSC) 1996, The Beauty Queen of Leenane (Druid Theatre Co at Royal Court) 1996, Silence Silence Silence (Mladinsko Theatre, Ljubljana) 1996, Oedipus Tyrannus (Epidaurus) 1996; *Opera* credits incl: La Voix Humaine and Savitri (Aix-en-Provence) 1990, Punch and Judy (Aldeburgh Festival) 1991, The Turn of the Screw (Bath and Wessex Opera) 1993, The Wildman (Aldeburgh Festival) 1995, The Mask of Orpheus (QEH/BBCSO) 1996; Baa Baa Black Sheep (Opera North and BBC 2); *Awards* TMA Best Design Award for Life is a Dream (jtly with Neil Warmington and Mic Pool); *Style*— Ben Ormerod, Esq; ✉ c/o Clare Vidal Hall, 28 Perrers Road, London W6 0EZ (☎ 0181 741 7647, fax 0181 741 9459, mobile 0385 954 000)

ORMEROD, Brig Denis Leonard; CBE (1976, MBE 1950); s of Harold Eric Ormerod, CBE (d 1959), and Kathleen Mary, *née* Bourke (d 1957); *b* 17 Feb 1922; *Educ* Downside; *m* 7 Oct 1950, Frances Mary Shewell, da of Brig Charles Edward Francis Turner, CBE, DSO, of Wadhurst, E Sussex; 2 s (Giles b 1957, Jonathan b 1962), 6 da (Jennifer (Mrs P Tolhurst) b 1951, Julia (Mrs A Wells) b 1953, Teresa (Mrs M Bromley Gardner) b 1959, Jessica (Mrs D Fields) b 1960, Clare (Mrs A Torrance) b 1964, Katherine (Hon Mrs Edward Wood) b 1968); *Career* cmmnd 1941 2 KEO Goorkhas (IA) served in India,

Italy, Greece 1941–47, transferred to RIrF 1947, served in Palestine, Egypt 1947–48, Malaya 1948–50 (seconded to 1/2 Goorkhas), (despatches 1949), Regt Serv RIrF N Ireland, BAOR, Berlin, Tripoli 1950–60, RN Staff Coll 1960–61, Staff Sch of Inf 1961–63, CO 1 Bn RIrF 1965–67 (BAOR, UK, Swaziland, Bechuanaland, Aden), asst Mil Sec Southern Cmd, Army Strategic Cmd 1967–69, Col GS MOD 1969–71, Cmd Ulster Def Regt (11 Bns) 1971–73 (despatches 1973), Brig Inf 1 (BR) Corps 1973–76, sec NW England and IOM TA and VR Assoc 1976–87; DL Merseyside 1983–87; *Recreations* country pursuits, horses, music, gardening; *Clubs* Army and Navy, Faugh-à-Ballagh (chm 1989–); *Style—* Brig Denis Ormerod, CBE; ✉ Kirkbank House, High Halden, Kent TN26 3JD (☎ 01233 850249)

ORMOND, Prof Leonée; *née* Jasper; *b* 27 Aug 1940; *Educ* Ware GS for Girls, St Anne's Coll Oxford (BA), Univ of Birmingham (MA); *m* 11 May 1963, Richard Louis Ormond, *qv*, s of Conrad Ormond (d 1979); 2 s (Augustus b 1972, Marcus b 1974); *Career* King's Coll London: asst lectr 1965–68, lectr 1968–85, sr lectr 1985–89, reader in English 1989–96, prof Victorian Studies 1996–; chair Tennyson Res Pubns Bd, tstee G F Watts Gallery Compton Surrey; *Books* George Du Maurier (1969), Lord Leighton (with Richard Ormond 1975), J M Barrie (1987), Alfred Tennyson: a Literary Life (1993); *Clubs* Univ Women's; *Style—* Prof Leonée Ormond; ✉ English Department, King's College, Strand, London WC2R 2LS

ORMOND, Richard Louis; s of Conrad Eric Ormond (d 1979), of Old Rectory, Cleggan, Co Galway, and Dorothea Charlotte (d 1987), da of Sir Alexander Gibbons, 7 Bt; *b* 16 Jan 1939; *Educ* Marlborough, Brown Univ USA, ChCh Oxford (MA); *m* 11 May 1963, Leonée Ormond, *qv*; 2 s (Augustus b 1972, Marcus b 1974); *Career* asst keeper Nat Portrait Gallery 1965–75, dep dir 1975–83, head of Picture Dept Nat Maritime Museum 1983–86, dir Nat Maritime Museum 1986–; chm: Tstees Watts Gallery Compton, Friends of Leighton House; dep chm Museums Training Inst 1994–, memb Cncl Maritime Tst; *Books* J S Sargent (1970), Early Victorian Portraits in the National Portrait Gallery (1973), Lord Leighton (with Leonée Ormond, 1975), Sir Edwin Landseer (1982), The Great Age of Sail (1986), F X Winterhalter and the Courts of Europe (1987); *Recreations* cycling, opera, theatre; *Clubs* Garrick; *Style—* Richard Ormond, Esq; ✉ National Maritime Museum, Greenwich, London SE10 9NF (☎ 0181 312 6611)

ORMONDE, 7 Marquess of (I 1825); James Hubert Theobald Charles Butler; MBE (1921); also Earl of Ormonde (I 1328), Earl of Ossory (I 1527), Viscount Thurles (I 1536), Baron Ormonde (UK 1821), and 31 Hereditary Chief Butler of Ireland (1177); s of Rev Lord James Butler (d 1929, 4 s of 2 Marquess, KP) and Annabella (d 1943), o da of Rev Cosmo Reid Gordon; 12 Earl cr Duke of Ormonde 1661 as reward for fidelity to the crown, 2 Duke was attainted 1715 for supporting the Stuarts; suc 1 cous, 6 Marquess, 1971; *b* 19 April 1899; *Educ* Haileybury, RMC Sandhurst; *m* 1, 1935, Nan (d 1973), da of Garth Gilpin, of USA; 2 da (Lady Ann Soukup b 1940, Lady Cynthia Robb b 1946); m 2, 1976, Elizabeth (d 1980), da of Charles Rarden, of USA; *Heir* to Marquessate, Viscountcy and Barony none, to Earldoms of Ormonde and Ossory and Hereditary Chief Butlership: 17 Viscount Mountgarret (descends from 8 Earl of Ormonde); *Career* served WWI, late Lt KRRC; US businessman, ret; *Clubs* Naval and Military; *Style—* The Most Hon the Marquess of Ormonde, MBE; ✉ 6101 S County Line, Burr Ridge, Illinois, USA 60521

ORNSBY, John Sidney; s of Leslie Sidney Ornsby (d 1996), of Plymouth, Devon, and Evelyn, *née* Buckland (d 1978); *b* 3 Oct 1936; *Educ* Bancroft's Sch Woodford Green Essex, QMC London (BSc); *m* 18 July 1959, Heather Doreen, da of Eric Stephen Padmore (d 1994), of Eastbourne, E Sussex; 1 da (Suzanne Doreen b 1963); *Career* graduate engr Mobil Oil Co 1958–60; Ready Mixed Concrete Group: joined 1960, dir UK Ltd and subsidiary cos 1971–95, ret; dir Hall Ham River Ltd 1968–71; pres Inst of Quarrying 1993–94 (chm 1979–81), chm Sand & Gravel Association of Great Britain Ltd 1988–90 (hon vice pres 1996–); memb Verney Ctee on Aggregates 1973–77; FIQ 1978, CEng 1983, MIMechE 1983, FRICS 1989; *Recreations* bridge, gardening; *Clubs* St George's Hill, Claremont Park Golf; *Style—* John Ornsby, Esq; ✉ Northfield House, Northfield Place, Weybridge, Surrey KT13 0RF (☎ 01932 847856)

O'RORKE, His Hon Judge; Richard Charles Colomb; s of Charles Howard Colomb O'Rorke (d 1986), and Jacqueline, *née* Prickett; *b* 4 June 1944; *Educ* Blundell's, Exeter Coll Oxford (open exhibitioner, MA); *m* 1965, Jane Elizabeth Phoebe, da of His Hon Judge Rowe Harding; 3 da (Kate b 1966, Rachel b 1969, Imogen b 1972), 1 s (Owen b 1978); *Career* called to the Bar Inner Temple 1968, in practice 1970–94, recorder (Midland & Oxford Circuit) 1987–94, circuit judge (Midland & Oxford Circuit) 1994–; *Recreations* gardening, Japanese art and culture; *Style—* His Hon Judge O'Rorke; ✉ c/o Midland & Oxford Circuit Office, 2 Newton Street, Birmingham B4 7LU

ORPEN-SMELLIE, Lt-Col Herbert John (Larry); OBE (1980); s of Maj William Archibald Smellie (ka 1940), and Elizabeth Staples, *née* Irwin, MBE (d 1995); *b* 18 Jan 1930; *Educ* Wellington, RMA Sandhurst, Staff Coll Quetta; *m* 6 March 1954, Jean Rackley, da of Abram Rackley Watson, MBE (d 1987); 1 s (Giles b 1959), 1 da (Jane b 1963); *Career* cmmnd Essex Regt 1949 (joined 1948), instr Small Arms Wing Sch of Inf 1952–54, Parachute Regt 1958, Adj 1 Para 1958–59, Staff Coll 1961, chief instr Small Arms Wing Sch of Inf 1977–80, ret 1984; RO III regtl sec 3 Royal Anglian Regt 1984–85, RO II G3 Trg HQ E Dist 1985–88, Maj OC 5 (HSF) Coy 10 Para 1985–90; various GB Teams rifle shooting 1952–96, Capt Army Eight 1968–82; memb Cncl Nat Rifle Assoc 1974–; pres: Essex County Rifle Assoc, SE Essex Branch Parachute Regt Assoc, Colchester Branch RBL; govr local sch; *Recreations* rifle shooting; *Style—* Lt-Col H J Orpen-Smellie, OBE

ORR, Craig Smith; *b* 4 Sept 1945; *Educ* Univ of Aberdeen (MA); *Career* asst ed Evening News until 1975, night ed and Scot exec ed Daily Express 1975–85, asst ed You Magazine 1985–86, managing ed Evening Standard 1986–96, exec ed Associated Electronic Publishing 1996–; *Recreations* working, sailing, films, talking to women; *Style—* Craig Orr, Esq; ✉ Associated Electronic Publishing, Northcliffe House, 2 Derry St, Kensington, London W8 5EE (☎ 0171 938 6000)

ORR, Sir David Alexander; kt (1977), MC (and Bar 1945); s of Canon Adrian William Fielder Orr (1964), of Dublin, and Grace, *née* Robinson (d 1967); *b* 10 May 1922; *Educ* Dublin HS, Trinity Coll Dublin (BA, LLB); *m* 1949, Phoebe Rosaleen, da of Harold Percival Davis (d 1980, late Indian Forest Service), of Dublin; 3 da (Catherine, Bridget, Paula); *Career* served WWII RE; Unilever plc: joined 1948, dir 1967–82, chm 1974–82; vice chm Unilever NV 1974–82; chm: Leverhulme Trust 1982–91 (tstee 1974–91), Armed Forces Pay Review Bd 1982–84; chm Inchcape plc 1983–86 and 1991–92 (dep chm 1986–91); non-exec dir: Rio Tinto Zinc 1981–92, Shell Transport 1982–92, CIBA-Geigy UK 1982–90, Bank of Ireland (memb Ct 1982–90); pres Liverpool Sch of Tropical Medicine 1981–89 (vice pres 1989–), chm Br Cncl 1985–92, pres The Children's Med Charity 1991–; pres Coll of Speech and Language Therapists 1991–95, chm The Shakespeare Globe Tst 1985–92; chllr Queen's Univ Belfast 1991–; Hon LLD: Univ of Dublin, Univ of Liverpool, Queen's Univ Belfast, Nat Univ of Ireland; Hon DUniv Surrey; Cdr Order of Orange Nassau 1979; FRSA; *Recreations* travel, golf, theatre; *Style—* Sir David Orr, MC; ✉ Home Farm House, Shackleford, Godalming, Surrey GU8 6AH (☎ 01483 810350); 81 Lyall Mews West, London SW1 (☎ 0171 235 7970); c/o Unilever plc, Unilever House, Blackfriars, London EC4P 4BQ

ORR, Deborah Jane; da of John Scott Orr, of Motherwell, and Winifred Meta, *née* Avis; *b* 23 Sept 1962; *Educ* Garrion Acad Wishaw, Univ of St Andrews (MA); *Career* dep ed City Limits magazine and contrib New Statesman until 1990, ed Guardian Weekend 1993– (joined The Guardian 1990); *Style—* Ms Deborah Orr; ✉ The Guardian, 119 Farringdon Road, London EC1R 3ER (☎ 0171 239 9826)

ORR, Gordon Inglis; s of John Inglis Orr (d 1993), of Broughty Ferry, Scotland, and Doris May, *née* Hoyle (d 1959); *b* 13 Dec 1946; *Educ* Audely Park Sch S Devon, S Devon Coll of Art (RSA bursary), Kingston Coll of Art (BA); *m* 1981, Susan Mary, yst da of James Hervey Hall; 1 da (Jenny Susanah Inglis b 1982), 1 s (Jonathon Inglis b 1985); *Career* interior designer Conran Design Group 1970–73, creative dir (interior design) Shuttleworth Farmer Orr Design Consultants 1973–76 (projects incl creation of Virgin Records retail chain), md Shuttleworth Orr Design Consultants London and Maclaren Orr Design Consultants Edinburgh 1976–83, creative dir (interiors) DIA Interiors (Lopex Group) 1984–86, jt md Sparkes Orr Design Consultants London 1986– (devpt of subsid companies Lighting Design House, Swain Communications and Rawcliffe & Associates since 1992), chm Robson Design Associates Bristol 1990–95; major design projects incl: Somerfield (new trading concept of Gateway) 1989–90 (winner Retail Environments category Design Week Awards 1991), Dales (new discount trading concept for Asda) 1992–93, Shoe Express (new discount trading concept for BSC) 1993; FRSA 1966, FInstD 1978; *Recreations* sailing, opera, Scottish country dance; *Style—* Gordon Orr, Esq; ✉ Elmhora, Upnor, Rochester, Kent ME2 4XE; Sparkes Orr Design Consultants Ltd, 1b Church Road, Croydon, Surrey CR0 1SG (☎ 0181 688 7499, fax 0181 688 7490)

ORR, Prof Robert Kemsley (Robin); CBE (1972); s of Robert Workman Orr (d 1942), and Florence Mary, *née* Kemsley (d 1943); *b* 2 June 1909; *Educ* Loretto Sch, RCM, Pembroke Coll Cambridge (MA, MusD); *m* 1, 1937 (m dis 1979), Margaret Ellen, da of late A C Mace; 1 s (David b 1940), 2 da (Alison (twin) b 1940, Jean b 1945 d 1995); m 2, 1979, Doris Ruth Orr, da of Leo Meyer-Bechtler (d 1977), of Zürich; *Career* Nat Serv RAFVR 1941–45, Flt Lt; composer; organist St John's Cambridge 1938–51, lectr Cambridge 1947–56; prof RCM 1950–56; prof of music: Univ of Glasgow 1956–65, Univ of Cambridge 1965–76 (emeritus 1976–); chm Scottish Opera 1962–76, dir Welsh Nat Opera 1977–83; fell St John's Coll Cambridge 1948–56 and 1965–76 (hon fell 1987–), hon fell Pembroke Coll Cambridge 1988–; Hon DMus Univ of Glasgow, Hon LLD Univ of Dundee; Freeman Worshipful Co of Musicians; FRCM, FRSAMD, Hon RAM; *Operas* Full Circle (1 act - 30 performances on TV and radio 1968–69), Hermiston (3 acts - Edinburgh Festival 1975), On The Razzle (3 acts - RSAMD cmmn and premiere Glasgow 1988), 3 Lyric Pieces for piano (Arts Cncl of England cmmn 1994); *Other compositions* incl: Oedipus at Colonus (Cambridge 1950), Rhapsody for String Orch (English Chamber Orch 1967), Symphony in One Movement (Edinburgh Festival 1965), Symphony No 2 (Edinburgh Festival 1975), Symphony No 3 (Llandaff Festival 1978), Sinfonietta Helvetica (BBC cmmn Glasgow 1991); *Recreations* gardening, mountain walks; *Style—* Prof Robin Orr, CBE; ✉ 16 Cranmer Rd, Cambridge CB3 9BL (☎ 01223 352858)

ORR EWING, Archibald Donald; s and h of Sir Ronald Archibald Orr Ewing, 5 Bt, *qv*; *b* 20 Dec 1938; *Educ* Gordonstoun, Trinity Coll Dublin (BA); *m* 1, 1965 (m dis 1972), Venetia Elizabeth, da of Maj Richard Turner; m 2, 1972, Nicola Jean-Anne, da of Reginald Baron (Barry) Black (d 1996), of Brook House, Fovant, nr Salisbury, Wiltshire, and (Eloise) Jean Horatia, *née* Innes-Ker, niece of 8 Duke of Roxburghe; 1 s (Alastair Frederick Archibald b 26 May 1982); *Career* landowner; memb Royal Co of Archers (Queen's Body Guard for Scotland); *Recreations* shooting, fishing, stalking, opera, theatre; *Clubs* New (Edinburgh), Pratt's; *Style—* Archibald Orr Ewing, Esq; ✉ 13 Warriston Cres, Edinburgh EH3 5LA (☎ 0131 556 9319)

ORR EWING, Maj Edward Stuart; s of Capt David Orr Ewing, DSO, DL (d 1964, s of Charles Orr Ewing, MP Ayr, 5 s of Sir Archibald Orr Ewing, 1 Bt), and Mary, da of late Benjamin Noaks, of Nylstroom, SA; *b* 28 Sept 1931; *Educ* Sherborne; *m* 1, 1958 (m dis 1981), Fiona Anne Bowman, da of Anthony Hobart Farquhar, of Hastingwood House (*see* Burke's Landed Gentry 18th edn 1965); 1 s (Alastair b 1964) 2 da (Jane b 1961, Victoria b 1962); m 2, 1981, Diana Mary, da of William Smith Waters, OBE, of Greenfoot, Dalston, Cumbria; *Career* serv The Black Watch 1950–69, Maj; landowner and farmer 1969–; Lord Lt Wigtown 1989– (DL 1970); *Recreations* country pursuits; *Clubs* New (Edinburgh); *Style—* Major Edward Orr Ewing; ✉ Dunskey, Portpatrick, Wigtownshire (☎ 0177 681 211)

ORR-EWING, Baron (Life Peer UK 1971), of Little Berkhamsted, Co Hertford; Sir (Charles) Ian Orr-Ewing; 1 Bt (UK 1963), OBE (Mil 1945); s of Archibald Ian Orr-Ewing (d 1942), and Gertrude Bertha, *née* Runge; *b* 10 Feb 1912; *Educ* Harrow, Trinity Coll Oxford (MA); *m* 1939, Joan Helen Veronica, da of William Gordon McMinnies (d 1982), of Stoke Orchard, nr Cheltenham; 4 s (Hon Simon, Hon Colin, Hon Malcolm, Hon Robert); *Heir* to Btcy only, s, Hon (Alistair) Simon Orr-Ewing; *Career* sits as Cons peer in House of Lords; serv WWII RAF, Wing Cdr 1941, Radar Branch, served N Africa and Italy 1943, chief radar offr Gen Eisenhower's Staff 1944–45; graduate apprentice EMI 1934–37, employed BBC TV 1937–39 and as dir Outside Bdcasts 1946–49; MP (C) Hendon N 1950–70; PPS to Min of Lab 1951–55, Parly under sec Air Miny 1957–59, Parly and fin sec to Admty 1959, civil lord of the Admty 1959–63; a vice chm Cons 1922 Ctee 1966–70, vice chm Assoc of Cons Peers 1978–86; chm: Ultra Electric Holdings 1965–79, Clayton Dewandre Ltd; dir: Carl Byoir plc 1977–86, Hill & Knowlton 1986–88, MK Holdings 1977–83, Dowty 1978–82; chm Metrication Bd 1972–77; pres: Harrow Wanderers 1983–92, Harrow Assoc 1986–87; pres Lords and Commons Cricket 1992– (vice pres 1988–92), fndr and pres Lords and Commons Ski Club; CEng, FIEE; *Books* A Celebration of Lords and Commons Cricket 1850–1988 (1989); *Recreations* tennis, cricket, skiing; *Clubs* Boodle's, MCC, Vincent's (Oxford), All England LTC (Wimbledon); *Style—* The Rt Hon Lord Orr-Ewing, OBE; ✉ 6 Caroline Terrace, London SW1W 8JS

ORR EWING, Maj Sir Ronald Archibald; 5 Bt (UK 1886), of Ballikinrain, Stirlingshire, and Lennoxbank, Co Dunbarton, JP (Perth 1956), DL (1963); s of Brig-Gen Sir Norman Archibald Orr Ewing, 4 Bt, CB, DSO (d 1960), and Laura Louisa, *née* Robarts (d 1968); *b* 14 May 1912; *Educ* Eton, RMC Sandhurst; *m* 6 April 1938, Marion Hester, da of late Col Sir Donald Walter Cameron of Lochiel, KT, CMG, and Lady Hermione Graham, da of 5 Duke of Montrose, KT; 2 s (Archibald Donald, *qv*, Ronald James (Jamie) b 9 Jan 1948), 2 da (Janet Elizabeth (Mrs John M Wallace) b 9 Nov 1940, Fiona Marion (Mrs Adrian P Drewe) b 3 March 1946); *Heir* s, Archibald Donald Orr Ewing, *qv*; *Career* Scots Guards 1932–53, ret as Maj; serv WWII, Middle E (POW 1942–45); memb Queen's Body Guard for Scotland (Royal Co of Archers); Grand Master Mason of Scotland 1965–69; *Recreations* travel, forestry; *Style—* Maj Sir Ronald Orr Ewing, Bt, JP, DL; ✉ Cardross, Kippen, Stirling FK8 3JY (☎ 01877 385220)

ORR-EWING, Hon (Alistair) Simon; eldest s of Baron Orr-Ewing, OBE (Life Peer and 1 Bt), *qv*; h to baronetcy; *b* 10 June 1940; *Educ* Harrow, Trinity Coll Oxford (MA); *m* 1968, Victoria, da of Keith Cameron (d 1981), of Fifield House, Oxon; 2 s (Archie Cameron b 1969, James Alexander b 1971), 1 da (Georgina Victoria b 1974); *Career* chartered surveyor; cncllr Royal Borough of Kensington and Chelsea 1982–90, chm Town Planning Ctee 1986–88; Lloyd's underwriter 1986–; FRICS; *Recreations* skiing, tennis, shooting; *Clubs* MCC, Boodle's; *Style—* The Hon Simon Orr-Ewing; ✉ 29 St James's Gardens, London W11 4RF (☎ 0171 602 4513)

ORRELL, His Hon Judge; James Francis Freestone; s of Francis Orrell (d 1994), of Rangemore, Staffordshire, and Marion Margaret, *née* Freestone (d 1988); *b* 19 March 1944; *Educ* Ratcliffe Coll, Univ of York (BA); *m* 1 Aug 1970, Margaret Catherine, da of Albert Bernard Benedict Hawcroft, of Derby; 2 s (James Benedict John b 27 Nov 1971, Patrick George Francis b 22 Jan 1981); *Career* called to the Bar Gray's Inn 1968, in practice Midland & Oxford Circuit 1969–89, recorder 1988–89, circuit judge (Midland and Oxford Circuit) 1989–; *Recreations* walking, reading; *Style*— His Hon Judge Orrell; ✉ c/o Derby Combined Court Centre, The Morledge, Derby DE1 2XE (☎ 01332 31841)

ORSON, Rasin Ward; CBE (1985); s of Rasin Nelson Orson, and Blanche, *née* Hyre; *b* 16 April 1927; *Educ* Stratford GS, LSE (BSc); *m* 1, 1950, Marie Goodenough; 2 s; m 2, 1979, Lesley Jean Vallance; *Career* memb The Electricity Cncl 1976–88; dir Chloride Silent Power Ltd 1974–88; companion IEE; *Style*— Rasin Orson, Esq, CBE; ✉ The Old Garden, Dunorlan Park, Tunbridge Wells TN2 3QA (☎ 01892 524027)

OSBORN, Fuller Mansfield; CBE (1972), DL (1975); s of Fuller Mansfield Osborn; *b* 1915; *Educ* Grocers' Co Sch Hackney Downs; *m* 1949, Mary Armstrong, da of William James Auld; *Career* WWII Maj RA SEAC; chm Northern Rock Building Soc 1982–87 (md 1949–78); chm: Northern Region Advsy Ctee of Land Cmmn, Newcastle upon Tyne Abbeyfield Soc 1959– (memb NE Regn), Cncl Bldg Socs Assoc 1969–71, Northern Rock Housing Tst 1986–91; pres: Euro Fedn of Bldg Socs 1979–82, Chartered Bldg Socs Inst 1984–85; memb Northern Econ Planning Cncl 1969–78, dep chm Washington New Town Corp 1973–88, memb Ct Univ of Newcastle upon Tyne; High Sheriff Tyne and Wear 1974–75; *Recreations* golf, beagling, cricket; *Clubs* Northern Counties (Newcastle upon Tyne); *Style*— Fuller Osborn Esq, CBE, DL; ✉ Arundel, 9 Furzefield Rd, Gosforth, Newcastle upon Tyne NE3 4EA (☎ 0191 285 7703; office: 0191 285 7191)

OSBORN, Sir John Holbrook; kt (1983); s of Samuel Eric Osborn (d 1951), and Aileen Decima (d 1994 in her 101st year), da of Col Sir Arthur Holbrook, KBE, MP (d 1946); *b* 14 Dec 1922; *Educ* Rugby, Trinity Hall Cambridge (MA), Nat Foundry Coll; *m* 1, 1952 (m dis), Molly Suzanne, *née* Marten; 2 da (Sallie, Rachel); m 2, 1976, Joan Mary MacDermot, *née* Wilkinson (d 1989); m 3, 1989, Patricia Felicity, *née* Read; *Career* RCS 1943–47, served Capt W Africa; RA TA 1948–1955, Maj; joined Samuel Osborn & Co Ltd 1947 (co founded by ggf Samuel Osborn): asst works mangr, prodn controller, cost controller in foundry and engrg subsid, dir Samuel Osborn and subsids 1951–79, gen mangr new precision casting foundry 1954–59; MP (Nat Lib and Unionist until 1964, whereafter C) Sheffield Hallam 1959–87; PPS to Sec of State for Cwlth Relations and Colonies (Duncan-Sandys) 1963–64, MEP 1975–79, hon assoc and former memb Assembly Cncl Europe and Western Euro Union 1973–75 and 1980–87, life memb Sheffield C of C; former memb: Assoc of Br C of C, CBI (Yorks and Humberside); memb: IOD, Exec Nat Union Cons Pty 1970–87 (jt hon sec 1922 Ctee 1968–87); vice chm Cons Energy Ctee 1979–81, chm Cons Tport Ctee and All-Pty Road Study Gp 1970–74, life memb (former offr and vice pres) Parly and Scientific Ctee 1960–87, memb Select Ctee on Sci and Technol 1970–73, sr (C) memb Select Ctee for Educn Sci and the Arts 1979–83, life memb and former chm Parly Gp for Energy Studies 1985–87; memb Cncl Br Branch Inter-Parly Union 1968–75 (now life memb); life memb Cwlth Parly Assoc; former chm Anglo-Swiss Parly Gp and Br Soviet Parly Gp; chm: All Pty Channel Tunnel Gp 1984–87, Friends of Progress 1990–94, Business In Devpt Ctee UK Chapter Soc of Int Devpt 1990–94; former memb Interim (formerly Voluntary) Licensing Authy 1987–91, hon life memb Industl Soc (memb Cncl 1963–79); Freeman (former Searcher) Cutlers' Co Hallamshire; FIM, FRSA; *Publications* Change or Decay; *Recreations* golf, tennis, photography, gardening, skiing; *Style*— Sir John Osborn; ✉ Newlands, 147 Hawton Road, Newark, Notts NG24 4QG

OSBORN, Neil Frank; s of George James Osborn, of Hemel Hempstead, and Georgina Rose, *née* Nash; *b* 24 Oct 1949; *Educ* St Albans Sch, Worcester Coll Oxford (MA); *m* 15 April 1975, Holly Louise, da of Lt-Col George Francis Smith, of McLean, Virginia, USA; *Career* reporter The Daily Progress Charlottesville Va USA 1972–74, freelance reporter Lloyd's List and Liverpool Daily Post 1975–77, sr ed Institutional Investor NY 1978–83, US ed Euromoney NY 1983–85, ed Euromoney London 1985–90, publisher Euromoney 1990–; dir: Euromoney Inc 1985–, Euromoney Publications plc 1988–; memb Exec Bd Family Welfare Assoc 1994–; *Style*— Neil Osborn, Esq; ✉ Flat 4, 16 Wetherby Gdns, London SW5 0JP; Euromoney Publications plc, Nestor House, Playhouse Yard, London EC4V 5EX (☎ 0171 779 8888, fax 0171 779 8653, telex 2907003 EUROMO G)

OSBORN, Sir Richard Henry Danvers; 9 Bt (E 1662), of Chicksands, Bedfordshire; s of Sir Danvers Lionel Rouse Osborn, 8 Bt (d 1983), and Constance Violette, *née* Rooke (d 1988); *b* 12 Aug 1958; *Educ* Eton; *Heir* kinsman, William Danvers Osborn, *qv*; *Career* Christie's 1978–83, ind fine paintings conslt P & D Colnaghi Ltd 1984–87, dir Paul Mitchell Ltd (antique framing and picture conservation business); *Recreations* real tennis, shooting, racing; *Clubs* Turf, MCC, Queen's, Pratt's; *Style*— Sir Richard Osborn, Bt; ✉ 25 Queen's Gardens, London W2 3BD

OSBORN, William Danvers; s of Danvers Osborn (d 1929), and Inez (d 1953), da of Henry Smith, of Victoria BC; hp of kinsman Sir Richard Henry Danvers Osborn, 9 Bt, *qv*; assumed names of William Danvers in lieu of christian names George Schomberg 1936; 1 Bt received Baronetcy in recognition of all the family had suffered in the cause of Charles I 1662, 3 Bt altered spelling of family name from Osborne to avoid confusion with the family of the Duke of Leeds. He was govr of NY and d there 1753; *b* 4 June 1909; *m* 1939, Jean Burns, da of R B Hutchinson, of Vancouver, BC; 1 da (Cheryl Elizabeth b 1945); *Style*— William Osborn, Esq

OSBORNE, Charles Thomas; s of Vincent Lloyd Osborne; *b* 24 Nov 1927; *Educ* Brisbane State HS; *m* 1970 (m dis 1975), Marie Korbelarova; *Career* author; lit dir Arts Cncl of GB 1971–86, chief theatre critic Daily Telegraph 1987–91; memb: PEN, Royal Philharmonic Soc; Hon DUniv Griffith Univ Brisbane Australia; FRSL 1996; *Books* The Complete Operas of Verdi (1969), The Concert Song Companion (1974), Wagner and His World (1977), The Complete Operas of Mozart (1978), W H Auden - the Life of a Poet (1979), The Complete Operas of Puccini (1981), Dictionary of the Opera (1983), Giving It Away - memoirs (1986), Verdi: a Life in the Theatre (1987), The Complete Operas of Richard Strauss (1988), The Complete Operas of Richard Wagner (1990), The Bel Canto Operas (1994); *Recreations* travel; *Clubs* Savile; *Style*— Charles Osborne, Esq, FRSL; ✉ 125 St George's Road, London SE1 6HY (☎ 0171 928 1534, fax 0171 401 9099)

OSBORNE, David Francis; s of William Henry Osborne (d 1969), of Surrey, and Beatrice Irene, *née* Hinge; *b* 24 Oct 1937; *Educ* Dulwich, Jesus Coll Oxford (MA); *children* 1 s (Martin b 1965), 2 da (Katharine b 1967, Juliet b 1968); *Career* Unilever Ltd 1960–66, PA International Management Consultants 1966–82, Hill Samuel & Co Ltd 1982–87, dir Electra Fleming Ltd 1987–; MIMgt, MICMA, MIMC; *Recreations* cricket, golf, reading, travel, languages, opera, bridge; *Clubs* MCC, United Oxford and Cambridge Univ; *Style*— David Osborne, Esq; ✉ Mayflower Cottage, Lower Assendon, Oxon RG9 6AH (☎ 01491 572004); Electra Fleming Ltd, 65 Kingsway, London WC2B 6QT (☎ 0171 831 6464, fax 0171 831 8014)

OSBORNE, Dr Denis Gordon; CMG (1990); s of Alfred Gordon Osborne, of Wooburn Common, Bucks, and Frances Agnes Osborne; *b* 17 Sept 1932; *Educ* Dr Challoner's GS Amersham Bucks, Univ of Durham (BSc, PhD); *m* 16 May 1970, Christine Susannah, da of Percy Rae Shepherd (d 1987); 2 da (Ruth b 1971, Sally b 1973); *Career* lectr in physics: Univ of Durham 1957, Fourah Bay Coll Freetown SA 1958, Univ of Ghana 1958–64; dean of sci Univ of Dar es Salaam 1968–70 (reader in physics 1964–66, prof of physics 1966–71), conslt World Bank Malaysia 1971 and Ethiopia 1972, res fell in physics UCL 1971–72; ODA London: princ 1972–80, asst sec natural resources 1980–84, asst sec Eastern and Western Africa 1984–87; High Cmmr in Malawi 1987–90; research advsr RIPA International 1990–; conslt and advsr on governance and development 1992–; reader St Barnabas Church Dulwich; author of papers on geophysics, technol, educn and devpt; govr Dulwich Coll Prep Sch; CPhys, FInstP 1966; *Books* Way Out: Some Parables of Science and Faith (1977); *Recreations* reading, writing, attempts at windsurfing; *Clubs* Athenaeum; *Style*— Dr Denis Osborne, CMG; ✉ 112 Dulwich Village, London SE21 7AQ (☎ 0181 693 7100, fax 0181 693 0906)

OSBORNE, Douglas Leonard; s of Leonard Osborne (d 1947), of Lincoln, and Gladys Ellen, *née* Ward; *b* 19 Oct 1940; *Educ* Royal Masonic Schs; *m* 22 March 1969, Barbara Helen, da of Ronald Bartrop; 1 s (Daniel James b 25 June 1972), 1 da (Emma Jane b 27 Aug 1974); *Career* Action for Blind People (formerly London Assoc for the Blind): asst sec 1965–76, dep dir 1976–79, dir 1979–83; exec dir Leukaemia Res Fund 1989– (admin 1983–89); dep chm Charities' Panel ICSA, memb Cncl Metropolitan Soc for the Blind; FCIS 1985 (ACIS 1967); *Books* Charities Administration (ed jtly, 1986, Supplements 1–16 1996); *Recreations* music, rugby football, swimming, cooking; *Style*— Douglas Osborne, Esq; ✉ Leukaemia Research Fund, 43 Great Ormond St, London WC1N 3JJ (☎ 0171 405 0101, fax 0171 405 3139)

OSBORNE, Prof John; s of Leonard Osborne (d 1947), and Gladys Ellen, *née* Ward; *b* 31 Dec 1938; *Educ* Royal Masonic Sch, Univ Coll Swansea (BA), Univ of Munich, Univ of Cambridge (PhD); *m* 7 Sept 1962, Janet Elizabeth, da of Alan George Hart, of Hove, Sussex; 1 s (Luke b 1979), 3 da (Helen b 1966, Josephine b 1968, Mary b 1975); *Career* lectr in German Univ of Southampton 1965–68, lectr and reader in German Univ of Sussex 1968–79, prof of German Univ of Warwick 1979–; Alexander von Humboldt res fell Univ of Göttingen 1972–73, 1976–77 and 1992, visiting prof Univ of Metz 1985–86; memb Cncl English Goethe Soc; DLitt Univ of Wales 1995; *Books* The Naturalist Drama in Germany (1971), J M R Lenz: The Renunciation of Heroism (1975), Die Meininger: Texte zur Rezeption (1980), Meyer or Fontane? (1983), The Meiningen Court Theatre (1988), Vom Nutzen der Geschichte (1994); *Recreations* listening to music, travel, swimming; *Style*— Prof John Osborne; ✉ 30 Waverley Rd, Kenilworth, Warwickshire CV8 1JN (☎ 01926 512126); Department of German Studies, University of Warwick, Coventry CV4 7AL (☎ 01203 524419)

OSBORNE, Col John Lander; CBE (1969, MBE 1943), TD (1947), DL (W Midlands 1975); s of Frank John Osborne, MC (d 1959), of Solihull, W Midlands, and Ida Marie, *née* Lander (d 1972); *b* 30 June 1917; *Educ* Solihull Sch, Villiars (Switzerland), Birmingham Sch of Architecture; *m* 1, 1942, Kate Honour (d 1980), da of Col Duncan Cameron, of Glasgow and Rawalpindi (d 1929); 1 da; m 2, 1981, Phyllis Mary Tipper, da of Harold Dyas James, of Little Aston, W Midlands (d 1964); *Career* WWII Lt-Col BEF Belgium and France 1939–40; served 1942–46: N Africa, Middle E, Sicily, Italy (despatches 1940, 1944 and 1945); rejoined TA 1947, Regt Cdr RE 1950–57, chief engr W Mids Dist 1958–66, Hon Col 48 Div Engrs 1957–66, ADC to HM The Queen 1968–72; ptnr The John Osborne Partnership Chartered Architects 1947–82, conslt 1982–87; pres Birmingham and Five Counties Architectural Assoc 1962–64; chm W Midlands Regn RIBA 1970–72; *Recreations* sailing, skiing, golf, horticulture; *Clubs* Army and Navy, Royal Thames Yacht, Birmingham, Little Aston Golf; *Style*— Col John Osborne, CBE, TD, DL; ✉ Maidenwell, Broad Campden, Chipping Campden, Glos GL55 6UR (☎ 01386 840772)

OSBORNE, John Leslie; s of Frederick James Osborne, of Lampeter, Wales, and May Doris, *née* Brown; *b* 20 March 1942; *Educ* The London Hosp Med Coll Univ of London (MB BS); *children* 2 s (Andrew b 1972, James b 1979), 2 da (Clare b 1969, Julia b 1981); *Career* lectr in obstetrics and gynaecology Inst of Obstetrics and Gynaecology 1974–79, conslt obstetrician and gynaecologist Queen Charlotte's and Chelsea Hosp for Women and combined Univ Coll and Middx Hosp 1979–; hon sr lectr: Inst of Urology, Inst of Obstetrics and Gynaecology; Freeman Worshipful Soc Apothecaries; FRCOG 1985 (MRCOG 1973), memb RSM; *Recreations* music, photography, old cars (Bentley); *Clubs* Bentley Drivers'; *Style*— John Osborne, Esq; ✉ 77 Harley House, Marylebone Road, London NW1 5HN (☎ 0171 935 1682)

OSBORNE, John Michael; s of Claudius Hase Osborne, and Irene Oliver, *née* Chaffé; *b* 30 Oct 1953; *Educ* Whitchurch GS, Univ of Sheffield (BSc); *m* 2 July 1983, Helen Elizabeth, da of Richard Derek Gommo; 1 da (Claire Hannah b 11 April 1986), 1 s (Nicholas John b 14 April 1988); *Career* Equity & Law (now AXA Equity & Law): joined 1975, devpt mangr 1986–86, planning mangr 1986–88, mangr Equity & Law Home Loans 1988–92, mangr and dir Equity & Law Unit Trust 1990–, actuary 1990–92, head of business devpt 1992–; FIA 1981; *Recreations* golf; *Style*— John Osborne, Esq; ✉ AXA Equity & Law, Amersham Road, High Wycombe, Bucks HP13 5AL (☎ 01494 466288)

OSBORNE, The Honourable Lord; Kenneth Hilton Osborne; QC (Scot) 1976; s of Kenneth Osborne and Evelyn Alice, *née* Hilton; *b* 9 July 1937; *Educ* Larchfield Sch Helensburgh, Merchiston Castle Sch Edinburgh, Univ of Edinburgh; *m* 1964, Clare Ann Louise Lewis; 1 s, 1 da; *Career* admitted to Faculty of Advocates in Scotland 1962, chm Local Govt Boundary Cmmn for Scot 1990–; chm: Disciplinary Ctee Potato Mktg Bd 1975–90, Legal Aid Ctee Supreme Ct 1979–81; advocate-depute 1982–84; pt/t legal memb Lands Tbnl for Scot 1985–87, chm Med Appeal Tbnls Scot 1988–90, sen Coll of Justice in Scot 1990–; standing jr counsel to Min of Def (Navy) in Scot 1974–76; *Clubs* New (Edinburgh); *Style*— The Honourable Lord Osborne, QC; ✉ 42 India St, Edinburgh EH3 6HB (☎ 0131 225 3094); Primrose Cottage, Bridgend of Lintrathen, by Kirriemuir, Angus DD8 5JH (☎ 01575 560316)

OSBORNE, Sir Peter George; 17 Bt (I 1629), of Ballintaylor, Co Tipperary; s of Lt-Col Sir George Francis Osborne, 16 Bt, MC (d 1960), and Mary, *née* Horn (d 1987); Richard Osborne cr 1 Bt of Ireland 1629, and supported Parl against the crown; 2, 7, 8, 9 and 11 Bts were MPs (8 Bt, PC); *b* 29 June 1943; *Educ* Wellington, Ch Ch Oxford; *m* 1968, Felicity, da of late Grantley Loxton-Peacock; 4 s (George Gideon Oliver b 1971, Benedict George b 1973, Adam Peter b 1976, Theo Grantley b 1985); *Heir* s, George Gideon Oliver Osborne b 23 May 1971; *Career* chm Osborne & Little plc; *Clubs* White's; *Style*— Sir Peter Osborne, Bt; ✉ 21 St Petersburgh Place, London W2; Vinnicks, Highclere, nr Newbury, Berks

OSBORNE, Richard Ellerker; s of William Harold Osborne (d 1984), and Georgina Mary, *née* Farrow; *b* 22 Feb 1943; *Educ* Worksop Coll, Univ of Bristol (BA, MLitt); *m* 18 Jan 1986, Hailz-Emily, da of Michael Ewart Wrigley, of Streetly, W Midlands; 1 s (Harry George Ellerker b 6 May 1992); *Career* head of English Bradfield Coll Berks 1982–88 (teacher 1967–88, head 6th form gen studies 1979–88); contrib: Records and Recording 1967–73, Gramophone 1974–, Opera, The Spectator, Times Literary Supplement; music critic The Oldie; presenter BBC Radio 3 Record Review 1988–; chm Music Section Critics' Circle 1984–87; *Books* Rossini (1986), Conversations with Karajan (1989); *Recreations* cooking, fell walking; *Style*— Richard Osborne, Esq; ✉ Old Rectory, Bradfield, Berks RG7 6AY (☎ and fax 0118 9744395)

OSBORNE, Robert (Bob); s of Walter Richard Osborne and Maud Osborne; *b* 18 April 1948; *Educ* Sedgehill Sch London, Univ of Warwick (BSc), Imperial Coll London (MSc, DIC); *m* 1970, Madeline, *née* Chatterton; 2 da (Tamsin b 20 March 1978, Jessica b 22 July 1982); *Career* dir Moon Enterprises (concert promotions) 1970, teacher 1970–71, commissioning ed mathematics and science Penguin Education 1971–74, commissioning ed rising to dep md Hutchinson Educational 1974–84, publishing dir then dep md Heinemann Educational Books 1984–88, md Heinemann Educational 1988–; FRSA 1988; *Recreations* music, sailing; *Style*— Bob Osborne; ✉ Heinemann Educational, Halley Court, Oxford 0X2 8EJ (☎ 01865 314120)

OSERS, Dr Ewald; s of Paul Osers (d 1923), of Prague, and Fini, *née* Anders (d 1942); *b* 13 May 1917; *Educ* schs in Prague Czechoslovakia, Prague Univ, Univ of London (BA);

m 3 June 1941, Mary, da of Arthur Harman (d 1959); 1 s (Richard b 1951), 1 da (Ann Margaret b 1947); *Career* translator/writer; BBC 1939–77, chm Translators' Assoc 1971, 1980–81 and 1983–84, chm Translators' Guild 1975–79; vice pres Int Fedn of Translators 1977–81 and 1984–87; Schlegel-Tieck Prize 1971, CB Nathhorst Prize 1977, Josef Dobrovsky Medal 1980, Gold Pin of Honour of the German Translators' Assoc, Silver Pegasus of the Bulgarian Writers' Union 1983, Dilia Medal Czechoslovakia 1986, European Poetry Translation Prize 1987, Vitezslav Nezval Medal of the Czech Literary Fndn 1987, P-F Caillé Medal 1987, Golden Pen of the Macedonian Translators' Union 1988, Austrian Translation Prize 1989; Hon PhD Olomouc Univ 1990; Officer's Cross of the Order of Merit of the Federal Republic of Germany 1991; FRSL 1984, FITI; *Books* translator of over 115 books, 33 of them poetry; Wish You Were Here (poems, 1976), Arrive Where We Started (poems, 1995); *Recreations* music, skiing; *Style*— Dr Ewald Osers, FRSL; ✉ 33 Reades Lane, Sonning Common, Reading RG4 9LL (☎ 0113 972 3196, fax 0118 972 4950)

O'SHEA, Chris; s of Frank Christopher Patrick O'Shea, and Lucy Alice O'Shea (d 1990); *b* 5 Dec 1947; *Educ* The Hewett Sch Norwich; *m* 15 Nov 1969, Suzanne, da of Peter Edwards; 2 s (Peter b 7 Dec 1978, Timothy b 23 May 1980), 1 da (Alice b 10 March 1975); *Career* various advtg agencies 1963–75, writer Abbott Mead Vickers 1975–84, copy chief then exec creative dir Lowe Howard-Spink 1984–89, exec creative dir Chiat Day 1989–91, fndr ptnr and creative dir Banks Hoggins O'Shea 1991–; award-winning work for various clients incl Heineken, Cow & Gate and Australian Tourist Cmmn; *Awards* 1 Gold (D&AD), 2 Gold, 2 Silver and 2 Bronze (Cannes), 6 Silver (Campaign Press), 2 Gold, 1 Silver and 3 Bronze (BTA), 2 Silver (Campaign Poster Awards), 1 Gold (Br Cinema Awards), 7 Gold (Clio), 2 Gold, 1 Silver and 2 Bronze (Creative Circle), 2 Gold (Int Bdcasting Awards), 5 Gold (Int Festival NY), 2 Gold (Eurobest Awards), 2 Gold (Irish TV Festival), 1 Silver (One Show Awards); *Recreations* family and sleeping; *Style*— Chris O'Shea; ✉ Banks Hoggins O'Shea, 54 Baker Street, London W1M 1DJ (☎ 0171 314 0000, fax 0171 314 0001)

O'SHEA, Prof Michael Roland; s of Capt Jack Arthur O'Shea, and Ellen, *née* Hughes; *b* 5 April 1947; *Educ* Forest Hill Sch London, Univ of Leicester (BSc), Univ of Southampton (PhD); *m* 1977 (m dis 1991), Barbara, *née* Moore; 1 da (Linda b 1978 d 1990); *Career* Univ of Calif Berkeley: NATO fell 1971–73, NIH fell 1973–75; SRC fell Univ of Cambridge 1975–77, asst prof Univ of Southern Calif Los Angeles 1977–79, assoc prof Brain Research Inst Univ of Chicago 1979–85, prof of neurobiology Univ of Geneva 1985–88, prof of molecular cell biology Univ of London 1988–91; Univ of Sussex: dir Interdisciplinary Research Centre Sussex Centre for Neuroscience 1991–, dir Centre for Computational Neuroscience and Robotics 1996–; author of numerous papers on neuroscience in learned jls; memb: NSPCC, Soc for Neuroscience; *Recreations* classical music, mountaineering, modern poetry, the public understanding of science, triathlons, restoration of classic Lotus, gardens; *Clubs* Club Lotus; *Style*— Prof Michael O'Shea; ✉ 29 Eldred Avenue, Brighton, East Sussex BN1 5EB; Sussex Centre for Neuroscience, School of Biological Sciences, University of Sussex, Brighton, East Sussex BN1 9QJ (☎ 01273 678055, fax 01273 678535, mobile 0402 069844, e-mail M.O-Shea@sussex.ac.uk)

OSLER, John Murray; s of Peter Alfred George Osler (d 1990), and Estelle Cordiner, *née* Murray (d 1981); *b* 1 March 1937; *Educ* Charterhouse, Gonville and Caius Coll Cambridge (MA); *m* 26 Oct 1963, Pamela Hilary, da of Robert Oliver Scott; 3 s (Jeremy Joseph Scott b 17 Sept 1971, Charles Samuel Scott b 27 July 1981, William Daniel Scott (twin) b 27 July 1981), 1 da (Rosemary Beatrice Scott b 10 Sept 1974); *Career* articled clerk Ryland Martineau & Co Birmingham 1960–63; asst slr: Frere Cholmeley London 1963–67, Stephenson Harwood London 1967–71; ptnr: Herbert Oppenheimer Nathan Vandyk 1972–88 (asst slr 1971), S J Berwin & Co London 1988–; memb: Worshipful Co of Slrs, Law Soc 1963; *Recreations* music, theatre, skiing; *Style*— John Osler, Esq; ✉ S J Berwin & Co, 222 Grays Inn Rd, London WC1X 8HB (☎ 0171 533 2222, fax 0171 533 2000)

OSMAN, David Antony; s of Colin Alfred Earnest Osman, of Cockfosters, Barnet, Herts, and Grace Florence, *née* White; *b* 13 April 1953; *Educ* Minchenden GS, Univ of Nottingham (BA); *m* 4 Sept 1976, Helen, da of Randall Jones-Pugh, of Roch, Dyfed; 2 da (Caroline b 15 Nov 1984, Nicola b 23 Jan 1988); *Career* dir RP Publishing Co Ltd 1975–78 (non-exec dir 1978–95), non-exec dir RP Typesetters Co Ltd 1980–96; UK economist Joseph/Carr Sebag & Co 1978–82, UK and int economist Laing & Cruickshank 1982–84, int economist James Capel & Co 1984–91; stockbroker: Sassoon (Europe) Ltd 1991–92, Smith New Court Far East/Merrill Lynch 1992–; fndr memb Enfield SDP 1981–87, SDP/Lib Alliance Pty candidate for Upminster 1983, vice chm (fndr memb and sec) City SDP 1984–88, fndr and memb Enfield Lib Democrats 1988–; sec City Democratic Forum 1988–89; memb City Lib Democrats 1990–; memb Soc of Business Economists, MSI; *Recreations* chess, cycling, football, golf, snooker; *Clubs* National Liberal, Old Minchendenians Football and Golf Soc; *Style*— David Osman, Esq; ✉ 10 Old Park Ridings, Winchmore Hill, London N21 2EU (☎ 0181 360 4343); Merrill Lynch, 20 Farringdon Road, London EC1M 3NH (☎ 0171 772 1000, fax 0171 772 2927, telex 945754)

OSMAN, Mat; *Career* bassist; fndr memb Suede 1989–; 3 top twenty singles (Metal Mickey 1992, We Are The Pigs 1994, The Wild Ones 1994), 3 top ten singles (Animal Nitrate 1993, Stay Together 1994, Trash 1996); albums: Suede (1993, UK no 1), Dog Man Star (1994), Coming Up (1996, UK no 1); Mercury Music Award 1993; *Style*— Mat Osman, Esq; ✉ c/o Interceptor Enterprises, 98 White Lion Street, London N1 9PF (☎ 0171 278 8001, fax 0171 713 6298)

OSMOND, Sir Douglas; kt (1971), CBE (1968, OBE 1958), QPM (1962); *b* 27 June 1914; *Educ* Univ of London (BSc); *Career* Metropolitan Police 1935, RN 1943, Control Cmmn for Germany 1944; chief constable: Shropshire 1946–62, Hampshire 1962–77; memb Royal Cmmn on Criminal Procedure 1978–81; pres Assoc of Chief Police Offrs 1967–69, chm Police Cncl for UK 1972 and 1974; memb: Bd of Govrs Police Coll 1968–72, Inter Departmental Ctee on Death Certification and Coroners 1964–71; OStJ 1971; *Style*— Sir Douglas Osmond, CBE, QPM, DL; ✉ The Pink House, 25 Broad Street, Alresford, Hants SO24 9AR (☎ 01962 734869)

OSMOND, Lady; Olivia Sybil; *née* Wells; JP (1971); da of Ernest Edward Wells, JP (d 1948), of Kegworth, Leics, and Olivia Maud, *née* Orton (d 1956); *Educ* St Elphin's Sch Darley Dale, Newnham Coll Cambridge (MA, MSc); *m* 5 Feb 1942, Sir Paul Osmond, CB, *qv*; 2 s (Oliver b 1944, Andrew b 1949); *Career* economist and statistician Nat Inst of Econ and Social Res 1938–39, Miny of Econ Warfare 1939–41, FO 1942–44, Int Fedn of Agric Prodrs 1951–60, econ advsr Miny of Health 1967; memb: Br Section Exec European Union of Women 1961–86, Bd of Govrs Bethlem Royal and Maudsley Hosp 1968–82 (vice chm 1980–82), Cncl Cambridge Soc 1980–94 (chm Exec Ctee 1988–91), Cncl Independent Schs Careers Orgn 1986–94; govr St Elphin's Sch 1967–94, Assoc Newnham Coll 1977–90; *Recreations* gardening, travel, theatre; *Clubs* Utd Oxford and Cambridge Univ; *Style*— Lady Osmond, JP; ✉ 20 Beckenham Grove, Shortlands, Bromley, Kent BR2 0JU (☎ 0181 460 2026)

OSMOND, Sir (Stanley) Paul; kt (1980), CB (1966); s of late Stanley C Osmond (d 1966), of Bristol; *b* 13 May 1917; *Educ* Bristol GS, Jesus Coll Oxford; *m* 1942, Olivia Sybil see Lady Osmond, JP, *qv*, da of late Ernest E Wells, JP; 2 s; *Career* WWII Glos Regt and staff 1940–46; Home Civil Serv 1939–75 (private sec to PM 1948–51, under sec 1959–65, dep sec 1965–75); sec to the Church Cmmrs 1975–80; chm Nat Marriage Guidance Cncl 1982–88; Royal Instn: hon treas 1981–86, chm Cncl 1989–92; *Recreations* travel, the theatre; *Clubs* Athenaeum (chm 1992–95); *Style*— Sir Paul Osmond, CB; ✉ 20 Beckenham Grove, Shortlands, Bromley, Kent BR2 0JU (☎ 0181 460 2026)

OSMOTHERLY, Edward Benjamin Crofton; CB (1992); s of Crofton Robert Osmotherly, of London, and Elsie May, *née* Sargent (d 1967); *b* 1 Aug 1942; *Educ* East Ham GS, Fitzwilliam Coll Cambridge (MA); *m* 6 June 1970, Valerie Ann, da of L R Mustill, CBE (d 1984); 1 s (John Nicholas b 1975), 1 da (Clare b 1972); *Career* asst princ Miny of Housing and Local Govt 1963–68 (private sec to Parly Sec and Min of State 1966–68), princ DOE 1968–76, asst sec DOE and Tport 1976–82, dep sec Dept of Tport 1989–93 (under sec 1982–88), chm Cmmn for Local Admin in England 1994–; Harkness fell Brookings Instn USA and exec fell Univ of California Berkeley 1972–73, sec Ctee on Railway Fin 1982; *Recreations* squash, reading; *Style*— Edward Osmotherly, Esq, CB; ✉ Commission for Local Administration in England, 21 Queen Anne's Gate, London SW1

OSTARHILD, Edda Hanna Flora; da of (Hans Herbert) Rudolf Ostarhild (d 1972), of Isle of Wight, and Hilde Franziska, *née* Spitzner-Kuhne (d 1991); *Educ* first degree in journalism Aachen (Germany), Univ of London (MA, CertEd/FE); *m* 1972, Dr Geoffrey Peter Jones; 1 da from previous m (Jasmine Diana Hilde); *Career* International Marketing 1960–65, lectr in mktg Harrow Coll 1965–74, sr/princ lectr Ealing Coll, West London Poly and Thames Valley Univ 1975–91, dir and chief exec Inst of Linguists 1992– (memb and chm Cncl 1986–91); visiting expert DG 13 Euro Cmmn 1976; chief examiner: RSA, Inst of Linguists; memb: Market Research Soc 1970, Bd of Govrs Richmond VIth Form Coll 1976–78, CNAA Postgraduate Panel of Linguistics 1990–92, Standing Conf of Heads of Modern Languages in HE, Univ Cncl for Modern Languages, Nat Cncl for Modern Languages, UK Centre for Euro Educn, Advsy Ctee Languages Lead Body, Nuffield Interpreter Project; convenor Educnl Tst Inst of Linguists 1989–91 (tstee 1988–91); FIL 1962, MInstD 1994; winner Speakers' Club Cup 1995; *Recreations* architecture, antiques, fine art, good food and wine in congenial company; *Clubs* Knightsbridge Speakers', Victorian Soc; *Style*— Ms Edda Ostarhild; ✉ Institute of Linguists, 24A Highbury Grove, London N5 2DQ (☎ 0171 359 7445, fax 0171 354 0202)

OSTELL, Richard John; s of Richard Davies Ostell (d 1990), and Gertrude Alice, *née* Carruthers; *Educ* Ulverston Victoria HS, Carlisle Coll of Art, St Martin's Sch of Art London (BA); *Career* fashion designer; Richard Ostell Ltd 1982–87, freelance working in films and fashion 1987–89, sr design asst Romeo Gigli Milan Italy 1989–90, Flyte Ostell Ltd (with Ellis Flyte, *qv*) 1990–; Fabrex Vyella Award 1985, New Generation Best Designer Award (British Fashion Awards) 1992; *Style*— Richard Ostell, Esq; ✉ Flyte Ostell, 30 Oval Road, Camden, London NW1 7DE (☎ 0171 284 2273, fax 0171 284 4211)

O'SULLEVAN, Peter John; CBE (1991, OBE 1977); s of late Col John Joseph O'Sullevan, DSO; *b* 3 March 1918; *Educ* Hawtreys, Charterhouse, Coll Alpin Switzerland; *m* 1951, Patricia, da of late Frank Duckworth of Manitoba Canada; *Career* racing commentator BBC TV since 1946 incl: Australia, S Africa, Italy, USA; racing corr Daily Express 1950–86; patron: Int League for the Protection of Horses, Brooke Hosp for Animals, Equine Rehabilitation Centre; *Books* Calling The Horses (autiobiog, 1989, on audio cassette 1996); *Recreations* racehorses, travel, reading, art, food and wine, supporting Compassion in World Farming; *Style*— Peter O'Sullevan, Esq, CBE; ✉ 37 Cranmer Court, Sloane Ave, London SW3 3HW (☎ 0171 584 2781)

O'SULLIVAN, Rt Rev Mgr James; CBE (1973, MBE 1963); s of Richard O'Sullivan (d 1957), and Ellen, *née* Ahern (d 1959); *b* 2 Aug 1917; *Educ* St Finnbarr's Coll Cork, All Hallows' Coll Dublin; *Career* cmmnd Royal Army Chaplain's Dept 1942, chaplain 49 Div Normandy 1944, sr chaplain (RC) Malaya 1952–54 (despatches 1953), chaplain Irish Gds 1954–56, princ chaplain MOD 1968–73, officiating chaplain to RAMC and QA Trg Centres 1973–; *Style*— The Rt Rev Mgr James O'Sullivan, CBE; ✉ Osgil, Vicarage Lane, Ropley, Alresford, Hants SO24 0DU

O'SULLIVAN, John Conor; s of James Vincent O'Sullivan (d 1976), of Harley St, London, and Maura O'Connor; *b* 25 Sept 1932; *Educ* Ampleforth, Oriel Coll Oxford (MA), Westminster Hosp Med Sch (BM BCh); *m* 26 April 1958, Maureen, da of Douglas Charles Mitchell (d 1977), of Wembley; 1 s (Hugh b 1966), 3 da (Marika b 1959, Claire b 1960, Catherine b 1962); *Career* Nat Serv RAMC 1960–62, dep asst dir Med Serv HQ London dist, T/Maj 1961; conslt obstetrician and gynaecologist Central Middx Hosp 1974–86, conslt in gynaecological oncology Hammersmith Hosp 1976–84, conslt gynaecologist Cromwell Hosp 1982–, sr lectr Royal Postgrad Sch Inst of Obstetrics and Gynaecology 1984–92; Freeman City of London 1955, Liveryman Worshipful Soc of Apothecaries; FRCS 1967, FRCOG 1983; *Recreations* golf, skiing; *Clubs* Royal Wimbledon Golf; *Style*— John O'Sullivan, Esq; ✉ 96 Arthur Rd, Wimbledon, London SW19 7DT (☎ 0181 946 6242); 8 Pennant Mews, London W8 (☎ 0171 580 6966/ 0171 370 4233, fax 0171 580 6966)

O'SULLIVAN, Michael Joseph; s of Patrick Joseph O'Sullivan, of Birmingham, and Mary Elizabeth, *née* Herbert; *b* 21 Dec 1958; *Educ* St Philip's Coll Birmingham, Univ of Oxford (BA), Univ of Cambridge (MPhil); *m* 17 July 1989, Moira, da of late James McDonald Boyd Grant; 2 da (Kira b 2 Oct 1990, Lara b 1 May 1992), 1 s (James b 23 June 1994); *Career* VSO English teacher Xiangtan China 1982–84; Br Cncl: asst dir Beijing 1987–90, UK corp planner 1991–93, dir S China 1993–; *Style*— Michael O'Sullivan, Esq; ✉ The British Council, South China Office, Room 1202, 255 Hennessey Road, Wanchai, Hong Kong

O'SULLIVAN, Sally Angela da of Albert James Lorraine (d 1995), of Jersey, Channel Islands, and Joan, *née* Crawley (d 1969); *b* 26 July 1949; *Educ* Ancaster House Sch Bexhill-on-Sea, Trinity Coll Dublin; *m* 2 Oct 1980, Charles Martin Wilson; 1 s (Luke b 18 Dec 1981), 1 da (Lily b 21 Aug 1985), 1 step da (Emma b 18 July 1970); *Career* freelance writer 1971–77, dep ed Women's World 1977–78, freelance writer NY 1978–80; women's ed: Daily Record 1980–81, Sunday Standard 1981–82; ed Options, launch ed and originator of Country Homes & Interiors 1986; ed: She 1989, Harpers & Queen 1989–91; ed in chief: Good Housekeeping 1991–95, Ideal Home, Woman & Home, and Homes & Ideas 1995–; Magazine Ed of the Year 1986 and 1994; memb: Bdcasting Standards Cncl 1994–, Nuffield Cncl on Bioethics 1995–, Advsy Cncl on the Misuse of Drugs 1996–; non-exec dir: London Transport 1995–, Anglia Water 1996–; *Books* Things My Mother Never Told Me, Looking Good; *Recreations* spending time with my family, riding; *Style*— Sally O'Sullivan; ✉ IPC Magazines, King's Reach Tower, Stamford Street, London SE1 9LS

O'SULLIVAN, Sonia; da of John O'Sullivan, and Mary, *née* Shealy; *b* 28 Nov 1969; *Educ* Cobh Vocational Sch, Villanova Univ; *Career* athlete; full int 1987–; achievements at 1500m: All Ireland Gold medal 1985, World Student Games champion 1991, Silver medal World Championships Stuttgart 1993; achievements at 3000m: Home Counties champion 1987, fourth Olympic Games Barcelona 1992, fourth World Championships 1993, Gold medal Euro Championships 1994, Gold medal 5000m World Championships Gothenburg 1995; World record holder 2000m (5:25.63) 1994, Euro record holder 3000m (8:21.64) 1994; Irish Sportsperson of the Year 1993, Women's Athlete of the Year 1995; *Recreations* movies, music, reading magazines, newspapers, books and drinking coffee; *Style*— Ms Sonia O'Sullivan; ✉ c/o Kim McDonald, 201 High Street, Hampton Hill, Middlesex TW12 1NL (☎ 0181 941 9732, fax 0181 941 9734)

OSWALD, Lady Angela Mary Rose; *née* Cecil; LVO (1993); 3 da of 6 Marquess of Exeter, KCMG (d 1981), and yst da by his 1 w, Lady Mary, *née* Montagu Douglas Scott (d 1984), da of 7 Duke of Buccleuch; *b* 21 May 1938; *m* 1958, (William Richard) Michael

Oswald, CVO, *qv*; 1 s (Capt William Alexander Michael b 1962), 1 da (Mrs Alexander Fergus Matheson); *Career* Woman of the Bedchamber to HM Queen Elizabeth, The Queen Mother 1983– (Extra Woman of the Bedchamber 1981–83); Freeman City of London 1995; *Style*— The Lady Angela Oswald, LVO; ✉ Flitcham Hall, King's Lynn, Norfolk PE31 6BY (☎ 01485 600319); Flat 6, St Olave's Court, St Petersburgh Place, London W2 4JY

OSWALD, Admiral of the Fleet Sir (John) Julian Robertson; GCB (1989, KCB 1987); s of Capt George Hamilton Oswald, RN (d 1971), of Newmore, Invergordon, and Margaret Elliot, *née* Robertson (d 1949); *b* 11 Aug 1933; *Educ* Beaudesert Park Sch, Britannia RNC Dartmouth, RCDS; *m* 25 Jan 1958, Veronica Therese Dorette, da of Eric James Thompson, OBE (d 1975); 2 s (Timothy b 1958, Christopher b 1960), 3 da (Elisabeth b 1963, Victoria b 1967, Samantha b 1970); *Career* Cadet RN 1947–51, Midshipman 1952–53 (HM Ships Vanguard and Verulam), Sub Lt 1953–55 (HMS Theseus), Lt 1955–63 (HM Ships Newfoundland, Jewel, Excellent (gunnery specialist course), Victorious and Yarnton), Lt Cdr 1963–68 (HM Ships Excellent, Naiad, MOD (Naval Plans)), Cdr 1969–73 (HMS Bacchante, MOD (Def Policy Staff)), Capt 1974–82 MOD (Asst Dir Def Policy), RCDS, HMS Newcastle, RN Presentation Team BRNC Dartmouth, Rear Adm 1982–86, Asst Chief of Def Staff (Programmes), Asst Chief of Defence Staff (Policy and Nuclear), Vice Adm 1986–87 (Flag Offr Third Flotilla and Cdr ASW Striking Force), Adm (C-in-C Fleet, Allied C-in-C Channel, C-in-C Eastern Atlantic 1987–89), First Sea Lord and Chief of Naval Staff 1989–93; First and Princ ADC to HM The Queen 1989–93; dir: SEMA Group plc 1993–, James Fisher & Sons plc 1993–, Marine and General Mutual Life Assurance Co 1994–; chm AeroSystems International 1995–; pres: Assoc of RN Officers 1993–, Destroyer Club 1992–, Frinton Soc 1990–, Sea Cadet Assoc; vice pres RUSI 1993–; chm: Maritime Tst, Nat Historic Ships Ctee, Ends of the Earth Club; tstee Nat Maritime Museum; govr Univ of Portsmouth; memb Cncl White Ensign Assoc; Liveryman Worshipful Co of Shipwrights (memb Ct of Assts); Hon MBA 1992; MInstD; *Recreations* gliding, tennis, fishing, family, stamps; *Clubs* Mensa; *Style*— Admiral of the Fleet Sir Julian Oswald, GCB; ✉ c/o Naval Secretary, Victory Building, HM Naval Base, Portsmouth, Hants PO1 3LS (☎ 01705 727401)

OSWALD, (William Richard) Michael; CVO (1988, LVO 1979); s of Lt-Col William Alexander Hugh Oswald, ERD (d 1974), of St George's Hill, Weybridge, Surrey, and Rose-Marie, *née* Leahy (d 1985); *b* 21 April 1934; *Educ* Eton, King's Coll Cambridge (MA); *m* 21 April 1958, Lady Angela Mary Rose, LVO, *qv*, da of 6 Marquess of Exeter, KCMG (d 1981); 1 s (Capt William Alexander Michael b 1962), 1 da (Katharine Davina Mary (Mrs Alexander Matheson) b 1959); *Career* 2 Lt 1 Bn King's Own Royal Regt 1953, BAOR and Korea, Lt 8 Bn Royal Fusiliers (TA) 1955, Capt 1958–61; pres The Thoroughbred Breeders Assoc 1997– (memb Cncl 1964–), chm Bloodstock Indust Ctee Animal Health Tst; mangr: Lordship and Egerton Studs Newmarket 1962–69, The Royal Studs 1970–; Liveryman Worshipful Co of Shipwrights; *Recreations* shooting, painting, military history; *Clubs* White's; *Style*— Michael Oswald, Esq, CVO; ✉ 6 St Olave's Court, St Petersburgh Place, London W2 4JY (☎ 0171 229 0773); Flitcham Hall, King's Lynn, Norfolk PE31 6BY (☎ 01485 600319); The Royal Studs, Sandringham, Norfolk (☎ 01485 540588, fax 01485 543272)

OSWALD, Richard Anthony; s of Denis Geoffrey Oswald, of Uppingham, and Dorothy Lettice Oswald (d 1990); *b* 12 Jan 1941; *Educ* The Leys Sch Cambridge; *m* 12 Oct 1963, Janet Iris, da of Charles Henry Penticost (d 1983), of Southborough, Tunbridge Wells; 3 s (James Anthony b 1966, Matthew Charles b 1967, William Andrew b 1973), 2 da (Helen Victoria b 1969 d 1971, Kathryn Elizabeth b 1971); *Career* admin trainee The London Hosp 1961–67, hosp sec Prince of Wales's Gen Hosp 1967–69, dep gp sec Ilford and Dist HMC 1969–72, hosp sec The London Hosp 1972–74, support servs mangr Camden and Islington AHA(T) 1974–77, dist gen mangr Leeds Western Health Authy 1985–89 (dist admin 1977–84), dep health serv cmmr 1989–96; MHSM, DipHSM 1967; *Recreations* classical music, ornithology, DIY; *Style*— Richard Oswald, Esq; ✉ The Orchard Cottage, Cripplegate Lane, Southwater, West Sussex RH13 7HN (☎ 01403 730467)

OTAKA, Tadaaki; s of Hisatada Otaka, conductor and composer, and Misaoko Otaka; *b* 8 Nov 1947; *Educ* Toho Gakuen Sch of Music (2nd prize Min-On Conducting Competition), Vienna Hochschule (Austrian State scholar); *m* 1978, Yukiko; *Career* conductor; began playing violin aged 5, studied conducting under Prof Hideo Saito and Prof Hans Swarowsky, student at NHK (Japanese Broadcasting Corp) Symphony Orch 1968–70; professional bdcasting debut 1971 with NHK Symphony Orch (asst conductor various int tours 1969–73), NY debut 1985 with American Symphony Orch; perm conductor Tokyo Philharmonic Orch 1971–91 (conductor laureate 1991–), conductor NHK New Year Opera Concert annually 1980–, chief conductor Sapporo Symphony Orch 1981–86, princ conductor BBC Nat Orch of Wales 1987–95 (conductor laureate 1996–), chief conductor Yomiuri Nippon Symphony Orch 1992–, music advsr and princ conductor Kioi Sinfonietta Japan 1995–; made various int tours incl: Vienna, Czechoslovakia, Germany, Russia, Indonesia, Australia, N America, Far East (BBC NOW); worked with other orchs incl: London Philharmonic, City of Birmingham Symphony, Royal Liverpool Philharmonic, Hallé, Brno State Philharmonic, Vancouver Symphony, Helsinki Philharmonic, Turku Philharmonic, Orchestre National de Lille, Dresden Philharmonic, Polish Nat Radio Symphony, Hong Kong Philharmonic, Melbourne and Sydney Symphony Orchs; *Opera* Salome (Welsh Nat Opera) 1991; *Recordings* various with BBC Welsh Symphony Orch; Suntory Music Award 1992, Hon Doctorate Univ of Wales 1993; *Recreations* fishing, tennis, cooking; *Style*— Mr Tadaaki Otaka; ✉ c/o Harold Holt Ltd, 31 Sinclair Road, London W14 ONS (☎ 0171 603 4600, fax 0171 603 0019)

O'TOOLE, Peter; s of Patrick Joseph O'Toole; *b* 2 Aug 1932; *Educ* RADA; *m* 1959 (m dis 1979) Sian Phillips, *qv*; 2 da; *Career* actor; with Bristol Old Vic Co 1955–58, assoc dir Old Vic Co 1980; *Theatre* incl: Major Barbara (Old Vic) 1956, Oh My Papa! (Garrick) 1957, The Long and the Short and the Tall (Royal Court and New) 1959, season with Shakespeare Memorial Theatre Company (Stratford-on-Avon) 1960, Baal (Phoenix) 1963, Hamlet (NT) 1963, Ride a Cock Horse (Piccadilly) 1965, Juno and the Paycock, Man and Superman, Pictures in the Hallway (Gaiety, Dublin) 1966, Waiting for Godot, Happy Days (Abbey, Dublin) 1969, Uncle Vanya, Plunder, The Apple Cart, Judgement (Bristol Old Vic) 1973, Uncle Vanya, Present Laughter (Chicago) 1978, Macbeth (Old Vic) 1980, Man and Superman (Haymarket) 1982, Pygmalion (Shaftesbury) 1984, Yvonne Arnaud (Guildford and NY) 1987, The Apple Cart (Haymarket) 1986, Jeffrey Bernard is Unwell (Apollo) 1989, Our Song (Apollo (Variety Club Best Stage Actor Award)) 1992; *Television* incl: Rogue Male 1976, Strumpet City 1979, Masada 1981, Svengali 1982, Pygmalion 1983, Kim 1983, Banshee 1986, The Dark Angel 1989; *Films* incl: Kidnapped 1959, The Day They Robbed the Bank of England 1959, The Savage Innocents 1960, Lawrence of Arabia 1962, Becket 1963, Lord Jim 1964, What's New Pussycat 1965, How to Steal a Million 1966, The Bible...in the Beginning 1966, The Night of the Generals 1967, Great Catherine 1968, The Lion in Winter 1968, Goodbye Mr Chips 1969, Brotherly Love 1970, Murphy's War 1971, Under Milk Wood 1971, The Ruling Class 1972, Man of La Mancha 1972, Rosebud 1975, Man Friday 1975, Foxtrot 1975, The Stunt Man 1977, Coup d'Etat 1977, Zulu Dawn 1978, Power Play 1978, The Antagonists 1981, My Favorite Year 1981, Supergirl 1983, Club Paradise 1986, The Last Emperor 1987, High Spirits 1988, Creator 1990; *Books* Loitering With Intent (autobiography, 1992), Loitering With Intent: The Apprentice (vol 2 of autobiography, 1996); *Clubs* Garrick; *Style*— Peter O'Toole Esq; ✉ c/o William Morris Agency (UK) Ltd, 31/32 Soho Square, London W1V 6DG (☎ 0171 434 2191, fax 0171 437 0238)

OTTAWAY, Richard Geoffrey James; MP (C) Croydon S (majority 20,425); s of Prof Christopher Wyndham Ottaway (d 1977), and Grace Ottaway; *b* 24 May 1945; *Educ* Backwell Secdy Mod Sch, Univ of Bristol (LLB); *m* 1982, Nicola Evelyn, da of John Kisch, CMG; *Career* Lt RN, Lt Cdr RNR; admitted slr 1977; MP (C): Nottingham N 1983–87, Croydon S 1992–; PPS to Baroness Young and Tim Renton, MP as Mins of State at FCO 1985–87, PPS to Michael Heseltine, MP as Pres of the Bd of Trade and then as Dep PM 1992–95, asst Govt whip 1995–96, a Lord Cmmr HM Treasy (Govt whip) 1996–; chm All Pty Gp on Population and Devpt 1992–95; ptnr Wm A Crump Slrs 1981–87, dir Coastal Europe 1988–95; *Books* Road to Reform, Thoughts for a Third Term (jtly, 1987), Less People, Less Pollution (1990); *Recreations* yacht racing, jazz, skiing; *Clubs* Royal Corinthian Yacht, Island Sailing; *Style*— Richard Ottaway, Esq, MP; ✉ c/o House of Commons, London SW1A 0AA

OTTER, Robert George (Robin); s of Francis Lewis Otter, MC (d 1946), of Ottershaw, Surrey, and Helen, *née* Stephens (d 1988); *b* 25 Feb 1926; *Educ* Marlborough, Univ Coll Oxford (BA, MA); *m* 16 Dec 1958, Elisabeth Ann, da of Eric Reginald St Aubrey Davies, MBE (d 1986); 2 s (Robert b 1960, David b 1966), 1 da (Lisette b 1968); *Career* RNVR 1944–47, cmmnd 1945, RNC Greenwich, served Minesweepers Far E 1945–46; dist offr/cmmr Kenya Colony Colonial Admin Serv 1951–62 (despatches 1957), slr and ptnr Moore, Brown & Dixon Tewkesbury 1963–96, conslt 1996–; govr Alderman Knight and Abbey Schs Tewkesbury, govr Three Counties Agric Soc; memb Cncl: Gloucester Cattle Soc 1973–95, Rare Breeds Survival Trust 1973–82 and 1994–; Parly candidate (Lib) 1966, 1970 and 1974, Euro Parly candidate 1979; memb: Law Soc, Glos & Wilts Law Soc, Glos Diocesan and Tewkesbury Deanery Synods 1969–95 (chm 1986–95), Cncl Friends of Tewkesbury Abbey 1966–, Exec Ctee Tewkesbury Soc (chm 1996–); *Books* Law - A Modern Introduction (contrib, ed Paul Denham, 1989); *Recreations* breeder of Gloucester cattle; *Clubs* Royal Cwlth Soc, Mombasa Club (Kenya), Oxford Union; *Style*— Robin Otter, Esq; ✉ Kemerton Grange, Tewkesbury, Glos GL20 7JE (☎ 01386 725253, fax 01684 295147)

OTTEWILL, Prof Ronald Harry; OBE (1989); s of Harry Archibald Ottewill (d 1976), of Bristol, and Violet Dorien, *née* Bucklee (d 1989); *b* 8 Feb 1927; *Educ* Southall Co Sch Middx, Queen Mary Coll London (BSc, PhD), Fitzwilliam Coll Cambridge (MA, PhD); *m* 31 Aug 1952, Ingrid Geraldine, da of Henry Roe (d 1963), of Frinton-on-Sea, Essex; 1 s (Adrian Christopher b 1958), 1 da (Geraldine Astrid b 1956); *Career* asst dir of res Univ of Cambridge 1958–63 (sr asst in res 1955–58); Univ of Bristol: lectr in physical chemistry 1964–66, reader in colloid sci 1966–70, prof of colloid sci 1971–81, head of Dept of Physical Chemistry 1973–92, Leverhulme prof of physical chemistry 1982–92 (emeritus prof 1992), dean Faculty of Sci 1988–90; memb various ctees SERC 1969–86, chm Neutron Beam Res Ctee 1982–86; pres Faraday Div Royal Soc of Chem 1989–91; FRS 1982; *Books* Surface Area Determination (1970), Science and Technology of Polymer Colloids (1983), Adsorption from Solution (1983), An Introduction to Polymer Colloids (1990), Scientific Methods for the Study of Polymer Colloids and their Applications (1990); *Recreations* gardening, music; *Style*— Prof Ronald Ottewill, OBE, FRS; ✉ School of Chemistry, University of Bristol, Cantocks Close, Bristol BS8 1TS (☎ 0117 928 7647, fax 0117 925 1295)

OTTLEY, Robert Jeremy Mark Linn; *Career* dir: Greenwell Montagu Stockbrokers 1968–92, Investmt Mgmnt Div James Capel Investment Management 1992–; *Style*— Robert Ottley; ✉ James Capel Investment Management, 6 Bevis Marks, London EC3A 7JQ

OTTO-JONES, John Alcwyn; s of Col Thomas Otto-Jones, CBE, TD, DL (d 1953), of Bredwardine, Hereford, and Kathleen Mary, *née* Hale (d 1979); *b* 7 Feb 1930; *Educ* Christ Coll Brecon, Univ of Cardiff (BA), Wadham Coll Oxford (MA); *m* 1 Oct 1960, Bridget Mary, da of Ernest Jackson, Mansfield, Nottinghamshire; 1 s (Justin b 1963), 1 da (Candida b 1966); *Career* cmmnd RAEC 1950; NP; Under Sheriff of Glamorgan 1985; *Recreations* vintage cars, reading; *Clubs* RAC, Cardiff and County; *Style*— John Otto-Jones, Esq; ✉ The Court, St Nicholas, Vale of Glamorgan; 29 Park Place, Cardiff (☎ 01222 225591)

OTTON, Sir Geoffrey John; KCB (1980, CB 1978); s of late John Alfred Otton; *b* 10 June 1927; *Educ* Christ's Hosp, St John's Coll, Cambridge (MA); *m* 1952, Hazel Lomas, *née* White; 1 s, 1 da; *Career* second permanent sec DHSS 1979–86; *Style*— Sir Geoffrey Otton, KCB; ✉ 72 Cumberland Rd, Bromley, Kent (☎ 0181 460 9610)

OTTON, The Rt Hon Lord Justice; Sir Philip (Howard); kt (1983), PC (1995); s of late Henry Albert Otton, of Kenilworth, and Leah Otton (d 1995); *b* 28 May 1933; *Educ* Bablake Sch Coventry, Birmingham Univ (LLB); *m* 1965, Helen Margaret, da of late P W Bates; 2 s (Charles, Christian), 1 da (Sophie (Mrs Euan Ambrose)); *Career* called to the Bar Gray's Inn 1955, dep chm Beds QS 1970–72, jr counsel to the Treasy (Personal Injuries) 1970–75, recorder of the Crown Court 1972–83, QC 1975, govr Nat Heart and Chest Hosps 1979–84, Master of the Bench Gray's Inn 1983–, judge of the High Court of Justice (Queen's Bench Div) 1983–95; a Lord Justice of the Court of Appeal 1995–; presiding judge: Midland and Oxford Circuit 1986–88, Official Referees' Court 1991–; chm: Royal Brompton & Nat Heart & Lung Hosps SHA 1991–, Nat Heart & Lung Inst 1991–95; pres Soc of Construction Law 1995–; tstee Migraine Tst 1992–; FCIArb 1995; *Recreations* theatre, opera, travel; *Clubs* Garrick, Pilgrims; *Style*— The Rt Hon Sir Philip Otton; ✉ Royal Courts of Justice, Strand, London WC2A 2LL

OTWAY, Mark McRae; s of Henry Arthur McRae Otway, of Surrey, and Ann, *née* Ingman; *b* 4 Oct 1948; *Educ* Dulwich, Churchill Coll Cambridge (MA); *m* 10 July 1973, Amanda Mary, da of Roland Stafford; 2 s (Miles Daniel b 1983, Paul David b 1985); *Career* ptnr (now managing ptnr business processing mgmnt Europe Middle East Asia and India) Andersen Consulting 1982– (joined 1970, mangr 1975, ptnr 1982); *Recreations* sailing, music, theatre; *Clubs* Royal Lymington Yacht; *Style*— Mark Otway, Esq; ✉ Andersen Consulting, 2 Arundel St, London WC2R 3LT (☎ 0171 438 3835)

OUGH, Dr Richard Norman; s of Rev Conrad Jocelyn Ough (d 1977), and Alice Louisa, *née* Crofts; *b* 25 Jan 1946; *Educ* Stamford Sch, St Mary's Hosp Med Sch Univ of London (MB BS), City Univ London (MA, Dip Law), London Business Sch (MSc); *m* 1, 1976 (m dis 1982), Shelley Jean Henshaw; 1 s (Geoffrey b 1977), 1 da (Elizabeth b 1978); m 2, 1984 (m dis 1988), Rona Mary Louise Hallam; m 3, 1991, Mary Jane Alison Payne; 2 s (Thomas b 1992, James b 1994); *Career* med practitioner Canada 1974–83; called to the Bar Inner Temple 1985; chm Social Security Appeal Tbnl 1993–, dep chm NHS Tbnl 1995–; non-exec dir Bedfordshire Health Authy 1996–; memb Hon Soc of Inner Temple; FCIArb 1993; *Books* The Mareva Injunction and Anton Piller Order (1987, 2 edn 1993); *Recreations* music, opera, walking; *Clubs* Reform; *Style*— Dr Richard N Ough; ✉ 4 Paper Buildings, Temple EC4Y 7EX (☎ 0171 353 3366, fax 0171 353 5778)

OUGHTON, Douglas Robert; *b* 1942; *Educ* MSc; *Career* Oscar Faber: joined as engr 1967, responsible for major projects in UK, Asia, Egypt and Nigeria, later assoc, currently dir Oscar Faber Consulting Engineers Ltd and Oscar Faber Applied Research; CIBSE: memb Tech Pubns Ctee 1975–85, memb External Affrs Ctee 1986–89, memb Professional Practices Ctee 1992–94, memb Cncl 1995–; memb: Cncl Building Servs Research and Info Assoc 1975–87, Br Standards Mech Engrg Standards Ctee 1980–84, Building Design and Construction Ctee CIRIA 1984–90; chm Euro Intelligent Building Gp 1992–95; author of numerous papers for professional jls; chartered engr, MACE, memb Inst of Refrigeration, memb Inst of Energy, FCIBSE, FEng 1995; *Books* Heating and Air Conditioning of Buildings (Faber & Kell); *Style*— Douglas Oughton, Esq, FEng; ✉ Oscar Faber Consulting Engineers, Marlborough House, Upper Marlborough Road, St Albans, Herts AL1 3UT (☎ 0181 784 5784, fax 0181 784 5700)

OUGHTRED, Peter Bentham; JP; s of Col John Alwyn Oughtred, MC (d 1958), and Phyllis Brown, *née* Jackson (d 1981); *b* 6 April 1921; *Educ* Leys Sch; *m* 1950, Lorna Agnes, da of John McLaren (d 1955); 3 s (Christopher, Angus, Nicholas), 1 da (Louise Jane (Mrs Adrian Mark Horsley)); *Career* WWII Capt E Yorks Regt UK and overseas 1940–47; pres William Jackson and Son plc, dir Beverley Race Co Ltd; farmer & landowner; High Sheriff of Humberside 1987–88; FIMgt, FInstD, FIGD; *Recreations* shooting, fishing, racing; *Clubs* Flyfishers'; *Style*— Peter B Oughtred, Esq, JP; ✉ Raby Lodge, 26 Cave Rd, Brough, East Yorkshire HU15 1HL (☎ 01482 667381); Wodencroft Lodge, Cotherstone, Barnard Castle, Co Durham (☎ 01833 650239); William Jackson & Son plc, 40 Derringham St, Hull HU3 1EW (☎ 01482 224131)

OULTON, Sir (Antony) Derek Maxwell; GCB (KCB 1984, CB 1979), QC (1985); s of late Charles Cameron Courtenay Oulton; *b* 14 Oct 1927; *Educ* St Edward's Sch Oxford, King's Coll Cambridge (MA, PhD); *m* 1955, Margaret Geraldine, JP (d 1989), da of late Lt-Col G S Oxley, MC; 1 s, 3 da; *Career* called to the Bar Gray's Inn 1952; dep sec Lord Chancellor's Office 1976–82, perm sec 1982–89; dep clerk of the Crown in Chancery 1977–82, clerk of the Crown in Chancery 1982–89; fell Magdalene Coll Cambridge 1990–95 (life fell 1995), visiting prof of law Univ of Bristol 1990–91; tstee Nat Gallery 1989–96; *Style*— Sir Derek Oulton, GCB, QC; ✉ Magdalene College, Cambridge CB3 0AG (☎ 01223 332100, fax 01223 359465)

OULTON, Therese; da of Robert Oulton, and Matilda, *née* Glover; *b* 20 April 1953; *Educ* St Martin's Sch of Art London, RCA London; *Career* artist; *Solo Exhibitions* incl: Fool's Gold: New Paintings (Gimpel Fils London) 1984, Recent Painting (MOMA Oxford) 1985, Letters to Rose (Galerie Krinzinger Vienna) 1986, Skin Deep (Galerie Thomas Munich, Galerie am Moritzplatz Berlin) 1986, Monoprints (Marlborough Graphics London) 1987, Lachrimae (Marlborough Fine Art London) 1988, Hirschl & Adler NY 1989, Therese Oulton - Works on Paper (Marlborough Graphics London) 1989, Paintings and Works on Paper (LA Louver Gallery Calif) 1991, Abstract with Memories (Marlborough Fine Art London) 1992, New Paintings (Marlborough Gallery NY) 1994; *Group Exhibitions* incl: John Moores (Walker Art Gallery Liverpool) 1982 and 1985, Landscape Memory and Desire (Serpentine Gallery) 1984, The Image as Catalyst (Ashmolean Museum Oxford) 1984, New Painters (Squire's Gallery Newcastle) 1985, How Much Beauty Can I Stand: Contemporary Landscape Painting (Aust Centre for Contemporary Art, S Yarra, Victoria) 1986, British Art and Design (Künstlerhaus Vienna) 1986, American/European: Painting and Sculpture (LA Louver Gallery Calif) 1986, Kunst aus den achtziger Jahren (All Art Forum Munich) 1987, Oulton Prangenberg Snyder (Hirschl & Adler NY) 1987, Turner Prize Display (Tate Gallery London) 1987, The Romantic Tradition in Contemporary British Painting (Sala de Exposiciones de Palacio de San Estelson Murcia and Circulo de San Estelson Madrid) 1988, 100 Years of Art in Britain (Leeds City Art Gallery) 1988, The British Picture (LA Louver Gallery Calif) 1988, Blasphemies Ecstasies Cries (Serpentine Gallery London and tour) 1989, The New British Painting (Contemporary Arts Center Cincinnati and tour) 1989, 3 Ways (Br Cncl/RCA touring exhibitions) 1990, Venice Bienale (Aperto) 1990, The Forces of Nature (Manchester City Art Galleries and Harris Museum and Art Gallery) 1990–91, Art at Broadgate (London) 1992, An American Passion: Contemporary British Art (Glasgow Museum of Art and RCA London) 1995, A Passion for the New (Tel Aviv Museum of Art) 1995; *Work in Public Collections* Arts Cncl of GB London, Br Cncl London, Harris Museum and Art Gallery Preston, Metropolitan Museum of Art NY, John Moores Liverpool, Tate Gallery, Leeds City Art Gallery, V&A, San Diego Museum California, Library of Congress Washington DC; *Style*— Ms Therese Oulton

OUSELEY, Duncan Brian Walter; QC (1992); s of Maurice Henry Ouseley (d 1978), Margaret Helen Irene, *née* Vagts; *b* 24 Feb 1950; *Educ* Trinity Sch Croydon, Fitzwilliam Coll Cambridge (MA, exhibitioner) UCL (LLM); *m* 27 April 1974, Suzannah Valerie, *née* Price; 3 s (Daniel b 18 Jan 1979, Jonathan b 24 May 1980, Robert b 2 March 1988); *Career* called to the Bar Gray's Inn 1973 (Atkin scholar 1972), jr counsel to Crown Common Law 1986–92, recorder 1994– (asst recorder 1991–94); chm examination in public of: Shropshire Structure Plan First Alterations 1985, Hampshire Structure Plan 1991; memb: Admin Law Bar Assoc, Local Govt, Planning and Environmental Law Assoc; *Recreations* family, sport, music, wine; *Style*— Duncan Ouseley, Esq, QC; ✉ 4–5 Gray's Inn Square, Gray's Inn, London WC1R 5AY (☎ 0171 404 5252)

OUTRAM, Sir Alan James; 5 Bt (UK 1858); s of late James Ian Outram (gs of 2 Bt), and late Evelyn Mary, *née* Littlehales; suc gt uncl, Sir Francis Davidson Outram, 4 Bt, OBE, 1945; Lt-Gen Sir James Outram, GCB, KBE, received Baronetcy 1858 for service in Persia and India; *b* 15 May 1937; *Educ* Marlborough, St Edmund Hall Oxford (MA); *m* 1976, Victoria Jean, da of late George Dickson Paton; 1 s, 1 da (Alison Catharine b 1977); *Heir* s, Douglas Benjamin James Outram b 15 March 1979; *Career* Hon Lt-Col TA & VR; schoolmaster Harrow Sch; *Recreations* bridge, golf, tennis, cycling; *Style*— Sir Alan Outram, Bt; ✉ Harrow School, Harrow-on-the-Hill, Middlesex HA1 3HR

OUTRAM, Christopher David; s of Joseph Outram (d 1972), and Vera Anne, *née* Ogden; *b* 4 April 1949; *Educ* King's SG, Atlantic Coll, Univ of Birmingham (BSc, BComm, Economics prize, Engineering prize), INSEAD Business Sch (MBA); *m* Anne Marie, da of Noel Leslie Costain; 2 da (Sophie Marie Elizabeth b 26 Sept 1981, Verity Clementine b 24 Nov 1983); *Career* Mobil Oil Company 1972–73, Air Products 1973–74, mktg mangr CCL Systems 1974–76, INSEAD Business Sch 1976–77, strategy conslt Boston Consulting Group 1977–79, strategic planning dir Van Gelder Papier 1979–81, strategy conslt Booz Allen & Hamilton 1981–86 (vice pres 1986), fndr and sr dir OC & C Strategy Consultants 1986–; dir PTRC; *Recreations* learning piano and golf and other leisure activities, reading, travelling; *Clubs* RAC; *Style*— Christopher Outram, Esq; ✉ OC & C Strategy Consultants, 65 Kingsway, London WC2B 6TD (☎ 0171 834 7447, fax 0171 400 6355)

OUTRAM, Robert Francis; s of Stephen Henry Outram, of Frimley, Surrey, and Wendy, *née* Palmer; *b* 8 May 1961; *Educ* France Hill Sch Camberley, St Catherine's Coll Oxford (BA, PPE), City of London Poly (Dip in Mgmnt Studies); *partner* Christina Cheong; *Career* admin offr: GLC 1983–85, ILEA 1985–88, trainee accountant Peat Marwick McLintock 1988–89; staff writer: Career Accountant magazine 1989–90, Accountancy Age 1990–92; ed Management Consultancy magazine Jan-July 1992, ed Accountancy Age July 1992–95; freelance 1995–; *Recreations* film, theatre, travel; *Style*— Robert Outram, Esq

OVENDEN, Graham Stuart; s of Henry Ovenden (d 1986), of Winchester, and Gwendoline Dorothy, *née* Hill (d 1988); *b* 11 Feb 1943; *Educ* Itchen GS, Southampton Coll of Art, Royal Coll of Music (ARCM), Royal Coll of Art (ARCA, MA); *m* 1 March 1969, Ann Dinah, da of George Walter Gilmore (d 1963), of Upper Winchendon, Bucks; 1 s (Edmund Dante b 1972), 1 da (Emily Alice b 1976); *Career* painter, poet, art historian; numerous exhibitions incl the Tate Gallery and Royal Acad, one man shows in most major western countries; fndr memb The Brotherhood of Ruralists 1976; *Books* Illustrators of Alice (1971), Victorian Children (with Robert Melville, 1972), Pre-Raphaelite Photography (1972), Hill and Adamson Photographs (1973), Alphonse Mucha Photographs (1973), Clementina Lady Hawarden (1973), Victorian Erotic Photography (1973), Aspects of Lolita (1975), A Victorian Family Album (with Lord David Cecil, 1976), Satirical Poems and Others (1983), The Marble Mirror (poetry, 1984), Lewis Carroll Photographer (1984), Monograph - Graham Ovenden (with essays by Laurie Lee, Clive Wainwright, Robert Melville and others, 1987), Sold With All Faults (poetry, 1991); *Recreations* music, architecture; *Style*— Graham Ovenden, Esq; ✉ Barley Splatt, Panters Bridge, Mount, Cornwall

OVENSTONE, Dr Irene Margaret Kinnear; da of David Ovenstone (d 1951), and Edith Margaret Ovenstone (d 1984); *b* 25 Oct 1929; *Educ* Harris Acad Dundee Scotland, Univ of St Andrews (MB ChB, DPH), Univ of Leeds (DPM), Univ of Dundee (MD); *Career* asst med offr of health Huddersfield 1957–61, registrar Huddersfield 1961–64, sr registrar in psychiatry Westminster Hosp London 1964–68, memb Scientific Staff and hon lectr MRC Unit for Epidemiological Studies in Psychiatry Edinburgh 1969–72, clinical teacher and conslt psychiatrist specialising in psychiatry of old age Univ of Nottingham 1973–94, sec and chm Nottingham Area Psychiatric Div 1974–79, emeritus conslt Nottingham City Hosp NHS Tst 1994; memb Working Parties on: Psychiatric Nurse Education 1974, Drug Custody and Admin 1977, Home for Elderly Project Notts Social Services Dept 1981; chm Notts Health Care Planning Team for Elderly 1981–82; memb: Mental Health Tbnls 1981–, Mental Health Cmmn 1983–86, Health Advsy Service 1989; author of papers on suicidal behaviour, marital neurosis, admissions to old people's homes in Nottingham; FRCPsych 1978 (MRCPsych 1973); *Recreations* ballet, music, theatre, archeology, art, wildlife; *Style*— Dr Irene Ovenstone; ✉ 10 Moor Road, Calverton, Nottingham NG14 6FW (☎ 0115 965 3309)

OVERBEEKE, Aernout Albert; *b* 17 May 1951; *Career* fashion photographer 1970–80, advertising photographer 1980–, dir film commercials 1995–; major works/exhbns incl: Mississippi (Amsterdam and Geneva) 1988, Portraits (Naarden) 1992, Garden of Eden (Amsterdam) 1994, Portraits (Cobra Museum Amsterdam) 1996; *Awards* photography awards of the Netherlands (PANL): silver award 1992, 1994 and 1995, merit and gold awards 1995; winner PANL/Kodak Award 1994 and 1995; Assoc of Photographers: silver award 1994–96, merit 1994 and 1996; German AD's Club Bronze Award 1992, 1994 and 1995, European AD's Club Gold Award 1995; *Books* A Overbeeke - The Newest Dutch Master (1990); *Style*— Aernout Overbeeke, Esq; ✉ Coen Cuserhof 39, 2012 GZ Haarlem, The Netherlands (☎ 00 31 23 5324000, fax 00 31 23 5320323); c/o Freddy Brazil, 312 Golden House, 29 Great Pulteney Street, London W1 (☎ 0171 494 4623, fax 0171 287 1255)

OVEREND, Prof (William) George; s of Harold George Overend (d 1986), of Shrewsbury, and Hilda, *née* Parry (d 1974); *b* 16 Nov 1921; *Educ* Priory Sch Shrewsbury, Univ of Birmingham (BSc, PhD, DSc); *m* 12 July 1949, Gina Olava, da of Horace Bertie Cadman (d 1980), of Birmingham; 2 s (George Edmund (Ted) b 1958, Desmond Anthony b 1963), 1 da (Sheila Hilda b 1961); *Career* assoc prof Pennsylvania State Coll 1951–52; Univ of London: reader in organic chemistry 1955–57, prof of chemistry 1957–87, emeritus prof 1987, Leverhulme emeritus fell 1987–89; Birkbeck Coll London: head Dept of Chemistry 1957–79, vice master 1974–78, master 1979–87; senator Univ of London 1978–87; conslt 1993–; memb: Br Pharmacopoeia Cmmn 1962–80, Home Office Poisons Bd 1966–; vice pres Perkin Div Royal Soc of Chemistry 1976–78, chm Cncl of Govrs S Bank Poly 1980–89 (memb Bd of Govrs 1970–91); memb Cncl Royal Soc of Chemistry 1972–78; Lampitt Medallist Soc of Chemical Indust 1965; Hon FCP 1986; hon fell: Birkbeck Coll 1987, S Bank Poly 1989; Hon DUniv Open Univ 1988; CChem, FRSC, FIMgt, FRSA; *Books* The Use of Tracer Elements in Biology (1951), Programmes in Organic Chemistry I-VIII (ed, 1966–73); *Recreations* rose growing; *Clubs* Athenaeum, RAC; *Style*— Prof George Overend; ✉ The Retreat, Nightingales Lane, Chalfont St Giles, Bucks HP8 4SR (☎ 01494 763996); Department of Chemistry, Birkbeck College (University of London), Gordon House, Gordon Street, London WC1E 7HX (☎ 0171 380 7479)

OVERSBY-POWELL, David John; s of George Herbert Oversby-Powell (d 1975), of Cranleigh, Surrey, and Eileen Mary Veronica, *née* Cornhill; *b* 13 Sept 1947; *Educ* Scotus Acad Edinburgh, John Fisher Sch Purley; *m* 10 June 1972, Jennifer Merlyn Isobel, da of Percival Sidney Bamber; 1 s (James David b 5 May 1981), 1 da (Kate Louise b 4 Feb 1984); *Career* trainee surveyor Huntingdonshire CC 1969, insur inspr and local mangr Guardian Royal Exchange Bedford 1974–77 (insur clerk 1970–73), pensions mangr Borg-Warner Ltd 1980–89 (asst insur mangr 1977–79), pension fund sec UAP Provincial Insurance plc 1989–; ACII 1973; *Recreations* oil painting, watercolour painting, hill walking; *Style*— David Oversby-Powell, Esq; ✉ UAP Provincial Insurance plc, Sand Aire House, Stramongate, Kendal, Cumbria LA9 4BE (☎ 01539 723415, fax 01539 731954, home ☎ 01539 724290)

OVERY, Paul Vivian; s of Arthur Frederick Overy (d 1992), of Hampstead, London, and Joan Vivien, *née* Major (d 1987); *b* 14 Feb 1940; *Educ* UCS London, King's Coll Cambridge (MA); *m* 1992, Theresa Ann Gronberg; *Career* art critic: The Listener 1966–68 and 1978–82, Financial Times 1968–71; book reviews ed New Society 1970–71, chief art critic The Times 1973–78, tutor in cultural history RCA London 1975–87, art critic The International Herald Tribune 1980–82, freelance art critic 1982–, contributing ed The Journal of Art 1990–91; currently lectr in art, architecture and design history: Univ of London, Middlesex Univ; guest lectr Slade Sch of Fine Art; exhibitions incl: 18 Artists from Hungary (Third Eye Centre Glasgow) 1985, Rietveld Furniture & the Schröder House (Warwick Univ Arts Centre) 1990, Whitworth Gallery Manchester, Collins Gallery Glasgow, City Art Gallery Southampton, Nat Museum of Modern Art Dublin 1991, Royal Festival Hall London 1991, Josef Albers (Nat Museum of Modern Art Dublin and touring) 1994; Italian Govt scholar to Italy 1970, Leverhulme Res fell Paris 1984–85; memb: Assoc Internationale des Critiques d'Art 1967, NUJ 1970, Assoc of Art Historians 1987; *Books* Kandinsky: The Language of the Eye (1969), De Stijl (1969), Concepts of Modern Art (contrib, 1974), The New Art History (contrib, 1986), The Rietveld Schröder House (jtly, 1988), De Stijl (1991), The Complete Rietveld Furniture (jtly, 1993), Investigating Modern Art (contrib, 1996); *Recreations* reading, walking; *Style*— Paul Overy, Esq; ✉ 92 South Hill Park, London NW3 2SN (☎ 0171 435 8725); c/o Andrew Hewson, John Johnson (Author's Agents Ltd), Clerkenwell House, 47 Clerkenwell Green, London EC1R 0HT (☎ 0171 251 0125, fax 0171 251 2172)

OWEN, Alan Charles; s of Thomas Charles Owen, and Florence Edith, *née* Blake; *b* 7 March 1939; *Educ* Elliot Central Sch Southfields London; *m* 11 Oct 1974, Janet Ann, da of William David Butcher; 1 s (Ian Charles), 1 da (Larraine Carol); *Career* mangr Gilbert Eliott & Co Stockbrokers 1970 (ptnr 1977), div dir Girozentrale Gilbert Eliott 1987–92, fndr dir Gilbert Eliott & Co Ltd 1993–; memb Stock Exchange 1976 (MSI); *Recreations* squash; *Style*— Alan Owen, Esq; ✉ Gilbert Eliott & Co Ltd, 277 Salisbury House, London Wall, London EC2M 5QQ (☎ 0171 369 0300, fax 0171 628 3500)

OWEN, His Hon Aron; *b* 16 Feb 1919; *Educ* Tredegar Co GS, Univ of Wales (BA, PhD); *m* 1946, Rose, JP, da of Solomon Alexander Fishman, Freeman City of London (d 1936); 1 s, 2 da; *Career* called to the Bar Inner Temple 1948; circuit judge (South Eastern Circuit) 1980–94 (retired); Freeman City of London; *Recreations* travel, gardening; *Style*— His Hon Aron Owen; ✉ 44 Brampton Grove, Hendon, London NW4 4AQ (☎ 0181 202 8151)

OWEN, Bill John; MBE; s of William George Davenport Rowbotham, and Louise Matthews; *b* 14 March 1914; *m* 1, 14 Feb 1946 (m dis 1964), Edith, da of Thomas Stevenson; 1 s (Thomas William Stevenson b 8 April 1949); m 2, 3 March 1977, Kathleen O'Donoghue; *Career* actor (1938–), director and writer; Nat Serv 2 Lt RPC 1940–42; vice pres London Fedn of Boys' Clubs (arts adviser); chm: Unity Theatre Tst; vice chm Yorks Soc London; *Theatre* roles incl: Touchstone in As You Like It (NY) 1949–50,

Mack the Knife in The Threepenny Opera 1956, Ko-Ko in The Mikado (Sadler's Wells Opera) 1963, Tommy Pasmore in March on Russia 1989; writer of book and lyrics for Matchgirls (Globe) 1966; *Television* numerous film and TV credits incl: Compo in Last of the Summer Wine (BBC), The Entertainer (BBC) 1993; *Books* Summer Wine And Vintage Years (autobiog, 1995); *Style*— Bill Owen, Esq, MBE; ✉ Bill Owen Ltd, c/o Saunders Wood & Co, 140a Tachbrook Street, London SW1V 2NE

OWEN, (Alfred) David; OBE (1997); s of Sir Alfred George Beech Owen, CBE (d 1975), and Eileen Kathleen Genevieve, *née* McMullan; *b* 26 Sept 1936; *Educ* Brocksford Hall, Oundle, Emmanuel Coll Cambridge (MA); *m* 1966, Ethne Margaret, da of Frank H Sowman, of Solihull; 2 s, 1 da; *Career* Nat Serv Lt RASC; chm Rubery Owen Group; dir: Blackwell Science Ltd, Brooke Tool Engineering (Holdings) plc, National Exhibition Centre Ltd, Castle Vale Housing Action Tst 1993–; tstee Community Development Fndn 1978–, memb BOTB 1979–83, pres Birmingham C of C 1980–81, vice pres SMMT 1987–90; pres Comité de Liaison de la Construction d'Equipments et de Pièces d'Automobiles 1988–90, pres Commercial Trailer Assoc; Liveryman Worshipful Co of Coachmakers & Coach Harness Makers; Hon DSc Univ of Aston 1988; *Recreations* industrial archaeology, ornithology, walking, photography, music; *Clubs* National; *Style*— A David Owen, Esq, OBE; ✉ Mill Dam House, Mill Lane, Aldridge, Walsall, WS9 0NB; Rubery Owen Holdings Ltd, PO Box 10, Darlaston, Wednesbury, W Midlands (☎ 0121 526 3131, fax 0121 526 2869)

OWEN, Baron (Life Peer UK 1992), of the City of Plymouth; David Anthony Llewellyn Owen; PC (1976), CH (1994); s of Dr John William Morris Owen (d 1994), and Molly Owen; *b* 2 July 1938; *Educ* Bradfield Coll, Sidney Sussex Coll Cambridge (hon fell 1977), St Thomas's Hosp (BA, MB BChir, MA); *m* 1968, Deborah (Mrs Deborah Owen, literary agent), da of late Kyrill Schabert, of Long Island, New York, USA; 2 s (Tristan Llewellyn b 1970, Gareth Schabert b 1972), 1 da (Lucy Mary b 1979); *Career* St Thomas's Hosp: house appts 1962–64, neurological and psychiatric registrar 1964–66, res fell med unit 1966–68; contested (Lab) Torrington 1964, MP (Lab) Plymouth Sutton 1966–74, MP (Lab until 1981, SDP 1981–92) Plymouth Devonport 1974–92; PPS to MOD (Admin) 1967, Parly under sec of state for def (RN) 1968–70, resigned over EEC 1972, Parly under sec of state DHSS 1974, min of state DHSS 1974–76 and FCO 1976–77, sec of state for foreign and Cwlth affairs 1977–79, oppn spokesman on energy 1979–81; fndr memb SDP 1981, chm SDP Parly Ctee 1981–82, dep leader SDP Oct 1982–83, elected SDP Leader following resignation of Rt Hon Roy Jenkins after election June 1983, resigned over merger with Liberals 1987, re-elected SDP leader 1988; memb: Palme Cmmn on Disarmament and Security Issues 1980–89, Ind Cmmn on Int Humanitarian Issues 1983–86; EU co-chm Steering Ctee Int Conf on Former Yugoslavia Aug 1992–95; chm Humanitas 1990–; exec chm: Middlesex Holdings 1995–, Abbott Laboratories 1995; non-exec dir Coats Viyella plc 1994–; chllr Univ of Liverpool 1996–; *Books* A Unified Health Service (1968), The Politics of Defence (1972), In Sickness and in Health (1976), Human Rights (1978), Face The Future (1981), A Future That Will Work (1984), A United Kingdom (1986), Personally Speaking (to Kenneth Harris) (1987), Our NHS (1988), Time to Declare (autobiography, 1991), Seven Ages (an anthology of poetry, 1992), Balkan Odyssey (1995); *Style*— The Rt Hon Lord Owen, PC, CH; ✉ 78 Narrow St, Limehouse, London E14 (☎ 0171 987 5441); 20 Queen Anne's Gate, London SW1H 9AA (☎ 0171 233 0278, fax 0171 233 0574)

OWEN, His Hon Judge (Francis) David Lloyd; TD (1967); s of Robert Charles Lloyd Owen, of Glanmorfa, Dolgellau, Meirionnydd, and Jane Ellen, *née* Francis; *b* 24 Oct 1933; *Educ* Wrekin Coll; *m* 28 Oct 1965, Jennifer Nan, da of Richard Eric Knowles Rowlands, of The Grange, Mickle Trafford, Chester; 2 da (Charis Jane b 7 May 1971, Anna Clare b 2 June 1974); *Career* Nat Serv 1952–54, cmmnd 22nd (Cheshire) Regt 1953, TA 1954–67, Maj 1963; admitted slr 1961; practising slr 1961–66, called to the Bar Gray's Inn 1967; practising Northern Circuit, actg stipendiary magistrate 1981, dep circuit judge, asst recorder 1977–88, recorder 1988–91, circuit judge (Northern Circuit) 1991–; *Recreations* country pursuits, walking, genealogy; *Clubs* Grosvenor (Chester), Royal Over-Seas (London and Edinburgh); *Style*— His Honour Judge Owen, TD; ✉ The Courts of Justice, Crown Square, Manchester

OWEN, Prof (David) Gareth; s of Oscar Vivian Owen (d 1988), and Mary Gwladys, *née* Davies (d 1961); *b* 6 Nov 1940; *Educ* Christ Coll Brecon, Downing Coll Cambridge (MA, PhD), Univ of London (BD); *m* 2 July 1966, Ann Valerie, da of Stanley Wilfred Owen Wright (d 1988); 2 da (Ceridwen b 1969, Rachel b 1971); *Career* graduate engr John Laing & Son 1966–67, sr engr Marconi Space and Defence Systems Portsmouth 1970–72, visiting assoc prof Univ of New Hampshire USA 1976; Heriot-Watt Univ: lectr Dept of Civil Engrg 1972–75, sr lectr Dept of Offshore Engrg 1977, head of dept 1981–91, prof of offshore engrg 1986–, seconded to Scottish Higher Educn Funding Cncl 1992–95, dir of quality 1995–96, dean of engrg 1996–; pres Edinburgh and Leith Petroleum Club 1991–92; FICE, CEng, FRSA; *Recreations* music, travel, languages; *Style*— Prof D Gareth Owen; ✉ 7 Oak Lane, Edinburgh EH12 6XH (☎ 0131 339 1740); Department of Civil and Offshore Engineering, Heriot-Watt University, Riccarton, Edinburgh EH14 4AS (☎ 0131 449 5111, fax 0131 451 5078, e-mail D.G.OWEN@hw.ac.uk)

OWEN, Dr Gareth; CBE (1988); s of John Richard Owen (d 1942), and Bronwen May, *née* Davies (d 1975); *b* 4 Oct 1922; *Educ* Pontypridd Boys' GS, Univ of Wales (BSc), Univ of Glasgow (DSc); *m* 28 March 1953, Beti, da of Rev Giraldus Jones (d 1978); 1 s (Geraint b 1958), 2 da (Shân b 1954, Gwyneth b 1956); *Career* Nat Serv pilot RAF 1942–47; lectr in zoology Univ of Glasgow 1950–64, pro vice chllr Queen's Univ Belfast 1974–79 (prof of zoology and head of dept 1964–79), princ UCW Aberystwyth 1979–89, vice chllr Univ of Wales 1985–87; memb: Royal Irish Acad 1976, Nature Conservancy Cncl 1984–91 (chm Welsh Ctee 1985–91); pres Welsh Centre for Int Affrs 1989–93; hon memb of the Gorsedd; Hon DSc Queen's Univ Belfast 1982, Hon LLD Univ of Wales 1989; FIBiol 1964; *Recreations* reading, photography; *Style*— Dr Gareth Owen, CBE; ✉ 6a St Margaret's Place, Whitchurch, Cardiff CF4 7AD (☎ 01222 692199)

OWEN, Gerald Victor; QC (1969); s of Samuel Owen (d 1972), and Ziporah Owen (d 1974); *b* 29 Nov 1922; *Educ* Kilburn GS, St Catharine's Coll Cambridge (MA), Queen Mary Coll London (sci scholarship), Univ of London (LLB); *m* 21 March 1946, Phyllis; 1 s (Michael b 15 Oct 1948), 1 da (Juliet b 26 Dec 1952); *Career* called to the Bar Gray's Inn 1949, ad eundem Inner Temple 1969; dep circuit judge 1971; recorder of the Crown Ct 1979–95; chm: Dairy Produce Quota Tribunal 1984–85, Med Appeal Tribunal 1984–94; FSS; *Recreations* music, winning Times crossword competition; *Style*— Gerald Owen, Esq, QC; ✉ 3 Paper Buildings, Temple, London EC4Y 7EU (☎ 0171 797 7000)

OWEN, Gordon Michael William; CBE (1991); s of Christopher Knowles Owen, and Margaret Joyce Milward, *née* Spencer (d 1986); *b* 9 Dec 1937; *Educ* Cranbrook Sch; *m* 2 Nov 1963, Jennifer Pearl, da of Basil John Bradford; 1 s (Timothy Derek b 14 Feb 1969), 1 da (Alison Carole b 29 Jan 1966); *Career* Cable & Wireless plc: joined 1954, md subsid co Mercury Communications Ltd 1984–90, dir 1986–91, jt md 1987, dep chief exec 1988, gp md 1990–91, chm Mercury Communications 1990–91; chm: Energis Ltd 1993–, Peterstar (Russia) 1992–94, MacIntyre Care 1993; non-exec chm Utility Cable plc 1994–; non-exec dir: Portals Group plc 1988–95, London Electricity plc 1990–, Verity plc 1992–, Acorn Computer PLC 1995–; vice chm Acad St Martins in the Field Orchestra Soc; CIMgt; *Recreations* golf (poor!), sailing, bee-keeping; *Style*— Gordon M W Owen, Esq, CBE; ✉ Little Hawksfold, Vann Road, Fernhurst, Sussex GU27 3NS; Energis Communications Ltd, Carmelite House, Victoria Embankment, London EC4 (☎ 0171 206 5555, fax 0171 936 5500)

OWEN, (John) Graham; s of (John) Hugh Owen, of Bridgend, and Mair Eluned, *née* Evans; *b* 30 Aug 1952; *Educ* Epsom Coll, Guy's Hosp (BDS, LDS, RCS); *m* Belle Steadman, da of Harry Mooney (d 1985), of Hounslow; 3 s (Robert b 28 Dec 1981, Jonathan b 27 June 1984, Martin b 17 Oct 1986), 1 da (Annabelle b 7 Feb 1983); *Career* Guy's Hosp: house offr 1977, sr house offr 1978, lectr in maxillofacial and oral surgery 1978–80 (pt/t 1980–); hon sec Dental Soc of London 1990–; md Owen Air Ltd (exec Air Charter Co); FRSM 1996; *Recreations* rugby, cricket, athletics, flying (private pilots licence); *Clubs* Rugby Club of London, Surrey CCC; *Style*— Graham Owen, Esq; ✉ High View, 339 Main Road, Westerham Hill, Kent TN16 2HP (☎ and fax 01959 573180); 142 Gipsy Hill, London SE19 (☎ 0181 761 8818); 84 Harley St, London W1 (☎ 0171 935 8084)

OWEN, Sir Hugh (Bernard Pilkington); 5 Bt (UK 1813); s of Sir John Arthur Owen, 4 Bt (d 1973), and Lucy, *née* Pilkington (d 1985); *b* 28 March 1915; *Educ* Chillon Coll Switzerland; *Heir* none; *Style*— Sir Hugh Owen, Bt; ✉ 63 Dudsbury Rd, Ferndown, Dorset BH22 8RD

OWEN, Hon and Rt Worshipful Mr Justice; Hon Sir John Arthur Dalziel; kt (1986); s of Robert John Owen (d 1940), and Olive Barlow, *née* Hall-Wright (d 1993); *b* 22 Nov 1925; *Educ* Solihull Sch, BNC Oxford (MA, BCL), DCL (Lambeth), Univ of Wales Coll of Cardiff (LLM in Canon Law 1996); *m* 26 July 1952, Valerie, da of William Ethell (d 1988), of Solihull; 1 s (James Alexander Dalziel b 1 June 1966), 1 da (Melissa Clare (Hon Mrs Michael-John Knatchbull) b 12 Nov 1960); *Career* cmmnd 2 King Edward's Own Gurkha Rifles 1945; called to the Bar Gray's Inn 1951, dep chm Warwickshire QS 1967–71, QC 1970, recorder of the Crown Court 1972–84, memb Senate of Inns of Court and Bar 1977–80, dep ldr Midland and Oxford Circuit 1979–84, Dean of the Arches and Auditor of Chancery Ct York 1980–, circuit judge at Old Bailey 1984–86, judge of the High Court of Justice (Queen's Bench Div) 1986–; chm W Midlands Area Mental Health Review Tribunal 1972–80; Hon Liveryman Worshipful Co of Scriveners; *Clubs* Garrick; *Style*— The Hon and Rt Worshipful Mr Justice John Owen; ✉ Royal Courts of Justice, Strand, London WC2A 2LL; 14 Gray's Inn Square, Gray's Inn, London WC1R 5LQ (☎ 0171 242 7722)

OWEN, John Aubrey; s of Douglas Aubrey Owen (d 1964), and Patricia Joan, *née* Griggs (d 1968); *b* 1 Aug 1945; *Educ* City of London Sch, St Catharine's Coll Cambridge (MA); *m* 8 May 1971, Julia Margaret, da of Thomas Gordon Jones, of Shrewsbury (d 1993); 1 s (Charles Aubrey b 1972), 1 da (Lucy Margaret b 1975); *Career* joined Miny of Tport 1969, asst private sec to Min for Tport Industs 1972, DOE 1972–75, Dept of Tport 1975–78, seconded to Cambs CC 1978–80; DOE 1980–: regnl dir Northern Regnl Office DOE and Dept of Tport 1987–91, dir of personnel mgmnt 1991–95, dir Regeneration Govt Office for London 1995–; FRSA; *Recreations* gardening, opera; *Style*— John Owen, Esq; ✉ 33 Valley Road, Welwyn Garden City, Herts AL8 7DH (☎ 01707 321768); Government Office for London, Room 6.1, River Walk House, 157–161 Millbank, London SW1P 4RR (☎ 0171 217 3092, fax 0171 217 3460)

OWEN, Prof John Bryn; s of Owen William Owen (d 1960), of Anglesey, Gwynedd, and Jane Owen (d 1953); *b* 23 May 1931; *Educ* Ffestiniog GS, Univ of Wales Bangor (BSc, PhD), Univ of Cambridge (MA); *m* 10 Aug 1955, Margaret Helen, da of Hugh James Hughes, MBE (d 1979), of Worcester; 2 s (Gareth b 1956, David b 1958), 1 da (Helen b 1964); *Career* farms mangr Huttons Ambo Estate Yorks 1956–58, lectr in agric UCW Aberystwyth 1958–62, lectr and dir of studies in agric Emmanuel Coll Cambridge 1962–72, prof of animal prodn and health Univ of Aberdeen 1972–78, prof of agric Univ of Wales Bangor 1978–, dean faculty of sci Bangor 1987–89, head Sch of Agric and Forest Sciences 1989–93; FIBiol 1970, FRSA 1975, FRAgS 1980; *Books* incl: Performance Recording in Sheep (1971), Detection and Control of Breeding Activity in Farm Animals (1975), Sheep Production (1976), Complete Diets for Cattle and Sheep (1979), Cattle Feeding (1983), Sheep (Defaid) (1984), New Techniques in Sheep Production (1987), Breeding for Disease Resistance in Farm Animals (1991); *Recreations* choral singing; *Clubs* Farmers'; *Style*— Prof John Owen; ✉ School of Agricultural and Forest Sciences, University of Wales Bangor, Deiniol Rd, Bangor, Gwynedd (☎ 01248 351151, fax 01248 354997)

OWEN, Maj-Gen John Ivor Headon; OBE (1963); s of Maj William Headon Owen, MC (d 1954), and Norita Alexandrina, *née* Morgan (d 1970); *b* 22 Oct 1922; *Educ* St Edmund's Sch Canterbury; *m* 1948, Margaret Jean, da of Edwin Hayes (d 1931); 3 da; *Career* RM commando 1942, Far East 1943–46, Constable Met Police 1946–47, rejoined RM, regtl serv to 1955, Staff Coll Camberley 1956, Bde Maj, MOD (Admty) 1962–64, JSSC 1966–67; CO 45 Commando 1967–69; RCDS 1971, Maj-Gen Commando Forces RM Plymouth 1972–73, Maj-Gen 1972; UK partnership sec to KMG Thomson McLintock 1974–87, Rep Col Cmdt RM 1985–86; dir Opus Resource Management Ltd 1991–93; vice chm Clergy Orphan Corp 1995–96 (treas 1980–94), memb Ctee of Sons of Clergy Corp; chm: Ctee Bowles Outdoor Centre, Tstees RM Museum, Govrs St Margaret's Sch Bushey; FIMgt; *Books* Brassey's Infantry Weapons of the World, and others; *Recreations* woodworking, gardening; *Clubs* Army and Navy; *Style*— Maj-Gen John Owen, OBE; ✉ Phoenix House, 25 High Street, Barrington, Cambs CB2 5QX

OWEN, John Wyn; CB (1994); s of Idwal Wyn Owen (d 1984), of Bangor, and Myfi, *née* Hughes; *b* 15 May 1942; *Educ* Friars Sch Bangor, St John's Coll Cambridge (BA, MA), King's Fund Hosp Admin Staff Coll (FHSM Dip HSM); *m* 1 April 1967, Elizabeth Ann, da of William MacFarlane (d 1980), of Bangor; 1 s (Dafydd b 1974), 1 da (Sian b 1971); *Career* hosp sec Glantawe HMC Swansea 1967–70, staff trg offr Welsh Hosp Bd Cardiff 1968–70, divnl admin Univ Hosp of Wales HMC Cardiff 1970–72, asst clerk St Thomas's Hosp London 1972–74, admin St Thomas's Health Dist 1974–79; exec dir United Medical Enterprises London 1979–85; dir: Allied Medical Group London 1979–85, Br Nursing Cooperations London 1979–85, Allied Med Gp Healthcare Canada 1982–85, Allied Shanning London 1983–85; chm Welsh Health Common Servs Authy 1985–94, dir Welsh NHS 1985–94, DG NSW Health Dept Aust, chm Australian Health Ministers' Advsy Cncl 1995–, dep chm Strategic Planning and Evaluation Ctee Nat Health & Research Cncl 1995–; tstee: Florence Nightingale Museum Tst 1983–90, Mgmnt Advsy Serv 1986–90; memb Personnel Standards Lead Body 1992–94; organist Utd Free Church Cowbridge 1985; fell Univ Coll of Wales Aberystwyth, fell Univ Coll of Wales Bangor; hon fell Faculty of Public Health Medicine, fell Australian Coll of Health Service Execs 1994; FHSM; *Recreations* organ playing, opera, travel; *Clubs* Athenaeum; *Style*— John Wyn Owen, Esq, CB; ✉ Newton Farm, Cowbridge, South Glamorgan CF7 7RZ (☎ 01446 775113)

OWEN, HE John Wynne; MBE (1979); s of Thomas David Owen (d 1977), of Pontardulais, S Wales, and Mair Eluned, *née* Richards (d 1988); *b* 25 April 1939; *Educ* Gowerton GS; *m* 1, 14 July 1962, Thelma Margaret (d 1987), da of Arthur James Gunton (d 1984), of Yarmouth, Isle of Wight; 1 s (David b 1970), 2 da (Sandra b 1963, Karen b 1969), 1 step da (Fiona Roberts b 1977); m 2, 19 March 1988, Carol, da of John Edmunds, of Wootton, IOW; *Career* HM Foreign Serv 1956–58, Nat Serv RS 1958–60, cmmnd 2 Lt 1959; HM Foreign Serv (later Dip Serv): Indonesia 1960–61, Vietnam 1961–62, Paris 1962–63, El Salvador 1963–67, resigned between 1967 and 1970 (to gain business experience), returned to FO 1970–73, 3 later 2 sec Br Embassy Tehran 1973–77, vice consul and later consul (commercial) Br Consulate Gen Sao Paulo Brazil 1978–80, 1 sec and consul Br Embassy Peking 1980–82, 1 sec FO 1983–85, special unpaid leave 1985–89, cnsllr FO 1990–92, HM consul gen Boston 1992–95, govr Cayman Islands 1995–; chm Gunham Plastics Ltd 1985–90 (dir since 1967), chm and md Gunham

Holdings Ltd 1987–90, chm Br Laminated Plastics Fabricators Assoc 1987–91; Freeman City of London, Liveryman Worshipful Co of Loriners; FIMgt 1985; *Recreations* swimming, flyfishing, walking; *Clubs* RAC, City Livery; *Style*— HE Mr John Wynne Owen, MBE; ✉ c/o FCO (Grand Cayman), King Charles Street, London SW1A 2AH

OWEN, Mark; *b* 27 Jan 1972; *Career* singer; memb Take That 1990–96, solo career 1996–; 11 top ten singles incl 6 no 1's (Pray 1993, Relight My Fire 1993, Babe 1993, Everything Changes 1994, Sure 1994, Back For Good 1995); albums with Take That: Take That and Party (1992, UK no 2), Everything Changes (1993, UK no 1), Nobody Else (1995); first solo CD Green Man (1996); *Awards* incl: Best British Single (for Could It Be Magic) BRIT Awards 1993, Nordoff Robbins Silver Clef Levi's Original Talent Award 1993, Best British Single and Best British Video (for Pray) BRIT Awards 1994, Best Group MTV Euro Pop Awards 1994; *Videos* incl: Take That and Party (1992, UK no 1), Take That - The Party Live At Wembley (1993, UK no 1), Everything Changes (1994, UK no 1), Take That - Berlin (1994, UK no 1); *Recreations* football, keeping fit; *Style*— Mark Owen, Esq

OWEN, Dr (J) Martin; *Career* chief exec NatWest Markets 1992–, dir National Westminster Bank plc 1992–; chm Advsy Bd Salvation Army; FCA, FCCA, FCIB, FCT; *Style*— Dr Martin Owen; ✉ NatWest Markets, 135 Bishopsgate, London EC2M 3UR (☎ 0171 375 4900)

OWEN, Brig Michael Charles; s of John Joseph Owen (d 1948), and Mary May, *née* McSweeney (d 1973); *b* 27 Nov 1936; *Educ* Aberdare GS, RMA Sandhurst; *m* 29 Dec 1960, Patricia Mary, da of George Tennant (d 1958); *Career* SOI (DS) Staff Coll 1975, CRAOC 1 Armoured Div 1976, AA and QMG AQ Ops and Plans 1979, Col Ord 1 1980, DACOS LOG HQ AFCENT 1983, Cdr RAOC Trg Centre 1988, Cmd Supply BAOR 1989; Anglican lay reader licenced 1978, selector C of E's Advsy Cncl for the Churches Ministry; sec RAOC Charitable Tst; MIMgt 1971, FInstPS 1988; *Recreations* walking, ornithology, sports (as a spectator); *Style*— Brig Michael Owen; ✉ RAOC Charitable Trust, Dettingen House, Deepcut, Camberley, Surrey GU15 2EJ

OWEN, (John) Michael Holland; s of Col Robert Leslie Owen, OBE, TD (d 1973), of Austwick, nr Settle, N Yorks, and Kathleen, *née* Steen (d 1989); *b* 4 March 1932; *Educ* St Edward's Sch Oxford; *m* 28 Jan 1968, (Patricia) Anne, da of Col J B Gartside, DSO, MC, TD, JP, DL (d 1964), of Crimble Cottage, Rochdale; 2 s (Robert b 15 Dec 1968, William b 11 March 1970), 1 da (Jennifer b 1 March 1972); *Career* Nat Serv 1950–52, appointed 2 Lt 1 Bn 22 (Cheshire) Regt, Capt 7 Bn 22 (Cheshire) Regt TA 1952–66; Whitecroft plc (formerly Bleachers Assoc Ltd) 1953–72; gen mangr: Ashworth & Smith Ltd 1960–63, River Etherow Bleaching Co Ltd 1963–64; md Chorley Bleaching Co Ltd and dir Inver Bleaching Co and Bulwell Dyeing Co Ltd 1964–71, Shiloh plc 1972–, non-exec dir WM Supplies UK Ltd 1974–91, md Amberguard Ltd 1977–; memb Ward Ctee Cons Pty 1975–85; *Style*— Michael Owen, Esq, TD; ✉ Amberguard Ltd, Elk Mill, Broadway, Chadderton, Oldham OL2 5HS (☎ 0161 620 4328)

OWEN, Dr Myrfyn; s of William Owen (d 1980), and Anne Mary, *née* Williams; *b* 8 April 1943; *Educ* Sir Hugh Owen GS Caernarfon, Dept of Agric Univ Coll of Wales Aberystwyth (BSc), Dept of Agric Univ of Leeds (DPhil); *m* March 1967, Lydia Marian Vaughan, da of Idris Goronwy Rees; 2 da (Nia Mair b 1971, Elen Gwenllian b 1973); *Career* The Wildfowl & Wetlands Trust (previously The Wildfowl Trust): joined as ecologist 1967, conservation research offr 1974–79, asst dir 1979–88, head of research 1988–92, dir of research and conservation 1992, DG 1992–; chm Wetlands Advisory Service Ltd 1992–; chm Severn Estuary Conservation Gp 1988–92; memb: Cncl Br Ornithologists' Union 1989–93, Conservation and Research Ctee Br Assoc for Shooting and Conservation 1990–95, Research and Surveys Ctee Br Tst for Ornithology 1990–93, Lead Poisoning in Waterfowl Working Gp DoE 1991–, Arctic Programme Steering Ctee Natural Environment Research Cncl 1991–; coordinator Threatened Waterfowl Research Gp and memb Bd Int Waterfowl and Wetlands Research Bureau 1991–92; memb: Br Ecological Soc 1966, Br Ornithologists' Union 1972; life memb Estuarine and Coastal Sciences Assoc 1972; *Publications* Wildfowl of Europe (1976), Wild Geese of the World (1980), Wildfowl in Great Britain (1986), Waterfowl Ecology (1990); also writer and collaborator on numerous popular articles, books and films; regular appearances on TV and radio; *Recreations* writing, cycling, walking, gardening, cooking and music; *Style*— Dr Myrfyn Owen; ✉ Woodleigh House, 62 Woodmancote, Dursley, Glos GL11 4AQ; The Wildfowl & Wetlands Trust, Slimbridge, Glos GL2 7BT (☎ 01453 890333, fax 01453 890827)

OWEN, Nicholas David Arundel; s of Tom Owen (d 1981), and Diana Owen; *b* 10 Feb 1947; *m* Brenda; 1 da (Rebecca b 22 Dec 1969), 1 s (Anthony b 2 Oct 1976); *Career* journalist: Surrey Mirror 1964–68, London Evening Standard 1968–70, Daily Telegraph 1970–72, Financial Times 1972–79, Now! Magazine 1979–81; reporter and presenter BBC Television News 1981–84, presenter ITN 1984–; *Books* History of the British Trolleybus (1972); *Recreations* reading, swimming, golf, piano; *Style*— Nicholas Owen, Esq; ✉ ITN Ltd, 200 Gray's Inn Road, London WC1X 8XZ (☎ 0171 430 4750)

OWEN, Nick Corbishley; *b* 1 Nov 1947; *Educ* Shrewsbury Sch, Univ of Leeds (BA); *m* Jill; 3 s (Andrew b 23 May 1979, Timothy b 30 March 1981, Christopher b 22 Nov 1986), 1 da (Jennifer b 8 Sept 1988); *Career* trainee reporter Doncaster Evening Post 1969–71, reporter Birmingham Post 1971–73, prodr BBC Radio Birmingham 1973–78, presenter/reporter (news and sport) ATV and Central TV 1978–83; presenter: TVam 1983–86, Sporting Triangles (ITV) 1986 and 1987, Midweek Sport Special ITV 1986–92 (plus World Athletics Championships 1987, Olympics 1988, World Cup 1990, and other maj sporting events UK and abroad), Wish You Were Here? (ITV) 1991–, Good Morning with Anne and Nick (BBC 1) 1992–96; *Recreations* children, watching cricket, football; *Style*— Nick Owen; ✉ c/o Knight Ayton Management, 10 Argyll Street, London W1V 1AB (☎ 0171 287 4405, fax 0171 434 3075)

OWEN, Norah Langton; da of William Albert Rogerson (d 1960), and Dorothy Mather, *née* Langton (d 1962); *b* 16 Feb 1918; *Educ* Farringtons Chislehurst Kent; *m* 1945 (m dis 1949), John H Y Owen; 1 da (Caroline (Mrs Masterton-Smith) b 1946); *Career* sec/asst J Baxter-Somerville Theatre Prodns 1937–40; War Serv: VAD nurse BRCS 1940, cmmnd RAF 1942 (served 1941–45); Clerke & Cochrane Publishers 1949, journalist Harper's Bazaar 1950–52, fashion ed The Sketch 1952–55, assoc dir PR Dept W S Crawfords 1955–63, sr ptnr Newslines PR 1963–75, assoc dir Charles Barker Ltd (after takeover) 1975–83, PR conslt and voluntary worker 1983–; pres AWPR 1974 (fndr memb 1960); IPR: assoc 1956, memb 1960, fell 1975, pres 1981–82, hon fell 1983, chm Benevolent Fund 1992; *Recreations* reading, gardening, grandchildren, writing; *Style*— Mrs Norah Owen; ✉ 34 Primrose Road, Thorpe Hamlet, Norwich, Norfolk NR1 4AS (☎ 01603 628718)

OWEN, Peter Francis; CB (1990); s of Arthur Owen (d 1988), and Violet, Winifred, *née* Morris; *b* 4 Sept 1940; *Educ* Liverpool Inst, Univ of Liverpool (BA); *m* 27 July 1963, Ann, da of William Henry Preece (d 1974); 1 s (David b 8 April 1969), 1 da (Poppy b 13 Sept 1973); *Career* joined Miny of Public Bldg and Works (now part of DOE) 1964, Cabinet Office and private sec to successive Ministers of Housing and Construction 1971–74, asst sec housing policy review DOE 1974–77, asst sec local govt fin DOE 1977–80, regnl dir Northern and Yorks and Humberside Regions DOE and Dept of Tport 1980–82, dir rural affrs DOE 1982–83, under sec local govt fin policy DOE 1983–86, dep sec housing and construction DOE 1986–90, dep sec Cabinet Office 1990–94, dep sec DFE 1994–95, director gen of Schs Directorate DFEE 1995–; *Recreations* gardening, French language and lit; *Style*— Peter Owen, Esq, CB; ✉ Department for Education and Employment, Sanctuary Buildings, Great Smith Street, London SW1P 3BT (☎ 0171 925 5800, fax 0171 925 5379)

OWEN, Philip Anthony; s of Alec Owen, ARIBA (d 1959), of Hornsea, East Yorks, and Katherine Mary, *née* Pink; *b* 25 Aug 1944; *Educ* Pitman's Coll Hull, Queens' Coll Cambridge; *m* 5 Sept 1984, Deborah Anne, da of Arthur Harry Lewin, of Auckland, NZ; 1 s (Simon b 1988), 1 da (Julia b 1987); *Career* admitted slr 1968; ptnr Allen & Overy 1982– (joined 1973); Liveryman Worshipful Co Slrs; memb Law Soc 1968, memb Cncl IOD; *Recreations* ocean racing, golf, skiing; *Clubs* Royal Ocean Racing, Royal Yorkshire Yacht, Royal Wimbledon Golf; *Style*— Philip Owen, Esq; ✉ Allen & Overy, One New Exchange, London EC4M 9QQ (☎ 0171 330 3000, fax 0171 330 9999)

OWEN, Philip Loscombe Wintringham; TD (1950), QC (1963); s of Rt Hon Sir Wintringham Stable, MC (d 1977), of Plas Llwyn Owen, Llanbrynmair, Powys, and Lucy Haden Stable (d 1976); assumed surname of Owen by deed poll 1942; *b* 10 Jan 1920; *Educ* Winchester, ChCh Oxford (MA); *m* 1949, Elizabeth Jane, da of Lewis Trelawny Widdicombe (d 1953); 3 s, 2 da; *Career* served WWII Royal Welch Fus, Maj TARO; received into RC Church 1943; called to the Bar Middle Temple 1949, memb Gen Cncl of Bar of Eng and Wales 1971–77; dep chm of QS: Montgomeryshire 1959–71, Cheshire 1961–71; bencher 1969; recorder: Merthyr Tydfil 1971, Crown Court 1972–85; ldr Wales and Chester circuit 1975–77; legal assessor to: Gen Med Cncl 1970–, Gen Dental Cncl 1970–, RICS 1970–; Parly candidate (C) Montgomeryshire 1945; JP: Montgomeryshire 1959, Cheshire 1961; dir Swansea City AFC Ltd 1975–86; tstee and memb Ctee Mgmnt Young Musicians Symphony Orchestra 1992–, vice pres Montgomeryshire Cons and Unionist Assoc, former pres Montgomeryshire Soc; *Recreations* shooting, fishing, forestry, music, association football; *Clubs* Carlton, Pratt's, Cardiff and County, Bristol Channel Yacht (Mumbles); *Style*— Philip Owen, Esq, TD, QC; ✉ Plas Llwyn Owen, Llanbrynmair, Powys SY19 7BE (☎ 01650 521542); Brick Court Chambers, 15–19 Devereux Court, Strand, London WC2R 3JJ (☎ 0171 583 0777)

OWEN, Dr Richard Charles; s of Alfred Roy Warren Owen (d 1978), of Rottingdean, Sussex, and Florence Mary, *née* Walker; *b* 14 July 1947; *Educ* Varndean GS, Univ of Nottingham (BA), LSE (MSc, PhD), Stanford Univ Calif (Harkness scholarship); *m* 1 May 1982, Julia Anne, da of Clive Raymond Crosse; 1 s (Laurence b 22 Aug 1988), 2 da (Eleanor Owen b 2 May 1983, Isabel Owen b 2 May 1983); *Career* script writer and prodr BBC External Servs 1973–79, asst prodr BBC TV Current Affrs 1979–80; The Times 1980–: ldr writer 1980–82, Moscow corr 1982–85, Brussels corr 1985–88, Jerusalem corr 1988–91, dep foreign ed 1991–92, foreign ed 1992–96, Rome corr 1996–; *Books* Letters from Moscow (1985), Crisis in the Kremlin (1986), The Times Guide to 1992, Britain in a Europe without Frontiers (1990), The Times Guide to World Organisations (1996); *Style*— Dr Richard Owen; ✉ The Times, 1 Pennington St, London E1 9BD (☎ 0171 782 5234)

OWEN, Richard Wilfred; s of Wilfred Arthur Owen (d 1974), and Ivy Ellen, *née* Gamble (d 1981); *b* 26 Oct 1932; *Educ* Gunnersbury Catholic GS; *m* 19 Feb 1966, Sheila Marie, *née* Kerrigan; 3 adopted s (b 1969, and 2 b 1971), 1 adopted da (b 1973), 1 foster da (b 1961), 1 foster s (b 1966); *Career* Lloyds Bank 1948–51, Russian translator RAF 1951–53, student accountant ICAEW 1953–58, Thomson McLintock 1958–62, Crompton Parkinson 1962–64; Touche Ross: joined 1964, ptnr 1969, seconded to Civil Serv 1970–71, ptnr i/c mgmnt consultancy 1974–87, nat dir of personnel 1987–93, Euro dir of mgmnt consultancy 1988–92, UK chm 1988–90, ret 1993; pres Mgmnt Consultancies Assoc 1987; tstee: Isabel Hospice; ACA 1958; *Style*— Mr Richard Owen; ✉ 92 Harmer Green Lane, Welwyn, Herts AL6 0EP

OWEN, Robert Frank; QC (1996); s of Tudor Owen (d 1994), of Clwyd, and (Alice) Pat, *née* Ferris; *b* 31 May 1953; *Educ* St Asaph GS, Prestatyn HS, PCL (Univ of London external LLB); *m* Anna Elizabeth, da of Richard Shaw; 3 s (Jonathan Robert b 31 Jan 1982, William Tudor b 25 May 1985, Thomas Rufus b 7 March 1989); *Career* called to the Bar Gray's Inn 1977; *Recreations* walking, gardening, sport; *Style*— R F Owen, Esq, QC; ✉ 24 The Ropewalk, Ropewalk Chambers, Nottingham NG1 5EF

OWEN, Robert Michael; QC (1988); s of Gwynne Llewellyn Owen (d 1986), of Fowey, Cornwall and Phoebe Constance Owen; *b* 19 Sept 1944; *Educ* Durham Sch Exeter Univ (LLB); *m* 9 Aug 1969, Sara Josephine, da of Sir Algernon Rumbold, KCMG, CIE, of Shortwoods, West Clandon, Surrey; 2 s (Thomas b 10 Nov 1973, Huw b 4 Jan 1976); *Career* called to the Bar 1968, recorder 1987–, dep High Ct judge 1994; chm London Common Law and Commercial Bar Assoc 1993–95 (vice-chm 1991–93), chm Gen Cncl of the Bar 1997 (vice-chm 1996); *Clubs* MCC, Royal Fowey Yacht; *Style*— Robert Owen, Esq, QC; ✉ 1 Crown Office Row, Temple, London EC4Y 7HH (☎ 0171 797 7500, fax 0171 797 9550)

OWEN, Prof (David) Roger Jones; s of Evan William Owen (d 1952), of Llanelli, and Margaret, *née* Jones (d 1990); *b* 27 May 1942; *Educ* Llanelli Boys' GS, Univ Coll Swansea (BSc, MSc), Northwestern Univ USA (PhD), Univ of Wales (DSc); *m* 12 Feb 1964, Janet Mary, da of William James Pugh (d 1983), of Llanelli; 2 da (Kathryn b 1967, Lisa b 1970); *Career* prof Univ of Wales 1982, dir Inst for Numerical Methods in Engrg Univ of Wales Swansea 1987–; chm Rockfield Software Ltd, dir Pineridge Press Ltd; author of numerous pubns; memb: Cncl Nat Assoc On Finite Element Methods and Standards, various SERC ctees; FICE 1983, FEng 1996; *Books* with E Hinton: Finite Element Programming (1977), An Introduction to Finite Element Computations (1979), Finite Elements in Plasticity (1980), A Simple Guide to Finite Elements (1980), Engineering Fracture Mechanics: Numerical Methods and Applications (1983); *Recreations* flying, golf, tennis; *Clubs* Langland Bay Golf, Swansea; *Style*— Prof Roger Owen, FEng; ✉ Department of Civil Engineering, University of Wales Swansea, Singleton Park, Swansea SA2 9PP (☎ 01792 295252, fax 01792 295676)

OWEN, Sally Ann; da of Robert James Owen, of Plas Llysyn, Carno, Powys, and Rhoda, *née* Betteridge; *b* 11 May 1952; *Educ* Hengrove Comp Sch Bristol, Bristol Sch of Dancing, Rambert Sch of Ballet London; *Career* dancer, actress and choreographer; soloist Ballet Rambert 1971–81; *Performances* with Second Stride 1983–91 incl: The Brilliant and the Dark, Java Jive, Minor Characters, Cosi Fan Tutti, New Tactics, Further and Further Into Night, Bösendorfer Walses, Weighing the Heart, Heaven Ablaze in his Breast, Lives of the Great Poisoners; with Direct Current 1985–88 incl: A Personal Appearance, Mary Mary, The Super Hero Project; also involved with: Secret Gardens (ICA and Micary Theatre Amsterdam) 1983, IQ of 4 (ICA) 1984, Lindsay Kemp (Italy, Sadler's Wells Theatre, Theatre Royal Brighton) 1985, Michael Matou (Barcelona 1985), Gateway to Freedom 1987–96, Fugue (Channel 4 TV) 1988, Of Shadows and Walls (Rosemary Butcher and Co) 1992, And The Ship Sailed On (London Mime Theatre) 1993–96, Cinderella, A Gothic Opera (Lindsay Kemp Co) 1994, The Ink Thief (Tyne Tees TV); *Choreography* works incl: Paper Sunday (Ballet Rambert) 1980, Unsuitable Case (Ballet Rambert) 1981, Mascaritas (Emma Dance Co) 1982, Giraffes and Jellyfish and Things (Extemporary Dance Theatre) 1982, We Shall Fight Them on the Beaches (English Dance Theatre) 1983, The Dead Moon (Junior Co of Nederlands Dance Theatre) 1984, Did Eat the Bait and Fisherman Beguile (Transitions Dance Co) 1987, The Tailor of Gloucester (National Youth Music Theatre) 1989, Midday Sun (ICA), Gormenghast (David Glass Ensemble) 1992; *Style*— Ms Sally Owen; ✉ c/o Second Stride, Sadler's Wells Theatre, Rosebery Ave, London EC1R 4TN (☎ 0171 278 2917, fax 0171 278 5927)

OWEN, Thomas Arfon; s of Hywel Peris Owen, of Tumble; *b* 7 June 1933; *Educ* Ystalyfera GS, Magdalen Coll Oxford (MA); *m* 1955, Mary Joyce, da of Tom Ellis Phillips, of Ystalyfera (d 1972); 3 s, 1 da; *Career* registrar Univ Coll of Wales

Aberystwyth 1967–84, dir Welsh Arts Cncl 1984–93, devpt and funding conslt 1993–; memb Consumer Ctee for GB 1975–90; High Sheriff of Dyfed 1976–77; memb Cncl: Health Authy S Glam 1984–87 (vice chm 1986–87), UWIST 1987–88, Univ of Wales Cardiff 1988–, Nat Library of Wales 1987– (vice pres 1992–), Univ of Wales Aberystwyth 1990–, Univ of Wales Coll of Med 1995–; master Welsh Livery Guild 1996–97; FRSA; *Recreations* reading, crosswords, public service; *Style*— Thomas Owen, Esq; ✉ Argoed, Ffordd-y-fulfran, Borth, Ceredigion SY24 5NN (☎ and fax 01970 871129)

OWEN, Trevor Bryan; CBE (1987); s of Leonard Owen, CIE (d 1965), of Gerrards Cross, and Dilys, *née* Davies Bryan; *b* 3 April 1928; *Educ* Rugby, Trinity Coll Oxford (MA); *m* 1955, Gaie, da of Cyril Dashwood Houston (d 1975), of Newark, Notts; 1 s (Jonathan b 1958), 1 da (Jane b 1956); *Career* dir Paints, Agric and Plastics Divs ICI 1955–78; md Remploy Ltd 1978–88; chm: Bethlem and Maudsley Special Health Authy 1988–94, Inst of Psychiatry 1990–, PHAB 1988–91; memb: Govt of N Ireland Higher Educn Review Gp 1979–81, Nat Advsy Cncl on the Employment of Disabled People 1978–88, CNAA 1973–79, Cncl CBI 1982–88, Cncl Ind Soc 1967–88, Cncl Inst of Manpower Studies 1975–87; chm Bd of Govrs, Nat Inst for Social Work 1985–91; *Books* Making Organisations Work (1978), The Manager and Industrial Relations (1979); *Style*— Trevor B Owen, CBE; ✉ 8 Rochester Terrace, London NW1 9JN (☎ 0171 485 9265)

OWEN, Tudor Wyn; s of Abel Rhys Owen (d 1974), of Aberdare, Glamorgan, and Mair, *née* Jenkins; *b* 16 May 1951; *Educ* Aberdare GS, King's Coll London (LLB Hons); *Career* called to the Bar Gray's Inn 1974, in practice South Eastern Circuit, recorder of the Crown Ct 1994; inspr DTI 1989; memb: Ctee Criminal Bar Assoc 1987–91 (treas 1988–91), Gen Cncl of the Bar 1988–94, Bar Professional Conduct Ctee 1989–91, Bar Ctee 1990–92 (vice chm 1991–92), Bar Public Affairs Ctee 1990–91, Gen Mgmnt Ctee 1992–93, Professional Standards Ctee 1992–93, S Eastern Circuit Ctee 1992–; *Recreations* motor racing, flying helicopters and WWII fighter aircraft, shooting, skiing, riding the Cresta Run, music; *Clubs* Garrick, Carlton, St Moritz Tobogganing; *Style*— Tudor Owen, Esq; ✉ 25 Dancer Road, Parsons Green, London SW6 4DU (☎ and fax 0171 731 7940); Chambers, 9–12 Bell Yard, London WC2A 2LF (☎ 0171 400 1800, fax 0171 404 1405)

OWEN-JONES, David Roderic; s of (John) Eryl Owen-Jones, CBE, JP, DL, *qv*, and Mabel Clara, *née* McIlvride; *b* 16 March 1949; *Educ* Llandovery Coll Dyfed, UCL (LLB, LLM); *Career* called to the Bar Inner Temple 1972, ad eundem Lincoln's Inn 1993; in practice S Eastern Circuit; Parly candidate: (Lib) Carmarthen Div Feb and Oct 1974, (Lib Alliance) Rugby and Kenilworth 1983 and 1987; govr Int Students Tst 1981–84 and 1992– (tstee 1981–), vice chm Assoc of Lib Dem Lawyers, memb Lord Chancellor's Advsy Ctee on the Appointments of JPs for Inner London 1986–91, actg Met stipendiary magistrate 1991–93; FRSA 1984; *Books* The Prosecutorial Process in England and Wales (jtly); *Recreations* theatre, historical biography; *Clubs* Nat Lib (tstee, chm 1988–91), Reform; *Style*— David Owen-Jones, Esq; ✉ 17 Albert Bridge Rd, London SW11 (☎ 0171 622 1280); 3 Temple Gdns, Temple, London EC4Y 9AU (☎ 0171 583 1155)

OWEN-JONES, (John) Eryl; CBE (1969), JP (1974), DL (Caerns 1971, Gwynedd 1974); s of John Owen-Jones (d 1962), of Colwyn Bay; *b* 19 Jan 1912; *Educ* Portmadoc GS, UCW Aberystwyth (LLB), Gonville and Caius Coll Cambridge (MA); *m* 1944, Mabel Clara, da of Grant McIlvride (d 1920), of Ajmer, Rajputana; 1 s (David Owen-Jones, *qv*), 1 da (Ann (Mrs Davies)); *Career* CO 8000 AMES (RAF Radar) Operation Torch N Africa 1942, Sqdn Ldr RAFVR 1945; admitted slr 1938, asst slr Chester Corp 1939, legal staff offr Judge Advocate General's Dept Med, dep clerk Caernarvonshire CC 1946; clerk of the Peace 1956–72; clerk to: Caernarvonshire CC 1956–74, N Wales Combined Probation Ctee, Gwynedd Police Authy 1956–67; dep clerk Snowdonia Park Jt Advsy Ctee, Clerk of Lieutenancy, memb Gorsedd y Beirdd Eisteddfod Genedlaethol 1990; vice pres Gwynedd Magistrates' Assoc 1982–; memb: Central Cncl Magistrates' Courts Ctees 1981, Bd Civic Tst for Wales 1982–, Bd Gwynedd Archaeological Tst Ltd 1982–; hon sec Caernarvonshire Historical Soc 1956–74, chm Caernarvon Civic Soc 1980–89; FRSA 1987; *Books* Caernarvonshire - A Choice of Celebrities (1993); *Recreations* music, photography, gardening; *Style*— Eryl Owen-Jones Esq, CBE, JP, DL; ✉ Rhiw Dafnau, Caernarfon, Gwynedd LL55 1LF (☎ 01286 673370)

OWEN-SMITH, Dr Brian David; s of Cyril Robert Smith, OBE (d 1993), and Margaret Jane, *née* Hughes (d 1994); *b* 29 May 1938; *Educ* Dulwich, Queens' Coll Cambridge (MA, MB BChir), Guy's Hosp London (DPhys, Med), MRCS, FRCP; *m* 24 Sept 1966, Hon Rose Magdalen Ponsonby, da of 2 Baron Ponsonby of Shulbrede (d 1976); 1 s (Timothy Clive b 25 April 1968), 1 da (Emma Elizabeth Jane b 22 Aug 1971); *Career* Lilly fell in clinical pharmacology Indiana Univ USA 1970, sr registrar rheumatic diseases Royal Nat Hosp Bath 1972; currently: conslt in rheumatics and rehabilitation St Richard's Hosp Chichester W Sussex, med dir Younger Disabled Unit Donald Wilson House, conslt in sports injuries BUPA Hosp Havant; fell Hunterian Soc, memb Chichester Soc; Freeman: City of London, Worshipful Soc of Apothecaries; LRCP, MRCS, FRCP; *Recreations* squash, tennis, sailing; *Clubs* RSM; *Style*— Dr Brian Owen-Smith; ✉ 48 Westgate, Chichester PO19 3EU (☎ 01243 786688)

OWENS, Bernard Charles; s of Charles Albert Owens (d 1992), and Sheila, *née* O'Higgins (d 1985); *b* 20 March 1928; *Educ* Solihull Sch, LSE; *m* 1954, Barbara Madeline, da of Thomas Murphy (d 1971); 2 s (Michael b 1955, Peter b 1960); 4 da (Jacqueline b 1955, Jennifer b 1957, Teresa b 1961, Susan b 1963); *Career* chm: Unochrome Int Ltd (now Unochrome Ind plc) 1964–79, Van der Horst worldwide and 70 other assoc cos; dep chm Hamdden Ltd 1991–93 (dir 1990); dir: Hobbs Savill & Bradford Ltd 1957–62, Trinidad Sugar Estates Ltd 1965–67, Cornish Brewery Co Ltd 1987–93, Br Jewellery and Giftware Fedn Ltd 1987–96 (pres 1991–92); md: Stanley Bros Ltd 1961–67, Coronet Industl Securities Ltd 1965–67; memb Monopolies and Mergers Cmmn 1981–93; memb: Order of Malta 1979, Lloyd's 1978, HAC 1984; life govr RNLI 1984, Parly candidate (Cons) Small Heath Birmingham 1959 and 1961; cncllr Solihull UDC and Borough Cncl 1954–64 (chm of finance 1957–64); Lord of the Manor of Southwood; Freeman City of London 1981; Liveryman: Worshipful Co of Gardeners 1982, Worshipful Co of Basketmakers 1995; FRSA; *Clubs* MCC, City Livery Yacht (Cdre), Wig and Pen, Stroud RFC; *Style*— Bernard Owens, Esq; ✉ The Vatch House, Stroud, Gloucestershire GL6 7JY (☎ 01453 763402)

OWENS, Prof David Howard; s of Maurice Owens, of Derby, and Joan, *née* Browes; *b* 23 April 1948; *Educ* Dronfield Henry Fanshawe, Imperial Coll London (BSc, PhD); *m* 18 July 1969, Rosemary, da of John Cecil Frost, of Sheffield; 1 s (Benjamin David b 1976), 1 da (Penelope Rosemary Jane b 1979); *Career* scientific offr UK AEA Atomic Energy Estab Winfrith 1969–73, reader in control engrg Univ of Sheffield 1982 (lectr 1973, sr lectr 1981), prof of dynamics and control Univ of Strathclyde 1988–90 (prof of engrg mathematics 1985); Univ of Exeter: prof of systems and control engrg 1990–, dir Sch of Engineering 1995–; ctee work and conference orgn: Inst of Electrical Engrs, IMechE, Inst of Mathematics and its Applications, Health and Safety Cmmn, UK Automatic Control Cncl; FIMA 1976, MIEE 1979, MIEEE 1990; *Books* Feedback and Multivariable Systems (1978), Multivariable and Optimal Systems (1981), Analysis and Control of Multipass Processes (with J B Edwards, 1982), Stability Analysis of Linear Repetitive Processes (with E Rogers, 1992); *Recreations* sketching, reading, guitar; *Style*— Prof David Owens; ✉ Centre for Systems and Control Engineering, School of Engineering, University of Exeter, North Park Rd, Exeter EX4 4QF (☎ 01392 263689, fax 01392 217965, telex 42894)

OWENS, John Ridland; s of Dr Ridland Owens (d 1968), of Lymington, and Elsie, *née* Smith (d 1990); *b* 21 May 1932; *Educ* Merchant Taylors', St John's Coll Oxford (MA); *m* 1, 1958 (m dis 1981), Susan Lilian, da of Cdr G R Pilcher, RN, of Yelverton; 2 s (David Ridland b 23 Feb 1962, James Graham b 27 Sept 1966), 1 da (Elizabeth Clare b 1 July 1960); m 2, 27 Sept 1985, Cynthia Rose, da of Sir Archibald Finlayson Forbes, GBE (d 1989); 1 s (Thomas Alasdair Ridland b 29 June 1987); *Career* Nat Serv 2 Lt RA served Germany 1951–52, Lt TA 1952–57, Gunner HAC 1957–61; section mangr ICI Ltd 1955–67 (founded Stokesley Civic Soc and the Civic Tst for the NE), md Cape Asbestos Fibres Ltd 1967–72, DG Dairy Trade Fedn 1973–83 (vice pres Assoc Industrie Laitière du Marché Commun, dir Nat Dairy Cncl, memb Food and Drink Indust Cncl, founded Nat Dairy Museum), dep DG CBI 1983–90, DG Building Employers' Confedn 1990–92, memb Bd UK Skills 1990–92, chm Owens Associates (ind conslt in strategic advice and govt rels) 1993–; chm: Haringey Healthcare NHS Tst 1993–, CBI Market Testing Gp 1994–; memb Tst Cncl and chm Procurement and Facilities Mgmnt Gp NAHAT 1995–; memb: Bd PRONED 1983–90, Indust Ctee RSA 1984–87, Assoc of Business Sponsorship of the Arts Cncl 1986–95, Advsy Bd RA 1987–91, Cncl City and Guilds Inst 1988–94, Ct City Univ 1988–, Cncl Franco-Br Cncl 1989–90, Cncl RSA 1995–; Freeman City of London, Liveryman Worshipful Co of Merchant Taylors (member Ct); FRSA; *Publications* Marketing in the NHS - Putting Patients First (1993), Strategic Procurement for the NHS - Working with Suppliers (1996); *Recreations* painting, music, walking; *Clubs* Reform; *Style*— John R Owens, Esq; ✉ 40 Blenheim Terrace, London NW8 0EG (☎ 0171 372 6993, fax 0171 372 7783)

OWENS, (John) Robin; s of Col Theobald David Cogswell Owens, MC (d 1984), of Chichester, West Sussex and Irene, *née* Hamilton (d 1949); *b* 26 May 1939; *Educ* Wellington, Welbeck Coll, RMA Sandhurst, Emmanuel Coll Cambridge (MA); *m* 1963, Margaret Ann, da of Harry Arthur Overton (d 1979), of Norfolk; 1 s (Nicholas b 1966), 1 da (Philippa b 1969); *Career* second in cmd Hong Kong Fortress Sqdn 1964–67, Projects Offr 1 Bn Royal Engrs 1966–68, ret with rank of Capt 1968; chm Airlease Int Fin 1977–78; dir: Midland Montagu Leasing Ltd 1978–80, Forward Tst Gp 1980–84, GATX Lease Fin Ltd 1984–85; md: Park Place Fin 1985–86, Medens Tst 1986–89; dir Brown Shipley & Co Ltd 1989–95, chm Willhire Group Ltd 1991–95, chief exec Building Centre Group Ltd 1996–; FCA 1972; *Recreations* tennis, sailing; *Clubs* The Utd Oxford and Cambridge Univ, Royal Engineers Yacht; *Style*— Robin Owens, Esq; ✉ Park Cottage, Teston, Maidstone, Kent (☎ and fax 01622 812208); Building Centre Group Ltd, 26 Store Street, London WC1E 7BT (☎ 0171 637 1022, fax 0171 580 3539)

OWERS, Anne Elizabeth; da of William Spark (d 1963), and Annie Smailes, *née* Knox (d 1969); *b* 23 June 1947; *Educ* Washington GS Co Durham, Girton Coll Cambridge (scholar, BA); *m* 13 July 1968, Rev Ian Humphrey Owers; 2 s (Nicholas William b 7 Dec 1970, Matthew Jonathan b 18 July 1972), 1 da (Rebecca Mary b 2 June 1974); *Career* teacher/researcher Zambia 1968–71, advice worker S London 1974–81, gen sec Joint Council for the Welfare of Immigrants 1986–92 (res offr 1981–86), dir Justice 1991–; memb C of E Race and Community Relations Ctee 1990–94, chair Tstees Refugee Legal Centre 1994–, memb Advsy Cncl NCVO; *Books* Human Rights in the UK (contrib, 1990), Strangers and Citizens (contrib, 1994); *Recreations* theatre, music, friends and family; *Style*— Ms Anne Owers; ✉ Justice, 59 Carter Lane, London EC4 (☎ 0171 329 5100)

OXFORD, Archdeacon of; *see:* Weston, Ven Frank Valentine

OXFORD, Sir Kenneth Gordon; kt (1988), CBE (1981), QPM (1976), DL (Co of Merseyside 1988–); s of Ernest George Oxford, and late Gladys Violet, *née* Seaman; *b* 25 June 1924; *Educ* Caldecot Sch, Lambeth; *m* 1954, Muriel, *née* Panton; *Career* RAFVR 1942–47, Bomber Cmd, SEAC; served Met Police 1947–69 (constable rising to detective chief supt), asst chief constable (crime) Northumbria Constabulary 1969–74, chief constable Merseyside Police 1976–89 (dep chief constable 1974–76), ret 1989; regnl dir Lloyds Bank plc 1988–91, chm Merseyside Community Tst 1988–, conslt dir Securicor Group plc 1989–90; Hon Col 156 (Merseyside and Gtr Manchester), Tport Regt RCT(V) 1989–93, Hon Col 156 (NW) Tport Regt The Royal Logistic Corps (Volunteers) 1993–95; chm: Crime Ctee Assoc of Chief Police Offrs of England, Wales and NI 1977–89, Jt Standing Ctee on Police Use of Firearms 1979–89, Assoc of Chief Police Offrs Sub-Ctee on Terrorism and Allied Matters 1982–89; rep ICPO (Interpol) 1983; pres: NW Police Benevolent Fund 1978–89, Assoc Chief Police Offrs of England, Wales and NI 1982–83; chm Merseyside Regnl Ctee of Prince's Tst 1978–82; pres Merseyside Branch Br Inst of Mgmnt 1983–93 (chm 1978–82); dep pres Merseyside Branch St John Ambulance Assoc 1985– (vice pres 1988–89, co dir 1976–84); Freeman City of London 1983; memb: Forensic Sci Soc 1970, Medico-Legal Soc 1975; CIMgt, FRSA; OStJ 1977; *Publications* author of various articles and papers on crime and kindred matters; *Recreations* shooting, cricket, music, books, roses; *Clubs* Royal Cwlth Soc, Special Forces, Artists (Liverpool), Surrey CCC, Lancs CCC, Liverpool St Helens Rugby Football; *Style*— Sir Kenneth Oxford, CBE, QPM, DL; ✉ c/o Chief Constable's Office, PO Box 59, Liverpool L69 1JD (☎ 0151 709 6010)

OXFORD, 41 Bishop of (1542) 1987–; The Rt Rev Richard Douglas Harries; patron of over 116 livings and the Archdeaconries of Oxford, Buckingham and Berks; the Bishopric was originally endowed with lands of dissolved monasteries by Henry VIII, but in Elizabeth I's reign many of these were removed from it; s of Brig William Douglas Jameson Harries, CBE (d 1991), and Greta Miriam, da of A Bathurst Brown, MB, LRCP; *b* 2 June 1936; *Educ* Wellington, RMA Sandhurst, Selwyn Coll Cambridge (MA), Cuddesdon Coll Oxford; *m* 1963, Josephine Bottomley, MA, MB BChir, DCH; 1 s, 1 da; *Career* Lt RCS 1955–58; curate Hampstead Parish Church 1963–69, chaplain Westfield Coll 1966–69, lectr Wells Theological Coll 1969–72, warden Wells, Salisbury and Wells Theological Coll 1971–72, vicar All Saints' Fulham 1972–81, dean King's Coll London 1981–87, conslt to Archbishop on Jewish Christian Relations 1986–92, chm The Johnson Soc 1988; chm Cncl of Christians and Jews 1992, chm C of E Bd of Social Responsibility 1996; The Sir Sigmund Sternberg award 1987; Hon DD London; FKC, FRSL; *Books* Prayers of Hope (1975), Turning to Prayer (1978), Prayers of Grief and Glory (1979), Being a Christian (1981), Should Christians Support Guerrillas? (1982), The Authority of Divine Love (1983), Praying Round the Clock (1983), Seasons of the Spirit (1984), Prayer and the Pursuit of Happiness (1985), Morning has Broken (1985), Christianity and War in a Nuclear Age (1986), CS Lewis - The Man and his God (1987), The One Genius (1987), Christ has Risen (1988), Is There a Gospel for the Rich? (1992), Art and the Beauty of God (1993), The Real God (1994), Questioning Belief (1995), A Gallery of Reflections: The Nativity of Christ (1995); contributor: What Hope in an Armed World (and ed, 1982), Reinhold Niebuhr and the issues of our Time (and ed, 1986), Stewards and the Mysteries of God (1975), Unholy Warfare (1983), The Cross and the Bomb (1985), Julian, Woman of our Time (1985), The Reality of God (1986); *Recreations* theatre, literature, sport; *Style*— The Rt Rev the Bishop of Oxford; ✉ Diocesan Church House, North Hinksey, Oxford OX2 0NB (☎ 01865 244566)

OXFORD AND ASQUITH, 2 Earl of (UK 1925); Julian Edward George; KCMG (1964, CMG 1961); also Viscount Asquith (UK 1925); s of Raymond Asquith (ka the Somme 1916; s of the Lib PM, Rt Hon Sir Herbert Henry Asquith, KG, later 1 Earl (d 1928)), and Katharine Frances (d 1976), da of Sir John Horner, KCVO (d 1927); *b* 22 April 1916; *Educ* Ampleforth, Balliol Coll Oxford (MA); *m* 28 Aug 1947, Anne Mary Celestine, CStJ, da of late Sir Michael Palairet, KCMG; 2 s, 3 da; *Heir* s, Viscount Asquith, OBE, *qv*; *Career* 2 Lt RE 1940; sits as Independent in House of Lords; asst dist cmmr Palestine Admin 1942–48, dep chief sec Br Admin Tripolitania 1949, dir of the Interior

Tripolitanian Govt 1951, advsr to PM of Libya 1952, admin sec Zanzibar 1955, admin St Lucia 1958–61, govr and C-in-C Seychelles 1962–67, and cmmr Br Indian Ocean Territory 1965–67, constitutional cmmr Cayman Islands 1971, constitutional cmmr Turks and Caicos Islands 1973–74; KStJ; *Style*— The Rt Hon the Earl of Oxford and Asquith, KCMG; ✉ The Manor House, Mells, Frome, Somerset (☎ 01373 812324)

OXFUIRD, 13 Viscount of (S 1651); Sir George Hubbard Makgill; 13 Bt (NS 1627), CBE (1997); also Lord Makgill of Cousland (S 1697); claim to Viscountcy admitted by Ctee for Privileges, House of Lords 1977; s of Sqdn Ldr Richard James Robert Haldane Makgill (d 1948, yr s of 11 Bt) and Elizabeth Lyman, *née* Hubbard (d 1981); suc uncle 1986; *b* 7 Jan 1934; *Educ* Wanganui Collegiate Sch NZ; *m* 1, 1967 (m dis 1977), Alison Campbell, da of late Neils Max Jensen, of Randers, Denmark; 3 s (Master of Oxfuird b 1969, Hon Robert Edward George b 1969 (twin), Hon Hamish Max Alistair b 1972); m 2, 1980, Venetia Cunitia Mary, da of Major Charles Anthony Steward, of The Platt, Crondall, nr Farnham, Surrey; 1 s (Hon Edward Anthony Donald b 1983); *Heir* s, Hon Ian Arthur Alexander Makgill, Master of Oxfuird b 14 Oct 1969; *Career* RAF GD Branch 1954–59, Ford Motor Co 1960–64, export mangr Lansing Bagnall 1965–88, external affrs mangr Lansing Linde 1989–93; dep chm 1992 and dep speaker 1993 House of Lords; memb: Jt Ctee on Statutory Instruments 1992, Personal Bills Ctee 1992–95, Hybrid Bills Ctee 1995, Offices Ctee 1995; dep chm Assoc of Conservative Peers 1993; *Recreations* shooting, gardening, fishing; *Clubs* Caledonian; *Style*— The Rt Hon the Viscount of Oxfuird, CBE; ✉ c/o The House of Lords, London SW1A 0PW

OXLADE, Roy; s of William Oxlade (d 1955), of Bexley Heath, Kent, and Emily, *née* Fenn; *b* 13 Jan 1929; *Educ* Bromley Coll of Art, RCA (PhD); *m* 10 Aug 1957, Rose, da of Alexander Forrest Wylie, OBE (d 1964), of Hythe, Kent; 1 s (Luke-John b 7 Aug 1958), 2 da (Elizabeth b 11 April 1960, Henrietta b 18 July 1966); *Career* painter; *Group Exhibitions* Young Contemporaries 1952, 1953 and 1954, Borough Bottega 1954 and 1955, Winnipeg Biennale 1960, John Moores Liverpool 1964 and 1991, Hayward Annual 1982, Odette Gilbert Gallery 1984 and 1990, Royal Acad Summer Exhibition 1984–, Rocks and Flesh 1985, Olympia Art Fair 1986, Chicago Art Fair 1987, Los Angeles Art Fair 1987, Waddington Schiel Toronto 1987, Jan Turner Los Angles 1988, Cleveland Int Drawing Biennale 1989, East 1991 and 1994, Seattle Art Fair 1996; *Solo Exhibitions* Vancouver Art Gallery 1963, Midland Gp Gallery 1975, New Metropole Gallery Folkestone 1983, Air Gallery 1983, Odette Gilbert Gallery 1985, 1987 and 1988, Gardner Centre Univ of Sussex 1990, Reed's Wharf Gallery 1993; *Publications* David Bomberg - RCA Papers III (1981), The Visual Arts in Adult Education and The Arts University of Nottingham (contrib, 1981), Modern Painters Magazine (contrib); *Clubs* Arts; *Style*— Roy Oxlade, Esq

OXLADE, Zena Elsie; CBE (1984); da of James Oxlade (d 1983), and Beatrice May, *née* Oliver (d 1962); *b* 26 April 1929; *Educ* Latymer GS, Univ of London; *Career* SRN and registered nurse tutor; chm Gen Nursing Cncl for England and Wales 1977–83 (memb 1975–83); area nursing offr Suffolk 1978–, regnl nursing offr East Anglia 1981–89, ret 1989; memb UK Cncl for Nurses Midwives and Health Visitors 1983–88; Hon Dr Univ of Surrey 1993; *Recreations* motoring, reading, handicrafts; *Clubs* Soroptimist Int; *Style*— Miss Zena Oxlade, CBE; ✉ 5 Morgan Court, Claydon, Ipswich, Suffolk IP6 0AN (☎ 01473 831895)

OXLEY, *see:* Rice-Oxley

OXLEY, David; OBE (1989); s of Robert Lacey Oxley (d 1980), of Hull, and Reena, *née* Stokes (d 1991); *b* 5 Jan 1938; *Educ* Hymers Coll Hull, Worcester Coll Oxford (BA, MA, DipEd); *m* 1, 1961 (m dis 1975), Elizabeth Mary Joan, *née* Walford; 1 s (Mark b 10 Jan 1968), 1 da (Alyson b 29 Aug 1965); m 2, 1977, Bridget Anne, da of Stanley Wisdom; 1 da (Lucy b 12 Sept 1979), 1 adopted s (Simon b 14 April 1966); *Career* chief exec Rugby Football League 1987–92 (sec-gen 1974–87); teacher: Merchant Taylors' Sch Northwood 1962–66, St Edward's Sch Oxford 1966–69; head of Eng Dept St Peter's Sch York 1969–72, dep headmaster Duke of York's Royal Military Sch Dover 1972–76; chm Yorks and Humberside Cncl for Sport & Recreation 1986–95, chm Br Assoc of Nat Sports Admins 1984–87, memb Exec CCPR 1988–95, vice chair and pres Fedn of Disability Sports Orgns (Yorks and Humberside), vice chair and govr Sports Aid Fndn (Yorks & Humberside), govr Bishop Burton Coll; hon fell Univ of Lincoln and Humberside 1990; memb: Lottery Awards Panel (Sport), English Sports Cncl; *Style*— David Oxley, Esq, OBE; ✉ 31 Leeds Road, Harrogate, N Yorkshire HG2 8AY

OXLEY, Julian Christopher; s of Horace Oxley (d 1958), of Newnham-on-Severn, Glos, and Lilian Alexandra Frances, *née* Harris (d 1985); *b* 23 Nov 1938; *Educ* Clifton (Open scholar), Oriel Coll Oxford (Organ scholar, MA); *m* 1, 1964, Carolyn, *née* Simpson; 2 da (Vivienne b 1966, Suzanne b 1967), 1 s (Martin b 1971); m 2, 1979, Carol, *née* Heath; 1 da (Joanna b 1985); *Career* articled clerk Deloitte Haskins & Sells (CAs) 1961–64 (audit mangr 1964–66), chief accountant and sec Pressweld Ltd 1966–68, fin dir and sec Williams & James Ltd (later plc) 1971–84 (fin controller 1968–71), DG The Guide Dogs for the Blind Association 1989– (dir of admin and sec 1984–89); chm Int Fedn of Guide Dog Schools 1990–; FCA 1965; *Recreations* music, old furniture, railways; *Clubs* Kennel; *Style*— Julian Oxley, Esq; ✉ Director-General, The Guide Dogs for the Blind Association, Hillfields, Burghfield, Reading, Berkshire RG7 3YG (☎ 0118 983 5555, fax 0118 983 5433)

OXMANTOWN, Lord; (Laurence) Patrick Parsons; s and h of 7 Earl of Rosse, *qv*; *b* 31 March 1969; *Educ* Aiglon Coll Switzerland, Univ of Beijing China; *Career* asst dir Land and Sky International Group Beijing; *Style*— Lord Oxmantown; ✉ Birr Castle, Birr, Co Offaly, Republic of Ireland

OXTOBY, David Jowett Greaves; s of John Henry Oxtoby (d 1972), of Horsforth, Yorks, and Ann Jowett, *née* Greaves (d 1978); *b* 23 Jan 1938; *Educ* Horsforth Cncl Sch, Bradford Coll of Art, RA Sch Piccadilly; *Career* artist, best known for visual interpretations of pop music, 44 one man shows, numerous exhibits in gp exhibitions; works in public collections incl: Br Museum, LA County Museum, Museum of Modern Art NY, Minneapolis Inst of Art, Tate Gallery, Victoria & Albert Museum; lectr numerous colls incl RA, visiting prof painting Minneapolis Inst of Art 1964–65, ret teaching 1972; *Books* painting reprod in: Oxtoby's Rockers (D Sandison 1978), V & A Museum Calendar (1985), Once Upon a Christmas (D Sandison 1986); *Recreations* cycling; *Style*— David Oxtoby, Esq; ✉ c/o David Sandison, 39 Glenthorne Road, London N11 3HU (☎ 0181 368 3683)

OZBEK, (Ibrahim Mehmet) Rifat; s of Abdulazim Mehmet Ismet Özbek, of Istanbul, and Melike, *née* Pekis; *b* 8 Nov 1953; *Educ* Isik Lisesi Istanbul, St Martin's Sch of Art (BA); *Career* fashion designer; Walter Albini for Trell Milan 1977–79, Monsoon Co 1979–84, formed own company and presented first collection 1984, launched O for Ozbek 1987 (now Future Ozbek); Br Fashion Cncl: Designer of the Year 1988 and 1992, Br Glamour Award 1989; *Style*— Rifat Ozbek, Esq; ✉ 18 Haunch of Venison Yard, London W1Y 1AF (☎ 0171 408 0625, fax 0171 629 1586)

ÖZVEREN, Ali Evrenay; s of Hamdi Özveren (d 1992), of Ankara, and Zehra, *née* Zincirci (d 1992); *b* 6 Oct 1945; *Educ* Ankara Coll, Dept of Architecture Middle East Tech Univ (BArch); *m* 13 Nov 1976, Susan Catherine, da of Arthur Frank William Gimbert; 1 s (Jan Emil b 28 Dec 1979); *Career* GMW Partnership London: joined as architectural asst 1970, completed univ educn in Turkey, assoc 1979, ptnr 1984, a sr ptnr 1991–; projects incl: Royal Mail (S London Postal Sorting Office, Battersea), Wates City of London Properties (City Tower, Basinghall St), Vestey Estates (34 Leadenhall St), Sun Alliance Group Properties (1 King William St and 24–30 St Swithin's Lane), Land Securities (Regis House, King William/Monument St); overseas projects incl: Wholesale Food Market Dubai (first prize int competition), Retail Food Market Dubai (commendation int competition); registered memb Chamber of Architects of Turkey 1971; FCSD 1992, FRSA 1995; *Recreations* modern art and architecture, travel, opera, photography, sport; *Style*— Ali Özveren, Esq; ✉ Senior Partner, GMW Partnership, PO Box 1613, 239 Kensington High Street, London W8 6SL (☎ 0171 937 8020, fax 0171 937 5815)

P

PACE, Franco Giustino; s of Edmondo Pace (d 1959); *b* 28 Sept 1927; *Educ* Bologna Univ (doctorate in industl engrg), Milan Univ (post grad specialisation in chemistry); *m* 1955, Maria Vittoria, da of Dr Ing Salvatore Picchetti, of Italy; 1 s (Valerio); *Career* dir: Montedison UK Ltd 1973–89, Polyamide Intermediates Ltd 1974–83, Farmitalia Carlo Erba Ltd 1990–93, Himont UK Subsidiary Ltd 1987–95, Montell Milton Keynes Ltd 1987–95, Accademia Italiana 1989–91; chm: Montefibre UK Ltd 1974–89, Acna UK Ltd 1976–88, Cedar Service UK Ltd 1982–88, Internike Ltd 1984–88, Selm International Ltd 1986–88, Rubber and Chemicals Ltd 1989–, Euroil Exploration Ltd 1989–, Ausimont UK Ltd 1991–; Italian C of C for GB: vice pres 1981–88, sec gen 1988–94; Commendatore al merito della Repubblica Italiana 1987; *Clubs* Hurlingham; *Style*— Franco G Pace, Esq; ✉ 10 Kensington Court Gardens, London W8 5QE (☎ 0171 937 7143); Euroil Exploration Ltd, 93–99 Upper Richmond Road, London SW15 2TG (☎ 0171 780 4000, fax 0171 780 2871)

PACEY, Albert Howard; CBE (1994), QPM; s of William Albert Pacey, of Lincoln, and Gwendoline Annie, *née* Quibell (d 1987); *b* 18 Dec 1938; *Educ* City Sch Lincoln, NDC Latimer, Police Staff Coll; *m* 20 Aug 1960, Ann Elizabeth, da of Alfred Hedley Wood (1985); 2 s (Mark b 1961, Simon b 1963), 1 da (Helen (Mrs Parker) b 1967); *Career* constable to chief superintendent Lincs Constabulary 1958–76 (police cadet 1955), staff offr to HM Inspr of Constabulary 1976, asst chief constable Humberside Police 1977–83, dep chief constable Lancs Constabulary 1983–87, chief constable Glos Constabulary 1987–93, DG Nat Criminal Intelligence Serv 1993–; advsr on police trg to Nigeria Govt; memb Assoc of Chief Police Offrs; *Recreations* golf, fell walking, gardening, reading; *Clubs* Cormorant; *Style*— Albert Pacey, Esq, CBE, QPM; ✉ Director General, National Criminal Intelligence Service, Spring Gardens, 2 Citadel Place, London SE11 5EF (☎ 0171 238 8204, fax 0171 238 8327)

PACHACHI, Reema; da of Dr Adnan Pachachi, and Selwa Ali, *née* Jawdat; *b* 10 April 1951; *Educ* Brearley Sch NY, UN Sch NY, Central Sch of Art & Design (BA), RCA (MA, Anstruther award); *m* 14 Dec 1977, John William Dennis; 2 s (Said b 26 Jan 1981, Kareem b 23 May 1986), 1 da (Aisha b 23 Nov 1983); *Career* jewellery designer; *Exhibitions* Passing Out (Goldsmiths' Hall London) 1979, Arnolfini Gallery Bristol 1979, Ehrman Gallery London 1980, Artwear NY 1980, New Faces (Br Crafts Centre London) 1981, Jungend Gestaltet Munich 1981, Loot (Goldsmiths' Hall London) 1981, British Women Artists (House of Commons) 1981, Dazzle (NT) 1981–82, New Ashgate Gallery Farnham Surrey 1982, Byzantium Gallery NY 1982 (Christman Exhbn) and 1993 (Spring/Christmas Exhbn), Nat Assoc of Decorative & Fine Art Socs' Clothes and Jewellery Show 1985, Precious Elements (Usher Gallery Lincoln) 1986, Sotheby's Decorative Arts Award Exhbn London 1988, History of Contemporary Jewellery Exhbn (Sheehan Gallery Washington) 1991; work in permanent collection of Crafts Cncl of GB (listed in their Index of Excellence 1982); jewellery designs for Arabella Pollen and Geoffrey Beene; sometime tutor various art colls incl RCA, Glasgow Sch of Art and Sir John Cass Sch of Art London (bd examiner BA course 1989–91); memb London Designer Collections Assoc 1988; *Recreations* reading, dancing, swimming; *Style*— Ms Reema Pachachi; ✉ 79 Elizabeth Street, London SW1W 9PJ (☎ 0171 730 8030)

PACK, Stephen Howard John; s of Leonard Pack (d 1992), of London, and Isabel, *née* Heiser; *b* 26 April 1950; *Educ* Univ of Manchester (MA); *m* Cheryl, da of Albert Klyne; 1 da (Susannah b 15 Nov 1976), 1 s (Anthony b 12 Feb 1979); *Career* ptnr Price Waterhouse 1984– (joined 1972); FCA 1975; *Style*— Stephen Pack, Esq; ✉ Price Waterhouse, Southwark Towers, 32 London Bridge Street, London SE1 9SY (☎ 0171 939 3000)

PACKARD, Lt-Gen Sir (Charles) Douglas; KBE (1957, CBE 1945, OBE 1942), CB (1949), DSO (1943); s of Capt C Packard, MC, of Copdock, Suffolk; *b* 17 May 1903; *Educ* Winchester, RMA Woolwich; *m* 1937, Marion Cargill Thomson (d 1981), da of Dr James Lochhead, of Edinburgh; 1 s, 2 da; m 2, 1982, Mrs Patricia Miles-Sharp; *Career* 2 Lt RA 1923, WWII ME and Italy, dep Chief of Staff 15 Army Gp 1944–45, temp Maj-Gen and Chief of Staff Allied Cmmn Austria 1945–46; dir Mil Intelligence War Office 1948–49, cmd Br Mil Mission to Greece 1949–51 chief of Staff GHQ MELF 1951–53, VQMG War Office 1953–56, mil advsr to W African Govts 1956–58, Lt-Gen 1957, GOC-in-C NI 1958–61; *Recreations* gardening and travel; *Style*— Lt-Gen Sir Douglas Packard, KBE, CB, DSO; ✉ Park Side, Lower Ufford, Woodbridge, Suffolk IP13 6DL (☎ 01394 460418)

PACKARD, Gilian Elizabeth; da of John Laurence Packard (d 1981), and Rachel Alice, *née* Kaye (d 1981); *b* 16 March 1938; *Educ* Claremont Sch Esher, Kingston Sch of Art, Central Sch of Arts and Crafts, RCA (DesRCA); *m* 6 March 1965 (m dis 1972), Dennis Nigel Johns Parris; *Career* jeweller; head Dept of Silversmithing and Jewellery Glasgow Sch of Art 1979–83, asst dir of design Worshipful Co of Goldsmiths 1983–87, project dir City of London Poly and Br Jewellers Assoc 1989–93; sr lectr Sir John Cass Dept of Art London Guildhall Univ 1987–; exhibitor of designs worldwide; winner: Diamonds-Int Awards 1963 and 1964, First Prize and commendation De Beers Competition for diamond engagement ring 1964; work in numerous collections incl: V & A, Goldsmiths Co, De Beers, Scottish Nat Museum; chm and Br rep World Crafts Cncl 1968–72, vice chm Soc of Designer-Craftsmen 1996–; memb: Crafts Advsy Ctee 1971–74, Scot Crafts Consultative Ctee 1979–83; Freeman: City of London, Worshipful Co of Goldsmiths 1971; FRSA, FCSD, FSDC; *Style*— Ms Gilian Packard; ✉ 8:2 Stirling Court, 3 Marshall St, London W1V 1LQ (☎ 0171 437 5902, fax 0171 437 5903); 195 High St, Aldeburgh, Suffolk IP15 5AL (☎ 01728 453903)

PACKARD, Richard Bruce Selig; s of John Jacob Packard (d 1992), of Delray Beach, Florida, and (Priscilla) Lilian, *née* Joseph; *b* 20 Feb 1947; *Educ* Harrow, Middlesex Hosp Med Sch (MD, DO); *m* 1, 21 March 1974 (m dis 1986), Veronica Susan, da of Michael Bird, CBE (d 1991), of Esher, Surrey; 2 s (Rupert Alexander b 1978, Hugo Philip b 1980), 1 da (Elvira Rose b 1984); m 2, 24 April 1986, Fiona Catherine, da of Walter F Kinnear, of Kilspindie, Perthshire; 1 s (Ian Charles b 1990), 1 da (Lucy Catherine b 1992); *Career* specialist trg in ophthalmology; house surgn in ophthalmology Middx Hosp 1970; held various jr med appointments 1971–75, res surgical offr Moorfields Eye Hosp 1975–78, sr registrar in ophthalmology Charing Cross Hosp Fulham 1978–82, conslt ophthalmic surgn and clinical dir Prince Charles Eye Unit King Edward VII Hosp Windsor 1982–; tstee Cyclotron Tst for Cancer Treatment; past chm Oxford RHA Ophthalmology Sub-Ctee, UK rep Int Med Panel for the Advance of Cataract Treatment 1992–; FRCS 1976, FRCOphth 1991; memb: American Acad of Ophthalmology, American Soc of Cataract and Refractive Surgery, Euro Soc of Cataract and Refractive Surgery; *Books* Cataract and Lens Implant Surgery (jtly, 1985), Emergency Surgery (jtly, 1986), Manual of Cataract and Lens Implant Surgery (jtly, 1991), Phacoemulsification (jtly, 1994); *Recreations* fly-fishing, wine, music; *Clubs* Garrick, MCC; *Style*— Richard Packard, Esq; ✉ 96 Harley Street, London W1 (☎ 0171 935 9555, fax 0118 934 3059, e-mail eyequack@vossnet.co.uk)

PACKER, Rt Rev John Richard; *see:* Warrington, Bishop of

PACKER, Kerry Francis Bullmore; AC (1983); s of late Sir Douglas Frank Hewson Packer, KBE (d 1974), and Gretel Joyce, *née* Bullmore (d 1960); *b* 17 Dec 1937; *Educ* Cranbrook Sch Sydney NSW, Geelong C of E GS Vic; *m* 1963, Roslyn Redman, da of late Dr F H Weedon; 1 s, 1 da; *Career* exec Australian Consolidated Press Ltd 1955, chm Consolidated Press Holdings Ltd and gp of cos 1974–; dir Publishing and Broadcasting Ltd (former chm); *Recreations* polo, golf, tennis, cricket; *Clubs* Royal Sydney Golf, Australian Golf, Elanora County, Tattersall's, Athenaeum (Melbourne); *Style*— Kerry F B Packer, Esq, AC; ✉ 54 Park St, Sydney, NSW 2000, Australia (☎ 00 61 29 282 8000, fax 00 61 29 267 2150)

PACKER, Linda Frances Jean; da of Frank Harold Packer (d 1973), and Jean Grace, *née* Row; *b* 18 June 1959; *Educ* Associated Arts Sch Wimbledon, Arts Educnl Sch London (Markova award for Ballet); *Career* princ dancer Scottish Ballet 1983– (joined 1978); princ roles incl: Sugar Plum Fairy in The Nutcracker, the Girl in John Gilpen's revival of Le Spectre de la Rose; title roles in: Giselle, Carmen, Cinderella, Juliet in John Cranko's Romeo & Juliet; *Recreations* astrology, alternative medicine; *Style*— Ms Linda Packer; ✉ Scottish Ballet, 261 West Princes St, Glasgow G4 9EE (☎ 0141 331 2931)

PACKER, Richard John; s of George Charles Packer (d 1979), and Dorothy May Packer (d 1993); *b* 18 Aug 1944; *Educ* City of London Sch, Univ of Manchester (BSc, MSc); *m* 1, Alison Mary, *née* Sellwood; 2 s (James b 1969, George b 1971), 1 da (Rachel b 1973); m 2, Lucy Jeanne, da of Edmund Neville-Rolfe, of Tisbury, Wilts; 4 s (Thomas b 1981, William b 1984, Harry b 1988, Samuel b 1994); *Career* MAFF: joined 1967, asst princ, 1 sec Office of UK Representative to EC 1973–76, princ private sec Minister 1976–78, asst sec 1979, under sec 1985, dep sec 1989, perm sec 1993–; dir ABM Chemicals 1985–86; *Recreations* many sporting and intellectual interests; *Style*— R J Packer, Esq; ✉ Ministry of Agriculture, Fisheries and Food, Whitehall Place, London SW1A 2HH (☎ 0171 270 8701)

PACKER, Robin John; s of Edwin James Packer, and Alma, *née* Lodge; *b* 6 May 1948; *Educ* Catford Sch; *m* 1 Aug 1970, Diane Irana, da of Kenneth Derek Jones; 2 da (Melanie b 28 Dec 1973, Natalie b 1 Aug 1977); *Career* de Zoete & Gordon 1964–66, Govett Sons 1966–74, Cazenove 1974–76; Wood MacKenzie & Co: joined 1976, ptnr 1984–87, dir 1986–87; currently a md UK equities UBS Phillips & Drew (joined 1987); memb local Cons Assoc; memb Stock Exchange; *Recreations* golf, game fishing; *Style*— Robin Packer, Esq; ✉ Southfields, Telegraph Hill, Higham by Rochester, Kent ME3 7NW (☎ 01634 721420); UBS Phillips & Drew, 100 Liverpool St, London EC2 (direct ☎ 0171 901 1386)

PACKER, William John; s of Rex Packer, and Molly Packer, *née* Wornham; *b* 19 Aug 1940; *Educ* Windsor GS, Wimbledon and Brighton Colls of Art; *m* 1965, Ursula Mary Clare, er da of Thomas Winn; 3 da (Charlotte, Claudia, Katherine); *Career* painter and art critic; first exhibited RA 1963, numerous gp exhibitions since; art critic Financial Times 1974–; selector of several exhibitions including Arts Cncl's first Br Art Show 1979–80; served on juries of many open exhibitions incl: John Moores Liverpool Exhibition, John Player Portrait Award, Hunting Prize; teacher 1964–77; memb: Fine Art Bd CNAA 1976–83, Advsy Ctee to Govt Art Collection 1977–84, Crafts Cncl 1980–87; hon fell RCA 1988, Hon RBA; *Books* The Art of Vogue Covers (1980), Fashion Drawing in Vogue (1983), Henry Moore, A Pictorial Biography (1985), René Bouët-Willaumez (1989), Carl Erickson (1989); *Recreations* hockey, bookshops, riding; *Clubs* Chelsea Arts; *Style*— William Packer, Esq; ✉ 39 Elms Rd, Clapham, London SW4 9EP (☎ 0171 622 1108)

PACKETT, (Charles) Neville; MBE (1974), JP (1964); s of Sydney Packett, JP (d 1980), and Alice Maude Packett (d 1972); *b* 25 Feb 1922; *Educ* Bradford GS, Queen Elizabeth GS Kirkby Lonsdale Cumbria, Ashville Coll Harrogate Yorks; *m* 1969, Audrey Winifred, da of Frank Vincent Clough (d 1975); *Career* WWII RAOC Middle E and N Africa; Sydney Packett & Sons: dir 1942–75, md 1975–87, conslt 1987–; pres Insurance Inst of Bradford 1959–60, hon vice pres The United Commercial Travellers' Assoc 1976– (nat pres 1975–76), chm House Ctee Ashville Coll Harrogate 1977–92 (govr 1970–96, hon govr 1996–), co cdr S and W Yorks St John Ambulance Bde 1984–90, memb Cncl City & Guilds of London Inst 1984–86 and 1991–96, memb Ct City Univ 1993–; Liveryman: Worshipful Co of Tin Plate Workers 1957 (Master 1986–87) Worshipful Co of Woolmen 1959 (Master 1979–80); Hon Historian City of London Lieutenancy 1987; Hon Adm Texas Navy USA 1978; Hon MA Univ of Bradford 1992; Grand Cross Order of St Agatha Repub of San Marino 1980, Tonga Royal Medal of Merit in silver 1976; KStJ 1985; chartered insurance practitioner 1989, FRSA, FRGS, ACII; *Books* The County Lieutenancy in the UK, Republic of San Marino, Tongatapu Island (Kingdom of Tonga), The Republic of Nauru, The Firm of Sydney Packett & Sons Ltd, The Texas Navy - A Brief History (1983), HM Commission of Lieutenancy for the City of London (1987), The Bradford Club - A Brief History (1986), Bradfords Around The World (1996); *Recreations* travel, amateur cine, heraldry, writing; *Clubs* City Livery, Nat Lib, The Bradford (pres 1985–86); *Style*— Neville Packett, Esq, MBE, JP; ✉ Flat 20, Wells Court, Wells Promenade, Ilkley, W Yorks LS29 9LG (☎ 01943 601398); Lloyds Bank Chambers, Hustlergate, Bradford, W Yorks BD1 1PA (☎ 01274 308755, fax 01274 732832)

PACKHAM, Jenny; da of Colin Packham, of Southampton, and Marion Rita, *née* Smith; *b* 11 March 1965; *Educ* Bitterne Park Sch Southampton, Southampton Art Coll (DA TEC) St Martin Sch of Art London (BA, RSA bursary award and fellowship); *partner* Mathew John Anderson; 1 da (Georgia Packham Anderson b 8 Nov 1993); *Career* started fashion design business with Mathew Anderson specialising in evening wear and bridal wear; clients incl: Harvey Nichols, Harrods, Bergdoff Goodman, Neiman Marcus, Saks (NY), Selfridges, Liberties, Joyce (Hong Kong); Condé Nast Brides and Setting Up Home: New Designer Award 1993, Informal Award 1996, New Direction Award 1996, New Glamour Couture Award 1997; FRSA; *Recreations* mothering; *Style*— Ms Jenny Packham;

✉ Jenny Packham London Ltd, The Courtyard, 44 Gloucester Avenue, Regent's Park, London NW1 8JD (☎ 0171 722 1415)

PACKMAN, Martin John; s of Ivan Desmond Packman, of Addington, Surrey, and Joan Emily, *née* Cook (d 1982); *b* 29 April 1949; *Educ* Simon Langton GS Canterbury, Univ of Lancaster (MA); *m* 17 Dec 1978, Lyn, da of James Green, of Holt, Norfolk; 1 s (Myles b 1980), 1 da (Charlotte b 1984); *Career* corp fin dir Baring Bros International Ltd 1987– (joined 1984); FCA 1973; *Books* UK Companies Operating Overseas - Tax and Financing Strategies (jtly, 1981); *Recreations* tennis, opera; *Style*— Martin Packman, Esq; ✉ Port Hill House, Bengeo, Hertford, Herts (☎ 01992 500950); Baring Bros Ltd, 60 London Wall, London EC2M 5TQ (☎ 0171 767 1000, fax 0171 767 7157)

PACKSHAW, Charles Max; s of Savile Packshaw (d 1969), and Muriel, *née* Newton; *b* 30 Jan 1952; *Educ* Westminster, Univ of Bristol (BSc), London Business Sch (MSc); *m* 9 July 1983, Helena Mary, da of Peter Youngman; 2 s (Harry b 1984, Edward b 1987), 1 da (Olivia b 1989); *Career* with Costain 1973–78, sr conslt Cresap 1980–84, exec dir Lazard Bros Co Ltd (joined 1984), non-exec dir City Centre Restaurants PLC 1996–; CEng, MICE 1978; *Style*— Charles Packshaw, Esq; ✉ c/o Lazard Brothers Co Ltd, 21 Moorfields, London EC2P 2HT (☎ 0171 588 2721)

PACKSHAW, Robin David; s of Savil Packshaw (d 1969), and Doris Mary (Fay), *née* Francis (d 1948); *b* 20 March 1933; *Educ* Diocesan Coll Cape Town, Bradfield Coll Berkshire; *children* 3 s ((Andrew) Giles David b 1957, Julian Robert b 1961, Justin James b 1966), 1 da (Amanda Jane (Mrs Cassar Toregiani) b 1956); *Career* Nat Serv Royal Marines Special Boat Service UK and Br Rhine Squadron 1951–53, Lt Royal Marines Reserve Special Boat Service 1953–58; Iraq Petroleum Company Ltd 1953–62 (Persuian Gulf Personnel and Industl Rels); dir: Long Till Colvin Ltd (local authy brokers) 1962–67, Guy Butler Company Ltd (sterling money brokers) 1967–69; founding md Packshaw and Associates (local authy brokers) 1969–73; chm: Fulton Packshaw (sterling money brokers) 1973–82, Charles Fulton Group 1982–85, International City Holdings plc 1985–89, Sterling Brokers Ltd 1993; conslt: Business in the Community 1990–92, London First 1992–93, Sterling Brokers 1993–; memb: Bank of England Jt Standing Ctee for Princs and Brokers in the Sterling Markets 1981–86, Steering Gp LIFFE 1981–82, Membership and Rules Ctee LIFFE 1983–89; chm Radionics Assoc 1990–; church warden All Saints Stour Row 1984–95, chm Stours Branch N Dorset Cons Assoc 1989–95, govr Stower Provost Co Primary Sch 1992–95; Freeman City of London 1983, memb Guild of Freeman of the City of London 1983; *Recreations* travel, people, Church of England; *Clubs* RAC, IOD; *Style*— Robin Packshaw, Esq; ✉ 10 Hurlingham Court, Ranelagh Gardens, London SW6 3SH (☎ 0171 736 6832, fax 0171 371 7576); Sterling Brokers Ltd, Colechurch House, 1 London Bridge Walk, London SE1 2SS (☎ 0171 962 9960, fax 0171 403 5377)

PADGETT, Robert Alan; s of William Thomas Padgett (d 1985), of Radlett, Herts, and Winifred Emily, *née* Duncan; *b* 27 May 1943; *Educ* Haileybury, Wadham Coll Oxford (MA), Univ of Pennsylvania (MBA); *m* 1, 6 June 1975 (m dis 1988), Gillian Diana, da of Stanley Arthur Herbert Hunn, of Rustington, Sussex; 1 s (Christopher b 1977); m 2, 23 Aug 1996, Diane Margaret, da of Gordon Alfred Pitt (d 1957), of Gt Staughton, Huntingdonshire; *Career* corp fin exec N M Rothschild and Sons Ltd 1970–73, dir Cripps Warburg Ltd 1973–75, mangr Brown Harriman and International Banks Ltd 1975–77; fin dir PO Staff Superannuation Fund 1977–83, dir and head of corp fin Hermes Investment Management Ltd 1993– (fin dir 1983–93); non-exec dir: Gateway Building Society 1985–88, The Beckenham Group plc 1987–92, Granville Private Equity Ltd 1993–, Intermediate Capital Group plc 1994–, Innisfree Ltd 1995–, LA Societe Fonciere Lyonnaise 1995–; memb Technical Directorate ICAEW 1995–; tstee The Hunger Project; FCA; *Books* Financial Reporting 1987–88 (contrib, 1988); *Recreations* ending world hunger, improving environment; *Style*— Robert Padgett, Esq; ✉ 2 Queen's Gate, London SW7 5EH (☎ 0171 589 2985); Hermes Investment Management Ltd, Standon House, 21 Mansell Street, London E1 8AA (☎ 0171 702 0888, fax 0171 702 9452, telex 8956577)

PADGHAM, Hugh Charles; s of Charles Arthur Padgham, of Aylesbury, Bucks, and Ursula Mary, *née* Samuelson; *b* 15 Feb 1955; *Educ* The Beacon Sch Chesham Bois, St Edward's Sch Oxford; *Career* asst Advision Studios 1974–75, engr/asst Lansdowne Studios 1975–77, engr Townhouse Studios 1977–80, record prodr and engr 1980–; produced and engineered: Split Enz' Conflicting Emotions (A&M 1980) and Time and Tide (A&M 1982), The Police's Ghost In The Machine (A&M 1981, Platinum disc) and Synchronicity (A&M 1983, Platinum disc), Phil Collins' Face Value (Virgin 1983, 6 Platinum discs), No Jacket Required (Virgin 1985, Platinum disc), Hello I Must Be Going (Virgin 1988, Platinum disc) and But Seriously (Virgin 1989, 8 Platinum discs), Genesis' Genesis (Virgin 1983, 2 Platinum discs) and Invisible Touch (Virgin 1986, 4 Platinum discs), XTC's English Settlement (Virgin 1983, Silver disc), Human League's Hysteria (Virgin 1984, Gold disc), David Bowie's Tonight (EMI 1985, Gold disc), Paul Young's Between Two Fires (CBS 1986, Platinum disc), Paul McCartney's Press To Play (Parlaphone 1988, Gold disc), tracks from Julia Fordham's Porcelain (Circa 1989, Silver disc) and Julia Fordham (Circa 1988, Gold disc), Sting's The Soul Cages (A&M 1991) and Ten Summoner's Tales (A&M 1993), Melissa Etheridge's Yes I Am (Island 1993, Grammy 1995), Billy Pilgrim's (debut album, Atlantic 1994), Melissa Etheridge's Your Little Secret (Island Records 1995), Phil Collins' Dance into the Light (Atlantic/EW 1996), Bee Gees' 3 Tracks (A&M 1996), Beth Hart Band's Immortal (Lava/143 Records 1996), Sting's Mercury Falling (A&M 1996), Clannad's Lore (BMG/Atlantic 1996); engineered: XTC's Drums and Wires (Virgin 1979) and Black Sea (Virgin 1980), Genesis' Abacab (Virgin 1983, Gold disc), Peter Gabriel's The Third (Virgin 1986, Gold disc); mixed numerous singles/tracks incl: Hall and Oates' H2O (RCA 1982, Platinum disc), Sting's Nothing Like The Sun (A&M 1987, Platinum disc), Phil Collins' In The Air Tonight (Virgin 1988 remix, Gold disc), remix of Joan Armatrading's Love & Affection (A&M 1991), Trisha Yearwood's Walkaway Joe (MCA Int 1994); recently worked with various other artists incl: Sheryl Crow, Tin Machine, Psychedelic Furs, Robbie Nevil; *Awards* Best British Producer Music Week Awards 1985 and 1990, Producer of the Year and Album of the Year Grammy Awards 1985, Best Producer nomination BPI Awards 1985 and 1986, Brit Awards Best Single 1989, Record of the Year Grammy Award 1990, Best Engineer Grammy Awards 1994; *Recreations* motor racing, tennis, windsurfing, skiing; *Style*— Hugh Padgham, Esq; ✉ c/o Dennis Muirhead, Muirhead Management, 202 Fulham Rd, Chelsea, London SW10 9JP (☎ 0171 351 5167, fax 0171 352 1514, e-mail 100625.1611@conpuserve.com)

PADMORE, Elaine Marguirite; da of Alfred Padmore (d 1971), and Florence, *née* Stockman; *b* 3 Feb 1947; *Educ* Newland HS Hull, Arnold Girls' Sch Blackpool, Univ of Birmingham (MA, BMus), Guildhall Sch of Music London; *Career* musician, singer, writer and broadcaster; ed Music Dept OUP 1970–71, lectr in opera RAM 1972–85, radio prodr Music Dept BBC 1971–76, chief prodr opera BBC Radio 1976–82, announcer BBC Radio 3 1982–90; artistic dir: Royal Danish Opera 1993–, Wexford Festival Opera (Ireland) 1982–94, Opera Ireland (formerly Dublin Grand Opera Soc) 1991–93, Classical Productions (UK) Ltd 1990–92, London Opera Festival 1991; Sunday Independent Award for servs to music in Ireland 1987; Hon ARAM 1984; Knight of the Royal Danish Dannebrog Order 1994; *Books* Wagner (Great Composers series), New Grove Dictionary of Music and Musicians (contrib); *Recreations* gardening, cats; *Style*— Miss Elaine Padmore; ✉ 11 Lancaster Ave, Hadley Wood, Herts EN4 0EP (☎ 0181 449 5369)

PADMORE, Peter Sheldon; s of Sheldon Leslie Padmore (d 1994), of Lyndhurst, Hants, and Eileen Mary, *née* Staley (d 1979); *b* 17 Sept 1940; *Educ* Southwell Minster GS, Brockenhurst County HS; *m* 19 Feb 1966, Jennifer Christobel, da of Harry Arthur Rice-Adams (d 1986); 1 s (Robert Sheldon), 1 da (Jane Elizabeth); *Career* Price Waterhouse: joined 1967, ptnr 1976–, managing ptnr Southampton 1992–; FCA, MIPA; *Recreations* golf, gardening, music; *Clubs* MCC, Reform, Royal Southampton Yacht; *Style*— Peter Padmore, Esq; ✉ Downsway, Dummer, Basingstoke, Hants (☎ 01256 397226); Price Waterhouse, 30 Channel Way, Ocean Village, Southampton, Hants SO14 3QG (☎ 01703 330077, fax 01703 236252, car 0860 716227)

PADOVAN, John Mario Faskally; s of Dr Umberto Mario Padovan (d 1966); *b* 7 May 1938; *Educ* St George's Coll Weybridge, King's Coll London (LLB), Keble Coll Oxford (BCL); *m* 1963, Sally Kay; 3 s; *Career* CA Price Waterhouse 1963; County Bank Ltd: chief exec 1976–83, dep chm 1982, chm 1984; exec dep chm Hambros Bank Ltd 1984–86, dep chm Barclays de Zoete Wedd Ltd 1986–91; chm: AAH plc 1993–95 (dep chm 1992), Gardner Merchant Services Group Ltd 1993–95; dir: Tesco plc 1982–94, de Zoete & Bevan Ltd 1986–92, Mabey Holdings Ltd 1989– (chm 1991–), The Hartstone Group plc 1991–, Whitbread plc 1992–, Planned Maintenance Engineering Ltd 1992–, Williams Lea Group Ltd 1992–, Schroder Split Fund plc 1993–, Evans of Leeds plc 1993–, Fairbairn European Smaller Company Index Trust PLC 1993–96, Broadgate Properties PLC 1994–96, London's Business Radio Ltd 1994 (chm), Tilbury Douglas PLC 1996–; memb Ct of Assts Worshipful Co of Drapers; *Style*— John Padovan, Esq; ✉ 15 Lord North Street, London SW1P 3LD

PAGAN, Dr Francis Stephen; s of Francis Edmund Pagan, of Piccadilly, London, and Margaret Jocelyn Neel (d 1971); *b* 22 July 1941; *Educ* Westminster, Univ of Cambridge (MA, MB BChir); *m* 12 Sept 1970, Nina Dilys, da of John Noël Mason Ashplant Nicholls, OBE, KPM (d 1987), of Stewards Hse, Pulham St Mary, Norfolk; 2 da (Isabel b 1975, Rosemary b 1978); *Career* house offr: surgery Royal Portsmouth Hosp 1968, med Medway Hosp Gillingham Kent 1968–69; sr house offr pathology Gen Hosp Nottingham 1969–70, registrar pathology Gen Hosp Southampton 1970–72, sr registrar microbiology Edgware Gen Hosp 1972–74, lectr bacteriology Middx Hosp London 1974–77, conslt microbiologist Meml Hosp Darlington 1977–; memb: BMA, Hosp Infection Soc, Br Soc of Antimicrobial Chemotherapy, Assoc of Med Microbiologists; FRCPath 1986; *Recreations* running, swimming, foreign travel, family life, herbs; *Style*— Dr Francis S Pagan; ✉ Elly Hill House, Barmpton, Darlington, Co Durham DL1 3JF (☎ 01325 464682)

PAGAN, Hugh Edmund; s of Francis Edmund Pagan, of Albany, Piccadilly, London, and Margaret Jocelyn, *née* Neel (d 1971); *b* 4 Oct 1944; *Educ* Westminster, ChCh Oxford (BA, MA); *m* 15 Feb 1974, Jill, da of Robert William Charles Catling, of Manchester; 2 s (Robert Edmund b 1974, Thomas Helier b 1978); *Career* antiquarian bookseller; dir B Weinreb Architectural Books Ltd 1978–87, md Hugh Pagan Ltd 1987–; jt ed Br Numismatic Jl 1971–76; Br Numismatic Soc: memb Cncl 1969–76 and 1979–, pres 1984–88, vice pres 1992–, John Sanford Saltus Gold medal 1989; vice chm Prep/Organising Ctee Int Numismatic Congress London 1986, memb Br Acad Ctee for Sylloge of Coinage of the Br Isles 1988–; fell Royal Numismatic Soc 1976 (memb Cncl 1981–84), FSA 1986; *Publications* Royal Numismatic Soc 150th Anniversary publication (jtly, 1986), contrib to volumes on Anglo-Saxon coinage, contrib articles in British Numismatic Journal; *Recreations* British political history; *Clubs* Garrick; *Style*— Hugh Pagan, Esq, FSA

PAGAN, Jill Catling; da of Robert William Charles Catling (d 1967), of Manchester, and Edna Catling (d 1978); *Educ* Loreburn Coll, Inns of Court Sch of Law; *m* 15 Feb 1974, Hugh Edmund, s of Francis Edmund Pagan, of Albany, London; 2 s (Robert b 27 Dec 1974, Thomas b 17 Jan 1978); *Career* called to the Bar Inner Temple 1972; int tax conslt: Tansley Witt & Co 1975–79, Thomson McLintock KMG 1980–82; practised at Revenue Bar 1982–89, int tax conslt J F Chown & Co Ltd 1989–92, memb Panel of Experts IMF 1992–, conslt OECD 1993; dir Hugh Pagan Ltd 1987–; contrib ed International Tax Report 1982–, founding ed Inner Temple Yearbook; author numerous articles on int fin, int and UK taxation; memb Bar Liaison Ctee Inner Temple 1985–90, ctee memb UK Branch Int Fiscal Assoc 1985–; *Books* Taxation Aspects of Currency Fluctuations (1 edn 1983, 2 edn 1992), Transfer Pricing Strategy in a Global Economy (with J Scott Wilkie, 1993), Borderless Income and Strategic Alliances - The New Age of Transfer Pricing (with J Scott Wilkie, 1997); *Recreations* family and travel; *Style*— Mrs Jill Pagan; ✉ 1 Trevor Street, Knightsbridge, London SW7 1DU (☎ 0171 581 9733)

PAGANO, Margareta; da of Gerald Pagano, and Bjørg Øyen; *b* 28 Aug 1955; *Educ* Friends' Sch Saffron Walden, SOAS London (BSc), Oslo Univ; *m* 26 Oct 1979, Jugurtha Yadi; 1 s (Hakim b 14 March 1984), 2 da (Hannah b 5 Jan 1987, Lydia b 5 Nov 1991); *Career* formerly trainee journalist Eastern Daily Press Norwich, business reporter The Times 1980–82; city corr: The Guardian 1982–87, The Daily Telegraph 1987, The Times 1987–88; city ed Sunday Correspondent 1988–90, fin ed Independent on Sunday 1991, business ed The European 1991–92, Euro business corr Sunday Telegraph 1992–; *Recreations* skiing; *Style*— Ms Margareta Pagano; ✉ The Sunday Telegraph, 1 Canada Square, Canary Wharf, London E14 5DT (☎ 0171 538 5000, fax 0171 538 1330)

PAGE, Prof Alan Chisholm; s of Samuel Chisholm Page, of Broughty Ferry, and Betsy Johnston, *née* Melville; *b* 7 April 1952; *Educ* Grove Acad Broughty Ferry, Univ of Edinburgh (LLB), City Univ (PhD); *m* 16 Aug 1975, Sheila Duffus, da of Ian Dunlop Melville, of Glasgow; 1 s (Michael b 1983), 1 da (Rebecca b 1986); *Career* lectr in law Univ of Cardiff 1975–80, dean Faculty of Law University of Dundee 1986–89 (sr lectr in law 1980–85, prof of pub law 1985–); memb Tax Law Review Ctee 1994–, lead assessor in law Scottish Higher Educn Funding Cncl 1995–96; *Books* Legislation (2 edn, 1990), Investor Protection (1992); *Recreations* mountaineering; *Style*— Prof Alan Page; ✉ Westlands, Westfield Road, Cupar, Fife (☎ 01334 655576); Department of Law, University of Dundee, Dundee DD1 4HN (☎ 01382 344633)

PAGE, Annette; da of James Lees Page (d 1979), and Margaret, *née* Johnson (d 1991); *b* 18 Dec 1932; *Educ* Altrincham GS, Sadler's Wells Ballet Sch; *m* 24 June 1957, Ronald Hynd, *qv*, s of William John Hens, of London; 1 da (Louise b 20 April 1968); *Career* ballerina; Sadler's Wells Royal Ballet 1950–55 (principal role in: Khadra, Les Rendevous, Les Sylphides, Beauty and the Beast, Lady and the Fool, Coppelia), Major Sadler's Wells Ballet (later Royal Ballet) 1955–67; major roles in: Symphonic Variations, Scenes de Ballet; title roles in: The Firebird, Sleeping Beauty, Swan Lake, Giselle, Fille Mal Gardee, Romeo and Juliet, Cinderella; after ret from stage: teacher Royal Acad of Dancing and London Contemporary Dance, choreographic asst to Ronald Hynd; asst dir of Bayerischestaats Ballet Munich 1984–86; memb Arts Cncl of GB (memb dance and music panels) 1967–84; *Recreations* singing, languages, travel, music, pottering around in Suffolk; *Style*— Ms Annette Page

PAGE, Anthony Frederick Montague; s of Brig F C G Page, of Oxford, and Pearl Valerie, *née* Montague Hall (d 1992); *b* 21 Sept 1935; *Educ* Winchester Coll (scholar), Magdalen Coll Oxford, Demy Neighbourhood Playhouse Sch of the Theatre New York; *Career* director; artistic dir Royal Court (various periods) 1964–73 (asst dir 1958 (co-dir Live Like Pigs 1962)); prodns incl: Inadmissible Evidence, Patriot for Me, Time Present, West of Suez, Time Present, Alpha Beta, Not I, Waiting for Godot, Uncle Vanya, Hedda Gabler, Krapp's Last Tape; RNT: The Rules of the Game, Mrs Warren's Profession, Absolute Hell; other prodn incl: Three Tall Women (West End), The Doll's House, Heartbreak House, Inadmissible Evidence (both Broadway), The Caretaker (The

Roundabout); *Television* USA: The Patricia Neal Story, Bill (Golden Globe Award), The Nightmare Years, Pack of Lies, Second Serve, Missiles of October, Pueblo Affair, Chernobyl - The Final Warning, The Parachute (Guild of Producers and Directors Award), Sheppy; UK: Z Cars, The Parachute, Sheppy, Absolute Hell, Middlemarch, The Human Bomb; *Films* incl: Inadmissible Evidence, Alpha Beta, Absolution, I Never Promised a Rose Garden; *Recreations* reading, swimming, sketching; *Style*— Anthony Page, Esq; ✉ c/o ICM Ltd, Oxford House, 76 Oxford Street, London W1N 0AX (☎ 0171 636 6565, fax 0171 323 0101)

PAGE, Ashley John; *né* Laverty; s of John Henry Laverty, of Gillingham, Kent, and Sheila Rachael, *née* Medhurst; *b* 9 Aug 1956; *Educ* St Andrew's Rochester Kent, Royal Ballet Lower and Upper Sch; *partner* Nicola Roberts; 1 s (Jordan Paris Gower Page b 14 July 1994); *Career* Royal Ballet: joined 1976 (after trg with Educnl Unit Ballet for All 1975), soloist 1980, principal dancer 1984; roles incl many created specially by resident & visiting choreographers plus a wide variety within Royal Ballet's repertoire incl: Romeo, Benvolio and Tybalt in Romeo and Juliet, Afternoon of a Faun, the Poet in Les Illuminations, The Prodigal Son, the Tutor in A Month in the Country, the boy with matted hair in Shadowplay, Ferdinand in The Tempest, Lescaut in Manon, Kings of the South and East in Prince of the Pagodas, Tirreneo in Ondine, the brother in My Brother My Sisters, Mars in the Planets, Troyte in Enigma Variations, the tango dancer in Isadora, the Angel of Light in Orpheus, Bruno in Valley of Shadows, Drum Major in Different Drummer, Solo Boy in Agon, Midsummer, Lysander in The Dream, Friday Night in Elite Syncopations, La Fin du Jour, an angel in Dances of Albion, pas de trois in Voluntaries, Rag Mazurka in Les Biches, Les Noces, the zebra in Still Life at the Penguin Cafe, 4 song in Song of the Earth, lead boy in Gloria, 6 song in Requiem, Paul in Wedding Bouquet, lead boy in Rhapsody, Apollo in Young Apollo, 3 song in Dark Elegies, Green and White Monotones, Saturday's child in Jazz calendar, pas de deux boy in Danses Concertantes, Duamutef in The Sons of Horus, Valvert and De Guiche in Cyrano, lead officer in Mayerling, The High Brahmin in La Bayadère, Carabosse in The Sleeping Beauty, the Count in La Ronde, Ugly Sister in Cinderella, Gamache in Don Quixote, Rothbart in Swan Lake; choreographer 1984–; work for Royal Ballet at Royal Opera House incl: A Broken Set of Rules 1984, Pursuit 1987, Piano 1989, Bloodlines 1990, Renard 1994, Fearful Symmetries 1994 (winner Time Out Dance Award 1994 and Olivier Award for best new dance prodn 1994), 2 or 3 Dialogues 1995, Ebony Concerto 1995, ... now languorous, now wild... 1996, Sleeping with Audrey 1996, Two-Part Invention 1996; work for Rambert Dance Company (under Richard Alston): Carmen Arcadiae 1986, Soldat 1988, Currulao 1990; choreographer: Savage Water dance film Channel 4 1989, numerous works for Dance Umbrella (incl collaborative work with Gaby Agis) 1983–87, Touch Your Coolness to my Fevered Brow (for Dutch National Ballet) 1992, Bisocosis Populi (for London Studio Centre) 1992, Quartet (for Irek Mukhamedov and Co) 1992, Heavenly Interior (for Istanbul State Ballet) 1992, 2011 and A Long Time Coming (for Turkuaz Dance Co) 1993, Escape at Sea (for Second Stride) 1993, Shirley Birly (for MDT Ankara) 1995, Mythologie Plastique (for Conservatoire de Paris) 1995; winner first Frederick Ashton Choreographic award 1982, first Frederick Ashton Meml Cmmn (which produced Currulao) 1990; *Style*— Ashley Page, Esq; ✉ Royal Ballet, Royal Opera House, Covent Garden, London WC2E (☎ 0171 240 1200)

PAGE, Maj-Gen Charles Edward; CB (1974), MBE (1944), DL (1986); s of late Sir (Charles) Max Page, KBE, CB, DSO; *b* 23 Aug 1920; *Educ* Marlborough, Trinity Coll Cambridge, Univ of London (BSc); *m* 1948, Elizabeth Marion, da of late Sir William Smith Crawford, KBE; 2 s, 1 da; *Career* Cdr Corps Royal Signals 1 (BR) Corps 1966–68, sec NATO Mil Ctee Brussels 1968–70, Dir Combat Devpt (A) 1971–74, ret 1974; Col Cmdt Royal Corps of Signals 1974–80; Hon Col Women's Tport Serv (FANY); *Recreations* shooting, fishing, golf; *Clubs* Royal and Ancient (St Andrews), Hurlingham; *Style*— Maj-Gen Charles Page, CB, MBE, DL

PAGE, Dr Christopher Howard; s of Ewert Lacey Page, and Marie Victoria, *née* Graham; *b* 8 April 1952; *Educ* Sir George Monoux Sch, Univ of Oxford (BA, MA), Univ of York (DPhil); *m* 15 Sept 1975, Régine, *née* Fourcade; *Career* currently lectr in Middle Eng Univ of Cambridge; fell Sidney Sussex Coll Cambridge (formerly fell Jesus Coll Oxford); presenter Radio 3 series Spirit of the Age; ldr of the ensemble Gothic Voices and prodr of acclaimed records; Gramophone Early Music Records of the Year: Hildegard of Bingen 1983 (also Guardian Choral Record of the Year), The Service of Venus and Mars 1988, A Song for Francesca (1989); chm Nat Early Music Assoc, chm Plainsong and Medieval Music Soc, fell Fellowship of Makers and Restorers of Historical Instruments; *Books* Voices and Instruments of the Middle Ages (1987), Sequences of Hildegard of Bingen (1986), The Owl and the Nightingale (1989), Summa Musice (1991), Discarding Images (1994); *Recreations* research and performance; *Style*— Dr Christopher Page; ✉ Sidney Sussex College, Cambridge CB2 3HU

PAGE, Christopher John (Chris); s of Albert Harold Page (d 1987), and Doris May, *née* Clarke; *b* 28 May 1947; *Educ* Eton House Sch, South Bank Poly (Dip Arch); *m* 7 July 1979, Janice Anne, da of Andrew John Sharman, of Wickford, Essex; 1 s (Richard b 1981), 1 da (Jacqueline b 1984); *Career* architect/program mangr; md: Atlanta Program Management 1986–, Atlanta Interiors 1987–; ptnr Chris Page Assocs, chm Atlanta Signs; *Recreations* sailing, sketching, pre-history in UK; *Clubs* Eton House Old Boys, Thorpe Bay Yacht; *Style*— Chris Page, Esq; ✉ 35 Challacombe, Thorpe Bay, Essex SS1 3TY (☎ 01702 585710); Raycastle Centre, 12 Devonshire Square, London EC2M 4TE

PAGE, David Norman; s of Bernard Page, of Edinburgh, and Catherine Page, *née* Adam; *b* 4 Sept 1957; *Educ* Bearsden Acad Strathclyde, Univ of Strathclyde (BSc, BArch); *m* 14 Dec 1982, Fiona Sinclair, da of Archibald Sinclair, of Helensburgh; *Career* sr ptnr Page and Park Architects 1981–; lectr Dept of Architecture and Building Science Univ of Strathclyde 1982–94; ARSA; *Style*— David N Page, Esq; ✉ Roseangle, 49A William St, Helensburgh (☎ 01436 676781); Page and Park Architects, The Italian Centre, 49 Cochrane Street, Glasgow, G1 (☎ 0141 552 0686)

PAGE, Dianne; da of William John Griffiths Bryce, of Walton, Wellesbourne, Warwickshire, and Audrey Jean, *née* Smith; *b* 14 May 1946; *Educ* Regis Sch Tettenhall Wolverhampton, Wolverhampton Poly (Dip); *partner* Paul Ronald Scott Lever; *Career* Sulzer Brothers Switzerland 1965–66, Alusuisse UK 1966–72, Tower Housewares 1972–80, md Barkers Public Relations 1980–; fell Inst of Home Economics 1978, MIPR 1974; *Books* Pressure Cooking Explained (1979), Slow Cooking Explained (1982), Food Processors Explained (1984); *Recreations* cooking, theatre, opera; *Style*— Mrs Dianne Page; ✉ Barkers Public Relations, Kennedy Tower, Snow Hill, Queensway, Birmingham B4 6JB (☎ 0121 236 9501, fax 0121 233 4156)

PAGE, Emma; *Educ* Univ of Oxford (MA); *children* 2 s, 1 da; *Career* detective writer; *Books* Final Moments (1987), A Violent End (1988), Deadlock (1991), Mortal Remains (1992), In The Event of My Death (1994), Murder Comes Calling (1995), Hard Evidence (1996) and others; *Style*— Ms Emma Page; ✉ c/o HarperCollins Publishers, 77–85 Fulham Palace Road, London W6 8JB (☎ 0181 741 7070, fax 0181 307 4440)

PAGE, Dr Ewan Stafford; s of late Joseph William Page; *b* 17 Aug 1928; *Educ* Wyggeston GS Leicester, Christ's Coll Cambridge (MA, PhD, Raleigh Prize 1952), London Univ (BSc); *m* 1955, Sheila Margaret Smith; 3 s, 1 da; *Career* instr RAF Tech Coll 1949–51, lectr in statistics Durham Colls 1954–57, dir Durham Univ Computing Lab 1957–63, Newcastle Univ Computing Lab 1963–78, visiting prof Univ of N Carolina 1962–63, prof of computing and data processing Univ of Newcastle upon Tyne 1965–78 (pro vice chllr 1972–78, acting vice chllr 1976–77); vice chllr Univ of Reading 1979–93; memb: West Berks District Health Authy 1981–93, Berks Health Authy 1993–95, Gen Optical Cncl 1984– (dep chm 1990–); chm: Review of Veterinary Manpower and Educn MAFF/DES 1989–90, Food Advsy Ctee MAFF 1989–94; CEng, CIMgt, fell Royal Statistical Soc (hon treas 1983–89); hon fell: Univ of Northumbria at Newcastle (formerly Newcastle upon Tyne Poly), American Statistical Assoc, Br Computer Soc; Chevalier dans l'Ordre des Palmes Académiques 1991; Hon DSc Univ of Reading; *Publications* approximately 50 papers in: Computer Jls, Jls of the Royal Statistical Soc, Biometrika, Technometrics, Applied Statistics; Information Representation and Manipulation in a Computer (with L B Wilson), Information Representation and Manipulation using Pascal (with L B Wilson), Computational Combinatories (with L B Wilson); *Style*— Dr E S Page; ✉ High View, Charlcombe Lane, Bath (☎ 01225 422073)

PAGE, Sir Frederick William; kt (1979), CBE (1961); s of late Richard Page, and Ellen Sarah Page; *b* 20 Feb 1917; *Educ* Rutlish Sch Merton, St Catharine's Coll Cambridge (MA); *m* 1940, Kathleen Edith de Courcy (d 1993); 3 s, 1 da; *Career* chief engr English Electric Aviation 1950, chief exec (Aircraft) 1959; dir Panavia Aircraft GmbH Germany 1969–83 (chm 1977–79), chm BAC Ltd 1977; jt chm Sepecat (France) 1966–73, chm and chief exec Aircraft Gp of Br Aerospace 1977–83; British Gold Medal Aeronautics 1962, RAeS Gold Medal 1974; Hon FRAeS 1980 hon fell UMIST 1970, Hon DSc Cranfield 1979; FRS, FEng 1977; *Clubs* United Oxford and Cambridge Univ; *Style*— Sir Frederick Page, CBE, FRS, FEng; ✉ Renvyle, 60 Waverley Lane, Farnham, Surrey GU9 8BN (☎ 01252 714999)

PAGE, Prof (John) Graham; s of George Ronald Page (d 1966), and Lilian Alice, *née* Kay (d 1982); *b* 16 Feb 1943; *Educ* Robert Gordon's Coll Aberdeen (MB ChB); *m* 30 Aug 1969, Sandra; 1 s (Andrew b 11 Jan 1972), 2 da (Caroline b 12 April 1974, Alison b 21 March 1977); *Career* prof of emergency med Aberdeen Royal Infirmary 1981– (house physician and surgn 1968–69, surgical registrar 1970–78), hon sr lectr in surgery Univ of Aberdeen 1981– (terminable lectr in pathology 1969–70), res fell Harvard Univ 1974–75, hon conslt Br Antarctic Survey Med Unit 1983–; memb: BMA, Edinburgh Royal Coll Surgns, Euro Undersea Baromedical Assoc; FRCS 1972, ChM 1977; *Books* with KLG Mills and R Morton: A Colour Atlas of Cardiopulmonary Resuscitation (1986), A Colour Atlas of Plaster Techniques (1986), A Colour Atlas and Text of Emergencies (1995); *Recreations* skiing, sailing; *Style*— Prof Graham Page; ✉ 16 Kingswood Ave, Kingswells, Aberdeen AB15 8AE (☎ 01224 742945); Aberdeen Royal Infirmary, Aberdeen Royal Hospitals NHS Trust, Accident and Emergency Department, Aberdeen AB25 2ZN (☎ 01224 681818 ext 53306, fax 01224 840718)

PAGE, Jennifer Anne; CBE (1994); da of Edward Page, and Olive Page; *b* 12 Nov 1944; *Educ* Barr's Hill GS Coventry, Royal Holloway Coll London (BA); *Career* Civil Serv: entered 1968, princ DOE 1974, asst sec Dept of Tport 1980; seconded: British National Oil Corporation 1981–83, London Dockland Development Corporation 1983–84; sr vice pres Pallas Invest SA 1984–89; chief exec: English Heritage 1989–95, The Millennium Cmmn March 1995–; non-exec memb: Br Railways Bd 1993–94, Railtrack Group plc 1994–, Equitable Life Assurance Soc 1994–; *Style*— Miss Jennifer A Page, CBE; ✉ Chief Executive, The Millennium Commission, 2 Little Smith Street, London SW1P 3DH (☎ 0171 340 2001, fax 0171 340 2000)

PAGE, Sir (Arthur) John; kt (1984); s of Sir Arthur Page, QC (d 1958), late Chief Justice of Burma, and Margaret Page, K-i-H, *née* Symes Thompson; *b* 16 Sept 1919; *Educ* Harrow, Magdalene Coll Cambridge; *m* 9 Dec 1950, Anne Gertrude, da of Charles Micklem, DSO, JP, DL (d 1957); 4 s (Hugo b 1951, Nathaniel b 1953, Henry b (twin) 1953, Rupert b 1963); *Career* served WWII, gunner RA 1939, Maj Norfolk Yeo 1945, served Middle East (wounded), France and Germany; contested (C) Eton and Slough Gen Election 1959, MP (C) Harrow 1960–87, chm Cons Parly Labour Affairs Ctee 1970–74 (sec 1960–61, vice chm 1964–69), memb Br Delegn to Cncl of Europe and WEU 1972–87; dir: Long & Hambly Ltd 1960–81, N Surrey Water Co 1988–; chm: Frederick Clarke (Furnishings) Ltd 1955–88, Colne Valley Water Co 1987–90 (dir 1984–90), Three Valleys Water plc 1990–; pres: Independent Schools Assoc 1971–83, Water Companies Assoc 1986–89; chm Cncl for Ind Educn 1974–80, vice pres British Insurance Brokers Assoc 1980–, elected substitute pres (Int) Inter-Party Union 1983, chm Groundwork Hertfordshire 1993–; Freeman City of London, Liveryman Worshipful Co of Grocers 1970; *Recreations* painting, politics, defending the Monarchy; *Clubs* Brooks's, MCC; *Style*— Sir John Page; ✉ Hitcham Lodge, Taplow, Maidenhead, Berks (☎ 01628 605056); Three Valleys Water Plc, PO Box 48, Bishop's Rise, Hatfield, Herts AL10 9HL (☎ 01707 268111)

PAGE, Maj-Gen John Humphrey; CB (1977), OBE (1967), MC (1952); s of Capt W J Page, JP (d 1961), of Devizes, and Alice Mary Page (d 1981); *b* 5 March 1923; *Educ* Stonyhurst; *m* 1956, Angela Mary, da of Bernard Bunting (d 1962); 3 s, 1 da; *Career* cmmnd RE 1942; Asst Cmdt RMA Sandhurst 1971–74, Dir of Personal Servs (Army) Miny of Def 1974–78, ret; dir London Law Tst 1979–88, vice chm Soldiers' Sailors' and Airmen's Families' Assoc 1983–87, chm Bd of Govrs St Mary's Sch Shaftesbury 1985–93, govr Stonyhurst Coll 1980–90, chm and tstee Home Start Consultancy 1981–90; KSG 1993; *Style*— Maj-Gen John Page, CB, OBE, MC; ✉ c/o Lloyds Bank, Devizes, Wiltshire

PAGE, Sir John Joseph Joffre; kt (1979), OBE (1959); s of William Joseph Page (d 1935), and Frances Page (d 1977); *b* 7 Jan 1915; *Educ* Emanuel Sch; *m* 1939, Cynthia Maynard, da of Lionel Maynard Swan, CBE (d 1969); 2 s; *Career* RAF 1933–38 and 1939–46 (despatches 1943), Gp Capt; Iraq Petroleum Gp of Cos: 1938–39 and 1946–70, gen mangr 1955–58, chief rep 1961–70; Mersey Docks and Harbour Co: chm 1972–77 and 1980–84, chief exec 1975–77; dep chm Br Ports Assoc 1974–77; chm: Nat Ports Cncl 1977–80, Chester Health Authy 1981–82, NW RHA 1982–88, Christie Hosp NHS Trust 1991–92; Liveryman Worshipful Co of Carmen; hon fell Manchester Metropolitan Univ 1993; *Recreations* music, fishing; *Clubs* Oriental, RAF, MCC; *Style*— Sir John Page, OBE; ✉ The Cottage, Hockenhull Lane, Tarvin, Chester CH3 8LB

PAGE, John Leslie Arthur; *b* 21 June 1940; *Educ* Halbutt St Secdy Mod Sch, SE Essex Tech Coll; *Career* fndr chm and dir: Phoenix Engineering Resources Ltd, Phoenix International Corporation Ltd (int recruitment conslts, manpower contractors for engrg, technical and associated personnel, servs to the engrg, energy, oil, gas, utilities, civil and construction industs worldwide); dir: Page International Corporation Ltd, Page International Engineering Ltd, Page International UK Ltd, Page Norway A/S, Page Engineering (PTY) Ltd; pres Page International Inc; IEng, MIED 1975, FFA 1978, MIMgt 1981, MECI 1981, MIED 1989, FInstD; *Style*— John L A Page, Esq; ✉ PO Box 44, Stanhope, Co Durham DL13 2DU (☎ 01388 526500, fax 01388 526800)

PAGE, Michael Brian; s of James Gourlay Page, of Chester-le-Street, Co Durham, and Mary Jane, *née* McTeague; *b* 14 April 1937; *Educ* Chester-le-Street GS Co Durham, Aston Univ (BSc Eng); *m* 1961, Jennifer Grace Elizabeth, da of Joseph Victor Wetton (d 1966); 3 da (Joanna b 1966, Kathryn b 1968, Sally b 1971); *Career* sales dir Brush Electrical Machines Ltd 1977–84; chm Hawker Siddeley Power Engrg Inc (USA) 1984–90, dir Hawker Siddeley Electric Ltd 1986–90, md Hawker Siddeley Power Engrg Ltd & assoc companies 1984–90 (conslt 1990–92); md: Allied Insulators Ltd 1992–, Doulton Insulators Ltd 1992–; chm Hopyard Foundries Ltd 1992–; CEng, FIEE, FIMgt, FInstD; *Recreations* golf, chess; *Clubs* Rothley Park Golf; *Style*— Michael Page, Esq; ✉ Blue Haze, 90 Station Rd, Cropston, Leicestershire LE7 7HE (☎ 0116 236 2527)

PAGE, Richard Lewis; MP (C) Hertfordshire South West (majority 20,107); s of Victor Charles Page (d 1968), and Kathleen Page; *b* 22 Feb 1941; *Educ* Hurstpierpoint Coll,

Luton Tech Coll; *m* 3 Oct 1964, Madeleine Ann, da of Geoffrey Ronald Brown; 1 s (Mark Lewis b 29 March 1968), 1 da (Tracey Louise b 25 April 1970); *Career* dir of family co 1964–95; cncllr Banstead UDC 1969–72; MP (C): Workington 1976–79, Herts SW 1979–; PPS to: Sec of State for Trade, Ldr of the House 1982–87; Parly under-sec DTI 1995–; memb Public Accounts Ctee 1987–95; nat treas Leukemia Research Fund 1988–95; Freeman City of London, Liveryman Worshipful Co of Pattenmakers 1979; *Recreations* riding, shooting; *Style*— Richard Page, Esq, MP; ✉ House of Commons, London SW1

PAGE, District Judge Simon Richard; s of Eric Rowland Page (d 1985), and Vera, *née* Fenton (d 1994); *b* 7 March 1934; *Educ* Lancing, LSE (LLB external); *m* 1, 1963 (m dis 1977); 3 s, 1 da; m 2, 1984; *Career* 2 Lt RA 1958–59; admitted slr 1957, in private practice 1959–75, recorder Crown Ct 1980–, dist judge High Ct of Justice, Guildford, Epsom and Reigate Co Courts; pres: W Surrey Law Soc 1972–73, Assoc of County Ct and Dist Registrars 1983–84; *Recreations* squash, lawn tennis, cricket, bridge; *Style*— District Judge Page; ✉ c/o The Law Courts, Guildford, Surrey

PAGE, Prof Trevor Francis; s of Cyril Francis Page (d 1980), of Lichfield, Staffs, and Gladys Mary, *née* Boston; *b* 6 Jan 1946; *Educ* King Edward VI GS Lichfield Staffs, Jesus Coll Cambridge (MA, PhD); *m* 7 Aug 1971, Andrea Gail, da of Cyril James Jones, of Cambridge; 1 s (Matthew Nicholas James b 1976), 1 da (Victoria Sophie Louise b 1979); *Career* Univ of Cambridge: SRC res fell 1971–72, demonstrator in metallurgy and materials sci 1972–76, lectr 1976–86, fndn fell Robinson Coll 1976–86; Cookson Gp prof of engrg materials Univ of Newcastle 1987– (head material div 1989–); author of numerous scientific papers, reviews and encyclopaedia articles on materials sci, the applications of microscopy, the devpt of ceramic materials and surface engrg; SERC: memb Materials Cmmn Equipment Ctee, memb Ceramics and Inorganic Materials Ctee 1985–90; memb American Ceramic Soc 1976; chm Tyne and Wear Metallurgical Soc 1988–90; fell: Royal Microscopical Soc 1971, Inst of Metals 1984, Inst of Ceramics 1987; FIM 1991; CEng; *Recreations* family, gardening, classical music, opera, theatre, cinema, food and wine, photography, riding, badminton; *Style*— Prof Trevor Page; ✉ Materials Division, Department Mechanical Materials & Manufacturing Engineering, Herschel Building, The University of Newcastle, Newcastle upon Tyne NE1 7RU (☎ 0191 222 7201, fax 0191 222 8563, e-mail T.F.Page@ncl.ac.uk)

PAGE WOOD, Sir Anthony John; 8 Bt (UK 1837), of Hatherley House, Gloucestershire; s of Sir David John Hatherley Page Wood, 7 Bt (d 1955); *b* 6 Feb 1951; *Educ* Harrow; *Heir* unc, Matthew Page Wood b 13 Aug 1924; *Career* dir Société Générale Strauss Turnbull (London) 1982; *Style*— Sir Anthony Page Wood, Bt; ✉ 77 Dovehouse St, London SW3

PAGE WOOD, Matthew Page; s of Sir John Stuart Page Wood, 6 Bt (d 1955), and hp of nephew, Sir Anthony Page Wood, 8 Bt; assumed by deed poll 1955 the additional surname of Page before his patronymic; *b* 13 Aug 1924; *Educ* Radley Coll; *m* 1947, Betsann, da of Lt-Col Francis Christesson Darby Tothill; 2 da (Belinda Jane b 1952 (m 1, Richard John Crowder; m 2, Charles Hoste; 1 s), Miranda Elizabeth b 1962 (m William Kendall; 2 da)); *Career* Capt Coldstream Gds, ret 1948; New York Stock Exchange; memb: London Stock Exchange 1949–60, CDN Investmt Banker 1960–79; chm Hammersmith Cons Assoc 1963–74 (pres 1974–83); *Recreations* golf, fishing; *Clubs* Brooks's, City of London, MCC; *Style*— Matthew Page Wood, Esq; ✉ 31 Halsey St, London SW3 2PT (☎ 0171 584 6008)

PAGEL, Prof Bernard Ephraim Julius; s of Traugott Ulrich Walter Pagel (d 1983), and Maria Magdalene Emilie Koll (d 1980); *b* 4 Jan 1930; *Educ* Merchant Taylors', Sidney Sussex Coll Cambridge (BA, PhD), Cambridge Observatories and Univ of Michigan; *m* Annabel Ruth, da of Edmond Scialom Tuby, of London; 2 s (David Benjamin b 1961, Jonathan Francis b 1966), 1 da (Celia Ann b 1959); *Career* res fell Sidney Sussex Coll Cambridge 1953–56, Radcliffe student Pretoria SA 1955, astrophysicist Sacramento Peak Observatory 1960; Royal Greenwich Observatory: princ scientific offr 1956–61, sr princ scientific offr 1961–71, dep chief scientific offr 1971–90; prof of astrophysics Nordita Copenhagen 1990–; Univ of Sussex: visiting reader in astronomy 1966–70, visiting prof of astronomy 1970–; Royal Astronomical Soc: jt ed Monthly Notices 1970–84, vice pres and foreign corr 1973–75, Gold medal 1990; served on ctees and panels of RAS and SERC concerned with grants and telescope time allocations, Kelvin lectr Br Assoc 1962; memb: RAS 1955, Int Astronomical Union 1958; FRS 1992; *Books* Théorie des Atmosphères Stellaires (1971), Evolutionary Phenomena in Galaxies (1989); *Recreations* music, cycling, skiing; *Style*— Prof Bernard Pagel, FRS; ✉ Groombridge, Lewes Road, Ringmer, East Sussex BN8 5ER (☎ 01273 812729); Nordita, Blegdamsvej 17, DK-2100 Copenhagen, Denmark (☎ 00 45 31 38 99 54, fax 00 45 31 38 91 57, telex 15216 NBI DK)

PAGET, David Christopher John; QC (1994); s of late Henry Paget, of Johannesburg, SA, and Dorothy, *née* Colenutt; *b* 3 Feb 1942; *Educ* St John' s Coll Johannesburg; *m* 21 March 1968, Dallas Wendy, da of Brian Thomas Hill; 2 da (Henrietta b 1975, Alexandra b 1987); *Career* called to the Bar Inner Temple 1967, sr prosecuting counsel to the Crown Central Criminal Ct 1989–94 (jr prosecuting counsel 1982, first jr 1988), recorder of Crown Ct 1986–; *Recreations* walking, bird watching, listening to music; *Style*— David Paget, Esq, QC; ✉ Queen Elizabeth Building, Temple, London EC4Y 9BS

PAGET, Henry James; s and h of Lt-Col Sir Julian Tolver Paget, 4 Bt, CVO, *qv*; *b* 2 Feb 1959; *Educ* Radley Coll; *m* 8 Sept 1993, Mrs Margrete E Varvill, da of late Halfdan Lynner; 1 s (Bernard Halfdan b 4 July 1994), 1 da (Daphne Ampuria b 9 Sept 1996); *Career* Coldstream Guards; ptnr J Rothschild Assurance; *Recreations* fishing, shooting and property renovation; *Style*— Henry Paget, Esq; ✉ Summerfield, Little London, Heathfield, Sussex TN21 0NU (☎ 01435 866119)

PAGET, Lt-Col Sir Julian Tolver; 4 Bt (UK 1871), of Harewood Place, Middlesex, CVO (1984); s of Gen Sir Bernard Charles Tolver Paget, GCB, DSO, MC (d 1961); suc unc, Sir James Francis Paget, 3 Bt (d 1972); *b* 11 July 1921; *Educ* Radley, ChCh Oxford (MA); *m* 1954, Diana Frances, da of late Frederick Spencer Herbert Farmer, of Lymington, Hants; 1 s (Henry James b 1959), 1 da (Olivia Jane (Mrs Nigel Cox) b 1957); *Heir* s, Henry James Paget, *qv*, b 2 Feb 1959; *Career* joined Coldstream Gds 1940, served NW Europe 1944–45, ret as Lt-Col 1968; extra gentleman usher to HM The Queen 1991– (gentleman usher 1971–91); author; *Books* Counter-Insurgency Campaigning (1967), Last Post-Aden 1964–67 (1969), The Story of the Guards (1976), The Pageantry of Britain (1979), The Yeomen of the Guard (1985), Wellington's Peninsular War (1990), Hougoumont: the Key to Victory at Waterloo (1992); *Clubs* Cavalry and Guards', Flyfishers'; *Style*— Lt-Col Sir Julian Paget, Bt, CVO; ✉ 4 Trevor St, London SW7 1DU (☎ 0171 584 3524)

PAGET, Sir Richard Herbert; 4 Bt (UK 1886), of Cranmore Hall, Co Somerset; s of Sir John Starr Paget, 3 Bt (d 1992), and Nancy Mary, JP, da of late Lt-Col Francis Woodbine Parish, DSO, MC, 60 Rifles; *b* 17 Feb 1957; *Educ* Eton; *m* 1985, Richenda Rachel, da of Rev Preb John Theodore Cameron Bucke Collins, formerly vicar of Holy Trinity, Brompton, London SW7; 3 da (Emma Rachel b 17 June 1986, (Richenda) Elizabeth b 29 Dec 1988, Camilla Mary b 5 May 1991); *Heir* bro, David Vernon John Paget b 1959; *Career* computer sales and marketing, currently runs own marketing consultancy (with emphasis on internet); pres Paget Gorman Soc; Liveryman Worshipful Co of Grocers; *Recreations* tennis, cricket, parachuting, carriage driving; *Style*— Sir Richard Paget, Bt; ✉ Burridge Heath Farm, Little Bedwyn, Marlborough, Wilts SN8 3JR (☎ 01672 870194, fax 01672 870994, personal no 07000 780555); Haygrass House, Taunton, Somerset TA3 7BS (☎ 01823 331779)

PAGET-WILKES, Ven Michael Jocelyn James; s of Rev Sqdn Ldr A H Paget-Wilkes (d 1956), of Freshford, nr Bath, and Bridget, *née* Perkins; *b* 11 Dec 1941; *Educ* Dean Close Sch Cheltenham, Harper Adams Agric Coll (NDA), London Coll of Divinity (ALCD); *m* 12 July 1969, (Ruth) Gillian, da of Dillon Macnamara (d 1967), of Dublin; 1 s (Rory b 1977), 2 da (Jessica b 1972, Claire b 1973); *Career* agric extension offr Lindi Tanzania 1964–66; curate All Saints Wandsworth 1969–74; vicar: St James Hatcham London 1974–82, St Matthews Rugby 1982–90, archdeacon of Warwick 1990; *Books* The Church and the Land (1968), Inside Out (1976), Poverty Revolution and the Church (1981); *Recreations* squash, gardening, tennis, skiing; *Style*— The Ven the Archdeacon of Warwick; ✉ 10 Northumberland Road, Leamington Spa, Warwicks CV32 6HA (☎ 01926 313337); Church House, Palmerston Rd, Coventry CV5 6FJ (☎ 01203 674328)

PAGETT, Nicola Mary; da of H W F Scott, of High Halden, Kent, and Barbara, *née* Black (d 1985); *b* 15 June 1945; *Educ* Convent Yokohama, The Beehive Bexhill on Sea, Ashford Secretarial Coll, RADA; *m* 9 July 1977, Graham Swannell, s of Maj William Swannell, MC (d 1982); 1 da (Eve Barbara Louise b 16 April 1979); *Career* actress; *Theatre* numerous roles incl: School for Scandal (Duke of York's), Ophelia Regina and Masha (Greenwich), Helen of Troy and Suzannah in The Marriage of Figaro (NT), A Voyage Round My Father (West End), Old Times in London and Los Angeles (West End), The Light of Day (Lyric) 1987, The Rehearsal (Garrick) 1991, Party Time, Rules of the Game (Almeida), What the Butler Saw (RNT) 1995, An Ideal Husband (Old Vic) 1996; *Television* incl: Upstairs Downstairs, Anna Karenina, A Bit of a Do, Ain't Misbehavin'; *Films* incl: Oliver's Story 1978, Privates on Parade 1982, An Awfully Big Adventure 1994; *Recreations* gardening, cooking; *Style*— Ms Nicola Pagett; ✉ c/o James Sharkey Associates Ltd, 21 Golden Square, London W1R 3PA (☎ 0171 434 3801, fax 0171 494 1547)

PAGNAMENTA, Peter John; s of Charles Francis Pagnamenta, of Richmond, and Daphne Isabel, *née* Kay (d 1990); *b* 12 April 1941; *Educ* Shrewsbury, Trinity Hall Cambridge; *m* 13 April 1966, Sybil, da of Frances Howard Healy, of New York, USA; 1 s (Robin b 1973), 1 da (Zoe b 1969); *Career* TV documentary prodr; joined BBC 1964, asst prodr Tonight 1965, prodr 24 Hours 1966, prodr New York office 1968, ed 24 Hours 1971, ed Midweek 1972, ed Panorama 1975; dir news and current affairs Thames Television 1977; BBC: prodr All Our Working Lives 1984, ed Real Lives series 1984, head of Current Affairs Group 1985, prodr Nippon 1990, prodr People's Century (26 part series) 1995–96; *Books* All Our Working Lives (with Richard Overy, 1984); *Style*— Peter Pagnamenta; ✉ 96 Elgin Crescent, London W11 2JL

PAGNI, Patrick Robert Marie; s of Robert Pagni, of Ville D'Avray, France, and Eliane, *née* Sanouiller; *b* 15 July 1949; *Educ* Ecole St Louis de Gonzague Paris, Université Paris IX Dauphine (Master in Management), Harvard Univ (MBA); *m* 2 Oct 1978, Viviane, da of Andre Guyot; *Career* Société Générale: joined 1970, asst mangr Paris 1974, dep branch mangr Paris 1976, vice pres NY Branch 1979, regnl mangr Western US 1981, gen mangr Hong Kong Branch 1984, UK gen mangr 1992–95, UK chief exec 1995–; Société Générale Strauss Turnbull Securities: exec dir 1988, chief exec 1990–92, UK chief exec 1995–; *Recreations* photography; *Clubs* Royal Hong Kong Jockey, City of London, London Capital; *Style*— Patrick Pagni, Esq; ✉ Société Générale, Exchange House, Primrose Street, London EC2A 2HT (☎ 0171 762 4444, fax 0171 638 6503)

PAHOR, Dr Ahmes Labib; s of Prof Pahor Labib (d 1994), of Cairo; *b* 15 Sept 1942, Cairo; *Educ* Cairo Univ (MB BCh, DLO), Ain Shams Univ Cairo (DMSc Path), MRCS LRCP (London), FRCSEd (Cert of Higher Surgical Trg in ENT), ECFMG (Philadelphia), Inst of Higher Coptic Studies Cairo (MA), DHMSA (Soc of Apothecaries London), Cert of Specialist Trg (EU); *Career* intern Cairo Univ Hosp (Teaching) 1964–65, sr house offr Miny of Health Cairo 1965–66, asst researcher (demonstrator) Pathology and Cytology Dept Nat Res Centre Miny of Scientific Res Cairo 1966–70, clinical attachment Surgical Dept Moyle Hosp Larne Co Antrim 1970, sr house offr ENT Dept Waveney Hosp Ballymena Co Antrim, sr house offr Birmingham and Midland Ear, Nose and Throat Hosp (Teaching) Birmingham 1972, registrar Eye and Ear Clinic Royal Victoria Hosp Belfast and Belfast City Hosp (Teaching) 1972–74; sr registrar Aug 1974–May 1975: Queen Elizabeth Hosp (Teaching), Birmingham Children's Hosp (Teaching), Birmingham Gen Hosp (Teaching); sr registrar June 1975–May 1976: Dudley Rd Hosp (Teaching) Birmingham, Birmingham Children's Hosp (Teaching); sr registrar June 1976–July 1977: Walsgrave Hosp Coventry, Coventry and Warwickshire Hosp Coventry, Gulson Hosp Coventry, St Cross Hosp Rugby, George Eliott Hosp Nuneaton Staffs; sr registrar Aug 1977–Nov 1978: City Gen Hosp, N Staffs Royal Infirmary Stoke-on-Trent; conslt ENT surgeon: City Hosp Dudley Rd (N Birmingham Health Authy - Teaching), Sandwell Dist Gen Hosp (Sandwell Dist Health Authy) 1978–; hon sr clinical lectr Med Sch Univ of Birmingham; memb: Ethical Ctee Sandwell Dist Gen Hosp 1981–92, Regnl Aural Servs Ctee, Regnl ENT Registrars and Sr Registrars Ctee; co-fndr, co-organiser and tutor: Temporal Bone Surgery Course Birmingham 1980–89, Combined Univs Advanced Otology Course 1987–; lectr on Operating Dept Assts' Trg Course Selly Oak Hosp Birmingham; examiner: ENT final yr med students Univ of Birmingham, Midland Inst of Otology Dip for Nurses 1979–89, fellowship examination (ENT) RCS(Ed); author of numerous articles and papers in professional jls and pubns in English and Arabic with translations into German and Flemish, abstracts in Spanish, Slovanic and French; various lectures to professional bodies worldwide incl: Inst d'Egypte Cairo 1981, RSM London 1995; fndr memb: Imhotep Scientific Soc Cairo, NY Acad of Scis; fndr sec British Soc for the History of ENT (organised meetings Birmingham Oct 1993, Oct 1994, Oct 1995 and Sept 1996); memb: Sandwell Social Evening Ctee, Rotary Club Birmingham (memb Int Ctee), BMA, RSM, BAOL, Midland Inst of Otology (hon librarian), Br Paediatric Otolaryngology Soc, Otology Research Soc, Soc of Authors 1979–82, Medical Writers' Gp 1980, Irish Otolaryngology Soc, European Rhinologic Soc, Int Hist of Medicine Soc, Int Hippocratic Fndn of Kos Greece, Int Assoc of Coptic Studies; *Recreations* travelling, reading, writing; *Style*— Dr Ahmes L Pahor; ✉ Department of ENT, Dudley Road Hospital, Birmingham B18 7QH (☎ 0121 554 3801 ext 4559, 0121 553 1831 ext 3213, fax 0121 551 5562)

PAIBA, His Hon Judge; Denis Anthony; s of Geoffrey Paiba (d 1974), of Belsize Park, London, and Geraldine Minnie, *née* Cohen (d 1978); *b* 10 Dec 1926; *Educ* Magdalen Coll Sch Oxford, Jesus Coll Cambridge 1944 - March 1945; *m* 1955, Lesley Patricia, da of Gerald Dresden, of Hove, East Sussex; 2 s (Giles Abraham b 29 Aug 1963, Piers Jonathan b 12 Feb 1967); *Career* serv Royal Marine Commandos 1945–47; called to the Bar Gray's Inn 1958, dep judge 1970–80, recorder 1980–82, circuit judge (SE Circuit) 1982–; *Recreations* music, theatre, wining and dining, general conviviality, nowadays watching rugby and cricket, collecting Blue and White china, pottery and porcelain (English up to approx 1840); *Style*— His Hon Judge Paiba; ✉ The Crown Court, Canbury Park Road, Kingston upon Thames, Surrey KT2 6JU (☎ 0181 549 5241)

PAICE, Dr Elisabeth Willemien; da of Ervin Ross Marlin, of Berkhamsted, and Hilda van Stockum, HRHA; *b* 23 April 1945; *Educ* Int Sch Geneva, Trinity Coll Dublin, Westminster Med Sch (BA, MB BCh, BAO); *m* 6 July 1968, Clifford Charles Dudley, s of Owen Paice (d 1973); 1 s (Malcolm b 1972), 2 da (Katharine b 1973, Joanna b 1977); *Career* sr registrar: Stoke Mandeville Hosp 1977–78, High Wycombe Hosp 1978–79, UCH 1980–82; conslt rheumatologist Whittington Hosp 1982–95, hon sr lectr UCL, assoc dean Postgrad Med NT(E) 1992–95, dean dir Postgrad Med and Dental Educn North Thames Univ of London 1995–; memb Br Soc of Rheumatology; MA 1995; FRCP 1989

(DipMedEd 1994); *Style—* Dr Elisabeth Paice; ✉ Thames Postgraduate Medical and Dental Education, 33 Millman Street, London WC1N 3EJ (☎ 0171 831 4566)

PAICE, James Edward Thornton; MP (C) Cambridgeshire South East (majority 23,810); s of Edward Percival Paice, of Trust Farm, Dennington, Suffolk, and Winifred Mary, *née* Thornton; *b* 24 April 1949; *Educ* Framlingham Coll Suffolk, Writtle Agric Coll (NDA); *m* 6 Jan 1973, Ava Barbara, da of late Robert Stewart Patterson, of Earl Soham, Suffolk; 2 s (Gordon b 1976, James b 1977); *Career* gen mangr/exec dir Framlingham Mgmnt and Training Services Ltd 1985–87 (non-exec dir 1987–89), non-exec dir United Framlingham Farmers Ltd 1989–94; MP (C) Cambs SE 1987–, memb Select Ctee on Employment 1987–89; PPS: to Min of State for Agric 1989–90, to Min for Agric Fisheries and Food then sec of state for environment 1990–94; Parly under-sec of state: Dept of Employment 1994–95, Dept for Educn and Employment 1995–; *Recreations* windsurfing, shooting; *Style—* James Paice, Esq, MP; ✉ House of Commons, London SW1A 0AA (☎ 0171 219 4101)

PAIGE, Elaine; OBE (1995); da of Eric Bickerstaff, of London; *b* 5 March 1957; *Career* actress and singer since 1968; *Theatre* musicals incl: created role of Eva Peron in Evita (London stage) 1978, created role of Grizabella in Cats 1981, created role of Florence in Chess 1986, Reno Sweeney in Anything Goes 1989, Edith Piaf in Piaf (West End and tour) 1993, Sunset Boulevard (Olivier Award nomination for Best Actress in a Musical 1996 (also Broadway 1996)) 1995; *Television* incl: Love Story, The Lady Killers, Phyllis Dixey, View of Harry Clark, Unexplained Laughter; *Films* incl: Oliver, Whatever Happened to What's His Name; *Recordings* incl: Stages (triple platinum) 1983, Cinema (gold) 1984, Chess 1985, I Know Him So Well (duet with Barbara Dickson, No 1 Hit Single) 1985, Love Hurts (platinum) 1985, Christmas 1986, Memories (compilation album, platinum) 1987, The Queen Album (8th consecutive gold album) 1988, Love Can Do That 1991, Romance and the Stage 1993, Elaine Paige - Piaf 1994, Encore 1995; UK concert tours 1985, 1987, 1991 and 1993; *Awards* Show Business Personality of the Year Variety Club of GB Award (for Evita), Swet Award for Best Actress in a Musical (for Evita), Rear of the Year Award 1984, Recording Artiste of the Year Variety Club of GB (for album Christmas), Head of the Year Award! 1987, Br Academy of Songwriters, Composers and Authors Gold Badge of Merit 1993; Olivier Award nomination for Outstanding Performance of the Year by an Actress in a Musical (for Chess and Anything Goes), Olivier Award nomination for Best Actress in a Musical (for Piaf); *Recreations* skiing, antiques; *Style—* Miss Elaine Paige, OBE; ✉ c/o M M & M, Pinewood Studios, Pinewood Road, Iver, Bucks SL0 0NH (☎ 01753 650808, fax 01753 650705)

PAIN, Gillian Margaret; da of Geoffrey Ernest Pain (d 1986), and Florence Agnes, *née* Marshall (d 1966); *b* 29 May 1936; *Educ* Felixstowe Coll Suffolk, Univ of St Andrews (MA), Univ Coll London (Dip Town Planning); *Career* teacher Northfield Sch Watford 1957–58, photogrammetrist Hunting Aerosurveys 1958–60, asst map research offr Directorate of Military Surveys 1960–62, planning asst rising to chief asst county planning adviser Essex CC 1962–73; Planning Inspectorate DOE: sr housing and planning inspr 1973–77, princ housing and planning inspr 1977–87, asst chief planning inspr 1987–93; chief reporter Scottish Office Inquiry Reporters Unit 1993–96, ret; pres Town and Country Planning Summer Sch 1992–94; MRTPI 1965; *Books* Planning and the Shopkeeper (1967); *Recreations* sailing, skiing, hill walking, tennis, classical music; *Clubs* Blackwater Sailing; *Style—* Miss Gillian Pain

PAIN, Hon Sir Peter (Richard); kt (1975); s of Arthur Richard Pain; *b* 6 Sept 1913; *Educ* Westminster, Christ Church Oxford; *m* 1941, Barbara Florence Maude Riggs; 2 s; *Career* called to the Bar Lincoln's Inn 1936, QC 1965, bencher 1972, a judge of the High Court of Justice Queen's Bench Div 1975–88; chm Race Relations Bd Conciliation Ctee for Greater London 1968–71, South Metropolitan Conciliation Ctee 1971–73, memb Parole Bd 1978–80, pres Holiday Fellowship 1977–83; *Style—* The Hon Sir Peter Pain; ✉ Loen, St Catherine's Rd, Frimley, Surrey

PAIN, Richard; s of Sir Peter Richard Pain, of Loen, St Catherines Rd, Frimley, Surrey, and Lady Barbara Florence Maud Pain, *née* Riggs; *b* 23 Sept 1942; *Educ* Westminster; *m* 6 Oct 1973, Adrienne Joyce, da of Myles Joseph Esmonde, of 18 Russell Sq, Longfield, Kent; 1 s (Peter b 1977), 1 da (Catherine b 1975); *Career* slr; ptnr Hyman Isaacs Lewis and Mills 1967–74, ptnr Beachcroft Hyman Isaacs 1974–88, ptnr Beachcroft Stanleys 1988–; memb City of London Law Soc; *Recreations* cricket, tennis; *Style—* Richard Pain, Esq; ✉ Beachcroft Stanleys, 20 Furnival St, London EC4A 1BN (☎ 0171 242 1011, fax 0171 430 1532, telex 264607 BEALAW G)

PAINE, Sir Christopher Hammon; kt (1995); s of Maj John Hammon Paine (d 1987), of Chapel House, Gt Coxwell, Faringdon, Oxon, and the Hon Mrs J Shedden, MBE, *née* Vestey (d 1991); *b* 28 Aug 1935; *Educ* Eton, Merton Coll Oxford (MA, MSc, DM); *m* 3 Nov 1959, Susan, da of late D Martin, of Bridgwater; 2 s (Edward b 1960, Simon b 1964), 2 da (Lucy b 1962, Alice b 1968); *Career* conslt in radiotherapy and oncology Oxford 1974–95, dir clinical studies Univ of Oxford 1980–84, gen mangr Oxfordshire Health Authy 1984–88; pres: Royal Coll of Radiologists 1992–95, Royal Soc of Med 1996–; med dir Advsy Ctee for Distinction Awards 1994–; Liveryman Worshipful Soc of Apothecaries; FRCP, FRCR; *Recreations* gardening; *Clubs* Farmers'; *Style—* Sir Christopher Paine; ✉ Kings Farm, Withypool, nr Minehead, Somerset TA24 7RE (☎ 01643 831381, fax 01643 831508)

PAINE, Graham Ernest Harley; s of Harley Joseph Paine, of Greywood, Coombe Hill Rd, Kingston on Thames, Surrey, and Ninette, *née* Sutch; *b* 2 Sept 1954; *Educ* Dulwich Coll, Univ of Bristol (LLB); *Career* admitted slr 1980; ptnr Wilde Sapte 1984– (articled clerk 1978–80, asst slr 1980–84); licensed insolvency practitioner; memb: Soc of Practitioners of Insolvency (memb London Region Ctee), Law Soc; *Recreations* golf, skiing, theatre, tennis; *Style—* Graham Paine, Esq; ✉ Wilde Sapte, 1 Fleet Place, London EC4M 7WS (☎ 0171 246 7000, fax 0171 246 7777)

PAINE, Jonathan; s of Cecil Finch Paine, and Freda Helen, *née* Weedon; *b* 3 Oct 1952; *Educ* Rugby, Merton Coll Oxford (BA); *m* 30 June 1979, Julie, da of Ronald Jork Barnes; *Career* with J Henry Schroder Wagg & Co Ltd 1975–82, dir Enskilda Securities 1982–87, exec dir then an md corporate fin Swiss Bank Corporation Investment Banking 1988–; *Style—* Jonathan Paine, Esq; ✉ Swiss Bank Corporation, 2 Finsbury Avenue, London EC2M 2PP (☎ 0171 395 2710)

PAINE, Peter Stanley; CBE (1980), DFC (1944); s of Arthur Bertram Paine; *b* 19 June 1921; *Educ* King's Sch Canterbury; *m* 1942, Sheila Mary (d 1994), da of late Frederick Wigglesworth; 2 s (Robin, Richard), 2 da (Jennifer, Alison); *Career* served 1940–46, Flt-Lt 2 Gp RAF; Punch Publishing Office 1946–48, sales promotion manager Newnes Pearson 1948–52, Odhams Press 1952–58; sales dir and dir: Tyne Tees Television 1958–67, Yorks Television 1967–74; md Tyne Tees Television 1974–83, dir Trident Television 1970–81, chm Oracle Teletext Ltd 1983–92; memb Cncl ITV Assoc 1974–82; *Style—* Peter Paine, Esq, CBE, DFC; ✉ Briarfield, Ashwood Rd, Woking, Surrey GU22 7JW (☎ 01483 773183, fax 01483 375 0007)

PAINES, Anthony John Cooper; s of Henry Wilfred Paines, KHS (d 1973), of Northwood, Middx, and Mary Agnes, *née* Cooper (d 1989); *b* 17 Nov 1925; *Educ* Mount St Mary's Coll, Lincoln Coll Oxford (MA); *m* 26 April 1952, Anne, da of Charles Philip Billot (d 1981), of St Martin, Jersey, CI; 2 s (Nicholas b 1955, Justin b 1963), 2 da (Caroline b 1957, Cathryn b 1959); *Career* RN 1944–47; admitted slr 1952, ptnr Allen & Overy 1958–88; JP 1967–77; memb Slrs' Disciplinary Tbnl 1974–92, cmmr of Tax Appeals (Jersey) 1988–; chm AIB Bank (CI) Ltd 1995–; dir AIB Grofund Currency Funds Ltd 1995–; *Recreations* boating, bridge, travel, reading; *Clubs* Victoria, St Helier Yacht; *Style—* Anthony J C Paines, Esq; ✉ La Chaumière, St Martin, Jersey JE3 6AD, CI (☎ 01534 862441, fax 01534 865156)

PAINES, Nicholas Paul Billot; s of Anthony John Cooper Paines, *qv*, and Anne, *née* Billot; *b* 29 June 1955; *Educ* Downside, Univ of Oxford (MA), Université Libre de Bruxelles (Licence Spéciale en Droit Européen); *m* 11 May 1985, Alison Jane, da of Eric Sargent Roberts (d 1969); 1 s (Rupert b 1986), 2 da (Emily b 1989, Katherine b 1992); *Career* called to the Bar: Gray's Inn 1978, NI; practising barr 1980–; memb Bar Cncl 1991–96; memb: Cncl St Christopher's Fellowship 1984–, Supplementary Panel of Counsel to the Crown (Common Law) 1993–; chm Bar European Gp 1996– (vice-chm 1994–96); *Books* Halsbury's Laws of England (contrib), Vaughan Law of the European Communities (contrib); *Recreations* family life; *Style—* Nicholas Paines, Esq; ✉ 4 Raymond Buildings, Gray's Inn, London WC1R 5BP (☎ 0171 405 7211, fax 0171 405 2084)

PAINTER, Michael William; s of William Bentley Painter (d 1984), of Coventry, and Maria, *née* Eggleton (d 1982); *b* 2 March 1938; *Educ* Bablake Sch Coventry; *m* 1, 23 Sept 1963, Jillian Margaret (d 1985), da of Harold Lane (d 1976); 1 s (Steven Michael b 1966), 2 da (Sarah b 1968, Rebecca b 1973); m 2, 26 Sept 1987, Susan Anne, da of Frederick Morley, of Swindon; 2 step da (Michelle b 1981, Rosanne b 1983); *Career* Nat Serv RAF 1958–60; dir Hogg Robinson UK Ltd 1973–85, chm Int Risk Mgmnt Div Bowring Marsh & McLennan Ltd 1992– (exec dir Main Bd 1985–), on secondment to Dept of Trade and Industry 1994–; FCII, FBIIBA, CIMgt; *Recreations* France, walking, cooking; *Clubs* RAC; *Style—* Michael Painter, Esq; ✉ c/o Department of Trade and Industry, 1 Victoria Street, London SW1H 0ET

PAINTER, Terence James; CB (1990); s of Edward Lawrence Painter (d 1971), and Ethel Violet Painter (d 1969); *b* 28 Nov 1935; *Educ* City of Norwich Sch, Downing Coll Cambridge (BA); *m* 12 Dec 1959, Margaret Janet, *née* Blackburn; 2 s (James b 30 May 1964, Ian b 17 Feb 1966), 2 da (Susan (Mrs Wallace) b 14 March 1963, Alison b 29 Oct 1968); *Career* Inland Revenue Bd: asst princ 1959, princ 1962, seconded Civil Service Selection Bd 1967–68, asst sec 1969, seconded HM Treasy 1973–75, under sec 1975–86, dep chm 1986–93; *Recreations* reading, hill walking, music, gardening; *Clubs* Reform; *Style—* Terence Painter, Esq, CB; ✉ Board of Inland Revenue, Somerset House, London WC2

PAINTING, Norman George; OBE (1976); s of Harry George Painting, and Maud Painting; *b* 23 April 1924; *Educ* Leamington Coll, King Edward VI Sch Nuneaton, Univ of Birmingham (BA), ChCh Oxford; *Career* Anglo-Saxon tutor Exeter Coll Oxford 1946–48, writer and dir BBC 1949–50, freelance writer, dir and performer 1945–; World's longest serving actor in a daily radio serial (Guinness record) as Philip Archer in The Archers 1950–, other radio work incl team capt Gardening Quiz BBC Radio 4; writing credits incl 1198 episodes of The Archers (as Bruno Milna), numerous TV films, radio scripts, plays and articles; TV appearances incl: chm of TV Quiz The Garden Game 1977–82, Wogan, Stop the Week, Quote Unquote, On the Air, subject of This is Your Life 1991, celebrity guest Countdown since 1992, Through the Keyhole 1993, judge Master Chef BBC1 1996; vice pres Tree Cncl; patron: Age Concern Warwickshire, First Steps to Freedom (Help for Phobics) 1991–; tstee: Warwicks and Coventry Historic Churches Tst (chm 1979–82), Birmingham Workshop for people with epilepsy; vice pres: Friends of Birmingham Cathedral, Friends of St Mary's Warwick; hon life govr RASE 1976, temp hon memb High Table ChCh Oxford 1985–; Hon MA Univ of Birmingham 1989; life fell RHS; life memb: CPRE, Nat Tst; *Books* Stories of the Saints (with M Day, 1956), More Stories of the Saints (with M Day, 1957), St Antony - The Man Who Found Himself (with M Day, 1958), Forever Ambridge (1975), Reluctant Archer (autobiography, 1982); *Recreations* music, poetry, swimming, gardens, being quiet; *Style—* Norman Painting, Esq, OBE; ✉ c/o BBC Broadcasting House, London W1A 1AA

PAIRMAN, (Lynda) Annette; *née* Miles; da of William John Edward Miles, of Edinburgh, and Sarah, *née* Carr; *b* 11 Feb 1958; *Educ* The Mary Erskine Sch Edinburgh, Univ of Edinburgh (LLB); *m* 20 Aug 1977, Gordon Alexander Pairman, s of Alexander George Pairman, of Glasgow; *Career* W & J Burness WS 1978–83, Herbert Smith & Co 1983–84, ptnr W & J Burness WS 1984–; memb: Law Soc of Scot, Soc of Writers to HM Signet, Royal Soc of Procurators of Glasgow, The Securities Institute; *Style—* Mrs Annette Pairman; ✉ W & J Burness WS, 242 West George Street, Glasgow G2 4QY (☎ 0141 248 4933, fax 0141 204 1601)

PAISH, Geoffrey Lane; MBE (1974); s of Arthur Paish (d 1957), and Florence Mary, *née* Lane (d 1957); *b* 2 Jan 1922; *Educ* Whitgift Middle Sch; *m* 18 Nov 1944, Sylvia Joan, da of John Frederick Carr (d 1972); 1 s (John b 1948), 1 da (Deborah (Mrs Miller, FCA) b 1955); *Career* Civil Serv Inland Revenue 1939–82; tennis player: memb Br Davis Cup team 1947–55, Br covered courts men's singles champion 1951, S of England champion 1951–55, Br veterans' men's singles champion over 60 1987, over 65 1988 and 1991 and over 70 1992–94; hon life cnsllr Int Tennis Fedn 1993; Lawn Tennis Assoc: memb Cncl 1970–79, chm 1979, vice pres 1980–92, hon life vice pres 1993; memb Ctee of Mgmnt The Championships Wimbledon 1979–90; Surrey Co Lawn Tennis Assoc: memb Cncl 1957–82, pres 1983–; *Recreations* tennis; *Clubs* All England LTC, Int LTC of GB, Shirley Park LTC; *Style—* Geoffrey Paish, Esq, MBE; ✉ 21 Cormorant Place, College Town, Sandhurst, Berks GU47 0XY

PAISLEY, Rev Ian Richard Kyle; MP (DUP) North Antrim (majority 14,936), MEP (Democratic Unionist) NI (DUP vote 160,110); s of late Rev J Kyle Paisley; *b* 6 April 1926; *Educ* Ballymena Model Sch, Ballymena Tech HS, S Wales Bible Coll, Reformed Presbyterian Theol Coll Belfast; *m* 1956, Eileen Emily Cassells; 2 s, 3 da; *Career* ordained 1946, minister Martyrs Memorial Free Presbyterian Church Belfast 1946–; MP (Protestant Unionist then DUP) Antrim N 1970–, Protestant Unionist memb Northern Ireland Parliament (Stormont) for Bannside 1970–72, MEP (DUP) Northern Ireland 1979–, DUP memb Northern Ireland Assembly for N Antrim 1982–86; co-fndr and ldr DUP 1971–; memb: Int Cultural Soc of Korea; FRGS; *Books* History of 59 Revival, Christian Foundations (1960, 2 edn 1985), Exposition of Epistle to Romans (1968, 2 edn 1985), Massacre of St Bartholomew (1972), Ulster the Facts (1981), No Pope Here (1982), Paisley's Pocket Preacher (1987), Be Sure - 7 rules for public speaking (1987); *Style—* The Rev Ian Paisley, MP, MEP; ✉ House of Commons, London SW1A 0AA; The Parsonage, 17 Cyprus Ave, Belfast BT5 5NT

PAISLEY, Bishop of (RC) 1988–; Rt Rev John Aloysius Mone; s of Arthur Mone (d 1964), and Elizabeth, *née* Dunn (d 1979); *b* 22 June 1929; *Educ* Holyrood Secdy Sch, Sulpician Seminaries in France of Issy-les-Moulineaux and Paris, Institut Catholique Paris; *Career* ordained priest Glasgow 1952, St Ninian's Glasgow 1952–75, Our Lady and St George 1975–79, St Joseph's Tollcross 1979–84, dir min to priests prog 1982–84, bishop of Abercorn and bishop auxiliary of Glasgow 1984–88; Scottish nat chaplain Girl Guides 1971–; chm: Scottish Catholic Int Aid Fund 1974–75 (pres/treas 1985–), Scottish Marriage Advsy Cncl 1982–84; pres: Justice and Peace Cmmn 1987–96, Pastoral and Social Care Cmmn 1996–; *Recreations* golf, piano playing; *Clubs* Hamilton Golf; *Style—* The Rt Rev the Bishop of Paisley; ✉ Diocesan Office, Cathedral House, 8 East Buchanan St, Paisley PA1 1HS (☎ 0141 889 3601, fax 0141 848 6136)

PAJARES, Ramon; s of Juan Antonio Pajares Garcia (d 1954), of Jaen Spain, and Rosario Salazar (d 1964); *b* 6 July 1935; *Educ* sr sch Jaen Spain, Madrid Inst of Hotel and Tourism Studies; *m* 13 July 1963, Jean Kathleen, 1 s (Roberto Javier b 17 March 1971), 2 da (Sofia Ramona b 14 June 1967, Maria del Rosario b 25 Aug 1969); *Career*

Spanish Nat Serv Spanish Navy 1955–57; Hotel Ritz Barcelona 1954–55, Hotel San Jorge Playa de Aro 1957, Hotel Parque Llavaneras 1957–59, Mansion Hotel Eastbourne 1959–61, Kleiner Reisen Koblenz Germany 1961, Hotel Feldbergerhof Feldberg Germany 1961–62, Le Vieux Manoir Morat Switzerland 1962, Hotel Reina Isabel Las Palmas Canary Is 1965–69, food and beverage dir Inn on The Park 1969–71, gen mangr San Antonio Lanzarate Canary Is 1972–74, gen mangr Inn On The Park London W1 1975–94, md The Savoy Group Nov 1994–; vice pres European Hotel Mangrs' Assoc 1992– (memb 1982–); memb: Académie Culinaire de France 1971–, Bd of Fells Skål 1972, Cookery and Food Assoc 1973, Confrerie de la Chaîne des Rotisseurs 1978–, Confrerie des Chevaliers du Sacavin 1979–, Caballeros del Vino 1987; medal of Merito Civil awarded by HM King of Spain 1984, Hotelier of the Year award of Br Hotel and Catering Industry 1984, Personalité de l'Année for The Hotel Indust 1986, medal of Oficial de la Orden de Isabel la Catolica awarded by HM King of Spain 1989; Freeman City of London 1988; officier de L'Ordre des Coteaux de Champagne, chev du Tastevin 1982, FHCIMA 1982, Master Innholder 1988; *Clubs* Les Ambassadeurs, Annabel's; *Style*— Ramon Pajares, Esq; ✉ The Savoy Hotel, 1 Savoy Hill, London WC2R 0BP (☎ 0171 836 1533)

PAKENHAM, Hon Kevin John Toussaint; yst s of 7 Earl of Longford, KG, PC, *qv*, and Countess of Longford, CBE, *qv*; *b* 1 Nov 1947; *Educ* Ampleforth, New Coll Oxford (MA), St Antony's Coll Oxford (MPhil); *Career* sr economist Rothschild Intercontinental Bank 1972–75, chief economist and vice pres American Express Bank 1975–83, md Foreign & Colonial Management 1983–88, chief exec John Govett & Co Ltd 1988 (currently chm), chief exec AIB Asset Management Holdings Ltd 1997–; *Clubs* MCC, Rye Golf, Hurlingham, City; *Style*— The Hon Kevin Pakenham; ✉ John Govett & Co Ltd, Shackleton House, 4 Battle Bridge Lane, London SE1 2HR (☎ 0171 378 7979)

PAKENHAM, Hon Michael Aidan; CMG (1993); 3 s of 7 Earl of Longford, KG, PC, *qv*, and Countess of Longford, CBE, *qv*; *b* 3 Nov 1943; *Educ* Ampleforth, Trinity Coll Cambridge, Rice Univ Texas; *m* 1980, Meta (Mimi) Landreth, da of William Conway Doak, of Maryland, USA; 2 da (Alexandra b 1981, Clio b 1985); *Career* reporter Washington Post 1965; HM Dip Serv: 3 sec FO 1966, 3 sec Nairobi, 3 later 2 sec Warsaw 1967, 2 sec FCO 1970, asst private sec later private sec to the Chllr of the Duchy of Lancaster 1971, on secondment to Cabinet Office 1972 (1 sec 1972), UK Delgn CSCE Geneva 1974, 1 sec New Delhi 1974, Washington 1978, cnsllr FCO 1983, cnsllr (external rels) Brussels 1987, HM ambass and consul-gen Luxembourg 1991–94, min Br Embassy Paris 1994–; *Recreations* tennis, golf, reading, bridge; *Clubs* MCC, Garrick, Golf St Nom-la-Bretèche (Paris); *Style*— The Hon Michael Pakenham, CMG; ✉ c/o Foreign and Commonwealth Office (Paris), King Charles St, London SW1A 2AH

PAKENHAM, Thomas Frank Dermot; s and h of 7 Earl of Longford, KG, PC, *qv*, but does not use courtesy title, and Countess of Longford, CBE, *qv*; *b* 14 Aug 1933; *Educ* Ampleforth, Magdalen Coll Oxford; *m* 1964, Valerie Susan, da of Maj Ronald Guthrie McNair Scott; 2 s, 2 da; *Career* writer; freelance 1956–58; on editorial staff of: TES 1958–60, Sunday Telegraph 1961, The Observer 1961–64; fndr memb: Victorian Soc 1958 (memb Ctee 1958–64), Historic Irish Tourist Houses and Gardens Assoc (HITHA) (memb Ctee 1968–72); treas Br-Irish Assoc 1972–, sec and co-fndr Christopher Ewart-Biggs Memorial Trust 1976–, chm Ladbroke Assoc 1988–91; sr assoc memb St Antony's Coll Oxford 1979–81; *Publications* The Mountains of Rasselas: An Ethiopian Adventure (1959), The Year of Liberty: The Story of the Great Irish Rebellion of 1798 (1969), The Boer War (1979, Cheltenham Prize 1980); selected and introduced (with Valerie Pakenham) Dublin: A Traveller's Companion (1988), The Scramble for Africa (1991, WH Smith Literary Award 1992, Alan Paton Award 1992), Meetings with Remarkable Trees (1996); *Style*— Thomas Pakenham, Esq; ✉ Tullynally, Castlepollard, Co Westmeath (☎ 00 353 44 61159)

PAKENHAM-WALSH, John; CB (1986), QC (1992); s of Rev Wilfrid Pakenham-Walsh (d 1974), and Guendolen Maud, *née* Elliott (d 1990); *b* 7 Aug 1928; *Educ* Bradfield Coll, Univ Coll Oxford (MA); *m* 29 Sept 1951, Deryn Margaret, da of Gp Capt Reginald Edgar Gilbert Fulljames, MC (d 1985); 1 s (John b 25 Nov 1961), 4 da (Carolyn 23 May 1953, Elizabeth b 19 Jan 1956, Sarah b 25 May 1965, Andrea b 7 Sept 1968); *Career* called to the Bar Lincoln's Inn 1951, Crown counsel Hong Kong 1953–57, Parly counsel Fedn of Nigeria 1958–61, joined Legal Advsrs Branch Home Office 1961, under sec (legal) Home Office 1980–88, standing counsel to Gen Synod C of E 1988–; *Style*— John Pakenham-Walsh, Esq, CB, QC; ✉ Crinken, Weydown Road, Haslemere, Surrey GU27 1DS (☎ 01428 642033); 36 Whitehall, London, SW1 (☎ 0171 210 6791)

PAKINGTON, Hon John Humphrey Arnott; s and h of 6 Baron Hampton, *qv*; *b* 24 Dec 1964; *Educ* Dyson Perrins C of E HS, Shrewsbury, Exeter Coll of Art and Design (BA); *m* 4 Oct 1996, Siena E E, yr da of Remo Caldato, of Rome; *Career* freelance photographer in London; *Style*— The Hon John Pakington

PALACHE, Robert; s of Ralph Palache, of London, and Rosalind, *née* Simons; *b* 11 Nov 1957; *Educ* JFS Sch, Magdalene Coll Cambridge (MA); *m* 28 July 1979, Johanne Helen, da of Michael George Barrett, MBE; 2 da (Abigail b 22 Aug 1984, Dora b 24 May 1987); *Career* slr Coward Chance 1982–87, ptnr Clifford Chance 1988– (slr 1987); *Recreations* reading, swimming; *Style*— Robert Palache, Esq; ✉ Clifford Chance, 200 Aldersgate Street, London EC1A 4JJ (☎ 0171 600 1000, fax 0171 600 5555)

PALFREEMAN, Neil; s of William Palfreeman, of Stockton on Tees, Cleveland, and Jean, *née* Cameron; *b* 11 Oct 1953; *Educ* Stockton GS, Univ of Bath (BSc); *m* 14 Oct 1983, Jane Alison, da of Bernard Longhurst; 2 s (Ben b 20 July 1984, Tom b 11 April 1987); *Career* export sales exec rising to regnl sales mangr Courtaulds Ltd 1976–81, non-food buying controller rising to non-food trading mangr Carrefour Hypermarkets Ltd 1981–86, mktg servs dir Gateway Foodmarkets Ltd 1986–88, mktg dir MFI Furniture Group plc 1988–; memb Mktg Soc 1989; *Recreations* golf, reading, football, cricket; *Style*— Neil Palfreeman, Esq; ✉ MFI Furniture Group plc, Southon House, 333 The Hyde, Edgware Road, London NW9 6TD (☎ 0181 913 5205, fax 0181 205 7197)

PALIA, Dr Satnam Singh; s of Daljit Singh Palia, of Punjab, India, and Pritam Kaur, *née* Harar; *b* 5 Oct 1952; *Educ* Govt Med Coll Amritsar India (MB BS); *m* 4 July 1976, Valwinder Kaur, da of Jaswant Karir of Southampton; 3 da (Satwinder Kaur b 4 Nov 1977, Navjinder (Dimple) b 12 Aug 1980, Rajinder (Rosie) b 13 Oct 1981); *Career* registrar in psychiatry St Annes Hosp Poole Dorset 1981–83, sr registrar in psychiatry Univ of Wales Hosp Cardiff 1983–85, conslt psychiatrist Glanrhyd and Penyfai Hosps 1986– (dep clinical dir Mental Health Services 1993–); author of papers on: water intoxication in psychiatric patients, mood disorders in epileptic patients, psychopharmacology; clinical tutor and course organiser RCPsych 1986–93; former chm Sikh Assoc of S Wales; DPM 1980, FRSH 1987, FRCPsych 1996 (MRCPsych 1981); *Recreations* music, reading, badminton; *Style*— Dr Satnam S Palia; ✉ Coity Clinic, Bridgend and District NHS Trust, Princess of Wales Hospital, Bridgend, Mid Glamorgan CF31 1RQ (☎ 01656 752252)

PALIN, Michael Edward; s of late Edward Palin, and late Mary Palin; *b* 5 May 1943; *Educ* Shrewsbury Sch, BNC Oxford (BA); *m* 16 April 1966, Helen Margaret, *née* Gibbins; 2 s (Thomas Edward b 8 Oct 1968, William Michael b 19 Nov 1970), 1 da (Rachel Mary b 13 Jan 1975); *Career* actor and writer; *Television* actor and writer: Monty Python's Flying Circus (BBC) 1969–74, Ripping Yarns (BBC) 1976–80; actor: Three Men in a Boat (BBC) 1975, GBH (Channel 4) 1991; presenter and writer of expedition series: Around the World in 80 Days (BBC) 1989, Pole to Pole (BBC) 1992; presenter Palin's Column (Channel 4) 1994; *Films* actor and writer: And Now for Something Completely Different 1970, Monty Python and The Holy Grail 1974, Monty Python's Life of Brian 1979, Time Bandits 1980, Monty Python's The Meaning of Life 1982, American Friends 1991; actor: Jabberwocky 1976, A Private Function 1984, Brazil 1985, A Fish Called Wanda 1989 (Best Supporting Actor BAFTA Awards); actor, writer and co-prodr The Missionary 1982; *Theatre* playwright The Weekend (Strand Theatre) 1994; *Books* Monty Python's Big Red Book (jtly, 1970), Monty Python's Brand New Book (jtly, 1973), Dr Fegg's Encyclopedia of All World Knowledge (jtly, 1984), Limericks (1985), Around the World in 80 Days (1989), Pole to Pole (1992), Pole To Pole - The Photographs (jtly, 1994), The Weekend (1994), Hemingway's Chair (novel, 1995); for children: Small Harry and the Toothache Pills (1981), The Mirrorstone (1986), The Cyril Stories (1986); co-writer Ripping Yarns (1978) and More Ripping Yarns (1980); *Style*— Michael Palin, Esq; ✉ c/o Mayday Management, 68a Delancey Street, Camden Town, London NW1 7RY (☎ 0171 284 0242, fax 0171 284 1004)

PALING, Her Hon Judge Helen Elizabeth (Mrs W J S Kershaw); da of A Dale Paling; *b* 25 April 1933; *Educ* Prince Henry's GS Otley, LSE (LLB); *m* 1961, William John Stanley Kershaw, PhD; 1 s, 3 da; *Career* called to the Bar Lincoln's Inn 1955, recorder of the Crown Court 1972–85, circuit judge (NE Circuit) 1985–, designated family judge Newcastle; *Style*— Her Hon Judge Paling

PALLANT, Jean; da of Victor Robinson Hodge (d 1968), of Surrey, and Ellen Rose, *née* Bragg; *Educ* Kingston Coll of Art (BA); *m* Martin Pallant, *qv*; *Career* fashion designer; cruisewear designer Jaeger 1965–66, lectr Kingston Coll of Art 1966–69; estab Jean & Martin Pallant Partnership (ladies designer fashion) 1969; jt md: Jean & Martin Pallant Ltd 1973–, Pallant (London) Ltd 1988–, Pallant Diffusion 1996–; consistently voted one of top ten UK fashion designers; *Style*— Mrs Jean Pallant; ✉ Jean & Martin Pallant Limited, Ferry Works, Summer Road, Thames Ditton, Surrey KT7 0QJ (☎ 0181 398 8865, fax 0181 398 8058); Pallant (London) Ltd, The Pantechnicon, Motcomb Street, London SW1W 8LB (☎ 0171 259 6046); Pallant Diffusion, 162a Sloane Street, London SW1X 9BS (☎ 0171 245 1145)

PALLANT, John; s of Dennis Pallant, of Southsea, Hants, and Doreen, *née* Hirst; *b* 10 Aug 1955; *Educ* St John's Coll Southsea, Univ of Reading (BA); *Career* copywriter: Griffin & George Ltd 1977, Acroyd Westwood Associates 1977, Boase Massimi Pollitt 1978, Collett Dickenson Pearce 1980, Gold Greenless Trott 1982; copywriter and creative gp head Boase Massimi Pollitt 1983; Saatchi & Saatchi: copywriter 1988, gp head 1991, dep creative dir and Exec Bd dir 1995, creative dir 1996–; *Awards* D & AD awards (for TV, press, public service and poster campaigns): Gold 1985, Silver 1981 (two), 1985 (three), 1989 and 1992; Br TV awards: Silver 1981, Gold 1992; Cannes Int Advtg awards: Silver 1981, Bronze 1988, Gold 1992; Campaign Press awards: Gold 1985, Silver 1985 (two), 1989 and 1990; Campaign Poster awards: Gold 1985, Silver 1983, 1985 (two), 1990 (two); Independent Radio awards Silver 1990; NY One Show awards Gold and Best of Show award 1992; IMSA Int Advtg awards Grand Prix for cinema 1992; *Style*— John Pallant, Esq; ✉ Saatchi & Saatchi Advertising, 80 Charlotte St, London W1A 1AQ (☎ 0171 636 5060 ext 3501, fax 0171 637 8489)

PALLANT, Martin; s of Frank Wilfred Pallant (d 1989), of Kent, and Irene Mary Claris, *née* Smyth; *b* 16 Feb 1943; *Educ* Kingston GS, Kingston Coll of Art (BA), RCA; *m* 1964, Jean Pallant, *qv*, *née* Hodge; *Career* fashion designer; freelance designer 1965–69, estab Jean & Martin Pallant Partnership (ladies designer fashion) 1969; jt md: Jean & Martin Pallant Ltd 1973–, Pallant (London) Ltd 1988–, Pallant Diffusion 1996–; consistently voted one of top ten UK fashion designers; *Style*— Martin Pallant, Esq; ✉ Jean & Martin Pallant Limited, Ferry Works, Summer Road, Thames Ditton, Surrey KT7 0QJ (☎ 0181 398 8865, fax 0181 398 8058); Pallant (London) Ltd, The Pantechnicon, Motcomb St, London SW1W 8LB (☎ 0171 259 6046); Pallant Diffusion, 162a Sloane Street, London SW1X 9BS (☎ 0171 245 1145)

PALLEY, Dr Claire Dorothea Taylor; da of Arthur Aubrey Swait, of Durban; *b* 17 Feb 1931; *Educ* Durban Girls' Coll, Univ of Cape Town (BA, LLB), Univ of London (PhD), Univ of Oxford (MA); *m* 1952 (m dis 1985), Ahrn Palley; 5 s; *Career* called to the Bar Middle Temple; advocate S Africa and Rhodesia; princ St Anne's Coll Oxford 1984–91; memb UN Sub Cmmn on Prevention of Discrimination and Protection of Minorities 1988–; constitutional advsr Republic of Cyprus 1980–94; Hon LLD Belfast; *Books* The Constitutional History and Law of S Rhodesia (1966), The United Kingdom and Human Rights (1991); *Style*— Dr Claire Palley; ✉ Pakhna Village, Limassol, Cyprus (☎ 00 357 5 242 077)

PALLEY, Eall Marcon (Marc); s of Dr Ahrn Palley, of Zimbabwe (d 1993), and Dr Claire, *née* Swait, *qv*; *b* 2 May 1954; *Educ* Clifton Coll, St John's Coll Oxford (MA); *m* 28 July 1979, Sabina Mary, da of Maj-Gen F W E Fursdon, *qv*; 3 s (Charles b 9 Dec 1982, Frederick b 6 June 1985, Harry b 15 May 1988); *Career* admitted slr 1978; Allen & Overy 1978–85, ptnr Berwin Leighton 1985– (currently head Banking Dept); *Style*— Marc Palley, Esq; ✉ Berwin Leighton, Adelaide House, London Bridge, London EC4R 9HA (☎ 0171 623 3144, fax 0171 623 4416)

PALLISER, Charles; *b* 11 Dec 1947; *Educ* Exeter Coll Oxford (BA), Wolfson Coll Oxford (BLitt); *Career* author; lectr: Huddersfield Poly 1972–74, Dept of Eng Studies Univ of Strathclyde 1974–90, Univ of Rutgers (spring semester) 1986; *Publications* The Journal of Simon Owen (BBC radio play, 1982), The Quincunx (1989, Sue Kaufman prize for first fiction 1991), The Sensationist (1991), Obsessions - Writing (1991), Betrayals (1994); also various scholarly articles published on George Eliot, Henry James and William Faulkner; *Style*— Charles Palliser, Esq; ✉ c/o Giles Gordon, Sheil Land Associates Ltd, 43 Doughty Street, London WC1N 2LF (☎ 0171 405 9351, fax 0171 831 2127)

PALLISER, Prof David Michael; s of Herbert Leslie Palliser (d 1973), and Doris Violet, *née* Brown (d 1969); *b* 10 Sept 1939; *Educ* Bootham Sch York, Worcester Coll Oxford (BA, MA, DPhil); *Career* asst princ Home Civil Serv 1961–64, res fell Univ of Keele 1967–73, lectr then sr lectr then reader in economic history Univ of Birmingham 1974–85, GF Grant prof of history Univ of Hull 1985–94, prof of medieval history Univ of Leeds 1994–; chm Urban Res Ctee Cncl for Br Archaeology 1978–84; memb Cncl Royal Historical Soc 1986–90 and 1991–95; FRHistS 1974, FSA 1977; *Books* The Staffordshire Landscape (1976), Tudor York (1979), York as They Saw It (with B M Palliser, 1979), York (with J H Hutchinson, 1980), The Age of Elizabeth (1983, 2 edn 1992); *Style*— Prof D M Palliser, FSA; ✉ School of History, University of Leeds, Leeds LS2 9JT (☎ 0113 233 3610)

PALLISER, Rt Hon Sir (Arthur) Michael; GCMG (1977, KCMG 1973, CMG 1966), PC (1983); s of Adm Sir Arthur Palliser, KCB, DSC (d 1956), and Margaret Eva, *née* King-Salter (d 1993); *b* 9 April 1922; *Educ* Wellington, Merton Coll Oxford (MA, hon fell 1986); *m* 1948, Marie Marguerite, da of Paul-Henri Spaak (d 1972), sometime PM of Belgium and sec gen NATO; 3 s; *Career* late Capt Coldstream Gds; entered FO 1947, private sec to PM 1966, min Paris 1969, ambass and head of UK Delgn to EEC Brussels 1971, ambass and UK perm rep to EEC 1973–75, perm under sec and head of Dip Serv FCO 1975–82; appointed PM's special advsr during Falklands Crisis 1982, assoc fell Harvard Univ Center for Int Affrs 1982; non-exec dir: Samuel Montagu & Co Ltd 1983–96 (chm 1984–93, vice chm 1993–96), Booker McConnell (now Booker plc) 1983–92, BAT Industries 1983–92, Eagle Star Holdings 1983–92, Shell Transport and Trading 1983–92, United Biscuits (Holdings) 1983–89, Ibec Inc (now Arbor Acres Farm Inc, agribusiness assoc of Booker plc based in Connecticut) 1983–91, XCL Ltd 1994–; dep chm: Midland Bank plc 1987–91, British Invisibles 1987–95; chm: Cncl Int Inst for Strategic Studies 1983–90, City and E London Confedn of Medicine and Dentistry 1989–95, Major Projects Assoc 1994–; memb: Cncl Royal Inst of Int Affairs 1982–89,

Bd Royal Nat Theatre 1988–96, Br Overseas Trade Bd 1992–96; pres: Br Section Int Social Servs 1982–95, China Britain Trade Gp (CBTG) 1992–96; memb: Security Cmmn 1983–92, Trilateral Cmmn 1982–96; govr Wellington Coll 1982–92; hon fell QMW 1990; Chevalier Order of Orange Nasssau 1944, Commandeur Légion d'Honneur 1996 (Chevalier 1957); FRSA 1983; *Recreations* travel, theatre; *Clubs* Buck's; *Style—* Rt Hon Sir Michael Palliser, GCMG; ✉ 12b Wedderburn Road, London NW3 5QG

PALLISTER, Gary Andrew; s of Ian Pallister, of Cleveland, and Jacqueline Patricia, *née* McKellar; *b* 30 June 1965; *Educ* Blakeston Comp Stockton, Billingham VIth Form Coll; *Career* professional footballer (defender); debut for Middlesbrough FC (vs Wimbledon) 1985, played 156 games, on loan to Darlington (7 games); Manchester United FC: joined for then record fee (£2.3m) 1989, winners FA Cup 1989/90, Euro Cup Winners' Cup 1990/91, Rumbelows Cup 1991/92, winners inaugural FA Premier League 1992/93, Charity Shield 1993 and 1994, winners League and FA Cup double 1994 and 1996 (setting record); England: debut vs Hungary 1988, over 15 full caps; PFA Player of the Year 1992; *Recreations* golf; *Style—* Gary Pallister, Esq; ✉ Manchester United FC, Old Trafford, Manchester M16 0RA

PALLISTER, Air Cdre Michael Alan; s of Dr Richard Alan Pallister, OBE (d 1996), of Berkhamsted, Herts, and Muriel Reay Pallister (d 1976); *b* 5 Oct 1930; *Educ* Guildford GS and Hale Sch Aust, Sedbergh, St John's Coll Cambridge (MA, MB BChir), St Thomas's Hosp, Univ of Liverpool (DTM&H), Univ of London (DPH, DIH); *m* 16 July 1955, Shelagh Patricia; 1 s (Simon Richard b 29 May 1956), 1 da (Julia b 26 July 1957); *Career* med branch RAF 1957–89; MOD 1965–69; offr i/c: RAF Inst of Community Med 1976–78, RAF Hosp Akrotiri Cyprus 1978–80; dep dir med orgn (RAF) and asst surgn gen personnel and trg MOD 1980–85, offr i/c Princess Alexandra Hosp RAF Wroughton 1986–89; conslt advsr in community med to RAF 1987–89; chm SE Somerset Archaeological Soc; Cdr (Bro) Order of St John; memb BMA 1956, MRCS and LRCP 1956, FRSTM&H 1960, MRCGP 1975, MFOM 1981, FFCM 1988; *Recreations* cabinet making; *Clubs* RAF; *Style—* Air Cdre Michael Pallister

PALLISTER, Timothy John Barry; s of John C Pallister (d 1973), of Woodbastwick, Norfolk, and Doreen Barry, *née* Drew (d 1984); *b* 2 July 1940; *Educ* Bloxham Sch Oxford, Coll of Law London; *m* 20 June 1970, Christine, da of The Hon and Mrs Richard Neville Cabbell-Manners; 2 s (James b 10 July 1971, Richard b 22 Nov 1976), 1 da (Charlotte b 16 June 1972); *Career* articled clerk Mills & Reeve 1958–62; Slaughter and May: asst slr 1963–71, ptnr 1972–96, first ptnr overseas Paris office 1973–80, New York office 1994–95; licensed as a legal conslt in the State of NY 1995; govr Beeston Hall Sch 1992–94; memb: Law Soc, Int Bar Assoc, UK Environmental Law Assoc, American Bar Assoc; *Recreations* motoring, tennis, theatre, country pursuits, golf; *Clubs* RAC, Norfolk, Sheringham Golf, Yale (NYC); *Style—* Timothy Pallister, Esq; ✉ The Old Vicarage, Tunstead, Norwich, Norfolk NR12 8HT (☎ 01692 536317); c/o Slaughter and May, 35 Basinghall St, London EC2V 5DB (☎ 0171 600 1200)

PALMANO, Cindy; da of Roger Rennels Palmano, and Jean Frances Palmano; *b* 30 Jan 1963; *Educ* Enfield Chace Sch for Girls, Central Sch of Art; *children* 1 s (Buster Luke Meeuwissen Palmano b 23 Dec 1987); *Career* photographer; work represented in the Nat Portrait Gallery and Nat Museum of Photography; magazine work incl: American, English Spanish and German Vogue, Tatler, Harpers & Queen, Face, Sunday Times, Vanity, Vanity Fair, Country Life; advtg work for clients incl: Fendi, Calugia & Giannelli, Jasper Conran, Georgina Godley, Fendissme, Shiseido International, Merloni, Tom Dixon, Kodak International, The Wool Board, Harvey Nichols, Debenham's, Pommery Champagne, Principals, Ignis, Kiss FM, Harrods; dir of music video for Tori Amos (four nominations MTV awards 1992), art dir 3 album campaigns for Tori Amos; *Exhibitions* 20th Century Aquisitions (Nat Portrait Gallery) 1986, First Int Photography Biennial (Nat Museum of Bradford) 1987, Fashion and Surrealism (NY Inst of Technol) 1988, The Photographers Gallery 1989, British Cncl 1989 and 1992, Arles 1991, Bliss (RCA) 1992, Positive View (Saatchi Gallery) 1994; *Style—* Miss Cindy Palmano; ✉ Top Floor, 56–58 Clerkenwell Rd, London EC1 5PX (☎ 0171 490 0630, fax 0171 490 3113)

PALMAR, Sir Derek James; kt (1986); o s of Lt-Col Frederick James Palmar (d 1978), and Hylda, *née* Smith; *b* 25 July 1919; *Educ* Dover Coll; *m* 1, 1946, Edith (d 1990), da of William Brewster (d 1948); 1 s (Alastair), 1 da (Caroline); m 2, 1992, Shuna Pyman; *Career* Nat Serv RA and Staff 1941–46, psc, Lt-Col 1945; Peat Marwick Mitchell & Co 1937–57, dir Hill Samuel Group 1957–70, advsr Dept of Econ Affrs 1965–67, memb BR Bd 1969–72, chm BR Southern Regnl Advsy Bd 1972–79; Bass plc: dir 1970, chm 1976–87, chief exec 1976–84, pres 1987–89; chm: Yorkshire Television plc (now Yorkshire Tyne Tees Television plc) 1982–93, Boythorpe 1986–, Zoological Soc of London Development Tst 1986–88, Univ of Leeds Fndn 1986–88, Nat Econ Devpt Ctee for Food and Drink Packaging Equipment 1986–88; dir: Grindlays Bank 1973–85, Grindlays Holdings 1979–85, Drayton Consolidated Tst 1982–93, Consolidated Venture Tst 1984–93; CM Group Holdings 1985–93; tstee Civic Tst 1982–89; memb Ct Brewers' Co 1980–87; vice-pres The Brewers' Soc 1982– (vice-chm 1978–80, chm 1980–82); Freeman City of London; FCA 1957 (ACA 1947), CIMgt; *Recreations* shooting, gardening; *Clubs* Boodle's; *Style—* Sir Derek Palmar

PALMER, 4 Baron (UK 1933), of Reading, Co Berks; Sir Adrian Bailie Nottage Palmer; 4 Bt (UK 1916); s of Col the Hon Sir Gordon William Nottage Palmer, KCVO, OBE, TD (d 1989), and Lorna Eveline Hope, DL, *née* Bailie; suc uncle, 3 Baron Palmer 1990; *b* 8 Oct 1951; *Educ* Eton, Univ of Edinburgh; *m* 7 May 1977, Cornelia Dorothy Katharine, da of Rohan Nicholas Wadham, DFC, of The Dog Kennel, Exning, nr Newmarket; 2 s (Hon Hugo Bailie Rohan b 1980, Hon George Gordon Nottage b 1985), 1 da (Hon Edwina Laura Marguerite b 1982); *Heir* s, Hon Hugo Bailie Rohan Palmer b 5 Dec 1980; *Career* mangr Assoc Biscuits Belgium 1974–77; farmer; sec Royal Caledonian Hunt 1989–, chm Historic Houses Assoc for Scotland 1994– (vice chm 1993–94); memb Cncl: Historic Houses Assoc for Scotland 1980–, Historic Houses Assoc 1981–, Scottish Landowners Fedn 1987–93; Scottish rep European Landowning Orgn 1986–92, memb Queen's Body Guard for Scotland (Royal Company of Archers) 1990–96, chm Country Sports Defence Tst 1994–; *Recreations* hunting, shooting, tennis, gardening; *Clubs* New (Edinburgh), MCC; *Style—* The Rt Hon the Lord Palmer; ✉ Manderston, Duns, Berwickshire TD11 3PP (☎ 01361 883450, fax 01361 882010)

PALMER, Dr Andrew Clennel; s of Gerald Basil Coote Palmer, of Duton Hill, Essex, and Muriel Gertrude, *née* Howes (d 1982); *b* 26 May 1938; *Educ* Royal Liberty Sch Romford, Univ of Cambridge (MA), Brown Univ USA (PhD); *m* 10 Aug 1963, Jane Rhiannon, da of George Ewart Evans; 1 da (Emily Abigail b 18 Sept 1971); *Career* lectr in mechanical engrg Univ of Liverpool 1965–67, lectr in engrg Univ of Cambridge 1967–75, chief engr R J Brown and Associates 1975–79, prof of civil engrg UMIST 1979–82, vice pres engrg R K Brown and Associates 1982–85, md Andrew Palmer and Associates 1985–93, tech dir SAIC Ltd 1993–; Jafar research prof of petroleum engrg Univ of Cambridge 1996–; CEng, memb Soc of Petroleum Engrs, FICE 1986, FEng 1990, FRS 1994; *Books* Structural Mechanics (1976); *Recreations* cooking, travel, languages; *Clubs* Athenaeum; *Style—* Dr Andrew Palmer, FRS, FEng; ✉ 49 Ashley Gardens, Ambrosden Avenue, London SW1P 1QF (☎ 0171 828 8843); Engineering Department, University of Cambridge, Cambridge CB2 1PZ (☎ 01223 332718, fax 01223 332662, e-mail acp24@eng.cam.ac.uk)

PALMER, Andrew Eustace; CMG (1987), CVO (1981); s of Lt-Col Rodney H Palmer, MC (d 1987), and Frances Pauline Ainsworth, *née* Gordon-Duff; gf and other ancestors, chm of Huntley & Palmer's Biscuits Reading; *b* 30 Sept 1937; *Educ* Winchester, Pembroke Coll Cambridge (MA); *m* 28 July 1962, Davina Cecil, da of Sir Roderick Barclay, GCVO, KCMG, of Latimer, Bucks; 2 s (Rodney b 1963, Michael b 1977), 1 da (Juliet (Viscountess Garmoyle) b 1965); *Career* Nat Serv 2 Lt The Rifle Bde 1956–58; HM Foreign Serv later Dip Serv: entered 1961, American Dept FO 1962–63, commercial sec La Paz 1963–65, second sec Ottawa 1965–67, Treasy Centre for Admin Studies 1967–68, Central Dept FO later Southern Euro Dept FCO 1968–72, first sec (press and information) Paris 1972–76, asst head of Def Dept FCO 1976–77, cnsllr Royal Coll of Def Studies Course 1978, head of chancery and consul-gen Oslo 1979–82, head Falkland Islands Dept FCO 1982–85, fell Harvard Center for Int Affrs 1985–86, HM ambass to Cuba 1986–88, seconded to Royal Household as private sec to TRH The Duke and Duchess of Kent 1988–90, HM ambass to The Holy See Rome 1991–95, ret 1996; extra equerry to HRH The Duke of Kent 1996–; memb Cncl Univ of Reading 1996–; *Recreations* photography, fishing, following most sports; *Clubs* Brooks's, MCC, Vanderbilt Tennis; *Style—* Andrew Palmer, Esq, CMG, CVO; ✉ Town Farm Cottage, Little Missenden, Amersham, Bucks HP7 0QX

PALMER, Andrew William; s of Victor Cecil Frederick Palmer (d 1991), of Singapore and Malaysia, and Joan, *née* Webster; *b* 14 Oct 1953; *Educ* Dulwich Coll; *m* 29 Nov 1975, Jane Caroline, da of Clyde Townrow; 2 s (Nicholas b 13 Sept 1982, Daniel b 6 Dec 1983); *Career* Brewer & Co (chartered accountants) 1973–77, Deloitte Haskins & Sells (chartered accountants) London and Oman 1977–82, Providence Capitol Life Assurance Co Ltd 1983–86, Commercial Union 1986–88; Legal & General Group plc: fin dir Investment Mgmnt 1988–91, fin dir Life & Pensions 1991–94, md Servs 1994–, gp dir Servs 1996–; memb: Auditing Practices Bd, The Children's Tst Tadworth Court; FCA 1977; *Recreations* game fishing, opera, watching motor racing; *Style—* Andrew Palmer, Esq; ✉ Legal & General Group plc, Legal & General House, Kingswood, Tadworth, Surrey KT20 6EU (☎ 01737 374273, fax 01737 376866)

PALMER, Anthony Wheeler; QC (1979); s of late Philip Palmer; *b* 30 Dec 1936; *Educ* Wrekin Coll Salop; *m* Jacqueline, da of late Reginald Fortnum, of Taunton; 1 s, 2 da; *Career* barr Gray's Inn 1962, recorder of the Crown Ct 1980–; *Style—* Anthony Palmer, Esq, QC; ✉ 17 Warwick Ave, Coventry CV5 6DJ

PALMER, Charles Stuart William; OBE (1973); s of Charles Edward Palmer, and Emma Byrne; *b* 15 April 1930; *Educ* Drayton Manor Co Sch; *Career* chm Br Olympic Assoc 1983–88 (vice chm 1977–83); represented GB in judo 1949–59, studied judo in Japan 1951–55, 1 Dan 1948, 4 Dan 1955, 9 Dan 1991, 10 Dan 1996; pres Int Judo Fedn 1965–79 (hon life pres 1979–), sec gen Gen Assoc of Int Sports Fedns 1975–84, pres Br Judo Assoc 1977– (chm 1962–85), govr Sports Aid Fndn 1979–, memb GB Sports Cncl 1983–93, chm Games and Sports Div CCPR, memb IOC Programme Cmmn; Olympic Order 1980, Gold medal Euro Judo Union 1982; memb Cncl Royal Albert Hall; Key of City of Taipei 1974, Key of City of Seoul 1981; *Recreations* judo, skiing, music, languages; *Style—* Charles Palmer, Esq, OBE; ✉ 4 Hollywood Road, London SW10 9HY (☎ 0171 352 6238, fax 0171 386 7766)

PALMER, Sheriff Charles William; s of Charles James Strachan Palmer (d 1961), of Estate Factor, Inverlochy, Castle Estate, Fort William, and Ida Patricia, *née* Miskimmin; *b* 17 Dec 1945; *Educ* Lochaber HS, Inverness Royal Acad, Univ of Edinburgh (UB); *m* 20 Dec 1969, Rosemary, da of Lt-Col Henry Walter Holt (d 1976), of Grantley Rd, Boscombe, Hants; 1 s (Richard James b 1971), 2 da (Lavinia Jayne b 1973, Emily Sarah b 1974); *Career* ptnr Allan McDougall & Co, slr Supreme Ct Edinburgh 1975; sheriff: N Strathclyde at Dunoon and Dumbarton 1986–92, Tayside Central & Fife at Dunfermline 1992–; memb Law Soc of Scotland; *Recreations* hill walking, music, photography, equestrian pursuits; *Style—* Sheriff Charles Palmer; ✉ c/o Dunfermline Sheriff's Clerk Office, Dunfermline KY12 7HJ

PALMER, Clifford Frederick; s of Charles Norman Palmer (d 1975), and Nora, *née* Drury (d 1991); *b* 7 Sept 1948; *Educ* Henley-in-Arden HS; *m* 1, 1 June 1974 (m dis 1984), Janet Mary, da of Frank Wilson, of Kettering, Northants; m 2, 22 Sept 1984, Jill Mary, da of Maurice James Steward (d 1980), of Dennington, Suffolk; 4 da (Charlotte b 1984, Victoria b 1985, Kathryn b 1987, Sarah b 1987); *Career* National Farmers' Union Mutual Insurance Society Stratford-upon-Avon 1965–69, SA Meacock & Co at Lloyd's 1969–79, dir Clifford Palmer Underwriting Agencies Ltd at Lloyd's 1979–92 (exec dir 1980); exec dir: Ashley Palmer Holdings 1984, Martin Ashley Underwriting Agencies Ltd 1984–92, Ashley Palmer & Hathaway Ltd 1987, ENAM Underwriting Franchises Inc 1991–96, Ashley Palmer Syndicates Ltd 1992, Vesta Insurance Group Inc 1993, F & G UK Agency Ltd 1995–; FCII; *Clubs* City of London; *Style—* Clifford Palmer, Esq; ✉ Croft Point, Links Rd, Bramley, Guildford, Surrey; Ashley Palmer Holdings Ltd, 27 Leadenhall Street, London EC3A 1AA (☎ 0171 488 0103, fax 0171 481 4995)

PALMER, David Erroll Prior; s of Brig Sir Otho Prior-Palmer DSO, and Mrs Sheila Mary Peers, *née* Weller-Poley; *b* 20 Feb 1941; *Educ* Eton, Christ Church Oxford (MA); *m* 1974, Elizabeth Helen, da of Tom Young, of Chichester; 2 s (James b 1975, Alexander b 1977), 1 da (Marina b 1978); *Career* Financial Times Group: features 1964–67, NY corr 1967–70, mgmnt ed 1970–72, news ed 1972–77, Frankfurt Project 1977–79, foreign ed 1979–80, dep ed 1981–83, gen mangr 1983–89, dep chief exec 1989–90, chief exec 1990–93, md Independent Newspapers (Ireland) 1994–; first Br finisher (third in class) Observer Transatlantic Race 1976; *Books* The Atlantic Challenge (1977); *Recreations* sailing (Sigma 33 - 'Honey of Bosham'); *Clubs* Itchenor Sailing, Oxford and Cambridge Sailing, Royal Saint George Yacht; *Style—* David Palmer Esq

PALMER, David Vereker; DL (Bucks 1995); s of Brig Julian William Palmer (d 1977), and Lena Elizabeth, *née* Vereker (d 1941); *b* 9 Dec 1926; *Educ* Stowe; *m* 10 June 1950, Mildred (Millie), da of Edward Asbury O'Neal (d 1977), of Alabama, USA; 3 da (Melanie (Mrs Rendall) b 29 June 1951, Alice (Mrs Parsons) b 12 May 1959, Katherine (Mrs Bentley) b 21 Feb 1962); *Career* Capt Life Gds 1944–49, served in Europe and ME; mangr NY office Edward Lumley & Sons 1953–59 (joined 1949); Willis Faber & Dumas Ltd: joined 1959, dir 1961, chief exec 1978, chm 1982, ret 1988; chm Syndicate Capital Tst plc 1993–96; cmmr Royal Hosp Chelsea 1980–88, pres Insur Inst of London 1985–86, chm Br Insur and Investmt Brokers' Assoc 1987–89; High Sheriff Bucks 1993–94; Freeman City of London 1980, memb Worshipful Co of Insurers (Master 1982); ACII 1950, memb Lloyd's 1953; *Recreations* farming, shooting; *Clubs* City of London, Cavalry and Guards'; *Style—* David Palmer, Esq, DL; ✉ Burrow Farm, Hambleden, nr Henley-on-Thames, Oxon RG9 6LT (☎ 01491 571256, fax 01491 571267); 18 Whaddon House, William Mews, London SW1X 9HG (☎ 0171 235 7900)

PALMER, Rev Canon Derek George; *b* 24 Jan 1928; *Educ* Clifton Coll, Selwyn Coll Cambridge, Wells Theol Coll; *m* 1952, June Cecilie; 4 c; *Career* served RA 1945–48; ordained (Bristol): deacon 1952, priest 1953; curate-in-charge Stapleton Bristol 1952–54, priest-in-charge Good Shepherd Bishopston 1954–58; vicar: New Parish Hartcliffe 1958–68, Christ Church Swindon 1968–76; hon canon Bristol Cathedral 1974–76, archdeacon and residentiary canon of Rochester 1977–83, team rector of Dronfield with Holmesfield Dio of Derby 1987–95, chaplain to HM the Queen 1991–, county ecumenical offr for Buckingham 1995–; memb: Gen Synod 1970–82, Gen Synod Bd of Educn, Ely Cmmn on Christian Initiation, Anglican Methodist Talks, Churches Cncl for Covenanting; fndr ed Contact Bristol and W Church newspaper, chm BBC Radio Kent, home sec Bd of Mission and Unity 1983, assoc sec Not Strangers But Pilgrims 1985, organiser Lent '86, chm The Christian Enquiry Agency 1987, Hon Canon Derby Cathedral 1992; *Publications* All Things New (on Estate Churches), Quest (on Confirmation Trg), Strangers No Longer (Hodder and Stoughton, 1990); *Recreations* family, canals (past and present), walking; *Style—* The Rev Canon Derek Palmer; ✉ 124 Bath Road, Banbury, Oxon OX16 0TR (☎ 01295 268201)

PALMER, Felicity Joan; CBE (1993); *Educ* Erith GS, Guildhall Sch of Music and Drama (AGSM, FGSM), Hochschule für Musik Munich; *Career* mezzo-soprano; Kathleen Ferrier Meml Prize 1970; major appearances at concerts in: Britain, America, Belgium, France, Germany, Italy, Spain, Poland, Czechoslovakia, Russia; operatic appearances: London and throughout England, La Scala Milan, Paris, Bordeaux, Houston, Chicago, NY, San Francisco, Geneva, Amsterdam, Toronto, Leipzig, Madrid, Berne, Zürich, Frankfurt, Hanover, Vienna; recordings with maj record cos incl recital records and two Victorian ballad records; *Style—* Miss Felicity Palmer, CBE; ✉ c/o AOR Management Ltd, Westwood, Lorraine Park, Harrow Weald, Middx HA3 6BX

PALMER, Geoffrey; *b* 4 June 1927; *Educ* Highgate Sch; *Career* actor; *Theatre* incl: Difference of Opinion (Garrick), West of Suez (Royal Court), Savages (Royal Court), On Approval (Haymarket), Eden End (NT), Private Lives (Globe), St Joan (Old Vic), Tishoo (Wyndhams), Kafka's Dick (Royal Court), Piano (NT); *Television* incl: The Fall and Rise of Reginald Perrin, Butterflies, The Insurance Man, The Last Song, Absurd Person Singular, Fairly Secret Army, Seasons Greetings, A Question of Attribution, As Time Goes By; *Films* incl: O Lucky Man, The Honorary Consul, Clockwise, A Zed and Two Noughts, A Fish Called Wanda, The Madness of George III, Her Majesty Mrs Brown; *Recreations* fly fishing; *Clubs* Garrick; *Style—* Geoffrey Palmer, Esq

PALMER, Sir Geoffrey Christopher John; 12 Bt (E 1660), of Carlton, Northamptonshire; s of Lt-Col Sir Geoffrey Frederick Neill Palmer, 11 Bt (d 1951), and Cicely Kathleen, *née* Radmall (d 1989); *b* 30 June 1936; *Educ* Eton; *m* 1957, Clarissa Mary, DL (Leics 1994), eldest da of Stephen Francis Villiers-Smith; 4 da (Sophia Mary (Mrs Michael H W Neal) b 1959, Celina Lucinda (Mrs William A M Francklin) b 1961, Isabella Anne (Mrs David W R Harrington) b 1962, Rosanna Jane (Mrs Edward J G Peel) b 1967); *Heir* bro, Jeremy Charles Palmer, *qv*; *Career* is a patron of two livings; *Recreations* shooting, golf; *Clubs* MCC, I Zingari, Free Foresters, Eton Ramblers, XL, Gentlemen of Leicestershire, Gentlemen of Lincolnshire, Butterflies, Frogs, Derby Friars CC, Northants Amateurs, Old Etonian Golfing Soc; *Style—* Sir Geoffrey Palmer, Bt; ✉ Carlton Curlieu Hall, Leicestershire LE8 0PH (☎ 0116 259 2656)

PALMER, Gerald Marley; s of Percy William Ernest Palmer (d 1932), of Bulawayo, S Rhodesia, and Esther, *née* Marley (d 1974); *b* 20 Jan 1911; *Educ* Milton HS S Rhodesia, Univ of London (BSc); *m* 6 May 1939, Diana Fleetwood (d 1991), da of Cornelius Percy Varley (d 1936), of Enfield; 1 da (Celia Fleetwood); *Career* Nat Serv Corpl Home Gd; apprenticeship Scammell Lorries Ltd 1927–38, Morris Motors Ltd 1938–42 (designed Oxford vaporiser anaesthetic apparatus), Jowett Cars Ltd (designed Jowett Javelin car) 1942–49, tech dir Morris Motors 1949–55, asst chief engr Vauxhall Motors Ltd 1955–72, dir F J Payne (Manufacturing) Ltd (designing equipment for disabled people) 1972–88; pres and chm Local Cons Assoc; CEng, FIMechE; *Recreations* sailing, vintage car racing; *Style—* Gerald Palmer, Esq; ✉ Orchard House, 4 Tree Lane, Iffley, Oxford (☎ 01865 779222)

PALMER, Professor Godfrey Henry Oliver (Geoff); s of Aubrey George Palmer (d 1985), of Jamaica and NY, and Ivy Georgina, *née* Larmond; *b* 9 April 1940, Jamaica; *Educ* Shelbourne Rd Secdy Modern London, Highbury Co Sch London, Univ of Leicester (BSc), Univ of Edinburgh (PhD), Heriot-Watt Univ (DSc); *m* 20 June 1969, (Margaret) Ann; 3 c; *Career* jr lab technician 1957–61, sr scientist Brewing Res Fndn 1968, inventor barley abrasion process for accelerating malt prodn in indust 1969, cereal conslt to various cos 1979, prof Heriot-Watt Univ 1992– (reader 1988–92); Kyoto Univ Japan: visiting prof and res scholar 1991, research assessor (food and sci) 1995; chm Scottish Section Inst of Brewing 1990–92; course chm Chivas Regel Acad 1992; convenor Church of Scotland Educn Ctee (dealing with multicultural educn) 1988–90, memb Edinburgh Lothian Community Relations Ctee 1989, chm E Mid Lothian Borders of Scot Ctee (involved in multicultural approach to racial incidence) 1990, chm Mid and E Lothian Race Relations Working Gps; fell Inst of Brewing 1985; *Books* Cereal Science and Technology (1989), contrib Reader's Digest: Complete Guide to Cooking (1989); *Recreations* reading, charity work, television; *Clubs* Staff, Univ of Edinburgh; *Style—* Prof Geoff Palmer; ✉ 23 Waulkmill Drive, Penicuik, Mid Lothian, Scotland (☎ 01968 675148); Department of Biological Sciences, International Centre for Brewing & Distilling, Heriot-Watt University, Riccarton, Edinburgh, Scotland (☎ 0131 449 5111)

PALMER, His Hon (Robert) Henry Stephen; s of Henry Alleyn Palmer (d 1965), and Maud Palmer, *née* Obbard (d 1973); *b* 13 Nov 1927; *Educ* Charterhouse, Univ Coll Oxford (MA); *m* 1955, Geraldine Elizabeth Anne, da of George Evan Evens (d 1950); 1 s (George), 2 da (Nicola, Katharine); *Career* 1972–78, circuit judge 1978–93, resident judge Harrow Crown Ct 1991–93; pres Mental Health Review Tbnl 1983–; regnl chm S Thames Mental Health Review Tribunal 1993–; *Recreations* self sufficiency; *Style—* His Hon Henry Palmer

PALMER, Hon Henry William; s of Viscount Wolmer (s of 3 Earl of Selborne, ka 1942), and Priscilla, *née* Egerton-Warburton, and bro of 4 Earl; *b* 12 July 1941; *Educ* Eton, Christ Church Oxford (MA); *m* 1968, Minette, da of Sir Patrick William Donner, of Hurstbourne Park, Whitchurch, Hants; 3 s, 1 da; *Career* Ford Motor Co 1963–66, Associated Industrial Consultants 1966–68, md The Centre for Interfirm Comparison 1985– (joined 1968, dep dir 1975); dep chm of govrs St Paul's Girls Sch, govr St Paul's Sch; Master Worshipful Co of Mercers 1992; FIMgt; *Clubs* Farmers'; *Style—* The Hon Henry Palmer; ✉ Burhunt Farm, Selborne, Alton, Hants GU34 3LP (☎ 01420 511209)

PALMER, Jeremy Charles; s of Lt-Col Sir Geoffrey Frederick Neill Palmer, 11 Bt (d 1951), and hp of bro, Sir Geoffrey Christopher John Palmer, 12 Bt, *qv*; *b* 16 May 1939; *Educ* Eton, Univ of Tours; *m* 24 July 1968, Antonia, da of late Astley Dutton; 2 s (Drew Herrick b 1974, Tom Jeremy b 1977); *Career* wine merchant Bull & Taylor; *Recreations* shooting, tennis; *Clubs* Queen's, Pratt's; *Style—* Jeremy Palmer, Esq; ✉ 6 Furber Street, London W6 (☎ 0181 748 1140)

PALMER, John; CB; s of William Nathaniel Palmer (d 1984), and Grace Dorothy May, *née* Procter (d 1979); *b* 13 Nov 1928; *Educ* Heath GS Halifax, Queen's Coll Oxford (MA); *m* 17 Dec 1958, Lyliane Anne Marthe, *née* Jeanjean; 2 da (Catherine b 1959, Sophie b 1962); *Career* joined admin class Home Civil Serv 1952, Cabinet Office 1963–65, asst sec 1965, under sec DOE 1971, ret as dep sec Dept of Tport 1989 (joined 1976); md Channel Tunnel BR 1990, chm European Passenger Services Ltd 1991–94, special advsr to Chm British Rail 1992–; Freeman City of London 1985, Liveryman Worshipful Co of Carmen 1985; FCIT; *Clubs* United Oxford & Cambridge Univ; *Style—* John Palmer, Esq, CB; ✉ British Railways Board, Euston House, 24 Eversholt Street, London NW1 1DZ

PALMER, John; *Career* Euro ed The Guardian 1975– (formerly business ed, chief econ ldr writer, industl ed); secondments: dir Gtr London Enterprise Bd 1983–86, memb Bd London Tport 1985–86; experienced radio tv broadcaster; *Style—* John Palmer, Esq; ✉ c/o International Press Centre, Box 12, No1 Boulevard Charlemagne, 1041 Brussels, Belgium (☎ 00 32 2 230 6879, fax 00 32 2 230 6850)

PALMER, Sir John Chance; kt (1979), DL (Devon 1984); s of Ernest Clephan Palmer (d 1954), and Claudine Pattie Sapey; *b* 21 March 1920; *Educ* St Paul's, St Edmund Hall Oxford (MA); *m* 1945, Mary Winifred, da of Arthur Sidney Ellyatt, OBE (d 1973); 4 s; *Career* served RNVR 1939–46, serv Atlantic and Med; admitted slr 1948, conslt Bevan Ashford (Tiverton, Exeter, Crediton, Taunton, Bristol, Swindon and London); Vice Lord-Lt Devon 1991–95; memb Cncl Law Soc of England and Wales 1963–83 (pres 1978–79), govr Coll of Law 1965–83; pres: Devon and Exeter Law Soc 1972, S Western Law Soc 1973; memb Cncl Univ of Exeter 1983–95; chm: Govrs Blundell's Sch 1980–91, Tstees London Sailing Project 1980–92, Tstees Int Technological Univ 1988–, Exmoor Calvert Tst 1991–94; memb: Criminal Injuries Compensation Bd 1981–92, SW Region Mental Health Tbnl 1983–92; hon memb: American Bar Assoc, Canadian Bar Assoc, Florida Defence Lawyers Assoc; Hon LLD Exeter 1980; *Clubs* Athenaeum, Royal Yacht Squadron, Naval, Royal Over-Seas League, Western (Glasgow); *Style—* Sir John Palmer, DL; ✉ Lower Withleigh Farmhouse, Tiverton, Devon EX16 8JJ (☎ 01884 252959); Sunnycote, Riverside, Shaldon, Devon (☎ 01626 872350) The Crannach Enochdhu, nr Blairgowrie, Perthshire (mobile 0850 794679)

PALMER, Sir John Edward Somerset; 8 Bt (GB 1791); s of Sir John Palmer, 7 Bt, DL (d 1963); *b* 27 Oct 1926; *Educ* Canford, Pembroke Coll Cambridge, Univ of Durham; *m* 1956, Dione Catharine, da of Charles Duncan Skinner; 1 s, 1 da; *Heir* s, Robert John Hudson Palmer; *Career* Lt RA serv India; Colonial Agric Serv N Nigeria 1952–61; sr exec R A Lister & Co Ltd Dursley Glos 1962–63, min Overseas Devpt 1964–68, ind conslt 1969–79, dir W S Atkins Agriculture 1979–88; *Recreations* sailing, fishing, shooting; *Style—* Sir John Palmer, Bt; ✉ Court Barton, Feniton, Honiton, Devon EX14 0BD (☎ 01404 851020)

PALMER, Prof John Michael; s of Henry William Palmer (d 1974), and Hilda May, *née* Ball (d 1955); *b* 24 April 1936; *Educ* Yeovil GS, Univ of Reading (BSc), Univ of Oxford (DPhil); *m* 16 July 1959, Irene Alice, da of Sidney Arthur Ricketts, of 16 Cromwell Rd, Yeovil, Somerset; 1 s (Stephen John b 1969), 2 da (Alison Hilary b 1965, Helen Melinda b 1967); *Career* NATO res fell Univ of California 1962–64, lectr in plant physiology KCL 1964–71, prof of plant biochemistry Imperial Coll London 1984– (reader in enzymology 1971–84); warden Kent Tst for Nature Conservation; fell: S London Botanical Inst, Br Mycological Soc, Soc for Experimental Biology; *Books* The Physiology and Biochemistry of Plant Respiration (1984); *Recreations* photography, natural history, music; *Clubs* Orpington Field, Kent Field; *Style—* Prof John Palmer; ✉ Imperial College of Science, Technology and Medicine, South Kensington, London SW7 2AZ (☎ 0171 589 5111, fax 0171 584 7596)

PALMER, Dr Keith Francis; s of Frank Palmer (d 1987), of Cardiff, and Gwenda Evelyn, *née* Merrick; *b* 26 July 1947; *Educ* Howardian HS Cardiff, Univ of Birmingham (BSc, PhD), Univ of Cambridge (Dip Devpt Econ); *m* 10 Aug 1974, Penelope Ann, *née* McDonagh; 4 da (Alexandra b 1977, Georgia b 1979, Katherine b 1981, Megan b 1982); *Career* NATO post doctoral res fell Lamont Geophysical Observatory NY 1971–73, first asst sec (fin) Miny Papua New Guinea 1974–78, with IMF/World Bank 1978–84, md corp fin N M Rothschild & Sons Ltd 1993– (dir corp fin 1984–93); chm Action Health Trust; govr Haberdashers' Aske's Sch; memb RIIA 1984, FGS 1987; *Recreations* geology, gemmology, music, running; *Clubs* IOD; *Style—* Dr Keith Palmer; ✉ N M Rothschild & Sons Ltd, New Court, St Swithins Lane, London, EC4 (☎ 0171 280 5000)

PALMER, Kenneth Ernest (Ken); s of Harry Palmer, of Taunton, Somerset, and Celia, *née* Rapps (d 1987); *b* 22 April 1937; *Educ* South Broom Secdy Modern Sch Devizes; *m* 1, 1962, Joy Valerie (d 1988), *née* Gilbert; 1 s (Gary b 1 Nov 1965); m 2, 24 Sept 1994, Jackie Jotcham; *Career* first-class cricket umpire; appointed 1972, selected for int panel 1978–; umpired: 22 Test matches 1978–89, 2 World Cups England, numerous domestic cup finals, 15 one day intsı player Somerset CCC 1955–69: awarded county cup 1958, testimonial 1968, 314 appearances, 7761 runs, 866 wickets; 1 Test cap England v SA 1964–65; coached in SA 1964–65, currently coaches youth teams; winner cricketers' double Somerset 1961, club record 102 not out batting at number eight, single wicket knockout champion Scarborough 1963; former semi-professional footballer: 2 seasons Bristol City, 1 season Exeter City; *Recreations* playing squash, coaching sports (cricket, squash, football); *Style—* Ken Palmer, Esq; ✉ c/o TCCB, Lords Cricket Ground, London NW8 8QN

PALMER, Malcolm John Frederick; *b* 22 Oct 1933; *Educ* Charterhouse, Queens' Coll Cambridge (MA); *m* 3 Nov 1962, Rachel M Phillips; 2 s (James b 10 Sept 1963, Stephen b 18 Jan 1965), 1 da (Melanie Ruth (Mrs Peter D Pryor) b 21 Feb 1968); *Career* Nat Serv REME 1952–54; articled Linklaters & Paines 1957–60, asst slr Rickerby & Mellersh Cheltenham 1960–62; Baker & McKenzie: asst slr London 1962–63, conslt Chicago 1963–65, ptnr London 1965–75, sr ptnr Hong Kong 1975–81, ptnr London 1981–93, chm London Mgmnt Ctee 1987–91; dep special cmmr and pt/t chm VAT and Duties Tbnl 1992–, memb Advsy Ctee Control Risks Gp 1996–; memb Law Soc 1960; *Recreations* bridge, bowls, buying and occasionally reading books; *Clubs* Reform, Hurlingham, RAC; *Style—* Malcolm Palmer, Esq; ✉ Woodsford Square, London W14 8DP (☎ 0171 602 6736)

PALMER, Sir (Charles) Mark; 5 Bt (UK 1886), of Grinkle Park, Co York, and of Newcastle-upon-Tyne; s of Sir Anthony Frederick Mark Palmer, 4 Bt (ka 1941), and Lady (Henriette Alice) Abel Smith, *qv*; *b* 21 Nov 1941, posthumously; *Educ* Eton; *m* 1976, Hon Catherine Elizabeth Tennant, da of 2 Baron Glenconner (d 1983); 1 s (Arthur Morris b 9 March 1981), 1 da (Iris Henriette b 1977); *Heir* s, Arthur Morris Palmer b 9 March 1981; *Career* was a page of honour to HM the Queen 1956–59; *Style—* Sir Mark Palmer, Bt; ✉ Mill Hill Farm, Sherborne, Northleach, Glos GL54 3DU (☎ 0145 14 395)

PALMER, Martin Giles; s of Rev Derek George Palmer, and Celilie June, *née* Goddard; *b* 14 Oct 1953; *Educ* Hartcliff Comp Sch Bristol, Commonweal Comp Sch Swindon, Selwyn Coll Cambridge (MA); *m* 27 Sept 1975, Sandra Ann, da of Rudi Fischer, of Aust; 1 s (James Richard b 25 June 1978), 1 da (Elizabeth Francis b 8 Dec 1981); *Career* Church Missionary Soc vol Christian Children's Home Hong Kong 1972–73, nat pres Student Christian Movement while student of theol and religious studies Cambridge 1973–76, res work on Hong Kong for World Cncl of Churches Prog to Combat Racism and Hong Kong Res Project 1976–77, regnl organiser Christian Educn Movement Gtr Manchester 1977–79, fndr dir Centre for the Study of Religion and Educn in the Inner City Manchester 1977–83, dir Int Consultancy on Religion, Educn and Culture (clients incl WWF) 1983–, religious advsr to HRH Prince Philip (pres WWF Int) 1986–; fndr: Christian Stateman magazine 1978–, International Labour Reports magazine 1983–; sec gen Alliance of Religions and Conservation 1995–, external advsr Sikh World Cncl India 1996–; lectr worldwide, contrib to various magazines and papers and to radio and TV progs incl being religious corr for This Sunday (ITV) 1993; Sandford Award for Religious Radio 1996; *Books* incl: Faiths and Festivals (1984), Worlds of Difference (1985), Genesis or Nemesis (1988), Contemporary I Ching (1989), Taoism (1991), Dancing to Armageddon (1992), Living Christianity (1993), Tao Te Ching (1993), Chuang Tzu (1995); *Recreations* brass rubbing, numismatics, cooking, icons, anything Chinese; *Style—* Martin Palmer; ✉ ICOREC, 9a Didsbury Park, Manchester M20 5LH (☎ 0161 434 0828, fax 0161 434 8374)

PALMER, Maj-Gen Sir (Joseph) Michael; KCVO (1985); s of late Lt-Col William Robert Palmer, DSO; *b* 17 Oct 1928; *Educ* Wellington, Sandhurst; *m* 1953, Jillean Monica Sherston; 2 s, 1 da; *Career* Def Servs sec 1982–85; dir: RAC 1978–81, ACS Allied Forces Central Europe 1976–78; Col 14/20 King's Hussars 1981–92, Hon Col Duke of Lancasters Own Yeo 1988–96; chm: Copley Marshall & Co, Bd of Tstees Sandroyd Sch; memb Ct of Assts Worshipful Co of Salters (Master 1989–90); FIMgt; *Recreations* riding, shooting, music, reading; *Clubs* Cavalry and Guards'; *Style—* Maj-Gen Sir Michael Palmer, KCVO; ✉ c/o The Cavalry and Guards' Club, 127 Piccadilly, London W1V 0PX

PALMER, Prof Nigel Fenton; s of James Terence Palmer, and Constance May, *née* Fenton; *b* 28 Oct 1946; *Educ* Hyde Co GS, Worcester Coll Oxford (MA, DPhil); *m* 1974, Susan Patricia, *née* Aldred; 1 da (Rachel Louise b 1975), 1 s (Rupert Oliver b 1979);

Career lectr in German Univ of Durham 1970–76; Univ of Oxford: lectr in Medieval German 1976–90, reader in German 1990–92, prof of German medieval and linguistic studies 1992–; fell Humboldt Fndn; *Publications* Visio Tnugdali (1982), Deutsche Handschriften 1100–1400 (ed, 1988), Latein und Volkssprache im Deutschen Mittlelatter (ed, 1992), Die lateinisch-deutschen Blockbücher des Berlin-Breslauer Sammelbandes (1992); *Style—* Prof Nigel F Palmer; ✉ St Edmund Hall, Oxford OX1 4AR

PALMER, Prof Norman Ernest; s of Norman George Palmer, of Grays Thurrock, Essex, and Muriel, *née* Walker; *b* 16 Aug 1948; *Educ* Palmer's Endowed Sch Grays Thurrock, Magdalen Coll Oxford (Ford Fndn scholar, exhibitioner, MA Jurisprudence, Shepherd Prize, BCL); *m* 1, 1971 (m dis), Judith Ann Weeks; 1 da (Victoria Olivia b 1974); m 2, 1994, Ruth Redmond-Cooper; *Career* called to the Bar Gray's Inn 1973, in practice SE Circuit; law reform cmmr Tasmania 1976–77, head Dept of Law Univ of Reading 1982–84 (prof of law 1981–84), prof of law Univ of Essex 1984–90 (dean Faculty of Law 1985–88), prof of law and dep dean Faculty of Law Univ of Southampton 1990–91, Rowe & Maw prof of commercial law UCL 1991–, head of chambers 2 Field Ct 1992–; Mallesons visiting fell Univ of Western Aust 1993, Ross Parsons visiting prof Univ of Sydney 1990 and 1991; sec and a dir Int Cultural Property Soc 1990–95, govr Inst of Art and Law 1995–, memb Treasure Trove Reviewing Ctee 1996–; ed-in-chief: Building Law Monthly 1983–, International Journal of Cultural Property 1990–95, Art and Antiquity Law Reports 1996–, Art Antiquity and Law 1996–; ACIArb 1983; *Publications include* Bailment (1979, 2 edn 1979), Halsbury's Laws of England (contrib, 1984–93), Emden's Construction Law (5 vols, jtly 1990), Product Liability in the Construction Industry (with E McKendrick, 1993), Interests in Goods (ed with E McKendrick and contrib, 1993, 2 edn 1997), Butterworth's Manual of Construction Law (with Ruth Redmond-Cooper and S Bickford-Smith, 1993), Encyclopaedia of Forms and Precedents (contrib, 1994), Laws of Australia (contrib, 1995); also author of numerous papers in various learned journals and periodicals; *Recreations* literature, archaeology, collecting antique motor cars, tombstone verse; *Style—* Prof Norman Palmer; ✉ chambers: 2 Field Court, Gray's Inn, London WC1R 5BB (☎ 0171 405 6114, fax 0171 831 6112); Faculty of Laws, University of London, Bentham House, 4–8 Endsleigh Gardens, London WC1H 0EG (direct ☎ 0171 391 1438, fax 0171 387 9597)

PALMER, Gen Sir (Charles) Patrick Ralph; KBE (1987, CBE 1982, OBE 1974); s of Charles Dudley Palmer (d 1965), and Catherine Anne, *née* Hughes-Buller (d 1981); *b* 29 April 1933; *Educ* Marlborough, RMA Sandhurst, Staff Coll Camberley, RCDS; *m* 1, 19 Dec 1960, Sonia (d 1965), da of Hardy Wigglesworth (d 1944); 1 s (Neil Patrick b 1962); m 2, 3 Sept 1966, Joanna Grace, da of Col Peter Stanhope Baines (d 1975); 2 da (Iona Catherine b 1967, Alison Joanna (Mrs Bruce Gilson) b 1969); *Career* cmmnd Argyll & Sutherland Highlanders 1953; served 1 Bn: Br Guiana, Berlin, Suez Operation, Cyprus, Borneo, Singapore, Aden; reformed and cmd 1 Bn A&SH 1972–74, COS to CBF Hong Kong 1974–76, Cdr 7 Armoured Bde 1977–80, Cdr Br Mil Advsy & Trg Team Zimbabwe 1980–82, GOC NE Dist & Cdr 2 Inf Div 1982–84, Cmdt Staff Coll 1984–86, Mil Sec 1986–89, C in C Allied Forces Northern Europe 1989–92, Col A&SH 1982–92; Constable and Governor of Windsor Castle 1992–; CIMgt 1988; *Recreations* travel, outdoor interests; *Clubs* Army and Navy; *Style—* Gen Sir Patrick Palmer, KBE; ✉ Norman Tower, Windsor Castle, Berks SL4 1NJ

PALMER, Richard John; JP (1961), DL (Berks 1994); s of Reginald Howard Reed Palmer (d 1970); *b* 5 Nov 1926; *Educ* Eton; *m* 1951, Hon Sarah Faith Georgina Spencer, da of 1 Viscount Churchill, GCVO (d 1934); 3 s, 1 da; *Career* served Grenadier Guards Lt 1944–48; dep chm GWR Group plc; chm: Thames Valley Broadcasting plc, Central European Broadcasting Ltd; dir Assoc of Biscuit Mfrs, chm Tstees Berkshire Community Tst, vice pres Berks Assoc of Young People; pres: Met Region YMCA, Reading E Cons Assoc; High Sheriff of Berks 1979–80; *Recreations* shooting, fishing; *Clubs* White's; *Style—* Richard Palmer, Esq, JP, DL; ✉ Queen Anne's Mead, Swallowfield, Berks RG7 1ST (☎ 0118 988 3264)

PALMER, Richard William (Dick); OBE (1986); s of Richard Victor Palmer (d 1983), of Llangwm, Pembrokeshire, and Mary Ellen, *née* Sambrook (d 1984); *b* 13 April 1933; *Educ* Haverfordwest GS, Trinity Coll Carmarthen, Chester Coll, Univ of Leicester (MEd); *Career* sports administrator; sec gen Br Students' Sports Fedn 1964–72 (pres 1979–86), organising sec World Univ Cross Country Championship 1970 and World Univ Judo Championship 1971; gen sec: Cwlth Games Cncl for England 1977–86, British Olympic Assoc 1977–; dep chef de mission GB Olympic teams Innsbruck and Montreal 1976; chef de mission GB Olympic teams: Lake Placid and Moscow 1980, Sarajevo and LA 1984, Calgary and Seoul 1988, Albertville and Barcelona 1992, Lillehamer 1994, Atlanta 1996; gen team mangr Eng Cwlth Games teams: Edmonton 1978, Brisbane 1982, Edinburgh 1986; memb: IOC Cmmn for New Sources of Fin 1981–95, Exec Bd Euro Nat Olympic Ctees 1989–, IOC Cmmn for 1996 Olympic Games Atlanta and 2000 Olympic Games Sydney 1990–; co-ordinator Assoc of Nat Olympic Ctees Cmmn for Olympic Games 1982–88 and 1992–, vice pres Euro Assoc of Nat Olympic Ctees 1990–; Award of Merit Assoc of Nat Olympic Ctees; physical educationalist and coach: track and field, rugby football, badminton; formerly rugby and athletics rep Pembrokeshire (club capt); Freeman of Pembroke; *Clubs* East India (life memb), Scribes, Fullwell and Haverfordwest Golf, Llangwm Boat; *Style—* Dick Palmer, Esq, OBE; ✉ British Olympic Association, 1 Wandsworth Plain, London SW18 1EH (☎ 0181 871 2677, fax 0181 871 9104)

PALMER, Dr Robert Leslie; s of Reginald John Freeman Palmer (d 1987), of Leamington Spa, and Marion May, *née* Sims (d 1988); *b* 15 March 1944; *Educ* Warwick Sch, St George's Med Sch, Univ of London (MB BS); *m* 19 July 1969, Mary Violet, da of Frank Carter, of Stamford Hill, London; 1 da (Rebecca 23 Oct 1971); *Career* res worker and hon lectr St George's Hosp Med Sch Univ of London 1971–73, lectr in psychiatry St Mary's Hosp Med Sch 1974–75, sr lectr in psychiatry Univ of Leicester 1975–; ed European Eating Disorders Review 1996–; author of papers on psychiatry and psychosomatic med especially clinical eating disorders; former examiner: for membership RCPsych, Univ of London final MB examination, Nat Univ of Singapore M Med Sci; MRCPsych 1972, FRCP 1984; *Books* Anorexia Nervosa: a guide for sufferers and their families (1980 and 1989); *Recreations* reading, jogging, birdwatching; *Style—* Dr Robert Palmer; ✉ University Department of Psychiatry, Leicester General Hospital, Gwendolen Rd, Leicester LE5 4PW (☎ 0116 258 4751, fax 0116 258 4751)

PALMER, Roger James Hume Dorney; s of Lt-Col Philip Dayrell Stewart Palmer (d 1979), of Dorney Court, Bucks, and Aileen Frances, *née* Cook (d 1983); *b* 21 March 1947; *Educ* Eton, Gonville and Caius Coll Cambridge (BA); *m* 30 June 1979, Teresa Mary (Tsa), da of Maj-Gen Reginald Henry Whitworth, CB, CBE, *qv*; 1 s (Jonathan b 27 Oct 1989), 2 da (Susannah b 28 June 1984, Lara b 28 April 1986); *Career* ptnr Grieveson Grant & Co 1980–86; dir: Kleinwort Benson Limited 1986–, Kleinwort Benson Securities 1988–; fndr: Palmer Milburn Beagles 1971, Berks & Bucks Draghounds 1974; memb London Stock Exchange 1980; *Recreations* wolves, beagling, draghunting, wildlife photography; *Clubs* Groucho; *Style—* Roger Palmer, Esq; ✉ Kleinwort Benson Group plc, 20 Fenchurch Street, London EC3P 3DB (☎ 0171 623 8000)

PALMER, Prof Stuart Beaumont; s of Frank Beaumont Palmer (d 1990), and Florence Beryl, *née* Wilkinson (d 1995); *b* 6 May 1943; *Educ* Ilkeston GS, Univ of Sheffield (BSc, PhD, DSc); *m* 1966, Susan Mary, da of Arthur Clay; 2 s (Richard Stuart b 30 May 1967, Anthony John b 7 May 1969), 1 da (Katherine Mary b 20 Dec 1993); *Career* reader in applied physics Univ of Hull 1967–87; Univ of Warwick: prof of experimental physics 1987–, chm Physics Dept 1989–, pro-vice-chllr 1995–; visiting prof: Univ of Grenoble 1982–83, Queen's Univ Ontario Canada 1986; ed Jl of Physics D: Applied Physics, ed-in-chief Nondestructive Testing and Evaluation (jl); FInstP 1978, FInstNDT 1982, FIEE 1992, CEng 1992; *Publications* Advanced University Physics (with M S Rogalski, 1995), Encyclopaedia Britannica (ed Physics section, 1968–89); also author of over 200 research papers; *Recreations* tennis, sailing, music; *Clubs* Hull Sailing; *Style—* Prof Stuart Palmer; ✉ Max Gate, Forrest Road, Kenilworth, West Midlands CV8 1LT; Department of Physics, University of Warwick, Coventry, West Midlands CV4 7AL (☎ 01203 523399, fax 01203 692016, e-mail phsaz@csv.warwick.ac.uk)

PALMER, Thomas Joseph (Joe); CBE (1994); *b* 11 Sept 1931; *Educ* Univ of Cambridge (MA); *Career* Legal and General plc: asst gen mangr planning 1969–72, gen mangr admin 1972–78, gen mangr international 1978–83, gp chief exec 1984–91; chm: Assoc of British Insurers 1989–91, Personal Investmt Authy (PIA) 1993–; non-exec dir: National Power plc 1991–, ProShare Ltd, Springman Tipper Campbell Partnership Ltd (chm), Halifax Building Society 1991–93, Securities and Investments Bd 1991–93, Investors' Compensation Scheme 1992–93, Sedgwick Group plc 1992–93 (now chm Pension Scheme Tstees); chm London Business Sch Assoc 1974–78, pres Insurance Inst of London 1982–83, memb Women's Econ Devpt Target Team Business in the Community 1988–91, sometime memb Hansard Soc Cmmns on Women at the Top and the Legislative System, chm Guildford WEA, govr King's Sch Bruton; hon fell London Business Sch; Liveryman Worshipful Co of Insurers; CIMgt; *Style—* Joe Palmer, Esq, CBE; ✉ The Personal Investment Authority, 1 Canada Square, Canary Wharf, London E14 5AZ (☎ 0171 538 8860, fax 0171 418 9300)

PALMER, Maj-Gen Tony Brian; CB (1984); s of Sidney Bernard Palmer, and Ann, *née* Watkins; *b* 5 Nov 1930; *Educ* Luton Technol Coll, Gen Motors Inst of Technol (USA); *m* 1953, Hazel Doris Robinson; 2 s; *Career* cmmnd REME 1954, held various cmd and staff appts 1954–74, head of Tech Intelligence (Army) 1974–76, dir Orgn and Trg 1977–79, Cdr Arborfield Garrison 1979–82, dir gen of Electrical and Mech Engrg (Army) 1983–86 (conslt 1986–92), ret; Col Cmdt REME 1985–91; chm Army Benevolent Fund Somerset 1988–; CEng, FIMechE, MIMgt; *Recreations* gardening, history; *Style—* Maj-Gen T B Palmer, CB; ✉ c/o Barclays Bank, Sunningdale Branch, PO Box 631, Ascot, Berks

PALMER, (Ann) Veronica Margaret; OBE (1993, MBE 1977); da of late Luke Murray, of Stone Hall, Trim, Co Meath, Ireland, and Mary, *née* Neville; *b* 20 March 1940; *Educ* Convent of Mercy Trim; *m* Barrie Palmer, s of Arthur Alfred and Dorothy Palmer; 3 da (Judith, Susan, Linda); *Career* student teacher 1958–61; RAF 1961–78, ret as Sqdn Ldr 1978; Parly sec Brewers' Soc 1981–88, Director General Confederation of Passenger Transport UK 1989–; FRSA 1993, FCIT 1993; *Recreations* hill walking, reading, theatre and horse racing; *Clubs* RAF; *Style—* Mrs Veronica Palmer, OBE; ✉ Confederation of Passenger Transport UK, Imperial House, 15–19 Kingsway, London WC2B 6UN (☎ 0171 240 3131, fax 0171 240 6565)

PALMER, William Alexander; CBE (1983), DL (Berks 1992); s of Reginald Howard Reed Palmer, MC, DL (d 1970), of Hurst Grove, nr Reading, Berks, and Lena Florence, *née* Cobham (d 1981); *b* 21 June 1925; *Educ* Eton; *m* 1949, Cherry Ann, da of late Arthur Gibbs (d 1945), of Sheffield Terrace, London; 2 s, 2 da; *Career* serv Grenadier Gds 1943–47, Capt, serv NW Europe and Palestine; dir Huntley & Palmers Ltd 1951 (chm 1980–83), dir Huntley & Palmers Foods plc 1971–83, chm Huntley Boorne & Stevens Ltd until 1983; pres: Flour Milling and Baking Res Assoc 1971–84, Royal Warrant Holders' Assoc 1976–77; chm Cake & Biscuit Alliance 1980–83; High Sheriff of Berks 1974–75; vice pres Univ of Reading 1995– (treas 1982–95); govr King Edward's Sch Whitley; *Recreations* shooting, tennis, gardening; *Clubs* Cavalry and Guards'; *Style—* William Palmer, Esq, CBE, DL; ✉ Bussock Wood, Snelsmore Common, nr Newbury, Berks RG14 3BT (☎ 01635 248203); Latheronwheel House, Caithness KW5 6DW (☎ 01593 741206)

PALMER-TOMKINSON, Charles Anthony; s of James A Palmer-Tomkinson (d 1952), and Doris, *née* Friedrich; *b* 4 July 1940; *Educ* Eton, Cirencester Agric Coll; *m* 1966, Patricia Mary, da of Ivan Dawson; 1 s (James b 15 Nov 1968), 2 da (Santa b 2 Feb 1970, Tara b 23 Dec 1971); *Career* farmer; High Sheriff for Co of Hampshire 1994–; memb Ski Club of Great Britain; memb Br Olympic Ski team (Innsbruck) 1964; *Recreations* skiing, mountains, shooting, stalking deer, fishing, tennis, golf, squash, racquets; *Clubs* Marks, Swinley Forest Golf, All England Tennis; *Style—* Charles Palmer-Tomkinson, Esq; ✉ Dummer Grange, Basingstoke, Hants RG25 2AT (☎ 01256 389331, fax 01256 389676, car 0860 253821)

PALUMBO, Baron (Life Peer UK 1991), of Walbrook in the City of London; Peter Garth Palumbo; s of late Rudolph Palumbo and Elsie Palumbo; *b* 20 July 1935; *Educ* Eton, Worcester Coll Oxford (MA); *m* 1, 1959, Denia (d 1986), da of late Maj Lionel Wigram; 1 s (Hon James Rudolph b 1963), 2 da (Hon Annabella Jane (Hon Mrs Adams) b 1961, Hon Laura Elizabeth (Hon Mrs Tikkoo) b 1967); m 2, 1986, Hayat, er da of late Kamel Morowa; 1 s (Hon Philip Rudolph b 1992), 2 da (Hon Petra Louise b 1989, Hon Lana Rose b 1991); *Career* chm: Tate Gallery Fndn 1986–87, Painshill Park Tst Appeal 1986–96, Arts Cncl of GB 1989–94, Serpentine Gallery 1994–; tstee: Mies van der Rohe Archive 1977–, Tate Gallery 1978–85, Whitechapel Art Gallery Fndn 1981–87, Natural History Museum 1994–, Design Museum 1995–; tstee and hon treas Writers' and Scholars' Educnl Tst 1984–; govr: LSE 1976–94, Royal Shakespeare Theatre 1995–; memb Cncl Royal Albert Hall 1995–; chllr Univ of Portsmouth 1992–; Hon DLitt Univ of Portsmouth 1993; Hon FRIBA, Hon FFB 1994, Hon FIStructE 1994; Nat Order of the Southern Cross Federal Republic of Brazil 1993; *Recreations* music, travel, gardening, reading; *Clubs* White's, Pratt's, Athenaeum, Knickerbocker; *Style—* The Lord Palumbo; ✉ Bagnor Manor, Bagnor, Newbury, Berks RG16 8AG (☎ 01635 40930)

PAMPLIN, Terence Michael; s of Leslie Cecil Pamplin, and Edith Mary, *née* Hayes; *b* 30 May 1941; *Educ* Middx Poly (BA), Hatfield Mgmnt Sch (DMS); *m* 15 March 1969, Elizabeth Ann, da of Richard Webb; 2 da (Iona b 1971, Kim b 1971); *Career* dir Arnold Dolmetsch Ltd 1973–77; head Dept of Music Technol Sir John Cass Faculty City of London Poly 1983–93 (joined 1977); London Guildhall Univ: faculty mktg mangr 1993–, reader in musical instrument technol 1996–; dir: Early Musical Instrument Makers' Assoc (former pres), Dolmetsch Fndn; fndr Nonsuch Guitar Soc (former chm); memb City & Guilds of London Inst, fndr chm Baryton Soc; Liveryman and memb Ct of Assts Worshipful Co of Musicians; MIOA, MIMgt, LRAM, LTCL, FIMIT (former pres), FRSA; *Recreations* playing viol and baryton, viol consorts and baroque trio sonatas, hill walking; *Clubs* City Livery; *Style—* Terence M Pamplin, Esq; ✉ Little Critchmere, Manor Crescent, Haslemere, Surrey GU27 1PB (☎ 01428 651158); Department of Communications and Music Technology, Sir John Cass Faculty, London Guildhall University, 41 Commercial Road, London E1 1LA (☎ 0171 320 1845, fax 0171 320 3114)

PANAYI, Prof Gabriel Stavros; s of Stavros Panayi, of Cyprus, and Maria, *née* Tarsides; *b* 9 Nov 1940; *Educ* Royal GS Lancaster, Gonville and Caius Coll Cambridge (Sir Lionel Whitby Medal), St Mary's Hosp Med Sch London (ScD, MD, FRCP, Max-Bonn Pathology Medal); *m* 11 March 1973, Alexandra, da of Alexander Jourrou; 2 s (Stavros b 5 July 1977, Alexander b 8 Feb 1982); *Career* house physician Queen Elizabeth Hosp Welwyn Garden City 1965–66, house surgn St Mary's Hosp London 1966, sr house offr in medicine Gen Hosp Nottingham 1966, sr house offr in pathology Central Middx Hosp London 1967, jr res fell MRC St Mary's and Kennedy Inst of Rheumatology London 1967–69, clinical res fell Northern Gen Hosp Edinburgh 1970–73; UMDS Guy's and St Thomas's Hosps: Arthritis and Rheumatism Cncl (ARC) lectr 1973–76, ARC sr lectr

1976–80, ARC prof of rheumatology 1980–; RSM: former sec Exec Ctee Section for Medicine, Experimental Medicine and Therapeutics, pres Section for Clinical Immunology and Allergy; former memb Exec Ctee Heberden Soc, memb Exec Ctee Br Soc of Rheumatology; Kave Berglund lectr Univ of Lund, Heberden orator BSR; memb: BSI, BSR, RSM, AASI, American Coll of Rheumatology; *Books* Annual Research Review of Rheumatoid Arthritis (1977–81), Immunopathogenesis of Rheumatoid Arthritis (1979), Essential Rheumatology for Nurses and Therapists (1980), Scientific Basis of Rheumatology (1982), Seronegative Spondyloarthropathies Clinics in Rheumatic Diseases (1985), Immunogenetics (1985); *Recreations* photography, painting, reading; *Style—* Prof Gabriel Panayi; ✉ Rheumatology Unit, Division of Medicine, United Medical and Dental Schools of Guy's and St Thomas' Hosps, St Thomas's St, London SE1 9RT (☎ 0171 955 4394, fax 0171 407 5134)

PANAYIOTOU, Panos; *b* 1953; *Educ* BSc (1st Class Hons), Dip Arch; *m* 1973 Svanhvit Olafsdottir; 1 da (Astria Lydia b 1985); *Career* architect; Scott Brownrigg & Turner Ltd: joined 1982, dir 1990, memb Bd of Dirs 1993, currently design dir; work incl: Lulu Leisure Island (Abu Dhabi), designs and implementation for regurbishment of Berkeley Square House (London) 1981, design and implementation 7 Dials residential devpt (Fairfield Court Covent Garden) 1988, designs for Digital's Southern Logistics Centre (Reading) 1988, design and implementation for offices and residential devpt Orange Street (London) 1989, design and implementation Jardin House (Crutched Friars, City of London), design and implementation BP Engineering HQ (Uxbridge), concept design BBC HQ (White City), masterplanning and design concept Camden Goods Yard, design proposals and implementation of office devpt Denison House (Victoria London) 1990, masterplan major office and retail park (Athens) 1994; RIBA 1981, ARCUK 1981; *Style—* Panos Panayiotou, Esq; ✉ Design Director, Scott Brownrigg & Turner Ltd, Langton Priory, Portsmouth Road, Guildford, Surrey GU2 5WA (☎ 01483 568686, fax 01483 575830)

PANDE, Dr Shiv Kumar; MBE (1989), JP (Liverpool 1982); *b* Jawad, India; *Educ* HS Bombay, Inter-Sci Jai Hind Coll Church Gate Bombay, Vikram Univ Ujjian (MB BS), Univ of Indore (MS); *Career* hosp appts Indore, Gwalior and Bombay India 1963–70 (lectr in surgery Med Coll Jabalpur 1968–71), SHO A&E Dept Royal Albert Edward Infirmary Wigan 1971; registrar in cardiothoracic surgery: London Chest Hosp 1972, Royal Liverpool Children's, Broadgreen and Fazakerley Hosps Liverpool 1972–74; A&E med asst various Liverpool hosps 1974, clinical med offr Child Health and Family Planning St Helens and Knowsley HA 1974–95, princ in gen practice Liverpool 1976– (trainee 1974–75, locum/ptnr 1975–76); chm int seminars Delhi (Family Planning in India) 1990 and Cairo (Recent Advances in Treatment of AIDS) 1992; memb GMC 1994–; Overseas Doctors Assoc: nat vice chm 1987–93, chm Merseyside and Cheshire Div 1994–96, nat gen sec 1996–; sec (N region) Indo-Br Assoc 1982–; advsr and presenter This is your Right? (Granada TV) 1980–92; memb Advsy Panel: Radio Merseyside 1982–87, BBC North TV 1983–88; interviewed variously for local, nat and int press, radio and TV; fndr memb Inter Faith Merseyside; memb (N Region) BAFTA, memb Med Journalists Assoc/Assoc of Bdcasting; FRIPHH 1988, MFCH 1990; *Recreations* cricket (doctor on duty at One Day Internationals and Test Matches at Lancs CCC since 1984), fundraising for charity; *Style—* Dr Shiv Pande, MBE, JP; ✉ Surgery, 14 North View, Edge Hill, Liverpool L7 8TS (☎ 0151 709 3779, fax 0151 709 6349, mobile 0802 483381)

PANDOR, Dr Shabir Ahmed Gulam; s of Gulam Mahomed Pandor, of Lusaka, Zambia, and Khadija Badat; *b* 1 Jan 1955; *Educ* Epsom Coll, UCL (LDS RCS, BDS), DGDP (UK), DDFHom; *m* 17 Dec 1985, (Maria) Suzy, da of Burghart Ferenc (d 1991), of Budapest, Hungary; 1 da (Aneesa b 21 Jan 1988); *Career* assoc dentist in practice: Chatham Kent 1980–81, Kingsway London 1979–80 and 1981–85; in own surgery Harley St 1985–; memb: BDA 1979, Faculty of Gen Dental Practioners (UK), British Endodontic Soc, British Homeopathic Dental Assoc, Br Med Acupuncture Soc, Int Assoc of Oral Med and Toxicology (IAOMT); *Recreations* golf, complementary med; *Style—* Dr Shabir Pandor; ✉ 44 Harley Street, London W1N 1AD (☎ 0171 580 1076/8702)

PANK, Maj-Gen (John) David Graham; CB (1988); s of Edward Graham Pank (d 1982), of Deddington, Oxon, and Margaret Sheelah, *née* Snowball (d 1989); *b* 2 May 1935; *Educ* Uppingham; *m* 27 July 1963, Julia Letitia, da of Col Michael Black Matheson, OBE, of Prosperous Farm, Hurstbourne Tarrant, Andover; 2 s (John William David b 1965, Edward Michael b 1970), 1 da (Victoria Katharine (Mrs Albemarle Cator) b 1964); *Career* cmmnd KSLI 1958, GSO3 ops HQ 99 Gurkha Bde 1965–66, Bde Maj HQ 24 Bde 1969–71, GSO1 Staff Coll 1973–74, CO 3 Bn LI 1974–76, asst dir def policy MOD 1977–79, cmd 33 Armd Bde 1979–81, RCDS 1982, Brig Inf BAOR 1982–83, cmd LF 1983–85, dir gen personal servs (Army) 1985–88, Col LI 1987–90, dir of infantry 1988–90; chief exec Newbury Racecourse 1990–; dir Racecourse Assoc 1994–; pres: Army Cricket 1987–90, Combined Servs Cricket 1988; *Recreations* racing, watching cricket, fishing; *Clubs* Army and Navy, I Zingari, Free Foresters, Mount, Mounted Infantry; *Style—* Maj-Gen David Pank, CB; ✉ Newbury Racecourse, Newbury, Berkshire RG14 7NZ (☎ 01635 40015)

PANK, Edward Charles; s of Charles Clifford Pank (d 1974), of Norwich, and Marjorie Eira, *née* Bringloe (d 1988); *b* 5 June 1945; *Educ* Framlingham Coll, Trinity Hall Cambridge (MA), St Thomas's Hosp Univ of London (MB BS); *m* 17 Sept 1983, (Judith) Clare, da of Anthony Pethick Sommerville (d 1988), of Minchinhampton; *Career* admitted slr 1969; dir Slater Walker Ltd 1974–76, co slr and sec Exco International plc 1987–; Liveryman Worshipful Co of Apothecaries 1986; MRCS, LRCP; *Style—* Edward Pank, Esq; ✉ Exco International plc, 119 Cannon Street, London EC4N 5AX

PANNETT, Juliet Kathleen; MBE (1993); da of Charles Somers (d 1958), and May Relph, *née* Brice (d 1960); *b* 15 July 1911; *Educ* Harvington Coll Ealing, Wistons Sch Brighton, Brighton Coll of Art; *m* 4 Oct 1938, Maj Maurice Richard Dalton Pannett (d 1980), s of late Richard Dalton Pannett, of London; 1 s (Denis b 7 Sept 1939), 1 da (Liz b 31 May 1947); *Career* portrait painter; official artist Qantas inaugural jet flights 1959 and 1964, special artist Illustrated London News 1957–64, freelance The Times, Daily Telegraph and Radio Times; portraits incl: HM The Queen (for Chartered Insurance Institute) 1989, HM The Queen (cmmnd by HRH The Duke of Edinburgh for Malta's 25th anniversary of independence), HRH The Duke of York and HRH Prince Edward (for HM The Queen), HRH Princess Marina, Lavinia Duchess of Norfolk (for Arundel Castle); London exhibitions: Royal Festival Hall 1957 and 1958, Cooling Gallery 1961, Fine Art Gallery 1969, Brotherton Gallery 1980, Royal Acad, Royal Soc of Portrait Painters, Royal Inst of Painters in Watercolours, Pastel Soc; other exhibitions in New York and Hong Kong; work in permanent collections of: Oxford and Cambridge colls, Maudsley Hosp, St Mary's Hosp, Painters' Hall, Univ of Edinburgh, Lincoln's Inn, Nat Portrait Gallery; Gold Medal Worshipful Co of Painter Stainers (for best exhibition painting) 1995; Freeman: City of London 1960, Worshipful Co of Painter Stainers 1960; FRSA 1960; *Style—* Mrs Juliet Pannett, MBE; ✉ Pound House, Roundstone Lane, Angmering Village, W Sussex BN16 4AL (☎ 01903 784446)

PANNICK, David Philip; QC (1992); s of Maurice Arthur Pannick, of London, and Rita Lois, *née* Cushcat; *b* 7 March 1956; *Educ* Bancroft's Sch Woodford Green, Hertford Coll Oxford (MA, BCL); *m* Denise, da of Maurice Sloam; 2 s (Samuel b 1983, Joel b 1985), 1 da (Shula b 1988); *Career* called to the Bar Gray's Inn 1978, jr counsel to the Crown Common Law 1988–92; fell All Souls Coll Oxford 1978–; *Books* Judges (Oxford Univ Press, 1987), Advocates (Oxford Univ Press, 1992); *Recreations* reading, watching television, theatre; *Style—* David Pannick, Esq, QC; ✉ 2 Hare Court, Ground Floor, Temple, London EC4Y 7BH (☎ 0171 583 1770, fax 0171 583 9269)

PANNONE, Rodger John; s of Cyril John Alfred Pannone (d 1982), and Violet Maud, *née* Weekes (d 1987); *b* 20 April 1943; *Educ* St Brendan's Coll Bristol, Manchester Coll of Law, London Coll of Law; *m* 13 Aug 1966, Patricia Jane, da of William Todd; 2 s (Mark b 24 Oct 1969, Richard b 7 Oct 1971), 1 da (Elizabeth b 19 July 1979); *Career* admitted slr 1969; sr ptnr Pannone & Partners; memb: Lord Chllr's Advsy Ctee on Civil Justice 1985–88; Law Soc: memb Cncl 1978–96, dep vice pres 1991–92, vice pres 1992–93, pres 1993–94; former memb Supreme Ct Rule Ctee; chm Manchester Concert Hall Ltd 1994–, memb Ct Univ of Manchester 1996–; vice pres: Acad of Experts 1992–, Manchester Community Tst 1992–; hon fell Manchester Metropolitan Univ 1994; Hon DLitt Univ of Salford 1993, Hon LLD (hc) Nottingham Trent Univ 1993; FRSA 1993; *Recreations* fell walking, wine and food, travelling; *Clubs* St James's (Manchester), Northern Lawn Tennis; *Style—* Rodger Pannone, Esq; ✉ Pannone and Partners, 123 Deansgate, Manchester M3 2BU (☎ 0161 832 3000, fax 0161 834 2067)

PANTON, Steve; s of John Robert Garner, MR (d 1985), and Frances Mary, *née* Bottomley; *b* 2 Dec 1947; *Educ* City Sch Lincoln; *m* 14 Sept 1968, Sheena Ann Mary, da of Eric Charles Bowler, of Harmston, Lincs; 1 s (James b 1 Sept 1972), 1 da (Lucy b 19 Oct 1974); *Career* prodr BBC Radio Nottingham 1971–77; managing ed: BBC Radio Solent 1987–93 (news ed 1977–81, prog organiser 1981–87), Greater London Radio 1993–; *Recreations* country sports; *Style—* Steve Panton, Esq; ✉ Coaklers, Lords Hill, Shamley Green, Guildford, Surrey GU5 0UZ (☎ 01483 892529); Greater London Radio, 35c Marylebone High Street, London W1A 4LG (☎ 0171 224 2424)

PANTON-LEWIS, Catherine Rita; da of John Panton, MBE, of Larbert, Stirlingshire, Scotland, and Elizabeth Renwick, *née* Seaton; *b* 14 June 1955; *Educ* Larbert HS, Univ of Edinburgh (MA), Thames Valley Univ (Post Graduate Dip in Hospitality Mgmnt); *m* 11 April 1991, Philip Lewis, of Llandybie, Dyfed, S Wales; *Career* golf player; Scot girls champion 1969, Br amateur champion 1976, Scot Sportswomen of the Year 1976, E of Scotland women's champion 1976; memb Br World Cup Amateur Team 1976, Vagliano Team 1977; winner: 1979 Women's Professional Golf Tour Order of Merit, 14 tournaments on the Women's Professional Golfers European Tour incl Portugese Open in 1986 and 1987 and S Women's Open in 1988, United Insurance section Ladies' Barbados Open 1993, Southern England Student Sports Assoc Championships 1994; former ctee memb Women's Professional Golfers' Assoc; exec dir McDonald's WPGA Championship 1996–; memb: PGA, WPGET 1978; *Recreations* scrabble, circuit training, current affairs, cinema, listening to music, horse racing; *Clubs* Glenbervie Golf, Pitlochry Golf, Silloth Golf, S Herts golf; *Style—* Mrs Catherine Panton-Lewis

PANTRIDGE, Prof (James) Francis (Frank); CBE (1978), MC (1942); s of Robert James Pantridge; *b* 3 Oct 1916; *Educ* Queen's Univ Belfast (MB ChB, BAO, MD); *Career* served RAMC 1940–45, RMO 2/Gordons; research fell Univ of Michigan 1948–49, hon prof of cardiology Queen's Univ of Belfast 1971, dir of Regnl Med Cardiology Centre NI 1977–82; pioneer of pre-hosp coronary care, developer of first portable defibrillator; Hon DSc Univ of Ulster 1981, Hon DUniv Open Univ 1981; FRCP 1962, FACC 1967, Hon FRCPI 1970; *Books* The Acute Coronary Attack (1975), An Unquiet Life (1989); *Recreations* fishing; *Clubs* Reform (NI); *Style—* Prof Frank Pantridge, CBE, MC

PAOLOZZI, Prof Sir Eduardo Luigi; kt (1989), CBE (1968); s of Rudolpho Antonio Paolozzi (d 1940), and late Carmella, *née* Rossi; *b* 7 March 1924; *Educ* Edinburgh Sch of Art, Slade Sch of Art; *m* 1951 (m dis 1988); 3 da; *Career* sculptor; tutor in ceramics RCA 1968–90 (visiting prof 1989–), lectr St Martin's Sch of Art 1955–56; prof of: ceramics Fachhochschule Cologne 1977–81, sculpture Akademie der Bildenden Kunste Munich 1981–90 (hon 1991–); maj works incl: fountain for Festival of Britain 1951, sculpture playground for Sir Terence Conran at Wallingford 1973, cast aluminium doors for Hunterian Gallery at Glasgow Univ 1977, cast iron sculpture (Piscator) at Euston Square 1981, mosaics for Tottenham Court Rd Underground station 1984, fountain for Garden Exhibition W Berlin 1984, set design for film Herschel and the Music of the Stars 1985, constructed wood relief in Queen Elizabeth II Conf Centre 1986, 26 bronze elements for Rhinegarten Cologne 1986, bronze self-portrait for 34–36 High Holborn London 1987, bronze sculpture for Kowloon Park Hong Kong 1988, bronze head for Design Museum London 1990, giant bronze hand and foot with stone for Edinburgh 1991, Newton After Blake for new Br Library London 1995; contrib to Spellbound (Hayward Gall) 1996; tstee Nat Portrait Gallery 1988–, HM Sculptor in Ordinary for Scotland 1986; corresponding memb Bayerische Akademie der Schönen Künste 1990; fell UCL 1986, hon fell Royal Incorporation of Architects in Scotland 1991; Hon DLitt: Glasgow 1980, London 1987, Heriot-Watt 1987, Birmingham 1996; Hon Dr RCA 1979, Univ of St Andrew's 1994, Jesus Coll Cambridge 1995; HRSA 1987, RA 1979 (ARA 1979); Cavalieri Ufficiale del Ordine al Merito della Repubblica Italiana 1991; *Awards* Br Critics' Prize 1953, David E Bright Award 1960, Purchase Prize Solomon Guggenheim Museum 1967, Norma and William Copley Fndn Award 1967, first prize Sculpture Carnegie Int Exhibition 1967, Saltire Soc Award 1975 and 1981, first prize Rhinegarten Competition Cologne 1980, Grand Prix d'Honneur Int Print Biennale Yugoslavia 1983, Goethe Medal 1991; *Clubs* Athenaeum; *Style—* Prof Sir Eduardo Paolozzi, CBE, RA; ✉ 107 Dovehouse St, London SW3; Akademie der Bildenden Kunste, Akadmiestrasse 2, 8000 Munchen 4, West Germany

PAPADAKIS, Prof Andreas Constantine; s of Constantine Paul Papadakis (d 1992), of Nicosia, Cyprus, and Natalia Christou (d 1978); *b* 17 June 1938; *Educ* Faraday House (DFH), Imperial Coll London (DIC), Brunel Univ (PhD); *Career* publisher; ed: Architectural Design 1977–92, Art and Design 1985–92; md Academy Group Ltd 1987–92 (imprint Academy Edns, founded 1968); dir Hellenic Centre London 1993–94, chm Hellenic Inst Royal Holloway Univ of London 1994–95 (pres 1995–), visiting prof Faculty of Architecture Univ of Lisbon Portugal, visiting prof History and Classics Depts Royal Holloway 1995–; md Papadakis Publishing 1996–; fndr and jt organiser Academy Forum at the Tate 1987–89, pres Academy Forum RA 1990–92, pres Windsor Hellenic Soc 1994–, fndr and jt organiser Annual Acad Architecture Lecture Royal Acad of Arts 1990–92, curator Theory and Experimentation - An Intellectual Extravaganza (RIBA and Whiteleys of Bayswater) 1992, memb Cncl for Hellenes Abroad 1995– (co-ordinator for educn and religion (Europe)), dir Orthodoxy and the Environment Project 1994–; Archon Protonotarios of the Ecumenical Patriarchate, sec-gen Archons of GB; *Books* edited jointly: Post Modern Design (1989), Deconstruction Omnibus (1989), New Classicism Omnibus (1990), Deconstruction Pocket Guide (1990), Decade of Architectural Design (1991), New Art - An International Survey (1991), The Free Spirit Omnibus Volume (1992); sole ed Theory and Experimentation (1992), Modern Classical Architecture (1996); numerous articles and editorials on architecture, art and the environment incl: Religion, Philosophy and Architecture Venice Biennale (1992), Architecture and City Form (1995), Philosophy and Architecture - A Partnership for the Future? (1996); *Recreations* horseriding, farming; *Clubs* IOD; *Style—* Prof Andreas C Papadakis; ✉ Kilbees Farm, Windsor Forest, Windsor, Berks SL4 2EH (☎ 01344 882040, fax 01344 882041)

PAPPIN, David Frederick; TD (1968); s of Eric Reginald Pappin (d 1979), of Eastbourne, and Evelyn Hope, *née* Pickering (d 1940); *b* 10 March 1935; *Educ* Melville Coll, Univ of Edinburgh (MA); *m* 1, 1958 (m dis 1977), Mary Elizabeth (now Mrs M E Towsey), da of George Trevor Norman Prideaux (d 1986), of Petersfield; 2 da (Amanda Ruth (Mrs Borthwick) b 1964, Belinda Claire b 1970); m 2, 30 Oct 1979, Maureen Grace, da of Malcolm Henry Harper (d 1979); 1 s (James Harper Sutcliffe b 1970 d 1990); *Career* Nat Serv REME 1953–55 (cmmnd 1954), TA REME 1955–73 (Capt 1961); trainee actuary Liverpool & London & Globe Insurance Co Ltd 1952–53 and 1958–61, Res Dept D A Bevan Simpson 1961–64; investment mangr: Minerals Separation Ltd 1964–66, Charterhouse Japhet Ltd 1966–67, Banque Belge Ltd 1967–70; ptnr: J & A Scrimgeour 1970–79, De Zoete & Bevan 1979–86; dir: Barclays de Zoete Wedd (Gilts) Ltd 1986–88, Streets Communications Ltd 1988–91; managing conslt of investmt servs Reeves Brown Assocs Ltd 1991–94, conslt Jardine Reeves Brown 1994–95, ret 1995; formerly chm Cobham Conservation Gp, pres Stoke d'Abernon CC; FFA 1963, AIIMR 1961, MSI 1991; *Recreations* golf, watching cricket and rugby; *Clubs* Gresham (formerly chm), MCC; *Style*— David Pappin, Esq, TD; ✉ Hatchford Farmhouse, Ockham Lane, Hatchford, Surrey KT11 1LS (☎ 01932 863020, fax 01932 868445); Passaro Amarelo, Dunas Douradas, Almancil, Portugal

PARAMOR, Roger Carlton; CBE (1992), QFSM; s of Albert Walter Alexander Paramor, CBE, of Bognor Regis, Sussex, and Marjorie Flora Maud, *née* Carlton; *b* 10 Nov 1938; *Educ* Churchers Coll Petersfield, Univ of Southampton, Warash, Southampton; *m* 30 Dec 1961, Angela Joan, da of Henry Gordon Harris; 1 s (Mark b 13 June 1965), 2 da (Joanna b 8 Dec 1967, Fiona b 1 March 1972); *Career* 2 offr MN 1956–62; fireman London Fire Bde 1962–64, leading fireman W Sussex Fire Bde 1964–66, divnl offr Lancashire Fire Bde 1966–72, dep chief fire offr Portsmouth Fire Bde 1972–73 and W Sussex Fire Bde 1973–76, chief offr Warwickshire Fire Bde 1976–79, chief fire offr Essex Co Fire and Rescue Serv 1979–93; Eastern area govr and voluntary relief skipper Ocean Youth Club, chm Squash Section Fire Servs Sports and Athletics Assoc; Freeman City of London 1986, memb Guild of Fire Fighters 1988; FIFireE 1985 (GIFireE 1966, MIFireE 1967); *Recreations* sailing, squash; *Clubs* West Mersea Sailing; *Style*— Roger Paramor, Esq, CBE, QFSM; ✉ Wendover, 8 Mersea Avenue, West Mersea, Essex CO5 8JL

PARASKEVA, Janet; JP (1993); da of Anthonis Paraskeva, and Doris Amanda, *née* Fowler (d 1986); *b* 26 May 1946; *Educ* Worcester Coll, Open Univ (BA); m (m dis 1988), Alan Richard Derek Hunt; 2 da (Amanda Joanne b 10 Feb 1970, Suzanne Maria b 19 Nov 1971); *Career* science teacher Shenley Court Comp Sch 1967–69, mathematics teacher St Thomas Aquinas GS 1969–71, pt/t Bromsgrove Club for the Mentally Handicapped 1969–71, dir Friday Toys 1970–73, sr youth worker Fillongley Youth Centre 1972–74, pt/t lectr N Warwicks Institute of Education 1973–74, field work co-ordinator Warwickshire Assoc of Youth Clubs 1973–74, projects offr NAYC (now Youth Clubs UK) 1974–78, head Youth Work Unit National Youth Bureau 1978–81, district inspr (Youth and Adult) Inner London Education Authy 1981–83, HMI (Youth and Community) DES 1983–88; dir: National Youth Bureau 1988–90, National Youth Agency 1990–95, Nat Lottery Charities Bd for England 1995–; non-exec dir Fosse Community Health Tst 1992–; Robert Schuman Silver medal for European Unity 1978; various contribs to TES and Educational pubns; *Style*— Ms Janet Paraskeva, JP; ✉ National Charities Lottery Board, 3rd Floor, Reasdon House, 96–98 Regent Road, Leicester LE1 7DZ (☎ 0116 258 7000, fax 0116 255 7398)

PARAVICINI, Dennis Stewart; OBE (1977); s of John Paravicini, JP (d 1961), and Winifred Marian, *née* Stewart-Brown (d 1964); *b* 1 Oct 1930; *Educ* Stowe, Gonville and Caius Coll Cambridge (MA); *m* 1963, Sallie Vivienne, da of Cdr H L Hayes, OBE, RN; 1 s (James b 1976), 2 da (Georgina b 1964, Olivia b 1966 (d 1974)); *Career* Nat Serv Cmmn 5 Royal Inniskilling Dragoon Gds; De La Rue plc: joined 1953, co sec 1980–85, md Royal Mint Servs 1986–94; chm N Hampshire Cons Assoc 1973–76, vice chm Anglo-Swiss Soc 1975–, tstee N Hampshire Med Fund 1978–, CBI London regnl cncllr 1980–86; *Recreations* travelling, sailing; *Clubs* Utd Oxford and Cambridge; *Style*— Dennis Paravicini, Esq, OBE; ✉ Street House, Bramley, Tadley, Hants RG26 5DE (☎ 01256 881283)

PARAVICINI, Nicolas Vincent Somerset; s of Col Vincent Rudolph Paravicini, TD (d 1989), and Elizabeth Mary (Liza) Maugham (now Baroness Glendevon); *b* 19 Oct 1937; *Educ* Eton, RMA Sandhurst; *m* 1, 4 April 1966 (m dis 1986), Mary Ann Parker Bowles; 2 s (Charles b 1968, Derek b 1979), 1 da (Elizabeth Ann b 1970); m 2, 18 Dec 1986 (Susan Rose) Sukie, da of Lt Alan Phipps, RN (ka 1943), and The Hon Lady Maclean; *Career* The Life Gds 1957–69, served Aden, Oman, Cyprus and Malaysia, ret Maj; dir Joseph Sebag & Co 1972–79, chm A Sarasin & Co Ltd 1980–89, chm and chief exec Sarasin Investment Management Ltd 1983, md Sarasin (UK) Ltd 1983–89, conslt Bank Sarasin & Co 1990, chief exec MacIntyre Investments Ltd 1990–92, chief exec Ely Place Investments Ltd 1992–; memb London Stock Exchange 1972–80; Freeman: City of London 1984, Worshipful Co of Bakers 1984; *Recreations* shooting, skiing; *Clubs* White's, Pratt's, Buck's; *Style*— Nicolas Paravicini, Esq; ✉ Glyn Celyn House, Brecon, Powys LD3 0TY (☎ 01874 624836); Ely Place Investments Ltd, 28 Ely Place, London EC1N 6RL (☎ 0171 242 0242, fax 0171 405 4786)

PARBHOO, Santilal Parag; s of Parag Parbhoo (d 1964), of Cape Town, and Jasoda Pemi, *née* Ramjee (d 1961); *b* 16 Jan 1937; *Educ* Livingstone HS Capetown, Univ of Cape Town (MB ChB), Queen's Univ Belfast (PhD); *m* 8 Jan 1969, (Constance) Ann, da of William Joseph Cedric Craig, of Belfast, NI; 2 s (Mark b 20 July 1970, Alan b 18 Feb 1977), 1 da (Kathryn b 1 Feb 1974); *Career* house surgn New Somerset Hosp Cape Town SA 1961, sr house surgn Edendale Hosp Pietermaritzburg 1961–62, tutor and registrar Royal Victoria Hosp Belfast 1964–65 (clinical asst 1962–64); surgical registrar: NI Hosp NI 1965–68, Frenchay Hosp Bristol 1973–74; conslt and sr lectr Royal Free Hosp and Sch London 1974–91 (res fell and lectr 1968–72); conslt: Bristol Myers Oncology UK 1984–86, Hospital of St John and St Elizabeth London 1991–; Royal Free Hosp London: chm Div of Surgery 1987–89, conslt surgn (general and breast) 1991–; hon conslt surgn Bart's London 1988–, chm surgical bd of studies Royal Free Hosp Sch of Med 1984–91; dir: Cancerkin London 1987–, Royal Free Hosp Breast Cancer Appeal; memb: Med Advsy Ctee Women's Nationwide Cancer Control Campaign, Euro Gp of Lymphology (GEL), Gujerati Arya Assoc London; NATO int res travelling fell 1991–92; hon fell: Hong Kong Soc of Surgns, Egyptian Soc of Hepatology 1989 (medal received 1989); fell: Surgical Res Soc, Br Assoc for Surgical Oncology, Assoc of Surgns of GB and I; FRCS 1967, FRCS (Eng); *Books* Bone Metastasis: Monitoring and Treatment (with B A Stoll, 1983); *Recreations* walking, gardening, philately; *Clubs* Consultant Staff (RFH); *Style*— Santilal Parbhoo, Esq; ✉ University Department of Surgery, Royal Free Hospital, Pond St, London NW3 2QG (☎ 0171 794 0500 ext 4651, private sec ☎ 0171 431 3845, fax 0171 431 4528)

PARDOE, Alan Douglas William; QC (1988); s of William Douglas Ronald Pardoe (d 1985), and Grace Irene, *née* Jones (d 1996); *b* 16 Aug 1943; *Educ* Victoria Sch Kurseong India, Oldbury GS, St Catharine's Coll Cambridge (LLB, MA, Winchester reading prize); *m* 1, 1972 (m dis 1976), Mary Ensor; m 2, 1991 (m dis 1994), Catherine Williams; *Career* Hardwicke scholar Lincoln's Inn 1964; lectr in law Univ of Exeter 1965–70, visiting lectr in law Univ of Auckland NZ 1970, lectr in law Univ of Sussex 1970–74; called to the Bar 1971, began practice at the Bar 1973, recorder of Crown Ct 1990–; *Recreations* mountain walking, cooking; *Clubs* Travellers'; *Style*— Alan Pardoe, Esq, QC; ✉ Devereux Chambers, Devereux Court, Temple, London WC2R 3JJ (☎ 0171 353 7534, fax 0171 353 1724)

PARDY, Bruce James; s of William Dryden Cribb Pardy (d 1979), and Mavis Irene Denize (d 1984); *b* 25 Nov 1939; *Educ* St Peter's Sch Cambridge NZ, Christ's Coll Christchurch NZ, Otago Univ NZ (MB BMedSc, ChM); *m* 26 April 1980, Kathleen Margaret, da of Leslie George Henry Townsend Robertson; 1 s (Robert James Dryden b 1985), 1 da (Caroline Anne b 1983); *Career* conslt vascular and gen surgn Newham Gen Hosp and St Andrew's Hosp London, late sr registrar in surgery St Mary's Hosp London; memb: Vascular Soc of GB & I, Surgical Res Soc, Assoc of Surgns UK and I, RSM; med advsr The Raynaud's Assoc; FRACS, FRCS; *Recreations* sailing, swimming, tennis; *Style*— Bruce Pardy, Esq; ✉ 49 Abingdon Villas, Kensington, London W8 6XA; 144 Harley St, London W1N 1AH (☎ 0171 935 0023)

PAREKH, Prof Bhikhu Chhotalal; s of Chhotalal Ranchhoddas Parekh, of Washington DC, USA, and Gajaraben Parekh; *b* 4 Jan 1935; *Educ* HDS HS India, Univ of Bombay (BA, MA), Univ of London (PhD); *m* 14 April 1959, Pramila, da of Kanaiyalal Keshavlal Dalal, of Baroda, India; 3 s; *Career* tutor LSE 1962–63, lectr Univ of Glasgow 1963–64; Univ of Hull: successively lectr, sr lectr then reader 1964–82, prof of politics 1982–; vice chllr Univ of Baroda 1981–84 (lectr 1957–59); visiting prof: Univ of Br Columbia 1967–68, Concordia Univ Montreal 1974–75, McGill Univ Montreal 1976–77; visiting prof Harvard Univ 1996; adjunct fell Centre for the Study of Developing Socs Delhi India 1990–; active in local cncl for racial equality, dep chm Cmmn for Racial Equality 1985–90; tstee: Runnymede Tst 1986–, Inst for Public Policy Res 1988–, Gandhi Fndn 1988–, Inst of Cwlth Studies 1991–; chm Nat Survey of the Ethnic Minorities in Britain Advsy Ctee 1993–; memb: Nat Cmmn on Equal Opportunities CVCP 1994–, Advsy Ctee Ofsted; Asian of the Year 1991; FRSA 1990; *Books* incl: Hannah Arendt (1981), Karl Marx's Theory of Ideology (1982), Contemporary Political Thinkers (1982), Gandhi's Political Philosophy (1989), Colonialism, Tradition and Reform (1989), Critical Assessments of Jeremy Bentham (4 Vols, 1993); *Recreations* reading, walking, music; *Style*— Prof Bhikhu Parekh; ✉ 211 Victoria Ave, Hull HU5 3EF (☎ 01482 345530); Deparment of Politics, University of Hull, Hull HU6 7RX (☎ and fax 01482 466208)

PARFECT, Maj John Herbert; MBE (1957); s of George Frederick Parfect (d 1970), and Hedwig, *née* Jordi (d 1948); *b* 9 April 1924; *Educ* Brentwood Sch, Univ of Manchester, Columbia Univ NY; *m* 14 Aug 1948, (Mercia) Heather, da of Brig John Lawrence Maxwell, CBE, MC (d 1972), 1 s (Jeremy John b 1963), 4 da (Penelope b 1951, Wendy b 1952, Jane b 1954, Louise b 1958); *Career* WWII cmmnd RE serv Sicily and Italy 1943; serv: Bengal Sappers and Miners India 1945–47, Gurkha Engrs Malaya 1948–50, 6 Armd Div Engrs BAOR 1951–53, Staff Coll Camberley 1954, GSO2 Northern Cmd York 1955–57, OC 40 Field Sqdn Cyprus 1957–58, ret 1958; personnel mangr ICI 1958–81, self employed fin planning conslt Allied Dunbar 1981–90; N Yorks CC 1977–93, chm N Yorks Police Authy 1986–93; FIPM; *Recreations* beagling, military history, investments; *Style*— Maj John Parfect, MBE; ✉ Colville Hall, Coxwold, York YO6 4AA (☎ 01347 868305)

PARFITT, Andrew (Andy); *b* 24 Sept 1958; *Educ* Bristol Old Vic Theatre Sch; *m* Laura; *Career* studio mangr BBC then prodr/presenter BFBS; BBC: rejoined as educn prodr, successively features prodr Radio 4, asst ed Radio 5, chief asst to controller of Radio 1, ed commissioning and planning Radio 1, managing ed Radio 1 1994–96, dep controller Radio 1 1996–; winner Sony Creative Award; *Style*— Andy Parfitt, Esq; ✉ BBC Radio 1, Yalding House, London W1A 1AA (☎ 0171 765 2147)

PARFITT, Judy Catherine Clare; da of Laurence Hamilton Parfitt (d 1973), and Catherine Coulton; *Educ* Notre Dame Convent, RADA; *m* 25 Aug 1963, Anthony Francis Steedman, s of Baron Anthony Ward; 1 s (David Lawrence b 29 Sept 1964); *Career* actress; *Theatre* incl: D H Lawrence trilogy (Royal Court), Annie in A Hotel in Amsterdam 1968, Queen Mary in Vivat! Vivat! Regina! (Piccadilly) 1970, Family Dance (Criterion), Cleopatra (Young Vic), Duchess of Malfi (Royal Court), Ranyevskya in The Cherry Orchard (Riverside Studios) 1978, Eleanor in Passion Play (Wyndham's) 1980, A Dream of People (RSC), Molière's The Sisterhood and Valentine's Day, Mrs Birling in An Inspector Calls (RNT prodn at Aldwych) 1993; *Television* incl: Villette, The Edwardians 1973, Shoulder to Shoulder, Malice Aforethought 1979, Pride and Prejudice, Death of a Princess, Secret Orchards, Jewel in the Crown 1984 (BAFTA Best Actress nomination), The Charmer 1987, The Charmings (USA series), Hilda Spearpoint in The Gravy Train 1989 and The Gravy Train Goes East 1992, The Borrowers (BBC), Lifeboat (BBC), Inspector Alleyn (BBC), September (mini-series), Harriet Collard in The Blackheath Poisonings (TV film), Loving (Screen Two), Heavy Weather (BBC), The Final Act (Granada), Element of Doubt; *Films* incl: Gertrude in Hamlet 1969, Madam Sarti in Galileo 1974, Getting it Right, Diamond Skulls, Maurice 1986, Vera Donovan in Dolores Claiborne, Lady Mount-Temple in Wilde, The Ruby Wing; *Recreations* needlepoint, gardening, antiques, talking; *Style*— Miss Judy Parfitt; ✉ c/o Conway van Gelder Robinson Ltd, 18–21 Jermyn Street, London SW1Y 6HP (☎ 0171 287 0077, fax 0171 287 1940)

PARFITT, Richard John (Rick); s of Richard Parfitt (d 1988), of Woking, and Lillian Rose, *née* Miller; *b* 12 Oct 1948; *Educ* Highlands County Secdy Woking Surrey; *m* 1, 1972, Marietta, da of Willie Böker; 1 s (Richard b 18 Oct 1974), 1 da (Heidi); m 2, Patricia, da of Stanley Beeden; 1 s (Harrison b 20 June 1989); *Career* Status Quo (originally known as the Spectres, joined 1966): co-fndr 1967, continual world touring 1967–, Gold and Silver discs every year since 1971; played at: launch of Prince's Tst 1983, Live Aid 1985, Knebworth 1990, Prince's Trust and Help a London Child charity performance Royal Albert Hall 1994; *Awards* Silver Clef award 1981, Ivor Novello award (for outstanding servs to music indust) 1984, World Music award Monaco 1991, BRIT award (for outstanding servs to music) 1991; ltd edn character jugs issued by Royal Doulton 1993; *Books* Just for the Record (autobiography, 1993); *Recreations* collecting miniature rare Porsches, boating; *Style*— Rick Parfitt, Esq; ✉ Handle Artists Management, 1 Albion Place, Galena Rd, Hammersmith, London W6 0QT (☎ 0181 846 9111)

PARGETER, Rt Rev Philip; s of Philip William Henry Pargeter, and Ellen, *née* Beards; *b* 13 June 1933; *Educ* St Bede's Coll Manchester, Oscott Coll Sutton Coldfield; *Career* ordained RC priest 1959, teacher and housemaster Cotton Coll North Staffs 1959–84 (rector 1983–85), admin St Chad's Cathedral Birmingham 1985–90 (canon 1986), aux bishop of Birmingham and titular bishop of Valentiniana 1989–, provost Birmingham Metropolitan Cathedral Chapter 1991; chm: Ctee for Community Relations RC Bishops Conf, Father Hudson's Soc (Coleshill Homes); *Recreations* listening to serious music, reading, walking; *Style*— The Rt Rev Philip Pargeter; ✉ Grove House, 90 College Rd, Sutton Coldfield, West Midlands B73 5AH (☎ 0121 354 4363)

PARIKH, Anu; da of Debesh Chandra Das, of Calcutta, India, and late Kamala, *née* Nag; *b* 16 March 1947; *Educ* Convent of Jesus and Mary New Delhi, Univ of Delhi (BA), King's Coll London (LLB); *m* 15 Feb 1972, Bharat Amritlal Parikh, s of Amritlal Vithaldas Parikh, of Calcutta, India; *Career* formerly practising barr Middle Temple, now slr; dir Grosvenor House Trading Ltd; formerly sub ed Atkins Court Forms for Butterworths Ltd; pt/t chm Social Security Appeals Tbnl; memb: Jt Cncl of Welfare for Immigrants, Slrs' Family Law Assoc, Law Soc; *Recreations* reading, gardening, theatres; *Style*— Mrs Anu Parikh; ✉ 179 Coombe Lane, London SW20 0RG (☎ 0181 947 4544, fax 0181 947 4644); Grosvenor House Trading Ltd, Dalton House, Windsor Avenue, London SW19 2RR

PARIS, Andrew Martin Ingledew; s of Vernon Patrick Paris, of Sussex, and Heather Constance Ingledew, *née* Dear; *b* 27 Nov 1940; *Educ* London Hosp Med Coll Univ of London (MB BS); *m* 1, 16 May 1964 (m dis), Anne Cardwell, da of Col Alleyn Cardwell Moore (d 1980), of NI; 1 da (Claire Elizabeth Ingledew Paris b 10 April 1966); m 2, 24 Dec 1975, Susan Philippa da of Perys Goodwin Jenkins (d 1969), of London; *Career* conslt urological surgn The Royal London Hosp 1976–, conslt urological surgn St Bartholomew's Hosp 1994–; hon conslt surgn The Italian Hosp 1979–90; hon surgn St

John Ambulance Air Wing (fndr memb), OStJ 1985; Liveryman Worshipful Soc of Apothecaries 1967 (memb Ct of Assts), Freeman City of London 1984; FRCS 1971, FRSM (vice pres section of urology 1988, 1989); *Recreations* sailing, skiing; *Clubs* Aldeburgh Yacht; *Style—* Andrew Paris, Esq; ✉ 121 Harley St, London W1N 1DM (☎ 0171 486 6324, fax 0171 935 5333)

PARIS, Judith; da of Thomas Henry Franklin (d 1990), of Cirencester, Glos, and Doris Mary, *née* Baker; *b* 7 June 1944; *Educ* Royal Ballet Sch; *m* 1 (m dis 1970), James Walters; m 2, 28 April 1977, John Kyle, s of Maj James Murphy (d 1971); 1 s (Benedict Kyle b 12 Dec 1979), 1 da (Tallis Kyle b 6 Sept 1986); *Career* actress: *Theatre* Broadway debut in Medea 1994; NT various periods 1974–86 incl: Juno in the Tempest, Ena Muller in Spring Awakening, Dottie in Jumpers, Joy Ferrett in Jean Seberg, Muriel in Animal Farm, Valoire in A Little Hotel on The Side; West End incl: Lady Fidget in Lust (Haymarket), Grace Farrell in Annie (Victoria), Slange in Ambassador (Her Majesty's), Nell in The Match Girls (Globe); other credits incl: Titania in A Midsummer Night's Dream (New Shakespeare Co), Celia in As you Like It (RSC (Best Actress nomination 1978)), Isabella in The White Devil (Bristol Old Vic); *Television* numerous roles incl: Irena in The Camomile Lawn (Zed Prodns), Mrs Somers in Lovejoy (Witzend Prodns), Celestia in 2.4 Children (BBC), Florence Allott in Touch of Frost (BBC); *Films* for Ken Russell incl: Sister Agnes in The Devils, Virginia Woolf in Savage Messiah, Miss Harby in The Rainbow, Madame Dreyfus in Prisoners of Honor, Mrs Marshall in Lady Chatterley; other credits incl: The Raging Moon, Pleasure; *Recreations* music, painting, rambling; *Style—* Miss Judith Paris; ✉ c/o David Daly Associates, Personal Management, 68 Old Brompton Road, London SW7 3LQ (☎ 0171 581 0121, fax 0171 589 2922)

PARISH, *see also:* Woodbine Parish

PARK, Andrew Edward Wilson; QC (1978), QC (NI, 1992); s of late Dennis Edward Park; *b* 27 Jan 1939; *Educ* Leeds GS, Univ Coll Oxford; *m* 1962, Ann Margaret Woodhead; 2 s (and 1 s decd), 1 da; *Career* called to the Bar Lincoln's Inn 1964, in practice at Revenue Bar 1965–, bencher 1986, recorder of the Crown Ct 1989–95; chm: Taxation and Retirement Benefits Ctee of the Bar Cncl 1978–82, Revenue Bar Assoc 1987–92; treas Senate of the Inns of Court and Bar 1982–85; *Style—* Andrew Park, Esq, QC; ✉ Gray's Inn Chambers, Gray's Inn, London WC1R 5JA (☎ 0171 242 2642)

PARK, Dr Gilbert Richard; TD (1985); *b* 17 May 1950; *Educ* Univ of Edinburgh (MB ChB, BSc, MD); *Career* Dept of Orthopaedic Surgery Royal Infirmary Edinburgh 1974, Dept of Med Bangor Gen Hosp 1974; Dept of Anaesthesia: Royal Infirmary Edinburgh 1975–80, Univ of Edinburgh 1980–83; dir of intensive care and conslt in anaesthesia Addenbrooke's Hosp Cambridge; TA: offr cadet 1968–74, Lt 1974–75, Capt 1975–80, Maj 1980–93; Hon MA Cambridge 1987; FFARCS 1978; *Books* Intensive Care: A Handbook (1988), The Management of Acute Pain (1991), Sedation and Analgesia (1993), Anaesthesia and Intensive Care for Patients with Liver Disease (1994), Sedation and Analgesia in the Critically Ill (1995), A Colour Atlas of Critical and Intensive Care (1995), Fighting for Life (1996), Tricks and Traps (1996), How to prescribe drugs in the critically ill (1996); *Recreations* writing, photography, sailing, cycling; *Style—* Dr G Park; ✉ The John Farman Intensive Care Unit, Addenbrooke's Hosp, Cambridge CB2 2QQ (☎ 01223 217433, fax 01223 217898)

PARK, (James) Graham; CBE; s of James Park, OBE, JP (d 1959), of Salford, and Joan Clay, *née* Sharp (d 1987); *b* 27 April 1941; *Educ* Malvern, Univ of Manchester (LLB); *m* 28 June 1969, Susan, da of Dr Charles Sydney Douglas Don (d 1973), of Manchester; 1 s (James b 1973); *Career* slr, ptnr H L F Berry & Co; Parly candidate (C) 1974 and 1979, chm Altrincham Sale Constituency Cons Assoc 1983–87, pres NW Area Cons 1995– (chm 1992–95), vice pres Nat Union Cons Pty 1996–; memb: Ct Univ of Salford 1987–, Parole Bd 1996–; *Recreations* cricket, motor racing; *Style—* Graham Park, Esq, CBE; ✉ HLF Berry & Co, Lancaster Buildings, 77 Deansgate, Manchester M3 2BZ (☎ 0161 834 0548)

PARK, Hon Sir Hugh Eames; kt (1965); s of late William Robert Park; *b* 24 April 1910; *Educ* Blundell's, Sidney Sussex Coll Cambridge; *m* 1938, Beryl Josephine, da of late Joseph Coombe; 3 da; *Career* called to the Bar Middle Temple 1936, QC 1960, bencher 1965, presiding judge Western Circuit 1970–75, judge of the High Ct of Justice Queen's Bench Div 1973–85 (Family Div 1965–73); hon fell Sidney Sussex Cambridge 1968; Hon LLD Univ of Exeter 1984; *Style—* Hon Sir Hugh Park; ✉ 34 Ordnance Hill, St John's Wood, London NW8 (☎ 0171 586 0417); Gorran Haven, Cornwall (☎ 01726 842333)

PARK, Ian Grahame; CBE (1995); s of William Park (d 1982), and Christina Wilson, *née* Scott; *b* 15 May 1935; *Educ* Lancaster Royal GS, Queens' Coll Cambridge; *m* 1965, Anne, da of Edward Turner (d 1979); 1 s (Adam); *Career* Nat Serv cmmnd Manchester Regt 1954–56; chm Northcliffe Newspapers Group (md 1982–95), dir Associated Newspapers Holdings 1983–95, dir Daily Mail and General Trust 1994–; md and ed in chief Liverpool Daily Post and Echo 1972–82, asst literary ed Sunday Times 1960–63; dir: Reuters 1978–82 and 1988–94, Press Assoc 1978–83 (chm 1978–79 and 1979–80); pres Newspaper Soc 1980–81; *Clubs* Reform; *Style—* Ian Park, Esq, CBE; ✉ Northcliffe Newspapers Group, 31 John Street, London WC1 (☎ 0171 400 1100)

PARK, (Ian) Michael Scott; CBE (1982); s of Ian Macpherson Park (d 1960), of Aberdeen, and Winifred Margaret, *née* Scott; *b* 7 April 1938; *Educ* Aberdeen GS, Univ of Aberdeen (MA, LLB); *m* 1964, Elizabeth Mary Lamberton, da of Alexander Marshall Struthers, OBE (d 1964), of Edinburgh; 2 s (Sandy b 1965 d 1996, William b 1972); *Career* slr; ptnr Paull & Williamsons Advocates Aberdeen 1964–91 (conslt 1991–); memb: Soc of Advocates Aberdeen 1962– (treas 1991–92, pres 1992–93), Cncl Law Soc of Scotland 1974–84 (vice pres 1979–80, pres 1980–81), Criminal Injuries Compensation Bd 1983–; frequent broadcaster on legal topics; *Recreations* golf, gardening, travel; *Clubs* New (Edinburgh); *Style—* Michael Park, Esq, CBE; ✉ Beechwood, 46 Rubislaw Den, South Aberdeen AB2 6AX (☎ 01224 313799); Paull & Williamsons Advocates, Investment House, 6 Union Row, Aberdeen AB9 8DQ (☎ 01224 621621)

PARK, Nicholas (Nick); *b* 1958; *Educ* Sheffield Sch of Art, National Film and Television Sch; *Career* producer/director of animated films; ptnr Aardman Animations (joined 1985); work incl: Archie's Concrete Nightmare (first bdcast BBC 1975), A Grand Day Out (BBC2 1989, BAFTA Best Animated Short 1990, Academy Award (Oscar) nomination 1990), Creature Comforts (Channel 4 1990, winner Academy Award for Best Animated Short 1990) and subsequent adaptation for series of 13 Heat Electric commercials (winners of various D&AD and other advtg industry awards), The Wrong Trousers (BBC2 1993, winner Academy Award for Best Animated Short and BAFTA Prodn Award for Best Short Animated Film 1994), A Close Shave (1995, BAFTA for Best Animated Film 1995, Emmy for Best Popular Arts Programme 1996, four British Animation Awards 1996, Academy Award (Oscar) 1996); *Style—* Nick Park, Esq; ✉ Aardman Animations Ltd, Gas Ferry Road, Bristol BS1 6UN (☎ 0117 922 7227, fax 0117 922 7225)

PARK, Richard Francis Hanbury; s of Jonathan Cyril Park, OBE (d 1979), and Frances Hanbury, *née* Dodds (d 1984); *b* 29 March 1933; *Educ* Winchester, Trinity Coll Cambridge (MA, LLM); *m* 3 July 1959, Patricia Zillah, da of Norman Louis Forrest (d 1988); of Barlaston, Stoke-on-Trent; 2 da (Caroline b 1963, Elizabeth b 1965); *Career* 1 Royal Dragoons 1951–53, Lanarkshire Yeo TA 1953–58; admitted slr 1959; slr with Blackett Hart and Pratt Darlington, ret 1994; clerk to Gen Cmmrs of Income Tax: Darlington, Bishop Auckland, Northallerton; chm: Social Security Appeals Tbnl 1984–, Disability Living Allowance Tbnls 1991–; pres Notaries Soc 1987–89; *Recreations* golf, tennis, walking, photography, music, pottery, gardening; *Style—* Richard Park, Esq; ✉ 28 The Green, Hurworth, Darlington, Co Durham DL2 2AA (☎ 01325 720321); 12 Houndgate, Darlington (☎ 01325 466794, fax 01325 55321)

PARK, William Dennis; s of Edward Park (d 1954), of Cockermouth, Cumbria, and Fanny Moyra, *née* Walker (d 1986); *b* 28 May 1934; *Educ* St Bees Cumbria; *m* 1 Jan 1959, Valerie Margaret, da of Wallace Rutherford Bayne, MD (d 1956), of Barrow-in-Furness, Cumbria; 1 s (Adam b 9 July 1961), 1 da (Claire (Mrs Banks) b 9 Jan 1963); *Career* Nat Serv RAOC, RASC 1955–57 (Army Legal Aid 1956–57); admitted slr 1955, ptnr Morrison & Masters Swindon 1961–66, sr litigation ptnr Linklaters & Paines London 1971–92; former pres London Slrs' Litigation Assoc, memb Cncl London Int Arbitration Tst, memb Cncl and Ctee of Mgmnt Br Inst of Int & Comparative Law, memb Bd of London Int Ct of Arbitration 1988–92, UK memb Ct of Arbitration of the Int Chamber of Commerce Paris 1991–93; memb various bodies associated with Lake Dist and local agriculture, subcriber to fell and beagle packs; Lord of the Manors of Whicham and Whitbeck Cumbria; memb: City of London Slrs' Co, Law Soc 1955; FCIArb 1991 (ACIArb 1980); *Books* Hire Purchase and Credit Sales (1958), Collection of Debts (1962), Discovery of Documents (1966), Documentary Evidence (1985), International Commercial Litigation (1990); *Recreations* Cumbrian history, country pursuits; *Style—* William Park, Esq; ✉ Yeomans, Upperton, Petworth, West Sussex GU28 9BG

PARK OF MONMOUTH, Baroness (Life Peer UK 1990), of Broadway in the County of Hereford and Worcester; Daphne Margaret Sybil Désirée Park; CMG (1971), OBE (1960); da of John Alexander Park (d 1952), and Doreen Gwynneth Park (d 1982); *b* 1 Sept 1921; *Educ* Rosa Bassett Sch, Somerville Coll Oxford, Newnham Coll Cambridge; *Career* WTS (FANY) 1943–47 (Allied Cmmn for Austria 1946–48); FO 1948, second sec Moscow 1954, first sec Leopoldville 1959, first sec Zambia 1964–67, consul-gen Hanoi 1969–70, chargé d'affaires Ulan Bator 1972, FCO 1973–79; princ Somerville Coll Oxford 1980–89, bd memb Sheffield Devpt Corp 1989–92, dir Devpt Tst Zoological Soc of London 1989–90, govr BBC 1982–87, former memb Br Library Bd, chm Legal Aid Advsy Ctee to Lord Chllr 1984–90, pro vice chllr Univ of Oxford, chm Royal Cmmn on the Historical Monuments of Eng 1989–94, pres Soc for the Promotion of the Trg of Women, memb Bd Britain Sasakawa Fndn 1994–, tstee The Jardine Fndn 1990–, govr Ditchley Fndn; Hon LLD: Univ of Bristol 1988, Mount Holyoke Coll 1992; fell Chatham House (RIIA), FRSA; *Recreations* good talk, politics and difficult places; *Clubs* Naval & Military, Cwlth Tst, Special Forces, United Oxford and Cambridge; *Style—* The Rt Hon the Lady Park of Monmouth, CMG, OBE; ✉ c/o House of Lords, London SW1A 0PW

PARKER, *see also:* Dodds-Parker

PARKER, (David) Alec; s of David Herbert Parker (d 1983), and Gertrude Alice, *née* Pipes (d 1978); *b* 3 Oct 1931; *Educ* Queen Elizabeth's GS Wimborne Dorset, Imperial Coll Univ of London (BSc, PhD, DSc (Eng)); *m* 24 March 1956, Mary, da of Henry John Gibbs (d 1986); 1 s (Adrian John b 17 March 1964), 2 da (Susan Jane b 8 Aug 1958, Helen June b 12 July 1960); *Career* Nat Serv Lieut REME 1950–51; ldr Mechanical Engrg Res Gp Engrg Div BTH Res Laboratory (AEI Central Res Laboratory 1960–) 1954–68, head Machinery Section Prodn Engrg Res Assoc 1968–69; Associated Engineering Developments Ltd (known as AE Developments Ltd since 1982) 1969–87: mangr Mechanical Engrg Dept 1972–77, dir 1977–78, acting md 1978–79, md 1979–87, memb AE Group Exec 1985–87; chm High Precision Equipment Ltd 1985–87, md T & N Technology 1987–93; conslt to T & N plc 1994–; visiting prof Univ of Bath 1994–; chm: Rugby Sub Branch IMechE 1977–79, Consortium for Ceramic Applications in Reciprocating Engines 1984–89, Materials Advsy Ctee DTI 1990–93; memb: Engine and Vehicle Ctee DTI 1982–85, Vehicle Advsy Ctee DTI 1985–88, Sci and Materials Bd SERC 1993–94; churchwarden All Saints Leamington Hastings Rugby 1969–94, chm govrs Leamington Hastings CE First Sch Rugby 1976–; awards: Design Cncl Commendation for AEconoguide piston design 1984, Herbert Akroyd Stuart prize (IMechE) for the best paper on diesel engines 1985, Design Cncl award for AEconoguide piston design 1989, Crompton Lanchester medal (Automobile Div IMechE) 1990, George Stephenson prize (IMechE) 1990; CEng 1968, FInstP 1968 (AInstP 1961), FIMechE 1981 (MIMechE 1968), CPhys 1985, FEng 1990; *Recreations* campanology, golf; *Style—* Alec Parker, Esq, FEng; ✉ Orchard Bungalow, Broadwell, Rugby, Warwickshire CV23 8HB (☎ 01926 812548, business ☎ and fax 01926 812541)

PARKER, Barrie Charles; s of Stanley Charles Digby Parker, of Southampton, and Betty Doreen, *née* Calverley; *b* 2 Oct 1940; *Educ* City of London Sch, Charing Cross Med Sch, Univ of London (MB BS); *m* 27 April 1968, Ann Teressa, da of William Rae Ferguson (d 1981), of Coventry; *Career* sr registrar Charing Cross and Royal Nat Orthopaedic Hosps 1973–76, conslt orthopaedic surgn Kingston Hosp 1976– (clinical tutor 1981–86), med dir Kingston Hosp NHS Tst; pres Kingston and Richmond Div BMA 1978–79; former memb Kingston and Esher Health Authy, former regnl advsr orthopaedics RCS England, Oxshott Heath conservator; fell: RSM 1974, Br Orthopaedic Assoc 1976 (memb Cncl); FRCS; *Recreations* rugby football, swimming, skiing and water skiing; *Clubs* London Irish RFC, Kingston Med, RAC, Pyrford Golf; *Style—* Barrie Parker, Esq, Delaval, Furzefield, Oxshott, Surrey KT22 0UR

PARKER, Bruce Rodney Wingate; s of Robert Parker (d 1988), and Doris Maud, *née* Wingate (d 1995); *b* 20 July 1941; *Educ* Elizabeth Coll Guernsey, Univ of Wales (BA), Univ of Reading (DipEd); *m* 16 Sept 1967 (m dis 1985), Anne, *née* Dorey; 2 s (James b 9 Aug 1968, Charles b 4 Aug 1974), 1 da (Sarah b 28 Dec 1969); *Career* house master Elizabeth Coll Guernsey 1964–67, BBC News and Current Affrs reporter, presenter and prodr 1967–; progs incl: Nationwide, Antiques Roadshow, Mainstream, Badger Watch, South Today; political corr BBC South 1991–, presenter BBC South of Westminster 1992–, frequent contribs to numerous radio and TV progs, rifle-shooting corr The Independent; former memb Educn Advsy Ctee Hampshire CC, former chm of govrs Harestock Sch Winchester; *Books* Everybody's Soapbox (with N Farrell, 1983); *Recreations* travel, gardening, rifle-shooting; *Clubs* Commonwealth Rifle; *Style—* Bruce Parker, Esq; ✉ 58 Canon Street, Winchester, Hants SO23 9JW 01962 866399, fax 01962 866993); c/o BBC Television, Havelock Road, Southampton SO14 7PU (☎ 01703 374202, fax 01703 374324)

PARKER, Cameron Holdsworth; OBE (1993), DL (Renfrewshire 1993); s of George Cameron Parker, MBE (d 1967), of Monifieth, Angus, and Mary Stevenson, *née* Houston (d 1985); *b* 14 April 1932; *Educ* Morrisons Acad Crieff, Univ of Glasgow (BSc); *m* 1, 20 July 1957, Elizabeth Margaret (d 1985), da of Andrew Sydney Grey Thomson (d 1957), of Dundee; 3 s (David b 1958, Michael b 1960, John b 1964); m 2, 23 May 1986, Marlyne, da of William Honeyman (d 1966), of Glasgow; *Career* chm John G Kincaid & Co Ltd 1976–80 (md 1967–80), chm and chief exec Scott Lithgow Ltd 1980–83, bd memb Br Shipbuilders Ltd 1977–80 and 1981–83, vice chm Lithgows Ltd 1991– (md 1984–92); dir: Campbeltown Shipyard Ltd 1984–94, J Fleming Engineering Ltd 1984–94, Lithgow Electronics Ltd 1984–94, Malak Off & Wm Moore Ltd 1984–94, McKinlay & Blair Ltd 1984–94, Prosper Engineering Ltd 1984–94, A Kenneth & Sons Ltd 1985–94, Landcatch Ltd 1985–94, Glasgow Iron and Steel Co Ltd 1985–94, Argyll and Clyde Health Bd 1991–95, Scottish Homes 1992–96, Clyde Shaw Ltd 1992–94; memb Cncl CBI Scotland 1986–92; Freeman City of London, Liveryman Worshipful Co of Shipwrights 1981, FIMarE 1965; *Recreations* golf, gardening; *Style—* Cameron Parker, Esq, OBE, DL; ✉ The Heath House, Rowantreehill Rd, Kilmacolm, Renfrewshire PA13 4PE (☎ 01505

873197); Lithgows Ltd, Netherton, Langbank, Renfrewshire PA14 6YG (☎ 01475 540692, fax 01475 540558, telex 779248)

PARKER, Charles David; s of David Parker (d 1961), of Bradford, Yorks, and Jane, *née* Homler (d 1970); *b* 2 May 1929; *Educ* Hanson HS Bradford, Univ of Leeds Dental Sch (BChD, Charles Rippon medalist); *m* 18 Sept 1954, Margaret Joyce, da of Robert Henry Hull Goss (d 1978), of Bournemouth; 2 s (Richard Martin b 1960, William George b 1963), 1 da (Sarah Caroline b 1958); *Career* Nat Serv Capt 1953–54 (1 Lt 1952–53) RADC, 18 Field Ambulance Hong Kong; Chapman Prize essayist Br Soc for the Study of Orthodontics 1963, pt/t memb Dental Estimates Bd Orthodontics 1975–84; conslt orthodontist Leicestershire HA Hosp and Community Dental Serv 1963–91, orthodontist emeritus to Leics HA 1991–, private practice 1966–96; past pres East Midlands Branch BDA, past chm and treas Conslt Orthondontics Gp; author of approximately 25 pubns of papers and letters and reports on orthodontics; LDS 1951, DOrthRCS 1957, FDSRCS 1958; memb: BDA, Br Soc for the Study of Orthodontics (past pres); life memb Euro Orthodontic Soc; *Recreations* skiing, swimming, public speaking, vegetable gardening; *Style*— Charles Parker, Esq; ✉ Stoke Dry Cottage, 2 Main St, Stoke Dry, nr Uppingham, Rutland LE15 9JG (☎ 01572 822805)

PARKER, Charles G A; DL (Oxfordshire 1992); s of Capt C E Parker, MC (d 1962), of Ewelme, Oxfordshire, and Hilda M Parker (d 1979), eld da of Sir John Starkey, 1 Bt, JP, DL (d 1940), of Norwood Park, Southwell, Notts; *b* 30 Jan 1924; *Educ* Eton, New Coll Oxford (MA); *m* 3 Nov 1958, Shirley, da of Col Frank Follett Holt, TD (d 1978), of Corrybrough, Tomatin, Inverness-shire; 1 da (Davina (Mrs John Walter)); *Career* Capt Rifle Bde 1942–46, served France (POW Germany); The Times Publishing Co 1949–56, Charringtons 1956–61, BMA Publications 1961–76, chm Court and Judicial Publishing Co Ltd 1976–; chm Tower Hill Improvement Tst, tstee Peter Samuel Royal Free Fund, pres Assoc of Learned and Professional Soc Publishers, vice pres Nettlebed Branch Royal Br Legion; JP: London W Central 1978–89, Oxford City 1990–94; High Sheriff of Oxfordshire 1989–90; Vice Lord-Lt Oxfordshire 1996; Liveryman Worshipful Co of Stationers & Newspaper Makers 1965; KStJ 1994 (chm St John Cncl for Oxfordshire 1988–95, Chapter Gen of St John 1994–); FRSA, FRGS; *Recreations* gardening, tennis; *Clubs* Beefsteak, White's, Garrick; *Style*— Charles Parker, Esq, DL; ✉ The White House, Nuffield, Oxon RG9 5SR; 19 Lennox Gardens, London SW1X 0DB

PARKER, Christopher John McKellen; s of late Alfred Derek McKellen Parker, of Beltinge, Herne Bay, Kent, and Muriel Joyce, *née* Hargreaves; *b* 25 July 1945; *Educ* Dulwich, LSE (BSc); *m* 27 Dec 1969, Alison Eyre, da of Robin Gordon Miller, of Shepherdswell, Dover, Kent, and Edith Jeane; 3 s (Thomas b 1972, Jonathan b 1974, Samuel b 1980); *Career* dir: Arbuthnot Latham & Co Ltd (merchant bankers) 1978–82, Caird Group plc (formerly A Caird & Sons plc) 1982–95 (chm 1982–87); FCA 1979 (ACA 1969); *Style*— Christopher Parker, Esq; ✉ Dennes House, Waltham, Canterbury, Kent CT4 5SD (☎ 01227 700389, fax 01227 700601); 163 Andrewes House, Barbican, London EC2Y 8BA (☎ 0171 638 5009)

PARKER, Hon David; yr s of 8 Earl of Macclesfield (d 1992); hp of bro, 9 Earl, *qv*; *b* 2 Jan 1945; *Educ* Stowe; *m* 1968, Lynne Valerie, da of George William Butler; 1 s (Timothy George b 1969), 2 da (Elizabeth Anne b 1971, Jessica b 1977); *Style*— The Hon David Parker; ✉ Model Farm, Shirburn, Watlington, Oxford OX9 5DX

PARKER, Dr David; s of late Hubert Eric Robert Parker, and Eileen Rose, *née* Goodson, of St Anne's Court, Buckland Rd, Maidstone, Kent; *b* 28 May 1940; *Educ* Maidstone GS for Boys, Univ of Nottingham (BA), Univ of Sheffield (PhD); *m* 24 Sept 1966, Elinor Sheila Halling, da of late Joseph Patrick Anthony Cheek, of Combwich, nr Bridgwater, Somerset; 1 s (Daniel b 1969), 1 da (Clare b 1972); *Career* lectr Univ of Sheffield 1966–68, assoc prof Univ of Malaya 1974–75 (lectr 1968–74), curator The Dickens House Museum 1978–; Freedom of Independence Missouri USA 1983; memb Int Cncl of Museums 1978; *Recreations* cooking, guitar playing; *Clubs* Dickens Fellowship; *Style*— Dr David Parker; ✉ The Dickens House Museum, 48 Doughty St, London WC1N 2LF (☎ 0171 405 2127, fax 0171 831 5175)

PARKER, Edward; s of Francis Parker (d 1943), and Lucy Maud, *née* Pritchard (d 1969); *b* 9 Aug 1933; *Educ* Central Manchester HS for Boys, Univ of Manchester (BSc, MSc); *m* 6 Aug 1960, Anne Marguerite, da of Alan Ewart Bracewell, of Heysham; 2 da (Susan Elizabeth b 1961, Katherine Jane b 1964); *Career* head of Aerothermodynamics Section A V Roe Woodford 1955–60, lectr Royal Coll of Advanced Technol 1960–67; Univ of Salford: lectr then sr lectr 1971–79, pro vice chllr 1979–93, dir of continuing educn 1981–87, dir CAMPUS 1987–, professorial fell 1993–; author of forty articles and papers on thermodynamics, continuing educn and industry-univ rels; memb Engrg Cncl: Continuing Educn Ctee 1985–94, Standing Ctee on Industry 1990–94; chm CONTACT Management Bd 1986–88, memb Salford Health Authy 1986–89, govr Bury GS 1987–94, chm Salford Family Practitioner Ctee 1988–90, memb Cncl Soc of Family Practitioner Ctees 1989–90, chm Salford Family Health Serv Authy 1990–93; memb: N Western Regnl Health Authy 1990–93 (vice chm 1992–93), Cncl Nat Assoc of Health Authys and Tsts 1990–93 (vice chm 1991–93); chm: Central Manchester Health Authy 1993–94, Manchester Purchasing Consortium 1993–94, Salford Community Health Care NHS Tst 1994–; Hon DSc Univ of Salford 1993; CEng 1964, FIMechE 1971; *Recreations* swimming, walking, music, church services, football (watching!); *Style*— Edward Parker, Esq; ✉ 12 Cove Rd, Silverdale, Lancs LA5 0RR (☎ 01524 701187); CAMPUS, The University of Salford, The Crescent, Salford M5 4WT (☎ 0161 743 1727, fax 0161 745 5999, telex 668680 SULIB)

PARKER, Elinor Sheila Halling; da of Joseph Patrick Anthony Cheek (d 1994), of New Malden, Surrey, and Joan Sheila Maude, *née* Halling (d 1996); *b* 21 Sept 1940; *Educ* Grey Coat Hosp Westminster, Univ of Sheffield (BDS); *m* 24 Sept 1966, Dr David Parker, s of Hubert Robert Parker (d 1990), Maidstone; 1 s (Daniel b 1969), 1 da (Clare b 1972); *Career* asst lectr Univ of Sheffield 1966–68; gen dental practitioner: Kuala Lumpur Malaysia 1969–74, New Malden Surrey 1975–87, Hersham Surrey 1987–; pt/t assoc ed Br Dental Jl 1992–; memb: Mgmnt Ctee Kingston Women's Centre 1984–87; Women's Ctee Kingston BC 1987–88, Br Dental Editors' Forum 1987–, Editorial Bd of The Probe 1990–92; memb Bd SW Thames Div Faculty of Gen Dental Surgery 1993–; chm Govrs Tiffin Girls' Sch 1987–88, chm Women in Dentistry 1989–90 (ed 1986–93); Dip in Gen Dental Practice of Faculty of Gen Dental Practice Royal Coll of Surgns 1992; chm Kingston and District Section Br Dental Assoc; memb: Br Dental Assoc, Gen Dental Practitioners' Assoc; *Recreations* writing, badminton, music; *Clubs* Kingston Feminists; *Style*— Mrs Elinor Parker; ✉ 16 Alric Avenue, New Malden, Surrey KT3 4JN (☎ 0181 949 2596); 5 The Green, Hersham, Walton on Thames, Surrey KT12 4HW (☎ 01932 248348, fax 01932 888248)

PARKER, Sir Eric Wilson; kt (1991); s of Wilson Parker (d 1983), and Edith Gladys, *née* Wellings; *b* 8 June 1933; *Educ* The Priory GS for Boys Shrewsbury; *m* 12 Nov 1955, Marlene Teresa, da of Michael Neale (d 1941); 2 s (Ian, Charles), 2 da (Karen, Sally Jane (Mrs Matthew Jessop)); *Career* Nat Serv RAPC Cyprus 1956–58; articled clerk with Wheeler Whittingham & Kent (CAs) 1950–55; with Taylor Woodrow 1958–64; Trafalgar House plc: joined 1965, fin dir 1969, dep md 1973, md 1977, chief exec 1983–92, dep chm 1988–93; dir: Hardy Oil & Gas plc, Caradon plc, Graham Consulting Group Ltd; dep chm Race Horse Owners Assoc; patron: Teenage Cancer Tst, Advsy Bd Phoenix Capital Devpt Fund; memb Lloyds; FCA 1967 (ACA 1956), FRSA, CIMgt; *Recreations* racehorse owner and breeder (Crimbourne Stud), golf, tennis, cricket, wine; *Clubs* RAC, West Sussex Golf, MCC; *Style*— Sir Eric Parker; ✉ Crimbourne House, Wisborough Green, Billingshurst, West Sussex RH14 0HR (☎ 01403 700400, fax 01403 700776)

PARKER, (James) Geoffrey; CBE (1996); s of Ian Sutherland Parker (d 1973), of Leicester, and Kathleen Lilian, *née* Cave (d 1976); *b* 27 March 1933; *Educ* Alderman Newton's Sch Leicester, Christ's Coll Cambridge (BA), Wadham Coll Oxford (CertEd); *m* 22 Sept 1956, Ruth, da of Edward Major, of Leicester; 2 da (Georgina b 1959, Katherine b 1960); *Career* RA 1954–56, Lance Bombardier 1955, 2 Lt 1955, Actg Capt 1956; asst master Bedford Modern Sch 1957–66, head History Dept Tonbridge Sch Kent 1966–75, head master Queen Elizabeth GS Wakefield 1975–85, high master Manchester GS 1985–June 1994; chm: National ISIS 1994–96, The Teacher Training Agency 1994–; memb: various HMC ctees (chm 1991), Advsy Cncl for Church's Miny; govr various schs and educnl bodies; *Recreations* sailing, coarse gardening; *Clubs* East India, Devonshire, Sports and Public Schs; *Style*— Geoffrey Parker, Esq, CBE; ✉ Ty Mawr, Carno, Powys SY17 5LL

PARKER, Prof (Noel) Geoffrey; s of late Derek Geoffrey Parker, and Kathleen Betsy, *née* Symon; *b* 25 Dec 1943; *Educ* Nottingham HS, Christ's Coll Cambridge (BA, MA, PhD, LittD); *Children* 3 s, 1 da; *Career* fell Christ's Coll Cambridge 1968–72; St Andrews Univ: reader in modern history 1978–82 (lectr 1972–78), prof of early modern history 1982–86; Br Acad Exchange fell Newberry Library Chicago 1981; visiting prof: Vrije Universiteit Brussels 1975, Univ of BC Vancouver Canada 1979–80, Keio Univ Tokyo 1984; Lees Knowles lectr in mil history Univ of Cambridge 1984, Charles E Nowell distinguished prof of history Univ of Illinois at Urbana-Champaign 1986–93 (chm of dept 1989–91), Robert A Lovett prof of mil and naval history Yale Univ 1993–96, Andreas Dorpalen Distinguished prof of history Ohio State Univ 1997–; corresponding fell Spanish Royal Acad of History 1988–; Hon Doctorate in History and Letters Vrije Universiteit Brussels 1990; Encomienda Order of Isabel the Catholic (Spain) 1988, Caballero Gran Cruz Order of Isabel the Catholic (Spain) 1992, Caballero Gran Cruz Order of Alfonso the Wise (Spain) 1996; FBA 1984; *Awards* American Military Inst's Best Book of the Year award for The Military Revolution (*see* Books) 1989, Dexter Prize for the best book pubd 1987–90 on the hist of technol for The Military Revolution 1990; *Books* The Army of Flanders and The Spanish Road 1567–1659 (1972, 3 edn 1990), The Dutch Revolt (1977, 3 edn 1985), Philip II (1978, 3 edn 1995), Europe in Crisis 1598–1648 (1979), Spain and the Netherlands 1559–1659 (1979, 2 edn 1990), The Thirty Years' War (1984, 3 edn 1996), The World - An Illustrated History (ed 1986, 4 edn 1995), The Military Revolution - Military Innovation and the Rise of the West 1500–1800 (1988, 3 edn 1996), The Spanish Armada (with Colin Martin 1988, 3 edn 1992), The Cambridge Illustrated History of Warfare (ed, 1995), The Times Compact Atlas of World History (ed, 1995), Spain, Europe and the Atlantic World - Essays in Honour of John H Elliott (ed, 1995), The Reader's Companion to Military History (ed, 1996); author of numerous articles and reviews and ed numerous books; *Recreations* travel, archaeology; *Style*— Prof Geoffrey Parker; ✉ The Ohio State University, 106 Dulles Hall, 230 West 17th Street, Columbus, Ohio 43210–1367, USA (☎ 00 1 614 292 2674)

PARKER, Prof Geoffrey Alan; s of Alan Parker (d 1989), and Gertrude Ethel, *née* Hill (d 1992); *b* 24 May 1944; *Educ* Lymm GS Cheshire, Univ of Bristol (BSc, Rose Bracher prize for biology, PhD), King's Coll Cambridge (MA); *m* 29 July 1967, Susan Mary (d 1994), da of Harold Alfred William Wallis; 1 da ((Nicola) Claire b 27 Aug 1973), 1 s (Alan Leslie b 4 April 1977); *Career* Univ of Liverpool: asst lectr in zoology 1968–69, lectr 1969–76, sr lectr 1976–80, reader 1980–89, prof Dept of Environmental and Evolutionary Biology 1989–96, prof Sch of Biological Scis 1996–; sr research fell King's Coll Research Centre Cambridge 1978–79, Nuffield Science research fell Univ of Liverpool 1982–83, SERC sr research fell Univ of Liverpool 1990–95; memb Editorial Bd: Heredity 1983–88, Ethology, Ecology and Evolution 1989–95, American Naturalist 1991–92, Journal of Evolutionary Biology 1991–96, Proceedings of the Royal Society of London, Series B 1991–; consulting ed Animal Behaviour 1977–78 and 1980–82; memb Cncl: Assoc for Study of Animal Behaviour 1979–82 (memb 1976–), Int Soc for Behavioural Ecology 1986–88 (memb 1986–); memb: Br Ecological Soc 1965–, American Soc of Naturalists 1978–, Euro Soc for Evolutionary Biology 1991–; FRS 1989; *Books* Evolution of Sibling Rivalry (co-author, 1997); also author of numerous scientific articles in learned jls; *Recreations* breeding, showing and judging exhibition bantams, playing jazz clarinet (mainly Dixieland) in local bands; *Style*— Prof Geoffrey Parker, FRS; ✉ School of Biological Sciences, Nicholson Building, University of Liverpool, Liverpool L69 3BX (☎ 0151 794 5018, fax 0151 794 5094, e-mail gap@liv.ac.uk)

PARKER, Geoffrey John; CBE (1984); s of Stanley John Parker (d 1983), of London, and Alice Ellen Parker (d 1984); *b* 20 March 1937; *Educ* Hendon Co GS; *m* 23 Nov 1957, Hazel Mary, da of Lawrence Edward; 2 s (Simon, Andrew), 2 da (Joanne, Amanda); *Career* Nat Serv RAF 1955–57; commercial dir Townsend Car Ferries Ltd Dover 1962–74, md Atlantic Steam Navigation Co Ltd 1974–86, chm and md Port of Felixstowe 1976–87, dir National Bus Company Ltd 1979–86, chm European Ferries plc 1986–87 (dir 1981), chief exec Highland Participants plc 1987–89, chief exec Maritime Transport Services Ltd 1989–, chm Thamesport (London) Ltd; FCIT 1982, FITA 1986; *Recreations* golf, opera; *Clubs* Ipswich Golf; *Style*— Geoffrey Parker, Esq, CBE; ✉ 101 Valley Rd, Ipswich, Suffolk IP1 4NF (☎ 01473 216003); Maritime Transport Services Ltd, Thamesport, Isle of Grain, Rochester, Kent ME3 0EP (☎ 01634 271511)

PARKER, Prof Eur Ing Graham Alexander; s of Joe Parker (d 1964), of Nuneaton, Warks, and Margaretta Annie, *née* Mawbey (d 1985); *b* 20 Nov 1935; *Educ* King Edward VI GS Nuneaton Warks, Univ of Birmingham (BSc, PhD, CEng, Eur Ing); *m* 7 Nov 1959, Janet Ada, da of Cecil Parsons (d 1963), of Nuneaton, Warks; 2 da (Joanne Marie b 1966, Louise Alessandra b 1968); *Career* Hawker-Siddeley Dynamics Ltd 1957–60, Cincinnati Milacron Inc USA 1963–64, Univ of Birmingham 1964–68, currently prof of mech engrg and head of dept Univ of Surrey (joined 1968); memb Cncl: Cranleigh Sch, St Catherines; govr Charterhouse Sch; memb Mfrg Systems Div IMechE; FIMechE, memb ASME; *Books* Fluidics - Components and Circuits (with K Foster, 1970), A Guide to Fluidics (contrib 1971); *Recreations* squash, tennis, walking; *Style*— Prof Eur Ing Graham Parker; ✉ Tall Chimneys, Malacca Farm, West Clandon, Guildford, Surrey GU4 7UG (☎ 01483 222328); Department of Mechanical Engineering, University of Surrey, Guildford, Surrey GU2 5XH (☎ 01483 259283, fax 01483 306039, e-mail g.parker@surrey.ac.uk)

PARKER, Prof Howard John; s of John Raymond Parker, and Doreen, *née* Taylor; *b* 2 Nov 1948; *Educ* Birkenhead Sch, Univ of Liverpool (BA, MA, PhD); *m* 4 Jan 1972, Diana Lesley; 2 s (James b 1977, Ben b 1980); *Career* reader in social work studies Univ of Liverpool 1987–88 (research fell 1972–74, lectr in applied social studies 1974–79, sr lectr in social work studies 1980–86), prof of social work Univ of Manchester 1988–; seconded on research work: to Home Office Res and Planning 1985, to Wirral Borough Cncl 1986; currently conducting research into alcohol and crime, organised child abuse and drug misuse; advsr on drugs policies in local, regnl and Govt depts (especially Home Office and Health Educn Authy 1993–96); memb Br Criminology Soc; *Books* View from the Boys (1979), Social Work and the Courts (1979), Receiving Juvenile Justice (1981), Living with Heroin (1988), Unmasking the Magistrates (1989), Drugs Futures: changing patterns of drug use amongst English Youth (1995); *Style*— Prof Howard Parker; ✉ Department of Social Policy and Social Work, University of Manchester, Manchester M13 9PL (☎ 0161 275 4783)

PARKER, James Mavin (Jim); s of James Robertson Parker (d 1983), of Hartlepool, and Margaret, *née* Mavin; *b* 18 Dec 1934; *Educ* Guildhall Sch of Music and Drama; *m* 1;

1 da (Louise b 1964); m 2, 2 Aug 1969, Pauline Ann, da of John George, of Reading; 2 da (Claire b 1974, Amy b 1976); *Career* musician 4/7 Dragoon Gds; composer and conductor, joined Barrow Poets 1963; composed music for: Banana Blush (John Betjeman), Captain Beaky (Jeremy Lloyd); printed music: Follow the Star (Wally K Daly), Muskett Fife and Drum (wind and brass band), The Golden Section (brass quintet), All Jazzed Up (flute and piano); childrens musicals: five Childrens Musicals (Tom Stanier), English Towns (flute and piano), A Londoner in New York (suite for brass), All Jazzed Up (oboe and piano), Mississippi Five (woodwind quintet); film and TV music: Mapp and Lucia, Wynne and Penkovsky, Good Behaviour, The Making of Modern London, Girl Shy (Harold Lloyd), The Blot, Wish Me Luck, Anything More Would be Greedy, House of Cards, Parnell and the Englishwoman, Soldier Soldier, The House of Eliott, Body and Soul, Goggle Eyes, To Play The King (BAFTA Award for Best TV Music 1993), The Final Cut; Hon GSM 1985; GSM (Silver medal) 1959, LRAM 1959; *Recreations* twentieth century art, literature; *Style*— Jim Parker, Esq; ✉ 19 Laurel Road, London SW13 OEE (☎ and fax 0181 876 8571)

PARKER, (Diana) Jean; *née* Morley; CBE (1989); da of Capt Lewis William Reeve Morley (d 1988), of Grantham, Lincolnshire, and Amy, *née* Southwood (d 1973); *b* 7 June 1932; *Educ* Kesteven and Grantham Girls' Sch, Univ of Birmingham (BCom); *m* 26 June 1959, Dudley Frost Parker (d 1971), s of Frederick Parker (d 1960), of Rugby; 1 s (Andrew b 1965), 1 da (Alison b 1960); *Career* dir: Vacu-Lug Traction Tyres Ltd 1957–, Langham Industries Ltd 1980–95, Central Independent TV Ltd (formerly plc) 1982– (chm Central Independent TV Regnl Advsy Cncl 1993–), British Steel (Industry) Ltd 1986–90, Goldsborough Healthcare plc 1994–; memb: Bd E Midlands Electricity 1983–90, Eastern Advsy Bd Nat West Bank plc 1985–92; CBI: memb Cncl 1985–89, memb Pres Ctee 1985–89, chm Smaller Firms Ctee 1986–88; chm: Lincolnshire Jt Devpt Ctee 1983–, N Lincolnshire Health Authy 1987–90, Middle England Fine Foods Ltd 1996–; dir Grantham and Dist Hosp NHS Tst 1995–; former chm: Age Concern Grantham, Grantham C of C; dir Lincs Ambulance & Health Tport Tst 1991–92, former memb E Midlands Econ Planning Cncl, sec Friends of St Wulfram's Church; CIMgt 1986; *Recreations* church architecture, reading fiction; *Clubs* University Women's; *Style*— Mrs Jean Parker, CBE; ✉ Vacu-Lug Traction Tyres Ltd, Londonthorpe Road, Grantham, Lincolnshire (☎ 01476 593095, fax 01476 513816, car tel 0836 693 389)

PARKER, Vice Adm Sir (Wilfred) John; KBE (1969, OBE 1953), CB (1965), DSC (1943); s of Henry Edmond Parker (d 1962), and Ida Mary Parker (d 1955); *b* 12 Oct 1915; *Educ* RNC Dartmouth, RNC Greenwich; *m* 1943, Marjorie Stuart, da of Alfred Nagle Jones (d 1961), of Halifax, Nova Scotia, Canada; 2 da; *Career* Capt RNC Dartmouth 1961–63, asst Chief of Def Staff (Operational Requirements) 1963–66, Flag Offr Medway and Adm Supt HM Dockyard Chatham 1966–69, ret 1969; *Clubs* Royal Navy; *Style*— Vice Adm Sir John Parker, KBE, CB, DSC; ✉ Flint Cottage, East Harting, Petersfield, Hants GU31 5LT (☎ 01730 825427)

PARKER, Dr (Thomas) John; s of Robert Parker (d 1957), and Margaret Elizabeth, *née* Bell; *b* 8 April 1942; *Educ* Belfast Coll of Technol, Queen's Univ Belfast; *m* July 1967, Emma Elizabeth, da of Alexander Blair, of Ballymena, NI; 1 s (Graham b 31 July 1970), 1 da (Fiona b 1 June 1972); *Career* shipbuilder and engr; Harland & Wolff Ltd: memb Ship Design Team 1963–69, ship prodn mangr 1969–71, prodn drawing office mangr 1971–72, gen mangr Sales and Projects Dept 1972–74; md Austin & Pickersgill (shipbuilders) Sunderland 1974–78, dep chief exec British Shipbuilders Corp 1980–83 (bd memb for shipbuilding mktg and ops 1978–80), chm and chief exec Harland & Wolff plc (became Harland & Wolff Holdings plc) 1983–93 (currently non-exec dir); Babcock International Group plc: dep chm and chief exec 1993–94, chm 1994–; bd memb: Indust Devpt Bd NI 1983–87, British Coal plc (formerly Corp) 1986–93, AS Quatro Norway 1989–93, AS Cinco Norway 1989–93; dir QUBIS Ltd Belfast 1984–93; non-exec dir GKN plc 1993–; memb: Cncl RINA 1978–80 and 1982– (vice pres 1985), Int Ctee Bureau Veritas Paris 1981–, Gen Ctee Lloyd's Register of Shipping 1983–, Br Ctee Det Norske Veritas Oslo 1984–94; memb Ct of Assts Worshipful Co of Shipwrights (Liveryman 1978); Hon DSc Queen's Univ of Belfast 1985, Hon ScD Trinity Coll Dublin 1986, Hon DSc Univ of Ulster 1992; FRINA 1978, FIMarE 1979, FEng 1982; *Recreations* sailing, reading, music; *Clubs* Royal Ulster Yacht; *Style*— Dr T John Parker, FEng; ✉ Babcock International Group plc, The Lodge, Badminton Court, Church Street, Amersham, Bucks HP7 0DD (☎ 01494 727296, fax 01494 721909)

PARKER, (Anthony) John; s of John Edward Parker (d 1976), of Nantwich, Cheshire, and Winnie May, *née* Bebbington; *b* 2 Oct 1942; *Educ* Nantwich Acton GS; *m* 21 June 1969, (Mary) Elizabeth, da of Frederick Langley (d 1990), of Audlem, Cheshire; 2 s (Simon b 1972, Stephen b 1974), 1 da (Ann-Marie b 1978); *Career* quantity surveyor Brown & Richmond 1959–65, sr quantity surveyor Allott & Lomax 1965–71, dir Sika Contracts Ltd 1974–86 (sr mangr 1971–74), jt md (following mgmnt buy out) Sika Contracts 1986– (now called SCL Group Ltd 1993–), chm SCL Group Ltd 1994; fndr memb and first chm Tech Ctee of Concrete Repair Assoc 1988–94, memb Working Pty of The Concrete Soc and CIRIA (on repairs to reinforced concrete structures) 1988–93, memb: EFNARC Euro Trade Fedn on Eurocodes, BSI Ctee on Euro Standards 1992–94; ARICS 1968, FInstD 1975; *Recreations* music, piano playing; *Clubs* IOD; *Style*— John Parker, Esq; ✉ SCL Group Ltd, Cuppin Street, Chester, Cheshire CH1 2BN (☎ 01244 312 553)

PARKER, (David) John; CBE (1997); s of Kenneth Kershaw Parker (d 1985), and Mary, *née* Moore; *b* 1 Feb 1938; *Educ* Churchill Sch Harare Zimbabwe, Univ of St Andrews (Maynard Tst scholar, MB ChB); *m* 1963, Veronica Ann, da of Russell Cary and Gertrud Good; 1 da (Jacqueline b 1965), 2 s (Andrew James b 1966, Simon Paul b 1968); *Career* lectr in surgery Univ of St Andrews 1967–68, sr registrar Nat Heart and Chest Hosps 1969–73, res fell Univ of Alabama Birmingham USA 1970, sr lectr and conslt cardiac surgn Nat Heart Hosp and Inst of Cardiology 1973–75, conslt cardiac surgn St George's Hosp 1985– (hon sr lectr Med Sch 1975–); Br Cardiac Soc: memb Cncl 1981–86, treas 1986–91, pres elect 1992, pres 1993–95; pres Cardiothoracic Section RSM 1993–94; memb: Ctee Soc of Thoracic and Cardiovascular Surgns 1980–83, Cardiology Ctee RCP 1981–85, Specialist Advsy Ctee on Higher Surgical Trg RCS 1983–89 (chm 1985–89); Hunterian prof RCS 1972; memb: Br Cardiac Soc 1973, Soc of Cardiothoracic Surgns 1973, Cardiac Res Club, Cardiac Muscle Res Gp; FRCSE 1967, FRCS 1967, FRCP 1986 (memb 1966), fell Euro Soc of Cardiology 1989, FACC 1994; *Recreations* sailing, skiing; *Clubs* Royal Lymington Yacht; *Style*— John Parker, Esq, CBE; ✉ Regional Cardiothoracic Unit, St George's Hospital, Blackshaw Rd, London SW17 0QT (☎ 0181 725 3552); 111 Harley Street, London W1N 1DG (☎ 0171 935 1590, fax 0171 224 2075)

PARKER, Dr John Richard Robert; s of Richard Robert Parker (d 1987), and Elsie Winifred, *née* Curtis; *b* 5 Nov 1933; *Educ* SE London Tech Coll, Regent St Poly (DipArch), UCL (DipTP), Central London Poly (PhD); *m* 1959, Valerie Barbara Mary, da of Edward James Troupe Duguid (d 1952); 1 s (Jonathan b 1965), 1 da (Joanna b 1968); *Career* Nat Serv 2 Lt RE served Canal Zone Cyprus 1952–54, TA (Lt) 1954–64; private architects and commercial firms 1954–59, architect LCC 1961–64, urban designer London Borough of Lambeth 1964–70, head central area team GLC 1970–86; fndr, md and sr ptnr Greater London Consultants 1986– (dir Environmental Appraisal Unit 1989–94), princ John Parker Associates (architectural and planning conslts) 1990–; originator of devpt nr tport interchanges related to pedestrian movement 1967–86, project mangr Piccadilly Circus redevpt 1972–86, planning conslt for Addis Ababa 1986; author of various pubns on subjects incl urban design, environmental planning and pedestrians and security; Winston Churchill fell 1967; RIBA Pearce Edwards Award 1969, Br Cncl Anglo-Soviet Award 1988; ARIBA, FRTPI, FRSA; *Recreations* tennis, golf, drawing, yoga; *Clubs* Cwlth Tst, Shortlands Golf, Catford Wanderers Sports (former chm); *Style*— Dr John Parker; ✉ 4 The Heights, Foxgrove Rd, Beckenham, Kent BR3 5BY (☎ 0181 658 6076); Greater London Consultants, 127 Beulah Road, Thornton Heath, Surrey CR7 8JJ (☎ 0181 768 1417, fax 0181 771 9384)

PARKER, John Stephen; s of Geoffrey Parker, CB (d 1985), and Janet Crawford, *née* Chidley (d 1982); *b* 20 March 1946; *Educ* Trinity Coll Cambridge (MA); *Career* civil servant; joined Miny of Tport 1969; princ: Dept of the Environment 1974–79, Dept of Tport 1979–80; asst sec: Dept of the Environment 1980–90, Dept of Tport 1990–93; princ fin offr Office of Passenger Rail Franchising 1993–95, head Government Offices Unit Dept of Tport 1995–; *Recreations* public administration; *Style*— John Parker, Esq; ✉ Department of Transport, Great Minster House, London SW1P 4DR (☎ 0171 271 5000)

PARKER, John Townley; s of Arthur Townley Parker, of Burnley, Lancashire, and Margaret Elizabeth, *née* Birchall, of Burnley, Lancashire; *b* 26 July 1959; *Educ* Nelson GS, Blackpool Coll of Art; partner, Trudy Parker; *Career* photographer; asst to: Ed Baxter 1980–82, Jerry Oke 1982–85; fndr and proprietor own studio 1986–; 2 Gold awards and 2 Silver awards Assoc of Photographers; memb: Assoc of Photographers 1987–, D&AD Assoc 1988–; *Recreations* football; *Style*— John Parker, Esq; ✉ 1 Warner House, 43–49 Warner Street, London EC1R 5ER (☎ 0171 278 9222)

PARKER, Hon Mr Justice; Hon Sir Jonathan Frederic; kt (1991); s of Sir (Walter) Edmund Parker (d 1981), and Elizabeth Mary, *née* Butterfield (d 1984); *b* 8 Dec 1937; *Educ* Winchester Coll, Magdalene Coll Cambridge (MA); *m* 1967, Maria-Belen, da of Thomas Ferrier Burns OBE; 3 s (James b 1968, Oliver b 1969, Peter b 1971), 1 da (Clare b 1972); *Career* called to the Bar Inner Temple 1962; QC 1979, bencher 1985, recorder of the Crown Court 1989–91, attorney gen Duchy of Lancaster 1989–91; judge of the High Court of Justice (Chancery Division) 1991–; vice-chllr County Palatine of Lancaster 1994–; *Recreations* painting, sailing; *Clubs* Garrick; *Style*— The Hon Mr Justice Parker; ✉ Royal Courts of Justice, Strand, London WC2A 2LL

PARKER, Keith John; OBE (1993); s of Sydney John Parker, of Tywyn, Gwynedd, N Wales, and Phyllis Mary, *née* Marsh; *b* 30 Dec 1940; *m* 25 Aug 1962, Marilyn Ann, da of Wilfred Frank Edwards; 1 s (Nicholas Edward b 18 July 1966); *Career* reporter: Wellington Journal and Shrewsbury News 1957–63, Express and Star Wolverhampton 1963–64; Shropshire Star: reporter, chief reporter, dep news ed 1964–72, ed and dir 1972–77; ed and dir Express and Star 1977–95, gen mangr Express and Star Jan-Dec 1995, md Shropshire Newspapers Limited 1996–; pres Guild of Br Newspaper Editors 1988–89 (chm Parly and Legal Ctee 1991–94), press memb Press Complaints Cmmn 1992–95, memb Data Protection Tbnl 1996–; *Style*— Keith Parker, Esq, OBE; ✉ 94 Wrottesley Rd, Tettenhall, Wolverhampton, West Midlands WV6 8SJ (☎ 01902 758595); Shropshire Newspapers, Ketley, Telford (☎ 01952 242424)

PARKER, Lynne Eleanor; da of Ronald Samuel Parker and Audrey Eleanor, *née* Tyler; *b* 30 June 1956; *Educ* Ashford Co GS Middx, London Coll of Fashion; *Career* journalist 1975–80, PR conslt in own business Parker Lightman Public Relations 1983–90, independent public relations and communications conslt 1991–; MIPR; memb Assoc of Women in PR; *Clubs* Groucho; *Style*— Ms Lynne Parker; ✉ 353 St Margaret's Road, St Margaret's, Twickenham, Middx TW1 1PW (☎ 0181 744 1750, fax 0181 744 0811)

PARKER, Malcolm Peter (Mal); s of William Harvey Parker, of Navenby, Lincs, and Mary Jean, *née* Spinks; *b* 4 June 1946; *Educ* Kings Sch Grantham, Oxford Sch of Architecture; *m* 21 June 1975, Linda Diane, da of Emmanuel Theodore, of London; 2 da (Charlotte b 1982, Georgina b 1984); *Career* architect; Tom Hancock Assocs 1972–73, John Winter Assocs 1973–74, Pentagram 1974–76, Richard Ellis 1976–78, founding ptnr Dunthorne Parker 1978–; projects incl: offices for BUPA, Brooke-Bond, Capital Radio and Swiss Life, industrial parks, Royal Bank of Scotland branches, historic shopping schemes in Oxford, Colchester, High Wycombe and Bury St Edmunds, retail stores for J Sainsbury, hotels in Central London, recording studios for Nat Bdcasting Sch and Chrysalis Records, hostel for High Cmmr for Malaysia, restoration of Grade I listed bldgs Golden Cross in Oxford and Red Lion in Colchester and Grade II offices in Clifton; awards incl: Robertson Award, Ideas in Architecture Award, Oxford Preservation Tst Award, Royal Tunbridge Wells Civic Soc Conservation Award, Civic Tst Award; RIBA 1973, MCSD 1986; *Recreations* golf, skiing, walking, philately, theatre, opera, concerts; *Clubs* Reform; *Style*— Mal Parker, Esq; ✉ Dunthorne Parker, 8 Seymour Place, London W1H 5AG (☎ 0171 258 0411, fax 0171 723 1329)

PARKER, His Hon Judge Michael Clynes; QC (1979); s of Herbert Parker; *b* 2 Nov 1924; *Educ* City of London Sch, Pembroke Coll Cambridge; *m* 1950, Molly Leila Franklin; 1 s, 2 da; *Career* called to the Bar Gray's Inn 1949, recorder of the Crown Ct 1972–78, circuit judge 1978–94; Parly candidate (L) S Kensington 1951; *Style*— His Hon Judge Parker, QC; ✉ 17 Courtnell Street, London W2 5BU

PARKER, Maj Michael John; CVO (1991), CBE (1996, MBE 1968); s of Capt S J Wilkins, and V S M Wilkins, *née* Parker; assumed his mother's maiden name in lieu of his father's patronymic by Deed Poll 1959; *b* 21 Sept 1941; *Educ* Dulwich, Hereford Cathedral Sch, RMA Sandhurst; *Career* Capt Queen's Own Hussars 1961–71, Maj TA Special List attached Queen's Own Hussars 1972–; deviser and prodr of large-scale civilian and mil events; antique dealer; vice-pres Morriston Orpheus Choir, vice-patron Int Music Centre for Blind Children Luberadz Poland; KStJ 1985 (OStJ 1982), Grand Offr Order of al Istiqlal (Jordan) 1987; *Main Productions* Becket 1963, Richard II (Berlin TV) 1964, Berlin Tatoo 1965, 1967, 1971, 1973, 1975, 1977, 1979, 1981, 1983, 1986, 1988 and 1992, British Week Brussels 1967, The Royal Tournament 1974–, The Edinburgh Military Tatoo 1992–94, The Aldershot Army Display 1974, 1975, 1977, 1979, 1981 and 1983, Wembley Musical Pageant 1979, 1981 and 1985, over 30 other mil events around the world; *Nat Events* The Queen's Silver Jubilee Celebrations 1977, The Great Children's Party (Int Yr of the Child) 1979, Carols for the Queen 1979, The Royal Fireworks 1981, The Great Children's Party Hyde Park 1985, The Queen Mother's 90th Birthday Celebrations 1990, Economic Summit Spectacular (G7) Buckingham Palace 1991, The Queen's 40th Anniversary Celebration 1992; *Other Events* Son et Lumière on Horse Guards Parade 1983 and 1985, Americas Cup Newport 1983, King Hussein of Jordan's 50th Birthday Celebrations 1985, Royal Weddings 1987 and 1993 and Coronation Celebration 1988 and 1993, Joy to the World (Christmas celebration Royal Albert Hall) 1988, 1989, 1990, 1991 and 1992, International Horse Shows Olympia, Wembley and Birmingham (variously), World Equestrian Games Stockholm, National Day Celebrations Oman (Royal Equestrian Day) 1990, Fortress Fantasia Gibraltar 1990, British National Day Expo'92 Seville Spain, P&O 150th Anniversary Celebration Greenwich 1992 (further 18 shows in Hong Kong, Cyprus, Jordan, USA, Canada, Germany and UK), Wedding of Prince Abdullah Bin Hussein of Jordan, Memphis in May International Festival Tattoo USA 1993 and 1994, Opening of The Queen Elizabeth Gate Hyde Park London 1993; *Recent Events* Firework Display to mark opening of The Channel Tunnel Folkestone 1994, The Spirit of Normandy (Royal Albert Hall) 1994, Multi-media Show for Normandy 50th Celebration Portsmouth 1994, The Army Benevolent Fund Drumhead Serv 1994, Pavarotti International Horse Show Modena Italy 1993 and 1994, P&O ship naming Shekou China 1994, P & O ship namings Portsmouth and USA 1995, VE Day Celebrations Hyde Park and Buckingham Palace 1995, Jersey Liberation Fireworks 1995, VJ Day Celebrations Horseguards and

Buckingham Palace 1995; *Clubs* Cavalry and Guards'; *Style*— Maj Michael Parker, CVO, CBE; ✉ c/o Cavalry & Guards' Club, 128 Piccadilly, London W1

PARKER, Michael Joseph Bennett; s of Henry Gordon Parker, CBE, MM, TEM (d 1980), of King's Lynn, Norfolk, and Alice Rose, *née* Bennett (d 1975); *b* 22 June 1931; *Educ* Eton, Magdalene Coll Cambridge (BA Agric); *m* 30 April 1960, Tania Henrietta, da of Peter Frank Tiarks (d 1975), of Beaminster, Dorset; 2 s (Stephen b 1960, Benjamin b 1962), 1 da (Naomi b 1964); *Career* dir: Favor Parker Ltd 1962–, Favor Parker Feeds Ltd 1963–, Favor Parker Farms Ltd 1965–, Sovereign Food Group Ltd 1977–, British Chicken Association Ltd 1983–88, British Poultry Meat Federation Ltd 1984–, Suffolk Sovereign Pulham Ltd, Rowywell Roasters Ltd, Pollohold Ltd, Sovereign Chicken Ltd, Sovereign Chicken Group (Essex) Ltd, BPF (Poultry Meat Inspection) Ltd, BCA (Co-operative and Export) Ltd; dir UKAEA 1985–88; *Recreations* country sports, windsurfing, lying in the sun; *Style*— Michael Parker, Esq; ✉ Gooderstone Manor, King's Lynn, Norfolk PE33 9BP (☎ 01366 328255); Favor Parker Ltd, The Hall, Stoke Ferry, King's Lynn, Norfolk PE33 9SE (☎ 01366 500911, fax 01366 500907, telex 81135 FPFEED G)

PARKER, Mike Howard; s of Michael Harding Parker, and Margaret Elfrida, *née* Armstrong; *b* 24 April 1956; *Educ* Chelmer Valley HS Chelmsford; *m* 31 May 1980, Teresa Marie, *née* Soler (d 1990); 1 da (Laura Michelle b 4 Dec 1980); *partner* Anna Marie Treacher; *Career* reporter Essex Chronicle 1973–77, freelance reporter 1977–82, reporter and feature writer News of the World 1982–87; Daily Star: reporter Jan-Sept 1987, night news ed 1987–88, dep news ed 1988–89, features ed 1989–94, asst ed 1994–; assignments covered in N and S America, W Indies, Africa, Middle East, Russia and throughout Europe; Nat Newspaper Consumer Journalist of the Year 1988; *Books* The World's Most Fantastic Freaks (1982); *Recreations* tennis, theatre, travel; *Style*— Mike Parker, Esq; ✉ The Daily Star, c/o Express Newspapers, Ludgate House, 245 Blackfriars Road, London SE1 9UX (☎ 0171 928 8000, fax 0171 620 1641)

PARKER, Sir Peter; KBE (1993), kt (1978), LVO (1985, MVO 1957); s of late Tom Parker and Dorothy S Parker; *b* 30 Aug 1924; *Educ* Bedford Sch, Univ of London, Lincoln Coll Oxford, Cornell Univ, Harvard Univ; *m* 1951, Gillian, da of Sir Ernest Rowe-Dutton, KCMG, CB (d 1965); 3 s, 1 da; *Career* Maj Intelligence Corps 1943–47; chm: Rockware Group 1971–76 and 1983–92 (dir 1971–, dep chm 1981), Br Rail Bd 1976–83, Whitehead Mann Group plc 1984–, Mitsubishi Electric UK Ltd 1984–96, Bardon Group plc 1989–94, Fidelity Japan OTC and Regional Markets Fund Ltd 1990–, Apricot Computers Ltd 1990–, Arcadian International plc 1990–, The Japan Festival 1990–92, Young Vic 1993–, Scruttons plc 1993–, Fidelity Japanese Values plc 1994–, CLM Insurance Fund plc 1995–, Mitsubishi Electric Europe BV 1996–; vice chm tstees of HRH The Duke of Edinburgh's Cwlth Study Conference (UK Fund) 1986–; dep chm: Group 4 Securitas Ltd 1984–96, Group 4 Securitas (UK) Ltd 1996–; dir: UK-Japan 2000 Gp 1986–, Royal National Theatre 1986–91, The Social and Liberal Democrats (Trustees) Ltd 1989–, Rebound IPD Ltd 1992–; dep chm Ct London Univ 1970–, chm Ct Govrs LSE 1988–; formerly with Booker McConnell, dir Booker Bros McConnell 1960–70; memb: BR Airways Bd 1971–81, Cncl BIM, Fndn Automation & Human Devpt 1971–, NEDC 1980–; Parly candidate (Lab) Bedford 1951; hon fell: SOAS, SIAD, London Business Sch, The Open Univ, Manchester Metropolitan Univ, RIBA, Lincoln Coll Oxford, Nuffield Coll Oxford, Nuffield Coll Oxford; Hon LLD: Bath 1983, Univ of London, Univ of Birmingham, Univ of Hull; Communicator of the Year Award Br Assoc of Industrial Editors 1981, Bicentenary Medal RSA 1990, Grand Cordon of the Order of the Sacred Treasure (Japan) 1991; CStJ 1982; *Books* For Starters: The Business of Life (autobiography, 1989 and 1991); *Recreations* rugby (played for Bedford and E Midlands), swimming, browsing; *Style*— Sir Peter Parker, KBE, LVO; ✉ Fountain House, 130 Fenchurch Street, London EC3M 5EE (☎ 0171 621 1472, fax 0171 283 7470)

PARKER, Sir (William) Peter Brian; 5 Bt (UK 1844), of Shenstone Lodge, Staffordshire; o s of Sir (William) Alan Parker, 4 Bt (d 1990), and Sheelagh Mary, *née* Stevenson; *b* 30 Nov 1950; *Educ* Eton; *m* 1976, Patricia Ann, da of late R and late Mrs D E Filtness, of Lea Cottage, Beckingham, Lincoln; 1 s (John Malcolm b 1980), 1 da (Lucy Emma b 1977); *Heir* s, John Malcolm Parker b 14 May 1980; *Career* FCA; sr ptnr Stephenson Nuttall & Co Newark Notts; *Style*— Sir Peter Parker, Bt; ✉ Apricot Hall, Sutton-cum-Beckingham, Lincoln LN5 ORE

PARKER, Peter William; TD (1966); s of William Nichol Parker (d 1978), of Burnley, and Muriel, *née* Constantine (d 1965); *b* 13 June 1933; *Educ* Winchester Coll, New Coll Oxford (MA); *m* 5 Oct 1963, Janet Pusey, da of Tom Rymer Till (d 1982), of Caerleon; 2 s (Tom b 1968, Daniel b 1971), 1 da (Lucy b 1966); *Career* Nat Serv; 2 Lt E Lancashire Regt 1952 (actg capt 1953), TA 4 E Lancashire Regt 1953–67 (Maj 1965); Phillips & Drew 1956–85: ptnr 1962, dep sr ptnr 1983; chm Phillips & Drew International Ltd 1980–85; tstee Tower of London Choral Fndn, vice chm Sidney Perry Fndn, treas Egypt Exploration Soc, govr Music Therapy Charity; Liveryman Worshipful Co of Actuaries (Master 1989–90); memb: Cncl Inst of Actuaries 1977–82 and 1986–92 (vice pres 1988–91), Cncl CGLI 1991–, Royal Patriotic Fund Corp 1991–, Ctee RUKBA 1996–; SBStJ; FIA 1963, MSI; *Recreations* music, gardening, travel, typography; *Clubs* City of London, Naval and Military; *Style*— Peter Parker, Esq, TD; ✉ 1 Turner Drive, London NW11 6TX (☎ 0181 458 2646, fax 0181 455 8498)

PARKER, Prof Ralph; s of Harry Parker (d 1950), of Swansea, and Dorothy Elizabeth, *née* Wilson; *b* 3 Dec 1926; *Educ* Univ of Wales (BSc, PhD, DSc); *m* 28 April 1951, Betty, da of late Thomas Frank, of Loughborough; 3 da (Susan b 6 Jan 1956, Helen b 22 May 1959, Margaret b 1 Dec 1961); *Career* Brush Electrical Engineering Co Ltd 1947–49, scientific civil serv MOS 1950–57, Rolls-Royce Ltd 1957–58, English Electric Co Ltd 1958–64; prof Dept of Mechanical Engrg Univ of Wales Swansea 1964–94 (now emeritus); FIMechE, MRAeS, FIOA, CEng; *Style*— Prof Ralph Parker; ✉ c/o Department of Mechanical Engineering, University of Wales, Swansea, SA2 8PP (☎ 01792 295221, fax 01792 295674)

PARKER, Sir Richard William; 12 Bt (E 1681), of Melford Hall, Suffolk; *see:* Hyde Parker, Sir Richard William

PARKER, Prof Robert Henry (Bob); s of Henry William Parker (d 1978), of London, and Gladys Mary, *née* Bunkell (d 1939); *b* 21 Sept 1932; *Educ* Paston Sch North Walsham Norfolk, UCL (BScEcon); *m* 5 Oct 1955, (Marie) Agnelle Hilda, da of Antoine Yves Laval (d 1962), of Mauritius; 1 s (Michael b 1956), 1 da (Theresa b 1959); *Career* accountant Cassleton Elliott and Co Lagos Nigeria 1958–59, lectr in commerce Univ of Adelaide 1960–61, sr lectr in commerce Univ of W Aust 1962–66, P D Leake res fell LSE 1966, reader in mgmnt accounting Manchester Business Sch 1966–68, assoc prof of finance INSEAD Fontainebleau 1968–70; prof of accountancy: Univ of Dundee 1970–76, Univ of Exeter 1976–; professorial fell Inst of CAs of Scotland 1991–96, ed Accounting and Business Research 1975–93; FCA 1968 (ACA 1958); *Books* Topics in Business Finance and Accounting (jtly, 1964), Readings in Concept and Measurement of Income (jtly, 1969, 2 edn 1986), Management Accounting - An Historical Perspective (1969), Understanding Company Financial Statements (1972, 4 edn 1994), Accounting in Scotland - A Historical Bibliography (jtly, 1974, 2 edn 1976), The Evolution of Corporate Financial Reporting (jtly, 1979), British Accountants - A Biographical Sourcebook (1980), Accounting Thought and Education (jtly, 1980), Bibliographies for Accounting Historians (1980), Comparative International Accounting (jtly, 1981, 4 edn 1995), Macmillan Dictionary of Accounting (1984, 2 edn 1992), Papers on Accounting History (1984), The Development of the Accountancy Profession in Britain to the Early Twentieth Century (1986), Issues in Multinational Accounting (jtly, 1988), A Dictionary of Business Quotations (jtly, 1990), Accounting in Australia - Historical Essays (1990), Consolidation Accounting (jtly, 1991), Collins Dictionary of Business Quotations (jtly, 1991), Accounting History - Some British Contributions (jtly, 1994), Financial Reporting in the West Pacific Rim (jtly, 1994), An International View of True and Fair Accounting (jtly, 1994), Accounting History from the Renaissance to the Present (jtly, 1996), Milestones in the British Accounting Literature (jtly, 1996), Readings in True and Fair (jtly, 1996), Accounting in France/ La comptabilité en France: Historical Essays/Etudes historiques (jtly, 1996); *Recreations* genealogy; *Style*— Prof Bob Parker; ✉ St Catherines, New North Road, Exeter EX4 4AG (☎ 01392 55154); Department of Economics, Amory Building, Rennes Drive, Exeter EX4 4RJ (☎ 01392 263201, fax 01392 263210, telex 42894 EXUNIV G)

PARKER, Robert John; s of Eric Robert Parker (d 1984), and Joan Marjorie Parker (d 1991); *b* 22 Feb 1952; *Educ* Whitgift Sch, St John's Coll Cambridge (MA); *m* 28 Aug 1982, Claudia Jane, da of Col Alexander Akerman; 3 s (Felix Alexander b 12 Feb 1987, Toby b 14 Oct 1991, Benjamin b (twin) 14 Oct 1991); *Career* asst dir NM Rothschild & Sons Ltd 1976–82, exec dir investmts Credit Suisse First Boston Group 1982–94, chief exec Credit Suisse Investment Management Ltd 1995–; Freeman City of London, Liveryman Worshipful Co of Farriers; *Style*— Robert Parker, Esq; ✉ Credit Suisse Investment Management, Beaufort House, 15 St Botolph Street, London EC3A 7JJ

PARKER, Robert Keith; s of Robert Y Parker (decd), of Hexham, Northumberland, and Catherine, *née* Cairns; *b* 6 Dec 1949; *Educ* St Mary's Sch Hexham, Hexham Gen Hosp (SRN), Royal Cornhill Hosp, Foresterhill Coll of Nursing Aberdeen (RMN), Sunderland Poly (Dip in Mgmnt Studies), Univ of Sunderland (BA); *m* 24 July 1971, Hazel Marjorie, da of Ian M Lakeman; 1 s (Keith Robert Parker b 22 June 1973), 1 da (Caroline Anne Parker b 3 March 1975); *Career* student nurse Hexham Gen Hosp 1969–71, post registered student Royal Cornhill Hosp Aberdeen 1971–73, charge nurse Hexham Gen Hosp 1973–75, nursing offr S Tyneside Health Authy 1975–79; sr nursing offr: Forth Valley Health Bd 1979–80, Greater Glasgow Health Bd 1980–82 (acting divnl nursing offr 1982–83); dir Patient Care Servs and dep unit gen mangr Sunderland Dist Gen Hosp 1986–90 (dir Nursing Servs 1983–86), dir Patient Care Servs and Quality Assurance and dep unit gen mangr Wearside Hosps Unit Sunderland 1990–93, dir of quality/chief nurse Priority Healthcare Wearside NHS Tst 1993–; memb: Nat Assoc of Quality Assurance in Health Care 1989–93, S Tyneside Health Authy 1987–90; memb RCN, MIMgt 1986; *Recreations* jogging, swimming, reading; *Style*— Robert Parker, Esq; ✉ Cherry Knowle Hospital, Ryhope, Sunderland SR2 0NB (☎ 0191 565 6256)

PARKER, Robert Stewart; s of Robert Arnold Parker, and Edna, *née* Baines; *b* 13 Jan 1949; *Educ* Brentwood Sch, Trinity Coll Oxford (BA, MA); *Career* called to the Bar Middle Temple 1975, ad eundem Lincoln's Inn 1977; Office of the Parliamentary Counsel 1980, Law Cmmn 1985–87, dep Parly counsel 1987–92, Parly counsel 1992–; Freeman City of London 1984, Liveryman Worshipful Co of Wheelwrights 1984; MIMgt 1984; *Books* Cases and Statutes on General Principles of Law (with C R Newton, 1980); *Recreations* the livery, cricket, bridge, books, music, computing; *Clubs* Athenaeum, City Livery, Langbourn Ward; *Style*— Robert Parker, Esq; ✉ Office of the Parliamentary Counsel, 36 Whitehall, London SW1A 2AY (☎ 0171 210 3000)

PARKER, Roger; s of Horace William Parker (d 1945), and Eliza Margaret, *née* Luckock (d 1959); *b* 27 April 1943; *Educ* King Edward VI Sch Aston Birmingham; *m* 19 Sept 1964, Anne, da of Douglas Archibald Maundrell; 2 s (Robin Gerard b 4 July 1965, Timothy Roger b 12 May 1969); *Career* sports photographer; Midlands Electricity Bd Birmingham 1960, govt serv Bd of Trade then Miny of Pensions (now DSS) 1960–64, key account exec then sales trainer Corn Products Co of USA 1965–68, freelance sports photographer for the press incl Daily Mail and Daily Mirror 1965–68, freelance press photographer 1969–74, The Sun Scotland 1974–75, The Sun London 1975–94; attended World Cup Soccer Finals 1966–94; memb: NUJ 1969–85, IOJ 1985–; *Books* SM (1986); *Recreations* golf, wines, Citröen SM cars, languages, private flying, American football; *Style*— Roger Parker, Esq; ✉ The Barn, Swanbourne, Buckinghamshire MK17 0SL (☎ 01296 720773, fax 01296 728181)

PARKER, Rt Hon Sir Roger Jocelyn Parker; kt (1977), PC (1983); s of Capt Hon T T Parker, DSC, RN (d 1975), and Marie Louise Leonie, *née* Kleinwort (d 1949); *b* 25 Feb 1923; *Educ* Eton, King's Coll Cambridge; *m* 1948, Ann Elizabeth Frederika, *née* White; 1 s, 3 da; *Career* serv Rifle Bde 1941–46; called to the Bar Lincoln's Inn 1948, QC 1961, bencher 1969, chm Bar Cncl and vice-pres Senate of the Four Inns of Ct 1972–73, High Ct judge (Queen's Bench) 1977–83, judge of the Cts of Appeal Jersey & Guernsey 1974–83, Lord Justice of Appeal 1983–92; pres Appeal Tribunal IMRO 1993–; *Style*— The Rt Hon Sir Roger Parker; ✉ The Old Rectory, Widford, nr Ware, Herts (☎ 01279 842593, fax 01279 843406)

PARKER, Prof Stella; da of James Parker (d 1976), and Gertrude, *née* Curley (d 1985); *b* 3 July 1944; *Educ* Brentwood Sch Southport Lancs, Imperial Coll London (BSc, PhD), Birkbeck Coll London (MSc), Garnett Coll London (CertEd); *m* (m dis); *Career* lectr Biology and Medical Lab Sci Hounslow Coll 1973–76, lectr Biological Educn and Medical Lab Sci Garnett Coll London 1976–83, seconded as advsy teacher Advanced Biology Alternative Learning Project 1978–80; City Univ: lectr continuing educn 1984–87, head Dept of Continuing Educn 1987–96, pro-vice-chllr 1993–96; Robert Peers chair in adult/continuing educn Univ of Nottingham 1997–; exec Univs Assoc of Continuing Educn 1987; co-opted memb City of London Educn Ctee; govr The City Lit 1995–; FRSA 1989; *Publications* jt ed ABAL Project books/manuals, also author of various pubns on sci and access; *Recreations* gentle exercise, Francophile; *Clubs* Reform; *Style*— Prof Stella Parker; ✉ Department of Continuing Education, City University, Northampton Square, London EC1V 0HB (☎ 0171 477 8250, fax 0171 477 8256, e-mail S.Parker@city.ac.uk)

PARKER-EATON, Robert George; OBE (1986, MBE (Mil) 1966); s of Leonard George Parker-Eaton (d 1956), of Wythall, nr Birmingham, and Phyllis Muriel, *née* Broome (d 1962); *b* 21 Nov 1931; *Educ* Solihull Sch Warwickshire, RAF Staff Coll; *m* 21 Dec 1962, Dorothy Elizabeth, da of Thomas Edgar Sharpe (d 1957), of Bletchley, Bucks; 2 s (Stephen Paul b 1963, Timothy Simon b 1968), 1 da (Sarah Frances b 1965); *Career* cmmnd supply branch RAF 1950, Wing Cdr 1966, controller civil air trooping MOD 1966–69, dep dir logistics prog Supreme Allied Cmd Atlantic 1969–72, OC air movements RAF Brize Norton 1972–74; Britannia Airways Ltd: controller customer servs 1974–78, dir customer servs and external affrs 1978–90, dep md 1990–; UK dir Ind Air Carriers Assoc (IACA) 1993–; memb: Exec Ctee Br Air Tport Assoc 1989–, Bd Duty Free Confedn 1993–; swimming rep: Cornwall 1955–56, Cumbria 1959–60, RAF 1959–69, Combined Services 1960–63, Berkshire 1961–62; FIMgt 1981 (MIMgt 1968), FCIT 1991 (MCIT 1982); *Recreations* swimming, model railways, reading; *Style*— Robert Parker-Eaton, Esq, OBE; ✉ 1 Kiln Lane, Clophill, Bedford MK45 4DA (☎ 01525 861128); Britannia Airways Ltd, Luton Airport, Luton, Bedfordshire (☎ 01582 424155, fax 01582 428000, telex 82239)

PARKES, Sir Edward Walter; kt (1982); s of Walter Parkes; *b* 19 May 1926; *Educ* King Edward's Birmingham, St John's Coll Cambridge; *m* 1950, Margaret Parkes, JP (chm Nat Cncl for Educnl Technol, former govr BBC), da of John Parr; 1 s, 1 da; *Career* head Engrg Dept Univ of Leicester 1960–65, prof of mechanics Univ of Cambridge 1965–74, vice chllr City Univ 1974–78; memb: Advsy Bd for Res Cncls 1974–83, Univ and Poly Grants Ctee Hong Kong 1974–; chm: University Grants Ctee 1978–83, Advsy Panel to sec of state for Environment on issues relating to Black Country limestone 1983–, Ctee of Vice Chllrs and Princs 1989–91 (vice chm 1985–89); vice chllr Univ of

Leeds 1983–91; ScD, FEng 1982; *Clubs* Athenaeum; *Style*— Sir Edward Parkes, FEng; ✉ The Cottage, Headington Hill, Oxford OX3 0BT

PARKES, Dr (Colin) Murray; OBE; s of late Eric William Parkes, of Herts, and Gwyneth Ann, *née* Roberts; *b* 26 March 1928; *Educ* Royal Med Coll Epsom, Westminster Med Sch Univ of London (MD); *m* 22 June 1957, Patricia Margaret Parkes, da of Rev Esmond Whitehall Patrick Ainsworth, CBE (d 1979), of Bromsash, Gloucestershire; 3 da (Elizabeth b 1958, Jennifer b 1960, Caroline b 1963); *Career* RAF Med Corp; memb res staff: Social Psychiatry Unit MRC, The Tavistock Inst of Human Relations; project offr Laboratory of Community Psychiatry Harvard Med Sch USA, sr lectr in psychiatry The London Hosp Med Coll, currently hon conslt psychiatrist St Christopher's Hospice Sydenham and St Joseph's Hospice Hackney; pres Cruse Bereavement Care; FRCPsych; *Books* Bereavement: Studies of Grief in Adult Life, Recovery from Bereavement (with R Weiss), Counselling in Terminal Care and Bereavement (with M Relf and A Couldrick); *Recreations* collecting antique blue and white transfer wares, Chiltern Choir; *Style*— Dr C Murray Parkes, OBE; ✉ 21 South Road, Chorleywood, Herts WD3 5AS (☎ 01923 282746, fax 01923 283628)

PARKES, Timothy Charles; TD (1988); s of Frank Leonard Parkes (d 1955), of Leamington Spa, Warwickshire, and Marie Joan Parkes, *née* Morris; *b* 13 Aug 1954; *Educ* Royal Masonic Sch, Wadham Coll Oxford (MA); *m* 31 Aug 1985, Wendy Patricia, da of Maj Vincent Reginald Hook, of Steep, Petersfield, Hants; 1 s (Charles Alexander Frederick b 1988), 2 da (Laura Claire Venetia b 1990, Eleanor Juliet Lucy b 1992); *Career* TACSC 1989 (Maj TA Royal Yeomanry 1984–); admitted slr 1980; currently ptnr Herbert Smith; memb: Judicial Studies Bd Hong Kong 1990–95, Civil Ct Users' Ctee Hong Kong 1993–95, Cncl Law Soc of Hong Kong 1993–95; Freeman Worshipful Co of Slrs 1982; memb: Int Bar Assoc, Inter-Pacific Bar Assoc, Law Soc of England and Wales; FCIArb; *Recreations* tennis, reading; *Clubs* Cavalry & Guards, Hong Kong, Royal Hong Kong Jockey; *Style*— Timothy Parkes, Esq, TD; ✉ Bergersh Place, Witnesham, Ipswich, Suffolk IP6 9EZ (☎ 01473 785504, fax 01473 785159)

PARKHOUSE, Peter; s of William Richard Parkhouse, MBE (d 1969), of Topsham, Devon, and Alice Vera, *née* Clarke (d 1981); *b* 22 July 1927; *Educ* Blundell's, Peterhouse Cambridge (organist 1944–45), Univ of Cologne (Br Cncl scholarship); *m* 1, 29 April 1950, Mary Alison Holland (d 1987); 1 da (Katharine Holland b 20 May 1953), 1 s (William John b 18 July 1955); m 2, 12 Feb 1994, Sally Isabel Squires; *Career* served RN as Instr Lt 1947–50, asst master Uppingham Sch 1951–52; Miny of Agric, Fisheries and Food (Miny of Food until 1955): joined as asst princ 1952, asst private sec to min 1954–58, princ 1958–67 (successively hd of branch Welsh Dept, External Relations (GATT) Div, Milk Div and princ private sec to min), asst sec 1967–73 (successively hd of Fisheries Div, Policy Planning Unit and EC Div), under sec 1973 (hd of EC Gp responsible for MAFF interests in Euro Community); dir European Cmmn Brussels 1973–79 (hd of Agric Economics Directorate then Agric Int Affrs Directorate), rejoined MAFF as under sec 1979–84 (successively hd of External Relations and Horticulture, Plant Health and Agric Resources Gps); chm Severn NHS Tst 1992–96; memb Tetbury Hosp Action Gp 1989–93, tstee Tetbury Hosp Tst Ltd 1992–93 and 1996–; memb Mgmnt Ctee Cheltenham Int Music Festival 1992–95, govr Barnwood House Tst 1996; *Recreations* music (especially opera, chamber music and the organ, sub-organist Tetbury Parish Church), fishing, gardening; *Clubs* United Oxford and Cambridge Univ; *Style*— Peter Parkhouse, Esq; ✉ Stafford House, The Chipping, Tetbury, Gloucs GL8 8ET (☎ 01666 502540)

PARKIN, Catherine Elizabeth (Kate); da of Ian Stuart Parkin, of Alderton, Glos, and Elizabeth, *née* Downey; *b* 9 April 1959; *Educ* Tewkesbury Comp, Cheltenham GS, St Catherine's Coll Oxford (BA); *m* 29 Aug 1983, William John Urwick Hamilton, s of Mark Hamilton; 2 da (Susannah Elizabeth Rose b 18 April 1989, Mary Isabel Angelica b 19 April 1993); *Career* grad trainee Thomson Publishing 1980–81, editorial controller Macmillan London Ltd 1981–85; Transworld Publishers Ltd: ed 1985–86, sr ed 1986–87 editorial dir 1987–89; editorial dir Collins Publishers 1989–91; Random House UK: publishing dir Century 1991–93, publisher Century Arrow 1993–; *Recreations* reading, cooking, gardening, music; *Style*— Ms Kate Parkin; ✉ Random House UK Ltd, Random House, 20 Vauxhall Bridge Road, London SW1V 2SA (☎ 0171 973 9000, fax 0171 233 6212)

PARKIN, Ian Michael; s of George Harold Parkin, of Worthing, W Sussex, and Ethel Mary, *née* Fullerton; *b* 15 Oct 1946; *Educ* Dorking Co GS, Open Univ (BA); *m* 30 April 1977, Patricia Helen, da of Maj Frederick James Fowles, MC (d 1982); 2 s (Andrew b 1978, Richard b 1984), 1 da (Jennifer b 1981); *Career* CA; formerly: sr ptnr Pannell Kerr Forster CI 1979–90, sr ptnr Brownes CAs Jersey, dir Citadel Trust Ltd Jersey 1990–93, ptnr Moores Rowland Jersey 1993–95; currently dir: Compass Trust Company Ltd Jersey, Cater Allen Trust Company (Jersey) Ltd; FCA 1979; *Recreations* golf, reading, sailing; *Style*— Ian Parkin, Esq; ✉ Le Petit Jardin, La Rue a la Pendue, Millais, St Ouen, Jersey (☎ 01534 483218, fax 01534 483795); Compass Trust Company Ltd, Thomas Edge House, Tunnell Street, St Helier, Jersey, CI

PARKIN, Sara Lamb; da of Dr George Lamb McEwan (d 1996), of Isle of Islay, Argyll, and Marie Munro, *née* Rankin; *b* 9 April 1946; *Educ* Barr's Hill GS Coventry, Bromsgrove Coll, Edinburgh Royal Infirmary (RGN), Univ of Michigan, Leeds Poly; *m* 30 June 1969, Donald Maxwell Parkin, s of Donald Harry Parkin, of Lincolnshire, and Lesley Mary, *née* Tyson; 2 s (Colin McEwan b 28 March 1974, Douglas Maxwell b 12 Sept 1975); *Career* staff nurse and ward sister Edinburgh Royal Infirmary 1970–74, nursing res asst and undergraduate tutor Univ of Edinburgh 1972–73, memb Cncl Brook Advsy Serv 1974–76, Leeds Area Health Authy 1976–80, self employed writer and speaker on green issues 1981–; Green Pty: memb Cncl 1980–81, int liaison sec 1983–90, chair of the Exec 1992; co-sec Euro Greens 1985–90 (ed Newsletter 1986–89); dir Forum For The Future 1995–; tstee: New Econs Fndn, Friends of the Earth Tst; companion ICE; *Publications* incl: Green Parties: An International Guide (1989), Green Light on Europe (ed, 1991), Green Futures (1991), The Life and Death of Petra Kelly (1994); also author of various nat and Euro Green Election manifestos; *Recreations* walking, gardening, theatre, opera; *Style*— Ms Sara Parkin; ✉ Forum for the Future, 227a City Road, London EC1V 1JT (☎ 0171 251 6070)

PARKINS, Brian James Michael; JP; s of Ronald Anthony Parkins (d 1979), of Ilford, Essex, and Adelaide Florence, *née* Percival; *b* 1 Nov 1938; *Educ* St Ignatius Coll London, King's Coll Hosp and Univ of London (BDS), Inst of Dental Surgery and RCS (LDS, FDS), Northwestern Univ Chicago (MS); *m* 1, 20 Oct 1966 (m dis 1980), Jill Elizabeth, da of James Dawson (d 1982), of Lytham St Annes; 1 s (Richard Mark b 1 March 1971), 1 da (Alison) Jane b 14 Nov 1967); m 2, 19 May 1988, Mary Saunders, *née* Burton; *Career* conslt dental surgn; sr clinical lectr Inst of Dental Surgery 1969–81, private practice 1970–, recognised teacher of the Univ of London 1972, conslt in restorative dentistry UCL and Middx Hosp Sch of Dentistry 1982–92; pres Br Soc for Restorative Dentistry 1987–88 (cncl memb 1982–84); sec: American Dental Soc of London (pres 1996–97), American Dental Soc of Europe (pres 1993–94); examiner 1977–86: BDS, RCS for LDS Final Part III FDS and MGDS; hon treas Dentist Provident Soc; hon memb American Dental Assoc; fell: Pierre Fouchard Acad, Int Coll of Dentists, American Coll of Dentists; *Recreations* reading, music, golf; *Clubs* Savage; *Style*— Brian Parkins, Esq, JP; ✉ 57 Portland Place, London W1N 3AH (☎ 0171 580 7146)

PARKINS, Graham Charles; QC (1990); *Educ* Univ of London (LLB); *Career* called to the Bar Inner Temple 1972, recorder of the Crown Court; *Style*— Graham Parkins, Esq, QC; ✉ 5 Kings Bench Walk, Temple, London EC4Y 7DN (☎ 0171 797 7600, fax 0171 797 7648)

PARKINSON, Baron (Life Peer UK 1992), of Carnforth in the County of Lancashire; Cecil Edward Parkinson; PC (1981); s of Sidney Parkinson, of Carnforth, Lancs; *b* 1 Sept 1931; *Educ* Royal Lancaster GS, Emmanuel Coll Cambridge; *m* 1957, Ann Mary, da of F A Jarvis, of Harpenden; 3 da (Hon Mary b 1959, Hon Emma (Hon Mrs Owrid) b 1961, Hon Joanna (Hon Mrs Bamber) b 1963); *Career* joined West Wake Price & Co 1956 (ptnr 1961–71); formerly with Metal Box Co, founded Parkinson Hart Securities Ltd 1967; chm: Hemel Hempstead Cons Assoc 1966–69, Herts 100 Club 1968–69; Parly candidate (C) Northampton 1970; MP (C): Enfield W Nov 1970–74, Herts S 1974–1983, Hertsmere 1983–92; sec Cons Parly Fin Ctee 1971–72, PPS to Michael Heseltine as min for Aerospace and Shipping DTI 1972–74, asst govt whip 1974, oppn whip 1974–76, oppn spokesman on trade 1976–79, min of state Dept of Trade 1979–81, chm Cons Pty and Paymaster-General 1981–83, chllr Duchy of Lancaster 1982–83, sec of state for trade and indust June-Oct 1983 (resigned), sec of state for energy 1987–89, sec of state for tport 1989–90; non-exec chm of various cos; *Style*— The Rt Hon the Lord Parkinson, PC

PARKINSON, Ewart West; s of Thomas Edward Parkinson (d 1958), of Leicester, and Lilian Esther West, *née* Hammond (d 1966); *b* 9 July 1926; *Educ* Wyggeston Sch Leicester, Coll of Tech Leicester, Univ of London (BSc, DPA); *m* 21 Aug 1948, Patricia Joan, da of Capt William John Lawson Wood (d 1985), of Leicester; 2 s (Mark b 1951, Michael b 1955), 1 da (Veronica b 1959); *Career* princ engr Bristol 1949–54, chief asst Dover 1954–57, dep borough engr Chelmsford 1957–60, dep city surveyor Plymouth 1960–64, city planning offr Cardiff 1964–74, dir Environment S Glam 1974–85; devpt advsr and company dir 1985–; projects incl: specialised rebuilding and regeneration war damaged cities 1948–64, urban regeneration Cardiff 1964–85, regeneration of Welsh towns 1988–; visiting lectr China Acad of Urban Planning and Design 1982–; chm and fndr: Star Leisure and Recreation Tst, Wales Sports Centre for the Disabled Tst; chm Facilities Ctee Sports Cncl for Wales 1966–78; managing tstee then chm Norwegian Church Preservation Tst, vice pres Wales Cncl for the Disabled, devpt dir Cardiff Action for the Single Homeless, fndr and first chm Co Planning Offrs Soc for Wales, chm Roald Dahl Arts Project Tst 1995–; hon life memb Int Fedn of Housing and Planning (The Hague); Miller Prize (Bridge Design) ICE, Nat Housing and Town Planning Cncl Diamond Jubilee Silver Medal, numerous awards for civic design; numerous papers presented worldwide; OStJ; FICE, FRTPI (pres 1975–76); *Recreations* working, being with friends and family; *Style*— Ewart Parkinson, Esq; ✉ 42 South Rise, Cardiff (☎ 01222 756394); W S Atkins & Partners, Longcross Court, Cardiff (☎ 01222 485159, fax 01222 485138)

PARKINSON, Graham Edward; s of Norman Edward Parkinson (d 1984), of Birstall, Leicestershire, and Phyllis, *née* Jaquiss; *b* 13 Oct 1937; *Educ* Loughborough GS; *m* 1963, Dinah Mary, da of Walter Bevan Pyper (d 1969), of Harrow on the Hill, Middx; 1 s (Nicholas b 1967), 1 da (Georgina b 1973); *Career* ptnr Darlington & Parkinson slrs 1969–82, Metropolitan Stipendiary Magistrate 1982–, recorder of the Crown Ct 1988–; *Recreations* music, theatre, reading; *Style*— Graham E Parkinson, Esq; ✉ Horseferry Road Magistrates Court, 70 Horseferry Road, London SW1P 2AX (☎ 0171 233 2000)

PARKINSON, Malcolm Ross; s of F C D Parkinson (d 1983), and Alexa St Clair, *née* Ross; *b* 20 April 1948; *Educ* Sutton Valence Sch; *m* 1972, Beatrice Maria, da of Prof C Schwaller; 1 da (b 1978), 1 s (b 1981); *Career* trainee navigation offr Cunard then actg 4th offr T & J Brocklebank Ltd 1964–69, trainee account exec BBD&O Ltd 1969–72, account dir Leo Burnett Inc 1972–74, jt md DWK Ltd 1974–76, dir B & Q Ltd 1976–84, chief exec F W Woolworth Ltd 1984–87; dir: Woolworth Holdings plc 1984–87, James Latham plc 1992–, Powerbreaker plc 1992–, Applied Chemicals Ltd 1992–; md: Retail Corporation plc 1989–92, Siegel & Gale Ltd (UK, Europe, Africa and ME) 1993–96; chm: Imatronic Ltd 1989–93, Latham Timber Centres Ltd 1992–, Malross Management Ltd; chm Sunday Trading Ctee, govr Capel Manor Coll; memb Worshipful Co of Gardeners; fell Mktg Soc; *Recreations* sailing, shooting; *Clubs* Royal Thames Yacht; *Style*— Malcolm Parkinson, Esq; ✉ Malross Management Ltd, Estate Office, Claywood House, Sway, Hampshire SO41 6DA (☎ 01590 683899); James Latham plc, Leeside Wharf, Mount Pleasant Hill Road, Clapton, London E5 9NG (☎ 0181 806 3333)

PARKINSON, (Robert) Michael; s of Robert Scott Parkinson, of Lancaster, and Rhoda, *née* Chirnside (d 1964); *b* 9 Aug 1944; *Educ* Wrekin Coll, Coll of Estate Mgmnt Univ of London (BSc); *m* 26 Oct 1968, Elizabeth Ann, da of Michael Moore, of Lancaster; 2 s (Duncan b 27 Nov 1969, Andrew b 4 Sept 1971); *Career* ptnr Ingham & Yorke (chartered surveyors, land agents, auctioneers and valuers) 1971–, dir Marsden Building Soc 1984– (vice chm 1994–); chm: Marsden Home Renovations Ltd 1991–, Marsden Homes (Pendle) Ltd 1994–; steward to the Honor of Clitheroe 1991–; memb (formerly sec and chm) Lancs Cheshire & Isle of Man Branch Rural Practice Div of RICS; FRICS 1976; *Recreations* mountaineering, country pursuits; *Clubs* Fell and Rock Climbing, Univ of London Graduate Mountaineering (pres), Rotary (Clitheroe), Clitheroe Ex-Tablers (41); *Style*— Michael Parkinson, Esq; ✉ Littlemoor House, Clitheroe, Lancs BB7 1HF (☎ 01200 422660); Ingham & Yorke, Littlemoor, Clitheroe, Lancs BB7 1HG (☎ 01200 423655, fax 01200 429160)

PARKINSON, Michael; *b* 28 March 1935, Yorkshire; *Educ* Barnsley GS; *m* 22 August 1959, Mary Heneghan; 3 s (Andrew, Nicholas, Michael); *Career* TV and radio presenter, journalist and writer; prodr/interviewer Granada TV 1964–68 (Granada's Scene, Granada in the North, World in Action, What The Papers Say), exec prodr and presenter LWT 1964–68; presenter: 24 Hours (BBC) 1964–68, Cinema (Granada TV) 1969–70, Tea Break and Where in the World (Thames TV) 1971; host Parkinson (BBC) 1972–82 (Channel 10 & ABC Australia 1979–85), co-fndr and presenter TV-AM 1983–84; presenter: Give Us A Clue (Thames TV) 1984–92, Desert Island Discs (BBC Radio 4) 1986–88; host: Parkinson One to One (Yorkshire TV) 1987–88, Parky (Thames TV) 1989, The Michael Parkinson Show (LBC) 1990–92; presenter: Help Squad (TVS) 1991–92, Ghostwatch (BBC) 1992, Parkinson on Sport (BBC Radio 5) 1994–; host Going For a Song (BBC) 1995–; fndr Pavilion Books 1980; sometime columnist: Sunday Times, Guardian, Daily Express, The People, The Listener, Daily Mirror, New Statesman, Mail on Sunday; currently columnist Daily Telegraph; Sports Feature Writer of the Yr (British Sports Journalism Awards) 1995; *Books* Football Daft (1968), Cricket Mad (1969), Pictorial History of Westerns (with Clyde Jeavons, 1969), Sporting Fever (1974), Best - An Intimate Biography (1975), A-Z of Soccer (with Willis Hall, 1975), Bats in the Pavilion (1977), The Woofits (1980), Parkinson's Lore (1981), The Best of Parkinson (1982), Sporting Lives (1992), Sporting Profiles (1995); *Recreations* sport (particularly cricket and golf); *Style*— Michael Parkinson, Esq; ✉ c/o James Kelly, IMG Artists, Axis House, Burlington Lane, Chiswick, London W4 2TH (☎ 0181 233 5805, fax 0181 233 5301)

PARKINSON, Ronald Dennis; s of late Albert Edward Parkinson, and late Jennie Caroline Clara, *née* Meagher; *b* 27 April 1945; *Educ* St Dunstan's Coll, Clare Coll Cambridge (MA); *Career* res asst V & A 1972–74, asst keeper Tate Gallery 1974–78, asst curator V & A 1978–; *Books* Catalogue of British Oil Paintings 1820–1860 in the V & A (1990); *Recreations* reading, shopping; *Clubs* Algonquin; *Style*— Ronald Parkinson, Esq; ✉ Victoria And Albert Museum, London SW7 2RL (☎ 0171 938 8474)

PARKINSON, Steven David; s of David K Parkinson, of Aberdeen, and Lilian, *née* Rannie; *b* 1 April 1967; *Educ* Robert Gordon's Coll Aberdeen, Queen Margaret Coll Edinburgh (Dip in Drama; *Career* mktg mangr Scottish Opera tours 1989, prodn mangr

P&O SS Canberra 1990, press and events offr National Garden Festival 1990, presenter Tyne Tees TV 1991; Metro Radio Group: charity fundraiser 1990, prodr Hallam FM Sheffield 1991–92, prog controller Great North Radio Newcastle 1992–94, prog controller Great Yorkshire Gold 1994–95, head of marketing and promotions Hallam FM and Great Yorkshire Gold 1995–; *Recreations* fencing, swimming, photography, theatre; *Style*— Steven Parkinson, Esq; ✉ Great Yorkshire Gold, 900 Herries Road, Sheffield, W Yorks S6 1RH (☎ 0114 285 2121, fax 0114 285 3159)

PARKS, Timothy Harold (Tim); s of Harold James Parks (d 1980), and Joan Elizabeth, *née* MacDowell; *b* 19 Dec 1954; *Educ* Westminster City Sch London, Downing Coll Cambridge (BA), Harvard Univ (MA); *m* 15 Dec 1979, Rita Maria, *née* Baldassarre; 1 s (Michele Roberto b 3 June 1985), 1 da (Stefania Angela b 20 Jan 1988); *Career* writer; marketing exec Tek Translation & International Print London 1979–80, freelance teacher and translator Verona 1981–85, lettore Univ of Verona 1985–, visiting lectr Istituto Universitario di lingue Moderne Milan 1992–; memb Soc of Authors 1986–; *Books* Tongues of Flame (1985, Somerset Maugham award, Betty Trask award), Loving Roger (1986, John Llewellyn Rhys award), Home Thoughts (1987), Family Planning (1989), Cara Massimina (as John MacDowell, 1990), Goodness (1991), Italian Neighbours (non-fiction, 1992) Shear (1993); series of trans from Italian incl work by Calvino, Moravia, Tabucchi and Calasso; *Recreations* fencing, cycling, squash; *Style*— Tim Parks; ✉ c/o Anthony Harwood, Aitken & Stone Ltd, 29 Fernshaw Road, London SW10 0TT (☎ 0171 351 7561, fax 0171 376 3594)

PARLETT, Michael Harold James; s of Lyall Mervyn Malzard Parlett (d 1995), of Trinity, Jersey, and Catherine McDougall, *née* Gray; *b* 16 Nov 1940; *Educ* Winchester, Millfield, St Andrews Univ (BSc); *m* 2 Sept 1967, Elizabeth Ann, da of Dr Frederick Roy Gusterson; 2 da (Lucinda b 1969, Clare b 1971); *Career* Shell International Petroleum 1965–68, Shell Sekiyu 1968–73; investmt mangr: Stewart Fund Managers 1973–74, Murray Johnstone Ltd 1974–77; exec dir Murray Johnstone Ltd 1977–83 and 1991–, vice pres and dir Kemper Murray Johnstone International Inc 1983–89, dir Murray Johnstone International Ltd 1989–, dir i/c Murray Johnstone Investment Tsts 1993–, chm Murray Universal Growth SICAV 1993–; *Recreations* skiing, hill-walking; *Style*— Michael Parlett, Esq; ✉ Glebe House, Manse Rd, Linlithgow EH49 6QP (☎ 01506 844247); Murray Johnstone Ltd, 7 West Nile St, Glasgow G1 2PX (☎ 0141 226 3131, fax 0141 248 5420)

PARLOUR, Ray; *b* 7 March 1973; *Career* professional footballer (midfielder); Arsenal FC: joined 1990, debut 1992, winners League and FA Cup double 1993, Cup Winners' Cup 1994 (runners up 1995); memb England under 21 team (12 under 21 caps), winners Toulon U21 Tournament 1994; *Style*— Ray Parlour, Esq; ✉ c/o Arsenal FC, Arsenal Stadium, Avenell Road, Highbury, London N5 1BU (☎ 0171 226 0304)

PARMINTER, Gail; da of Francis Parminter, of Maidenhead, Berks, and Barbara Helen, *née* Cox; *b* 29 Nov 1964; *Educ* Holt Sch Wokingham Berks, Berkshire Coll of Art & Design; *partner* Peter Gunn; 4 s (Joseph William Parminter-Gunn, Theo James Parminter-Gunn, George Henry Parminter-Gunn, Henry Alexander Parminter-Gunn); *Career* copywriter BSB Dorland 1986–91; TV commercial and press work; accounts incl: Eden Vale, Ski, Austin Rover, Heinz, Electricity Cncl, Feminax, Castrol, Halifax Building Society, Woolworths; winner: Silver Campaign Poster award for Austin Rover Mini, D & AD award for Flowers Bitter, Clio award for Eden Vale, Campaign Press award for Austin Rover; fndr memb Notman Parminter advertising 1991–94; accounts incl: Bernard Matthews plc, Larkhall Natural Health, Ann Summers Ltd, Totes; copywriter Bates Dorland 1994–; shortlisted Cosmopolitan magazine Achievements Awards 1992; *Style*— Ms Gail Parminter; ✉ Bates Dorland, 121–141 Westbourne Terrace, London W2 6JR (☎ 0171 262 5077)

PARMOOR, 4 Baron (UK 1914); (Frederick Alfred) Milo Cripps; s of 3 Baron Parmoor, DSO, TD, DL (d 1977), and of Violet Mary Geraldine (d 1983), da of Sir William Nelson, 1 Bt; *b* 18 June 1929; *Educ* Ampleforth, Corpus Christi Coll Oxford; *Heir* cous, (Matthew) Anthony Leonard Cripps, *qv*; *Style*— The Rt Hon the Lord Parmoor; ✉ Dairy, Duck Street, Sutton Veny, Wilts

PARNELL, Alexandra; da of Cyril Henry Parnell (d 1985), of Dorking, Surrey, and Heather, *née* Beasley; *b* 3 May 1952; *Educ* Purley Co GS for Girls; *m* 1, 20 April 1974 (m dis 1982), Geoffrey Willis; m 2, Aug 1996, Adam Hipkin; *Career* asst sec to The Hon David Astor ed The Observer 1970–72, sec to Betty Reyburn, features ed Woman's Journal 1972–73, fashion asst Woman's Journal 1973–75, asst fashion ed Country Life 1975–78, fashion ed Woman's Journal 1978–; *Recreations* riding, foreign travel; *Style*— Ms Alexandra Parnell; ✉ IPC Magazines Ltd, King's Reach Tower, London SE1 (direct ☎ 0171 261 6064, fax 0171 261 7061)

PARNELL, Hon John Patrick Christian; s and h of 8 Baron Congleton, *qv*; *b* 17 March 1959; *m* 1985, Marjorie-Anne, o da of John Hobdell, of The Ridings, Cobham, Surrey; 2 s (Christopher John Edward b 1987, Harry Gustav Willem b 1990), 1 da (Phoebe Anna Hedvig b 1992); *Career* Liveryman Worshipful Co of Gunmakers; *Style*— The Hon John Parnell

PARR, Anthony Stephen; s of Stephen Valentine Parr, of Preston, Lancs, and Brenda, *née* Carter-McGrath (d 1970); *b* 27 Aug 1949; *Educ* Balshaws GS Leyland Lancs; *m* Jan 1985, Jannette Marie, da of Rudi Becker; 2 s (Jamie Anthony b 6 June 1986, Daniel Andrew b 14 June 1988), 1 da (Sally Jane b 26 June 1990); *Career* accountant Lancs CC 1967–72, accountant Shropshire CC 1973–77, asst treas Somerset CC 1977–85, treas Bristol and Weston Health Authy 1987–91 (dep treas 1985–87), chief exec South Devon Healthcare NHS Tst 1991–; CIPFA 1972; *Recreations* golf, former rugby player; *Style*— Anthony Parr, Esq; ✉ South Devon Healthcare NHS Trust, Hengrave House, Torbay Hospital, Lawes Bridge, Torquay, Devon TQ2 7AA (☎ 01803 655703, fax 01803 616334)

PARR, Christopher Serge (Chris); *b* 25 Sept 1943; *Educ* High Sch for Boys Chichester, Queen's Coll Oxford (Open scholar, Classics); *m* 23 Dec 1985, Anne Maria Devlin; 1 s (Connal Sebastian Devlin Parr b 23 Oct 1984); *Career* ABC trainee dir's bursary Nottingham Playhouse 1965–66, freelance theatre dir 1966–69, fell in theatre Univ of Bradford 1969–72, freelance (incl Royal Court Theatre) 1972–75, artistic dir Traverse Theatre Club 1975–81, prodr TV Drama BBC Northern Ireland, Pebble Mill, London and Scotland 1981–93, head of TV drama BBC Pebble Mill 1993–95, head of drama series BBC TV 1995–96, exec prodr BBC TV Drama Gp 1996–; *Awards* two RTS Serial Awards (for Nice Work and Children of the North), ACE Award (for The Rainbow), BAFTA Award (Drama Serial, for Takin' Over the Asylum), Celtic Film and TV Festival Drama Award (for Naming the Names), Michael Powell Award Edinburgh Festival (for You, Me and Marley); *Style*— Chris Parr, Esq; ✉ BBC Centre House, Wood Lane, London W12 7RJ (☎ 0181 743 8000 ext 69460)

PARR, (Thomas) Donald; CBE (1986); s of Thomas Parr (d 1975), of Bramhall, Cheshire, and Elizabeth Parr; *b* 3 Sept 1930; *Educ* Burnage GS; *m* 1954, Gwendoline Mary, da of Frank Lawton Chaplin, of Cheadle, Cheshire (d 1969); 3 s, 1 da; *Career* chm William Baird PLC (textile and industl gp) 1981–; non exec dir: Vendome Luxury Group PLC, Hepworth PLC, Kwiksave plc; *Recreations* sailing (yacht 'Quailo'); *Clubs* Boodle's, Royal Yacht Sqdn, Royal Ocean Racing; *Style*— Donald Parr, Esq, CBE; ✉ Homestead, Homestead Rd, Disley, Stockport, Cheshire SK12 2JP; Broadstone House, Broadstone Rd, Reddish, Stockport, Cheshire SK5 7DL (☎ 0161 442 8118); William Baird PLC, 79 Mount St, London W1Y 5HJ (☎ 0171 409 1785, fax 0171 499 6271)

PARR, John Robert; s of Henry George Parr (d 1982), and Hilda Frances, *née* Pattison (d 1992); *b* 25 Sept 1934; *Educ* Dulwich Coll, Merton Coll Oxford (open scholar, MA); *m* June 1993, Margaret Dolores, da of Charles Michael O'Reilly; *Career* British Iron and Steel Fedn 1959–64, Industl Policy Div Dept of Economic Affairs 1965–67; British Steel Corporation: joined 1968, co-ordinator European Community Affairs 1972–73; DG British Footwear Manufacturers Fedn 1973–76; General Secretariat of the Cncl of the European Communities: joined 1976, head of Div for Air Tport and Shipping 1986–89, hon dir 1989–96; DG Air Tport Users Cncl 1989–; chm Airline-Consumer Forum Geneva 1995–; MCIT; *Recreations* theatre, concert and opera going, 20th c European history; *Style*— John Parr, Esq

PARRATT, Prof James Roy; s of James John Parratt, and Eunice Elizabeth Parratt; *b* 19 Aug 1933; *Educ* St Clement Danes Holborn Estate GS, Univ of London (BPharm, MSc, PhD), Univ of Strathclyde (DSc); *m* 7 Sept 1957, Pamela Joan Lyndon, da of Stanley Charles Marels; 2 s (Stephen John Lyndon b 14 March 1960, Jonathan Mark b 21 March 1969), 1 da (Deborah Joy b 3 Sept 1965); *Career* sr lectr Dept of Physiology Univ of Ibadan Nigeria 1958–66, chm and head Dept of Physiology and Pharmacology Univ of Strathclyde 1986–90 (sr lectr then reader Dept of Pharmacology 1966–74, personal chair in pharmacology 1975, newly established chair in cardiovascular pharmacology 1983–); former chm Br Soc Cardiovascular Res, hon memb Pharmacological Soc Hungary 1976; Polish Physiological Soc Medal 1989, J Purkinje Gold Medal Acad of Scis of the Czech Republic 1995; Hon MD Albert Szent-Györgyi Med Univ Szeged Hungary 1989; memb Br Cardiac Soc, FRSE 1986, FIBiol, FRCPath, FRPharmS; *Books* Early Arrhythmias Resulting From Myocardial Ischaemia; Mechanisms and Prevention by Drugs (1982), Calcium Movement and its Manipulation by Drugs (1984), Myocardial Response to Acute Injury (1992), Ischaemic Preconditioning (1996); *Recreations* music; *Style*— Prof James Parratt, FRSE; ✉ 16 Russell Drive, Bearsden, Glasgow G61 3BD (☎ 0141 942 1461); Department of Physiology and Pharmacology, University of Strathclyde, Royal College, 204 George St, Glasgow G1 1XW (☎ 0141 552 4400 ext 2858, fax 0141 552 2562, telex 77472)

PARRIS, Matthew Francis; s of Leslie Francis Parris, and Theresa Eunice, *née* Littler; *b* 7 Aug 1949; *Educ* Waterford Sch Swaziland, Clare Coll Cambridge, Yale Univ USA; *Career* author, journalist and broadcaster; FO 1974–76, Cons Research Dept 1976–79, MP (C) West Derbyshire 1979–86, presenter Weekend World LWT 1986–88, currently freelance broadcaster and columnist The Times; Edgar Wallace Outstanding Reporter of the Year Award 1990, Columnist of the Year Br Press Awards 1991, 1993 and 1996, What the Papers Say Columnist of the Year 1992; *Books* Inca-Kola (1990), So Far So Good (1992), Look Behind You (1993), Scorn (1994), Great Parliamentary Scandals (1995), Read My Lips (1996); *Recreations* running, travelling, reading; *Style*— Matthew Parris, Esq; ✉ c/o The Times, 1 Virginia Street, London E1 9XN

PARRITT, Clive Anthony; s of Allan Edward Parritt, MBE, and Peta, *née* Lloyd; *b* 11 April 1943; *Educ* privately; *m* 1, 28 Sept 1968 (m dis 1984), Valerie Joyce, da of Jesse Sears, of Reigate, Surrey; 2 s (James b 1977, Daniel b 1980); m 2, 5 Oct 1985, Deborah, da of Kenneth Jones, of Ashtead, Surrey; 2 s (Matthew b 1987, Thomas b 1989); *Career* CA; successively ptnr 1973–82: Fuller Jenks Beecroft, Mann Judd, Touche Ross & Co; Baker Tilly: ptnr 1982–, managing ptnr 1987–96, chm 1996–; dir: Pilot Investment Trust plc 1983–, Herald Investment Trust plc 1984–; chm: Baronsmead Investment Trust plc 1984–, European Region BKR International Accounting Group; memb Advsy Panel to Enterprise and Deregulation Unit DTI 1986–88; memb: Nat Assoc of CA Students Soc 1965–67 (chm London Branch 1965–66), Cncl ICAEW 1983–; chm London Soc of CAs 1982–83 (treas 1980–82); chm Redhill and Reigate Round Table 1976–77, treas Br Theatre Assoc 1984–87; Liveryman Worshipful Co of Chartered Accountants; FCA 1966; *Recreations* theatre, entertaining, gardening; *Style*— Clive Parritt, Esq; ✉ 3 Howitt Road, London NW3 4LT (☎ 0171 722 8551, fax 0171 586 6777); Baker Tilly, 2 Bloomsbury St, London WC1B 3ST (☎ 0171 413 5100, fax 0171 413 5101)

PARROTT, Andrew Haden; s of Reginald Charles Parrott, BEM (d 1979), of Walsall, and Edith Dora Parrott; *b* 10 March 1947; *Educ* Queen Mary's GS Walsall, Merton Coll Oxford (open postmastership, BA); *m* 1 (m dis); m 2, 23 June 1986, Emily, da of William Payne Van Evera, of Duluth, Minnesota; 1 da (Kate b 3 Aug 1995); *Career* conductor; fndr and artistic dir Taverner Choir, Consort and Players 1973–; guest conductor: Europe, Scandinavia, USA, Canada, Mexico, Israel; appeared at festivals incl: Bath, Lucerne, Salzburg, Tanglewood, Proms; memb Royal Musical Assoc, hon research fell Royal Holloway Univ of London; *Recordings* approx 50 incl works by: Josquin, Taverner, Tallis, Gabrieli, Monteverdi, Purcell, Vivaldi, Bach, Handel, Mozart; *Publications* New Oxford Book of Carols (jt ed), various articles; *Style*— Andrew Parrott, Esq; ✉ c/o Allied Artists, 42 Montpelier Square, London SW7 1JZ (☎ 0171 589 6243, fax 0171 581 5269)

PARROTT, Graham Joseph; *b* 17 Aug 1949; *Career* gp commercial dir Granada Group PLC; FCIS; *Style*— Graham Parrott, Esq; ✉ Granada Group PLC, Stornoway House, 13 Cleveland Row, London SW1A 1GG (☎ 0171 451 6407, fax 0171 451 3008)

PARROTT, Prof (Horace) Ian; s of Horace Bailey Parrott (d 1953), and Muriel Annie, *née* Blackford (d 1958); *b* 5 March 1916; *Educ* Harrow, RCM, New Coll Oxford (MA, DMus); *m* 1, 1 June 1940, Elizabeth Olga (d 1994), da of Edwin Cox (d 1956); 2 s (Michael b 16 Sept 1942, Richard b 16 Dec 1945); m 2, 8 June 1996, Jeanne Peckham; *Career* WWII Capt Royal Signals Africa 1940–45; lectr Univ of Birmingham 1946–50, Gregynog prof of music UCW Aberystwyth 1950–83 (prof emeritus 1983–); examiner Trinity Coll of Music 1949–; recordings incl: String Quartet No 4 1971, Trombone Concerto 1974, Songs etc 1997; vice pres: Elgar Soc 1973–, Guild for the Promotion of Welsh Music 1979–, Peter Warlock Soc 1984–; Symphonic Impression Luxor 1947, first prize Royal Philharmonic Soc 1949, Harriet Cohen Int Musicology Medal 1966; fell: Trinity Coll of Music London 1953, London Coll of Music 1983; ARCO, ISM; *Books* Pathways to Modern Music (1947), A Guide to Musical Thought (1955), Method in Orchestration (1957), The Music of An Adventure (1966), The Spiritual Pilgrims (1969), Elgar Master Musicians (1971), The Music of Rosemary Brown (1978), The Story of The Guild for the Promotion of Welsh Music (1980), Cyril Scott and His Piano Music (1992), The Crying Curlew Peter Warlock: Family and Influences (1994); *Clubs* New Cavendish; *Style*— Prof Ian Parrott; ✉ Henblas Abermad, Aberystwyth, Ceredigion SY23 4ES (☎ 01974 241660)

PARROY, Michael Picton; QC (1991); s of Leopold Gerald May Parroy (d 1982), and Elizabeth Mary, *née* Picton-Bayton (d 1979); *b* 22 Oct 1946; *Educ* Malvern, Brasenose Coll Oxford (MA); *m* 18 Nov 1978, Susan Patricia Blades Winter; *Career* called to the Bar Middle Temple 1969 (Winston Churchill exhibitioner), recorder 1990– (asst recorder 1986), head of chambers; memb Hon Soc of the Middle Temple; *Books* Halsbury's Law of England (co-author, 4 edn vol 40); *Recreations* dog-walking, gardening; *Style*— Michael Parroy, Esq, QC; ✉ Lorne Park Chambers, 20 Lorne Park Road, Bournemouth, Dorset BH1 1JN (☎ 01202 292102, fax 01202 298498)

PARRY, Alan; s of George Henry Edgar James Parry (d 1984), of Upper Gatton Park, Reigate, Surrey, and Jessica, *née* Cooke; *b* 30 Oct 1927; *Educ* Reedham Sch; *m* 17 April 1954, Shirley Ann, da of Esmonde Plunkett Yeoman (d 1962), of Tadworth, Surrey; 1 s (Simon), 1 da (Alannah); *Career* RN 1946–48; dir Sedgwick Group 1960–81; chm: Carter Brito e Cunha Ltd 1982–87, Johnson & Higgins Ltd 1987–88; pres Johnson & Higgins (Holdings) Ltd 1989–; dep chm Lloyd's 1987–88; past chm Ctee City of London Chamber Orch; Freeman City of London, Liveryman Worshipful Co of Insurers 1981; FBIBA, FRSA; *Recreations* flyfishing, music, drama; *Style*— Alan Parry, Esq; ✉ The Quarry, Fir Toll Road, Mayfield, East Sussex TN20 6NG 01435 872120)

PARRY, Alan; s of Alexander Parry (d 1985), of Liverpool, and Margaret Helen, *née* Duff (d 1960); *b* 20 Aug 1948; *Educ* Hillfoot Hey GS for Boys Liverpool; *m* (m dis); 2 s (Simon b 1972, Mark b 1983); *Career* jr reporter rising to sports ed The Weekly News Group Merseyside 1965–69, journalist Mercury Press Agency 1969–70, asst features ed Lancs Evening Post Wigan 1970–72, reporter (later sports ed) BBC Radio Merseyside 1972–73, sports commentator BBC Radio Sport 1973–81, commentator/reporter BBC TV Sport (Match of the Day, Football Focus, Sportsnight) 1981–84, athletics and football commentator ITV Sport 1984–96, sports commentator Sky TV 1996–; covered 4 Olympic Games and 4 World Cup Finals; memb: Football Writers' Assoc, Athletics Writers' Assoc; *Recreations* jogging, playing and watching football; *Clubs* Wycombe Wanderers FC (dir); *Style—* Alan Parry, Esq; ✉ c/o John Hockey Associates, 106 Gloucester Place, London W1H 3DB (☎ 0171 935 2506)

PARRY, Chris N; s of Thomas Sydney Parry (d 1985), of Welshpool, and Kathleen, *née* Pomfret (d 1989); *b* 23 May 1952; *Educ* Welshpool HS, Shrewsbury Tech Sch; *m* Vivien Christina Parry; 1 s (Richard Michael b 4 Dec 1974); *Career* lighting designer; dep head of lighting RSC (Stratford-upon-Avon) 1976–88, freelance lighting designer 1980–, prof of lighting design Univ of California 1988–; memb: Assoc of Lighting Designers (UK), Illuminating Engineering Soc (USA), United Scenic Artists (USA); *Theatre* for RSC Stratford 1986–94 (prodns transfering to London) incl: Flight, Les Liaisons Dangereuses, A Question of Geography, Macbeth, King John, The Plantagenets, Othello, King Lear, The Blue Angel, The Winters Tale, A Midsummer Night's Dream; other RSC prodns incl: Hamlet (UK tour) 1986, Comedy of Errors (UK tour) 1986, Barbarians (London) 1990, Measure for Measure (Stratford and tour) 1991; for RNT: The Crucible 1990, Piano 1990, Way of the World 1995; *Broadway* Les Liaisons Dangereuses (The Music Box) 1987, Search and Destroy (Circle-in-the-Square) 1992, Tommy (St James Theatre (tours: USA nat tour 1993–94, Toronto 1995–96, Germany 1995–96)) 1993, Translations (Plymouth) 1993, A Midsummer Night's Dream (Lunt Fontayne Theatre and tour) 1996; recent regnl rep incl: The Misanthrope (South Coast Rep) 1995, Hysteria (Mark Taper Forum) 1995, The Seagull (Milwaukee Rep) 1996, Camping with Henry and Tom (Pasadena Playhouse) 1996; *Opera* for Buxton Festival 1987: L'Occasione fa il Ladro, Don Quixote in Sierra Morena, Il Pygmalioni; for Los Angeles Opera 1993: La Boheme, Un Ballo in Mashera; *Film* Renaissance Man (Henry V 2nd Unit) 1994; *Awards* Lighting Designer of the Year Award (Lighting Dimensions Int Magazine USA) 1993; Dramalogue Awards for Best Lighting incl: Search & Destroy (South Coast Rep) 1990, Twelfth Night (La Jolla Playhouse) 1990, Twelfth Night (Old Globe, San Diego) 1994; Awards for Tommy incl: NY Drama Desk Award for Best Lighting 1993, NY Outer Critics' Circle Award for Best Lighting 1993, Tony Award for Best Lighting on Broadway 1993, Dora Mavor Moore Award (Canadian Tony) 1995, LA Drama Critics' Circle Award for Distinguished Achievement 1995; *Nominations* for Best Lighting incl: Tony Award (for Les Liaisons Dangereuses) 1987, San Diego Critics' Circle Award (for Macbeth) 1989, American Theatre Wing Design (for Tommy) 1993, LA Theatre Ovation Award (for Hysteria) 1995, Olivier Award (for A Midsummer Night's Dream and Way of the World) 1995, New York Drama Desk Award (A Midsummer Night's Dream) 1996; *Recreations* windsurfing, dancing; *Style—* Chris Parry, Esq; ✉ c/o agent, Richard Haig, Performing Arts, 6 Windmill Street, London W1P 1HF (☎ 0171 255 1362, fax 0171 631 4631); 3450 3rd Ave, Apt 206, San Diego, CA 92103, USA (☎ 00 1 619 291 1818)

PARRY, Christopher Douglas; s of Louis Douglas Parry (d 1980), of Pinner, Middx, and Norah Eileen, *née* Sheard; *b* 24 July 1946; *Educ* Orly Farm Sch Harrow, Queen's Coll Taunton; *m* 19 June 1981, Alison Jane, da of Noel Lewis; 1 s (Luke), 1 da (Lucie); *Career* Despatch Dept Griggs Lander Advertising 1963–64, account exec S H Benson Advertising 1967–71 (prodn exec 1964–67), account mangr Interlink Advertising 1971–74, account dir Lonsdale Advertising 1975–77 (account mangr 1974–75), dep md Childs Greene Advertising 1977–78; md: PPP Ltd 1978–81, Nutford Promotions 1981–82; chm Chris Parry Promotions Ltd 1982–91 (sold to Holmes & Marchant PLC on 5 yr earn-out 1987/88), retirement in France 1991–93, chm Impact FCA! 1993–; memb: Inst of Sales Promotion, Euro Assoc of Advtg Agencies, Inst of Practitioners in Advtg, SPCA; *Recreations* golf, swimming, photography, France, public speaking; *Style—* Christopher Parry, Esq; ✉ Impact FCA! 110 St Martin's Lane, London WC2N 4DY (☎ 0171 240 0888, fax 0171 836 3965)

PARRY, His Hon Judge; David Johnston; s of Kenneth Johnston Parry (d 1942), and Joyce Isobel, *née* Burt (now Mrs Cooper); *b* 26 Aug 1941; *Educ* Merchant Taylors', St Catharine's Coll Cambridge (MA), Higher Cts (Criminal Proceedings) Advocacy qualification 1994; *m* 20 April 1968, Mary, da of George Percy Harmer; 1 s (Andrew Kenneth b 4 Feb 1970), 3 da (Susanna b 25 Feb 1971, Annette b 26 Nov 1973, Marita b 12 July 1976); *Career* articled clerk Turberville Smith & Co Uxbridge Middx, admitted slr 1968, ptnr (then co sr ptnr) Dixon Ward Slrs 1969–95; asst recorder of the Crown Ct 1986–91, recorder of the Crown Court 1991–95, circuit judge (SE Circuit) 1995–; pt/t chm Ind Tbnl Serv 1993–96, admin Richmond and Twickenham Duty Slr Scheme 1990–95, co-chm Richmond Legal Advice Serv 1969–95; memb Merchant Taylors' Co, Freeman City of London; memb: Law Soc, London Criminal Cts Slrs' Assoc; *Recreations* music, literature, theatre, travel, DIY and (whenever possible) lying in the sun doing nothing!; *Clubs* Old Merchant Taylors'; *Style—* His Hon Judge Parry; ✉ Dixon Ward, 16 The Green, Richmond, Surrey TW9 1QD (☎ 0181 940 4051)

PARRY, Prof Eldryd Hugh Owen; OBE (1982); s of Owen Brynog Parry (d 1954), of Cardiff, and Constance Lilian, *née* Griffiths (d 1974); *b* 28 Nov 1930; *Educ* Shrewsbury, Emmanuel Coll Cambridge (MA, MD), WNSM; *m* 26 Aug 1960, Helen Madeline, da of (Arthur) Humphry House (late Maj RAC WWII, d 1955), of Wadham Coll, Oxford; 1 s (David b 1962), 3 da (Julia b 1964, Anna b 1965, Victoria b 1968); *Career* jr appts Cardiff Royal Infirmary, Nat Heart Hosp and Hammersmith Hosp 1956–65; assoc prof of med: Haile Sellassie I Univ Addis Ababa 1966–69, Ahmadu Bello Univ Zaria Nigeria 1969–77; foundation dean Faculty of Health Scis Univ of Ilorin Nigeria 1977–80, dean Sch of Med Scis Univ of Sci and Technology Kumasi Ghana 1980–85, dir Wellcome Tropical Inst 1985–90, sr res fell London Sch of Hygiene and Tropical Med 1990–95 (visiting prof 1995–); Albert Cook meml lectr Kampala 1974; memb: Med and Dental Cncl Ghana 1980–85, Cncl All Nations Christian Coll 1986–; chm Tropical Health and Educn Tst 1989–; Frederick Murgatroyd prize RCP 1974; hon fell Royal Soc of Tropical Med and Hygiene 1993, hon fell London Sch of Hygiene and Tropical Med 1997; FRCP 1970, fell W African Coll of Physicians 1976; *Books* Principles of Medicine in Africa (2 edn, 1984); *Recreations* tennis, Welsh furniture, study of The Bible; *Style—* Prof Eldryd Parry, OBE; ✉ 21 Edenhurst Avenue, London SW6 3PD (☎ 0171 736 4685); THET, 1 Park Square West, London NW1 4LJ (☎ 0171 486 1725, fax 0171 486 1724)

PARRY, District Judge Emyr Owen; s of Ebenezer Owen Parry; *b* 26 May 1933; *Educ* Caernarfon GS, Univ Coll of Wales Aberystwyth; *m* 1959, Enid Griffiths; 1 s, 1 da; *Career* admitted slr 1957, dep circuit judge 1975, recorder Crown Ct 1979, district judge Bangor gp of county courts and District Registry of the High Court at Bangor, Caernarfon and Rhyl 1992; chm Nat Insur Appeals Tbnl Holyhead Area 1969–92, slr memb Lord Chllr's Co Ct Rule Ctee 1975; *Style—* District Judge Emyr Parry

PARRY, Baron (Life Peer UK 1975), of Neyland, Co Dyfed; Gordon Samuel David Parry; DL (Dyfed 1993); s of Rev Thomas Lewis Parry, Baptist Minister (d 1965), and Anne Parry (d 1958); *b* 30 Nov 1925; *Educ* Neyland Sch, Pembroke Co Intermediate Sch, Trinity Coll Carmarthen, Inst of Educn, Univ of Liverpool; *m* 1948, Glenys Catherine, da of Jack Leslie Incledon; 1 da (Hon Catherine Anne b 1955); *Career* sits as Lab peer in House of Lords; teacher and journalist; house master and librarian Co Secdy Sch Haverfordwest 1952–68, warden Pembrokeshire Teachers' Centre 1968–78; chm: Milford Leisure, Taylor Plan Services; dir Seacon Holdings plc; chm Wales Tourist Bd 1978–83, memb Br Tourist Authy 1978–83, pres Br Inst of Cleaning Sci, chm British Cleaning Cncl, pres Tidy Britain Gp, chm Britain in Bloom, chm Clean World Int, pres Milford Docks Co; hon fell: James Cook Univ Queensland Australia, Inst of Wastes Management, Trinity Coll Carmarthen, Univ of Glamorgan; fell: Tourism Soc, Br Inst of Cleaning Sci, Hotel and Catering and Industl Mgmnt Assoc; Hon DEd Swansea Inst of HE; hon fell: Univ of Glamorgan, Trinity Coll Carmarthen; FRSA; *Recreations* watching rugby football; *Clubs* Neyland Rugby, Neyland Yacht; *Style—* The Rt Hon Lord Parry, DL; ✉ Willowmead, 52 Port Lion, Llangwm, Haverfordwest, Pembrokeshire, Dyfed SA62 4JT (☎ 01646 600667); House of Lords, London SW1A 0PW

PARRY, Jann; da of John Hywel Parry (d 1992), of Cambridge, and Evelyn Florence, *née* Upton; *Educ* Kingsmead Coll Johannesburg, Univ of Cape Town (BA), Girton Coll Cambridge (BA, Cwlth scholar); *m* 15 April 1994, Richard Ruegg Kershaw, *qv*; *Career* prodr BBC Radio World Service 1970–89; dance critic: The Listener 1981, The Spectator 1982 and 1995–96, The Observer 1983–; memb: Dance Panel Arts Cncl 1988–90, Exec Ctee Dance UK 1991–, Critics' Circle; *Style—* Ms Jann Parry; ✉ 82 Prince of Wales Mansions, Prince of Wales Drive, London SW11 4BL (☎ and fax 0171 738 8732)

PARRY, John Kelsall; s of Edward Parry (d 1983), of Birmingham, and Kathleen Mary, *née* Allen; *b* 28 Aug 1936; *Educ* Loughborough GS, London Sch of Journalism (Dip); *m* 18 Dec 1960, Judy Valerie Cornwell, *qv*, da of late Darcy Nigel Barry Cornwell, of Gympie, Qld, Aust; 1 s (Edward Dylan Parry b 20 June 1965); *Career* reporter Evening Argus Brighton 1960–62, feature writer then William Hickey diarist Daily Express London 1962–67, reporter Tomorrow's World BBC TV 1967–70; BBC Radio News and Current Affrs: reporter and presenter World at One, PM and The World This Weekend 1971–82, arts corr 1982–95; writer for The Times, columnist The Spectator 1996–; *Recreations* theatre, opera, cooking; *Clubs* Garrick; *Style—* John Parry, Esq

PARRY, John Richard; s of David Parry (d 1957), of Thetford, Norfolk, and Alma Harriet, *née* Fuller (d 1990); *b* 3 May 1934; *Educ* The GS Thetford, Fitzwilliam Coll Cambridge (MA); *m* 9 Sept 1961, Mary, da of William Dorrington, of Pinner, Middx; 1 s (Simon David William b 1964), 1 da (Anne-Louise b 1968); *Career* Nat Serv Bombadier RA 1952–54 (Suez Canal Zone); Commercial Union Properties Ltd: dir 1971, md 1978; Hammerson Property Investment and Development Corporation plc: dir 1984–93, dep md 1985, jt md 1986, md 1988–93; pres Br Property Fedn 1992–93 (memb Cncl 1986–); memb: Telford Devpt Corp 1980–82 (dep chm 1982–86), Property Advsy Gp DOE 1980–93; JP Gore Div Middx Petty Sessions 1980–84; tstee Douglas Haig Memorial Homes; Freeman: City of London, Worshipful Co of Chartered Surveyors 1985; FRICS 1962; Coll of Estate Mgmnt Reading: memb The Charter Soc 1987, hon fell 1988, memb 1993, chm 1995–; *Recreations* keeping fit, eating out, opera and ballet; *Clubs* Arts, Athenaeum; *Style—* John Parry, Esq; ✉ ASDA Property Holdings plc, 58 Queen Anne Street, London W1M 9LA (☎ 0171 224 1030)

PARRY, (George) Mervyn; s of George Alwyn Parry, of E Horsley, Surrey, and Aileen Maude, *née* Long; *b* 16 March 1951; *Educ* King's Coll Sch Wimbledon, Downing Coll Cambridge (Squire scholar, BA, 3 badminton half-blues); *m* 1 Aug 1987, Jill Patricia, da of William Odiam; 2 da (Imogen Sophie b 21 June 1989, Annabel Rose b 1 Sept 1992); *Career* Allen & Overy: articled clerk 1973–75, asst slr 1975–85, ptnr 1985–; memb Law Soc 1973; *Recreations* photography, mountain walking, wine, opera, family, sport; *Style—* Mervyn Parry, Esq; ✉ Allen & Overy, One New Change, London EC4M 9QQ (☎ 0171 330 3000, fax 0171 330 9999)

PARRY, Richard Nicholas (Rick); s of Nicholas Albert Parry (d 1987), of Chester, and Kathleen Stuart, *née* Howard; *b* 23 Feb 1955; *Educ* Ellesmere Port GS, Univ of Liverpool (BSc); *m* 12 Aug 1978, Catherine Mary, da of Dr Malcolm Vivian John Seaborne; 3 s (James Robert b 27 Oct 1982, Thomas William b 3 April 1985, Jonathan b 4 Nov 1994); *Career* trainee chartered accountant Arthur Young McClelland Moores 1976–79, mktg accountant Haulfryn Estate Co 1979–81, fin controller Hoseasons Holidays 1981–83, mgmnt conslt Arthur Young 1983–92, seconded (as full-time dir) Manchester Olympic Bid Ctee 1988–90, chief exec FA Premier League 1992–96 (chief exec designate 1991), chief exec Liverpool FC 1996–; FCA 1979; *Recreations* watching sport; *Style—* Rick Parry, Esq; ✉ c/o Liverpool FC, Anfield Road, Anfield, Liverpool L4 0TH

PARRY, Robert; MP (Lab) Liverpool Riverside (majority 17,437); s of Robert Parry; *b* 8 Jan 1933; *Educ* Bishop Goss RC Sch Liverpool; *m* 1956, Marie, *née* Hesdon; *Career* MP (Lab): Liverpool Exchange 1970–74, Liverpool Scotland Exchange 1974–83, Liverpool Riverside 1983–; chm Merseyside Gp of Labour MPs 1976–89, fndr memb Campaign Gp of Labour MPs 1982–, memb Lab Delgn Cncl of Europe and Western Euro Union 1984–92 (chief whip 1987–91); patron UN Assoc Hong Kong 1976, memb Int Ctee for Human Rights Syria 1985, vice pres Ctee for the Independence and Peaceful Reunification of Korea 1986–, fndr pres Human Right Int 1994–, memb Exec Nord Sud XXI Non Governmental Orgn Geneva 1995–, exec memb Br-Afro-Asian Solidarity Orgn, judge Int Tribunal against Child Labour; pres: Liverpool Transport Amateur Boxing Club 1978–, Rotunon Boxing Club 1996–; memb House of Commons jazz and opera gps; *Style—* Robert Parry, Esq, MP; ✉ House of Commons, SW1A 0AA

PARRY, Roger; *b* 4 June 1953; *Educ* Univ of Bristol (BSc), Jesus Coll Oxford (MLitt); *m* 1990, Johanna; 1 s (Benjamin b 1993); *Career* broadcaster BBC and ITV 1977–85, conslt McKinsey & Co 1985–88; devpt dir: WCRS Group 1988–90, Aegis Group 1990–94; pres Carat North America 1994–95, chief exec offr More Group 1995–; non-exec dir Gold Rose Communications, dir Globe Theatre; *Books* People Businesses (1991); *Clubs* MCC, United Oxford & Cambridge; *Style—* Roger Parry, Esq; ✉ More Group plc, 33 Golden Square, London W1R 3PA (e-mail rparry@moregroup.com)

PARRY-EVANS, Air Chief Marshal Sir David; GCB (1991, KCB 1985), CBE (1978); s of Gp Capt John Parry-Evans (d 1978), and Dorothy Parry-Evans; *b* 19 July 1935; *Educ* Berkhamsted; *m* 1960, Ann, da of Charles Reynolds (d 1966), and Gertrude Reynolds (d 1995); 2 s; *Career* RAF 1956–92: OC 214 Sqdn 1974–75, OC RAF Marham 1975–77, Air Cdre 1979, Dir Def Policy MOD 1979–81, Cmdt RAF Staff Coll Bracknell 1981–82, Air Vice-Marshal 1982, AOC No 1 and 38 Gps 1982–85, Air Marshal 1985, CinC RAF Germany, Cdr 2 Allied Tactical Air Force 1985–87, Dep Chief of Defence Staff 1987–89, Air Chief Marshal 1989, Air Memb for Personnel 1989–91; Chief Cdr St John Ambulance 1992–; govr Royal Star & Garter Home 1990–; *Clubs* RAF; *Style—* Air Chief Marshal Sir David Parry-Evans, GCB, CBE

PARRY EVANS, Mary Alethea (Lady Hallinan); da of Dr Evan Parry Evans, MD, JP; *b* 31 Oct 1929; *Educ* Malvern Girls' Coll, Somerville Coll Oxford (BCL, MA); *m* 1955, Sir (Adrian) Lincoln Hallinan, *qv*; 2 s, 2 da; *Career* called to the Bar Inner Temple 1953, in practice Wales and Chester circuit, a recorder of the Crown Ct 1978–; *Style—* Mary Parry-Evans

PARSLOE, John; s of (Charles) Guy Parsloe (d 1985), and (Mary) Zirphie (Munro), *née* Faiers; *b* 14 Oct 1939; *Educ* Bradfield, Queen's Coll Oxford (MA); *m* 6 Oct 1973, (Helen) Margaret, da of Dr (Daniel) Arnold Rolfe (d 1985); 2 s (Thomas b 1974, William b 1979), 1 da (Alice b 1976); *Career* admitted slr 1971; dir: Mercury Asset Management plc 1990–, S G Warburg Trust Co Ltd 1992–; memb Law Soc 1971; *Style—* John Parsloe, Esq; ✉ Mercury Asset Management plc, 33 King William St, London EC4R 9AS (☎ 0171 280 2800)

PARSONAGE, Jennifer Lilian (Jenny); da of late Arthur Lowe, of Southport, Merseyside, and late Lilian Bentham, *née* Finch; *b* 21 Feb 1950; *Educ* Southport Sch of Nursing (RGN), Preston HA (Registered Midwife), Stevenage Coll (Registered Health Visitor), Thames Coll (Dip in Mgmnt Studies), Barrow-in-Furness Coll (Dip in Computing and Mgmnt Info), Canterbury Business Sch Univ of Kent; *m* Robert Arthur Parsonage, s of Arthur Parsonage; 1 s (Martin Andrew b 15 Sept 1979); *Career* cadet nurse then student nurse 1966–71, student midwife 1971–73, staff nurse Sefton Hosp Liverpool 1973–74, sr ward sister Fazakerly Hosp Liverpool 1974–79, health visitor 1979–82, sr nurse Furness Hosp Barrow 1982–84, asst dir of nursing servs Kent and Canterbury Hosp 1984–85, dir of planning Acute Servs Canterbury and Thanet HA 1985–87, dir of nursing servs and dir of business mgmnt Medway HA 1987–90, unit gen mangr Community and Priority Care Dartford and Gravesham HA 1990–91, chief exec Thameslink Healthcare Servs NHS Tst 1991–; author of various papers on health-related subjects; AHSM 1987; *Style*— Mrs Jenny Parsonage; ✉ Brambles, Norwood Lane, Meopham, Kent (☎ 01474 812054); ISIS, 18/20 Bis Rue de Vieux, Ceret, France 66400 (☎ 00 33 68 87 11 47); Thameslink Healthcare Services NHS Trust, Archery House, Bow Arrow Lane, Dartford, Kent DA2 6PB (☎ 01322 622222, fax 01322 622215)

PARSONS, (Thomas) Alan; CB (1984); s of late Arthur and Laura Parsons; *b* 25 Nov 1924; *Educ* Clifton, Bristol Univ (LLB); *m* 1, 1947, Valerie Vambeck; 1 s; m 2, 1957, Muriel Lewis; 2 s; *Career* served WWII RM 1943–46; called to the Bar Middle Temple 1950, legal asst Miny of Nat Insur 1950, sr legal asst Miny of Pensions and Nat Insur 1955; DHSS: asst slr 1968, princ asst slr 1977, chief adjudication offr 1984–86; *Style*— Alan Parsons Esq, CB; ✉ 11 Northiam Street, Pennethorne Place, London E9 7HX

PARSONS, Charles Andrew (Charlie); s of Anthony Maxse Parsons, of Tunbridge Wells, and Rosamund, *née* Hurst; *b* 7 Aug 1958; *Educ* Tonbridge, Pembroke Coll Oxford (MA, pres JCR); *Career* reporter Ealing Gazette 1980–82, researcher London Weekend Television 1982–87, series ed Network 7 (Channel Four) 1988 (prodr 1987), series ed Club X (Channel Four) 1989; exec prodr for Planet 24 Productions Ltd (formerly 24 Hour Productions Ltd): The Word 1990, Handel's Messiah at The Point Dublin 1991, The Big Breakfast 1992–, Gaytime TV 1995–, Desire 1996–; jt md Planet 24 Ltd 1992–, ceo Planet 24 (America); Freeman: City of London, Worshipful Co of Haberdashers; memb: RTS, BAFTA, IOD; *Awards* Royal Instn of Chartered Surveyors Best News Award for The London Programme 1985–86, BAFTA Originality Award 1987 and Gold Hugo Chicago Film Festival 1988 for Network 7, Silver Medal NY Int Film Festival for The Word 1991, RTS Best Team Award for The Big Breakfast 1992; *Recreations* listening to books on tape, Coronation Street; *Style*— Charlie Parsons, Esq; ✉ Planet 24 Ltd, The Planet Building, Thames Quay, 195 Marsh Wall, London E14 9SG (☎ 0171 512 5063, fax 0171 987 8469)

PARSONS, Prof (John) David; s of Oswald Parsons (d 1976), and Doris Anita, *née* Roberts (d 1986); *b* 8 July 1935; *Educ* Ebbw Vale GS, Univ Coll Cardiff (BSc), King's Coll London (MSc Eng, DScEng); *m* 19 July 1969, Mary Winifred Stella, da of Frederick Stanley Tate (d 1959); *Career* Nat Serv RAF 1954–56; GEC Applied Electronics Laboratories 1959–62, Regent St Poly 1962–66, City of Birmingham Poly 1966–68, reader in electronic engrg (former lectr and sr lectr) Univ of Birmingham 1969–82, UN expert in India 1977, hon sr princ scientific offr Royal Signals and Radar Establishment Malvern 1978–82, visiting prof Univ of Auckland 1982; Univ of Liverpool: David Jardine prof of electrical engrg, head Dept of Electrical Engrg and Electronics 1983–86 and 1996–, dean Faculty of Engrg 1986–89, pro vice-chllr 1990–96; visiting res engr NTT Japan 1987; memb: Communications Sub-Ctee Sci and Engrg Res Cncl 1983–87, Cncl Inst of Electronic and Radio Engrs 1985–88, Cncl Inst of Electrical Engrs 1988–89; FIEE 1985, FEng 1988; *Books* Electronic and Switching Circuits (with Bozic and Cheng, 1975), Mobile Communication Systems (with Gardiner, 1989), The Mobile Radio Propagation Channel (1992); *Recreations* golf, bridge, skiing; *Style*— Prof David Parsons, FEng; ✉ Department of Electrical Engineering and Electronics, University of Liverpool, PO Box 147, Liverpool L69 3BX (☎ 0151 794 4503, fax 0151 794 4540, telex 627095 UNILPOL G, e-mail jdp@liv.ac.uk)

PARSONS, Prof Ian; s of Arthur Alan Parsons (d 1992), and Doris Marion, *née* Ivins (d 1942); *b* 5 Sept 1939; *Educ* Beckenham and Penge GS, Univ of Durham (BSc, PhD); *m* 8 Aug 1963, Brenda Mary, da of William Spence Reah; 3 s (Mark Ian b 10 July 1967, John Richard b 8 March 1969, Andrew James (twin) b 8 March 1969); *Career* DSIR res fell Univ of Manchester 1963–64, personal prof Univ of Aberdeen 1983–88 (asst lectr 1964–65, lectr 1965–77, sr lectr 1977–83), prof of mineralogy Univ of Edinburgh 1988– (head of dept 1993–96); pres Mineralogical Soc of Great Britain and Ireland 1994–96 (vice pres 1980); memb Cncl Int Mineralogical Assoc 1995–; Schlumberger medal Mineralogical Soc 1993 (Hallimond lectr 1977); memb: Mineralogical Soc of Great Britain 1962, Mineralogical Soc of America 1980, American Geophysical Union 1983, Euro Union of Geosciences 1988; FRSE 1984; *Books* Geological Excursion Guide to the Assynt District of Sutherland (with M R W Johnson, 1979), Origins of Igneous Layering (1987), Feldspars and their Reactions (1994); *Recreations* walking, skiing, music; *Style*— Prof Ian Parsons, FRSE; ✉ Department of Geology and Geophysics, University of Edinburgh, West Mains Road, Edinburgh EH9 3JW (☎ 0131 650 8512, fax 0131 668 3184)

PARSONS, John Anthony; s of Leslie Norman Parsons, of Oxford, and Marian Eunice, *née* Evans; *b* 20 Feb 1938; *Educ* Magdalen Coll Sch Oxford; *Career* journalist; Oxford Mail 1946–64, Daily Mail 1964–80, Daily Telegraph 1980– (lawn tennis corr); sec: Lawn Tennis Writers' Assoc 1983– (chm 1980–81), Int Tennis Fedn Media Cmmn; chm Oxford-Leiden City Link 1973–92, dep pres 1992–; *Awards* Golden Pin of Honour City of Leiden Holland (for servs to Twin-City links), Tennis Writer of the Year (Lawn Tennis Assoc) 1987, Media Person of the Year (Women's Tennis Assoc) 1990, Ted Tinling award for Services to Tennis 1991; *Books* The Championships Wimbledon 1983–96; *Recreations* theatre; *Style*— John Parsons, Esq; ✉ Daily Telegraph, 1 Canada Square, Canary Wharf, London E14 5DT (☎ 0171 538 5000, fax 0171 513 2507)

PARSONS, John Christopher; LVO (1992); s of Arthur Christopher Parsons, of Odiham, Hants, and Veronica Rosetta de Courcy, *née* Glover; *b* 21 May 1946; *Educ* Harrow, Trinity Coll Cambridge (BA); *m* 20 Feb 1982, Hon Anne Constance Manningham-Buller, da of 1 Viscount Dilhorne, PC; 2 s (Michael b 1983, David b 1985), 1 da (Lilah b 1988); *Career* CA; Dowty Group Ltd 1968–72, Peat Marwick Mitchell & Co 1972–85; asst treas to HM The Queen 1985–87, dep keeper of the Privy Purse and dep treas to HM The Queen 1988–, dep dir (fin) Royal Collection 1992–93; FCA, FIMC; *Clubs* Brooks's, Pratt's; *Style*— John Parsons, Esq, LVO; ✉ The Old Stables, Kensington Palace, London W8 4PU (☎ 0171 937 8272); Buckingham Palace, London SW1A 1AA (☎ 0171 930 4832)

PARSONS, John William; CBE (1988); s of Frederick John Parsons (d 1988), of Wareham, Dorset, and Dorothy Ellen, *née* Toop; *b* 24 July 1936; *Educ* Poole GS, Porthcurno Engrg Coll; *m* 1, 1958 (m dis 1979); 1 s (Christopher), 1 da (Yasmin); m 2, 1981, Sally-Anne, da of Robert St Vincent Parker-Jervis (d 1972); 2 s (Timothy, Dominic), 1 da (Victoria); *Career* Actg Capt Royal Signals; Cable and Wireless: joined 1960, head of business (Caribbean) 1966–72, md Euro cos 1972–78; md ITR International Time Ltd 1979–82, chm and chief exec Time and Data Systems International (TDSI Ltd) 1982–96 (dir of gp 1996–); chm: Talbot Assocs Ltd, Albion Controls Ltd 1996–, Sok-Lok UK Ltd 1996–; memb BOTB 1985–93; chm: BOTB Small Firms Ctee 1987–93, CBI Smaller and Medium Enterprise Cncl 1994–96; dir: Assoc Br Chambers of Commerce 1990–94, Dorset TEC, Dorset C of C; former pres Dorset C of C and Indust; cncllr: Purbeck DC 1983–91, Corfe Castle Parish Cncl 1988–; govr Poole GS; CEng, FIEE, FInstD, FIMgt; *Clubs* IOD, Exiles, RAC; *Style*— John Parsons, Esq, CBE; ✉ Townsend House, Corfe Castle, Wareham, Dorset BH20 5EG (☎ and fax 01929 480265); Albion Controls Ltd, 27 Albion Close, Poole, Dorset BH12 3LL (☎ 01202 666222, fax 01202 679730)

PARSONS, Dr Malcolm; s of Rev Dr Eric Parsons, and late Ina, *née* Robson; *b* 3 March 1933; *Educ* Kingswood Sch Bath, St Catharine's Coll Cambridge (MA), UCH (MB BChir); *m* 8 June 1972, Diana Margaret, da of late William Hill; 2 da (Fiona b 1973, Georgina b 1975); *Career* Nat Serv cmmnd RAMC 1960–62; Nat Hosp Queen Square 1964, Hammersmith Hosp 1965, Maida Vale UCH 1966–69; conslt neurologist Gen Infirmary Leeds, sr clinical lectr in neurology Univ of Leeds 1969–96; memb: Assoc of Physicians, Assoc of Br Neurologists; FRCP; *Books* Diagnostic Picture Tests in Clinical Neurology (1987), Tuberculous Meningitis (2 edn, 1988), Colour Atlas of Clinical Neurology (2 edn 1993); *Style*— Dr Malcolm Parsons; ✉ 1 Ancaster View, Leeds LS16 5HR

PARSONS, Sir (John) Michael; kt (1970); s of late Rt Rev Richard Godfrey Parsons, DD, Bishop of Hereford (d 1948), and Dorothy Gales Streeter (d 1956); *b* 29 Oct 1915; *Educ* Rossall, Univ Coll Oxford; *m* 1, 1946 (m dis 1964), Hilda Mary Frewen; 1 s, 2 da; m 2, 1964, Caroline Inagh Margaret, da of Col Laton Frewen, DSO (d 1976), of Ross-on-Wye; *Career* Barry & Co Calcutta 1937–39; Royal Garhwal Rifles 1939–46 (POW Singapore); Macneill & Barry Ltd 1946–70 (chm and md 1964–70), chm Macdonald Hamilton & Co Pty Ltd Australia 1970–72; Inchcape & Co Ltd: dir 1971–81, sr md 1976–81, dep chm and chief exec 1979–81; chm and dir Assam Investments 1976–81, dir Commonwealth Development Finance Co Ltd 1973–80; vice chm Indian Jute Mills Assoc 1960–61, pres Bengal C of C 1968–69, pres Associated Cs of C of India 1969, memb Advsy Cncl Bd of Trade India 1968–69; chm: UK Ctee Cwlth Cs of C 1974, Cncl of Royal Cwlth Soc 1976–81; dep chm Utd World Colls 1982–86; *Recreations* golf; *Clubs* Oriental; *Style*— Sir Michael Parsons; ✉ Tall Trees, Warren Hill Lane, Aldeburgh, Suffolk IP15 5QB (☎ 01728 452917)

PARSONS, (Christopher) Nicholas; s of Dr Paul Frederick Nigel Parsons (d 1981), of Hampstead, London, and Nell Louise, *née* Maggs (d 1980); *b* 10 Oct 1928; *Educ* St Paul's, Univ of Glasgow; *m* 1, 21 Aug 1954 (m dis 1989), Denise Pauline Rosalie, da of Claud Bryer; 1 da (Suzy Zuleika (Mrs James Buchanan) b 13 June 1958), 1 s (Justin Hugh b 24 Dec 1960); m 2, 1995, Ann Reynolds; *Career* actor, solo performer; Variety Club Radio Personality of the Year 1967, entered in the Guinness Book of Records for longest after dinner humorous speech 1978; involved with children's charities incl The Lord's Taverners (memb Cncl) and NSPCC (govr), Barker of The Variety Club of GB; memb: Soc of Stars, Sparks, Living Earth conservation charity; Rector Univ of St Andrews 1988–91, Hon LLD Univ of St Andrews; *Theatre* The Hasty Heart (London), Jack in Charley's Aunt (Palace Theatre), Arsenic and Old Lace (tour), in repertory Bromley 1949–51, in cabaret (Quaglinos, Colony, Cafe de Paris, Blue Angel, Pigalle, Society), as comedian (Windmill Theatre) 1952, revues (London fringe theatres and Lyric Revue) 1953, 1st and 2nd Edition (Watergate Theatre) 1954, Swing Along with Arthur Haynes (Palladium) 1963, starred in Boeing Boeing (Duchess Theatre) 1967, Say Who You Are (Vaudeville Theatre) 1968, Uproar in the House (Whitehall Theatre) 1968, Darling I'm Home (tour) 1978, Stage Struck (tour) 1980, Keeping Down with the Joneses (tour) 1981, Charlie Girl (Victoria Palace and nat tour) 1987–88, the Narrator in Into the Woods (Stephen Sondheim musical, Phoenix Theatre) 1990–91, Rocky Horror Show (Duke of York's Theatre) 1994 and 1995, numerous pantomimes and 3 one-man shows (Edward Lear Show performed at Edinburgh Festival 1990); *Television* comedy work in partnership with Eric Barker 1952–55, straight man in partnership with Arthur Haynes 1956–66, Last Train to Surbiton (comedy series, BBC) 1966, Benny Hill Show 1969–70, host of Sale of the Century (Anglia TV) 1971–84 and The Alphabet Game (LWT Night Network) 1988, Mr Jolly Lives Next Door (for Comic Strip) 1988, The Curse of Fenric (Dr Who story, BBC) 1989, host of Laughlines (BSB) 1990, Just a Minute (Carlton TV) 1994 and 1995; *Films* Brothers-in-Law, Carlton Browne of the FO, Happy is the Bride, Don't Raise the Bridge Lower the River, Spy Story, Simon and Laura, Upstairs Downstairs, Too Many Crooks, Eyewitness, Carry On Regardless; writer and dir of 5 comedy documentaries for cinema and TV for own production co; *Radio* since 1952 incl: various prodns for BBC Drama Repertory Company 1953, host of Just a Minute 1966–, Listen to This Space (first radio satire show) 1967–92, How Pleasant to Know My Lear (solo show) 1995; *Books* Egg on the Face (1985), The Straight Man - My Life in Comedy (autobiography, 1994); *Recreations* cricket, golf, gardening, photography; *Style*— Nicholas Parsons; ✉ c/o Susan Shaper, Billy Marsh Associates Ltd, 174–178 North Gower Street, London NW1 2NB (☎ 0171 388 6996, fax 0171 388 6848)

PARSONS, Peter Frank; s of Frank Leslie John Parsons, of Fleet, and Margaret, *née* Wing; *b* 24 Aug 1950; *Educ* Farnborough GS, City of London Coll; *children* 2 da (Amy Carol b 18 July 1977, Zoe Gemma b 16 Oct 1978); *Career* chartered accountant; ptnr Temple Gothard 1977–85, nat dir business devpt Touche Ross (now Deloitte & Touche) 1995– (ptnr 1985–); FCA; *Style*— Peter Parsons, Esq; ✉ Deloitte & Touche, Stonecutter Court, 1 Stonecutter Street, London EC4A 3TR (☎ 0171 936 3000, fax 0171 583 8517)

PARSONS, Prof Peter John; s of Robert John Parsons, and Ethel Ada, *née* Frary; *b* 24 Sept 1936; *Educ* Raynes Park Co GS, ChCh Oxford (Craven scholar, de Paravicini scholar, Derby scholar, Dixon and sr scholar, Passmore Edwards scholar, MA, Chancellor's prize for Latin verse, Gaisford prize for Greek verse); *Career* Univ of Oxford: lectr in documentary papyrology 1960–65, lectr in papyrology 1965–89, regius prof of Greek 1989–, student of Christ Church 1964–; J H Gray lectr Univ of Cambridge 1982, Heller lectr Univ of Calif Berkeley 1988; Hon PhD Bern 1985, Hon DLitt Milan 1993, Hon PhD Athens 1995; fell Academia Europaea 1990, FBA 1977; *Books* The Oxyrhynchus Papyri: XXXI (jtly, 1966), XXXIII and XXXIV (jtly, 1968), XLII (1973), LIV (jtly, 1987), LIX (jtly, 1992), LX (jtly, 1993); Supplementum Hellenisticum (with H Lloyd-Jones, 1983); *Recreations* music, cinema, cooking, eating; *Style*— Prof Peter Parsons, FBA; ✉ Christ Church, Oxford OX1 1DP (☎ 01865 276223)

PARSONS, Sir Richard Edmund Clement Fownes; KCMG (1982, CMG 1977); s of Dr Richard A Parsons (d 1960), of Kirkbeck House, Coniston, Cumbria (d 1960), and Mrs Richard Parsons (d 1977); *b* 14 March 1928; *Educ* Bembridge Sch, Brasenose Coll Oxford (BA); *m* 1960, Jenifer Jane (d 1981), da of Charles Reginald Mathews; 3 s; *Career* Nat Serv 1949–51; HM Dip Serv; joined FO 1951; formerly served: Buenos Aires, Ankara, Washington, Vientiane; former cnsllr Lagos, head personnel ops dept 1972–76; ambassador: Hungary 1976–79, Spain 1980–84, Sweden 1984–87 (ret); author of six published novels and plays (professionally produced in London and at Brighton and Edinburgh Festivals); *Clubs* Garrick; *Style*— Sir Richard Parsons, KCMG; ✉ 152 De Beauvoir Road, London N1

PARSONS, Robin Edward; s of Anthony Maxse Parsons, of Southcombe, Tunbridge Wells, Kent, and Rosamund, *née* Hurst; *b* 30 Dec 1948; *Educ* Uppingham, UCL (LLB); *m* 27 May 1972, Elizabeth Hamilton Floyd; 2 da (Sonia Katharine Elizabeth, Alexandra Geraldine); *Career* asst slr Coward Chance 1973–75 (articled clerk 1971–73); Cameron Markby Hewitt (formerly Cameron Kemm Nordon): asst slr 1975–77, ptnr 1977– (estab Paris Office 1980); lectr at numerous legal conferences and seminars incl series given to Chartered Inst of Bankers 1988–95, author of articles for legal jls; Freeman and Liveryman Worship Co of Haberdashers, Freeman Worshipful Co of Slrs; memb Law Soc (memb City of London Banking Law Sub-Ctee); *Recreations* tennis, squash, skiing,

French; *Style*— Robin Parsons, Esq; ✉ Cameron Markby Hewitt, Sceptre Court, 40 Tower Hill, London EC3N 4BB (☎ 0171 702 2345, fax 0171 702 2303)

PARSONS, Prof Roger; s of Robert Harry Ashby Parsons (d 1966), and Ethel, *née* Fenton (d 1973); *b* 31 Oct 1926; *Educ* King Alfred Sch London, Strathcona HS Edmonton Alberta, Imperial Coll London (BSc, ARCS, PhD, DIC), Univ of Bristol (DSc); *m* 8 June 1953, Ruby Millicent, da of Malcolm Turner (d 1971); 3 s (Gavin Christopher b 1954, Colin Mark b 1959, Magnus Frank b 1961), 1 da (Celia Janet b 1957); *Career* Deedes fell Univ of St Andrews 1951–54, lectr Univ of Bristol 1954–63 (reader in electrochemistry 1963–79), dir Laboratoire d'Electrochimie Interfaciale du CNRS Meudon France 1977–84, prof of chemistry Univ of Southampton 1985–92 (now emeritus), ed in chief Jl of Electroanalytical Chemistry 1963–; FRS 1980; Palladium medal (USA) 1979, Bruno Breyer medal Aust 1980, Paul Pascal prize France 1983, Galvani medal Italy 1986; *Books* Electrochemical Constants (1959), Interfacial Electrochemistry (1972), Electrochemistry in Research and Development (1985), Standard Potentials in Aqueous Solution (1985); *Recreations* listening to music, going to the opera; *Style*— Prof Roger Parsons, FRS; ✉ 16 Thornhill Rd, Bassett, Southampton SO16 7AT (☎ 01703 790143); 64 Ferguson Avenue, Milngavie G62 7TE (☎ 0141 956 1332); Department of Chemistry, University of Southampton, Southampton SO9 5NH (☎ 01703 593371, fax 01703 676960, e-mail rp3@soton.ac.uk)

PARSONS, Roger Wentworth; s of Sir Maurice Parsons, KCMG (d 1978), and Daphne, *née* Warner (d 1979); *b* 16 Feb 1942; *Educ* Marlborough, St John's Coll Cambridge; *m* 1969, Julie, *née* Deli; 2 da; *Career* Citibank NA 1963–73, European Banking Company Ltd 1973–77, dir Grindlay Brandts Ltd 1977–81, md Grindlays Bank Ltd 1981–85, dir Wentworth Parsons Ltd 1985–88, md Rea Brothers Group plc 1988–, non-exec dir American Standard Companies Inc 1994–; *Clubs* Brooks's; *Style*— Roger Parsons, Esq; ✉ Rea Brothers Group plc, Aldermans House, Aldermans Walk, London EC2M 3XR (☎ 0171 623 1155, fax 0171 623 2692)

PARSONS, Terry; *Educ* Cardiff Art Coll, Central Sch of Art London; *Career* set and costume designer; previous appts as head of design: Theatre Royal Plymouth, Haymarket Leicester, Belgrade Coventry (Arts Cncl Scholarship); over 33 West End Prodns incl: Present Laughter, Out of the Blue, Radio Times, Annie Get Your Gun, Some Like it Hot, Sophisticated Ladies (costume only), Silly Cow, Gasping, South Pacific (also tour), Can-Can, Lend me a Tenor, When we are Married, Charlie Girl, Two into One, Grease (also tour), What a Show, Marlene (costumes only); other credits incl: No Trams on Lime Street (Liverpool Playhouse), John Paul George Ringo and Bert (Denmark), A View from the Bridge, Time and the Conways (Old Vic), Miranda (Chichester), Underneath the Arches, Singin' in the Rain (tour); recent foreign tours incl: Alone Together, The Secretary Bird, California Suite, A Touch of Spring, Lloyd George knew my Father, You Must be the Husband, Not in Front of the Children, Key for Two, Oh' Coward!, The Reluctant Debutante, The Last of the Red Hot Lovers; numerous pantomime incl: Cinderella, The Sleeping Beauty, Mother Goose; *Style*— Terry Parsons, Esq; ✉ c/o Stella Richards Management, 42 Hazebury Road, London SW6 2ND (☎ 0171 736 7786, fax 0171 731 5082)

PARTINGTON, Prof (Thomas) Martin; s of Thomas Paullet Partington (d 1980), and Alice Emily Mary, *née* Jelly (d 1970); *b* 5 March 1944; *Educ* King's Sch Canterbury, Univ of Cambridge (BA, LLB); *m* 1, 15 Aug 1969 (m dis 1973), Marcia Carol, *née* Leavey; 1 s (Daniel b 1971); m 2, 21 Oct 1978, Daphne Isobel, *née* Scharenguivel; 1 s (Adam b 1979), 1 da (Hannah b 1980); *Career* lectr: Univ of Warwick 1969–73, LSE 1973–80; dean Faculty of Social Sciences Brunel Univ 1985–87 (prof of law 1980–87); Univ of Bristol: asst lectr 1966–69, prof of law 1987–, dean Faculty of Law 1988–92, pro-vice-chllr 1995–; called to the Bar Middle Temple 1984, barr Arden Chambers London 1993–; memb: Lord Chllr's Advsy Ctee on Legal Aid 1988–91, Law Soc Trg Ctee 1989–93, Judicial Studies Bd 1992–94, Cncl on Tbnls 1994–; chm: Ctee Heads of Univ Law Schs 1990–92, Socio-Legal Studies Assoc 1993–95, Social Security Appeal Tbnls 1990–94 (pt/t), Med Appeal Tbnls and Disability Appeal Tbnls 1992–94 (pt/t); *Books* Landlord and Tenant (1975), Housing Law: Cases, Materials and Commentary (with Jonathan Hill, 1991), Claim in Time (1994), Housing Law (with Andrew Arden and Caroline Hunter, 1994); *Recreations* music, walking, cooking, gardening, foreign travel; *Style*— Prof Martin Partington; ✉ Little Court, Grib Lane, Blagdon, North Somerset BS18 6SA (☎ 01761 462916); Faculty of Law, University of Bristol, Bristol BS8 1RJ (☎ 0117 928 7443, fax 0117 925 1870, telex 445938)

PARTINGTON, Robin Courtland; s of Dr James Ernest Partington (d 1967), of Bolton, and June, *née* Whittenbury; *b* 5 Aug 1960; *Educ* Bolton Sch Bolton, Univ of Liverpool Sch of Architecture (BA, BArch); *m* 22 Sept 1990, Sally Maurice, da of Maurice Owen Jones; *Career* training (year out) Scott Brownrigg and Turner Guildford 1981–82; Foster & Partners (formerly Sir Norman Foster & Partners): joined 1984, assoc 1987, project dir 1988, dir 1992–; RIBA 1985, ARCUK 1985, RIAS 1996; *Recreations* sailing, shooting; *Clubs* Royal Philatelic Soc; *Style*— Robin Partington, Esq; ✉ Foster & Partners, Riverside 3, 22 Hester Road, London SW11 4AN (☎ 0171 738 0455, fax 0171 738 1107/1108)

PARTON, Geoffrey Paul; s of Walter St John Parton (d 1962), and Betty Mary, *née* Herring; *b* 25 April 1947; *Educ* Belfairs HS; *m* 1973, Patrika Anne, da of John McClemont; 1 s (John Vivian Henry b 1981), 2 da (Hannah Mary b 1978, Frances Anne b 1980); *Career* dir Marlborough Fine Art London (joined 1969); numerous exhibitions organised incl those of R B Kitaj and Frank Auerbach; memb Exec Ctee Soc of London Art Dealers 1991–; *Style*— Geoffrey Parton, Esq; ✉ Marlborough Fine Art, 6 Albemarle Street, London W1X 3HF (☎ 0171 629 5161, fax 0171 629 6338)

PARTON, Nicholas George; s of Maj Michael Henry Parton, and Jean Mary, *née* Saxby; *b* 1 June 1954; *Educ* Haileybury, Grenoble Univ, Liverpool Poly (BA); *m* 12 Sept 1981, (Elizabeth) Querida, da of His Hon Judge John Wilfred da Cunha, of Churchill, nr Bristol, Avon; 2 s (Sam b 1984, John (Jack) b 1996), 3 da (Amy b 1983, Phoebe b 1986, Felicity b 1988); *Career* admitted slr 1979; articled clerk Bremmer Sons & Corlett 1977, Holman Fenwick & Willan 1980, Middleton Potts 1983; ptnr: Taylor Garrett 1985–89, Taylor Joynson Garrett 1989–92, Jackson Parton 1992–; memb Law Soc 1979; *Recreations* skiing and sailing; *Clubs* Lansdowne, Broadgate; *Style*— Nicholas Parton, Esq; ✉ 31 Ambleside Ave, London SW16 1QE (☎ 0181 769 0127); Pant y Llin, Ravenspoint Road, Trearddur Bay, Anglesey, N Wales (☎ 01407 861099); Le Mazuet, Bellentre, Aime, Savoie, France; Jackson Parton, 5th Floor, 18 Mansell Street, London E1 8AA (☎ 0171 702 0085, fax 0171 702 0858, telex 8812084 SEALAW G)

PARTRIDGE, Andrew John (Andy); s of John Kenneth Partridge, and Vera Joyce Dolce, *née* Reeves; *b* 11 Nov 1953; *Educ* Penhill Secdy Sch, Merton Fields Sch, Swindon Coll; *m* 28 Aug 1979 (m dis 1993), Marianne, da of Edward Bargrave Wyborn, and Nora Wyborn; 1 da (Holly Victoria b 9 June 1985), 1 s (Harry Scott b 17 Aug 1987); *Career* musician and record prodr; joined first band Stray Blues 1970, memb of numerous bands until forming Helium Kidz 1972 (became XTC 1975); recording and publishing contract Virgin Records 1977; XTC albums: White Music (1978), Go 2 (1978), Drums & Wires (1979, Canadian & NZ gold records), Black Sea (1980), English Settlement (1982, silver record), Waxworks (compilaton, 1982), Mummer (1983), The Big Express (1984), Skylarking (1986), Oranges and Lemons (1989), Nonsuch (1992); XTC albums under name The Dukes of the Stratosphear: 25 O'Clock (1985), Psonic Psunspot (1987), Chips From the Chocolate Fireball (compilation, 1987); also Takeaway/The Lure of Salvage (as Mr Partridge) and compilation albums incl: The Compact XTC, Rag and Bone Buffet, Drums and Wireless, BBC Sessions '77–'89, Fossil Fuel 1996; extensive touring 1977–82; nominated Grammy and Ivor Novello awards 1993; *Recreations* collecting (and making) toy soldiers, books and occasional painting; *Style*— Andy Partridge, Esq; ✉ c/o Suite 59, The Pall Mall Deposit, 124–128 Barlby Road, London W10 6BL (☎ 0181 960 5707, fax 0181 960 4431)

PARTRIDGE, Prof Derek; *b* 24 Oct 1945; *Educ* UCL (BSc), Imperial Coll London (DIC, PhD); *m* 27 Aug 1971, Mehrazar; 2 da (Mischa b 1974, Morgan b 1976); *Career* lectr in computer sci Univ of Nairobi Kenya 1972–74, asst prof, assoc prof then full prof Dept Computer Sci New Mexico State Univ USA 1975–86, prof of computer sci Univ of Exeter 1987–; visiting fell Univ of Essex 1981–82, visiting lectr Univ of Queensland 1983–84; involved with Nat Youth Theatre 1966–68; FRSA, AAAI, AISB; *Books* incl: Artificial Intelligence: Applications in the Future of Software Engineering (1986), Computers for Society (contrib, 1986), The Encyclopaedia of Microcomputers (contrib, 1988), Machine Learning (contrib, 1989), The Foundations of Artificial Intelligence: A Source Book (contrib, 1989); *Recreations* reading, writing, natural history, football; *Style*— Prof Derek Partridge; ✉ University of Exeter, Department of Computer Science, Exeter EX4 4PT (☎ 01392 264069, fax 01392 264067)

PARTRIDGE, Derek William; CMG (1987); s of Ernest Partridge (d 1984), of Wembley, Middx, and Ethel Elizabeth, *née* Buckingham (d 1985); *b* 15 May 1931; *Educ* Preston Manor Co GS Wembley; *Career* RAF 1949–51; HM Dip Serv: FO 1951–54, Oslo 1954–56, Jedda 1956, Khartoum 1957–60, Sofia 1960–62, Manila 1962–65, Djakarta 1965–67, FCO 1967–72, Brisbane 1972–74, Colombo 1974–77; FCO 1977–86, head Migration and Visa Dept 1981–83, head Nat and Treaty Dept 1983–86, Br high cmmr Freetown Sierra Leone 1986–91; cncllr (Lib Dem) London Borough of Southwark 1994–; memb Royal African Soc; *Clubs* National Liberal; *Style*— Derek W Partridge, Esq, CMG; ✉ 16 Wolfe Crescent, Rotherhithe, London SE16 1SF (☎ and fax 0171 231 2759)

PARTRIDGE, Frances Catherine; da of William Cecil Marshall (d 1921), of London, and Margaret Anna, *née* Lloyd (d 1941); *b* 15 March 1900; *Educ* Bedales Sch, Newnham Coll Cambridge (BA); *m* 2 March 1933, Maj Reginald Sherring Partridge, MC (d 1960); 1 s (Lytton Burgo b 1935, d 1963); *Career* antiquarian bookseller 1922–28; edited Greville diaries with husband 1928–38 (8 vols), translator of French and Spanish works; FRSL; *Books* A Pacifist's War (1978), Memories (1981), Julia (1983), Everything To Lose (1985), Friends in Focus (1987), The Pasque Flower (1990), Hanging On (1990), Other People (1993), Good Company (1994); *Recreations* travel, music, reading, botany; *Clubs* Int PEN; *Style*— Mrs Frances Partridge; ✉ 15 West Halkin St, London SW1X 8JL (☎ 0171 235 6998)

PARTRIDGE, Frank; s of John Partridge, of Inverness, and Flora Partridge; *b* 16 Aug 1953; *Educ* Abbey Sch Fort Augustus Inverness-shire, Univ of Edinburgh (BA), Univ Coll Cardiff (Dip in Journalism); *Career* BBC: presenter Newsbeat Radio One 1982–88, sports corr 1988–91, presenter PM Radio 4 1991–93; presenter with Sky Television 1993–; *Recreations* squash, swimming, cricket playing, watching and collecting; *Style*— Frank Partridge, Esq; ✉ Presenter, Sky Television PLC, 6 Centaurs Business Park, Grant Way, Isleworth, Middx TW7 5QD (☎ 0171 705 3000)

PARTRIDGE, Ian Harold; CBE (1992); s of Harold William (d 1972), and Eugenia Emily, *née* Stinson (d 1992); *b* 12 June 1938; *Educ* New Coll Oxford (chorister), Clifton, RCM, Guild Sch of Music (LGSM); *m* 4 July 1959, Ann Pauline, da of William Maskell Glover (d 1965), of Bexhill, Sussex; 2 s (Daniel b 1964, Jonathan b 1967); *Career* tenor; concert singer and recitalist, repertoire ranges from early baroque to new works; operatic debut as Iopas in Les Troyens (Covent Garden) 1969, title role in Britten's St Nicolas (Thames TV, winner Prix Italia 1977), regular appearances at London's concert halls with major orchestras and conductors and at int festivals throughout the world, frequent broadcaster on BBC Radio 3; over 200 performances worldwide of An Evening with Queen Victoria (with Prunella Scales), given masterclasses on Lieder, English Song and Early Music at festivals incl Aldeburgh, Dartington, Trondheim and Vancouver; prof of singing RAM; govr RSM 1994–, pres ISM 1996–97, dir PAMRA 1996–; Hon RAM 1996; *Recordings* incl: Schubert's Die Schöne Müllerin and Winterreise, Schumann Dichterliebe, Vaughan Williams' On Wenlock Edge, Warlock's The Curlew, Britten's Winter Words; *Recreations* theatre, bridge, horse racing; *Clubs* Garrick; *Style*— Ian Partridge, Esq, CBE; ✉ 127 Pepys Rd, Wimbledon, London SW20 8NP (☎ 0181 946 7140, fax 0181 241 8544)

PARTRIDGE, (Walter Michael) James; TD (1992); s of Maj Michael Harry Partridge, of Betchworth, Surrey, and Diana Marjorie, *née* Chamberlain; *b* 14 March 1958; *Educ* Lancing, Trinity Coll Cambridge (BA); *m* 16 July 1983, Sarah Mercy, da of Wallace Barrie Page, of Killearn, Scotland; 1 s (Harry Michael James b 1989), 1 da (Georgiana Diana Margaret b 1987); *Career* admitted slr 1983; asst slr Lawrence Graham 1983–86, ptnr Thomson Snell & Passmore 1987–; memb Law Soc; cmmnd RA (Vol) 1979, Lt-Col 1996–, 100 (Yeo) Regt RA; *Recreations* sailing, walking, reading; *Clubs* Cavalry and Guards'; *Style*— James Partridge, Esq, TD; ✉ Thomson Snell & Passmore, 3 Lonsdale Gardens, Tunbridge Wells, Kent TN1 1NX (☎ 01892 510000, fax 01892 549884)

PARTRIDGE, John Arthur; s of Claude Partridge (d 1958), of Brompton Square, London, and Iris Florence, *née* Franks (d 1982); *b* 6 July 1929; *Educ* Elstree Sch, Harrow; *m* 1, 1954 (m dis), Hon Caroline Elizabeth Maud Cust, da of 6 Baron Brownlow, of Belton House, Lincs (d 1978); 2 s (Frank David Peregrine b 14 Sept 1955, Claude Edward b 29 Aug 1962), 1 da (Sophia Josephine (Mrs Anthony Waltham) b 12 May 1969); m 2, Rosemary FitzGibbon, da of Maj Robert Tyrrell (d 1975), of Litcham, Norfolk; *Career* ADC to Govr of S Aust Gen Lord Norrie 1952–53; chm and md Partridge Fine Art plc 1958–, chm Fine Art and Antique Export Ctee 1979–; *Recreations* hunting, fishing, shooting, gardening; *Clubs* Brooks's; *Style*— John Partridge, Esq; ✉ Prebendal House, Empingham, Rutland, Leicestershire (☎ 01780 460234); Partridge Fine Art plc, 144/146 New Bond St, London W1Y 0LY (☎ 0171 629 0834)

PARTRIDGE, Prof Linda; da of George Albert Partridge, of Bath, and Ida, *née* Tucker; *b* 18 March 1950; *Educ* Convent of the Sacred Heart, Univ of Oxford (Christopher Welch scholar, BA, DPhil); *m* 1983 (m dis 1990), V French; *Career* NERC post-doctoral fell Univ of York 1974–76; Univ of Edinburgh: demonstrator 1976–78, lectr 1978–87, reader 1987–92, prof of evolutionary biology and Darwin res fell 1992–93; Weldon prof of biometry UCL 1994–; memb: Genetical Soc, Br Ecological Soc; pres: Int Soc for Behavioural Ecology 1990–92, Assoc for the Study of Animal Behaviour 1995–97; FRSE 1992, FRS 1996; *Recreations* gardening, painting, tennis; *Style*— Prof Linda Partridge, FRS, FRSE

PARTRIDGE, Dr Martyn Richard; s of Maj Raymond John Bruce Partridge, RA, of Loughton, Essex, and Grace, *née* Darch; *b* 19 May 1948; *Educ* Pocklington Sch, Univ of Manchester (MB ChB, MD); *m* 23 June 1973, Rosemary Jane Emily, da of Lt (John) Dennis Radford, of Hove, Sussex; 1 s (Richard John Oliver b 15 Feb 1979), 2 da (Judith Stephanie Louise b 10 June 1977, Philippa Rachel Jane b 26 Feb 1981); *Career* resident med offr Nat Heart Hosp London 1975–76, med registrar Royal Post Grad Med Sch London 1976–78, sr Jules Thorne res fell Middx Hosp 1978–80; sr med registrar: London Chest Hosp 1980–81, UCH 1981–82; conslt physician Whipps Cross Hosp London 1982–, author of various pubns of respiratory med and terminal care; chm Editorial Ctee: British Thoracic Soc, Nat Asthma Campaign (chm Bd of Mgmnt); FRCP, FRSM; *Recreations* travel, railways, music, church and family; *Style*— Dr Martyn Partridge; ✉ Whipps Cross Hosp, Whipps Cross Rd, London E11 1NR (☎ 0181 539 5522 ext 16, fax 0181 558 8115)

PARTRIDGE, Sir Michael John Anthony; KCB (1990, CB 1983); s of Dr John Henry Partridge (d 1956), and Ethel, *née* Green (d 1993); *b* 29 Sept 1935; *Educ* Merchant Taylors', St John's Coll Oxford (MA); *m* 1968, Joan Elizabeth, da of Trevor Grattan Hughes (d 1953); 2 s, 1 da; *Career* civil servant; dep sec DHSS 1981–83, dep sec Home Office with responsibility for Police Dept 1983–87, second perm sec DHSS 1987–88, perm sec DSS 1988–95; hon fell St John's Coll Oxford 1991–; chm Bd of Govrs Middx Univ 1996–, dir Norwich Union 1996–, dir Stationery Office 1996–; govr Merchant Taylors' Sch 1993–; Liveryman Worshipful Co of Merchant Taylors; *Recreations* skiing, reading, DIY; *Clubs* United Oxford and Cambridge; *Style*— Sir Michael Partridge, KCB; ✉ 27 High View, Pinner, Middx HA5 3NZ (☎ 0181 868 0657, fax 0181 429 4532)

PASCO, Richard Edward; CBE (1977); s of Cecil George Pasco (d 1982), and Phyllis Irene, *née* Widdison (d 1989); *b* 18 July 1926; *Educ* King's Coll Sch Wimbledon, Central Sch of Speech and Drama; *m* 1 (m dis), Greta, *née* Watson; 1 s; m 2, 1967, Barbara Leigh-Hunt, *qv*; *Career* Army Serv 1944–48; actor; many leading roles RSC, London, West End Theatre, film, radio and TV, concert and recital work; hon assoc artist RSC, Royal Nat Theatre player; tstee Shakespeare's Birthplace Tst 1992, dir Royal Theatrical Fund 1995; *Recreations* music, gardening, reading; *Clubs* Garrick; *Style*— Richard Pasco, Esq, CBE; ✉ c/o Michael Whitehall Ltd, 125 Gloucester Road, London SW7 4TE (☎ 0171 244 8466, fax 0171 244 9060)

PASCO, Rowanne; da of John Pasco (d 1992), and Ann, *née* MacKeonis; *b* 7 Oct 1938; *Educ* Ursuline Convent HS, Open Univ (MA); *m* 1994, Rev William FitzGerald; *Career* travel rep in Tuscany Horizon Holidays 1961–64, various radio and TV commercials whilst res in Hollywood California 1964–66; BBC 1966–79 (reporter radio news, TV ed staff newpaper Ariel, prodr/presenter religious programmes radio), ed Catholic newspaper The Universe 1979–87, first religious ed TV-AM 1987–92, presenter religion GMTV 1993–94, currently freelance bdcaster and journalist specialising in religion, editorial advsr Cncl of Christians and Jews; memb NUJ; *Books* Faith Alive (ed jtly, 1988, New Catechism edn 1994), One Hundred and One Questions on the New Catechism (1995), Why I am a Catholic (1995); *Recreations* Italy, cooking, cats; *Clubs* BBC; *Style*— Ms Rowanne Pasco; ✉ The Dell, Blockley, Glos GL56 9DB

PASCOE, Alan Peter; MBE; s of Ernest George Frank Pascoe, of Portsmouth, and Joan Rosina Pascoe; *b* 11 Oct 1947; *Educ* Portsmouth Southern GS, Borough Rd Coll, Univ of London (BEd Hons); *m* 15 Aug 1970, Della Patricia, da of Douglas Charles Albert James; 1 s (Daniel James b 1983), 1 da (Lucy Joanna b 1979); *Career* int athlete 1967–78; GB rep in: 110m hurdles, 400m hurdles, 200m, 2 4x100 and 4x400m relay; GB team capt 1971 and 1972, Euro indoor champion 1969, bronze medallist 110m hurdles Euro Championships Athens 1969, Olympic silver medallist 4x400m relay 1972, Euro Cup winner 1973 and 1975, Cwlth Games and Euro champion 1974 (set record in both events), Cwlth silver medallist 4x400m 1974, Euro gold medallist 4x400m relay 1974, ranked No 1 in World 1975, Cwlth bronze medallist 400m hurdles 1978; represented Europe in World Cup Cwlth v USA and USSR; memb: Sports Cncl 1974–80, BBC Advsy Cncl 1975–79; chm The Sponsorship Group, md Alan Pascoe Associates Ltd (sports sponsorship) 1986–; *Recreations* theatre; *Style*— Alan Pascoe, MBE; ✉ Alan Pascoe Associates, 141–143 Drury Lane, London WC2B 5TB (☎ 0171 379 5220)

PASCOE, Dr Michael William; s of Canon W J T Pascoe (d 1974), and Daisy, *née* Farlow; *b* 16 June 1930; *Educ* St John's Sch Leatherhead, Selwyn Coll Cambridge (BA, PhD); *m* 1, 24 March 1957 (m dis 1974), Janet, da of John Clark (d 1962), of Naphill, Bucks; 3 da (Katherine Jane (Mrs Burrows) b 1957, Joanna Mary (Mrs Evans) b 1959, Madeline Bridget (Mrs Robinson) b 1961); m 2, 23 Dec 1974, Brenda Reed; 1 da (Josephine Lucy b 1980); *Career* med physicist Mt Vernon Hosp 1955–57, textile scientist Br Nylon Spinners Ltd 1957–60, surface coating scientist ICI Paints 1960–67, lectr in material science Brunel Univ 1967–76; The Br Museum: princ scientific offr 1976–79, keeper of conservation and technical services 1979–81; tutor Open Univ 1973–84, visiting prof ICCROM Rome (conservation centre), visiting lectr Brunel Univ 1995; author of numerous publications on friction, textiles, engineering, conservation; conslt and advsr: Royal Acad of Arts, Science Museum, Mary Rose Tst, Public Record Office, Cncl for the Care of Churches, Madame Tussauds, Parliament of Guyana; former memb Historic Wrecks Ctee, former govr Camberwell Sch of Art and Crafts; FRSA 1969, MInstP 1958–83; *Recreations* painting and drawing, travel, museums; *Style*— Dr Michael Pascoe; ✉ 15 Parkfield Rd, Ickenham, Uxbridge UB10 8LN (☎ 01895 674723, fax 01895 633399)

PASCOE, Nigel Spencer Knight; QC (1988); s of Ernest Sydney Pascoe (d 1970), and Cynthia, *née* Holtom (d 1992); *b* 18 Aug 1940; *Educ* Epsom; *m* 1964, Elizabeth Anne, da of Bryan Walter; 4 da (Gillie, Jemma, Dimity, Miranda), 2 s (Hallam, Tristan); *Career* called to the Bar Inner Temple 1966 (bencher 1996), in practice Western Circuit (ldr 1995–), recorder of the Crown Court 1979–; fndr ed All England Quarterly Law Gazettes; memb Hampshire CC 1979–83; The Trial of Penn and Mead (one man show, Edinburgh Fringe Festival) 1994; *Books* The Trial of Penn and Mead (1994); *Recreations* acting, cricket, theatre, writing, presenting legal anthologies with Elizabeth Pascoe, after dinner speaking; *Clubs* Garrick; *Style*— Nigel Pascoe, Esq, QC; ✉ 3 Pump Court, Upper Ground, Temple, London EC4Y 7AJ (☎ 0171 353 0711)

PASCOE, Ronald Rowe (Ron); s of Victor Pascoe (d 1975), and Catherine, *née* Rowe (d 1935); *b* 12 Jan 1935; *Educ* Falmouth GS, Fitzwilliam Coll Cambridge (MA); *m* 25 March 1972, Patricia Lilian, da of William Ellis; 2 s (Stephen b 19 Jan 1974, Richard b 1 June 1976); *Career* Nat Serv 1954–56; sales rep Hadfields Ltd 1959–67, called to the Bar 1967; asst co sec: James Booth Aluminium Ltd 1967–70, Alcan Booth Aluminium Ltd 1970–72; legal mangr Ada Halifax Ltd 1972–75, sec Mullard Ltd 1975–80, div sec of maj divs Philips 1980–87, co sec and UK gp counsel Philips UK Ltd 1987–96 (dir Philips Pension Fund Ltd); jr C of C 1960–65; memb Companies Ctee CBI; tstee Pye Fndn; *Recreations* singing, acting, skiing, swimming; *Style*— Ron Pascoe, Esq; ✉ c/o Philips Electronics UK Ltd, The Philips Centre, 420–430 London Road, Croydon CR9 3QR

PASLEY, Sir (John) Malcolm Sabine; 5 Bt (GB 1794), of Craig, Dumfriesshire; s of Sir Rodney Marshall Sabine Pasley, 4 Bt (d 1982), and Aldyth (d 1983), da of Maj Lancelot Hamber; *b* 5 April 1926; *Educ* Sherborne, Trinity Coll Oxford (MA); *m* 1965, Virginia Killigrew, da of Peter Lothian Killigrew Wait, of Kew, Surrey; 2 s; *Heir* s, Robert Pasley, *qv*; *Career* fellow Magdalen College Oxford; *Style*— Sir Malcolm Pasley, Bt; ✉ 25 Lathbury Rd, Oxford

PASLEY, Robert Killigrew Sabine; er s and h of Sir Malcolm Pasley, 5 Bt, *qv*; *b* 23 Oct 1965; *Style*— Robert Pasley, Esq; ✉ 25 Lathbury Rd, Oxford

PASMORE, (Edwin John) Victor; CH (1982), CBE (1959); s of Edwin Stephen Pasmore, MD, MRCP (d 1926), and Gertrude Eva, *née* Screech (d 1974); *b* 3 Dec 1908; *Educ* Harrow; *m* 3 June 1940, Wendy, da of Capt John Lloyd Blood (d 1956), of The Old Rectory, White Colne, nr Colchester, Essex; 1 s (John b 1941), 1 da (Mary b 1943); *Career* artist; visiting teacher LCC Camberwell Sch of Art 1945–49, Central Sch of Arts and Crafts 1949–53; master of painting Univ of Durham 1954–61; conslt urban and architectural designer SW Area Peterlee New Town 1955–77; memb: London Artists Assoc 1932–34, The London Gp 1935–52, Euston Road Gp 1937–40; tstee Tate Gallery 1963–66; *Retrospective Exhibitions* Venice Biennale 1960, Musee des Arts Decoratifs Paris 1961, Stedelijle Copenhagen 1962, Kestner-Gesellschaft Hanover 1962, Kunsthalle Berne 1963, Tate Gallery 1965, Sao Paolo Biennale 1965, Cartwright Hall Bradford 1980, Royal Acad London 1980, Yale Center of British Art USA 1988, Tate Gallery 1994; *Recent Exhibitions* incl: London, NY, Rome, Milan, Zurich, Lubjlana, Messina, Oslo, Osaka, Tokyo, Delhi, Toronto; works represented in public museums incl: GB, Canada, Australia, NZ, Holland, Italy, France, Austria, Portugal, Switzerland, S America and the USA; Carnegie Prize, Pittsburgh Int USA 1964; Grand Prix d' Honneur, Graphics Biennale, Lubjlana 1977; Wollaston Award Royal Acad 1984; hon degrees: Univ of Newcastle 1967, Univ of Surrey 1969, Univ of Warwick 1985, RCA 1969; *Publications* Burning Waters (poem with visual images, 1988); subject of: Monograph and Catalogue Raisonné 1926–79 (Alan Bowness, 1980), Monograph, Paintings and Graphics 1980–92 (Norbert Lynton, 1992); *Recreations* animals, natural philosophy; *Clubs* Arts; *Style*— Victor Pasmore, Esq, CH, CBE, RA; ✉ 12 St Germans Place, Blackheath, London SE3; Dar Gamri, Gudja, Malta; Marlborough Fine Art Ltd, 6 Albemarle Street, London W1X 3HF (☎ 0171 629 5161); Marlborough Gallery Inc, 40 West 57th Street, New York, NY 10018, USA

PATCH, Donald; s of Samuel Harry Patch, of Seaford, Sussex, and Lillian Gertrude, *née* Dean; *b* 19 June 1930; *m* 29 Sept 1956, Pamela Doreen, da of George Ely Cullingford (d 1996); 2 s (Trevor Samuel b 5 Sept 1962 d 1963, Matthew John b 21 Oct 1968), 2 da (Deborah Grace (Mrs Kew) b 21 June 1960, Madeleine Louise b 25 Oct 1964); *Career* Nat Serv Air History Branch Chelsea RAF 1952–53; architecture and civil engrg Air Miny London and Northwood 1947–53, asst architect Cameroons Devpt Corp W Africa 1953–56, project architect Mulago Teaching Hosp Kampala Uganda Miny of Health 1956–62, assoc architect Watkins Gray London (specialist in hosp design London Teaching Hosps) 1963–73; Norman & Dawbarn: joined 1973, ptnr 1977–91, conslt 1991–94; projects incl hosps in: Nigeria, India, Tanzania, Ethiopia, Oman, Uganda, Malawi, London; other projects incl: cancer res labs, health centres, TV studios, theatre studies for Elmbridge Arts Cncl; numerous MOD projects for the Army, Navy and RAF in UK, Ascension Island and The Falkland Islands; promoter of arts devpts incl Kampala Nat Theatre and arts facilities in Elmbridge, memb Borough of Elmbridge Arts Forum 1988–90 (Theatre Working Pty 1993–95), architectural advsr Elmbridge Arts Cncl 1988–; memb Malawi Inst of Architects 1983; ARIBA 1971; *Recreations* walking, music, travel, theatre (both tech and artistic aspects); *Clubs* Walton and Weybridge Amateur Operatic Soc, Kampala, Cameroon Motor and Social; *Style*— Donald Patch, Esq; ✉ Highlands, The Coombe, Betchworth, Surrey RH3 7BT (☎ 01737 844138)

PATEL, Dr Hasmukh Rambhai; s of Rambhai Patel, of London, and Shardaben Patel; *b* 1 Jan 1945; *Educ* King's Coll London, King's Coll Hosp Med Sch (MB BS, MRCS); *m* 16 July 1969, Mrudula Hasmukh, da of Revabhai Patel, of Baroda, India; 1 s (Veran b 31 July 1972), 1 da (Nesha b 7 May 1975); *Career* conslt paediatrician Joyce Green Hosp Dartford 1976–, SE Thames regnl postgrad associate dean Univ of London 1991–; coll tutor RCP 1986–; memb: Royal Med Benevolent Fund, BPA; FRCPE 1985, FRCP 1986; *Recreations* travel, swimming, photography; *Style*— Dr Hasmukh Patel; ✉ 10 Northumberland Gardens, Bickley, Bromley, Kent BR1 2XD; Postgraduate Medical Centre, Joyce Green Hospital, Dartford, Kent (☎ 01322 283430)

PATEL, Dr Indraprasad Gordhanbhai; Hon KBE (1990); s of Gordhanbhai Tulsibhai Patel, and Kashiben Jivabhai Patel; *b* 11 Nov 1924; *Educ* Baroda Coll Univ of Bombay (BA), King's Coll Cambridge (BA, PhD), Harvard Univ Grad Sch; *m* 28 Nov 1958, Alaknanda, da of Prof A K Dasgupta; 1 da (Rishiparna Rehana); *Career* prof of econs and head of dept Univ of Baroda 1949–50 (princ Baroda Coll), economist later asst div chief Res Dept IMF Washington DC 1950–54, dep econ advsr Miny of Fin Govt of India 1954–58, alternate exec dir for India IMF Washington DC 1958–61, econ advsr Planning Cmmn 1961–63, visiting prof Delhi Sch of Econs 1964, chief econ advsr Miny of Fin 1961–64 and 1965–67, special sec and sec Dept of Econ Affrs Miny of Fin 1967–72, dep admin UN Devpt Prog NY 1972–77; govr Reserve Bank of India 1977–82; dir: Indian Inst of Mgmnt Ahmedabad 1982–84, LSE 1984–90; chm Aga Khan Rural Support Prog 1990–, hon advsr to chm Indian Petrochemicals Corp Ltd 1990–, hon advsr planning Govt of Gujarat 1991–, memb New Int Cmmn on Global Governance 1992–; formerly (1961–67): memb Monopolies Cmmn, chm Managing Agency Ctee, sec Ctee on Gold Control, memb UN Gp of Experts on Int Monetary Reform, memb Gp of Experts to advise first UNCTAD Meeting; formerly memb (1967–72): Atomic Energy Cmmn Govt of India, Space Cmmn Govt of India, Tata Inst of Fundamental Res, Nat Cncl of Applied Econ Res, Inst of Economic Growth, Indian Red Cross; memb: UN Ctee for Devpt Planning 1977–86, Gp of Thirty 1978–90, Governing Body Int Inst of Econs 1983–, Advsy Gp Gen Agreement Trade and Tariffs 1984–85, Governing Body World Inst Devpt Econs Res 1987–90; hon fell: King's Coll Cambridge 1986, LSE 1990; Hon DLitt Sardar Patel Univ India 1980, Hon DCL Univ of Mauritius 1990, Hon DLitt Univ of Baroda 1993; Padma Vibhushan 1991; *Publications incl* Inflation in Relation to Economic Development (1952), Monetary Policy in Post-War Years (1953), Selective Credit Controls in Underdeveloped Economies (1954), Limits of Economic Policy (1964), Foreign Capital and Domestic Planning from Capital Movements and Economic Development (ed J Handler, 1967), Essays in Economic Policy and Economic Growth (1986); *Recreations* music, reading, watching cricket; *Style*— Dr Indraprasad Patel, KBE; ✉ 12 Amee Society, Diwalipura, Old Padra Road, Baroda 390015, India (☎ 00 91 265 339026, fax 00 91 265 333658)

PATEL, Prof Minoo Homi; s of Homi Edalji Patel, of Hounslow, Middlesex, and Doly Homi Patel; *b* 28 July 1949; *Educ* Univ of London (BSc, PhD); *m* Irene Veronica, da of Harry Kay, of Basildon, Essex; 2 s (Zubin Homi b 1973, Darren Lindsay b 1975); *Career* res engr Queen Mary Coll London 1973–76, UCL 1976– (lectr, reader, currently Kennedy prof of mechanical engrg and head of dept); dir: BPP Ocean Technology Ltd 1983–, Pamec Technology Ltd 1986–, BPP Technical Services Ltd 1989–, UCLi Ltd 1990–; FRINA, FIMechE, CEng; *Books* Dynamics of Offshore Structures (1989), Compliant Offshore Structures (1990); *Recreations* gliding, jogging; *Style*— Prof Minoo Patel; ✉ Head Department of Mechanical Engineering, University College London, Torrington Place, London WC1E 7JE (☎ 0171 380 7178, fax 0171 388 0180, telex 296273)

PATEMAN, Jack Edward; CBE (1970); s of William Edward Pateman; *b* 29 Nov 1921; *Educ* Gt Yarmouth GS; *m* 1949, Cicely Hope Turner; 1 s, 1 da; *Career* md GEC Avionics Ltd 1971–86; dir: Canadian Marconi Co 1971–87, GEC Computers Ltd 1971–89, Elliott Brothers (London) Ltd 1979–89, GEC Marconi (China) Ltd 1979–89, Marconi Electronic Devices Ltd 1980–87, GEC Information Systems Ltd 1982–86, GEC Avionics Projects (UK) Ltd 1984–89, GEC Plc 1986–88; dep chm GEC Avionics Ltd 1986–92; chm Kent County Engrg Soc 1989–96; Br Gold medal RAeS 1981; FEng 1981; *Style*— Jack Pateman, Esq, CBE, FEng; ✉ Spindles, Ivy Hatch, Sevenoaks, Kent TN15 0PG

PATERSON, Prof Alan Keith Gordon; s of Maj Albert Paterson (d 1946), of Kinmundy House, Aberdeenshire, and Helen, *née* Horne; *b* 8 March 1938; *Educ* Aberdeen GS, Univ of Aberdeen (MA), Univ of Cambridge (PhD); *m* 28 June 1965, Anna, da of Tage Holm, of Malmö, Sweden; 1 s (Andrew); *Career* lectr Queen Mary Coll Univ of London 1964–84, prof of Spanish St Andrews Univ 1985– (dean Faculty of Arts 1991–94); author of specialist pubns on theatre, poetry and prose of seventeenth century Spain; memb Scottish Examination Bd; *Books* Tirso De Molina, La Venganza De Tamar (1967), Calderón, The Painter of His Dishonour (1992); *Recreations* cooking, hill-walking, motor-cycling; *Style*— Prof Alan Paterson; ✉ Spanish Department, The United College, St Andrews, Scotland KY16 9AL (☎ 01334 476161, fax 01334 476474, telex 9312110846 SAG)

PATERSON, Alastair Craig; CBE (1987); s of Duncan McKellar Paterson, and Lavinia, *née* Craig; *b* 15 Jan 1924; *Educ* Glasgow HS, RCST (ARCST), Univ of Glasgow (BSc); *m* 1947, Betty *née* Burley; 2 s 2 da; *Career* cmmnd REME 1944, served India and Burma, attached Indian Army 1944–47; engr; Merz and McLellan 1947–58, Taylor Woodrow 1958–60; Bullen and Partners consulting engrs: ptnr 1960–69, sr ptnr 1969–88, ret; Inst of Structural Engrs: memb Cncl 1976–89, vice pres 1981–84, pres 1984–85; Inst of Civil Engrs: memb Cncl 1978–91, vice pres 1985–88, pres 1988–89; chm Br Conslts Bureau 1978–80, pres Br Section Societe des Ingenieurs et Scientifiques de France, 1980–81; memb: Cncl Br Bd of Agrément 1982–, Overseas Projects Bd 1984–87, Engrg Cncl 1987–90; fndr memb: Hazards Forum, Br Nat Ctee for Int Engrg Affairs; former Br delegate to Fédération Européenne d'Associations Nationales d'Ingénieurs and WFEO Congresses; Hon DSc Univ of Strathclyde 1989; FICE 1963, FIMechE 1964, FCIArb 1968, FIStructE 1970, FEng 1983; *Style*— Alastair Paterson, Esq, CBE, FEng

PATERSON, Anthony John; s of John McLennan Paterson (d 1978), and Isobel Margaret, *née* Reichwald; *b* 16 May 1951; *Educ* Winchester, Worcester Coll Oxford (LLB); *Career* slr; special constable 1976–79; Parly candidate (Lib) for Finchley 1979, press offr Cons Bow Group 1983–84, Parly liaison offr 1984–85, res sec 1985–87, Parly candidate (C) for Brent S 1987; currently immigration conslt; author of 3 Bow Group papers; sec Bow Group Environment Ctee; memb: Cncl World Wildlife Fund 1985–91, Exec Green Alliances 1987–90; *Books* The Green Conservative (1989); *Recreations* politics, reading, languages; *Style*— Anthony J Paterson, Esq; ✉ office: (☎ and fax 0181 748 8532)

PATERSON, Dame Betty Fraser Ross; DBE (1981, CBE 1973), JP (1950), DL (Herts 1980); da of Robert Ross Russell (d 1934), and Elsie Marian Fraser (d 1918); *b* 14 March 1916; *Educ* Harrogate Coll, Western Infirmary Glasgow (MCSP); *m* 1940, Ian Douglas Paterson, s of George Stanley Vaughan Paterson (d 1935); 1 s (Ross), 1 da (Rosemary); *Career* memb: Chartered Soc of Physiotherapy 1938, NE Met Regnl Hosp Bd 1960–73, Cmmn for the New Towns 1961–74 (dep chm 1970–74), Govrs St Bartholomew's Hosp 1961–73, Govrs Bishop Stortford Coll 1966–81; chm: Herts CC 1969–73 (memb 1952–74, alderman 1959–74), NW Thames RHA 1973–84, Nat Staff Ctee for Nurses and Midwives 1974–84, Tstees Nat Health Service Pensioners' Tst 1991–96; pres Herts Assoc of Local Cncls 1978–90; vice pres: Herts Magistrates Assoc 1987, Community Devpt Agency for Hertfordshire 1987 (formerly Herts Community Cncl); *Recreations* music, cooking, foreign travel; *Style*— Dame Betty Paterson, DBE, JP, DL; ✉ 52 Free Trade Wharf, The Highway, London E1 9ES (☎ 0171 791 0367)

PATERSON, Bill; *b* 3 June 1945; *Career* actor; also asst dir Glasgow Citizen's Theatre for Youth Co, Mongrel's Heart (Edinburgh Lyceum) 1994; *Theatre* for 7:84 Theatre Co Scotland: incl: Willie Rough (Royal Lyceum), Great Northern Welly Boat Show (Edinburgh Festival), The Game's a Bogey, Little Red Hen and The Cheviot, The Stag and The Black Black Oil; London prodns incl: Treetops (Riverside), Writer's Cramp (Hampstead/Bush), Ella (ICA), Whose Life Is It Anyway? (Savoy), And Me Wi' A Bad Leg Tae (Royal Court), A Man With Connections (Royal Court/Traverse), Crime and Punishment (Lyric Hammersmith), Guys and Dolls (NT), title role in Schweyk In The Second World War (NT), Good Person of Sezuan (NT), Death and the Maiden (Royal Court/Duke of York's), Misery (Criterion) 1992–93; *Television* for BBC: The Cheviot, The Stag and The Black Black Oil, Licking Hitler, The Vanishing Army, The Lost Tribe, United Kingdom, The Cherry Orchard, Smiley's People, Stan's Last Game, One of Ourselves, Lily My Love, The Singing Detective, The Interrogation of John, Yellowbacks, It's My City, Tell Tale Hearts, Wall of Silence, Oliver's Travels, Ghostbusters of East Finchley, The Writing on the Wall; other credits incl: Aufwiedersehen Pet (Central), Boon (Central), Traffik (Channel 4) 1993, Shrinks (Euston Films), God On The Rocks (Channel 4); The Crow Road 1996; *Radio* incl: Byline, A Man With Connections, Flowers in the Sky, Hiroshima The Movie, A Good Man in Africa, Hedda Gabler, The Caucasian Chalk Circle; *Films* incl: The Ploughman's Lunch, The Killing Fields, Comfort and Joy, A Private Function, Defence of the Realm, Hidden City, Friendships Death, The Witches, Baron Munchausen, Charlie, Truly Madly Deeply, Victory, Richard III; *Style*— Bill Paterson, Esq; ✉ c/o Marina Martin Associates, 12–13 Poland Street, London W1V 3DE (☎ 0171 734 4818, fax 0171 734 4832)

PATERSON, Christopher John; s of John MacDonald Paterson, and Mary Kathleen, *née* Body; *b* 9 Jan 1947; *Educ* Peterhouse S Rhodesia, Univ of Exeter (BA), Graduate Interne Prog UN Geneva 1970, Stanford Exec Prog 1994; *m* 15 Dec 1973, Gillian Diana, da of Geoffrey Piper, of Christchurch, Dorset; 1 s (Timothy b 1981), 1 da (Sarah b 1978); *Career* Nat Serv Royal Rhodesia Regt 1965–66; Macmillan: joined 1970, publisher Nature 1980–81, md College Press Zimbabwe 1983–85, chm Macmillan Southern African companies 1983–, md The Macmillan Press 1985–91, dir Macmillan Publishers Ltd 1989–, md Macmillan Publishers-International 1995–; memb: Chllr's Advsy Cncl Univ of Exeter 1994–, Southern Africa Assoc Exec 1995–; *Recreations* tennis, gardening, watching and coaching rugby football; *Clubs* Harare, Henley RFC; *Style*— Christopher Paterson, Esq; ✉ Sarum House, Mead Lane, Upper Basildon, Berkshire RG8 8NA (☎ 01491 671515); Macmillan Publishers Ltd, 25 Eccleston Place, London SW1W 9NF (☎ 0171 881 8000, fax 0171 881 8001)

PATERSON, Don; s of Russell Leslie Paterson, of Dundee, and Jean Louise, *née* Cougan; *b* 30 Oct 1963; *Educ* Kirkton HS; *Career* poet and musician; writer in residence Univ of Dundee 1993; Eric Gregory Award 1990, winner Arvon/Observer Poetry competition 1994; memb Jazz band Lammas (Young Jazz Ensemble of the Year BBC Jazz Awards 1993); *Recordings* Talisker 1987, Lammas 1992, Lammas: This Morning 1994, Lammas: The Broken Road 1995, Lammas: Elsewheres 1997; *Publications* Nil Nil (1993, Forward prize for Best First Collection, Scottish Arts Cncl Book Award), God's Gift to Women (1997); *Recreations* badminton, origami, supporting Dundee Utd FC; *Style*— Don Paterson, Esq; ✉ Faber & Faber Ltd, 3 Queen Square, London WC1N 3AU (☎ 0171 465 0045, fax 0171 465 0034)

PATERSON, Douglas Gordon James; s of Gordon Mellish Paterson, of Moor Park, Herts, and Anne Barbara Bolam, *née* Mason; *b* 24 Oct 1943; *Educ* George Watson's Coll Edinburgh, Univ Coll Sch, Univ of St Andrews (MA); *m* 29 May 1972, Pamela Jane, da of William Taylor Rollo (d 1984); 2 s (Christopher Douglas Mark b 18 Oct 1973, Nicholas Gordon William b 13 May 1975), 1 da (Alice Elspeth Jane b 21 March 1977); *Career* Coopers & Lybrand: qualified CA 1968, Cologne office 1970–72, London office 1972–77, ptnr Switzerland 1977–79, ptnr UK 1979, currently audit ptnr and chm German Sector Group; FCA 1968, ATII 1968; *Recreations* tennis, squash, photography, walking, reading; *Clubs* Caledonian; *Style*— Douglas Paterson, Esq; ✉ Coopers & Lybrand, 1 Embankment Place, London WC2N 6NN (☎ 0171 212 4572, fax 0171 212 5280)

PATERSON, His Hon Frank David; s of David Paterson, of Liverpool (d 1956); *b* 10 July 1918; *Educ* Quarry Bank HS Liverpool, Univ of Liverpool (LLB); *m* 1953, Barbara Mary, da of Oswald Ward Gillow (d 1949), of Formby, Lancs; 1 s, 2 da; *Career* called to the Bar Gray's Inn 1941, asst dep coroner Liverpool 1960–68; chm: Miny of Pensions and Nat Insur Tbnl Liverpool 1957–68, Mental Health Review Tbnl SW Lancs and Cheshire 1963–68 and 1983–93; circuit judge (formerly County Court judge) 1968–93; pres Merseyside Branch Magistrates' Assoc 1978–92; Hon LLD Univ of Liverpool 1993; *Clubs* Athenaeum (Liverpool); *Style*— His Hon Frank Paterson; ✉ Vailima, 2 West Lane, Formby, Liverpool L37 7BA (☎ 01704 874345)

PATERSON, Graham Julian; s of Peter James Paterson, *qv*, and Beryl, *née* Johnson; *b* 7 June 1955; *Educ* Dulwich, Magdalen Coll Oxford (BA); *Career* journalist Daily Telegraph 1977–86, ed 7 Days Section Sunday Telegraph 1988–89 (assoc ed 1987–88, home ed 1986–87); The Times: asst ed 1989–, chief asst to the Ed and Features Ed 1993–95, Foreign Ed 1995–; *Clubs* Travellers'; *Style*— Graham Paterson, Esq; ✉ The Times, 1 Pennington St, London E1 9XN

PATERSON, Lt-Col Howard Cecil; TD (two clasps); s of Henry John Paterson (d 1969), of Romanno Bridge, Peeblesshire, and Margaret Isobel, *née* Eunson (d 1983); *b* 16 March 1920; *Educ* Daniel Stewart's Coll Edinburgh, Edinburgh Coll of Art; *m* 21 July 1945, Isabelle Mary, da of Frederick Augustus Edward Upton (d 1960), of 28 College Rd, Southampton; 1 s (Colin Howard b 7 Aug 1948); *Career* Lt-Col RA (TA), serv Europe, ret 1970; asst personnel mangr Jute Industries Ltd 1949–51, dep dir Scot Co Indust Devpt Tst 1951–66, sr dir Scot Tourist Bd 1966–81, ind tourism conslt 1981–; chm: Taste of Scot Scheme 1976–86, Scot Int Gathering Tst 1982–92, Trekking and Riding Soc of Scot 1995– (vice chm 1990–95); vice chm: Scot Aircraft Collection Tst 1982–89 (chm 1989–90), John Buchan Soc 1988–95; memb: Br Horse Soc Scot Ctee, Lothian Area Ctee of Scot Lowland T&AVR, Royal Artillery Assoc, Royal Artillery Institution, City of Edinburgh Artillery Officers' Assoc, Reserve Forces Assoc, Royal Artillery Heritage Campaign (fndr memb), Tweedale Branch British Red Cross, Scot Landowners' Fedn; FSA Scot, FRSA; *Books* Tourism in Scotland (1969), Flavour of Edinburgh (with Catherine Brown, 1986); *Recreations* fishing, shooting, drawing and painting, writing, wild life study, food; *Clubs* Caledonian, 52 Lowland Division Officers'; *Style*— Lt-Col Howard Paterson, TD; ✉ Dovewood, West Linton, Peeblesshire EH46 7DS (☎ and fax 01968 660346)

PATERSON, James Rupert; s of Maj R E Paterson, MC, of Seaforth Highlanders, late of Palazzo Bonlini, Venice, Italy (d 1964), and Josephine Mary, *née* Bartlett (d 1986); *b* 7 Aug 1932; *Educ* St Augustine's Abbey Sch Ramsgate, The Nautical Coll Pangbourne, RMA Sandhurst; *m* 18 Aug 1956, Kay, da of Patrick Dinneen, of Rathmore, Co Kerry; 2 s (Dominic b 1961, Sean b 1963), 2 da (Sara b 1958, Helen b 1959); *Career* cmmnd RA 1953, serv Hong Kong, Cambridge (attached to Univ Faculty of Slavonic Languages), Paris, Singapore, Berlin (twice); HM Dip Serv: FCO 1970–71, first sec Islamabad 1972–75, dep high cmmr Trinidad and Tobago 1975–78, FCO 1979–81, ambass Ulan Bator 1982–84, consul-gen Istanbul 1985–88, consul-gen Geneva 1988–92, ret; *Recreations* reading, writing, golf; *Style*— James Paterson, Esq; ✉ c/o Barclays Bank, 4 Broad St, Deal, Kent

PATERSON, Sheriff James Veitch; s of John Robert Paterson; *b* 16 April 1928; *Educ* Peebles HS, Edinburgh Acad, Lincoln Coll Oxford, Edinburgh Univ; *m* 1956, Ailie, da of Lt Cdr Sir (George) Ian Clark Hutchison; 1 s, 1 da; *Career* admitted to Faculty of Advocates 1953; Sheriff of the Lothian and Borders (formerly Roxburgh, Berwick and Selkirk) at Jedburgh, Selkirk and Duns 1963–; *Style*— Sheriff James Paterson; ✉ Sheriff Court House, Ettrick Terrace, Selkirk TD7 4LE

PATERSON, John Mower Alexander; OBE (1985), JP, DL (Bucks 1982); s of Leslie Martin Paterson (d 1969), and Olive Harriette, *née* Mower (d 1980); *b* 9 Nov 1920; *Educ* Oundle, Queens' Coll Cambridge (MA); *m* 1944, (Daisy) Miriam Ballanger (d 1993), da of Cdr Hugh Haddow Darroch Marshall, RNR (d 1958), of Dover; 1 s (Martin), 2 da (Rosemary, Lisa); m 2, 1995, Jean Kennard, da of late Eric Irving-Prior; *Career* Lt RE 1941–46; Cincinnati Milling Machines (Birmingham) 1946–48, dir and works mangr The Bifurcated and Tubular Rivet Co Aylesbury 1948–60 (chm and md 1960–69), chm and md Bifurcated Engrg Ltd 1969–73, chm Bifurcated Engrg plc (now Clayhithe plc) 1974–85 (dir 1974–88), gen cmmr of Taxes Aylesbury Div 1959–95; memb: Governing Body Aylesbury Coll of Further Educn 1961–89 (chm 1977–88), Grand Cncl CBI 1971–84, Southern Regnl Cncl CBI 1971–85 (chm 1974–76), Mgmnt Ctee of Waddesdon Manor 1980–; memb Chapter General Order of St John 1992– (chm of the Order in Bucks 1981–); pres Aylesbury Div Cons and Unionist Assoc 1984–85, dir Rickmansworth Water Co 1984–90 (chm 1988–90), dir Three Valleys Water Services PLC 1990–92; High Sheriff of Bucks 1978, Vice Lord Lt of Bucks 1984–; KStJ 1990 (OStJ 1981, CStJ 1985); *Recreations* sailing (yacht "Gallivanter"), veteran cars, gardening; *Clubs* Royal Ocean Racing, Royal Yacht Squadron (Cowes), Royal Lymington Yacht, St John; *Style*— John Paterson, Esq, JP, DL; ✉ Park Hill, Potter Row, Great Missenden, Bucks HP16 9LT (☎ 01494 862995)

PATERSON, Martin James Mower; s of John Mower Alexander Paterson, of Park Hill, Great Missenden, Bucks, and Miriam Daisy Ballinger Paterson; *b* 14 March 1951; *Educ* Oundle, Univ of Birmingham (BSc), Cranfield Inst of Techol (MBA), Inst of Mktg (DipM); *m* 9 July 1977 (m dis 1996), Anne Vivien, da of Vivian Erroll, DSC; 2 s (David Mower Erroll, Andrew James), 1 da (Victoria Katharine); *Career* Metal Box 1973–81: graduate trainee 1973–74, devpt technician 1974–76, mfrg mangr 1975–78, works mangr Thailand 1978–81; Betec plc: dir and gen mangr Black and Luff Ltd 1981–82, divnl mfrg dir 1982–84; Cranfield Inst of Technol 1984–85, special assignments exec TI Group plc 1985–86, md Seals Div Aeroquip Ltd 1986–89, chm STS Ltd 1989–90, chm Manufacturing Investments Ltd 1991–, chm and chief exec Gallery Home Fashions Ltd 1991–; MIEE, MCIM, CEng; *Recreations* sailing; *Clubs* Royal Lymington Yacht, RORC; *Style*— Martin Paterson, Esq; ✉ Westoe Llysworney, Vale of Glamorgan CF71 7NQ (☎ 01446 772188); Gallery Home Fashion Ltd, Pant Glas Industrial Estate, Bedwas, Gwent NP1 8DR (☎ 01222 868311, fax 01222 869664)

PATERSON, Maurice Dinsmore; s of Maurice Sidney Paterson (d 1977), of Glasgow, and Agnes Dinsmore, *née* Joss (d 1995); *b* 28 Aug 1941; *Educ* Glasgow HS; *m* 3 Oct 1967, Avril Grant, da of John Gordon Barclay (d 1984), of Glasgow; 2 s (Michael b 11 Sept 1970, Colin b 28 May 1974); *Career* Scottish Amicable 1959–94: asst sec 1968, gen mangr sales and mktg 1978, dir 1985, dep md 1990–94; dir Refuge Group plc 1994–; dir LAUTRO 1990–94; chm Glasgow Life and Pensions Group 1972–73, non exec chm Origo Services Ltd 1989–91; pres Insur and Actuarial Soc of Glasgow 1987–88; FFA 1967 (memb Cncl 1996–); *Recreations* golf, badminton, jogging, genealogy; *Clubs* Pollok Golf, Western Gailes Golf; *Style*— Maurice Paterson, Esq; ✉ 8 Merrylee Rd, Glasgow G43 2SH (☎ 0141 637 2690)

PATERSON, Peter James; *b* 4 Feb 1931; *Educ* Spurgeon's Orphan Home, Balham and Tooting Sch of Commerce, LCC evening classes; *children* see Graham Julian Paterson; *Career* reporter: Fulham Gazette 1948–49, Fulham Chronicle 1951–52, Western Daily Press 1952–54; Parly reporter Exchange Telegraph News Agency 1954–59, industl corr Daily Telegraph 1959–62, industl corr Sunday Telegraph 1962–68, asst ed New Statesman 1968–70, political columnist Spectator 1970, TV critic Daily Mail 1987– (industl ed 1985–87); *Books* The Selectorate (1967), Tired and Emotional - The Life of Lord George Brown (1993); *Recreations* dog walking, collecting old typewriters; *Clubs* Academy, Travellers'; *Style*— Peter Paterson, Esq; ✉ Daily Mail, Northcliffe House, 2 Derry Street, London W8 5TT (☎ 0171 938 6362, fax 0171 937 3251)

PATERSON, Ronald McNeill; s of Ian McNeill Paterson, of Glasgow, and Doris MacNicol, *née* Dunnett (d 1980); *b* 1 Aug 1950; *Educ* Hillhead HS Glasgow, Univ of Aberdeen (LLB); *m* 31 Dec 1988, Frances Ann Early, da of Hon Mr Justice Kenneth David Potter, QC (d 1986); *Career* CA 1974; ptnr Arthur Young 1982–89 (joined 1970), ptnr and dir of accounting Ernst & Young 1989–; memb: Accounting Standards Ctee 1987–90, Urgent Issues Task Force Accounting Standards Bd 1991–; *Books* UK GAAP - Generally Accepted Accounting Practice in the United Kingdom (jt author 1989), Off Balance Sheet Finance (1993); *Recreations* rowing, tennis, travel; *Clubs* Deeside Scullers; *Style*— Ronald Paterson, Esq; ✉ 5 Sudeley St, Islington, London N1 8HP (☎ 0171 278 2789); Ernst & Young, Rolls House, 7 Rolls Buildings, Fetter Lane, London EC4A 1NH (☎ 0171 928 2000)

PATERSON, Prof William Edgar; s of William Edgar Paterson (d 1978), of Comrie, Perthshire, and Williamina, *née* McIntyre; *b* 26 Sept 1941; *Educ* Morrison's Acad, Univ of St Andrews (MA, class medallist), LSE (S H Bailey scholar, MSc, PhD); *m* 1, 1964, Jacqueline, *née* Cramb (d 1974); 2 s (William b 1970, John b 1973); m 2, 10 July 1979, Phyllis MacDowell; 1 da (Alison b 1980), 1 step s (Colin b 1970), 1 step da (Catherine b 1975); *Career* lectr in int relations Univ of Aberdeen 1967–70; Univ of Warwick: Volkswagen lectr in German politics 1970–75, sr lectr 1975–82, reader 1982–89, prof and chm of dept 1989–90; Salvesen prof of European Insts and dir Europa Inst Univ of Edinburgh 1990–94, prof of German politics and fndn dir Inst for German Studies Univ of Birmingham 1994–; memb Königswinter Conf Steering Ctee; chm: Assoc for the Study of German Politics 1974–76, Univ Assoc for Contemporary European Studies 1989–94; memb ESRC Research Priorities Bd; assoc fell Royal Inst of Int Affairs 1994; FRSE 1994; *Books* incl: Federal Republic of Germany and the European Community (with Simon Bulmer, 1987), Government and the Chemical Industry (with Wyn Grant, 1988), Developments in German Politics II (jtly, 1996); co-ed German Politics and also author of numerous articles in learned jls; *Recreations* walking; *Style*— Prof William Paterson, FRSE; (☎ 0121 414 7183, fax 0121 414 7329)

PATERSON-BROWN, Dr June; CBE (1991), DL (Roxburgh, Ettrick and Lauderdale 1990); da of Wing Cdr Thomas Clark Garden (d 1978), of South Esk Lodge, Temple, Gorebridge, Midlothian, and Jean Martha Garden, BEM, *née* Mallace (d 1976); *b* 8 Feb 1932; *Educ* Esdaile Coll Edinburgh, Univ of Edinburgh Med Sch (MB ChB); *m* 29 March 1957, Peter Neville Paterson-Brown s of Keith Paterson-Brown (d 1981), of Edinburgh; 3 s (Simon b 1958, Timothy b 1960, William b 1965), 1 da (Sara b 1959); *Career* med offr Family Planning and Well Woman Clinics Hawick 1960–85, non-exec dir Border TV plc 1979–; former memb Roxburghshire Co Educn Ctee; chm: Roxburghshire Co Youth Ctee, Roxburgh Dist Duke of Edinburgh Award Ctee; co cmmr: Roxburghshire Girl Guides Assocs 1971–77, Peebleshire Girl Guides Assoc 1973–75; chief cmmr UK and Cwlth Girl Guides 1985–90 (Scot chief cmmr 1977–82); chm: Borders Region Children's Panel Advsy Ctee 1982–85, Scot Standing Conf Voluntary Youth Orgns 1982–85; tstee: Prince's Tst 1980–94 (vice chm Tst 1980–92), MacRoberts Tsts 1987–; Queen's Silver Jubilee Medal 1977, Paul Harris fell Rotary Int 1990; *Recreations* skiing, golf, tennis, music, reading, fishing; *Clubs* Lansdowne; *Style*— Dr June Paterson-Brown, CBE, DL; ✉ Norwood, Hawick, Roxburghshire TD9 7HP (☎ 01450 372352)

PATHY, Prof (Mohan Sankar) John; OBE (1991); s of Dr Conjeveram Pathy (d 1977), and Agnes Maud Victoria, *née* Purchel (d 1992); *b* 26 April 1923; *Educ* King's Coll Univ of London, King's Coll Hosp London; *m* 27 Sept 1949, Norma Mary, da of John Gallwey (d 1959); 2 s (Aidan b 13 May 1951, Damian b 3 Nov 1963), 3 da (Anne b 21 April 1952, Sarah b 29 Nov 1956, Helen b 4 May 1959); *Career* asst physician Oxford Regnl Hosp Bd 1958–60, conslt physician in geriatric med S Glamorgan Health Authy 1960–79, prof of geriatric med Univ of Wales Coll of Med 1979–90, emeritus prof Univ of Wales 1990, res dir Health Care Res Unit St Woolos Hosp Newport 1991–; memb: Exec Ctee Int Assoc of Gerontology, Scientific Ctee Fedn Int des Assoc de Personnes Agées; chm Age Concern Wales; memb: BMA 1943, BGS 1958, BSRA 1976; FRCPE 1967, FRCP 1973; *Books* Principles and Practice of Geriatric Medicine (2 edn, 1991), Geriatric Medicine: Problems and Practice (1989); *Recreations* creative gardening; *Style*— Prof John Pathy, OBE; ✉ Mathern Lodge, Cefn Coed Crescent, Cardiff CF2 6AT (☎ 01222 755476); University of Wales College of Medicine, Heath Park, Cardiff CF4 4XN (☎ 01222 747747, fax 01222 742914)

PATIENT, Matthew Le May; CBE (1994); s of Cyril Mortimer Patient (d 1981), and Joan Mary Christine Grace Lemay (d 1989); *b* 16 March 1939; *Educ* Brighton Coll; *m* 10 June 1967, Susan Elizabeth (Sue), da of Geoffrey Ernest Soar; 1 s (Jonathan b 1 Feb 1971), 2 da (Joanna Elizabeth b 1 April 1969, Alexandra Louise b 23 Nov 1973); *Career* CA; sr tech ptnr Coopers & Lybrand 1981–94 (ptnr 1966–94); dep chm FRC Review Panel 1996– (memb 1995–); dir: Lioncover Insurance Co Ltd 1992–, CLM Insurance Fund PLC 1993–, Global Insurance Ltd (Barbados) 1985–; memb Company Affrs Ctee IOD 1974–91; ICAEW: memb Parly and Law Ctee 1974–81, memb Cncl 1984–88; CCAB: memb Accounting Standards Ctee 1981–86, memb Auditing Practices Ctee 1981–88 (chm 1986–88); memb: International Auditing Practices Ctee 1989–95 (chm 1993–95), Auditing Practices Bd 1991–95, Urgent Issues Task Force Accounting Standards Bd 1991–94; ind memb Retail Trades (Non-Food) Wages Cncl 1982–93, nominated memb Cncl Lloyd's of London 1989–92; govr and vice pres Brighton Coll, govr St Andrews Sch Woking; Liveryman Worshipful Co of Chartered Accountants; FCA 1973 (ACA 1963), ATII, FRSA; *Books* Licensed Dealers Rules & Regulations 1983 (1983), Accounting Provisions of The Companies Act 1985 (1985), Auditing Investment Businesses (1989), Manual of Accounting (1990), various professional articles; *Clubs* RAC, IOD, City University, Wig and Pen; *Style*— Matthew Patient, Esq, CBE; ✉ Woodlands, Cedar Road, Hook Heath, Woking, Surrey GU22 0JJ (☎ 01483 762143, business ☎ and fax 01483 728214)

PATNICK, Sir (Cyril) Irvine; kt (1994), OBE (1980), MP (C) Sheffield Hallam (majority 6,741); *Career* MP (C) Sheffield Hallam 1987–; *Style*— Sir Irvine Patnick, OBE, MP; ✉ House of Commons, London SW1A 0AA (☎ 0171 219 3000)

PATON, Alasdair Chalmers; s of David Paton, of Tighnabruaich Argyll, and Margaret Elizabeth, *née* Chalmers; *b* 28 Nov 1944; *Educ* John Neilson Instn Paisley, Univ of Glasgow (BSc, DMS); *m* 5 June 1969, Zona, *née* Gill; 1 da (Nicola Jane b 11 Dec 1973), 1 s (Richard Alasdair b 22 Oct 1976); *Career* asst engr Clyde Port Authy 1967–71, asst engr Dept of Agric and Fisheries for Scotland 1971–72, engr then sr engr Scottish Devpt Dept 1972–77, seconded to Public Works Dept Hong Kong Govt 1977–80; Scottish Devpt Dept: sr engr (structures) 1980–82, sr engr (marine works, water supplies, sewerage) 1982–84, princ engr 1984–87, dep chief engr 1987–91; SO: chief engr Environment Dept 1991–92, dir and chief engr Engineering Water and Waste Directorate 1992–95; chief exec The Scottish Environment Protection Agency 1995–; memb Inst Civil Engrs Water Gp Board 1988–91; CEng, MICE (1972), FICE (1989), FCIWEM (1991, memb 1984, memb ctee Scottish Branch 1988–, chm 1993–94); *Recreations* sailing, golf; *Clubs* Rotary, golf, various sailing; *Style*— Alasdair C Paton, Esq; ✉ Chief Executive, The Scottish Environment Protection Agency, Erskine Court, The Castle Business Park, Stirling FK9 4TR (☎ 01786 457700)

PATON, Sir (Thomas) Angus Lyall; kt (1973), CMG (1960); s of Thomas Lyall Paton (d 1962), of St John, Jersey, CI, and Janet, *née* Gibb (d 1959); *b* 10 May 1905; *Educ* Cheltenham, UCL (BSc); *m* 7 June 1933, (Eleanor) Joan Medora (d 1964), da of Maj George Arthur Delmé-Murray, DSO (d 1944); 2 s (Alan b 1942, John b 1952), 2 da (Janet b 1934, Anne b 1937); *Career* sr conslt Sir Alexander Gibb & Ptnrs 1977–84 (sr ptnr 1955–77); pres Inst of Civil Engrs 1970–71, vice pres Royal Soc 1977–78; fell: UCL 1962, Imperial Coll London 1978; Hon DSc: London 1978, Bristol 1981; FRS 1969, Hon FICE 1975, FIStructE, FRSA, FEng 1976, Foreign Assoc Nat Acad of Engrg (USA) 1979; *Books* Power From Water (jtly, 1960); *Recreations* gardening, DIY; *Style*— Sir Angus Paton, CMG, FRS, FEng; ✉ L'Epervier, Route Orange, St Brelade, Jersey, Channel Islands JE3 8GQ (☎ 01534 45619)

PATON, David Romer; OBE (1997); s of John David Paton, JP (d 1982), of Grandhome, Aberdeen, and Mary Fenella, *née* Crombie (d 1949); *b* 5 March 1935; *Educ* Gordonstoun, Keble Coll Oxford; *m* 2 July 1975, Juliette, da of Capt Christopher Arthur Geoffrey Burney (d 1980), of Kensington; 2 s (William John Burney b 1976, (Christopher) Matthew George b 1979); *Career* chartered surveyor in practice on own account; chm: Gordon Cons and Unionist Assoc 1986–88, Royal Northern and Univ Club 1984–85, Aberdeen Civic Soc 1982–91, Scottish Chambers of Commerce 1990–93, Grampian Cancer Care Project 1989–90, Grampian-Houston Assoc 1991–94; Sec of State appointee NE River Purification Bd 1984–96, Min of State appointee HMG Salmon Advsy Ctee 1986–96, Sec of State appointee N of Scotland Water Authy, Sec of State appointee SO Salmon Strategy Task Force; pres Aberdeen C of C 1987–90 (currently dir), memb Bd of Mgmnt Assoc of Br Chambers of Commerce 1990–93; chm: NE Scotland Preservation Tst, Don Dist Salmon Fishery Bd, Aberdeen Harbour Bd; jt chm Grampian MacMillan Nurse Appeal; pres: Friends of Grampian Stones, Aberdeen Civic Soc; chm NE Ctee and vice pres Scottish Cncl Devpt and Indust, patron Scottish Conservation Projects Tst; memb: Ctee Architectural Heritage Soc of Scotland, Cncl Assoc of Scottish Dist Salmon Fisher Bds, Grampian Initiative Working Pty, Grampian Ctee Epilepsy Assoc of Scotland, Order of St John (chm Aberdeen Ctee, chm St John's Assoc Aberdeen); dir: Aberdeen Maritime Museum Appeal Co Ltd, Aberdeen Salmon Co Ltd; Burgess of Guild City of Aberdeen 1983; SBStJ 1992; FRICS 1976, IRRV 1971, FSA (Scot) 1989; *Recreations* fishing, bridge, conservation; *Clubs* Royal Northern and Univ (Aberdeen); *Style*— David Paton, Esq, OBE; ✉ Grandhome, Aberdeen AB22 8AR (☎ 01224 722202); Estates Office, Grandhome, Aberdeen AB22 8AR (☎ 01224 722202, fax 01224 724546)

PATON, Maj-Gen Douglas Stuart; CBE (1983); s of Stuart Paton, and Helen Kathleen, *née* Hooke (d 1953); *b* 3 March 1926; *Educ* Sherborne, Univ of Bristol (MB ChB, FFCM, FFPHM); *m* 1957, Jennifer Joan, da of Maj Edward Loxley Land (d 1968), of Great Bookham, Surrey; 2 da; *Career* cmmnd RAMC 1952, CO CMH Aldershot 1973–76, RCDS 1977, DDMS HQ 1 (BR) Corps 1978–80, DDGAMS MOD 1981–83, Cdr Med Servs BAOR with rank of Maj-Gen 1983–86; Hon Col 221 (S) Field Ambulance RAMC (V) 1988–92; QHP 1981–86, chm RAMC Assoc 1988–, govr Moorfields Eye Hosp 1988–90; CStJ 1986; *Recreations* opera, gardening, travel; *Style*— Maj-Gen Douglas Paton, CBE; ✉ Brampton, Springfield Road, Camberley, Surrey GU15 1AB

PATON, Maureen Virginia; da of William Harney, and Blanche, *née* Adams (later Mrs Paton); *Educ* Watford Tech HS, Univ of Leicester (BA); *m* 21 May 1977, Liam Michael Maguire, s of William Maguire; *Career* journalist; trainee with British Printing Corporation on various pubns, subsquently with IPC Business Press; Daily Express 1979–: successively sub ed, show business writer, TV critic, video critic, drama critic, sr feature writer; freelance work incl: BBC Radio broadcaster GLR, presenter What the Papers Say Granada TV, drama critic The Stage & Television Today, The Independent, UK Press Gazette; memb: NUJ, Critics' Circle 1989, Women In Journalism; *Books* Alan Rickman: The Unauthorised Biography; *Recreations* house-hunting, writing; *Style*— Maureen Paton; ✉ Daily Express, Ludgate House, 245 Blackfriars Rd, London SE1 9UX (☎ 0171 922 7036)

PATON-PHILIP, Philip; VRD (1957); s of Dr Wilfrid Paton-Philip, MC, MA, MB, DPH, DMRE, FCCP (USA) (d 1956), of Cambridge, and Mary Isobel, *née* Simpson (d 1985); *b* 12 Sept 1926; *Educ* St John's Coll Cambridge (MA, MB BChir, MChir, FRCS, LRCP); *m* 1, 1959 (m dis 1970), Julia, da of Stephen Vaux (d 1985), of Birchington, Kent; 1 s (Charles Philip b 1960); m 2, 1978, Christina, da of Dr Carl Henri Bernhardson, of Stockholm, Sweden; 2 s (Richard b 1980, James b 1982); *Career* surgn Lt Cdr RN and RNVR 1947–52, surgn in charge RN Surgical Chest Unit; conslt urological surgn: St George's Hosp London (hon sr lectr St George's Med Sch), St Helier Hosp Carshalton, Epsom Dist Hosp; sr consltg urological surgn: St Anthony's Hosp Cheam Surrey, Ashtead Private Hosp Ashtead Surrey; teaching hosps: St Bartholomew's, St Thomas's Denver Med Coll Colorado USA; *Recreations* riding, showjumping, skiing, sailing, carriage driving; *Clubs* Garrick, Savage, BHS, BSJA, British Driving Soc, Royal Naval Med; *Style*— Philip Paton-Philip, Esq, VRD; ✉ The Ship, Hurst Drive, Walton-on-the-Hill, Tadworth, Surrey; 149 Harley St, London W1 (☎ 0171 935 4444)

PATON WALSH, Gillian (Jill); CBE (1996); da of John Llewellyn Bliss (d 1979), and Patricia, *née* Dubern (d 1977); *b* 29 April 1937; *Educ* St Michael's Convent Sch N Finchley, St Anne's Coll Oxford (BA, MA, DipEd); *m* 1961, Anthony Edmund Paton Walsh; 1 s (Edmund Alexander b 1963), 2 da (Margaret Anne b 1965, Helen Clare b 1966); *Career* teacher Enfield Girls GS 1959–62, Arts Cncl Creative Writing Fellowship 1976–78, perm visiting faculty memb Centre for Children's Literature Simmons Coll Boston Mass 1978–86, Gertrude Clarke Whittall lectr Library of Congress 1978, judge Whitbread prize 1984, chm Cambridge Book Assoc 1987–89, ptnr Green Bay Pubns; memb: Ctee Children's Writers Gp, Mgmnt Ctee Soc of Authors; adjunct Br Bd memb Children's Literature New England; FRSL 1996; *Books* Hengest's Tale (1966), The Dolphin Crossing (1967), Wordhoard (1969), Fireweed (1970), Farewell, Great King (1972), Goldengrove (1972), Toolmaker (1973), The Dawnstone (1973), The Emperor's Winding Sheet (1974), The Butty Boy Macmillan (1975), The Island Sunrise: Prehistoric Britain (1975), Unleaving (1976), Crossing to Salamis, The Walls of Athens, Persian Gold (1977–78), A Chance Child (1978), The Green Book (1981), Babylon (1982), Lost & Found (1984), A Parcel of Patterns (1984), Gaffer Samson's Luck (1985), Five Tides (1986), Lapsing (1986), Torch (1987), A School for Lovers (1989), Birdy and The Ghosties (1989), Can I Play? (1990), Grace (1991), When Grandma Came (1992), Matthew and The Seasingers (1992), The Wyndham Case (1993), Knowledge of Angels (1994, Booker Prize nominee), A Piece of Justice (1995), Connie Came to Play (1995), The Serpentine Cave (1997); *Recreations* reading, walking, sewing, photography; *Style*— Mrs Jill Paton Walsh, CBE, FRSL; ✉ c/o Bruce Hunter, David Higham Associates, 5–8 Lower John Street, Golden Square, London W1R 3PE

PATRICK, Andrew Graham McIntosh; s of Dr James McIntosh Patrick, RSA, ARE, RDI, LLD, of Dundee, Angus, Scotland, and Janet, *née* Watterston (d 1983); *b* 12 June 1934; *Educ* Harris Acad Dundee; *Career* The Fine Art Soc: joined 1954, dir 1966, md 1976–; has presented hundreds of exhibitions, mostly of Br artists but covering all aspects of the visual arts; memb: Exec Ctee Soc of London Art Dealers (chm 1983–86), Cncl The Br Antique Dealers' Assoc 1986–93, Curatorial Ctee Nat Tst for Scot 1986–89; *Recreations* collecting: pictures, Japanese prints, camels, works by Christopher Dresser, old shoes, etc; *Clubs* Marks; *Style*— Andrew McIntosh Patrick, Esq; ✉ The Fine Art Society Plc, 148 New Bond St, London W1Y 0JT (☎ 0171 629 5116)

PATRICK, Andrew John; s of Patrick John Charles, of Hockley Heath, W Midlands, and Norma, *née* Harris (d 1987); *b* 23 Nov 1955; *Educ* Dartmouth HS, Univ of Birmingham (BA); *m* 3 Dec 1981, Petrice Janice, da of Edward Blackmore; 1 da (Joanna Norma b 8 Sept 1985), 1 s (Matthew John b 29 Jan 1988); *Career* actor 1975–76 (stage credits incl Black and White Minstrel Show, Another Bride Another Groom and The National Health, TV credits incl Angels, Penda's Fen, Looking for Clancy, Crossroads and Trinity Tales), asst mangr Birmingham Hippodrome Theatre 1976–78; British Film and TV Producers Assoc (now PACT): accountant 1978–80, asst sec 1980–83, sec 1983–86, dir Admin and Mktg 1986–88, dep chief exec 1988–91; chief exec British Film Commission 1992–; memb: BAFTA 1992–, European Film Financiers and Insurers Assoc 1993–; dir Medicinema (registered charity); *Recreations* board games, squash, football, watching cricket, cinema; *Style*— Andrew Patrick, Esq; ✉ British Film Commission, 70 Baker Street, London W1M 1DJ (☎ 0171 224 5000, fax 0171 224 1013)

PATRICK, Bruce Robertson; s of Francis Wheatly Patrick, of Edinburgh, and Isobel, *née* Spencer; *b* 26 Nov 1945; *Educ* Glasgow Acad, Edinburgh Acad, Exeter Coll Oxford (BA), Univ of Edinburgh (Green Prize for criminal law, Millar Prize for Scots law, LLB); *m* 9 Feb 1980, Hilary Jane, eld da of Richard Alan Sutton; 2 da (Ruth b 5 Nov 1980, Catherine b 4 July 1982), 1 s (Robert James b 9 July 1984); *Career* apprentice Mitchells

Johnston Solicitors Glasgow 1971–73; asst: Maclay Murray & Spens Glasgow 1973–75, Coward Chance Solicitors London 1975–76; Maclay Murray & Spens: ptnr Company Dept 1976– (Glasgow office 1976–77, Edinburgh office 1978–), managing ptnr 1991–94; pt/t tutor in law Univ of Edinburgh 1980–84; completed Glasgow marathon 1985; memb: Law Soc of Scotland 1973 (vice-convenor Company Law Ctee), Royal Faculty of Procurators Glasgow 1976, Soc of WS 1980; *Books* IBA Handbook on Maritime Law (contrib Scottish section, 1983); *Recreations* golf, hill walking, rugby (now spectator), occasional gardening; *Clubs* New (Edinburgh), Luffness Golf, Prestwick Golf; *Style*— Bruce Patrick, Esq; ✉ Maclay Murray & Spens, 3 Glenfinlas Street, Edinburgh EH3 6AQ (☎ 0131 226 5196, fax 0131 226 3174)

PATRICK, (Katherine) Emily (Mrs Michael Perry); da of William Pitt Patrick, of Folkestone, Kent, and Rosemary Martha, *née* Pulvertaft; *b* 4 Oct 1959; *Educ* Folkestone GS, Architectural Assoc, Univ of Cambridge (MA); *m* 16 Oct 1986, Michael Luke Perry, s of David Edward Perry, of Hitchin, Herts; 2 da (Beatrice Lillian b 9 Sept 1987, Isabel Eliza b 5 March 1990), 1 s (Alfred Oberon Patrick b 4 April 1994); *Career* artist; exhibited at: King St Gallery, Wraxall Gallery, Long & Ryle Int, Maine Gallery, Mall Galleries, Lefevre Gallery, The Nat Portrait Gallery, The Napier Gallery; one man shows at Agnew's 1986, 1989, 1992 and 1995; painted HRH The Princess of Wales, portrait for Royal Hants Regt 1987; first winner of Royal Soc of Portrait Painters' Caroll Prize 1988; *Recreations* walking; *Style*— Emily Patrick; ✉ 2 St John's Park, London SE3 7TG

PATRICK, John Howard; s of George Edward Patrick (d 1994), of Shrewsbury, Shropshire, and Emmeline Swindells, *née* Brierley; *b* 17 June 1943; *Educ* Haberdashers' Aske's, St Thomas' Hosp Med Sch Univ of London; *m* 9 Sept 1972, Patricia, da of Geoffrey Thornton-Smith, of Wokingham, Berks; 3 da (Tamsyn b 1975, Abigail b 1977, Bryony b 1989); *Career* RAF 1963–72 (ret sqdn ldr); various house appts St Thomas's Hosp, sr lectr and hon conslt orthopaedic surgn Univ of Liverpool, dir Orthotic Res and Locomotion Assessment Unit, conslt orthopaedic surgn 1980–; papers published in med jls incl British Medical Journal, Euro ed Gait and Posture; memb Int Standards Orgn; former Master Shrewsbury Drapers' Co; FRCS 1972; *Recreations* skiing, sailing, travel; *Clubs* RAF; *Style*— John Patrick, Esq; ✉ Orthotic Research and Locomotion Assessment Unit, Robert Jones and Agnes Hunt Orthopaedic Hospital, Oswestry, Shropshire SY10 7AG (☎ 01691 655311)

PATRICK, Keith Ian; s of Hubert Eric Patrick (d 1983), of Watford, and Edna May, *née* Hart; *b* 23 Feb 1952; *Educ* Watford Boys' GS, Watford Sch of Art, Hockerill Coll, Camberwell Sch of Art (BA); *m* 1989, Maria Teresa Lorés Bergua (Maite Lorés); 1 step s (Fabian Hutchinson b 25 July 1973), 1 step da (Anna Nuria Smythe b 4 May 1981); *Career* worked and exhibited as practising artist 1974–83, art critic 1983–; works published in numerous art jls at home and abroad, guest ed Studio International 1984, ed Art Line Magazine 1990–; curator of exhibitions incl: The Romantic Tradition in Contemporary British Painting (Spain and England touring) 1988, Romantic Visions (Camden Arts Centre) 1988, Critics' View (Royal Festival Hall) 1991, From Bacon to Now - The Outsider in British Figuration (Palazzo Vecchio Florence) 1991–92, Contemporary Br Sculpture - Henry Moore to the 90s (Spain and Portugal touring) 1995; Int Assoc of Art Critics: assoc 1984, sec Br Section 1986–89, pres Br Section 1991–94, vice pres Int Section 1993–; *Publications* Aspects of British Sculpture in the 20th Century (1997), Oil on Canvas (1997); *Style*— Keith Patrick, Esq; ✉ 49 Priory Gardens, Highgate, London N6 5QU (☎ 0181 340 1640, fax 0181 342 8623)

PATRICK, Peter Laurence; s of Anthony Frederick Herbert Patrick, of St Peters, Broadstairs, Kent, and Joyce Stanley, *née* Sowerby; *b* 11 July 1946; *Educ* Alleyne's Sch Stevenage, Univ Coll Durham (BA); *m* 22 April 1972, Teresa Mary Patrick, JP, da of William Roland Mills, MBE, of Billericay, Essex; 1 s (Edward William b 4 Nov 1973), 1 da (Frances Elizabeth b 10 July 1975); *Career* CA 1972; Price Waterhouse & Co: Newcastle 1967–70, London 1970–73, Paris 1973–76; computer audit mangr Howard Tilly & Co 1976–78, head of inspection Hambros Bank Ltd 1978–86, co sec Hambros plc and Hambros Bank Ltd 1986–; cncllr Billericay East Basildon DC 1984–96 (dep ldr Cons Gp of cncllrs 1985–90 and 1993–95, ldr 1995); chm Fin Ctee Basildon DC 1992–95; treas Billericay Cons Assoc (chm 1990–92), chm Towngate Theatre Co Basildon Essex 1988–89, tstee Adventure Unlimited (Chelmsford Dio Youth Charity), tstee Burstead Foundation (local educnl charity); govr: Quilters Sch Billericay, Briscoe Sch Basildon, memb choir St Mary Magdalene Gt Burstead Essex; memb Inst of Bankers, assoc memb Br Computer Soc; *Recreations* singing, gardening, politics, history, architecture; *Style*— Peter Patrick, Esq; ✉ 6 Highland Grove, Billericay, Essex (☎ 01277 651137); Hambros Bank Ltd, 41 Tower Hill, London EC3N 4HA (☎ 0171 480 5000)

PATTEN, Brian; *b* 7 Feb 1946; *Career* poet and author; poetry: Little Johnny's Confessions (1967), The Mersey Sound (with Adrian Henri and Roger McGough, 1967), Penguin Modern Poets (1967), Notes to the Hurrying Man (1969), The Irrelevant Song (1971), The Unreliable Nightingale (1973), Vanishing Trick (1976), The Shabby Angel (1978), Grave Gossip (1979), Love Poems (1981), Clares Countryside (1978), New Volume (1983), Storm Damage (1988), Grinning Jack (Selected Poems, 1990); novels: Mr Moon's Last Case (1975); plays: The Pig and the Junkle (1975), The Mouth Trap (with Roger McGough, 1982), Blind Love (1983), Gargling with Jelly - The Play! (1989); for younger readers: The Elephant and the Flower (1969), Jumping Mouse (1971), Emma's Doll (1976), The Sly Cormorant and the Fish (1977), Gangsters Ghosts and Dragonflies (1981), Gargling with Jelly (1985), Jimmy Tag-along (1988), Thawing Frozen Frogs (1990), The Puffin Book of Twentieth Century Children's Verse (ed, 1991), Grizzelda Frizzle (1992), The Magic Bicycle (1993), Impossible Parents (1994), The Utter Nutters (1994); Armada (1996); *Clubs* Chelsea Arts; *Style*— Brian Patten, Esq; ✉ c/o Penguin Books, 27 Wrights Lane, London W8 5TZ (☎ 0171 416 3000, fax 0171 416 3099)

PATTEN, Rt Hon Christopher Francis (Chris); PC (1989); s of late Francis Joseph Patten; *b* 12 May 1944; *Educ* St Benedict's Ealing, Balliol Coll Oxford; *m* 1971, (Mary) Lavender St Leger, da of late Maj John Thornton, by his late wife Joan Coulton, *née* Walker-Smith, sister of 1 Baron Broxbourne; 3 da (Kate, Laura, Alice); *Career* CRD 1966–70, dir 1974–79; worked in Cabinet Office 1970–72, Home Office 1972, PA to Chm Cons Party 1972–74, MP (C) Bath 1979–92; PPS to: Norman St John-Stevas as Chllr Duchy of Lancaster and Leader House of Commons 1979–81, Patrick Jenkin as Sec of State for Social Servs 1981; jt vice chm Cons Fin Ctee Nov 1981–83, under sec of state NI Office 1983–85; min of state DES 1985–86, min of state for Overseas Devpt 1986–July 1989, sec of state for the Environment July 1989–Nov 1990, chm Cons Pty and Chancellor of the Duchy of Lancaster 1990–92, govr and C-in-C of Hong Kong 1992–97; Hon FRCPE 1994; *Recreations* reading, tennis; *Clubs* Beefsteak, RAC; *Style*— The Rt Hon Chris Patten; ✉ c/o Conservative Central Office, 32 Smith Square, London SW1

PATTEN, H; s of Hubert Patten, of Birmingham, and Agnes, *née* Johnson (d 1986); *b* 20 Jan 1961; *Educ* Lea Mason C of E Sch Birmingham, Bournville Sch of Art and Craft Birmingham (City & Guilds Pt 1), South Glamorgan Inst of Higher Educn Cardiff (BA Hons), Univ of Legon Ghana; *m* 1 s (Kwesi Yaadi b 26 July 1987), 2 da (Mawuena Esi b 16 March 1986, Onayomi Ayokunle b 22 August 1994); *Career* dancer; Danse de L'Afrique 1982–86: fndr memb, princ male dancer, drummer English tour 1983, Moroccan tour 1984 organised and performed Midlands tour with Jean Binta Breeze 1985; participant Mayfest Festival Glasgow with Pepsi Poet and Benjamin Zephania 1983; Inst of African Studies Univ of Legon Ghana 1983: trg with Ghana National Danse Ensemble, tutor of Caribbean dance, participant in Accra and Hogbetsocho Festival Angola Volta Region; dep dir and community arts worker The CAVE (Community and Village Entertainment) Birmingham 1983–86; freelance artiste, tutor of Caribbean and African music and dance and visual arts, painter, sculptor, photographer, storyteller 1986–; performer and teacher of dance Int Lit Festival Lecce Italy (for Cwlth Inst) 1990, lead dancer Adaniloro nat tour (with Sakoba Prodns) 1991; Adzido Pan African Dance Ensemble: joined 1986, re-joined 1987, In the Village of Africa tour 1987, Coming Home tour 1988, performances at Queen Elizabeth Festival Hall South Bank 1988, Edinburgh Festival 1988, performances at Sadler's Wells 1988, Irish tour 1989, Montpellier Dance, Festival France 1989, Under Africa Skies tour 1990, educn outreach liasion co-ordinator 1990; Dis Ya Set Up (dance, drama, story telling prodn, which toured nationally) prodr/choreographer/performer 1994, dance conslt Africa 95 (an int festval of African arts), Panafest (workshops, Ghana) 1994; Black Dance Development Trust: tstee Bd 1987, performed at first and second annual awards 1987 and 1989, planned and co-ordinated prog for Summer School III 1988, received Creativity in Music & Dance award 1989, East Midlands educn outreach devpt worker 1989; choreographer of: Carnival Fire (Third Dimension Theatre Co) 1987, Devil Going to Dance (Staunch Poets & Players) 1988, Mother Poem (Temba Theatre Co) 1989, Round Heads and Peak Heads (Tara Arts Theatre Co) 1989, Soul-Less-Game (Kokuma Performing Arts) 1989, Flying Costumes, Floating Tombs (by Keith Khan for London Int Festival of Arts) 1991 (Dance Umbrella award), Ina De Wildanis (one man theatre prodn touring nationally and internationally) 1992 (also prodr), Journey From Jourouvert (for Costume Designers Club and LIFT Festival) 1993 (designed and cmmnd making of costumes for Irie Dance Theatre Co in The Gambia), The Story Behind the Song - Torie Bac a De Song (Irie Dance Theatre) 1993; involved with: UK Black by Karen Wheeler (music video) 1990, Black Voices film 1990, Ama (Efirititi Film Co) 1990; British Council sponsored tours: to Malawi (choreographed Ndakula prodn with Kwacha Cultural Troupe, led troupe on first nat tour) 1990, to Zambia (choreographed one hour showcase with Zambia National Dance Troupe and The Univ of Zambia Dance Ensemble) 1992, to Malawi (to work with Kwacha Cultural Troupe) and to Kenya 1993; research tour to Ghana, Senegal, The Gambia, Jamaica, Trinidad, Tobago, Carriacou and Greneda (with Irie Dance Theatre for The Story Behind the Song) 1992; also extensive teaching in UK and abroad, work with numerous nat and int tutors of African and Caribbean dance; Black Dance Devpt Tst Summer Schs 1 2 3 4 & 5; solo storytelling performance Guildhall Gloucester 1989; has exhibited extensively in Britain and the Caribbean; *Recreations* basketball, music, research into Folk Culture; *Style*— H Patten, Esq; ✉ 28A Tressillian Rd, Brockley, London SE4 1YB (☎ 0181 692 0297)

PATTEN, James; s of James Arthur Patten (d 1973), and Edith Veronica Patten (d 1989); *b* 30 July 1936; *Educ* St Mary's Coll Liverpool, Trinity Coll of Music London (FTCL, GTCL, LTCL), Die Hochschule für Musik Berlin; *m* (m dis 1990); 3 s (Clovis, Dominic, Samuel); *Career* Duke of Wellington's Regt 1956–59; Die Hochschule Fur Music Berlin DAAD scholarship, Royal Philharmonic Composition Prize 1963, lectr in theory of music Ealing Coll of Further Educn 1965–69, prof of composition Trinity Coll of Music London 1965–70, tutor Open Univ 1970–76, freelance lectr and composer, head of music SWGS Salisbury 1976–78, music tutor and composer in residence Downside Sch 1981–90; pt/t lectr: Bristol Univ Dept of Continuing Educn 1987–91, Wells Community Educn Dept 1991–93; visiting lectr Birmingham Conservatoire 1991–, conductor Frome and Dist Choral Union 1992–; compositions (published by Kevin Mayhew Publishers) incl works for guitar, piano, string quartet, organ, various chamber ensembles, saxophone, solo cello, choir and orchestra; memb: Ctee SEAC 1989–92, Univ of Oxford Delegacy Music Panel (chief examiner and sr moderator A and AS Level Music) 1989–96, Horningham Parish Cncl 1979–90, Creys Charity; PRS 1965; memb: Composers' Guild of GB 1965, APC 1991, MCPS 1987, BASCA 1987, RSM 1987, Nat Fedn of Music Socs (SW Region) 1994; *Recreations* reading; *Style*— James Patten, Esq; ✉ 1 Crown Cottages, Cats Ash, Shepton Mallet, Somerset BA4 5EL (☎ 01749 344859, fax 01749 343445)

PATTEN, Rt Hon John Haggitt Charles; PC (1990), MP (C) Oxford West and Abingdon (majority 3,539); s of lateJack Patten, and late Maria Olga, *née* Sikora; *b* 17 July 1945; *Educ* Wimbledon Coll, Sidney Sussex Coll Cambridge (MA, PhD); *m* 1978, Louise Alexandra Virginia, da of late John Rowe; 1 da (Mary-Claire b 10 June 1986); *Career* MP (C): Oxford 1979–83, Oxford W and Abingdon 1983–; PPS to Leon Brittan and Timothy Raison as Mins of State at the Home Office 1980–81; Parly under sec of state: NI Office 1981–83, DHSS 1983–85; min of state: for housing, urban affrs and construction 1985–87, Home Office 1987–92; sec of state for education 1992–94; advsr to the Bd Charterhouse Bank 1995–; fell Hertford Coll Oxford 1972–94 (Univ of Oxford lectr 1969–79); Liveryman Worshipful Co of Drapers; *Books* The Conservative Opportunity (with Lord Blake), Things to Come: The Tories in the 21st Century, and four other books; *Recreations* talking with my wife and daughter; *Style*— The Rt Hon John Patten, MP; ✉ House of Commons, London SW1A 0AA (☎ 0171 219 4436)

PATTEN, Prof Thomas Diery (Tom); CBE (1981); s of William Patten (d 1965), of Midlem, Selkirkshire, and Isabella, *née* Hall (d 1986); *b* 1 Jan 1926; *Educ* Leith Acad, Univ of Edinburgh (BSc, PhD); *m* 29 March 1950, Jacqueline McLachlan; 1 s (Colin), 2 da (Diane, Gail); *Career* Capt REME 1946–48, served Palestine and Greece; chartered mechanical engr; prof and head Dept of Mechanical Engrg Heriot-Watt Univ 1967–82, dir Inst of Offshore Engrg 1972–79, actg princ Heriot-Watt Univ 1980–81; chm MTD Ltd 1982–; non-exec dir: Melville Street Investments plc 1983–95, Sealand Industries plc 1987–94, Benson Group plc 1991–96, Edinburgh Petroleum Services 1992–; past pres IMechE; Hon DEng Heriot-Watt Univ; hon fell Napier Univ, Hon DSc Edinburgh Univ, Dr hc Universidad Politecnica de Madrid; FEng 1986, FIMechE, FRSE 1967; *Recreations* music, squash; *Clubs* New (Edinburgh), Caledonian; *Style*— Prof Tom Patten, CBE, FEng, FRSE; ✉ 67/7 Grange Loan, Edinburgh EH9 2EG (☎ 0131 662 1101)

PATTENDEN, Prof Gerald; s of Albert James Pattenden, and Violet Eugene, *née* Smith; *b* 4 March 1940; *Educ* Brunel Univ, Univ of London (BSc, PhD, DSc); *m* 3 Aug 1969, Christine Frances, da of Charles Leo Doherty; 3 da (Caroline Sarah b 1971, Rebecca Jane b 1974, Katherine Rachael b 1977); *Career* lectr Univ Coll Cardiff 1966, Sir Jesse Boot prof of organic chemistry and head of dept Nottingham Univ 1988– (lectr 1972, reader 1975, prof 1980); chem conslt; pres Perkin Div Royal Soc of Chemistry 1995–97; scientific ed J Chem Soc, Perkin Trans I; also author of 350 res pubns and editor of over 20 books; FRSC, CChem, FRS; *Recreations* sport, gardening, entertainment; *Style*— Prof Gerald Pattenden, FRS; ✉ Chemistry Department, Nottingham University, Nottingham NG7 2RD (☎ 0115 951 3530, fax 0115 951 3535)

PATTERSON, Aaron Joseph; s of William Patterson, of The Oystercatcher Inn, The Cross, Belgooly, Oysterhaven, Co Cork, and Elizabeth, *née* Leach (d 1979); *b* 10 June 1969; *Educ* St Paul's Comp Sch, Southfields Coll (City & Guilds); *m* 10 Oct 1992, Clare Anna, da of William George Parker; *Career* chef; successively apprentice chef, commis chef, chef de partie, sr chef de partie then pastry chef Hambleton Hall Hotel Leics 1985–90, successively commis chef, demi chef de partie, chef de partie then sr chef de partie Le Manoir Aux Quat' Saisons Oxon 1990–92 (employee of the year 1991); staigiare 1985–90: Le Crocodile Strazbourg, La Tante Claire London, The Belfry London; head chef Hambleton Hall Hotel 1992– (4/5 Good Food Guide 1996); *Recreations* reading, sport, travelling; *Style*— Aaron Patterson, Esq; ✉ Hambleton Hall Hotel, Hambleton Village, nr Oakham, Rutland, Leics LE15 8TH (☎ 01572 756991, fax 01572 724721)

PATTERSON, Anthony James (Tony); *b* 17 Nov 1951; *Educ* St Joseph's Coll Blackpool, UCL (LLB); *m* (m dis); 2 s (James, Thomas), 1 da (Sophie); *Career* Frere

Cholmeley: articled clerk 1973–75, admitted slr 1975, ptnr 1980–, head Property Dept 1994–, memb Exec Ctee 1987–93 and 1994–; *Style—* Tony Patterson, Esq; ✉ Frere Cholmeley Bischoff, 4 John Carpenter Street, London EC4Y 0NH (☎ 0171 615 8000, fax 0171 615 8080)

PATTERSON, Edward McWilliam; s of Samuel Patterson (d 1962), of Kirkbymoorside, and Emily Elisabeth Wright (d 1975); *b* 30 July 1926; *Educ* Univ of Leeds (BSc, PhD); *m* 1, 10 Aug 1950, Joan Sibald (d 1981), da of Thomas Maddick (d 1965), of Goole; 1 da (Christine b 1952); m 2, 16 Sept 1982, Elizabeth McAllan, da of George James Hunter (d 1967), of Aberdeen; *Career* res demonstrator in mathematics Univ of Sheffield 1949–51; lectr: Univ of St Andrews 1951–56, Univ of Leeds 1956–59; prof Univ of Aberdeen 1965–89 (sr lectr 1960–64); Royal Soc visiting prof Univ of Malaya 1973, pres Edinburgh Mathematical Soc 1964–65, chm AUT Scotland 1964–66, vice pres IMA 1973–74, chm Scottish Mathematical Cncl 1974–80; FRSE 1959, FIMA 1964; *Books* Topology (1959), Elementary Abstract Algebra (jtly 1965), Solving Problems in Vector Algebra (1968); *Recreations* music, walking, mathematical problems; *Clubs* Commonwealth Trust; *Style—* Edward Patterson, Esq, FRSE; ✉ Department of Mathematical Sciences, University of Aberdeen, The Edward Wright Building, Dunbar St, Aberdeen AB24 3QY

PATTERSON, George Benjamin (Ben); s of Prof Eric James Patterson (d 1972), of Stonehedge, Alphington Cross, Exeter, Devon, and Dr Ethel Patterson, *née* Simkins (d 1993); *b* 21 April 1939; *Educ* Westminster, Trinity Coll Cambridge (MA), LSE; *m* 5 Dec 1970, Felicity Barbara Anne, da of Gordon W Raybould, of Little Combe Bank, Sundridge, Sevenoaks, Kent; 1 s (Alexander b 6 Dec 1974), 1 da (Olivia b 15 April 1977); *Career* tutor Swinton Coll Masham Yorks 1961–65, ed CPC Monthly Report 1965–73, dep head Euro Parly London Office 1973–79, dir Wiltenbridge Ltd 1980–93; MEP (EDG until 1992, now EPP) Kent West 1979–94, spokesman on economic monetary and industl policy 1984–89, bureau memb EDG/EPP 1989–94, vice pres Euro Parl Econ, Monetary and Industl Ctee 1992–94, Secretariat Euro Parliament 1994–; cncllr London Borough of Hammersmith 1968–71; MInstD; *Books* The Character of Conservatism (1973), Direct Elections to the European Parliament (1974), The Purse-strings of Europe (1979), Vredeling and All That (1984), VAT: The Zero Rate Issue (1988), European Monetary Union (1991), A European Currency (1994), Optims for a Definitive VAT Systems (1995); *Recreations* squash, walking; *Clubs* IOD, Bow Group; *Style—* Ben Patterson, Esq; ✉ Elm Hill House, Hawkhurst, Kent TN18 4XU; 9 rue de la Chapelle, L-8017 Strassen, Luxembourg (☎ 00 352 310783, office 00 352 4300 4114)

PATTERSON, Glenn; s of Phares Patterson, of Belfast, and Agnes Alexandra (Nessie), *née* Murphy; *b* 9 Aug 1961; *Educ* Methodist Coll Belfast, UEA (BA, MA); *partner* Ali Fitzgibbon, of Cork; *Career* writer; Artist in the Community Arts Cncl of NI 1989–91, creative writing fell UEA 1992, writer in residence UC Cork Oct 1993–April 1994, currently writer in residence Queen's Univ Belfast; memb Arts Cncl NI 1996–; Rooney Prize for Irish Literature 1988, secdy Betty Trask Award 1988; *Books* Burning Your Own (1988), Fat Lad (1992), Monday Night, Little Ireland, North of England (play, 1994), Black Night at Big Thunder Mountain (1995); *Style—* Glenn Patterson; ✉ Aitken & Stone, 29 Fernshaw Road, London SW1D 0TG (☎ 0171 351 7561)

PATTERSON, Dr Linda Joyce; da of Thomas William Matthew Patterson (d 1981), of Liverpool, and Mary Frances, *née* Patterson; *b* 12 April 1951; *Educ* Liverpool Inst HS for Girls, Middx Hosp Med Sch London (MB BS, MRCP); *partner* Christopher Stephen Green; *Career* pre-registration house offr Stoke-on-Trent and Gloucester 1975–76, SHO/registrar in pathology Charing Cross Hosp 1976–77, SHO in gen med Manchester Royal Infirmary 1978–80, tutor in med Univ of Manchester 1980–82, sr registrar in gen and geriatric med Withington Hosp Manchester and Bolton 1982–84, asst prof of geriatric med Univ of Saskatchewan Canada 1985, conslt physician in geriatric med Burnley Gen Hosp 1986–, clinical dir of med for the elderly Burnley Gen Hosp 1992–95, med dir Burnley Health Care NHS Tst 1995–; King's Fund travelling scholar; memb: Standing Ctee of Membs RCP 1986–89, Geriatric Med Speciality Ctee RCP 1987–90 and 1994–, Audit Ctee Br Geriatrics Soc 1990–, NW Region Speciality Trg Ctee in Geriatric Med 1992–, Exec Ctee Manchester Med Soc 1993–, GMC 1994–; FRCPE 1991, FRCP 1993; *Recreations* active member of Labour Party, Medical Practitioners Union, MSF, CND and MEDACT, feminist (attends weekly women's group), playing the piano and enjoying opera; *Style—* Dr Linda Patterson; ✉ Knott Hall, Charlestown, Hebden Bridge, West Yorkshire HX7 6PE (☎ 01422 845390); Burnley General Hospital, Casterton Avenue, Burnley, Lancs BB10 2PQ (☎ 01282 474543, fax 01282 474444)

PATTERSON, Dr Mark Jonathan David Damian Lister; s of Alfred Patterson (d 1972), and Frederica Georgina Mary Hammersley, *née* Lister Nicholson; *b* 2 March 1934; *m* 25 Oct 1958, Jane Teresa Mary Scott, da of David Dominic Scott Stokes, of London; 1 s (Damian b 1967), 2 da (Rebecca b 1972, Victoria b 1977); *Career* NHS, Univ of London and MRC 1959–67, conslt haematologist NHS and sr lectr Univ of London 1967–84; conslt haematologist: Bradford Royal Infirmary 1990–94, Royal Conwall Hosps 1994–96, Leighton District Gen Hosp 1996–; Parly candidate (Cons) Ealing N 1974, memb GLC 1969–73 and 1977–81; memb Worshipful Soc of Apothecaries 1965; MB BS, MRCS, LRCP, MRCP; *Recreations* historic restoration of ancient buildings; *Style—* Dr Mark Patterson; ✉ Wolverton Manor, Shorwell, Newport, Isle of Wight PO30 3JS (☎ 01983 740609, fax 01983 740977, e-mail MLPATTE@ibm.net)

PATTERSON, Neil Michael; s of Robin Shanks Patterson (d 1964), and Nancy Mearns, *née* Milne; *b* 22 March 1951; *Educ* Trinity Coll Glenalmond, Watford Art Sch; *m* 23 July 1983, Doris Karen, da of Ceferino William Boll, of Saguier, Province of Santa Fe, Argentina; 1 s (Robin William); *Career* sr writer Saatchi & Saatchi 1973; river columnist: Trout & Salmon 1976–78, Trout Fisherman 1982; exec creative dir: TBWA 1983–85, Young & Rubicam 1985–90; creative ptnr Mitchell Patterson Grime Mitchcell (formerly Mitchell Patterson Aldred Mitchell) 1990–; columnist Fly-Fishing & Fly-Tying 1992–; *Books* Chalkstream Chronicle, The Complete Fly Fisher, The Art of the Trout Fly, The One That Got Away; *Recreations* fly fishing, guitar, cooking; *Clubs* Flyfishers, D & AD; *Style—* Neil Patterson, Esq; ✉ Rose Cottage, 59 Bute Gardens, London W6 7DX (☎ 0171 603 6931); Wilderness Lodge, Elcot, Newbury, Berks RG20 8NH; Mitchell Patterson Grime Mitchell, 31 Kingly Street, London W1R 5LA (☎ 0171 734 8087, fax 0171 434 3081)

PATTERSON, Noel Anthony; s of Arthur Patterson (d 1975), and Doreen Violet, *née* Smith; *b* 29 Dec 1952; *Educ* Penarth GS, Univ of Wales Coll of Cardiff (BScEcon), LSE (MSc), Queens' Coll Cambridge (MPhil, coach Univ Amateur Boxing Club); *m* Janet Susan, da of Leonard George Frederick Boyle; 2 s (Frederick James b 12 June 1990, Arthur Henri b 4 July 1994); *Career* furniture remover Lyon France 1974–75, exec offr PO Telecommunications London 1977–78, industl rels offr Alcan Aluminium (UK) Ltd Rogerstone Gwent 1978–80; Mobil Oil Co Ltd: employee rels advsr London 1980–85, terminals mangr Midlands and West 1985–86, gen mangr Gatwick Refuelling Servs Gatwick 1986–87, industl rels mangr Coryton Refinery 1987–88; employee rels mangr Watney Truman Ltd London 1988–89, human resources mangr Grand Metropolitan Brewing Ltd London 1989–91, employee rels mangr Courage Ltd London 1991–92, dir Patterson James Management Consulting 1993–, assoc Harold Whitehead & Partners Ltd 1994–95, dir of personnel Matthew Clark plc 1995–; memb Nat Examining Bd for Supervision and Mgmnt (steering ctee) 1994–, lectr in mgmnt Richmond upon Thames Coll 1994; regular contrib to: Modern Management, Professional Manager, Progress and numerous other mgmnt jls; assoc memb IOD 1990, MIMgt 1990, FIPD 1990, MCIM 1994 (dip); *Recreations* reading, writing, sports and fatherhood; *Clubs* Glamorgan CCC (vice pres), Actors Anonymous Cricket, Dinas Powis RFC (vice pres); *Style—* Noel Patterson, Esq; ✉ 16 St Pauls Road, Richmond, Surrey TW9 2HH (☎ and fax 0181 948 2045); Matthew Clark plc, Whitchurch Lane, Bristol BS14 0JZ (☎ 01275 836100, fax 01275 890693)

PATTERSON, Paul Leslie; s of Leslie Patterson, of Exeter, and Lilian Anne, *née* Braund; *b* 15 June 1947; *Educ* RAM; *m* 12 Dec 1981, Hazel Rosemary, da of Dr Alexander Wilson, of Winchester; 1 s (Alastair b 1986), 1 da (Philippa b 1983); *Career* dir twentieth century music Univ of Warwick 1976–81, head of composition RAM 1985– (prof of composition 1972–), artistic dir Exeter Festival 1991–; composer of large-scale choral music incl: Mass of the Sea, Stabat Mater, Te Deum, Requiem, Voices of Sleep, Little Red Riding Hood, Magnificat; other compositions incl: orchestral music, symphony, concertos, chamber music, organ music, film and TV music; performances world-wide by leading musicians; featured composer at festivals incl: Llandaff 1985, Greenwich 1985, PLG 1987, Cheltenham 1988, Three Choirs 1988, Patterson South Bank 1988, Peterborough 1989, Southwark 1989–91, Cheltenham 1990, Exeter 1991; composer in residence: Eng Sinfonia Nottingham 1969–70, SE Arts Canterbury 1981–83, Truro Festival 1992–94; cmmns incl: BBC, RPO, LPO, Polish Chamber Orchestra, Kings Singers, Eng Chamber Orchestra, London Sinfonietta, Bach Choir, Acad of Saint Martins in the Field; memb: Arts Cncl Recordings Ctee, BBC Reading Panel, RPS Award Panel; pres RAM Club 1992–94, pres numerous choral socs and choirs; ARAM 1978, memb SPNM, FRAM 1982, FRSA 1989; Medal of Honour Miny of Culture Poland 1987; *Recreations* sailing, swimming; *Style—* Paul Patterson, Esq; ✉ 31 Cromwell Ave, Highgate, London N6 5HN (☎ 0181 348 3711, fax 0181 340 6489); Royal Academy of Music, London NW1 5HT (☎ 0171 873 7373, fax 0171 873 7374, telex COUNTER POINT); Exeter Festival, Civic Centre, Exeter EX1 1JN (☎ 01392 265095, fax 01392 265366)

PATTIE, Sir Geoffrey Edwin; kt (1987), PC (1987), MP (C) Chertsey and Walton (majority 22,819); o s of late Alfred Edwin Pattie, LDS, of Hove, Sussex, and Ada Olive, *née* Carr; *b* 17 Jan 1936; *Educ* Durham Sch, St Catharine's Coll Cambridge; *m* 1 Oct 1960, Tuëma Caroline, er da of Charles William Eyre-Maunsell (d 1989); 1 s (Andrew Edwin Charles b 1966), 1 da (Jessica Tuëma b 1963, decd); *Career* served TA Queen Victoria's Rifles, later Queen's Royal Rifles then 4 Royal Green Jackets (Capt, Hon Col 1996); called to the Bar Gray's Inn 1964; Parly candidate (C) Barking 1966 and 1970, MP (C) Chertsey and Walton Feb 1974–; former memb GLC (Lambeth) and chm ILEA Fin Ctee; vice chm: All-Pty Ctee on Mental Health 1977–79, Cons Parly Def Ctee 1978–79; Parly under-sec of state: for the RAF 1979–81, for defence procurement 1981–83; min of state: for defence procurement 1983–84, for industry and IT 1984–87; dir Fairey Group 1987–93, dep chm Cambridge Instruments 1988–91; chm: CDP Nexus 1988–92, GEC Marconi 1990–; *Clubs* Reform, Royal Green Jackets; *Style—* The Rt Hon Sir Geoffrey Pattie, MP; ✉ House of Commons, London SW1A 0AA (☎ 071 219 4055)

PATTINSON, The Rev Sir (William) Derek; kt (1990); s of Thomas William Pattinson (d 1970), and Elizabeth, *née* Burgess (d 1986); *b* 31 March 1930; *Educ* Whitehaven GS, Queen's Coll Oxford (BA, MA); *Career* Civil Serv 1952–70 (asst sec 1961): Inland Revenue Dept 1952–62 and 1965–68, HM Treasy 1962–65 and 1968–70; sec-gen of the Gen Synod of the C of E 1972–90 (assoc sec-gen 1970–72); ordained: deacon 1991, priest 1992; memb: Archbishops' Cmmn on Church and State 1966–70, Br Cncl of Churches 1972–90; vice chm Grosvenor Chapel Ctee 1973–81, vice pres SPCK; chm: Liddon Tstees 1972–, English Friends of Anglican Centre in Rome 1985–; princ Soc of the Faith 1991–, govr Greycoat Fndn; memb: Parish Clerks' Co (Master 1986–87), Woolmens' Co; Freeman City of London 1973; *Style—* The Rev Sir Derek Pattinson; ✉ 9 Strutton Ct, Great Peter Street, London SW1P 2HH (☎ 0171 222 6307)

PATTISON, Douglas Roderick (Doug); s of Joseph Roderick Pattison, of Bognor Regis, and Andrée Gabrielle, *née* Martin; *b* 17 Jan 1945; *Educ* Chichester HS for Boys, RNEC Manadon, RNC Greenwich (Cert in Naval Architecture (1st class)); *m* 1 April 1967, Gail Mary, da of Ronald Arthur Foster, OBE; 2 s (Adrian Robert b 14 April 1978, Simon Richard b 8 Sept 1981); *Career* probationary asst constructor Royal Corps of Naval Constructors (RCNC) 1963, RNEC Manadon 1963–65, RNC Greenwich 1965–68, Ship Dept Bath 1968, Constructor Lt RN Far East Fleet 1968–69; MOD: asst constructor Ship Dept Bath 1969–71, Admty Experiment Works (now DRA) Haslar 1971–73, constructor (now grade 7) on secondment as lectr in naval architecture UCL 1973–76, constructor HM Dockyard Portsmouth 1976–79, constructor Design Computing Gp Ship Dept Bath 1979–83, chief constructor (now grade 6) and asst dir design computing Warship Dept 1983–85, chief constructor MOD London 1985–88, seconded as prof of naval architecture Dept of Mechanical Engrg UCL 1989–93, dir Frigate and Mine Countermeasures (grade 5) MOD(PE) Bath and Abbey Wood 1993–; memb Cncl Royal Instn of Naval Architects 1991–96; hon naval architect RNSA; tstee Priston Village Hall; CEng 1973, FRINA 1986 (MRINA 1973), FEng 1996; *Publications include* Surface Piercing versus Fully submerged Foils for Sailing Hydrofoils (with J B Wynne, 1980), The Computer Aided Ship Design System GODDESS and its Application to the Structural Design of Royal Navy Warships (jtly, 1982), The Design of a Sailing Hydrofoil-FORCE 8 (1983, RINA Silver Medal), Technology Transfer in Computer Aided Ship Design (with R Carr, 1992), Trimaran Ships (with J W Zhang, 1995, RINA Gold Medal); *Recreations* sailing: small boat racing, design and cruising; Morris dancing, music, playing Greek auloi; *Clubs* Chew Valley Lake Sailing; *Style—* Doug Pattison, Esq, FEng; ✉ Director Frigates & Mine Countermeasures, DSSC, MOD, Abbey Wood 51a, PO Box 702, Bristol BS12 7DU (☎ 0117 913 6190, fax 0117 913 6913)

PATTISON, Rev Dr George Linsley; s of George William Pattison (d 1981), and Jean, *née* Allan; *b* 25 May 1950; *Educ* Perse Sch Cambridge, Univ of Edinburgh (MA, BD), Univ of Durham (PhD); *m* 25 Feb 1971, Hilary Christine, da of Robert Gilchrist Cochrane; 2 da (Charlotte Ann b 14 April 1972, Elisabeth Linsley b 20 Feb 1980), 1 s (Neil John Robert b 15 Aug 1976); *Career* ordained: deacon 1977, priest 1978; curate St James Newcastle upon Tyne 1977–80, priest-in-charge St Philip and St James Kimblesworth Co Durham 1980–83, rector Badwell Ash Great Ashfield Hunston and Stowlangtoft with Langham Suffolk 1983–91, dean of chapel King's Coll Cambridge 1991–; ed Modern Believing 1994–; *Books* Art, Modernity and Faith (1991), Kierkegaard: The Aesthetic and the Religious (1992), Kierkegaard on Art and Communication (ed, 1993), Pains of Glass (with Wendy Beckett, 1995), Spirit and Tradition (with Stephen Platten, 1996), Agnosis: Theology in the Void (1996); *Style—* The Rev Dr George Pattison; ✉ King's College, Cambridge CB2 1ST (☎ 01223 331100, fax 01223 331315)

PATTISON, Ian Frank; s of Frank Marsden Pattison, of Bradford, West Yorkshire, and Esther, *née* Williams (d 1958); *b* 8 Dec 1943; *Educ* Thornton GS Bradford; *m* 1, 1966 (m dis 1988), Kathleen Brenda Terry; 1 da (Annabel Claire b 29 July 1971); m 2, 1988, Maralyn Fox, da of Leslie Bould; *Career* articled clerk Williamson Butterfield & Roberts (now Grant Thornton) 1960–66, ptnr Grant Thornton 1971–91; pres Kirkless Jr C of C 1975, memb Cncl Kirkless & Wakefield C of C and Indust 1980– (pres 1985); dep chm Assoc of Yorks & Humberside Cs of C 1987; chm: Kirkless Enterprise Agency 1987–89, Wakefield Enterprise Agency 1987–89; chm Dewsbury Health Authy 1986–93, non-exec dir W Yorks Health Authy 1993–94; memb Exec N Kirkless Enterprise Gp 1987–, dir Enterprise House Ltd 1989–, chm Kenmore Cheshire Home 1994–; ACA 1966, ATII 1962; *Recreations* golf, cricket, rugby; *Clubs* Cleckheaton and District Rotary;

Style— Ian Pattison, Esq; ✉ Hollybank, 81 Bramley Lane, Lightcliffe, Halifax, West Yorkshire HX3 8NS (☎ 01422 201212)

PATTISON, Michael Ambrose; CBE (1996); s of Osmond John Pattison, of Charlecote Mill House, Hampton Lucy, Warwickshire, and Eileen Susannah, *née* Cullen; *b* 14 July 1946; *Educ* Sedbergh, Univ of Sussex; *m* 16 July 1975, Beverley Jean, da of Hugh E Webber (d 1988), of Florida; 1 da (Jennifer b 1977); *Career* civil serv: Miny of Overseas Devpt 1968, asst private sec to Minister for Overseas Devpt 1970–72, 1 sec UK perm mission to the UN NY 1974–77, private sec to successive PMs 1979–82, estab offr ODA 1983–85; chief exec RICS 1985–95, dir The Sainsbury Family Charitable Tsts 1995–; dir: Surveyors Holdings Ltd 1985–95, Battersea Arts Centre Tst 1988–94; Univ of Greenwich (formerly Thames Poly): govr 1989–, pro-chllr 1994–; memb Advsy Bd Univ of Nottingham Inst of Engrg Surveying and Space Geodesy 1990–95; hon visiting fell Dept of Valuation and Property Mgmnt City Univ 1990–; FRSA; *Recreations* cricket, real tennis, countryside, cinema; *Style*— Michael Pattison, Esq, CBE; ✉ Director, The Sainsbury Family Charitable Trusts, 9 Red Lion Court, London EC4A 3EB (☎ 0171 410 0330)

PATTISSON, John Harmer; s of Frederick Edward Pattisson (d 1946), of Meyricks Bidborough, Tunbridge Wells, and Louise Mary, *née* Dalton (d 1973); *b* 24 April 1931; *Educ* Radley, Trinity Coll Oxford (MA); *m* 29 March 1958 (m dis 1975), Julia Jane, da of Maj Percy Montagu Nevile (d 1957), of Skelbrooke Park, Yorks and Yerdley House, Long Compton, Warwicks; 2 s (Edward b 1960, William b 1963); *Career* Nat Serv 2 Lt Oxford & Bucks LI 1950–52, Capt TA 1952–63; Dawnay Day Group Ltd 1955–80 (dir 1964–69, md 1969–80), dir Hanson Trust Ltd (formerly Wiles Group Ltd) 1960–74; dir: Target Trust Group Ltd 1973–81, J Rothschild & Co Ltd 1980–81, Hanson plc 1981–89, New Court Property Fund Managers Ltd 1984–92, Imperial Group Pension Trust Ltd 1986–96 (chm 1989–96), Imperial Investments Ltd 1987–96 (chm 1989–96), Wassall plc 1988–, Allders plc 1993– (chm 1994–), Blenheim Group plc 1994–96; memb Cncl Radley Coll 1965– (vice-chm 1992–), vice-chm of Govrs City Technol Coll Kingshurst 1988–, memb Cncl Aims of Industry 1990–; FRSA 1995; *Clubs* Boodle's, City of London; *Style*— John H Pattisson, Esq; ✉ 1c Elm Place, London SW7 3QH (☎ 0171 370 4652); MacMillan House, 96 Kensington High Street, London W8 4SG (☎ 0171 376 1322, fax 0171 376 1366, mobile 0830 224626)

PATTISSON, Rodney Stuart; MBE (1969); s of Lt Cdr Kenneth Pattisson, DSC, RN, of Poole, and Margaret, *née* Collett; *b* 5 Aug 1943; *Educ* Pangbourne Coll, Br Royal Naval Coll Dartmouth; *Career* international yachtsman; achievements incl: Cadet world champion 1960, public schs Firefly champion 1960–61, Gold medal Flying Dutchman Olympic Games Mexico 1968 and W Germany 1972 (Silver Canada 1976), Flying Dutchman World champion (1969, 1970 and 1971), Flying Dutchman Euro champion (1968, 1970, 1972 and 1975), Quarter Ton World Cup champion Finland 1976, co-skipper Victory '83 Americas Cup 1983, One Ton World Cup champion England 1984; in Guinness Book of Records for lowest number of penalty points by winner of any class in Olympic Games (3 points 1968); RN Submariner Lt 1961–71, co dir Marine Yachting Conslts 1971; *Books* Tactics, Boat Speed; *Recreations* aero and nautical modelling, squash, skiing, cars; *Style*— Rodney Pattisson, Esq, MBE

PATTMAN, Dr Richard Stewart; s of Robert Pearson Pattman, VRD, of Milngavie, and Joyce Mary, *née* Long (d 1989); *b* 19 April 1950; *Educ* Glasgow Acad, Sedbergh, Univ of Glasgow (MB ChB); *m* 27 April 1976, (Mary) Geraldine, da of John Purcell (d 1983), of Glasgow; 1 s (Stewart John b 1979); *Career* house offr and registrar in gen med Western Infirmary Gartnavel Glasgow 1976–76, sr registrar in genito-urinary med Royal Infirmary Glasgow 1976–79, conslt in genito-urinary med and clinical lectr to Univ of Newcastle upon Tyne 1979–; memb Editorial Ctee of Genito-urinary Med; MRCP 1976, MFFP 1995, FRCPG 1986, FRCP 1991; *Recreations* gardening, fishing; *Style*— Dr Richard Pattman; ✉ Department of Genito-Urinary Medicine, Newcastle General Hospital, Westgate Rd, Newcastle upon Tyne NE4 6BE (☎ 0191 273 3320)

PATTON, Edwin Galbraith; s of Hugh Ferguson Patton, of Newtownards, Co Down, NI, and Sarah, *née* Galbraith (d 1987); *b* 29 June 1942; *Educ* Sullivan Upper Sch Holywood NI, Queen's Univ Belfast (LLB); *m* 1965, Margaret Elizabeth Victoria, da of Samuel Simpson Smyth (d 1979); 1 s (Dominic Edwin b 29 March 1973), 2 da (Siobhan Victoria b 4 Jan 1971, Susannah Jane b 11 April 1978); *Career* lectr in law Univ of Bristol 1964–67; Clifford Chance (formerly Coward Chance): articled clerk 1968–70, slr 1970–, ptnr 1974–; memb City of London Solicitors' Co; supporting memb London Maritime Arbitrators' Assoc; memb: Law Soc 1970, Int Bar Assoc; *Recreations* theatre, golf, skiing; *Style*— Edwin Patton, Esq; ✉ 10 Park Hill, Ealing, London W5 2JN (☎ 0181 997 1541); Clifford Chance, 200 Aldersgate Street, London EC1A 4JJ (☎ 0171 600 1000, fax 0171 600 5555)

PATTON, Dr Michael Alexander; s of Henry Alexander Patton, of Donaghadee, and Margaret Murray, *née* Drennan; *b* 15 April 1950; *Educ* Campbell Coll Belfast, Pembroke Coll Cambridge (MA), Univ of Edinburgh (MB ChB, MSc); *m* 4 June 1977, Jaqueline Heidi, da of John Pickin, OBE, of Wyck Rissington, Glos; 1 s (Alistair b 10 April 1979), 1 da (Rebecca b 21 Sept 1983); *Career* dir Regnl Genetics Serv SW Thames RHA; St George's Hosp Med Sch: conslt 1986–, sr lectr 1986–92, reader 1992–; med advsr to various parent gps for inherited disease, med dir Scientific Ctee Birth Defects Fndn; co dir Birth Defects Trading Co; examiner: RCPath 1990, Univ of London 1986–, Univ of Sheffield 1994; inspr Human Fertilisation and Embryology Authy 1991–96; memb Ctee: Genetic Interest Gp, Clinical Genetic Soc; FRCP 1993 (MRCP 1979); *Recreations* skiing, sailing, watercolour painting; *Style*— Dr Michael Patton; ✉ 126 Woodlands Rd, Little Bookham, Surrey KT23 4HJ (☎ 01372 456327, fax 01372 453151); SW Thames Regnl Genetic Service, St George's Hospital Medical School, Cranmer Terrace, London SW17 0RE (☎ 0181 767 8150, fax 0181 725 3444)

PATTULLO, Sir (David) Bruce; kt (1995), CBE (1989); s of Colin Arthur Pattullo; *b* 2 Jan 1938; *Educ* Rugby, Hertford Coll Oxford; *m* 1962, Fiona Jane Nicholson; 3 s, 1 da; *Career* Bank of Scotland: dep treas 1978–79, treas and chief exec 1979–88, dep govr and gp chief exec 1988–91, govr and gp chief exec 1991–96, govr 1996–; dir: Standard Life Assurance Co 1985–96, British Linen Bank Ltd 1977–, Bank of Wales plc 1986–, NWS Bank plc 1986–, Countrywide Banking Corporation Ltd 1987–; chm Ctee Scottish Clearing Bankers 1981–83 and 1987–89, pres Chartered Inst of Bankers in Scotland 1990–92; Hon LLD Univ of Aberdeen 1995, Hon DUniv Stirling 1996; FRSE 1990; *Recreations* tennis, hill walking; *Clubs* New (Edinburgh), Caledonian; *Style*— Sir Bruce Pattullo, CBE, FRSE; ✉ PO Box 5, The Mound, Edinburgh EH1 1YZ (☎ 0131 243 5555)

PAUK, Gyorgy; s of Imre Pauk (d 1944), and Magda Pauk; *b* 26 Oct 1936; *Educ* Franz Liszt Music Acad Budapest; *m* 19 July 1959, Susan, *née* Mautner; 1 s (Thomas b 19 April 1962), 1 da (Catherine b 13 June 1966); *Career* violinist; as the youngest pupil of the Franz Liszt Music Acad toured numerous countries incl Hungary and Eastern Europe; first prize winner: The Paganini Competition, Marguerite Long/Jacques Thibauld Competition, Munich Sonata Competition; London orchestral and recital debuts 1961; currently performs with maj orchestras of the world under such conductors as: Sir Colin Davies, Antal Dorati, Kondrashin, Lorin Maazel, Rozhdestvensky, Rattle, Previn, Tennstedt, Haitink, Sir George Solti; American debut with the Chicago Symphony Orch leading to subsequent return visits playing with: Cleveland Philadelphia, Los Angeles Philharmonic, Boston Symphony Orch; festival appearances incl: Aspen, Ravinia, Hollywood Bowl, Saratoga; many prizewinning recordings incl works by Bartok (new recording nominated for Grammy 1995), Schubert, Mozart, Brahms; hon memb Guildhall Sch, prof of music RAM 1986 (hon memb), artistic dir Mozart Festival in London Wigmore Hall 1991; *Style*— Gyorgy Pauk, Esq; ✉ c/o Tennant Artists, Unit 2, 39 Tadema Road, London SW10 0PY (☎ 0171 376 3758, fax 0171 351 0679)

PAUL, Alan; *b* 19 July 1954; *Educ* St Paul's, Univ Coll Oxford (MA); *m*; 3 s, 1 da; *Career* ptnr Allen & Overy 1985– (seconded to Panel on Takeovers and Mergers 1985–88); memb Law Soc; *Style*— Alan Paul, Esq; ✉ Allen & Overy, One New Change, London EC4M 9QQ (☎ 0171 330 3000, fax 0171 330 9999)

PAUL, Geoffrey David; OBE (1991); s of Reuben Goldstein; *b* 26 March 1929; *Educ* Liverpool, Kendal, Dublin; *m* 1, 1952 (m dis 1972), Joy Stirling; 1 da; m 2, 1974, Rachel Mann; 1 s; *Career* ed Jewish Chronicle 1977–90, ed US Affairs 1990–96; *Books* Living in Jerusalem; *Style*— Geoffrey Paul, Esq, OBE; ✉ 1 Carlton Close, West Heath Road, London NW3 7UA (☎ and fax 0181 458 6948)

PAUL, George William; DL (Suffolk 1991); s of William Stuart Hamilton Paul (d 1984), of Freston Lodge, Ipswich, and Diana Violet Anne, *née* Martin; *b* 25 Feb 1940; *Educ* Harrow, Wye Coll Univ of London (BSc); *m* 1, 1963, Mary Annette (d 1989), da of Col Frank Mitchell, DSO, MC (d 1985); 2 s (Stuart, Oliver), 1 da (Bridget); m 2, 1991, Margaret Joyce, da of F J Hedges (d 1984); *Career* chm: Pauls plc 1985–95, Harrisons and Crosfield plc 1994– (chief exec 1987–94, dir 1985–), Norwich Union 1994– (dir 1990–), Jockey Club Estates Ltd 1991–; ptnr William Paul and Sons Farmers; chm Essex and Suffolk Foxhounds (master 1978–85), High Sheriff Suffolk 1990; *Recreations* country pursuits, travel, sailing; *Clubs* The Jockey Club, Boodle's, Farmers'; *Style*— George Paul, Esq, DL; ✉ Harrisons & Crosfield plc, The Havens, Ipswich, Suffolk IP3 9SJ (☎ 01473 272700, fax 01473 322347)

PAUL, Eur Ing Prof John Poskitt; s of William Boag Paul (d 1962), of Old Kilpatrick, and Maude Meikle, *née* Poskitt (d 1972); *b* 26 June 1927; *Educ* Aberdeen GS, Allan Glens Sch Glasgow, Royal Tech Coll Glasgow (BSc, PhD), Univ of Glasgow; *m* 7 Sept 1956, Elizabeth Richardson, da of James Richardson Graham (d 1962), of Dalmuir; 1 s (Graham William b 1962), 2 da (Gillian Anne b 1960, Fiona Helen b 1968); *Career* Univ of Strathclyde: lectr in mechanical engrg 1952, sr lectr 1964, personal prof of bioengrg 1972, prof of bioengrg 1978–94 (now emeritus), head of Bioengrg Unit 1980–92; visiting prof West Virginia Univ Morgantown 1969–70; Donald Julius Groen lectr Instn of Mech Engrs 1991; pres Int Soc of Biomechanics 1987–89; memb Ctee: BSI (chm Ctee for Bone and Joint Replacements), ISO (chm Ctee for Bone and Joint Replacements), CEN, MRC, SERC, SHHD; FIMechE 1971, FISPO 1979, FRSA 1974, FBOA 1975, FRSE 1984, Eur Ing 1990, FEng 1992; membre d'Honneur Societé de Biomecanique, Medal of Honour Czechoslovak Soc for Mechanics 1990; *Books* Disability (co-ed, 1979), Computing in Medicine (sr ed, 1982), Biomaterials in Artificial Organs (sr ed, 1984), Influence of New Technology in Medical Practice (sr ed, 1984), Total Knee Replacement (co-ed, 1988), Progress in Bioengineering (sr ed, 1989), Influence of New Technologies in Medical Practice (sr ed, 1991); *Recreations* gardening, bridge, formerly rugby and refereeing; *Style*— Eur Ing Prof John P Paul, FRSE, FEng; ✉ 25 James Watt Rd, Milngavie, Glasgow G62 7JX (☎ and fax 0141 9563221); Bioengineering Unit, Wolfson Centre, Univ of Strathclyde, Glasgow G4 ONW (☎ 0141 5524400, fax 0141 5526098, telex 77472 UNSLIBG)

PAUL, Sir John Warburton; GCMG (1965, KCMG 1962), OBE (1959), MC (1940); s of Walter George Paul; *b* 29 March 1916; *Educ* Weymouth Coll Dorset, Selwyn Coll Cambridge (MA); *m* 1946, Kathleen Audrey, da of Dr A D Weeden, of Weymouth; 3 da; *Career* commissioned RTR 1937–47; called to the Bar Inner Temple 1947; colonial admin service Sierra Leone 1947–61; govr and C-in-C: The Gambia 1962–65 (govr gen 1965–66), Br Honduras 1966–72, The Bahamas 1972–73; govr gen The Bahamas July-Oct 1973, Lt-Govr Isle of Man 1974–80; dir of overseas rels St John Ambulance 1981–89, chm St Christopher's Motorists' Security Assoc 1980–93; hon fell Selwyn Coll Cambridge; Chapter Gen Order of St John 1981–91 (memb Cncl Hampshire 1990–95), KStJ 1962; *Clubs* Athenaeum, MCC, Hawks (Cambridge); *Style*— Sir John Paul, GCMG, OBE, MC; ✉ Sherrens Mead, Sherfield on Loddon, Hampshire RG27 0ED (☎ 01256 882 331)

PAUL, Julian Braithwaite; s of Michael Braithwaite Paul, MD, of Orchard House, Newchurch, Burton-on-Trent, Staffs, and Patricia Elisabeth Ann, *née* Mumm; *b* 18 May 1945; *Educ* Wrekin Coll Shrops, St John's Coll Oxford (BA, MA); *m* 3 Nov 1973, Diana, da of Ernest Trevor Davies (d 1981), of Epsom, Surrey; 1 s (Rupert b 1981), 2 da (Arabella b 1975, Henrietta b 1978); *Career* Arthur Andersen & Co CAs 1966–71, Citibank NA 1971–74, dep md Banco Hispano Americano Ltd 1974–87, md Guinness Mahon & Co Ltd 1987–90, princ Julian Paul & Co Chartered Accountants 1990–, dep chm Castle Communications plc 1991–; non-exec chm Tele-Cine Cell Group plc 1994–; non-exec dir: Tiger Books International plc 1994–, Sleepy Kids plc 1996–; chm of govrs Valence Sch Westerham Kent; cncllr Kent County Cncl (Sevenoaks West) 1985–93; FCA 1979; *Recreations* politics, travel; *Clubs* Carlton; *Style*— Julian Paul, Esq; ✉ The Mount House, Brasted, Westerham, Kent TN16 1JB (☎ 01959 563617, fax 01959 561296)

PAUL, Dr (Peter) Michael; s of Thomas James Paul, of Woore, Shropshire, and Nora, *née* Wilcox; *b* 26 Sept 1947; *Educ* Queen Elizabeth GS Wakefield Yorkshire, St Andrews Univ Scotland (MB), Univ of Manchester (MB ChB), DObstRCOG, FPA Cert, MRCGP; *m* 22 June 1974, Susan Margaret, da of Frank Pickles; *Career* house offr Wythenshaw Hosp Manchester 1973–74, sr house offr Casualty Dept Westminster Hosp London 1974, vocational trg scheme Aylesbury Buckinghamshire 1974–77, ptnr in practice White Bungalow Surgery Sunninghill 1977–86, private GP and med dir Gen Med Clinics Ltd London 1986; memb Ctee Ascot Volunteer Bureau 1981–86, med offr Ascot Priory Convent 1977–86, memb Ctee and hon treas Thames Valley Faculty RCGP 1980–86, fndr and hon sec Independent Doctors Forum 1989–, gen practice trainer, pt/t lectr Red Cross; FRSM, memb BMA; *Recreations* theatre, reading, walking; *Clubs* RAC; *Style*— Dr Michael Paul; ✉ 285a Kings Rd, Chelsea, London SW3 5EW (☎ 0171 351 6210); General Medical Clinics Ltd, 74 London Fruit Exchange, Brushfield Street, London E1 6EN (☎ 0171 522 0011, fax 0171 972 9975)

PAUL, Nancy Catherine Trask; da of Frank Stone Trask (d 1983), of Deer Lodge, Montana, USA, and Cora Nichols (d 1964); *b* 1 June 1936; *Educ* Powell County HS, DL Montana, Univ of Montana USA (BA, MA); *m* 17 Sept 1960 (m dis 1982), William J Paul, Jr; 2 s (William James Paul, III b 19 Nov 1962, Michael Justin Paul b 18 June 1971), 1 da (Elisa Anne Paul b 7 Sept 1969); *Career* lectr in psychology Univ of Montana 1958–60, assoc mgmnt prof Brunel Univ 1979–; dir: Paul Mgmnt Ltd 1979–89, Excel International Ltd 1989–; author of pubns on: the effects of divorce on men and women, orgns and work in the UK and USA; maker of numerous award winning videos; fndr memb Inst of Transactional Analysis, hon memb Int Inst of Transactional Analysis Assoc; memb: American Acad of Mgmnt, Int OD Network; *Books* The Right to Be You (1985), The Principles of Project Management (1991), Meetings, Your Guide to Making Them Work (1991); *Recreations* mountaineering, classical music; *Style*— Mrs Nancy Paul; ✉ Excel International Ltd, Excel House, 35 Lind Road, Sutton, Surrey SM1 4PP (☎ 0181 770 0465)

PAUL, Philip; *Educ* privately, DipCAM; *Career* various news/editorial appts with regnl and nat newspapers until 1960, asst PRO CEGB 1960–68, assoc dir Eric White & Partners PR conslts 1968–70, dep dir of PR The Post Office 1970–76; dir of PR: RICS 1976–78, Royal Pharmaceutical Soc of GB 1978–86; freelance author, journalist and PR/public affrs conslt 1986–, chm Health & Med PR Assoc (HAMPRA) 1992–; memb: Chartered Inst of Journalists, Br Assoc of Journalists, RSM, Crime Writers' Assoc, Soc of Authors; FIPR 1986 (MIPR 1960); *Books* City Voyage (1967), Some Unseen Power (1985), Murder Under the Microscope: the story of Scotland Yard's forensic science laboratory (1990); *Recreations* video and still photography, target shooting, motor racing; *Style*— Philip Paul, Esq; ✉ Upper Benchwood, Guestling Thorn, Hastings, East Sussex TN35 4LU (☎ and fax 01424 812847)

PAUL, Robert Cameron (Robin); CBE (1996); *b* 7 July 1935; *Educ* Rugby, Corpus Christi Coll Cambridge (BA, MA, MEng); *m* 1 May 1965, Diana Kathleen, *née* Bruce; 2 da (Caroline b 1966, Juliet b 1968); *Career* Nat Serv 2 Lt RE BAOR 1953–55; ICI 1959–86 (dep chm ICI Mond Div 1979), dep chm and md Albright & Wilson Ltd 1986–95, chief exec Albright & Wilson plc 1995–; non-exec dir Courtaulds plc 1994–; pres: Inst of Chemical Engrs 1990–91, Chemical Industries Assoc 1995–; Hon DEng Univ of Birmingham; FEng 1990 (memb Cncl until 1994); *Recreations* music, golf; *Clubs* Oriental; *Style*— R C Paul, Esq, CBE, FEng; ✉ Albright & Wilson plc, 210–222 Hagley Road West, Oldbury, Warley, W Midlands B68 0NN (☎ 0121 429 4942, fax 0121 420 5151)

PAUL, Baron (Life Peer UK 1996), of Marylebone in the City of Westminster; Swraj Paul; s of Payare Paul (d 1944), and Mongwati, *née* Lal; *b* 18 Feb 1931; *Educ* Univ of Punjab (BSc), MIT (BSc, MSc); *m* 1 Dec 1956, Aruna; 3 s (Hon Ambar b 20 Dec 1957, Hon Akash b (twin) 20 Dec 1957, Hon Angad b 6 June 1970), 2 da (Hon Anjli b 12 Nov 1959, Ambika b 1963, d 1968); *Career* dir family owned Apeejay-Surrendra Gp India 1952–66, came to England 1966, estab Natural Gas Tubes Ltd 1968; chm: Caparo Group Ltd 1978–, Caparo Industs plc 1980–, Caparo Inc USA 1988–; Hon PhD American Coll of Switzerland 1986, Hon DSc Univ of Hull 1992, Hon DHL Chapman Univ California 1996; Order of Padma Bhushan India 1983; *Books* Indira Gandhi (1985); *Clubs* MCC, RAC; India: Royal Calcutta Turf, Royal Calcutta Golf, Cricket of India (Bombay); *Style*— The Rt Hon Lord Paul; ✉ Caparo Group Ltd, Caparo House, 103 Baker St, London W1M 2LN (☎ 0171 486 1417, fax 0171 935 3242)

PAUL, William Halkerston Clunie; s of John Litster Wallace Paul (d 1979), of Fife, Scotland, and Margaret White, *née* Clunie (d 1982); *b* 21 March 1955; *Educ* Bell Baxter HS, Univ of Aberdeen (MA); *m* 2 Nov 1978, Linda Anne, *née* Forsyth; 2 s (Andrew Halkerston Clunie b 26 March 1983, William James Forsyth b 18 Sept 1985); *Career* trainee reporter Press and Journal Aberdeen 1976–80, sr reporter The Scotsman Edinburgh 1980–88, news ed Scotland on Sunday Edinburgh 1995– (chief reporter 1988–95); *Books* Seasons of Revenge (1985), Mummy's Boy (1987), The Hindmost (1988), The Lion Rampant (1989), Dance of Death (1991), Sleeping Dogs (1993), Sleeping Pretty (1995), Sleeping Partner (1996); *Recreations* rugby, golf; *Style*— William Paul, Esq; ✉ Scotland on Sunday, 20 North Bridge, Edinburgh EH1 1YT (☎ 0131 243 3486, fax 0131 220 2443)

PAULSON-ELLIS, Jeremy David; s of Christian William Geoffrey Paulson-Ellis (d 1982), and Vivien Joan Paulson-Ellis (d 1966); *b* 21 Sept 1943; *Educ* Sherborne; *m* 27 April 1973, Jennifer Jill, da of Harry Milne (d 1958); 2 s (Nicholas b 1976, Matthew b 1984), 1 da (Vivien b 1974); *Career* Citicorp Scrimgeour Vickers International Ltd (formerly Vickers da Costa & Co): joined 1964, ptnr 1970, dir 1974, chm 1985–88; chm: Genesis Investment Management Ltd, Genesis Emerging Markets Fund Ltd, Genesis Chile Fund Ltd, Genesis Malaysia Maju Fund Ltd, Genesis Condor Fund Ltd; dir: Fleming Japan Investment Tst PLC, Vietnam Fund Ltd, Second India Investment Fund Ltd, Korea Asia Fund Ltd 1991–96; memb Investmt Advsy Cncl: Korea International Trust 1982–87, Seoul International Trust (chm) 1985–87, Thailand Fund 1986–88; ind memb Heathrow Airport Consultative Ctee 1984–88; MSI 1970; AMSIA; *Recreations* tennis, travel; *Style*— Jeremy Paulson-Ellis, Esq; ✉ Broomlands, Langton Green, Tunbridge Wells, Kent TN3 0RA (☎ 01892 863 555); Genesis Investment Management Ltd, 21 Knightsbridge, London SW1X 7LY (☎ 0171 235 5040, fax 0171 235 8065, telex 919062 GIML)

PAULUSZ, Jan Gilbert; s of Jan Hendrik Olivier Paulusz, of Tanglewood, Westbury, Wiltshire, and Edith, *née* Gilbert; *b* 18 Nov 1929; *Educ* The Leys; *m* 18 April 1973, Luigia Maria, da of Luigi Attanasio; *Career* Nat Serv 2 Lt 1 Bn S Lancs Regt 1951–53, Lt TA 1953–60 (Capt 1955); called to the Bar Lincoln's Inn 1957, recorder of the Crown Court 1980–; *Recreations* photography, mountain walking; *Style*— Jan Paulusz, Esq; ✉ 50 Royston Gardens, Redbridge, Ilford, Essex 1G1 3SY (☎ 0181 554 9078); 10 King's Bench Walk, Temple, London EC4Y 7EB (☎ 0171 353 7742)

PAUNCEFORT-DUNCOMBE, David Philip Henry; s and h of Sir Philip Digby Pauncefort-Duncombe, 4 Bt, *qv*; *b* 21 May 1956; *Educ* Gordonstoun, RAC Cirencester; *m* 1987, Sarah Ann, er da of late Reginald T G Battrum; 1 s (Henry Digby b 16 Dec 1988), 1 da (Laura Mary b 15 Jan 1991); *Style*— David Pauncefort-Duncombe, Esq; ✉ Westfield Farm, Great Brickhill, Bletchley, Bucks MK17 9BG (☎ 01525 261479)

PAUNCEFORT-DUNCOMBE, Sir Philip Digby; 4 Bt (UK 1859), of Great Brickhill, Buckinghamshire, DL (Bucks 1971); s of Maj Sir Everard Philip Digby Pauncefort-Duncombe, 3 Bt, DSO (d 1971); *b* 18 May 1927; *Educ* Stowe; *m* 4 April 1951, Rachel Moyra, yr da of Maj Henry Gerald Aylmer, gggs of 2 Baron Aylmer; 1 s (David Philip Henry b 1956), 2 da (Diana (Mrs Jeremy D T West) b 1953, Charlotte b 1967); *Heir* s, David Philip Henry Pauncefort-Duncombe b 21 May 1956; *Career* 2 Lt Grenadier Guards 1946, Hon Maj (ret 1960), RARO, County Cmdt Bucks ACF 1967–70, memb HM Body Guard of Hon Corps of Gentlemen-at-Arms 1979–, Harbinger 1993; High Sheriff of Buckinghamshire 1987–88; KASG; CStJ 1992 (OStJ 1986); *Style*— Sir Philip Pauncefort-Duncombe, Bt, DL; ✉ Great Brickhill Manor, Milton Keynes, Bucks MK17 9BE (☎ 01525 261205)

PAUSON, Prof Peter Ludwig; s of Stefan Pauson (d 1964), and Helene Dorothea, *née* Herzfelder (d 1989); *b* 30 July 1925; *Educ* Univ of Glasgow (BSc), Univ of Sheffield (PhD); *m* 7 June 1952, Lai-ngau, da of Pak Yun Wong (d 1971); 1 s (Alfred b 1956), 1 da (Hilary b 1954); *Career* asst prof Duquesne Univ Pittsburgh PA 1949–51; res fell: Univ of Chicago 1951–52, Harvard Univ 1952–53; reader Univ of Sheffield 1959 (lectr 1953–59), Freeland prof of chemistry Univ of Strathclyde (formerly Royal Coll of Sci and Technol) 1959–90, prof emeritus 1990–; memb Deutsche Akademie der Naturforscher Leopoldina 1976; FRSE 1961; *Books* Organometallic Chemistry (1967); *Recreations* skiing, hill-walking, gardening, listening to music; *Style*— Prof Peter Pauson, FRSE; ✉ 40A Station Road, Bearsden, Glasgow G61 4AL (☎ 0141 942 5213); Department of Pure and Applied Chemistry, University of Strathclyde, Glasgow G1 1XL (☎ 0141 552 4400, fax 0141 552 5664)

PAVANE, Lisa; *Educ* Australian Ballet Sch; *m* Greg Horsman, sr princ with English National Ballet; 1 da (Cassandra b 1992); *Career* ballet dancer; studied with Tessa Maunder, coached by Galina Ulanova; The Australian Ballet: joined 1981, soloist 1983–86, princ artist 1986–94; roles with The Australian Ballet incl: Spartacus, Romeo and Juliet, Coppelia, Tales of Hoffman, La Fille Mal Gardée, Suite en Blanc, The Sleeping Beauty, Odette/Odile in Swan Lake, the Sylph in La Sylphide, Kitri in Don Quixote, Black Queen in Checkmate, Katherina in The Taming of the Shrew, Tatiana in Onegin, Hanna in The Merry Widow, Milady in The Three Musketeers, Nikiya in La Bayadère, title role in Giselle, title role in Manon; sr princ English National Ballet 1994–; roles incl: Juliet in Nureyev's Romeo and Juliet, title role in Derek Deane's Giselle, Lichine's Graduation Ball, Balachine's Square Dance, Queen of Hearts in Derek Deane's Alice in Wonderland, title role in Michael Corder's Cinderella; guest appearances with: Boston Ballet, Kirov Ballet, Birmingham Royal Ballet, sixth and seventh World Ballet Festivals Japan (with Greg Horsman); *Style*— Ms Lisa Pavane; ✉ English National Ballet, Markova House, 39 Jay Mews, London SW7 2ES (☎ 0171 581 1245, fax 0171 225 0827)

PAVEY, Martin Christopher; s of Archibald Lindsay Pavey, MC (d 1977), of Sherborne, Dorset, and Margaret Alice, *née* Salsbury; *b* 2 Dec 1940; *Educ* Magdalen Coll Sch Oxford, UCL (BA), Univ of Cambridge (PGCE), Univ of Nottingham (MA); *m* 9 April 1969, Louise Margaret, da of Dr Joseph Charles Henry Bird (d 1985), of Cambridge; 2 s (Nicholas b 1972, Robert b 1974); *Career* headmaster: Fairham Sch Nottingham 1976–81, Cranbrook Sch Kent 1981–88, Latymer Upper Sch London 1988–91; educn conslt, lectr and inspr 1991–; *Clubs* East India; *Style*— Martin Pavey, Esq; ✉ 5 Vineyards, Bath BA1 5NA (☎ 01225 444269)

PAVEY, Terence Joseph (Terry); s of Joseph Pavey, and Margaret Honora, *née* Byfield; *b* 29 May 1943; *Educ* Univ of Public Libraries; *m* 2 Sept 1967, Carole Andrea; 2 s (James Robert b 4 Nov 1972, Nicholas Paul b 25 Nov 1974); *Career* early career with local newspapers, reporting agencies and court reporting agencies; sub ed Morning Advertiser; freelance with: Daily Mirror, The Sun, News of the World; TVTimes: chief sub ed features and programmes, asst ed, assoc ed, managing ed, dep ed, ed 1991–94; freelance ed 1995–; *Recreations* watching TV!, reading, walking, animal welfare; *Style*— Terry Pavey, Esq; ✉ The Retreat, 90 Elmfield Road, Potters Bar, Herts EN6 2JL (☎ 01707 657646)

PAVIA, Michael James; s of Cyril Victor Felix Pavia (d 1994), and Barbara, *née* Fulk; *b* 7 Oct 1946; *Educ* King James I Sch IOW; *m* 1986, Judith Elizabeth, *née* Shepherd; 2 s (William James, Christopher James), 2 da (Katherine Elizabeth, Lucy Elizabeth); *Career* articled clerk Allen Baldry Holman & Best 1964–69, audit sr rising to sr mangr Price Waterhouse 1969–79; LASMO plc: chief accountant 1980–82, controller 1982–86, treas 1986–88, fin dir 1988–93; gp fin dir Seeboard plc 1994–; also dir: Seeboard Share Scheme Trustees Ltd, Felix Pavia & Sons Ltd; memb: Tech Ctee ICAEW 1986–88, Oil Industry Accounting Ctee 1988–94; FCA; *Recreations* sport, home, family; *Style*— Michael J Pavia, Esq; ✉ Seeboard plc, Forest Gate, Brighton Road, Crawley, West Sussex RH11 9BH (☎ 01293 657450)

PAVITT, Prof Keith Leslie Richard; *b* 13 Jan 1937; *Educ* Hackney Downs GS, Trinity Coll Cambridge (BA), Harvard Univ; *m* 29 March 1964, Michelle Simone, *née* Rouffigmac; 1 s (Richard Robert b 21 Aug 1965), 1 da (Isabelle Catherine b 6 April 1969); *Career* PO RAF 1955–57; staff memb OECD Paris 1961–70; Univ of Sussex: sr fell 1971, prof of sci and technol policy 1984–, actg dir Sci Policy Res Unit Univ of Sussex 1988; visiting prof: Princeton Univ USA 1970, Université Louis Pasteur Strasbourg 1983, Univ of Padua 1987, Univ of Nice 1991 and 1993, Stanford Univ 1992, Univ of Aalborg 1992, Univ of Paris-Dauphine 1993 and 1994, Univ of Lyon 1994, Univ of Reading 1994; vice-chm Res Grants Bd, memb Econ and Social Res Cncl; memb Schumpeter Soc 1989; *Books* Technical Innovation and British Economic Performance (ed, 1980), The Comparative Economics of Research, Development And Innovations in East and West: A Survey (with P Hanson, 1987); *Recreations* tennis, food, visits to France; *Clubs* Royal Air Force; *Style*— Prof Keith Pavitt; ✉ Science Policy Research Unit, Mantell Building, University of Sussex, Brighton, E Sussex BN1 9RF (☎ 01273 678173, fax 01273 685865)

PAVORD, Anna; da of Arthur Vincent Pavord (d 1989), of Abergavenny, Gwent, and Christabel Frances, *née* Lewis (d 1978); *b* 20 Sept 1940; *Educ* Abergavenny HS for Girls, Univ of Leicester (BA); *m* Trevor David Oliver Ware, s of John Ronald Ware; 3 da (Oenone b 15 Dec 1967, Vanessa b 7 June 1970, Tilly b 8 Dec 1974); *Career* copywriter Lintas Advertising Agency 1962–63, Line-Up BBC TV 1963–70 (prodn asst rising to dir), contrib Observer 1970–92, gardening corr The Independent 1986–, assoc ed Gardens Illustrated 1993–; writer and presenter Flowering Passions (10–part series, Channel 4) 1991; memb Gardens Panel Nat Tst 1996–; *Books* Growing Things (1982), Foliage (1990), The Flowering Year (1991), Gardening Companion (1992), The Border Book (1994), The New Kitchen Garden (1996); *Recreations* gardening, sailing, rainforests in Central America, Evelyn Waugh, black and white films; *Style*— Ms Anna Pavord; ✉ The Independent, 1 Canada Square, Canary Wharf, London E14 5DL (☎ 0171 293 2000, fax 0171 293 2435)

PAWLEY, Prof (Godfrey) Stuart; s of George Charles Pawley (d 1956), of Bolton, Lancs, and Winifred Mary, *née* Wardle (d 1989); *b* 22 June 1937; *Educ* Bolton Sch, Univ of Cambridge (MA, PhD); *m* 29 July 1961, Anthea Jean, da of Rev Alan Miller (d 1981), of Northwich, Cheshire; 2 s (Philip b 1963, Graham b 1967), 1 da (Alison b 1965); *Career* prof of computational physics Univ of Edinburgh 1985– (lectr 1964–69, reader 1970–85), guest prof Aarhus Univ of Denmark 1969–70; FRSE 1975, FRS 1992; *Books* An Introduction to OCCAM-2 Programming (jtly); *Recreations* choral singing, hill-walking; *Style*— Prof Stuart Pawley, FRS, FRSE; ✉ Physics Department, Kings Buildings, University of Edinburgh, Edinburgh EH9 3JZ (☎ 0131 650 5300, fax 0131 650 5212)

PAWLOWSKI, Mark; s of Kazimierz Pawlowski, of London, and Maria Zwienislawa, *née* Konkol; *b* 15 Sept 1953; *Educ* Wetherby Sch, St Benedict's Sch Ealing, Univ of Warwick (LLB), Wadham Coll Oxford (BCL); *m* 19 April 1986, Lidia Maria, da of Capt Jerzy de Barbaro (of the Barbaro family, Venice); 1 da (Joanna Veronica b 9 Feb 1980); *Career* called to the Bar Middle Temple 1978; in practice at Chancery Bar 1980–91; Univ of Greenwich (formerly Thames Poly): pt/t lectr 1980–83, lectr 1983–84, sr lectr 1984–95, reader in property law 1995–; visiting lectr UCL 1990–, memb convocation Wadham Coll Oxford 1983; ed: Journal of Rent Review and Lease Renewal, Landlord and Tenant Review; author of numerous articles in learned jls on property, landlord and tenant law 1984–; Sweet & Maxwell Law prizewinner 1974; memb: Middle Temple, Soc of Public Teachers of Law, Assoc of Law Teachers, Br Polish Legal Assoc; ACIArb 1990; *Books* Casebook on Rent Review and Lease Renewal (with Diana Brahams, 1986), The Forfeiture of Leases (1993), Casebook on Landlord and Tenant (with James Brown, 1995), Law Q & A, Landlord and Tenant (with James Brown, 1995), The Doctrine of Proprietary Estoppel (1996); *Recreations* tennis, scuba diving, gardening, walking, travel; *Style*— Mark Pawlowski, Esq; ✉ School of Law, University of Greenwich, Avery Hill Campus, Bexley Road, Eltham, London SE9 2PQ (☎ 0181 331 9040, fax 0181 331 8473); Pepys' Chambers, 17 Fleet Street, London EC4Y 1AA (☎ 0171 936 2710, fax 0171 936 2501)

PAWSEY, James Francis (Jim); MP (C) Rugby and Kenilworth (majority 13,247); s of Capt William John Pawsey (d 1941), of Coventry, and Mary Victoria, *née* Mumford (d 1958); *b* 21 Aug 1933; *Educ* Coventry Tech Sch, Coventry Tech Coll; *m* 1956, Cynthia Margaret, da of Arthur John Francis (d 1990), of Coventry; 6 s (Mark, Michael, Gregory, Clive (twin), Philip, Adrian (twin)); *Career* MP (C): Rugby 1979–83, Rugby and Kenilworth 1983–; memb Exec Ctee 1922 Ctee 1989–; chm Select Ctee of the Parly Cmmn for Admin; PPS: DES 1982–83, DHSS 1983–84, NI Office 1984–86; vice chm Int Parly Union, chm Cons Backbench Educn Ctee 1985–, chm W Midlands Gp of Cons MPs; memb: Rugby RDC 1964–73, Rugby Borough Cncl 1973–75, Warwickshire CC 1974–79; *Books* The Tringo Phenomenon; *Recreations* gardening; *Style*— Jim Pawsey, Esq, MP; ✉ Rugby and Kenilworth Cons Assoc, Albert Buildings, Albert St, Rugby (☎ 01788 569556); House of Commons, London SW1A 0AA (☎ 0171 219 5127)

PAWSEY, Karol Anne; da of Hubert Sydney Pawsey, of Thurrock, Essex, and Kathleen Ada, *née* Jordan; *b* 26 July 1963; *Educ* Grays Sch Essex, Glos Coll of Art Cheltenham (BA, CNAA distinction for thesis); *Career* art dealer; with Fischer Fine Art London 1985–87, dir Curwen Gallery 1988– (joined 1987); *Style*— Ms Karol Pawsey; ✉ 361 Queenstown Rd, Battersea, London SW8 (☎ 0171 627 1659); Curwen Gallery, 4 Windmill St, off Charlotte St, London W1P 1HF (☎ 0171 636 1459, fax 0171 436 3059)

PAWSON, Anthony John Dalby; s of Donald Pawson, and Kathleen, *née* Goodwin; *b* 14 Oct 1946; *Educ* Kent Coll Canterbury, City Univ (BSc); *m* 1969, Kathleen, *née*

Chisholm; 1 s, 1 da; *Career* MOD: joined 1967, private sec to Chief of Air Staff 1978–80, first sec UK Delgn to NATO 1981–83, private sec to Sec of State for N Ireland 1990–92, RCDS 1992, asst under sec of state (Fleet Support) 1993–95; under sec Cabinet Office 1995–; *Recreations* cricket, rugby; *Style*— Anthony Pawson, Esq; ✉ Cabinet Office, 70 Whitehall, London SW1A 2AS

PAWSON, Henry Anthony (Tony); OBE (1988); s of Albert Guy Pawson, CMG, of Penshurst, and Helen Humphrey, *née* Lawson; *b* 22 Aug 1921; *Educ* Winchester, Ch Ch Oxford (MA); *m* Hilarie Anne, da of Lt-Col Tarn Prichard Bassett, DSO (d 1977), of Chilcomb; 2 s (Anthony James, John Henry), 1 da (Sarah Anne); *Career* Rifle Bde N Africa/Italy 1940–46, Maj (despatches); master at Winchester 1949–50, personnel dir Reed Paper Gp 1950–71, Southern sec Paper and Board Employers Fedn 1972–74, arbitration final stage HMSO procedure 1974–75, industl rels advsr Brewers Soc 1976–87, memb Southampton Industl Tbnl 1977–89, currently corr for Observer on cricket, soccer and angling; world and Euro flyfishing champion, only man since WWII to play as an amateur in Co Cricket (Kent) and First Div Soccer (Charlton); played in: MCC v S Africa 1947, Gentlemen v Players 1948; 12 rep caps for England amateur soccer team, 1952 GB Olympic soccer team; Royal Humane Soc Life Saving Commendation 1985; *Books* 100 Years of FA Cup, Official History (1971), Football's Managers, The Goalscorers, Runs and Catches, Competitive Fly Fishing, The Observer on Soccer, Fly Fishing Around the World, Kingswood Book of Fishing, Two Game Fishermen (jtly with s); *Recreations* fishing, cricket; *Style*— Tony Pawson, Esq, OBE; ✉ Manor House, Chilcomb, nr Winchester, Hants SO21 1HR (☎ 01962 861482); c/o The Sports Desk, The Observer, 119 Farringdon Road, London EC1R 3ER

PAWSON, Kenneth Vernon Frank; s of Capt Arnold Gilderdale Pawson (d 1937), and Freda Eunice Pawson; *b* 24 Sept 1923; *Educ* Rugby, Trinity Hall Cambridge; *m* 1950, Nicolette Vivian, da of Mervyn Thoresby (d 1965); 1 s, 2 da; *Career* Capt Rifle Bde BAOR 1942–47; called to the Bar Gray's Inn 1949; md Joseph Hobson & Son Ltd (Brewers) 1954–74, exec dir Mount Charlotte Investments plc (now Thistle Hotels plc) 1974–95, chm and md Gale Lister & Co Ltd 1975–95; *Recreations* shooting, fishing, farming, old cars; *Style*— Kenneth Pawson, Esq; ✉ Haggas Hall, Weeton, nr Leeds, Yorkshire LS17 0BH (☎ 01423 734200, fax 01423 734731); 59 St Dunstans Rd, London W6 8RE

PAWSON, Michael Edward; s of Edward Basil Pawson (d 1942), of Dyserth, Gwent, and Mary Bertha Batson, *née* Stephens (d 1979); *b* 10 June 1937; *Educ* Marlborough, St Thomas's Hosp Med Sch (MB BS); *m* 12 Aug 1961, Carolyn, da of Robert Cruickshank Handasyde (d 1979), of Kingsmead Cottage, Weybridge, Surrey; 1 s (Robert b 5 Nov 1964), 2 da (Alexandra b 8 Sept 1966, Lara b 23 Jan 1968); *Career* sr lectr Univ of London; Chelsea and Westminster Hosp London: lectr 1970–74, conslt obstetrician (formerly conslt obstetrician and gynaecologist) 1974–, currently clinical dir Assisted Conception Unit; examiner Univ of London and RCOG; chm Br Soc of Psychosomatic Obstetrics, Gynaecology and Andrology 1995–96, memb Exec Ctee Int Soc of Psychosomatic Obstetrics and Gynaecology; memb: Br Fertility Soc, Br Holistic Med Assoc; LRCP, MRCS, MRCOG 1970, FRCOG 1981; *Books* numerous pubns on infertility; *Recreations* first edition book collecting, gardening; *Style*— Michael Pawson, Esq; ✉ 55 Wimpole St, London W1M 7DF (☎ 0171 935 1964)

PAXMAN, Jeremy Dickson; s of Arthur Keith Paxman, formerly of Yorkshire, now resident Queensland, Aust, and Joan McKay, *née* Dickson, of Yorkshire; *b* 11 May 1950; *Educ* Malvern, St Catharine's Coll Cambridge (exhibitioner); *Career* television presenter; journalist Northern Ireland 1974–77, BBC Tonight 1977–79, Panorama (BBC 1) 1979–84, presenter Six O'Clock News (BBC 1) 1985–86, presenter and interviewer Breakfast Time (BBC 1) 1986–89, presenter and interviewer Newsnight (BBC 2) 1989–; presenter: Did You See? (BBC 2) 1991–93, University Challenge (BBC 2) 1994–, You Decide - with Paxman (BBC 1) 1995–96; numerous contribs to newspapers and magazines; RTS Award 1984, Richard Dimbleby Award BAFTA 1996; *Books* A Higher Form of Killing (jtly, 1982), Through the Volcanoes (1985), Friends in High Places (1990), Fish, Fishing and the Meaning of Life (1994); *Recreations* fly fishing, mountains; *Style*— Jeremy Paxman, Esq; ✉ c/o Simpson Fox Associates, 52 Shaftesbury Avenue, London W1V 7DE

PAY, Antony Charles; s of Arthur Morris Pay, of London, and Charlotte Pay; *b* 21 Feb 1945; *Educ* Leyton Co HS, Corpus Christi Coll Cambridge; *m* 14 April 1980, Suki, da of Louis Towb, of Newcastle; 2 s (Sam b 24 April 1981, Mungo b 20 Aug 1984); *Career* principal clarinet and fndr memb London Sinfonietta 1968–83; principal clarinet: Royal Philharmonic Orch 1968–78, Acad of St Martin-in-the-Fields 1979–84; memb: Nash Ensemble 1968–83, Tuckwell Wind Quintet 1973–77; soloist with many orchestras incl: RPO, LPO, Philharmonia, Berlin Radio Orch, San Francisco Symphony, RAI Torino, Acad of St Martin-in-the-Fields, London Sinfonietta; conducted: London Sinfonietta, Acad of St Martin-in-the-Fields, Philharmonia, Royal Philharmonic, San Diego Symphony, Stockholm Philharmonic; *Recordings* Spohr Clarinet Concerti (Atherton, London Sinfonietta, Argo 1978), Mozart Clarinet Concerto (Hogwood, AAM, Decca 1984), Weber Clarinet Concerti (soloist and dir, Orch of Age Enlightenment, Virgin 1988), Crusell Clarinet Concerti (soloist and dir, OAE, Virgin 1990), various chamber music discs; *Recreations* reading, computers; *Style*— Antony Pay, Esq; ✉ c/o Allied Artists, 42 Montpelier Square, London SW7 1JZ (☎ 0171 589 6243, fax 0171 581 5269)

PAYKEL, Prof Eugene Stern; s of Joshua Paykel (d 1962), and Eva, *née* Stern; *b* 9 Sept 1934; *Educ* Auckland GS NZ, Univ of Otago (MB ChB, MD), Univ of Cambridge (MD), Univ of London (DPM); *m* 7 July 1969, Margaret, da of John Melrose (d 1966); 2 s (Nicholas b 1971, Jonathan b 1973); *Career* registrar then sr registrar Maudsley Hosp London 1962–65, asst prof of psychiatry and co-dir (later dir) Depression Res Unit Yale Univ 1966–71, prof of psychiatry St George's Hosp Med Sch Univ of London 1977–85 (consIt and sr lectr 1971–75, reader 1975–77), prof of psychiatry Univ of Cambridge and fell Gonville and Caius Coll 1985–; ed Psychological Med 1994–; pres: Br Assoc for Psychopharmacology 1982–84 (hon sec 1979–82), Marce Soc 1992–94; chief scientist advsr Mental Illness Res Liaison Gp DHSS 1984–88, memb Neuro Sciences Bd MRC 1981–85 and 1995–, tstee Mental Health Fndn 1988–95, chm Jt Ctee on Higher Psychiatric Trg 1991–95 (hon sec 1988–90), chm Pharmacopsychiatry Section and memb Cncl World Psychiatric Assoc 1992–; ed Jl of Affective Disorders 1979–93; formerly examiner: Univ of Edinburgh, Univ of Nottingham, Univ of Manchester, Univ of London, Chinese Univ of Hong Kong; vice pres RCPsych 1994–96 (examiner, chm Social and Community Psychiatry Section 1984–88, cncl memb, memb Exec and Fin Ctee and various other ctees); Foundations Fund Prize for Res in Psychiatry 1978, second prize Anna Monika Stiftung 1985; Maudsley lectr RCPsych 1988; MRCPEd 1960, MRCP 1961, MRCPsych 1971, FRCP 1977, FRCPEd 1978, FRCPsych 1977; *Books* The Depressed Woman (1971), Psychopharmacology of Affective Disorders (1979), Monoamine Oxidase Inhibitors - the State of the Art (1981), Handbook of Affective Disorders (1982, 2 edn 1992), Community Psychiatric Nursing for Neurotic Patients (1983), Depression - an Integrated Approach (1989), Prevention in Psychiatry (1994); *Recreations* opera, music, theatre; *Style*— Prof Eugene Paykel; ✉ Department of Psychiatry, University of Cambridge, Addenbrooke's Hospital, Hills Rd, Cambridge CB2 2QQ (☎ 01223 336961, fax 01223 336968)

PAYMASTER, Dr Nalin Jagmohandas; s of Jagmohandas Varajdas Paymaster, of Bombay, India, and Champa, *née* Shah; *b* 13 April 1933; *Educ* St Teresa's HS Bombay, Univ of Bombay (MB BS, DA), Univ of London (DA), Royal Coll of Anaesthetists (FRCA); *m* 30 Sept 1967, (Marjorie) Elaine, *née* Bankes; 1 s (Rajan b 1972), 1 da (Asha b 1969); *Career* res physician KEM Hosp Bombay 1957–59 (house physician 1956–57), sr house offr in anaesthesia United Liverpool Hosps 1959–60, anaesthetic registrar Liverpool Regnl Hosp Bd 1960–61, sr anaesthetic registrar Newcastle Regnl Hosp Bd 1961–62, fell in anaesthesiology Univ of Pennsylvania Philadelphia 1962–63 and Univ of Washington Seattle 1963–64, consIt anaesthetist Mersey RHA 1965–; author of publications on anaesthetic equipment, local anaesthetic toxicity, pre-medication, intravenous nutrition, post-operative pain, magnesium metabolism, intra cellular pH; presented papers at med confs in USA, Brazil, Sweden, India, Hong Kong, Belgium, Holland and France; memb: Liverpool Soc of Anaesthetists, Birkenhead Med Soc; *Recreations* philately, numismatics, travel, photography, mountain walking, bridge, chess, cricket, table tennis and swimming; *Style*— Dr Nalin J Paymaster; ✉ The Close, Chantry Walk, Lower Heswall, Wirral, Merseyside L60 8PX (☎ 0151 342 4143); Clatterbridge Hospital, Clatterbridge Road, Bebington, Wirral, Merseyside L63 4JY (☎ 0151 334 4000, fax 0151 334 9299)

PAYNE, Alan Jeffrey; CMG (1988); s of Sydney Ellis Payne (d 1967), of Enfield, Middx, and Lydia Ethel, *née* Sweetman (d 1980); *b* 11 May 1933; *Educ* Enfield GS, Queens' Coll Cambridge (exhibitioner); *m* 6 June 1959, Emily Letitia, da of Frank Hodgkinson Freeman (d 1985); 3 s (Richard Andrew b 1960, David Jeffrey b 1963, Jeremy Martin b 1966); *Career* Nat Serv RN 1955–57; EMI Ltd 1957–62, NATO Secretariat Paris 1962–64; HM Dip Serv: entered 1965, first sec Kuala Lumpur 1967–70, asst head SW Pacific Dept FCO 1970–72, head Commercial Dept Br Embassy Budapest 1972–75, dep head Mission on promotion to cnsllr Br Embassy Mexico City 1975–79, head Mexico and Caribbean Dept FCO then Mexico and Central America Dept FCO 1979–82, consul general Lyons 1982–87, Br high cmmr Kingston Jamaica and non resident ambass Port-au-Prince Haiti 1987–89; sec gen International Primary Aluminium Inst (IPAI) 1989–; FIL 1962; *Recreations* theatre, music, restoring old cars; *Style*— Alan Payne, Esq, CMG; ✉ IPAI, 8 Floor, New Zealand House, Haymarket, London SW1Y 4TE

PAYNE, Anthony Edward; s of Edward Alexander Payne (d 1958), and Muriel Margaret Elsie, *née* Stroud (d 1991); *b* 2 Aug 1936; *Educ* Dulwich, Univ of Durham (BA); *m* 24 Sept 1966, Jane Marian, da of Gerald Manning (d 1987); *Career* composer; visiting Milhaud prof of music Mills Coll Oakland California 1983, teacher in composition NSW Conservatorium Sydney Aust 1986; memb: Soc for the Promotion of New Music (chm 1969–71), Macnaghten Concerts Soc (chm 1965–67), Myra Hess Tst, Boise Mendelssohn Fndn, Composers' Guild of GB, Assoc of Professional Composers; artistic dir Spitalfields Festival; *Works* incl: Phoenix Mass 1968–72, Paean (for solo piano, 1971), Concerto for Orchestra (1974), The World's Winter (for soprano and 8 players, 1976), String Quartet (1978), The Stones and Lonely Places Sing (for 7 players, 1979), The Song of the Clouds (for oboe and orchestra, 1980), A Day in the Life of a Mayfly (for 6 players 1981), Evening Land (for soprano and piano, 1981), Spring's Shining Wake (for orchestra 1981), Songs and Seascapes (for strings 1984), The Spirit's Harvest (for orchestra 1985), The Song Streams in the Firmament (for 6 players 1986), Half Heard in the Stillness (for orchestra, 1987), Consort Music for String Quintet (1987), Sea Change (for 7 players, 1988), Time's Arrow (for orchestra, 1990), Symphonies of Wind and Rain (for chamber orchestra, 1991), A Hidden Music (for orchestra, 1992), The Seeds Long Hidden..... (orchestral variations, 1994), Empty Landscape - Heart's Ease (for 6 players, 1995); *Books* Schoenberg (1968), Frank Bridge Radical and Conservative (1984); *Recreations* films, British countryside; *Style*— Anthony Payne, Esq; ✉ 2 Wilton Square, London N1 3DL (☎ 0171 359 1593, fax 0171 226 4369)

PAYNE, Prof Anthony Philip; s of Philip Charles Payne, and Pamela Burgoyne, *née* Daniels (d 1982); *b* 9 July 1947; *Educ* Eastbourne GS, Univ of Reading (BSc), Univ of Birmingham (PhD); *m* 28 July 1970, Ruth Mary, da of Donald Jack Beake; 2 s (Christopher Jeremy b 7 Nov 1977, Alexander Richard b 24 Jan 1980); *Career* MRC jr res fell Dept of Anatomy Univ of Birmingham 1971–73; Dept of Anatomy Univ of Glasgow: temp lectr 1973–76, lectr 1976–84, sr lectr 1984–94, head 1993– (acting head 1990–92), prof 1994–; memb: The Anatomical Soc (memb Cncl 1993–), Euro Neuroscience Assoc, Soc for Endocrinology, Soc for the Study of Fertility; *Books* Social Behaviour in Vertebrates (1976), Animal Behaviour (consulting ed, 1976 and 1980); *Recreations* reading, ornithology; *Style*— Prof Anthony Payne; ✉ 16 St Kilda Drive, Jordanhill, Glasgow G14 9JN (☎ 0141 959 3927); Laboratory of Human Anatomy, University of Glasgow, Glasgow G12 8QQ (☎ 0141 339 8855 ext 5869, fax 0141 330 4299)

PAYNE, Prof Christopher Charles; OBE (1997); s of Rupert George Payne (d 1990), and Evelyn Violet, *née* Abbott (d 1981); *b* 15 May 1946; *Educ* Bexley GS, Wadham Coll Oxford (Minor scholar, MA, Christopher Welch scholar, Sr scholar, DPhil Forestry); *m* 1 Sept 1969, Margaret Susan, da of William Roy Street; 1 da (Katherine Ruth b 11 Nov 1970), 1 s (Robert James b 22 Dec 1971); *Career* post doctoral fell Dept of Microbiology Univ of Otago NZ 1972–73, sr scientific offr Unit of Invertebrate Virology NERC Oxford 1973–77; Glasshouse Crops Res Inst (GCRI) Littlehampton: head Insect Virus Section 1977–83, head Entomology and Insect Pathology Dept 1983–87; head Crop and Environment Protection Div AFRC E Malling 1987–90, chief exec Horticulture Res Int Wellesbourne 1990–; hon prof: Dept of Biological Sciences Univ of Warwick 1991–, Sch of Biological Sciences Univ of Birmingham 1995–; pres: Soc for Invertebrate Pathology 1992–94, Assoc of Applied Biologists 1995–96; FIHort 1991, FIBiol 1995; *Books* Dictionary and Directory of Animal, Plant and Bacterial Viruses (with F Brown and R Hull, 1989); *Recreations* cycling, walking, gardening; *Clubs* Farmers', Cyclists' Touring, Audax UK; *Style*— Prof Christopher Payne, OBE; ✉ 25 Chapel Street, Wellesbourne, Warwick CV35 9QU (☎ 01789 842562); Horticulture Research International, Wellesbourne, Warwick CV35 9EF (☎ 01789 472041, fax 01789 470363, car 0850 717388)

PAYNE, Christopher Frederick; CBE (1987), QPM (1975), DL (Cleveland 1983 and N Yorks 1996); s of Cdr Gerald Frederick Payne, OBE, BEM, QPM (d 1979), of Wallington, Surrey, and Amy Florence Elizabeth, *née* Parker (d 1989); *b* 15 Feb 1930; *Educ* Christ's Coll Finchley, Hendon Tech Coll; *m* 4 Oct 1952, Barbara Janet, da of Herbert Charles Saxby (d 1944), of Hampstead Way, Hampstead; 1 s (Roger b 1961), 3 da (Gillian b 1954, Adrianne b 1956, Valerie b 1965); *Career* Nat Serv Intelligence Corps 1948–50; Met Police: joined 1950, chief inspector Ops Branch 1963, supt and chief supt Hammersmith 1965–68, sr command course 1965, HO R and D Branch 1968–70, chief supt D Dist 1970–71, cdr X Dist 1971–74, cdr Airport Dist 1974–76, chief constable of Cleveland Constabulary 1976–90, chm Public Order Ctee ACPO 1981–88, dep regnl police cdr (designate) no 2 Home Def Region 1984–90, consIt Disaster Planning & Mgmnt 1990–, sr visiting res fell Univ of Bradford 1991–, advsr Queensland Govt Chemical Hazards Unit 1989–90, memb UNDRO External Servs 1990–, emergency planning advsr Br Red Cross Cleveland 1990–; pres Teesside Branch Inst of Mgmnt 1991–, memb Cncl Inst of Mgmnt 1994–; dep chm Met Police Friendly Soc 1971–76, police advsr to ACC Social Servs Ctee 1979–90, cdr St John Ambulance Cleveland 1985–89 (co dir 1978–85); chm: Cleveland Mental Health Support Gp 1981–86, St John Cncl Cleveland 1986–89, Castlegate Quay Heritage Tst 1992–; vice pres Cleveland Youth Assoc 1983–, vice chm Royal Jubilee and Prince's Tsts Ctee for Durham and Cleveland 1984–90; pres Chief Constables' Club 1989–90; author of various articles on contingency planning and management; CStJ 1985; Freeman City of London 1987; CIMgt 1988; *Recreations* painting, philately, gardening; *Clubs* Cleveland; *Style*— Christopher Payne,

Esq, CBE, QPM, DL; ✉ c/o The Chief Constable's Office, PO Box 70, Ladgate, Middlesbrough, Cleveland TS8 9EH

PAYNE, David John Allen; s of late Harry Payne, and late Edith Mary, *née* Kirby; *b* 29 July 1928; *Educ* Canterbury, Farnham, Brighton Coll of Art, Royal Acad Schs; *m* 11 Aug 1951, Iris Jean, da of late James Freeman; 1 s (Mark Allen b 21 April 1961), 1 da (Mary Anne b 30 Dec 1956); *Career* oil and watercolour artist; former sr lectr Bedford Coll of Higher Education; exhibited: Ash Barn Gallery Petersfield 1978–80, Bedford Sch 1973–76, The Gallery Wellingborough 1983–85, Ellingham Mill 1979–82, sponsored exhibition at Sotheby's 1981, Portal Gallery 1986, RA 1976, 1978–87, 1989, 1991, 1992 and 1995, New Ashgate Gallery Farnham 1987, Singer & Friedlander/Sunday Times Watercolour Exhibition 1991, 1992, 1993 and 1994, RWS 1992–95, NEAC 1992–94; work in permanent collections incl Beds CC Educn Loan Serv; *Style*— David Payne, Esq

PAYNE, Harold Lloyd; CBE (1996, OBE 1972); s of Horace Frederick Payne (d 1956), of Blackheath, and Dora Kate, *née* Lloyd (d 1972); *b* 16 Oct 1920; *Educ* City of London Sch; *m* 12 June 1947, Mary Mildred, da of William George Hill (d 1951), of Blackheath; 1 da (Lorna b 1949); *Career* TA HAC 1939, II Regt RHA 1939, cmmnd 137 FD Regt RA 1941 (Japanese POW 1942–45); dir Lloyd's Insurance Brokers 1937–80, memb Lloyd's 1949–88; forest owner 1974–; vice chm Far East Fund, memb Cncl Br Serv and Ex-Serv Orgns (vice chm 1982–92); vice chm and tstee Queen Mary's Roehampton Tst, pres Nat Fedn of Far Eastern POW Assocs 1973–; memb: Bd of Govrs Westminster Hosp Gp 1970–74, Central Advsy Ctee War Pensions, Br Membs' Cncl World Veterans Fedn; vice chm Kent War Pensions Ctee 1992 (chm 1991–92); Freeman City of London 1951, Liveryman Worshipful Co of Carmen 1952; *Recreations* rugby, gardening; *Clubs* City Livery, Guild of Freemen; *Style*— Harold L Payne, Esq, CBE; ✉ Long View, 18 Whybourne Crest, Tunbridge Wells, Kent TN2 5BS (☎ 01892 527024); Foresters, Girnwood, Hawick, Roxburghshire, Scotland TD9 7PN (☎ 01450 880203)

PAYNE, Keith Howard; s of Sydney William John Payne (d 1990), and Jean Emily, *née* Blower (d 1966); *b* 16 July 1937; *Educ* Shooters Hill GS; *m* 1, Dec 1972 (m dis); m 2, 23 Nov 1984, Tania Jeannette, da of Frank John Trevisani; 1 da (Francesca Jean b 13 April 1987); *Career* Nat Serv personal staff Dep SACEUR SHAPE Paris 1955–57; fin journalist The Times 1958–68 (first banking 1965–68); Charles Barker City 1968–91: dir 1970–74, asst md 1974–76, md 1976–80, dep chief exec and vice chm 1980–84, dep chm 1984–91; dir Charles Barker Ltd 1988–92; dep chm: Georgeson & Co Ltd 1992–95, Tavistock Communications Ltd 1995–; Freedom Nova Scotia Province (following journalistic visit with The Times) 1965; MIPR; *Recreations* swimming, walking, theatre; *Style*— Keith Payne, Esq; ✉ Tavistock Communications Limited, 1 Angel Court, London EC2R 7HX (☎ 0171 600 2288, fax 0171 600 5084)

PAYNE, Kevin Jacques; s of Arthur Harold Payne (d 1982), and Margarita, *née* Bussell; *b* 6 May 1956; *Educ* Chelsea Coll London (BSc); *m* 5 May 1990, Jacqueline Kim, *née* Setchell; *Career* scientific res Immunology Dept Chelsea Coll 1977–80, asst ed Golf Illustrated 1980–82, md Kempsters PR 1987–91 (joined 1982), jt md De Facto Consultants 1991–, dir Genus Communications 1994–; MIPR 1985 (vice chm Wessex Branch 1990–91); *Recreations* scouting (medal of merit 1991, long service medal 1991, asst leader trainer 1992); *Style*— Kevin Payne, Esq; ✉ De Facto Consultants, Essex House, Essex Road, Basingstoke, Hants RG21 8SU (☎ 01256 842274, fax 01256 469308)

PAYNE, Michael Anthony; s of late Albert John Payne, and Beryl Kathleen Cavey, *née* Slater; *b* 2 Sept 1939; *Educ* Stowe, City of Westminster Coll, Open Univ (BA); *m* 1965, Elizabeth Harvieston, da of Alan Brown, of Scotland; 1 s (Toby b 1970), 1 da (Sophie b 1968); *Career* Nat Serv 2 Lt Royal Regt of Artillery 1960–62, gunner HAC TA, Capt 254 FD Regt RA TA; co sec: Hill Samuel and Co (Jersey) Ltd 1978–88, Hill Samuel Jersey Ltd 1984–95, Hill Samuel Bank (Jersey) Ltd; dir: Hill Samuel (CI) Tst Co Ltd 1979–95, Hill Samuel Fund Mangrs (Jersey) Ltd 1982–95; mangr private clients Mourant du Feu & Jenne 1995–; MIMgt, fell Chartered Assoc of Certified Accountants; Hon ADC to Lieut Govr of Jersey 1990–95; *Recreations* historical reading, glass engraving; *Clubs* Honorable Artillery Co, United (Jersey); *Style*— Michael Payne, Esq; ✉ 3 Ashley Close, Bagatelle Rd, St Saviour, Jersey, CI JE2 7TY; Mourant du Feu & Jenne, 22 Grenville Street, St Helier, Jersey, CI JE4 8PX (☎ 01534 609220, fax 01534 609330)

PAYNE, Michael William; s of Albert Leonard Payne, MM, RFC (d 1955), of Orpington, Kent, and Grace Maud, *née* Lyon (d 1974); *b* 18 April 1927; *Educ* Dulwich; *m* 2 June 1951, Angela Margaret Westmacott, da of Hugh Sherwood Leary (d 1955); 2 s (Thomas b 1965, William b 1968), 2 da (Susan b 1952, Sally b 1956); *Career* Sgt RAF 1945–48; underwriter 1948–68; active underwriter: Sir William Garthwaite & Others 1969–71, Michael Payne & Others 1973–91; sr ptnr Michael Payne & Partners 1967–; exec chm Janson Payne Management Ltd 1986–90, dir Janson Green Ltd 1986–92 (dep chm 1990–92); exec chm: Oakwood Underwriting Agencies Ltd 1991–96 Sedgwick Oakwood Lloyd's Underwriting Agencies Ltd 1996–; dir HIH Winterthur Australia 1992–; chm and chief exec: HIH (UK) Ltd, HIH European Holdings Ltd; chm 'Integer' Lloyd's Underwriting Members Mutual Club Ltd 1992–, dir Gerling Global Reinsurance (UK) Ltd 1994–; memb Lloyd's Law Reform Ctee 1968–95 (jt chm 1973–84, chm 1991–95); vice pres Insur Inst of London 1969; Freeman City of London 1979, memb Worshipful Co of Insurers 1980; *Books* Modern Requirements in Liability Insurance (1968); *Recreations* golf, sailing, opera, music; *Clubs* City of London; *Style*— Michael Payne, Esq; ✉ Wroughton, 47 Sundridge Ave, Bromley, Kent (☎ 0181 460 4924, fax 0181 313 3536); Shene Cottage, Vicarage St, Colyton, Devon (☎ 01297 552621); Sedgwick Oakwood Lloyd's Underwriting Agencies Ltd, Sackville House, 143–152 Fenchurch Street, London EC3M 6BN (☎ 0171 825 7200, fax 0171 825 7212)

PAYNE, (Geoffrey John) Nicholas; s of John Laurence Payne (d 1961), and Dorothy Gwendoline, *née* Attenborough; *b* 4 Jan 1945; *Educ* Eton, Trinity Coll Cambridge (BA); *m* 6 Jan 1986, Linda Jane, da of Donald Wallace Adamson (d 1992), of Bristol; 2 s (Ralph John Anthony b 1986, Oliver Nicholas Pearsall b 1988); *Career* fin asst Royal Opera House 1968–70, subsid offr Arts Cncl of GB 1970–76, fin controller WNO 1976–82, gen admin Opera North 1982–93, artistic co-ordinator Leeds Festival 1990, dir Royal Opera 1993–; *Style*— Nicholas Payne, Esq; ✉ Royal Opera House, Covent Garden, London WC2E 9DD (☎ 0171 240 1200, fax 0171 497 0070)

PAYNE, Sir Norman John; kt (1985), CBE (1976, OBE 1956, MBE 1944); s of late Frederick Payne, of Folkestone; *b* 9 Oct 1921; *Educ* John Lyon Sch Harrow, City and Guilds Coll London; *m* 1946 (sep), Pamela Vivien, *née* Wallis; 4 s, 1 da; *Career* Capt RE (despatches twice), served India and Burma; ptnr Sir Frederick Snow & Ptnrs 1955 (joined 1949); chm: Br Airports Authy 1977–87 (chief exec 1972–77), BAA plc 1987–91, ret; Hon DTech Loughborough Univ, fell Imperial Coll 1989; FEng 1984, FCGI, FICE, FCIT, FIHT, Companion RAeS 1987; *Recreations* gardening, swimming; *Style*— Sir Norman Payne, CBE, FEng; ✉ L'Abri, La Route des Merriennes, St Martin, Guernsey GY4 6NS, Channel Islands (☎ 01481 37302, fax 01481 39786)

PAYNE, Richard; s of Capt Matt Payne (d 1937), and Ellen Rosina, *née* Burdett (d 1989); *b* 26 June 1935; *Educ* Lancing, De Havilland Aeronautical Sch; *m* 30 Nov 1957, Ann Helen, da of Cyril Philip de Muschamp Porritt (d 1976); 2 s ((Peter) Matt, (Alexander) Richard de Muschamp), 1 da ((Helen) Annabel); *Career* supplies engr De Havilland's 1958–60, design and project engr Norris Bros consulting engrs 1961–62, tech mangr Kluber GmbH 1963–65, consulting engr 1966–68, chm Thurne Engineering Co Ltd 1970–93 (fndr 1969, md 1969–85), md Edward Hines (engineers) Ltd 1970–89, md and chm Bronpole Group 1975–93; fndr 1985: Thurne GmbH Germany, Thurne Corporation; chm Estuary Engineering 1989–93 (bought out by Thurne Engineering Co 1975); dir: Richard Payne & Associates Ltd 1994–, Production Performance Ltd 1994–; GIMechE; *Recreations* sailing, skiing, gardening, reading; *Clubs* Norfolk; *Style*— Richard Payne, Esq; ✉ Bale Hall, Bale, Norfolk NR21 9DA (☎ 0132 877 467); Richard Payne & Associates Ltd, Field Dalling Road, Bale, Norfolk NR21 0QS

PAYNE, Richard William Newth; s of Stuart Dean Payne (d 1954), of Surrey, and Kathleen Amelia, *née* Newth (d 1981); *b* 14 Dec 1930; *Educ* Tonbridge, Univ of Bristol (BA); *m* 30 May 1964, Ann, da of David Windover Millard, of Surrey; 2 s (William b 1965, Timothy b 1967), 1 da (Annabel b 1971), 1 step s (Andrew b 1956), 1 step da (Sarah b 1959); *Career* CA; W H Payne & Co: ptnr 1955–95, sr ptnr 1974–95, conslt 1995–; dir: Marlowe Investments (Kent) Ltd 1962–, Millard Estates Ltd 1980–; *Recreations* golf, gardening, bridge; *Clubs* MCC, Croham Hurst Golf; *Style*— Richard Payne, Esq; ✉ Broadway, 11 Landscape Rd, Warlingham, Surrey CR6 9JB; W H Payne & Co, Sandringham House, 199 Southwark Bridge Rd, London SE1 0HA (☎ 0171 407 7752)

PAYNE, Lt-Col Robert Arnold; OBE (1996), JP (1963); s of Robert William Tom Payne (d 1974), and Esther Victoria, *née* Elliott (d 1967); *b* 21 Sept 1919; *Educ* Finchley HS, Finchley Co GS; *m* 20 May 1950, Audrey Mary Jean, da of David Bradford; 2 da (Jean Elizabeth b 6 July 1952, Patricia Mary (twin) b 6 July 1952); *Career* WWII Duke of Cornwall's LI 1939–40, cmmnd Beds Herts Regt 1940, Inf Signals Instr 1940, Orkney & Shetland Def Force 1941–42, Instr 160 Sp Gp OCTU 1942–43, 2 Bn Essex Regt 1944–45, Q staff 49 Inf Div HQ 1945–46; RARO 1949, Herts ACF 1953–61; Dep Co Cadet Cmdt 1958–61; memb: ACF Nat Trg Ctee 1961–63, Advsy Panel ACF Duke of Edinburgh's Award 1963–87; hon first aid trg advsr Army and Combined Cadet Forces 1961–87; sr sec and accountancy asst Br Iron and Steel Corp 1948–52, sec and dir subsid co Int Aeradio Ltd 1952–77, sec and fin conslt 1977–84; memb: Middx branch Magistrates Assoc Exec Ctee 1977–87 (chm 1984–87), St John Ambulance 1936–93 (dep cmmr London (Prince of Wales's) Dist 1969–78); Cdr Co of Buckinghamshire 1978–93, memb Cncl Order of St John Bucks 1978– (vice chm 1978–93), memb Branch Ctee Royal Br Legion 1983– (chm 1985–89), memb Royal Soc of St George 1990–, hon sec Chiltern Open Air Museum Enterprises Ltd 1991–; hon treas: Middlesex Victoria Fund 1989–, Middlesex King Edward VII Meml Fund 1989–; Freeman City of London 1974, Liveryman Worshipful Co of Scriveners 1978; FCIS 1952, FIMgt 1970, FFA 1977; Offr Cross of Merit Sovereign Military Order of Malta 1971; KStJ 1975; *Recreations* voluntary community activities, stamp collecting; *Style*— Lt-Col Robert Payne, OBE, JP; ✉ 72 Amersham Rd, Little Chalfont, Amersham, Bucks HP6 6SL (☎ and fax 01494 764900)

PAYNE, Robert Gardiner; s of Dr Robert Orlando Payne (d 1989), and Frances Elisabeth, *née* Jackson (d 1987); *b* 12 July 1933; *Educ* Lady Barn House Sch, Packwood Haugh, Clifton, Trinity Hall Cambridge (MA); *m* 11 April 1964, Diana Catalina, da of Rupert Henry Marchington, of Wilton Crescent, Alderley Edge, Cheshire; 1 s (Philip Robert b 1968), 2 da (Frances Patricia b 1967, Emily Diana b 1972); *Career* Nat Serv 2 Lt RA 1952–54; admitted slr 1961; ptnr: Skelton and Co (Manchester) 1963–66, March Pearson and Skelton 1966–91, Pannone March Pearson (now Pannone & Partners) 1992–; chm: FWA (Family Welfare Assoc), Lady Barn House Sch; memb Law Soc; *Recreations* opera, tennis, skiing, walking; *Style*— Robert Payne, Esq; ✉ Bradford Lodge, Bradford Lane, Over Alderley, Macclesfield, Cheshire SK10 4UE (☎ 01625 583156); Pannone & Partners, 123 Deansgate, Manchester M3 2BU (☎ 0161 832 3000, fax 0161 834 2067, telex 668172)

PAYNE, Roger Jeremy; JP; s of Gordon Edgar Payne, OBE, JP (d 1988), and Dorothy Esther Payne (d 1995); *b* 14 Dec 1937; *Educ* Wycliffe Coll Stonehouse Glos, Birmingham Sch of Architecture (DipArch); *m* 22 Aug 1964, Mary Nanette (d 1996), da of William Henry Davis (d 1984); 1 s (Mark b 1969), 1 da (Sarah b 1972); *Career* sr ptnr Preece Payne Partnership, proprietor Roger Payne Associates; dir: Abbeybridge Property Group Ltd, West Country Motor Hotel Services, Preece Payne Consultant (Gibraltar); memb Br Equity, RIBA; *Recreations* theatre, power boating; *Clubs* Royal Yachting Assoc; *Style*— Roger Payne, Esq, JP; ✉ 323 Painswick Road, Gloucester GL4 4QJ; 39 Garbinell, Punta Montgo, L'Escala, Gerona, Spain; Roger Payne Associates, St Luke's House, 3 Llanthony Road, Gloucester GL1 5QT (☎ 01452 386518, fax 01452 387518, mobile 0374 249481)

PAYNTER, Cecil de Camborne Pendarves; s of late Col E Pendarves Paynter, TD, and late Cicely Marion, *née* Hadow; *b* 17 July 1930; *Educ* Summer Fields, Wellington Coll, RMA Sandhurst; *m* 29 July 1961, Fiona Marion Naismith; 2 s (Michael John Pendarves b 1963, Andrew Francis de Camborne b 1965); *Career* Capt 3 King's Own Hussars, airborne trg offr N Somerset Yeo 1951–54; regnl retail mangr RHM 1955–60, md Magnet Signs and Joinery 1960–63, chm LGT Co 1963–96, dir English Wine Consortium 1989–93; formerly dir Wine Standards Bd 1989–92, formerly memb Bd of Tstees Wine and Spirits Educn Tst 1984–90, Cncl memb South of England Agric Show and Soc 1988–96, gp chm Royal Br Legion W Kent 1986–93; vice pres Riverpoint (care of homeless people London); memb Ct of Assts Worshipful Co of Vintners (Master 1993); *Recreations* country pursuits, golf, cricket, fishing, viticulture; *Clubs* Army and Navy; *Style*— C de C P Paynter, Esq; ✉ Rookery Cottage, Hever, nr Edenbridge, Kent TN8 7LR (☎ 01342 850350, fax 0171 236 8177)

PAYNTER, Prof John Frederick; OBE (1985); s of Frederick Albert Paynter (d 1968), and Rose Alice, *née* Garbutt (d 1963); *b* 17 July 1931; *Educ* Emanuel Sch London, Trinity Coll of Music London, Univ of York (DPhil); *m* 25 July 1956, Elizabeth, da of Matthew George Hill; 1 da (Catherine Elizabeth b 12 Aug 1957); *Career* teacher primary and secdy schs 1954–62, lectr in music City of Liverpool Coll of Educn 1962–65, princ lectr in music Bishop Otter Coll Chichester 1965–69; Dept of Music Univ of York: lectr 1969, sr lectr 1974–82, prof 1982–94 (pt/t 1994–), head of dept 1983–94; dir Schs Cncl Project Music in the Secdy Sch Curriculum; int lectures in music educn, books translated into numerous languages; compositions incl: Landscapes (1972), The Windhover (1972), Galaxies for Orchestra (1977), String Quartet no 1 (1981), The Inviolable Voice (1982), Piano Sonata (1987), String Quartet no 2 (1991), Four Sculptures of Austin Wright (for viola and orchestra, 1991, revised 1994), Time After Time (1991); Hon GSM Guildhall Sch of Music London; FRSA 1987; *Books* Sound and Silence (1970), Hear and Now (1972), The Dance and the Drum (1974), Music in the Secondary School Curriculum (1982), Sound and Structure (1992); *Style*— Prof John Paynter, OBE; ✉ Department of Music, University of York, Heslington, York YO1 5DD (☎ 01904 432453, fax 01904 432450)

PAYTON, Roger Louis; s of Leonard Joseph Payton (d 1984), and Vera Mary, *née* Crepin; *b* 18 Oct 1930; *Educ* Caterham, Univ of London (LLB); *m* 10 May 1958, Geraldine Eyre, da of Wilfrid Farley (d 1974); 1 s (Christopher b 1961), 1 da (Jane b 1959); *Career* admitted slr 1958; dir: Baring Bros & Co Ltd 1969–84, Davies & Newman Holdings plc 1985–92, Morland & Co plc 1985–95, Stewart Underwriting plc 1985–, Roskel plc 1986–; dep chm Great Portland Estates plc 1991–; chm: Richardsons Westgarth plc 1988– (dir 1972–), Rothsay Holdings Ltd 1993– (dir 1985–), Jarvis plc 1994–; also chm: Bishopsgate Fndn 1979–81, Metropolitan Public Gardens Assoc 1991–; Master Worshipful Co of Gardeners 1981–82, Liveryman City of London Solicitors' Co; FRSA, FInstD; *Recreations* gardening, tennis; *Clubs* Savile; *Style*— Roger L Payton, Esq; ✉ Little Bedwell, Essendon, Hatfield, Herts AL9 6JA (☎ 01707 642623); Great Portland Estates plc, Knighton House, 56 Mortimer Street, London W1N 8BD (☎ 0171 580 3040, fax 0171 631 5169)

PEACE, Dr David Brian; MBE (1977); s of Herbert W F Peace (d 1951), of Sheffield, and Mabel, *née* Hammond (d 1915); *b* 13 March 1915; *Educ* Mill Hill Sch, Univ of Sheffield; *m* 2 Sept 1939, Jean Margaret, da of Rev McEwan Lawson, of Mill Hill; 2 da (Rachel (Mrs D Davies) b 1942, Juliet (Mrs C R Johnson) b 1946); *Career* WWII Airfield Construction Serv RAF Sqdn Ldr 1942–46; town planner: Staffs CC 1948–61, dep co planning offr and head of environmental planning Cambs CC 1961–80, DOE Appeals Inspectorate 1980–82; glass engraver specialising in lettering and heraldry; 12 one man shows since 1956, retrospective exhibition 1990; 26 works in public collections incl: V & A, Fitzwilliam & Kettle's Yard Cambridge, Broadfield House Nat Museum of Glass Stourbridge, Corning Museum USA, Keatley Tst collection; windows, screens, doors and other glass in over 40 churches incl: St Nicholas Liverpool, St Albans Cathedral, Manchester Cathedral, Westminster Abbey, St Nicholas Whitehaven, St Botolph Aldgate, Gray's Inn Chapel, St Mary's Cambridge; coll and church work since 1986 with Sally Scott incl Westminster Abbey, Lancaster and Sheffield Univs, St John's Coll Cambridge, Lincoln Coll Oxford, Norwich Cathedral, Burwell Church Cambs, Christ the Cornerstone Milton Keynes; memb: Ely Diocesan Advsy Ctee 1963–, Cncl for Br Archaeology 1965–85; Master Art Workers' Guild 1973, Liveryman Worshipful Co of Glaziers 1977, first chm Guild of Glass Engravers 1975–80 (pres 1980–86), pres Assoc for Studies in Conservation of Historic Bldgs 1994, vice pres Betjeman Soc 1996; Hon DScTech Univ of Sheffield 1991; ARIBA 1938, RTPI 1948 (memb Cncl 1961–62 and 1972–73), FSA 1975; *Publications* Glass engraving: Lettering and Design (1985), The Engraved Glass of David Peace - the Architecture of Lettering (1990), Historic Buildings Maps and Guides: Peak District (1954), North Wales (1958), A Guide to Historic Buildings Law 'The Cambridgeshire Guide' (originator, 1965), Eric Gill: The Inscriptions - A Descriptive Catalogue (1994); various publications on historic conservation; *Recreations* townscape, heraldry; *Clubs* Arts; *Style—* Dr David Peace, MBE, FSA; ✉ Abbots End, Hemingford Abbots, Huntingdon, Cambs PE18 9AA (☎ 01480 462472)

PEACE, Prof Richard Arthur; s of Herman Peace (d 1991), of Otley, W Yorks, and Dorothy, *née* Wall (d 1993); *b* 22 Feb 1933; *Educ* Ilkley GS, Keble Coll Oxford (MA, BLitt); *m* 18 Oct 1960, (Shirley Mary) Virginia, da of Capt William George Wright (d 1969), of London; 1 s (Henry Richard b 24 April 1964, d 25 Sept 1975), 2 da (Mary b 7 April 1967, Catherine b 14 Jan 1969); *Career* prof of Russian: Univ of Hull 1975–84, Univ of Bristol 1984–94 (lectr 1963, sr lectr 1972–75); prof emeritus Univ of Bristol 1994–; pres Br Univs Assoc of Slavists 1977–80; *Books* Dostoevsky: An Examination of The Major Novels (1971), The Enigma of Gogol (1981), Chekhov: A Study of The Four Major Plays (1983), Oblomov: A Critical Examination of Goncharov's Novel (1991), Dostoevsky's Notes from Underground (1993), Gogol: Village Evenings near Dikanka (introduction and bibliography, 1994), Dostoevsky: Crime and Punishment (introduction and notes, 1995); *Recreations* fishing; *Style—* Prof Richard Peace; ✉ Department of Russian Studies, University of Bristol, 17 Woodland Road, Bristol BS8 1TE (☎ 0117 930 3030 ext 3516, fax 0117 928 8188)

PEACEY, Col John Capel (Charles); *b* 11 Dec 1928; *Educ* Marlborough, Bournemouth Municipal Coll (Dip Mech Eng); *m* 17 July 1954, Dr Jean Menzies Peacey, *née* Thirlby; 2 da (Susan (Mrs Graves), Diana (Mrs Taine)); *Career* cmmnd RE 1949; various professional engrg appts UK, Malaya, Germany and Singapore 1950–71, SO I Logistics Petroleum AFSOUTH Naples Italy 1971–73, chief instr Electrical and Mechanical Sch RSME Chatham 1973–75, CRE specialist team RE acting as consltg engrs for Govt of Malta 1975–77, cdr RE team Br Mil Mission to Saudi Nat Guard Riyadh Saudi Arabia 1978–80, chief of infrastructure progs and SACEUR's rep on NATO Infrastructure Ctee 1980–83, ret; dep sec Assoc of Consulting Engrs 1984–94 (conslt 1994–95); memb Mgmnt Ctee ICE Benevolent Fund 1994–96, hon treas RE Assoc 1995; Freeman City of London, Liveryman Worshipful Co of Engrs 1986; FICE, FIMechE; *Recreations* golf, family bridge, gardening, conservation, local history; *Style—* Col Charles Peacey; ✉ 46 Riverside Court, Nine Elms Lane, London SW8 5BY (☎ 0171 627 2818); The Old Grain House, 27 High Street, Bourn, Cambs CB3 7SQ (☎ 01954 718310)

PEACH, Prof (Guthlac) Ceri Klaus; s of Wystan Adams Peach, and Charlotte Marianne, *née* Klaus; *b* 26 Oct 1939; *Educ* Howardian HS Cardiff, Merton Coll Oxford (MA, DPhil); *m* 1964, Susan Lesley, *née* Godfrey; 2 s, 1 da; *Career* Univ of Oxford: demonstrator 1964–66, faculty lectr in geography 1966–92, prof of social geography 1992–, head of dept Sch of Geography 1995–; fell and tutor St Catherine's Coll Oxford 1969– (sometime dean, sr tutor and bursar, pro-master 1993–94); visiting fell Dept of Demography Australian Nat Univ 1973, visiting prof Dept of Sociology Yale Univ 1977, Fulbright visiting prof Dept of Geography Univ of California Berkeley 1985; *Books* West Indian Migration to Britain: a social geography (1968), Urban Social Segregation (ed, 1975), Ethnic Segregation in Cities (co-ed, 1981), South Asians Overseas (co-ed, 1990), The Ethnic Minority Populations of Great Britain (1996); *Recreations* travelling, reading, computing; *Style—* Prof Ceri Peach; ✉ St Catherine's College, Oxford OX1 3UJ (☎ 01865 271700)

PEACH, Denis Alan; CB (1985); s of Richard Peach (d 1979), of Worthing, and Alice Ellen, *née* Fraser (d 1982); *b* 10 Jan 1928; *Educ* Selhurst GS; *m* 1957, Audrey Hazel, da of Allan Chamberlain (d 1970); *Career* Home Office 1946–82 (asst under-sec of state 1974–82); chief charity cmmr 1982–88; *Recreations* painting, gardening; *Clubs* Reform; *Style—* Denis Peach, Esq, CB

PEACH, Sir Leonard Harry (Len); s of Harry Peach (d 1985), of Walsall, Staffs, and Beatrice Lilian, *née* Tuck (d 1978); *b* 17 Dec 1932; *Educ* Queen Mary's GS Walsall, Pembroke Coll Oxford (MA), LSE (Dip Personnel Mgmnt); *m* 15 March 1958, Doreen Lilian, da of John Roland Barker (d 1979), of W Molesey, Surrey; 2 s (Mark Philip b 1964, David John b 1967); *Career* Nat Serv 1951–53, 2 Lt 1 Bn S Lancs Regt 1952; Capt TA 5 Bn S Staffs Regt 1953–65; res asst to Randolph S Churchill 1956, various personnel mgmnt appts 1956–71; dir IBM: UK Rentals 1971–76, UK Holdings 1976–85 and 1989–92, Pensions Trust 1976–85 and 1989–92; gp dir personnel IBM (Europe, Africa, ME) 1972–75, dir of personnel and corp affrs IBM UK Ltd 1975–85 and 1989 (dir of personnel 1971–72), pres IPM 1983–85, seconded to DHSS as dir of personnel NHS Mgmnt Bd 1985–86, chief exec NHS Mgmnt Bd and memb NHS Supervisory Bd 1986–89; chm: IPM Services Ltd, NHS Trg Authy 1986–91, Skillbase Ltd 1990–94, IPD Enterprises Ltd 1994–; cmmr for public appts (first appointee) Dec 1995–; dir: Nationwide Building Society 1990–93, Coutts Consulting Group plc 1993–, Personal Investment Authy 1993–; chm: Policy Studies Institute 1991–, Police Complaints Authy 1992–95, Univ of Westminster 1993–; dep chm Nationwide Pension Fund 1991–; pres: Manpower Soc 1991–, Assoc of Business Schs 1991–; memb Data Protection Tbnl 1985–; memb Civilian Trg Bd MOD 1992–; govr Portsmouth GS; Hon DSc Aston Univ; hon fell: Thames Poly (now Univ of Greenwich), Pembroke Coll Oxford 1996; FRSA 1979, CIPM 1983, CIMgt 1988, Hon FFOM 1994; *Recreations* opera, theatre, cricket, gardening; *Style—* Sir Len Peach; ✉ Crossacres, Meadow Rd, Wentworth, Virginia Water, Surrey GU25 4NH (☎ 01344 842258); Commissioner for Public Appointments, Cabinet Office, Horse Guards Road, London SW1P 3AL (☎ 0171 270 6472, fax 0171 270 1981)

PEACOCK, Prof Sir Alan Turner; kt (1987), DSC (1945); s of Prof Alexander David Peacock (d 1976), and Clara Mary, *née* Turner (d 1983); *b* 26 June 1922; *Educ* Dundee HS, Univ of St Andrews (MA); *m* 23 Feb 1944, Margaret Martha, da of Henry John Astell Burt (d 1960); 2 s (David Michael b 1945, Richard Alan b 1947); 1 da (Helen Mary Charlton b 1950); *Career* Lt RNVR 1943–45; reader in economics LSE 1951–56; prof of economics: Univ of Edinburgh 1956–62, Univ of York 1962–77, Univ of Buckingham 1978–84 (princ vice chllr 1980–84); res prof of public fin Heriot-Watt Univ 1984–; chief econ advsr and dep sec DTI 1973–76, chm Ctee on Financing BBC 1985–86; chm Scottish Arts Cncl 1986–92, exec dir David Hume Inst Edinburgh 1985–90, managing tstee IEA 1987–93, memb Panel of Econ Advsrs Sec of State for Scotland 1987–91; non-exec dir Caledonian Bank 1990–96; hon doctorates: Stirling 1974, Zürich 1984, Buckingham 1986, Brunel 1989, St Andrews, Edinburgh, Dundee 1990, Catania 1991, York; hon fell: LSE, IEA, Italian Acad of Arts and Scis; FBA 1979, FRSE 1989; *Books* numerous books and publications in professional journals mainly on economics topics and occasionally on music; *Recreations* trying to write serious music, wine spotting; *Clubs* Reform, New (Edinburgh); *Style—* Prof Sir Alan Peacock, DSC, FBA, FRSE; ✉ 146/4 Whitehouse Loan, Edinburgh EH9 2AN (☎ 0131 447 5917); c/o David Hume Institute, 21 George Square, Edinburgh EH8 9LD (☎ 0131 650 4633, fax 0131 667 9111)

PEACOCK, Annette; da of Miles Coleman (d 1969), and Frieda, *née* Morell (d 1990); *b* 8 Jan 1941; *Educ* El Cajon HS, LACC, Mill Brook, Juillard Sch of Music; *m* 1, 1960 (m dis 1967), Gary Peacock; 1 da (Solo b 5 Aug 1966); m 2, 31 Aug 1983, Jeremy Belshaw, s of Prof D G R Belshaw; 1 da (Avalon b 15 Oct 1983); *Career* originator of Free-Form Songform and Philosetry and voice plus band through prototype synthesizers, electronic arranger, prodr, record company proprietor; works incl LPs: Revenge 1969, Improvisie 1971, Dual Unity 1972, I'm The One 1972, X-Dreams 1978, The Perfect Release 1979, Sky-Skating 1982, Been in the Streets Too Long 1983, I Have No Feelings 1986, Abstract-Contact 1988; performances incl: Wired For Sound, Philharmonic Hall, Lincoln Center NYC 1970, Montreux Jazz Festival 1972, holographic actress in show with Salvador Dali on Broadway NYC 1973; WOMAD 1982 and 1986, MCPS, PRS; *Style—* Ms Annette Peacock; ✉ Ironic Records, PO Box 58, Wokingham, Berks RG11 7HN

PEACOCK, Christopher Arden (Chris); s of Ralph Warren Peacock (d 1987), and Phyllis Emily Alice, *née* Hardwicke (now Rostron); *b* 9 April 1945; *Educ* Wellington; *m* 1, 1968 (m dis); 2 da (Julie b 1971, Susannah b 1973); m 2, 1979; 3 c (Samantha b 1980, Charles b 1982, Thomas b 1986); *Career* Kemsley Whiteley Ferris 1963–66, Daniel Smith Briant & Done 1966–72; Jones Lang Wootton: joined 1972, ptnr 1974, chm and head Ptnr Agency 1988, managing ptnr Continent of Europe 1992–96, chief exec Jones Lang Wootton Europe 1996–; memb Bd of Mgmnt Br Cncl for Offices; Freeman City of London, memb Ct Worshipful Co of Pewterers; FRICS 1982 (ARICS 1970); *Recreations* golf, sailing, tennis, travel, motorbiking; *Clubs* Walton Heath Golf; *Style—* Chris Peacock, Esq; ✉ Jones Lang Wootton, 22 Hanover Square, London W1A 2BN (☎ 0171 457 3859, fax 0171 457 3999, mobile 0370 306140, e-mail cap@jlw.co.uk)

PEACOCK, Darren; *b* 3 Feb 1968; *Career* professional footballer (defender); 28 appearances Newport County 1984–88, 59 appearances Hereford Utd 1988–90, transferred to Queen's Park Rangers 1990–94, joined Newcastle Utd 1994; *Style—* Darren Peacock, Esq; ✉ c/o Newcastle United FC, St James Park, Newcastle upon Tyne NE1 4ST (☎ 0191 232 8361)

PEACOCK, Elizabeth Joan; JP (1975), MP (C) Batley and Spen (majority 1,408); da of late John William Gates, and Dorothy Gates; *b* 4 Sept 1937; *Educ* St Monica's Convent Skipton; *m* 1963, Brian David Peacock, s of late David Peacock, of East Marton, Skipton, N Yorks; 2 s (Jonathan, Nicholas); *Career* MP (C) Batley and Spen 1983–; memb Select Ctees on: Employment 1983–87, House of Commons Services 1988–91; PPS to: Rt Hon Angela Rumbold as Min of State Home Office 1991–92, Rt Hon Nicholas Scott as Min for Social Security and Disabled People 1992; chm All Party: Wool Textile Gp 1989–, Transpennine Gp 1989–95; vice chm All Party Water Gp 1995–, jt sec All Pty Pro Life Gp; vice chm Cons Back Bench Party Orgn Ctee 1984–86, memb Exec Ctee 1922 Ctee 1987–91; hon sec Yorks Cons Membs Gp 1983–87, vice pres Yorks Area Young Cons 1984–87, pres Yorks Cons Trade Unionists 1988–, vice pres Cons Trade Unionists 1995–; memb UK Fedn of Business and Professional Women 1965–, hon pres Nat Assoc of Approved Driving Instrs 1984–88, memb Gen Advsy Cncl BBC 1988–93; vice pres: Yorks and Humberside Devpt Assoc, W Yorks Pre-Retirement Assoc; Liveryman Worshipful Co of Woolmen; FRSA 1991; *Recreations* motoring, theatre; *Clubs* House of Commons Motor (chm); *Style—* Mrs Elizabeth J Peacock, JP, MP; ✉ House of Commons, London SW1A OAA (☎ 0171 219 4092)

PEACOCK, Geraldine; *b* 26 Jan 1948; *Educ* Redland HS for Girls Bristol, Univ of Durham (BA), Univ of California (Rotary Int fell), Univ of Newcastle-upon-Tyne (CQSW, post grad dip in Applied Social Work Studies); *Career* 1969–1989; sr social work practitioner, lectr Social Policy and Social Work Theory and Practice, trg conslt to Govt Depts and Local Authys, dep dir of London Training for Care; chief exec Nat Autistic Soc 1989–, chm ACENVO 1996– (vice chm 1995–96); govr Whitfields Sch; FRSA; *Books* Social Work and Received Ideas (with C Rojek and S Collins, 1989), The Haunt of Misery (with C Rojek and S Collins, 1990); author of numerous articles and conference papers; *Style—* Ms Geraldine Peacock; ✉ National Autistic Society, 276 Willesden Lane, London NW2 5RB (☎ 0181 451 1114, fax 0181 451 5865)

PEACOCK, Ian Douglas; s of Andrew Inglis Peacock (d 1981), of Sevenoaks, Kent, and Minnie Maria, *née* King (d 1978); *b* 9 April 1934; *Educ* Sevenoaks Sch; *m* 21 July 1962, Joanna Hepburn, da of George Milne MacGregor, of Strathaven, Lanarkshire; 1 s (Colin Michael b 8 Sept 1963), 1 da (Susan Jean b 2 May 1965); *Career* PO RAF 1953–54, Flying Offr RAuxAF 1955–58; md: Slazenger Ltd 1976–83 (mktg dir 1973–76), Sports Mktg Surveys Ltd 1983–85; chief exec Lawn Tennis Assoc 1986–96; chm Golf Ball 1975–96, pres Br Sports and Allied Industs Fedn 1983–85, cncllr and dir Golf Fndn 1984–, chm Golf Fndn 1996–; *Recreations* golf, painting; *Clubs* RAF, Royal Ashdown Forest Golf, Queens; *Style—* Ian Peacock, Esq; ✉ Moat End House, Church Lane, Burstow, Surrey RH6 9TG (☎ 01342 842262), The Lawn Tennis Association, Queens Club, Palliser Road, London W14 (☎ 0171 381 7000)

PEACOCK, Ian Rex; s of Mervyn George Peacock, of Bristol, and Evelyn Joyce, *née* Gay; *b* 5 July 1947; *Educ* Trinity Coll Cambridge; *m* 31 March 1973, Alyanee, da of Lt-Gen Amnuay Chya-Rochana; 1 s (Christopher b 5 May 1982); *Career* economist Unilever Ltd 1968–72, Cripps Warburg Ltd 1972–75; Kleinwort Benson Limited: asst mangr Credit Dept 1976–77, mangr Hong Kong Office 1978–81, asst dir of corporate banking London 1981–82, dir North American Dept London 1984–85 (asst dir 1983–84), dir NY Office 1985–87, dir of corporate banking London 1987–90, jt head of fin div 1990–94, dir Kleinwort Benson Group plc 1990–94; co-head of Merchant Banking Barclays de Zoete Wedd New York 1994–; *Clubs* United Oxford and Cambridge Univ; *Style—* Ian Peacock, Esq; ✉ Barclays de Zoete Wedd, 11th Floor, 222 Broadway, New York, NY 10038, USA

PEACOCK, Trevor Edward; s of Victor Edward Peacock (d 1970), of Enfield, Middx, and Alexandra Victoria, *née* Mathews (d 1986); *b* 19 May 1931; *Educ* Enfield GS, Univ of Oxford (Dip Ed); *m* 1, Sept 1957 (m dis 1978), Iris, da of Charles Jones; 1 s (Daniel b 2 Oct 1958), 1 da (Sally Georgia b 16 Feb 1960); m 2, 10 Aug 1979, Victoria Tilly, *née* Sanderson; 1 s (Harry Lemuel Xavier b 25 Aug 1978), 1 da (Maudie Mary b 21 Jan 1982); *Career* actor; Nat Serv 1949–51; composer: Erb, Leaping Ginger, Andy Cap, Class K; fndr memb Royal Exchange Theatre Manchester, Ivor Novello award; memb: Amnesty Int, Oxfam, Performing Rights Soc, Writers' Guild; *Theatre* incl: Titus in Titus Andronicus, Nathan Detroit in Guys and Dolls, Willy Mossop in Hobson's Choice, Estragon in Waiting for Godot, Tony Lumpkin in She Stoops To Conquer, Oliver in The Blue Ball (RNT) 1995; *Television* incl: Born and Bred (Thames), The Old Curiosity Shop (BBC), Wish Me Luck (LWT), The Riff Raff Element, The Vicar of Dibley; *Recreations* cricket, music, reading, rolling (down grassy slopes); *Style—* Trevor

Peacock, Esq; ✉ c/o Scott Marshall Personal Management, 44 Perryn Road, London W3 7NA (☎ 0181 749 7692, fax 0181 743 1669)

PEACOCKE, Rev Dr Arthur Robert; MBE (1993); s of (Arthur) Charles Peacocke (d 1961), of Watford, Herts, and Rose Elizabeth, *née* Lilly (d 1967); *b* 29 Nov 1924; *Educ* Watford Boys' GS, Exeter Coll Oxford (BA, BSc, MA, DPhil, DSc, DD), Univ of Cambridge (ScD by incorporation), Univ of Birmingham (BD); *m* 7 Aug 1948, Rosemary Winifred, da of Edgar Mann (d 1970), of Cheltenham; 1 s (Christopher b 1950), 1 da (Jane b 1953); *Career* successively asst lectr, lectr then sr lectr Univ of Birmingham 1948–59, univ lectr in biochemistry and fell and tutor St Peter's Coll Oxford 1959–73, dean, fell, tutor and dir of studies in theol Clare Coll Cambridge 1973–84, prof Judeo-Christian Studies Tulane Univ 1984, dir Ian Ramsey Centre St Cross Coll Oxford 1985–88 and 1995–, Royden B Davis prof of interdisciplinary studies Georgetown Univ 1994; lay reader Oxford Dio 1960–71, ordained 1971; pres Science and Religion Forum 1995– (chm 1972–78, vice pres 1978–92); warden Soc of Ordained Scientists 1987–92 (warden emeritus 1992–); Christ Church Cathedral Oxford: hon chaplain 1988–96, hon canon 1995–; Univ of Oxford: Bampton lectr 1978, select preacher 1973 and 1975; Hulsean preacher Univ of Cambridge 1976, Gifford lectr Univ of St Andrews 1993; sec then chm Br Biophysical Soc 1965–69; Lecomte du Nouy Prize 1983; Hon DSc De Pauw Univ Indiana 1983, Hon DLitt Hum Georgetown Univ of Washington 1991; Academic Fell Inst on Religion in an Age of Sci 1986; *Books* Molecular Basis of Heredity (with J B Drysale, 1965), Science and the Christian Experiment (1971), Osmotic Pressure of Biological Macromolecules (with M P Tombs, 1974), From Cosmos to Love (with J Dominian, 1974), Creation and the World of Science (1974), Intimations of Reality (1984), God and the New Biology (1986, reprinted 1994), The Physical Chemistry of Biological Organization (1983, reprint 1989), Persons and Personality (ed with G Gillet, 1987), Theology for a Scientific Age (1990, 2 edn 1993, Templeton Fndn prize 1995), Chaos & Complexity (with R J Russell and N Murphy, 1995, Templeton Fndn prize 1996), From DNA to DEAN (1996), God and Science (1996); *Recreations* music, hill walking, churches; *Style—* The Rev Canon Arthur Peacocke, MBE; ✉ 55 St John St, Oxford, OX1 2LQ (☎ 01865 512 041, fax 01865 54791); Exeter College, Oxford, OX1 3DP

PEACOCKE, Prof Christopher Arthur Bruce; s of Arthur Robert Peacocke, and Rosemary Winifred Mann; *b* 22 May 1950; *Educ* Magdalen Coll Sch Oxford, Exeter Coll Oxford (MA, BPhil, DPhil); *m* 3 Jan 1980, Teresa Anne, *née* Rosen; 1 s, 1 da; *Career* jr res fell Queen's Coll Oxford 1973–75, prize fell All Souls Coll Oxford 1975–79, fell and tutor and CUF lectr in philosophy New Coll Oxford 1979–85, Susan Stebbing prof of philosophy KCL 1985–88; visiting prof: Univ of California Berkeley 1975, Univ of Michigan Ann Arbor 1978, UCLA 1981, Univ of Maryland 1987; visiting fell ANU 1981, fell Centre for Advanced Study in the Behavioural Sciences Stanford 1983–84, Waynflete prof of metaphysical philosophy Univ of Oxford 1989–, fell Magdalen Coll Oxford 1989–, Leverhulme personal res prof 1996–2001, visiting prof New York Univ 1996–98; Euro Soc for Philosophy and Psychology: memb Steering Ctee 1991–95, memb Advsy Bd 1992–; papers on philosophy of mind, language and logic and metaphysics; pres Mind Assoc 1986; FBA 1990; *Books* Holistic Explanation: Action, Space, Interpretation (1979), Sense and Content (1983), Thoughts: an Essay on Content (1986), A Study of Concepts (1992); *Recreations* music, visual arts; *Style—* Prof Christopher Peacocke, FBA; ✉ Magdalen Coll, Oxford (☎ 01865 276000, fax 01865 276103)

PEAFORD, Alan James; s of James William Thomas Peaford (d 1986), and Iris Maud, *née* Tustain; *b* 31 Oct 1952; *Educ* Ockendon Court, Harlow Coll, Cranfield (Mktg Mgmnt Dip); *m* 17 Dec 1978, Jane Elizabeth, da of John Donald Saxton; 1 s (Thomas James Charles b 16 Feb 1982), 2 da (Sara Jane b 20 Aug 1980, Victoria Lesley b 28 March 1985); *Career* journalist; Express Newspapers 1971–74, Westminster Press 1975–76, Times Newspapers 1977–, night ed Arab Times 1977–78, dep ed Gulf Daily News 1978–79, PR and communications mangr British Petroleum 1980–88, md Charles Barker 1988–90, chief exec Barkers Trident Communications 1990–, dir Communication Europe Ltd; awards: Foreign Corr of the Year 1977, Safety Writer of the Year 1982; nat chm BAIE 1989–90 (memb 1981, fell 1986), memb Bd Nat Youth Theatre 1988, chm Cornelia de Lange Syndrome Fndn 1990–, vice pres CdLS Fndn Inc (USA), pres Fedn of European Editors; *Recreations* cricket, racing, tennis, watching West Ham; *Clubs* Wig & Pen, Oil Industries, National Sporting Club, Ward of Cheap; *Style—* Alan Peaford, Esq; ✉ Barkers Trident Communications, Trident House, 31–32 Cock Lane, London EC1A 9BU (☎ 0171 236 2727, fax 0171 236 4740)

PEAKE, David Alphy Edward Raymond; s of Sir Harald Peake (d 1978), and his 1 w Resy, OBE, *née* Countess de Baillet Latour; *b* 27 Sept 1934; *Educ* Ampleforth, ChCh Oxford; *m* 1962, Susanna, da of Sir Cyril Kleinwort (d 1980); 1 s, 1 da; *Career* 2 Lt Royal Scots Greys 1953–55; chm: Hargreaves Group plc 1974–86, Kleinwort Benson Group plc 1989–93; dir: Kleinwort Benson Ltd 1971–93, BNP plc 1974–, The British Library 1990–96, British Overseas Trade Bd 1993–96, Life Educn Centres 1994–; chm The Educn 2000 Tst 1994–; memb Ct of Assts Worshipful Co of Goldsmiths 1992; *Clubs* Brooks's, Cavalry and Guards', Pratt's; *Style—* David Peake, Esq; ✉ Sezincote House, Moreton-in-Marsh, Glos GL56 9AW (☎ 01386 700 444); 15 Ilchester Place, London W14 8AA (☎ 0171 602 2375)

PEAKE, Air Cdre Dame Felicity Hyde (Lady Peake); DBE (1949, MBE 1941), AE, JP; da of late Col Humphrey Watts, OBE, TD; *b* 1 May 1913; *Educ* St Winifred's Eastbourne, Les Grands Huguenots (Vaucresson, Seine et Oise, France); *m* 1, 1935, John Charles Mackenzie Hanbury (ka 1939); m 2, 1952, as his 2 w, Sir Harald Peake, AE (d 1978); 1 s (Andrew b 1956); *Career* joined ATS Co of RAF 1939, cmmnd WAAF 1939, served at home and M East; dir: WAAF 1946–49, WRAF (from its inception) 1949–50, ret 1950; Hon ADC to King George VI 1949–50; memb RAF Benevolent Fund 1946– (vice-pres 1978), tstee Imperial War Museum 1963–85, re-elected govr London House 1978–91, pres The Friends of the Imperial War Museum 1988–92 (fndr memb and chm 1986–88), tstee St Clement Danes Central Church of the RAF 1989–; *Books* Pure Chance (1993); *Style—* Air Cdre Dame Felicity Peake, DBE, AE, JP

PEAKE, John Morris; CBE (1986); s of Albert Edward Peake (d 1977), of Cambridge, and Ruby, *née* Morris (d 1978); *b* 26 Aug 1924; *Educ* Repton, Clare Coll Cambridge (Mech Sci Tripos, MA), RNC Greenwich (Dip Naval Arch); *m* 9 May 1953, Elizabeth, da of Arthur Rought, MC (d 1972), of Lympstone, Devon; 1 s (Christopher b 1956), 1 da (Catharine b 1954); *Career* RCNC 1944–50; Personnel Admin Ltd 1950–51, dir Baker Perkins 1956–87 (joined 1951), jt md Baker Perkins Ltd 1963–66, md Baker Perkins Pty Aust 1969–74, pres Baker Perkins Inc USA 1975–77, md Baker Perkins Hldgs 1980–85 (dep md 1978–79), chm Baker Perkins PLC 1984–87; memb Chemicals and Minerals Requirements Bd 1978–81; CBI Cncl 1980–89: chm Overseas Scholarships Bd 1981–87, chm Educn and Trg Ctee 1986–88; cmmr Manpower Servs/Trg Cmmn 1986–88, chm Bd for Engrg BTEC 1985–91 (memb BTEC Cncl 1986–89); chm: Nene Park Tst Peterborough 1988–93, RSA Examinations Bd 1989–93 (joined 1987), RSA Educn and Assessment Fndn 1993, Greater Peterborough Partnership 1994–95; vice pres RSA Cncl 1989–93, vice chm Greater Peterborough Trg and Enterprise Cncl 1990–94, chm Design Cncl Educn and Trg Ctee 1990–93, chm Cambridgeshire Careers Guidance Ltd 1995–; memb: Design Cncl 1991–93, British Library Advsy Cncl 1990–92; Silver medal (hockey) Olympic Games London 1948; Hon DTech CNAA 1986; FInstD 1956, FIMA 1967, FIMechE 1969, CIMgt 1978, FRSA 1984; *Recreations* sport, travel; *Clubs* East India, MCC; *Style—* John Peake, Esq, CBE; ✉ Old Castle Farmhouse, Stibbington, Peterborough PE8 6LP (☎ 01780 782683)

PEAKE, Michael I'Anson; s of Alfred I'Anson Peake (d 1981), of Hillside, Benllech, Anglesey, and Eileen Constance Peake; *b* 25 Nov 1949; *Educ* Rydal Sch, Univ of London (LLB); *m* 11 July 1981, Mrs Dilys Shone; 2 s (Christopher I'Anson b 1981, Daniel Michael b 1984), 1 step s (Richard Arthur Shone b 1977), 1 step da (Nicole Louise Shone b 1968); *Career* slr, managing ptnr Forshaw Spittles; dep dist judge; chm Contentious Sub Ctee of local Law Soc, memb Slrs' Complaints Panel; *Recreations* golf; *Clubs* Warrington Golf; *Style—* Michael Peake, Esq; ✉ Forshaw Spittles, 1 Palmyra Square, Warrington, Cheshire WA1 1BZ (☎ 01925 230000)

PEAKER, Prof Malcolm; s of Ronald Smith Peaker, of Stapleford, Nottingham, and Marian, *née* Tomasin; *b* 21 Aug 1943; *Educ* Henry Mellish GS Nottingham, Univ of Sheffield (BSc, DSc), Univ of Hong Kong (PhD); *m* 23 Oct 1965, Stephanie Jane, da of Lt Cdr J G Large, DFC; 3 s (Christopher James Gordon, Alexander John, Nicholas Edward); *Career* ARC Inst of Animal Physiology 1968–78, head Dept of Physiology Hannah Res Inst 1978–81, dir and Hannah prof Univ of Glasgow 1981–; FZS 1969, FIBiol 1979, FRSE 1983, FRS 1996; *Books* Salt Glands in Birds and Reptiles (1975), Avian Physiology (ed, 1975), Comparative Aspects of Lactation (ed, 1977), Physiological Strategies in Lactation (ed, 1984), Intercellular Signalling in the Mammary Gland (ed, 1995); *Recreations* zoology, natural history, golf; *Clubs* Farmers', Royal Troon Golf, Zoological; *Style—* Prof Malcolm Peaker, FRSE, FRS; ✉ Hannah Research Institute, Ayr KA6 5HL (☎ 01292 476013, fax 01292 671052)

PEARCE, (John) Allan Chaplin; yr s of John William Ernest Pearce (d 1951), and Irene, *née* Chaplin; bro of Baron Pearce (Life Peer, d 1990); *b* 21 Oct 1912; *Educ* Charterhouse, Brasenose Coll Oxford; *m* 18 Nov 1948, Raffaella, da of Avv Umberto Baione, of Florence; 2 s (Laurence b 1949, Charles b 1952); *Career* cmd 4 Co of London Yeo, served Libya, Egypt, Sicily, Italy 1941–44, Maj, Mil Mission to Italian Army Rome 1945–46; admitted slr 1947; sr ptnr Sandilands Williamson Hill & Co 1952–70, asst Legal Dept Church Cmmrs for England 1970–78; memb Ctee Br Italian Soc 1967–92, memb Ctee Venice in Peril Fund 1970– (hon treas 1986–93); Turner Soc (whose call for a Turner Gallery was answered in 1987): fndr memb and chm 1976–80, vice-pres 1980–; Liveryman Worshipful Co of Skinners 1937, Liveryman City of London Solicitors' Co, Freeman City of London; Cavaliere of the Order of Merit of the Italian Republic 1978; *Recreations* travel, opera, painting; *Clubs* Travellers', Hurlingham; *Style—* Allan Pearce, Esq; ✉ 32 Brompton Square, London SW3 2AE (☎ 0171 584 9429); 11 Quartiere Duca D'Aosta, Viareggio, Italy

PEARCE, Andrew; s of Henry Pearce (d 1964); *b* 1 Dec 1937; *Educ* Rydal Sch Colwyn Bay, Univ of Durham; *m* 1966, Myra, da of Kevin Whelan, of Co Wexford; 3 s, 1 da; *Career* formerly mgmnt servs exec; princ admin Cmmn of the Euro Communities Brussels 1974–79, fndr and vice pres Br Cons Assoc Belgium; Euro Community advsr Littlewoods Orgn Liverpool 1989–93; chm Int Trade Ctee Br Retail Consortium 1990–93, vice chm Euro Business Devpt Gp Liverpool C of C 1991–93; Parly candidate (C) Islington North 1969 and 1970, MEP (C) Cheshire West 1979–89, Euro Parly candidate (C) Cheshire W 1989, Parly candidate (C) Ellesmere Port and Neston 1992; currently dep head Tourism Unit Euro Cmmn Brussels; govr: Archway Comp Sch 1967–70, Woodchurch HS Birkenhead 1985–90, Nugent Sch Liverpool 1992–94; *Style—* Andrew Pearce, Esq; ✉ 13 Lingdale Rd, W Kirby, Wirral L48 5DG (☎ and fax 0151 632 3191 and ☎ 00 322 296 3018, fax 00 322 296 1377)

PEARCE, Sir Austin William; kt (1980), CBE (1974); s of William Thomas Pearce (d 1970); *b* 1 Sept 1921; *Educ* Devonport HS for Boys, Univ of Birmingham (BSc, PhD); *m* 1, 1947, Maglona Winifred Twinn (d 1975); 3 da; m 2, 1979, Dr Florence Patricia Grice (d 1993), da of John Walter Forsythe; *Career* chm and chief exec Esso Petroleum Co Ltd 1972–80 (joined Esso when called Agwi Petroleum 1945, dir 1963, md 1968–71); chm: British Aerospace 1980–87 (dir 1977–87, memb Organising Ctee 1976), Williams & Glyn's Bank 1983–85 (dir 1974–85), Oxford Instruments 1987–91; vice chm Royal Bank of Scotland Group 1985–92 (dir 1978–92); non-exec dir: Pearl Assurance plc 1985–91, Jaguar plc (now Ltd) 1986–93, Smiths Industries plc 1986–92; chm CBI Industl Policy Ctee 1982–86; memb Takeover Panel 1987–92, former pres Inst of Petroleum, chm UK Petroleum Indust Assoc, pt/t memb NRDC 1973–76, memb Standing Cmmn on Energy and Environment 1978–81, pres Soc of Br Aerospace Cos 1982–83, pro chllr Univ of Surrey 1985–93 (pro chair emeritus 1994–), chm Bd of Tstees Science Museum 1986–95, treas Royal Soc of Arts Mfrs and Commerce (RSA) 1988–93, chm Warden Housing Assoc 1994–; Br Assoc of Industl Eds Communicator of the Year award 1983; Hon DSc: Southampton 1978, Exeter 1985, Salford 1987, Cranfield 1987; Hon DEng Birmingham 1986, Hon DUniv Surrey 1993; FEng 1978; *Clubs* Royal Wimbledon Golf; *Style—* Sir Austin Pearce, CBE, FEng; ✉ Treeps House, 2 High Street, Hurstpierpoint, W Sussex BN6 9TY (☎ and fax 01273 832927)

PEARCE, (John) Brian; s of George Frederic Pearce (d 1963), of Wakefield and Sidmouth, and Constance Josephine, *née* Seed (d 1967); *b* 25 Sept 1935; *Educ* Queen Elizabeth GS Wakefield, Brasenose Coll Oxford (BA); *m* 30 June 1960, Michelle, da of Alfred Starr Etcheverry (ka 1944); 4 s (Christopher David b 1963, Colin Alexander b 1965, Jonathan Edward b 1969, James Frederic Lauriston b 1970); *Career* Nat Serv RAF 1954–56, Pilot Offr 1955–56; Miny of Power 1959–60, Colonial Office 1960–67, Dept of Econ Affrs 1967–69, Civil Serv Dept 1969–81, HM Treasy 1981–84 (under sec 1976–84), dir Inter Faith Network for UK 1987–; *Recreations* reading (mainly theology), travel; *Style—* Brian Pearce, Esq; ✉ 124 Court Lane, London SE21 7EA; 5–7 Tavistock Place, London WC1H 9SN (☎ 0171 388 0008)

PEARCE, Brian Harold; CBE (1995); s of (John) Harold George Pearce (d 1982), of Sevenoaks, and Dorothy Elsie Pearce (d 1994); *b* 30 July 1931; *Educ* Tonbridge, UCL (BSc(Eng)); *m* 1, 3 Sept 1955, Jean Isabel, *née* Richardson (d 1985); 2 s (Nicholas Michael John b 1959, Jonathan Brian Miles b 1966), 1 da (Gillian Sarah (Mrs Mueller-Pearce) b 1961); m 2, 2 Aug 1988, Veronica Mary, *née* Maund, formerly Mrs Magraw; *Career* Nat Serv RE 1953–55 (cmmnd 2 Lt 1954); gp chm Pearce Signs Group and subsids 1981–96 (joined 1955, gp md 1975); memb Bd London First 1992–96; dir: London First Centre 1992–, Business Link London 1995–; pres London C-of-C and Indust 1994–96; former pres: Br Sign Assoc, Euro Fedn of Illuminated Signs; chm: Stag Theatre Sevenoaks, Royal London Soc for the Blind; govr New Beacon Sch Sevenoaks; Freeman: City of London, Worshipful Co of Lightmongers; *Recreations* sailing, flying (helicopter), country interests; *Clubs* RAC, Little Ship; *Style—* Brian Pearce, Esq, CBE; ✉ Hamptons Farm House, Hamptons, Shipbourne, Kent TN11 9SR (☎ 01732 810547, fax 01732 810862)

PEARCE, Prof Eur Ing Christopher Michael; s of Glyndwr Pearce (d 1975), and Inis Mary, *née* Kenniford; *b* 23 Oct 1952; *Educ* Newent Sch, Univ of Bath (prizewinner, BSc); *m* 20 Sept 1975, Janice, da of Frank Holman; 2 da (Gillian Louise b 15 Aug 1980, Catherine Ruth b 29 Oct 1984); *Career* Dowty Group plc: apprentice 1970–74, designer and ldr Dowty Rotol Ltd 1974–79, propeller project engr Dowty Rotol Ltd 1979–84, gp trg mangr Dowty Group plc 1984–86, chief engr Dowty Fuel Systems Ltd 1986–87, dir of engineering Dowty Fuel Systems Ltd 1987–89, dir of ops Dowty Fuel Systems Ltd 1989–90, dir and gen mangr Dowty Aerospace Hydraulics 1990–93, dir of Dowty Aerospace 1993–94; tech dir Ricardo Aerospace Ltd, Ricardo Hitec Ltd and Geschäftsführer Ricardo Technology GmbH (Ricardo Group plc) 1994–; visiting fell Univ of Bristol, visiting prof Xi'an Jiaotong Univ (People's Republic of China), Royal Academy visiting prof Univ of Salford; Sir George Dowty prizewinner, Sir Roy Fedden prizewinner; CEng 1981, FEng 1993, MRAeS 1981, FIMechE 1991; *Recreations* active church memb, fell walking, running, table tennis (former rep Univ of Bath); *Style—* Prof

Eur Ing Christopher Pearce, FEng; ✉ Ricardo Aerospace Ltd, Brunswick House, Upper York Street, Bristol BS2 8QN (☎ 0117 924 0088, fax 0117 924 4640)

PEARCE, Christopher Thomas; s of Thomas Neill Pearce, OBE (d 1994), of Worthing, and Stella Mary, *née* Rippon (d 1978); *b* 13 Jan 1941; *Educ* Christ's Hospital Sch; *m* 1972, Jennifer Jane, da of Guy Stephen Carlton; 1 s (Marcus b 1976), 1 da (Tiffany b 1978); *Career* articled clerk Cole Dickin & Hills CAs 1960–65, CA Coopers & Lybrand London and New York 1965–70, with J Henry Schroder Wagg & Co Ltd and Schroder Group in London, Hong Kong and Brazil 1970–84 (dir 1981–84), dir County NatWest London 1984–87, fin dir Rentokil Group plc 1987–; FCA 1964; *Recreations* sailing, skiing, reading, music; *Style*— Christopher Pearce, Esq; ✉ Rentokil Group plc, Felcourt, East Grinstead, West Sussex RH19 2JY (☎ 01342 833022)

PEARCE, David John; s of Dr Raymond Maplesden Pearce (d 1976), and Ivy, *née* Shingler (d 1960); *b* 25 March 1928; *Educ* Manchester GS, Univ of Manchester (BSc); *m* 1, 24 Feb 1954, Doreen (d 1977), da of John Valentine (d 1964), of Brindle Heath, Salford; 1 s (Andrew b 1959), 1 da (Shiela b 1962); m 2, 7 June 1986, Eileen, da of John Alfred Corlett (d 1961), of Wigan; 2 step s (Paul b 1953, Barry b 1954), 1 step da (Tina-Ann b 1959); *Career* Nat Serv Lance Corpl HQ RE BAOR 1951–53; graduate engr Oscar Faber and Partners consltg engrs 1949–51, res engr Spillers Ltd 1949–51, asst engr Merz and McLellan 1953–54, sr devpt engr Matthews and Mumby Ltd (asst engr, pt/t lectr) 1954–71; ptnr: Dennis Matthews and Partners 1972–79 (sr engr 1971–72), Pearce Matthews Partnership 1979–88, res ptnr Wallace Evans and Ptnrs Northern office (incorporating Pearce Matthews) 1988–90, divnl md Wallace Evans Ltd N Western Office 1990–92, ind conslt 1992, ptnr Pearce Larsson Partnership 1992–; chm Lancs and Cheshire branch IStructE 1983; AMIStructE 1953, MICE 1958, FIStructE 1969, MConsE 1977; *Recreations* travel, walking, swimming, crafts; *Clubs* Rotary (Worsley); *Style*— David Pearce, Esq; ✉ The Chimes, 19 Bellpit Close, Ellenbrook Grange, Worsley M28 7XH (☎ 0161 799 4965)

PEARCE, Prof David William; s of William Henry Pearce, and Gladys Muriel, *née* Webb; *b* 11 Oct 1941; *Educ* Harrow Weald Co GS, Lincoln Coll Oxford; *m* 27 Aug 1966, Susan Mary, da of William Federick Reynolds; 2 s (Daniel Benjamin b 1972, Corin Gareth b 1976); *Career* lectr in economics Univ of Lancaster 1964–67, sr lectr Univ of Southampton 1967–74, dir Public Sector Economics Research Centre Univ of Leicester 1974–77; prof: Univ of Aberdeen 1977–83, UCL 1983–; dir: London Environmental Economics Centre 1988–90, Centre for Social and Economic Research on the Global Environment 1990–; special advsr to the Sec of State for the Environment 1989–92; winner of UN Global 500 Award for servs to environmental improvement, winner Giuseppi Mazzotti Prize for Literature; FRSA 1988; *Books* Economic Analysis (with S G Sturmey, 1966), Cost Benefit Analysis (1971), The Economics of Natural Resource Depletion (ed, 1975), Decision Making for Energy Futures - A Case Study of the Windscale Inquiry (with L Edwards and G Beuret, 1979), Waste Paper Recovery (1979), Social Projects Appraisal (with C A Nash, 1981), The Macmillan Dictionary of Economics (gen ed, 1981), Economics and the Environment - A Contribution to the National Conservation Strategy for Botswana (with C Perrings, J Opschoor, J Arntzen and A Gilbert, 1988), Blueprint for a Green Economy (with A Markandya and E Barbier, 1989), Economics of Natural Resources and the Environment (with R K Turner, 1989), Sustainable Development (with A Markandya and E Barbier, 1990), Blueprint 2 (jtly, 1991), Economic Values and the Natural World (1993), World Without End: Economics, Environment and Sustainable Development (with J Warford, 1993), Economics of Biodiversity (1994), Blueprint 3 (jtly, 1993), Blueprint 4 (1995), Blueprint 5 (jtly, 1996); *Recreations* bird watching in Africa, collecting English porcelain; *Style*— Prof David Pearce; ✉ White Friars Farm, Duddenhoe End, nr Saffron Walden, Essex CB11 4UU (☎ 01763 838332, fax 01763 837106); Centre for Social and Economic Research in the Global Environment, University College London, Gower St, London WC1E 6BT (☎ 0171 380 7874, fax 0171 916 2772)

PEARCE, Gareth David; s of Howard Spencer Pearce, of Cardiff, and Enid Norma, *née* Richards (d 1994); *b* 13 Aug 1953; *Educ* Abingdon Sch, Balliol Coll Oxford (MA); *m* Virginia Louise, da of late Desmond Campbell Miller; 4 da (Caroline, Emma, Davina, Leonora); *Career* CA: Peat Marwick Mitchell & Co 1975–81, Electra Investment Trust plc 1982–86, Smith & Williamson 1986–; ACA 1979; *Clubs* Hurlingham; *Style*— Gareth Pearce, Esq; ✉ Smith and Williamson, 1 Riding House Street, London W1A 3AS (☎ 0171 637 5377, fax 0171 323 2714)

PEARCE, Sir (Daniel Norton) Idris; kt (1990), CBE (1982), TD (1972), DL (Greater London 1986); s of Lemuel George Douglas Pearce (d 1988), and Evelyn Mary Pearce (d 1987); *b* 28 Nov 1933; *Educ* West Buckland Sch, Coll of Estate Mgmnt; *m* 1 June 1963, Ursula Helene, *née* Langley; 2 da (Sara b 30 April 1965, Claire Mary (Mrs Simon C Thomsett) b 8 Dec 1968); *Career* chartered surveyor; Nat Serv RE 1957–59, cmd 135 Ind Topographic Sqdn TA 1970–73, Hon Col 1989–91; Richard Ellis: joined 1959, ptnr 1961, managing ptnr 1981–87, conslt 1992–; chm English Estates 1989–94, dep chm Dusco Ltd 1992–; non-exec dir: National Mortgage Bank plc 1992–, Higgs & Hill plc 1993–; chm: Varsity Funding 1995–, Redburgh Ltd 1996–; dir: Innisfree Ltd 1996–, Millenium & Copthorne plc 1996–; RICS: memb Gen Cncl 1980–94, chm of Parly and public affairs 1984–89, memb Bd of Mgmnt 1984–91, vice pres 1986–90, pres 1990–91; memb Advsy Bd for Institutional Fin in New Towns 1974–80, chm Int Assets Valuation Standards Ctee 1981–86, memb Inquiry of Sec of State for Health and Social Security into Surplus Land in NHS 1982, property advsr NHS 1985–89; dep chm English Partnerships 1993–; HEFC: chm Wales 1992–96, memb England 1992–; memb: Advsy Bd PSA 1981–86, Advsy Panel on Dip Estate FCO 1985–, Ct City Univ 1987–, Cncl Univ of Surrey 1993– (pro vice-chllr 1994–), Univs Funding Cncl 1991–92, Fin Reporting Review Panel 1991–92, Bd London First Centre 1992–; vice chm Gtr London TA&VRA 1991–94 (memb 1970–, chm Works and Bldgs Sub-Ctee 1983–91); chm Bd of Govrs Stanway Sch Dorking 1982–85; Parly candidate (C) Neath W Glam 1959; Freeman: Worshipful Co of Tylers and Bricklayers 1973, Worshipful Co of Chartered Surveyors 1977; Hon DSc: City Univ 1991, Univ of Salford 1992, Oxford Poly 1991; Hon DEng Univ of the West of England 1994; hon fell Coll of Estate Mgmnt 1987, centenary fell Thames Poly 1991, companion De Monfort Univ 1993; FRICS, FRSA; *Recreations* reading, opera, ballet, travel; *Clubs* Brooks's, City of London; *Style*— Sir Idris Pearce, CBE, TD, DL; ✉ c/o Richard Ellis, Berkeley Square House, Berkeley Square, London W1X 6AN (☎ 0171 629 6290, fax 0171 629 3975)

PEARCE, Prof John Barber; s of Arnold Porteous Pearce (d 1979), and Ruth, *née* Parry; *b* 27 Oct 1940; *Educ* Michael Hall (Rudolph Steiner Sch), UCL, UCH (MB BS, DCH, MPhil, FRCP, FRCPsych); *m* 1965, (Jean) Mary, da of Derek Wynne Bogle; 3 da (Rachel Christina b 1 Dec 1966, Clare Judith b 10 Oct 1968, Anna Jane b 19 March 1971); *Career* postgraduate: Bart's 1967–71, Maudsley Hosp 1971–75; conslt child and adolescent psychiatrist Guy's Hosp London 1975–87, sr lectr in child and adolescent psychiatry Univ of Leicester 1987–91, prof of child and adolescent psychiatry Univ of Nottingham 1991–; formerly examiner (MSc in Human Communication) Univ of London, examiner (DCH) RCP 1989–; RCPsych: formerly sec Child and Adolescent Psychiatry Speciality Advsy Ctee, formerly examiner membership exam, sec Child and Adolescent Section 1993–95 (formerly academic sec), memb Jt Ctee for Higher Psychiatric Trg 1993–; team memb Exploring Parenthood (advice serv for parents) 1989–, regnl advsr Med Cncl on Alcoholism 1992–; expert on childhood problems for nat and local radio and TV and for nat newspapers and mags, weekly columnist Nottingham Evening Post; memb: BMA, Br Paediatric Assoc, Assoc of Psychologists and Psychiatrists, Assoc for the Psychiatric Study of Adolescence; *Books* The 'Kids Work Out' Guide for Parents (1987), Worries and Fears (1989), Bad Behaviour (1989), Tantrums and Tempers (1989), Fighting, Teasing and Bullying (1989), Food: Too Faddy Too Fat (1991), Family and Friends (1991), Bad Behavious, Tantrums and Tempers (1993), Good Habits - Bad Habits (1994), Growth and Development - Too Fast Too Slow (1994); also author of book chapters and scientific papers concerning childhood depression and suicide, the psychiatric consequences of physical illness, bullying and general child psychiatric topics; *Recreations* narrowboating and sailing, playing the cello occasionally, restoring anything, travelling with my wife; *Style*— Prof John Pearce; ✉ Queen's Medical Centre, Nottingham NG7 2UH (☎ and 0115 952 9455)

PEARCE, (Ann) Philippa; OBE (1997); da of Ernest Alexander Pearce; *Educ* Perse Girls' Sch Cambridge, Girton Coll Cambridge; *m* 1963, Martin James Graham Christie (decd); 1 da; *Career* prodr/scriptwriter schs bdcasting BBC Radio 1945–58, ed Educn Dept Clarendon Press 1958–60, children's ed Andre Deutsch Ltd 1960–67, freelance writer of children's fiction 1967–; Hon DLitt Univ of Hull 1995; FRSL 1994; *Books* incl: Tom's Midnight Garden (Carnegie medal, 1959), A Dog So Small, The Elm Street Lot, The Battle of Bubble and Squeak (Whitbread award, 1978), The Way to Sattin Shore (1983), Here Comes Tod! (1992), Dread and Delight (ed, 1995); *Style*— Philippa Pearce, OBE, FRSL; ✉ c/o Viking-Kestrel Books, 27 Wrights Lane, London W8 5TZ

PEARCE, Reynold (Ren); *Educ* Trent Poly Nottingham (BA Fashion), Central St Martin's Sch of Art London (MA); *Career* fashion designer; former asst to designers incl John Galliano and Roland Klein, fndr ptnr own label Pearce Fionda (with Andrew Fionda, *qv*) 1994–; New Generation Designers of the Yr (Br Fashion Awards) 1995, Newcomers Award for Export (Br Knitting and Clothing Export Cncl/Fashion Weekly) 1995, World Young Designers Award (Int Apparel Fedn Istanbul) 1996; worldwide stockists incl: Liberty, Harrods, Harvey Nichols and Selfridges (UK), Saks 5th Avenue and Bergdorf Goodman (USA), Lidia Shopping (Italy), CRC (Thailand), Brown Thomas (Ireland); gp exhbns incl: Design of the Times (RCA) 1996, The Cutting Edge of British Fashion 1947–1997 (V&A) 1997; *Style*— Ren Pearce; ✉ Pearce Fionda, 27 Horsell Road, Highbury, London N5 1XL (☎ and fax 0171 609 6470)

PEARCE, Shaun David; s of David Pearce, of Newbury, Berks, and Jenifer Ann, *née* Mason; *b* 13 Dec 1969; *Educ* Park House Sch, Newbury Coll of Further Educn; *Career* canoeist (slalom K1 class); began competing aged 11; memb: GB jr team 1984–87, GB sr B team 1988–90, GB sr A team 1991–; achievements incl: nat under 16 champion 1985, winner Jr World Championship 1987, runner up Jr Euro Championship 1987, nat under 18 champion 1987, winner World Cup canoe slalom 5th leg USA 1990, world champion 1991, Br champion 1991, third place World Cup canoe slalom 3rd leg France 1991, first and third place Champion Int Whitewater Series USA 1992 (third place overall), fourth place World Championships Italy 1993, first place World Team Championships Italy 1993, Br champion 1993, fourth world ranking 1993, ninth place World Cup 1993, World Cup champion 1994, world ranked number one 1994, Br champion 1995, tenth place World Championships 1995, third place World Team Championships 1995, 25th place Olympic Games Atlanta 1996; Notts Sports Personality 1991; *Recreations* watching football; *Style*— Shaun Pearce, Esq; ✉ 3 The Hollies, Sandiacre, Nottingham NG10 5HN

PEARCE, Stuart; *b* 24 April 1962; *Career* professional footballer; 51 league appearances Coventry City 1983–85, joined Nottingham Forest 1985–, England: 72 caps and 5 goals (as at Jan 1997), memb squad World Cup 1990 and European Championships 1992 and 1996; honours: League Cup 1989 and 1990 (Nottingham Forest, runners up 1992); *Style*— Stuart Pearce, Esq; ✉ Nottingham Forest FC, City Ground, West Bridgford, Nottingham NG2 5FJ

PEARCE, Prof Susan Mary; *b* 20 March 1942; *Educ* Wycombe HS for Girls, Somerville Coll Oxford (MA), Univ Southampton (PhD); *m*; *Career* curatorial asst Dept of Archaeology Nat Museums of Merseyside 1965; Exeter City Museum: curator of antiquities 1965–78, sr curator (dep dir post) 1978–84; tutor Univ of Exeter 1972–84; Dept of Museum Studies Univ of Leicester: sr lectr 1984–89, dir and head of dept 1989–96, dean of arts 1996–, personal professorship in museum studies 1992–; tutor and examiner dip of Museum Assoc 1976–79; visiting lectr: Dept of Rhetoric Univ of Calif Berkeley 1982, Dept of Museum Studies Univ of Brno Czechoslovakia 1988; memb: Area Archaeological Advsy Ctee 1976–81, Archaeology Advsy Ctee Exmoor Nat Park 1979–84, Nat Trust Archaeological Advsy Ctee 1979–84, Govt Ctee for Reviewing Works of Art for Export 1990–92, Scholarship Assessment Panel Cwlth Inst 1991–; sec, chm and pres Devon Archaeological Soc 1973–79, exec sec Devon Ctee for Rescue Archaeology 1978–83, chm Leicester Univ Press Ctee 1991–, treas and chm Museums Ethnographers Gp 1976–83; Museums Assoc: Cncl memb 1989–, vice chair Educnl Bd 1989–, professional vice pres 1990–92, pres 1992–; Winston Churchill Travelling Fellowship (to visit Central Arctic) 1975, Catherine and Leonard Woolley Fellship grant Somerville Coll Oxford (res Balearic Isles) 1984; FSA 1979, FMA 1980 (AMA 1973); *Books* The Kingdom of Dumnonia - Studies in History and Tradition in SW Britain AD 350–1150 (1978), The Archaeology of SW Britain (1981), The Early Church in W Britain and Ireland (ed, 1982), The Bronze Age Metalwork of SW Britain (pts 1 and 2, 1983), Museum Studies in Material Culture (ed, 1989), Archaeological Curatorship (1990), Objects of Knowledge (ed, 1990), Museum Economics and the Community (ed, 1991), Museum Studies Bibliography (ed, 1991), Museums and Europe (ed, 1992), Museums, Objects and Collections - A Cultural Study (1992), Museums and the Appropriation of Culture (ed, 1993), Art in Museums (ed, 1994), Collecting in the European Tradition (1995); author of numerous papers for confs and jls; *Style*— Prof Susan M Pearce, FSA; ✉ Department of Museum Studies, University of Leicester, 105 Princess Road East, Leicester LE1 7LG (☎ 0116 252 3963)

PEARCEY, Leonard Charles; s of Leonard Arthur Pearcey (d 1992), of Dorset, and Jessie Sinclair, *née* Millar (d 1965); *b* 6 June 1938; *Educ* Christ's Hosp, CCC Cambridge (MA); *Career* PA to md Hargreaves Group 1957–59, dir of studies Rapid Results Correspondence Coll 1962–63, teacher Wimbledon 1964–65, arts admin Harold Holt Ltd 1965–66, music dir Guildhall Sch of Music and Drama 1966–70, competition sec Int Violin Competition 1966–70, dir Merton Festival 1972–76, involved in numerous major arts and religious radio and TV programmes incl BBC Radio 2 Young Musician competition, also own series as singer and guitarist (Gold disc 1990), composer numerous songs and arrangements; prodr and presenter: P & O Liner naming ceremonies, various other major presentations, conferences and award ceremonies, audio communication cassettes; admin BBC Radio Times Drama Awards and Comedy Awards 1972–90, stage co-ordinator and compere World Travel Market, dir Forte Hotels Music at Leisure Series; ed Music Teacher Magazine 1980–85, feature columnist Classical Music Magazine 1979–85; Mayoress (sic) London Borough of Merton 1973–74; memb Actors Equity; *Books* The Musician's Survival Kit (1979); *Recreations* travel; *Style*— Leonard Pearcey, Esq; ✉ 53 Queens Road, Wimbledon, London SW19 8NP (☎ 0181 947 2555)

PEAREY, Capt Michael Alan; s of William Scott Pearey (d 1940), of Newcastle upon Tyne, and Harriet Pringle, *née* Rochester (d 1972); *b* 3 June 1933; *Educ* Christ's Hosp; *m* 1957, Thelma Joy, da of Edward Hugh Owen, of Portsmouth; 3 s (Michael Scott b 1959, Richard Pringle b 1960, Alan Quentin b 1964), 2 da (Susan Adrienne (Mrs White) b 1957, Julia Heriot b 1966); *Career* joined RN 1951, Cdr 1970, Capt 1979, dir Fleet

Supply Duties 1982–84, dir Naval Offr Appts (S and S Offrs and WRNS) 1984–86, ret 1986; clerk Christ's Hosp Horsham 1986–; chm London HCIMA 1983–85; pres: RFU 1990–91 (memb Ctee 1968–95), England Schs RFU 1995–; Freeman: Newcastle upon Tyne 1952, City of London 1986, Worshipful Co of Shipwrights 1995; FHCIMA 1991 (MHCIMA 1978); *Recreations* rugby union, tennis; *Clubs* Devonshire, East India and Public Sch Sports; *Style*— Capt Michael Pearey; ✉ Counting House, Christ's Hospital, Horsham, W Sussex RH13 7YP (☎ 01403 211297, fax 01403 211580)

PEARL, David Brian; s of Leonard Pearl (d 1983), past Lord Mayor of Westminster; *b* 6 Aug 1944; *Educ* Wellington Coll; *m* 1972, Rosamond Mary Katharine, da of Lt Cdr C G de L'isle Bush, of Frampton-upon-Severn, Glos; 2 s, 1 da; *Career* articled clerk Coopers & Lybrand (qualified CA); md: Meru Group Ltd 1972–76, Promotions House plc 1976–84; chm London Securities plc 1984–94; currently: chm Gabriel Trust plc, non-exec dir Stanley Leisure plc; underwriting memb Lloyds of London 1977–90; vice chm Medway Ports Authy (Dept of Tport appointment) 1987–93, chm The Crown Suppliers (Dept of Environment appointment) 1989–90; cncllr Westminster City Cncl 1974–82 (served on most ctees, local sch govr, London Tourist Bd rep, dep Lord Mayor, chief whip, vice chm Fin and Scrutiny Ctee, chm Contracts Sub-ctee and Investments Sub-ctee); past chm: St Marylebone Cons Assoc, London Central Euro Cons Assoc, Cons Party Property Advsy Ctee SE Region; FCA, MInstM; *Recreations* PPL - Helicopters, greyhound breeding, sports, travel; *Clubs* White's, Reform, Royal St George's Golf; *Style*— David B Pearl, Esq; ✉ Ockwells Home Farm, Cox Green, Berks SL6 3AB (☎ 01628 20197); 7 Norfolk Road, St John's Wood, London NW8

PEARL, His Hon Judge; David Stephen; s of late Chaim Pearl, and Anita, *née* Newman; *b* 11 Aug 1944; *Educ* George Dixon's Sch Birmingham, Westminster City Sch, Univ of Birmingham (LLB), Queens' Coll Cambridge (LLM, MA, PhD); *m* 1, 7 April 1967 (m dis 1983), Susan, da of late Joseph Roer, of Croydon, Surrey; 3 s (Julian Kim b 1969, Daniel Benjamin Meir b 1971, Marcus Alexander Jethro b 1974); m 2, 4 Oct 1985, Gillian, da of Ryzard Maciejewski, of Melbourn, Royston, Herts; *Career* called to the Bar Gray's Inn 1968, recorder of the Crown Court 1992–94 (asst recorder 1985–92), circuit judge 1994–; fell and dir studies in law Fitzwilliam Coll Cambridge 1969–89 (life fell 1989), univ lectr Cambridge 1972–89, prof of law and dean Sch of Law UEA 1989–94; city cncllr Cambridgeshire 1972–74, co cncllr Cambridge 1974–77, asst dep coroner Cambridge 1978–89, pt/t adjudicator Immigration Act 1980–92, pt/t chm Immigration Appeal Tbnl 1992–94, chief adjudicator Immigration Appeals 1994–; gen sec Int Soc on Family Law 1985–91 (vice pres 1991–), memb Civil and Family Ctee Judicial Studies Bd 1994–; *Books* A Textbook on Muslim Personal Law (1979, 2 edn 1987), Social Welfare Law (with K Gray, 1981), Interpersonal Conflict of Laws (1981), Family Law and Society (with B Hoggett, 1983, 2 edn 1987, 3 edn 1991, 4 edn 1996), Family Law and Immigrant Communities (1986), Blood Testing, Aids and DNA Profiling (with A Grubb, 1990), Frontiers of Family Law (jt ed with A Bainham, 1993), Butterworths Immigration Law Service (ed); *Recreations* long distance running (badly); *Style*— His Hon Judge Pearl; ✉ Thanet House, 231 The Strand, London WC2R 1DA (☎ 0171 353 8060)

PEARL, Prof Valerie Louise; da of Cyril R Bence, MP (d 1992), and Florence Bence (d 1974); *b* 31 Dec 1926; *Educ* King Edward VI HS Birmingham, St Anne's Coll Oxford (BA, MA, DPhil); *m* 1949, Morris Leonard Pearl, s of Nathan Pearl (d 1961); 1 da; *Career* prof of history of London UCL 1976–81, pres New Hall Cambridge 1981–95; govr Museum of London 1978; syndicate: Cambridge Univ Library 1983, CUP 1984; cmmr Royal Cmmn on Historical Manuscripts 1984; FRHistS, hon fell St Anne's Coll Oxford; FSA; *Style*— Prof Valerie Pearl; ✉ New Hall, Huntingdon Road, Cambridge CB3 0DF

PEARLMAN, Joseph Joshua (Jerry); s of Samuel Myer Pearlman, MM (d 1981), and Sarah Rachael Pearlman (d 1983); *b* 26 April 1933; *Educ* Keighly GS, King James VI GS Bishop Auckland, Univ of London (LLB); *m* 18 June 1962, Bernice; 2 da (Kate, Debbie); *Career* Nat Serv Lt RASC; admitted slr 1956; fndr Pearlman Grazin & Co (became Godlove Pearlman) 1958–95, conslt Brooke North and Goodwin 1996–; advsr to Omukama of Bunyoro-Katara Uganda 1960–61; hon slr: Sikh temple Leeds 1965–, Ramblers' Assoc 1980–; pres: Leeds and W Riding Medico Legal Soc 1975–76, Leeds Law Soc 1985–86; ministerial appointed memb Yorkshire Dales Nat Park Ctee 1983–92, memb Adjudication Ctee Slrs' Complaints Bureau 1986–88, chm Open Spaces Soc 1988, vice chm Yorkshire Dales Millenium Tst 1996–; *Recreations* rambling, eating, drinking; *Clubs* Royal Over-Seas League; *Style*— Jerry Pearlman, Esq; ✉ 10 Lakeland Crescent, Leeds LS17 7PR (☎ 0113 267 1114); Bells Cottage, Stalling Busk, Askrigg via Leyburn, N Yorks; Brooke North and Goodwin Solicitors, Crown House, Great George Street, Leeds LS1 3BR (☎ 0113 283 2100, fax 0113 283 3999, car tel 0860 311600)

PEARLMAN, Her Honour Judge; Valerie Anne Pearlman; da of Sidney Pearlman, and Marjorie Pearlman; *b* 6 Aug 1936; *Educ* Wycombe Abbey; *m* 1972; 1 s, 1 da; *Career* called to the Bar Lincoln's Inn 1958, recorder (SE Circuit) 1982–85, circuit judge (SE Circuit) 1985–; chm Home Sec's Advsy Bd on Restricted Patients 1991–; memb: Parole Bd 1989–94, Civil and Family Ctee Judicial Studies Bd 1992–, Mental Health Fndn Ctee on the Mentally Disordered Offender 1992–95; memb Cncl Marlborough Coll 1989–; patron Suzy Lamplugh Tst; *Style*— Her Honour Judge Pearlman; ✉ Southwark Crown Court, English Grounds, London SE1 2HU

PEARS, David; s of Reginald Pears (d 1979); *b* 6 Dec 1967; *Educ* Moorclose Secdy Workington, Workington GS; *Career* Rugby Union fly-half Harlequins FC and England; clubs: Aspatria RUFC 1984–88, Sale FC 1989, Harlequins FC 1990; rep: Eng U21 1989, Eng B 1989–91 (6 caps); England: debut v Argentina 1990, tour Argentina 1990, memb team to S Africa 1994; *Recreations* tennis, golf; *Style*— David Pears, Esq; ✉ Harlequins FC, Stoop Memorial Ground, Craneford Way, Twickenham, Middlesex

PEARSALL, Dr Fiona Jean Burns; da of Dr Ian Stewart Pearsall (d 1982), and Jean Dawson, *née* Burns; *b* 5 May 1963; *Educ* Craigholme Sch for Girls Glasgow, Hutchesons' GS Glasgow, Univ of Glasgow (MB ChB, MSc), FRCA (Dip); *Career* house offr (med and surgery) Western Infirmary Glasgow 1986–87, registrar (anaesthesia) Victoria Infirmary Glasgow 1988–91 (SHO (anaesthesia) 1987–88), research asst Univ of Glasgow 1991–93, SHO (anaesthesia) Western Infirmary Glasgowy 1993; Glasgow Royal Infirmary: registrar (anaesthesia) 1993–94, sr registrar 1994–96, conslt anaesthetist 1996–; memb: GMC, BMA; *Recreations* drawing and watercolour painting, music, ornithology, swimming; *Clubs* RSM; *Style*— Dr Fiona Pearsall; ✉ Directorate of Anaesthesia, Glasgow Royal Infirmary, Castle Street, Glasgow (☎ 0141 211 4620/1, fax 0141 211 4622)

PEARSE, William Richard George (Bill); s of Richard John Pearse (d 1946), of Taunton, and Daisy May, *née* Thomas (d 1982); *b* 23 Feb 1924; *Educ* Taunton Sch; *Career* RASC 1944–46; CA 1951, memb Exec Ctee Robson Rhodes 1981–84, managing ptnr Apsleys 1987–90 (conslt 1990–); pres and co-fndr SW Soc of CAs 1978–79; recorder Taunton Ct Leet; govr Bishop Foxes Sch, memb Cncl Taunton Sch, vice pres Somerset CCC; RFU: memb Mgmnt Ctee Somerset County 1968–96, Somerset rep 1981–96, chm SW Div 1988–89; Freeman: City of London 1978, Worshipful Co of CAs in England & Wales 1978; FCA (1961, ACA 1951); *Recreations* sport, cricket, rugby football; *Clubs* E India, Victory Service; *Style*— Bill Pearse, Esq; ✉ 11 Highlands, Taunton, Somerset TA1 4HP (☎ 01823 284701); Apsleys, Apsley House, Tower Street, Taunton, Somerset TA1 4BJ (☎ 01823 259101, fax 01823 334459)

PEARSE WHEATLEY, Robin John; s of John Edward Clive Wheatley, MC, JP, of Exeter, and Rosemarie Joy, *née* Malet-Veale; *b* 23 May 1949; *Educ* Leys Sch Cambridge, Inns of Court Sch of Law; *m* 9 April 1979, Victoria Eugenia Perez de Ascanio y Zuleta de Reales, da of Nicolas Perez de Ascanio Ventoso, of Tenerife, Spain; 1 s (Edward Victor Francisco de Borga b 23 Dec 1988), 2 da (Victoria-Eugenia Amabel b 16 Dec 1983, Rafaela Eleanor b 11 Jan 1986); *Career* called to the Bar Inner Temple 1971, recorder Crown Ct 1992– (asst recorder 1987–92); councillor RBK and C 1974–78; Cons Parly candidate Lewisham Deptford 1983; chm London Area Nat Fedn Self Employed and Small Business 1989–92; Cons Euro candidate London South Inner 1989; Knight of Grace Constantinian Order of St George; *Recreations* swimming, bridge; *Clubs* Annabel's; *Style*— Robin Pearse Wheatley, Esq; ✉ 30 Edenhurst Avenue, London SW6 3PB (☎ 0171 736 7060); 2 Paper Buildings, London EC4Y 7ET (☎ 0171 936 2611, fax 0171 583 3423, car tel 0831 306562)

PEARSON, Barrie; s of Albert James Pearson (d 1987), of Selby, Yorks, and Mary Pearson (d 1980); *b* 22 Aug 1939; *Educ* King's Sch Pontefract Yorks, Univ of Nottingham (BSc); *m* 1, 1962 (m dis), Georgina Ann; 1 s (Gavin Charles Livingstone b 1968), 1 da (Philippa Jane Antonia b 1965); m 2, 1984, Catherine Campbell; *Career* Dexion-Comino Int Ltd 1960, The Plessey Co 1967, The De La Rue Co 1973; non-exec chm Info Transmission Ltd 1985–87, exec chm Livingstone Guarantee plc 1976–; visiting fell in corporate acquisitions and disposals City Univ Business Sch 1989–; non-exec dir Universal Salvage plc 1995–; seminar presenter for: Inst of CAs, Inst of Dirs, CIMA; video films: Business Strategy 1989, Time Management 1990, for Accountancy TV 1993; *Books* Successful Acquisition of Unquoted Companies (1983, 3 edn 1989), Common Sense Business Strategy (1987), Common Sense Time Management for Personal Success (1988), Realising The Value of a Business (1989), The Profit Driven Manager (1990), The Shorter MBA (1991), Manage Your Own Business (1991), How to Buy and Sell a Business (1995); *Recreations* food guide inspector, theatre, ballet, tennis, outstanding hotels, travel; *Style*— Barrie Pearson, Esq; ✉ Campbell House, Weston Turville, Bucks HP22 5RQ (☎ 01296 613828); Livingstone Guarantee plc, 11–15 William Rd, London NW1 3ER (☎ 0171 388 4242)

PEARSON, David Compton Froome; s of Compton Edwin Pearson, OBE (d 1977), and Marjorie Pearson (d 1994); *b* 28 July 1931; *Educ* Haileybury, Downing Coll Cambridge; *m* 1966 (m dis 1994), Venetia Jane, *née* Lynn; 2 da (Arabella, Cressida); *Career* admitted slr 1957; ptnr Linklaters & Paines 1961–69 (joined 1957); dir: Robert Fleming & Co Ltd 1969–90, The Fleming Enterprise Investment Trust plc 1971–84, Blue Circle Industries plc 1972–87, Robert Fleming Holdings Ltd 1974–90, Lane Fox & Partners Ltd 1987–91, The Fleming Income & Growth Investment Trust plc 1994–, Chesterton International plc 1994–; chm: The Fleming Property Unit Trust 1971–90, Channel Tunnel Investments plc 1981–86, Gill & Duffus Group plc 1982–85 (dir 1973–85), Robert Fleming Securities 1985–90; dep chm: Austin Reed Group plc 1977–96 (dir 1971–96), Robert Fleming Holdings Ltd 1986–90; memb Fin Act 1960 Tbnl 1978–84; *Recreations* walking, gardening; *Clubs* Brooks's; *Style*— David C F Pearson, Esq; ✉ The Manor, Berwick St John, Shaftesbury, Dorset SP7 0EX (☎ 01747 828363)

PEARSON, Dr David John; s of Eric Pearson (d 1977), of Eccleston, Chester, and Winifed Mary Pearson (d 1988); *b* 29 Jan 1946; *Educ* Ampleforth, St George's Hosp Med Sch London (MB BS), Univ of Manchester (PhD); *Career* house offr St George's Hosp 1968, sr house offr Manchester Royal Infirmary 1970, visiting scientist US Pub Health Serv 1977, asst prof of med Univ of W Virginia 1977, sr lectr in med Univ of Manchester 1979– (res fell 1972, lectr in med 1976), hon conslt physician S Manchester DHA 1979–; author of numerous res papers on allergy, immunology, food and health; memb: Br Soc for Immunology, Br Soc for Allergy and Clinical Immunology, Soc for Free Radical Res; FRCP 1987; *Recreations* skiing, windsurfing, sailing; *Style*— Dr David Pearson; ✉ Department of Medicine, University Hospital of South Manchester, Nell Lane, Manchester M20 8LR (☎ 0161 447 3828)

PEARSON, Dr Donald William Macintyre; s of William Clark Gilmour Pearson (d 1982), of New Cumnock, Ayshire, and Morag Macrae, *née* Macintyre (d 1961); *b* 5 Sept 1950; *Educ* Cumnock Acad Cumnock Ayrshire, Univ of Glasgow (BSc, MB ChB, MRCP); *m* 26 Sept 1972, Margaret Jessie Kennedy, da of James Harris, of Auchenleck, Ayrshire; 2 s (Andrew b 1979, Donald b 1984), 1 da (Gillian b 1977); *Career* registrar Univ Dept of Med Glasgow Royal Infirmary 1979–81, sr registrar in med diabetes and endocrinology Grampian Health Authy 1982–84, hon sr lectr Univ of Aberdeen 1984– (lectr in med 1981–82), conslt physician Aberdeen Royal Hosps NHS Tst 1984–; memb: Br Diabetic Assoc, Scottish Soc for Experimental Med, Aberdeen Medico-Chirurgical Soc, Scottish Soc of Physicians, BMA; MRCP 1979, FRCPGlas 1988, FRCPEd 1990; *Books* Carbohydrate Metabolism in Pregnancy and the New Born (ed with Sutherland and Stowers, 1989); *Recreations* golf; *Style*— Dr Donald Pearson; ✉ Diabetic Clinic, Woolman Hill, Aberdeen Royal Infirmary, Aberdeen, Scotland (☎ 01224 681818)

PEARSON, Dr Graham Scott; CB (1990); s of Ernest Reginald Pearson, and Alice, *née* Maclachlan (d 1987); *b* 20 July 1935; *Educ* Woodhouse Grove Sch Bradford Yorks, Univ of St Andrews (BSc, PhD); *m* 10 Sept 1960, Susan Elizabeth Meriton, da of Dr John Meriton Benn, CB (d 1992); 2 s (Gavin b 1963, Douglas b 1965); *Career* Univ of Rochester NY 1960–62, princ scientific offr Rocket Propulsion Estab 1967–69 (sr sci offr Westcott 1962–67), explosives and propellants liaison offr Br Embassy Washington DC 1969–72, asst dir Naval Ordnance Servs Bath 1973–76, tech advsr explosives and safety Chevaline 1976–79, princ superintendent Perme Westcott 1979–80, dep dir 1 and 2 Rarde Fort Halstead 1980–83, dir gen R & D Royal Ordnance Factories 1983–84, dir Chemical Def Estab Porton Down 1984–91, DG and chief exec Chemical and Biological Def Estab MOD Porton Down 1991–95, asst chief scientific advsr (non-proliferation) MOD 1995, hon sr visiting research fell in peace studies Univ of Bradford 1996–; FBIS 1967, CChem, FRSC 1985, FRSA 1989; *Books* contrib: Advances in Inorganic and Radiochemistry Vol 8 (1966), Advances in Photochemistry Vol 3 (1964), Oxidation and Combustion Reviews Vol 3 and 4 (second edn, 1969), Biological Weapons: Weapons of the Future (1993), Non-Conventional Weapons Proliferation in the Middle East (1993), US Security in an Uncertain Era (1993), Control of Dual Threat Agents: The Vaccines for Peace Programme (1994), Weapons Proliferation in the 1990s (1995); *Recreations* reading, long distance walking, photography, foreign travel; *Style*— Dr Graham S Pearson, CB; ✉ Department of Peace Studies, University of Bradford, Bradford, West Yorkshire BD7 1DP (☎ 01274 384186, fax 01274 385240)

PEARSON, John; *Career* early career experience with Thomson regional newspaper gp, sales exec Radio Luxembourg 1979–80, sales gp head Capital Radio 1984–87 (joined 1980), sales controller i/c women's mags IPC Magazines 1987–89, sales controller rising to sales dir LBC 1989–92; Virgin Radio: joined as launch sales dir 1992, appointed to Bd 1994, md 1995–; *Style*— John Pearson, Esq; ✉ Virgin Radio, 1 Golden Square, London W1R 4DJ (☎ 0171 434 1215, fax 0171 434 9005, pager 0941 103262, e-mail jpearson@vradio.co.uk)

PEARSON, (Hugh) John Hampden; s of Lt-Col Hugh Henry Pearson (d 1975), and Sybil Monica, *née* Dunn (d 1994); *b* 22 March 1947; *Educ* Charterhouse, King's Coll London (LLB); *m* 12 Oct 1974, Jacqueline Anne, da of Maj Harold Arthur Bird, of Goring, Sussex; 1 s (Daniel b 1982), 2 da (Alice b 1976, Juliet b 1978); *Career* admitted slr 1971, Stephenson Harwood 1971–73, Coward Chance 1973–86; ptnr: Durrant Piesse 1986–88, Lovell White Durrant 1988–; treas S African Townships Health Fund; memb: City of London Slrs Co, Law Soc, Assoc of Pension Lawyers; *Recreations* reading, hill walking, tennis, bridge, opera; *Clubs* MCC, Roehampton; *Style*— John Pearson, Esq; ✉ 15 Howard's Lane, London SW15 6NX; Providence Cottage, Buckland Newton, Dorset DT2

7BU; Lovell White Durrant, 65 Holborn Viaduct, London EC1A 2DY (☎ 0171 236 0066, fax 0171 248 4212, telex 887122)

PEARSON, Keith Philip; s of Fred Goring Pearson (d 1979), of Preston Lancs, and Phyllis, *née* Fryer; *b* 5 Aug 1941; *Educ* Preston GS, Madrid Univ, Univ of Cambridge (MA, DipEd); *m* 26 Aug 1965, Dorothy, da of Albert Edward Atkinson, of Woolley, Wakefield; 2 da (Lisa b 20 Nov 1968, Sally 13 May 1970); *Career* asst teacher then head of languages Rossall Sch 1964–72, dep princ George Watson's Coll 1979–83 (head of languages 1964–79), headmaster George Heriot's Sch 1983–; memb Scottish Consultative Cncl 1987–91; memb: HMC, SHA; FRSE 1995; *Recreations* sport, hill walking, music, DIY, foreign travel; *Style*— Keith Pearson, Esq, FRSE; ✉ George Heriot's School, Lauriston Place, Edinburgh EH3 9EQ (☎ 0131 229 7263, fax 0131 229 6363)

PEARSON, Mark Hadden; s of Dr Robert William Laird Pearson (d 1984), and Florence Margaret Kathleen, *née* Ashcroft (d 1977); *b* 1 Nov 1943; *Educ* St Bees Sch Cumberland; *m* 10 May 1969, Gaynor, da of George Clifford Rogers; 1 s (Thomas Hadden b 20 march 1981); *Career* chm and chief exec Neilson Cobbold Ltd 1988–; dir Rathbone Brothers PLC 1996–; vice chm Ctee Liverpool Local Unit Stock Exchange 1988–91 (memb 1983–91); memb: Northern Regnl Ctee Stock Exchange 1988–91, NW Regnl Advsy Panel London Stock Exchange 1991–92; MSI (memb Stock Exchange 1966); *Recreations* cricket, golf, walking; *Style*— Mark Pearson, Esq; ✉ The Hollies, Vyner Rd South, Bidston, Birkenhead, Merseyside L43 7PW (☎ 0151 653 9372); Neilson Cobbold Ltd, Martins Building, 4 Water St, Liverpool L2 3UF (☎ 0151 236 6666, fax 0151 236 4996, car 0831 637221)

PEARSON, Sir (Francis) Nicholas Fraser; 2 Bt (UK 1964), of Gressingham, Co Palatine of Lancaster; o s of Sir Francis Fenwick Pearson, 1 Bt, MBE (d 1991), and Katharine Mary, *née* Fraser; *b* 28 Aug 1943; *Educ* Radley; *m* 1978, Henrietta, da of Cdr Henry Pasley-Tyler, of Coton Manor, Guilsborough, Northants; *Heir* none; *Career* 3 Bn RB 1961–69 (ADC to C-in-C Far East 1969); Cons party candidate Oldham West 1975–78; dir: Voyager Travel Holdings Ltd 1988–92, Inter-Continental Hotels Group Ltd 1989–92, Saison Holdings BV 1990–92, Passport Hotels 1992, Ecofin Group Ltd 1993, Robert Langley & Co Ltd 1994; chm Euro-Asia Group Ltd 1994; *Recreations* shooting, fishing, tennis, opera; *Clubs* Carlton; *Style*— Sir Nicholas Pearson, Bt; ✉ 9 Upper Addison Gardens, Holland Park, London W14 8AL

PEARSON, Nicholas (Nick); *b* 24 March 1951; *Educ* King Edward Sch Birmingham, Lincoln Coll Oxford (BA Jurisprudence); *m* 1982, Chooi Yong Fong; 1 s (Oliver b 1985), 1 da (Sarah b 1989); *Career* Herbert Smith & Co 1974–79; Baker & McKenzie: based Hong Kong 1979–88, ptnr 1982–, based London 1988–, currently head Insolvency Dept; insolvency practitioner 1990–; memb Law Soc; *Recreations* tennis, cricket, walking; *Clubs* MCC; *Style*— Nick Pearson, Esq; ✉ Baker & McKenzie, 100 New Bridge Street, London EC4V 6JA (☎ 0171 919 1000, fax 0171 919 1999, e-mail nick.pearson@bakermck.com)

PEARSON, Richard John Crewdson; s of Maj R A R B Pearson (d 1983), and Evelyn Katherine, *née* Crewdson; *b* 4 May 1940; *Educ* Packwood Haugh, St Edward's Oxford, Univ of St Andrews (MA); *m* 30 Nov 1968, Catriona Wallace, da of Robert S Angus; 1 s (Richard b 25 Sept 1971), 1 da (Sarah Catriona b 13 April 1973); *Career* CA; chm Pannell Kerr Forster 1990– (ptnr 1970–); auditor Corp of London; cmmr of taxes 1988; Freeman City of London, Liveryman Worshipful Co of Barbers 1971; FCA 1975 (ACA 1965); *Recreations* golf, walking, sporting and country pursuits; *Clubs* Reform; *Style*— Richard Pearson, Esq; ✉ 6 The Lindens, Stock, Essex CM4 9NH; Pannell Kerr Forster, New Garden House, 78 Hatton Garden, London EC1N 8JA (☎ 0171 831 7393, fax 0171 405 6736)

PEARSON, Dr Richard Martin; s of late Leonard Louis Pearson, of Bournemouth, and late Anne, *née* Tobias; *b* 9 April 1943; *Educ* Royal GS High Wycombe, Gonville and Caius Coll Cambridge, St Mary's Hosp London; *Career* house surgn Addenbrooke's Hosp Cambridge 1967, house physician St Mary's Hosp London 1968, res fell and registrar Hammersmith Hosp 1971–73, sr registrar Royal Free Hosp 1977–80; conslt physician: Victoria and Kilton Hosps Bassetlaw 1980–81, Harold Wood and Bart's Hosps 1981–, Musicians' and Keyboard Clinic 1986–; *Recreations* opera, keep fit, walking; *Clubs* Savile; *Style*— Dr Richard Pearson; ✉ 152 Harley Street, London W1N 1HH (☎ 0171 935 3834, fax 0171 224 2574)

PEARSON, (Geoffrey) Stuart; s of Geoffrey William Pearson, of Ilkley, W Yorkshire, and Joan, *née* Richardson; *b* 17 Aug 1947; *Educ* Bradford GS; *m* 27 June 1970, Jean Barbara, da of Capt Charles Raymond Clegg, of Ilkley; 1 s (James Stuart b 1974), 1 da (Emma Jane b 1972); *Career* sr ptnr: Rawlinsons CAs 1976–85, G S Pearson & Co CAs 1989–96, Pearson Hudson CAs 1996–; chm: PCP International Ltd 1986–, Thornton and Pearson (Holdings) Ltd 1992–; pres KGL International Inc 1996–; FCA 1970, FCCA 1974; *Recreations* reading, opera, squash; *Style*— Stuart Pearson, Esq; ✉ Beech Cottage, Arthington, W Yorks (☎ 0113 284 2387); Pearson Hudson, Realtex House, Leeds Road, Rawdon, Leeds LS19 6AX (☎ 0113 250 0537, fax 0113 239 1629)

PEARSON, Gen Sir Thomas Cecil Hooke; KCB (1967, CB 1964), CBE (1959, OBE 1953), DSO (1940, and bar 1943), DL (Hereford and Worcester 1983); s of Vice Adm J L Pearson, CMG (d 1965), and Phoebe Charlotte, *née* Beadon (d 1973); *b* 1 July 1914; *Educ* Charterhouse, RMC Sandhurst; *m* 1947, Aud, da of Alf Skjelkvale (d 1953), of Oslo; 2 s (Anthony, Thomas); *Career* cmmnd RB 1934, Staff Coll 1942, Cdr 2 Bn RB 1942–43, Dep Cdr 2 Para Bde and 1 Airlanding Bde 1944–45, Cdr 1 and 7 Para Bns 1945–47, Jt Servs Staff Coll 1950, GSO 1 HQ Malaya and GHQ FARELF 1950–53, dir staff Jt Servs Staff Coll 1953–55, Cdr 45 Para Bde (TA) 1955–56, Nat Def Coll Canada 1957, Cdr 16 Para Bde 1957–59, COS to dir of Ops Cyprus 1960, chief Br Mil Mission to Soviet Forces in Germany 1960–61, Maj-Gen cmd 1 Div BAOR 1961–63, COS Northern Army Gp 1963–67, Cdr FARELF 1967–68, mil sec MOD 1969–72, C-in-C Allied Forces Northern Europe 1972–74, Col Cmdt Royal Green Jackets 1973–77, ADC Gen to HM The Queen 1974, ret; fisheries memb Welsh Water Authy 1980–83; Haakon VII Liberty Cross 1945, Norwegian Defence Association Medal 1973; *Recreations* yachting, shooting, fishing; *Clubs* Naval and Military, Kongalig Norsk Seilforening; *Style*— Gen Sir Thomas Pearson, KCB, CBE, DSO, DL

PEARSON, Wayne Clive; s of Clive William Howard Pearson, of Princetown, Devon, and Cynthia Rosemary, *née* Lake (d 1977); *b* 8 March 1969; *Educ* Tavistock Community Coll, Plymouth Coll of FE; *Career* chef; Old Police Station Restaurant Princetown Devon 1984–86, commis chef Dormy Hotel Ferndown 1986–88; sous chef: The Plough Clanfield 1989–91 (commis chef 1988–89), Well House St Keyne 1991–92, Chateau La Chaire Jersey 1992–93, Calcot Manor Tetbury May-Oct 1993; head chef Well House St Keyne 1993–; Masterchef of GB 1996; *Awards* Employee of the Year Hatton Hotel Gp 1989, Young Talent of the Year 1994, Good Food Guide 3* out of 5 1994 and 1995, AA Guide 3 Rosettes 1994–; *Recreations* football (following Liverpool FC), pool, snooker, eating out; *Style*— Wayne Pearson, Esq; ✉ Well House Hotel, St Keyne, Liskeard, Cornwall PL14 4RN (☎ 01579 342001, fax 01579 343891)

PEARSON LUND, Peter Graham; s of Douglas Pearson Lund, CBE (d 1974), of Springfields, Fetcham, Surrey, and Honor Winifred; *b* 9 Sept 1947; *Educ* Shiplake Coll Henley, Guildford Sch of Art; *m* 16 Nov 1968, Isabelle McLachlan; 2 s (Piers b 19 Oct 1969, Oliver b 10 Dec 1971); *Career* Tilney & Co 1969–70, Cazenove and Co 1970–73, Antony Gibbs 1973–75; md: Henderson Unit Trust Management (dir Henderson Administration Ltd) 1975–85, Gartmore Fund Managers Ltd (dir Gartmore plc) 1985–; *Recreations* tennis, skiing, sailing; *Style*— Peter Pearson Lund, Esq; ✉ Gartmore plc, Gartmore House, 16–18 Monument St, London EC3R 8QQ (☎ 0171 782 2411, fax 0171 782 2061)

PEARSON OF RANNOCH, Baron (Life Peer UK 1990), of Bridge of Gaur in the District of Perth and Kinross; Malcolm Everard MacLaren Pearson; s of late Col John MacLaren Pearson; *b* 20 July 1942; *Educ* Eton; *m* 1, 1965 (m dis 1970), Francesca Frua, da of Giuseppe Frua de Angeli; 1 da (Hon Silvia Maria Francesca (Hon Mrs Le Marchant) b 1966); 2, 1977 (m dis 1995), Hon (Francesca) Mary Charteris, o da of Baron Charteris of Amisfield, GCB, GCVO, QSO, OBE, PC, *qv*; 2 da (Hon Marina b 1980, Hon Zara Alexandra Mary b 1984); *Career* chm PWS Holdings plc; hon treas CNAA 1986–93; memb House of Lords Select Ctee on the European Communities, memb House of Lords Sub Ctee C on Environment and Social Affairs; Hon Pres of RESCARE (Nat Soc for Mentally Handicapped People in Residential Care 1994–; Hon LLD from CNAA; *Clubs* White's; *Style*— The Rt Hon the Lord Pearson of Rannoch; ✉ House of Lords, London SW1A 0PW

PEART, Michael John; CMG (1995), LVO; s of Joseph Albert William Peart (d 1993), and Thelma Theresa, *née* Rasmussen (d 1990); *b* 15 Dec 1943; *Educ* Gillingham Co GS; *m* 16 March 1968, Helena Mary, da of William Stuttle (d 1991); 1 s (Christopher John Stuttle b 23 Aug 1975); *Career* Prison Dept Home Office 1960–66; HM Dip Serv: FE and Pacific Dept FCO 1966–67, Scientific Rels Dept FCO 1967, Security Dept FCO 1967–69, commercial attaché Blantyre 1969–72, Polish language trg FCO 1973, third sec (commercial) Warsaw 1973–75, second sec (aid/political) Mexico City 1975–80, Personnel Ops Dept FCO 1980–83, first sec sur place 1982, head of Chancery Dhaka 1983–87, asst head S Pacific Dept FCO 1987–89, asst head Migration and Visa Dept FCO 1990–91, ambass Vilnius 1991–94, ambass to Fiji and concurrently non-resident high cmmr to Kiribati and to Nauru and Tuvalu 1995–; *Recreations* music, reading, walking; *Style*— Michael Peart, Esq, CMG, LVO; ✉ c/o FCO (Suva), King Charles Street, London SW1A 2AH

PEART, Prof Sir (William) Stanley; kt (1985); s of John George Peart (d 1950), of London, and Margaret Joan, *née* Fraser (d 1977), of London; *b* 31 March 1922; *Educ* King's Coll Sch Wimbledon, St Marys Hosp Med Sch, Univ of London (MB BS, MD); *m* Peggy, da of Col Walter Parkes, DSO, MC; 1 s (Robert b 1955), 1 da (Celia b 1953); *Career* MRC res student Dept of Pharmacology Univ of Edinburgh 1946–48; St Mary's Hosp Med Sch: lectr in med 1950–54, sr lectr 1954–56, prof of med 1956–87; res fell Nat Inst Med Res 1950–52, master Hunterian Inst RCS 1988–92; dep chm Wellcome Tst 1991–94 (tstee 1975–94), tstee Beit Tst; Hon DSc Univ of Edinburgh 1993; fell Imperial Coll 1988, hon fell Royal Australasian Coll of Physicians 1995; FRCP, FRS 1969; *Recreations* walking, skiing, reading, gardening; *Style*— Prof Sir Stanley Peart, FRS; ✉ 17 Highgate Close, Highgate, London N6 4SD (☎ 0181 341 3111)

PEART, Susan Rhona; *b* 31 July 1956; *Educ* Felixstowe Coll Suffolk; *Career* Cosmopolitan magazine: editorial asst 1979–81, sub ed 1981–82, asst features ed 1982–83, features ed 1983–84; dep features ed Daily Express 1985–87 (dep women's ed 1984–85), ed Sunday Express Magazine 1989–91 (dep ed 1987–89), ed Weekend Times 1992–93, dep ed YOU magazine 1993–; runner up Catherine Pakenham Award 1981; memb Br Soc of Magazine Eds 1987; *Recreations* entertaining, theatre, films, cooking, reading; *Style*— Ms Susan Peart; ✉ 1 Hollingbourne Road, Dulwich, London SE24 9NB (☎ 0171 274 6497)

PEASE, Alexander Michael; s of Nicholas Edwin Pease (d 1975), and Anne Raikes (d 1985); *b* 14 March 1956; *Educ* Malvern, Mansfield Coll Oxford (MA); *m* 22 April 1989, Lucy Jane, da of (George) Anthony Slater, of Guildford; 2 da (Claudia Catherine Anne b 14 April 1992, Marina Lily Jane b 16 July 1994); *Career* Allen & Overy: asst slr 1981, ptnr 1989–; memb: Law Soc Int Bar Assoc, City of London Law Soc; *Clubs* Cavalry and Guards'; *Style*— Alexander Pease, Esq; ✉ Allen & Overy, One New Change, London EC4M 9QQ (☎ 0171 330 3000, fax 0171 330 9999, telex 8812081)

PEASE, Joseph Gurney; s of Sir Alfred Edward Pease, 2 Bt (d 1939), and hp of bro, Sir (Alfred) Vincent Pease, 4 Bt, *qv*; *b* 16 Nov 1927; *Educ* Bootham Sch York; *m* 1953, Shelagh Munro, da of Cyril G Bulman; 1 s, 1 da; *Career* memb Guisborough UDC 1950–53; Lib candidate (gen elections): Bishop Auckland 1959, Darlington 1964, Westmoreland 1970, Penrith and the Border 1974; pres NE Young Lib Fedn 1961, memb Cncl Lib Pty 1969, pres NW Regnl Lib Pty 1970 and 1971; *Style*— Joseph Pease, Esq; ✉ Oak Tree House, Woodhall, Askrigg, Leyburn, N Yorks DL8 3LB

PEASE, Richard Peter; s and h of Sir Richard Thorn Pease, 3 Bt, *qv*, of Hindley House, Stocksfield, Northumberland and Anne, *née* Heyworth; *b* 4 Sept 1958; *Educ* Eton, Univ of Durham; *Career* formerly investmt fund mangr with Central Bd of Fin for the C of E, currently with Jupiter Tyndall; *Recreations* chess, bridge, backgammon, tennis, squash; *Clubs* Brooks's, Queen's; *Style*— Richard Pease, Esq; ✉ Jupiter Tyndall Ltd, 197 Knightsbridge, London SW7 1RB (☎ 0171 412 0703)

PEASE, Sir Richard Thorn; 3 Bt (UK 1920); s of Sir Richard Arthur Pease, 2 Bt (d 1969); *b* 20 May 1922; *Educ* Eton; *m* 9 March 1956, Anne, o da of Lt-Col Reginald Francis Heyworth (d 1941), and formerly w of David Henry Lewis Wigan; 1 s, 2 da; *Heir* s, Richard Peter Pease b 4 Sept 1958, *qv*; *Career* served WWII 60 Rifles 1941–46; vice chm Barclays Bank Ltd 1970–82, vice chm Barclays Bank UK Mgmnt 1971–82, chm Yorkshire Bank 1987–90, dir Grainger Tst plc; *Recreations* fishing; *Clubs* Brooks's, Pratt's, Army and Navy; *Style*— Sir Richard Pease, Bt; ✉ Hindley House, Stocksfield-on-Tyne, Northumberland (☎ 01661 842361)

PEASE, Rosamund Dorothy Benson (Dora); da of Michael Stewart Pease (d 1966), and Helen Bowen, *née* Wedgwood (d 1981); *b* 20 March 1935; *Educ* Mount Sch York, Newnham Coll Cambridge (BA); *Children* 1 s (Josiah Nodder b 27 May 1976); *Career* Dept of Health: asst princ 1958–63, private sec to Parly Sec 1963–64, princ 1965–73; asst sec Pay Bd 1973–74, Office of Manpower Economics 1974–75, Cabinet Office 1975–76, DHSS (personnel, trg, juvenile delinquency, security, children's residential servs) 1976–83, Office of Population Censuses and Surveys 1983–85, under sec NI Office 1985–88, under sec Dept of Health 1989–95 (food safety, nutrition, environmental health 1988–92, health care client gps and strategic issues 1992–95), ret; *Recreations* tennis, gardening, music, house; *Clubs* University Women's; *Style*— Miss R D B Pease

PEASE, Dr (Rendel) Sebastian; s of Michael Stewart Pease, OBE, JP (d 1966), of Reynolds Close, Girton, Cambridge, and Hon Helen Bowen, *née* Wedgwood, JP (d 1981); *b* 2 Nov 1922; *Educ* Bedales, Trinity Coll Cambridge (MA, ScD); *m* 9 Aug 1952, Susan (d 1996), da of Capt Sir Frank Todd Spickernell, KBE, CB, CVO, DSO, RN (d 1956), of Deane, Kintbury, Berkshire; 2 s (Christopher b 1956, Roland b 1959), 3 da (Rosamund (Mrs Chalmers) b 1953, Sarah (Mrs Kimbell) b 1955, Rowan (Mrs Zhao) b 1963); *Career* asst sci offr op res Miny Aircraft Prodn 1942–46, Sci Civil Serv Harwell 1947–54; UKAEA 1954–87: sci offr 1954–61, dir Culham laboratory 1967–81, dir fusion res programme 1981–87; pres Inst of Physics 1978–80; cons[illegible] Pease Partners 1988–; Royal Soc assessor Nuclear Physics Bd SERC 1987–93, visiting [illegible]of Univ of NSW 1991, memb Bd of Visitors Blackett Laboratory Imperial Coll Lon[illegible]91–; chm Br Pugwash Gp 1988–; memb: Newbury Symphony Orch 1947–92, [illegible]Parish Cncl 1987–, Euro Physical Soc, Royal Soc, Euro-Atlantic Gp, Fa[illegible]Univ Surrey 1973, Hon ScD Aston 1981, Hon DSc City 1987; Hon FINucE, [illegible]res 1978–80), CPhys, FIEE 1978, FRS 1977 (vice pres 1986–87); *Recreations* [illegible]Dr Sebastian Pease, FRS; ✉ The Poplars, W Ilsley, Newbury, Berks RG20 7A[illegible]5 281237)

PEASE, Sir (Alfred) Vincent; 4 Bt (UK 1882), of Hutton Lowcross and Pinchinthorpe, Co York; s of Sir Alfred Edward Pease, 2 Bt (d 1939), of Pinchinthorpe House,

Guisborough, Cleveland, and Emily Elizabeth, *née* Smith (d 1979); half-bro of Sir Edward Pease, 3 Bt (d 1963); *b* 2 April 1926; *Educ* Bootham Sch York, Durham Sch of Agric; *Heir* bro, Joseph Gurney Pease, *qv*; *Style*— Sir Vincent Pease, Bt; ✉ 149 Aldenham Road, Guisborough, Cleveland TS14 8LB (☎ 0287 636453)

PEASE, Hon William Simon; s of 1 Baron Wardington (d 1950), and Dorothy Charlotte (d 1983), da of 1 Baron Forster (d 1936, when title became extinct); hp of bro, 2 Baron Wardington; *b* 15 Oct 1925; *Educ* Eton, New Coll Oxford (MA), St Thomas's Hosp Medical Sch (MB BS); *m* 26 Oct 1962, Hon Elizabeth Jane Ormsby Gore, da of 4 Baron Harlech, KG, GCMG, PC (d 1964); *Career* Capt Grenadier Gds 1944–47; former conslt surgn ENT Dept Central Middx and Northwick Park Hosps; FRCS; *Recreations* sailing, gardening; *Clubs* Royal Yacht Sqdn; *Style*— The Hon William Pease; ✉ 29 Upper Addison Gardens, London W14 8AJ (☎ 0171 371 1776); Lepe House, Exbury, Southampton SO45 1AD (☎ 01703 893724)

PEASNELL, Prof Kenneth Vincent (Ken); *b* 2 Feb 1945; *Educ* Univ of Sheffield (postgrad dip in business studies), LSE (MSc), Lancaster Univ (PhD); *m*; 2 c; *Career* trainee accountant Melman Pryke & Co London 1961–67, fin analyst IBM (UK) Ltd 1968–69; Lancaster Univ: P D Leake res fell Dept of Accounting and Fin 1970–72, research fell ICRA 1972–75, lectr in accounting and fin 1976–77, Wolfson prof of accounting and fin 1977–87, head Dept of Accounting and Fin 1978–83, assoc dean Mgmnt Sch 1987–91 and 1994–, research prof of accounting and dir ICRA 1987–; memb Lancaster Univ: Fin Ctee 1980–83 and 1990–91, Academic Promotions Ctee 1986–87, Ctee for Research 1986–, Ctee for Colleges 1991, Budgeting and Monitoring Ctee 1994–, Senate 1978–83 and 1990–91, Univ Cncl 1987–91; visiting prof: Dept of Accounting Univ of Sydney 1983–84, Graduate Sch of Business Stanford Univ April-July 1984; memb Editorial Bd: Accounting Review 1977–82 and 1989–93, Journal of Business Fin and Accounting 1980–84, Accounting and Business Res 1981–80; ed Accounting and Business Research 1993–; external examiner: Univ of Birmingham 1979–80, Univ of Bristol 1979–82, Univs of Manchester and Warwick 1981–83, Manchester Business Sch 1987–90, LSE 1993–; external assessor for professorial or readership appointments at numerous univs; memb Exec Ctee Cncl of Depts of Accounting Studies 1979–84, chm Assoc of Univ Teachers of Accounting 1981–82; ICAEW: memb Res Sub-Ctee of Tech and Res Ctee 1979–82, memb Tech Ctee 1985–87, memb Educn and Training Advsy Gp 1987–90; memb Academic Accountants' Panel Accounting Standards Bd 1990– (Accounting Standards Ctee 1987–90), academic advsr to Accounting Standards Ctee on Off-Balance Sheet Financing 1988–90, memb Business and Mgmnt Studies Sub-Ctee of Univ Grants Ctee 1984–89; Univs Funding Cncl: chm Accountancy Panel 1989, Accountancy Subject advsr 1989–91; dir and hon treas Dukes Playhouse Ltd 1988–93; Distinguished Academic of the Year Award Chartered Assoc of Cert Accountants and Br Accounting Assoc 1996; FCA 1975 (ACA 1967); *Publications* author of numerous articles in academic, professional and miscellaneous publications and contribs to books; British Financial Markets and Institutions (with C W R Ward, 1985, 2 edn with J Piesse and C W R Ward, 1995), Off-Balance Sheet Financing (with R A Yaansah, 1988), Discounting in Corporate Financial Reporting (with C J Lovejoy, M Y Talukdar and P A Taylor, 1989); *Style*— Prof Ken Peasnell; ✉ International Centre for Research in Accounting, Management School, Lancaster University, Lancaster LA1 4YX (☎ 01524 593977)

PEAT, Adam Erskine; s of Raymond B B Peat, and Cynthia Elisabeth Peat, of Barham, Suffolk; *b* 30 Nov 1948; *Educ* Stowmarket County GS, Pembroke Coll Oxford (open exhbn, MA); *m* 1973, Christine Janet, da of James Huzzard Champion; 1 s (Andrew James b July 1979), 1 da (Joanna Jane b Nov 1982); *Career* Welsh Office: joined 1972, princ 1977, private sec to Sec of State 1982–83, asst sec 1984; acting dir CADW 1984–85, head Housing Div Welsh Office 1985–89, chief exec Housing for Wales 1989–; *Style*— Adam Peat, Esq; ✉ Chief Executive, Housing for Wales, 25–30 Lambourne Crescent, Llanishen, Cardiff CF4 5RS (☎ 01222 741500, fax 01222 741501)

PEAT, Sir Gerrard Charles; KCVO (1988); s of Charles Urie Peat, MC, MP (d 1979), and Ruth Martha, *née* Pulley (d 1979); *b* 14 June 1920; *Educ* Sedbergh; *m* 17 June 1949, Margaret Josephine Collingwood, da of Cyril Wylam-Walker (d 1965); 1 s (Michael Charles Gerrard b 1949); *Career* served WWII pilot RAF and ATA 1940–45, pilot 600 City of London Aux Sqdn 1948–51; ptnr Peat Marwick Mitchell & Co 1956–87, underwriting memb Lloyd's 1973–, auditor to Queen's Privy Purse 1980–88 (asst auditor 1969–80); memb: Ctee of Assoc of Lloyd's Membs 1983–88, Corp of City of London 1973–78, Cncl Lloyd's of London 1989–92; hon treas Assoc of Cons Clubs 1971–79; Liveryman Worshipful Co of Turners; FCA 1951; *Recreations* travel, shooting, fishing, golf; *Clubs* Boodle's, MCC; *Style*— Sir Gerrard Peat, KCVO; ✉ Home Farm, Mead Lane, Upper Basildon, Berks RG8 8ND (☎ 01491 671241); Flat 10, 35 Pont Street, London SW1X OBB (☎ 0171 245 9736); Suite 607, Britannia House, Glenthorne Rd, London W6 0LF (☎ 0181 748 9898, fax 0181 748 4250)

PEAT, Sir Henry; KCVO (1980, CVO 1973), DFC; s of late Sir Harry (William Henry) Peat, GBE, KCVO; *b* 1913; *Educ* Eton, Trinity Coll Oxford; *Career* served WWII, Flt Lt RAF Bomber Cmd Europe 1939–45; FCA; *Style*— Sir Henry Peat, KCVO, DFC; ✉ c/o Cadenham Manor, nr Chippenham, Wiltshire SN15 4NL

PEAT, (William Wood) Watson; CBE (1972), JP (Stirlingshire 1963); s of William Peat (d 1988), of Kirkland Farm, Denny, and Margaret, *née* Hillhouse (d 1986); *b* 14 Dec 1922; *Educ* Denny Public Sch; *m* 4 Oct 1955, Jean Frew Paton, da of James McHarrie, JP (d 1966), of Westwood, Stranraer; 2 s (James, William), 1 da (Margaret); *Career* served Lt RCS NW Europe and India 1940–46; farmer 1946–86 (ret); memb Nat Cncl of Scottish Assoc of Young Farmers' Club 1949–85 (chm 1953–54, pres 1979–81); gen cmmr of Income Tax 1962–; memb: Cncl of Nat Farmers' Union of Scotland 1959–78 (pres 1966–67), Stirling CC 1955–74 (vice convenor 1967–70); chm BBC Scottish Agric Advsy Cmmn 1971–77; dir: Agri-Finance (Scotland) Ltd 1968–79, FMC plc 1974–83, Islay Farmers Ltd 1974–86; pres Cncl Scottish Agriculture Organisations Ltd 1974–77, vice pres Assoc of Agric 1978–; memb: Scottish River Purification Advsy Ctee 1960–79, Cncl Hannah Res Inst 1963–82, Br Farm Produce Cncl 1964–87 (vice chm 1974–87), Central Cncl for Agric and Horticultural Co-operation 1967–83, Co-operative Devpt Bd Food From Britain 1983–89; govr W of Scotland Agric Coll 1964–90 (vice chm 1975–83, chm 1983–88); chm: Bd of Dirs Scottish Agriculture Colleges Ltd 1984–90, Scottish Advsy Ctee Assoc of Agric 1974–79 (vice pres 1979–); dir Fedn of Agric Co-operatives (UK) Ltd 1974–77; memb: Br Agric Cncl 1974–84, Govt Ctee of Enquiry into Acquisition and Occupancy of Agric Land 1977–79; BBC nat govr for Scotland, chm Broadcasting Cncl for Scotland 1984–89; pres Ariel Radio Gp BBC 1985–; OStJ 1987; MRTS, memb Radio Soc of GB, FRAgS 1987, hon fell Scottish Agric Coll 1990; *Recreations* amateur radio, flying, photography, gardening; *Clubs* Farmers', BBC; *Style*— Watson Peat, Esq, CBE, JP; ✉ Carbro, 61 Stirling Rd, Larbert, Stirlingshire FK5 4SG (☎ 01324 562420)

PEATTIE, Ian Harry; s of Thomas Wilmshurst Peattie (d 1972), and Lillie Beatrice, *née* Gregory (d 1984); *b* 12 June 1942; *Educ* St John's Sch Leatherhead, St Chad's Coll Durham; *m* 1964 (m dis 1981), Elizabeth Anne, da of William George Parsons; 2 da (Tracey Jayne b 16 Nov 1963, Adelle Theresa b 24 Jan 1965); *Career* Civil Service: joined as clerical offr Public Works Loan Bd 1965–67, in charge mechanised accounting 1967–74 (installed first computer in 1972), sec to Cmmrs 1987– (asst sec 1978–87), comptroller gen Nat Debt Office 1987–, dir Nat Investment and Loans Office 1987–, asst paymaster gen Office of HM Paymaster General 1996–; memb: Treasy Ctee on Local Authy Borrowing, Treasy Mgmnt Panel CIPFA, Capital Fin Forum DOE/Audit Cmmn; author of articles in specialist magazines incl Local Govt Chronicle and Public Finance; Liveryman Worshipful Co of Glass Sellers 1996, Freeman City of London 1996; *Recreations* family, friends, golf; *Clubs* Abbotsley Golf (capt); *Style*— Ian Peattie, Esq; ✉ The National Investment and Loans Office, 1 King Charles Street, London SW1A 2AP (☎ 0171 270 3855, fax 0171 270 3860)

PECK, Alan Charles Weston; s of Awdry Francis Weston Peck (d 1980), and Marjory, *née* Taylor; *b* 13 April 1949; *Educ* Sherborne, Univ of Oxford (BA); *m* 1974, Anne Carolyn, da of Sir Herbert Ingram, 3 Bt (d 1980); 1 s (Alexander Robin Weston b 12 Feb 1981), 1 da (Frances Miranda Weston b 17 Sept 1978); *Career* admitted slr 1974; Freshfields: joined 1972, ptnr 1980–86 and 1989–, managing ptnr 1993–96, chief exec 1996–; dir S G Warburg & Co Ltd 1986–88; *Recreations* shooting, fishing, gardening; *Clubs* Turf, MCC; *Style*— Alan Peck, Esq; ✉ Hurst Lodge, Hurst, nr Reading, Berks RG10 0RB (☎ 0118 934 1088); Freshfields, 65 Fleet St, London EC4Y 1HS (☎ 0171 936 4000, fax 0171 832 7001)

PECK, David Arthur; s of Frank Archibald Peck, of Wellingborough, Northants, and Molly, *née* Eyels (d 1995); bro of Maj-Gen Richard Peck, CB, , *qv*; *b* 3 May 1940; *Educ* Wellingborough Sch, St John's Coll Cambridge (MA); *m* 3 Feb 1968, Jennifer Mary, da of late Frederick William Still, and late Heather Mary Still, of Liphook, Hants; 2 da (Emma b 2 Oct 1970, Sophie b 11 Oct 1973), 1 s (Mark b 12 June 1975); *Career* admitted slr 1966, sr ptnr Birkbeck Montagu's 1985–91 (ptnr 1967), ptnr Penningtons 1991–95; Clerk to Worshipful Co of Merchant Taylors 1995–; memb: Cncl Radley Coll, Law Soc, Euro Slrs' Gp, Int Bar Assoc, Soc of English and American Lawyers; *Clubs* MCC, Hawks; *Style*— David Peck, Esq; ✉ 26 Chepstow Place, London W2 (☎ 0171 229 9674)

PECK, Sir Edward Heywood; GCMG (1974, KCMG 1966, CMG 1957); s of Lt-Col Edward Surman Peck, IMS (d 1934), and Doris Louise Heywood (d 1934); *b* 5 Oct 1915; *Educ* Clifton, Queen's Coll Oxford (MA); *m* 1948, Alison Mary, da of late John MacInnes, of Sevenoaks; 1 s, 2 da; *Career* entered Consular Serv 1938, served Turkey, Greece, India and Singapore 1940–60, dep cmdt Br Sector Berlin 1955–58; asst under sec of state for SE Asia and Far Eastern Affrs FCO 1960–65, high cmmr Kenya 1966–68, dep under sec of state FCO 1968–70, Br perm rep to N Atlantic Cncl 1970–75, ret; hon visiting fell Def Studies Univ of Aberdeen 1976–85; memb Cncl of Nat Tst for Scot 1982–87; FRGS; *Publications* North-East Scotland, Avonside Explored, The Battle of Glenlivet; *Recreations* hill walking, travel, reading history, writing guide-books; *Clubs* Alpine; *Style*— Sir Edward Peck, GCMG; (☎ 01807 580 318)

PECK, Maj-Gen Richard Leslie; CB (1990); s of Frank Archibald Peck, of Wellingborough, Northants, and Molly, *née* Eyels (d 1995); bro of David Arthur Peck, *qv*; *b* 27 May 1937; *Educ* Wellingborough Sch, RMA Sandhurst, RMCS Shirvenham (BSc); *m* 4 Aug 1962, Elizabeth Ann (Liz), da of Maj Denis James Bradley, of Shrivenham; 2 s (David b 1967, Simon b 1972), 1 da (Sarah b 1965); *Career* cmmnd RE 1957, Troop Cdr Cyprus 1962, instr RMAS 1965, Staff Coll 1968, Bde Maj 1969, Sqdn Cdr BAOR 1972, DS Staff Coll 1973, CO BAOR 1977, MOD Col (MS) 1979, Bde Cdr 1981, RCDS 1984, Dir of Personnel MOD 1985, Engr-in-Chief MOD 1988–91, Col Cmdt RE 1991–, Col Queen's Gurkha Engineers 1991–96; tstee: Gurkha Welfare Tst 1991–96, Lord Kitchener Nat Meml Fund 1992–; dir The Churches Conservation Tst (formerly Redundant Churches Fund) 1992–; CEng, FICE, FRGS; *Recreations* cricket, golf, shooting, swimming; *Clubs* Army and Navy, Royal Mid-Surrey Golf, MCC, I Zingari, Free Foresters, Band of Brothers; *Style*— Maj-Gen Richard Peck, CB

PECK, Robert (Bob); s of Ernest Lambert Peck, of Leeds, and Millicent, *née* McBain (d 1971); *b* 23 Aug 1945; *Educ* Leeds Modern Sch, Leeds Coll of Art (Dip AD); *m* 11 Sept 1982, Gillian Mary, da of Jack Roderick Baker; 1 s (George Edward b 22 July 1985), 2 da (Hannah Louise b 9 Feb 1982, Emily Helena (Milly) b 17 July 1990); *Career* actor; began in repertory theatre in Birmingham, Scarborough Library Theatre and Exeter Northcott Theatre 1969, appeared Royal Court Theatre and West End in Life Class 1974; numerous radio plays and readings; *Theatre* RSC 1975–84 (appearing in numerous prodns of classical and contemporary work in UK, NY and three European countries (from Gravedigger and The Player-King in Hamlet to the title role in Lear)), other RSC roles incl: Macduff, Macbeth, Iago, Kent, Malvolio, Caliban, Enobarbus, Sir Mullberry Hawk and John Browdie in Nicholas Nickleby; other roles incl: The Road to Mecca and A Chorus of Disapproval (both NT) 1985, Two Way Mirror (Young Vic) 1989, In Lambeth (The Warehouse) 1989, The Price (Young Vic) 1990, The Birthday Party (RNT), Rutherford and Son (RNT) 1994; *Television* incl: Macbeth, Three Sisters, Nicholas Nickleby, Bavarian Night (BBC) 1981, Edge of Darkness (BBC, winner BAFTA Best Television Actor of the Year Award 1985) 1984, After Pilkington 1986, The Soldier and Death (ITV) 1987, A TV Dante (Channel 4) 1988, One Way Out (BBC) 1988, Children Crossing (BBC) 1989, Centrepoint (ITV) 1989, In Lambeth (BBC) 1990, The Black Velvet Gown (ITV) 1990, Shoot the Revolution 1990, Children of the Dragon (ABC/BBC) 1991, Natural Lies (BBC) 1992, An Ungentlemanly Act (BBC) 1992, Tuesday (BBC) 1993, Hard Times (BBC) 1993; *Films* incl: Parker 1984, The Kitchen Toto 1986, On The Black Hill 1987, Slipstream 1988, Ladder of Swords 1988, Jurassic Park 1993, The Merchant of Venice 1995, Surviving Picasso 1996, Miss Smillas Sense of Snow 1996, Illuminations 1996, The Opium Wars 1996; *Style*— Bob Peck, Esq; ✉ c/o Pippa Markham, Markham & Froggatt Ltd, 4 Windmill Street, London W1P 1HF (☎ 0171 636 4412, fax 0171 637 5233)

PECK, Stanley Edwards; CBE (1974), BEM (1954), QPM (1964), DL (Staffs 1962); s of Harold Edwards Peck, of Shanghai and Edgbaston (d 1962), and Mabel Beatrice Bevan, *née* Bell (d 1966); *b* 24 Jan 1916; *Educ* Solihull Sch, Univ of Birmingham; *m* 1, 1939, Yvonne Sydney Edwards (d 1994), da of John Edwards Jessop (d 1965); 2 s (John, Timothy), 2 da (Josephine, Angela); m 2, 31 August 1996, Elizabeth Beddows; *Career* Flt Lt RAF 1941–45; Met Police 1935–54, supt New Scotland Yard 1950, chief constable Staffs 1960–64 (asst and dep chief constable 1954–60), HM inspector of constabulary 1964–78, memb Br Rail Bd Police Ctee 1978–87; pres Royal Life Saving Soc (UK) 1969–74; OStJ; *Recreations* golf, dog walking; *Clubs* RAF; *Style*— Stanley Peck, Esq, CBE, BEM, QPM, DL; ✉ Lodge Gardens, Walnut Grove, Radcliffe-on-Trent, Notts (☎ 0115 933 2361)

PECKER, Morley Leo; s of Alec Pecker (d 1975), of London; *b* 7 April 1937; *Educ* Epsom Coll; *Career* Nat Serv 2 Lt RA 1960–63; CA; articles Charles Eves Lord and Co 1954–60, mangr RF Frazer & Co 1963–65, sr advsr accountant Bd of Inland Revenue 1965–73, princ admin Euro Cmmn Brussels 1973–; memb Int Hockey Fedn, hon treas Euro Hockey Fedn, memb Br Olympic Assoc, hon life memb The Cricket Soc, past hon treas Middx Cricket Union; Olympic Hockey judge: Munich 1972, Montreal 1976, Moscow 1980, Los Angeles 1984; memb Inst of Taxation 1964; ACA 1960, FCA 1970; *Recreations* hockey, cricket, music, photography; *Clubs* Chateau St Anne (Belgium), MCC, Lord's Taverners, The Cricket Society; *Style*— Morley Pecker, Esq; ✉ Le Grand Forestier, Ave du Grand Forestier 26 (Box 10), B-1160 Brussels, Belgium (☎ and fax 00 32 2 672 57 85); European Commission, 200 Rue de la Loi, B-1049 Brussels, Belgium (☎ 00 32 2 295 53 79, fax 00 32 2 295 28 44)

PECKHAM, Prof (Lady); Catherine Stevenson; da of Dr Alexander King, CBE, CMG, of 168 Rue de Grenelle, Paris, and Sarah Maskell, *née* Thompson; *b* 7 March 1937; *Educ* St Paul's Girls' Sch London, Univ of London (MB BS, MD); *m* 7 Oct 1958, Prof Sir Michael John Peckham, *qv*, s of William Stuart Peckham (d 1981); 3 s (Alexander b 1962, Daniel Gavin b 1964, Robert Shannan b 1965); *Career* reader in community med Charing Cross Hosp Med Sch 1977–85, prof of paediatric epidemiology Inst of Child

Health and hon conslt Hosp for Sick Children Great Ormond St 1985– (sr lectr and hon conslt 1975–77), hon conslt Public Health Laboratory 1985–; memb: US Fulbright Cmmn 1987–95, Med Advsy Ctee Br Cncl 1992–, Advtg Standards Authy 1993–; FFM 1980, FRCP 1988, FRCPath 1992, FRCOG 1994; *Recreations* flute; *Style*— Prof Catherine Peckham; ✉ 59 Onslow Square, London SW7 3LR (☎ 0171 589 2826); Institute of Child Health, Guilford St, London WC1

PECKHAM, Prof Sir Michael John; kt (1995); s of William Stuart Peckham (d 1981), and Gladys Mary, *née* Harris; *b* 2 Aug 1935; *Educ* William Jones W Monmouthshire Sch, St Catharine's Coll Cambridge (MA, MD), UCH Med Sch; *m* 7 Oct 1958, Prof Catherine Stevenson Peckham, *qv*, da of Dr Alexander King, CMG, CBE, of 168 Rue de Grenelle, Paris; 3 s (Alexander b 1962, Daniel Gavin b 1964, Robert Shannan b 1965); *Career* Capt RAMC 1960–62; clinical res cncl scholar MRC Paris 1965–67, dean Inst of Cancer Res London 1984–86 (sr lectr 1972–74, prof 1974–86), civilian conslt to RN 1975–86, dir Br Postgrad Med Fedn 1986–90, dir of res and devpt Dept of Health 1991–95, dir Sch of Public Policy UCL 1996–; special tstee Guy's Hosp & St Thomas' Hosp Bd of Special Tstees 1996–; pres: Euro Soc of Therapeutic Radiology and Oncology 1984–85, Br Oncology Assoc 1986–88, Fedn of Euro Cancer Socs 1989–91; ed-in-chief European Journal of Cancer 1990–95, fndr Bob Champion Cancer Tst; former memb special health authy: Hosps for Sick Children Gt Ormond St, Brompton and Nat Heart Hosp, Hammersmith Hosp, Imperial Cancer Res Fund (vice chm Cncl); Hon DSc Loughborough Univ of Technol 1992; Dr (hc): Université de Franche-Compté Besançon 1991, Katholieke Universiteit Leuven 1993; foreign assoc memb Nat Acad of Sciences Inst of Med Washington 1994; FRCP, FRCR, FRCPath, FRCPG, FRCS; *Recreations* painting; *Style*— Prof Sir Michael Peckham; ✉ 59 Onslow Square, London SW7 3LR

PECKOVER, Richard Stuart; s of late Rev Cecil Raymond Peckover, and Grace Lucy, *née* Curtis; *b* 5 May 1942; *Educ* King Edward VII Sch King's Lynn, Wadham Coll Oxford (MA), CCC Cambridge (PhD); *Career* UKAEA 1969–: res scientist Culham Laboratory 1969–81, res assoc MIT 1973–74, branch head Safety and Reliability Directorate 1983–87 (gp ldr 1982), site dir Winfrith Technology Centre 1990–92 (asst dir 1987, dep dir 1989), UKAEA safety dir 1992–; chm SIESO 1989–93; FIMA, FInstP, FRAS, FRMetS, FIMgt, FSaRS; *Recreations* walking, talking, listening to music; *Clubs* United Oxford and Cambridge; *Style*— Richard Peckover; ✉ The Barn, Pallington, Dorchester, Dorset DT2 8QU; Winfrith Technology Centre, Winfrith, Dorchester, Dorset DT2 8DH

PEDDER, Air Marshal Sir Ian Maurice; KCB (1982), OBE (1963), DFC (1949); s of Maurice Albert Pedder (d 1967), and Elsie Pedder (d 1981); *b* 2 May 1926; *Educ* Royal GS High Wycombe, Queen's Coll Oxford; *m* 1949, Jean Mary, da of Tom and Clara Kellett; 1 s, 2 da; *Career* served RAF Far East, Germany and UK 1944–64, directing staff RAF Staff Coll 1964–67, staff and cmd appts 1967–80; Nat Air Traffic Servs: dep controller 1977–81, controller 1981–85; Air Marshal 1981; memb Bd CAA 1981–85; co dir Davies and Newman plc 1986–92, chm Dan-Air Services Ltd 1988–90, sr aviation conslt 1993–; *Clubs* Royal Air Force, Victory Services; *Style*— Air Marshal Sir Ian Pedder, KCB, OBE, DFC; ✉ The Chestnuts, Cheddar, Somerset

PEDDIE, (Hon) Ian James Crofton; QC (1992); s of Baron Peddie, MBE, JP (Life Peer; d 1978), and Lady Hilda Peddie (d 1985); *b* 1945; *Educ* Gordonstoun, Univ Coll London (LLB); *m* 1976, Susan Renée, da of Edmund John Brampton Howes; 2 s, 2 da; *Career* called to the Bar Inner Temple 1971, asst recorder 1992–; *Style*— Ian Peddie, Esq, QC; ✉ 22 Old Buildings, Ground Floor, Lincoln's Inn, London WC2A 3UJ

PEDDIE, Peter Charles; CBE (1983); s of Ronald Peddie, CBE, JP (d 1986), of Springwater Farm, Mudgley, Wedmore, Somerset, and Vera, *née* Nicklin (d 1981); *b* 20 March 1932; *Educ* Canford, St John's Coll Cambridge (MA); *m* 25 June 1960, Charlotte Elizabeth, da of Ernest Pierce Ryan (d 1982), of Betchworth, Surrey; 2 s (Andrew b 20 Sept 1963, Jonathan b 5 May 1968), 2 da (Emma b 20 June 1961, Rachel b 9 Aug 1965); *Career* admitted slr 1957; Freshfields: asst slr 1957–60, ptnr 1960–92, conslt 1992; advsr to Govr and first head Legal Unit Bank of England 1992–96; govr Canford Sch 1981–94, special tstee Middx Hosp 1977–92, memb Cncl Middx Hosp Med Sch 1977–88; Freeman Worshipful Co of Slrs; memb: Law Soc, Slrs' Benevolent Assoc; *Recreations* gardening; *Clubs* City of London; *Style*— Peter Peddie, Esq, CBE; ✉ Bannisters Farmhouse, Mattingley Green, Hook, Hants RG27 8LA (01734 326570)

PEDERSEN, Cecil Ivan; s of Ivan Pedersen (d 1963), of London, and Ethel Mary, *née* McCormick; *b* 31 May 1931; *Educ* Owen's Sch London; *m* 4 June 1960, (Ann) Isabel, da of Samuel James Curry, OBE, JP, of Coleraine, Co Londonderry, NI; 2 da (Catherine b 1961, Hilary b 1964); *Career* RAF: Nat Serv Cmmn 1949, short serv cmmn; sponsored to study Russian Univ of London 1953, instr in Russian Jt Servs Sch for Linguists 1956–58, sr editorial asst The Iron and Steel Inst 1959–61; press offr: DSIR 1961–62, PR Prodn Engrg Res Assoc (PERA) 1962–66, Decca Radar Ltd 1966–67; asst sec The Inst of Physics 1967–84 (managing ed 1967–70, dir of publishing 1970–84, md Adam Hilger Ltd 1976–84), publishing conslt 1985–, chief exec Br Assoc of Industl Eds 1986–92; fell Br Assoc of Communicators in Business; *Recreations* languages, bridge, outdoor activites, photography; *Clubs* Danish, Remenham (Henley); *Style*— C I Pedersen

PEDLER, Garth; s of Thomas Wakeham Pedler (d 1984), of Exeter, and Ruby, *née* Cornish (d 1996); *b* 21 Feb 1946; *Educ* King's Coll Taunton (memb Old Boys' Ctee 1972–); *partner* Jane Domaille Palmer, of Guernsey; *Career* with Touche Ross & Co 1969–73, now independent taxation conslt; occasional contributor on fiscal matters: Sunday Telegraph 1991–, Sunday Times 1993–; FCA, ATII; *Books* The 9.5mm Vintage Film Encyclopaedia (ed and jt author), biography of Joan Morgan, *qv*; regular contributor to Classic Images USA 1982–; *Recreations* vintage film research and associated journalism, genealogy, large collections of hardback books and vintage films, alpine hiking in summer; *Style*— Garth Pedler, Esq; ✉ Hay Hill, Totnes, Devon TQ9 5LH

PEDLEY, Roger Keith; s of Thomas Kenneth Fitzgeorge Pedley (d 1976), and Winifred Gordon, *née* Smith; *b* 12 Oct 1944; *Educ* King's Sch Worcester; *m* 26 Oct 1970, Paula Lesley, da of George Holland; 1 s (Rupert b 1980), 1 da (Helen b 1977); *Career* CA; Peat Marwick Mitchell (now KPMG): joined 1968, Paris 1969–72, Nottingham 1973–75, London 1975–76, ptnr Nottingham 1976, sr ptnr Derby 1980–; dir St John Ambulance Assoc for Derbyshire; *Recreations* flyfishing, windsurfing; *Style*— Roger K Pedley, Esq; ✉ Pear Tree House, Church Street, Ockbrook, Derbyshire DE72 3SL; KPMG, 5 Stuart Street, Derby DE1 2EQ (☎ 01332 636100)

PEDLEY, Rev (Geoffrey) Stephen; QHC (1985); s of Rev Prebendary Geoffrey Heber Knight Pedley (d 1974), and Muriel, *née* Nixon (d 1972); *b* 13 Sept 1940; *Educ* Marlborough, Queens' Coll Cambridge (MA), Cuddesdon Coll Oxford; *m* 9 Jan 1970, Mary Frances, da of Rev Canon Alexander Macdonald (d 1980); 2 s (Mark Alexander b 1974, Andrew Francis b 1976), 1 da (Philippa Rose b 1979); *Career* asst curate: Liverpool Parish Church 1966, Holy Trinity Coventry 1969; rector Kitwe Zambia 1971–77, vicar St Peter's Stockton 1977–88, rector Whickham 1988–93, canon residentiary of Durham Cathedral 1993–; *Style*— The Rev Canon Stephen Pedley, QHC; ✉ 6A The College, Durham DH1 3EQ (☎ 0191 384 5489)

PEDLEY, Prof Timothy John; s of Richard Rodman Pedley (d 1973), and Jean Mary Mudie Pedley, *née* Evans; *b* 23 March 1942; *Educ* Rugby, Trinity Coll Cambridge (Wrangler, Mayhew Prize, MA, PhD, ScD 1982); *m* 1965, Avril Jennifer Martin Uden, da of B G Grant-Uden (d 1990); 2 s (Jonathan Richard b 1968, Simon Grant b 1969); *Career* post-doctoral fell Mechanics Dept Johns Hopkins Univ 1966–68, lectr Physiological Flow Studies Unit and Dept of Mathematics Imperial Coll London 1968–73, successively asst dir of research, lectr then reader in biological fluid dynamics Dept of Applied Mathematics and Theoretical Physics (DAMTP) Univ of Cambridge 1973–89, prof of applied mathematics Univ of Leeds 1990–96 (head Dept of Applied Mathematics 1991–94), G I Taylor prof of fluid mechanics DAMTP Univ of Cambridge 1996–; Gonville & Caius Coll Cambridge: fell and dir of applied mathematics 1973–89, professorial fell 1996–; sometime govr: Perse Sch Cambridge, Batley GS; Adams Prize Univ of Cambridge 1977; EPSRC sr fell 1995–; memb: American Soc of Mechanical Engrg 1990, Soc for Experimental Biology 1993; FIMA 1981, FRS 1995; *Books* Scale effects in animal locomotion (ed, 1977), The mechanics of the circulation (jtly, 1978), The fluid mechanics of large blood vessels (1980), Biological fluid dynamics (co-ed, 1995); *Recreations* bird watching, running, reading, crosswords; *Style*— Prof Timothy Pedley; ✉ Department of Applied Mathematics & Theoretical Physics, University of Cambridge, Silver Street, Cambridge CB3 9EW (☎ 01223 339842, fax 01223 337918, e-mail tjp3@damtp.cam.ac.uk)

PEEBLES, Robert Andrew (Andy); s of Robert Peebles (d 1961), and Mary Jean, *née* Simmonds (d 1992); *b* 13 Dec 1948; *Educ* Bishop's Stortford Coll, Bournemouth Coll Of Tech; *Career* radio presenter: BBC Radio Manchester 1973, Piccadilly Radio Manchester 1974–78, BBC World Serv 1978–88, BBC Radio One 1978–92, BBC Schools Radio 1983–87, BBC Radio Sport 1983–, BBC Radio Lancashire 1992–; *Books* The Lennon Tapes (1981), The Elton John Tapes (1981); *Recreations* sport, cinema, photography; *Clubs* Harlequins Rugby Football Club, Lancashire County Cricket Club; *Style*— Andy Peebles, Esq; ✉ BBC Radio Lancashire, Darwen St, Blackburn, Lancs BB2 2EA (☎ 01254 262411)

PEEK, Sir William Grenville; 5 Bt (UK 1874), of Rousdon, Devon; s of Capt Roger Grenville Peek (d 1921), and Hon Joan Penelope Sclater-Booth (d 1976), da of 2 Baron Basing; suc cousin Sir Francis Henry Grenville Peek, 4 Bt (d 1996); *b* 15 Dec 1919; *Educ* Eton; *m* 8 July 1950, Lucy Jane, yst da of late Maj Edward Dorrien-Smith, DSO, KSLI, of Weir Point, Restronguet, Falmouth, Cornwall; 1 s (Richard Grenville b 1955), 3 da (Jane Elizabeth (Mrs James Robertson) b 27 Nov 1952, Mary Susannah (Mrs Malcolm Robertson) b 1957, Katherine Julia (Mrs James Hughes) b 20 July 1960); *Heir* s, Richard Grenville Peek b 3 Feb 1955; *Career* Capt late 9 Lancers WWII serv 1939–45 (despatches); *Clubs* Royal Western Yacht; *Style*— Sir William Peek, Bt; ✉ Weekemoor, Loddiswell, Kingsbridge, S Devon TQ7 4DY

PEEL, David Alexander Robert; s of Maj Robert Edmund Peel (d 1951), of London, and Sheila Mary, *née* Slattery (d 1992); *b* 12 Nov 1940; *Educ* St Edmund's Coll Herts, Univ Coll Oxford (BA); *m* 1971, Patricia Muriel, da of Albert Essery; 2 s (Robert b 2 June 1973, William b 29 Feb 1976); *Career* private sec to Min of State Miny of Tport 1967–68 (asst princ 1964–67), seconded as first sec Office of the UK Rep to EC FCO 1972–75, private sec to Min for Tport DOE 1975–76, asst sec Dept of Tport and DOE 1976–82, head Road Prog and Highways Policy Div Dept of Tport 1982–86, head of support servs Dept of Tport and DOE 1986–90, under sec and dir of admin resources DOE 1990–96; reference sec (pt/t) MMC 1996–; *Recreations* allotment gardening, opera and ballet, Baroque architecture; *Style*— David Peel, Esq; ✉ c/o Lloyds Bank, Pall Mall St James's, 8 Waterloo Place, London SW1Y 4BE

PEEL, Jane Elizabeth; da of William Richard Peel (d 1994), and Josephine Irene, *née* Stewart (d 1995); *b* 4 Oct 1960; *Educ* Highbury Hill HS London, Harlow Tech Coll (NCTJ Cert), Fletcher Sch of Law and Diplomacy Medford Mass; *Career* reporter Barnet Press/Enfield Gazette 1981–84, sr reporter Lincolnshire Echo 1984–85; BBC: reporter BBC Radio Lincolnshire 1985–86, news prodr BBC Essex 1986–87, news ed BBC Essex 1987–89, reporter BBC national radio 1989–90 (assignments incl Romanian revolution 1989–90), home and legal affrs corr 1990–; *Recreations* waterskiing, snow skiing; *Style*— Ms Jane Peel; ✉ BBC News & Current Affairs, Broadcasting House, London W1A 1AA (☎ 0802 496927, fax 0171 636 4295)

PEEL, Sir (William) John; kt (1973); s of late Sir William Peel, KCMG, KBE; *b* 16 June 1912; *Educ* Wellington Coll, Queens' Coll Cambridge; *m* 1936, Rosemary Mia Minka, da of late Robert Readhead; 1 s (Quentin), 3 da (Joanna, Alethea, Lynda); *Career* Colonial Admin Serv 1933–51, Br resident Brunei 1946–48, res cmmr Gilbert and Ellice Islands 1949–51; Parly candidate (C) Meriden Div of Warwicks 1955, MP (C) Leicester SE 1957–74; PPS to: Econ Sec to Treasy 1958–59, Min State BOT 1959–60; asst govt whip (unpaid) 1960–61, Lord Cmmr Treasy Nov 1961–64; pres: N Atlantic Assembly 1972–73, WEU Assembly 1972–74; memb Br Delgn to Euro Parl 1973–74, hon dir Cons Party Int Office 1975–76; chm Victoria League for Cwlth Friendship 1982–83; memb Ct of Assts Worshipful Co of Framework Knitters (Master 1983–84); *Clubs* Carlton, Hurlingham, Hawks (Cambridge); *Style*— Sir John Peel; ✉ 51 Cambridge St, London SW1 (☎ 0171 834 8762)

PEEL, Prof John David Yeadon; s of Prof Edwin Arthur Peel (d 1992), of Birmingham, and Nora Kathleen, *née* Yeadon (d 1988); *b* 13 Nov 1941; *Educ* King Edward's Sch Birmingham, Balliol Coll Oxford (MA), LSE (PhD), Univ of London (DLit); *m* 4 Sept 1969, Jennifer Christine Ferial, da of Maj Kenneth Nathaniel Pare; 3 s (David Nathaniel Yeadon b 16 March 1972, Timothy James Olatokunbo b 27 Jan 1974, Francis Edwin b 30 March 1977); *Career* asst lectr and lectr in sociology Univ of Nottingham 1966–70, lectr in sociology LSE 1970–73, visiting reader in sociology and anthropology Univ of Ife Nigeria 1973–75, Charles Booth prof of sociology Univ of Liverpool 1975–89 (dean of Faculty of Social and Environmental Studies 1985–88), visiting prof of anthropology and sociology Univ of Chicago 1982–83, prof of anthropology and sociology with reference to Africa SOAS Univ of London 1989– (dean of undergraduate studies 1990–94); ed Africa (jl of Int African Inst) 1979–86, gen ed Int African Library 1985–; writer of numerous scholarly articles in Africanist, anthropological and sociological jls; Amaury Talbot Prize for African Anthropology 1983, Herskovits Award for African Studies (USA) 1984; memb Assoc of Social Anthropologists 1979, pres African Studies Assoc of UK 1996–98; FBA 1991; *Books* Aladura: A Religious Movement among the Yoruba (1968), Herbert Spencer: The Evolution of a Sociologist (1971), Ijeshas and Nigerians: The Incorporation of a Yoruba Kingdom (1983); *Recreations* gardening, fell walking, old churches; *Style*— Prof J D Y Peel, FBA; ✉ Bryn Tirion, 23 Mount Rd, Upton, Wirral, Merseyside L49 6JA (☎ 0151 678 6783); Department of Anthropology and Sociology, School of Oriental and African Studies (University of London), Thornhaugh St, London WC1H 0XG (☎ 0171 323 6217)

PEEL, Sir John Harold; KCVO (1960); s of Rev John Edward Peel and Katherine Hannah Peel; *b* 10 Dec 1904; *Educ* Manchester GS, Queen's Coll Oxford (MA, BM BCh), King's Coll Hosp Med Sch; *m* 1, 1935 (m dis 1945), Muriel Elaine Pellow; 1 da (Diana); m 2, 1947, Freda Margaret Mellish (d 1993); m 3, Sally Barton; *Career* obstetric and gynaecological surgn King's Coll Hosp 1936–69, surgn-gynaecologist Princess Beatrice Hosp 1936–66, emeritus lectr King's Coll Hosp Med Sch 1969–; surgn-gynaecologist to HM The Queen 1961–73; fell King's Coll London; pres: RCOG 1966–69 (hon treas 1959–66), BMA 1970–71, Int Fedn of Obstetrics and Gynaecology 1970–73; Liveryman Worshipful Soc of Apothecaries; Hon DSc Birmingham 1971, Hon DM Southampton 1973, Hon DCh Newcastle 1980; Hon FACOG, Hon FACS, Hon FRCS (Canada), Hon FCM (SA), Hon FRSM, FRCS, FRCOG, FRCP; *Books* Textbook of Gynaecology (1943), Lives of the Fellows of Royal College of Obstetricians and Gynaecologists (1976), William Blais-Bell Father and Founder (1988); *Recreations* fishing, gardening; *Clubs* Naval and Military; *Style*— Sir John Peel, KCVO; ✉ 11 Harnwood Road, Salisbury, Wilts SP2 8DD

PEEL, Jonathan Sidney; CBE (1994), MC (1957), DL (1976); s of Maj David Arthur Peel (ka 1944, s of late Rev the Hon Maurice Berkeley Peel, MC, 4 s of 1 Visc Peel), and Hon Sara Vanneck, da of 5 Baron Huntingfield; *b* 21 June 1937; *Educ* Norwich Sch, Eton, St John's Coll Cambridge (MA); *m* 20 Jan 1965, Jean Fulton, da of Air Chief Marshal Sir Denis Hensley Fulton Barnett, GCB, CBE, DFC; 1 s (Robert b 1976), 4 da (Ruth b 1966, Emily b 1967, Anne b 1970, Delia b 1974); *Career* page of honour to HM King George VI 1951–52 and to HM the Queen 1952–53; cmmnd RB Royal Green Jackets 1956, served Malaya 1956–57, UN Forces Congo (Zaire) 1960–61, Cyprus 1962–63, Capt 1966, resigned; dir Norwich Union Insurance Group 1973–, chm Pleasureworld 1985–89; National Trust: memb Cncl, memb Exec Ctee, chm Ctee for E Anglia 1980–90, chm Properties Ctee 1990–, dep chm 1992–; memb Norfolk CC 1974–; dep pres Norfolk Naturalists Tst 1982–; chm: How Hill Tst for Environmental Studies 1985–, Norwich Sch 1985–, Police Authy 1985–89, Broads Authy 1985–, Planning and Transport Ctee 1989–93; Vice Lord-Lt Norfolk 1981–, High Sheriff; Liveryman Worshipful Co of Fishmongers; *Books* Towards a Rural Policy (with M J Sayer, 1973); *Recreations* music, forestry; *Clubs* Norfolk, Boodle's; *Style*— Jonathan Peel, Esq, CBE, MC, DL; ✉ Barton Hall, Barton Turf, Norwich NR12 8AU

PEEL, Richard Martin; s of Robert Horace Peel, of Boston, Lincs and Joan Ella, *née* Martin; *b* 23 April 1952; *Educ* Boston GS, Lanchester Poly (BA); *m* 26 May 1984, Diane Joan, da of Laurie Almond, of Perth, Ontario, Canada; 1 da (Charlotte Emma b 1976); *Career* cricket corr Northampton Chronicle and Echo 1976–79 (journalist 1973–79), press offr Milton Keynes Devpt Corp 1979–83; BBC: press offr 1983, sr press offr 1983–85, chief press offr 1985–87, chief asst info 1987–88, head of publicity and PR BBC News and Current Affrs 1988–93, head of communications and info BBC News and Current Affrs 1993–96, controller of communication and info BBC News 1996–; memb: Media Soc, RTS, Radio Acad, American Mgmnt Assoc; *Recreations* golf, walking, reading, music; *Style*— Richard Peel, Esq; ✉ Pinetree Cottage, 30 Startops End, Marsworth, Bucks (☎ 01442 827568); Room 3008, BBC Television Centre, Wood Lane, London W12 7RJ (☎ 0181 576 1410, fax 0181 576 1271, car 0860 317785)

PEEL, (Kenneth) Roger; s of Kenneth Galloway Peel (d 1966), and Elizabeth Margaret, *née* Watson (d 1989); *b* 9 Sept 1935; *Educ* Aireborough GS, Univ of Leeds Med Sch (MB ChB, FRCSEd, FRCOG); *m* 1959, Doreen; 2 s (Simon Charles b 19 Dec 1961, Andrew James b 15 April 1964); *Career* formerly GP and holder of jr hosp appts in obstetrics, gynaecology, urology and gen surgery, conslt obstetrician and gynaecologist St James's Univ Hosp and St Mary's Hosp 1968–72, surgn to the Hosp for Women Leeds and the Maternity Hosp Leeds 1968–80, conslt gynaecological surgn to Gen Infirmary Leeds (with responsibilities in gynaecological oncology) 1980–; post graduate advsr in obstetrics and gynaecology Yorks region 1977–83, memb then chm Dept of Health Ctee on Gynaecological Cytology 1981–89, memb Cncl Royal Coll of Obstetricians and Gynaecologists 1984–90 and 1991–95 (sr vice pres and overseas offr 1992–95), invited memb Cncl Royal Coll of Surgns of England 1990–92, sometime external examiner to RCOG, Arab Bds, Coll of Physicians and Surgns of Pakistan and Univs of Khartoum and W Indies; Sims Black travelling prof to Pakistan, India, Sri Lanka and Nepal 1996; memb GMC 1995–; former chm Central Yorks Scout Assoc; Freeman City of London; fndr memb: Br Soc of Colposcopy and Cervical Pathology, Gynaecological Cancer Gp (later Br Gynaecological Cancer Soc); memb: Soc of Apothecaries, BMA; *Publications* Dewhurst's Postgraduate Textbook of Obstetrics and Gynaecology (contrib chapters on gynaecological oncology, 1995); *Recreations* sailing, skiing, fell walking and vintage cars; *Style*— Roger Peel, Esq; ✉ North Grange, North Road, Horsforth, Leeds, West Yorkshire LS18 5HG (☎ 0113 258 4375); The General Infirmary, Great George Street, Leeds LS1 (☎ 0113 243 2799)

PEEL, 3 Earl (UK 1929); Sir William James Robert Peel; 8 Bt (GB 1800); Viscount Peel (UK 1895) and Viscount Clanfield (UK 1929); s of 2 Earl Peel (d 1969, himself gs of 1 Viscount, who was in turn 5 s of Sir Robert Peel, 2 Bt, the distinguished statesman); *b* 3 Oct 1947; *Educ* Ampleforth, Tours Univ, RAC Cirencester; *m* 1, 1973, Veronica Naomi Livingston, da of Alastair Timpson; 1 s (Viscount Clanfield), 1 da (Lady Iona Joy Julia b 1978); m 2, 1989, Hon Charlotte Clementine, *née* Soames, da of Baron Soames, GCMG, GCVO, CH, CBE, PC (Life Peer, d 1987), and formerly w of (Alexander) Richard Hambro, *qv*; 1 da (Lady Antonia Mary Catherine b 14 Dec 1991); *Heir* s, Ashton Robert Gerard, Viscount Clanfield b 16 Sept 1976; *Career* chm The Game Conservancy, pres Yorkshire Wildlife Tst; memb: Prince's Cncl 1993–, Exec Ctee The Moorland Assoc, The Cncl for English Nature, Bd The Countryside Movement; former memb Yorkshire Dales National Park Ctee; Lord Warden of the Stannaries and Keeper of the Privy Seal of the Duke of Cornwall 1994–; *Style*— The Rt Hon the Earl Peel; ✉ Kilgram Grange, Jervaulx, Ripon, N Yorkshire HG4 4PQ

PEERS, Charles Oliver; s of (Charles John) Jack Peers (d 1977), of Stadhampton, Oxford, and Rotha, *née* de Selincourt; *b* 16 Oct 1937; *Educ* Wennington Sch Wetherby Yorks, Northamptonshire Coll of Agric; *m* 8 Oct 1963, Heather Myrtle, da of William James Ridgway (d 1975), of Waterstock, Oxon; 2 s (Robert b 1967, Thomas b 1973); *Career* Nat Serv NCO 1956–58; farmer 1963; chm Stadhampton and Great Milton Parish Cncls 1968–82, dist cncllr 1970–78, chm NFU Parly Ctee 1980–87 (branch chm 1979–80), chm Bd of Dirs Organic Farmers and Growers 1993–, memb UK Register Organic Food Standards 1994–; chm Bd of Govrs Peers Sch Littlemore Oxford 1978 (govr 1971–); hon treas Berks Bucks and Oxon Co Branch NFU 1989–91, hon treas Central Region NFU; *Recreations* shooting, classic vehicle restoration, agricultural buildings preservation; *Style*— Charles Peers, Esq; ✉ Views Farm, Great Milton, Oxford 0X9 7NW (☎ 01844 279 352)

PEET, Ronald Hugh (Ron); CBE (1974); s of late Henry Leonard Peet, and late Stella Peet, of Manchester; *b* 12 July 1925; *Educ* Doncaster GS, Queen's Coll Oxford; *m* 1, 1949, Winifred Joy (d 1979), da of late Ernest Adamson; 2 s, 2 da; m 2, 1981, Lynette Judy Burgess Kinsella; *Career* Legal & General Assurance Society Ltd: dir 1969–84, chief exec 1972–80, chm 1980–84; Legal & General Group plc: gp chief exec 1979–84, dir 1979–84; chm Aviation & General Insurance Co Ltd 1978–80, dir Watling Street Properties 1971–84, chm City Arts Trust Ltd 1980–87; dir: Royal Philharmonic Orch Ltd 1977–88, ENO 1978–95; chm Stockley plc 1984–87, dir AMEC plc 1984–96; chm The Howard Group plc 1985–86, dep chm PWS Holdings plc 1986–88, dir New Scotland Insurance Group plc 1987–; memb Ct of Assts Worshipful Co of Insurers; FIA; *Recreations* music, opera; *Clubs* Hurlingham, City of London; *Style*— Ron Peet, Esq, CBE; ✉ 9 Marlowe Court, Petyward, London SW3 3PD (☎ 0171 581 3686)

PEGDEN, Jeffrey Vincent; QC (1996); s of George Vincent Pegden (d 1994), and Stella Blanche Katherine, *née* Maxted; *b* 24 June 1950; *Educ* Wallington County GS, Univ of Hull (LLB, pres Univ Law Soc); *m* 5 Sept 1981, Delia Mary, da of Paul and Lucy Coonan; 1 s (Oliver Roderick William b 30 May 1982), 1 da (Antonia Catherine Lucy b 15 Aug 1985); *Career* called to the Bar Inner Temple 1973, Bar Cncl of England and Wales rep Criminal Bar Assoc 1993–95, recorder 1996–; memb: SE Circuit, Criminal Bar Assoc, Br Acad of Forensic Sciences; FRSA; *Recreations* music, reading, walking; *Style*— Jeffrey Pegden, Esq, QC; ✉ 3 Temple Gardens, Ground Floor, Temple, London EC4Y 9AU (☎ 0171 353 3102, fax 0171 353 0960)

PEGG, Dr Michael Stuart; s of Gilbert Seaton Pegg, of Reigate, Surrey and Waldy Greta, *née* Jonsson; *b* 15 June 1948; *Educ* The Grammar Sch Reigate Surrey, UCL, Westminster Med Sch (BSc, MB BS), Cardiff Law Sch (LLM); *m* 17 Jan 1983, Kaija Kaarina, da of Niilo Sarolehto, of Espoo, Finland; 1 s (Justin William b 12 June 1986), 1 da (Antonia Alexandra b 9 Aug 1984); *Career* conslt anaesthetist Royal Free Hosp 1981–, hon sr lectr Royal Free Hosp Med Sch 1981–; memb: BMA, Assoc of Anaesthetists; FRCA; *Style*— Dr Michael Pegg; ✉ Newstead, 3 Canons Close, Radlett, Herts WD7 7ER (☎ 01923 856640, fax 01923 858430); Department of Anaesthetics, Royal Free Hospital, Pond Street, London NW3 2QG

PEIN, Malcolm; s of Norman Pein, and Linda Pein (d 1990); *b* 14 Aug 1960; *Educ* Quarry Bank Comp, UCL (BSc); *m* 20 Jan 1991, Philippa, da of Leslie Vides; *Career* chess corr: The European 1990–91 and 1992–, Daily Telegraph 1991–; purchased Maxwell McMillan Chess & Bridge Ltd 1992 (publishing Chess Monthly and Bridge Monthly); Br jr chess champion 1977, int chess master 1985; *Books* Grunfeld Defence Exchange Variation (1981), Trends in the Marshall Attack (1991), Blumenfeld Gambit (1991), Bobby Fischer $5 Million Comeback (1992), Daily Telegraph Guide to Chess (1995); *Recreations* football, classical music, BBC World Service; *Style*— Malcolm Pein, Esq; ✉ Chess & Bridge Ltd, 369 Euston Road, London NW1 3AR (☎ 0171 388 2404, fax 0171 388 2407)

PEIRCE, Rev Canon (John) Martin; s of Martin Westley Peirce (d 1966), and Winifred Mary, *née* Bennett; *b* 9 July 1936; *Educ* Brentwood Sch, Jesus Coll Cambridge (MA, CertEd), Westcott House Cambridge; *m* 8 June 1968, Rosemary Susan, da of George Duncan Nicholson Milne, of Kingston upon Thames; 2 s (Richard b 1969, Michael b 1971); *Career* RAF 1954–56, PO; teacher and housemaster St Stephen's Coll Hong Kong 1960–64; asst curate: St John the Baptist Croydon 1966–70, Holy Trinity Fareham 1970–71; team vicar St Columba Fareham 1971–76, team rector of Langley Slough 1976–85, diocesan dir of ordinands Oxford 1985–, canon residentiary of Christ Church Oxford 1987–; memb Gen Synod C of E 1985–95; *Recreations* walking, gardening; *Style*— The Rev Canon Martin Peirce; ✉ Christ Church, Oxford OX1 1DP (☎ 01865 721330)

PEIRSE, Air Vice-Marshal Sir Richard Charles Fairfax; KCVO (1988), CB (1984); s of late Air Chief Marshal Sir Richard Peirse, KCB, DSO, AFC (d 1970), and late Lady (Mary Joyce) Peirse, *née* Ledgard; the Peirses were once great landowners in N Riding of Yorks, being descended from Peter Peirse, who fought for the House of York as a standard-bearer at Bosworth Field 1485 (where he lost a leg); the pedigree is first recorded in the Visitation of 1634; John Peirse (1593–1658) is thought to have been the purchaser of the manor of Bedale, where the family resided for many generations, until it descended through m to the Beresford-Peirse family; *b* 16 March 1931; *Educ* Bradfield, RAF Coll Cranwell; *m* 1, 1955 (m dis 1963), Karalie Grace Cox; 2 da (Amanda, Susan); m 2, 1963, Deirdre Mary O'Donovan (d 1976); 1 s (Richard d 1989); m 3, 1977, Anna Jill Margaret Long, da of Rt Hon Sir John (Brinsmead) Latey, MBE, *qv*; *Career* cmmnd 1952, served various sqdns and HQ in Germany, UK, Malta 1952–68, graduate RAF Staff Coll Andover 1963, Jt Servs Staff Coll 1968, cmd No 51 Sqdn 1968–69, Dep Capt of the Queen's Flight 1969–72, cmd RAF Waddington 1973–75, MOD 1975–82, AOC and Cmdt RAF Coll Cranwell 1982–85, Defence Servs Sec 1985–88, ret 1988; qualified flying instr 1956; RCDS 1972; Gentleman Usher of the Scarlet Rod Order of the Bath 1990–; *Clubs* RAF; *Style*— Air Vice-Marshal Sir Richard Peirse, KCVO, CB; ✉ The Old Mill House, Adderbury, nr Banbury, Oxon (☎ 01295 810196)

PEIRSON, Margaret Ellen; CB; eld da of late David Edward Peirson, CBE, and Norah Ellen, *née* Corney; *b* 28 Nov 1942; *Educ* N London Collegiate Sch Canons Edgware Middx, Somerville Coll Oxford (BA), Yale USA; *Career* joined HM Treasy 1965, seconded to Bank of England 1982–84, under sec HM Treasy 1986–, transferred DSS 1990–; *Recreations* choral singing, theatre; *Style*— Miss Margaret Peirson, CB; ✉ Room 11–13, DSS, Adelphi, 1–11 John Adam Street, London WC2N 6HT

PEIRSON, Richard; s of Geoffrey Peirson (d 1986), of Purley, Surrey, and Beryl Joyce, *née* Walder; *b* 5 March 1949; *Educ* Purley GS, Univ of Liverpool (BSc); *m* 1, 31 May 1975 (m dis), Jennifer Margaret, da of late F E Fernie; 1 s (James Richard b 1978), 1 da (Caroline Jane b 1980); m 2, 16 Feb 1991, Victoria, da of R P Steiner; 2 s (Charles Hamilton b 1993, George Alexander b 1996); *Career* Arthur Andersen & Co 1970–72, Colegrave & Co 1972–73, J & A Scrimgeour Ltd 1973–75, Carr Sebag & Co (formerly W I Carr Sons & Co) 1975–82, Grieveson Grant & Co 1982–86, Kleinwort Benson Investment Management Ltd 1986–94, Framlington Investment Management Ltd 1994–; MSI; *Recreations* tennis, squash, reading, collecting watercolours; *Style*— Richard Peirson, Esq; ✉ 13 Kings Road, Richmond, Surrey TW10 6NN (☎ 0181 940 2013); Framlington Investment Management Ltd, 155 Bishopsgate, London EC2M 3XJ (☎ 0171 374 4100, fax 0171 330 6643)

PEISER, Graham Allan; s of Eric George Peiser (d 1991), of Bucks, and Honor, *née* Greenwood (d 1988); *b* 26 March 1940; *Educ* Aldenham, Coll of Estate Mgmnt; *m* 26 Sept 1970, Jennifer Ann, da of Dr John Richard Cooper; 2 da (Georgina b 1972, Lucy b 1976); *Career* chartered surveyor and arboriculturalist; ptnr: Fuller Peiser 1970–91, Graham Peiser Properties 1991–, Hyrons Trees 1992–; Liveryman Worshipful Co of Glass Sellers; FRICS; *Style*— Graham A Peiser, Esq; ✉ Pear Tree Cottage, The Green, Sarratt, Rickmansworth, Herts WD3 6BL (☎ 01923 269136, fax 01923 270625)

PELHAM, Dr Hugh Reginald Brentnall; s of Reginald Arthur Pelham, (d 1981), and Pauline Mary, *née* Brentnall; *b* 26 Aug 1954; *Educ* Marlborough, Christ's Coll Cambridge (MA, PhD); *Career* res fell Christ's Coll Cambridge 1978–84, postdoctoral fell Dept of Embryology Carnegie Inst of Washington Baltimore Maryland 1979–81, staff memb MRC Laboratory of Molecular Biology Cambridge 1981–, visitor Univ of Zürich Switzerland 1987–88; awards: Colworth medal of the Biochemical Soc 1988, EMBO medal 1989, Louis Jeantet prize for med 1991, King Faisal International prize for science 1996; memb: Euro Molecular Biology Orgn 1985, Academia Europaea 1990; FRS 1988; *Style*— Dr Hugh Pelham, FRS; ✉ MRC Laboratory of Molecular Biology, Hills Rd, Cambridge CB2 2QH (☎ 01223 248011, fax 01223 412142)

PELHAM, Michael Leslie; s of Cyril Hall Pelham (d 1967), and Clare Elizabeth (d 1981); *b* 27 Dec 1939; *Educ* St Edward's Sch Oxford, St Edmund Hall Oxford (BA); *m* Elizabeth Vivien, *née* Mott; 1 s (Hugh b 1967), 1 da (Georgina b 1970); *Career* Richard Costain Limited 1961–69: grad engr, posts overseas, asst to Chief Exec UK; mgmnt conslt McKinsey & Co Inc 1969–72, responsible for industl acquisitions for jt venture between Consolidated African Selection Tst and Baird & Lane Ltd 1972–76, md Seltrust CBO (subsid of Selection Trust Ltd) 1976–78, chm and md CBO International 1978–86, md Conder Group plc 1988–91 (dir gp devpt 1987–88); conslt 1991–92; chm: Westminster Scaffolding Group plc 1992–, Shafer Group Ltd 1996–; fndr chm Br Int Rowing Fund, tstee Oxford Univ Boat Club Tst; *Recreations* producing wine and olive oil, squash, reading; *Clubs* Leander, Vincent's; *Style*— Michael Pelham, Esq

PELHAM, Richard Anthony Henry; s of Maj Anthony George Pelham (d 1969); kinsman and hp of 9 Earl of Chichester; *b* 1 Aug 1952; *Educ* Eton; *m* 1987, Georgina, da of David Gilmour, of Ringshall Grange, Suffolk; 2 s (Duncan b 1987, Christopher b 1990); *Recreations* vintage motor cycle racing; *Clubs* The Motor Cycling Club; *Style*— Richard Pelham, Esq; ✉ c/o Lloyds Bank, Warminster, Wilts

PELHAM BURN, Angus Maitland; JP (Kincardine and Deeside 1984), DL (1978); s of Brig-Gen Henry Pelham Burn, CMG, DSO (d 1958), and Katherine Eileen, *née* Staveley-Hill (d 1989); *b* 13 Dec 1931; *Educ* Harrow, N of Scotland Coll of Agric, LLD; *m* 19 Dec 1959, Anne Rosdew, da of Sir Ian Algernon Forbes-Leith, 2 Bt, KT, MBE (d 1973); 4 da (Amanda b 1961, Lucy b 1963, Emily b 1964, Kate b 1966); *Career* Hudson's Bay Co 1951–58; chm and dir MacRobert Farms (Douneside) Ltd 1970–87, chm Pelett Administration Ltd 1973–95; dir: Aberdeen and Northern Marts Ltd 1970–86 (chm

1974–86), Aberdeen Meat Marketing Co Ltd 1973–86 (chm 1974–86), Bank of Scotland 1977– (dir Aberdeen and North Local Bd chm 1973–), Prime Space Design Ltd 1981–87, Taw Meat Co 1984–86, Skeendale Ltd 1987–88, Status Timber Systems 1986–90, Abtrust Scotland Investment Co plc 1989–96; chm: Aberdeen Trust plc (formerly Aberdeen Fund Managers then Aberdeen Trust Holdings Ltd) 1993– (dir 1985–); chm Scottish Provident Institution 1995– (dir 1975–, dep chm 1991–95); memb: Kincardine CC 1967–75 (vice convener 1973–75), Grampian Regnl Cncl 1974–94; memb: Aberdeen Assoc for the Prevention of Cruelty to Animals 1975–96 (dir 1984–94, chm 1984–89), Accounts Cmmn 1980–94 (dep chm 1987–94), Cncl Winston Churchill Meml Tst 1984–93, Exec Cncl Scottish Veterans' Residences; chm: Aberdeen Airport Consultative Ctee 1986–, Order Ctee Order of St John (Aberdeen) Ltd (formerly OStJ Aberdeen) 1992– (memb 1987–); tstee The Gordon Highlanders Regimental Tst; memb Queen's Body Guard for Scotland (The Royal Co of Archers) 1968–; Vice Lord Lt for Kincardineshire 1978–; Liveryman Worshipful Co of Farmers until 1988; Hon FInstM 1987; *Recreations* vegetable gardening, photography; *Clubs* New (Edinburgh), Royal Northern & Univ (Aberdeen); *Style*— Angus Pelham Burn, Esq, JP, DL; ✉ 68 Station Rd, Banchory, Kincardineshire AB31 5YJ (☎ 01330 823343, fax 01330 823749); Knappach, Banchory, Kincardineshire AB31 6JS (☎ 01330 844555)

PELL, Marian Priscilla; *née* Leak; da of Anthony Edward Leak, and Elsie Ellen, *née* Chellingworth; *b* 5 July 1952; *Educ* Watford GS for Girls, Univ of Southampton (LLB); *m* 4 Aug 1973, Gordon Francis Pell, s of Lt-Col Denis Herbert Pell (d 1987); 2 s, 1 da; *Career* ptnr Herbert Smith 1984– (asst slr 1976–84); memb Law Soc; *Recreations* music, walking, tennis, riding; *Style*— Mrs Marian Pell; ✉ Herbert Smith, Exchange House, Primrose St, London EC2A 2HS (☎ 0171 374 8000, fax 0171 496 0043)

PELLEGRINI, Anthony; s of Victor Pellegrini (d 1985), of London, and Marika, *née* Tachtari (d 1987); *b* 18 May 1940; *Educ* St James' HS Barnet, LSE (BA); *Career* Cardinal Vaughan Memorial Sch: asst master 1962–63, master in charge of discipline Lower Sch 1963–68, dir Schola Cantorum 1965–90, head of Economics Dept and master in charge of discipline Upper Sch 1968–69, dep headmaster 1969–76, headmaster 1976– (in charge of transition from Grammar to Comp Sch 1977, introduced girls to sixth form 1981, guided sch from Voluntary Aided to Grant Maintained Status 1990); memb: Educn Cmmn Diocese of Westminster 1978–85, Sch Examinations and Assessment Cncl 1992–95, Cncl for the Accreditation of Teacher Trg 1993–95, Strategic Forum Exec Gp CENTEC 1993–95; *Recreations* travel, organ playing (organist and choirmaster St Joseph's Church Wembley 1961–79), cooking; *Style*— Anthony Pellegrini, Esq; ✉ Cardinal Vaughan Memorial School, 89 Addison Road, Kensington, London W14 8BZ (☎ 0171 603 8478, fax 0171 602 3124)

PELLEW, Mark Edward; LVO (1980); s of Anthony Pownoll Pellew, RN (d 1992), of Wimbledon, and Margaret Julia Critchley, *née* Cookson; *b* 28 Aug 1942; *Educ* Winchester, Trinity Coll Oxford (BA); *m* 1965, Jill Hosford, da of Prof Frank Thistlethwaite, CBE, of Cambridge; 2 s (Adam Lee b 1966, Dominic Stephen b 1968); *Career* HM Dip Serv 1965–; FO 1965–67, Singapore 1967–69, Saigon 1969–70, FCO 1970–76, first sec Rome 1976–80, asst head Personnel Ops Dept FCO 1981–83, cnsllr (political) Washington DC 1983–89, on secondment to Hambros Bank Ltd 1989–91, head N America Dept FCO 1991–96; *Recreations* tennis, singing, playing the horn; *Clubs* Hurlingham; *Style*— Mark Pellew, Esq, LVO; ✉ 51 St George's Square, London SW1V 3QN

PELLING, Anthony Adair; s of Brian Pelling, and Alice, *née* Lamb; *b* 3 May 1934; *Educ* Purley GS, LSE (BSc), NW Poly London, Wolverhampton Coll of Technol (MIPM); *m* 1, Margaret Rose, *née* Lightfoot; 1 s (Andrew John), 1 da (Sarah Margaret); m 2 Virginia, *née* Glen-Calvert; 1 da (Amanda); *Career* War Office 1955–57, NCB 1957–67; Civil Serv 1967–93: princ 1967–69, asst sec 1969–81, under sec 1981–93, dep dir Business in the Community 1981–83, dir Highways Contracts and Maintenance Dept of Tport 1983–85, dir Construction Indust, Sports and Recreation Directorates DOE 1985–87, dir London Region DOE 1987–91, dir Construction Policy Directorate DOE 1991–93; dir GJW Government Relations Ltd 1993–95; conslt Trade and Regulatory Intelligence 1995–; dir: Cities in Schools, Croydon Business Venture; memb Croydon Family Health Servs Authy; *Clubs* Reform; *Style*— Anthony Pelling; ✉ 3814 Seminary Ave, Richmond, Virginia, USA (☎ 00 1 804 262 7387)

PELLING, Dr Henry Mathison; s of late Douglas Langley Pelling, of Birkenhead, Cheshire, and late Maud Mary, *née* Mathison; *b* 27 Aug 1920; *Educ* Birkenhead Sch, St John's Coll Cambridge (BA, MA, PhD, LittD); *Career* RA 1941–42, cmmnd 2 Lt then Lt RE 1942, Capt Educn Corps 1945; Queen's Coll Oxford: fell 1949–65, tutor 1950–65, dean 1963–64, supernumerary fell 1980; St John's Coll Cambridge: fell 1966, asst dir of res History Faculty 1966–77, reader in recent Br history 1977–80; Smith-Mundt Sch Univ of Wisconsin USA 1953–54, fell Woodrow Wilson Center Washington DC 1983, author of pieces written for various jls; Hon DLitt New Sch for Social Res NY 1983; FBA; *Books* Origins of the Labour Party (1954), Challenge of Socialism (1954), America and the British Left (1956), British Communist Party (1958), Labour and Politics (with Frank Bealey, 1958), American Labor (1960), Modern Britain 1885–1955 (1960), Short History of the Labour Party (1961, 11 edn 1996), History of British Trade Unionism (1963, 5 edn 1992), Social Geography of British Elections (1967), Popular Politics and Society in Late Victorian Britain (1968, 2 edn 1979), Britain and the Second World War (1970), Winston Churchill (1974, 2 edn 1989), The Labour Governments 1945–51 (1984), Britain and the Marshall Plan (1988); *Recreations* theatre, cinema; *Clubs* Nat Lib, Royal Cwlth Soc; *Style*— Dr Henry Pelling, FBA; ✉ St John's College, Cambridge CB2 1TP (☎ 01223 338600)

PELLOW, Marti; *b* 23 March 1966; *Career* lead singer with Wet Wet Wet; 14 top twenty singles incl 3 no 1's (With A Little Help from my Friends 1988 (raised over £600,000 for Childline), Goodnight Girl 1992, Love Is All Around 1994); albums with Wet Wet Wet: Popped In Souled Out (1987, UK no 1), The Memphis Sessions (1988, UK no 3), Holding Back The River (1989, UK no 2), High On The Happy Side (1992, UK no 1), End of Part One (compilation, 1994, UK no 1), Picture This (1995); participated in: Prince's Trust Rock Gala 1988, 1989 and 1990, concert for Nelson Mandela's 70th birthday 1988, John Lennon Tribute concert 1990; *Style*— Marti Pellow, Esq; ✉ c/o Wet TM Ltd, 14/16 Speirs Wharf, Port Dundas, Glasgow G4 9TB (☎ 0141 353 1515, fax 0141 353 3852)

PELLY, Derek Roland (Derk); s of Arthur Roland Pelly (d 1966), of Ballygate House, Beccles, Suffolk, and Phyllis Elsie, *née* Henderson (d 1973); *b* 12 June 1929; *Educ* Marlborough, Trinity Coll Cambridge (MA); *m* 20 June 1953, Susan, da of John Malcolm Roberts (d 1986), of Felpham, Sussex; 1 s (Sam b 1960), 2 da (Rosemary b 1955, Catherine b 1958); *Career* 2 Lt RA 1947–49; Barclays Bank 1952–88: local dir Chelmsford Dist 1959–68 (asst to chm 1968–69), local dir Luton Dist 1969–79, dir Barclays Int 1974 (vice chm 1977–86, chm 1986–87), dir Barclays plc 1974 (vice-chm 1984–86, dep chm 1986–88); dir Private Bank and Tst Co Ltd 1989–94, memb Ctee Family Assur Soc 1988–91, chm City Commuter Gp 1987–88, dir Milton Keynes Devpt Corpn 1976–85, memb Cncl Overseas Devpt Inst 1984–89; govr London House for Overseas Graduates 1985–91, treas Friends of Essex Churches 1989–96, memb Chelmsford Diocesan Bd of Fin 1989–96; JP Chelmsford 1965–68; FCIB, FRSA; *Recreations* painting; *Style*— Derk Pelly, Esq; ✉ Kenbank, St John's Town of Dalry, Kirkcudbrightshire DG7 3TX (☎ 01644 430424)

PELLY, Frances Elsie; da of Russell Steele Pelly (d 1993), and Agnes Mysie, *née* MacPherson; *b* 21 July 1947; *Educ* Morrison's Acad, Duncan of Jordanstone Coll of Art (Scottish Educn scholar, Carnegie scholar, DA), Moray House Coll of Educn (CertEd); *Career* sculptor; *Exhibitions* Loomshop Gall 1973, Torrance Gall 1975, Three Perthshire Artists (Perth Festival) 1976, Open Eye Gall 1978, Royal British Sculptors (Artspace) 1981, Five From Aberdeen (Third Eye Gall) 1982, Scottish Sculpture Open 1983, 1989 and 1993, A Survey of Scottish Sculpture (Talbot Rice) 1984, Hands Off (Crawford Art Centre) 1985, Paper, Wood and Stone (Collective Gall) 1985, Sculpture on Paper (Talbot Rice) 1985, Four Sculptors in Charlotte Square (Edinburgh Festival) 1985, Stirling Smith Biennial 1985 and 1987, One Cubic Foot (Artspace) 1985, Spring Fling 1986, retrospective (Crawford Art Centre) 1987, Artist in Industry Exhbn (Seagate Gall) 1987, Scottish Sculpture Tst (tour) 1988, Glasgow Garden Festival 1988, State of Art (Fine Art Soc) 1989, Ten Years On 1989, Directions in Scottish Sculpture (Barbican) 1990, Open Exhbn (Pier Art Gall) 1990, Five Thousand Years of Orkney Art (tour) 1990, Contemporary Sculpture (Open Eye Gall) 1990, Nousts (tour) 1992, Scottish Sculpture Open No 7 (Kildrummy Castle) 1993, Scandex Exhbn (tour) 1994–96, Glasgow Mayfest 1994, Shoreline Exhbn (tour) 1995–96, New Work at the Yards St Magnus Festival (Kirkwall) 1996, Island (Crawfords Arts Centre St Andrews) 1996, RSA Festival Exhbn 1996; *Work in Collections* Dundee Coll of Commerce, Fine Art Soc (Edinburgh and London), Scottish Arts Cncl, RSA, Royal Glasgow Concert Hall, Museum of Scotland, Fort William, Banff, Perth, Kirkwall, Glasgow; artist in residence: Stromness Acad 1990, Fort William Library 1991, RSA 1991; artist in indust Highland Park Distillery 1987; pt/t lectr Duncan of Jordanstone Coll of Art 1974–78, lectr Gray's Sch of Art 1979–83; memb Scottish Soc of Artists; RSA 1990; *Awards* Gleichen Award Royal British Sculptors 1970, Guthrie Award RSA 1971, Ottillie Helen Wallace Award RSA 1972, William J Macaully Award RSA 1977, Benno Schotz Award Royal Glasgow Inst 1980, Gillies Award RSA 1982, Ireland Alloys Award RSA 1983; *Recreations* riding, gardening, studying wildlife, travelling; *Style*— Frances Pelly, RSA; ✉ Costa Schoolhouse, Evie, Orkney KW17 2NJ (☎ 01856 751326)

PELLY, Sir Richard John; 7 Bt (UK 1840), of Upton, Essex; s of Richard Heywood Pelly (d 1988), and Mary Elizabeth, *née* Luscombe; *b* 10 April 1951; *Educ* Wellington, Wadham Coll Oxford (BA); *m* 1983, Clare Gemma, da of late Harry Wilfred Dove, of Winchester, Hants; 3 s (Anthony Alwyne b 1984, James Richard b 1986, Harry Philip b 1988); *Heir* s, Anthony Alwyne Pelly b 30 Oct 1984; *Career* farmer; *Style*— Sir Richard Pelly, Bt; ✉ The Manor House, Preshaw, Upham, Southampton SO32 1HP

PEMBERTON, Sir Francis Wingate William; kt (1976), CBE (1970), DL (Cambs 1979); s of late Dr William Warburton Wingate (assumed Arms of Pemberton, by Royal Licence, 1921), and Viola Patience, *née* Hudson; *b* 1 Oct 1916; *Educ* Eton, Trinity Coll Cambridge; *m* 19 April 1941, Diana Patricia, da of late Reginald Salisbury Woods, and late Irene Woods, CBE, TD; 2 s; *Career* former sr ptnr Bidwells Chartered Surveyors; dir: Agricultural Mortgage Corporation Ltd 1969–91, Barclays Bank UK Management Ltd 1977–81; High Sheriff Cambs and Isle of Ely 1965–66; Liveryman Worshipful Co of Farmers; FRICS; *Style*— Sir Francis Pemberton, CBE, DL; ✉ Trumpington Hall, Cambridge (☎ 01223 841941); Business: Enterprise House, Maris Lane, Trumpington, Cambridge (☎ 01223 840840)

PEMBERTON, Dr James; s of Tom Winstanley Pemberton, of Sheffield, and Marjorie, *née* Chesney; *b* 21 Dec 1940; *Educ* King Edward VII Sch Sheffield, St Bartholomew's Hosp Med Sch (MB BS, MRCP, BSc scholarship, Hayward prize); *m* Sylvia Ann, *née* Finnigan; 4 c (Philippa Louise b 12 Sept 1968, Tom Winstanley b 12 Oct 1969, James Wentworth b 25 June 1971, Sam b 28 April 1981); *Career* St Bartholomew's Hosp: house physician 1968, house surgn 1969, registrar Pathology Dept 1970, registrar in med 1970–71, registrar in diagnostic radiology 1971–73; sr registrar in diagnostic radiology King's Coll Hosp 1973–74, conslt radiologist St Thomas's Hosp 1974–; admin head Radiology Dept Lambeth and S Western Hosps 1975–77; organiser Scientific Exhibition Jl Annual Congress of the Combined Royal Colls of UK, Netherlands and BIR 1978 and 1979; chm: Radiology Sub Ctee St Thomas's Hosp 1978–80 and 1984–86, Dist Working Pty on Jr Hosp Med and Dental Staff Hours of Work 1988; St Thomas's Hosp: chm Dist Working Pty on Junior Doctors' Rotas (Safety Nets), memb Dist Manpower Ctee 1986–92, chm Med and Surgical Offrs Ctee 1993–95, pres Sch of Radiography; memb: Regnl Manpower Ctee 1986–90, Regnl Radiology Specialists Sub Ctee 1984–90; tstee Symposium Mammo Graphicum; memb BIR: Prog Ctee 1976–79, Med Ctee 1977–79 and 1990–92, Cncl 1990–93, Radiation Protection Ctee 1990–92; med lectr for: RCR, Br Cncl, FRCS Course and FRCR Course in Radiotherapy St Thomas's Hosp; author of numerous pubns in learned jls; MRCS 1967, LRCP 1967, DMRD 1972, FFR 1974, FRCR 1976; *Recreations* watching Arsenal FC, horseracing; *Style*— Dr James Pemberton; ✉ 18 Village Way, Dulwich, London SE21 7AN (☎ 0171 737 2220); St Thomas's Hospital, London SE1 (☎ 0171 928 9292); 148 Harley St, London W1 (☎ 0171 486 8685)

PEMBERTON, Jeremy; s of Sidney Charles Pemberton (d 1974), and Levina Beatrice (d 1974); *b* 17 Oct 1948; *Educ* Hampton GS; *m* 25 July 1969, Anne Marie Therese Antoinette, da of Adrien Croughs; *Career* dep chm and creative dir Yellowhammer plc 1972–92; Darcy Masius Benton & Bowles advtg: creative dir 1992–, dep chm 1994–; *Recreations* squash, chess; *Clubs* RAC; *Style*— Jeremy Pemberton, Esq; ✉ D'Arcy Masius Benton & Bowles, 123 Buckingham Palace Road, London SW1W 9DZ (☎ 0171 630 0000, fax 0171 630 0033)

PEMBROKE, Dr Andrew Charles; s of Geoffrey Vernon Worth Pembroke (d 1983), of Bexhill-on-Sea, E Sussex, and Mary Constance, *née* Purkis (d 1978); *b* 1 June 1947; *Educ* Winchester (scholar), King's Coll Cambridge (scholar and sr scholar, MA, MB BChir), Bart's Med Coll; *m* 1977, Jacqueline Beatrice, da of Percival Henry Gage Hall; 3 s (Thomas Peter Ignatius b 1980, Charles Dominic b 1985, Theodore Philip Gervase b 1987), 2 da (Beatrice Mary b 1978, Olivia Constance b 1982); *Career* med registrar Hackney Hosp 1974–75, sr registrar in dermatology London Hosp 1975–78; conslt dermatologist: King's Coll Hosp 1981–94 (sr registrar in dermatology 1978–81), Bromley Hosps NHS Tst 1994–; hon treas Br Assoc of Dermatologists 1987–92, chm SE Thames Regnl Specialty Sub-Ctee for Dermatology 1987–91; FRCP 1988; *Style*— Dr A C Pembroke; ✉ 28 Dartford Road, Sevenoaks, Kent TN13 3TQ (☎ 01732 450197); 152 Harley St, London W1N 1HH (☎ 0171 935 2477)

PEMBROKE, Ann Marjorie Francesca; *Educ* Holy Trinity Convent Kent, Sorbonne Paris; *Career* Foreign Office London and Paris 1956–58, Pembroke & Pembroke fin recruitment conslts London 1969–; memb: Ct of Common Cncl City of London, Care, IOW Soc, War Widows Reception Ctee; dep Ward of Cheap, asst Irish Soc, govr City of London Sch; tstee: Dr Johnson's House, Dickens House Museum; Freeman City of London 1977, Liveryman Worshipful Co of Horners 1978; *Recreations* travel, horticulture, country pursuits; *Clubs* City Livery, Guildhall, Ward of Cheap; *Style*— Mrs A M F Pembroke; ✉ Pembroke & Pembroke, The Green House, 41–42 Clerkenwell Green, London EC1R 0DE

PEMBROKE AND MONTGOMERY, 17 Earl of (E 1551) and 14 Earl of (E 1605) respectively; Henry George Charles Alexander Herbert; also Baron Herbert of Cardiff (E 1551), Baron Herbert of Shurland (E 1605), and Baron Herbert of Lea (UK 1861); o s of 16 Earl of Pembroke and Montgomery, CVO (d 1969), and Lady Mary Dorothea Hope, CVO (d 1995), da of 1 Marquess of Linlithgow, KT, GCMG, GCVO, PC; *b* 19 May 1939; *Educ* Eton, ChCh Oxford; *m* 1, 1966 (m dis 1981), Claire Rose, o da of Douglas Gurney Pelly; 1 s, 3 da (Lady Sophia Elizabeth b 1966, Lady Emma Louise b 1969, Lady Flora Katinka b 1970); m 2, 16 April 1988, Miranda Juliet, da of Cdr John Somerville Kendal Oram, of Bulbridge House, Wilton, Salisbury, Wilts; 2 da (Lady

Jemima Juliet b 4 Oct 1989, Lady Alice Mary b 10 Nov 1991); *Heir* s, William Alexander Sidney, Lord Herbert b 18 May 1978; *Career* hereditary grand visitor of Jesus Coll Oxford; Royal Horse Gds 1958–60; owner of Wilton House (Inigo Jones, built around 1650, with additional work by James Wyatt 1810); *Style—* The Rt Hon the Earl of Pembroke and Montgomery; ✉ Wilton House, Salisbury, Wilts

PENDER, Anthony Reginald (Tony); CBE; *b* 26 Aug 1942; *Educ* Cardiff HS, Queens' Coll Cambridge (BA); m; 1 da, 1 s; *Career* Valuation Office Inland Revenue 1964–72, British Airports Authy 1973–76, Welsh Development Agency 1976–79, chief exec English Estates 1979–94, ptnr Ryder, Chambers Surveyors 1995–; memb: Arts Cncl Nat Lottery Panel, Carnegie Third Age Programme Ctee, Cncl Univ of Newcastle upon Tyne, Bd of Govrs Univ of Teeside, Court of Govrs RSC, Bd Newcastle Theatre Royal Trust Ltd, Cncl Assoc for Business Sponsorship in the Arts; tstee Captain Cook Birthplace Tst; chm: Economic Research Services Ltd, Northern Sinfonia Concert Soc; vice chair: Northern Arts, Business in the Arts; CIMgt, FRICS; *Recreations* music, theatre, fishing, walking; *Style—* Tony Pender, Esq, CBE

PENDER, Cmmr Dinsdale Leslie; s of Lt Col (Salvation Army) Leslie Pender (d 1977), and Lilian, *née* Widdowson (d 1984); *b* 22 March 1932; *Educ* Colfe's GS Lewisham, Bradford GS, William Booth Meml Trg Coll; *m* 29 Sept 1955, Winifred Violet, da of Wilfred Robinson Dale; 2 da (Ruth Lilian b 1956, Catherine Joy b 1958), 1 s (Christopher Leslie b 1960); *Career* Nat Serv RAF 1950–52 (sr aircraftsman); The Salvation Army: offr cadet trg William Booth Meml Coll 1952–54 (cmmnd 1954), cmdg offr various corps appts (Crowland, Bridlington, Manchester, Bath, Coventry, London (Wood Green)) 1954–73, divnl cdr Northern Div (Newcastle upon Tyne) 1973–77, asst field sec Nat HQ 1977–80, chief sec NZ and Fiji Territory 1980–82, chief sec (later territorial cdr) Southern Africa 1982–86, territorial cdr Scot Territory 1986–90, territorial cdr Aust Southern Territory 1990–93, territorial cdr UK & Ireland Territory 1993–; chm Manchester Cncl of Churches 1960, supervisor relief work Lockerbie (following Pan AM air disaster) 1988; *Recreations* keyboard, sport (tennis, golf, jogging), writing; *Style—* Cmmr Dinsdale Pender; ✉ The Salvation Army, UK Territory, 101 Queen Victoria Street, London EC4P 4EP (☎ 0171 236 5222, fax 0171 236 6272)

PENDER, 3 Baron (UK 1937); John Willoughby Denison-Pender; s of 2 Baron Pender, CBE (d 1965), and Camilla Lethbridge, da of late Willoughby Arthur Pemberton; *b* 6 May 1933; *Educ* Eton; *m* 1962, Julia, da of Richard Nevill Cannon, OBE, of Coombe Place, Lewes, Sussex; 1 s, 2 da (Hon Emma Charlotte (m Matthew Brett, gs of Visc Esher) b 1964, Hon Mary Anne Louise b 1965); *Heir* s, Hon Henry John Richard Denison-Pender b 19 March 1968; *Career* formerly Lt 10 Royal Hussars and Capt City of London Yeo; former dir Globe Trust Ltd, chm J J & D Frost plc; vice pres The Royal Sch for Deaf Children 1992–; sits as Cons in House of Lords; steward Lingfield Park Folkestone; *Recreations* golf, racing, gardening; *Clubs* White's, Pratt's; *Style—* The Rt Hon the Lord Pender; ✉ North Court, Tilmanstone, Kent CT14 0JP

PENDER, Reginald Robinson (Robin); s of Reginald George Pender (d 1967); *b* 23 March 1934; *Educ* Harrow; *m* 1958, Elizabeth, da of Charles Joseph Meager (d 1968); 2 s, 1 da; *Career* Nat Serv Capt (Army) 1952–54; co sec; dir Standard Building Soc; FCIS, ACIArb; *Recreations* gardening; *Clubs* Sunderland; *Style—* Robin Pender, Esq; ✉ Bark Mill, West Hall, Brampton, Cumbria CA8 2BS (☎ 016977 47289)

PENDLETON, Alan George; *b* 26 May 1929; *Educ* UMIST (MSc); *m* 10 Nov 1956, Joan, *née* Royle; 2 da (Jennifer b 29 April 1958, Susan b 28 May 1961), 1 s (Andrew b 17 April 1960); *Career* md West's Group International plc 1977–86; non-exec dir: United Utilities plc (formerly North West Water Group plc) 1987–, Chieftain Group plc 1988–94, Nord Anglia Education PLC 1989–; FRSC 1981, FRSA 1984; *Recreations* golf, gardening; *Clubs* Hale Golf, Manchester Naval Officers' Assoc; *Style—* Alan Pendleton, Esq; ✉ 12 Harrop Road, Hale, Altrincham, Cheshire WA15 9BX (☎ 0161 928 2805); United Utilities plc, Dawson House, Great Sankey, Warrington, Cheshire WA5 3LW (☎ 01925 234000, fax 01925 233361)

PENDRILL, (Alfred) Malcolm; s of A A Pendrill (d 1970), of Redhill, Surrey, and Olive Rose, *née* Sutton (d 1989); *b* 14 Feb 1926; *Educ* Reigate GS; *m* 11 Dec 1948, Phyllis Margaret, *née* Bryant (d 1993); 1 da (Christine Ann b 8 June 1956); *Career* aerial photographer/printer Aero Pictorial Ltd Redhill Surrey 1955–60, industrial staff photographer and film maker Morfax Ltd Mitcham Surrey 1960–63; fndr Malcolm Pendrill Ltd offering a serv to industl clients in aerial photography, industl photography and documentary films 1963, now specialises in aerial photography and film making; lectr to various professional bodies and amateur gps; former external assessor at various colls: former memb Bd of Govrs Reigate Sch of Art and Design; pres Surrey and S London Centre of Inst of Incorporated Photographers 1972; hon memb Rotary Club of Reigate (memb 1967); FBIPP 1972, FRPS 1973, FRSA 1987; *Books* Reflections of Yesterday (1982), Memories of Yesterday (1983); *Recreations* music, films, travel, family history, sailing; *Style—* Malcolm Pendrill, Esq; ✉ 24 West Street, Reigate, Surrey RH2 9BX (☎ 01737 246576)

PENDRY, Prof John Brian; s of Frank Johnson Pendry (d 1978), and Kathleen, *née* Shaw; *b* 4 July 1943; *Educ* Ashton-under-Lyne GS, Downing Coll Cambridge (BA, MA, PhD); *m* 15 Jan 1977, Patricia, da of Frederick Gard, of London; *Career* res fell in physics Downing Coll Cambridge 1969–75, memb tech staff Bell Laboratories USA 1972–73, sr asst in research Cavendish Lab Cambridge 1973–75 (postdoctoral fell 1969–72), SPSO and head Theory Gp SERC Daresbury Laboratory 1975–81, prof of theoretical solid state physics Imperial Coll London 1981– (assoc head of dept 1981–92), dean Royal Coll of Sci 1993–96; memb: SERC Physics Ctee (chm Panel Y) 1985–88, SERC Sci Bd 1992–93, Royal Soc Cncl 1992–94; FRS 1984, FInstP 1984; *Recreations* music, piano playing, gardening, photography; *Style—* Prof John Pendry, FRS; ✉ Metchley, Knipp Hill, Cobham, Surrey KT11 2PE (☎ 01932 864306); The Blackett Laboratory, Imperial College, London SW7 2BZ (☎ 0171 594 7603, fax 0171 594 7604)

PENDRY, Thomas (Tom); MP (Lab) Stalybridge and Hyde (majority 8,831); s of L E Pendry, of Broadstairs; *b* 10 June 1934; *Educ* St Augustine's Ramsgate, Univ of Oxford; *m* 1966 (sep 1983), Moira Anne, da of A E Smith, of Derby; 1 s, 1 da; *Career* Nat Serv RAF 1955–57; joined Lab Pty 1950, NUPE official 1960–70, memb Paddington Cncl 1962–65, chm Derby Lab Pty 1966; MP (Lab) Stalybridge and Hyde 1970–, oppn whip 1971–74, a Lord Cmmr of the Treasy (Govt whip) 1974–77 (resigned), parly under sec of state NI Office 1978–79; oppn spokesman: on NI 1979–81, on overseas devpt 1981–82, on devolution and regnl affrs 1982, on Sport 1992; shadow min for sport and tourism 1992–; chm: PLP Sports Ctee 1984–92, All Pty Football Ctee 1980–92; co-chm All Pty Jazz Ctee, steward Br Boxing Bd of Control 1987–; Freeman Borough of Tameside 1975, Lordship of Mottram in Longdendale 1975; *Recreations* sports of all kinds; *Clubs* Stalybridge Labour, Wig and Pen, Scribes, Lord's Taverners; *Style—* Tom Pendry, Esq, MP; ✉ The Lodge, 131a Woolley Lane, Hollingworth, Hyde, Cheshire SK14 8NN; House of Commons, London SW1A 0AA (☎ 0171 219 3000)

PENFOLD, Derek John; s of Joseph Penfold, of Tiverton, Devon, and Catherine, *née* O'Sullivan; *b* 17 July 1948; *Educ* Clapham Coll, City of Westminster Coll, NW London Poly (LLB); *Career* features ed Estates Times 1975–78, dep ed Estates Gazette 1980–86 (news ed 1978–80), property analyst Alexanders Laing & Cruickshank 1986–87; dir: Streets Communications 1987–89, Phillips Communications 1990–91, Derek Penfold Associates 1991–94; ed Estates Times 1994–; chm Greenwich Theatre 1976–87 (dir 1975–90), dir Greenwich Young People's Theatre 1980–88 (tstee 1990–), former chm Greenwich Festival; London Borough of Greenwich cncllr 1971–78, (chm Leisure Ctee, chief whip); vice pres The Story of Christmas Charity Appeal; Freeman City of London; fell Land Inst; *Recreations* theatre, architecture; *Clubs* Wig & Pen, Globe Rowing, Walbrook and Broad Street Wards, Architecture; *Style—* Derek Penfold, Esq; ✉ 42 Owenite Street, Abbey Wood, London SE2 0NQ (☎ and fax 0181 311 6039)

PENFOLD, HE Peter Alfred; CMG (1995), OBE (1986); s of Alfred Penfold (d 1991), and Florence Maud Penfold; *b* 27 Feb 1944; *Educ* Sutton Co GS; *m* 1, 1972 (m dis 1983), Margaret Quigley; 2 da (b 1963 and 1974), 2 s (b 1973 and 1980); m 2, 1992, Celia Dolores Koenig; *Career* Foreign Serv (later HM Dip Serv); joined 1963, Bonn 1965–68, Kaduna 1968–70, various posts Mexico City, Quito, San Juan, Montevideo, Asuncion and St Vincent 1970–72, Canberra 1972–75, second sec Addis Ababa 1975–78, Port of Spain 1978–81, FCO 1981–84, dep high cmmr Kampala 1984–87, FCO 1987–91, govr Br Virgin Islands 1991–97, high cmmr to Sierra Leone 1997–; Queen's scout; *Recreations* travel, mountaineering, reading; *Style—* HE Mr Peter Penfold, CMG, OBE; ✉ c/o Foreign and Commonwealth Office (Freetown), King Charles Street, London SW1A 2AH

PENHALIGON, Susan; da of William Russell Penhaligon, of San Francisco, USA, and Muriel Jean Mickleborough; *Educ* The Collegiate Sch Winterbourne, Rustington House Sch Sussex, The Webber-Douglas Sch London; *Career* actress; *Theatre* Painting Churches (Nuffield Southampton), David Lodge's The Writing Game (Birmingham Rep), The Girl In Melony Klein (Palace Watford), A Dolls House (Palace Watford), The Three Sisters (Albery), The Maintenance Man (Comedy), Of Mice And Men (Southampton & Mermaid), The Formation Dancers (Yvonne Arnaud Theatre), Tom Stoppard's The Real Thing (Strand), Sylvia Plath's Three Women (Old Red Lion), Mrs Warren's Profession (Gardner Centre Brighton), The Cherry Orchard (Royal Exchange Manchester), The Lower Depths (Royal Exchange Manchester), Time And The Conways (Royal Exchange Manchester), Picasso's Four Little Girls (Open Space), Painting Churches (Nuffield Theatre Southampton), Abducting Diana (Edinburgh Festival), The Statement (Watermans Art Centre), Dangerous Corner (Whitehall); *Television* Trouble In Mind, Fay Weldon's Heart Of The Country, Seven Faces Of Women, Andrew Davies' Fearless Frank, Phillip Saville's Dracula, Country Matters, Jonathan Miller's The Taming Of The Shrew, A Fine Romance, A Kind Of Loving, Bouquet Of Barbed Wire, Casualty; *Films* The Last Chapter, The Soldier Of The Queen, The Uncanny, The Confessional, Miracles Still Happen, No Sex Please We're British, Patrick, Nasty Habits, Leopard In The Snow, Under Milk Wood, The Land That Time Forgot, Private Road; *Style—* Ms Susan Penhaligon; ✉ c/o Jeremy Conway, 18–21 Jermyn Street, London SW1Y 6HP

PENN, Christopher Arthur; s of Lt-Col Sir Eric Charles William Mackenzie Penn, GCVO, OBE, MC (d 1993), and Prudence Stewart-Wilson, da of Aubyn Wilson (d 1934); *b* 13 Sept 1950; *Educ* Eton; *m* 1976, Sabrina Mary, 2 da of Timothy Colman, DCL, of Bixley Manor, Norwich; 1 s (Rory b 1980), 1 da (Louisa b 1983); *Career* chartered surveyor; ptnr Jones Lang Wootton; *Clubs* White's, Buck's; *Style—* Christopher Penn, Esq; ✉ Jones Lang Wootton, 22 Hanover Square, London W1A 2BN (☎ 0171 493 6040, fax 0171 408 0220)

PENN, Dr Christopher Robert Howard; s of John Howard Penn (d 1977), of Southend-on-Sea, Essex, and Kathleen Mary, *née* Dalton; *b* 24 Aug 1939; *Educ* Felsted, QMC, Trinity Hall Cambridge (MA, MB BCh); *m* 27 May 1966, Elizabeth, da of John Henry Griffin, of Bishopsteignton, Devon; 3 da (Katherine Clare, Sarah Elizabeth, Charlotte Mary); *Career* sr house offr in med Lincoln Co Hosp 1966–67, sr house offr in surgery Scartho Rd Infirmary Grimsby 1967–68; The London Hosp Dept of Radiotherapy 1968–73: sr house offr, registrar, sr registrar; sr conslt Dept of Radiotherapy and Oncology Royal Devon and Exeter and Torbay Hosps 1982– (conslt 1973–82); numerous pubns in jls; chm Bd of Govrs Trinity Sch Teignmouth, churchwarden St Gregory's Dawlish; memb Br Inst Radiology; Freeman City of London 1960; FRCR 1972; *Books* Radiotherapy in Modern Clinical Practice (contrib 1975); *Recreations* sailing, naval history; *Style—* Dr Christopher Penn; ✉ 1 Holcombe Road, Teignmouth, Devon TQ14 8UP (☎ 01626 778448); Dept of Radiotherapy and Oncology, Royal Devon and Exeter Hosp (Wonford), Barrack Rd, Exeter (☎ 01392 402102)

PENN, David John; s of late Surgn Capt Eric Arthur Penn, DSC, of W Mersea, Essex, and Catherine, *née* Dunnett; *b* 2 Jan 1945; *Educ* Dulwich, St Catherine's Coll Oxford (MA); *m* 1993, Catherine Janet Davidson; 1 s (Alexander Eric Davidson b 12 Jan 1995); *Career* keeper Imperial War Museum: Dept of Info Retrieval 1970–77, Dept of Firearms 1973–76, Dept of Exhibits and Firearms 1976–; vice pres Muzzle-Loaders Assoc of GB, hon sec Hist Breechloading Smallarms Assoc; memb: Br Shooting Sports Cncl, Home Office Firearms Consultative Ctee 1989, National Historic Ships Ctee 1995; Freeman City of London 1982, Liveryman Worshipful Co of Gunmakers 1982; FSA 1989; *Books* Imperial War Museum Film Cataloguing Rules (with R B N Smither, 1976); *Recreations* shooting; *Style—* David Penn, Esq, FSA; ✉ Imperial War Museum, Lambeth Rd, London SE1 6HZ (☎ 0171 416 5270, fax 0171 416 5374)

PENN-SMITH, Derek John; s of Major Sydney Penn-Smith, RE, FRIBA (d 1987), of Leicester, and Olive Amelia, *née* Kinton; *b* 21 Feb 1934; *Educ* Wyggeston Sch Leics, Sch of Architecture Leicester (DipArch), Univ of Durham (Dip Town Planning, Sailing colours); *m* 1, 19 July 1968 (m dis), Eva Margaret; 2 da (Fiona b 1964, Sally b 1966); m 2, 2 Dec 1972, Molly, da of John Berkin (d 1985), of Leics; *Career* Nat Serv 2 Lt RE Gibraltar; ptnr and conslt: Penn-Smith & Wall Peterborough 1961–87, Penn-Smith & Weston Derby 1961–88; ptnr S Penn-Smith Son & Ptnrs Leicester 1961–88 (sr ptnr 1980–88), dir Douglas Smith Stimson Partnership Ltd (incorporating S Penn-Smith Son & Ptnrs) 1988–89, town planning conslt 1989–; Freeman City of London, Liveryman Worshipful Co of Pewterers; FRIBA, FRTPI; *Recreations* sailing, aviation (gliding and light aircraft), orchid growing; *Style—* Derek J Penn-Smith, Esq; ✉ Delphi, High St, Naseby, Northants NN6 6DD (☎ 01604 740326)

PENNA, Colin Eric; s of John Henry Penna (d 1988), of Willington, Crook, Co Durham, and Ruth, *née* Collin (d 1966); *b* 1 Nov 1935; *Educ* King James I Sch Bishop Auckland Co Durham, King's Coll London (LLB); *Career* slr; conslt Marquis Penna & Hewitt Brown-Humes & Hare of Co Durham; HM coroner S Dist Durham Co 1980; *Recreations* music, theatre; *Clubs* RAC; *Style—* Colin Penna, Esq; ✉ 28 Briardene, Durham City (☎ 0191 386 8030); Marquis Penna & Hewitt Brown-Humes & Hare, 5 Market Place, Bishop Auckland, Co Durham (☎ 01388 604691)

PENNANT-REA, Rupert Lascelles; s of Peter Athelwold Pennant-Rea, MBE, of Bourton-on-the-Water, Glos, and Pauline Elizabeth, *née* Creasy; *b* 23 Jan 1948; *Educ* Peterhouse Zimbabwe, Trinity Coll Dublin (BA), Univ of Manchester (MA); *m* 1, 3 Oct 1970 (m dis 1975), (Elizabeth) Louise, da of Rt Rev William Derrick Lindsay Greer (d 1972), sometime Bishop of Manchester; m 2, 18 Aug 1979 (m dis 1986), Jane Trevelyan, da of John Hamilton, of Isles of Scilly; 1 s (Rory b 1983), 1 da (Emily b 1982); m 3, 24 June 1986, Hon Helen, er (twin) da of late Baron Jay, PC (Life Peer), and former w of David Kennard; 1 s (Edward b 1986), 2 step da; *Career* with Confedn of Irish Indust 1970–71, Gen & Municipal Workers Union 1972–73, Bank of England 1973–77; The Economist: economics corr 1977–81, economics ed 1981–85, ed 1986–93; dep govr Bank of England 1993–95; chm: Caspian (investmt bank Luxembourg) 1995–, The Stationery Office 1996; non-exec dir BAT Industries 1995–, dir Sherritt International 1995–; *Books* Gold Foil (1978), Who Runs The Economy? (jtly, 1979), The Pocket Economist (jtly, 1982), The Economist Economics (jtly, 1986); *Recreations* music, tennis, fishing, family; *Clubs* MCC, Reform, Harare; *Style—* Rupert Pennant-Rea, Esq; ✉ c/o BAT Industries plc, Windsor House, 50 Victoria Street, London SW1H ONL (☎ 0171 222 7979)

PENNEY, Malcolm Olaf; s of John William Penney (d 1983), of Bridport, Dorset, and Phyllis Gertrude, *née* Radnor; *b* 24 June 1939; *Educ* City of London Sch; *m* 28 Dec 1973, Marian Joyce, da of Leslie Edward Johnson (d 1989); 1 s (Martin Edward b 19 Aug 1976), 1 da (Caroline Phyllis b 10 Sept 1980); *Career* Lord Foster & Co: articled clerk 1956–61, sr clerk 1961–64, ptnr 1964–86 (latterly ptnr i/c Int Tax); ptnr i/c Newbury office and tax ptnr Thames Valley Dearden Farrow (latterly Binder Hamlyn) 1986–88, tax ptnr Reading office Ernst & Young 1988–; chm Fiscal Ctee of the Confédération Fiscal Européenne 1991–93, memb Tax Ctee ICAEW 1978–91, memb Cncl Inst of Taxation 1987– (vice chm Tech Ctee 1992–93, chm Int Tax Sub Ctee 1995–); Plender prize ICAEW 1959, Stephens prize ICAEW 1961; Freeman City of London 1973, Under Warden Worshipful Co of Glovers (Liveryman 1973); FCA (ACA 1961), FTII (ATII 1964); *Books* Capital Transfer Tax Planning (with E K Wright and others, 1974), Taxation of Capital Gains (with P W Elliott, 1982); *Recreations* travelling, walking; *Clubs* City Livery; *Style—* Malcolm Penney, Esq; ✉ Greenways, Fawley, Berkshire OX12 9NQ (☎ 01488 638784); Ernst & Young, Apex Plaza, Reading RG1 1YE (☎ 0118 950 0611, fax 0118 950 7744)

PENNEY, Penelope Anne; da of Richard Chamberlain, and (Lydia) Joan, *née* Kay, of Highgate, London; *b* 30 Sept 1942; *Educ* Chatelard Sch Les Avants Switzerland, Univ of Bristol (BA); *m* 27 July 1963, Rev William Affleck Penney, s of Robert Affleck Penney; 1 s (Christopher James Affleck b 25 Sept 1964), 2 da (Margaret Clare b 10 Feb 1966, Alison Joan b 27 April 1971); *Career* pt/t English teacher 1967–74, head of languages and communications Astor of Hever Sch Maidstone 1975–79; headmistress: Prendergast Sch Catford 1980–86, Putney HS (GPDST) 1987–91, Haberdashers' Aske's Sch for Girls 1991–; memb SHA 1980–, memb Professional Ctee GSA 1991– (memb 1987–), chm London Region GSA 1992–, pres GSA 1994–95); Freeman of the City of London 1993; memb IOD 1991, FRSA 1994, FIMgt 1994; *Recreations* fast cars; *Style—* Mrs Penelope Penney; ✉ Haberdashers' Aske's School for Girls, Aldenham Road, Elstree, Herts WD6 3BT (☎ 0181 953 4261, fax 0181 953 5663)

PENNINGTON, Malcolm Read; s of Capt Stanley Read Pennington (d 1975), and Esther Elsie, *née* Hall; *b* 6 Feb 1947; *Educ* Repton Sch; *m* 24 April 1971, Jillian Elizabeth, da of James Shepherd (d 1977); 1 s (James b 1976), 1 da (Sarah b 1977); *Career* CA fndr ptnr Pennington Williams CAs of Bromborough and Chester 1975; Chevalier de l'Ordre des Coteaux de Champagne 1982; FCA 1979; *Recreations* golf, cricket, badminton, gastronomy; *Clubs* Delamere Forest Golf, Heswall Golf, Oxton CC, Wirral Wine Soc; *Style—* Malcolm Pennington, Esq; ✉ Horbury, 74 Osmaston Rd, Prenton, Birkenhead, Merseyside L42 8LP (☎ 0151 608 1578)

PENNINGTON, Michael Vivian Fyfe; s of Vivian Maynard Cecil Pennington (d 1984), and Euphemia Willock Fyfe (d 1987); *b* 7 June 1943; *Educ* Marlborough, Trinity Coll Cambridge (BA); *m* 10 Oct 1964 (m dis 1967), Katharine, da of Peter Barker; 1 s (Mark Dominic Fyfe b 12 Aug 1966); *Career* actor; memb RSC 1964–66; freelance, West End and TV plays 1966–73: The Judge, Hamlet, A Woman of No Importance, Savages; leading memb RSC 1974–81: Angelo in Measure for Measure, Mercutio in Romeo and Juliet, Edgar in King Lear, Berowne in Love's Labours Lost, Mirabell in Way of the World, title role in Hippolytus, title role in Hamlet, Donal Davoren in Shadow of a Gunman; NT 1984: title role in Strider, Jaffier in Venice Preserved, title role in Anton Chekhov; subsequent credits: The Real Thing (West End) 1985, Oedipus The King (BBC) 1985; artistic dir English Shakespeare Co until 1993 (fndr and leading actor 1986–92, participated in four round the world tours); roles incl: Richard II, Henry V, Coriolanus, Leontes in The Winter's Tale, Macbeth; other credits: Summer's Lease (BBC) 1989, Playing with Trains (RSC Barbican) 1989, Vershinin in Three Sisters (Gate Theatre Dublin) 1990, Edward Damson in The Gift of the Gorgon (RSC Barbican and Wyndham's) 1993, Old Times and One for the Road (Dublin Pinter Festival), Claudius and the Ghost in Hamlet (Peter Hall Co) 1994, Taking Sides (Chichester Festival, Criterion) 1995, Archie Rice in The Entertainer (Hampstead) 1996; dir Twelfth Night (English Shakespeare Co 1991, Haiyuza Co Tokyo 1993, Shakespeare Repertory Co Chicago 1996); *Books* Rossya: A Journey Through Siberia (1977), English Shakespeare Company: The Story of the Wars of The Roses (1990), Hamlet: A User's Guide (1995); *Recreations* reading, music; *Style—* Michael Pennington, Esq; ✉ c/o Marmont Management Ltd, Langham House, 308 Regent Street, London W1R 5AL (☎ 0171 637 3183, fax 0171 323 4798)

PENNINGTON, Prof Robert Roland; s of Roland Alexander Pennington (d 1952), of Warley, W Mids, and Elsie Davis (d 1977); *b* 22 April 1927; *Educ* Holly Lodge Smethwick W Mids, Univ of Birmingham (LLB, LLD); *m* 14 March 1968, Patricia Irene, da of Cecil Allen Rook (d 1968), of Alcester, Warwickshire; 1 da (Elisabeth Anne b 1974); *Career* admitted slr 1951; reader Law Soc's Sch of Law London 1955 (sr lectr 1951), memb Bd of Mgmnt Coll of Law London 1962; Univ of Birmingham sr lectr in law 1962–68, prof of commercial law 1968–94, emeritus prof 1994–; visiting prof Univ of London 1995–; govt advsr on co legislation Trinidad 1967 and Seychelles 1970, special legal advsr on commercial law harmonisation Cmmn of the Euro Communities 1973–79; Hon LLD Univ of Exeter 1994; memb Law Soc 1951; *Books* Company Law (1959, 7 edn 1995), Companies in the Common Market (1962, 3 edn as Companies in the European Communities 1982), The Investor and the Law (1967), Stannary Law - A History of the Mining Law of Cornwall and Devon (1973), Commercial Banking Law (1978), The Companies Acts 1980 and 1981 - A Practitioner's Manual (1983), Stock Exchange Listing - The New Requirements (1985), Jura Europa - Gesellschaftsrecht: Vereinigtes Königreich (1986), Directors' Personal Liability (1987), Company Liquidations - The Substantive Law, The Procedure (2 vols, 1987), The Law of the Investment Markets (1990), Corporate Insolvency Law (1990); *Recreations* travel, walking, history, archaeology; *Style—* Prof Robert Pennington; ✉ Gryphon House, Langley Road, Claverdon, Warwicks (☎ 0192 684 3235); Faculty of Law, Univ of Birmingham, Birmingham B15 2TT (☎ 0121 414 6296)

PENNOCK, Dr Charles Anthony; s of Sydney Pennock, and Edith Anne, *née* Oliver; *b* 26 Dec 1937; *Educ* Varndean Sch Brighton, Univ of Bristol (MB ChB, BSc, MD); *m* 1 April 1961, Patricia Ann (Paddy), da of Charles Ross Haller; 1 s (Christopher b 3 March 1965), 1 da (Sarah b 30 Sept 1963); *Career* conslt Paediatric Chem Path Dept United Bristol Hosps Healthcare NHS Tst 1972–, sr lectr in child health Univ of Bristol 1975–, conslt in biochemical genetics Southmead Hosp NHS Tst 1993–; visiting prof of science Sheffield Hallam Univ 1994–, hon fell Univ of Bath 1980; govr Inst of Child Health Univ of Bristol, chm Br Inherited Metabolic Disease Gp; FRCPath 1982 (MRCPath 1970); *Recreations* photography, fiscal philately; *Style—* Dr Charles Pennock; ✉ Warners Cottage, Chewton Keynsham, Bath & NE Somerset BS18 2SU (☎ 0117 986 2320); Paediatric Chem Pathology Department, St Michael's Hospital, Southwell Street, Bristol BS2 8EG (☎ 0117 928 5318, fax 0117 928 5312)

PENNY, Nicholas Beaver; s of Joseph Noel Bailey Penny, QC, of Lingfield, Surrey, and Agnes Celia, *née* Roberts (d 1969); *b* 21 Dec 1949; *Educ* Shrewsbury Sch, St Catharine's Coll Cambridge (MA), Courtauld Inst London (MA, PhD); *m* 1971 (m dis), Anne Philomel, *née* Udy; 2 da (Caroline Emily and Elizabeth Joan (twins) b 26 Jan 1977); *Career* Leverhulme fell Clare Coll Cambridge, lectr Dept of History of Art Univ of Manchester 1975–82, sr res fell King's Coll Cambridge 1982–84, keeper of Western art Ashmolean Museum and professorial fell Balliol Coll Oxford 1984–89, Clore curator of Renaissance painting National Gall 1990–; Slade prof of fine art Univ of Oxford 1980–81; Cavaliere dell Ordine al merito della Repubblica Italiana 1990; *Books* Church Monuments in Romantic England (1977), Piranesi (1978), Taste and the Antique (with Francis Haskell, 1981), Mourning (1981), The Arrogant Connoisseur (ed with Michael Clarke, 1982), Raphael (with Roger Jones, 1983), Reynolds (ed, 1986), Alfred and Winifred Turner (1988), Lucian Freud, Works on Paper (with Robert Flynn Johnson, 1988), Ruskin's Drawings (1988), From Giotto to Dürer (with Jill Dunkernon et al, 1991), The Materials of Sculpture (1993); *Style—* Nicholas Penny, Esq; ✉ The National Gallery, Trafalgar Square, London WC2N 5DN (☎ 0171 747 2801, fax 0171 753 8179)

PENNY, Norman James; s of Santiago Penny, and Phyllis Muriel, *née* Buckley (d 1989); *b* 11 April 1948; *Educ* Inverness Royal Acad, Inverness Tech Coll, Napier Coll Edinburgh, Watford Coll of Technol (HNC); *m* 1, 1970 (m dis 1976), Francis, *née* Brooker; 1 da (Tara Samantha b 3 Oct 1971); m 2, 1977, Annie, da of Donald MacDonald (d 1992); 1 da (Melody Anne b 13 April 1983); *Career* trainee technician Post Office Telephones Inverness 1965–68, x-ray service technician Profexray Cincinnati 1968–69; British Telecom 1969–: private circuit network designer and systems analyst London 1969–75, gp mangr (Maintenance and Training) Scottish Highlands and Islands Inverness 1975–83, head various engrg and sales divs Canterbury 1983–91, mangr Global Customer Serv Product Launch Unit 1991–; chm IEEIE Cncl 1987–88 (Publications award for Decision Dynamics - A Systems Approach to Implementing Change 1980), memb Engrg Cncl 1991–95, memb British Nat Ctee for Int Engrg Affairs 1993–95; FIEIE 1981 (memb 1973), MIMgt 1984, FSE 1990 (memb 1975); *Recreations* swimming, horse riding, hill walking, DIY; *Style—* Norman Penny, Esq; ✉ Fore, The Fairway, Herne Bay, Kent CT6 7TW (☎ 01227 740740); British Telecom, Rutland House, St George's Place, Canterbury, Kent CT1 1GA (☎ 01227 474200, fax 01227 450037)

PENNY, Hon Peter George Worsley; s and h of 3 Viscount Marchwood, *qv*; *b* 8 Oct 1965; *Educ* Winchester; *m* 1995, Annabel C, yr da of Rex Cooper, of E Bergholt, Suffolk; *Career* assoc dir The HMG Group plc 1990; *Recreations* racing, tennis, cricket, shooting; *Style—* The Hon Peter Penny; ✉ 37 Coniger Road, London SW6 (☎ 0171 736 6834)

PENRHYN, 6 Baron (UK 1866); Malcolm Frank Douglas-Pennant; DSO (1945), MBE (1943); s of 5 Baron Penrhyn (d 1967, himself gn of 17 Earl of Morton and ggs of Lady Frances Lascelles, da of 1 Earl of Harewood), and Alice Nellie (d 1965), da of Sir William Charles Cooper, 3 Bt; *b* 11 July 1908; *Educ* Eton, RMC Sandhurst; *m* 1954, Elisabeth Rosemary, da of late Brig Sir Percy Laurie, KCVO, CBE, DSO, JP; 2 da (*see* Thomas Richard Troubridge); *Heir* bro, Hon Nigel Douglas-Pennant; *Career* Col (ret) KRRC, served WWII 1939–45 in N Africa and NW Europe; *Style—* The Rt Hon the Lord Penrhyn, DSO, MBE; ✉ Littleton Manor, Winchester, Hants SO22 6QU (☎ 01962 880205)

PENRITH, Bishop of 1994–; Rt Rev Richard Garrard; s of Charles John Garrard, of Northampton, and Marjorie Louise Garrard; *b* 24 May 1937; *Educ* Northampton GS for Boys, KCL (BD, AKC, Wichelow Prize for elocution); *m* 1961, Elizabeth Ann, da of Vern E Sewell; 1 s (James Richard b 14 Dec 1964), 1 da (Charlotte Ann b 1 May 1969); *Career* ordained: deacon 1961, priest 1962; curate: Woolwich PC 1962–66, St Mary the Great Cambridge 1966–68; chaplain/lectr Keswick Hall Coll of Educn 1968–74, princ Wilson Carlile (Church Army Coll) 1974–79, canon chllr Southwark Cathedral and diocesan dir of trg 1979–87, canon residentiary St Edmundsbury Cathedral and advsr for clergy trg 1987–91, archdeacon of Sudbury 1991–94; MIMgt 1987; *Books* Lent with St Mark (1993), A Time to Pray (1993), Love on the Cross (1995); *Recreations* cats and crosswords, Italy and the fells; *Style—* The Rt Rev the Bishop of Penrith; ✉ 13 Castle Road, Kendal, Cumbria LA9 7AU (☎ 01539 727836, fax 01539 734380)

PENROSE, Prof Oliver; s of Lionel S Penrose, FRS, and Margaret, *née* Leathes; *b* 6 June 1929; *Educ* Central Collegiate Inst London Ontario, UCL (BSc), Univ of Cambridge (PhD); *m* 1953, Joan Lomas, *née* Dilley; 2 s (and 1 s decd), 1 da; *Career* mathematical physicist English Electric Co Luton 1952–55, res asst Yale Univ 1955–56, lectr rising to reader in mathematics Imperial Coll London 1956–69; prof of mathematics: Open Univ 1969–86, Heriot-Watt Univ 1986–94; author of numerous papers in physics jls; FRS 1987, FRSE 1989; *Books* Foundations of Statisical Mechanics (1970); *Recreations* making music, chess; *Style—* Prof Oliver Penrose, FRS, FRSE; ✉ 29 Frederick St, Edinburgh EH2 2ND (☎ 0131 225 5879); Department of Mathematics, Heriot-Watt University, Riccarton, Edinburgh EH14 4AS (☎ 0131 451 3225)

PENROSE, Dr Richard James Jackson; s of Walter James Pace (d 1944), and Gertrude May, *née* Penrose (d 1981); name changed by deed poll 1968; *b* 12 Oct 1941; *Educ* Haberdashers' Aske's, Charing Cross Hosp Med Sch London (MB BS, LRCP, MRCS); *m* 1 May 1976, Lynda Elisabeth, da of Dr Reginald John Alcock, of The Pigeon House, Kemble; 2 s (James b 1977, William b 1980); *Career* Charing Cross Hosp: house surgn in ENT 1966, house physician in gen med and neurology 1967, sr house offr in psychiatry 1968; sr registrar in psychiatry St George's Hosp London 1971–75 (sr house offr and registrar 1968–71); conslt psychiatrist: St George's Hosp 1975–89, West Park Hosp Epsom 1975–81, Springfield Hosp 1981–89, Epsom Gen Hosp 1989–; memb Assoc of Behavioral Clinicians, fndr Br Assoc for Psychopharmacology; DPM 1970, MRCPsych 1973; *Books* various articles in jls on life events, brain haemorrhage, depression and drug treatment; *Recreations* music, gardening, reading; *Style—* Dr Richard Penrose; ✉ Department of Psychiatry, Epsom General Hospital, Epsom, Surrey (☎ 01372 735735)

PENROSE, Roger Ian; s of Edward Charles Penrose, of Plymouth, and Grace Feltis, *née* Bond; *b* 15 Sept 1953; *Educ* Plymouth Coll, Univ of Bath (BSc, BArch); *m* 7 Aug 1976, Janet Elaine, da of Richard Alan Harvey, RN; 2 s (Richard Merrick b 1984, Simon Tristan b 1987), 1 da (Laura Jane b 1989); *Career* princ Ian Penrose and Associates (chartered architects), md Ian Penrose Architects Ltd 1987–; *Recreations* motorcycling, sailing, cycle, swimming; *Clubs* OPM, IMTC, Exeter Golf and Country; *Style—* R I Penrose, Esq; ✉ Ian Penrose Architects Ltd, The Park House, 13 Queens Terrace, Exeter EX4 4HR (☎ 01392 53000)

PENRY-DAVEY, David Herbert; QC (1988); s of Samuel Saunders Watson Penry-Davey (d 1991), and Almary Lorna, *née* Patrick, of Rochester, Kent; *b* 16 May 1942; *Educ* Hastings GS, King's Coll London (LLB); *m* 1970, Judith Ailsa Nancy, da of John Walter, of Morley St. Botolph, Norfolk; 2 s (Matthew b 1972, James b 1979), 1 da (Caroline b 1974); *Career* called to the Bar Inner Temple 1965; recorder Crown Ct 1986, ldr SE Circuit of the Bar 1992–95, chm Gen Cncl of the Bar 1996– (vice-chm 1995–96); *Recreations* music, golf, cycling; *Style—* David Penry-Davey, Esq, QC; ✉ 2–3 Gray's Inn Square, London WC1R 5JH (☎ 0171 242 4986, fax 0171 405 1166)

PENSON, Alan Anthony; *b* 30 Jan 1952; *Educ* Dulwich, St Catharine's Coll Cambridge (MA); *m* 1976, Jane; 1 s (Alexander b 1983), 1 da (Mary b 1985); *Career* Price Waterhouse 1974–85, gp chief exec Clarke Hooper plc 1992 (fin dir 1986–92), gen mangr Interwood Marketing (UK) plc 1993, gp fin dir Grey Communications Group Ltd 1994–95, princ Penson Associates 1996–; ACA; *Style—* Alan Penson, Esq; ✉ Penson Associates, Fairfield House, Dodds Lane, Chalfont St Giles, Bucks HP8 4EL (☎ 01494 872546, fax 01494 870046)

PENTLAND, Dr Brian; s of George Hodge Pentland (d 1985), and Irvine Wilson, *née* Booth (d 1991); *b* 24 June 1949; *Educ* Gracemount Secdy Sch, Liberton HS, Univ of Edinburgh (BSc, MB ChB, MRCP), Euro Bd of Physical Med and Rehabilitation (Dip); *m* 21 July 1973, Gillian Mary, da of Cecil John Duggua; 4 s (Malcolm Keith b 16 Sept 1977, Gordon Neil b 17 Nov 1978, Duncan Roy b 14 Dec 1981, Kenneth Brian b 1 March 1984); *Career* house physician Royal Infirmary Edinburgh 1974–75, house surgn West Cumberland Hosp Whitehaven Feb-July 1975, SHO Northern Gen Hosp Edinburgh

1975–76, registrar Ninewells and Kings Cross Hosps Dundee 1976–78, registrar Northern Gen Hosp Edinburgh Jan-Sept 1979, lectr in med neurology Univ of Edinburgh 1979–82, conslt neurologist (rehabilitation med) Astley Ainslie Hosp Edinburgh 1982–, dir Scottish Brain Injury Rehabilitation Serv Edinburgh 1991–, head Rehabilitation Studies Unit Univ of Edinburgh 1991–, head of rehabilitation servs Edinburgh Healthcare NHS Tst 1994–; visiting lectr Queen Margaret Coll Edinburgh 1979–; memb Assoc of Br Neurologists 1982, Scottish Soc of Physicians 1986; FRCPEd 1986; *Books* Parkinson's Disease: diagnosis and management (1986); over 100 published articles or chapters in scientific jls; *Recreations* hill walking, gardening; *Style*— Dr Brian Pentland; ✉ Edinburgh Healthcare NHS Trust, Astley Ainslie Hospital, Grange Loan, Edinburgh EH9 2HL (☎ 0131 537 9039, fax 0131 537 9030)

PENTON, John Howard; MBE (1987); s of Richard Howard Penton (d 1960), of London N1, and Ciceley Urmson, *née* Heinekey (d 1966); *b* 12 Feb 1938; *Educ* Merchant Taylors', Architectural Assoc Sch of Architecture (AADip), Open Univ (BA); *m* 2 Nov 1963 (sep), (Elizabeth) Diana, da of (Henry) Harold King (d 1985), of 1 Summerhill Ct, Avenue Rd, St Albans, Herts; 1 da (Ciceley Rebecca Clare b 1975); *Career* chartered architect; assoc D E Pugh & Assocs 1963–72, fndr ptnr Penton Smart & Grimwade 1972–91, independent conslt 1994–; consultancies: LT, London Housing Consortium, Irish Nat Rehabilitation Bd, The Inst for Rehabilitation & Res Houston Texas, The English Tourist Bd, Perkins Sch & Inst for the Blind Boston USA, The Nordic Ctee on Deaf/Blindness Dronninglund Denmark, St Albans Cathedral, The Leonard Cheshire Fndn; hon architect Herts Assoc for Disabled; awards: RIBA/DOE Housing Design award 1985 and 1991, RIBA res fellowship 1984–85; Liam McGuire Memorial Lecture Dublin 1986, res fell Hull Sch of Architecture 1987, expert witness damage actions of disabled; fndr chm Herts and Beds Constructions Indust Liaison Gp, former chm Herts Assoc of Architects, chm Centre for Accessible Environments, fndr memb The Access Ctee for England, memb Prince of Wales Advsy Gp on Disability, memb Grants Ctee King Edward VII's Hosp Fund; memb Ct of Assts Worshipful Co of Merchant Taylors (Warden 1988/1991), Renter Warden Worshipful Co of Chartered Architects; RIAS, ACIArb, FBEng, FCSD, FRSA; *Recreations* reading, sketching, swimming, target rifle shooting, carving chessmen; *Clubs* Reform; *Style*— John Penton, Esq, MBE; ✉ 5A George Street, St Albans, Hertfordshire AL3 4ER; 8 Spicer St, St Albans, Herts AL3 4PQ (☎ 01727 868873, fax 01727 852376)

PENTREATH, (Richard) John; s of John Alistair Dudley Pentreath (ka Burma 1945), and Mary Lena, *née* Gendall; *b* 28 Dec 1943; *Educ* Sir Humphry Davy GS, Univ of London (BSc, DSc), Univ of Auckland (Commonwealth scholar, PhD); *m* Elisabeth Amanda, *née* Leach; 2 da (Tamsin Sarah b 22 Feb 1971, Lamorna Kate b 7 Nov 1974); *Career* MAFF: science res cncl fell 1969 and memb scientific staff 1969–89, head Radiobiological Res 1985–87, head Aquatic Environment Protection Div and Res Support Gp and dep dir Fisheries Res 1988–89; chief scientist and dir of water quality National Rivers Authy 1989–95, chief scientist and dir of environmental strategy Environment Agency 1995–; memb: Nat Environment Res Cncl 1992–, Advsy Bd Centre for Social and Economic Res on the Global Environment 1994–, Higher Educn Funding Cncl Res Assessment Panel 1995–96; hon prof Univ of E Anglia 1996–; CBiol, FIBiol, FSRP; *Books* Nuclear Power, Man and the Environment (1980); *Recreations* visual arts, Cornish history, tall ship sailing; *Style*— Dr John Pentreath; ✉ Environment Agency, Rio House, Waterside Drive, Aztec West, Almondsbury, Bristol BS12 4UD (☎ 01454 624400)

PENYCATE, John William (Jack); CBE (1988); s of Walter John Penycate (ka Jutland 1916), and Emily, *née* Puttock (1944); *b* 10 March 1913; *Educ* Royal GS Guildford; *m* 1, 9 Sept 1939, Dorothy Gladys Crawt (d 1969); 1 s (John), 1 da (Prudence (Mrs Goodwin); m 2, 10 Jan 1970, Mary Doreen (Mollie) Liggett, MBE; *Career* journalist; gp editorial dir The Surrey Advertiser 1960–74 (ed); playwright; plays: Peacock in a Dovecot, Ordeal by Marriage, A Killing in Oils; Yvonne Arnaud Theatre Guildford: tstee Bldg Appeal Ctee 1958–61 (memb), chm Bd of Dirs 1972–88 (vice chm 1961–72); Nat Fedn of Playgoers' Socs: jt fndr, hon sec 1957–75, vice pres; chm Middx and Surrey League for the Hard of Hearing, chm Broadcasting Ctee Br Assoc for the Hard of Hearing 1987–93; Hon DUniv Surrey 1974; *Recreations* formerly cricket, currently The Times and The Independent crosswords; *Style*— Jack Penycate, Esq, CBE; ✉ 11 Josephs Road, Guildford, Surrey GU1 1DN (☎ 0438 66943)

PEPLOE, Guy; s of Denis Frederick Neil Peploe, RSA, and Elizabeth Marion, *née* Barr; *b* 25 Jan 1960; *Educ* The Edinburgh Acad, Univ of Aberdeen (MA); *m* Rosanne Claire, *née* Munro; *Career* exhibition offr Royal Scottish Acad 1983, res asst Scottish Nat Gallery of Modern Art 1983–85, managing dir The Scottish Gallery 1991– (dir 1984–); *Recreations* golf, mycology; *Clubs* Scottish Arts (Pictures Convenor 1988–89); *Style*— Guy Peploe, Esq; ✉ The Scottish Gallery, 16 Dundas Street, Edinburgh EH3 6HZ (☎ 0131 558 1200, fax 0131 558 3900)

PEPPARD, Nadine Sheila; CBE (1970); da of Joseph Anthony Peppard (d 1960), of Tunbridge Wells, and May, *née* Barber (d 1963); *b* 16 Jan 1922; *Educ* Macclesfield HS, Univ of Manchester (BA, Dip in teaching); *Career* teacher Maldon GS 1943–46, Spanish ed George G Harrap & Co 1946–55, Training Dept Marks & Spencer 1955–57, dep gen sec London Cncl of Social Service 1957–64, nat advsy offr for cwlth immigrants 1964–65, gen sec Nat Ctee for Cwlth Immigrants 1965–68, chief offr Community Rels Cmmn 1968–72, race rels advsr Home Office 1972–83, race rels conslt 1983–89, dir of admin Equalities Associates 1989–90, race relations conslt 1991–; author of various professional articles on race rels 1957–, race rels training articles for New Community 1972–85; *Publications* Primitive India (trans 1954), Toledo (trans 1955); *Recreations* writing, travel, cookery; *Style*— Ms Nadine Peppard, CBE

PEPPER, Donald John; s of Cdr Frank Sydney Charles Pepper, RN (d 1940), and Beatrice Mary, *née* Trevor (d 1952); *b* 7 Aug 1921; *Educ* Frobisher RN Coll Dartmouth, RN Engrg Coll Plymouth, RN Coll Greenwich; *m* 7 June 1946, Maureen, da of Robert MacKenzie im Thurn (d 1956), of Friern Barnet; 3 s (John Robert b 1948, David MacKenzie b 1952, Mark im Thurn b 1957); *Career* naval engrg offr: HMS King George V, HMS Indefatigable; Staff Naval Engrg Coll, invalided 1947; head Nuclear Energy Dept Foster Wheeler Ltd, fndr dir Rolls Royce & Associates 1959 (md 1962–66), memb Rolls Royce Bd 1969 (vice chm 1976–83), ret; currently: chm Metropolitan Safe Deposits, dir Chilworth Centre Limited, devpt tstee Univ of Southampton; Gold medallist NCIES; Freeman City of London, memb Worshipful Co of Coach Makers and Coach Harness Makers; MIMechE 1962, MIMarE 1960, NCIES 1961, CIMgt 1969; *Recreations* golf, sailing; *Clubs* Royal Southern, Army and Navy; *Style*— Donald Pepper, Esq; ✉ Hard Cottage, Swanwick Shore, Southampton SO3 7EF (☎ 01489 572107)

PEPPER, Prof Gordon Terry; CBE; s of Harold Terry Pepper (d 1973), and Jean Margaret Gordon, *née* Furness (d 1963); *b* 2 June 1934; *Educ* Repton, Trinity Coll Cambridge (MA); *m* 30 Aug 1958, Gillian Clare, da of Lt-Col William Helier Huelin (d 1978); 3 s (Alasdair b 1960, Harry b 1967, Mark b 1969), 1 da (Linda (Ninna) b 1961); *Career* Nat Serv cmmnd RCS 1952–54; Equity and Law Life Assurance Soc 1957–60; W Greenwell & Co: joined 1960, ptnr 1962, jt sr ptnr 1980; chm Greenwell Montagu & Co 1986–87, dir and sr advsr Midland Montagu (Holdings) Ltd 1987–90, chm Payton Pepper & Sons Ltd 1987– (dir 1986–); City Univ Business Sch: dir Centre For Financial Markets 1988–, prof 1991– (hon visiting prof 1987–90); memb: Ctee on Indust and Fin Nat Econ Devpt Cncl 1988–90, Econ and Social Res Cncl 1989–93; FIA 1961, FIIMR; *Publications* Money, Credit and Inflation (1990), Money, Credit and Asset Prices (1994), articles in various econ and fin jls; *Recreations* sailing, tennis, walking, family; *Clubs* Reform, Royal Ocean Racing, Royal Channel Islands Yacht; *Style*— Prof Gordon Pepper, CBE; ✉ Staddleden, Sissinghurst, Cranbrook, Kent TN17 2AN (☎ and fax 01580 714853); City University Business School, Frobisher Crescent, Barbican Centre, London EC2Y 8HB (☎ 0171 477 8000, fax 0171 477 8880)

PEPPER, Prof Michael; s of Morris Pepper (d 1982), and Ruby, *née* Bloom; *b* 10 Aug 1942; *Educ* St Marylebone GS, Univ of Reading (BSc, PhD); *m* Oct 1973, Dr Jeannette Denise, da of Albert Josse, of London; 2 da (Judith Leah, Ruth Jennifer); *Career* res physicist The Plessey Co Ltd 1969–82, res Cavendish Lab 1973–, princ res fell GEC plc 1982–87, prof of physics Univ of Cambridge 1987–; Warren res fell Royal Soc 1978–86, fell Trinity Coll Cambridge 1982–; md Toshiba Cambridge Research Centre Ltd 1990–; awarded: Guthrie Prize and Medal Inst of Physics 1985, Hewlett-Packard Europhysics Prize 1985, Hughes Medal of Royal Soc 1987; ScD Cambridge 1989; FRS 1983; *Recreations* travel, music, walking, whisky tasting; *Clubs* Arsenal FC, Athenaeum; *Style*— Prof Michael Pepper, FRS; ✉ Cavendish Laboratory, Madingley Rd, Cambridge CB3 0HE (☎ 01223 337330, fax 01223 337271); Toshiba Cambridge Research Centre, 260 Cambridge Science Park, Milton Rd, Cambridge CB4 4WE (☎ 01223 424666, fax 01223 424341)

PEPPERCORN, David James Creagh; s of James Kenneth Peppercorn (d 1991), and Ida Alice Knight (d 1985); *b* 25 Aug 1931; *Educ* Beaumont Coll, Trinity Coll Cambridge (MA); *m* 1, 11 April 1959, Susan Mary Sweeney; 3 da (Caroline b 1961, Sarah b 1963, Frances b 1964); m 2, 10 June 1977, Serena Sutcliffe, *qv*; *Career* int wine conslt; dir: French Wine Farmers Ltd 1993–, Wine Standards Bd of the Vintners' Co 1987–93, Morgan Furze & Co Ltd 1958–74, Peter Dominic 1964–74, Gilbey Vintners 1969–74; memb Inst of Masters of Wine 1962 (chm 1968–70); judge at Premier Concours Mondial (Budapest 1972); Liveryman Worshipful Co of Vintners 1952, memb Worshipful Co of Watermen and Lightermen of the River Thames; André Simon Meml Prize 1983; Chevalier de l'Ordre des Arts et des Lettres 1988; *Books* Drinking Wine (with Bryan Cooper, 1979), Bordeaux (1982, 2 edn 1991), Pocket Guide to the Wines of Bordeaux (1986 and 1996, translated into German 1986 and 1996, French 1987 and 1993, Danish 1987, Swedish 1988, Japanese 1990, also American edn 1987); *Recreations* music, walking, travelling; *Clubs* Garrick, MCC, Saintsbury; *Style*— David Peppercorn, Esq; ✉ 2 Bryanston Place, London W1H 7FN (☎ 0171 262 9398)

PEPPIATT, Michael Henry; s of Edward George Peppiatt (d 1983), of Stocking Pelham, Herts, and Elsa Eugène, *née* Schlaich; *b* 9 Oct 1941; *Educ* Brentwood Sch, Göttingen Univ, Trinity Hall Cambridge (MA); *m* 1989, Jill Patricia Lloyd, da of Dr John Barnes; 1 da (Clio Patricia b 16 Feb 1991), 1 s (Alexander Michael b 23 April 1994); *Career* art critic The Observer 1964, arts ed Réalités Paris 1966–68, art and literary ed Le Monde 1969–71; Paris arts corr: New York Times, Financial Times 1972–76, Art News 1973–86; ed and publisher Art International 1987–, fndr The Archive Press (fine art edns) 1987–; regular contrib to: New York Times, Town & Country, Architectural Digest; author: Imagination's Chamber - Artists and Their Studios (1983), Francis Bacon: Anatomy of an Enigma (1996); numerous catalogue introductions and essays on modern and contemporary art; art film conslt Musée D'Art Moderne Paris, exhibition organiser, co-curated Francis Bacon retrospective at Museo d'Arte Moderna Lugano 1993; memb Vasari Prize Jury Paris 1988–; memb: Int Art Critics Assoc, Soc of Authors, Royal Soc of Lit; *Clubs* Jeu de Paume (Paris), Oxford and Cambridge, RAC; *Style*— Michael Peppiatt, Esq; ✉ 56 St James's Gardens, London W11 4RA (☎ and fax 0171 603 6249); 77 rue des Archives, 75003, Paris, France (☎ 00 33 14804 84 54)

PEPPITT, His Hon Judge John Raymond; QC (1976); s of Reginald Peppitt, MBE (d 1962), and Phyllis Claire, *née* French (d 1978); *b* 22 Sept 1931; *Educ* St Paul's, Jesus Coll Cambridge (BA); *m* 2 April 1960, Judith Penelope, da of Maj Lionel Frederick Edward James, CBE; 3 s (Matthew b 1962, William b 1964, Edward b 1968); *Career* Nat Serv 2 Lt RA 1950–51; called to the Bar Gray's Inn 1958; recorder Crown Court 1976–91, bencher 1982, circuit judge (SE Circuit) 1991–; *Recreations* collecting watercolours; *Style*— His Hon Judge John Peppitt, QC; ✉ The Law Courts, Chaucer Road, Canterbury, Kent CT1 1ZA

PERCEVAL, John Dudley Charles Ascelin; s of Lt-Col John Francis George Perceval (d 1981), of Vancouver, Br Columbia, and Diana Madeleine Scott, *née* Pearce; *b* 8 April 1942; *Educ* Eton; *m* 11 Sept 1971, Tessa Mary, da of Geoffrey Bruce Dawson, OBE, MC (d 1984), of Caerleon; 2 s (Oliver Charles b 1972, Christopher Geoffrey John b 1978), 1 da (Candida Mary b 1974); *Career* Unilever 1961–69, Save & Prosper Group Ltd 1969–95 (exec dir 1985–95), Omnium Group Limited 1995–; *Style*— John Perceval, Esq; ✉ The Forge House, Monk Sherborne, Tadley, Hants RG26 5HS (☎ 01256 850073)

PERCEVAL, Viscount; Thomas Frederick Gerald Perceval; s of 11 Earl of Egmont, *qv*; *b* 17 Aug 1934; *Style*— Viscount Perceval

PERCHARD, Colin William; OBE (1985); s of William George Perchard, of La Chasse, St Martin, Jersey, and Winifred Sarah, *née* Horn; *b* 19 Oct 1940; *Educ* Victoria Coll Jersey, Univ of Liverpool (BA), Int Inst for Educn Planning UNESCO Paris (Advanced Dip Educn Planning and Admin); *m* 4 April 1970, Elisabeth Penelope Glynis, da of Sir Glyn Jones, GCMG, MBE (d 1992); 3 s (Nicholas b 1972, Jonathan b 1976, Adam b 1985); *Career* Br Cncl: asst rep Blantyre Malawi 1964–68, regnl offr Africa S of Sahara 1968–71, asst rep Calcutta 1971–72, offr i/c Dhaka 1972, rep Seoul 1973–76, dir Tech Co-op Trg Dept 1976–79, Int Inst for Educn Planning Paris 1979–80, rep Harare 1980–86, controller Africa Div 1986–90, dir Turkey 1990–93, min (cultural affrs) New Delhi 1993–; *Recreations* theatre, music, cooking; *Style*— Colin Perchard, Esq, OBE; ✉ The British Council, 10 Spring Gardens, London SW1A 2BN (☎ 0171 930 8466, fax 0171 839 6347, telex 8952201)

PERCHARD, Peter John; s of Stanley Drelaud Perchard, of Wadhurst, E Sussex, and Shirley Gwendoline, *née* Twyman, of Worcester Park, Surrey; *b* 4 Nov 1943; *Educ* Sevenoaks Sch Kent, Bromley Tech Coll; *m* 1, 19 March 1966, Paula Bennett; 1 da (Lorna Melanie b 27 April 1967); m 2, 2 March 1982, Lorraine Eve, da of Thomas Victor Frederick Cooper; 1 s (Oliver James b 10 Aug 1983), 1 da (Lucy Grace b 11 Aug 1985); *Career* copy ed George Newnes Ltd 1962–64, advtg/features New Musical Express 1964–66, Penguin Books Ltd 1967–85 (sometime exhibitions mangr, fieldwork mangr, mktg prodn mangr); The Cricketer: joined as dep ed 1986, exec ed 1988, managing ed 1991–; co-author and prodr Virgin Warrior (rock opera, Epsom Playhouse) 1986; memb Performing Right Soc 1976; *Books* Virgin Warrior: The Rock Opera (1986), Cricket (1988); *Recreations* cricket, soccer, theatre, music, song writing, books, cinema, photography; *Clubs* Cricket Writers'; *Style*— Peter Perchard, Esq; ✉ 21 Burgh Heath Road, Epsom, Surrey KT17 4LP (☎ 01372 813401); The Cricketer, Third Street, Langton Green, Tunbridge Wells, Kent TN3 0EN (☎ 01892 862551, fax 01892 863755)

PERCIVAL, Prof Alan; s of Harold Percival (d 1948), and Hilda, *née* Twyford (d 1970); *b* 22 May 1932; *Educ* Manchester GS, BNC Oxford (MA, BM), St Mary's Hosp Med Sch (BCh); *m* 1, 15 Sept 1962, Audrey Gillian, *née* Hughes (d 1979); 1 s (David b 1963), 1 da (Sally b 1964); m 2, 14 Oct 1983, (Pauline) Jill, *née* Gillett; 2 step da (Alison b 1962, Karen b 1964); *Career* house surgn Radcliffe Infirmary Oxford 1958–59, house physician med unit St Mary's Hosp London 1959, registrar in pathology Edgware Gen Hosp 1959–63, lectr in bacteriology Wright-Flemming Inst St Mary's Hosp 1963–67; Univ of Liverpool: sr lectr in bacteriology 1967–79, prof in clinical bacteriology 1979–81 and 1988–; prof of bacteriology Univ of Manchester 1981–88; memb: Assoc of Med Microbiologists (chm 1985–87), W Lancs Health Authy 1985–88, Southport and Formby

DHA 1988–; Hon MSc Univ of Manchester 1982; MRCPath 1970 (cncl memb 1982–85); *Recreations* golf, music; *Clubs* Royal Birkdale Golf; *Style—* Prof Alan Percival; ✉ Dept of Medical Microbiology, Duncan Building, Royal Liverpool Hosp, PO Box 147, Liverpool L69 3BX (☎ 0151 709 0141, ext 4415)

PERCIVAL, Anthony Henry; s of William Potter Percival, of Westcliff-on-Sea, and Iris, *née* Hiller (d 1973); *b* 11 Jan 1940; *Educ* Felsted Sch; *m* 30 May 1964, Sally Angela, da of Owen Buckland; 2 s (Jonathan Clive b 14 July 1966, James Owen b 28 Dec 1968), 1 da (Anna Catherine b 19 April 1977); *Career* Coopers & Lybrand (formerly Deloitte Haskins & Sells): articled clerk 1957–62, ptnr 1966–95, ptnr in charge London Audit Div 1982–87, managing ptnr Deloitte Haskins & Sells Singapore 1988–90; gp fin dir Kingfisher plc 1995–; Liveryman Worshipful Co of Chartered Accountants; FCA 1973 (ACA 1963); *Recreations* tennis, theatre, gardening; *Clubs* RAC; *Style—* Anthony Percival, Esq; ✉ Pollards, Bardfield Saling, Braintree, Essex CM7 5EG (☎ 01371 850396); Kingfisher plc, North West House, 119 Marylebone Road, London NW1 5PX (☎ 0171 724 7749, fax 0171 724 1160)

PERCIVAL, Rt Hon Sir Ian; kt (1979), PC (1983), QC (1963); s of Eldon Percival (d 1947), and Chrystine, *née* Hoyle (d 1979); *b* 11 May 1921; *Educ* Latymer Upper Sch, St Catharine's Coll Cambridge (MA); *m* 1942, Madeline Buckingham, da of Albert Cooke (d 1928); 1 s (Robert), 1 da (Jane); *Career* serv WWII Maj The Buffs N Africa and Burma 1940–46; called to the Bar Inner Temple 1948, bencher 1970; recorder of Deal, later of the Crown Court 1971–94, slr gen 1979–83, master treas Inner Temple 1990; vice pres N American Cncl of London Ct of Int Arbitration 1989–; memb Sidley and Austin USA and Int Attorneys 1984–92; MP (C) Southport 1959–87; landowner; memb Royal Econ Soc, pres Masonic Trust for Girls and Boys 1989–93; sole tstee Bhopal Hosp Tst 1992–; Master Arbitration Co 1993–94 (Jr Warden 1991–92, Sr Warden 1992–93); FTII, FCIArb; *Recreations* tennis, golf, windsurfing, parachuting, abseiling; *Clubs* Carlton, Rye Golf, City Livery; *Style—* The Rt Hon Sir Ian Percival, QC; ✉ Oxenden, Stone-in-Oxney, nr Tenterden, Kent TN30 7HD (☎ 01233 758321); 2 Harcourt Buildings, Temple, London EC4Y 9DB (☎ 0171 583 2939); 5 Paper Buildings, Temple, London EC4Y 7HB (☎ 0171 583 4555, telex 8956431 ANTON G, fax 0171 583 1926)

PERCIVAL, Prof John; s of Walter William Percival, and Eva, *née* Bowers; *b* 11 July 1937; *Educ* Colchester Royal GS, Hertford and Merton Colls Oxford (MA, DPhil); *m* 1, 11 Aug 1962, Carole Ann (d 1977), da of Eric John Labrum; 2 da (Alice Mary Ann b 28 June 1963, Jessica Jane b 29 Dec 1964); m 2, 10 Sept 1988, Jacqueline Anne, da of Terence Donovan; *Career* Univ Coll Cardiff: asst lectr 1962–64, lectr 1964–72, sr lectr 1972–79, reader 1979–85, prof 1985–, dep princ 1987–90, head of Sch of History and Archaeology 1987–96, pro-vice-chllr 1996–; chm and vice pres The Classical Assoc; FSA; *Books* The Reign of Charlemagne (with H R Loyn, 1975), The Roman Villa (2 edn, 1988); *Recreations* music; *Style—* Prof John Percival, FSA; ✉ 26 Church Road, Whitchurch, Cardiff CF4 2EA (☎ 01222 617869); School of History and Archaeology, University of Wales College of Cardiff, PO Box 909, Cardiff CF1 3XU (☎ 01222 874260, fax 01222 874929)

PERCIVAL, John; s of late Cecil Ernest Percival and late Mua Phoebe, *née* Milchard; *b* 16 March 1927; *Educ* Sir George Monoux GS Walthamstow, St Catherine's Coll Oxford (MA); *m* 1, 1953 (m dis), Betty, *née* Thorne-Large; m 2, 1972, Judith, *née* Cruickshank; *Career* dance critic The Times 1965–94; Dance & Dancers magazine: contrib 1950–, assoc ed 1964–80, ed 1981–; London corr Ballet Review (New York) 1996–; contrib numerous other dance magazines and newspapers incl Ballet Annual, Ballett (Germany) and Dance Magazine (NY); memb and past pres The Critics' Circle; *Books* Antony Tudor, Modern Ballet, The World of Diaghilev, Experimental Dance, Nureyev, Facts About A Ballet Company, Theatre In My Blood (biog of John Cranko), Men Dancing (with Nigel Gosling); *Style—* John Percival; ✉ 36 Great James Street, London WC1N 3HB (☎ 0171 405 0267); Dance & Dancers, 214 Panther House, 38 Mount Pleasant, London WC1X 0AP (☎ and fax 0171 837 2711)

PERCIVAL, Michael John; s of John William Percival (d 1971), of Northampton, and Margery Edith, *née* Crawford; *b* 11 July 1943; *Educ* Berkhamsted Sch Herts; *m* 11 June 1966, Jean Margaret, da of Vincent Everard Dainty, of Northampton; 3 da (Katie b 1968, Alison b 1970, Linda b 1973); *Career* admitted slr London 1966, ptnr Howes Percival Slrs (sr ptnr 1984–); memb Cncl of Northants Law Soc 1982–94 (pres 1992–93), pres Northampton and Dist Branch MS Soc 1988; tstee: Northants Nat Hist Soc and Field Club, St Christopher's Church of England Home for the Elderly Northampton; govr Northampton HS for Girls 1993–; registrar High Ct and Co Ct 1983–88, memb Northampton DHA 1987–90, clerk to Gen Cmmrs of Taxes for Northampton Dist 1 and 2 1988–; memb Law Soc 1966–; *Recreations* rugby, tennis, sailing; *Style—* Michael Percival, Esq; ✉ Messrs Howes Percival Solicitors, Oxford House, Cliftonville, Northampton NN1 5PN (☎ 01604 230400, fax 01604 20956, telex 311445)

PERCY, Humphrey Richard; s of Adrian John Percy, of Tunbridge Wells, Kent, and Maisie, *née* Gardner; *b* 2 Oct 1956; *Educ* Winchester; *m* 27 April 1985, Suzanne Patricia Spencer, da of Maj Bruce Holford-Walker, of London; 2 s (Luke, Christopher), 2 da (Daisy, Emma); *Career* J Henry Schroder Wagg & Co Ltd 1974–80, dir Barclays Merchant Bank Ltd 1985–86 (joined 1980), dir Barclays de Zoete Wedd Ltd 1986–94, md Europe Global Swaps and Options Group Barclays Bank plc 1989–92, global head Foreign Exchange Barclays Bank plc 1992–94, dir Barclays de Zoete Wedd Capital Markets Ltd until 1994, dir Barclays de Zoete Wedd Futures Ltd until 1994, divnl md Barclays Bank PLC until 1994; exec dir Strategic Asset Management Ltd Bermuda 1994–95, head of treasury Europe and jt md Westdeutsche Landesbank Girozentrale London 1995–; *Recreations* tennis, reading, travel; *Clubs* Capital; *Style—* Humphrey Percy, Esq; ✉ The Old House, Goodley Stock Rd, Crockham Hill, Edenbridge, Kent TN8 6TA (☎ 01732 865826, fax 01732 865827); Westdeutsche Landesbank Girozentrale (WestLB), 51 Moorgate, London EC2R 6AE (☎ 0171 638 6141, fax 0171 374 8672)

PERCY, Prof John Pitkeathly (Ian); CBE (1997); s of John Percy (d 1984), of Edinburgh, and Helen Glass, *née* Pitkeathly (d 1988); *b* 16 Jan 1942; *Educ* Edinburgh Acad, Univ of Edinburgh; *m* 26 June 1965, Sheila Isobel, da of Roy Toshack Horn (d 1957), of Edinburgh; 2 da (Jill Sheila b 12 April 1969, Sally Charlotte b 24 Dec 1972); *Career* CA; asst Graham Smart & Annan 1960–68, ptnr Martin Currie & Scott 1969–71; Grant Thornton: ptnr 1971–95, London managing ptnr 1981–88, Scottish sr ptnr 1991–95; hon prof of accountancy Univ of Aberdeen; chm Macdonald Orr Ltd 1991–; non-exec dir: Morgan Grenfell (Scotland) Ltd 1992–, William Wilson Holdings Ltd 1993–; dep chm: Scottish Provident Institution 1993–, Scottish Water and Sewerage Customers Cncl 1995–; chm: Accounts Cmmn for Scotland 1992–, ICMG Corporate Governance Cmmn; vice chm UK Auditing Practices Bd 1991–, UK memb Int Audit Practices Cmmn, memb Steering Bd Companies House 1995–; pres ICAS 1990–91; chm Govrs The Edinburgh Acad 1992–; elder St Cuthbert's Church of Scotland; Freeman: City of London 1982, Worshipful Co of Painter-Stainers 1982; CA 1967, MBAE 1989, FRSA 1989; *Recreations* golf, trout fishing; *Clubs* Hon Co of Edinburgh Golfers, Royal and Ancient Golf, RAC, New (Edinburgh), Caledonian; *Style—* Prof Ian Percy, CBE; ✉ 30 Midmar Drive, Edinburgh EH10 6BU (☎ 0131 447 3645, fax 0131 447 6233); office: 1/4 Atholl Crescent, Edinburgh (☎ 0131 229 9181, fax 0131 229 4560)

PERCY, Keith Edward; s of Cyril Edward Percy, of London, and Joyce Rose Percy; *b* 22 Jan 1945; *Educ* Wanstead Co HS, Univ of Manchester (BA); *m* 14 Feb 1970, (Rosemary) Pamela, da of Thomas William Drake, of London; 1 s (Nicholas b 1977), 1 da (Elizabeth b 1974); *Career* head res Phillips & Drew 1976–83 (joined 1967), exec chm Phillips & Drew Fund Management 1983–90; chief exec: UBS Asset Management (UK) Ltd 1989–90, Morgan Grenfell Asset Management Ltd 1990–96; non-exec dir: Smiths Industries Med Systems 1977–, IMRO 1987–95; memb Cncl Soc of Investmt Analysts 1976–87, chm FTSE Actuaries Share Indices Steering Ctee, dir FTSE Int 1995–; *Recreations* tennis, rugby, music; *Clubs* The City; *Style—* Keith Percy, Esq

PERCY, His Hon Rodney Algernon; 3 s of late Hugh James Percy, of Alnwick; *b* 15 May 1924; *Educ* Uppingham, BNC Oxford (MA); *m* 1948, Mary Allen, da of late J E Benbow, of Aberystwyth; 1 s, 3 da; *Career* Lt RCS 1942–46, served Burma, India, Malaya and Java; called to the Bar Middle Temple 1950, ad eundum Lincoln's Inn 1987; dep coroner N Northumberland 1957, asst recorder Sheffield QS 1964, dep chm Co Durham QS 1966–71, recorder of the Crown Ct 1972–79, circuit judge NE Circuit 1979–93; fndr memb and hon pres Conciliation Serv for Northumberland and Tyneside 1982–93, pres Northumberland and Tyneside Marriage Guidance Cncl 1983–87; Caravan Park op 1993–; *Publications* ed: Charlesworth on Negligence (4 edn 1962, 5 edn 1971, 6 edn 1977), Charlesworth & Percy on Negligence (7 edn 1983, 8 edn 1990, 9 edn 1996); *Recreations* golf, gardening, hill walking, beachcombing, King Charles Cavalier spaniels; *Style—* His Hon Rodney Percy; ✉ Brookside, Lesbury, Alnwick, Northumberland NE66 3AT (☎ 01665 830326, fax 01665 830000)

PERCY-ROBB, Prof Iain Walter; s of Capt Ian Ernest Percy-Robb (d 1967), and Margaret Drysdale Carrick, *née* Galbraith (d 1991); *b* 8 Dec 1935; *Educ* George Watson's Coll Edinburgh, Univ of Edinburgh (MB ChB, PhD); *m* 22 May 1961, Margaret Elizabeth, da of Dr Ronald Leslie Cormie, of Pollokshields, Glasgow; 2 s (Michael Iain b 1964, Stephen Leslie b 1966), 2 da (Jane Elizabeth b 1962, Claire Margaret b 1971); *Career* MRC int travelling res fell Cornell Univ 1972–73; Univ of Edinburgh: res scholar 1963–65, lectr 1965–68, sr lectr 1968–76, reader 1976–84; prof of pathological biochemistry Univ of Glasgow 1984– (assoc dean of educn Faculty of Med); chm Informed Software Ltd 1987–; memb Scot Swimming Team Empire and Cwlth Games Cardiff 1958; FRCPE, FRCPath; *Books* Lecture Notes on Clinical Chemistry (jtly, 1984), Diseases of the Gastrointestinal Tract and Liver (jtly, 1989), Muir's Textbook of Pathology (jtly, 1992); *Recreations* golf; *Clubs* Royal Burgess Golfing Soc (Edinburgh), The Glasgow GC; *Style—* Prof Iain Percy-Robb; ✉ Rossendale, 7 Upper Glenburn Road, Bearsden, Glasgow G41 4DW (☎ 0141 934 1481); Department of Pathological Biochemistry, Glasgow West Hospitals University NHS Trust, Glasgow G11 6NT (☎ 0141 211 2652, fax 0141 357 4547)

PEREGRINE, Prof (Dennis) Howell; *b* 30 Dec 1938; *Educ* Univ of Oxford (BA), Univ of Cambridge (PhD); *Career* Sch of Mathematics Univ of Bristol: lectr 1964–77, reader 1977–87, prof 1987–; FIMA; *Style—* Prof D H Peregrine; ✉ School of Mathematics, University Walk, Bristol BS8 1TW (☎ 0117 928 7971, fax 0117 928 7999)

PEREIRA, Sir (Herbert) Charles; kt (1977); s of Herbert John Pereira (d 1952); *b* 12 May 1913; *Educ* St Alban's Sch, Univ of London (BSc, PhD, DSc); *m* 1941, Irene Beatrice, da of David James Sloan (d 1916); 3 s, 1 da; *Career* RE 1939–46; Colonial Serv 1946–67, dep dir E Africa Agric and Forestry Res Orgn 1955–61; dir: ARC of Rhodesia and Nyasaland 1961–63, ARC of Central Africa (Rhodesia Zambia and Malawi) 1963–67; chm ARC of Malawi 1967–74, dir E Malling Res Station 1969–72, chief scientist (dep sec) MAFF 1972–77, res conslt in tropical agric to World Bank and other orgns 1978–; memb Bd of Tstees: Royal Botanic Gdns Kew 1983–86, Marie Stopes Int 1992–; pres Tropical Agric Assoc 1990–; Haile Selassie Prize for Res in Africa 1966; Hon DSc Cranfield Univ 1977; Chevalier du Merite Agricole 1991; FRS 1969; *Books* Land Use and Water Resources (1973), Policy and Practice in the Management of Tropical Watersheds (1989); *Recreations* sailing, swimming, mountain walking; *Clubs* Athenaeum, Harare; *Style—* Sir Charles Pereira, FRS; ✉ Peartrees, Nestor Court, Teston, Maidstone, Kent ME18 5AD (☎ 01622 813333)

PEREIRA, Dr (Raul) Scott; s of Dr Helio Gelli Pereira, FRS (d 1994), and Dr Marguerite Pereira, *née* Scott (d 1988); *b* 14 April 1948; *Educ* Mill Hill Sch, Trinity Coll Cambridge, Univ of Oxford Med Sch; *m* 14 April 1972, Hilary Glen, da of Prof Vernon Rycroft Pickles, of Oxford; 1 s (Thomas b 1979), 1 da (Penelope b 1977); *Career* pathology trainee Northwick Park Hosp Harrow 1973–76, res sr registrar Westminster Hosp and Med Sch 1976–79, clinical scientist MRC Clinical Res Centre Harrow 1979–83, res fell West Middlesex Univ Hosp 1983–86; conslt and sr lectr in immunology: St Helier Hosp, Carshalton and St George's Hosp Med Sch Tooting 1986–96; sr lectr and conslt immunologist Chelsea & Westminster Hosp (Charing Cross & Westminster Med Sch) 1996–; vice pres Residential Boat Owners' Assoc; *Recreations* offshore cruising, boating; *Style—* Dr Scott Pereira; ✉ Division of Immunology, Chelsea & Westminster Hospital, 369 Fulham Road, London SW10 9NH (☎ 0181 746 8243, fax 0181 746 5997, e-mail s.pereira@cxwms.ac.uk)

PEREIRA GRAY, Prof Denis John; OBE (1981); s of Dr Sydney Joseph Pereira Gray (d 1975), of Exeter, and Alice Evelyn, *née* Cole; *b* 2 Oct 1935; *Educ* Exeter Sch, St John's Coll Cambridge (MA), Bart's Med Sch (MB BChir); *m* 28 April 1962, Jill Margaret, da of Frank Carruthers Hoyte (d 1976), of Exeter; 1 s (Peter b 1963), 3 da (Penelope b 1965, Elizabeth b 1968, Jennifer b 1970); *Career* in gen med practice 1962–, prof of gen practice Univ of Exeter 1986– (sr lectr 1973–86), regnl advsr in gen practice Univ of Bristol 1975–, ed Med Annual 1983–87, conslt advsr in gen practice to CMO DHSS 1984–87, dir Postgraduate Med Sch Exeter 1987–, assoc med postgraduate dean Univ of Bristol 1992–; hon ed RCGP journal 1972–80 and pubns 1976–, governing tstee Nuffield Provincial Hosps Tst 1993–, chm Jt Ctee on Postgrad Trg for Gen Practice 1994–; Hunterian Soc Gold Medal 1966 and 1969, Sir Charles Hastings Prize 1967 and 1970, James Mackenzie Lecture 1977, George Abercrombie Award 1978, RCGP Fndn Cncl Award 1980, Sir Harry Platt Prize 1981, Gale Memorial Lecture 1979, Haliburton Hume Memorial Lecture 1988, McConaghey Memorial Lecture 1988, Northcott Memorial Lecture 1988, Harvard Davis Lecture 1988, Murray Scott Lecture 1990, Harben Lecture 1994, Sally Irvine Lecture 1995; elected memb: Cncl RCGP 1991– (chm 1987–90), GMC 1994–; MRCGP 1967, FRCGP 1973, FRSA 1989; *Books* Training for General Practice (1981), Running a Practice (jtly, 1978), Forty Years On: The Story of the First 40 Years of the Royal College of General Practitioners (ed, 1992); *Recreations* reading, walking; *Clubs* RSM; *Style—* Prof Denis Pereira Gray, OBE; ✉ Alford House, 9 Marlborough Rd, Exeter, Devon EX2 4TJ (☎ 01392 218080, 01392 413449); Director, Postgraduate Medical School, University of Exeter, Barrack Road, Exeter EX2 5DW (☎ 01392 403020)

PERELMAN, Alan Steven; *b* 30 April 1948; *Educ* Ashville Coll Harrogate, Christ's Coll Cambridge (MA), London Business Sch (MSc); *m* 30 Jan 1977, Christine, *née* Thomas; 1 s (Richard b 1 March 1978), 1 da (Elizabeth); *Career* controller Bougainville Copper 1980–82, dep gen mangr mktg and devpt Hamersley Iron 1984–85 (controller ops 1982–84); gp fin dir The Gateway Corporation 1986–89, gp fin dir Whitbread and Co 1990– (also human resources dir 1994–); *Recreations* theatre, bridge, squash; *Style—* Alan Perelman, Esq; ✉ Whitbread plc, The Brewery, Chiswell St, London EC1Y 4SD (☎ 0171 606 4455)

PERERA, Dr Bernard Sarath; s of Vincent Perera (d 1985), of Colombo, Sri Lanka, and Patricia, *née* Fernando; *b* 20 Feb 1942; *Educ* St Joseph's Coll Colombo Sri Lanka, Univ of Ceylon (MB BS), Univ of Manchester (DipBact); *m* 1 June 1971, late Dr Piyaseeli Perera, da of Piyasena Jayatilake, of Colombo; 1 s (Shamira b 10 Aug 1973), 1 da (Lakshika b 7 June 1975); *Career* registrar Med Res Inst Colombo 1972–75, registrar in pathology Manchester Royal Infirmary 1976–78, sr registrar Northwest Regnl HA 1978–82; conslt microbiologist: Scarborough Hosp 1983, Royal Oldham Hosp 1984–;

memb: BMA, Assoc of Med Microbiologists, Assoc of Clinical Pathologists, Manchester Med Soc; MRCPath 1982, FFPath RCPI 1985; *Clubs* St Joseph's Coll Old Boys', Sri Lankan Doctors'; *Style*— Dr Bernard S Perera; ✉ Consultant Microbiologist, Dept of Microbiology, Royal Oldham Hospital, Oldham OL1 2JH (☎ 0161 6240420)

PERERA, Prof Katharine Mary; da of Arnold Lacey, of Wallasey, and Eileen, *née* Haylock; *b* 12 Dec 1943; *Educ* Wallasey HS for Girls, Bedford Coll Univ of London (BA), Univ of Manchester (MA, PhD); *m* 1967, Suria Perera; *Career* VSO Malaysia 1965–66, teacher Merseyside 1967–72, lectr Padgate Coll of HE 1973–76; Univ of Manchester: lectr 1977–91, prof 1991–, pro-vice-chllr 1994–; memb: Linguistics Assoc of GB 1977, Int Assoc for the Study of Child Language 1991; *Books* Children's Writing and Reading (1984), Understanding Language (1987), Growing Points in Child Language (1994); *Recreations* walking, reading, music (memb Hallé Concerts Soc); *Style*— Prof Katharine Perera; ✉ Department of Linguistics, University of Manchester, Oxford Road, Manchester M13 9PL (☎ 0161 275 3190, fax 0161 275 3187)

PERETZ, David Lindsay Corbett; CB (1996); *Career* exec dir (UK) Int Monetary Fund and World Bank 1990–94, dep dir Int Finance HM Treasy 1994–; *Style*— David Peretz, Esq, CB; ✉ HM Treasury, Parliament Street, London SW1P 3AG (☎ 0171 270 3000)

PERGANT, Jean-Jacques; s of Jean Pergant (d 1974), and Anne-Marie, *née* François; *b* 24 Feb 1949; *Educ* Coll Episcopal St Etienne Strasbourg, Lycée Technique Hotelier de Strasbourg, McGill Univ Mgmnt Inst Montreal Quebec (Sr Mgmnt Prog), Exec TV Worshop NY (media trg); *m*; 2 c; *Career* hotelier; served French Forces 1969–70; various jr managerial positions in hotel business London, Paris and Canary Islands 1968–74, various mgmnt positions within Four Seasons Hotels and Resorts Group 1974–91 (latterly gen mangr Four Seasons Hotel Ottawa Ontario 1986–91); gen mangr: Hanbury Manor Hotel, Golf & Country Club Herts 1991–94; dir and gen mangr The Berkeley Hotel (Savoy Group) London 1994–; memb London Divnl Ctee Br Hospitality Assoc; Officier/Maitre de Table La Chaine des Rotisseurs, Grand Officer L'Ordre Illustre des Chevaliers de Meduse, Cdr La Commanderie de Bordeaux, Chev Chancellerie Franco-Britannique; *Recreations* triathlons, photography, watercolours, the visual arts; *Style*— Jean-Jacques Pergant, Esq; ✉ The Berkeley Hotel, Wilton Place, London SW1X 7RL (☎ 0171 235 6000, fax 0171 235 4330)

PERHAM, Prof Richard Nelson; s of Cyril Richard William Perham (d 1948), of London, and Helen Harrow, *née* Thornton (d 1992); *b* 27 April 1937; *Educ* Latymer Upper, St John's Coll Cambridge (BA, MA, PhD, ScD), MRC Laboratory of Molecular Biology Cambridge (MRC scholar); *m* 22 Dec 1969, Dr Nancy Jane Lane, *qv*, da of Maj Temple Haviland Lane; 1 s (Quentin Richard Haviland b 1973), 1 da (Temple Helen Gilbert b 1970); *Career* Nat Serv RN 1956–58; fell St John's Coll Cambridge 1964– (res fell 1964–67, tutor 1967–77), Helen Hay Whitney fell Yale Univ 1966–67; Univ of Cambridge: lectr in biochemistry 1969–77 (demonstrator 1964–69), reader in biochemistry of macromolecular structures 1977–89, head of dept 1985–96, pres St John's Coll 1983–87, prof of structural biochemistry 1989–; govr Latymer Upper Sch; syndic Cambridge Univ Press; pres Lady Margaret Boat Club; memb Sci Bd SERC 1985–90; chm Biological Sci Ctee SERC 1987–90, pres Section D Br Assoc for Advancement of Sci 1987–88, memb Exec Cncl CIBA Fndn 1989–; Fogarty int scholar Nat Insts of Health USA 1990–93, Max Planck Prize 1993; memb: Biochemical Soc 1965, Euro Molecular Biology Orgn 1983, Royal Inst of GB 1986; FRS 1984, FRSA 1988, Academia Europaea 1992; *Books* Instrumentation in Amino Acid Sequence Analysis (ed 1975), numerous papers in scientific jls; *Recreations* gardening, theatre, rowing, nosing around in antique shops; *Clubs* Hawks (Cambridge), United Oxford and Cambridge; *Style*— Prof Richard Perham, FRS; ✉ 107 Barton Rd, Cambridge CB3 9LL (☎ and fax 01223 363752); Department of Biochemistry, University of Cambridge, Tennis Ct Road, Cambridge CB2 1QW (☎ 01223 333663, fax 01223 333345, e-mail rnp1@mole.bio.cam.ac.uk)

PERKIN, (George) David; s of Alan Spencer Perkin (d 1996), of Leeds, and Vera Perkin (d 1958); *b* 16 Aug 1941; *Educ* Leeds Modern Sch, Pembroke Coll Cambridge, Kings Coll Hosp; *m* 11 July 1964, Louise Ann, da of Sqdn Ldr John Boston, of Sevenoaks; 2 s (Michael b 1968, Matthew b 1971), 1 da (Emma b 1969); *Career* conslt neurologist Charing Cross Hosp 1977–; memb Part 2 Bd Royal Coll of Physicians; FRCP, FRSM; *Books* Optic Neuritis and its Differential Diagnosis (1978), Basic Neurology (1986), Slide Atlas of Neurology (1986, 2 edn 1993), Diagnostic Tests in Neurology (1988), Clinical Examination (1993); *Recreations* music; *Style*— David Perkin, Esq; ✉ Department of Neurology, Charing Cross Hospital, London W6 (☎ 0181 846 1153)

PERKINS, *see also:* Steele-Perkins

PERKINS, Alice Elizabeth; da of Derrick Leslie John Perkins (d 1965), and Elsa Rose, *née* Rink (d 1986); *b* 24 May 1949; *Educ* North London Collegiate Sch, St Anne's Coll Oxford (BA); *m* 10 Nov 1978, Jack Straw, MP, *qv*; 1 s (William David John Straw b 21 Sept 1980), 1 da (Charlotte Alice b 18 Aug 1982); *Career* DSS (formerly DHSS): joined as admin trainee 1971, private sec to Min of State 1974–75, princ 1975, asst to Chm of Supp Benefits Cmmn 1975–77, asst sec 1984–90, under sec and dir of personnel 1990–93; HM Treasy: head Def and Material Gp 1993–95, dep dir of public spending 1995–; *Recreations* gardening, riding, looking at pictures; *Style*— Ms Alice Perkins; ✉ HM Treasury, Parliament Street, London SW1P 3AG (☎ 0171 270 4510)

PERKINS, Hon Mrs (Celia Mary); da (by 1 m) of Baron Duncan-Sandys, CH, PC (d 1987), and Diana Churchill (d 1963; da of Rt Hon Sir Winston Churchill, KG, OM, CH, FRS); *b* 18 May 1943; *m* 1, 1965 (m dis 1970), George Michael Kennedy; 1 s (Justin b 1967); m 2, 1970 (m dis 1979), Sir Dennis Walters, MBE, *qv*; 1 s (Dominic b 1971); m 3, 1985, Maj-Gen Kenneth Perkins, CB, MBE, DFC, *qv*; 1 s (Alexander b 1986), 1 da (Sophie b 1988); *Career* writer; tstee Int Churchill Soc; *Books* From Winston with Love and Kisses (1994), The Young Churchill (1995); author of various newspaper articles; *Style*— The Hon Mrs Perkins; ✉ 4 Bedwyn Common, Marlborough, Wiltshire SN8 3HZ (☎ 01672 87008, fax 01672 871066)

PERKINS, David Charles Langrigge; s of Charles Samuel Perkins, OBE (d 1987), of Newcastle upon Tyne, and Victoria Alexandra Ryan (d 1991); *b* 31 May 1943; *Educ* Uppingham, Univ of Newcastle (LLB); *m* Sept 1971, Sandra Margaret, da of Frank Gerard Buck; 4 s (Benedict William Charles Heritage b 21 June 1972, Rory Philip Francis b 12 Oct 1979, Guy Ranulf David Westbury b 27 Jan 1983, Rupert Alexander David Langrigge b 19 Nov 1973 d 1981), 1 da (Davina Helen Alexandra b 20 May 1978); *Career* admitted slr 1969; Theodore Goddard & Co 1967–72, Clifford-Turner 1972–87, ptnr Clifford Chance 1987–; memb Cncl The Intellectual Property Inst; memb: Law Soc, City of London Slrs' Co, Intellectual Property Lawers' Assoc, Int Bar Assoc, Euro Communities Trade Mark Practitioners' Assoc, Union of Euro Practitioners in Industl Property, Association Internationale pour la Protection de la Propriété Industrielle, American Bar Assoc; assoc memb: Chartered Inst of Patent Agents, Inst of Trade Mark Agents; foreign memb: Int Trade Mark Assoc, American Intellectual Property Law Assoc (chm Int Sub-Ctee Anti-Tst Law Ctee, co-chm Int Devpts Sub-Ctee ADR Ctee May 1–3 1996); *Publications* incl: Rights of Employee Inventors in the United Kingdom under the Patents Act 1977 (1979), Know-How/Confidential Information: an EEC Perspective (1984), Intellectual Property Protection for Biotechnology (1983), Copyright and Industrial Designs (1985), Intellectual Property and the EEC: 1992 (1988), EEC Aspects of Patent/Anti-Trust (1989), Intellectual Property Aspects of 1992 (1989), Transnational Legal Practice in Europe (1991), Foreign Principles of Intellectual Property/Anti-Trust (1992), Proving Patent Infringement in the United Kingdom (1993), The European Community's draft Technology Transfer Regulation (1995), Foreign Principles of Intellectual Property/Anti-Trust (with M van Kerckhove, 1995), A New EC Block Exemption for Patent Licenses and Know-How Licenses (with M van Kerckhove, 1996), Patent Infringement and Forum Shopping in Europe (1996), Claim Interpretation: the United Kingdom and Germany - A Comparative Study (with D Rosenberg, 1996), The WIPO Perspective on Resolution of Intellectual Property Disputes (1996), The EU Technology Transfer Block Exemption for Patent and Know-How Licenses (1996); *Recreations* golf, tennis; *Clubs* Northumberland Golf, Northern RFC, Hurlingham; *Style*— David Perkins, Esq; ✉ Clifford Chance, 200 Aldersgate Street, London EC1A 4JJ (☎ 0171 600 1000, fax 0171 600 5555)

PERKINS, Geoffrey Howard; s of Wilfred Jack Perkins, and Peggy, *née* Patterson; *b* 22 Feb 1953; *Educ* Harrow Co GS, Lincoln Coll Oxford (exhibitioner, MA); *m* 1986, Lisa Braun; 1 da (Charlotte b 1988), 1 s (Arthur b 1989); *Career* writer, producer and performer; dir Hat Trick Productions Ltd 1988–95, head of comedy BBC TV 1995–; former prodr of over 20 programmes and 200 individual shows incl The Hitch-Hikers Guide to the Galaxy for BBC Radio Light Entertainment (latterly chief prodr new comedy); TV prodn credits: Spitting Image (Central) 1986–88, Saturday Live and Friday Night Live (Channel 4), The Robbie Coltrane Special (LWT), Norbert Smith...A Life (Hat Trick/Channel 4, also co-writer (Int Emmy, Banff Light Entertainment Award, Silver Rose of Montreux)), Ben Elton: The Man From Auntie (BBC1), Harry Enfield's Television Programme (2 series, BBC2), Montreal Comedy Festival Tenth Anniversary Gala (Channel 4) 1992, Game On (BBC 2) 1996; writer: Stand By Your Man (for series About Face, awarded American Blue Riband), Radio Active 1980–87 (BBC Radio, winner BPG, Sony and Premier Onda Barcelona awards), Uncyclopaedia of Rock (Capital Radio, also prodr) 1986–87 (Monaco Radio award 1986), KYTV (BBC2) 1989–92 (Grand Prix and Silver Rose of Montreux 1992); performer: Radio Active (BBC Radio 4), KYTV (BBC2), Don't Quote Me (host, Channel 4); *Style*— Geoffrey Perkins, Esq; ✉ BBC Television Centre, Woodlane, London W8

PERKINS, Ian Richard Brice; s of Francis Layton Perkins, CBE, DSC (d 1994), of London, and Josephine Louise, *née* Brice; *b* 15 Nov 1949; *Educ* Charterhouse; *m* 5 April 1975, Melissa Anne, da of Sir John Milne; 1 s (Roderick John Bloomfield b 2 Oct 1984), 2 da (Lisa Elizabeth b 5 Feb 1980, Tania Catherine Brice 29 Jan 1982); *Career* W I Carr 1968–70 and 1971–72, Fergusson Bros Johannesburg 1970–71, Greenshields Inc 1972–79; James Capel and Co: joined 1979, pres James Capel Inc NY 1986–88, dir 1988–91; dir King & Shaxson Holdings plc 1991– (chief exec offr 1994); Freeman City of London 1973, memb Ct of Assts Worshipful Co of Skinners (Freeman 1975); *Recreations* golf, tennis, skiing; *Clubs* Boodle's, The Berkshire, Honourable Co of Edinburgh Golfers (Muirfield), Swinley Forest; *Style*— Ian Perkins, Esq; ✉ Moth House, Brown Candover, Alresford, Hants SO24 9TT (☎ 01256 389260); King & Shaxson Holdings plc, 52 Cornhill, London EC3V 3PD (☎ 0171 623 5433)

PERKINS, Prof (Michael) John; s of George Karl Perkins (d 1987), and Eva, *née* Richardson (d 1990); *b* 29 Sept 1936; *Educ* Warwick Sch, King's Coll Univ of London (BSc, PhD, DSc); *m* 24 March 1962, Pauline Mary, da of Herbert Edwin Attwood (d 1948); 3 da (Inger b 1963, Georgina b 1964, Alexandra b 1971); *Career* lectr Kings Coll London 1960–72; prof: Chelsea Coll London 1972–84, Royal Holloway and Bedford New Coll London 1985–92 (head of dept 1985–92); assoc prof Dept of Chemistry Brunel Univ, prof emeritus Univ of London; author of papers published in various jls incl Journal of the Chemical Soc, sometime co author and co ed Organic Reaction Mechanisms series; Corday-Morgan medallist Chem Soc 1972; FRSC, CChem; *Books* Radical Chemistry (1994); *Recreations* hill walking, photography; *Style*— Prof John Perkins; ✉ Department of Chemistry, Brunel University, Uxbridge, Middlesex UB8 3PH (☎ 01895 274000, fax 01895 256844)

PERKINS, Prof John Douglas; s of Douglas Herbert Perkins, of Kent, and Isobel Mary Perkins; *b* 18 March 1950; *Educ* Royal GS Guildford, Univ of London (BSc, MA, PhD, ACGI, DIC, Dip TCDHE, Hinchley Meml Medal); *m* 11 June 1975 (m dis 1992), Chantal Marie, da of Claude Paul Ernest Lestavel; 1 s (Matthew John b 1987); *Career* univ demonstrator in chem engrg Univ of Cambridge 1973–77, seconded to ICI Agric Div as res engr 1975–76, sr lectr in chemical engrg Imperial Coll London 1983–85 (lectr 1977–83), ICI prof of process systems engrg Univ of Sydney 1985–88; Imperial Coll London: prof of chem engrg 1988–, dir Centre for Process Systems Engrg 1992–, head Dept of Chem Engrg 1996–; fell Inst of Mathematics and its Applications 1992 (assoc fell 1976), FIChemE 1986, FEng 1993; *Recreations* orienteering, reading; *Style*— Prof John Perkins, FEng; ✉ Department of Chemical Engineering, Imperial College of Science, Technology and Medicine, London SW7 2BY (☎ 0171 594 5556, fax 0171 594 5604)

PERKINS, Maj-Gen Kenneth (Ken); CB (1977), MBE (1955), DFC (1953); s of George Samuel Perkins, and Arabella Sarah, *née* Wise; *b* 15 Aug 1926; *Educ* Lewes Co Sch for Boys, New Coll Oxford; *m* 1, 1949 (m dis 1984), Anne Theresa, da of John Barry (d 1960); 3 da; m 2, 1985, Hon Celia Mary Sandys, *qv*, 2 da of Baron Duncan-Sandys, CH, PC (d 1987), and Diana (d 1963), da of Rt Hon Sir Winston Churchill, KG, OM, CH, FRS); 1 s (b 1986), 1 da (b 1988); *Career* enlisted in the ranks 1944, cmmnd RA 1946, held various appts worldwide 1946–66 (incl army aviation during Korean War and Malayan Emergency), Staff Coll Quetta 1958, jssc 1963, cmd 1 Regt Royal Horse Artillery 1967–69, GS01 Far East Land Forces 1970, Cdr 24 Airportable Bde 1971–72, RCDS 1973, dir Operational Plans MOD 1974, Cdr Sultan of Oman's Armed Forces 1975–77, ACDS (Ops) 1977–79, dir Mil Assistance Office 1980–82, Col Cmdt RA 1980–82, ret 1982; def advsr: British Aerospace 1982–86, The Sun 1991–; memb Cncl: RUSI 1978–81, Res Inst Study of Conflict 1992–; chm SAF Assoc 1985–93 (vice pres 1994–); Order of Oman 1977, Hashemite Order of Independence 1975, Selangor Distinguished Conduct medal 1955; *Books* Weapons and Warfare (1987), A Fortunate Soldier (1988), Khalida (1991); *Recreations* writing, painting (exhibited Royal Academy), cycling; *Clubs* Army and Navy; *Style*— Maj-Gen Ken Perkins; ✉ 4 Bedwyn Common, Marlborough, Wilts SN8 3HZ (☎ 01672 870087, fax 01672 871066)

PERKINS, Michael John; s of Phillip John Broad Perkins, OBE, DL (d 1982), of Lymington, Hants, and Jane Mary, *née* Hope; *b* 31 Jan 1942; *Educ* Eton, RNC Dartmouth; *m* 9 Nov 1968, Nicola Margaret, da of Air Cdre William Vernon Anthony Denney, of Amersham, Bucks; 1 s (Robert b 1971), 1 da (Caroline b 1973); *Career* RN 1961–66, Sub Lt 1963, Lt 1965; sr ptnr Westlake Clerk & Co CAs 1996– (ptnr 1981–96), dir Southern Newspapers plc 1981–; Freeman City of London 1964, Liveryman Worshipful Co of Haberdashers 1964; CA (Canada) 1973, FCIS 1982; *Recreations* sailing, skiing, shooting; *Clubs* Royal Lymington Yacht, Royal Naval Sailing Assoc; *Style*— Michael Perkins, Esq; ✉ Critchells Farmhouse, Lockerley, Romsey, Hants SO51 0JD (☎ 01794 340281); Westlake Clark & Co Chartered Accountants, Newcourt House, New St, Lymington, Hants SO41 9BQ (☎ 01590 672674, fax 01590 674272)

PERKS, David Rowland; s of Rowland Loftus Perks, OBE, formerly of Leeds, now of Saffron Walden, and Doris Mary, *née* Whitfield; *b* 16 May 1948; *Educ* The Leys Sch Cambridge, Univ of Bristol (LLB); *m* 4 Jan 1975, Susan Lesley, da of Ernest Riddlough, MBE, of Heysham, Lancs; 2 da (Emma, Clare); *Career* admitted slr 1973; ptnr Ashurst Morris Crisp 1980–; *Recreations* shooting; *Clubs* Lysander Boat, Castle Camps Gun; *Style*— David Perks, Esq; ✉ Broadwalk House, 5 Appold St, London EC2A 2HA (☎ 0171 638 1111, fax 0171 972 7990, telex 887067)

PERKS, (Charles) Roger; OBE (1993); s of Leonard Perks (d 1992), and Vivienne Clare, *née* Gallatley; *b* 24 Nov 1939; *Educ* Rugeley GS (head boy), St Peter's Teacher Training

Coll (CertEd); *m* 17 August 1961, Christine Evelyn, da of James Selby Bond; 3 da (Debra Derryn b 28 July 1962, Alison b 5 Feb 1965, Victoria Louise b 9 Oct 1968), 1 s (Roger Leonard b 1 Aug 1973); *Career* probationary teacher Stockland Green Bilateral Sch 1961–64, head of history Moseley Comp Sch Birmingham 1964–69, head of English Aston Manor Comp Sch Birmingham 1969–72, dep head Ladywood Comp Sch Birmingham 1972–77, head Naseby Comp Sch Birmingham 1977–83, head Baverstock Grant Maintained Sch Birmingham (formerly Baverstock Comp Sch until 1989) 1983–; head Selly Park Ladywood and Aston Manor adult educn centres 1969–77; winner City of Birmingham Avis "We try harder" Award 1979; fndr memb: Nat Advsy Cncl for the Educn and Trg Targets, Grant Maintained Schs' Advsy Cncl, Nat Schs Improvement Ctee; memb NAHT (memb Grant Maintained Schs Ctee); FRSA; *Books* Clearway English 1–5 (1972–74), Clearway English Workshop 1–5 (1972–75), Opting Out: The Challenge for Schools in the 1990's (contrib, 1992); *Recreations* coastal path walking, rock pool fishing, hockey, Wolverhampton Wanderers FC, theatre, motor cars, family; *Clubs* Yardley Hockey; *Style*— Roger Perks, Esq, OBE; ✉ 1a Russell Road, Moseley, Birmigham B13 8RA (☎ 0121 449 5174); Baverstock GM School, 501 Bells Lane, Druids Heath, Birmingham B14 5TL (☎ 0121 430 7924, fax 0121 474 5313)

PEROWNE, Rear Adm James Francis; OBE (1983); s of Lt Cdr John Herbert Francis Perowne, of Saundersfoot, Dyfed, and (Mary) Joy, *née* Dibb; *b* 29 July 1947; *Educ* Sherborne, BRNC Dartmouth; *m* 1, 22 May 1971 (m dis 1990), Susan Anne, da of Cdr Peter John Holloway, of Western Australia; 4 s (Julian b 1972, Samuel b 1975, Roger b 1977, Timothy b 1977); m 2, 15 Feb 1992, Caroline Nicola, da of Dr T Grimson, of Co Durham; *Career* CO: HMS Opportune 1976–77, HMS Superb 1981–83, HMS Boxer 1986–88, Second Submarine Sqdn 1990–92, HMS Norfolk and 6 Frigate Sqdn 1992–94; sr naval memb RCDS 1995–96, Flag Offr Submarines 1996–; *Recreations* shooting, gardening, classic cars; *Clubs* Army and Navy, IOD; *Style*— Rear Adm James Perowne, OBE; ✉ Flag Officer Submarines, Eastbury Park, Northwood, Middlesex HA6 3HP

PEROWNE, John Florian Canning; s of Sir Victor Perowne, KCMG (d 1951), and Hon Agatha Violet, *née* Beaumont (d 1994), da of 1 Viscount Allendale; *b* 20 Aug 1942; *Educ* Eton, Corpus Christi Coll Cambridge (MA); *m* 12 Oct 1968, Elizabeth Mary, da of Rev S B Freeman, formerly Rector of Long Bredy, Dorset; 1 s (Matthew b 1983), 2 da (Anastasia b 1975, Clementine b 1979); *Career* admitted slr 1968, ptnr Eversheds Norwich; *Clubs* Norfolk (Norwich); *Style*— John Perowne, Esq; ✉ The White House, Bramerton, Norwich NR14 7DW (☎ 01508 538673); Eversheds, Paston House, 13 Princes St, Norwich NR3 1BD (☎ 01603 272727)

PERRAUD, Michel Bernard; s of René Perraud (d 1989), of Vendée, France, and Jeanne, *née* Brebion; *b* 30 Jan 1957; *children* 1 s (Cédric b 16 Dec 1985), 1 da (Sabrina b 23 Oct 1987); *Career* French Nat Serv 1978–79; chef; apprentice Restaurant Dagorno Paris 1975–77; commis de cuisine: Hotel St Paul Noirmoutier 1977, Restaurant Chez Albert Cassis 1977–78; chef de partie: Hotel St Paul Noirmoutier 1979, Restaurant Trois Gros Roanne 1979–80; demi-chef de partie Restaurant Taillevent Paris 1980–81; chef de cuisine: Hotel St Paul Noirmoutier 1981, Restaurant Le Bressan London 1981, Waterside Inn Restaurant Bray Berks 1982–87; assistant de direction conseiller en sous vide Ecole de Cuisine Georges Pralus Briennon 1988, chef de cuisine Les Alouettes Restaurant Claygate Surrey 1988–92, chef des chefs Le Cordon Blue London 1992, opened own restaurant Fleur de Sel 1994; memb Académie Culinaire de France in UK 1983–; *Awards* first prize Mouton Cadet Rothschild Menu Competition 1983–84, 3 Michelin Stars (Waterside Inn) 1985, 1 Michelin Star (Les Alouettes) 1990, 1 Michelin Star (Fleur de Sel) 1995, Diplôme MOGB (Meilleur Ouvrier de Grande Bretagne) 1987; *Style*— Michel Perraud; ✉ Fleur de Sel, 23–27 Lower Street, Haslemere, Surrey GU27 2NY (☎ 01428 651462)

PERRETT, His Hon Judge; Desmond Seymour; QC (1980); s of His Honour Judge John Perrett, JP (d 1992), and Elizabeth Mary, *née* Seymour; *b* 22 April 1937; *Educ* Westminster; *m* 1961, Pauline Merriel, da of late Paul Robert Buchan May, ICS; 1 s, 1 da; *Career* RN 1955–57; called to the Bar Gray's Inn 1962, bencher 1989, recorder Crown Ct 1978–92, circuit judge (Midland and Oxford Circuit) 1992–; *Style*— His Hon Judge Perrett, QC; ✉ Midland and Oxford Circuit Office, The Priory Courts, 33 Bull Street, Birmingham B4 6DW (☎ 0121 627 1700)

PERRIAM, Wendy Angela; da of Edward Francis Leopold Brech, of Esher, Surrey, and Irene Ella, *née* Thompson; *b* 23 Feb 1940; *Educ* Combe Bank Convent Kent, St Anne's Coll Oxford (BA, MA), LSE; *m* 1, 22 Aug 1964, Christopher Hugh Tyack, s of Dr Norman Tyack; 1 da (Pauline Maria b 31 Dec 1965); m 2, 29 July 1974, John Alan Perriam, s of John Perriam; *Career* author; formerly copywriter: Colman Prentis & Varley, Notley & Pritchard Wood; various articles and stories published in magazines and newspapers incl: She, Cosmopolitan, Penthouse, Esquire, Sunday Times, Daily Mail, Evening Standard; poems and stories included in Arts Cncl Anthology and SE Arts anthologies; memb: Soc of Authors, PEN, Br Actors Equity; *Books* Absinthe for Elevenses (1980, reissued 1991), Cuckoo (1981, reissued 1992), After Purple (1982, reissued 1993), Born of Woman (1983, reissued 1993), The Stillness The Dancing (1985, reissued 1994), Sin City (1987, reissued 1994), Devils, for a Change (1989), Fifty-Minute Hour (1990), Bird Inside (1992), Michael, Michael (1993), Breaking and Entering (1994), Coupling (1996); *Style*— Wendy Perriam; ✉ c/o Jonathan Lloyd, Curtis Brown, 4th Floor, Haymarket House, 28–29 Haymarket, London SW1Y 4SP (☎ 0171 396 6600)

PERRICK, Penny; da of Ben Perrick, of London, and Eve *née* Spitter (d 1995); *b* 30 June 1941; *Educ* S Hampstead HS, Alliance Française Paris; *m* 1, 1962 (m dis 1973), Clive Labovitch (d 1994); 1 s (Mark b 1963), 1 da (Emmy b 1965); m 2, 1977 (m dis 1988), Frank Copplestone (d 1996); *Career* fashion writer Vogue 1959–61, columnist The Sun 1974–79, columnist The Times 1983–89, fiction ed The Sunday Times 1989–94; memb: Soc of Authors 1992, English PEN 1993, Royal Soc of Literature 1993; *Books* Malina (1993), Impossible Things (1995); *Recreations* mooching about the west of Ireland, gardening; *Style*— Ms Penny Perrick; ✉ c/o A P Watt Ltd, 20 John Street, London WC1N 2DR (☎ 0171 405 6774, fax 0171 831 2154)

PERRIN, Brian Hubert; s of Charles Hubert Perrin (d 1975), of Norbury, and Beatrice, *née* Beckley (d 1973); *b* 19 Aug 1932; *Educ* Whitgift Middle Sch, Croydon Sch of Art, Royal Coll of Art (ARCA), Rome scholar; *m* 20 Oct 1962, Elisabeth Jane, da of Denis Lisle; 2 s (Alexander Thomas b 29 Sept 1963, Jason Timothy b 22 Aug 1965); *Career* artist and lectr; Rome scholar 1954, Ealing Sch of Art 1956–64, Hornsey Coll of Art 1959–64, head of printmaking Wimbledon Sch of Art 1964–; specialist advsr Fine Art Bd CNAA 1983–89 (memb Bd 1978–83), specialist advsr Cncl for Educnl Awards Dublin 1983–91, memb Cncl Royal Soc of Painter Printmakers; works in public collections incl: Museum of Modern Art New York, Metropolitan Museum New York, NY Public Library, Cincinatti Art Museum, Library of Congress Washington, Boston Public Library, Boston Museum of Art, Benzalei Museum Jerusalem, Perth Art Gallery, V&A, Arts Cncl of GB, Br Cncl, City Art Galleries Glasgow, All Union Soc of Bibliophiles Moscow; represented in major print biennales incl Cincinatti, Llubljiana, Krakow and Bradford 1962–; RE 1988; *Prizes* Christie Galleries Royal Acad of Arts 1987, Open Print Exhbn RE 1988; *Style*— Brian Perrin, Esq; ✉ 293 Kings Road, Kingston-upon-Thames, Surrey KT2 5JJ (☎ 0181 546 3640); Wimbledon School of Art, Merton Hall Road, Wimbledon SW19 (☎ 0181 540 0231, fax 0181 543 1750)

PERRIN, Charles John; s of Sir Michael Perrin, CBE (d 1988), of London, and Nancy May, *née* Curzon (d 1992); *b* 1 May 1940; *Educ* Winchester, New Coll Oxford; *m* 1966, Gillian Margaret, da of late Rev M Hughes-Thomas (d 1969); 2 da (Felicity Margaret Roche b 1970, Nicola May Roche b 1973); *Career* Hambros Bank Ltd: joined 1963, dir 1973, dep chm 1986–, chief exec 1995–; dir: Hambros PLC, Hambro Pacific Ltd Hong Kong, Hambros Trust Co (formerly Hambros Bank Executor & Tstee Co Ltd), Harland & Wolff plc Belfast (non-exec 1984–89); memb Exec Ctee UK Ctee UNICEF 1970–91 (vice chm 1972–91); hon treas UK Assoc for Int Year of the Child 1979; memb: Royal Brompton Nat Heart and Lung Hosps SHA 1993–94, Royal Brompton Hosp NHS Tst 1994–, Cncl Univ of London 1994–; govr: Queen Anne's Sch Caversham 1981–, London Hosp Med Coll 1991–95; Liveryman Worshipful Co of Shipwrights; *Clubs* Athenaeum; *Style*— Charles Perrin, Esq; ✉ Hambros plc, 41 Tower Hill, London EC3N 4HA (☎ 0171 480 5000, fax 0171 702 9262)

PERRING, Dr Franklyn Hugh; OBE (1988); s of Frank Arthur Perring (d 1982), of Oundle, and Avelyn Millicent Newsum (d 1987); *b* 1 Aug 1927; *Educ* Forest Sch, Snaresbrook London, Harlow Coll, Earls Colne GS, Queens' Coll Cambridge; *m* 1, 16 June 1951 (m dis 1972), Yvonne Frances Maud, da of Harold Matthews; 1 s (Neil Stephen b 1954); m 2, Margaret Dorothy, da of Harold Barrow; 1 da (Emma Frances b 1972); *Career* Nat Serv 1945–48 (2 Lt RA 1947–48); dir Botanical Soc of Br Isles Distribution Maps Scheme Botanic Garden Cambridge 1959–64 (asst 1954–59), head of Biological Records Centre Monks Wood Experimental Station Huntingdon 1964–79, gen sec Royal Soc for Nature Conservation Lincoln 1979–87, chm Wildlife Travel Ltd 1988–; botanical sec of Linnean Soc 1972–78; memb: Cncl Inst of Biology 1973–77, Cncl Ray Soc 1990–94; pres Botanical Soc of Br Isles 1993–95 (vice pres 1987–91); chm: Exec Cambridgeshire Wildlife Tst 1968–70, Northamptonshire Wildlife Tst 1985–87, Peterborough Wildlife Gp 1987–90; pres Peterborough Wildlife Gp 1990–94; Hon DSc Univ of Leicester 1989; FLS 1964, FIBiol 1979; *Books* Atlas of British Flora (co-ed, 1962), Critical Supplement to the Atlas of British Flora (1968), English Names of Wild Flowers (co-ed, 1974), RSNC Guide to Wild Flowers (1984), Conservation Heritage (1991); *Recreations* opera going, reading, plant hunting abroad; *Style*— Dr Franklyn Perring, OBE; ✉ Green Acre, Wood Lane, Oundle, Peterborough PE8 5TP (☎ 01832 274892, fax 01832 274568)

PERRING, John Raymond; TD (1965); s and h of Sir Ralph Edgar Perring, 1 Bt, *qv*, by his late w Ethel Mary, da of Henry Theophilus Johnson, of Putney; *b* 7 July 1931; *Educ* Stowe; *m* 1961, Ella Christine, da of late Maj Anthony George Pelham; 2 s (John b 1962, Mark b 1965), 2 da (Emma (Mrs Christian Heyman) b 1963, Anna (Mrs Edward Standish) b 1968); *Career* chm: Perring Furnishings Ltd 1981–88, Perrings Finance Ltd 1986–, Ranyard Nursing Home 1992–; cncl memb Retail Consortium 1972–91 (hon treas 1973–78); Master: Worshipful Co of Furniture Makers 1978–79, Merchant Taylors' Co 1988–89 and 1994–95; one of HM Lieutenants of the City of London 1963–, Sheriff City of London 1991–92; OStJ, FRSA; *Style*— John Perring, Esq, TD; ✉ 21 Somerset Rd, Parkside, Wimbledon, London SW19 5JZ

PERRING, Sir Ralph Edgar; 1 Bt (UK 1963), of Frensham Manor, Surrey; kt (1960), JP (London 1943); s of Col Sir John Ernest Perring, JP, DL (d 1948), and Florence, *née* Higginson (d 1960); *b* 23 March 1905; *Educ* Univ Coll Sch London; *m* 20 June 1928, (Ethel) Mary, OStJ (d 1991), da of late Henry Theophilus Johnson; 2 s (and 1 s decd); *Heir* s John Raymond Perring, *qv*; *Career* Lt RA (TA) 1938–40; JP Co of London 1943, memb Ct of Common Cncl (Ward of Cripplegate) 1948–51, alderman City of London (Langbourn Ward) 1951–75, one of HM Lts of City of London and Sheriff 1958–59, Lord Mayor of London 1962–63; chm Perring Furnishings Ltd 1948–81, dir Confederation Life Insurance Co of Canada 1969–82; vice-pres Royal Bridewell Hosp 1964–73, tstee Morden Coll Blackheath 1970– (chm 1979–95), memb Bd of Govrs ESU 1976–81; former Master Worshipful Co of: Tin Plate Workers (memb Ct of Assts), Painter-Stainers, Furniture Makers (tstee and memb Ct of Assts); Hon Memb Worshipful Co of Builders Merchants, Hon Asst Worshipful Co of Marketors; FRSA, KStJ; *Clubs* City Livery (sr former pres), RAC (sr hundred roll); *Style*— Sir Ralph Perring, Bt, JP; ✉ 15 Burghley House, Somerset Road, Wimbledon, London SW19 5JB (☎ 0181 946 3433)

PERRIS, Sir David Arthur; kt (1977), MBE (1970), JP (Birmingham 1961); s of Arthur Perris; *b* 25 May 1929; *Educ* Sparkhill Commercial Sch Birmingham; *m* 1955, Constance Parkes; 1 s, 1 da; *Career* sec Birmingham Trades Cncl 1966–83; chm: Birmingham RHB 1970–74, W Midlands RHA 1974–82; regnl sec TUC W Midlands 1974–94, chm Nat Trg Cncl NHS 1975–82; vice chm ATV Midlands Ltd 1980–81, dir Central Independent TV plc and vice chm W Midlands Regnl Bd 1981–83; pres Community Media Assoc 1983–, chm Birmingham Hosp Saturday Fund 1985–, pres Birmingham Magistrates' Assoc 1986– (chm 1975–86), chm Central Telethon Tst 1988–, pres Br Health Care Assoc 1995–; Hon LLD Univ of Birmingham; *Style*— Sir David Perris, MBE, JP; ✉ Broadway, 21 Highfield Rd, Moseley, Birmingham B13 9HL (☎ and fax 0121 449 3652)

PERROTT, Prof Ronald Henry; *b* 27 Dec 1942; *Educ* Queen's Univ Belfast (BSc, PhD); *m* 4 April 1974, Valerie Mary Perrott; 1 s (Simon b 2 March 1976); *Career* prof of software engrg: Univ of Wisconsin 1968–69, NASA Res Centre California 1977–78, CERN Geneva 1984–85, Queen's Univ Belfast 1985–; memb: EC Working Gp on High Performance Computing, IT Advsy Bd to DTI and SERC; ed Jl of Scientific Programming; NI BCS IT Professional of the Year 1993; FBCS, FRSA; *Books* Operating Systems Techniques (1972), Software Engineering (1978), Pascal for Fortran Programmers (1983), Parallel Programming (1987), Software for Parallel Computers (1991); *Recreations* skiing, squash; *Style*— Prof Ronald Perrott; ✉ Department of Computer Science, The Queen's University of Belfast, Belfast BT7 1NN (☎ 01232 335463, fax 01232 683890)

PERRY, Alan Joseph; s of Joseph George Perry (d 1957), of London, and Elsie May, *née* Lewis (d 1963); *b* 17 Jan 1930; *Educ* John Bright Sch LLandudno, Dartford GS Kent; *m* 1961, Vivien Anne, da of Lt-Col Ernest Charles Ball, of London (d 1968); 2 s (Howard b 1968, Myles b 1974); *Career* serv RE 1948–50; HM Treasy 1951–86 (princ 1968, asst sec 1976), cnsllr (Econ) Br Embassy Washington 1978–80, chm Review of BBC External Servs 1984, dir Public Sector Servs Ernst & Young Accountants and Consultants 1986–92, dir Whitehall Strategic Management Consultants Ltd 1992–95; *Recreations* tennis, painting, golf; *Style*— Alan Perry, Esq; (☎ 01883 653195)

PERRY, Hon Alan Malcolm; s of Baron Perry of Walton (Life Peer), *qv*, and Anne Elizabeth, *née* Grant; *b* 6 Feb 1950; *Educ* George Heriot's Sch Edinburgh, Trinity Coll Oxford (MA); *m* 1976, Naomi Melanie, da of Dr Abraham Freedman, MD, FRCP, of London; 3 s (Daniel b 1980, Guy b 1982, Edmund b 1986); *Career* Harmsworth scholar, admitted slr 1982, currently ptnr D J Freeman; *Recreations* painting, making music, gardening; *Style*— The Hon Alan Perry; ✉ 43 Meadway, London NW11 7AX; D J Freeman, 43 Fetter Lane, London EC4A 1NA (☎ 0171 583 4055, telex 894579)

PERRY, David Andrew; s of Peter Nelson Perry, of Bridport, Dorset, and Margaret Adeleine, *née* Murrell; *b* 10 Nov 1945; *Educ* Colfox Sch Bridport, LSE (BScEcon); *m* 1970, Mary Jane, *née* Pratt; 1 s ((Anthony John) Julian b 1976), 1 da (Helen Elizabeth b 1985); *Career* Arthur Andersen: articled clerk 1967–70, CA 1970, ptnr 1979–, fndr and managing ptnr Reading Office 1984, managing ptnr Southern Region 1986–91, head Audit and Business Advsy Practice South 1986–94, ptnr Arthur Andersen Moscow 1994–; Freeman City of London 1982, memb Worshipful Co of Weavers 1982; FCA (ACA 1970); *Recreations* music, choral singing, reading, family pursuits; *Clubs* City Livery; *Style*— David Perry, Esq; ✉ c/o Arthur Andersen, Abbots House, Abbey Street, Reading, Berkshire RG1 3BD (☎ 0118 950 8141, fax 0118 950 8101)

PERRY, David Gordon; s of Elliott Gordon Perry (d 1994), of Kemble, nr Cirencester, and Lois Evelyn, *née* Allen; *b* 26 Dec 1937; *Educ* Clifton, Christ's Coll Cambridge (Rugby blue); *m* 16 Sept 1961, Dorne Mary, da of Edwin Timson Busby (d 1980), of Braybrooke,

Market Harborough; 4 da (Belinda b 1963, Philippa b 1964, Rebecca b 1967, Joanna b 1970); *Career* Nat Serv 2 Lt Parachute Regt 1956–58; Br Printing Corp (BPC) Ltd: md Fell & Briant Ltd (subsid) 1966–78, chief exec Packaging and Paper Products Div 1978–81, dir 1981; John Waddington plc: md 1981–88, chief exec 1988–92, chm 1993–; chm Anglian Group plc 1996–; non-exec dir: Dewhirst Group plc, Yorkshire Water plc; fifteen caps England Rugby XV 1963–66 (Capt 1965); Liveryman Worshipful Co of Makers of Playing Cards; CIMgt 1986, FIP; *Recreations* golf, music; *Clubs* United Oxford & Cambridge Univ, MCC; *Style—* David Perry, Esq; ✉ Deighton House, Deighton, Nr Escrick, York YO4 6HQ; John Waddington plc, Wakefield Road, Leeds LS10 3TP (☎ 0113 277 0202, fax 0113 271 3503)

PERRY, Sir David Howard; KCB (1986); s of Howard Dace Perry (d 1971), and Annie Evelyn (d 1976); *b* 13 April 1931; *Educ* Berkhamsted Sch, Pembroke Coll Cambridge (MA); *m* 1961, Rosemary, da of Alfred Seymour Grigg (d 1982); 1 s, 2 da; *Career* Royal Aircraft Estab 1954–78; MOD: procurement exec Air Systems Controllerate 1978–82, chief of Def Procurement 1983–85, chief of Def Equipment Collaboration 1985–87, ret; FRAeS; *Style—* Sir David Perry, KCB

PERRY, George Cox; s of George Cox Perry (d 1962), of Berkhamsted, Herts, and Hortense Irene Emily Sadler (d 1983); *b* 7 Jan 1935; *Educ* Tiffin Sch, Trinity Coll Cambridge (BA, MA, ed Varsity); *m* 1 (m dis 1976), Susanne Puddefoot; m 2, 1976, Frances Nicola, da of Sidney Murray Scott (d 1987); 1 s (Matthew Richard Scott b 1977); *Career* advtg (creative) T Eaton Co Montreal 1957, sub ed The Sphere 1957–58, copywriter J Walter Thompson 1958–62; The Sunday Times: sub ed 1962–63, asst to the Ed (magazine) 1963–65, projects ed 1965–69, asst ed 1967–77, sr ed 1977–85, films ed 1985–; managing ed Crossbow 1965–70; film critic: The Illustrated London News 1982–88 and 1992–, Jazz-FM 1990–92; presenter Radio 2 Arts 1990–; chm (film) The Critics' Circle 1991–94 (vice chm 1987–91); *Books* incl: The Films of Alfred Hitchcock (1965), The Penguin Book of Comics (1967), The Great British Picture Show (1974), Movies from the Mansion (1976), Forever Ealing (1981), Life of Python (1983), Rupert - A Bear's Life (1985), Bluebell (adapted as BBC drama serial, 1986), The Complete Phantom of the Opera (1987), Sunset Boulevard: from Movie to Musical (1993), The Life of Python (1994); *Recreations* watching movies, travelling, taking pictures; *Style—* George Perry, Esq; ✉ The Sunday Times, 1 Pennington St, London E1 9XW (☎ 0171 782 5776, fax 0181 878 8727)

PERRY, George Edward (Ted); s of William Walter Perry (d 1973), and Olive Mary Monica, *née* Salt; *b* 15 May 1931; *m* 1959 (m dis), Doreen Audrey; 2 da (Nicola Jane b 1959, Victoria Louise b 1963), 1 s Simon Edward (b 1961); *Career* buyer/asst ed The Monthly Letter EMG Handmade Gramophones Ltd London 1949–56, asst sales mangr Heliodor Record Co DGG London 1956–57, distributor NSW Festival Records Australia 1958–60, A & R mangr then dir Saga Records 1961–63, A & R mangr Saga Records 1972–77, ptnr Meridian Records 1977–80, fndr/md Hyperion Records 1980–; hon memb Robert Simpson Soc; memb IOD 1993; *Recreations* astronomy, gardening; *Style—* Ted Perry, Esq; ✉ The Coach House, 112 Hervey Road, Blackheath, London SE3 8BX (☎ 0181 319 1544); Hyperion Records Ltd, PO Box 25, London SE9 1AX (☎ 0181 294 1166, fax 0181 294 1161, e-mail ted@hyperion.records.co.uk)

PERRY, Dr Ian Charles; s of Capt Sidney Charles Perry (d 1984), of Bush Hill Park, Enfield, Middx, and Marjorie Ellen, *née* Elliott; *b* 18 April 1939; *Educ* Highgate, Guy's Hosp (MB BS, MRCS, LRCP), RAF Inst of Aviation Med (Dip in Aviation Med), Univ of London (MFOM), RCP; *m* 27 July 1963, Janet Patricia, da of Maj Albert Edward Watson, of Burton Bradstock, Dorset; 2 da (Johanna Elizabeth b 18 Oct 1964, Helen b 7 July 1967); *Career* Lt RAMC 1963, Capt 2 i/c 24 Field Ambulance Aden 1965 and 1967 (SMO Aden Bde 1966), SMO (specialist in aviation med) Army Air Corps Centre 1967–68, 200 Army Pilots Course 1968–69, Maj SMO Conslt Aviation Med Army Air Corps Centre 1969, chm NATO (AG ARD) Aircrew Fatigue Panel 1969–72, ret 1973, RARO 1973–, TA (AAC) 1989–94; princ aviation and occupational med practice 1973–; med dir Int Aviation Med Centre London, sr conslt Avimed Ltd, md Fireseal International Ltd; hon conslt: IAOPA, Br Helicopter Advsy Bd; conslt: Twinings Tea, Jt Aviation Authy Med Gp; former chm: Br Assoc of Aviation Conslts, Grateley PC, Grateley PTA; memb: Army Air Corps Museum Friends, Preservation of Rural Eng; sec Nurdling Assoc of England; author of papers on aviation med; Freeman City of London 1973, Liveryman Worshipful Co of Gunmakers, Master Guild of Air Pilots and Navigators 1996; FRSM, FRAeS, FAMA, MBAC, MIMgt 1986, MIOSH 1988; *Recreations* orchids, golf, shooting; *Clubs* Cavalry and Guards', Sloane, Tidworth Golf; *Style—* Dr Ian Perry; ✉ The Old Farm House, Grateley, Hants SP11 8JR (☎ 01264 889659/639, fax 01264 889639, mobile 0836 664670); 19 Cliveden Place, London SW1W 8HD (☎ 0171 730 8045/9328, fax 0171 730 1985); The Lister Hospital, Chelsea Bridge Rd, London SW1 (☎ 0171 730 1985/9328); The Cromwell Hospital, Cromwell Rd, London SW3 (☎ 0171 730 1985/9328)

PERRY, Dr J David; *b* 21 April 1946; *Educ* Bristol GS, Middx Hosp Med Sch (MB), Univ of London (BSc, MB BS, FRCP (London) 1986); *Career* house physician Oldchurch Hosp Romford then house surgn Middx Hosp 1971, casualty MO Middx Hosp and SHO in gen and chest med The London Hosp 1972–74, registrar in gen and chest med The London Hosp 1975–76 (SHO and registrar Dept of Rheumatology 1974–75), sr registrar in rheumatology The London Hosp and Prince of Wales Hosp Tottenham 1976–77, sr registrar in rheumatology Colchester and The London Hosp 1977–79, conslt rheumatologist The London Hosp (now Royal Hosps Tst) 1979–, clinical dir Musculoskeletal Directorate Royal Hosps Tst; univ teacher Univ of London; hon sr lectr Bart's London Hosp Med Coll and Queen Mary Westfield Coll, MO BAAB, med dir Crystal Palace Nat Sports Centre, co-organiser and treas Therapy Pool Appeal The London Hosp (pool opened by HRH The Princess Royal), memb Hispanic Soc Goldsmiths' Coll, former sec NE Thames Regnl Advsy Sub-ctee on Rheumatology and Rehabilitation, hon sec Med Cncl Royal London Hosp; *Books* Hutchison's Clinical Methods (contrib chapter The Locomotor System, 18 edn, 1984 and 1995), Rheumatology Examination and Injection Techniques (jtly, 1992); chapters in: Sports Medicine (ed J B King, 1992), Rheumatology (eds Klippel & Dieppe, 1994); *Style—* Dr J David Perry; ✉ The Royal London Hospital, Mile End, London E1 1BB (☎ 0171 377 7859, fax 0171 377 7807)

PERRY, Jane; da of Evan Morgan Perry (d 1989), of Brighton, E Sussex, of Hilda Ellen, *née* Webb; *b* 28 Sept 1948; *Educ* Brighton and Hove HS for Girls (GPDST), Univ of Exeter (BA History and Archaeology); *m* 4 Nov 1972 (sep 1983), Derek John Brandon; 2 s (James Martin b 24 Dec 1977, Thomas Henry b 21 April 1980); *Career* advtg exec; research exec BMRB 1969–71, research assoc J Walter Thompson NY 1971–72, research mangr Manchester Evening News 1972–77, UK mangr IMS London 1977–82, media research mangr Davidson Pearce (now BMP) 1982–87: Young & Rubicam: media research mangr 1987–89, Euro media research dir 1989–; FIPA 1995; *Books* European Marketing and Media Pocket-Book (annually 1991–), European Media Cost Comparison (1991, 1993 and 1995), European Media Overspill (1992); *Style—* Ms Jane Perry; ✉ Young & Rubicam Ltd, Greater London House, Hampstead Road, London NW1 7QP (☎ 0171 611 6739, fax 0171 611 6368)

PERRY, Rt Rev John Freeman; *see:* Chelmsford, Bishop of

PERRY, Prof John Grenville; s of Frederick Perry (d 1974), of Stoke-on-Trent, and Elsie, *née* Till; *b* 21 May 1945; *Educ* Longton HS Stoke-on-Trent, Univ of Liverpool (BEng, MEng), Univ of Manchester (PhD); *m* 20 April 1968, Ruth Katharine, da of Eric Stanley Forrester (d 1989), of Fulford, Staffs; 2 s (Jonathan b 17 Nov 1970, Timothy b 10 June 1972); *Career* engr Costain Ltd 1967–70, project engr ICI Ltd 1970–74, sr lectr UMIST 1984–88 (lectr 1974–84); Univ of Birmingham: Beale prof and head of Sch of Civil Engrg 1988–, dep dean Faculty of Engrg 1995–; former chm local branch Lib Pty; MAPM 1988, FICE 1993 (MICE 1975); *Recreations* tennis, golf, fell walking; *Style—* Prof John Perry; ✉ School of Civil Engineering, The University of Birmingham, Edgbaston, Birmingham B15 2TT (☎ 0121 4145048)

PERRY, John Hill; s of Archie John Hill Perry (d 1982), and Evelyn Blanche, *née* Dalton (d 1978); *b* 11 May 1928; *Educ* Charterhouse, Ecole Hôtelière Lausanne Switzerland; *m* 12 April 1958, Patricia Stuart, da of Frederick Charles Gatcombe Fry; 2 s (James Hill b 5 April 1963, Andrew Hill b 29 Oct 1965); *Career* asst mangr Imperial Hotel Torquay 1950–53; P & H Hotels Ltd: Raven Hotel Shrewsbury 1953–60, Livermead House Hotel Torquay 1960–89, Livermead Cliff Hotel Torquay 1968–; West Country Tourist Bd: memb Exec Ctee 1974–96, vice chm 1978–95, vice pres 1995–, first chm of the commercial membs; fndr govr Sports Aid Fndn (SW Region); memb: Rotary Club of Torquay 1972–, Nat Cncl Br Hotels Restaurants and Caterers Assoc 1972–86 and 1990–91, Hotel and Catering Advsy Ctee Torquay Tech Coll 1976–93, Howell Ctee of Inquiry into Sponsorship in Sport (CCPR) 1981–83, Econ Planning Cncl for SW DOE (cncl terminated 1979), BHA Membership and Communications Ctee 1991–, Torbay Tourism Forum 1992–; vice chm Concord Hotels Trg Scheme 1989– (memb 1972–); memb: BHA/AA Liaison Ctee 1973–, BHA/RAC Liaison Ctee 1994–; past nat chm Best Western Hotels (formerly Interchange Hotels), pres Skal Club of Devon and Cornwall 1980, dir Torquay United FC 1970–87; Master Innholder 1981; Freeman City of London 1981, Liveryman Worshipful Co of Butchers 1981; Chevalier du Tastevin (Cdr) 1962; fell Tourism Soc, FHCIMA; *Recreations* golf, watching sports; *Clubs* MCC, Cardiff & County, Churston Golf; *Style—* John Perry, Esq; ✉ P & H Hotels (Torquay) Ltd, Livermead Cliff Hotel, Seafront, Torquay, Devon TQ2 6RQ (☎ 01803 299666, fax 01803 294496)

PERRY, John William; s of John Perry, and Cecilia Perry; *b* 23 Sept 1938; *Educ* Wallington GS, Brasenose Coll Oxford (BA, MA); *m* 4 Feb 1961, Gillian Margaret; 2 da (Jane (Mrs Wernette) b 1963, Sarah b 1965); *Career* Burroughs: dir of mktg Burroughs Machines Ltd 1967–71, dir of mktg Europe & Africa Div 1977–78, gp dir int mktg 1978–80, vice pres strategic planning 1981–83, vice pres Fin Systems Gp 1983–85, vice pres Central USA 1985–86, md UK 1986; chm and md Unisys Ltd 1987–94 (corp offr Unisys Corporation 1990, pres fin line of business (worldwide) Unisys Corp 1993); chm Trace Computers 1996–; memb: Nat Enterprise Team CBI, Bd of Govrs Poly of E London 1989–91; involved with Business in the Community; *Recreations* reading, gardening, golf, music; *Style—* John Perry, Esq; ✉ c/o Trace Computers PLC, 224–232 St John Street, London EC1V 4PH

PERRY, Jonathan Peter Langman; s of Thomas Charles Perry, and Kathleen Mary Perry; *b* 6 Sept 1939; *Educ* Peter Symonds Sch Winchester; *Career* chartered accountant; articled Butler, Viney & Childs 1956–62, Coopers & Lybrand 1962–66; Morgan Grenfell Group plc: joined 1966, dir Morgan Grenfell & Co Limited 1973, jtly i/c banking 1973–77, i/c New York office 1977–80, i/c banking and capital markets 1980–87, i/c overseas offices 1987–88, dir Morgan Grenfell Holdings 1987; fin advsr and proprietor Perry & Associates 1988–90, chm and chief exec Ogilvy Adams & Rinehart Ltd 1990–92, exec chm National Home Loans Holdings plc 1992– (non-exec dir 1991–92); non-exec dir Comcast UK Cable Partners Ltd 1994–; memb Cncl of Int Stock Exchange 1986–88; yachtsman, memb Br Team Int 14s 1973, 1977 and 1983 (capt 1983), team capt Br Americas Cup Team 1986; FCA; *Recreations* sports (yacht racing, tennis, golf), music, painting, writing; *Clubs* Brooks's, Itchenor Sailing, Vanderbilt Racquet, Royal Yacht Squadron; *Style—* Jonathan Perry, Esq; ✉ National Home Loans Holdings plc, 28 King Street, London EC2V 8EH (☎ 0171 726 4054)

PERRY, Kenneth; s of Ernest William James Perry (d 1950), and Florence May, *née* Shurley (d 1984); *b* 24 June 1946; *Educ* Royal Free Boys' Sch Windsor, LSE (NGA Scholarship, Dip in Trade Union Studies), Univ of Kent at Canterbury (BA); *m* 26 June 1971, Sandra Anne, da of William Wanmer, of Hawkhurst, Kent; 1 s, 1 da (Matthew Kenneth, Julia Sandra (twins) b 28 Sept 1975); *Career* apprentice compositor Windsor Slough & Eton Express 1962–67, involved in intro of new technol in magazine printing 1968–76, studies at LSE and Univ of Kent 1976–80, with Prudential Assurance Co 1981–84; Nat Union of Insurance Workers: asst gen sec 1984–89, actg gen sec 1989–90, gen sec 1990–; sec Confedn of Insurance Trade Unions 1994– (chair 1990–94); *Recreations* family, current affrs, walking, gardening; *Style—* Kenneth Perry, Esq; ✉ National Union of Insurance Workers, 27 Old Gloucester St, London WC1N 3AF (☎ 0171 405 6798, fax 0171 404 8150)

PERRY, Rev Canon Michael Charles; s of Charlie Perry (d 1972), and Kathleen Farmer (d 1991); *b* 5 June 1933; *Educ* Ashby-de-la-Zouch Boys' GS, Trinity Coll Cambridge (MA), Westcott House Cambridge; *m* 13 July 1963, Margaret, da of Maj J M Adshead (d 1965); 2 s (Andrew b 1965, David b 1968), 1 da (Gillian b 1973); *Career* archdeacon of Durham 1970–93, canon residentiary of Durham Cathedral 1970–, sub dean 1985–, sr chaplain to Bishop of Durham 1993–; chm: Lord Crewe's Charity 1982–96, Churches' Fellowship for Psychical and Spiritual Studies 1986–95; memb: Cncl Soc for Psychical Res 1984–89, General Synod 1974–90; author; ed: The Church Quarterly 1968–71, The Christian Parapsychologist 1978–; *Books* incl: The Easter Enigma (1959), Sharing in One Bread (1973), The Resurrection of Man (1975), The Paradox of Worship (1977), Handbook of Parish Finance (1981), Psychic Studies (1984), Deliverance (1987, 2 edn 1996), Gods Within (1992); *Style—* The Rev Canon Michael Perry; ✉ 7 The College, Durham DH1 3EQ (☎ 0191 386 1891, fax 01388 605264)

PERRY, Sir Michael Sydney; kt (1994), CBE (1990, OBE 1973); s of Lt Cdr Sydney Albert Perry, RNVR (d 1979), of Douglas, IOM, and Jessie Kate, *née* Brooker; *b* 26 Feb 1934; *Educ* King William's Coll IOM, St John's Coll Oxford (MA); *m* 18 Oct 1958, Joan Mary, da of Francis William Stallard (d 1948), of Worcester; 1 s (Andrew b 1967), 2 da (Carolyn b 1962, Deborah b 1963); *Career* Nat Serv RN 1952–54; Unilever plc: joined 1957, dir 1985–, vice chm 1991–92, chm and chief exec 1992–96; non-exec chm Dunlop Slazenger Group Ltd 1996–; dep chm Bass plc 1996–; non-exec dir: British Gas plc 1994–, Marks and Spencer PLC 1996–; chm: Japan Trade Gp BOTB 1986–, Shakespeare Globe Tst 1993–, The Mktg Cncl 1996–, Sr Salaries Review Body; vice pres: Chartered Inst of Mktg, Liverpool Sch of Tropical Medicine; tstee: Leverhulme Tst 1992–, HFT Development Tst 1993–; *Recreations* music (choral), golf; *Clubs* Oriental, Wentworth; *Style—* Sir Michael Perry, CBE; ✉ Bridges Stone Mill, Alfrick, Worcs WR6 5HR (☎ 01886 833290); 35/3 Queen's Gate Gardens, London SW7 5RR (☎ 0171 581 9839)

PERRY, Dr Nicholas Mark; s of (Sidney) Arthur Perry, of S Kensington, and Constance Frances, *née* Sheere; *b* 23 Oct 1950; *Educ* Westminster, Bart's Med Sch (MB BS); *m* 12 May 1979, Angela Judith, da of Anthony Hillier Poil; 1 s (Alexander William Mark b 10 Oct 1983), 1 da (Francesca Elizabeth Sarah b 21 Feb 1987); *Career* house surgn Bart's 1975, house physician St Leonard's Hosp Hoxton 1976, SHO A/E Bart's 1976–78, SHO Hackney Hosp 1978–79, SHO in urology Bart's 1979–80; registrar in diagnostic radiology: St Thomas' Hosp 1980–82, Bart's 1982–83; sr registrar Bart's, Chase Farm Hosp and N Middx Hosp 1983–85, sr registrar Bart's, Great Ormond Street, Hackney and Homerton Hosps 1985–88; conslt radiologist: Bart's 1988–, King Edward V11 Hosp, 108 Harley St Breast Clinic, London Imaging Centre, Unilever; conslt in breast screening Europe Against Cancer Euro Cmmn 1991–, chm Advsy Ctee Euro Network of Reference Assessment Centres (EUREF) 1996–; quality assurance mangr N Thames Breast

Screening Prog 1988–, clinical dir Central and E London Breast Screening Serv 1990–; Nat Breast Screening Prog: chm Quality Assurance Mangrs Gp 1989–, chm Equipment Ctee 1989–95; memb: Euro Gp for Breast Cancer Screening, BMA, British Assoc of Surgical Oncology, Euro Soc of Mastology; FRCS 1980, FRCR 1984; *Books* Radiological Casebook (1988); *Recreations* country pursuits, antiquarian books, lawn tennis (capt English Public Schs 1967, British Universities' Doubles champion 1976, vice pres United Hospitals Lawn Tennis Club, pres Bart's and Royal London Hosps Lawn Tennis Club); *Clubs* Queen's; *Style*— Dr Nicholas Perry; ✉ 4 Chudleigh Road, Brondesbury Park, London NW6 7AH; Breast Assessment Centre, St Bartholomew's Hospital, London EC1 (☎ 0171 601 8841, fax 0171 601 7895)

PERRY, Nick; *b* 1961; *Educ* Univ of Hull, Nat Film and TV Sch; *Career* playwright and dramatist; TV dramas and stage plays incl: Arrivederci Millwall (prod 1985, jt winner of Samuel Beckett Award 1986), Smallholdings (performed Kings Head 1986), Rockliffe's Babies (contrib to BBC series), Tales of Sherwood Forest (for Central TV), Mamma (for BBC), Clubland (for BBC); awarded Euro Script Fund Devpt Prize for screen adaptation of Paddy The Cope; *Style*— Nick Perry, Esq; ✉ c/o Rochelle Stevens & Co, 2 Terretts Place, Upper Street, London N1 1QZ (☎ 0171 359 3900, fax 0171 354 5729)

PERRY, Dr Norman Henry; s of Charles Perry (d 1984), of London, and Josephine, *née* Ehrlich (d 1986); *b* 5 March 1944; *Educ* Quintin Sch London, UCL (BA, PhD); *m* 7 Aug 1970, Barbara Ann, da of James Harold Marsden, and Margaret, *née* Lütkemeyer, of Sheffield; 2 s (Ben b 1974, Tom b 1977); *Career* lectr in geography UCL 1965–69, sr res offr GLC 1969–73, sr res fell Social Sci Res Cncl Survey Unit 1973–75; DOE: princ London & Birmingham 1975–79, princ London 1979–80, asst sec W Midlands 1980–86; Grade 4 head of Inner Cities Unit Dept of Employment and DTI 1986–88, Grade 3 regnl dir DTI W Midlands 1988–90; chief exec: Wolverhampton Metropolitan Borough Cncl 1990–96, Solihull Metropolitan Borough Cncl 1996–; dir Wolverhampton Trg and Enterprise Cncl Ltd 1990–96; co sec Solihull Business Partnership 1996–; govr Univ of Wolverhampton 1993–96; FIMgt 1983, FRSA 1996; *Books* Demands for Social Knowledge (with Elisabeth Crawford, 1976), Vols in European Glossary of Legal and Administrative Terminology: German/English, Vol 18 Regional Policy (1974), Vol 29 Environmental Policy (1979), Public Enterprise (1989); *Recreations* reading history; *Clubs* Solihull Municipal; *Style*— Dr Norman Perry; ✉ Council House, PO Box 18, Solihull B91 3QS (☎ 0121 704 6016, fax 0121 704 8341)

PERRY, Peter Sinclair; s of Edward Perry (stage name Edward Sinclair, d 1977), of Kingston-upon-Thames, and Gladys Ethel, *née* Green; *b* 12 March 1948; *Educ* Surbiton County GS; *m* 20 Jan 1973, Janice May, da of Cyril Frederick White (d 1989); *Career* professional television and stage actor 1965–72, sales dir Felix Rosenstiel's Widow & Son Ltd fine art publishers Chelsea 1972–81, gp sales head Independent Radio Sales Ltd London 1981–83, fndr memb Radio Mercury (Reigate and Crawley) 1983–91, stn dir Ocean Sound Classic Hits, Power FM and South Coast Radio (all Southern Radio Group) 1991–92, md Allied Radio PLC (owners of Radio Mercury and Fortune 1458 Ltd) 1992–96; dir: Surrey CrimeStoppers 1992–, Fortune 1458 Ltd 1994–96, Country 1035 Ltd 1992–94; *Recreations* music, guitar, motor racing, cycling; *Style*— Peter Sinclair Perry, Esq; ✉ Dell O Dene, Tuckey Grove, Ripley, Surrey GU23 6JG (☎ 01483 224834)

PERRY, Robert; s of Robert Perry, of Glasgow, and Margaret, *née* Wright; *b* 2 June 1964; *Educ* Cranhill Secdy Sch, Glasgow Coll of Bldg and Printing (HND in Photography); *m* 23 Feb 1990, Margaret, da of Joseph Gilligan (d 1977); *Career* staff photographer (fashion/editorial) Gloss Magazine 1989–90, freelance press photographer (reg clients incl The Independent, The Financial Times, The Daily Telegraph, Scotland on Sunday and The Herald) 1992, staff photographer Scotland on Sunday 1994–; Nikon Regnl Photographer of the Yr 1993, Scottish Sports Photographer of the Yr (Portfolio Merit and Sports Picture of the Yr Merit) 1993; memb NUJ; *Recreations* sports, music, reading; *Style*— Robert Perry, Esq; ✉ Scotland on Sunday, 20 North Bridge, Edinburgh EH1 1YT (mobile ☎ 0836 580673)

PERRY, Dr Robert Henry; s of Frank Perry (d 1992), of Sileby, Loughborough, Leics, and Lois Ellen, *née* Harriman; *b* 20 Aug 1944; *Educ* Loughborough GS, Univ of St Andrews (DSc), FRCP, FRCPath; *m* 5 June 1971, Elaine King, da of James Cyril King Miller, WS (d 1979), of Collinton, Edinburgh; 1 s (Jonathan b 1972), 1 da (Nicolette b 1973); *Career* Newcastle Gen Hosp: sr registrar in neuropathology 1975–79, clinical scientist MRC Neuroendocrinology Unit, conslt neuropathologist 1980–; reader in neurochemical pathology Univ of Newcastle upon Tyne 1991– (sr lectr in neuropathology 1986–91); author of res pubns on neuropathological correlations of dementia, Alzheimer's disease, Parkinson's disease and related topics; memb Br Neuropathological Soc; *Recreations* sailing, skiing, salads; *Style*— Dr Robert Perry; ✉ Dilston Mill House, Corbridge, Northumberland NE45 5QZ (☎ 01434 623 2308); Neuropathology Department, Newcastle General Hospital, Westgate Road, Newcastle upon Tyne NE45 5QZ (☎ 0191 273 8811 ext 22373)

PERRY, Robert John; s of Idris James Perry (d 1975), and Betty, *née* Davies; *b* 23 March 1948; *Educ* Exeter Sch, Univ of Warwick (BSc); *Career* Arthur Andersen & Co 1969–76, N M Rothschild & Sons Ltd 1976– (dir 1987–), dir Bumiputra Merchant Bankers Berhad Malaysia 1988–; FCA; *Recreations* tennis, travel; *Clubs* Hurlingham; *Style*— Robert Perry, Esq; ✉ N M Rothschild & Sons Limited, New Court, St Swithin's Lane, London EC4P 4DU (☎ 0171 280 5000, fax 0171 929 1643)

PERRY, Rodney Charles Langman (Rod); s of Thomas Charles Perry, of Felpham, Bognor Regis, West Sussex, and Kathleen Mary, *née* Moojen; *b* 23 July 1941; *Educ* Peter Symonds Sch Winchester; *m* 5 March 1965, Susan Geraldine, da of John Reginald Quertier, of East Boldre, Brockenhurst, Hants; 1 s (James Quertier b 20 Sept 1968), 1 da (Sarah De Moulpied b 23 Feb 1967); *Career* CA; articles Charles Comins & Co 1960–65, Coopers & Lybrand Zimbabwe 1965–69, ptnr Coopers & Lybrand UK 1976–; ICAEW: memb Cncl 1984–86, chm Technology Gp 1984–86; Freeman: City of London, Worshipful Co of Information Technologists; FCA 1975; *Books* An Audit Approach To Computers (1986); *Recreations* squash, tennis, golf, boating, painting; *Clubs* Royal Lymington Yacht, Brockenhurst Manor Golf; *Style*— Rod Perry, Esq; ✉ East Boldre House, East Boldre, Brockenhurst, Hants (☎ 01590 612407); Flat 19, 87 St George's Court, St George's Drive, Pimlico, London SW1 (☎ 0171 630 7968); Coopers & Lybrand, Embankment Place, London (☎ 0171 822 4575, fax 0171 212 4968)

PERRY, Roy James; MEP (Cons) Wight and Hampshire S (majority 5,101); s of George Charles Perry (d 1979), of Herts, and Dora Emily Perry; *b* 12 Feb 1943; *Educ* Tottenham County Sch (head boy), Univ of Exeter (BA); *m* 1 June 1968, Veronica Grace Winifred, *née* Haswell; 2 da (Elisabeth Helene Veronica b 5 April 1971, Caroline Fiona Ellen b 26 June 1972); *Career* Marks & Spencer PLC 1964–66, sr lectr Southampton Tech Coll 1966–94; MEP (C) Wight and Hampshire S 1994–; memb Eastleigh BC 1970–74; Test Valley BC: memb 1979–, chm Planning Ctee 1983–85, ldr 1985–94; *Recreations* French joie de vivre, French cuisine, keep fit (to compensate for the latter); *Clubs* Royal Naval and Royal Albert Yacht; *Style*— Roy Perry, Esq, MEP; ✉ Tarrants Farmhouse, Maurys Lane, West Wellow, Romsey, Hants SO51 6DA (☎ 01794 322472, fax 01794 323498)

PERRY, Simon James; s of James Anthony Perry, of Oxfordshire and Pauline, *née* Bezani; *b* 9 June 1962; *Educ* Croydon Sch of Art, Chelsea Sch of Art (BA), Royal Acad Sch (MA); *m* 14 Oct 1986, Elise, da of Andrew Terry Fraser; 1 s (Oscar Fraser b 15 April 1988), 1 da (Mathilda Fraser b 6 Feb 1991); *Career* artist and sculptor; *Solo Exhibitions* Nicola Jacobs Gallery London 1988, Linden SArt Centre Melbourne 1993; *Gp Exhibitions* incl: ILEA at the Barbican (London) 1983, Portland Bill Sculpture Park 1983, Quarries Exhibition (Camden Art Centre London) 1983, Christie's Inaugural Exhibition (London) 1983, Summer Exhibition (Nicola Jacobs Gallery London) 1983, New Sculpture Exhibition (Royal Acad London) 1984, Interbuild Exhibition (NEC Birmingham) 1985, Nicola Jacobs Gallery London 1986, 1987 and 1990, Germinations IV (touring) 1988, Work in Progress (Br Sch at Rome) 1988, Dieci Artisti (Br Sch at Rome) 1988, Ten Years of the Br Sch at Rome (RCA London) 1990, Lynne Stern Associates Gallery London 1990, Summer '91 exhibition (Benjamin Rhodes Gallery); subject of several catalogues and other pubns incl The History of the British School at Rome (1990); sculpture cmmn City of Brunswick Melbourne 1993–94, artists seat cmmn Linden Gallery St Kilda Melbourne 1993; *Awards* Landseer scholarship award 1985, Edward Stott Tst travel scholarship 1986, Royal Acad Gold medal for sculpture 1986, Rome scholar in sculpture Br Sch at Rome 1987, awarded Australia Cncl Grant 1992; *Style*— Simon Perry, Esq; ✉ 111 Baston Road, Hayes, Kent BR2 7BS; 25 Glenmorgan Street, East Brunswick 3057, Victoria, Melbourne, Australia (☎ 013 383 3329)

PERRY, Stephen Laurence Andrew; s of Jack Perry (d 1996), of London, and Doris-Kate Perry (d 1985); *b* 12 Sept 1948; *Educ* UCL (LLB); *m* 24 Dec 1980, Wendy Janet, da of Joseph Bond (d 1957), and Lillian Bond; 1 s (Jack b 1984), 1 da (Jodie b 1981); *Career* md London Export Ltd, chm Millennium Tableware Ltd; dir International Shakespeare Globe Tst Ltd; vice pres China-Br Trade Gp, chm 48 Group Club; *Recreations* football, tai-chi; *Clubs* RAC, Wentworth, IOD, Hendon Golf, Academicals FC (pres); *Style*— Stephen Perry, Esq; ✉ London Export Limited, 49 Berkeley Square, London W1X 5DB (☎ 0171 493 4009, fax 0171 491 7420)

PERRY, Dr Wayne; s of William Perry (d 1947), of Hayes, Middlesex, and Margery Rideley, *née* Wilson; *b* 30 June 1944; *Educ* Royal Hosp Sch Ipswich, Univ of Birmingham Med Sch (MB ChB, MRCP), Accreditation by Jt Ctee on Higher Med Trg (RCP) in Gen (Internal) Med with a special interest in Metabolic Med; *m* 1980, Siew Mui Lee; *Career* house physician Queen Elizabeth Hosp Birmingham 1968, house surgn Dudley Rd Hosp Birmingham 1969; sr house offr: Dept of Med Harari Hosp Univ of Salisbury Rhodesia 1969 (Dept of Paediatrics), Chest Diseases King Edward VII Hosp Warwick 1971; registrar in med The Med Professorial Unit King's Coll Hosp London 1972, sr med registrar Dept of Metabolic Med Royal Nat Orthopaedic Hosp Stanmore 1974, asst prof Dept of Internal Faisal Univ Saudi Arabia 1979 (conslt physician and endocrinologist King Fahad Univ Hosp, hon conslt endocrinologist King Fahad Univ Hosp, hon conslt endocrinologist King Abdul Aziz Airbase Hosp); conslt endocrinologist: Harley St 1983, Metabolism and Bone Disease The Endocrine and Dermatology Centre Harley St 1987; author numerous learned articles in med jls; Sir Herbert Seddon Gold Medal and prize for origional res (Inst of Orthopaedics Univ of London and Royal Nat Orthopaedic Hosp); medals awarded at VI and VII Saudi Med Confs 1981, 1982, and for the first graduating students from King Faisal Fahad Univ Dammam Saudi Arabia; FRSM; memb: BMA, Med Defence Union; registered Med Practioner Gen Med Cncl; approved conslt for UK: BUPA, PPP; *Recreations* violoncello, poetry, arcadian landscapes, France; *Style*— Dr Wayne Perry; ✉ The Endocrine Centre, 69 Wimpole St, London W1M 7DE (☎ 0171 935 2440); 57a Wimpole Street, London W1M 7DF (☎ 0171 486 1095)

PERRY OF SOUTHWARK, Baroness (Life Peer UK 1991), of Charlbury in the County of Oxfordshire; Pauline Perry; *née* Welch; da of John George Embleton Welch (d 1963), of Sunderland, and Elizabeth, *née* Cowan (d 1982); *b* 15 Oct 1931; *Educ* Wolverhampton Girls' HS, Girton Coll Cambridge (MA); *m* 26 July 1952, George Walter Perry, s of Percy Walter Perry (d 1939), of Wolverhampton; 3 s (Hon Christopher b 1953, Hon Timothy b 1962, Hon Simon b 1966), 1 da (Hon Hilary (Hon Mrs Winstone) b 1955); *Career* teacher various secdy schs UK, USA and Canada 1953–56 and 1959–61; lectr in philosophy: Univ of Manitoba 1956–59, Univ of Mass 1961–62; lectr in educn: Univ of Exeter (pt/t) 1963–66, Univ of Oxford (pt/t) 1966–70; Access Course tutor 1966–70, HM Chief Inspr of Schs 1981–86 (inspr 1970–74, staff inspr 1975–81), vice-chllr South Bank Univ (formerly South Bank Poly) 1987–93, pres Lucy Cavendish Coll Univ of Cambridge 1994–; freelance journalist and broadcaster; author of various books, chapters in books and numerous published articles, various radio and TV appearances; memb Prime Minister's Advsy Panel for the Citizen's Charter 1993–; memb House of Lords Select Ctee: on Sci and Technol 1992–95, on the Scrutiny of Delegated Powers 1994–, on Relationships of Local and Nat Govt 1995–; chm: South Bank Univ Enterprise Ltd 1988–93, DTI Export Group for Educn and Training Sector 1993–; memb: Governing Body Inst of Devpt Studies 1987–95, British Cncl's Ctee on Int Co-operation in Higher Educn 1987–, Econ and Social Res Cncl 1988–91, Cncl Fndn for Educn Business Partnerships 1990–91, Bd South Bank Centre 1992–94, Ct Univ of Bath 1992–, Bd of Patrons of the Royal Soc 1996–; rector's warden Southwark Cathedral 1990–94; vice pres: British Youth Opera 1993–, Alzheimer's Research Tst 1993–, Soc for Res in Higher Educn 1993–, City & Guilds of London Inst 1994–; Hon FCP 1987, Hon FRSA 1988, hon fell Sunderland Poly 1990; Hon LLD: Univ of Bath 1991, Univ of Aberdeen 1994, South Bank Univ 1994; Hon DLitt Univ of Sussex 1992, Hon DEd Univ of Wolverhampton 1994, Hon DUniv Surrey 1995; Freeman City of London 1992, Liveryman Worshipful Co of Bakers 1992; *Recreations* music, walking; *Clubs* IOD; *Style*— The Rt Hon Baroness Perry of Southwark; ✉ c/o House of Lords, London SW1A 0PW; Cambridge (☎ 01223 332192, fax 01223 332178)

PERRY OF WALTON, Baron (Life Peer UK 1979), of Walton, Co Bucks; Walter Laing Macdonald Perry; kt (1974), OBE (1957); s of Fletcher Smith Perry (d 1960), and Flora Macdonald Macdonald (d 1966); *b* 16 June 1921; *Educ* Ayr Acad, Dundee HS, Univ of St Andrews (MBChB, MD, DSc); *m* 1, 1946 (m dis 1971) Anne Elizabeth Grant; 3 s (Hon Michael John b 1948, Hon Alan Malcolm b 1950, Hon Niall Fletcher b 1953); m 2, 1971, Catherine Hilda, da of Ambrose Crawley; 2 s (Hon Robin Charles Macdonald b 11 June 1973, Hon Colin Stuart Macdonald b 12 Aug 1979), 1 da (Hon Jennifer Joan Macdonald b 6 Feb 1981); *Career* dep leader SDP in House of Lords 1981–83; dir Dept of Biological Standards Nat Inst for Med Res 1952–58; prof of pharmacology Univ of Edinburgh 1958–68 (vice princ 1967–68); vice chllr The Open Univ 1969–80 (fell 1981–); memb: Foundation for Science and Technology, Bd of Editors of Encyclopaedia Britannica; pres: Videotel Internat, Research Defence Soc; FRCPE, FRCP, FRSE 1959, FRS; *Recreations* making music and playing games; *Clubs* Scottish Arts; *Style*— The Rt Hon the Lord Perry of Walton, OBE, FRS, FRSE; ✉ The Open University Scotland, 10 Drumsheugh Gardens, Edinburgh EH3 7QJ (☎ 0131 260 4173, fax 0131 226 6730)

PERRYMAN, Stephen John (Steve); MBE (1986); s of Ronald Edward Perryman, and Joyce, *née* Barwick; *b* 21 Dec 1951; *Educ* Elliots Green GS Northolt; *m* (m dis); 1 s (Glenn Richard b 29 Sept 1977), 2 da (Loren Ann b 5 Feb 1974, Elena-Rose b 9 July 1995); *Career* professional football manager; schoolboy player: Ealing District, Middlesex County, London and England Schs; professional player: 864 appearances Tottenham Hotspur 1969–86, 17 appearances Oxford Utd 1986, 66 appearances Brentford 1986–90; manager: Brentford 1987–90, Watford 1990–93; asst manager Tottenham Hotspur 1993–94; head coach I K Start (Norway) 1995–; England caps: under 18, 17 under 23, 1 full v Iceland 1982; honours as player Tottenham Hotspur: FA Cup twice, League Cup twice, UEFA Cup twice, capt for 10 years; records: most appearances Tottenham Hotspur, most England under 23 caps; Football Writers' Player of the Year 1982; *Books* A Man For All Seasons (autobiography, 1985); *Recreations* own sports shops, tennis, travel; *Style*— Steve Perryman, Esq, MBE; ✉ I K Start, Postboks 1533, Valhalla, 4602 Kristiansand, Norway (☎ 00 47 3809 6091)

PERSAUD, Prof Bishnodat; s of Dhwarka Persaud, and Dukhni, *née* Surujbali; *b* 22 Sept 1933, Guyana; *Educ* Univ of Reading (postgrad dip in agric econs, PhD), Queen's Univ Belfast (BScEcon); *m* Aug 1962, Lakshmi; 3 c (Rajendra, Avinash, Sharda); *Career* res fell Inst of Social and Econ Res Univ of WI 1965–74; Cwlth Secretariat: chief econs offr Commodities Div 1974–76, asst dir Econ Affrs Div 1976–81, dir and head Economic Affrs Div 1981–92; Univ of the West Indies Jamaica: prof of sustainable devpt 1992–, dir and Alcan prof Centre for Environment and Devpt 1993–; co-leader IDB Team on Socio-Economic Reform in Guyana 1994, memb Bd of Tstees Guyana Rainforest Programme 1992–93; memb: Univ of Guyana Review Cmmn 1991 and 1996, UN Ctee for Devpt Planning 1995–, Cmmn on Cwlth Studies 1995–96; numerous speeches and lectures incl address to Euro Foreign and Security Policies Conf of the Euro Movement 1991, numerous radio bdcasts and TV appearances in Cwlth countries, author of two books on econ devpt and contrib articles to professional and learned jls; FRSA; *Books* Developing with Foreign Investment (jtly, 1987), Economic Policy and the Environment (jtly, 1995); *Clubs* RAC; *Style—* Prof Bishnodat Persaud; ✉ University of the West Indies, Mona, Kingston, Jamaica

PERSSON, Rt Rev William Michael Dermot; s of Leslie Charles Grenville Alan Persson (d 1948), and Elizabeth Mercer, *née* Chambers; *b* 27 Sept 1927; *Educ* Monkton Combe Sch, Oriel Coll Oxford (MA); *m* 27 April 1957, Ann, da of Reginald Charles Ward Davey (d 1983), of Heronsgate; 2 s (Matthew b 1960, Adam b 1966), 1 da (Rachel (Mrs C A Johnstone-Burt) b 1958); *Career* Royal Signals 1945–48, served in Germany, cmmnd 2 Lt; deacon 1953, priest 1954, vicar Christ Church Barnet 1958–67, rector of Bebington 1967–79, vicar of Knutsford 1979–82, bishop of Doncaster 1982–92; proctor in convocation 1975–82, examining chaplain to Bishop of London 1981–82, del to WCC Vancouver Assembly 1983; memb: BCC Assembly 1977–80 and 1984–90, chm C of E Cncl for Christian Unity 1991–92, asst bishop Dio of Bath and Wells 1993–; *Style—* The Rt Rev William Persson; ✉ Ryalls Cottage, Burton Street, Marnhull, Sturminster, Newton, Dorset DT10 1PS (☎ 01258 820452)

PERT, Michael; QC (1992); s of Lt Henry McKay Pert, RN (ret), and Noreen Margaret Mary, *née* Murphy; *b* 17 May 1947; *Educ* St Boniface's Coll Plymouth, Univ of Manchester (LLB); *m* 29 July 1971, Vivienne Victoria, da of Ernest George Braithwaite; 2 da (Lucy Claire b 27 Aug 1975, Katherine Olivia b 10 Feb 1979), 1 s (Benjamin McKay b 4 March 1977); *Career* called to the Bar Gray's Inn 1970, recorder 1988–; *Recreations* bee keeping, sailing; *Style—* Michael Pert, Esq, QC; ✉ 36 Bedford Row, London WC1R 4JH (☎ 0171 421 8000, fax 0171 421 8080)

PERTH, 17 Earl of (S 1605); (John) David Drummond; PC (1957); also Lord Drummond of Cargill and Stobhall (S 1488), Lord Maderty (S 1609), Viscount Strathallan (S 1686), and Lord Drummond of Cromlix (S 1686); s of 16 Earl of Perth, GCMG, CB, PC (d 1951), and Hon Angela Constable-Maxwell (d 1965), da of 11 Lord Herries of Terregles; *b* 13 May 1907; *Educ* Downside, Trinity Coll Cambridge; *m* 4 Aug 1934, Nancy Seymour (d 1996), da of Reginald Fincke, of New York City; 2 s; *Heir* s, Viscount Strathallan, *qv*; *Career* Lt Intelligence Corps, seconded to War Cabinet Offices 1942–43 and to Min of Production 1944–45; a representative peer for Scotland 1952–63, Hereditary Thane of Lennox and Hereditary Steward of Menteith and Strathearn; memb Malta Round Table Conf 1956, min of state for Colonial Affairs 1957–62, first crown estate cmmr 1962–77, chm of the Reviewing Ctee on the Export of Works of Art 1972–76, tstee Nat Library of Scotland until 1995, chm Hosp of St John and St Elizabeth 1982–92; Hon LLD Univ of St Andrews; Hon FRIBA 1978, Hon FRIAS 1988, FSA 1994; *Clubs* White's, Puffins (Edinburgh); *Style—* The Rt Hon the Earl of Perth, PC; ✉ Stobhall, by Perth PH2 6DR (☎ 01821 640332)

PERTWEE, Christopher Ferens; DL (Essex 1996); s of Norman Frank Pertwee, of Frinton-on-Sea, Essex, and Eileen Pertwee (d 1982); *b* 25 Nov 1936; *Educ* Tonbridge; *m* 1960, Carole, da of A G (Jim) Drayson, of Sutton Valence, Kent; 3 s (Mark, Julian, Nicholas); *Career* chm Pertwee Holdings Ltd 1970–, dep chm Willmott Pertwee Ltd 1993–; pres UK Agric Supply Trade Assoc 1982–83; memb Cncl Univ of Essex 1990–, chm Colchester Catalyst Charity 1993–, dir Essex Community Fndn 1996–; High Sheriff Co of Essex 1995–96, Jr Warden Worshipful Co of Farmers 1996–97; *Recreations* sport, gardening, antiques; *Clubs* Farmers'; *Style—* Christopher Pertwee, Esq, DL; ✉ The Bishops House, Frating, Colchester, Essex CO7 7HQ; office: Lodge Lane, Langham, Colchester, Essex CO4 5NE (☎ 01206 231000, fax 01206 231132)

PERTWEE, Richard James Charles Drury; s of Capt James Waddon Martyn Pertwee, CBE, of Cintra House, 5 Christchurch Rd, Winchester, Hants, and Margaret Alison, *née* Elliott; *b* 2 May 1955; *Educ* Sherborne, Worcester Coll Oxford (BA); *m* 15 Aug 1981, Gail, da of Wilfred McBrien Swain, OBE (d 1983); 2 da (Laetitia b 1984, Sophie b 1987); *Career* joined RNR 1978, Sub Lt 1980, res 1982; Richards Butler & Co: articled clerk 1978–80, slr 1980–82; asst then ptnr: Trevor Robinson & Co 1982–85, Joynson-Hicks 1985–89; ptnr Taylor Joynson Garrett 1989– (managing ptnr 1993–95); *Recreations* tennis, squash, shooting, cricket; *Clubs* Sherborne Pilgrims, Vincent's (Oxford), MCC; *Style—* Richard Pertwee, Esq; ✉ Taylor Joynson Garrett, Carmelite, 50 Victoria Embankment, Blackfriars, London EC4Y 0DX (☎ 0171 353 1234, fax 0171 936 2666, telex 268014)

PERUTZ, Dr Max Ferdinand; OM (1988), CH (1975), CBE (1963); s of Hugo Perutz, and Adele Perutz; *b* 19 May 1914; *Educ* Theresianum Vienna, Vienna Univ, Peterhouse Cambridge (hon fell 1962); *m* 1942, Gisela Peiser; 1 s, 1 da; *Career* chm MRC Laboratory of Molecular Biology Cambridge 1962–79 (memb Scientific Staff 1979–), Fullerian prof of physiology at the Royal Institution 1973–79, Nobel prize for Chemistry 1962, Royal Medal of Royal Society 1971, Copley medal of Royal Soc 1979, Pour le Mérite 1988; Hon FRCP 1993; *Style—* Dr Max Perutz, OM, CH, CBE, FRS; ✉ 42 Sedley Taylor Rd, Cambridge CB2 2PN (☎ 01223 246041); MRC Laboratory of Molecular Biology, Cambridge CB2 2QH (☎ 01223 248011, fax 01223 213556, telex 81532)

PESARAN, Prof (Mohammad) Hashem; s of Jamal Pesaran (d 1973), and Effat Pesaran; *b* 30 March 1946; *Educ* Univ of Salford (BSc, Athletics colours), Harvard Univ, Univ of Cambridge (PhD, Basketball half-blue); *m* 1969, Marion Fay, *née* Swainston; 3 s (Bijan b 12 Oct 1973, Jamal b 5 Jan 1975, Hassan Ali b 30 Dec 1992), 2 da (Eva-Leila b 24 Sept 1978, Natasha-Guiti b 19 March 1990); *Career* 1 Lt Farahabad Barracks Tehran 1976; jr res offr Dept of Applied Economics Univ of Cambridge and lektor Trinity Coll Cambridge 1971–73, head Econ Res Dept Central Bank of Iran 1974–76 (asst to Vice Govr 1973–74), under sec Miny of Educn Iran 1977–78; Univ of Cambridge: teaching fell and dir of studies in economics Trinity Coll 1979–88, lectr in economics 1979–85, reader in economics 1985–88, prof of economics and professorial fell Trinity Coll 1988–; prof of economics and dir Prog in Applied Econometrics UCLA 1989–93; visiting lectr Harvard 1982, visiting fell ANU 1984 and 1988; visiting prof: Univ of Rome 1986, UCLA 1987–88, Inst of Advanced Studies Vienna 1991, Univ of Pennsylvania 1993; dir: Camfit Data Ltd 1986–, Acorn Investment Trust 1987–89 and 1991–93, Cambridge Econometrics 1985, 1988–89 and 1992–96 (hon pres 1996–); memb: HM Treasy Academic Panel 1993–, Advsy Ctee UK Meteorological Office, Bd of Tstees Economic Research Forum of Arab Countries, Iran and Turkey 1996–; memb Editorial Bd: Cambridge Jl of Economics 1981–89, Econometric Theory 1984–87, Cyprus Jl of Economics 1990–, Hellenic Review 1993–; assoc ed: Econometrica 1984–85, Jl of Economic Dynamics and Control 1995–; fndr ed Jl of Applied Econometrics 1986–; memb Advsy Bd Jl of Economic Surveys 1995–, George Sell Prize Inst of Petroleum 1990, Royal Econ Soc Prize for 1990–91 1992; Hon DLitt Salford 1993; fell: Econometric Soc 1989, Jl of Econometrics 1990; *Books* World Economic Prospects and the Iranian Economy - a Short Term View (1974), Dynamic Regression - Theory and Algorithms (with L J Slater, 1980), Keynes' Economics - Methodological Issues (ed with T Lawson, 1985), The Limits to Rational Expectations (1987), Data-FIT - an Interactive Software Econometric Package (with B Pesaran, 1987), Disaggregation in Economic Modelling (ed with T Barker, 1990), Microfit 3.0 - an Interactive Software Econometric Package (with B Pesaran, 1991), Non-Linear Dynamics, Chaos and Econometrics (ed with S Potter, 1993), Handbook of Applied Econometrics Vol 1 (ed with M Wickens, 1995); *Recreations* basketball, swimming, squash, jogging; *Style—* Prof Hashem Pesaran; ✉ 283 Hills Road, Cambridge CB2 2RP (☎ 01223 500639); Trinity College, Cambridge CB2 1TQ (☎ 01223 338403, fax 01223 335471)

PESCHARDT, Michael Mogens; s of Mogens Jan Hagbarth Peschardt, and Betty Joyce, *née* Foster; *b* 17 Nov 1957; *Educ* Merchant Taylors', Univ of Sussex; *m* 9 July 1977, Sarah Louise, da of Tom James Vaughan; 3 s (Joseph Mogens b 1980, Jack Oliver b 1982, Samuel Thaddeus b 1984), 1 da (Lily Mae b 1993); *Career* news prodr BBC Radio Manchester 1980–82, chief parly journalist BBC Regnl Broadcasting until 1986, sports reporter BBC TV News, currently Australia corr BBC TV; *Recreations* surfing, football; *Style—* Michael Peschardt, Esq; ✉ BBC Level H, 50 Berry Street, N Sydney 2060, NSW, Australia

PESCOD, Peter Richard; s of Philip Pescod (d 1965), of Darlington, and Elsie, *née* Parnaby; *b* 29 June 1951; *Educ* Queen Elizabeth GS Darlington, Univ of Newcastle (LLB); *m* 15 April 1978, Barbara Jane, da of John Magoveny King, of Morpeth, Northumberland; 1 s (Henry b 12 April 1983), 1 da (Jennifer b 21 May 1981); *Career* admitted slr 1975; ptnr Hay and Kilner 1976–; memb Northumberland CC 1989–93; Parly candidate (C) Blaydon 1987 and 1992; vice pres Forum of Insurance Lawyers 1993–95; dep district judge 1995–; memb: Northumberland FPC 1985–90 (chm Med Serv Ctee 1988–96), Family Health Services Appeal Authy 1996–, Nat Tst, Eng Heritage, Law Soc; chm of govrs Ovingham Middle Sch 1993–96; *Recreations* politics, auction sales, building, landscape gardening, architecture; *Clubs* Anglo Belgian, Newcastle upon Tyne Lit and Phil; *Style—* Peter Pescod, Esq; ✉ Ovington Cottage, Ovington, Northumberland NE42 6DH (☎ 01661 832358); Hay & Kilner, 33 Grey St, Newcastle upon Tyne NE1 6EH (☎ 0191 232 8345, fax 0191 261 7704)

PESCOD, Prof (Mainwaring Bainbridge) Warren; OBE (1977); s of Bainbridge Pescod (d 1979), and Elizabeth, *née* Brown (d 1973); *b* 6 Jan 1933; *Educ* Stanley GS Co Durham, King's Coll Univ of Durham (BSc), MIT (SM); *m* 16 Nov 1957, (Mary) Lorenza, da of John Francis Coyle (d 1970); 2 s (Duncan Warren b 1959, Douglas James b 1961); *Career* teaching and res assoc MIT 1954–56, res assoc Dept of Civil Engrg King's Coll Univ of Durham 1956–57, lectr and actg head Dept of Engrg Fourah Bay Coll, Univ Coll of Sierra Leone W Africa 1957–61, asst engr Babtie Shaw and Morton Glasgow 1961–64, prof and chm Environmental Engrg Div Asian Inst of Technol Bangkok 1964–76; Univ of Newcastle upon Tyne: Tyne & Wear prof of environmental control engrg 1976–, head Dept of Civil Engrg 1983–; memb Northumbrian Water Authy 1986–89, dir Northumbrian Water Group PLC 1989–, chm and md Environmental Technology Consultants Ltd 1988–; CEng, FICE 1973, FCIWEM (formerly FIPHE) 1962, MIWM 1985, MRSH 1964; *Books* Water Supply and Wastewater Disposal in Developing Countries (ed, 1971), Treatment and Use of Sewage Effluent for Irrigation (ed with A Arar, 1988); *Recreations* squash, golf, reading; *Clubs* British and Royal Bangkok Sports (Bangkok); *Style—* Professor Warren Pescod, OBE; ✉ Tall Trees, High Horse Close Wood, Rowlands Gill, Tyne & Wear NE39 1AN (☎ 01207 542 104); Department of Civil Engineering, University of Newcastle upon Tyne, Newcastle NE1 7RU (☎ 0191 222 6410, fax 0191 222 6502, telex 53654 UNINEW G)

PESEK, Libor; *b* 22 June 1933; *Career* fndr Prague Chamber Harmony 1958, chief conductor Slovak Philharmonic 1980–81, conductor-in-residence Czech Philharmonic Orch 1982–, music dir Royal Liverpool Philharmonic Orch 1987–; worked as guest conductor with orchs incl: London Symphony, The Philharmonia, Los Angeles Philharmonic and St Louis Symphony Orchs, Moscow and Japan Philharmonic Orchs, La Scala Milan, Oslo Philharmonic, Orchestre National de France, Orchestre de Paris, Berlin Symphony, Dresden Staatskapelle, Pittsburgh, Montreal, Indianapolis and Philadelphia Orchs; *Recordings* incl: Dvorak's Symphony Cycle, Britten's Sinfonia da Requiem, Peter Grimes and the Young Person's Guide to the Orchestra, Strauss' Ein Heldenleben, Berg's Chamber Concerto, Stravinsky's symphonies for wind instruments, Ravel's Daphnis and Chloe, Suk's Asrael Symphony, Suk's Summer's Tale, Suk's Ripening, Mahler's Symphonies 9 and 10, various works by Haydn, Mozart, Janacek and Martinu; *Recreations* physics, Eastern philosophy, literature (especially Kafka, Tolstoy and Dostoyevsky); *Style—* Libor Pesek, Esq; ✉ c/o Nicola Eaton, IMG Artists (Europe), Media House, 3 Burlington Lane, Chiswick, London W4 2TH (☎ 0181 233 5800, fax 0181 233 5801)

PESKIN, Richard Martin; s of Leslie Peskin (d 1980), and Hazel Pauline Peskin (d 1980); *b* 21 May 1944; *Educ* Charterhouse, Queens' Coll Cambridge (MA, LLM); *m* 6 Feb 1979, Penelope Ann Elizabeth Howard, *née* Triebner; 1 s (Michael b 1966), 2 da (Elizabeth b 1969, Virginia b 1979); *Career* Great Portland Estates PLC: dir 1968–, dep md 1972–85, md 1985–, chm 1986–; FRSA 1989, CIMgt 1989; *Recreations* crosswords, composing limericks, fine wine, racing, golf; *Clubs* MCC, RAC, Mark's, Annabel's, Wentworth; *Style—* Richard Peskin, Esq; ✉ 41 Circus Road, London NW8 9JH (☎ 0171 289 0492); Great Portland Estates PLC, Knighton House, 56 Mortimer Street, London W1N 8BD (☎ 0171 580 3040, fax 0171 631 5169)

PESTELL, John Edmund; s of Edmund Ernest Pestell (d 1965), and Isabella Cummine, *née* Sangster (d 1987); brother of Catherine Eva Hughes, *qv*; *b* 8 Dec 1930; *Educ* Roundhay Leeds, New Coll Oxford (MA); *m* 19 April 1958, Muriel Ada, da of William Norman Whitby (d 1971); 3 s (James b 1962, Hugh b 1963, Charles b 1966); *Career* admin Staff Coll Henley 1963; MOD 1953–72: private sec to Parly Under sec of State 1958–60, private sec to Min of Equipment 1969–70; press sec (co-ordination) PMs Office 1972–74, under sec Civil Service Dept 1976–81 (asst sec 1974–76), HM Treasy 1981–84, MOD 1984–88, chm Civil Service Selection Bd, Cabinet Office 1988–90, partnership sec Linklaters & Paines 1990–94; govr Cranleigh Sch 1975–95; *Clubs* Athenaeum; *Style—* John Pestell, Esq; ✉ New House, Bridge Road, Cranleigh, Surrey GU6 7HH

PESTELL, Sir John Richard; KCVO (1969); s of late Lt-Cdr Frank Lionel Pestell, RN (d 1947), and Winifred Alice Pestell (d 1983); *b* 21 Nov 1916; *Educ* Portsmouth Northern Secdy Sch; *m* 1951, Betty, da of Reuben Parish (d 1955); 3 da; *Career* British SA Police S Rhodesia 1939–65, Cyrenaica Def Force 1944–49, Maj; sec and comptroller to Govr of S Rhodesia (Rt Hon Sir Humphrey Gibbs) 1965–69, adjudicator Immigration Appeals Harmondsworth 1970–87; *Recreations* walking; *Style—* Sir John Pestell, KCVO; ✉ Batch Cottage, North Road, Charlton Horethorne, Sherborne, Dorset DT9 4NS (☎ 01963 220719)

PESTON, Baron (Life Peer UK 1987), of Mile End, Greater London; Maurice Harry Peston; s of Abraham Peston; *b* 19 March 1931; *Educ* Bellevue Bradford, Hackney Downs London, LSE (BScEcon), Princeton Univ USA; *m* 17 Nov 1958, Helen, da of Joseph Conroy; 2 s (Hon Robert James Kenneth b 1960, Hon Edward Charles Richard b 1964), 1 da (Hon Juliet Claire Elaine b 1961); *Career* prof of economics Queen Mary and Westfield Coll Univ of London; *Style—* The Rt Hon Lord Peston; ✉ c/o House of Lords, London SW1A 0PW

PETCH, Dr Michael Charles; s of Dr Charles Plowright Petch (d 1987), of Wolferton, Norfolk, and Edna Margaret, *née* Stirling; *b* 15 July 1941; *Educ* Gresham's, St John's Coll Cambridge, St Thomas's Hosp (MA, MD, MB BChir); *m* 19 April 1965, Fiona Jean Shepheard, da of Cdr David George Fraser Bird, of the Nyewood, Sussex; 2 s (Tom b 1966, Simon b 1968), 1 da (Amanda b 1971); *Career* sr registrar Nat Heart Hosp 1971–77, conslt cardiologist Papworth and Addenbrooke's Hosps 1977–, assoc lectr Univ of Cambridge; memb: cncl Br Cardiac Soc 1985–89, various ctees Coll of Physicians; contrib: British Med Jl, Lancet, British Heart Jl; MRCP 1967, FRCP 1980, fell American Coll of Cardiology 1980; *Books* Heart Disease (1989); *Recreations* natural history, sailing, opera; *Style*— Dr Michael Petch; ✉ 20 Brookside, Cambridge CB2 1JQ (☎ 01223 365226, fax 01223 302858); Papworth Hosp, Cambridge CB3 8RE (☎ 01480 830541, fax 01480 831083)

PETCH, Simon Geoffrey Filby; s of Eric Petch (d 1986), of Cirencester, Glos, and Nancy Mary, *née* Lamplough (d 1988); *b* 6 May 1943; *Educ* Dean Close Sch Cheltenham, St Peter's Coll Oxford; *m* 1969, Patricia Ann, da of William James Burton (d 1983); 1 s (Jack b 1975); *Career* research offr Union of Construction Allied Trades and Technicians 1969–73, nat research offr Electrical Power Engrs Assoc 1973–76; dep gen sec: Engrs Managers Assoc, Electrical Power Engrg Assoc 1976–85; gen sec Soc of Telecom Executives 1986–; *Recreations* horse racing, reading, walking; *Style*— Simon Petch, Esq; ✉ 3 Walpole Gardens, Strawberry Hill, Twickenham, Middx TW2 5SL (☎ 0181 894 1316); 1 Park Road, Teddington, Middx TW11 0AR (☎ 0181 943 5181)

PETCHEY, Mark Rodney James; s of Rodney John Petchey, of Loughton, Essex, and Avril Rosemary Petchey; *b* 1 Aug 1970; *Educ* Forest Sch Snaresbrook; *Career* tennis player; turned professional 1988; nat champion: under 14, under 18; represented GB: int events at various levels, Euro Cup, Davis Cup; *Recreations* reading, playing golf and sitting on a beach; *Style*— Mark Petchey, Esq; ✉ c/o Lawn Tennis Association, Queens Club, Palliser Road, London W14

PETER, John Anthony; s of Dr András Péter (d 1944), and Veronika, *née* Nagy (d 1977); *b* 24 Aug 1938; *Educ* various state schools in Hungary, Campion Hall Oxford (MA), Lincoln Coll Oxford (BLitt); *m* 1978, Linette Katharine, da of Rai Bahadur Amar Nath Purbi; *Career* reporter and editorial asst Times Educational Supplement 1964–67; The Sunday Times: editorial staff 1967–79, dep arts ed 1979–84, chief drama critic 1984–; *Books* Vladimir's Carrot: Modern Drama and the Modern Imagination (1987); *Style*— John Peter, Esq; ✉ The Sunday Times, 1 Pennington St, London E1 9XW (☎ 0171 782 5000)

PETERBOROUGH, Very Rev Dean of; *see:* Bunker, Very Rev Michael

PETERBOROUGH, Bishop of 1996–; Rt Rev Ian Patrick Martyn Cundy; s of Dr Henry Martyn Cundy, and Kathleen Ethel, *née* Hemmings; *b* 23 April 1945; *Educ* Monkton Combe Sch, Trinity Coll Cambridge (MA), Tyndale Hall Bristol; *m* 1969, Josephine Katherine, *née* Boyd; 2 s, 1 da; *Career* ordained: deacon 1969, priest 1970; curate Christ Church New Malden 1969–73, lectr in church history and Christian doctrine Oak Hill Coll 1973–77, team rector of Mortlake with E Sheen 1978–83, examining chaplain to Bishop of Southwark 1978–83, warden Cranmer Hall St John's Coll Durham 1983–92, bishop of Lewes 1992–96; memb: Anglican Old Catholic Int Theol Conf 1980–, Faith & Order Advsy Gp 1981–, Advsy Bd of Miny 1991–92, Ct Univ of Sussex 1992–96; govr: Monkton Combe Sch 1986–, Eastbourne Coll 1993–96, Lancing Coll 1994–; *Recreations* music, walking, photography; *Style*— The Rt Rev the Bishop of Peterborough; ✉ Bishop's Lodging, The Palace, Peterborough PE1 1YA (☎ 01735 62492)

PETERKEN, Laurence Edwin; CBE (1990); s of Edwin James Peterken (d 1971), of Banstead, Surrey, and Constance Fanny, *née* Giffin (d 1973); *b* 2 Oct 1931; *Educ* Harrow, Peterhouse Cambridge (scholar, MA); *m* 10 Dec 1955, (Hanne) Birgithe (d 1968), da of Harald von der Recke (d 1960), of Copenhagen; 1 s (Oliver b 1956), 1 da (Camilla b 1959); m 2, 29 May 1970, Margaret Raynal Blair; 1 s (Alexander b 1974), 1 da (Jemima b 1977); *Career* Nat Serv 1950–52, Pilot Offr RAF Regt, Sqdn Adjt No 20 LAA Sqdn 1952; mangr Serv Div 1961–63 and commerical dir Hotpoint Ltd 1963–66, gp md Br Domestic Appliances 1966–68, dir Br Printing Corp Ltd 1969–73, md Debenhams Fashion Multiple Div 1974–75, mgmnt auditor Debenhams Ltd 1975–77, controller of operational servs GLC 1977–85, gen mangr Gtr Glasgow Health Bd 1986–93, dir of special projects NHS in Scotland 1993–; chm Glasgow and West of Scotland Inst of Public Administration 1993–; *Recreations* golf, opera; *Clubs* Athenaeum; *Style*— Laurence Peterken, Esq, CBE

PETERS, Andi; *b* 29 July 1970, London; *Educ* Emmanuel Sch Battersea; *Career* television presenter, producer and director; presented for BBC: But First This (BFT) 1989, CBBC 2 1989, The Broom Cupboard 1990–92, Smash Hits Awards 1993, 1994 and 1995, Children In Need 1993 and 1994, The Ozone (also prodr/dir) 1993–96, Live and Kicking (with Emma Forbes, *qv*) 1993–96, The Travel Quiz 1994, Take Two 1995, EEK 1995, Good Fortune 1995, Short Change 1996; for ITV as presenter: Free Time 1988, The Noise 1996–; as prodr Train 2 Win; twice winner Top Personality on TV (voted by Newsround); *Style*— Andi Peters, Esq; ✉ c/o James Grant Media Group Ltd, Syon Lodge, London Road, Syon Park, Middlesex TW7 5BH (☎ 0181 232 4100, fax 0181 232 4101)

PETERS, Prof Andrew Raymond; s of Raymond Barlow Peters, of Shepshed, Leics, and Dorothy Ellen, *née* Sparrow; *b* 10 Dec 1949; *Educ* Ashby de la Zouch Boys' GS, RVC (BVetMed, MRCVS), Open Univ (BA), Univ of Nottingham (PhD), DVetMed (London); *m* Jean Elizabeth, *née* Pallett; 3 s (Daniel Joseph b 13 July 1980, Thomas Michael b 13 June 1982, Robert James b 1 Jan 1987); *Career* practising vet surgn 1972–74, demonstrator in animal physiology Univ of Nottingham 1974–79, sr vet offr Meat and Livestock Cmmn 1979–87, sr exec (pharmaceuticals) British Technology Group 1987–88, regulatory mangr Hoechst Animal Health 1989–93, prof of animal health and prodn and head Dept of Farm Animal and Equine Med and Surgery RVC Univ of London 1993–; memb Animal Welfare Ctee RZS, UK rep Standing Ctee Int Congress on Animal Reproduction; memb: Assoc of Vet Teachers and Research Workers, Br Soc of Animal Sci, BVA, Br Cattle Vet Assoc, Pig Vet Soc; FRCVS 1982, FIBiol 1983; *Books* Reproduction in Cattle (1986), Vaccines for Veterinary Applications (1993); also author of approx 80 published papers in animal/vet sci journals, reg contrib to scientific and indust confs; *Recreations* hill walking, running, swimming, DIY building; *Style*— Prof Andrew Peters; ✉ Royal Veterinary College, Department of Farm Animal and Equine Medicine and Surgery, Boltons Park Farm, Potters Bar, Herts EN6 1NB (☎ 01707 666333, fax 01707 647085)

PETERS, Frank David; s of Alfred George Charles Peters (d 1985), and Georgina, *née* Robins; *b* 7 Jan 1952; *Educ* Kings Heath Boys' Tech Sch, Birmingham Coll of Art & Design, Lanchester Poly (Cert in Design Visual Communication (3 Dimensions)); *partner* Carmen Martinez-Lopez; 1 da (Christina Onesireosan-Martinez b 15 Aug 1976); *Career* exhbn designer 1975–77, proprietor own co 1977–80 (sold to Badger Graphics), freelance designer 1980–84; fndr: Creative Facility Associates (gp mktg, PR & translation servs) 1984–, Sherborne Group (interior design & build contractors and exhbn contractors) 1994–; currently involved in design mgmnt and mktg in leisure, entertainment and educn sectors (work incl Euro motor show stands for Land Rover/Rover motor show stand Geneva, etc); memb Policy Ctee Birmingham Design Innitiative; co-creator Birmingham Contemporary Music Gp (under artistic direction of Sir Simon Rattle); FRSA, MCSD (chm Midlands Region); *Recreations* cooking, film, classical music; *Clubs* Edgbaston Priory; *Style*— Frank Peters, Esq; ✉ 29 Blenheim Road, Moseley, Birmingham B13 9TY (☎ 0121 449 5928); Creative Facility Associates Ltd, Number One, of Sherborne Gate, Sherborne Street Wharf, Birmingham B16 8DE (☎ 0121 608 6000, fax 0121 608 2223)

PETERS, Prof George Henry; *b* 2 Sept 1934; *Educ* Mold GS Clwyd, UCW Aberystwyth (BSc, MSc), King's Coll Cambridge, MA by decree (Oxon); *Career* Inst for Research in Agricultural Economics Univ of Oxford: research asst 1959–61, departmental demonstrator 1961–64, lectr 1964–67; pt/t lectr Dept of Land Economy Univ of Cambridge 1963–65; Dept of Economics and Commerce Univ of Liverpool: lectr 1967–69, sr lectr 1967–70, Brunner prof of economic sci 1970–79, head of Dept 1976–79 (acting head 1975–76); dir Inst of Agricultural Economics Univ of Oxford 1980–86; Queen Elizabeth House Univ of Oxford: research prof in agricultural economics 1986–, dep dir 1991–; Wolfson Coll Oxford: professorial fell 1980–, vicegerent 1991–93; pres Agricultural Economics Soc 1991–92; memb Exec Ctee and ed proceedings Int Assoc of Agricultural Economists 1991–; *Books* Cost Benefit Analysis and Public Expenditure (1966, 2 edn 1968, 3 edn 1973, trans into German 1968), Private and Public Finance (1971, 2 edn 1975), Agriculture: Review of United Kingdom Statistical Sources (1988), Sustainable Agricultural Development: The Role of International Cooperation (ed with B F Stanton, 1992), Agricultural Competitiveness: Market Forces and Policy Choice (ed with D Hedley, 1995), Agricultural Economics: International Library of Critical Writings in Economics (ed, 1995); also author of numerous book chapters and of articles in learned jls; *Style*— Prof George Peters; ✉ Queen Elizabeth House, International Development Centre, University of Oxford, 21 St Giles, Oxford OX1 3LA (☎ 01865 273600, fax 01865 273607)

PETERS, John Edgar Norris; CBE (1988, MBE (mil) 1945); *b* 18 Jan 1919; *Educ* Emanuel Sch; *m* 14 Nov 1994, Mrs Joan G Ellis, widow of Dr Dennis Ellis; *Career* Royal Artillery 1939–46; Gillette Industries Ltd 1946–68 (bd memb 1955–68), dir Partridge & Love Colour Printers Bristol 1966–70, chm and md British American Optical Co 1968–73, gen mangr Euro operations American Optical Corp 1968–73, dir J R Gill & Sons newspaper publishers 1976–86, dir TSW Television 1980–92 (chm Political Advsy Bd), dir Central Livestock Auction Satellite Sales Ltd 1992–95; memb S Hams Police Liaison Consultative Ctee 1986–94, non-exec memb Plymouth and Torbay HA 1993–96; memb LLoyd's 1968–; chm Totnes Cons Assoc 1980–83 (vice chm 1974–80), memb Cons Western Provincial Area Exec Ctee and Cncl 1980–94, chm S Hams Cons Assoc Selection Ctee, chm S Hams Cons Assoc 1983–86 (pres 1986–93, patron 1993–95), past memb Devon Cons Euro Constituency Selection Ctee; memb Kingsbridge Town Cncl 1974–76, memb Devon Local Valuation Panel 1976–91, Devon CC rep to Bd of Govrs and Tstees St Thomas More's Sch Totnes 1983–91; licensed reader Church of England 1975–, vice chm Stokenham Parochial Church Cncl 1976–95; churchwarden Stokenham Parish Church 1995–96, vice chm Stokenham Parochial Church Cncl 1996–; memb The Pilgrims 1970–; Liveryman Worshipful Co of Broderers 1970–; *Clubs* Army & Navy; *Style*— John E N Peters, Esq, CBE; (☎ 01548 531 292, fax 01548 531 046)

PETERS, Prof Sir (David) Keith; kt (1993); s of Herbert Lionel Peters, of Baglan, Port Talbot, and Olive Mainwaring, *née* Hare; *b* 26 July 1938; *Educ* Glanafan GS Port Talbot, Welsh Nat Sch of Med Univ of Wales (MB BCh); *m* 1, 1961 (m dis 1976), Jean Mair Garfield; 1 s (Andrew b 1961), 1 da (Katharine b 1969); m 2, 1979, Pamela, da of Norman Wilson Ewan, of Cambridge; 2 s (James b 1980, William b 1989), 1 da (Hannah b 1982); *Career* prof of med Royal Postgraduate Med Sch 1977– (lectr 1969–75, reader 1975–77), regius prof of physic Univ of Cambridge Sch of Clinical Med 1987– (fell Christ's Coll); memb: MRC 1984–88, Advsy Cncl Sci and Technol 1988–91; chm: Nat Kidney Res Fund 1980–86, Nat Radiological Protection Bd; Hon MD Univ of Wales 1986, Hon DSc Aberdeen 1994; FRCP 1975, FRCPath 1991, FRCPEd 1995, FRS 1995; *Books* Clinical Aspects of Immunology (jt ed, 1982 and 1993); *Recreations* tennis; *Clubs* Garrick; *Style*— Prof Sir Keith Peters; ✉ Office of the Regius Professor of Physic, University of Cambridge School of Clinical Medicine, Addenbrooke's Hosp, Hills Rd, Cambridge CB2 2QP (☎ 01223 336738, fax 01223 336721)

PETERS, Kenneth Jamieson; CBE (1979), JP (City of Aberdeen 1961), DL (Aberdeen 1978); s of William Jamieson Peters (d 1966), and Edna Rosa, *née* Hayman (d 1980); *b* 17 Jan 1923; *Educ* Aberdeen GS, Univ of Aberdeen; *m* 1951, Arunda Merle Jane Jones; *Career* serv WWII, Capt/Adj 2 Bn King's Own Scottish Borderers; ed: Evening Express Aberdeen 1953–56, The Press and Journal Aberdeen 1956–60; dir Highland Printers Ltd (Inverness) 1968–83, md Aberdeen Journals Ltd 1960–80, chm 1980–81; dir: Thomson Regional Newspapers 1974–81, Thomson North Sea 1981–88, Thomson Scottish Petroleum Ltd 1981–86, Aberdeen Journals Ltd 1960–90, National Girobank Scotland 1984–90; chm Aberdeen and NE Scotland Ctee The Scottish Cncl for Devpt and Industry 1982–88; memb Bd: British Rail (Scotland) 1982–92, Peterhead Bay Authority 1983– (vice chm 1989–); Burgess of Guild City of Aberdeen 1963; assoc memb CIT 1985, FSA (Scot) 1980, FRSA 1989; *Clubs* MCC, Royal Northern and University (Aberdeen); *Style*— Kenneth Peters Esq, CBE, DL; ✉ 47 Abergeldie Rd, Aberdeen AB1 6ED (☎ 01224 587647)

PETERS, Mary Elizabeth; CBE 1990 (MBE 1973); da of Arthur Henry Peters (d 1990), of Australia, and Hilda Mary Ellison (d 1956); *b* 6 July 1939; *Educ* Ballymena Acad, Portadown Coll, Belfast Coll of Domestic Science; *Career* formerly home economics teacher Graymount Girls' Secondary Sch; int athlete 1961–74, represented N Ireland at every Cwlth Games 1958–74; achievements incl: fourth place pentathlon Olympic Games 1964, Silver medal shot Cwlth Games 1966, Gold medal pentathlon and shot Cwlth Games 1970, Gold medal pentathlon Olympic Games 1972 (world record), Gold medal pentathlon Cwlth Games 1974; memb NI Sports Cncl 1973–93, vice chm NISC 1977–80, chm NI Ctee of Sport for the Disabled 1984–91, memb Sports Cncl (GB) 1974–77 (re-elected 1987–93), memb Sports Aid Fndn, patron NI Amateur Athletic Fedn, formerly pres NI Women's AAA, team mangr Br Women's Athletics Team 1979–84 (incl Moscow and LA Olympic Teams), pres NI Paraplegic Assoc 1993–, memb Women's Ctee Int Amateur Athletic Fedn, tstee Ulster Sports & Recreation Tst; pres British Athletics Fedn 1996–; chm: Ulster Games Fndn 1990–93, Belfast 1991 Sports Ctee; dep chm NI Tourist Bd 1996–; md Mary Peters Sports Ltd, columnist Irish edition Daily Mail 1994–; patron Friends of The Royal (Royal Victoria Hosp); Hon DSc New Univ of Ulster 1974; *Recreations* fitness training, patchwork; *Style*— Mary E Peters, CBE; ✉ Willowtree Cottage, River Rd, Dunmurry, Belfast BT17 9DP; Mary Peters Health Club, 37 Railway Street, Lisburn BT28 1XP (☎ 0184 66 76411)

PETERS, Michael Harold Barry; OBE (1990); s of Hyman Peters (d 1986), of London, and Claire Peters; *b* 12 Feb 1941; *Educ* Luton GS, London Coll of Printing (NDD), Yale Univ Sch of Architecture (Euro fell, MFA); *m* 1963, Josephine, da of Alfred and Rachel Levy; 1 s (Gary b 1964), 1 da (Sarah b 1967); *Career* graphic designer; Cato Peters O'Brien 1965–66, Klein Peters 1966–68, Michael Peters & Partners (became Michael Peters Group plc 1983 then Michael Peters Ltd 1990) 1970–92, fndr chm and creative dir Identica (now The Identica Partnership) 1992–; life pres DBA (fndr 1986); lectr worldwide, author of numerous pubns; visiting prof Bezalel Sch of Art Jerusalem; memb Alliance Graphique Internationale 1985, fell Royal Charter of Designers 1986; *Projects* incl: identities for numerous govt depts, Conservative Pty identity, numerous other worldwide corp identity projects, packaging design projects and worldwide literature systems; *Awards* D&AD, Clio, NY Art Dirs' Club, Los Angeles Art Dirs' Club, Stock Exchange (for annual report design), numerous other graphic and typographic awards worldwide; *Recreations* walking, gardening, music, collector of contemporary British crafts; *Style*— Michael Peters, Esq, OBE; ✉ The Identica Partnership, 30 Queensway, London W2 3SA (☎ 0171 221 9900, fax 0171 221 2225)

PETERS, Robert Byron; MBE (1977); s of Geofrey Halsted Peters, of Eddington Mill House, Hungerford, Berks, and Edith Frances *née* Scott; *b* 3 May 1926; *Educ* Marlborough, RAF Short Course Trinity Coll Oxford; *m* 15 Jan 1959, Jean Eileen Meredith, da of George Thomas Edwards, of Hornsey; 1 s (Laurence Geofrey Byron b 1963); 2 da (Rebecca Frances b 1965, Victoria Louise b 1967); *Career* served RAF aircrew 1943–45; chief exec and sec Inst of Advanced Motorists until 1956–94; former dir IAM Fleet Training Ltd; dir: Advanced Mile-Posts Publications Ltd, Clearshift Ltd, College of Driver Education Ltd; chm Kentex Estates Ltd; chm Advsy Ctee Hosp and Med Care Assoc (HMCA); memb HAC; Liveryman Worshipful Co of Wheelwrights; *Recreations* amateur radio, swimming, tennis, computers, travel, aviation; *Style*— Robert Peters, Esq, MBE; ✉ Hospital and Medical Care Association, 184 Fleet Street, London EC4A 2HD (☎ 0171 242 8322, fax 0171 831 9080, car 0589 006877)

PETERS, Prof Timothy John; s of Stanley Frederick Peters (d 1993), of Uley, Dursley, Gloucester, and Paula, *née* March (d 1973); *b* 10 May 1939; *Educ* King's Sch Macclesfield Cheshire, Univ of St Andrews (MB ChB, MSc, DSc), Univ of London (PhD), The Rockefeller Univ NY; *m* 21 Sept 1965, Judith Mary, da of Dr William Basil Bacon (d 1983), of Manchester; 1 s (Christopher b 1983), 2 da (Carolyne b 1967, Sarah b 1969); *Career* successively lectr, sr lectr then reader Royal Postgrad Med Sch Univ of London 1972–79, head Div of Clinical Cell Biology Clinical Res Centre Harrow 1979–88, prof and head of Dept of Clinical Biochemistry King's Coll London 1988–, dir of pathology King's Healthcare 1992–, sub-dean for research and higher degrees King's Coll Sch of Med and Dentistry 1992–; Raine visiting prof 1994, Br Cncl visiting prof Dept of Biochemistry Univ of West Australia 1995; ed Alcohol and Alcoholism 1991–94, ed in chief Addiction Biology 1995–; tstee and memb Cncl Sir Richard Stapley Educational Tst 1992–; FRCP 1974, FRCPEdin 1981, FRCPath 1984, FRSA 1996; *Recreations* baroque recorders; *Clubs* RSM; *Style*— Prof Timothy J Peters; ✉ Dept Clinical Biochemistry, King's Coll Sch of Medicine and Dentistry, Bessemer Rd, London SE5 9PJ (☎ 0171 346 3008, fax 0171 737 7434)

PETERS, William; CMG (1980), LVO (1961), MBE (1959); s of John William Peters (d 1983), of Morpeth, Northumberland, and Louise, *née* Woodhouse (d 1965); *b* 28 Sept 1923; *Educ* King Edward VI GS Morpeth, Balliol Coll Oxford (MA), LSE, SOAS; *m* 1944, Catherine Bertha, da of Daniel Bailey (d 1928), of Edinburgh and Paisley; *Career* HM Dip Serv (ret); served WWII Britain and Far East Queen's Royal Regt, KOSB, 9 Gurkha Rifles, demobbed as Capt 1946; joined HM Overseas Colonial Serv as asst dist cmmr Gold Coast (now Ghana) 1950, ret as acting sec/regnl cmmr (Cabinet rank) Northern Ghana; asst princ then princ CRO 1959; first sec: Dacca 1960–63, Cyprus 1963–67; head: Zambia and Malawi Dept CRO 1967–68, Central African Dept FCO 1968–69; dir Int Affrs Div Cwlth Secretariat 1969–71, cnsllr and head Chancery Canberra 1971–73, dep high cmmr Bombay 1974–77, ambass Uruguay 1977–80, high cmmr Malawi 1980–83, ret; chm: LEPRA 1984–92, Tibet Soc of UK 1985–93 (vice pres 1994–), Tibet Relief Fund 1985–93, Abbeyfield Ethnic Minorities Sub-Ctee 1989–96, Abbeyfield (Walmer) Soc; United Soc for the Propagation of the Gospel: chm Cncl 1991–94, vice pres 1995–, govr 1996–; tstee Jubilee 2000, pres Royal Br Legion (Downs Branch); memb: Cncl South Atlantic Cncl, Deal Soc, Editorial Bd Royal Soc for Asian Affairs; past pres Deal Rotary Club 1989–90, govr Walmer Secdy Sch; FIMgt; *Books* Diplomatic Service: Formation and Operation (1972); articles and reviews in Asian Affairs and Army Quarterly and Defence Review; *Recreations* music, archaeology; *Clubs* Oxford & Cambridge, Commonwealth Trust, Royal Soc for Asian Affairs; *Style*— William Peters, Esq, CMG, LVO, MBE; ✉ 12 Crown Court, Middle St, Deal, Kent CT14 7AG (☎ 01304 362822, fax 01304 380821, e-mail j2000@gn.apc.org)

PETERSEN, Sir Jeffrey Charles; KCMG (1978, CMG 1968); s of Charles Petersen; *b* 20 July 1920; *Educ* Westcliff HS, LSE; *m* 1962, Karin Kristina Hayward; 2 s, 4 da; *Career* RN 1939–46; HM Dip Serv 1948–80; ambass to: Republic of Korea 1971–74, Romania 1975–77, Sweden 1977–80; chm: British Materials Handling Board 1981–95, Barclays Bank SAE (Spain) 1982–87, Åke Larson Ltd 1987–93, North Sea Assts plc 1988–94; pres Anglo-Korean Soc; vice pres: Anglo-Swedish Soc, Swedish C of C for the UK; Knight Grand Cross Royal Order of the Polar Star Sweden 1984, Order of Diplomatic Merit South Korea 1984; *Clubs* Travellers', Kent and Canterbury; *Style*— Sir Jeffrey Petersen, KCMG; ✉ 32 Longmoore St, London SW1V 1JF (☎ 0171 834 8262); Crofts Wood, Petham, Kent (☎ 01227 700537)

PETERSEN, Prof Ole Holger; s of Rear Adm Jorgen Petersen (d 1986), and Elisabeth, *née* Klein; *b* 3 March 1943; *Educ* Med Sch Copenhagen Univ (MB ChB, MD); *m* 1, 1968 (m dis 1995), Nina Bratting, da of Wilhelm Jensen, of Copenhagen, Denmark; 2 s (Jens b 26 May 1969, Carl b 25 Dec 1970); m 2, June 1995, Nina Burdakova, da of Nikolay Kolichev, of Grozny, Russia; *Career* Lt Royal Danish Army Med Corps 1970–71; sr lectr in physiology Univ of Copenhagen 1973–75 (lectr 1969–73), prof of physiology Univ of Dundee 1975–81, subject ed Pflügers Archiv (Euro jl of physiology) 1978–, George Holt prof of physiology Univ of Liverpool 1981–; foreign sec Physiological Soc 1992–; memb Scientific Advsy Bd Max Planck Inst for Molecular Physiology Dortmund 1995–, fndn memb Academia Europaea (chair Physiology and Med Section 1996–); memb: Royal Danish Acad of Sciences and Letters 1988, Int Faculty Danish Res Acad 1993; Jacobaeus Prize (Novo Nordic Fndn) 1994; *Books* The Electrophysiology of Gland Cells (1980); *Recreations* music; *Style*— Prof Ole Petersen; ✉ MRC Secretary Control Research Group, The Physiological Laboratory, University of Liverpool, Brownlow Hill, Liverpool L69 3BX (☎ 0151 7945322, fax 0151 7945327)

PETERSEN, Richard Eli; s of Eli Ezra Petersen, and Alice Margaret, *née* Wolfe; *b* 22 Nov 1940; *Educ* Lewiston Senior HS Idaho, Univ of Idaho (BArch); *m* 28 Dec 1968, Hylda Margaretta, da of James Noel Green; 1 s (Christian James b 30 Nov 1972), 1 da (Anna Sophia b 14 Jan 1971); *Career* architect: Payne & Settecase Salem Oregon 1963–66, Borough Architect's Dept Southend-on-Sea 1966–67, Noel Tweddle & Park London 1967–68, Shavey & Schmidt Seattle 1968–69; architect and interior designer Benaroya Co Seattle 1969–71, interior designer Henry End Assoc London 1971–72, architectural assoc Tributus Design Group 1972–75, architect and interior design assoc Michael Aukett Assocs 1975–79, architect and interior design ptnr Knox Design Bremerton Washington 1979–81, interior design ptnr Aukett Assocs 1981–87, dir of design mgmnt BAA plc 1987–92, sr lectr in design mgmnt de Montfort Univ 1992–95, sr lectr in design mgmnt Surrey Inst of Art and Design 1995–; memb SID, assoc memb D&AD, FCSD, FRSA; *Recreations* golf, swimming, fitness, squash; *Clubs* RAC, Architecture; *Style*— Richard Petersen, Esq; ✉ The Garden House, Burley Orchard, Staines Lane, Chertsey, Surrey KT16 8PS (☎ 01932 560508)

PETERSHAM, Viscount; Charles Henry Leicester Stanhope; s and h of 11 Earl of Harrington, *qv*, and Eileen, *née* Grey; *b* 20 July 1945; *Educ* Eton; *m* 1, 1966 (m dis), Virginia Alleyne Freeman, da of Capt Harry Freeman Jackson (d 1993), of Cool-na-Grena, Co Cork; 1 s (Hon William b 1967), 1 da (Hon Serena (Viscountess Linley) b 1970); m 2, 1984, Anita Robsahm, formerly w of 21 Earl of Suffolk and Berkshire, and yr da of Robin Robsahm Fuglesang (d 1991), of Lacock, Wiltshire; *Career* FRGS; *Recreations* shooting, sailing (circumnavigation 1983–85 SY Surama), hunting (Master of the Limerick Hounds 1974–77 and 1990–93), carriage driving, fishing; *Clubs* House of Lords Yacht; *Style*— Viscount Petersham; ✉ Mount St John, Felixkirk, Thirsk, N Yorks YO7 2DT (☎ 01845 537205, fax 01845 537048)

PETERSON, Col Sir Christopher; kt (1994), CBE (1983), TD (1956), JP (1973), DL (1978); s of Oscar Peterson (d 1923), and Minnie Dee; *b* 22 Feb 1918; *Educ* St Illtyd's Coll Cardiff, Cardiff Tech Coll; *m* 1945, Grace Winfred, da of John McNeil (d 1940); 3 children (and 1 child decd); *Career* Capt RASC 1940–46; Shipbroker Office Cardiff Docks 1936–39; chm SWIRCO-Newton Gp 1968–79 (joined 1952 when S Wales India Rubber Co), dir Dorado Holdings plc 1979–83; chm: Wales Local Bd Commercial Union Assurance Co 1972–77, J McNeil (Cameras) 1983–92, Randall Cox (photography) 1984–92, Cox & Tarry Ltd 1984–89, Stanton-King Orgn 1985–89, Taff Ely Enterprise Partnership 1989–91, SWIRCO-Hall 1990–92; memb: Cardiff City Cncl 1968–71, S Glam CC 1973–85; TA: serv 1946–65, CO 1961–65, Hon Col 1972–77; High Sheriff S Glamorgan 1981; OStJ 1991; *Recreations* walking; *Clubs* Cardiff County, Army and Navy; *Style*— Col Sir Christopher Peterson, CBE, TD, JP, DL; ✉ 51 Rannoch Drive, Cyncoed, Cardiff CF2 6LP (☎ 01222 754062); 15 Castle Pill Crescent, Milford Haven SA73 1HD

PETHER, Dr John Victor Sebastian; s of Dr Geoffrey Charles Pether, TD (d 1972), of South Petherton, Somerset, and Margaret Joan, *née* Broderick (d 1985); *b* 13 Aug 1934; *Educ* Haileybury, ISC, Pembroke Coll Oxford (MA, BM BCh, DipBact, DTM&H); *m* 1, 12 April 1961, Anne (d 1984), da of George Boys (d 1953), of Huddersfield; 2 s (Michael b 1963, Thomas b 1969), 1 da (Suky b 1965); m 2, Sonia Jane, *née* David; *Career* house physician St Luke's Hosp Guildford 1960, pathologist Middx Hosp 1961–64 (house surgn 1960), Public Health Laboratory Serv Colindale 1965–68, dir Taunton Public Health Laboratory 1969–95; FRCPath; *Recreations* climatology, travel; *Style*— Dr John Pether; ✉ The Old School, Church Lane, Kingston St Mary, Somerset TA2 8HR (☎ 01823 451 311)

PETHICK, Jan Stephen; s of Maj Thomas Francis Henry Pethick (d 1981), of Ventnor, IOW, and Denise Joyce, *née* Clark (d 1994); *b* 16 Sept 1947; *Educ* Clifton, Jesus Coll Oxford (MA); *m* 20 Dec 1974, Belinda Patricia, da of Douglas Collins, of Hare Hatch, Reading, Berks; 1 s (Benjamin b 18 May 1981), 2 da (Emily b 26 May 1975, Nancy b 15 April 1977); *Career* stock jobber/trader Pinchin Denny & Co 1969–74, Midland Doherty Eurobond Trading 1975–77, exec dir Bonds Lehman Bros Kuhn Loeb 1977–84, md Shearson Lehman Hutton International Inc 1986–90, dir Luthy Baillie Dowsett Pethick & Co Ltd 1990–; dir Bibendum Wine Limited 1991–; tstee The Peper Harow Orgn; *Recreations* golf, tennis; *Clubs* New Zealand Golf, Vanderbilt Racquet, Queen's, Turf; *Style*— Jan Pethick, Esq; ✉ 71 Kew Green, Kew, Richmond, Surrey TW9 3AH (☎ 0181 940 2426); Luthy Baillie Pethick & Co Ltd, Fitzwilliam House, 10 St Mary Avenue, London EC3A 8BS (☎ 0171 600 1739)

PETHIG, Prof Ronald; s of Charles Edward Pethig, of Sanderstead, Surrey, and Edith Jane, *née* Jones; *b* 10 May 1942; *Educ* Purley GS, Univ of Southampton (BSc, PhD, DSc), Univ of Nottingham (PhD); *m* 10 Aug 1968, Angela Jane, da of John Stephen Sampson, of Tibshelf, Derbyshire (d 1973); 1 s (Richard John b 16 June 1971), 1 da (Helen Jane b 17 Jan 1976); *Career* ICI Fell Univ of Nottingham 1968–71, corpn memb Marine Biological Laboratory Woods Hole USA 1982–, adjunct prof of physiology Med Univ S Carolina USA 1984–90; Univ of Wales: reader 1982–86, personal chair 1986–, dir Inst of Molecular and Biomolecular Electronics 1986–, dean Faculty of Sci 1991–93; dir P & B (Sciences) Ltd 1989–; memb: SERC Molecular Electronics Ctee 1991–94, Int Evaluation Ctee of Swedish Nat Bd for Industl and Tech Devpt 1991–92, Exec Ctee Snowdonia National Park Soc 1991–94; CEng 1975, FIEE 1986; *Books* Dielectric and Electronic Properties of Biological Materials (1979); *Recreations* mountain walking, restoring old scientific instruments; *Style*— Prof Ronald Pethig; ✉ Inst of Molecular and Biomolecular Electronics, Univ of Wales at Bangor, Dean St, Bangor, Gwynedd LL57 1UT (☎ 01248 382682, fax 01248 361429)

PETHYBRIDGE, Prof Roger William; s of Arthur Pethybridge (d 1981), and Sadie Isobel, *née* Renshaw; *b* 28 March 1934; *Educ* Sedbergh, Univ of Oxford (MA), Univ of Geneva; *Career* prof and dir centre of Russian studies Univ of Wales Swansea 1974–; visiting professorships incl: Australian Nat Univ at Canberra, Chinese Acad Peking, Hungarian Acad, Univ of Otago; former memb: ESRC Politics Ctee, Nat Assoc for Soviet & E European Studies, Br Cncl Ctee for Cultural Exchange with Russia, various editorial boards; Rockefeller Fndn fell, Kennan Inst fell; *Publications incl* A Key to Soviet Politics - The Crisis of the Anti-Party Group (1962), Witnesses to the Russian Revolution (ed 1964), The Development of the Communist Bloc (ed 1965), A History of Postwar Russia (1966), The Spread of the Russian Revolution: Essays on 1917 (1972), The Social Prelude to Stalinism (1974), One Step Backwards, Two Step Forwards, Soviet Society and Politics under the New Economic Policy (1990); over 30 chapters and papers; *Clubs* Athenaeum; *Style*— Prof Roger Pethybridge; ✉ Centre of Russian Studies, University of Wales, Swansea (☎ 01792 205678)

PETIT, Sir Dinshaw Manockjee; 4 Bt (UK 1890), of Petit Hall, Island of Bombay; né Nasserwanjee Dinshaw Petit but obliged, under a trust created by Sir Dinshaw Manockjee Petit, 1 Bt, to adopt the name of the first Bt; s of Sir Dinshaw Manockjee Petit, 3 Bt (d 1983), and Sylla (d 1963); *b* 13 Aug 1934; *m* 1, 1964 (m dis 1985), Nirmala Mody (surname of stepfather assumed by Deed Poll 1964), *née* Nanavati; 2 s (Jehangir b 1965, Framjee b 1968); m 2, Elizabeth Maria Tinkelenberg; *Heir* s, Jehangir b 21 Jan 1965; *Career* pres: NM Petit Charities, Sir D M Petit Charities, F D Petit Sanatorium, Persian Zoroastrian Amelioration Fund, Petit Girls' Orphanage, D M Petit Gymnasium, JN Petit Inst, Native Gen Dispensary; tstee Soc for Prevention of Cruelty to Animals and memb Managing Ctee B D Petit Parsi Gen Hosp; *Style*— Sir Dinshaw Petit, Bt; ✉ Petit Hall, 66 Nepean Sea Rd, Bombay 400 006, India

PETO, Henry Christopher Morton Bampfylde; s and h of Sir Michael Henry Basil Peto, 4 Bt, *qv*, of Cliddesden, Basingstoke, and Sarah Susan Worthington, *née* Stucley; *b* 8 April 1967; *Educ* Eton; *Recreations* tennis, psychology, football; *Style*— Henry Peto, Esq; ✉ Court Hall, North Molton, Devon EX36 3HP (☎ 01598 740 224)

PETO, Sir Henry George Morton; 4 Bt (UK 1855); s of Cdr Sir Henry Francis Morton Peto, 3 Bt, RN (d 1978); *b* 29 April 1920; *Educ* Sherborne, CCC Cambridge; *m* 1947, Frances Jacqueline, JP, da of late Ralph Haldane Evers; 2 s; *Heir* s, Francis Michael Morton Peto; *Career* RA 1939–46; manufacturing industry 1946–80; *Style*— Sir Henry Peto, Bt; ✉ Stream House, Selborne, Alton, Hants GU34 3LE (☎ 01420 511246)

PETO, Sir Michael Henry Basil; 4 Bt (UK 1927); s of Brig Sir Christopher Henry Maxwell Peto, 3 Bt, DSO (d 1980); *b* 6 April 1938; *Educ* Eton, Ch Ch Oxford (MA); *m* 1, 1963 (m dis 1970), Sarah Susan, da of Maj Sir Dennis Stucley, 5 Bt; 1 s, 2 da; m 2, 1971, Lucinda Mary, da of Maj Sir Charles Douglas Blackett, 9 Bt; 2 s; *Heir* s, Henry Christopher Morton Bampfylde Peto b 8 April 1967; *Career* called to the Bar Inner Temple 1960, memb Stock Exchange 1965–; dir Barnett Consulting Group 1985–; *Clubs* Pratt's; *Style*— Sir Michael Peto, Bt; ✉ Kirknewton House, Wooler, Northumberland NE71 6XF

PETRE, His Hon Judge; Francis Herbert Loraine; s of late Maj-Gen R L Petre, CB, DSO, MC, and Katherine Petre; *b* 9 March 1927; *Educ* Downside, Clare Coll Cambridge; *m* 1958, Mary Jane, da of Everard Charles Xavier White, and Sydney Mary Carlton, *née* Holmes, of Masterton, NZ; 3 s, 1 da; *Career* called to the Bar Lincoln's Inn 1952, dep chm E Suffolk QS 1970, dep chm Agric Lands Tbnl (Eastern area) 1972, circuit judge (SE Circuit) 1972–, regular judge central criminal court 1982–92; chm Police Complaints Authy 1989–92; *Style*— His Hon Judge Petre; ✉ The Ferriers, Bures, Suffolk CO8 5DL

(☎ 01787 227254); Chelmsford Crown Court, PO Box 9, New Street, Chelmsford CM1 1EL

PETRE, 18 Baron (E 1603); John Patrick Lionel Petre; DL (Essex 1991); o s of 17 Baron Petre (d 1989), and Marguerite Eileen, *née* Hamilton; *b* 4 Aug 1942; *Educ* Eton, Trinity Coll Oxford (MA); *m* 16 Sept 1965, Marcia Gwendolyn, o da of Alfred Plumpton, of Portsmouth; 2 s (Hon Dominic William, Hon Mark Julian b 1969), 1 da (Hon Clare Helen b 1973); *Heir* s, Hon Dominic William Petre b 9 Aug 1966; *Career* pres Essex St John Ambulance 1992–; *Style*— The Rt Hon the Lord Petre, DL; ✉ Writtle Park, Highwood, Chelmsford, Essex

PETRIE, Charles James; s and h of Sir Peter Petrie, 5 Bt, CMG; *b* 16 Sept 1959; *Educ* American Coll Paris (BA), INSEAD Fontainebleau (MBA); *m* 1981, France, yr da of Comte Bernard de Hauteclocque, of Château d'Etrejust, Picardie; 3 s (Arthur Cecil b 15 Feb 1987, Oliver Bernard b 12 July 1989, Victor Francis b 14 Aug 1992), 1 da (Cecilia Marie Bernard b and d 1985); *Career* 2 Lt 67 French Inf Regt; sr conslt Coopers & Lybrand, mgmnt conslt assignments in French W Africa, Liberia and Sudan 1987–90; chief of UN Emergency Unit Sudan 1991–92, sr humanitarian advsr UNOSOM Somalia 1992–94, dep UN humanitarian co-ordinator Rwanda 1994–95, chief of E & Central Africa Unit, Complex Emergency Division, UN Dept of Humanitarian Affairs, New York 1995–96, special asst to Cmmr Gen of UNRWA Gaza Strip; *Style*— Charles Petrie, Esq; ✉ c/o Sir Peter Petrie, Bt, CMG, 16a Cambridge Street, London SW1V 4QH

PETRIE, Prof James Colquhoun; CBE (1996); s of Dr James Beattie Petrie (d 1966), and Dr Cairine Ross Petrie; *b* 18 Sept 1941; *Educ* Robert Gordon's Coll Aberdeen, Univ of Aberdeen (MB ChB); *m* 16 July 1964, Dr (Margaret) Xanthe Patricia, da of Col Sir John Stewart Forbes, 6 Bt, DSO (d 1984); 2 s (Dr John Ross Petrie b 1965, Dr Mark Colquhoun Petrie b 1969), 2 da (Dr Rachel Xanthe Ann Petrie b 1967, Dr Paula Jane Petrie b 1970); *Career* hon conslt physician Aberdeen Teaching Hosps 1971–, prof of clinical pharmacology Univ of Aberdeen 1985– (head Dept of Med and Therapeutics 1994–); memb Ctee on the Safety of Meds Meds Control Agency; chm Lecht Ski Co; FRCP, FRCPE (assessor Cncl), FRCPI, FFPM; *Books* The Problem Orientated Medical Record (with N McIntyre, 1979), Clinically Important Adverse Drug Interactions vol 1–3 (1985), Textbook of Medical Treatment (ed with R H Girwood, 1988); *Recreations* ski, golf, fishing; *Clubs* Royal Aberdeen Golf; *Style*— Prof James Petrie, CBE; ✉ Department of Medicine and Therapeutics, University of Aberdeen, Polwarth Building, Fosterhill, Aberdeen AB2 4DQ (☎ 01224 681818, fax 01224 699884)

PETRIE, Sir Peter Charles; CMG (1980); 5 Bt (UK 1918); s of Sir Charles Petrie, 3 Bt (d 1977), and of Cecilia, Lady Petrie (d 1987); suc his half-bro, Sir Richard Petrie, 4 Bt 1988; *b* 7 March 1932; *Educ* Westminster, Ch Ch Oxford (MA); *m* 1958, Countess Lydwine Maria Fortunata, da of Count Charles Alphonse von Oberndorff, of The Hague and Paris; 2 s, 1 da; *Heir* s, Charles James Petrie b 16 Sept 1959; *Career* 2 sec UK Delegation NATO Paris 1958–61, 1 sec New Delhi 1961–64, chargé d'affaires Katmandu 1963, Cabinet Office 1965–67, UK Mission to UN (NY) 1969–73, cnsllr (head of Chancery) Bonn 1973–76, head of Euro Integration Dept (Int) FCO 1976–79, min Paris 1979–85; ambass to Belgium 1985–89; advsr to govr Bank of England on Euro and Parly affairs 1989–; memb: Franco-British Cncl 1995–, Institut de l'Euro Lyon Conseil d'Administration 1995–; corresponding memb Académie de Comptabilité Paris 1996–; *Clubs* Brooks's, Beefsteak, Jockey (Paris); *Style*— Sir Peter Petrie, Bt, CMG; ✉ 16A Cambridge St, London SW1V 4QH; Bank of England, Threadneedle Street, London EC2R 8AH (☎ 0171 601 5221)

PETTERSSON, Dr Rosemary Winifred; da of Arthur Reginald Atkinson (d 1980), and Marjorie Edith Sarah, *née* Orchard (d 1985); *b* 23 May 1939; *Educ* St Joseph's Convent Wanstead, Wanstead Co HS, Royal Free Hosp Univ of London (MB BS, LRCP, MRCS); *m* 9 May 1964, Dr Michael Jollius Pettersson, s of Dr Max Leopold Robert Pettersson (d 1995), of Whitstable, Kent; 2 da (Hannah b 1 Dec 1966, Elizabeth b 20 July 1968); *Career* conslt physician in med for the elderly; memb Hosp and Health Bd Ctees; memb Soc of Med and Dental Hypnosis; *Recreations* reading, walking, cooking, gardening, cats; *Style*— Dr Rosemary Pettersson; ✉ Greenrig, Hawksland, Lesmahagow, Lanark ML11 9QB (☎ 01555 664866); Department of Medicine for the Elderly, Law Hospital, Carluke, Lanarkshire ML8 5ER (☎ 01698 361100)

PETTIFER, Brian Warren Bowers; s of Fred Tyler Pettifer (d 1965), of Alfryn House, Grimsby, S Humberside, and Chrystine, *née* Thompson; *b* 10 Oct 1935; *Educ* Oundle; *m* 2 Oct 1965, Veronica Mary, da of Dr Georg Tugendhat (d 1973), of Greensted Hall, Greensted, Ongar, Essex; 3 s (Crispin b 1967, Adam b 1969, Daniel b 1970), 1 da (Teresa b 1974); *Career* served HAC 1963–66; admitted slr 1963; in own practice 1966–92, ptnr Rollit Farrell & Bladon 1992–; underwriter Lloyd's 1977–; pt/t lectr Univ of Hull 1994–; cncllr: Lindsey CC 1970–74, Humberside CC 1974–77; chief whip Cons Pty and shadow chm for planning 1974–77; chm: Humberside Youth Assoc 1974–75, Barton on Humber Youth Centre Mgmnt Ctee 1974–88, Humberside Euro Cons Cncl 1983–86; capt Law Soc Golf Club 1985–86, hon steward Wimbledon Tennis tournament 1989–; Liveryman Worshipful Co of Makers of Playing Cards 1991–; NP, FCIArb; *Recreations* skiing, golf, tennis; *Clubs* Oriental, Ski Club of GB, Kandahar Ski; *Style*— Brian Pettifer, Esq; ✉ Cob Hall, Priestgate, Barton-on-Humber, N Lincolnshire DN18 5ET (☎ 01652 632248, fax 01652 660077); Rollit Farrell & Bladon, Wilberforce Court, High Street, Hull HU1 1YJ (☎ and fax 01482 323239)

PETTIFER, Julian; s of Stephen Henry Pettifer (d 1980), of Malmesbury, Wilts, and Diana Mary, *née* Burton; *b* 21 July 1935; *Educ* Marlborough, St John's Coll Cambridge (BA); *Career* television broadcaster and author; Nat Serv 1953–55, basic trg with Rifle Bde, cmmnd Northamptonshire Regt, served as 2 Lt in Korea and Hong Kong; TV series incl: BBC Tonight, Panorama, 24 Hours, Diamonds in the Sky, The Living Isles, Missionaries, Nature, Biteback, Assignment, British Steel Challenge, ITV's Nature Watch, Automania; awarded BAFTA Reporter of the Year 1968–69, Royal Geographical Soc Cherry Kearton Award for Wildlife Films 1990; pres: BBONT, RSPB; vice pres Royal Soc for Nature Conservation, tstee Royal Botanic Gardens Kew; *Books* Diamonds in the Sky (with Kenneth Hudson, 1979), Automania (with Nigel Turner, 1984), Nature Watch (with Robin Brown, 1981), The Nature Watchers (with Robin Brown, 1985), Missionaries (with Richard Bradley, 1990), Nature Watch (with Robin Brown, 1994); *Recreations* music, theatre, tennis, gardening, books; *Clubs* Queen's; *Style*— Julian Pettifer, Esq; ✉ c/o Curtis Brown, 28/29 Haymarket, London SW1Y 4SP

PETTINGELL, (Peter) John Partington; s of Hubert Edmund Pettingell (d 1980), and Avril Leah Nancy Pettingell (d 1985); *b* 28 Jan 1934; *Educ* Leeds GS, London Univ (BD); *m* 31 July 1965, Phyllis Margaret, da of Charles Chamberlain (d 1983); 1 s (John Stephen Edmund b 3 Jan 1973), 2 da (Julie Margaret b 5 Oct 1966, Susan Jane b 2 April 1968); *Career* Nat Serv RAF 1956–58; audit mangr WL Gallant & Co 1958–60, audit supervisor Price Waterhouse 1960–63, chief accountant GLC London 1963–65, sr lectr SW London Coll 1973–77, princ lectr Hong Kong Poly 1977–80, sr lectr Dorset Inst of Higher Educn 1980–86, princ Partington Pettingell & Co 1983–; min Stockwell Baptist Church 1973–77; Lord of the Manor of Donhead Wilts; FCA 1956; *Books* Then the Spirit Came (1975), Jesus is Coming (1974); *Recreations* sailing, badminton, tennis; *Style*— John Pettingell, Esq; ✉ 41A Southern Rd, Bournemouth, Dorset (☎ 01202 431 406)

PETTIT, Sir Daniel Eric Arthur; kt (1974); s of Thomas Edgar Pettit (d 1940), of Liverpool, and Pauline Elizabeth, *née* Kerr (d 1957); *b* 19 Feb 1915; *Educ* Quarry Bank HS Liverpool, Fitzwilliam Coll Cambridge (MA); *m* 1940, Winifred, da of William Standing Bibby, of Liverpool (d 1951); 2 s (Richard, Michael); *Career* Mil Serv 1940–46, Maj RA; serv: UK, Africa, India, Burma; TA Hon Col (movement); UK team Olympic Games 1936; sch master 1938–39 and 1946–47; Unilever MGT 1948–59; chm: SPD Ltd (Unilever) 1960–70, Nat Freight Corp 1970–78; dir: Bransford Farmers Ltd 1973–, Bransford Leisure Pursuits Ltd 1973–, Lloyds Bank Ltd 1977–78; chm Birmingham and W Midlands Lloyds Bank Ltd 1978–85, dir Lloyds Bank (UK) Ltd 1979–85, chm Post Office Staff Superannuation Fund 1979–83; pres and chm Incpen 1979–90, chm PosTel Investment Ltd 1982–83; dir: Black Horse Ltd 1984–85, Lloyds Bank Unit Tst 1984–85; chm RDC Properties Ltd 1987–; memb: Nat Ports Cncl 1971–80, Freight Integration Cncl 1971–78, Fndn of Mgmnt Educn 1973–78; chm Econ Devpt Ctee for Distributive Trades 1974–78, pres Chartered Inst of Tport 1972, vice pres and fell Inst of Packaging; Freeman City of London 1971, Liveryman Worshipful Co of Carmen 1971; hon fell Fitzwilliam Coll Cambridge 1985; CIMgt, FCIT, FIM, FRSA, FIP, MIPM; *Recreations* watching cricket and football, fishing, country pursuits; *Clubs* Hawks' (Cambridge), MCC, Farmers'; *Style*— Sir Daniel Pettit; ✉ Bransford Court Farm, Worcester WR6 5JL (☎ 01905 830098)

PETTIT, Rosemary; da of G H N Pettit, and Ruby, *née* Garner; *b* 22 May 1944; *Educ* Bury St Edmunds GS, Bedford Coll London (BSc); *Career* copy ed Penguin Books 1971–73, researcher LWT 1973–74, section ed Marshall Cavendish 1974–75; sec: Ind Publishers' Guild 1979–89, Book Packagers' Assoc 1985–, Directory Publishers' Assoc (also dir) 1989–; jt ed Traditional Acupuncture Journal 1982–90, jt ed Clarion (jl of Gladstone Club) 1982–86, proprietor Blenheim Books 1992–; dir Paddington Industrial Association Ltd 1984–86, memb Mgmnt Ctee Paddington Law Centre 1984–86, traditional crafts organiser Art in Action 1984–89, memb Publishing Assessment Section Nat Cncl for Vol Qualifications 1989, memb Books-across-the-Sea Ctee ESU 1989–, memb Cncl Advtg Standards Bd of Fin 1991–, memb PPA Parly and Legal Consultative Gp 1994–; memb Liberal Party 1979, Westminster N Lib Democrat Assoc (sec, membership sec, vice-chm, chm) 1979–90; Social and Liberal Democrat candidate for By Election 1989 (Cncl elections 1982), chm Kensington Liberal Democrat Assoc 1993–95; *Books* The Craft Business (1975), Occupation Self Employed (2 edn, 1981); *Style*— Ms Rosemary Pettit; ✉ 93A Blenheim Crescent, London W11 2EQ (☎ 0171 221 9089)

PETTMAN, Prof Barrie Owen; s of Matthew Mark Pettman (d 1967), and Ivy, *née* Warcup; *b* 22 Feb 1944; *Educ* Hull GS, Hull Tech Coll (BSc), City Univ Business Sch (MSc, PhD), International Mgmnt Centres (DLitt); *m* 1, 1970 (m dis 1986), Heather Richardson; m 2, 1987, Norma (d 1991); m 3, 1992, Maureen, da of George Crowther (d 1944); *Career* lectr Dept of Social Admin Univ of Hull 1970–82, dir Manpower Unit Univ of Rhodesia 1978–79, registrar Int Mgmnt Centres 1983–; dir: MCB Univ Press 1970–, Int Inst of Social Econ 1972–; ed: International Journal of Social Economics 1973–79, International Journal of Manpower 1980–84, Management Research News 1981–, Equal Opportunities International 1981– (asst ed 1982–), International Journal of Manpower 1980–84, International Journal of Sociology & Social Policy 1984–, International Journal of New Ideas 1992–; jt ed Managerial Law 1975–; asst ed: Employee Relations 1978–82, Archives of Economic History 1983–; visiting prof Canadian Sch of Mgmnt 1983–, hon vice pres Br Soc of Commerce 1975–; chm: Inst of Sci Business 1972–79, Inst of Trg and Devpt Humberside Branch 1990–; memb: Manpower Soc 1977–91, Int Inst of Social Econs; FCI, FRGS, FRSA, FIManf, FIMS, FIPD, FIMgt, MIAM; *Books* Training and Retraining (1973), Labour Turnover and Retention (1975), Equal Pay (1975), Manpower Planning Workbook (1976, 1984), Industrial Democracy (1984), Discrimination in the Labour Market (1980), Management: A Selected Bibliography (1983); *Recreations* golf, shooting; *Clubs* The Reform; *Style*— Prof Barrie Pettman; ✉ Enholmes Hall, Patrington, Hull HU12 0PR (☎ 01964 630033); MCB University Press, 62 Toller Lane, Bradford, W Yorkshire BD8 9BY (☎ 01274 777700, fax 01274 785200, car 0860 813688)

PETTY, Very Rev John Fitzmaurice; s of Dr Gerald Fitzmaurice Petty, TD, MRCS, LRCP, FRCGP (d 1986), and Edith Stuart, *née* Knox (d 1977); *b* 9 March 1935; *Educ* King's Sch Bruton, RMA Sandhurst, Trinity Hall Cambridge (MA), Cuddesdon Theol Coll Oxford; *m* 10 Aug 1963, Susan, da of Sir Geoffrey Peter Shakerley (d 1982); 3 s (Simon b 1967, Mark b 1969, Jeremy b 1972), 1 da (Rachel b 1965); *Career* cmmnd RE 1955, seconded Gurkha Engrs Malaya/Borneo 1959–62, resigned cmmn as Capt 1964; ordained Sheffield Cathedral: deacon 1966, priest 1967; curate St Cuthbert's Fir Vale Sheffield 1966–69, priest i/c Bishop Andrewes' Church Southwark 1969–75, area dean Ashton-under-Lyne 1983–87, vicar St John's Hurst Ashton-under-Lyne 1975–87, hon canon Manchester Cathedral 1986, provost of Coventry 1988–; hon chaplain RAPC (Offrs Accounts) Ashton-under-Lyne 1977–87; memb Ctee St Helier Artificial Kidney Fund (SHAK) 1967–69, chm Tameside Aids and Services for the Handicapped (TASH) 1981–87; co-ordinator: Home for Homeless Girls Tameside 1977–87, Ambulance for the Elderly 1976–87, Holidays for Belfast Families 1977–86; Hon DLitt Coventry Univ 1996; *Recreations* cycling, skiing; *Style*— The Very Rev the Provost of Coventry; ✉ Provost's House, Priory Row, Coventry CV1 5ES (☎ 01203 221835); Coventry Cathedral, 7 Priory Row, Coventry CV1 5ES (☎ 01203 227597, fax 01203 631448)

PEYTON, Kathleen Wendy; da of William Joseph Herald, and Ivy Kathleen, *née* Weston; *b* 2 Aug 1929; *Educ* Wimbledon HS, Manchester Sch of Art (ATD, Carnegie medal, Guardian award); *m* Sept 1950, Michael Peyton; 2 da (Hilary b 1956, Veronica b 1958); *Career* author; art teacher Northampton HS 1953–55; memb Soc of Authors; *Publications incl* as Kathleen Herald: Sabre the Horse from the Sea (1947), The Mandrake (1949), Crab the Roan (1953); as K M Peyton: Flambards (Guardian award, 1967), The Edge of the Cloud (Carnegie medal, 1969), Flambards in Summer (1969), Pennington's Seventeenth Summer (1970), A Pattern of Roses (1972), Prove Yourself a Hero (1977), A Midsummer Night's Death (1978), Flambards Divided (1981), Dear Fred (1981), Who, Sir? Me, Sir? (1983), The Sound of Distant Cheering (1985), Darkling (1989), No Roses Round the Door (1990), Poor Badger (1990), Late to Smile (1992), The Wild Boy and Queen Moon (1993), Snowfall (1994); *Recreations* riding, walking, gardening, sailing; *Style*— Mrs Kathleen Peyton; ✉ Rookery Cottage, North Fambridge, Chelmsford, Essex CM3 6LP (☎ 01621 828 545)

PEYTON-JONES, Julia; da of Jeremy Norman Peyton-Jones (d 1985), and Rhona Gertrude Jean, *née* Wood; *b* 18 Feb 1952; *Educ* Byam Shaw Sch of Drawing and Painting (dip, LCAD Distinct), RCA (MA, John Minton travelling scholar); *m* 1975 (m dis 1985), Prosper Riley-Smith; *Career* fndr cataloguer 20 Century Pictures Dept Phillips Auctioneers London 1974–75, lectr in painting and humanities Edinburgh Sch of Art 1978–79, curator Atlantis Gallery 1980–81, exhibition organiser Wapping Artists Open Studios Exhibition 1981–82, exhibition organiser Tolly Cobbold Eastern Arts 4th Nat Exhibition 1982–84, exhibition organiser Raoul Dufy 1877–1953 (Hayward Gallery) 1983–84, exhibitions sponsorship offr Arts Cncl and S Bank Bd 1984–87, exhibition organiser Linbury Prize for Stage Design 1986–87; curator Hayward Gallery 1988–91 (exhibitions incl: Leonardo da Vinci - Artist Scientist Inventor 1989, Andy Warhol - A Retrospective 1989, The Drawings of Jasper Johns 1990, Garry Winogrand - Figments of the Real World 1990, (Henri de) Toulouse-Lautrec 1991); dir Serpentine Gallery 1991– (exhibitions incl: Broken English, Objects for the Ideal Home, Four Rooms, Gordon Matta-Clark, Robert Gober, Agnes Martin, Rebecca Horn, Man Ray); tstee: PADT 1987–88, Chisenhale Tst 1987–89, New Contemporaries 1988–90; memb: Exec Ctee Linbury Prize for Stage Design 1988–95, Visual Arts Projects Ctee Arts Cncl 1991–94, Visual Arts and Photography Panel Arts Cncl 1994–95, Film and Television Panel Arts Cncl 1996–; purchaser Arts Cncl Collection 1989–90; *Recreations* opera, theatre, dance, cinema; *Style—* Ms Julia Peyton-Jones; ✉ Serpentine Gallery, Kensington Gardens, London W2 3XA (☎ 0171 402 6075, fax 0171 402 4103)

PEYTON OF YEOVIL, Baron (Life Peer UK 1983), of Yeovil, Co Somerset; John Wynne William Peyton; PC (1970); s of Ivor Eliot Peyton (d 1938), of Englemere Wood, Ascot, and Dorothy Helen, *née* Elphinstone (d 1977); *b* 13 Feb 1919; *Educ* Eton, Trinity Coll Oxford (MA); *m* 1, Dec 1947 (m dis 1966), Diana, da of Douglas Clinch, of Durban, S Africa; 1 s (Hon Thomas (Tom) Richard Douglas b 1950), 1 da (Hon Sarah Grenville (Hon Mrs Chester) b 1948), and 1 s decd; m 2, 27 July 1966, Mary Constance, only da of Col Hon Humphrey Wyndham, MC (6 s of 2 Baron Leconfield), and former w of Ralph Hamilton Cobbold; *Career* served 15/19 Hussars WWII (POW 1940–45); called to the Bar Inner Temple 1945; MP (C) Yeovil 1951–83, Parly sec Miny of Power 1962–64, min of Transport 1970, min for Transport Industries DOE 1970–74, chm Texas Instruments Ltd 1974–90; dir: British Alcan Aluminium plc 1974 (chm 1987–91), Alcan Aluminium Ltd 1985–91; treas Zoological Soc of London 1984–91, chm Zoo Operations Ltd 1988–91; pres Devon Guild of Craftsmen 1988–; *Clubs* Boodle's, Pratt's, Beefsteak; *Style—* The Rt Hon the Lord Peyton of Yeovil, PC; ✉ The Old Malt House, Hinton St George, Somerset TA17 8SE (☎ 01460 73618); 6 Temple West Mews, West Square, London SE11 4TJ (☎ 0171 582 3611)

PFEFFER, Dr Jeremy Michael; s of Maurice Leslie Pfeffer, of Manchester, and Hannah, *née* Posen; *b* 23 Sept 1946; *Educ* Manchester GS, UCH London (MB BS, BSc); *m* 5 Sept 1972, Vivian Barbara, da of Dr Eric Norman, of Liverpool; 2 s (James b 1978, Paul b 1979), 1 da (Kate b 1992); *Career* house surgn Professorial Surgical Unit UCH London 1972, house physician Newmarket Gen Hosp 1972–73, sr house offr and registrar chest med Papworth Hosp Cambridge 1973–74, sr house offr psychiatry Fulbourn Hosp Cambridge 1974–75, sr house offr and registrar psychiatry Bethlem Royal and Maudsley Hosp 1975–78, sr registrar psychiatry The London and Bethlem Royal and Maudsley Hosps 1978–80; conslt psychiatrist: The Royal London Hosp 1980–96, Royal Brompton Hosp 1994–; former hon sr lectr London Hosp Med Coll, sr lectr Nat Heart and Lung Inst Imperial Coll of Sci, Technology and Med 1996–; former examiner RCPsych, variously offr and memb psychiatric ctees at local regnl and nat level; memb RSM, FRCPsych 1988 (MRCPsych 1977), FRCP 1990 (MRCP 1974); *Books* Medicine and Psychiatry: A Practical Approach (ed with Francis Creed, 1982), Psychiatric Differential Diagnosis (with Gillian Waldron, 1987); *Recreations* music, reading, food, football; *Style—* Dr Jeremy M Pfeffer; ✉ 97 Harley Street, London W1N 1DF (☎ 0171 935 3878)

PFIRTER, HE Rogelio; *b* 25 July 1948, Santa Fé, Argentina; *Educ* Colegio Inmaculada Conepción SJ, Universidad Nacional del Litoral (law), Inst of the Foreign Serv (graduate); *m*; *Career* Argentine diplomat; Miny of Foreign Affrs: third sec Brazil Desk S America Dept 1974, second then first sec Perm Mission to the UN 1975–80, first sec Undersecretariat of Foreign Affrs 1980–81, cnsllr London 1982, cnsllr Perm Mission to the UN 1982–90 (alternate perm rep to the UN 1989), min plenipotentiary and dep head Foreign Min's Cabinet 1990–91, dir of int security, nuclear and space affrs 1991–92, under sec of foreign policy 1992–93, memb Posting and Promotion Bd 1993–95, ambass to the Ct of St James's 1995–, perm rep to IMO 1995–; memb: UN Advsy Bd on Disarmament Matters 1993–96, Bd of Dirs Nat Cmmn of Space Activities 1994–95; head Argentine Delgn: to various bilateral negotiations with UK 1992–94, to Conf on Amendments to the treaty of Tlatelolco and the VII Extraordinary Meeting of the Gen Conf of OPANAL 1992 and 1994; dir Argentine-Brazilian Agency for Accounting and Control of Nuclear Materials 1992–95, pres 19 Gen Assembly Int Maritime Orgn 1994–96; Order of Merit Cavalieri di Gran Croce (Italy) 1992, Order of Merit (Chile) 1992, Order of Isabel la Cátolica (Spain) 1994; *Style—* HE Mr Rogelio Pfirter; ✉ Embassy of the Argentine Republic, 53 Hans Place, London SW1X 0LA (☎ 0171 584 6494, fax 0171 589 3106)

PFLEGER, Martin Charles; *b* 5 May 1948; *m* 1995, Amanda Jane Dolphin; 2 s (David b 6 June 1967, Matthew b 21 Feb 1972) and 1 da (Alison b 22 Feb 1974) from previous m; *Career* National Audit Office: joined 1967, private sec to Sir Douglas Henley 1979–80, trg mangr 1980–83, assoc dir Audit DOE 1985–86 (audit mangr 1983–85), dir IT Audit 1986–88, dir Corp Policy and Fin 1988–93, asst auditor general and princ estab and fin offr 1993–; visiting fell Nottingham Trent Univ; CIPFA; *Recreations* golf, hill walking, bridge; *Clubs* IOD; *Style—* Martin Pfleger, Esq; ✉ National Audit Office, 157–197 Buckingham Palace Road, Victoria, London SW1W 9SP (☎ 0171 798 7314, fax 0171 931 8303)

PHAIR, Michael Keith; s of George Carlton Phair, of Ontario, Canada, and Mary Lucille, *née* Munro; *b* 24 June 1950; *Educ* Univ of Western Ontario (BA), Graduate Sch of Business Univ of Western Ontario (MBA); *m* 21 July 1973, Margaret Noreen (Margot), da of Charles Alexander Joseph Rogers, of Buenos Aires; 1 s (Nicholas b 20 Aug 1982), 1 da (Stephanie b 16 Aug 1978); *Career* sr rep Mexico Toronto Dominion Bank 1975–79, pres Banque Anval S A 1979–84, sr investmts offr Capital Mkts Dept International Finance Corp Washington DC 1984–87, exec dir N M Rothschild & Son Ltd 1988–96, md UBS Ltd 1996–; *Recreations* skiing, tennis, sailing; *Clubs* Hurlingham; *Style—* Michael K Phair, Esq

PHAM, Prof Duc-Truong; s of Van-Xam Pham, of Ho Chi Minh City, Vietnam and ThiNinh, *née* Vu; *b* 16 Feb 1952; *Educ* Univ of Canterbury NZ (BEng, PhD, DEng); *m* 19 May 1979, Paulette Thi Nga, da of Pierre Laforet, of Lyon, France; 1 da (Kim-Anh b 1982); *Career* lectr Univ of Birmingham 1979–88, prof of engrg Univ of Wales 1988–; CEng, FIEE; *Books* Robot Grippers (ed with WB Heginbotham, 1986), Expert Systems in Engineering (ed, 1988), Artificial Intelligence in Design (ed, 1990), Neural Networks for Identification, Prediction and Control (with X Liu, 1995), Intelligent Quality Systems (with E Oztenmel, 1996); *Style—* Prof Duc-Truong Pham; ✉ School of Engineering, University of Wales, PO Box 917, Cardiff CF2 1XH (☎ and fax 01222 874429)

PHARAOH, Paul Grenville; s of late Morton Grenville Pharaoh, of Salt, Staffs, and Kathleen Jean, *née* Bishop; *b* 16 April 1947; *Educ* Chesterfield GS, Bishop Vesey's GS, Univ of Manchester (LLB), Liverpool Coll of Commerce; *m* 27 Oct 1969, Lynn Margaret, da of Alan Edward Francis; 1 da (Claire Rachael b 9 Oct 1973), 1 s (Richard Paul b 13 Jan 1976); *Career* admitted slr 1971; ptnr Bettinsons 1973–90 (asst slr 1971–73); Shakespeares: ptnr 1990–96, memb Mgmnt Bd 1990–93, head of practice devpt 1990–93, head of Commercial Dept and Quality Team 1992–96; ptnr Educn Dept Martineau Johnson 1996–; Law Society: memb Cncl 1990–, chm Entry Casework Ctee 1992–94, vice-chm Trg Ctee 1992–94, chm Legal Practice Course Bd 1993–95, memb Strategy Ctee 1993–96, chm Conf Ctee 1994–95, chm Adjudication & Appeals Ctee 1995–96, chm Compliance & Supervision Ctee 1996–; Birmingham Law Soc: chm Young Slrs' Gp 1978–82, memb Cncl 1981–, jt hon sec 1983–88; hon sec W Midland Assoc of Law Socs 1988–90; hon sec Birmingham Settlement 1986–90 (hon treas 1973–86), memb Ct Univ of Birmingham 1980–90, memb Cncl Birmingham Medico-Legal Soc 1989–91, chm Advsy Ctee Ind Inquiry into W Mids Police Serious Crime Squad 1989–91, memb Competences in Undergraduate Law Courses Advsy Ctee CNAA 1990–93, memb Membership Ctee City 2000 1992–94, memb Lottery Working Gp Birmingham Repertory Theatre 1996–; author of various articles in legal jls; memb Law Soc 1971; FRSA; *Recreations* theatre, reading, hill walking, tennis; *Style—* Paul Pharaoh, Esq; ✉ 45 Pilkington Avenue, Sutton Coldfield, West Midlands B72 1LA (☎ and fax 0121 354 4099); Martineau Johnson, St Philip's House, St Philip's Place, Birmingham B3 2PP (☎ 0121 200 3300, fax 0121 200 2667, mobile 0468 796203, e-mail Education@martjohn.com)

PHARO-TOMLIN, Col John Axel; s of Axel Christian Pharo-Tomlin (d 1965), of Dane Court, St Peter's-in-Thanet, Kent, and Edith Madelaine Quayle, *née* Tomlin (d 1974); *b* 8 April 1934; *Educ* Radley, RMA Sandhurst; *m* 19 Dec 1964, Joanna Marguerite Kate (d 1991), da of Lt-Col John Boileau Pemberton (d 1974), of Coaxdon Hall, Axminster, Devon; 1 s (Edward b 1968), 2 da (Sally b 1965, Alice b 1975); *Career* cmmnd 14/20 King's Hussars 1954, Adj 1961, instr RMA Sandhurst 1963, RNSC 1966, Sqdn Ldr 14/20 King's Hussars 1967, GSO 2 Singapore Dist 1968, Second-in-Cmd Duke of Lancaster's Own Yeo 1971, Bde Major 11 Armoured Bde 1972, GSO 1 Operational Requirements MOD 1975, CO 14/20 King's Hussars 1977 (despatches 1979), Col AG 16/17/18 MOD 1980, Col M1 (A) MOD 1984, ret 1986; mangr Banque Paribas London 1986–92; memb Mole Valley DC 1992–; Freeman City of London 1987; FIMgt 1984; *Recreations* country pursuits, music; *Clubs* Cavalry and Guards'; *Style—* Col John Pharo-Tomlin; ✉ Peverel, Leigh, nr Reigate, Surrey RH2 8NX (☎ and fax 01306 611247)

PHAROAH, Prof Peter Oswald Derrick; s of Oswald Higgins Pharoah (d 1941), and Phylis Christine, *née* Gahan (d 1991); *b* 19 May 1934; *Educ* Lawrence Meml Royal Mil Sch Lovedale India, Palmer's Sch Grays Essex, Univ of London (MD, MSc); *m* 17 May 1960, Margaret Rose, da of James McMinn (d 1978); 3 s (Paul b 1962, Mark b 1966, Timothy b 1975), 1 da (Fiona b 1961); *Career* med offr Dept of Public Health Papua New Guinea 1963–74, sr lectr London Sch of Hygiene and Tropical Med 1974–79, prof of public health Univ of Liverpool 1979–; FFPHM 1980; *Recreations* philately, squash, walking; *Style—* Prof Peter Pharoah; ✉ 11 Fawley Road, Liverpool L18 9TE (☎ 0151 724 4896); Department of Public Health, University of Liverpool, Liverpool L69 3BX (☎ 0151 794 5577)

PHEASANT, Victor Albert; MBE (1983); s of Albert George Pheasant (d 1976), of Bexleyheath, Kent, and Margaret, *née* Williams; *b* 2 July 1940; *Educ* Erith Tech Sch; *m* 21 Oct 1961, Susan Mary, da of Arthur Waldron Slade, of Rothwell, Northamptonshire; 2 s (Andrew Victor b 1962, Richard Michael b 1965); *Career* RAF 1960–84: air crew Strike Cmd 1960–80, RAF Central Tactics and Trials Orgn CTTO 1980–84, ret as Sqdn Ldr; dir countermeasure progs Chemring Group plc 1985–; dir: Pains-Wessex Ltd 1992–, Chemring Ltd 1992–, Alloy Surfaces Inc 1992–; *Recreations* carpentry; *Clubs* RAF; *Style—* Victor A Pheasant, Esq, MBE; ✉ Heathcote, Purbrook Heath, Waterlooville, Hants PO7 5RX (☎ 01705 263249); Chemring Group plc, 1480 Parkway, Whiteley, Fareham, Hants PO15 7AF (☎ 01489 881880, fax 01489 881123)

PHELAN, His Hon Andrew James; s of Cornelius Phelan, of Clonmel, Ireland; *b* 25 July 1923; *Educ* Clongowes Wood Co Kildare, Nat Univ of Ireland, Trinity Coll Cambridge; *m* 1950, Joan Robertson, OBE (1996), da of John McLagan (d 1978), of Callender, Perthshire; 1 s, 2 da; *Career* called to the Bar: (Ireland) King's Inn 1945, Gray's Inn 1949; jr fell Univ of Bristol 1948–50, circuit judge (SE Circuit) 1974–95; *Recreations* skiing, sailing (yacht 'Sarakiniko'); *Clubs* Royal Cruising, Bar Yacht; *Style—* His Hon Andrew James Phelan; ✉ 17 Hartington Rd, Chiswick, London W4 3TL (☎ and fax 0181 994 6109)

PHELAN, Dr Martin Kennedy; s of John Lazarian Phelan (d 1986), of Ballymullen, Abbeyleix, Ireland, and Mary Prisca, *née* Kennedy (d 1964); *b* 24 Oct 1938; *Educ* Finchley Catholic GS, UCH London (BDS, LDSRCS, DOrth, FDSRCS, capt and colours for football), Clare Coll and Addenbrookes Hosp Cambridge (LMSSA, MB BChir), London Coll of Osteopathic Med (MLCOM); *m* 10 June 1967, Almut Brigitte, da of Johannes Karl Wünsche; 3 s (Sean b 22 May 1968, Timothy b 11 Nov 1970, Patrick b 24 July 1976), 2 da (Marianne b 8 Sept 1969, Annette b 13 Jan 1981); *Career* various hosp jobs London and Univ of Cambridge, asst surgn Queen Elizabeth II Hosp Welwyn Garden City 1970, orthopedic physician UCH and Middlesex Hosp 1988–90; formerly: orthopedic physician Royal London Homeopathic Hosp, tutor London College of Osteopathic Medicine; currently private practitioner in orthopaedic, osteopathic and sports medicine Harley St, med offr Newmarket Race Course, lectr in psychosomatic med and history of med; sr memb list Clare Coll Cambridge, sec then vice pres Anglo American Med Soc; FRSM; Freeman City of London 1979, Yeoman then Liveryman Worshipful Soc of Apothecaries 1984; memb: BMA, Ctee Byron Soc, Euro Atlantic Gp, Inst of Agric Med, Br Assoc of Manipulative Med, Br Osteopathic Assoc, Cambridge Med Soc, Cambridge Philosophical Soc, Hunterian Soc, Inst of Sports Med; former memb Cncl Inst of Orthopaedic Med; KM; *Recreations* horse riding, skiing, tennis, fishing, farming, country sports; *Clubs* Royal Society of Medicine London; *Style—* Dr Martin Kennedy Phelan; ✉ 148 Harley St, London W1N 1AH (☎ 0171 224 0557, fax 0171 935 3356); home (fax 01582 713815)

PHELAN, Terry; *b* 13 March 1967; *Career* professional footballer (defender); clubs: Leeds Utd 1984–86, Swansea City 1986–87, Wimbledon 1987–92 (FA Cup 1988), joined Manchester City FC 1992 (for £2.5m), transferred Chelsea FC Nov 1995–; Republic of Ireland: debut 1991, over 15 full caps, memb World Cup squad 1994; *Style—* Terry Phelan, Esq; ✉ Chelsea Football Club, Stamford Bridge, Fulham Road, London SW6 1HS (☎ 0171 385 5545, fax 0171 381 4831)

PHELPS, Prof Charles Frederick; s of Capt Seth Arthur Rose Phelps, MBE (d 1978), of Peaslake, Surrey, and Rigmor Louise, *née* Kaae (d 1984); *b* 18 Jan 1934; *Educ* Bromsgrove, BNC Oxford (BSc, MA, DPhil, DSc); *m* 29 Feb 1960, Joanna, da of Eric Lingeman, CBE (d 1966), of Eaton Square, London; 1 s (Anthony John Rose b 8 Sept 1960), 1 da (Amanda Louise Barnett b 26 Sept 1962); *Career* Univ of Bristol: lectr in chem physiology 1960–63, reader in biochemistry 1970–74 (lectr 1963–70); prof of biochemistry Univ of Lancaster 1974–80, princ Chelsea Coll Univ of London 1980–84, pro-rector Imperial Coll of Sci Technol and Med 1984–89 (advsr to rector on int affrs); memb: Res Ctee Arthritis and Rheumatism Cncl 1974–78, Ctee Br Biophysical Soc 1974–84 (chm 1983–84), Editorial Bd Biochem Biophys ACTA 1976–80, Ctee Biochemical Soc 1980–84, Editorial Bd Int Res Common Systems 1980–; govr: Furzedown Sch Battersea 1980–85, King Edward's Sch Witley 1984–, Mill Hill Sch 1985–, Royal GS Guildford 1988–, Royal Postgrad Med Fndn 1986–93; fell King's Coll London 1985; *Books* Messenger RNA (ed with H R V Arnstein), Biotechnology (ed with P Clarke), Molecular Variants of Proteins (with P Campbell); *Recreations* landscape gardening, cooking, birdwatching; *Clubs* Athenaeum; *Style—* Prof Charles Phelps; ✉ Brockhurst, The Green, Chiddingfold, Surrey GU8 4TU (☎ 01428 683092, fax 01428 685297)

PHELPS, Howard Thomas Henry Middleton; s of Ernest Henry Phelps (d 1981), of Gloucester, and Harriet Maria Ann, *née* Middleton (d 1978); *b* 20 Oct 1926; *Educ* Crypt GS Gloucester, Hatfield Coll Univ of Durham (BA); *m* 1949, Audrey, da of Thomas Ellis (d 1972); 1 da; *Career* dep dir industl rels NCB until 1972, dir of ops British Airways 1979–86 (personnel dir 1972–79), dir P & O Steam Navigation Co plc 1986–89; chm: Earls Court and Olympia Ltd 1986–89, Sutcliffe Catering Gp Ltd 1986–89, QA Training Ltd 1989–94; dir: Alden Press Ltd 1990–, Brewery Arts Ltd 1994– (chm 1991–94); chm: Govrs Cirencester Coll 1990–, Cncl Univ of Durham 1992–, Rendcomb Coll; dir: Chedworth Village Tst 1987–, Assoc of Colls 1996; Hon DCL Univ of Durham 1995; FRAeS, FCIT, CIMgt; *Recreations* music, gardens; *Clubs* Royal Over-Seas; *Style—* Howard Phelps, Esq; ✉ Tall Trees, Chedworth, nr Cheltenham, Glos (☎ and fax 01285 720324)

PHELPS, John Christopher; s of Anthony John Phelps, CB, of London, and Sheila Nan, *née* Rait (d 1967); *b* 25 May 1954; *Educ* Whitgift Sch S Croydon, Univ of Liverpool (LLB); *m* 13 April 1985, Isabelle Michele Jeanine, da of Maurice Albert Haumesser (d

1987), of Nancy, France; 1 s (Christopher b 1988), 1 da (Jessica b 1991); *Career* admitted slr 1978; ptnr Beachcroft Stanleys 1986–; Freeman City of Oxford; *Books* VAT for Solicitors (with Julian Gizzi, 1993); *Recreations* football, rugby and cricket spectator, tennis and squash; *Clubs* MCC; *Style*— John Phelps, Esq; ✉ Beachcroft Stanleys, 20 Furnival St, London EC4A 1BN (☎ 0171 242 1011, fax 0171 430 1532)

PHELPS, Maurice; s of Harry Thomas Phelps (d 1973), and Lilian Carter; *b* 17 May 1935; *Educ* Wandsworth Sch, CCC Oxford (BA); *m* 1960, Elizabeth Anne Hurley; 2 s, 1 da; *Career* personnel dir Heavy Vehicle Div Leyland Vehicles 1977–80, Bd memb personnel British Shipbuilders 1980–87, Br Ferries Ltd 1987–89, managing ptnr Emslie Phelps Associates and Value Through People Ltd, chm Saratoga (Europe) Ltd; Freeman City of London, Freeman Worshipful Co of Watermen and Lightermen; *Recreations* surfing, sailing, squash; *Style*— Maurice Phelps, Esq; ✉ Abbotsfield, Goring Heath, South Oxfordshire RG8 7SA (☎ 01491 681916); Maurice Phelps Associates and Emslie Phelps Assocs, Bix Manor, Broadplat Lane, Henley-on-Thames, Oxfordshire RG9 4RS (☎ 01491 411949)

PHELPS, Dr Peter David; s of Donald Percy (d 1944), of Little Chalfont, Bucks, and Phyllis Mabel, *née* Willis; *b* 22 May 1939; *Educ* Merchant Taylors', Charing Cross Hosp Med Sch Univ of London (MB BS, DMRD, MD); *Career* Charing Cross Hosp 1962–63, sr house offr of surgery Leicester Royal Infirmary 1964, radiology trg Radcliffe Infimary Oxford 1969–72 (surgical training ENT 1966–68), conslt radiologist to Coventry Gp Hosp 1974–, conslt radiologist to Royal Nat ENT Hosp 1987–, hon conslt to Gt Ormond St Children's Hosp London 1988–; contrib numerous chapters in radiology and ENT text books; memb: Inland Water Ways Assoc, Kennet and Avon Canal Tst, BMA, MDU; FRCS 1968, FRCR 1973; *Books* Diagnostic Imaging of the Ear (with Dr G A S Lloyd, 1989), Clinical ENT Radiology (with J M Stansbie, 1993); *Recreations* vintage cars, canals, rugby football; *Clubs* Vintage Sports Car; *Style*— Dr Peter Phelps; ✉ Doric House, Easenhall, Rugby, Warwickshire CV23 0JA (☎ 01788 832347); Department of Radiology, Royal National Throat Nose and Ear Hospital, Gray's Inn Rd, London (☎ 0171 837 8855); Radiology Department, Walsgrave Hospital, Clifford Bridge Rd, Coventry

PHELPS, Richard Lawson; s of John Graham Phelps, and Barbara Phelps; *b* 19 April 1961; *m* Teresa, *née* Purton; 2 s (Aarron, Jason); *Career* athlete (modern pentathlon); jr nat champion 1979, 1981 and 1982, sr nat champion 1979, 1981, 1982, 1983, 1984, 1986, 1988, 1990, 1991, 1992, 1993 and 1995; ranked UK no 1; world champion 1993; team Bronze medallist (modern pentathlon) Seoul Olympics 1988, team Silver medallist World Championships 1994; memb Br team: Barcelona Olympics 1992, Atlanta Olympics 1996; life memb: Modern Pentathlon Assoc of GB 1984, Gloucester City Swimming Club 1988; proprietor iron reclamation business; *Style*— Richard Phelps, Esq; ✉ c/o British Olympic Assoc, 1 Wandsworth Plain, London SW18 1EH

PHELPS, Richard Wintour; CBE (1986); s of late Rev H Phelps, of Sidmouth, Devon, and Elsie, *née* Pearce; *b* 26 July 1925; *Educ* Kingswood Sch Bath, Merton Coll Oxford (MA); *m* 12 Feb 1955, Pamela Marie Phelps; 2 da (Hilary Susan b 25 Oct 1957, Diana Gillian b 15 March 1961); *Career* Lt 14 Punjab Regt Indian Army 1944–46; HM Overseas CS Nigeria 1948–57 and 1959–61, princ home CS HM Treasy 1957–59 and 1961–65, gen mangr Skelmersdale New Town Devpt Corp 1967–71, gen mangr Central Lancs Devpt Corp 1971–86, sr admin Hants CC 1963–65; pt/t advsr on housing to: Govt of Vanuatu 1986–88, Govt of Falkland Islands 1988 and 1989; Parly candidate (Alliance) Barrow in Furness 1987, chm Examinations in Public of Cambs, Derbys, Hants Leics, Notts, Northants and W Sussex CCs Structure Plans 1989–96, appointed to carry out ind inquiry into abuses of the planning system in Bassetlaw DC 1995–96; FRSA; *Recreations* travel, reading, bridge; *Clubs* Royal Cwlth Soc; *Style*— Richard Phelps, Esq, CBE; ✉ 38 Wharncliffe Road, Highcliffe, Christchurch, Dorset (☎ 01425 272242)

PHILIP, The Hon Lord; Alexander Morrison Philip; s of Alexander Philip, OBE (d 1979), and Isobel Thomson Morrison; *b* 3 Aug 1942; *Educ* HS of Glasgow, Univ of St Andrews (MA), Univ of Glasgow (LLB); *m* 9 Oct 1971, Shona Mary, da of Kenneth Macrae, of St Andrews; 3 s (Jamie b 24 Oct 1977, Colin b 8 June 1979, Tom b 25 June 1983); *Career* slr 1967–72, admitted to Faculty of Advocates 1973, QC (Scot) 1984, advocate depute 1982–85, chm Med Appeal Tbnls 1987–92, chm Scottish Land Court and pres Lands Tbnl for Scotland 1993–96, Senator Coll of Justice in Scotland (Lord of Session) 1996–; *Recreations* piping, golf; *Clubs* Scottish Arts, Royal Scottish Pipers' Soc (Edinburgh); *Style*— The Hon Lord Philip; ✉ Parliament House, Edinburgh EH1 1RQ (☎ 0131 225 2595)

PHILIP SORENSEN, (Nils Jorgen) Philip; s of Erik Philip Sorensen, of Lillon, Skane, Sweden, and Brita Hjordis Bendix, *née* Lundgren (d 1984); *b* 23 Sept 1938; *Educ* Herlufsholm Kostskole Naestved Denmark, Niels Brock Commercial Sch (CPH); *m* 1962, Ingrid, da of Eigil Baltzer-Andersen (d 1965); 1 s (Mark b 1973), 3 da (Annette b 1963, Christina b 1965, Louisa b 1968); *Career* estab modern security indust in Europe; chm and fndr Group 4 Securitas cos: Albania, Australia, Austria, Belgium, Bulgaria, Canada, Cyprus, Czech Republic, Greece, Hungary, India, Ireland, Kuwait, Luxembourg, Malta, Morocco, Nepal, Netherlands, NZ, NI, Poland, Slovak Repub, Turkey, UK, USA, Ukraine, UAE, and associated and affiliated cos in France, Japan, Sri Lanka, Singapore, Thailand; pres Ligue Internationale des Societes de Surveillance; memb Cncl Br Security Indust Assoc; owner: Dormy House Hotel Broadway, Strandhotellet Skagen Denmark; Soldier of the Year award Sweden; hon citizen of Cork 1985, ambass of Skagen Denmark 1994; *Recreations* sailing (fishing vessel "Oke"; sponsoring chm yacht "Group 4" British Steel Challenge 1992/3, "Group 4" Global Challenge 1994/5, sponsor Br Team Admiral's Cup 1995, British Telecom Challenge 1996/7), photography, travelling, book collecting; *Clubs* Hurlingham, Annabel's, Harry's Bar, Mosimann's; *Style*— Philip Sorensen, Esq; ✉ Group 4 Securitas Ltd, Farncombe House, Broadway, Worcestershire WR12 7LJ (☎ 01386 858585, fax 01386 858833); Prinsevinkenpark 2, PO Box 85911, 2508 Den Haag, The Netherlands (☎ 00 31 70519191)

PHILIPP, Elliot Elias; s of Oscar Isaac Philipp (d 1965), of Geneva, Switzerland, and Clarisse, *née* Weil (d 1971); *b* 20 July 1915; *Educ* St Paul's, St John's Coll Cambridge (MA), Middlesex Hosp (MB BCh, MRCS, LRCP), Univ of Lausanne; *m* 22 March 1939, Lucie Ruth (d 1988), da of Zacharias Max Hackenbroch (d 1937); 1 s (Alan Henry b 24 Oct 1943), 1 da (Ann Susan (Mrs Hills) b 7 Jan 1941); *Career* Sqdn Ldr (med) RAFVR 1940–46, Bomber Cmd (despatches twice); registrar Addenbrooke's Hosp 1947, anatomical demonstrator Middlesex Hosp 1948 (house surgn 1939–40, house surgn and registrar in obstetrics and gynaecology 1946–47); sr registrar: St Thomas's Hosp 1948–49, Royal Free Hosp 1949–50; first asst Dept of Obstetrics and Gynaecology Univ Coll Hosp 1951; conslt obstetrician and gynaecologist: Old Church Hosp Romford 1952–64, Royal Northern Hosp and City of London Maternity Hosp 1964–80, Whittington Hosp 1980–; pres Hunterian Soc 1988–89 (orator 1987), pres Med Soc of London 1993–94; chev Légion d'Honneur 1971, Gold Medal City of Milan 1972; Freeman City of London, Liveryman Worshipful Soc of Apothecaries; memb RSM (pres Section of History of Med 1996–97); FRCS, FRCOG; *Books* Scientific Foundations of Obstetrics and Gynaecology (co-ed 1970, 4 edn 1991), Infertility (1981), Caesareans (1988), Obstetrics and Gynaecology Combined for Students (1962, 2 edn 1970), A History of Obstetrics and Gynaecology (jtly, 1994); *Recreations* walking (particularly along sea walls), formerly mountaineering and skiing; *Style*— Elliot Philipp, Esq; ✉ 166 Rivermead Court, Ranelagh Gardens, London SW6 3SF (☎ and fax 0171 736 2851)

PHILIPPS, Hon Roland Alexander; s of 3 Baron Milford, *qv*, of Llanstephan, Powys, and Viscountess Norwich, *née* Mary Makins, of London; *b* 20 Sept 1962; *Educ* Eton, Trinity Coll Cambridge (BA, MA); *m* 1991, Felicity Kate, da Hilary Rubinstein; 1 s (Nathaniel Alexander b 19 Dec 1996); *Career* publishing dir Macmillan London 1989–94, publisher Hodder and Stoughton 1994–; *Recreations* reading; *Style*— The Hon Roland Philipps; ✉ 231 Westbourne Park Road, London W11 1EB

PHILIPS, Prof Sir Cyril Henry; kt (1974); s of William Henry Philips; *b* 27 Dec 1912; *Educ* Rock Ferry HS, Univ of Liverpool (MA), Univ of London (PhD); *m* 1, 1939, Dorcas (d 1974), da of John Rose Wallasey; 1 da (1 s decd); m 2, 1975, Joan Rosemary, da of William George Marshall; *Career* Univ of London: prof of Oriental history 1946–80, dir Sch of Oriental and African Studies 1957–76, vice-chllr 1972–76; chm: Royal Cmmn on Criminal Procedure 1978–80, Police Complaints Bd 1980–85, Cncl on Tribunals 1986–89; *Clubs* Athenaeum; *Style*— Prof Sir Cyril Philips; ✉ c/o School of Oriental and African Studies, Malet Street, London WC1E 7HP (☎ 0171 637 2388)

PHILIPS, Justin Robin Drew; s of Albert Lewis Philips (d 1978), of Pinner, London, and Henrietta, *née* Woolfson; *b* 18 July 1948; *Educ* John Lyon Sch Harrow, Coll of Law London; *Career* called to the Bar Gray's Inn 1969, practised Criminal Bar 1970–89, met stipendiary magistrate 1989–, chm Inner London Youth Courts 1992–, asst recorder of the Crown Ct 1994–; hon sec Hendon Reform Synagogue 1990–94, tstee Tzedek Charity; memb Br Acad of Forensic Scis; *Recreations* music, reading, attempting to keep fit; *Style*— Justin Philips, Esq; ✉ Tower Bridge Magistrates Court, Tooley Street, London SE1 2JY (☎ 0171 407 4232)

PHILIPSON, Maj Christopher Roland; s of Major Thirlwell Philipson, MC (d 1952), of Fordham Abbey, Cambridgeshire, and Daphne, *née* Gladstone (d 1971); *b* 4 March 1929; *Educ* Eton, Sandhurst; *m* 1 Jan 1958, Mary, da of Sir Reginald MacDonald-Buchanan, KCVO, MC (d 1981), of Cottesbrooke Hall, Northampton; 2 da (Caroline b 1959, Joanna b 1961); *Career* Maj Life Gds, served in Germany, Cyprus, Egypt, Aden 1947–61; chm British Bloodstock Agency plc 1992– (md 1980–92); *Recreations* shooting, gardening; *Clubs* Turf; *Style*— Maj Christopher Philipson; ✉ Queensberry House, Newmarket, Suffolk (☎ 01638 665021)

PHILIPSON, (John) Trevor Graham; QC (1989); s of William Arnold Philipson, of Morpeth, Northumberland, and Rosalind Amy, *née* Mood; *b* 3 March 1948; *Educ* Newcastle Royal GS, Wadham Coll Oxford (BA, BCL); *m* 13 July 1974 (m dis 1982), Victoria Caroline, da of Oliver Haskard, of Vermont, USA; *Career* called to the Bar Middle Temple 1972; *Recreations* The Pyrenees; *Clubs* RAC, Savile; *Style*— Trevor Philipson, QC; ✉ 239 Knightsbridge, London SW7 1DJ (☎ 0171 581 2214); Fountain Court, Temple, London EC4Y 9DH (☎ 0171 583 3335, fax 0171 353 0329, telex 8813408 FONLEG G)

PHILIPSON-STOW, Sir Christopher; 5 Bt (UK 1907), of Cape Town, Cape of Good Hope, and Blackdown House, Lodsworth, Co Sussex, DFC; s of late Henry Matthew Philipson Philipson-Stow, JP (3 s of Sir Frederic Philipson-Stow, 1 Bt), and Elizabeth, da of Sir Thomas Chitty, 1 Bt; suc 1 cous, Sir Edmond Cecil Philipson-Stow, 4 Bt, MBE, 1982; *b* 13 Sept 1920; *Educ* Winchester; *m* 1952, Elizabeth Nairn, da of late James Dixon Trees, of Toronto, and widow of Maj Frederic George McLaren, of 48th Highlanders of Canada; 2 s (Robert Matthew b 29 Aug 1953, Rowland Frederic b 2 Sept 1954); *Heir* er s, Robert; *Career* late Flt Lt RAFVR, served WWII; *Style*— Sir Christopher Philipson-Stow, Bt, DFC

PHILIPSON-STOW, Robert Nicholas; o s of Guyon Philipson Philipson-Stow (d 1983; 6 and yst s of Sir Frederick Samuel Philipson Stow, 1 Bt), and Alice Mary, *née* Fagge (d 1989); *b* 2 April 1937; *Educ* Winchester; *m* 25 Sept 1963, Nicolette Leila, er da of Hon Philip Leyland Kindersley; 2 s (Robert Rowland b 23 Sept 1970, Edward Miles b 30 April 1972), 1 da (Georgina Mary b 28 Oct 1976); *Career* Nat Serv 2 Lt RHG 1955–57; co sec Miles Druce & Co Ltd 1966–68; ptnr: George Henderson & Co stockbrokers 1970–74, Henderson Crosthwaite & Co stockbrokers 1974–86; dir of admin and ops Guinness Mahon Holdings plc 1986–; chm Crown and Manor Boys' Club Hoxton, govr Malvern Girls' Coll 1993–; FCA 1963; *Clubs* White's; *Style*— Robert Philipson-Stow, Esq; ✉ Priors Court, Long Green, Gloucester GL19 4QL (☎ 01684 883221); Guinness Mahon Holdings plc, 32 St Mary-at-Hill, London EC3P 3AJ (☎ 0171 772 7934)

PHILLIMORE, 5 Baron (UK 1918); Sir Francis Stephen Phillimore; 6 Bt (UK 1881); o s of 4 Baron Phillimore (d 1994), and Anne Elizabeth, *née* Smith-Dorrien-Smith (d 1995); *b* 25 Nov 1944; *Educ* Eton, Trinity Coll Cambridge; *m* 1971, Nathalie, da of late Michel Anthony Pequin, of Paris, France; 2 s (Hon Tristan Anthony Stephen b 18 Aug 1977, Hon Julian Michel Claud b 3 Nov 1981), 1 da (Hon Arabella Maroussia b 22 Feb 1975); *Heir* s, Hon Tristan Anthony Stephen Phillimore b 18 Aug 1977; *Career* called to the Bar Middle Temple 1972; *Recreations* polo, real tennis, sailing, shooting; *Clubs* Royal Yacht Sqdn, Brooks's, Pratt's; *Style*— The Rt Hon the Lord Phillimore; ✉ Coppid Hall, Binfield Heath, nr Henley-on-Thames, Oxon RG9 4JR

PHILLIPPS, Ian Hugh; DL (Notts 1990); s of Dr Frederick Alfred Phillipps, MBE (d 1975), of Jersey, and Gwendolen Herbert, *née* Smith (d 1980); *b* 15 Nov 1924; *Educ* Winchester, Trinity Coll Cambridge (MA); *m* 14 Oct 1958, Jennifer, da of Capt Harold Freeman Robinson, of Little Hallingbury, Essex; 1 s (Vere b 1961), 2 da (Victoria b 1959, Christina (Mrs Henry Jodrell) b 1968); *Career* dir: Humphreys & Glasgow Ltd 1960–67, Radiation Group Ltd 1967–70, Tube Investments Ltd 1970–81, Chamberlain Phipps plc 1982–89; chm and chief exec Raleigh Industries Ltd Nottingham 1974–81; chm: Wests Group International plc 1983–86, The BSS Group plc 1986–95; chm Cncl Soc of Br Gas Industs 1970–72, pres The Bicycle Assoc of GB 1977–79, chm E Midlands Regnl Cncl CBI 1983–84 (memb 1978–); memb Cncl: CBI 1980–95, Univ of Nottingham 1979–95; govr Welbeck Coll MOD 1987–95, chm Indust Year E Mids 1986; memb: Pay Review Body for Nurses Midwives and the Professions Allied to Med 1984–91, Probation Ctee for Notts 1990–96; pres British Assoc for Cricketers with Disabilities 1991–95; pres CUBC 1945; High Sheriff of Nottinghamshire 1992–93; FEng 1982, FICE 1950, FIGE 1951; *Recreations* fishing, rowing, brass band playing; *Clubs* Leander, London Rowing; *Style*— Ian Phillipps, Esq, DL, FEng; ✉ Grange Farm, Rempstone, Loughborough, Leics LE12 6RW (☎ 01509 880071)

PHILLIPPS, Sandra Ann; da of Samuel Charles Vivian Phillipps, of Falmouth, Cornwall, and Stephanie Mamie Phillipps (d 1986); *b* 6 Feb 1962; *Educ* Falmouth Sch, London Coll of Fashion (HND in fashion design); *partner* Paul Bennett; 1 da (Daisy Bennett b 27 Sept 1992), 1 s (Edward Bennett b 18 Feb 1995); *Career* milliner; in-house designer The Hat Shop London 1984–85, ptnr in own design co 1985– (private cmmns until 1987, ready to wear 1987–); currently exhibits twice seasonally; stockists incl Harvey Nichols, Selfridges, Harrods, Fenwicks, Liberty's and various retailers abroad; *Recreations* windsurfing, horse riding; *Style*— Ms Sandra Phillipps; ✉ Sandra Phillipps Hats, Noblesgate Yard, Bells Yew Green, Tunbridge Wells, Kent TN3 9AT (☎ 01892 750 592, fax 01892 750 387, e-mail 100773.1350@compuserve.com)

PHILLIPS, Prof Adrian Alexander Christian; s of Eric Lawrance Phillips, CMG, of London, and Phyllis Mary, *née* Bray (d 1991); *b* 11 Jan 1940; *Educ* The Hall Sch, Westminster, Ch Ch Oxford (MA), UCL (DipTP); *m* 16 Feb 1963, Cassandra Frances Elais, da of late David Francis Hubback, CB, of London; 2 s (Oliver b 1965, Barnaby b 1968); *Career* Planning Serv Miny of Housing 1962–68, sr res offr then asst dir Countryside Cmmn 1968–74, asst to Exec Dir then head of Programme Co-ordination Unit UN Environment Programme Nairobi 1974–78, programme dir Int Union for Conservation of Nature & Natural Resources Switzerland 1978–81, dir gen Countryside

Cmmn 1981–92, prof of countryside and environmental planning Univ of Wales Coll of Cardiff 1992–; chm: Int Cmmn on Nat Parks and Protected Areas 1994–, Wales Ctee RSPB 1992–; advsr National Heritage Meml Fund 1995–; hon fell Landscape Inst; MRTPI 1966, RSA 1982, FRGS 1983; *Recreations* walking, stroking the cats; *Clubs* Royal Over-Seas League; *Style*— Prof Adrian Phillips; ✉ 2 The Old Rectory, Dumbleton, nr Evesham, Worcs WR11 6TG (☎ and fax 01386 882094)

PHILLIPS, His Hon (David) Alan; s of Stephen Thomas Phillips, MC (d 1971), and Elizabeth Mary, *née* Williams (d 1963); *b* 21 July 1926; *Educ* Llanelli GS, Univ Coll Oxford (MA); *m* 1960, Jean Louise, da of Frederick Edmund Godsell (d 1963); 2 s (Stephen, David); *Career* served WWII 1944–48, Capt GS (Far East); lecturer 1952–59; called to the Bar Gray's Inn 1960, barr 1960–75, recorder of the Crown Court 1974, stipendiary magistrate for Mid-Glamorgan 1975–83, circuit judge (Wales and Chester Circuit) 1983–95; chllr Diocese of Bangor 1988–95; *Recreations* music, computers, swimming; *Style*— His Hon Alan Phillips

PHILLIPS, Andrew Bassett; s of William George Phillips (d 1972), and Doreen May, *née* Harris (d 1983); *b* 26 Sept 1945; *Educ* Newport HS, Univ of Reading (BA, ALA); *m* 1976, Valerie Christine, da of Alexander Cuthbert; 2 s (Edward b 1978, Simon b 1983), 1 da (Jocelyn b 1980); *Career* British National Bibliography Ltd 1969–70, National Libraries ADP Study 1970–71, Nat Cncl for Educational Technol 1971–73; British Library: various positions in bibliographic servs and reference divs 1973–90, dir Humanities and Social Sciences 1990–96, head of Br Library's Review of Legal Deposit 1996–; dir: Cedar Audio Ltd 1992–94, Saga Continuation Ltd 1993–; memb Governing Body City Literary Inst 1982–97; tstee Shakespeare's Birthplace 1991–; author of various reviews and articles; *Style*— Andrew Phillips, Esq; ✉ 23 Meynell Road, London E9 7AP (☎ 0181 985 7413); The British Library, Great Russell Street, London WC1B 3DG (☎ 0171 412 7491, fax 0171 412 7730)

PHILLIPS, Rev Canon Dr Anthony Charles Julian; s of Arthur Reginald Phillips (d 1965), of Mawnan Smith, Falmouth, Cornwall, and Esmee Mary, *née* Aikman (d 1987); *b* 2 June 1936; *Educ* Kelly Coll Tavistock, King's Coll London (BD, AKC), Gonville and Caius Coll Cambridge (PhD), Coll of the Resurrection Mirfield; *m* 11 April 1970, Victoria Ann, da of Vernon Bruce Stainton, OBE (d 1946), of Rawalpindi, Punjab; 2 s (Christopher Charles Withiel b 6 Aug 1971, James Alexander Withiel b 27 June 1973), 1 da (Lucy Karenza Withiel b 10 Feb 1975); *Career* curate of Good Shepherd Cambridge 1966–69, dean chaplain and fell of Trinity Hall Cambridge 1969–74; St John's Coll Oxford: chaplain and fell 1975–86, domestic bursar 1982–84; lectr in theol: Jesus Coll Oxford 1975–86, Hertford Coll Oxford 1984–86; SA Cook Bye fell Gonville and Caius Coll Cambridge 1984, hon chaplain to Bishop of Norwich 1970–71; examining chaplain to: Bishop of Oxford 1979–86, Bishop of Manchester 1980–86, Bishop of Wakefield 1984–86; inter faith conslt for Judaism Archbishops of Canterbury and York 1984–86; headmaster The King's Sch Canterbury 1986–96, canon theologian Dio of Truro 1986–, hon canon of Canterbury Cathedral 1987–96; author of various articles in learned jls; *Books* Ancient Israel's Criminal Law (1970), Deuteronomy (1973), God BC (1977, and 1996), Israel's Prophetic Tradition (ed, 1982), Lower than the Angels (1983), Preaching from the Psalter (1987), The Passion of God (1995); contributor: Words and Meanings (ed P R Ackroyd and B Lindars, 1968), Witness to the Spirit (ed W Harrington, 1979), The Ministry of the World (ed G Cuming, 1979), Heaven and Earth (ed A Linzey and P Wexler, 1986), Tradition and Unity (ed D Cohn-Sherbok, 1991), Glimpses of God (ed D Cohn-Sherbok, 1994); *Recreations* gardening, beachcombing; *Style*— The Rev Canon Dr Anthony Phillips; ✉ The Old Vicarage, 10 St Peter's Road, Flushing, Falmouth, Cornwall (☎ 01326 377217)

PHILLIPS, (William) Bernard; s of Stanley George Phillips (d 1968), of Sutton Coldfield, and Enid Effie, *née* Eades; *b* 26 April 1944; *Educ* Bishop Vesey GS Sutton Coldfield, Hertford Coll Oxford (MA); *m* 1, 13 May 1967 (m dis 1986), Christine Elizabeth, da of Arthur Charles Wilkinson, of Maidstone; 3 s (Andrew b 1968, Simon b 1972, William b 1974); m 2, 1 Aug 1987, Deborah Grace, da of Ellis Green (d 1975), of Sheffield; *Career* schoolmaster 1966–67, lectr 1967–70, called to the Bar Inner Temple 1970, in practice NE Circuit 1971–, recorder 1989– (asst recorder 1984–89); memb Inner Temple 1964; *Recreations* cookery, gardening, collecting books; *Style*— Bernard Phillips, Esq; ✉ Padley Croft, Nether Padley, Grindleford, Derbyshire (☎ 01433 631359); 12 Paradise Square, Sheffield (☎ 0114 273 8951, fax 0114 276 0848)

PHILLIPS, Prof Calbert Inglis; s of Rev David Horner Phillips, and Margaret Calbert Phillips; *b* 20 March 1925; *Educ* Glasgow HS, Robert Gordon's Coll Aberdeen, Univ of Aberdeen (MB ChB, MD), Univ of Edinburgh (DPH), Univ of Bristol (PhD), Univ of Manchester (MSc); *m* 1962, Christina Anne, *née* Fulton; 1 s; *Career* Nat Serv Lt and Capt RAMC 1947–49; house surgn: Aberdeen Royal Infirmary 1946–47 (house physician 1951), Aberdeen Maternity Hosp 1949, Glasgow Eye Infirmary 1950–51; asst Anatomy Dept Univ of Glasgow 1951–52, resident registrar Moorfields Eye Hosp 1953–54, sr registrar St Thomas's Hosp (and res asst Inst of Ophthalmology) 1954–58, conslt surgn Bristol Eye Hosp 1958–63, Alexander Piggott Wernher travelling fell Dept of Ophthalmology Harvard Univ 1960–61, conslt ophthalmic surgn St George's Hosp 1963–65, prof of ophthalmology Univ of Manchester 1965–72, hon conslt ophthalmic surgn to United Manchester Hosps 1965–72, prof of ophthalmology Univ of Edinburgh 1972–90, ophthalmic surgn Royal Infirmary Edinburgh 1972–90, now prof emeritus; Hon FBOA 1975; FRCS 1955, FRCSE 1973; *Books* Clinical Practice and Economics (jt ed, 1977), Basic Clinical Ophthalmology (1984), Ophthalmology: a primer (first author, 1994), Logic in Medicine (ed, 1995); author of numerous papers on ophthalmological and related topics for Br and American jls; *Style*— Prof Calbert Phillips; ✉ Princess Alexandra Eye Pavilion, Chalmers St, Edinburgh EH3 9HA (☎ 0131 536 3769)

PHILLIPS, Caryl; *b* 13 March 1958; *Educ* Queen's Coll Oxford (BA); *Career* author and stage/screen writer; author of articles in various jls; writing instructor Arvon Fndn 1983–; writer in residence: The Factory Arts Centre 1980–82, Literary Criterion Centre Univ of Mysore 1987, Univ of Stockholm 1989, Amherst Coll MA 1992– (visiting writer 1990–92, prof of English 1994–), Nat Inst of Educn Singapore 1994; visiting lectr: Univ of Ghana 1990, Univ of Poznan 1991; visiting prof of English New York Univ 1993; visiting writer Humber Coll Toronto 1992 and 1993, conslt ed Faber Inc 1992–94, contrib ed Bomb Magazine 1993, series ed Faber & Faber 1996–, co-prodr The Final Passage (C4) 1996; memb: Drama Panel Arts Cncl 1982–85, Prodn Bd BFI 1985–88, Bd Bush Theatre 1985–89, Bd The Caribbean Writer 1989; hon sr memb Univ of Kent 1988; *Awards* Arts Cncl Bursary in Drama 1984, BBC Giles Cooper Award (for The Wasted Years) 1984, Malcolm X Prize for Literature (for The Final Passage) 1985, Martin Luther King Meml Prize (for The European Tribe) 1987, Sunday Times Young Writer of the Year (for Cambridge) 1992, Rockefeller Fndn Bellagio Residency 1994, James Tait Black Meml Prize (for Crossing the River) 1994, Lannan Literary Award 1994; Br Cncl Fiftieth Anniversary fell 1984, Guggenheim Fndn fell 1992; *TV Dramas* Lost in Music (BBC, 1984), The Hope and the Glory (BBC, 1984), The Record (C4, 1985), Playing Away (film on 4, 1986), The Final Passage (C4, 1996); *TV and Radio Documentaries* Welcome to Birmingham USA (Central, 1983), Black on Black (LWT, 1983), St Kitt's Independence (Radio 4, 1983), Bookmark (BBC, 1984), Sport and the Black Community (Radio 4, 1984), No Complaints - James Baldwin at 60 (Radio 4, 1985), Darker Than Blue: Curtis Mayfield (BBC 1995), The Spirit of America (Radio 4, 1995), These Islands Now: Transformations in British Culture (Radio 3, 1995); *Fiction* The Final Passage (1985), A State of Independence (1986), Higher Ground (1989), Cambridge (1991), Crossing the River (1993); *Non-Fiction* The European Tribe (1987); *Plays* Strange Fruit (1981), Where There is Darkness (1982), The Shelter (1984), The Wasted Years (radio play) 1985; *Style*— Caryl Phillips, Esq; ✉ c/o Antony Harwood, Aitken & Stone, 29 Fernshaw Road, London SW10 0TG (☎ 0171 351 7561)

PHILLIPS, Dr Celia Mary; er da of Percival Edmund Phillips (d 1989), and Marjorie, *née* Hughes; *b* 16 Dec 1942; *Educ* Dunfermline HS, Windsor Sch Hamm, High Wycombe HS, LSE (BSc, PhD); *m* 23 June 1973, Rev Preb Ronald Frederick Swan, o s of Frederick William Swan (d 1975), of Southampton; 1 s (Toby b May 1978), 1 da (Elly b Dec 1974); *Career* LSE: lectr 1967–, dean of undergraduate studies 1986–89, sr tutor Interdisciplinary Inst of Mgmnt 1994–; memb Educn Ctee ILEA 1975–78, tstee St Catherine's Cumberland Lodge Windsor 1987–; FRSS; *Books* Changes in Subject Choice at School and University (1969), Statistical Sources in Civil Aviation (1979), The Risks in Going to Work (with J Stockdale, 1989), Violence at Work (with J Stockdale, 1991); *Recreations* choral singing (Chelsea Opera Group and others), walking, reading; *Style*— Dr Celia Phillips; ✉ Statistics Department, London School of Economics, Houghton Street, London WC2A 2AE (☎ 0171 955 7644)

PHILLIPS, Prof David; s of Stanley Phillips (d 1979), of South Shields, Tyne and Wear, and Daphne Ivy, *née* Harris; *b* 3 Dec 1939; *Educ* South Shields Grammar Tech Sch, Univ of Birmingham (BSc, PhD); *m* 21 Dec 1970, (Lucy) Caroline, da of Clifford John Scoble, of Plymouth, Devon; 1 da (Sarah Elizabeth b 1975); *Career* Fullbright fell Univ of Texas Austin USA 1964–66, exchange fell Royal Soc/Acad of Sciences USSR 1966–67; Univ of Southampton: lectr 1967–73, sr lectr 1973–76, reader 1976–80; The Royal Inst of GB: Wolfson prof of natural philosophy 1980–89, dep dir 1986–89; prof of physical chemistry Imperial Coll London 1989– (head of dept 1992–); res scientist in applications of lasers in chemistry biology and med, author of 410 scientific papers reviews and books in this field, various appearances on BBC TV and Radio incl Royal Inst Christmas Lectures for Young People with JM Thomas 1987 and 1988; vice pres and gen sec Br Assoc for the Advancement of Science 1988–89; RSC Nyholm lectr 1994; FRSC 1976; *Books* Time-correlated Single-photon Counting (with D V O'Connor), Time-resolved Vibrational Spectroscopy (with G H Atkinson), Jet-Spectroscopy and Molecular Dynamics (with J M Hollas); *Recreations* music, theatre, popularisation of science; *Clubs* Athenaeum; *Style*— Prof David Phillips; ✉ 195 Barnett Wood Lane, Ashtead, Surrey KT21 2LP (☎ 01372 274385); Department of Chemistry, Imperial College of Science Technology and Medicine, Exhibition Rd, London SW7 2A2 (☎ 0171 594 5716, fax 0171 594 5801)

PHILLIPS, David Anthony; OBE (1994); *b* 27 April 1943; *Educ* Cardiff HS, Univ of Bristol Dental Sch (BDS, Paediatric Dentistry Prize, Prosthetics Prize, American Soc of Paedodontics Award); *m*; 1 da; *Career* house offr (oral surgery) Bristol Royal Infirmary 1965–66, dental practitioner 1966–81; Med Protection Soc: dental sec 1981–85, dep sec Dental Div 1985–89, sec Bd of Dental Proctection 1989–, dental dir 1989–; non-exec dir Herts NHS Tst 1994–95, chm Wellhouse NHS Tst 1995–; specialist advsr House of Commons Select Ctee on Health Oct 1992; memb Advsy Bd: Denplan Ltd 1988–, Nat Soc of Dental Practitioners USA 1988–; pres Metropolitan Branch BDA 1991–92; memb Bd: Cordent Tst 1989–, Dental Update Magazine 1991–, The Dentist Magazine 1991–; chm Five Plus Charity Bd 1975–81; supporting memb FDI, FRSM, fell Int Coll of Dentists, fndr memb Cwlth Dental Assoc; *Recreations* golf, gardening, oil painting, sculpture; *Clubs* East India; *Style*— David Phillips, Esq, OBE; ✉ Medical Protection Society, 50 Hallam Street, London W1N 6DE (☎ 0171 323 6555, fax 0171 323 1031)

PHILLIPS, David George Hedges; s of Francis George Hedges Phillips (d 1962), and Doris Mary Gyles, *née* Hepworth (d 1993); *b* 14 July 1945; *Educ* St Peter's Sch Huntingdon; *m* 1967, Margaret Jean Lindsay, *née* Lucksford; 1 s (Richard George Hedges b 1969), 1 da (Lindsay Jane Hedges b 1974); *Career* organiser and constituency agent Cons Pty 1966–79, PR mangr Lancer Boss Group 1979–84, md Klein PR 1984–85, princ Phillips and Company PR Consultancy 1985–; md Media Measurement Ltd 1992–; ed Bradford Onlooker 1968–70, fndr and sec S Beds Co Show 1978–86, memb Bd Prince's Youth Business Tst 1991–; FIPR 1993 (MIPR 1980); *Books* Evaluating Press Coverage; *Recreations* praying for high winds, sailing; *Style*— David Phillips, Esq; ✉ Phillips and Company, 62 High Street, Stony Stratford, Milton Keynes, Bucks MK11 1AQ (☎ 01908 262411, fax 01908 262455)

PHILLIPS, Prof Dewi Zephaniah; s of David Oakley Phillips (d 1978), of Morriston, Swansea, and Alice Frances, *née* Davies (d 1982); *b* 24 Nov 1934; *Educ* Swansea GS, Univ Coll of Swansea (BA, MA), St Catherine's Coll Oxford (BLitt); *m* 2 Sept 1959, (Margaret) Monica, da of Frederick John Hanford (d 1951), of Swansea; 3 s (Aled b 1962, Steffan b 1965, Rhys b 1971); *Career* lectr in philosophy Queen's Coll Dundee 1964–65 (asst lectr 1963–64), lectr in philosophy Univ Coll Bangor 1963–65; Univ of Wales Swansea: lectr in philosophy 1965–67, sr lectr 1967–70, prof 1971–96, Rush Rhees research prof 1996–, dean of arts 1982–85, vice-princ 1989–92; Danforth prof Claremont Grad Sch Calif 1992–; *Books* The Concept of Prayer (1969), Faith and Philosophical Enquiry (1970), Death and Immortality (1970), Moral Practices (with H O Mounce, 1970), Sense and Delusion (with Ilham Dilman, 1971), Athronyddu am Grefydd (1974), Religion Without Explanation (1976), Through a Darkening Glass (1982), Dramau Gwenlyn Parry (1982), Belief Change and Forms of Life (1986), R S Thomas: Poet of the Hidden God (1986), Faith After Foundationalism (1988), From Fantasy to Faith (1991), Interventions in Ethics (1992), Wittgenstein and Religion (1993), Writers of Wales: J R Jones (1995), Introducing Philosophy (1996); *Recreations* lawn tennis, supporting Swansea City AFC; *Style*— Prof D Z Phillips; ✉ 45 Queen's Rd, Sketty, Swansea (☎ 01792 203935); Department of Philosophy, University of Wales Swansea, Singleton Park, Swansea (☎ 01792 295189, fax 01792 295893)

PHILLIPS, Lt-Col Edward Courtenay; MC (1945), JP (Hereford 1965), DL (Hereford 1987); s of Gerald Courtenay Phillips (d 1938), of St Ct, Kingsland, Leominster, Hereford, and Dorothy Phillips (d 1975); *b* 6 June 1922; *Educ* Marlborough; *m* 9 Aug 1947, Anthea Mary, da of Capt R F J Onslow, MVO, DSC, RN, of The Cat and Fiddle, Presteigne, Radnorshire; 2 da (Sarah (Mrs Corbett) b 1948, Harriet (Mrs Cheney) b 1953); *Career* KRRC: joined 1940, cmmnd 1941, Capt 1945, Temporary Maj 1946–54, mil attaché Khartoum 1959–61, ret 1961, Co Cmdt ACF Hereford 1970–75; conslt dir Sun Valley Poultry 1987–95 (joined 1961, chm 1983–87); chm: Herefordshire Co PSD 1987, South Hereford PSD 1988–90, Hereford Diocesan Appeal 1976–81; High Sheriff Hereford and Worcester 1977–78; Gen Cmmr of Income Tax 1983–; *Recreations* field sports, racing; *Clubs* Army and Navy; *Style*— Lt-Col Edward Phillips, MC, JP, DL; ✉ Chase House, Monnington-on-Wye, Hereford HR4 7NL (☎ 01981 500282)

PHILLIPS, Edward Thomas John (Jack); CBE (1985); s of Edward Emery Kent Phillips (d 1984), and Margaret Elsie, *née* Smith (d 1986); *b* 5 Feb 1930; *Educ* Exmouth GS Devon, UCL (BA), Inst of Educn London Univ (postgraduate Cert Ed), SOAS (Dip Linguistics); *m* 27 Sept 1952, Sheila May, da of Thomas Henry Abbott (d 1978); 2 s (Christopher b 11 Dec 1957, Jonathan b 8 May 1965), 2 da (Nicola b 11 Sept 1960, Deborah b 3 July 1962); *Career* Nat Serv RAF 1948–49; educn offr Colonial Serv Nigeria 1953–62; The British Cncl: head of centre unit London overseas students dept 1962–65, trg at SOAS 1965–66, English language offr Enugu Nigeria 1966–67, sr lectr dept of educn Lagos Univ Nigeria 1967–70, English language teaching advsr Miny of Educn Nicosia Cyprus 1970–72, chief inspr English teaching div inspectorate 1974–75 (inspr 1972–74), rep Bangladesh 1975–77, dir personnel dept and dep controller personnel and staff recruitment div 1977–80, rep Malaysia 1980–85, controller English language and lit div 1985–89, ret 89; conslt on recruitment British Exec Serv Overseas 1990–, dir

Project Mala (educnl charity for formerly illegally-employed children in India) 1992–; memb: IATEFL, Br-Malaysia Soc, Anti-Slavery Soc, Br-Nigeria Assoc; *Books* Organised English Books I and II (jt ed 1973); *Recreations* sport, music, theatre; *Style*— Edward Phillips, Esq, CBE; ✉ 1 Bredune, Kenley, Surrey CR8 5DU (☎ 0181 660 1929); Westcott, Westwood, nr Starcross, Devon

PHILLIPS, Sir Fred Albert; kt (1967), CVO (1966), QC; s of Wilbert A Phillips, of Brighton, St Vincent; *b* 14 May 1918; *Educ* Univ of London (LLB), Toronto Univ, McGill Univ (MCL); *Career* called to the Bar Middle Temple; cabinet sec West Indies Fedn 1960–62, govr St Kitts, Nevis & Anguilla 1967–69; Cable & Wireless plc: sr legal advsr 1969–91, sr govt relations conslt 1992–; chm: Grenada Telecommunications Ltd, Agricultural Venture Tst; dir: Barbados External Telecommunications, Barbados Telephone Co, St Kitts and Nevis Telecommunications Ltd; Hon LLD Univ of the W Indies; KStJ 1968; *Recreations* writing; *Style*— Sir Fred Phillips, CVO, QC; ✉ PO Box 206, Bridgetown, Barbados (☎ 00 1 246 42 90448/42 90427)

PHILLIPS, (Gerald) Hayden; CB (1989); s of Gerald Phillips (d 1995), of Tunbridge Wells, and Dorothy Florence, *née* Joyner (d 1992); *b* 9 Feb 1943; *Educ* Cambridgeshire HS Clare Coll Cambridge (MA), Yale USA (MA); *m* 1, 23 Sept 1967, Dr Ann Watkins, da of Prof S B Watkins (d 1966); 1 s (Alexander b 1970); 1 da (Rachel b 1974); m 2, 11 July 1980, Hon Laura Grenfell (*see* Hon Mrs Phillips), da of 2 Baron St Just (d 1984); 1 s (Thomas Peter b 1987), 2 da (Florence b 1981, Louisa Henrietta b 1984); *Career* princ private sec to Home Sec 1974–76, dep chef de cabinet to Pres the Euro Communities 1977–79, asst sec Home Office 1979–81, under sec of state Home Office 1981–86, dep under sec of state Cabinet Office 1986–88, dep sec HM Treasy 1988–92, perm sec Dept of National Heritage 1992–; *Clubs* Brooks's; *Style*— Hayden Phillips, Esq, CB; ✉ Department of National Heritage, 2–4 Cockspur Street, London SW1 (☎ 0171 211 6255)

PHILLIPS, Capt Hedley Joyce; OBE (1980), QPM (1972), DL (Hants 1987); s of Francis Hedley Joyce Phillips (d 1928), and Constance Daisy, *née* Bigg (d 1986); *b* 12 March 1925; *Educ* Aldworth's Hosp (Reading Blue Coat Sch); *m* 22 March 1947, Brenda Marjorie, da of Herbert Walter Horner (d 1968); 1 s (Michael Hedley Joyce b 1948); *Career* WWII serv: enlisted RM 1942, cmmnd 1944, 48 RM Commando NW Europe 1944–45, 44 RM Commando SE Asia 1945–46, demobbed with rank of Capt 1946; cmmnd RM Forces Vol Res 1948, ret Capt 1953; Berks Constabulary 1946–64, asst chief constable Hants Constabulary 1964–67 (dep chief constable 1967–83), ret 1983; chm Winchester & Dist VSO Ctee 1965–70, vice pres RLSS 1985– (chm S Region 1980–89), treas Southampton Travellers' Aid 1972–80; *Recreations* golf, swimming, chess, military history; *Clubs* Bramshaw Golf; *Style*— Capt Hedley Phillips, OBE, QPM, DL

PHILLIPS, Sir Henry Ellis Isidore; kt (1964), CMG (1960), MBE (Mil 1946); s of Harry Joseph Phillips, MBE (d 1961), and Rachel Love Trachtenberg (d 1961); *b* 30 Aug 1914; *Educ* Haberdashers' Sch Hampstead, UCL (MA), Inst of Historical Res; *m* 1, 1941 (m dis 1965), Vivien, da of Albert M Hyamson, OBE (d 1954); 2 s, 1 da; m 2, 1966, Philippa, da of Michael Cohen (d 1965); *Career* cmmnd Bedfs and Herts Regt 1939, Capt and Adj 5 Bn (POW Singapore 1942–45); Colonial Admin Serv 1946: devpt sec Nyasaland 1952, seconded to Fed Treasy Rhodesia and Nyasaland 1953–57 (dep sec 1956–57); fin sec Nyasaland Govt 1957–64, min of fin Nyasaland 1961–64; md Standard Bank Finance and Development Corporation 1966–72, dir (latterly hon vice chm) SIFIDA Investment Co SA 1970–, dir National Bank of Malawi 1983–88; chm: Ashley Industrial Trust 1986–88, Assured Property Trust plc 1988–96; advsr Air Tport Users' Cncl 1981–; bd memb Civil Aviation Authy 1975–80, fndr memb (latterly hon pres) Stonham Housing Assoc 1976–, hon treas (latterly vice chm) Stonham Meml Tst 1977–; memb: Fin Ctee UCL 1986–, Cncl SOS Sahel Int UK 1987–; chm Urban Aid Africa 1992–; fell UCL 1992; FRHistS 1965; *Clubs* MCC; *Style*— Sir Henry Phillips, CMG, MBE; ✉ 34 Ross Ct, Putney Hill, London SW15 3NZ (☎ 0181 789 1404)

PHILLIPS, Sir Horace; KCMG (1973, CMG 1963); s of Samuel Phillips; *b* 31 May 1917; *Educ* Hillhead HS Glasgow; *m* 1944, Idina Doreen Morgan; 1 s, 1 da; *Career* Br later Indian Army (Maj) 1940–47; Dip Serv 1947–; ambass to Indonesia 1966–68, high cmmr in Tanzania 1968–72, ambass to Turkey 1973–77; resident rep Taylor Woodrow International Ltd: Iran 1978–79, Hong Kong 1979–83, Bahrain 1983–84, China (at Peking) 1985–87; lectr in diplomatic history Bilkent Univ Ankara Turkey 1988–96; Hon LLD Glasgow 1977; Order of the Taj (Iran) 1961; *Publications* Envoy Extraordinary: A Most Unlikely Ambassador (1995); *Recreations* languages, long distance car driving; *Clubs* Travellers', Hong Kong; *Style*— Sir Horace Phillips, KCMG; ✉ 34a Sheridan Rd, Merton Park, London SW19 3HP (☎ 0181 542 3836)

PHILLIPS, Prof Ian; s of Stanley Phillips (d 1942), of Whitworth, Lancashire, and Emma, *née* Price (d 1960); *b* 10 April 1936; *Educ* Bacup and Rawtenstall GS, St John's Coll Cambridge (MA, MD), St Thomas' Hosp Med Sch; *Career* clinical dean and prof of med microbiology United Med and Dental Schs of Guy's and St Thomas' Hosps, hon conslt microbiologist Guy's and St Thomas' Hosp Tst, civil conslt microbiology RAF 1979–; memb Cncl Royal Coll of Pathologists 1974–76 and 1987–90, chm Dist Med Team St Thomas' Hosp 1978–79, chm Br Soc for Antimicrobial Chemotherapy 1979–82, memb Veterinary Products Ctee 1981–85, chm Assoc of Med Microbiologists 1990–91, pres European Soc of Clinical Microbiology and Infectious Disease 1995–96, memb S London Botanical Inst; Freeman City of London 1975, Liveryman Worshipful Soc of Apothecaries; MFPHM, FRCP, FRCPath; *Books* Laboratory Methods in Antimicrobial Chemotherapy (ed with D S Reeves, J D Williams and R Wise, 1978), Microbial Disease (with D A J Tyrell, GS Goodwin and R Blowers, 1979); *Clubs* Athenaeum, Royal Soc of Med; *Style*— Prof Ian Phillips; ✉ Department of Microbiology, St Thomas' Hospital, Lambeth Palace Rd, London SE1 7EH (☎ 0171 928 9292)

PHILLIPS, John; s of John Tudor Phillips (d 1981), of Finchley, London N12, and Bessie Maud, *née* Cork (d 1989); *b* 25 Nov 1926; *Educ* Christ's Coll Finchley, Northern Poly Holloway; *m* 24 Sept 1955, Eileen Margaret, da of Lt-Col Robert Fryer (d 1946), of Finchley; *Career* Nat Serv 1945–48, cmmnd 2 Lt RE 1947; architect; studied under Romilly B Craze architect 1948–52; surveyor to the fabric: Truro Cathedral 1960–79 (conslt architect 1979–), Westminster Cathedral 1976–96, RIBA 1979–96; conslt architect Brisbane Cathedral 1988–; pres Ecclesiastical Architects' and Surveyors' Assoc 1982, chm Christian Enterprise Housing Assoc 1964–82; RIBA 1954; *Recreations* steeple crawling, choral singing; *Style*— John Phillips, Esq; ✉ 8 Friary Way, N Finchley, London N12 9PH (☎ 0181 445 3414); office: 1 Greenland Place, London NW1 0AP (☎ 0171 284 0077, fax 0171 284 0447)

PHILLIPS, John Edward; s of Stanley Edward Phillips (d 1987), of London, and Elsie Evelyn Ruth, *née* Wilson; *b* 12 May 1938; *Educ* Haileybury and ISC; *m* 29 Dec 1967, Mary Isabelle, da of Colin Bootra Taylor; 1 s (Michael John b May 1972 d 16 Oct 1980), 1 da (Sarah Jane b 14 Sept 1969); *Career* Trade Indemnity plc: joined 1961, gen mangr and dir 1978–90; chm Advent Management Ltd; pres Int Credit Insur Assoc 1986–88, memb Mgmnt Ctee Inst of Credit Mgmnt; chm: Nat Head Injuries Assoc (Headway) 1991–94, Headway Surrey Head Injuries Assoc 1995–; tstee Old Haileyburians RFC; Freeman City of London 1980, memb Ct of Assts Worshipful Co of Insurers (Sr Warden 1996–97); fell Inst of Credit Mgmnt, FInstD; *Recreations* tennis, golf; *Clubs* MCC, Worplesdon Golf, Royal Melbourne Golf, Athenaeum (Melbourne); *Style*— John E Phillips, Esq; ✉ Heather Court, Whitmoor Common, Worplesdon, Guildford, Surrey GU3 3RP (☎ 01483 232615, fax 01483 236469)

PHILLIPS, John Francis; CBE (1977, OBE 1957), QC (1981); s of late F W Phillips; *b* 1911; *Educ* Cardinal Vaughan Sch, Univ of London, Trinity Hall Cambridge (LLB, LLM); *m* 1937, Olive M Royer; 1 s, 2 da; *Career* arbitrator; called to the Bar Gray's Inn 1944; chm London Ct of Int Arbitration 1985–88; Private Patients Plan: dir 1958–, vice chm 1972–77, chm 1977–84, currently pres; dep chm Eggs Authy 1971–80; Associated Examining Bd: chm 1986–92, pres 1992–; DCL City Univ 1985; Hon Ct Asst: Worshipful Co of Scriveners (master 1982–83), Worshipful Co of Arbitrators (master 1981); Hon Asst Worshipful Co of Chartered Secretaries & Administrators (master 1978–79 and 1987–88); CStJ 1995 (OStJ 1985); FCIArb (pres 1976–77), FICSA (pres 1977–78), CIMgt; *Clubs* Athenaeum, Oxford and Cambridge; *Style*— John Phillips, Esq, CBE, QC; ✉ 17 Ossulton Way, Hampstead Garden Suburb, London N2 0DT (☎ 0181 455 8460)

PHILLIPS, Prof John Hartley; s of Frederick Hartley Phillips, of Dorking, Surrey, and Winifred Joan, *née* Francis (d 1972); *b* 19 Feb 1941; *Educ* Leighton Park Sch Reading, Christ's Coll Cambridge (Darwin Prize, MA, PhD); *m* 1965, Kerstin Birgitta, da of Nils Bruno Halling; 2 da (Ingrid Kristina b 24 June 1968, Karin Anne b 8 April 1970); *Career* lectr in biochemistry Makerere Univ Kampala Uganda 1967–69, on MRC scientific staff Laboratory for Molecular Biology Cambridge 1969–74; Univ of Edinburgh: lectr in biochemistry 1974–92, prof of biology teaching 1992–, head Dept of Biochemistry and head of Biomedical Scis 1993–; memb Biochemical Soc 1972; *Style*— Prof John Phillips; ✉ 46 Granby Road, Edinburgh EH16 5NW (☎ 0131 667 5322); Department of Biochemistry, University of Edinburgh, Hugh Robson Building, George Square, Edinburgh EH8 9XD (☎ 0131 650 3720, fax 0131 650 3711)

PHILLIPS, Jonathan; s of Gilbert Reginald Phillips, of Walsall, W Mids, and Ruby May, *née Hughes; b* 21 May 1952; *Educ* Queen Mary's GS Walsall, St John's Coll Cambridge (BA, PhD), Inst of Educn Univ of London (PGCE); *m* 31 Aug 1974, Amanda Rosemary, da of Ivor William Broomhead; 2 s (Ian Benjamin b 25 Oct 1980, Alexander Thomas b 22 May 1982); *Career* DTI 1977–: seconded to Economics Directorate CBI 1982–83, seconded as sec to Cmmn of Inquiry into Regulatory Arrangements at Lloyd's 1986–87, asst sec DTI 1987–93; under sec and head Exec Agencies Directorate Dept of Transport 1993–96, dir of investigations and enforcement DTI 1996–; *Recreations* music, walking; *Style*— Jonathan Phillips, Esq; ✉ Investigations and Enforcement Directorate, Department of Trade and Industry, 10 Victoria Street, London SW1H 0NN (☎ 0171 215 3199, fax 0171 215 3225)

PHILLIPS, Josephine Marian (José); da of late William Norman Phillips, of Durban, South Africa, and Eileen Helen, *née* Callaghan; *b* 21 Oct 1947; *Educ* Convent HS Durban South Africa, Univ of Natal; *Career* info offr SE Arts 1975–78; Sadler's Wells Royal Ballet: press offr 1978–82, press and mktg offr 1983–87; mktg mangr Royal Opera House 1987–92, mktg dir The London Philharmonic 1992–94, freelance arts marketing conslt 1994–95, public affrs mangr The Nat Trust Thames and Chiltern Region 1995–; vice chm Exec Ctee Convent Garden Marketing Group until 1990; *Recreations* theatre, music, reading, cooking, gardening; *Style*— Ms José Phillips; ✉ 16 Dorchester Court, Herne Hill, London SE24 9QX (☎ and fax 0171 737 1666)

PHILLIPS, Hon Mrs (Laura Clare); *née* Grenfell; da of 2 and last Baron St Just (d 1984), and his 1 w Leslie, Lady Bonham Carter, da of Condé Nast; *b* 17 July 1950; *Educ* Univ of London (BA); *m* 1980, Hayden Phillips, CB, *qv*; 1 s (Thomas Peter b 1987), 2 da (Florence Leslie b 1981, Louisa Henrietta b 1984); *Career* with Private Office of Rt Hon Lord Jenkins of Hillhead at EC 1977–79, ed Becket Pubns (Becket's Directory of the City of London) 1984–90; bd dir: Rambert Dance Company 1992–, Cncl Griffin Soc 1993–, Nat Assoc of Probation and Bail Hostels 1993–, Siobhan Davies Dance Co 1994–; *Style*— The Hon Mrs Phillips

PHILLIPS, Leslie Samuel; s of Frederick Arthur Phillips (d 1934), and Cecelia Margaret, *née* Newlove (d 1984); *b* 20 April 1924; *Educ* Chingford Sch, Italia Conti; *m* (m dis), Penelope Noel, da of Richard Thorpe Bartley (d 1963); 2 s (Andrew Richard Bartley b 21 Nov 1954, Roger Quentin b 16 Nov 1959), 2 da (Caroline Elizabeth b 30 Oct 1949, Claudia Mary b 4 Oct 1951); m 2, 31 July 1982, Angela Margaret, da of Lt-Col Alexander Scoular (d 1978); 1 step s (Daniel Alexander Scoular b 6 Sept 1970); *Career* actor, director and producer; Mil Serv DLI; dir Royal Theatrical Fund; began acting 1935, numerous comedy and serious roles; *Theatre* incl: Dear Octopus, On Monday Next, For Better For Worse, The Man Most Likely To..., Chapter 17, Pride and Prejudice, Merry Wives of Windsor, Camino Real, Love for Love, The Cherry Orchard, Passion Play, Painting Churches, August; *Television* incl: Our Man At St Mark's, Summer's Lease, Chancer, Life After Life, Who Bombed Birmingham?, Rumpole, Mr Palfrey, Thacker, The Oz Trial, Lovejoy (BBC) 1994, The Changeling, Bermuda Grace, Royal Celebration, Vanity Dies Hard, Love on a Branch Line, Honey for Tea, 2 Golden Balls 1994, The Pale Horse, Canterville Ghost, Edgar Wallace (series, Germany) 1995; *Radio* incl: The Navy Lark, Round the World in 80 Days, Wind in the Willows, Philip and Rowena, England Their England; *Films* over one hundred incl: Ferdinando, Les Girls, Carry On Nurse, Doctor in Love, The Longest Day, Out Of Africa, Empire of the Sun, Scandal, King Ralph, August; *Style*— Leslie Phillips, Esq; ✉ c/o Harriet Robinson, ICM Ltd, Oxford House, 76 Oxford Street, London W1N 0AX (☎ 0171 636 6565, fax 0171 323 0101)

PHILLIPS, Malcolm John; s of Thomas John Phillips (d 1978), of Pembroke Dock, Dyfed, and Hilda Mary, *née* Morse (d 1978); *b* 18 Jan 1945; *Educ* Pembroke GS, Univ Coll of Wales Aberystwyth (BSc), Univ of Salford (PhD); *m* 1970, Ena Christine; 1 da (Ceri b 4 June 1981); *Career* product devpt mangr Van Den Berghs & Jurgens plc 1969–71 (brand mgmnt 1971–74), mktg mangr New Product Devpt Cadbury plc 1974–78, Crookes Healthcare Ltd 1978–93 (mktg mangr Cosmetics and Toiletries then all brands, head of mktg Healthcare, dir sales and mktg), mktg dir Pfizer Consumer Healthcare 1994–; memb The Proprietory Assoc of GB, memb Mktg Soc; *Recreations* food, wine, relaxation; *Style*— Malcolm Phillips; ✉ Marketing Director, Pfizer Consumer Healthcare, Wilsom Road, Alton, Hants GU34 2TJ (☎ 01420 84801)

PHILLIPS, Capt Mark Anthony Peter; CVO (1974), ADC(P); s of Maj Peter William Garside Phillips, MC, late 1 King's Dragoon Gds, and Anne Patricia, *née* Tiarks (d 1988); *b* 22 Sept 1948; *Educ* Marlborough, RMA Sandhurst; *m* 1973 (m dis 1992), HRH The Princess Royal (*see* Royal Family section); 1 s (Peter b 15 Nov 1977), 1 da (Zara b 15 May 1981); *Career* 1 The Queen's Dragoon Gds 1969, Regtl Duty 1969–74, co instr RMA Sandhurst 1974–77, Army Trg Directorate MOD 1977–78, ret; student RAC Cirencester 1978–79; personal ADC to HM The Queen 1974–; in Three Day Equestrian Event GB winning teams; team championships: World 1970, European 1971, Olympic Gold Medallists (Team) Olympic Games Munich 1972, memb Equestrian Team (Reserve) Olympic Games Mexico 1968 and Montreal 1976, Olympic Silver Medal (Team) Olympic Games Seoul 1988; dir: Gleneagles Mark Phillips Equestrian Centre 1988–92, Gloucestershire TEC, Equiland, Equiscot Management Ltd; govr Hartbury Coll; second person ever to win Badminton Horse Trials four times; memb Royal Caledonian Hunt; patron Young Glos; int trainer and course designer; chm British Equestrian Olympic Fund 1989–, chef d'equipe and coach US Equestrian Team 1993–; farmer; Liveryman Worshipful Cos of: Farriers, Saddlers, Loriners; Hon Liveryman Worshipful Co of Farmers; Freeman: Worshipful Co of Carmen, City of London; *Clubs* Buck's (hon memb); *Style*— Captain Mark Phillips, CVO, ADC(P); ✉ Aston Farm, Cherington, Tetbury, Glos GL8 8SW

PHILLIPS, Mark Paul; s of Norman John Phillips, of Beaconsfield, Bucks, and Wendy Sharon, *née* Cashman; *b* 28 Dec 1959; *Educ* The John Hampden Sch High Wycombe, Univ of Bristol (LLB, LLM); *m* 11 Aug 1984, Deborah Elizabeth, da of Norman Fisher, of Castleton, Derbs; 1 s (Jack Nathan Robert b 7 April 1996), 2 da (Kathryn Mary b 22 Oct 1990, Sarah Olivia Enid b 4 Aug 1993); *Career* called to the Bar Inner Temple 1984; practising commercial law and specialising in insolvency and city work at the chambers of Michael Crystal, QC 1986–; memb: Nat Youth Theatre of GB 1977–82, Br Debating Team to USA Speaking Union 1983; *Books* Byles on Bills of Exchange (contrib, 1988), Paget's Law of Banking (contrib, 1989), Butterworth's Insolvency Law Handbook (co ed, 1990 and 1994); *Style*— Mark Phillips, Esq; ✉ 3/4 South Square, Gray's Inn, London WC1R 5HP (☎ 0171 696 9900, fax 0171 696 9911)

PHILLIPS, Michael David; s of Frank Phillips, and Cynthia Margaret, *née* Bond; *b* 22 June 1955; *Educ* Rickmansworth GS, Univ of Bath (BSc), PCL (DipArch); *m* 23 Aug 1986, Jane Louise, *née* Hamon; 2 s (James b 28 April 1988, Harry b 9 May 1991), 1 da (Sarah b 6 April 1995); *Career* architect; DeVerre Urban Design prize PCL 1981; Casson Conder 1974, Ralph Erskine 1975, Moxley Jenner 1978, Powell Moya 1978–79, Hutchison Locke & Monk 1981–85; ptnr Michael Phillips Assocs 1985–; prizewinner: IBA Int Soc Housing Competition Berlin, Edinburgh Royal Mall urban regeneration competition, Arndale Centre redevelopment competition; RIBA; *Style*— Michael Phillips, Esq; ✉ 80 Drakefield Road, London SW17 8RR (☎ 0181 672 6247)

PHILLIPS, Mike; s of George Milton Phillips (d 1972), and Marjorie Phillips, of New York; *Educ* Highbury Sch London, Univ of London (BA), Univ of Essex (MA), Goldsmiths Coll Univ of London (PGCE); *ptnr* Dr J Owen; 2 s (Akwesi George b 17 Oct 1974, Ivan Akojo Romario b 12 July 1994); *Career* writer; teacher and community worker, ed Westindian World, educn offr BBC 1977–79, tv prodr Diverse Productions, sr lectr in media studies Univ of Westminster 1983–93, currently writer in res Royal Festival Hall South Bank Centre; freelance journalist and broadcaster BBC World Service, Radio Four, Guardian, Sunday Times, Observer; memb Film Prodn Bd BFI; winner Silver Dagger The Crime Writers Assoc 1990, current holder Arts Fndn Thriller Writing Fellowship; FRSA; *Books* Community Work and Racism (1982), Smell of the Coast (short stories, 1987), Blood Rights (1989), The Late Candidate (1990), Boyz N The Hood (1991), Notting Hill in the Sixties (1991), Whose Cities? (contrib, 1991), Shelter Anniversary Book (contrib, 1991), Point of Darkness (1994), An Image to Die For (1995), The Dancing Face (1997); as Joe Canzius: Fast Road To Nowhere (1996), Dead Men Also Dream (1997), Kill and Make Up (1997); screenplays: Bloodrights (BBC Television, 1990), The Late Candidate, Yardie (BBC), Expendable Man; *Recreations* gardening, reading, contemporary music; *Style*— Mike Phillips, Esq; ✉ c/o Anthony Harwood, Aitken & Stone, 29 Fernshaw Road, London SW10 0TG; South Bank Centre London SE1 8XX (☎ 0171 921 0619)

PHILLIPS, (David) Nicholas; s of (David) Cecil Phillips (d 1988), of Sandwich, Kent, and Megan, *née* Davey; *b* 13 Jan 1953; *Educ* Dover Coll; *m* 13 Sept 1980, Anne Rosemary, da of Ernest Frank Robert Cross (d 1980), of Salfords, Surrey; 1 s (Oliver Nicholas b 1984), 2 da (Lucy Vanessa b 1987, Amelia Fleur b 1991); *Career* admitted slr 1977; ptnr Stephenson Harwood 1987–; Freeman Worshipful Co of Slrs 1980; memb Law Soc 1977; *Recreations* sailing, tennis; *Clubs* Royal Corinthian Yacht; *Style*— Nicholas Phillips, Esq; ✉ The Thatched House, The Street, Bolney, W Sussex (☎ 01444 881405); Stephenson Harwood, One St Paul's Churchyard, London EC4M 8SH (☎ 0171 329 4422, fax 0171 606 0822, telex 886789)

PHILLIPS, Rt Hon Lord Justice; Rt Hon Sir Nicholas Addison Phillips; kt (1987); *b* 21 Jan 1938; *Educ* Bryanston, King's Coll Cambridge; *m* 1972, Christylle Marie-Thérèse Rouffiac, *née* Doreau; 2 da, and 1 step s, 1 step da; *Career* RNVR 1956–58; called to the Bar Middle Temple 1962, jr counsel to MOD and to Treasy in Admty matters 1973–78, QC 1978, recorder of the Crown Ct 1982, judge of High Court of Justice (Queen's Bench Div) 1987–95, a Lord Justice of Appeal 1995–; chm Cncl of Legal Educn 1992–; govr Bryanston Sch 1975– (chm 1981); *Style*— The Rt Hon Lord Justice Phillips; ✉ Royal Courts of Justice, Strand, London WC2A 2LL

PHILLIPS, Nicolas Hood (Nick); s of John Henry Hood Phillips (d 1977), and Winifred Marion, *née* Shovelton (d 1994); *b* 7 Aug 1941; *Educ* St Paul's, St John's Coll Oxford (MA); *m* June 1969, Katherine, da of late Robert Kirk; 2 s (Christopher b June 1973, Benedict b June 1976), 1 da (Clare b Dec 1971); *Career* early posts in mktg and res (Fisons Ltd, S H Benson, AGB Research and EMI Ltd) 1962–67, res controller Granada Television 1967–73, head of res COI 1973–78, mktg servs dir Beecham Products 1978–84, dir Granada Television 1984–89, DG IPA 1989–; other directorships incl: National Readership Surveys Ltd, Audit Bureau of Circulation Ltd, Radio Joint Audience Research Ltd, Broadcasters Audience Research Bd, Advtg Standards Bd of Fin, Euro Assoc of Advtg Agencies; memb UK Govt's Advsy Ctee on Advtg; author of conf papers and articles on advtg, res and media; FRSA 1992; *Recreations* travel, opera, bridge, family; *Clubs* RAC; *Style*— Nick Phillips, Esq; ✉ 1 Nassau Road, Barnes, London SW13 9QF (☎ 0181 741 3326); Institute of Practitioners in Advertising, 44 Belgrave Square, London SW1X 8QS (☎ 0171 235 7020, fax 0171 245 9904)

PHILLIPS, (Jeremy) Patrick Manfred; QC (1980); s of Manfred Henry Phillips (d 1963), and Irene Margaret, *née* Symondson (d 1970); *b* 27 Feb 1941; *Educ* Charterhouse; *m* 1970, Virginia Gwendolyn Dwyer; 2 s (Rufus b 1969, d 1989, Marcus b 1970); m 2, 1976, Judith Gaskell Hetherington; 2 s (Tobias b 1982, Seamus b 1985), 2 da (Rebekah b 1979, Natasha b 1980); *Career* articled clerk Thomson McLintock & Co CAs 1958–61, called to the Bar 1964, head of Chambers 2 Temple Gardens EC4 1991–; DTI inspr into affairs of Queens Moat House PLC 1993–; owner of Kentwell Hall; contrib to successive ed of Cooper's Manual of Auditing and Cooper's Students' Manual of Auditing; deviser and originator of Kentwell Hall's Annual Re-Creation of Tudor Domestic Life 1978–; landowner (900 acres); dir Care International UK (pt of Care Int, the Third World devpt agency); *Books* author of various articles and pamphlets on Kentwell Hall, Tudor domestic life and heritage educn; *Recreations* Kentwell Hall, Tudor buildings, Tudor domestic life; *Style*— Patrick Phillips, Esq, QC; ✉ Kentwell Hall, Long Melford, Suffolk; 2 Temple Gardens, London EC4Y 9AY

PHILLIPS, (Ian) Peter; JP (Inner London); s of Bernard Phillips (d 1996), of Ferring-on-Sea, Sussex, and Constance Mary Clayton (d 1984); *b* 13 Oct 1944; *Educ* Highgate Sch London, Sorbonne; *m* 2 May 1970, Wendy, da of Maurice Samuel Berne, of London NW11; 1 s (Leo b 1972), 1 da (Kira b 1974); *Career* ptnr Bernard Phillips & Co London 1968–82, ptnr and UK head of corporate recovery services Arthur Andersen & Co 1982–88, chm Buchler Phillips 1988–; treas North Kensington Neighbourhood Law Centre 1972, dir Hampstead Theatre 1990–; pres Insolvency Practitioners Assoc 1988–89; FCA 1968, FIPA 1981, FCCA 1983, MICM 1974; *Recreations* horse riding, skiing, modern jazz, baroque music, photography; *Style*— Peter Phillips, Esq, JP; ✉ Buchler Phillips, 84 Grosvenor St, London W1X 9DF (☎ 0171 518 5201, fax 0171 629 6444)

PHILLIPS, Peter; *Educ* Univ of Oxford (organ scholar); *Career* fndr and dir The Tallis Scholars (choral gp specialising in Renaissance sacred music) 1973–, also co-fndr and dir Gimell Records Ltd (affiliated to Philips Classics 1996–) 1981–; music columnist The Spectator (also cricket corr 1989) 1983–, also contrib to Musical Times (proprietor 1995–), Early Music, New Republic, Guardian, Music and Letters, Music and Musicians and The Listener; numerous TV and radio bdcasts on progs incl Music Weekly (BBC Radio 3 and World Service) and Kaleidoscope and Today (Radio 4), Tallis Scholars and Gimell Records subject of South Bank Show documentary (LWT) 1990 and cover feature Gramophone magazine 1994; live bdcasts from BBC Proms 1988 and Aldeburgh, Bath and Cheltenham Festivals, regular tours of Europe, US and Far East, around eighty concerts a year; bdcast from Sistine Chapel featured on Japanese and Italian TV to mark cleaning of Michelangelo's Last Judgement; *Recordings* incl: Josquin des Près' Missa Pange lingua and Missa La sol fa re mi (Gramophone Magazine Record of the Year 1987), Palestrina's Missa Assumpta est Maria and Missa Sicut lilium (Gramophone Early Music Award 1991), Josquin's L'Homme armé Masses (Prix Diapason d'Or 1989, International Record Critics' Award 1990), Lassus' Missa Osculetur me (Prix Diapason d'Or 1989), Victoria Requiem (Ritmo Early Music Award Spain, 1988), Rore's Missa Praeter rerum seriem (Gramophone Early Music Award and Classic FM People's Choice 1994); *Books* English Sacred Music 1549–1649, Companion to Medieval and Renaissance Music (contrib, 1992); *Recreations* Romantic music, cricket, philology, Arabia; *Clubs* Chelsea Arts, MCC, Athenaeum; *Style*— Peter Phillips, Esq; ✉ c/o Gimell Records Ltd, 4 Newtec Place, Magdalen Road, Oxford OX4 1RE; 22 Gibson Square, London N1 0RD (☎ 0171 354 0627); 48 rue des Francs-Bourgeois, 75003 Paris, France (☎ 00 33 1 42 72 44 61)

PHILLIPS, Peter Anthony; s of Thomas George Phillips, of Cardiff, and Hilda Maud, *née* Connolly (d 1962); *b* 21 June 1938; *Educ* Howardian HS Cardiff, Cardiff Coll of Art (Cert commercial art), Welsh Coll of Advanced Technol (HNC Building); *Career* television and theatre designer; Nat Serv Gunner RA 1960–62; trainee Co Design Studio 1955–60, designer for int co 1962–63; BBC: design asst 1963–66, designer 1966–80, sr designer 1980–82, mangr design resources BBC Wales 1982–93; design conslt 1993–; MCSD 1970 (licentiate 1960), memb Nat Cncl CSD 1989; *Theatre* My People and Solidarity (Theatr Clwyd), War Music and Pity of War (Lyric Hammersmith); *Television* incl: Hawkmoor, Dylan, Enigma Files, The Rajah's Diamond (TV opera, RTS winner Wales Award Design Award); *Recreations* gardening, travel; *Style*— Peter Phillips, Esq; ✉ Telynfa, Gwaelod-y-Garth, nr Cardiff CF4 8HJ (☎ 01222 810791)

PHILLIPS, Sir Peter John; kt (1990), OBE (1983); s of Walter Alfred Phillips (d 1972), of Cardiff, and Victoria Mary Phillips (d 1974); *b* 18 June 1930; *Educ* Radley, Pembroke Coll Oxford (MA); *m* 9 June 1956, Jean Gwendoline, da of Sydney Essex Williams of Cardiff; 1 s (Jeremy Essex b 30 May 1957), 1 da (Louise Victoria b 7 May 1960); *Career* Nat Serv 2 Lt Welch Regt 1948–49; md Aberthaw & Bristol Channel Portland Cement plc 1964–83; chm: AB Electronic Products Group plc 1987–93, Principality Building Society 1991–; former memb Cncl CBI Wales (chm 1982–83); memb Cncl Univ of Wales Coll of Cardiff, govr Univ of Glamorgan 1993– (dep chm 1996–), chm University of Glamorgan Commercial Services Ltd 1995–; *Recreations* fishing, walking, reading; *Clubs* Cardiff & County; *Style*— Sir Peter Phillips, OBE; ✉ Great House, Llanblethian, Cowbridge, S Glamorgan CF7 7JG (☎ 01446 775163)

PHILLIPS, Richard Charles Jonathan; QC (1990); s of Air Cdre M N Phillips (d 1986), and Dorothy Ellen, *née* Green (d 1987); *b* 8 Aug 1947; *Educ* King's Sch Ely Cambridge (King's scholar), Sidney Sussex Coll Cambridge (exhibitioner); *m* 9 Sept 1978, Alison Jane (Annie), OBE, da of David Arthur Francis; 1 da (Ella Rose b 31 March 1995); *Career* called to the Bar 1970, specialises in town and country planning and local govt; asst Parly boundary cmmr for England; *Recreations* natural history, travel, photography; *Style*— Richard Phillips, Esq, QC; ✉ 2nd Floor, 2 Harcourt Bldgs, Temple, London EC4Y 9DB (☎ 0171 353 8415, fax 0171 353 7622)

PHILLIPS, Robert Sneddon; s of William James Phillips (d 1982), and Mary Jane Sneddon (d 1983); *b* 15 Sept 1932; *Educ* George Heriot's Sch Edinburgh, Univ of Edinburgh (MB ChB); *m* 2 Oct 1957, Isabella Newlands (Ella), da of George Forrest (d 1969); 1 s (Graeme Robert b 2 Nov 1964), 1 da (Gillian Moir b 16 March 1961); *Career* Surgn Lt RNVR 1957–59; conslt orthopaedic surgn 1967–; contrib to numerous pubns on orthopaedic matters; memb: Methodist Church, Leonard Cheshire Fndn, local ctee Oakwood Cheshire Home; public speaker on works of Robert Burns; fell Br Orthopaedic Assoc, FRCSEd, FRCS; *Recreations* cricket, golf; *Clubs* Stockport Cricket, Hazel Grove Golf, Forty, MCC; *Style*— Robert Phillips, Esq; ✉ 3 Milverton Drive, Bramhall, Stockport SK7 1EY (☎ 0161 440 8037); 11 St John St, Manchester M3 4DW (☎ 0161 832 9999)

PHILLIPS, Sir Robin Francis; 3 Bt (UK 1912); s of Sir Lionel Francis Phillips, 2 Bt (d 1944); *b* 29 July 1940; *Educ* Aiglon Coll Switzerland; *Heir* none; *Career* owner of Ravenscourt Theatre Sch Ltd Hammersmith London; *Style*— Sir Robin Phillips, Bt; ✉ 12 Manson Mews, Queen's Gate, London SW7 5AF

PHILLIPS, Siân; da of David Thomas Phillips (d 1961), and Sally Thomas (d 1985); *Educ* Pontardawe GS, Cardiff Coll Univ of Wales (BA), RADA (Meggie Albanesi scholarship, Bancroft Gold medal); *m* 1, 1959 (m dis 1979), Peter O'Toole, *qv*; 2 da (Kate b 1961, Pat b 1964); m 2, 1979 (m dis 1992), Robin David Sachs, s of Leonard Sachs (d 1990); *Career* actress; former BBC News reader/announcer Wales; memb: Gorsedd of Bards 1960, Drama Ctee Arts Cncl 1970–75; govr Welsh Coll of Music and Drama, former govr St David's Theatre Tst, dir Film Wales, fell Welsh Coll of Music and Drama 1991; Hon DLitt Univ of Wales 1983; hon fell: Cardiff Coll Univ of Wales 1980, Polytechnic of Wales 1988; delivered RTE annual (Huw Wheldon) lecture on BBC TV 1993; *Theatre* London prodns incl: Hedda Gabler 1959, Ondine, Duchess of Malfi 1961, Lizard on the Rock 1961, Gentle Jack 1963, Maxibules 1964, Night of the Iguana 1964 (best actress nomination), Ride a Cock Horse 1965, Man and Superman (best actress nomination), Man of Destiny 1966, The Burglar 1967, Epitaph for George Dillon 1972, A Nightingale in Bloomsbury Square 1973, The Gay Lord Quex 1975, Spinechiller 1978, You Never Can Tell 1979, Pal Joey 1979–81 (best actress in a musical nomination), Dear Liar 1982, Major Barbara (NT) 1983, Peg 1984, Gigi 1985, Thursday's Ladies 1987, Brel 1988, Paris Match 1989, Vanilla 1990, The Manchurian Candidate 1991, Painting Churches (Playhouse), Ghosts 1993, Marlene (RNT Studio) 1994, An Inspector Calls (Royale Broadway) 1995, A Little Night Music (RNT, Olivier Award nomination for Best Supporting Performance in a Musical 1996) 1995–96, Marlene (nat tour) 1996; *Television* drama series incl: Shoulder to Shoulder, How Green was my Valley (BAFTA Best Actress Award), Crime and Punishment, Tinker Tailor Soldier Spy, Barriers, The Oresteia of Aeschylus, I Claudius (BAFTA Best Actress Award and Best Performance Royal TV Soc), Vanity Fair, Shadow of the Noose, Snow Spider, Emlyns Moon (1990, BAFTA Best Actress nomination), Perfect Scoundrels (1991), The Chestnut Soldier 1991, The Borrowers 1992; *Films* incl: Becket 1963, Goodbye Mr Chips 1968 (Best Supporting Actress awards), Murphy's War 1970, Under Milk Wood 1971, Dune (dir David Lynch) 1984, Valmont (dir Milos Forman) 1989, Dark River, A Painful Case (RTE), Age of Innocence (dir Martin Scorsese) 1992, Heidi (Disney), House of America; *Radio* incl: Bequest to a Nation, Antony and Cleopatra, Henry VIII, All's Well That Ends Well, Oedipus, Phaedra, The Maids; *Records* Pal Joey, Gigi, Peg, Bewitched Bothered and Bewildered (single), I Remember Mama, A Little Night Music; *Books* Sian Phillips' Needlepoint (1987); *Recreations* gardening, drawing, needlepoint; *Style*— Miss Sian Phillips; ✉ c/o Saraband Associates, 265 Liverpool Road, London N1 1LX (☎ 0171 609 5313, fax 0171 609 2370)

PHILLIPS, Dr Simon Jeremy; s of late Basil Montagu Phillips, LVO, of Wells, Somerset, and Sheila Monica, *née* Redding; *b* 13 April 1943; *Educ* Sherborne, St Bartholomew's Hosp and Univ of London (MB BS, MRCS, LRCP, DCH, DObstRCOG), Univ of Bath (MPhil); *m* 30 Sept 1967, (Susan) Jennifer, da of Albert Hugh Thompson (d 1969), of Leeds, Yorkshire; 2 s (Jeremy David Hugh b 29 Oct 1970, Charles James Aston b 24 Oct 1973); *Career* GP 1970–96 (recently ptnr in practice); dir Inst of Refugee Health Care Studies Bath, hon med advsr Returning Aid Workers Tst London; res grant from Bath Area Med Res Tst for work with refugees from Indo-China 1981–83; author of numerous papers, articles in major journals and contribns to med books; Freeman City of London 1968, Liveryman Worshipful Co of Gardeners 1976 (Freeman 1968); memb: BMA 1966, Clinical Soc of Bath; FRGS 1993; *Recreations* cooking, fishing, walking and mountaineering, backpacking, cross country skiing, photography, painting; *Style—* Dr Simon Phillips; ✉ Church Holding, Etchilhampton, Devizes, Wilts SN10 3JL (☎ 01380 860291)

PHILLIPS, Terence Anthony; s of Walter Edwin Phillips (d 1991), and Mary Elizabeth, *née* Gallagher (d 1991); *b* 18 Nov 1934; *Educ* St Mary's Coll Middlesbrough, St Boniface Coll Plymouth, St Thomas Univ Rome (Baccalaureatus, Licentia), Birkbeck Coll London (BA, MA), Inst of Educn Univ of London (post grad cert in educn); *m* Barbara Anne, da of James Henry Allison; 2 da (Claire Elizabeth b 20 May 1978, Katherine Isabel 21 March 1980); *Career* teacher and relief worker Zaire 1962–70, asst master Maidstone GS 1976–81, head of VI form The Margaret Dane Sch Bishop's Stortford 1981–83; Hemel Hempstead Sch: dep headmaster 1984–89, acting headmaster 1989–90, headmaster 1990–; chm Dacorum Evironmental Forum; memb SHA; FRSA; *Recreations* sailing, visiting art galleries and collections, travel, reading; *Style—* Terence Phillips, Esq; ✉ Hemel Hempstead School, Heath Lane, Hemel Hempstead, Herts HP1 1RP (☎ 01442 390100, fax 01442 233706)

PHILLIPS, Thomas Bernard Hudson (Tom); s of late Prof Arthur Phillips OBE, and Kathleen, *née* Hudson; *b* 12 Aug 1938; *Educ* King's Sch Canterbury; *m* 14 July 1979, Rosemary Eleanor, da of Maj R A D Sinclair (ret), of Burnham-on-Crouch, Essex; 1 s (Roland b 12 Dec 1980), 1 da (Laura b 9 May 1982); *Career* slr; State Counsel Kenya 1967–70; Herbert Smith: joined 1970, ptnr 1977–96, conslt 1996–; memb Law Soc; *Recreations* sailing, skiing, golf; *Style—* Tom Phillips, Esq; ✉ c/o Herbert Smith, Exchange House, Primrose St, London EC2A 2HS (☎ 0171 374 8000)

PHILLIPS, (Mark) Trevor; s of George Milton Phillips (d 1972), of Georgetown, Guyana and New York, and Marjorie Eileen, *née* Canzius; *b* 31 Dec 1953; *Educ* Wood Green Sch N London, Queen's Coll Georgetown Guyana, Imperial Coll London (BSc); *m* 25 July 1981, Asha Aline Francine, da of Padmashree Jehangir Bhownagary, of Bombay and Paris; 2 da (Sushila Melody b 11 July 1984, Holly May b 7 Jan 1988); *Career* pres NUS 1978–80; LWT: researcher (Skin, The London Programme) 1980–82, prodr (Black on Black, Club Mix, The Making of Britain) 1982–86; reporter This Week Thames TV 1986–87; LWT: presenter The London Programme 1987– (ed 1987–93), anchor Eyewitness 1988–90, presenter Nation 1992–93, head of current affairs 1993–94, exec prodr factual progs 1995–; dir Pepper Productions 1995–; presenter: The Midnight Hour (BBC) 1994–, In Living Colour (BBC) 1996–, Crosstalk (LNN) 1996–; also presenter: US Prized Pieces Winner (public affrs/news) 1985, RICS Journalist and Broadcasters Award 1988, Royal Television Soc Awards 1988 and 1993; memb: Film Video and Broadcasting Panel The Arts Cncl, Dirs Inst of Citizenship Studies, London Arts Bd, London First, Greenwich Millenium Tst; chm: The Runnymede Trust, Hampstead Theatre; Hon MA; RTS 1990, ARCS, FRSA; *Books* Partners In One Nation (1986); *Recreations* music, gardening, America; *Clubs* The Groucho; *Style—* Trevor Phillips, Esq; ✉ London Weekend Television, London TV Centre, Upper Ground, London SE1 9LT (☎ 0171 620 1620 and fax 0181 600 5200)

PHILLIPS, Trevor Thomas (Tom); s of David John Phillips, and Margaret Agnes, *née* Arnold; *b* 24 May 1937; *Educ* Henry Thornton GS, St Catherine's Coll Oxford (MA), Camberwell Sch of Arts and Crafts (NDD); *m* 1, 12 Aug 1961 (m dis 1988), Jill Purdy; 1 s (Conrad Leofric (Leo) b 26 Jan 1965), 1 da ((Eleanor) Ruth b 25 Jan 1964); m 2, 26 Oct 1995, Fiona Maddocks, *qv*; *Career* artist; visiting artist and Josep Lluis Sert practitioner in the arts Carpenter Center Harvard 1993; composer of the opera IRMA (recorded twice by Obscure Records 1977 and Matchless Recordings 1988, performed at Bordeaux Festival, Istanbul Festival and ICA); writer and critic for TLS and regular writer for BBC Music Magazine and RA Magazine; translated, illustrated, printed and published Dante's Inferno 1983, TV dir of A TV Dante for Channel 4 with Peter Greenaway (first prize Montreal Festival 1990, Prix Italia 1991); chm Royal Acad Library 1989–94, currently chm of Exhbs Royal Acad, vice chm copywright Cncls 1984–88, hon pres S London Art Soc 1988–; hon fell: St Catherine's Coll Oxford 1992, Bretton Hall Univ of Leeds 1994; RE 1987, RA 1989 (ARA 1984) *Work in Collections* Tate Gallery, V & A Museum, Br Museum, Nat Portrait Gallery, Br Cncl, MOMA NY, Philadelphia Museum, Library of Congress, Bibliothèque Nationale Paris, Aust Nat Gallery Canberra, Museum of Fine Arts Budapest; *Exhibitions* worldwide since 1969 incl: retrospective exhibition (Kunsthalle Basel, Gemeente Museum The Hague, Serpentine Gallery London) 1974–75, portrait retrospective (Nat Portrait Gallery) 1989, N Carolina Museum 1990, retrospective (Royal Academy) 1992, new works (V&A) 1992, retrospective (Yale Center for British Art) 1993, Univ of Penn 1993, South London Gallery 1997, Dulwich Picture Gallery 1997; curator Africa: The Art of a Continent (Royal Acad) 1993–95; *Designed Tapestries* St Catherine's Coll Oxford, HQ Channel 4, Morgan Grenfell Office, The Ivy Restaurant; *Books* Trailer (1971), Works and Texts to 1974 (1975), A Humument (revised edns, 1987 and 1997), Heart of a Humument (1985), Where Are They Now - The Class of '47 (1990), Works and Texts Vol II (1992), A Humument - Variants and Variations (1992), Merely Connect (with Salman Rushdie, 1994), Aspects of Art (1996); *Recreations* watching cricket, collecting African art; *Clubs* Chelsea Arts, The Groucho, SCCC; *Style—* Tom Phillips, Esq, RA; ✉ 57 Talfourd Rd, London SE15 (☎ 0171 701 3978, fax 0171 703 2800)

PHILLIPS OF ELLESMERE, Baron (Life Peer UK 1994), of Ellesmere in the County of Shropshire; Sir David Chilton Phillips; KBE (1989), kt (1979); s of Charles Harry Phillips (d 1963), of Ellesmere, Shropshire, and Edith Harriet, *née* Finney (d 1972), da of Samuel Finney, MP 1916–22; *b* 7 March 1924; *Educ* Oswestry Boys' HS, Univ Coll Cardiff (BSc, PhD); *m* 1960, Diana Kathleen, da of Maj Edward Maitland Hutchinson, RA (d 1957), of Chalfont St Giles; 1 da (Hon Sarah); *Career* Sub Lt RNVR 1944–47; post doctoral fell Nat Res Cncl of Canada 1951–53, res offr Nat Res Labs Ottawa Canada 1953–55, res worker Royal Instn London 1956–66, prof of molecular biophysics Univ of Oxford 1966–90 (emeritus prof 1990–), fell CCC Oxford 1966–90 (hon fell 1990–); chm Finsbury Communications Ltd 1992–; Fullerian prof of physiology Royal Instn 1979–83; dir Celltech Ltd 1982–, biological sec The Royal Soc 1976–83; memb MRC 1974–78, Royal Soc assessor 1976–83, chm Advsy Bd Res Cncls 1983–93; tstee Wolfson Fndn 1988–, govr De Montfort Univ 1993–; Hon DSc: Univ of Leicester 1974, Univ of Wales 1975, Univ of Chicago 1978, Univ of Warwick 1982, Univ of Exeter 1982, Univ of Birmingham 1987, Univ of Glasgow 1990, Univ of Glamorgan 1993, Univ of Bath 1993; Hon DUniv: Univ of Essex 1983, Univ of Stirling 1995; Hon PhD Weizmann Inst of Science 1990; Biochemical Soc Biochemical Soc CIBA medal 1971, Royal Soc Royal medal 1975, Prix Charles Léopold Mayer French Académie des Sciences (jtly, 1979), Wolf prize (jtly, 1987), Aminoff prize Royal Swedish Acad 1991; hon memb American Soc Biological Chemists, foreign hon memb American Acad Arts and Sciences; foreign associate US Nat Acad of Sciences, foreign memb Royal Swedish Acad; FInstP, FRS 1967 (vice pres 1972–73 and 1976–83); *Style—* The Rt Hon Lord Phillips of Ellesmere, KBE, FRS; ✉ 35 Addisland Court, Holland Villas Road, London W14 8DA (☎ 0171 602 0738, fax 0171 602 5346)

PHILLIS, Michael John; s of Francis William Phillis, and Gertrude Grace, *née* Pitman; bro of Robert Weston Phillis, *qv*; *b* 6 March 1948; *Educ* Archbishop Tennyson's GS Croydon; *m* 30 Aug 1969, Janice Susan, da of George Horne (d 1963); 1 s (Marc Weston b 26 Aug 1973), 1 da (Michelle b 18 Feb 1976); *Career* Bank of London & S America Ltd 1967–73, asst dir London & Continental Bankers 1973–81, regnl vice pres Marine Midland Bank 1981–83; dep gen mangr (Treasy) Kansallis Osake Pankki 1983–94; dep gen mangr and treas Merita Bank (formed upon merger of Kansallis Banking Group and Union Bank of Finland) 1995–; dir: Kansallis Gota Securities Ltd 1989–90, Kansallis Securities Ltd 1990–95, Merita Securities Ltd; memb Chicago Mercantile Exchange Interest Rate Advsy Ctee (London) 1990–94; *Recreations* golf, music, family, gardening; *Clubs* South Weald Golf, Pinheiros Altos Golf; *Style—* Michael Phillis, Esq; ✉ Merita Bank, 19 Thomas More Street, London E1 9YW (☎ 0171 265 3333, fax 0171 709 7003, telex 887820)

PHILLIS, Robert Weston (Bob); s of Francis William Phillis, and Gertrude Grace, *née* Pitman; bro of Michael John Phillis, *qv*; *b* 3 Dec 1945; *Educ* John Ruskin GS, Univ of Nottingham; *m* 16 July 1966, Jean, da of Herbert William Derham; 3 s (Martin b 1971, Benjamin b 1974, Timothy b 1974); *Career* lectr Univ of Edinburgh and Scottish Business Sch 1971–75; md: Sun Printers Ltd 1976–79, Independent Television Publications Ltd 1979–81, Central Independent Television plc 1981–87; dir: ITVA 1982–87, ITN Ltd 1982–87; chm: Zenith Productions Ltd 1984–91, ITV Network Programming Ctee 1984–86; gp md Carlton Communications plc 1987–91, chief exec ITN Ltd 1991–93, dir World Television News Ltd 1991–93, dep dir gen BBC 1993–, md BBC World Service 1993–94; chm: BBC Enterprises Ltd 1993–94, BBC Worldwide 1994–; dir and tstee TV Tst for the Environment 1984–, chm RTS 1989–92 (and vice pres), vice pres Int Cncl Nat Acad of TV Arts and Sciences 1994– (dir 1985–); vice pres European Broadcasting Union 1995–; FRSA 1984, FRTS 1988; *Recreations* golf, skiing, sport, travel, music; *Style—* R W Phillis, Esq; ✉ BBC Broadcasting House, London W1A 1AA (☎ 0171 580 4468)

PHILLPOTTS, Simon Vivian Surtees; s of Christopher Louis George Phillpotts, CMG (d 1985), and Vivian Chanter, *née* Bowden; *b* 9 Feb 1947; *Educ* Abberley Hall, Harrow, Georgetown Univ USA; *m* 1 June 1991, Emma Rose Dymock, da of William Ashe Dymoke Windham, of Parc Gwynne, Glasbury-on-Wye, Radnorshire; 1 s (Archie Christopher Louis b 29 Dec 1992), 1 da (Lara Georgina Windham b 21 April 1995); *Career* mangr: Shiro (China) Ltd Hong Kong 1968–74, Jardine Matheson & Co Hong Kong 1974–82; gen mangr Anglo Swiss Trading Hong Kong 1982–84, dir Daks-Simpson Ltd UK 1985–; *Style—* Simon Phillpotts, Esq; ✉ The White House, White Street, Maryet Lavington, nr Devizes, Wiltshire SN10 4DP (☎ 01380 813236, fax 01380 816236); Daks-Simpson, 34 Jermyn Street, London SW1 6HS (☎ 0171 439 8781, fax 0171 437 3633)

PHILPOT, Elizabeth; *née* Devereux Massey; da of William Edmund Devereux Massey, CBE (d 1991), of Dorking, Surrey, and Ingrid, *née* Glad-Block; *b* 8 April 1943; *Educ* Heathfield, Courtauld Inst Univ of London (BA), Johann Wolfgang Goethe-Universität Frankfurt am Main (Dip); *m* 10 Sept 1977, Timothy Stephen Burnett Philpot, s of Christopher Burnett Philpot (d 1971), of Pickering, Yorks; *Career* local govt offr LCC (later GLC and ILEA) 1962–65, asst keeper of the muniments Westminster Abbey 1968–69, admin asst Bedford Coll London 1969–70; HM Dip Serv 1970–82: third sec Brasilia Embassy, info attaché Paris Embassy; freelance lectr and art historian 1982–, assoc lectr in history of art Univ of Surrey 1990–, lectr Assoc for Cultural Exchange Study Tours Cambridge 1993–; chm Reigate Branch Nat Cncl of Women of GB 1990–93, memb Nat Cncl of Women of GB Health Ctee 1988–94; Freeman City of London 1975, Liveryman Worshipful Co of Clockmakers 1983 (Steward 1989); *Publications* Judith and Holofernes: Changing Images in the History of Art (essay included in Translating Religious Texts, ed D Jasper, 1993); *Recreations* art history, travel, photography, horology, theatre, swimming, sailing, skiing; *Style—* Mrs Timothy Philpot; ✉ Ivinghoe, 9 Croft Ave, Dorking, Surrey RH4 1LN (☎ 01306 882739, fax 01306 885938)

PHILPOTTS, Paul; s of Raymond Dennis Philpotts (d 1987), and Ruby Elizabeth May, *née* Richards (d 1973); *b* 22 July 1957; *Educ* Eton, Univ of Durham (BSc Engrg Sci); *m* 22 May 1982, Joanna Stephanie, da of Gerald Hearley; 1 da (Alexandra Lucy b 29 Oct 1987); *Career* asst ed: Control & Instrumentation 1979–81, Computer Systems 1981–82; ed Food Processing 1983; mktg mangr Techpress Publishing 1983–85, account gp dir Hill & Knowlton 1986–88, sr conslt Shandwick Consultants 1988–89, mktg dir IML Group 1989–92, dir Shandwick Consultants 1992–94, divnl md Burson-Marsteller 1994–96, md Burson-Marsteller UK 1996–, dir Burson-Marsteller Europe 1996–; *Recreations* opera, tropical fish, computing; *Style—* Paul Philpotts, Esq; ✉ Camden Cleve, 39 Yester Road, Chislehurst, Kent BR7 5HN (☎ 0181 467 5485, fax 0181 467 4944); Burson-Marsteller, 24–28 Bloomsbury Way, London WC1A 2PX (☎ 0171 831 6262, fax 0171 831 5510, mobile 0468 457249, e-mail paul@yester.demon.co.uk)

PHIN, Dr Nicholas Fulton; *b* 5 May 1958; *Educ* Kilmarnock Acad, Univ of Glasgow (MB ChB), Univ of Wales Cardiff (LLB (Legal Aspects of Med)); *Career* dir of public health: Grimsby HA 1991–92, Scunthorpe and Grimsby 1992–96, Dyfed Powys HA 1996–; MFPHM 1991; *Style—* Dr Nicholas Phin; ✉ Dyfed Powys Health Authority, PO Box 13, Carmarthen SA31 3YH (☎ 01267 234501)

PHIPPIN, Eric Thomas; s of Thomas William Phippin (d 1979), and Margaret Anne, *née* Preston; *b* 9 Oct 1931; *Educ* Loughborough Central Sch London, City of London Coll; *m* 18 July 1953, Patricia Ann, da of Sidney Henry Collins (d 1982), of London; 3 s (Paul Jeremy b 31 Aug 1957, Stephen Christopher b 2 May 1960, Andrew Michael b 7 Sept 1966); *Career* Nat Serv RAF (movement control) 1950–52; RAFVR: Pilot Offr 1952, Flying Offr (orgn and supply) 1955; mgmnt trainee Union-Castle Mail Steamship Co Ltd 1952–63 (seconded to S and E Africa 1956–58); dir: Chandris Cruises Ltd 1963–77 (passenger mangr 1963), Ocean Travel Devpt 1967–75, Chandris Tours 1971–77, CTC Lines 1977–89, CTC (Air Sea Holidays) Ltd 1977–89, CTC (Hellas) SA 1984–89, Celebrity Cruises (UK) Ltd 1989–; chm Passenger Shipping Assoc 1994– (dir 1975–); Freeman: City of London 1974, Worshipful Co of Basket Makers 1974; FCIT 1963; *Recreations* cricket, music; *Style—* Eric Phippin, Esq; ✉ Celebrity Cruises (UK) Ltd, 17 Old Park Lane, London W1Y 3LH (☎ 0171 412 0290, fax 0171 412 0908, telex 290708)

PHIPPS, Dr Colin Barry; s of Edgar Reeves Phipps; *b* 23 July 1934; *Educ* Acton Co Sch, Swansea GS, UCL, Univ of Birmingham; *m* 1956, Marion May, da of Clifford Harry Lawrey; 2 s, 2 da; *Career* dep chm and chief exec Clyde Petroleum Ltd 1979–83, chm Clyde 1983–94, chm Greenwich Resources plc 1989–, chm Universal Ceramic Materials plc 1993–; MP (Lab) Dudley W 1974–79; memb: Cncl of Europe 1976–79, Western Euro Union 1976–79; chm Falkland Islands Fndn 1990–92; FGS 1956, FInstPet 1972, MIGeol 1978, CGeol 1992; *Clubs* Reform; *Style—* Dr Colin Phipps; ✉ Mathon Court, Mathon, Malvern WR13 5NZ (☎ 01684 892267); 24 Old Burlington Street, London W1X 1RL (☎ 0171 734 5575)

PHIPPS, Air Vice-Marshal Leslie William; CB (1983), AFC (1959); s of late Frank Walter Phipps; *b* 17 April 1930; *Educ* SS Philip and James Sch Oxford; *Career* successively fighter pilot, Sqdn Cdr and Station Cdr 1951–70, dir RAF Staff Coll 1971–72, Cdr RAF (Oman) 1973–74, RCDS 1975, Cdr UK MOD team Saudi Arabia 1976–78, dir of Air Def and Overseas Ops 1978–79, dir-gen Personnel Mgmnt RAF 1980–82, sr directing staff RCDS 1983; British Aerospace (Mil Aircraft Div) 1984–91, ret; service with charitable orgns throughout Berkshire 1991–; *Style—* Air Vice-Marshal Leslie Phipps, CB, AFC; ✉ 33 Knole Wood, Devenish Rd, Sunningdale, Berks SL5 9QR

PHIPSON, John Norman; TD (1975); s of N H W Smith, and Margaret Helen, *née* Brown; descendant of Oliver Cromwell, via mother's family; *b* 29 Nov 1940; *Educ* Rugby; *m* 2 Feb 1974, Harriet Jane Maxwell, da of late Hugh Hamilton McCleery; 2 s, 2 da; *Career* slr; ptnr Linklaters & Paines Slrs, London, Moscow, Paris, New York, Hong

Kong, Brussels, Tokyo, Singapore and Frankfurt; Maj HAC (TA) 1959–75, memb Ct of Assts HAC 1972, treas 1984–87, vice pres 1988–90; *Recreations* family; *Clubs* Players' Theatre; *Style*— John N Phipson, Esq, TD; ✉ Linklaters & Paines, Barrington House, 59–67 Gresham St, London EC2V 7JA (☎ 0171 606 7080, fax 0171 606 5113, telex 884 349)

PHIZACKERLEY, Ven Gerald Robert; s of John Dawson Phizackerley (d 1980), and Lilian Mabel Ruthven, *née* Falloon (d 1983); *b* 3 Oct 1929; *Educ* Queen Elizabeth GS Penrith, Univ Coll Oxford (MA), Wells Theol Coll; *m* 1959, Annette Catherine, da of Cecil Frank Baker, MBE (d 1982); 1 s (David b 1963), 1 da (Mary b 1961); *Career* curate St Barnabas Carlisle 1954–57, chaplain Abingdon Sch 1957–64, rector Gaywood with Bawsey and Mintlyn Norwich 1964–78, rural dean Lynn 1968–78, hon canon Norwich Cathedral 1975–78, archdeacon Chesterfield and hon canon of Derby Cathedral 1978–96, ret; memb Gen Synod 1985–95, fell Woodard Corpn 1981–; JP Norfolk 1972–78; *Recreations* theatre, travel, border collies; *Style*— The Ven Gerald Phizackerley; ✉ Archway Cottage, Hall Road, Leamington Spa, Warwickshire CV32 5RA (☎ 01926 332740)

PHYSICK, John Frederick; CBE (1984); s of Nino William Physick (d 1946), of London, and Gladys, *née* Elliott (d 1978); *b* 31 Dec 1923; *Educ* Battersea GS; *m* 28 May 1954, Eileen Mary, da of Cyril Walter Walsh (d 1970), of London; 2 s (Alastair b 2 Dec 1955, Nigel b 9 June 1958), 1 da (Helen b 6 Jan 1960); *Career* WWII Petty Offr Airman RN (Fleet Air Arm) 1942–46, AFHQ Algiers/Caserta 1942–45, RNVR until 1956; V & A Museum: joined 1948, sec to Advsy Cncl 1973–83, asst to Dir 1974–83, keeper of museum servs 1975–83, dep dir 1983; pres Church Monuments Soc 1984–86 and 1996–; chm: Monuments Sub-Ctee Cncl for the Care of Churches 1984– (memb 1978–), Conservation Ctee Cncl for the Care of Churches 1993–; vice chm: Rochester Diocesan Advsy Ctee for the Care of the Churches 1987–91 (memb 1964–91), Rochester Cathedral Advsy Fabric Ctee 1992– (memb 1987–); memb: Drawings Ctee RIBA 1975, Cathedrals Advsy Ctee 1977–81, Ctee Friends of Kent Churches 1980– (chm Grants Ctee 1984–94), Westminster Abbey Architectural Advsy Panel 1985–, Cncl Br Archaeological Assoc 1985–87, Canterbury and Rochester Jt Diocesan Books and Documents Ctee 1989–, Canterbury and Rochester Jt Diocesan Archaeological Sub Ctee 1989–, Cncl Soc of Antiquaries 1991–93; DrRCA, DLitt (Lambeth); FSA; *Books* Catalogue of the Engravings of Eric Gill (1965), Designs for English Sculpture 1680–1860 (1969), The Wellington Monument (1970), Marble Halls (1975), The Victoria and Albert Museum: the History of its Building (1982), Sculpture in Britain 1530–1830 (ed 2 edn, 1988), The Royal College of Art (contrib, 1987), Westminster Abbey: The Monuments (jtly, 1989), Design of the Times: one hundred years of the Royal College of Art (contrib, 1996); *Style*— John Physick, Esq, CBE, FSA; ✉ 49 New Rd, Meopham, Kent DA13 0LS (☎ 01474 812301); 14 Park St, Deal, Kent CT14 6AG (☎ 01304 381621)

PIATKUS, Judith (Judy); da of Raphael Emmanuel Assersohn (d 1988), and Estelle Freda, *née* Richenberg (d 1993); *b* 16 Oct 1949; *Educ* South Hampstead HS; *m* 1, 5 Dec 1971 (m dis 1985), Brian John Piatkus; 1 s, 2 da; m 2, 30 Dec 1990, Cyril Bernard Ashberg; 1 step da; *Career* md and publisher Piatkus Books 1979–; *Recreations* reading; *Style*— Ms Judy Piatkus; ✉ Piatkus Books, 5 Windmill St, London W1P 1HF (0171 631 0710, fax 0171 436 7137)

PICARDA, Hubert Alistair Paul; QC (1992); s of Pierre Adrien Picarda (d 1985), and Winifred Laura, *née* Kemp (d 1988); *b* 4 March 1936; *Educ* Seaford Coll W Worthing, Westminster, Magdalen Coll Oxford (MA, BCL, open exhibitioner), UCL (Bunnell Lewis prize for Latin verse); *m* 4 March 1976 (m dis 1995), Ann Hulse, da of Stanley Stone; 1 s (Dominic Nicholas Piers b 7 March 1977), 1 da (Claudia Caroline Holly b 19 Feb 1979); *Career* called to the Bar Inner Temple 1962, Profumo scholar 1963, admitted ad eundem Lincoln's Inn and Gray's Inn 1965, night lawyer with Daily Express and Sunday Express (Beaverbrook Newspapers) 1964–72, in practice Chancery Bar 1964–; memb Senate of Inns of Ct and Bar Cncl 1978–81; managing ed: Charity Law and Practice Review 1992–, Receivers Administrators and Liquidators Quarterly 1993–; memb Editorial Bd: Butterworths Jl of Int Banking and Fin Law, Tst Law Int, Jl of Business Law; visiting lectr in receivership law Malaysian Bar Cncl, Sabah Law Assoc and Law Socs of Singapore and Hong Kong 1994, visiting lectr in banking and derivative trading law Malaysian Bar Cncl and Advocates Assoc of Sarawak 1995; hon pres Charity Law Assoc 1992–; memb: Insolvency Lawyers' Assoc, Chancery Bar Assoc, Inst of Conveyancers; *Books* Picarda Law and Practice Relating to Charities (1977, 2nd edn 1995), Picarda Law Relating to Receivers Managers and Administrators (1984, 2nd edn 1990); *Recreations* Andalusian baroque, Latin, Spain in WWII, Early Romantic music, conversation; *Clubs* Beefsteak, Pratt's; *Style*— Hubert Picarda, Esq, QC; ✉ 3 New Square, Lincoln's Inn, London WC2A 3RS (☎ 0171 405 5577, fax 0171 404 5032)

PICK, Charles Samuel; s of Samuel Pick; *b* 22 March 1917; *Educ* Masonic Sch Bushey; *m* 1938, Hilda Beryl Hobbs; 1 s, 1 da; *Career* served WWII 1939–46, cmmnd RA, AA Cmd, apptd Staff Capt; served ALFSEA: India, Ceylon, Singapore; started in publishing with Victor Gollancz Ltd 1933, fndr memb Michael Joseph Ltd 1935 (jt md 1959–62), md William Heinemann Ltd 1962, dir Heinemann Group of Publishers 1962 (md 1979–85), dir Pan Books 1968, chm Secker & Warburg 1973, ret from Heinemann in 1985; started Charles Pick Consultancy 1985 acting as sole literary agent for Wilbur Smith; chm and pres Heinemann Holdings Inc 1980–85, memb Cncl Publishers' Assoc 1980–83; *Recreations* walking, reading, theatre; *Clubs* Savile, MCC; *Style*— Charles Pick, Esq; ✉ Littlecot, Lindfield, W Sussex RH16 2JZ (☎ 01444 482218); 3 Bryanston Place, London W1 (☎ 0171 402 8043)

PICK, Prof John Morley; s of John Mawson Pick, of Ripon, Yorks, and Edith Mary, *née* Morley; *b* 12 Oct 1936; *Educ* King Edward VI Sch Retford, Univ of Leeds (BA, PGCE), Univ of Birmingham (MA), City Univ London (PhD); *m* 19 April 1960, Ann Clodagh, da of Sydney Simmons Johnson (d 1983), of Eastbourne; 1 s (Martyn b 1963), 1 da (Catherine b 1965); *Career* dir Dillington House Coll of Adult Educn and Arts Centre 1973–76, head of arts policy and mgmnt studies City Univ 1976–90, Gresham prof of rhetoric Gresham Coll City Univ 1983–88, prof of arts mgmnt City Univ 1985–91, dir Gresham Coll Res Project 1988–; prof emeritus City Univ 1991–; *Books* Arts Administration (1980), The State of The Arts (1981), The West End: Mismanagement And Snobbery (1983), The Theatre Industry (1984), The Modern Newspeak (1985), Managing The Arts? (1987), Arts in a State (1988), Vile Jelly (1991), Arts Administration: Politics, Bureaucracy and Management in the Arts (1995); *Recreations* gardening, theatre, writing, comedy; *Style*— Prof John Pick; ✉ Willow Cottage, 20 High St, Sutton on Trent, Newark NG23 6QA (☎ 01636 822102); Department of Arts Policy and Management, Level 7, Frobisher Crescent, The Barbican, Silk St, London EC2Y 8HB (☎ 0171 253 4399 and 0171 628 5641/2)

PICK, Robert David Arthur; s of Werner Rolf Theodor Pick, of Claygate, Surrey, and Margaret Hermine, *née* Fischer; *b* 13 June 1942; *Educ* Charterhouse, Pembroke Coll Oxford (Holford scholar, MA); *m* 1969, Christine Elizabeth, da of John Hardy Layton Royle; 1 s (Rupert b 1974), 2 da (Isabel b 1972, Rebecca b 1976); *Career* articled clerk Biddle & Co London 1965–88, admitted slr 1969, asst slr Macfarlanes London 1969–72; Baker & McKenzie: asst slr London 1972–74, Hong Kong 1974–76, ptnr Hong Kong 1976–81, sole res ptnr Singapore 1981–83, ptnr London 1983–; memb Bar: Hong Kong 1974, Brunei 1981, Victoria Aust 1983; NP Hong Kong 1977–81; memb Bd of Govrs: Kellett Sch Hong Kong 1978–81, Tanglin Sch Singapore 1981–83, SOAS 1993–; Liveryman Worshipful Co of Tallow Chandlers 1992, Freeman City of London Slrs' Co 1993; memb Law Soc; *Recreations* gardening, tennis, golf, choral singing; *Clubs* United Oxford and Cambridge Univ, St George's Hill Golf, Hong Kong Club, Shek-O (Hong Kong); *Style*— Robert Pick, Esq; ✉ The Old Vicarage, Shamley Green, Guildford, Surrey GU5 0UD (☎ 01483 892071); Baker & McKenzie, 100 New Bridge Street, London EC4V 6JA (☎ 0171 919 1000, fax 0171 919 1999)

PICKARD, Brian Harold; s of Alfred Harold Pickard (d 1954), of London, and Winifred Sarah, *née* Cockrill (d 1982); *b* 14 Feb 1922; *Educ* Eltham Coll, Guy's Hosp and London Univ (MB BS, DLO, swimming colours); *m* 1, 13 May 1944, Joan Daisy, da of Harry Packham, of London; 2 s (Geoffrey b 1952, William b 1958), 2 da (Diane (Mrs Yeo) b 1945, Celia (Mrs Greetham) b 1947); m 2, Diana Sylvia, da of John William Stokes, of Frinton; 1 da (Lucy b 1981); *Career* RAF 1948–50, ENT specialist RAF Hosp Cosford; Sqdn Ldr RAFVR 1950–55; sr registrar ENT: Hosp for Sick Children Great Ormond St, King's Coll Hosp London; conslt surgn ENT: St George's Hosp London, Moorfields Eye Hosp London, Dispensaire Français London; visiting ENT specialist St Helena; private pilot 1948–, med advsr Guild of Air Pilots and Air Navigators; conslt: All Nippon Airline, JAL, Japanese Aviation Authy (former conslt Br Airways); memb Med Panel CAA (authorised aviation med examiner), former pres and sec Br Med Pilots Assoc; Freeman: City of London, Worshipful Soc of Apothecaries; Past Master Guild of Air Pilots and Air Navigators; Chevalier de l'Ordre National du Mérite France; FRCS, LMSSA, MRAeS; *Recreations* sailing, flying; *Clubs* RAF, United Hosps Sailing (vice cdre), St George's Hosp Sailing (former cdre), Royal Corinthian Yacht; *Style*— Brian Pickard, Esq; ✉ Shandon, 19 Waltham Way, Frinton-on-Sea, Essex CO13 9JE (☎ and fax 01255 674808); Cromwell Hospital, Cromwell Rd, London SW5; Blackheath Hospital, 40 Lee Terrace, London SE3 (☎ and fax 01255 674808, telex 8951182 GECOMS G)

PICKARD, Dr John; *b* 11 Sept 1963; *Educ* Univ of Wales at Bangor (BMus, PhD), Royal Conservatory The Hague (Dutch govt scholarship); *Career* composer; studied with William Mathias then Louis Andriessen; lectr Univ of Wales at Bangor 1989–93, lectr Univ of Bristol 1993–; compositions incl: 3 symphonies (No 3 cmmnd by BBC 1996), Piano Sonata, The Flight of Icarus (cmmnd by BBC 1991, London première BBC Proms 1996), Channel Firing (premièred BBC Nat Orch of Wales) 1993, String Quartets Nos 1 and 3 (cmmnd by Britten Quartet), String Quartet No 2 (cmmnd by Allegri Quartet), various orchestral and chamber works; *Recreations* astronomy (memb Bristol Astronomical Soc), gardening, swimming; *Style*— Dr John Pickard; ✉ c/o Bardic Edition, 6 Fairfax Crescent, Aylesbury, Buckinghamshire HP20 2ES (☎ and fax 01296 28609, e-mail at Univ of Bristol john.pickard@bristol.ac.uk)

PICKARD, Sir (John) Michael; kt (1997); s of John Stanley Pickard (d 1979), of Epsom, Surrey, and Winifred Joan Pickard; *b* 29 July 1932; *Educ* Oundle; *m* 1959, Penelope Jane, da of Christopher Catterall; 3 s, 1 da; *Career* fin dir Br Printing Corp Ltd 1965–68, md: Trust Houses Ltd, Trust House Forte 1968–71; chm: Happy Eater Ltd (fndr) 1972–86, Grattan plc 1978–84, Courage Ltd and Imperial Brewing & Leisure Ltd 1981–86; dep chief exec Imperial Group plc 1985–86, chief exec Sears plc 1988–92 (dep chief exec 1986–88), chm London Docklands Development Corporation 1992–; non-exec dir: Brown Shipley Holdings Ltd 1986–93, Electra Investment Trust 1989–, Nationwide Building Society 1991–94, Wates Leisure Ltd 1992–, Bentalls plc 1993–, Docklands Light Railway Ltd 1994–, London First 1992–, Bullough plc 1995– (chm 1996–); memb Ctee The Automobile Assoc 1994–; chm Roedean Cncl 1981–90, govr Oundle 1987–; Master Worshipful Co of Grocers 1995–96; FCA; *Recreations* sport, education; *Clubs* Walton Heath, MCC, Pilgrims'; *Style*— Sir Michael Pickard; ✉ 16 Grosvenor Hill Court, Bourdon St, London W1X 9HG; London Docklands Development Corporation, 191 Marsh Wall, London E14 9TJ (☎ 0171 512 3000)

PICKARD, Michael John; s of Denis Luther Pickard; *b* 9 July 1939; *Educ* Christ's Hosp; *m* 1965 (sep 1992), Heather Jill; 1 s, 1 da; partner Lynn Furmark; *Career* The Royal London Mutual Insurance Society Ltd: actuary 1974–82, dir 1977–, chief gen mangr 1983–87, chm 1988–; dir: Essex Rivers Healthcare NHS Tst 1991–96, Personal Investment Authy 1994–; chm Life Insur Cncl of Assoc of Br Insurers 1990–92; memb Ct of Assts Worshipful Co of Insurers; FIA; *Recreations* golf, reading; *Style*— Michael Pickard, Esq; ✉ The Royal London Mutual Insurance Soc Ltd, Royal London House, Middlesborough, Colchester, Essex CO1 1RA (☎ 01206 761761)

PICKARD, Paul Ian; s of Ivan Pickard, of Doxey, Stafford, and Mary, *née* Sutcliffe; *b* 10 Aug 1958; *Educ* King Edward VI GS Stafford, Stradbrooke Coll Sheffield (NCTJ Cert Photography, winner NCTJ Student of the Year Award); *Career* Stafford Newsletter 1980–84, sr photographer Derby Evening Telegraph and Coventry Evening Telegraph (each for 3 months) 1984, currently chief photographer Express & Star Wolverhampton (joined as sr photographer 1984); *Awards* Kodak Royal Picture of the Year 1984, Canon/UK Press Gazette Sports Picture of the Year 1986, News Picture of the Year Ilford Photographic Awards 1989, Feature Picture of the Year Ilford Photographic Awards 1990, highly commended various awards 1991, runner up Press Photographer of the Year Ilford Photographic Awards 1991; *Recreations* croquet, Cajun music, cinema; *Style*— Paul Pickard, Esq; ✉ c/o Picture Desk, Express & Star, Queen Street, Wolverhampton WV1 3BU (home ☎ 01785 282637, work ☎ 01902 313131, fax 01902 319431)

PICKARD, Dr Willis Ritchie Sturrock; s of William Sturrock Pickard (d 1973), and Anne Ogilvy Gall, *née* Ritchie; *b* 21 May 1941; *Educ* Daniel Stewart's Coll Edinburgh, Univ of St Andrews (MA); *m* 27 Dec 1969, Ann Marie; 2 da (Gillian Fleur b 1970, Rebecca Jane b 1974); *Career* leader writer and features ed The Scotsman 1963–77, ed Times Scottish Education Supplement 1977–; rector Univ of Aberdeen 1988–90, memb Scottish Arts Cncl 1982–88; chm: Children's Book Ctee for Scotland, Book Tst Scotland 1989–95; fell Scot Vocational Eduncl Cncl 1996, Hon LLD Univ of Aberdeen 1991; *Clubs* Scottish Lib; *Style*— Dr Willis Pickard; ✉ Times Scottish Education Supplement, 37 George St, Edinburgh (☎ 0131 220 1100, fax 0131 220 1616)

PICKEN, Ralph Alistair; s of Dr David Kennedy Watt Picken, TD, JP, DL, of Cardiff, and Liselotte Lore Inge, *née* Regensteiner; *b* 23 May 1955; *Educ* Shrewsbury, Univ of Birmingham (LLB); *Career* admitted slr 1980; managing ptnr Trowers & Hamlins London 1996– (joined 1981, resident Muscat 1981–86, ptnr 1984–); memb: Law Soc 1980, Int Bar Assoc, Anglo-Omani Soc; FRSA; *Recreations* bridge and The Baroque, Bordeaux and Bangkok; *Clubs* MCC, Cardiff & County, Chatham Dining; *Style*— Ralph Picken, Esq; ✉ 15 Jeffreys Street, London NW1 9PS (☎ 0171 485 5121); Trowers & Hamlins, 6 New Square, Lincoln's Inn, London WC2A 3RP (☎ 0171 269 2000, fax 0171 269 1234)

PICKERING, Prof Brian Thomas; s of Thomas Pickering (d 1952), and Dorothy May, *née* Rourk (d 1984); *b* 24 May 1936; *Educ* Haberdashers' Aske's Hatcham, Univ of Bristol (BSc, PhD, DSc); *m* 4 Sept 1965, Joan, da of Frederick Charles Robinson Perry (d 1984), of Gävle, Sweden; 2 da (Francesca b 1966, Veronica b 1969); *Career* jr res biochemist Hormone Research Laboratory Univ of California 1961–62 (Wellcome Res travelling fell 1961), memb Scientific Staff MRC Nat Inst for Med Res Mill Hill 1963–65, memb MRC Gp for Res in Neurosecretion, visiting prof Dept of Physiology Univ of Geneva Switzerland 1977; Univ of Bristol: lectr in biochemistry and pharmacology 1965–70, lectr in anatomy and biochemistry 1970–72, reader 1972–78, prof of anatomy and head of dept 1978–92, dean Faculty of Med 1985–87, pro vice chllr 1990–92, dep vice chllr 1992–; contrib numerous papers on neuroendocrinology in scientific jls; non-exec dir United Bristol Healthcare NHS Tst, pres Euro Soc for Comparative Endocrinology 1990–94, sec Br Neuroendocrine Gp 1988–92, annual review lectr Anatomical Soc of GB and Ireland 1984; MD (hc) Carol Davila Univ Bucharest 1994; memb: Anatomical Soc,

Biochemical Soc, Physiological Soc, Soc for Endocrinology (Society medallist 1977), Euro Neuroscience Assoc, Euro Soc for Comparative Endocrinology; *Books* ed: Pharmacology of the Endocrine System and Related Drugs: The Neurohypophysis (with H Heller, 1970), Stimulus Secretion Coupling in Neuroendocrine Systems (with D Ganten and D Pfaff, 1988), Neurosecretion: Cellular Aspects of the Production and Release of Neuropeptides (with J B Wakerley and A J S Summerlee, 1988); *Recreations* gardening; *Style*— Prof Brian Pickering; ✉ University of Bristol, Bristol BS8 1TH (☎ 0117 928 8254, fax 0117 930 4263)

PICKERING, Donald Ellis; s of John Joseph Pickering (d 1978), of Newcastle-upon-Tyne, and Edith, *née* Ellis (d 1983); *b* 15 Nov 1933; *Educ* private; *Career* actor; trained Old Vic Theatre Sch under Michel St Denis 1950–52, Old Vic Co 1952, Stratford 1954, Bristol Old Vic 1957–59, RNT 1987–90 and 1995; *Theatre* West End incl: Poor Bitos, School for Scandal (and NY), Case in Question, Conduct Unbecoming (nominated Tony Award), Male of the Species, Hay Fever; *Television* incl: The Pallisers, Private Lives, Irish RM, Yes Prime Minister, Return to Treasure Island; *Films* incl: Nothing but the Best, Thirty Nine Steps, Half Moon St; *Recreations* gardening, riding, tennis; *Style*— Donald Pickering, Esq; ✉ Back Court, Manor House, Eastleach Turville, Cirencester, Glos GL7 3NQ; (☎ 0136 785 476)

PICKERING, Dr Errol Neil; s of Russell Gordon Pickering (d 1985), of Australia, and Sylvia Mary, *née* Bennett; *b* 5 May 1938; *Educ* York Univ Toronto (BA), Univ of Toronto (Dip Hosp Admin, Robert Wood Johnston award), Univ of NSW (PhD); *Career* exec dir: Aust Cncl on Hosp Standards 1974–80, Aust Hosp Assoc 1980–87; dir gen Int Hosp Fedn 1987–; dir Healthcare Risk Solutions Ltd 1993–; past pres UNICEF Aust, past chm Int Assoc Forum RSM; FRSM; *Recreations* bridge, classical music, reading biographies; *Style*— Dr Errol Pickering; ✉ International Hospital Federation, 4 Abbot's Place, London NW6 1NP (☎ 0171 372 7181, fax 0171 328 7433)

PICKERING, Prof John Frederick; s of William Frederick Pickering (d 1973), of Slough, and Jean Mary, *née* Clarke; *b* 26 Dec 1939; *Educ* Slough GS, UCL (BSc, PhD, DSc); *m* 25 March 1967, Jane Rosamund, da of Victor William George Day (d 1993), of Bristol; 2 da (Rachel b 1970, Catherine b 1974); *Career* industl market res exec 1961–62; lectr: Univ of Durham 1964–66, Univ of Sussex 1966–73; sr directing staff Admin Staff Coll Henley 1974–75; UMIST: prof of industl econ 1975–88, vice princ 1983–85, dean 1985–87; Univ of Portsmouth (formerly Portsmouth Poly): vice pres 1988–90, acting pres 1990–91, dep pres 1991–92, dep vice chllr 1992–94; consit economist 1994–, visiting prof Univ of Durham Business Sch 1995–; memb: Royal Econ Soc 1973, Retail Prices Index Advsy Ctee 1974–, Gen Synod C of E 1980–90; church cmmr 1983–90, pres BCMS-Crosslinks 1986–92; memb MMC 1990–; non-exec dir Staniland Hall Ltd 1987–94; FIMgt 1987; *Books* Resale Price Maintenance in Practice (1967), The Small Firm in the Hotel and Catering Industry (jtly, 1971), Industrial Structure and Market Conduct (1974), The Acquisition of Consumer Durables (1977), The Economic Management of the Firm (jt ed, 1984); *Recreations* cricket, classical music, theatre; *Clubs* Royal Cwlth Soc; *Style*— Prof J F Pickering; ✉ 1 The Fairway, Rowlands Castle, Hants PO9 6AQ (☎ 01705 412007, fax 01705 413385)

PICKERING, John Michael; s of late John Dennis Pickering, of Rough Hill, Lache, Chester, and Margaret, *née* Owen; *b* 25 Jan 1941; *Educ* Rossall Sch Fleetwood Lancs; *m* 20 Sept 1947, Elizabeth Josephine, *née* Tatton; 1 s (John Alexander b 3 Nov 1970), 1 da (Christine Elizabeth b 10 July 1972); *Career* farmer (900 acres with 800 cows Cheshire, 1500 acres Anglesey), dairy food processor and property developer; High Sheriff of Cheshire 1995–96; memb Worshipful Co of Farmers; *Recreations* rugby, shooting, skiing and all country sports; *Style*— John Pickering, Esq; ✉ Rough Hill, Lache, Chester, Cheshire CH4 9JS (☎ 01244 671011)

PICKERING, Karen Denise; MBE (1994); da of Derek James Pickering, of Hove, E Sussex, and Dain Irene, *née* Sixma; *b* 19 Dec 1971; *Educ* Brighton & Hove HS; *Career* swimmer; memb: Ipswich Swimming Club, Eng and GB jr team 1986; sr int debut 1986; nat freestyle titles (summer): 50m 1992 and 1993, 100m 1989–93, 200m 1990, 1992,1993,1994 and 1995, 400m 1992; nat freestyle titles (winter): 50m 1991, 1992 and 1993, 100m 1988, 1991, 1992 and 1993, 200m 1991 and 1992, 400m 1990 and 1991, 800m 1991 (first woman to win all five freestyle titles Nat Winter Championships 1991); int honours: Silver medal medley team and Bronze medal freestyle team Cwlth Games 1990, Silver medal 200m freestyle and Bronze medal 100m freestyle Euro Open Championships 1990, Bronze medal 200m freestyle, 4 x 100m medley relay and 4 x 200m freestyle relay Euro Championships Sheffield 1993, Gold medal 4 x 100m freestyle relay Cwlth Games 1994; also competed in World Championships 1991 and 1994 and Olympic Games Barcelona 1992; World champion (short course) 200m freestyle Palma 1993, Bronze medal 100m freestyle; Commonwealth Games Victoria 1994: Gold medal 100m freestyle, Bronze medal 200m freestyle, Gold medal 4 x 100m freestyle relay, Silver medal 4 x 200m freestyle relay, Silver medal 4 x 100m medley relay; Euro Championships Vienna 1995: Bronze medal 100m freestyle, Bronze medal 200m freestyle, Bronze medal 4 x 100m freestyle relay, Bronze medal 4 x 200m freestyle relay; records: Cwlth/Br/English 100m freestyle long course (55:79) 1992, English 50m freestyle short course (25:74) 1992, Br/English 100m freestyle short course (54:39) 1993, Cwlth/Br/English 200m freestyle short course (1.56:25) 1993, Br 4 x 200m freestyle relay, Br 4 x 100m freestyle relay, Br 4 x 100m medley relay, short course and long course; ranked 1 in world 200m freestyle short course 1994; Alan Hime and Pat Besford Trophies Winter Nationals 1991, BSCA British Female Swimmer of the Year 1992, 1993 and 1994, Bill Juba Memorial Trophy 1992, Ipswich Sports Personality of the Year 1991 and 1993, ASA British Swimmer of the Year 1994; swimwear and gymwear model; *Recreations* art and design, writing for local paper, designing and printing T-shirts; *Style*— Miss Karen Pickering, MBE; ✉ c/o ASA, Harold Fern House, Derby Square, Loughborough, Leics LE11 0AL (☎ 01509 230431)

PICKERING, Paul Granville; s of Arthur Samuel Pickering (d 1962), of Rotherham, S Yorks, and Lorna Cynthia, *née* Groocock; *b* 9 May 1952; *Educ* Royal Masonic Schs Bushey Herts, Univ of Leicester (BA, Sports colours); *m* 11 Dec 1983, Alison, da of Albert Leslie Beckett; 1 da (Persephone Alyce b 1 Feb 1993); *Career* Thomson Graduate Trg Scheme 1974, Latin America corr Now! magazine, columnist Times, Sunday Times and Punch 1981–84, novelist 1984–; memb: NUJ, Soc of Authors; FRGS; *Novels* Wild About Harry (1985), Perfect English (1986), The Blue Gate of Babylon (1989), Charlie Peace (1991); *Anthologies* Winter's Tales (contrib short story, 1989); *Plays* After Hamlet (New Grove Theatre, 1994); *Recreations* scuba-diving, birdwatching; *Clubs* Groucho; *Style*— Paul Pickering, Esq; ✉ 20 Brackenbury Gardens, London W6 0BP (☎ and fax 0181 743 9406); c/o Alexandra Pringle, Toby Eady Associates Ltd, 9 Orme Court, London W2 (☎ 0171 792 0092)

PICKERING, His Hon Judge; Richard Edward Ingram; s of Richard Pickering (d 1961), and Dorothy Elizabeth Craze Pickering (d 1991); *b* 16 Aug 1929; *Educ* Birkenhead Sch, Magdalene Coll Cambridge (MA); *m* 1962, Jean Margaret, *née* Eley; 2 s; *Career* called to the Bar Lincoln's Inn 1953; elected jr of N Circuit 1960, legal chm Miny of Pensions and Nat Insurance Appeals Tbnl Liverpool 1967–77, hon memb Manx Bar (Summerland Fire Enquiry) 1973–74, pt/t chm Liverpool Industl Tbnl 1977–79, recorder Crown Ct 1977–81, regnl chm Merseyside Mental Health Review Tbnl 1979–81, circuit judge (N Circuit) 1981–, N Circuit rep on Cncl HM Circuit Judges 1984–89, nominated judicial memb Merseyside Mental Health Review Tbnl 1984–; cncllr Hoylake UDC 1961–64; *Recreations* study of military history, walking, gardening; *Clubs* Athenaeum (Liverpool), United Oxford & Cambridge Univ; *Style*— His Hon Judge Pickering; ✉ Crown Court, Derby Square, Liverpool

PICKERING OF KINTRADWELL, Ralph Bernard; s of George Cecil Pickering, of Broomhill, Lockerbie, Dumfriesshire, and Janet, *née* McEachern; *b* 21 Feb 1958; *Educ* Dumfries Acad, Napier Univ; *m* 26 April 1986, Fiona Margaret, da of Dr John Richard Campion Stubbs, of Arncliffe, Dumfries; 1 s (Lewis John Fitzyork b 28 Oct 1990), 1 da (Ellen Mary Elizabeth b 5 May 1993); *Career* landowner and land manager; 5th laird of Kintradwell 1986–; land mangr Smiths Gore 1979–85, sr ptnr Pickering Gordon & Co 1985–91, with Norwich Union 1991–93, United Friendly Insurance plc 1993–94; ptnr Fitzyork Estates 1986–; dir: Nith Tyne Developments Ltd 1988–91, Galloway Ancestry Ltd 1996–, Harp Art Records USA 1996–; patron Sutherland and Dist Sheepdog Trials 1987–89, sec Kirkbean Branch Galloway Cons & Unionist Assoc 1990–93 (treas 1987–89), elder Kirkbean Church 1990– (memb Congregational Bd 1987–, property convenor 1995–), treasurer Kirkbean Sch Bd 1996–, Kirkcudbrightshire co-ordinator Action Aid 1991–92, chm Kirkbean Hall and Amenity Ctee 1993–; memb: Dumfries and Lockerbie Agric Soc 1978–, Scottish Landowners' Fedn 1987–, Regional Liaison Offr 1996–, Kirkbean Community Cncl 1988–, Huddersfield and Dist Family History Soc 1989–, Dumfries and Galloway Family History Soc 1996–; author of various articles on architecture; *Recreations* painting, fishing, gardening, domestic architecture; *Clubs* Royal Smithfield; *Style*— Ralph Pickering of Kintradwell; ✉ Grovewood House, Kirkbean, Dumfries DG2 8DW (01387 880215); Kintradwell, Brora, Sutherland

PICKERSGILL, Monica; da of Howard Horton (d 1956), and Agatha Louise, *née* Alleyne, of Sutton Coldfield; *b* 29 May 1933; *Educ* Sutton Coldfield HS for Girls, City of Worcester Trg Coll (DipEd); *m* 28 July 1956, Peter Pickersgill, s of Leonard Pickersgill; *Career* teacher of PE and English West Park Secdy Sch Leeds 1953–55, head of girls' PE Mirfield Secdy Modern Sch W Yorks 1955–62, head of PE Dept Greenhead HS Huddersfield 1962–66, head of PE Dept Wakefield Girls' HS W Yorks 1966–70, dep head Colne Valley HS Huddersfield 1970–93; pres: All England Women's Hockey Assoc 1992–, Northern Counties Women's Hockey Assoc 1988–92; former pres North Schoolgirls' Hockey Assoc; memb: Great Britain Women's Olympic Hockey Ctee 1992–, Great Britain Olympic Hockey Bd 1994–; former hockey player: Yorks 1st XI (capt for 16 years), N of England, England triallist; memb Secdy Heads Assoc; *Recreations* sport, modern languages, reading, walking, gardening; *Clubs* Wakefield Hockey, Bradford Ladies' Hockey; *Style*— Mrs Monica Pickersgill; ✉ 7 Furnbrook Gardens, Kirkheaton, Huddersfield, West Yorks HD5 0DY (☎ 01484 428911); All England Women's Hockey Association, The Stadium, Silbury Boulevard, Milton Keynes MK9 1NR (☎ 01908 689290, fax 01908 689286)

PICKETT, Joy Rosina; da of James William Bishop Woodford (d 1982), of Bushey, Herts, and Ivy, *née* Maskell; *b* 15 April 1950; *Educ* Bushey GS, Cassio Coll, Universite de Nanterre, Watford Coll of Technol; *m* 28 March 1978 (m dis), Graham John Pickett; *Career* Friends Provident Life Office 1969–71, Sun Alliance Insurance Group (life and pensions) 1971–76, sr pensions admin Noble Lowndes Pension Consultants 1977–79, pensions funds mangr British Waterways Board and co sec British Waterways Pensions Trustees Ltd 1979–87; IMI plc 1988–: gp pensions mangr, dir IMI Pensions Trust Ltd, dir IMI Investment Management Ltd 1988–94; Nat Assoc of Pensions Funds: dir 1989–95, memb Membership Ctee 1983–88 (co-opted) and 1990–95, memb Sifting Panel of Golden Pen Awards 1986 (chm 1989), memb Ctee W Midlands Gp 1988– (chm 1995–), memb Nat Cncl 1989–95, memb Parly Ctee 1990–; Nationalised Industs Pension Gp: memb 1980–87, memb Gen Purposes Ctee 1982–87, sec 1985–87; Occupational Pensions Advsy Serv: regnl organiser London NW Region 1987–88, advsr W Midlands Region 1988–94; memb CBI Pensions Panel 1989–91; Pensions Mgmnt Inst Midlands Region: memb Ctee 1993–, chm Educn Ctee 1994–; FPMI (APMI prizewinner); *Recreations* dogs, literature, music, art; *Style*— Mrs Joy Pickett; ✉ IMI plc, Kynoch Works, PO Box 216, Birmingham B6 7BA (☎ 0121 356 4848, fax 0121 344 4655)

PICKETT, Thomas; CBE (1972); s of John Joseph Pickett (d 1985), and Caroline, *née* Brunt (d 1970); *b* 22 Nov 1912; *Educ* Glossop GS, Univ of London (LLB); *m* 29 June 1940, (Winifred) Irene (d 1993), yr da of Benjamin Buckley (d 1945); *Career* served Army 1939–50, Maj; dep asst dir Army Legal Servs 1948, called to the Bar Lincoln's Inn 1948; Judge Pres of Ct of Appeal for Zambia 1965–71; sr regional chm NW Area Industl Tbnls (England and Wales) 1972–85 (ret); *Recreations* walking, swimming; *Clubs* County (Llandudno), Victoria (Llandudno); *Style*— Thomas Pickett, Esq, CBE; ✉ Bryn Awelon, Aber Place, Craigside, Llandudno, Gwynedd LL30 3AR (☎ 01492 544244)

PICKFORD, Anthony James; s of Frederick Pickford, and Ethel Alice, *née* Hart; *b* 12 May 1925; *Educ* Univ Coll Sch Hampstead, King's Coll London (LLB); *m* 1 Sept 1956, Bettine Eleanor Marion Casson, da of Kenneth Casson Smith; *Career* served Army 1943–49; called to the Bar Lincoln's Inn 1951; practice in: London 1951–57, Nigeria 1957–59; legal asst George Wimpey & Co Ltd 1959–64, legal advsr Smithkline & French Laboratories Ltd 1964–90 (dir 1970–90); practising barrister; memb Patent County Ct Users' Ctee; memb: Standing Advsy Ctee (trade marks) DTI 1970–88, Ctees ABPI 1964–91, Ctees UNICE; assoc memb Chartered Inst of Patent Agents, assoc MCIA; former sec Cons Ctee for W Africa Affrs, Parly candidate (C) East Ham Gen Election 1955, former chm and pres Harlow Cons Assoc; *Books* The Taxation of Intellectual Property (jtly); *Recreations* conservative politics; *Clubs* East India; *Style*— Anthony Pickford, Esq; ✉ Prince Henry's Chambers, 17 Fleet Street, London EC4Y 1AA (☎ 0171 353 1183, fax 0171 353 1204)

PICKFORD, David Michael; s of Aston Charles Corpe Pickford (d 1945), of London, and Gladys Ethel, *née* May (d 1981); *b* 25 Aug 1926; *Educ* Emanuel Sch London, Coll of Estate Mgmnt; *m* 1956, Elizabeth Gwendoline, da of John Hooson, of Segrwyd Hall, Denbigh (d 1972); 1 s (Charles John Norcliffe b 1960), 2 da (Penelope Anne b 1952, Elizabeth Jane b 1958); *Career* chartered surveyor; chm: Haslemere Estates plc 1983–86 (md until 1983), Lilliput Property Unit Trust 1984–, Compco Holdings plc 1986–, Gulliver Developments Property Unit Trust 1989–, Wigmore Property Investment Trust plc 1993–96, Swift Balanced Property Unit Trust 1993–; dir: London and Nationwide Missions Ltd 1980–, Youth With A Mission 1987–, Care Campaigns Ltd 1988–, Louth Estates Ltd 1990–, and many others; chm: Mission to London 1981–, Prison Fellowship England & Wales 1989–93; hon life pres The Boys' Bde London, pres Christians In Property, vice pres London City YMCA 1993–, organizer of Residential Christian Conference Centre for 15–25 year-olds (2000 visitors each year), dir Billy Graham Evangelistic Association Ltd 1987–; FRICS; *Recreations* sheep farming, youth work; *Style*— David Pickford, Esq; ✉ Elm Tree Farm, Mersham, Nr Ashford, Kent TN25 7HS (☎ 01233 720200, fax 01233 720522); 33 Grosvenor Square, Mayfair, London W1X 9LL (☎ 0171 493 1156)

PICKFORD, Prof John Aston; OBE (1964); s of late Aston Charles Pickford, of London, and Gladys Ethel, *née* May (d 1981); *b* 28 Dec 1924; *Educ* Emanuel Sch London, Imperial Coll London (BSc, MSc); *m* 27 Sept 1947, Daphne Annie, da of William Edmund Ransom (d 1972), of London; 3 s (Robert Aston b 1950, William John b 1952, Ian Charles b 1952), 1 da (Helen Dorothy (Mrs Sheard) b 1959); *Career* REME 1943–47, Lt 1944, Capt 1946; with Boroughs of Sutton and Cheam, Southall and Gravesend 1945–54, town engr Sekondi-Takoradi Municipal Cncl Ghana 1954–60; Loughborough Univ: lectr 1960–66, sr lectr, dir Water Engrg and Development Centre 1971–90, head of Dept of Civil Engrg 1983–87, prof 1985–90 (prof emeritus 1990–); conslt: WHO, UNICEF, ODA, World Bank, ITDG; pres IPHE 1981–82 (memb Cncl 1971–87); Hon DTech Loughborough Univ of

Technol 1991; Hon FCIWEM 1987, FICE 1977; *Books* Analysis of Surge (1969), Developing World Water (ed Vols 1–5, 1985–90), Low-cost Sanitation (1995); *Recreations* travel, DIY, history of Africa and the Indian subcontinent; *Style—* Prof John Pickford, OBE; ✉ 5 Forest Rd, Loughborough, Leics LE11 3NW (☎ 01509 215035); WEDC (Water, Engineering and Development Centre), Loughborough University, Leicestershire LE11 3TU (☎ 01509 222390, fax 01509 211079, telex 24319 UNITEC G, e-mail j.a.pickford@lut.ac.uk)

PICKFORD, Robert William Granville; s of late Col Richard Ellis Pickford, TD, DL, of Hathersage, Derbyshire, and late Mary Avice, *née* Glossop; *b* 26 Nov 1941; *Educ* Rugby, Univ of Sheffield (LLB); *m* 11 Oct 1980, Heather Elizabeth, da of Francis Ernest Woodings, of Chesterfield, Derbyshire; 1 s (Bartholomew b 9 Sept 1985), 1 da (Olivia b 21 Dec 1981); *Career* admitted slr 1966; ptnr W & A Glossop Sheffield, NP 1966; dir The Notaries Soc 1979–, dir William Cook plc 1995–, dep chm Sheffield Children's Hosp NHS Tst; memb Law Soc; *Style—* Robert Pickford, Esq; ✉ 66 Wilkinson St, Sheffield S10 2GQ (☎ 0114 273 7776)

PICKLES, David; s of Jim Pickles, of Christchurch, Dorset, and Jean Emily, *née* Doughty; *b* 18 Oct 1945; *Educ* Elmhurst GS Street Somerset; *m* 15 April 1972, Maureen Hazel, da of Clifford Anson Rayner; 1 s (Andrew Thomas b 9 June 1973), 1 da (Jennifer Helen b 23 Dec 1975); *Career* fin mgmnt and branch mgmnt until 1980, youth and community work Dorset CC 1980–85, gen sec British Ice Hockey Assoc 1985–; live vice pres (former memb Cncl and chm) Bournemouth FA, chm Bournemouth Ice Hockey Club 1985–89; former co level football and cricket rep; hon sec Bournemouth and Dist Cricket Assoc; *Recreations* local league football referee; *Style—* David Pickles, Esq; ✉ British Ice Hockey Association, 2nd Floor Suite, 517 Christchurch Rd, Boscombe, Bournemouth BH1 4AG (☎ 01202 303946, fax 01202 398005)

PICKLES, Eric; MP (C) Brentwood and Ongar (majority 15,145); *b* 20 April 1952; *Educ* Greenhead GS, Leeds Poly; *m* Sept 1976, Irene; *Career* Bradford Met DC: cncllr 1979–91, chm Social Servs Ctee 1982–84, chm Educn Ctee 1984–86, ldr Cons Gp 1987–91, ldr of the Cncl 1988–90; MP (C) Brentwood and Ongar 1992–, memb Commons Select Ctee on the Environment 1992–93, PPS to Min for Indust DTI 1993, vice chm Cons Pty 1993–, memb Select Ctee on Tport 1996–; memb Cons Pty Nat Union Exec Ctee 1975–91, nat chm Young Conservatives 1980–81, chm Cons Pty Nat Local Govt Advsy Ctee 1992– (memb 1985–); dep ldr Cons Gp on the Assoc of Met Authorities 1989–91, local govt ed Conservative Newsline 1990–; memb Yorks RHA 1982–90; *Recreations* films, opera, serious walking; *Style—* Eric Pickles, Esq, MP; ✉ House of Commons, London SW1A 0AA

PICKLES, His Honour James; s of Arthur Pickles, OBE, JP; *b* 18 March 1925; *Career* circuit judge 1976–91; *Books* Straight from the Bench (1987), Judge for Yourself (1992), Off the Record (1993); *Style—* His Hon James Pickles

PICKLES, John George; s of William Pickles (d 1972), of N Wales, and Kathleen Pickles, *née* Cathcart; *b* 29 Nov 1935; *Educ* Ruthin Sch, Univ of Liverpool (MCD, BArch); *m* 15 July 1961, Susan Rosemary (d 1985), da of Dr William Webb (d 1955), of Liverpool; 1 s (Charles b 1965), 1 da (Caroline b 1962); *Career* architect and town planner; ptnr in Holford Associates 1972–, dir Meridian Office Servs; artist exhibitions in NW England 1984–; ARIBA, MRTPI, MSAI, FRSA; *Recreations* watercolour painting, skiing, travel; *Style—* John G Pickles, Esq; ✉ Holford Associates, Queen Building, 8 Dale Street, Liverpool (☎ 0151 227 2881, fax 0151 236 1329)

PICKSTOCK, Samuel Frank (Sam); CBE (1989); s of Francis John Pickstock (d 1981), of Stafford, and Hilda Jane, *née* Billington; *b* 10 Aug 1934; *Educ* King Edward VI GS Stafford; *m* 1957, Edith, da of Joseph Lawton (d 1980), of Hanley; *Career* dir: John McLean & Sons Ltd and its subsids 1976–94, Tarmac Properties Ltd and its subsids 1977–91, Tarmac plc 1984–94, Tarmac Atlantic Wharf Developments Ltd 1985–94; chief exec John McLean & Sons Ltd (chm subsids) 1981–94; dir: Countryside Properties plc 1994–, Eco Energy Controls Ltd 1995–, Stonepine Management Services Ltd; CIMgt, FInstLEx, FInstD; *Recreations* weeding and thinking (occasionally); *Style—* Sam Pickstock, Esq, CBE; ✉ The Crows Nest Holding, Coton End, Gnosall, Stafford (☎ 01785 822755); The Lodge at Crows Nest, Coton End, Gnosall, Stafford (☎ 01785 823173)

PICKTHALL, Colin; MP (Lab) Lancashire West (majority 2,077); s of Francis Pickthall, and Edith Pickthall; *b* 13 Sept 1944; *Educ* Ulverston GS, Univ of Wales, Univ of Lancaster; *m* 1973, Judith Ann, *née* Tranter; 2 da; *Career* asst master Ruffwood Comp Sch Kirkby 1967–70, lectr in English then head of modern Euro cultural studies Edge Hill Coll Ormskirk 1970–92; cncllr Lancs CC 1989–92, MP (Lab) Lancs W 1993– (also contested 1987); memb Select Ctee on Agriculture, sec Parly All-Pty Gp on Diabetes, sec NW Gp of Lab MPs; former memb NW Regnl Advsy Ctee and Lancs Consultative Ctee on Higher Educn, former chm Bd of Govrs Skelmersdale Coll of FE; memb USDAW (formerly NATFHE); dir First Bite Theatre, pres W Lancs Arthritis Care, chm W Lancs Forum; *Recreations* fell walking, cricket, Shakespeare, gardening; *Style—* Colin Pickthall, Esq, MP; ✉ House of Commons, London SW1A 0AA

PICKTHORN, Henry Gabriel Richards; s of Rt Hon Sir Kenneth William Murray Pickthorn, 1 Bt (d 1975), and Nancy Catherine Lewis, *née* Richards (d 1982); hp of nephew Sir James Francis Pickthorn, 3 Bt, *qv*; *b* 29 Sept 1928; *Educ* Eton, Trinity Coll Cambridge (BA); *m* 9 July 1955, Mary, da of Juxon Barton, CMG, OBE (d 1980); 3 s (John b 1957, Andrew b 1961, Thomas b 1967), 1 da (Henrietta b 1959); *Career* Nat Serv 1946–48, 2 Lt Northants Regt; TA 1952–61, Capt Queen's Westminsters (KRRC); admitted slr 1955; ptnr Linklaters & Paines 1959–90; *Style—* Henry Pickthorn, Esq; ✉ 54 Chelsea Park Gdns, London SW3 6AD (☎ 0171 352 8905);

PICKTHORN, Sir James Francis; 3 Bt (UK 1959), of Orford, Co Suffolk; s of Sir Charles William Richards Pickthorn, 2 Bt (d 1995), and Helen Antonia, *née* Mann; *b* 18 Feb 1955; *Educ* Eton; *Heir* unc, Henry Gabriel Richards Pickthorn, *qv*; *Career* ptnr Kinney & Green chartered surveyors and estate agents 1991–94, fndr Pickthorn estate agent and chartered surveyor 1994–; memb: Hon Artillery Co 1978–, City Concern over Maastricht 1993–; *Style—* Sir James Pickthorn, Bt; ✉ 45 Ringmer Ave, London SW6 5LP; Pickthorn (☎ 0171 621 1380)

PICKUP, Col Christopher John; OBE (1984); s of Wing Cdr K H Pickup, and Vera, *née* Halliwell (d 1943); *b* 26 Aug 1942; *Educ* Abingdon Sch, RMA Sandhurst; *m* 16 Dec 1967, Elizabeth Anne, da of Robert Geoffrey Spencer (d 1971); 1 s (Charles b 1970), 1 da (Lucy b 1971); *Career* cmmnd RA 1962, transferred Army Air Corps 1972, Army Staff Coll 1972–74; various cmd and staff appts UK, Borneo, Germany incl Chief of Staff and Regimental Col Army Air Corps 1990–92, ret 1994; sec The Royal Warrant Holders Assoc 1996–; *Recreations* sailing, skiing, fishing; *Clubs* Army and Navy; *Style—* Col Christopher Pickup, OBE; ✉ The Royal Warrant Holders Association, 7 Buckingham Gate, London SW1E 6JP (☎ 0171 828 2268)

PICKUP, Ronald Alfred; s of Eric Pickup (d 1981), of Chester, and Daisy, *née* Williams; *b* 7 July 1940; *Educ* King's Sch Chester, Leeds Univ (BA), RADA; *m* 9 Aug 1964, Lans Talbot, da of Claude Traverse, of Encino, CA, USA; 1 s (Simon b 1971), 1 da (Rachel b 1973); *Career* actor; in rep Leicester 1964, first title role Shelley (Royal Court) 1965, Nat Theatre Co 1966–72; memb Global Co-operative for a Better World; *Theatre* roles incl: Rosalind in all-male As You Like It (NT), Edmund in Long Day's Journey Into Night (NT), title role in Richard II (NT), Gaev in The Cherry Orchard 1989–90; *Television* incl: Jennie, Orwell, Fortunes of War, Behaving Badly 1988, Not with a Bang 1988, Time to Dance 1991, The Riff-Raff Element (BBC) 1992–93, The Rector's Wife (film for TV) 1993, The Cold Light of Day (Screen 2, BBC) 1994, Message for Posterity (BBC revival of Dennis Potter's work), Ruth Rendell's Case of Coincidence 1994, The Dying Day 1995, title role in Henry IV (adapted by John Caird for BBC) 1995; other credits incl: Hetty Wainthropp Investigates, Casualty, Fitzursein in Ivanhoe (6 part series); *Films* incl: Day of the Jackal, The Mission, Eleni, title role in My Friend Walter, Percy in Bring Me The Head of Mavis Davis; *Recreations* walking, reading, listening to music; *Clubs* BAFTA; *Style—* Ronald Pickup, Esq; ✉ c/o London Management, 2–4 Noel Street, London W1V 3RB (☎ 0171 287 9000, fax 0171 287 3036)

PICKWOAD, Michael Mervyn; s of William Mervyn Pickwoad (d 1976), of Windsor and Ludham, and Anne Margaret, *née* Payne Cook (d 1992); *b* 11 July 1945; *Educ* Charterhouse, Univ of Southampton (BSc); *m* 27 Oct 1973, Vanessa Rosemary, da of Leslie William Orriss, of Cookham, Berks; 3 da (Zoë b 1975, Katharine b 1977, Amy b 1979); *Career* film production designer; exhibition design Treasures of the Mind (Trinity Coll Dublin Quatercentenary Exhibition) 1992, exhibitor Directors Eye (Museum of Modern Art Oxford) 1996; *Television* incl: Ex 1991, Murder Most Horrid 1991, Running Late 1992, Class Act 1993, The Dying of the Light (YTV) 1994, Cruel Train (Screen 2) 1994, Witness Against Hitler (Screen 2) 1995, Kavanagh QC 1995, Element of Doubt (Carlton) 1996; *Films* incl: Comrades 1985, Withnail and I 1986, The Lonely Passion of Judith Hearne 1987, How to Get Ahead in Advertising 1988, The Krays 1989, Let Him Have It 1990, Century 1992, Food of Love 1996; memb: Georgian Gp, BECTU, BAFTA, GBFD; *Recreations* architectural history, drawing, photography, sailing, carpentry, history of transport; *Clubs* Rolls Royce Enthusiasts; *Style—* Michael Pickwoad, Esq; ✉ 3 Warnborough Rd, Oxford OX2 6HZ (☎ 01865 511106)

PICOZZI, Gerard Louis; s of Louis Picozzi, of Coatbridge, and Madeleine, *née* Lagorio; *b* 2 Oct 1949; *Educ* St Patrick's HS, Univ of Glasgow (MB ChB); *m* 20 Sept 1975, Joan, da of Joseph McCue, of Glasgow; 1 s (Christopher b 1977, d 1981), 2 da (Natalie b 1976, Madeleine b 1983); *Career* registrar ENT surgery Glasgow Royal Infirmary 1978–80, sr registrar ENT surgery Gtr Glasgow Health Bd 1980–84, conslt otolaryngolgist Lanarkshire Health Bd 1984–; FRCS 1980, RCPSGlas 1980, RSM 1980; *Recreations* running, cycling, motoring, skiing, shooting; *Style—* Gerard Picozzi, Esq; ✉ Department of Ear Nose & Throat Surgery, Law Hospital, Carluke, Lanarkshire ML8 5ER (☎ 01698 361100)

PICTON, Jacob Glyndwr (Glyn); CBE (1972); s of David Picton (d 1960), of Aberdare, and Elen Evans (d 1937); *b* 28 Feb 1912; *Educ* Aberdare Boys' Co Sch, Univ of Birmingham (MCom); *m* 2 Sept 1939, Rhiannon Mary (d 1978), harpist, da of late Arthur James, and Megan James, harpist, of Swansea; 1 s (Arthur Gwynfor b 1943), 1 da (Eira Myfanwy b 1946); *Career* Chance Bros Ltd 1933–47 (asst sec 1945–47); Univ of Birmingham: sr lectr in industl econs 1947–79, sub dean Faculty of Commerce and Social Scis 1952–58; govr United Birmingham Hosps 1953–74 (vice chm 1958–74), chm Birmingham Children's Hosp 1956–66, vice chm W Midlands Regnl Health Authy 1974–82; pres W Midlands Rent Assessment Panel, teaching hosps rep on Whitley Cncls of NHS, vice chm Nat Staff Ctee NHS; chm Birmingham Industl Therapy Assoc Ltd, chm several Wages Cncls; sole cmmr of enquiry into S Wales Coalfield Dispute 1965 (report introduced concept of Constructive Tension, this idea attributable to late Rhiannon Picton); *Publications* A Glimpse of the American Hospital Scene (1961), Independent Members in the Hospital Service and Elsewhere (published in the Lancet, 1961), South Wales Coalfield Dispute (1965), General Sir Thomas Picton and The Pictons of Pembrokeshire, The Pictons of Pembrokeshire 1066–1995; *Recreations* music, gardening, Pembrokeshire history; *Clubs* Univ of Birmingham Academic Staff; *Style—* Glyn Picton, Esq, CBE; ✉ Maes Y Tannau, 54 Chesterwood Rd, Birmingham B13 0QE (☎ 0121 444 3959)

PICTON, John Douglas; RD (1969, Clasp 1979); s of Dr Norman Picton (d 1960), of Saltcoats, Ayrshire, and Margaret Brown, *née* McGinn (d 1988); *b* 8 April 1934; *Educ* Loretto, Univ of St Andrews (BSc); *m* 23 Sept 1960, Elizabeth Mary, da of Douglas Clark Wallace, OBE (d 1989), of Lundin Links, Fife; 1 s (Simon b 1970), 3 da (Jane b 1961, Nicola b 1963, Sarah b 1966); *Career* Nat Serv RN 1955–57, CO Tay Div RNR 1978–81 (joined 1952, former cdr); md Robert L Fleming Ltd 1974–91 (joined 1957), ret 1991; *Recreations* golf; *Clubs* Naval; *Style—* John Picton, Esq, RD; ✉ Farthings, Station Road, Longforgan, Dundee DD2 5EX

PICTON-TURBERVILL, Geoffrey; s of Wilfrid Picton-Turbervill, and Shirley, *née* Masser; *b* 11 May 1959; *Educ* Marlborough, Christ Church Oxford (MA), Guildford Coll of Law; *m* 27 June 1987, Mary Teresa, da of David Mowbray Balme; 2 s (Harry David b 23 Oct 1990, Thomas Joshua b 11 Nov 1995), 1 da (Lucy Charlotte b 19 Sept 1992); *Career* trainee slr Farrer & Co 1983–85; Ashurst Morris Crisp 1986–: asst slr 1986–90, assoc ptnr 1990–94, ptnr 1994– (currently memb Energy and Major Projects Gp specialising in oil and gas, electricity, mining and other infrastructure projects and related fin transactions), resident ptnr New Delhi Office 1994–95; memb: Law Soc, Int Bar Assoc, Inst of Petroleum, RIIA; *Recreations* family, music, sport; *Clubs* MCC, Vincent's (Oxford); *Style—* Geoffrey Picton-Turbervill, Esq; ✉ Ashurst Morris Crisp, Broadwalk House, 5 Appold Street, London EC2A 2HA (☎ 0171 638 1111, fax 0171 972 7990)

PIDD, Prof Michael; s of Ernest Pidd, of Sheffield, and Marion, *née* Clark; *b* 3 Aug 1948; *Educ* High Storrs GS Sheffield, Brunel Univ (BTech), Univ of Birmingham (MSc); *m* 2 Jan 1971, Sally Anne, da of Eric Victor Nutt, of London; 2 da (Karen b 18 Aug 1977, Helen b 22 Jan 1981); *Career* team leader operational res Cadbury Schweppes Ltd 1971–75, lectr in operational res Univ of Aston 1975–79; Univ of Lancaster: lectr then sr lectr in operational res 1979–92, prof of mgmnt studies 1992–96, prof of mgmnt sci 1996–; winner President's medal OR Soc; memb: St Thomas Church Lancaster, Operational Res Soc (memb Cncl, memb Educn and Research Ctee), INFORMS; *Books* Computer Simulation in Management Sciences (1984, 1988, 1992), Computer Modelling for Discrete Simulation (1989), Tools for Thinking: modelling in management science (1996); *Recreations* fell-walking, church activities; *Style—* Prof Michael Pidd; ✉ The Management School, Lancaster Univ, Bailrigg, Lancaster LA1 4YX (☎ 01524 593870, fax 01524 592417, e-mail M.Pidd@lancaster.ac.uk)

PIDGLEY, Anthony William; s of William Pidgley (d 1967), of Hersham, Surrey, and Florence, *née* Smith (d 1990); *b* 6 Aug 1947; *Educ* Ambleside Sch, Hersham Surrey; *m* 7 May 1966, Ruby Theresa, da of Walter John Williams, of East Molesey, Surrey; 1 s (Tony b 17 Sept 1968), 1 da (Tania b 12 June 1966); *Career* fndr P & J Plant Hire 1963 (sold business 1968), dir Crest Nicholson plc (formerly Crest Homes) 1968–75, jt fndr The Berkeley Group plc 1976–; tstee Princess Alice Hospice; SBStJ 1987; *Recreations* gardening; *Clubs* Ritz, Peak Carlton Towers, Tramps; *Style—* Anthony Pidgley, Esq; ✉ The Berkeley Group plc, Berkeley House, 19 Portsmouth Road, Cobham, Surrey KT11 1JG (☎ 01932 868555, fax 01932 868667)

PIERCE, David Glyn; s of Gwilym John Pierce, of London, and Hilda Alice, *née* Webster; *b* 25 July 1942; *Educ* Stationers' Co Sch London, Univ of Exeter (BA); *m* 1, 1963, Anne Valerie Sherwood; 1 s (Adam b 7 Dec 1967), 1 da (Rebecca b 18 Aug 1970); m 2, 9 Feb 1991, Victoria Isobel, da of Samuel Seymour, of Seattle, Washington, USA; 1 da (Alexandra b 27 June 1988), 1 s (Marcus b 1 Sept 1992); *Career* TV time buyer Garland Compton 1964–68 (media trainee 1963), head of Media Gp Foote Cone & Belding 1968–77, head of TV buying Everetts 1977–82; Media Campaign Services: joined 1982, bd dir 1986–, dir planning and res 1987–; occasional lectr Coll for Distributive Trades; MCAM 1981, memb Publicity Club of London 1982; *Recreations* competitive cycling, memb Velo Club des Londres; *Style—* David Pierce, Esq; ✉ Media Campaign Services, 3 St Peter's Street, Islington Green, London N1 8JD (☎ 0171 359 6696, fax 0171 354 5735)

PIERCY, 3 Baron (UK 1945); James William Piercy; s of 2 Baron Piercy (d 1981), and Oonagh Lavinia, JP (d 1990), da of Maj Edward John Lake Baylay, DSO; *b* 19 Jan 1946; *Educ* Shrewsbury, Univ of Edinburgh (BSc); *Heir* bro, Hon Mark Edward Pelham Piercy, *qv*; *Career* AMIEE, FCCA; *Style—* The Rt Hon the Lord Piercy; ✉ 13 Arnold Mansions, Queen's Club Gdns, London W14 9RD

PIERCY, Hon Mark Edward Pelham; s of 2 Baron Piercy (d 1981), and hp of bro, 3 Baron; *b* 30 June 1953; *Educ* Shrewsbury, New Coll Oxford (BA); *m* 1979, Vivien Angela, da of His Hon Judge Monier-Williams; 1 s (William Nicholas Pelham b 1989), 3 da (Katherine Henrietta b 1982, Olivia Charlotte b 1984, Harriet Lavinia b 1987); *Career* called to the Bar Lincoln's Inn 1976; *Style—* The Hon Mark Piercy; ✉ 39 Carson Rd, W Dulwich, London SE21 8HT

PIERCY, Prof Nigel Francis; s of Gilbert Piercy (d 1984), of Cambridge, and Helena Gladys, *née* Sargent; *b* 13 Jan 1950; *Educ* Cambridge GS for Boys, Heriot-Watt Univ (BA), Univ of Durham (MA), Univ of Wales (PhD); *m* 1, 1971 (m dis 1985), (Patricia) Jean Piercy; 1 s (Niall Christopher b 1979); m 2, Stephanie Monica, da of Eric James Oscar Burges (d 1991); m 3, 1996, Nikala; *Career* planner Amersham International 1974–77; sr lectr Newcastle Poly 1977–81 (lectr 1972–74); Univ of Wales: lectr 1981–83, sr lectr 1983–86, reader 1986–88, prof of mktg and strategy Cardiff Business Sch 1988–96, Sir Julian Hodge chair in mktg and strategy Cardiff Business Sch 1996–; visiting prof: Neeley Sch of Business Texas Christian Univ 1993–94, Haas Sch of Business Univ of Calif at Berkeley 1994; Author of the Year UK Inst of Mktg 1980–82; FCIM 1988; *Books* Export Strategy (1982), Managing Marketing Information (with M Evans, 1983), The Management Implications of New Information Technology (ed, 1984), Marketing Organisation (1985), Management Information Systems (ed 1986), Marketing Budgeting (1986), Preparing Marketing for the New Millenium (ed, 1991), Market-Led Strategic Change (1991); *Recreations* cycling, badminton; *Style—* Prof Nigel Piercy; ✉ 23 Campbell Drive, Windsor Quay, Cardiff CF1 7QE (☎ 01222 842185); Marketing and Strategy Group, Cardiff Business School, University of Wales College of Cardiff, Colum Drive, Cardiff CF1 3EU (☎ 01222 874275, fax 01222 874419, mobile 0836 751042, e-mail PIERCY@CARDIFF.AC.UK)

PIERRE, Antony David (Tony); s of Jean Pierre, of Chislehurst, Kent, and Sara Fajga, *née* Libchaber; *b* 25 Feb 1956; *Educ* Alleyn's Sch Dulwich, City Univ Business Sch (BSc); *m* 27 May 1990, Michelle Linda, da of late Bernard Langdon; 1 s (Magnus George b 11 May 1995), 1 da (Klara Sophie b 2 Aug 1991); *Career* CA 1981, currently ptnr i/c Nat Corp Fin Baker Tilly; FCA 1992 (ACA 1982); *Recreations* skiing, squash, tennis, theatre, opera; *Clubs* RAC; *Style—* Tony Pierre, Esq; ✉ Baker Tilly, 2 Bloomsbury Street, London WC1B 3ST (☎ 0171 413 5100, fax 0171 413 5101)

PIERS, Sir Charles Robert Fitzmaurice; 10 Bt (I 1661), VRD; s of Sir Charles Piers, 9 Bt (d 1945); *b* 30 Aug 1903; *Educ* RNCs Osborne and Dartmouth; *m* 1936, Ann Blanche Scott (d 1975), da of late Capt Thomas Ferguson; 1 s, 1 da (decd); *Heir* s, James Desmond Piers, *qv*; *Career* mangr Midland Doherty Ltd of Duncan BC, ret; *Style—* Sir Charles Piers, Bt; ✉ 6709 Chisholm Trail, RR1 Duncan, British Columbia V9L 1M3, Canada

PIERS, James Desmond; s and h of Sir Charles Robert Fitzmaurice Piers, 10 Bt, *qv*; *b* 24 July 1947; *m* 1975, Sandra Mae Dixon; 1 s (Stephen James b 1979); 1 da (Christine Sarah b 1976); *Style—* James Piers, Esq

PIERS, Martin James; s of Karl Piers, of Ewell, Surrey, and Meryl Menzies; *b* 12 Sept 1954; *Educ* Hertford GS, Univ of Southampton (LLB); *m* 26 Feb 1993, Ana Maria, da of Raphael Ortega, of Malaga, Spain; *Career* admitted slr 1979, admitted licensed insolvency practitioner 1992; ptnr Gouldens 1983–; lectr on dir personal liability at insur and insolvency confs; contrib business law section Financial Times; memb insurance ctee section of business law Int Bar Assoc; memb: Int Bar Assoc, Br Insur Law Assoc, Br and American Chamber of Commerce, Soc Eng and American Lawyers, Insol, The City Forum; *Books* Guide to Directors and Officers Liability and Loss Prevention (1989); *Recreations* skiing, tennis, walking; *Clubs* Roof Garden; *Style—* Martin Piers, Esq; ✉ Gouldens, 22 Tudor St, London EC4Y 0JJ (☎ 0171 583 7777, fax 0171 583 3051, telex 21520)

PIGGOT, (Thomas) Alan; TD (1967); s of Thomas Piggot (d 1957), and Elizabeth Winifred, *née* Spence (d 1996); *b* 8 March 1930; *Educ* Methodist Coll Belfast, Queens Univ Belfast (MB ChB, BAO), RCS Edinburgh; *m* 16 Sept 1961, Mary Simpson, da of Robert Sprott (d 1993), of Randalstown, Co Antrim; 1 s (Alan b 1962), 1 da (Dawn b 1964); *Career* joined TA: Queens Univ OTC 1950–68, Lt-Col 201(N) Gen Hosp RAMC(V) 1969–80; sr registrar plastic surgn Wythenshave Hosp Manchester 1966–68, clinical lectr in plastic surgery Univ of Newcastle upon Tyne 1968–95, conslt plastic surgn Newcastle Health Authy 1968–95; memb: BMA 1953, Br Assoc Plastic Surgns 1976, Br Assoc Aesthetic Plastic Surgns 1981; FRCS 1961; *Recreations* golf, photography; *Style—* Alan Piggot, Esq, TD; ✉ Ardlui, 3 Osbaldeston Gardens, Gosforth, Newcastle upon Tyne, Tyne & Wear NE3 4JE (☎ 0191 285 8934); Newcastle Nuffield Hospital, Clayton Road, Jesmond, Newcastle upon Tyne, Tyne and Wear NE2 1JP (☎ 0191 281 6131, fax 0191 212 0163)

PIGGOTT, Harold Ebenezer; s of Percy Henry Heath Piggott (d 1979), and Mary Gertrude, *née* Saunders (d 1962); *b* 14 April 1937; *Educ* Worthing HS for Boys, Brighton Tech Coll (City & Guilds); *m* 5 Sept 1959, Barbara Ethel, da of William John Tunbridge, of Cornwall; 3 da (Susan b 17 July 1960, Clare b 8 Aug 1965, Amanda b 29 April 1968); *Career* fndr Harold E Piggott Ltd 1962; Hearts of Oak Friendly Society Ltd: dir 1977–, currently fin dir, chm Hearts of Oak Insurance Group Staff Pension Scheme 1987–88 and 1995–96, vice-chm 1986, 1991 and 1994, chm of society 1991–93; dir Hearts of Oak Trustees Ltd 1979– (chm 1991–93); dir London Aberdeen & Northern Mutual Assurance Society Ltd 1978– (chm 1990–91, vice chm 1995–97), pres Worthing Hard of Hearing Club, govr C of E Sch 1974–93; vice pres Sussex Parkinson's Disease Soc, fndr chm City of London Freeman Assoc of Sussex; life memb: Guild of Freeman of City of London, Nat Tst, Worthing Civic Soc; chm Legislation Sub-Ctee Friendly Association Soc and pres Assoc of Friendly Socs Ltd 1996–97 (vice pres 1995–96); inc exec accountant Worthing Borough Sussex Police Consultative Ctee 1989–92; co cncllr W Sussex 1974–85, chm catering County Hall 1980–85; Worthing Borough Cncl: cncllr Heene Ward 1974–95, mayor 1982–83, ldr of Cncl 1989–94 (dep ldr 1982–89), chm Worthing Centenary Ctee 1990; chm W Sussex Branch Assoc of Dist Cncls 1992–93 (vice chm 1991–92); memb DHSS Appeals Tbnl 1975–87; Hon Alderman of Worthing 1995–, Lord of the Manor of Netherhall Old Newton Suffolk; Liveryman City of London 1977– (Freeman 1972), Liveryman Worshipful Co of Basketmakers (Steward 1988); FInstD 1965, FIMgt 1983, FCEA 1983, FFA 1987, FRSA 1988, memb Chartered Insurance Inst 1990; *Books* Beauty & History in the South East (article in Hearts of Oak Magazine, 1978); *Recreations* swimming, chess, snooker, golf, reading; *Clubs* The Manorial Soc of GB, The United Wards Club of City of London, Offington Park Golf; *Style—* Harold Piggott, Esq; ✉ Netherhall, Upper Brighton Rd, Worthing, W Sussex BN14 9HY (☎ and fax 01903 235510); Apartment at Playa Sol, 11–15 Avenida Gola D'estany, Santa Margarita, Rosas; Hearts of Oak Friendly Society Ltd, Hearts of Oak House, Registered Office, 84 Kingsway, London WC2B 6NF (☎ 0171 430 1714, fax 0171 831 4490)

PIGNATELLI, Frank; *b* 22 Dec 1946; *Educ* St Mungo's Acad Glasgow, Univ of Glasgow (MA, MEd); *m* 23 Aug 1969, Rosetta; 1 s (Paul b 4 Sept 1970), 1 da (Angela b 13 Oct 1973); *Career* dir of educn Strathclyde Regnl Cncl 1988–96, gp dir of human resources Assoc Newspapers Ltd 1996–; visiting prof Univ of Glasgow 1990; memb: Advsy Scottish Cncl for Educn and Trg Targets, Bd Scottish Vocational Educn Cncl; chm: Nat Technol Review Gp, Nat Curriculum Gp on Educn and Trg; formerly dir and memb Scottish Consultative Cncl on the Curriculum; conslt to: Egyptian Govt on vocational educn, Queensland Catholic Educn Cmmn; pres Renfrewshire Branch Inst of Mgmnt (formerly BIM) 1988–93, chm Glasgow and W of Scot Branch RIPA 1989–93; Hon DUniv Univ of Paisley; FIMgt, FRSA; *Books* World Yearbook of Education (contrib, 1987); *Recreations* genealogy, reading, swimming, DIY; *Style—* Frank Pignatelli, Esq; ✉ Northcliffe House, 2 Derry Street, Kensington, London W8 5TT (☎ 0171 938 6601, fax 0171 937 9188)

PIGOT, Sir George Hugh; 8 Bt (GB 1764), of Patshull, Staffordshire; s of Maj-Gen Sir Robert Anthony Pigot, 7 Bt, CB, OBE (d 1986), and his 1 w, Honor, *née* Gibbon (d 1964); *b* 28 Nov 1946; *Educ* Stowe; *m* 1, 2 Dec 1967 (m dis 1973), Judith Sandeman, er da of late Maj John Hele Sandeman Allen, RA; 1 da (Melanie Barbara b 4 Dec 1969); m 2, 2 Feb 1980 (m dis 1993), Lucinda Jane, yr da of Donald Charles Spandler, of Chiddingfold, Surrey; 2 s ((George) Douglas Hugh b 17 Sept 1982, (Robert) Edward Richard b 26 Sept 1984); *Heir* s, (George) Douglas Hugh Pigot b 17 Sept 1982; *Career* with Coutts & Co 1965–67, Hogg Robinson & Gardner Mountain 1967–69; freelance photographer 1970–77, founded Padworth Fisheries (trout farm) 1977, chm and md Padworth Fisheries Ltd 1981–95, dir Southern Trout Ltd 1993–95 (man dir 1994–95); memb Cncl British Trout Assoc 1986–93 (hon treas 1990–92); management conslt 1995–; *Recreations* promotion of fish farming, trout, classic cars, golf; *Clubs* British Trout Assoc, NFU; *Style—* Sir George Pigot, Bt; ✉ Mill House, Mill Lane, Padworth, nr Reading, Berks RG7 4JX (☎ 0118 971 2322, fax 0118 971 3015)

PIGOTT, David John Berkeley; er s and h of Sir (Berkeley) Henry Sebastian Pigott, 5 Bt; *b* 16 Aug 1955; *Educ* Moor Park Ludlow, Hurn Court Bournemouth; *m* 1, 1981 (m dis 1984), Alison Fletcher; m 2, 19 Nov 1986, Julie, da of Eric Gordon Wiffen, of 28 Fitzroy Close, Bassett, Southampton; 1 da (Christabel Maria b 18 Aug 1989); *Career* neon glassbender Pearce Signs 1980–87, production mangr Signwise (Scotland) Ltd 1987–89, proprietor Neon Light Co 1989–; memb local Conservative Assoc; *Recreations* flying model helicopter/plane, rebuilding Jensen cars; *Clubs* Model Helicopter/Plane, Jensen Owners'; *Style—* David Pigott, Esq; ✉ 91 Bellemoor Road, Upper Shirley, Southampton SO15 7QW (☎ 01703 777168)

PIGOTT, Sir (Berkeley) Henry Sebastian; 5 Bt (UK 1808), of Knapton, Queen's County; s of Maj Sir Berkeley Charles Pigott, 4 Bt (d 1982), and Christabel, *née* Bowden-Smith (d 1974); *b* 24 June 1925; *Educ* Ampleforth; *m* 4 Sept 1954, (Olive) Jean, o da of John William Balls (d 1975), of Holly Lodge, Surlingham, Norfolk; 2 s (David John Berkeley b 1955, Antony Charles Philip b 1960), 1 da (Sarah Jane Mary b 1964); *Heir* s, David John Berkeley Pigott, *qv*; *Career* served WWII RM 1944–45; farmer; Freeman of City of Baltimore USA; *Recreations* sailing (in Guinness Book of Records (1988 edn) for smallest single-handed circumnavigation); *Style—* Sir Henry Pigott, Bt; ✉ Brook Farm, Shobley, Ringwood, Hants BH24 3HT

PIGOTT, Hugh Sefton; s of Alfred Sefton Pigott, OBE (d 1979), of Dean Hill, Wilmslow, Cheshire, and Frances Ann, *née* Mills (d 1984); *b* 21 Dec 1929; *Educ* Oundle, King's Coll Cambridge (BA, MA); *m* 1, 31 Aug 1957 (m dis 1984), Venetia Caroline Mary, da of Derric John Stopford Adams, of Ansty Hall, Coventry, Worcs; 4 s (Charles b 1958, Francis b 1960, Edward b 1963, Philip b 1966); m 2, 1 Nov 1986, Fiona Margaret Miller, da of John McDermid, of The Old Rectory, Hickling, Norfolk; *Career* Clifford Chance (formerly Coward Chance): articled clerk 1952–55, asst slr 1955–60, ptnr 1960–92; memb: Law Soc's Standing Ctee on Co Law 1972–85, Advsy Working Pty on Europe 1976–79; hon legal advsr to Accounting Standards Ctee 1986–90, memb Review Body on Senior Salaries 1988–93; memb Jt Disciplinary Scheme of the UK Accountancy Profession 1992; ed Butterworths Jl of International Banking and Financial Law 1996; sr visiting fell Centre for Commercial Law Studies Queen Mary and Westfield Coll London 1994; Liveryman Worshipful Co of Slrs; *Recreations* poetry, the visual arts, piano playing, cooking; *Style—* Hugh Pigott, Esq; ✉ 28 Marlborough Road, Richmond, Surrey TW10 6JR (☎ 0181 940 1960, fax 0181 332 9348)

PIGOTT-SMITH, Timothy Peter (Tim); s of Harry Thomas Pigott-Smith, of Stratford-upon-Avon, and Margaret Muriel, *née* Goodman; *b* 13 May 1946; *Educ* Wyggeston Boys GS Leicester, King Edward VI GS Stratford-upon-Avon, Univ of Bristol (BA Hons), Bristol Old Vic Theatre Sch; *m* 1972, Pamela, da of Alfred Miles; 1 s (Tom Edward b 1976); *Career* actor and director; *Theatre* numerous tours and rep incl: Birmingham, Cambridge, Nottingham and Bristol; Bristol Old Vic 1969 incl: Major Barbara, As You Like It; Prospect Theatre 1970–71 incl: Much Ado, Boswell's Johnson, Hamlet (tour and West End); RSC 1972–75 incl: Roman Plays, Cymbeline, Dr Watson in Sherlock Holmes (London and Broadway); RNT 1987–88 incl: Coming into Land, Octavius Caeser in Antony & Cleopatra, Henry Moule in Entertaining Strangers, Winter's Tale, Cymbeline, Tempest; other roles incl: Traps (Royal Court) 1977, Benefactors (Vaudeville) 1984, Bengal Lancer (Leicester Haymarket and Lyric Hammersmith) 1985, Old Times 1993, Mr Rochester in Jane Eyre (Playhouse) 1993–94, Robert Ross in The Picture of Dorian Gray (Lyric Hammersmith) 1994, Retreat (Orange Tree) 1995, The Letter (Lyric Hammersmith) 1995, The Alchemist, Mary Stuart (RNT) 1996; Compass Theatre (artistic dir 1989–92) incl: Julius Caesar, Amadeus, Royal Hunt of the Sun (dir) 1989, Playing the Wife (dir); also dir Company by Samuel Beckett (Edinburgh, Fringe First Award) 1987, Hamlet (Regent's Park) 1994; *Television* BBC incl: Glittering Prizes, North and South, Wings, Eustace and Hilda, The Lost Boys, Henry IV (part 1), Measure for Measure, Fame is the Spur, School Play, Francis Crick in Life Story, The True Adventures of Christopher Columbus, The Bullion Boys (winner Emmy 1994), The Shadowy Third, Calcutta Chronicles; ITV incl: No Mama No, I Remember Nelson, The Traitor, Struggle, Wilderness Years, Ronald Merrick in Jewel in the Crown (BAFTA, TV Times, Broadcasting Press Guild Best Actor Awards), The Chief 1989–91; Channel Four: Calcutta (documentary) 1995; *Films* incl: Aces High, Joseph Andrews, Sweet William, The Hunchback of Notre Dame, The Day Christ Died, Richard's Things, Clash of the Titans, Escape to Victory, State of Emergency, Remains of the Day; *Recreations* music, reading, Lord's Taverners Cricket; *Style—* Tim Pigott-Smith, Esq; ✉ c/o Michael Whitehall Ltd, 125 Gloucester Road, London SW7 4TE (☎ 0171 244 8466, fax 0171 244 9060)

PIHL, Brig the Hon Dame Mary Mackenzie; *née* Anderson; DBE (1970, MBE 1958); da of 1 Viscount Waverley, PC, GCB, OM, FRS (d 1958), and Christina, *née* Mackenzie (d 1920); *b* 3 Feb 1916; *Educ* Sutton HS, Villa Brillantmont Lausanne Switzerland; *m* 8 July 1973, Frithjof Pihl (d 1988), s of Carl Pihl (d 1936); *Career* joined ATS 1941, transfd WRAC 1949; dir WRAC 1967–70; Hon ADC to HM The Queen 1967–70, ret 1970; *Style—* Brig the Hon Dame Mary Pihl, DBE

PIKE, Claude Drew; OBE (1970), DL (Devon 1979); s of Ivan Samuel Pike (d 1934), and Alice, *née* Goodhead (d 1956); bro of The Rt Hon the Baroness Pike of Melton, DBE, *qv*; *b* 4 July 1915; *Educ* Silcoates Sch Wakefield, Jesus Coll Cambridge (MA, LLM); *m* 23 May 1941, Margaret, da of George Thomas Hirst (d 1965); 1 s (John), 1 da (Penelope); *Career* WWII serv 1940–45, promoted Capt Paymaster; dir Watts Blake Bearne plc 1945–95 (chm 1964–86, pres 1995–); dir: F J Reeves Ltd 1969–75, Lloyds Bank (Devon and Cornwall) 1973–86, Graham Group Ltd 1974–78, Hepworth Ceramic Holdings plc 1974–87, Westbrick Products Ltd 1977–81, Morwellham Recreational Tst 1979–90; CBI: memb Cncl 1968–83, chm SW Regnl Cncl 1974–76, memb Fin and Gen Purposes Ctee 1977–83; chm Exeter Cathedral Preservation Tst, former pres Men of the Trees Devon, chm Torbay Hosp Med Research Tst 1970–96, govr Blundells Coll 1980–90, patron Teignbridge Constituency Cons Assoc 1995– (pres 1993–95), pres Devon Historic Buildings Tst Ltd (also former dir), pres Devon Co Agric Assoc 1988; landowner; Hon LLD Exeter 1988; CIMgt 1976; *Books* Heathercombe - The History of a Dartmoor Valley; *Recreations* forestry, dendrology; *Clubs* Utd Oxford & Cambridge Univ; *Style*— Claude Pike, Esq, OBE, DL; ✉ Dunderdale Lawn, Penshurst Rd, Newton Abbot TQ12 1EN (☎ 01626 54404); Manwood, Heathercombe, Newton Abbot, Devon TQ13 9XE; Watts Blake Bearne & Co plc, Park House, Courtenay Park, Newton Abbot, Devon TQ12 4PS (☎ 01626 332345, telex 428 24 WBB G)

PIKE, Dr Derek; s of Harold Pike, of Cheltenham, and Frances Christina, *née* Williams (d 1990); *b* 24 Jan 1944; *Educ* Harrow Weald Co GS, Univ of Leeds (BSc, PhD); *m* 14 Dec 1979, Thirza Guté, da of Lionel Kotzen, of Johannesburg, SA; *Career* jr engr Harris & Sutherland London 1970–73, engr Arup Associates 1973–77; project engr: John Herrick CSE Oregon USA 1977–79, Michael Barclay Partnership London 1979–82; assoc Ove Arup & Partners 1982–90, currently ptnr Building Design Partnership; memb Cncl IStructE 1992–, chm N Thames Branch IStructE 1995–96; registered civil engr USA; MICE, MConsE, FIStructE, MASCE; *Recreations* pottery, travel; *Style*— Dr Derek Pike; ✉ Building Design Partnership, PO Box 4WD, 16 Gresse Street, London W1A 4WD (☎ 0171 631 4733, fax 0171 631 0393)

PIKE, Douglas Charles McDonald; s of Douglas William Pike (d 1974), and Rachel Brunton, *née* McDonald (d 1979); *b* 25 Aug 1938; *Educ* City of London Sch, Univ of Bristol (BDS); *m* 1965, Julia Margaret, *née* Summers; 2 da (Rebecca b 1966, Amelia b 1968), 1 s (Mathew b 1972); *Career* gen dental practitioner Sudbury Suffolk; elected memb GDC; memb: BDA, Gen Dental Practitioners Assoc, SAAD; *Recreations* walking, sailing, gardening; *Style*— Douglas Pike, Esq; ✉ Scotland Place, Stoke by Nayland, Colchester CO6 4QG (☎ 01206 262098, fax 01206 263339); The Dental Practice, 5 Bank Buildings, Sudbury, Suffolk CO10 6SX (☎ 01787 881100)

PIKE, Prof Edward Roy; s of Anthony Pike (d 1968), of Abercarn, Monmouth, and Rosalind, *née* Davies (d 1982); *b* 4 Dec 1929; *Educ* Southfield Sch Oxford, Univ Coll Cardiff (BSc, PhD); *m* 1955, Pamela, da of William Henry Spearing Sawtell (d 1978); 1 s, 2 da; *Career* served RCS (SHAPE HQ France) 1948–50; Fulbright scholar Faculty of Physics MIT USA 1958–60, chief scientific offr Scientific Civil Serv 1960–91, visiting prof of mathematics Imperial Coll London 1984–86, Clerk Maxwell prof of theoretical physics KCL 1986–, head Sch of Physical Scis and Engrg KCL 1991–94; chm Adam Hilger Ltd 1981–85, dir Richard Clay plc 1985–86; vice pres Inst of Physics 1981–85; FInstP, CPhys, FIMA, CMath, FRS; *Recreations* languages, music; *Style*— Prof E R Pike, FRS; ✉ 8 Bredon Grove, Malvern, Worcs WR14 3JR (☎ 01684 574910); King's College London, Strand, London WC2R 2LS (☎ 0171 873 2155)

PIKE, Francis Bruce; s of Esmund Francis Victor Wallace Pike, of Old Brow, Bimport, Shaftesbury, Dorset, and Elizabeth Rosemary, *née* Dun; *b* 13 Feb 1954; *Educ* Uppingham, Univ of Paris, Selwyn Coll Cambridge (MA); *m* 7 Oct 1993, India-Jane Romaine, da of Marcus Oswald Hornby Lecky Birley, and Lady Annabel Goldsmith; *Career* INVESCO MIM: md Tokyo 1983–87, dir INVESCO MIM Management Ltd 1987–90, pres INVESCO MIM Asset Management (Japan) Ltd 1990–92, chm INVESCO MIM Investment Trust Management Ltd 1992–93; dir: OUB Investment Management Ltd 1986–93, MIM Britannia Okasan Investment Management Ltd 1986–93, Nippon Warrant Fund 1987–93, Drayton Far Eastern Trust plc 1988–, Drayton Asia Tst plc 1989–93, Euro Warrant Fund 1990–93, East Europe Development Fund; chm: Asia Supergrowth Fund 1987–93, Asia Tiger Warrant Fund 1990–93, Central European Asset Management 1990, Peregrine Asset Management 1993–, Drayton Korea Trust 1991–, Indonesian Strategic Development Fund 1991–, Peregrine Capital Ltd 1994–, Peregrine Indian Smaller Companies Fund 1994–; *Recreations* reading; *Style*— Francis Pike, Esq; ✉ Villar Ville, 2nd Floor, 16 Ramchandani Marg, Apollo Bunder, Bombay 400 039, India

PIKE, Baroness (Life Peer UK 1974), of Melton, Co Leics; Irene Mervyn Parnicott Pike; DBE (1981); da of Ivan Samuel Pike (d 1934), and Alice Pike (d 1956); sis of Claude Drew Pike, *qv*; *b* 16 Sept 1918; *Educ* Hunmanby Hall, Univ of Reading; *Career* MP (C) Melton, Leics Dec 1956–Feb 1974, asst postmaster-gen 1959–63, jt parly under-sec state Home Office 1963–64; dir Watts Blake Bearne plc 1964–89; memb Robens Ctee on Health and Safety of Workers 1970–72; chm: IBA Gen Advsy Cncl 1974–79, WRVS 1974–81, Broadcasting Complaints Ctee 1981–86; dir Dunderdale Investmts; *Style*— The Rt Hon the Baroness Pike of Melton, DBE; ✉ Hownam, nr Kelso, Roxburgh

PIKE, John Douglas; s of Rev Horace Douglas Pike, of Rufforth, nr York, and Phyllis Joyce, *née* Langdon; *b* 4 Oct 1947; *Educ* QEGS Wakefield, Keighley Sch, Jesus Coll Cambridge (MA), De Montfort Univ (MA); *m* 11 Oct 1975, Rosemary Elizabeth, da of Archibald Richard Harlow (d 1985), of Wetherby; 2 s (Richard b 28 April 1983, Stephen b 18 July 1985), 1 da (Alison b 23 July 1981); *Career* Booth and Co: articled clerk 1969–71, slr 1972–76, ptnr 1976, head Commercial Property Dept 1991–, mktg ptnr 1993–94, head Environmental Unit 1992–; NP; memb: Law Soc, Slrs Benevolent Assoc; dir Leeds Enviromnental Business Forum and Urban Mines; govr Moorlands Sch Leeds; *Recreations* walking, swimming, rugby football, skiing, gardening; *Style*— John Pike, Esq; ✉ Booth & Co, Sovereign House, South Parade, Leeds LS1 1HQ (☎ 0113 283 2000, fax 0113 283 2060, car 0860 500507, telex 557439)

PIKE, Michael Edmund; KCVO, CMG (1984); *b* 4 Oct 1931; *Educ* Wimbledon Coll, LSE, BNC Oxford (MA); *m* 1962, Catherine, *née* Lim; 1 s, 2 da; *Career* former cnsllr Washington and Tel Aviv, RCDS, ambass to Vietnam 1982–85, min and dep perm rep NATO 1985–87, high cmmr Singapore 1987–90 (ret); special rep of the Sec of State for Foreign and Cwlth Affairs; non-exec dir John Govett's Asian Smaller Companies Investment Trust; memb Manchester 2002 Cwlth Games Bid Ctee, dir Greenwich Millenium Tst; *Style*— Sir Michael Pike, KCVO, CMG

PIKE, Peter Leslie; MP (Lab) Burnley (majority 11,491); s of Leslie Henry Pike (d 1980), and Gladys Pike (d 1971); *b* 26 June 1937; *Educ* Hinchley Wood Secdy Sch; *m* 1962, Sheila Lillian, da of Hubert John Bull (d 1964); 2 da; *Career* served RM 1955–57; Midland Bank 1954–62, pty organiser Lab Pty 1963–73, Mullard (Simonstone) Ltd 1973–83; MP (Lab) Burnley 1983–, memb Environment Select Ctee 1985–90, chm Lab Pty Environment Ctee 1987–90, front bench spokesperson on rural affrs 1990–92, front bench spokesperson on housing 1992–94, chair All-Pty Romania Gp, vice chair All-Pty Homelessness Gp, jt chair All-Pty Tport Forum; memb: Deregulation Ctee, Procedural Ctee; vice pres Burnley Youth Theatre; memb: Nat Tst, CND, Anti-Apartheid; *Recreations* Burnley FC supporter; *Clubs* Byerden House Socialist; *Style*— Peter Pike, Esq, MP; ✉ 73 Ormerod Rd, Burnley, Lancs BB11 2RU (☎ 01282 434719); House of Commons, London SW1A 0AA (☎ 0171 219 3514/6488); Constituency Office (☎ 01282 450840, fax 01282 839623)

PIKE, Dr Richard Andrew; s of Tudor Morgan Pike, of Gosport, Hants, and Eileen Mary, *née* Oxley; *b* 2 April 1950; *Educ* Gosport County GS, Downing Coll Cambridge (scholar, pres Anglo-Japanese Soc, MA, PhD); *m* 26 April 1986, Fiona Elizabeth, da of Murdoch MacLean Henry; 1 s (Stuart Richard b 13 Dec 1993), 2 da (Emma Elizabeth b 1 Sept 1987, Claire Fiona b 10 March 1990); *Career* British Petroleum 1975–93: devpt engr Engrg Dept London 1975–80, area commissioning engr Shetland 1980–82, business devpt co-ordinator Joint Ventures London 1982–83, devpt superintendent Pipelines and Facilities Div Aberdeen 1984–85, offshore prodn engr North Sea 1985–86, mangr (tech) Shetland 1986–88, mangr Joint Venture Japan 1988–89, gen mangr (chemicals) Tokyo 1989–93, pres BP Chemicals Japan 1991–93, dir Samsung-BP Chemicals S Korea 1989–91; DG Inst of Mechanical Engineers 1993–; Award to Excellence Inst of Plant Engineers 1991; FIMechE 1988, FIChemE 1991, FInstPet 1992, FIEE 1996; *Recreations* reading, swimming (swam from Yell to Unst and Mainland to Yell Shetland Islands 1980); *Style*— Dr Richard Pike; ✉ Institution of Mechanical Engineers, 1 Birdcage Walk, London SW1H 9JJ (☎ 0171 222 7899, fax 0171 222 4557)

PIKETT, Christopher; s of Maj Cecil Charles Pikett, and Joan Madeleine Pikett; *b* 15 Oct 1952; *Educ* West Bridgford GS Nottingham, Univ of Southampton (LLB); *m* 18 Sept 1976, Geraldine Barbara, da of Derek Alan Stopps; 2 s (Oliver James b 1980, Edward Guy b 1983); *Career* called to the Bar Middle Temple 1976, legal advsr in indust 1976–82; dir of legal servs and co sec Varity Holdings and subsidaries 1987–89; co sec and gen mangr Legal Affairs 3M United Kingdom PLC 1989–; memb Hon Soc of Middle Temple; FRSA; *Style*— Christopher Pikett, Esq; ✉ 3M United Kingdon PLC, 3M House, Bracknell, Berks RG12 1JU (☎ 01344 858565, fax 01344 858553)

PILBROW, Richard Hugh; s of Arthur Gordon Pilbrow; *b* 28 April 1933; *Educ* Cranbrook Sch, Central Sch of Speech and Drama; *m* 1, 1958, Viki Brinton; 1 s, 1 da; m 2, 1974, Molly Friedel; 1 da; *Career* chm Theatre Projects Consultants 1957–, theatre conslt prodr and lighting designer for prods in London, Moscow, New York, Paris; vice pres: Assoc of Br Theatre Technicians, memb: Cncl Nat Youth Theatre, Cncl London Acad of Music and Drama; FRSA; *Books* Stage Lighting (1970); *Clubs* Garrick; *Style*— Richard Pilbrow, Esq; ✉ 78 Barrack Hill Road, Ridgefield, Connecticut 06877, USA (☎ 00 1 203 438 7879)

PILCH, (Anthony) Michael; CBE (1984); s of Lt-Col George Harold Pilch (d 1943); *b* 6 July 1927; *Educ* Shrewsbury, Balliol Coll Oxford (BA); *m* 1950, Betty Christine, da of Franklin John Skinner (d 1976); 1 da; *Career* dir Noble Lowndes & Partners Ltd 1968–85 (ret); chm: Nat Assoc of Pension Funds 1979–81 (vice pres 1981–83), New Horizon Tst, Park Hill Tst; fndr Miller Centre Caterham; *Recreations* theatre, photography, writing; *Style*— Michael Pilch, Esq, CBE; ✉ 10 Timber Hill Rd, Caterham, Surrey CR3 6LD (☎ 01883 346671)

PILCHER, David Richard; s of Archibald Bertram Pilcher, of West Chiltington, Sussex, and Sylvia, *née* Adlard (d 1995); *b* 26 March 1937; *Educ* Aldenham; *m* 4 April 1970, Veronica Betty, da of George Brown (d 1983), of Wimborne; 1 s (Jonathan David b 21 July 1973), 1 da (Sarah Elizabeth b 26 Feb 1972); *Career* CA with Pridie Brewster & Gold 1957–67; The Royal Opera House: chief accountant 1968–95, head of fin 1995–96; project accountant RNT 1996–; ATII 1966, FCA 1977 (ACA 1966); *Recreations* music, theatre, amateur dramatics; *Style*— David Pilcher, Esq; ✉ 16 Church Lane, Kimpton, Hitchin, Herts SG4 8RS (☎ 01438 832493); Royal National Theatre, South Bank, London SE1 9PX (☎ 0171 928 2033, fax 0171 620 1197)

PILDITCH, John Richard; s and h of Sir Richard Edward Pilditch, 4 Bt, *qv*; *b* 24 Sept 1955; *Style*— John Pilditch, Esq; ✉ c/o 4 Fisherman's Bank, Mudeford, Christchurch, Dorset

PILDITCH, Sir Richard Edward; 4 Bt (UK 1929); s of late Sir Philip Harold Pilditch, 2 Bt, and bro of Sir Philip John Frederick Pilditch, 3 Bt (d 1954); *b* 8 Sept 1926; *Educ* Charterhouse; *m* 7 Oct 1950, Pauline Elizabeth Smith; 1 s, 1 da; *Heir* s, John Richard Pilditch, *qv*; *Career* RN 1944–47 India and Ceylon; *Style*— Sir Richard Pilditch, Bt; ✉ 4 Fishermans Bank, Mudeford, Christchurch, Dorset

PILE, Col Sir Frederick Devereux; 3 Bt (UK 1900), of Kenilworth House, Rathgar, Co Dublin; MC (1945); s of Gen Sir Frederick Alfred Pile, 2 Bt, GCB, DSO, MC (d 1976), and his 1 w Vera, da of Brig-Gen Frederick Lloyd, CB; *b* 10 Dec 1915; *Educ* Weymouth Coll, RMC Sandhurst; *m* 1, 1940, Pamela (d 1983), da of late Philip Henstock; 2 da; m 2, 1984, Violet Josephine Andrews, da of Alfred Denys Cowper; *Heir* n, Anthony John Devereux Pile; *Career* served WWII 1939–45, Col Royal Tank Regt, Korea 1953, Suez Expedition 1956; Br Jt Servs Mission Washington DC 1957–60, Cmdt RAC Driving and Maintenance Sch 1960–62, distribution mangr Vaux and Associated Breweries 1963–65, gen sec Royal Soldiers Daughters Sch 1965–72; *Books* Better Than Riches; *Recreations* fishing, cricket, travelling; *Clubs* MCC; *Style*— Col Sir Frederick Pile, Bt, MC; ✉ Beadles, Cowbeech, nr Hailsham, East Sussex

PILE, Sir William Dennis; GCB (1978, KCB 1971, CB 1968), MBE (1944); s of James Edward Pile; *b* 1 Dec 1919; *Educ* Royal Masonic Sch, St Catharine's Coll Cambridge; *m* 1, 1939 (m dis 1947), Brenda Skinner; m 2, 1948, Joan Marguerite Crafter; 1 s, 2 da; *Career* perm sec DES 1970–76, chm Bd of Inland Revenue 1976–79; dir: Nationwide Building Society 1980–89, Distillers' Co Ltd 1980–86; *Clubs* United Oxford & Cambridge, Hawks (Cambridge); *Style*— Sir William Pile, GCB, MBE; ✉ The Manor House, Riverhead, nr Sevenoaks, Kent TN13 2AS (☎ 01732 454498)

PILGER, John Richard; s of Claude Harold Pilger (d 1989), and Elsie, *née* Marheine (d 1989), of Sydney; *b* 9 Oct 1939, Sydney; *Educ* Sydney HS; *m* (m dis), Scarth Flett; *partner* Jane Hill; 1 s (Sam b 1973), 1 da (Zoe b 1984); *Career* journalist, film-maker, playwright and author; trained with Sydney Daily Telegraph and Sunday Telegraph; formerly with: Reuter London, Daily Mirror, World in Action (Granada TV), ATV/Central TV; has written for: Daily Mirror, New Statesman, New York Times, Los Angeles Times, Guardian, Independent, The Age; war corr: Vietnam, Cambodia, Indo-Pakistan, Biafra, Middle East; has made 42 documentary TV films, many with David Munro, notably Year Zero - The Silent Death of Cambodia (1979), Death of a Nation, the Timor Conspiracy (1994) and Inside Burma: Land of Fear (1996); awards incl: Descriptive Writer of the Year 1966, Reporter of the Year 1967, Journalist of the Year 1967, International Reporter of the Year 1970, News Reporter of the Year 1974, Campaigning Journalist of the Year 1977, Journalist of the Year 1979, Reporter Sans Frontieres 1980, UN Media Peace prize 1980, UN Media Gold Medal 1981, George Foster Peabody Award (US) 1990, Richard Dimbleby Award (BAFTA) 1991, Emmy (US) 1991; Hon DLitt Staffordshire Univ 1994, Hon DPhil Dublin City Univ 1995; Edward Wilson fell Deakin Univ Aust 1995; memb NUJ; *Books* The Last Day (1975), Aftermath: the Struggle of Cambodia and Vietnam (1983), The Outsiders (1984), Heroes (1986), A Secret Country (1989), Distant Voices (1992); *Recreations* swimming, sunning, mulling; *Style*— John Pilger, Esq; ✉ 35–38 Portman Square, London W1 (☎ 0171 486 6688, fax 0171 612 7555)

PILKINGTON, Sir Antony Richard; kt (1990), DL; only s of Maj Arthur Cope Pilkington, MC (yr bro of late Sir Richard Pilkington, KBE, MC), and Otilia Dolores, *née* Reed-Cook; *b* 20 June 1935; *Educ* Ampleforth, Trinity Coll Cambridge; *m* 1960, Alice Kirsty, er da of Sir Thomas Calderwood Dundas, 7 and last Bt, MBE (d 1970); 3 s (Jerome b 1961, David b 1963, Simon b 1972), 1 da (Miranda b 1966); *Career* chm Pilkington plc 1980–95; non-exec dir: GKN plc 1982–91, National Westminster Bank plc 1984–94, Nat West Investment Bank Ltd 1989–91, Imperial Chemical Industries PLC 1991–; chm: Community of St Helens Tst 1978–95, St Helens Housing Assoc Ltd 1995–, Holties Sci & Arts Centre Ltd 1996–; High Sheriff of Cheshire 1996–97; pres St Helens C of C Trg and Enterprise 1996–; hon fell John Moores Univ Liverpool 1996, memb Ct Univ of Manchester 1996–; Liveryman Worshipful Co of Glaziers & Painters of Glass; *Style*— Sir Antony Pilkington, DL; ✉ c/o Pilkington plc, Prescot Rd, St Helens WA10

3TT (☎ 01744 28882); Imperial Chemical Industries plc, Group Headquarters, No 9 Millbank, London SW1P 3JF (☎ 0171 834 4444, fax 0171 834 2042)

PILKINGTON, (Richard) Godfrey; s of Col Guy Reginald Pilkington, DSO, TD (d 1970), of St Helens, Merseyside, and Margery, *née* Frost (d 1973); *b* 8 Nov 1918; *Educ* Clifton, Trinity Coll Cambridge (MA); *m* 14 Oct 1950, Evelyn Edith (Eve), da of Philip Robert Stanley Vincent (d 1933), of Gerrards Cross, Bucks; 2 s (Andrew b 1955, Matthew b 1964), 2 da (Penny b 1956, Clarissa b 1958); *Career* WWII Lt (Temp Actg Capt) Anti-Tank and Medium Gunners RA, served BNAF I Army and CMF Italy 1940–46; art dealer Frost and Reed Ltd 1947–53, fndr and ptnr Piccadilly Gallery London 1953–, ed Pictures and Prints 1951–60; Master Fine Art Trade Guild 1964–66, chm Soc of London Art Dealers 1974–77; govr Wimbledon Sch of Art 1990–; *Recreations* walking, gardening, tennis, golf, boating; *Clubs* Athenaeum, Garrick, Hurlingham; *Style—* Godfrey Pilkington, Esq; ✉ 45 Barons Court Rd, London W14 9DZ (☎ 0171 385 8278); The Old Vicarage, Lamb Lane, Buckland, Faringdon, Oxfordshire; Piccadilly Gallery, 16 Cork St, London W1X 1PF (☎ 0171 629 2875, fax 0171 499 0431)

PILKINGTON, Baroness; Mavis Joy Doreen; DL (Merseyside 1985); er da of Gilbert Caffrey, of Woodleigh, Lostock Park, Bolton; formerly Mrs Wilding; *m* 2, 17 Feb 1961, as his 2 w, Baron Pilkington (Life Peer, d 1983); *Career* pres: The Lung Cancer Fund, St Helens Amateur Operatic Soc; patron Southport Flower Show, vice patron Nat Rose Soc; *Style—* The Rt Hon the Lady Pilkington; ✉ Windle Hall, St Helens, Merseyside

PILKINGTON, Muriel Norma; da of Norman Herbert Fosbury (d 1987), of Guildford, and Lilian Alice, *née* Gilbey (d 1996); *b* 1 Jan 1941; *Educ* Woking Co GS for Girls, Helene Lange Oberschule Hamburg, Lady Margaret Hall Oxford (MA, organ scholarship); *m* 1, 1962, Anthony Leonald Andrews; 1 s (David Leonard Neil b 1966); m 2, 1983, Derek Brogden Pilkington; 1 step da (Sarah Louise b 1965), 1 step s (Charles Edward Brogden b 1967); *Career* asst teacher modern history Shephalbury Sch Stevenage 1962–64, second in Modern History Dept Hatfield Girls' GS 1964–66, home tutor gen subjects Herts CC 1966–70; Sir James Altham Sch Watford: asst teacher modern history 1970–72, head of Modern History Dept 1972–76, head of Humanities Faculty 1976–81; dep headteacher Francis Bacon Sch St Albans 1981–86, headteacher Wycombe HS 1986–; examiner AEB (O Level) and EAEB (CSE) 1976–82; cert of advanced professional study Univ of Cambridge 1982 and 1985; contrib to TES 1977–; govr: Chiltern Gate Sch High Wycombe, Buckinghamshire Coll (Brunel Univ); memb: SHA, NAHT, Royal Choral Soc 1962–80; tstee: Whitmore Vale Housing Assoc, London Art Sch; FRSA 1991; *Recreations* classical music, ballet, opera, ardent Francophile, cordon bleu cookery; *Clubs* London Schools and Colleges Dining; *Style—* Mrs Muriel Pilkington; ✉ Wycombe High School, Marlow Hill, High Wycombe, Bucks HP11 1TB (☎ 01494 523961, fax 01494 510354)

PILKINGTON, Dr Roger Windle; s of (Richard) Austin Pilkington (d 1951), of St Helens, and The Hon Hope Cozens-Hardy (d 1947); *b* 17 Jan 1915; *Educ* Rugby, Univ of Freiburg, Magdalene Coll Cambridge (MA, PhD); *m* 1, 27 July 1937 (m dis 1973), Theodora Miriam, da of Dr Farris Nasser Jaboor (d 1940); 1 s (Hugh Austin b 1942, d 1986), 1 da (Cynthia Miriam b 1939); m 2, 11 Oct 1973, Ingrid Maria, da of Herman Gustaf Geijer (d 1961), of Brattfors; *Career* res in genetics 1937–45; freelance writer and author of 57 books; contrib to: Time and Tide, Family Doctor, Sunday Telegraph; chm: London Missionary Soc 1962, Tstees of Homerton Coll Cambridge 1962–74, The Hall Sch 1962–73; life memb Eugenics Soc 1951; Master Worshipful Co of Glass Sellers 1967 (memb 1957); Chevalier Confrérie du Minervois (France) 1987; *Books* incl: scientific works: The Ways of the Sea (1957), Robert Boyle, Father of Chemistry (1959); for children: The Boy from Stink Alley (1966), The Ormering Tide (1974), I Sailed on the Mayflower (1990); The Small Boat Series in 20 volumes, Small Boat in the Midi (1988), Small Boat Down The Years (1988); One Foot in France (1992), View from the Shore (1995); *Recreations* inland navigation, walking; *Style—* Dr Roger Pilkington; ✉ 4 Links Court, Grouville, Jersey (☎ 01534 851350); Les Cactus, 34310 Montouliers, France (☎ 00 33 67 89 49 98)

PILKINGTON OF OXENFORD, Baron (Life Peer UK 1995), of West Dowlish, Co Somerset; Rev Canon Peter Pilkington; s of Frank Pilkington (d 1977), of Newcastle-upon-Tyne, and Doris Pilkington (d 1985); *b* 5 Sept 1933; *Educ* Dame Allan's Sch Newcastle upon Tyne, Jesus Coll Cambridge (BA, MA); *m* 1966, Helen, da of Charles Wilson, of Risseholme, Lincoln and Elleron Lodge, N Yorks; 2 da (Hon Celia b 1970, Hon Sarah b 1972); *Career* schoolmaster St Joseph's Coll Chidya Tanganyika 1955–58, ordained 1959, curate of Bakewell Derbys 1959–62, schoolmaster Eton Coll 1965–75, headmaster King's Sch Canterbury 1975–86, high master St Paul's Sch London 1986–92; hon canon of Canterbury Cathedral 1975–90, canon emeritus 1990–; memb Parole Bd 1990–95; chm Broadcasting Complaints Cmmn 1992–96; *Clubs* Garrick, Beefsteak; *Style—* The Rev the Rt Hon Lord Pilkington of Oxenford; ✉ Oxenford House, nr Ilminster, Somerset TA19 0PP

PILL, Rt Hon Lord Justice; Rt Hon Sir Malcolm Thomas; kt (1988), PC (1995); s of Reginald Thomas Pill, MBE (d 1987), and Anne Elizabeth, *née* Wright (d 1982); *b* 11 March 1938; *Educ* Whitchurch GS, Trinity Coll Cambridge (MA, LLM), Hague Acad of Int Law (Dip); *m* 19 March 1966, Roisin Mary, da of Dr Thomas Prior Riordan, of Swansea; 2 s (John b 1967, Hugh b 1968), 1 da (Madeleine b 1971); *Career* serv RA 1956–58, Glamorgan Yeo (TA) 1958–67; called to the Bar Gray's Inn 1962; third sec FO 1963–64, recorder of the Crown Court 1976–87, QC 1978, bencher Gray's Inn 1987, judge of the High Court of Justice (Queen's Bench Div) 1988–95 (presiding judge Wales and Chester Circuit 1989–93), a Lord Justice of Appeal 1995–; judge of the Employment Appeal Tribunal 1992–95; dep chm Boundary Cmmn for Wales 1993–95, Euro Parly Constituency Ctee for Wales 1993; chm: UNA (Welsh Centre) Tst 1969–77 and 1980–87, Welsh Centre for Int Affairs 1973–76, UK Ctee Freedom from Hunger Campaign 1978–87; *Clubs* Army & Navy, Cardiff and Co; *Style—* The Rt Hon Lord Justice Pill; ✉ Royal Courts of Justice, Strand, London WC2A 2LL

PILLAR, Adm Sir William Thomas; GBE (1983), KCB (1980); s of William Thomas Pillar (d 1960), of Dartmouth, and Lily, *née* Woolnough (d 1932); *b* 24 Feb 1924; *Educ* Blundell's, RNEC; *m* 1946, Ursula Winifred, da of Arthur Benjamin Ransley, MC (d 1965); 3 s, 1 da; *Career* joined RN 1942, Capt RNEC 1973–75, Port Adm Rosyth 1976–77, Asst Chief Fleet Support 1977–79, Chief Fleet Support and memb Admty Bd 1979–82, Adm 1982, Cmdt RCDS 1982–83, Lt-Govr and C-in-C Jersey 1985–90; nat pres Forces Help Soc and Lord Roberts Workshops 1991–; pres RNVR: Officers' Assoc and Naval Club 1991–, Youth Sail Training Tst 1994–; memb Cncl RUSI 1984–87 (vice-chm 1986–87), vice-pres Blundell's Sch 1987–, pres Square Rigger Club (support of training ship Royalist) 1988–; chm Zeals Parish Cncl 1992–; KStJ 1985; FIMechE 1969, CEng, FIMarE 1972; *Recreations* sailing, rough gardening, fixing things; *Clubs* Naval, Royal Naval Sailing Assoc (Cdre 1980–83, Life Vice Cdre 1990), Royal Yacht Sqdn; *Style—* Adm Sir William Pillar, GBE, KCB; ✉ Selwood, Zeals Row, Zeals, Warminster, Wilts BA12 6PE (☎ 01747 840577)

PILLAY, HE J Y; *b* 30 March 1934, Malaysia; *Educ* Imperial Coll London (BSc); *m*; 1 da; *Career* Singapore diplomat; Singapore Civil Serv: joined 1961, subsequently seconded to Economic Devpt Bd until 1965, dep sec Economic Devpt Div Miny of Fin 1965–68, perm sec 1968–70, second perm sec Miny of Defence 1970–72, perm sec Miny of Fin (Revenue) 1972–85, md Monetary Authy of Singapore and Government of Singapore Investment Corporation 1985–89, perm sec Miny of Nat Devpt 1989–95, ret 1995; Singapore high cmmr to the Ct of St James's 1996–; non-exec chm: Singapore Airlines 1972–96, Temasek Holdings Pte Ltd 1974–86, Petrochemical Corporation of Singapore Pte Ltd 1977–86, Development Bank of Singapore 1979–86, Singapore Technologies Holding Pte Ltd 1991–94; dir Singapore Symphony Orchestra 1979–96, pres Singapore Indian Devpt Assoc 1991–96; *Style—* HE Mr J Y Pillay; ✉ High Commission for the Republic of Singapore, 9 Wilton Crescent, London SW1X 8RW (☎ 0171 235 8315, fax 0171 245 6583)

PILLEY, John Cyril Dorland; s of Capt Eric Charles Pilley, and Elsa Celeste, *née* Henderson; *b* 25 Jan 1935; *Educ* Charterhouse, ChCh Oxford; *m* 1 Feb 1985, Caroline Yvonne, da of Ian Gillett Gilbert; *Career* ADC to CINC Far East 1960–61, ADC to CIGS 1961–62, Adj 1 Bn Coldstream Guards 1964–66, ret as Capt; dir: Henderson Unit Trust Management 1982, Henderson Administration Ltd 1987; chm Russell Wood Ltd 1989; *Recreations* tennis, fishing, riding; *Clubs* Boodle's, City of London; *Style—* Capt John Pilley; ✉ Trotton Old Rectory, Near Petersfield, Hampshire (☎ 01730 813612); Russell Wood Ltd, 30 Great Guildford St, London SE1 (☎ 0171 928 0505, fax 0171 928 893) and 1 Hay Hill, Berkeley Square, London W1X 7LF (☎ 0171 409 3202)

PILLING, Christopher Robert; s of Robert Granville Pilling (d 1992), of Applethwaite, Cumbria, and Florence Mary, *née* Pollard (d 1966); *b* 20 April 1936; *Educ* King Edward's Sch Birmingham, Univ of Leeds (BA), Loughborough Coll (CertEd); *m* 6 Aug 1960, Sylvia, da of Willam Edward Hill, and Gladys Hill; 1 s (Mark Christopher 24 Dec 1961), 2 da (Zoë Rachel b 2 Sept 1963, Ceri Susannah b 23 April 1966); *Career* writer and teacher; asst d'Anglais Ecole Normale d'Instituteurs Moulins 1957–58; asst teacher of French and PE: Wirral GS 1959–61, King Edward's Sch for Boys Birmingham 1961–62, Ackworth Sch Pontefract 1962–73 (house master); head of modern languages and house master Knottingley HS W Yorks 1973–78, tutor in literature Univ of Newcastle Dept of Adult Educn 1978–80, head of French, teacher of German, Latin, Italian and gen studies Keswick Sch Cumbria 1980–88; reviewer TLS 1973–74; numerous broadcasts BBC Radio 3; rep Cumbria vintage squash team 1990–; *Awards* Arts Cncl Grant 1971, Arts Cncl Translator's Grant 1977, Northern Playwrights' Soc Award for verse play 1983, Northern Arts Writers' Award 1985, prizewinner Concours Européen de Création Littéraire Centre Culturel du Brabant Wallon 1992, Tyrone Guthrie Centre Residency (awarded by Northern Arts) 1993, Euro Poetry Translation Network Residency (awarded by Northern Arts) 1995, Bourse des Communautés Européennes 1996; *Poetry* Snakes & Girls (1970, New Poets Award), Fifteen Poems (New Poets Award, 1970), In All the Spaces on All the Lines (1971), Wren & Owl (1971), Andrée's Bloom and the Anemones (1973), Light Leaves (1975), War Photographer from the Age of 14 (1983), Foreign Bodies (1992), Cross your Legs and Wish (1994), Glitter When You Jump (1996); anthologies incl: Arts Cncl Anthologies, PEN New Poetry, Adam's Dream: Poems from Cumbria and Lakeland (1981), The Oxford Book of Christmas Poems (1983), Lancaster Literature Festival Anthologies (1983, 1984, 1986, 1990, 1992, 1993), Between Comets: for Norman Nicholson at 70 (1984), Speak to the Hills (1985), Voices of Cumbria (1987), New Christian Poetry (1990), The New Lake Poets (1991), Northern Poetry Two (1991), The Poetry Book Society Anthology 3 (1992), The Forward Book of Poetry (1994), A Squillet of Wise Fool's Gold (Nat Autistic Soc, 1994), Swarthmoor Anthology (1995), Critical Survey (1996); translations incl: in The Oxford Book of Verse in English Translation (1980), These Jaundiced Loves: A Translation of Tristan Corbière's Les Amours Jaunes (1995), Modern Poetry in Translation 8: French issue (with David Kennedy, 1995), Modern Poetry in Translation 9 (1996); poems in: The Spectator, The Observer, The New Statesman, TLS, Poetry Review, The London Magazine, Encounter, Critical Quarterly, Ambit, Lettres d'Europe and others; *Recreations* playing squash (capt Keswick 2nd team), listening to classical music and jazz, going to the theatre, reading poetry, fiction and philosophy, looking at wildlife and art; *Style—* Christopher Pilling, Esq; ✉ 25 High Hill, Keswick, Cumbria CA12 5NY (☎ 017687 73814)

PILLINGER, Prof Colin Trevor; s of Alfred Pillinger (d 1985), and Florence, *née* Honour; *b* 9 May 1943; *Educ* Kingswood GS, Univ of Wales (BSc, PhD), Univ of Bristol (DSc); *m* Judith Mary, da of late (Gordon) Jack Hay; 1 da (Shusanah Jane b 30 Jan 1976), 1 s (Nicolas Joseph b 11 Aug 1977); *Career* res assoc Dept of Chemistry Univ of Bristol 1972–76 (post doctoral res asst 1968–72), sr res assoc Dept of Earth Sciences Univ of Cambridge 1978–84 (res assoc 1976–78, at Trinity Hall 1981–84); Open Univ: sr res fell 1984–90, personal chair in planetary sciences Dept of Earth Sciences Open Univ 1990–, Gresham Prof of Astronomy 1996–; British Steel Corporation fell 1972–74, SERC Special Replacement Award 1984–89, Wolfson Research Award 1990–93; memb: British Mass Spectrometry Soc 1981, Int Astronomical Union 1991; fell Meteoritical Soc 1986 (memb 1972), FRAS 1981, FRS 1993, FRGS 1993; author of over 160 papers in refereed jls and numerous book reviews; *Recreations* farming, soccer, animals; *Style—* Prof Colin Pillinger, FRS; ✉ Planetary Sciences Research Institute, Department of Earth Sciences, The Open University, Walton Hall, Milton Keynes MK7 6AA (☎ 01908 652119, fax 01908 655910, e-mail psri@open.ac.uk)

PILLMAN, Joseph Charles; s of Lt-Col Joseph Robert Pillman, TD (d 1977), of Clwyd; *b* 7 July 1952; *Educ* Rugby, Cambridge (MA); *children* 2 da (Katherine Avril b 1985, Harriet Emma b 1987); *Career* admitted slr 1977, ptnr Cole and Cole Oxford 1983–; *Clubs* MCC; *Style—* Joseph Pillman, Esq; ✉ Cole and Cole, Buxton Court, 3 West Way, Oxford OX2 0SZ (☎ 01865 791122, fax 01865 721367)

PILSWORTH, Michael John; s of Alwyne Pilsworth, of Retford, Notts, and Catherine, *née* Silverwood; *b* 1 April 1951; *Educ* King Edward VI GS Retford Notts, Univ of Manchester (BA, MA); *m* 7 Oct 1972, Stella Frances, da of Donald Lionel Hore, of Bristol; 1 s (Thomas James b 18 Dec 1984), 1 da (Rosa Grace b 8 March 1977); *Career* res asst Inst of Advanced Studies Manchester Poly 1972–73, lectr in adult educn Univ of Manchester 1976–78 (res fell 1973–75), res assoc Centre for TV Research Univ of Leeds 1979, prog devpt exec London Weekend TV 1983–84 (researcher 1979–82), gp devpt controller TVS Entertainment plc 1987–88 (head of prog planning and devpt 1985–86), chief exec MGMM Communications Ltd 1988–89; md: Alomo Productions Ltd 1990–93, SelecTV plc 1993 (dir 1990–93); chief exec Chrysalis Visual Entertainment and dir Chrysalis plc 1993–; memb: BAFTA, RTS; *Books* Broadcasting in The Third World (1977); *Recreations* swimming, tennis, cinema, reading; *Clubs* Groucho, 2 Brydges Place; *Style—* Michael Pilsworth, Esq; ✉ Chrysalis Group plc, The Chrysalis Building, Bramley Road, London W10 6SP (☎ 0171 221 2213, fax 0171 465 6159)

PILTON, Patrick William; s of William Alfred Pilton (d 1982), and Ethel Violet Pilton (d 1988); *b* 24 Oct 1938; *Educ* Raines Fndn GS Whitechapel; *m* 1963 (m dis), Mellanie Harrington; 1 s (Simon Mark b 4 Nov 1963), 1 da (Trudi b 1 Jan 1969); *Career* journalist; trainee reporter Pontypridd Observer 1960–61, reporter East London News Agency 1961–62; sub-ed: Western Mail & Echo Cardiff 1964–65 (reporter 1962–64), Evening Post Reading 1965–67; sub-ed Daily Mirror 1968–69, chief sub-ed Evening Post Hemel Hempstead 1969–71 (dep chief sub 1967–68), asst ed (night) The Journal Newcastle upon Tyne 1971–73; The Sun: asst night ed 1973–76, dep night ed 1976–79, assoc features ed 1979; ed Sunday Sun Newcastle upon Tyne 1980–81, night ed Daily Express 1983–85 (dep night ed 1981–83), exec ed (prodn) Today 1985–86, dep ed London Daily News 1986–87, leader Publishers Planning Team Mirror Group Newspapers 1987, asst ed Today 1989–91 (night ed 1987–89), ed South Wales Echo Cardiff 1991–93, gp managing ed Mirror Group Newspapers 1993–; *Books* Every Night at the London Palladium (1976), Page Three: Story of the Sun's Page Three Girls (1978); *Recreations* cricket, watching rugby, walking, theatre; *Clubs* Surrey CCC; *Style—* Patrick Pilton, Esq; ✉ Mirror Group Newspapers, 1 Canada Square, Canary Wharf, London E14 5AP

PIMLOTT, Prof Benjamin John (Ben); s of John Alfred Ralph Pimlott, CB (d 1969), of Wimbledon, London, and Ellen Dench Pimlott, *née* Howes (d 1976); *b* 4 July 1945; *Educ* Marlborough, Worcester Coll Oxford; *m* 2 July 1977, Jean Ann, da of Albert William Seaton; 3 s; *Career* lectr Univ of Newcastle 1970–79 (Br Acad Thank Offering to Britain fell 1972–73, Nuffield Fndn res fell 1977–78), res assoc LSE 1979–81, prof of politics and contemporary history Birkbeck Coll Univ of London 1987– (lectr 1981, reader 1986); columnist: Today 1986–87, The Times 1987–88, New Statesman 1987–88, Sunday Times 1988–89; ed Samizdat 1988–90; Parly candidate (Lab): Arundel 1974, Cleveland and Whitby 1974 and 1979; exec The Fabian Soc 1987– (chm 1993–94); FRHistS 1993; FBA 1996; *Books* Labour and the Left in the 1930s (1977), Hugh Dalton (Whitbread Biography award, 1985), Harold Wilson (1992), Frustrate Their Knavish Tricks (1994), The Queen (1996); *Style—* Prof Ben Pimlott, FBA; ✉ Birkbeck College, Malet St, London WC1 (☎ 0171 631 6780)

PIMLOTT, Graham; *Career* admitted slr 1976, later ptnr Lovell White Durrant slrs, sec Takeover Panel 1981–83, corp fin dir Kleinwort Benson 1986–89, head of corp fin then chief exec Merchant Banking Div Barclays de Zoete Wedd 1989–96, dir of planning, ops and technol Barclays PLC 1997–; non-exec dir: Tesco plc 1993–, Hammerson plc; *Style—* Graham Pimlott, Esq; ✉ Barclays plc, 54 Lombard Street, London EC3P 3AH (☎ 0171 699 5000)

PIMLOTT, Steven Charles; s of Arthur Pimlott (d 1994), of Manchester, and Marian, *née* Whittaker; *b* 18 April 1953; *Educ* Manchester GS, Univ of Cambridge; *m* Daniela Beckly, opera singer; 3 c (Oskar b 22 Nov 1990, Raphael b 6 April 1992, Phoebe b 4 Aug 1993); *Career* director of theatre, opera and musicals; began career as staff prodr ENO 1976 (revivals incl: Rigoletto, A Night in Venice, Gianni Schicchi); joined Opera North 1978; assoc dir Crucible Theatre 1987–88 season; *Theatre* early prodns incl: Ring Around the Moon (Manchester Royal Exchange), Entertaining Mr Sloane (Harrogate), Deathtrap (Northcott), On the Razzle (Leeds Playhouse), Amadeus (Harrogate), A Patriot for Me (Leeds), The Daughter in Law (Sheffield), Carousel (Manchester Royal Exchange); recent RSC prodns (assoc dir 1996–) incl: Julius Caesar 1991, Murder in the Cathedral 1993, Measure for Measure 1994, Richard III 1995, As You Like It 1996, Molière's Les Femmes Savantes 1996; also recently dir world premiere of Michael Hastings' Unfinished Business and world premiere of two plays by Phyllis Nagy: Butterfly Kiss (Almeida) 1994, The Strip (Royal Court) 1995; also dir Vieux Carre (Nottingham Playhouse) 1995; *Musicals* recent prodns incl: Sunday in the Park with George 1991 (Olivier Award for Best Musical), Joseph and the Amazing Technicolor Dreamcoat 1991 (West End, Broadway, UK tour, Canada, Aust); *Opera* prodns for Opera North incl: Tosca, Nabucco, Bartered Bride, Werther, Cavalleria Rusticana; other credits incl: The Pearl Fishers (Scottish Opera), Samson et Dalila (Bregent), La Bohème (ENO), Don Giovanni (Victoria State Opera), Manon Lescaut (Aust Opera), La Traviata (Jerusalem Festival), Un Ballo in Maschera (Flanders Opera), Eugenie Onegin (New Israeli Opera); arena prodn of Carmen 1988– (Earls Ct, Tokyo, Melbourne, Sydney, Birmingham, Dortmund, Zurich, Munich, Berlin); *Recreations* playing the oboe; *Style—* Steven Pimlott, Esq; ✉ c/o Harriet Cruickshank, 97 Old South Lambeth Road, London SW8 1XU (☎ 0171 735 2933, fax 0171 820 1081)

PINCHER, (Henry) Chapman; s of Maj Richard Chapman Pincher (d 1964), and Helen, *née* Foster (d 1960); *b* 29 March 1914; *Educ* Darlington GS, King's Coll London (BSc, Carter medallist), Inst of Educn; *m* 16 Nov 1965, Constance Sylvia Wolstenholme; 1 s (Michael b 1949), 1 da (Patricia b 1947); *Career* RAC 1940, Mil Coll of Sci 1942, Tech SO Rocket Div Min of Supply 1943–46; staff Liverpool Inst 1936–40, defence sci and medical ed Daily Express 1946–73 (Journalist of the Year 1964, Reporter of the Decade 1966), asst ed Daily Express and chief def corr Beaverbrook Newspapers 1973–79, freelance writer and business conslt 1979–, regular fishing corr Country magazine; Hon DLitt Univ of Newcastle, fell King's Coll London 1979; *Books* Breeding of Farm Animals (1946), A Study of Fishes (1947), Into the Atomic Age (1947), Spotlight on Animals (1950), Evolution (1950), It's Fun Finding Out (with Bernard Wicksteed, 1950), Sleep and How to Get More of It (1954), Not with a Bang (1965), The Giantkiller (1967), The Penthouse Conspirators (1970), Sex in our Time (1973), The Skeleton at the Villa Wolkonsky (1975), The Eye of the Tornado (1976), The Four Horses (1978), Inside Story (1978), Dirty Tricks (1980), Their Trade is Treachery (1981), The Private World of St John Terrapin (1982), Too Secret Too Long (1984), The Secret Offensive (1985), Traitors (1987), A Web of Deception (1987), Contamination (1989), The Truth About Dirty Tricks (1990), One Dog and Her Man (1991), A Box of Chocolates (1993), Pastoral Symphony (1993), Life's a Bitch! (1996); *Recreations* fishing, shooting, natural history, music; *Style—* Chapman Pincher, Esq; ✉ The Church House, 16 Church St, Kintbury, nr Hungerford, Berks RG15 9TR (☎ and fax 01488 658855)

PINCHES, Rosemary Vivian; *née* Bidder; da of Lt-Col Harold Francis Bidder, DSO, JP (d 1971), formerly of Ravensbury Manor, Morden, Surrey, and Lilias Mary Vivian, *née* Rush (d 1973); ggf was George Parker Bidder 'The Calculating Boy', illustrious engineer with Robert Stephenson and others, pres Inst of Civil Engineers, etc (*see* DNB and George Parker Bidder, by E F Clark (1983)); *b* 19 Jan 1929; *Educ* Glendower Sch London, Westonbirt Sch Glos; *m* 26 July 1952, John Harvey Pinches, MC, s of John Robert Pinches (d 1968), of Holland Park Ave, London; 2 da (Joanna Harriet (Mrs Charles Hansard) b 1954, Sarah Carolan Rosemary b 1956); *Career* personal asst to Sir John Heaton-Armstrong Chester Herald Coll of Arms 1948–52; heraldic publisher and author, genealogist, proprietor of Heraldry Today (publishing house and bookshop specialising in heraldry and genealogy) 1954–; memb: Heraldry Soc, AGRA, Soc of Genealogists, Wilts Archaeological Inst, Wilts Family History Soc; *Books* Elvin's Mottoes Revised (1971), A European Armorial (with Anthony Wood, 1971), The Royal Heraldry of England (with John H Pinches, 1974), A Bibliography of Burke's 1876–1976 (1976); *Recreations* horse-racing, browsing in old bookshops, playing bridge; *Style—* Mrs John Pinches; ✉ Parliament Piece, Ramsbury, Marlborough, Wiltshire SN8 2QH (☎ 01672 520613/520617, fax 01672 520183)

PINCHES, Stuart John Allison; s of George Arthur Pinches (d 1993), and Marjorie Allison; *b* 2 April 1947; *Educ* Friern Barnet GS, Poly of Central London (Dip Photography & Film); *m* 18 Dec 1970 (m dis 1991), (Brigid) Imelda, da of Patrick Behan (d 1969), of Edenderry, Co Offaly, Eire; m 2, 21 June 1994, Sandie, da of Stanley Montague, of London; *Career* gen mgmnt exec United Artists Corporation Ltd 1968–70, project mangr Organon International BV Holland 1971–73, md Viscom Ireland Ltd Dublin 1974–77, assoc dir Purchasepoint Group London 1978–79, divnl md Viscom Group London 1979–81, head of Programme Servs TVS plc 1981–85; md: AKA Ltd London 1986–87, Interface Design Ltd 1988; jt md Roach and Partners Ltd 1989–93, dir The Management Channel Television Company Ltd 1991–, fndr SP Management Consulting (UK) 1993–, launch dir VH-1 1993–94, pres and chief exec offr Pinches Management Consulting USA Inc 1995–; conslt: MTV Networks (Europe), Village Roadshow (Aust); *Recreations* personal development and fitness, collecting music, motor sport, photography, tennis; *Style—* Stuart Pinches, Esq; ✉ 913 Euclid Street 3, Santa Monica, CA 90403, USA (☎ 00 1 310 458 1240, fax 00 1 310 395 3965); 4 Clarence Road, Southsea, Hampshire PO5 2LG (☎ 01705 731462)

PINCKNEY, David Charles; s of Dr Charles Percy Pinckney (d 1982), of Park House, Ascot, Berks, and Norah Manisty, *née* Boucher (d 1988); *b* 13 Sept 1940; *Educ* Winchester, New Coll Oxford (MA); *m* 25 May 1974, Susan Audrey, da of Col Austin Richards (d 1974), of Pump House, Writtle, Essex; 1 s (Charles b 1977), 2 da (Katherine b 1974, Caroline b 1976); *Career* sr audit ptnr Peat Marwick Mitchell CAs France 1977–83 (London 1963–67, Paris and Lyons 1968–83), md Wrightson Wood Financial Services Ltd 1984–86, gp fin dir Thornton and Co Ltd 1987–; dir East Hampshire Housing Assoc 1995–; govr Br Sch Paris 1981–83; memb Ctee of Mgmnt Inst of Child Health 1992–96; FCA (ACA 1966); *Recreations* skiing, tennis, classic cars, opera; *Clubs* Brooks's, The Hurlingham, Vincent's (Oxford); *Style—* David Pinckney, Esq; ✉ Rake Hanger House, Hill Brow, Liss, Hampshire GU33 7NW (☎ 01730 893775); Thornton Management Ltd, Swan House, 33 Queen Street, London EC4R 1AX (☎ 0171 246 3000, fax 0171 246 3003, telex 923061 THORN G)

PINCKNEY, Jeremy Gerald; s of Gerald Henry Pinckney; *b* 17 Oct 1935; *Educ* Eton; *m* 1960, Helen Belinda, da of Maj M H Gold, MC; 2 s, 1 da; *Career* served 9 Lancers; dir: Guardian Corporate Finance Ltd, Risk Decisions Ltd, various other cos; *Style—* Jeremy Pinckney Esq; ✉ 45 Black Lion Lane, London W6; Garden House, Balthayock, Perth PH2 7LG

PINCOTT, Leslie Rundell; CBE (1978); s of Hubert George Pincott; *b* 27 March 1923; *Educ* Mercers' Sch Holborn; *m* 1944, Mary Mae Tuffin (d 1996); 2 s (Anthony, David), 1 da (Mandy); *Career* articled to firm of City CAs 1940; served RN 1941–46 (Lt RNVR); oil company exec 1950–78, md Esso Petroleum Co Ltd 1970–78; vice chm Remploy Ltd 1970–87, chm Edman Communications Group plc 1983–87, memb Investmt Ctee London Devpt Capital Fund (Guinness Mahon) 1985–; dep chm Price Cmmn 1978–80, pres Dist Heating Assoc 1977–79; chm: Printing Indust Econ Devpt Ctee 1982–87, Stone-Platt Industs 1980–82; dir: Canada Permanent Trust Co (UK) Ltd 1978–79, BR SR Bd 1977–89, George Wimpey & Co Ltd 1978–85, Highlands Fabricators Ltd 1985–91; memb The Pilgrims 1971–; chm: Hundred Gp of Fin Dirs 1978–79, Oxford Univ Summer Sch 1975–78; memb Cncl Ind Sch Careers Orgn 1978–; involved with housing assocs and other vol work 1989–; FCA, CIMgt; *Recreations* tennis; *Clubs* Hurlingham (chm 1988–92); *Style—* Leslie R Pincott, Esq, CBE; ✉ 6 Lambourne Ave, Wimbledon, London SW19 7DW

PINCUS, George Bernard; s of Dr Joseph Victor Pincus (d 1946), of Brighton, and Ruth, *née* Burns; *b* 13 Nov 1942; *Educ* Epsom Coll; *m* 1, 21 May 1965 (m dis); 2 s (Benjamin b 1969, Damian b 1970); m 2, 20 Dec 1986, Carolyn, *née* Shaljean; *Career* md: PVAF 1974–84, BBDO Ltd 1984–90, Interpartners 1990–; dir Retail Marketing Partnership 1990–, ptnr Chance Jarosz 1993–, chm Lighthouse Communications Ltd 1994–; memb Cncl Epsom Coll 1965– (chm Devpt Ctee 1986–); *Recreations* visual arts, theatre, history, travel; *Style—* George B Pincus, Esq; ✉ Willoughbys West, Wrens Hill, Oxshott, Surrey KT22 0HN; office (☎ 01372 844406)

PINDAR, George Thomas Ventress (Tom); OBE (1986), DL; s of George Kyte Grice Pindar (d 1959), and Mary Ann, *née* Ventress (d 1973); *b* 30 Jan 1928; *Educ* Scarborough HS, Leeds Coll of Technol; *m* 22 May 1953, Margery Joyce Pointer; 1 da (Margaret Ann b 17 Nov 1954), 1 s (George Andrew b 27 Oct 1957); *Career* chm G A Pindar & Son Ltd (family printing business, various positions since joining 1949); former chm Scarborough and NE Yorks Healthcare NHS Tst, chm Yorkshire Coast Radio Ltd; dir: Scarborough Building Society, G Harmsworth & Co Ltd, St Catherine's Hospice Trust; govr Univ Coll Scarborough, memb Co of Merchant Adventurers of the City of York; *Recreations* theatre, music, swimming, hill walking, gardening; *Clubs* RAC; *Style—* Tom Pindar, Esq, OBE, DL; ✉ Court Close, 10 High St, Scalby, Scarborough, N Yorks YO13 0PT (☎ 01723 372414); G A Pindar & Son Ltd, Thornburgh Road, Eastfield, Scarborough YO11 3UY (☎ 01723 581581, fax 01723 371068); Scarborough Building Society, PO Box 6, Prospect House, Scarborough (☎ 01723 368155)

PINDER, Dr Jennifer Marion; da of John Raymond Pinder (d 1988), of Doncaster, and Elizabeth Ross, *née* Ward (d 1991); *b* 15 Dec 1947; *Educ* Queen Ethelburga's Sch Harrogate, Doncaster Tech Coll, Univ of Sheffield (BDS), RCS England (MGDS), Birkbeck Coll London (BSc); *partner* Ross Henderson; *Career* in gen dental practice in various locations incl City of London 1971–75, Sunnybrook Hosp Univ of Toronto 1976–78, assoc in gen dental practice City of London 1978–88, in own practice 1988–; chm and pres Gen Dental Practitioners Assoc 1983–87, fndr chm Women in Dentistry 1985–87, pres Metropolitan Branch BDA 1990–91 (sec 1987–94); memb: GDC 1984–, Standing Dental Advsy Ctee 1990–93, Standing Ctee on Dental and Surgical Materials 1992–94, Bd Faculty of Gen Dental Practitioners 1992– (vice dean 1995–96); govr Eastman Dental Hosp 1986–91; *Recreations* cookery, tapestry, Burmese cats, computing; *Style—* Dr Jennifer Pinder; ✉ 16 Chelsfield Gardens, London SE26 4DJ (☎ 0181 291 0063, fax 0181 291 0016); Jennifer Pinder Practice, 36b Old Street, London EC1V 9AE (☎ 0171 250 3554, fax 0171 490 2896)

PINDER, Margaret Lilian; o da of Brig Harold Senhouse Pinder, CBE, MC, Royal Leics Regt (d 1973), of Burghclere Grange, Newbury, Berks, and Lilian Edith Murray (d 1975); *b* 4 May 1920; *Educ* Privately; *Career* vice-chm and vice-pres Arthritis Care (formerly Br Rheumatism and Arthritis Assoc), memb since 1953; fndr of first recuperative holiday hotel for arthritis sufferers (later named Margaret Pinder House by Arthritis Care) 1960; fndr and tstee of The Pinder Centre for hydrotherapy and physiotherapy treatment of temporarily and physically disabled 1973; tstee the Lady Hoare Tst 1985–87 (now amalgamated with Arthritis Care); *Recreations* painting, racing (first owner to have horses trained under Nat Hunt in France after war); *Style—* Margaret Pinder; ✉ The Pinder Centre, Avington, Nr Winchester, Hants SO21 1DD (☎ 01962 779498)

PINE, Courtney; *b* 18 March 1964; *Career* saxophonist and fndr memb Jazz Warriors 1985–; fndr memb The Abiba Jazz Arts 1985–; solo albums incl: Journey To The Urge Within (1986, Silver Award), Destiny's Song & The Image Of Pursuance (1988), The Vision's Tale (1989), Closer To Home (1990), Within The Realm Of Our Dreams (1991), To The Eyes Of Creation (1993), Modern Day Jazz Stories (1996); featured on Out Of Many One People with Jazz Warriors (album, 1987), guest appearances with Mick Jagger on Wandering Spirit (album) and with Guru on Jazzmattaz (album), featured artist on The Glory of Gershwin (Larry Adler tribute album); *Style—* Courtney Pine, Esq; ✉ c/o Nicky Neave, John Reid Enterprises, Singes House, 32 Galena Road, London W6 0LT (☎ 0181 741 9933, fax 0181 741 3938)

PINHORN, Margaret (Maggie) (Mrs Martin Dyke-Coomes); da of George Herbert Pinhorn (d 1996), and Mary Elizabeth Suther (d 1963); *b* 1 Nov 1943; *Educ* Walthamstow Hall Sch for Girls Sevenoaks, Central Sch of Art and Design London; *m* 24 June 1978, Martin Dyke-Coomes, *qv*, s of Ernest Thomas Dyke-Coomes, of Crawley, Sussex; 1 s (Ned Alexander b 1981), 1 da (Amy Elizabeth b 1983), 2 adopted s (Anthony b 1967, Claude b 1973); *Career* artist, dir, designer, prodr; fndr of Alternative Arts 1971– and dir: Covent Garden St Theatre 1975–88, Soho Street Theatre 1988–93; started career in films in 1968 at Pinewood Studios in Art Dept of James Bond movie; worked on Br feature films incl: Chitty Chitty Bang Bang, Otley, Till Death Us Do Part; ind film maker, made Dynamo (1970), and Tunde's Film (1973); started Basement Community Arts Workshop in Cable Street 1972; made one of the first 'Open Door' progs for BBC TV and went on to res and present the first BBC TV series 'Grapevine' for Community Programmes Unit; nat co-ordinator of the Assoc of Community Artists 1974–79; vice-chm Tower Hamlets Arts Ctee 1975–79; memb: Arts Cncl Community Art Ctee 1975–79, Gtr London Arts Community Arts Ctee 1979–81; dir: Circus UK 1985–, Alternative Art Galleries 1991–, Spitalfields Arts Devpt Prog 1993–; *Recreations* playing with my children, creative cooking, collecting wines, travel, philosphy, the arts; *Clubs* West Ham Football, Soho Society; *Style—* Ms Maggie Pinhorn; ✉ Alternative Arts, 47a Brushfield Street, Spitalfields, London E1 6AA (☎ 0171 375 0441, fax 0171 375 0484)

PINKER, Sir George Douglas; KCVO (1990, CVO 1983); s of late Ronald Douglas Pinker and late Queenie Elizabeth Pinker; *b* 6 Dec 1924; *Educ* Reading Sch, St Mary's Hosp London Univ (MB BS), DObst; *m* Dorothy Emma, *née* Russell; 3 s, 1 da; *Career* surgn-gynaecologist to the Queen 1973–90, consltg gynaecological surgn and obstetrician St Mary's Hosp Paddington and Samaritan Hosp 1958–90, consltg gynaecological surgn Middx and Soho Hosps 1969–80, conslt gynaecologist King Edward VII Hosp for Officers 1974–94; chief med advsr BUPA 1983–90; pres Royal Coll of Obstetricians and Gynaecologists 1987–90 (hon treas 1970–77, vice pres 1980–83), memb Bd Modern Med 1980 (chm 1988–91); cncl memb Winston Churchill Tst, vice pres London Choral Soc 1988, chm Antisoma 1990–94, pres Royal Soc of Med 1992–94; Hon FRCSI 1987, hon memb British Paediatric Assoc 1988; Hon FRACOG (Aust) 1989, Hon FACOG (America) 1990, Hon FRSM 1995; FMCSA 1991, MRCOG, FRCS(Ed), FRCOG, FRCS 1989,; *Clubs* Garrick; *Style—* Sir George Pinker, KCVO; ✉ Top Flat, 96 Harley St, London W1N 1AF (☎ 0171 935 7254)

PINKER, Prof Robert Arthur; s of Joseph Pinker (d 1976), and Dora Elizabeth, *née* Winyard (d 1987); *b* 27 May 1931; *Educ* Holloway Co Sch, LSE (Cert Soc Sc), Univ of London (BSc, MSc); *m* 24 June 1955, Jennifer Farrington (1994), da of Fred Boulton (d 1941); 2 da (Catherine b 1963, Lucy b 1965); *Career* Nat Serv, 2 Lt Royal Ulster Rifles 1951–52; TA, Lt London Irish Rifles 1952–54; head of Sociology Dept Goldsmiths' Coll London 1964–72, Lewisham prof of social admin Goldsmiths' and Bedford Colls London 1972–74, prof of social studies Chelsea Coll London 1974–78; LSE: prof of social work studies 1978–93, prof of social admin 1993–96 (prof emeritus 1996–), pro-dir 1985–88; pro vice chllr for social sci Univ of London 1988–90; chm: Social Admin Assoc 1974–77, Advsy Cncl Centre for Policy on Ageing 1971–81 (chm of govrs 1981–94), Jl of Social Policy 1981–86 (ed 1977–81), Editorial Bd Ageing and Soc 1981–91; scientific advsr Nursing Res DHSS 1974–79 and 1980–82; memb: Social Sci Res Cncl 1972–76, Working Pty on Role and Tasks of Social Workers Barclay Ctee 1981–82, Cncl Advertising Standards Authy 1988–96, Cncl Direct Mail Accreditation and Recognition Centre 1995–; privacy cmmr Press Complaints Cmmn 1994– (memb 1991–); *Recreations* reading, writing, travel, unskilled gardening; *Style—* Prof Robert Pinker; ✉ 76 Coleraine Rd, Blackheath, London SE3 7PE (☎ 0181 858 5320); LSE, Houghton St, Aldwych, London WC2A 2AE (☎ 0171 405 7686)

PINNELL, Raoul Michael; s of David Andrew Pinnell, OBE, of London, and Madeleine Laura, *née* Farrell; *b* 13 June 1951; *Educ* Bradfield, Ealing Sch of Mgmnt (HND Business Studies), Poly of Central London (Dip Mktg), Imede Switzerland (PED); *m* 31 Aug 1976, Judith Jane, da of John Goslett, MBE; 2 s (Henry b 19 May 1983, Philip b 8 July 1985); *Career* salesman H J Heinz 1971–72, product mangr Findus 1972–75, gp product mangr Table Top S Africa 1975–77; Nestlé (Findus): regnl sales mangr 1977–79, gp product mangr new product devpt 1979–80, mktg mangr new product devpt 1981–83, mktg mangr existing brands 1983–85, gen mktg mangr 1985–89; The Prudential Assurance Co Ltd: nat mktg mangr 1989–90, mktg dir 1991–94; first dir of mktg National Westminster Bank plc 1994–96, new cmmns branding dir Shell International Petroleum Co Ltd 1996–; FCIM; *Awards* Mktg Soc award and Supermarketing award for Findus Lean Cuisine; *Recreations* theatre, reading, travel, good food, good company; *Clubs* IOD; *Style—* Raoul Pinnell, Esq; ✉ Shell International Petroleum Co Ltd, Shell Centre, Waterloo, London SE1 7NA (☎ 0171 934 1234)

PINNER, Hayim; OBE (1989); s of late Simon Pinner, and Annie, *née* Wagner; *b* 25 May 1925; *Educ* Davenant Fndn Sch, Univ of London, Yeshiva Etz Hayim, Bet Berl Coll Israel; *m* 1956 (m dis 1980), Rita, *née* Reuben; 1 s, 1 da; *Career* RAOC 1944–48; ed Jewish Vanguard 1950–74, exec dir B'nai B'rith 1957–77, hon vice pres Zionist Fedn of GB and Ireland 1975– (hon treas 1971–75), sec gen Bd of Deputies of Br Jews 1977–91, vice pres Lab Zionist Movement, dir Stenberg Charitable Fndn 1991–96; memb: Jewish Agency and World Zionist Orgn, Cncl Christians and Jews (hon sec), Exec Inter-Faith Network, Advsy Cncl World Congress of Faiths, Trades Advsy Cncl, Hillel Fndn, Jt Israel Appeal, British Technion Soc, Lab Pty Middle East Ctee, UNA, Imperial War Museum; on B List of Lab Party Candidates; contrib to: BBC radio and TV, LBC, Radio London; Freeman City of London; Cdr Order of Civil Merit (Spain) 1993; FRSA; *Recreations* travelling, swimming, reading, talking; *Style—* Hayim Pinner, Esq, OBE; ✉ 62 Grosvenor Street, London W1X 9DA (☎ 0171 485 2538)

PINNINGTON, Christopher John; s of William F Pinnington, of Cheshire, and Dorothy Joan Pinnington (d 1970); *b* 22 Aug 1956; *Educ* Stonyhurst, Univ of Bristol (BSc); *m* 1986, Fiona Mary, da of D N A McLure; 2 s (James Oliver b 8 March 1989, Benjamin William b 13 Feb 1995), 1 da (Harriet Anna b 31 May 1991); *Career* graduate trainee rising to assoc dir D'Arcy Masius Benton & Bowles 1978–82, dir Wight Collins Rutherford Scott 1982–88, managing ptnr Ball WCRS Sydney 1988–90, managing ptnr FCO Ltd 1990–93, md Euro RSCG (now Euro RSCG Wnek Gosper) 1993–; MIPA; *Recreations* sailing, tennis, advertising; *Clubs* Hurlingham, RAC; *Style—* Christopher Pinnington, Esq; ✉ Euro RSCG Wnek Gosper, 11 Great Newport Street, London WC2H 7JA (☎ 0171 240 4111)

PINNINGTON, Roger Adrian; TD; s of William Austin Pinnington (d 1979), of Alderley Edge, Cheshire, and Elsie Amy Pinnington (d 1983); *b* 27 Aug 1932; *Educ* Rydal Sch Colwyn Bay, Lincoln Coll Oxford (MA); *m* (Marjorie) Ann, da of George Alan Livingstone Russell, of Beverley, Yorks; 1 s (Andrew b 1967), 3 da (Suzanne b 1963, Sally-Ann b 1964, Nikki b 1975); *Career* 2 Lt RA 1952, Maj Royal Mil Police 1960; dir: William E Cary Ltd 1964–74, Jonas Woodhead & Sons plc 1968–74; md TRW Cam Gears Ltd 1974–82, vice pres TRW Europe Inc 1980–82, dep chm and chief exec UBM Group plc 1982–85, dir Norcros plc 1985–86; dir and chief exec: Royal Ordnance plc 1986–87, Pilgrim House Group 1987–89; chm: Blackwood Hodge plc 1988–90, Petrocon Group plc 1989–91, Aqualisa Products Ltd 1991–93, Jenbacher Holdings (UK) plc 1991–95, Toleman Holdings Co Ltd 1992–94; dir Swithland plc 1993–94; currently chm: Harford Consultancy Services Ltd, Lynx Holdings plc, Montanaro & Co Ltd, Cortworth plc, British World Aviation Ltd, Huntingdon International Holdings plc; Freeman City of London, Liveryman Worshipful Co of Glaziers 1977; CIMgt 1988, FRSA 1983; *Recreations* gardening, debate, collecting silver sauce bottle labels; *Clubs* Vincent's, RAC; *Style—* Roger A Pinnington, Esq, TD; ✉ 15 Lennox Gardens Mews, London SW1X 0DP (☎ 0171 581 9684, fax 0171 589 3614)

PINNOCK, Trevor David; CBE (1992); s of Kenneth Alfred Thomas Pinnock, of Canterbury, Kent, and Joyce Edith, *née* Muggleton; *b* 16 Dec 1946; *Educ* Canterbury Catheral Choir Sch, Simon Langton GS Canterbury, RCM (winner maj performance prizes organ and harpsichord); *Career* harpsichordist and conductor; London début with Galliard Harpsichord Trio (jt fndr) 1966, solo début Purcell Room London 1968, NY début Metropolitan Opera conducting Giulio Cesare 1988; formed The English Concert 1972 (dir 1973–), London début of the English Concert English Bach Festival 1973; artistic dir and princ conductor Nat Arts Centre Orchestra Ottawa 1991–96; conductor The English Conert BBC Proms 1996; recordings: CRD Records 1974–78, DGG (Archiv) 1978–; tours of Europe, USA, Canada, Japan, South America (solo, with The English Concert, and as orchestral conductor); Hon RAM; *Style—* Trevor Pinnock, Esq, CBE; ✉ 8 St George's Terrace, London NW1 8XJ (☎ 0171 911 0901, fax 0171 911 0903)

PINSENT, Sir Christopher Roy; 3 Bt (UK 1938); s of Sir Roy Pinsent, 2 Bt (d 1978); *b* 2 Aug 1922; *Educ* Winchester; *m* 27 June 1951, Susan Mary, da of John Norton Scorer, of Walcot Lodge, Fotheringhay; 1 s, 2 da; *Heir* s, Thomas Benjamin Roy Pinsent b 21 July 1967; *Career* lectr Camberwell Sch of Art, ret 1986; *Style—* Sir Christopher Pinsent, Bt; ✉ The Chestnuts, Castle Hill, Guildford, Surrey GU1 3SX

PINSENT, Matthew Clive; MBE (1993); s of Rev Ewen Macpherson Pinsent, of Child Okeford, Dorset, and Jean Grizel, *née* McMicking; *b* 10 Oct 1970; *Educ* Eton, St Catherine's Coll Oxford (BA); *Career* amateur rower; memb Leander Club 1989–; sr int debut 1989 (jr debut 1987); honours incl: Gold medal coxless pairs Jr World Championships 1988, Bronze medal coxed fours World Championships 1989, Gold medal coxless pairs World Championships 1991 (set world record 6 mins 21 secs), Gold medal coxless pairs Olympic Games Barcelona 1992 (set Olympic record 6 mins 27 secs), Gold medal coxless pairs World Championships 1993, 1994 (new World record 6 mins 18 secs) and 1995, Gold Medal coxless pairs Olympic Games Atlanta 1996; pres Oxford Univ Boat Club 1992–93 (twice univ boat race winner); winner Team of the Year (with S Redgrave) BBC Sports Personality of the Year Awards 1996; *Recreations* golf; *Style—* Matthew Pinsent, Esq, MBE; ✉ c/o Leander Club, Henley-on-Thames, Oxon RG9 2LP (☎ 01491 575782)

PINSON, Barry; QC (1973); s of Thomas Alfred Pinson; *b* 18 Dec 1925; *Educ* King Edward's Sch, Univ of Birmingham; *m* 1, 1950, Miriam Mary; 1 s, 1 da; m 2, 1977, Anne Kathleen Golby; *Career* called to the Bar Gray's Inn 1949, bencher 1981; tstee RAF Museums 1980–; *Publications* Revenue Law (17 edns); *Recreations* music, photography; *Clubs* Arts; *Style—* Barry Pinson, Esq, QC; ✉ 11 New Square, Lincoln's Inn, London WC2A 3QB (☎ 0171 242 3981, fax 0171 831 2391)

PINTER, Harold; CBE (1966); s of J Pinter; *b* 10 Oct 1930; *Educ* Hackney Downs GS; *m* 1, 1956 (m dis 1980), Vivien Thompson (Vivien Merchant) (d 1982); 1 s; m 2, 1980, Lady Antonia Fraser, *qv*; *Career* playwright, director, actor; Hon DLitt: Univ of Reading 1970, Univ of Birmingham 1971, Univ of Glasgow 1974, Univ of East Anglia 1974, Univ of Stirling 1979, Brown (USA) 1982, Univ of Hull 1986, Univ of Sussex 1990, Univ of East London 1994, Univ of Sofia (Bulgaria) 1995; Cwlth Award 1981, David Cohen Prize for Lifetime Achievement in Literature 1995; hon memb: American Acad and Inst of Arts & Letters 1984, American Acad of Arts and Sciences 1985; hon fell: Modern Language Assoc, Queen Mary Coll London 1987; FRSL; *Directed* The Collection (Aldwych) 1962, The Lover and The Dwarfs (Arts) 1963, The Birthday Party (Aldwych) 1964, Exiles (Mermaid) 1970, Butley (Criterion, film 1973) 1971, Next of Kin (NT) 1974, Otherwise Engaged (Queen's) 1975 (NY 1977), The Innocents (NY) 1977, Blithe Spirit (NT) 1977, The Rear Column (Globe) 1978, Close of Play (NT) 1979, The Hothouse (Hampstead) 1980, Quartermaine's Terms (Queen's) 1981, Incident at Tulse Hill (Hampstead) 1982, The Trojan War Will Not Take Place (NT) 1983, The Common Pursuit (Lyric Hammersmith) 1984, One for the Road (Lyric Studio) 1984, Sweet Bird of Youth (Haymarket) 1985, Circe and Bravo (Hampstead, Wyndham's) 1986, Mountain Language (NT) 1988, Vanilla (Lyric) 1990, The New World Order (Royal Court) 1991, The Caretaker (Comedy) 1991, Party Time (Almeida, televised 1992) 1991, Oleanna (Royal Court, Duke of York's) 1993, Landscape (Gate, Dublin, RNT, televised 1995) 1994, Taking Sides (Chichester Festival and Criterion) 1995, Twelve Angry Men (Comedy) 1996; *Acting* Anew McMaster Company (Ireland) 1951–53, Donald Wolfit Company 1953, rep at Chesterfield, Whitby, Huddersfield, Colchester, Bournemouth, Torquay, Birmingham, Palmers Green, Worthing and Richmond 1953–59, Mick in The Caretaker (London) 1960, Lenny in The Homecoming (Watford) 1969, Deeley in Old Times (Los Angeles) 1985, Hirst in No Man's Land (London) 1992–93, Roote in The Hothouse (Chichester, London) 1995; *Plays* The Room (1957), The Birthday Party (1957), The Dumb Waiter (1957), The Hothouse (1958), A Slight Ache (1958), A Night Out (1959), The Caretaker (1959), Night School (1960), The Dwarfs (1960), The Collection (1961), The Lover (1962), Tea Party (1964), The Homecoming (1964), The Basement (1966), Landscape (1967), Silence (1968), Night (1969), Old Times (1970), Monologue (1972), No Man's Land (1974), Betrayal (1978), Family Voices (1980), Victoria Station (1982), A Kind of Alaska (1982), One For the Road (1984), Mountain Language (1988), The New World Order (1991), Party Time (1991), Moonlight (1993); *Screenplays* The Caretaker (1962), The Servant (1962), The Pumpkin Eater (1963), The Quiller Memorandum (1965), Accident (1966), The Birthday Party (1967), The Homecoming (1969), The Go-Between (1969), Langrishe Go Down (1970), A la Recherche du Temps Perdu (1972), The Last Tycoon (1974), The French Lieutenant's Woman (1980), Betrayal (1981), Victory (1982), Turtle Diary (1984), The Handmaid's Tale (1987), Reunion, The Heat of the Day (1988), The Comfort of Strangers (1989), The Trial (1989); *Clubs* Groucho; *Style—* Harold Pinter, Esq, CBE, FRSL; ✉ c/o Judy Daish Associates, 2 St Charles Place, London W10 6EG (☎ 0181 964 8811, fax 0181 964 8966)

PINTO, George Richard; s of Maj Richard James Pinto, MC (d 1969), of London, and Gladys, *née* Hirsch (d 1985); *b* 11 April 1929; *Educ* Eton, Trinity Coll Cambridge (MA); *Career* Nat Serv Coldstream Gds 1947–49 (2 Lt); Cooper Bros and Co (now Coopers & Lybrand) 1953–56, Model Roland and Stone 1957–58, banker Kleinwort Benson Ltd 1958–96 (dir 1968–85, advsr 1985–96); hon treas: Anglo-Israel Assoc 1987–, Israel/Diaspora Tst 1992–; chm Central Cncl for Jewish Community Serv 1975–78 (vice chm 1972–75), chm of Fin Ctee Jewish Blind Soc 1962–89, vice pres Jewish Care 1990–; govr Oxford Centre for Hebrew and Jewish Studies 1987–; FCA; *Recreations* reading, listening to classical music, golf, bridge; *Clubs* Brooks's, Cavalry and Guards', Portland; *Style—* G R Pinto, Esq; ✉ c/o 127 Piccadilly, London W1V 0PX

PINTUS, Matthew; s of Ronald Pintus, of Surrey, and Carmel, *née* Corcoran; *b* 14 Sept 1956; *Educ* Ampleforth, Univ of Warwick, Guildford Coll of Law; *Career* Russell Cooke Potter and Chapman 1981–85, Macfarlanes 1985– (currently ptnr i/c of probate); memb Soc of Tst and Estate Practitioners; *Publications* Butterworths Wills Probate and Administration (ed Contentious Matters section); *Recreations* bridge, opera, sailing; *Style—* Matthew Pintus, Esq; ✉ 3 Pembridge Square, London W2; Macfarlanes, 10 Norwich Street, London EC4A 1BD (☎ 0171 831 9222, fax 0171 831 5607)

PIPE, Martin Charles; s of D A C Pipe, of Somerset, and B A Pipe; *b* 29 May 1945; *Educ* Queen's Coll Taunton; *m* Mary Caroline, 1 s (David Edward b 7 Feb 1973); *Career* racehorse trainer; major wins incl: Champion Hurdle, Grand National, Welsh National, Irish National, Scottish National, Midlands National, Hennessy Gold Cup, Mackieson Gold Cup; trained 4 winners at Royal Ascot; only trainer to train over 200 winners in a season, champion trainer Nat Hunt 6 times; subject of book Martin Pipe - The Champion Trainer's Story; *Style—* Martin Pipe, Esq; ✉ Pond House, Nicholashayne, Wellington, Somerset TA21 9QY (☎ 01884 840715, fax 01884 841343)

PIPER, Geoffrey Steuart Fairfax; DL (Merseyside 1993); s of Sqdn Ldr Donald Steuart Piper (d 1972), of Bakewell, and Nancy Fairfax, *née* Robson (d 1990); *b* 8 June 1943; *Educ* Repton, Pembroke Coll Cambridge (MA); *m* 29 July 1967, Susan Elizabeth, da of Roswell Douglas Arnold; 1 s (Charles b 1980), 3 da (Jennifer (Mrs William Simms) b 1968, Angela (Mrs Daniel King) b 1970, Caroline b 1973); *Career* ptnr i/c Deloitte Haskins & Sells: CI 1980–86, Liverpool 1986–90; pres Jersey Soc of Chartered and Certified Accountants 1983–85, chm Business Opportunities on Merseyside 1987–93; dir: Mersey Partnership 1993–, Coral Products plc 1995–; chief exec NW Business Leadership Team 1990–; FCA 1973; *Recreations* golf, cricket, choral music; *Clubs* Royal and Ancient, MCC; *Style—* Geoffrey Piper, Esq, DL; ✉ The Croft, Thornton Hough, Wirral, Merseyside L63 1JA (☎ 0151 336 4830); North West Business Leadership Team, Alexandra House, Borough Road, St Helens, Merseyside WA10 3RN (☎ 01744 755440, fax 01744 754865)

PIPER, Thomas Stephen Towry (Tom); s of Sir David Towry Piper, CBE (d 1990), and Anne Horatia, *née* Richmond; *b* 24 Nov 1964; *Educ* Magdalen Coll Sch Oxford, Trinity Coll Cambridge (scolar, BA), Slade Sch UCL; *m* 1992, Caroline Rohais, da of William Millar; 2 da (Rachel b 29 Dec 1993, Claire b 29 July 1995); *Career* theatre designer; asst: Voytek 1988–90, Chloe Obolensky (for Peter Brook's prodn Tempest) 1990; *Theatre* major projects incl: The Birthday Party, Blinded by the Sun (both RNT), Much Ado About Nothing, Spring Awakening, Broken Heart (all RSC), The Crucible, Six Characters in Search of an Author (both Abbey Theatre Dublin), Macbeth, Endgame (both The Tron Glasgow), Duchess of Malfi (Greenwich and Wyndhams), KinderTransport (Soho Theatre and Vaudeville), Master Builder (Edinburgh Lyceum), The Philanderer, Sweet Panic (both Hampstead), The Way of The World (Lyric Hammersmith), Cherry Orchard (Nottingham Playhouse); *Awards* London Fringe Design Award 1989, 1990, 1992, 1993; *Style*— Tom Piper, Esq; ✉ c/o Society of British Theatre Designers, 47 Bermondsey Street, London SE1 3XT

PIPPARD, Prof Sir (Alfred) Brian; kt (1975); s of Prof Alfred John Sutton Pippard (d 1969), and Frances Louisa Olive Field (d 1964); *b* 7 Sept 1920; *Educ* Clifton, Clare Coll Cambridge (MA, PhD, ScD, hon fell 1973); *m* 1955, Charlotte Frances, da of Francis Gilbert Dyer (d 1948); 3 da; *Career* Univ of Cambridge: demonstrator, lectr, reader, J H Plummer prof, Cavendish prof of physics 1971–82; pres Clare Hall Cambridge 1966–73; FRS; *Recreations* music; *Style*— Prof Sir Brian Pippard, FRS; ✉ 30 Porson Rd, Cambridge CB2 2EU (☎ 01223 358713)

PIPPARD, Prof Martin John; s of Dr John Sutton Pippard, of Woodford Green, Essex, and Kathleen Marjorie, *née* Fox; *b* 16 Jan 1948; *Educ* Buckhurst Hill Co HS Essex, Univ of Birmingham (BSc, MB ChB); *m* 15 May 1976, Grace Elizabeth, da of Wallace Swift, of Guisley, Leeds; 2 s (Timothy b 1980, Benjamin b 1983), 1 da (Helen b 1977); *Career* conslt haematologist MRC Clinical Res Centre Harrow 1983–88, prof of haematology Univ of Dundee 1989–; memb: Br Soc for Haematology, Assoc of Clinical Pathologists, assoc ed Bd British Journal of Haematology; FRCPath 1994 (MRCPath 1982), FRCP 1988; *Recreations* hill walking, gardening; *Style*— Prof Martin Pippard; ✉ 10 Balnacarron Avenue, 118 Hepburn Gardens, St Andrews, Fife KY16 9LT (☎ 01334 476234); University of Dundee, Dept of Haematology, Dundee DD1 9SY (☎ 01382 660111, fax 01382 645748)

PIRIE, David Alan Tarbat; s of Maj Halyburton Berkeley Pirie, MC, TD, DM (d 1984), and Joyce Elaine, *née* Tarbat; *b* 4 Dec 1946; *Educ* Trinity Coll Glenalmond, Univ of York (BA); *m* 21 June 1983, Judith Leslie, da of Maj William Leslie Harris (d 1985); 1 s (Jack b 1987), 1 da (Alice b 1984); *Career* writer, film and TV critic; Time Out: TV critic 1970–74, film critic 1974–80, film ed 1981–84; film critic 1976–: Kaleidoscope (BBC Radio 4), BBC World Service, Capital Radio; contrib 1976–: The Times, Sunday Times, The Media Show, Did You See?, The South Bank Show, Sight and Sound, Movie Magazine; film columnist Options Magazine 1981–92, literary ed Event Magazine 1980–81; film and TV screenwriter 1984–; works incl: Rainy Day Women 1984 (winner Drama Prize NY Film and TV Festival), Total Eclipse of the Heart (screenplay), Mystery Story (screenplay from own novel), Wild Things (BBC TV film) 1989, Never Come Back (winner Best Mini-series prize Chicago Film Festival) 1990, Ashenden (TV series) 1991, Natural Lies (TV series) 1992, Black Easter (winner Best TV Feature Prize Chicago Film Festival), The Woman in White (feature film), The Element of Doubt (TV film) 1996; sr tutor Br Film and TV Prodrs Assoc Advanced Screenwriting Course 1990–; *Books* Heritage of Horror (1973), Mystery Story (1980), Anatomy of the Movies (1981); *Recreations* running, walking; *Clubs* Writers' Guild; *Style*— David Pirie, Esq; ✉ c/o The Agency, 24 Pottery Lane, Holland Park, London W11 (☎ 0171 727 1346, fax 0171 727 9037, telex 27618 AUTHOR G)

PIRIE, Gp Capt Sir Gordon Hamish; kt (1984), CVO (1987), CBE (1946), JP (London 1962), DL (London 1962); s of Harold Victor Campbell Pirie; *b* 10 Feb 1918; *Educ* Eton, RAF Coll Cranwell; *m* 1, 1953, Margaret Joan Bomford (d 1972); m 2, 1982, Joanna Marian, wid of John C Hugill; *Career* perm cmmn RAF 1938, serv WWII (despatches), Gp Capt 1946, ret; contested (LNat&U) Dundee W 1955; memb Westminster City Cncl 1949–82 (Mayor 1959–60, ldr 1961–69, alderman 1963–78, Lord Mayor 1974–75); dep high bailiff Westminster 1978–87; chm Servs Sound and Vision Corp 1979–90, dir Parker Gallery; Master Worshipful Co of Girdlers 1996–97; KStJ 1969; Cdr Cross of Merit SMO Malta 1971; *Recreations* motoring, bird-watching; *Clubs* Carlton, RAF; *Style*— Gp Capt Sir Gordon Pirie, CVO, CBE, JP, DL; ✉ Cottage Row, Tarrant Gunville, Blandford, Dorset DT11 8JJ (☎ 01258 830212)

PIRIE, Dr (Duncan) Madsen; s of Douglas Gordon Pirie, and Eva, *née* Madsen; *b* 24 Aug 1940; *Educ* Univ of Edinburgh (MA), Univ of St Andrews (PhD); *Career* prof of philosophy and logic Hillsdale Michigan USA 1975–78, pres Adam Smith Institute 1978–, memb PM's Citizen's Charter Panel 1991–95; *Books* Trial and Error & The Idea of Progress (1978), Test Your IQ (with Eamonn Butler, 1983), Book of the Fallacy (1985), Micropolitics (1988), Privatization (1988), Boost Your IQ (with Eamonn Butler, 1991), Blueprint for a Revolution (1992), The Sherlock Holmes IQ Book (with Eamonn Butler, 1995); *Recreations* calligraphy; *Style*— Dr Madsen Pirie; ✉ Adam Smith Institute, 23 Great Smith St, London SW1P 3BL (☎ 0171 222 4995, fax 0171 222 7544)

PIRIE-GORDON OF BUTHLAW, (George) Patrick; yr s of Lt-Col Charles Pirie-Gordon, OBE, DSC, GCStJ, FSA, FRGS, sometime ed *Burke's Landed Gentry* and Dir of Ceremonies Ven Order of St John, by his w Mabel, CStJ, herself da of George Buckle, sometime ed *The Times*; suc er bro as 15th Laird of Buthlaw 1980; *b* 24 May 1918; *Educ* Winchester, Oriel Coll Oxford; *m* Catherine Grace, da of Alfred Rickard Taylor, of Lymington, and widow of Maj Jack Childerstone Colebrooke; 2 da (Penelope b 1948, Jean b 1950); *Career* serv WWII RA, rising to Lt-Col 2 Survey Regt (despatches twice); local dir Glyn Mills & Co bankers (now Royal Bank of Scotland) 1949–78; dir: Anglo-American Securities Corporation 1973–80, Montagu Boston Investment Tst 1982–85; tstee Transantarctic Assoc 1962–94, chm Mount Everest Fndn 1966, hon vice pres RGS 1982–93; govr Tonbridge Sch 1963–, vice pres Queen's Nursing Inst 1980–93; memb Royal Co Archers (Queen's Body Guard for Scotland) 1948–; Master Worshipful Co of Skinners 1963–64; hon fell Oriel Coll Oxford 1988; KStJ, FRGS; *Recreations* gardening, cooking, bird-watching; *Clubs* Athenaeum; *Style*— Patrick Pirie-Gordon of Buthlaw; ✉ Waterton, Paddock Field, Chilbolton, Stockbridge, Hants SO20 6AU

PIRNIE, HE Graham John Campbell; s of Ian Campbell Pirnie (d 1963), and Emily Elizabeth, *née* Lee; *b* 9 Aug 1941; *Educ* Surbiton GS, Univ of Birmingham (BSocSc); *m* 1967, Kathleen, da of Norman Gunstone (d 1994); 2 s (Julian Campbell b 1968, Andrew Campbell b 1971), 1 da (Sian Marie Campbell b 1983); *Career* HM Dip Serv: joined FCO 1966, third sec and vice consul Phnom Penh 1968–70, commercial offr Paris 1970–74, second sec (commercial) The Hague 1974–77, second later first sec FCO 1977–82, HM consul Geneva 1982–86, JSDC 1986, first sec FCO 1986–89, HM consul and dep head of mission Quito 1989–92, first sec FCO 1992–95, HM ambass to Paraguay 1995–; *Recreations* reading, skiing, antiques restoration; *Style*— HE Mr Graham Pirnie; ✉ c/o Foreign and Commonwealth Office (Asuncion), King Charles Street, London SW1A 2AH

PIRRET, David John; s of George Riddle Pirret, of Edinburgh, and Marion, *née* Taylor Maxwell; *b* 29 Dec 1952; *Educ* Eastwood HS Glasgow, Univ of Strathclyde (BA); *m* 1 March 1980, Patricia Zoe Frances, da of Maj Patrick Dennis Warren; 1 da (Heather Marion Joy b 30 Nov 1981), 2 s (Andrew George Nigel b 5 Jan 1985, James Patrick Gordon (twin) b 5 Jan 1985); *Career* Shell Chemicals UK Ltd 1974–79 (UK market devpt mangr 1977–79), product mangr Shell International Chemical Co Ltd 1979–81, gen mangr Shell Cyprus Trading Co Ltd 1981–84, divnl planning mangr Shell International Chemical Co Ltd 1984–87, divnl gen mangr Shell Chemicals UK Ltd 1987–89, gen mangr (Retail Div) Shell UK Ltd 1992–96 (gen mangr Lubricants Div 1989–92), head of mktg (Oil Products) Shell International Petroleum Co Ltd 1996–; *Recreations* golf, sailing, skiing; *Clubs* RAC; *Style*— David Pirret, Esq; ✉ Shell International Petroleum Co Ltd, Shell Centre, London SE1 7NA (☎ 0171 934 2922, fax 0171 934 6541)

PIRRIE, David Blair; *Educ* Strathallan Sch Perthshire, Harvard Univ (PMD); *m* Angela; 1 da, 3 s; *Career* Lloyds TSB Group plc (formerly Lloyds Bank plc): joined 1959, gen mangr Brazil 1974–81, exec dir Lloyds Bank International 1981–83, sr gen mangr International Banking Div 1983–86, dir UK retail banking 1987–92, main bd dir 1989–, dir of international banking and private banking & financial servs 1992–; FCIB; *Recreations* sport generally and golf in particular, opera, ballet; *Style*— David Pirrie, Esq; ✉ Lloyds TSB Group plc, 71 Lombard Street, London EC3P 3BS (☎ 0171 626 1500)

PISSARIDES, Prof Christopher Antoniou; s of Antonios Pissarides, of Cyprus, and Eudokia, *née* Georgiades; *b* 20 Feb 1948; *Educ* Pancyprian Gymnasium Nicosia Cyprus, Univ of Essex (BA, MA), LSE (PhD); *m* 24 July 1986, Francesca Michela, da of Antonio Cassano, of Rome; 1 s (Antony b 1987), 1 da (Miranda b 1988); *Career* LSE: lectr 1976–82, reader 1982–86, prof 1986–, dir Nat Economic Performance Res Prog 1990–, dir Int Summer Sch in Economics 1993–; res fell Centre for Economic Policy Res 1994–; visiting prof Univs of: Harvard 1979–80, Princeton 1984, Berkeley 1989–90; visiting prof Euro Univ Inst 1989, Houblon-Norman fell Bank of England 1994; memb Interim Governing Bd Univ of Cyprus 1989–95, memb Bd Review of Economic Studies 1983–92; ed Economica 1980–83; conslt: World Bank, EU, OECD; memb: Royal Economic Soc, Euro Economic Assoc, American Economic Assoc; *Books* Labour Market Adjustment (1976), Equilibrium Unemployment Theory (1990); also author of articles in professional jls; *Recreations* gardening, cooking; *Style*— Prof Christopher Pissarides; ✉ London School of Economics, Houghton St, London WC2A 2AE (☎ 0171 955 7513, fax 0171 831 1840, telex 24655 BLPES G)

PITBLADO, Sir David Bruce; KCB (1967, CB 1955), CVO (1953); s of Robert Bruce Pitblado, and Mary Jane, *née* Sear; *b* 18 Aug 1912; *Educ* Strand Sch, Emmanuel Coll Cambridge; *m* 1941, Edith (d 1978), da of Capt J T Rees Evans; 1 s, 1 da; *Career* civil servant 1935–71: Dominions Office, Treasy, private sec to PM 1951–56, Miny of Power (perm sec), Comptroller and Auditor Gen 1971–76, ret; hon treas SSAFA 1978–90, chm Davies's 1979–89; memb: Victoria County Histories Ctee 1976–, Fin and GP Ctee Royal Postgrad Med Sch 1980–; hon fell Emmanuel Coll Cambridge 1972; memb Middle Temple; *Clubs* Athenaeum; *Style*— Sir David Pitblado, KCB, CVO; ✉ 23 Cadogan Street, London SW3 2PP (☎ 0171 589 6765); Pengoitan, Borth, Dyfed SY24 5LN

PITCHER, Sir Desmond Henry; kt (1992), DL; s of George Charles Pitcher (d 1968), of Liverpool, and Alice Marion, *née* Osborne (d 1985); *b* 23 March 1935; *Educ* Liverpool Coll of Technol; *m* 1, 1961 (m dis 1973), Patricia, *née* Ainsworth; 2 da (Stephanie b 18 May 1965, Samantha (twin) b 18 May 1965); m 2, 1978 (m dis 1984), Carol Ann, *née* Rose; 2 s (George b 1 Oct 1978, Andrew b 1 March 1981); m 3, 1 June 1991, Norma Barbara, *née* Niven; *Career* devpt engr A V Roe & Co 1957–58, systems engr Automatic Telephone & Electrical Co 1958–60, nat mangr engrg Sperry Univac Ltd 1961–66; md: MDS (Data Processing) Ltd 1966–71, Sperry Univac Ltd 1971–73; dep chm Sperry Rand Ltd 1973–76 (dir 1971–73), vice pres Int Div Sperry Univac Corp 1973–76; md: Truck and Bus Div BL Ltd 1976–78, Plessey Telecommunications and Office Systems 1978–83; dir Plessey Co 1979–83, chief exec The Littlewoods Organisation 1983–93 (non-exec vice chm 1993–95), chm United Utilities plc (formerly North West Water Group PLC) 1993– (dir 1990–, dep chm 1991–93); non-exec dir: Nat West Bank (Northern Advsy Bd) 1989–92, National Westminster Bank plc 1994–; dep chm Everton FC Ltd 1990– (dir 1987–), chm Merseyside Development Corporation 1991–; Faraday lectr 1973–74; visiting prof of business policy Univ of Manchester 1993, hon fell Liverpool John Moores Univ 1993; Freeman: City of London 1987, Worshipful Co of Info Technologists 1987; CEng, FIEE 1968, FBCS 1975, Hon FIDE 1977, CIMgt 1985, FRSA 1987; *Recreations* football, opera, golf; *Clubs* Brooks's, Royal Birkdale Golf, RAC, Moor Park Golf, Delamere Golf, Lancashire CC; *Style*— Sir Desmond Pitcher, DL; ✉ Onston Hall, Onston, Cheshire CW8 2RG (☎ 01606 854649); United Utilities plc, Birchwood Point Business Park, Birchwood Boulevard, Birchwood, Warrington WA3 7WB (☎ 01925 285011, fax 01925 285040)

PITCHFORD, Christopher John; QC (1987); *b* 28 March 1947; *Educ* Dyffryn Comp Newport, Queen's Coll Taunton, Queen Mary Coll (LLB); *Career* called to the Bar Middle Temple 1969; recorder 1987–; arbitrator Motor Insurers' Bureau 1994–; *Style*— Christopher Pitchford, Esq, QC; ✉ Farrar's Building, Temple, London EC4Y 7BD (☎ 0171 583 9241, fax 0171 583 0090)

PITCHFORD, David; s of Joseph Robert Heal Pitchford, of Wolverhampton, and Daphne Gladys, *née* Bond; *b* 26 May 1949; *Educ* Meole Brace Secdy Sch Shrewsbury, Wolverhampton Poly (City & Guilds), Ealing Hotel Sch (pt/t City & Guilds), Garnett Coll Univ of London (CertEd); *m* 1975, Rona Caroline, da of Albert Samuel North; 2 s (Samuel Joseph b 4 June 1977, Alexander b 9 July 1980); *Career* chef BBC Television Centre 1967, first commis Mayfair Hotel London 1968, chef tournant Dorchester Hotel 1968–73, lectr in professional cookery Ealing Hotel Sch 1974–77, chef/patron Reads Restaurant Faversham Kent 1977–; promotional tours incl: USA 1987 and 1988, S Africa 1988 and 1991; judge Chef of the Year Hotelympia 1992, Br rep Azalea Festival Virginia USA 1995; memb Academie Culinaire de France 1987, memb Craft Guild of Chefs; *Awards* Chef of the Year 1986 and 1987, Good Food Guide Co Restaurant of the Year (Reads) 1992, Michelin Star 1992; *Recreations* golf, classic cars; *Clubs* Clermont, Faversham Golf; *Style*— David Pitchford, Esq; ✉ Read's Restaurant, Painters Forstal, Faversham, Kent ME13 0EE (☎ 01795 535344, fax 01795 591200, mobile 0850 484705)

PITCHFORK, Air Cdre Graham Ralph; MBE (1972); s of Ralph Pitchfork, of Sheffield, and Margaret Agnes, *née* Wragg; *b* 4 Feb 1939; *Educ* High Storrs GS Sheffield, RAF Coll Cranwell (BA); *m* 5 June 1965, Marlane Margaret-Rose, da of Gareth Weadick (d 1939), of Dublin; 1 s (Paul b 1971), 2 da (Siobhan b 1966, Joanna b 1968); *Career* RAF: navigator 1961; served Malay Peninsula 1965–66, S Arabia 1965–66; OC 208 Sqdn RAF Honington 1979–81, stn cdr RAF Finningley 1987–89; AOC and Cmdt OASC Biggin Hill 1989–91, Air Cdre MOD 1991–94; chm: Br Schs Exploring Soc, Buccaneer Aircrew Assoc; pres Clevelands Gliding Club; FRAeS 1991; *Recreations* gliding, RAF history, ornithology; *Clubs* RAF; *Style*— Air Cdre Graham Pitchfork, MBE

PITFIELD, Michael; s of Edward George Pitfield (d 1976), and Robina Heslop (d 1996); *b* 22 May 1945; *Educ* Univ of London (BSc), Univ of Reading (MA); *m* 12 Aug 1972, Angela May, da of Albert Victor McCallin (d 1969); 2 s (Alexander b 1975, Alastair b 1982), 1 da (Anna b 1979); *Career* asst dir Inst of Personnel Mgmnt 1978–89 (special advsr 1989–), dir Thames Valley Business Sch 1989–90, dir of corp affrs Henley Mgmnt Coll 1990–; memb: European Business Govt Rels Cncl 1993–, Bd UNICON (USA) 1994– (vice chm 1996); FIPD 1980; FRSA 1992, MIPRA 1994; *Books* How To Take Exams (1980), Developing International Managers (1996); *Recreations* genealogy, history, travel; *Style*— Michael Pitfield, Esq; ✉ Henley Management College, Greenlands, Henley-on-Thames, Oxon RG9 3AU (☎ 01491 571454, fax 01491 571635, e-mail michaelp@heuleymc.ac.uk)

PITFIELD, Thomas Baron; s of Thomas Baron Pitfield (d 1925), and Mary, *née* Fallows; *b* 5 April 1903; *Educ* Bolton Municipal Sch, Bolton Tech Coll, Royal Manchester Coll of Music, Bolton Sch of Art; *m* 26 Dec 1934, Alice Maud, da of William Astbury (d 1945); *Career* composer, artist and writer; millwright draughtsman 1917–24, teacher of cabinet work to unemployed Wolverhampton Cncl of Social Serv 1934–36, p/t and supply teacher, later sr art and music master Tettenhall Coll 1935–47, freelance designer and composer and prof of composition Royal Northern (formerly Royal Manchester) Coll of Music 1947–73; exhibited in Royal Acad of Art, numerous one man exhibitions in municipal and other galleries; 4 exhibitions of life and works for 90th birthday; written articles in: The Listener, Country Life, The Countryman, The Artist, Musical Times, Musical Opinion; numerous broadcasts, numerous musical pubns for chorus, orchestra chamber, piano and other ensembles and combinations; CD of chamber music and songs issued by RNCM; A Short Community Service (BBC); memb: Bd of Profs Royal Manchester Coll of Music, Cheshire Community Cncl, SCAM, Composers' Guild of GB, Performing Right Soc, NRD; hon fell Vegetarian Soc UK, hon memb Assoc of Professional Composers, Hon FRNCM; *Books* The Poetry of Trees (1945), Words without Songs, Musicianship for Guitarists, Art Teaching Course, No Song No Supper (autobiography, Vol 1), A Song after Supper (autobiography, Vol 2), A Cotton Town Boyhood (3rd autobiography), My Words (50 poems), Limusics (40 limericks and linocuts), From a Wayfarer's Sketchbook, Johnnyrobins (nonsense verse and illustrations); *Recreations* country walking, bird watching, wood carving; *Style—* Thomas Pitfield, Esq; ✉ Lesser Thorns, 21 East Downs Road, Bowdon, Altrincham, Cheshire WA14 2LG (☎ 0161 928 4644)

PITHER, Dr Charles Edward Pither; s of David E Pither, of Garston, Herts, and June, *née* Cadisch; *b* 21 July 1953; *Educ* Aldenham Sch Elstree, St Thomas' Hosp Med Sch London (MB BS); *m* 22 Sept 1979, Jane Patricia Anne, da of Cdr David Roberts, MBE, RN; 3 da (Claire Elizabeth Wensley b 12 July 1982, Kate Victoria b 14 Nov 1984, Sephanie Jane Eleanor b 22 Dec 1986); *Career* instr in anaesthesia Univ of Cincinnati Med Center Ohio 1984 (fell in pain control and regnl anaesthesia 1983–84), lectr and hon sr registrar St Thomas' Hosp 1984–85; currently: conslt pain specialist St Thomas' Hosp, med dir INPUT Pain Mgmnt Unit St Thomas' Hosp, hon conslt anaesthetist and pain specialist Nat Hosp for Neurology and Neurosurgery Queen Square, med dir (pain servs) Powys Health Care Tst, med dir Unsted Park Hosp Pain Mgmnt Prog Godalming Surrey; fndr chm CAMPAIN - the Nat Pain Charity; co-winner: King's Fund maj grant 1987, Evian Health Award 1993; FRCA 1982; *Recreations* gardening, country sports, old motor cars, travel; *Style—* Dr Charles Pither; ✉ 18 Corkran Road, Surbiton, Surrey KT6 6PN (☎ 0181 399 8455); St Thomas' Hospital, London SE1 7EH (☎ 0171 922 8107, fax 0171 922 8229)

PITHER, Jon Peter; s of Philip John Pither (d 1965), and Vera, *née* Roth (d 1980); *b* 15 June 1934; *Educ* Dauntsey's, Queens' Coll Cambridge (MA); *m* 1961, Karin Jutta, da of Werner Gropp; 1 s (Michael Gordon Carsten b 1963), 1 da (Brigitte Clare b 1965); *Career* cmmnd Royal Sussex Regt 1969–; dir: Glynwed International plc 1988–91, Suter plc 1991–96, Eurokit UK Limited 1991–, Alumasc Group plc 1992–, Avon Holdings plc 1992–, Wisley Golf Club plc 1992–, City Technology Ltd 1994–, World Telecom plc 1994–, Wessex Traincare (Holdings) Ltd 1995–, Lady in Leisure Group plc 1996–, Aim Trust plc 1996–; chm: Primary Industries Ltd 1992–, Equinox International Ltd 1992–; md Surrey Management Services Ltd 1991–; underwriter Lloyd's of London; Liveryman Worshipful Co of Fanmakers; *Recreations* sailing, skiing, golf; *Clubs* Athenaeum, Mitre, Wisley Golf, NZ Golf, St George's Hill Golf; *Style—* Jon P Pither, Esq; ✉ Surrey Management Services, South House, Claremont Park, Esher, Surrey (☎ 01372 470279, fax 01372 470541)

PITMAN, Sir Brian Ivor; kt (1994); s of Ronald Ivor Pitman, and Doris Ivy, *née* Short; *b* 13 Dec 1931; *Educ* Cheltenham GS; *m* 1954, Barbara Mildred Ann; 2 s (Mark, David), 1 da (Sally); *Career* chief exec and dir Lloyds Bank Plc 1983–97 (dep chief exec 1982–83), chm Lloyds TSB Group plc 1997– (gp chief exec 1996–97); dir: Lloyds Bank California 1982–86, The National Bank of New Zealand 1982–, Lloyds Bank International Ltd 1985–87 (dep chief exec 1978–81), Lloyds Merchant Bank Holdings Ltd 1985–88, NBNZ Holdings Ltd 1990–; pres: British Bankers' Assoc 1996–97, Chartered Inst of Bankers 1997–; (Hon) DSc City Univ 1996; *Recreations* golf, cricket, music; *Style—* Sir Brian Pitman; ✉ Lloyds TSB Group plc, 71 Lombard Street, London EC3P 3BS (☎ 0171 626 1500)

PITMAN, Giles William; s of Capt John Pitman (ka 1943), and Elizabeth Cattanach Pitman; *b* 5 Sept 1938; *Educ* Eton, ChCh Oxford (MA); *m* 1961, Jane, da of Maj George De Pree; 2 s, 1 da; *Career* jt gp md Pitman plc 1981–85, fin dir Really Useful Group plc 1988–89, chief exec Summer International plc 1989–91, chm Spectral Technology Group Ltd 1991–96, ops dir The Financial Training Company 1993–94; non-exec dir: Marine & General Mutual Life Assurance Society 1976–96, Oxford House Group plc 1991–92, Hambro Insurance Services Group plc 1993–, BFSS Investments Ltd 1993–; chm Chant Group PLC 1995–; md Market Link Publishing 1996–; hon treas: BFSS 1992–96; FCA, ACMA; *Recreations* country sports; *Clubs* Cavalry and Guards'; *Style—* Giles Pitman, Esq; ✉ Heath House, Albury, Ware, Herts SG11 2LX (☎ 01279 771293, fax 01279 771820)

PITMAN, Jennifer Susan (Jenny); da of George Harvey, and Mary Harvey; *b* 11 June 1946; *Educ* Sarson Secdy Girls' Sch; *m* 1965 (m dis), Richard Pitman; 2 s (Paul Richard, Mark Andrew Pitman, *qv*); *Career* national hunt racehorse trainer 1975–; dir Jenny Pitman Racing Ltd 1975–; major races won incl: Midlands National 1977 (Watafella), Massey Ferguson Gold Cup 1980 (Bueche Giorod), Welsh National 1982 (Corbiere), 1983 (Burrough Hill Lad) and 1986 (Stearsby), Grand National 1983 (Corbiere), King George VI Gold Cup 1984 (Burrough Hill Lad), Hennessey Gold Cup 1984 (Burrough Hill Lad), Cheltenham Gold Cup 1984 (Burrough Hill Lad) and 1991 (Garrison Savannah), Whitbread Trophy 1985 (Smith's Man), Ritz Club National Hunt Handicap 1987 (Gainsay), Sporting Life Weekend Chase 1987 (Gainsay), Philip Cornes Saddle of Gold Final 1988 (Crumpet Delite), Welsh Champion Hurdle 1991 (Wonderman) and 1992 (Don Valentino), Grand National 1995 (Royal Athlete), Scottish Grand National 1995 (Willsford), Sun Alliance Chase 1996 (Nahthen Lad), Supreme Novice Hurdle 1996; first woman to train Grand National and Gold Cup winners, trainer of Esha Ness (winner of the aborted Grand National 1993); awards incl: Golden Spurs Racing Personality of the Year 1983, Cwlth Sports awards 1983 and 1984, Piper Heidsieck Trainer of the Year 1983–84 and 1989–90, Variety Club of GB Sportswoman of the Year 1984, Golden Spurs Best Nat Hunt Trainer 1984; *Books* Glorious Uncertainty (autobiography, 1984); *Style—* Mrs Jenny Pitman; ✉ Weathercock House, Upper Lambourn, nr Newbury, Berks (☎ 01488 71714, fax 01488 72196)

PITMAN, Mark Andrew; s of Richard Thomas Pitman, and Jennifer Susan (Jenny) Pitman, *qv*; *b* 1 Aug 1968; *Educ* Wycliffe Coll; *m* 1995, Natasha Susan Cowen; *Career* national hunt jockey; debut 1983, professional 1984–; second yst jockey to complete the National Course 1984, second place Conditional Jockey Championship 1986–87; asst trainer to Mrs Jenny Pitman 1993– (retained jockey 1988–93); career best of 57 winners in a season 1989–90 (incl second place in Cheltenham Gold Cup and won Ritz Club Jockey of the Meeting Aintree), second in Grand National Aintree 1991; maj races won incl: Tote Cheltenham Gold Cup 1991, Welsh Champion Hurdle 1991, The Martell Cup Steeple Chase, The Mumm Club Novices Steeple Chase, The Larchlap Chase, The Midlands Grand National, The EBF Hurdle Final, The Charterhouse Mercantile Chase, The Swish Hurdle, The John Bull Chase, The Sporting Life Weekender HCP Chase, The Old Road Securities Novice Chase, The Souter of Stirling Novices Chase; *Recreations* keeping fit incl aerobics and circuit training, squash, water-skiing; *Style—* Mark Pitman, Esq; ✉ Penny Cottage, Wantage Road, Great Shefford, Berks; Weathercock House, Upper Lambourn, Berkshire (☎ 01488 71714, fax 01488 721986)

PITT, Barrie William Edward; yr s of John Pitt, and Ethel May, *née* Pennel; *b* 7 July 1918; *Educ* Portsmouth Southern GS; *m* 1, 1943, Phyllis Kate, *née* Edwards; 1 s (decd); m 2, 1953 (m dis 1971), Sonia Deirdre, *née* Hoskins; m 3, 1983, Frances Mary, *née* Moore; *Career* WWII Army 1939–45; bank clerk 1935, surveyor 1946, info offr UKAEA 1961, historical conslt to BBC series The Great War 1963; author and ed of mil histories, contrib to Encyclopaedia Britannica and The Sunday Times; *Books* The Edge of Battle (1958), Zeebrugge, St George's Day 1918 (1958), Coronel and Falkland (1960), 1918 The Last Act (1962), Purnell's History of the Second World War (ed, 1964), Ballantine's Illustrated History of World War 2 (ed-in-chief, 1967), Purnell's History of the First World War (ed, 1969), Ballantine's Illustrated History of the Violent Century (ed-in-chief, 1971), British History Illustrated (ed, 1974–78), The Battle of the Atlantic (1977), The Crucible of War: Western Desert 1941 (1980), Churchill and the Generals (1981), The Crucible of War: Year of Alamein 1942 (1982), Special Boat Squadron (1983), The Military History of World War II (1986), The Chronological Atlas of World War II (with Frances Pitt, 1989); *Recreations* golf; *Clubs* Savage; *Style—* Barrie Pitt, Esq; ✉ 10 Wellington Rd, Taunton, Somerset TA1 4EG (☎ and fax 01823 337188)

PITT, Hon Bruce Michael David; o s of Baron Pitt of Hampstead (Life Peer, d 1994), and Dorothy Elaine, *née* Alleyne; *b* 18 June 1945; *Educ* King Alfred Sch Hampstead, Univ Coll London (LLB); *Career* called to the Bar Gray's Inn 1970; memb: Sub-Ctee Criminal Bar Assoc Advsy Body to Law Cmmn on Special Defence - Duress and Entrapment Coercion 1974, Bar Cncl Young Barristers' Ctee 1974–75, Senate Inns of Court and Bar Cncl 1975–76, Attorney-Gen's List of Counsel 1981–, Race Relations Ctee Bar Cncl 1990–93; recorder S Eastern Circuit 1993– (asst recorder 1985–92); memb: Hampstead Lab Pty 1960–69, Campaign Against Racial Discrimination 1964–67; memb Bars of Jamaica, Trinidad and Tobago, Barbados, and West Indies Associated States; *Recreations* swimming, arts, watching cricket; *Clubs* MCC; *Style—* The Hon Bruce Pitt

PITT, Brig John Keith; OBE (1979); s of Herbert William Pitt (d 1972), of East Ashling, Chichester, and Beatrice Irene, *née* Reeve; *b* 5 April 1934; *Educ* Highgate Sch; *m* 21 Dec 1968, Yvette Anne Barbara, da of Charles Edward Emile Cormeau (d 1940), of London; 1 s (Keith Charles William b 8 April 1970), 1 da (Natasha Anne Barbara b 10 Nov 1971); *Career* cmmnd RASC 1953, RCT 1965, ret Brig 1988 (despatches 1981); dep dir Wandsworth Borough Cncl 1988–96; Freeman City of London 1988, Liveryman Worshipful Co of Carmen 1988; FCIT; *Recreations* marathon running, music, military history, golf, fly fishing; *Clubs* Milford Golf; *Style—* Brig John Pitt, OBE; ✉ Robin House, Old Park Lane, Farnham, Surrey GU10 5AA (☎ 01252 714965)

PITT, Nicholas John; s of George Stanhope Pitt (d 1983), of East Horsley, Surrey, and Lesley Henrietta, *née* Bayley; *b* 21 Oct 1950; *Educ* Aldenham, Lancaster Univ; *partner* since 1984, June Williamson, da of late Wilfrid Mansfield; *Career* sub ed Stratford Express 1977–79, sports writer The Sunday Times 1979–87, chief sports writer London Daily News 1987; The Sunday Times: dep sports ed 1988–94, sports ed 1994–96, sports writer 1996–; special award Br Sports Journalism Awards 1985; *Recreations* golf, tennis; *Clubs* Priory Park Lawn Tennis, Wimbledon Park Golf, Magdalen Park Lawn Tennis; *Style—* Nicholas Pitt, Esq; ✉ Sports Editor, The Sunday Times, 1 Pennington Street, London E1 9XW (☎ 0171 782 5714, fax 0171 782 5720)

PITT, Peter Clive Crawford; TD (1976); s of Norman Pitt (d 1987), of High Trees Ct, High Trees, Reigate, and Emily, *née* Crawford (d 1994); *b* 7 Sept 1933; *Educ* Epsom Coll, Guy's Hosp (MB BS, DTM&H, MRCP); *m* 23 Jan 1965, Anna Catherine, da of Frederick William Markham Pratt (d 1965), of Pewsey, Wilts; 2 s (James Peter William b 22 Jan 1966, Daniel Crawford b 12 Sept 1969), 1 da (Rachel Louise b 6 Sept 1967); *Career* (mentioned in despatches 1956), QA Mil Hosp 1959–61; surgical specialist Br Mil Hosp Kaduna Nigeria 1961–63, Cambridge Mil Hosp Aldershot 1963–65; sr surgical specialist: Br Mil Hosp Rinteln BAOR 1965–66, Br Mil Hosp Dharan Nepal 1966–68; Regtl MO TA 1969–93; house surgn: Guy's 1957, (Paediatric) Guy's 1958; house physician Addenbrooke's Cambridge 1958, registrar Redhill 1968–70, sr registrar Guy's and Chase Farm 1970–72, conslt surgn Havering Hosps 1972–, dir Garnish Hall Tutorial Centre 1983–; pres Barking and Brentwood branch BMA 1981; cmmr Inland Revenue 1988– (dep chm); hon memb Rotary Club of Dagenham 1994–; memb: BMA, RSAA 1973, Hunterian Soc; fell PEN 1985; FRCS 1963, FRSM; *Books* Surgeon in Nepal: John Murray (1970); *Recreations* gardening, tennis; *Style—* Peter Pitt, Esq, TD; ✉ Garnish Hall, Margaret Roding, Dunmow, Essex (☎ 0124 5231 209); 3 Lake Rise, Romford, Essex (☎ 01708 747255, fax 01708 741172)

PITT-KETHLEY, (Helen) Fiona; da of Rupert Singleton Pitt-Kethley (d 1975), of England, and Olive, *née* Banfield; *b* 21 Nov 1954; *Educ* Haberdashers' Aske's Girls' Sch Acton, Chelsea Sch of Art (BA, Biddulph painting prize); *m* 1995, James Plaskett; 1 s (Alexander Michael b 15 Sept 1996); *Career* poet, travel writer, novelist and journalist; memb: Film Artistes' Assoc, Sussex Book Group; *Books* poetry collections: Sky Ray Lolly (1986), Private Parts (1987), The Perfect Man (1989), Dogs (1993), Double Act (1996); others: Journeys to the Underworld (travel book, 1988), The Misfortunes of Nigel (novel, 1991), The Literary Companion to Sex (anthology, 1992), The Maiden's Progress (novella, 1992), Too Hot to Handle (essays and letters, 1992), The Pan Principle (travel book, 1993), The Literary Companion to Low Life (anthology, 1995); *Recreations* singing Baroque arias, weight-training, herbalism, painting, sex, playing the spinet, swimming in the sea, allotment gardening, yoga; *Clubs* Chelsea Arts; *Style—* Ms Fiona Pitt-Kethley; ✉ 7 Ebenezer Rd, Hastings, East Sussex TN34 3BS

PITTAWAY, David Michael; s of Eric Michael Pittaway, of Coventry, and Heather Yvette, *née* Scott; *b* 29 June 1955; *Educ* Uppingham, Sidney Sussex Coll Cambridge (MA); *m* 26 March 1983, Jill Suzanne, da of Dr Ian Douglas Bertie Newsam, of Cambridge; 2 s (James Frederick Henry b 9 July 1986, Charles Edward Bennet b 22 July 1989); *Career* called to the Bar Inner Temple 1977, practising Midland and Oxford circuit 1979–; FCIArb 1991; *Recreations* country life, gardening, music, skiing, travel; *Clubs* RAC; *Style—* David Pittaway, Esq; ✉ 43 Canonbury Park North, London N1 2JU (☎ 0171 226 3060); No 1 Serjeants' Inn, London EC4Y 1LL (☎ 0171 353 9901)

PITTEWAY, Prof Michael Lloyd Victor; s of Lloyd Sydney Pitteway (d 1990), and Elsie Maud, *née* Hall (d 1947); *b* 10 Feb 1934; *Educ* Felsted, Queens' Coll Cambridge (MA, PhD, ScD); *m* 2 April 1955, Cynthia Ethel Patricia, da of Percival Henry Wilkins (d 1955), of Leicester; *Career* Harkness fell USA 1959–61, sr res fell Space and Sci Res Lab Slough 1961–63, computer dir Univ of Nottingham 1963–67, res prof Brunel Univ 1985– (head of Computer Sci Dept 1967–85); assoc conslt Intera Information Technologies 1991–; FBCS 1968, FIMA 1972, FInstP 1978; *Recreations* music, duplicate bridge, golf; *Clubs* Castle Royle Golf and Country; *Style—* Prof Michael Pitteway; ✉ Hedgerows, Star Lane, Knowl Hill, Berks RG10 9XY; Computer Science Department, Brunel University, Uxbridge UB8 3PH (☎ 01895 274000 ext 2233, fax 01895 251686, e-mail MIKE.PITTEWAY@UK.AC.BRUNEL)

PIZZEY, Erin Patria Margaret; *née* Carney; da of Cyril Carney, MBE (d 1980), and Ruth Patricia Last; *b* 19 Feb 1939; *Educ* Leweston Manor Sherborne Dorset; *m* 1, 1961 (m dis 1979), John Leo Pizzey; 1 s (Amos b 1967), 1 da (Cleo b 1961), 5 stepchildren (Francis, Trevor, Annie, Richard, Daren); *Career* author, journalist and social reformer; fndr of the Int Shelter Movement for Battered Men, Women and Children; memb: Royal Soc of Literature, Author's Club; Int Order of Volunteers for Peace Diploma of Honour 1981, Nancy Astor Award for Journalism 1983, Distinguished Leadership Award (World

Congress of Victimology) 1987, Valentino Palm d'Oro Award for Literature 1994; hon citizen of San Ginani D'Asso Italy 1993; has contributed to many leading newspapers and journals; author of articles: Choosing a Non-Violent Relationship, Sexual Abuse Within the Family; TV documentaries incl: Scream Quietly (1975), Chiswick Women's Aid (1977), That Awful Woman (1987), Cutting Edge: Sanctuary (1991); *Non-Fiction* Scream Quietly or the Neighbours Will Hear, Infernal Child, Sluts Cookbook, Erin Pizzey Collects, Prone To Violence, All In The Name of Love, The Wicked World of Women (1996), Wild Child (autobiography); *Fiction* The Watershed, In the Shadow of the Castle, The Pleasure Palace, First Lady, The Consul General's Daughter (1988), The Snow Leopard of Shanghai (1989), Other Lovers (1991), Morningstar (1992), Swimming With Dolphins (1993), For the Love of a Stranger (1994), Kisses (1995); *Short Stories* The Man in the Blue Van, The Frangipani Tree, Addiction, Dancing; *Recreations* reading, cooking, antiques, violin, wine, travel; *Style—* Erin Pizzey; ✉ c/o Il Molino di Trove, 23 San Giovanni d'Asso, Siena 53020, Italy (☎ 00 39 577 823170); c/o PO Box 2420, Georgetown, Grand Cayman, British West Indies

PLAISTOWE, Alan David; s of David Plaistowe, of Connemara, Co Galway, and Rhona Elizabeth, *née* ffrench; *b* 18 June 1932; *Educ* Marlborough, Ramsey Labs UC London (BSc); *m* 14 June 1957, Jane, da of Donovan Candler, of London; 1 da (Victoria b 1966); *Career* Lt RE Libya 1950–52; with Design Engrs Foster Wheeler (gas processing, oil refining) 1955–58; Stone and Webster Engrg 1958–65; fndr and md Chem Systems Ltd 1965–92, chm Chem Systems Group 1992– (pres 1986–92); FIChemEng, FInstPet, CEng; *Recreations* flying, golf, gardening, jazz; *Clubs* RAC; *Style—* Alan Plaistowe, Esq; ✉ Wanden, Egerton, Kent

PLAISTOWE, (William) Ian David; s of David William Plaistowe (d 1975), and Julia, *née* Ross Smith; *b* 18 Nov 1942; *Educ* Marlborough, Queens' Coll Cambridge; *m* 1968, Carolyn Anne Noble, da of Tom Kenneth Noble Wilson; 2 s (Richard William Ian b 1969, Peter David Alexander b 1972), 1 da (Nicola Louise b 1977); *Career* Arthur Andersen: joined 1964, ptnr 1976, head of Accounting & Audit Practice London 1984–87, managing practice dir Audit and Business Advsy Practice Europe 1992–; chm London Soc of Chartered Accountants 1981–82, pres ICAEW 1992–93 (currently memb Cncl), chm Auditing Practices Bd 1994–; memb Ct of Assts Worshipful Co of CAs; FCA; *Recreations* golf, tennis, squash, skiing, gardening; *Clubs* Carlton, Moor Park Golf; *Style—* Ian Plaistowe, Esq; ✉ Arthur Andersen, 1 Surrey St, London WC2R 2PS (☎ 0171 438 3572, fax 0171 831 1133)

PLANER, Nigel George; s of George Victor Planer, and (Margaret) Lesley, *née* Weeden; *b* 22 Feb 1953; *Educ* Westminster, Univ of Sussex, LAMDA; *m* 19 Aug 1989, Anna, da of Michael Lea; 1 s (Stanley b 5 Sept 1988); *Career* actor; memb: Equity 1977, Writers' Guild 1987, Musicians' Union 1987; *Theatre* incl: Leeds Playhouse, Lyric, Young Vic, Oxford Playhouse, Globe; memb original cast Evita, Man of the Moment, Angry Old Men; *Television* leading roles incl: Shine on Harvey Moon, Rollover Beethoven, King and Castle, The Young Ones, Filthy Rich and Catflap, Number Twenty Seven, Blackeyes, Frankenstein's Baby, The Comic Strip Presents, The Naked Actor, Bonjour La Classe 1993, Wake Up With; narrator The Magic Roundabout (Channel 4) 1993; *Films* incl: The Supergrass, Brazil, Yellowbeard, More Bad News, The Strike; *Scripts* incl: Radio 4 sketches, Not the Nine O'Clock News, Funseekers (Channel 4 film), King and Castle (Thames); *Live appearances* incl: fndr memb Comic Strip, Comedy Store, Edinburgh Festival, MTV NY, Adelaide Festival (Aust), Hammersmith Odeon; other work incl two comedy LPs; *Awards* winner BPI Award Best Comedy Record 1984; *Books* Neil's Book of the Dead (1983), I, An Actor (1987), A Good Enough Dad (1992), Let's Get Divorced (1994), Therapy and How to Avoid It (1996); *Style—* Nigel Planer, Esq; ✉ c/o Peters Fraser & Dunlop Ltd, 503 The Chambers, Chelsea Harbour, Lots Road, London SW10 0XF (☎ 0171 344 1010, fax 0171 352 7356)

PLANT, (Ronald Arthur) Derek; JP (Herts 1993); s of Arthur Plant (d 1982), and Edith Frances, *née* Brock (d 1985); *b* 13 Jan 1935; *Educ* Rothesay Acad Isle of Bute, Scottish Hotel Sch Glasgow (Dip Hotel Mgmnt); *m* 22 Dec 1960, Christina Ann Murray, da of John Craig, of Cardross, Scotland; 2 da (Alison Christina (Mrs Carlton) b 1964, Isla Edith b 1966); *Career* Nat Serv 1955–57; Br Tport Hotels Ltd 1957–83: hotel gen mangr 1964–79, div dir 1979–80, company ops dir 1980–83; joint md Compass Hotels Ltd 1983–, non-exec dir Andrew Weir Hotels Ltd 1993–; Freeman: City of London 1978, Worshipful Co of Distillers 1979–; FHCIMA 1975; *Recreations* music, cricket, travel, reading; *Clubs* MCC; *Style—* Derek Plant, Esq, JP; ✉ Mapledurham, Bishops Rd, Tewin Wood, Herts AL6 0NR (☎ 01438 798493)

PLANT, John David; *b* 22 May 1944; *Career* Lloyd's underwriter; Claremount Underwriting Agency Ltd: dep underwriter Non-Marine Syndicate 558 1970–78, active underwriter Non-Marine Syndicate 507 1978–83, jt active underwriter Non-Marine Syndicate 558 1983–87, active underwriter Non-Marine Syndicate 506 1987–92, dep chm 1992–93, actg chm 1993–94, chief exec 1993–; memb: Lloyd's Disciplinary Panel, Lloyd's European Working Gp; former dir Lloyd's Underwriters' Technical Services Ltd; *Recreations* boating; *Style—* J D Plant, Esq; ✉ Claremount Underwriting Agency Ltd, Mint House, 77 Mansell Street, London E1 8AN (☎ 0171 464 1502, fax 0171 481 8928)

PLANT OF HIGHFIELD, Baron (Life Peer UK 1992), of Weelsby in the County of Humberside; Raymond Plant; s of Stanley Plant (d 1983), and Marjorie Plant; *b* 19 March 1945; *Educ* Havelock Sch Grimsby, King's Coll London (BA), Univ of Hull (PhD); *m* 27 July 1967, Katherine Sylvia, da of Jack Dixon (d 1989); 3 s (Hon Nicholas b 1969, Hon Matthew b 1971, Hon Richard b 1976); *Career* sr lectr in philosophy Univ of Manchester 1967–69, prof of politics Univ of Southampton 1979–94, master St Catherine's Coll Oxford 1994–; Stevenson lectr Univ of Glasgow 1981, Agnes Cumming lectr Univ Coll Dublin 1988, Stanton lectr Univ of Cambridge 1989–90 and 1990–91, Sarum lectr Univ of Oxford 1991; chm Lab Pty Cmmn on Electoral Systems 1991–; author and contrib to New Statesman and Society, The Independent, The Times, etc; memb: Fabian Soc, Political Studies Assoc UK; Hon DLitt: Univ of Hull, London Guildhall Univ; FRSA 1992; *Books* Social and Moral Theory in Social Work (1970), Hegel: An Introduction (1973), Community and Ideology (1974), Political Philosophy And Social Welfare (1981), Philosophy Politics and Citizenship (1984), Equality Markets And the State (1984), Conservative Capitalism in Britain And The United States: A Critical Appraisal (1988), Citizenship Rights and Socialism (1989), Modern Practical Thought (1991); *Recreations* ornithology, opera, Bach, Mozart; *Style—* The Rt Hon Lord Plant of Highfield; ✉ 6 Woodview Close, Bassett, Southampton SO2 3P2 (☎ 01703 769529); St Catherine's College, Oxford OX1 3UJ (☎ 01865 271762)

PLANTEROSE, Rowan Michael; s of Anthony Ernest Charles Planterose, of Chedworth, Glos, and Jean D'Arcy, *née* Palmer; *b* 19 Feb 1954; *Educ* Eastbourne Coll, Downing Coll Cambridge (MA, LLB); *Career* called to the Bar 1978; FCIArb 1989 (memb Cncl 1991–); *Recreations* squash, skiing, gliding; *Style—* Rowan Planterose, Esq; ✉ 12 Gray's Inn Square, Gray's Inn, London WC1R 5JP (☎ 0171 404 4866, fax 0171 404 4812, mobile 0860 593743)

PLANTIN, Marcus; *Career* various positions rising to exec prodr light entertainment BBC TV until 1985; London Weekend Television: controller of entertainment 1985–91, dir of progs and md LWT Programmes 1991–92; network dir ITV Network Centre 1992–; FRTS 1996; *Style—* Marcus Plantin, Esq; ✉ Network Director, ITV Network Centre, 200 Gray's Inn Road, London WC1X 8HF (☎ 0171 843 8000)

PLASKETT, Maj-Gen Frederick Joseph; CB (1980), MBE (1966); s of Frederick Joseph Plaskett (d 1982), and Grace Mary Plaskett (d 1988); *b* 23 Oct 1926; *Educ* Wallasey GS, Chelsea Poly; *m* 1, 9 Sept 1950, Heather (d 1982), da of Maurice William Kington (d 1976), of Salisbury, Wilts; 4 da (Helen b 1951, Wendy b 1954, Kate b 1960, Lucy b 1965); m 2, 1984, Mrs Patricia Joan Healy, da of Richard Upton, of Wimborne, Dorset; *Career* Army 1945–81; regtl and staff appts: India, Korea, Japan, Malaya, W Africa, Germany, UK; ret as Maj-Gen; dir gen Tport and Movements (Army) 1981; Col Cmdt RCT 1981–91; cmmr Royal Hosp Chelsea 1985–88; dir gen Road Haulage Assoc Ltd 1981–88; dir: Paccar UK (Foden Trucks) 1981–, Road Haulage Insurance Services 1983–88, Br Road Fedn 1982–88, BR London Midland Regn 1986–92 (chm 1989–92); Freeman City of London 1979, Liveryman Worshipful Co of Carmen 1979; FCIT; *Recreations* sailing, fishing, gardening; *Clubs* Army and Navy, Royal Motor Yacht; *Style—* Maj-Gen Frederick Plaskett, CB, MBE; ✉ c/o National Westminster Bank plc, The Commons, Shaftesbury, Dorset SP7 8JY

PLASTOW, Sir David Arnold Stuart; kt (1986); s of James Stuart Plastow (d 1987), of Grimsby, Lincs, and Marie Plastow (d 1975); *b* 9 May 1932; *Educ* Culford Sch Bury St Edmunds; *m* 1954, Barbara Ann, da of Ralph May, of Luton, Beds; 1 s, 1 da; *Career* mktg dir Motor Car Div Rolls-Royce Ltd 1967–70 (md 1971), md Rolls-Royce Motors Ltd 1972 (gp md 1974–80); Vickers plc: non-exec dir 1975–80, md and chief exec 1980–87, chm and chief exec 1987–92; chm Inchcape plc 1992–95; dep chm: Guinness plc 1987–94 (dir 1986–94), TSB Group plc 1991–95 (non-exec dir Lloyds TSB Group plc following merger 1995–); also non-exec dir: GKN plc 1978–84, Legal and General Group plc 1985–87, F T Everard & Sons Ltd 1991–, Cable and Wireless plc 1991–93, Tenneco Inc 1996–; non-exec govr and dep chm BUPA 1990–; pres: Soc of Motor Manufacturers and Traders 1976–78, Motor Indust Res Assoc 1978–81; memb: Bd Tenneco Inc Houston 1985–92, Offshore Energy Technol Bd 1985–86, Engrg Cncl 1980–83; dep chm Listed Cos Advsy Ctee 1987–90; chm: Cncl Indust Soc 1983–87, MRC 1990–; chllr Univ of Luton 1993–; Liveryman Worshipful Co of Coachmakers & Coach Harness Makers; Hon DSc Cranfield 1978; *Recreations* golf, music; *Clubs* Royal and Ancient (St Andrews), Royal St George's (Sandwich), Pine Valley Golf (Philadelphia); *Style—* Sir David Plastow; ✉ Lloyds TSB Group plc, 71 Lombard Street, London EC3P 3BS (☎ 0171 626 1500)

PLATA, Rick; *b* 12 May 1958; *Educ* Haliford GS, Kingston Coll Surrey; *m* 20 Sept 1987, Robin Beth, da of Joseph Moskowitz, of NY; 1 s Matthew b 14 June 1992); *Career* sr planner/buyer Foote Cone and Belding 1980–82 (asst media planner/media planner 1979–80), media mangr The Leagas Delaney Partnership 1982–84; Laing Henry Advertising: dir of media planning 1984–86, media/bd dir (concurrently md Communique Media ind media co within agency) 1986–89; sr vice pres/dir of business devpt Hill Holliday Connors Cosmopolus Advertising Inc NY 1992–93 (sr vice pres/media dir 1989–92), media dir/Euro media co-ordinator Burkitt Weinreich Bryant Clients and Co Ltd 1993–95; head of sales NBC Europe 1996– (head of strategic planning NBC Super Channel 1995–96); sometime memb: Educn Ctee IPA, Media Ctee American Assoc of Advtg Agencies, Editorial Bd Agency Magazine; recipient: Media Week award, recognition and distinction for work performed on behalf of NYC (given by Mayor David Dinkins) 1991; memb: NY Advtg Club, Soc of Advtg Media Professionals, D&AD; *Recreations* tennis, golf, theatre, music; *Clubs* Groucho's; *Style—* Rick Plata, Esq; ✉ 18 Onslow Gardens, London SW7 3AL (☎ 0171 589 7254)

PLATELL, Amanda Jane; da of Francis Ernest Platell, and Norma June, *née* Malland; *b* 12 Nov 1957; *Educ* Penrhos Methodist Ladies Coll, Univ of Western Aust (BA Hons); *Career* reporter Perth Daily News 1978–81, Woman's ed Western News 1981, Sydney Bureau chief Perth Daily News 1983; sub ed: Sydney Sun 1984, Harpers Bazaar 1985, Today Newspaper 1986; metro dep ed London Daily News 1987, dep ed Today 1987–92 (features prodn ed 1987), gp managing ed Mirror Group Newspapers 1993, also dir of marketing MGN 1993, mktg dir Independent 1993–95, md Independent and Independent on Sunday 1995–96, ed Sunday Mirror 1996–; *Style—* Miss Amanda Platell; ✉ Sunday Mirror, 1 Canada Square, Canary Wharf, London E14 5AP (☎ 0171 293 3000, fax 0171 293 3939)

PLATER, Alan Frederick; s of Herbert Richard Plater, and Isabella Scott Plater; *b* 15 April 1935; *Educ* Kingston HS Hull, King's Coll Newcastle upon Tyne; *m* 1, 1958 (m dis 1985), Shirley Johnson; 2 s, 1 da; m 2, 1986, Shirley Rubinstein; 3 step s; *Career* architect until 1961, writer 1961–; pres Writers' Guild of GB 1991–95 (co chm 1986–87), writer in residence Aust Film Television & Radio Sch Sydney 1988; hon fell Humberside Coll of FE 1983, Hon DLitt Univ of Hull 1985; FRSL 1985, FRSA 1990; *Theatre* A Smashing Day, Close the Coalhouse Door, And a Little Love Besides, Swallows on the Water, Trinity Tales, The Fosdyke Saga, Fosdyke Two, On Your Way, Riley!, Skyhooks, A Foot on the Earth, Prez, In Blackberry Time, Rent Party, Sweet Sorrow, Going Home, I Thought I Heard A Rustling, Shooting the Legend; *Television* plays: So Long Charlie, See the Pretty Lights, To See How Far It Is (trilogy), Land of Green Ginger, Willow Cabins, The Party of the First Part, The Blacktoft Diaries, Thank You Mrs Clinkscales, Misterioso; biographies: The Crystal Spirit, Pride of our Alley, Edward Lear - On the Edge of the Sand, Coming Through, Selected Exits, Doggin' Around; series and serials: Z Cars, Softly Softly, Shoulder to Shoulder, Trinity Tales, The Good Companions, The Consultant, Barchester Chronicles, The Beiderbecke Affair, The Fortunes of War, The Beiderbecke Tapes, A Very British Coup, The Beiderbecke Connection, Oliver's Travels, Dalziel & Pascoe; *Radio* The Journal of Vasilije Bogdanovic, All Things Betray Thee; *Films* The Virgin & the Gypsy, It Shouldn't Happen to a Vet, Priest of Love; *Awards* Writer's Guild Radio Award 1972, Sony Radio Award 1983, RTS Writer's Award 1984/5, Broadcasting Press Guild Award 1987 and 1988, BAFTA Writer's Award 1988, Banff Television Festival Grand Prix 1989, RTS Regional Award 1994, BAFTA Cymru Wrtiers Award 1994; *Books* The Beiderbecke Affair (1985), The Beiderbecke Tapes (1986), Misterioso (1987), The Beiderbecke Connection (1992), Oliver's Travels (1994); plays and short pieces in various anthologies, contrib The Guardian, New Statesman & others; *Recreations* reading, theatre, jazz, snooker, talking, listening; *Clubs* Dramatists', Ronnie Scott's; *Style—* Alan Plater, Esq; ✉ c/o Alexandra Cann, 200 Fulham Road, London SW10 9PN (☎ 0171 352 6266, fax 0171 352 2294)

PLATFORD, Richard John; s of Eric Roy Platford, of Great Warley, Essex, and Joan Mary, *née* Willis; *b* 20 Jan 1945; *Educ* Felsted Sch, Trinity Hall Cambridge (MA), London Business Sch (MBA); *m* 29 Dec 1973, Marie Renee, da of Rene Louis de Peyrecave; 4 s (James Alexander b 11 July 1976, Giles Richard b 26 April 1978, Edward William b 14 April 1983, Thomas Henry (twin)); *Career* mgmnt trainee Rolls Royce Aero Engines 1963–64, systems implementation offr Rolls Royce 1967–69; Otis Elevator 1971–75: trainee Paris, prodn controller then materials mangr Milan; dir of materials Clark Equipment 1976–78; Coopers & Lybrand: conslt 1978–79, ptnr Manufacturing Europe 1983–87 (mangr 1979–83), ptnr Manufacturing UK 1987–91, chm Int Pharmaceutical Sector Programme 1991–; memb Bd of Govrs Amesbury Sch; memb Ct of Assts Worshipful Co of Needlemakers, fell British Prodn and Inventory Control Soc 1978; Freeman City of London; CEng, MIEE 1978, MIMgt 1979, MIMC 1985; *Recreations* golf, tennis, skiing, opera, music; *Style—* Richard Platford, Esq; ✉ The Farmery, Darlings Lane, Pinkneys Green, Berks SL6 6PB (☎ 01628 24873); Coopers & Lybrand, 1 Embankment Place, London WC2N 6NN (☎ 0171 583 5000, fax 01895 256413)

PLATT, Adrian; s of Clifford Lowe Platt, OBE (d 1982), of Chislehurst, Kent, and Katharine Eileen, *née* Everington (d 1975); *b* 28 Nov 1935; *Educ* Marlborough, Univ of Lyons; *m* 24 Sept 1960, Valerie, da of Richard Bois (d 1956); 2 da (Emma b 1965, Katie b 1967); *Career* Nat Serv 4 RHA 1954–56, TA HAC 1956–62; dir Sedgwick Collins Ltd

1964–; chm: Sedgwick Forbes Marine Ltd 1968–69, Sedgwick Forbes Bland Payne Marine Ltd 1969–; dir: Sedgwick Group PLC 1981–93 (md special projects 1991–93), Sedgwick Group Development Ltd 1993–; chm: Sedgwick Marine and Aviation Group 1986–88, Sedgwick Ltd Development Group 1988–, Sedgwick James Overseas Cos Ltd 1990–91; tstee Mary Rose Tst, memb Cncl for Music in Hospitals; Liveryman: Worshipful Co of Vintners 1956 (memb Ct), Worshipful Co of Shipwrights 1988; *Recreations* skiing, tennis, golf, shooting, reading; *Clubs* HAC, IOD; *Style*— Adrian Platt, Esq; ✉ Hatchfield Cottage, Butlers Hill, West Horsley, Surrey KT24 6AZ (☎ 014865 3448); Sedgwick Group PLC, Sedgwick House, 10 Whitechapel High St, London E1 (☎ 0171 377 3411, fax 0171 377 3199, telex 882131)

PLATT, Anthony Michael Westlake; CBE (1991); s of James Westlake Platt, CBE (d 1972), and Veronica Norma Hope, *née* Arnold (d 1987); *b* 28 Sept 1928; *Educ* St George's Coll and Belgrano Day Sch Buenos Aires, Stowe, Institut auf dem Rosenberg St Gallen, Balliol Coll Oxford (BA); *m* 1, 12 April 1952 (m dis 1982), (Jennifer) Susan, *née* Scott-Fox; 3 s (Michael b 1953, Timothy b 1961, Robin b 1962); m 2, 14 April 1984, Heather Mary (formerly Mrs Stubbs), *née* McCracken (d 1986); 1 step s (Rupert Stubbs b 1960), 1 step da (Imogen Stubbs b 1961); m 3, 18 Dec 1987, Sarah Elizabeth, *née* Russell; *Career* 2 Lt RA 1947–49, pilot offr RAFVR 1949–51; FO 1951–56: Br Embassy Prague 1953–54, Perm Delgn to UN 1955–56; various positions Shell Group (UK and abroad) 1956–84; chief exec London C of C and Indust 1984–91, advsr to Cncl Br C of C in Continental Europe 1992–95; Freeman City of London 1991; *Recreations* gliding, walking, opera, languages; *Style*— Anthony Platt, Esq, CBE; ✉ 114 Castelnau, Barnes, London SW13 9EU

PLATT, Prof Colin Peter Sherard; s of James Westlake Platt, CBE (d 1972), of Jersey, CI, and Veronica Norma Hope, *née* Arnold (d 1987); *b* 11 Nov 1934; *Educ* Collyers Sch Horsham Sussex, Balliol Coll Oxford (BA, MA), Univ of Leeds (PhD); *m* 1, 8 Feb 1963 (m dis), Valerie, da of Thomas Ashforth (d 1976), of Cannock, Staffs; 2 s (Miles b 9 April 1965, Theo b 20 Dec 1971), 2 da (Emma b 17 July 1963, Tabitha b 3 Jan 1967); m 2, 14 June 1996, Claire, da of Hugh Donovan; *Career* Nat Serv RN Leading Coder Special 1953–54; lectr in medieval archaeology Univ of Leeds 1962–64; Dept of History Univ of Southampton: lectr 1964–74, sr lectr 1974–79, reader 1979–83, prof of history 1983–; awarded Wolfson Prize for History for 1990; FSA 1968, FRHistS 1971; *Books* The Monastic Grange in Medieval England (1969), Medieval Southampton: The Port and Trading Community, AD 1000–1600 (1973), Excavations in Medieval Southampton 1953–1969 (1975), The English Medieval Town (1976), Medieval England: A Social History and Archaeology from the Conquest to 1600 AD (1978), The Atlas of Medieval Man (1979), The Parish Churches of Medieval England (1981), The Castle in Medieval England and Wales (1982), The Abbeys and Priories of Medieval England (1984), Medieval Britain from the Air (1984), The Traveller's Guide to Medieval England (1985), The National Trust Guide to Late Medieval and Renaissance Britain (1986), The Architecture of Medieval Britain: A Social History (1990), The Great Rebuildings of Tudor and Stuart England (1994), King Death: The Black Death and its Aftermath in Late-Medieval England (1996); *Recreations* reading fiction, visiting antiquities, entertaining friends; *Style*— Prof Colin Platt, FSA; ✉ Department of History, University of Southampton, Southampton, Hants SO17 1BJ (☎ 01703 592211, fax 01703 593939, telex 47661)

PLATT, David Andrew; s of Frank Platt, and Jean, *née* Jackson; *b* 10 June 1966; *Educ* South Chadderton Comp Sch; *m* 1992, Rachel Vaughan; *Career* professional footballer; Manchester Utd 1983–85 (no appearances), Crewe Alexandra 1985–88 (145 appearances, 60 goals), transferred for £200,000 to Aston Villa 1988–91 (over 125 appearances, over 60 goals), transferred for £5.5m to Bari Italy 1991–92, transferred for £6.5m to Juventus Italy 1992–93, transferred to Sampdoria Italy for £5.2m 1993–95, transferred to Arsenal for £4.75m 1995–; England: 3 under 21 caps, 3 B caps, 62 full caps and 27 goals (as at Jan 1997) (15 as capt), played in World Cup Italy 1990 (scoring 3 goals), played in Euro Championship Sweden 1992 (scoring 1 goal) and Euro 96, capt England March 1994–96; UEFA Cup winner with Juventus 1993, Italian Cup winner with Sampdoria 1994; PFA Player of the Year 1990; *Books* David Platt: Achieving the Goal (1995); *Recreations* horse racing, films; *Style*— David Platt, Esq; ✉ c/o Arsenal Football Club, Highbury, London N5 1BU

PLATT, David Wallace; s of Christopher Platt, of Knock, Ulster, and Susan Harriette La Nauze, *née* Wallace; *b* 13 Sept 1964; *Educ* Campbell Coll, Trinity Hall Cambridge (MA); *Career* called to the Bar Middle Temple 1987; TV presenter BBC N Ireland; chm Cambridge Univ Cons Assoc 1986, vice chm Westminster Cons Assoc, formerly political res asst and aide House of Commons and Cons Central Office; former memb Exec CPRE; *Books* Educating Our Future (1986); *Recreations* politics, skiing, architecture, conservation, Greek history; *Clubs* Carlton; *Style*— David Platt, Esq; ✉ 1 Paper Buildings, Temple, London EC4Y 7EP (☎ 0171 583 1227, fax 0171 834 8348)

PLATT, Denise; CBE (1996); da of Victor Platt (d 1980), of Cheshire, and May, *née* Keeling; *b* 21 Feb 1945; *Educ* Congleton GS for Girls, Univ Coll Cardiff (BSc Econ); *Career* social worker Middx Hosp 1968–73, sr social worker Guy's Hosp 1973–76, gp ldr Southwark Social Servs 1976–78, princ social worker Hammersmith Hosp 1978–83, dir of Social Serv London Borough Hammersmith and Fulham 1986–94 (asst dir 1983–86), under sec social servs Assoc of Metropolitan Authorities (AMA) 1994–97, head of social servs Local Government Assoc 1997–; pres Assoc of Dirs of Social Servs 1993–94, vice chair Nat Cncl for Domiciliary Care Servs until 1995, memb Advsy Gp Policy Studies Inst until 1994, memb Academic Cncl Royal Postgrad Med Sch until 1994, tstee and vice chm Nat AIDS Tst; memb: Ministerial Action Gp on AIDS 1991–93, Dept of Health Steering Gp Community Care Devpt Prog (formerly Dept of Health Caring for People Advsy Group), Cncl Central Cncl for Educn and Trg in Social Work (CCETSW); govr Nat Inst for Social Work, chair NISW Research Consultative Ctee; AIMSW 1968; *Recreations* music, watercolours, walking; *Clubs* Royal Over-Seas League; *Style*— Miss Denise Platt, CBE; ✉ 13 Hillmore Court, Belmont Hill, Lewisham, London SE13 5AZ (☎ 0181 852 9556)

PLATT, Derrick James Branscomb; OBE (1988); s of James Ernest Platt (d 1969), of Ramsgate, and Doris May, *née* Puncher (d 1981); *b* 13 Sept 1923; *Educ* Stationers' Co Sch London, Dartford GS, LSE; *m* 1972, Muriel Joan Cooke, *née* Bedman (d 1989); 2 step s (Stephen Cooke b 1943, Colin Cooke b 1947); *Career* with Balfour Williamson Ltd London 1947–52, asst sec IBE Group Ltd Slough 1952–55; T R Beckett Ltd Eastbourne (regnl newspaper publishers): sec 1955–62, fin dir 1962–72, chief exec and dep chm 1972–92; vice chm E Sussex AHA 1974–81 (memb 1972–81); chm: Eastbourne Health Authy 1981–90, Eastbourne Hosps NHS Tst 1991–93; memb Cncl Fedn of NHS Tsts 1992–93; chm: Eastbourne Assoc of Vol Servs 1972–, Community Housing and Therapy (formerly Fellowship Charitable Fndn) 1994–95, Cncl of Tstees St Wilfrid's Hospice Eastbourne 1995– (memb 1981–); Freeman City of London 1992, Liveryman Worshipful Co of Chartered Secretaries & Administrators 1992; FCIS 1958 (ACIS 1950), ATII 1958, FInstD 1961; *Recreations* gardening, music, walking; *Clubs* RAC; *Style*— Derrick Platt, Esq, OBE; ✉ Eastbourne Association of Voluntary Services, 8 Saffrons Road, Eastbourne, East Sussex BN21 1DG (☎ 01323 639373, fax 01323 410977)

PLATT, Eleanor Frances; QC (1982); er da of Dr Maurice Leon Platt (d 1966), of Sussex, and Sara, *née* Stein (d 1983); *b* 6 May 1938; *Educ* Univ of London (LLB); *m* 1963, Frederick Malcolm; 1 s (Jonathan b 1969), 1 da (Amanda b 1965); *Career* called to the Bar Gray's Inn 1960; recorder SE circuit 1982–, jt head of chambers, memb Matrimonial Causes Rule Ctee 1986–90, treas Family Law Bar Assoc 1990–95 (acting chm 1995); chm Law Parly and General Purposes Ctee Bd of Deputies of British Jews 1988–94, New London Synagogue 1994–, dep chm NHS Tbnl 1995–, legal assessor Gen Med Cncl and Gen Dental Cncl 1995–; *Recreations* the arts, travel, skiing; *Style*— Miss Eleanor Platt, QC; ✉ 1 Garden Court, Temple, London EC4Y 9BJ (☎ 0171 797 7900, fax 0171 797 7929)

PLATT, Martin Philip; s and h of Hon Prof Sir Peter Platt, 2 Bt, *qv*; *b* 9 March 1952; *m* 1971, Frances Corinne Moanna, da of Trevor Samuel Conley; 2 s, 2 da; *Style*— Martin Platt, Esq

PLATT, Norman; OBE (1985); s of Edward Turner Platt (d 1956), and Emily Jane Platt (d 1972); *b* 29 Aug 1920; *Educ* Bury GS, King's Coll Cambridge (BA); *m* 1, 1942, Diana Franklin, da of Sir Charles Travis Clay, CB (d 1975); 1 s (Tristan), 1 da (Marianna); m 2, 1963, Johanna Sigrid, da of Jesse Stewart Bishop; 1 s (Benjamin b 1965), 2 da (Rebecca b 1966, Lucinda b 1969); *Career* singer, actor, teacher; translator of: The Coronation of Poppea, Don Giovanni, Fidelio; opera prodr: L'Incoronazione di Poppea (Lisbon), Iphigenia in Tauris (Edinburgh Festival), Il Seraglio (Metz), Agrippina (Sadler's Wells), Don Giovanni (Singapore and Valencia), Peter Grimes (Bath Festival); princ: Sadler's Wells Opera 1946–48, Eng Opera Gp 1948; memb Deller Consort; fndr and artistic dir Kent Opera 1969–89, co-fndr (with Robin Jessel) The Canterbury Theatre and Festival Tst, refounded Kent Opera 1992 (artistic dir until 1996); chm Canterbury Festival Planning Ctee 1984–86; dir Acting in Opera course 1989; Hon DCL Kent 1981, Hon DMus Univ of Greenwich 1996; *Recreations* listening to music, being read to by my wife; *Style*— Norman Platt, OBE; ✉ Pembles Cross Farmhouse, Egerton, Ashford, Kent TN27 9BN (☎ 01233 756237)

PLATT, Hon Sir Peter; 2 Bt (UK 1959); s of Baron Platt (Life Peer and 1 Bt, d 1978), and Margaret Irene, *née* Cannon (d 1987); *b* 6 July 1924; *Educ* Abbotsholme Sch Derbyshire, Magdalen Coll Oxford (MA, BMus, BLitt), RCM; *m* 1948, Jean Halliday, da of late Charles Philip Brentnall, MC; 1 s (Martin), 2 da (Margaret, Katherine); *Heir* s, Martin Philip Platt, *qv*; *Career* served WWII RNVR (despatches), ret 1989; prof of music: Univ of Otago NZ 1957–75, Univ of Sydney 1975–89 (emeritus prof 1990); memb bd The Australian Music Centre; Hon FGSM 1973, Hon MMus Univ of Sydney 1990, Hon Life Memb The Musicological Soc of Australia; *Style*— The Hon Sir Peter Platt, Bt; ✉ 1 Ellison Place, Pymble, NSW 2073, Australia (☎ 00 612 449 4372, fax 00 612 660 6093)

PLATT, Richard Andrew; *b* 26 May 1947; *Educ* Samuel Pepys Secdy Modern Sch Brockley; *m* Jocelyn; 3 s (Stephen b 28 Aug 1977, James b 1 April 1980, Nicholas b 6 Oct 1983), 2 da (Rebecca b 29 May 1988, Georgin b 6 Jan 1994); *Career* media buyer Masius Wynne Williams 1970–76, dep md Tape Consultancy 1976–82, asst programmer Network 10 Sydney 1982–84, head of programming Sky Channel 1984–88, dir of progs Maxwell Entertainment 1988–89, controller of progs Scansat 1989–92; Meridian Television: controller of programming 1992–93, controller of bdcasting 1993–, dir 1994–; dir of bdcasting MAI Media 1995–, dir ITFC Ltd 1995–, dir of ITV bdcasting United Broadcast Entertainment 1996–; *Recreations* soccer, photography, cinema, theatre; *Style*— Richard Platt, Esq; ✉ Meridian Broadcasting Ltd, Television Centre, Northam Road, Southampton SO2 0TA (☎ 01703 222555)

PLATT, Stephen; s of Kenneth Norman Platt, of Stoke-on-Trent, and Joyce, *née* Pritchard; *b* 29 Sept 1954; *Educ* Longton HS Stoke-on-Trent, Wade Deacon Sch Widnes, LSE (BSc Econ); *partner*, Anna Elizabeth Sutton; 1 da by prev partner (Rachel Louise b 22 Sept 1977); *Career* teacher Moss Brook Special Sch 1972–73, dir Self Help Housing Resource Library 1977–79, co-ordinator Islington Community Housing 1979–83, various writing and journalism 1983–85, ed Roof 1986, news ed New Society 1986–87 (actg ed 1988); ed: Midweek 1988–89, Enjoying the Countryside 1989–, New Statesman and Society 1990–96; *Recreations* countryside, walking, football, frogs and Paddington Bear; *Clubs* Red Rose, Port Vale; *Style*— Stephen Platt, Esq; ✉ 46 Tufnell Park Road, London N7 0DT (☎ 0171 263 4185); New Statesman and Society, Foundation House, Perseverance Works, 38 Kingsland Road, London E2 8DQ (☎ 0171 739 3211)

PLATT OF WRITTLE, Baroness (Life Peer UK 1981), of Writtle, Co Essex; Beryl Catherine Platt; CBE (1978), DL (Essex 1983); da of Ernest Myatt (d 1950); *b* 18 April 1923; *Educ* Westcliff HS for Girls, Girton Coll Cambridge (MA); *m* 1949, Stewart Sydney Platt, s of Sydney Rowland Platt (d 1946); 1 s (Hon Roland Francis b 1951), 1 da (Hon Victoria Catherine (Hon Mrs Davies) b 1953); *Career* tech asst Hawker Aircraft Ltd 1943–46, BEA 1946–49; memb Chelmsford RDC 1959–74; Essex CC: elected 1965, alderman 1969–74, chm Educn Ctee 1971–80, chm Further Educn Sub-Ctee 1969–71, vice chm 1980–83, memb Advsy Ctee on Women's Employment 1984–88; chm Equal Opportunities Cmmn 1983–88; memb House of Lords Select Ctee: on Murder and Life Imprisonment 1988–89, on Sci and Technol 1982–85 and 1990–94; vice pres Parly Sci Ctee 1996–; memb Ct: Univ of Essex 1968–, City Univ 1968–78, Brunel Univ 1985–92, Cranfield Inst of Technol 1989–; memb: Cncl City and Guilds of London Inst 1974–95, Univ of Cambridge Appts Bd 1975–79; vice pres UMIST 1985–92, chllr Univ of Middlesex 1993–; memb: Engrg Cncl 1982–90, Cncl Royal Soc of Arts 1983–88, Cncl Careers Res and Advsy Ctee 1983–93, Engrg Trg Authy 1990–92, Ctee on the Public Understanding of Sci 1990–93, Cncl Fndn for Sci and Technol 1991–, Meteorological Advsy Ctee 1992– (chm 1995–); pres: Nat Soc for Clean Air and Environmental Protection 1991–93, Pipeline Industries Guild 1994; vice pres Assoc of CCs 1992–; non-exec dir British Gas plc 1988–94, dir Smallpiece Tst 1989–94 (fell 1988); Freeman City of London 1988, Liveryman Worshipful Co of Engrs 1988 (memb Ct of Assts 1996–); hon fell: Women's Engrg Soc 1988, Girton Coll Cambridge, Univ of Glamorgan (formerly Poly of Wales), Manchester Metropolitan Univ (formerly Poly of Manchester), UMIST 1992; Hon Insignia Award City and Guilds London Inst 1988; Hon LLD Univ of Cambridge 1988, Hon DTech Loughborough Univ; Hon DSc: Cranfield Inst, City Univ, Nottingham Trent Univ; Hon DUniv: Univ of Salford, Open Univ, Univ of Bradford (Eng), Univ of Essex, Brunel Univ (Tech), Univ of Middlesex 1993; Hon FCP, Hon FIMechE, Hon FIStructE 1991, Hon FICE 1991, Hon FRAeS 1994; Eur Ing, FEANI 1988, FEng 1987, FRSA, FITD, FIGasE; *Recreations* reading, swimming for pleasure, cooking, sailing (yacht 'Corydalis'); *Clubs* United Oxford and Cambridge Univ; *Style*— The Rt Hon the Baroness Platt of Writtle, CBE, DL, FEng; ✉ House of Lords, London SW1

PLATTEN, Very Rev Stephen George; s of Capt George Henry Platten, RM (d 1969), of Enfield, Middx, and Marjory Agnes, *née* Sheward; *b* 17 May 1947; *Educ* Stationers' Co's Sch, Univ of London (BEd), Trinity Coll Oxford (DipTheol), Cuddesdon Theol Coll; *m* 1 April 1972, Rosslie, da of David Robert Thompson, of Newbury, Berks; 2 s (Aidan Stephen George b 1976, Gregory Austin David b 1978); *Career* with Shell International Petroleum Co Ltd 1966–68; ordained: deacon 1975, priest 1976; asst curate St Andrew Headington Oxford 1975–78, chaplain and tutor Lincoln Theol Coll 1978–82, diocesan dir of ordinands and canon residentiary Portsmouth Cathedral 1983–89, dir of post-ordination trg and continuing ministerial educn Dio of Portsmouth 1984–89, hon canon Canterbury Cathedral 1990–95, Archbishop of Canterbury's sec for ecumenical affairs 1990–95, anglican sec Anglican-RC International Cmmn (II) 1990–95, dean of Norwich 1995–; min provincial Euro Province 3 Order Soc of St Francis 1991–96; chm Soc for Study of Christian Ethics 1983–88, guestmaster Nikaean Club 1990–95, dir SCM Press 1990–; *Books* Deacons in the Ministry of the Church (contrib, 1987), Ethics - Our Choices (sr ed, 1989), Say One for Me (contrib, ed A W Carr, 1992), Pilgrims (1996), Spirit and Tradition: An Essay on Change (with George Pattison, 1996), Augustine's

Legacy: Authority and Leadership in Anglicanism (1997), New Soundings (ed with Graham James and Andrew Chandler, 1997); author of contribs to theol and educnl jls; *Recreations* reading, music, walking, Northumberland; *Clubs* Athenaeum; *Style*— The Very Rev Stephen Platten; ✉ The Deanery, The Close, Norwich NR1 4EG (☎ 01603 219483, fax 01603 766032)

PLATTS, Graham John; s of Joseph Henry Platts (d 1992), and Lois, *née* Brown; *b* 1 June 1950; *Educ* Christ's Coll Finchley, Portsmouth Poly (BSc); *m* 13 Sept 1975, Sandra Doreen, da of Kenneth Sidney Dark; 1 da (Deborah Suzanne b 16 Nov 1979), 1 s (Christopher David b 25 March 1981); *Career* supervisor Farrow Middleton & Co CAs 1977–78 (trainee 1971–75); Dearden Farrow (following merger): mangr 1979–81, sr mangr 1981–85, managing ptnr Poole office 1986–87 (ptnr 1985); BDO Stoy Hayward (following merger): managing ptnr Poole office 1987–90, regnl managing ptnr 1990–; memb: Dorset C of C and Indust, CBI; FCA 1980 (ACA 1975); *Recreations* most sports especially tennis, theatre, films, cycling, reading; *Style*— Graham Platts, Esq; ✉ 17 Heath Road, St Leonards, Ringwood, Hants BH24 2PZ (☎ 01425 475355); BDO Stoy Hayward, Old Orchard, 39–61 High Street, Poole, Dorset BH15 1AE (☎ 01202 681221, fax 01202 687211, car 0860 747087)

PLATTS, Nigel Landsbrough; s of Francis Arthur Platts, and Mabel Landsbrough, *née* Williams; *b* 20 Oct 1945; *Educ* Whitgift Sch, Oriel Coll Oxford (MA); *m* 26 July 1969, Anne Christine, da of Samuel Walker; 1 s (Thomas b 22 May 1978), 2 da (Philippa b 8 Feb 1972, Hannah b 8 April 1980); *Career* CA 1970; KPMG (formerly Peat Marwick Mitchell & Co then KPMG Peat Marwick): successively articled clerk, sr mangr, ptnr (managing ptnr Int Markets 1992–95); FCA; *Recreations* collecting books, watching rugby, playing, coaching and organising cricket; *Clubs* Naval & Military; *Style*— Nigel Platts, Esq; ✉ KPMG, 1 Puddle Dock, Blackfriars, London EC4V 3PD (☎ 0171 311 6098, fax 0171 311 5860)

PLATTS-MILLS, John Faithful Fortescue; QC (1964); s of John F W Mills, of NZ, and Dr Daisy Platts-Mills; *b* 4 Oct 1906; *Educ* Nelson Coll NZ, Victoria Univ NZ (Rhodes scholar, LLM (Double First), 4 Blues), Balliol Coll Oxford (MA (First), BCL); *m* 1936, Janet Katherine Cree (d 1992); 6 s (Timothy, Jonathan (Jo) Platts-Mills, *qv*, Thomas, Barney, Benjamin, Mark Platts-Mills, QC, *qv*); *Career* served WWII, pilot offr RAF; collier 1944–45; called to the Bar NZ 1928, Inner Temple 1932, appeared in 20 foreign jurisdictions; bencher Inner Temple 1970; MP and borough cncllr: (Lab) Finsbury 1945–48, (Lab Ind) Finsbury 1948–50; pres: Haldane Soc of Socialist Lawyers, Soc for Cultural Rels with USSR; vice pres Int Assoc of Democratic Lawyers; Liveryman Worshipful Co of Ironmongers, common councilman City of London 1995–; memb: TGWU, NUM; *Clubs* Athenaeum, Vincent's (Oxford), Leander; *Style*— John Platts-Mills, Esq, QC; ✉ Cloisters, Temple, London EC4Y 7AA (☎ 0171 583 0303, fax 0171 583 5597)

PLATTS-MILLS, Jonathan Lewis (Jo); s of John Faithful Fortescue Platts-Mills, *qv*, and Janet Katherine, *née* Cree (d 1992); bro of Mark Platt-Mills, QC, *qv*; *b* 11 March 1939; *Educ* Bryanston (capt rowing 1st eight), Balliol Coll Oxford (BA, head of Torpids); *m* 21 Nov 1966, Marioara Jercan; 1 s (Thomas Tiberius b 17 March 1968), 1 da (Ioana Patricia b 19 Nov 1970); *Career* graduate apprentice Davy United Sheffield 1960–62, plate mill project engr Romania 1965–67, cold rolling mill project mangr Algeria 1969–73, project mangr Humphreys and Glasgow London 1973–76; Lonrho plc gp: various appts incl sr exec project mangr Volkswagen UK HQ, sugar mills in Benin, re-estab Lonrho ops in Tanzania, started Lonrho business in USSR 1989, assoc dir 1990–91, main bd dir i/c new projects, CIS, Zaire, Angola and Belgium 1991–; Yeoman Worshipful Co of Ironmongers; FIMechE 1992; *Recreations* hill walking, occasional rowing and sailing; *Clubs* Athenaeum, Leander (Henley); *Style*— Jo Platts-Mills, Esq; ✉ 10 Warwick Road, Ealing, London W5 3XJ (☎ 0181 579 3293); Lonrho plc, 4 Grosvenor Place, London SW1 7DL (☎ 0171 201 6000, fax 0171 201 6100)

PLATTS-MILLS, Mark Fortescue; QC (1995); s of John Faithful Fortescue Platts-Mills, *qv*, and Janet Katherine, *née* Cree (d 1992); bro of Jonathan (Jo) Platts-Mills, *qv*; *b* 17 Jan 1951; *Educ* Bryanston, Balliol Coll Oxford (BA); *m* 1982, Dr Juliet Anne Britton; 1 s (John Mark Fortescue b 1987); *Career* called to the Bar Inner Temple 1974; memb Lincoln's Inn; *Recreations* sailing, hockey, gardening; *Style*— Mark Platts-Mills, Esq, QC; ✉ 8 New Square, Lincoln's Inn, London WC2A 3QP (☎ 0171 405 4321)

PLAYFAIR, Sir Edward Wilder; KCB (1957, CB 1949); s of late Dr Ernest Playfair; *b* 17 May 1909; *Educ* Eton, King's Coll Cambridge; *m* 1941, Dr Mary Lois Rae; 3 da; *Career* serv Treasy 1934–46 and 1947–56, control office Germany and Austria 1946–47, perm under sec of state for War 1956–59, perm sec MOD 1960–61; chm Int Computers and Tabulators Ltd 1961–65; tstee National Gallery 1967–74 (chm 1972–74), fell Imperial Coll of Science and Technol 1972; hon fell: UCL 1969, King's Coll Cambridge 1986; Hon FBCS; *Clubs* Brooks's; *Style*— Sir Edward Playfair, KCB; ✉ 62 Coniger Rd, London SW6 3TA (☎ 0171 736 3194)

PLAYFORD, Jonathan Richard; QC (1982); s of Maj Cecil Roche Bullen Playford (d 1977), of London, and Euphrasia Joan, *née* Cox; *b* 6 Aug 1940; *Educ* Eton, Univ of London (LLB); *m* 1978, Jill Margaret, da of William Herbert Dunlop, MBE (d 1982), of Doonside, Ayr; 1 s (Nicholas b 1981), 1 da (Fiona b 1985); *Career* called to the Bar Inner Temple 1962, bencher 1991, recorder of the Crown Ct 1985–; memb Criminal Injuries Compensation Bd 1995–; *Recreations* music, country pursuits; *Clubs* Garrick; *Style*— Jonathan Playford, Esq, QC; ✉ 2 Harcourt Buildings, Temple EC4Y 9DB (☎ 0171 583 9020)

PLAZAS, Mary; da of Francisco Plazas, and Albertina, *née* de Oliveira; *b* 9 Sept 1966; *Educ* RNCM (dip professional performance, GMus (Hons), Alexander Young Award, Curtis Gold Medal, Claire Croiza Prize for French Song), Nat Opera Studio (The Friends of Covent Garden scholarship, Peter Moores Fndn Award, Peter Stuyvesant Award); *Career* soprano; studied with Ava June RNCM, Eric Tappy Geneva 1994; operatic debut ENO 1992; co princ ENO 1995–; *Performances* solo recitals incl: Wigmore Hall, Purcell Room, Birmingham Town Hall, The Royal Exchange Theatre Manchester, Herbert von Karajan Centre Vienna; festivals incl: Cheltenham Festival, Aldeburgh Festival, Chester Festival 1995; roles incl: The Voice from Heaven in Verdi's Don Carlos (ENO 1992, Royal Opera BBC Proms 1996), Peep Bo in Mikado (ENO), Frasquita in Carmen (ENO), title role in The Cunning Little Vixen (ENO), Gypsy in Roberto Gerhard's The Duenna (Opera North), Susanna in Le Nozze di Figaro (Opera North), Tebaldo in Don Carlos (Opera North), Elisetta in Il Matrimonio Segreto (Opera North), Adina (English Touring Opera), Anne Truelove (Opera Factory, London, Birmingham and Lisbon), Poulenc's La Voix Humaine (Aix-en-Provence, RNCM), Nannetta in Falstaff (Aldeburgh Festival), Despina (Mid-Wales Opera), Adele and Norina in Don Pasquale (Clonter Opera), Echo in Ariadne auf Naxos (Garsington Opera), Madame Silvaklang in Die Schauspieldirektor (Garsington Opera), title role in Cesti's Le Disgrazie d'Amore (Batignano), Marzelline in Fidelio (ENO), Mimi in La Bohème (ENO), Leila in The Pearl Fishers (ENO), second angel in Pfitzner's Palestrina (Royal Opera House); concerts incl: Haydn's Creation (conducted by Sir David Willcocks, Royal Albert Hall), Tippett's A Child of our Time (Royal Festival Hall), Handel's Messiah (with Ulster Orch conducted by John Lubbock), Mozart Concert Arias, J Strauss's Voices of Spring (with Hallé Orch conducted by Kent Nagano); *Television* Le Nozze di Figaro (Opera Factory prodn for Channel 4), First Enchantress in Dido and Aeneas (conducted by Richard Hickox, BBC Television, also recorded for Chandos); *Recordings* Mercadante's Emma d'Antiocchia (A Hundred Years of Italian Opera/Opera Rara), Pacini's Maria d'Ingilterra (Opera Rara with Philharmonia under David Parry); *Awards* winner Nat Fedn Music Socs/Esso Award for Young Singers 1989, Isobel Baille Performance Award 1990, Kathleen Ferrier Memorial Scholarship 1991; *Recreations* cinema, tennis, cross stitch, listening to Radio 2, meeting friends, godchildren; *Style*— Ms Mary Plazas; ✉ c/o Owen/White Management, 14 Nightingale Lane, London N8 7QU (☎ 0181 340 9571, fax 0181 340 4056)

PLEAT, David Jonathon; *b* 15 Jan 1945; *Educ* Mundella GS Nottingham; *m* 14 June 1969, Maureen, *née* Brown; 1 s (Jonathon b 8 Oct 1970), 1 da (Joanne b 26 April 1973); *Career* professional football manager; player: debut Nottingham Forest v Cardiff 1962 (youngest debutant at time aged 17), transferred to Luton Town for a fee of £8,000 1964, Shrewsbury Town 1967–68, Exeter City 1968–70 (PFA rep 1967–70), Peterborough Utd 1970–71; mangr: Nuneaton 1971–74 (also player), Luton Town 1978–86 (coach 1975–78) and 1991–95, Tottenham Hotspur 1986–87, Leicester City 1987–91, Sheffield Wednesday 1995–; England: 5 schoolboy caps 1959–60, youth caps 1961–63 (memb World Cup Youth Winner's Squad 1963); FA full coaching award 1968; Div 2 Championship Luton Town 1982, FA Cup runners-up Tottenham Hotspur v Coventry City 1987; various Bells Mangr of the Month Awards, Sportsman of the Year award Canon Football League 1983, mangr Endsleigh League v Italian League (3–2) 1995; commentator and analyst: ITV 1983–89, Sky TV 1990, BBC Radio 2 and 5, covered World Cup Mexico 1986, Italy 1990 and USA 1994 (for Radio 5), European Championships 1996 (for BBC TV); judge Barclays performance of the week award, memb Football League Exec Staff Assoc 1982– (dep chm 1984); contrib football articles: Inside Football 1965–68, Luton News 1978–86, Sports Argus Birmingham 1985–87, Leicester Mercury 1988–90, Daily and Sunday Telegraph (currently); *Style*— David Pleat, Esq; ✉ Sheffield Wednesday FC, Hillsborough, Sheffield S6 1SW (☎ 0114 221 2122)

PLEDGE, Michael; s of Frederick Herbert Pledge, of Southend, Essex, and Marjorie Evelyn, *née* Abbott (d 1978); *b* 26 May 1946; *Educ* Westcliff HS for Boys; *m* 16 June 1973, Gillian Sara; 2 s (Andrew b 25 Feb 1977, David b 10 Nov 1982), 1 da (Julie b 20 Sept 1974); *Career* CA; Spicer & Pegler: articled 1964–68, qualified 1968, remained until 1971; audit sr Johannesburg Peat Marwick Mitchell 1971–73, mgmnt accountant Cassell Collier MacMillan (publishers) 1973–74, fin accountant Thermos Ltd Brentwood 1974–75; Cape Industries Ltd: ops accountant Cape Contracts Ltd 1975–78, fin dir and co sec Cape Contracts International Ltd 1978–80; fin dir Ogilvy & Mather PR Ltd 1980–89, Euro fin dir Burson Marsteller Ltd 1989–; FCA (ACA 1968); *Recreations* golf, tennis, bridge; *Clubs* Welwyn Garden City Golf; *Style*— Michael Pledge, Esq; ✉ Burson-Marsteller Ltd, 24–28 Bloomsbury Way, London WC1A 2PX (☎ 0171 831 6262)

PLEETH, William; OBE (1989); s of John Pleeth, né Plicht (d 1973), of Warsaw, and Edith, *née* Gold (d 1971); *b* 12 Jan 1916; *Educ* Leipzig Conservatoire Germany; *m* 28 Jan 1944, (Alice) Margaret, da of Frank Leonard Good; 1 s (Anthony Michael b 1948), 1 da (Janet Elizabeth b 1946); *Career* concert cellist until 1980; debut in Leipzig 1931, London debut 1933; prof of cello Guildhall Sch of Music 1948–78; visiting prof: Menuhin Sch 1981–, Royal Coll of Music 1986–; frequent broadcasts and recordings 1933–80; FGSM 1952 (emeritus 1978), FRCM 1988; *Books* Cello (1982); *Recreations* cooking, researching antiques, reading; *Style*— William Pleeth, Esq, OBE

PLEMING, Nigel Peter; QC (1992); s of Rev Percy Francis Pleming (d 1978), of Lincolnshire, and Cynthia Myra, *née* Cope, now Mrs Tuxworth; *b* 13 March 1946; *Educ* Tupton Hall GS Clay Cross Derby, King Edward VI GS Spilsby Lincs, Liverpool Coll of Commerce, Kingston Poly (LLB), UCL (LLM); *m* 22 Sept 1979, Evelyn Carol Joan, *née* Hoffmann; 2 da (Joanna b 10 April 1985, Katherine b 11 Jan 1989), 1 s (William b 29 Oct 1986); *Career* lectr in law 1969–73, called to the Bar Inner Temple 1971, in practice at the Bar 1973–; *Recreations* cricket, chess, guitar; *Clubs* Nat Liberal; *Style*— Nigel Pleming, Esq, QC; ✉ 39 Essex Street, London WC2R 3AT (☎ 0171 583 1111, fax 0171 353 3978)

PLENDER, (William) John Turner; s of William Plender (d 1977), of Wiltshire, and Avril Maud, *née* Turnbull; *b* 9 May 1945; *Educ* Downside, Oriel Coll Oxford; *m* (m dis 1989), Sophia Mary, *née* Crombie; 1 s, 2 da; *Career* CA and writer; Deloitte Plender Griffiths & Co 1967–70, Investors' Chronicle 1970–71, The Times 1972–74, fin ed The Economist 1974–79, FCO 1980–81, freelance journalist, publisher and broadcaster (leader writer Financial Times) 1982–; chm Pensions Investment Research Consultants Ltd (PIRC) 1992–; FCA 1970; *Books* That's The Way The Money Goes (1981), The Square Mile (with Paul Wallace, 1985), A Stake In The Future (1997); *Clubs* Travellers'; *Style*— John Plender, Esq; ✉ Financial Times, 1 Southwark Bridge, London SE1 9HL (☎ 0171 873 3000, fax 0171 873 3194)

PLENDER, Richard Owen; QC (1989); s of George Plender, and Louise Mary, *née* Savage; *b* 9 Oct 1945; *Educ* Dulwich, Queens' Coll Cambridge (BA, LLB, LLD, Rebecca Squire Prize), Univ of Illinois (LLM, JSD, Coll of Law Prize), Univ of Sheffield (PhD); *m* 16 Dec 1978, Patricia Clare, da of Wing Cdr John Lawson Ward (d 1974); 2 da (Sophie Clare b 31 Aug 1986, Amy Louise b 30 May 1991); *Career* called to the Bar Inner Temple 1974 (Berridale Keith prize); legal advsr UN High Cmmr for Refugees 1976–78, referendaire Euro Ct 1980–83; dir Centre of Euro Law Kings Coll London 1988–90, prof assoc Univ of Paris II; hon sr memb Robinson Coll Cambridge, hon visiting prof City Univ; *Books* International Migration Law (1972, 2 edn 1988), Fundamental Rights (1973), Cases and Materials on the Law of the European Communities (1980, 3 edn 1993), A Practical Introduction to European Community Law (1980), Introduccion al Derecho Comunitario (1985), Basic Documents on International Migration Law (1988, 2 edn 1996), Legal History and Comparative Law (1990), The European Contracts Convention - The Rome Convention on the Choice of Law for Contracts (1991), The European Courts Practice and Precedents (gen ed and contrib, 1996); *Recreations* classical music, writing light verse; *Style*— Richard Plender, Esq, QC; ✉ 20 Essex Street, London WC2R 3AL (☎ 0171 583 9294, fax 0171 583 1341, telex 893468 SXCORT G)

PLENDERLEITH, Ian; s of Raymond William Plenderleith, and Louise Helen, *née* Martin; *b* 27 Sept 1943; *Educ* King Edward's Sch Birmingham, Christ Church Oxford (MA), Columbia Business Sch NY (MBA, Beta Gamma Sigma medal); *m* 1 April 1967, Kristina Mary, da of John Hardy Bentley, OBE (d 1980); 1 s (Giles b 1972), 2 da (Melanie b 1969, Cressida b 1976); *Career* Bank of England: joined 1965, seconded as tech asst to UK Exec Dir International Monetary Washington DC 1972–74, private sec to Govr 1976–79, alternate dir Euro Investment Bank 1980–86, head Gilt Edged Div 1982–90, govt broker 1989–, assoc dir i/c market operations 1990–94, exec dir i/c monetary operations 1994–, alternate dir Bank for International Settlements Basle 1994–; dir London Stock Exchange 1989–; chm: Stock Borrowing and Lending Ctee 1990–95, Editorial Bd OECD Study on Debt Mgmnt 1990–93; co-chm Government Borrowers Forum 1991–94; hon sec Tillington CC; memb: Advsy Bd Inst of Archaeology Devpt Tst UCL 1987–, Euro Bd of Overseers Columbia Business Sch 1991–, Legal Risk Review Ctee 1991–92, Fin Law Panel 1992–94, Fundraising Planning Gp St Bartholomew's Hosp 1992–94, Cncl Br Museum Soc 1993–; Liveryman Worshipful Co of Innholders 1977; fell Assoc of Corp Treasurers 1989; *Recreations* archaeology, theatre, cricket, skiing; *Clubs* Tillington CC; *Style*— Ian Plenderleith, Esq; ✉ Bank of England, London EC2R 8AH (☎ 0171 601 4444)

PLESS, Mary, Princess of; (Dorothea) Mary Elizabeth; da of Lt-Col Richard George Edward Minchin (d 1985), of Busherstown, Co Offaly and Annagh, Co Tipperary, and Elizabeth Eve, *née* McKerrell-Brown (d 1985); *Educ* St Leonards Sch St Andrews;

m 23 July 1958 (m dis 1971), Henry, Prince of Pless (d 1984), eld s of Hans Heinrich XV, 3 Prince of Pless, Imperial Count of Hochberg by his 1 w Daisy, *née* Cornwallis-West; *Recreations* theatre, animal life; *Style*— Mary, Princess of Pless; ✉ 14 Campden House, Sheffield Terrace, London W8

PLEWES, Jeremy John Lawrence; s of Lawrence William Plewes, CBE, of Kensworth, Beds, and Faith Sybil Etrenne, *née* Downing; *b* 5 Sept 1940; *Educ* Marlborough, ChCh Oxford (MA, BM BCh); *m* 12 Feb 1966, Jenna Rose, da of Lt Cdr Vernon Judge Glassborow (d 1971), of Yelverton, Devon; 1 da (Caryl Robin b 1969), 1 s (Andrew Burns b 1970); *Career* conslt orthopaedic surgn South Birmingham Health Authy 1982–, sr clinical lectr in surgery Univ of Birmingham 1982–; FRCS, FRSM; *Recreations* photography, oenology, sailing; *Style*— Jeremy Plewes, Esq; ✉ Selvas Cottage, Withybed Green, Alvechurch, Worcs B48 7PR (☎ 0121 445 1624); 81 Harborne Rd, Edgbaston, Birmingham B15 3HG; Royal Orthopaedic Hospital, Birmingham B31 2AP (☎ 0121 627 1627)

PLEWS, Nigel Trevor; s of Isaac Plews (d 1975), of Nottingham, and Minnie, *née* Stanley (d 1968); *b* 5 Sept 1934; *Educ* Mundella GS Nottingham; *m* 24 Sept 1956, Margaret Mary, da of Francis George Ley; 1 s (Douglas b 21 April 1964), 1 da (Elaine b 24 Feb 1961); *Career* cricket umpire; former club and league cricketer Nottinghamshire; appointed to: First Class Cricket Umpires List 1982, Int Panel 1986, Test Panel 1988; umpire: 11 Test Matches (England v West Indies Old Trafford 1988, England v Australia Lords and Trent Bridge 1989, England v India Lords and The Oval 1990, England v Australia Headingly 1993, England v New Zealand Lords 1994, India v West Indies Nagpur 1994, New Zealand v West Indies Christchurch 1995, England v West Indies Trent Bridge 1995, Pakistan v Sri Lanka Faisalabad 1995), 16 One Day Internationals (England v New Zealand Old Trafford 1986, England v West Indies Lords 1988, England v Australia Lords 1989, England v New Zealand Headingly 1990, England v New Zealand Edgbaston 1994, England v West Indies Trent Bridge 1995, India v Bangladesh Sharjah 1995, Sri Lank v Bangladesh Sharjah 1995, Pakistan b Bangladesh Sharjah 1995, India v Sri Lanka Sharjah 1995, India v Sri Lanka (Asia Cup Final) Sharjah 1995, Pakistan v Sri Lanka Sharjah 1995, Pakistan v West Indies Sharjah 1995, Sri Lanka v West Indies Sharjah 1995, Pakistan v Sri Lanka Sharjah 1995, England v Pakistan Old Trafford 1996), 5 Cup Finals Lords (1988, 1989, 1990, 1994 and 1995); memb MCC (toured as umpire with MCC in 1991 in Namibia); appointed one of four English umpires to the first National Grid Int Cricket Umpires Panel to officiate in test matches abroad 1994–96, ret from int cricket; former Detective Sgt Company Fraud Squad Nottingham City Police Force; *Recreations* hill walking, reading, travel; *Style*— Nigel Plews, Esq

PLIATZKY, Sir Leo; KCB (1977, CB 1972); s of Nathan Pliatzky; *b* 1919; *Educ* Manchester GS, City of London Sch, CCC Oxford (hon fell); *m* 1948, Marian Jean (d 1979), da of late Capt James Elias, MN; 1 s, 1 da; *Career* Sgt REME and Capt RAOC in ME and Central Med 1940–45 (despatches); second perm sec Treasy 1976–77, perm sec Dept of Trade 1977–79, ret, retained for special duties 1979–80; non-exec dir: BA 1980–85, Assoc Communications Corp plc 1980–82, Central Independent TV 1981–89, Ultramar plc 1981–90; visiting prof City Univ 1980–84, assoc fell LSE 1982–85, treas History of Parl Tst 1985–94 (currently tstee), govr Charles Dickens Primary Sch 1995; hon fell CCC Oxford 1980; Hon DLitt Salford 1983; *Books* Getting and Spending: Whitehall memoirs (revised edn 1984), Paying and Choosing - The Intelligent Person's Guide to the Mixed Economy (1985), The Treasury Under Mrs Thatcher (1989); *Clubs* Reform; *Style*— Sir Leo Pliatzky, KCB; ✉ 27 River Ct, Upper Ground, London SE1 9PE (☎ 0171 928 3667)

PLOUVIEZ, Peter William; s of Charles Plouviez; *b* 30 July 1931; *Educ* Sir George Monoux GS, Hasting GS; *m* 1978, Alison Dorothy Macrae; 2 da (by former m); *Career* gen sec Br Actors' Equity Assoc 1974–91; chm: Radio and TV Safeguards Ctee 1974–91, Festival of Br Theatre 1983–91; cncllr St Pancras 1962–65, Parly candidate (Lab) St Marylebone By-Election 1963; vice chm Confedn of Entertainment Unions 1974–91, vice pres Int Fedn of Actors 1989–92, treas Entertainment Charities Fund, memb Theatres Tst (dep chm 1992–); chm: Fedn of Entertainment Unions 1991, Nat Cncl for Drama Training 1991–, Equity Tst Fund 1991–, Dancers Resettlement Tst; *Style*— Peter Plouviez, Esq; ✉ National Council for Drama Training, 5 Tavistock Place, London WC1H 9SN (☎ 0171 387 3650)

PLOWDEN, Hon Anna Bridget; CBE (1997); da of Baron Plowden (Life Peer); *b* 1938; *Educ* New Hall Chelmsford, Inst of Archaeology Univ of London; *Career* md Plowden & Smith Ltd, chm Art Services Ltd, dir Recollections Ltd 1986–93; chm Conservation Ctee Crafts Cncl 1979–83, memb Ctee Conservation Unit Museums and Galleries Cmmn, tstee: V&A Museum, Edward James Fndn; memb Cncl Royal Warrant Holders Assoc, fell Int Inst for Conservation of Historic and Artistic Works; *Books* Looking after Antiques (co-author, 1987); *Style*— The Hon Anna Plowden, CBE; ✉ Plowden & Smith Ltd, 190 St Ann's Hill, London SW18 2RT (☎ 0181 874 4005, fax 0181 874 7248)

PLOWDEN, Baroness; Bridget Horatia; *née* Richmond; DBE (1972); da of late Adm Sir Herbert Richmond, KCB (2 s of Sir William Richmond, KCB), and Elsa Florence, 2 da of Sir Hugh Bell, 2 Bt, CB, JP, DL, by his 2 w Florence, DBE, JP, da of Sir Joseph Olliffe; *Educ* Downe House; *m* 1933, Baron Plowden, *qv*; 2 s, 2 da; *Career* dir Trust Houses Forte Ltd 1961–72; govr and vice chm BBC 1970–75, chm IBA 1975–80; vice chm ILEA Schools Sub-Ctee 1967–70; Advsy Ctee for the Educn of Romany and Other Travellers: memb 1969–, chm 1969–84, pres 1984; pres: Pre-School Playgroups Assoc 1972–82 (vice pres 1982–), Nat Assoc of Adult Educn 1980–88, Nat Marriage Guidance Cncl (RELATE) 1983–93, Voluntary Orgn Liaison Cncl for Under-Fives 1983– (chm 1974–83), Br Accreditation Cncl for Independent Further and Higher Educn 1985–90; memb Nat Theatre Bd 1976–88, pres Coll of Preceptors 1987–94 (vice pres 1983–87), JP Inner London Area Juvenile Panel 1962–71; Liveryman Worshipful Co of Goldsmiths 1979, Hon LLD: Univ of Leicester 1968, Univ of Reading 1970, Univ of London 1976; Hon DLitt Loughborough Univ 1976, DUniv Open Univ 1974; FRTS 1980; *Style*— The Rt Hon the Lady Plowden, DBE; ✉ Martels Manor, Dunmow, Essex (☎ 01371 872141)

PLOWDEN, Baron (Life Peer UK 1959), of Plowden, Co Shropshire; Edwin Noel Plowden; GBE (1987, KBE 1946), KCB (1951); s of late Roger H Plowden; *b* 6 Jan 1907; *Educ* Switzerland, Pembroke Coll Cambridge; *m* 1933, Bridget Horatia (*see* Plowden, Baroness); 2 s, 2 da; *Career* sits as Independent in House of Lords; temp civil servant Miny of Econ Warfare 1939–40, Miny Aircraft Prodn 1940–46 (chief exec and memb Aircraft Supply Cncl 1945–46), chief planning offr and chm Econ Planning Bd, HM Treasy 1947–53, vice chm Temp Cncl Ctee of NATO 1951–52; chm: UKAEA 1954–59, various Ctees of Inquiry 1959–79, Tube Investments Ltd 1963–76 (pres 1976–90), London Graduate Sch of Business Studies 1964–76 (pres 1976–90), Equity Capital for Indust Ltd 1976–82, Police Complaints Bd 1976–81, Top Salaries Review Body 1981–89 (memb 1977–81); independent chm Police Negotiating Bd 1979–82; memb: Ford Euro Advsy Cncl 1976–83, Engrg Industs Cncl 1976, Int Advsy Bd Southeast Bank NA 1982–86; chm CBI Companies Ctee 1976–80, vice chm President's Ctee CBI 1977–80; visiting fell Nuffield Coll Oxford 1956–64, hon fell Pembroke Coll Cambridge 1958; Hon DSc Pennsylvania State Univ 1958, Hon DSc Aston 1972, Hon DLitt Loughborough 1976; *Books* An Industrialist in the Treasury: The Post War Years; *Style*— The Rt Hon the Lord Plowden, GBE, KCB; ✉ Martels Manor, Dunmow, Essex (☎ 01371 872141)

PLOWDEN, Hon Francis John; s of Baron Plowden (Life Peer); *b* 1945; *Educ* Eton, Trinity Coll Cambridge; *m* 1984, Geraldine Wickman, er da of late Gerald Wickman, of Orton Longueville, Peterborough; 1 s (George Frederick Wickman b 25 May 1995); *Career* CA 1969; ptnr Coopers and Lybrand (Nigeria) 1976–79, seconded to Fin Mgmnt Unit HM Treasy/MPO 1981–82; Coopers and Lybrand: ptnr 1983–, ptnr i/c Govt Servs Div 1986–94, managing ptnr Int Affrs and Bd memb 1995–; govr Royal Ballet Sch 1989–, tstee Royal Armouries 1989–; *publications* The State under Stress (with C D Foster, 1996); *Clubs* RAC, Powerstock & Hooke Cricket; *Style*— The Hon Francis Plowden; ✉ 4 Highbury Road, London SW19 7PR; Coopers and Lybrand, 1 Embankment Place, London WC2N 6NN (☎ 0171 583 5000)

PLOWDEN, William Francis Godfrey; JP (Shropshire 1953); o s of Roger Edmund Joseph Plowden, JP (d 1946), and his 1 w, Mary Florence, *née* Cholmondeley (d 1930); the Plowden family has been seated at Plowden since the C12, when Roger de Plowden is believed to have been present at the siege of Acre 1191 (*see* Burke's Landed Gentry, 18 edn, vol III, 1972); *b* 4 Dec 1925; *Educ* Beaumont, RAC Cirencester; *m* 17 July 1951, Valerie Ann, o da of Cdr Athelstan Paul Bush, DSO, RN (d 1970), of Tockington Court, nr Bristol; 3 s (Roger Godfrey Paul b 8 Feb 1953, Francis Richard Piers b 12 Jan 1957, Charles Edmund Philip b 31 Dec 1960), 1 da (Jacqueline Mary Prudence b 27 Feb 1954); *Career* serv WWII in Rifle Bde 1943–46; farmer on family estate; High Sheriff of Shropshire 1967; *Recreations* hunting, fishing, shooting; *Style*— William Plowden, Esq, JP; ✉ The Old Farmhouse, Choulton, Lydbury North, Shropshire SY7 8AH (☎ 01588 680639)

PLOWDEN, Hon William Julius Lowthian; s of Baron Plowden (Life Peer); *b* 1935; *Educ* Eton, King's Coll Cambridge (BA, PhD), Univ of California; *m* 1960, Veronica Mary, da of Lt-Col Derek Ernest Frederick Orby Gascoigne; 2 s, 2 da; *Career* Central Policy Review Staff Cabinet Office 1971–77, under sec Dept of Indust 1977–78, dir-gen Royal Inst of Public Admin 1978–88; visiting prof Dept of Govt LSE 1982–88, exec dir UK Harkness Fellowships New York 1988–91 (sr advsr London 1991–), visiting sr res fell London Business Sch 1993–94, assoc dir Atlantic Fellowships 1995–; tstee CSV 1984–, Southern African Advanced Educn Project 1986–; *Style*— The Hon William Plowden; ✉ 49 Stockwell Park Rd, London SW9 (☎ 0171 274 4535)

PLOWDEN ROBERTS, (Hugh) Martin; s of Stanley Plowden Roberts, OBE (d 1968), and Joan Aline Mary, *née* Mawdesley; *b* 6 Aug 1932; *Educ* St Edward's Sch Oxford, St Edmund Hall Oxford (BA, MA); *m* 22 Sept 1956, Susan Jane (d 1996), da of Andrew Patrick (d 1979), of Ferriby, Humberside; 2 da (Alexandra b 1961, Caroline b 1964); *Career* dir Payne & Son Meat Group Ltd 1958–60, asst gen mangr CWS Meat Group 1960–67; dir: Allied Suppliers Ltd 1967–82, Cavenham Ltd 1979–82 (chm 1981–82); dep chm Argyll Stores Ltd 1983–85; dir: Argyll Group plc 1983–95, Plowden Roberts Associates Ltd 1984–96, Lawson Mardon Group Ltd 1987–91; chm Dairy Crest Ltd 1985–88; memb Milk Mktg Bd 1983–89; Liveryman Worshipful Co of Butchers 1958; FIGD 1983; *Clubs* Farmers'; *Style*— Martin Plowden Roberts, Esq; ✉ Barn Cottage, Fulking, Henfield, West Sussex BN5 9NH (☎ 01273 857622)

PLOWMAN, John Patrick; s of late Robert Gilbee Plowman, of Bolter End, Bucks, and Ruth Wynn, *née* Dutton; *b* 20 March 1944; *Educ* St Edward's Sch Oxford, Univ of Grenoble, Univ of Durham (BA); *m* 8 Sept 1973, Daphne Margaret, da of Dr Alexander Kennett (d 1984), of Swanage, Dorset; 2 s (Hugo b 1977, William b 1981), 1 da (Katherine b 1974); *Career* Lt Royal Marines Res 1967–70; MOD: joined 1967, Private Office Ministers of State for Def 1969–71; on secondment: Civil Service Selection Bd 1975, Cabinet Office 1976–78; memb Bd of Property Servs Agency (Supplies) 1982–84, DOE 1984–87 and 1990–93, UK permanent rep to the European Communities 1987–90, regnl dir Depts of Environment and Tport NW 1993–94, dir Wildlife and Countryside DOE 1994–; FIMgt 1984; *Recreations* tennis, cricket, fishing, music; *Clubs* Royal Over-Seas League; *Style*— John Plowman; ✉ Department of the Environment, 2 Marsham Street, London SW1P 3EB (☎ 0171 276 3000)

PLOWMAN, Sir John Robin; kt (1979), CBE (1970, OBE 1949); s of Owen Plowman; *b* 18 Sept 1908, Bermuda; *Educ* Bermuda and England; *m* 1936, Marjorie Hardwick (d 1989); 2 s; *Career* various Govt boards and cmmns 1942–68, Miny of Organisation 1968–77 and 1980–82, Min of Marine & Air 1977–80; govt leader Legislative Cncl (now Senate) 1968–82; *Style*— Sir John Plowman, CBE; ✉ Chiswick, Paget, Bermuda

PLOWMAN, Jon; *Educ* Univ Coll Oxford; *Career* former asst dir Royal Court Theatre, then freelance theatre dir; currently head of comedy entertainment BBC; work incl: French and Saunders (BAFTA winner), Murder Most Horrid, Absolutely Fabulous (both series, Int Emmy for Best Popular Arts Prog 1993 and 1994), A Bit of Fry & Laurie (4th series), Smith & Jones (2 series), The Vicar of Dibley; *Style*— Jon Plowman; ✉ c/o BBC TV Light Entertainment Group, Television Centre, Wood Lane, London W12 7RJ (☎ 0181 743 8000)

PLOWRIGHT, David Ernest; CBE (1996); s of William Ernest Plowright; *b* 11 Dec 1930; *Educ* Scunthorpe GS; *m* 1953, Brenda Mary, *née* Key; 1 s, 2 da; *Career* Granada Television: joined as news ed 1958 (from Yorkshire Post), prog prodr 1960, exec prodr of news and current affrs 1966 (incl World In Action), prog controller 1969–79, md Granada TV Ltd 1976–87 (jtly 1976–81), exec responsibility for drama including Brideshead Revisited and Laurence Olivier's King Lear, chm Granada TV Ltd 1987–92, dir Granada Group plc 1981–92; visiting prof Univ of Salford 1992–, dep chm Channel Four 1992–; chm Assoc of Independent TV Cos 1984–86; dir: British Screen Ltd until 1992, Inward until 1991; chm Development Ctee Manchester City of Drama 1992–94; memb: Tate in the North Advsy Ctee until 1992, International Cncl of European Film and TV Forum until 1992, Manchester Olympic Bid Ctee (and chm Design Panel until 1994), Hulme Regeneration Bd; former memb International Cncl US Nat Acad of TV Arts and Sciences, vice pres Royal TV Soc, fell BAFTA 1992 (also tstee 1992); *Recreations* sailing, theatre, television; *Style*— David Plowright, Esq, CBE; ✉ Westways, Wilmslow Rd, Mottram St Andrew, Prestbury, Cheshire SK10 4QT (☎ 01625 820948, fax 01625 820709)

PLOWRIGHT, Joan Ann; (Lady Olivier), CBE (1970); da of William Ernest Plowright; *b* 28 Oct 1929; *Educ* Scunthorpe GS, Laban Art of Movement Studio, Old Vic Theatre Sch; *m* 1, 1953 (m dis), Roger Gage; m 2, 1961, Sir Laurence Olivier, later Baron Olivier (Life Peer, d 1989); 1 s, 2 da; *Career* leading actress stage, film and television; memb Cncl RADA; Int Award 18th Annual Crystal Awards Women in Film USA 1994; *Theatre* first stage appearance If Four Walls Told (Croydon Rep Theatre) 1948, with Bristol Old Vic and Old Vic Co S Africa Tour 1952, first London stage appearance in The Duenna (Westminster) 1954, Moby Dick (Duke of York's) 1955, with Nottingham Playhouse 1955–56, with English Stage Co (Royal Court) 1956, The Crucible, Don Juan, The Death of Satan, Cards of Identity, The Good Woman of Setzuan, The Country Wife (transferred to Adelphi 1957), The Chairs, The Making of Moo (Royal Court) 1957, The Entertainer (Palace) 1957, The Chairs, The Lesson (Phoenix NY) 1958, The Entertainer (Royale NY) 1958, The Chairs, The Lesson, Major Barbara (Royal Court) 1958, Hook Line and Sinker (Piccadilly) 1958, Roots (Royal Court and Duke of York's) 1959, Rhinoceros (Royal Court) 1960, A Taste of Honey (Lyceum NY) 1960 (Tony Award for Best Actress); leading actress with NT 1963–74; opening season 1963: St Joan, Uncle Vanya, Hobson's Choice; The Master Builder 1964, Much Ado About Nothing 1967 and 1968, Three Sisters 1967 and 1968, The Advertisement 1968, Love's Labours Lost 1968, The Merchant of Venice 1979, A Woman Killed With Kindness 1971, The Rules of the Game 1971, Eden End 1974; Rosmersholm (Greenwich) 1973, Saturday, Sunday, Monday

(Queen's) 1974–75, The Sea Gull (Lyric) 1975, The Bed Before Yesterday (Lyric) 1975 (Variety Club of GB Award 1977), Filumena (Lyric) 1977 (SWET Award 1978), Enjoy (Vaudeville) 1980, The Cherry Orchard (Haymarket) 1983, The House of Bernarda Alba (Globe) 1986; Chichester Festival: Uncle Vanya, The Chances 1962, St Joan (Evening Standard Award for Best Actress), Uncle Vanya 1963, The Doctor's Dilemma, The Taming of the Shrew 1972, Cavell 1982, The Way of the World 1984, If we are Women (Greenwich Theatre) 1995; directed: A Prayer for Wings 1985, Married Love 1988, Time and The Conways 1990/91; *Films* The Entertainer 1960, Equus, Britannia Hospital 1962, Three Sisters 1970, Wagner, Revolution 1985, Drowning by Numbers 1988, The Dressmaker 1988, I Love You to Death 1989, Avalon 1989, Denis, Last Action Hero 1992, Driving Miss Daisy 1992, A Place for Annie 1993, Widows Peak 1993, A Pin for the Butterfly 1993, On Promised Land 1994, Hotel Sorrento 1994, A Pyromaniacs Love Story 1994, The Scarlet Letter 1994, Jane Eyre 1995, Mr Wrong 1995, 101 Dalmations 1996; films for TV incl: The Merchant of Venice, Brimstone and Treacle, A Dedicated Man, House of Bernada Alba (1991), Stalin (Best Supporting TV actress Golden Globe 1993), Enchanted April (BBC Screen Two, Best Supporting Film Actress Golden Globe 1993, Best Supporting Film Actress Oscar Nomination 1993) 1992, Clothes in The Wardrobe 1992; *Recreations* reading, music, entertaining; *Style*— Miss Joan Plowright, CBE; ✉ c/o ICM Ltd, Oxford House, 76 Oxford Street, London W1N 0AX (☎ 0171 636 6565, fax 0171 323 0101)

PLOWRIGHT, Rosalind Anne; da of Robert Arthur Plowright, and Celia Adelaide Plowright; *b* 21 May 1949; *Educ* Notre Dame HS Wigan, Royal Northern Coll of Music Manchester; *m* 1984, James Anthony Kaye; 1 s (Daniel Robert), 1 da (Katherine Anne); *Career* soprano; London Opera Centre 1974–75, debut as Agathe in Der Freischutz (Glyndebourne Chorus and Touring Co) 1975, with ENO, WNO and Kent Opera 1975–78, Miss Jessel in Turn of the Screw (ENO) 1979, Ortlinde in Die Walküre (Royal Opera House debut) 1980; 1980–81: Bern Opera (Adriadne, Alceste), Frankfurt Opera (Ariadne, Aida, Il Trovatore), Munich Opera (Ariadne); debuts: USA, Paris, Madrid and Hamburg 1982, La Scala, Milan, Edinburgh Festival, San Francisco and Carnegie Hall NY 1983, Berlin, Houston, Pittsburgh, San Diego and Verona 1985, Rome, Florence and Holland 1986, Tulsa, NY Philharmonic, Buenos Aires, Santiago, Chile, Israel, Paris Opera and Bonn 1987, Lausanne, Geneva, Oviedo and Bilbao 1988, Zurich, Copenhagen and Lisbon 1989, Vienna, Torre del Lago and Bregenz 1990, Athens 1995; *Roles* principal roles incl: Amelia in Un Ballo in Maschera, Desdemona in Otello, Elisabetta in Don Carlos, title role in Norma, Leonora in La Forza del Destino, title role in Tosca, Lady Macbeth in Macbeth, title role in Ariadne auf Naxos, Abigaille in Nabucco, Giorgetta in Il Tabarro, title role in La Giaconda (Opera North) 1993; *Recordings* for EMI: Mary Stuart, Otello, Les Contes d'Hoffman; for Deutsche Grammophon: Il Trovatore, La Forza del Destino, Mahler Resurrection Symphony; La Vestale for Orfeo Records; *Awards* incl: First Prize Int Competition for Opera Singers (Sofia 1979), Prix Fndn Fanny Heldy (Nat Acad du Disque Lyrique 1985); *Recreations* fell walking; *Style*— Miss Rosalind Plowright; ✉ c/o Victoria Smith Management Ltd, 2 Fir Hill Villas, Hollywater Road, Bordow, Hants GU35 0AG

PLOWRIGHT, Dr Walter; CMG (1974); s of Jonathan Plowright, and Mahala Plowright; *b* 20 July 1923; *Educ* Moulton and Spalding GS, RVC London; *m* 1959, Dorothy Joy, *née* Bell; *Career* with Colonial Vet and Res Servs (Kenya and Nigeria) 1950–63, Animal Virus Res Inst Pirbright 1963–71, prof of vet microbiology RVC 1971–78, head Dept of Microbiology Inst for Res on Animal Diseases 1978–83; King Baudouin Int Devpt prize 1984; Hon DSc: Univ of Nairobi 1984, Univ of Reading 1986; Gold Award Office Int des Epizooties 1988, Theiler Memorial Trust Award (SA) 1994; FRCVS, FRS; *Style*— Dr Walter Plowright, CMG, FRS; ✉ Whitehill Lodge, Reading Rd, Goring, Reading RG8 OLL (☎ 01491 872891, fax 01491 872567)

PLUMB, Baron (Life Peer UK 1987), of Coleshill, Co Warwicks; (Charles) Henry Plumb; kt (1973), DL (Warwicks 1977), MEP (EDG) The Cotswolds (majority 4,268); s of Charles Plumb, of Ansley, Warwicks, and Louise, *née* Fisher; *b* 27 March 1925; *Educ* King Edward VI Sch Nuneaton; *m* 1947, Marjorie Dorothy, da of Thomas Victor Dunn, of Bentley, Warwicks; 1 s (Hon John Henry b 1951), 2 da (Hon Mrs Holman, Hon Mrs Mayo); *Career* MEP (Cons) The Cotswolds 1979–, chm Agric Ctee Euro Parl 1979–82, ldr (Cons) EDG Euro Parl 1982–87, pres Euro Parl 1987–89; pres NFU 1970–79 (dep pres 1966–69, vice pres 1964–66, memb Cncl 1959–), chm Br Agric Cncl 1975–79; pres Warwicks County Fedn of Young Farmers' Clubs 1974–, pres Nat Fedn 1976–86; memb Cncl: CBI, Animal Health Tst; pres: COPA 1975–77, RASE 1977 (dep pres 1978), Int Fedn of Agric Prodrs 1979–; chllr Univ of Coventry 1995–; hon pres Ayrshire Cattle Soc; non-exec dir Midland Marts Ltd; chm Int Policy Cncl on Agriculture, Food and Trade; memb Ct of Assts Worshipful Co of Farmers; hon fell Wye Coll, Hon Liveryman Worshipful Co of Fruiterers 1991; Hon DSc Cranfield 1983; FRSA 1970, FRAgS 1974; Order of Merit (Fed Repub of Germany) 1976, Gd Cross Order of Merit (Portugal) 1987, Order of Merit (Luxembourg) 1988, Grand Cross Order of Civil Merit (Spain) 1989, Knight Cdr Cross of the Order of Merit (Fed Repub of Germany) 1990; *Clubs* Farmers', St Stephen's, Coleshill Rotary (hon memb); *Style*— The Rt Hon Lord Plumb, DL, MEP; ✉ Maxstoke, Coleshill, Warwickshire B46 2QJ (☎ 01675 463133, telex 01675 464156); 2 Queen Anne's Gate, London SW1 (☎ 0171 222 0411)

PLUMB, Prof Sir John Harold; kt (1982); s of late James Plumb, of Leicester; *b* 20 Aug 1911; *Educ* Alderman Newton's Sch Leicester, Univ Coll Leicester, Christ's Coll Cambridge (PhD, LittD); *Career* historian; prof of modern English history Univ of Cambridge 1966–74, master Christ's Coll Cambridge 1978–82, chm Centre of E Anglian Studies 1979–82; tstee Nat Portrait Gallery 1961–82; Hon DLitt: Univ of Leicester 1968, UEA 1973, Bowdoin Coll 1974, Univ of S California 1978, Westminster Coll 1983, Washington Univ, St Louis 1983, Bard Coll 1987; FRHistS, FBA; *Clubs* Brooks's; *Style*— Prof Sir John Plumb, FBA; ✉ Christ's College, Cambridge CB2 3BU (☎ 01223 334918, fax 01223 334919)

PLUMBE, (Philip) Graham; s of John Philip Hubert Plumbe (d 1980), of Crookham Village, Hants, and Winifred, *née* Roberts; *b* 28 Sept 1933; *Educ* Berkhamsted Sch, Coll of Estate Management Univ of Reading; *m* 6 Nov 1965, Rachel Mary, da of Noel Cattell Kemp; 1 s (Timothy Guy b 28 June 1970), 1 da (Joanna Mary b 28 Oct 1967); *Career* RAF pilot Fighter Cmmd then Flt Lt 1952–56; clerk Dalgety & Co Ltd 1950–51, trainee surveyor Edward Erdman & Co 1957–63; Gooch & Wagstaff (Chartered Surveyors): joined 1963, ptnr 1972, chm Management Bd 1988–90, sr ptnr 1990–92; regular arbitration appointments and memb sundry professional ctees and working parties; Freeman City of London 1976, Liveryman Worshipful Co of Gold and Silver Wyre Drawers 1976; FRICS 1973, FCIArb 1975; *Recreations* golf, squash, gardening; *Clubs* North Hants Golf; *Style*— Graham Plumbe, Esq; ✉ Gooch & Wagstaff, 73 Watling St, London EC4M 9BL (☎ 0171 248 2044, fax 0171 236 4659)

PLUMBLY, Derek John; CMG (1991); s of John Cecil Plumbly (d 1987), and Jean Elizabeth, *née* Baker; *b* 15 May 1948; *Educ* Brockenhurst GS, Magdalen Coll Oxford (BA); *m* 10 Nov 1979, Nadia, da of Youssef Gohar, of Cairo, Egypt; 2 s (Samuel b 1985, Joseph b 1987), 1 da (Sara b 1983); *Career* VSO Pakistan 1970–71, FCO 1972, second sec Jedda 1975, first sec Cairo 1977, FCO 1980, first sec Washington 1984, cnsllr and dep head of mission Riyadh 1988–92, counsellor and head of chancery UKMIS NY 1992–96, sr int drugs coordinator and dir Drugs and Int Crime FCO 1996–; *Style*— Derek Plumbly, Esq, CMG; ✉ Foreign & Commonwealth Office, Downing Street, London SW1A 2AL (☎ 0171 270 3000)

PLUMMER, Maj-Gen Leo Heathcote; CBE (1974); s of Lt-Col Edmund Waller Plummer, DSO (d 1958), of Farnham, Surrey, and Mary Dorothy, *née* Brookesmith (d 1984); *b* 11 June 1923; *Educ* Canford Sch, Queens' Coll Cambridge; *m* 13 April 1955, Judyth Ann, da of Edward Victor Dolby, OBE (d 1973), of Eardisley, Hereford and Worcester; 3 da (Virginia, Sara, Nicola); *Career* cmmnd RA 1943, 17 Field Regt served N Africa, Sicily, Italy, Austria 1943–47, Adj LAA Regt RA TA 1947–49, 66 Airborne Light Regt 1949–50, 4 RHA 1950–51, Staff Coll Camberley 1952, GSO 2 HQ Anti-Aircraft Cmd 1953–54, BMRA 7 Armd Div 1957–59, Jt Servs Staff Coll 1959, battery cdr 39 Missile Regt 1960–61, brevet Lt-Col 1961, directing staff Staff Coll Camberley 1961–63, Cmdt Sudan Armed Forces Staff Sch 1963–65, CO 20 Heavy Regt 1965–67, Col Gen Staff MOD 1967, Brig Cdr 1 Artillery Bde 1967–70, dep dir Manning Army MOD 1971–74, asst chief staff ops HQ Northern Army Gp 1974–76, ADC to HM the Queen 1974–76, Maj-Gen Chief Jt Servs Liaison Orgn Bonn 1976–78, ret 1979; chm Civil Serv Cmmn Panel 1983–90; churchwarden: All Saints' Cologne 1976–78, All Saints' Icklesham E Sussex 1981–85; memb SSAFA Canterbury 1987–91, tstee and sec Old Meeting House Tst Helmsley 1993–, pres 78 Div Battleaxe Club 1995–; *Recreations* gardening; *Clubs* Army and Navy; *Style*— Maj-Gen Leo Plummer, CBE; ✉ Vivers Lodge, Old Rd, Kirkbymoorside, N Yorks YO6 6BD (☎ 01751 432230)

PLUMMER OF ST MARYLEBONE, Baron (Life Peer UK 1981), of the City of Westminster; Sir (Arthur) Desmond (Herne) Plummer; kt (1971), TD (1950), JP (London 1958), DL (Greater London 1970); s of late Arthur Herne Plummer, and late Janet McCormick; *b* 25 May 1914; *Educ* Hurstpierpoint Coll, Coll of Estate Mgmnt; *m* 1941, Ella Margaret (Pat), da of Albert Holloway, of Epping; 1 da (Hon Sally Jane); *Career* sits as Cons peer in House of Lords; memb: St Marylebone Borough Cncl 1952–65 (mayor 1958–59), LCC St Marylebone 1960–65, ILEA 1964–76; GLC: memb for Cities of London and Westminster 1964–73, memb for St Marylebone 1973–76, ldr of oppn 1966–67 and 1973–74, ldr of Cncl 1967–73; memb Ct Univ of London 1967–77; chm National Employers' Life Assurance Co 1983–89; chm: Portman Building Society 1983–90 (pres 1990–), Horserace Betting Levy Bd 1974–82, Epsom and Walton Downs Trg Grounds Mgmnt Bd 1974–82, Nat Stud 1975–82; pres: Met Assoc of Bldg Socs 1983–89, London Anglers' Assoc 1976–; memb Order of St John Cncl for London 1971–94; FAI 1948, FRICS 1970, FRSA 1974, Hon FFAS 1966, KStJ 1986; *Clubs* Carlton, RAC; *Style*— The Rt Hon the Lord Plummer of St Marylebone, TD, DL; ✉ 4 The Lane, Marlborough Place, St Johns Wood, London NW8 OPN

PLUMPTON, Alan; CBE (1980), JP (Monmouthshire 1971); s of John Plumpton (d 1978), of Sunderland, Co Durham, and Doris, *née* Barrett; *b* 24 Nov 1926; *Educ* Sunderland Tech Sch, Univ of Durham (BSc), Henley Admin Staff Coll; *m* 9 Dec 1950, Audrey; 1 s (Nigel b 5 July 1953), 1 da (Jill (Mrs Stiel) b 3 Oct 1956); *Career* N Eastern Electricity Bd: graduate engr 1948–49, asst distribution engr 1949–57, dist commercial engr Stockton 1957–60; S Wales Electricity Bd: dist mangr E Monmouthshire Dist 1961–64, dep chief commercial engr 1964–67, chief commercial engr 1967–72; London Electricity Bd: dep chm 1972–76, chm 1976–80; dep chm Electricity Cncl 1981–86; chm: Manx Electricity Cncl 1985–, Ewbank Preece Group Ltd 1986–91, Schlumberger Measurement and Systems (UK) Ltd 1988–92 (dir 1985–87), Schlumberger plc 1992–, Beaufort Management Consultants 1992–; dir Eleco Holdings plc 1993–; memb: Cncl Inst of Electrical Engrs UK 1983–87, Jt Ctee of Princs Electricity Bd/Br Electrical & Allied Mfrs Assoc UK 1981–86, Br Nat Ctee of CIGRE 1981–85, Directing Ctee of UNIPEDE 1975–81, Br Nat Ctee and Exec Ctee World Energy Conf 1981–, Industl Policy Ctee CBI Industs 1981–85; chm Euro Panel of Nationalised Industs 1983–85; formerly: chm Pontypool RDC, memb Gwent Water Authy; Liveryman Worshipful Co of Gardeners 1978; FEng 1991, FIEE, CIMgt; *Recreations* golf, gardening; *Clubs* City Livery, IOD, Harewood Downs Golf; *Style*— Alan Plumpton, Esq, CBE, JP, FEng; ✉ Lockhill, Stubbs Wood, Amersham, Bucks HP6 6EX (☎ 01494 433791)

PLUMPTRE, Hon (Wyndham) George; 3 s of 21 Baron FitzWalter, and Margaret Melesina, *née* Deedes; *b* 24 April 1956; *Educ* Radley, Jesus Coll Cambridge; *m* 1984, Alexandra Elizabeth, da of Prince Michael Cantacuzene, Count Speransky and Mrs James Edwards; 2 s (Wyndham James Alexander b 1986, Piers Harry Constantine b 1987), 1 da (Hermione Amy Katherine b 1991); *Career* Sotheby's rep in Kent 1991–, gardening corr The Times 1994–, ed Sotheby's magazine Preview 1996–; author; *Books* Royal Gardens (1981), Collins Book of British Gardens (1985), The Fast Set (1985), Homes of Cricket (1988), The Latest Country Gardens (1988), Cricket Caricatures and Cartoons (1989), Garden Ornament (1989), The Golden Age of Cricket (1990), Barclays World of Cricket (ed, 1986), Back Page Cricket (ed, 1987), Back Page Racing (ed, 1989), The Water Garden (1993), The Garden Makers (1993), Great Gardens, Great Designers (1994), Edward VII (1995); *Clubs* Beefsteak, Pratt's; *Style*— The Hon George Plumptre; ✉ Godinton House, Near Ashford, Kent TN23 3BW (☎ 01233 620773)

PLUMPTRE, Hon Julian Brook; s and h of 21 Baron FitzWalter, and Margaret Melesina, *née* Deedes; *b* 18 Oct 1952; *Educ* Radley, Wye Coll London (BSc); *m* March 1988, (Alison) Sally, o da of late I M T Quiney; 3 s (Edward Brook b 26 April 1989, Tom Alexander b 14 June 1991, Max Eustace Ian b 17 April 1993); *Career* land agency; *Style*— The Hon Julian Plumptre; ✉ Crixhall Court, Staple, Canterbury, Kent

PLUNKET, 8 Baron (UK 1827); Robin Rathmore Plunket; s of 6 Baron Plunket (d 1938), and bro of 7 Baron (d 1975); *b* 3 Dec 1925; *Educ* Eton; *m* 1951, Jennifer, da of late Bailey Southwell, of S Africa; *Heir* bro, Hon Shaun Albert Frederick Sheridan Plunket; *Career* formerly Capt Rifle Bde; forester; *Recreations* fishing; *Clubs* Boodle's; *Style*— The Rt Hon the Lord Plunket; ✉ Rathmore, Chimanimani, Zimbabwe (☎ 00 263 26 2281); 39 Lansdowne Gardens, London SW8 2EL (☎ 0171 622 6049)

PLUNKET, Hon Shaun Albert Frederick Sheridan; s of 6 Baron Plunket, and Dorothé, *née* Lewis (both died in aircrash in USA 1938); hp of bro, 8 Baron Plunket; *b* 5 April 1931; *Educ* Eton, L'Institut de Touraine; *m* 1, 1961, Judith Ann, er da of late Gerard Patrick Power, of Lapworth, Warwickshire; 1 s (Tyrone Shaun Terence b 1966), 1 da (Loelia Dorothé Alexandra b 1963); m 2, 1980, Mrs Elisabeth de Sancha (d 1986), da of late Helge Drangel, of Stockholm, formerly w of T de Sancha (d 1986); m 3, 1989, Mrs Andrea Reynolds, da of late André Milos; *Career* formerly Lt Irish Gds, ADC to GOC Rhine Army 1951–52, dist cmdt Kenya Police Res Mau Mau 1953; Hambros Bank: dir Garrod & Lofthouse Ltd 1956–68, chm and md Wilmington Overseas Security Ltd 1978–94: dir: Pannonia Farms Inc USA, Rathmore Forests (PVT) Ltd Zimbabwe; vice pres Arthritis Care, patron Mary Hoare Tst; *Recreations* tennis, fly-fishing; *Clubs* White's; *Style*— The Hon Shaun Plunket; ✉ Livingston Farm, Livingston Manor, New York 12758, USA (☎ 00 914 439 4000, fax 00 914 439 3344); c/o White's, 37 St James's St, London SW1

PLUNKETT, Hon Jonathan Oliver; s and h of 16 Baron Louth; *b* 4 Nov 1952; *Educ* De La Salle Coll Jersey, Hautlieu Sch Jersey, Hull Univ (BSc); *m* 1981, Jennifer, da of Norman Oliver Hodgetts, of Weston-super-Mare; 1 s (Matthew Oliver b 22 Dec 1982), 1 da (Agatha Elizabeth b 17 Aug 1985); *Career* electronics engr; AMIEE; *Style*— The Hon Jonathan Plunkett; ✉ Les Sercles, La Grande Pièce, St Peter, Jersey, CI

PLUNKETT-ERNLE-ERLE-DRAX, Henry Walter; JP (1971), DL (1979); s of Adm the Hon Sir Reginald Aylmer Ranfurly Plunkett-Ernle-Erle-Drax (2 s of 17 Baron Dunsany); *b* 18 March 1928; *Educ* RNC Dartmouth; *m* 6 April 1957, Hon Pamela Rose; 5 s; *Career* served RN 1945–68; landowner, farmer, forester, company director; govr: Milton Abbey Sch, Canford Sch; *Recreations* skiing, shooting, fishing, tennis, golf;

Style— H W Drax, Esq, JP, DL; ✉ Charborough Park, Wareham, Dorset BH20 7EW (☎ 01258 857368, office 01258 857484)

PLYMOUTH, Archdeacon of; *see:* Ellis, Ven Robin Gareth

PLYMOUTH, Bishop of (RC) 1986–; Rt Rev (Hugh) Christopher Budd; s of John Alfred Budd (d 1993), and Phyllis Mary, *née* Pearson (d 1978); *b* 27 May 1937; *Educ* Salesian Coll Chertsey Surrey, Cotton Coll N Staffs, Ven English Coll Rome, Pontifical Univ Gregoriana Rome (PhL, STL, STD); *Career* tutor in theol Rome 1965–71, lectr in theol Newman Coll Birmingham and asst priest St Brigid's Northfield 1971–76, head of trg Catholic Marriage Advsy Cncl 1976–79, rector St John's Seminary Wonersh Guildford 1979–85, admin Brentwood Cathedral 1985–86; *Recreations* walking, watching cricket; *Style*— The Rt Rev the Bishop of Plymouth; ✉ Bishop's House, 31 Wyndham Street West, Plymouth, Devon PL1 5RZ (☎ 01752 224414, fax 01752 223750)

PLYMOUTH, 3 Earl of (UK 1905); Other Robert Ivor Windsor-Clive; DL (Salop 1961); Viscount Windsor (UK 1905), Baron Windsor (E 1529); s of 2 Earl of Plymouth, DL, PC (d 1943), and Lady Irene Corona, *née* Charteris (d 1989), da of 11 Earl of Wemyss; *b* 9 Oct 1923; *Educ* Eton; *m* 1950, Caroline Helen, da of Edward Rice, of Dane Court, Eastry, Kent; 3 s, 1 da; *Heir* s, Viscount Windsor; *Career* late Coldstream Gds; memb Standing Cmmn on Museums and Galleries 1972–82, chm Reviewing Ctee on Export of Works of Art 1982–85; FRSA; KStJ; *Style*— The Rt Hon the Earl of Plymouth, DL; ✉ The Stables, Oakly Park, Ludlow, Shropshire

POBERESKIN, Louis Howard; *b* 16 Aug 1948; *Educ* Case Western Reserv Univ (BS, MD); *m* 28 Nov 1980; 2 da (Sarah b 1983, Lisa b 1983); *Career* sr registrar in neurosurgery Addenbrooke's Hosp Cambridge 1981–85, conslt neurosurgeon Derriford Hosp 1985–; FRCSEd 1987; *Style*— Louis Pobereskin, Esq; ✉ Department of Neurosurgery, Derriford Hospital, Plymouth (☎ 01752 792539, fax 01752 784027)

POCKNEY, Penrhyn Charles Benjamin; s of Maj Ronald Penrhyn Pockney (d 1969), of Bishopthorpe, York, and Catherine Helen Margaret, *née* Dodsworth (d 1992); *b* 22 May 1940; *Educ* Winchester; *m* 15 May 1965, (Patricia) Jane, da of Sir Richard William de Bacquencourt des Voeux, Bt (d 1944), of Burghclere, Newbury, Berks; 2 s (Richard b 1968, James b 1969); *Career* dir J & A Scrimgeour Ltd 1972–80 (ptnr 1968–72), ptnr Mullens & Co 1980–86; dir: S G Warburg Securities Ltd 1986–95, Hiscox Select Insurance Fund plc 1993–; extra memb Ct Worshipful Co Skinners 1977 (Freeman 1963); FCA; *Recreations* gardening, fishing, golf; *Clubs* Boodle's, Lansdowne, MCC; *Style*— Penrhyn Pockney, Esq; ✉ Flat 14, 47 Courtfield Road, London SW7 4DB (☎ 0171 244 7293)

POCOCK, Air Vice-Marshal Donald Arthur; CBE (1975, OBE 1957); s of Arthur Pocock (d 1970), of Hampstead, and E Pocock, *née* Broad; *b* 5 July 1920; *Educ* Crouch End; *m* 1947, Dorothy Monica, da of D Griffiths; 2 s, 3 da; *Career* cmmnd RAF 1941; cmd RAF Regt Wing 1957–58, MOD 1958–59, HQ AAFCE 1959–62, sr ground def SO NEAF 1962–63, MOD 1963–66, sr ground def SO FEAF 1966–68, ADC to HM The Queen 1967, Cmdt-Gen RAF Regt 1973–75; gen mangr (Iran) British Aerospace Dynamics Group 1976–79; dir Br Metallurgical Plant Constructors' Assoc 1980–85; *Style*— Air Vice-Marshal Donald Pocock, CBE; ✉ 16 Dence Park, Herne Bay, Kent CT6 6BQ (☎ 01227 374773)

PODGER, Geoffrey John Freeman; s of Leonard Podger, and Beryl Enid, *née* Freeman; *b* 3 Aug 1952; *Educ* Worthing HS for Boys, Pembroke Coll Oxford (open scholar, MA); *Career* MOD: admin trainee 1974–77, seconded to Int Staff NATO HQ Brussels 1977–79, princ 1979–82; DHSS 1982–88, on loan as sec to Port Stanley Hosp Fire Inquiry Falkland Islands 1985; Dept of Health: private sec to Chm NHS Management Bd 1985–87, asst sec 1987, princ private sec to Sec of State for Social Servs 1987–88, project mangr NHS Review 1988–92, head International Relations Unit 1992–93, under sec for Health Promotion 1993–96; under sec (Food Safety and Science Group) MAFF 1996–; *Style*— Geoffrey Podger, Esq; ✉ MAFF, Ergon House, c/o Nobel House, Room 423, 17 Swire Square, London SW1P 3JR (☎ 0171 238 6430)

PODMORE, Keith; s of Fredrick Podmore, of Birmingham, and Gladys, *née* Etheridge; *b* 6 June 1944; *Educ* Silvermere Secdy Modern Sheldon Birmingham; *m* 25 Nov 1972, Edith Sadie, da of Ronnie Mackie; 2 s (Jonathan Mark b 12 June 1975, Simon David b 3 Dec 1977); *Career* chef; apprentice Queens Hotel Birmingham 1960–65, Turnberry Hotel Jan-June 1966, Hotel des Alps Loche Les Bains Switzerland July-Oct 1966, Restaurant Bürterhaus Bern 1966–67, La Reserve de Beaulieu Cote d'Azur April-Sept 1967, Queens Hotel Leeds 1967–68, Tregenna Castle Hotel St Ives April-Oct 1968, Manor House Hotel Moretonhampstead Devon 1968–70, Turnbury Hotel 1970–71, Central Hotel Glasgow April-Sept 1971, Caledonian Hotel Edinburgh 1971–73, Grand Hotel Hartlepool 1973–77, Station Hotel Perth 1977–81, Charing Cross Hotel London 1981–82, chef de cuisine Boodle's 1983–; Académie Culinaire de France: memb 1985, currently vice chm, chm MOGB, chm Educn Ctee; memb Assoc Culinaire de France 1977; *Recreations* golf, gardening, cooking, antiques; *Clubs* Nizels Golf (Hildenborough); *Style*— Keith Podmore, Esq; ✉ Boodle's, 28 St James's Street, London SW1A 1HJ (☎ 0171 930 7166, fax 0171 839 5669)

POETON, William George; CBE (1991); s of George Edward Poeton (d 1963), and Gladys Maude, *née* Jewill (d 1974); *b* 24 Dec 1926; *Educ* Bristol GS; *m* 1, 1947 (m dis 1970), Jean Rankin Poeton; 3 s (Anthony b 1948, Barrie b 1952, Timothy b 1956); m 2, 21 Oct 1971, Barbara, da of Frederick Bevis; *Career* fndr A T Poeton and Son Ltd (high tech electroplating) 1954–, dir of admin and lab affrs HTV Ltd 1969–72, former chm and chief exec Eddington Poeton Video Productons Ltd, currently chm Poeton Group of Cos; pres Bristol W of England Mfrs Assoc 1960, regnl chm SW CBI 1974–76; memb: Nat Cncl CBI President's Advsrs Panel 1974–76, Mgmnt Bd W of England Employers Assoc 1974–83, SW RHA; vice pres Econ and Social Ctee of the Euro Communities 1986–89 (memb 1982–89), former pres Gloucester Cons Assoc, former cncllr Univ of Bristol, fndr Bristol Arts Centre; former chm: Bristol-Hanover Soc, Bristol Round Table, The Everyman Theatre Cheltenham; former int convenor Round Table, current pres Union of Ind Cos, current dep chm Small Business Bureau, memb Cncl European Policy Forum; FInstD; *Recreations* sailing, theatre; *Clubs* Reform, Royal Thames Yacht; *Style*— William Poeton, Esq, CBE; ✉ 9 Pelham Place, London SW7 2NQ (☎ 0171 589 2120, 0171 589 1945, fax 0171 225 0444)

POGMORE, John Richard; s of Edward Richard Fry Pogmore, MBE (d 1986), and Edith Mary, *née* Trevitt; *b* 12 June 1942; *Educ* Southwell Minster GS, Univ of London (MB BS); *m* 18 June 1966, Trina Ann Leigh, da of Frederick Waterman; 2 s (Simon b 1970, James b 1972); *Career* cmmnd RAF 1963, ret 1980 with rank of Wing Cdr; currently conslt obstetrician and gynaecologist Birmingham Women's Health Care NHS Tst; former chm Hosp Recognition Ctee RCOG; FRCOG 1988; *Recreations* rugby, cartography, wine; *Clubs* RAF; *Style*— Mr John Pogmore; ✉ Priory Hospital, Priory Rd, Edgbaston, Birmingham B5 7UG (☎ 0121 440 2323, fax 0121 446 5686)

POHL, Dr Jürgen Ernst Friedrich (George); s of Dr Ernst Richard Albert Pohl (d 1985), of Kronberg, Germany, and Hildegard Anneliese, *née* Gorschlüter (d 1990); *b* 14 March 1935; *Educ* Melbourne Boys' HS, Univ of Melbourne (BSc, MB BS); *m* 24 Aug 1963, Irene Jean, da of Thomas Wickham, of London; 2 s (John b 1964, David b 1971), 3 da (Julia b 1966, Andrea b 1969, Deborah b 1975); *Career* lectr in therapeutics and materia medica Univ of Manchester 1968–74, conslt physician Manchester Royal Infirmary 1972–74, sr lectr in med Univ of Leicester 1974–, conslt physician and cardiologist United Leicester Hosps 1974–, univ memb South Lincs Dist Health Authy 1982–90, priv memb 1992–93; memb: MENSA 1966–, Assoc of Physicians, Med Res Soc, Br Euro and Int Cardiac Soc, Int and Br Hypertension Soc, Renal Assoc; MRCP, FRCP; *Recreations* chess, bridge, reading; *Style*— Dr George Pohl; ✉ Department of Medicine, Leicester General Hospital, Gwendolen Rd, Leicester LE5 4PW (☎ 0116 249 0490, fax 0016 249 0064)

POLAK, Prof Julia Margaret; da of Carlos Polak, and Rebeca, *née* Mactas; *b* 29 June 1939; *Educ* Univ of Buenos Aires (MD, Dip Histopathology), Univ of London (DSc); *m* 1961, Daniel Catovsky, s of Felix Catovsky; 2 s (Elliot Sebastian b 1973, Michael David b 1976), 1 da (Marina b 1963); *Career* Buenos Aires: demonstrator 1961–62, SHO in surgery and med 1962, registrar and sr registrar 1963–67; London Royal Postgrad Med Sch: res asst Dept of Histochemistry 1968–69, asst lectr 1970–73, lectr 1973–79, sr lectr 1979–82, reader 1982–84; Dept of Histopathology Hammersmith Hosp: hon conslt 1979–, prof of endocrine pathology 1984–, dep dir 1988–91, head Dept of Histochemistry 1991–; ed of numerous med jls and organiser of int and nat med meetings; memb numerous ctees within Royal Postgrad Med Sch; external ctees incl: chm Immunocytochemistry Club, chm Br Endocrine Pathologists Club, memb Exec Ctee Cncl Circulation of American Heart Assoc, memb Cncl Histochemical Soc of GB 1984–86, memb Bd of Studies on Pathology; memb learned socs incl: American Thoracic Soc, Br Cardiac Soc, Br Neuroendocrine Gp, Cwlth Assoc for Devpt, IBRO, NY Acad of Sciences; memb: BMA, RSM, American Assoc of Pathologists; FRCPath 1986 (memb 1974); Benito de Udaondo Cardiology prize 1967; *Books* incl: Gut Hormones (with S R Bloom, 1981), Basic Science in Gastroenterology, Vol I: Structure of the Gut (jtly, 1982), The Systematic Role of Regulatory Peptides (with S R Bloom and E Lindenlaub, 1983), Immunolabelling for Electron Microscopy (with I M Varndell, 1984), Endocrine Tumours - The Pathobiology of Regulatory Peptide-producing Tumours (with S R Bloom, 1985), Regulatory Peptides (1989), In Situ Hybridization: Principles and Practice (with J O D McGee, 1990), Electron Microscopic Immunocytochemistry: Principles and Practice (with J V Priestley, 1992), Diagnostic Histopathology of Neuroendocrine Tumours (1993), Clinical Gene Analysis and Manipulation - Tools, Techniques and Troubleshooting (with J A Z Jankowski and Sir David Weatherall, 1996); *Style*— Prof Julia Polak; ✉ Department of Histochemistry, Royal Postgraduate Medical School, Du Cane Rd, London W12 0NN (☎ 0181 740 3231, fax 0181 743 5362)

POLAND, Michael Desmond; s of Kenneth Gordon Poland (d 1970), of Downlands, Liphook, Hants, and Hester Mary Beatrice, *née* Chichele-Plowden (d 1993); *b* 9 Aug 1937; *Educ* Downside; *m* 1 (m dis 1981), Elizabeth, da of late Philip Asprey; 4 da (Lara b 1969, Emma b 1970, Lisa b 1973, Anna b 1974); m 2, 20 Feb 1981, Carolyn Mary, da of late Wing Cdr William James Maitland Longmore, CBE (d 1988), of Bishops Waltham, Southampton; *Career* dir: Ajax Insurance Holdings Ltd (formerly The Ajax Insurance Association Ltd) 1964–91, John Poland & Co Ltd 1968–89 and 1991–, The Ajax Insurance Association Ltd 1980–91; chief exec HP Motor Policies at Lloyd's 1974–82; chm: Poland Insurance Brokers Ltd (formerly Cannon Rogers Ltd) 1974–, Radio Victory Ltd 1984–85 (dir 1982–85), Beechbourne Ltd 1989; dir A H Worth Ltd 1990–; Master IOW Foxhounds 1983–95; *Recreations* foxhunting, thoroughbred horse breeding, conservation; *Style*— Michael Poland; ✉ Lower Preshaw House, Upham, Southampton SO32 1HP (☎ 01489 892652, fax 01489 891331)

POLAND, Rear Adm (Edmund) Nicholas; CB (1967), CBE (1962); s of Maj Raymond Alfred Poland, RMLI (ka 1918), and Frances Olive Bayly Jones, *née* Weston (d 1976); *b* 19 Feb 1917; *Educ* RNC Dartmouth; *m* 1 Sept 1941, Pauline Ruth Margaret, da of Maj Hugh Charles Pechell (d 1955), of Manor Close, Felpham, Bognor Regis, Sussex; 3 s (Raymond Anthony b 1942, Roger b 1949, Andrew b 1960), 2 da (Elizabeth b 1944, d 1948, Celia b 1947); *Career* Midshipman HMS Hood and Shropshire 1935–37, Sub Lt HMS Beagle and Hermes 1938–40, Lt HMS Eclipse Norwegian Campaign 1940, MTB serv in Channel and Med 1940–43, qualified torpedo offr HMS Vernon 1943, HMS Furious 1943–44, staff offr ops to Naval Force Cdr Burma HMS Nith 1944, HMS Royalist 1945, MTBs HMS Hornet 1945–46, Lt Cdr HMS Osprey 1946, Flotilla Torpedo Anti-Submarine Offr 3 Submarine Flotilla 1947–50, Cdr 1950, Naval Staff Course Admty Naval Staff Air Warfare Div 1950–53, Br Jt Servs Mission Washington DC 1953–55, Jt Servs Staff Course 1956, Admty Tactical and Ship Requirements Div 1957, Capt 1957, Cmd RN Air Station Abbotsinch 1957–59, NATO Standing Gp Washington DC 1959–62, dir of underseas warfare MOD 1963–66, Rear Adm 1966, Chief of Staff to C in C Western Fleet 1966–68, ret 1968; md: Wellman Incandescant (Africa) Pty Ltd Johannesburg 1968–70, John Bell Fabrics of Scot Ltd Biggar Lanarkshire 1970–72; vice pres Scot Assoc for the Care and Resettlement of Offenders 1979 (dir 1974–79), vice pres Int Prisoners Aid Assoc 1980; pres local branch Royal Br Legion 1982–88; Alliance candidate CC; FIMgt 1958–70; *Books* Majumba's Survival Trail (1992), The Torpedomen (1993); *Recreations* gardening; *Style*— Rear Adm Nicholas Poland, CB, CBE; ✉ 39 Limmer Lane, Felpham, Bognor Regis, W Sussex PO22 7HD (☎ 01243 824258)

POLANI, Prof Paul Emanuel; s of Enrico Polani (d 1945), of Trieste, Italy, and Elsa, *née* Zennaro (d 1962); *b* 1 Jan 1914; *Educ* Classical Lyceum F Petrarca Trieste, Univ of Siena, Scuola Normale Superiore Pisa (MD); *m* 24 Aug 1944, Nina Ester, da of Samuel Sullam, of London; *Career* ships surgn 1939–40, MO i/c First Aid Post Borough of Southwark 1941–45; sr med and surgical offr Evelina Children's Hosp London 1941–48; Guy's Hosp and Med Sch London: Nat Birthday Tst res fell 1948–50, asst dir of paediatrics 1950–55, hon conslt paediatrician 1960–83, Prince Philip prof of paediatric res 1960–80, dir Paediatric Res Unit (now div of Medical and Molecular Genetics) 1960–83, geneticist 1961; res physician and dir Res Unit The Spastics Soc (now Scope) London 1955–60, seconded WHO conslt Nat Inst of Health USA 1959–60, visiting prof of human genetics and devpt Coll of Physicians and Surgns Columbia Univ NY 1977–85; Int Sanremo award for Genetic Res 1984, Baly medal RCP 1985, Gold medal Int Cerebral Palsy Soc 1988; chm Bd of Studies in Genetics Univ of London 1976–78, chm Ctee of Mutagencity DHSS 1978–86, chm Study Gp on Med Biology GEC 1984–87; hon fell UMDS Guy's and St Thomas's Hosp 1994; Cdr Order of Merit Italian Republic 1981; DCH 1945, MRCP 1948, FRCP 1961, FRCOG 1971, FRS 1973, FRCPath 1984, FRCPI 1989; *Recreations* reading, horse riding; *Style*— Prof Paul Polani, FRS; ✉ Little Meadow, Clandon Road, West Clandon, Guildford, Surrey GU4 7TL (☎ 01483 222436); Division of Medical and Molecular Genetics, United Schools of Guy's and St Thomas's Hospitals, Guy's Tower, Guy's Hospital, London SE1 9RT (☎ 0171 955 5000 ext 2524, fax 0171 407 1706)

POLE, *see also:* Carew Pole

POLE, Prof Jack Richon; s of Joseph Pole (d 1985), and Phoebe Louise, *née* Rickards (d 1989); *b* 14 March 1922; *Educ* King Alfred Sch London, Kings Coll London, Queen's Coll Oxford (BA), Princeton (PhD); *m* 31 May 1952 (m dis 1988), Marilyn Louise, da of John Glenn Mitchell (d 1968); 1 s (Nicholas), 2 da (Ilsa, Lucy); *Career* RCS 1941–42, 2 Lt RA 1942, served E Surrey Regt seconded to Somali Scouts 1944–46, ret Capt; instr in history Princeton Univ 1952–53, asst lectr (later lectr) in American history UCL 1953–63, fell Commonwealth Fund American Studies 1957; visiting prof: Berkeley 1960–61 (Jefferson Meml lectr 1971), Ghana 1966, Chicago 1969, Peking 1984; fell Center for Advanced Study in Behavioral Sciences Stanford California 1969; Univ of Cambridge: reader in American history and govt 1963–79, fell Churchill Coll 1968–79, vice master Churchill Coll 1975–79, memb Cncl of Senate 1970–74; guest scholar Woodrow Wilson Int Center Washington 1978–79; Univ of Oxford: Rhodes prof of American history and institutions, fell of St Catherine's Coll 1979–89 (emeritus fell 1989–); Goleib fell NY Univ Law Sch 1990, sr res fell Cwlth Center for Study of American Culture Coll of William and Mary Virginia 1991, Leverhulme emeritus fell 1991–93; memb Amnesty Int, hon vice pres Int Cmmn for the History of Representative and Parly Inst (1990); New Jersey prize Princeton Univ 1953, Ramsdell prize Southern Hist Assoc USA 1960; hon fell Hist Soc of Ghana; FBA 1985, FRHistS; *Books* Political Representation in England & The Origins of the American Republic (1966), The Advance of Democracy (ed, 1967), The Seventeenth Century: The Origins of Legislative Power (1969), Foundations of American Independence (1972), The Revolution in America: Documents of the Internal Development of America in the Revolutionary Era (1971), The Decision for American Independence (1975), The Pursuit of Equality in American History (1978, 2 revised edn 1993), Paths to the American Past (1979), The Gift of Government (1983), Colonial British America (co-ed, 1983), The American Constitution For and Against (ed, 1987), The Blackwell Encyclopedia of the American Revolution (co-ed, 1991); *Recreations* cricket, writing, painting; *Clubs* MCC, Trojan Wanderers' Cricket; *Style*— Prof J R Pole; ✉ 20 Divinity Rd, Oxford OX4 1LJ (☎ 01865 246950); St Catherine's College, Oxford OX1 3UJ (☎ 01865 271 700, fax 01865 271768)

POLE, Peter John Chandos; s and h of Sir Peter Van Notten Pole, 5 Bt; *b* 27 April 1952; *m* 1973, Suzanne Norah, da of Harold Raymond Hughes; 2 s (Michael b 1980, Andrew b 1986), 1 da (Naomi b 1983); *Style*— Peter Pole, Esq; ✉ 41 Webster St, Nedlands 6009, W Australia

POLE, Sir Peter Van Notten; 5 Bt (GB 1791); s of late Arthur Chandos Pole and kinsman of Sir Cecil Pery Van-Notten-Pole, 4 Bt (d 1948); *b* 6 Nov 1921; *Educ* Guildford GS; *m* 1949, Jean Emily, da of late Charles Douglas Stone; 1 s, 1 da; *Heir* s, Peter John Chandos Pole, *qv*; *Career* 1939–45 war as Flt Sgt RAAF; accountant, ret; FASA, ACIS; *Style*— Sir Peter Pole, Bt; ✉ 130/60 Kalinda Drive, City Beach, WA 6015, Australia

POLIZZI DI SORRENTINO, (Hon) (Olga); *née* Forte; CBE (1990); eldest da of Baron Forte (Life Peer), *qv*; *b* 1947; *Educ* St Mary's Ascot; *m* 1, 26 Sept 1966, Marchese Alessandro Polizzi di Sorrentino (decd), s of Gen Polizzi di Sorrentino (d 1980); 2 da (Alexandra b 28 Aug 1971, Charlotte b 8 April 1974); m 2, Oct 1993, (Hon) William Hartley Hume Shawcross, *qv*, son of Baron Shawcross, GBE, PC, QC (Life Peer); *Career* exec dir Forte plc until 1996; elected to Westminster City Cncl 1989–94; govr St Mary Sch Ascot; co-chm The Grosvenor House Antiques Fair; memb Cncl Royal Coll of Music; *Style*— Mrs Olga Polizzi, CBE; ✉ Forte plc, 166 High Holborn, London WC1 (☎ 0171 301 2250)

POLKINGHORNE, Rev Dr John Charlton; s of George Baulkwill Polkinghorne (d 1981), and Dorothy Evelyn, *née* Charlton (d 1983); *b* 16 Oct 1930; *Educ* Elmhurst GS Street Somerset, Perse Sch Cambridge, Trinity Coll Cambridge (BA, PhD, MA, ScD), Westcott House Cambridge; *m* 26 March 1955, Ruth Isobel, da of Hedley Gifford Martin (d 1979); 2 s (Peter b 1957, Michael b 1963), 1 da (Isobel Morland b 1959); *Career* Nat Serv RAEC 1948–49; fell Trinity Coll Cambridge 1954–86; lectr: Univ of Edinburgh 1956–58, Univ of Cambridge 1958–65 (reader 1965–68, prof of mathematical physics 1968–79); ordained: deacon 1981, priest 1982; curate: Cambridge 1981–82, Bristol 1982–84; vicar Blean Kent 1984–86, fell, dean and chaplain Trinity Hall Cambridge 1986–89 (hon fell 1989), pres Queens' Coll Cambridge 1989–96 (fell 1996–), Proctor in Convocation 1990–; chm: Ctee on Use of Foetal Material 1988–89, Nuclear Physics Bd 1978–79, Task Force to Review Servs for Drug Misusers 1994–96, Advsy Ctee on Genetic Testing 1996–; memb: SRC 1975–79, Doctrine Cmmn 1989–96; chm govrs Perse Sch 1972–81; Hon DD Univ of Kent 1994, Hon DSc Univ of Exeter 1994, Hon DSc Univ of Leicester 1995; FRS 1974; *Books* The Analytic S-Matrix (1966), The Particle Play (1979), Models of High Energy Processes (1980), The Quantum World (1984), The Way the World Is (1983), One World (1986), Science and Creation (1988), Science and Providence (1989), Rochester Roundabout (1989), Reason and Reality (1991), Science and Christian Belief (1994), Serious Talk (1995), Scientists on Theologians (1996), Beyond Science (1996); *Recreations* gardening; *Style*— The Rev Dr John Polkinghorne, FRS; ✉ 74 Hurst Park Avenue, Cambridge CB4 2AF (☎ 01223 360743, fax 01223 335566)

POLL, Prof (David) Ian Alistair; s of Ralph Poll, of Macclesfield, Cheshire, and Mary, *née* Hall; *b* 1 Oct 1950; *Educ* Heckmondwike GS Yorks, Imperial Coll London (BSc), Cranfield Inst of Technol (PhD); *m* 31 May 1975, Elizabeth Mary, da of Ewart John Read (d 1968), of Painswick, Gloucestershire; 2 s (Edward b 1977, Robert b 1980), 1 da (Helen b 1984); *Career* Future Projects Dept Hawker Siddeley Aviation 1972–75, sr lectr in aerodynamics Cranfield Inst of Tech 1985–87 (res asst 1975–78, lectr 1978–85); Univ of Manchester: prof of aeronautical engrg and dir Goldstein Laboratory 1987–95, head Engrg Dept 1991–94, head Aerospace Div 1994–95; md Flow Science Ltd 1990–95; head Coll of Aeronautics Cranfield Univ 1995–, md Cranfield Aerospace Ltd 1996–; visiting scientist: DFVLR Göttingen W Germany 1983, NASA Langley Res Centre Virginia USA 1983, 1989 and 1990, NASA Ames Research Centre California 1995; memb Fluid Dynamics Panel NATO Advsy Gp for Aerospace R & D 1991–; Royal Aeronautical Soc: memb Cncl 1987–89 and 1996–, chm Accreditation Panel 1989–91; author of over 100 papers on aerodynamics; ACGI 1972; CEng 1978, FRAeS 1987, AFAIAA 1993, FEng 1996; *Recreations* fell walking, DIY, political debate; *Style*— Prof Ian Poll, FEng; ✉ College of Aeronautics, Cranfield University, Cranfield, Bedfordshire MK43 0AL (☎ 01234 754743, fax 01234 752149, e-mail D.I.A.POLL@CRANFIELD.AC.UK)

POLLACCHI, Derek Albert Paterson; s of Dr Alberto Giovanni Pollacchi (d 1969), and Kathleen Mary, *née* Paterson (d 1980); *b* 23 July 1951; *Educ* St Mungo's Acad Glasgow, Inst of Health Servs Mgmnt (DipHSM); *m* 25 July 1975, Jean Lindsay, da of John Charles Mullan; 2 da (Christine Maria b 7 June 1980, Julie Kathleen Margaret b 12 Jan 1982); *Career* Scottish Management Training Scheme 1969–72, various jr mgmnt posts 1972–79; sector admin: Mearnskirk Gen Hosp Glasgow 1979–83, Leverndale Hosp Glasgow 1983–84; dir of admin servs Lennox Castle Hosp/Stobhill Gen Hosp and assoc community health servs 1984–87, gen mangr Mental Handicap Servs Forth Valley Health Bd 1987–92; chief exec: Royal Scottish Nat Hosp and Community NHS Tst 1993–94, The Central Scotland Healthcare NHS Tst 1994–; assoc memb Inst Health Servs Mgmnt; *Style*— Derek A Pollacchi, Esq; ✉ The Central Scotland Healthcare NHS Trust, The Royal Scottish National Hospital, Old Denny Rd, Larbert FK5 4SD (☎ 01324 570700, fax 01324 562367)

POLLACK, Anita Jean; MEP (Lab) London SW (majority 30,975); da of John Samuel Pollack, of Sydney, Australia, and Kathleen, *née* Emerson; *b* 3 June 1946; *Educ* Sydney Tech Coll (Dip in Advertising), City of London Poly (BA), Birkbeck Coll London (MSc); *m* Philip Stephen Bradbury; 1 da (Katherine Louise Pollack Bradbury b 4 Sept 1986); *Career* former advtg copywriter Aust, book ed London 1970–74, res asst to Rt Hon Barbara Castle 1981–89; MEP (Lab) London SW 1989–; *Recreations* family; *Style*— Ms Anita Pollack, MEP; ✉ 177 Lavender Hill, London SW11 5TE (☎ 0171 228 0839, fax 0171 228 0916)

POLLARD, Prof Arthur; s of George Arthur Pollard (d 1992), of Clitheroe, Lancs, and Nellie, *née* Smith (d 1977); *b* 22 Dec 1922; *Educ* Clitheroe Royal GS, Univ of Leeds (BA), Lincoln Coll Oxford (BLitt); *m* 1, 2 Sept 1948, Ursula Ann Egerton (d 1970), da of Nathan Jackson (d 1973), of Congleton, Cheshire; 2 s (John Stanley b 1952, Andrew Michael b 1958); m 2, 9 April 1973, Phyllis Mary, da of John Richard Pattinson (d 1958), of Cartmel, Cumbria; *Career* 161 (RMC) OCTU 1943, cmmnd E Lancs Regt, served 1 Bn 1943; overseas serv, seconded on intelligence to FO 1943–45, Staff Capt (Movements), Kilindini E Africa 1945–46; Univ of Manchester: asst lectr in Eng literature 1949–52, lectr 1952–64, sr lectr 1964–67, dir of gen studies Faculty of Arts 1964–67; Univ of Hull: prof of Eng 1967–84, dean Faculty of Arts 1976–78; conslt prof of Eng Univ of Buckingham 1983–89; Congleton BC: cncllr 1952–65, ldr 1963–67, alderman 1965–67; Humberside CC: cncllr 1979–96, Cons educn spokesman 1981–96; cncllr E Riding of Yorks Cncl 1995–; memb: Secdy Examinations Cncl 1983–88, Assoc of CCs Educn Ctee 1985–89, Funding Agency for Schs 1996–; contrib to Black Papers on educn; reader: St Peter's Congleton 1951–67, All Saints North Ferriby 1968–74, All Saints South Cave 1974–; memb Gen Synod C of E 1990–; Hon DLitt Univ of Buckingham 1982; *Books* Charles Simeon 1759–1836 (with M M Hennell, 1959), New Poems of George Crabbe (1960), English Hymns (1960), English Sermons (1963), Mrs Gaskell Novelist and Biographer (1965), Richard Hooker (1966), The Letters of Mrs Gaskell (with J A V Chapple, 1966), The Victorians (1970, revised and enlarged 1987), Satire (1970), Crabbe: The Critical Heritage (1972), Anthony Trollope (1978), The Landscape of the Brontës (1988), Complete Poetical Works of George Crabbe, 3 vols (with Norma Dalrymple-Champneys, 1988), Richard Hooker: Ecclesiastical Polity (1990); *Recreations* cricket, railway history; *Style*— Prof Arthur Pollard; ✉ Sand Hall, North Cave, Brough, E Yorks HU15 2LA (☎ 01430 422202, fax 01430 424850); County Hall, Beverley, E Yorks (☎ 01482 885011, fax 01482 885009)

POLLARD, Maj-Gen (Charles) Barry; s of Leonard Charles Pollard (d 1980); *b* 20 April 1927; *Educ* Ardingly, Selwyn Coll Cambridge; *m* 1954, Mary, da of Jack Sydney Heyes (d 1970); 3 da; *Career* RE 1947, GSO 1 MOD 1967, DS Staff Coll 1967–68, CRE 3 Div 1969–71, Col GS 3 Div 1971–72, CCRE 1 (Br) Corps 1972–74, RCDS 1975, chief engr BAOR 1976–79, Col Cmdt RE 1982–87; nat dir Project Trident (Trident Tst) 1980–84, dir Solent Business Fund 1984–91, md Westgate Fund Mgmnt Ltd 1985–89; tstee Douglas Haig Meml Homes 1987–; *Recreations* ocean sailing, golf; *Style*— Maj-Gen Barry Pollard; ✉ Yateley, Coombe Rd, Salisbury, Wilts SP2 8BT (☎ 01722 335493)

POLLARD, Chief Constable Charles; QPM (1990); s of Humphrey Charles Pollard (d 1990), and Margaret Isobel, *née* Philpott (d 1986); *b* 4 Feb 1945; *Educ* Oundle, Univ of Bristol (LLB); *m* 13 July 1972, Erica Jane, da of Gordon Daniel Jack; 2 s (Jonathan Christopher), 1 da (Rosemary); *Career* Met Police 1964–66, travelled abroad 1967, Met Police 1968–80 (latterly chief inspr); Sussex Police: supt i/c Eastbourne Sub-Div 1980–84, chief supt i/c Operational Support Dept HQ Lewes 1984–85; asst chief constable Thames Valley Police 1985–88, dep asst cmmr i/c Plus Programme and later SW Area Met Police 1988–91, chief constable Thames Valley Police 1991–; visiting fell Nuffield Coll Oxford 1993–; memb ACPO (chm Quality Serv Ctee 1991–94), chm Oxford Common Purpose 1996–; *Recreations* walking, bridge, tennis, family pursuits; *Clubs* Royal Over-Seas League; *Style*— Chief Constable Charles Pollard, QPM; ✉ Thames Valley Police HQ, Oxford Road, Kidlington, Oxon OX5 2NX (☎ 01865 846002, fax 01865 846057)

POLLARD, Christopher Leslie; OBE (1989); s of Sidney Samuel Pollard (d 1975), and Gertrude Winifred, *née* Skipper (d 1987); *b* 18 June 1939; *Educ* Thames Valley GS Twickenham, Ealing Sch of Hotel Mgmnt, post graduate City & Guilds Technical Teachers Certificate (UWIST); *m* 13 April 1963, Vivien Mary, da of Edwin Hornby (d 1982); 1 da (Rebecca b 27 June 1966); *Career* lectr hotel mgmnt and assoc studies Cardiff Coll of Food Technol and Commerce 1960–63; proprietor Mount Sorrel Hotel Barry 1963–74; md Hamard Catering Gp 1968–86 (chm 1974–86), dir Hamard Catering Saudi Arabia Ltd 1978, chm and md Dramah Investments Ltd and Dramah Developments Ltd 1986; dir: Middlepatch Ltd 1987, Cardiff Marketing Ltd 1991–92, Welsh Food Promotions Ltd 1991–93; memb Wales Tourist Bd appointed by Sec of State for Wales 1983–92; chm: Taste of Wales - Blas ar Gymru Ltd 1988–91, Attractions Advsy Ctee Wales Tourist Bd 1986, Hotels Advsy Ctee Wales Tourist Bd 1986; memb Help the Aged Jubilee Appeal for Wales 1986, hon treas UK Freedom from Hunger Campaign 1977–87; High Sheriff of South Glamorgan 1989–90; Freeman City of London 1986, Liveryman Worshipful Co of Tinplate Workers alias Wire Workers 1986; FHCIMA; *Clubs* Leander Rowing; *Style*— Christopher Pollard, Esq, OBE; ✉ Penarth House, Cliff Parade, Penarth, South Glamorgan CF6 2BP (☎ 01222 709065)

POLLARD, Dr Corinna Mary; da of Air Vice-Marshal Henry Lindsay Roxburgh, CBE (d 1989), and Hermione Babington, *née* Collard; *b* 16 Oct 1951; *Educ* Farnborough Hill Convent Coll, St George's Hosp Med Sch London (MB BS); *m* 16 Aug 1975, Timothy William, s of Kenneth John Pollard (d 1979); 2 da (Amy b 1984, Sophie b 1986); *Career* currently conslt haematologist Mayday Hosp Surrey; memb Br Soc for Haematology 1985; memb Med Advsy Panel to Anthony Nolan Bone Marrow Tst; MRCP 1979, MRCPath 1983, FRCP 1995, FRCPath 1995; *Recreations* art, skiing; *Style*— Dr Corinna Pollard; ✉ Department of Haematology, Mayday Hospital, Mayday Rd, Thornton Heath, Surrey CR7 7YE (☎ 0181 401 3000)

POLLARD, Eve (Lady Lloyd); da of Ivor Pollard, and Mimi Pollard; *m* 1, 8 Dec 1968 (m dis), Barry Winkleman, *qv*; 1 da (Claudia b 15 Jan 1972); m 2, 23 May 1979, Sir Nicholas Lloyd, *qv*; 1 s (Oliver b 6 Aug 1980); *Career* fashion ed: Honey 1967–68, Daily Mirror Magazine 1968–69; reporter Daily Mirror 1969–70; women's ed: Observer Magazine 1970–71, Sunday Mirror 1971–81; asst ed Sunday People 1981–83, features ed and presenter TV-am 1983–85; ed: Elle (launch, USA) 1985–86, Sunday Magazine (News of the World) 1986, You Magazine (Mail on Sunday) 1986–88, Sunday Mirror and Sunday Mirror Magazine 1988–91, Sunday Express and Sunday Express magazine 1991–94; devised two series Frocks on the Box for ITV 1985; chair - Women in Journalism (launch) 1995–, 1Editor of the Year Newspaper Focus Awards 1990; memb English Tourist Bd 1993–; *Books* Jackie: Biography of Mrs J K Onassis (1971), Splash (jtly Val Corbett and Joyce Hopkirk, 1995), Best of Enemies (1996); *Style*— Miss Eve Pollard; ✉ c/o Simpson Fox Associates Ltd, 52 Shaftesbury Avenue, London W1V 7DE (☎ 0171 434 9167, fax 0171 494 2887)

POLLARD, (Andrew) Garth; s of Rev George Pollard, of 44 Vernon Rd, Sheffield, and Elizabeth Beatrice, *née* Briggs; *b* 25 April 1945; *Educ* Queen's Coll Taunton, King's Coll London (LLB); *m* 26 May 1973, Lucy Petica, da of Prof Charles Martin Robertson, of Cambridge; 3 s (Finn b 1978, Tam b 1980, Liam b 1982); *Career* admitted slr 1969; ptnr Clifford-Turner 1975–87 (slr 1969–75), exec ptnr Clifford Chance 1991– (ptnr 1987–); AKC; *Recreations* music, walking; *Style*— Garth Pollard, Esq; ✉ Clifford Chance, 200 Aldersgate Street, London EC1A 4JJ (☎ 0171 600 1000, fax 0171 600 5555, telex 887847)

POLLARD, Ian Douglas; s of Douglas Pollard, DFC (ka 1945), and Peggy, *née* Murfitt (d 1989); *b* 9 June 1945; *Educ* Perse Sch Cambridge; *m* 25 July 1964, Dianna, da of Prof Alexander Deer, of Cambridge; 3 da (Juliette b 1964, Samantha b 1966, Arushka b 1987), 2 s (Rufus b 1992, Kian b 1995); *Career* chm and md Flaxyard plc 1972–; architectural designer of: Marcopolo (Observers Bldg) 1987, Sainsbury's Homebase Kensington 1988, Martin Ryan Inst for Marine Scis Galway 1991; memb Nat Gdns Scheme; ARICS; *Recreations* gardening, cycling, diving; *Style*— Ian Pollard, Esq; ✉ The Abbey House, Market Cross, Malmesbury, Wilts SN16 9AS (☎ 01666 822212)

POLLARD, John Stanley; s of Prof Arthur Pollard, of N Cave, Humberside, and Ursula Ann Egerton, *née* Jackson (d 1970); *b* 4 Jan 1952; *Educ* King's Sch Macclesfield, Hymer's Coll Hull, Univ of Leeds (LLB); *m* 14 Sept 1974, Clare Judith, da of Arnold Walter George Boulton (d 1992), of Cookham Dean, Berkshire; 3 s (Samuel John b 1979, Joseph William b 1981, Edward George b 1984); *Career* admitted slr 1977; HM dep coroner Cheshire, HM coroner Manchester South District; memb Congleton Town Cncl 1983–; Parly candidate (SDP) Crewe and Nantwich 1983; dir and tstee Astbury Mere Tst; dir Congleton Town FC, pres Vale Juniors FC; memb: Law Soc, Coroners Soc of England and Wales; *Recreations* football, sport, gardening, politics; *Style*— John Pollard, Esq;

✉ The Old Vicarage, Brook Street, Congleton, Cheshire; HM Coroner, First Floor, Greenhale House, Piccadilly, Stockport

POLLEN, Sir John Michael Hungerford; 7 Bt (GB 1795), of Redenham, Hampshire; s of late Lt Cdr John Francis Hungerford Pollen, RN; suc father's 2 cous, Sir John Lancelot Hungerford Pollen, 6 Bt, 1959; *b* 6 April 1919; *Educ* Downside, Merton Coll Oxford; *m* 1, 1941 (m dis 1956), Angela Mary Oriana (d 1990), da of Maj F J Russi, MC; 1 s, 1 da; m 2, 1957, Mrs Diana Alice Jubb (d 1995), da of late A E Timbrell; *Heir* s, Richard John Hungerford Pollen, *qv*; *Career* served WWII (despatches), Capt RA; *Style*— Sir John Pollen, Bt; ✉ Manor House, Rodbourne, Malmesbury, Wilts

POLLEN, Richard John Hungerford; s and h of Sir John Michael Hungerford Pollen, 7 Bt, *qv*; *b* 3 Nov 1946; *Educ* Worth Abbey; *m* 2 Oct 1971, Christianne Mary, da of Sir (William) Godfrey Agnew, KCVO, CB (d 1995); 5 s (William Richard Hungerford b 1976, Jonathan Charles b 1979, Andrew Francis b 1982, Alexander Christian b 1986, Joseph Anthony b and d 1991), 3 da (Isabel Mary Ruth b 1975, Alice Charlotte Mary b 1984, Beatrice Veronica Mary b 1992); *Career* Capel-Cure Myers 1964–68; overseas 1969–70; Charles Barker 1971–79, Valin Pollen 1979–89, Richard Pollen & Company (corp and fin communications and PR consultancy) 1989–94, Ludgate Group 1994–; memb: BHS, CGA; MIPR, MInstD; *Recreations* equestrianism, skiing, tennis, walking; *Style*— Richard J H Pollen, Esq; ✉ Dunsfold Ryse, Chiddingfold, Surrey GU8 4YA (☎ 01483 200354); Ludgate Group, 111 Charterhouse Street, London EC1M 6AA (☎ 0171 216 4500, fax 0171 216 4501)

POLLER, Prof Leon; s of Nathan Kristian Poller (d 1975), of Southport, Lancs, and Helena, *née* Minshull (d 1987); *b* 16 April 1927; *Educ* Univ of Manchester (DSc, MD); *m* 9 July 1955, Jean Mavis, da of James Albert Dier, MBE (d 1989), of Bolton, Lancs; 2 s (David b 1962, John b 1965); *Career* Lt, Capt, Maj RAMC 1953–55, CDEE Porton Down Miny of Supply; jr hosp appts Manchester 1957–61, conslt haematologist and dir UK Ref Lab for Anticoagulant Reagents and Control Collaborating Centre WHO 1961–92, currently hon conslt haematologist Withington Hosp and hon prof Univ of Manchester; over 200 published papers, books and reviews on blood coagulation and thrombosis; currently: chm Int Ctee Standardization in Haematology Task Force Blood Coagulation 1972–, chm Nat and Int Med Scientific Ctees, project ldr Euro Community Concerted Action on Anticoagulation, co-chm ISHT Sub-Ctee on Anticoagulant Control; sec Manchester Thrombosis Res Fndn; chm: ICSH Task Force on Quality Control in Blood Coagulation, WHO IEQAS in Blood Coagulation Advsy Group; currently chm Manchester and Dist Home for Lost Dogs; FRCPath 1968; *Books* Theory and Practice of Anticoagulant Treatment (1962), Recent Advances in Blood Coagulation 1–7 (ed, 1968–96), Recent Advances in Thrombosis (ed, 1972), Thrombosis and its Management (ed, 1993), Oral Anticoagulants (ed, 1996); *Recreations* forestry, cricket (playing), music (listening); *Clubs* Athenaeum; *Style*— Prof Leon Poller; ✉ 5 Oakwood Ave, Gatley, Cheadle, Cheshire SK8 4LR (☎ 0161 428 7621, fax 0161 428 0763); Department of Pathological Sciences, Medical School, University of Manchester (☎ and fax 0161 275 5316)

POLLINGTON, Viscount; John Andrew Bruce Savile; s and h of 8 Earl of Mexborough, *qv*; *b* 30 Nov 1959; *Style*— Viscount Pollington; ✉ Arden Hall, Hawnby, York YO6 5LS

POLLINS, Martin; s of Harry Pollins (d 1969), of London, and Hetty Pollins; *b* 11 Dec 1938; *Educ* Brighton Tech Sch; *m* 1, March 1963 (m dis 1980); m 2, 13 Dec 1980, Susan Elizabeth, da of Arthur Edwin Hines, of Brighton; 4 s (Andrew, Richard, Nicholas, Matthew), 1 da (Anna); *Career* CA; ptnr PRB Martin Pollins 1968–, chm Professional Enterprise Gp plc 1986–, chm Maltrace Plc 1995–, dir Network Technology Plc 1995–; cncl memb ICAEW 1987–96; FCA 1964, ATII 1964; *Recreations* spectator of sport; *Style*— Martin Pollins, Esq; ✉ Forest Ridge, Maresfield, E Sussex TN22 3ER; PRB Martin Pollins, 5 Bridge Rd Business Park, Bridge Rd, Haywards Heath, W Sussex RH16 1TX (☎ 01444 458252, fax 01444 458184)

POLLITT, Prof Christopher John; s of Almora John Pollitt, and Freda Hebbert, *née* Ashcroft; *b* 7 Feb 1946; *Educ* Oriel Coll Oxford (MA), LSE (PhD); *partner* Hilkka Helena Summa; 2 s from prev m (Thomas John b 22 April 1971, Jack Christopher b 12 Aug 1972); *Career* asst princ then princ Home Civil Serv (MOD, Miny of Technol, DTI) 1967–73, sr lectr Middx Poly 1973–75, lectr then sr lectr in govt Open Univ 1975–90; Brunel Univ: prof of govt and co-dir Centre for the Evaluation of Public Policy and Practice 1990–, dean Faculty of Social Scis 1994–; hon jt ed Public Admin 1980–88, dir Study Gp for Quality and Productivity in Public Servs Euro Gp for Public Admin 1988–94, non-exec dir Hillingdon Hosp Tst 1995–; numerous research grants and consultancies with public and govt bodies incl: ESRC, EC, HM Treasy, OECD; memb Cncl RIPA 1990–92, pres Euro Evaluation Soc 1996–98; *Books* incl: Managerialism and the Public Service (2 edn, 1993), Controlling Health Professionals (with Steve Harrison, 1994), Quality in European Public Services (with Geert Bouckaert, 1995); *Recreations* squash, walking, owl-watching; *Style*— Prof Christopher Pollitt; ✉ Dean Faculty of Social Sciences and Co-Director Centre for the Evaluation of Public Policy and Practice, Brunel University, Uxbridge, Middx UB8 3PH (☎ 01895 203334, fax 01895 274697)

POLLITT, Dr John Deryk; s of Charles Edwin (d 1968), of Plumstead, London, and Sarah Jane, *née* Fisher (d 1976); *b* 24 Aug 1926; *Educ* City of London Sch, St Thomas's Hosp Med Sch London (Peacock scholar, MB BS, MD, FRCP, FRCPsych, DPM, Planck prize in Psychiatry, Gold and Bronze medallist RCPsych); *m* 1953, Erica Elizabeth, da of Arthur Ratzkowski; 2 da (Angela Elizabeth b 10 Feb 1957, Daphne Jane b 26 June 1958); *Career* chief asst to Sr Registrar Dept of Psychological Med St Thomas's Hosp London 1958–59, Rockefeller travelling res fell in med 1959–60, res fell Harvard Med Sch Mass Mental Health Centre Boston (conslt Advsy Bd Drug Res Project); St Thomas's Hosp London: physician in psychological med 1961–85, physician i/c Dept of Psychological Med 1972–79; regnl postgraduate dean SE Thames RHA 1979–83, asst dir Br Postgraduate Med Fedn 1979–83; dir of med educn and hon clinical advsr Hayes Grove Priory Hosp 1986–88 (med dir 1983–86); recognised teacher of psychological med Univ of London 1961–85, advsr in psychiatry to CMO Metropolitan Police 1977–82, advsr in psychiatry to CMO Imperial Chemical Industries 1986–90; postgrad advsr RCP SE Thames Region 1977–79; memb: Bd of Postgrad Studies in Med Univ of London 1972–85, Advsy Cmmn of Deans Cncl of Postgrad Med Educn 1979–83, Conf of Postgrad Deans and Dirs of Postgrad Educn in UK 1979–83, Jt Med Advsy Ctee of Academic and Collegiate Cncls Univ of London 1979–83; chm Regnl Postgrad Ctee of SE Thames Region 1979–83; pres Section of Psychiatry RSM 1976–77 (vice pres 1973–76), vice pres Br Assoc for Social Psychiatry 1974–76; *Books* Depression and its Treatment (1965), Psychological Medicine for Students (1973), Psychiatric Emergencies in Family Practice (1987); *Recreations* landscape, painting in watercolour, architectural drawing, letterpress printing, etching and drypoint, antiquarian horology; *Style*— Dr John Pollitt; ✉ 152 Harley St, London W1N 1HH (☎ 0171 935 8868)

POLLOCK, *see:* Montagu-Pollock

POLLOCK, Sheriff Alexander; s of Robert Faulds Pollock, OBE, and Margaret Findlay, *née* Aitken; *b* 21 July 1944; *Educ* Rutherglen Acad, Glasgow Acad, BNC Oxford (Domus exhibitioner, MA), Univ of Edinburgh (LLB), Perugia Univ; *m* 1975, Verena Francesca Gertraud Alice Ursula, da of late J Reginald Critchley, of Patmore Lodge, Patmore Heath, Albury, Ware, Herts; 1 s (Andrew b 1979), 1 da (Francesca b 1976); *Career* slr 1970–73, advocate Scottish Bar 1973–91; MP (C): Moray and Nairn 1979–83, Moray 1983–87; memb Commons Select Ctee on Scottish Affrs 1979–82; PPS to George Younger: as Sec of State for Scotland 1982–86, as Sec of State for Def 1986–87; sec Br Austrian Parly Gp 1979–87, Advocate Depute 1990–91; Floating Sheriff of Tayside, Central and Fife at Stirling 1991–93, Sheriff of Grampian, Highland and Islands at Aberdeen and Stonehaven 1993–; memb Queen's Body Guard for Scotland (Royal Co of Archers) 1984–; *Clubs* New (Edinburgh), Highland (Inverness); *Style*— Sheriff Alexander Pollock; ✉ Drumdarrach, Forres, Moray, Scotland IV36 ODW

POLLOCK, His Hon Judge (Peter) Brian; s of Brian Treherne Pollock (d 1994), of Dial Cottage, Rolvenden Layne, Kent, and Helen Evelyn, *née* Holt-Wilson (d 1995); *b* 27 April 1936; *Educ* St Lawrence Coll; *m* 1, 1966 (m dis 1981), Joan Maryon, da of late Maj Charles Eustace Maryon Leggett; 2 s (Robin b 1967, Guy b and d 1969, Richard b 1971); m 2, 22 June 1988, Jeannette Mary Nightingale, da of Cdr Wilfrid Farrell, MBE, RN (d 1996); 1 step da (Anna (Mrs Lee-Emery) b 1967), 2 step s (Paul b 1969, Jim b 1972); *Career* called to the Bar Middle Temple 1958; recorder of the Crown Court 1986, circuit judge (SE Circuit) 1987–; *Recreations* playing tennis, watching cricket, travel, walking, cooking, gardening; *Clubs* MCC, Roehampton; *Style*— His Hon Judge Pollock; ✉ Croydon Combined Court, The Law Courts, Altyre Road, Croydon CR0 3NE

POLLOCK, David (Charles) Treherne; s of Brian Treherne Pollock (d 1994), and Helen Evelyn (d 1995), da of Brig-Gen Sir Eric Holt-Wilson, CMG, DSO (d 1950); *b* 7 April 1938; *Educ* St Andrew's Pangbourne, Nowton Ct, The Hill Sch, St Lawrence Coll; *m* 1961, Lisbeth Jane, da of Maj Peter Scratchley (d 1974); 2 s (Piers, Blair), 1 da (Sophie-Jane); *Career* 2 Lt The Gordon Highlanders 1956–59; The Economist 1961–68; dir: Mathers & Streets Ltd 1968–69, Charles Barker (City) Ltd 1969–70, Dewe Rogerson Ltd 1970–88, Dewe Rogerson Group Ltd 1975–88, Maxwell Stamp plc 1988–, Seal Ice Ltd 1995–; chm: Corporate Television Broadcasting Ltd 1988–92, The Bloxham Group Ltd 1992–; tstee Restoration of Appearance and Function Tst 1994–; *Clubs* City of London; *Style*— David Treherne Pollock, Esq; ✉ Maxwell Stamp plc, 2 Hat and Mitre Court, St John St, London EC1M 4EL (☎ 0171 251 0147, fax 0171 251 0140); 9 The Chase, London SW4 0NP (☎ 0171 622 1535, fax 0171 498 6400)

POLLOCK, David Frederick; s and h of Sir George Frederick Pollock, 5 Bt, *qv*; *b* 13 April 1959; *m* 14 Sept 1985, Helena R, o da of late L J Tompsett, OBE, of Tadworth, Surrey; 1 da (Anna-Lisa Frances b 7 May 1989); *Career* md Pollock Audio Visual Ltd 1983–; dir: Cloud 9 (Video Film Prodns) Ltd 1987–91, Friends Travel Ltd 1993–, Hatton Farm Estates Ltd 1995–; md Cloud 9 Television (Facilities) Ltd 1991–; *Style*— David Pollock, Esq; ✉ 21 Meare Close, Tadworth, Surrey KT20 5RZ

POLLOCK, David Raymond John; s of Eric John Frank Pollock (d 1992), of Dulwich, and Beryl Olive, *née* Newens (d 1982); *b* 22 Oct 1949; *Educ* Dulwich, Univ of Keele (BA); *m* 30 July 1975, Barbara Ann, da of Henry Chambré, MBE, of Hendon; 1 da (Sarah Charlotte Chambré b 23 Aug 1980), 1 s (Thomas Hugo John b 19 March 1984); *Career* MOD: admin trainee 1972, higher exec offr 1975 (private sec to Chief Sci Advsr), princ 1978; asst dir Primary Mkts Div Int Stock Exchange 1989–91 (head of Industry Policy Unit 1986, head of Business Devpt Primary Mkts Div 1988), dir Newspaper Publishers Assoc 1992– (dir designate 1991); memb: Cncl and Fin Ctee Royal Inst of GB, Soc of Archer Antiquaries; Liveryman Worshipful Company of Stationers and Newspaper Makers; *Recreations* country pursuits, drawing and painting, books, conviviality; *Style*— David Pollock, Esq; ✉ 46 Dacres Rd, London SE23 2NR (☎ 0181 699 3883); The Newspapers Publishers Association Ltd, 34 Southwark Bridge Road, London SE1 9EU (☎ 0171 928 6928, fax 0171 928 2067)

POLLOCK, Ellen Clara; da of Hedwig Elizabeth Kahn (d 1958); *Educ* St Mary's Coll London, Convent of The Blessed Sacrament Brighton; *m* 1, 13 July 1928, Lt-Col Leslie Frank Coventry Hancock, OBE (d 1944); 1 s (Michael Coventry); m 2, 1945, James Proudfoot, RP, ROI (d 1971); *Career* actress 1920–; theatre incl: Hit the Deck 1927, Her First Affaire 1930, The Good Companions 1931, Finished Abroad 1934, The Dominant Sex 1935; seasons of Shaw's plays 1944–53, Mrs Warren's Profession (Royal Ct Theatre) 1960, Six Characters in Search of an Author 1963, Lady Frederick 1969–70, Pygmalion 1974, Tales from Vienna Woods (NT) 1976, The Dark Lady of the Sonnets 1977, The Woman I Love 1979, Country Life 1980, Harlequinade (NT); numerous film and TV appearances incl: Forsyte Saga, The Pallisers, World's End, The Nightingale Saga, The Old Men at the Zoo; pres The Shaw Soc; *Recreations* antiques; *Style*— Miss Ellen Pollock; ✉ 9 Tedworth Square, Chelsea, London SW3 4DU (☎ 0171 352 5082)

POLLOCK, Sir George Frederick; 5 Bt (UK 1866), of Hatton, Middx; s of Sir (Frederick) John Pollock, 4 Bt (d 1963); *b* 13 Aug 1928; *Educ* Eton, Trinity Coll Cambridge (MA); *m* 1951, Doreen Mumford, da of Norman Ernest Keown Nash, CMG (d 1966); 1 s (David Frederick b 1959), 2 da (Charlotte Anne b 1952, Catherine Frances Jill b 1955); *Heir* s, David Frederick Pollock, *qv*, b 13 April 1959; *Career* 2 Lt 17/21 Lancers 1948–49; admitted slr 1956; artist-photographer and audio-visual creator 1963–; hon vice pres: Disabled Photographers' Soc, Croydon Camera Club; Hon FRPS (pres 1978), FRSA, EFIAP; *Clubs* DHO; *Style*— Sir George F Pollock, Bt; ✉ 83 Minster Way, Bathwick, Bath BA2 6RL (☎ 01225 464692)

POLLOCK, Prof Griselda Frances Sinclair; da of Alan Winton Seton Pollock (d 1986), and Kathleen Alexandra, *née* Sinclair (d 1964); *b* 11 March 1949; *Educ* Queen's Coll London, Lady Margaret Hall Oxford (MA), Courtauld Inst of Art (MA, PhD); *m* 30 Oct 1981, Prof Antony Bryant, s of Paul and Leonie Bryant, of London; 1 s (Benjamin b 22 March 1983), 1 da (Hester b 7 Feb 1986); *Career* lectr in art history Univ of Manchester 1974–77; Univ of Leeds: lectr in art history and film 1977–85, sr lectr 1985–90, prof of social and critical histories of art 1990–, dir Centre for Cultural Studies, exec Centre for Jewish Studies 1995–; author of numerous articles in jls; memb Tate Gallery Liverpool Advsy Bd 1988–94; FRSA 1996; *Books* Millet (1977), Vincent Van Gogh (1978), Mary Cassatt (1980), Old Mistresses Women Art and Ideology (1981), The Journals of Marie Bashkirtseff (1985), Framing Feminism Art and the Women's Movement (1987), Vision and Difference Feminism, Femininity and the Histories of Art (1988), Dealing with Degas (co-ed with R Kendall, 1992), Avant-Garde Gambits 1888–1893: Gender and the Colour of Art History (1992, Walter Neurath Meml Lecture), Generations and Geographies in the Visual Arts (1996), Avant-Gardes and Partisans Reviewed (with Fred Orton, 1996); *Recreations* running, skiing, opera, music; *Style*— Prof Griselda Pollock; ✉ Department of Fine Art, University of Leeds, Leeds LS2 9JT (☎ 0113 233 5267/0, fax 0113 245 1977, telex 556473 UNILDS G)

POLLOCK, Jason Charles Stuart; s of Rev N S Pollock, and Josephine, *née* Reddie; *b* 20 April 1947; *Educ* Pierrepont Sch, Northampton Coll; *Career* formerly: worked on BBC Radio 1, TV/radio reporter and disc jockey San Francisco, PR exec for launch of LBC 1973 (later arts ed), fndr Ladbroke Radio (first syndicated radio feature co in UK), showbiz ed Thames TV, prodr Southern TV, fndr PSA PR co; head of entertainment TV-am plc 1990–92 (show business ed 1983–90), chm Entertainment Partnership Ltd (incl TV prodn co), currently md Pulse Productions; *Clubs* RAC; *Style*— Jason Pollock, Esq; ✉ Pulse Productions, 44 Earlham Street, London WC2H 9LA

POLLOCK, John C; s of Alfred Kenneth Pollock (d 1994), of Bexhill, Sussex, and Ruby Nora Kathleen, *née* Briggs; *b* 4 June 1940; *Educ* Dulwich Coll; *m* 3 March 1972, Renee Mary Desborough; 1 s (James Martin b 2 June 1978); *Career* sr Layton Bennett Billingham & Co CAs 1963–64 (articled clerk 1958–63), chartered accountant Ernst & Whinney The Hague 1965–66 (London 1966–67), Litton Industries Zurich 1968–70, md MCA/Universal Pictures Amsterdam 1970–74, estab Netherlands office Josolyne Layton-Bennett & Co 1974–82 (ptnr UK firm), following merger estab Leeds office Arthur Young 1982–85 (returned as UK desk ptnr in the Netherlands 1985–89), equity ptnr Moret Ernst & Young Netherlands 1990– (following merger with Ernst & Whinney Int Sector 1989), currently ed Moret Ernst & Young's Netherlands Briefing (Eng language bulletin); memb Cncl Netherlands-Br C of C, treas and sec Br Business Assoc (Netherlands), treas Netherlands branch IOD; MBCS (fndr memb), FCA; numerous articles published and lectures given; *Recreations* skiing, walking, photography, travel, gardening, formerly a keen alpinist; *Style*— John C Pollock, Esq; ✉ Moret Ernst & Young Accountants, Drentestraat 20, 1083 HK Amsterdam, The Netherlands (☎ 00 31 20 549 7500, fax 00 31 20 646 2553)

POLLOCK, Rev John Charles; s of Robert Pollock (d 1957), of Syresham Priory, Brackley, Northants, and Ethel Mary Purefoy, *née* Powell (d 1970); *b* 9 Oct 1923; *Educ* Charterhouse, Trinity Coll Cambridge (MA); *m* 4 May 1949, Anne, da of Sir Richard Barrett-Lennard, 5 Bt, OBE, of Horsford Manor, Norwich, Norfolk (d 1977); *Career* Coldstream Gds 1943–45, 2 Lt 1943, Lt 1944, Capt 1945, GSO III Staff of Supreme Allied Commander SE Asia (Mountbatten); asst master Wellington Coll 1947–49; ordained C of E: deacon 1951, priest 1952; curate St Paul's Portman Square London 1951–53, rector Horsington Somerset 1953–58, chaplain to High Sheriff of Devon 1990–91; biographer and historian; *Books* incl: Hudson Taylor and Maria (1962), Moody without Sankey (1963), Billy Graham (3 edn, 1984), The Apostle (1969), Wilberforce (1977), Amazing Grace (1981), Shaftesbury (1985), John Wesley (1989), Fear No Foe (1992), Gordon: the Man Behind the Legend (1993), Way to Glory: the Life of Havelock of Lucknow (2 edn, 1996); *Recreations* tennis, mountain and moorland walking; *Clubs* English-Speaking Union; *Style*— The Rev John Pollock; ✉ Rose Ash House, South Molton, Devonshire EX36 4RB (☎ 01769 550403)

POLLOCK, Adm of the Fleet Sir Michael Patrick; GCB (1971, KCB 1969, CB 1966), LVO (1952), DSC (1944); s of Charles Albert Pollock (d 1937), of, Lydham, Shrops, and Gladys Mason; *b* 19 Oct 1916; *Educ* RNC Dartmouth; *m* 1, 1940, Margaret Mary (d 1951), da of late W E Steacy, of Kingston, Ontario; 2 s, 1 da; m 2, 1954, Marjory Helen Reece, da of late F H Bissett; 1 step da; *Career* RN 1930, Cdr 1950, Capt 1955, cmd HMS Ark Royal 1963–64, Rear Adm 1964, Asst Chief of Naval Staff 1964–66, 2 i/c Home Fleet 1966–67, Vice Adm 1968, Flag Offr Submarines and NATO Cdr Submarines Eastern Atlantic 1968–69, Adm 1970, Controller of the Navy 1970–71, Chief of Naval Staff and First Sea Lord 1971–74, first and princ Naval ADC to The Queen 1972–74, Adm of the Fleet 1974; chm Naval Insur Tst 1975–85; Bath King of Arms 1976–85; *Style*— Adm of the Fleet Sir Michael Pollock, GCB, LVO, DSC; ✉ The Ivy House, Churchstoke, Montgomery, Powys SY15 6DU

POLLOCK, Peter Glen; s of Jack Campbell Pollock (d 1953), and Rebecca Shields Marshall, *née* Clarke (d 1985); *b* 6 Sept 1946; *Educ* Nautical Coll Pangbourne, Univ of St Andrews (MA); *m* 3 Sept 1977, Nicola Sara, da of Derek William Bernard Clements, of Cirencester, Glos; 2 s (Jonathan William Campbell b 1982, Matthew Charles Simon b 1984), 1 da (Antonia Rebecca b 1991); *Career* fin dir: Hawker Siddeley Power Transformers Ltd 1978–83, Fisher Controls Ltd 1983–85; gp chief exec ML Holdings plc 1985–92, mgmnt conslt Peter Pollock & Co 1992–94; dir: Faversham Oyster Fishery Co 1993–94, Menvier Swain Group PLC 1993–, Mentmore Abbey Plc (formerly Platignum Plc) 1994–, Lionheart PLC 1996–; chm: Second Phase Industries Ltd 1994–, Valetmatic Holdings Ltd 1994–; memb: Ctee RUKBA 1985–, Cncl SBAC 1989–92; FCA; *Recreations* country pursuits, skiing; *Clubs* Knole, Knole Park Golf; *Style*— Peter G Pollock, Esq; ✉ Filston Oast, Filston Lane, Shoreham, nr Sevenoaks, Kent TN14 5JU (☎ 01959 524724, fax 01959 525391)

POLLOCK, Hon Richard Charles Standish; TD (1986); yr s of 2 Viscount Hanworth (d 1996); bro and hp of 3 Viscount; *b* 6 Feb 1951; *Educ* Wellington, Trinity Coll Cambridge (MA); *m* 1982, Annette Louise, da of Peter Lockhart, of Daisy Cottage, Studham, Common Road, nr Dunstable, Beds; 2 s (Harold William Charles b 30 April 1988, Frederick Thomas Charles b (twin) 30 April 1988); *Career* Maj R Yeo T & AVR; slr Simmons and Simmons; *Recreations* hot air ballooning, Maj Royal Yeo TAVR; *Style*— The Hon Richard Pollock, TD; ✉ Brook House, North End, Dunmow, Essex CM6 3PQ; Simmons and Simmons, 21 Wilson St, London EC2M 2TQ (☎ 0171 628 2020, fax 0171 628 2070, telex 888562)

POLLOCK-HILL, Stephen David; s of Malcolm William Lyttleton Pollock-Hill (d 1995), of San Pedro, Malaga, Spain, and Jeanne, *née* Beale; *b* 22 March 1948; *Educ* Harrow, Sorbonne, Univ de Madrid, Univ de Vienna, Hatfield Poly (HND); *m* 18 June 1983, Samantha Ann Maria Russell, da of Sir William Russell Lawrence, QC; 1 s (Robert b 1977), 1 da (Talitha Louise b 1985); *Career* documentalist Mead Carney France (mgmnt conslts) 1970–71; Nazeing Glass Works: sales liaison offr 1972, sales rep 1973, sales mangr 1975, export mangr 1976, sales dir 1980–91, jt md 1990–, chm 1992–; chm and md Nazeing Glass Investments 1990–; memb Euro Domestic Glass Ctee 1978–, chm Sci Museum Glass Gallery Ctee 1978–90, memb Cncl Glass Mfrs' Cncl 1980–88, chm GMF Domestic and Handmade Glass Ctee 1980–88, tstee Br Glass Educnl Tst 1990–, Euro domestic glass advsr EEC-CPIV Ctee Brussels 1985–90; memb Int Crystal Fedn; chm: Herts Conservation Soc 1993–96 (now vice pres), Herts Business Link Lea Valley Branch; memb Mgmnt Ctee and Fin and Gen Purposes Ctee Tree Cncl; life memb: Nat Tst, Int Wine & Food Soc, RHS, Soc of Glass Technol; Freeman City of London, Liveryman Worshipful Co of Glass Sellers; *Recreations* conservation, lawn tennis, real tennis, gardening, trees, fine wine; *Clubs* Hatfield House Real Tennis, The October (hon sec); *Style*— Stephen Pollock-Hill, Esq; ✉ Nazeing Glass Works Ltd, Broxbourne, Herts EN10 6SU (☎ 01992 464485, fax 01992 450966)

POLTIMORE, 7 Baron (UK 1831); Sir Mark Coplestone Bampfylde; 12 Bt (E 1641); s of Capt the Hon Anthony Gerard Hugh Bampfylde (d 1969), er s of 6 Baron, and Brita Yvonne (now Mrs Guy Elmes), *née* Baroness Cederström; suc his gf 6 Baron, Poltimore 1978; *b* 8 June 1957; *Educ* Radley; *m* 12 June 1982, Sally Anne, da of Dr Norman Miles, of Caythorpe, Lincs; 2 s (Hon Henry, Hon Oliver Hugh Coplestone b 15 April 1987), 1 da (Lara Fiona Brita b 14 May 1990); *Heir* s, Hon Henry Anthony Warwick Bampfylde, b 3 June 1985; *Career* Christie's: associate dir Picture Dept 1984, dir and head of 19th Century Picture Dept 1987–; *Books* Popular 19th Century Painting, A Dictionary of European Genre Painters (1986, co-author with Philip Hook); *Clubs* White's; *Style*— The Rt Hon the Lord Poltimore; ✉ Ridgemoor Farm House, West Street, Burghclere, Newbury, Berks RG15 9LD; Christie's, 8 King St, St James's, London SW1Y 6QT (☎ 0171 839 9060)

POLUNIN, Prof Nicholas; CBE (1975); s of Vladimir Polunin (d 1957), of Chiswick Mall, London, and Elizabeth Violet, *née* Hart; *Educ* Latymer Upper Sch, ChCh Oxford (BA, MA, DPhil, DSc), Yale Univ (MS), Harvard Univ; *m* 3 Jan 1948, Helen Eugenie, da of late Douglas Argyle Campbell, of Toronto and Montreal; 2 s (Dr Nicholas Vladimir Campbell, Douglas Harold Hart), 1 da (April Xenia); *Career* WWII Intelligence Offr Home Guard E Oxford; New Coll Oxford 1939–47 (univ demonstrator and lectr in botany, Fielding curator and keeper of univ herbaria, earlier sr scholar and latterly sr res fell), Macdonald prof of botany McGill Univ Montreal Canada 1947–52, various appts Harvard and Yale Univs 1952–55, prof of plant ecology and taxonomy and head of Dept of Botany while helping to plan Univ of Baghdad Iraq until revolution 1956–58; guest prof Univ of Geneva 1959–61 and 1975–76, fndr prof and head Dept of Botany Univ of Ife Nigeria 1962–66 (founding dean Faculty of Science), established Fndn for Environmental Conservation 1975, fndr and pres World Cncl For The Biosphere 1984– (initiator Biosphere Day 1991–), sec gen and ed fourth Int Conf on Environmental Future Budapest 1990 (fndr and ed first Finland 1971, organiser and ed second Reykjavik 1977, sec gen and ed third Edinburgh 1987); fndr and ed: Environmental Conservation 1974–95 (Biological Conservation 1967–74), Environmental Monographs & Symposia 1979–88; chm Cambridge Studies in Environmental Policy 1984–; discovered: descendants of plants introduced to Greenland from North America by Vikings some thousand years previously 1936, in arctic Canada the last major islands to be added to the world map (later named Prince Charles Island and Air Force Island) 1946; demonstrated the existence of microbial life over North Pole and correlated spora with air-mass provenance 1948; awards: US Order of Polaris 1948, Canadian Marie Victorin Medal 1957, Indian Ramdeo Medal for Environment Sci 1986, Int Sasakawa Environment Prize 1987, UN Sec Gen's illuminated and signed certificate in recognition of most outstanding contribution in the field of the environment, Chinese Academy of Sciences' Pres Quo Mo-Jo Medal 1987, USSR Academy of Sciences' Vernadsky Medal 1988 and 1989, Hungarian Academy of Sciences' Founder's (Zéchenyi) Medal 1990, Netherlands Order of the Golden Ark (Officer) 1990, UNEP Global 500 Roll of Honour 1991; FLS, FRGS, FRHS; *Publications* author of over 550 res and sci papers, editorials, reports, comments and books, incl: Botany of the Canadian Eastern Arctic (3 vols 1940, 1947, 1948), Circumpolar Arctic Flora (1959), Introduction to Plant Geography and some Related Sciences (1960, various later translations), Eléments de Géographie Botanique (1967), The Environmental Future (ed 1972), Growth Without Ecodisasters? (ed 1980), Ecosystem Theory and Application (ed, 1986), Maintenance of the Biosphere (ed with Sir John Burnett, 1990), Environmental Challenges: From Stockholm to Rio and Beyond (ed with Mohammad Nazim, 1993), Surviving with the Biosphere (ed with Sir John Burnett, 1993), Population and Global Security (ed with Mohammad Nazim, 1994), World Who Is Who and Does What in Environment & Conservation (1996); *Recreations* mountain scrambling, maintaining a multiplicity of serious joblets; *Clubs* Reform (life memb), Harvard (NY USA, life memb); *Style*— Prof Nicholas Polunin, CBE; ✉ President Foundation for Environmental Conservation, 7 Chemin Taverney (7th and 8th floors), 1218 Grand-Saconnex, Geneva, Switzerland (☎ 00 41 22 798 2383 and 4, fax 00 41 22 798 2344)

POLWARTH, Master of; Hon Andrew Walter Hepburne-Scott; s and h of 10 Lord Polwarth; *b* 30 Nov 1947; *Educ* Eton, Trinity Hall Cambridge; *m* 1971, (Isabel) Anna, da of Maj John Freville Henry Surtees, OBE, MC; 2 s, 2 da; *Career* asst dir Baring Bros 1982–91; Liveryman Worshipful Co of Grocers; *Style*— The Master of Polwarth; ✉ Harden, Hawick, Roxburghshire TD9 7LP

POLWARTH, 10 Lord (S 1690); Henry Alexander Hepburne-Scott; TD, DL (Roxburgh 1962); s of Master of Polwarth, JP, DL (d 1942), and Elspeth, JP (da of Rt Rev Archibald Campbell, DD, DCL, sometime Bishop of Glasgow and Galloway, by his w, Hon Helen, *née* Brodrick, da of 8 Visc Midleton, JP); suc gf (9 Lord Polwarth, CBE, JP, DL) 1944; *b* 17 Nov 1916; *Educ* Eton, King's Coll Cambridge; *m* 1, 1943 (m dis 1969), Caroline (d 1982), da of Capt Robert Hay (d 1939), er bro of Sir Bache Hay, 11 Bt (d 1966, since when Btcy dormant); 1 s, 3 da; m 2, 1969, Jean, da of Adm Sir Angus Cunninghame Graham of Gartmore and of Ardoch, KBE, CB, and formerly w of Charles Jauncey, QC; 2 step s, 1 step da; *Heir* s, Master of Polwarth; *Career* sits as Cons Peer in House of Lords, Rep Peer for Scotland 1945–63; Maj Lothians and Border Horse NW Europe 1944–45; CA; govr Bank of Scotland 1966–72 (dir 1974–87), chm General Accident Gp 1968–1972, min of State for Scotland 1972–74; dir: ICI 1974–81, Canadian Pacific Ltd 1975–86, Sun Life Assurance of Canada 1975–84, Halliburton Co (USA) 1974–87; memb Queen's Body Guard for Scotland (Royal Co of Archers), Vice Lord-Lieut Borders Region (Roxburgh, Ettrick and Lauderdale) 1975–91, chllr Aberdeen Univ 1966–86, memb Franco-Br Cncl (Br section); Hon LLD: St Andrews, Aberdeen; Hon DLitt Heriot-Watt, Hon DUniv Stirling; FRSA, FRSE 1966, Hon FRIAS; *Recreations* country pursuits and the arts; *Clubs* New (Edinburgh); *Style*— The Rt Hon the Lord Polwarth, TD, DL, FRSE; ✉ Wellfield Parva, Hawkchurch, Axminster, Devon EX13 5UT (☎ 01297 678 735)

POMEROY, Brian Walter; *b* 26 June 1944; *Educ* The King's Sch Canterbury, Magdalene Coll Cambridge (MA); *m* 7 Aug 1974, Hilary Susan; 2 da (Gabriela b 1975, Alisa b 1977); *Career* ptnr Touche Ross (now Deloitte & Touche): ptnr 1975, seconded as under sec in DTI 1981–83, sr ptnr Touche Ross Management Consultants 1995– (nat dir 1987–95); non-exec dir BL (now Rover Group plc) 1985–88; memb Ctee of Enquiry into Regulatory Arrangements at Lloyd's 1986, nominated memb of Cncl of Lloyd's 1987–92 and 1996–, dep chm Lloyd's Regulatory Bd 1996–; chm: Centrepoint Soho 1993–, AIDS Awareness Tst 1993–; FCA 1978, FRSA, FIMC; *Recreations* photography, tennis, cycling; *Style*— Brian Pomeroy, Esq; ✉ Deloitte & Touche, Stonecutter Court, 1 Stonecutter Street, London EC4A 4TR (☎ 0171 936 3000)

POMEROY, Maj Hon Robert William; yst s of 8 Viscount Harberton, OBE (d 1956), and Mary Katherine, *née* Leatham (d 1971); bro of 9 Visc (d 1980) and bro and hp of 10 Visc; *b* 29 Feb 1916, (twin); *Educ* Eton; *m* 28 April 1953, (Winifred) Anne, da of Sir Arthur Colegate, MP (d 1956); 2 s (Henry Robert b 1958, Richard Arthur b 1960); *Career* Maj Welsh Gds 1945, ret 1960; *Books* Nunney Church; *Recreations* beagling; *Clubs* Bembridge Sailing; *Style*— Maj The Hon Robert Pomeroy; ✉ Rockfield House, Nunney, nr Frome, Somerset BA11 4NP (☎ 01373 836208)

POMMIER, Pascal; s of Jean-Jacques Marcel Pommier, of Paray-le-Monial, France, and Yvette Renee Monique, *née* Gonnin; *b* 15 Dec 1964; *Educ* Ces Cours Jean Jeaures (DEFO Dip), CFA Mercurey Coll (CAP); *Career* chef; apprenticeship Hotel Moderne Charolles France 1980–82, Hotel Belvedere du Pelvoux Pelvoux France 1982–83, Mil Serv Macon France 1983–84, Restaurant Alain Raye Albertville France 1985–86, The Mill House Hotel Kingham Oxon 1986–88, The Normandie Hotel Gtr Manchester 1988–96; Lancashire Life Restaurant of the Yr 1988, Ackerman Clover Award annually awarded 1989–94, AA Rosettes annually awarded 1990–, County Restaurant of the Yr Good Food Guide 1993 and 1994, Egon Ronay Star annually awarded 1990–, Michelin Star 1995; *Recreations* rugby, football, squash, snooker, travel; *Style*— Pascal Pommier, Esq; ✉ The Normandie Hotel Ltd, Elbut Lane, Birtle, Bury, Greater Manchester BL9 6UT (☎ 0161 764 3869, fax 0161 764 4866)

POMPA, Prof Leonardo (Leon); s of Dominic Albert Pompa (d 1976), of Edinburgh, and Maria Annunziata Pompa (d 1956); *b* 22 Feb 1933; *Educ* Bournemouth Sch, Univ of Edinburgh (MA, PhD); *m* 9 Aug 1962, (Juliet) Caroline, da of Sir Rupert Leigh Sich, CB (d 1995); 1 s (Nicholas b 1963), 1 da (Antonia b 1965); *Career* lectr in philosophy Univ of Edinburgh 1961–77; Univ of Birmingham: prof of philosophy 1977–, dean of arts 1984–87 and 1989–92, head Sch of Philosophy and Theol 1993–94; memb Cncl: Hegel Soc of GB (former pres), Nat Ctee for Philosophy; chm Philosphy Panel Higher Educn Funding Cncl for England's Research Assessment Exercise 1995–96; memb: Br Soc for History of Philosophy (former memb Mgmnt Ctee), Aristotelian Soc 1964–; *Books* Vico: A Study of the New Science (1975, 2 edn 1990), Substance and Form in History (ed with W H Dray, 1982), Vico: Selected Writings (trans and ed, 1982), Human Nature and Historical Knowledge: Hume Hegel Vico (1990); *Recreations* music, sport, literature, foreign travel, wine; *Clubs* Edgbaston Golf, Murrayfield Golf; *Style*— Prof Leon Pompa; ✉ 155 Russell Rd, Moseley, Birmingham B13 8RR (☎ 0121 449 3623); University of Birmingham, Birmingham B15 2TT (☎ 0121 414 6052, fax 0121 414 6866)

PONCE-VIVANCO, HE (José) Eduardo; s of Eduardo Ponce-Mendoza, and Laura Vivanco de Ponce-Mendoza; *b* 8 March 1943; *Educ* Colegio Jesuita de San José de Arequipa Peru, Univ Nacional de San Agustín de Arequipa, Pontificia Univ de Hautes Etudes Internationale Geneva; *m* 1969, Clemencia Hilbck; 1 da; *Career* Peruvian diplomat; third sec to Int Orgns Under-Secretariat 1967–68, Tokyo 1968–70, second sec Quito 1971–75, prof of Peruvian Diplomatic History Diplomatic Acad Peru 1976, asst to Advsr for Legal and Maritime Affrs Min's Office 1976–77, head Dept for Ecuador, Colombia and Venezuela Under-Secretariat for Political Affrs 1977, asst dir for planning Miny of Foreign Affrs 1978–79, perm alternate rep to UN and Int Orgns Geneva 1979–83, min London 1984, perm rep to Int Commodities Orgns London 1984, dir of territorial sovereignty Miny of Foreign Affrs 1985, dir America Dept Miny of Foreign Affrs 1986, asst under-sec Bilateral Policy for American Affrs 1987–88, perm rep to Latin American Integration Assoc Montevideo 1988–89, ambass to Ecuador 1990–94, vice-min Int Policy and sec gen of foreign affrs 1994–95, ambass to the Ct of St James's and perm rep to the Int Maritime Orgn 1995–; pres Peruvian Delgn to UN World Water Conf 1977, memb numerous Peruvian delgns to UN, Geneva and other int orgns; Grand Cross: Orden El Sol del Peru 1995, Orden Al Mérito Naval (Peru) 1996; Cdr: Orden por Servicios Distinguidos (Peru) 1979, Defensor Calificado de la Patria (Peru) 1995; recipient other decorations from Japan, Brazil and Bolivia; *Publications* The Resolutions of the United Nations General Assembly (1969); *Recreations* tennis, music, ballet; *Clubs* Queen's, Travellers', Naval and Military, Nacional Terrazas (Lima), Arequipa; *Style*— HE Mr J Eduardo Ponce-Vivanco; ✉ Embassy of Peru, 52 Sloane Street, London SW1X 9SP (☎ 0171 235 4451)

PONCIA, Dr John; s of Anthony Edward Poncia (d 1982), of Warks, and Mary Winifred, *née* Tams; *b* 15 April 1935; *Educ* Ratcliffe Coll, Univ of Edinburgh Med Sch (MB ChB); *m* 1, 1959, Elizabeth Madaleine (d 1972), da of late Alexander Birrell Grosset, of Fife; 4 s (Jonathan, MBE, b 1960, Gavin b 1962, Fergus b 1964, Hugo b 1970); m 2, 1994, Rosamond, da of late Brig Charles Wynn-Pope, OBE; *Career* house offr Royal Infirmary Edinburgh, registrar St George's Hosp London, sr registrar Westminster Hosp, conslt psychotherapist Broadmoor Hosp; DPM, MRCPsych; *Recreations* yachting; *Clubs* Savile, Royal Thames Yacht, Lloyds Yacht; *Style*— Dr John Poncia; ✉ 40 Harley St, London W1N 1AB (☎ and fax 0171 323 3061)

POND, Edward Charles (Eddie); s of Nathan James Pond (d 1965), and Mary Elizabeth, *née* Seabrook (d 1983); *b* 12 March 1929; *Educ* Royal Coll of Art (Royal scholar, Silver medal); *m* 1954, Grace Nina Primrose, *née* Sparks; 1 s (Christopher b 1960), 2 da (Rebecca b 1963, Hannah b 1965); *Career* Nat Serv Parachute Regt; dir: Bernard Wardle (Everflex) Ltd 1958–61, Bernard Wardle (Fabrics) Ltd 1961–65, The Wall Paper Manufacturers Ltd 1965–76, Polycell Products Ltd, Polypops Products Ltd 1969–71; owner and dir Paperchase Products Ltd; fndr Edward Pond Associates Ltd 1976; awards: COID Design of the Year award 1959, Public Arts Devpt Tst competition winner 1988, prizewinner Nat Paperbox and Packing Assoc of America, 3 Excellence awards 1988, Bronze medal NY Advertising Festival 1990; design projects incl: BR Network SE, Boots The Chemist plc, Defeat of the Armada (ceramic mural, Plymouth) fabric hangings BAA; author of various articles in jls and magazines; chm Metropolitan Police Consultative Ctee 1993–96; Voluntary Service Cross 1996; pres CSD 1981–83 (memb 1959), memb DIA; FRSA; *Recreations* painting, writing, rugby, genealogy, jazz; *Clubs* Blackheath FC; *Style*— Eddie Pond, Esq; ✉ Long Loft, Cadgwith, Helston, Cornwall TR12 7JY (☎ 01736 736562)

PONDER, Prof Bruce Anthony John; s of Anthony West Ponder, and Dorothy Mary, *née* Peachey; *b* 25 April 1944; *Educ* Charterhouse, Jesus Coll Cambridge (open scholar, MA), St Thomas' Hosp Med Sch (open scholar, MB BChir), UCL (PhD); *m* 2 Aug 1969, Margaret Ann, da of John Eliot Hickinbotham; 3 da (Jane b 2 March 1971, Katherine b 20 March 1973, Rosamund b 10 Sept 1975), 1 s (William b 5 June 1976); *Career* house physician St Thomas' Hosp 1968, house surgn Kent and Canterbury Hosp 1969, house physician Brompton Hosp 1969, sr house offr Lambeth and St Thomas' Hosp 1969, med registrar St Thomas' and Worthing Hosps 1970–73, clinical res fell Imperial Cancer Research Fund 1973–77, Hamilton Fairley fell Cancer Research Campaign (CRC) Harvard Med Sch 1977–78, clinical scientific offr Imperial Cancer Research Fund Bart's 1978–80, CRC fell and sr lectr in med Inst of Cancer Research and Royal Marsden Hosp 1980–86, head of human cancer genetics Inst of Cancer Research 1987–89, reader in cancer genetics and hon conslt physician Royal Marsden, St George's and Guy's Hosps 1987–89, hon conslt physician Addenbrooke's and Royal Marsden Hosps 1989–; Univ of Cambridge: dir CRC Human Cancer Genetics Group 1989–, CRC prof of human cancer genetics 1992–, prof of clinical oncology 1995–; Gibb fell CRC 1990, fell Jesus Coll Cambridge 1992; treas Br Assoc for Cancer Research 1983–86; Int Public Service Award Nat Neurofibromatosis Fndn 1991; FRCP 1988 (MRCP 1970); *Books* Cancer Biology and Medicine (series ed with M J Waring, 1989–); *Recreations* gardening, golf, travel, wine; *Clubs* Royal Ashdown Forset Golf; *Style*— Prof Bruce Ponder; ✉ CRC Human Cancer Genetics Group, Box 238, Addenbrookes Hospital, Hills Road, Cambridge CB2 2QQ (☎ 01223 336900, fax 01223 336902)

PONSONBY, Sir Ashley Charles Gibbs; 2 Bt (UK 1956), of Wootton, Co Oxford; KCVO (1993), MC (1945); s of Col Sir Charles Edward Ponsonby, 1 Bt, TD, DL (d 1976), and Hon Winifred Gibbs, da of 1 Baron Hunsdon (d 1935); *b* 21 Feb 1921; *Educ* Eton, Balliol Coll Oxford; *m* 14 Sept 1950, Lady Martha, *née* Butler, da of 6 Marquess of Ormonde, CVO, MC (d 1971); 4 s (Charles Ashley b 1951, Rupert Spencer b 1953, Luke Arthur b 1957, John Piers b 1962); *Heir* s, Charles Ashley Ponsonby b 10 June 1951; *Career* Schroder Wagg & Co Ltd (dir 1962–80); chm Colville Estate Ltd; dir: Equitable Life Assur Soc 1969–86, Rowntree Mackintosh Ltd 1974–86, Schroder Global Tst plc 1963–89 (chm 1964–87); church cmmr 1963–80; memb Cncl Duchy of Lancaster 1979–93; Lord-Lt of Oxfordshire 1980–96; Liveryman Worshipful Co of Grocers; KStJ 1989; *Clubs* Pratt's; *Style*— Sir Ashley Ponsonby, Bt, KCVO, MC; ✉ Woodleys, Woodstock, Oxon OX20 1HJ (☎ 01993 811422); 120 Cheapside, London EC2V 6DS (☎ 0171 382 6000)

PONSONBY, Charles Ashley; s and h of Sir Ashley Charles Gibbs Ponsonby, 2 Bt, KCVO, MC, of Woodleys, Woodstock, Oxford, and Lady Martha Ponsonby, yr da of 6 Marquess of Ormonde; *b* 10 June 1951; *Educ* Eton, Ch Ch Oxford (MA); *m* 1983, Mary Priscilla, yr da of Maj Arthur Richard Bromley Davenport (d 1982), of Knutsford, Cheshire; 2 s (Arthur Ashley b 1984, Frederick Edward b 1986), 1 da (Alice Elizabeth b 1988); *Career* Deloitte Haskins & Sells 1973–77, Price Waterhouse 1977–79, Kleinwort Benson 1980–87, Barclays de Zoete Wedd 1987–92, Curzon Financial 1993–, Walter Judd Public Relations 1993–; non-exec dir South Uist Estates Ltd 1985– (non-exec chm 1985–89); Liveryman Worshipful Co of Grocers; FCA; *Clubs* Pratt's, Turf; *Style*— Charles Ponsonby, Esq; ✉ Grim's Dyke Farm, Woodstock, Oxford OX20 1HJ (☎ 01993 811717, fax 01993 812966); Flat 3, 5 Ralston St, London SW3 4DT (☎ 0171 376 4178); Walter Judd Public Relations, 64 Queen Street, London EC4R 1AJ (☎ 0171 236 6230, fax 0171 329 8941)

PONSONBY, Robert Noel; CBE (1985); s of Noel Edward Ponsonby (d 1928), and Mary Adela, *née* White-Thomson; *b* 19 Dec 1926; *Educ* Eton, Trinity Coll Oxford (MA); *Career* Glyndebourne 1951–55, dir Edinburgh Festival 1955–60, gen mangr Scottish Nat Orchestra 1964–72, controller music BBC 1972–85; artistic dir Canterbury Festival 1986–88; conslt Friends of Musicians Benevolent Fund 1987; Hon RAM 1973; *Recreations* walking, bird watching, photography, music; *Style*— Mr Robert Ponsonby, CBE

PONSONBY, Thomas Charles George; s of George Thomas Ponsonby (d 1984), of Kilcooley Abbey, Thurles, Co Tipperary, and Elizabeth Penelope Melville, *née* Wills; *b* 23 Aug 1950; *Educ* Eton, Trinity Coll of Music, Eurocentre Neuchatel Switzerland, Br Inst Florence Italy; *m* 1980 (m dis 1985), Elisabeth Marie Philippine, da of Jean Masurel, of Paris; 1 s (Sebastian Jean b 1983); *Career* asst Foreign Tours Dept Ibbs & Tillett 1974–78, asst to Victor Hochhauser 1978–81, tour mangr Euro Community Youth Orch and Chamber Orch of Europe 1982–83, Music Dept Br Cncl 1983–89, exec dir Br Assoc of Concert Agents 1989–94, Business Relations Dept British Cncl 1995–; memb: King Edward VII British-German Fndn, Stefan Zweig Ctee Br Library; tstee Colin Keer Tst; *Recreations* mountains, food, architecture; *Style*— Thomas Ponsonby, Esq; ✉ Flat 2, 31 Ladbroke Gardens, London W11 2PY

PONSONBY, Hon Thomas Maurice; TD, DL (Glos); s of 5 Baron de Mauley; hp to bro, 6 Baron; *b* 2 Aug 1930; *Educ* Eton; *m* 1956, Maxine Henrietta, da of late William Dudley Keith Thellusson; 2 s; *Career* Lt-Col The Royal Wessex Yeo 1970–72, Brevet Col TA 1972–; High Sheriff of Glos 1978; *Style*— The Hon Thomas Ponsonby, TD, DL; ✉ The Common, Little Faringdon, Lechlade, Glos

PONSONBY OF SHULBREDE, 4 Baron (UK 1930), of Shulbrede, Sussex; Frederick Matthew Thomas Ponsonby; o s of 3 Baron Ponsonby of Shulbrede (d 1990), and his 1 w, Ursula Mary, *née* Fox-Pitt; *b* 27 Oct 1958; *Educ* Holland Park Comprehensive Sch, Univ Coll Cardiff, Imperial Coll London; *Heir* none; *Career* cncllr London Borough of Wandsworth 1990–94; Lab Pty educn spokesman House of Lords 1992–; FIMM 1996; *Style*— The Rt Hon Lord Ponsonby of Shulbrede; ✉ c/o House of Lords, London SW1

PONTEFRACT, Bishop of 1993–; Rt Rev John Thornley Finney; s of Arthur Frederick Finney (d 1964), and Elaine, *née* Bowcock (d 1959); *b* 1 May 1932; *Educ* Charterhouse, Hertford Coll Oxford (BA, DipTheol); *m* 25 April 1959, Sheila Elizabeth, da of Charles Russell (d 1961); 3 da (Elizabeth Ann b 1960, Catherine Hilary b 1961, Helen Rachel b 1965); *Career* Nat Serv Pilot Offr 92 Sqdn RAF 1950–52; ordained 1958, curate All Saints Highfield Oxford 1958–61, curate i/c Church of the Holy Spirit Bedgrove Aylesbury 1961–65, rector Tollerton Notts 1965–71, vicar St Margaret's Aspley Nottingham and sec Diocesan Synod and Bishop's Cncl 1971–80, advsr in evangelism Dio of Southwell 1980–89; freelance lectr and writer 1989–93; offr for the Decade of Evangelism C of E 1990–, adjunct prof Fuller Seminary Calif USA; *Books* Understanding Leadership (1989), The Well Church Book (1991), Church on the Move (1992), Finding Faith Today (1992), Stories of Faith (1995), Recovering the Past (1996); *Recreations* relaxing; *Style*— The Rt Rev the Bishop of Pontefract; ✉ Pontefract House, 181a Manygates Lane, Wakefield WF2 7DR (☎ 01924 250781, fax 01924 240490)

PONTER, Prof Alan Robert Sage; s of Arthur Tennyson Ponter (d 1964), of Bath, and Margaret Agatha Ponter (d 1974); *b* 13 Feb 1940; *Educ* King Henry VIII GS Abergavenny, Imperial Coll London (BSc, ARCS, PhD), Univ of Cambridge (MA); *m* 12 Sept 1962, Sonia, da of Robert Hutchinson Valentine, of Workington, Cumbria; 1 s (David Robert Arthur b 25 Nov 1964, d 1986), 3 da (Ruth Virginia b 1964, Kathryn Emma b 1968, Alexandra Margaret Valentine b 1980); *Career* visiting lectr Iowa Univ 1964, res fell Brown Univ USA 1964–65, lectr Univ of Glasgow 1965–66, sr asst researcher Engrg Dept Univ of Cambridge 1966–69, fell Pembroke Coll Cambridge 1967–69, prof of engrg Brown Univ USA 1976–78; Univ of Leicester: lectr 1969–74, reader 1974–76, prof of engrg 1978–, pro-vice chllr 1987–91 and 1993–96; visiting prof Univ of Calif Santa Barbara 1991–92, conslt prof Univ of Chongqing People's Repub of China 1991–; memb several SERC ctees and working parties on mechanical engrg, conslt to EEC and others on structural integrity of structures particularly at high temperatures; *Books* Creep of Structures (1982), about 100 articles in applied mathematics and engrg literature; *Recreations* reading, music and walking; *Style*— Prof Alan Ponter; ✉ Oak Lodge, 10 Elmsleigh Ave, Stoneygate, Leicester LE2 2DF (☎ 0116 270 4395); University of Leicester, University Rd, Leicester LE1 7RH (☎ 0116 252 2323, fax 0116 252 2525, telex 347250 LEICHN G)

PONTIFEX, Brig David More; CBE (1977, OBE 1965, MBE 1956); s of Cdr John Weddall Pontifex (d 1977), of Cloudes Lodge, Lilliput, Poole, Dorset, and Monica Melangell Rosewall, *née* Matthews (d 1970); *b* 16 Sept 1922; *Educ* Downside; *m* 6 Aug 1968, Kathleen Betsy (Kate), da of Maxwell Heron Matheson (d 1978), of Widelands, Waldringfield, Woodbridge, Suffolk; 1 s (John b 1975), 4 da (Catherine b 1969, Emily b 1971, Louise b 1973, Rosalind b 1975); *Career* cmmnd Rifle Bde 1942, Lt then Capt 10 and 2 Bn Italy 1944–45 (despatches 1945), Capt adjt 2 Bn BAOR 1946–48, Capt instr Eaton Hall OCS 1948–50, Staff Coll Camberley 1951, Maj DAA and QMG 16 Ind Para Bde Gp Egypt 1952–54, 1 Bn Kenya 1954–56, WO (MO 4) 1956–58, Armed Forces Staff Coll Norfolk Virginia 1958–59, 1 Bn BAOR 1959–61, Bde Maj 63 Gurkha Bde Gp Malaya 1961–62, Lt-Col 1 Bn Fed Regular Army Aden 1962–64, GSO1 2 Div BAOR 1965–67, Col GS Staff Coll Camberley 1967–69, Brig the Light Div Winchester 1969–73, DDSD Army 1973–75, Dep Cdr and COS SE Dist Aldershot 1975–77; ADC to HM The Queen 1975–77, gen sec ACF Assoc, sec CCF Assoc, ed The Cadet Journal 1977–87; govr Farnborough Sixth Form Coll 1977–81; *Recreations* travel, history; *Clubs* Naval and Military; *Style*— Brig David Pontifex, CBE; ✉ 68 Shortheath Rd, Farnham, Surrey GU9 8SQ (☎ 01252 723284)

PONTIN, Sir Frederick William (Fred); kt (1976); s of Frederick William Pontin (d 1945), of Bristol; *b* 24 Oct 1906; *Educ* Sir George Monoux GS Walthamstow; *m* 1929, Dorothy Beatrice Mortimer (decd); 1 da; *Career* London Stock Exchange 1920–39, work in catering and welfare for Admty WWII; Pontins Ltd: chm and md 1946–79, hon fndr pres 1987–; dir: Pontinental Ltd 1963–79, Belhaven Brewery until 1981; dep chm Kunick Leisure Gp plc 1985–87 (chm 1983–85); memb: Variety Club of GB (chief barker 1968), Grand Order of Water Rats; MInstD; *Clubs* Farmers', Saints and Sinners, Derby; *Style*— Sir Fred Pontin; ✉ Flat 127, 3 Whitehall Court, London SW1A 2EL (☎ 0171 839 5251)

PONTIUS, His Hon Judge; Timothy Gordon; s of Gordon Stuart Malzard Pontius (d 1993), and Elizabeth Mary, *née* Donaldson (d 1996); *b* 5 Sept 1948; *Educ* Boroughmuir Sr Secdy Sch Edinburgh, Univ of London (LLB, external); *Career* called to the Bar Middle Temple 1972, in practice at Criminal Bar 1972–88, judge advocate 1988, asst judge-advocate gen HM Forces 1991, recorder 1993–95, circuit judge (SE Circuit) 1995–; *Recreations* music, swimming, travel; *Clubs* Naval & Military; *Style*— His Hon Judge Pontius; ✉ The Crown Court, 1 Pocock Street, London SE1 0BT (☎ 0171 922 5800)

PONTON, Prof John Wylie (Jack); s of John Ronald Ponton, of Berwickshire, and Nancy, *née* Wylie; *b* 2 May 1943; *Educ* Melville Coll Edinburgh, Univ of Edinburgh (BSc, PhD); *m* 1973, Katherine Jane Victoria, da of Jack Eachus; *Career* Univ of Edinburgh 1967– (successively lectr, sr lectr, ICI prof of chemical engrg), res fell McMaster Univ Canada 1969–70, NATO fell and assoc prof Case Western Reserve Univ 1975, process engr ICI Mond Div 1979; contribs to jls of chemical, mech, electrical and info engrg; foreign fell Russian Acad of Technological Scis 1992; FIChemE, FEng 1991, FRSA 1993; *Recreations* music, walking, amateur radio (GM0RWU); *Style*— Prof Jack Ponton, FEng; ✉ Legerwood, Earlston, Berwickshire TD4 6AS; Department of Chemical Engineering, University of Edinburgh, King's Buildings, Edinburgh EH9 3JL (☎ 0131 650 4858, fax 0131 650 6551)

PONTON, Michael Thomas John; s of Thomas Bevan Ponton (d 1991), and Zena May, *née* Bennett; *b* 11 July 1946; *Educ* Canton HS for Boys Cardiff, Inst of Health Servs Mgmnt (Dip), Inst of Health Record Info and Mgmnt (Dip), Harvard Grad Business Sch (Alumna); *m* 1; 2 da (Lisa Meirwen b 13 April 1972, Karen Jane b 16 Oct 1975); m 2, 26 Feb 1983, Patricia Ann, da of Richard James Taylor; 2 s (Richard Michael Thomas b 25 Jan 1984, David Michael James b 17 Feb 1987); *Career* clerk: Ely Hosp Cardiff 1962–63, Utd Cardiff Hosps 1963–65, Cardiff Royal Infirmary 1965–68; admin asst St Mary's Hosp London 1968–72, dep hosp sec Leicester Gen Hosp 1972–74, sector admin

Swansea North Hosps 1974–77; asst gen mangr W Glamorgan HA 1982–85 (area planning offr 1977–82), unit gen mangr Swansea North Unit 1988–90, asst dist gen mangr E Dyfed HA 1990–92, jt md E Dyfed and Pembrokeshire HAs 1992–95, md Dyfed HA 1995–96, chief exec Health Promotion Wales 1996–; FHSM; *Recreations* reading, walking, music, gardening, rugby football; *Style—* Michael Ponton, Esq; ✉ Health Promotion Wales, Tŷ Glas Avenue, Llanishen, Cardiff CF4 5DZ (☎ 01222 752222)

POOLE, Dame Anne Avril Barker; DBE (1992); *b* 11 April 1934; *m* John Poole; *Career* asst chief nursing offr City of Westminster 1967–69, chief nursing offr London Borough of Merton 1969–74, area nursing offr Surrey AHA 1974–81, chief nursing offr Dept of Health 1982–92 (dep chief nursing offr 1981–82); non-exec dir Western Surrey Health Cmmn 1993–96; tstee and memb Cncl Marie Curie Cancer Care; memb NHS Policy Bd, expert advsr to WHO; memb: RCN, Health Visitors' Assoc; RSM; CIMgt; *Recreations* gardening, embroidery, entertaining; *Style—* Dame Anne Poole, DBE; ✉ Ancaster House, Church Hill, Merstham, Surrey RH1 3BL (☎ 01737 644332, fax 01737 643040)

POOLE, Hon Mr Justice; Hon Sir David Anthony; kt (1995); s of William Joseph Poole (d 1956), and Lena Thomas; *b* 8 June 1938; *Educ* Ampleforth, Jesus Coll Oxford (MA), Univ of Manchester (Dip Tech Sci); *m* 1974, Pauline, da of James O'Flaherty; 4 s (William, Alexander, Gareth, Simon); *Career* called to the Bar Middle Temple 1968, recorder of the Crown Court 1982–95, QC 1984, bencher Middle Temple 1992; judge of the High Court of Justice (Queen's Bench Div) 1995–; chm Assoc of Lawyers for the Defence of the Unborn 1985–91; govr St Bede's Coll Manchester; *Recreations* reading, walking, watching rugby; *Clubs* Vincent's, London Irish, Heaton Mersey Cricket; *Style—* The Hon Mr Justice Poole; ✉ c/o Royal Courts of Justice, Strand, London WC2A 2LL

POOLE, 2 Baron (UK 1958); David Charles Poole; s of 1 Baron Poole, PC, CBE, TD (d 1993), and his 1 w, Betty Margaret, *née* Gilkison (d 1988); *b* 6 Jan 1945; *Educ* Gordonstoun, ChCh Oxford, INSEAD Fontainebleau; *m* 1, 21 Sept 1967 (m dis), Fiona, da of John Donald; 1 s (Hon Oliver John b 1972); m 2, 1975, Philippa, da of late Mark Reeve, of Lower Brook House, King's Somborne, Hants; m 3, 6 Jan 1995, Mrs Lucinda Edsell; *Heir* s, Hon Oliver John Poole b 30 May 1972; *Career* formerly: chm James Capel Corporate Finance Ltd, exec dir James Capel & Co Ltd, memb Policy Unit Prime Minister's Office; currently chief exec offr Ockham Holdings plc; *Clubs* Brooks's, Royal Yacht Squadron, City; *Style—* The Rt Hon the Lord Poole; ✉ Ockham Holdings plc, 9 Devonshire Square, London EC2M 4YL

POOLE, David James; s of Thomas Herbert Poole (d 1978), and Catherine, *née* Lord (d 1980); *b* 5 June 1931; *Educ* RCA; *m* 5 April 1958, Iris Mary, da of Francis Thomas Toomer (d 1968); 3 s (Edward b 1959, Vincent b 1960, Bruce b 1964); *Career* served RE 1949–51; sr lectr in painting and drawing Wimbledon Sch of Art 1961–77; featured in series Portrait (BBC TV) 1976, featured in magazine Frankfurter Allgemeine W Germany 1986; pres Royal Soc of Portrait Painters 1983–91; ARCA 1954, RP 1968; cmmnd by the City of London Corp to paint the official portrait group of the Royal Family to commemorate HM Queen Elizabeth II's Silver Jubilee Luncheon; *Portraits* incl: HM The Queen, HRH Prince Philip, HM Queen Elizabeth the Queen Mother, HRH The Princess Royal, HRH The Prince of Wales, HRH The Duke of York, HRH Prince Edward, Earl Mountbatten, distinguished membs of govt, HM Forces, industry, commerce, medical, the academic and legal professions; *Solo Exhibitions* London 1978, Zürich 1980; *Work in Private Collections* HM The Queen, Australia, Bermuda, Canada, France, Germany, Italy, S Africa, Saudia Arabia, Switzerland, USA; *Recreations* travel, being in the country; *Style—* David J Poole, Esq, PPRP, ARCA; ✉ Trinity Flint Barn, Weston Lane, Weston, Petersfield, Hants GU32 3NN; 01730 265075); Studio 6, Burlington Lodge, Rigault Rd, Fulham, London SW6 4JJ (☎ 0171 736 9288)

POOLE, (Francis) Henry Michael; s of Charles Frederick John Kaitting Poole (d 1976), of Lanteglos-by-Fowey, Cornwall, and Stella Mary Grant, *née* Morris; *b* 23 Sept 1949; *Educ* Eton, Trinity Hall Cambridge; *m* 20 Sept 1975, Diana Mary Olga, da of Eric Arthur Parker (d 1983), of Headcorn, Kent; 1 s (Frederick Henry Eric b 1983), 2 da (Angelica Lucy Daphne b 1978, Stella Antonia Felicity b 1980); *Career* dir Credit Lyonnais Laing (formerly Laing and Cruickshank Institutional Equities) 1985– (joined 1971, ptnr 1979), non-exec dir Rockware Gp 1986–87; memb Kensington Cons Assoc, MSI (dip, memb London Stock Exchange 1979); *Books* European Paper Directory (1988); *Recreations* bridge, history, riding, mountain walking; *Style—* Henry Poole, Esq; ✉ 74 Hornton St, London W8 4NU; Gibbet Oast, Leigh Green, Tenterden, Kent TN30 7DH; Credit Lyonnais Laing, Broadwalk House, 5 Appold St, London EC2A 2DA (☎ 0171 588 4000, telex 888397/8, fax 0171 588 0290)

POOLE, Sheriff Isobel Anne; da of John Cecil Findlay Poole (d 1985), and Constance Mary, *née* Gilkes (d 1992); *b* 9 Dec 1941; *Educ* Oxford HS for Girls, Univ of Edinburgh (LLB); *Career* advocate 1964, former standing jr counsel to the Registrar Gen for Scot; Sheriff of: Lothian and Borders 1979–, Edinburgh 1986–; memb: Sheriffs' Cncl 1980–85, Scot Lawyers' Euro Gp; *Recreations* country, the arts, houses, gardens, friends; *Clubs* Scottish Arts; *Style—* Sheriff Isobel Anne Poole; ✉ Sheriffs' Chambers, Sheriff Court House, 27 Chambers Street, Edinburgh EH1 1LB

POOLE, James; *Educ* Univ of Cambridge (BA Natural Scis Tripos); *m* Jenny; 2 c; *Career* former journalist (10 yrs at Sunday Times and ed Multinational Business jl for EIU), subsequently head of corp affrs Barclays Bank, currently dir Shandwick Consultants Ltd; advsr to: Dept of Tport (on privatisation of BR), British Gas (on demerger plans), Marks & Spencer and Shell (on critical issues); judge Financial Journal's Fin Journalist and Young Fin Journalist of the Yr 1993, 1994 and 1995; memb: Euro Public Affrs Forum, Spokesman Gp IIMR; MIPR; *Style—* James Poole, Esq; ✉ Shandwick Consultants Ltd, Aldermary House, 10–15 Queen Street, London EC4N 1TX (☎ 0171 329 0096, fax 0171 919 9079, mobile 0860 314855)

POOLE, (Jeremy) Quentin Simon; s of Graham Poole, of Kingswear, S Devon, and Dr Jill Poole, *née* Prichards; *b* 7 Jan 1955; *Educ* Epsom Coll, Univ of Warwick (LLB); *Career* admitted slr 1981; managing ptnr Wragge & Co 1995– (ptnr 1985–); memb: Birmingham Law Soc 1981, Law Soc 1981; *Recreations* cricket; *Style—* Quentin Poole, Esq; ✉ Wragge & Co, 55 Colmore Row, Birmingham B3 2AS (☎ 0121 233 1000, fax 0121 214 1099, telex 338728 WRAGGE G)

POOLE-WILSON, Prof Philip Alexander; s of Denis Smith Poole-Wilson, CBE, and Monique Michelle, *née* Goss (d 1985); *b* 26 April 1943; *Educ* Marlborough, Trinity Coll Cambridge (MA, MB BChir, MD), St Thomas's Med Sch; *m* 25 Oct 1969, Mary Elizabeth, da of Dr William Horrocks Tattersall; 2 s (William, Michael), 1 da (Oenone); *Career* prof of cardiology Nat Heart and Lung Inst Imperial Coll London 1984– (sr lectr and reader 1976–84, vice dean 1981–84), Simon Marks Br Heart Fndn prof of cardiology 1988–, hon conslt physician Royal Brompton Nat Heart & Lung Hosp 1976–, visiting prof Charing Cross and Westminster Med Sch 1988–; memb Cncl Br Heart Fndn, pres Euro Soc of Cardiology 1994–96 (sec 1990–92); FESC, FACC, FRCP 1978; *Recreations* sailing, gardening, countryside; *Style—* Prof Philip Poole-Wilson; ✉ 174 Burbage Rd, London SE21 7AG (☎ 0171 274 6742); National Heart and Lung Institute, Imperial College, Dovehouse Street, London SW3 6LY (☎ 0171 351 8179, fax 0171 351 8113)

POOLER, Amanda Elizabeth (Mandy); da of Kenneth Hindley Pooler, of Bolton, Lancs, and Adrianne, *née* Sherlock; *b* 23 May 1959; *Educ* Bolton Sch, Jesus Coll Oxford (MA); *m* Paul Andrew Eden; 2 c (Max and Eleanor (twins) b 18 June 1990); *Career* grad recruit (mktg) Thomson Organisation 1980–82; Ogilvy & Mather advtg agency: joined 1982, bd dir 1989–, media dir 1990–94, md The Network (formerly O&M Media) 1994–; Advertising Woman of the Yr (Adwomen) 1994; memb Mktg Soc; *Style—* Ms Mandy Pooler; ✉ The Network, 10 Cabot Square, Canary Wharf, London E14 4QB (☎ 0171 345 3000, fax 0171 345 9027)

POOLEY, Dr Derek; CBE (1995); s of Richard Pike Pooley (d 1988), of Port Isaac, Cornwall, and Evelyn, *née* Lee (d 1985); *b* 28 Oct 1937; *Educ* Sir James Smith's Sch Camelford, Univ of Birmingham (BSc, PhD); *m* 1961, Jennifer Mary, da of William Arthur Charles Davey (d 1980), of Birmingham; 2 s (Michael Bruce b 1967, Benjamin John b 1969), 1 da (Miriam Jane b 1973); *Career* head Materials Devpt Div Harwell 1976–81, dir energy res Harwell 1981–83, chief scientist Dept of Energy 1983–86, dir Winfrith Technology Centre 1989–90, md AEA Nuclear Business Group 1991–94, chief exec UKAEA 1996–; *Recreations* photography, walking, history, gardening; *Style—* Dr Derek Pooley, CBE; ✉ 11 Halls Close, Drayton, Abingdon, Oxfordshire 0X14 4LU; UKAEA Harwell, Oxfordshire OX11 0RA (☎ 01235 436880)

POOLEY, Prof Frederick David; s of Frederick Pooley (d 1964), and Ellen, *née* Dix (d 1996); *b* 3 Feb 1939; *Educ* Univ of Wales Coll of Cardiff (BSc, MSc, PhD); *m* 18 Aug 1962, Patricia Mary, da of John Boyt Williams (d 1992), of Abergavenny, Gwent; 2 s (Anthony John b 1964, Andrew David b 1966), 1 da (Susan Elizabeth b 1968); *Career* res fell MRC 1966–69; Univ of Wales Coll of Cardiff: lectr in minerals engrg Dept of Mineral Exploitation 1969–76, sr lectr 1976–77, reader 1977–87, prof Sch of Engrg 1987–; author of numerous papers and articles on dust disease, res and biological treatment of minerals; fell Minerals Engrg Soc 1986; CEng 1977, MAIME 1979, FIMM 1994, MCIWEM 1995; *Recreations* sailing; *Clubs* PH Yacht; *Style—* Prof Frederick Pooley; ✉ School of Engineering, University of Wales College of Cardiff, Newport Rd, PO Box 917, Cardiff CF2 1XH (☎ 01222 874825, fax 01222 874939, telex 498635)

POOLEY, Graham Howard John; s of John Henry William Pooley, of Loughton, Essex, and Joan Margaret, *née* Price (d 1983); *b* 11 March 1949; *Educ* Brentwood Sch, Oriel Coll Oxford (MA); *m* 8 May 1971 (m dis 1993); 1 s (Oliver Edward b 1973), 1 da (Laura Kathleen May b 1976); *Career* dir Barclays de Zoete Wedd Ltd 1986–89, md Chase Investment Bank 1989–92, in own consultancy co 1993–; Chelmsford borough cncllr 1995–; memb: Lib Dem Pty (prospective candidate Maldon and E Chelmsford), Friends of the Earth, Voting Reform Gp, Charter '88, Nat Campaign for Nursery Educn; *Style—* Graham Pooley; ✉ 100 School Lane, Broomfield, Chelmsford, Essex CM1 7DS (☎ 01245 443721, fax 01245 442951)

POOLEY, Joseph; s of Arthur Edward Pooley, of Richmond, Yorks, and Marjorie, *née* Lister; *b* 8 Dec 1946; *Educ* Barnard Castle Sch, Univ of Newcastle upon Tyne (MB BS, MD); *m* 2 July 1977, Jane Elizabeth, da of Ronald George Mills; 1 s (Nicholas James b 21 Sept 1985), 1 da (Victoria Jane b 15 Aug 1988); *Career* house surgn and house physician Royal Victoria Infirmary Newcastle upon Tyne 1971–72, demonstrator in anatomy Med Sch Univ of Newcastle 1972–73, sr surgical house offr Royal Victoria Infirmary 1973–74, registrar in surgery Newcastle Surgical Rotation 1974–77, orthopaedic surgical registrar Royal Victoria Infirmary 1978, res assoc Dept of Surgical Science Univ of Newcastle 1978–80, sr registrar in orthopaedic surgery Northern Region 1980–83, sr lectr in orthopaedics Univ of Newcastle 1985– (lectr 1983–85), conslt orthopaedic surgn Royal Victoria Infirmary and Freeman Hosp 1985–; British Orthopaedic Research Soc: President's medal 1978–80, travelling fell 1983; British Orthopaedic Assoc: Robert Jones Gold medal and prize 1983, Euro travelling scholar 1984; memb: BMA 1972, British Orthopaedic Research Soc 1980, British Orthopaedic Oncology Soc 1988; FRCS (MRCS 1977); *Recreations* tennis, walking, music; *Style—* Joseph Pooley, Esq; ✉ University Department of Orthopaedics, Royal Victoria Infirmary, Queen Victoria Road, Newcastle upon Tyne NE1 4LP (☎ 0191 231 5131)

POOLEY, Moira Helen; *née* Lewis; da of Roger Francis Lewis (d 1978), of Chadwell Heath, Essex, and Kathleen, *née* Kingseller; *b* 17 June 1950; *Educ* Ursuline Convent Brentwood Essex, QMC London (LLB); *m* 1, May 1971 (m dis); 1 s (Oliver Edward b 24 March 1973), 1 da (Laura Kathleen May b 10 Nov 1976); m 2, 16 April 1993, Anthony Goldstaub, QC; *Career* called to the Bar Middle Temple 1974; memb local govt and planning bar assocs; vice chm: Little Baddow Parish Cncl 1981–84, Barnston Parish Cncl 1988–92; chm: Social Security Appeal Tbnl 1986–, Nat Insur Tbnl 1986–; *Recreations* poultry keeping, archaeology, cookery; *Style—* Mrs Moira Pooley; ✉ 4 King's Bench Walk, Temple, London EC4Y 9DL (☎ 0171 353 3581)

POOLEY, Peter; CMG (1996); *b* 1936; *m* 1966, Janet Mary, er da of Jack Pearson, of Banbury; 1 s, 1 da; *Career* agric min Office of UK Perm Rep to Euro Community Brussels 1979–82, fisheries sec Miny of Agric London 1982–83; Euro Cmmn Brussels: dep DG (Agric) 1983–89, dep DG (Devpt) 1989–92, acting DG (Devpt) 1993–95, hon DG (Devpt) 1995–; *Style—* Peter Pooley, Esq, CMG; ✉ Commission of the European Communities, Rue de la Loi 200, B1049, Brussels, Belgium; Dereymaekerlaan 53, 3080 Tervuren, Belgium

POOLEY, Robert John; s of Sydney John Pooley (d 1972), and Hilda Vera, *née* Salmon; *b* 9 Feb 1935; *Educ* Medburn Sch; *m* 1, 24 Feb 1962 (m dis 1973), Yvonne Margaret, da of William Pereiva (d 1976), of Hatfield, Herts; 1 s (Julian David John b 26 Feb 1964), 1 da (Katharine Yvonne 12 March 1966); m 2, 5 July 1974, Carolyn, da of Dr J Alfred Lee, of Westcliff, Essex; 1 s (Sebastian Robert John b 3 May 1979), 1 da (Samantha Carolyn Merlyn b 30 July 1974); *Career* RAF SAC 4 Sqdn 1953–57; De Havilland Aircraft Co 1957–61; chm: Airtour Int Ltd, Airtour Flight Equipment Ltd, Airlife Publishing Ltd, Robert Pooley Ltd, Pooleys Ltd; ed and publisher Pooley Flight Guides 1961; chm Soc of the St John Ophthalmic Hosp Jerusalem 1987–91, tstee Museum of Army Flying Devpt Tst; dir Middle Wallop Int Air Show (AAC); vice pres: Helicopter Club of GB, Guild of Aviation Artists, Br Precision Pilots' Assoc; vice chm Royal Aero Club, tstee Boxmoor Tst, pres 1187 Sqdn ATC, St John Ambulance Bde Hemel Hampstead; memb Cncl Herts Order of St John 1986, chm The Ballon Club; Freeman City of London 1971, Liveryman Guild of Air Pilots and Air Navigators 1971 (Master 1987–88); CStJ 1992 (OStJ 1987), FRIN 1979, FRAS 1981; *Books* Pooleys Flight Guides (1962–1997), Pilots Information Guide (1982 and 1986); *Recreations* flying, ballooning, riding, sub-aqua, skiing; *Clubs* Royal Aero, City Livery, Cavalry & Guards'; *Style—* Robert Pooley, Esq; ✉ Forter Castle, Glenisla, Angus PH11 8QW (☎ 01575 82305); Pooleys Ltd, Elstree Aerodrome, Herts WD5 3AW (☎ 0181 953 4870, fax 0181 953 5219)

POORE, Dr (Martin Edward) Duncan; s of Thomas Edward Deverell Poore (d 1966), of Coshieville, Aberfeldy, and Elizabeth, *née* MacMartin (d 1965); *b* 25 May 1925; *Educ* Trinity Coll Glenalmond, Clare Coll Cambridge (MA, PhD), Oxford (MA by incorpn); *m* 3 Sept 1949, Judith Ursula (Judy), da of Gen Sir Treffry Owen Thompson, KCSI, CB, CBE (d 1979), of Chulmleigh, N Devon; 2 s (Robin b 1952, Alasdair b 1954); *Career* prof of botany Univ of Malaya 1959–65, dir Nature Conservancy 1966–74, sci dir then DG IUCN 1974–78, prof of forest sci and dir Cwlth Forestry Inst Univ of Oxford 1980–83, conslt in land use and conservation 1983–; sr fell IIED; memb Thames Water Authy 1981–84, chm Advsy Ctee on Sci Nature Conservancy Cncl 1982–84, chm Cwlth Forestry Assoc 1986–88 (vice pres 1988–), pres Br Assoc of Nature Conservationists 1983–93 (vice-pres 1993–); hon memb Botanical Soc of Scotland; memb: Inst of Chartered Foresters, Inst of Ecology and Environmental Mgmnt; FIBiol, FRGS 1967, FRSA 1974; *Books* No Timber Without Trees: Sustainability in the Tropical Forest (1989), Protected Landscapes in the United Kingdom (with Judy Poore, 1992), The Management of Tropical Moist Forest Lands: Ecological Guidelines (with Jeffrey Sayer, 1991); *Recreations* gardening, hill walking, music; *Clubs* Royal Over-Seas League; *Style—* Dr Duncan Poore; ✉ Balnacarn, Glenmoriston, Inverness-shire IV3 6YJ (☎ 01320 340261)

POORE, Sir Herbert Edward; 6 Bt (GB 1795), of Rushall, Wilts; s of Sir Edward Poore, 5 Bt (d 1938); *b* 1930; *Heir* unc, Nasionceno Poore b 1900; *Style*— Sir Herbert Poore, Bt; ✉ Curuzu Cuatia, Corrientes, Argentina

POPAT, Surendra (Andrew); CBE (1997); s of Dhirajlal Kurji Popat (d 1989), of Putney, London, and Kashiben Chitalia (d 1963); *b* 31 Dec 1943; *Educ* Govt Secdy Sch Dar Es Salaam Tanzania, Univ of London (LLB), Univ of California (LLM); *Career* called to the Bar Lincoln's Inn 1969, apptd list of the dir of public prosecutions by the then attorney gen Sir Michael Havers 1984, admitted memb Inner Temple 1985, asst recorder Crown Ct 1992–; contested (Cons) Palewell Ward E Sheen 1978, Parly candidate (Cons) Durham N general election 1983, Parly candidate (Cons) Bradford S 1992 gen election, treas Surbition Cons Assoc 1985, dir John Patten's election campaign 1987; chm Disraeli Club (Cons Pty orgn to promote intellectual dialogue and raise funds) 1993–; Freeman City of London 1987, Liveryman Worshipful Co of Plaisterers 1987; *Recreations* travel, theatre, cricket, tennis; *Clubs* Carlton; *Style*— Andrew Popat, Esq, CBE; ✉ 9 King's Bench Walk, Temple, London EC4Y 7DX (☎ 0171 353 7202, fax 0171 583 2030)

POPE, Anthony; s of Lt Col Albert Victor Pope (d 1976), and Barbara, *née* Shaw (d 1982); *b* 25 April 1933; *Educ* Melbourne GS Victoria Aust; *m* 1965, Cynthia Margaret, da of Wing-Cdr Alexander Walker (d 1976); 1 s, 1 da; *Career* dir Eldridge Pope & Co plc 1960–; FHCIMA, FRSH; *Recreations* shooting, farming; *Clubs* Cavalry and Guards'; *Style*— Anthony Pope, Esq; ✉ Hamlet House, Hamlet, nr Sherborne, Dorset (☎ 01935 872325); Eldridge Pope & Co plc, Dorchester Brewery, Dorchester, Dorset (☎ 01305 251251)

POPE, Cathryn Mary; *b* 6 July 1957; *Educ* RCM, Nat Opera Studio; *m* 1981, Stuart Petersen; *Career* soprano; debut Sophie in Werther (ENO) 1982, int debut Gretel in Hansel and Gretel (Netherlands Opera Amsterdam); *Roles* with ENO incl: Gretel in Hansel and Gretel 1987 and 1990, Despina in Cosi fan Tutte 1988, Oskana in Christmas Eve 1988, Leila in The Pearl Fishers 1988, Mélisande in Pelléas and Mélisande 1990, Pamina in The Magic Flute 1990, Donna Elvira in Don Giovanni 1991, Susanna in The Marriage of Figaro 1991 and 1993, Goosegirl in Königskinder 1992, Tatyana in Eugene Onegin 1994; other performances incl: Marguerite in Faust (New Sussex Opera) 1989, Nedda in Pagliacci, Emma in Khovanshchina, Micaela in Carmen; *Recordings* incl Anne Truelove in The Rake's Progress (Decca); *Style*— Miss Cathryn Pope; (☎ and fax 01932 227191)

POPE, Dudley Bernard Egerton; s of Sidney Broughton Pope (d 1926), and Alice Egerton, *née* Meehan; *b* 29 Dec 1925; *Educ* Ashford GS; *m* 17 March 1954, Kathleen Patricia, da of Edward Reginald Hall (d 1983); 1 da (Jane Clare Victoria b 17 Feb 1965); *Career* Midshipman MN 1942–43 (wounded); London Evening News: naval corr, sub-ed, dep foreign ed 1944–59; naval historian and author 1959–; *Non-fiction* Flag 4, the Battle of Coastal Forces in the Mediterranean (1954), The Battle of the River Plate (1956), 73 North (1958), England Expects (1959), At 12 Mr Byng Was Shot (1962), The Black Ship (1963), Guns (1965), The Great Gamble (1972), Harry Morgan's Way (1977), Life in Nelson's Navy (1981), The Devil Himself (1987); *Fiction* the Ramage series: Ramage (1965), Ramage and the Drum Beat (1967), Ramage and the Freebooters (1969), Governor Ramage, RN (1973), Ramage's Prize (1974), Ramage and the Guillotine (1975), Ramage's Diamond (1976), Ramage's Mutiny (1977), Ramage and the Rebels (1978), The Ramage Touch (1979), Ramage's Signal (1980), Ramage and the Renegades (1981), Ramage's Devil (1982), Ramage's Trial (1984), Ramage's Challenge (1985), Ramage at Trafalgar (1986), Ramage and the Saracens (1988), Ramage and the Dido (1989); The Yorke Series: Convoy (1979), Buccaneer (1981), Admiral (1982), Decoy (1983), Galleon (1986), Corsair (1987); *Recreations* sailing, shell collecting; *Style*— Dudley Pope, Esq; ✉ Le Pirate 379, 97150 Marigot, St-Martin, French West Indies (☎ 00 1 809 690 872428)

POPE, Vice Adm Sir (John) Ernle; KCB (1976); s of Cdr Rowland Cecil Kyrle Pope, DSO, OBE, DL, RN (d 1976), and late Agnes Jessie, *née* MacDonald; bro of Rear Adm Michael Kyrle Pope, CB, MBE, DL (*see* Kyrle Pope, Michael); *b* 22 May 1921; *Educ* RNC Dartmouth; *m* 21 Dec 1968, Phyllis Mary Webber; *Career* joined RN 1935, Capt 1960, CO HMS Decoy 1962–64, dir Naval Equipment 1964–66, CO HMS Eagle 1966–68, Rear Adm 1969, Flag Offr Flotillas Western Fleet 1969–71, COS to C in C Western Fleet 1971–74, Vice Adm 1972, Cdr Allied Naval Forces S Europe 1974–76; *Clubs* Army and Navy; *Style*— Sir Ernle Pope, KCB; ✉ Homme House, Much Marcle, Ledbury, Hereford

POPE, Dr Geoffrey George; CB (1986); s of Sir George Reginald Pope (d 1982), and Susie Annie, *née* Hendy (d 1995); *b* 17 April 1934; *Educ* Epsom Coll, Imperial Coll London (MSc, PhD); *m* 1, 1961, Rosemary Frances Harnden (d 1989); 2 s; *m* 2, 1991, Helen Vernon Brewis; *Career* dep dir (Weapons) Royal Aircraft Estab 1979–81, asst chief scientific advsr (Projects) MOD 1981–82, dep controller and advsr (Res and Technol) MOD 1982–84, dir Royal Aircraft Estab 1984–89, dep chief scientific advsr MOD 1989–94; FEng 1988, FRAeS (pres 1993–94), FCGI; *Recreations* music, photography, walking; *Style*— Dr Geoffrey Pope, CB, FEng; ✉ 3 Silver Street, Thorverton, Exeter, Devon EX5 5LT

POPE, Gregory (Greg); MP (Lab) Hyndburn (majority 1,960); s of late Samuel Pope, and Sheila Pope; *b* 29 Aug 1960; *Educ* St Mary's Coll RC GS Blackburn, Univ of Hull (BA); *m* 2 Aug 1985, Catherine, *née* Fallon; 2 s, 1 da; *Career* vice pres Hull Univ Students' Union 1981–82, co-ordinator Blackburn Trade Union Centre for the Unemployed 1983–85, with Star newspaper Blackburn 1985–87, local govt offr Lancs CC 1987–92; cncllr: Hyndburn BC 1984–88, Blackburn BC 1989–91; Parly candidate (Lab) Ribble Valley 1987, MP (Lab) Hyndburn 1992–; opposition whip 1995–; *Recreations* walking, chess, music; *Style*— Greg Pope, Esq, MP; ✉ House of Commons, London SW1A 0AA

POPE, Jeremy James Richard; OBE (1985); s of Philip William Rolph Pope (d 1996), of Dorchester, Dorset, and Joyce Winifred Harcourt, *née* Slade; *b* 15 July 1943; *Educ* Charterhouse, Trinity Coll Cambridge (MA); *m* 1969, Hon Jacqueline Dorothy Mametz Best, da of Lt-Col 8 Baron Wynford, MBE, DL, of Dorchester; 3 s (Rory b 1970, Rupert b 1973, Toby b 1977); *Career* admitted slr 1969; dir: Eldridge Pope & Co plc 1969– (md 1988, dep chm 1987–), Winterbourne Hosp plc 1981–89 (fndr chm), JB Reynier Ltd 1984–; chm: Realstream Ltd 1987–92, Highcliff Hotel (Bournemouth) Ltd 1988–; memb Exec Ctee Brewers' Soc 1977–88, memb Dept of Trade Advsy Panel on Co Law 1980–81, chm Smaller Firms' Cncl CBI 1981–84, memb NEDC 1981–85, govr Forres Sch Swanage 1983–92, chm Wessex Medical Tst 1992– (tstee 1991–); memb: Royal Cmmn on Environmental Pollution 1984–92, Exec Ctee Food and Drinks Fedn (dep pres 1987–90), Top Salary Review Body 1986–93; chm management ctee Devonshire and Dorset Regimental Museum 1995–; tstee Devonshire and Dorset Regiment's Regimental Charities; memb Law Soc; Liveryman: Worshipful Co of Innholders, Worshipful Co of Gunmakers; FRSA 1989; *Recreations* gardening, field sports, cooking, beekeeping; *Style*— Jeremy Pope, Esq, OBE; ✉ Field Cottage, West Compton, nr Dorchester, Dorset DT2 0EY; Eldridge, Pope & Co plc, The Dorchester Brewery, PO Box 2, Dorchester, Dorset DT1 1QT (☎ 01305 251251)

POPE, Sir Joseph Albert; kt (1980); s of Albert Henry Pope, and Mary Pope; *b* 18 Oct 1914; *Educ* Sch of Arts and Crafts Cambridge, King's Coll London; *m* 1940, Evelyn Alice, da of Rev Robert Henry Gallagher; 1 s, 2 da; *Career* Whitworth scholarship 1935, prof of mechanical engrg Nottingham Univ 1949–60, vice chllr Univ of Aston in Birmingham 1969–79, chm TecQuipment Gp Nottingham 1975–88; dir John Brown plc 1970–82, gen treas Br Assoc 1975–82, chm W Midlands Econ Planning Cncl 1977–79, dir Royal Worcester plc 1979–84; Hon LLD Univ of Birmingham 1979, Hon DUniv Heriot-Watt 1979; Hon DSc: Aston Univ 1979, Univ of Belfast 1980, Univ of Salford 1980, Univ of Nottingham 1987; FIMgt, CEng, FIMechE; *Style*— Sir Joseph Pope; ✉ 3 Mapperley Hall Drive, Nottingham NG3 5EP (☎ 0115 962 1146); TecQuipment Ltd, Bonsall Street, Long Eaton, Nottingham NG10 2AN (☎ 0115 972 2611, fax 0115 973 1520, telex 377 828)

POPE, Martin John; s of Anthony Peter Pope, and Patricia, *née* Servant; *b* 8 Aug 1963; *Educ* Dame Alice Owen Sch Potters Bar Herts, Barnet Art Coll, Stradbroke Coll Sheffield (NCTJ); *Career* chief photographer: The Hendon Times 1987–90, Katz Pictures 1990–; assignments incl: Romania 1990 and 1991, Albanian elections 1992, Somalia famine 1992, Iraqi Kurdistan 1993, gold panning/AIDS Zimbabwe 1993, South Africa in transition 1993–94, life after the Zapatista rebellion Chiapas Mexico 1995; work included in World Press Exhbn 1994; *Awards* Fuji Feature award 1992, Canon Press Photo of the Yr 1992, Kodak Portfolio award 1993; *Style*— Martin Pope, Esq; (☎ and fax 01945 860244, mobile 0850 656962)

POPE, Timothy Patrick; s of Bryan George Patrick Pope, of Walton-on-Thames, and Mary Margaret, *née* Knoyle; *b* 23 March 1948; *Educ* Glynn GS; *m* Dec 1980, Gerda Hendrika Maria, da of L T M Rokebrand; 3 s (Alexander b Sept 1983, Michael b Aug 1985, William b Feb 1988); *Career* ptnr Deloitte Haskins & Sells 1979 (articled clerk 1966–70), currently ptnr and chm Professional Standards Ctee Coopers & Lybrand and memb Auditing Practices Bd; FCA (ACA 1970); *Recreations* golf, photography; *Clubs* Brooks's, RAC, St George's Hill Lawn Tennis, The Wisley Golf; *Style*— Timothy Pope, Esq; ✉ Coopers & Lybrand, 1 Embankment Place, London WC2N 6NN (☎ 0171 583 5000)

POPESCU, Christine Pullein-Thompson; da of late Capt H J Pullein-Thompson, and Joanna, *née* Cannan; sis of Josephine Pullein-Thompson, *qv*, and Diana Farr, *qv*; *Educ* Pneu Sch, Wychwood Sch; *m* 1954, Julian John Hunter Popescu; 2 s (Philip b 1955, Mark, *qv* b 1960), 2 da (Charlotte b 1957, Lucy b 1966); *Career* writer; work trans into 12 languages incl Catalan, Bulgarian and Estonian; dir Grove Riding Schools Ltd 1946–52; chm Parish Cncl, chm Riding for the Disabled Henley-on-Thames 1975–79; memb Soc of Authors, memb PEN; *Books* We Rode to the Sea, We Hunted Hounds, I Carried the Horn, Goodbye to Hounds, Phantom Horse, Phantom Horse Comes Home, Phantom Horse Goes to Ireland, Phantom Horse Goes to Scotland, Phantom Horse in Danger, Wait for Me Phantom Horse, Riders From Afar, The First Rosette, The Second Mount, Three to Ride, The Open Gate, The Empty Field, The Pony Dopers, A Day to Go Hunting, Ride By Night, The Horse Sale, The Lost Pony, For Want of a Saddle, The Impossible Horse, Stolen Ponies, Riders on the March, They Rode to Victory, Strange Riders at Black Pony Inn, Mystery At Black Pony Inn, Secrets At Black Pony Inn, Prince At Black Pony Inn, Good Deeds At Black Pony Inn, Catastrophe At Black Pony Inn, Pony Patrol, Pony Patrol S.O.S., Pony Patrol Fights Back, Pony Patrol and The Mystery Horse, Black Velvet, Ponies In The Park, Ponies In The Blizzard, Ponies In The Forest, I Rode A Winner, Father Unknown, A Home for Jessie, Please Save Jessie, Come Home Jessie, Across The Frontier, The Long Search, The Big Storm, The Road Through The Hills, Smoke In The Hills, Stay At Home Ben, Careless Ben, Runaway Ben, Candy Goes To The Gymkhana (Ladybird), Candy Stops A Train (Ladybird), I Want That Pony (Ladybird, 1993); books for 4–10 year olds: Granny Comes to Stay, The Lost Cow, Little Black Pony, The Gipsy Children, The Stolen Car, Robbers In The Night, Bandits In The Hills, Homeless Katie, Room To Let, A Day To Remember, No-One At Home, The Boys From The Cafe; books for 6–10 year olds: Giles And The Elephant, Giles And The Greyhound, Giles And The Canal, The Eastmans In Brittany, The Eastmans Find A Boy, The Eastmans Move House, Nigel Eats His Words; equine anthologies: Pony Scrap Book, Second Pony Scrap Book, Book of Pony Stories, Second Book of Pony Stories, Horse and Pony Stories (1992), Thundering Hooves (1996, UK and USA), Fair Girls on Gray Horses (autobiography in collaboration with sisters, 1996); instructional pony books: Good Riding, A Pony to Love, Riding for Fun, Improve Your Riding, The Follyfoot Horse and Pony Quiz Book; I Want that Pony (1993), The Best Pony for Me (1995), The Pony Test (1997); *Recreations* riding, travelling, conversation; *Style*— Christine Pullein-Thompson

POPESCU, Mark Cannan; s of Julian John Hunter Popescu, of Old Parsonage, Mellis, nr Eye, Suffolk, and Christine Pullein-Thompson Popescu, *qv*; *b* 9 Sept 1960; *Educ* King James Coll Henley, Univ of Exeter (BA); *partner*, Lesley Pauline, da of David Trevor Hugh Tring; 2 s (Oliver Jack b 2 April 1989, Daniel Edward b 3 Jan 1991); *Career* reporter Devonair Radio Exeter 1983–84, news ed GWR Radio Swindon 1984–86, prodr BBC Radio News London 1986–87; ITN: prodr News at One 1987–88, home news ed 1988–89, ed Forward Planning 1989–91, political news ed Westminster 1991–94, ed The Lunchtime News 1994–96, ed News at Ten and head of Special Progs ITN for ITV 1996–; maj assignments incl: Romanian Revolution 1990 (sr prodr), Kuwait City 1991 (sr prodr), General Election 1992 (campaign news ed), Party Confs 1991, 1992 and 1993 (ed); *Recreations* kite flying, cooking and oneirology; *Style*— Mark Popescu, Esq; ✉ ITN, 200 Gray's Inn Road, London WC1X 8XZ (☎ 0171 833 3000)

POPHAM, Maj-Gen Christopher John; CB (1982); s of Gordon F B Popham (d 1949), and Dorothy A L, *née* Yull (d 1990); *b* 2 April 1927; *Educ* Merchant Taylors'; *m* 1950, Heather Margaret, da of Lt-Col H Reginald W Dawson (d 1937); 2 s; *Career* asst COS (Intelligence) Supreme HQ Allied Powers Europe 1979–82, ret 1982, Col Cmdt Corps of RE 1982–87; dir Br Atlantic Ctee 1982–92; *Recreations* photography, railways, music; *Style*— Maj-Gen Christopher Popham, CB; ✉ c/o Barclays Bank plc, High St, Andover, Hants

POPLE, Andrew Howard; *Educ* BA, MPhil, MBA; *Career* with Bank of England 1983–88; Abbey National plc: regnl dir 1992–94, dir Life Assurance Div and chief exec subsid Scottish Mutual 1994–96, md Retail Div 1996–; *Style*— Andrew Pople, Esq; ✉ Abbey National plc, Abbey House, Baker Street, London NW1 6XL (☎ 0171 612 4000)

POPPLEWELL, Nicholas James; s of Newton J Popplewell, of Gory, Co Wexford, and Olive, *née* Gregory; *b* 6 April 1964; *Educ* Newtown Sch Waterford; *Career* rugby union prop forward; clubs: Gorey RFC, Greystones RFC 1984–95, Newcastle RFC 1995–, Barbarians RFC (v Newport 1989); rep: Leinster 1987–, Ireland U25 (debut v Italy 1988); Ireland: tour France 1988, tour USA and Canada 1989, debut v NZ 1989, reserve Five Nations 1990, memb squad World Cup 1991 and 1995, 39 caps; memb British Lions' team touring NZ 1993; retail mangr Argus Furniture; *Recreations* golf, squash, reading, eating; *Style*— Nicholas Popplewell, Esq; ✉ Newcastle RFC, New Ground, Great North Road, Gosforth, Newcastle upon Tyne NE3 2DT (☎ 0191 214 0422); c/o MP Associates, 156 Sutherland Avenue, London W9 1HP (☎ 0171 286 1793)

POPPLEWELL, Hon Mr Justice; Hon Sir Oliver Bury Popplewell; kt (1983); s of Frank Popplewell, OBE (d 1965), and Nina, *née* Sydney (d 1979); *b* 15 Aug 1927; *Educ* Charterhouse, Queens' Coll Cambridge (exhibitioner, MA, LLB); *m* 1954, Catharine Margaret (DL Bucks 1993), da of Alfred John Storey (d 1941); 4 s (and 1 s decd); *Career* served RN 1946–48; called to the Bar Inner Temple 1951 (bencher 1978), QC 1969, dep chm Oxon QS 1970–72, recorder of Burton 1970–72, recorder of the Crown Court 1970–83, judge of the High Court of Justice (Queen's Bench Div) 1983–; memb: of Home Office Advsy Bd on Restricted Patients 1980–82, Carlisle Ctee of Inquiry into Parole 1988; chm and ind memb Wages Cncls, vice chm Parole Bd 1986–87 (memb 1985); pres: Employment Appeal Tbnl 1986–88, MCC 1994–96; chm Ctee of Inquiry into Crowd Control Safety and Control at Sports Grounds 1985; *Recreations* sailing, tennis, bridge; *Clubs* MCC (memb Ctee 1972 and 1987–, tstee 1983–94, pres 1994–96), Hawks

(Cambridge), Blakeney Sailing, Garrick; *Style*— The Hon Mr Justice Popplewell; ✉ Royal Courts of Justice, Strand, London WC2A 2LL

POPPLEWELL, Richard John; MVO (1990); s of Norman Stanley Popplewell (d 1941), and Eileen Mary Louise, *née* Jagger (d 1975); *b* 18 Oct 1935; *Educ* King's Coll Cambridge (chorister, organ scholar), Clifton Coll (organ scholar, Sawyer prize, ARCO), RCM (organ scholar, ARCM); *m* 1963, Margaret, da of Frank Lawrence Conway; 1 s (James David b 1970); *Career* asst organist St Paul's Cathedral 1958–66, dir of music St Michael's Cornhill 1966–79, organist, choirmaster and composer HM Chapels Royal St James's Palace 1979–; prof of organ RCM 1962–; examiner: RCO (memb Cncl), King's Coll London, RCM, Assoc Bd of the Royal Schs of Music; accompanist and asst conductor The Bach Choir 1966–79; soloist Proms 1965; special cmmr RSCM; memb: NATFHE, Musicians' Union, Assoc of Cathedral Organists, ISM, RSM; memb Ctee Friends of Kent House Richmond; FRCM, FRCO; *Compositions* published choral works incl: There Is No Rose 1974, The National Anthem (dedicated by Gracious Permission to HM Queen Elizabeth II) 1984, Two Final Amens 1989, O How Amiable 1992, A Vast Cloud of Love 1996, various anthems for royal baptisms; published organ works incl: Suite for Organ 1974, Puck's Shadow 1976, Easter Hymn 1977, Chants d'oiseaux, des poules, des moutons et des vaches 1977, Elegy 1980, Concerto in D 1981, Prelude on Down Ampney 1982, Romance 1986, Triumphal March 1993; *Recreations* swimming, reading; *Style*— Richard Popplewell, Esq, MVO; ✉ 23 Stanmore Gardens, Richmond, Surrey TW9 2HN (☎ 0181 332 7301); HM Chapel Royal, St James's Palace, London SW1 (☎ 0171 930 3007)

PORCHESTER, Lord; George (Geordie) Reginald Oliver Molyneux Herbert; s and h of 7 Earl of Carnarvon, *qv*; *b* 10 Nov 1956; *Educ* Eton, St John's Coll Oxford (BA); *m* 16 Dec 1989, Jayne M, eldest da of K A Wilby, of Cheshire, and Princess Frances Colonna di Stigliano, of Ashford, Co Wicklow; 1 s (George b 13 Oct 1992), 1 da (Saoirse b 2 June 1991); *Career* a page of honour to HM The Queen 1969–73; PA to Hon Peter Morrison, MP 1986–87, computer conslt/estate mgmnt 1976–92, founder shareholder of Telecom Express Ltd 1992–96; *Style*— Lord Porchester

PORRITT, (Hon Sir) Jonathon Espie; 2 Bt (UK 1963), of Hampstead, Co London; does not use title; er s of Baron Porritt, GCMG, GCVO, CBE (Life Peer and 1 Bt; d 1994), and his 2 w, Kathleen Mary, *née* Peck; *b* 6 July 1950; *Educ* Eton, Magdalen Coll Oxford; *m* 1986, Sarah, da of Malcolm Staniforth, of Malvern, Worcs; 2 da (Eleanor Mary b 1988, Rebecca Elizabeth b 1991); *Heir* bro, Hon Jeremy Charles Porritt b 19 Jan 1953; *Career* dir Friends of the Earth 1984–90; dir Forum for the Future, co fndr Real World; author and broadcaster; writer and presenter: Where On Earth Are We Going? (BBC) 1991, How To Save The World (Channel 4) 1992; *Books* Seeing Green: the Politics of Ecology Explained, The Friends of the Earth Handbook, The Coming of the Greens, Where On Earth Are We Going?, Save the Earth, Captain Eco; *Style*— Jonathon Porritt; ✉ 9 Lypiatt Terrace, Cheltenham, Glos GL50 2SX

PORRITT, Sheila; da of Lt Cdr Geoffrey Arthur Stephen Cowley, MBE (d 1979), and Linda, *née* Dessberg; *b* 14 June 1948; *Educ* Portsmouth HS for Girls, Univ of Bristol (BSc); *m* 11 April 1970 (m dis 1988), Stephen John Porritt, s of Sidney Sherwood Porritt (d 1966); 1 s (Eliot b 1979), 1 da (Luisa b 1987); *Career* scientific asst nuclear physics statistical res CEGB 1969–72, dept head of radio programming IBA 1987–89 (broadcasting exec: TV scheduling 1972–77, radio programming 1977–89), prog mangr Channel Four TV 1989–90, md Melody Radio 1990–; dir Assoc of Independent Radio Cos; memb Radio Acad Festival Ctee 1989; *Recreations* tennis, film, theatre, gardening, interior design; *Style*— Ms Sheila Porritt; ✉ Melody Radio, 180 Brompton Road, London SW3 1HF (☎ 0171 581 1054)

PORTAL, Sir Jonathan Francis; 6 Bt (UK 1901), of Malshanger, Church Oakley, Co Southampton; s of Sir Francis Spencer Portal, 5 Bt (d 1984), and his 2 w, Jane Mary, da of late Albert Henry Williams, OBE; *b* 13 Jan 1953; *Educ* Marlborough, Edinburgh Univ (BCom); *m* 9 Oct 1982, Louisa Caroline, er da of Sir (Frederick) John Charles Gordon Hervey-Bathurst, *qv*; 3 s (William Jonathan Francis b 1987, Robert Jonathan b 1989, John Arthur Jonathan b 1993); *Heir* s, William Jonathan Francis Portal b 1 Jan 1987; *Career* chartered accountant; chief accountant Seymour Int Press Distributors 1986–89, gp fin controller Henderson Administration Group plc 1989–91, fin dir Grosvenor Venture Managers Ltd 1992–93, mangr int 3i Group plc 1995–; govr Old Malthouse School Swanage; Liveryman Clothworkers' Co; ACA 1977; *Recreations* travel, music, country sports; *Style*— Sir Jonathan Portal, Bt; ✉ Burley Wood Ashe, Basingstoke, Hants RG25 3AG (☎ 01256 770269)

PORTARLINGTON, 7 Earl of (I 1785); George Lionel Yuill Seymour Dawson-Damer; Baron Dawson (I 1770), Viscount Carlow (I 1776); s of Air Cdre Viscount Carlow (k on active serv 1944) and gs of 6 Earl of Portarlington (d 1959); *b* 10 Aug 1938; *Educ* Eton; *m* 26 July 1961, Davina, eldest da of late Sir Edward Henry Windley, KCMG, KCVO; 3 s (Viscount Carlow b 1965, Hon Edward Lionel Seymour b 1967, Hon Henry Lionel Seymour b 1971), 1 da (Lady Marina Davina b 1969); *Heir* s, Viscount Carlow, *qv*; *Career* Page of Honour to HM The Queen 1953–55; dir: G S Yuill & Co Pty Ltd Sydney, Clyde Agriculture Ltd Sydney; *Recreations* skiing, fishing; *Clubs* Union (Sydney); *Style*— The Rt Hon the Earl of Portarlington; ✉ 118 Wolseley Road, Point Piper, NSW 2027, Australia (☎ 00 612 9363 9725, fax 00 612 327 4691); Gledswood, Melrose, Roxburghshire TD6 9DN (☎ 01896 822558, fax 01896 823324)

PORTAS, Mary; da of Samuel Edward Newton (d 1980), of Watford, Herts, and Mary Theresa, *née* Flynn (d 1977); *b* 28 May 1960; *Educ* Watford Coll of Art (HND in visual merchandising); *m* 5 Sept 1987, Graham Charles Portas; 1 s (Mylo b 19 Jan 1994), 1 da (Verity b 23 Nov 1995); *Career* leading visual merchandiser and window designer; visual merchandiser Harrods dept store until 1984, visual mangr Top Shop (150 stores) 1984–91; Harvey Nichols: head of visual merchandising 1989–91, mktg dir 1991–; most notable window designs for Harvey Nichols incl Financial Times newspaper sculptures and empty charity Christmas windows; recipient various awards for best window design, int lectr on the art of visual mktg; MInstD 1994; memb: RSA 1994, Mktg Gp of GB 1995; *Books* currently preparing a worldwide critical survey of contemporary visual merchandising for Thames and Hudson; *Recreations* keen dramatist and set designer for The Abbey Theatre (The Company of Ten) and The Pump House Theatre; *Style*— Mrs Mary Portas; ✉ Harvey Nichols, Knightsbridge, London SW1X 7RJ (☎ 0171 584 0011, fax 0171 235 9507, mobile 0585 437374)

PORTEN, Anthony Ralph; QC (1988); s of Ralph Charles Porten (d 1976), and Joan, *née* Edden; *b* 1 March 1947; *Educ* Epsom Coll, Emmanuel Coll Cambridge (BA); *m* 17 Oct 1970, Kathryn Mary, da of John Rees Edwards, JP (d 1988); 2 da (Lucinda b 1973, Deborah b 1976); *Career* called to the Bar Inner Temple 1969, recorder of the Crown Ct 1993–; *Recreations* family, walking, motoring; *Clubs* RAC; *Style*— Anthony Porten, Esq, QC; ✉ Clive Cottage, Claremont Drive, Esher, Surrey KT10 9LU (☎ 01372 467513); 2–3 Gray's Inn Square, London WC1R 5JH (☎ 0171 242 4986, fax 0171 405 1166, telex 21785 ADVICE G, car 0836 215935)

PORTEOUS, Christopher Selwyn; CBE (1993); s of Selwyn Porteous (d 1972), of Dulwich, and Marjorie Irene, *née* Glover (d 1958); *b* 8 Nov 1935; *Educ* Dulwich Coll; *m* 27 Feb 1960, Brenda, da of William Stanley Wallis (d 1977); 4 da (Catherine b 1961, Judith b 1963, Gillian b 1965, Anne b 1969); *Career* admitted slr 1960; articled clerk local govt 1954–60, slr London CC 1960–62; New Scotland Yard: legal asst 1962–68, sr legal asst 1968–76, asst slr 1976–86, slr to the Cmmr of Police 1987–95; author of articles in law magazines; reader of C of E, former memb Pastoral Ctee Rochester Dio; memb: Law Soc, Cwlth Law Soc; hon pres Assoc of Police Lawyers, hon memb ACPO; *Recreations* writing, gardening, walking, listening to music; *Style*— Christopher Porteous, Esq, CBE; ✉ c/o Solicitor's Department, New Scotland Yard, Broadway, London SW1H 0BG

PORTEOUS, John (Robin); OBE (1994); s of Charles Frederick Porteous (d 1941), of London, and Mary Grace, *née* Wooster (d 1995); *b* 29 July 1934; *Educ* Westminster, ChCh Oxford (MA); *m* 16 June 1956, Catherine Eleanor, da of John Traill Christie; 2 s (Matthew b 1957, Tom b 1960), 1 da (Rebecca b 1969); *Career* with Baring Brothers & Co Ltd 1955–57, Philip Hill Higginson Ltd 1957–60, ptnr Pember & Boyle Stockbrokers 1966–86 (joined 1960), dir Morgan Grenfell Govt Securities Ltd 1986, fell and bursar Gonville and Caius Coll Cambridge 1987–; memb: Royal Mint Advsy Ctee 1968, Syndic of Fitzwilliam Museum Cambridge 1989; Liveryman Worshipful Co of Skinners 1956; memb Stock Exchange 1966–87; FSA 1980; *Books* Coins (1963), Coins in History (1969), Aangemunt En Nagemunt (Amsterdam 1970); *Recreations* numismatics, foreign travel, second hand bookshops; *Style*— John Porteous, Esq, OBE; ✉ 52 Elgin Crescent, London W11 2JJ (☎ 0171 727 6915); 7 Summerfield, Newnham, Cambridge (☎ 01223 363947); Gonville and Caius College, Cambridge CB2 1TA (☎ 01223 332455, fax 01223 332406)

PORTEOUS, Col Patrick Anthony; VC (Dieppe 1942); s of Brig-Gen C McL Porteous (d 1936); *b* 1 Jan 1918; *Educ* Wellington, RMA Woolwich; *m* 1, 1943, Lois Mary (d 1953), da of Maj-Gen Sir Horace Roome, KCIE (d 1970); 1 s, 1 da; *m* 2, 1955, Deirdre, da of late Eric King; 3 da; *Career* 2 Lt RA 1937, 6 AA Regt 1938, served France, Belgium, Dunkirk 1939–40, joined Commandos 1940, Dieppe 1942, Normandy 1944; instr RMA Sandhurst 1950–53, DAQMG FARELF 1953–56, 14 Field Regt RA 1956, RAF Staff Coll 1958, AMS HQ Southern Cmd 1959–60, Lt-Col Junior Leaders Regt RA 1960–63, Col Gen Staff War Office then MOD 1963–66, Cdr Rheindahlen Garrison 1966–69, ret 1970; *Recreations* sailing, gardening; *Style*— Col Patrick Porteous, VC; ✉ Christmas Cottage, Funtington, Chichester, W Sussex PO18 9LQ (☎ 01243 575315)

PORTER, *see also:* Horsbrugh-Porter

PORTER, Anita; MBE (1963); da of Stanley Lonsbrough, of 82 Briarlyn Rd, Birchencliffe, Huddersfield, and Maud, *née* Elwood; *b* 10 Aug 1941; *Educ* St Mary's Coll Leeds, St Joseph's Convent Bradford; *m* 17 June 1965, Hugh William Porter, MBE, s of late Joseph Porter; *Career* former international swimmer; currently: swimming corr Daily Telegraph and Sunday Telegraph, swimming conslt Sports and Outside Bdcasting Dept BBC Radio; nat 220 yds breaststroke champion 1958–62, nat 440 yds medley champion 1963–64, nat 220 yds freestyle champion 1963; first represented GB 1958; Cwlth Games: Gold medal 220 yds (Br and Games record) 1958, Gold medal 4 x 100 yds medley relay (world record) 1958, Gold medals 110 yds breaststroke, 220 yds breaststroke (world record) and 400m medley (Br and Cwlth record) 1962, Silver medal 4 x 110 yds medley relay 1962; Euro Championships: Silver medal 200m breaststroke and Bronze medal 4 x 100m medley relay 1958, Gold medal 200m breaststroke 1962, Silver medal 400m medley 1962, Bronze medal 4 x 100m medley relay 1962; Olympic Games: Gold medal 200m breaststroke Rome 1960 (world record, first swimmer under 2 min 50 sec), finalist 400m medley Tokyo 1964; Sportswoman of the Year Daily Express and Sports Writers' Assoc 1960 and 1962, Personality of the Year BBC Sportsview (first woman to win award) 1962; *Style*— Mrs Anita Porter, MBE; ✉ Roma, 6 Rivendell Gardens, Tettenhall, Wolverhampton, West Midlands WV6 8SY (☎ 01902 758802)

PORTER, Bruce Scott; s of Eric Andrew Porter (d 1981), and Helen, *née* Spooner (d 1964); *b* 12 Dec 1937; *Educ* Christ's Hosp, Trinity Coll Oxford (BA, MA, 1st XV Rugby); *m* Jan 1963, Marion, da of Sydney Herbert Allard; *Career* Baker & McKenzie: articled clerk 1961–64, admitted slr 1965, admitted slr New South Wales and Victoria 1967, slr Sydney 1967–72, ptnr 1969, admitted slr Hong Kong 1977, slr Hong Kong 1977–80, managing ptnr London 1991–94, memb Int Exec Ctee (memb Exec Ctee 1985–88), chm Policy Ctee 1990–91; memb Law Soc; *Recreations* tennis, walking, travel; *Style*— Bruce Porter, Esq; ✉ Baker & McKenzie, 100 New Bridge Street, London EC4V 6JA (☎ 0171 919 1000, fax 0171 919 1999)

PORTER, Colin Grant; s of William Graham Porter (d 1973), and Edna May, *née* Wilson; *b* 18 March 1951; *Educ* Syon Sch Isleworth, Harrow Sch of Art, Wolverhampton Sch of Art (BA); *m* 15 July 1972, Janice Ann, da of Albert Edward Manning; 4 s (Joel Edward William b 26 Oct 1976, James Henry b 30 Aug 1978, William Alexander b 11 Feb 1982, Theo Hugh b 2 April 1989); *Career* jr graphic designer Fitch & Company 1977, graphic designer Murdoch Design Associates 1973–74, assoc dir Fitch & Company 1978–79 (sr designer 1974–79), founding ptnr Coley Porter Bell 1979– (chm 1994–); clients incl: British Gas, Lego, BBC, Ross Youngs, A & P, Woolworths; regular tutor and speaker on design and design management for various orgns incl Design Cncl and Market Res Soc; awarded: 3 Clios (US) 1989, 1 Clio (US) 1990, 3 Clios (US) 1991, Design Business Assoc Design Effectiveness Award 1990, various D & AD Awards; one-man painting exhibition (Smith's Gallery Covent Garden) 1991; fndr memb and bd dir Design Business Assoc; memb: D & AD 1975, FCSD 1986; *Recreations* painting, collecting paintings and ephemera; *Style*— Colin Porter, Esq; ✉ Coley Porter Bell, 11A West Halkin Street, London SW1X 8JL (☎ 0171 470 4000)

PORTER, David Andrew; s of Michael Robert Porter, OBE, of Hereford, and Cecile Jane Graeme, *née* Stuart (d 1988); *b* 22 April 1960; *Educ* Dulwich; *Career* media exec Garrott Westbourne Ltd 1977–78, media mangr Woolward Royds (Edinburgh) Ltd 1980–82, co dir Yellowhammer Advertising Co 1986–89 (media exec 1978–80, dep md 1982–89), md Axle Media Ltd 1989–90; media dir: Generator Advertising and Marketing Ltd 1989–90, The Leisure Process Ltd 1990; subsequently asssoc dir Media Campaign Services, media dir Lansdown Conquest 1994–95, press assoc dir The Media Business Group plc 1995–; MIPA 1987; *Recreations* music, cinema, passive smoking; *Style*— David Porter, Esq; ✉ The Media Business Group plc, 70 North Row, Park Lane, London W1R 1DE (☎ 0171 408 4400)

PORTER, David John; MP (C) Waveney (majority 6,702); s of George Edward Porter (d 1964), of Lowestoft, and Margaret Elizabeth, *née* Robinson; *b* 16 April 1948; *Educ* Lowestoft GS, New Coll of Speech and Drama London; *m* 25 March 1978, Sarah Jane, da of Rev Peter Shaw (d 1979); 2 s (Thomas Edward b 1982, Samuel George b 1986), 2 da (Victoria Louise b 1979, Alice Elizabeth b 1988); *Career* teacher London 1970–72, dir and co-fndr Vivid Children's Theatre 1972–78, head of drama Benjamin Britten HS Lowestoft 1978–81; Cons party agent: Eltham 1982–83, Norwich North 1983–84, Waveney 1985–87; MP (C) Waveney 1987–; memb Select Ctee: on Social Security 1991–92, on Educn 1992–96, on Educn and Employment 1996–; cncllr Waveney DC; *Recreations* writing, Waveney past present and future, family; *Style*— David Porter, Esq, MP; ✉ House of Commons, Westminster, London SW1A OAA (☎ 0171 219 6235)

PORTER, Henry Christopher Mansel; s of Maj Harry Robert Mansel Porter, MBE, of Pershore, Worcs, and Anne Victoria, *née* Seymour; *b* 23 March 1953; *Educ* Wellington, Univ of Manchester (BA), Perugia Univ Italy; *m* Elizabeth Mary Elliot; 2 da (Miranda Victoria Elliot b 30 Oct 1985, Charlotte Mary Clementine Elliot b 22 Oct 1988); *Career* journalist; Evening Standard 1979–81, feature writer Sunday Times 1981–83 (columnist 1983–87); ed: Illustrated London News 1987–89, Sunday Correspondent Magazine 1989–90; exec ed Independent on Sunday 1990–91, currently London ed Vanity Fair; *Books* Lies, Damned Lies and Some Exclusives (1984); *Recreations* sailing, fishing, painting, art galleries, reading; *Style*— Henry Porter, Esq; ✉ Vanity Fair, Conde Nast Publications Ltd, 1 Hanover Square, London W1R 0AD (☎ 0171 499 9080)

PORTER, James Forrest; CBE (1991); s of Ernest Porter, and Mary Violetta Porter; *b* 2 Oct 1928; *Educ* Salford GS, Dudley Trg Coll, LSE, London Univ Inst of Educn; *m* 1952, Dymphna, da of Leo Francis Powell; 2 da (Louise, Alison); *Career* princ Bulmershe Coll of Higher Educn 1967–78, dir gen Cwlth Inst 1978–91; Univ of London Inst of Educn: visiting fell Dept of Int & Comparative Educn 1991–92, Nuffield res fell 1992–, head of int affrs 1993, actg dean 1994–95; conslt UN 1975–; Cwlth fell Aust 1977, chm World Educn Fellowship 1979–; memb: UGC 1970–76, James Ctee on Teacher Educn 1972–, IBA 1973–80, BBC Educn Cncl 1987–92; chm Newsconcern International 1983–91 and 1994–, memb Bd Round Table Magazine 1986–; Hon FCP; *Clubs* Phyllis Court; *Style—* James Porter, Esq, CBE; ✉ The House by the Water, Bolney Road, Shiplake, Oxon RG9 3NS (☎ and fax 0118 940 2187)

PORTER, Prof John Alan; OBE (1971); s of Alan Porter (d 1979), and Etta, *née* Ward (d 1952); *b* 29 Sept 1934; *Educ* Lawrence Sheriff Rugby, Bristol Univ (BSc), Southampton Univ; 2 s (Alan, David); *Career* cmmnd RAF 1953, appts in UK, USA and Cyprus 1953–79, RCDS 1980, dep gen mangr NATO MRCA Devpt and Prodn Agency (NAMMA) Munich 1981–84, dir-gen Aircraft 2 Procurement Exec MOD 1984–89, ret RAF as Air Vice-Marshal 1989; dir Sci & Technol GCHQ Cheltenham 1991–94; dep vice chllr Univ of Glamorgan 1994–; CEng, FRAeS, FIEE; *Recreations* the arts, skiing; *Style—* Prof John Porter, OBE; ✉ University of Glamorgan, Pontypridd CF37 1DL

PORTER, John Andrew; TD, JP (Kent 1952), DL (Kent); s of Horace Augustus Porter, DFC, JP (d 1948), of Kent, and Vera Marion, *née* Andrew (d 1967); *b* 18 May 1916; *Educ* Radley, Sidney Sussex Coll Cambridge (MA); *m* 1941, Margaret Isobel, da of Samuel Alexander Wisnom (d 1944), of London; 2 da (Jocelyn, Angela); *Career* served WWII, Lt-Col RA; past chm: Anglia Building Society, Hastings and Thanet Building Society; sr ptnr Porter & Cobb Chartered Surveyors 1948–81, sr Cobbs 1981–; chm Gravesham PSD 1976–83; pres Gravesend Cons Assoc 1966–78, cmmr of Income Tax; FRICS; *Recreations* cricket, gardening, reading; *Clubs* RAC, Hawks (Cambridge), Kent CCC (pres 1985–86); *Style—* John Porter, Esq, TD, JP, DL; ✉ Leader, Hodsoll St, nr Wrotham, Kent TN15 7LH (☎ 01732 822260)

PORTER, Air Marshal Sir (Melvin) Kenneth Drowley; KCB (1967, CB 1959), CBE (1945, OBE 1943); s of Flt Lt Edward Ernest Porter, MBE, DCM (d 1927), and Helen Porter (d 1920); *b* 19 Nov 1912; *Educ* No 1 Sch of Tech Trg Halton, RAF Coll Cranwell; *m* 1940, Elena (d 1993), da of F W Sinclair (d 1961); 2 s (Evan, Simon), 1 da (Judith); *Career* RAF 1928, cmmnd 1932, served WWII 1939–45 (despatches 3); chief signals offr: Balloon Cmd 1939–40, 11 Gp 1940–42, 2 Tactical AF 1943–45 (Actg Air Cdre 1944), Bomber Cmd 1945–46, (Actg Air Cdre) 2 TAF 1955–56, Fighter Cmd 1956–59 (Air Cdre 1958), IDC 1959, Cmdt No 4 Sch of Tech Trg RAF St Athan and Air Offr Wales 1960–61, dir-gen of Ground Trg Air Miny 1961–63, Air Vice-Marshal 1962, dir-gen of Signals (Air) MOD 1963–66, AOC-in-C Maintenance Cmd 1966–70, Air Marshal 1966, ret 1970; dir Tech Educn Projects Dept of Educn Univ Coll Cardiff 1970–74; CEng, FRAeS, FIEE, FIMgt; Offr Legion of Merit (USA); *Recreations* reading; *Clubs* RAF; *Style—* Air Marshal Sir Kenneth Porter, KCB, CBE

PORTER, Sir Leslie; kt (1983), TD; s of Henry Alfred Porter (d 1955), and Jane, *née* Goldstein (d 1983); *b* 10 July 1920; *Educ* Holloway Co Sch; *m* 1949, Dame Shirley Porter, *qv*, da of Sir John Edward Cohen (d 1980); 1 s (John), 1 da (Linda); *Career* TA 1 Bn The Rangers KRRG 1938, served WWII 1 Bn KRRC TQMS; served: Egypt, Greece, Lybia, Algeria, Sicily, Italy; chm Tesco plc 1973–85 (pres 1985–90); landowner (8200 acres); memb Lloyd's 1964–; hon vice pres Sports Aid Fndn, chllr and hon chm Bd of Govrs Tel Aviv Univ (hon PhD 1973), vice pres NPFA; past pres Inst of Grocery Distribution, International V P Museum of the Diaspora; OStJ; CIMgt, FIGD; *Recreations* yachting, golf, bridge, swimming; *Clubs* City Livery, Coombe Hill Golf, Dyrham Park Co, Frilford Heath Golf, RAC, Valderrama Golf; *Style—* Sir Leslie Porter

PORTER, Marguerite Ann (Mrs Henson); da of William Albert Porter, and Mary Maughan; *b* 30 Nov 1948; *m* 1, 1970 (m dis 1978), Carl Myers; *m* 2, 1 Aug 1986, Nicholas Victor Leslie Henson, *qv*, s of Leslie Henson; 1 s (Keaton Leslie b 24 March 1988); *Career* Royal Ballet Co: joined 1966, soloist 1973, princ 1978–85, guest artist 1985–; *Publications* Ballerina - A Dancer's Life (1989); Marguerite Porter's Balletcise (video, 1992); *Recreations* motherhood, reading, friends, theatre, teaching Balletcise (a ballet-based exercise class), choreography (recently choreographed play Dancing at Lughnasa, Royal Lyceum Edinburgh); *Style—* Ms Marguerite Porter; ✉ c/o Linda Ronan, Richard Stone Partnership, 25 Whitehall, London SW1A 2BS (☎ 0171 839 6421)

PORTER, Michael James Robert; *b* 18 Jan 1945; *Educ* Marlborough; *m*; 2 c; *Career* audit clerk Arthur Young & Co Paris Jan - July 1963, audit sr Peat Marwick Mitchell & Co 1968–71 (articled clerk 1963–68), Main Bd dir and gp co sec Allied Polymer Group Ltd 1976–78 (gp co sec 1972–76); BTR plc: admin dir Miles Redfern-Dunstable 1978–81, admin mangr 1981–83, mangr Special Projects April - Sept 1983, md BTR Insurance Services 1983–86; gp co sec Stone International PLC 1986–87, gp co sec FKI plc 1987– (asst co sec 1987–89); *Recreations* stamp collecting, music, theatre; *Style—* Michael Porter, Esq; ✉ FKI plc, West House, King Cross Road, Halifax, W Yorkshire HX1 1EB (☎ 01422 330267, fax 01422 320547)

PORTER, Peter Neville Frederick; s of William Ronald Porter (d 1982), of Brisbane, Australia, and Marion, *née* Main (d 1938); *b* 16 Feb 1929; *Educ* C of E GS Brisbane, Toowoomba GS; *m* 1, 24 March 1961, Shirley Jannice (d 1974), da of Dr Richard Nichol Henry; 2 da (Katherine Sybilla Marion b 1962, Clarissa Jane b 1965); *m* 2, 2 Nov 1991, Christine Berg, da of John Donovan; *Career* poet; journalist Brisbane 1947–48, warehouseman Brisbane until 1951, clerk London 1951–53 and 1955–56, bookseller London 1956–59, advertising copywriter 1959–68, freelance writer 1968–; author of: Collected Poems (1983, contents of 9 previously published volumes), Fast Forward (1984), The Automatic Oracle (1987), Possible Worlds (1989), The Chair of Babel (1992); awarded: London Magazine Poetry prize 1962, Duff Cooper Memorial prize 1984, Whitbread Poetry award 1988; Hon DLitt: Univ of Melbourne 1985, Univ of Loughborough 1986; Australian Literature Gold medal 1990; former memb Literature Panel Arts Council; *Recreations* music, Italy; *Style—* Peter Porter, Esq; ✉ Flat 3, 42 Cleveland Square, London W2 6DA (☎ 0171 262 4289)

PORTER, Richard Bruce; s of Maynard Eustace Prettyman Porter (d 1984), and Irene Marjorie, *née* Turner (d 1994); *b* 20 Jan 1942; *Educ* St Joseph's Coll Ipswich, City of London Coll (BSc Econ); *m* 1965, Susan Mary, da of Philip Early; 2 da (Anna Lucie b 10 Feb 1970, Kitty b 10 Jan 1972); *Career* market researcher: A C Nielsen 1965–70, Brooke Bond Oxo 1970–75; mgmnt conslt Peat Marwick 1975–81 (incl postings as project dir and devpt economist India and SE Asia), environmental conslt Africa and Far East Environmental Resources Ltd 1981–84, ptnr Strategy Consltg Unit KPMG 1984–94, exec dir Sight Savers (charity) 1994–; *Books* jt author: Energy from Waste, Science Parks and the Growth of High Technology Firms; *Recreations* cinema, theatre, hockey, tennis, reading, bridge; *Style—* Richard Porter, Esq; ✉ 15 Park Road, Burgess Hill, West Sussex RH15 8EU (☎ 01444 232602); Sight Savers, Grosvenor Hall, Bolnore Road, Haywards Heath, West Sussex RH16 4BX (☎ 01444 412424, fax 01444 440899)

PORTER, Richard James; s of Capt James Graham Porter, of Conwy, Gwynedd, and Ann, *née* Wharry; *b* 28 Nov 1951; *Educ* Eton, Univ Coll Oxford (MA, MSc, BM BCh); *m* 26 July 1974, Diana Isabel, da of Douglas James Roper Austin (d 1979); 2 da (Charlotte b 1977, Alice b 1980); *Career* sr registrar in obstetrics and gynaecology St Mary's Hosp London and Addenbrooke's Hosp Cambridge 1984–88, conslt in obstetrics and gynaecology Bath DHA 1989–, med dir Wilts Health Care NHS Trust 1992–; MRCOG 1982; *Recreations* wine, theatre; *Style—* Richard Porter, Esq; ✉ Weston Lea, Weston Park, Bath BA1 4AL (☎ 01225 425618); Bath Clinic, Claverton Down Rd, Bath BA2 7BR (☎ 01225 835555)

PORTER, Prof Richard William; s of Joseph Luther Porter, and Mary, *née* Field; *b* 16 Feb 1935; *Educ* Oundle, Univ of Edinburgh (MD); *m* Christine Margaret, da of Wilfred Brown; 4 s (Daniel, William, Matthew, James); *Career* formerly: conslt orthopaedic surgn Doncaster, prof of orthopaedics Forester Hill Med Sch Aberdeen; currently dir of educn and trg Royal Coll of Surgns of Edinburgh; pres Br Soc for Back Pain Res; FRCS, FRCSEd; *Books* Understanding Back Pain (1985), Management of Back Pain (1993); *Style—* Prof Richard Porter; ✉ (home ☎ 01302 538888); c/o Royal College of Surgeons of Edinburgh, Nicolson Street, Edinburgh EH8 9DW (fax 0131 557 6406)

PORTER, Richard William; s of Dr W A Porter, of Hove, Sussex, and Phyllis May, *née* Richardson; *b* 25 March 1946; *Educ* Brighton Coll; *m* 1 Oct 1988, Tracy Jane Vallis-Porter, da of Stanley Vallis; *Career* insur broker: Halford Shead Lloyd's Broker 1965–71, G P Turner 1971–73; Alexander and Alexander Ltd (formerly Alexander Stenhouse UK Ltd): joined 1973, mangr Reading Branch 1974–78, unit dir City Branch 1978–81, exec dir mktg London and Lloyd's 1981–82, devpt dir City Branch 1983–86, divnl dir Central Insur 1987–88, exec dir 1989–94, chief exec offr Alexander and Alexander Europe Ltd 1995–; memb: Canada-UK C of C, Royal Inst of Int Affairs, CBI; FCII 1971, MIMgt 1984; *Recreations* squash, rugby; *Style—* Richard Porter, Esq; ✉ Holmgarth, Betchworth Ave, Earley, Berks RG6 7RJ (☎ 01734 265637); Alexander and Alexander Europe Ltd, 10 Devonshire Square, London EC2M 4LE (☎ 0171 621 9990, fax 0171 621 9950)

PORTER, Rt Hon Sir Robert Wilson; kt (1971), PC (NI 1969), QC (NI 1965); s of late Joseph Wilson Porter; *b* 23 Dec 1923; *Educ* Model Sch, Foyle Coll Londonderry, Queen's Univ Belfast (LLB); *m* 1953, Margaret Adelaide, da of late F W Lynas; 1 s, 1 da (and 1 da decd); *Career* RAFVR 1943–46, RA (TA) 1950–56; called to the Bar: NI 1950, Republic of Ireland 1975, Middle Temple 1988; counsel to Attorney-Gen for NI 1963–64 and 1965; min of Health and Social Services NI 1969, Parly sec 1969 and min of Home Affairs NI 1969–70; chm War Pensions Appeal Tbnl for NI 1961–66 (vice chm 1959–61); MP (U): Queen's Univ of Belfast 1966–69, Lagan Valley 1969–73; County Court Judge NI 1978–95, recorder of Belfast 1993–95; *Clubs* RAF; *Style—* The Rt Hon Sir Robert Porter, QC; ✉ Larch Hill, Church Close, Ballylesson, Belfast, N Ireland BT8 8JX

PORTER, Robin Anthony; s of Maurice Malcolm Porter (d 1986), and Danuta, *née* Monitz; *b* 15 Sept 1945; *Educ* Highgate Sch, Univ of Leeds (LLB); *m* 14 Sept 1974 (d 1992), Monica Jolan, da of Péter Dénes Halász, of Munich, Germany; 2 s (Adam b 1978, Nicholas b 1983); *Career* articled clerk Titmuss Sainer & Webb 1968–70; admitted slr 1971; asst slr: Commercial Property Dept Clifford-Turner & Co 1971–72, Company and Commercial Dept McKenna & Co 1972–73, Company and Commercial Dept Penningtons 1974; Wilde Sapte 1974–91: asst slr Commercial Property Dept 1974–75 ptnr Commercial Property Dept 1975–84 and 1987–91 (ptnr i/c New York Office 1984–87); ptnr Banking Group Waltons & Morse 1991–95; projects dir International Tax and Investment Centre 1996–; Freeman City of London 1987, Liveryman Worshipful Company of Musicians 1990, Freeman Worshipful Co of Solicitors 1993; memb: Law Soc 1971, Int Bar Assoc 1984; *Recreations* music, theatre, tennis, skiing, cycling; *Style—* Robin Porter, Esq; ✉ 18 Cholmley Gardens, Aldred Road, London NW6 1AE (☎ 0171 435 4564); International Tax and Investment Centre, 326 High Holborn, London WC1V 7PT (☎ 0171 611 1952, fax 0171 611 4635)

PORTER, Prof Rev Canon (Joshua) Roy; s of Joshua Porter (d 1945), of Marple, Cheshire, and Bessie Evelyn, *née* Earlam (d 1976); *b* 7 May 1921; *Educ* King's Sch Macclesfield, Merton Coll Oxford (BA), St Stephen's House Oxford (BA, MA); *Career* ordained: deacon 1945, priest 1946; curate St Mary Portsea 1945–47, resident chaplain to Bishop of Chichester 1947–49, fell chaplain and tutor Oriel Coll Oxford 1949–62, prof of theology and head of dept Univ of Exeter 1962–86 (emeritus prof 1986–), dean of arts Univ of Exeter 1968–71, canon and prebendary Wightring and theol lectr Chichester Cathedral 1965–88, Wiccamical canon and prebendary of Exceit 1988–, visiting prof South Eastern Seminary Wake Forest N Carolina 1967, Ethel M Wood lectr Univ of London 1979, Michael Harrah Wood lectr Univ of the S Sewanee 1984, lectr in Holy Scriptures Holyrood Seminary New York 1986–94; examining chaplain to: Bishop of Chichester 1950–, Bishop of Gibraltar in Europe 1989–93; proctor in convocation Canterbury Exeter Diocese 1964–75 (and other Univs incl Canterbury) 1975–90; memb Gen Synod 1970–90 (Panel of Chairmen 1984–86); memb: Soc for Old Testament Study 1952 (pres 1983), Soc of Biblical Lit 1967, Folklore Soc (hon memb 1988), Anglican Assoc (pres), Prayer Book Soc (vice chm 1984–96), Anglican Soc (vice pres); FAMS 1989; *Books* World in the Heart (1944), Moses and Monarchy (1963), The Extended Family in the Old Testament (1967), Proclamation and Presence (with J I Durham, 1970), The Non-Juring Bishops (1973), Leviticus (1976), The Crown and the Church (1978), Animals in Folklore (with W M S Russell, 1978), C Westermann, The Living Psalms (translated 1989), Synodical Government in the Church of England (1990), The Illustrated Guide to the Bible (1995); *Recreations* theatre, opera, book collecting, travel; *Clubs* Athenaeum; *Style—* Prof the Rev Canon Roy Porter; ✉ 36 Theberton St, Barnsbury, London N1 0QX (☎ 0171 354 5861); 68 Sand St, Longbridge Deverill, nr Warminster, Wilts BA12 7DS (☎ 01985 840311)

PORTER, Dame Shirley; DBE (1991); da of Sir John Edward Cohen (d 1980), and Sarah Fox (d 1989); *b* 29 Nov 1930; *Educ* Warren Sch Worthing, La Ramée Lausanne Switzerland; *m* 1949, Sir Leslie Porter, *qv*, s of Henry Alfred Porter (d 1955); 1 s (John), 1 da (Linda); *Career* ldr Westminster City Cncl 1983–91 (memb until 1993), Lord Mayor of Westminster 1991–92; chm: LBC 1993–94, Bd of Govrs Oxford Centre for Hebrew & Jewish Studies 1993–; memb Bd of Govrs Tel Aviv Univ; pres The London Parade 1993–94; dir and memb Bd TBG (Tidy Britain Group), pres Br Inst of Cleaning Servs, pres European Standing Conf on the Environment and Tourism 1992–; former dir: Capital Radio, English National Ballet; vice pres LUYC; past Master Worshipful Co of Environmental Cleaners; JP (Inner London) 1972–84; *Recreations* golf, tennis, promoting talent, ballet, theatre, caring for London; *Clubs* Queen's, Coombe Hill, Frilford Heath, Wentworth, Dyrham Park Golf, RAC; *Style—* Dame Shirley Porter

PORTER OF LUDDENHAM, Baron (Life Peer 1990), of Luddenham in the Co of Kent; Sir George; OM (1989), kt (1972); s of late John Smith Porter, and Alice Ann, *née* Roebuck; *b* 6 Dec 1920; *Educ* Thorne GS, Univ of Leeds (BSc), Emmanuel Coll Cambridge (MA, PhD, ScD); *m* 12 Aug 1949, Stella Jean, da of Col George Arthur Brooke (d 1973), of Caring, Leeds, nr Maidstone, Kent; 2 s (Hon John Brooke b 22 Sept 1952, Hon Andrew Christopher George b 17 Aug 1955); *Career* Radar Offr RNVR Western Approaches and Med 1941–45; demonstrator in physical chemistry Univ of Cambridge 1949–52, asst dir of res physical chemistry and fell Emmanuel Coll Cambridge 1952–54, asst dir Br Rayon Res Assoc 1954–55, Firth prof of chemistry and head Dept of Chemistry Univ of Sheffield 1963–66 (prof of physical chemistry 1955–63); The Royal Instn of GB: dir 1966–85, dir The Davy Faraday Res Laboratory 1966–85, Fullerian prof of chemistry 1966–87; chllr Univ of Leicester 1986–95, res prof and fell Imperial Coll London and chm Centre for Photomolecular Sciences 1987–, Gresham prof of astronomy and physical sciences 1990–93; chm Editorial Advsy Bd IC Press 1995–; visiting prof: Pennsylvania State Univ 1961, UCL 1967–86, Caltech 1974, Univ of California at Berkeley 1978, Imperial Coll London 1978–; hon fell: Emmanuel Coll Cambridge 1967, Royal Scot Soc of Arts 1975, Royal Med Soc Edinburgh 1987, Imperial

Coll London 1987; fell: Royal Soc of Edinburgh 1983, Queen Mary and Westfield Coll London 1986; awarded: Corday-Morgan Medal of Chem Soc 1955, Nobel Prize for Chemistry 1967, Silvanus Thompson Medal of Br Inst of Radiology 1968, Davy Medal of Royal Soc 1971, 1976, Kalinga Prize (UNESCO) for Popularisation of Sci 1977, Robertson Prize of Nat Acad of Sci 1978, Rumford Medal of Royal Soc 1978, Communications Award of Euro Physical Soc 1978, Faraday Medal of Chem Soc 1980, Longstaff Medal of RSC 1981, Melchett Medal of Inst of Energy 1987, Porter Medal 1988, Michael Faraday Medal of RS 1991, Soc's Medal of SCI 1991, Copley Medal of Royal Soc 1992; author of over 300 scientific papers, many lectures given on scientific subjects, numerous TV and radio appearances, presenter of scientific films and videos; pres: Comité International de Photobiologie 1968–72, Chem Soc 1970–72 (Faraday Div 1973–74), Nat Assoc for Gifted Children 1975–80, Res and Devpt Soc 1977–82, Assoc for Sci Educn 1985, Br Assoc for Advancement of Sci 1985–86, Royal Soc 1985–90, London Int Youth Sci Fortnight 1987–89; vice pres UK Soc for Promotion of Sci and Technol in Pakistan 1989–; memberships incl: Res Grants Ctee DSIR 1963–65, Aeronautical Res Cncl 1964–66, BBC Sci Consultative Gp 1967–75, Open Univ Cncl 1969–75, Advsy Cncl Sci Museum 1970–73, Cncl RSA 1978–80, Advsy Cncl on Sci & Technol 1987–91, Lords Select Ctee on Sci & Technol 1991; pres Nat Energy Fndn 1991–; hon memb Royal Inst of GB; foreign memberships incl: NY Acad of Sciences 1968, Chem Soc of Japan 1982, Russian Acad of Sciences (formerly Soviet) 1989, Japan Acad 1988, Academia Lincei 1987, Pontifical Acad of Sciences 1974, La Real Academia de Ciencias Madrid 1978, Indian Nat Acad of Sciences 1986; foreign assoc: Nat Acad of Sciences Washington 1974, Göttingen Acad 1974, Hungarian Acad 1988; tstee: Br Museum 1972–74, The Bristol Exploratory 1986–; Hon Liveryman Worshipful Co of Salters 1981 (Master 1993–94), Freeman City of London 1981; Hon Doctorate of 34 Univs (incl Hon LLD Univ of Cambridge), Hon Professorship of 2 Univs and 2 Insts; FRS 1960, PRS 1985; *Books* Chemistry for the Modern World (1962), Chemistry in Microtime (1995); *Recreations* sailing; *Clubs* Athenaeum; *Style—* The Rt Hon Lord Porter of Luddenham, OM, FRS; ✉ The Old Rectory, Luddenham, nr Faversham, Kent ME13 0TE; 53 Princes Gardens, Exhibition Road, London SW7; Chairman of the Centre for Photomolecular Sciences, Departments of Chemistry and Biochemistry, Imperial College of Science and Technology, South Kensington, London SW7 2AZ (☎ 0171 594 5786, fax 0171 594 5812, e-mail g.porter@ic.ac.uk)

PORTES, Prof Richard David; s of Herbert Portes; *b* 10 Dec 1941; *Educ* Yale Univ, Balliol and Nuffield Colls Oxford (Rhodes Scholar); *m* 1963, Barbara Frank; children; *Career* fell Balliol Coll 1965–69; prof of economics: Princeton Univ 1969–72, Univ of London 1972–94, London Business Sch 1995–; dir Centre for Econ Policy Res 1983–, sec gen Royal Econ Soc 1992–; *Books* Planning and Market Relations (1971), Deficits and Detente (1983), Threats to International Financial Stability (1987), Global Macroeconomics (1987), Blueprints for Exchange Rate Management (1989), External Constraints on Macroeconomic Policy (1991), Economic Transformation of Central Europe (1993), European Union Trade with Eastern Europe (1995), Crisis? What Crisis? Orderly Workouts for Sovereign Debtors (1995); *Recreations* swimming, squash; *Clubs* Groucho; *Style—* Prof Richard Portes; ✉ Department of Economics, London Business School, Sussex Place, Regent's Park, London NW1 4SA (☎ 0171 706 6886, fax 0171 724 1598, e-mail RPortes@LBS.LON.AC.UK)

PORTILLO, Rt Hon Michael Denzil Xavier; PC (1992), MP (C) Enfield Southgate (majority 15,563); yst s of Luis Gabriel Portillo (d 1993), and Cora Waldegrave, *née* Blyth; *b* 26 May 1953; *Educ* Harrow Co Sch for Boys, Peterhouse Cambridge (MA); *m* 12 Feb 1982, Carolyn Claire, da of Alastair G Eadie; *Career* Ocean Transport and Trading Co 1975–76, Cons Res Dept 1976–79, special advsr to Sec of State for Energy 1979–81, Kerr McGee Oil (UK) Ltd 1981–83, special advsr to Sec of State for Trade and Indust 1983, special advsr to Chllr of the Exchequer 1983–84; Parly candidate Birmingham Perry Barr 1983, MP (C) Enfield Southgate 1984–, asst Govt whip 1986–87, Parly under sec of state for social security 1987–88, min of state for tport 1988–90, min for local govt and inner cities 1990–92, chief sec to the Treasy 1992–94, sec of state for employment 1994–95, sec of state for defence 1995–; *Clubs* Carlton; *Style—* The Rt Hon Michael Portillo, MP; ✉ House of Commons, Westminster, London SW1A 0AA (☎ 0171 219 4014)

PORTLAND, 11 Earl of (GB 1689); Henry Noel Bentinck; also Viscount Woodstock, Baron Cirencester (both GB 1689), and Count Bentinck (Holy Roman Empire); s of Capt Count Robert Bentinck (d 1932), and Lady Norah Ida Emily Noel (d 1939), da of 3 Earl of Gainsborough; suc his kinsman 9 and last Duke (and 10 Earl) of Portland, CMG (d 1990); *b* 2 Oct 1919; *Educ* Harrow; *m* 1, 1940, Pauline (d 1967), da of late Frederick William Mellowes, of Penn House, Renolds Close, Hampstead, London; 1 s, 2 da; m 2, 1974, Jenifer, o da of late Reginald Hopkins, of 91 Kingsley Way, London; *Heir* s, Viscount Woodstock, *qv*; *Career* formerly Lt Coldstream Guards; served WWII (twice wounded); author; *Style—* The Rt Hon the Earl of Portland

PORTMAN, Hon Christopher Edward Berkeley; s and h of 9 Viscount Portman; *b* 30 July 1958; *m* 1, 30 July 1983, Caroline, da of Terence Ivan Steenson, of Caversham, Berks; 1 s (Luke Oliver Berkeley b 31 Aug 1984); m 2, 7 Dec 1987, Patricia Martins, da of Bernardino Pim, of Rio de Janeiro, Brazil; 2 s (Matthew Bernardo Berkeley b 24 Sept 1990, Daniel Edward Berkeley b 27 July 1995); *Career* computer sci, molecular nanotechnology, psychology; 8th collegue of The Foresight Inst for Molecular Nanotechnology Palo Alto Calif; *Style—* The Hon Christopher Portman; ✉ 38 Seymour St, London W1H 6BP

PORTMAN, 9 Viscount (UK 1873); Edward Henry Berkeley Portman; Baron Portman (UK 1873); s of Hon Michael Berkeley Portman (d 1959) (yr s of 7 Viscount) and n of 8 Viscount (d 1967); *b* 22 April 1934; *Educ* Canford, RAC Cirencester; *m* 1, 1956 (m dis 1965), Rosemary Joy, er da of Charles Farris, of Coombe Bissett, Wilts; 1 s, 1 da; m 2, 1966, Penelope Anne Hassard, yr da of Trevor Robert William Allin, of North Moreton, Berks; 4 s (Hon Alexander b 1967, Hon Justin b 1969, Hon Piers b 1971, Hon Matthew b 1973, d 1990); *Heir* s, Hon Christopher Edward Berkeley Portman, *qv*; *Career* farmer; *Recreations* music, motorsport, fishing, shooting; *Clubs* White's, British Racing Drivers'; *Style—* The Rt Hon the Viscount Portman; ✉ Clock Mill, Clifford, Herefordshire (☎ 01497 831235)

PORTMANN, Dr Bernard Claude; s of late Henry Paul Portmann, and Emilie Emma, *née* Jaques; *b* 6 Feb 1940; *Educ* Calvin Coll Geneva Switzerland, Geneva Univ (MB, Swiss Med Dip, MD); *m* 1, 11 Sept 1963 (m dis 1969), Arlette Andree, da of Walter Ernst Kress; 1 da (Sandra b 7 Aug 1964); m 2, 23 Sept 1970, Hermine Elisabeth, da of Leo Bertholdt Neumann; 2 c (Barbara b 8 Feb 1971, Jan b 26 Oct 1972); *Career* lectr in pathology Univ Hosp Geneva 1968–72 (house offr 1966–67); King's Coll Hosp London: res fell Liver Unit 1973–75, res histopathologist 1975–78, hon sr lectr 1978–, conslt; hon sr lectr Univ of London 1978–; travelling fellowship Mount Sinai Med Center NY 1982; former memb Ctee Br Assoc for Study of the Liver; MRCPath 1977, FRCPath 1989; *Recreations* skiing, woodwork; *Style—* Dr Bernard Portmann; ✉ 20 Ewelme Rd, Forest Hill, London SE23 3BH (☎ and fax 0181 699 6717); Institute of Liver Studies, King's College Hospital, Denmark Hill, London SE5 9RS (☎ 0171 346 3369, fax 0171 346 3760)

PORTNO, Dr Antony David (Tony); *b* 30 May 1938; *Educ* Accrington GS, Univ of London (BSc, PhD); *Career* joined Bass 1961, Brewing Research Fndn 1964, devpt mangr Pfizer 1969; rejoined Bass PLC as quality control mangr Bass Production Ltd Burton on Trent 1971, princ sci Bass Brewers Runcorn 1975, gp research scientist Bass PLC Burton on Trent 1975, dir of res Bass PLC 1976, dir Britannia Soft Drinks 1983, main bd dir Bass PLC 1985– (memb Exec Ctee 1989–), dir Bass UK Ltd 1988–93, chm Britvic Soft Drinks 1990–96, chm Bass Brewers 1991–, chm Bass Leisure 1996–; Liveryman Worshipful Co of Brewers; fell Inst of Brewing; *Recreations* fishing, antiquarian book collecting, gardening; *Style—* Dr Tony Portno; ✉ Bass PLC, 20 North Audley Street, London W1Y 1WE (☎ 0171 409 1919, fax 0171 409 8503)

PORTNOY, Leslie Reuben; s of Israel Portnoy, and Miriam Portnoy; *b* 27 May 1939; *Educ* Manchester GS, Univ of Manchester (LLB); *m* 7 March 1961, Stephanie, da of Nathan Swift; 1 s (Jonathan b 10 May 1966), 1 da (Naomi b 25 Oct 1969); *Career* called to the Bar Gray's Inn 1961; dep circuit judge 1978, memb Panel and Jewish Tbnl (Shops Act) 1980, asst recorder 1981, recorder 1988; *Style—* Leslie Portnoy, Esq; ✉ 95 Cavendish Rd, Salford, Manchester M7 4NB (☎ 0161 740 2286); 9 St John Street, Manchester M3 4DN (☎ 0161 955 9000, fax 0161 955 9001)

PORTSMOUTH, Archdeacon of; *see:* Knowles, Ven Graeme Paul

PORTSMOUTH, Bishop of (RC) 1988–; Rt Rev (Roger Francis) Crispian Hollis; s of (Maurice) Christopher Hollis (d 1977), of Mells, Somerset, and Margaret Madelaine, *née* King (d 1984); *b* 17 Nov 1936; *Educ* Stonyhurst, Balliol Coll Oxford, Pontifical Gregorian Univ Rome; *Career* Nat Serv 2 Lt Somerset LI 1954–56; ordained priest 1965, asst priest Amesbury Wilts 1966–67, asst RC chaplain Oxford Univ 1967–70 (sr RC chaplain 1970–77), RC asst to Head of Religious Broadcasting BBC 1977–81, admin Clifton Cathedral and vicar gen Clifton Diocese 1981–87, auxiliary bishop Archdiocese of Birmingham 1987–88; *Recreations* golf, cricket-watching; *Style—* The Rt Rev the Bishop of Portsmouth; ✉ Bishops House, Edinburgh Road, Portsmouth PO1 3HG (☎ 01705 820 894)

PORTSMOUTH, Dr (Owen Henry) Donald; s of Oliver Spencer Portsmouth (d 1970), of Swansea, and Gwendolen Anne, *née* Trevor Owen (d 1991); *b* 24 May 1929; *Educ* Blundell's, St Thomas's Med Sch Univ of London (MB BS, DTM and H), Univ of Keele (MA in med ethics, 1993); *m* 1, 18 Sept 1954, Moira Heloise (d 1979), da of Alan John Sinclair (d 1967), of Kenya; 3 s (Charles b 1956, Richard b 1958, Andrew b 1961), 1 da (Helen b 1964); m 2, 3 Jan 1981, Glennis Cook, *née* Weddle; 1 step da (Esther b 1975); *Career* jr hosp appointments 1953–56, med serv Kenya Govt 1956–66 (med specialist 1960–66), conslt physician in geriatric med E Birmingham Hosp 1966–94, hon conslt physician Birmingham Heartlands Hosp 1994–, sr clinical lectr in biomedical ethics Univ of Birmingham 1994–; pres W Midlands Inst of Geriatric Med (dir 1975–93), vice chm Solihull Health Authy 1984–90, chm of tstees Solihull Frail Ambulant Unit, Dawson meml lectr Queens Univ Kingston Ontario 1984, Kirk Meml lectr Birmingham Heartlands Hosp 1996, President's Medal Br Geriatrics Soc 1996; FRCP 1977, FRCPEd 1971; *Recreations* heraldry, architecture, history, foreign travel; *Style—* Dr Donald Portsmouth; ✉ Oakfield, 12 Paddock Drive, Dorridge, Solihull, W Midlands B93 8BZ (☎ and fax 01564 775032); Department of Biomedical Science and Ethics, The Medical School, University of Birmingham, Edgbaston, Birmingham B15 2TT (☎ 0121 414 3616, fax 0121 414 6979)

PORTSMOUTH, Bishop of 1995–; Rt Rev Dr Kenneth William Stevenson; s of Frederick Robert Stevenson (d 1993), of E Linton, E Lothian, and Margrete, *née* Hoffmeyer; *b* 9 Nov 1949; *Educ* Edinburgh Acad, Univ of Edinburgh (MA), Salisbury/Wells Theol Coll, Univ of Southampton (PhD), Univ of Manchester (DD); *m* 1970, Sarah Julia Mary, da of John Morton Glover; 3 da (Elisabeth Helen b 29 Nov 1971, Katharine Anne b 30 April 1974, Alexandra Margrete b 25 Jan 1984), 1 s (James Christian William b 6 July 1979); *Career* curate Grantham 1973–76, sr curate Boston 1976–80, pt/t tutor Lincoln Theol Coll 1975–80, chaplain and lectr Univ of Manchester 1980–86, visiting prof Univ of Notre Dame Indiana 1983, rector Holy Trinity and St Mary Guildford 1986–95; *Books* Nuptial Blessing: a Study of Christian Marriage Rites (1982), Eucharist and Offering (1986), Jerusalem Revisited (1988), The First Rites (1989), Covenant of Grace Renewed: a vision of the Eucharist in the 17th century (1994), Handing On: Borderlands of Worship and Tradition (1996); *Recreations* music (horn and piano), historical biographies; *Style—* The Rt Rev the Bishop of Portsmouth; ✉ Bishopswood, Fareham, Hants PO14 1NT (☎ 01329 280247, fax 01329 231538)

PORTSMOUTH, Provost of; *see:* Yorke, Very Rev Michael Leslie

PORTSMOUTH, 10 Earl of (GB 1743); Quentin Gerard Carew Wallop; also Baron Wallop (GB 1720), Viscount Lymington (GB 1720); Hereditary Bailiff of Burley in the New Forest; s of Viscount Lymington (d 1984) and his 2 w Ruth Violet, née Sladen (d 1978); suc gf 9 Earl (d 1984); *b* 25 July 1954; *Educ* Eton, Millfield; *m* 1, 1981 (m dis 1985), Candia Frances Juliet, only da of Colin McWilliam, and Margaret, *née* Henderson; 1 s (Oliver Henry Rufus, Viscount Lymington b 22 Dec 1981), 1 da (Lady Clementine Violet Rohais b 20 Nov 1983); m 2, 16 March 1990, Annabel, eldest da of Dr Ian Fergusson, and Rosemary, *née* Howard, of Tudor Place, Richmond Green, Surrey; 1 da (Lady Rose Hermione Annabel b 23 Oct 1990); *Heir* s, Viscount Lymington, *qv*; *Career* pres Basingstoke Cons Assoc; patron Hampshire Branch British Red Cross; dir Grainger Tst plc; *Recreations* shooting, sailing; *Clubs* Buck's, Royal Yacht Sqdn, Int Assoc of Cape Horners; *Style—* The Rt Hon the Earl of Portsmouth; ✉ Farleigh House, Farleigh Wallop, Basingstoke, Hants RG25 2HT (☎ 01256 21026)

PORTWIN, Guy Lyster; s of Edwin Thomas Portwin, of Herts, and Elizabeth Emily Louise, *née* Gadd; *b* 28 Dec 1949; *Educ* Merchant Taylors'; *m* 6 May 1979, Kathleen, da of John Joseph Skerritt, of Eire; 4 children (Liza, Emma, Guy, John); *Career* dir: Wheatland Journals Ltd 1973–90, Turret Press (Holdings) Ltd 1979–84; md Turret-Wheatland Ltd 1984–88; chm: Turret Group plc 1988–90, Hill Media Ltd 1991–, Trophex Ltd 1991–, Hill Communications Ltd 1992–, Toy News Ltd 1992–95; dir: European Toy Fair Ltd, Millhouse Publishing International Ltd 1992–94, Association Publishing Ltd 1995–; FInstD 1985; *Recreations* riding, reading; *Clubs* Durrants; *Style—* Guy Portwin, Esq; ✉ Hill Media Group, 119 High Street, Berkhamsted, Herts HP4 2DJ (☎ 01442 878787, fax 01442 870888)

POSNANSKY, Jeremy Ross Leon; QC (1994); s of Anthony Victor Posnansky, of London, and Evelyn Davis, JP, *née* Leon; *b* 8 March 1951; *Educ* St Paul's, Coll of Law London; *m* 31 Dec 1974, Julia Mary, da of Richard Sadler, MBE (d 1967), of Bournemouth; 2 da (Charlotte b 1976, Zoë b 1979); *Career* called to the Bar Gray's Inn 1972, asst recorder 1993–; memb Inner London Family Cts Servs and Business Ctees 1991–94; memb Hon Socs of Gray's Inn and Lincoln's Inn, admitted to the Bar of Antigua and Barbuda; *Recreations* scuba diving, travels with my family, computers; *Style—* Jeremy Posnansky, Esq, QC; ✉ 1 Mitre Court Buildings, Temple, London EC4Y 7BS (☎ 0171 797 7070, fax 0171 797 7435)

POSNER, Lindsay Steven; s of Dennis Posner, and Pauline Posner; *b* 6 June 1959; *Educ* Latymer GS, Univ of Exeter (BA), RADA; *Career* assoc dir Royal Court Theatre 1986–92; plays directed: The Treatment, Death and the Maiden (Best Play Olivier Awards), American Bagpipes, Colquhoun and MacBryde, Blood, Downfall, Ambulance, Ficky Stingers, The Doctor of Honour, Cheek By Jowl, Leonce and Lena; dir of The Maitlands (BBC), dir of Jenufa; *Style—* Lindsay Posner; ✉ c/o Peters Fraser & Dunlop Ltd, 503 The Chambers, Chelsea Harbour, Lots Road, London SW10 0XF (☎ 0171 352 4446, fax 0171 352 7356)

POSNER, Michael Vivian; CBE (1983); s of Jack Posner; *b* 1931; *Educ* Whitgift Sch, Balliol Coll Oxford; *m* 5 Aug 1953, Prof Rebecca Posner, *qv*, da of William Reynolds (d 1958); 1 s (Christopher Nicholas b 14 Sept 1965), 1 da (Barbara Virginia b 7 July 1968); *Career* dir econs Miny of Power 1966–67, conslt IMF 1971–72, reader econs Univ of

Cambridge 1974–75 (fell Pembroke Coll 1960–83), memb Energy Conservation Advsy Cncl 1974–76, dep chief econ advsr Treasy 1975–76 (econ advsr 1967–69, econ consIt 1969–71); memb: BR bd 1976–84, Standing Cmmn on Energy and Environment 1978–82; chm SSRC 1979–83, dir Tech Change Centre 1981–86, econ dir Nat Econ Devpt Office 1984–86, sec gen Euro Sci Fndn Strasbourg 1986–93, a dir British Rail Pension Trustee Company 1986–; Hon DLitt Univ of Bristol 1992; *Style*— Michael Posner, Esq, CBE; ✉ Rushwood, Jack Straw's Lane, Oxford OX3 0DN (☎ 01865 63578)

POSNER, Prof Rebecca; da of William Reynolds (d 1958), and Rebecca, *née* Stephenson (d 1988); *b* 17 Aug 1929; *Educ* Nuneaton HS for Girls, Somerville Coll Oxford (BA, DPhil); *m* 5 Aug 1953, Michael Vivian Posner, CBE, *qv*, s of Jack Posner (d 1978); 1 s (Christopher Nicholas b 14 Sept 1965), 1 da (Barbara Virginia b 7 July 1968); *Career* res fell Girton Coll Cambridge 1960–63, prof of French studies and head of Dept of Modern Languages Univ of Ghana 1963–65, reader in linguistics Univ of York 1965–78, professorial fell St Hugh's Coll Oxford 1978–96, assoc prof of the romance languages Univ of Oxford 1978–96 (emeritus prof 1996–), research assoc Oxford Univ Centre for Linguistics & Philology 1996–, Leverhulme emeritus fell 1997; pres Philological Soc 1996–; memb: Linguistic Soc of America, Société de Linguistique Romane, Linguistics Assoc of GB, Modern Humanities Res Assoc, Soc for French Studies, Assoc for French Language Studies; *Books* Consonantal Dissimilation in the Romance Languages (1960), The Romance Languages (1966), Introduction to Romance Linguistics (1970), Trends in Romance Linguistics and Philology (with J N Green, 1980–93), The Romance Languages (Cambridge Language Survey, 1996), Linguistic Change in French (1997); *Recreations* gardening, walking, music, travel; *Style*— Prof Rebecca Posner; ✉ Rushwood, Jack Straw's Lane, Oxford (☎ 01865 63578)

POSNETT, Sir Richard Neil; KBE (1980, OBE 1963), CMG (1976); s of Rev Charles Walker Posnett, K-i-H of Medak, India, and Phyllis, *née* Barker; *b* 19 July 1919; *Educ* Kingswood, St John's Coll Cambridge (MA); *m* 1; 2 s, 1 da; m 2, 1959, Shirley Margaret, da of Claude Hudson; 2 s, 1 da; *Career* lawyer, colonial admin, diplomat; admin offr Uganda 1941; first ascent South Portal Peak Ruwenzori Mountains 1942; called to the Bar Gray's Inn 1951, chm Uganda Olympic Ctee 1955–58, Colonial Office London 1958, perm sec for External Affrs Uganda 1962–63; joined British Foreign Serv 1964, UK mission to UN 1966–70, govr and C-in-C of Belize 1972–76, Dependent Territories advsr FCO 1977–79, UK cmmr Br Phosphate Cmmrs 1978–81, Br high cmmr Kampala 1979, govr and C-in-C of Bermuda 1980–83; memb Lord Chllr's Panel of Ind Insprs 1984–89, pres Kingswood Assoc 1983; govr Kingswood Sch 1985–93; pres Godalming-Joigny Friendship Assoc 1988–; memb RIIA; KStJ 1972; *Recreations* skiing, golf, trees; *Clubs* Royal Cwlth Soc, Royal Forestry Soc, Achilles, West Surrey GC, Privateers Hockey; *Style*— Sir Richard Posnett, KBE, CMG; ✉ Bahati, Old Kiln Close, Churt, Surrey GU10 2JH (☎ 01428 714147)

POSNETTE, Prof Adrian Frank; CBE (1976); s of Frank William Posnette (d 1956), of Cheltenham, Glos, and Edith Mary, *née* Webber (d 1969); *b* 11 Jan 1914; *Educ* Cheltenham GS, Christ's Coll Cambridge (BA, MA, ScD), Imperial Coll of Tropical Agric (AICTA), Univ of London (PhD); *m* 15 July 1937, Isabelle (d 1991), da of Dr Montgomery De Forest La Roche (d 1958), of New York City; 1 s (John b 1950), 2 da (Jane b 1939, Suzanne b 1942); *Career* Colonial Agric Serv Gold Coast 1937–55: appointed botanist 1937–44, head of botany and plant pathology W African Cocoa Res Inst 1944–49, seconded to E Malling Res Station Maidstone Kent 1949, appointed princ scientific offr 1955; dir E Malling Res Station 1972–79 (head Plant Pathology Section 1957–69, dep dir 1969–72, dir 1972–79), hon prof of plant sciences Wye Coll Univ of London 1971–78; author of: series of eight res pubns on virus diseases of cocoa trees 1947–55, numerous pubns on virus diseases of fruit trees and strawberries 1953–80; govr Redhill Sch E Sutton; awarded Ridley medal of the Worshipful Co of Fruiterers 1978 (Hon Freeman 1982), VMH 1982; FIBiol 1963, FRS 1971; *Recreations* ornithology; *Clubs* Hawks (Cambridge); *Style*— Prof Adrian Posnette, CBE, FRS; ✉ Gwyn, Sutton Valence, Maidstone, Kent ME17 3AD (☎ 01622 843234)

POST, Herschel; s of Herschel E Post (d 1973), and Marie, *née* Connelly; *b* 9 Oct 1939; *Educ* Yale (AB), New Coll Oxford (BA, MA), Harvard Law Sch (LLB); *m* 24 Aug 1963, Peggy, da of Charles H Mayne (d 1963); 1 s (Herschel Day b 1969), 3 da (Clarissa b 1975, Eliza b 1977, Olivia b 1982); *Career* dep admin Parks Recreation and Cultural Affrs Admin City of NY 1972–73, vice pres Morgan Guaranty Trust Co Brussels and London 1974–84, pres and dir Posthorn Global Asset Management and Shearson Lehman Global Asset Management 1984–90, chief operating offr Lehman Bros and Lehman Bros Securities 1990–95, chief exec and dep chm Coutts & Co 1995– (chief operating offr Coutts Gp 1995); dep chm London Stock Exchange 1989–95; *Clubs* Vanderbilt Racquet; *Style*— Herschel Post, Esq; ✉ Coutts & Co, 440 Strand, London WC2R 0QS (☎ 0171 753 1000)

POSTE, Dr George H; *Educ* Univ of Bristol (BSc, PhD); *Career* SmithKline Beecham plc: joined Smith Kline & French Laboratories 1980, various sr R&D appts, chm research and devpt and research prof Dept of Pathology and Laboratory Med SmithKline Beecham Pharmaceuticals 1992–, main bd dir 1992–; co-ed Cancer and Metastasis Reviews, co-ed Advanced Drug Delivery Reviews, former chm Editorial Bd Bio/Technology, memb editorial bd various other jls; former memb US Govt Ctees on: Nat Insts of Health, NASA, Office of Technol Assessment, State Dept, Commerce Dept, Defense Dept; former chm: R&D Steering Ctee Pharmaceutical Mfrs' Assoc Washington DC, Scientific Ctee Asso of the British Pharmaceutical Industry; sometime memb governing body: Gordon Research Confs, Nat Fndn for Biomedical Research, Life Scis Research Fndn, Center for Molecular Genetics and Med Stanford Univ, Philadelphia Coll of Pharmacy and Sci, Alliance for Ageing, Keystone Center, Royal Soc of Med Fndn, US Nat Center for Genome Resources; Hon DSc Univ of Bristol 1987, Hon LLD Univ of Bristol 1995; FRCVS 1987, FRCPath 1989, Hon FRCP 1993; *Recreations* military history, photography, motor racing; *Style*— Dr George Poste; ✉ SmithKline Beecham Pharmaceuticals, New Frontiers Science Park, Third Avenue, Harlow, Essex CM19 5AW (☎ 01279 644333, fax 01279 644400, internet GEORGE_POSTE%SBPHRD.COM)

POSTGATE, Prof John Raymond; s of Raymond William Postgate (d 1971), of Canterbury, and Daisy (d 1971); *b* 24 June 1922; *Educ* Kingsbury Co Sch and others, Balliol Coll Oxford (BA, MA, DPhil, DSc); *m* 20 Oct 1948, (Muriel) Mary, da of Leslie Gordon Stewart (d 1963), of Whetstone, London; 3 da (Selina b 1955, Lucy (Mrs Timothy Duffield) b 1956, Joanna (Mrs Timothy Foulsham) b 1958); *Career* Nat Chem Laboratory: sr res investigator 1949–50, sr and later princ sci offr 1950–59; princ then sr princ sci offr Microbiological Res Estab 1959–63, asst dir ARC Unit of Nitrogen Fixation RVC 1963–65 (Univ of Sussex 1965–80); Univ of Sussex: dir AFRC Unit of Nitrogen Fixation 1980–87, prof of microbiology 1965–87, emeritus prof 1987–; visiting prof: Univ of Illinois 1962–63, Oregon State Univ 1977–78; hon memb: Soc for Applied Bacteriology 1981, Soc for Gen Microbiology 1988 (pres 1984–87); Hon DSc Univ of Bath 1990; FIBiol (pres 1982–84), FRS 1977; *Books* A Plain Man's Guide to Jazz (1973), The Sulphate-Reducing Bacteria (1979, 2 edn 1984), The Fundamentals of Nitrogen Fixation (1982), Microbes and Man (3 edn 1992), The Outer Reaches of Life (1994), A Stomach for Dissent: The Life of Raymond Postgate (with Mary Postgate, 1994); *Recreations* hearing and playing jazz music; scientific, jazz and biographical writing; *Style*— Prof John Postgate, FRS; ✉ Houndean Lodge, 1 Houndean Rise, Lewes, E Sussex BN7 1EG (☎ 01273 472 675)

POSTGATE, Prof (John) Nicholas; s of Ormond Oliver Postgate (d 1989), of Winchester, Hants, and Patricia Mary, *née* Peet; *b* 5 Nov 1945; *Educ* Winchester, Trinity Coll Cambridge (BA); *m* 1968, Carolyn June, da of Dr Donald Arthur Prater; 1 s (Richard Laurence b 30 March 1973), 1 da (Elizabeth Anne b 14 July 1975); *Career* asst lectr in Akkadian SOAS London 1967–71; fell Trinity Coll Cambridge 1970–74; dir British Sch of Archaeology in Iraq 1975–81 (asst dir 1972–75); Univ of Cambridge: lectr in history and archaeology of the ancient Near East 1982–85, reader in Mesopotamian studies 1985–94, prof of Assyriology 1994–; FBA 1993; *Books* Early Mesopotamia: Society and Economy at the Dawn of History (1992); *Style*— Prof Nicholas Postgate, FBA; ✉ Trinity College, Cambridge CB2 1TQ (☎ 01223 338443); Faculty of Oriental Studies, University of Cambridge, Sidgwick Avenue, Cambridge CB3 9DA (☎ 01223 335120)

POSTLETHWAITE, Dr Harvey Ernest; s of William Stanley Postlethwaite (d 1956), of London, and Lilly, *née* Ringer; *b* 4 March 1944; *Educ* Royal Masonic Schs Bushey, Univ of Birmingham (BSc, PhD); *m* Cherry Ruth, *née*, Thompson; 1 s (Ben Thomas b 9 Dec 1980), 1 da (Amey Jane b 1 Jan 1984); *Career* race car designer; formerly: res scientist Petrochemical and Polymer Lab ICI, devpt engr March Engineering, chief designer Hesketh Racing, chief designer Wolf Racing, chief chassis engr Ferrari Racing Dept Italy, md Tyrrell Racing; MIMechE; *Recreations* skiing, collecting and driving Ferraris; *Style*— Dr Harvey Postlethwaite; ✉ Tyrrell Racing Organisation, Long Reach, Ockham, Surrey (☎ 01483 284955)

POSWILLO, Prof David Ernest; CBE (1989); s of Ernest Joseph Poswillo, JP (d 1979), of Gisborne, NZ, and Amelia Mary, *née* McCormick; *b* 1 Jan 1927; *Educ* Gisborne Boys' HS, Univ of Otago NZ (BDS, DDS, DSc), Westminster Med Sch Univ of London (MRCPath); *m* 27 June 1956, Elizabeth Alison, da of John Whitworth Russell (d 1982), of Nelson, NZ; 2 s (Stephen b 22 Nov 1962, Mark b 10 Dec 1964), 2 da (Jane (Mrs Caton) b 13 Oct 1958, Jill (Mrs Battye) b 8 Jan 1960); *Career* OC Southern Dists Hosp RNZDC 1948–50, 30 Field Ambulance RAMC BAOR 1951; dir of oral surgery N Canterbury Hosp Bd NZ 1953–68, prof of teratology RCS 1969–77, consIt oral surgn Queen Victoria Hosp E Grinstead 1969–77, prof of oral pathology and oral surgery Univ of Adelaide South Aust 1977–79, sr oral and maxillofacial surgn Royal Adelaide and Children's Hosp South Aust 1977–79, prof of oral surgery Royal Dental Hosp London 1979–83, prof of oral and maxillofacial surgery Guy's Hosp London 1983–92 (prof emeritus 1992); memb: Cncl Royal Dental Hosp London 1977–83, Govrs' Cncl UMDS Guy's and St Thomas's Hosps 1983–92; memb Human Task Force WHO 1976–78, consIt advsr to chief MO DHSS 1979–86; chm Dept of Health: Working Pty on Anaesthesia, Sedation and Resuscitation in Dentistry (Poswillo Report) 1990, Ctee on Dental and Surgical Materials 1993, Scientific Ctee on Tobacco and Health 1994; tstee Tobacco Products Research Tst 1980–95; RCS: memb Bd of Faculty of Dental Surgery 1981–89, Hunterian tstee 1994–; sec gen Int Assoc of Oral and Maxillofacial Surgeons 1983–90 (hon fell 1992); dir and memb Cncl Med Def Union 1983–; RSM: pres Odontology Section 1989–90, memb Cncl 1990–94, hon treas 1994–, hon fell 1995; dir RSM Services 1994–; pres Br Assoc of Oral and Maxillofacial Surgns 1990–91; Hunterian prof RCS 1968 and 1976, Regent's prof Univ of California 1987; lectures: Arnott Demonstrator 1972, Erasmus Wilson 1973, Darwin-Lincoln Johns Hopkins 1975, Waldron Harvard 1976, Richardson Harvard 1981, Tomes RCS 1982, President's BAOMS 1985, Sarnat UCLA 1989, William Guy RCSEd 1990, Chalmers Lyons AAOMS 1996; RNZADC Prize 1948, Tomes Prize 1966, Down Medal 1973, Kay-Kilner Prize 1975, ASOMS Res Award 1976, Hunter Medal and Triennial Prize 1976, Orthog Surgery Award Univ of Texas 1982, Hon MD Univ of Zurich 1983, Edison Award Univ of Michigan 1987, Colyer Gold Medal RCS of England 1990, Goldman Lecture and Medal BPMF 1992; memb: German Acad of Natural Scis Leopoldina 1988, Inst of Med Nat Acad of Sci Washington USA 1989; FDSRCS 1952, FRACDS 1966, Hon FFDRCSI 1974, FRCPath 1981, FIBiol, CBiol; *Recreations* gardening, DIY, skiing, sailing; *Style*— Prof David Poswillo, CBE; ✉ Ferndale, Oldfield Road, Bickley, Kent BR1 2LE (☎ 0181 467 1578); Keats House, Guy's Hospital, London SE1 9RT

POTTER, *see:* Lee-Potter

POTTER, Christopher John; s of Frank Potter (d 1995), and Catherine, *née* Kerr; *b* 1 April 1959; *Educ* King's Coll London (BSc, AKC, MSc), London Coll of Music (ALCM); *partner* Peter Parker; *Career* publishing dir Fourth Estate 1994–; titles commissioned incl: The Stone Diaries by Carol Shields (winner Pulitzer Prize 1994), The Shipping News by E Annie Proulx (winner Pulitzer Prize 1995); columnist Convivium (quarterly food magazine); Ed of the Year (NIBBIES) 1994; *Recreations* piano (playing); *Style*— Christopher Potter, Esq; ✉ 14 Aubrey Road, London E17 4SL (☎ and fax 0181 521 3910); Fourth Estate Ltd, 6 Salem Road, London W2 4BU (☎ 0171 727 8993)

POTTER, David Roger William; s of William Edward Potter, of Durweston, Dorset, and Joan Louise, *née* Frost; *b* 27 July 1944; *Educ* Bryanston, Univ Coll Oxford (MA); *m* 1, 1966 (m dis 1984), Joanna Trollope, *qv*, da of A G C Trollope; 2 da (Louise (Mrs Paul Ansdell) b 1969, Antonia b 1971); m 3, 1991, Jill, da of James Benson; 1 da (Harriet b 1993); *Career* National Discount Co 1964–69; md: Credit Suisse First Boston 1969–81, Samuel Montagu and various subsidiaries 1981–87, Midland Montagu Corporate Banking 1987–89, David Potter Consultants 1989–90; chm and chief exec Guinness Mahon & Co Ltd 1990–, gp chief exec Guinness Mahon Holdings 1990–; dir Thomas Cook Group 1989–91; chm Bd London Film Cmmn; memb Bd of Advsrs The Capital Club of London; UMDS Med Sch: govr, chm, chm of Fin Ctee; govr Bryanston Sch; tstee: ORBIS, Youth for Britain; Liveryman Worshipful Co of Wheelwrights; *Recreations* shooting, golf, theatre, wine; *Clubs* Oxford and Cambridge, City, Vincent's (Oxford); *Style*— David R W Potter, Esq; ✉ Guinness Mahon & Co Ltd, 32 St Mary at Hill, London EC3P 3AJ (☎ 0171 772 7401, fax 0171 982 9253)

POTTER, Donald Charles; QC (1972); s of late Charles Potter; *b* 24 May 1922; *Educ* St Dunstan's Coll, LSE; *Career* asst lectr in law LSE 1947–49, called to the Bar Middle Temple 1948, in practice 1950–88, bencher Lincoln's Inn 1979; chm Revenue Bar Assoc 1978–88, special cmmnr of income tax 1986–95, gen cmmnr of income tax 1988–, pt/t chm VAT Tribunal 1986–95; *Clubs* Garrick; *Style*— D C Potter, Esq, QC; ✉ 27 Old Buildings, Lincoln's Inn, London WC2A 3UJ

POTTER, Edward; s of Flt Lt Edward Josef Data (d 1974), of Krakow, Poland, and Eleanor, *née* Bolton (d 1976); *b* 15 Sept 1941; *Educ* Bolton Tech Sch, Manchester Regnl Coll of Art, Oxford Sch of Arch (Dip Arch); *Career* architect; RIBA Thesis Prize Winner 1968; ptnr Edward Potter Assocs (chartered architects in gen practice and specialists in restoration of historic buildings); chm: S London Soc of Architects 1993–95, Wandsworth Society Open Spaces Ctee 1993–; RIBA rep Wandsworth Conservation Advsy Ctee 1995; RIBA, FIAS; *Recreations* railways; *Clubs* Chelsea Arts; *Style*— Edward Potter, Esq; ✉ 59 Westover Rd, London SW18 2RF (☎ 0181 870 7595, fax 0181 870 8683)

POTTER, Jennifer; da of Desmond Potter (d 1961), and Mavis, *née* Sutter; *b* 24 Jan 1949; *Educ* Univ of Sussex (BA); *m* 24 Jan 1981, Dennis Svoboda, s of Emil Svoboda; *Career* public relations exec; PR offr: Hong Kong Tourist Association 1972, Peter Whelpton Associates 1973, FJ Lyons (acquired by Charles Barker 1976) 1975; md Charles Barker-Marketing 1988–; dir: Charles Barker Holdings Ltd 1989–, Charles Barker plc 1992–; dep chief exec Charles Barker plc 1996–; *Style*— Ms Jennifer Potter; ✉ Charles Barker plc, 56 Dean Street, London W1V 5HJ (☎ 0171 494 1331, fax 0171 439 1071)

POTTER, Maj-Gen Sir (Wilfrid) John; KBE (1968, CBE 1963, OBE 1951), CB (1966); s of late Maj Benjamin Henry Potter, OBE, MC; *b* 18 April 1913; *m* 1, 1943, Vivienne Madge (d 1973), da of late Capt Henry D'Arcy Medlicott Cooke; 1 s, 1 da; m 2, 1974,

Mrs D Ella Purkis; 1 step s, 1 step da; *Career* Maj-Gen 1962, dir of Supplies and Tport (Army) 1963–65, Tport Offr in Chief (Army) 1965–66, dir of movements (Army) MOD 1966–68, ret; chm Traffic Cmmrs and Licensing Authy Western Traffic Area 1973–83; *Style*— Maj-Gen Sir John Potter, KBE, CB; ✉ Orchard Cottage, The Orchard, Freshford, Bath BA3 6EW (☎ 01225 722594)

POTTER, John McEwen; s of Alistair Richardson Potter, JP (d 1951), of Hazeldene, Bexley, Kent, and Mairi Chalmers, *née* Dick (d 1954); *b* 28 Feb 1920; *Educ* Clifton, Emmanuel Coll Cambridge (BA, MB BChir, MA), Univ of Oxford (MA, BM, BCh, DM); *m* 21 April 1943, Kathleen, da of Rev Dr Herbert Shaw Gerrard (d 1969), of Manchester; 3 s (James b 1944, Andrew b 1949, Simon b 1953); *Career* RAMC 1944–47, Lt 1944, active serv 8 Army Europe, Capt 1945, served India and Burma, graded neurosurgeon 1946; lectr in physiology and jr chief asst surgical professorial unit Bart's 1948–51, graduate asst to Nuffield prof of surgery Oxford 1951–56, EG Fearnsides scholar Cambridge 1954–56, Hunterian prof RCS 1955; conslt neurosurgeon: Manchester Royal Infirmary 1956–61, Radcliffe Infirmary Oxford 1961–87; clinical lectr in neurosurgery Univ of Oxford 1962–68, fell Linacre Coll 1967–69, univ lectr in neurosurgery 1968–87; Wadham Coll Oxford: fell 1969, professorial fell 1974–87, sub warden 1978–81, dean of degrees 1983–96, emeritus fell 1987–; dir of postgrad med educn Oxford Univ 1972–87, memb Bd of Govrs Utd Oxford Hosps 1973; memb: Gen Med Cncl 1973–89 (chm Registration Ctee 1979–89), Gen Bd of Faculties Univ of Oxford 1975–83, Oxon Health Authy 1982–89, Hebdomadal Cncl Univ of Oxford 1983–89, Med Appeals Tbnl 1987–92; former examiner Univs of Oxford and Cambridge; vice pres Fourth Int Congress of Neurological Surgery, pres Neurology Section Royal Soc of Med 1975–76, sr memb Soc of Br Neurological Surgns (former hon sec and archivist); corresponding memb: American Assoc of Neurological Surgns, Deutsche Gesellschaft für Neurochirurgie, Sociedad Luso-Espanhola de Neurocirurgia; hon memb Egyptian Soc of Neurological Surgns; memb BMA, FRCS 1951, FRSM; *Books* The Practical Management of Head Injuries (fourth edn 1984), contrib books and jls on subjects mostly relating to neurology and med educn; *Recreations* fishing; *Style*— Mr John Potter, Esq; ✉ 47 Park Town, Oxford OX2 6SL (☎ 01865 557875); Myredykes, Newcastleton, Roxburghshire TD9 0SR

POTTER, Jon Nicholas; s of Robert Edward Potter, and June, *née* Rosemayer; *b* 19 Nov 1963; *Educ* Burnham GS, Univ of Southampton (BA), Aston Business Sch (MBA); *m* Tracy Clare, *née* Holland; *Career* hockey player; memb Hounslow Hockey Club (capt Nat League winners 1990); Bronze medal Olympic Games LA 1984, Silver medal World Cup London 1986, Silver medal Euro Cup Moscow 1987, Gold medal Olympic Games Seoul 1988, Bronze medal Euro Cup 1991, 6th Olympic Games Barcelona 1992; 234 int caps; England capt World Cup 1994; most capped male GB player; Hockey Player of the Year 1987–88; mktg mangr: KP Foods 1988–92, Nestlé Rowntree 1992–95, Čokoládovny (Nestle Prague) 1995–; *Recreations* skiing, tennis, films, music; *Clubs* Ladykillers; *Style*— Jon Potter, Esq; ✉ Jánský Vršek 350, 110 00 Praha 1, Czech Republic (☎ 00 42 2 532 452); Čokoládovny AS, Modřanská 27, 143 20 Praha 4, Czech Republic (☎ 00 42 2 4091 512, fax 00 42 2 4091 111)

POTTER, His Hon Judge (Francis) Malcolm; s of Francis Martin Potter; *b* 28 July 1932; *Educ* Rugby, Jesus Coll Oxford; *m* 1970, Bertha Villamil; 1 s, 1 da; *Career* called to the Bar Lincoln's Inn 1956, recorder of the Crown Ct 1974–78, circuit judge (Midland and Oxford Circuit) 1978–; *Recreations* painting; *Clubs* Army & Navy; *Style*— His Hon Judge Malcolm Potter; ✉ Queen Elizabeth II Law Courts, Birmingham

POTTER, Rt Hon Lord Justice; Rt Hon Sir Mark Howard; kt (1988); s of Prof Harold Potter (d 1951), and Beatrice Spencer, *née* Crowder (d 1978); *b* 27 Aug 1937; *Educ* Perse Sch Cambridge, Gonville and Caius Coll Cambridge (MA); *m* 1962, Undine Amanda Fay, da of Maj James Eric Miller (Rajputana Rifles); 2 s (Nicholas b 6 Sept 1969, Charles b 27 Dec 1978); *Career* cmmnd 15 Medium Regt RA 1958, 289 Light Para Regt RHA (TA) 1960–65; asst supervisor legal studies Univ of Cambridge (Gonville and Caius, Queen's, Sydney Sussex, Girton) 1961–68; called to the Bar Gray's Inn 1961, practised Fountain Court, QC 1980, bencher 1987, judge of the High Court of Justice (Queen's Bench Div) 1988–96, presiding judge Northern Circuit 1991–94, judge in charge Commercial Ct 1994–95, a Lord Justice of Appeal 1996–; chm Bar Public Affrs Ctee 1987; vice chm: Cncl of Legal Educn 1989–91, Advsy Ctee Lord Chllr's Civil Justice Review 1985–88; memb Cncl Univ of Nottingham; govr Hall Sch Hampstead; *Recreations* family, sporting; *Clubs* Garrick, Saintsbury, St Enedoc Golf; *Style*— The Rt Hon Lord Justice Potter; ✉ Royal Courts of Justice, Strand, London WC2 (☎ 0171 936 6000)

POTTER, Raymond; CB (1990); *b* 26 March 1933; *Career* joined Lord Chancellor's Dept Central Office Royal Courts of Justice 1950, Western Circuit of Assize 1962; called to the Bar Inner Temple 1971, bencher 1989; chief clerk Bristol Crown Ct 1972, dep circuit admin Western Circuit 1976, circuit admin Northern Circuit 1982, dep sec Cts and Legal Servs 1986–93, dep clerk of the Crown in Chancery 1989–93, pres S Western Rent Assessment Panel 1995–; *Recreations* painting; *Clubs* Athenaeum; *Style*— Raymond Potter, Esq, CB; ✉ 8 Robinson Way, Backwell, Bristol BS19 3BP

POTTERTON, Homan; s of Thomas Edward Potterton (d 1960), and Eileen, *née* Tong (d 1990); *b* 9 May 1946; *Educ* Kilkenny Coll, Trinity Coll Dublin (BA, MA); *Career* cataloguer Nat Gallery of Ireland 1971–73, asst keeper Nat Gallery London 1974–80, dir Nat Gallery of Ireland 1980–88, ed Irish Arts Review 1993–; contrib to Burlington Magazine, Apollo, Connoisseur, Country Life, Financial Times; FSA, HRHA; *Books* Irish Church Monuments 1570–1880 (1975), A Guide to the National Gallery (1976), The National Gallery, London (1977), Reynolds and Gainsborough - Themes and Painters in the National Gallery (1976), Pageant and Panorama - The Elegant World of Canaletto (1978), Irish Art and Architecture (with Peter Harbison and Jeanne Sheehy, 1978, reissued 1993), Venetian Seventeenth Century Painting (1979), Dutch Seventeenth and Eighteenth Century Paintings in the National Gallery of Ireland - a complete catalogue (1986) The Golden Age of Dutch Paintings from the National Gallery of Ireland (exhibition catalogue, 1986); *Style*— Homan Potterton, Esq; ✉ 119 West 71 St, New York, NY 10023 (☎ 00 1 212 721 0510); 3 Westmoreland Terrace, London SW1V 4AG (☎ 0171 834 8279)

POTTINGER, Frank; *b* 1932; *Educ* Edinburgh Coll of Art (DA); *Career* artist and sculptor; engrg apprenticeship 1948–53; art teacher 1965–73, lectr in art Aberdeen Coll of Educn 1973–85, visiting lectr Aberdeen, Dundee, Glasgow and Edinburgh Colls of Art 1982–90, pt/t lectr Edinburgh Coll of Art 1990–93; *Exhibitions* 57 Gall 1965, Richard Demarco Gall 1971, Peterloo Gall 1975, Compass Gall 1976, Yorkshire Sculpture Park 1979 and 1984, Scottish Sculpture Workshop 1981, 1983, 1987, 1991 and 1993, Scottish Sculpture Trust 1982, Fruitmarket Gall 1983, Aberdeen Art Gall 1983, Camden Arts Centre 1983, Pier Art Centre 1984, Hands Off (Crawford Arts Centre) 1985, Sculptors' Drawings (Scottish Arts Cncl) 1985, Peacock Ten 1985, Landscapes (Open Eye Gall) 1987, Kingfisher Gall 1988, Twin City (Aberdeen and Regensburg) 1988, Waverley Taylor Gall 1989, Decorated Ceramics (Open Eye Gall) 1989, Inverclyde Print Biennial 1989, Scottish Sculpture Now (Aberdeen Art Gall) 1989, 21 Years of Contemporary Art (Compass Gall) 1990, Ceramic Sculpture (Open Eye Gall) 1990, Haldane Connections (Glasgow Sch of Art) 1990, Scottish Art in the 20th Century (Royal West of England Acad) 1991, Shoebox Sculpture Exhbn (Univ of Hawaii) 1993; *Work in Collections* Hunterian Gall, Univ of Dundee, Paisley Museum Gall, Scottish Arts Cncl, IBM, Leeds Educn Authy; *Awards* Scottish Arts Cncl 1978, William J Macaulay prize RSA 1979, IBM award Soc of Scottish Artists 1986, Mobil North Sea award Scottish Sculpture Workshop 1991; chm Scottish Sculpture Workshop 1980–90; RSA 1991; *Style*— Frank Pottinger, Esq, RSA; ✉ 30/5 Elbe Street, Leith, Edinburgh EH6 7HW (☎ 0131 553 5082)

POTTINGER, Martin Neil; s of Peter Jamieson Henry Pottinger (d 1987), of Edinburgh, and Gladys May, *née* Crafer; *b* 14 March 1948; *Educ* Royal HS Edinburgh, Scott Sutherland Sch of Architecture Aberdeen, Thames Poly London (Dip Arch); *m* 1, 10 Sept 1976 (m dis 1985), Caroline Mary, *née* Moresco; m 2, 30 Sept 1985, Harriet St Bride Ram, da of Sir David Burdett Money-Coutts, KCVO, *qv*; 3 s (William b 19 Nov 1985, Thomas b 6 Jan 1989, Robin b 21 Sept 1990), 1 da (Flora b 25 April 1987); *Career* architect; ptnr Hutchinson & Ptnrs 1979–81, princ Martin Pottinger Chartered Architect 1982–85, princ Martin Pottinger Associates Architects 1986–; RIBA 1980; *Recreations* carpentry, walking, my children; *Style*— Martin Pottinger, Esq; ✉ 1 Old Coach House, Upottery, Honiton, Devon EX14 9PN (☎ 01404 861689); Martin Pottinger Associates, 11 Eton Garages, Lambolle Place, London NW3 4PE (☎ 0171 586 9372)

POTTS, James Richardson; s of James Kenneth Potts (d 1973), of Somerset, and Nina Kathleen, *née* Hayman; *b* 13 Nov 1944; *Educ* King's Sch Bruton Somerset, Wadham Coll Oxford (MA), Univ of London (PGCE), Univ of Bristol (postgrad cert in film and drama); *m* 13 Aug 1969, Maria, *née* Strani; 1 da (Nina-Maria Penelope b 30 Sept 1972), 1 s (Alexander James Kenneth b 11 June 1976); *Career* British Council: English language teacher and educnl TV and radio prodr 1969–71, TV prodr Addis Ababa 1971–75, TV and film prodr Nairobi 1975–77, educnl TV/technol conslt London 1977–80, regnl dir N Greece 1980–85, cultural attaché Prague 1986–89, head East and Central Europe Dept and dep dir Europe Div London 1990–92, dir Aust 1993–; *Recreations* film-making, poetry, blues guitar, walking and watersports, foreign cultures and literatures; *Style*— James Potts, Esq; ✉ The British Council, PO Box 88, 203 New South Head Road, Edgecliff, NSW 2027, Australia (☎ 00 61 29 326 2022, fax 00 61 29 3274868)

POTTS, Michael Stuart; s of late Thomas Edmund Potts, ERD, of Bray on Thames, and Phyllis Margaret, *née* Gebbie; *b* 2 Sept 1938; *Educ* Hilton Coll S Africa, Repton; *m* 23 May 1964, Virginia May Lindsay, da of late Gp Capt Hugh Whittall Marlow, OBE, AFC, of Cape Town, S Africa; 3 s (Andrew b 1966, Alexander b 1968, Rupert b 1970); *Career* CA; ptnr Coopers & Lybrand: Ireland 1968–70, UK 1970–92 (sr ptnr Liverpool Office 1971–92); dir: H J Uren & Sons Ltd 1993–, W O & J Wilson Ltd 1994–; chm North West Cancer Research Fund 1993–, dir Mersey Regional Ambulance Service (NHS Tst) 1993–; pres Liverpool Soc of CAs 1982–83; memb Cncl: Merseyside C of C and Indust 1974–92 (hon treas 1974–82), Univ of Liverpool 1979–89 (dep treas 1986–89, hon treas 1993–), ICAEW 1988–92; Liveryman: Worshipful Co of Clockmakers, Worshipful Co of Chartered Accountants; FCA; *Recreations* sailing, golf, motoring, horology; *Clubs* Dee Sailing (Commodore 1979–80), Royal Liverpool Golf (treas 1992–96), Aston Martin Owners, Antiquarian Horological Soc; *Style*— Michael Potts, Esq; ✉ Brooke House, The Parade, Parkgate, Cheshire L64 6RN (☎ 0151 336 1494, office ☎ and fax 0151 353 0701)

POTTS, Paul John; s of Michael Henry Potts (d 1960), of Sheffield, and Sylvia Brenda Potts; *b* 21 Jan 1950; *Educ* Worksop Coll Nottingham; *m* Aug 1994, Judith Fielding; *Career* gen reporter Sheffield Star 1967–74, lobby corr Yorkshire Post 1974–78; gen reporter: Daily Telegraph 1978–81, Mail on Sunday 1981–82; political ed News of the World 1982–86, dep ed Daily Express 1988– (political then asst ed 1986–88); *Recreations* all sports, horse racing; *Style*— Paul Potts, Esq; ✉ The Daily Express, Ludgate House, 245 Blackfriars Road, London SE1 9UX (☎ 0171 928 8000, fax 0171 620 1643)

POTTS, Robin; QC (1982); s of Flt Lt William Potts (d 1971), and Elaine Muriel, *née* Winkle (d 1958); *b* 2 July 1944; *Educ* Wolstanton GS, Magdalen Coll Oxford (BA, BCL); *m* 1 (m dis 1982), Eva Rebeca, *née* Giwercer; 1 s (James Rupert b 1970); m 2, 8 March 1985, Helen Elizabeth, da of Neville Duncan Sharp, of IOW; 2 s (Timothy Edward b 1986, Christopher William b 1988), 1 da (Emma Clare b 1990); *Career* called to the Bar Gray's Inn 1968, Bencher 1993; *Recreations* gardening, reading, wine; *Style*— Robin Potts, Esq, QC; ✉ The Grange, Church Lane, Pinner, Middx HA5 3AB; Windmill Cottage, Queen's Rd, Freshwater, IOW PO40 9ES

POTTS, Prof William Taylor Windle; s of Ronald Windle Potts (d 1983), and Kathleen Anne, *née* Cole (d 1983); *b* 10 July 1928; *Educ* The Perse Sch Cambridge, St Catharine's Coll Cambridge (MA, PhD), DSc (Birmingham); *m* 17 Sept 1955, Margaret Taylor; 3 s (Aidan b 1957, Thomas b 1959, Malcolm b 1963); *Career* lectr Univ of Birmingham 1955–56, prof Univ of Lancaster 1966–95; *Books* Osmotic & Ionic Regulation in Animals (1964), Practical Exercises in Biology (1988), Queen Victoria's Gene (1995); *Recreations* archaeology; *Style*— Prof William Potts; ✉ The Nook, Caton, Lancaster (☎ 01524 770500); Department of Biological Sciences, University, The Lancaster LA1 4YQ (☎ 01524 65201, fax 01524 843854)

POULSEN, HE Ole Lønsmann; *b* 14 May 1945; *Educ* Copenhagen Univ (LLB); *m*; 2 s; *Career* Danish diplomat; head of dept Danchurchaid 1969–73, head of section Miny of Foreign Affrs 1973–76, advsr Asian Development Bank Manila 1976–77, first sec Danish Embassy New Delhi and trade cmmr Bombay 1977–80, alternate exec dir World Bank Washington 1980–83, head Dept of Int Devpt Co-operation 1983–88, under-sec for multilateral affrs/ambass Miny of Foreign Affrs 1988–92, ambass to Austria and perm rep to IAEA, UNIDO and the UN in Vienna 1992–93, state sec/ambass Miny of Foreign Affrs 1993–96, ambass to the Ct of St James's 1996–; chm Bd: Scandinavian Seminar Coll 1975–76, Nordic Devpt Fund 1990–91; chm Industl Devpt Bd UNIDO 1990–91; Order of the Dannebrog (first class); *Style*— HE Mr Ole Lønsmann Poulsen; ✉ Royal Danish Embassy, 55 Sloane Street, London SW1X 9SR (☎ 0171 333 0200, fax 0171 333 0270)

POULTER, Brian Henry; s of William Henry Poulter (d 1971), of Dundonald, Co Down, and Marjorie Elizabeth Everett, *née* McBride (d 1972); *b* 1 Sept 1941; *Educ* Regent House GS Newtownards Co Down; *m* 8 June 1968, (Margaret) Ann, da of Henry Dodds, of Dundonald; 1 s (Richard b 1975), 2 da (Andrea b 1972, Suzanne (twin) b 1972); *Career* Hill Vellacott and Bailey CAs 1959–62; NI Civil Serv: Miny of Health and Local Govt 1962–65, Miny of Health and Social Servs 1965–71, Miny of Commerce 1971–75, dir Exchequer and Audit Dept 1982–87 (princ auditor 1975–81, dep dir 1981–82), sec NI Audit Office 1989– (dir 1987–89); assoc CACA 1967; *Recreations* reading, walking, cricket; *Style*— Brian Poulter, Esq; ✉ Northern Ireland Audit Office, 106 University Street, Belfast BT7 1EU (☎ 01232 251129)

POULTER, Graham George; s of George Henry Poulter (d 1980), and Mavis Kathleen, *née* Shipman; *b* 5 May 1942; *Educ* Art Coll Wakefield; *m* 1, 29 March 1967 (m dis), Patricia Ann, *née* Dickinson; 2 s (Jason b 1970, James b 1975); m 2, 18 Nov 1995, Kathryn Mary, *née* Rignall; *Career* art dir/copywriter Kidds Advertising, account mangr Cravens Advertising, branch mangr Taylor Advertising (London), dir Leeds Office Goddard Watts; currently chm: Poulter plc (fndr memb 1969), On Demand Information plc (fndr memb 1993); *Recreations* skiing, jogging, gym; *Style*— Graham G Poulter, Esq; ✉ The Old Wives House, Trip Lane, Wood Hall, Wetherby, West Yorkshire LS22 4HZ; On Demand Information plc, Poulter House, 2 Burley Road, Leeds LS3 1NJ (☎ 0113 233 0000, fax 0113 234 3574)

POULTON, Christopher Geoffrey; s of Sqdn Ldr Geoffrey Poulton, DFC (decd), and Margery, *née* Hillman; *b* 4 June 1943; *Educ* Dulwich Coll, Churchill Coll Cambridge (MA); *m* 2 Sept 1967, Judith, *née* Barton; 3 da (Annabel, Rebecca, Victoria); *Career* Baring Bros & Co 1972–75, asst dir Charterhouse Japhet 1975–84, dir Cadogan Oakley 1984–86, divnl md Credit Lyonnais Securities 1986–; *Recreations* fishing, music, tennis; *Style*— Christopher G Poulton, Esq; ✉ Bells Farm, Bells Farm Lane, Hadlow, Kent; Credit

Lyonnais Securities, Broadwalk House, 5 Appold St, London EC2A 2DA (☎ 0171 588 4000)

POULTON, Richard Christopher; s of Rev Christopher John Poulton (d 1988), and Aileen Muriel, *née* Sparrow (d 1977); *b* 21 June 1938; *Educ* Kings Coll Taunton, Wesleyan Univ Middleton Connecticut USA, Pembroke Coll Cambridge (DipEd, MA); *m* 3 April 1965, Zara Irene Mary, da of Prof Peter Charles Crossley-Holland, of Llangeler, Llandysul; 2 s (Anthony b 1969, Benedict b 1971), 1 da (Elizabeth b 1966); *Career* asst master: Bedford Sch 1962–63, Beckenham and Penge GS 1963–66; head of dept and housemaster Bryanston Sch 1966–80; headmaster: Wycliffe Coll 1980–86, Christ's Hosp 1987–96; fndr headmaster Int Sch of the Regents Thailand 1996–; JP S Glos 1985–86, govr Oxford and Cambridge Exam Bd 1987–90; memb: HMC 1980, SHA 1980; Freeman City of London 1987, Liveryman Worshipful Co of Ironmongers 1993; FRSA 1994; *Books* Victoria, Queen of a Changing Land (1975), Kings and Commoners (1977), A History of the Modern World (1980); *Recreations* choral music, walking, watching sport, writing; *Clubs* East India, Public Schs; *Style*— Richard Poulton, Esq; ✉ PO Box 33, Naklua, Banglamung, Chonburi 20150, Thailand (☎ 00 66 38 734777, fax 00 66 38 734778)

POULTON, His Hon Judge; William Dacres Campbell; s of Maj Arthur Stanley Poulton (d 1981), of Battle, Sussex, and Winifred Evelyn, *née* Montgomery Campbell; *b* 15 Dec 1937; *Educ* Dover Coll, New Coll Oxford (BA, MA); *m* 3 Jan 1970, Carolyn Frances, da of Flt Lt Francis Macken (d 1961); 2 s (Charles b 1970, Andrew b 1976), 1 da (Elinor b 1972); *Career* Nat Serv 1956–58, 2 Lt Royal Sussex Regt 1957, Somaliland Scouts 1957–58; lectr in law New Coll Oxford 1963–68; called to the Bar Middle Temple 1965, in practice SE Circuit, recorder 1992–94, circuit judge (SE Circuit) 1994–; *Recreations* gardening, walking, skiing; *Style*— His Hon Judge Poulton; ✉ Provender Oast, Norton, Nr Faversham, Kent TN13 3SF (☎ 01795 521176); Canterbury Combined Court, Canterbury, Kent

POUND, Sir John David; 5 Bt (UK 1905), of Stanmore, Co Middlesex; s of Sir Derek Allen Pound, 4 Bt (d 1980); Sir John Pound, 1 Bt, was head of the firm John Pound & Co, Portmanteau Manufacturers, and Lord Mayor of London 1904–05; *b* 1 Nov 1946; *Educ* Burebank Sch Aylsham Norfolk; *m* 1, 20 July 1968 (m dis 1978), Heather Frances O'Brien, o da of Harry Jackson Dean; 1 s; m 2, 1978, Penelope Ann, da of Grahame Arthur Rayden; 2 s (Christopher James b 1982, Nicholas Edward b 1986); *Heir* s, Robert John Pound b 2 Feb 1973; *Career* Liveryman Leathersellers' Co; *Style*— Sir John Pound, Bt; ✉ Brooklands, Yarnborough Hill, Old Swinford, Stourbridge DY8 2EB

POUND, Rev Canon Keith Salisbury; s of Percy Salisbury Pound (d 1946), of Charlton, London, and Annie Florence, *née* Button (d 1979); *b* 3 April 1933; *Educ* Roan Sch for Boys Blackheath, St Catharine's Coll Cambridge (BA, MA), Cuddesdon Coll Oxford; *Career* curate St Peter St Helier Morden Surrey 1957–61, warden Hollowford Training Centre Diocese of Sheffield 1964–68 (trg offr 1961–64), rector Holy Trinity with St Matthew Southwark 1968–78, rural dean Southwark and Newington 1973–78, team rector Thamesmead 1978–86, sub dean of Woolwich 1984–86, dean of Greenwich 1985–86, hon canon Southwark Cathedral 1985–, chaplain gen and archdeacon to HM Prison Serv 1986–93, chaplain HM Prison Grendon and Springhill 1993–; chaplain to HM The Queen 1988–; *Books* Creeds and Controversies (1966); *Recreations* theatre, music, reading, crosswords; *Clubs* Civil Service; *Style*— The Rev Canon Keith Pound; ✉ 1 Park Road, Grendon Underwood, Aylesbury, Bucks HP18 0TD (☎ 01296 770494); 28 Tackleway, Hastings, E Sussex (☎ 01424 716745); Chaplain's Office, HM Prison Grendon, Grendon Underwood, Aylesbury, Bucks HP18 0TL (☎ 01296 770301)

POUNDER, Prof Derrick John; s of Wilfred Pounder, of Penycoedcae, Wales, and Lilian, *née* Jones; *b* 25 Feb 1949; *Educ* Pontypridd Boys GS, Univ of Birmingham (MB, ChB); *m* 28 Nov 1975, Georgina, da of Patrick Kelly, of Tullamore, Co Offaly, Ireland; 1 s (Emlyn b 18 May 1989), 2 da (Sibéal b 30 March 1985, Sinéad b 9 Sept 1991); *Career* lectr then sr lectr in forensic pathology Univ of Adelaide S Aust, dep chief med examiner Edmonton Alberta Canada and assoc prof Univs of Alberta and Calgary 1985–87, prof of forensic med Univ of Dundee Scotland 1987–; memb SNP; chm Physicians for Human Rights; Freeman Llantrisant; FRCPA, FFPathRCPI, FCAP, FRCPath, FHKCPath; *Recreations* photography, medieval architecture, almost-lost causes; *Style*— Prof Derrick Pounder; ✉ Department of Forensic Medicine, The Royal Infirmary, Dundee, Scotland DD1 9ND (☎ 01382 200794, fax 01382 322094)

POUNDS, Prof Kenneth Alwyne; CBE (1984); s of Harry Pounds (d 1976), and Dorothy Louise, *née* Hunt (d 1981); *b* 17 Nov 1934; *Educ* Salt Sch Shipley Yorks, UCL (BSc, PhD); *m* 1, 29 Dec 1961, Margaret Mary (d 1976), da of Patrick O'Connell (d 1969); 2 s (David Edwin b 12 May 1963, John Michael b 13 April 1966), 1 da (Jillian Barbara b 12 June 1964); m 2, 10 Dec 1982, Joan Mary, da of Samuel Millit (d 1983); 1 s (Michael Andrew b 5 Aug 1983), 1 da (Jennifer Anne b 22 Feb 1987); *Career* Univ of Leicester: asst lectr 1960, lectr 1962, sr lectr in physics 1989, dir X-Ray Astronomy Gp 1969–94, reader in physics 1971, prof of space physics 1973–, head of physics 1986–93; chief exec Particle Physics and Astronomy Res Cncl 1994–; author of over 175 publications worldwide; playing memb Oadby Town CC; fndr memb BNSC Mgmnt Bd; cncl memb: SERC (chm Astronomy, Space and Radio Bd 1980–84), Royal Soc 1986–87; pres Royal Astronomical Soc 1990–92; Hon DUniv York 1984, Hon DSc Loughborough 1992; FRS 1981; *Recreations* cricket, football, music; *Style*— Prof Kenneth Pounds, CBE, FRS; ✉ 12 Swale Close, Oadby, Leics (☎ 0116 271 9370); Particle Physics and Astronomy Research Council, Polaris House, North Star Avenue, Swindon SN2 1ET (☎ 01793 442067, fax 01793 442106)

POUNTAIN, Christopher Charles; s of Charles Alfred Pountain, of Edinburgh, and Jean Mary, *née* Stanfield; *b* 4 May 1953; *Educ* Royal High Sch Edinburgh, Univ of St Andrews (BSc); *m* 29 July 1988, Joyce Margaret, da of William Thomson, of Balrownie, nr Brechin; 2 s (Andrew William, David Charles); *Career* actuary student Scottish Widows Fund 1975–79, insur analyst Wood Mackenzie 1979 (dir 1985, merger with County NatWest 1988), London Office County NatWest 1988, Morgan Stanley International 1989, corp fin and planning mangr rising to overseas dir Commercial Union plc 1992–; FFA 1978; *Recreations* hill walking, skiing, cinema going, reading; *Style*— Christopher Pountain, Esq; ✉ Commercial Union plc, CU House, 69 Park Lane, Croydon CR9 1BG (☎ 0171 662 8035)

POUNTAIN, Sir Eric John; kt (1985), DL (Staffs 1985); *b* 5 Aug 1933; *Educ* Queen Mary's GS Walsall; *m* 1960, Joan Patricia, *née* Sutton; 1 s, 1 da; *Career* jt princ F Maitland Selwyn & Co auctioneers and estate agents 1959 (joined 1956), fndr Midland & General Developments 1964 (acquired by John McLean & Sons Ltd 1969), chief exec John McLean & Sons Ltd 1969 (acquired by Tarmac plc 1974); Tarmac plc: chief exec Housing Div until 1979, dir 1977–, gp chief exec 1979–92, exec chm 1983–92, chm 1992–94, ret; non-exec chm: James Beattie plc 1987– (dir 1984–), IMI plc 1989– (dir 1988–); non-exec dir: Lloyds Chemists plc, United News & Media plc (formerly United Newspapers plc), John Maunders Group plc; patron Staffs Agric Soc; Liveryman Worshipful Co of Gunmakers; hon fell Univ of Wolverhampton (formerly Wolverhampton Poly); CIMgt, FIHE, FRSA; *Style*— Sir Eric Pountain, DL; ✉ Edial House, Edial, nr Lichfield, Staffordshire; c/o James Beattie plc, 71–80 Victoria Street, Wolverhampton WV1 3PQ (☎ 01902 22311)

POUNTNEY, David Willoughby; CBE (1994); s of Edward Willoughby Pountney, of Clevedon, Avon, and Dorothy Lucy, *née* Byrt (d 1984); *b* 10 Sept 1947; *Educ* St John's Coll Choir Sch Cambridge, Radley, St John's Coll Cambridge (MA); *m* 23 Feb 1980, Jane Rosemary, da of Maj James Emrys Williams (d 1978); 1 s (James b 1984), 1 da (Emilia b 1981); *Career* dir of productions: Scottish Opera 1976–80, ENO 1983–93; dir of operas in: Ireland, Holland, Germany, Italy, Aust and USA, all maj Br cos; princ productions incl: Janacek cycle (Scot Opera, WNO), Bussoni's Dr Faust (ENO, Deutsche Opera), The Lady Macbeth of Mtensk (ENO), Hansel and Gretel (ENO, received the Evening Standard award), Wozzeck, Pelleas et Mélisande, world première of Philip Glass' The Voyage (Met Opera NY) 1992; translated numerous opera incl: Smetana's The Bartered Bride, Two Widows, Die Fledermaus, From the House of the Dead, The Flying Dutchman, La Traviata, Christmas Eve, Il Seraglio, The Excursions of Mr Broucek, Fidelio; Chev Ordre des Arts et Lettres (France) 1993; *Recreations* croquet, cooking, gardening; *Clubs* Garrick; *Style*— David Pountney, Esq, CBE; ✉ 35 Brookfield Mansions, Highgate West Hill, London N6 6AT (☎ 0181 342 8900, fax 0181 342 8901)

POUT, Harry Wilfred; CB (1978), OBE (1959); *b* 11 April 1920; *Educ* East Ham GS, Imperial Coll London; *m* 1949, Margaret Elizabeth, *née* Nelson; 3 da; *Career* dep controller (MOD): Guided Weapons 1973, Guided Weapons and Electronics 1973–75, Air Systems 1975–79, Aircraft Weapons and Electronics 1979–80; def conslt 1980–82 and 1986–, Marconi Underwater Weapons Systems Ltd 1982–86; treas Guildford Gem Mineral and Lapidary Club; FCGI, FIEE, FIMgt; *Recreations* mountaineering, geology; *Style*— Harry Pout, Esq, CB, OBE; ✉ Oakmead, Fox Corner, Ash Road, Worplesdon, Guildford, Surrey GU3 3PP (☎ 01483 232223)

POVER, Alan John; CMG (1990); s of John Pover (d 1978), and Anne, *née* Hession, of Atherton, Manchester; *b* 16 Dec 1933; *Educ* Salesian Coll Bolton; *m* 31 Oct 1964, Doreen Elizabeth, da of James Dawson (d 1988); 1 s (David b 1966), 2 da (Jane b 1965, Claire b 1971); *Career* Nat Serv Army 1952–54; Civil Serv Miny Pensions and Nat Insur 1954–61; HM Dip Serv: CRO London 1961–62, second sec Lagos 1962–66, second sec Tel Aviv 1966–69, first sec and consul Karachi and Islamabad 1969–73, FCO 1973–76, consul Cape Town 1976–80, cnsllr Dip Serv Inspr FCO 1983–86 (first sec 1980–83), cnsllr and consul gen Washington DC 1986–90, high cmmr Banjul 1990–93; *Recreations* golf, historical research, gardening, cricket; *Style*— Alan Pover, Esq, CMG; ✉ 6 Farriers Lane, East Ilsley, Newbury, Berks RG20 7JB

POVEY, Chief Constable Keith; QPM (1991); s of Trevor Roberts Povey (d 1983), and Dorothy, *née* Parsonnage (d 1965); *b* 30 April 1943; *Educ* Abbeydale GS Sheffield, Univ of Sheffield (Bramshill scholar, BA); *m* 1964, Carol Ann, da of late Albert Harvey; 2 da (Allyson Patricia b 11 Sept 1965, Louise Ann b 23 Feb 1970); *Career* Sheffield City Police 1961–84; posts incl: cadet 1961, constable 1962, chief inspr HM Inspector of Constabulary NE Region 1981–82 (memb Secretariat Home Office Enquiry into Yorkshire Ripper case), FBI Academy USA 1982, supt and sub-divnl cdr Sheffield City Centre 1982–84 (ground cdr for policing during miners' dispute at Orgreave Coking Plant); staff offr HM Chief Inspector of Constabulary Home Office 1984–86 (reported on Zimbabwe Republic Police 1984), asst chief constable Humberside 1986–90, deputy chief constable Northants 1990–93, chief constable Leicestershire Constabulary 1993–; ACPO: chm General Purposes Ctee, chm Crime Prevention Sub-Ctee, head Working Gp on Police Patrol, rep Home Office Working Party on Special Constabulary; *Recreations* jogging, flying; *Style*— Chief Constable Keith Povey, QPM; ✉ Leicestershire Constabulary HQ, St Johns, Narborough, Leicester LE9 5BX (☎ 0116 248 2005, fax 0116 248 2004)

POVEY, Robert Frederick Donald; s of Donald James Frederick Povey (d 1987), and Ellen Lillian, *née* Nye (d 1987); *b* 8 July 1944; *Educ* Strand GS, Brixton Sch of Bldg; *m* 1, 23 March 1966 (m dis 1970), Pauline, da of Ernest John Wise; m 2, 22 June 1974 (m dis 1996), Karen Moira, da of late Arthur Reginald Whitfield; m 3, 16 Nov 1996, Lynda, da of late Lester Harvey; *Career* engr; ptnr Mitchell McFarlane and Ptnrs (dir and co sec); formerly chm Surrey Branch of Inst of Structural Engrs, memb ctees of CIRIA and SCI producing pubns for structural engrs; FIStructE; *Recreations* golf, amateur dramatics; *Clubs* Puttenham Golf; *Style*— Robert Povey, Esq; ✉ Mitchell McFarlane & Ptnrs, 137–143 High Street, Sutton Surrey SM1 1JH (☎ 0181 661 6565, fax 0181 643 9136)

POWE, Ian Wilton; s of Herbert Lungley Powe (d 1976), and Gertrude Isabella, *née* Morton (d 1980); *b* 17 Oct 1932; *Educ* Royal Naval Coll; *m* 10 Sept 1955, Deirdre Ann, da of Derek Fuller; 3 s (Julian b 8 Feb 1957, Jonathan b 21 Nov 1958, Rory b 10 May 1963), 1 da (Sally b 1 June 1960); *Career* joined RN as cadet 1946, served Korean War 1950–51, jr appts at sea 1953–57, anti-submarine trg 1957–58, served anti-submarine helicopter front line sqdn and minesweeping Malta 1958–60, on staff RNC Dartmouth 1960–62, served submarines and frigates 1962–66, served variously at sea, as dir of trg Anti-Submarine Sch, at MOD and at Jt Serv Staff Trg 1967–77 (incl disaster relief work following Sicilian earthquake 1968, cmd HMS Yarmouth during Cod War), variously on staff of Fleet Cdr, dir of RN staff trg RNC Greenwich, i/c Fleet Support Establishment Rosyth, naval asst to chief of naval personnel then COS to FO Plymouth until 1986, ret as Capt 1986; dir Gas Consumers Cncl 1986–; Freeman: Montevago Sicily (where street Via Commandante Powe named in honour of earthquake relief work), Great Yarmouth (following cmd of HMS Yarmouth); MInstE 1992, FInstD; *Recreations* family, trout fishing, collecting modern first editions, pictures, antiques, theatre; *Clubs* IOD; *Style*— Ian Powe, Esq; ✉ The Gas Consumers Council, Abford House, 15 Wilton Road, London SW1V 1LT (☎ 0171 931 0977, fax 0171 630 9934, mobile 0850 704587)

POWELL, Anthony; s of Arthur Lawrence Powell (d 1939), of Manchester, and Alice, *née* Woodhead; *b* 2 June 1935; *Educ* William Hulmes GS Manchester, St Andrew's Coll Dublin, Central Sch of Arts and Crafts London; *Career* costume and set designer for theatre and film; served Royal Corps of Signals (Br Army occupation of the Rhine) 1953–55; asst to Sir Cecil Beaton and Oliver Messel; lectr in theatre design Central Sch of Art and Design 1958–71, RSA scholar 1958, freelance design conslt Sabre Sportwear and Jantzen Swimwear 1960–69, Br Colour Cncl 1965–67, numerous building interior designs incl Sutton Place 1981–83; numerous books written about him and his work; *Theatre* Women Beware Women (RSC) 1961, School for Scandal (Haymarket and NY) 1961, Comedy of Errors (RSC and world tour) 1963, The Rivals (Haymarket) 1966, Fish Out of Water (London) 1971, Private Lives (London, NY, USA tour) 1972, Ring Round the Moon (Ahmanson Theatre LA) 1975, Amadeus (Paris) 1981, Lettice and Lovage (Maggie Smith's costumes, NY) 1990, Hay Fever (London and provincial tour) 1992, Trelawny of the Wells (RNT) 1992, Sunset Boulevard (London/LA 1993, Broadway 1994, Frankfurt/Toronto 1995, Aust and US tour 1996); *Opera* Rinaldo (Sadlers Wells Opera and Komischesopera Berlin) 1960, La Belle Helene (Sadlers Wells Opera) 1962, Il Seraglio (Sadlers Wells Opera) 1962, Capriccio (Glydebourne Festival Opera) 1963, Mortis Lie (for US TV) 1965; *Films* Royal Hunt of the Sun 1968, Joe Egg 1969, A Town Called Bastard 1970, Nicholas and Alexandra 1971, Travels with my Aunt 1972, Papillon 1973, That Lucky Touch 1974, Buffalo Bill and the Indians, Sorcerer 1976, Death on the Nile 1977, Tess 1978–79, Priest of Love 1980, Evil Under the Sun 1981, Indiana Jones and the Temple of Doom 1983, Pirates 1984–85, Ishtar 1985–86, Nostromo (preparation) 1986–87 and 1989, Frantic 1987, Indiana Jones and the Last Crusade 1988, Hook 1990–91, Walt Disney's 101 Dalmatians (costumes for Glenn Close) 1996; *Awards* for Best Costume Design incl: Tony Award for School for Scandal 1963, US Academy Award for Travels with my Aunt 1973, LA Drama Critics' Circle Award for Ring Around the Moon 1975, Br and US Academy Awards for Death on the Nile 1979, US Academy Award for Tess 1981, Cesar Award (France) for Pirates 1987, Drama-logue Critics Award and LA Drama Critics' Circle Award for Sunset Boulevard 1993; US Academy nominations for Pirates 1987, Hook 1992; *Recreations* music, gardening, collecting, laughing; *Style*— Anthony Powell, Esq; ✉ c/o Andrew S P Glynne, Glynnes

Solicitors, 37 Marylebone Lane, London W1M 5FN (☎ 0171 486 3166, fax 0171 486 2164)

POWELL, Anthony Dymoke; CH (1988), CBE (1956); s of late Lt-Col P L W Powell, CBE, DSO, and Maud Mary, *née* Wells-Dymoke; *b* 21 Dec 1905; *Educ* Eton, Balliol Coll Oxford; *m* 1934, Lady Violet Pakenham, 3 da of 5 Earl of Longford, KP, MVO (ka 1915); 2 s (Tristram, John); *Career* writer; served Welch Regt and Intelligence Corps WWII, Maj; tstee Nat Portrait Gallery 1962–76; hon fell: Balliol Coll Oxford 1974, Modern Language Assoc of America 1981; hon memb American Acad of Arts and Letters 1977; Hon DLitt: Univ of Sussex 1971, Univ of Leicester 1976, Univ of Kent 1976, Univ of Oxford 1980, Univ of Bristol 1982, Univ of Wales 1992, Univ of Bath 1996; Order of the White Lion (Czech), Order of the Oaken Crown and Croix de Guerre (Luxembourg), Order of Leopold II (Belgium); *Books* incl: Agents and Patients (1936), A Dance to the Music of Time (12 Vol series), A Question of Upbringing (1951), At Lady Molly's (1957, James Tait Black Memorial Prize), Temporary Kings (1973, W H Smith Prize), Hearing Secret Harmonies (1975), To Keep the Ball Rolling (memoirs, 4 vol series 1976–82), The Fisher King (1986), The Album of Music of Time (ed Violet Powell, 1987), Miscellaneous Verdicts (1990), Under Review, Journals of Anthony Powell 1982–86 (1995) and 1987–89 (1995); *Plays* Afternoon Men (adapted from book of 1931), Arts Theatre Club, The Garden God, The Rest I'll Whistle; *Clubs* Travellers', Pratt's; *Style*— Anthony Powell, Esq, CH, CBE; ✉ The Chantry, nr Frome, Somerset BA11 3LJ (☎ 01373 836314)

POWELL, Sir Charles David; KCMG (1990), kt (1990); s of Air Vice-Marshal John Frederick Powell, OBE, AE *qv*, and Geraldine Ysolda, *née* Moylan; bro of Jonathan, *qv*; *b* 6 July 1941; *Educ* King's Sch Canterbury, New Coll Oxford (BA); *m* 24 Oct 1964, Carla, da of Domingo Bonardi, of Italy; 2 s (Hugh b 1967, Nicholas b 1968); *Career* memb HM Dip Serv, Helsinki, Washington, Bonn and EEC Brussels, private sec and advsr on foreign affrs and defence to PM 1984–91 (under sec 1987); dir: Jardine Matheson (and subsids and associates) 1991–, National Westmister Bank plc 1991– (chm International Advsy Bd), Arjo Wiggins Appleton plc 1992–, Louis Vuitton-Moet Hennessy SA; dep chm Trafalgar House plc until 1996; vice pres China-Britain Trade Gp, chm Singapore-British Business Cncl; *Recreations* walking; *Clubs* Turf, Beefsteak; *Style*— Sir Charles Powell, KCMG; ✉ Matheson & Co Ltd, 3 Lombard Street, London EC3V 9AQ

POWELL, (John) Christopher; s of Air Vice-Marshal John Frederick Powell, and Geraldine Ysolda Moylan; *b* 4 Oct 1943; *Educ* Canterbury Cathedral Choir Sch, St Peter's Sch, York, LSE (BSc); *m* 1973, Rosemary Jeanne, da of Ralph Symmons; 2 s (Ben b 1974, Jamie b 1977), 1 da (Lucy b 1980); *Career* account mgmnt trainee Hobson Bates 1965–67, account mangr Wasey's 1967–69; BMP DDB: account mangr 1969–75, jt md 1975, sole md 1986–95, chief exec 1986–; pres IPA 1993–95; non-exec dir: Riverside Studios 1989–, Riverside Community Healthcare NHS Trust 1994–, United News & Media plc 1995–; *Recreations* tennis, walking, riding, reading; *Style*— Christopher Powell, Esq; ✉ BMP DDB, 12 Bishops Bridge Rd, London W12 (☎ 0171 258 3979)

POWELL, Daryl Anthony; s of Garry Powell, and Jean, *née* Simpson; *b* 21 July 1965; *Educ* Carlton HS Pontefract, Castleford HS; *m* Janice, *née* Collins; 2 da (Kegan Jay, Briana Dee); *Career* rugby league player; amateur Redhill Castleford, professional Sheffield Eagles 1984–95 (over 300 appearances), Keithley Cougers 1995–; represented Yorkshire v Lancashire 1988; GB: debut v France 1990, toured NZ and Papua New Guinea 1990, Aust NZ and Papua New Guinea 1992, 3 Test matches v Aust 1990, 28 full caps; overseas clubs: Glenora NZ 1986, Balmain Aust 1988, Gold Coast Aust 1991; rep England (5 full caps); Player of the Year Sheffield Eagles 1985, Players' Player of the Year Sheffield Eagles 1988–89, Fellow Professionals' Div 2 Player of the Year 1988–89, Journalists Div 2 Star Man of the Year 1988–89; rugby league coaching scheme: regnl coach 1989–90, staff coach 1990–; *Recreations* golf, squash, football, physical training, spending time with Janice; *Style*— Daryl Powell, Esq; ✉ Keithley Cougers Rugby League Club, Couger Park, Royd Ings Avenue, Keithley, West Yorkshire BD21 3NB (☎ 01535 213111)

POWELL, David Beynon; s of David Eynon Powell (d 1942), and Catherine Ada, *née* Beynon; *b* 9 Feb 1934; *Educ* Gowerton GS, Christ's Coll Cambridge (MA, LLB), Yale Law Sch (LLM), Harvard Business Sch (SMP 18); *m* 1973 (m dis); *Career* Nat Serv Flying Offr RAF 1952–54; slr Supreme Ct, dep legal advsr BLMC Ltd 1970–73, dir of legal servs BL Ltd (British Leyland) 1974–83, gp legal dir Midland Bank plc 1984–91, dir of gp legal servs Guinness plc 1992–94, legal advsr PA Consulting Group 1994–96, currently legal advsr Domino Printing Sciences plc; non-exec dir Ross Group plc; *Recreations* reading, music, bridge; *Style*— David Powell, Esq; ✉ 20c Randolph Crescent, London W9 1DR (☎ 0171 289 2326)

POWELL, David (Dick); s of Arthur Barrington Powell, CMG, of Pwllmeyni, Gwent, and Jane, *née* Weir; *Educ* Ampleforth Coll, Manchester Poly (DipAD), RCA (MDesRCA, Burton award 1975 and 1976); *m* (Jennifer) Lucy, da of Peter Talbot Willcox; 1 da (Jemma b 25 July 1980), 3 s (Oscar b 1 Sept 1983, Freddie b 24 Feb 1985, Gus b 5 Dec 1992); *Career* product designer; co-fndr CAPA Partnership 1976–79, freelance designer 1980–83, fndr (with Prof Richard Seymour, *qv*) Seymour-Powell 1984– (clients incl British Rail, Yamaha, Tefal, Casio and MZ); pt/t lectr in industl and automotive design RCA 1980–83, other teaching experience at Leicester, Newcastle, Birmingham and Lanchester Polytechnics, Glasgow Sch of Art, Napier Coll Edinburgh and Central Sch of Art, external assessor BA Hons degree course Manchester Poly 1990–; contrib BBC Design Classics, Designs on Britain and LWT Design Education series 1986; main speaker and contrib British Design in Vienna seminar and Design Cncl conf Sweden 1987, main speaker Blueprint Moving Up seminars 1988, main speaker Design Means Business conf Hong Kong and Int Sales conf IBM 1993, main speaker DTI organised design conf Delhi 1994; FRSA 1993, FCSD 1993, memb Design Cncl 1995; *Awards* Best Overall Design and Product Design (for Norton F1 motorcycle) Design Week Awards 1990, D&AD Silver Award (for Technophone Cellular Telephone) 1991, ID Award and D&AD Silver Award (for MuZ Skorpian motorcycle) 1993, winner Product Design category BBC Design Awards 1994, CSD Minerva Award (for MuZ Skorpian) 1994, ID Award (for Sun Voyager) 1994, D&AD President's Award (for outstanding contribution to design) 1995; *Books* Presentation Techniques (1985, revised edn 1988, translations in Dutch and Spanish); *Recreations* motorcycles; *Style*— Dick Powell, Esq; ✉ Seymour Powell, The Chapel, Archel Road, London W14 9QH (☎ 0171 381 6433, fax 0171 381 9081)

POWELL, His Hon Dewi Watkin; JP (Mid Glamorgan); s of W H Powell; *b* 29 July 1920; *Educ* Penarth GS, Jesus Coll Oxford; *m* 1951, Alice, da of William Williams; 1 da; *Career* called to the Bar Inner Temple 1949, dep chm Merioneth and Cardigan QS 1966–71, dep recorder 1965–71 (Cardiff, Birkenhead, Merthyr Tydfil, Swansea), a circuit judge and official referee for Wales and Chester 1972–92, liaison judge for Dyfed 1974–84 and Mid Glamorgan 1984–91, designated judge for Merthyr Tydfil 1986–90; vice pres: Mid and S Glamorgan Branch Magistrates' Assoc 1973–, Gwynedd Branch Magistrates' Assoc 1990–; Univ Coll Cardiff: memb of Ct and Cncl 1976–88, vice pres 1982–88, hon fell and chm of Cncl 1987–88; vice pres hon fell and vice chm Cncl UCW Cardiff 1988–; memb: Ct and Cncl Univ Coll of Wales Aberystwyth 1972–91, Cncl Univ of Wales Coll of Med 1989–93, Ct Univ of Wales 1974–, Cncl Univ of Wales 1990; chm Cncl of Hon Soc of Cymmrodorion 1979–86 (vice pres 1986–), pres Cymdeithas Theatr Cymru 1983–89, memb Gorsedd of Bards, Nat Eisteddfod lectr (Language, Nation and Legislation: Towards New Attitudes) 1990; pres: Baptist Union of Wales 1993–94 (vice pres 1992–93), Free Church Cncl of Wales 1995– (vice pres 1993–95); chm Draft Govt of Wales Bill Working Gp Parliament for Wales Movement 1995–; *Clubs* Oxford Union; *Style*— His Hon Dewi Watkin Powell, JP; ✉ Nanmor, Morannedd, Cricieth

POWELL, Rt Hon (John) Enoch; MBE (1943), PC (1960); s of Albert Enoch Powell, and Ellen Mary Breese; *b* 16 June 1912; *Educ* King Edward's Sch Birmingham, Trinity Coll Cambridge (MA); *m* 1952, Margaret Pamela, da of Lt-Col L E Wilson, IA; 2 da; *Career* fell Trinity Coll Cambridge 1934–38, prof of Greek Sydney Univ NSW 1937–39; serv Royal Warwickshire Regt WWII, Brig 1944; MP: (Cons) Wolverhampton SW 1950–74, (UU) Down S 1974–83, (UU) S Down 1983–87; contested (UU) S Down 1987; Parly sec Miny of Housing and Local Govt 1955–57, fin sec to the Treasy 1957–58, min of Health 1960–63; author; *Clubs* Athenaeum; *Style*— The Rt Hon Enoch Powell, MBE; ✉ 33 South Eaton Place, London SW1 (☎ 0171 730 0988)

POWELL, (Richard) Guy; s of Richard Albert Brakell Powell (d 1957), of 2 King's Bench Walk, London, and Stella Float, *née* Young (d 1990); *b* 28 April 1927; *Educ* The King's Sch Canterbury, Hertford Coll Oxford (MA); *Career* admitted slr 1953; ptnr: Rooper & Whately 1960–70, Lee & Pembertons 1970–92 (conslt 1992–96); clerk Prowdes Educnl Fndn 1974–94 (tstee 1994–); memb Cncl Private Libraries Assoc 1963–; Freeman City of London 1948, Liveryman Worshipful Co of Drapers 1952; FRSA 1952, memb Vereinigung der Freunde Antiker Kunst (Switzerland) 1960; *Recreations* book collecting, Anglican church music; *Clubs* Travellers', United Oxford and Cambridge; *Style*— R Guy Powell, Esq

POWELL, James Richard Douglas; s and h of Sir Nicholas Folliott Douglas Powell, 4 Bt, *qv* and his 1 w, Daphne Jean, *née* Errington; *b* 17 Oct 1962; *Educ* Peterhouse Zimbabwe, RAC Cirencester; *m* 14 Dec 1991, Susanna Frances, eld da of David Murray Threipland; 1 s (Douglas James Folliott b 22 Oct 1992), 1 da (Cordelia Catherine b 16 March 1995); *Career* farmer; *Style*— James Powell, Esq; ✉ Oxford Farm, Box 49, Marondera, Zimbabwe

POWELL, Jane; da of Anthony Alfred Edward Powell, of Sheffield, and Barbara, *née* Jackson; *b* 19 Jan 1957; *Educ* Abbeydale Girls' GS Sheffield, Chelsea Coll of PE, Univ of Sussex (BEd); *Career* memb Eng Women's Cricket Squad 1979–91, Eng Women's Cricket Capt 1988–91, memb Eng Women's Hockey Squads 1978–80; hockey coach: Eng Univs, Midland Seniors, Midland Under 21; coach England under 18; advanced coach in hockey and cricket; exec memb English Hockey Coaching Assoc (EHCA); coaching sec Midlands Women's Hockey Assoc; memb: Christians in Sport, Nat Coaching Fndn, Inst of Leisure and Amenity Mgmnt, Hockey Rules Advsy Gp, National Assoc of Sports Coaches (SNASC); *Recreations* all sports, golf, active Christian work; *Style*— Miss Jane Powell; ✉ 24 Alicante Close, Malvern, Worcs WR14 2SH (☎ 01684 565361); The Chase High School, Geraldine Road, Malvern, Worcs WR14 3NZ (☎ 01684 572096, fax 01684 566643)

POWELL, Jeffrey Richard (Jeff); s of Alfred William John Powell, of Canvey Island, Essex, and late Dorothy Faith, *née* Parkin; *b* 21 Feb 1942; *Educ* Buckhurst Hill Co HS, The Poly Regent St; *m* 1 (m dis); 2 da (Natalie Jane b 22 May 1972, Natasha Dawn b 14 April 1974); m 2, 20 Feb 1987, Maria del Consuelo Ortiz de Powell, da of Gen Jose Ortiz Avila; 1 s (Jeffrey Jose b 17 March 1988); *Career* Walthamstow Guardian 1959–66 (jr reporter, sports ed); Daily Mail: sports sub-ed 1966–69, football reporter 1969–71, chief soccer corr 1971–89, chief sports feature writer 1989–; Br Sports Reporter of the Year 1978, 1983 and 1985, Br Sports Journalist of the Year 1985, Br Sports Feature Writer of the Year 1995; memb: Football Writers' Assoc 1969 (chm 1982–83 and 1989–90), Sportswriters' Assoc 1969; *Books* Bobby Moore, The Authorised Biography; *Recreations* golf, tennis, theatre, opera, chess; *Clubs* RAC, Tramp, Scribes, Morton's; *Style*— Jeff Powell, Esq; ✉ Daily Mail, Northcliffe House, 2 Derry St, Kensington, London W8 5TT (☎ 0171 938 6229, fax 0171 938 4053)

POWELL, Air Vice-Marshal John Frederick; OBE (1956), AE (1946); s of Rev Morgan Powell (d 1951), of Limpley Stoke, nr Bath, and Edith Susannah, *née* David (d 1964); *b* 12 June 1915; *Educ* King's Coll Choir Sch Cambridge, Lancing, King's Coll Cambridge (BA, MA); *m* 16 Sept 1939, (Geraldine) Ysolda, da of Sir John Moylan, CB, CBE (d 1967), of Bury, Sussex; 4 s (Sir Charles Powell, KCMG, *qv* b 1941, Christopher b 1943, Roderick b 1948, Jonathan, *qv* b 1956); *Career* lectr RAF Coll Cranwell 1938, controller coastal cmd (ops) RAFVR 1939–45 (despatches), RAF (Educn Branch) 1946, instr later sr tutor RAF Coll 1946–59, educn staff FEAF 1959–62, MOD 1962–64, Gp Capt 1964, cmd educn offr HQ Bomber Cmd 1964–66, OC RAF Sch of Educn 1966–67, Air Cdre 1967, dir RAF Educn Servs 1967–72, Air Vice-Marshal 1968; warden and dir of studies Moor Park Coll Farnham 1972–77; *Recreations* choral music, gardening, walking; *Clubs* RAF; *Style*— Air Vice-Marshal John Powell, OBE, AE; ✉ Barkers Hill Cottage, Donhead St Andrew, Shaftesbury, Dorset SP7 9EB (☎ 01747 828505)

POWELL, John Frederick; s of Alfred John Powell, of Greenford, Middlesex, and Ethel Mary, *née* Levy; *b* 22 Sept 1934; *Educ* Univ Coll Sch; *m* 1, 5 Oct 1957, Ena Deirdre, *née* Leeland; 2 s (Richard John, Neil Andrew), 2 da (Sandra Jane, Susan Mary); m 2, 25 April 1980, Cecilia Mary Theresa, *née* Relph; 1 da (Danielle Ida); *Career* Nat Serv RAPC; articled clerk Elles Reeve; Coopers & Lybrand (merged with Cork Gully 1980): joined 1963, ptnr 1977, sr insolvency ptnr West Midlands 1986–93, managing partner Newcastle upon Tyne 1993–96, ret; FCA (ACA 1957), fell Insolvency Practitioners Assoc; *Books* Liquidation Manual (1988); *Recreations* golf, football (spectator), walking; *Clubs* Copt Heath Golf; *Style*— John F Powell, Esq; ✉ c/o Coopers & Lybrand, Hadrian House, Higham Place, Newcastle upon Tyne NE1 8BP

POWELL, John Lewis; QC (1990); s of Gwyn Powell (d 1981), of Ammanford, Dyfed, and Lilian Mary, *née* Griffiths; *b* 14 Sept 1950; *Educ* Christ Coll Brecon, Amman Valley GS, Trinity Hall Cambridge (MA, LLB); *m* 1 Sept 1973, Eva Zofia, da of Dr Adam J Lomnicki; 3 c (Sophie Anna b 14 Feb 1980, Catrin Eva (Katie) b 3 Jan 1982, David John b 3 Feb 1985); *Career* called to the Bar Middle Temple (Harmsworth scholar) 1974; Parly candidate (Lab) Cardigan 1979; pres Soc of Construction Law 1991–, memb Commercial Bar Assoc; *Books* Encyclopedia of Financial Services Law (with Eva Lomnicki), Professional Negligence (with R Jackson, 3 edn 1992), Palmer's Company Law (jt ed, 25 edn 1991), Issues and Offers of Company Securities: The New Regimes (1988); *Recreations* travel, sheep farming in Black Mountain Dyfed, walking; *Style*— John L Powell, Esq, QC; ✉ 2 Crown Office Row, Temple, London EC4Y 7HJ (☎ 0171 797 8000, fax 0171 797 8001)

POWELL, Jonathan Leslie; s of James Dawson Powell, and Phyllis Nora, *née* Sylvester; *b* 25 April 1947; *Educ* Sherborne, Univ of E Anglia; *m* 29 Dec 1990, Sally Brampton, *qv*; *Career* script ed then prodr Granada TV 1969–77; BBC TV: prodr 1977–84 (prodr of classic serials incl The Mayor of Casterbridge, Tinker Tailor Soldier Spy, Testament of Youth, The Barchester Chronicles and The Old Men at the Zoo), head of drama series and serials 1984–87, head Drama Group 1987, controller of BBC1 1988–92; dir of drama and international devpt Carlton Television 1993–; exec prodr Peak Practice 1995–; memb Exec Ctee Edinburgh Int Television Festival; *Recreations* fishing; *Style*— Jonathan Powell, Esq; ✉ Carlton Television, 35–38 Portman Square, London W1H 0NU (☎ 0171 486 6688)

POWELL, Jonathan Nicholas; s of Air Vice-Marshal John Frederick Powell, OBE, AE, *qv*, and Geraldine Ysolda, *née* Moylan; bro of Sir Charles Powell, KCMG, *qv*; *b* 14 Aug 1956; *Educ* Univ Coll Oxford (BA); *m* Karen Drayne; 2 s (John b 10 Sept 1982, Charles b 14 Aug 1985); *Career* with Granada TV Manchester 1979–80; second sec Br Embassy Lisbon 1981–84; first sec: FCO London 1984–86, CDE Stockholm 1986, CSCE Vienna 1986–89; FCO London (Reunification of Germany) 1989–91, first sec Br Embassy

Washington 1991–95; chief of staff to Rt Hon Tony Blair, MP as Leader of Opposition 1995–; *Style—* Jonathan Powell, Esq; ✉ Chief of Staff to Rt Hon Tony Blair, MP, The Office of the Leader of The Opposition, House of Commons, London SW1A 0AA

POWELL, (Geoffrey) Mark; s of Francis Turner Powell, MBE, of W Clandon, Surrey, and Joan Audrey, *née* Bartlett; *b* 14 Jan 1946; *Educ* Tonbridge, St Chad's Coll Univ of Durham (BA); *m* 24 July 1971, Veronica Joan, da of Paul Frank Rowland (d 1993), of Langford, Clymping, Sussex; 2 da (Jessica b 1973, Catriona b 1976); *Career* ptnr Powell Popham Dawes & Co 1972–77, dir Laing & Cruickshank 1977–86; chief exec: CL-Alexanders Laing & Cruickshank Holdings Ltd 1987–89 (dir 1986–89), Laurence Keen 1989–; jt gp md Rathbone Brothers plc 1995–; dir Assoc of Private Client Investment Managers and Stockbrokers; Freeman City of London 1967, memb Ct Worshipful Co of Haberdashers 1989–; memb Cncl REACH 1996–; memb London Stock Exchange 1971, MSI; FRSA; *Clubs* MCC, City of London; *Style—* Mark Powell, Esq; ✉ Creedhole Farm, High Button, Thursley, Surrey GU8 6NR (☎ 01428 683163); Laurence Keen Ltd, 49/51 Bow Lane, London EC4M 9LX (☎ 0171 489 9493, fax 0171 489 8638, telex 916966)

POWELL, Michael Peter; s of Arthur Owen Powell (d 1967), of Oxford, and Jane, *née* Mustard; *b* 24 July 1950; *Educ* Wellington Berks, New Coll Oxford (MA), Middx Hosp Med Sch (MB BS); *m* 13 Jan 1979, Dr Jennifer Shields, da of (Leslie) Stuart Shields, QC; 3 da (Ruth b 29 May 1981, Alice b 27 Sept 1983, Penny b 13 Sept 1986); *Career* registrar and research registrar Neurosurgery Dept Frenchay Hosp Bristol 1980–83; currently neurosurgn: The Nat Hosp for Neurology and Neurosurgery (sr registrar 1983–85), UCH, RNOH London; hon conslt: Whittingdon Hosp, St Thomas' Hosp, St Luke's Hosp for the Clergy, King Edward VII Hosp for Offrs; civilian advsr in neurosurgery to the RAF; FRCS; *Style—* Michael Powell, Esq; ✉ The National Hospital, Queen Square, London WC1N 3BG (☎ 0171 837 3611 ext 3176)

POWELL, Neil Ashton; s of late Ian Otho James Powell, of Orford, Suffolk, and Dulcie Delia, *née* Lloyd; *b* 11 Feb 1948; *Educ* Sevenoaks Sch Kent, Univ of Warwick (BA, MPhil); *Career* ed Tracks 1967–70, English teacher Kimbolton Sch Huntingdon 1971–74, head of English St Christopher Sch Letchworth 1978–86 (English teacher 1974–78), owner The Baldock Bookshop 1986–90; winner Soc of Authors Gregory Award 1969, writer in residence Samuel Whitbread Sch Shefford 1988, resident tutor Arvon Fndn Totleigh Barton Devon 1989, tutor Bd of Extra Mural Studies Univ of Cambridge 1991, tutor WEA Eastern Region 1994–, visiting tutor Norwich Sch of Art 1995–; contrib poetry, fiction, essays and reviews to: Critical Quarterly, Encounter, The Guardian, The Listener, London Magazine, New Statesman, PN Review, Poetry Review, Times Literary Supplement, various anthologies, BBC Radio Three; memb Soc of Authors 1974; *Books* Suffolk Poems (1975), At the Edge (1977), Carpenters of Light (1979), Out of Time (1979), A Season of Calm Weather (1982), Selected Poems of Fulke Greville (ed, 1990), True Colours: New and Selected Poems (1991), Unreal City (1992), The Stones on Thorpeness Beach (1994), Roy Fuller: Writer and Society (1995); *Style—* Neil Powell, Esq; ✉ Delhi Cottage, Crabbe Street, Aldeburgh, Suffolk IP15 5BW (☎ 01728 452677)

POWELL, Sir Nicholas Folliott Douglas; 4 Bt (UK 1897); s of Sir Richard George Douglas Powell, MC, 3 Bt (d 1980); descends from Walter Powell (d 1567), descendant of Rhys ap Tewdwr Mawr, King of South Wales; kinsman of William R Powell, MP, *qv*; *b* 17 July 1935; *Educ* Gordonstoun; *m* 1, 26 May 1960 (m dis 1987), Daphne Jean, yr da of Maj George Henry Errington, MC; 1 s (James Richard Douglas b 17 Oct 1962), 1 da (Catherine Mary b 1961); m 2, 10 July 1987, Davina Hyacinth Berners, er twin da of Michael Edward Ranulph Allsopp, *qv*; 2 s (Benjamin Ranulph Berners b 5 Jan 1989, Oliver Michael Folliott b 4 Nov 1990), 1 da (Mamie Josephine Berners b 21 April 1992); *Heir* s, James Richard Douglas Powell; *Career* Lt Welsh Gds 1953–57; co dir; *Style—* Sir Nicholas Powell, Bt; ✉ Hillside Estate, Bromley, Zimbabwe

POWELL, Paul Douglas; *b* 6 May 1939; *Career* qualified chartered accountant 1963; fin accountant: with wine importer and wholesaler 1964–66, with industrial manufacturer 1966–68; Moore Stephens: joined 1968, ptnr 1974, currently sr ptnr Shipping Indust Gp; speaker at: Seatrade Acad Cambridge, The City Univ Business Sch, various shipping confs in London, Pireaus, New York, Beijing, Vienna, Latvia and CIS; expert witness before arbitration and High Court proceedings; contrib articles to shipping media; rep memb Int Maritime Industries Forum; memb: Soc for Nautical Res, Baltic Exchange, Br Acad of Experts, Int Assoc of Marine Economists; AInstT, FCA; *Style—* Paul Powell, Esq; ✉ Moore Stephens, St Paul's House, Warwick Lane, London EC4P 4BN

POWELL, Peter James; s of James Powell Moore Montague (d 1981), and Margaret, *née* Jones; *b* 24 March 1951; *Educ* Uppingham; *m* 31 Jan 1990, Anthea Turner, *qv*, da of Brian Turner; *Career* presenter BBC Radio Birmingham 1970–77, disc jockey BBC Radio 1 1977–89 (UK's Top Live Disc Jockey Carl Alan Awards 1980); ptnr and dir James Grant Media Group Ltd; mangr: Phillip Schofield 1985–, Anthea Turner 1985–, Simon Mayo 1986–, Mark Goodier 1986–, Caron Keating 1987–, Darren Day 1990–, Toby Anstis 1993–, Andi Peters 1993–, Emma Forbes 1994–, Zöe Ball 1994–, Tim Vincent 1995–, Mike Read 1996–, Kevin Greening 1996–, Lawrence Dallaglio 1996–, Phil de Glanville 1996–, Andy Gomarsall 1996–, Alex King 1996–; hon vice pres Nat Assoc of Youth Clubs, assoc dir main bd Radio Lollipop UK; *Recreations* sailing, skiing; *Clubs* RORC, RYA, RAC; *Style—* Peter Powell, Esq; ✉ James Grant Media Group Ltd, Syon Lodge, London Road, Middx TW7 5BH (☎ 0181 232 4100, fax 0181 232 4101)

POWELL, Sir (Arnold Joseph) Philip; CH (1984), kt (1975), OBE (1957); s of Rev Canon Arnold Cecil Powell (d 1963), of Chichester, and (Mary) Winnifred, *née* Walker (d 1954); *b* 15 March 1921; *Educ* Epsom Coll, AA Sch of Architecture; *m* 17 Jan 1953, Philippa June, da of Lt-Col Charles Chevalier Eccles (d 1977), of Tunbridge Wells; 1 s (Benjamin James b 1957), 1 da ((Harriet) Dido b 1955); *Career* architect; ptnr Powell and Moya Architects 1946–91; works incl: Skylon for festival of Britain 1951 (won in open competition), Plumstead Manor Sch Woolwich 1970, dining rooms Bath Acad of Art Corsham 1970 and Eton Coll 1974, Br Pavilion Expo 70 Osaka Japan; houses and flats at: Churchill Gdns Westminster 1948–62 (won in open competition), Chichester 1950, Gospel Oak St Pancras 1954, Toys Hill 1954, Oxshott 1954, Baughurst Hants 1954, Vauxhall Park Lambeth 1972, Covent Gdn 1983; extension to Brasenose Coll Oxford 1961, Chichester Festival Theatre 1962, picture gallery and undergraduate rooms Christ Church Oxford 1967, Cripps Bldg St John's Coll Cambridge 1967, Swimming Baths Putney 1967, extension to Corpus Christi Coll Oxford 1969, Wolfson Coll Oxford 1974, Cripps Court Queens' Coll Cambridge 1976, Museum of London 1976, London and Manchester Assurance HQ nr Exeter 1978, Sch for Advanced Urban Studies Univ of Bristol 1981, NatWest Bank Shaftesbury Ave London 1982, Queen Elizabeth II Conf Centre Westminster 1986, laboratories incl Queen's Bldg Royal Holloway and Bedford New Coll Egham 1986; hosps in: Swindon, Slough, High Wycombe, Wythenshawe, Woolwich, Maidstone, Hastings, Gt Ormond St Children's Hosp extension; has won numerous medals and awards for architectural work incl Royal Gold Medal for Architecture RIBA 1974; memb Royal Fine Art Cmmn 1969–94, tstee Sir John Sloane's Museum 1984–, treas RA 1985–95; RA 1977 (ARA 1972), FRIBA; *Recreations* travel, listening to music; *Style—* Sir Philip Powell, CH, OBE, RA; ✉ 16 The Little Boltons, London SW10 9LP (☎ 0171 373 8620)

POWELL, Philip B; s of Frank James Powell (d 1987), of London, and Elizabeth Anne, *née* Hamel (d 1977); *b* 3 Nov 1951; *Educ* Highbury Co GS, LSE, Univ of E Anglia (BA); *m* 10 March 1978, Jacqueline Anne, da of Frank Lloyd; 2 s (Matthew Frank b 16 Jan 1982, Christopher James b 22 May 1984), 1 da (Joanne Alice b 4 Jan 1988); *Career* Unilever plc: grad mgmnt trainee Walls Ice Cream 1974–76, sr product mangr Walls Ice Cream 1976–80, gp product mangr Iglo Ola Netherlands 1980–81, sr brand mangr Lever Brothers 1982–83; mktg mangr Colmans of Norwich Reckitt & Colman plc 1983–86, fndr The Marketing House Norwich 1986–88, head of mktg Goodman Fielder Wattie NZ 1989–91, business devpt mangr Cow & Gate 1991–93, mktg dir Central Statistical Office 1994–; fndr chm Canned Food Info Serv NZ 1990–91; memb: Infant & Diatetic Food Assoc 1991–92, Dissemination Ctee Govt Statistical Serv, EC Statistical Dissemination Gp; MCIM; *Recreations* carpentry, painting, tennis, squash, family, travelling, food and wine (eating and cooking); *Style—* Philip B Powell, Esq; ✉ Central Statistical Office, Government Offices, Rm 1/08, 1 Drummond Gate, London SW1V 2QQ (☎ 0171 233 9233)

POWELL, Sir Raymond; kt (1996), MP (Lab) Ogmore (majority 23,827); s of Albert Powell; *b* 19 June 1928; *Educ* Pentre GS, Nat Cncl of Labour Colls, LSE; *m* 1951, Marion Grace Evans; 1 s, 1 da; *Career* sec/agent Ogmore CLP 1965–79, chm Lab Pty Wales 1977–78, chm S Wales Euro-Constituency Lab Pty 1979–80 (memb Exec Ctee 1965–79 and 1983–); MP (Lab) Ogmore 1979–, memb Select Ctee on: Employment 1979–82, Wales 1982–85, HOC Servs 1987–, HOC Servs Accomodation 1987–; oppn whip Wales 1983–87, accommodation whip 1987–95, pairing whip 1987–95; chm New Building Ctee 1987–91, chm Accommodation Ctee 1991–, chm Wales Ctee 1991–; sec Anglo-Bulgaria All Pty Parly Gp 1982–, sec Welsh Gp Lab MP's 1985–, vice-chm PLP Agriculture Ctee 1987–88, sec/organiser All Party Parly Gp on Fairs and Showgrounds 1987–; *Style—* Sir Raymond Powell, MP; ✉ House of Commons, London SW1A 0AA (☎ 0171 219 3000)

POWELL, Sir Richard Royle; GCB (1967, KCB 1961, CB 1951), KBE (1954), CMG (1946); s of Ernest Hartley Powell; *b* 30 July 1909; *Educ* Queen Mary's GS Walsall, Sidney Sussex Coll Cambridge; *Career* dep sec: Admty 1948–50, MOD 1950–56; perm sec: MOD 1956–59, BOT 1960–68; dep chm Perm Ctee on Invisible Exports 1968–76; chm: Alusuisse (UK) Ltd 1969–84, Sandoz Gp of cos 1972–87, Wilkinson Match Ltd 1979–80 (hon pres 1981–83); dir: Hill Samuel Group 1968–79, General Electric Company 1968–79, Whessoe plc 1968–87, Philip Hill Investment Tst 1968–81, Ladbroke Group plc 1980–86, Bridgewater Paper Co Ltd 1983–90, Aero-Print Ltd 1969–84, Clerical Medical and General Life Assurance Society 1972–85, BPB Industries plc 1973–83, Philip Hill & Partners 1981–86; chm Civil Service Security Appeals Panel until 1982; hon fell Sidney Sussex Coll Cambridge 1972; *Clubs* Athenaeum; *Style—* Sir Richard Powell, GCB, KBE, CMG; ✉ 56 Montagu Sq, London W1H 1TG (☎ 0171 262 0911)

POWELL, Robert; *b* 1 June 1944; *Career* actor; *Theatre* incl: repertory Stoke-on-Trent 1964–65, Hamlet (Leeds) 1971, Travesties (RSC) 1975, Terra Nova (Watford) 1982, Private Dick 1982–83, Tovarich (Chichester Festival Theatre, nat tour then Piccadilly Theatre) 1991, Sherlock Holmes - The Musical (Bristol Old Vic and nat tour) 1993; *Television* incl: Doomwatch 1969–70, title role in Shelley (BBC film) 1971, Jude the Obscure (BBC series) 1971, Mrs Warren's Profession 1972, Mr Rolls and Mr Royce 1972, Looking for Clancy (serial) 1975, title role in Zefirelli's Jesus of Nazareth 1976 (Best Actor TV Times and Italian TV Times Awards, Int Arts Prize Fiuggi Film Festival, Grand Prize St Vincent Film Festival Italy), You Never Can Tell (BBC) 1977, The Four Feathers (NBC) 1978, Pygmalion 1981, The Hunchback of Notre Dame (CBS) 1982, Frankenstein (Yorkshire) 1984, Shaka Zulu (series) 1985, Richard Hannay in Hannay (Thames, 2 series) 1987–88, Ambrosius in Merlin and the Crystal Cave (Noel Gay/BBC) 1991, Cortez in The Golden Years (Brook/Channel 4) 1992, DC Dave Briggs in The Detectives (BBC series) 1992; *Films* incl: Secrets 1971, Running Scared 1972, The Asphyx 1972, Asylum 1972, title role in Ken Russell's Mahler 1974, Capt Walker in Ken Russell's Tommy 1975, Beyond Good and Evil 1977, The Thirty-Nine Steps 1978, Harlequin 1980 (Best Actor Paris Film Festival), Jane Austen in Manhattan 1980, The Survivor 1980, Imperative 1981 (Best Actor Venice Film Festival 1982), The Jigsaw Man 1982, What Walts Below 1983, D'Annunzio and I 1986, Down There in the Jungle (Venezuela) 1987, The Sign of Command 1989, The Long Conversation with a Bird 1990, The First Circle 1990, Once on Chunuk Bair 1991, The Mystery of Edwin Drood 1992; *Style—* Robert Powell, Esq; ✉ c/o Jonathan Altaras Associates Ltd, 27 Floral Street, London WC2E 9DP (☎ 0171 836 8722, fax 0171 836 6066)

POWELL, (Stephen) Roy; s of Edward Powell, of Didsbury, nr Manchester, and Miriam Powell; *b* 2 March 1958; *Educ* Parrs' Wood Sch Manchester, Univ of Warwick (BA); *Career* articled clerk Arthur Andersen 1979–83, analyst Esmark Inc 1983–85, Euro fin dir Saatchi & Saatchi Co Plc 1985–86, gp fin dir BSB Dorland Ltd 1986–93, sr vice pres commercial devpt BSB Worldwide 1993–; memb Fin Policy Gp IPA 1990–; ACA 1982, MIPA 1989; *Publications* Agency Remuneration (in-house, 1991); *Recreations* Formula One; *Style—* Roy Powell, Esq; ✉ BSB Worldwide Inc, Chrysler Building, 405 Lexinton Avenue, New York, NY 10174, USA (☎ 00 1 212 297 8325)

POWELL, Roy Colin; s of Fred Johnson, of Florida, and Mildy Powell (d 1986); *b* 30 April 1965; *Educ* Batley HS for Boys; *m* 9 July 1993, Helen, *née* Browell; 1 s (Lewis Spencer b 26 Oct 1995); *Career* rugby league second row forward Featherstone Rovers RLFC; formerly with Leeds RLFC and Bradford Northern RLFC; 4 caps Yorkshire; GB: 5 under 21 caps, 19 full caps, toured 1988 and 1990; Carryfast 1981–82, Co-op Maintenance Dept 1982–83, Cave and Gerrald 1983, Walter West Builders 1983, Plastering Div Miller Construction 1983–85, Simmons & Wainwright Plasterers 1985–86, self-employed plasterer 1986–; *Recreations* photography, learning to play the piano; *Style—* Roy Powell, Esq

POWELL, Sandy; *b* 7 April 1960; *Educ* St Martin's Coll of Art and Design, Central Sch of Art; *Career* costume and set designer; costume designer for Mick Jagger on The Rolling Stones European Urban Jungle tour 1990 and for all shows by The Cholmondoleys and The Featherstonehaughs; *Theatre* numerous credits incl: Edward II (dir Gerard Murphy, RSC), Rigoletto (dir Wagtmachers, Netherlands Opera); *Film* costume design incl: Cobachan (dir Lindsay Kemp), The Last of England (dir Derek Jarman), Stormy Monday (dir Mike Figgis), The Pope Must Die (dir Peter Richardson), Edward II (dir Derek Jarman, recipient Evening Standard Award), Caravaggio (dir Derek Jarman), Venus Peter (dir Ian Sellar), The Miracle (dir Neil Jordan), The Crying Game (dir Neil Jordan), Orlando (dir Sally Potter, winner Best Technical Achievement Award Evening Standard Awards 1994, Oscar nomination 1994), Being Human (dir Bill Forsyth), Interview with a Vampire (dir Neil Jordan), Rob Roy (dir Michael Caton Jones), Michael Collins (dir Neil Jordan), The Butcher Boy (dir Neil Jordan), The Wings of the Dove (dir Iain Softley); *Style—* Ms Sandy Powell; ✉ c/o London Management, 2–4 Noel Street, London W1V 3RB (☎ 0171 287 9000, fax 0171 287 3036)

POWELL, Stephen Joseph; s of Joseph Thomas Powell (d 1958), of Goffs Oak, Herts, and Dorothy May, *née* Welch; *b* 26 May 1943; *Educ* Cheshunt GS, The Royal Dental Hosp of London Sch of Dental Surgery (BDS); *m* 6 July 1968, Yvonne Heather, da of Sydney Frederick Williams, of Pucklechurch, nr Bristol; 2 da (Rebecca b 1986, Charlotte b 1991); *Career* sr registrar in orthodontics Hosp for Sick Children Gt Ormond St and The Royal Dental Hosp London 1972–74; conslt in orthodontics: The Royal Dental Hosp London and St George's Hosp London 1975–, King's Coll Hosp Sch of Med and Dentistry 1986–; memb: BDA, Br Soc for the Study of Orthodontics, European Orthodontic Soc, American Assoc of Orthodontists; cncl memb Soc of St Augustine of Canterbury; FDS RCS, MOrth RCS; *Recreations* swimming, music, theatre, French culture; *Clubs* Athenaeum; *Style—* Stephen Powell, Esq; ✉ 5 Hood Rd, Wimbledon, London SW20 0SR (☎ 0181 946 3401); St George's Hospital, Blackshaw Rd, Tooting, London SW17

0LT; 2A Barham Rd, Wimbledon, London SW20 0EU (☎ 0181 946 3064, car 0385 291182)

POWELL, Timothy Douglas; s of Mr R J Powell, of Radwell, Herts, and Mrs W A Powell, *née* Bray; *b* 31 Dec 1966; *Educ* Barnfield Coll Luton Beds 1984–86; *Career* commis chef rising to first commis The Mansion House Middx 1986–87, first commis rising to demi chef de partie Ettington Park Hotel Stratford upon Avon 1987–88, premier commis rising to demi chef de partie The Ritz Hotel London 1988–89, chef de partie La Tante Claire London 1989–90, chef de partie Hotel des Rochers France 1990–91, sous chef Midsummer House Cambridge 1991–92, sous chef The Hampshire Hotel London 1992–93, sr sous chef Le Pont de la Tour London 1993–95, chef The Canteen Chelsea Harbour 1995–; *Awards* 3 medals West of England Salon Culinaire 1988, English finalist Pierre Taittinger Int Culinary Prize, winner Caterer & Hotelkeeper Menu of the Year 1996; *Style*— Timothy Powell, Esq; ✉ The Canteen, Unit G4, Harbour Yard, Chelsea Harbour, London SW10 0XD (☎ 0171 351 7330, fax 0171 351 6189)

POWELL, Timothy Martin (Minnow); s of Arthur Barrington Powell CMG, and Jane, *née* Weir; *b* 17 Sept 1954; *Educ* Ampleforth, Jesus Coll Oxford (BA); *m* Victoria Elizabeth, da of Peter Geoffrey Holmes; 2 s (Alexander James Barrington b 26 June 1987, Toby Peter Johnathan b 3 Aug 1990); *Career* Touche Ross (now Deloitte & Touche): joined 1976, CA 1979, ptnr 1985–; FCA; *Recreations* golf; *Clubs* Northern Counties, Woking Golf, Royal Porthcawl Golf, Rye Golf, Royal St Georges Golf, Royal and Ancient Golf, Royal West Norfolk, Northumberland Golf; *Style*— Minnow Powell, Esq; ✉ Deloitte & Touche, Hill House, 1 Little New Street, London EC4A 3TR (☎ 0171 936 3000, fax 0171 583 8517)

POWELL, William Rhys; MP (C) Corby (majority 342); Pst s of Rev Canon Edward Powell, formerly Vicar and Lord of the Manor of Belchamp St Paul, Sudbury, Suffolk, and Anne Woodhouse, *née* Newton; descends from Walter Powell (d 1567), of Bucknell, Salop who descended from Rhys ap Tewdwr Mawr, King of South Wales; kinsman of Sir Nicholas Powell, 4 Bt, *qv*; *b* 3 Aug 1948; *Educ* Lancing, Emmanuel Coll Cambridge (MA); *m* 1973, (Mary) Elizabeth, da of Adolphus Henry Vaudin, of Great Bookham, Surrey; 3 da; *Career* called to the Bar Lincoln's Inn 1971; MP (C) Corby 1983–; PPS to: Timothy Raison as Min for Overseas Devpt 1985–86, Rt Hon Michael Heseltine as Sec of State for the Environment 1990–92; memb Select Ctees on: Commons Procedure 1987–90, Foreign Affrs 1990–91, Science and Technol 1992–95, Agriculture 1995–; chm: Br-Italian Parly Gp 1992–92, Br-Taiwan Parly Gp 1992–, Br-Mongolia Parly Gp 1993–, Br-Tunisia Gp 1994; *Clubs* Corby Cons; *Style*— William Powell, Esq, MP; ✉ House of Commons, London SW1A 0AA; Lynch House, Fowlmere, Cambs

POWELL-JONES, John Ernest; CMG (1974); s of late Walter James Powell-Jones, and Gladys Margaret, *née* Taylor; *b* 14 April 1925; *Educ* Charterhouse, Univ Coll Oxford; *m* 1, 1949 (m dis 1967), Ann Murray; 2 s, 1 da; m 2, 1968, Pamela Sale; *Career* HM Foreign Serv: entered 1949, ambass Phnom Penh 1973–75, RCDS 1975; ambass: Senegal, Guinea, Mali, Mauritania and Guinea-Bissau 1976–79, Cape Verde 1977–79, Switzerland 1982–85; ret 1985; ambass and perm rep UN Conf on Law of the Sea (concluded Dec 1982) 1979–82; chm Inter Counsel (UK) Ltd 1986–93; cncllr Waverley Borough Cncl 1987–95, vice chm Wonersh Parish Cncl 1990–; memb: Ctee Hurtwood Control 1987–95, Bd Surrey Historic Bldgs Tst 1988–92, Ctee Winkworth Arboretum 1988–, Cncl Cranleigh and SE Eng Agric Soc 1991–95; *Clubs* Travellers'; *Style*— John Powell-Jones, Esq, CMG; ✉ Gascons, Gaston Gate, Cranleigh, Surrey (☎ 01483 274313)

POWELL-JONES, Robert James; s of John Ernest Powell-Jones, CMG, of Cranleigh, Surrey, and Ann Elizabeth, *née* Murray; *b* 6 Jan 1954; *Educ* Winchester, Wadham Coll Oxford (BA); *m* 1980 (m dis 1992), Flora Elizabeth, da of Rt Hon Maj Sir Hugh Charles Patrick Joseph Fraser, MBE, MP, PC (d 1984); 1 da (Stella Elizabeth b 1987); *Career* called to the Bar Middle Temple 1978; *Style*— Robert Powell-Jones, Esq; ✉ 13 Old Square, Lincoln's Inn, London WC2 (☎ 0171 404 4800, fax 0171 405 4267)

POWELL-SMITH, Christopher Brian; s of Edgar Powell-Smith (d 1970), of Horley, Surrey, and Theodora Kirkham Baker (d 1984); *b* 3 Oct 1936; *Educ* City of London Sch, Law Soc's Sch of Law (Travers-Smith scholar, Clements Inn Prize); *m* 1964, Jenny, da of Douglas Goslett; 2 da (Amanda b 1968, Emily b 1972), 2 s (Giles b 1970, Edward b 1975); *Career* McKenna & Co: ptnr 1964–, managing ptnr 1984–88, head Corp Dept 1988–92, sr ptnr 1992–; non-exec dir Carlsberg Brewery Ltd 1987–92, non-exec chm Black & Decker Group Inc 1988– (non-exec dir 1970–); memb Ctee of Mgmnt Thames Valley Housing Assoc 1995–; TA: cmdg offr HAC 1976–78, regtl Col and master gunner HM Tower of London 1978–80; memb: Law Soc 1959, Int Bar Assoc 1975, City of London Slrs' Co 1987; *Recreations* golf, choral singing, walking; *Clubs* City of London, Brooks's, Royal Mid-Surrey Golf; *Style*— Christopher Powell-Smith, Esq, TD; ✉ McKenna & Co, Mitre House, 160 Aldersgate Street, London EC1A 4DD (☎ 0171 606 9000, fax 0171 606 9100)

POWELL-TUCK, Dr Jeremy; s of late Dr Geoffrey Alan Powell-Tuck, and Catherine Gwendoline, *née* Kirby, of Cleeve Hill, nr Cheltenham; *b* 20 May 1948; *Educ* Epsom Coll, Univ of Birmingham (MB ChB, MD); *m* Fiona Caroline, da of Charles William Sandison Crabbe (d 1969); 1 s (Thomas b 1984), 2 da (Amy b 1987, Rosie b 1988); *Career* res fell St Mark's Hosp 1974–80, res fell Dept of Nutrition London Sch of Hygiene and Tropical Med 1980–81, sr registrar of med and gastroenterology Charing Cross, W Middx and Westminster Hosps 1981–88, head Rank Dept of Human Nutrition London Hosp Med Coll and conslt physician The Royal London Hosp 1988–; contrib chapters on nutritional therapy and gastro-intestinal disease; dep chm Bd of Studies in Nutrition and Food Science Univ of London; memb: Ctee WHO Steering Gp, Network for Nutrition Educn in Med Schs, Cncl Euro Soc for Parenteral and Enteral Nutrition, Cncl Br Assoc for Parenteral and Enteral Nutrition; FRSM 1976, FRCP 1992 (MRCP 1973); *Recreations* choral music, tennis; *Style*— Dr Jeremy Powell-Tuck; ✉ 9 Horbury Crescent, London W11 3NF (☎ 0171 727 2528); Department of Human Nutrition, London Hospital Medical College, Turner Street, London E1 (☎ 0171 377 7794)

POWER, Sir Alastair John Cecil; 4 Bt (UK 1924), of Newlands Manor, Milford, Southampton; s of Sir John Patrick McLannahan Power, 3 Bt (d 1984), and Melanie, adopted da of Hon Alastair Erskine (d 1987; s of 6 Baron Erskine); *b* 15 Aug 1958; *Heir* bro, Adam Patrick Cecil Power b 22 March 1963; *Style*— Sir Alastair Power, Bt

POWER, Dr Anne; MBE; *Career* Martin Luther King Southern Christian Leadership Conference 1966, warden Africa Centre London 1966–67, co-ordinator Friends Neighbourhood House 1967–72, co-ordinator North Islington Housing Rights Project 1972–78, nat conslt DOE Priority Estates Project 1979–87, advsr Welsh Office and Rhondda BC 1989–93; LSE: successively academic visitor, pt/t research offr Dept of Social Admin then visiting research assoc Dept of Social Policy 1981–88, currently reader in social policy, course dir of postgraduate MSc/dip in housing and co-ordinator Housing Research Centre; dir Bootstrap Enterprise; fndr dir Nat Tenants Resource Centre; advsy memb panel of experts to EC on urban problems and social segregation in cities, co-opted memb Ctee Holloway Tenant Co-op; assoc LSE: Welfare State Prog, Inter-disciplinary Centre for Mgmnt; *Books* Property before people: the management of twentieth century council housing (1987), Housing Management - A Guide to Quality and Creativity (1991), Hovels to High-rise - State Housing in Europe since 1850 (1993), Estates on the Edge - The social consequences of mass housing in Northern Europe (1996); also author of numerous governmental reports and articles in the press on social policy and housing issues; *Style*— Dr Anne Power, MBE; ✉ Department of Social Policy and Administration, London School of Economics and Political Science, Houghton Street, London WC2A 2AE (☎ 0171 405 7686, fax 0171 955 7415)

POWER, Gordon Robert; s of Robert Alfred Power, of Northborough, Cambs, and Amelia Barbara, *née* Jukes; *b* 24 June 1953; *Educ* Romford Tech HS; *m* 1977, Brigid Sheilagh, *née* Collins; 1 s (Christopher Michael b 1980), 1 da (Helen Elizabeth b 1983); *Career* audit mangr H Graham King & Co CAs London 1969–73, asst internal audit mangr Thomas Borthwick & Sons UK plc (meat wholesalers) 1973–77, divnl accountant London Meat Wholesaling Div Spillers Ltd 1977–78, gp financial controller Guinness Peat Group plc 1978–88, md Guinness Mahon Development Capital Ltd 1988– (following demerger of Guinness Mahon from GPG); ACEA 1978, MIMgt 1989, MInstD 1989; *Recreations* tennis, sailing; *Style*— Gordon Power, Esq; ✉ Guinness Mahon Development Capital Ltd, 32 St Mary at Hill, London EC3P 3AJ (☎ 0171 623 6222, fax 0171 623 4313)

POWER, John Graham; s of Lawrence David Power (d 1953), and (Pamela) Joy, *née* Stanley; *b* 4 Oct 1946; *Educ* Eastbourne GS, Univ of Bristol (BA); *m* 27 March 1986, Fiona Elizabeth, da of David Greg; 1 s (Oliver Lawrence b 13 Jan 1987), 1 da (Megan Louise b 26 Oct 1989); *Career* Touche Ross (now Deloitte & Touche): joined 1975, tax ptnr 1979, tax ptnr corp fin 1991–; FCA 1971, FTII 1973; *Books* Tax Aspects of Going Public (1989); *Recreations* walking, reading; *Style*— John Power, Esq; ✉ Deloitte & Touche, Stonecutter Court, 1 Stonecutter Street, London EC4A 4TR (☎ 0171 936 3000, fax 0171 583 1198)

POWER, Jonathan Richard Adrian; s of Patrick Power (d 1994), of Boars Hill, Oxford, and Dorothy Power (d 1984); *b* 4 June 1941; *Educ* Liverpool Inst HS, Univ of Manchester (BA), Univ of Wisconsin (MA); *m* 1, 22 Dec 1964 (m dis 1988), Anne Elizabeth, da of Dennis Hayward, of Southampton; 3 da (Carmen b 18 Jan 1966, Miriam b 23 May 1968, Lucy b 24 Nov 1978); m 2, Jean-Christine, da of Arvid Eklund, of Gothenburg, Sweden; 1 da (Jenny b 25 June 1990); *Career* foreign affrs columnist International Herald Tribune 1974–91, independent foreign affrs columnist 1991– (column syndicated to 16 princ US, Canadian and European papers and 20 African, Asian and Australasian papers); memb Int Inst for Strategic Studies 1980, memb Common Room Queen Elizabeth House Univ of Oxford 1996–; *Film* It's Ours Whatever They Say (Silver Medal Venice Film Festival 1972); *Books* Development Economics, World of Hunger, The New Proletariat, Against Oblivion, Vision of Hope - 50 Years of the United Nations; *Recreations* walking, cycling, opera; *Style*— Jonathan Power, Esq; ✉ Little House, Lincombe Lane, Boars Hill, Oxford OX1 5DU (☎ and fax 01865 735645)

POWER, Vince; s of John Power (d 1972), and Brigid Power (d 1986); *b* 29 April 1947; *Educ* Dungarvan Vocational Coll; *m* 1967 (m dis 1979); 3 c; 2 c from 1 ptnr; 3 c from current ptnr; *Career* owner chain furniture shops N London 1964–82; opened The Mean Fiddler Harlesden 1982 (became The Mean Fiddler Organisation 1987); also fndr: Subterania 1989, The Grand Clapham 1991, The Jazz Cafe 1992, The Forum 1993, The Garage 1993, Upstairs at the Garage 1994, The Crossbar 1995, The Mean Fiddler Dublin 1995, The Palace Luton 1995, The Powerhaus 1996, The Complex 1996, The Cube 1996; promoter: Reading Festival 1989–, London Fleadh 1990–, Phoenix Festival 1993–, Tribal Gathering 1995–, Madstock 1992, 1994 and 1996, Neil Young 1993, Paul Weller 1996, The Sex Pistols 1996 (first UK performance for 20 years); patron UNICEF, involved with Cradle (Bosnian children's charity); Irish Post Award 1995; *Style*— Vince Power, Esq; ✉ The Mean Fiddler Organization, 22–28A High Street, Harlesden, London NW10 4LX (☎ 0181 961 5490, fax 0181 961 9414)

POWERS, Dr Anthony Jonathan William; s of Michael Powers (d 1994), and Frances, *née* Wilson; *b* 13 March 1953; *Educ* Marlborough, The Queen's Coll Oxford (BA), Univ of York (DPhil), private study with Nadia Boulanger; *m* 1984, Helen Frances, da of late Dr C Priday; 1 s (Richard b 1991), 1 da (Camilla b 1993); *Career* lectr in music Dartington Coll of Arts 1978–80, composer in res Southern Arts 1980–82, tutor in composition Univ of Exeter and Dartington Coll of Arts 1983–86, composer in res Univ of Wales Cardiff 1989–; chm Assoc of Professional Composers 1995– (memb 1985); *Compositions* incl: Stone, Water, Stars (BBC Symphony Orch) 1987, Horn Concerto (Royal Liverpool Philharmonic Orch) 1990, Cello Concerto (Kings Lynn Festival) 1990, Terrain (BBC Nat Orch of Wales) 1993, Symphony (BBC Nat Orch of Wales, premièred BBC Proms) 1996; *Clubs* Savile; *Style*— Dr Anthony Powers; ✉ c/o Music Department, Oxford University Press, 70 Baker Street, London W1M 1DJ (☎ 0171 616 5900, fax 0171 616 5901)

POWERS, Dr Michael John; QC (1995); s of late Reginald Frederick Powers, of Parkstone, Poole, and Kathleen Ruby, *née* Whitmarsh; *b* 9 Feb 1947; *Educ* Poole GS, Middx Hosp Med Sch London (BSc, MB BS, DA), Poly of Central London (Dip Law); *m* 16 Nov 1968 (sep 1989), Meryl Julia, da of Frank Edward Hall, of Queen's Park, Bournemouth; 1 s (Andrew b 1982), 1 da (Julia b 1972); *Career* registered med practitioner 1972–, house surgn Middx Hosp 1972–73, house physician Royal S Hants Hosp 1973–74, sr house offr Royal Utd Hosp Bath 1974–75, registrar (anaesthetics) Northwick Park Hosp Harrow 1975–77; called to the Bar Lincoln's Inn 1979, practising at Common Law Bar specialising in med and pharmaceutical law, HM asst dep coroner Westminster 1981–87; pres SE Eng Coroners Soc 1987–88; students' cnsllr to Hon Soc Lincoln's Inn 1983–90, memb: Soc of Doctors in Law, BMA, Medico-Legal Soc; FRSM 1972; *Books* The Law and Practice on Coroners (with Paul Knapman 1985), Casebook on Coroners (with Paul Knapman, 1989), Medical Negligence (with Nigel Harris, 1990 and 1994); *Recreations* sailing, hill walking, painting, and music; *Clubs* Bar Yacht, Royal Yachting Assoc, Nat Liberal, Royal Thames; *Style*— Dr Michael Powers, QC; ✉ 1 Paper Buildings, Temple, London, EC4Y 7EP (☎ 0171 583 7355, fax 0171 353 2144)

POWERS, William; MBE (1982), JP, DL (Beds 1989); s of Capt John Powers (d 1974), and Doris Gladys, *née* Rickard; *b* 2 Sept 1924; *m* 27 June 1953, Janet Elsie Elisabeth, da of Archibald Fletcher; 2 da (Lynda Elisabeth b 1954, Jane Alison b 1957); *Career* Beds & Herts Regt 1941, 9 Commando 2 Special Serv Bde 1942–45 (despatches 1943), Mounted Police Palestine 1945–47, appointed Dist Supt 1947, Trans-Jordan Frontier Force 1947–49, seconded Maj; chief exec Shaw & Kilburn Luton 1968–86, chm S Bedfordshire Health Care Tst 1990–; patron: Luton & Dist Royal Br Legion, Luton & Dunstable Burma Star Assoc; vice pres: Luton Household Div Assoc, Luton Royal Naval Assoc; dir Bedfordshire Musical Pageant, pres Luton and Dunstable Operatic Soc, JP and dep chm Luton Magistrates' Ct, chm S Beds Cmmrs of Taxes, memb The Lord Chancellor's Advsy Ctee, High Sheriff of Beds 1987; FIMI 1965; *Clubs* The Household Div Luton; *Style*— William Powers, Esq, MBE, JP, DL; ✉ The Old Vicarage, Ludham, Norfolk NR29 5QA (☎ 01692 678663)

POWERS-FREELING, Laurel Claire; da of Lloyd Marion Powers, of Bloomfield Hills, Michigan, and Catharine Joyce, *née* Berry (d 1992); *b* 16 May 1957; *Educ* Bloomfield Andover HS Michigan, Barnard Coll Columbia Univ NY (AB), Alfred P Sloan Sch MIT (MS); *m* 28 Jan 1989, Dr Anthony Nigel Stanley Freeling, s of Prof Paul Freeling, OBE; 1 s (Matthew Charles Powers-Freeling b 26 Dec 1991), 1 da (Catharine Grace Powers-Freeling b 1 March 1994); *Career* sr conslt Price Waterhouse Boston and NY 1983–85 (conslt 1980–85), mangr McKinsey & Co Inc London and NY 1987–89 (conslt 1985–87), corp fin offr Morgan Stanley International London 1989–91; Prudential Corporation plc: dir of corp strategy 1991–93, dir of private financial planning servs 1993–94; gp fin dir Lloyds Abbey Life plc 1994–; *Recreations* classical music, cookery; *Clubs* Cliveden, Riverside; *Style*— Mrs Laurel Powers-Freeling; ✉ Lloyds Abbey Life plc, 205 Brooklands Road, Weybridge, Surrey KT13 0PE (☎ 01932 850888)

POWERSCOURT, 10 Viscount (I 1743); Mervyn Niall Wingfield; also Baron Wingfield (I 1743), and Baron Powerscourt (UK 1885, title in House of Lords); s of 9 Viscount Powerscourt (d 1973), and Sheila Claude, *née* Beddington (d 1992); *b* 3 Sept 1935; *Educ* Stowe; *m* 1, 1962 (m dis 1974), Wendy Ann Pauline, da of Ralph C G Slazenger; 1 s, 1 da; m 2, 1979 (m dis 1995), Pauline, da of W P Van, of San Francisco, Calif; *Heir* s, Hon Mervyn Anthony Wingfield; *Style—* The Rt Hon the Viscount Powerscourt

POWIS, 8 Earl of (UK 1804); Dr John George Herbert; also Baron Powis, of Powis Castle, Co Montgomery, Baron Herbert of Chirbury, Co Salop, and Viscount Clive, of Ludlow, Co Salop (all UK 1804), Baron Clive, of Walcot, Co Salop (GB 1794), and Baron Clive of Plassey, Co Limerick (I 1762); eldest s of 7 Earl of Powis (d 1993), and Hon Katharine Odeyne de Grey, yst da of 8 Baron Walsingham, DSO, OBE (d 1965); *b* 19 May 1952; *Educ* Wellington Coll, McMaster Univ Ontario (MA, PhD); *m* 1977, Marijke Sophia, eldest da of Maarten N Guther, of Ancaster, Ontario, Canada; 2 s (Jonathan Nicholas William, Viscount Clive, Hon Alexander Sebastian George b 1994), 2 da (Lady Stephanie Moira Christina b 1982, Lady Samantha Julie Esther b 1988); *Heir* s, Viscount Clive b 5 Dec 1979; *Career* asst prof of English lit Redeemer Coll Ancaster Ontario 1989–92; *Style—* The Rt Hon the Earl of Powis; ✉ Powis Castle, Welshpool, Powys

POWIS, Russell John; s of George Henry Powis, of Birmingham, and Nellie, *née* Croft; *b* 6 Aug 1947; *Educ* Yardley GS; *m* 30 May 1970, Susan Mary, da of Ernest John Cotterill; 3 s (Richard James Andrew b 27 Feb 1973, David Russell James b 1 Oct 1974, Stephen Robert Edward b 1 Jan 1983); *Career* articled clerk Russell Durie Kerr Watson and Co 1965–70; Coopers & Lybrand: joined 1976 (Birmingham), tax ptnr (Cardiff) 1982–, ptnr i/c tax practice 1990–; FCA (ACA 1970); *Recreations* spectator sports, golf; *Clubs* Cardiff and County; *Style—* Russell Powis, Esq; ✉ Coopers & Lybrand, Churchill House, Churchill Way, Cardiff CF1 4XQ (☎ 01222 237000, fax 01222 223361)

POWLES, Dr Raymond Leonard; s of Leonard William David Powles (d 1989), and Florence Irene, *née* Conolly; *b* 9 March 1938; *Educ* Eltham Coll, Bart's Med Sch London (BSc, MB BS, MD); *m* 1980, Louise Jane, da of Roy Frederick Richmond; 3 s (Sam Tristan Richmond b 2 Feb 1982, Luke Alexander Richmond (twin) b 2 Feb 1982, Max Ashley Richmond b 30 May 1989), 1 da (Gabriella Louise b 12 April 1985); *Career* house physician Bart's London 1965–66, resident med offr Royal Marsden Hosp London 1967–68, Leukaemia Fund fell to Prof George Mathe Ville Juif Paris 1968, Tata Meml Fund leukaemia fell Royal Marsden Hosp and Inst of Cancer Res Sutton Surrey 1969–72, Imperial Cancer Res Fund sr scientific offr Bart's 1972–74, currently chief of haemato-oncology and head/physician-in-charge Leukaemia Unit and Myeloma Unit Royal Marsden Hosp; recognised teacher Univ of London 1977–, clinical tutor RCP 1990–; invited lectures throughout world on leukaemia res and treatment, author of over 583 scientific papers and book chapters on leukaemia; variously memb: Royal Marsden Special Health Authy, MRC Working Pty on Leukaemia, UK Cancer Co-Ordinating Sub-Ctee on Leukaemia and Bone Marrow Transplantation (UKCCCR), Dept of Health Standing Med Advsy Sub-Ctee on Cancer, Br Assoc for Cancer Res, American Cancer Soc Sci Writers' Alumni, Euro Bone Marrow Transplantation Soc Working Pty for Leukaemia, Int Bone Marrow Transplant Registry Advsy Ctee, WHO Ctee Int Prog of Leukaemia Effects of the Chernobyl Accident, EORTC Anti-Fungal Ctee, SW Thames Regional Negotiating Team (Drugs and Supplies), London Bone Marrow Transplant Gp; sometime hon conslt CEGB; med advsr: The Bud Flanagan Leukaemia Fund, Leukaemia Soc of Ireland; specialist leukaemia advsr to BACUP; variously memb Editorial Bd: Leukaemia Research, Bone Marrow Transplantation, Indian Jl of Cancer Chemotherapy, Indian Jl of Med and Paediatric Oncology, Experimental Haematology; memb Int Advsy Panel: for virus infections Wellcome Ltd, on fungus infections Pfizer Ltd, on leukaemia Pharmitalia Carlo Erba Ltd; memb: Bd Euro Soc for Med Oncology, Euro Bone Marrow Transplantation Soc, Int Soc for Experimental Haematology, Int Transplantation Soc, American Soc of Haematology, Int Immunocompromised Host Soc, Euro Haematology Assoc, Br Soc of Haematology, Br Transplantation Soc, Assoc of Cancer Physicians, Br Soc of Pharmaceutical Med, Br Acad of Forensic Scis, BMA; FRCP 1980, FRCPath 1993; *Recreations* sport, cinema, cooking; *Style—* Dr Raymond Powles; ✉ Little Garratts, 19 Garratts Lane, Banstead, Surrey SM7 2EA (☎ 01737 353632); The Royal Marsden Hospital, Downs Road, Sutton, Surrey SM2 5PT (☎ 0181 642 6011, fax 0181 770 7313)

POWLES, Stephen Robert; QC (1995); s of Andrew Frederick Arthur Powles, and Nora, *née* Bristol; *b* 7 June 1948; *Educ* Westminster, Univ Coll Oxford (MA); *m* 12 April 1975, Geraldine Patricia Hilda, da of Dr Campbell Millar Taggart Adamson; 1 s (Henry b 1979), 1 da (Olivia b 1981); *Career* called to the Bar Middle Temple 1972 (Harmsworth maj exhibitioner, Astbury law scholar), Lincoln's Inn 1976, legal assessor UK Central Cncl for Nurses & Midwives 1987–, asst recorder of the Crown Court 1993–; *Recreations* sailing, hill walking, joinery; *Clubs* Royal Solent Yacht; *Style—* Stephen Powles, Esq, QC; ✉ 2 Harcourt Buildings, Middle Temple Lane, Temple, London EC4Y 9DB (☎ 0171 583 9020, fax 0171 583 2686)

POWLES, Dr Trevor James; s of Leonard William David Powles (d 1989), and Florence Irene, *née* Conolly; *b* 8 March 1938; *Educ* Eltham Coll, Bart's Med Coll (BSc, MB BS, MRCP, PhD); *m* Penelope Margaret, da of Walter and Doreen Meyers, of Durban, SA; 2 s (James Watson b 19 Dec 1969, Thomas Bartholomew b 10 April 1971), 1 da (Lucy Alexandra b 31 Jan 1975); *Career* house physician and registrar Royal Postgrad Med Sch Hammersmith Hosp 1967–68, med registrar Bart's 1969–70, MRC clinical res fell Inst of Cancer Res London 1971–73; Royal Marsden Hosp London and Sutton: sr registrar and lectr 1974, sr lectr 1974–78, conslt physician 1978–, head Breast Cancer Unit; invited lectures throughout world on various aspects of breast cancer biology, diagnosis and treatment; breast cancer advsr Br Assoc for Cancer United Patients, tstee Breast Cancer Res Tst; memb: Cancer Res Campaign Adjuvant Breast Trial Working Pty, Soc of Endocrinology, Br Breast Gp, UK Cancer Coordinating Sub-Ctee on Breast Cancer, Assoc of Cancer Physicians, Int Soc for Cancer Chemoprevention (vice pres), Euro Soc for Med Oncology, American Soc of Clinical Oncology, American Assoc for the Advancement of Sci; FRCP 1983; *Books* Breast Cancer Management (jtly, 1981), Prostaglandins and Cancer (jtly, 1982), Medical Management of Breast Cancer (jtly, 1991); *Recreations* horse riding, skiing, reading; *Style—* Dr Trevor Powles; ✉ The Royal Marsden Hospital, London & Sutton, Downs Road, Sutton, Surrey SM2 5PT (☎ 0181 642 6011, fax 0181 770 7313)

POWLEY, Roger Peter; s of Frank William Powley (d 1991), of 17 King's Court, Beddington Gardens, Wallington, Surrey, and Jessie Ethel, *née* Shaw; *b* 6 May 1947; *Educ* St Joseph's Coll London; *m* 26 July 1975, Diana Mary, da of George Harrison Wray; 1 s (Adam Oliver b 18 Aug 1984), 2 da (Imogen Louise b 15 Sept 1982, Alannah Corinne b 2 June 1988); *Career* PA to sr ptnr Hays Allan (chartered accountants) 1973–75 (articled clerk then jr accountant 1966–73), asst to Gp Chief Accountant Courtaulds 1975–76, fin controller Mktg Servs Subsids Kimpher plc 1976–1978, fin dir TMD Advertising Ltd 1978–88; gp fin dir: TMD Advertising plc 1985–91, Carat UK Ltd 1991–; dir: Manning Gottlieb Media Ltd, Meridian Outdoor Ltd; FCA 1971; *Recreations* motor boating, sailing; *Clubs* Chichester Yacht, Bosham Sailing; *Style—* Roger Powley, Esq; ✉ Carat UK Ltd, New London House, 172 Drury Lane, London WC2B 5QR (☎ 0171 611 7654)

POWNALL, His Hon Judge; Henry Charles; QC (1979); s of John Cecil Glossop Pownall, CB (d 1967), and Margaret Nina, *née* Jesson (d 1992); *b* 25 Feb 1927; *Educ* Rugby, Trinity Coll Cambridge; *m* 1955, Sarah Bettine, da of Maj John Latham Deverell (d 1978); 1 s (Nicholas C D b 1959), 2 da (Emma M E b 1956 d 1957, Charlotte S J (Mrs Edward Mountain) b 1963); *Career* called to the Bar Inner Temple 1954; jr prosecuting counsel to the Crown at the Central Criminal Ct 1964–71, recorder of the Crown Ct 1972–84, bencher 1976, sr later second sr prosecuting counsel 1976–79, hon legal advsr ABA 1976–86, judge Cts of Appeal Jersey and Guernsey 1980–86, circuit judge (SE Circuit) 1984– (sr judge Knightsbridge Crown Ct 1984–88); pres Orders and Medals Res Soc 1971–75 and 1977–81 (memb Ctee 1961–69, 1970–71, 1975–76 and 1981–95); *Recreations* travel, medals and medal ribbons; *Clubs* Pratt's, Hurlingham, Ebury Court; *Style—* His Hon Judge Pownall, QC; ✉ Central Criminal Court, Old Bailey, London EC4M 7EH

POWNALL, Brig John Lionel; OBE (1972); s of John Cecil Glossop Pownall, CB (d 1967), and Margaret Nina, *née* Jesson (d 1992); *b* 10 May 1929; *Educ* Rugby, RMA Sandhurst; *m* 1962, Sylvia Joan Cameron, da of James Cameron Conn, WS (d 1957), of Hawick, Roxburghshire; 2 s (Richard b 1967, Edward b 1972); *Career* enlisted 1947, cmmnd 16/5 Lancers 1949, served in Egypt, Cyrenaica, Tripolitania, BAOR, Hong Kong, Cyprus; psc, jssc; cmd 16/5 The Queen's Royal Lancers 1969–71, Adj-Gen's Secretariat 1971–72, offr i/c RAC Manning and Records 1973–75, Col GS Near East Land Forces/Land Forces Cyprus 1975–78, asst dir def policy MOD 1978–79, Brig RAC UK Land Forces 1979–82, Brig MOD 1982–84, ret 1984, Col 16/5 The Queen's Royal Lancers 1985–90; dep chm Police Complaints Authy 1986–93 (memb 1985); *Recreations* country pursuits, opera, arts; *Clubs* Cavalry and Guards'; *Style—* Brig John Pownall, OBE; ✉ Sweatmans, Milland, Liphook, Hampshire GU30 7JT

POWNALL, Michael Graham; s of Raymond Pownall (d 1984), and Elizabeth Mary, *née* Robinson; *b* 11 Oct 1949; *Educ* Repton, Univ of Exeter (BA); *m* 14 Sept 1974, Deborah Ann, da of Thomas Hugh McQueen; 2 da (Sarah Elizabeth b 20 Aug 1978, Rebecca Claire b 19 May 1980); *Career* Parliament Office House of Lords: joined 1971, seconded as private sec to Leader of House of Lords and Govt Chief Whip 1980–83, establishment offr and sec to Chm of Ctees 1983–88, princ clerk Private Bill Office and examiner of petitions for private bills 1988–90, princ clerk of ctees and Overseas Office 1991–95, clerk of the jls and of Info Office 1995–97, reading clerk 1997–; *Recreations* birdwatching, tennis; *Clubs* Riverside Racquet; *Style—* Michael Pownall, Esq; ✉ 13 Flanders Road, London W4 1NQ (☎ 0181 994 0797); Journal Office, House of Lords, London SW1A 0PW (☎ 0171 219 3187)

POWNER, Prof Edwin Thomas (Eddie); s of Thomas Powner (d 1989), of Stoke on Trent, and Evelyn, *née* King; *b* 22 April 1938; *Educ* Univ of Durham (BSc), Univ of Manchester (MSc, PhD); *m* 8 Sept 1962, Barbara, da of William Henry Turner (d 1963), of Stoke on Trent; 2 s (Stephen John b 25 Dec 1966 d 13 March 1987, Peter David b 30 May 1972), 1 da (Suzanne b 18 March 1969); *Career* Inst of Sci and Technol Univ of Manchester: electronics engr 1960–63, lectr 1963–74, sr lectr 1974–79, reader 1979–80, prof of electronic engrg 1980–92, vice princ 1986–88, dean of technol 1989–92; Univ of Sussex: prof of electronic engrg 1992–, dean of engrg 1996–; author of numerous tech pubns; Inst of Nat Electrical Engrs: memb Cncl, chm Library Ctee, memb Professional Bd, memb Qualifications Bd, memb Membership Bd, memb Accreditation Bd, local chm NW Centre 1988–89; CEng, FIEE 1987 (memb 1965); *Books* Digital Simulation (jtly), Digital Signal Processing (jtly); *Recreations* photography, mechanisms and clocks, railways; *Style—* Prof Eddie Powner; ✉ School of Electric Engineering, University of Sussex, Falmer, Brighton BN1 9QT (☎ 01273 678622, fax 01273 678399)

POWNER, John; s of John Reginald Powner, of Kensington, London, and Jean, *née* McLeish; *b* 18 May 1962; *Educ* The Campion GS Hornchurch, Southend Coll of Technol, Brighton Poly (BA); *Career* graphic designer: Mitchell Beazley Publishing Ltd, The Advtg Bureau Sussex, Pentagram Design Ltd; fndr Atelier Works Ltd; Gold Award Lahti Biennale Competition 1989, Bronze Award TIA Typographic Excellence Competition 1993; *Recreations* classic motorcycles; *Clubs* D&AD, VMCC; *Style—* John Powner, Esq; ✉ Atelier Works, 14 The Dove Centre, 109 Bartholomew Road, London NW5 2BJ (☎ 0171 284 2215, fax 0171 284 2242)

POYNTER, Kieran Charles; s of Kenneth Reginald Poynter, of Sanderstead, Surrey, and Catherine Elizabeth, *née* Reilley; *b* 20 Aug 1950; *Educ* Salesian Coll, Imperial Coll London (BSc, ARCS); *m* 20 Aug 1977, Marylyn, da of Cmdt Thomas Melvin (d 1969), of Athlone, Ireland; 3 s (Dominic b 1979, Benedict b 1980, Andrew b 1983), 1 da (Louise b 1981); *Career* CA 1974; Price Waterhouse: joined 1971, ptnr 1982, sr ptnr 1993–, memb Supervisory Bd 1993–, memb Exec 1994–, managing ptnr 1996–, responsible for servs to insur sector in UK 1983–94 and in Europe 1989–94, memb Price Waterhouse World Firm Insurance Group 1986–94; memb: Insur Ctee ICAEW 1983–95, Standing Inter-Professional Liaison Gp Accounting and Actuarial Professions 1987–, Accounting and Auditing Standards Ctee Lloyd's of London 1988–90, Life Insur Accounting Ctee ABI 1992–94, HM Govt Task Force on Deregulation of Fin Servs Sector 1993–94; chm: Gooda Walker Loss Review Ctee at Lloyd's 1991–92, Syndicate 387 Loss Review at Lloyd's 1992–93, Solvency and Reporting Ctee at Lloyd's 1994–95; FCA 1979, FRSA 1994; *Recreations* golf, skiing, tennis; *Clubs* IOD, London Capital Club, Surrey Tennis and Country; *Style—* Kieran Poynter, Esq; ✉ Cranbrook, The South Border, Woodcote, Purley, Surrey CR8 3LL (☎ 0181 660 4723, fax 0181 660 5999); Price Waterhouse, Southwark Towers, 32 London Bridge Street, London SE1 9SY (☎ 0171 939 3000, fax 0171 939 2989, telex 884657/8)

POYNTON, Robert Alan (Joe); s of Alan Poynton, of Lelant, Cornwall, and Mabel Winifred, *née* Evans; *b* 28 Jan 1943; *Educ* King Edward's Sch Bath, Univ of Bath (BSc); *m* 14 Aug 1970, Jane Elizabeth, da of Leonard East, of The Manor, Cannington, Somerset; 3 da (Susan b 1971, Jenny b 1973, Sally b 1976); *Career* architect; sr ptnr Poynton Bradbury Wynter St Ives Cornwall, chm Poynton Bradbury Wynter Ltd; projects incl: The Barbara Hepworth Museum 1975, Lands End Visitor Centre 1982, Isles of Scilly Centre 1984, Nat Lighthouse Museum 1987; architect to Curry Mallet Village Community Project initiated by HRH The Prince of Wales 1985; memb The Nat Community Architecture Gp 1982–87, chm Cornwall Branch RIBA 1984–86; winner: CPRE/RIBA Housing Design Award 1987, Cwlth Fndn Award 1989, RIBA Regnl Design Award 1991; *Recreations* sailing, windsurfing; *Clubs* St Ives Sailing (pres), Penzance Sailing, RIBA Sailing; *Style—* Joe Poynton, Esq; ✉ The Old Sail Lofts, The Harbour, St Ives, Cornwall TR26 1PB (☎ 01736 797828, fax 01736 798464)

POYNTZ, Rt Rev Samuel Greenfield; s of Rev James Poyntz (d 1968), and Katharine Jane Poyntz; *b* 4 March 1926; *Educ* Portora Royal Sch Enniskillen, Univ of Dublin (MA, BD, PhD); *m* 1952, Noreen Henrietta Armstrong; 1 s, 2 da; *Career* deacon 1950, priest 1951, archdeacon of Dublin and examining chaplain to Archbishop of Dublin 1974–78, bishop of Cork Cloyne and Ross 1978–87, bishop of Connor 1987–95; chm Irish Cncl of Churches 1986–88, vice pres Br Cncl of Churches 1987–90; DLitt honoris causa Univ of Ulster 1995; *Style—* The Rt Rev Samuel Poyntz; ✉ 10 Harmony Hill, Lisburn, Co Antrim BT27 4EP

POYSER, Dr Norman Leslie; s of George Clifford Poyser (d 1987), and Marjorie Ellis, *née* Knight (d 1982); *b* 9 Aug 1947; *Educ* High Pavement GS Nottingham, Sch of Pharmacy Univ of London (BPharm), Univ of Edinburgh (PhD, DSc, Sandoz prize); *m* 1, 1976, Valerie Lesley (d 1985), da of Dr James Rennie Whitehead; 1 s (Timothy James), 1 da (Natalie Claire); m 2, 1990, Moira Anderson Scott; 2 step da (Carolyn Scott, Beverley Scott); *Career* Univ of Edinburgh: ICI research fell 1971–73, MRC research fell 1973–75, lectr 1975–87, sr lectr 1987–, head Dept of Pharmacology 1995–; memb: Soc for

Endocrinology 1972, Br Pharmacological Soc 1974, Soc for the Study of Fertility 1975; *Books* Prostaglandins in Reproduction (1981); numerous pubns incl original articles, contribs to books and review articles; *Recreations* tennis, bridge, theatre-going, concert-going, watching sport on TV; *Clubs* Colinton Lawn Tennis (Edinburgh); *Style*— Dr Norman Poyser; ✉ University of Edinburgh, 1 George Square, Edinburgh EH8 9JZ (☎ 0131 650 3502, fax 0131 650 6530, mobile 0802 810056, e-mail Norman.Poyser@ed.ac.uk)

PRAG, Derek Nathan; s of late Abraham J Prag, and Edith Prag (d 1992); *b* 6 Aug 1923; *Educ* Bolton Sch, Emmanuel Coll Cambridge (MA); *m* 1948, Dora Weiner; 3 s; *Career* econ journalist Reuters 1950–55, freelance ed Financial Times Business Letter from Europe 1975–77, i/c Anglo-American Section of Info Serv of High Authy of the Euro Coal and Steel Community 1955–59, head Pubns Div Jt Info Serv of Euro Communities 1959–67, dir London Press and Info Office of Euro Communities 1965–73, ran own consultancy on rels with EEC 1973–79; MEP (EDG 1979–92, EPP 1992–94) Hertfordshire 1979–94; Cons spokesman Institutional Ctee 1982–84 and 1987–94 (first vice chm 1987–94 (elected chm 1993 but stood down)), Cons spokesman Political Affrs Ctee 1984–87, sr vice chm Ctee of Enquiry into Fascism and Racism 1986, sr vice chm Euro Parl ASEAN Delgn 1979–87; memb: Tport Ctee 1991–94, Euro Parl Israel Delgn 1991–94, Security Sub-ctee 1984–94; vice pres Israel-Euro Parly Intergroup 1987–94; memb or alternate memb Foreign Affrs and Security Ctee 1979–94; rapporteur: on EU's int relations for draft treaty on Euro Union adopted 1984, on Seat of the EC Insts and working-place of the Euro Parl (Prag Report, adopted 1989 by 223 votes to 173, decided on gradual concentration of Euro Parl's work and staff in Brussels); chm: Euro Parl's All-Party Gp on Disablement 1980–94, London Europe Soc 1968–; fndr memb Cons Gp for Europe (dep chm 1974–77 and 1991–93); Cdr Order of Leopold II (Belgium) 1996; hon dir EEC Cmmn 1974, Silver Medal of Euro Merit 1974, Hon DLitt Herts 1993, Hon MEP 1994; *Publications* Businessman's Guide to the Common Market (with late E D Nicholson, 1973); many booklets and articles on Euro subjects; *Recreations* listening to music, reading, swimming, gardening, languages (speaks seven); *Clubs* Royal Over-Seas League, Anglo-Belgian, RAC (Brussels); *Style*— Derek Prag, Esq; ✉ Pine Hill, 47 New Rd, Digswell, Herts AL6 0AQ (☎ 01438 712999, fax 01438 840422)

PRAG, Dr (Andrew) John Nicholas Warburg; s of Adolf Prag, of The Old Prebendal House, Shipton-under-Wychwood, Oxon, and Dr Frede Charlotte Prag, *née* Warburg; *b* 28 Aug 1941; *Educ* Westminster, BNC Oxford (Domus exhibitioner, hon scholar, BA, Dip in Classical Archaeology, sr Hulme scholar, MA, DPhil); *m* 6 July 1969, Dr Kay Prag, da of Douglas James Wright (d 1979), of Sydney, NSW; 1 s (Jonathan Ralph Warburg b 1975), 1 da (Kate Susannah b 1977); *Career* temp asst keeper Dept of Antiquities Ashmolean Museum Oxford 1966–67; Univ of Manchester: keeper of archaeology Manchester Museum 1969–, sr lectr 1977, hon lectr Dept of History 1977–83, hon lectr in archaeology 1984–; visiting prof Dept of Classics McMaster Univ Hamilton Ontario 1978, ed Archaeological Reports 1975–87, visiting fell British Sch at Athens 1994; family rep Mgmnt Ctee Warburg Inst Univ of London, ind assessor Office of Arts & Libraries Review Ctee for the Export of Works of Art; FSA 1977; *Books* The Oresteia: Iconographic & Narrative Tradition (1985); *Recreations* walking, music, cooking, travel; *Style*— Dr A J N W Prag, FSA; ✉ The Manchester Museum, The University, Manchester M13 9PL (☎ 0161 275 2665, fax 0161 275 2676, e-mail john.prag@man.ac.uk)

PRAG, Thomas Gregory Andrew; s of Adolf Prag, of Shipton-under-Wychwood, Oxon, and Frede Charlotte, *née* Warburg; *b* 2 Jan 1947; *Educ* Westminster, Brasenose Coll Oxford (MA); *m* 4 April 1971, Angela Mary, da of late Leslie Hughes; 3 s (Benjamin David b 18 Nov 1972, Henry John b 17 Feb 1975, Nicholas Timothy b 18 Nov 1977); *Career* trainee studio mangr BBC Radio Bush House 1968–70, BBC Radio Oxford 1970–78, prog organiser BBC Highland Inverness 1978–81; md and prog controller Moray Firth Radio 1981–; pres Inverness C of C, dir Highland Festival, tstee Highland Community Fndn; memb Commercial Radio Companies Assoc (CRCA); FIMgt; *Recreations* home and family and elderly Daimler convertible; *Clubs* Inverness Rotary, Inverness Choral Soc; *Style*— Thomas Prag, Esq; ✉ Windrush, Easter Muckovie, Inverness IV1 2BN (☎ 01463 791697); Moray Firth Radio, PO Box 271, Inverness IV3 6SF (☎ 01463 224433, fax 01463 243224)

PRAGNELL, Anthony William; CBE (1982, OBE 1960), DFC (1944); s of late William Hendley Pragnell, and late Silvia Mary Pragnell; *b* 15 Feb 1921; *Educ* Cardinal Vaughan Sch London, Univ of London (LLB external); *m* 1955, Teresa Mary (d 1988), da of late Leo Francis Monaghan, of Maidstone; 1 s, 1 da; *Career* served RAF 1942–46, Flt Lt Bomber Cmd; asst examiner Inland Revenue 1939–50, GPO 1950–54; dep dir gen Independent TV Authority (became IBA 1972, now ITC) 1961–83 (joined 1954, sec 1955–61), dir Channel 4 TV 1983–88; Emile Noël Europe prize 1987; memb BBC Radio Kent Religious Advsy Gp 1988–, chm Sevenoaks and Dist Cncl of Churches 1990–92 and 1995–96; FRTS 1980, fell Euro Inst for the Media 1983; *Recreations* reading, listening to music, watching TV; *Clubs* RAF, Kent CCC; *Style*— Anthony Pragnell, Esq, CBE, DFC; ✉ Ashley, Grassy Lane, Sevenoaks, Kent TN13 1PL (☎ 01732 451463)

PRAGNELL, Michael; *b* 1946; *Educ* Douai Sch Berks, St John's Coll Oxford (BA), INSEAD Fontainebleau (MBA); *Career* branded fibre mktg exec Courtaulds Ltd London 1968–71, INSEAD 1971–72, sales mangr imported yarns Courtaulds North America Inc NYC 1972–74, asst officer International Dept First National Bank of Chicago 1974–75, commercial mangr marine rising to md packaging and coil coatings International Paint plc 1975–85, md National Plastics Ltd (subsid of Courtaulds plc) 1985–86, md International Paint plc (now Courtaulds Coatings Ltd) 1986–90; Courtaulds plc: exec dir responsible for coatings business worldwide 1990–92, fin dir 1992–94, exec dir responsible for polymer products 1994–95; chief exec offr Zeneca Agrochemicals 1995–, memb Bd Zeneca Group PLC 1997–; *Style*— Michael Pragnell, Esq; ✉ Zeneca Group PLC, 15 Stanhope Gate, London W1Y 6LN

PRAIN, Philip James Murray; s of (John) Murray Prain, DSO, OBE, TD, DL (d 1985), and (Lorina) Helen Elspeth, *née* Skene (d 1993); *b* 14 Nov 1936; *Educ* Eton, Clare Coll Cambridge (MA); *m* 28 Sept 1972, Susan Ferrier, da of Andrew Munro Marr (d 1955); 1 da (Philippa Victoria b 1975); *Career* 2 Lt Black Watch 1955–57, Lt TARO, memb The Queen's Body Guard for Scot (Royal Co of Archers) 1966; called to the Bar Inner Temple 1963; currently asst dir Group Services Kleinwort Benson Ltd (joined 1962), dir Kleinwort Benson (Hong Kong) Ltd 1979–83; underwriting memb Lloyd's; chm: Manor Gardens Enterprise Centre Islington, Westminster Amalgamated Charity, Nat Canine Def League; memb: Cncl Utd World Coll of the Atlantic S Wales, Fin Ctee Br Red Cross; tstee: St Clement Dane's Holborn Estate Charity, All Saints' Fndn Margaret St; dir E London Small Business Centre; Freeman City of London 1978, Liveryman Worshipful Co of Founders 1978; *Recreations* travel, photography; *Clubs* Beefsteak, MCC, Hurlingham, Royal and Ancient Golf, Downhill Only (Wengen), Leander (Assoc), Hong Kong, Royal Hong Kong Jockey; *Style*— Philip Prain, Esq; ✉ 73 Woodsford Square, London W14 8DS (☎ 0171 603 7767, fax 0171 602 9609); Kleinwort Benson Ltd, 20 Fenchurch St, London EC3P 3DB (☎ 0171 956 5828, fax 0171 621 1481)

PRAIS, Prof Sigbert Jon; s of Samuel Prais, and Bertha Prais; *b* 19 Dec 1928; *Educ* King Edward's Sch Birmingham, Univ of Birmingham (MCom), Univ of Cambridge (PhD, ScD), Univ of Chicago; *m* 1971, Vivien Hennessy; 1 s, 3 da; *Career* Dept of Applied Economics Cambridge 1950–57, res offr NIESR 1953–59, UN Tech Assistance Orgn 1959–60, IMF Washington 1960–61, fin dir Elbief Co 1961–70, sr res fell NIESR 1970–, visiting prof of econ City Univ 1975–; memb: Cncl Royal Econ Soc 1979–83, Cncl City Univ 1990–93, Mathematics Ctee Schs Examination and Assessment Cncl 1991–93; Hon DLitt City Univ 1989; FBA 1985; *Books* Analysis of Family Budgets (co-author, 1955), Evolution of Giant Firms in Britain (1976), Productivity and Industrial Structure (1981), Productivity, Education and Training (1995); articles in economic and statistical jls, esp on influence of educn and training on economic growth; *Style*— Prof Sigbert Prais, FBA; ✉ 83 West Heath Rd, London NW3 (☎ 0181 458 4428); office (☎ 0171 222 7665)

PRANCE, Prof Sir Ghillean (Iain) Tolmie; kt (1995); s of Basil Camden Prance, CIE, OBE (d 1947), and Margaret Hope, *née* Tolmie (d 1970); *b* 13 July 1937; *Educ* Malvern, Univ of Oxford (BA, MA, DPhil); *m* 13 July 1961, Anne Elizabeth, da of Rev Archibald MacAlister Hay (d 1980); 2 da (Rachel b 1963, Sarah b 1966); *Career* NY Botanical Gardens: res asst 1963–68, BA Krukoff curator Amazonian Botany 1968–75, dir res 1975–81, vice pres 1977–81, sr vice pres 1981–88, dir Inst Econ Botany 1981–88; adjunct prof City Univ NY 1968–; visiting prof: tropical studies Univ of Yale 1983–88, Univ of Reading 1988–; dir Royal Botanic Gardens Kew 1988–; author of numerous papers and books; memb Bd of Dirs: Margaret Mee Amazon Tst 1988–, Lovaine Tst 1989–, Royal Botanic Gardens Kew Fndn 1990–; exec dir Orgn Flora Neotropica (UNESCO) 1975–88, memb Mayor's Cmmn on Cable TV White Plains NY 1981–88; tstee: Au Sable Inst of Environmental Studies 1984–, WWF 1989–93, Horniman Museum 1990–, World Humanities Action Tst 1994–, New Island Tst 1995–; ldr Amazonian Exploration Prog 1965–88; Dr (hc) Goteborgs Univ 1983; DSc (hc): Univ of Kent 1994, Portsmouth Univ 1994, Kingston Univ 1994, Univ of St Andrews 1995, Bergen Univ Norway 1996; Patrons Medal RGS 1994; FLS 1963, FRGS 1989, FRS 1993; fell AAAS 1990; foreign memb Royal Danish Acad Scis and Letters 1988, corr memb Brazilian Acad of Scis 1976, foreign memb Royal Swedish Acad Sci 1989; International Cosmos prize 1993, hon fell Royal Botanic Garden Edinburgh 1995; *Books* Arvores De Manaus (1975), Extinction Is Forever (1977), Biological Diversification in the Tropics (1981), Leaves (1986), Amazonia (1985), Wild Flowers for all Seasons (1988), White Gold (1989), Out of the Amazon (1992), Bark (1993), The Earth Under Threat (1996); *Recreations* squash, music; *Clubs* Explorers' (fell 1978); *Style*— Prof Sir Ghillean Prance, FRS; ✉ Royal Botanic Gardens, Kew, Richmond, Surrey, TW9 3AB (☎ 0181 332 5112, fax 0181 948 4237, e-mail g.prance@rbgkew.org.uk)

PRASHAR, Usha; CBE (1995); *b* 29 June 1948; *Educ* Univ of Leeds (BA), Univ of Glasgow (Dip in Social Admin); *m* 21 July 1973, Vijay Sharma; *Career* conciliation offr Race Rels Bd 1971–76, dir Runnymede Tst 1976–84, res fell Policy Studies Inst 1984–86, dir Nat Cncl for Voluntary Orgn 1986–91; memb: Arts Cncl of GB 1979–81 and 1994–, Study Cmmn on the Family 1980–83, Social Security Advsy Ctee 1980–83, Exec Ctee Child Poverty Action Gp 1984–85, Gtr London Arts Assoc 1984–86, London Food Cmmn 1984–90, BBC Educnl Broadcasting Cncl 1987–88, Advsy Cncl Open Coll 1987–88, Elfrida Rathbone Soc 1988–, Slrs' Complaints Bureau 1989, Lord Chllr's Advsy Ctee on Legal Educn 1991–, Royal Cmmn on Criminal Justice 1991–93, Bd Energy Saving Tst 1992–, Ealing Hounslow and Hammersmith HA 1993–96, Cncl Royal Holloway Coll London 1992–; non-exec dir Channel Four Television Corporation, vice pres Cncl for Overseas Student Affrs 1986–, patron Sickle Cell Soc 1986–, vice chm Br Refugee Cncl 1987–90, chm English Advsy Ctee Nat AIDS Tst 1988–89, vice pres Patients' Assoc 1990–91, pt/t Civil Serv cmmr 1990–96, dep chm Nat Literacy Tst 1993–; tstee: Thames Help Tst 1984–86, Charities Aid Fndn 1986–91, Independent Broadcasting Telethon Tst 1987–93; hon assoc Nat Cncl of Women of GB 1989–; hon fell Goldsmiths' Coll Univ of London 1992; Hon LLD: De Montfort Univ, South Bank Univ; FRSA 1989; *Books* contrib to: Britain's Black Population (1980), The System - A Study of Lambeth Borough Council's Race Relations Unit (1981), Scarman and After (1984), Sickle Cell Anaemia Who Cares? A Survey of Screening Counselling Training and Educational Facilities in England (1985), Routes or Road Blocks - A Study of Consultation Arrangements Between Local Authorities and Local Communities (1985), Acheson and After - Primary Health Care in the Inner City (1986); *Recreations* painting, country walks, golf, music; *Style*— Miss Usha Prashar, CBE; ✉ 142 Buckingham Palace Road, London SW1W 9TR

PRATCHETT, Terence David John (Terry); s of David and Eileen Pratchett, of Hay-on-Wye; *b* 28 April 1948; *Educ* High Wycombe Tech HS, Beaconsfield Public Library; *m* Lyn Marian, da of Jean and Richard Purves; 1 da (Rhianna Katie b 1976); *Career* writer; various regnl journalism 1965–80, press offr Central Electricity Generating Bd 1980–87, full time writer 1987–; memb Soc of Authors (memb Mgmnt Ctee 1991–); *Books* The Carpet People (1971), The Dark Side of the Sun (1976), Strata (1981), The Colour of Magic (1983), The Light Fantastic (1986), Equal Rites (1987), Mort (1987), Sourcery (1988), Wyrd Sisters (1988), Pyramids (1989), Truckers (1989), Guards! Guards! (1989), The Unadulterated Cat (illustrated by Gray Jolliffe, 1989), Eric (illustrated by Josh Kirby, 1989), Good Omens (with Neil Gaiman, 1990), Moving Pictures (1990), Diggers (1990), Wings (1990), Reaper Man (1991), Witches Abroad (1991), Small Gods (1992), Only You Can Save Mankind (1992), Lords and Ladies (1992), Johnny and the Dead (1993), Men at Arms (1993), Soul Music (1994), Interesting Times (1994), The Discworld Companion (with S Briggs, 1994), Maskerade (1995), Johnny and the Bomb (1996), Feet of Clay (1996); *Recreations* writing, walking, computers, life; *Style*— Terry Pratchett, Esq; ✉ c/o Colin Smythe, PO Box 6, Gerrards Cross, Bucks SL9 8XA (☎ 01753 886000, fax 01753 886469)

PRATLEY, Alan Sawyer; s of Frederick Pratley (d 1970), and Hannah, *née* Sawyer (d 1981); *b* 25 Nov 1933; *Educ* Latymer Upper Sch, Sidney Sussex Coll Cambridge (BA); *m* 1, 29 Aug 1960 (m dis 1979), Dorothea, da of Walter Rohland; 2 da (Christiane b 14 Nov 1961, Alexa b 5 Jan 1963); m 2, 22 Dec 1979, Josette Kairis; 1 da (Fiona b 3 Feb 1981); *Career* head of German Dept Stratford GS 1958–60, asst dir examinations Civil Service Cmmn 1960–68, asst sec Home Office 1971–73 (princ 1968–71); Cmmn of the European Communities: head of Individual Rights Div 1973–79, dep head of cabinet to Christopher Tugendhat as UK EEC cmmr 1979–80, advsr to Michael O'Kennedy as EEC cmmr for Republic of Ireland 1981, dir-gen admin 1981–86, dep fin controller 1990– (dir fin control 1986–90); *Recreations* tennis; *Clubs* Travellers'; *Style*— Alan Pratley, Esq; ✉ Commission of the European Communities, 200 rue de la Loi, CSM2, 8th floor, Bureau no 100, 1049 Brussels, Belgium (☎ 00 32 2 295 2686, fax 00 32 2 295 0141)

PRATLEY, David Illingworth; s of Arthur George Pratley, of Dorset, and Olive Constance, *née* Illingworth; *b* 24 Dec 1948; *Educ* Westminster, Univ of Bristol (LLB); *m* 1996, Caryn Loise Faure Walker; *Career* PR offr Thorndike Theatre Leatherhead 1970–71, press and publicity offr Queen's Univ Belfast 1971–72, dep dir Merseyside Arts Assoc 1972–76, dir Gtr London Arts Assoc 1976–81, regnl dir Arts Cncl of GB 1981–86, arts mgmnt conslt 1986–87, dir Dance Umbrella Ltd 1986–92, chief exec Royal Liverpool Philharmonic Soc 1987–88, md Trinity Coll of Music 1988–91, chm Nat Campaign for the Arts 1988–92, dir of leisure, tourism and economic devpt Bath City Cncl 1992–96, lottery policy advsr Arts Cncl of England 1996–; *Books* Culture for All (1981), Cumbria Arts & Museums Strategy (1987), The Pursuit of Competence - the Arts and the European Community (1987), Musicians Go To School (1993); *Recreations* arts, travel, gardens, countryside; *Clubs* Athenaeum; *Style*— David Pratley, Esq; ✉ 16 Guinea Lane, Lansdown, Bath BA1 5NB (☎ 01225 461503)

PRATT, Anthony Richard (Tony); s of Arthur Edward Pratt (d 1976), of Brentwood, Essex, and Marjorie Louise, *née* Wright; *b* 21 June 1940; *Educ* Brentwood Sch; *m* 9 Sept 1961, Barbara Ann Grace, da of Herbert Edward Richardson (d 1989); 1 da (Susan b 1 Aug 1965), 1 s (David b 21 Jan 1967); *Career* reporter: Brentwood Review 1956–62,

Romford Recorder 1962–64, sub ed then diary writer Sun 1964–70; Daily Mirror: diary writer 1970–76, TV and showbusiness feature writer and TV critic 1976–84, TV critic and TV listings ed 1984–89; TV listings ed and critic Mirror Group (incl Daily Mirror, Sunday Mirror, The People) 1989–, memb NUJ; *Recreations* cricket, reading, gardening, music, walking; *Clubs* Wig and Pen, Essex County Cricket; *Style*— Tony Pratt, Esq; ✉ Mirror Group Newspapers Limited, 1 Canada Square, Canary Wharf, London E14 5AP (☎ 0171 293 3000, fax 0171 293 3062, direct 0171 293 3496)

PRATT, (Richard) Camden; QC (1992); s of Richard Sheldon Pratt, of 108 Manthorpe Rd, Grantham, Lincs, and late Irene Gladys, *née* Whalley; *b* 14 Dec 1947; *Educ* Boston GS, Westcliff HS, Lincoln Coll Oxford (MA, Hanbury law scholar); *m* 4 Aug 1973, Dorothy Jane Marchia, da of late Capt William Paul Allsebrook, of Athens; *Career* called to the Bar Gray's Inn 1970, recorder of the Crown Court 1993–; chm: Sussex Cts Liaison Ctee 1993–, Sussex Sessions Bar Mess 1995–; *Recreations* sailing, walking, theatre, cinema; *Style*— Camden Pratt, Esq, QC; ✉ 1 King's Bench Walk, Temple, London EC4 (☎ 0171 583 6266, fax 0171 583 2068)

PRATT, (Ewart) George; CVO (1986); s of George William Pratt (d 1955), of Harrow on the Hill, and Florence Edith, *née* Redding (d 1957); *b* 10 Oct 1917; *Educ* LSE (Dip); *m* 9 Oct 1948, Margaret, da of William Heath (d 1977), of Letchworth; 2 s (Christopher John Ewart b 1950, Martin Andrew b 1953); *Career* Inner London Probation Serv 1949–81: probation offr, sr probation offr, asst chief probation offr then dep chief probation offr; chm Assoc of Social Workers 1959–70, treas Br Assoc of Social Workers 1970–73; fndr govr Nat Inst for Social Work 1961–71, sec Voluntary Housing Assoc 1964–81, memb Ctee on the Voluntary Worker in the Social Servs 1966–69, memb Home Office Working Pty on Community Serv by Offenders 1971–72; The Prince's Tst: tstee 1976–94, hon admin 1976–78, chm 1978–86; tstee REACT 1990–, elder United Reformed Church, formerly UK delegate to World Cncl of Churches, memb Social Responsibility Ctees of the Baptist Union and the Br Cncl of Churches; memb numerous governmental, professional and charitable advsy gps; *Recreations* music, theatre, travelling, lecturing and talking about the needs of disadvantaged and potentially terminally-ill children and young people; *Style*— George Pratt, Esq, CVO; ✉ 14 The Squirrels, 24A The Avenue, Branksome Park, Poole, Dorset BH13 6AF (☎ 01202 767552)

PRATT, (Edmund) John; s of Edmund Addison Pratt (d 1970), and Ruth Marie Erneste, *née* Wilkinson; *b* 14 Oct 1944; *Educ* Warwick Sch, Imperial Coll London (BSc(Eng) Civil Engrg, MSc(Eng) Tport); *m* 21 Dec 1968, Jennifer Grace, *née* Reynolds; 2 da (Polly Louise b 22 Nov 1972, Sophie Alice b 2 May 1974); *Career* engr Sir William Halcrow & Partners 1966–70, civil engr The Gostain Group 1970–73, conslt P-E Consulting Group 1973–76, dir and gen mangr George Longden Construction Ltd (subsid of Whitecroft plc) 1976–79, northern UK gen mangr Damp Proofing Div Rentokil plc 1979–81, sales and mktg dir Steetley Brick Ltd 1981–85, gp mktg dir David Webster Ltd 1986–88, md Leading Edge Management Consultancy Ltd 1994– (sr ptnr 1988–94); MCIM (memb Nat Cncl, past chm Construction Indust Gp); *Recreations* classic cars, family history, cycling; *Style*— John Pratt, Esq; ✉ Leading Edge Management Consultancy Ltd, Bridge Chambers, 28 High Street, Welwyn, Herts AL6 9EQ (☎ 01438 840880, fax 01438 840884, mobile 0831 827603, e-mail consult@ledge.telme.com)

PRATT, (Edward Roger) Michael; JP (Norfolk 1969), DL (Norfolk 1974); s of Lt-Col Edward Roger Pratt, MC (d 1966), and Beatrix Elaine, *née* Thynne (d 1969); *b* 28 Sept 1926; *Educ* Eton, Univ of Cambridge; *m* 28 July 1955, Sarah Constance Neville, da of Very Rev Hedley Robert Burrows (Dean of Hereford, d 1983); 2 s ((Edward Roger) Piers b 1956, Nicholas Julian Hedley b 1958), 1 da ((Lavinia Mary) Claire (Mrs Bunting)); *Career* Nat Serv Lt in Coldstream Gds 1944–47; chm Downham Bench 1984–89 (dep chm 1976), memb Lord Chllr's Advsy Sub-Ctee 1986–92; Downham Rural Dist Cncl: elected 1952, vice chm 1964, chm 1967–74; memb Norfolk CC 1970–74, chm Norfolk Valuation Tribunal 1973–; memb: W Norfolk Dist Cncl 1975–76 (Hon Alderman 1976), Lord Chllr's Advsy Ctee for Gen Cmmrs 1980– (joined as gen cmmr for Income Tax 1965, chm King's Lynn Div); *Recreations* shooting, photography; *Clubs* Army and Navy; *Style*— Michael Pratt, Esq, JP, DL; ✉ Stonehills House, Ryston, Downham Market, Norfolk PE38 0AB (☎ and fax 01366 382059); Estate Office, Ryston Hall, Downham Market, Norfolk PE38 0AA (☎ 01366 383322, fax 01366 387149)

PRATT, Michael John; QC (1976); o s of W Brownlow Pratt; *b* 23 May 1933; *Educ* West House Sch Edgbaston, Malvern Coll (LLB Birmingham); *m* 1960, Elizabeth Jean Hendry; 2 s, 3 da; *Career* 2 Lt 3 Carabiniers (Prince of Wales's Dragoon Gds), Staff Capt; called to the Bar Middle Temple 1954, bencher 1986; recorder of the Crown Ct 1974–; *Clubs* Cavalry and Guards', Birmingham Cons; *Style*— Michael Pratt, Esq, QC; ✉ 2 Fountain Court, 1st Floor, Steelhouse Lane, Birmingham B4 6DR (☎ 0121 236 3882)

PRATT, Peter Charles; s of Charles Frederick Pratt (d 1982), of Sunningdale, and Edith Hilda, *née* Appleton (d 1983); *b* 24 Sept 1931; *Educ* Salesian Coll, Clapham Coll, Univ of Reading (BSc); *m* 1, 29 Sept 1956, Pamela Mary (d 1969), da of Alfred Smith (d 1960) of Colchester; 1 s (Julian b 1957), 1 da (Nicola b 1961); m 2, 8 July 1982, Fay Jameson, *née* Wright (d 1993); *Career* Nat Serv Lance-Corpl RE 1950–52 (works servs Cyprus 1951–52); Overseas Civil Serv 1955–60: trainee surveyor Sch of Mil Survey 1955–56, surveyor Dept of Lands and Surveys Govt of Tanganyika 1956–60; Ellerman Lines plc: investmt mgmnt and admin 1960–74, co sec 1967–84, divnl chief exec 1979–82, dir Main Bd 1982–84; chm and md New Cavendish Street Investment Co Ltd 1990–94 (dir 1984–94); memb: Investmt Ctee Merchant Navy Ratings Pension Fund 1982–96 (chm of Tstees 1996–), MNOPF Tstees Ltd (chm Investmt Ctee 1991–), dir Argosy Asset Management plc 1989–91; dir and sec The John Ellerman Fndn 1994–96 (tstee 1996–), tstee Burgh House Tst Hampstead (chm Mgmnt Ctee 1990–93); Freeman City of London 1967, Liveryman Worshipful Co of Shipwrights 1968 (memb Ct 1992); FRGS 1952, FCIS 1966; *Recreations* swimming, clay-pigeon shooting, theatre, music, reading, watching cricket; *Clubs* Carlton, Royal Automobile, Surrey CCC, MCC; *Style*— Peter C Pratt, Esq; ✉ 25 Willoughby Rd, Hampstead, London NW3 1RT (☎ 0171 794 9040, fax 0171 431 7138); Suite 10, Aria House, 23 Craven St, London WC2N 5NT (☎ 0171 930 8566, fax 0171 839 3654)

PRATT, Sandy Robert Gammack; s of Alexander Robert Pratt (d 1976), of Elgin, Scotland, and Daphne Lesley Crofton, *née* McCann; *b* 25 Dec 1951; *Educ* Blairmore Sch Aberdeenshire, Fettes Coll Edinburgh, Christ's Coll Cambridge (MA, LLM); *m* 8 Jan 1977, Helen, da of Joseph Aubrey Pritchard (d 1963), of Chester; 1 s (James b 21 Oct 1983), 1 da (Samantha b 13 June 1980); *Career* admitted slr Supreme Court 1978; authorised insolvency practitioner 1987–, ptnr Corporate and Financial Dept Norton Rose 1988– (trainee slr 1976–78, asst slr 1978–88); Freeman: City of London, Worshipful Co of Slrs; memb: Law Soc, City of London Law Soc, Insolvency Practitioners' Assoc, Soc of Practitioners' of Insolvency, Insolvency Lawyers' Assoc, Int Bar Assoc, Assoc Européenne des Praticiens des Procédures Collectives; *Books* Norton Rose "Corporate Insolvency Law and Practice" booklet (ed, 3 edn, 1993); *Recreations* rugby (Cambridge blues 1973 and 1974), genealogy, golf, shooting, fishing, woodturning; *Clubs* London Scottish FC, The Whale, Hawk's, Denham Golf; *Style*— Sandy Pratt, Esq; ✉ The Mount, Rookery Hill, Ashtead Park, Ashtead, Surrey KT21 1HY (☎ 01372 273420); Norton Rose, Kempson House, Camomile Street, London EC3A 7AN (☎ 0171 283 6000, fax 0171 283 6500)

PRATT, Timothy Jean Geoffrey; CB (1993); s of Geoffrey Cheeseborough Pratt (d 1975), and Elinor Jean, *née* Thomson (d 1934); *b* 25 Nov 1934; *Educ* Brighton Coll, Trinity Hall Cambridge (MA); *m* Pamela Ann, *née* Blake; 2 da (Eleanor Jane b 1965, Lucy Ann b 1967); *Career* called to the Bar Middle Temple 1959, practiced in Lincoln's Inn 1959–61; Treasury Solicitor's Dept: legal asst 1961–67, sr legal asst 1967–72, Law Officers Dept 1972–74; asst slr DTI 1974–79; legal advsr: Office of Fair Trading 1979–85, Cabinet Office (European Secretariat) 1985–90; dep treasy slr 1990–93, counsel to the Speaker (European Legislation & Co) 1993–; *Clubs* Oxford and Cambridge; *Style*— Timothy Pratt, Esq, CB; ✉ House of Commons, London SW1A 0AA (☎ 0171 219 5561, fax 0171 219 2509)

PRAWER, Prof Siegbert Salomon; s of Marcus Prawer, and Eleonora Prawer; *b* 15 Feb 1925; *Educ* King Henry VIII Sch Coventry, Jesus Coll and Christ's Coll Cambridge (MA, LittD), Univ of Birmingham (PhD), Univ of Oxford (MA, DLitt); *m* 1949, Helga Alice; 1 s (1 s decd), 2 da; *Career* asst lectr, lectr, sr lectr Univ of Birmingham 1948–63, prof of German Westfield Coll Univ of London 1964–69; Univ of Oxford: prof of German Lit and Lang 1969–86 (now emeritus), professorial fell Queen's Coll 1969–86 (dean of degrees 1978–93, now hon fell); visiting prof: City Coll NY 1956–57, Univ of Chicago 1963–64, Harvard Univ 1968, Univ of Hamburg 1969, Univ of Calif Irvine 1975, Univ of Otago 1976, Univ of Pittsburgh 1977; visiting fell: Knox Coll Dunedin 1976, Humanities Res Centre ANU 1980, Tauber Inst Univ of Brandeis 1981–82, Russell Sage Fndn 1988; hon dir Univ of London Inst of Germanic Studies 1966–68 (hon fell 1988), pres Br Comparative Lit Assoc 1984–87 (hon fell 1987), hon memb Modern Language Assoc of America 1986; English Goethe Soc: pres 1990–95, vice pres 1995–; co-ed: Oxford German Studies 1971–75, Anglica Germanica 1973–79; Hon DPhil Cologne 1984, Hon DLitt Birmingham 1988, Goethe medal 1973, Friedrich Gundolf Prize 1986, Gold medal Deutsch Goethe Gesellschaft 1995; hon memb Modern Languages Assoc of America 1985; corresponding fell German Acad of Language and Literature 1988, hon fell Jesus Coll Cambridge 1996; FBA 1981; *Books* German Lyric Poetry (1952), Mörike und seine Leser (1960), Heine: The Tragic Satirist (1962), The Penguin Book of Lieder (1964), The Romantic Period in Germany (1970), Comparative Literary Studies (1973), Karl Marx and World Literature (1976, Isaac Deutscher meml Prize, 1977), Caligari's Children (1980, 2 edn 1989), Heine's Jewish Comedy (1983), Frankenstein's Island (1986), Israel at Vanity Fair. Jews and Judaism in the Writings of W M Thackeray (1992); *screenplay* Das Kabinett des Dr Caligari (co-ed and intr, 1996); *Recreations* portrait drawing; *Style*— Prof Siegbert Prawer, FBA; ✉ The Queen's College, Oxford OX1 4AW

PREBBLE, David Lawrence; s of George Wilson Prebble (d 1983), of Eastbourne, Sussex, and Margaret Jessie, *née* Cuthbertson (d 1993); *b* 21 Aug 1932; *Educ* Cranleigh Sch, ChCh Oxford (MA); *m* 9 May 1959, Fiona Winifred, da of Thomas Hudspith Melville (d 1986); 3 da (Sarah Lorne Melville (Mrs Kollias) b 1960, Catriona Jean b 1963, Alison Fiona b 1966); *Career* Nat Serv cmmnd 3 Carabiniers Prince of Wales's Dragoon Guards 1950–52; practising barrister 1957–81, Master of The Queen's Bench Div Supreme Court of Justice 1981–; Capt TA 1952–61, City of London Yeomanry (Rough Riders); *Recreations* food, music, horses, hounds and dogs (especially Salukis and Border Collies), books; *Clubs* Royal Wimbledon Golf; *Style*— David Prebble, Esq; ✉ 16 Wool Road, Wimbledon, London SW20 OHW (☎ 0181 946 1804); Royal Courts of Justice, Strand, London WC2

PREBBLE, Stuart Colin; s of Dennis Stanley, and Jean Margaret, *née* McIntosh (d 1981); *b* 15 April 1951; *Educ* Beckenham & Penge GS, Univ of Newcastle upon Tyne (BA); *m* 25 Aug 1978, Marilyn Anne, da of George Charlton, of Newcastle upon Tyne; 2 da (Alexandra Juliette b 1979, Claire Samantha b 1982 d 1996); *Career* reporter BBC TV 1973–79; Granada TV: ed World in Action 1986–89 (prodr 1981–86), head of regnl progs 1989–92; controller of network factual programmes ITV Network Centre 1992–96, chief exec Granada Sky Broadcasting 1996–; dir Parliamentary Broadcasting Ltd; fndr Campaign for Quality TV, memb Cncl BAFTA, tstee Broadcast Support Servs, advsr Victim Support; *Books* A Power in the Land (1988), The Lazarus File (1989); *Recreations* music, writing, travel; *Style*— Stuart Prebble, Esq; ✉ Granada Sky Broadcasting, 16 Hatfields, London SE1 8DJ (☎ 0171 578 4002)

PREECE, Andrew Douglas; s of Bernard Charles Preece, of Beechfield Drive, Walton on the Hill, Stafford, and Joyce Mary, *née* Clayton; *b* 28 Sept 1944; *Educ* King Edward V1 GS Stafford, Selwyn Coll Cambridge (MA); *m* 5 Oct 1968, Caroline Jane, da of Edmund Arthur Bland (d 1988); 1 s (James Douglas b 4 Aug 1976), 2 da (Victoria Jane b 31 March 1972, Joanna Mary b 19 Jan 1981); *Career* articled clerk asst slr Hall Collins 1968–71, ptnr Herbert Smith 1977– (asst slr 1971–74, assoc ptnr 1974–77); memb UK Energy Lawyers Gp; Freeman Worshipful Co of Slrs; memb: Law Soc, IBA; *Recreations* sailing, golf; *Clubs* Moor Park Golf, RAF Yacht, RNVR Yacht; *Style*— Andrew Preece, Esq; ✉ Hyde Farm, Hyde Lane, Great Missenden, Bucks HP16 0RF; Flat 20, President's Quay House, 72 St Katherine's Way, London E1; Herbert Smith, Exchange House, Primrose St, London EC2A 2HS (☎ 0171 374 8000, fax 0171 496 0043)

PREECE, Anthony John; s of John Henry Preece (d 1977), and Ivy, *née* Rhodes; *b* 11 May 1945; *Educ* Batley GS, Univ of Loughborough; *m* 1, 30 Sept 1967 (m dis 1986), Caroline Betty, da of Thomas Harold Keston Edwards (d 1962); 3 s (David b 23 Nov 1971, Christopher b 6 March 1975, Adam b 23 March 1977); m 2, Esme Irene, da of Jacques Sadler (d 1971); 1 da (Sarah b 18 June 1986); *Career* asst dir Stock Exchange 1972–85, md Scrimgeour Vickers Services 1985–86; ops dir Citicorp Scrimgeour Vickers 1986–89, dir Stock Exchange 1989–90, head of business devpt London Stock Exchange 1991–94, dir global operations Barclays Securities Services 1994–95, head of mkt ops Euro Assoc of Securities Dealers Automated Quotations System (EASDAQ) 1995–; *Recreations* wine, food, travel, theatre; *Clubs* Royal Institution; *Style*— Anthony Preece; ✉ Bowman Lodge, Warren Lane, Oxshott, Surrey KT22 0ST (☎ 01372 842461)

PREECE, Ralph Stephen; s of John Raymond Preece, of 1 Ashgrove, Dinas Powis, South Glamorgan, and Doris, *née* Derrick; *b* 14 May 1946; *Educ* King's College Sch, Cathays HS Cardiff; *m* 27 Dec 1969, Marilyn Preece, JP, da of Edwin Ralph Gardener Thomas; 2 da (Justine Claire b 28 Sept 1973, Natalie Jane b 27 Feb 1976); *Career* articled clerk Richard Davies & Co Cardiff 1965–70, qualified chartered accountant 1970, Coopers & Lybrand 1970–76 (Johannesburg, London, Cardiff), insolvency specialist Mann Judd Cardiff 1976–79; Deloitte & Touche (formerly Touche Ross): moved to Birmingham Office 1979, ptnr 1983, ptnr i/c Corp Special Servs (now Corp Recovery) 1983–, ptnr i/c London Office 1994–; memb Transvaal Soc of CAs 1972, FCA 1979 (ACA 1970), MICM 1986, MIPA 1988, memb Assoc Européene des Practiciens des Procedures Collectives 1988, MSPI 1990; *Recreations* gardening; *Clubs* Leeds; *Style*— Ralph Preece, Esq; ✉ Deloitte & Touche, PO Box 810, Cedric House, 8–9 East Harding Street, London EC4A 3AS (☎ 0171 936 3000)

PREISKEL, Harold Wilfred; s of David Preiskel (d 1983), of London NW6, and Lili, *née* Wick; *b* 1 June 1939; *Educ* St Paul's, Guy's Med and Dental Sch (LDSRCS, BDS, FDSRCS, MDS), Ohio State Univ (MSc); *m* 22 Aug 1962, Nira, da of Joshua Orenstein (d 1977), of Tel Aviv; 3 s (Daniel b 1965, Ronald b 1969, Alon b 1976), 1 da (Daphne b 1979); *Career* house surgn 1962, lectr in restorative dentistry Royal Dental Hosp Sch of Surgery 1966–69, hon conslt Guy's Hosp 1971, chm London Dental Study Club 1971, examiner in dental prosthetics RCS 1972, staff examiner in prosthetic dentistry Univ of London 1974 (examiner 1969), pt/t conslt in prosthetic dentistry Guy's Hosp Dental Sch 1974 (sr lectr 1969, lectr 1962–66); Thomas Hinman award Atlanta Georgia 1975, Int Circuit Course award of the American Coll of Prosthodontists 1988; pres: Int Coll of Prosthodontists 1987–91, The American Dental Soc of London, BDA metropolitan branch 1981–82; chm: Editorial Bd of Int Jl of Prosthodontists 1988, tstees of Alpha Omega Charitable Tst; fell Int Coll of Dentists; memb: Editorial Bd Jl of Dentistry 1972–,

Br Soc for Restorative Dentistry, Br Soc for Study of Prosthetic Dentistry, Euro Prosthodontic Assoc, Euro Dental Soc, American Dental Soc of London, American Dental Soc of Europe, Carl O Boucher Prosthodontic Soc, American Acad Esthetic Dentistry (fndr), American Equilibration Soc, Federation Dentair International; hon citizen of New Orleans 1978; *Books* author of numerous pubns in the field of prosthodontic dentistry incl: Precision Attachments in Dentistry (1968, 1973, 1979), Precision Attachments in Prosthodontics Vol 1 & 2 (1985, trans in six languages), Overdentures Made Easy; *Recreations* classical music, general aviation; *Style—* Harold Preiskel, Esq; ✉ 25 Upper Wimpole St, London W1M 7TA (practice) (☎ 0171 935 4525, fax 0171 486 8337, car 0836 223194); Department of Prosthetic Dentistry, United Medical and Dental Schools of Guy's and St Thomas', London Bridge SE1 9RT (☎ 0181 955 4027)

PRENDERGAST, (Christopher) Anthony; CBE, DL (1980); s of Maurice Prendergast; *b* 4 May 1931; *Educ* Falmouth GS; *m* 1959, Dame Simone Ruth Prendergast, DBE, JP, DL, *qv*; 1 s; *Career* chm Dolphin Square Trust Ltd 1967–, dir London Electricity plc 1990; Lord Mayor and dep high steward of Westminster 1968–69, High Sheriff of Gtr London 1980, DL Gtr London 1988; memb Ct of Assts Worshipful Co of Pattenmakers; Lloyd's underwriter; *Recreations* shooting, fishing, photography; *Clubs* Carlton, Brooks's, Irish, MCC; *Style—* Anthony Prendergast, Esq, CBE, DL; ✉ Flat C, 52 Warwick Square, London SW1V 2AJ (☎ 0171 821 7653)

PRENDERGAST, Brig John Hume; DSO (1946), MC (1937, bar 1940); s of Maj-Gen Charles Gordon Prendergast, CB (d 1930), of Jersey, and Marguerite Egbertha, *née* Hume (d 1970); *b* 15 Nov 1910; *Educ* Victoria Coll Jersey; *m* 3 April 1939, (Rose Ann) Peggy, da of Henry Norton Hutchinson, OBE, ICS (d 1947); 2 s (John b 1942, Rollo b 1947), 1 da (Caroline (Mrs Priestly) b 1944); *Career* cmmnd Royal Sussex Regt 1931, 4/15 Punjab Regt Razmak Waziristan 1932, seconded N Waziristan Transborder Armed Police 1936–39, active serv Ipi Ops, Capt 1939, mountain warfare advsr Norway Expedition 1940, returned IA 1940, Maj 1940, instr in mountain warfare Sch of Inf Poona 1941–42, raised and cmmd 1 Western Tribal Legion 1943, 2 i/c 1/15 Punjab Regt in first Arakan ops 1943–44, joined 19 (Dagger) Indian Div in reconquest of Burma 1944, cmd first river recrossing of Irawaddy (despatches), recapture of Mandalay, CO 3/6 Rajputana Rifles 1945, continued in Burma until 1947, Staff Coll Quetta 1947, 1 Yorks and Lancaster Regt 1948, mil attaché Kabul Embassy Afghanistan 1948–50, 1 Yorks and Lancaster Regt Brunswick 1951 (cmd 1952), served Khartoum and Canal Zone 1952, GSO1 BAOR 1955, cmd 147 Midland Bde TA 1957–60, ret 1960; long distance motor exploration (incl voluntary work for wild life conservaton): Iran, Afghanistan, Pakistan, India; pres 15 Punjab Regt Assoc 1983–88; *Books* The Road to India (1977), Prender's Progress (1979), A Plume of Dust (1993); *Recreations* long distance motor travel, fly-fishing, painting, writing; *Style—* Brig John Prendergast, DSO, MC; ✉ Barton Mead, Tisbury, Wilts SP3 6JU (☎ 01747 870542)

PRENDERGAST, Sir (Walter) Kieran; KCVO (1991), CMG (1990); s of Lt Cdr Joseph Henry Prendergast (d 1989), and Mai, *née* Hennessy (d 1988); *b* 2 July 1942; *Educ* St Patrick's Coll Sydney Aust, Salesian Coll Chertsey Surrey, St Edmund Hall Oxford; *m* 10 June 1967, Joan, da of Patrick Reynolds (d 1974); 2 s (Damian b 1968, Daniel b 1976), 2 da (Siobhain b 1971, Brigid b 1973); *Career* FO 1962, Istanbul (Turkish language student) 1964, Ankara 1965, FO 1967, second sec Nicosia 1969, Civil Serv Coll 1972, first sec FCO 1972, first sec (info, later economic) The Hague 1973, asst private sec to 2 foreign secs (Rt Hon Anthony Crosland and Rt Hon Dr David Owen) 1976, UK Mission to UN New York 1979, cnsllr, head of chancery and consul-gen Tel Aviv 1982, head of Southern African Dept FCO 1986–89; Br high cmmr: to Zimbabwe 1989–92, to Kenya 1992–95; Br ambass to Turkey 1995–; *Recreations* family, walking, reading, shooting, wine; *Clubs* Beefsteak, Muthaiga (Nairobi); *Style—* Sir Kieran Prendergast, KCVO, CMG; ✉ c/o Foreign and Commonwealth Office (Ankara), King Charles Street, London SW1A 2AH

PRENDERGAST, His Hon Judge; Robert James Christie Vereker; s of Capt Richard Henry Prendergast (d 1965), of Roehampton, London, and Jean, *née* Christie (d 1988); *b* 21 Oct 1941; *Educ* Downside, Trinity Coll Cambridge (MA); *m* 16 Apr 1971, Berit, da of Wilburg Thauland (d 1982), of Oslo, Norway; 1 da (Victoria b 1973); *Career* called to the Bar Middle Temple 1964, recorder (SE Circuit) 1987–89, circuit judge (SE Circuit) 1989–; *Recreations* most gentle pursuits; *Style—* His Hon Judge Prendergast; ✉ 5 Paper Buildings, Temple, London, EC4Y 7HB (☎ 0171 353 5638, fax 0171 353 6166)

PRENDERGAST, Dame Simone Ruth; DBE (1986, OBE 1981), DL (Greater London 1982), JP (Inner London 1971); da of Norman Laski (d 1968), and Elaine Blond, *née* Marks, OBE (d 1985); *b* 2 July 1930; *Educ* Queen's Coll London, Cheltenham Ladies' Coll; *m* 1, 1953 (m dis 1957), Albert Kaplan; m 2, 21 Sept 1959, (Christopher) Anthony Prendergast, CBE, *qv*, s of Maurice Anthony Prendergast (d 1961); 1 s (Christopher Hugh b 6 June 1960); *Career* chm: Cities of London and Westminster Cons Assoc 1971–75, London Central Euro Constituency 1976, Gtr London Area Nat Union of Cons Assocs 1984–87; dep chm Gtr London Area Cons Party Nat Union 1981–84; pres Westminster Homes 1985–90; Lady Mayoress Westminster 1968; chm: Blond McIndee Centre Med Res 1986–, Jewish Refugees Ctee 1980–91, Westminster Childrens Soc 1980–90; vice chm Age Concern Westminster 1988; cmdt Jewish Lads' and Girls' Bde 1996–; memb: Cncl Central Br Fund for Jewish Relief 1969– (jt treas 1991–), St John Cncl for London 1975–82, Bethnal Green and E London Housing Assoc 1990–92; memb: Lord Chllr's Advsy Ctee 1981–91, Slrs Disciplinary Tbnl 1986–; asst cmmr St John 1982; pt/t memb CRE 1996–; memb Ct of Patrons RCS 1987, hon FRSA 1988; *Recreations* reading, walking, gardening; *Style—* Dame Simone Prendergast, DBE, JP, DL; ✉ 52 Warwick Square, London SW1V 2AJ

PRENN, Oliver Simon; s of Daniel Dan Prenn (d 1991), and Charlotte Prenn (d 1977); *b* 26 Sept 1937; *Educ* St Paul's, Hertford Coll Oxford (MA); *m* 27 Sept 1958, Nyda Margaret McDonald; 1 s (Alexis b 18 March 1962), 1 da (Natasha b 11 April 1964); *Career* private family companies 1959–65, dep md Controls & Communications Ltd 1965–69, dep chm Racal Electronics Ltd (now plc) 1974–77 (dep md 1969–77); chm: Derritron plc 1980–82, Magellan Industries plc 1988–94, Fii Group plc 1995–96; vice chm Serpentine Gallery until 1993, memb Devpt Cncl Royal Nat Theatre, hon patron of New Art Tate Gallery, dir Youth and Music Ltd, chm Amadeus Scholarship Fund; Jr Wimbledon Tennis Champion 1955, played Wimbledon Championships 1956–59; FRSA; *Recreations* spectator, listener and occasional patron of theatre, music and art; *Clubs* Queen's; *Style—* Oliver Prenn, Esq; ✉ 47 Hyde Park Gate, London SW7 5DU (☎ 0171 584 8870); Vicarage House, 58–60 Kensington Church Street, London W8 4DB (☎ 0171 938 3440)

PRENTICE, Bridget; JP (1985), MP (Lab) Lewisham East (majority 1,095); da of late James Corr, and Bridget Corr; *b* 28 Dec 1952; *Educ* Our Lady and St Francis Sch Glasgow, Univ of Glasgow (MA), Univ of London (PGCE), South Bank Univ (LLB); *m* 20 Dec 1975, Gordon Prentice, *qv*, MP for Pendle; *Career* rector's assessor Univ of Glasgow 1972–73, teacher London Oratory Sch 1974–86 (head of careers 1984–86), head of careers John Archer Sch 1986–88; London Borough of Hammersmith and Fulham: cncllr 1986–92, chm Lab Gp 1986–90, chm Public Servs Ctee 1987–90; MP (Lab, GMB sponsored) Lewisham E 1992–; memb Select Ctee on Parly Admin (ombudsman) 1992–95, oppn whip 1995–; memb: GMB, NUT, Lab Women's Network, Women's Legal Defence Fund, Lab Campaign for Criminal Justice; *Recreations* knitting, reading, music, crosswords, gardening, badminton (qualified coach), my two cats; *Style—* Bridget Prentice, JP, MP; ✉ House of Commons, London SW1A 0AA (☎ 0171 219 3503, fax 0171 219 5581)

PRENTICE, Hon Mrs (Eve-Ann); da of Baron Whaddon (Life Peer); *b* 1952; *m* 1972, Patrick Prentice; *Career* journalist Guardian 1978–87; production ed Sunday Telegraph 1988–89 (dep production ed 1987–88); production ed The Sunday Correspondent 1989–90 (asst ed 1990); asst foreign ed The Times 1991–, diplomatic corr The Times 1993–; *Recreations* science, foreign affairs; *Style—* The Hon Mrs Prentice; ✉ The Times, 1 Pennington Street, London E1 9XN (☎ 0171 782 5000, fax 0171 488 3242)

PRENTICE, Gordon; MP (Lab) Pendle (majority 2,113); s of late William Prentice, and Esther Prentice; *b* 28 Jan 1951; *Educ* George Heriot's Sch Edinburgh, Univ of Glasgow (MA); *m* 20 Dec 1975, Bridget Prentice, *qv*, MP for Lewisham East, da of late James Corr; *Career* with Lab Pty Policy Directorate 1982–92, Lab Pty local govt offr 1985–92, MP (Lab) Pendle 1992–; London Borough of Hammersmith and Fulham: cncllr 1982–90, ldr Lab Gp 1984–88 (dep ldr 1982–84), ldr of Cncl 1986–88; *Style—* Gordon Prentice, Esq, MP; ✉ House of Commons, London SW1A 0AA

PRENTICE, Graham Noel; *b* 7 March 1955; *Educ* Peter Symonds Winchester, Churchill Coll Cambridge (BA); *m* 15 Sept 1975, Beverley Annette Prentice; 2 da (Katy b 1987, Alice b 1989); *Career* admitted slr 1980; articled clerk Wragge & Co 1978–80, ptnr Freshfields 1986– (joined 1981); *Publications* Irregular Resolution of Unincorporated Association May Not be a Nullity (1980), The Enforcement of Outsider Rights (1980), Protected Shorthold Tenancies: Traps for the Unwary (I, II, III, 1982), Remedies of Building Sub-Contractors against Employers (1983); *Recreations* photography, reading; *Style—* Graham Prentice, Esq; ✉ Freshfields, 65 Fleet St, London EC4Y 1HT (☎ 0171 936 4000, fax 0171 832 7001)

PRENTICE, Nicholas John (Nick); s of Norman Frank Prentice, of Eastbourne; *b* 14 Feb 1956; *Educ* Mount Grace Sch Potters Bar, Queens' Coll Cambridge (MA); *m* 28 Dec 1978, Jane Patricia; 2 da (Philippa Mary b 3 Dec 1981, Kate Victoria b 22 June 1983); *Career* Arthur Andersen: joined 1978, CA 1981, mangr Tax 1983–88, ptnr 1988–, head of South Tax Practice 1989–94, managing ptnr South Practice 1991–, UK managing ptnr Tax 1995–; memb Ethics Ctee ICAEW 1984–87; FCA 1981, ATII 1981, memb Int Fiscal Assoc 1986, FInstD 1992; *Recreations* squash, tennis, bridge, theatre, travel, genealogy; *Style—* Nick Prentice, Esq; ✉ Arthur Andersen, Abbots House, Abbey Street, Reading, Berks RG1 3BD (☎ 0118 950 8141, fax 0118 950 8101)

PRENTICE, Baron (Life Peer UK 1992), of Daventry in the County of Northamptonshire; Sir Reginald Ernest Prentice; kt (1987), PC (1966), JP (Croydon 1961); s of Ernest George Prentice, of Thornton Heath, Surrey; *b* 16 July 1923; *Educ* Whitgift Sch, LSE (BSc); *m* 1948, (Vera May) Joan, da of Rosa Godwin, of Hatfield Heath, Essex; 1 da (Hon Christine Ann b 1951); *Career* MP (Lab): East Ham North 1957–74, Newham North East 1974–77; MP (C): Newham North East 1977–79, Daventry 1979–87 (ret); min of state Dept of Educn and Sci 1964–66, min for Public Building and Works 1966–67, min for Overseas Devpt 1967–69, oppn spokesman on Employment 1972–74, sec of state for Educn and Sci 1974–75, min for Overseas Devpt 1975–76, min for Social Security 1979–81; alderman GLC 1970–71; pres: Assoc of Business Execs 1983–94, Devizes Constituency Conservative Assoc; co dir and conslt on public affrs; *Clubs* Carlton; *Style—* The Rt Hon Lord Prentice, PC

PRENTICE, Hon Sir William Thomas; kt (1977), MBE (1945); s of Claud Stanley Prentice (d 1931); *b* 1 June 1919; *Educ* St Joseph's Coll Sydney, Univ of Sydney (BA, LLB); *m* 1946, Mary Elizabeth Beresford, da of Frank Beresford Dignam (d 1946); 3 s, 1 da; *Career* Staff Capt 25 Aust Inf Bde PNG Campaigns 1942–43 and 7 Aust Inf Bde Bougainville Campaign 1944–45; barr NSW 1947–70, Judge Supreme Ct PNG 1970, sr puisne judge 1975, dep chief justice on independence PNG 1975, chief justice 1978–80, sr memb Admins Appeals Tribunal (Australia) 1981–87; *Recreations* bush walking, swimming, reading; *Clubs* Tattersall's (Sydney), Cricketers; *Style—* The Hon Sir William Prentice, MBE; ✉ 16 Olympia Rd, Naremburn, NSW 2065, Australia

PRENTICE, Dame Winifred Eva; DBE (1977, OBE 1972); da of Percy John Prentice, and Anna Eva Prentice; *b* 2 Dec 1910; *Educ* Northgate Sch for Girls Ipswich E Suffolk and Ipswich Hosp, W Middx Hosp, Queen Elizabeth Coll Univ of London; *Career* principal tutor Stracathro Hosp 1947–61, matron 1961–72; pres Royal Coll of Nursing 1972–76; *Style—* Dame Winifred Prentice, DBE; ✉ Marleish, 4 Duke Street, Brechin, Angus DD9 6JY (☎ 01356 622606)

PRESCOT, Kenrick Warre; s of late Brig C P Prescot, CBE, and Constance Margaret, *née* Stewart; *b* 21 Nov 1920; *Educ* Eton, Worcester Coll Oxford; *m* 1948, Angharad Joanna, da of Brig C R M Hutchison, DSO, MC (ka 1942); 2 s (Colin b 1950, Jeremy b 1952), 1 da (Caroline (Mrs Gordon Dewar) b 1955); *Career* served WWII RA, India, Burma and UK 1942–46, Capt; Bank of England 1947–59, vice pres Bankers' Trust Company 1959–83; dir: Bankers' Trust Int Ltd 1970–76, AMEV Life Assurance Ltd 1973–80, AMEV (UK) Ltd 1980–91; dep chm Bankers' Trustee Co Ltd 1993– (dir 1983–); hon fell Worcester Coll Oxford 1993; *Recreations* tennis, bowls, croquet; *Clubs* MCC, Hurlingham; *Style—* Kenrick Prescot, Esq; ✉ 13 The Little Boltons, London SW10 9LJ

PRESCOTT, Jeremy Malcolm; s of Rev Malcolm Crosby Prescott, CF, QHC, and Mary, *née* Webber (d 1974); *b* 26 March 1949; *Educ* Ampleforth, Fitzwilliam Coll Cambridge; *m* 20 March 1982, Jacqueline Mary Elizabeth, *née* Kirk; 1 s (John Edmund Philip), 1 da (Katherine Mary); *Career* CA; with Peat Marwick Mitchell & Co 1970–76, dir of corp fin HSBC Samuel Montagu 1987– (joined Samuel Montagu & Co Ltd 1976); FCA 1979, MSI; *Books* How to Survive the Recession (1982); *Style—* J M Prescott, Esq; ✉ HSBC Samuel Montagu, Vintner's Place, 68 Upper Thames Street, London EC4V 3BJ (☎ 0171 336 9000, fax 0171 336 9500)

PRESCOTT, Prof John Herbert Dudley; s of Herbert Prescott (d 1959), of Barrow-on-Humber, Lincs, and Edith Vera, *née* Crowder (d 1993); *b* 21 Feb 1937; *Educ* Haileybury, Univ of Nottingham (BSc, PhD); *m* 23 July 1960, Diana Margaret, da of Frank Mullock, of Poulton Hall, Chester; 2 s (Ian b 26 May 1961, Tony b 22 Aug 1962), 2 da (Joanna b 8 July 1965, Sarah-Vivien b 24 April 1968); *Career* dir H Prescott (Goxhill) Ltd 1959–78 (chm 1970–78), demonstrator in agric Univ of Nottingham 1960–63, lectr in animal prodn Univ of Newcastle-upon-Tyne 1963–74, animal prodn offr FAO UN (Argentina) 1972–74, head of animal prodn and devpt East of Scotland Coll of Agric 1974–78, prof of animal prodn Univ of Edinburgh 1978–84, dir Grassland Res Inst Hurley 1984–86, dir Animal & Grassland Res Inst 1986, dir of res Grassland & Animal Prodn 1986–88, princ Wye Coll Univ of London 1988–; memb Cncl Br Grassland Soc 1984–87, pres Br Soc of Animal Prodn 1988; FIBiol 1983, FRAgS 1986; *Recreations* walking, wildlife, country pursuits; *Clubs* Farmers'; *Style—* Prof John Prescott; ✉ Wye College, University of London, Wye, Ashford, Kent TN25 5AH (☎ 01233 812401, fax 01233 813320, e-mail J.Prescott@Wye.ac.uk)

PRESCOTT, Rt Hon John Leslie; PC (1994), MP (Lab) Hull East (majority 18,719); s of John Herbert Prescott, JP, of Chester, and Phyllis Prescott; *b* 31 May 1938; *Educ* Ellesmere Port Secondary Modern Sch, Ruskin Coll Oxford, Univ of Hull (BSc(Econ)); *m* 1961, Pauline, da of Ernest Tilston, of Chester; 2 s; *Career* joined Lab Pty 1956; former trainee chef & merchant seaman (NUS official 1968–70); Parly candidate (Lab) Southport 1966, MP (Lab) Hull East 1970–, delegate Cncl of Europe 1973–75, PPS to Sec of State for Trade 1974–76, ldr Lab Pty Delegn European Parl 1976–79 (memb 1975–79); oppn spokesman on: tport 1979–81, regional affrs 1981–Nov 1983; memb Shadow Cabinet 1983–; oppn front bench spokesman on: tport Nov 1983–84 and 1988–93, employment

1984–87, energy 1987–88, employment 1993–94; candidate Lab Pty dep leadership election 1988 and 1992, dep ldr Lab Pty 1994– (also candidate leadership election); *Publications* Alternative Regional Strategy: A Framework for Discussion (1982), Planning for Full Employment (1985), Real Needs - Local Jobs (1987), Moving Britain into the 1990s (1989), Moving Britain into Europe (1991), Full Steam Ahead (1993), Financing Infrastructure Investment (1993), Jobs and Social Justice (1993); *Style*— The Rt Hon John Prescott, MP; ✉ House of Commons, London SW1A 0AA (☎ 0171 219 4612)

PRESCOTT, Prof Laurie Francis; s of Dr F Prescott (d 1989), of Coombe Ridge, Churt, Surrey, and J Prescott, *née* Raison (d 1983); *b* 13 May 1934; *Educ* Hitchin Boys' GS Herts, Downing Coll Cambridge (MA, MB BChir, MD); *m* 1, 1957 (m dis 1978), Josephine Anne, da of Nicholas Carpentieri, of White Plains, NY; 1 s (Nicholas David b 8 Jan 1962), 3 da (Katherine Elizabeth b 16 Oct 1964, Caroline Fiona b 8 Jan 1967, Christina Rachel b 26 July 1970); m 2, 6 Sept 1980, Jennifer Anne, da of Charles Gorvin, of Garden Cottages, Tapeley Park, Westleigh, N Devon; *Career* cmmnd pilot RAF 1952–54; res fell Johns Hopkins Hosp Baltimore USA 1963–65, lectr Univ of Aberdeen 1965–69, prof of clinical pharmacology Univ of Edinburgh 1985– (sr lectr and conslt physician 1969–74, reader 1974–85); former memb Ctee on Safety of Med, memb RSM; FRCPE, FRCP, FFPM, FRSE 1989; *Books* Drug Absorption (ed 1981), Handbook of Clinical Pharmacokinetics (ed 1983), Rate Control in Drug Therapy (1985), Novel Drug Delivery (1989), Paracetamol: A Critical Bibliographic Review (1996); *Recreations* gardening, sailing, music; *Style*— Prof Laurie Prescott, FRSE; ✉ 24 Colinton Road, Edinburgh EH10 5EQ (☎ 0131 447 2571); Clinical Pharmacology Unit, Western General Hospital, Crewe Road, Edinburgh EH4 2XU (☎ 0131 537 1826)

PRESCOTT, Sir Mark; 3 Bt (UK 1938), of Godmanchester, Co Huntingdon; s of Maj (William Robert) Stanley Prescott (d 1962, yr s of Col Sir William Prescott, 1 Bt), by his 1 w (Hylda) Gwendolen, *née* Aldridge (d 1992), and n of Sir Richard Stanley Prescott, 2 Bt (d 1965); *b* 3 March 1948; *Educ* Harrow; *Heir* none; *Career* racehorse trainer; *Style*— Sir Mark Prescott, Bt; ✉ Heath House, Moulton Rd, Newmarket, Suffolk CB8 8DU (☎ 01638 662117, fax 01638 666572)

PRESCOTT, Peter Richard Kyle; QC (1990); s of Capt Richard Stanley Prescott (d 1987), of Cordoba, Argentina, and Sarah Aitchison, *née* Shand; *b* 23 Jan 1943; *Educ* St George's Coll Argentina, Dulwich, UCL (BSc), QMC (MSc); *m* 23 Sept 1967, Frances Rosemary, da of Wing Cdr Eric Henry Bland (d 1980), of Tonge Corner, Sittingbourne; 2 s (Richard Julyan Kyle b 1973, Thomas Alexander Kyle b 1975), 1 da (Miranda Katherine b 1971); *Career* called to the Bar Lincoln's Inn 1970; *Books* The Modern Law of Copyright (with Hugh Laddie and Mary Vitoria, 1980, 2 edn 1995); *Recreations* flying, music, cooking, reading; *Style*— Peter Prescott, Esq, QC; ✉ residential: London and Isle of Purbeck, Dorset; chambers: 8 New Square, Lincoln's Inn, London WC2A 3QP (☎ 0171 405 4321, fax 0171 405 9955)

PRESCOTT THOMAS, John Desmond; RD (1977, clasp 1987); s of William Prescott Thomas (d 1973), and Beatrice Isobel, *née* Jones; *b* 28 May 1942; *Educ* Rhyl GS Clwyd, Whitchurch GS Glamorgan, Jesus Coll Oxford (BA, MA); *m* 1, 7 Oct 1967 (m dis 1993), Bridget Margaret, da of Rev Canon Adrian Denys Somerset-Ward (d 1976); 2 da (Viveka Ruth b 1969, Bronwen Jane b 1971); m 2, 14 Oct 1994, Heather Elizabeth Graham; *Career* BBC: gen trainee 1963–65, asst prodr sch TV 1965–68, prodr 1968–76, sr prodr modern languages and European studies 1976–81, head of schs bdcasting TV 1981–84, head Bristol network prodn centre 1984–86, head of bdcasting South and West 1986–91; md Westcountry Television Ltd 1991–95; ind bdcasting conslt 1995–; wrote and produced: radiovision prog on Stanley Spencer's Burghclere paintings (Japan Prize nomination 1965), TV adaptation of Peter Carter's The Black Lamp; three BAFTA/RTS award nominations, twelve Euro documentary and language series; articles in: TES, Br Language Teaching Jl, Le Français dans le Monde; Bolland Lecture (Bristol Poly 1984); govr Univ of West of England Bristol, tstee: Bath In Festival (memb Cncl of Mant), The Exploratory, St George's Music Tst Bristol, Bristol Cathedral Tst; memb: Euro Bd CIRCOM Regional, Royal TV Soc, BAFTA, ABE, Assoc for Language Learning; RNR: cmmnd 1963, qualified ocean cmd 1974, Cdr 1978, exec offr London Div 1983–84, Severn Div 1984–92; *Books* Two EFL stories for children, Encounter: France (1980), Dès le Début, Dicho y Hecho, Alles Klar (1983); *Recreations* languages, sailing, photography, industrial archaeology, model engineering, heraldry, playing the alto saxophone; *Clubs* Naval, Royal Western Yacht; *Style*— John Prescott Thomas, Esq; ✉ Earl's Pool, Ladymead Lane, Lower Langford BS18 7EQ (☎ 01934 852606)

PRESLAND, Frank George; *b* 27 Feb 1944; *Educ* Univ of London (Fairbridge Cwlth scholar, BSc), Univ Coll of Rhodesia and Nyasaland; *m* 16 April 1968, Julia Mary Bronwen; 1 s (Anthony Charles b 1980), 1 da (Linda Mary b 1975); *Career* articled clerk Kerly Sons & Keruth/Prestons & Kerlys 1970–72, admitted slr 1973; Frere Cholmeley Bischoff: joined 1973, ptnr 1976–, head Litigation Dept 1985–88, memb Exec Ctee 1988–, chm 1992–; *Recreations* yachting; *Style*— Frank Presland, Esq; ✉ Frere Cholmeley Bischoff, 4 John Carpenter Street, London EC4Y 0NH (☎ 0171 615 8000, fax 0171 615 8080)

PRESLEY, Prof John Ralph; s of Ralph Presley, of Dinnington, Sheffield, and Doris, *née* Edson; *b* 17 Sept 1945; *Educ* Woodhouse GS Sheffield, Univ of Lancaster (BA), Univ of Loughborough (PhD); *m* 15 July 1967, Barbara, da of Kenneth Mallinson, of Kegworth, Derby; 1 s (John Robert Ralph b 9 June 1981), 2 da (Joanne Marie b 29 July 1968, Catherine Jane b 2 Sept 1972); *Career* Univ of Loughborough: lectr 1969–76, sr lectr 1976–81, reader 1981–84, prof of economics 1984–, dir Banking Centre 1985–89, head Dept of Economics 1991–; sr economic advsr Miny of Planning Saudi Arabia 1979–80, visiting scholar Harvard 1982–, visiting professorial fell Univ of Nottingham 1989–90; DTI: memb Ctee for ME Trade 1993–, chm Area Action Ctee for Gulf Cooperation Countries and Yemen; memb exec ctee Saudi-British Soc, memb Omani-British Friendship Assoc; *Books* European Monetary Integration (with P Coffey, 1971), Currency Areas: Theory and Practice (with G E J Dennis, 1976), Robertsonian Economics (1978), Pioneers of Modern Economics Vol 1 (ed with D O'Brien, 1983), Directory of Islamic Financial Institutions (1988), Pioneers of Modern Economics Vol 2 (ed with D Greenaway, 1989), A Guide to the Saudi Arabian Economy (with A J Westaway, 1983, 2 edn 1989), Banking in the Arab Gulf (with R Wilson, 1991), Essays on Robertsonian Economics (ed, 1992), Robertson on Economic Policy (ed with S R Deunison, 1992); *Recreations* gardening, reading, music, travel; *Style*— Prof John Presley; ✉ Department of Economics, Loughborough University, Loughborough, Leics (☎ 01509 222702, fax 01509 223910, telex 34319)

PRESS, John Bryant; s of Edward Kenneth Press (d 1951), and Gladys May Smith, *née* Cooper (d 1980); *b* 11 Jan 1920; *Educ* King Edward VI Sch Norwich, CCC Cambridge (MA); *m* 20 Dec 1947, Janet Nellie, da of Oliver Crompton (d 1982), of Cardiff; 1 s (Roger b 1948), 1 da (Judith b 1953); *Career* WWII RA 1940–45: Gunner 1940–41, 2 Lt 1942, Lt 1943, Staff Capt 1944–45; Br Cncl 1946–80: Athens 1946–47, Salonika 1947–50, Madras 1950–51, Colombo 1951–52, Birmingham 1952–54, Cambridge 1955–62, London 1963–65, Paris 1966–71, Oxford 1972–78, London 1979–80; author; FRSL 1959; *Books* The Fire and the Fountain (1955), Uncertainties (1956), The Chequer'd Shade (1958), Guy Fawkes Night (1959), Rule and Energy (1963), A Map of Modern English Verse (1969), The Lengthening Shadows (1971), A Girl with Beehive Hair (1986), Palgrave's Golden Treasury (ed, 6 edn 1994); *Recreations* the arts, travel; *Style*— John Press, Esq, FRSL; ✉ 5 South Parade, Frome, Somerset BA11 1EJ (☎ 01373 461142)

PRESS, Dr (Christopher) Martin; s of Gp Capt Charles Henry Press, of Gt Gormellick, Liskeard, Cornwall, and Christina, *née* Hindshaw; *b* 24 Jan 1944; *Educ* Bedales Sch, King's Coll Cambridge (BA), UCH (MB BChir, MA), Chelsea Coll London (MSc); *m* 10 June 1967, Angela Margaret, da of Charles Douglas Lewis, of Church Farm, Dibden, Southampton; 5 s (Matthew b 1970, Joseph b 1972, Samuel b 1974, Benjamin b 1980, Daniel b 1984); *Career* med registrar Royal Post Grad Med Sch Hammersmith Hosp 1971–73, MRC res fell Univ of California 1973–75, asst prof of med and paediatrics Yale Univ Sch of Med 1981–87, currently conslt physician and hon sr lectr Royal Free Hosp Med Sch; memb: BMA, Br Diabetic Assoc, American Diabetic Assoc, Southampton Canal Soc; *Recreations* orienteering, bell ringing, canal cruising; *Style*— Dr Martin Press; ✉ 99 Highfield Lane, Southampton SO17 1NN (☎ 01703 55 1617); Department of Endocrinology, Royal Free Hospital, London NW3 3QG (☎ 0171 830 2171)

PREST, Nicholas Martin; s of Prof Alan Richmond Prest (d 1984), of Wimbledon, and Pauline Chasey, *née* Noble; *b* 3 April 1953; *Educ* Manchester GS, ChCh Oxford (MA); *m* 1985, Anthea Joy Elisabeth, da of Stuart John Guthrie Neal, of Wales; 1 s (Frederick George Alan b 1989), 2 da (Clementine Joy Chasey b 1987, Tabitha Rose Florence b 1992); *Career* entered civil serv MOD 1974 admin trainee, princ offr 1979; joined United Scientific Instruments Ltd 1982; Alvis plc (formerly United Scientific Holdings plc); dir 1985–, chief exec 1989–, chm and chief exec 1996–; *Recreations* tennis; *Style*— Nicholas Prest, Esq; ✉ Alvis plc, 215 Vauxhall Bridge Rd, London SW1 (☎ 0171 821 8080)

PRESTIGE, Colin Gwynne; s of Harold Haldane Calder Prestige, CBE (d 1982), of Chislehurst, Kent, and Lydia Ellen Neville, *née* Edwards (d 1983); *b* 19 Nov 1926; *Educ* Bradfield Coll, Oriel Coll Oxford (MA); *Career* Supply and Secretarial Div RN 1945–48; admitted slr 1954, poor man's lawyer Islington 1954–60, second sr ptnr Lawrence Graham London 1987–89 (articled clerk and asst slr 1950–59, ptnr 1959–89, conslt 1989–); cmmr for oaths 1961–, chm Rent Assessment Appeals Ctee Greater London 1965–68; Law Soc: memb 1954, chm Young Slrs' Gp 1960–61, memb Working Pty on Modernisation of Conveyancing 1964–69, memb Cncl 1967–92, chm Library Ctee 1970–85, chm Non-contentious Business Ctee 1974–77 (vice chm 1971–74), vice chm Professional Purposes Ctee 1980–82 and 1983–84, chm Accounts Rules and Compensation Fund Sub-ctee 1981–86, father of Cncl 1987–92; fndr memb and memb Ctee Holborn Law Soc 1962– (hon treas 1963–71, vice pres 1971–73, pres 1973–74); fndr memb and memb Exec Ctee Oriel Law Soc 1993–; memb Cncl: Incorporated Cncl of Law Reporting England and Wales 1984– (vice chm 1996–), The Selden Soc 1988–, Slrs Staff Pension Fund 1988–92; memb: Land Registration Rules Ctee 1972–92, Standing Jt Ctee of Insurance Agents 1970–77 (chm 1976–77), Investigation Ctee Slrs' Complaints Bureau 1986–92, Br Records Assoc (Records Preservation Section) 1986–, Disciplinary Bd Br Psychological Soc 1990– (chm 1995–); dir Royal Theatrical Fund 1967–79 and 1989–; tstee: D'Oyly Carte Opera Tst 1964–, Friends of D'Oyly Carte 1981–; Sherlock Holmes Soc of London: fndr memb 1951, memb cncl 1951–82, hon sec 1954–71, chm 1977–80, hon treas 1980–82, hon memb 1995–; memb Ctee Oriel Soc 1968–72, memb Provost of Oriel's Fundraising Task Force 1986–90; memb Worshipful Co of Slrs 1988, FRSA 1967; *Books* D'Oyly Carte and the Pirates: Original New York Productions 1875–96 (1971), Conveyancing: Who Buys Your House? (1977); over 300 articles on legal, theatrical and literary subjects; *Recreations* Gilbert and Sullivan, the plays of William Shakespeare (has seen all 37 professionally performed), literary research; *Clubs* Garrick; *Style*— Colin Prestige, Esq; ✉ c/o Lawrence Graham, 190 Strand, London WC2R 1JN (☎ 0171 379 0000, fax 0171 379 6854, telex 22673 LAWGRA G)

PRESTON, Dr Frank Samuel; OBE (1988), VRD (1963); s of Frank Anderson Baillie Preston (d 1978), of Milngavie, Scotland, and Rachel, *née* McDonald (d 1968); *b* 13 March 1923; *Educ* Glasgow Acad, Univ of Glasgow (MB ChB, DA); *m* 2 Oct 1954, Margaret, da of Norman McGregor (d 1974), of Falkirk, Scotland; 1 s (Frank Alan b 1955), 2 da (Jacqueline Ann (Mrs G Murray) b 1961, Kathryn Frances b 1962); *Career* marine engr small vessels pool Admty 1943–45, Surgn Lt RNVR - Surgn Capt RNR 1947–73, QHP 1972–73, regn med offr BEA 1954–65, princ air med offr BEA and BOAC 1965–78, dir med serv BA 1981–87 (dep dir med serv 1978–81), med spokesman Br Heart Fndn 1987–90, conslt in aviation and occupational med 1987–, memb Med Cmmn for Accident Prevention 1987–; sr med examiner CAA and Fed Aviation Authy USA; memb Anglo-American Med Soc (former pres); numerous articles on aviation and travel; med dir (aeromedical) St John Ambulance; Freeman Guild of Air Pilots and Air Navigators 1979; memb Int Acad Aviation and Space Med, fell Aerospace Med Assoc (formerly vice pres), FRAeS, FFOM RCP; *Books* contrib to: Oxford Textbook of Medicine (1988), Textbook of Aviation Medicine (1988); *Recreations* golf, diving, sailing; *Clubs* Naval; *Style*— Dr Frank Preston, OBE, VRD; ✉ Wynn Institute for Metabolic Research, 21 Wellington Rd, St John's Wood, London NW8 9SQ (☎ 0171 935 2266)

PRESTON, (John) Hugh Simon; JP (West Berkshire 1990); s of Rev Cecil George Armitage Preston (d 1966), and Dr Maureen Evans; *b* 28 April 1937; *Educ* Marlborough; *m* 10 Oct 1964 (m dis 1993), Julia Deborah, da of Richard Glover Hubbard (d 1969); 1 s (Guy b 1968), 1 da (Olivia b 1972); m 2, 24 June 1995, Hilary Gay Jackson, da of Jack Douglas Shepard; *Career* chartered surveyor, ptnr Strutt & Parker; FRICS; *Recreations* reading, golf, gardening, music; *Clubs* Farmers'; *Style*— Hugh Preston, Esq, JP; ✉ Summerdown House, Malshanger, Basingstoke, Hampshire RG23 7ES; 55 Northbrook St, Newbury, Berks RG14 1AN

PRESTON, Dr Ian Mathieson Hamilton; CBE (1993); s of John Hamilton Preston (d 1978), and Edna Irene Paul (d 1992); *b* 18 July 1932; *Educ* Kilmarnock Acad, Univ of Glasgow (BSc, PhD); *m* 5 Aug 1958, Sheila Hope, da of Robert Johnston Pringle; 2 s (Colin John b 10 Feb 1960, Ewan Robert b 5 Dec 1961); *Career* asst lectr Univ of Glasgow 1957–59; South of Scotland Electricity Bd: asst reactor physicist 1959–65, sr asst engr 1965–67, res projects mangr 1967–69, tech servs mangr 1969–70, mangr generation and design Tech Servs Div 1970–72, chief engr Generation Design and Construction Div 1972–77; dir gen Generation Devpt and Construction Div CEGB 1977–83, dep chm South of Scotland Electricity Bd 1983–90, chief exec Scottish Power 1990–95; chm: Mining (Scotland) Ltd 1995–, Scottish Coal Co Ltd 1995–, East of Scotland Water Authority 1995–, Motherwell Bridge Holdings Ltd 1996– (non-exec dir 1994–96); non-exec dir Deutsche Morgan Grenfell (Scotland) 1994–, Clydeport plc 1994–, Hub Power Co (Pakistan) 1995; chm Scottish Cncl Devpt and Indust 1993–; MInstP 1959, FIEE 1974, FEng 1982; *Recreations* fishing, gardening; *Clubs* Western; *Style*— Dr Ian Preston, CBE, FEng; ✉ Scottish Coal Company Ltd, 160 Glasgow Road, Corstorphine, Edinburgh EH12 8LT (☎ 0131 317 7300, fax 0131 317 7197)

PRESTON, Jeffrey William; CB (1989); s of William Preston, and Sybil Grace, *née* Lawson; *b* 28 Jan 1940; *Educ* Liverpool Collegiate Sch, Hertford Coll Oxford (MA); *Career* asst princ Miny of Aviation 1963, private sec to Perm Sec BOT 1966, princ BOT 1967, HM Treasy 1970, DTI 1973, asst sec Dept of Trade 1975–82, under sec and regnl dir Yorks and Humberside Region DTI 1982–85, dep sec Welsh Office 1985–90, dep dir gen OFT 1990–96 (acting dir gen 1995), dir gen Energy DTI 1996–; chm Hertford Soc 1986–95; *Recreations* motoring, opera, swimming; *Clubs* United Oxford and Cambridge Univ; *Style*— Jeffrey Preston, Esq, CB; ✉ DTI, 1 Victoria Street, London SW1H 0ET (☎ 0171 215 5000)

PRESTON, John Anthony Russell; s of late Dennis Anthony Gurney Preston, and Margaretta Constance, *née* Higson; *b* 9 Sept 1953; *Educ* Marlborough; *m* 23 Nov 1991, Maria, *née* Djurkovic; *Career* stage mangr Open Space Theatre 1973, asst film ed 1974–78, freelance journalist 1981–83, TV ed Time Out 1983–86, ed Arts Section

Evening Standard 1986–90, arts ed The Sunday Telegraph 1990–; *Books* Touching the Moon (1990), Ghosting (1996); *Recreations* walking; *Style*— John Preston, Esq; ✉ The Sunday Telegraph, 1 Canada Square, Canary Wharf, London E14 5DT (☎ 0171 538 7391)

PRESTON, John O'Driscoll; s of Maj Ian Preston, of Aboyne, Aberdeenshire; *b* 29 Aug 1950; *Educ* Shrewsbury Sch, Trinity Coll Oxford (scholar, MA Modern History), Univ of Liverpool (BPhil Latin American Studies); *m* Rosalind Helen; *Career* shop mangr rising to mktg dir Brock's Record Shops 1973–76, artist devpt mangr rising to Harvest Label mangr EMI Records 1977–80, gen mangr Decca Records Ltd 1980–83, mktg dir Decca Records then md Polydor Records Ltd (both pt of Polygram Records Ltd) 1983–85, md REA Records Ltd 1985–89, chm BMG Entertainment International UK & Ireland Ltd 1989–; chm BPI 1995; memb Lab Party; *Recreations* sailing, tennis, golf, reading; *Style*— John Preston, Esq; ✉ BMG Entertainment International Ltd, Bedford House, 69–79 Fulham High Street, London SW6 3JW (☎ 0171 384 7517, fax 0171 973 0354)

PRESTON, Michael David; s of Richard Preston, and Yetta, *née* Young (d 1958); *b* 12 Dec 1945; *Educ* St Paul's, Exeter Coll Oxford (Sr Open Scholar, MA); *m* 13 April 1969 (m dis 1994), Stephanie Ann, *née* Levy; 2 s (Matthew b 1972, Robert b 1975); *Career* articled clerk Price Waterhouse London; fndr shareholder and dir Sterling Publishing Group plc until 1995 (dep chm 1990–94), former dir Debrett's Peerage Ltd, vice pres Long Distance Direct Holdings Inc 1991–, ptnr Alberdale Holdings; former pres Oxford Univ Cons Assoc; FCA 1971; *Recreations* music, painting, wine, real tennis, lawn tennis, golf; *Clubs* MCC, Utd Oxford and Cambridge, New York Racquet and Tennis; *Style*— Michael Preston, Esq; ✉ Alberdale Holdings, 11 Cross Keys Close, London W1M 5FY (☎ 0171 935 2070, fax 0171 935 2680); Long Distance Direct Holdings Inc, 1 Blue Hill Plaza, Pearl River, New York 10965, USA (☎ 00 1 914 620 0765, fax 00 1 914 620 0709)

PRESTON, Michael Richard; s of Maj Frederick Allen Preston, MC, TD (d 1972), of Carshalton, Surrey, and Winifred Gertrude, *née* Archer (d 1987); *b* 15 Oct 1927; *Educ* Whitgift Sch, Sutton and Cheam Sch of Art Surrey, Guildford Sch of Art (NDD), Goldsmiths' Coll London (ATD, Dip Humanities); *m* 1, 13 Aug 1955 (m dis 1975), Anne, da of Dr Ralph Gillespie Smith (d 1959), of Kirdford, Sussex; m 2, 22 Aug 1980, Judith Gaye James, da of Alec Warden Hopkins (d 1989), of Blenheim, NZ; *Career* volunteer Queen's Royal Regt 1944–48, Queen's Royal Regt TA 1948–52, HAC 1952–61; asst master Whitgift Sch 1954–55, drawing master Dulwich Coll 1955–64, head of design and later keeper Dept of Museum Servs Science Museum 1964–87; exhibitions designed incl: Centenary of Charles Babbage 1971, A Word to the Mermaids 1973, Tower Bridge Observed 1974, The Breath of Life 1974, Science and Technology of Islam 1976, Stanley Spencer in the Shipyard 1979, Science and Technology of India 1982, The Great Cover-Up Show 1982, Beads of Glass 1983, Louis Pasteur and Rabies 1985; designed many permanent galleries incl: Science Museum 1964–86, Nat Railway Museum York 1971–75, Wellcome Museum of the History of Medicine 1975–80, Nat Museum of Photography Film and Television Bradford 1977–83; advsy assignments on museum projects: Iran 1976–79, Spain 1977–80, Germany 1978–79, Canada 1979–82, Expo '86 Vancouver BC 1984–86, Trinidad 1982–83, Turkey 1984–94, Hong Kong 1985, ret; conslt designer 1987–; consultancies to: The Wellcome Fndn 1986–95, Dean and Chapter of Canterbury 1987–95, TAVRA 1988–94, Design Expo '89 Nagoya Japan 1988–89, Bank of England Museum 1989, Tricycle Theatre 1989–94, Royal National Theatre 1988–90, Norwich Tourist Agency 1989–90, Scottish Office 1990, Richmond Theatre Surrey 1990, Academia Italiana 1990–94, English Heritage 1990, Société Generale 1992–94, Castrol International 1994–95; keeper of pictures and works of art The Arts Club 1992–96; chm Greenwich Soc 1961–64, examiner UEI 1959–64, examiner first degrees Univ of London 1970–74, Panel memb BTEC 1982–93, memb Int Advsy Panel Tubitak (Sci Res Cncl of Turkey) 1984–90; visiting prof Nat Inst of Design India 1989–, tstee Vivat Tst 1989–92; FRSA 1955–68, memb ICOM 1964, FCSD 1972 (MCSD 1953), hon memb Guild of Glass Engravers 1976 (hon fell 1980, pres 1986–92); *Recreations* looking at buildings, travel, food, jazz; *Clubs* Arts; *Style*— Michael Preston, Esq

PRESTON, (Christopher) Miles (Cary); s of Alan Tomlinson Preston, TD, and Audrey Anne Flint, *née* Wood, of Shrewsbury, Shropshire; *b* 12 April 1950; *Educ* Shrewsbury; *m* 5 June 1974, Jane Mowbray, da of Norman Seddon Harrison (d 1988), and Jeanne, *née* Peirce, of Blackheath, London; 2 da (Caroline Mowbray b 28 Dec 1978, Georgina Clare b 20 Nov 1986); *Career* admitted slr 1974; ptnr Radcliffes & Co 1980–94, sr ptnr Miles Preston & Co 1994–; served on Sir Gervais Sheldon's Family Law Liaison Ctee 1982; Slrs' Family Law Assoc: fndr memb 1982, memb Main Ctee 1982–88, chm Working Pty on Procedure 1982–88; Int Acad of Matrimonial Lawyers: fndr memb 1986, govr 1986–92, pres English Chapter 1989, pres Euro Chapter 1989–92, parliamentarian to Main Ctee 1989–92, pres Main Acad 1994–96 (pres elect 1992); chm: Old Salopian Ctee 1992–94, Osteopathic Educnl Fndn 1994–; memb The President's Int Family Law Ctee 1994–; *Recreations* food, travel and classic cars; *Clubs* Turf, Leander; *Style*— Miles Preston, Esq; ✉ Miles Preston & Co, Eldon Chambers, 30 Fleet Street, London EC4Y 1AA (☎ 0171 583 0583, fax 0171 583 0128)

PRESTON, (Bryan) Nicholas; OBE (1985); s of Bryan Wentworth Preston, MBE (d 1965), and Jean Brownlie, *née* Reid (d 1991); *b* 6 Feb 1933; *Educ* Eton, RAC Cirencester; *m* 1955, Elsbeth, *née* Hostettler; 1 s, 2 da; *Career* farmer; dir Stone Manganese Marine Ltd, chm Br Marine Equipment Cncl 1966–68 and 1976–78; memb: BOTB E Euro Trade Cncl 1979–82, BOTB Euro Trade Ctee 1972–89; Liveryman Worshipful Co of Shipwrights; *Recreations* field sports, skiing; *Clubs* Boodle's, Farmers'; *Style*— Nicholas Preston, Esq, OBE; ✉ Park Farm, Beverston, nr Tetbury, Glos GL8 8TT (☎ and fax 01666 502435)

PRESTON, Prof Paul; s of Charles Ronald Preston (d 1973), and Alice, *née* Hoskisson (d 1956); *b* 21 July 1946; *Educ* St Edward's Coll Liverpool, Oriel Coll of Oxford (BA, DPhil), Univ of Reading (MA); *m* 24 March 1983, Gabrielle, da of William Anthony Ashford-Hodges; 2 s (James Mark William b 20 Jan 1987, Christopher Charles Thomas b 2 April 1989); *Career* lectr in history Univ of Reading 1974–75; Queen Mary Coll: lectr 1975–79, reader 1979–85, prof 1985–91; LSE: prof of international history 1991–94, Principe de Asturias prof 1994–; Comendador de la Orden de Mérito Civil 1987; FRHistS 1982, FBA 1994; *Books* The Coming of the Spanish Civil War (1978), The Triumph of Democracy in Spain (1986), The Spanish Civil War (1986), The Politics of Revenge (1990), Franco: A Biography (1993, Yorkshire Post Book of the Year); *Recreations* opera, classical music, modern fiction, wine; *Clubs* Spanish (Cavendish Square); *Style*— Prof Paul Preston, FBA; ✉ Department of International History, London School of Economics, Houghton Street, London WC2A 2AE (☎ 0171 955 7107, fax 0171 955 6757)

PRESTON, Peter John; s of John Whittle Preston; *b* 23 May 1938; *Educ* Loughborough GS, St John's Coll Oxford; *m* 1962, Jean Mary Burrell; 2 s, 2 da; *Career* editor The Guardian 1975–95, editor-in-chief Guardian and Observer April 1995–April 1996, ed dir Guardian Media Group April 1996–; memb Press Complaints Cmmn until 1994; *Style*— Peter Preston, Esq; ✉ The Guardian, 119 Farringdon Road, London EC1R 3ER (☎ 0171 278 2332)

PRESTON, Brig Roger St Clair; CBE (1986, OBE 1979); s of Col Geoffrey William Preston (d 1976), of Menethorpe, Malton, N Yorks, and Daphne Jane Preston, OBE, *née* St Clair-Ford; *b* 24 Oct 1935; *Educ* Eton, RMA Sandhurst; *m* 29 Aug 1964, Polly Mary, da of Robin George Marriott (d 1943), of Malton, N Yorks; 2 s (Mark b 20 Jan 1968, Hugh b 21 Oct 1970), 1 da (Sarah (Mrs Alexander Guthe) b 5 March 1966); *Career* cmmnd KOYLI 1955, serv in Kenya, Cyprus, Malaya, Brunei and Germany 1955–66, Indian Staff Coll 1966, CO 2 LI 1976–79, Col AG2 1981–84, Brig cmd UDR 1984–86; regnl dir (N Region) Br Heart Fndn 1986–96, pt/t farmer 1986–, church warden; *Recreations* shooting, gardening, fishing; *Clubs* Army and Navy; *Style*— Brig Roger Preston, CBE; ✉ Whitegrounds, Thornthorpe, Malton, N Yorkshire YO17 9LX (☎ 01653 658305)

PRESTON, Sir Ronald Douglas Hildebrand; 7 Bt (UK 1815), of Beeston St Lawrence, Norfolk; s of Sir Thomas Hildebrand Preston, OBE, 6 Bt (d 1976), and Ella, Lady Preston (d 1989); *b* 9 Oct 1916; *Educ* Westminster, Trinity Coll Cambridge (MA), Ecole des Sciences Politiques Paris; *m* 1, 1954 (m dis 1971), Smilya Stefanovic; m 2, 1972, Pauleen Jane, da of late Paul Lurcott; *Heir* kinsman, Philip Charles Henry Hulton Preston; *Career* served WW II, with 8 Army in Mid East and Italy, Austria and Allied Control Cmmn to Bulgaria, late Maj Intelligence Corps; Reuter's corr in Belgrade 1948–53; Times corr: Vienna and E Europe 1953–60, Tokyo 1960–63; HM Dip Serv 1963–76; *Recreations* tennis, shooting; *Clubs* Travellers', Norfolk (Norwich), Tokyo (Tokyo); *Style*— Sir Ronald Preston, Bt; ✉ 68 Saxmundham Road, Aldeburgh, Suffolk IP15 5PA (☎ 01728 454063)

PRESTON, Simon Douglas Nelson; s of Jocelyn Panizzi Preston (d 1970), of Romsey, and Emily Geraldine Morval Kirby, *née* Nelson (d 1995), of Mawgan, Cornwall; *b* 5 Aug 1933; *Educ* Sherborne, Trinity Coll Cambridge (MA); *m* 30 June 1962, Celia Mary, da of Frank Bodenham Thornely, MC (d 1958), of Tunbridge Wells; 4 s (Rupert b 1963, Adam b 1966, John b 1975, Charles b 1975), 1 da (Emma b 1965); *Career* Nat Serv Lt RM Commandos Austria special duties 1952–54; PR offr Stock Exchange 1959–64, info offr Lazard Bros & Co Ltd 1964–66; dir: Financial PR Ltd 1966–68, Charles Barker City Ltd 1968–71, Mixed Media Ltd 1982–87; fin dir Leo Burnett Ltd 1971–74, md and dir Dewe Rogerson Ltd 1974–81, dep chm St James PR Ltd 1987–90; chm Financial Public Relations Ltd 1990–; chm: City Liaison Gp 1973–74 and 1979–83, Br Enterprise Award Ctee 1981–84; memb Cncl Assoc of Ind Business 1978–79, dir Think British Campaign 1982–87; MIPR (hon treas 1981–82); *Recreations* farming, sailing, entomology; *Clubs* Travellers'; *Style*— Simon Preston, Esq; ✉ Bohemia, Old Kennels, Bunny Lane, Frant, Tunbridge Wells, Kent TN3 9HA (☎ 01892 750936); Financial Public Relations Ltd, 76 Shoe Lane, London EC4A 3JB (☎ 0171 353 8907, fax 0171 353 7550)

PRESTON, Thomas Davis; s of Thomas William Samuel Lane Preston (d 1952), of Eastbourne, Sussex, and Madeleine Irene, *née* Davis (d 1966); *b* 1 Dec 1932; *Educ* Gillingham Sch; *m* 23 March 1963, Jennifer Katherine, da of Dr James Anderson, OBE; 2 da (Carolyn b 1969, Lesley b 1971); *Career* Colonial Serv Kenya: dist offr 1954–62, dist cmmr 1962–63, ret 1963; Phillips Harrisons & Crosfield Kenya: mktg mangr 1963–69, mktg dir 1970–73, chm and md 1974–79, chm 1979–88; dir Harrisons & Crosfield plc London 1981–94, chm and chief exec Harrisons & Crosfield Aust 1982–94; chm: Harcros Chemicals Aust 1982–94, Harrisons & Crosfield Papua New Guinea 1982–96, New Britain Palm Oil Development Papua New Guinea 1982–96, Linatex Aust 1984–85, Kapiura Plantations Papua New Guinea 1986–96, Hudson Timber & Hardware 1994–96, Asia Pacific Speciality Chemicals 1995–; pres Aust-Papua New Guinea Business Cncl 1991–93; FCIM; *Recreations* golf, opera; *Clubs* Carlton, Elanora Country (Sydney), Royal Sydney Yacht Sqdn (Sydney); *Style*— Thomas Preston, Esq; ✉ Hamptons, Shipbourne, Kent; Elamang Ave, Kirribilli, Sydney, Australia

PRESTON, Timothy William; QC (1982); s of Charles Frank Preston; *b* 3 Nov 1935; *Educ* Haileybury, Jesus Coll Oxford (BA); *m* 1965, Barbara Mary Haygarth; *Career* 2 Lt 16/5 Lancers 1955, Capt Staffs Yeo, ret; called to the Bar Inner Temple 1964, recorder of the Crown Ct 1979–; *Recreations* golf, hunting; *Clubs* Cavalry and Guards'; *Style*— Timothy Preston, Esq, QC; ✉ 2 Temple Gardens, London EC4Y 9AY (☎ 0171 583 6041)

PRESTON-DUNLOP, Dr Valerie Morthland; *née* Preston; da of Arthur Llewellyn Preston (d 1936), Bishop of Woolwich, and Nancy Robina, *née* Napier (d 1977); *b* 14 March 1930; *Educ* Downe House Newbury, Art of Movement Studio (Dip), Univ of London (Dip Ed, MA), Laban Centre (PhD); *m* 16 Sept 1961, John Henderson Dunlop, s of Sir John Kinninmont Dunlop, KBE, CMG, MC (d 1976), of Ridge Lea, Sevenoaks; 1 s (Roger Napier b 1965), 1 da (Emma Preston b 1971); *Career* sr lectr Dartford Coll of PE 1954–63, dir Beechmont Movement Study Centre 1965–73, currently advsr on postgrad studies and res Laban Centre for Movement and Dance, int lectr and writer on dance (princ areas of res Rudolf Laban and Choreology), pioneer of practice dance scholarship; *Books* Practical Kinetography (1969), Dancing and Dance Theory (1979), Dance in Education (1980), Point of Departure (1984), Schrifttanz: a view of German dance in the Weimar Republic (1990), Rudolf Laban: an introduction (1990), Dance Words (1995); *Clubs* Royal Society of Arts; *Style*— Dr Valerie Preston-Dunlop; ✉ Corners, The Street, Ightham, Kent (fax 01732 886764); Laban Centre, Newcross, London SE14 (☎ 0181 692 4070)

PRESTRIDGE, Jeffrey John; s of Stanley Prestridge, of Sutton Coldfield, W Mids, and Helen Joyce, *née* Carpenter; *b* 8 April 1959; *Educ* Bishop Vesey GS, Loughborough Univ (BSc); *m* 10 Sept 1983, Susan, *née* Dove; 3 s (Matthew Stanley George b 25 March 1991, Mark Christopher Jeffrey b 21 Sept 1992, James David Luke b 11 Feb 1994); *Career* articled clerk Price Waterhouse CAs 1980–82, res asst Debenham Tewson Chinnocks 1982–84, self-employed 1984–86, dep ed World Investor 1986–87, economist Bristol & West Building Society 1987, dep ed Money Management Magazine 1987–90; family fin ed: The Sunday Telegraph 1990–94, The Mail on Sunday 1994–; winner of several awards for personal fin journalism; *Recreations* swimming, photography, squash, WBA FC, walking in the Lakes; *Style*— Jeffrey Prestridge, Esq; ✉ 10 Upper Hitch, Carpenders Park, Herts WD1 5AW (☎ 0181 428 5190); The Mail on Sunday, Northcliffe House, 2 Derry Street, London W8 5TS (☎ 0171 938 6000)

PRESTT, His Hon Arthur Miller; QC (1970); s of Arthur Prestt (d 1959), and Jessie, *née* Miller (d 1978); bro of Ian Prestt, CBE (d 1995); *b* 23 April 1925; *Educ* Bootham Sch York, Trinity Hall Cambridge; *m* 1949, Jill Mary, da of Graham Richards Dawbarn, CBE (d 1977); 1 s, 1 da; *Career* served WWII 13 Bn Parachute Regt: NW Europe, Malaya, Java; war crimes prosecutor Far E, Hon Maj Parachute Regt; called to the bar Middle Temple 1949; JP Cumberland 1966, chm Cumberland QS 1969–70 (dep chm 1966–69), circuit judge 1971–90, sr circuit judge Manchester (N Circuit) and recorder of Manchester 1982–90; previously active in Scout Assoc (Silver Acorn 1970); *Recreations* golf, gardening; *Style*— His Hon Arthur Prestt, QC; ✉ 10 Heigham Grove, Norwich, Norfolk NR2 3DQ (☎ 01603 622631)

PRESTWICH, Prof Michael Charles; s of John Oswald Prestwich, of Oxford, and Menna, *née* Roberts (d 1990); *b* 30 Jan 1943; *Educ* Charterhouse, Magdalen Coll Oxford, ChCh Oxford (MA, DPhil); *m* 11 May 1973, Margaret Joan, da of Herbert Daniel (d 1980), of Glossop; 2 s (Robin b 1974, Christopher b 1976), 1 da (Kate b 1980); *Career* res lectr Christ Church Oxford 1965–69, lectr in medieval history Univ of St Andrews 1969–79; Univ of Durham: reader in medieval history 1979–86, prof of history 1986–, pro-vice chllr 1992–; FRHistS 1972, FSA 1980; *Books* War, Politics and Finance under Edward I (1972), The Three Edwards: War and State in England 1272–1377 (1980), Documents Illustrating the Crisis of 1297–8 in England (1980), Edward I (1988), English Politics in the Thirteenth Century (1990), Armies and Warfare in the Middle Ages: The English Experience (1996); *Recreations* skiing; *Style*— Prof Michael Prestwich, FSA; ✉ 46 Albert Street, Western Hill, Durham DH1 4RJ (☎ 0191 3862539); Department of History, 43/46 North Bailey, Durham DH1 3EX

PRETTY, Dr Katharine Bridget (Kate); da of Maurice Walter Hughes (d 1975), of Birmingham, and Bridget Elizabeth Whibley, *née* Marples; *b* 18 Oct 1945; *Educ* King Edward VI HS for Girls Birmingham, New Hall Cambridge (scholar, MA, PhD); *m* 1,

1967 (m dis), Graeme Lloyd Pretty; m 2, 1988, Prof Tjeerd Hendrik van Andel; *Career* Univ of Cambridge: fell and lectr in archaeology New Hall 1972, admissions tutor New Hall 1979–82, sr tutor New Hall 1985–91 (emeritus fell 1995–), princ Homerton Coll 1991–, memb Univ Fin Bd 1986–, chm Faculty Bd of Archaeology and Anthropology 1991–, memb Univ Gen Bd 1997, chm Cncl Sch of Humanities and Social Scis 1997–; sec Cambs Archaeological Ctee 1974–79, chm RESCUE Br Archaeological Tst 1978–83; *Recreations* archaeology in the Arctic, botany and gardening; *Style—* Dr Kate Pretty; ✉ Homerton College, Hills Road, Cambridge CB2 2PH (☎ 01223 507131, fax 01223 507130)

PREVETT, Geoffrey James (Geoff); s of James William Prevett, of Ewell, Surrey, and Helen Lillian, *née* Luckett; *b* 30 Nov 1944; *Educ* Westminster; *m* 25 June 1966, Joan, da of Thomas Bevan, of Maesteg, South Wales; 1 s (Christopher b 31 Jan 1980), 1 da (Melanie b 6 Feb 1973); *Career* admitted slr 1978; Travers Smith Braithwaite 1963–79, Lewis Lewis and Co 1979–82 (ptnr 1981), ptnr Eversheds (Jaques and Lewis before merger) 1982–; memb: Law Soc, Holborn Law Soc; FCIArb; *Recreations* music, theatre, reading, cricket; *Style—* Geoff Prevett, Esq; ✉ 22 Northcliffe Close, Worcester Park, Surrey KTF4 7DS (☎ 0181 337 3377); Eversheds, Senator House, 85 Queen Victoria Street, London EC4V 4JL (☎ 0171 919 4500, fax 0171 919 4919)

PREVETT, John Henry; OBE (1974); s of Frank George Harry Prevett (d 1981), and Florence Emily, *née* Wilson (d 1968); *b* 6 April 1933; *Educ* Oxted Co GS, John Ruskin GS; *m* 28 March 1959, Joy Maureen, da of Martin Josiah Goodchild (d 1947); 2 s (David b 1961, Steven b 1962); *Career* actuary; ptnr Bacon & Woodrow Consultants 1962–; chm: Assoc of Consltg Actuaries 1983–85, Br Def and Aid Fund for Southern Africa 1983–94; memb: (Lab) Reigate Borough Cncl 1963–69 and 1971–73, Reigate and Banstead Borough Cncl 1973–84 and 1986–; Freeman: City of London 1980, Worshipful Co of Actuaries 1980; FIA 1955, FPMI 1977; *Books* Actuarial Valuations of Interests in Settled Property (with C O Beard, 1973); *Recreations* wining and dining; *Clubs* Lunchtime Comment; *Style—* John Prevett, Esq, OBE; ✉ 62 Gatton Rd, Reigate, Surrey RH2 OHL (☎ 01737 246629); Bacon & Woodrow, St Olaf House, London Bridge City, London SE1 2PE (☎ 0171 357 7171, fax 0171 378 8428/8470)

PREVITE, His Hon Judge John Edward; QC (1989); s of late Lt-Col Kenneth E Previte, OBE, and (Edith) Frances, *née* Capper (d 1995); *b* 11 May 1934; *Educ* Wellington Coll, Christ Church Oxford (MA); *m* 1959, Hon Phyllida Browne, da of 6 Baron Kilmaine (d 1978); 2 s (Andrew Capper b 1961, Matthew John b 1963); *Career* called to the Bar Inner Temple 1959, bencher 1986; recorder W Circuit 1987–92, circuit judge (SE Circuit) 1992–; Liveryman Worshipful Co of Salters; *Recreations* sailing, Nordic skiing; *Style—* His Hon Judge Previte, QC; ✉ Knightsbridge Crown Court, 1 Pocock Street, London SE1 0BT

PREVOST, Brian Trevor George; s of Raymond George Prevost (d 1974), and (Winifred) Grace, *née* White (d 1981); *b* 2 May 1932; *Educ* Bradfield, Imede Lausanne Switzerland; *m* 16 June 1956, Margaret Anne, da of Lt-Col John Douglas Allder Vincent (d 1964); 3 da (Sally b 1958, Wendy b 1960, Jacky b 1964); *Career* 2 Lt RA 1951–53, Lt HAC (RHA) 1955–63; dir Sedgwick Collins & Co Ltd 1964–72, dir Sedgwick Forbes Ltd and chm Sedgwick Forbes Reinsurance Brokers Ltd 1972–79; Swiss Reinsurance Co (UK) Ltd: dep chief exec 1979–83, dir and gen mangr 1983–89, md 1989–92, dep chm 1993–; dir: THG Holdings Ltd 1988–96, Audatex (UK) Ltd 1987–; chm: Reinsurance Offices Assoc 1988–90 (memb Exec Ctee 1983–90, dep chm 1987–88), Orchard Way Residents Ltd 1996–; memb Cncl London Insurance and Reinsurance Market Assoc 1991–92; underwriting memb Lloyd's 1969–79; Freeman City of London, Liveryman Worshipful Co of Insurers 1982; FInstD; *Recreations* golf, bridge; *Clubs* Burhill Golf, Insurance Golfing Soc of London; *Style—* Brian T G Prevost, Esq; ✉ Rickstones, 8 Orchard Way, Esher, Surrey KT10 9DY (☎ 01372 462318); Swiss Reinsurance Co (UK) Ltd, Swiss Re House, 71–77 Leadenhall St, London EC3A 2PQ (☎ 0171 623 3456, fax 0171 929 4282, telex 884380)

PREVOST, Sir Christopher Gerald; 6 Bt (UK 1805); s of Sir George James Augustine Prevost, 5 Bt (d 1985), and Muriel Emily, *née* Oram (d 1939); *b* 25 July 1935; *Educ* Cranleigh; *m* 1964, Dolores Nelly, o da of Dezo Hoffmann; 1 s, 1 da; *Heir* s, Nicholas Marc Prevost b 13 March 1971; *Career* late 60 Regt; fndr Mailtronic Ltd manufacturers and suppliers of mailroom equipment (chm and md 1977–91); memb Exec Cncl Huguenot Soc; *Recreations* squash, jet-skiing; *Style—* Sir Christopher Prevost, Bt; ✉ Caixa 307Z, Vale Rabelho (Guia), 8200 Albufeira, Portugal

PRICE, *see also:* Rugge-Price

PRICE, (Alan) Anthony; s of Walter Longsdon Price (d 1942), and Kathleen Lawrence (d 1937); *b* 16 Aug 1928; *Educ* The King's Sch Canterbury, Merton Coll Oxford (MA); *m* 1953, Ann, da of Norman George Stone (d 1968); 2 s (James, Simon), 1 da (Katherine); *Career* mil serv 1947–49, Capt; journalist and author; ed The Oxford Times 1972–88; *Books* The Labyrinth Makers (1970, CWA Silver Dagger), The Alamut Ambush (1971), Colonel Butler's Wolf (1972), October Men (1973), Other Paths to Glory (1974, CWA Gold Dagger 1974, Swedish Acad of Detection Prize 1978), Our Man in Camelot (1975), War Game (1976), The '44 Vintage (1978), Tomorrow's Ghost (1979), The Hour of the Donkey (1980), Soldier No More (1981), The Old Vengeful (1982), Gunner Kelly (1983), Sion Crossing (1984), Here Be Monsters (1985), For the Good of the State (1986), A New Kind of War (1987), A Prospect of Vengeance (1988), The Memory Trap (1989), The Eyes of The Fleet (1990); *Recreations* military history, gardening, travelling; *Clubs* Detection; *Style—* Anthony Price, Esq; ✉ Wayside Cottage, Horton-cum-Studley, Oxford OX33 1AW (☎ 01865 351 326)

PRICE, Antony; *b* Yorkshire; *Educ* Bradford Coll of Art (Dip), RCA (MA); *Career* fashion designer; initial experience with Stirling Cooper mens and womenswear retailers, subsequent designs of covers, sets and clothes for Roxy Music and The Rolling Stones and numerous Hollywood stars, opened first shop under own label Plaza in King's Road Chelsea 1977, expanded to South Molton Street Mayfair 1986; currently specialises solely in exclusive haute couture business from own salon for an international clientele; Glamour Designer of the Year Award Br Fashion Awards 1989; *Style—* Antony Price, Esq; ✉ 468 Kings Road, London SW10

PRICE, Barrie; s of Albert Price (d 1978), of Bradford, and Mary, *née* Melvin (d 1982); *b* 13 Aug 1937; *Educ* St Bede's GS Bradford; *m* 15 April 1963, Elizabeth, da of William Murphy (d 1979); 4 s (Nicholas Becket b 1963, Joseph b 1965, Gerard b 1968, Mark b 1974), 1 da (Catherine b 1966); *Career* trainee accountant 1953–58, sr ptnr Lishman Sidwell Campbell and Price 1974– (ptnr 1962–), chm and md Lishman Sidwell Campbell & Price Ltd (formerly Slouand Ltd) 1968–; cncllr: Ripon City Cncl 1968–91 (Mayor 1980–81, dep Mayor 1974–75, 1982–83 and 1987–88), Harrogate Borough DC 1974–91 (dep leader 1987–88 and 1990–91, chm Econ Devpt Ctee); chm: Ripon Life Care and Housing Tst, Ripon City and Dist Devpt Assoc 1969–90; govr St Wilfrid's RC Sch Ripon 1970–91; tstee: City of Ripon Festival (chm 1981–), Yorks Film Archive, Ripon Cathedral Appeal; memb: Ripon Chamber of Trade and Commerce 1962–83 (pres 1975–77, life memb 1983–), RC Diocese of Leeds Finance Ctee & Bd 1989–94, Ripon Improvement Tst 1994– (chm Fin Ctee 1994–); FCA 1968 (ACA 1959), FCCA, FIMgt; *Recreations* opera, football, racing, farm animals; *Clubs* Opera North, Ripon Race Course Members; *Style—* Barrie Price, Esq; ✉ Prospect House, 54 Palace Road, Ripon, North Yorks HG4 1HA (☎ 01765 602058); Lishman Sidwell Campbell & Price Ltd, John Aislabie House, 68 North Street, Ripon, North Yorks (☎ 01765 690890); Lishman Sidwell Campbell & Price, Becket's House, Market Place, Ripon, North Yorks (☎ 01765 600681)

PRICE, Barry David Keith; CBE (1991), QPM (1981); s of John Leslie Price, and Lena, *née* Morgan; *b* 28 June 1933; *Educ* Southall GS; *m* 4 July 1953, Evelyne Jean Horlick; 3 da (Gaynor b 8 Aug 1954, Alison b 29 Aug 1956, Kathryn b 28 Aug 1964); *Career* Constable through ranks to Detective Chief Supt Metropolitan Police 1954–75, Asst Chief Constable Northumbria Police 1975–78, Dep Chief Constable Essex Police 1978–80, Chief Constable Cumbria Constabulary 1980–87, coordinator Nat Drugs Intelligence Unit 1987–93, ret; currently private conslt; author of articles in law enforcement and med pubns; co dir St John Ambulance Assoc 1981–87, pres English Police Golf Assoc 1981–92, memb Advsy Cncl on Misuse of Drugs 1982–87, advsr to ACPO Crime Ctee on Drugs Matters 1985–92 (former chm and sec), memb Drugs Intelligence Steering Gp 1987–92; *Recreations* golf, painting, gardening; *Style—* Barry Price, Esq, CBE, QPM

PRICE, Bernard Albert; CBE (1997); s of Albert Price (d 1952), of Calverhall, Shrops, and Doris, *née* Whittingham (d 1959); *b* 6 Jan 1944; *Educ* Whitchurch GS Shrops, King's Sch Rochester Kent, Merton Coll Oxford (MA); *m* 4 June 1966, Christine Mary, da of Roy William Henry Combes (d 1979), of Chelmsford, Essex; 2 s (David b 1971, John b 1976), 1 da (Emma b 1973); *Career* co clerk and chief exec Staffs CC 1983– (sr dep clerk 1980–83), clerk to the Lieutenancy Staffs 1983–, sec and chief exec W Mids Forum of Local Authys 1985–; *Recreations* sailing, walking; *Style—* Bernard Price, Esq, CBE; ✉ The Cottage, Yeatsall Lane, Abbots Bromley, Rugeley, Staffs (☎ 01283 840269); County Buildings, Martin St, Stafford, Staffs (☎ 01785 223121)

PRICE, Brian Derek; s of Gp Capt Derek Price (d 1988), and Lorna Mary MacMullen, *née* Bulleid (d 1995); *b* 2 Oct 1939, Ayr; *Educ* Tonbridge; *m* 18 June 1966, Juliet Elisabeth Rosamund, yr da of Maj Sir Reginald Lawrence William Williams, Bt, MBE, ED (d 1970); 2 s (Edmund Hugh Owain b 1969, Henry William Frederick b 1973); *Career* CA; ptnr Kidsons Impey (formerly Hodgson Impey and Hodgson Harris) 1974–90, seconded as dep sec DOE 1988–89; md Michael Else and Co Ltd 1991–93, dir Aero-Print Ltd 1991–; chm London Soc of CAs 1979–80 (ctee memb 1967–80), memb Cncl ICAEW 1987–93; fndr Founding Societies Centenary Award 1980, tstee and treas Fight for Sight 1980–95, treas Fight for Sight Special Appeal 1987–91, govr Royal Nat Coll for the Blind Hereford 1982–90, treas Putney Cons Assoc 1995–; Liveryman Worshipful Co of Curriers; ACA 1962, FCA 1967; *Recreations* history, walking; *Clubs* Athenaeum, City of London, Leander, London Rowing; *Style—* Brian Price, Esq; ✉ 52 Hazlewell Rd, Putney, London SW15 6LR

PRICE, Charles Beaufort; s of Mervyn Beaufort Price, and Jessie Price; *b* 7 Nov 1945; *Educ* King's Coll Taunton, Queen Mary Coll London (BA); *m* 29 May 1971, Patricia Ann; 1 s (Gareth Charles b 29 March 1978), 1 da (Isabelle Louise b 8 Sept 1981); *Career* md N M Rothschild & Sons (Singapore) Limited 1976–79, dir N M Rothschild & Sons Limited 1985–96 (chm Wales 1992–96); memb Lombard Assoc; AIB; *Recreations* gardening, rugby, opera; *Clubs* Tanglin (Singapore); *Style—* Charles Price, Esq

PRICE, The Hon Charles H; s of Charles Harry Price and Virginia, *née* Ogden; *b* 1 April 1931; *Educ* Univ of Missouri; *m* Carol Ann, *née* Swanson; 2 s, 3 da; *Career* pres Linwood Securities 1960–81; chm Mercantile Bank of Kansas City 1992–96; chm, chief exec offr and pres Ameribanc Inc 1990–92 (chm 1989–); chm: Price Candy Co 1969–81, American Bank Corpn 1973–81, American Bank and Tst Co 1973–81, American Mortgage Co 1973–81; US ambass: Belgium 1981–83, UK 1983–89; dir: US Industries Inc NJ, Hanson plc London, New York Times Co, Texaco Inc NY, Sprint Kansas City, 360° Communications Inc Chicago; Midwest Res Inst Kansas City; hon fell Regent's Coll 1986; Hon Doctorate: Westminster Coll Missouri 1984, Univ of Missouri 1988, Baker Univ Baldwin City Kansas 1991; Salvation Army's William Booth award 1985; Univ of Missouri Kansas City Chancellor's Medal 1992; Tstee Citation award Midwest Res Inst 1987 (William F Yates Medallion for Distinguished Service 1996); *Recreations* golf, tennis, shooting; *Clubs* White's, Mark's, Swinley Forest Golf, The Brook (NY), Cypress Point (Calif), Eldorado (Calif), Castle Pines Golf (Colorado), Kansas City Country; *Style—* The Hon Charles H Price II; ✉ One West Armour, Suite 300, Kansas City, Missouri 64111, USA

PRICE, Christopher; s of Stanley Price (d 1988), of Sheffield, and Katherine Phyllis, *née* Thornton; *b* 26 Jan 1932; *Educ* Leeds GS, Queen's Coll Oxford; *m* 26 June 1956, Annie Grierson, da of James Ross (d 1987), of Edinburgh; 2 s (Anthony Ross b 1959, Michael John b 1962), 1 da (Jennifer Margaret b 1957); *Career* ed New Education 1966–68, educn corr New Statesman 1968–74, princ Leeds Metropolitan Univ (formerly Leeds Poly) 1986–93 (princ-emeritus 1994); MP (Lab): Birmingham Perry Barr 1966–70, Lewisham West 1974–83; chm Select Ctee on Educn Sci and the Arts 1979–83, co-chm Campaign for Freedom of Info 1988–94, memb Bd Yorks and Humberside Arts 1993–; pres Br Educnl Mgmnt and Admin Soc 1992–94; fell Int Inst of Biotechnology 1984; Hon DUniv Leeds Met Univ 1994; FRSA 1987; *Books* The Confait Confessions (1979); *Style—* Christopher Price; ✉ 17 Albert Hill, Settle, North Yorkshire BD24 9HE (☎ 0802 754071)

PRICE, Christopher John Stuart; s of John Eric Price (d 1994), of Weymouth Park, Salcombe, S Devon, and Mary Stuart, *née* Hicks; *b* 16 March 1939; *Educ* Brentwood Sch; *m* 8 Sept 1962, Elizabeth Kay, da of Geoffrey Egerton Gilbert; 1 s (Matthew Stuart b 28 Dec 1965), 1 da (Emma Ruth b 22 Jan 1968); *Career* chm Sedgwick Credit Europe Ltd; Freeman City of London, Liveryman Worshipful Co of Insurers; CIMgt; *Recreations* gardening, walking, hunting, music; *Style—* Christopher Price, Esq; ✉ The Oasts, Lower Cousley Wood, Wadhurst, East Sussex TN5 6HF (☎ 01892 783106); Sedgwick Credit Europe Ltd, Sedgwick House, The Sedgwick Centre, London E1 8DX (☎ 0171 481 5229, fax 0171 377 3199, telex 882131)

PRICE, Brig Christopher Keith; s of Col David Keith Price, MC, TD (d 1981), and Barbara Christian, *née* Naumann; *b* 12 July 1947; *Educ* Charterhouse; *m* 6 April 1974, Michele, da of Edward Asa-Thomas, TD (d 1983); 1 s (Andrew b 21 Nov 1980); *Career* cmmnd 4/7 Royal Dragoon Guards 1966, Troop Ldr 1966–70, Regtl Signals Offr/Asst Adj 1970–71, ADC to Cdr Land Forces NI 1971–73, 2 i/c Sqdn 4/7 DG 1973–75, GSO3 3 Div 1975–77, Staff Offr to Res Cmmr Designate to Rhodesia 1977–78, Chief of Staff HQ 33 Armd Bde 1980–81, Sqdn Cdr 4/7 DG 1982–83, Directing Staff Army Staff Coll 1984–86, CO 14/20 King's Hussars 1987–89, BAOR Trg Review 1989–90, ACOS HQ 1 (BR) Corps 1990–93, COS RMAS 1993–94, Chief External Affrs Div and Jt Services Liaison Orgn Br Forces Germany 1995–; memb Grand Military Race Ctee; Freeman: City of London, Worshipful Co of Grocers 1975; *Recreations* hunting, shooting, fishing, skiing; *Clubs* Cavalry and Guards'; *Style—* Brig Christopher Price

PRICE, Prof Christopher Philip; s of Philip Bright Price (d 1955), and Frances Gwendoline Price (d 1986); *b* 28 Feb 1945; *Educ* Univ of London (BSc), Univ of Birmingham (MSc, PhD), MA(Cantab) 1983; *m* 1968, Elizabeth Ann, da of late Frederick Dix; 2 da (Carolyn Sarah b 2 Jan 1974, Emma Jane b 21 Nov 1975); *Career* basic grade biochemist Coventry & Warwick Hosp 1967–72, sr grade then princ grade biochemist E Birmingham Hosp 1972–76; conslt biochemist: Southampton Gen Hosp 1976–80, Addenbrooke's Hosp Cambridge 1980–88; prof of clinical biochemistry St Bartholomew's & The Royal London Sch of Med & Dentistry (formerly London Hosp Med Coll) 1988–, clinical dir for biochemistry Royal Hosp NHS Tst 1988–; memb: Assoc of Clinical Biochemists (chm 1991–94), American Assoc for Clinical Chemistry, Biochemical Soc, American Soc for Bone and Mineral Research, Int Soc for Clinical Enzymology; CChem, FRSC, FRCPath; *Publications* ed 5 books incl Principles & Practice of Immunoassay (2 edn), over 200 research papers and reviews; *Recreations* walking, gardening, reading; *Style—* Prof Christopher Price; ✉ Department of Clinical Biochemistry, St

Bartholomew's & The Royal London School of Medicine & Dentistry, Turner Street, London E1 2AD (☎ 0171 377 7241, fax 0171 377 1544, e-mail C.P.Price@mds.qmw.ac.uk)

PRICE, Sir David Ernest Campbell; kt (1980), DL (Hants 1982); s of Maj Villiers Price (d 1982), and Margaret Campbell Currie (d 1930); *b* 20 Nov 1924; *Educ* Eton, Trinity Coll Cambridge, Univ of Yale USA; *m* 1960, Rosemary Eugénie Evelyn, da of Cyril F Johnston, OBE (d 1950); 1 da (Arabella); *Career* WWII served 1 Bn Scots Gds, HQ 56 (London) Div, Italy; with ICI 1949–62; MP (C) Eastleigh 1955–92, Parly del to Western European Union and Cncl of Europe 1958–61, Parly sec BOT 1962–64, oppn front bench spokesman on Sci and Technol 1964–70, Parly sec Miny of Technol June-Oct 1970, Parly sec Miny of Aviation Supply 1970–71, Parly under sec state Aerospace DTI 1971–72; memb Select Ctee on: Science and Technol 1974–79, Tport 1979–83, Social Servs 1984–90, Health 1990–92; conslt Western United Investment Company Ltd 1973–92, vice pres Inst of Industl Mangrs 1973–90, chm Parly and Scientific Ctee 1973–74 and 1979–82; non-exec dir Southampton Univ Hosps Tst 1992–, chm Hants Community Care Forum 1993–, tstee Wessex Medical Tst 1988–96, govr Middlesex Hosp 1960–62; FIMgt; *Recreations* wine, history of art, music, cooking, gardening; *Clubs* Athenaeum, Beefsteak; *Style*— Sir David Price, DL; ✉ Forest Lodge, Moonhills Lane, Beaulieu, Hampshire S042 7YW (☎ 01590 612537)

PRICE, David William James; s of Richard J E Price (d 1983), of Quinta da Romeira, Bucelas, Portugal, and Miriam Joan, *née* Dunsford; *b* 11 June 1947; *Educ* Ampleforth, CCC Oxford (MA); *m* 1971, Shervie Ann Lander, da of Sir James Whitaker, 3 Bt, *qv*; 1 s (William b 1973), 1 da (Hesther b 1971); *Career* farmer and merchant banker; dir: Warburg Investment Management Ltd 1978, S G Warburg & Co Ltd 1982–87; chm Mercury Asset Management plc 1983–, dep chm Mercury Asset Management Group plc 1987–; non-exec dir: Mercury European Privatisation Trust 1994–, Equitable Life Assurance Soc 1996–; cncllr London Borough of Lambeth 1979–82; *Clubs* Brooks's, Lincolnshire; *Style*— David Price, Esq; ✉ Harrington Hall, Spilsby, Lincs; 39 Old Town, Clapham, London SW4 0JL; Mercury Asset Management plc, 33 King William St, London EC4 (☎ 0171 280 2800)

PRICE, Eric Hardiman Mockford; s of Frederick Hardiman Price, and Florence Nellie Hannah; *b* 14 Nov 1931; *Educ* St Marylebone GS, Christ's Coll Cambridge (BA, MA); *m* 3 Feb 1963, Diana Teresa Anne Mary Stanley, da of Stanley Joseph Leckie Robinson (d 1962), of Harbury Hall, Warwicks; 1 s (Julian b 27 Feb 1969), 3 da (Caroline b 29 Jan 1964, Nichola b 28 March 1966, Ashling b 6 July 1970); *Career* Nat Serv Army 1950–52, HAC 1952–57; economist: Central Electricity Authy Electricity Cncl 1957–58, Br Iron and Steel Fedn 1958–62; chief economist Port of London Authy 1962–67; Miny of Tport: sr econ advsr 1966–69, chief econ advsr 1967–71, dir of econs 1971–75; DOE: under sec econs 1972–76, dir of econs and statistics 1975–76; under sec econs and statistics: Depts of Trade Indust and Consumer Protection 1977–80, Dept of Energy 1980–92; under sec and chief economic advsr DTI 1992–93; special conslt National Economic Research Associates 1993–; dir Robinson Bros (Ryders Green) Ltd 1985–; proprietor The Energy Economics Consultancy 1995–; Br Inst of Energy Econs: memb Cncl 1980–, vice chm 1981–82 and 1988–89, chm 1982–85; FREconS, FRSS, FInstD, MInstPet; *Recreations* squash, tennis, local history; *Clubs* Moor Park Golf, Batchworth Park Golf; *Style*— Eric Price, Esq; ✉ Batchworth House, Batchworth Heath Farm, London Rd, Rickmansworth, Herts WD3 1QB (☎ 01927 824471), fax 01923 841002)

PRICE, Sir Francis Caradoc Rose; 7 Bt (UK 1815), QC (1992); s of Sir Rose Francis Price, 6 Bt (d 1979), and Kathleen June, yr da of Norman William Hutchinson, of Melbourne, Aust; *b* 9 Sept 1950; *Educ* Eton, Trinity Coll Univ of Melbourne, Univ of Alberta; *m* 1975, (Hon Madam Justice) Marguerite Jean, da of Roy Samuel Trussler, of Victoria, BC; 3 da (Adrienne Calantha Rose b 1976, Megan Kathleen Rose b 1977, Glynis Nicola Rose b 1982); *Heir* bro, Norman William Rose Price, *qv*; *Career* barr and slr Canada, ptnr Reynolds Mirth Richards & Farmer; chartered arbitrator; *Books* Pipelines in Western Canada (1975), Mortgage Actions in Alberta (1985); *Recreations* cricket, jogging, theatre, opera; *Clubs* Centre, Faculty; *Style*— Sir Francis Price, Bt, QC; ✉ 9626 95 Ave, Edmonton, Alberta T6C 2A4, Canada (☎ home 00 1 403 469 9555, work 00 1 403 497 3388, fax 00 1 403 429 3044)

PRICE, Frank Christopher (Chris); s of Geoffrey Arthur Price, of Wilmslow, Cheshire, and Celia, *née* Fixter; *b* 1 Aug 1946; *Educ* Uppingham, Univ of Nottingham (indust scholar, BSc), Leicester Poly (DMS); *m* 1, 1970 (m dis 1992), Catherine; 1 s (Geoffrey Michael b 19 Sept 1974), 1 da (Anne Elisabeth b 17 Dec 1976); m 2, 1995, Sylvia; *Career* British Shoe Machinery Ltd: graduate apprentice, mangr Machinery Res and Devpt Dept, memb Bd of Mgmnt 1981–85; engrg dir Rearsby Automotive Ltd Leicester 1985–87; USM TEXON Ltd (formerly United Machinery Gp Ltd): dir Res and Devpt 1987–93, dir Product and Process Development 1993–; named inventor on 20 patents; hon sr indust fell and hon visiting prof de Montfort Univ 1992–; Inst of Mech Engrs: chm E Midlands Branch 1986–88, vice pres 1991–93, dep pres 1993–94, pres 1995–96; memb Senate Engrg Cncl; Freeman City of London 1995, Liveryman Worshipful Co of Engrs 1995; FIMechE 1985 (MIMechE 1976), FEng 1993, FIEE 1995; *Recreations* skiing, theatre, walking, gardening; *Style*— Chris Price, Esq, FEng; ✉ 15 Southland Road, Leicester LE2 3RJ (☎ and fax 0116 270 4614); USM TEXON Ltd, PO Box 88, Ross Walk, Belgrave, Leicester LE4 5BX (☎ 0116 261 0111, fax 0116 261 0423)

PRICE, Sir Frank Leslie; kt (1966), DL; s of George Frederick Price (d 1978), and Lucy Price (d 1978); *b* 26 July 1922; *Educ* St Mathias Sch Birmingham, Vittoria St Arts Sch; *m* 1, 1944 (m dis 1976), Maisie Edna, da of Albert Davis, of Handsworth Wood, Birmingham; 1 s (Noel Bayley); m 2 (m dis 1984), Veronica, da of Zubadri Singh; m 3, Daphne, da of John Ling (d 1947), of Highgate; *Career* md Murrayfield Real Estate Co Ltd 1958–68; chm: Midlands Arts Centre for Young People 1960–66, Birmingham and Midlands Investments Ltd 1967–74, Telford New Town Corp 1968–72, Br Waterways Bd 1968–84, Wharf Holdings 1968–72, M L Alkan Ltd 1972–75, Sir Frank Price and Compania Sociedad Colectiva 1985–; dir: Comp Devpts Assoc 1968–80, National Exhibition Centre Ltd 1970–76, Butlers and Colonial Wharfs Ltd 1971–76; cncllr and alderman Birmingham City Cncl 1949–84, Lord Mayor of Birmingham 1964–65; DL: Warwickshire 1970–77, W Mids 1974–82, Hereford & Worcs 1973–82; memb: Cncl Town and Country Planning Assoc 1954–74, Lord Chllr's Advsy Ctee 1967–72, Nat Water Cncl 1975–79, English Tourist Bd 1975–82; pres Br Assoc of Industl Eds 1979–83; Freeman City of London; FSVA, FCIT, FRSA; *Clubs* Reform; *Style*— Sir Frank Price, DL; ✉ Casa Non Such Apartado, 534 Mojacar Playa, Almeria 04638, Spain (☎ 00 34 50 478915, fax 00 34 50 478963)

PRICE, Gerald Alexander Lewin; QC (1992); s of Denis Lewin Price, of Cowbridge, S Glam, and Patricia Rosemary, *née* Metcalfe; *b* 13 Sept 1948; *Educ* Haileybury, Coll of Law, Inns of Ct Sch of Law; *m* 28 Dec 1974, Theresa Elizabeth, da of Hilary Baldwin Iremonger-Watts; 2 s (Alexander Baldwin Lewin b 27 Feb 1981, Lawrence Christopher b 3 Dec 1983); *Career* called to the Bar Middle Temple 1969, private practise at Bar Cardiff 1969–77, resident magistrate Bermuda 1977–81, chm Price Control Cmmn 1979, registrar of Supreme Ct Bermuda 1980, chief magistrate Bermuda, sr coroner, chm Land Valuation Appeals Tbnl, chm Liqour Licensing Bd and chm Jury Revising Ctee 1981–84, private practise at Bar Cardiff 1984–, recorder 1990–; Parly candidate (C) Newport Gwent Feb and Oct 1974, Gower 1987; Anglican lay preacher 1969–; FRCS; *Recreations* travel, motorboats, Menorca, sunshine, tennis, classical music, comedy; *Clubs* RYA, Royal Commonwealth Soc, Glamorgan Lawn Tennis & Croquet; *Style*— Gerald Price, Esq, QC; ✉ 33 Park Place, Cardiff CF1 3BA (☎ 01222 233313, fax 01222 228294, DX 50755)

PRICE, Hon Mrs (Rosalind (Lindy) Helen Penrose); *née* Lewis; CBE (1994); da of 1 Baron Brecon, PC (d 1976, when title became extinct), and Baroness Brecon, CBE, *qv*; *b* 1938; *Educ* Cheltenham Ladies' Coll; *m* 1963, (Arthur) Leolin Price, CBE, QC, *qv*; 2 s, 2 da; *Career* Radio and TV Dept Conservative Central Office 1959–61, Br Consul-General's Office NY 1962, dir Bulldog Manpower Services Ltd 1975–87; dir Norland Nursery Trg Coll 1964–86, chm Governing Body N London Collegiate Sch 1968–87 (co-chm of the fndn 1977–87), memb Governing Body Frances Mary Buss Fndn 1969–87, memb Parole Bd for England and Wales 1969–74, co-opted memb Inner London Probation Ctee 1971–91 (memb sub ctees regarding community serv), former chm Bd of Visitors Brixton Prison (memb 1972–80), memb Cncl Nat Assoc for the Care and Resettlement of Offenders 1974–79, former vice chm Jellicoe Ctee (memb 1974–75), memb Cons Pty Ctee 1977, dep chm Camden Sch for Girls 1981; memb: Police Complaints Bd 1983–85, Midwifery Ctee UK Central Cncl 1983–88, Social Security Advsy Ctee DSS 1987–96; chm: Powys Dist Health Authy 1986–92, Powys Health Care NHS Tst 1992–96, Gwent Health Authy 1996–; dir Powys TEC 1990–95; The Griffins Soc: memb 1965–79, hon sec 1966–70, vice-chm 1970–74, chm 1974–79; *Style*— The Hon Mrs Price, CBE; ✉ 32 Hampstead Grove, London NW3 6SR (☎ 0171 435 9843); Moor Park, Llanbedr, Crickhowell, Powys NP8 1SS (☎ 01873 810443, fax 01873 810659)

PRICE, James Richard Kenrick; QC (1995); s of Lt-Col Kenrick Jack Price, DSO, MC (d 1982), and Juliet Hermione, *née* Slessor (now Mrs de Laszlo, wid of John de Laszlo); *b* 14 Sept 1948; *Educ* Eton, St Edmund Hall Oxford (BA); *m* 1983, Hon Virginia Yvonne, da of Lord Mostyn, MC; *Career* called to the Bar Inner Temple 1974; *Recreations* gardening, skiing, hill walking, fine and decorative arts, dogs; *Clubs* Brooks's, Beefsteak; *Style*— James Price, Esq, QC; ✉ 26 Seymour Walk, London SW10 9NF (☎ 0171 352 8973); Pettifers, Lower Wardington, Nr Banbury, Oxon OX17 1RU (☎ 01295 750232); 5 Raymond Buildings, Gray's Inn, London WC1R 5BP (☎ 0171 242 2902)

PRICE, John Alan (Jack); QC (1980); s of Frederick Leslie Price (d 1976); *b* 11 Sept 1938; *Educ* Stretford GS, Univ of Manchester (LLB Hons); *m* 1, 1964 (m dis 1982), Elizabeth Myra, da of Stanley Priest; 1 s, 1 da; m 2, 1984, Alison Elizabeth, da of Stanley Ward; *Career* called to the Bar Gray's Inn 1961, in practice on Northern Circuit, dep circuit judge 1975–, recorder Crown Court 1980–; *Recreations* tennis, golf; *Style*— Jack Price, Esq, QC; ✉ 25 Byrom St, Manchester M3 4PF (☎ 0161 834 5238)

PRICE, John Philip; s of Eifion Wyn Price, of Rhayader, Powys, and Kathleen, *née* Woodfield; *b* 11 Dec 1949; *Educ* Monmouth Sch, CCC Oxford (MA, BPhil); *Career* called to the Bar Inner Temple 1974; dir gen Dairy Industry Fedn (formerly Dairy Trade Fedn) 1986–; *Books* The English Legal System (1979); *Style*— John Price, Esq; ✉ 20 Rossmore Court, Park Rd, London NW1 6XX (☎ 0171 723 9485); Dairy Industry Federation, 19 Cornwall Terrace, London NW1 4QP (☎ 0171 486 7244, fax 0171 487 4734, telex 262027)

PRICE, Air Vice-Marshal John Walter; CBE (1979, OBE 1973), DL (Hereford & Worcs 1995); s of Henry Walter Price (d 1984), and Myrza, *née* Griffiths (d 1958); *b* 26 Jan 1930; *Educ* Solihull Sch, RAF Coll Cranwell; *m* 1956, Margaret Sinclair (d 1989), da of John McIntyre (d 1960), of Sydney, Aust; *Career* cmmnd from RAF Coll Cranwell 1950; Sqdn flying appts: Vampires and Venoms Germany, Meteors with 77 Sqdn RAAF Korea (despatches 1953), Vampires and Meteors Aust; staff appts in Air Miny 1961–64, cmd No 110 Sqdn Sycamores and Whirlwinds Malaya and Borneo 1964–66, DS RAF Staff Coll 1967, PSO to CAS 1968–70, cmd No 72 Sqdn Wessex 1970–72, dep dir Ops MOD Air 1973–75, cmd RAF Laarbruch (Buccaneers and Jaguars) Germany 1976–78, Gp Capt Ops HQ Strike Cmd 1979, dir Ops Strike MOD Air 1980–82, ACAS Ops 1982–84, ret as Air Vice-Marshal 1984; Clyde Petroleum plc 1984–95; memb Bd of Govrs Solihull Sch 1979– (elected chm 1982); MRAeS, MInstPet, FIMgt (memb Nat Cncl 1994–); *Recreations* golf, cabinet making, motor cycling; *Clubs* RAF; *Style*— Air Vice-Marshal John Price, CBE, DL; ✉ 2 Palace Yard, Hereford (☎ and fax 01432 272292)

PRICE, (Arthur) Leolin; CBE (1996), QC (1968, Bahamas 1969, NSW 1987); s of Evan Price (d 1959), and Ceridwen Price (d 1974); *b* 11 May 1924; *Educ* Judd Sch Tonbridge, Keble Coll Oxford (scholar, MA); *m* 1963, Hon Rosalind (Lindy) (Hon Mrs Price, CBE, *qv*), da of 1 and last Baron Brecon, PC (d 1976); 2 s, 2 da; *Career* called to the Bar Middle Temple 1949 (bencher 1970, treas 1990), ad eundem Lincoln's Inn 1959; head of chambers; barr: Br Virgin Islands 1994, Gibraltar 1996; chllr Diocese of Swansea and Brecon 1982–; vice chm Soc of Cons Lawyers 1987–; dir: Marine Adventure Sailing Trust plc 1982–89, Thornton Asian Emerging Markets Investment Trust plc 1989–95; chm SR Pan-European Investment Trust (formerly Child Health Res Investment Trust plc) 1987– (dir 1980–); chm Ctee of Mgmnt Inst of Child Health 1976–; govr and tstee Great Ormond St Hosp for Sick Children 1972–; govr: Br Postgraduate Med Fedn 1976–96, Christ Coll Brecon 1977–; *Clubs* Carlton; *Style*— Leolin Price, Esq, CBE, QC; ✉ 32 Hampstead Grove, London NW3 6SR (☎ 0171 435 9843); 10 Old Square, Lincoln's Inn, London WC2A 3SU (☎ 0171 405 0758, fax 0171 831 8237); Moor Park, Llanbedr, Crickhowell, Powys NP8 1SS (☎ 01873 810443, fax 01873 810659); Selborne Chambers, 174 Phillip Street, Sydney 2000, Australia (☎ 00 61 2 233 5188)

PRICE, Lionel Dennis Dixon; s of Harold Price (d 1988), of Birkenhead, and Florence Mitchley, *née* Thompson (d 1996); *b* 2 Feb 1946; *Educ* Bolton Sch, CCC Cambridge (MA); *m* 19 Oct 1968, Sara Angela, da of Ronald William Holt (d 1991), of Gerrards Cross, Bucks; 3 s (Matthew b 1972, Edward b & d 1974, James b 1975); *Career* Bank of England 1967–79, alternate exec dir IMF 1979–81; Bank of England: head Info Div 1981–84, head Int Div 1985–90, head Economics Div 1990–94, dir of Central Banking Studies 1994–; dir Rocol Ltd 1991–93; treas Policy Studies Inst 1993–; *Recreations* genealogy, walking; *Style*— Lionel D D Price, Esq; ✉ Bank of England, London EC2R 8AH (☎ 0171 601 4444, fax 0171 601 5650)

PRICE, Dame Margaret Berenice; DBE (1993, CBE 1982); da of late Thomas Glyn Price; *b* 13 April 1941; *Educ* Pontllanfraith Secondary Sch, Trinity Coll of Music London (hon fellow); *Career* opera singer; debut with Welsh Nat Opera 1962; has appeared in all major opera houses incl: La Scala, Vienna State, Munich, Paris, Hamburg, San Francisco, Met Opera NY, Chicago Lyric Opera; also concert and Lieder career, renowned for her interpretation of Mozart, performed first recital in re-opened Wigmore Hall 1992; winner Elizabeth Schumann Prize for Lieder, Ricordi Prize for Opera, Silver Medal Worshipful Co of Musicians, Bayerische Kammersängerin 1979; Hon DMus Univ of Wales 1983, hon fell UCW Aberystwyth 1991, Hon RAM; *Style*— Dame Margaret Price, DBE; ✉ Bayerisch Staatsoper München, Max-Joseph-Platz 2, 80539 München, Germany

PRICE, Mary Elizabeth; da of David Oglesby, of Slough, Berks, and Dora, *née* Mason; *b* 27 Aug 1943; *Educ* Bishop Otter Teacher Training Coll; *m* 5 April 1969, Peter Edwin Price, s of Herbert George William Price, of Burnham, Bucks; *Career* bowls player; formerly: Br Isles Indoor Pairs champion, Br Isles Indoor Singles champion, Nat Pairs Indoor and Outdoor champion; Nat Singles and Fours winner 1996, Br Isles Indoor Pairs champion 1996, Br Isles Indoor Pairs champion 1996, World Championships Triples and Fours bronze 1996, Euro Indoor Champions England team; Cwlth Games Pairs bronze, Atlantic Rim Games bronze; teacher: Bartholomew Tipping Sch Stokenchurch Bucks 1964–65, Lynch Hill Sch Slough 1965–79; self employed supplier and engraver of sports trophies 1979–; memb: Eng Women's Bowls Assoc, Eng Women's Indoor Bowls Assoc; *Recreations* bowls; *Clubs* Burnham Bowls (Bucks), Desborough Bowls (Maidenhead); *Style*— Mrs Peter Price

PRICE, Nicholas Peter Lees; QC (1992); s of Frank Henry Edmund Price, MBE (Mil) (d 1991), and Agnes Lees, *née* Brittlebank; *b* 29 Sept 1944; *Educ* Prince of Wales Sch Nairobi, Univ of Edinburgh; *m* 4 Jan 1969, Wilma Ann Alison, *née* Steel; 1 s (James Alexander Lees b 9 March 1971), 1 da (Nicola Catherine Lees b 3 Nov 1973); *Career* called to the Bar Gray's Inn 1968, recorder 1987–; memb Bar Cncl 1993–95 (vice chm Legal Servs Ctee 1993, vice chm Public Affrs Ctee 1995); *Style*— Nicholas Price, Esq, QC; ✉ 3 Raymond Buildings, Gray's Inn, London WC1R 5BH (☎ 0171 831 3833)

PRICE, Dr Norman George; JP (1961); s of George Strongitharm Price (d 1942), and Kate, *née* Hopkins (d 1939); *b* 14 Nov 1922; *Educ* Rockferry HS, Univ of Liverpool (DipSocSci), Birkbeck Coll London (MSc), LSE (PhD 1991); *m* 1945, Grace Dorothy (d 1995), da of Sydney Russell Barrett-Melling; 2 da (Christine Ann (Mrs Thorne) b 1946, Janice Helen (Mrs Clarke) b 1951); *Career* Merchant Navy 1940–46, Miny of Supply 1950–54, Colonial Serv Fiji 1954–58, Granada Group Ltd 1958–62; personnel dir: Carreras Ltd 1962–71, J Bibby Sons Ltd 1971–81; educn conslt Assoc of Business Execs 1981–82; chm Boleyns Estate Ltd 1971–94; chm: Domestic Ct 1987–91, Dunmow Bench 1990–93; memb: Essex Magistrates' Cts Ctee, Essex Probation Ctee, Central Cncl of Magistrates' Cts Ctees 1990–93; govr Birkbeck Coll Univ of London 1990– (chm Audit Ctee 1991–), clerk Great Easton PC 1993–95; vice pres Inst of Personnel Mgmnt 1969–71; sec Donkey Breed Soc 1982–85; CIPM 1970, FIM 1972; *Recreations* racing, gardening, reading; *Clubs* Reform, Newmarket Race; *Style*— Dr Norman Price, JP; ✉ Boleyns, Duton Hill, Dunmow, Essex CM6 2DU (☎ 01371 870419)

PRICE, Norman William Rose; s of Sir Rose Francis Price, 6 Bt (d 1979), and Kathleen June, yr da of Norman William Hutchinson, of Melbourne, Australia; hp of bro, Sir Francis Caradoc Rose, 7 Bt; *b* 17 March 1953; *Educ* Eton, Gordonstoun; *m* 1987, Charlotte Louise, da of Randolph Rex Bivar Baker, of Yelverton, Devon; 2 s (Benjamin William Rose b 16 Sept 1989, Timothy Charles Rose b 27 October 1991); *Career* restaurateur; *Style*— Norman Price, Esq; ✉ 73 Fawnbrake Avenue, London SE24 0BE

PRICE, Dr Patricia M; da of Michael Hogan, of Coventry, and Jane, *née* Quill; *b* 13 Aug 1957; *Educ* Newnham Coll Cambridge (MA), King's Coll Hosp Med Sch (MB BChir, MRCP), MD (Cambridge, Lionel Whitby medal); *m* 1, 1984 (m dis), Dr C G A Price; 2 s (Oliver b 8 Oct 1986, Rory b 24 Sept 1988); m 2, 1994, Prof Terry Jones; *Career* house surgn Professorial Surgical Unit then house physician Professorial Med Unit King's Coll Hosp 1981–82; SHO in med: A & E Dept Middx Hosp 1982–83, Professorial Med Unit Addenbrooke's Hosp Cambridge 1983–84, Regional Cardiology Unit Papworth Hosp Cambridge 1984; SHO Radiotherapy and Oncology Dept Addenbrooke's Hosp Cambridge 1983–84, hon sr registrar Radiotherapy and Oncology Unit Royal Marsden Hosp 1988–89 (registrar 1984–88), CRC clinical scientist Inst of Cancer Research 1988–89, reader in clinical oncology Royal Postgraduate Med Sch Hammersmith Hosp and hon conslt oncologist Hammersmith, St Mary's and Ealing Hosps 1989–; currently: head PET Oncology Gp MRC Cyclotron Unit Hammersmith Hosp Clinical Scis Centre, teacher in radiotherapy and oncology Faculty of Med Univ of London Bd of Studies; Varian Clinical Research Award Euro Soc for Therapeutic Radiology and Oncology 1985, Sterling Oncology Award 1989; memb: BMA 1981, Br Oncological Assoc 1987 (sec 1991–93); FRCR 1987, FRCP 1995; *Books* Treatment of Cancer (3 edn, 1995); *Style*— Dr Patricia Price; ✉ Department of Clinical Oncology, Hammersmith Hospital, 150 Du Cane Road, London W12 0HS (☎ 0181 740 3357, fax 0181 743 8766)

PRICE, Dr Paul Anthony; s of Wolf Price, of London, and Dinah, *née* Shafar; *b* 15 May 1949; *Educ* Christ's Coll GS Finchley, UCL (BSc), UCH Med Sch (MB BS); *m* 15 March 1985, Sandra Margaret, *née* Miller; *Career* sr house offr physician: Brompton Hosp, Enfield Dist Gen Hosp 1973–75; hon registrar and Parkinson's Disease Soc res fell KCH 1977–78, registrar UCH 1978–79, hon sr registrar Bart's 1979–83, sr registrar St George's Hosp Gp London 1983–85, conslt physician Princess Margaret Hosp Swindon 1985–; cncl memb Section of Endocrinology RSM; FRCP, FRSM, memb BMA; *Books* chapters in books on neurology and endocrinology; *Recreations* music, playing the bassoon; *Style*— Dr Paul Price; ✉ Department of Medicine, Princess Margaret Hospital, Okus Rd, Swindon SN1 4JU (☎ 01793 536231 ext 6343)

PRICE, Rev Canon Peter Bryan; s of Rev Capt Alec H Price (d 1983), late RA, and Phyllis E M, *née* Bryan (d 1983); *b* 17 May 1944; *Educ* Glastonbury Sch Morden, Redland Coll Bristol (CertEd), Oak Hill Theol Coll London (Dip in Patoral Studies), Heythrop Coll London (Research Studies); *m* Edith Margaret, da of Samuel Munro Burns; 4 s (David b 6 Aug 1968, Patrick b 26 Feb 1970, Neil b 5 Nov 1971, John-Daniel b 13 Sept 1982); *Career* asst teacher Ashton Park Sch 1966–70, sr tutor Lindley Lodge Young People's Centre 1970, head of religious studies Cordeaux Sch Louth 1970–72, student Oakhill Coll 1972–74, community chaplain Crookhorn and curate Christchurch Portsdown 1974–78, chaplain Scargill Community 1978–80, vicar of St Mary Magdalene Addiscombe 1980–88, chair Diocese of Southwark Bd of Mission 1987–92 (Bishop's advsr on church devpt 1980–86), chllr and residentiary canon Southwark Cathedral 1988–91, gen sec United Soc for the Propagation of the Gospel 1992–; *Books* Church as Kingdom (1987), Seeds of the Word (1996); *Recreations* painting, walking, gardening, reading, conversation; *Clubs* New Cavendish; *Style*— The Rev Canon Peter Price; ✉ 14 Oakwood Road, London SW20 0PW (☎ 0181 946 3814); United Society for the Propagation of the Gospel, Partnership House, 157 Waterloo Road, London SE1 8XA (☎ 0171 928 8681, fax 0171 928 2371)

PRICE, Peter Nicholas; s of late Rev Dewi Emlyn Price, and Kate Mary Price; *b* 19 Feb 1942; *Educ* Worcester Royal GS, Aberdare Boys' GS, Univ of Southampton; *m* 30 July 1988, Joy; 1 da (Myfanwy Angharad b 29 Feb 1992); *Career* slr, freelance broadcaster 1960–67; sr ptnr Peter Price & Ptnrs 1969–80; MEP (Cons): Lancashire West 1979–84, London SE 1984–94; Hon MEP 1994–; memb External Econ Relations Ctee Euro Parl and rapporteur on aid for the former USSR 1992–94; memb Delegation for Relations with US Congress, chm Budgetary Control Ctee 1989–92 (vice chm 1979–84); EDG spokesman: on Legal Affrs Ctee 1984–87, on Budgets Ctee 1986–89; rapporteur for several budgetary, single market and legal reports; former nat vice chm: Young Cons, Cons Political Centre; former sec Foreign Affrs Forum; former memb Cons Nat Exec Ctee; memb: EPP, ACP-EEC Jt Assembly, RIIA; govr Thames Valley Univ; non-exec dir Bureau Veritas Quality International (BVQI) Ltd; Euro strategy counsel; *Recreations* theatre, music, photography; *Style*— Peter Price, Esq; ✉ 60 Marlings Park Ave, Chislehurst, Kent BR7 6RD (☎ 01689 820681, fax 01689 890622)

PRICE, Philip John; QC (1989); s of Ernest Price, and Sarah Eunice, *née* Morgan; *b* 16 May 1943; *Educ* Cardiff HS, Pembroke Coll Oxford; *m* 27 March 1967, Mari Josephine, da of Thomas Stanley Davies; 1 s (Matthew Huw Caradog b 1978), 2 da (Alexandra Ruth b 1973, Harriet Angharad b 1975); *Career* lectr in law Univ of Leeds 1966–70, called to Bar Gray's Inn 1969, practising on Wales and Chester Circuit 1971–93, Temple 1991–93; circuit judge (Wales and Chester Circuit) 1993–; chllr Diocese of Monmouth 1992–, memb Governing Body Church in Wales 1992–; *Recreations* books, buildings, cricket; *Clubs* Cardiff and County; *Style*— His Hon Judge Philip Price, QC; ✉ 2nd Floor, Churchill House, Churchill Way, Cardiff CF1 4HH (☎ 01222 396925)

PRICE, (Llewelyn) Ralph; CBE (1972); s of Llewelyn David Price (d 1962); *b* 23 Oct 1912; *Educ* Quarry Bank Sch Liverpool; *m* 1939, Vera Patricia, da of C H Harrison (d 1935); 1 s, 2 da; *Career* chm: Honeywell Ltd 1972–88, ML Hldgs Ltd 1975–87, Honeywell Advsy Cncl 1981–88; dir American Chamber of Commerce 1976–81; former memb NEDC Electronics Ctee, pres Br Indust Measurement and Control Trade Assoc 1972–77; FCA 1935; *Recreations* golf, music, bridge; *Clubs* Temple Golf; *Style*— Ralph Price, Esq, CBE; ✉ Nascot, Pinkneys Drive, Pinkneys Green, Maidenhead, Berks (☎ 01628 28270)

PRICE, Richard Lloyd Duffield; s of David Henderson Price, and Janet Helen, *née* Duffield; *b* 13 April 1949; *Educ* Royal GS Newcastle upon Tyne, Magdalen Coll Oxford (BA), Univ of London (Postgrad Dip in Applied Social Studies); *m* 1981, Joanna Mary, da of William Murray; 2 s (Gregory Richard Murray b 10 Sept 1982, Alastair Joseph Murray b 4 Oct 1985); *Career* probation offr Inner London Probation Serv 1973–77, info offr Personal Social Serv Cncl 1977–78, dep dir Int Yr of the Child (UK) 1978–80, communications mangr Nexos Office Systems Ltd 1980–83, md European Marketing Consultants Ltd 1984– (dir 1983–84); MIPR 1984, memb PRCA 1985; *Recreations* singing, cricket, family activities; *Clubs* United Oxford & Cambridge Univ; *Style*— Richard Price, Esq; ✉ European Marketing Consultants, Spa House, 11–17 Worple Road, London SW19 4JS (☎ 0181 879 3033, fax 0181 946 9072)

PRICE, Richard Mervyn; OBE (1995), QC (1996); s of William James Price (d 1987), of Sheffield, and Josephine May, *née* Preston; *b* 15 May 1948; *Educ* King Edward VII Sch Sheffield, King's Coll London (LLB); *m* 1971, Caroline Sarah, da of Geoffrey and Mary Ball, of Surrey; 1 s (Timothy George b 13 Jan 1975), 2 da (Kathryn Sara b 3 Dec 1977, Emma Charlotte Louisa b 28 July 1983); *Career* called to the Bar Gray's Inn 1969, standing counsel on election law Cons Central Office 1986–; *Recreations* politics, theatre, films, music, walking, cycling; *Clubs* RAC, St Stephen's Constitutional, Scribes Cellar; *Style*— Richard Price, Esq, OBE, QC; ✉ Littleton Chambers, 3 King's Bench Walk North, Temple, London EC4Y 7HR (☎ 0171 797 8600, fax 0171 797 8699)

PRICE, His Hon Judge Richard Neville Meredith; s of Christopher Price (d 1980), and Valerie Ruby, *née* Greenham (d 1992); *b* 30 May 1945; *Educ* Marsh Court Stockbridge, Sutton Valence Kent, Coll of Law Guildford; *m* Oct 1971, Avril Judith, da of Edward Purser Lancaster (d 1954), and Dorothy Margaret, *née* Collins; 3 s (Andrew b 10 Nov 1974, Simon b 24 Sept 1979, David b 10 June 1986); *Career* slr 1970–90, called to the Bar Middle Temple 1990, recorder 1990–96 (asst recorder 1986–90), appointed to Circuit Bench 1996; *Recreations* choral singing, sailing, reading, listening to music; *Clubs* Royal Victoria Yacht, Seaview Yacht; *Style*— His Hon Judge Richard Price; ✉ Portsmouth Combined Court Centre, Courts of Justice, Winston Churchill Avenue, Portsmouth, Hants

PRICE, Richard Shirvell; *b* 1933; *Educ* Milton Acad Mass, Leeds GS, Liverpool Inst Sch, Univ of Leeds; *m* 1963, Joan, *née* Silk; 1 s, 1 da; *Career* served RNVR and RNR 1951–64; Nat Serv Supply Offr RN 1955–57; PRO Benger Laboratories Ltd 1957–59, freelance journalist 1957–59, sr PRO PIDA (Agricultural Authy) 1959, PRO, orgn mangr then sales controller Bayer (UK) 1960–62, fndr and ed PULSE (the GP newspaper, now published by Morgan Grampian) 1960–62, md Pharmacia (UK) Ltd 1962–65, sales dir Granada Television (Overseas) Ltd 1965–67, chm Primetime plc gp (includes RPTA Ltd largest ind UK prog distributor) founded 1968; dir Television Enterprise & Asset Management plc (TEAM plc); memb Cncl RTS 1975–83; BAFTA: memb Cncl 1982–, hon treas 1984–91, chm and tstee 1991–93, dep chm 1993–95; local cncllr Paddington 1963–65 (later vice chm Health Ctee): Parly candidate (C) N Paddington 1969 and 1970; chm CPC study gps on Traffic and Broadcasting 1965–68; chm local MENCAP Soc 1980–86; govr: Parkwood Hall Sch 1986– (chm of govrs 1990–94), Home Farm Tst for Learning Difficulties 1993– (bd govr 1994–); memb: Blue Planet Project Steering Ctee 1994–, Fulbright Advsy Ctee 1995–; chm LSE Media Advsy Gp 1995–; FRTS 1984; *Style*— Richard Price, Esq; ✉ Primetime plc, Seymour Mews House, Seymour Mews, Wigmore Street, London W1H 6PQ (☎ 0171 935 9000, fax 0171 935 1992)

PRICE, Richard Stephen; s of Dr David Brian Price, OBE, of Bridgend, Mid Glamorgan, and Menna Myles, *née* Jones (d 1988); *b* 27 May 1953; *Educ* Cowbridge GS, Univ of Leeds (Hons); *m* 3 May 1980, Nicola Mary, da of Philip Griffin, of Henstridge, Nr Templecombe, Somerset; 1 s (Nicholas b 13 Sept 1988), 2 da (Roseanna b 4 Dec 1986, Susannah Kate Rhiannon b 1 Feb 1993); *Career* admitted slr 1977, ptnr McKenna and Co 1984– (i/c ME practice 1984–88); memb City of London Slrs' Co, memb Law Soc; *Recreations* golf; *Style*— Richard Price, Esq; ✉ McKenna & Co, Mitre House, 160 Aldersgate Street, London EC1A 4DD (☎ 0171 606 9000, fax 0171 606 9100, telex 27251)

PRICE, Robert Thomas; s of Richard James Price (d 1978), of Criccieth, Gwynedd, and Laura Jane, *née* Thomas; *b* 10 Oct 1932; *Educ* Porthmadog GS, Univ Coll of Wales Aberystwyth (LLB); *m* 14 Oct 1978, Ann Wyn, da of Hugh John Hughes (d 1978), of Bryneglwys Ynys Talsarnau, Gwynedd; 1 da (Anna Eluned b 1981); *Career* RAF 1958–60; admitted slr 1957, ptnr William George & Son Porthmadog Gwynedd, coroner Lleyn and Eifion Dist of Gwynedd 1984–96, dep coroner N W Wales 1996–; chm: Criccieth Town Cncl 1967, 1973, 1980 and 1989, Dwyfor DC 1980, Govrs Ysgol Eifionydd Secdy Sch 1993–; capt Criccieth GC 1968; pres Gwynedd Law Soc 1992; *Recreations* yachting, golf, angling; *Style*— Robert Price, Esq; ✉ Monfa, Beach Bank, Criccieth, Gwynedd LL52 0HW (☎ 01766 522717); 103 High St, Porthmadog, Gwynedd (☎ 01766 512474, fax 01766 514363)

PRICE, Robin Mark Dodgson; s of Wilfred Barrie Price, of Knowle, West Midlands, and Jocelyn Mary, *née* Berry; *b* 30 April 1956; *Educ* The Leys Sch Cambridge, Univ of Bristol (LLB); *m* 27 Sept 1986, Jane, da of Vyvian Hugh Reginald Rawson; 1 s (Joe Gulliver b 19 Nov 1990), 1 da (Eleanor Alice b 22 Sept 1992); *Career* Arthur Young McClelland Moores 1978–82 (articled clerk, chartered accountant), md Frontline Video Ltd 1983–87, jt managing ptnr HHCL and Partners (formerly Howell Henry Chaldecott Lury) 1987–; ACA, MIPA; *Recreations* tennis, golf, swimming; *Clubs* Roehampton; *Style*— Robin Price, Esq; ✉ HHCL and Partners, Kent House, 14–17 Market Place, London W1N 7AJ (☎ 0171 436 3333, fax 0171 436 2677)

PRICE, Roland John Stuart; s of Philip Stuart Price, of Tamworth, and Rowena Mary, *née* Jones; *b* 29 July 1961; *Educ* Sydney GS Aust, Royal Ballet Sch London; *Career* ballet dancer; Gold Medal Adeline Genée award 1978; princ dancer: Sadler's Wells Royal Ballet (now Birmingham Royal Ballet) 1984– (joined 1979), Boston Ballet USA 1990–94, freelance 1995–; princ roles incl: The Two Pigeons, La Fille Mal Gardée, Coppelia, Giselle, Romeo and Juliet, Swan Lake, The Sleeping Beauty, The Snow Queen, Abdallah, The Nutcracker, Etudes, many one act ballets incl creations by Macmillan and Bintley; Lawrence Olivier Award nominee 1980 and 1985; *Recreations* opera; *Style*— Roland Price, Esq

PRICE, Dr Timothy James Carlyle; s of Dr James Alan Price (d 1992), and Elizabeth, *née* Donnan (d 1995); *b* 3 Dec 1941; *Educ* Rugby, Clare Coll Cambridge (BA, MB BChir), Middx Hosp Med Sch (DMRD); *m* 26 June 1970, Anne, da of Frederick Robinson (d 1984); 1 s (Henry James b 3 May 1976), 1 da (Melissa Catherine b 23 Dec 1970); *Career* conslt radiologist Calderdale Health Authy 1974–; *Recreations* gardening, tapestry; *Clubs* Hebden Bridge Constitutional; *Style*— Dr Timothy Price; ✉ Hollingsgate, Broad Lane, Luddendenfoot, Halifax, West Yorkshire HX2 6JY (☎ 01422 882955)

PRICE, Vivian William Cecil; QC (1972); s of late Evan Price; *b* 14 April 1926; *Educ* Judd Sch Tonbridge, Trinity Coll Cambridge, Balliol Coll Oxford; *m* 1961, Elizabeth Anne, da of late Arthur Rawlins; 3 s, 2 da; *Career* RN 1946–49; called to the Bar: Middle Temple 1954, Hong Kong 1975, Singapore 1979; bencher Middle Temple 1979, dep judge Chancery Div High Ct 1975–; *Clubs* Travellers'; *Style*— Vivian Price, Esq, QC; ✉ Redwall Farmhouse, Linton, Kent (☎ 01622 743682)

PRICHARD, (Francis) Anthony (Tony); s of Francis Leo Prichard, and Dorothy Joanne; *b* 10 June 1949; *Educ* Ratcliffe Coll, Univ of Liverpool (LLB); *m* 21 Dec 1974, Elizabeth Ann, da of Joseph Prescott (d 1991); 3 s (Mark b 10 Aug 1979, Paul b 6 April

1981, James b 28 Dec 1983); *Career* admitted slr 1974; ptnr Weightmans Liverpool 1976–; Notary Public; memb Law Soc; *Recreations* tennis, skiing, squash, golf, bridge; *Clubs* Racquet, Blundellsands Lawn Tennis, Formby Golf; *Style*— Tony Pritchard, Esq; ✉ Merrywood, Dowhills Road, Blundellsands, Liverpool L23 8SP (☎ 0151 931 2315); Weightmans, Richmond House, 1 Rumford Place, Liverpool L3 9QW (☎ 0151 227 2601, fax 0151 227 3223, telex 627538)

PRICHARD, Prof Brian Norman Christopher; CBE (1996); s of Sir Norman George Mollett Prichard (d 1972), of London, and Winifred, *née* Just (d 1989); *b* 7 Nov 1932; *Educ* Merton House Sch, Battersea GS, St George's Hosp Univ of London (BSc, MSc, MB BS), FRSM, FRCP 1977, FFPM 1989, FESC 1996; *m* 8 Sept 1956, Denise Margaret, da of Edward Stoneham (d 1982), of Ewell; 2 s (Andrew J N Prichard, FRCS, Rev Ian E B Prichard), 2 da (Ruth (Mrs Bowers), Catherine (Mrs Bonnington)); *Career* sr house offr in surgery Dorking Gen Hosp 1958–59, registrar St George's Hosp 1959–61 (house offr posts 1957–58); Univ Coll Hosp Med Sch: res asst 1961–62, lectr in clinical pharmacology 1962–68, sr lectr 1968–75, reader 1975–80, prof 1980–, conslt physician 1973–; author of about 150 reviews and papers, winner of Astra Award Int Soc of Hypertension (for the introduction of beta adrenergic blocking drugs into the treatment of hypertension) 1979; vice pres Cons Med Soc, cncllr London Borough of Wandsworth; chm: Inst of Alcohol Studies, Action on Drinking and Driving; memb: Exec Bd Int Soc of Cardiovascular Therapy, Br Cardiac Soc, Br Pharmacological Soc, Med Soc of London, Assoc of Physicans, Med Res Soc, Int Soc of Hypertension; *Books* Biological Effects of Drugs in Relation to their Plasma Concentration (ed with D S Davies, 1973), Prescribing - What, When, Why? (with J Fry and M Godfrey, 1986), Beta Blockers in Clinical Practice (with J M Cruickshank, 2 edn 1994); *Recreations* photography, walking; *Clubs* Carlton, RAC; *Style*— Prof B N C Prichard, CBE; ✉ 24 Lyford Road, Wandsworth Common, London SW18 3LG (☎ 0181 870 3066); Division of Clinical Pharmacology, University College London Medical School, University College, 5 University St, London WC1E 6JJ (☎ 0171 209 6204)

PRICHARD, David; s of Richard Euan Prichard, of Bodmin, and Phyllis, *née* Hiscock; *b* 23 Sept 1948; *Educ* Kingston GS, Bartlett Sch of Architecture (BSc, DipArch, Sir Andrew Taylor Prize); *m* 23 Sept 1988, Catherine Jamison, da of Ian McCarter; 1 da (Isobel b 13 Nov 1984), 2 s (Charlie b 28 Feb 1986, George b 16 Dec 1988); *Career* architect; assoc Richard MacCormac and Peter Jamieson 1974–79 (joined 1972), ptnr MacCormac Jamieson Prichard Architects 1979–; *Projects* masterplan and six projects Queen Mary and Westfield Coll 1986, responsible for masterplans at Spitalfields Market, Docklands, Bow, Univ of Westminster and Fitzwilliam Coll Cambridge 1985, Cable and Wireless Coll Coventry 1990–94 (Building of the Year Award 1994); visiting lectr: UCL, RCA, Brighton Poly; RIBA examiner 1981–94: Univ of Kent, UCL, Univ of North London; RIBA Awards for: housing in Milton Keynes and Newport, Informatics Laboratory Queen Mary and Westfield Coll; Civic Tst Awards for: student residences Queen Mary Coll, sheltered housing in Croydon, housing in Brixton and Docklands; RIBA 1974; *Recreations* family, walking, gardening; *Style*— David Prichard, Esq; ✉ Wilmot Cottage, Mote Road, Ivy Hatch, Sevenoaks, Kent TN15 0NT (☎ 01732 810063); MacCormac Jamieson Prichard, 9 Heneage Street, Spitalfields, London E1 5LJ (☎ 0171 377 9262)

PRICHARD, David Colville Mostyn; s of Rev George Mostyn Prichard (d 1972), of Kensington, and Joan Mary, *née* Wild (d 1978); *b* 26 May 1934; *Educ* Radley, Pembroke Coll Oxford (MA); *m* 11 July 1992, C Elizabeth Major; *Career* CO CCF Monkton Combe Sch 1955, fndr first UK Volunteer Police Cadets 1965; headmaster: Port Regis Sch 1969–93, Wycliffe Coll Glos 1994–; organiser Nat Conf of Govrs Bursars and Heads 1981–92 (lectr 1974–, Aust Bicentenary lectr 1988), chm Incorporated Assoc of Prep Schs 1990–91 (memb Cncl 1986); Industl Soc lectr 1991–92; memb Ctee Pembroke Coll Oxford, fndr memb Sci Exploration Soc, dir Smallpiece Tst, dir Smallpiece Enterprises Ltd, co-chm Operation New World; govr: Swanbourne House, Holmwood House, Orwell Park, St Johns Chepstow; Liveryman Worshipful Co of Loriners; FIMgt, FRSA, FCP; *Books* Training for Service (1968); *Recreations* travel, management, gardening; *Clubs* Leander, National (Carlton), East India; *Style*— David Prichard, Esq; ✉ Castleton House, Sherborne, Dorset DT9 3SA (☎ 01935 816539); Headmaster's House, Wycliffe College, Stonehouse, Glos GL10 2JQ (☎ 01453 823217, fax 01453 827634)

PRICHARD, Mathew Caradoc Thomas; CBE (1992), DL (1994); s of Maj Hubert de Burgh Prichard, of Pwllywrach, Cowbridge (ka 1944), and Rosalind Margaret Clarissa Hicks, *née* Christie; *b* 21 Sept 1943; *Educ* Eton, New Coll Oxford (BA); *m* 20 May 1967, Angela Caroline, da of Thomas Craddock Maples, of Symonds Farm House, Childrey, nr Wantage; 1 s (James b 1970), 2 da (Alexandra b 1968, Joanna b 1972); *Career* chm: Agatha Christie Ltd 1977–, Booker Entertainment 1987–; chm Welsh Arts Cncl 1986–94, memb Arts Cncl GB 1983–94, pres Nat Museum of Wales 1996– (vice-pres 1992–96), chm Cardiff Bay Opera House Tst 1993–94, chm Cardiff Old Library Tst 1993–; High Sheriff Co of Glam 1973–74; *Recreations* golf, cricket, bridge; *Clubs* Boodle's, Cardiff and County, R & A, Royal Porthcawl Golf, MCC; *Style*— Mathew Prichard, Esq, CBE, DL; ✉ Booker Entertainment, 141 Sloane St, London SW1X 9AY (☎ 0171 730 7778, fax 0171 259 9940)

PRICHARD, Paul John; s of John Prichard, of Colchester, Essex, and Margaret Anne, *née* Richardson; *b* 7 Jan 1965; *Educ* Brentwood Co HS; *m* 1992, Jo-Anne, *née* Black; 1 da (Danielle Jade b 23 April 1993), 1 s (Alexander James b 16 Aug 1995); *Career* professional cricketer; Essex CCC: joined 1981, first class debut 1984, awarded county cap 1986, shared record partnership of 403 with Graham Gooch scoring career best 245 v Leics 1990, appointed capt 1995– (vice capt 1993); memb England A team Australia tour 1993; represented: Young England under 19s 1981–83, Sutherland Dist CC Sydney off-seasons 1983, 1984 and 1985, Waverley Dist CC Sydney off-seasons 1988, 1989 and 1990; honours with Essex CCC: County Championship 1984, 1986, 1991 and 1992, John Player League 1984 and 1985, NatWest Trophy 1985, runners-up Benson & Hedges Cup 1985 and 1989, Refuge Assurance Cup 1989; Britannic Assurance Player of the Season 1992; mktg exec Ridley's Brewery; *Recreations* horse racing, golf, Sydney beaches; *Style*— Paul Prichard, Esq; ✉ Essex CCC, New Writtle St, Chelmsford, Essex CM2 0PG (☎ 01245 252420, fax 01245 491607)

PRICHARD-JONES, David John Walter; s and h of Sir John Prichard-Jones, 2 Bt, *qv*, and his 1 w, Heather Vivian Mary, da of Sir Walter Richard Nugent, 4 Bt, MP (d 1955); *b* 14 March 1943; *Educ* Ampleforth, ChCh Oxford (BA); *Style*— David Prichard-Jones, Esq

PRICHARD-JONES, Sir John; 2 Bt (UK 1910), of Bron Menai, Dwyran, Llangeinwen, Anglesey; s of Sir John Prichard-Jones, 1 Bt, JP, DL (d 1917); *b* 20 Jan 1913; *Educ* Eton, ChCh Oxford (MA); *m* 1, 1937 (m dis 1950), Heather Vivian Mary, da of late Sir Walter Richard Nugent, 4 Bt; 1 s; m 2, Feb 1959, Helen Marie Thérèse, da of late J F Liddy, of Drogheda; 1 da (Susan Marie b Nov 1959); *Heir* s, David John Walter Prichard-Jones, *qv*, b 14 March 1943; *Career* called to the Bar Gray's Inn 1936; former Capt The Queen's Bays; farmer and bloodstock breeder; *Style*— Sir John Prichard-Jones, Bt; ✉ Allenswood House, Lucan, Co Dublin, Republic of Ireland

PRICHARD JONES, Kenneth Victor; s of John Victor Jones, MBE (d 1981), and Eunice Aldwyn Marie, *née* Prichard (d 1976); *b* 12 Sept 1946; *Educ* Clifton, Univ of Kent at Canterbury (BA); *m* 26 Sept 1967, Dagmar Eva, da of Col Pavel Svoboda (d 1993), of Putney, London; 3 s (Sebastian b 1973, Piers b 1975, Christian b 1980), 1 da (Lucy b 1978); *Career* admitted slr 1972; chm: Clifton Charterhouse Securities Ltd 1976–, Network Corporate Holdings PLC 1993–, Club Radio Ltd 1996–; friend of Keats-Shelley Meml Assoc; Medal of Honour for Conservation Europa Nostra 1994; memb Law Soc; *Books* The Law and Practice of Franchising (with Prof John Adams, 3 edn 1990), F is for Franchising (2 edn, 1983), Encyclopaedia of Forms and Precedents (Agency Documents vol, 1984, revised edn 1992), Merchandising (contrib, 1987), Commercial Hiring and Leasing (contrib, 1989), Encyclopaedia of Forms and Precedents (Food vol, 1995); *Recreations* swimming, shooting; *Clubs* Café de Paris; *Style*— Kenneth Prichard Jones, Esq; ✉ Field Place, Warnham, West Sussex RH12 3PB (☎ 01403 265004); 34 James Street, London W1M 5HS (☎ 0171 486 9957, car 0836 768596)

PRICKETT, (Robert) Andrew; *b* 2 Aug 1948; *Educ* Univ of Sheffield (LLB), Coll of Law Guildford; *m* 1976, Margaret; *Career* articled clerk with private practice Sheffield 1969–71, admitted slr 1971, prosecutor Chief Prosecuting Slr's Dept Notts 1971–73, ptnr in private practice (specialising in criminal advocacy) Nottingham 1973–76, princ prosecutor Chief Prosecuting Slr's Dept Notts 1976–80, area prosecuting slr Chief Prosecuting Slr's Dept Lancs 1980–85, first chief prosecuting slr Wilts 1985–86, first chief crown prosecutor (on inception of CPS) Glos and Wilts 1986–93, first chief crown prosecutor Area of CPS Wales (following reorganisation of CPS) 1993–; memb Cncl Law Soc 1996–; *Style*— Andrew Prickett, Esq; ✉ Crown Prosecution Service, Tudor House, 16 Cathedral Road, Cardiff CF1 9LJ (☎ 01222 783000, fax 01222 783097)

PRICKETT, Prof (Alexander Thomas) Stephen; s of Rev William Ewart Prickett (d 1975), of Canterbury, Kent, and Barbara Browning, *née* Lyne; *b* 4 June 1939; *Educ* Kent Coll Canterbury, Trinity Hall Cambridge (scholar, BA, MA, PhD, T H prize for English, Edward George Harwood prize for English, Cambridge Univ Membs' prize), Univ Coll Oxford (DipEd); *m* 17 Aug 1966 (m dis 1981), Diana Joan, da of George Mabbutt; 1 s (Mark Thomas b 1974), 1 da (Ruth Charlotte b 1970); m 2, 1984, Maria Angelica Alvarez; *Career* teacher of English: Methodist Coll Uzuakoli E Nigeria 1962–64, Univ of Sussex 1967–82, Aust Nat Univ Canberra Australia 1983–89; Regius prof of English language and literature Univ of Glasgow 1990–; govr Bishop Otter Coll of Educn 1974–77, tstee Fernley Hartley Tst 1978–83; chm: Higher Educn Gp 1971–82, Higher Educn Fndn 1991–95; fell Australian Acad of Humanities 1986; *Books* Do It Yourself Doom (1962), Coleridge and Wordsworth: The Poetry of Growth (1970), Romanticism and Religion (1976), Victorian Fantasy (1979), Words and the Word (1986), The Bible (1991), Origins of Narrative (1996); *Recreations* walking, skiing, tennis, attending conferences; *Style*— Prof Stephen Prickett; ✉ Department of English Literature, University of Glasgow, Glasgow G12 8QQ (☎ 0141 339 8855, fax 0141 330 4601)

PRICKETT, Air Chief Marshal Sir Thomas Other; KCB (1965, CB 1957), DSO (1943), DFC (1942); s of late Eric G Prickett, of Bedford; *b* 31 July 1913; *Educ* Stubbington House Sch, Haileybury; *m* 1, 1942, Elizabeth Gratian (d 1984), da of late William Galbally, of Laguna Beach, California, USA; 1 s, 1 da; m 2, 1985, Shirley Westerman, former w of William Westerman; *Career* joined RAF 1937, served Desert Air Force and Bomber Cmd 1939–45, Gp Capt 1952, idc 1956, Air Cdre 1956, COS Special Air Task Force (Suez Operations), SASO 1 Group, Air Vice-Marshal 1960, asst chief Air Staff (Ops) Air Miny 1960–63 (Policy and Planning 1963–64); AOC-in-C NEAF and Cdr Br Forces Cyprus (administrator Sovereign Base Area) 1964–66, Air Marshal 1966, AOC-in-C RAF Transport and Air Support Cmds 1967–68, Air Chief Marshal 1969, Air memb for Supply and Organisation MOD (RAF) 1968–70, ret; dir Goodwood Estate 1970–78, md Goodwood Terrena 1970–78, pres Sussex Co Br Legion 1989; *Clubs* RAF; *Style*— Air Chief Marshal Sir Thomas Prickett, KCB, DSO, DFC; ✉ 46 Kingston Hill Place, Kingston upon Thames, Surrey KT2 7QY

PRIDAY, Charles Nicholas Bruton; s of Christopher Bruton Priday, QC (d 1992), and Jill Holroyd, *née* Sergeant; *b* 17 July 1959; *Educ* Radley, Univ Coll Oxford, City Univ London; *m* 17 July 1982, Helen Elizabeth, da of M M Jones; 2 da (Elizabeth b 1987, Emma b 1989); *Career* called to the Bar Middle Temple 1982; *Recreations* escaping to the Cotswolds, golf, tennis; *Clubs* Oxford Unicorns Real Tennis, Moreton Morrell Real Tennis; *Style*— Charles Priday, Esq; ✉ 7 King's Bench Walk, Temple, London EC4Y 7DS (☎ 0171 583 0404, fax 0171 583 0950, telex 887491 KBLAW)

PRIDAY, Helen Elizabeth; da of Michael Montague Jones (d 1995), of Radley, Oxon, and Alison Priscilla, *née* Shepherd (d 1993); *b* 24 Sept 1957; *Educ* Dragon Sch, Radley; *m* 17 July 1982, Charles Nicholas Bruton Priday, *qv*, s of Christopher Bruton Priday, QC (d 1992), of London; 2 da (Elizabeth b 1987, Emma b 1989); *Career* publicity and promotions mangr W H Freeman & Co Oxford 1978–82, ed Pitkin Pictorials London 1982–83, mktg and publicity dir Times Books Angus and Robertson London 1983–, promotions dir The Times Supplements 1990– (The Times Literary Supplement, The Times Educational Supplement, The Times Higher Education Supplement); memb Exec Bd Music for Youth, memb Exec Cncl BESA; *Recreations* walking in the Cotswolds, tennis, golf, good food and wine, travelling in France; *Clubs* St Enodoc Golf; *Style*— Mrs Helen Priday; ✉ The Times Supplements, Admiral House, 66–68 East Smithfield, London E1 9XY (☎ 0171 782 3000, fax 0171 782 3398)

PRIDDIS, Rt Rev Anthony Martin; *see:* Warwick, Bishop of

PRIDE, Prof Stephen James; s of George William Pride (d 1989), of NSW, Aust, and Winifred Agnes Mary, *née* Whittaker; *b* 8 Jan 1949; *Educ* Hampton HS Melbourne, Monash Univ (BSc), Aust Nat Univ (PhD, Peter Stroud prize); *Career* res fell Open Univ 1974–78, lectr in mathematics KCL 1978–79, prof of mathematics Univ of Glasgow 1992– (lectr 1979–87, reader 1987–92); memb: Australian Mathematical Soc 1971, London Mathematical Soc 1975 (memb Ed Bd 1989–), Edinburgh Mathematical Soc 1979; author of over 60 articles on group and semigroup theory in learned jls; FRSE 1992; *Recreations* outdoor activities (especially cycling), gardening, travelling, cinema; *Style*— Prof Stephen Pride, FRSE; ✉ 54 Airlie Street, Glasgow G12 9SN (☎ 0141 339 7395); Department of Mathematics, University of Glasgow G12 8QW (☎ 0141 339 8855, ext 6528, fax 0141 330 4111, e-mail sjp@maths.gla.ac.uk)

PRIDEAUX, Sir Humphrey Povah Treverbian; kt (1971), OBE (1945), DL (Hants 1983); s of Walter Treverbian Prideaux (d 1958), of Elderslie, Ockley, Dorking, Surrey, and Marion Fenn, *née* Arbuthnot (d 1958); bro of Sir John Francis Prideaux, OBE, DL (d 1993) and Walter Arbuthnot Prideaux, CBE, MC, TD (d 1995); *b* 13 Dec 1915; *Educ* St Aubyns Rottingdean, Eton, Trinity Coll Oxford; *m* 1939, Cynthia, da of late Lt-Col H Birch Reynardson, CMG; 4 s; *Career* Jt Planning Staff War Office 1945, Naval Staff Coll 1948, Cmdt Sch of Admin 1948, Chiefs of Staff Secretariat 1950–53, ret; dir: NAAFI 1956–73 (chm 1963–73), The London Life Assoc Ltd 1964–88 (vice pres 1965–72, pres 1973–84), Brooke Bond Liebig Ltd 1968–81 (chm 1972–81), W H Smith & Son Ltd 1969–77 (vice chm 1977–81), Morland & Co 1981–93 (chm 1983–93), Grindlays Bank 1982–85; chm Lord Wandsworth Fndn 1966–92; Liveryman Worshipful Co of Goldsmiths; *Clubs* Cavalry & Guards'; *Style*— Sir Humphrey Prideaux, OBE, DL; ✉ Kings Cottage, Buryfields, Odiham, Hants RG29 1NE (☎ 01256 703658)

PRIDEAUX, Dr John Denys Charles Anstice; CBE (1994); s of Denys Robert Anstice Prideaux (d 1966), and Francis Hester Dorothy, *née* Glaze (d 1992); *b* 8 Aug 1944; *Educ* The Hall Hampstead, St Paul's, Univ of Nottingham (BSc, PhD); *m* 3 June 1972, Philippa Mary Anstice; 1 s (John Piers Grahame Anstice b 1976), 1 da (Sophia Mary Louise Anstice b 1974); *Career* BR: area mangr Newton Abbot 1972–74, strategic planning offr BR Bd 1974–80, divnl mangr Birmingham 1980–83, dir Policy Unit BR Bd 1983–86, dir and then md InterCity 1986–90, md New Ventures and chm Union Railways Ltd 1992–93; non-exec dir Docklands Light Railway Ltd 1994–; chm: Prideaux and Associates Ltd 1994–, Angel Train Contracts Ltd 1996–; memb: Advsy Ctee on Trunk Road Assessment 1977, Transport Ctee Science & Engrg Research Cncl 1982, Environment Ctee ESRC 1985, Cncl Manchester Business Sch; Liveryman Worshipful Co of Carmen; MCIT, FRSA; *Books* Five Railway Histories (1964–1980), author of many professional papers; *Recreations* riding, hunting, shooting, skiing, sailing, design; *Style*— Dr John Prideaux, CBE; ✉ 17 Highgate West Hill, London N6 6NP (☎ 0181 340 3038)

PRIDEAUX, Julian Humphrey; OBE (1995); s of Sir Humphrey Povah Treverbian Prideaux, OBE, DL, *qv*, and Cynthia, *née* Birch-Reynardson; *b* 19 June 1942; *Educ* St Aubyn's Rottingdean, Eton, RAC Cirencester (Dip); *m* 5 Aug 1967, Rosamund Jill, da of Richard Patrick Roney Dougal (d 1993), of Bridgnorth, Shropshire; 2 s (Adam b 1968, Nigel b 1971); *Career* land agent; Burd and Evans Chartered Surveyors Shrewsbury 1964–67; Col the Hon GC Cubitt and Others 1967–69; The National Trust: land agent Cornwall Region 1969–77, dir Thames and Chilterns Region 1978–86, chief agent 1987–; FRICS 1974, FRSA 1975; *Recreations* walking, fishing; *Clubs* Farmers'; *Style*— Julian Prideaux, Esq, OBE; ✉ The National Trust, 36 Queen Annes Gate, London SW1H 9AS (☎ 0171 447 6421, fax 0171 447 6424)

PRIDEAUX, Michael Charles Terrell; s of Sir John Francis Prideaux, OBE, DL (d 1993), and Joan Terrell, *née* Pigott-Brown; *b* 23 Oct 1950; *Educ* Eton, Trinity Coll Cambridge (MA); *m* 1975, Susan Henriette, da of Charles Peto Bennett (d 1977); 1 s (John b 1979), 1 da (Laura b 1976); *Career* fin advertisement mangr Financial Times 1979–80 (UK advertisement dir 1980–83), chief exec Charles Barker City 1983–89; dir: Charles Barker Group 1983–89, Charles Barker plc 1987–89; dir of gp public affrs BAT Industries plc 1989–; *Recreations* gardening, shooting; *Clubs* Brooks's; *Style*— Michael Prideaux Esq; ✉ Selehurst, Lower Beeding, nr Horsham, Sussex (☎ 01403 891501); BAT Industries plc, Windsor House, 50 Victoria Street, London SW1H ONL (☎ 0171 222 7979)

PRIDEAUX, Brig Nicholas Mark; s of Sir Humphrey Povah Treverbian Prideaux, OBE, DL, of Odiham, Hants, and Cynthia Violet, *née* Birch-Reynardson; *b* 23 July 1940; *Educ* St Aubyns, Eton, Army Staff Coll, US Armed Forces Staff Coll; *m* 23 July 1966, Amanda Fiona, da of Cdr Donald Cameron, VC (d 1961); 1 s (William James Nicholas b 1974), 2 da (Victoria b 1967, Henrietta b 1970); *Career* cmmnd 1 Green Jackets 43 and 52 1959, ADC to GOC Northumbrian Dist 1961–63, MOD 1975–77, second in cmd and CO 2 Bn The Royal Green Jackets 1979, CO The Rifle Depot The Royal Green Jackets 1980–82, Mil Asst to DSACEUR SHAPE 1982–85, Col GS Live Oak 1985–88, Army Dir NAAFI Bd of Mgmnt 1988–91, def and mil attaché Athens 1993–95; appeals dir Army Benevolent Fund 1995–; Freeman: Worshipful Co of Goldsmiths 1986, City of London 1987; FIMgt 1989; *Recreations* outdoor pursuits; *Clubs* Army & Navy; *Style*— Brig Nicholas Prideaux; ✉ Rose Cottage, Barton Stacey, Winchester, Hants SO21 3RL

PRIDEAUX, Walter Michael Cokayne; er s of Walter Arbuthnot Prideaux, CBE, MC, TD (d 1995); *b* 19 Nov 1937; *Educ* Eton, Trinity Coll Cambridge (MA); *m* 19 Sept 1964, Lenore Mary Jaqueline, da of Brig Richard Hugh Rossiter Cumming (d 1982), of Weybridge, Surrey; 1 s (Walter Edward Cumming b 25 July 1971), 2 da (Rebecca Lenore b 20 Aug 1965, Belinda June b 20 June 1969); *Career* 2 Lt Queen's Royal Rifles (TA) 1961, Lt 1963, TARO 1964–87; admitted slr 1964; White & Bowker (formerly White Brooks & Gilman) Winchester Southampton and Eastleigh: asst slr 1964, ptnr 1966, sr ptnr 1983–; memb Winchester City Cncl 1976–90; govr: Perin's Community Sch Alresford 1976–92 (chm 1981–88), Peter Symond's Sixth Form Coll Winchester 1981–; Freeman City of London 1958, Liveryman Worshipful Co of Goldsmiths 1961; memb Law Soc 1964; *Clubs* Green Jackets; *Style*— Walter Prideaux, Esq; ✉ High Stoke, Beauworth, Alresford, Hants (☎ 01962 771434); White & Bowker, 19 St Peter St, Winchester, Hants (☎ 01962 844440, fax 01962 842300)

PRIEST, Christopher McKenzie; s of Walter Mackenzie Priest, and Millicent Alice, *née* Haslock; *b* 14 July 1943; *Educ* Cheadle Hulme Sch; *m* Laura Lee, *née* McClure; 1 s (Simon Walter b 23 Oct 1989), 1 da (Elizabeth Millicent (twin) b 23 Oct 1989); *Career* writer; memb Soc of Authors; *Books* Indoctrinaire (1970), Real-Time World (short stories, 1974), Fugue for a Darkening Island (1972), Inverted World (1974), The Space Machine (1976), A Dream of Wessex (1977), An Infinite Summer (short stories, 1979), The Affirmation (1981), The Glamour (1984), The Quiet Woman (1990), The Prestige (1995); *Style*— Christopher Priest, Esq; ✉ c/o Aitken and Stone Ltd, 29 Fernshaw Road, London SW10 0TG (☎ 0171 351 7561, fax 0171 376 3594)

PRIEST, David James; s of James George Priest (d 1945), and Phoebe Young, *née* Logan; *b* 20 March 1937; *Educ* Kingston Coll; *m* 23 May 1959, Carol-Ann, da of Arthur Basham, of Westcliff-on-Sea, Essex; 1 s (Christopher David b 1961), 1 da (Melanie Jayne b 1966); *Career* engr: Vicker Armstrongs Aircraft Ltd Weybridge 1954–61, Br United Airways 1961–65; various positions Standard Telephones and Cables Ltd (subsid of ITT) 1965–75; md: Barking-Grohe Ltd (ITT) 1975–79, ITT Jabsco Ltd 1979–83, Woods of Colchester Ltd (subsid of GEC) 1983–; past pres: Fedn of Environmental Trade Assocs, Heating and Ventilation Mfrs Assoc; memb Essex Trg and Enterprise Cncl Bd, dir Wivenhoe Enterprises Ltd, dep chm and memb Bd Colchester Institute Corp, memb Eastern Region Industl Devpt Bd, memb Ct Univ of Essex; memb local advsy gp: Community Hospitals Ltd, E Anglian Radio; tstee Winsley's Charity (Alms Houses); memb Rotary Int; hon fell South Bank Univ; CEng, FIMechE; *Recreations* swimming, tennis; *Clubs* Colchester Garrison Officers; *Style*— David Priest, Esq; ✉ 44 Lexden Rd, Colchester, Essex CO3 3RF (☎ 01206 48398); Woods of Colchester Ltd, Tufnell Way, Colchester, Essex CO4 5AR (☎ 01206 44122, fax 01206 574434)

PRIEST, Prof Eric Ronald; s of Ronald Priest, of Halesowen, Worcs, and Olive Vera, *née* Dolan; *b* 7 Nov 1943; *Educ* King Edward VI Birmingham, Univ of Nottingham (BSc), Univ of Leeds (MSc, PhD); *m* 25 July 1970, Clare Margaret, da of Rev William Henry Wilson, of St Andrews; 3 s (Andrew Nicholas b 1973, David Mark b 1978, Matthew Aidan b 1978), 1 da (Naomi Clare b 1982); *Career* prof of theoretical solar physics Univ of St Andrews 1983– (lectr in applied mathematics 1969, reader 1977); memb Norwegian Acad of Scis and Letters 1994; FRSE 1985, FInstP 1989, FRAS; *Books* Solar Flare Magnetohydrodynamics (1981), Solar Magnetohydrodynamics (1982), Solar System Magnetic Fields (1985), Dynamics and Structure of Solar Prominences (1989), Magnetic Flux Ropes (1990), Basic Plasma Processes on the Sun (1990), Advances in Solar System MHD (1991), Mechanisms of Chromospheric and Coronal Heating (1991), Dynamics of Solar Flares (1991); *Recreations* bridge, swimming, hill walking, aerobics, children; *Style*— Prof Eric Priest, FRSE; ✉ Mathematical & Computational Sciences Department, The University, St Andrews, Scotland KY16 9SS (☎ 01334 463709)

PRIEST, Keith; s of William John Priest, of Sunderland, and Christina, *née* Black; *b* 26 April 1950; *Educ* Bede Sch Sunderland, AA Sch of Architecture (AADipl); *Career* architect; Sir Dennys Lasdun & Partners until 1973, design dir Wolff Olins design conslts 1973–78, fndr ptnr Fletcher Priest Architects 1978–; responsible for projects incl: IBM UK Laboratories, Sony Pictures London, London Planetarium, Powergen HQ, Leo Burnett, Bartle Bogle Hegarty, BBC Broadcast House, UNUM Headquarters, DLR Stations and cinema projects; memb: D&AD, AA; RIBA, FRSA; *Recreations* skiing, reading; *Style*— Keith Priest, Esq; ✉ Fletcher Priest Architects, 23–27 Heddon Street, London W1R 7LG (☎ 0171 439 8621, fax 0171 439 8526); Fletcher Priest Bösl Architekten, Sudermanplaz 3, 50670 Koln, Germany (☎ 00 49 221 726818, fax 00 49 221 7327608)

PRIEST, Margaret Diane (Mrs Tony Scherman); da of Arthur Edmund Priest (d 1995), of Toronto, Ontario, Canada, and Gertrude, *née* Tommason; *b* 15 Feb 1944; *Educ* Dagenham Co HS Essex, SW Essex Tech Coll and Sch of Art Walthamstow, Maidstone Coll of Art (DipAD), RCA (John Minton scholar, MA, Silver medallist); *m* 1 Sept 1972, Tony Scherman, s of Paul Scherman (d 1996); 1 s (Leo b 2 April 1975), 2 da (Georgia Donna b 13 Jan 1978, Claudia Eve b 3 April 1980); *Career* artist; teacher of art: Harrow Sch of Art 1970–74, St Martin's Sch of Art London 1972–76, Univ of Waterloo Sch of Architecture Ontario 1982–83, Univ of Toronto Sch of Architecture 1983–95; currently tenured assoc prof of fine art Univ of Guelph Ontario (joined Dept of Fine Art 1983), visiting critic to schs of art and architecture UK, USA and Canada; work in numerous public and private collections; design and installation of The Monument to Construction Workers (Bay/Adelaide Park Toronto) 1993; memb: Univ Art Assoc of Canada, Bd Gershon Iskowitz Fndn 1988–; *Exhibitions* major solo exhibitions incl: Arnolfini Gallery Bristol 1970 and 1974, Garage Art Limited London 1974, Felicity Samuel Gallery London 1976, Theo Waddington Gallery London, Toronto, New York and Montreal 1980–83, Marianne Friedland Gallery Toronto 1985 and 1987, Albemarle Gallery London 1989, To View from Here Gallery Hamilton and Macdonald Stewart Art Centre Guelph 1996; numerous gp exhibitions since 1969 in England, Yugoslavia, Switzerland, Belgium, Canada, USA, West Germany and Italy; *Awards* Arts Cncl of GB 1969, Internationale Jugendtriennale Drawing Award 1979, Ontario Arts Cncl Drawing award 1981, Governor Gen's Award for Architecture 1994; *Style*— Ms Margaret Priest; ✉ 38 Dunvegan Rd, Toronto, Ontario M4V 2P6, Canada (☎ 00 1 416 922 9699, fax 416 944 0814); Department of Fine Art, University of Guelph, Guelph, Ontario NIG 2WI, Canada (☎ 00 1 519 824 4120 ext 2413, fax 00 1 519 837 1315)

PRIEST, Prof Robert George; s of James George Priest (d 1945), of South Benfleet, Essex, and Phoebe, *née* Logan; *b* 28 Sept 1933; *Educ* Westcliff HS, UCL (MB BS, MD); *m* 24 June 1955, Marilyn, da of Baden Roberts Baker, JP (d 1979), of Westcliff-on-Sea; 2 s (Ian b 1956, Roderick b 1960); *Career* Capt RAMC 1958–61 (acting Maj 1960–61), Sch of Infantry Warminster 1958–59, GHQ Far ELF Singapore 1960–61; house physician to Lord Amulree 1956–57, house surgn Edgware Gen Hosp 1957, SHO registrar Royal Edinburgh Hosp 1961–64, lectr in psychiatry Univ of Edinburgh 1964–67, visiting lectr Univ of Chicago 1966–67, sr lectr St George's Hosp Med Sch Univ of London 1967–73, prof and head Dept of Psychiatry Imperial Coll Sch of Med at St Mary's 1973–96, chm Bd of Studies in Med Univ of London 1987–89, senator Univ of London 1989–93; chm Psychiatric Advsy Ctee NW Thames RHA 1976–79, memb Cncl Br Assoc for Psychopharmacology (chm Membership Ctee 1977–81), pres Soc for Psychosomatic Res 1980–81, vice chm Regnl Manpower Ctee NW Thames RHA 1980–83, chm Mental Health Gp Ctee BMA 1982–85, memb Ctee World Psychiatric Assoc 1985–93 (memb Cncl 1989–93); Int Coll of Psychosomatic Med: fell 1977, memb Governing Body and UK delegate 1978–81, treas 1981–83, sec 1981–85, vice pres 1985–87; Royal Coll of Psychiatrists: memb Cncl 1982–88, registrar 1983–88, chm Public Policy Ctee 1983–88, memb Ct of Electors 1983–88, chm Gen Psychiatry Ctee 1985–88, chm Fellowship Sub-Ctee; memb Central Ctee for Hosp Med Servs 1983–92 (chm Psychiatric Sub Ctee 1983–87); FRCPE 1974, FRCPsych 1974; *Books* Insanity: A Study of Major Psychiatric Disorders (1977), Sleep Research (jt ed, 1979), Benzodiazepines Today and Tomorrow (jt ed, 1980), Psychiatry in Med Practice (ed, 1982), Anxiety and Depression (1983), Anxiety and Depression: A Practical Guide to Recovery (e edn, 1988), Sleep: An International Monograph (1984), Nomifensine Pharmacological and Clinical Profile (jt ed, 1984), Psychological Disorders in Obstetrics and Gynaecology (ed, 1985), Handbook of Psychiatry (jtly, 1986), Trastornos psicologicos en obstetricia y ginecologia (1987), Oro och depression (1987), Anxiety and Depression (1988), Sleepless Nights (Insomnia): What To Do (jtly, 1990), Depression and Anxiety (jtly, 1992), Ansiedad y Depresion (1992), Depression in General Practice (jtly, 1996); *Recreations* squash, tennis, foreign languages, nature study; *Style*— Prof Robert Priest; ✉ 29 Old Slade Lane, Richings Park, Iver, Bucks SL0 9DY

PRIESTLEY, Clive; CB (1983); s of Albert Ernest Priestley (d 1985), of Bournemouth, Dorset, and Annie May Priestley (d 1974); *b* 12 July 1935; *Educ* Loughborough GS, Univ of Nottingham (BA, MA), Harvard Univ; *m* 1, 1961 (m dis 1984), Barbara Anne, *née* Wells; 2 da (Rebecca, Alison); m 2, 1985, Daphne June Challis Priestley, OBE, JP, DL, da of Walter Challis Franks, JP (d 1969); *Career* civil serv 1960–83 (under sec PM's office 1979–83), divnl dir BT plc 1983–88, conslt on orgn and mgmnt; govr: RSC 1984–, City Literary Inst 1994–96; memb: Bart's Med Coll Cncl 1990–95 (vice pres 1993–95, acting pres 1995), Arts Cncl of GB 1991–95, Arts Cncl of England 1996–, Cncl Queen Mary and Westfield Coll 1995–; chm London Arts Bd 1991–; Freeman City of London 1989, Liveryman Worshipful Co of Glaziers 1989; Hon FTCL; *Clubs* Army and Navy; *Style*— Clive Priestley, Esq, CB; ✉ c/o London Arts Board, 133 Long Acre, London WC2E 9AF (☎ 0171 240 1313)

PRIESTLEY, Hugh Michael; s of James Frederick Priestley, MC, of Headbourne Worthy, nr Winchester, and Honor Purefoy, *née* Pollock; *b* 22 Aug 1942; *Educ* Winchester, Worcester Coll Oxford (MA); *m* 9 July 1968, Caroline Clarissa Duncan, da of Brig John Hume Prendergast, DSO, MC, of Tisbury, Wilts; 2 da (Alexandra b 1971, Susannah b 1974); *Career* The Times Newspaper 1964–66, Henderson Admin 1972–93, dir Laurence Keen Ltd 1993–; dir of four quoted investment tst companies; treas UCL 1981–; fell UCL; *Recreations* shooting, skiing, fishing; *Clubs* City of London, Boodle's, MCC; *Style*— Hugh Priestley, Esq; ✉ 52 Stanford Rd, London W8 5PZ (☎ 0171 937 5554); Laurence Keen Ltd, 49/51 Bow Lane, London EC4M 9LX (☎ 0171 489 9493, fax 0171 489 8640, telex 916966)

PRIESTLEY, Rev John Christopher; s of Ronald Priestley (d 1994), and Winifred Mary, *née* Hughes (d 1968); *b* 23 May 1939; *Educ* William Hulme GS Manchester, Trinity Coll Oxford (BA, MA), Wells Theol Coll, Univ of Sheffield (MMin 1994); *m* 26 Dec 1964, Margaret Ida, da of Edward Machan, of Prestwich, Gtr Manchester; 1 s (Andrew John b 1970), 1 da (Rosemary Jane b 1967); *Career* asst master St James' Sch Clitheroe 1961–64, dep headmaster The Green Sch Padiham 1964–70; ordained deacon then priest Blackburn Cathedral 1968; curate: All Saints Burnley 1968–70, St Leonard's Padiham 1970–75; vicar Christ Church Colne 1975–, chaplain to HM The Queen 1990–, rural dean Pendle 1991–96, dir Post Ordination Trg Diocese of Blackburn 1996–; chaplain Colne Branch Royal Br Legion 1975–; memb: RSPB 1974–, Rotary Club of Colne 1976–86, Movement for the Ordination of Women 1982–94; *Recreations* long distance walking, music, people watching, flying light aircraft; *Style*— The Rev John Priestley; ✉ Christ Church Vicarage, Colne, Lancs BB8 7HF (☎ 01282 863511)

PRIESTLEY, John Philip; s of Walter Priestley (d 1980), and Edith, *née* Moss; *b* 4 July 1937; *Educ* Barnsley GS, Univ of Oxford (BA); *m* Kathleen Margaret, da of late Raymond Arthur Foord; 1 s (Julian b 1982), 2 da (Alison b 1978, Jennifer b 1980 (decd)); *Career* CA 1965; Arthur Andersen: ptnr London 1972, managing ptnr Bristol Office 1978–85, managing ptnr Manchester Office 1985–92, ptnr 1992–94; fin and operational conslt 1994–; FCA; *Style*— John Priestley, Esq; ✉ 8th Floor, Bank House, 9 Charlotte St, Manchester M1 4EU (☎ 0161 228 2121)

PRIESTLEY, Leslie William; TD (1974); s of George Priestley (d 1947), and Winifred, *née* Young (d 1994); *b* 22 Sept 1933; *Educ* Shooters Hill GS; *m* 8 Oct 1960, Audrey Elizabeth, da of Sidney Humber (d 1978); 1 s (Ian b 1967), 1 da (Jane b 1970); *Career* head of mktg Barclaycard 1966–73, local dir Barclays Bank 1978–79 (asst gen mangr 1974–77), sec gen Ctee of London Clearing Bankers 1979–83, dir Banker's Automated Clearing Servs Co 1979–83, md Barclays Insurance Services 1983–84, regnl gen mangr Barclays Bank 1984–85, chief exec TSB England & Wales plc 1985–89 (also dir TSB

Group and Trustcard Ltd 1985–89); chm: Hill House Hammond Ltd 1988–89, Mortgage Express 1988–89, Caviapen Investments Ltd 1993–, Caviapen Trustees Ltd 1993–, Financial Telemarketing Services plc 1995–; dir Civil Aviation Authy 1990–96; dir: London Electricity plc (formerly LEB) 1984–, Pearce Group Holdings Ltd 1989–, Pinnacle Insurance plc 1990–, Omnia ICL Ltd 1992–94, Prudential Banking plc 1996–; banking advsr Touche Ross & Co 1990–96; memb: Monopolies & Mergers Commision 1990–96, London C of C and Industry 1992–96; visiting fell Univ Coll of N Wales 1989–95, conslt ed Bankers Magazine 1972–81; FCIB, CIMgt, FCIM, FRSA; *Recreations* reading, gardening, golf, theatre; *Clubs* Wig and Pen, RAC, Sundridge Park Golf; *Style—* Leslie Priestley, Esq, TD; ✉ c/o The Civil Aviation Authority, CAA House, 45–59 Kingsway, London WC2B 6TE (☎ 0171 832 5371, fax 0171 832 6478)

PRIESTLEY, Prof Maurice Bertram; s of Jack Priestley (d 1990), of Manchester, and Rose Priestley (d 1966); *Educ* Manchester GS, Jesus Coll Cambridge (MA, Dip Math Stat), Univ of Manchester (PhD); *m* 24 June 1959, Nancy, da of Ralph Norman Nelson (d 1959); 1 s (Michael Richard b 1963), 1 da (Ruth Nicola b 1961); *Career* scientific offr Royal Aircraft Estab 1955–56, lectr Univ of Manchester 1960–65 (asst lectr 1957–60), prof UMIST 1970– (sr lectr 1965–70, head Dept of Mathematics 1973–75, 1980–85 and 1986–89), dir Manchester-Sheffield Sch of Probability and Statistics 1976–79, 1988–89 and 1991–92, visiting prof Princeton and Stanford Univs USA 1961–62; Cncl memb Manchester Statistical Soc; hon prof of probability and statistics Univ of Sheffield; fell of Royal Statistical Soc 1955, memb Int Statistical Inst 1972, fell Inst of Mathematical Statistics 1978; *Books* Spectral Analysis and Time Series (vols I and II, 1981), Essays in Time Series and Allied Processes (jt ed 1986), Non-Linear and Non-Stationary Time Series Analysis (1988); *Recreations* music, Hi-Fi, amateur radio, golf; *Style—* Prof Maurice Priestley; ✉ Department of Mathematics, UMIST, Manchester, M60 1QD (☎ 0161 200 3660)

PRIESTLEY, Philip John; CBE; s of Frederick Priestley (d 1963), and Caroline, *née* Rolfe (d 1982); *b* 29 Aug 1946; *Educ* Boston GS Lincs, Univ of E Anglia (BA); *m* 14 Nov 1972, Christine, da of Mrs M Sanders (d 1987); 1 s (Max b 1 Nov 1978), 1 da (Maya b 30 March 1976); *Career* Foreign & Commonwealth Office 1969–71, 3 sec Sofia 1971–73, 3 later 2 sec Kinshasa 1973–76, 1 sec FCO 1976–79, head of Chancery Wellington 1979–83, 1 sec FCO 1984–87, commercial cnsllr/dep head of mission Manila 1987–90, HM ambass Libreville 1990–91, fell Center for International Affairs Harvard Univ 1991–92, HM consul-gen Geneva 1992–95, head N America Dept FCO 1996–; *Recreations* golf, tennis, theatre; *Style—* Philip Priestley, Esq, CBE; ✉ c/o Foreign & Commonwealth Office, King Charles St, London SW1A 2AH (☎ 0171 270 2658, fax 0171 270 2560)

PRIESTLEY, Dr Robert Henry; s of Henry Benjamin Priestley, of Nantwich, Cheshire, and Margaret Alice, *née* Lambert; *b* 19 March 1946; *Educ* Brunts GS Mansfield, Univ of Southampton (BSc), Univ of Exeter (PhD); *m* 1970, Penelope Ann, da of Sydney Fox; 2 da (Rosalind Jane b 8 Sept 1975, Jessica Mary b 28 May 1978); *Career* plant pathologist Lord Rank Res Centre Rank Hovis McDougal Research Ltd 1970–73; National Institute of Agricultural Botany: cereal pathologist 1973–78, head Cereal Pathology Section 1978–82, head Plant Pathology Dept 1982–88; gen sec Institute of Biology 1989–; memb: Cncl Fedn of British Plant Pathologists 1980–81, British Nat Ctee for Microbiology 1982–89, Ctee of Mgmnt Biological Cncl 1989–91, Parly and Scientific Ctee 1989–, Bd Cncl for Science and Technology Insts 1989–, Nominations Ctee Int Union of Biological Sciences 1994–; sec UK Cereal Pathogen Virulence Survey 1974–82, chm EC Biologists' Assoc 1992–96, memb Br Soc for Plant Pathology 1980 (treas 1981–87, UK rep 1988–92); CBiol, FIBiol; *Books* Identification and Control of Diseases (1982), Diseases of Oilseed Rape and Fodder Brassicas (1985), Diseases of Grasses and Herbage Legumes (1988); author of numerous scientific papers on crop diseases; *Recreations* music, gardening, collecting, football, swimming; *Style—* Dr Robert Priestley; ✉ Institute of Biology, 20–22 Queensberry Place, London SW7 2DZ (☎ 0171 581 8333, fax 0171 823 9409)

PRIESTMAN, Dr Jane; OBE (1991); da of Reuben Stanley Herbert (d 1986), and Mary Elizabeth, *née* Ramply (d 1957); *b* 7 April 1930; *Educ* Northwood Coll, Liverpool Coll of Art (NDD, ATD); *m* 1954 (m dis), Arthur Martin Priestman; 2 s (Matthew Temple b March 1958, Paul Dominic b June 1961); *Career* designer; own design practice 1954–75, design mangr BAA 1975–86, dir of architecture and design British Railways Board 1986–91, ind design mgmnt conslt 1991–; govr: Cwlth Inst, Kingston Univ; chm RIBA Awards Gp; dir London Open House 1996–; memb Design Cncl 1996–; Hon DDes De Montfort Univ 1994; Hon FRIBA, FCSD, FRSA; *Recreations* opera, city architecture, textiles, travel; *Clubs* Architecture; *Style—* Dr Jane Priestman, OBE; ✉ 30 Duncan Terrace, London N1 8BS (☎ 0171 837 4525, fax 0171 837 4525)

PRIESTMAN, Richard John; s of Cecil Priestman, of Liverpool, and Mary, *née* Gray; *b* 16 July 1955; *Educ* Maghull GS, Liverpool Poly; *Career* target archer (international 1984–); honours incl team Bronze medal Olympic Games Seoul 1988 and Barcelona 1992; Br archery record holder FITA round 1988, ranked number 1 in GB 1989, Br indoor champion 1976 and 1992, Br outdoor champion 1993, Br record holder Double York round 1993, Br record holder indoors at 18 and 25 metres; nat coaching organiser Grand National Archery Soc 1994–; bank clerk National Westminster Bank plc; *Clubs* Nethermoss Archers, Grand National Archery Soc; *Style—* Richard Priestman, Esq

PRIESTMAN, Dr Terrence James; s of Francis Dennis Priestman (d 1980), of Bournemouth, and Vera Mercy, *née* Jackman (d 1962); *b* 1 Jan 1945; *Educ* King Henry VIII Sch Coventry, King's Coll London, Westminster Med Sch London (MB BS, Frederick Bird prize); *Career* house offr: in radiotherapy and oncology Westminster Hosp London 1968, in gen surgery Bolingbroke Hosp London 1968–69; SHO: in gen med Willesden Gen Hosp 1969–70, in cardiology London Chest Hosp 1970, in radiotherapy and oncology Westminster Hosp 1970–71; registrar in radiotherapy and oncology Christie Hosp and Holt Radium Inst Manchester 1973–74, conslt in radiotherapy and oncology Velindre Hosp Cardiff 1974–77, med advsr in oncology Wellcome Research Labs and hon conslt in radiotherapy and oncology Westminster Hosp 1977–81, conslt in radiology and oncology Queen Elizabeth and Dudley Road Hosps Birmingham 1981–89 (chm Div of Radiotherapy and conslt in administrative charge Dept of Radiotherapy and Oncology Queen Elizabeth Hosp 1982–87), conslt clinical oncologist Royal Hosp Wolverhampton 1989–; memb Med Exec Ctee Central Birmingham HA 1984–87; W Midlands RHA: memb Regnl Scientific Ctee 1986–91, chm Regnl Advsy Ctee on Radiotherapy and Oncology 1990–94; Royal Coll of Radiologists: memb Faculty Bd (Radiotherapy and Oncology) 1984–87 (elected) and 1987– (ex-officio), memb Cncl 1987–89, rep Br Assoc for Radiation Protection 1989–93 (chm 1990–91), rep Standing Intercollegiate Ctee on Nuclear Med 1989–94, registrar Faculty of Clinical Oncology 1994–96, dean Faculty of Clinical Oncology 1996–; memb: Cncl Section of Oncology RSM 1986–87, Nat Ctee Br Assoc of Surgical Oncology 1981–84; Twining Medal for Research Royal Coll of Radiologists; MRCP 1971 DMRT 1972, FRCR (FFR) 1973, MD 1981, FRCP 1984; *Books* Cancer Chemotherapy: an introduction (3 edn, 1989); author of various book chapters and numerous original articles; ed Clinical Oncology 1989–94 (dep ed 1987–89); *Recreations* watercolour painting (portraits); *Style—* Dr Terrence Priestman; ✉ New Cross Hospital, Wolverhampton WV10 0QP (☎ 01902 642978, fax 01902 642994)

PRIMAROLO, Dawn; MP (Lab) Bristol South (majority 8,919); *b* 2 May 1954; *Educ* Thomas Bennett Comprehensive Sch Crawley, Bristol Poly (BA), Univ of Bristol; *m* 7 Oct 1972 (m dis), Michael Primarolo; 1 s (Luke b 24 Jan 1978); m 2, 29 Nov 1990, Ian Ducat; *Career* legal sec and advice worker 1972–75, sec Resources for Learning Avon CC 1975–78 (cncllr 1985–87); MP (Lab) Bristol S 1987–, memb Select Ctee on Members' Interests 1990–92, shadow min for health, shadow spokesperson for treasy 1994–; *Style—* Ms Dawn Primarolo, MP; ✉ PO Box 1002, Bristol BS99 1WH (☎ 0117 909 0063); House of Commons, London SW1A 0AA (☎ 0171 219 3000)

PRIME, Brian Salisbury; s of George Henry Luke Prime (d 1975), of Northwood, Middx, and Dilys Salisbury, *née* Jones (d 1978); *b* 14 Aug 1932; *Educ* Harrow GS, LSE (BSc); *m* 10 March 1962, Susan Mary Eveline, da of Thomas Holdstock (d 1983), of Redhill; 2 s (Jonathan b 1965, Richard b 1967), 1 da (Sally-Ann b 1963); *Career* Lt RA 1954–56; trained as CA and mgmnt accountant; md: Kingsway Group plc 1985–93 (dir 1967–93), Celcon Blocks Ltd 1975–93, Ryarsh Brick Ltd 1980–93, Eurospace Furniture Packs Ltd 1983–93, New Horizon Furniture Ltd 1985–93, Nymoelle Stenindustri Ltd 1986–93, Bushboard Parker Ltd 1986–93, Brantham Engineering Ltd 1987–93, Elremco Products Ltd 1987–93, Hormigones Celulares SA 1989–93, Essex Electronics Ltd 1989–93, Earthspan plc 1990–93, Brulynco BV (Netherlands) 1990–93, Bald BV (Netherlands) 1990–93, Bald NV (Belgium) 1990–93, Bald UK Ltd 1992–93, Kayplan Windows Ltd 1990–93, Compton Aggregates Ltd 1978–94; mgmnt conslt 1993–; memb Cncl Chartered Inst of Mgmnt Accountants 1985–92; CIMgt, FCA, FCMA; *Recreations* skiing, gardening; *Clubs* IOD, Danish; *Style—* Brian S Prime, Esq; ✉ Oakwood Cottage, Oakwood Close, Chislehurst, Kent BR7 5DD

PRIMOST, Norman Basil; s of Sydney Simon Primost (d 1976), of London, and Regina, *née* Bader (d 1991); *b* 25 June 1933; *Educ* St Paul's, LSE (LLB), Trinity Hall Cambridge; *m* 30 Aug 1965, Debbie Doris, da of Chaim Ferster; 1 da (Belinda Rosemary (Mrs Mindell) b 10 April 1967), 3 s (Mark Stephen Adam b 12 July 1969, David Jonathan Andrew b 23 Jan 1975, Simon Henry William b 29 Sept 1977); *Career* Nat Serv censoring mail RASC Military Corrective Estab Colchester 1954–56; called to the Bar Middle Temple 1954, pupillage with Montague Waters QC 1956–57, gen common law practice specialising in property law, with particular emphasis on landlord and tenant law 1957–, head of chambers 1 Temple Gardens Temple 1986–94; legal corr Stock Exchange Jl 1967–69, ed Restrictive Practices Reports 1969–71; *Recreations* theatre, chess, modern literature, classical music; *Clubs* Wig & Pen, King's Head Theatre; *Style—* Norman Primost, Esq; ✉ Grande Vue, 98 West Heath Road, Hampstead, London NW3 7TU (☎ 0181 458 9757); 39 Crag Head, Manor Road, Bournemouth, Dorset; 5 Pump Court, Temple, London EC4Y 7AP (☎ 0171 353 2532, fax 0171 353 5321)

PRIMROSE, Andrew Hardie; s of Kenneth Alexander (d 1939), of Glasgow, and Mary Dougall, *née* Campbell (now Mrs Primrose); *b* 25 Sept 1939; *Educ* Glenalmond, Univ Coll Oxford (Open scholar, BA), Univ of Glasgow (Cunninghame bursar in Scots law, LLB); *m* 1, 1964, Helen Mary (d 1986), da of David Clark Banks; 1 s (David Alexander b 1965), 1 da (Alison Clare b 1968); m 2, Margaret (Meg), da of John Royston Laidlaw; *Career* Maclay Murray & Spens: apprentice 1961–64, admitted slr in Scot 1964, ptnr 1966–, NP 1967, convener Conveyancing Dept 1976–78, managing ptnr 1978–85, moved to open first London office 1989, chm Environmental Law Unit 1994–, returned to Glasgow 1995; external examiner in conveyancing Univ of Glasgow 1984–88, chm Real Estate Ctee Int Bar Assoc 1988–92, memb Working Party Euro Environmental Law Assoc (addressing EC Green Paper on Civil Liability for Damage to the Environment) 1994; chm Glasgow Jr C of C 1971–72 (senator Jr Chamber Int), Rotary Fndn Exchange scholar to Indiana USA 1974, memb Bd Scottish Industl Estates Corp 1973–75, former tstee West of Scotland TSB (then TSB Scotland), dir Glasgow C of C 1987–89, fndr chm Glasgow City Ctee Macmillan Cancer Relief Fund; memb Incorporation of Hammermen in Glasgow (deacon 1985–86), Liveryman City of London Slrs' Co 1995; memb: Law Soc of Scotland 1964, Royal Faculty of Procurators in Glasgow 1966, Int Bar Assoc 1978, UK Environmental Law Assoc 1991, Law Soc of Eng 1994; *Books* Drafting and Negotiating Commercial Leases in Scotland (co-author 1985, 2 edn 1993); *Recreations* playing and watching sport, active sports: golf, curling, hill-walking, riding, cycling, skiing; *Clubs* Western (Glasgow), Royal Scottish Automobile (Glasgow), East Renfrewshire Golf (Glasgow), Vincent's (Oxford); *Style—* Andrew Primrose, Esq; ✉ Maclay Murray & Spens, 151 St Vincent Street, Glasgow G2 5NJ (☎ 0141 248 5011, fax 0141 248 5819)

PRIMROSE, Sir John Ure; 5 Bt (UK 1903), of Redholme, Dumbreck, Co of City of Glasgow; s of Sir (Alasdair) Neil Primrose, 4 Bt (d 1986), and (Elaine) Noreen, o da of Edmund Cecil Lowndes, of Buenos Aires, Argentina; *b* 1960; *m* 1983 (m dis 1987), Marion Cecilia, da of Hans Otto Altgelt, of Buenos Aires, Argentina; 2 da (Christine Anne b 1984, Jennifer Diana b 1986); *Heir* bro, Andrew Richard Primrose b 19 Jan 1966; *Style—* Sir John Primrose, Bt; ✉ Puerto Victoria, Alto Parana Misiones, Argentina

PRINCE, Dr Alan; s of Harold Bernard Prince (d 1971), and Amy, *née* Williamson (d 1975); *b* 9 Sept 1927; *Educ* Holgate GS Barnsley, Univ of Sheffield (BMet, DMet); *m* 27 Jan 1951, Sheila Mary, da of William Foster Jacklin (d 1969); 4 s (Neil b 1957, Ian b 1958, Simon b 1961, Howard b 1965), 1 da (Christine (Mrs Maltby) b 1955); *Career* tech offr ICI 1949–52, lectr Univ of Southampton 1953–55; chief metallurgist: GEC-Simon Carves Atomic Energy Div 1956–61, Hirst Res Centre GEC 1961–87; prof assoc Brunel Univ 1987–91; consulting engr 1987–; FIM 1954 (pres 1972–73), FEng 1986; *Books* The Constitution of Alloys: a Bibliography (1956), Alloy Phase Equilibria (1966), Multicomponent Alloy Constitution Bibliography 1955–73 (1978), Multicomponent Alloy Constitution Bibliography 1974–77 (1981), Handbook of Precious Metals (ed, 1989), Phase Diagrams of Ternary Gold Alloys (jtly, 1990), Handbook of Ternary Alloy Phase Diagrams (10 vols, jtly, 1995); *Style—* Dr Alan Prince, FEng; ✉ 90 Station Road, Harpenden, Herts AL5 4TY (☎ 01582 712335)

PRINCE, Dominic Clech; s of late John Clech Prince, of Chipping Warden, Oxfordshire, and Joyce Elizabeth, *née* Hazzard; *b* 8 Jan 1961; *Educ* Chiswick Sch London, Witney Agric Coll Oxfordshire; *m* 17 July 1993, Hon Rose Amanda Jeffreys, yr da of 2 Baron Jeffreys; *Career* freelance journalist, writer and TV producer; Evening Standard, Daily Mail and Daily Express 1985–88, obituaries Daily Telegraph 1987–; investigative reporter: Sunday Times (also business diarist) 1990–91, Independent on Sunday 1991; City ed Sunday Express 1992–94 (City writer and dep City ed 1991–92), freelance journalist, writer and TV prodr 1994–; prodr The Totter (Channel 4) 1990 (nominated best documentary Bdcast Awards 1991), reporter and co-prodr Despatches prog on fund mgmnt (Channel 4); prodr: The Big Deal (series, BBC 2) 1996, The Headhunter, In the Blood; commended Journalist of the Year 1990; *Books* Guide Book to Covent Garden (ed, 1986), Last of a Kind - the Sinking of Lew Grade (co-author, 1987); *Recreations* horses, drinking, shooting; *Style—* Dominic Prince, Esq; ✉ 177 Battersea Bridge Road, London SW11 3AS (☎ 0171 223 9709, fax 0171 350 1336)

PRINCE, Harold Smith; s of Milton Prince (d 1966), and Blanche Stern (d 1984); *b* 30 Jan 1928; *Educ* Univ of Pennsylvania (BA); *m* 26 Oct 1962, Judith Chaplin Prince, da of Saul Chaplin; 1 s (Charles b 1963), 1 da (Daisy b 1965); *Career* theatre dir and prodr; memb Nat Cncl for the Arts 1976–82, pres League of NY Theatres; recipient: 20 Tony Awards, Drama Critics' Circle Awards, Obi Awards, Plays and Players Best Dir Award, Evening Standard Award, Commonwealth Award; Hon DFA: Univ of Pennsylvania, Pratt Inst, Wagner Coll; Hon DLitt Franklin and Marshall Emerson Coll; honoree Kennedy Center 1994; *Theatre* co-produced: The Pajama Game (Tony Award) 1954, Damn Yankees (Tony Award) 1955, New Girl in Town 1957, West Side Story 1957, A Swim In the Sea 1958, Fiorello! (Tony Award, Pulitzer Prize) 1959, Tenderloin 1960, A Call On Kuprin 1961, They Might Be Giants 1961, Side by Side by Sondheim 1977; produced: Take Her, She's Mine 1961, A Funny Thing Happened on the Way to the Forum (Tony Award) 1962, Fiddler on the Roof 1964, Poor Bitos 1964, Flora, The Red

Menace 1965; directed: Family Affair 1962, Baker Street 1965, The Great God Brown 1972, The Visit 1973, Love for Love 1974, Some of My Best Friends 1977, On the Twentieth Century 1978, Evita (London 1979, USA 1979–83, Aust, Vienna 1980, Mexico City 1981, Tony Award Best Dir, SWET Award) 1978, Sweeney Todd (Tony Award Best Dir) 1979, Play Memory 1984, End of the World 1984, Diamonds 1984, Phantom of the Opera (NY 1988, Tokyo 1989, LA 1989, Toronto 1989, London 1992, Tony Award Best Dir 1986), Roza 1987, Cabaret 1987, Kiss of the Spider Woman (Toronto, London and Broadway) 1993, Show Boat (Toronto and Broadway) 1993 and 1994; produced and directed: She Loves Me (Broadway 1963, London 1964), Superman 1966, Cabaret (Tony Award Best Dir, Best Musical) 1966, Zorba 1968, Company (Tony Award Best Musical) 1970, Follies (co-dir, Tony Award Best Dir) 1971, A Little Night Music 1973, Candide (co-prodr, Tony Award Best Dir) 1974, Pacific Overtures 1976, Merrily We Roll Along (co-prodr) 1981, A Doll's Life 1982, Grind (co-prodr) 1985; directed and co-wrote: Grandchild of Kings (Off-Broadway) 1992; *Opera* directed: Ashmedai (NYC Opera) 1976, La Fanciulla del West (Chicago Lyric Opera) 1978, Silverlake (NYC Opera) 1980, Willie Stark (Houston Grand Opera) 1981, Candide (NYC Opera) 1982, Madama Butterfly (Chicago Lyric Opera) 1983, Turandot (Vienna Staatsoper) 1983, Sweeney Todd (NYC Opera) 1984, Don Giovanni (NYC Opera) 1989, Faust (Metropolitan Opera NY) 1990; *Films* co-produced: The Pajama Game 1957, Damn Yankees 1958; directed: Something for Everyone 1970, A Little Night Music 1978; *Books* Contradictions (1974); *Clubs* Players, SSD & C; *Style—* Harold Prince, Esq; ✉ 10 Rockefeller Plaza, Suite 1009, New York, NY 10020 (☎ 00 1 212 399 0960, fax 00 1 212 974 8426)

PRINCE, Dr John Anthony; s of Flt Lt Allan Leslie Prince (ka 1944), and Mary Pamela, *née* Paul; *b* 5 Nov 1941; *Educ* Giggleswick, ChCh Oxford (MA, BM BCh, DIH, MRCGP, MFOM); *Career* conslt occupational physician: Occidental Oil Inc 1977–83, London Borough of Tower Hamlets 1983–, Tower Hamlets Health Authy London Hosp 1983, News International 1985–86; memb Tower Hamlets DHA, sr ptnr Tower Med Centre, special advsr on disablement to DSS; memb: BMA, Soc of Occupational Med; FRSM; *Recreations* literature, history, antiquarianism, natural history, walking; *Style—* Dr John Prince; ✉ 69 Philpot St, London E1 2JH

PRINCE, Oscar Peter; s of Peter E Prince, MBE (d 1972), of Heliopolis St, Nicosia, Cyprus, and Minnie Prince; *b* 3 Sept 1934; *Educ* Mount St Mary's Coll Spinkhill, Univ of Hull; *m* 12 June 1976, Patricia, da of Donald Reilly, and Ruby Reilly, of Macandrew Bay, Dunedin, NZ; *Career* called to the Bar Gray's Inn 1966; Thos R Miller & Son London 1960–64, BISC London 1965–66, Constructors John Brown Ltd London 1966–68, legal advsr RMC Group plc 1968–; memb: Ctee T (construction), Ctee M (sale of goods), Int Bar Assoc 1982–, Gen Ctee BACFI 1985–91, Cncl of Legal Educn 1987–92, Gen Cncl of the Bar 1988–94, Int Relations Ctee Bar Cncl 1989–; *Recreations* bibliophile, gardening, theatre; *Style—* Oscar Prince, Esq; ✉ The First House, Midway, Walton-on-Thames, Surrey KT12 3HY (☎ 01932 228472); RMC Group plc, RMC House, Coldharbour Lane, Thorpe, Egham, Surrey TN20 8TD (☎ 01932 568833, fax 01932 568933, telex 918150)

PRINCE, Roger Graham; s of Graham Stanley Prince, of Norwich, and Lilian Mary, *née* Gee; *Educ* Avenue Road Sch, City of Norwich Sch, Downing Coll Cambridge (MA, LLB); *Career* called to the Bar: Inner Temple 1977, New South Wales 1989, Ireland 1992; practises trust and personal law; fndr and princ World Law Centre devoted to establishing liberty through the rule of law; fndr memb World Bar 1993; inventor of: the Rotarower 1993, Extendarigger, Extendanoar and Extendascull 1994; memb MENSA 1983, MRIN; *Books* The Law of Fact - A Comprehensive and Coherent Theory of Evidence (1990); *Recreations* instr Amateur Rowing Assoc, riding, sailing; *Clubs* Downing Coll Boat, London Rowing, Bar Yacht; *Style—* R G Prince, Esq; ✉ World Law Chambers, 268 Earlham Road, Norwich NR2 3RH (☎ 01603 453354)

PRINCE-SMITH, James William; s and h of Sir (William) Richard Prince-Smith, 4 Bt, *qv*; *b* 2 July 1959; *Educ* Wellesley House, Gresham's, Univ of Buckingham; *Career* Capt 13/18 Royal Hussars (Queen Mary's Own) 1979–87, Yorks Sqdn QOY; *Recreations* farming, mountaineering, photography, riding, travelling; *Clubs* Cavalry and Guards'; *Style—* James Prince-Smith, Esq; ✉ Morton Hall, Norwich NR9 5JS (☎ 01603 880165)

PRINCE-SMITH, Sir (William) Richard; 4 Bt (UK 1911), of Hillbrook, Keighley, W Riding of Yorks; s of Sir William Prince-Smith, 3 Bt, OBE, MC (d 1964), and Marian Marjorie (d 1970); *b* 27 Dec 1928; *Educ* Charterhouse, Clare Coll Cambridge (MA); *m* 1, 11 Oct 1955, Margaret Ann, o da of late Dr John Carter, of Loughton, Essex; 1 s (James William, *qv*), 1 da (Elizabeth Ann (Mrs Colin Earl) b 1957); m 2, 1975, Ann Christina, da of late Andrew Faulds, OBE, of Colchester, Essex; *Heir* s, James William Prince-Smith b 2 July 1959; *Career* former farmer and agric landowner, ret; *Clubs* The Springs (Rancho Mirage); *Style—* Sir Richard Prince-Smith, Bt; ✉ 40–735 Paxton Drive, Rancho Mirage, Calif 92270, USA (☎ 619 321 1975)

PRINDL, Dr Andreas; *b* 1939; *Career* banker; various posts Morgan Guaranty NY, Europe and Japan from 1964 incl secondment as chief exec Saudi International Bank; joined Nomura International 1984, fndr chm Nomura Bank International plc (London) 1986–97 (non-exec dir 1997–); pres: Chartered Inst of Bankers 1994–95 (vice pres 1995–), Assoc of Corp Treasurers 1996– (dir 1995–); chm Banking Indust Trg and Devpt Cncl 1994–96; memb Cncl: Gresham Coll 1995– (provost 1996–), City & Guilds of London Inst 1995– (hon memb 1995); hon fell Omicron Delta Kappa 1989, hon yeoman Worshipful Co of Musicians 1996, Hon DSc City Univ 1996; FCIB 1980, FRSA 1991; *Style—* Dr Andreas Prindl; ✉ Nomura Bank International plc, Nomura House, 1 St Martin's-le-Grand, London EC1A 4NP (☎ 0171 521 2000)

PRING-MILL, Dr Robert Duguid Forrest; s of Maj Richard Pring-Mill, RA (d 1961), and Nellie, *née* Duguid (d 1967); *b* 11 Sept 1924; *Educ* Colegio de Montesión Palma de Mallorca, New Coll Oxford (MA, DLitt); *m* 19 Aug 1950 (Maria) Brigitte, da of Ludwig Heinsheimer (d 1960); 1 s ((Andrew) Francis b 1952), 1 da ((Mary) Monica Sophia b 1954); *Career* The Black Watch RHR: enlisted 1941, cmmnd 1942, temp Capt 1945, demobbed 1947; sr Demyship Magdalen Coll Oxford 1950–52, lectr in Spanish Univ of Oxford 1952–88 (New Coll 1956–88, Exeter Coll 1963–81); English ed: Romanistisches Jahrbuch 1953–, Estudios Lulianos 1957–; corresponding memb Inst d'Estudis Catalans 1966, emeritus fell St Catherine's Coll Oxford 1991– (fell and tutor 1965–88, fell by special election 1988–91); Magister Maioricensis Schola Lullistica 1957; Premi Pompeu Fabra 1956, Premi Ciutat de Palma 1979, Premi Catalònia 1991, Premi Crítica Serra d'Or 1992; Creu de Sant Jordi (Generalitat de Catalunya) 1990, Comendador Orden de Isabel la Católica (Spain) 1990, Officer Orden de Bernardo O'Higgins (Chile) 1992; FBA 1988; *Books* Chinese Triad Societies (1946), Lope de Vega: Five Plays (ed, 1961), El Microcosmos Lul·lià (1961), Neruda: The Heights of Macchu Picchu (with N Tarn, 1966), Neruda Poems (with Katya Kohn, 1969), Lullus: Quattuor Libri Principiorum (ed, 1969), Neruda: A Basic Anthology (1975), Cardenal: Marilyn Monroe & Other Poems (ed and trans, 1975), Cardenal: Apocalypse & Other Poems (ed with Donald D Walsh, 1977), The Scope of Spanish-American Committed Poetry (1977), Studies in Honour of P E Russell (jt ed, 1981), Hacia Calderón (jt ed, 1982), Cantas - Canto - Cantemos (1983), Gracias a la vida: The Power and Poetry of Song (1990), Estudis sobre Ramon Llull (1991, awarded Premi Crítica Serra d'Or), A Poet for All Seasons (Neruda) (1993); *Recreations* travel, field-recording & photography in Latin America, glass engraving; *Style—* Dr Robert Pring-Mill, FBA; ✉ 11 North Hills, Brill, Bucks HP18 9TH (☎ 01844 237481); St Catherine's College, Oxford OX1 3UJ (fax 01865 271768)

PRINGLE, Alexandra Jane Reina; da of Alexander James Sommerville Pringle, and Natalie May, *née* Afriat; sis of John Richard Pringle, *qv*; *b* 13 March 1953; *Educ* Kensington HS, Putney HS, Cambridgeshire Coll of Arts & Technol (BA), Univ Coll London (post grad res); *m* 1984, Tim Hilton, s of Prof Rodney Hilton, *qv*; 1 s (Daniel b 30 April 1986); *Career* editorial asst Art Monthly 1976–78; editorial dir: Virago Press 1978–90 (dir 1984–), Hamish Hamilton 1990–94; dir Toby Eady Associates (literary agency) 1994–; *Recreations* reading, gardening, partying; *Clubs* Chelsea Arts Club, Groucho; *Style—* Ms Alexandra Pringle; ✉ Toby Eady Associates, 9 Orme Court, London W2 4RL (☎ 0171 792 0092)

PRINGLE, Air Marshal Sir Charles Norman Seton; KBE (1973, CBE 1967); s of Seton Pringle, OBE (d 1955), of Dublin, and Ethel Louisa, *née* McMunn (d 1938); *b* 6 June 1919; *Educ* Repton, St John's Coll Cambridge (MA); *m* 1946, Margaret Elisabeth, da of Bertie Sharp (d 1956), of Baildon, Yorks; 1 s (Andrew Charles Seton b 30 April 1949); *Career* RAF: joined 1941, dir gen of engrg MOD 1969–70, AO Engrg Strike Cmd 1970–73, dir gen of engrg 1973, controller of engrg and supply 1973–76, ret 1976; sr exec Rolls Royce Ltd 1976–78, dir Hunting Engrg 1976–78, dir and chief exec Soc of Br Aerospace Cos 1979–85; dir: FR Gp plc 1985–89, Aeronautical Tsts 1987–; Cncl memb: RAeS 1968–87 (pres 1975–76), Air League 1976–92, CBI 1978–84, RSA 1978–83 and 1986–92; sec Def Industs Cncl 1978–84, pres Inst of Mechanical & Gen Tech Engrs 1979–82; chm: CEI 1977–78 (treas 1980–83), Governing Body Repton Sch 1987–92 (memb 1985–92); Liveryman Worshipful Co of Coachmakers & Coach Harness Makers; CIMgt, FEng 1977, Hon FRAeS 1989; *Recreations* photography, ornithology; *Clubs* Buck's, RAF; *Style—* Air Marshal Sir Charles Pringle, KBE, FEng; ✉ Appleyards, Fordingbridge, Hampshire SP6 3BP; K 9 Sloane Avenue Mansions, London SW3 3JP

PRINGLE, Derek Raymond; s of Donald James Pringle (d 1975) of Nairobi, Kenya, and Doris May, *née* Newton; *b* 18 Sept 1958; *Educ* St Mary's Sch Nairobi Kenya, Felsted, Fitzwilliam Coll Cambridge (Cricket blue); *Career* professional cricketer; Essex CCC: joined 1978, awarded county cap 1982, benefit 1992; England: schs tour India 1978, full debut 1982 v India, 30 test matches 1982–, 40 one day ints, 2 Man of the Match awards v W Indies, memb tour NZ 1992, memb World Cup squad Aust 1992; cricket corr Independent; author of various articles for Daily Telegraph, The Times and The Cricketer; *Recreations* art, music, conchology, photography, travel; *Style—* Derek Pringle, Esq; ✉ c/o The Independent, 1 Canada Square, Canary Wharf, London E14 5AP (☎ 0171 293 2000, fax 0171 293 2435)

PRINGLE, Hamish Patrick; s of Robert Henry Pringle (d 1990), of Nassau, Bahamas, and Pamela Ann, *née* Molloy; *b* 17 July 1951; *Educ* Trinity Coll Glenalmond Perthshire, Trinity Coll Oxford (BA); *m* 24 July 1977, Vivienne Elizabeth, da of Dr H Michael Lloyd (d 1976), of Ripley, Surrey; 3 s (Sebastian b 1983, Benedict b 1985, Tristan b 1989), 1 da (Arabella Elizabeth Lloyd b 1993); *Career* grad trainee Ogilvy & Mather advtg 1973–74, account exec McCormick Richards 1974–75, account dir Boase Massimi Pollitt 1975–79, new business dir Publicis 1979–82, dir Abbott Mead Vickers/SMS 1982–86, md Madell Wilmot Pringle 1986–90, dir Leagas Delaney Partnership 1990–92; K Advertising (formerly KHBB): new business dir 1992–93, gp account dir 1993, jt md 1993–, chm and ceo 1994–; IPA: memb Cncl 1985–86 and 1992–, chm Advertising Effectiveness Awards Ctee 1994–; chm NABS Gen Mgmnt Ctee; MIPA 1985; *Recreations* sport, gardening, property development, art, family; *Style—* Hamish Pringle, Esq; ✉ K Advertising, 89 Whitfield Street, London W1A 4XA (☎ 0171 462 7777, fax 0171 462 7766)

PRINGLE, John Brown (Jack); s of John Pringle, of Nottingham, and Grace Mason, *née* Cowler; *b* 13 March 1952; *Educ* Nottingham HS for Boys, Univ of Bristol (BA, DipArch, professors' prize/travelling scholarship for arch); *m* 1992, Claire; 2 da (Maxine, Francesca); *Career* architect; Powell Moya and Partners 1973 and 1975–82; ptnr: Jack Pringle Architects 1982–85, Pringle Brandon Architects 1986–; RIBA: memb Cncl 1981–87, vice pres 1982–83, rep Br Cncl visit to Romania 1982, memb Educn Visiting Bd to Schs of Arch 1985–, memb visiting gp to China 1992 and 1993, chm Visiting Bd to Sri Lanka Sch of Architects 1995; memb CNAA Architecture Bd 1986–87; RIBA 1975, FRSA 1981; *Recreations* flying; *Style—* Jack Pringle, Esq; ✉ Pringle Brandon Architects, 10 Bonhill Street, London EC1 (☎ 0171 377 6782, fax 0171 247 5600)

PRINGLE, Hon Mr Justice; Hon Sir John Kenneth; kt (1993); s of Robert Henry Kenneth Pringle (d 1953), of Belfast, and Katie, *née* Batchen (d 1991); *b* 23 June 1929; *Educ* Campbell Coll Belfast, Queen's Univ Belfast (Open scholar, BSc, LLB); *m* 31 March 1960, Jennifer Ruth, da of Robert Ferguson Henry; 1 da (Susan Marjorie (Mrs Benjamin Robinson) b 21 Dec 1961), 2 s (Kenneth Henry b 24 April 1964, James Robert b 10 Sept 1965); *Career* called to the Bar NI 1953, QC 1970, bencher 1973, chm Bar Cncl NI Bar 1975–80, recorder of Belfast 1984–93, judge of the High Court of Justice NI 1993–; dep chm Boundary Cmmn 1993–; *Recreations* gardening and being outdoors; *Style—* The Hon Mr Justice Pringle; ✉ Royal Courts of Justice, Belfast, Northern Ireland BT1 3JF (☎ 01232 235111)

PRINGLE, John Richard; s of Alexander James Sommerville Pringle, of London, and Natalie May, *née* Afriat; bro of Alexandra Pringle, *qv*; gs of W M R Pringle, MP; *b* 30 May 1951; *Educ* Shrewsbury, Architectural Association (AADipl); *m* 1975, Penny, da of Denis George Richards, OBE; 1 s (Patrick b 1982), 1 da (Georgina b 1984); *Career* architect; Mario Pérez De Arce L Santiago de Chile 1972–73, Pascall & Watson London 1976–77, Scott Brownrigg & Turner Guildford 1977–78, ptnr Michael Hopkins & Partners 1981–96 (joined 1978), fndr ptnr Pringle Richards Sharratt 1996–; work incl: Schlumberger Res Centre Cambridge 1985, Mound, Compton and Edrich Stands Lord's Cricket Ground 1987, David Mellor Buildings Hathersage and London 1989–91, Bracken House City of London 1991, Glyndebourne Opera House 1994, New Parly Building and Underground Station Westminster 1995–; lectr: Europe 1987–, N America 1995; RIBA external examiner Univ of N London 1991–94; memb Bd Architectural Educn ARCUK 1986–93; Architectural Assoc: memb 1969, memb Cncl 1987–, hon treas 1991–93, pres 1993–95; RIBA 1983; *Recreations* travel, Italian, restoring pinball machines; *Style—* John Pringle, Esq; ✉ Pringle Richards Sharratt, Unit 12, 90 Lots Road, London SW10 0PQ (☎ 0171 352 8001)

PRINGLE, Margaret Douglas (Maggie); da of John Douglas Pringle, of Sydney, Australia, and Celia, *née* Carroll; *Educ* Convent of the Holy Child London, Convent of the Sacred Heart Sydney, Lady Margaret Hall Oxford (MA); *Career* journalist; former asst on: diary Evening Standard, Pendennis column Observer; former fiction ed: Nova, Woman; London ed Doubleday 1979–81, sr ed John Murray 1981–82, commissioning ed Michael Joseph 1983–, literary ed Today 1987–92, books conslt Sunday Express 1992–93, books ed Daily Mirror 1993–95, books ed The Sun 1995–96, books conslt Daily Telegraph and Punch 1996–; *Books* Dance Little Ladies (1977); *Recreations* reading, travel; *Style—* Ms Maggie Pringle; ✉ Michael Joseph, 27 Wrights Lane, London W8 5TZ (☎ 0171 416 3200)

PRINGLE, Simon Robert; s and h of Sir Steuart Robert Pringle, 10 Bt, *qv*; *b* 6 Jan 1959; *Educ* Worth Abbey, Trinity Coll Oxford (BA); *m* 1992, Pamela Margaret, da of George Hunter, of Belfast; 1 da (Siena Evangeline b 1994); *Career* oil and gas insur broker; *Clubs* Oxford & Cambridge; *Style—* Simon Pringle, Esq; ✉ 5 Hyde Vale, Greenwich, London SE10 8QQ

PRINGLE, Lt Gen Sir Steuart Robert; 10 Bt (NS 1683), KCB (1982); o s of Sir Norman Hamilton Pringle, 9 Bt (d 1961), and Winifred Olive, *née* Curran; *b* 21 July 1928; *Educ* Sherborne; *m* 5 Sept 1953, Jacqueline Marie, o da of late Wilfrid Hubert Gladwell; 2 s,

2 da; *Heir* s, Simon Robert Pringle b 6 Jan 1959; *Career* RM 1946, Lt 1949, Capt 1957, Maj 1964, Lt-Col 1971, Col 1975, Maj-Gen RM Commando Forces 1978–79, COS to Cmdt Gen RM 1979–81, Cmdt Gen RM 1981–84, Col Cmdt RM 1989–90, Rep Col Cmdt RM 1991–92; chm and chief exec Chatham Historic Dockyard Tst 1984–91; pres: St Loyes Coll Exeter 1984–, City of London Branch RM Assoc 1984–; vice pres Royal Naval Benevolent Tst 1984–, dir Medway Enterprise Agency 1986–89; memb Ct of Assts Worshipful Co of Plaisterers; Hon DSc City Univ 1982; Hon LLD Exeter Univ 1994; Man of the Year Awards 1982; CIMgt 1984; *Clubs* Royal Thames Yacht, MCC, Army and Navy; *Style*— Lt Gen Sir Steuart Pringle, Bt, KCB; ✉ 76 South Croxted Rd, Dulwich, London SE21 8BD

PRIOR, Venerable Christopher; CB (1968); s of Ven William Henry Prior (d 1969), and Mary Prior (d 1956); *b* 2 July 1912; *Educ* King's Coll Taunton, Keble Coll Oxford (MA), Cuddesdon Coll; *m* 1945, Althea Stafford, da of Lt-Col Cuthbert Harold Coode, RM; 2 da; *Career* clerk in Holy Orders; chaplain RN 1941–, chaplain of the Fleet and archdeacon for the RN 1966–69, archdeacon of Portsmouth 1969–77, emeritus 1977–; QHC 1966–69; *Style*— The Venerable Christopher Prior, CB; ✉ Ponies End, West Melbury, Shaftesbury, Dorset SP7 OLY (☎ 01747 811239)

PRIOR, Baron (Life Peer UK 1987), of Brampton, Co Suffolk; James Michael Leathes Prior; PC (1970); 2 s of Charles Bolingbroke Leathes Prior (d 1964), of Norwich; *b* 11 Oct 1927; *Educ* Charterhouse, Pembroke Coll Cambridge; *m* 30 Jan 1954, Jane Primrose Gifford, 2 da of Air Vice-Marshal Oswin Gifford Lywood, CB, CBE (d 1957); 3 s (Hon David, Hon Simon, Hon Jeremy), 1 da (Hon Mrs Roper); *Career* farmer and land agent in Norfolk and Suffolk; MP (C): Lowestoft (Suffolk) 1959–83, Waveney 1983–87; PPS to: Pres of BOT 1963, Min of Power 1963–64, Rt Hon Edward Heath (leader of the oppn) 1965–70; min of Agric Fisheries and Food 1970–72, a dep chm Cons Pty 1972–74 (vice chm 1965), lord pres of Cncl and ldr of House of Commons 1972–74, oppn front bench spokesman on employment 1974–79; sec of state: Employment 1979–81, NI 1981–84; chm: Indust and Parl Tst 1990–93, Rural Housing Tst, Great Ormond Street Hosp Special Tstees until 1994, Royal Vet Coll; memb: Tenneco Euro Advsy Cncl, American Int Gp Advsy Bd; chm The General Electric Co plc 1984–, non-exec dir United Biscuits (Holdings) plc until 1994, non-exec chm Allders Ltd until 1994, chm Arab-British C of C 1996–; *Books* A Balance of Power; *Recreations* cricket, gardening, philately, field sports, golf; *Style*— The Rt Hon Lord Prior, PC; ✉ House of Lords, London SW1

PRIOR, Baroness; Jane Primrose Gifford Prior; da of Air Vice-Marshal Oswin Gifford Lywood, CB, CBE (d 1957), and Hilda Jessie, *née* Foster; *b* 5 Oct 1930; *Educ* St Agnes Sch Alexandria Virginia USA, St Felix Southwold; *m* 30 Jan 1954, Baron Prior), *qv*; 3 s (David b 3 Dec 1954, Simon b 17 July 1956, Jeremy b 7 March 1962), 1 da (Sarah Jane b 5 Sept 1959); *Career* non-exec dir: Tate & Lyle plc 1985–, TSB Group plc 1985–95; JP 1977–89; memb Cncl Prince's Youth Business Tst 1987–, tstee Charities Aid Fndn 1990–95; govr: Atlantic Coll 1986– (chm govrs 1995–), Bradfield Coll 1989–; chm Govrs St Felix Sch Southwold 1982–90, chm Church Schs Co 1992–; vice-chm United World Colleges 1994–; *Style*— The Rt Hon Lady Prior; ✉ 36 Morpeth Mansions, Morpeth Terrace, London SW1

PRIOR, Michael John; JP (1983); s of Harold Prior (d 1989), and Nellie, *née* Cochrane; *b* 22 July 1945; *Educ* St Ambrose Coll; *m* 19 June 1976, Angela Elizabeth, wid of John Elland, da of Roger Stephen Popplewell; 4 c (Catherine Mary b 21 Aug 1966, Mathew Roger Percy b 5 April 1969, David Michael Harold b 13 July 1977, Elizabeth Margaret Helen b 25 Nov 1978); *Career* articled clerk Joseph W Shepherd & Co 1961–66, qualified CA 1966, ptnr Heywood Shepherd 1969–89, chm Manchester area Kidsons Impey 1990– (ptnr 1989–); dep chm of the Bench Trafford 1994–; pres: Manchester CAs Students Soc 1979–80, Manchester Soc of CAs 1988–89; memb Cncl ICAEW 1993–; FCA (ACA 1966); *Recreations* my family, golf, walking in the Lake District, watching Manchester Utd; *Clubs* St James's, Ringway Golf; *Style*— Michael Prior, Esq, JP; ✉ The Oaks, 4 Kings Acre, Bowdon, Altrincham, Cheshire WA14 3SE; Kidsons Impey, Devonshire House, 36 George St, Manchester M1 4HA (☎ 0161 236 7733, fax 0161 236 7020, car 0860 579883)

PRIOR, Peter James; CBE (1980), DL (1983); s of Percy Prior (d 1954), and Eleanora Prior (d 1976); *b* 1 Sept 1919; *Educ* Royal GS High Wycombe, Univ of London (BSc Econ); *m* 1957, Prinia Mary, da of Reginald Ernest Moreau (d 1970); 2 s; *Career* fin dir Br Aluminium Co 1961–64, chm H P Bulmer Holdings 1973–82, dep chm Holden Hydroman plc 1982–87, dir Trebor Ltd 1982–86; named Communicator of the Year by Br Assoc of Industrial Editors 1982; chm Govt Inquiries into: Potato Processing 1970, Motorway Servs 1980, Prison Discipline 1984; Croix de Guerre 1944; FCA, CIMgt, FIMC; *Books* Leadership is not a Bowler Hat; *Recreations* flying, motorcycling, music; *Clubs* Army & Navy, Special Forces; *Style*— Peter J Prior Esq, CBE, DL; ✉ Highland, Holbach Lane, Sutton St Nicholas, Hereford HR1 3DF (☎ 01568 797222)

PRIOR-WILLEARD, Christopher Howard; s of Peter Arnold Prior-Willeard, of Kent, and Anne Jocelyn, *née* Prior; *b* 7 March 1956; *Educ* Gresham's; *m* 18 Oct 1980, Penelope Jane, da of David John Steen, of Sevenoaks, Kent; 1 s (Mark b 1982), 2 da (Annabel b 1984, Emily Camilla b 1992); *Career* fndr London Meat Futures Exchange; head of depositary receipts HSBC Group; *Books* Farming Futures; *Recreations* shooting, country pursuits; *Clubs* Farmers'; *Style*— Christopher H Prior-Willeard, Esq; ✉ Crookfoot, Rye Lane, Otford, Kent TN14 5JF

PRITCHARD, (Arthur) Alan; CB (1979), JP (1981); s of Arthur Henry Standfast Pritchard; *b* 3 March 1922; *Educ* Wanstead HS Essex; *m* 1949, Betty Rona Nevard, *née* Little; 2 s, 1 da; *Career* BOT 1939, pilot RAFVR 1941–52, Admty 1952, asst under sec of State Naval Personnel and Op Requirements MOD 1972–76, seconded as dep sec NI office 1976–78, dep under sec of state (Navy) MOD 1978–81; mgmnt conslt 1984–88; chm Ringwood Bench 1991–92, pres Fordingbridge and District Community Assoc 1996– (chm 1990–95); *Style*— Alan Pritchard, Esq, CB, JP; ✉ Courtlands, Manor Farm Rd, Fordingbridge, Hants

PRITCHARD, Prof Colin; s of Sydney William Pritchard (d 1986), and Doris (d 1947); *b* 24 Feb 1936; *Educ* Univ of Manchester (Postgrad Cert), Univ of Bradford (MA), Univ of Southampton (PhD); *m* 15 Sept 1962, Beryl, da of Ivor William Harrison (d 1968); 2 da (Rebecca Anne Harrison b 26 Feb 1967, Claire Elizabeth b 23 Dec 1968); *Career* RAF 1954–56, serv in Cyprus and Suez 1956; lectr Dept of Psychiatry Univ of Leeds 1970–76, dir of social work Univ of Bath 1976–80, fndn prof of social work Univ of Southampton 1980–; memb: Central Cncl Educn and Training in Social Work 1974–81, Southampton Health Authy 1981–86; advsr (mental health) UN PREDEP Macedonia 1996; memb: Assoc of Child Psychiatry and Psychology 1965, Br Assoc of Social work 1970, American Assoc of Suicidology 1988, Int Assoc of Social Work (BR rep and bd memb 1988–); FRSA 1994; *Books* Social Work Reform or Revolution? (with R K S Taylor, 1978), The Protest Makers: The British Anti-Nuclear Movement Twenty Years On (with R K S Taylor, 1980), Social Work with Adolescents (with R Jones, 1980), Social Work with the Mentally Ill (with A J W Butler, 1986), Maintaining Staff Morale (1987), Suicide the Ultimate Rejection: A Psycho-Social Study (1995); contrib to comparisons of: Suicide and Violent Death in the Western World 1964–86, Suicide and Unemployment in UK and EEC, Elderly Suicide: Salutary or Disregarded Neglect 1964–90; *Recreations* family, friends, fell walking, squash, mourning Yorkshire and English Cricket; *Clubs* Hemsworth Miners Welfare, Fitzwilliam (hon life memb); *Style*— Prof Colin Pritchard; ✉ 33 Bassett Avenue, Bassett, Southampton SO1 7DP (☎ 01703 769169); Dept of Social Work Studies, University of Southampton, Southampton SO9 5NH (☎ 01703 594000, fax 01703 593939, telex 47661)

PRITCHARD, David Peter; s of Norman Pritchard, of Brampton, Cambs, and Peggy, *née* Fotherby; *b* 20 July 1944; *Educ* Read GS, Univ of Southampton (BSc); *m* 1 (m dis); 1 s (James b 1978), 1 da (Louisa b 1971); m 2, 5 May 1993, Elizabeth, *née* Cresswell; *Career* Hawker Siddeley Aviation 1966–71, William Brandt's Sons & Co 1971–72, Edward Bates & Sons Ltd 1972–78, md Citicorp Investment Bank Ltd 1978–86, sr vice pres and gen mangr Europe Royal Bank of Canada 1986–95, gp treas and md TSB Hill Samuel Markets 1995–96; FRSA; *Recreations* bicycle racing, cross country skiing, photography; *Style*— David Pritchard, Esq; ✉ 17 Thorney Crescent, London SW11 3TT (☎ 0171 585 2253)

PRITCHARD, Capt Eric; s of Robert Pritchard (d 1980), of Rhos-on-Sea, and Catherine, *née* Roberts (d 1962); *b* 24 Jan 1921; *Educ* George Dixon GS; *m* 20 March 1946, Bernice Catherine, da of William Frederick Stuart Henderson (d 1963), of Calgary, Alberta, Canada; 2 da ((Mary Catherine) Erica (Mrs Bryant) b 16 Aug 1947, (Elizabeth Anne) Sherran (Mrs Tye) b 25 May 1951); *Career* RAFVR serv wireless operator 1939, pilot 1941, pilot No 45 Gp Tport Cmd Montreal (ferrying aircraft across N and S Atlantic) 1942, cmmnd Flt-Lt RAFVR 1943, posted to No 46 Gp on close support air tport 1944 (despatches 1945), Tport Cmd Trg Gp detached to Central Flying Sch Little Rissington, completed serv as Flying Instr Tport Cmd 1945; 1 Offr BOAC 1946, transferred to Euro div (later BEA) 1946, appointed to Cmd BEA 1950; aircraft flown incl: Vickers Viking, Douglas Dakota, Vickers Viscount, A W Argosy, DH Comet IVB, HS Trident, Boeing 707; ret 1976; memb: BEA modification ctee and mgmnt/pilot tech liaison ctee, tech ctee Br Airline Pilots Assoc for 25 years (chm accident investigation study gp for 7 years), panel World Aerospace Med Conf Miami 1976; chm accident investigation study gp Int Fedn Airline Pilots Assoc for 7 years (sec tech sub-ctee D at 6 int confs, rep at Accident Investigation Panel Meeting Int Civil Aviation Orgn Montreal), chm Air Safety Gp 1976–92; visiting lectr on accident investigation and prevention Coll Aeronautics Cranfield, presented various papers at air safety and tech confs; awards: Certificate of Appreciation Flight Safety Fndn 1969, Master Air Pilot Certificate No 500, Guild Air Pilots and Air Navigators 1972, Scroll of merit IFALPA 1974, Silver Medal BALPA 1976; Freeman City of London 1976, Liveryman Guild of Air Pilots and Air Navigators 1976; *Recreations* walking, gardening; *Style*— Capt Eric Pritchard

PRITCHARD, (Iorwerth) Gwynn; s of Rev Robert Islwyn Pritchard (d 1988), and Megan Mair, *née* Lloyd; *b* 1 Feb 1946; *Educ* schs in Eng and Wales, King's Coll Cambridge (MA); *m* 17 Oct 1970, Marilyn Patricia (d 1994); 2 s (Matthew Osian b 1975, Dafydd Islwyn b 1989), 1 da (Nia Siân b 1977); *Career* prodr and dir BBC OU Productions 1970–77; prodr: BBC Wales 1977–82, HTV Wales 1982–85; commissioning ed Channel 4 TV 1985–88, sr commissioning ed educn Channel 4 TV 1989–92, head of progs BBC Wales 1992–; tstee: Welsh Writers Trust, Coleg Harlech; memb Bd Welsh Int Film Festival; pres Int Bd INPUT 1992–93; memb: RTS, BAFTA; Winston Churchill Meml Fellowship 1973, Sir Huw Weldon Broadcasting Fellowship 1990; Chevalier de L'Ordre des Arts et des Lettres (France) 1990; *Recreations* reading, swimming, walking; *Style*— Gwynn Pritchard, Esq; ✉ BBC Cymru/Wales, Broadcasting House, Llandaff, Cardiff CF5 2YQ (☎ 01222 572096, fax 01222 572532)

PRITCHARD, Ven John Lawrence; s of Neil Lawrence Pritchard, of Lyndhurst, Hants, and Winifred Mary Coverdale, *née* Savill (d 1991); *b* 22 April 1948; *Educ* Arnold Sch Blackpool, St Peter's Coll Oxford (MA), Ridley Hall Cambridge (DipTh, Cert in Pastoral Theol), St John's Coll Durham (MLitt Theol); *m* 1972, Susan Wendy, da of George Edward Claridge; 2 da (Amanda Kate b 27 May 1976, Nicola Clare b 3 Nov 1977); *Career* asst curate St Martin's in the Bull Ring Birmingham 1972–76, diocesan youth chaplain and asst dir of religious educn Bath and Wells Dio 1976–79, vicar Wilton Parish Taunton 1980–88, warden Cranmer Hall St John's Coll Durham 1993–96 (dir of pastoral studies 1989–93), archdeacon of Canterbury 1996–; memb Br and Irish Assoc of Practical Theol; *Books* Practical Theology in Action (1996); *Recreations* fell walking, photography, music, travel, reading, writing, cricket, badminton; *Style*— The Ven the Archdeacon of Canterbury; ✉ 29 The Precincts, Canterbury, Kent CT1 2EP (☎ 01227 463036, fax 01227 785209)

PRITCHARD, Rev John Ralph; *b* 15 April 1941; *Educ* Wade Deacon GS Widnes, Manchester GS, Univ of Bristol (BA), Univ of Cambridge (BA); *m* 3 July 1965, Patricia Ann (Pat); 1 da, 1 s; *Career* methodist min: Côte d'Ivoire 1966–75, Sheffield 1975–80, Portchester Hants 1980–86; general sec Methodist Church Overseas Division 1991–96 (Africa sec 1986–91), currently world devpt offr Methodist Church; *Books* Graines D'Evangile (ed, 1973), Travelling Along (jtly with John Simmonds, 1982); *Style*— Rev John R Pritchard; ✉ Methodist Church House, 25 Marylebone Road, London W1R 5JR (☎ 0171 486 5503, fax 0171 935 1507)

PRITCHARD, Dr Jon; *b* 7 March 1942; *Educ* Manchester GS, St John's Coll Cambridge (BA, capt Univ Lacrosse Team, played for England 1963–65), St Thomas' Hosp Med Sch (MB BChir), FRCP 1981 (MRCP 1971); *children* 2 c (Adam b 1970, Alex b 1972), 3 step c (Sian b 1977, Kate b 1980, Charlotte b 1982); *Career* house surgn St Thomas' Hosp London 1966–67, house physician Scarborough Hosp Yorks 1967, paediatric house physician St Thomas' Hosp 1967–68, paediatric SHO Univ of Rhodesia Med Sch Harare Hosp Salisbury 1968, SHO in gen med Harare Hosp Salisbury 1968–69, SHO in gen med and paediatrics Burton-on-Trent Gen Hosp Staffs 1969–70, registrar in paediatrics with haematology/oncology Alder Hey Hosp and in neonatology Mill Rd Maternity Hosp Liverpool 1970–71, res fell Dept of Haematology Univ of Liverpool and Liverpool Royal Infirmary 1971–74, hon sr registrar in paediatric haematology/oncology Alder Hey Hosp Liverpool 1973–74, res fell in haematology Children's Hosp Med Center and fell in med Harvard Univ Boston (MRC travelling fell) 1974–75, clinical fell in paediatric oncology Sidney Farber Cancer Center and Children's Hosp Med Center Boston 1975–76; Inst of Child Health London: lectr 1976–78, sr lectr (Leukaemia Res Fund 1978–83, sr lectr (Imperial Cancer Res Fund) 1983–95, hon conslt in paediatric oncology 1983–, clinical conslt Imperial Cancer Res Fund Lab of Molecular Genetics 1985–95; conslt in paediatric oncology: Hosp for Sick Children Gt Ormond St London 1978–, Bart's 1980–, SE/South Thames RHA 1985–; visiting prof: Postgrad Inst of Med Educn and Res Chandigarh India and All India Inst of Med Scis New Delhi 1993, Univ of Malaysia 1995; memb: UK Children's Cancer Study Gp and Children's Solid Tumour Gp/London Paediatric Haematology-Oncology Gp 1977–; RCP: memb Res Ctee 1980–87, memb Med Oncology Ctee 1980–86; fndr memb and tstee: Neuroblastoma Soc 1981–, Sick Children's Tst 1982–90, Histiocyte Soc 1985–, Nikolas Symposia 1989–; tstee: Emma Killingback Neuroblastoma Res Fund 1986–, RICC Fund 1990–, Histiocytosis Res Tst 1991–; dir Br Assoc of Children's Hosps 1992–; sub-ed Euro Jl of Cancer 1995–; memb Editorial Bd: Paediatric Haematology and Oncology 1987–92, Br Jl of Cancer 1988–, Euro Jl of Cancer 1990–95; examiner PhD degrees Univs of Cambridge, Louvain (Brussels), Leuven and Newcastle-upon-Tyne; co-chm Int Neuroblastoma Consortium 1992–; memb: Br Paediatric Assoc 1978, American Soc of Clinical Oncology 1981, Br Assoc of Paediatric Surgns 1984–92, Assoc of Cancer Physicians 1986, Int Soc of Paediatric Oncology 1986; hon fell American Acad of Paediatrics 1991; *Books* Practical Paediatric Oncology (jt ed, 1992), Proceedings of Nikolas Symposium on the Histiocytoses (Br Jl of Cancer, 1994), A Colour Atlas of Paediatric Haematology (jtly, 1983, 3 edn 1996); also author of numerous orginal articles, chapters and reviews; *Recreations* music (especially piano playing), photography, walking and tennis; *Style*— Dr Jon Pritchard; ✉ Department of

Haematology and Oncology, Great Ormond Street Hospital for Children NHS Trust, London WC1N 3JH (☎ 0171 829 8832, fax 0171 813 8588)

PRITCHARD, Kenneth William; OBE (1992), WS; s of Dr Edward Kenneth Pritchard (d 1976), of Uxbridge, and Isobel Mary, *née* Broom (d 1948); *b* 11 Nov 1933; *Educ* Dundee HS, Fettes, Univ of St Andrews (BL); *m* 18 Oct 1962, Gretta, da of late Robert Broadfoot Stitt Murray, of Lochranza, Isle of Arran; 2 s (Kenneth b 1963, Gavin b 1964), 1 da (Katharine b 1968); *Career* Nat Serv Argyll & Sutherland Highlanders 1955–57, Capt TA 1957–62; sr ptnr J & J Scrimgeour Dundee 1970–76 (joined 1957); memb: Sheriff's Court & Rules Cncl 1973–76, Lord Dunpark's Ctee on Reparation Reporting, Nat Tst for Scotland Jubilee Ctee 1980–82; pres Dundee HS Old Boys' Club 1975–76 (capt RFC 1959–62), sec Law Soc of Scot 1976–, Temp Sheriff Dundee 1978, govr Moray House Coll of Educn 1978–80; hon visiting prof of law Univ of Strathclyde 1986–94, memb Ct Univ of Dundee 1989–93; *Recreations* golf; *Clubs* New (Edinburgh), Hon Co of Edinburgh Golfers, Bruntsfield Links Golfing Soc; *Style*— Kenneth Pritchard, Esq, OBE, WS; ✉ 36 Ravelston Dykes, Edinburgh EH4 3EB (☎ 0131 332 8584); Law Society of Scotland, 26 Drumsheugh Gardens, Edinburgh EH3 7YR (☎ 0131 226 7411, fax 0131 225 2934)

PRITCHARD, Sir Neil; KCMG (1962, CMG 1952); s of late Joseph Pritchard; *b* 14 Jan 1911; *Educ* Liverpool Coll, Worcester Coll Oxford; *m* 1943, Mary Burroughes (d 1988); *Career* high cmmr Tanganyika 1961–63, dep under sec of state Cwlth Office 1963–67, ambass Bangkok 1967–70, ret; *Style*— Sir Neil Pritchard, KCMG; ✉ Little Garth, Daglingworth, Cirencester, Glos GL7 7AQ (☎ 01285 652353)

PRITCHARD, Prof Robert Hugh; s of Henry Ambrose Pritchard, OBE (d 1932), of London, and Fiorenza Rozina, *née* Napolitano (d 1981); *b* 25 Jan 1930; *Educ* Emmanuel Sch London, Kings Coll London (BSc), Univ of Glasgow (PhD); *m* 1 (m dis), Jacqueline, *née* Thompson; 2 s (John David b 1960 d 1966, Simon Niel b 1961); m 2, 3 Nov 1974, Susan Beth, da of Sidney Rosenberg (d 1983), of Chicago; 1 step da (Naomi Rose b 1966); *Career* lectr in genetics Univ of Glasgow 1956–59, Scientific Staff MRC 1959–64, prof of genetics Univ of Leicester 1964–84; city cncllr Leicester, co cncllr Leicestershire (ldr Lib Democrats); memb: Genetic Soc, Soc for Genetic Microbiology, American Soc for Microbiology; *Books* Basic Cloning Techniques (1985); *Recreations* politics, gardening; *Style*— Prof Robert Pritchard; ✉ 8 Knighton Grange Rd, Leicester LE2 2LE (☎ 0116 270 5210); Leicestershire County Council, County Hall, Glenfield, Leicester LE3 8RJ (☎ 0116 265 6190)

PRITCHARD-GORDON, Giles William; s of William Herbert Alexander Pritchard-Gordon (d 1987), and Lesley Pamela Joy, *née* Blackburn (d 1996); *b* 22 May 1947; *Educ* Radley; *m* 19 Nov 1971, Veronica, da of Ronald Victor Smyth, of Clear Height, Downs Rd, Epsom, Surrey; 4 da (Alice Clare b 1974, Emily Kate b 1979, Lucy Clementine b 1983, Eliza Mary 1986); *Career* dir H Clarkson & Co Ltd 1972–73, fndr Giles W Pritchard-Gordon & Co Ltd 1973 (dir Giles W Pritchard-Gordon subsids Shipbroking 1981, Farming 1981, Shipowning 1981, Property 1984, Futures 1985, Tankers 1996); memb Lloyd's; Freeman City of London, Liveryman Worshipful Co of Fishmongers 1983; *Recreations* horse racing and breeding, stalking, golf; *Clubs* Royal & Ancient, MCC, Seaview Yacht; *Style*— Giles Pritchard-Gordon, Esq; ✉ Slaugham Park, Slaugham, Sussex (☎ 01444 400388)

PRITCHETT, Matthew (Matt); s of Oliver Pritchett, feature writer, and Joan, *née* Hill, of Eastling, Kent; gs of Sir V S Pritchett, *qv*; *b* 14 July 1964; *Educ* Addey & Stanhope GS, St Martin's Sch of Art (graphics degree); *m* 12 Dec 1992, Pascale Charlotte Marie Smets, *qv*; 2 da (Edith b 13 April 1994, Mary b 29 Jan 1996); *Career* freelance cartoonist for New Statesman, Punch, Daily Telegraph and Spectator, front page cartoonist Daily Telegraph 1989–; Cartoonist of the Year What the Papers Say (Granada TV) 1992, Cartoon Arts Tst Award 1995, Cartoonist of the Year UK Press Awards 1996; *Books* Best of Matt 1991 (1991), Best of Matt 1992 (1992), Best of Matt 1993 (1993), Best of Matt 1994 (1994), Best of Matt 1995 (1995), Best of Matt 1996 (1996); *Style*— Matt Pritchett, Esq; ✉ The Daily Telegraph, 1 Canada Square, Canary Wharf, London E14 5DT

PRITCHETT, Sir Victor Sawdon; CH (1993), kt (1975), CBE (1968); s of Sawdon Pritchett; *b* 16 Dec 1900; *Educ* Alleyn's; *m* 1936, Dorothy, da of Richard Samuel Roberts; 1 da, 1 s (Oliver Pritchett, the journalist); gf of Matt Pritchett, *qv*; *Career* author and literary critic; Christian Gauss lectr Princton Univ 1953, Beckman prof Univ of California Berkeley 1962, writer-in-residence Smith Coll Mass 1966; visiting prof: Univ of Brandeis Mass, Univ of Columbia, Vanderbilt Univ Nashville Tennessee (Clark lectr 1969); foreign memb: American Acad and Inst 1971, American Acad Arts and Sci 1971; pres: Int PEN 1974–76, Soc of Authors 1977–; CLit 1987; Hon DLitt Univ of Leeds, Hon DLitt Univ of Columbia and Sussex, Hon DLitt Harvard Univ 1985; winner ST Dupont Golden Pen Award for Long Service to Literature PEN 1993; *Books* Marching Spain (1928), Clare Drummer (1929), The Spanish Virgin (1930), Shirley Sanz (1932), Nothing Like Leather (1935), Dead Man Leading (1937), You Make Your Own Life (1938), In My Good Books (1942), It May Never Happen (1946), The Living Novel (1946), Why Do I Write? (1948), Mr Beluncle (1951), Books In General (1953), The Spanish Temper (1954), Collected Stories (1956), When My Girl Comes Home (1961), London Perceived (1962), The Key To My Heart (1963), Foreign Faces (1964), New York Proclaimed (1965), The Working Novellist (1965), Dublin - A Portrait (1967), A Cab at the Door (autobiography, 1968), Blind Love (1969), George Meredith and English Comedy (1970), Midnight Oil (autobiography, 1971), Balzac (1973), The Camberwell Beauty (1974), The Gentle Barbarian (1977), Selected Stories (1978), The Myth Makers (1979), On the Edge of the Cliff (1980), The Tale Bearers (1980), The Oxford Book of Short Stories (ed, 1981), The Turn of the Years (1982), Collected Stories (1982), More Collected Stories (1983), The Other Side of a Frontier (1984), Man of Letters (1985), Chekhov (1988), A Careless Widow and Other Stories (1989), At Home and Abroad (1990), The Complete Short Stories (1990), Lasting Impressions (1990), The Complete Essays (1991); *Clubs* Savile, Beefsteak; *Style*— Sir Victor Pritchett, CH, CBE; ✉ 12 Regent's Park Terrace, London NW1 7ED

PRITTY, Dr Paul Edmund; s of Charles Pritty, and Kathleen, *née* Ellenthorpe; *b* 29 Nov 1945; *Educ* Spalding GS, St George's Med Sch, Selwyn Coll Cambridge (MB BChir, MA); *m* 1 Dec 1973, Carole, da of William Thomas; 2 da (Emma Louise b 5 Nov 1976, Amy Clare b 27 Feb 1979); *Career* conslt in accident and emergency med Derbyshire Royal Infirmary 1980–, jt site med offr Kegworth M1 air crash 1989; conslt in charge Flying Squad Emergency Med Team; Derbyshire Red Cross: MO Derby City Centre, asst branch MO; FRCS 1978, memb Casualty Surgns Assoc 1980; *Recreations* DIY, butterfly breeder; *Style*— Dr Paul Pritty; ✉ Accident and Emergency Department, Derbyshire Royal Infirmary, London Rd, Derby DE1 2QY (☎ 01332 347141)

PROBERT, David Henry; CBE (1996); s of William David Thomas Probert, of Birmingham, and Doris Mabel, *née* Mayell (d 1987); *b* 11 April 1938; *Educ* Bromsgrove HS; *m* 14 June 1968, Sandra Mary, da of John Howard Prince (d 1988); 1 s (Russell b 1979), 1 da (Jane b 1974); *Career* various posts: ICI Metals Div 1960–66, Coopers & Lybrand 1966–71; gp fin dir: BSA Ltd 1971–73, Mills & Allen International Ltd 1974–75; W Canning plc: gp fin dir 1976–, chief exec 1979–85, chm and chief exec 1986–; non-exec dir: Linread plc 1983–90, ASD plc 1984–90, Sandvik Ltd 1986–90, Beatson Clark plc 1987–88, Rockwool Ltd 1988–90 and 1992–95; chm: PPP Healthcare Group plc 1996– (dir 1988–), Leigh Interests plc 1996– (dir 1995–); chm Crown Agents 1990– (crown agent 1981–, dep chm 1985–90); memb: W Midlands Regnl Cncl CBI 1978–84 and 1988–90, Br Hallmarking Cncl 1983–90, Cncl Birmingham C-of-C 1990– (vice pres 1991–94, pres 1994–95); chm W Midlands Lord's Taverners 1996– (memb Ctee 1985–); Freeman: City of London, Worshipful Co of Secs and Administrators (memb Ct of Assts); CIMgt, FCMA, FCCA, FCIS; *Recreations* reading, music, theatre; *Clubs* RAC; *Style*— David Probert, Esq, CBE; ✉ W Canning plc, 133 Great Hampton Street, Birmingham B18 6AS (☎ 0121 236 8621, fax 0121 236 3320)

PROBERT, Peter W; *b* 16 Sept 1932; *Educ* Tweedale Sch Carshalton, King's Coll Birmingham, Wimbledon Tech Coll, Henley Business Centre, CAM Educn Fndn (DipCAM); *m*; 1 s; *Career* Nat Serv 1950–52; writer on industl and trade jls Swift Press and Publications 1952–55, account exec Jack Fallon Public Relations 1955–57, asst to MD Print Processes Ltd 1957–61, press offr Central Office of Information 1960–63, sr exec offr MPBW 1963–70, princ information offr DOE 1970–72, asst controller Central Office of Information 1972–78, seconded as head of mktg and information Manpower Services Cmmn 1979, head of press and PR BOTB 1979–86, account dir John Stewart Public Relations and freelance advsr to Operation Raleigh 1986–90, dir Invicta Communications and independent PR conslt 1990–; pt/t lectr in PR Coll for Distributive Trade, chief examiner CAM 1981–83; IPR: memb Cncl 1981–84 and 1986–89, memb Int Ctee 1980– (chm 1984); memb Riverhead (Sevenoaks) Parish Cncl 1988–92; FIPR 1987 (MIPR 1970); *Recreations* amateur dramatics (memb Westerham Amateur Dramatics Soc), music, theatre, reading and writing, playing golf, watching cricket and football; *Style*— Peter Probert, Esq; ✉ Invicta Communications, 15 Bessels Way, Bessels Green, Sevenoaks, Kent TN13 2QG (☎ 01732 457306)

PROBERT, Lt-Col Richard Harlackenden Carwardine; OBE (1959), DL (Suffolk 1983); s of Col (Geoffrey) Oliver Carwardine Probert, CBE (d 1987), of Great Bevills, Suffolk, and Ruby Margaret Alexandra, *née* Marc (d 1992), with collateral family links with Bures and Earls Colne dating back to 14 century (*see* Burke's Landed Gentry 18 edn, Vol I, 1965); *b* 19 April 1922; *Educ* Eton, RMCS; *m* 25 April 1945, Elisabeth Margaret, da of Donald Boase Sinclair, OBE, WS, (d 1972), of Edinburgh; 1 s (Geoffrey b 1953), 2 da (Camilla (m Tim Melville-Ross, *qv*) b 1946, Anne (Mrs Edward Tozer) b 1948); *Career* served WWII RHA 1940–45, Normandy and NW Europe 1944–45, instr in gunnery 1945–46, Royal Armament Res and Design Estab 1948–51 (Tripartite Conf Washington 1951), 3 RHA BAOR 1951–54, staff Dir-Gen of Artillery 1954–56, Br Nuclear Def Trials Australia 1957; Dir Staff Lt-Col RMCS 1956–59; md Bexford Ltd (a subsid of ICI 1968) 1962–76 (Queen's award to Industry 1966, 1969, 1971 and 1973); farmer; Freeman City of London 1956, Liveryman Worshipful Co of Ironmongers (Master 1977–78); High Sheriff of Suffolk 1980–81; hon lay canon St Edmundsbury Cathedral 1984–91; memb: Ct Essex Univ 1966–, Suffolk Ctee TAVR & ACF 1980–, Suffolk Ctee CLA 1981–94 (pres 1991–94); FRSA 1964; *Recreations* countryside, conservation, walking, travel; *Clubs* Army and Navy; *Style*— Lt-Col Richard Probert, OBE, DL; ✉ Chapel Barn Cottage, Bevills Farm, Bures, Suffolk CO8 5LD

PROBY, Sir Peter; 2 Bt (UK 1952), of Pottle Green, Elton, Cambs; s of Sir Richard George Proby, 1 Bt, MC (d 1979), and Betty Monica (d 1967), er da of Alexander Henry Hallam Murray, of Sandling, Hythe, Kent; *b* 4 Dec 1911; *Educ* Eton, Trinity Coll Oxford (BA); *m* 15 Jan 1944, Blanche Harrison, da of Col Henry Harrison Cripps, DSO (d 1960), of Bath Lodge, Ballycastle, Co Antrim; 1 s (and 1 s decd), 3 da (Sarah (Mrs Mills) b 1945, Charlotte (Mrs Hay) b 1957, Christine (Mrs Dobbs) b 1957); *Heir* s, William Henry Proby, *qv*; *Career* serv 1939–45, Capt Irish Gds; bursar of Eton Coll 1953–71; land agent; Lord-Lt Cambs 1981–85 (DL 1980); KStJ 1983; Liveryman Worshipful Co of Grocers; FRICS; *Clubs* Travellers'; *Style*— Sir Peter Proby, Bt; ✉ No 2 St Botolph's Green, Elton, Peterborough PE8 6SG (☎ 01832 280434)

PROBY, William Henry; DL (Cambs 1995); s and h of Sir Peter Proby, 2 Bt; *b* 13 June 1949; *Educ* Eton, Lincoln Coll Oxford (MA), Brooksby Coll of Agric; *m* 1974, Meredyth Anne, da of Timothy David Brentnall, of Preston, Rutland; 4 da (Alexandra b 1980, Alice b 1982, Frances Rose b 1986, Isabella b 1991); *Career* farmer; asst dir Morgan Grenfell 1980–82, md M W P Ltd 1980–82; dir: M M & K Ltd 1986, Ellis & Everard plc 1988, Booker Countryside Ltd 1994; pres Historic Houses Assoc 1993; Liveryman Worshipful Co of Grocers; FCA 1975; *Recreations* skiing, shooting, music; *Clubs* Brooks', Boodle's; *Style*— William Proby, Esq, DL; ✉ Elton Hall, nr Peterborough PE8 6SH (☎ 01832 280310, fax 01832 280584); Flat 3, 4 Lyall Street, London SW1 (☎ 0171 235 7801)

PROBYN, Jeffrey Alan (Jeff); s of Charles Probyn, of Udimore, Sussex, and Patricia Rachel Thomas; *b* 27 April 1956; *Educ* London Nautical GS; *m* 27 December 1975, Jennifer Christine, da of late Victor Gordon Thomas; 3 c (Jeffrey-Paul b 8 July 1976, Steven James Victor Charles b 3 September 1977, Rebecca Faye Jennifer b 14 May 1980); *Career* rugby union prop forward; Surrey Sch U15 and U18, London Cos U15 and U18, U15 Eng triallist; clubs: Old Albanians 1971–77, Streatham & Croydon 1977–80, Richmond 1980–84, Wasps 1984– (over 120 appearances); county: Hertfordshire 1976, Surrey Club 1979, Middlesex 1982, Surrey 1984–85; London Division: v Aust as replacement, appeared in every game in Divnl Championship 1985–; England: reserve World Cup 1987, debut v France Parc des Princes 1988, toured Australia 1988, first try v Queensland 1988, first test try v Romania 1989, first Five Nations try v Ireland Twickenham 1990, memb Grand Slam winning team 1991 and 1992, memb runners-up team World Cup 1991, 38 caps; toured S Africa with World XV 1989, memb British Lions v France bicentennial 1989; memb: RFU Ctee, English Sports Cncl; litigation clerk Durrant Piesse Solicitors 1975–77, dir Probros Ltd 1977–, occasional TV rugby pundit; *Recreations* sailing, shooting, scuba diving; *Style*— Jeff Probyn, Esq; ✉ Probros Ltd, 2–4 Chance St, Bethnal Green, London E1 6JT (☎ 0171 739 3887, fax 0171 729 4403)

PROCHASKA, Dr Alice Marjorie Sheila; da of John Harold Barwell (d 1983), of Cambridge, and The Hon Sheila Margaret Ramsay, *née* McNair; *b* 12 July 1947; *Educ* Perse Sch for Girls Cambridge, Somerville Coll Oxford (BA, MA, DPhil); *m* 25 June 1971, Franklyn Kimmel Prochaska, s of Franklin Anton Prochaska (d 1952), of Cleveland, Ohio, USA; 1 s (William b 1982), 1 da (Elizabeth b 1980); *Career* asst keeper: London Museum 1971–73, Public Record Office 1975–84; sec and librarian Inst of Historical Res Univ of London 1984–92, dir of special collections British Library 1992–; author of numerous articles on archives and various aspects of Br history ca 1800 to present; organiser of special expos incl: London in the Thirties 1973, Young Writers of the Thirties 1976; memb: Nat Cncl on Archives (chm 1991–95), Steering Gp History at the Univs Def Gp 1987–92, Nat Curriculum History Working Gp Dept of Educn and Sci 1989–90, Heritage Educn Tst, Bd of Govrs London Guildhall Univ 1995–, Sir Winston Churchill Archive Tst 1995–; FRHistS 1987 (memb Cncl 1991–95, vice-pres 1995–); *Books* London in the Thirties (1973), History of the General Federation of Trade Unions, 1899–1980 (1982), Irish History from 1700 - A Guide to Sources in the Public Record Office (1986), Margaretta Acworth's Georgian Cookery Book (ed with Frank Prochaska, 1987); *Recreations* family life, cookery, travel, reading; *Style*— Dr Alice Prochaska; ✉ The British Library, Great Russell St, London WC1B 3DG (☎ 0171 412 7501, fax 0171 412 7745)

PROCTER, Herbert Gerald; s of Herbert George Procter (d 1974), of N Ferriby, Humberside, and Phyllis, *née* Charlesworth (d 1985); *b* 28 May 1931; *Educ* Hull GS; *m* 14 April 1956, Pauline, da of Frederick Charles McKeigh Heath (d 1964); 2 s (Andrew b 1958, Nicholas b 1964), 1 da (Deborah b 1960); *Career* Capt (TA) 1959–61, Flying Offr RAF 1955–57; slr; sr ptnr Stamp Jackson & Procter 1968–, coroner for Holderness 1965–74; dep chm Humberside CC 1980–81 (chm Planning and Tport Ctee 1977–81); pres: Hull Jr C of C & Shipping 1966–67, Hull Incorporated Law Soc 1978–79, Kingston upon Hull Cons Fedn 1980–89, Bridlington Cons Assoc 1991–95, Hull C of C 1995–96;

dir W A Holdings plc 1973–87; dir Hull C of C and Shipping 1991–, chm Assoc of Yorks & Humberside C of C 1996–; *Recreations* flying, music, languages; *Clubs* Carlton, Royal Air Force; *Style—* H Gerald Procter, Esq; ✉ The Paddock, Souttergate, Hedon, Hull HU12 8JS (☎ 01482 897640); 5 Parliament St, Hull HU1 2AZ (☎ 01482 24591, telex 597001, fax 01482 224048)

PROCTER, Jane Hilary Elizabeth (Mrs Goldstaub); da of Gordon Heslop Procter, and Florence Henrietta, *née* Bibby; *Educ* Queen's Coll Harley St; *m* 4 June 1985, Thomas Charles Goldstaub, *qv*, s of Werner Fritz Goldstaub; 1 s (Rollo Alexander b 1989), 1 da (Tabitha Sophie b 1985); *Career* fashion asst Vogue 1974–75, asst fashion ed Good Housekeeping 1975–77, actg fashion ed Woman's Journal 1977–78, fashion writer Country Life 1978–80; freelance fashion ed: Times, Sunday Times, Daily Express 1980–87; ed British W 1987–88, ed Tatler 1990–; *Books* Dress Your Best (1983), Celebrity Knitting (1984), What do you call a kid? (1985); *Style—* Miss Jane Procter; ✉ Tatler, Vogue House, 1 Hanover Square, London W1 (☎ 0171 499 9080); 34 The Chase, London SW4 0NH

PROCTER, (Mary) Norma; da of John Procter (d 1977), of Grimsby, and Edith Clarice, *née* Hockney; *b* 15 Feb 1928; *Educ* Wintringham Secdy Sch; *Career* int concert singer (contralto); vocal studies with Roy Henderson, musicianship with Alec Redshaw, lieder with Hans Oppenheim and Paul Hamburger, London debut at Southwark Cathedral 1948, specialist in concert works oratorio and recitals, appeared with all the major orchestras and in all the major festivals in UK; operatic debut Lucretia in Britten's Rape of Lucretia Aldeburgh Festival 1957–58, Covent Garden debut in Gluck's Orpheus 1960; performed in: Germany, France, Spain, Portugal, Norway, Holland, Belgium, Sweden, Denmark, Finland, Austria, Israel, Luxembourg, S America; recordings incl: Messiah, Elijah, Samson, Mahler's 2, 3 and 8 Symphonies, Das Klagende Lied, Hartmann 1 Symphony, Juluis Caesar Jones, Nicholas Maw's Scenes and Arias, Hermann Suter Le Laudi, BBC Last Night of the Proms; pres Grimsby Philharmonic Soc; Hon RAM; *Recreations* sketching, painting, tapestry, TV; *Style—* Miss Norma Procter; ✉ 194 Clee Rd, Grimsby, S Humberside DN32 8NG (☎ 01472 691210)

PROCTER, Sidney; CBE (1986); s of Robert Procter; *b* 10 March 1925; *Educ* Ormskirk GS; *m* 1952, Isabel, *née* Simmons; 1 da; *Career* RAF 1943–47; dir: Williams & Glyn's Bank 1976–85 (chief exec 1978–82), Royal Bank of Scotland 1979–85; Royal Bank of Scotland Group: dir 1978–86, dep gp md 1979–82, gp chief exec 1982–85, vice chm 1986–87; advsr to Govr Bank of England 1985–87; chm Exeter Trust Ltd 1985–, dir Provincial Group 1985–96 (dep chm 1991–95), chm Provincial Holdings Ltd 1995–96; cmmr Bldg Socs Cmmn 1986–93; FIB; *Style—* Sidney Procter, Esq, CBE; ✉ The Piece House, Bourton-on-the-Water, Glos

PROCTOR, His Hon Judge Anthony James; s of James Proctor (d 1967), of Harrogate, Yorks, and Savina Maud, *née* Horsfield (d 1981); *b* 18 Sept 1931; *Educ* Mexborough GS Yorkshire, St Catharine's Coll Cambridge (BA, LLB, MA, LLM); *m* 12 Sept 1964, Patricia Mary, da of George William Bryan, of Sheffield (d 1981); 1 da (Susan Jane b 1966); *Career* Nat Serv Flying Offr RAF 1953–55; articled clerk to Sir Bernard Kenyon, clerk W Riding CC 1955–58, admitted slr 1958, asst slr Barnsley Corporation 1958–60, sr prosecuting and Common Law slr Sheffield Corporation 1960–64, ptnr Neals and Shelley Barkers Slrs 1964–74, dist registrar and registrar of Co Ct 1974–88, recorder Crown Ct 1985–88, circuit judge (Northern Circuit) 1988–; memb Law Soc 1958–, pres Soc of Dist and Co Registrars 1985; *Recreations* fell walking, photography, genealogy; *Style—* His Hon Judge Anthony Proctor; ✉ The Law Courts, Ringway, Preston, Lancs PR1 2LL

PROCTOR-BEAUCHAMP, Sir Christopher Radstock; 9 Bt (GB 1745), of Langley Park, Norfolk; s of Rev Sir Ivor Cuthbert Proctor-Beauchamp, 8 Bt (d 1971); *b* 30 Jan 1935; *Educ* Rugby, Trinity Coll Cambridge (MA); *m* 1965, Rosalind Emily Margot, da of Gerald Percival Wainwright, of St Leonards-on-Sea; 2 s (Charles Barclay b 1969, Robert Ivor b 1971), 1 da (Rosalind Caroline b 1967); *Heir* s, Charles Barclay Proctor-Beauchamp b 7 July 1969; *Career* slr with Gilbert H Stephens & Sons Exeter; *Style—* Sir Christopher Proctor-Beauchamp, Bt; ✉ The Coach House, Balfour Mews, Sidmouth EX10 8XL

PRODGER, John Alan; ERD (1964), JP (Bucks 1982); s of Alan St George Cuthbert Prodger (d 1983), and Rona Ethel Prodger; *b* 19 Jan 1932; *Educ* Merchant Taylors', Worcester Coll Oxford (MA, Rugby blue); *m* 1971, Tessa Mary Colthurst, da of Capt Gerald Oulton Colthurst Davies, RN (d 1989); 1 s, 1 da; *Career* served 9 Queen's Royal Lancers (now 9/12 Royal Lancers); Tate and Lyle Ltd 1957–73, dir Personnel Bd Carreras Rothmans Ltd 1973–84, dir of personnel Rothmans International plc 1984–88, mgmnt conslt 1988–; chm: Tobacco Indust Employers' Assoc 1979–84, Cncl Southern Region CBI 1979–88; gen cmmr for income tax 1989–, chm Oxford Diocesan Bd of Fin 1990–96, govr Aylesbury GS 1990–, memb Cncl Open Univ and tstee Open Univ Fndn 1990–, memb Cncl and Fin and Gen Purposes Ctee Univ of Buckingham 1991–; tstee Maj Stanley's Tst OURFC 1990–, vice pres OURFC 1996–, dir and tstee Freemantle Tst 1991–96; FIPD, FInstD, FRSA; *Recreations* fishing, cricket, gardening, watching rugby; *Clubs* Cavalry and Guards', MCC, Vincent's; *Style—* John Prodger, Esq, ERD, JP; ✉ Granborough Lodge, Granborough, Buckingham MK18 3NJ (☎ 01296 670349)

PROES, Capt Richard Geoffrey; s of Maj Geoffrey Ernest Sullivan Proes (ka 1941), and Nancy Madeleine, *née* Churcher (d 1983); *b* 18 Aug 1937; *Educ* Wellington, RMA Sandhurst; *m* 28 May 1970, Victoria Margaret, da of Maj Arthur Michael Temple Trubshawe (d 1985); *Career* Capt Grenadier Gds 1957–68; salmon farmer; dir: Kyles of Bute Salmon Ltd 1981–, Scottish Salmon Growers Assoc 1983–, Scottish Salmon Bd 1990–; *Recreations* shooting, fishing; *Style—* Capt Richard Proes; ✉ West Glen Caladh, Tighnabruaich, Argyll PA21 2EH (☎ 01700 811224)

PROFUMO, John Dennis; CBE (1975, OBE (Mil) 1944); 5 Baron of Italy; s of Baron Albert Peter Anthony Profumo, KC (d 1940), and Martha Thom, *née* Walker; bro of Mary Baroness Balfour of Inchrye; *b* 30 Jan 1915; *Educ* Harrow, BNC Oxford (MA); *m* 1954, Valerie Louise Hobson, *qv*, da of late Capt Robert Gordon Hobson, RN, and former w of Anthony James Allan Havelock-Allan (now 4 Bt); 1 s; *Career* MP (Cons): Kettering Div Northants 1940–45, Stratford-on-Avon Div Warwicks 1950–63; jt Parly sec Miny of Tport and Civil Aviation 1952–57, Parly under of sec state Colonies 1957–58, Parly under of sec state Foreign Affrs 1958–59, min of state Foreign Affrs 1959–60, sec of state for War 1960–63; dep chm Provident Life Assoc of London 1978–82 (dir 1975–), pres Toynbee Hall 1985– (chm 1982–84); *Clubs* Boodle's; *Style—* John Profumo, Esq, CBE

PROOPS, Greg; *Career* comedian, improvisor, actor; Edinburgh Festival 1993–96, nat tour 1994, 1995 and 1996; *Television* Whose Line Is It Anyway? (Hat Trick/Channel 4) 1989–, Clive Anderson Talks Back (Hat Trick/Channel 4) 1992, Viva Cabaret (TV 21/Channel 4) 1993, Martin Mayhew in Anna Lee 1993, Edinburgh Nights (BBC) 1993–95, presenter The Unforgetable Memory Show (BBC) 1994, presenter Potted Histories (BBC) 1994, Gag Tag (BBC) 1994, That's Showbusiness (BBC) 1994 and 1996, Comedy Rules (STV) 1994, The Clothes Show (BBC) 1994, writer/presenter Astounding Science Theatre (BBC) 1994, Special on the London Comedy Festival (Carlton) 1994, Jack Dee Variety Show (TV21/ITV) 1995, Good Stuff (Carlton) 1996, Have I Got News for You (Hat Trick/BBC 2) 1996; *Radio* The Usual Suspects (BBC) 1993, Comedy DJ (BBC Radio 1) 1994, guest and stand-in presenter The Mark Radcliffe Show (BBC Radio 1) 1994 and 1995, Seymour the Fractal Cat (2 series, BBC) 1994 and 1996, Worldy Wise (2 series, BBC) 1994 and 1995, Five Live Command (BBC) 1994, co-presenter The Big Red Mug Show (Virgin Radio) 1994, presenter Bits From Last Week's Radio (BBC Radio 1) 1995 and 1996, Darling You Were Marvellous (BBC) 1995, Conversations in a Rock Pool (BBC) 1996, Wizard of Oz (BBC Radio 4) 1996; *Film* various voices in Tim Burton's Nightmare Before Christmas 1993; *Awards* nominated Edinburgh Festival Perrier Award 1993; *Recreations* spawning, sunning, pressing flowers, shining, kickin' it; *Clubs* 9 Iron, 3 Wood, Niblick; *Style—* Greg Proops, Esq; ✉ c/o Francesca Pashby, The Richard Stone Partnership, 25 Whitehall, London SW1A 2BS (☎ 0171 839 6421, fax 0171 839 5002)

PROSSER, David John; s of Ronald Thomas Prosser, of Penarth, S Wales, and Dorothy, *née* Denham; *b* 26 March 1944; *Educ* Ogmore GS, Univ Coll Wales at Aberystwyth; *m* Nov 1971, Rosemary Margaret, da of Alan Snuggs; 2 da (Charlotte Jane b Aug 1976, Claire Elizabeth b July 1979); *Career* Sun Alliance Group 1965–69, Hoare Govett 1969–73, CIN Management 1973–88; Legal & General Group plc: investment dir 1988–91, chief exec 1991–; chm Life Insurance Cncl, dep chm ABI; FIA 1971; *Recreations* golf, family activities; *Clubs* RAC; *Style—* David Prosser; ✉ Legal & General Group plc, Temple Court, 11 Queen Victoria Street, London EC4N 4TP (☎ 0171 528 6000, fax 0171 528 6224)

PROSSER, Sir Ian Maurice Gray; kt (1995); s of Maurice Clifford Prosser (d 1992), and Freda Prosser; *b* 5 July 1943; *Educ* King Edward's Sch Bath, Watford GS, Univ of Birmingham (BComm); *m* 1964, Elizabeth Herman; 2 da (Sarah, Joanna); *Career* Coopers and Lybrand (accountants) 1964–69, joined Bass Charrington Ltd (now Bass plc) 1969: memb Bd 1978, vice chm 1982–87, gp md 1984–87, chm and chief exec 1987–; dir: Brewers' Soc 1983–, Lloyds TSB Group plc 1988–; Liveryman Worshipful Co of Brewers; FCA; *Recreations* bridge, golf, gardening; *Clubs* RAC; *Style—* Sir Ian Prosser; ✉ Bass PLC, 20 North Audley Street, London W1Y 1WE (☎ 0171 409 1919)

PROSSER, Prof James Anthony William (Tony); s of James Allan Prosser (d 1968), and Flora Gertrude, *née* Evans; *b* 3 May 1954; *Educ* Ludlow GS, Univ of Liverpool (LLB); *Career* res asst in law Univ of Southampton 1974–76; lectr in law: Univ of Hull 1976–79, Univ of Sheffield 1980–89; sr lectr in law Univ of Sheffield 1989–92, John Millar prof of law Univ of Glasgow 1992–; visiting prof: European Univ Inst 1990 (Jean Monnet fell 1987–88), Univ of Rome 1992; memb: Soc of Public Teachers of Law 1976, Socio-Legal Studies Assoc 1990; *Books* Test Cases for the Poor (1983), Nationalised Industries and Public Control (1986), Waiving the Rules (with C Graham, 1988), Privatizing Public Enterprises (with C Graham, 1991), Privatisation and Regulatory Change in Europe (with M Moran, 1994); *Recreations* walking, listening to jazz, travel; *Style—* Prof Tony Prosser; ✉ Flat 1/R, 21 Botanic Crescent, Glasgow G20 8QJ (☎ 0141 946 9487); School of Law, Stair Building, University of Glasgow, Glasgow G12 8QQ (☎ 0141 330 4180, fax 0141 330 5140)

PROSSER, His Hon Judge; (Elvet) John; QC (1978); s of David Prosser; *b* 10 July 1932; *Educ* Pontypridd GS, King's Coll London; *m* 1957, Mary Louise Cowdry; 2 da; *Career* Flt Lt RAF 1957–59; called to the Bar Gray's Inn 1956, recorder Crown Court 1972–88, bencher 1986, circuit judge (Wales and Chester Circuit) 1988–, resident judge Newport Crown Court; pt/t chm of Industl Tbnls 1975–81, asst boundary cmmr for Wales 1977–, memb Senate of Inns of Court and the Bar 1980–87, ldr Wales and Cheshire Circuit 1984–87; *Recreations* cricket, golf; *Clubs* East India, Cardiff and County; *Style—* His Hon Judge Prosser, QC; ✉ Hillcroft, Mill Rd, Lisvane, Cardiff CF4 5XL

PROSSER, Brig (William) Keith Lloyd; CBE (1982, MBE 1973), MC (1958); s of William George Prosser (d 1985), of Bath, and Maud, *née* Lloyd (d 1989); *b* 7 March 1936; *Educ* City of Bath Sch, Sandhurst, Army Staff Coll Camberley, RCDS London; *m* 10 Feb 1962, May Ruth, da of Jacob Elias (d 1973), of Singapore; 1 s (David b 1963), 1 da (Amanda b 1966); *Career* cmmnd The 22 (Cheshire) Regt 1956, CO 1 Bn The 22 (Cheshire) Regt 1976–78, Bde Cdr 8 Inf Bde 1980–82, dir Army Reserves and cadets MOD (A) 1986–89, Col The 22 (Cheshire) Regt 1985–91, ADC 1988; Clerk Worshipful Co of Tallow Chandlers 1990 (Liveryman 1992), Freeman City of London 1991; *Recreations* rugby, skiing, tennis, walking; *Style—* Brig Keith Prosser, CBE, MC; ✉ Tallow Chandlers' Hall, 4 Dowgate Hill, London EC4R 2SH (☎ 0171 248 4726)

PROSSER, Margaret Theresa; da of Frederick James (d 1973), of London, and Lilian Mary, *née* Barry (d 1983); *b* 22 Aug 1937; *Educ* St Philomena's Convent Carshalton Surrey, NE London Poly (postgrad dip); *m* 15 Feb 1957 (m dis); 1 s (Jeffrey Jonathan b 1958), 2 da (Carol Ann b 1960, Stella Jane b 1963); *Career* advice centre organiser Home Office Funded Community Devpt Project 1974–77, law centre advsr 1977–83; TGWU: dist organiser 1983–84, nat women's sec 1984–, nat organiser 1992–; pres TUC 1995–96 (memb Gen Cncl 1985–96), treas Lab Pty 1996–; assoc memb Inst of Legal Execs 1981–83; *Recreations* walking, cooking; *Style—* Mrs Margaret Prosser; ✉ 154 Moffat Rd, Thornton Heath, Surrey CR7 8PX (☎ 0181 771 5487); TGWU, Transport House, 16 Palace Street, Victoria, London SW1E 5JB (0171 828 7788, fax 0171 630 5861)

PROSSER, Hon Lord; William David Prosser; s of David G Prosser, MC, WS, of Edinburgh; *b* 23 Nov 1934; *Educ* Edinburgh Acad, Corpus Christi Oxford (MA), Univ of Edinburgh (LLB); *m* 1964, Vanessa, da of Sir William O'Brien Lindsay, KBE; 2 s, 2 da; *Career* passed advocate 1962, QC (Scot) 1974, dean Faculty of Advocates 1983–86 (vice dean 1979–83), senator Coll of Justice in Scotland (a Lord of Session) 1986–; chm: Royal Lyceum Theatre Co Edinburgh 1987–92, Scottish Historic Bldgs Tst 1988–, Royal Fine Art Cmmn for Scotland 1990–95, Chamber Gp of Scotland 1993–, Scottish Architectural Educn Tst 1994–; Hon FRIAS 1995; *Clubs* New (Edinburgh), Scottish Arts; *Style—* The Hon Lord Prosser; ✉ 7 Randolph Crescent, Edinburgh EH3 7TH (☎ 0131 225 2709); Netherfoodie, Dairsie, Fife (☎ 01334 870438)

PROTHERO, Dr David; s of Lewis Thomas Prothero (d 1992), of Church Stretton, Shropshire, and Gwyneth Mary, *née* Jenkyn-Owen (d 1986); *b* 10 April 1937; *Educ* Bembridge Sch IOW, Univ Coll London, UCH Sch (MB BS, MRCS, LRCP, DPM); *m* 1, 1963 (m dis), Dr Yolanda Glaser; 1 s (Alan Neil b 6 July 1964), 1 da (Caroline Marion (Mrs Kelly) b 16 Sept 1966); *m* 2, 5 Sept 1973, Dianne, da of William Wells; 1 s (William b 8 Sept 1989), 2 da (Claudia Elizabeth b 10 Oct 1981, Louise b 17 Oct 1984); *Career* UCH and Shenley Hosp Herts 1960–66, clinical lectr in psychiatry London Hosp Med Coll 1966–69, conslt psychiatrist Claybury Hosp Woodford Green Essex 1969–86, conslt psychiatrist and med dir Grovelands Priory Hosp 1986–; memb BMA 1969, FRCPsych 1985 (MRCPsych 1972); *Style—* Dr David Prothero; ✉ 152 Harley St, London W1N 1HH (☎ 0171 935 8868); Grovelands Priory Hospital, The Bourne, London N14 6RA (☎ 0181 882 8191, fax 0181 447 8138)

PROTHERO, Dr William Bernard Francis; s of Huw Prothero (d 1986), of Haverfordwest, Pembrokeshire, and Hannah Falmai Mary, *née* Mathias; *b* 12 July 1953; *Educ* Aberaeron CS, Univ of Wales Cardiff (MB BCh); *Career* registrar Guy's Hosp London 1980–83; sr registrar: Westminster Hosp 1983–85, Charing Cross Hosp 1986–88; conslt psychiatrist Ashford Hosp 1988–; MRCPsych; *Recreations* theatre, reading, golf, travel; *Style—* Dr William Prothero; ✉ Department of Psychiatry, Ashford Hospital, Ashford, Middx (☎ 01784 884488)

PROTHEROE, Col Alan Hackford; CBE (1991, MBE 1980), TD (and Bar), DL (Bucks 1993); s of Rev B P Protheroe (d 1971); *b* 10 Jan 1934; *Educ* Maesteg GS Glam; *m* 1956, Anne Miller, da of H M Watkins (d 1984); 2 s; *Career* Nat Serv 2 Lt Welch Regt 1954–56, Col TA; reporter: Glamorgan Gazette 1951–53, BBC Wales 1957–70; industl corr Wales BBC 1959–64, ed Wales News and Current Affrs 1964–70; BBC TV News: asst ed 1970–72, dep ed 1972–77, ed 1977–80, asst dir BBC News and Current Affrs 1980, asst dir-gen 1982–87; dir: Visnews Ltd 1982–87, Defence Public Affairs Consultants Ltd

1988–, Europac Group 1989– (chm 1991–), TRBL Training Company; md The Services Sound and Vision Corp 1988–94; chm Eastern Wessex Reserve Forces Assoc, memb Cncl RUSI 1984–87, fndr memb Assoc of Br Eds (chm 1987); lectr and contrib to jls on def and media affrs; memb Mgmt Bd Royal British Legion; Hon Col Pool of Army Information Offrs 1991–96; FIMgt, MIPR; *Recreations* pistol and rifle shooting, scuba diving; *Clubs* Savile, Army & Navy; *Style*— Col Alan Protheroe, CBE, TD, DL; ✉ Amberleigh House, 60 Chapman Lane, Flackwell Heath, Bucks HP10 9BD (☎ 01628 528492, fax 01628 533209)

PROTHEROE, Dr David Trevelyan; s of Dr Harry Trevelyan Protheroe, of Gilwern, Gwent, and Ruby, *née* Davies; *b* 22 Feb 1937; *Educ* King Edwards Sch Sheffield, Trinity Coll Oxford, St Thomas' Hosp Med Sch (BA, MA, BM BCh); *m* 22 Oct 1963, Margaret Catherine, *née* Cooke; 2 s (Richard Trevelyan b 22 June 1965, Andrew Simon b 21 Sept 1966); *Career* sr registrar in anaesthetics Bristol 1968–72, conslt anaesthetist Bath 1972; chm Br Standards Instn Ctee on Infusion Pumps, rep and del of Int Electrotechnical Commission 65D; memb: BMA, Assoc of Anaesthetics 1966, RCS 1968, Intensive Care Soc 1974, RSM 1985; FFARCS 1968; *Recreations* golf; *Clubs* Bath & County; *Style*— Dr David Protheroe; ✉ Long Barn, Charlton, Kilmersden, Somerset BA3 5TN (☎ 01761 432326); Royal United Hospital, Combe Park, Bath (☎ 01225 428331); The Bath Clinic, Claverton Down Rd, Bath (☎ 01225 835555)

PROUD, George; s of Albert Proud (d 1972), of Durham, and Frances, *née* Sigworth; *b* 23 Aug 1943; *Educ* Newcastle Royal GS, Univ of Durham (BDS), Univ of Newcastle (MB BS, MD); *m* 25 July 1970, Janet Mary, da of Joseph Davies (d 1978), of Worthing; 1 s (Stuart James b 1 April 1976), 1 da (Kathryn Siân b 8 Sept 1973); *Career* conslt surgn Royal Victoria Infirmary Newcastle 1981– (and clinical director of Surgery), former gen sec Br Transplantation Soc; memb: Assoc of Surgns of GB and I, Vascular Surgical Soc, Euro Soc for Vasular Surgery, Exec Ctee Northern Cos Kidney Res Fund, Ct of Examiners RCS; gen surgical rep Nat Confidential Enquiry into Peri Operative Death (NCEPOD) Ctee; fndr memb: Weardale Ski Club, NE Ski Assoc; former pres Heaton on Tyne Rotary Club; Hunterian prof of surgery RCS 1979; winner Jacksonian Prize for Surgery RCS 1981; FRCS, memb BMA; *Publications* many papers on surgical topics; *Recreations* skiing, fell walking, photography; *Style*— George Proud, Esq; ✉ Royal Victoria Infirmary, Queen Victoria Rd, Newcastle upon Tyne NE1 4LP (☎ 0191 232 5131, fax 0191 232 5278, car 0860 440290)

PROUDFOOT, Prof (Vincent) Bruce; OBE (1997); s of Bruce Falconer Proudfoot (d 1993), and Cecilia, *née* Thompson (d 1996); *b* 24 Sept 1930; *Educ* Royal Belfast Academical Inst, Queen's Univ Belfast (BA, PhD); *m* 16 Dec 1961, Edwina Valmai Windram, da of Edwin Alexander Field, of 15 Liberton Brae, Edinburgh; 2 s (Bruce b 1962, Malcolm b 1964); *Career* lectr in geography: Queen's Univ Belfast 1958–59 (res offr Nuffield Quaternary Res Unit 1954–58), Univ of Durham 1959–67; coll librarian Hatfield Coll Univ of Durham 1963–65 (tutor 1960–63), visiting fell Univ of Auckland NZ 1966, prof Univ of Alberta Canada 1970–74 (assoc prof 1967–70), co-ordinator and staff conslt Alberta Human Resources Res Cncl 1971–72, prof of geography Univ of St Andrews 1974–93 (head Dept of Geography 1974–85), prof emeritus 1993–; Br Assoc Advancement of Sci: jt sec Section H (Anthropology and Archaeology) 1958–62 (memb Ctee 1957–58 and 1986–), rec 1962–65, pres 1985; tstee Nat Museum of Antiquities of Scotland 1982–85; Soc of Antiquaries of Scotland: memb Res Ctee 1979–82, vice pres 1982–85; Royal Scot Geographical Soc: memb Cncl 1975–78 and 1992–93, memb Scot Geog Mag Ctee 1975–78, hon ed and convenor Pubns Ctee 1978–93, memb Business Ctee 1978–93, vice chm 1980–81, chm Dundee Centre 1993–, vice pres 1993 , chm Cncl 1993–; Royal Soc of Edinburgh: memb Cncl 1982–85 and 1990–91, convenor Earth Sciences Ctee 1983–85, memb Awards Ctee 1984–85, vice pres 1985–88, convenor Grants Ctee 1988–91, gen sec 1991–96; FSA 1963, FRSE 1979, FRGS, FRSA, FSA Scotland 1979, FRSGS 1991; *Books* The Downpatrick Gold Find (1955), Frontier Settlement Studies (jtly, 1974), Site, Environment and Economy (ed, 1983); *Recreations* gardening; *Clubs* New (Edinburgh); *Style*— Prof Bruce Proudfoot, OBE, FSA, FRSE; ✉ Westgate, Wardlaw Gardens, St Andrews, Scotland KY16 9DW (☎ 01334 473293)

PROUDMAN, Sonia Rosemary Susan; QC (1994); da of Kenneth Oliphant Proudman, of London, and Sati, *née* Hekimian; *b* 30 July 1949; *Educ* St Paul's Girls' Sch, Lady Margaret Hall Oxford (MA); *m* 19 Dec 1987, David Crispian Himley Cartwright, s of Himley Cartwright, of Henley-on-Thames; 1 da; *Career* called to the Bar Lincoln's Inn 1972, bencher 1996, in practice at the Chancery Bar 1972; *Recreations* cinema, jazz, food, fashion; *Clubs* Hurlingham, CWIL; *Style*— Miss Sonia Proudman, QC; ✉ 11 New Square, Lincoln's Inn, London WC2A 3QB (☎ 0171 831 0081, fax 0171 405 2560/0798)

PROUT, David John; s of Donald Cornell Prout, of Budleigh Salterton, Devon, and Kathleen Susan Constance, *née* Miller; *b* 13 Nov 1947; *Educ* Rugby, Hatfield Coll Durham, Univ of Reading (BA); *m* 17 July 1971, Amanda Jane, da of late Clifford Sherwood Nell; 2 s (Oliver Samuel b 13 June 1981, Jonathan Benedict b 9 Dec 1984); *Career* photographer; trained at GEC 1965, started Creed Lane Studio 1975; clients incl: William Collins, Jonathan Cape, Grant Thornton, Schlumberger, Touche Ross, Arthur Andersen, Vauxhall Motors, BT, Esso, CEPEC, Rank Xerox, Dept of Health; Creed Lane nominated for Eurobest and AGR Graduate Recruitment awards; former teacher Canterbury Coll of Art; memb Graphics Gp and various ctees Chartered Soc of Designers 1976–94; FCSD 1985 (MCSD 1976), FRSA 1994; *Recreations* restoring pre-war cars, skiing, avoiding gardening, projects in Romania; *Clubs* MG Car, Octagon Car; *Style*— David Prout, Esq; ✉ Creed Lane Graphic Communication, 82–84 Clerkenwell Rd, London EC1M 5RJ (☎ 0171 608 1122, fax 0171 608 1127)

PROVAN, James Lyal Clark; MEP (Cons) S Downs W (majority 21,067); s of John Provan, and Jean, *née* Clark; *b* 19 Dec 1936; *Educ* Oundle, RAC Cirencester; *m* 1960, Rowena Adele, da of Andrew H S Lewis; 1 da (Pepita Clare b 1961), 2 s ((John) Lyal, Andrew James (twins) b 1963); *Career* cncllr Tayside 1978–82, MEP NE Scot 1979–89, chm McIntosh Donald 1989–94, exec dir Scot Financial Enterprise 1990–92, chm McIntosh of Dyce 1991–94, MEP (C) S Downs W 1994–; currently non-exec dir: New Holland Holdings NV, New Holland NV; chm Rowett Research Inst 1992–; memb AFRC 1990–94, memb Lloyds; ARAgS; FAAV, FRSA; *Recreations* country pursuits, flying, sailing, music; *Clubs* Royal Perth, Farmers', East India; *Style*— James Provan, Esq, MEP; ✉ Middle Lodge, Barnes Green, Horsham, West Sussex RH13 7NL (☎ 01403 733700, fax 01403 733588)

PROWSE, Dr Keith; s of Valentine Prowse, of Rugby, and Irene Ellen, *née* Rogers (d 1989); *b* 23 Dec 1937; *Educ* Lawrence Sheriff GS Rugby, Univ of Birmingham (BSc, MB ChB, MD); *m* 22 Sept 1962, Hilary Ann, da of Reginald Varley (d 1971), of Sutton Coldfield; 1 s (Robert b 1975), 1 da (Carolyn b 1972); *Career* lectr in med Univ of Birmingham 1968–71, Inserm res fell unité 14 Centre Hospitalier Universitaire Nancy France 1971–72, conslt physician N Staffs Hosps Centre 1972–, sr clinical lectr in respiratory med Dept of Postgrad Med Univ of Keele 1986–, med dir North Staffordshire Hosp NHS Tst; chm Br Thoracic Soc, fndr memb Cncl Br Lung Fndn, UK rep UEMS Monospeciality Ctee Pneumology; FRCP 1977; *Recreations* castles, owls, walking, music, France; *Clubs* Y; *Style*— Dr Keith Prowse; ✉ Kyriole Pinewood Road, Ashley Heath, Nr Market Drayton, Shropshire TF9 4PP (☎ 01630 87 2879); Department of Respiratory Medicine, North Staffordshire Hospital, City General Site, Newcastle Rd, Stoke on Trent, Staffs ST4 6QG (☎ 01782 718328)

PROWSE, Philip; s of late Alan William Auger Prowse, and Violet Beatrice, *née* Williamson; *b* 29 Dec 1937; *Educ* King's Sch Worcester, Malvern Coll of Art, Slade Sch of Fine Art; *Career* director and designer for opera, ballet and theatre; sr lectr UCL, head of theatre design dept Slade Sch 1995–; professional debut with Royal Ballet's Diversions (ROH) 1961; worked with numerous cos incl: Glasgow Citizens' Theatre (dir 1970–), RNT, RSC, Old Vic, Royal Opera, Royal Ballet, ENO, Sadler's Wells Royal Ballet, WNO, Scottish Opera, Opera North, English Nat Ballet (Festival Ballet), Scottish Ballet; worked extensively in Europe and USA; *Theatre* prodns as dir incl: Chinchilla (NY), Phedra (with Glenda Jackson, Old Vic and Aldwych), The Duchess of Malfi (with Ian McKellen, RNT and Chicago); for Greenwich Theatre incl: The White Devil, The Seagull, The Orphan; recent works for Citizens' Theatre Glasgow: The Picture of Dorian Gray, Private Lives, The Milk Train Doesn't Stop Here Anymore, The Soldiers, Don Carlos (both at Edinburgh Int Festival); other recent prodns incl: A Woman of No Importance (RSC), The White Devil (RNT), Lady Windermere's Fan (Albery and tour), The Vortex (also designer, Garrick, with Rupert Everett); *Opera* prodns as dir incl: La Gioconda (Opera North), Giovanna D'Arco (ROH), Tamburlaine (WNO), The Pearl Fishers (ENO); for Opera North: Orpheus, The Threepenny Opera, Aida, Daphne; *Ballet* as designer incl: The Sleeping Beauty (Dutch Nat Ballet/Vienna State Opera), Swan Lake (Munich); for Royal Ballet: The Sleeping Beauty, Swan Lake, Carmina Burana; *Style*— Philip Prowse, Esq; ✉ c/o Cruickshank Cazenove, 97 Old South Lambeth Road, London SW8 1XU (☎ 0171 735 2933, fax 0171 820 1081)

PROWTING, Peter Brian; s of Arthur Edwin Alfred Prowting (d 1977), of Littlehampton, and Edith Kate, *née* Jones (d 1987); *b* 19 Dec 1924; *Educ* Ickenham HS, Frays Coll Uxbridge; *m* 1, 22 Oct 1948 (m dis 1965), Phyllis; 1 da (Wendy b 9 Sept 1956); m 2, 24 Nov 1966, Elizabeth Anne (Liz), da of Wing Cdr Leslie George Mobsby, RAF (d 1966), of Chenies, Bucks; *Career* chm: Prowting plc 1955– (dir 1948–), Estates & General plc 1982– (dir 1974–); *Recreations* gardening, golf, jazz; *Clubs* Beaconsfield Golf, Mill Reef (Antigua); *Style*— Peter Prowting, Esq; ✉ Prowting plc, Breakspear House, Bury St, Ruislip, Middx HA4 7SY (☎ 01895 633344, fax 01895 677190)

PRYCE, Carmen Vanessa Jackson; da of Edward Alderman Pryce, of Nottingham, and Theresa Leonora Jackson; *b* 7 Feb 1961; *Educ* Manvers Pierrepont Comp Sch Nottingham, Notts Coll of Agric (OND), Univ of Reading (BSc), City Univ London (Dip Journalism); *Career* television presenter; trainee reporter Central News Birmingham 1985–86; researcher/asst prodr: MotorMouth (TVS) 1988, Get Fresh (Tyne Tees) 1988, 7–Sport (LWT), Q & A (BBC Schools) 1991–92; presenter: Get Fresh (Tyne Tees) 1987, Search Out Science (BBC2) 1989–90, Advice Shop (BBC2) 1990, Tomorrow's World (BBC1) 1991–94; narrator BBC Open Univ 1994–; memb Br Assoc for the Advancement of Sci; *Recreations* running (former junior international athlete); *Style*— Miss Carmen Pryce; ✉ c/o Blackburn Sachs Associates, Eastgate House, 16–19 Eastcastle Street, London W1N 7PA (☎ 0171 636 7744)

PRYCE, Jonathan; s of Isaac Price (d 1976), of N Wales, and Margaret Ellen, *née* Williams (d 1986); *b* 1 June 1947; *Educ* Holywell GS, Sch of Art Kelsterton, Edge Hill Coll of Educn, RADA; *Career* actor; patron Friends United Network, fell Welsh Coll of Music and Drama; *Theatre* Everyman Theatre Liverpool 1972, Nottingham Playhouse 1974, RSC 1979 and 1986, Royal Court 1980, NT 1981, Lyric Hammersmith, Queens Theatre, Vaudeville Theatre, Drury Lane Theatre Royal 1989–90, Music Box and Belasco NY, Broadway Theatre NY; roles incl: Richard III, Hamlet, Macbeth, Petruchio, Angelo, Octavius Caesar, Mick in the Caretaker, Gethin Price in Comedians, Tallys Folly, Trigorin, Astrov, Engineer in Miss Saigon, Fagin in Oliver (London Palladium) 1994–95; *Television* incl: Daft as a Brush, Playthings, Glad Day, Roger Doesn't Live Here Anymore, The Caretaker, Comedians, Timon of Athens, Martin Luther Heretic, Praying Mantis, Two Weeks in Winter, The Man from the Pru, Selling Hitler, Mr Wroe's Virgins, Thicker than Water; *Films* incl: Voyage of the Damned, Breaking Glass, Loophole, Ploughmans Lunch, Something Wicked This Way Comes, Brazil, Man on Fire, Jumpin' Jack Flash, Doctor and the Devils, Haunted Honeymoon, Consuming Passions, The Adventures of Baron Munchausen, The Rachel Papers, Glengarry Glen Ross, The Age of Innocence, Barbarians at the Gate, Great Moments in Aviation, A Business Affair, Deadly Advice, Shopping, Carrington, Evita; *Recordings* Under Milk Wood, Miss Saigon, Nine, Cabaret, Oliver, Evita; *Awards* Tony Award and Theatre World Award (for Comedians) 1977, SWET/Olivier Award (for Hamlet) 1980, Olivier Award (for Miss Saigon) 1990, Variety Club of GB Stage Actor of 1990, Tony Award for Best Actor in a Musical 1991, Drama Desk Award, Cannes Film Festival Award for Best Actor (for Carrington) 1995, Evening Standard Award for Best Actor (for Carrington) 1995; *Style*— Jonathan Pryce, Esq; ✉ c/o James Sharkey Associates, 21 Golden Square, London W1R 3PA (☎ 0171 434 3801– 6, fax 0171 494 1547)

PRYCE, (George) Terry; CBE (1994); s of Edwin Pryce (d 1951), and Hilda, *née* Price; *b* 26 March 1934; *Educ* Welshpool GS, Nat Coll of Food Technol; *m* 1957, Thurza Elizabeth, da of Arthur Denis Tatham (d 1942); 2 s (Simon Charles Conrad b 1961, Timothy John Robert b 1965), 1 da (Sarah Jane b 1970); *Career* Dalgety plc: dir 1972, md 1978–81, chief exec 1981–89; chm Solway Foods Ltd 1990–94, chm York House Gp Ltd 1996–; dir: HP Bulmer Holdings plc 1984–94, Jas Bowman & Sons Ltd 1991–; former chm Bd for Food Sci and Technol Univ of Reading, chm Horticultural Res Int 1991–; memb: Cncl AFRC 1986–94, Advsy Bd Inst of Food Res 1988–94; MFC, CIMgt, FIFST; *Recreations* sport (golf), reading; *Style*— G Terry Pryce, Esq, CBE

PRYDE, Roderick Stokes; s of William Gerard Pryde (d 1955), and Patricia Mary, *née* Stokes (d 1959); *b* 26 Jan 1953; *Educ* George Watson's Coll Edinburgh, Univ of Sussex (BA), UCNW (PGCE, TEFL); *m* 1, 16 July 1976 (m dis), Dominique, *née* Cavalier; 1 da (Claire Patricia b 12 Sept 1979); m 2, 25 March 1989, Susanne Mona Graham, da of George Hamilton; 2 da (Beatrice Grace Hamilton b 14 Oct 1989, Madeleine Eve Hamilton b 20 July 1993), 1 s (Frederick William Hamilton b 1 June 1991); *Career* lectr Univ of Dijon 1975–76, mgmnt trainee and English language co-ordinator Societé Française des Pneumatiques Michelin 1977–81; British Council: asst regnl language offr 1981–83, dir of studies Milan 1983–87, regnl dir Seville 1987–88, regnl dir Bilbao 1988–89, Japanese language trg SOAS 1989–90, dir Kyoto 1990–92, dir Western Japan 1992–94, dir English Language Centre Hong Kong 1994–; *Recreations* reading, walking, children, canoeing; *Clubs* Kobe, Watsonian (Edinburgh), HK Fringe, Royal Asiatic Soc; *Style*— Roderick Pryde, Esq; ✉ The British Council, 255 Hennessy Road, Wanchai, Hong Kong (☎ 00 852 2879 5138, fax 00 852 2507 5731)

PRYER, (Eric) John; CB (1986); s of Edward John Pryer (d 1970), of Pickhurst Mead, Hayes, Kent, and Edith Blanche, *née* Jordan (d 1943); *b* 5 Sept 1929; *Educ* Beckenham & Penge County GS, Birkbeck Coll London (BA); *m* 20 Oct 1962, Moyra Helena, da of James Townley Cross (d 1942), of Blackburn, Lancs; 1 s (Andrew b 26 May 1968), 1 da (Sarah b 23 Aug 1971); *Career* called to the Bar Gray's Inn 1957; exec offr Treasy Slrs Dept 1948, legal asst HM Land Registry 1959, asst land registrar 1965, dist land registrar Durham 1976, dep chief land registrar 1981–83, chief land registrar 1983–90, legal offr Cncl for Licensed Conveyancers 1991–92; conslt (land registration) 1992–; assoc memb RICS; *Publications* Ruoff & Roper's The Law and Practice of Registered Conveyancing (co-ed 6 edn), Land Registration Handbook; various articles in professional jls; *Recreations* reading; *Style*— John Pryer, Esq, CB; ✉ Sprangewell, Poles Lane, Thundridge, Ware, Herts SG12 0SQ (☎ 01920 462595, fax 01920 463212)

PRYKE, Sir David Dudley; 3 Bt (UK 1926); s of Sir (William Robert) Dudley Pryke, 2 Bt (d 1959), and Dame Majorie Pryke (d 1936); gf Lord Mayor of London 1925–26; *b* 16 July 1912; *Educ* St Lawrence Coll Ramsgate; *m* 1945, Doreen Winifred, da of late Ralph Bernard Wilkins; 2 da (Madge b 1946, Anita b 1949); *Heir* nephew, Christopher Dudley

Pryke b 17 April 1946; *Career* dir: Pryke & Palmer Ltd 1945–62, Pryke & Scott Ltd 1963–86; former common cnclman Queenhithe Ward 1960–74; Liveryman Worshipful Co of Turners 1961 (Renter Warden 1983, Upper Warden 1984, Master 1985); *Recreations* photography; *Clubs* Guildhall, Queenhithe Ward (former chm); *Style*— Sir David Pryke, Bt; ✉ 27 Wantz Haven, Princes Road, Maldon, Essex CM9 5HA (☎ 01621 840 473)

PRYNNE, Andrew Geoffrey Lockyer; QC (1995); s of Maj-Gen Michael Whitworth Prynne, CB, CBE (d 1977), and Jean Violet, *née* Stewart (d 1977); *b* 28 May 1953; *Educ* Marlborough, Univ of Southampton (LLB); *m* 30 July 1977, Catriona Mary, da of Maj Henry Gordon Brougham (d 1958); 3 da (Jessica Jean, Miranda Wendy, Natasha Sally); *Career* called to the Bar Middle Temple 1975; *Recreations* sailing, fishing, shooting, theatre, music; *Clubs* Royal Yacht Sqdn, Royal Solent Yacht, Island Sailing; *Style*— Andrew Prynne, Esq, QC; ✉ Mount Le Hoe, Benenden, Kent; 107 Elm Park Mansions, Park Walk, London SW10; 2 Harcourt Buildings, Middle Temple Lane, Temple, London EC4Y 9DB

PRYOR, Dr Arthur John; CB (1997); s of late Quinton Arthur Pryor, of Budleigh Salterton, and Elsie Margaret, *née* Luscombe; *b* 7 March 1939; *Educ* Harrow County GS, Downing Coll Cambridge (MA, PhD); *m* 1964, Marilyn Kay, da of Sidney Petley; 1 da (Clare Marianne b 1969), 1 s (Mark John b 1973); *Career* asst lectr then lectr in Spanish and Portuguese Univ Coll Cardiff 1963–66, asst princ then princ DTI 1966–73, first sec Civil Aviation and Shipping British Embassy Washington DC 1973–75; DTI: princ Commercial Rels and Exports Div 1975–77, asst sec (Shipping Policy, Air Div, Int Trade Policy) 1977–85, regnl dir W Midlands 1985–88; DG Br Nat Space Centre 1988–93, under sec Competition Policy Div DTI 1993–96; memb Inter-Agency Ctee on Global Environmental Change 1990–93, contrib to modern languages and space pubns; *Recreations* tennis, golf, book collecting; *Style*— Dr Arthur Pryor, CB; ✉ c/o Department of Trade and Industry, 1 Victoria Street, London SW1H 0ET

PRYOR, His Hon Judge Brian Hugh; QC (1982); s of Lt-Col Ronald Ernest Pryor (d 1984), and Violet Kathleen, *née* Steele (d 1978); *b* 11 March 1931; *Educ* Chichester HS for Boys, Univ Coll Oxford (exhibitioner, BA); *m* 1955, Jane Mary, da of Albert Edward Smith; 2 da (Elizabeth Jane (Mrs McConnell) b 31 Dec 1959, Helen Margaret (Mrs Hausmann) b 12 Jan 1963), 1 s (Matthew Robert b 16 April 1964); *Career* called to the Bar Lincoln's Inn 1956 (Sir Thomas More bursary), recorder 1981–86, circuit judge (SE Circuit) 1986– resident judge Woolwich Crown Ct 1993–; memb SE Circuit Bar Mess 1957–86, chm Kent Co Bar Mess 1979–82 (memb 1957–82); memb Camberwell DHA and King's Coll Hosp Trust Res Ethics Ctee 1990–95; *Recreations* gardening; *Style*— His Hon Judge Pryor, QC; ✉ Woolwich Crown Court, 2 Belmarsh Road, London SE28 0EY

PRYOR, John Pembro; s of (William) Benjamin Pryor, and Kathleen Martha Amelia, *née* Pembro (d 1959); *b* 25 Aug 1937; *Educ* Reading Sch, King's Coll London, King's Coll Hosp Medical Sch (MS); *m* 25 July 1959, Marion, da of Illtyd Thomas Hopkins; 4 s (Andrew b 1962, Damian b 1964, Justin b 1966, Marcellus b 1968); *Career* conslt urological surgn with special interest in andrology King's Coll Hosp and St Peter's Hosp 1974–94; Inst of Urology London Univ: dean 1978–85, sr surgn 1992–, reader 1996–; Hunterian prof RCS 1994–95; first chm Br Andrology Soc 1978–85, memb Ctee British Assoc of Urological Surgeons 1979–82 (St Peter's Medal 1995), chm Euro Assoc of Gen Microsurgeons 1992–96; treas Br Jl of Urology 1991–; Liveryman Worshipful Soc of Apothecaries; FRCS; *Books* Andrology (1987), Urological Prostheses, Appliances and Catheters (1992), Impotence: An Integrated Approach to Clinical Practice (1993); *Style*— John Pryor, Esq; ✉ The Lister Hospital, Chelsea Bridge Rd, London SW1W 8RH (☎ 0171 730 3417)

PRYOR, His Hon Judge Robert Charles; QC (1983); s of Charles Selwyn Pryor (d 1977), of Suffolk, and Olive, *née* Woodall (d 1977); *b* 10 Dec 1938; *Educ* Eton, Trinity Coll Cambridge (BA); *m* 1969, Virginia, da of Lt-Col Peter Thomas Wellesley Sykes, of Wilts; 1 s (Michael b 1969), 1 da (Caroline b 1971); *Career* Nat Serv 2 Lt KRRC 1957–59; called to the Bar Inner Temple 1963, recorder of the Crown Court 1989–91, circuit judge (Western Circuit) 1991–; dir Sun Life Assurance plc 1977–91; *Style*— His Hon Judge Robert Pryor, QC

PRYS-DAVIES, Baron (Life Peer UK 1982), of Llanegryn in the Co of Gwynedd; Gwilym Prys Prys-Davies; s of William and Mary Matilda Davies; assumed by deed poll 1982 the surname Prys-Davies in lieu of his patronymic; *b* 8 Dec 1923; *Educ* Towyn Sch, Univ Coll of Wales Aberystwyth; *m* 1951, Llinos, da of Abram Evans; 3 da (Hon Catrin Prys (Hon Mrs Waugh) b 1957, Hon Ann Prys b 1959, Hon Elin Prys b 1963); *Career* RN 1942–46; slr 1956, ptnr Morgan Bruce and Nicholas slrs 1957–87 (conslt 1987–93), special advsr to Sec of State for Wales 1974–78; chm Welsh Hosp Bd 1968–74; memb: Welsh Cncl 1967–69, Econ and Social Ctee EEC 1978–82; oppn front bench spokesman on: NI 1982–, Welsh affrs 1987–95; hon fell Univ of Wales Aberystwyth, Trin Coll Carmarthen, Cardiff Inst of Higher Educn; Hon LLD Wales; OStJ; *Publications* A Central Welsh Council 1963, Y Ffermwr a'r Gyfraith (1967); *Style*— The Rt Hon The Lord Prys-Davies; ✉ Lluest, 78 Church Rd, Tonteg, Pontypridd, Mid Glam; c/o House of Lords, London SW1A 0PW

PRYS-ROBERTS, Prof Cedric; s of William Prys Roberts (d 1992), of Exeter, and Winifred, *née* Osborne Jones (d 1990); *b* 8 Aug 1935; *Educ* Dulwich, Bart's Med Sch (MB BS), MA, DM (Oxon), PhD (Leeds); *m* 1961, Linda Joyce, da of Tom Bickerstaff; 2 da (Kathryn Rachel b 1 May 1962, Lesley Elaine b 17 July 1965), 2 s (Simon Alastair b 25 March 1964, Dr Curig Owen Prys-Roberts b 25 Sept 1968); *Career* SHO/registrar Middx Hosp London and research fell Univ of Leeds 1964–67, clinical reader in anaesthetics Univ of Oxford 1967–76, hon conslt anaesthetist Radcliffe Infirmary Oxford 1967–76, fell Worcester Coll Oxford 1970–76; prof of anaesthesia: Univ of California San Diego 1973–74, Univ of Bristol 1976–; hon conslt anaesthetist Bristol Royal Infirmary and Bristol Royal Hosp for Sick Children 1976–; pres Royal Coll of Anaesthetists 1994– (vice pres 1990–92); Hunterian prof Royal Coll of Surgns of England 1978; senator Euro Acad of Anaesthesiology 1984–92, pres Soc of Anaesthetists of the SW Regn 1992, fell (by election) Aust and NZ Coll of Anaesthetists 1986; founding ed Current Opinion in Anaesthesiology 1988–95, author of numerous articles in learned jls on physiology and pharmacology related to anaesthesia and intensive therapy; FRCA, FANZCA; *Books* The Circulation of Anaesthesia (ed, 1980), Pharmacokinetics of Anaesthesia (ed, 1984), Monitoring in Anaesthesia and Intensive Care (ed, 1994), International Practice of Anaesthesia (ed, 2 vols, 1995); *Recreations* mountaineering, skiing, philately, music (playing trumpet); *Style*— Prof Cedric Prys-Roberts; ✉ Sir Humphry Davy Department of Anaesthesia, University of Bristol, Bristol Royal Infirmary, Bristol BS2 8HW (☎ 0117 928 2103); Royal College of Anaesthetists, 48/49 Russell Square, London WC1B 4JY (☎ 0171 813 1900)

PSYLLIDES, Milton Nicholas; s of Nicholas Milton Psyllides, of Chislehurst, Kent, and Loulla, *née* Christophides; *b* 30 Oct 1953; *Educ* Brockley Co GS, Univ of Liverpool (LLB); *m* 16 April 1976, Lynne Josephine, da of Horace Walter Rutherford, of Birmingham; 2 s (Paul b 4 Oct 1986, d 27 July 1988, Andrew b 11 May 1989), 1 da (Louise b 11 Aug 1984); *Career* slr; Evershed & Tomkinson (now Eversheds): asst slr 1978, assoc 1981, ptnr 1984; chm Roman Rentals 001–055 plc; non-exec dir: Shire plc, Burgmann (UK) Ltd; Birmingham Law Soc: sec Co and Commercial Law Ctee, memb Cncl; memb Law Soc 1978; *Recreations* family life, keep fit; *Style*— Milton N Psyllides, Esq; ✉ 1 Halloughton Road, Sutton Coldfield, West Midlands B74 2QG (☎ 0121 354 7694); Eversheds, 10 Newhall St, Birmingham B3 3LX (☎ 0121 233 2001, fax 0121 236 1583, telex 336688)

PUCKRIN, Arthur William; s of Thomas William Puckrin (d 1977), of Middlesbrough, and Eleanor Mary, *née* Cumiskey; *b* 5 May 1938; *Educ* Middlesbrough HS, Univ of London (LLB Hons, BL); *m* 2 April 1966, Patricia Ann, da of Charles Henry Dixon (d 1972), of Middlesbrough; 2 s (Geoffrey Arthur b 1984, James William b 1986); *Career* called to the Bar 1966; legal advsr Dorman Long Steel Ltd 1966–71, Parly advsr to City of London Corp 1971; memb Bar Assoc for Commerce Fin and Indust 1967–; athlete, long distance runner and long distance swimmer; record holder for: Pennine Way 250 miles, Southern Highlands of Scotland 170 miles, Welsh 14 Peaks over 3000 feet, N Yorks Moors 80 miles, Lyke Walk N Yorks Moors 120 miles; defeated 50 horses over 44 miles at Wolsingham Horse Trials, record holder for 110 mile walk Middlesbrough to York and back in 23 hours 40 mins; represented GB playing bridge on 8 occasions incl 2 World Championships and four Euro Championships; life memb: Fell Runners' Assoc, Darlington HF Walking Club, Br Long Distance Swimming Assoc; life master English Bridge Union; FCIS 1977, MIMgt 1980; *Clubs* Hartlepool Bridge, Middlesbrough and Cleveland Harriers, Lyke Wake; *Style*— Arthur W Puckrin, Esq; ✉ 3 Romanby Gardens, Middlesbrough, Cleveland (☎ 01642 593807); 257 Acklam Rd, Middlesbrough (☎ 01642 240215)

PUDDEPHATT, Andrew Charles; s of Andrew Ross Puddephatt, and Margaret, *née* Deboo; *b* 2 April 1950; *Educ* Kingsbury Sch Dunstable, Sidney Sussex Coll Cambridge (BA), Architectural Assoc (dip); *children* 2 da (Leni Joanne Wild, Kelly Wild); *Career* teacher ILEA 1979, computer programmer CAP/CPP 1979–81, researcher Jt Action Docklands Gp 1985–89, gen sec Liberty - The Nat Cncl for Civil Liberties 1989–95, dir Charter 88 1995–; London Borough of Hackney: councillor 1982–90, dep ldr 1984–85, ldr 1986–89; *Recreations* music, literature, escaping from work; *Style*— Andrew Puddephatt; ✉ Director, Charter 88, Exmouth House, 3–11 Pine Street, London EC1R 0JH (☎ 0171 833 1988, fax 0171 833 5895)

PUGH, Prof Alan; s of Albert Pugh (d 1989), and Stella, *née* Gough (d 1991); *b* 7 March 1936; *Educ* Whitchurch GS, UC of S Wales and Monmouthshire (BSc, Page Prize in Engrg), Univ of Nottingham (PhD); *m* Alison Jean (d 1995), da of Robert Lindsay; 1 s (Simon David b 7 Nov 1962), 1 da (Judith Caroline (Mrs Watson) b 30 Oct 1961); *Career* postgrad apprenticeship BBC 1957–59, design engr on Br nuclear submarine prog Rolls Royce 1959–61, lectr then sr lectr in electrical engrg Univ of Nottingham 1961–78 (J Langham-Thompson Premium 1968), prof of electronic engrg Univ of Hull 1978– (head of dept 1978–90, dean 1987–90, pro-vice-chllr 1990–93); memb NATO Collaborative Research Grant Ctee 1995–; FIEE 1979 (MIEE 1964), FRSA 1982, FEng 1992; *Books* Robot Vision (1983), Robot Sensors (Vol 1 - Vision, Vol 2 - Tactile and Non-Vision, 1986), Machine Intelligence and Knowledge Engineering for Robotic Applications (with A K C Wong, 1987); *Recreations* hill walking, flying, pottering around the house and garden; *Style*— Prof Alan Pugh, FEng; ✉ Cherry Tree Cottage, Wateringdike Lane, Goodmanham, York YO4 3JD (☎ 01430 871225)

PUGH, Alastair Tarrant; CBE (1986); s of Sqdn Ldr Rev Herbert Cecil Pugh, GC (d 1941), and Amy Lilian Pugh (d 1956); *b* 16 Sept 1928; *Educ* Tettenhall Coll Staffs, De Havilland Aeronautical Tech Sch; *m* 1957, Sylvia Victoria Marlow; 2 s (Giles, Duncan), 1 da (Emma); *Career* md British Caledonian Airways 1978–85, exec vice chm British Caledonian Group 1985–88, conslt Goldman Sachs International Ltd; memb Air Worthiness Requirements Bd 1982–92, tstee Brooklands Museum 1988, pres Chartered Inst of Tport 1988–89; FCIT, FRAeS; *Recreations* vintage sports cars; *Clubs* Reform; *Style*— Alastair Pugh, Esq, CBE; ✉ England's Cottage, Sidlow Bridge, Reigate, Surrey (☎ 01737 243456, fax 01737 224145)

PUGH, Andrew Cartwright; QC; s of Lewis Gordon Pugh (d 1989), and Erica, *née* Cartwright; *b* 6 June 1937; *Educ* Tonbridge, New Coll Oxford (MA); *m* 28 April 1984, Chantal Helene, da of Andre Langevin (d 1987); 2 da (Alexandra b 21 Nov 1985, Sophie b 16 Sept 1987); *Career* Nat Serv Royal Sussex Regt 1955–57; called to the Bar Inner Temple 1961; SE Circuit: bencher 1989, recorder 1990–; legal assessor: GMC, GDC; Liveryman Worshipful Co of Skinners; *Recreations* tennis, gardening, reading; *Clubs* United Oxford and Cambridge; *Style*— Andrew Pugh, Esq, QC; ✉ 2 Hare Court, Temple, London EC4, (☎ 0171 583 1770, fax 2 & 3 071 583 9269, telex 27139 LIN LAW)

PUGH, Dennis; OBE (1988), JP (Gwynedd 1982); s of Rhys Pugh (d 1963), and Elizabeth, *née* Vaughan (d 1971); *b* 27 July 1930; *Educ* Ffestiniog Co Sch; *m* 20 Dec 1952, Annie Lloyd, da of William George Rees (d 1951); 2 da (Carolyn b 1958, Judith b 1961); *Career* Nat Serv RAF 1948–50, BAFO Berlin 1949–50; entered Civil Serv 1947, Miny of Pensions Blackpool, Newcastle upon Tyne and Wales 1947–66, DTI (formerly Bd of Trade) 1966–72, Customs and Excise 1972–76, Welsh Office 1976–90; special advsr Welsh Devpt Int 1990–; dir Kronospan Ltd; dep chm Llandudno Div Magistrates' Cts; *Recreations* tennis, hill walking, swimming; *Style*— Dennis Pugh, Esq, OBE, JP; ✉ Moelwyn, Tyn y Groes, Conwy, Gwynedd LL32 8SZ (☎ 01492 650438)

PUGH, Sir Idwal Vaughan; KCB (1972, CB 1967); s of late Rhys Pugh; *b* 10 Feb 1918; *Educ* Cowbridge GS, St John's Coll Oxford (hon fell 1979); *m* 1946, Mair Lewis (d 1985); 1 s, 1 da; *Career* second perm sec DOE 1971–76, Parly cmmr for admin and health serv, cmmr for England Wales and Scotland 1976–79; chm Chartered Trust Ltd 1979–88; dir: Standard Chartered Bank 1979–88, Halifax Building Soc 1979–88; chm Devpt Corp of Wales 1980–83, vice pres Univ Coll Swansea 1988–94 (hon fell 1995), chm Cncl RNCM 1988–93 (MRNCM 1983); pres: Coleg Harlech 1990–, Cardiff Business Club 1992–; Hon LLD Univ of Wales 1988; *Clubs* Brooks's, Cardiff and County; *Style*— Sir Idwal Pugh, KCB; ✉ 5 Murray Court, 80 Banbury Road, Oxford OX2 6LQ (☎ 01865 510015)

PUGH, Michael James; s of Patrick James Pugh (d 1974), of Redruth, and Daphne Pamela, *née* Webber; *b* 23 April 1948; *Educ* Downside; *m* 11 July 1970, Shirley Condliffe, da of Matthew Douglas Reginald Legg (d 1990), of Portsmouth; *Career* articled clerk G C Davies & Ptnrs Redruth 1967–72, admitted slr 1972, ptnr Barlow Lyde and Gilbert 1975–92 (asst slr 1972–75), ptnr Coopers & Lybrand 1992–; chm: Insur Ctee of Int Bar Assoc 1984–88, Br Insur Law Assoc 1990–92; admitted slr Hong Kong 1986; vice chm Ctee on Int Tort and Insur Law American Bar Assoc; memb: Law Soc 1972, Int Bar Assoc 1981, Br Insur Law Assoc 1982, Law Soc of Hong Kong 1986, City of London Law Soc 1986; *Recreations* mountain walking, bird watching, music, classic motor cars, wine; *Clubs* Reform, Worcestershire CCC; *Style*— Michael Pugh, Esq; ✉ Coopers & Lybrand, 1 Embankment Place, London WC2N 6NN (☎ 0171 583 5000, fax 0171 822 4652, telex 887470)

PUGH, Richard Henry Crommelin; DL (Hereford and Worcester 1991); s of John James Edgar Pugh (d 1944), of Buxton, Derbyshire, and Charlotte Winifred Crommelin, *née* Sadler (d 1977); *b* 9 Sept 1927; *Educ* Buxton Coll, Univ of London (LLB); *m* 15 Aug 1953, Ann, da of Roy Waddington Swales (d 1979), of Fernilee, Derbyshire; 1 s (Stephen b 1958), 1 da (Helen b 1956); *Career* Nat Serv RAF 1947–49; qualified CA; Grattan Warehouses Ltd 1951–56; chm Kay & Co Ltd (Home Shopping Div of Great Universal Stores) 1968–96, dep chm The Great Universal Stores plc 1990–96; fell Worcester Coll of Further Educn, tstee Worcester Cathedral Appeal, co chm Order of St John; memb Ct of Assts Worshipful Co of Chartered Secretaries 1984, Freeman City of London 1984; FCA 1951, ACIS 1951, ACMA 1959, FRGS; *Recreations* golf, swimming, genealogy; *Clubs* City Livery; *Style*— Richard Pugh, Esq, DL; ✉ c/o Kay & Co Ltd, Elgar Suite, 250 Bransford Rd, Worcester WR99 1AA (☎ 01905 23411)

PUGH-THOMAS, Anthony; s of Dr John Pugh-Thomas (d 1968), of The Wirral, and Gladys, *née* Dugdale (d 1989); *b* 14 July 1939; *Educ* Repton, Jesus Coll Cambridge (MA, LLM); *m* 20 May 1967, Rosemary Dennys, da of Michael Bernard Clarke Butler-Cole; 2 da (Antonia Francesca b 18 June 1970, Claudia Rachel b 19 Oct 1972); *Career* admitted slr 1965; articled clerk Simmons & Simmons Solicitors, ptnr Durrant Cooper & Hambling 1967 (joined as asst slr), currently ptnr Lovell White Durrant (formerly Durrant Cooper Hambling and then Durrant Piesse); author of various articles on topics of legal interest; memb Cncl and treas Justice; nominated memb Ct of Appeal (Civil Div) Users' Ctee and Commercial Ct Users' Ctee, pres London Slrs' Litigation Assoc 1980–82; hon slr to The Georgian Gp; chm City of London Law Soc; memb: Law Soc (memb Consumer and Commercial Law Ctee and Banking Law Sub-Ctee); *Recreations* growing unusual plants; *Clubs* Oriental, Travellers'; *Style*— Anthony Pugh-Thomas, Esq; ✉ Lovell White Durrant, 65 Holborn Viaduct, London EC1A 2DY (☎ 0171 236 0066, fax 0171 236 0084)

PUGHE, Brig Neville Morris; s of Maj Morris George Pughe (d 1951), and Dorothy Edith, *née* Goss; *b* 10 Jan 1936; *Educ* Exeter Sch, RMA Sandhurst, RMCS Shrivenham, RAF Staff Coll Bracknell; *m* 19 Jan 1963, Linda Jane, da of Denis Carr Chetwood (d 1974); 3 s (David Michael Stephen b 9 Jan 1964, Richard Neville Iain b 31 July 1965, Jonathan Owen b 7 Feb 1967); *Career* cmmnd RA 1955, Bde Maj 16 Parachute Bde 1972–74, instr Staff Coll Camberley 1974–76, CO 26 Field Regt RA 1976–78, Col GS MOD 1980–82, AMA Washington 1983–85, def attaché Bonn 1986–88, dep cdr SW Dist 1988–89; ADC to HM The Queen 1988–90; currently chief exec Surrey Heath Borough Cncl; warden Woodland Tst; sec Anglo-German Officers' Assoc, govr RNLI; FIMgt 1988, FIPD 1996; Officer's Cross Order of Merit of Federal Republic of Germany 1993; *Recreations* walking, gardening, music, writing, environment; *Style*— Brig Neville Pughe; ✉ Woodstock's, 22 Paddock Close, Camberley, Surrey GU15 2BN (☎ 01276 686238); Surrey Heath Borough Council, Knoll Rd, Camberley, Surrey (☎ 01276 686252, fax 01276 22277)

PUGSLEY, Sir Alfred Grenvile; kt (1956), OBE (1944); s of Herbert William Pugsley, of Wimbledon, and Marian, *née* Clifford; *b* 13 May 1903, May; *Educ* Rutlish Sch, Univ of London; *m* 1928, Kathleen Mary (d 1974), da of Laban Warner, of Aldershot; *Career* civil engrg apprentice Royal Arsenal Woolwich 1923–26, Royal Airship Works Cardington 1926–31, RAE Farnborough 1931–45, prof of civil engrg Univ of Bristol 1944–68 (pro vice chllr 1961–64, emeritus prof); chm Aeronautical Res Cncl 1952–57; hon fell Univ of Bristol 1986; Hon DUniv Surrey 1968; Hon DSc: Belfast 1965, Cranfield 1978, Birmingham 1982; emeritus memb Smeatonian Soc of Civil Engrs 1989; Structural Engrs Gold medal 1968, Civil Engrs Ewing Gold medal 1979; FRS 1952, FEng 1976; Hon: FRAeS 1963, FICE 1981; *Clubs* Athenaeum; *Style*— Sir Alfred Pugsley, OBE, FRS, FEng; ✉ St Angelas, 5 Litfield Place, Clifton, Bristol BS5 3LU (☎ 0117 923 8278)

PUGSLEY, His Hon Judge David Philip; s of Rev Clement Harry Howell Pugsley (d 1967), and Edith Alsop, *née* Schofield (d 1956); *b* 11 Dec 1944; *Educ* Shebbear Coll, St Catharine's Coll Cambridge (MA); *m* 31 Dec 1966, Judith Mary, da of John S Mappin, 2 da (Joanna Hazel b 28 March 1972, Alison Jane b 12 Feb 1974); *Career* called to the Bar Middle Temple 1968, chm Birmingham Region Industl Tbnls 1985–, recorder Midland and Oxford Circuit 1991–92 (practised until 1985), circuit judge (Midland and Oxford Circuit) 1992–; Hon MPhil Univ of Birmingham 1995; *Books* Industrial Tribunals - Compensation for Loss of Pension Rights (jtly, 1990); *Recreations* fishing, golf, walking; *Clubs* Birmingham; *Style*— His Hon Judge Pugsley; ✉ 3 Fountain Court, Steelhouse Lane, Birmingham B4 6DR (☎ 0121 236 5854); Regional Office of Industrial Tribunals, Phoenix House, Newhall House, Newhall St, Birmingham (☎ 0121 236 6051)

PULESTON JONES, Haydn; s of Iago Oliver Puleston Jones (d 1971), and Elizabeth Ann, *née* Morris; *b* 16 Sept 1948; *Educ* Welshpool HS, King's Coll London (LLB, AKC); *m* 9 June 1973, Susan Elizabeth, da of Lt Cdr George Karn (d 1969); 2 s (Simon b 1975, Nicholas b 1978); *Career* ptnr Linklaters & Paines 1979– (joined 1971); chm Banking Law Sub Ctee City of London Law Soc 1994– (memb Sub Ctee 1980–); vice pres Montgomeryshire Soc 1993– (memb Ctee 1974–91); tstee Montgomeryshire Soc Charitable Tsts 1983–; memb: Law Soc 1973–, City of London Slrs' Co 1980–; *Recreations* gardening, classical music, genealogy; *Style*— Haydn Puleston Jones, Esq; ✉ Ducks Farm, Dux Lane, Plaxtol, nr Sevenoaks, Kent TN15 0RB; Linklaters & Paines, Barrington House, 59/67 Gresham St, London EC2V 7JA (☎ 0171 606 7080, fax 0171 606 5113, telex 884349)

PULLEIN-THOMPSON, Christine; *see:* Popescu, Christine

PULLEIN-THOMPSON, Diana; *see:* Farr, Diana

PULLEIN-THOMPSON, Josephine Mary Wedderburn; MBE (1984); da of Harold James Pullein-Thompson (d 1958), and Joanna Cannan (novelist, d 1961); sis of Diana Farr, *qv*, and Christine Popescu, *qv*; *Educ* Wychwood Sch Oxford, and educated at home; *Career* author; gen sec Eng Centre of Int PEN 1976–93 (pres 1993–, official delegate of many int confs); published 41 books from 1946, first novel It Began with Picotee (juvenile work, written jtly with sisters); crime novels: Gin and Murder (1959), They Died in the Spring (1960), Murder Strikes Pink (1963); Ernest Benn award (for All Change) 1961; latest works incl: Black Swift (children's book, 1991), A Job with Horses (teenage novel, 1994), Fair Girls and Grey Horses: memories of a country childhood (jtly with sisters, 1996); horsewoman; has competed in horse trials and showjumping, dressage judge; memb: Ctee Crime Writers' Assoc 1971–73, Ctee of Children's Writers' Group (Soc of Authors) 1973–78; *Recreations* reading, travel; *Style*— Miss Josephine Pullein-Thompson, MBE; ✉ Jennifer Luithlen Agency, 88 Holmfield Rd, Leicester LE2 1SB (☎ 0116 273 8863, fax 0116 273 5697)

PULLEN, Janice Annette; da of Albert Henry Pullen, of Bow, London, and Joan, *née* Morgan (d 1985); *b* 3 Jan 1951; *Educ* Lewes County GS for Girls; *Career* wardrobe sec Glyndbourne Festival Opera 1966–72, wardrobe mistress Scottish Opera 1974–77, wardrobe dir Royal Opera House 1979–92, currently freelance costume designer and supervisor; *Recreations* reading, cooking and entertaining, writing; *Style*— Miss Janice Pullen; ✉ Muffin Cottage, 6 Little East St, Lewes, East Susex BN7 2NU (☎ and fax 01273 479373, mobile 0378 181580)

PULLEN, Trevor Keith; s of Ronald Pullen, of Bexley, Kent, and Pamela Ann, *née* Berry; *b* 22 Nov 1948; *Educ* Roan GS Greenwich, Lanchester Poly Coventry (BA); *m* 1, 13 Sept 1969 (m dis 1980), Glenise May; 1 s (Andrew b 1973), 1 da (Samantha b 1971); m 2, 31 March 1988, Pauline; *Career* Prudential Portfolio Mangrs: UK equity dir 1982, global securities dir 1988; investmt dir Prudential Holborn 1987, ops dir Prudential Financial Services 1991, md Prudential Life and Pensions 1992–94, md GHN 1994–; *Recreations* golf, squash, skiing; *Clubs* Addington Golf; *Style*— Trevor Pullen, Esq; ✉ 9 Prince Consort Drive, Chislehurst, Kent (☎ 0171 467 9522); GHN, 16 Hanover Square, London W1R 9AJ (☎ 0171 493 5239)

PULLEY, (Henry John) Campbell; s of William Laurie Pulley (d 1992), of Shenfield, Essex, and Janet Fairley, *née* Jackson (d 1985); *b* 26 Oct 1939; *Educ* Lancing, Magdalene Coll Cambridge (MA); *m* 25 April 1964, Margaret Anne (Nan), da of Walter Roy Nieland (d 1962), of Hutton, Essex; 2 da (Nicola b 8 April 1965, Deborah b 3 Nov 1967); *Career* memb Lloyd's 1972–, dir Anderson Finch Villiers Ltd 1977–80, dir of risk mgmnt Minet Group 1985–, chm Hutton Mount Ltd; govr Alleyn's Sch; Freeman City of London 1961, memb Ct of Assts Worshipful Co of Saddlers (Liveryman 1961, Master 1994); FCII 1975; *Style*— H J C Pulley, Esq; ✉ Bow End, 9 Bowhay, Hutton Mount, Brentwood, Essex CM13 2JX (☎ 01277 214072); Minet Ltd, Minet House, 66 Prescot Street, London E1 8HG (☎ 0171 481 0707, fax 0171 464 3337)

PULLINGER, Sir (Francis) Alan; kt (1977), CBE (1970), DL (Herts 1982); s of William Pullinger; *b* 22 May 1913; *Educ* Marlborough, Balliol Coll Oxford; *m* 1, 1946, Felicity Charmian Gotch Hobson (d 1964); 2 s (Martin d 1968, Anthony, *qv*), 1 da (Clare); m 2, 1966, Jacqueline Louise Anne Durin (d 1992); *Career* chm Haden Carrier Ltd 1961–79, pres Inst of Heating and Ventilating Engrs 1972–73; vice chm Cncl of Benenden Sch, chm Herts Scout Cncl 1968–91; Hon FCIBS 1977; *Recreations* mountaineering, sailing, beagling; *Clubs* Alpine, Travellers'; *Style*— Sir Alan Pullinger, CBE, DL; ✉ Barnhorn, Meadway, Berkhamsted, Herts HP4 2PL (☎ 01442 863206)

PULLINGER, Anthony Giles Broadbent; s of Sir Alan Pullinger, CBE, *qv*, of Barnhorn, Meadway, Berkhamstead, Herts, and his 1 w, Felicity Charmian Gotch, *née* Hobson (d 1964); *b* 24 May 1955; *Educ* Dragon Sch, Marlborough, Balliol Coll Oxford; *m* 2 Oct 1982, Henrietta Mary Conyngham, da of Maj Richard Conyngham Corfield, of Hill Cottage, Radway, Warwicks; 1 s (Jack b 1985), 2 da (Rosanna b 1988, Isla b 1992); *Career* stockbroker Laing & Cruickshank 1978–90, seconded to the Panel on Takeovers and Mergers 1982–84, ptnr Laing & Cruickshank 1984–87, dir Alexanders Laing & Cruickshank 1985–89, dep DG Panel on Takeovers and Mergers 1990–; Freeman: City of London 1986, Worshipful Co of Grocers 1986; *Recreations* fishing, shooting, walking, music, travel, natural history; *Style*— Anthony Pullinger, Esq; ✉ The Panel on Takeovers and Mergers, PO Box No 226, The Stock Exchange Building, London EC2P 2JX (☎ 0171 382 9026, fax 0171 638 1554)

PULLMAN, Bruce John; s of Bernard John Pullman, of Brockenhurst, Hants, and Dorothy Jean, *née* Hayes; *b* 4 April 1957; *Educ* Canford, Merton Coll Oxford (BA); *m* 14 July 1979, Joanna Alexis Hamilton, da of John Edward Hamilton Davies, of Whitby, N Yorks; 1 s (Joshua b 1989), 2 da (Rebecca b 1984, Abigail b 1985); *Career* NM Rothschild & Sons Ltd 1979–81, dir County NatWest Investment Management 1987–93 (joined 1981, responsible for quantitative investmt research and product devpt), md Hill Samuel Investment Management 1993, dir QUANTEC Ltd (investment consultancy) 1993–94, head of fin engrg Smith New Court 1995, head of asset mgmnt consulting Merrill Lynch 1995–; MSI 1993; *Books* Portfolio Insurance (contrib, ed Donald L Luskin, 1988); *Recreations* Baptist Church, humanitarian aid to Eastern Europe and the former Soviet Union; *Style*— Bruce Pullman, Esq; ✉ Merrill Lynch International Ltd, 20 Farringdon Road, London EC1M 3NH (☎ 0171 772 1046, fax 0171 867 4190)

PULVERMACHER, (Francis) Michael; s of Francis Howard Pulvermacher (d 1978), of Pentyrch, Glamorgan, and Marjorie Constance Denman, *née* Wheatley; *b* 26 July 1938; *Educ* Framlingham, Univ of London (LLB, LLM); *m* 17 Sept 1966, Diana, da of Lt-Col James William Randall Penrose (d 1966), of Shernal Green, Droitwich, Worcs; 1 s (Francis b 1975), 3 da (Joanna b 1968, Isobel b 1969, Helen b 1971); *Career* admitted slr 1961; ptnr Alms and Young 1968–93, conslt Risdon Hosegood 1994–; hon sec Somerset Law Soc 1971–84, lectr Notaries Soc 1983– (memb Cncl); NP 1961; memb: Scout Assoc, Lord Chllr's Legal Aid Advsy Ctee 1986–93; pres Assoc of SW Law Socs 1977–78, tstee St James Pool Taunton Charity, memb Bd of Mgmnt Nationwide Ind Slrs' Gp 1989–93; memb Law Soc 1961; *Recreations* hill walking, sailing, beekeeping, campanology; *Style*— Michael Pulvermacher, Esq; ✉ 6 Higher Vexford, Lydeard Saint Lawrence, Taunton, Somerset TA4 3QF

PULVERTAFT, Rear Adm David Martin; CB (1990); s of Captain William Godfrey Pulvertaft, OBE, RN (d 1971), and Annie Joan Martin (d 1988); *b* 26 March 1938; *Educ* Canford, Brittania RNC Dartmouth, RN Engrg Coll Manadon (BSc); *m* 25 July 1961, Mary Rose, da of Frederick John Jeacock (d 1973), of Hong Kong; 1 s (Rupert James b 1964), 2 da (Sarah Jane b 1965, Lucy Michelle b 1966); *Career* HMS Anchorite 1963–66, HMS Dreadnought 1967–71, 10th Submarine Sqdn 1971–72, HM Dockyard Devonport 1973–75 and 1979–82, NDC Latimer 1975–76, MOD 1976–78, RCDS 1983, chm Naval Nuclear Tech Safety Panel 1984–85; dir: Ship Refitting 1986–87, Gen Aircraft (Navy) 1987–90, Gen Procurement and Support Orgn (Navy) 1990–92, sec Defence, Press and Bdcasting Advsy Ctee 1992–; FIMechE 1989 (MIMechE 1974); *Recreations* genealogy, printing and bookbinding; *Clubs* Naval; *Style*— Rear Adm David Pulvertaft, CB; ✉ Sec DPBAC, Ministry of Defence, Main Building, London SW1A 2HB

PUMPHREY, Christopher Jonathan; TD, DL; s of Col Jonathan Moberly Pumphrey, OBE, TD, DL (d 1992), and Violet Frances, *née* Bosanquet (d 1984); *b* 2 Nov 1933; *Educ* Winchester, Magdalene Coll Cambridge (MA); *m* 1960, Joanna Jane, da of (Frederic) Howard Aykroyd (d 1978), of The Lodge, Kirkby Overblow, nr Harrogate; 2 s (Edward b 1963, Andrew b 1965), 1 da (Sara Rose (Mrs Alexander) b 1962); *Career* chm Wise Speke Ltd stockbrokers 1987–93 (ptnr 1960–87); dir: Sturge Holdings plc 1987–93, Northern Rock Building Society 1991–; chm Northumberland Community Health NHS Tst 1993–; Hon Col Northumberland Hussars Sqdns Queen's Own Yeo 1992–; *Clubs* Northern Counties (Newcastle upon Tyne), Leander; *Style*— Christopher Pumphrey, Esq, TD, DL; ✉ Bolam West Houses, Middleton, Morpeth, Northumberland (☎ 01661 881232)

PUMPHREY, Sir (John) Laurence; KCMG (1973, CMG 1963); s of late Charles Ernest Pumphrey (d 1950), of W Bitchfield, Belsay, Northumberland, and Iris Mary, *née* Moberly-Bell (d 1968); *b* 22 July 1916; *Educ* Winchester, New Coll Oxford; *m* 1945, Jean, da of Sir Walter Riddell, 12 Bt, of Hepple, Morpeth, Northumberland; 4 s (Matthew b 1946, Charles b 1948, Jonathan b 1954, James b 1964), 1 da (Laura b 1951); *Career* served WWII, Lt Northumberland Hussars (POW 1941–45); joined Foreign Serv 1945, dep high cmmr Nairobi 1965–67, high cmmr Zambia 1967–71, ambass to Pakistan 1971–76, ret; *Recreations* walking; *Clubs* Royal Cwlth Soc; *Style*— Sir Laurence Pumphrey, KCMG; ✉ Caistron, Thropton, Morpeth, Northumberland NE65 7LG (☎ 01669 640244)

PUNUKOLLU, Dr Nageswara Rao; s of Gopalakrishnaiah Punukollu, of India, and Bhaskaramba Punukollu; *b* 28 Dec 1942; *Educ* Osmania Univ India (MB BS), Univ of Dublin (DPM); *m* 22 May 1972, Krishna Kumari Parvataneni, da of Venktaratnam Parvataneni (d 1980); 1 s (Bhaskar b 4 July 1976), 1 da (Mallika b 21 July 1973); *Career* conslt psychiatrist NHS UK 1980– (trainee 1973–80), dir Nat Inst of Crisis Intervention Therapy and Research 1988–; developed: crisis intervention team in Huddersfield, comprehensive community based mental health services in Huddersfield Dist, transcultural psychiatry serv in Huddersfield Dist; estab: Nat Inst of Crisis Intervention Therapy and Res in UK, Mental Handicap Prevention Gp Huddersfield; FRCPsych 1992 (MRCPsych 1979); *Style*— Dr Nageswara Rao Punukollu; ✉ National Institute of Crisis Intervention Therapy and Research, 63 Nabcroft Lane, Crosland Moor, Huddersfield HD4 5RQ (☎ 01484 654711, fax 01484 425699)

PURBECK, Luca G; s of Herbert Gutmann (d 1942, former dir of Dresdner Bank Berlin, and London stockbroker), and Daisy (d 1959), da of Maj Kurt von Frankenberg und Ludwigsdorf (d 1932); Mr Purbeck's (1) paternal gf Gutmann founded Dresdner Bank 1872; (2) maternal gggf Gen von Porbeck was ka at Talavera on Napoleon's side, whilst (3) maternal gggf Frankenberg fought under the Duke of Brunswick with Wellington in Spain and at Waterloo and was severely wounded; *b* 13 July 1914; *Educ* Realgymnasium Potsdam, Berlin Univ; *m* 1, 1954, Vera (d 1979), da of Arthur Doughty, of London (d 1961); 1 s (and 1 s decd); m 2, 1982, Monica Pelissier, da of Arthur Greey (d 1974), of Birmingham; *Career* Hambros Bank Ltd London 1936–37, dir Brieger & Co Ltd London 1938–39, news ed Assoc Press of America (London) 1944–46, fndr md Mayborn Products Ltd London and Dylon International Ltd 1946–86, pres Dylon-France Safco SA, ret 1986; dir: Dylon-Japan KK, ret 1986, Dylon-Nederland NV 1946–79,

Mayborn Group Ltd 1983–86 (non-exec vice chm 1980–82); Silver medallist Soc of Dyers and Colourists; paintings and sculpture accepted by Royal Acad; FCIM, FInstD; *Publications* Selected Poems (1982), Ausgewaehlte Gedichte (1982); *Recreations* golf, painting, sculpting, writing; *Clubs* RAC, Directors'; *Style*— Luca Purbeck, Esq; ✉ 14 Langford Place, St John's Wood, London NW8 0LL (☎ 0171 624 9492)

PURCELL, Roger Bernard Allan; s of Bernard George Purcell (d 1982), of Leatherhead, and Hazel Cecily, *née* Roseberry; *b* 27 April 1945; *Educ* Shrewsbury, Pembroke Coll Cambridge (MA); *Career* CA; Binder Hamlyn 1966–72, First Investors and Savers 1972–74, Save & Prosper Gp 1974–86; dir: County Securities 1986–87, Securities and Investmts Bd 1987–; FCA 1969; *Recreations* walking, jogging, bridge, singing; *Style*— Roger Purcell, Esq; ✉ 202 Old Brompton Rd, London SW5 (☎ 0171 370 3028); Securities and Investments Board, Gavrelle House, 2–14 Bunhill Row, London EC1 (☎ 0171 638 1240, fax 0171 382 5900)

PURCHAS, Christopher Patrick Brooks; QC (1990); s of The Rt Hon Sir Francis Purchas, *qv*, and Patricia Mona Kathleen, *née* Milburn; bro of Robin Purchas, QC, *qv*; *b* 20 June 1943; *Educ* Marlborough, Trinity Coll Cambridge; *m* 7 Dec 1974 (m dis 1995), Bronwen Victoria Mary, da of Lt-Col Charles Peter Vaughan, DSO, DL (d 1975); 2 da (Léonie Melissa b 2 Aug 1978, Domino Octavia b 5 April 1983); *Career* called to the Bar Inner Temple 1966; recorder of the Crown Ct 1986–, bencher Inner Temple 1995; *Recreations* golf, tennis, shooting; *Style*— Christopher Purchas, Esq, QC; ✉ 2 Crown Office Row, Temple London EC4 (☎ 0171 797 8100, fax 0171 797 8101)

PURCHAS, Rt Hon Sir Francis Brooks; kt (1974), PC (1982); s of late Capt Francis Purchas; *b* 19 June 1919; *Educ* Summerfields Sch Oxford, Marlborough, Trinity Coll Cambridge; *m* 1942, Patricia Mona Kathleen, *née* Milburn; 2 s (Christopher Patrick Brooks Purchas, QC, *qv*, Robin Michael Purchas, QC, *qv*); *Career* called to the Bar Inner Temple 1948, QC 1965, cmmr Central Criminal Ct 1970–71, bencher 1972, recorder 1969–72 (hon recorder of Canterbury 1972–74), ldr SE Circuit 1972–74, High Court judge (Family Div) 1974–82, presiding judge SE Circuit 1977–82, a Lord Justice of Appeal 1982–93; judicial memb City Disputes Panel 1994–, dep appeal cmmr Personal Investments Authy 1994–; Liveryman Worshipful Co of Broderers; *Recreations* shooting, golf, fishing; *Clubs* Boodle's, Hawks (Cambridge); *Style*— The Rt Hon Sir Francis Purchas; ✉ Parkhurst House, nr Haslemere, Surrey GU27 3BY (☎ 01428 707280); 1 Temple Gardens, Temple, London EC4Y 9BB (☎ 0171 353 5124)

PURCHAS, Robin Michael; QC (1987); s of The Rt Hon Sir Francis Purchas, *qv*, and Patricia Mona Kathleen, *née* Milburn; bro of Christopher Purchas, QC, *qv*; *b* 12 June 1946; *Educ* Marlborough, Trinity Coll Cambridge (MA); *m* 3 Sept 1970, (Denise) Anne Kerr, da of Capt David Finlay, RN; 1 s (James Alexander Francis b 27 Sept 1973), 1 da (Charlotte Robin b 3 Nov 1975); *Career* called to the Bar Inner Temple 1968, recorder of the Crown Ct 1989–, bencher 1996; *Recreations* tennis, golf, fishing, skiing, opera, theatre, shooting; *Clubs* Queen's, Lansdowne, Boodle's; *Style*— Robin Purchas, Esq, QC; ✉ 2 Harcourt Buildings, Temple, London EC4 (☎ 0171 353 8415, fax 0171 353 7622)

PURCHASE, Kenneth; MP (Lab) Wolverhampton North East (majority 3,939); s of late Albert Purchase, and late Rebecca Purchase; *b* 8 Jan 1939; *Educ* Springfield Secdy Modern, Wolverhampton Poly (BA); *m* 1960, Brenda, *née* Sanders; *Career* apprentice toolmaker foundry indust 1956–60, experimental component engr aerospace indust 1960–68, toolroom machinist British Leyland 1968–76, in Property Div Telford Devpt Corp 1977–80, housing mangr Housing Dept Walsall Met BC 1981–82, business devpt advsr Black Country Devpt Agency 1982–92, MP (Lab, Co-op Pty sponsored) Wolverhampton NE 1992– (also contested 1987); memb Trade & Industry Select Ctee 1995–; chm PLP Backbench Trade & Industry Ctee 1993–; jt chm Commons Export Gp; cncllr: Wolverhampton County BC 1970–74, Wolverhampton MBC 1973–90; memb: Wolverhampton DHA 1985–87 and 1988–90, Wolverhampton Community Health Cncl 1990–96, DSS Benefits Tbnl, Wolverhampton and Dist Manpower Bd; *Recreations* jazz, swimming; *Style*— Ken Purchase, Esq, MP; ✉ House of Commons, London SW1A 0AA

PURDEN, Roma Laurette (Laurie); MBE (1973); da of George Cecil Arnold Purden (d 1964), and Constance Mary Sheppard (d 1952); *b* 30 Sept 1928; *Educ* Harecroft Sch Tunbridge Wells; *m* 1957, John Keith Kotch (d 1979), s of Harold James Kotch, OBE (d 1962); 2 da (Emma, Sophie); *Career* asst ed Home Notes 1951–52 (fiction ed 1948–51), asst ed Woman's Own 1952, sr asst ed Girl 1952–54; ed: Housewife 1954–57, Home 1957–62, House Beautiful 1963–65, Good Housekeeping 1965–73; ed-in-chief: Good Housekeeping and Womancraft 1973–77, Woman's Journal 1978–88 (Periodical Publishers Assoc Consumer Magazine of the Year award 1985), Woman & Home 1982–83; dir Brickfield Pubns Ltd 1978–80; Magazine Editor of the Year 1979 (Br Soc of Magazine Editors); *Style*— Laurie Purden, MBE; ✉ 174 Pavilion Rd, London SW1X 0AW (☎ 0171 730 4021)

PURDIE, Prof David Wilkie; s of Robert Wilkie Purdie (d 1990), and Jean Wilson Purdie, of Prestwick, Scotland; *b* 13 Aug 1946; *Educ* Ayr Acad, Univ of Glasgow (MB ChB); *m* 24 June 1983, Dr Katherine Ann Purdie, da of Maj Thomas Arklay Guthrie, of Windyedge Farm, by Tibbermore, Perthshire; 1 s (Arklay b 1984), 2 da (Catriona b 1986, Mhairi-Rose b 1988); *Career* ship's surgn SS Canberra RNR 1970–72, MRC res registrar Univ of Glasgow 1973–75, registrar Queen Mother's Hosp and W Infirmary Glasgow 1975–78, lectr Univ of Dundee 1978–83, sr lectr Univ of Leeds 1983–89, hon conslt gynaecologist Royal Hull Hosps Tst 1989–, prof and dir of postgrad med educn Univ of Hull 1989–94, fndn dean Postgraduate Med Sch Univ of Hull 1994–95, clinical coordinator Centre for Metabolic Bone Disease Hull Royal Infirmary/Univ of Hull 1995–; memb Cncl Nat Osteoporosis Soc, chm Br Menopause Soc; author of scientific articles on osteoporosis, medical educn and menopause related subjects; FSA Scot 1981, FRCOG 1988, MD (commendation) 1990; *Recreations* classical rhetoric, golf; *Clubs* Caledonian; *Style*— Prof David W Purdie; ✉ The Old Rectory, Rowley, Little Weighton, E Yorkshire HU20 3XR (☎ 01482 875987); Centre for Metabolic Bone Disease, Hull Royal Infirmary, Kingston upon Hull (☎ 01482 328541)

PURDON, Maj-Gen Corran William Brooke; CBE (1970), MC (1945), CPM (1982); s of Maj-Gen (William) Brooke Purdon, DSO, OBE, MC, and Dorothy Myrtle, *née* Coates; *b* 4 May 1921; *Educ* Rokeby Sch Wimbledon, Campbell Coll Belfast, RMC Sandhurst; *m* 28 July 1945, (Maureen) Patricia, da of Maj James Francis Petrie (d 1952), and Betty, *née* Dundas (d 1984); 2 s (Patrick b 1947, Timothy b 1949), 1 da (Angela (Mme Zerrouck) b 1959); *Career* cmmnd Royal Ulster Rifles 1939, Army Commandos, France and Germany 1940–45 (wounded, MC), Palestine Emergency 1945–46, Egypt 1949–51, Malayan Emergency 1956–58, Cyprus Emergency 1958; CO 1 Bn Royal Ulster Rifles, BAOR and Borneo War 1962–65, GSO1 and chief instr Sch of Inf Warminster 1965–67, Cdr Sultan's Armed Forces Sultanate of Oman and Dir of Ops Dhofar War 1967–70, Cmdt Sch of Inf Warminster 1970–72; GOC: NW Dist 1972–74, Near East Land Forces 1974–76, ret as Maj-Gen; dep cmmr Royal Hong Kong Police 1978–81; currently freelance mil advsr; dir: Falconstar Ltd (Mil Trg Teams) 1983–85, Defence Systems Ltd 1985–89; govr Royal Humane Soc 1984–, Hon Col Queen's Univ Belfast OTC 1975–78, pres Army Gymnastic Union 1973–76, patron Small Arms Sch Corps Old Comrades Assoc 1985–90; St John Ambulance: cdr Wiltshire 1981–83, memb Cncl 1981–86, pres Devizes Div 1993–; Hon Col D Co (London Irish Rifles) The London Regt 1986–93; KStJ 1983; MIMgt; Bravery Medal (Oman) 1968, Distinguished Service Medal (Oman) 1969, Commendation Medal (Oman) 1970; *Publications* List the Bugle - Reminiscences of an Irish Soldier (1993); *Recreations* physical fitness, writing, swimming, military biographies, St Nazaire Society, English bull terriers and German shepherd dogs; *Clubs* Army and Navy, Hong Kong; *Style*— Maj-Gen Corran Purdon, CBE, MC, CPM; ✉ Old Park House, Devizes, Wiltshire SN10 5JR (☎ 01380 724876);

PURDUM, Richard Curtis; s of Rufus Purdum (d 1970), of Blawenberg, New Jersey, USA, and Mary Louise, *née* Reed (d 1970); *b* 26 Feb 1943; *Educ* Princeton HS Princeton New Jersey, Chouinard Art Inst Los Angeles; *m* 6 Dec 1976, Jill, da of Ralph Thomas; *Career* served US Navy 1965–69; MGM Animation/Chuck Jones Enterprises 1965, dir and animator Richard Williams Animation London 1969–79, fndr Richard Purdum Productions 1980 (studio produces traditional character animation primarily for advertising and title sequences); awards for animated commercials incl: Grand Prix Cinema 24 Int Advertising Festival 1977, Clio Award for Craftsmanship in Animation 1977, Gold award Int Film and TV Festival of New York 1984, Br Animation Awards for best design in animation and best advertising concept in animation 1988, Br Animation Award best animated commercial 1990; *Recreations* cats; *Style*— Richard Purdum, Esq; ✉ Richard Purdum Productions, Kings Court, 2–16 Goodge St, London W1P 1FF (☎ 0171 636 5162, fax 0171 436 5628)

PURDY, Dr Martin Terence; s of Gordon Purdy, OBE (d 1976), and Margaret Mary Purdy (d 1950); *b* 22 Feb 1939; *Educ* Oakham Sch, Lancing Coll, Poly of Central London, Univ of York (MA), Univ of Birmingham (PhD); *Career* ptnr APEC Architects 1969–; formerly teaching and res positions at Birmingham Sch of Architecture and Univ of Aston; foremost designs incl: Ecumenical Centre Skelmersdale, St Bartholomew's Church and Centre East Ham, Froud Centre Manor Park; currently architect to Sheffield Cathedral; memb RIBA; *Books* Housing on Sloping Sites (with Barry Simpson, 1984), Churches and Chapels - a design and development guide (1991), author of numerous articles on church architecture; *Style*— Dr Martin Purdy; ✉ APEC Architects, The Custard Factory, Gibb Street, Digbeth, Birmingham B9 4AA (☎ 0121 683 7771)

PURDY, Quentin Alexander; s of Gordon Purdy, OBE (d 1976), and Margaret Dorothy Annie, *née* Stokes; *b* 23 Aug 1960; *Educ* Gresham's, Leicester Poly (BA), UCL (LLM), Inns of Court Sch of Law (Bar exams); *m* 3 Sept 1988, Elizabeth Audrey, da of William Alfred Hazelwood, of Paddock Wood, Kent; 2 da (Anna Elizabeth b 10 Oct 1992, Helen Sophie b 4 Oct 1994); *Career* called to the Bar Gray's Inn 1983 (A Band Tst Award); practising in Common Law Chambers London and on S Eastern circuit, cmmr for oaths, memb: Criminal Bar Assoc, Ecclesiastical Law Soc; *Recreations* reading, foreign travel, walking; *Style*— Quentin Purdy, Esq; ✉ 2 Paper Buildings, Temple, London EC4Y 7ET (☎ 0171 936 2613, fax 0171 353 9439, DX 210 CHANCERY LANE)

PURKIS, Dr Andrew James; s of Clifford Henry Purkis, OBE (d 1994), of Trevone, N Cornwall, and Mildred Jeannie, *née* Crane (d 1993); *b* 24 Jan 1949; *Educ* Highgate Sch, CCC Oxford (BA), St Antonys Coll Oxford (DPhil); *m* 18 July 1980, Jennifer Harwood, da of Francis Harwood Smith, of Willaston, Wirral, Cheshire; 1 s (Henry b 1982), 1 da (Joanna b 1980); *Career* princ NI Office 1977–80 (admin trainee 1973–76, private sec 1976– 1977), asst dir Nat Cncl for Voluntary Orgns 1986–87 (head of policy analysis 1980–84, head of policy planning 1984–86); dir Cncl for the Protection of Rural England 1987–91, public affrs sec to the Archbishop of Canterbury 1992–; dir Green Alliance; FRSA 1989; *Books* Housing and Community Care (jtly, 1982), Health in the Round (jtly, 1984); *Recreations* walking, birdwatching, surf riding, travel, theatre, music; *Style*— Dr Andrew Purkis; ✉ 38 Endlesham Rd, Balham, London SW12 8JL (☎ 0181 675 2439); Lambeth Palace, London SE1 7JV (☎ 0171 928 8282, fax 0171 261 9836)

PURLE, Charles Lambert; QC (1989); s of Robert Herbert Purle (d 1982), and Doreen Florence, *née* Button; *b* 9 Feb 1947; *Educ* King Edward VII GS Retford Notts, Univ of Nottingham (LLB), Worcester Coll Oxford (BCL); *m* 1, 1969 (m dis 1990), Lorna Barbara, da of Roy Sinclair Brown; 1 da (Sally b 12 Sept 1972), 1 s (William b 5 March 1977); m 2, 1991, Virginia Dabney Hopkins, da of Charles Peter Rylatt; 2 s (Charles Carter Lee b 19 June 1992, Harry George Hopkins b 13 Sept 1993), 1 da (Nancy Elizabeth Lambert b 5 Oct 1995); *Career* called to the Bar Gray's Inn 1970, in practice 1974–; *Recreations* opera, music, food and wine, my children; *Style*— Charles Purle, Esq, QC; ✉ 12 New Square, Ground Floor, Lincoln's Inn, London WC2A 3SW (☎ 0171 405 3808, fax 0171 831 7376)

PURNELL, Paul Oliver; QC (1982); s of Oliver Cuthbert Purnell (d 1948), and Pauline Purnell; *b* 13 July 1936; *Educ* Oratory Sch, Jesus Coll Oxford (MA); *m* 1966, Celia Consuelo Ocampo; 3 c (Elizabeth b 1968, Richard b 1971, Catherine b 1974); *Career* called to the Bar Inner Temple 1963, treasy counsel Central Criminal Court 1976–82, recorder 1984–, bencher Inner Temple 1992; *Recreations* windsurfing, gardening; *Clubs* Cavalry, Hurlingham; *Style*— Paul Purnell, Esq, QC; ✉ 1 Crown Office Row, Temple, London EC4Y 7HH (☎ 0171 797 7111)

PURSER, George Robert Gavin; s of Dr Joseph Alexander Purser (d 1968), of Charlwood, Surrey, and Constance Katherine, *née* Back; *b* 31 May 1936; *Educ* Lancing; *m* 4 June 1966, Mary-Ruth, da of Harold Lowe, of Charlwood Surrey; 2 da (Harriet b 1968, Philippa b 1969); *Career* Lt served Cyprus; sr ptnr Lawrence Graham slrs; *Recreations* freemasonry, golf, shooting, gardening; *Clubs* Athenaeum; *Style*— G R G Purser, Esq; ✉ Halesbridge House, Blanks Lane, Newdigate, Surrey RH5 5ED; Lawrence Graham, 190 Strand, London WC2R 1JN (☎ 0171 379 0000, fax 0171 379 6854, telex 22673)

PURSER, Simon Edmund Kinross; s of Lt Edmund Kinross Purser, RN (ret), of Exeter, Devon, and Pamela Mary, *née* Scanes; *b* 21 Feb 1947; *Educ* Sherborne; *Career* audit supervisor Cooper Bros 1971–73, exec Old Broad Street Securities 1973–75, dir County NatWest Ltd 1975–89, chief exec Buckland Corporate Finance Ltd 1990–96, ptnr Simon Purser & Associates 1996; non-exec dir: McCarthy & Stone plc, Pascoes Group plc, South West Assured Tenancies plc; FCA 1970; *Recreations* sailing, power boats, bridge, classic cars; *Style*— Simon Purser, Esq; ✉ 16 Monmouth Hill, Topsham, Exeter, Devon (☎ 01392 877013, fax 01392 874209)

PURSLOW, Christopher George (Chris); s of George Ellis Purslow (d 1985), and Lillian Rose, *née* Embrey; *b* 27 March 1946; *Educ* The High Sch Newcastle under Lyme, Univ of Bristol (BA, BArch); *m* 12 Aug 1970 (m dis 1977), (Sally) Louise, da of Dr Carl Basch, of South Orange, New Jersey; *Career* architect; Courtaulds Ltd Coventry 1967–68, Tarmac Ltd Wolverhampton 1968–69, Philip Johnson (Architect) NY 1969–72, Rice/Roberts (Architects) London 1972–74, London Borough of Islington 1974–88 (borough architect 1983–88), dir of architecture Glasgow 1988–96; RIBA, RIAS, FRSA; *Recreations* theatre, music, architecture, skiing and making waves; *Style*— Chris Purslow, Esq; ✉ Rosslyn House, 1a Victoria Circus, Glasgow G12 9LH (☎ 0141 334 8162); 20 Trongate, Glasgow G1 6EY (☎ 0141 227 5379, fax 0141 227 5551)

PURTON, Peter John; *b* 18 July 1933; *Educ* Aldwickbury, Aldenham; *m* 6 Sept 1958, Mary, da of Lawrence Fone, of Chipperfield, Herts; 2 s (William b 1962, Thomas b 1965), 1 da (Catherine b 1960); *Career* 3 Regt RHA 2 Lt Germany 1951–53, 290 (City of London) Field Regt RATA, Capt UK 1953–60; admitted slr 1958; Norton Rose: joined 1953, ptnr 1961–92, conslt 1992–94; memb Cncl Law Soc 1969–86, dep pres Family Welfare Assoc 1990– (chm 1983–90), chm Wine Standards Bd of Vinters Co 1993– (memb 1990–); memb Bd of Govrs Aldenham Sch 1981–94; Liveryman Worshipful Co of Tallow Chandlers 1983, Master Worshipful Co of Slrs 1983–84; memb: American Bar Assoc, Int Bar Assoc, Anglo-American Real Property Institute; FRSA, LMRTPI; *Books* The Organisation and Management of a Solicitors Practice (gen ed, 1979), Butterworths Planning Law and Practice (jt gen ed, 1990), Cordery on Solicitors (conslt ed, 1995); *Recreations* swimming, shooting, stalking, walking, heritage, jigsaw puzzles and family; *Clubs* Union Soc of

Westminster, Special Forces; *Style*— Peter Purton, Esq; ✉ Bodicote Mill, Bodicote, Nr Banbury, Oxon OX15 4DR (☎ 01295 251239, fax 01295 251269)

PURVES, Elizabeth Mary (Libby); da of James Grant Purves, CMG (d 1984), of Suffolk, and Mary, *née* Tinsley; *b* 2 Feb 1950; *Educ* Sacred Heart Tunbridge Wells, St Anne's Coll Oxford; *m* 1980, Paul Heiney, the broadcaster, s of Norbert Wisniewski (d 1970), of Sheffield; 1 s (Nicholas b 1982), 1 da (Rose b 1984); *Career* journalist and broadcaster; presenter: Radio 4 Today, Midweek; radio documentaries incl: Street Gospel, Holy Bones, Seven about Seven; *Books* Britain at Play (1982), Adventures Under Sail (1982), Sailing Weekend Book (with Paul Heiney, 1985), How Not To Be A Perfect Mother (1986), One Summer's Grace (1989), How Not to Raise a Perfect Child (1991), How Not To Be The Perfect Family (1994); Novels: Casting Off (1995), A Long Walk in Wintertime (1996); *Recreations* yachting, walking, writing; *Clubs* Ocean Cruising, Royal Cruising; *Style*— Ms Libby Purves; ✉ LE, 26a Rochester Square, London NW1 9SA

PURVES, (Andrew) Geoffrey; s of Maj Andrew Purves (d 1967), of High Heaton, Newcastle upon Tyne, and Blanche, *née* Lawson; *b* 12 June 1944; *Educ* Heaton GS, Univ of Durham (BA), Univ of Newcastle (BArch); *m* 12 Oct 1968, (Elizabeth) Ann, da of James Campbell Finlay, of Newcastle upon Tyne; *Career* architect; sr ptnr: Geoffrey Purves Partnership, Purves Robinson Partnership, Purves Project Management; dir: RIBA Companies Ltd, Newcastle Arch Workshop Ltd, Saunders and Purves Ltd, Purves Ltd, Geoffrey Purves and Partners (Project Management) Ltd, Clayton Development Ltd; chm Northern Architecture Centre; RIBA: chm Northumbria Branch 1981–83, chm Northern Regn 1988–89, memb Nat Cncl 1991–, hon treas 1995–; memb Cncl ARCUK; Freeman City of London 1993, memb Worshipful Co of Chartered Architects 1993; RIBA, FRIAS, FRSA; *Recreations* sailing; *Clubs* Clyde Cruising; *Style*— Geoffrey Purves, Esq; ✉ Hawthorn House, Kirkwhelpington, Northumberland NE19 2RT (☎ and fax 01830 540376); Geoffrey Purves Partnership, 8 North Terrace, Newcastle upon Tyne NE2 4AD (☎ 0191 232 0424, fax 0191 232 8131)

PURVES, Peter John; s of (John) Kenneth Purves (d 1987), of Swanage, Dorset, and Florence, *née* Patton (d 1976); *b* 10 Feb 1939; *Educ* Arnold Sch Blackpool, Alsager Teachers Training Coll (DipEd); *m* 1, 29 Sept 1962 (m dis 1981), Gillian Diane Emmett; 1 s (Matthew b 1963), 1 adopted da (Lisa b 1963); m 2, 5 Feb 1982, Kathryn Lesley Evans; *Career* producer, writer, director, actor and presenter; began in repertory theatre Barrow in Furness 1961–63, London Theatre and TV 1963–65; md Purves Wickes Video Projects Ltd 1984–; specialist presenters trainer BBC Elstree 1993–; pres: Rugby Animal Tst, Radio Nene Valley 1996; patron Southern Newfoundland Activity Gp; *Theatre* incl: various pantomimes 1978–, Once in a Lifetime (Blackpool) 1981, prodr Bobby Davro's Not in Front of the Children 1993; *Television* BBC incl: Dr Who 1965–66, Blue Peter 1967–78, Special Assignments 1976–79, Crufts Dog Show 1976–, We're Going Places 1978–80, Stopwatch 1978–81, Kickstart 1978–92, darts presenter 1979–84, Ten Glorious Years 1989, Superdogs 1990–93, Crimewatch Midlands 1989–91; other credits incl: Makers 1983–84, Work Out (both HTV) 1985, Babble (Channel 4) 1985–87; *Radio* presenter BBC Radio Northampton 1995–; *Books* Tess, The Story of a Guide Dog (1980); *Clubs* Vaudeville Golf Soc; *Style*— Peter Purves, Esq; ✉ c/o Arlington Enterprises, 1–3 Charlotte Street, London W1P 1HD (☎ 0171 580 0702)

PURVES, Thomas Finlayson Grant (Tom); s of Thomas Finlayson Purves (d 1968), and Christine Home Grant (d 1983); *b* 25 Nov 1948; *Educ* Daniel Stewart's Coll Edinburgh; *m* 10 July 1976, Hilde, da of Ornulf Boye Hansen, of Oslo, Norway; 1 s (Thomas Alexander), 1 da (Christine Ragnhild); *Career* Rolls Royce: student engrg apprentice (Car Div Crewe) 1967–70, various positions Rolls Royce Motors at home and later export sales, joined Euro Distribution Office Lausanne 1979, Kuwait Office 1979 (area mangr ME and Africa), returned to Lausanne 1981 (sales mangr Europe, ME and Africa), returned to UK as dir sales ops 1983; md BMW (GB) Ltd 1990–96 (joined as sales dir UK 1985), md Sales and Mktg Rover Group Ltd 1996–; *Recreations* golf, music, family; *Clubs* RAC; *Style*— Tom Purves, Esq; ✉ Rover Group Ltd, International HQ, Warwick Technology Park, Warwick CV34 6RG (☎ 01926 482000)

PURVES, Sir William; kt (1993), CBE (1988), DSO (1951); s of Andrew Purves (d 1945), and Ida Purves; *b* 27 Dec 1931; *Educ* Kelso HS; *m* 1958 (m dis 1988), Diana Troutbeck, da of Nicholas Gosselin Pepp Richardson (d 1944); 2 s, 2 da; m 2, 9 Feb 1989, Rebecca Jane, *née* Lewellen; *Career* served Cwlth Division Korea; formerly with National Bank of Scotland (now Royal Bank of Scotland); Hongkong and Shanghai Bank: Germany, Singapore, Sri Lanka, mangr Japan, chief accountant Hong Kong, gen mangr international 1979–82, exec dir banking 1982–84, dep chm 1984–86, dep chm and chief exec 1986, chm The Hongkong and Shanghai Banking Corporation Limited 1986–92 (now dir), chm HSBC Holdings plc 1990– (also chief exec 1990–92), chm Midland Bank plc 1993– (dir 1987–93), chm The British Bank of the Middle East, dir Marine Midland Bank; non-exec dir: Shell Transport and Trading Co plc 1993–, East Asiatic Company Ltd A/S 1995–; pres Int Monetary Conf Toronto 1992; vice pres Chartered Inst of Bankers; Hon DUniv: Stirling, Sheffield, Strathclyde, Hong Kong; Dr (hc) Hong Kong Poly; FCIB, FCIB (Scotland); *Recreations* golf; *Clubs* Hong Kong, Hong Kong Jockey (hon steward), Hong Kong Golf, New (Edinburgh), RAC, East India; *Style*— Sir William Purves, CBE, DSO; ✉ HSBC Holdings plc, 10 Lower Thames Street, London EC3R 6AE (☎ 0171 260 0012, fax 0171 260 6686)

PURVIS, Christopher Thomas Bremner; s of Dr Victor Bremner Purvis (d 1995), and Joanna Isabel, *née* Gibbs (d 1995); *b* 15 April 1951; *Educ* Bradfield Coll, Keble Coll Oxford (MA); *m* 21 June 1986, Phillida Anne, *née* Seaward; 1 s (Lucian Annesley Bremner b 31 May 1992), 3 da (Kerensa Toura Isabel b 26 March 1988, Xenobe Eva Wendela b 8 March 1990, Ella Blanche Honor b 27 Aug 1993); *Career* SBC Warburg (formerly S G Warburg & Co Ltd): joined 1974, dir Warburg Investment Management International Ltd 1980, dir S G Warburg & Co Ltd 1983, mangr Tokyo office 1982–87 and 1989–92, md SBC Warburg 1995–; dir UK-Japan High Technol Indust Forum 1994–; memb: Ctee Tokyo Stock Exchange Membership 1990–92, Ctee Br Invisibles Japan 1993–, Cncl Japan Soc 1994–; *Recreations* opera, wine, reading; *Clubs* Oriental; *Style*— Christopher Purvis, Esq; ✉ 19 Norland Square, London W11 4PU (☎ 0171 221 6985); SBC Warburg, 1 Finsbury Avenue, London EC2M 2PA (☎ 0171 606 1066)

PURVIS, John Robert; CBE (1990); s of Lt-Col Robert William Berry Purvis, MC; *b* 6 July 1938; *Educ* Cargilfield Barnton Edinburgh, Glenalmond Coll Perths, St Salvator's Coll, Univ of St Andrews; *m* 1962, Louise S Durham; 1 s, 2 da; *Career* md Gilmerton Mgmnt Servs Ltd 1973–92, managing ptnr Purvis & Co 1986–; dir: James River (UK) Holdings Ltd 1988–95, Edgar Astaire & Co Ltd 1993–94, Johnson NV 1994–95, Johnson Fry European Utilities Trust Plc 1994–, Crown Vantage Ltd 1995–, Curtis Fine Papers Ltd 1995–; MEP (EDG) Mid Scotland and Fife 1979–84; memb: Scottish Landowners' Fedn Taxation Ctee 1978–, IBA London (chm for Scotland) 1985–89, Scottish Advsy Ctee on Telecommunications 1990–; chm SCUA Econ Ctee 1986–, vice pres Scottish Cons & Unionist Assoc 1987–89; FInstD; *Clubs* Cavalry and Guards', Farmers', New (Edinburgh), Royal and Ancient (St Andrews); *Style*— John Purvis, Esq, CBE; ✉ Gilmerton, Dunino, St Andrews, Fife KY16 8NB (☎ 01334 473275)

PURVIS, Brig Richard Hopkins (Dick); CBE; s of Albert Hopkins Purvis (d 1968), and Mabel Hope, *née* Fendick (d 1931); *b* 16 Dec 1920; *Educ* Aldenham; *m* 2 Oct 1948, Jean (d 1991), da of William Douglas Walker (d 1957); 2 s (Nicholas Hopkins b 1952, Paul Richard b 1956); *Career* trainee chartered surveyor 1937–39; memb HAC 1938–40, cmmnd Royal Regt of Artillery 1940, Royal Artillery pilot Air Observation Post 654 Sqdn RAF 1942–44, ME Staff Coll 1944, Royal Naval Staff Coll 1957, CO 1963–65, Cmdt Sch of Artillery Manorbier 1969–70, Def Sales Orgns MOD 1970–75; fndr Def Mfrs Assoc of GB 1976 (dir gen 1976–87, vice pres 1987); pres Guildford Branch Royal Artillery Assoc; Freeman City of London 1947, Liveryman Worshipful Co of Painters and Stainers 1947–88; *Clubs* Army and Navy; *Style*— Brig Richard H Purvis, CBE; ✉ c/o Army and Navy Club, 36 Pall Mall, London SW1Y 5JN

PURVIS, Stewart Peter; s of Peter Purvis, and Lydia, *née* Stewart; *b* 28 Oct 1947; *Educ* Dulwich, Univ of Exeter (BA); *m* 2 Sept 1972 (m dis 1993), Mary, da of Arthur Presnail; 1 da (Helen b 1974); partner, Jacqui Marson; 1 s (Tom b 1994); *Career* formerly presenter Harlech TV, news trainee BBC 1969; ITN: journalist 1972, prog ed News at Ten 1980–83, ed Channel Four News 1983, dep ed ITN 1983–89, ed ITN 1989–91, editor-in-chief 1991–95, chief exec 1995–; RTS awards for: The Pope in Poland 1979, Return of the Canberra 1982; Bdcasting Press Guild Award for Best News or Current Events Prog (Channel Four News) 1984, BAFTA award for Best News or Outside Broadcast (Channel Four News) 1987 and 1988; FRTS; *Style*— Stewart Purvis, Esq; ✉ Independent Television News Ltd, 200 Gray's Inn Road, London WC1X 8XZ (☎ 0171 833 3000)

PUTTERGILL, Graham Fraser; s of Henry William Puttergill (d 1984), of Gonubie, SA, and Elizabeth Blanche, *née* McClelland (d 1991); *b* 20 March 1949; *Educ* St Patrick's Coll Port Elizabeth SA; *m* 7 Aug 1976, Susan Jennifer, da of Victor James Wilkinson, of Dorchester; 2 s (Miles b 1982, David b 1987), 2 da (Robyn b 1985, Lucy b 1989); *Career* 1 Lt Cape Town Highlanders 1967–68; chm HSBC Gibbs Benefit Consultants Ltd 1982– (md 1977–82), exec chm HSBC Gibbs Ltd 1985–, dep chm HSBC Insurance Holdings Ltd 1993–; ACII 1973, FPMI 1983; *Recreations* family, golf, tennis; *Clubs* City, Wisley Golf; *Style*— Graham Puttergill, Esq; ✉ Kisdon, Puers Lane, Jordans, Bucks HP9 2TE; HSBC Gibbs Ltd, Bishops Court, 27–33 Artillery Lane, London E1 7LP (☎ 0171 247 5433, fax 0171 377 2139)

PUTTNAM, Sir David Terence; kt (1995), CBE (1983); s of Capt Leonard Arthur Puttnam, RA (d 1981), of Winchmore Hill, and Marie Beatrice, *née* Goldman; *b* 25 Feb 1941; *Educ* Minchenden GS London; *m* 22 Sept 1961, Patricia Mary, da of Maj John Frederick Jones, of Folkestone, Kent; 1 s (Alexander David b 5 April 1966), 1 da (Deborah Jane (m Loyd Grossman, *qv*) b 25 Jan 1962); *Career* film prodr; chief exec Enigma Productions Ltd 1978–; chm Nat Film & TV Sch Ltd; dir: Anglia TV Group plc, Chrysalis Group until 1996; chm and chief exec offr Columbia Pictures 1986–88; pres Cncl for Protection of Rural England 1985–92; tstee: Tate Gallery 1985–92, National Energy Foundation, Landscape Fndn; vice pres BAFTA, memb Technol Foresight Ctee DTI; LWT London Lecture 1994; Hon LLD Bristol 1983, Hon DLitt Leicester 1986, Hon LittD Leeds 1992, hon fell Manchester Univ; Hon DLitt: Univ of Bradford 1993, Humberside 1996, Sunderland 1996; Officieur dans l'Ordre des Arts et des Lettres (France) 1991; visiting prof Film Dept Univ of Bristol 1985–; FRGS, FRSA, FRPS; *Awards* Special Jury Prize (Cannes) for The Duellists 1977, two Academy Awards and four Br Academy Awards for Midnight Express 1978, four Acadamy Awards (incl Best Film) and three Br Academy Awards (incl Best Film) for Chariots of Fire 1981, three Academy Awards and eight Br Academy Awards (incl Best Film) for The Killing Fields 1985, Palme D'Or for The Mission 1986, Michael Balcon Award for outstanding contrib to the Br film industry Br Academy Awards 1982; *Books* The Third Age of Broadcasting (co-author, 1982), Rural England (co-author, 1988); *Recreations* fishing, reading; *Clubs* MCC, Chelsea Arts; *Style*— Sir David Puttnam, CBE; ✉ Enigma Productions, 13–15 Queen's Gate Place Mews, London SW7 5BG (☎ 0171 581 0238, fax 0171 584 1799)

PUXON, Dr (Christine) Margaret; QC (1982); da of Reginald Wood Hale (d 1960), of Bournemouth, and Clara Lilian, *née* Poulton (d 1947); *b* 25 July 1915; *Educ* Abbey Sch Malvern Wells, Univ of Birmingham (MRCS, LRCP, MB ChB), MD(Obst), MRCOG; *m* 1, Sept 1937, Ralph Weddell; 1 da (Imogen Margaret b 1 Dec 1938), 1 s (Adrian John Goldsbrough b 8 Nov 1941); m 2, 1945, Francis Edward Mortimer Puxon; 1 s (Paul b 23 Dec 1948); m 3, 15 Sept 1955, Frederick Morris Williams (d 6 Feb 1986); *Career* house surgn appts 1941–42, gynaecological registrar Queen Elizabeth Hosp Birmingham 1942–43, cnslt to Essex CC 1945–48; called to the Bar Inner Temple 1954, practised in criminal, family and civil work SE Circuit, head of East Anglian Chambers 1978–85, recorder 1983–89, dep circuit judge 1970–89; currently non-practising barr actg as medical legal conslt; memb Genetic Manipulation Advsy Gp, Privy Cncl appointed memb of Cncl of Royal Pharmaceutical Soc 1975–89, memb Clinical Res Ethics Ctee RCGP 1985–90, chm Ethics Ctee Assisted Reproducton Unit Lister Hosp 1987–, chm Soc of Doctors in Law; Liveryman Worshipful Soc of Apothecaries; hon memb Royal Pharmaceutical Soc; FRSM, FRCOG 1976; *Books* The Family and the Law (Penguin, 1972), numerous contribs to medical jls and text books, consulting ed Medical Law Reports; *Recreations* opera, travel, gardens; *Style*— Dr Margaret Puxon, QC; ✉ 19 Clarence Gate Gardens, Glentworth Street, London NW1 6AY (☎ 0171 723 7922, fax 0171 258 1038)

PYANT, Paul; s of Leonard Vincent Pyant (d 1976), of Croydon, and Jean Pheobe, *née* Frampton; *b* 22 July 1953; *Educ* Haling Manor High Croydon, RADA (1973 Charles Killic Award); *Career* lighting designer; prodn electrics and asst lighting mangr Glyndebourne Opera 1974–87, freelance 1988–; memb: Labour Party, CND, Nat Tst, Woodland Tst, Brit Actors Equity 1975, Assoc of Lighting Designers, United Artists 829 (USA) 1994; *Theatre* RNT (dir Nicholas Hytner, *qv*) incl: Wind in the Willows 1990, The Madness of George III 1991, Carousel 1992; Arcadia (dir Trevor Nunn, *qv*) 1993; Donmar Warehouse (dir Sam Mendes, *qv*) incl: Assassins 1992, Cabaret 1993, Company 1995; other credits incl: Orpheus Descending (London and New York (Broadway debut)) 1988, The Tempest (RSC) 1993; *Opera* incl: King Priam (Kent Opera) 1984, Xerxes (ENO) 1985, Lady Macbeth of Mtsensk (ENO) 1987, Death in Venice (Glyndebourne) 1990, Le Nozze De Figaro (Wien Festival) 1991, Gawain (ROH) 1991, Fedora (Wien Staatsoper debut) 1994, Stiffelio (La Scala debut) 1995, Pique Dame (Metropolitan Opera debut) 1995; *Awards* winner: Olivier Award for Lighting Designer of the Year (for Wind in the Willows) 1990, New York Critics' Award (for Carousel) 1994; numerous nominations incl: Tony Award for Best Lighting (Orpheus Descending) 1988; *Recreations* steam locomotives, walking; *Clubs* Friends of Nat Railway Museum, Great Western Soc, The Severn Valley Railway; *Style*— Paul Pyant, Esq; ✉ c/o Jeffrey Campbell Management, 18 Queen Annes Street, London W1M 0HB (☎ 0171 637 0993, fax 0171 637 0985)

PYBUS, William Michael; s of Sydney James Pybus (d 1972), and Evelyn Mary, *née* Wood (d 1976); *b* 7 May 1923; *Educ* Bedford Sch, New Coll Oxford (MA); *m* 12 Sept 1959, Elizabeth Janet, da of Peter Percy Whitley (ka 1942); 2 s (Peter b 1961, Charles b 1965), 2 da (Sarah b 1962, Elizabeth b 1967); *Career* cmmnd 1 King's Dragoon Gds 1942, attached II Hussars Normandy (wounded), Egypt and ME; admitted slr 1950; ptnr Herbert Oppenheimer Nathan & Vandyk 1953–88; chm: AAH Holdings plc 1968–92, British Fuel Co 1968–88, Inter-Continental Fuels Ltd 1975–88, Overseas Coal Developments Ltd 1979–88, Leigh Interests plc 1982–89, British Rail (London Midland) 1977–89 (pt/t memb BR Midlands and W Bd 1975–77); dir: Siebe plc 1972– (chm 1980–90), National Westminster Bank plc (Outer London Region) 1977–88, Cornhill Insurance plc 1977–96, Bradford & Bingley Building Society 1983–95; dep chm R Mansell Ltd 1980–85, chm Homeowners Friendly Society Ltd 1991–96 (dir 1980–96); conslt Denton Hall Burgin & Warrens (now Denton Hall) 1988–94; dir Coal Trade Benevolent Assoc 1969–, pres Coal Indust Soc 1976–81 (vice pres 1981–); chm Ashdown House Sch Tst Ltd 1975–89, chm City Univ Club 1975–76, govr Harpur Tst 1979–87;

Master Worshipful Co of Pattenmakers 1972–73, Master Worshipful Co of Fuellers 1994–95; CIMgt, FCIM, FRSA; *Recreations* fishing; *Clubs* Cavalry and Guards', MCC, RAC, Yorkshire CCC; *Style—* William M Pybus, Esq

PYE, Prof (John) David; s of Wilfred Frank Pye (d 1972), of Mansfield, Notts, and Gwenllian, *née* Davies (d 1993); *b* 14 May 1932; *Educ* Queen Elizabeth's GS for Boys Mansfield, UCW Aberystwyth (BSc), Bedford Coll for Women Univ of London (PhD); *m* 27 Dec 1958, Ade Pye, sr lectr in audiology UCL, da of August Kuku, and Olga Kuku, of Valga, Estonia; *Career* Univ of London: res asst Inst of Laryngology and Otology 1958–64, lectr in zoology King's Coll 1964–70, reader in zoology King's Coll 1970–73, prof of zoology Queen Mary Coll 1973–91 (emeritus 1991), head Dept of Zoology and Comparative Physiology Queen Mary Coll 1977–82; fndr dir QMC Instruments Ltd 1976–89, delivered the six televised Royal Instn Christmas Lectures 1985–86 and two Friday Evening Discourses 1979 and 1983, co-organiser (with wife), RI Discussion Evenings (RIDE) 1994–; memb IEE Professional Gp Ctee E15 (Radar, Sonar, Navigation and Avionics) 1983–86; memb Editorial Bds: Zoological Soc 1972–77, 1978–83 and 1985–90, Journal of Experimental Biology 1974–78, Journal of Comparative Physiology 1978–96, Bioacoustics 1987–; memb: Linnean Soc (ed Zoological Journal 1981–85, editorial sec 1985–91, vice pres 1987–90), Zoological Soc 1957, Soc for Experimental Biology 1958, Assoc for Study of Animal Behaviour 1963, Mammal Soc 1964, Royal Hort Soc 1988; *Books* Bats (1968), Ultrasonic Communication by Animals (with G D Sales, 1974), Sound Reception in Mammals (ed with R J Bench and A Pye, 1975); *Recreations* brewing, baking, DIY, arts, travel; *Style—* Prof David Pye; ✉ 24 St Mary's Ave, Finchley, London N3 1SN (☎ 0181 346 6869); School of Biological Sciences, Queen Mary and Westfield College, Mile End Road, London E1 4NS (☎ 0171 775 3293)

PYE, Brig Hugh William Kellow; s of Brig Randall Thomas Kellow Pye, DSO, OBE, of Horsted Keynes, W Sussex, and Peggy Muriel, *née* Sagar-Musgrave-Brooksbank; *b* 23 May 1938; *Educ* Wellington Coll, RMA Sandhurst; *m* 8 June 1968, Mary Ann, da of Cdr The Hon David Edwardes, DSC, RN (d 1983), of Wincanton, Somerset; 1 s (Robert Alec Kellow b 1970), 1 da (Victoria Ann b 1973); *Career* cmmnd 12 Royal Lancers (POW) 1958, Cdr Berlin Armd Sqdn 1968, Staff Coll Camberley 1971, GSO2 INT JSIS Hong Kong 1972, Armed Forces Staff Coll Norfolk Virginia USA 1976, cmdg 9/12 Royal Lancers (POW) 1977–79 (despatches), AMS MS 4 1979–82, dep Chief of Staff (DCOS) and Cdr Br Contingent UNFICYP 1982–84, Col Coordination Staff Coll Camberley 1984–85, project mangr, Dep Cdr and advsr Oman Cmd and Staff Coll 1986–89, Dep Cdr SW dist and Cdr Br Element AMF (L) 1990–92, ret; Hon Col: Leicestershire and Derbyshire Yeo (PAO) TA 1992–, 9/12 Royal Lancers (POW) 1995–; treas Soc of Merchant Venturers Bristol 1992–; govr: Colston's Collegiate Sch 1992– (chm 1994–), Colston's Girls' Sch 1992–; tstee Gtr Bristol Fndn 1993–; awarded Sultan of Oman's Commendation medal 1989; *Recreations* shooting, fishing; *Clubs* Cavalry and Guards', Clifton (Bristol); *Style—* Brigadier Hugh Pye; ✉ Tuxwell Farm, Spaxton, Bridgwater, Somerset TA5 1DF (☎ 01278 671833)

PYE, Nigel Lindsay; s of Herbert Francis Pye, Cuckfield, Sussex, and Doreen Mary, *née* Star; *b* 1 May 1945; *Educ* Whitgift Sch Croydon; *m* 1, 1972 (m dis 1985), Frances Jean Fermor; 1 s (Matthew Francis b 1976), 1 da (Alexandra Claire b 1978); m 2, 1988, Hilary, da of John Thomas Carroll; *Career* articled clerk James Edwards Dangerfield & Co London 1964–69, assigned to Alexander Grant & Co Chicago 1970–71, London office Tansley Witt & Co (successor firm of James Edwards Dangerfield & Co) 1971–79 (ptnr 1976); Arthur Andersen: ptnr London office 1979–85, managing ptnr Cambridge office 1985–91, managing ptnr Manchester office 1991–96, ptnr St Albans office 1996–; chm Croydon Soc of Chartered Accountants 1984–85, dir S Cambridge Training and Enterprise Cncl 1989–91, memb Cncl CBI 1989–91, dir Cambridge Arts Theatre 1991; ACA 1969; *Recreations* squash, country walking, travel, theatre; *Clubs* St James's (Manchester); *Style—* Nigel Pye, Esq; ✉ Arthur Andersen, 3 Victoria Square, Victoria Street, St Albans, Herts AL1 3TF (☎ 01727 815570, fax 01727 815535)

PYE, William Burns; s of Sir David Pye, CB, FRS (d 1959), of Elstead, Surrey, and Virginia Frances, *née* Kennedy; *b* 16 July 1938; *Educ* Charterhouse, Wimbledon Sch of Art, Sch of Sculpture RCA; *m* 1963, Susan Marsh; 1 s (Tristram b 18 March 1966), 2 da (Rebecca Jane b 2 June 1968, Alexandra Virginia b 4 Aug 1973); *Career* sculptor; visiting prof California State Univ 1975–76; made films Reflections 1971, From Scrap to Sculpture 1971; FRBS, Hon FRIBA, *Cmmns and Sculptures on Public Sites* Zemran (South Bank London), King's Cross House Cmmn (Pentonville Rd London), water sculpture (Aston Univ Campus), mural at Vauxhall railway stn, Slipstream and Jetstream water sculptures (Gatwick North Terminal), Curlicue (Greenland Dock London Docklands), Alpheus (Gatwick Forte Crest Hotel), Chalice (Fountain Square, 123 Buckingham Palace Rd), Orchid (The Peacocks Woking), Aventino (Mercury House London), Epidavros (Dolby Laboratories Wootton Bassett Wilts), Cristos (St Christopher's Place London), Flyover (M25 Clacket Lane Service Station), Downpour (Br Embassy Muskat Oman), Derby Cascade (Market Square Derby), Colisée Pyramid (Le Colisée St Ouen Paris), Jefferson (Louisville Kentucky), Mesa (Phoenix Arizona), Eastgate (Cincinatti Ohio), Regency (Racine Wisconsin), San-Mateo (California); *Work in Public Collections* incl: Arts Cncl of GB, Museum of Modern Art NY, Contemporary Art Soc, Royal Albert Museum Exeter, Birmingham City Art Gallery, Szepmuveszeti Museum Budapest, Graves Art Gallery Sheffield, National Museum of Wales, Utsukushi-ga-hara Open Air Museum Japan, Nat Portrait Gallery; *Solo Exhibitions* incl: Redfern Gallery London 1966, 1969, 1973 and 1975, Bertha Schaefer Gallery NY 1970, Bear Lane Gallery Oxford 1972, Ikon Gallery Birmingham 1975, Morgan Thomas Gallery LA 1976, Yorkshire Sculpture Park 1978, Winchester Great Hall 1979, Welsh Touring Exhbn 1980, London Business Sch 1986, The Rotunda One Exchange Square Hong Kong 1987; *Group Exhibitions* incl: Towards Art II (Arts Cncl Gallery), Internationale der Zeichnung (Darmstadt), Middleheim 10th Biennale of Sculpture (Antwerp), British Sculptors '72 (RA), British Painting and Sculpture Today (Indianapolis Museum of Art), Royal Jubilee Exhbn of Contemporary British Sculpture (London), Budapest International Exhbn of Small Sculpture (Prix de Sculpture), British Sculpture in the 20th Century (Whitechapel Art Gallery), Welsh Sculpture Tst Inaugural Exhbn (Margam Park, Port Talbot), 6th Henry Moore Grand Prize Exhbn (Br nomination, Utsukushi-ga-hara Museum Japan), Chelsea Harbour Sculpture '93; *Awards* Prix de Sculpture Budapest In Sculpture Exhbn 1981, Vauxhall Mural Competition 1983, Peace Sculpture Competition (for Ackers Park Small Heath Birmingham) 1984, Art at Work Award Wapping Arts Tst (for Sculpture at Gatwick Airport) 1988, Assoc of Business Sponsorship of the Arts Award 1988, Royal UENO Award Japan 1989; *Recreations* playing the flute; *Style—* William Pye; ✉ 43 Hambalt Road, Clapham, London SW4 9EQ (☎ 0181 673 2318, office ☎ 0181 682 2727, office fax 0181 682 3218)

PYM, Baron (Life Peer UK 1987), of Sandy, Co Beds; Francis Leslie Pym; PC (1970), MC (1945), DL (Cambs 1973); o s of Leslie Ruthven Pym, JP, DL (d 1945), sometime MP for Monmouth and Lord Cmmr of the Treasy, and Iris Rosalind (d 1982), da of Charles Somerville Orde; *b* 13 Feb 1922; *Educ* Eton, Magdalene Coll Cambridge (hon fell); *m* 25 June 1949, Valerie Fortune, er da of Francis John Heaton Daglish; 2 s (Hon (Francis) Jonathan, *qv*, Hon Andrew Leslie), 2 da (Hon Charlotte Hazell (Hon Mrs Lightbody) b 1950, Hon Sarah Lucy (Hon Mrs Walton) b 1958); *Career* served WWII 9 Queen's Royal Lancers (despatches twice), Capt; served in African and Italian campaigns; memb Herefordshire CC 1958–62; contested (C) Rhondda 1959, MP (C) Cambs 1961–83 and SE Cambs 1983–87; parly sec to the Treasy and govt chief whip 1970–73, sec of state NI 1973–74; oppn spokesman: agric 1974–76, House of Commons affrs and devolution 1976–78, foreign and cwlth affrs 1978–79; sec of state for defence 1979–81; chllr of the Duchy of Lancaster, paymaster gen and ldr House of Commons 1981, lord pres of the Cncl and Ldr House of Commons 1981–82, Foreign and Cwlth sec 1982–83; chm: Diamond Cable Communications, St Andrew's (Ecumenical) Tst; dir: Christie Brockbank Shipton Ltd, The Landscape Fndn; memb Cncl Br Exec Serv Overseas, vice pres Register of Engrs for Disaster Relief, pres Atlantic Treaty Assoc 1985–88, chm English Speaking Union 1987–92; *Books* The Politics of Consent (1984); *Clubs* Buck's; *Style—* The Rt Hon the Lord Pym,; ✉ Everton Park, Sandy, Beds SG19 2DE (☎ 01767 681640, fax 01767 683129)

PYM, (Hon) (Francis) Jonathan; er s of Baron Pym, MC, PC (Life Peer), *qv*; does not use courtesy prefix of Hon; *b* 21 Sept 1952; *Educ* Eton, Magdalene Coll Cambridge (MA); *m* 25 June 1981, Laura Elizabeth Camille, yr da of Robin Alfred Wellesley; 2 s ((Francis) Matthew b 1984, Oliver Quintin b 1988), 1 da (Katie Camille b 1985); *Career* ptnr Travers Smith Braithwaite slrs 1984–; memb: Law Soc, City of London Law Soc, Int Bar Assoc; *Clubs* Garrick, City of London, Roehampton; *Style—* Jonathan Pym, Esq; ✉ 53 Ridgway Place, London SW19 4SP (☎ 0181 946 3583); Travers Smith Braithwaite, 10 Snow Hill, London EC1A 2AL (☎ 0171 248 9133, fax 0171 236 3728, telex 887117 TRAVER G)

PYMAN, Avril; *see:* Sokolov, Dr Avril

PYMONT, Christopher Howard; QC (1996); s of John Pymont, of Penn, Bucks, and Joan, *née* Marmoy; *b* 16 March 1956; *Educ* Marlborough (scholar), Christ Church Oxford (scholar, MA); *Career* called to the Bar Gray's Inn 1979, specialist in chancery and commercial law; *Style—* Christopher Pymont, Esq, QC; ✉ 13 Old Square, Ground Floor, Lincoln's Inn, London WC2A 3UA

PYPER, Mark Christopher Spring-Rice; s of Arthur Spring-Rice Pyper (d 1994), of Seaford, Sussex, and Rosemary Isobel, *née* Ferguson; *b* 13 Aug 1947; *Educ* Winchester, Balliol Coll Oxford, Univ of London (BA); *m* 7 April 1979, Jennifer Lindsay, da of Raymond James Gilderson (d 1975), of Seaford; 1 s (Robin Spring-Rice b 1983), 2 da (Sarah Katharine b 1986, Alice Rosemary b 1989); *Career* asst headmaster St Wilfrid's Prep Sch Seaford Sussex 1977–79 (asst master 1972–77), dep headmaster Sevenoaks Sch Kent 1988–90 (asst master then registrar 1979–88), headmaster Gordonstoun Sch 1990–; dir Sevenoaks Summer Festival 1979–90; *Clubs* MCC; *Style—* Mark Pyper, Esq; ✉ Gordonstoun School, Elgin, Moray IV30 2RF (☎ 01343 830445)

PYRAH, Malcolm John; s of late Flt-Lt Stanley Pyrah, and Joyce Evelyne, *née* Hall; *b* 26 Aug 1941; *Educ* Kingston HS Hull; *m* 22 Oct 1973, (Suzanne) Judy, da of Leigh Boulter, of Manor Farm, Queniborough, Leics; 1 da (Niki Jane b 1982); *Career* showjumper; team world Gold 1978, team Euro Gold 1979, individual Euro Silver 1981, individual world Silver 1982, team Euro Gold 1985 and 1987; trainer Br showjumping team 1992–; memb Exec Br Showjumping Assoc; *Style—* Malcolm Pyrah, Esq; ✉ Keyworths Farm, Granby, Nottingham NG13 9PS (☎ 01949 850599, fax 01949 851246, car 0385 727272)

PYTCHES, Rt Rev (George Edward) David; 6 s of Rev Thomas Arthur Pytches (d 1953), of Woodbridge, Suffolk (see Burke's Landed Gentry 1937 edn), and Eirene Mildred, *née* Welldon (d 1947); *b* 9 Jan 1931; *Educ* Old Buckenham Hall Norfolk, Framlingham Coll Suffolk, Univ of Bristol (BA), Univ of Nottingham (MPhil), Trinity Coll Bristol; *m* 8 Jan 1958, Mary, da of Albert Trevisick (d 1984), of Bishopstawton, N Devon; 4 da (Charlotte Mary (Mrs Cocksworth) b 24 Dec 1958, Deborah Jane (Mrs Wright) b 13 Dec 1961, Rebecca Anne (Mrs Hopper) b 10 July 1963, Natasha Clare (Mrs Shaw) b 18 Feb 1965); *Career* ordained: deacon 1955, priest 1956; asst curate: St Ebbe's Oxford 1955–58, Holy Trinity Wallington 1958–59; missionary priest: Chol Chol Chile 1959–62, Valparaiso Chile 1962–70 (rural dean 1966–70); asst bishop and vicar-gen Diocese of Chile Bolivia and Peru 1970–72, bishop of the Anglican Dio of Chile, Bolivia and Peru 1972–76, vicar St Andrew's Chorleywood 1977–96; dir: Kingdom Power Tst, New Wine (annual week-long christian family conf at Royal Bath and W Showground) 1989, 1990, 1991, 1992, 1993, 1994, 1995 and 1996, Soul Survivor (youth w/e at Royal Bath and W Showground) 1993, 1994, 1995 and 1996 (combined attendance 17,000); *Books* Come Holy Spirit (1985), Does God Speak Today? (1989), Some Said It Thundered (1990), New Wineskins (jtly 1991), Prophecy in the Local Church (1993), Recovering the Ground (contrib, 1995); *Recreations* travel, pottering about, collecting semi-precious stones; *Style—* The Rt Rev David Pytches; ✉ Red Tiles, Homefield Road, Chorleywood, Herts WD3 5QJ (☎ 01923 283763, fax 01923 283762)

PYTEL, Walenty; s of Wladislaw Pytel, of Bath, and Jadwiga Pytel; *b* 10 Feb 1941; *Educ* Leominster Minster Sch, Hereford Coll of Art (NDD); *m* 7 Oct 1963, Janet Mary, da of William Sidney Spencer (d 1973), of Westington Court; 1 s (Jeremy Walenty Spencer b 1964), 1 da (Victoria Catharine Mary b 1968); *Career* sculptor in steel, bronze, bone china; works incl: mural Lord Montague Beaulieu 1972, Le Perroquet Berkeley Hotel London 1973, Chanel Perfume Paris 1975, Sculpture cmmnd by MPs to commemorate Queen's Silver Jubilee New Palace Yard Westminster 1977, unicorn from HRH Princess Anne to Portuguese Govt 1979, Cwlth beasts for Sir Edward du Cann MP and Sir John Hall MP 1980, Take Off Birmingham Int Airport 1985, unicorn representing coat of arms for Lord and Lady Leigh Stoneleigh Abbey 1989, 5 vikings for Anders Wilhelmsen & Co 1996, 2 15ft cranes for Mazak Europe Machine Tools; exhibitions: Marbella 1985, New Jersey 1987, San Diego 1987, Tokyo 1987, Soc of Wildlife Artists Mall Galleries 1988 (award winner), Essen Germany 1989, Couvent de Recollets Cognac France 1992; work in various private collections; memb Soc of Br Sculptors; ARBS; *Recreations* salmon fishing, game shooting, sailing; *Style—* Walenty Pytel, Esq; ✉ Hartleton, Bromsash, Ross on Wye HR9 7SB (☎ 01989 780536), Wyebridge Interiors, Bridge Street, Hereford HR4 9DG (☎ 01432 350722, fax 01432 344076)

Q

QESKU, HE Pavli; s of Mihal Qesku (d 1985), of Elbasan, Albania, and Vasilika, *née* Gjerasi; *b* 16 June 1943; *Educ* Gen Secdy Sch Elbasan, Beijing Univ (one yr language course), Univ of Tirana; *m* 2 Sept 1973, Lidia, da of Dhimiter Daka; 1 s (Martin b 12 June 1978), 1 da (Afërdita b 14 Jan 1981); *Career* translator and ed of English pubns for state publishing house Albania 1968–75 and 1978–93, English teacher Albania 1975–78, ambass extraordinary and plenipotentiary of the Republic of Albania to the Ct of St James's 1993–; hon patron Anglo-Albanian Assoc 1993–; *Books* trans of numerous books from English to Albanian, compiler of 100,000 entry English-Albanian dictionary; *Recreations* reading and music; *Style*— HE Mr Pavli Qesku; ✉ Albanian Embassy, 4th Floor, 38 Grosvenor Gardens, London SW1W 0EB (☎ 0171 730 5709, fax 0171 730 5747)

QUALLINGTON, (Herbert) Timothy; s of Herbert Edward Quallington (d 1959), and Dorothy, *née* Smith (d 1971); *b* 2 Nov 1935; *Educ* Kent Coll Canterbury (BA), Brunel Univ (MA); *m* 16 Sept 1961, Jean Frances, da of Frank Loudonsack Barker (d 1992); 1 s ((Herbert) Philip b 20 Sept 1962), 2 da ((Brenda) Elizabeth 4 Jan 1965, Rachel Mary b 16 March 1966); *Career* Nat Serv Armament Fitter RAF 1954–57; photographer Jack Harley Ltd Cranleigh 1961–62, photographer Central Electricity Res Laboratories Leatherhead 1962–63, sr photographer and studio mangr Cncl of Industl Design (now Design Cncl) 1964–88 (photographer 1963–64), self employed commercial social and editorial photographer 1988–, lectr in photography Farnborough Coll of Technol 1988–; work published in various local and nat newspapers and magazines incl Design Magazine and Engineering Magazine, paper on The Photography of Lighting Installation presented to Illuminating Engrg Soc 1971; former external course and student assessor SIAD and external assessor for BIPP at W Surrey Coll of Art Farnham; asst Scout master and asst Rover Scout ldr 1st Oxshott Scout Gp 1957–60; FRSA 1969, FBIPP 1970, FRPS 1971, FCSD 1974; *Recreations* family, local church, interior design, gardening, caravanning and photography; *Clubs* Rotary Int (past pres local Rotary); *Style*— Timothy Quallington, Esq; ✉ 2 Woodland Grange, Cranleigh, Surrey GU6 7HY (☎ 01483 273361)

QUANT, Air Cdre John Antony (Tony); s of John Henry Quant (d 1968), and Mildred Gwenllian, *née* Jones (d 1988); *b* 19 Jan 1933; *Educ* Taunton Sch, Eltham Coll, Univ of London, Guy's Hosp (BDS, MB BS); *m* 11 Feb 1956, Valerie Kathleen, da of Ernest James Goose (d 1970); 2 da (Sarah (Mrs Allen) b 1958, Amanda (Mrs Chandler) b 1961); *Career* Nat Serv RAF 1957, perm cmmn Dental Offr 1958–90, RAF Lyneham 1957, Prince Rupert Sch Wilhelmshaven 1958, RAF Sundern 1959, RAF Gütersloh 1961, RAF Halton 1961, oral surgn PMRAF Hosp Halton 1962, RAF Hosp Nocton Hall 1962, registrar oral surgn RAF Hosp Cosford 1963, sr registrar TPH RAF Hosp Akrotiri 1965; med student Guy's 1966–70, house surgn Guy's 1971, house physician Willesborough Hosp Ashford Kent, sr registrar/conslt (oral surgery and med) RAF Hosp Wegberg 1972, conslt PM RAF Hosp Halton 1978, conslt advsr (oral surgery and med) RAF 1979–90; formerly sec and chm Defence Med Servs Post Grad Cncl Speciality Bd in Oral Surgery and Oral Med, formerly dental advsr RAF Aviation Forensic Pathology Team, chm RAF LTA 1985–88; CStJ 1987; FDSRS 1963, MRCS 1970, LRCP 1970, FBAOMS, memb Oral Surgery Club of GB; *Recreations* tennis, golf, bridge; *Clubs* RAF; *Style*— Air Cdre Tony Quant; ✉ Witsend, 54 Clay Lane, Wendover, Bucks HP22 6NS (☎ 01296 624714); The Paddocks Private Hosp, Princes Risborough, Bucks HP17 0JS (☎ 0184434 6951); BMH Rinteln, BFPO 29 (☎ 00 49 5751 701216); 8 Hohe Wanne, 31737 Rinteln, Germany (☎ 00 49 5751 76633)

QUANT, Mary (Mrs A Plunket Greene); OBE (1966); da of Jack Quant, and Mildred Quant; *b* 11 Feb 1934; *Educ* Goldsmiths' Coll of Art London; *m* 1957, Alexander Plunket Greene; 1 s; *Career* fashion designer; estab Mary Quant Gp of Cos 1955, currently co-chm Mary Quant Ltd; memb: Design Cncl 1971, Br and USA Bicentennial Liaison Ctee 1973, Advsy Cncl V & A 1976–78; hon fell Goldsmith's University 1993; winner: Maison Blanche Rex Award 1964, Sunday Times Int Award 1964, Piavola d'Oro Award 1966, Annual Design Medal Inst of Industl Artists and Designers 1966, Hall of Fame Award Br Fashion Cncl 1990; sr fell RCA 1991; FSIA 1967, RDI 1969, FRSA 1995; *Style*— Miss Mary Quant, OBE; ✉ 3 Ives Street, London SW3 2NE (☎ 0171 584 8781, fax 0171 589 9443)

QUANTRILL, Prof Malcolm William Francis; s of Arthur William Quantrill (d 1976), of Norwich, and Alice May, *née* Newstead (d 1979); *b* 25 May 1931; *Educ* City of Norwich Sch, Univ of Liverpool (BArch), Univ of Pennsylvania (MArch), Tech Univ of Wroclaw (DSc); *m* 1 (m dis 1965), Arja Irmeli Nenonen; *m* 2, 18 Dec 1971, Esther Maeve, da of James Brignell Dand (d 1982), of Chester; 2 s (Christopher b 1961, Jan b 1962), 2 da (Francesca b 1974, Alexandra b 1978); *Career* dir Architectural Assoc London 1967–69, dean Sch of Architecture North London Poly 1973–80, prof of architecture Univ of Jordan Amman 1980–83, distinguished prof of architecture Texas A & M Univ 1986–; dep ed Art International Lugano 1978–83, ed-in-chief Studies in Architecture and Culture (CASA) 1988–; Thomas Cubitt lectr 1993, Kivett lectr 1994; fndr memb The Thomas Cubitt Tst London (tstee 1977, sec 1977–80); RIBA 1961, ASCA (Assoc of Collegiate Schs of Architecture) Distinguished Prof 1990; Knight Cdr of the Order of Knights of the Finnish Lion 1988; *Books* Gotobed Dawn (1962), Gotobedlam (1964), John Gotobed Alone (1965), Ritual and Response in Architecture (1974), Monuments of Another Age (1976), On the Home Front (novel, 1977), Alvar Aalto: A Critical Study (1983), Reima Pietilä: Architecture, Context and Modernism (1985), The Environmental Memory (1987), Reima Pietilä: One Man's Odyssey in Search of Finnish Architecture (1988), Constancy and Change in Architecture (1991), Urban Forms, Suburban Dreams (1993), Finnish Architecture and the Modernist Tradition (1995), The Norman Foster Office: Consistency through Diversity (1997); *Recreations* photography, travel, tennis, broadcasting; *Clubs* Garrick; *Style*— Prof Malcolm Quantrill; ✉ College of Architecture, Texas A & M University, Texas 77843-3137, USA (☎ 00 1 409 845 7878, fax 00 1 409 845 4491)

QUARMBY, Dr Arthur; s of Harold Quarmby (d 1981), of Lane House, Holmfirth, and Lucy May, *née* Barrow; *b* 18 March 1934; *Educ* Pocklington Sch, Leeds Sch of Architecture and Town Planning (Dip Arch); *m* 13 Aug 1957, Jean Valerie, da of Herbert Mitchell, of Hebble Drive Holmfirth; 1 s (Jonathan Hugh, b 1961), 1 da (Rachel Jane b 1964); *Career* architect; plastics structures in Europe and the Antarctica, world's largest transparent inflated dome (for 20th Century Fox), assault craft for Rotork Marine, conslt on structural plastics, world authy on earth-sheltered architecture, architectural journalist; chief constable of the Graveship of Holme; memb: Huddersfield Choral Soc, Colne Valley Male Voice Choir; Hon DSc 1996; RIBA 1959, FRIBA 1985, FRSA; *Books* The Plastics Architect (1974); *Recreations* music, archaeology, watersports, hill walking; *Clubs* Inigo Jones; *Style*— Dr Arthur Quarmby; ✉ Underhill, Holme, W Yorks (☎ 01484 682372); 83 Fitzwilliam St, Huddersfield (☎ 01484 536553, fax 01484 432586)

QUARMBY, David Anthony; s of Frank Reginald Quarmby (d 1983); *b* 22 July 1941; *Educ* Shrewsbury, King's Coll Cambridge (MA), Univ of Leeds (PhD, Dip Industl Mgmnt); *m* 1968, Hilmary, da of Denis Hilton Hunter; 4 da; *Career* md London Tport Exec Buses 1978–84 (memb 1975–84), jt md J Sainsbury plc 1988–96 (dir 1984–96); memb Sch Curriculum and Assessment Authy 1993–95, chm British Tourist Authy and English Tourist Bd 1996–; non-exec dir Central Mgmnt Bd Dept of Tport 1996–; pres Inst of Logistics 1996–; govr and dep chm James Allen's Girls' Sch Dulwich (chm 1995–), dir Blackheath Concert Halls 1990–94, chm Retail Action Gp for Crime Prevention 1995–96, memb Crime Prevention Agency Bd 1995–, chm S London Business Leadership 1996–; FCIT, FILog, FRSA, CIMgt, CORS; *Recreations* music, singing, photography, walking, family life; *Style*— David Quarmby, Esq; ✉ British Tourist Authority, Thames Tower, Blacks Road, London W6 9EL (☎ 0181 846 9000)

QUARREN EVANS, His Hon (John) Kerry; s of Hubert Royston Quarren Evans, MC (d 1967), and Violet Soule Quarren Evans (d 1993); *b* 4 July 1926; *Educ* King Henry VIII Sch Coventry, Cardiff HS, Trinity Hall Cambridge (MA, LLM); *m* 1958, Jane Shaw, da of Neil Lawson (d 1985); 1 s, 1 da; *Career* Army 1944–48, Capt Royal Welch Fus; slr of Supreme Ct 1953; ptnr: Lyndon Moore & Co of Newport Gwent 1954–71, T S Edwards & Son 1971–80; recorder Wales and Chester circuit 1974–80, circuit judge (SE Circuit) 1980–95; *Recreations* golf, rugby football, music, staurologosophy, oenology, old things; *Clubs* Denham Golf, Royal Porthcawl Golf, Crawshays Welsh RFC; *Style*— His Hon Kerry Quarren Evans; ✉ 2 Mount Park Crescent, Ealing, London W5 2RN

QUASTEL, Dr Anthony Stephen; s of Gerald Quastel, of London, and late Rita Joy Leonora Quastel; *b* 14 Nov 1955; *Educ* St Dunstan's Coll Catford, Middx Hosp Med Sch Univ of London (MB BS); *Career* princ in gen practice 1984; res appts in med and surgery 1980–81, sr house offr in psychiatry Middx Hosp 1982, currently med dir of four private practices in SE England; *Recreations* gardening, politics, talking; *Style*— Dr Anthony Quastel; ✉ Hightrees House, Highclere Close, Kenley, Surrey CR8 5JU (☎ 0181 668 1998); 204 High St, Bromley, Kent (☎ 0181 464 4599, fax 0181 464 3471, car 0836 201725); 12 Parsons Mead, Croydon, Surrey (☎ 0181 680 9853); 100–104 King St, Maidstone, Kent (☎ 01622 688188); 67 Victoria Way, Woking, Surrey (☎ 01483 750465)

QUAYLE, (Thomas) David Graham; CB (1990); s of Dr Thomas Quayle, CIE (d 1962), and Phyllis Gwendolen, *née* Johnson (d 1977); *b* 7 April 1936; *Educ* Repton, Trinity Coll Oxford (BA); *m* 2 Aug 1962, Susan Jean, da of Brig F W P Bradford, MBE (d 1977); 3 da (Lucy b 1963, Sophie b 1964, Emma b 1966); *Career* cmmnd RA 1958, cmdg 40 Field Regt (The Lowland Gunners) RA 1976–79, Cdr Artillery 4 Armd Div and Herford Garrison 1981–83, Def Attaché Br Embassy Bonn 1983–86, Cdr Artillery 1 Br Corps 1987–90, ret as Maj-Gen 1990; Ombudsman for Corporate Estate Agents 1990–; FRSA 1992; *Recreations* shooting, fishing, bridge, travel; *Style*— David Quayle, Esq, CB; ✉ PO Box 1114, Salisbury SP1 1YQ (☎ 01722 333306)

QUAYLE, John Bryant; s of late George Quayle, and Christina, *née* Lonsdale (d 1994); *b* 13 Oct 1945; *Educ* Llandovery Coll, Fitzwilliam Coll Cambridge (MA, MB BChir), St George's Hosp Med Sch London (MChir); *m* 4 March 1972, Prudence Margaret, da of (John) Denis Smith; 3 da (Tamsin Elinor b 4 Jan 1975, Ruth Elizabeth b 26 Oct 1976, Anna Margaret 27 March 1979); *Career* sr surgical registrar (rotation) St George's Hosp London 1978–82 (house physician 1970), conslt surgn Royal Shrewsbury Hosp 1982–89, conslt surgn Princess Royal Hosp Telford 1989–; memb Cncl Surgical Section RSM 1980–; memb Worshipful Soc of Apothecaries 1974; FRCS 1974; *Recreations* riding, sailing, music, walking; *Clubs* RSM; *Style*— John Quayle, Esq; ✉ Shropshire Nuffield Hospital, Shrewsbury; Princess Royal Hospital, Telford (☎ 01743 353441)

QUAYLE, John Douglas Stuart; s of Douglas Quayle (d 1957), of London, and Katherine, *née* Parke; *b* 21 Dec 1937; *Educ* Challoners St Albans, RADA; *m* 20 Oct 1966, Petronell Emily, da of Arthur Thomas Pickard (d 1972), of Torquay; *Career* actor; Nat Serv RCS 1956–58, Cyprus and NI; Pitlochry Festival Theatre 1966; repertory: in Colchester, Salisbury, Richmond, tours, London plays incl Donkeys Years and Habeas Corpus 1967–78; NT player 1980–82; West End plays incl: Noises Off (Savoy) 1983–85, Theatre of Comedy (Ambassadors and Criterion) 1986–88, Don't Dress for Dinner (Apollo) 1991–92, Runs in the Family (Playhouse) 1993, Travels with My Aunt (Whitehall) 1994; various radio, TV and film performances; *Recreations* riding, shooting, walking; *Clubs* Garrick, Farmers'; *Style*— John Quayle, Esq; ✉ c/o Barry Burnett Organisation Ltd, Suite 42–43, Grafton House, 2–3 Golden Square, London W1R 4AA (☎ 0171 437 7048/9, fax 0171 734 6118)

QUAYLE, Robert Brisco MacGregor; s of John Pattinson Quayle, of South Petherton, Somerset, and Doreen Helen MacGregor, *née* MacMullen; *b* 6 April 1950; *Educ* Monkton Combe Sch, Selwyn Coll Cambridge (MA); *m* 30 Sept 1972, (Deborah) Clare, da of Sir (Francis) Alan Pullinger, CBE, of Barnhorn, Meadway, Berkhamsted, Herts; 3 s (Jonathan b 1981, William b 1985, Thomas b 1988), 2 da (Hannah b 1976, Eily b 1978); *Career* admitted slr 1978; Linklaters & Paines 1974–76, clerk of Tynwald and sec House of Keys 1976–87, ptnr Travers Smith Braithwaite 1987–90 (conslt 1990–); dir: Isle of Man Steam Packet Co, Singer & Friedlander (Isle of Man) Ltd, Total (Isle of Man) Ltd, Bradford & Bingley (Isle of Man) Ltd; memb Manx Heritage Fndn, dir Manx Radio; author of various articles on Parly affrs and history of IOM; *Recreations* family, church (licensed lay reader); *Style*— Robert Quayle, Esq; ✉ Mullen Beg, Patrick, IOM (☎ 01624 842912); 4 Upper Church St, Douglas, IOM (☎ 01624 625515, fax 01624 624625)

QUAYLE, Prof (John) Rodney; s of John Martin Quayle, and Mary Doris Quayle; *b* 18 Nov 1926; *Educ* Alun GS, UCNW Bangor (BSc, PhD), Univ of Cambridge (PhD); *m* 1951, Yvonne Mabel, da of Albert Sanderson; 1 s, 1 da; *Career* West Riding prof of microbiology Univ of Sheffield 1965–83 (sr lectr in biochemistry 1963–65), vice chllr Univ of Bath 1983–92; FRS; *Style*— Prof Rodney Quayle, FRS; ✉ The Coach House, Vicarage Lane, Compton Dando, Bristol BS18 4LA

QUEENSBERRY, 12 Marquess of (S 1682); Sir David Harrington Angus Douglas; 11 Bt (S 1668); also Viscount Drumlanrig, Lord Douglas of Hawick and Tibbers (both S 1628), and Earl of Queensberry (S 1633); s of 11 Marquess (d 1954), by his 2 w Cathleen, *née* Mann (d 1959); *b* 19 Dec 1929; *Educ* Eton; *m* 1, 1956 (m dis 1969), Ann, da of Maurice Sinnett Jones and formerly w of George Arthur Radford; 2 da (Lady Emma Cathleen b 1956, Lady Alice (Lady Alice Melia) b 1965); m 2, 1969 (m dis 1986), Alexandra Mary Clare Wyndham, da of Guy Wyndham Sich; 2 s (Viscount Drumlanrig, Lord Milo Luke Dickon b 1978), 1 da (Lady Kate Cordelia Sasha b 1969); *Heir* s, Viscount Drumlanrig b 1 June 1967; *Career* late 2 Lt RHG; prof of ceramics RCA 1959–83; pres Design and Industs Assoc 1976–78; fndr and sr ptnr Queensberry Hunt design group; dir Poole Pottery; *Style*— The Most Hon the Marquess of Queensberry; ✉ Queensberry Hunt, 24 Brook Mews North, London W2 3BW (☎ 0171 724 3701, fax 0171 723 0508)

QUELCH, Prof John Anthony; s of Norman Quelch, of Stratford St Mary, Suffolk, and Laura Sally, *née* Jones; *b* 8 Aug 1951; *Educ* King Edward VI Sch Norwich, Exeter Coll Oxford (BA), Univ of Pennsylvania (MBA), Harvard Univ (MS, DBA); *m* 17 June 1978, Joyce Ann, da of Harold Loring Huntley; *Career* asst prof Univ of Western Ontario Canada 1977–79; Harvard Business Sch: asst prof 1979–84, assoc prof 1984–88, prof of business admin 1988–93, Sebastian S Kresge prof of mktg 1993–; dir: Reebok International Ltd, WPP Group plc, European Communication Management Ltd, US Office Products, US Cncl of Better Business Bureaus; *Books* Advertising and Promotion Management (1987), Multinational Marketing Management (1988), Sales Promotion Management (1989), How to Market to Consumers (1989), The Marketing Challenge of Europe 1992 (1991), Ethics in Marketing (1992), Marketing Management (1993), European Cases in Marketing Management (1994), Cases in Product Management (1995); *Recreations* tennis, squash; *Clubs* Harvard (Boston); *Style*— Prof John Quelch; ✉ Harvard Business School, Soldiers Field, Boston, Massachusetts 02163, USA (☎ 00 1 617 495 6433, fax 00 1 617 496 5637)

QUENBY, John Richard; s of Richard Quenby (d 1942), of Bedford, and Margaret, *née* Wyse (d 1991); *b* 30 Oct 1941; *Educ* Bedford Modern Sch, Open Univ (BA); *m* 9 April 1965 (sep 1993), Sandra, da of Col Noel Frederick Charles King (d 1974), of Sydney, Aust; 2 da (Georgia Margaret b 1970, Fiona Elizabeth b 1971); *Career* dir Granada Computer Servs Ltd 1983–85, md Granada Overseas Hldgs Ltd 1985–89, dir and chm of various subsidiaries and assoc companies; chief exec and dir RAC Motor Sports Assoc 1990–, non-exec dir Beds and Shires Health and Care NHS Tst 1992– (chm 1994–), dir Trireme Tst 1994– (chm 1994–95), dir Auto Cycle Union 1995–, dir Speedway Control Bd 1995–, dir Motorcycle Circuit Racing Control Bd 1995– (chm 1995–); *Recreations* rowing, photography; *Clubs* RAC, Bedford, Bedford Rowing; *Style*— John Quenby, Esq; ✉ RAC Motor Sports Association Ltd, Motor Sports House, Riverside Park, Colnbrook (☎ 01753 681736)

QUICKE, Sir John Godolphin; kt (1988), CBE (1978), DL (Devon 1985); s of Capt Noel Arthur Godolphin Quicke (d 1943), and Constance May Quicke; *b* 20 April 1922; *Educ* Eton, New Coll Oxford; *m* 1953, Prudence Tinné, da of Rear Adm Charles Pierre Berthon, CBE (d 1965); 3 s, 3 da; *Career* farmer and landowner; chm SW Regnl Panel Miny of Agric 1972–75, pres CLA 1975–77, memb SW Regnl Bd Natwest Bank 1973–92, chm Exeter Local Bd Commercial Union Assurance Co 1980–92; memb: Consultative Bd Jt Consultative Orgn for R & D, Food & Agric 1980–84, Countryside Cmmn 1981–88, Properties Ctee Nat Tst 1984–; vice chm N Devon Meat Ltd 1982–86; chm: Agric EDC, NEDO 1983–88, Agric Sector Gp NEDO, Soc for the Responsible Use of Resources in Agric and on the Land 1983–, Estates Panel Nat Tst 1984–92; memb Bd Univ of Plymouth (formerly Poly of the South West) 1989–93; pres Royal Bath and West of England Soc 1989–90, hon fell Royal Agric Soc of England 1989; Hon DSc: Univ of Exeter 1989, Univ of Plymouth 1991; RASE Bledisloe Gold Medal 1985; *Recreations* music, gardening, travel; *Clubs* Boodle's; *Style*— Sir John Quicke, CBE, DL; ✉ Sherwood, Newton St Cyres, Exeter, Devon (☎ 01392 851216)

QUIGLEY, Anthony Leslie Coupland (Tony); s of Leslie Quigley (d 1990), and Vera Barbara Rodaway, *née* Martin; *b* 14 July 1946; *Educ* Apsley GS Hemel Hempstead, Queen Mary Coll Univ of London (BSc); *m* 1968, Monica, da of Ronald Frewin Dean; 2 da (Angela Victoria b 1972, Rachel Helen b 1980), 1 s (Geoffrey Richard b 1974); *Career* res scientist ASWE (exchange scientist US Naval Surface Weapons Centre 1976–79) 1967–81, head Command, Control and Assessment RARDE 1981–87, head Science and Technol Assessment Cabinet Office 1987–90, dir Strategic Def Initiative Participation Office 1990–93, asst chief scientific advsr (Nuclear) 1993–95, dir Sci & Engrg Base Gp Office of Science and Technology 1995–; CEng, FIEE 1986; *Recreations* umpiring cricket, golf, flying models; *Style*— Tony Quigley, Esq; ✉ Director Science & Engineering Base Group, Office of Science and Technology, Albany House, 94–98 Petty France, London SW1H 9ST (☎ 0171 271 2071, fax 0171 271 2018)

QUIGLEY, Ian Spiers; s of John Spiers Quigley, of Inverness, and Celia, *née* Bennett; *b* 29 Nov 1946; *Educ* Aberdeen GS, Oban HS, Univ of Glasgow (LLB); *m* 6 July 1973, Elizabeth Ann, da of Tom Rutherford Lindsay; 2 da (Claire Lee b 8 March 1975, Victoria Lindsay b 24 June 1977); *Career* apprentice Wright Johnston & MacKenzie Glasgow; Maclay Murray & Spens: joined 1975, seconded to Linklaters & Paines London 1976, ptnr Maclay Murray & Spens 1977–, currently head Commercial Property Dept; memb Advsy Bd Outward Bound Scotland; memb: Law Soc of Scotland, Soc of HM Writers to the Signet; NP; *Recreations* hillwalking, cross-country skiing, cycling, gardening; *Clubs* New (Edinburgh); *Style*— Ian Quigley, Esq; ✉ Pomathorn Cottage, Howgate, Midlothian, Scotland EH26 8PJ (☎ 01968 672334); Maclay Murray & Spens, 3 Glenfinlas Street, Edinburgh EH3 6AQ (☎ 0131 226 5196, fax 0131 226 3174)

QUIGLEY, Sir William George Henry; kt (1993), CB (1982); s of William George Cunningham Quigley (d 1969), and Sarah, *née* Martin (d 1987); *b* 26 Nov 1929; *Educ* Ballymena Acad, Queen's Univ Belfast (fndn scholar, BA, PhD); *m* 5 May 1971, Moyra Alice, da of Frank Munn (d 1970); *Career* NI Civil Serv: joined 1955, perm sec Dept of Manpower Servs 1974–76, perm sec Dept of Commerce 1976–79, perm sec Dept of Fin 1979–82, perm sec Dept of Fin and Personnel 1982–88; chm Ulster Bank Ltd 1989– (dep chm 1988–89); dir: Short Brothers PLC 1989–, National Westminster Bank PLC 1990–; professorial fell Queen's Univ Belfast 1988–92; memb: Fair Employment Cmmn for NI 1989–93, Cncl NI C of C and Indust 1989–92, Cncl CBI (NI div) 1990–94; chm: IOD (NI div) 1990–, Royal Hosps Gp NHS Tst 1992–, NI Econ Cncl 1994–, Co-Operation North 1994–; CIMgt 1977; *Books* Registrum Johannis Mey (co-author with Dr E F D Roberts, 1972); *Recreations* historical research, reading, music, gardening; *Style*— Sir George Quigley, CB; ✉ Ulster Bank Limited, 47 Donegall Place, Belfast BT1 5AU (☎ 01232 244744, fax 01232 898588)

QUILLEY, Denis Clifford; s of Clifford Charles Quilley (d 1968), and Ada Winifred, *née* Stanley; *b* 26 Dec 1927; *Educ* Bancroft's Sch Woodford Essex; *m* 1949, Stella Jean, *née* Chapman; 1 s, 2 da; *Career* actor; first stage appearance Birmingham Repertory Theatre 1945; Nat Theatre 1971–76; *Theatre* incl: Privates on Parade (Aldwych 1977, SWET Award 1977, Piccadilly 1978), Morell in Candida (Albery) 1977, Deathtrap (Garrick) 1978, title role in Sondheim's Sweeney Todd (Drury Lane, SWET Award 1980), Molokov in Chess (Barbican) 1985, Antony in Antony and Cleopatra (Chichester) 1985, Fatal Attraction (Haymarket) 1985, La Cage aux Folles (Palladium) 1986, title role in Sweeney Todd (RNT) 1994, Falstaff in The Merry Wives of Windsor (RNT) 1995, A Patriot for Me (RSC) 1995; *Television* incl: The Merchant of Venice, The Crucible, Masada, Anno Domini, Rich Tea and Sympathy, The Marriage of Figaro; *Films* incl: Murder on the Orient Express 1974, Evil Under the Sun 1982, Privates on Parade 1982, Mr Johnson 1990, A Dangerous Man: Lawrence After Arabia 1991; *Recreations* playing the piano, flute and cello, walking; *Style*— Denis Quilley, Esq; ✉ c/o Bernard Hunter Associates, 13 Spencer Gardens, London SW14 7AH (☎ 0181 878 6308, fax 0181 392 9334)

QUILLIAM, Prof Juan Pete (Peter); OBE (1986); s of Thomas Alfred Quilliam (d 1953), of N Finchley, London, and Caroline Maude, *née* Pavitt (d 1958); *b* 20 Nov 1915; *Educ* Univ Coll Sch Hampstead, UCL (BSc, MSc, MB BS, DSc); *m* 1, Melita Kelly (d 1957); 1 s (Jonathan Peter b 1953), 1 da (Penelope Sally Ann (Mrs Walker) b 1950); m 2, 28 March 1958, Barbara Lucy, da of Rev W Kelly, of Pelynt, Cornwall; *Career* MO RAFVR 1942–46; Univ of London: prof of pharmacology St Bartholomew's Hosp Med Coll 1962–83, memb Senate 1968–90, memb Ct 1973–90, memb Mil Educn Ctee, chm Convocation 1973–90, tstee Convocation Tst 1990– (chm 1973–90); memb: Advertising Advsy Ctee ITC (formerly IBA) 1984–92, Jt Charity Appeals Advsy Ctee ITC/BBC 1987–92; dep chm Gen Optical Cncl 1975–88 (memb 1960–88), tstee City Parochial Fndn 1977–89; Help the Hospices Tst: chm of tstees and co-chm 1986–94, chm Bd of Dirs 1994–; Nat Forum of Coronary Heart Disease: memb Exec Ctee 1988–, hon treas 1990–94; chm Crouch Harbour Authy 1988–92 (memb 1985–), chm Crouch Area Yachting Fedn 1984–, memb Grants Cncl Charities Aid Fndn 1990–; BMA: chm Med Academic Staff Ctee 1978, 1980 and 1982, memb Cncl 1971–85, chm Bd of Sci 1982–85, vice-pres 1988–; memb: Physiological Soc 1948, Br Pharmacological Soc 1950; Univ of London Rowing purple 1938–40, pres Univ of London Boat Club 1939–40; FRCP (London) 1975; *Books* Experimental Pharmacology (1954, 1989), Medical Effects of Nuclear War (jtly, 1983); *Recreations* sailing; *Clubs* United Hosps Sailing (Essex, Cdre 1973–); *Style*— Prof Peter Quilliam, OBE; ✉ Hornbeams, 34 Totteridge Common, London N20 8NE

QUILTER, David Cuthbert Tudway; DL (Somerset 1970); s of Percy Cuthbert Quilter (d 1947), and Gladys Clare Alice, *née* Tudway (d 1973); *b* 26 March 1921; *Educ* Eton; *m* 30 Oct 1953, Elizabeth Mary, da of Col Sir John Carew Pole, 12 Bt, DSO, TD, JP, DL (d 1993); 1 s (Simon b 26 March 1955), 2 da (Susan b 9 July 1957, Lucy b 6 May 1961); *Career* served Coldstream Gds WWII, Capt; Barclays Bank Ltd: local dir Pall Mall Dist 1957–62, Bristol Dist 1962–84, dir 1971–81; dir Bristol Evening Post 1982–91; chm of tstees Wells Cathedral Preservation Tst 1976–, treas Univ of Bristol 1976–88, govr Wells Cathedral Sch 1968–; memb: Cncl Outward Bound Tst 1959–92, Garden Soc 1973–; life tstee Carnegie UK Tst 1981–, tstee The American Museum in Britain 1985–90, chm Somerset Gardens Tst 1991–; master Soc of Merchant Venturers Bristol 1984; JP London Juvenile Courts 1959–62, Mayor of Wells 1974–75, High Sheriff Somerset 1974–75, Vice Lord-Lt Somerset 1978–96; Liveryman Worshipful Co of Fishmongers 1964; Hon LLD Univ of Bristol; *Books* No Dishonourable Name (1947), History of Wells Cathedral School (1985); *Recreations* gardening, shooting, travel; *Clubs* Boodle's, Pratt's; *Style*— David Tudway Quilter, Esq, DL; ✉ Milton Lodge, Wells, Somerset BA5 3AQ (☎ 01749 672168)

QUILTER, Jeffrey Derek (Jeff); s of Alfred Stanley Quilter (d 1984), and Dorothy Lillian, *née* Rainbird (d 1976); *b* 7 Sept 1950; *Educ* St Martin's Sch for Boys; *m* 4 Aug 1984, Alison Judith, da of John Stout; 3 s (James b 30 Aug 1970, Joel b 24 June 1994, Finn b 3 Aug 1996), 1 da (Nicola b 22 Aug 1974); *Career* Doyle Dane Bernbach advtg agency 1970–74, French Gold Abbott 1974–78, Grey Advertising 1978–82, Publicis 1982–86, Ted Bates Advertising 1986–88, creative servs dir Simons Palmer Clemmow Johnson 1988–; MIPA 1985, memb Cartophillic Soc 1985; *Recreations* golf, cartophilly, cricket; *Clubs* Lancashire CCC; *Style*— Jeff Quilter, Esq; ✉ Farthing Hill, Langley Road, Chipperfield, Herts WD4 9JQ (☎ 01923 260525); Simons Palmer Clemmow Johnson Ltd, 19–20 Noel Street, London W1V 3PD (☎ 0171 287 4455, fax 0171 437 0415)

QUIN, Joyce Gwendolen; MP (Lab) Gateshead East (majority 18,530); *b* 1944; *Career* MEP (Lab) Tyne and Wear 1979–89; MP (Lab) Gateshead E 1987–, memb Select Ctee on Treasy and the Civil Serv 1987–89; oppn spokesperson: on trade and indust 1989–92, on employment 1992–, on Europe 1993–; memb Cncl RCVS 1992–96; hon fell Univ of Sunderland 1986, hon fell St Mary's Coll Univ of Durham 1993; *Style*— Joyce Quin, MP; ✉ Constituency Office: 1A Collingwood Street, Sunderland Road, Felling, Gateshead NE10 9NA (☎ 0191 469 606, fax 0191 469 6009); House of Commons, London SW1A 0AA

QUINE, Hector; s of Herbert Leigh Quine (d 1951), of London, and Gladys, *née* Foster (d 1934); *b* 30 Dec 1926; *Educ* Hextable Coll Kent; *m* 10 Oct 1960, Penelope Mary, da of Francis Henry Arnold Engleheart (d 1963), of The Priory, Stoke-by-Nayland, Suffolk; 1 s (Adrian b 1967), 1 da (Francesca b 1972); *Career* serv RASC 1944–48, Norway, Egypt, Palestine; guitarist Royal Opera House Covent Garden 1958–87; prof: RAM 1959–87, Guildhall Sch of Music and Drama 1967–78, Trinity Coll of Music London 1958–78; advsr Assoc Bd of the Royal Schs of Music 1967–; Hon RAM, Hon FTCL; *Recreations* cricket, carpentry, photography; *Clubs* Chelsea Arts, Royal Philharmonic Soc, Royal Soc of Musicians, Performing Rights Soc; *Style*— Hector Quine, Esq; ✉ 22 Limerston St, Chelsea, London SW10 0HH (☎ 0171 352 4419)

QUINION, David William; s of Frederick William Quinion (d 1984), and Muriel Elizabeth, *née* Price (d 1980); *b* 29 Sept 1926; *Educ* Watford GS for Boys, Northampton Engrg Coll (Hons Dip), Univ of London (BSc); *m* 1951, Joan Leonora, da of Percival Philip Parker; 2 s (Graham Robert b 3 June 1953, Malcolm David b 25 April 1956), 1 da (Sharon Fiona b 11 Jan 1965); *Career* indentured engr Sir Robert McAlpine 1946–49, design engr Oscar Faber Ptnrs 1949, section engr Marples Ridgway 1950–52, contracts mangr Taylor Woodrow Construction 1952–67, chief engr Tarmac Construction Ltd 1967–88, conslt Tarmac Construction 1988–91; vice pres: Concrete Soc 1982–84 (chm W Midlands Branch 1976–77), Int Assoc for Bridge & Structural Engrg 1990– (chm Br Gp 1988–); chm Tech Advsy Ctee FCEC 1984–; memb Cncl: BBA 1982–, CIRIA 1978–88, IStructE 1975–80 (chm Midland Cos Branch 1975–76); memb Standing Ctee on Structural Safety 1989–95; FIStructE 1963, FICE 1963, FEng 1988; *Recreations* walking and countryside; *Style*— David Quinion, Esq, FEng; ✉ 4 Netheravon Close, Salisbury, Wiltshire SP1 3BE (☎ and fax 01722 333378)

QUINLAN, Chris Charles; s of Edward Charles Quinlan, of Betchworth, Surrey, and June, *née* Richiardi; *b* 21 Dec 1954; *Educ* Alleyn's Sch Dulwich, Univ of Sheffield (LLB); *m* 4 April 1987 (m dis 1994); *Career* slr Wilkinson Kimbers 1981–83, advtg control offr IBA 1983–84, asst sec Beecham Group plc 1984–85, controller of advtg The Cable Authy 1985–90, mktg dir Carlton Cabletime Limited (subsid of Carlton Communications plc) 1990–92, dir Media Matrix Ltd 1992–; memb: Jt Indust Ctee for Cable Audience Res, Cable TV Assoc Mktg Gp, Bd of Mgmnt Gp 64 Theatre London; memb: Law Soc 1981, Mktg Soc 1992; *Books* Making Sense of Computers in General Practice (jtly, 1995); *Recreations* ballooning, directing plays, games inventing; *Style*— Chris Quinlan, Esq; ✉ Media Matrix Ltd, Glen House, 200–208 Tottenham Court Road, London W1P 9LA (☎ 0171 573 4580)

QUINLAN, Sir Michael Edward; GCB (1991, KCB 1985, CB 1980); s of late Gerald Andrew Quinlan, of Hassocks, Sussex, and late Roseanne Quinlan; *b* 11 Aug 1930; *Educ* Wimbledon Coll, Merton Coll Oxford; *m* 1965, (Margaret) Mary, *née* Finlay; 2 s, 2 da; *Career* RAF 1952–54; civil servant 1954–92: def cnsllr UK delgn to NATO 1970–73, under sec Cabinet Office 1974–77, dep under sec of State (policy and programmes) MOD 1977–81, dep sec (indust) Treasy 1981–82, perm sec Dept of Employment 1983–88, MOD 1988–92; dir: Lloyds Bank plc 1992–, Pilkington plc 1992–, Ditchley Fndn 1992–; tstee

Science Museum 1992–; visiting prof KCL 1992–; hon fell Merton Coll Oxford 1989; author of various articles on defence and public serv; *Recreations* golf, watching cricket, listening to music; *Clubs* RAF, MCC, Chipping Norton CC; *Style*— Sir Michael Quinlan, GCB; ✉ Ditchley Park, Enstone, Chipping Norton, Oxon OX7 4ER

QUINLAN, Timothy Edward; s of Edward John Quinlan (d 1959), of Essex, and Emma Louise, *née* Norrie (d 1974); *b* 12 Aug 1935; *Educ* St Ignatius Coll, Harvard Business Sch; *m* 1961 (m dis 1981), Maryann, da of Arthur Barron (d 1976), of Essex; 2 s (James b 1962, Edward b 1975), 1 da (Sarah b 1964); m 2, 22 July 1988, Susan, da of Raymond Lindley, of Moorland House, Epworth, nr Doncaster, South Yorkshire; 2 da (Emma Louise b 1989, Chloe Ann b 1991); *Career* dir and gp gen mangr: Brent Walker Group plc, Brent Walker Holdings plc, Brent Walker Ltd, Brent Walker Casinos Division Ltd, Brent Walker Catering Division Ltd, Brent Walker Film Distributors Ltd, Brent Walker Film Productions Ltd, Brent Walker Restaurants Ltd, Brent Walker Concessionaires Ltd, Brent Walker Finance Ltd, Brent Walker Casinos Northern Ltd, Basildon Astrodome Ltd, Radio Mercury, Essex Radio, Widcombe Basin Ltd, Curzon Restaurants Ltd, Peter Evans Holdings Ltd, Peter Evans Eating Houses Ltd, La Boheme (Chelsea) Ltd, Focus Cinemas Ltd, Garons Agencies Ltd, Isow's Restaurants Ltd, Marlowe Rooms Ltd, Network Cinema (UK) Ltd, Waldair (Chancery Lane) Ltd, Waldair (Foster Lane) Ltd, Waldair (High Holborn) Ltd, Waldair (Tower Hill) Ltd, Westcliff Leisure Centre Ltd, Manorlike Ltd, Fillfore Ltd; Baron of Balrothery; *Recreations* skiing, golf, tennis; *Clubs* Thorpe Hall Golf, Thorpe Bay Tennis, St James's; *Style*— Timothy Quinlan, Esq; ✉ 121 Thorpe Bay Gdns, Thorpe Bay, Southend on Sea, Essex SS1 3NW (☎ 01702 296310); The Brent Walker Group, 53–54 Brooks Mews, London W1Y 2NY (☎ 0171 629 6944, fax 0171 629 6955)

QUINN, (James Steven) Brian; s of James Joseph Quinn (d 1977), of Lancs, and Elizabeth, *née* Thomas; *b* 16 June 1936; *Educ* Waterpark S Ireland, Univ Coll Dublin, King's Inn Dublin (LLB, BCL); *m* 1963, Blanche Cecilia, da of Richard Francis James (d 1986), of Spain; 2 s (James b 1963, Alexander b 1969), 1 da (Susannah b 1965); *Career* head of Industl Activities Prices and Incomes Bd 1969–71, dir M L H Conslts 1971–79, corporate devpt advsr Midland Bank Int 1977–80, chief industl advsr Price Cmmn 1977–78; chm: Brightstar Communications 1983–85, BAJ Holdings 1985–87, Harmer Holbrook 1987–88; chm and chief exec Digital Computer Services 1989–96 (dir 1985–96); memb Exec Ctee Inst of Euro Trade and Technol 1983–, pres Int Inst of Communications 1988–91 (tstee 1982–, chm Exec Ctee 1984–87), chm Gtr London Regnl Cncl Inst of Mgmnt (formerly BIM) 1990–93, tstee Int Communications Centre San Diego State Univ 1990–, chm Editorial Bd The Professional Manager 1991–; *Recreations* golf, reading, poetry, veteran vehicles; *Clubs* Athenaeum; *Style*— Brian Quinn, Esq; ✉ Craiglea House, Austenwood Lane, Gerrards Cross, Bucks

QUINN, Brian; CBE; *b* 18 Nov 1936; *Educ* Univ of Glasgow (MA), Univ of Manchester (MA(Econ)), Cornell University (PhD); *m* 1961, Mary, *née* Bradley; 2 s (Aidan Thomas b 1962, David Bradley b 1969), 1 da (Fiona Anne b 1965); *Career* economist African Dept IMF 1964–70, IMF rep Sierra Leone 1966–68; Bank of England: Economics Div 1970–74, Chief Cashier's Dept 1974–77, head of Info Div 1977–82, asst dir Banking Supervision Div 1982–84, asst dir and head Banking Supervision Div 1984, asst dir and head of banking supervision 1986, exec dir i/c banking supervision and banking ops 1988–96, actg dep govr 1995, ret Bank 1996; non-exec chm Nomura Bank International plc 1996–; *Recreations* football, fishing, golf, cycling, listening to music; *Style*— Brian Quinn, CBE; ✉ Nomura Bank International plc, Nomura Houe, 1 St Martin's-le-Grand, London EC1A 4NP (☎ 0171 521 2000, fax 0171 626 0851)

QUINN, James Charles Frederick; s of Rev Chllr James Quinn (d 1962), and Muriel Alice May, *née* MaGuire (d 1973); *b* 23 Aug 1919; *Educ* Shrewsbury, Trinity Coll Dublin, ChCh Oxford (MA); *m* 1941, Hannah, da of Rev Robert Malcolm Gwynn (Vice Provost Trinity Coll Dublin); 1 s (Gough), 1 da (Christina); *Career* served WWII Maj Irish Gds Italy and NW Europe 1941–46, Br Army Staff France, and Town Major Paris 1946; film prodr and exhibitor; dir BFI 1955–64, memb Gen Advsy Cncl BBC 1960–64; Foreign Leader award US State Dept 1962, Cncl of Europe fellowship 1966; tstee: Imperial War Museum 1968–78, Nat Life Story Collection 1986–91; chm Nat Panel for Film Festivals 1966–83; films produced incl: Herostratus 1966, Overlord 1975 (Silver Bear Berlin Film Festival); memb Film TV and Video Advsy Ctee Br Cncl 1984–90; chm The Minema Ltd 1984–94; Chevalier de l'Ordre des Arts et des Lettres (France 1979); *Recreations* lawn tennis; *Clubs* Cavalry and Guards', Vincent's (Oxford); *Style*— James Quinn, Esq; ✉ 108 Marine Parade, Brighton, East Sussex

QUINN, (Thomas) Richard; s of Thomas Quinn (d 1994), of Banffshire, and Helen, *née* McDonald; *b* 2 Dec 1961; *Educ* Bannockburn HS; *m* 17 Feb 1990 (m dis 1994), Fiona Christine, da of Frank David Johnson; 1 s (Joshua Burns b 18 Nov 1990), 1 da (Robyn Helen b 12 Sept 1989); *Career* jockey; first ride 1978, first winner Kempton 1981, Euro champion apprentice 1983, Br champion apprentice 1984, most winners 123 in 1993; major races won (all Group One): Dewhurst Stakes, Irish St Leger, Grosser Preis der Berliner Bank, 214th St Leger, Irish Oaks, Yorkshire Oaks, Cheiveley Park, Prix de la Foret, Derby Italiano, Gran Premio d'Italio, R & V Europe Preis, Gran Premio de Milano, Faith Sultan Mehmet II Trophy, Brent Walker Fillies Mile, Ciga Prix Marcel Boussac, French 1000 Guineas, Kenya 2000, Rothmans Int (Canada), Prix Royal Oak (Franch Leger); second place Derby Italiano 1994; ridden winners in: GB, France, Ireland, Italy, Germany, USA, Canada, Aust, S Africa, Denmark, Holland, Sweden, Spain, Turkey, Belgium, Kenya, Saudi Arabia and Hong Kong; *Recreations* gardening, skiing; *Style*— Richard Quinn, Esq; ✉ 2 Cherry Grove, Hungerford, Berkshire RG17 0HP

QUINN, Dame Sheila Margaret Imelda; DBE (1987, CBE 1978); da of Wilfred Amos Bairstow Quinn (d 1963); *b* 16 Sept 1920; *Educ* Layton Hill Convent Sch Blackpool, Univ of London; *Career* regnl nursing offr Wessex RHA 1978–83, UK rep Standing Ctee of Nurses EEC 1979–91, pres Royal Coll of Nursing 1982–86 (chm Cncl 1974–79, dep pres 1980–82), nursing advsr Br Red Cross 1983–88; memb EEC Advsy Ctee on Trg in Nursing 1983–90 (pres 1979–82), first vice pres Int Cncl of Nurses 1981–85 (memb Bd of Dirs 1977–81); Hon DSc Univ of Southampton 1986; *Recreations* reading, walking, gardening; *Clubs* St John's House, RSM; *Style*— Dame Sheila Quinn, DBE; ✉ 31 Albany Park Court, Winn Road, Southampton, Hants SO17 1EN (☎ 01703 676592)

QUINN, Terry; *b* 17 Nov 1951; *Educ* St Aloysius Coll Glasgow, Langside Coll; *m* Pat; 1 s, 1 da; *Career* ed-in-chief M Publications Scotland 1975–79, asst ed Buckinghamshire Advertiser 1979–81; ed: Bedfordshire Times & Express Series and N Herts Gazette & Express Series 1982–84, Telegraph & Argus 1984–89, Evening News Edinburgh 1989–92; editorial dir Thomson Regional Newspapers March-Sept 1994 (dep editorial dir 1992–March 1994), ed Daily Record Oct 1994–; *Recreations* newspapers, books, music, football, tennis, travel; *Style*— Terry Quinn, Esq; ✉ Scottish Daily Record & Sunday Mail Ltd, Anderson Quay, Glasgow G3 8DA (☎ 0141 248 7000, fax 0141 204 0770)

QUINNEN, (Paul) Nigel Andrew; s of John Norman Quinnen (d 1986), of Ealing, London, and Elisabeth, *née* Clark; *b* 10 Oct 1953; *Educ* St Benedict's Ealing, Wadham Coll Oxford (Rugby blue); *m* 16 Dec 1977, Dinah Mary, da of Rear Adm Derek Hetherington, of Christmas Common, Oxon; 1 s (Bruno b 1986), 2 da (Romy b 1987, Sarah b 1991); *Career* articles Coopers & Lybrand 1976–80, fund mangr J Henry Schroder Wagg 1980–85, investmt dir and head of UK equities Lazard Investors Ltd 1985–91, dir UK equities Lincoln Investment Management 1991–; ACA 1980; *Recreations* golf; *Clubs* Royal Mid Surrey Golf; *Style*— Nigel Quinnen, Esq; ✉ The Red House, Cranham Woods, Cranham, Glos (☎ 01452 864760)

QUINTON, Baron (Life Peer UK 1982), of Holywell in City of Oxford and Co of Oxfordshire; Anthony Meredith Quinton; s of Surgn Capt Richard Frith Quinton, RN (d 1935), and Gwenllyan Letitia Quinton; *b* 25 March 1925; *Educ* Stowe, Christ Church Oxford (BA); *m* 1952, Marcelle, da of late Maurice Wegier, of New York; 1 s, 1 da; *Career* served WWII RAF; fell: All Souls Coll Oxford 1949–55, New Coll Oxford 1955–78; pres Trinity Coll Oxford 1978–87, memb Arts Cncl of GB 1979–82; vice pres Br Acad 1985–86, chm Br Library Bd 1985–90; pres Royal Inst of Philosophy 1991–; FBA; *Books* Political Philosophy (ed, 1967), The Nature of Things (1973), Utilitarian Ethics (1973), The Politics of Imperfection (1978), Francis Bacon (1980), Thoughts and Thinkers (1982); *Clubs* Garrick; *Style*— The Rt Hon the Lord Quinton, FBA; ✉ The Mill House, Turville, Henley-on-Thames, Oxon RG9 6QL (☎ 01491 638777); A11 Albany, Piccadilly, London W1V 9RD (☎ 0171 287 8686)

QUINTON, Sir John Grand; kt (1990); s of William Grand Quinton (d 1968), and Norah May, *née* Nunn (d 1969); Freeman City of Norwich (by inheritance since 1702) and City of London; *b* 21 Dec 1929; *Educ* Norwich Sch, St John's Coll Cambridge (MA 1954); *m* 1954, Jean Margaret, da of Donald Chastney (d 1950); 1 s (Michael), 1 da (Joanna); *Career* Barclays Bank plc: joined 1953, seconded to Miny of Health 1966, asst gen mangr 1968, local dir Nottingham 1969, regnl gen mangr 1971, gen mangr 1975, dir and sr gen mangr 1982–84, dep chm 1985–87, chm 1987–92; non-exec chm: FA Premier League 1991–, George Wimpey plc 1992–95; non-exec dir Norwich and Peterborough Building Society 1993–; dep chm Mercantile Credit Co Ltd 1975–79, chm Motability Finance Ltd 1978–85; chm: Chief Exec Offrs Ctee of London Clearing Bankers 1982–83, Advsy Cncl London Enterprise Agency 1986–91, Office of the Banking Ombudsman 1987–92, Ctee of London and Scot Bankers 1989–91; memb: City Capital Markets Ctee 1981–86, NE Thames RHA 1974–87, Accounting Standards Ctee 1982–85, Econ and Fin Policy Ctee CBI 1985–88 (chm 1987–88); treas Chartered Inst of Bankers 1980–86 (pres 1989–90), hon treas and bd memb Business in the Community 1986–90, chm Br Olympic Appeal 1988, tstee Royal Acad Tst 1987–93, chm Bd of Tstees Botanic Gardens Conservation Int, chm Metropolitan Police Ctee 1995–; govr: Motability 1985–, Ditchley Fndn 1987–92; memb: Ct of Govrs Royal Shakespeare Theatre 1986–, Ct Henley Coll 1987–92; FRSA 1988; *Recreations* gardening, opera; *Clubs* Reform; *Style*— Sir John Quinton; ✉ c/o FA Premier League, 16 Lancaster Gate, London W2 3LW

QUIRICI, Daniel; s of Ernest Quirici, of Cannes, France, and Candide, *née* Postai; *b* 8 June 1948; *Educ* Ecole des Hautes Etudes Commerciales Paris (MBA), Stanford Univ California (PhD); *m* 1 Sept 1972, Margaret, da of Donald Wright Mann, of NY; 2 s (Alexandre b 15 Aug 1973, Francois b 23 May 1979), 1 da (Florence b 14 Feb 1978); *Career* assoc prof HEC 1970–76, assoc Arthur D Little 1976–82, sr vice pres Credit Commercial de France (CCF) Paris 1983–91, md CCF Holdings Ltd (formerly Laurence Prust & Co Ltd) 1986–91, chief exec Deloitte & Touche (D & T) Corporate Finance Europe Ltd 1991–; memb Traffic Ctee Knightsbridge Assoc; *Recreations* tennis, golf; *Clubs* RAC, Hurlingham; *Style*— Daniel Quirici, Esq; ✉ 8 Montpelier Square, London SW7 1JU; Deloitte & Touche (D & T) Corporate Finance Europe Ltd, Stonecutter Court, 1 Stonecutter Street, London EC4A 4TR (☎ 0171 303 6615, fax 0171 303 5920)

QUIRK, Hon Eric Randolph; s of Baron Quirk, CBE, FBA (Life Peer), *qv*, and Jean, *née* Williams (d 1995); *b* 30 Dec 1951; *Educ* Highgate Sch, UCL (LLB); *m* 30 July 1977 (m dis 1995), Patricia Anne, da of Stanley Lawrence Hemsworth; 1 s (Richard b 2 April 1983), 2 da (Catharine b 25 May 1979, Sara b 14 Nov 1980); *Career* admitted slr 1975; asst slr: Slaughter & May 1973–77, Alexander Tatham & Co 1978–81; ptnr: Alsop Wilkinson Manchester (formerly Lee Lane-Smith) 1981–93 (trg ptnr 1982–92), Laytons 1993– (trg ptnr); memb: Legal Resources Gp Educn Ctee 1988–93, UCL Alumnus Soc, Univ of Manchester Careers Serv Bd, Law Soc; corp memb MCCI; friend Hallé Orch, friend Royal Exchange Theatre Co; *Recreations* violin, string quartets, squash, fell walking, opera, political banter, finding humour in life; *Clubs* Brooklands Sports; *Style*— The Hon Eric Quirk; ✉ Laytons, 22 St John Street, Manchester M3 4EB (☎ 0161 834 2100, fax 0161 834 6862)

QUIRK, Michael William (Mike); s of Frederick Charles Quirk, of Plymouth, and Beatrice May Quirk; *b* 6 March 1938; *Educ* Warwick Business Sch (MSc); *m* Joyce Mary, *née* Tull; 2 s (Jason b 19 May 1967, Ross b 1 May 1971); *Career* Miny of Supply London 1953–57, Nat Serv RAF Tengah Singapore 1957–59, volume planning mangr Rootes Motors/Chrysler Motors 1961–74, undergraduate 1974–76, Young & Rubicam Advertising 1976–95 (latterly head of strategic devpt); *Style*— Mike Quirk, Esq; ✉ 54 Crescent Lane, Clapham, London SW4 9PU (☎ 0171 720 2889)

QUIRK, Baron (Life Peer UK 1994), of Bloomsbury in the London Borough of Camden; Sir (Charles) Randolph Quirk; kt (1985), CBE (1976); s of late Thomas Quirk and Amy Randolph Quirk; *b* 12 July 1920; *Educ* Cronk y Voddy Sch, Douglas HS IOM, UCL (MA, PhD, DLitt), Yale Univ; *m* 1, 1946 (m dis 1979), Jean (d 1995), da of Ellis Gauntlett Williams; 2 s (Hon Eric Randolph Quirk, *qv*, Hon Robin Antony b 1955); m 2, 1984, Gabriele, da of Judge Helmut Stein; *Career* prof of Eng language: Univ of Durham 1958–60, Univ of London 1960–68, Quain prof of Eng language and lit UCL 1968–81, vice chllr Univ of London 1981–85; memb: Bd Br Cncl 1983–91, Cncl RADA; govr English Speaking Union; pres: Br Acad 1985–89, Inst of Linguists 1983–86, Coll of Speech and Language Therapists 1987–91; chm: Br Library Advsy Ctee, Hornby Educnl Tst 1979–93; tstee Wolfson Fndn; Hon Doctorate Univs of: Lund, Uppsala, Paris, Liège, Nijmegen, Salford, Reading, Leicester, Newcastle, Durham, Bath, Open, Essex, Bar Ilan, Southern California, Westminster, Brunel, Sheffield, Glasgow, London, Poznan, Aston, Richmond Coll; foreign fell: Royal Belgian Acad of Sci, Royal Swedish Acad, Finnish Acad of Sci, American Acad of Arts and Sci; fell and res fell UCL; hon master of the Bench Gray's Inn 1983; FBA, fell Academia Europaea; *Books* A University Grammar of English (1973), Style and Communication in the English Language (1982), English in the World (1985), A Comprehensive Grammar of the English Language (1985), Words at Work (1986), English in Use (1990), A Student's Grammar of the English Language (1990), An Introduction to Standard English (1993), Grammatical and Lexical Variance in English (1995); ed English Language Series (Longman); *Clubs* Athenaeum; *Style*— The Rt Hon the Lord Quirk, CBE, FBA; ✉ University College London, Gower St, London WC1E 6BT (☎ 0171 387 7050)

QURESHI, (Abdul) Saleem; s of Sheikh Muhammad Qureshi Qadi (d 1969), of Khanpur, Pakistan, and Amina Begum, *née* Ameer (d 1972); *b* 15 Jan 1938; *Educ* Punjab Univ (BA), Karachi Univ (LLB); *m* 1, 15 Sept 1970 (m dis 1978), Joy Edith, da of Thomas Gordon Falconer (d 1945), of Chichester, Essex; m 2, 6 Jan 1980, Khadeer Unnisa Sajida, da of Mohammed Ehsan-ul-Haq (d 1970), of Hyderabad, India; 1 s (Arif b 25 May 1986), 2 da (Sara b 7 Oct 1981, Asma b 12 April 1983); *Career* asst ed weekly Satluj Bahawalpur Pakistan 1955–57, ed Nationalism and Internationalism Pakistan 1957, teacher govt sch Noorpur Pakistan 1958–59, sub ed Daily Rehbar Bahalvapur Pakistan 1959; teacher: Mary Claco Sch for Girls and Boys Karachi 1961–62, Cantonment Public Sch Karachi Cantonment 1962–64; called to the Bar Middle Temple 1972, practising SE Circuit 1973–; hon advsr to UK Pakistan Cultural Fndn, convenor and sec gen Nat Youth Cncl Bahawalpur Pakistan 1957, author of law articles and lectures and contrib Hum Log magazine; sec Public Speaking Union and memb Drama Club SM Law Coll Karachi 1963–64, fndr memb World Assoc Muslim Jurists Lahore Pakistan 1978, fndr and sec gen MA Jinnah Soc London 1984, chm Police Monitoring Gp Waltham Forest

London 1982–83; memb: Med and Dental Serv Ctee City and E London Family Health Serv Authy; *Books* Jinnah - the Founder of Pakistan (ed, 1995); *Recreations* swimming, lawn tennis, badminton, participation in poetic symposia; *Style*— Saleem Qureshi, Esq; ✉ 2A Barclay Road, London E11 3DG (☎ 0181 558 2289)

QURESHI, Dr Shakeel Ahmed; s of Mohammed Aslam Qureshi, of Luton, Beds, and Sara Begum Qureshi; *b* 20 March 1952; *Educ* Thomas Rotherham Coll, Rotherham GS, Univ of Manchester Med Sch (MB ChB); *m* 29 Dec 1968, Azra Siddique, da of Mohammed Siddique Qureshi, of Rawalpindi, Pakistan; 3 s (Sajid Shakeel b 21 May 1977, Abid Shakeel b 14 Feb 1980, Imran Shakeel b 29 July 1982), 1 da (Noreen b 14 April 1971); *Career* house physician Luton and Dunstable Hosp Luton 1976–77, house surgn Manchester Royal Infirmary Feb-July 1977, sr house physician Joyce Green Hosp Dartford 1977–79, med registrar Barnet Gen Hosp Herts 1979–80, cardiology res registrar Harefield Hosp Middx 1980–83, conslt paediatric cardiologist Rawalpindi Pakistan 1983–85; conslt paediatric cardiologist: Royal Liverpool Children's Hosp 1987–88 (sr registrar paediatric cardiology June-Dec 1986), Guy's Hosp 1988–; memb: BMA 1976, Br Cardiac Soc, Br Paediatric Cardiac Assoc, Assoc of European Paediatric Cardiologists; FRCP 1994 (MRCP 1979); *Recreations* squash, cricket; *Style*— Dr Shakeel Qureshi; ✉ Department of Paediatric Cardiology, Guy's Hospital, St Thomas Street, London SE1 9RT (☎ 0171 955 4616)

QUYSNER, David William; s of late Charles William Quysner, of Mildenhall, Suffolk, and Marjorie Alice, *née* Partington; *b* 26 Dec 1946; *Educ* Bolton Sch, Selwyn Coll Cambridge (MA), London Business Sch; *m* 11 Sept 1971, Lindsay Jean Parris, da of Sir Norman Biggs, *qv*, of Hurstpierpoint, Sussex; 1 s (Simon James b 1980), 2 da (Sarah Louise b 1976, Deborah Helen b 1977); *Career* Investors in Indust plc 1968–82, dir Abingworth plc (now Manakin Holdings plc) 1986–91; chm Cncl Br Venture Capital Assoc 1996–97 (memb 1992–), memb London Stock Exchange AIM Advsy Ctee 1995–96; *Recreations* opera, golf; *Style*— David Quysner, Esq; ✉ Abingworth Management Ltd, 26 St James's Street, London SW1A 1HA (☎ 0171 839 6745, fax 0171 930 1891)

R

RABAGLIATI, Duncan Charles Pringle; s of Brig (Charles) Ian Evershed Rabagliati (d 1991), of Menston, Yorkshire, and Joan, *née* Pringle; *b* 3 Jan 1945; *Educ* Sedbergh; *m* Mair Alethea, da of (Christopher) Ivor Williams; 2 s (Alastair James b 15 Jan 1974, Jonathan Stuart b 5 Oct 1975), 1 da (Sarah Louise b 9 June 1980); *Career* articled clerk Booth & Co Leeds 1964–69; McKenna & Co London: asst slr 1969–73, ptnr 1973–91, conslt 1991–94; ptnr: Payne Hicks Beach 1991–92 (conslt 1992), Wedlake Bell 1992–; *Books* The Formula One Record Book (jtly, 1971), The History of Grand Prix and Voiturette Racing (10 vols, jtly, 1985–96), The Asian Buyers' Guide to UK Property (contrib, 1996); contrib to numerous motoring books and magazines; *Recreations* motoring history, classic motor racing, genealogy; *Style*— Duncan C P Rabagliati, Esq; ✉ Wedlake Bell, 16 Bedford Street, London WC2E 9HF (☎ 0171 379 7266, fax 0171 836 6117)

RABAN, Jonathan; s of Rev Peter J C P Raban, and Monica, *née* Sandison; *b* 14 June 1942; *Educ* Univ of Hull (BA); *m* 1985 (m dis 1992), Caroline Cuthbert; m 2, 1992, Jean Lenihan; 1 da (b 1992); *Career* lectr in Eng and American Lit UCW 1965–67, UEA 1967–69, professional writer 1969–; FRSL; *Books* The Technique of Modern Fiction (1969), Mark Twain: Huckleberry Finn (1969), The Society of the Poem (1971), Soft City (1973), Arabia Through The Looking Glass (1979), Old Glory (1981, Heinemann award RSL 1982, Thomas Cook award 1982), Foreign Land (1985), Coasting (1986), For Love and Money (1987), God, Man and Mrs Thatcher (1989), Hunting Mister Heartbreak (1990, Thomas Cook Award 1991), The Oxford Book of the Sea (ed, 1992), American Gothic: A Place in the West (1996); *Recreations* sailing; *Clubs* Groucho, Cruising Assoc; *Style*— Jonathan Raban, Esq, FRSL; ✉ Aitken & Stone Ltd, 29 Fernshaw Road, London SW10 0TG (☎ 0171 351 7561, fax 0171 376 3594)

RABIN, Prof Brian Robert; s of Emanuel Rabin (d 1973), and Sophia, *née* Neshaver (d 1982); *b* 4 Nov 1927; *Educ* Latymer's, UCL (BSc, MSc, PhD); *m* 29 Aug 1954, Sheila Patricia, da of Charles Patrick George (d 1972); 1 s (Paul Robert b 27 Jan 1958), 1 da (Carol (Mrs Costa) b 23 Sept 1959); *Career* UCL 1954–: asst lectr then lectr 1954–63, reader in biochemistry 1963–67, prof of enzymology 1967–70, head of Biochemistry Dept 1970–88, fell UCL 1984, prof of biochemistry 1988–94 (prof emeritus 1994); fndr dir London Biotechnology Ltd 1985–, dir Cogent Ltd and Cogents Holdings Ltd 1986–89; FZS 1972, FIBiol 1972, EMBO 1980, memb Academie Für Umuweltfragen 1987; *Recreations* travel, carpentry; *Clubs* Athenaeum; *Style*— Prof Brian Rabin; ✉ 34 Grangewood, Potters Bar, Herts EN6 1SL (☎ 01707 654576)

RABINOWITZ, Harry; MBE (1978); s of Israel Rabinowitz (d 1960), and Eva, *née* Kirkel (d 1971); *b* 26 March 1916; *Educ* Athlone HS SA, Witwatersrand Univ, London Guildhall Sch of Music; *m* 15 Dec 1944, Lorna Thurlow, da of Cecil Redvers Anderson (d 1970); 1 s (Simon Oliver b 1951), 2 da (Karen Lesley b 1947, Lisa Gabrielle b 1960); *Career* Corpl SA Forces 1942–43; conductor BBC Radio 1953–60; head of music: BBC TV Light Entertainment 1960–68, LWT 1968–77; currently freelance conductor/composer; conductor: Hollywood Bowl 1983–84, Boston Pops 1985–92, London Symphony Orchestra, Royal Philharmonic Orchestra; conductor for films: Chariots of Fire, Manhattan Project, Heat & Dust, The Bostonians, Maurice, Time Bandits, Return to Oz, L'Argent, Camile Claudel, Ballad of the Sad Cafe, J'Embrasse Pas, La Voix, Pour Sacha, Les Carnassiers, Howard's End, The Ark and the Flood, Tractions, The Remains of the Day, Shirley Valentine, Business Affair, Grosse Fatigue, Le Petit Garçon, The Flemish Board, Mantegna et Fils, La Fille de d'Artagnan, Death and the Maiden, Jefferson in Paris, Nelly and Mr Arnold, Secret Agent, The Stupids, The Proprietor, Star Command, La Belle Verte, Surviving Picasso, The English Patient; TV: New Faces 1987–88, Paul Nicholas Special 1987–88, Julia MacKenzie Special 1986, Nicholas Nickleby, Drummonds, The Insurance Man, Absent Friends, Simon Wiesenthal Story, Marti Caine Special, Alien Empire (BBC), Memento Mori (BBC); composer TV: Agatha Christie Hour, Reilly Ace of Spies, The Great Depression, Memento Mori, DW Griffiths Father of Film; conductor theatre: World Premieres of "Cats" and "Song and Dance"; Discs: Michael Crawford, Sarah Brightman, The Music of Duke Ellington (with Johnny Mathis), The Music of George Gershwin (with Jack Jones), Radio City Christmas Album, 11 Japanese song hits (with RPO); awards: Br Acad of Songwriters, Composers and Authors (BASCA) Gold award 1986, Radio and TV Industries award 1984, Allmusic Lifetime Contrib Gold award 1990, Freeman City of London 1996; *Recreations* wine tasting, gathering edible fungi; *Clubs* Holmbury St Mary Village; *Style*— Harry Rabinowitz, Esq, MBE; ✉ Yellow Cottage, Walking Bottom, Peaslake, Surrey GU5 9RR (☎ 01306 730605)

RACE, Russell John; s of Russell Edgar Race (d 1982), and Winifred Olive, *née* Clissold (d 1996); *b* 28 May 1946; *Educ* Sir Joseph Williamson's Mathematical Sch Rochester, Univ of Liverpool (BA); *Career* economist White Fish Authy 1967–70, dir ABN AMRO Hoare Govett 1985– (investmt analyst 1970–76, corp fin 1976–); memb: Securities Inst, Inst of Investment Management and Research; Liveryman Worshipful Co of Glaziers & Painters of Glass; *Recreations* music, hockey, cricket; *Clubs* Naval and Military, London Capital; *Style*— Russell Race, Esq; ✉ 86 Ingle Rd, Chatham, Kent ME4 5SE (☎ 01634 406 347); ABN AMRO Hoare Govett Corporate Finance Ltd, 4 Broadgate, London EC2M 7LE (☎ 0171 374 1861, fax 0171 374 1388)

RACE, Stephen Russell (Steve); OBE (1992); s of Russell Tiniswood Race (d 1926), of Lincoln, and Robina Race (d 1964); *b* 1 April 1921; *Educ* Christ's Hosp Sch (formerly Lincoln Sch), RAM; *m* 1, 7 June 1944, Clair Leng (d 1969); 1 da (Nicola b 1946); m 2, 14 April 1970, Leonie Rebecca Govier Mather; *Career* RAF 1941–46; freelance pianist arranger and composer 1946–55, light music advsr Assoc-Rediffusion Ltd 1955–60, TV conductor Tony Hancock and Peter Sellers Shows; radio and TV appearances incl: My Music, A Good Read, Jazz in Perspective, Any Questions?, Music Now, Music Weekly, Kaleidoscope, Look What They've Done to My Song, Jazz Revisited, With Great Pleasure, Desert Island Discs, Jerome Kern Among Friends, Gershwin Among Friends, Irving Berlin Among Friends; compositions incl: Nicola (Ivor Novello Award), Faraway Music, The Pied Piper, incidental music for Richard III, Cyrano de Bergerac, Twelfth Night (BBC); cantatas: Song of King David, The Day of the Donkey, Song of Praise, My Music - My Songs; numerous other works incl: ITV advertising soundtracks (Venice Award 1962, Cannes Award 1963); film music: Calling Paul Temple, Three Roads to Rome, Against The Tide, Land of Three Rivers; author of radio reviews in The Listener 1975–80; Wavenden Allmusic Media Personality of the Year 1987, TV and Radio Industs Club Award 1988, British Acad of Songwriters Composers and Authors Gold Badge of Merit 1991; dep chm Performing Rights Soc 1966–68, memb Royal Albert Hall Cncl of Arts and Sci 1976–95, govr Tokyo Metropolis Prize for Radio 1979, memb Exec Cncl Musicians' Benevolent Fund 1985–95; Freeman City of London 1982; ARAM 1968, FRSA 1975, FRAM 1978; *Books* Musician at Large (autobiography, 1979), My Music (1979), Dear Music Lover (1981), Steve Race's Music Quiz (1983), The Illustrated Counties of England (contrib, 1984), You Can't be Serious (1985), The Penguin Masterquiz (1985), With Great Pleasure (contrib, 1986), The Two Worlds of Joseph Race (1988); *Style*— Steve Race, Esq, OBE; ✉ Martins End Lane, Great Missenden, Bucks HP16 9HS

RADCLIFFE, David Andrew; s of Clinton Bower Radcliffe, and Margaret, *née* Turnbull; *b* 13 June 1942; *Educ* The Leys Sch Cambridge, Univ of Cambridge (MA); *m* 22 May 1971, Elisabeth Mary, da of David Scotson Bramley; 2 s (James b 11 Nov 1975, Matthew b 5 Jan 1981), 1 da (Emily b 7 Feb 1978); *Career* cmmnd RM Reserve 1967, ret 1971; called to the Bar Inner Temple 1966; recorder Crown Court 1987–; vice pres Putney Soc 1987– (chm 1983–85); *Recreations* golf, tennis, squash, swimming, walking; *Clubs* Roehampton; *Style*— David Radcliffe, Esq; ✉ 5 King's Bench Walk, Temple, London EC4Y 7DN (☎ 0171 797 7600)

RADCLIFFE, John Peter; s of John Maurice Radcliffe (d 1949), of Almondsbury, Bristol, and Margery Bloomfield Lumsden (d 1974); *b* 9 Jan 1935; *Educ* Cheltenham (open scholar), Clare Coll Cambridge (exhibitioner, MA); *m* 5 Sept 1959, Bridget Jane, da of Dr William Leslie Cuthbert, of Stirling; 2 da (Virginia Frances b 10 Oct 1961, Polly Clare b 10 Dec 1965), 1 s (Jonathan James b 31 July 1963); *Career* asst to commercial mangr (economics) UKAEA Industrial Group 1960–61; BBC: prodr World Service Current Affairs 1961–64, prodr responsible for history BBC Schools Television 1965–70, sr prodr responsible for social sciences BBC Open Univ Prodns 1970–72, exec prodr BBC Continuing Educn Television 1972–84, exec prodr BBC Computer Literacy Project 1980–83, head of BBC Open Univ Prodn Centre 1984–89, md BBC Subscription Television 1990–93; exec prodr The MultiMedia Corp 1994–; *Recreations* hill walking, photography, literature, computing, conversation; *Style*— John Radcliffe, Esq; ✉ 106 Richmond Avenue, Islington, London N1 0LS (☎ 0171 837 5039)

RADCLIFFE, Julian Guy Yonge; TD; s of Maj Guy Lushington Yonge Radcliffe, MBE, and Anne Marigold, *née* Leyland; *b* 29 Aug 1948; *Educ* Eton, New Coll Oxford; *m* Francis Harriet Thompson; 2 s, 1 da; *Career* Lloyd's broker and underwriting memb of Lloyd's; md: Investmt Insurance Int 1973–81, Control Risks Ltd 1976–81; dir: Credit Insurance Assoc Ltd 1975–83, Hogg Group plc 1986–94, Bain Hogg International 1994–, Loss Management Group 1994–; chm International Art and Antique Loss Register Ltd 1991–; cmmnd Royal Yeomanry 1971, Lt-Col 1993; upper bailiff Worshipful Co of Weavers 1995–96; *Recreations* farming, shooting, military and strategic studies; *Clubs* City of London, Cavalry and Guards'; *Style*— Julian Radcliffe, Esq, TD; ✉ 32 Brynmaer Rd, SW11 4EW; Lower Stanway, Much Wenlock, Shropshire TF13 6LD

RADCLIFFE, Mark Hugh Joseph; s of Hugh John Reginald Joseph Radcliffe, MBE (d 1993), of Andover, Hants, and Marie-Thérèse (Mariquita), *née* Pereira; bro of Most Rev Timothy Radcliffe, *qv*; cousin and hp of Sir Sebastian Everard Radcliffe, 7 Bt, *qv*; *Educ* Downside; *m* 20 Feb 1963, Anne, da of Maj-Gen Arthur Evers Brocklehurst, CB, DSO; 3 da (Lucinda b 1964, Emily Marie Louise b 1968, Camilla Mary b 1971); *Career* 2 Lt Coldstream Gds 1956–58; mktg mangr Cape Asbestos Ltd 1958–68, chief exec Lancer Boss Group Ltd 1968–74, md Triang Pedigree Ltd 1974–78, dir TI Group plc 1978–92; CBI: dep dir gen 1991–93, estab National Manufacturing Cncl 1991, advsr on industl affrs 1991–94; non-exec chm Metsec PLC 1993–; non-exec dir: London Stock Exchange 1993–, William Jacks plc 1994–, Reliance Security Group PLC 1995–; independent dir Securities and Futures Authority Ltd 1993–, chm Upton Management Services Ltd 1992–; High Sheriff of Hampshire 1996–97; FInstD; *Recreations* shooting, golf, tennis, gardening; *Clubs* Cavalry and Guards'; *Style*— Mark Radcliffe, Esq; ✉ The Malt House, Upton, Andover, Hants SP11 0JS (☎ 01264 736266)

RADCLIFFE, Sir Sebastian Everard; 7 Bt (UK 1813), of Milnesbridge House, Yorkshire; s of Capt Sir (Joseph Benedict) Everard Henry Radcliffe, 6 Bt, MC (d 1975), and Marcia Helen, *née* Turville-Constable-Maxwell (now Mrs Howard M S Tanner); *b* 8 June 1972; *Heir* cousin, Mark Hugh Joseph Radcliffe, *qv*; *Style*— Sir Sebastian Radcliffe, Bt

RADCLIFFE, Most Rev Timothy Peter Joseph; s of Hugh John Reginald Joseph Radcliffe, MBE (d 1993), of Andover, Hants, and Marie-Thérèse (Mariquita), *née* Pereira; bro of Mark Hugh Joseph Radcliffe, *qv*; *b* 22 Aug 1945; *Educ* Downside, St John's Coll Oxford (MA); *Career* entered Dominican Order 1965, chaplain Imperial Coll London 1976–78, prior Blackfriars Oxford 1982–88 (teacher 1978–88), provincial English Province of the Order of Preachers (Dominicans) 1988–92, pres Conf of Major Religious Superiors of England and Wales 1991–92, Master of the Order of Preachers 1992–; grand chllr: Pontifical Univ of St Thomas Aquinas Rome, Univ of St Thomas Manila Philippines, Faculty of Theology Univ of Fribourg Switzerland, Ecole Biblique Jerusalem; former John Tookey scholar-in-residence Univ of Sydney; Hon STD Providence Coll RI; Hon LLD Barry Univ Florida, Hon DHL Ohio Dominican Coll; hon fell: St John's Coll Oxford, John XXIII Coll Australian Nat Univ; hon citizen of Augusta Italy; *Recreations* walking, reading very long novels; *Style*— The Most Rev Timothy Radcliffe; ✉ Convento di S Sabina, Piazza Pietro d'Illiria 1, Aventino, 00153 Roma, Italy (☎ 00 39 6 57 94 1, fax 00 39 6 57 50 675)

RADCLYFFE, Sarah; da of Capt Charles Raymond Radclyffe, of Lew House, Lew, Nr Bampton, Oxon, and Helen Viola Egerton, *née* Cotton; *b* 14 Nov 1950; *Educ* Heathfield Sch Ascot Berks; *children* 2 s (Sam Charles Radclyffe b 30 March 1989, Callum b 7 Feb 1995); *Career* film prodr 1978–; films incl: My Beautiful Laundrette 1985, Caravaggio 1985, Wish You Were Here 1986, Sammy and Rosie Get Laid 1987, A World Apart 1988, Paperhouse 1989, Fools of Fortune 1990, Robin Hood 1991, Sirens 1993, Second Best 1993; *Style*— Miss Sarah Radclyffe; ✉ Sarah Radclyffe Productions, 83 Berwick Street, London W1V 3PJ (☎ 0171 437 3128, fax 0171 437 3129)

RADDA, Prof George Karoly; CBE (1993); *b* 9 June 1936, Gyor, Hungary; *Educ* Pannonhalma Hungary, Eotvos Univ Budapest, Merton Coll Oxford (MA, DPhil); *m*; 3 c (from previous m); *Career* research assoc Univ of Calif Berkeley 1962–63; Univ of Oxford: jr research fell Merton Coll 1961–64, lectr in organic chemistry St John's Coll 1963–64, deptl demonstrator in biochemistry 1964–66, fell and tutor in organic chemistry Merton Coll 1964–84, univ lectr in biochemistry 1966–84, dir Br Heart Fndn NMR

Research Gp 1983–, Br Heart Fndn prof of molecular cardiology 1984–, professorial fell Merton Coll 1984–, hon dir MRC Biochemical and Clinical Magnetic Resonance Unit 1988–96, head Dept of Biochemistry 1991–96; chief exec MRC 1996–; memb: various panels SRC, various panels and sub-ctees MRC (memb Cncl and Strategy Ctee 1988–92, memb Cell Bd 1982–87, chm Cell and Disorders Bd 1988–92, chm Human Genome Mapping Directed Prog Ctee 1993–96, chm Human Genome Mapping Coordinating Ctee 1994–96); memb Cncl: Royal Soc 1990–92, ICRF 1991–96 (chm Scientific Advsy Ctee 1994–96); pres Soc of Magnetic Resonance in Med 1985–86; memb: Fachbeirat Max Planck Institut fur Systemphysiologie Dortmund 1987–92, Int Advsy Bd Euro Soc for Magnetic Resonance in Med and Biology (ESMRMB) 1994–; conslt: ICI Pharmaceuticals 1978–95, Oxford Magnet Technology 1985–87, CIBA Geigy UK Ltd 1985–90, Otsaka Electronics 1987–88; author of over 700 pubn in reviewed scientific and med jls worldwide, ed Clinical Cardiology 1994–; Colworth Medal 1969, Feldberg Fndn Prize 1981, Br Heart Fndn Gold Medal and Prize for Cardiovascular Research 1982, CIBA Medal and Prize Biochemical Soc 1983, Gold Medal Soc of Magnetic Resonance in Med 1984, Buchanan Medal Royal Soc 1987, Skinner Lecture Medal Royal Coll of Radiology 1989, Rank Prize in Nutrition 1991; numerous named lectures incl most recently: Welbeck Meml Lecture Coll of Radiographers London 1990, ICI Canada Distinguished Lectureship Ottawa 1992, Louise Bertram Abraham Lecture RCP London 1993, Linacre Lecture St John's Coll Cambridge 1994; Hon DM Bern 1985, Hon DSc (Med) London 1991; Hon FRCR 1985, hon fell American Heart Assoc (Citation for Int Achievement) 1987, Hon FRCP 1987; memb: Chemical Soc 1961–79, Biochemical Soc 1964, Br Photobiology Soc 1964–76, Br Biophysical Soc 1967–78; FRS 1980, fell Soc of Magnetic Resonance 1994; *Style*— Prof George K Radda, CBE, FRS; ✉ Chief Executive, Medical Research Council, 20 Park Crescent, London W1N 4AL (☎ 0171 637 6037, fax 0171 580 4396); Merton College, Oxford OX1 4JD

RADFORD, Prof Colin Buchanan; OBE (1994); s of Walter Buchan Radford (d 1995), of London, and Elizabeth Robertson, *née* Collie (d 1990); *b* 28 May 1931; *Educ* Ashby-de-la-Zouch Boys' GS, RMA Sandhurst, Univ of Nottingham (BA, MA, PhD); *m* 5 April 1958, Ingeborg Sara (Inge), da of Chaim Frenkel (d 1938), of Vienna; 1 s (Tim b 23 Feb 1963), 1 da (Katy b 24 April 1961); *Career* cmmnd RA 1952, served until 1957; asst head of recruitment for employee rels Esso Petroleum 1961–62, head of modern languages Up Holland GS 1962–66; Queen's Univ Belfast: prof of French 1975–93 (prof emeritus 1994), dir Sch of Modern and Medieval Languages 1987–92; author of books incl four on French lit; chm Arts Cncl of NI 1991–94, memb Bd Br Inst in Paris 1988–92, memb and hon treas Soc of French Studies 1972–92; tstee Grand Opera House Belfast 1993–; FIL; Commandeur dans l'Ordre des Palmes Académiques France 1989 (Officier 1986); *Recreations* theatre, gardener's mate; *Style*— Prof Colin Radford, OBE; ✉ The Hill, Woburn Rd, Millisle, Co Down (☎ 01247 861361, fax 01247 862310)

RADFORD, His Hon Judge; David Wyn; s of Robert Edwin Radford, CB, of Guildford, Surrey, and Eleanor Margaret, *née* Jones; *b* 3 Jan 1947; *Educ* Cranleigh Sch, Selwyn Coll Cambridge (MA, LLM); *m* 23 Sept 1972, Nadine, da of Joseph Poggioli, of London; 2 s (Simon b 1982, Peter b 1983), 2 da (Carina b 1975, Lauren b 1986); *Career* called to the Bar Gray's Inn 1969, recorder 1993–96 (asst recorder 1988–93), circuit judge (SE Circuit) 1996–; Lib Parly candidate Hampstead 1975–83; *Recreations* following soccer, politics, theatre; *Style*— His Hon Judge Radford; ✉ Snaresbrook Crown Court, Hollybush Hill, Snaresbrook, London E11 1QW

RADFORD, Jonathan Vaughan; s of Patrick Vaughan Radford, CBE, MC, TD, DL, *qv*, of Langford Hall, Newark, Notts, and Evelyn, *née* Wilkinson; *b* 11 June 1959; *Educ* Eton, Univ of Bristol (BA); *Career* accountant; Peat Marwick Mitchell and Co London 1981–86, fin dir Stag Furniture Holdings plc 1992–95 (various mgmnt positions 1986–92), chief exec Elit International Limited 1995–; former memb Governing Bd Young NACF; Freeman City of London 1987, Liveryman Worshipful Co of Furniture Makers 1987; ACA 1984, ACIS 1990, FCA 1994; *Recreations* shooting, skiing, tennis, art, travel; *Clubs* Annabel's; *Style*— Jonathan Radford, Esq; ✉ Elit International Limited, Cavendish House, 128–134 Cleveland Street, London W1P 5DN (☎ 0171 388 6222, fax 0171 388 7555, mobile 0836 671993)

RADFORD, Matthew; *b* 1953; *Educ* Camberwell Sch of Art (BA); *Career* artist; teacher: Camberwell Sch of Art 1981–84, Drawing Center NY 1985–86, NY Studio Sch 1989–93; *Solo Exhibitions* Letchworth Museum and Art Gallery 1980, Kettle's Yard 1984, Chuck Levitan NY 1985, Donald Wren Gallery NY 1987, Frank Bernarducci Gallery NY 1988 and 1990, CVII NY 1989, Tatistcheff Gallery Los Angeles 1993 (NY 1991), Grace Borgenicht Gallery NY 1993 and 1994, Houldsworth Fine Art London 1994; *Group Exhibitions* Royal Festival Hall 1980, 1981 and 1983, RA Diploma Galleries 1980, Stock Exchange Gallery 1981, British Drawing (Hayward Gallery) 1982, The Drawing Center 1985 and 1993, Donald Wren Gallery 1987, New York Observed (Frank Bernarducci Gallery) 1988, Downtown Perspectives (Adelphi Univ NY) 1988, New York Art Now (Helander Gallery Palm Beach) 1989, Visions and Visionaries (Tavelli Gallery Aspen) 1989, Quest (NY Studio Sch) 1989, Social Studies (Lintas Worldwide NY) 1989, Art and Law (Minnesota Museum of Art and tour) 1990, New York at Night (Helander Gallery) 1990, Four Artists (Houldsworth Fine Art) 1990, New Faces, New Work (Tatistcheff & Co NY) 1991, On the Move (Champion Gallery Stamford) 1991, ICAF91, Houldsworth Fine Art 1991, 1992, 1993 and 1994, City (Martin County Cncl of the Arts Florida) 1992, Mall Galleries 1992, People (Gallery Three Zero NY) 1992, Art92, Isolation (Tatistcheff Gallery) 1992, Art93, Mostyn Open Exhibition 1993, Art94, Lew Allen Horwich Gallery Santa Fe 1994, Grace Borgenicht Gallery 1994; *Work in Collections* incl: Arthur Andersen Inc, Amerada Hess NY, Morgan Grenfell, McDonalds Corporation, Mercer Inc, Champion International Corporation, Fidelity Insurance Co, New Sch of Social Research, New York Public Library, Yale Center for British Art, Metropolitan Museum of Art; *Awards* Jeffrey Archer Prize 1981, GLC Award 1982, Eastern Arts Major Award 1983, Honarium-Drawing Center 1985, ED Fndn 1989; *Recreations* cricket, literature and old films; *Style*— Matthew Radford, Esq; ✉ c/o Houldsworth Fine Art, Pall Mall Deposit, 124–128 Barlby Road, London W10 6BL (☎ 0181 969 8197, fax 0181 964 3595)

RADFORD, (Oswald) Michael James; s of Oswald Charles Radford, of Haslemere, Surrey, and Ruth, *née* Presser; *b* 24 Feb 1946; *Educ* Bedford Sch, Worcester Coll Oxford (BA), Nat Film and TV Sch; *m* 4 Aug 1990, Iseult Joanna, *née* St Aubin de Teran; *Career* director; freelance film dir 1979–; govr Nat Film and TV Sch 1982–90; memb BAFTA; *Televison* documentary films for BBC incl: The Madonna and The Volcano (Grand Prix Nyon Documentary Film Festival 1979), The Last Stronghold of the Pure Gospel, La Belle Isobel, The White Bird Passes (Scot Acad Award 1980); *Films* Another Time, Another Place (Best Film Award Cannes Film Festival 1983, Special Jury Prize Celtic Film Festival 1983, George Sadoul Prize Paris for Best Foreign Film 1982, Nineteen Eighty Four (Standard Best Film of the Year Award 1984) 1984, White Mischief 1988, Ilpostino (The Postman (David Lean Award for Best Direction 1996)) 1994; *Recreations* fishing, skiing, snooker; *Clubs* Groucho's; *Style*— Michael Radford, Esq; ✉ c/o Seifert-Dench Associates, 24 D'Arblay Street, London W1V 3FH (☎ 0171 437 4551, fax 0171 439 1355)

RADFORD, Neal Victor; s of Victor Reginald Radford, of Johannesburg, SA, and Joyce Edith, *née* Osler; *b* 7 June 1957; *Educ* Athlone Boys HS Johannesburg SA; *m* 20 April 1985, Lynne Mary, da of Lawrence Middleton; 2 s (Luke Anthony b 3 June 1988, Josh Deckland b 12 Feb 1990); *Career* professional cricketer; schoolboy teams: Transvaal SA 1974–75, SA Schs 1975–76; SA Army 1978, first class Transvaal 1978–89; Lancs League: Bacup 1979–80, Nelson 1981, Ramsbottom 1983; Lancashire CCC 1980–84; Worcestershire CCC 1985–95: awarded county cap 1985, 192 first class appearances (296 career), 218 one day appearances (over 333 career), 653 first class wickets (994 career), 297 one day wickets (457 career); completed 1000 runs/100 wickets Sunday League career double during last match 1993 season; England: 3 Test matches (v India Edgbaston 1986, NZ Lords 1986, NZ Auckland 1987), 6 one day Ints (4 v NZ 1987, 1 v Aust 1987, 1 v W Indies 1988); honours with Worcestershire CCC: County Champions 1988 and 1989, NatWest Trophy runners up 1988, Refuge Assurance League winners 1987 and 1988, Benson & Hedges winners 1991 (runners up 1990), Refuge Cup winners 1991, runners-up Benson & Hedges 1994, Nat West winners 1994; holds record for most wickets in a season 1985 (101) and 1987 (109); Esso/Mail on Sunday bowler of the year 1985, Cricketers' cricketer of the year 1985, Wisden cricketer of the year 1985, Mail on Sunday bowler of the year 1987, Worcestershire CCC player of the year 1987; SA Army 1977–78, auditor SA 1979–81, cricket coach SA 1981–89, PR and promotional work Spectrum Organisation Wilts 1990–91, indoor cricket for Stumps Birmingham, sales exec Nationwide Boards 1991–92, salesman Filter Supply 1992–93, own business Radford Ezy Net 1993–, currently dir of cricket Banbury CC; *Recreations* enjoying home comforts with my family, pottering around in the garden, playing golf; *Style*— Neal Radford, Esq; ✉ Banbury CCC, Banbury, Oxon (☎ 01295 264368)

RADFORD, Patrick Vaughan; CBE (1983), MC (1945), TD, DL (1987); s of Vaughan Nattrass Radford (d 1988), and Beatrice Mary, *née* Bullivant (d 1978); *b* 16 Nov 1920; *Educ* Oundle; *m* 1, 1945 (m dis 1956), Nancy Madeline, *née* Shaw; 1 da (Carol b 1946); m 2, 1956, Evelyn Lily, da of George Herbert Wilkinson (d 1971); 4 s (Nicholas b 1957, Jonathan, *qv*, b 1959, Timothy b 1960, Anthony b 1962), 1 step da (Anthea b 1947); *Career* Nat Serv WWII, joined RAC 1941, cmmnd 2 Lt 1942, served 1 Derby Yeo in UK, N Africa, Italy, Austria 1942–46, joined Derby Yeo TA 1947 (Maj), 2i/c Leics and Derbys Yeo TA 1956, Lt-Col 1958–61; called to the Bar Gray's Inn 1954; chm Stag Furniture Holdings PLC 1971–91; dir Project Telecommunications Ltd 1992–; memb Ct of Assts and Tstee Worshipful Co of Furniture Makers (Liveryman 1963, Master 1982–83); FCIS; *Recreations* fishing, gardening; *Clubs* Cavalry & Guards', Nottingham United Servs; *Style*— Patrick Radford, Esq, CBE, MC, TD, DL; ✉ Langford Hall, Newark, Notts NG23 7RS (☎ 01636 76802)

RADFORD, Prof Peter Frank; s of Frank Radford (d 1994), and Lilian, *née* Marks (d 1981); *b* 20 Sept 1939; *Educ* Tettenhall Coll, Cardiff Coll of Educn, Purdue Univ USA, Univ of Glasgow (Dip in Physical Educn, MSc, PhD); *m* 1961, Margaret, da of Richard Beard; 1 da (Elizabeth Anne b 18 Dec 1967); *Career* lectr and asst prof McMaster Univ Hamilton Ontario Canada 1967–75; Univ of Glasgow: dir and head Dept of Physical Educn and Recreation 1976–87, prof and head Dept of Physical Educn and Sports Sci 1987–94; exec chm Br Athletic Fedn 1994– (vice-chm 1992–93, chm 1993–94); chm: Scottish Consultative Gp on Sports Med and Sports Sci 1984–90, Sports Cncl Drug Advsy Gp 1991–95 (memb 1988–91), Sport Cncl's Review of Coaching in Sport (coaching matters) 1991–93, Cncl of Europe's Int Anti-Doping Convention 1994– (memb Monitoring Gp 1990–95, vice-chm 1992–94); memb: Scottish Sports Cncl 1983–90, Int Working Gp on Anti-Doping in Sport 1991–93, Mgmnt Ctee Nat Sports Med Inst 1991–94; contrb to various jls, conf proceedings and books on sport educn, sports sci, sports history and doping control; *Athletics achievements* memb GB athletics teams 1958–64, winner bronze medal 100m and 4 x 100m Olympic Games Rome 1960; former world record holder: 200m/220yds 1960, 4 x 110yds relay 1963, indoor 50m 1959, junior 100m and 200m 1958; Br 100m record set in Paris 1958 remained unbroken for 20 years; *Recreations* sports history 1650–1850, 18th & 19th century sporting art, gardening; *Style*— Prof Peter Radford; ✉ British Athletic Federation, 225a Bristol Road, Edgbaston, Birmingham B5 7UB (☎ 0121 440 5000, fax 0121 440 0555)

RADFORD, Roger George; s of Ernest Reginald Radford (d 1977), and Evelyn, *née* Lamont (d 1985); *b* 17 March 1944; *Educ* City of London Sch; *m* 29 May 1971, Susan, da of Geoffrey Mitchell; 2 s (Andrew b 15 July 1974, James b 20 August 1980), 1 da (Juliette b 27 May 1977); *Career* Clerical Medical & General Life Assurance Society 1963–84, sec The Church of England Pensions Board 1984– (joined as dep sec 1984); chm of govrs St Nicholas Sch Elstree; AIA 1975; *Recreations* cricket, golf, gardening, reading; *Clubs* John Carpenter, Jesters, Fifty Nine; *Style*— Roger Radford, Esq; ✉ Secretary, The Church of England Pensions Board, 7 Little College Street, Westminster, London SW1P 3SF (☎ 0171 222 2091, fax 0171 233 1763)

RADICE, Giles Heneage; MP (Lab) Durham North (majority 19,637); s of Lawrence Wallace Radice (d 1996; himself s of Evadio Radice) and Patricia, eldest da of Sir Arthur Pelham Heneage, DSO, JP, DL, sometime MP for Louth; *b* 4 Oct 1936; *Educ* Winchester, Magdalen Coll Oxford; *m* 1, 1959 (m dis 1969), Penelope, er da of late Robert Angus, JP, DL, of Ladykirk, Ayrshire, by his w (subsequently Lady Moore); 2 da (Adele b 1961, Sophia b 1964); m 2, 1971, Lisanne, *née* Gervis; *Career* former head Res Dept GMWU; MP (Lab): Chester-le-Street 1973–83, Durham N 1983–; chm Manifesto Gp in Labour Party 1980–81, oppn front bench spokesman on employment 1981–83, memb Shadow Cabinet 1983–87, memb Select Ctees on: Treasy and Civil Service 1987–, Public Service 1996–; memb Cncl Policy Studies Institute 1978–82, chm European Movement 1995–; *Style*— Giles Radice Esq, MP; ✉ House of Commons, London SW1A 0AA

RADNOR, Dowager Countess of; Anne Isobel Graham Pleydell-Bouverie; OBE (1961), DL (Wiltshire 1987); da of Lt-Col Richard Oakley, DSO, JP (d 1948), and Enid Elizabeth (d 1980), da of James Noble Graham, JP, DL (of the senior cadet branch of the Ducal family of Montrose); *b* 6 Sept 1908; *m* 1, 1931, Richard Sowerby (d 1939), er s of Lt-Col Thomas Sowerby, JP, of The Manor House, Lilley, Herts; m 2, 1943, as his 2 w, 7 Earl of Radnor, KG, KCVO, JP, DL (d 1968); 1 s (Richard Oakley); *Career* memb: Historic Buildings Cncl for England 1953–68, Advsy Bd for Redundant Churches 1969–79; tstee Historic Churches Preservation Tst; pres: Health Visitors' Assoc 1963–84, Salisbury League of Hosp Nurses, Wilts Assoc of Beekeepers, South Wilts Girl Guides, Salisbury Civic Soc; former pres: Assoc of Wilts Parish Cncls, Wilts Assoc of Youth Clubs, Wilts Tst for Nature Conservation, Wilts Community Cncl; patron: Salisbury & South Wilts Museum, Salisbury Hospice Tst, Wiltshire Historic Buildings Tst Ltd; *Style*— The Rt Hon the Dowager Countess of Radnor, OBE, DL; ✉ Avonturn, Alderbury, Salisbury (☎ 01722 710235)

RADNOR, 8 Earl of (GB 1765); Sir Jacob Pleydell-Bouverie; 11 Bt (GB 1714); also Viscount Folkestone, Baron Longford (both GB 1747), and Baron Pleydell-Bouverie (GB 1765); patron of two livings; s of 7 Earl of Radnor, KG, KCVO (d 1968), and his 1 w, Helena (who m 2, 1943, Brig Montacute William Worrell Selby-Lowndes, and d 1985), da of late Charles Adeane, CB (whose w Madeline, CBE, JP, was gda of 1 Baron Leconfield); *b* 10 Nov 1927; *Educ* Harrow, Trinity Coll Cambridge; *m* 1, 1953 (m dis 1962), Anne, da of Donald Seth-Smith, MC; 2 s; m 2, 1963 (m dis 1985), Margaret, da of Robin Fleming, of Catter House, Drymen; 4 da; m 3, 1986, Mrs A C Pettit; *Heir* s, Viscount Folkestone; *Career* landowner and farmer; chm Br Dyslexia Assoc 1971–76, pres Dyslexia Inst 1972–94, govr French Hospital (La Providence) 1971–, memb House of Lords Select Ctee (agriculture, food and consumer affrs) 1985–90 and 1991–93, co-opted House of Lords Sub Ctee (science and technology - "Sustainable Fisheries") 1995; *Recreations* field sports, fly-tying, fishing, bird-watching; *Clubs* Farmers'; *Style*— The Rt Hon the Earl of Radnor; ✉ House of Lords, London SW1A 0PW

RADO, Gabor Andras (Gaby); s of Joseph Rado, of Chislehurst, Kent, and Eva, *née* Varnai; *b* 17 Jan 1955; *Educ* King's Coll Sch, Christ's Coll Cambridge (BA); *m* 1980, Carol

Louise, da of Colin Watson; 3 s (Thomas James b 17 April b 1985, Nicholas Alexander b 22 Nov 1986 d 1991, Michael-Louis b 3 Aug 1992); *Career* reporter: Kentish Times 1976–78, BBC Radio Leicester 1978–79; scriptwriter BBC TV News 1979–83, freelance reporter Thames TV and BBC 1984–85, prodr ITN 1985–88, reporter Channel 4 News and ITN 1988–90, foreign affrs corr Channel 4 News 1992– (Moscow corr 1991–92); memb NUJ 1976; *Recreations* tennis, cinema, literature, music; *Clubs* Knockholt Tennis; *Style*— Gaby Rado, Esq; ✉ Channel 4 News, ITN Ltd, 200 Gray's Inn Road, London WC1X 8XZ (☎ 0171 430 4481, fax 0171 430 4609)

RAE, Allan Alexander Sinclair; CBE (1973); s of John Rae (d 1969), of Ayr, and Rachel Margaret, *née* Sinclair (d 1969); *b* 26 Nov 1925; *Educ* Ayr Acad, Univ of Glasgow (LLB); *m* 1, 1 June 1955, Shelia Grace (d 1985), da of Capt Geoffrey Saunders, OBE, RN (d 1948); 2 s (Nigel b 1956, David b 1961), 1 da (Susan b 1962); m 2, 7 April 1986, Gertrud, da of Arnold Dollinger (d 1972), of Basle, Switzerland; *Career* Staff Capt RA JAG Dept 1944–47; admitted slr; sr ptnr Crawford Bayley & Co Bombay 1959–64 (joined 1948, ptnr 1950–59), dir and head of Legal and Patents Dept CIBA Ltd Basle 1964–69, dir and head of Regnl Servs CIBA-Geigy Ltd Basle 1969–72, memb Exec Ctee CIBA-Geigy AG Basle 1972–88, chm: CIBA-Geigy Gp of Cos UK 1972–90, Ilford Ltd 1972–88; dir: ABB Power Ltd 1973–89, Williams & Glyn's Bank 1974–85, T & N plc 1979–94, ABB Kent (Hldgs) plc 1980–94, Mettler Instruments Ltd 1985–89, Riggs AP Bank Ltd 1986–91; pres Chemical Industs Assoc Ltd 1986–88 (vice pres 1984–86, memb Cncl 1975–95); vice pres Business and Industry Advsy Ctee OECD 1985–93; CIMgt; *Recreations* sailing, skiing, golf; *Clubs* Royal Thames Yacht; *Style*— Allan Rae, Esq, CBE; ✉ Bryn Dulas, Llanddulas, Conwy LL22 8NA (☎ 01492 517501, fax 01492 518088)

RAE, Barbara Davis; da of James Rae, Provost, of Crieff, Perthshire (d 1982), and Mary, *née* Young; *b* 1943; *Educ* Morrisons Acad Crieff, Edinburgh Coll of Art, Moray House Coll of Educn; *Career* artist; art teacher: Ainsie Park Comp Edinburgh 1968–69, Portobello Secdy Sch Edinburgh 1969–72; lectr in drawing painting and printmaking Aberdeen Coll of Educn 1972–74, lectr in drawing and painting Glasgow Sch of Art 1975, exchange teacher Fine Art Dept Univ of Maryland 1984; memb: Art Panel CNAA 1986–, Cncl RSW 1986–90 (vice-pres for East 1992–), Royal Fine Art Cmmn for Scotland 1995–; pres Soc of Scottish Artists 1982–84; tstee Arts Educn Tst 1986–90; assoc: RSA, RSW, RGI; *Exhibitions* New '57 Gall Edinburgh 1967 and 1971, Univ of York 1969, Univ of Aberdeen and Aberdeen Art Gall 1974, Peterloo Gall Manchester 1975, Stirling Gall Stirling 1976, Greenock Arts Guild 1976, Gilbert Parr Gall London 1977, Univ of Edinburgh 1978 and 1979, The Scottish Gall Edinburgh 1979, 1983, 1987, 1988, 1990 and 1995, Wright Gall Dallas Texas USA 1985, Leinster Fine Art London 1986, Glasgow Print Studio 1987, The Scottish Gall London and Edinburgh 1989–90, Earth Pattern (William Jackson Gall London) 1992, Altandhu to Atejate (Glasgow Print Studio 1992, Hunt/Jennings Gallery London 1993, Jorgensen Fine Art Dublin 1993), The Reconstructed Landscape (Highland regn touring exhbn Scotland) 1993, Art First (Cork Street Gall) 1994, Edinburgh Festival Exhbn (Aitken Dott) 1995, Jorgensen Fine Art Dublin 1995; *Collections* work in numerous private and public collections incl: Bank of England, Arts Cncl of Scotland, HRH Prince Philip, Br Museum, Royal Bank of Scotland, Nat Gall of Modern Art Edinburgh; tapestry cmmn for Edinburgh Festival Theatre 1994; *Awards* Arts Cncl Award 1968, maj Arts Cncl Award 1975–81, Guthrie Medal RSA 1977, May Marshall Brown Award (RSW Centenary Exhibition) 1979, RSA Sir William Gillies Prize 1983, Calouste Gulbenkian Printmaking Award 1983, Alexander Graham Munro Award RSW 1989, Hunting Gp Prize 1990, Scottish PO Bd Award RSA 1990, Scottish Amicable Award RGI 1990, W J Burness Award RSA 1990; *Style*— Ms Barbara Rae; ✉ Glasgow School of Art, 167 Renfrew Street, Glasgow (☎ 0141 353 4500)

RAE, Fiona; *b* 10 Oct 1963, Hong Kong; *Educ* Croydon Coll of Art (Fndn Course), Goldsmiths' Coll of Art London (BA); *Career* artist; shortlisted Turner Prize 1991, shortlisted Eliette Von Karajan Prize for Young Painters (Austria) 1993; *Solo Exhibitions* Third Eye Centre Glasgow 1990, Pierre Bernard Gallery Nice 1990, Waddington Galleries London 1991, Kunsthalle Basel 1992, ICA London 1993–94, John Good Gallery NY 1994, Galerie Nathalie Obadia Paris 1994, Waddington Galleries London 1995, Contemporary Fine Arts Berlin 1996; *Group Exhibitions* incl: Freeze (Surrey Docks London) 1988, Anderson O'Day Gallery London 1989, Promises promises (Serpentine Gallery London and Ecole de Nimes) 1989, Br Art Show (McLellan Galleries Glasgow, Leeds City Art Gallery, Hayward Gallery London) 1990, Aperto (Venice Biennale) 1990, Witte de With Center for Contemporary Arts Rotterdam 1990, Anthony Reynolds Gallery London 1990, Who Framed Modern Art or The Quantitative Life of Roger Rabbit (Sidney Janis Gallery NY) 1991, Br Art from 1930 (Waddington Galleries London) 1991, A View of London (Salzburger Kunstverein) 1991, John Moores Liverpool Exhbn XVII (Walker Art Gallery) 1991, La Metafisica della Luce (John Good Gallery NY) 1991, Abstraction (Waddington Galleries) 1991, Turner Prize Exhbn (Tate Gallery London) 1991, The Contemporary Art Society: 80 Years of Collecting (Hayward Gallery and UK tour) 1991–92, Play between Fear and Desire (Germans van Eck Gallery NY) 1992, New Voices: Recent Paintings from the British Council Collection (Euro tour) 1992–95, A Decade of Collecting: Patrons of New Art Gifts 1983–93 (Tate Gallery) 1993–94, Moving into View: Recent British Painting (Arts Cncl Collection, Royal Festival Hall and UK tour) 1993–95, Unbound: Possibilities in Painting (Hayward Gallery) 1994, Chance, Choice and Irony (Todd Gallery London and John Hansard Gallery Univ of Southampton) 1994, Here and Now (Serpentine Gallery) 1994, Repicturing Abstraction (Marsh Art Gallery Univ of Virginia Richmond Va) 1995, From Here (Waddington Galleries and Karsten Schubert London) 1995, Malerei: Sechs Bilder, Sechs Positionen (Galerie Bugdahn und Kaimer Düsseldorf) 1995, Des limites du tableau: les possibles de la peinture (Musée Départemental de Rochechouart Haute-Vienne) 1995, Nuevas Abstracciones (Museo Nacional Centro de Arte Reina Sofia Madrid and also touring) 1996; *Collections* work in public collections incl: Arts Cncl of GB, Br Cncl, Contemporary Art Soc, Fonds Régional d'Art Contemporain d'Ile de France, Hamburger Bahnhof - Museum für Gegenwart Berlin SMPK Marx Collection, Musée Départemental de Rochechouart Haute-Vienne, Tate Gallery, Walker Art Gallery Liverpool; *Style*— Ms Fiona Rae; ✉ c/o Waddington Galleries Ltd, 11 Cork Street, London W1X 2LT

RAE, Dr John; s of John Rae (d 1976), of Rutherglen, Lanarkshire, and Marion, *née* Dow; *b* 29 Sept 1942; *Educ* Rutherglen Acad, Univ of Glasgow (BSc, PhD); *m* 11 May 1968, Irene Isabella, da of William Cassels, of Glasgow; 1 s (Philip John b 23 March 1974), 1 da (Helen Janet b 13 May 1976); *Career* teaching and res in theoretical physics: Univ of Glasgow 1964–68, Univ of Texas Austin 1968–70, Univ Libre Brussels 1970–72, QMC London 1972–74; acting div head theoretical physics div Harwell 1985 (industl fell 1974–76, gp leader theory of fluids 1976–86), chief scientist Dept of Energy 1986–89; chief exec AEA Environment and Energy 1990–93, business devpt dir (Govt) AEA Technology 1993–95, dir Nat Environmental Technol Centre 1993–95, md NPL Management Ltd 1995–; memb: SERC 1986–89, NERC 1986–89, BNES 1985; FInstE 1986; *Recreations* music (singing), gardening; *Style*— Dr John Rae; ✉ National Physical laboratory, Teddington, Middlesex TW11 0LW (☎ 0181 977 3222, fax 0181 943 1350)

RAE, Dr John Malcolm; s of Dr Lawrence John Rae (d 1979), of Walton on the Hill, Surrey, and Annie Blodwen, *née* Williams (d 1977); *b* 20 March 1931; *Educ* Bishop's Stortford Coll, Sidney Sussex Coll Cambridge (MA), King's Coll London (PhD); *m* 31 Dec 1955, Daphne Ray, da of John Phimester Simpson (d 1939), of Edinburgh; 2 s (Shamus, Jonathan (twins)), 4 da (Siobhan, Penelope, Alyce, Emily); *Career* 2 Lt Royal Fus 1950–51; history master Harrow Sch 1955–66, headmaster Taunton Sch 1966–70, headmaster Westminster Sch 1970–86, chm HMC 1977; dir The Laura Ashley Fndn 1986–89, Gresham prof of rhetoric 1988–90; dir: The Portman Group 1989–96, The Observer Ltd 1986–93; author of film script Reach for Glory 1961 (UN award), contrib to nat newspapers; JP Middx 1961–66; memb Nat Bd for Crime Prevention 1993–95, govr of Schs and Colls; Freeman City of London; Hon FCP 1984; *Books* The Custard Boys (1960), Conscience and Politics (1970), The Public School Revolution (1980), Letters from School (1987), Too Little, Too Late? (1989), Delusions of Grandeur (1993); five books for children; *Recreations* cinema, swimming; *Clubs* Hawks (Cambridge), RAC; *Style*— Dr John Rae; ✉ 2s Cedar Lodge, Lythe Hill Park, Haslemere, Surrey GU27 3TD (☎ 01428 652616)

RAE, John William; er s of Lt-Col William Rae, DSO, CD, VD (d 1973) of Victoria, British Columbia, and Edith Marion, *née* Brodrick (d 1988); *b* 16 Dec 1938; *Educ* Charterhouse, Queen's Coll Oxford (MA); *Career* TA: 2 Lt 5 Bn Queen's Royal Regt 1959–60, Lt 3 Bn Queen's Royal Surrey Regt 1961–63, TA Reserve of Offrs 1963–67; Regular Army Reserve of Offrs (II) 1967–85 and 1988–, Hon Artillery Co (HSF) 1985–88; called to the Bar Inner Temple 1961; worked way around world 1962–64; int commercial lawyer (German speaker) 1965–78, practising barr 1979–95; dir Campden Hill Court Ltd 1995–; memb: Exec Ctee Oxford Soc (chm West London Branch 1968–96), Guild Church Cncl and Ctee of Friends of St Botolph-without-Aldersgate Church City of London, Aldersgate Ward Club, Royal United Services Inst, St Bart's Hosp Choral Soc, Friends of Holland Park Kensington; Freeman City of London, memb Ct of Assts Worshipful Co of Plumbers (Master 1982–83), Liveryman Worshipful Co of Painter-Stainers; *Recreations* beagling, cycling, skiing, walking, travel, current affairs, music, photography; *Clubs* Athenaeum, Beefsteak, Canada, Coningsby; *Style*— John W Rae, Esq; ✉ 16A Campden Hill Court, Campden Hill Rd, London W8 7HS (☎ 0171 937 3492)

RAE, Rita Emilia Anna; QC (Scot 1992); da of Alexander Smith Cowie Rae (d 1993), and Bianca Angela Carmela Ermanna, *née* Bruno; *b* 20 June 1950; *Educ* St Patrick's HS Coatbridge Strathclyde, Univ of Edinburgh (LLB); *Career* apprentice Biggart Lumsden & Co Glasgow (solicitors) 1972–74, asst slr Biggart Baillie & Gifford Glasgow 1974–76, asst then ptnr Ross Harper & Murphy Glasgow 1976–81, admitted to Faculty of Advocates 1982, temp sheriff 1988–; memb: Scot Assoc for Study of Delinquency, SACRO, Soc for Computers & Law, Amnesty International; *Recreations* walking, music, opera, theatre, reading, travelling to Italy; *Style*— Miss Rita E A Rae, QC; ✉ c/o Advocates' Library, Parliament House, Edinburgh EH1 1RF (☎ 0131 226 5071)

RAEBURN, Ashley Reinhard George; CBE (1976); s of Dr Adolf Alsberg (d 1933), of Kassel, Germany, and Elisabeth, *née* Hofmann (d 1949); *b* 23 Dec 1918; *Educ* UCS, Balliol Coll Oxford (MA); *m* 6 Nov 1943, Esther Letitia Vivonne, da of Alfred Johns, of Goodwick, Pembs (d 1957); 1 s (Richard b 1946), 3 da (Ursula b 1944, Joanna b 1949, Charlotte (Mrs Barney), *qv*, b 1954); *Career* WWII RA (Capt) served in UK and India 1940–46; Miny of Food and HM Treasy 1946–54, Royal Dutch Shell Group 1955–77 (gp treas 1962), dir Shell International Petroleum Co Ltd (responsible for Africa, India and Pakistan) 1968–72, chief rep Shell Cos in Japan 1972–77, dir Rolls Royce Ltd 1978–82 (vice chm 1979–82), dir Boosey & Hawkes plc 1983–88 (chm 1984–86), dir Amalgamated Metal Corporation plc 1983–; endowment tstee Balliol Coll Oxford 1966–, memb Cncl of Mgmnt Studies Oxford (now Templeton Coll) 1965– (chm 1978–85), dir Euro Centre for Public Affrs 1987–93; hon fell Templeton Coll 1992– (Barclay fell 1995–); *Recreations* walking, gardening, music; *Clubs* United Oxford and Cambridge Univ; *Style*— Ashley Raeburn, Esq, CBE

RAEBURN, David Antony; s of Walter Augustus Leopold Raeburn, QC (d 1972), of London, and Dora Adelaide Harvey, *née* Williams; *b* 22 May 1927; *Educ* Charterhouse, ChCh Oxford (MA); *m* 8 April 1961, Mary Faith Fortescue, da of Arthur Hubbard (d 1977), of Harare, Zimbabwe; 2 s (Mark b 1965, Martin b 1967), 1 da (Fiona b 1969); *Career* Nat Serv 1949–51, cmmnd RAEC 1950; asst master: Bristol GS 1951–54, Bradfield Coll 1955–58; head of classics Alleyns Sch Dulwich 1958–62; headmaster: Beckenham and Penge GS (renamed Langley Pk Sch for Boys 1969) 1963–70, Whitgift Sch Croydon 1970–91; grammatikos (tutor in Ancient Greek) Univ of Oxford 1991–96, Grocyn lectr Univ of Oxford 1992–96; treas of HMC 1983–89, pres Jt Assoc of Classical Teachers 1983–85 (dir Summer Sch in Ancient Greek 1968–85); FRSA 1969; *Recreations* play production; *Style*— David Raeburn, Esq; ✉ 13a St Anne's Rd, Eastbourne, E Sussex BN21 2AJ (☎ 01323 724696)

RAEBURN, Maj-Gen Sir (William) Digby Manifold; KCVO (1979), CB (1966), DSO (1945), MBE (1941); s of late Sir Ernest Manifold Raeburn, KBE, s of 1 Bt; *b* 6 Aug 1915; *Educ* Winchester, Magdalene Coll Cambridge (MA); *m* 1960, Adeline Margaret, da of late Thomas Selwyn Pryor, MC; *Career* Maj-Gen (ret), late Scots Gds; dir of Combat Devpt (Army) 1963–65, Chief of Staff Allied Forces N Europe 1965–68, Chief Army Instructor Imperial Defence Coll 1968–70, resident govr and keeper of Jewel House of HM Tower of London 1971–79; *Style*— Maj-Gen Sir Digby Raeburn, KCVO, CB, DSO, MBE; ✉ 25 St Ann's Terrace, London NW8 6PH

RAEBURN, Prof John Alexander (Sandy); TD (1978); s of Lt-Col Hugh Adair Raeburn, RAMC (d 1975), and Christine Constance, *née* Forbes; *b* 25 June 1941; *Educ* Loretto, Univ of Edinburgh (MB ChB, PhD); *m* 1, 12 Aug 1967 (m dis 1980); 1 s (Hugh Alasdair b 1974), 2 da (Morag Elspeth Jean b 1969, Alison Forbes b 1971); m 2, 17 May 1980, Arlene Rose, da of George Conway, MBE, of Edinburgh; 2 step s (Kenneth Robert Aitchison b 1970, Ian George Aitchison b 1972); *Career* Maj TA & VR RAMC; sr res fell Univ of Leiden 1972–73, sr lectr in human genetics Univ of Edinburgh 1973–89, prof of clinical genetics Univ of Nottingham; former chm: Scot Downs Syndrome Assoc, Scot Cncl Cystic Fibrosis Res Tst; FRCPE 1976; *Recreations* Scottish literature, fishing; *Style*— Prof Sandy Raeburn, TD; ✉ Centre for Medical Genetics, City Hospital, Hucknall Road, Nottingham NG5 1PB (☎ 0115 962 7712, fax 0115 962 7711)

RAEBURN, (Sir) Michael Edward Norman; (4 Bt, UK 1923, but does not use his title); s of Sir Edward Alfred Raeburn, 3 Bt (d 1977), and Joan, da of Frederick Hill, of Boston, USA; *b* 12 Nov 1954; *m* 1979, Penelope Henrietta Theodora, da of Alfred Louis Penn (d 1963), of London; 2 s, 3 da; *Heir* s, Christopher Edward Alfred Raeburn b 4 Dec 1981; *Career* civil servant; *Style*— Michael Raeburn, Esq; ✉ Little Spring Cottage, Fletching Street, Mayfield, East Sussex TN20 6TN; HM Land Registry, Curtis House, Forest Rd, Hawkenbury, Tunbridge Wells, Kent

RAEBURN, Sheriff Susan Adiel Ogilvie; QC (Scot 1991); da of George Ferguson Raeburn (d 1993), of Aberdeenshire, and Rose Anne Bainbridge, *née* Morison; *b* 23 April 1954; *Educ* St Margaret's Sch for Girls Aberdeen, Univ of Edinburgh (LLB); *Career* apprentice Messrs Fyfe Ireland 1974–76, admitted to Faculty of Advocates 1977, sheriff of Glasgow and Strathkelvin 1993– (temporary sheriff 1988–93); pt/t chm: Social Security Appeal Tbnls 1985–92, Medical Appeal Tbnls 1992–93; *Recreations* the arts, travel, salmon fishing; *Clubs* Scottish Arts; *Style*— Sheriff S A O Raeburn, QC; ✉ Sheriffs Chambers, Sheriff Court of Glasgow and Strathkelvin, 1 Carlton Place, Glasgow (☎ 0141 429 8888)

RAFFAN, Mark Thomas; s of Albert Smith Raffan, of Langley, Nr Maidstone, and Joan, *née* Martin; *b* 12 May 1963; *Educ* Knoll Sch for Boys Hove, Brighton Tech Coll (City & Guilds); *m* 1993, Paula Georgia, da of George Kyriacou, of Limassol, Cyprus; 1 da (Georgia Naomi b 1993), 1 s (Charlie Laithe b 1995); *Career* trainee The Eaton Restaurant Hove 1978–81, chef de partie Gravetye Manor Hotel & Country Club 1984–85 (commis chef 1981–83), chef tournant Wahper Terrace Hotel Kitchener Ontario Feb-June 1985, chef tournant Le Gavroche London 1985–86, chef Gravetye Manor Hotel 1988–91 (jr sous chef 1986–87, sous chef 1987–88), exec chef The Royal Palaces of HM King Hussein of Jordan 1991–95, head chef Gravetye Manor Hotel 1995–; memb Acorn Club 1995–96; *Awards* Cookery and Food Assoc Gold Medal, Acorn Award 1990, Egon Ronay 1 star; *Recreations* shooting, the countryside; *Style*— Mark Raffan, Esq; ✉ Gravetye Manor Hotel, Vowels Lane, Nr East Grinstead, West Sussex RH19 4LJ (☎ 01342 810496, fax 01342 810080)

RAFFE, Prof David James; s of John Neish Raffe (d 1992), of Norwich, and Elizabeth Constance, *née* Kendrew; *b* 5 May 1951; *Educ* The Leys Sch Cambridge, New Coll Oxford (BA), Nuffield Coll Oxford (BPhil); *m* 1979, Shirley Sandra, *née* Paine; 1 s (Alasdair b 1982), 1 da (Sonia b 1984); *Career* Univ of Edinburgh: prof of sociology of educn 1992– (lectr in educn 1979–85, reader 1985–92), dir Centre for Educnl Sociology 1995– (research fell 1975–79, dep dir 1979–87, co-dir 1987–95); dir Inst for the Study of Educn and Society 1996–; occasional conslt OECD and Euro Cmmn; chm Euro Sci Fndn Network on Transitions in Youth 1993–; Scot Educnl Res Assoc (SERA) Medal for educnl research 1984; memb: Br Sociological Assoc, BERA, SERA; *Books* Reconstructions of Secondary Education (co-author, 1983), Fourteen to Eighteen (1984), Education and the Youth Labour Market (1988), A British Baccalaureat (co-author, 1990); *Style*— Prof David Raffe; ✉ 128 Comiston Drive, Edinburgh EH10 5QX (☎ 0131 447 2844); Centre for Educational Sociology, University of Edinburgh, 7 Buccleuch Place, Edinburgh EH8 9LW (☎ 0131 650 4191, fax 0131 668 3263)

RAFFERTY, Anne Judith; QC (1990); da of John Rafferty (d 1953), of Lancashire, and Helena, *née* Marchant (d 1987), of London; *Educ* Wolverhampton Girls' HS, Univ of Sheffield (LLB), Inns of Ct Sch of Law; *m* 1977, Brian Barker, QC, eld s of William Barker; 4 da (Anne Camilla Frances b 11 April 1980, Helen Davina Gillow b 31 Aug 1981 d 5 July 1983, Edwina Mary Gillian b 6 Oct 1983, Felicity Abigail Clare b 5 June 1985); *Career* called to the Bar Gray's Inn 1973, pupillage with Simon Evans (now His Hon Judge Evans) at 4 Brick Ct 1974, recorder SE Circuit 1991–, head of chambers 4 Brick Ct 1993–; Criminal Bar Assoc: sec 1989–91, vice chm 1993–95, chm 1995–; memb: Pigot Ctee 1988–89, Royal Cmmn on Criminal Justice 1991–93, Cncl Eastbourne Coll 1994–; govr: St Andrews Prep Sch Eastbourne 1990–, Expert Witness Inst 1996–; FRSA 1993; *Style*— Miss Anne Rafferty, QC; ✉ 4 Brick Court, First Floor, Temple, London EC4Y 9AD (☎ 0171 583 8455, fax 0171 353 1699)

RAFFERTY, John Campbell; *b* 30 June 1951; *Educ* Edinburgh Acad, Univ of Edinburgh (LLB); *Career* W & J Burness: trainee slr 1973–75, asst slr 1975–77, ptnr 1977–, also currently head Co Dept; tutor in taxation Univ of Edinburgh 1973–77; memb Soc of HM Writers to the Signet 1979, MSI 1994; *Recreations* hill walking, skiing, gardening; *Clubs* New (Edinburgh); *Style*— John Rafferty, Esq; ✉ W & J Burness, 16 Hope Street, Edinburgh EH2 4DD (☎ 0131 226 2561, fax 0131 225 3949, mobile 0370 236430)

RAFTERY, Andrew Thomas; s of Andrew Raftery (d 1987), of York, and Nora Maria, *née* Kelly; *b* 29 June 1943; *Educ* St Michael's Jesuit Coll, Univ of Leeds Sch of Med (BSc, MB ChB, MD); *m* 6 Aug 1980, Anne Christine, da of Norman Turnock, of Buxton; 2 s (Andrew b 1985, Dominic b 1989), 1 da (Catherine b 1981); *Career* lectr in anatomy Univ of Leeds 1970–73, surgical registrar Yorkshire Health Authy 1974–75, lectr in surgery Univ of Manchester 1976–80, lectr in surgery and hon conslt Univ of Cambridge 1980–83, conslt surgn (vascular surgery and transplantation) Sheffield Health Authy 1983–; external examiner in surgery Univ of Cambridge 1983–; examiner Primary FRCS: England 1985–91, Glasgow 1989–; memb Ct of Examiners RCS 1991– (chm Ct of Examiners 1994–97), invited memb Cncl RCS 1994–97, pres Br Assoc of Clinical Anatomists 1996–; numerous contribs to books and jls; MIBiol, FRCS; *Recreations* horse racing, theatre, watercolour painting; *Style*— Andrew Raftery, Esq; ✉ Renal Unit, Northern General Hospital, Herries Rd, Sheffield S5 7AU (☎ 0114 243 4343)

RAGGATT, Timothy Walter Harold; QC (1993); s of Walter George Raggatt (d 1976), and Norah Margaret Raggatt (d 1987), of Redditch, Hereford and Worcester; *b* 13 April 1950; *Educ* Redditch Co HS, King's Coll London (LLB); *m* 1991, Carol Marion, da of Wilfred Carl Overton; *Career* called to the Bar 1972, tutor at Inns of Ct Sch of Law 1972–73, pupillage 3 Fountain Ct Birmingham 1973–74, recorder of the Crown Court 1994– (asst recorder 1991); memb Midland and Oxford Circuit 1974–; *Style*— Timothy Raggatt, Esq, QC; ✉ 36 Bedford Row, London WC1R 4JH (☎ 0171 421 8000, fax 0171 421 8080)

RAGLAN, 5 Baron (UK 1852); FitzRoy John Somerset; JP (Monmouthshire, now Gwent, 1958), DL (1971); s of 4 Baron Raglan, JP (d 1964, who was descended from 5 Duke of Beaufort), and Hon Julia Hamilton, da of 11 Lord Belhaven and Stenton; *b* 8 Nov 1927; *Educ* Westminster, Magdalen Coll Oxford, RAC Cirencester; *m* 1973 (m dis), Alice, yr da of Peter Baily, of Gt Whittington, Northumberland; *Heir* bro, Hon Geoffrey Somerset, *qv*; *Career* sits as ind peer in House of Lords; Capt Welsh Gds; chm: Cwmbran New Town Devpt Corpn 1970–83, Courtyard Arts Tst 1974–83, Bath Preservation Trust 1975–77, Bath Soc 1977–, Bugatti Owners' Club 1988–; pres: Bath Centre Nat Tst, UK Housing Trust 1982– (chm S Wales Region 1976–89), Usk Civic Soc; memb Sub-Ctee D (Food and Agric) of House of Lords Ctee on European Communities 1974–85 and 1987–92 (chm 1976–78); patron: Usk Farmers' Club, Raglan Baroque Players; memb UK Housing Assoc (later Tst) 1974–90 (pres 1982–89, chm Welsh Region 1975–89), chm United Welsh Housing Assoc 1989–91 (pres 1991–); *Style*— The Rt Hon the Lord Raglan, JP, DL; ✉ Cefntilla, Usk, Gwent (☎ 01291 672050)

RAI, Dr Gurcharan Singh; s of Gurdev Singh Rai, of London, and Kartar Kaur Rai; *b* 30 July 1947; *Educ* Tollington GS London, Univ of Newcastle upon Tyne (MB BS, MD), Univ of London (MSc); *m* 8 Nov 1977, Harsha, da of Shri Lal Bhatia (d 1980), of India; 2 s (Sandeep b 30 Sept 1978, Gurdeep b 18 Nov 1981); *Career* house offr Nottingham Gen Hosp 1971–72, registrar in med Newcastle Univ Hosp 1974–76 (sr house offr 1972–73), sr res assoc Univ of Newcastle upon Tyne 1976–78, sr registrar in geriatric med Chesterton Hosp Cambridge 1978–80; consIt physician: Whittington Hosp 1980–, Royal Northern Hosp 1980–, sr lectr Univ Coll Med Sch 1980–; prof in geriatric med Univ of Nijmegen The Netherlands 1991–92; chm Regnl Advsy Cmmn Geriatric Med NE Thames Region; FRCP 1988; *Books* Databook On Geriatrics (1980), Case Presentations In Clinical Geriatric Medicine (1987), Manual of Geriatric Medicine (1991); *Recreations* chess, stamp collecting; *Style*— Dr Gurcharan Rai; ✉ Whittington Hospital, Highgate Hill, London N19 5NF (☎ 0171 272 3070)

RAIKES, Vice Adm Sir Iwan Geoffrey; KCB (1976), CBE (1967), DSC (1943), DL (Powys 1983); s of Adm Sir Robert Henry Taunton Raikes, KCB, CVO, DSO and bar (d 1953), and Ida Guinevere, *née* Evans (d 1983); *b* 21 April 1921; *Educ* RNC Dartmouth; *m* 1947, Cecilia Primrose, da of Philip Gerald Benedict Hunt (d 1958), of Woodhayes, Woodlands, Southampton; 1 s, 1 da; *Career* RN 1935, HMS Beagle Atlantic convoys 1941, submarines Atlantic, Mediterranean and North Sea 1942–45; cmd HM Submarines: H43 1943–44, Varne 1944–45, Virtue 1945–46, Talent 1948–49, Aeneas 1951–52; Cdr 1952, staff of C-in-C Allied Forces Mediterranean 1953–55, exec offr HMS Newcastle (Far East) 1955–57, JSSC 1957, Capt 1960, cmd HMS Loch Insh (Persian Gulf) 1961–62, dep dir Undersurface Warfare MOD 1962–64, dir plans and Operations (Singapore) on staff of C-in-C Far East 1965–66, IDC 1967, cmd HMS Kent 1968–69, ADC to HM The Queen 1969–70, Rear Adm 1970, naval sec MOD 1970–72, flag offr First Flotilla 1973–74, flag offr Submarines and cdr Submarines Eastern Atlantic 1974–76, Vice Adm 1973, ret 1977; chm Utd Usk Fishermen's Assoc 1978–92, memb Governing Body and Representative Body Church in Wales 1980–93; *Recreations* fishing, shooting, gardening; *Clubs* Naval & Military; *Style*— Vice Adm Sir Iwan Raikes, KCB, CBE, DSC, DL; ✉ Aberyscir Ct, Brecon, Powys LD3 9NW

RAILTON, David; QC (1996); s of Andrew Scott Railton, and Margaret Elizabeth, *née* Armit; *b* 5 June 1957; *Educ* Balliol Coll Oxford (MA); *m* 1996, Sinéad Major; *Career* called to the Bar Gray's Inn 1979; *Recreations* cricket, golf; *Style*— David Railton, Esq, QC; ✉ Fountain Court Chambers, Temple, London EC4Y 9DH (☎ 0171 583 3335)

RAILTON, Dame Ruth; DBE (1966, OBE 1954); da of Rev David Railton, MC (d 1955; rector of Liverpool and originator of the idea of the Unknown Warrior's Tomb, his flag, used in WWI, hangs in the Warriors' Chapel in Westminster Abbey), and Ruby Marion de Lancey Willson; *b* 14 Dec 1915; *Educ* St Mary's Sch Wantage, Royal Acad of Music London (FRAM); *m* 1962, Cecil Harmsworth King (d 1987); *Career* dir of music or choral work for various schools and societies 1937–49, adjudicator Fedn of Music Festivals 1946–74, fndr and musical dir of the Nat Youth Orchestra of GB and Nat Jr Music Sch 1946–65, pres Ulster Coll of Music 1960–, govr Royal Ballet Sch 1966–74, vice pres Cork Int Festival 1960–85, fndr and pres Irish Children's Theatre 1978–81, memb Bd of Dirs Nat Concert Hall Dublin 1981–86, chm Nat Children's Orch 1991–94, patron European Pianoforte Teachers' Assoc, fndr Cecil King Meml Fndn 1991; Hon LLD Univ of Aberdeen 1960; hon prof: Chopin Conservatoire Warsaw 1960, Conservatoire of Azores (Lisbon) 1966; Hon RMCM 1959, Hon FRCM 1965, Hon FTCL 1969; *Books* Daring to Excel - The Story of the National Youth Orchestra of Great Britain (1992); *Clubs* University Women's; *Style*— Dame Ruth King, DBE; ✉ 34 Elizabeth Court, Milman's Street, London SW10 0DA (☎ 0171 351 0089)

RAINE, Craig Anthony; s of Norman Edward Raine, and Olive Marie Raine, *née* Cheeseborough; *b* 3 Dec 1944; *Educ* Barnard Castle Sch, Exeter Coll Oxford; *m* 1972, Elisabeth Ann Isabel, da of Dr Eliot Slater, OBE (d 1982); 3 s (Isaac b 1979, Moses b 1984, Vaska b 1987), 1 da (Nina b 1975); *Career* poet; fell New Coll Oxford; *Publications* The Onion Memory (1978), A Martian Sends A Postcard Home (1979), Rich (1984), The Electrification of the Soviet Union (1986), A Choice of Kipling's Prose (ed, 1987), 1953 (1990, staged Almeida Theatre 1996), Haydn and the Valve Trumpet (1990), Rudyard Kipling: Selected Poetry (ed, 1992), History: The Home Movie (1994), Clay. Whereabout Unknown (1996); *Recreations* music; *Style*— Craig Raine, Esq; ✉ New College, Oxford OX1 3BN

RAINE, George Edward Thompson; s of Reginald Thompson Raine, MC (d 1960), of Stocksfield, Northumberland, and Mary Dorothy, *née* Tomlinson (d 1976); *b* 1 Aug 1934; *Educ* Rugby, Emmanuel Coll Cambridge (MA), St Thomas' Hosp Med Sch (MB BChir); *m* 11 June 1960, Ena Josephine, da of Joseph Noble; 1 da (Meriel b 1965); *Career* sr consIt orthopaedic surgn W Middlesex Univ Hosp 1974–96; orthopaedic surgn Royal Masonic Hosp London, orthopaedic surgn to Brunel Univ Coll Sports and Dance Injuries Clinic; orthopaedic surgn to: Brentford FC, various sporting bodies; formerly sr orthopaedic registrar: St George's Hosp London, Rowley Bristow Orthopaedic Hosp Pyrford Surrey, Centre for Hip Surgery Wrightington; govr The Lady Eleanor Holles' Sch Hampton; memb Cncl Nat Back Pain Assoc; Freeman City of London 1987; fell British Orthopaedic Assoc, FRCS; *Recreations* English Lake District, foreign travel; *Clubs* Whitefriars; *Style*— George E T Raine, Esq; ✉ Pelham's View, 32 Pelhams Walk, Esher, Surrey KT10 8QD (☎ 01372 466656, fax 01372 470265); 144 Harley St, London W1N 1AH (☎ 0171 935 0023)

RAINE, Sandra Margaret; da of Charles Kitchener Lovell (d 1976), and Mary Rosamund, *née* O'Hare; *b* 7 March 1958; *Educ* Convent of the Sacred Heart Hammersmith, Univ of Newcastle upon Tyne (BA); *m* 9 Aug 1980, Ian Henry Raine, s of Joseph Raine; *Career* pensions asst Dunlop Ltd 1980, admin offr NE Cncl on Alcoholism 1980–82, sr admin asst Newcastle Poly 1982–85, urban prog asst Gateshead MBC 1985–86, asst divnl dir admin, finance and personnel Royal Co of Berks 1986–90, asst co sec AA 1990–91, benevolent fund sec Chartered Inst of Building 1992–94, sec and chief exec Inst of Gas Engrs 1994–; ACIS; *Recreations* gymnasium, swimming; *Clubs* Royal Thames Yacht, Nirvana Sport and Leisure; *Style*— Mrs Sandra Raine; ✉ Institution of Gas Engineers, 21 Portland Place, London W1N 3AF (☎ 0171 636 6603, fax 0171 636 6602)

RAINEY, Christopher John (Chris); s of late Alec Barnard Rainey, of Bishops Lydeard, Taunton, and Hilda Edith (Sally), *née* Edmonds; *b* 22 Jan 1946; *Educ* Westwoods GS, Polytechnic of the South Bank (HNC); *m* 20 July 1967, Christel, da of late Hermann Carl Wilhelm Laartz; 2 s (Mark Andrew b 23 Dec 1970, Paul Simon b 24 Feb 1973); *Career* currently engineer, inventor, problem solver; Signal Dept London Transport Board (involved with design of trackside electronics for world's first automatic passenger train Victoria Line) 1964–69, devpt of UK's first cash dispensers with Burroughs Machines and Lead Electronics Team (patent assigned relating to Credit Card security) 1969–72, whilst self-employed jtly invented and patented Endfield/Rainey keyboard (now called Microwriting System) 1973, consIt on Microwriter projects; awarded British Design Award 1990 for design of Agenda electronics (current microwriters machine); *Recreations* vintage car restoration, video production; *Style*— Chris Rainey, Esq; ✉ Bellaire Electronics, 4 Broadgate, Pilton, Barnstaple, N Devon EX31 1QZ (☎ 01271 43296, fax 01271 24759)

RAINGER, Peter; CBE (1982); s of Cyril Frederick Rainger (d 1973), and Ethel, *née* Wilson (d 1983); *b* 17 May 1924; *Educ* Northampton Engrg Coll, Univ of London (BSc); *m* 1, 1953, Josephine Dorothy (decd), da of Joseph Campbell, of Northolt, London; 2 s (John b 1957, David b 1960); m 2, Barbara Gibson; 1 step da (Pamela b 1946); *Career* Nat Serv RAF 1942–47; BBC: designer TV equipment 1951–69, head Designs Dept 1969–71, head Res Dept 1971–76, asst dir of engrg 1976–78, ret as dep dir engrg responsible for all R & D 1984 (devpts incl conversion of TV pictures between different tech standards and introduction of teletext broadcasting); currently consIt to broadcasting indust; Freeman City of London; memb Soc of Motion Picture and TV Engrs (US), FIEE, FEng 1979, FRTS 1969, FRS 1982; *Books* Satellite Broadcasting (1985); *Recreations* computing, model engineering, sculpture; *Style*— Peter Rainger, Esq, CBE, FRS, FEng; ✉ 22 Mill Meadow, Milford on Sea, Hants SO41 0UG

RAINGOLD, Gerald Barry; s of Henry Raingold (d 1979), of 19 Hanover House, London NW8, and Frances Raingold (d 1992); *b* 25 March 1943; *Educ* St Paul's, Inst of CAs, London Graduate Sch of Business Studies (MBA); *m* 12 July 1978, Aviva, da of Henry Petrie (d 1962), of London; 1 s (Andrew b 18 Sept 1981), 2 da (Nina b 2 Aug 1979, Karen b 23 July 1983); *Career* CA; articled clerk then CA Cole Dicken & Hills 1963–68, Cooper Bros 1968–72 (mangr 1972), sr mangr corporate fin Wallace Brothers Bank 1972–76, sr consIt Midland Montagu Group 1976–78, dep md Banque Paribas London 1978–95 (formerly mangr, sr mangr, asst gen mangr), dep chm Dawnay Day Corporate Finance Ltd 1995–, dir Dawnay Day & Co Ltd 1995–; memb: London Business Sch Alumni, City Ctee Inst of Mgmnt 1980–83, IOD City Branch, Royal Inst Int Affrs, Bus Graduates Assoc; dir Br Francophone Business Group (trade assoc); Sloan fell London Business Sch; Freeman City of London 1987; FCA 1968, FInstD 1987, FRSA 1993; *Recreations* opera, ballet, tennis, reading; *Clubs* Overseas Bankers; *Style*— Gerald Raingold, Esq; ✉ 12 Marston Close, London NW6 4EU (☎ 0171 328 5800, fax 0171 328 0286); Dawnay Day & Co Ltd, 15 Grosvenor Gardens, London SW1W 0BD (☎ 0171 411 4570, fax 0171 411 4575, car 0385 281308)

RAINS, Prof Anthony John Harding; CBE (1986); s of Robert Harding Rains (Capt RAMC, d 1920), of Bexhill, and Florence Eleanor, *née* Rapson (d 1962); *b* 5 Nov 1920; *Educ* Christ's Hosp, St Mary's Hosp Med Sch London (MB BS, MS); *m* 30 Oct 1943,

Mary Adelaide, da of Edward Henry Lillywhite (d 1963), of London; 3 da (Margaret b 1944, Diana b 1948, Charlotte b 1963); *Career* med offr RAF 1944–47; lectr in surgery Univ of Birmingham 1950–59, hon conslt surgn Utd Birmingham Hosps 1954–59, prof of surgery Charing Cross Hosp Med Sch (Univ of London) 1959–81, hon conslt surgn Charing Cross, West London and Fulham Hosps 1959–81; RCS: memb Cncl 1972–84, dean Inst Basic Med Sci 1976–83, vice pres 1983–84; postgrad dean SW Met RHA 1981–85, asst dir Br Postgrad Med Fedn 1981–85, ed Jl RSM 1986–94; chm Med Cmmn Accident Prevention 1972–84, tstee Smith and Nephew Fndn 1974, first chm Child Accident Prevention Ctee, cncllr Kings Norton Birmingham 1953–59; Freeman Worshipful Soc of Apothecaries 1965; FRCS 1948; *Books* The Treatment of Cancer in Clinical Practice (with PB Kunkler, 1959), Bailey and Love's Short Practice of Surgery (ed 13–20 edns, 1965–88), Joseph Lister and Antisepsis (1977); *Recreations* reading; *Style*— Prof Anthony Rains, CBE; ✉ 39A St Cross Road, Winchester, Hants SO23 9PR (☎ 01962 869419)

RAISMAN, John Michael; CBE (1983); s of Sir Jeremy Raisman, GCMG, GCIE, KCSI (d 1978), and Renée Mary, *née* Kelly (d 1989); *b* 12 Feb 1929; *Educ* Dragon Sch Oxford, Rugby, Queen's Coll Oxford (MA); *m* 22 Aug 1953, (Evelyn) Anne, da of Brig James Ingram Muirhead, CIE, MC (d 1964); 1 s (Andrew Jeremy b 1969), 3 da (Angela (Mrs Denniss) b 1955, Valerie (Mrs Kelleher) b 1957, Alison (Mrs Brady) b 1960); *Career* Nat Serv 1951–53, Lt Kings Dragoon Guards; chm Shell UK Ltd 1979–85 (chief exec 1978–85), dep chm British Telecom plc 1987–91; dir: Vickers plc 1981–90, Glaxo Holdings plc 1982–90, Lloyds Bank plc 1985–, Candover Investments plc 1990–, Tandem Computers Ltd 1991–, British Biotech Plc 1993– (chm 1995–); chm: Oil Indust Emergency Ctee 1980–85, Advsy Cncl London Enterprise Agency 1980–85, Cncl Indust for Mgmnt Educn 1979–85, Electronics EDC 1985–87, Cncl for Industry and Higher Educn 1991–, Bd of Tstees Royal Acad 1985–, Languages Lead Body 1990–, Business Forum Euro Movement 1990–; dep chm Nat Cmmn on Educn 1991–95; CBI: memb Cncl, chm Europe Ctee 1980–88, memb President's Ctee 1980–88; memb: Governing Body Business in the Community 1982–85, Cncl Inst for Fiscal Studies, Royal Cmmn on Environmental Pollution 1985–87; govr Henley Mgmnt Coll 1988–93, pro chllr Aston Univ 1987–93; Hon DUniv Stirling 1983; Hon LLD: Aberdeen 1985, Manchester 1986, Univ of West of England 1994; Hon DSc Aston 1992; CIMgt 1980; *Recreations* golf, skiing, travel, opera; *Clubs* Brooks's, Royal Mid-Surrey, Sunningdale Golf; *Style*— John Raisman, Esq, CBE; ✉ Netheravon House, Netheravon Road South, Chiswick, London W4 2PY (☎ 0181 742 1000, fax 0181 994 3731)

RAISON, Rt Hon Sir Timothy Hugh Francis; kt (1991), PC (1982); s of late Maxwell Raison, of Theberton; *b* 3 Nov 1929; *Educ* Eton, Christ Church Oxford; *m* 1956, Veldes Julia, er da of John Arthur Pepys Charrington; 1 s, 3 da; *Career* formerly journalist with: Picture Post, New Scientist; formerly ed: Crossbow, New Society; MP (C) Aylesbury 1970–92; PPS to NI Sec 1972–73, Parly under sec DES 1973–74, oppn spokesman environment 1975–76, min of state Home Office 1979–83, min for overseas devpt 1983–86; chm Advtg Standards Authy 1991–94; memb: Central Advsy Cncl on Educn 1963–66, ILEA 1967–70, Richmond Cncl 1967–71, Home Office Advsy Cncl on Penal System 1970–74, Cncl Policy Studies Inst 1978–79; chm Aylesbury Vale Community Healthcare Tst 1992–; *Clubs* Beefsteak, MCC; *Style*— The Rt Hon Sir Timothy Raison

RAITT, Prof Alan William; s of William Raitt (d 1968), of Morpeth, Northumberland, and Mary Davison (d 1970); *b* 21 Sept 1930; *Educ* King Edward VI GS, Morpeth, Magdalen Coll Oxford (MA, DPhil); *m* 1, 29 July 1959 (m dis 1971), Janet Suzanne Taylor; 2 da (Suzanne b 1961, Claire b 1964); m 2, 16 Dec 1974, Lia Noémia Rodrigues Correia, da of Cdr Virgilio Lopes Correia (d 1985), of Parede, Portugal; *Career* Univ of Oxford: fell by examination Magdalen Coll 1953–55, fell and lectr Exeter Coll 1955–66, fell and tutor Magdalen Coll 1966–, univ reader in French literature 1979–92, gen ed French Studies 1987–, univ prof of French literature 1992–; prof associé à la Sorbonne 1987–88, memb Exec Ctee Soc for French Studies 1987–; Grand Prix du Rayonnement de la Langue Française (Médaille d'Argent) French Acad 1987, Commandeur dans l'Ordre des Palmes Académiques (France) 1995; FRSL 1971, FBA 1992; *Books* Villiers de l'Isle-Adam et le Mouvement Symboliste (1965), Life and Letters in France, The Nineteenth Century (1966), Prosper Mérimée (1970), The Life of Villiers de l'Isle-Adam (1981), Villiers de l'Isle-Adam: Oeuvres Complètes (ed with P-G Castex, 1986), Villiers de l'Isle-Adam Exorciste du Réel (1987), Flaubert: Trois Contes (1991), Gustave Flaubert: Pour Louis Bouilhet (1994), A C Friedel et 'Le Nouveau Théâtre allemand': un intermédiaire reconnu (1995); *Recreations* music, watching football; *Style*— Prof Alan Raitt, FBA; ✉ Magdalen College, Oxford OX1 4AU (☎ 01865 276024)

RAJA RAYAN, Raj Kumar; s of Ramanathan Chelvarayan Raja Rayan, of Ceylon, and Lingamani, da of Prof C Suntharalingam; *b* 6 April 1953; *Educ* Harrow, Guy's Hosp Dental Sch (BDS), Eastman Dental Hosp (MSc); *m* Ahila, da of Sanmugam Arumugam, of Ceylon; 1 da (Dipa Lakshmi b 3 Nov 1980), 2 s (Darshan Kumar b 3 Aug 1982, Ravi Kumar b 11 Dec 1987); *Career* currently: practice Harley St, dental surgn to Bush Boake Allen Ltd, sr res fell Inst of Dental Surgery; former assoc advsr Br Postgrad Med Fndn, accredited teacher Univ of London; emeritus examiner RCS for memb in Gen Dental Surgery; examiner RCS for Diploma in Gen Dental Practice, fellowship examiner Examining Bd for Dental Surgery Assts; pres Br Soc for General Dental Surgery; chm: Inst of Transcultural Oral Health, Fin Ctee Faculty of Gen Dental Practitioners UK (also vice dean), Royal Coll of Surgeons of England (first ever elected nat memb); elected memb Gen Dental Cncl; former memb Conf of UK Advsrs NW Thames, past pres Anglo Asian Odontological Gp, fndr Central London MGDS Study Gp, fndr memb BDA Young Practitioner Gp; Cottrell Award 1990, Ahmed Oration Indian Dental Assoc 1991, various nat and int lectures; life memb: Nat Autistic Soc, Music Acad of India, Int Inst of Tamil Studies; memb: Lord Chllr's Advsy Ctee on JPs and Judicial Appointments Ctee, Standing Advsy Ctee to Sec of State for Health, Exec Ctee of Dentists Provident Soc (Friendly Soc), Dental & Dental Servs Ctee of Medical Defence Union, Dental Advsy Panel BUPA Dental Care; LDS RCS, MGDS RCS, MRD RCS, RCPS, DRD RCS; *Books* Self Assessment Manual and Standards (manual of clinical standards in dental practice, contrib 1991), Path Ways in Practice (distance learning manual in dental practice, contrib 1993), Dentists Patients & Minorities - Towards the new Millennium (co-ed); contributions to numerous learned jls; *Recreations* cricket, chess, bridge, golf; *Clubs* MCC, Magpies Cricket; *Style*— Raj K Raja Rayan, Esq; ✉ 46 Harley St, London W1N 1AD (☎ and fax 0171 631 5213)

RAJANI, Shashi Haridas; s of Haridas Savji Rajani (d 1989), and Gomtiben, *née* Suchak; *b* 24 May 1934; *Educ* HR Meml Central Sch Tabora Tanzania, Govt Secdy Sch Dar es Salaam Tanzania; *m* Chandrika (Sandra), da of Gordhandas Tulshidas Modi; 3 da (Rita b 24 June 1961, Priya b 13 March 1967, Nina Karen b 18 April 1973); *Career* called to the Bar Lincoln's Inn 1955, admitted slr 1975; advocate Tanzania 1956–70: in private practice 1956–64, asst then sr asst administrator-gen (incl official receiver in bankruptcies and company liquidations and several other statutory positions) Govt of Tanzania 1964–70, public prosecutor for bankruptcy offences 1964–70, public prosecutor for company law offences 1965–70, state attorney (criminal prosecutions and appeals) 1967–70, legal conslt Nat Bank of Commerce 1968–70; mangr Insolvency Dept Coopers & Lybrand CAs London 1970–76, sr asst slr Linklaters & Paines London 1977–88, sr asst slr Cameron Markby London 1988, ptnr Cameron Markby Hewitt 1989–93, ptnr and head Corp Rescue and Insolvency Gp Nicholson Graham & Jones 1994–; Freeman City of London 1984; Freeman City of London Solicitors' Co 1984; memb: Tanzania Law Soc 1956–70 (memb Cncl 1963–64), Law Soc 1976–, City of London Law Soc 1984– (memb Insolvency Law Sub-ctee 1991–, dep chm 1995–), Euro Assoc of Insolvency Practitioners 1980–, INSOL Int 1980–, Insolvency Lawyers' Assoc 1990– (cncl memb 1992–), Soc of Practitioners in Insolvency 1991–, Soc of English and American Lawyers 1992–, Soc of Asian Lawyers 1993– (memb Ctee 1993–); visiting prof London Guildhall Univ 1992–; *Publications* Tolley's Corporate Insolvency Handbook (1991), Tolley's Company Law (contrib insolvency and other chapters, 1983–), Insolvency Law & Practice (jl, jt ed 1989–), Tolley's Corporate Insolvency (1994); *Recreations* tennis, table tennis, badminton, chess, music (electronic organ); *Style*— Shashi Rajani, Esq; ✉ Tudor Heights, Mill Lane, Broxborough, Herts EN10 7AZ (☎ 01992 466806, fax 01992 460707); Nicholson Graham & Jones, 110 Cannon Street, London EC4N 6AR (☎ 0171 648 9000, fax 0171 648 9001)

RAJECKAS, HE Prof Raimundas; *Educ* Kaunas Poly Inst Lithuania (MS), Moscow State Univ (DEcon), Central Economic Mathematical Inst of the USSR Acad of Scis (DSocSc); *Career* Lithuanian diplomat; mangr of prodn and ops Nat Rubber Products Factory Lithuania 1959–61, dir of Metal Products Factory 1961–64, grad student Moscow State Univ 1964–66, asst prof of economics Kaunas Poly Inst Lithuania 1966–67; Lithuanian State Planning Ctee: dept head 1967–71, dir of The Computer Center 1971–73; research dir Inst for Planning and Economics 1973–78; Lithuanian Acad of Scis: academician sec Social Scis Div 1987–89, vice pres 1989–92; prof of economics Vilnius Univ 1972–, chief advsr to the Pres of the Republic of Lithuania 1993–94, Lithuanian ambass to the Ct of St James's and to Ireland 1994–96; Harvard Univ: visiting scholar 1967–68, hon research assoc in economics by special invitation 1974–75, Fulbright scholar 1988; visiting scholar Univ of Calif at Berkeley 1991–92, Mary Whitin Calkins prof of economics (visiting professorship) Wellesley Coll Wellesley MA 1992; guest lectr at numerous univs across USA incl Harvard, Stanford, Chicago and Michigan; pres Lithuanian Cncl of Scientific and Tech Socs 1972–82, chm Cncl of Experts for fundamental problems in economics Lithuanian Acad of Scis 1987–92; co-ed The Jl of Sci and Technol 1972–; author of over 200 scholarly pubns incl 17 books; Honored Scientist of Lithuania 1981, Lithuanian State Prize in Sci 1989; memb (academician) Lithuanian Acad of Scis 1987; *Style*— Prof Raimundas Rajeckas

RAKE, Michael Derek Vaughan; s of Derek Shannon Vaughan Rake, and Rosamund, *née* Barrett; *b* 17 Jan 1948; *Educ* Wellington Coll Crowthorne Berks; *m* 1, 5 Sept 1970 (m dis), Julia, *née* Cook; 3 s (Matthew b 5 Dec 1972, Jamie b 12 March 1974, Piers b 19 Dec 1976); m 2, Caroline, *née* Thomas; 1 s (Ashley b 1 July 1985); *Career* Turquands Barton Mayhew London and Brussels 1968–74; KPMG: joined Brussels 1974, made ptnr 1979, ptnr i/c audit Belgium and Luxembourg 1983–86, resident sr ptnr Middle East 1986–89, ptnr London 1989–, memb Bd KPMG Peat Marwick UK 1991, regnl managing ptnr SE Region 1992–96, chief operating offr UK 1996–; FCA; *Recreations* golf, riding, shooting; *Clubs* Carlton; *Style*— Michael Rake, Esq; ✉ Highclere, Haw Lane, Bledlow Ridge, Bucks HP14 4JJ (☎ 01494 481740); KPMG, 8 Salisbury Square, London EC4Y 8BB (☎ 0171 311 1000, fax 0171 311 8499)

RAKOFF, Alvin Abraham; s of Samuel Rakoff (d 1970), of Toronto, Canada, and Pearl Himmelspring (d 1986); *Educ* Ryerson Public Sch Toronto Canada, Harbord Collegiate, Univ of Toronto (BA); *m* 4 June 1958, Jacqueline Hill (d 1993); 1 s (John Dmitri b 27 Jan 1970), 1 da (Sasha Victoria b 27 Aug 1967); *Career* freelance director/writer/producer; journalist: New Toronto Advertiser, The Globe and Mail Toronto; memb BBC Contract Staff 1954–57; memb: Dirs' Guild of GB (pres 1988–90), Dirs' Guild of Canada, Writers' Guild of GB; directed: Requiem for a Heavyweight (Sean Connery, Michael Caine) 1957, On Friday at Eleven (Rod Steiger) 1960, The Comedy Man (Kenneth More) 1963, The Seekers 1964, Hamlet (Bristol Old Vic) 1965, Call Me Daddy (Donald Pleasance), Hoffman (Peter Sellers) 1969, Say Hello to Yesterday (Jean Simmons) 1970, Summer and Smoke (Lee Remick) 1971, The Adventures of Don Quixote (Rex Harrison) 1972, Shadow of a Gunman 1973, Cheap in August 1974, In Praise of Love (Claire Bloom, Kenneth More) 1975, The Dame of Sark (Celia Johnson) 1976, The Kitchen (BBC) 1977, Mr Halpern and Mr Johnson (Laurence Olivier, Jackie Gleeson) 1981, A Voyage Round My Father (Laurence Olivier, Alan Bates) 1982, The First Olympics (Angela Lansbury, Louis Jordan) 1983, Royal Albert Hall Cruise Charity Concert (before HM Queen) 1984, Paradise Postponed 1986, The Best of Friends (John Gielgud) 1991, Sam Saturday (devised series) 1992; prodr and dir: A Dance to the Music of Time (Channel 4) 1996/97; *Awards* Nat TV Award 1964, Emmy Int Award Nat Acad of TV Arts and Scis US 1967 and 1982, Best in Festival Award and Best Film Award Banff TV Festival 1982; various nominations incl: Monte Carlo Festival, BAFTA, Prix Italia; *Novel* & Gillian (1996); *Recreations* photography, literature, music, skiing, boats, swimming, cricket, baseball; *Style*— Alvin Rakoff, Esq; ✉ Table Top Productions, Dance Time Ltd; c/o Nyman Libson Paul, 124 Finchley Rd, London NW3 5JS (☎ 0171 794 5611, fax 0171 431 1109)

RALLI, David Charles; s and h of Sir Godfrey Ralli, 3 Bt, TD; *b* 5 April 1946; *Educ* Eton, Harper Adams Agric Coll; *m* 1975, Jacqueline Cecilia, da of David Smith; 1 s (Philip Neil David b 31 March 1983), 1 da (Marina Louise b 15 May 1980); *Career* farmer; chm Dereham Farm Servs 1985–87, dir Mid Norfolk Farmers 1985–93; Breckland DC: cncllr 1987–95, chm Environmental Health 1990–95; chm Game Conservancy Norfolk Gp 1993–; chm Govrs St Andrews First Sch North Pickenham 1995–; Liveryman Worshipful Co of Farmers 1985–; *Recreations* golf, shooting, fishing; *Clubs* White's, Farmers; *Style*— David Ralli, Esq; ✉ The Old Hall, Hardingham, Norwich, Norfolk NR9 4EW

RALLI, Sir Godfrey Victor; 3 Bt (UK 1912), of Park Street, City of Westminster; TD; s of Sir Strati Ralli, 2 Bt, MC (d 1964); *b* 9 Sept 1915; *Educ* Eton; *m* 1, 24 June 1937 (m dis 1947), Nora Margaret, o da of late Charles Forman, of Lodden Court, Spencers Wood, nr Reading; 1 s, 2 da; m 2, 24 March 1949, Jean, da of late Keith Barlow, of 3 Vicarage Gate, London W8; *Heir* s, David Charles Ralli; *Career* Ralli Brothers Ltd 1936–62 (apart from Army Serv 1939–45); chm: G & L Ralli Investment & Tstee Co Ltd 1962–75, Greater London Fund for the Blind 1962–82; *Recreations* golf, fishing, gardening; *Clubs* Naval and Military; *Style*— Sir Godfrey Ralli, Bt, TD; ✉ Great Walton, Eastry, Sandwich, Kent CT13 0DN

RALLING, (Antony) Christopher; OBE (1992); s of Harold St George Ralling, and Dorothy Blanche, *née* Williams; *b* 12 April 1929; *Educ* Charterhouse, Wadham Coll Oxford (BA); *m* Angela Norma, da of John Henry Gardner (d 1985); 1 da (Joanna Margaret b 1965); *Career* television writer, producer and director; British Memorial Fndn fell in Australia 1959; BBC: radio scriptwriter and prodr External Services 1955–59, dep ed Panorama 1965–66 (prodr 1962–65); BBC TV Documentary Department 1966–82: prodr and dir Revolution in Hungary 1966, prodr One Pair of Eyes 1967, dir Tokyo - the Fifty First Volcano 1969 (Blue Ribbon NY Film Festival), prodr Australia - Last of Lands 1970, prodr and dir The Search for the Nile 1972 (2 US Emmys, UK Critic's Guild Award), prodr and dir The Fight Against Slavery 1973 (Martin Luther King Award), prodr and dir Everest The Hard Way 1975, prodr The Voyage of Charles Darwin 1978 (2 Br Acad Awards), head of documentaries 1980–82; fndr Dolphin Productions 1982, dir and sr conslt Worldview International Fndn 1994–; freelance: scriptwriter Shackleton (BBC) 1983, prodr Everest the Unclimbed Ridge 1983, dir The History of Africa (Channel 4) 1984 (Gold medal NY Film Festival), writer and dir Chasing a Rainbow 1985 (US Emmy, Gold medal NY Film Festival), dir Vintage (Channel 4) 1987, dir Charles At Forty (LWT) 1988, writer and prodr The Kon-Tiki Man

(BBC) 1989, dir The Buried Mirror (2 episodes, BBC) 1992, writer and dir A Diplomat in Japan (BBC) 1992, dir Return to Everset (Channel 4) 1993; FRGS 1978; *Books* Muggeridge Through the Microphone (1967), The Voyage of Charles Darwin (1987), Shackleton (1983), The Kon-Tiki Man (1990); *Recreations* tennis, skiing; *Clubs* BAFTA, Alpine; *Style—* Christopher Ralling, Esq, OBE

RALLS, Keith John; s of Bernard Joseph Ralls (d 1983), of Wylye, Wilts, and Annie Ellen, *née* Bennett; *b* 29 Sept 1938; *Educ* Bishops Wordsworth's Sch Salisbury, Bournemouth Tech Coll (ONC Mechanical Engrg, ONC Electrical Engrg), Univ of Southampton (BSc Electrical Engrg), E Mids Mgmnt Centre Derby (Sr Exec Prog); *m* 19 May 1962, Patricia Maureen, *née* Webb; 4 c; *Career* engrg apprentice De Haviland Aircraft Co Christchurch 1956–60, graduate trainee rising to sr analytical engr English Electric Co (later part of GEC) 1963–70; GEC: asst sales mangr Power Transmission Div 1970–74, commercial dir Power Transformer Co 1974–77; gen mangr Herbert Morris Heavy Crane and Conveyor Div Davy Corporation Loughborough (also memb Commercial Exec Ctee Davy Corporation) 1977–79, gen mangr Adamson Butterley Crane Div Norcross Telford 1979–80; GEC (now GEC Alsthom): project dir Power Transmission Div 1981–85, mktg dir GEC Transmission & Distribution Projects Ltd Jan-July 1986, md GEC Alsthom T & D Power Electronic Systems Ltd 1986–, md GEC Alsthom T & D Systems Group 1975–; also dir various GEC Alsthom subsids UK and Europe; IEE: memb Bd Power Div 1987–90 and 1991–97 (chm 1994–95), memb Learned Soc Bd 1993–95, memb Cncl 1993–96; FIEE, FEng 1996; *Recreations* badminton, swimming, golf, grandchildren; *Clubs* GEC Overseas (life vice pres 1995); *Style—* Keith Ralls, Esq, FEng; ✉ GEC Alsthom T & D Systems Group, PO Box 27, Stafford ST17 4LN (☎ 01785 274796, fax 01785 274472, mobile 0831 506564)

RALPH, Prof Brian; s of Reginald James (d 1960), of Norwich, and Gwenthellian Anne, *née* Thomas (d 1990); *b* 4 Aug 1939; *Educ* City of Norwich Sch, Jesus Coll Cambridge (BA, MA, PhD, ScD); *m* 22 June 1961, Anne Mary, da of Leslie Ernest Perry, of Bath; 1 da (Zoanna); *Career* lectr Dept of Metallurgy and Material Sci Univ of Cambridge 1966–83 (demonstrator 1964–66, fell and tutor Jesus Coll 1964–83); prof and head Dept of Metallurgy and Material Sci Univ Coll Cardiff 1984–87, prof and head Dept of Materials Technol Brunel Univ 1987–93 (dean of technol 1991–96); hon prof Warsaw Univ of Technol 1994; co-ed over twenty res monographs in the field of microscopy and physical metallurgy; FIM, FInstP, Hon FRMS, CEng, CPhys, Eur Ing; *Recreations* sailing, woodwork, music; *Clubs* Cardiff and Country; *Style—* Prof Brian Ralph; ✉ Ty Carrog, St Brides-Super-Ely, Cardiff CF5 6EY (☎ 01446 760469); Department of Materials Engineering, Brunel, The University of West London, Uxbridge, Middx UB8 3HP (☎ 01895 274000, fax 01985 812636)

RALPH, Philip Pyman; s of Leslie Philip Ralph, VRD (d 1994), of Rossland, Hatch Beauchamp, Somerset, and (Christian) Doreen, *née* Pyman (d 1973); *b* 4 Aug 1931; *Educ* Fettes, Clare Coll Cambridge; *m* 20 Aug 1960, Joan Francis (Jill), da of Dr John Scott Brown; 2 s (Charles Ralph b 1962, Nicholas Ralph b 1963); *Career* Nat Serv 1950–52; articled clerk Albert Goodman & Company 1955–58, accountant Peat Marwick Mitchell & Company 1958–62, exec Corp Fin Dept Hill Samuel & Company Ltd 1962–71 (dir 1968–71), jt md Spey Investments Ltd 1971–76; dir and head Corp Fin Dept: William Brandt & Company Ltd 1973–76, Charterhouse Japhet Ltd 1976–81; dir corp fin The General Electric Company plc 1981–88, vice chm The Summit Group plc 1988–; non-exec dir: Chamberlin & Hill plc 1971–, Olim Convertible Trust plc 1989–, McDonnell Information Systems Group Plc 1996–; *Recreations* tennis, skiing, sailing; *Style—* Philip Ralph, Esq; ✉ The Summit Group plc, Summit House, 84 St Katherine's Way, London E1 9YS (☎ 0171 480 5588)

RALPH, HE Richard Peter; CVO (1992); s of Mr Peter Ralph, of Walmer, Kent, and late Evelyn Marion, *née* Horsley; *b* 27 April 1946; *Educ* King's Sch Canterbury, Univ of Edinburgh (MSc); *m* 1969, Margaret Elisabeth; 1 s (James Patrick Eveleigh b 14 Aug 1970), 1 da (Lucy Katharine b 4 Jan 1974); *Career* HM Dip Serv: third sec FCO 1969, third later second sec Vientiane Laos 1970–73, second later first sec Lisbon Portugal 1974–77, FCO 1977–81, head of Chancery Br High Cmmn Harare Zimbabwe 1981–84, FCO 1984–89, head of Chancery and congressional cnsllr Br Embassy Washington DC 1989–93, HM ambass Latvia 1993–95, govr of the Falkland Is (concurrently cmmr of S Georgia and the S Sandwich Is) 1996–; *Recreations* outdoor sports, motorcycling; *Style—* HE Mr Richard Ralph, CVO; ✉ Government House, Stanley, Falkland Islands

RALPHS, Lady; Enid Mary; CBE (1984), JP, DL (Norfolk 1981); da of Percy William Cowlin (d 1929), and Annie Louise, *née* Willoughby (d 1977); *b* 20 Jan 1915; *Educ* Camborne GS, Univ of Exeter (BA), Univ of Cambridge (DipEd); *m* 1938, Sir Lincoln Ralphs (d 1978), sometime chief educn offr Norfolk; 1 s, 2 da; *Career* teacher Penzance GS 1937–38; staff tutor Univ of Oxford 1942–44, pt/t sr lectr Keswick Hall Coll of Educn 1948–80; chm Norwich Bench 1977, vice pres Magistrates' Assoc of England and Wales, chm Cncl of Magistrates' Assoc 1981–84, memb Home Office Advisory Bd on Restricted Patients 1985–91, ret; Hon DCL Univ of E Anglia 1989; *Books* The Magistrate as Chairman (co-author, 1987, 2 edn 1992); *Recreations* gardening, travel; *Clubs* Royal Over-Seas League, Norfolk; *Style—* Lady Ralphs, CBE, JP, DL; ✉ Jesselton, 218 Unthank Rd, Norwich NR2 2AH (☎ 01603 53382)

RAMEL, Baron (Axel) Knut Stig Malte; yr (twin) s of Baron Stig Urban Malte Ramel, of Stockholm, Sweden, and Ann-Marie, *née* Countess Wachtmeister af Johanneshus; *b* 4 April 1954; *Educ* Stockholm Sch of Economics; *Career* Beijer Invest AB Stockholm 1978–80, Credit Suisse First Boston Ltd 1980–84, md Merrill Lynch Int & Co 1984–; *Style—* Baron Knut Ramel; ✉ 49A Britannia Rd, London SW6 (☎ 0171 384 1081); 25 Ropemaker St, London EC2 (☎ 0171 867 2805, fax 0171 867 2040)

RAMPHAL, Hon Sir Shridath Surendranath; OM (1990), GCMG (1990, CMG 1966), Hon AC (1982), QC (Guyana 1965); s of James I Ramphal, and Grace Ramphal; *b* 3 Oct 1928; *Educ* Queen's Coll Georgetown, King's Coll London, Harvard Law Sch; *m* 1951, Lois Winifred, *née* King; 2 s, 2 da; *Career* called to the Bar Gray's Inn 1951, crown counsel Br Guyana 1953–54, asst to AG 1954–56; legal draftsman: Br Guyana 1956–58, W Indies 1958–59; slr-gen Br Guyana 1959–61, asst AG W Indies 1961–62, AG Guyana 1965–73, memb Nat Assembly 1965–75, min of state for External Affrs 1967–72, min of Foreign Affrs 1972–75 (held concurrently with attorney-generalship until 1973), min of Justice 1973–75, sec-gen Cwlth 1975–90; chm: W Indian Cmmn 1990–92, Int Steering Ctee LEAD Program Rockefeller Fndn 1991–, Advsy Ctee Future Generations Alliance Fndn Kyoto 1994–, Bd Int Inst for Democracy and Electoral Assistance (IDEA) 1995–; co-chm Cmmn on Global Governance 1992–; pres The World Conservation Union 1991–93; memb: Int Cmmn Jurists 1970–, Ind (Brandt) Cmmn on Int Devpt Issues 1977–, Ind (Palme) Cmmn on Disarmament and Security Issues 1980–89, Ind Cmmn on Int Humanitarian Issues 1983–, World Cmmn on Environment and Devpt 1984–, Int Bd Utd World Colls 1984–94, Ind Cmmn of the South on Devpt Issues 1987–, Cncl of Int Negotiation Network Carter Center Georgia 1991–, Carnegie Cmmn on Preventing Deadly Conflict 1994–, Bd Int Devpt Res Center Canada; advsr to Sec-Gen UNCED 1992; chllr: Univ of Guyana 1988–92, Univ of Warwick 1989, Univ of W Indies 1989; hon fell: King's Coll London 1975, LSE 1979, Magdalen Coll Oxford 1982; visiting prof: Univ of Exeter 1986, Faculty of Laws King's Coll London 1988; Hon LLD: Punjab Univ 1975, Univ of Southampton 1976, Univ of W Indies 1978, St Francis Xavier 1978, Univ of Aberdeen 1979, Cape Coast Univ 1980, Univ of London 1981, Benin Univ 1982, Univ of Hull 1983, Univ of Cambridge 1985, Yale 1985, Univ of Warwick 1988, Univ of York 1988, Malta Univ 1989, Otago Univ 1990, Univ of Staffordshire 1993; Hon DLitt: Univ of Bradford 1985, Indira Gandhi Open Univ 1989; Hon DUniv: Surrey 1979, Essex 1980; Hon DCL: Univ of Oxford 1982, Univ of East Anglia 1983, Univ of Durham 1985; Hon DSc Cranfield Inst of Technol 1987; companion De Monfort Univ (formerly Leicester Poly) 1991; Int Educn award Richmond Coll London 1988, Albert medal RSA 1988; Hon Master of Bench Gray's Inn 1981, Hon FRSA 1981; SC Guyana 1966, OE 1983, ONI 1989, ONZ 1990, GCON 1990, GCOCF 1990, NQA 1990, OCC 1991, COGA 1994; *Books* One World to Share: selected speeches of the Commonwealth Secretary-General 1975–79, Inseparable Humanity: An Anthology of Reflections of Shridath Ramphal (ed R Sanders, 1988), An End to Otherness: eight speeches by the Commonwealth Secretary-General (1990), Our Country, The Planet (1992); *Recreations* photography, cooking; *Style—* The Hon Sir Shridath Ramphal, OE, OM, OCC, GCMG, QC; ✉ 1 The Sutherlands, 188 Sutherland Ave, London W9 1HR (☎ 0171 266 3409, fax 0171 286 2302)

RAMPLING, Dr Anita M (Mrs Anita M Darbyshire); *née* Larcher; *b* Liverpool; *Educ* Erdington GS for Girls, Univ of Nottingham (BSc Dairying), Univ of Birmingham Med Sch (PhD, MB ChB, William Thorpe Prize in Biochemistry, Leith-Neumann Prize in Pathology, Queen's scholar (fifth yr)), Univ of Cambridge (MA), FRCPath 1992 (MRCPath 1981); *m*; 1 s; *Career* asst bacteriologist Northern Regnl Bd Raigmore Hosp Inverness 1957–58, dairy bacteriologist Dept of Agric Brisbane Aust 1959–62, vet bacteriologist Dept of Agric Port Moresby Papua New Guinea 1962–66, sr microbiologist Queen Elizabeth Hosp Birmingham 1968–72, house physician Bromsgrove Gen Hosp Worcs 1978 (house surgn 1977–78), assoc lectr Dept of Pathology Univ of Cambridge 1984–91 (clinical lectr 1978–84), conslt med microbiologist/dep dir Public Health Lab Cambridge 1984–91 (actg dir 1988–91), consit med microbiologist/dir Public Health Lab Dorchester 1991–; infection control doctor for the W Dorset Tsts 1991– (chm Control of Infection Ctee); Public Health Lab Serv: chm Dairy Working Gp, dep chm Standing Scientific Ctee on Food and Dairy Products; memb Speciality Advsy Ctee on Med Microbiology and Cncl Royal Coll of Pathologists, inspr Clinical Pathology Accreditation Scheme; memb: Assoc of Clinical Pathologists, Br Soc for the Study of Infection, Hosp Infection Soc, Br Soc for Antimicrobial Chemotherapy, Assoc of Med Microbiologists, Soc for Anaerobic Microbiology, Med Research Club, Royal Soc of Med; research interests: hosp infections and public health microbiology incl dairy products and food; *Style—* Dr Anita M Rampling; ✉ Clinical Microbiology and Public Health Laboratory, West Dorset Hospital, Damers Road, Dorchester, Dorset DT1 2JY (☎ 01305 251150)

RAMPLING, Dr Roy Peter; s of Alan William Rampling (d 1984), and Lorenza, *née* Camilleri (d 1966); *b* 13 Sept 1946; *Educ* Clacton Co HS, Imperial Coll (BSc, PhD, DIC), Chelsea Coll (MSc), UCL (MB BS); *m* 27 Dec 1975, Susan Mary, da of Richard Erskine Bonham-Carter, of Knebworth; 2 s (Thomas William b 1979, Jack Richard b 1984), 1 da (Laura Elizabeth b 1977); *Career* currently sr lectr Dept of Radiation Oncology Univ of Glasgow; ARCS, memb Inst of Physics 1972, MRCP 1981, FRCR 1984, FRCPGlas 1992; *Style—* Dr Roy Rampling; ✉ Beatson Oncology Centre, Western Infirmary, Glasgow G11 6NT (☎ 0141 339 8822)

RAMPRAKASH, Mark Ravindra; s of Deonarine Ramprakash, and Jenifer, *née* Walker; *b* 5 Sept 1969; *Educ* Gayton HS for Boys, Harrow Weald Sixth Form Coll; *Career* professional cricketer; Middlesex CCC: debut 1987, 78 first class appearances, awarded county cap 1990; England: rep schools under 15 and under 19, rep Young Eng under 19, memb B tour to Pakistan and Sri Lanka 1991, 17 test matches (debut v W Indies at Headingley 1991), 7 one day ints, memb sr tour NZ 1992, memb A tour Bermuda and W Indies 1992, memb team touring W Indies 1993/94 and S Africa 1995/96; Gray Nicholls Young Player of the Year 1985 (under 15) and 1987 (under 19), Cricket Sportswriters' Young Cricketer of the Year 1991; *Recreations* playing snooker, watching old cowboy films; *Style—* Mark Ramprakash, Esq; ✉ Middlesex CCC, Lord's Cricket Ground, London NW8 8QN (☎ 0171 289 1300)

RAMPTON, (Anthony) James Matthew; s of John Richard Anthony Rampton, of London, and Carolyn Mary, *née* Clarke; *b* 22 May 1964; *Educ* St Paul's Davidson Coll N Carolina US (scholar), Exeter Coll Oxford (BA); *m* 1992, Mary Anne Howlett Jones; 1 da (Helen Catherine); *Career* dep film ed (listings) The Independent 1988–89, TV writer The Independent on Sunday 1990–93, contributing features ed The Independent 1993–95, freelance feature writer 1995–; *Recreations* rugby, cricket, *not* watching television; *Style—* James Rampton, Esq; ✉ c/o The Independent, 1 Canada Square, Canary Wharf, London E14 5AP (☎ 0171 293 2000, fax 0171 293 2435)

RAMSAY, Sir Alexander William Burnett; 7 Bt (UK 1806), of Balmain, Kincardineshire; s of late Sir Alexander Burnett Ramsay, 6 Bt (d 1965); is the presumed heir to the Baronetcy of Burnett of Leys (cr 1626); *b* 4 Aug 1938; *m* 1963, Neryl Eileen, da of J C Smith Thornton, of Trangie, NSW; 3 s (Alexander David b 1966, Ian John b 1968, David Burnett b 1971); *Heir* s, Alexander David Ramsay b 20 Aug 1966; *Style—* Sir Alexander Ramsay, Bt

RAMSAY, Andrew Charles Bruce; s of Norman Bruce Ramsay (d 1952), and Marysha Octavia, *née* Skrynska (d 1960); *b* 30 May 1951; *Educ* Cheam Sch, Winchester Coll, Univ of London (BA); *m* 9 July 1983, Katharine Celia, da of David Marsh; 2 da (Isobel Daisy b 22 Dec 1985, Octavia Beatrice b 5 July 1988); *Career* HM Civil Service: joined DOE and Dept of Tport 1974, private sec to Jr Tport Min 1978–80, princ DOE and Dept of Tport 1980–85, asst sec DOE 1986–93, under sec and head Arts, Sport and Lottery Gp Dept of National Heritage 1993–96, head Fin, Lottery and Personnel Gp Dept of National Heritage 1996–; *Recreations* gardening, opera, birds; *Style—* Andrew Ramsay, Esq; ✉ Department of National Heritage, 2–4 Cockspur Street, London SW1Y 5DH (☎ 0171 211 6189)

RAMSAY, Andrew Vernon; s of Douglas Charles Ramsay, of Glos, and Dorothy Isobel, *née* Shankland; *b* 7 July 1948; *Educ* Chosen Hill Sch, Churchill Coll Cambridge (MA); *m* 3 July 1971, Ruth Irene, da of Francis James Mullen; 1 s (William James b 27 Oct 1975), 1 da (Elizabeth Jean b 9 Jan 1978); *Career* apprentice AEI Rugby 1966–70, contract engr GEC Electrical Projects 1970–72; CEGB: exec offr Legal and Insur Dept 1972–74, princ Engrg Servs Dept 1974–79; sec Chartered Instn of Bldg Servs Engrs (CIBSE) 1985– (dep sec 1979–84); Freeman Worshipful Co of Fanmakers 1995; MIEE 1980, FCIS 1985; *Recreations* opera, rowing; *Clubs* Rumford; *Style—* Andrew Ramsay, Esq; ✉ CIBSE, Delta House, 222 Balham High Road, London SW12 9BS (☎ 0181 675 5211, fax 0181 673 0822)

RAMSAY, Maj-Gen Charles Alexander; CB (1989), OBE (1979); s of Adm Sir Bertram Home Ramsay, KCB, KBE, MVO (Allied Naval C in C Invasion of Europe 1944, ka 1945), and Helen Margaret Menzies (d 1993); descended from Sir Alexander Ramsay, 2nd Bart of Balmain, Kincardineshire; *b* 12 Oct 1936; *Educ* Eton, Sandhurst; *m* 1967, Hon Mary, da of 1 Baron MacAndrew, TD, PC (d 1979); 2 s, 2 da; *Career* cmmnd Royal Scots Greys 1956, Staff Coll, Canada 1967–68, cmd Royal Scots Dragoon Gds 1977–79, Cdr 12 Armd Bde and Osnabruck Garrison 1980–82, dep DMO MOD 1983–84, GOC Eastern Dist 1984–87; dir gen TA and Army Orgn 1987–89, resigned from Army 1989; chm: Eagle Enterprises Ltd (Bermuda) 1990–95, The Wine Co (Scotland) Ltd 1991–93, Cockburns of Leith plc 1993–; dir: John Menzies plc 1990–, Potomac Holdings Inc (USA) 1990–, Edinburgh Military Tattoo Ltd 1991–, Grey Horse Properties Ltd 1991–, Morningside Developments Ltd (USA) 1993–, Morningside Holdings Ltd (USA) 1996–; chief exec Caledonian Eagle (GB) 1991–; farmer and landowner; Col The Royal Scots Dragoon Gds 1992–; memb Queen's Body Guard for Scotland (The Royal Co of Archers); *Recreations* field sports, equitation, travel, motor yachting; *Clubs* Boodle's, Cavalry &

Guards', New (Edinburgh), Pratt's; *Style*— Maj-Gen C A Ramsay, CB, OBE; ✉ Bughtrig, Coldstream, Berwickshire TD12 4JP; Chesthill, Glenlyon, Perthshire PH15 2NH

RAMSAY, Gordon James; *b* 8 Nov 1966, Glasgow; *Educ* Oxford Tech Coll; *Career* apprentice footballer Glasgow Rangers FC until 1983; hotel and catering mgmnt course Oxford Tech Coll 1983–85; chef: Mayfair Intercontinental Hotel (under Michael Coker) 1985, Harvey's Restaurant London (under Marco Pierre White) 1985–87, Le Gavroche Restaurant London 1987–89, Hotel Diva Isola 2000 South of France (under Albert Roux) 1989–91, kitchens of Guy Savoy Paris 1991–93, Le Jamin Restaurant Paris (under Joel Robuchon) 1993; chef/proprietor Aubergine Restaurant Chelsea Sept 1993–; Chef of the Year 1992, Newcomer of the Year (The Independent) 1993, 1 star Michelin Guide 1995, 16/20 Gault Mileau Guide 1995, 4 rosettes AA Guide 1994/95, London Restaurant of the Year (Good Food Guide) 1995, Newcomer of the Year Catey Awards 1995, 4 out of 5 Good Food Guide 1996; *Style*— Gordon Ramsay, Esq; ✉ Aubergine Restaurant, 11 Park Walk, London SW10 (☎ 0171 352 3449)

RAMSAY, Lord; James Hubert Ramsay; DL (1993 Angus); s and h of 16 Earl of Dalhousie, KT, GBE, MC, by his w Margaret, da of late Brig-Gen Archibald Stirling of Keir (2 s of Sir John Stirling-Maxwell, 10 Bt, KT, DL, which Btcy has been dormant since 1956) and Hon Margaret Fraser, OBE, da of 13 Lord Lovat; *b* 17 Jan 1948; *Educ* Ampleforth; *m* 1973, Marilyn, 2 da of Maj Sir David Henry Butter, KCVO, MC, and Myra Alice, da of Sir Harold Wernher, 3 and last Bt, GCVO, TD, by his w Lady Zia, *née* Countess Anastasia Mikhailovna, er da Lady Ramsay is hence 1 cous of the Duchess of Abercornia; *qv*); 1 s, 2 da (Hon Lorna b 1975, Hon Alice b 1977); *Heir* s, Hon Simon David Ramsay b 18 April 1981; *Career* cmmnd 2 Bn Coldstream Gds 1968–71; dir Hambros Bank 1981–82; exec dir Enskilda Securities 1982–87; dir: Jamestown Investments Ltd 1987–, Central Capital Ltd 1987–91, Capel-Cure Myers 1987–91; chm William Evans 1990–, Alex Brown & Sons Holdings Ltd 1993–, Scottish Woodlands Ltd 1993–, Edinburgh Japan Trust plc (formerly Dunedin Japan Investment Trust plc until 1996) 1993–; pres: British Deer Soc 1987, Caledonian Club 1990–; *Clubs* White's, Pratt's, Turf, Caledonian; *Style*— Lord Ramsay, DL; ✉ Dalhousie Lodge, Edzell, Angus DD9 7TU; Flat 15, 41 Courtfield Road, London SW17 4DB (☎ 0171 727 2800)

RAMSAY, Prof Lawrence Eccles; s of William Ramsay (d 1970), of Ayrshire, Scotland, and Margaret Cables, *née* Eccles (d 1989); *b* 11 June 1943; *Educ* Cumnock Acad, Univ of Glasgow (MB ChB); *m* 17 Sept 1965, Mary Helen, da of Harry Hynd (d 1971), of Lanark, Scotland; 3 s (William b 1972, Alan b 1974, Iain b 1983), 1 da (Helen b 1970); *Career* Surgn Lt RN 1968–73, HMS Osprey 1968–69, HMS Jufair 1969–70, Admty Med Bd 1970–71, RNH Haslar 1971–73; lectr in medicine Univ of Glasgow 1977–78, conslt physician Royal Hallamshire Hosp 1978–, prof of clinical pharmacology and therapeutics Univ of Sheffield 1991– (reader in clinical pharmacology 1985–91); ed British Journal of Clinical Pharmacology 1988–94; visiting memb to Australasia for Br Pharmacological Soc 1989; memb: Cncl World Hypertension League 1989, Br Pharmacopoeia Cmmn 1980–, Ctee on Review of Medicines 1982–91, Sub Ctee on Pharmacovigilance CSM 1992–, Assoc of Physicians 1987; vice-pres Br Hypertension Soc 1995– (sec 1985–89); FRCP 1985 (memb 1970); *Recreations* soccer, golf, travel; *Style*— Prof Lawrence Ramsay; ✉ 85 Redmires Rd, Lodge Moor, Sheffield S10 4LB (☎ 0114 276 6222)

RAMSAY, Sheriff Norman James Gemmill; s of James Ramsay (d 1940), of Kilmarnock and Buenos Aires, and Christina Emma, *née* Sheppard (d 1950); *b* 26 Aug 1916; *Educ* Merchiston Castle Sch, Univ of Edinburgh (MA, LLB); *m* 5 Jan 1952, Rachael (Ray) Mary Berkeley, da of Sir Herbert Charles Fahie Cox; 2 s (David James b 10 Jan 1954, Alexander Malcolm b 4 March 1957); *Career* WS 1939; WWII RN 1940–46; serv: E Indies Station, Eastern Fleet Aden; writer, leading writer, Petty Offr Writer, Paymaster Sub Lt, Paymaster Lt, Lt (S) RNVR; admin gen Northern Rhodesia 1947–56, advocate (Scotland) 1956–, res magistrate 1956–58, sr res magistrate 1958–64, puisne judge High Ct of Northern Rhodesia (later Zambia) 1964–68; Sheriff Substitute/Sheriff Dumfries and Galloway (later South Strathclyde, Dumfries and Galloway) 1971–85 (now Hon Sheriff); *Recreations* gardening; *Clubs* Royal Cwlth Soc; *Style*— Sheriff Norman Ramsay; ✉ Mill of Borgue, Kirkcudbright DG6 4SY (☎ 01557 870211)

RAMSAY, Richard Alexander McGregor; s of Alexander John McGregor (d 1986), of Ramsay, and Beatrice Kent, *née* De La Nauze; *b* 27 Dec 1949; *Educ* Trinity Coll Glenalmond, Univ of Aberdeen (MA); *m* 19 July 1975, Elizabeth Catherine Margaret, da of Robert Cecil Blackwood (d 1969); 1 s (Alistair Robert Blackwood b 19 Feb 1983), 1 da (Catherine Anne Blackwood b 1 Feb 1981); *Career* CA; articled clerk Price Waterhouse 1972–75, Grindlay Brandts Ltd 1975–78, Hill Samuel and Co Ltd 1979–88 (dir 1984–88, seconded as dir Industl Devpt Unit DTI 1984–86); Barclays de Zoete Wedd Ltd: dir 1988–93, md Corp Fin Div 1990–93; dir Ivory & Sime Investment Management 1993–; FCA; *Recreations* skiing, mountain walking, gardening, historic and classic cars; *Clubs* Caledonian, City; *Style*— Richard Ramsay, Esq; ✉ Ivory & Sime Investment Management, 14th Floor, One Angel Court, London EC2R 7HJ (☎ 0171 600 6655, fax 0171 600 4371)

RAMSAY, Roderick Thomas (Rod); s of Thomas Ramsay (d 1979), of Birmingham, and Barbara, *née* Dunicliffe; *b* 27 April 1945; *Educ* Bournville Tech Sch, LSE (BScEcon); *m* Litsa, da of Alfred Hill; 2 da (Christina b 2 Jan 1972, Kate b 20 May 1981); *Career* Mfrg Dept (prodn material control) Austin Morris 1968–72, Sales and Mktg Dept 1972–76, orgn planning mangr Leyland International 1976–78, various positions Austin Morris/Austin Rover (incl programming mangr, Euro mktg servs mangr, UK sales planning dir) 1978–87, regnl dir Scotland, NI and Northern England Rover Cars 1987–90, mktg progs dir 1990–91, dir Rover Cars Marketing 1991–93, dir Rover Group Marketing 1994–; *Recreations* reading, motor racing (spectator); *Style*— Rod Ramsay, Esq; ✉ Rover Group, Longbridge, Birmingham

RAMSAY, William Marcus Raymond; s of Raymond Ramsay, MBE (d 1996), and Lillian, *née* Bateman; *b* 24 July 1956; *Educ* The Royal GS High Wycombe, Univ of London (BA), Henley Mgmnt Coll, Brunel Univ (MPhil); *m* 11 Oct 1980, Fiona, da of Peter Gray, of Lothersdale, N Yorks; 2 s (William b 1981, James b 1985), 1 da (Sophie b 1989); *Career* asst dir Morgan Grenfell & Co Ltd 1985 (grad entrant 1979, mangr 1984), memb Mgmnt Ctee Rothschild Asset Management (joined 1986, dir 1987), memb Occupational Pensions Bd (appointed by Sec of State) 1989; Freeman: City of London 1980, Worshipful Co of Fletchers 1980 (memb Ct of Assts); MSI 1993; *Recreations* theatre (memb Br Actors' Equity), swimming; *Clubs* Brooks's; *Style*— William Ramsay, Esq; ✉ Rothschild Asset Management Ltd, Five Arrows House, St Swithin's Lane, London EC4N 8NR (☎ 0171 280 5000, fax 0171 929 1643, telex 888031)

RAMSAY OF MAR, Capt Alexander Arthur Alfonso David Maule; DL (Aberdeenshire 1971); s of Adm the Hon Sir Alexander Ramsay, GCVO, KCB, DSO (d 1972, s of 13 Earl of Dalhousie), and Lady Patricia (d 1974, da of HRH 1 Duke of Connaught and Strathearn, 3 s of Queen Victoria), who on her marriage renounced, by Royal permission, the style and title of HRH and Princess and assumed that of Lady; *b* 21 Dec 1919, (King Edward VIII and King Alfonso XIII of Spain sponsors); *Educ* Eton, Trinity Coll Oxford (MA); *m* 1956, The Rt Hon the Lady Saltoun, *qv*; 3 da; *Career* page of honour at Coronation of George VI 1937; Grenadier Gds 1938–47 (wounded N Africa 1943), Capt 1941, ADC to HRH the Duke of Gloucester 1944–47; chartered surveyor; memb Forestry Soc of GB (now Inst of Chartered Foresters) 1957–, vice patron Braemar Royal Highland Soc 1959–, Laird of Mar 1963–87, chm Exec Ctee Scottish Life Boat Cncl RNLI 1965–89 (hon life govr RNLI 1989), memb Nat Bd SWOA (later TGUK) 1966–91 (chm NE Region 1967–82); FRICS; *Recreations* shooting, sailing, travel, Scottish and family history, heraldry; *Clubs* Cavalry and Guards', New (Edinburgh), Household Div Yacht (Warsash), Island Sailing (Cowes), Royal Northern and Univ (Aberdeen); *Style*— Capt Alexander Ramsay of Mar, DL; ✉ Cairnbulg Castle, Fraserburgh, Aberdeenshire AB43 5TN (☎ 01346 513149); Inverey House, Braemar, Aberdeenshire AB35 5YB; Flat 8, 25 Onslow Square, London SW7 3NJ

RAMSBOTHAM, Gen Sir David John; GCB (1993, KCB 1987), CBE (1980, OBE 1974); s of Rt Rev Bishop John Alexander Ramsbotham (d 1989), of Hexham, Northumberland, and Eirian Morgan, *née* Morgan Owen (d 1988); *b* 6 Nov 1934; *Educ* Haileybury, CCC Cambridge (BA, MA); *m* 26 Sept 1958, Susan Caroline, da of Robert Joicey Dickinson, of Corbridge, Northumberland (d 1980); 2 s (James David Alexander b 30 Aug 1959, Richard Henry b 8 June 1962); *Career* cmmnd Rifle Bde 1958, Royal Green Jackets CO 2 RGJ 1974–76, Cdr 39 Inf Bde 1978–80, RCDS 1981, dir PR (Army) 1982–84; Cdr: 3 Armd Div 1984–87, UK Field Army 1987–90; inspr gen TA 1987–90, Adj Gen 1990–93, ADC Gen 1990–93; HM Inspr of Prisons for England and Wales 1995–; dir International Affairs Defence Systems Ltd 1994–; memb Cncl IISS 1996–; CIMgt 1993; *Recreations* shooting, gardening, sailing; *Clubs* MCC; *Style*— Gen Sir David Ramsbotham, GCB, CBE; ✉ Home Office, 50 Queen Anne's Gate, London SW1H 9AT

RAMSBOTHAM, Hon Sir Peter Edward; GCMG (1978, KCMG 1972, CMG 1964), GCVO (1976), DL (Hants); yr s of late 1 Viscount Soulbury, GCMG, GCVO, OBE, MC, PC (d 1971), and his 1 w, Doris Violet (d 1954), da of Sigmund de Stein; hp of bro, 2 Viscount; *b* 8 Oct 1919; *Educ* Eton, Magdalen Coll Oxford; *m* 1, 30 Aug 1941, Frances Marie Massie (d 1982), da of late Hugh Massie Blomfield; 2 s (Oliver b 1943, Simon b 1950), 1 da (Mary b 1945); m 2, 1985, Dr Zaïda Hall, da of Maurice Henry Megrah, QC; *Career* served HM Forces 1943–46, Lt Col Intelligence Corps; entered FO 1948, Br high cmmr Cyprus 1969–71, ambass to Iran 1971–73, ambass to USA 1974–77, govr and C-in-C Bermuda 1977–80; dir: Commercial Union Assurance Co 1981–90, Lloyds Bank plc 1981–90; chm Southern Regnl Bd Lloyds Bank 1983–89; tstee Leonard Cheshire Fndn 1981–94; chm: Ryder-Cheshire Fndn for Relief of Suffering 1982–, World Meml Fund for Disaster Relief 1990–; govr King's Sch Canterbury 1981–91, hon fell Magdalen Coll Oxford 1991; Hon LLD: Akron Univ 1975, Coll of William and Mary Coll 1975, Univ of Maryland 1976, Yale Unv 1977; Croix de Guerre; KStJ 1976; *Recreations* gardening, fishing; *Clubs* Garrick; *Style*— The Hon Sir Peter Ramsbotham, GCMG, GCVO, DL; ✉ East Lane, Ovington, nr Alresford, Hants SO24 0RA (☎ and fax 01962 732515)

RAMSBOTTOM, Roy Frederic; s of Harry Ramsbottom, of The Paddocks, Davenham, Northwich, Cheshire, and Stella, *née* Walton; *b* 11 Aug 1943; *Educ* Sir John Deanes GS Northwich; *m* 21 Oct 1972, Susan Mary (Su); *Career* sr ptnr Murray Smith and Co CAs Northwich Cheshire 1985– (ptnr 1970–85), dir Walthamstow Building Society 1985–90, local dir Cheltenham & Gloucester Building Society 1990–92; non-exec dir West Cheshire NHS Trust 1993–; hon treas Cheshire Agric Soc 1977–93, chm Chester and N Wales Soc of CAs 1978–79; FCA; *Recreations* cricket; *Clubs* Pitt, Oulton Park CC; *Style*— Roy Ramsbottom, Esq; ✉ Helensmere, Little Budworth, Tarporley, Cheshire CW6 9EL; Murray Smith and Co, Darland House, 44 Winnington Hill, Northwich, Cheshire CW8 1AU (☎ 01606 79411, fax 01606 782878)

RAMSBURY, Bishop of 1989–; Rt Rev Peter St George Vaughan; s of late Dr Victor St George Vaughan, of St Leonards-on-Sea, E Sussex, and Dorothy Marguerite, *née* Longworth-Dames; *b* 27 Nov 1930; *Educ* Dean Close Jr Sch, Charterhouse, Selwyn Coll Cambridge (MA), Ridley Hall Cambridge, Univ of Oxford (MA); *m* 2 Sept 1961, Elisabeth Fielding, da of late Dr Fielding Parker, of Auckland, NZ; 1 s (Richard b 1969), 2 da (Sarah b 1963, Merle b 1966); *Career* Army NS RHA and RAPC (Lt) 1949; asst curate Birmingham Parish Church 1957–62, chaplain Oxford Pastorate, asst chaplain Brasenose Coll Oxford 1963–67, vicar Christ Church Galle Face Colombo Sri Lanka 1967–72, precentor Auckland Cathedral NZ 1972–75, princ Crowther Hall Selly Oak Coll 1975–83, archdeacon of Westmorland and Furness and hon canon of Carlisle 1983–89, preb of Salisbury 1989–; *Recreations* swimming, walking, gardening, reading; *Style*— The Rt Rev the Bishop of Ramsbury; ✉ Bishop's House, High St, Urchfont, Devizes, Wilts SN10 4QH (☎ 01380 840373)

RAMSDEN, Rt Hon James Edward; PC (1963); only s of Capt Edward Ramsden, MC, JP, and Geraldine Ramsden, OBE, yst da of Brig-Gen John Wilson, CB, JP, DL, and great n of 13 Baron Inchiquin; *b* 1 Nov 1923; *Educ* Eton, Trinity Coll Oxford; *m* 1949, Juliet Barbara Anna, yst da of Col Sir Charles Ponsonby, 1 Bt, TD, by his w Hon Winifred Gibbs, eld da of 1 Baron Hunsdon; 3 s (Thomas b 1950, George b 1953, Richard b 1954), 2 da (Emma b 1957, Charlotte b 1960 d 1991); *Career* KRRC, served WWII NW Europe, with RB (despatches); MP (C) Harrogate 1954–74, PPS to Home Sec 1959–60, under sec and fin sec WO 1960–63, sec of state for war 1963–64, min of def (Army) April-Oct 1964; dir: Colonial Mutual Life Assur (UK Bd) 1966–72, Standard Telephones & Cables 1971–81, London Clinic 1973–96 (chm 1984–96), Prudential Corp 1979–91 (dep chm 1979–82); memb Historic Bldgs Cncl England 1971–72; *Recreations* foxhunting, forestry, woodturning; *Clubs* Pratt's; *Style*— The Rt Hon James Ramsden; ✉ Old Sleningford Hall, Ripon, N Yorks (☎ 01765 635229, fax 01765 635485)

RAMSDEN, Lady; (Jennifer) Jane; *née* Bevan; yr da of Rear Adm Christopher Martin Bevan, CB, and Patricia Constance, *née* Bedford; *b* 4 Jan 1953; *Educ* Winchester County HS, Newnham Coll Cambridge (MA), LGSM; *m* 14 Dec 1985, Sir John Charles Josslyn Ramsden, 9 Bt, *qv*; 2 da (Isobel Lucy b 27 April 1987, Stella Evelyn b 4 Aug 1989); *Career* professional musician (violinist and pianist) 1974–79, broadcaster; memb HM Dip Serv 1979–85 (third sec rising to first sec); prodr Music Dept BBC Radio 3 1985–95; *Recreations* music, writing, family; *Style*— Lady Ramsden

RAMSDEN, Sir John Charles Josslyn; 9 Bt (E 1689), of Byram, Yorks; o s of Sir Caryl Oliver Imbert Ramsden, 8 Bt, CMG, CVO (d 1987), and Anne, Lady Ramsden; *b* 19 Aug 1950; *Educ* Eton, Trinity Coll Cambridge (MA); *m* 14 Dec 1985, (Jennifer) Jane, *qv*, da of Rear Adm Christopher Martin Bevan, CB; 2 da (Isobel Lucy b 27 April 1987, Stella Evelyn b 4 Aug 1989); *Heir* undetermined; *Career* Dawnay Day & Co Ltd (merchant bankers) 1972–74; HM Dip Serv: entered 1975, second sec Dakar 1976–78, first sec Delgn to MBFR Talks Vienna 1979, head of chancery and HM consul Hanoi 1980–82, FCO 1982–90, cnsllr and dep head of Mission Embassy to GDR 1990, cnsllr and dep head of Br Embassy Berlin Office 1990–93, head of Information Dept FCO 1993–96, dep perm rep UK Mission to UN Geneva 1996–; *Style*— Sir John Ramsden, Bt; ✉ c/o Foreign and Commonwealth Office, King Charles St, London SW1

RAMSDEN, (John) Michael; s of John Leonard Ramsden (d 1967), and Edith Alexandra, *née* Hartley (d 1979); *b* 2 Oct 1928; *Educ* Bedford Sch, de Havilland Aeronautical Tech Sch; *m* 26 Sept 1953, Angela Mary, da of Walter Mortimer; 1 s (James b 1956), 1 da (Annabel b 1960); *Career* ed in chief Flight 1981–89 (ed 1964–81), ed Aerospace 1989–93, editorial contrib Royal Aeronautical Soc; vice chm D-Notice Ctee 1980–89, dir de Havilland Aircraft Museum; CEng, FRAeS; *Books* The Safe Airline (1978), Caring for the Mature Jet (1981); *Recreations* flying, water-colour painting, squash; *Clubs* London Sch of Flying, D H Moth; *Style*— Michael Ramsden, Esq; ✉ The Royal Aeronautical Soc, Hamilton Place, Park Lane, London W1V 0BQ (☎ 0171 499 3515, fax 0171 499 6230)

RAMSDEN, Prof Richard Thomas; s of Thomas William Ramsden, of Balmerino, Fife, and Elaine Napier, *née* Meikle; *b* 30 Dec 1944; *Educ* Madras Coll St Andrews, Univ of St Andrews (MB ChB), FRCS; *m* 1, 1968 (m dis 1984), Wendy Margaret, *née* Johnson; 1 s (Alistair b 1974), 2 da (Helen b 1972, Fiona b 1977); m 2, 21 June 1985, (Eileen)

Gillian, da of Clifford Whitehurst, of Knutsford, Cheshire; *Career* consIt otolaryngIogist and hon visiting prof in otolaryngology Manchester Royal Infirmary; hon lectr: Dept of Surgery Victoria Univ of Manchester, Dept of Audiology Speech Pathology and Educn of the Deaf Victoria Univ of Manchester 1977; author of chapters and articles on aspects of ear surgery; asst ed Jl of Laryngology and Otology; memb Editorial Bd: American Jl of Otology, Revue de Laryugologie Otologie Rhinologie, ENT Jl; memb Nat Ctee of Enquiry into Perioperative Deaths; memb Cncl, vice pres and treas Otology Section Royal Soc of Medicine 1985– (pres 1994/95), examiner and bd memb Intercollegiate Bd in Otolaryngology, memb Ct of Examiners RCPSGlas 1987–, chm Br Cochlear Implant Gp 1989–, memb Collegium Oto-Rhino-Laryngologicum Amicitiae Sacrum, memb UK Cncl on Deafness; winner Dalby Prize Royal Soc of Med 1992, Wilde Medal 1994, VS Subramaniam lectr and Gold Medal 1995; FRCS 1973, memb BMA 1977; *Recreations* golf, otology; *Clubs* St Andrews New; *Style*— Prof Richard Ramsden; ✉ Lake House, Legh Rd, Knutsford, Cheshire WA16 8LP (☎ 01565 650936); 9/11 Lorne St, Manchester M13 0EZ (☎ 0161 273 4231, fax 0161 273 8124); Manchester Royal Infirmary, Oxford Road, Manchester M13 9WL (☎ 0161 276 4639, fax 0161 276 8511, e-mail rramsden@fsl.mci.man.ac.uk)

RAMSDEN, Stephen; *b* 2 March 1957; *Educ* Smithills Moor GS Bolton; *Career* trainee NW RHA 1975–83 (IHSA 1981), dep unit gen mangr Oldchurch Hosp Romford Essex 1983–88; chief exec: Mount Vernon Hosp NHS Tst 1991–93 (unit gen mangr 1988–91), Mount Vernon & Watford Hosps NHS Tst 1994– (project offr 1993–94); tstee Gray Lab Cancer Research Tst, memb King's Fund Organisational Audit Cncl; MHSM; *Style*— Stephen Ramsden, Esq; ✉ Mount Vernon & Watford Hospitals NHS Trust, Watford General Hospital, Vicarage Road, Watford, Herts WD1 8HB (☎ 01923 244366, fax 01923 217440)

RAMSDEN, Prof Stuart Abbott; s of Arnold Richardson Ramsden (d 1984), of Walkington, Humberside, and Helen, *née* Abbott (d 1979); *b* 17 Sept 1930; *Educ* West Leeds HS Leeds, Keble Coll Oxford (BA, DPhil); *m* 17 Dec 1955, Eileen Nancy, da of Vernon Harcourt Richardson (d 1988), of Leconfield, Humberside; 2 s (Nigel Christopher b 1957, Simon Nicholas b 1960), 1 da (Caroline Jane b 1963); *Career* sr scientific offr AERE Harwell 1956–62, gp leader laser and plasma physics section Nat Res Cncl Ottowa Canada 1962–67, prof of applied physics Univ of Hull 1967–86, co-ordinator of laser prog Rutherford Appleton Laboratory 1986–94, ret; memb Euro Physical Soc, FInstP; *Recreations* walking, golf, piano and organ; *Style*— Prof Stuart Ramsden; ✉ Sarren House, Buckland, Faringdon, Oxon (☎ 01367 870381)

RAMSEY, Vivian Arthur; QC (1992); s of Ian Thomas Ramsey (d 1972 former Bishop of Durham), and Margretta, *née* McKay; *b* 24 May 1950; *Educ* Abingdon Sch, Harley Sch Rochester NY USA, Oriel Coll Oxford (MA), City Univ (Dip Law); *m* 14 Aug 1974, Barbara, da of Lt-Col Gerard Majella Walker, of Hitchin, Herts; 2 s (Nicholas b 1981, James b 1986), 2 da (Helen b 1980, Katharine b 1984); *Career* graduate engr Ove Arup & Ptnrs 1972–77, called to the Bar Middle Temple 1979; practising barr 1981–, ctee official referee Bar Assoc 1986–91, arbitrator (incl ICC arbitration) 1988– (mediator 1991–); ed Construction Law Jl 1984–, special prof Dept of Civil Engrg Univ of Nottingham 1990–; treas: St Swithuns Hither Green 1977–84, Swanley Village Sports and Social Club 1986– (chm 1990–); chm Swanley Action Gp 1990–; MICE 1977; *Recreations* pantomime, building renovation; *Style*— Vivian Ramsey, Esq, QC; ✉ 10 Essex St, Outer Temple, London WC2R 3AA (☎ 0171 240 6981, fax 0171 240 7722, telex 8955650)

RAMSHAW, Prof Colin; *b* 12 Oct 1936; *Educ* Univ of Newcastle (BSc, PhD); *Career* sr scientific offr Miny of Aviation 1962–66, scientific offr Central Instrument Res Laboratories ICI Plc 1966–74, sr staff and section mangr ICI Corporate Laboratory 1974– (res assoc, memb Fluid Separation Panel); fndr jt res scheme Univ of Newcastle (with John Porter) 1981, jt fndr ICI/ETSU project Heriot Watt Univ (with Prof K Cornwell), consIt EEC Joule 1 programme on energy conservation 1990–; prof of chem engrg Univ of Newcastle 1991– (visiting prof 1989–91), EPSRC chair of Responsive Processing Univ of Newcastle 1996–; author of various papers in learned journals; memb Inst of Chemical Engrs Res Ctee 1984–86; FEng 1989; *Style*— Prof Colin Ramshaw, FEng; ✉ 20 High View, Ponteland, Newcastle upon Tyne NE20 9ET (☎ 01661 872436, office 0191 222 7270)

RAND, Gerald Frederick; s of William Frederick Rand (d 1960), of Herts, and Elsie Mary White (d 1926); *b* 10 Nov 1926; *Educ* Merchant Taylors'; *m* 1, 13 July 1949, Eileen Margaret, da of William Alexanda Winson (d 1975), of Herts; 1 s (Stephen b 1953); m 2, 1 Nov 1972, Clarissa Elizabeth, da of Thomas William Barker (d 1956), of Hull; *Career* ret master builder; chm Rand Contractors Ltd 1952–68, md Power Plant Int 1962–71, chm Manor Minerals (UK) Ltd 1985–; landowner, owner of the Lynford Hall Estate Norfolk; memb CLA, elected to Société Jersiaise 1967; memb Governing Cncl The Manorial Soc of GB 1985–, regnl chm Domesday Nat Ctee 1986–; Lord of the Manor of: Lynford, Mundford, Cranwich Norfolk; Freeman City of London 1986; FSA(Scot) 1993; *Recreations* shooting, hunting, studies in medieval history, historic buildings; *Style*— Gerald F Rand, Esq; ✉ Lynford Hall, Thetford, Norfolk IP26 5HW (☎ 01842 878351, fax 01842 878252); Westmill, Ashwell, Herts (☎ 01462 742568)

RANDALL, Adrian John Laurence; s of Robert Bennet Randall (d 1950), of London, and Ivy Ellen, *née* French (d 1986); *b* 4 Dec 1944; *Educ* Harrison Coll Barbados, Univ of Hull (BSc); *m* 1, 5 Sept 1970 (m dis 1990), Suzanne, da of William Marshall, of Morpeth; 2 da (Nicola Jane b 6 Oct 1973, Emma Louise b 3 June 1976); m 2, 18 March 1995, Jennifer LeSbirel, da of Cecil Henry Sturgess; *Career* articled clerk Harper Smith Bennett & Co Norwich 1964–68; Tate & Lyle plc: accountant Zambia Sugar Co Ltd 1971–76, accountant Tate & Lyle plc 1976–78, fin controller Tate & Lyle Agribusiness Ltd 1978–79, fin dir Unalco Div 1980–84; Hays Group: chief exec Anti-Pollution Chemicals Ltd 1984–85, gen mangr Gen Chemicals Div London 1986–87 (fin mangr 1985–86); dir of fin and resources Cancer Research Campaign 1987–94, dir Charities Group Moores Rowland 1994–; pres Essex Soc of CAs 1988–89, co-fndr and past chm The Charity Fin Dirs Gp 1988–92, chm The Charities Tax Reform Gp 1992–94, visiting prof to the Chair of Charity Fin S Bank Univ 1992–; memb: Bd Chartered Accountants in Business 1988–92, Charity Cmmn Ctee to review Charities SORP; ICAEW: chm Career Devpt Gp 1988–92, memb Charity Accounts Working Pty; ACA 1968; *Recreations* camping, swimming, watching cricket, reading, theatre, music, charity activities; *Clubs* Essex CCC; *Style*— Adrian Randall, Esq; ✉ 23 Plumberow Mount Ave, Hockley, Essex SS5 5AU; Moores Rowland, Clifford's Inn, Fetter Lane, London EC4A 1AS (☎ 0171 831 2345, fax 0171 831 6123, telex 283 LONDON WC2, mobile 0589 749755)

RANDALL, Alan William; s of William Edward Randall, of Portugal, and Joan Dorethia, *née* Way; *b* 1 Nov 1944; *Educ* Hornsey Coll of Art (BA); *Career* photographer and director; directed numerous films and TV commercials for major advtg agencies UK and Europe incl: Saatchi & Saatchi, J Walter Thompson, Ogilvy & Mather, McCann-Erickson, Young & Rubicam, Dorlands, Leo Burnett; still and commercial work for clients incl: Ford, Heinz, Dubonnet, Schweppes, Burberry's, Saab, Barclays Bank, British Telecom; major shoots directed incl: General Motors in NZ, American Express in NY; dir: 30 minute drama for Hitachi, Royal Tournament commercial (nomination Cannes Film Festival Awards); *Recreations* martial arts, horse riding, drawing, reading; *Clubs* Chelsea Arts, Groucho; *Style*— Alan Randall, Esq; ✉ Canonbury Studio, 36a Canonbury Square, London N1 2AN (☎ 0171 226 1642)

RANDALL, Gwendolen Mary; da of Albert Joseph Benjamin and Emily Amelia Triggs; *b* 30 Dec 1950; *Educ* Mary Datchelor Girls' Sch Camberwell, Univ of Bristol (open scholar, Clothworkers' Co exhbn, BA); *m* 7 July 1973, David John Randall, s of Eric Frank Randall, MBE; 1 da (Katherine b 3 Nov 1979); *Career* teacher of French Ridgeway Sch Wroughton 1973–74, head of Modern Languages St Mary's Sch Calne Wilts 1974–76, teacher of French and English Gymnasium Andreanum Hildesheim Germany 1977–79, teacher of French and head of Drama St Mary's Sch Calne 1980–85, dep head Dauntsey's Sch W Lavington Devizes Wilts 1985–94, head Framlingham Coll and jr section Brandeston Hall 1994–; *Recreations* drama, tennis, piano, debating, keen interest in equestrian pursuits; *Style*— Mrs Gwendolen Randall; ✉ Framlingham College, Framlingham, Suffolk IP13 9EY (☎ 01728 723789, fax 01728 724546)

RANDALL, Jeff William; s of Jeffrey Charles Randall, and Grace Annie Randall; *b* 3 Oct 1954; *Educ* Royal Liberty GS Romford, Univ of Nottingham (BA), Univ of Florida; *m* 8 Feb 1986, Susan Diane, da of H W Fidler; 1 da (Lucy Susan b 10 Jan 1989); *Career* research economist Wolverhampton Poly 1980–82, Hawkins Publishers 1982–85, asst ed Financial Weekly 1985–86, city corr The Sunday Telegraph 1986–88, city ed The Sunday Times 1989–95 (joined 1988), dir Times Newspapers 1994–95, jt dep chm Financial Dynamics 1995–96, asst ed Sunday Times April 1996 - Sept 1996, sports ed Sunday Times Sept 1996–; winner FT Analysis Financial Journalist of the Year 1991; *Recreations* golf, horseracing; *Clubs* Wentworth, Stock Brook Manor Golf; *Style*— Jeff Randall, Esq; ✉ The Sunday Times, 1 Pennington Street, London E1 9XW (☎ 0171 782 5000, fax 0171 782 5658)

RANDALL, John Yeoman; QC (1995); s of Dr Richard Francis Yeoman Randall, of Royal Leamington Spa, and Jean Evelyn, *née* Child; *b* 26 April 1956; *Educ* Rugby, Loomis Inst Connecticut, Jesus Coll Cambridge (MA); *m* 1982, Christine, da of late (Gordon) Keith Robinson and Shirley Grace, *née* Temple, of Sydney; 1 s (Oliver Yeoman b 1985), 1 da (Sally Jenine b 1988); *Career* called to the Bar Lincoln's Inn 1978, called to the Bar NSW 1979, asst recorder of the Crown Court 1995–; *Recreations* travel, sports, music; *Style*— John Randall, Esq, QC; ✉ 7 Fountain Court, Steelhouse Lane, Birmingham B4 6DR (☎ 0121 236 8531, fax 0121 236 4408)

RANDALL, Paul Nicholas; s of Jack Sidney Randall, of Sunbury-on-Thames, and Grace Ruth, *née* Fletcher; *b* 26 Jan 1960; *Educ* City of London Sch, KCL (LLB, AKC), Coll of Law; *m* 27 April 1985, Anamaria Dans Randall, da of William Enrique Dans Coath; 2 s (James William Alexander b 6 Oct 1987, William Henry Charles b 7 Nov 1990); *Career* asst slr Wedlake Bell 1984–87 (articled to Sir John Welch Bt 1982–84); Ashurst Morris Crisp: asst slr 1987–90, sr assoc 1990–95, ptnr and head Employment Dept 1995–; *Style*— Paul Randall, Esq; ✉ Ashurst Morris Crisp, Broadwalk House, 5 Appold Street, London EC2A 2HA (☎ 0171 638 1111)

RANDALL, Stuart Jeffrey; MP (Lab) Hull West (majority 10,585); *b* 22 June 1938; *Educ* Univ of Wales (BSc); *m* 1963, Gillian Michael; 3 da (Jennifer, Joanna, Emma); *Career* MP (Lab) Hull West 1983–, PPS to Rt Hon Roy Hattersley as dep ldr of the Lab Pty and shadow Chllr of the Exchequer 1984–85; front bench spokesman: on agric, fisheries and food 1985–87, on home affairs 1987–92; *Style*— Stuart Randall, Esq, MP; ✉ House of Commons, London SW1A 0AA (☎ 0171 219 3583 and 01276 471686)

RANDALL-PAGE, Peter; s of Charles Randall-Page, of Crowborough, Sussex, and Joan Mary, *née* Teale; *b* 2 July 1954; *Educ* Eastbourne Coll, Bath Acad of Art (BA); *m* 10 March 1984, Charlotte Eve, da of Philip Harry Hartley; 1 s (Thomas Charles b 16 Sept 1984), 1 da (Florence Ruth b 7 Aug 1987); *Career* sculptor; recent solo exhibitions incl Sculpture & Drawings 1980–1992 (Leeds City Art Galleries, Yorkshire Sculpture Park, Royal Botanic Garden Edinburgh and Arnolfini Gallery Bristol, organised by Henry Moore Centre Leeds), Boulders and Banners (Wenlock Priory, Shropshire and Reed's Wharf Gallery London) 1994, In Mind of Botany (Royal Botanic Gardens Kew) 1996; recent commissions incl: National Trust Derwentwater 1995, LDDC Butlers Wharf London 1996, Manchester City Cncl St Ann's Square 1996, Lothian Regional Cncl and others Hunters Square Edinburgh 1996, BUPA House London 1996; work in collections incl Tate Gallery (acquired sculpture Where the Bee Sucks 1993); FRSA; *Style*— Peter Randall-Page, Esq; ✉ c/o Clive Adams, The Two Brewers, 60 High Street, Ashwell, Herts SG7 5NR (☎ 01462 743251, fax 01462 743085)

RANDLE, Guy Hawksworth; s of James Randle (d 1965), and Emma, *née* Hawksworth (d 1978); *b* 10 July 1937; *Educ* Hitchin GS, St Bartholomew's Hosp Med Coll London (MB BS), Liverpool Med Sch; *m* 26 June 1965, Diana Suzanne, da of Brian Wright (d 1971); 1 s (Marcus b 1970), 2 da (Katherine b 1966, Louisa b 1975); *Career* med dir E Yorkshire Hosps Tst, consIt obstetrician and gynaecologist Beverley E Yorks; memb Worshipful Soc of Apothecaries; memb: Hull Med Soc, NINES O & G Soc; MRCS, LRCP, LMSSA, DObstRCOG, MRCOG, FRCOG; *Recreations* squash, golf, mountaineering; *Clubs* Beverley Squash, Beverley and Ganton Golf, Alpine, Wayfarers; *Style*— Guy Randle, Esq; ✉ Walkington Grange, Walkington, E Yorkshire HU17 8SZ (☎ 01430 827210)

RANDLE, Prof James Neville; s of James Randle (d 1989), and Florence, *née* Wilkins (d 1980); *b* 24 April 1938; *Educ* Waverley GS Birmingham, Aston Tech Coll Birmingham; *m* 1963, Jean Violet, da of Alfred Robert Allen; 1 s (Steven James b 1966), 1 da (Sally Joanne b 1968); *Career* Rover Co Ltd: apprentice 1954–61, tech asst 1961–63, project engr 1963–65; Jaguar Cars Ltd: project engr 1965–72, chief vehicle research engr 1972–78, dir of vehicle engrg 1978–80, dir of product engrg 1980–90, dir of vehicle and concept engrg 1990–91, leader of team that produced Jaguar XJ40 (winner Top Car award 1986) and Jaguar XJ220 (winner Turin and Horner prize 1988); independent engrg consIt 1991–; chm and chief exec Randle Engineering and Design 1994–; dir Automotive Engineering Centre Univ of Birmingham 1993–; hon prof of automobile engrg Univ of Birmingham 1992–, visiting prof of engrg design Royal Acad of Engrg, visiting prof of mfrg engrg De Montford Univ; non-exec dir United Turbine UK Ltd; former memb Cncl IMechE (chm Automobile Div 1987–88), fndr memb Autotech, memb Prince Philip Design Award Ctee 1992–; *Awards* Crompton Lanchester Medal 1986, James Clayton Prize 1986, Sir William Lyons International Award 1987; FEng 1988, FIMechE, FInstD, FRSA, RDI 1994; *Recreations* flying, sailing, skiing, hill walking; *Style*— Prof James Randle, FEng; ✉ Downwind House, Ryton Road, Bubbenhall, Coventry CV8 3BH (home ☎ and fax 01203 306730, Univ ☎ 0121 414 4162, fax 0121 414 2688, Co ☎ 01203 690446, fax 01203 690448)

RANDLE, Prof Sir Philip John; kt (1985); s of Alfred John Randle (d 1952), of Nuneaton, and Nora Annie, *née* Smith (d 1968); *b* 16 July 1926; *Educ* King Edward VI GS Nuneaton, Univ of Cambridge (MA, PhD, MD), UC Hosp Med Sch; *m* 1952, Elizabeth Ann, da of Dennis Arthur Harrison (d 1974); 1 s (Peter d 1971), 3 da (Rosalind, Sally, Susan); *Career* res fell Sidney Sussex Coll Cambridge 1954–57, fell Trinity Hall Cambridge 1957–64, lectr in biochemistry Univ of Cambridge 1955–64, prof of biochemistry Univ of Bristol 1964–75, prof of clinical biochemistry Univ of Oxford 1975–93 (emeritus prof 1993–); fell: Hertford Coll Oxford 1975–93 (emeritus 1993), UCL 1991–; hon fell Trinity Hall Cambridge 1988–; FRCP, FRS; *Style*— Prof Sir Philip Randle, FRS; ✉ 11 Fitzherbert Close, Iffley, Oxford (☎ 01865 773115); Dept of Clinical Biochemistry, Radcliffe Infirmary, Oxford (☎ 01865 224001)

RANDLE, Thomas John; s of Norvell Lee Randle (d 1989), and Mary Sylvia O'Connell; *b* 21 Dec 1958; *Educ* Orange Coast Coll, Chapman Coll, Univ of Southern Calif; *partner* Toni Racklin; 1 da (Bella Sidney Randle Racklin b 14 July 1992); *Career* tenor; solo concert debut Bach Weinachtsoratorium (Leipzig Rundfunksinfonie) 1987, operatic debut as Tamino in The Magic Flute (ENO) 1988; *Performances* incl: Tippett Songs for Dov (LA Philharmonic) 1985, Rossini Stabat Mater (London Philharmonic) 1988, Tamino in the Magic Flute (ENO 1988, 1989 and 1990, Glyndebourne Opera 1991), Handel Messiah (Royal Philharmonic) 1989, 1990 and 1991, Borodin La Mer (LSO) 1989, Haydn Die Jahreszeiten (Boston Symphony Orch) 1989, Beethoven Ninth Symphony (Scottish Chamber Orch 1989, Bergen Philharmonic Orch 1991, Prague Spring Festival 1996), Pelleas in Pelleas et Melisande (ENO) 1989, title role in Oedipus Rex (Madrid Opera) 1989, title role in L'Orfeo (Valencia 1989, Oviedo Opera Festival 1990), Haydn Die Schöpfung (Tivoli Festival Copenhagen 1990), Liszt Faust Symphony (BBC Scottish Symphony Orch (1990), Tippett The Ice Break (London Sinfonietta) Proms 1990, Ferrando in Cosi fan Tutte (Scottish Opera and Brussels Opera 1990, Geneva Opera 1992), Purcell Fairy Queen (Aix-en-Provence) 1989, Mozart Requiem (Acad of London) 1991, Paul McCartney Liverpool Oratorio 1992 (Ravinia Festival Chicago Aug, Helsinki Festival Finland Sept, Munich Symphony Orch Oct), Ferrando in Cosi fan Tutte (Geneva Opera) 1992, Pelleas in Pelleas et Melisande (with Peter Brook) Theatre Les Bouffes du Nord Paris (and Euro tour) 1992/93, Mozart Die Zauberflöte (Schleswig-Holstein Festival Hamburg 1993/94, Deutsche Oper Berlin 1996), Magic Flute (Auckland Opera NZ) 1993/94, Britten Gloriana, Earl of Essex (Opera North and Royal Opera House Covent Garden) 1993/94, Peter Schat World Premiere Opera Symposion (Netherlands Opera) 1993/94, Haydn L'Incontro Improviso (Garsington Opera Festival) 1993/94, Taverners' Apocalypse (world premiere, London Proms) 1993/94, Mozart Don Giovanni (Los Angeles Music Center Opera 1993/94, Munich Staatsoper 1995), Achilles in King Priam (ENO) 1995, Tippett The Mask of Time (LSO under Sir Colin Davis) 1995, Mendelssohn Elijah (Radio Orch France under Richard Hickox) 1995, Don Ramiro in La Cenerentola (Garsington Opera) 1995, Britten War Requiem (with BBC Scottish Symphony under Martyn Brabbins) 1995, title role in Handel Samson (with The Sixteen under Harry Christophers, Spanish tour) 1995, Mozart Requiem and Nono Canti di Vita e d'amore (concert tour with Bundesjugendorchester for Int Physicians for the Prevention of Nuclear War on 50th anniversary of Hiroshima bombing) 1995, Requiem der Versöhnung/Requiem of Reconciliation (world premiere with Israel Philharmonic under Helmuth Rilling) 1995, Mahler Das Klagende Lied (BBC Symphony under Alexander Lazarev, BBC Proms) 1995, Oberon in The Fairy Queen (ENO new prodn) 1995/96, Paris in La Belle Hélène (ENO new prodn) 1995/96, Gerald in Lakmé (Victoria State Opera Australia) 1996, title role in Idomeneo (Scottish Opera) 1996; *Recordings* incl: set of a cappella choral settings of sacred texts (Pater Noster, Stabat Mater, Vinea Mea, Electa, Benediction Amen, Ave Maria, Ave Verum Corpus) 1981–83, Purcell Fairy Queen (with Les Arts Florrisants under William Christie, from the Aix-en-Provence Festival) 1989, Tippett The Ice Break (with London Sinfonietta under David Atherton) 1990, complete Handel Messiah (with RPO under Owain Arwel Hughes), Handel Esther (with The Sixteen under Harry Christophers, Collins Classics) 1995, Britten War Requiem (with BBC Scottish Symphony under Martyn Brabbins, Naxos) 1995, Non Canti di Vita e d'amore (with Bamberg Symphony under Ingo Metzmacher, EMI) 1995, Handel Samson (with Harry Christopher and The Sixteen); *Recreations* motorsports (especially Formula One); *Style—* Thomas Randle, Esq; ✉ c/o IMG Artists Europe, Media House, 3 Burlington Lane, London W4 2TH (☎ 0181 747 9977, fax 0181 747 9131)

RANDOLPH, David John; JP (Wilts 1991); s of Thomas Berkeley Randolph (d 1987), of Midhurst, Sussex, and Margaret, *née* Jenner; *b* 25 April 1939; *Educ* Marlborough, Univ of Reading (BSc); *m* 4 April 1964, Elizabeth Mary, da of Thomas John Williams; 2 s (Gwyn John b 4 Aug 1965, Hugh Charles b 21 Feb 1969); *Career* farmer: Wenvoe Glamorgan 1960–74, Wiltshire 1974–; pt/t lectr/instr Lackham Coll 1976–90, assessor City and Guilds London 1984–85, instr Agric Trg Bd 1972–92; memb Wilts CC 1977–81, memb Managing/Advsy Body Cotswold Community at Ashton Keynes 1977–, tstee Cotswold Community Tst; govr: Burton and Nettleton Primary Sch 1977–81, Hardenhuish Sch Chippenham 1977–85 (chm of Govrs 1979–85); former church warden Leigh Delamere Church, lay vice-chm Grittleton PCC, memb Grittleton Village Hall Ctee 1987–91, chm Grittleton Cricket Club 1991–; memb Wilts Ctee Game Conservancy 1990–; pres Wilts Branch CLA 1995 (chm 1985–87), High Sheriff of Wilts 1995–96; *Recreations* shooting, environmental issues, theatre, gardening, reading, travel, antiques; *Clubs* Farmers; *Style—* David Randolph, Esq; ✉ West Foscote Farm, Grittleton, Chippenham, Wiltshire SN14 6AH (☎ 01249 782413)

RANFURLY, 7 Earl of (I 1831); Gerald François Needham Knox; also Baron Welles (I 1781), Viscount Northland (I 1791), and Baron Ranfurly (UK 1826, which he sits as in House of Lords); er s of Capt John Needham Knox, RN (d 1967, ggs of Hon John Knox, 3 s of 1 Earl of Ranfurly), and Monica, *née* Kitson (d 1975); suc kinsman, 6 Earl of Ranfurly, KCMG 1988; *b* 4 Jan 1929; *Educ* Wellington; *m* 22 Jan 1955, Rosemary Beatrice Vesey, o da of Air Vice-Marshal Felton Vesey Holt, CMG, DSO (d 1931); 2 s (Viscount Northland, *qv*, Hon Rupert Stephen b 5 Nov 1963), 2 da (Lady Elizabeth Marianne (Mrs Empson) b 24 Feb 1959, Lady Frances Christina (Mrs Gordon-Jones) b 13 Feb 1961); *Heir* s, Viscount Northland; *Career* former Lt Cdr RN; memb London Stock Exchange 1963–94; *Style—* The Rt Hon the Earl of Ranfurly; ✉ Maltings Chase, Nayland, Colchester, Essex (☎ 01206 262224)

RANFURLY, Hermione, Countess of; Hermione; *née* Llewellyn; OBE (1970); eldest da of Griffith Robert Poyntz Llewellyn, of Baglan Hall, Abergavenny; *m* 17 Jan 1939, 6 Earl of Ranfurly, KCMG (d 1988); 1 da (Lady Caroline Simmonds); *Career* WWII PA to Supreme Allied Cdr Med; fndr pres The Ranfurly Library Serv, which sends donated English books to developing countries; received Rotary Award for World Understanding 1987; CStJ; *Style—* The Rt Hon Hermione, Countess of Ranfurly, OBE; ✉ Great Pednor, Chesham, Bucks HP5 2SU (☎ 01494 862155)

RANG, Dr Humphrey Peter; *b* 13 June 1936; *Educ* Univ Coll Sch Hampstead, UCL (BSc, MSc), UCH Med Sch (MB BS), Balliol Coll Oxford (DPhil, MA); *Career* Univ of Oxford: J H Burn research fell Dept of Pharmacology 1961–64, research asst Dept of Pharmacology 1964–65, lectr 1965–72, fell and tutor in physiology Lincoln Coll 1967–72; prof of Pharmacology Univ of Southampton 1972–74; prof and head Dept of Pharmacology: St George's Hosp Med Sch London 1974–79, UCL 1979–83; dir Sandoz Inst for Med Research 1983–; visiting research assoc Dept of Pharmacology Albert Einstein Coll of Med NY USA 1966–67; organizing sec Symposia on Drug Action Biological Cncl 1979–; conslt Sandoz Ltd Basle 1981–83; memb Editorial Bd Br Jl of Pharmacology 1968–74; memb Editorial Advsy Bd: Molecular Pharmacology 1975–, Archives of Pharmacology 1977–; memb: Neurosciences Bd MRC 1974–77, Govt Grant Bd Royal Soc 1980–, Exec Ctee Int Congress of Pharmacology 1981–84, Senate Univ of London 1981–, Wellcome Tst Neurosciences Panel 1988–90; Poulsson Medal Norwegian Pharmacological Soc 1994; Br Pharmacological Soc: Gaddum Medal 1972, memb Ctee 1977–80; memb Academia Europaea 1991; FRS 1980; *Style—* Dr Humphrey Rang, FRS; ✉ Sandoz Institute for Medical Research, 5 Gower Place, London WC1E 6BN (☎ 0171 387 4445, fax 0171 387 4116)

RANGER, Sir Douglas; kt (1978); s of William Ranger, and Hatton Thomasina Ranger; *b* 5 Oct 1916; *Educ* Brisbane CE GS, Middx Hosp Med Sch (MB BS); *m* 1943, Betty, da of Capt Sydney Harold Draper, and Elsie Draper; 2 s; *Career* temp Maj and surgical specialist RAMC 1945–48; surgical registrar Middx Hosp 1942–44; otolaryngologist: Middx Hosp 1950–82, Mt Vernon Hosp 1958–74, London Chest Hosp 1952–75, King Edward VII's Hosp for Officers 1966–86; dean Middx Hosp Med Sch 1974–83; memb: Cncl RCS 1967–72, Ct of Examiners 1966–72; civil conslt in otolaryngology RAF 1965–83, advsr in otolaryngology to DHSS 1971–83, hon civil conslt RAF 1983–; hon sec Br Assoc of Otolaryngologists 1965–71, dir Ferens Inst of Otolaryngology 1965–83; pres: Br Assoc of Head and Neck Oncologists 1974–77, Section of Laryngology Royal Soc of Med 1976–77, United Servs Section Royal Soc of Med 1991–93; Liveryman Worshipful Soc of Apothecaries; FRCS 1943; *Books* The Middlesex Hospital Medical School, Centenary to Sesquicentary; *Style—* Sir Douglas Ranger; ✉ Wisteria House, Bayshill Lane, Cheltenham, Gloucestershire GL50 3AX

RANK, John Rowland; s of Capt Rowland Rank, RFA (d 1939), of Aldwick Place, W Sussex, and Margaret, *née* McArthur (d 1988); n of late J Arthur Rank (Baron Rank, d 1972), fndr of Rank Orgn, and gs of late Joseph Rank, fndr of Rank Flour Milling; *b* 13 Jan 1930; *Educ* Stowe; *Career* property owner; Lord of Manor of Saham Toney Norfolk; Rank Ltd 1948–50; patron: Pallant House Gallery Tst, Wessex Cancer Help Centre; tstee: Stansted Park Fndn (ret), Chichester Festival Theatre, Chichester Centre of Arts (former chm), Ian Askew Charitable Tst; former memb Cncl: Sussex Diocese, Friends of Chichester Cathedral, Funtington Parish; sometime on Ct of Corp of Sons of Clergy; memb and hon sec Sennicotts Church Advsy Cncl; hon pres Bognor Regis Drama Club, vice pres Chichester Fencing Club; Freeman City of London 1989; *Recreations* theatre, architectural, gardening, travelling, art exhibitions; *Clubs* Georgian Gp, Regency Soc of Brighton and Hove; *Style—* John Rank, Esq; ✉ Sennicotts, Chichester, W Sussex PO18 9AJ; 16 King's Quay, Chelsea Harbour, London SW10 0XF

RANK, Nicholas John; s of late John Stephen Rank, OBE, of Cheshire, and Hilda, *née* Hammerton; *b* 5 Nov 1950; *Educ* Stockport Sch, Univ of Manchester (BA, BArch); *m* 28 July 1973, Janet Elizabeth, da of Sidney Silcock, of Cheshire; 3 da (Naomi b 1976, Anna b 1978, Sarah b 1981); *Career* architect: ptnr Nicholas Rank Assocs 1983–93, ptnr Buttress Fuller Alsop Williams practice (architects, historic bldgs conslts) 1993, conslt architect Manchester Dio and Salford RC Dio, sr lectr in architecture Manchester Poly 1978–88; chm Assoc of Christians in Planning and Architecture; memb: Ecclesiastical Architects and Surveyors' Assoc, Cncl Care of Churches, Cathedral Architects Assoc; RIBA, FRSA; *Recreations* music, reading; *Style—* Nicholas Rank, Esq; ✉ 68 Parsonage Rd, Heaton Moor, Stockport, Cheshire SK4 4JR (☎ 0161 442 7086, 0161 236 3303)

RANKEILLOUR, 4 Baron (UK 1932); Peter St Thomas More Henry Hope; s of 3 Baron Rankeillour (d 1967; descended from Gen The Hon Sir Alexander Hope, of Craighall, in the Kingdom of Fife, GCB, 4 s of 2 Earl of Hopetoun, also the ancestor of the Marquesses of Linlithgow), and Mary Sybil, da of late Col Wilfred Ricardo, DSO; *b* 29 May 1935; *Educ* Ampleforth; *Heir* kinsman, Michael Hope; *Career* farmer and landowner; grand-scale landscaping; agricultural and horticultural equipment inventor and designer, freelance; former dep chm Br Sailors' Soc (North of Scotland); currently Rear Cdre House of Lords Yacht Club; *Style—* The Rt Hon the Lord Rankeillour; ✉ Achaderry House, Roy Bridge, W Inverness-shire (☎ 0139 781 206); House of Lords, London SW1A 0PW

RÁNKI, Dezsö; *b* 1951; *Educ* Franz Liszt Acad; *Career* pianist; appeared with numerous major orchs incl: Berlin Philharmonic, London Philharmonic, Concertgebouw Amsterdam, Eng Chamber Orch, Orchestre National de France, NHK Tokyo; worked with numerous leading conductors incl: Zubin Mehta, Kurt Sanderling, Sir Georg Solti, Vaclav Neumann, Kyrill Kondrashin, Jeffrey Tate; appeared at venues incl: London, Paris, Amsterdam, Berlin, Vienna and Milan; festivals: Lucerne, Vienna, Prague Spring, Berlin, Helsinki, Bath, BBC Proms; various recordings on Hungaraton, Teldec and Quint Records; first prize Robert Schumann Competition Zwickau 1969, first prizec Int Liszt Competition Budapest 1973, Kossuth Prize Hungary 1978, Grand Prix de l'Academie Charles-Cros; *Style—* Dezsö Ránki, Esq; ✉ c/o Sue Lubbock Concert Management, 25 Courthope Road, London NW3 2LE (☎ 0171 485 5932, fax 0171 267 0179)

RANKIN, Sir Alick Michael; kt (1992), CBE (1987), DL (City of Edinburgh 1996); s of Col Niall Rankin (d 1965), and Lady Jean Margaret Rankin, DCVO (woman of the bechamber to HM Queen Elizabeth The Queen Mother), da of 12 Earl of Stair; *b* 23 Jan 1935; *Educ* Eton, Univ of Oxford; *m* 1, 1958 (m dis 1976), Susan, da of Hugh Dewhurst, of Dungarthill, Dunkeld; 1 s, 3 da; m 2, 1976, Suzetta, da of Patrick Nelson, of Seafield, IOM; *Career* served Scots Gds 1953–55; investmt banking Wood Gundy Toronto Canada 1956–59; Scottish & Newcastle plc (formerly Scottish & Newcastle Breweries): joined 1960, gp md 1983–85, chief exec 1985–91, dep chm 1987–89, chm 1989–; chm: Christian Salvesen plc 1992– (dir 1986–), Scottish Financial Enterprise 1992–95; dep chm General Accident plc 1995– (dir 1986–), Scottish Financial Enterprise ... dir: Bank of Scotland 1987–, Sears plc 1991–, Securities Trust of Scotland plc 1991–, BAT Industries plc 1993–95, James Finlay plc 1994–; chm The Brewers Soc 1990–91 (vice pres 1991–), chm Holyrood Brewery Fndn; memb Cncl Edinburgh Int Festival; memb Ct of Assts Worshipful Co of Brewers; FRSA; *Recreations* fishing, shooting, golf, tennis, ornithology; *Clubs* Royal and Ancient (St Andrews), Hon Co of Edinburgh Golfers (Muirfield), Boodle's, New (Edinburgh), Vanderbilt Tennis, I Zingari (cricket), Eton Ramblers, Butterflies; *Style—* Sir Alick Rankin, CBE, DL; ✉ 3 Saxe Coburg Place, Edinburgh EH3 5BR (☎ 0131 332 3684); Scottish & Newcastle plc, Abbey Brewery, Holyrood Rd, Edinburgh EH8 8YS (☎ 0131 556 2591)

RANKIN, Andrew; QC (1968); s of William Locke Rankin (d 1963), and Mary Ann, *née* McArdle; *b* 3 Aug 1924; *Educ* Royal HS Edinburgh, Univ of Edinburgh (BL), Downing Coll Cambridge (BA); *m* 1, 1944 (m dis 1963), Winifred, da of Frank McAdam, of Edinburgh; 5 children, 1 decd; m 2, 1964, Veronica (d 1990), da of George Aloysius Martin, of Liverpool (d 1965); m 3, 1991, Jenifer Margaret, da of Alfred George Hodges, of Bebington, Wirral; *Career* lectr Faculty of Law Univ of Liverpool 1948–52; called to the Bar Gray's Inn 1950, recorder of the Crown Ct 1970–; *Style—* Andrew Rankin, Esq, QC; ✉ Chelwood, Pine Walks, Prenton, Birkenhead, Merseyside L42 8LQ (☎ 0151 608 2987, fax 0151 608 0068); 69 Cliffords Inn, Fetter Lane, London EC4A 1BX (☎ 0171 405 2932); 4 Field Court, Gray's Inn, London WC1R 5EA (☎ 0171 440 6900, fax 0171 242 0197)

RANKIN, (Herbert) David; s of Walter Rankin (d 1980), of Newtownards, Co Down, and Anna, *née* Douglas; *b* 21 June 1931; *Educ* Belfast Royal Acad, Trinity Coll Dublin (BA); *m* 1 Nov 1957, Anne Margaret Isobel, da of Ebenezer Vannan (d 1964), of Ewell, Surrey; 1 s (Aidan b 1966); *Career* asst lectr in classics QMC 1955–58, asst lectr and lectr in classics Univ of Sheffield 1958–65, fndn prof of classical studies and chm of Dept Monash Univ Aust 1965–72; Univ of Southampton: prof of classics and head of Dept 1972–88, prof of ancient philosophy 1988, head Dept of Philosophy 1989–92; *Books* Plato and the Individual (1964), Petronius the Artist (1971), Archilochus of Paros (1978), Sophists Socratics and Cynics (1983), Antisthenes Sokratikos (1985), Celts and the Classical World (1987); *Recreations* Celtic studies, model railways, photography; *Style—* David Rankin, Esq; ✉ Department of Philosophy, Univ of Southampton, Southampton S09 5NH (☎ 01703 595000 ext 3400, fax 01703 593344, telex 47661)

RANKIN, Gavin Niall; s and h of Sir Ian Niall Rankin, 4 Bt; *b* 19 May 1962; *Educ* Eton, Buckingham Univ (LLB); *m* Alexandra, da of Dr Jürgen von Knieriem and Mrs Monica von Pott; 1 da (Xenia Sophia b 21 May 1996); *Career* 2 Lt Scots Gds 1981; Price Waterhouse 1984–88, CA Panfida Group 1989–90, md Lonpra AS Prague 1991–95; Troika Dialogue Moscow 1995–; Page of Honour to HM Queen Elizabeth The Queen Mother 1977–79; ACA, FRGS; *Clubs* Annabel's, Brooks's; *Style—* Gavin Rankin, Esq; ✉ 13 Addison Road, London W14 8DJ

RANKIN, Sir Ian Niall; 4 Bt (UK 1898), of Bryngwyn, Much Dewchurch, Co Hereford; s of late Lt-Col (Arthur) Niall Talbot Rankin, yr s of 2 Bt; s unc, Sir Hugh Rankin, 3 Bt 1988; *b* 19 Dec 1932; *Educ* Eton, ChCh Oxford (MA); *m* 1, 1959 (m dis 1967),

Alexandra, da of Adm Sir Laurence George Durlacher, KCB, OBE, DSC; 1 s (Gavin Niall), 1 da (Zara Sophia b 1960); m 2, 1980, June, er da of late Capt Thomas Marsham-Townshend, and former w of Bryan Montagu Norman; 1 s (Lachlan John b 1980), 1 step da; *Heir* s, Gavin Niall Rankin b 19 May 1962; *Career* Lt Scots Gds (Res); dir of indust cos: B S Group plc, New Arcadia Explorations Ltd, Slumberfleece Ltd, I N Rankin Oil Ltd; patron The Samaritans; FRGS; *Recreations* tennis, shooting, yachting; *Clubs* Royal Yacht Sqdn, Pratt's, Car Clamp Recovery, Beefsteak, White's; *Style*— Sir Ian Rankin, Bt; ✉ Rankin House, 97 Elgin Avenue, London W9 2DA

RANKIN, James Deans (Hamish); s of James Deans Rankin (d 1963), of Barnoldswick, Yorks, and Florence Elizabeth, *née* Wight; *b* 17 Feb 1943; *Educ* Merchiston Castle Sch, Gonville and Caius Coll Cambridge (MA); *m* 6 Oct 1973, Susan Margaret, da of Francis Eric Adams; 1 s (Andrew Deans b 15 May 1975), 1 da (Sally Margaret b 5 May 1977); *Career* Agric Div ICI: res 1965–68, projects and engineering 1968–71, plant commissioning and management Ammonia Works 1971–77, res management 1977–83; process technol gp mangr ICI New Science Gp 1983–88, res & devpt mangr ICI Films 1988–93, ICI Engineering 1993–94, ICI sr science and technol assoc 1994; FEng 1987, FIChE 1987; *Recreations* domestic engineering, motoring, church bell ringing, photography; *Style*— Hamish Rankin, Esq, FEng; ✉ ICI Engineering Technology, PO Box 8, The Heath, Runcorn, Cheshire WA7 4QF (☎ 01928 515679, fax 01928 515660)

RANKIN, (Christopher) Paul; s of Hugh Rankin, of Bangor, Co Down, and Iris, *née* Gracey; *b* 1 Oct 1959; *Educ* Royal Belfast Academical Instn, Hutcheson GS Glasgow, Queen's Univ Belfast; *m* 22 March 1984, Jeanne Marie, da of Prof Richard Allen Lebrun, of Winnipeg; 2 da (Claire Nasya b 19 Aug 1986, Emily Paige b 25 March 1989); *Career* worked as waiter while travelling world 1981–83; chef: Le Gavroche 1984–86, Club 19 Saskatchewen Aug-Dec 1986, (tournant) Four Seasons Hotel Vancouver 1987, Mount View Hotel Calistoga Napa Valley Calif 1988; chef/proprietor Roscoff Restaurant Belfast 1989–; Michelin star 1991, Caterer and Hotelkeeper Newcomer of the Yr 1991, included in Gault Milau 300 best restaurants in Europe, Britain's Best Restaurant Courvoisier's Book of the Best 1994, and Great British Chefs II 1995, 4/5 Good Food Guide 1996; TV appearances on Hot Chefs 1991 and Gourmet Ireland (BBC) 1993, Ready Steady Cook (BBC) 1994–95; memb Acadamie Culinaire de Grande Bretagne; *Books* Hot Chefs (1991), Gourmet Ireland (1993), Hot Food, Cool Jazz (1994), Goumet Ireland II (1995); *Recreations* yoga, cycling, playing with the kids; *Style*— Paul Rankin, Esq; ✉ Roscoff, 7 Lesley House, Shaftesbury Square, Belfast BT2 7DB (☎ 01232 331532)

RANKIN, Dr Robert Alexander; s of Prof Oliver Shaw Rankin (d 1954), of Edinburgh, and Olivia Theresa, *née* Shaw (d 1963); *b* 27 Oct 1915; *Educ* Fettes, Clare Coll Cambridge (BA, MA, PhD, ScD); *m* 25 July 1942, Mary Ferrier (d 1996), da of William Morgan Llewellyn (d 1959), of Cardiff; 1 s (Charles Richard Shaw b 1947), 3 da (Susan Mary Llewellyn b 1943, Fenella Kathleen Clare b 1950, Olivia Roberta Mary b 1954); *Career* WWII work on rockets MOS 1940–45; asst tutor and praelector Clare Coll Cambridge 1947–51 (res fell 1939–47), lectr Univ of Cambridge 1947–51 (former asst lectr), Mason prof of maths Univ of Birmingham 1951–54, dean of faculties Univ of Glasgow 1985–88 (prof of maths 1954–82, dean Faculty of Science 1967–68, clerk of senate 1971–78); chm: Scot Maths Cncl 1967–73, Clyde Estuary Amenity Cncl 1969–81; memb Glasgow Incorporation of Hammermen 1984; FRSE 1955, FRSAMD 1982; *Books* Introduction to Mathematical Analysis (1963), Lectures on The Modular Group (1969), Modular Forms and Functions (1977); *Recreations* hill walking, organ music, Gaelic studies; *Style*— Dr Robert Rankin, FRSE; ✉ 98 Kelvin Court, Glasgow G12 0AH (☎ 0141 339 2641); University of Glasgow, Department of Maths, Glasgow G12 8QW (☎ 0141 339 8855, e-mail rar@maths.gla.ac.uk)

RANKIN-HUNT, Maj David; MVO (1993), TD (1990); s of James Rankin-Hunt, of Wales, and Edwina Anne, *née* Blakeman; *b* 26 Aug 1956; *Educ* Christ Coll Brecon, St Martin's Sch; *Career* Lt Scots Gds, Maj The London Scottish Regt (51 Highland Vol) 1989– (a regimental tstee); Lord Chamberlain's Office 1981–: registrar 1987–89, employed in The Royal Collection 1989– (administrator 1993–); Norfolk Herald of Arms Extraordinary 1994–, dep inspr of Regtl Colours 1995–; county pres Berks St John Ambulance, dir of ceremonies Priory for Wales Order of St John; lay steward St George's Chapel Windsor Castle; curatorial advsr Berkshire Yeomanry Museum; received various foreign orders; OStJ; *Recreations* military history, conservation issues, dogs, music, books; *Clubs* Army and Navy; *Style*— Maj David Rankin-Hunt, MVO, TD; ✉ 7 Cumberland Lodge Mews, The Great Park, Windsor, Berks (☎ 01784 437269); The Royal Collection, Stable Yard House, St James's Palace, London SW1 (☎ 0171 930 4832)

RANKINE, Jean Morag; da of Alan Rankine (d 1988), of Whitley Bay, and Margaret Mary Sloan, *née* Reid; *b* 5 Sept 1941; *Educ* Central Newcastle HS, UCL (BA, MPhil), Copenhagen Univ; *m* 17 Nov 1992, Norman Anthony Hall; *Career* British Museum: res asst Dept of Printed Books 1967–73, asst keeper Dir's Office 1973–78, head of public servs 1978–83, dep dir 1983–; fell UCL 1990; *Recreations* rowing, skiing, walking, opera; *Clubs* Thames Rowing; *Style*— Miss Jean Rankine; ✉ British Museum, London WC1B 3DG (☎ 0171 323 8490, fax 0171 323 8480)

RANSLEY, Philip Goddard; *b* 17 Aug 1942; *Educ* Northgate GS Ipswich, Gonville and Caius Coll Cambridge (MA, annual prize), Guy's Hosp Med Sch London (MB BChir, Treas's medal and prize in clinical surgery); *Career* demonstrator Dept of Physiology Univ of Queensland Brisbane 1963, postgrad research surgn Univ of Calif San Francisco 1966, house surgn Guy's Hosp 1967, casualty offr Lewisham Hosp 1968–69 (house physician 1967), clinical asst St Mark's Hosp 1969–70, jr surgical registrar Guy's Hosp 1969–70, surgical registrar Harold Wood Hosp 1970–72, sr surgical registrar St Peter's Hosps 1972–73 and 1975–76, research fell in paediatric urology Dept of Paediatric Surgery Inst of Child Health 1973–75, sr surgical registrar Hosp for Sick Children Great Ormand St 1976–77, conslt urological surgn Hosp for Sick Children and St Peter's Hosps 1977–, sr lectr in paediatric urology Inst of Child Health and hon sr lectr in paediatric urology Inst of Urology London 1977–; *awards* Registrar's Prize NE Metropolitan Region Surgical Soc 1972, Simpla Prize for Research Br Assoc of Eurological Surgns 1975, John Latimer Lecture American Urological Assoc 1982, Inaugural Nils Ericsson Meml Lecture 1984, Dantec Prize Br Assoc of Urological Surgns 1985, distinguished overseas guest Section of Surgery and hon fell American Acad of Pediatrics 1989, Dantec Prize Br Assoc of Urological Surgns 1991; FRCS 1971; *Publications* author of numerous pubns in learned jls; *Style*— Philip Ransley, Esq; ✉ 29A Orde Hall Street, London WC1N 3JL (☎ 0171 405 9791, fax 0171 405 3707)

RANSOM, David; s of Wallace Charles Ransom, of Ilkeston, Derbyshire, and Betty Florence, *née* Goodson; *b* 2 Sept 1947; *Educ* Hallcroft Sch, City of Sheffield Coll, Univ of Nottingham, Sheffield Poly; *m* 5 Jan 1978, Susan; 1 s (Joseph b 11 Jan 1987), 1 da (Jessica b 1 Dec 1981); *Career* Nat Basketball League coach Doncaster Panthers, Leeds Athletic Inst, Calderdale and Nottingham clubs 1976–87, head coach English Basketball Team 1989–91 (asst coach 1987–89; 53 int caps, team qualified for semi-finals Euro Championships Turkey 1987 and Norway 1989), coach English Cwlth Championship winning team 1991; nat dir of coaching English Basketball Assoc 1990 (first chief exec 1991–95); college lectr 1970–79 and 1984–87; MSC: projects mangr 1980–82, local govt mangr 1982–84, dir of mktg 1987–88, asst princ with responsibility for mktg 1988–90; frelance conslt 1995–96, chief exec S Yorks People United Against Crime 1996–; *Recreations* management training and consultancy; *Style*— David Ransom, Esq; ✉ 41 Mylor Rd, Sheffield S11 7PF (☎ 0114 266 1895)

RANT, His Hon Judge James William; CB (1995), QC (1980); s of Harry George Rant (d 1989), of Gerrards Cross, Bucks, and Barbara, *née* Veale (d 1989); Grant of Arms to William Rant of Yelverton 1574 (Robert Cooke, Clarenceaux King of Arms); *b* 16 April 1936; *Educ* Stowe, Univ of Cambridge (MA, LLM); *m* 1963, Helen, da of Percival George Adnams (d 1964), of IOM; 1 s and 1 s decd, 2 da; *Career* called to the Bar Gray's Inn 1961 (bencher 1996), pupillage with the late J N Dunlop 1962–63, in Chambers of Dorothy Waddy QC until 1968, head of Chambers 1968–84, dep circuit judge 1975, recorder of the Crown Ct 1979, circuit judge (SE Circuit) 1984, judge of Central Criminal Ct 1986, Judge Advocate General of the Army and RAF 1991; Freeman: City of London, Worshipful Co of Clockmakers; FRSA 1996; *Recreations* cookery, music; *Style*— His Hon Judge James Rant, CB, QC; ✉ 3 Temple Gdns, Middle Temple Lane, Temple, London EC4

RANTZEN, Esther Louise (Mrs Desmond Wilcox); OBE (1991); da of Henry Barnato (Harry) Rantzen (d 1992), of London, and Katherine, *née* Leverson; *b* 22 June 1940; *Educ* N London Collegiate Sch, Somerville Coll Oxford (MA); *m* 22 Dec 1977, Desmond Wilcox, *qv*, s of John Wilcox; 1 s (Joshua b 1981), 2 da (Emily b 1978, Rebecca b 1980); *Career* television prodr and presenter; studio mangr BBC Radio 1963; BBC TV: researcher 1965, dir 1967, researcher and reporter Braden's Week 1968, presenter and prodr That's Life 1973–94, prodr documentary series The Big Time 1976; presenter: That's Family Life, Hearts of Gold 1988–94, Drugwatch, Childwatch, Esther 1994–; chm Childline, pres Meet-a-Mum Assoc; vice pres ASBAH; hon memb NSPCC 1989; memb: Consumer Cncl 1981–90, Health Educn Authy 1989–, Health Visitors Assoc, Spastics Soc (now Scope), Contact-a-Family (families of disabled children), DEMAND (furniture for the disabled), Downs Children Assoc; patron Addenbrookes Kidney Patients Assoc, tstee Ben Hardwick Meml Fund; Special Judges Award RTS 1974, BBC Personality of 1975 Variety Club of GB, Euro Soc for Organ Transplant Award 1985, Richard Dimbleby award BAFTA 1988; *Books* Kill the Chocolate Biscuit (with Desmond Wilcox, 1981), Baby Love (with Desmond Wilcox, 1985), Ben - the Story of Ben Hardwick (with Shaun Woodward, 1985); *Recreations* walking the dogs; *Style*— Miss Esther Rantzen, OBE; ✉ BBC TV, White City, 201 Wood Lane, London W12 7TS; Childline, London N1 0QW; c/o Noel Gay Artists, 76 Oxford St, London W1N 0AT (☎ 0171 836 3941)

RAPER, Dr Alan Humphrey; CBE (1989); s of Frederick George Raper (d 1977), and Beatrice May, *née* Humphrey; *b* 11 Aug 1927; *Educ* Acklam Hall Middlesbrough, Univ of Leeds (BSc, PhD, Akroyd scholar); *m* 1955, Audrey, *née* Baker; 1 s, 2 da; *Career* dir: Glaxo Holdings Ltd (ret 1987), Glaxo Group Ltd (ret 1987), Glaxochem (Pte) Ltd Singapore, Glaxo Nigeria Ltd, Glaxo Laboratories (India) Ltd, Glaxo Far East (Pte) Ltd, Glaxo Orient (Pte) Ltd, Glaxo Australia Pty Ltd, Glaxo Bangladesh Ltd, Glaxo Canada Ltd, Glaxo Laboratories (Pakistan) Ltd, Glaxo Philippines Inc, Glaxo NZ Ltd, Glaxo (1972) Charity Tst, Scholeds Ltd; chm Macfarlan Smith Ltd (ret 1987), pres Br & S Asian Trade Assoc 1986–88; memb: Cncl Chemical Industs Assoc 1974–87, Health and Safety Cmmn 1983–90; *Recreations* skiing, hill walking, history; *Clubs* The Oriental; *Style*— Dr Alan Raper, CBE; ✉ The White House, Husthwaite, York YO6 3TA (☎ 01347 868688)

RAPHAEL, Adam Eliot Geoffrey; s of Geoffrey George Raphael (d 1969), of London, and Nancy May, *née* Rose; *b* 22 April 1938; *Educ* Charterhouse, Oriel Coll Oxford (MA); *m* 16 May 1970, Caroline Rayner, da of George Ellis (d 1954), of Cape Town, SA; 1 s (Thomas Geoffrey b 1971), 1 da (Anna Nancy b 1974); *Career* 2 Lt RA 1956–58; political corr The Guardian 1974–76 (foreign corr Washington 1969–73 and S Africa 1973), exec ed The Observer 1988–93 (political corr 1976–81, political ed 1981–87), presenter Newsnight BBC TV 1987–88, writer on home affairs The Economist 1994–; Investigative Reporter of the Year Granada 1973, Journalist of the Year British Press Awards 1973; *Books* My Learned Friends (1990), Grotesque Libels (1993), Ultimate Risk (1994); *Recreations* tennis, skiing, reading; *Clubs* RAC, Hurlingham, SCGB; *Style*— Adam Raphael, Esq; ✉ 50 Addison Ave, London W11 4QP (☎ 0171 603 9133)

RAPHAEL, Frederic Michael; s of Cedric Michael Raphael, TD (d 1979), and Irene Rose, *née* Mauser; *b* 14 Aug 1931; *Educ* Charterhouse, St John's Coll Cambridge (MA); *m* 17 Jan 1955, Sylvia Betty, da of Hyman Glatt; 2 s (Paul b 1958, Stephen b 1967), 1 da (Sarah b 1960); *Career* author; FRSL 1964; *Books* Obbligato (1956), The Earlsdon Way (1958), The Limits of Love (1960), A Wild Surmise (1961), The Graduate Wife (1962), The Trouble with England (1962), Lindmann (1963), Orchestra and Beginners (1967), Like Men Betrayed (1970), Who Were You With Last Night? (1971), April, June and November (1972), Richard's Things (1973, screenplay 1981), California Time (1975), The Glittering Prizes (1976, TV plays 1976, Writer of the Year Award), Heaven and Earth (1985), After The War (1988), The Hidden I (1990), Of Gods and Men (1992), A Double Life (1993), Old Scores (1995); short stories: Sleeps Six (1979), Oxbridge Blues (1980, TV plays 1984), Think of England (1986), The Latin Lover (1994); screenplays: Nothing but the Best (1964), Darling (Acad Award, 1965), Two for the Road (1967), Far From the Madding Crowd (1967), A Severed Head (1972), Daisy Miller (1974), Rogue Male (1976), Something's Wrong (dir, 1978), School Play (1979), The Best of Friends (1979), Richard's Things (1980), Oxbridge Blues (1984), After the War (1989), The Man In The Brooks Brothers Shirt (dir 1990, ACE Award), Armed Response (1995), Coast to Coast (1997); biography: Somerset Maugham and his World (1977), Byron (1982); essays: Bookmarks (ed, 1975), Cracks in the Ice (1979), The Necessity of Anti-Semitism (1997); From the Greek (play, 1979); translations (with Kenneth McLeish): Poems of Catullus (1976), The Oresteia (1978, televised as The Serpent Son BBC 1979), Complete plays of Aeschylus (1991), Euripides' Medea (1994), Sophokles Aias (1996), Euripides Hoppolytos (1997); *Recreations* tennis, skiing; *Clubs* Savile, The Queen's; *Style*— Frederic Raphael, Esq, FRSL; ✉ Lagardelle, St Laurent-La-Vallée 24170 Belves, France; c/o Deborah Rogers, 20 Powis Mews, London W11 1JN

RAPHAEL, Ven Timothy John; s of Hector Carisbrook Raphael (d 1987), and Emily Alexandrina, *née* Kirk (d 1975); *b* 26 Sept 1929; *Educ* Christ's Coll Christchurch NZ, Univ of Leeds (BA), Coll of the Resurrection Mirfield; *m* 29 June 1957, Anne Elizabeth, da of John Lees Shepherd; 1 s (Julian Peter b 18 March 1958), 2 da (Caroline Mary b 8 Sept 1960, Bridget Clare b 18 April 1963); *Career* curate St Stephen with St John Westminster 1955–60; vicar: St Mary Welling (Dio of Southwark) 1960–63, St Michael Christchurch NZ 1963–65, dean of Dunedin NZ 1965–73, vicar St John's Wood London 1973–83, area dean of St Marylebone 1982–83, archdeacon of Middx 1983–96; *Recreations* contemporary poetry, beachcombing; *Style*— The Ven the Archdeacon of Middlesex; ✉ 121 Hales Road, Cheltenham, Gloucestershire GL52 6ST (☎ 01242 256075)

RAPLEY, Prof Christopher Graham (Chris); s of Ronald Rapley, of Bath, and Barbara Helen, *née* Stubbs; *b* 8 April 1947; *Educ* King Edward's Sch Bath, Jesus Coll Oxford (MA), Victoria Univ of Manchester Jodrell Bank (MSc), Univ of London (PhD); *m* 13 June 1970, Norma, da of Y Khan, of Georgetown, Guyana; 2 da (Emma Jane, Charlotte Anne (twins) b 1971); *Career* project scientist/princ investigator UCL Instrument NASA Solar Maximum Mission 1975–81; princ investigator: NASA Shuttle Imaging Radar-C 1988–94, ESA ERS-1 Radar Altimetry 1988–94; memb Science Team NASA Cassini Titan Radar 1990–; UCL Dept of Space and Climate Physics: lectr 1981–87, reader 1988–91, prof of remote sensing science 1991–; MSSL: head Remote Sensing Gp 1982–94, assoc dir 1990–94; exec dir Int Cncl of Scientific Unions Int Geosphere-Biosphere Prog Royal Swedish Acad of Sciences Stockholm Sept 1994–; author of over 90 research pubns on space astronomy and earth observation; memb: Remote Sensing Soc, American Geophysical Union; FRAS; *Recreations* jogging, windsurfing, photography; *Style—* Prof Chris Rapley; ✉ Executive Director, International Geosphere-Biosphere Programme, The Royal Swedish Academy of Sciences, Box 50005, Lilla Frescativägen 4, S-104 05 Stockholm, Sweden (☎ 00 46 8 16 64 48, fax 00 46 8 16 64 05, mobile 00 46 708 605777, e-mail cgr@igbp.kva.se)

RAPLEY, Jane Margaret; da of John Edward Robert Rapley, of Wisborough Green, W Sussex, and Ella Mary, *née* Jones (d 1970); *b* 10 July 1946; *Educ* Ickenham HS, Ealing Sch of Art, Nottingham Coll of Art (DipAD), RCA (MA); *partner* since 1977, Peter David Towse; 1 da ((Crystal) Bella Towse b 31 Oct 1984); *Career* design mangr (men's knitwear) Sabre International Textiles 1971–76, design and design mgmnt conslt Chateau Stores of Canada 1977–78, dir (men's casualwear) J R Associates 1977–81, retail dir South Molton Clothing Depot 1981–83, dir (men's retail and design collections) Burrows & Hare 1984–87, dir Peter Towse Design Servs 1983–; lectr on design history, design mgmnt, knitwear and menswear 1970–80: Middlesex, Brighton, Kingston, Trent and Lancashire Polys, Textile Inst, Costume Soc; lectr on: knitwear Central Sch of Art & Design 1977–81, menswear RCA 1981–84; head of Textile Dept Central Sch of Art & Design 1987–89, dean of fashion and textiles Central Saint Martin's Coll of Art & Design 1989–; ACSD 1977–; *Books* The Art of Knitting (Collins); *Recreations* reading the early works of Sergei Kaplovitch, collecting back copies of School Friend; *Clubs* Kit Kat (St Petersburg), The Union (London); *Style—* Ms Jane Rapley; ✉ School of Fashion & Textiles, Central Saint Martin's College of Art & Design, 109 Charing Cross Road, London WC2 (☎ 0171 514 7000, fax 0171 514 7152)

RAPLEY, Raymond Herbert; s of Richard Herbert Rapley (d 1928), and Olive Evelyn, *née* Riddiford (d 1979); *b* 13 Jan 1929; *Educ* Huntingdon GS, Open Univ (BA); *m* 6 May 1950, Betty, da of Harry Gregory, MM (d 1946), of Dronfield, Derbys; 2 s (Martin b 1957, David b 1965), 2 da (Elizabeth Frances, b 1955, Yvonne Linda b 1958); *Career* Rapleys Surveyors and Planning Conslts London 1951–89, md Yelcon Ltd Housebuilders Cambs 1961–; former memb Cncl Int Soc of Valuers and Auctioneers 1968–69, regnl pres Housebuilders Fedn (E Anglia Region) 1986–87, pres Bldg Employers' Confedn (Cambridge Branch) 1986–87; *Style—* Raymond Rapley, Esq; ✉ Misty Meadows, Gore Tree Rd, Hemingford Grey, Cambs

RAPPORT, Cecil Herbert; CBE (1994), JP, DL (South Glamorgan); s of Maurice Aaron Rapport (d 1953), and Phoebe Annie, *née* Jacobs (d 1960); *b* 12 Oct 1915; *Educ* Monkton House Coll Cardiff, City of Cardiff Tech Coll; *m* 25 Nov 1942, Audrey Rachel, da of Sidney Fligelstone; 1 s (Derek Ivor), 2 da (Valerie Avery Gee, Heather Hockley); *Career* Welch Regt 1939–45; pres: Cardiff Inst for the Blind, Royal Br Legion Cardiff, Friends of Cardiff Royal Infirmary, Cardiff Central Cons Assoc; chm Wales Festival of Rememberance; High Sheriff S Glamorgan 1984–85, former Dep Lord Mayor City of Cardiff, former Alderman City of Cardiff; Freeman City of London 1959; Jr Warden Welsh Livery Guild; memb: Worshipful Co of Horners 1958, Guild of Freemen of the City of London 1969; MInstD; KStJ; *Recreations* swimming, sailing, music; *Clubs* City Livery, RAC; *Style—* Cecil Rapport, Esq, CBE, JP, DL; ✉ Cefn Coed House, Cefn Coed Rd, Cyncoed, Cardiff, South Glam CF2 6AP (☎ 01222 757375); Ivor House, Bridge St, Cardiff, South Glam CF1 2TH (☎ 01222 373737 or 01222 231444, fax 01222 220121)

RASCH, Sir Simon Anthony Carne; 4 Bt (UK 1903), of Woodhill, Danbury, Essex; s of Sir Richard Guy Carne Rasch, 3 Bt (d 1996), and his 1 w, Anne Mary, *née* Dent-Brocklehurst (d 1989); *b* 26 Feb 1948; *Educ* Eton, RAC Cirencester; *m* 31 Oct 1987, Julia, er da of Maj Michael Godwin Plantagenet Stourton and Lady Joanna Stourton, *née* Lambart, da of Field Marshal 10 Earl of Cavan; 1 s (Toby Richard Carne b 28 Sept 1994), 1 da (Molly Clare Anne b 10 Sept 1990); *Heir* s, Toby Richard Carne Rasch b 28 Sept 1994; *Career* page of honour to HM 1962–64; chartered surveyor; Liveryman Worshipful Co of Grocers; *Clubs* Pratt's; *Style—* Sir Simon Rasch, Bt; ✉ The White House, Manningford Bruce, nr Pewsey, Wilts

RASH, Dr Ramakant Maganlal; s of Maganlal Bhanji Rash, of Heaton Moor, Stockport, and Kasturben Maganlal, *née* Mirani; *b* 30 Jan 1937; *Educ* Govt Secdy Sch Kampala Uganda, Plymouth and Davenport Coll, Univ of Manchester (BSc, MB ChB, MRCP); *m* 6 June 1964, Bena Aruna, da of Narshidas Liladhar Ghelani (d 1962); 1 s (Amar b 28 Jan 1971); *Career* Wythenshawe Hosp Manchester: house physician 1962–63, house surgn 1963, sr house offr 1963–66, med registrar 1966–70, sr registrar 1971–75, conslt physician in geriatric med 1975–93, hon assoc lectr in geriatric med 1985–93; conslt geriatrician Withington Hosp Manchester 1993–; fell Manchester Med Soc; memb: Br Geriatric Soc, BMA; FRCP 1984; *Recreations* gardening, reading, watching football (supporter of Manchester City FC); *Style—* Dr Ramakant Rash; ✉ 46 Leegate Rd, Heaton Moor, Stockport SK4 4AX (☎ 0161 432 1085); Department of Geriatric Medicine, Burton House, Withington Hospital, Manchester M20 8LR (☎ 0161 291 3299)

RASHBASS, Dr Barbara; da of Leonard Cramer (d 1972), and Sarina, *née* Klinger; *Educ* Godolphin Sch Salisbury, Univ Coll London (MB BS); *m* 9 Oct 1956, Cyril Rashbass (d 1982); 2 s (Jem b 1961, Andrew b 1965), 1 da (Pen b 1964); *Career* called to the Bar 1969, sec Wolfson Family Charitable Tst 1989–, dir Wolfson Fndn 1990– (dep dir 1987–90); PMO MRC 1983–87, dept chm Harrow Health Authy 1982–84; memb Med Legal Soc; DCH 1961, DPH 1968; FRSM 1989, FRCP 1995; *Recreations* walking; *Style—* Dr Barbara Rashbass; ✉ The Wolfson Foundation, 18 Haymarket, London SW1Y 4DQ (☎ 0171 930 1057, fax 0171 930 1036)

RASHID, Dr Abutaleb Muhammed Fazlur (Faz); s of Dr A M M A Rouf (d 1972), of Barisal, Bangladesh, and Shamse Ara, *née* Ahmed; *b* 29 Dec 1937; *Educ* Univ of Dhaka Bangladesh (MB BS, MSc); *m* 9 June 1968, Faozia Sultana, da of M Habibullah (d 1987), of Chandpur, Bangladesh; 2 da (Tina Farzana b 1971, Samantha Fahima b 1972); *Career* various trg posts in pathology Dhaka Med Coll and Hosp Bangladesh 1962–70, asst prof of pathology Inst of Post Grad Med and Res Dhaka Bangladesh 1970–74, asst in pathology Inst of Pathology Free Univ of Berlin W Germany 1974–75, registrar in pathology Royal Sussex Co Hosp 1975–78, sr registrar in pathology Southampton Gen Hosp and Poole Gen Hosp 1978–80, conslt pathologist Joyce Green Hosp 1980–, clinical dir pathology servs Dartford & Gravesham NHS Trust; coll tutor RCPath; past pres Dartford Bengali Assoc, past chm and treas London and SE Branch Bangladesh Med Assoc in UK; former memb Central Exec Ctee Bangladesh Med Assoc in UK; chm Regnl Exec Ctee BMA Dartford and Medway; memb: ACP, BSCC, ODA; FRCPath; *Recreations* swimming, jogging, snooker, gardening, DIY, computers; *Style—* Dr Faz Rashid; ✉ Joyce Green Hospital, Dartford, Kent DA1 5PL (☎ 01322 283531)

RASHID, Dr Aly; *b* 14 Oct 1958; *Educ* Burnage HS Manchester, Univ of Manchester (MB ChB, DRCOG, MD); *m* Claire; 1 da (Eleanor); *Career* house physician in gen med and rheumatology N Manchester Gen Hosp 1982–83, house surgn in gen surgery and urology Royal Preston Hosp 1983, vocational trg scheme in gen practice Hope Hosp Salford 1983; SHO: in obstetrics and gynaecology Hope Hosp 1984, in paediatrics Royal Manchester Children's and Hope Hosps 1984–85, in gen med Hope and Ladywell Hosps 1985; trainee GP Swinton 1985–86; princ in gen practice: St Matthews Med Centre Leicester 1986–92, Counteshorpe Health Centre Leicester 1992–; Univ of Leicester: RCGP research fell in gen practice Dept of Community Health 1987–90, clinical tutor in gen practice Med Sch 1987–, assoc advsr in gen practice 1996–; postgrad trainer in gen practice Leicester Vocational Trg Scheme 1988–; Royal Coll of Gen Practitioners: memb Faculty Bd 1987–, memb Nat Cncl 1991–, memb Exec Ctee Nat Cncl 1993–, nat chm of educn 1993–; RCGP observer Assoc of Univ Depts of Gen Practice 1993–; memb: Conf of Postgrad Advsrs in Gen Practice Univs of the UK 1993–, Jt Ctee on Postgrad Trg for Gen Practice (JCPTGP) 1996–, Advsy Gp on Med Educn and Trg in Gen Practice Dept of Health 1996–, Med Audit Advsy Gp (MAAG) 1996–; med writer Leicester Mercury 1989–92, also author of numerous pubns in academic jls; FRCGP 1991 (MRCGP 1986); *Recreations* tennis, cricket (former rep Manchester and Lancashire Colleges and capt Manchester Med Sch Cricket Team, currently player for village team Willoughby Waterleys); *Clubs* Carisbrooke Lawn Tennis (Leicester); *Style—* Dr Aly Rashid; ✉ The Health Centre, Central Street, Countesthorpe, Leicester LE8 5QJ (☎ 0116 277 6336)

RASHLEIGH, Jonathan Michael Vernon; s of Nicholas Vernon Rashleigh, of Rodmell, Lewes, Sussex, and Rosalie Mary, *née* Matthews; *b* 29 Sept 1950; *Educ* Bryanston; *m* 5 April 1975, Sarah, da of John Norwood, of Knowle, Solihull, W Midlands; 3 s (Charles b 1979, Hugh b 1986, Philip b 1988), 1 da (Julia b 1982); *Career* Ernst and Whinney 1968–76, 3i Group 1976–90 (dir 3i plc 1986–90); dir: Legal & General Investment Management Ltd 1991–93, National Australia Group 1993–95, Henderson Crosthwaite Ltd 1995–; Freeman City of London, Liveryman Worshipful Co of Tobacco Pipe Makers and Tobacco Blenders 1972; MSI 1993; FCA 1979 (ACA 1974), FRSA 1995; *Recreations* chess, theatre, cricket, music; *Style—* Jonathan Rashleigh, Esq; ✉ Longeaves, Norton Lindsey, Warwick CV35 8JL (☎ 01926 842523); Henderson Crosthwaite Ltd, 32 St Mary at Hill, London EC3P 3AJ (☎ 0171 772 7367)

RASHLEIGH, Sir Richard Harry; 6 Bt (UK 1831), of Prideaux, Cornwall; s of Sir Harry Evelyn Battie Rashleigh, 5 Bt (d 1984), and Honora Elizabeth, *née* Sneyd; *b* 8 July 1958; *Educ* All Hallows Sch Dorset; *m* 3 Feb 1996, Emma F C, eldest da of John McGougan, of London, and Lady Acland (*see* Sir Antony Acland); *Heir* none; *Career* mgmnt accountant; with Arthur Guinness Son & Co plc 1980–82, Dexion-Comino International Ltd 1982–84, United Biscuits plc 1985–88, Wessex Housing 1988–90, self-employed 1990–; *Recreations* sailing, tennis, shooting; *Clubs* Royal Fowey Yacht; *Style—* Sir Richard Rashleigh, Bt; ✉ Menabilly, Par, Cornwall PL24 2TN

RASKIN, Susan; da of John Cary Abbatt (d 1988), of Bath, and Sybil Eileen, *née* Lympaney; *b* 28 March 1942; *Educ* Plymouth HS, Tiffin Girls' Sch Kingston upon Thames; *m* 18 Aug 1966, James Leo Raskin, s of Meyer Raskin (d 1971); 1 da (Joanna b 1967), 2 s (Benjamin Leo 1969, Thomas John b 1972); *Career* admitted slr 1967; ptnr: Raskin & Raskin 1969–88, Russell Jones & Walker 1988–94, Ledbury Raskin 1994–; dep dist judge 1992–; sr law lectr Bristol Poly 1980–83 (lectr 1974–80); memb Bath Assoc of Graduate Women, govr Bath HS (GPDST) 1983–; FRSA 1993, AIL 1994; *Recreations* singing, foreign languages, reading, hill-walking, swimming; *Style—* Mrs Susan Raskin; ✉ Ledbury Raskin, 370 Two Mile Hill Road, Kingswood, Bristol BS15 1AQ (☎ 0117 967 9395, fax 0117 961 8202)

RATCLIFF, Christopher John Raven; s of John Henry Raven Ratcliff (d 1989), of Hertford, Herts, and Kathleen Mary, *née* Viall (d 1956); *b* 4 July 1931; *Educ* The Leys Sch Cambridge, Clare Coll Cambridge (MA), Architectural Assoc Sch of Architecture (AADipl); *m* 29 Oct 1955, Josephine Celia, da of Alexander Delap (d 1962), of Eastergate, Chichester; 2 s (Jeremy b 1959, Jonathan b 1961), 2 da (Diana b 1956, Melanie b 1963); *Career* Nat Serv 2 Lt RE 1957–59; architect; ptnr Building Design Ptnrship 1980–93 (architect 1959, assoc 1963, ret 1993); examiner: Sch of Architecture Univ of Liverpool 1986–91, North West Schs of Architecture 1992–; memb: Cncl ARCUK 1980–82, Cncl RIBA 1982–88; chm RIBA NW region 1988–90, chm of govrs Beaumont Coll of FE (Spastics Soc) Lancaster 1992–; design and mktg conslt 1993–; *Recreations* genealogy, calligraphy, music, fell walking; *Style—* Christopher Ratcliff, Esq; ✉ 4 Ribblesdale Place, Preston, Lancs PR1 3NA (☎ and fax 01772 258427)

RATCLIFFE, Anne Kirkpatrick; da of Dr John Kirkpatrick Ratcliffe, and Alice Margaret, *née* Vaughan-Jones; *b* 19 April 1956; *Educ* Cheltenham Ladies' Coll, Univ of Southampton (BSc), City Univ (Dip Law); *Career* called to the Bar Inner Temple 1981, in practice S Eastern Circuit 1981–; memb: Exec Ctee Family Law Bar Assoc, Soc of Cons Lawyers; *Recreations* collecting modern art, gardening; *Style—* Miss Anne Ratcliffe; ✉ 51 Waldemar Avenue, London SW6 5LN; 5 Pump Ct, Temple, London EC4 (☎ 071 353 2532, fax 071 353 5321)

RATCLIFFE, Dr Frederick William; CBE (1994), JP (Cambridge 1981); s of Sidney Ratcliffe (d 1964), of Leek, Staffs, and Dora, *née* Smith (d 1975); *b* 28 May 1927; *Educ* Leek HS, Univ of Manchester (BA, MA, PhD), Univ of Cambridge (MA); *m* 20 Aug 1952, Joyce, da of Thomas Edwin Brierley (d 1993), of Harrogate; 2 s (George, John), 1 da (Helen); *Career* WWII N Staffs Regt 1945–48; asst librarian Univ of Manchester Library 1954–62, sub librarian Univ of Glasgow Library 1962–63, dep univ librarian Univ of Newcastle upon Tyne 1963–65, librarian Univ of Manchester 1965–80 (dir John Rylands Univ Library of Manchester 1972–80), hon lectr in historical bibliography Univ of Manchester 1970–80, univ librarian Univ of Cambridge 1980–94 (emeritus 1994–); Corpus Christi Coll: fell 1980–94, life fell 1994–, Parker librarian 1995–; visiting prof Univ of Loughborough 1982–86, Sandars reader in bibliography Univ of Cambridge 1989; JP Stockport 1972–80; tstee: St Deiniol's Library Hawarden, George Fearn Tst Stockport, FC Pybus Tst Newcastle, Malaysian Cwlth Studies Centre, Cambridge Fndn 1987–92; fell Woodard Corp 1981–; chm: Advsy Ctee Nat Preservation Office 1984–94, Wellcome Inst for the History of Med Library Panel 1988–93; memb UK Delgn CSCE Cultural Forum Budapest 1985, patron Soc of Bookbinders and Restorers; memb: Library Assoc, Bibliographical Soc, Cambridge Bibliographical Soc; Hon FLA 1987; FRSA 1986; Encomienda de la Orden del Merito Civil (Spain) 1988; *Books* numerous articles in literary jls; *Recreations* book collecting, gardening, handprinting; *Clubs* Sette of Odd Volumes; *Style—* Dr Frederick Ratcliffe, CBE, JP; ✉ Ridge House, Rickinghall Superior, Diss, Norfolk IP22 1DY (☎ 01379 898232); 84 Church Lane, Girton, Cambridge CB3 0JP (☎ 01223 277512); Corpus Christi College, Cambridge

RATCLIFFE, Jason David; s of David Philip Ratcliffe, of Shirley, Solihull, and Sheila Mary, *née* O'Donnell; *b* 19 June 1969; *Educ* Sharmans Cross Secdy Sch, Solihull Sixth Form Coll; *Career* professional cricketer (opening bastman and off spin bowler); Warwickshire CCC: first class debut 1988, 50 first class appearances; joined Surrey CCC 1995; overseas teams: West End Kimberley SA 1987–88, Belmont NSW 1990–91, Penrith DCC Sydney 1992–93 and 1993–94; off-seasons incl memb mktg staff Birmingham City FC; NCA staff coach; memb Warwickshire Nat West Trophy winning side 1993; *Style—* Jason Ratcliffe, Esq; ✉ Surrey CCC, Fosters Oval, Kennington, London SE11 5SS (☎ 0171 582 6660)

RATCLIFFE, (John) Michael; s of Donald Ratcliffe (d 1988), and Joyce Lilian, *née* Dilks; *b* 15 June 1935; *Educ* Cheadle Hulme Sch, Christ's Coll Cambridge (BA); *Career* journalist; graduate trainee Sheffield Telegraph 1959–61, asst literary and arts ed Sunday Times 1962–67; The Times: literary ed 1967–72, chief book reviewer 1972–82; freelance writer 1982–83; The Observer: theatre critic 1984–89, literary ed 1990–95, contrib ed 1995–96; commended in critic of the year section Br Press Awards 1989; memb NUJ 1959–; *Books* The Novel Today (1967), The Bodley Head 1887–1987 (with J W Lambert, 1987); *Recreations* music, travel, walking, cycling, architecture, art, gardening; *Style—* Michael Ratcliffe, Esq; ✉ 4 Elia Street, London N1 8DE (☎ 0171 837 1687, fax 0171 713 6286)

RATCLIFFE, Col Peter Jocelyn Carne; OBE (1972); s of Jocelyn Vivian Ratcliffe (d 1973), of Penhellis, Helston, Cornwall, and Daphne Naylor, *née* Carne (d 1992); *b* 17 Nov 1926; *Educ* Harrow; *m* 7 Oct 1950, Ann Pamela, da of Leonard Forsell, of Bosrhyn, Port Navas, Cornwall; 1 s (David b 1953), 1 da (Susan b 1956); *Career* Grenadier Gds 1944, cmmnd 2 Lt 1945; serv: Germany, Egypt, Cyprus (despatches 1958), Belgium; Adj Gds Depot 1952, Adj 2 Bn Gren Gds 1954, SD Directorate WO and MOD 1962–64, Regtl Adj Gren Gds 1964–67, 2 i/c 1 Bn 1967, Cmdt Gds Depot 1967, GSOI HQ London Dist

1970–73, Dep Cdr 3 Inf Bde 1973–74, chief Mil Personnel Branch SHAPE 1974, ret 1974; City Marshal 1974–75, admin stock exchange firm 1978, exec dir Cinema and TV Benevolent Fund 1983–95; Freeman City of London 1974; *Recreations* sailing, gardening, radio; *Clubs* Royal Yacht Sqdn, Household Division Yacht; *Style*— Col Peter J C Ratcliffe, OBE; ✉ c/o Barclays Bank Ltd, 6 Killigrew St, Falmouth, Cornwall TR11 3RD

RATCLIFFE, (James) Terence; MBE (1987), JP (1972); s of John Ratcliffe (d 1995), of Bury, and Alice, *née* Bennet (d 1981); *Educ* Bury HS, Univ of Manchester (DipArch); *m* 8 Sept 1956, Mary Grundy (Molly), da of Reginald Victor Adlem (d 1990), of Bury; 3 s (Mark b 1961, Jonathon b 1964, Nicholas b 1965), 1 da (Elisabeth (twin) b 1965); *Career* architect, md Ratcliffe Groves Partnership, dir Carter Design Consultants, dir KM Project Management; pres Euro Area of YMCAs; ARIBA; *Recreations* athletics, YMCA; *Style*— Terence Ratcliffe, Esq, MBE, JP; ✉ Ivy House, Bolton Rd, West, Holcombe Brook, Bury, Lancs; 105 Manchester Rd, Bury, Lancs (☎ 0161 797 6000); Ratcliffe Groves Partnership, 83/84 Long Acre, Covent Garden, London WC2 (☎ 0171 240 9827)

RATFORD, David John Edward; KCMG (1994, CMG 1984), CVO (1979); s of late George Ratford, and Lilian, *née* Jones; *b* 22 April 1934; *Educ* Trinity Sch of John Whitgift, Selwyn Coll Cambridge; *m* 1960, Ulla Monica, da of late Oskar Jerneck, of Stockholm; 2 da; *Career* Nat Serv Intelligence Corps 1953–55; joined FO 1955, 3 sec Prague 1959–61, 2 sec Mogadishu 1961–63, 2 then 1 sec FO 1963–68, 1 sec (commercial) Moscow 1968–71, FCO 1971–74, cnsllr (agric and econ) Paris 1974–78, cnsllr Copenhagen 1978–82, min Moscow 1983–86, asst under-sec of state (Europe) and dep political dir FCO 1986–90, HM ambass Oslo 1990–94, ret; Cdr Order of The Dannebrog Denmark 1979; *Recreations* music, tennis; *Clubs* Travellers'; *Style*— Sir David Ratford, KCMG, CVO; ✉ Wisborough Cottage, Wisborough Green, West Sussex RH14 0DZ; 47404 Käringön, Bohuslän, Sweden

RATH, James Winston; s of Maj Joseph Rath (d 1983), and Mary, *née* Futterweit (d 1988); *b* 12 May 1944; *Educ* St Marylebone GS, Univ of St Andrews (MA); *m* 1991, Pamela Posner, *née* London; 1 step da; *Career* CA; Coopers & Lybrand 1969–73; sec Assoc of Investment Tst Companies 1988– (asst sec 1973–88); ACA 1972, FCA 1978; *Style*— James Rath, Esq; ✉ 28 Alba Gardens, Golders Green, London NW11 9NR (☎ 0181 458 3790); Association of Investment Companies, Durrant House (3rd Floor), 8–13 Chiswell Street, London EC1Y 4YY (☎ 0171 588 5347, fax 0171 638 1803)

RATHBONE, Brian Benson; s of Brig Reginald Blythe Rathbone, OBE (d 1987), of Arreton, Blockley, Glos, and Eileen, *née* Wakeley (d 1930); *b* 15 Oct 1924; *Educ* Bradfield Coll Berks, Trinity Coll Dublin; *m* 20 Feb 1971 (m dis 1974), (Amelda) Jane, da of late Cdr Redvers Prior, DSO, RN, of Highland, St Lawrence, Jersey, CI; *Career* joined RE 1943, cmmnd RASC 1947, ret as Lt 1950; in business 1952–57, called to the Bar Lincoln's Inn 1960; in practice: Oxford Circuit 1960–71, Western Circuit 1972–; examiner of the court 1977–87, pt/t judge advocate 1981–; memb Criminal Bar Assoc; Parly candidate (C) Smethwick 1970; memb: Birmingham City Cncl 1967–70, Camden Borough Cncl 1982–86; *Recreations* riding, swimming, travelling, bridge, chess; *Clubs* Brooks's, Royal Naval & Royal Albert Yacht (Portsmouth); *Style*— Brian Rathbone, Esq; ✉ 33 Colley Close, Winchester, Hants SO23 7ES (☎ 01962 866779); Southsea Chambers, PO Box 148, Portsmouth, Hants PO5 2TU (☎ 01705 291261, fax 01705 753152, DX 2266)

RATHBONE, John Rankin (Tim); MP (C) Lewes (majority 12,175); s of J Rathbone, MP (ka 1940), and Beatrice, later Lady Wright (m Sir Paul Wright, *qv*); *b* 17 March 1933; *Educ* Eton, ChCh Oxford, Harvard Business Sch; *m* 1, 1960 (m dis 1981), Margarita Sanchez y Sanchez; 2 s (John Paul, Michael), 1 da (Tina (Mrs Anton Mueller)); m 2, 1982, Susan Jenkin, da of Jenkin Coles (d 1969) and former w of Lionel Geoffrey Stopford Sackville; 2 step s (Charles, Thomas); *Career* 2 Lt KRRC 1951–53; with Robert Benson Lonsdale & Co 1956–58, trainee rising to vice pres Ogilvy & Mather Inc NY 1958–66, chief publicity and PR offr Cons Central Office 1966–68; dir: Charles Barker Group 1968–87, Ayer Barker Ltd (md 1970–74, dep chm 1974–79), Charles Barker City 1981–87; MP (C) Lewes Feb 1974–; PPS to: Min of Health 1979–82, Min for Trade (consumer affrs) 1982–83, Min for the Arts 1985; fndr memb and chm All Pty Drug Misuse Gp 1984–, chm Parly Engrg Devpt Gp 1992–; chm All Pty: Br-Lebanese Gp 1994–, S Africa Gp 1995–; memb: Br-China-Japan Gps, Parly Human Rights Gp, Br-Iraqi Shia Gp, All Pty Franchise Gp, Br-S American Gp, Br-American Gp, Tory Reform Gp, Euro Movement; delegate to Cncl of Euro and Western Euro Union 1987–; Liveryman Worshipful Company of Drapers; FRSA (memb Cncl 1984–88); *Publications* Nursery Schooling - too long the overlooked ingredient in education for life (Tory Reform Group, 1990), It's My Problem As Well - Drugs Prevention and Education (Business Against Drugs, 1992); *Clubs* Brooks's, Pratt's, Sussex, Soc of Sussex Downsmen; *Style*— Tim Rathbone, Esq, MP; ✉ House of Commons, London SW1A 0AA (☎ 0171 219 3460, fax 0171 219 2578)

RATHBONE, Julian Christopher; s of Christopher Fairrie Rathbone (d 1960), and Decima Doreen, *née* Frost (d 1984); *b* 10 Feb 1935; *Educ* Clayesmore Sch Dorset, Magdalene Coll Cambridge (BA); *Career* author; English teacher: Ankara Coll and Univ of Ankara 1959–62, various Schs UK 1962–73 (head English Dept Bognor Regis Comp Sch 1970–73); full time author 1973–; contrib: The Guardian, New Statesman, Literary Review; Southern Arts bursary 1977, literary advsr Royal Berks Library Servs 1981; Deutsches Krimi Preis (Grnfinger) 1989, Crime Writers' Assoc Best Short Story Award 1993, Swanage Int Poetry Competition First Prize 1994; memb Crime Writers' Assoc; *Books* incl: Diamonds Bid (1967), Trip Trap (1971), Bloody Marvellous (1975), King Fisher Lives (1976, nominated Booker Prize for Fiction), A Raving Monarchist (1977), Joseph (1979, nominated Booker Prize for Fiction), A Last Resort (1980), A Spy of the Old School (1982), Wellington's War (1984), Lying in State (1985), ZDT (1986), The Crystal Contract (1988), The Pandora Option (1990), Dangerous Games (1991, TVM screenplay 1994), Sand Blind (1993); *Radio plays* Albert and the Truth About Rats (Suddeutscher Rundfunk 1990), Intimacy (1995), Accidents Will Happen (1995); *Recreations* painting, music, skiing, cycling; *Style*— Julian Rathbone; ✉ Sea View, School Rd, Thorney Hill, Christchurch, Dorset BH23 8DS (☎ 01425 673313)

RATHBONE, Robert; s of Roger Anthony Rathbone, of Keswick, Cumbria, and Jean, *née* Sander; *b* 19 Aug 1962; *Educ* Keswick GS Cumbria, Teeside Poly Middlesbrough, Richmond Coll Sheffield; *m* 23 July 1990, Lorraine Susan, da of John Broadley; 2 s (Robert Anthony b 24 June 1988, Ryan George b 3 Jan 1992), 1 da (Megan Jade b 2 March 1994); *Career* photographer; trainee press photographer West Cumberland Times and Star Workington Cumbria 1983–85, freelance photographer working through East Midlands Picture Service Nottingham 1986–87, chief photographer East Midlands Picture Service Nottingham 1987, photographer News Team Birmingham 1988, self-employed Robert Rathbone Photography Nottingham 1988–; Sports Picture award Kodak Black and White Photography Awards 1987, Photographic Printer award (Sport Section) Kodak Black and White Photography Awards 1987, Sports Photographer of the Year British Press Awards 1989; memb NUJ 1983; *Recreations* football, cricket, squash, music, walking; *Clubs* Derwent, Keswick, Keyworth Cricket; *Style*— Robert Rathbone, Esq; ✉ Robert Rathbone Photography, 15 Dorchester Gardens, West Bridgford, Nottingham NG2 7AW (☎ 0115 945 2335, fax 0115 945 2337, mobile 0973 411598)

RATHBONE, William; s of William Rathbone (d 1992), of Charlbury, Oxon, and Margaret Hester (Peggie), *née* Lubbock (d 1986); *b* 5 June 1936; *Educ* Radley, Christ Church Oxford (MA), IMEDE Lausanne (Dip Business Studies); *m* 1960, Sarah Kynaston, da of Brig Hugh S K Mainwaring, CB, CBE, DSO, TD; 1 da (Lucy Elena b 17 April 1970), 1 s (William b 19 July 1974); *Career* Nat Serv cmmnd 2 Lt Royal Artillery 1954–56 (served Malaya 1955–56); The Ocean Group plc 1959–88: Elder Dempster Lines 1959–69 (based Nigeria and Ghana for 4 years), started up tanker and bulk carrier div 1969–71, IMEDE Lausanne 1972, dir Wm Cory & Sons Ltd 1973–74, gen mangr Ocean Inchcape Ltd 1974–79, exec dir Gastranco Ltd 1979–88; dir and chief exec Royal United Kingdom Beneficent Association and Universal Beneficent Soc 1988–; non-exec dir Rathbone Brothers plc (fund mgmnt and banking gp) 1994–; currently: vice chm and tstee Queen's Nursing Inst, memb Ct New England Co, tstee Honeywood Tst, memb Cncl St Peter's Convent Woking, tstee North Waltham Village Tst, govr Crossways Tst Ltd, vice pres Christ Church (Oxford) United Clubs; Freeman City of London, Liveryman Worshipful Co of Skinners; *Recreations* the arts, opera, theatre, fishing, shooting, rowing, friends; *Clubs* Brooks's, Leander; *Style*— William Rathbone, Esq; ✉ Director, RUKBA, 6 Avonmore Road, London W14 8RL (☎ 0171 602 6274, fax 0171 371 1807)

RATHCAVAN, 3 Baron (UK 1953); Hugh Torrens O'Neill; 3 Bt (UK 1929); o s of 2 Baron Rathcavan, PC (d 1994), and his 1 w, Clare Désirée, *née* Blow (d 1956); *b* 14 June 1939; *Educ* Eton; *m* 1983, Sylvie Marie-Thérèse, da of late Georges Wichard, of Provence, France, and formerly w of Hilary Chittenden; 1 s (Hon François b 1984); *Heir* s, Hon François Hugh Nial O'Neill b 26 June 1984; *Career* Capt Irish Gds; journalist: Irish Times, Observer, Financial Times; dir: Lamont Holdings plc, Northern Bank Ltd, The Old Bushmills Distillery Co Ltd, The Berkeley Hotel; chm: NI Tourist Bd, FRX International Ltd; *Recreations* food, travel; *Clubs* Beefsteak; *Style*— The Rt Hon the Lord Rathcavan; ✉ 14 Thurloe Place, London SW7 2RZ (☎ 0171 584 5293); Cleggan Lodge, Ballymena, Co Antrim BT43 7JW (☎ 01266 862222, fax 01266 862000)

RATHCREEDAN, 3 Baron (UK 1916), of Bellehatch Park, Oxon; Christopher John Norton; s and h of 2 Baron Rathcreedan, TD (d 1990), and Ann Pauline, *née* Bastian; *b* 3 June 1949; *Educ* Wellington, RAC Cirencester; *m* 1978, Lavinia Anne Ross, da of Alan George Ross Ormiston, of Coln Orchard, Arlington, Bibury, Glos; 2 da (Hon Jessica Charlotte b 13 Nov 1983, Hon Serena Clare b 12 Aug 1987); *Heir* br, Hon Adam Gregory Norton; *Career* pedigree livestock auctioneer; Liveryman Worshipful Co of Founders; *Recreations* horse racing, gardening; *Clubs* Turf; *Style*— The Rt Hon Lord Rathcreedan; ✉ Stoke Common House, Purton Stoke, Swindon, Wiltshire SW5 9LL (☎ 01793 772492)

RATHDONNELL, 5 Baron (I 1868); Thomas Benjamin McClintock-Bunbury; s of 4 Baron Rathdonnell (d 1959); *b* 17 Sept 1938; *Educ* Charterhouse, RNC Dartmouth; *m* 2 Oct 1965, Jessica Harriet, o da of George Gilbert Butler (eighth in descent from 2 Baron Dunboyne) and Norah Pomeroy Colley, gggda of 4 Viscount Harberton; 3 s (Hon William, Hon George b 26 July 1968, Hon James b 21 Feb 1972), 1 da (Hon Sasha b 10 Feb 1976); *Heir* s, Hon William Leopold McClintock-Bunbury, b 6 July 1966; *Style*— The Rt Hon the Lord Rathdonnell; ✉ Lisnavagh, Rathvilly, Co Carlow, Republic of Ireland (☎ 00 353 503 61104)

RATLEDGE, Prof Colin; s of Fred Ratledge (d 1975), of Preston, Lancs, and Freda Smith Proudlock (d 1986); *b* 9 Oct 1936; *Educ* Bury HS, Univ of Manchester (BSc, PhD); *m* 25 March 1961, Janet Vivien, da of Albert Cyril Bottomley (d 1977), of Preston, Lancs; 1 s (Stuart b 15 March 1968), 2 da (Alison b 7 July 1964, Jane b 15 July 1971); *Career* res fellowship MRC Ireland 1960–64, res scientist Unilever plc 1964–67; Univ of Hull: lectr 1967–73, sr lectr 1973–77, reader 1977–83, personal chair 1983, head of Dept of Biochemistry 1986–88, prof of microbial biochemistry 1988–; memb Euro Fedn of Biotechnol (Sci Advsy Ctee 1984–90), vice-pres Soc of Chem Industry 1993–; chm: Food Res Grant Bd and memb Food Res Ctee AFRC 1989–92, Soc of Chemical Industry 1989–91, Inst of Biology Biotechnol Gps 1989–93, Br Co-ordinating Ctee for Biotechnol 1989–91, Inst of Biology Industrial Biology Ctee 1993–96; memb: Int Union of Biochemistry Biotechnol Ctee 1984–, Int Cncl of Scientific Unions Press Ctee 1994–; sec Int Ctee of Environmental and Applied Microbiology 1990–94; Kathleen Barton-Wright Meml lectr (Soc for Gen Microbiology and Inst of Biology) 1994, Australian Soc of Microbiology visiting lectr 1986, NZ Soc of Microbiology visiting lectr 1986; memb: Soc for Gen Microbiology, Soc of Chem Industry, Biochemical Soc, American Microbiological Soc, American Oil Chemists Soc; FRSC 1970, FIBiol 1983, FRSA 1987, fell Int Inst of Biotechnology 1993; *Books* The Mycobacteria (1977), Microbial Technology: Current State, Future Prospects (1979), The Biology of the Mycobacteria (vol 1 1982, vol 2 1983, vol 3 1989), Biotechnology for the Oils and Fats Industry (1984), Microbial Technology in the Developing World (1987), Microbial Lipids (vol 1 1988, vol 2 1989), Microbial Physiology and Manufacturing Industry (1988), Biotechnology: Economic and Social Aspects (1992), Industrial Applications of Single Cell Oils (1992), Biochemistry of Microbial Degradation (1993); World Journal of Microbiology and Biotechnology (ed-in-chief), Biotechnology Techniques (exec ed), Biotechnology Letters (exec ed); *Recreations* hill walking, bonsai gardening, chess; *Style*— Prof Colin Ratledge; ✉ 49 Church Drive, Leven, Beverley, East Yorkshire (☎ 01964 542690); Department of Biological Sciences, University of Hull, Hull HU6 7RX (☎ 01482 465243, fax 01482 465458, e-mail c.ratledge@biosci.hull.ac.uk)

RATLIFF, John Harrison; s of Anthony Hugh Cyril Ratliff, and Jean, *née* Harrison; *b* 13 Jan 1957; *Educ* Clifton, Univ Coll Oxford (BA), Univ of Amsterdam (DIEI); *m* 27 July 1985, Pascale, da of Pierre Bourgeon; *Career* called to the Bar Middle Temple 1980; winner of Hon Sir Peter Bristow Award 1981, young lawyers prog Germany 1981–82, J C Goldsmith and Assoc Paris 1983–84, ptnr Stanbrook and Hooper Brussels 1987–; memb: Int Bar Assoc, Anglo Germany Lawyers Assoc, Rheinischer Internationaler Juristen Verein; *Recreations* music, travel; *Clubs* Reform; *Style*— John Ratliff, Esq; ✉ 42 Rue Du Taciturne, 1000 Brussels, Belgium (☎ 00 32 2 230 5059, fax 00 32 2 230 5713)

RATNER, Gerald Irving; s of Leslie Manuel Ratner, and Rachelle Ezra, *née* Moses; *b* 1 Nov 1949; *Educ* Hendon County GS; *m* 1, (m dis 1989), Angela Nadine Trup; 2 da (Suzanne b 1975, Lisa Karen b 1977); m 2, Kathleen Moira, *née* Day; 1 s (Jonathan b 1991), 1 da (Sarah Charlotte b 1989); *Career* Ratners plc: dir 1970, jt md 1978, md 1984, chm and chief exec 1986–92, chief exec until Nov 1992; former dir Norweb plc, conslt Tobacco Dock discount retail co 1995–; former memb: Crime Concern, Business in the Community; *Recreations* tennis, scrabble; *Style*— Gerald Ratner, Esq; ✉ Hampton Lodge, Church Road, Bray, Berks SL6 1UP

RATNER, Richard Anthony; TD (1981); s of Jack Louis Ratner (d 1970), of Bryanston Court, London, and Vivienne, *née* Salbstein (d 1976); *b* 21 Sept 1949; *Educ* Epsom Coll, Univ of Leeds (LLB); *m* 27 July 1974, (Silvia) Jane, da of Maj A C Hammond, TD (d 1990); 2 s (James Anthony Mark b 1975, Christopher Piers Alexander b 1980), 1 da (Katie Emma Jayne b 1979); *Career* textiles indust (latterly chm U U Textiles plc) 1972–81, dir institutional sales and ptnr Kitcat & Aitken & Co 1981–91, dir and head of institutional sales Carr Kitcat & Aitken Ltd 1991–93, sr vice pres Williams de Broe 1993–96, dir Mees Pierson Securities 1996–; conslt: Owen & Robinson plc 1986–, Seasons Garden Centres 1988–92; ptnr West St Antiques Dorking 1990–; Maj The Queen's Own Hussars (TA) 1968–85; memb Court of Common Cncl for the Ward of Broad St 1981–91; former chm: Broad St Ward Club, Soc of Young Freeman, Bd of Govrs City of London Sch; former govr Bridewell Royal Hosp and Christ's Hosp, govr Abinger Hammer Village Sch; chm Mitchell City of London Charity; memb: City Branch TA & VRA, HAC; Freeman City of London 1976, Liveryman Worshipful Co of Gunmakers 1979; memb: Lloyd's 1975–84, Stock Exchange 1984, MSI (Dip) 1992; *Books* The English Civil War (contrib, 1971); *Recreations* antique firearms, antiques, model railways; *Clubs* Cavalry and Guards'; *Style*— Richard Ratner, Esq, TD; ✉ Hill House, Hammerfield,

Abinger Hammer, Dorking, Surrey (☎ 01306 730182); Mees Pierson Securities, Camomile Court, 23 Camomile Street, London EC3 (☎ 0171 444 8436)

RATSEY, Dr David Hugh Kerr; s of Capt Franklin Ratsey, and Mary Gwendoline Lucy, *née* Walduck; *b* 7 June 1944; *Educ* Sherborne, St Bartholomew's Hosp (MB BS, MRCS, LRCP); *m* 6 Sept 1969, Christine, da of Arthur William Tutt-Harris; 3 s (Matthew David, Timothy James, Nicholas Paul), 1 da (Anna Mary); *Career* pre-registration post Prince of Wales Hosp Tottenham then house surgn Whipps Cross Hosp Leytonstone 1968–69, sr house offr in anaesthesia St Bartholomew's Hosp 1970–71, Alwyn bursar and res registrar in anaesthesia St Bartholomew's Hosp 1971–72, anaesthetic registrar St George's Hosp 1973–75, trainee then princ Gen Practice 1975–80, pt/t clinical asst Royal Homeopathic Hosp 1975–82 and 1986–, consltg Homeopathic practice Kensington 1980–; recognised as having conslt status for benefit payment by PPP 1984, BCWA 1987, BUPA 1988, Orion and Sun Alliance 1989; Faculty of Homeopathy: elected Cncl 1983, offr 1984, external examiner 1984, founder memb official Ct of Examiners 1987, vice pres 1987 and 1988, pres 1992–; *Recreations* sailing; *Clubs* Medical Soc of London; *Style*— Dr David Ratsey; ✉ 2 Harley St, London W1N 1AA (☎ 0171 589 2776, fax 0171 323 5743)

RATTANSI, Prof Pyarally Mohamedally (Piyo); s of Mohamedally Rattansi (d 1957), of Nairobi, Kenya, and Mani Hirji, *née* Ladha (d 1965); *b* 15 Oct 1930; *Educ* Duke of Gloucester Sch Nairobi, LSE (BSc, PhD), Univ of Cambridge (MA); *m* 11 June 1966, Zarin Pyarally, da of Mirali Bhimji Charania (d 1953), of Kisumu, Kenya; 2 s (Afshin b 13 Jan 1968, Shihab b 25 Aug 1971); *Career* lectr Dept of Philosophy Univ of Leeds 1964–67 (Leverhulme Res Fell 1962–64), visiting assoc prof Univ of Chicago 1966, fell King's Coll Cambridge 1967–71, visiting lectr Princeton Univ 1969–70, memb Inst for Advanced Study Princeton 1969, prof and head of Dept of History and Philosophy of Science UCL 1971–95, emeritus prof 1996–; vice pres Br Soc for History of Sci 1974–77 (memb 1972–74), vice pres History of Sci Section Br Assoc for the Advancement of Science 1993–94 (pres 1991–92), UK delegate to numerous int scientific confs and symposia; *Books* incl: Science and Society 1600–1900 (contrib, 1972), Isaac Newton and Gravity (1974), History and Imagination - Essays in Honour of H R Trevor-Roper (contrib, 1981), The Physical Sciences Since Antiquity (contrib, 1986), Revolutions in Science - Their Meaning and Relevance (contrib, 1988), Let Newton Be! (contrib, 1988), Teaching the History of Science (contrib, 1989), Alchemy and Chemistry in the 16th and 17th Centuries (co-ed, 1994); *Recreations* swimming; *Style*— Prof Piyo Rattansi; ✉ 6 Hillersdon Avenue, Edgware, Middx HA8 7SQ (☎ and fax 0181 958 9442); Department of History & Philosophy & Communication of Science, University College London, Gower St, London WC1E 6BT (☎ 0171 387 7050, fax 0171 916 2425)

RATTEE, Hon Mr Justice; Hon Sir Donald Keith; kt (1989); s of Charles Ronald and Dorothy Rattee; *b* 9 March 1937; *Educ* Clacton Co HS, Trinity Hall Cambridge (MA, LLB); *m* 1964, Diana Mary, da of John Leslie and Florence Elizabeth Howl; 4 da; *Career* called to the Bar Lincoln's Inn 1962, QC 1977, bencher Lincoln's Inn 1985, attorney gen Duchy of Lancaster 1986–89, recorder of the Crown Court 1989, judge of the High Court of Justice (Chancery Div) 1993– (Family Div 1989–93); *Recreations* golf, music, gardening; *Clubs* RAC, Banstead Downs Golf; *Style*— The Hon Mr Justice Rattee; ✉ Royal Courts of Justice, Strand, London WC2A 2LL

RATTLE, Sir Simon Denis; kt (1994), CBE (1987); *b* 19 Jan 1955, Liverpool; *Educ* Royal Acad of Music; *m* 1, Elise Ross; 2 s; m 2, 1996, Candace Allen; *Career* conductor; played percussion with the Royal Liverpool Philharmonic Orch aged 15, asst conductor Bournemouth Symphony Orch and Sinfonietta 1974–76, assoc conductor Royal Liverpool Philharmonic and BBC Scottish Symphony Orchs 1977–80; City of Birmingham Symphony Orch: princ conductor and artistic advsr 1980–, music dir 1990–; guest conductor LA Philharmonic 1979– (princ guest conductor 1979–94); princ guest conductor: Rotterdam Philharmonic 1981–84, Orch of the Age of Enlightenment 1992–; artistic dir South Bank Summer Music Festival 1981–84; worked with various other major orchs incl: London Sinfonietta, The Philharmonia, London Philharmonic, Berlin Philharmonic, Rotterdam Philharmonic, Stockholm Philharmonic, Philadelphia Orch, Chicago, San Francisco, Toronto, Cleveland and Boston Symphony Orchs; Festival Hall début 1976, Glyndebourne debut 1977, US debut 1979, NY debut 1985, Concertgebouw Amsterdam debut 1986, US operatic debut 1988, Royal Opera House Covent Garden debut 1990, Vienna Philharmonic debut 1993; Hon DMus: Univ of Birmingham, Univ of Leeds, Univ of Liverpool; Officier des Arts et Lettres 1995; *Operas* conducted incl: The Cunning Little Vixen (Glyndebourne 1977 and Covent Garden 1990), Ariadne auf Naxos (Glyndebourne, 1981), Der Rosenkavalier (Glyndebourne, 1982), The Love for Three Oranges (Glyndebourne, 1983), Idomeneo (Glyndebourne, 1985), Katya Kabanova (ENO, 1985), Porgy and Bess (Glyndebourne, 1986), L'heure escagnole and L'enfant et les sortilèges (Glyndebourne, 1987), The Marriage of Figaro (Glyndebourne, 1989), Cosi fan Tutte (Glyndebourne, 1991), Pelléas et Mélisande (Netherlands Opera, 1993), Don Giovanni (Glyndebourne, 1994); *Recordings* over 60 for EMI incl: Mahler's 2nd (with CBSO, 1987, Gramophone Record of the Year and Best Orchestral Recording 1988), Turanglila Symphony (with CBSO, 1987, winner Grand Prix du Disque and Grand Prix Caecilia 1988), Porgy and Bess (with London Philharmonic, 1988, winner Gramophone Opera Award 1989, Int Record Critics' Award 1990, Grand Prix in Honorem de l'Academie Charles Cros 1990, Prix Caecilia, Br Phonographic Industry Classical Award, Edison Award), Szymanowski Litany for the Virgin Mary (Germany's Echo Award for best symphonic recording 1994), Schoenberg Chamber Symphony No 1 and Variations and Erwartung (with Birmingham Contemporary Music Gp and CBSO, winner Gramophone Best Orchestral Recording Award 1995), Szymanowski Stabat Mater (with City of Birmingham Symphony Chorus and CBSO, Gramophone Best Choral Award and Best Engrg Award 1995); *Awards* Gramophone Artist of the Year 1993, Mountblanc de la Culture Award (for private vision) 1993; *Style*— Sir Simon Rattle, CBE; ✉ c/o Harold Holt Ltd, 31 Sinclair Road, London W14 0NS (☎ 0171 603 4600, fax 0171 603 0019)

RAUTER, Peter Karl; s of Ferdinand Rauter (d 1987), of London, and Claire, *née* Kosten; *b* 15 April 1948; *Educ* Michael Hall Sch Sussex, London Coll of Printing (dip); *m* 30 Aug 1992, Rebecca Mary, da of Stewart Washbourne Money, MBE; *Career* photographer; asst to Terence Donovan 1971–73, worked from Cornel Lucas' studio Chelsea 1973–77, Rossetti Studios 1978–83, in own studio Kilburn 1984–; editorial work (travel features, still life, life style, food, etc) for magazines incl: Vogue, Brides, Country Life, Country Homes and Interiors; advtg work for clients incl: BTA, Ford, Jaguar, Range Rover, Marks & Spencer, Seagram, Air Canada, Peaudouce; currently directing TV commercials (Ponds, Vaseline, local work, etc) and working on personal photographic projects in Istanbul; AFAEP Merit award winner (for advtg) 1992, AFAEP Silver award winner (for portraits) 1993, D&AD award winner 1993; *Books* English Cottage Interiors; *Recreations* travel and good food, dinner and friends; *Style*— Peter Rauter, Esq; ✉ Peter Rauter Ltd, The Priory Works, 252 Belsize Road, London NW6 (☎ 0171 372 0069)

RAVEN, James (Jim); s of Patrick Raven, and Irene, *née* Cossan; *b* 23 June 1953; *Educ* William Penn Secdy Sch London; *m* 15 June 1975, Wendy Margaret; 3 da (Lyanne b 21 Sept 1976, Ellie b 17 Aug 1979, Jodie b 1 Nov 1985); *Career* trainee reporter Press Association 1969–70; reporter: SE London Mercury 1970–73, freelance 1973–75, Fleet St News Agency 1975, The Sun and freelance 1975–77, Sevenoaks Chronicle 1977–78, Kent Evening Post 1978–81; TVS Television: joined as scriptwriter 1981, later prodr, ed Coast to Coast (regnl news magazine prog) 1989–92 (formerly dep ed); controller of news, sport and current affrs Meridian Broadcasting 1992–; London Young Journalist of the Year 1972; *Books* Pinnacle of Ice, The Triad Consignment, When Strangers Came, The Venice Ultimatum; *Recreations* painting, travelling, reading, writing; *Style*— Jim Raven, Esq; ✉ Meridian Broadcasting, Television Centre, Northam Road, Southampton SO14 0PZ (☎ 01703 222555)

RAVEN, Dame Kathleen Annie (Dame Kathleen Ingram); DBE (1968); o da of Fredric William Raven (d 1952), and Annie Williams, *née* Mason (d 1973); sis of Ronald William Raven, OBE, TD (d 1991, *see* 1991 edn); *b* 9 Nov 1910; *Educ* Ulverston GS, privately, St Bartholomew's Hosp London, City of of London Maternity Hosp; *m* 1959, Prof John Thornton Ingram (d 1972); *Career* asst matron St Bartholomew's Hosp 1946–49, matron The General Infirmary Leeds 1949–57, chief nursing offr DHSS 1958–72; memb: Gen Nursing Cncl for England and Wales 1950–57, Exec Ctee Assoc of Hosp Matrons for England and Wales 1955–57, Cncl Royal Coll Nursing 1950–57, Cncl Central Health Services 1957–58, Cncl and Nursing Advsy Bd BRCS 1958–72, Nat Florence Nightingale Meml Ctee of GB and NI 1958–72, WHO Expert Advsy Panel on Nursing 1961–79 (fell 1960); vice pres Royal Coll of Nursing 1972–, chief nursing advsr United Medical Enterprises 1973–91, memb Distressed Gentlefolks Aid Assoc 1973–89 (chm Exec Ctee 1981–87), chm Interviewing Panels Civil Serv Cmmn 1974–80, fndn govr Aylesbury GS 1986–; memb Cncl and vice pres Epsom Coll 1991–, tstee The Ronald Raven Chair in Clinical Oncology Tst 1992–; memb Ct of the Patrons RCS England 1994; Hon Freewoman Worshipful Co of Barbers 1981, Freeman City of London 1986; Hon DLitt Keele Univ 1992, Hon Dr of Laws Univ of Leeds 1996; SRN 1936, SCM 1938, FRSA 1970 FRCN 1986; OStJ 1963; *Recreations* painting, reading, travel; *Clubs* Royal Commonwealth Soc; *Style*— Dame Kathleen Raven, DBE; ✉ Jesmond, Burcott, Wing, nr Leighton Buzzard, Beds LU7 0JU (☎ 01296 688 244)

RAVEN, Simon Arthur Noel; s of Arthur Godart Raven, and Esther Kate, *née* Christmas; *b* 28 Dec 1927; *Educ* Charterhouse, King's Coll Cambridge (MA); *m* 1951 (m dis), Susan Mandeville, *née* Kilner; 1 s (Adam); *Career* novelist, dramatist and critic; works incl: The Pallisers (BBC), Edward & Mrs Simpson (Thames); FRSL; *Books* Arms for Oblivion (10 vols), The First-Born of Egypt (7 vols); *Style*— Simon Raven, Esq, FRSL; ✉ c/o Curtis Brown, 4th Floor, Haymarket House, 28–29 Haymarket, London SW1Y 4SP (☎ 0171 396 6600)

RAVENSCROFT, Ven Raymond Lockwood; s of Cecil Ravenscroft, and Amy Gwendoline, *née* Beatty; *b* 15 Sept 1931; *Educ* Sea Point Cape Town, Univ of Leeds (BA), Coll of the Resurrection Mirfield; *m* 24 June 1957, Ann, da of James Peter Stockwell; 1 s (David b 1960), 1 da (Gillian b 1958); *Career* ordained 1955; asst curate: St Alban's Goodwood Cape SA 1955–58, St John's Pro-Cathedral Bulawayo S Rhodesia 1958–59; rector Francistown Bechuanaland 1959–62, asst curate St Ives Cornwall 1962–64; vicar: All Saints Falmouth 1964–68, St Stephen by Launceston with St Thomas 1968–74; team rector Probus Team Miny 1974–88, rural dean Powder 1977–81, hon canon Truro Cathedral 1982–88, archdeacon of Cornwall 1988–96, canon librarian of Truro Cathedral 1988–96; *Style*— The Ven Raymond Ravenscroft

RAVENSDALE, 3 Baron (UK 1911); Sir Nicholas Mosley; 7 Bt (GB 1781), of Ancoats, Lancashire, and of Rolleston, Staffordshire, MC (1944); s of Sir Oswald Mosley, 6 Bt (d 1980), and (first w) Lady Cynthia Blanche, *née* Curzon, da of 1 Marquess of Curzon Kedleston and 1 Baron Ravensdale (she d 1933); suc aunt, Baroness Ravensdale (who was also cr a Life Peer as Baroness Ravensdale of Kedleston 1958) 1966; suc father as 7 Bt 1980; *b* 25 June 1923; *Educ* Eton, Balliol Coll Oxford; *m* 1, 1947 (m dis 1974), Rosemary Laura (d 1991), da of late Marshal of the RAF Sir John Maitland Salmond, GCB, CMG, CVO, DSO, by his 2 w, Hon Monica Grenfell (da of 1 Baron Desborough and Ethel, da of Hon Julian Fane, 4 s of 11 Earl of Westmorland, by Julian's w Lady Adine Cowper, da of 6 Earl Cowper); 3 s (Hon Shaun Nicholas b 1949, Hon Ivo Adam Rex b 1951, Hon Robert b 1955), 1 da (Hon Clare Imogen b 1959); m 2, 1974, Verity Elizabeth, 2 da of late N J B (Jack) Raymond, of Basingstoke, and former w of (John) Adrian Bailey; 1 s (Hon Marius b 1976); *Heir* s, Hon Shaun Nicholas Mosley b 5 Aug 1949; *Career* Capt Rifle Bde WW II; author (as Nicholas Mosley); *Books* include Accident (1966, filmed by Joseph Losey), Impossible Object (1968), Assassins (1967), The Assassination of Trotsky (1972, also filmed), Julian Grenfell (1976), Catastrophe Practice (1979), Imago Bird (1980), Serpent (1981), Rules of the Game: Sir Oswald and Lady Cynthia Mosley 1896–1933 (1982), Beyond the Pale, Sir Oswald Mosley 1933–80 (1983), Judith (1986), Hopeful Monsters (Whitbread Book of the Year, 1990); *Recreations* gardening; *Style*— The Rt Hon the Lord Ravensdale, MC; ✉ 2 Gloucester Crescent, London NW1 7DS (☎ 0171 485 4514); c/o Peters Fraser & Dunlop, The Chambers, Chelsea Harbour, London SW10

RAVENSWORTH, 8th Baron (UK 1821); Sir Arthur Waller Liddell; 13th Bt (E 1642), JP (Northumberland 1959); s of Hon Cyril Liddell, JP, DL (2 s of 5th Baron Ravensworth); suc cous, 7th Baron, 1950; is 2 cous once removed of late Guy Liddell, CB, CBE, MC, sometime civil asst War Office. Lord Ravensworth's gf, the 5th Baron, was second cousin to Alice Liddell, whose Adventures in Wonderland and through the Looking Glass were immortalised by Lewis Carroll; *b* 25 July 1924; *Educ* Harrow; *m* 1950, Wendy, adopted da of J Stuart Bell, of Cookham; 1 s, 1 da; *Heir* s, Hon Thomas Liddell, *qv*; *Career* former radio engr BBC; *Style*— The Rt Hon The Lord Ravensworth, JP; ✉ Eslington Park, Whittingham, Alnwick, Northumberland (☎ 0166 574 239)

RAVIV, HE Moshe; *b* 1935, Bukovina, Romania; *Educ* Youth Aliyah, Hebrew Univ Jerusalem, Univ of London (BA (Int Rels)); *m*; 3 c; *Career* Israeli diplomat; second sec London 1961–63, Office of Foreign Min (Mrs Golda Meir) 1964–65, political sec to Foreign Min (Abba Eban) 1966–68, political cnsllr Washington DC 1968–74, dir N American Div Miny of Foreign Affrs 1976–78 (dir E Europe Div 1974–76), ambass to Philippines 1978–81, dir Economic Div Miny of Foreign Affrs 1981–83, min plenipotentiary London 1983–88, dep DG i/c info Miny of Foreign Affrs 1988–93, ambass to Ct of St James's 1993–; *Style*— HE Mr Moshe Raviv; ✉ Embassy of Israel, 2 Palace Green, Kensington, London W8 4QB (☎ 0171 957 9500, fax 0171 957 9555)

RAW, Peter Michael; s of George Raw, of Ewell, and Florence May, *née* Elliott (d 1990); *b* 17 May 1939; *Educ* Queen Elizabeth's GS Wakefield, Downing Coll Cambridge (BA, MA); *m* 1 July 1972, Mary Angela, da of John Smith (d 1977), of Leicester; 3 s (James Edward b 1973, Simon David b 1975, John Peter b 1977), 1 da (Catherine Jane b 1981); *Career* BICC Ltd 1963–79, devpt dir Engelhard-CLAL Ltd Chessington Surrey 1983–96, conslt (precious metals) 1996–; MIM 1979, CEng 1984; *Recreations* long distance running, cricket, travel; *Style*— Peter Raw, Esq; ✉ Orchard House, Bushy Rd, Bookham, Surrey KT22 9SX (☎ and fax 01372 457546)

RAWCLIFFE, Roger Capron; s of Brig James Maudsley Rawcliffe, OBE, MC, TD (d 1965), and Margaret Duff Capron (d 1982); *b* 2 Aug 1934; *Educ* Rossall Sch, Trinity Coll Cambridge (Open Exhibitioner, Henry Arthur Thomas Travelling Scholarship, BA, MA); *m* 1960, Mary Elizabeth White, da of Maurice White; 1 s (James Maurice b 1966); *Career* Nat Serv 1952 Grenadier Guards and E Lancs Regt, 2 Lt 1953, Lt 1954, Capt Stowe CCF 1963, Maj 1964, OC 1966, Hon Col IOM ACF 1987 (Cadet Forces Medal and Bar); articled to Sir Thomas Robson at Price Waterhouse; Stowe Sch: asst master 1960–80, head of dept 1967, housemaster 1969, OC CCF 1966; lectr School of Extension Studies Univ of Liverpool 1981–; guest lectr Swan Hellenic Cruises 1967–; ptnr Pannell Kerr Forster 1982–91; dir: Rothschild Asset Management (Isle of Man) 1987–91, Isle of Man Breweries (now Heron and Brearley Ltd) 1992–, Singer & Friedlander (Isle of Man) 1992–; chm IOM Soc of Chartered Accountants 1993–94; govr Rossall Sch 1981–; tstee:

King William's Coll 1987–94, Manx Museum & Nat Tst 1991–; memb Hon Artillery Co 1960; FCA 1970 (ACA 1960); *Style*— Roger Rawcliffe, Esq; ✉ The Malt House, Bridge Street, Castletown, Isle of Man IM9 1ET (☎ 01624 825667)

RAWLINGS, Keith John; s of Jack Frederick Rawlings (d 1985), and Eva, *née* Mullis; *b* 24 April 1940; *Educ* Kent Coll Canterbury; *m* 21 Dec 1963, Susan Mary, da of Thomas Johnson (d 1967); 1 s (Jonathan James Ashley b 27 March 1965), 1 da (Sarah Louise (Mrs Watson) b 15 Feb 1967); *Career* insur broker and ind fin advsr; chm Burlington Insurance Group 1969–91; dir: London & Edinburgh Trust plc 1986–87, Rutland Trust plc 1987–91; group business development dir Bain Hogg Ltd 1991–95; dep chm: GN Bishop (Insurance Brokers) Ltd 1995–, AFPS Ltd 1995–; FCII; *Recreations* golf, tennis, skiing, sailing, bridge, travel; *Clubs* St James's, Carnegie; *Style*— Keith Rawlings, Esq; ✉ Summerhayes, Cliff Road, Hythe, Kent CT21 5XQ (☎ 01303 267014); AFPS Ltd, 15–16 Dover Street, Canterbury, Kent CT1 3HD (☎ 01227 762380, fax 01227 760726)

RAWLINGS, Baroness (Life Peer UK 1994), of Burnham Westgate in the County of Norfolk; Patricia Elizabeth Rawlings; da of late Louis Rawlings, and Mary, *née* Boas de Winter; *b* 27 Jan 1939; *Educ* Oak Hall Surrey, Le Manoir Lausanne Switzerland, Univ of Florence, UCL (BA), LSE (Post Grad Dip in Int Rels); *m* 1962 (m dis 1967), David Wolfson (later Baron Wolfson of Sunningdale, *qv*); *Career* Parly candidate (C): Sheffield 1983, Doncaster 1987; special advsr to Min on Inner Cities DOE 1987–88; MEP (C) Essex SW 1989–94; memb Euro Parl Ctee on: Youth, Educn, Culture, Media, Sport, Political Affrs; memb Euro Parl's Delgn to Romania, Bulgaria, and Albania; BRCS: memb 1964–, chm Appeals London Branch 1964–88, Nat Badge of Hon 1981, hon vice pres 1988–; memb: Children's Care Ctee LCC 1959–61, WMHNR Nursing Westminster Hosp to 1968, Br Bd of Video Classification, Cncl Peace Through NATO, IISS, RIIA, Euro Union Women; dir Eng Chamber Orchestra and Music Soc; Bulgarian Order of the Rose Silver Class 1991; *Recreations* music, art, architecture, golf, skiing, travel, gardening; *Clubs* Queen's, Grillions, Royal West Norfolk; *Style*— The Rt Hon Baroness Rawlings

RAWLINS, Brig Gordon John; OBE (1986); s of Arthur James Rawlins, of New Milton, Hants, and Joyce Rosemary, *née* Smith; *b* 22 April 1944; *Educ* Welbeck Coll, RMA Sandhurst, RMCS (BSc); *m* 1, 28 Aug 1965, Ann Rose (d 1986), da of Alfred George Beard (d 1981); 1 s (Richard James b 1968); m 2, 25 Oct 1986, Margaret Anne (Meg), da of James Martin Edward Ravenscroft; 1 step s (Hamish Richmond Haddow b 1970), 1 step da (Islay Elizabeth Haddow b 1972); *Career* cmmnd REME 1964; recent career: Staff Coll (Maj) 1977–78, Maj GSO2 ASD 1 MOD 1978–80, Maj 21C 5 Armd Workshop 1981–82, Lt-Col CO 7 Armd Workshop 1982–84, Lt-Col Mil Asst to MGO MOD 1984–86, Col PB21 MOD 1986, Col Sec to COS Ctee MOD 1987, Brig Cmd Maint 1 (BR) Corps 1988; served Aden, Oman, Jordan, UK, Hong Kong and BAOR, ret as Brig 1989; sec Inst of Mfrg Engineers and chief exec Instn of Industl Mangrs (now Inst of Mgmnt) 1988–91, dep sec Instn of Electrical Engrs 1991–, sec National Electronics Cncl 1991–; Liveryman Worshipful Co of Turners 1991; CEng 1982, FIEE 1991; *Recreations* rugby, cricket, music; *Clubs* Army and Navy; *Style*— Brig G J Rawlins, OBE; ✉ Institution of Electrical Engineers, Savoy Place, London WC2R 0BL (☎ 0171 240 1871, fax 0171 240 7735)

RAWLINS, Surgn Vice Adm Sir John Stuart Pepys; KBE (1978, OBE 1960, MBE 1956); s of Col Cmdt Stuart William Hughes Rawlins, CB, CMG, DSO (d 1927), and Dorothy Pepys, *née* Cockerell (d 1937); *b* 12 May 1922; *Educ* Wellington, Univ Coll Oxford (MA), Bart's London (BM BCh); *m* 1944, Diana Margaret Freshney (d 1992), da of Charles Freshney Colbeck, ISO (d 1966); 1 s, 3 da; *Career* Surgn Lt RNVR 1947, Surgn Lt RN, RAF Inst Aviation Med 1951, RN Physiology Laboratory 1957, Surgn Cdr RAF Inst Aviation Med 1961, HMS Ark Royal 1964, US Naval Med Res Inst 1967, Surgn Capt 1969, Surgn Cdre dir of health and res (Naval) 1973, Surgn Rear Adm 1975, Dean of Naval Medicine and MO i/c Inst of Naval Medicine 1975–77, Actg Surgn Vice Adm 1977, Med Dir-Gen (Navy) 1977–80; QHP 1975–80; chm: Deep Ocean Technology Inc, Deep Ocean Engineering Inc 1984–91, Trident Underwater (Systems) Ltd, Medical Express Ltd; dir: Under Sea Industries Inc 1981–83, Diving Unlimited International Ltd; past pres Soc for Underwater Technology; conslt in underwater technol, hon res fell Univ of Lancaster Dept of Psychology, hon fell Univ Coll Oxford; Hon DTech Robert Gordons Univ; CStJ, FRCP, FFPHM, FRAeS; *Recreations* stalking, shooting, riding, judo; *Clubs* Vincent's (Oxford); *Style*— Surgn Vice Adm Sir John Rawlins, KBE; ✉ Little Cross, Holne, Newton Abbot, S Devon TQ13 7RS (☎ 01364 631249/400, fax 01364 631400)

RAWLINS, Prof Michael David; s of Rev Jack Rawlins (d 1946), of Kingswinford, Staffs, and Evelyn Daphne, *née* Douglas-Hamilton; *b* 28 March 1941; *Educ* Hawtreys nr Marlborough Wilts, Uppingham, St Thomas' Hosp Med Sch London (BSc, MB BS, MD); *m* 3 Aug 1963, Elizabeth Cadbury Rawlins, JP, da of Edmund Hambly (d 1985), of Seer Green, Bucks; 3 da (Vicky b 1964, Lucy b 1965, Suzannah b 1972); *Career* lectr in med St Thomas' Hosp Med Sch London 1968–71, sr registrar Hammersmith Hosp London 1971–73, MRC visiting res fell Karolinska Inst Stockholm 1972–73, Ruth and Lionel Jacobson prof of clinical pharmacology Univ of Newcastle upon Tyne 1973– (public orator 1990–93), visiting prof Royal Perth Hosp Western Aust 1980, Bradshaw lectr RCP London 1987, William Withering lectr RCP London 1994, Dixon Medal Ulster Med Soc 1994; author of papers on clinical pharmacology and therapeutics; memb: Nat Ctee Pharmacology 1977–83, Cncl St Oswalds Hospice 1977–, Ctee on Toxicity of Chemicals in Food Consumer Prods and Environment 1989–92; chm: Sub Ctee Safety Efficacy and Adverse Reactions 1987–92, Ctee Safety of Meds 1993– (memb 1980–); vice chm Northern Regnl Health Authy 1990–94, pres NE Cncl on Addictions 1990–; MRCP 1968, FRCP London 1977, FRCPE 1987, FFPM 1989, fell RSM; *Books* Variability in Human Drug Response (with S E Smith, 1973); *Recreations* music, golf; *Clubs* Northern Counties; *Style*— Prof Michael Rawlins; ✉ 29 The Grove, Gosforth, Newcastle upon Tyne NE3 1NE; Shoreston House, Shoreston, Seahouses, Northumberland; University of Newcastle, Wolfson Unit of Clinical Pharmacology, Newcastle upon Tyne NE2 4HH (☎ 0191 222 8041, fax 0191 232 3613, e-mail m.d.rawlins@ncl.ac.uk)

RAWLINS, Peter Jonathan; *b* 30 April 1951; *Educ* St Edward's Sch Oxford, Keble Coll Oxford (MA); *m* 1973, Louise, *née* Langton; 1 da (Juliette b 2 Sept 1978), 1 s (Oliver b 19 Feb 1981); *Career* Arthur Andersen: articled clerk 1972–75, ptnr 1983–85, seconded as PA to dep chm and chief exec Lloyd's of London 1983–84; md R W Sturge & Co and dir Sturge Holdings plc (and subsids) 1985–89, chief exec London Stock Exchange 1989–93, independent conslt 1993–96, md (Europe, Middle E and Africa) Siegel & Gale Ltd 1996–; chm Assoc for Research into Stammering in Children; dir Covent Garden Festival Ltd; memb: Royal Nat Theatre Devpt Cncl, Quality of Life Team London First, Advsy Cncl Keble Coll; FCA, FRSA; *Recreations* tennis, squash, clay pigeon shooting, travelling; *Clubs* City of London, MCC; *Style*— Peter Rawlins, Esq; ✉ 15 Lancaster Gardens, London SW19 5DG (☎ 0181 947 3970, fax 0181 944 8497); Siegel & Gale Ltd, 27 Fitzroy Street, London W1P 5AP (☎ 0171 580 0202)

RAWLINSON, Alexander Noel; s and h of Sir Anthony Rawlinson, 5 Bt, *qv*; *b* 15 July 1964; *Style*— Alexander Rawlinson Esq

RAWLINSON, Sir Anthony Henry John; 5 Bt (UK 1891); s of Sir (Alfred) Frederick Rawlinson, 4 Bt (d 1969), and Bess, *née* Emmatt (d 1996); *b* 1 May 1936; *Educ* Millfield; *m* 1, 1960 (m dis 1967), Penelope Byng, da of Rear Adm Gambier John Byng Noel, CB; 1 s, 1 da; m 2, 1967 (m dis 1976), Pauline Strickland, da of John Holt Hardy, of Sydney, NSW; 1 s; m 3, 1977 (separated 1988), Helen Leone, da of Thomas Miller Kennedy, of Glasgow; 1 s; *Heir* s, Alexander Noel Rawlinson, *qv*; *Career* fashion photographer (portraits); *Recreations* tennis, cricket; *Style*— Sir Anthony Rawlinson, Bt; ✉ Heath Farm, Guist, Dereham, Norfolk

RAWLINSON, Charles Frederick Melville; s of Capt Rowland Henry Rawlinson (d 1980); *b* 18 March 1934; *Educ* Canford, Jesus Coll Cambridge (MA); *m* 1962, Jill Rosalind, da of John Wesley; 3 da (incl Julia Caroline b 1964, m 1988, James Ogilvy, s of Hon Sir Angus Ogilvy, and HRH Princess Alexandra); *Career* banker; chm API Group plc 1979–91, dir Willis Faber plc 1981–89, jt chm Morgan Grenfell & Co Ltd (London) 1983–87 (dir 1970–87); sr advsr Morgan Grenfell Group plc 1988–93 (vice chm 1985–88), hon pres Morgan Grenfell Asia Ltd Singapore 1989–93, chm Boxford (Suffolk) Holdings Ltd 1992–; sr advsr West Merchant Bank 1993–; ICAEW: chm IMACE (Industrial Members Advsy Ctee on Ethics) 1991–, memb Chartered Accountants' Jt Ethics Ctee 1994–, memb Jt Disciplinary Scheme Exec Ctee 1995–, memb Cncl 1995–; dir Britten Sinfonia 1989–; Nat Assoc of Boys' Clubs (now NABC - Clubs for Young People): chm 1992–94, hon vice pres 1995–; chm: The Hundred Gp of Finance Directors 1985–86, The Peache Advowson Tst 1982–; FCA 1958, FCT 1984; *Recreations* music, shooting, sailing; *Clubs* Brooks's; *Style*— Charles Rawlinson, Esq; ✉ The Old Forge, Arkesden, Saffron Walden, Essex CB11 4EX (☎ 01799 550315)

RAWLINSON, William; CBE (1978); s of David Rawlinson (d 1950), of London, and Ann Markus (d 1974); *b* 10 Sept 1916; *Educ* Balliol Coll Oxford (MA); *m* 29 July 1954, Marietta, *née* Pordes; *Career* Nat Serv Flt Lt RAF 1941–46; called to the Bar Inner Temple 1939; memb Govt Legal Serv 1948–81; since 1972 deals with EEC Law and policy; lectr on EEC Civil Serv Coll, lectr Univ of Southern California, California State Univ and Bar Ilan Univ 1982; contrib: Int Fin Law Review 1982–90, Fordham Int Law Jl 1989–90; stipendiary mt magistrate London (sitting periodically) 1970–79; *Books* European Community Law (now second expanded edn); *Recreations* reading, music; *Clubs* Reform; *Style*— William Rawlinson, Esq, CBE; ✉ 11 Kings Bench Walk, Temple, London EC4Y 7EQ (☎ 0171 583 0610, fax 0171 583 9123)

RAWLINSON OF EWELL, Baron (Life Peer UK 1978), of Ewell, Co Surrey; Peter Anthony Grayson Rawlinson; kt (1962), PC (1964), QC (1959, NI 1972); s of Lt-Col Arthur Richard Rawlinson, OBE (d 1984), of Ferring, Sussex, and Ailsa, eldest da of Sir Henry Grayson, 1 Bt, KBE; *b* 26 June 1919; *Educ* Downside, Christ's Coll Cambridge (exhibitioner 1938, hon fellow 1981); *m* 1, 1940 (m annulled by Sacred Rota Rome 1954), Haidée, da of Gerald Kavanagh, of Dublin; 3 da; m 2, 1954, his 1 cous, Elaine, da of Vincent Dominguez, of Rhode Island, and Angela, 6 da of Sir Henry Grayson, 1 Bt, KBE; 2 s, 1 da; *Career* sits as Cons peer in House of Lords; Maj Irish Gds WWII (despatches); called to the Bar Inner Temple 1946, bencher 1962, reader 1983, treas 1984; recorder of Salisbury 1960–62, called to the Bar NI 1972, recorder of Kingston upon Thames 1975, ldr Western Circuit 1975–82, ret from Bar 1985; chm of the Bar 1975–76, pres Senate Inns of Courts and Bar 1986–87; Parly candidate (C) Hackney S 1951; MP (C): Surrey Epsom 1955–74, Epsom and Ewell 1974–78; slr-gen 1962–64, attorney-gen 1970–74; author 1989–; *Books* incl: A Price Too High (autobiog, 1989), 4 novels; *Clubs* White's, Pratt's, RAC, MCC; *Style*— The Rt Hon the Lord Rawlinson of Ewell, PC, QC; ✉ 9 Priory Walk, London SW10 9SP

RAWNSLEY, Andrew Nicholas James; s of Eric Rawnsley, and Barbara, *née* Butler; *b* 5 Jan 1962; *Educ* Rugby, Sidney Sussex Coll Cambridge (MA); *Career* writer and broadcaster; BBC 1983–85, The Guardian 1985–93 (political columnist 1987–93), assoc ed and political columnist The Observer 1993–; presenter: Channel 4 TV series A Week in Politics 1989–, ITV series The Agenda 1996–; Student Journalist of the Year 1983, Young Journalist of the Year 1987; *Recreations* House of Commons; *Style*— Andrew Rawnsley, Esq; ✉ The Guardian Newspaper, 119 Farringdon Rd, London EC1R 3ER (☎ 0171 278 2332, fax 0171 837 2114, telex 8811746 GUARDN G)

RAWSON, Christopher Selwyn Priestley; s of Cdr S G C Rawson, OBE, RN (d 1974), and Dr Doris Rawson, *née* Brown (d 1979); *b* 25 March 1928; *Educ* The Elms Sch Colwall Worcs, The Nautical Coll Pangbourne; *m* 24 Jan 1959, Rosemary Ann, da of Alex R Focke (d 1983); 2 da (Gina b 16 Jan 1961, Caroline b 22 March 1964); *Career* navigating apprentice Merchant Serv T & J Brocklebank Ltd 1945–48, mangr John Crossley & Sons Ltd Halifax 1948–53, London rep of Milford Docks Ltd 1953–60, chm and md Christopher Rawson Ltd 1960–80; Sheriff City of London 1961–62, common councilman Ward of Bread St 1963–72, JP City of London Bench 1972–92 and Inner London 1967–72, Alderman Ward of Lime St 1972–83, HM Lt City of London 1980–83, CStJ; Master Worshipful Co of Clothworkers 1988 (Liveryman 1952, Asst 1977), Master Co of Watermen and Lightermen 1982–84 (Freeman 1966, Asst 1974), Yr Bro Trinity House 1988; assoc Textile Inst 1953; Cdr Order of: Senegal 1961, Ivory Coast 1961, Liberia 1962; *Recreations* shooting, sailing; *Clubs* Garrick, Royal London Yacht (Cdre 1990–91), City Livery Yacht (Cdre 1987–90); *Style*— Christopher Rawson, Esq; ✉ 23 Cristowe Road, London SW6 3QF

RAWSON, Dr Jessica Mary; *née* Quirk; CBE (1994); da of Roger Nathaniel Quirk, CB (d 1964), and Paula, *née* Weber; *b* 1 Jan 1943; *Educ* St Paul's Girls' Sch, New Hall Cambridge (BA, MA, LittD), SOAS London (BA); *m* May 1968, John Graham Rawson, s of Graham Stanhope Rawson (d 1953); 1 da (Josephine b 1972); *Career* asst princ Miny of Health 1965–67; Dept of Oriental Antiquities Br Museum: asst keeper II 1967–71, asst keeper I 1971–76, dep keeper 1976–87, keeper 1987–94; warden Merton Coll Oxford 1994–; guest prof Heidelberg Univ Kunst Historiches Institut 1989, visiting prof Dept of Art Univ of Chicago 1994; vice-chm GB China Centre 1985–87, chm Oriental Ceramic Soc 1993–; Barlow Lecture Univ of Sussex 1979 and 1994, Levintritt Meml Lecture Harvard Univ 1989, British Acad Albert Reckitt Archaeological Lecture 1989, A J Pope Meml Lecture Smithsonian Inst Washington 1991, Harvey Buchanan Lecture Cleveland Museum of Art 1993; FBA 1990; *Books* Animals in Art (1977), Ancient China, Art and Archaeology (1980), Chinese Ornament, the Lotus and the Dragon (1984), Chinese Bronzes, Art and Ritual (1987), Ancient Chinese Bronzes in the Collection of Bella and PP Chiu (1988), Western Zhou Bronzes from the Arthur M Sackler Collections (1990), Ancient Chinese and Ordos Bronzes (with Emma Bunker, 1990), British Museum Book of Chinese Art (ed, 1992), Chinese Jade from the Neolithic to the Qing (1995), Mysteries of Ancient China: New Discoveries from the Early Dynasties (1996); *Style*— Dr Jessica Rawson, CBE, FBA; ✉ 19 Merton Street, Oxford OX1 4JE (☎ 01865 276368); Merton College, Oxford OX1 4JD (☎ 01865 276351, fax 01865 276282)

RAWSON, Prof Kenneth John; s of Arthur William Rawson (d 1949), and Beatrice Annie, *née* Standing (d 1990); *b* 27 Oct 1926; *Educ* Northern GS Portsmouth, RNC Greenwich, UCL, Brunel Univ (MSc); *m* 29 July 1950, Rhona Florence, *née* Gill, da of William Henry Gill, MBE (d 1992), of Norton St Philip; 2 s (Christopher John b 1955, Timothy James b 1981), 1 da (Hilary Anne b 1958); *Career* at sea 1950–51, structural research 1951–53, forward design Admty 1953–57, with Lloyd's Register of Shipping 1957–59, ship designer MOD 1959–69, naval staff 1969–72, prof UCL 1972–77, head of forward design MOD 1977–79, chief naval architect MOD 1979–83; Brunel Univ 1983–89 (prof, dean of educn and design, pro vice chllr); William Froude Gold Medal 1994, Hon DEng Univ of Portsmouth 1996; hon vice pres RINA 1993; FEng 1983, FRINA 1961, FCSD 1984, FRSA 1984; *Style*— Prof Kenneth Rawson, FEng; ✉ Moorlands The Street, Chilcompton, Bath BA3 4HB (☎ 01761 232793)

RAWSON, Dr Malcolm David; s of Stanley Ronald Rawson, OBE (d 1977), and Phyllis Elizabeth, *née* Birkin (d 1988); *b* 26 June 1933; *Educ* Leeds GS, Univ of Leeds Med Sch (MD); *m* 8 June 1963 (m dis 1988), Janet Elizabeth Rees, da of Clifford Lodge (d 1981);

1 s (James b 1966), 2 da (Edwina b 1965, Felicity b 1970), 2 step da (Clare b 1956, Caroline b 1961); *Career* sr registrar in neurology (former registrar) Manchester Royal Infirmary 1963–70, sr res fell in neurology Yale Univ Med Sch New Haven Conn USA 1966–67, conslt neurologist Hull Royal Infirmary Yorks RHA 1969–; memb Cncl N of England Neurological Assoc, pres Hull Med Soc 1980, dir Postgrad Educn Hull 1984–89; FRCR 1976, FRCP 1977; *Recreations* salmon and trout fishing, fell walking, skiing; *Style*— Dr Malcolm Rawson; ✉ 19 The Paddocks, Kirk Ella, Hull HU10 7PF (☎ 01482 655351); Hull Royal Infirmary, Anlaby Road, Hull HU3 2KZ (☎ 01482 28541)

RAWSTHORNE, Anthony Robert; s of Frederic Leslie Rawsthorne (d 1991), and Nora, *née* Yates, of Blundellsands, nr Liverpool; *b* 25 Jan 1943; *Educ* Ampleforth, Wadham Coll Oxford (MA); *m* 18 Dec 1967, Beverley Jean, da of Richard Osborne, and Jean; 1 s (Richard Anthony b 1968), 2 da (Josephine Alice b 1969, Mary-Anne b 1969); *Career* Home Office 1966–: various positions incl Prison Dept, Race Relations Div, Criminal Dept 1966–77, head Crime Policy Planning Unit 1977–79, head Personnel Div 1979–82, sec Falkland Islands Review Ctee 1982, princ private sec to Home Sec 1983, head of div Immigration and Nationality Dept 1983–86, head Establishment Dept 1986–91, head Equal Opportunities and General Dept 1991, under sec/dep DG Policy and Nationality Immigration and Nationality Dept 1991–; *Recreations* bridge, cycling, squash, looking at pictures; *Style*— Anthony Rawsthorne, Esq; ✉ Immigration and Nationality Directorate, Home Office, Apollo House, 36 Wellesley Road, Croydon CR9 2BY (☎ 0181 760 8524, fax 0181 760 8529)

RAY, Edward Ernest; CBE (1988); s of Walter James Ray (d 1968), of London, and Cecilia May, *née* Hampton; *b* 6 Nov 1924; *Educ* Holloway Co Sch, Univ of London (BCom); *m* 2 July 1949, Margaret Elizabeth, da of (Stanley) George Bull (d 1964), of Kettering, Northants; 2 s (Andrew John b 26 Nov 1952, Patrick Charles b 17 March 1956); *Career* Petty Offr RN 1943–46; CA, sr ptnr Spicer and Oppenheim (formerly Spicer and Pegler) 1984–88 (ptnr 1957–88), chm London CAs 1972–73, inspr DTI, bd memb Securities and Investmt Bd 1984–90, chm Investors Compensation Scheme 1988–90; memb: Worshipful Co of CAs 1975, Freeman City of London; FCA (pres ICAEW 1982 and 1983); *Books* VAT for Businessmen (1972), Partnership Taxation (3 edn 1987); *Recreations* golf, tennis, walking and bird watching; *Clubs* City of London; *Style*— Edward Ray, Esq, CBE; ✉ Southgate, Wiveton Rd, Blakeney, Norfolk NR25 7NJ (☎ 01263 740603)

RAY, Elizabeth Mary; da of Rev Henry Cleeve Brocklehurst (d 1942), of Chalfont St Giles, Bucks, and Gwenna Maud, *née* Jones (d 1971); *b* 1 Oct 1925; *Educ* privately, LSE (Dip Soc Sci and Admin); *m* 22 May 1953, Cyril Ray (d 1991), s of Albert Benson Ray (d 1954), of Lytham St Annes; 1 s (Jonathan Cleeve b 1960); *Career* food writer; contrib: Homes and Gardens, A La Carte, numerous other magazines; cookery corr Observer 1969–79, contrib Sunday Telegraph 1990–92; social worker: LCC 1956–60, GLC 1964–68, Kent CC Social Servs 1972–83; freelance study supervisor Social Servs Course (Sussex) 1983–87; JP: Kent 1968–81, E Sussex 1981–94; memb: Bd of Visitors HM Prison Lewes 1984–89, Mgmnt Cncl Kent Opera 1970–89, E Sussex Probation Ctee 1989–94; memb Guild of Food Writers; *Books* Wine with Food (with Cyril Ray, 1976), Best of Eliza Acton (1968), Resourceful Cook (1975), Country Cooking (1978), Alexis Soyer - Cook Extraordinary (1991); *Recreations* travel, listening to music, cooking; *Clubs* University Women's (chm 1993–95); *Style*— Mrs Elizabeth Ray, JP; ✉ Flat 2, 66 Regency Square, Brighton BN1 2FF (☎ 01273 726171)

RAY, Malcolm John; s of George Henry Ray (d 1985), and Lucy, *née* Roberts (d 1985); *b* 27 Aug 1938; *Educ* Bilston GS, Univ of Aston (BSc, MSc); *m* 6 Sept 1962, Betty Maria, da of Whitmore Nicholls (d 1968), of Staffs; 1 s (Jonathan b 1974); *Career* GKN Technology Ltd 1953–70, Hycast Ltd (tech dir) 1970–75, sales dir Rylands Whitecross Ltd Warrington 1976–81, md Catton & Co Ltd Leeds 1981–87; chm and md: Birmid Holdings Ltd 1990–, Birmid Components Ltd; chm: PBM Components Ltd 1987–, Darcast Components Ltd 1987–, Thyssen Industrie Holdings (UK) Plc 1990–, Birmid Holdings Pension Trustees Ltd 1990–; dir: QDF Components Ltd 1995–, Thyssen Guss (Essen Germany) 1996–; vice pres The Inst of Br Foundrymen; govr Solihull Sixth Form Coll; Liveryman Worshipful Co of Founders 1991; MIBF 1964, MIMgt 1974, FIM 1975, CEng 1976, MInstM 1976; *Recreations* golf, game fishing, walking; *Style*— Malcolm Ray, Esq; ✉ Thatched Cottage, Hill Wootton, Warwick CV35 7PP (☎ 01926 50 309); Birmid Holdings Ltd, 6 The Quadrangle, Cranmore Ave, Shirley, Solihull, West Midlands B90 4LE (☎ 0121 711 4555, fax 0121 711 4447)

RAY, Robin; s of Ted Ray, and Sybil, *née* Stevens; *Educ* Highgate Sch, RADA; *m* 1960, Susan, da of Alan Stranks; 1 s (Rupert b 1979); *Career* actor, author, broadcaster; West End debut The Changeling (Royal Court) 1960, extensive work in theatre, radio and TV, especially music and arts, stage play Café Puccini (Wyndhams) 1986, drama critic Punch 1986–87, music conslt Classic FM Radio 1989–, co-author/narrator Let's Do It (Chichester) 1994, creative dir Performance Channel TV 1996–; *Style*— Robin Ray, Esq; ✉ c/o David Wilkinson Associates, 115 Hazlebury Road, London SW6 2LX (☎ 0171 371 5188, fax 0171 371 5161)

RAY, Sidney; *b* 5 Oct 1939; *Educ* Owen's Sch London, North London Poly (BSc), The Polytechnic Regent St, City Univ London (MSc); *m*; 2 s; *Career* cadet instr and RAF civilian instr ATC 1956–68; photographer and lectr in photography; asst chemist Res Laboratories Gas Cncl 1959–60, photographic chemist Johnsons of Hendon Ltd 1960–66, pt/t lectr 1962–66, lectr Univ of Westminster (formerly Poly of Central London) 1966–, examiner various colls and courses 1972–, organiser of confs 1978–, conslt for govt depts, industry, publishers and others; regular contributor Br Jl of Photography, contributing ed Photoresearcher magazine; regular book reviewer: British Book News, The Photographer, The Photogrammetric Record, Jl of Photographic Science, Photoresearcher, Professional Photographer; numerous articles in photographic jls, many hundreds of photographs published, author of 14 photographic textbooks and contributor to 8 others; accredited sr imaging scientist 1994; memb: NATFHE, Photogrammetric Soc, Euro Soc for the History of Photography, The Steroscopic Soc, Cinema Theatre Assoc, Greater London Industl Archaeology Soc, Assoc of Historical and Fine Art Photographers; FRPS 1972, FBIPP 1974, fell Master Photographers Assoc 1986, fell Royal Microscopical Soc 1992; *Style*— Sidney Ray, Esq; ✉ University of Westminster, Faculty of Communication, Watford Road, Northwick Park, Harrow HA1 3TP (☎ 0171 911 5000 ext 4531, fax 0171 911 5939)

RAYANANONDA, HE Vidhya; *b* 2 March 1942; *Educ* BA Int Rels (Thammasat Univ Thailand), MA (USA), Nat Def Coll Thailand; *m* Nantana; 2 da; *Career* Thai diplomat; successively: third sec Royal Thai Embassy Washington DC, second sec SE Asian Div Political Affrs Dept, first sec Royal Thai Embassy Manila, dir Far East Div Political Affrs Dept, dep DG Political Affrs Dept, dep DG Info Dept, consul-gen Los Angeles, ambass attached to Miny of Foreign Affrs, dep sec-gen then sec-gen to PM, DG Protocol Dept Miny of Foreign Affrs, ambass to Swiss Confedn and Holy See, ambass to the Ct of St James's Nov 1994–; *Style*— HE Mr Vidhya Rayananonda; ✉ The Royal Thai Embassy, 1/3 Yorkshire House, Grosvenor Crescent, London SW1X 7EP

RAYER, Michael Anthony; s of Alick Anthony Rayer, of Cardiff, and Carole Mary, *née* Hill; *b* 21 July 1965; *Educ* Bishop Hannon RC HS, Rumney Tech Coll; *m* 14 July 1990, Debra Ann, da of Leonard Charles Tout; 1 da (Abigail Ann b 5 Jan 1991), 1 s (Lloyd Anthony b 4 Nov 1992); *Career* Rugby Union fullback; clubs: Llandudno, Cardiff; Wales: 19 full caps (debut v W Samoa 1991), Five Nations debut 1992; capt Wales B Baseball team 1990–91; former sheetmetal worker, currently salesman; *Recreations* golf; *Style*— Michael Rayer, Esq; ✉ c/o Cardiff RFC, Cardiff Arms Park, Westgate Street, Cardiff, South Glamorgan (☎ 01222 383546)

RAYFIELD, Tom; JP (1993); s of Alfred John Rayfield, and Doris Caryl, *née* Lyons; *b* 15 Feb 1941; *Educ* Watford GS, Queens' Coll Cambridge (exhibitioner, MA); *m* 15 Oct 1971, Rosemary Jean, da of John Fearon; 2 s (Tobias Stephen Fearon b 3 Jan 1974, Joe Daniel Fearon b 9 June 1977); *Career* J Walter Thompson: joined as copywriter 1963, transferred NY office 1966–67, creative gp head London 1967–73, creative dir and bd memb 1973–74; creative dir/bd dir: Lintas 1974–75, The Kirkwood Company 1975–77; J Walter Thompson: rejoined as creative dir/bd dir 1978–95, chm and creative dir JWT Direct 1988–95; freelance writer 1996–; memb and former vice pres Advertising Creative Circle; memb: D&AD 1969, BDMA; MIPA 1973; *Publications* Dear Personalised (1992), Great Call Reports (1992), Dear Sir or Madam (1993), Fifty in Forty (1996); *Recreations* collecting signed first editions, golf; *Clubs* Weston Turville Golf; *Style*— Tom Rayfield, Esq, JP; ✉ The Blacksmiths, Radnage Common, Bucks HP14 4DH (☎ 01494 483986, fax 01494 484458)

RAYLEIGH, 6 Baron (UK 1821) John Gerald Strutt; s of Hon Charles Richard Strutt (d 1981; s of 4 Baron Rayleigh), and Hon Mrs (Jean Elizabeth) Strutt; suc uncle 5 Baron Rayleigh 1988; *b* 4 June 1960; *Educ* Eton, RAC Cirencester; *m* 2 May 1991, Annabel Kate, yst da of Maj William Garry Patterson, Life Guards, and Hon Sandra Debonnaire, *née* Monson, da of 10 Baron Monson; 2 s (Hon John Frederick b 29 March 1993, Hon William Hedley Charles b 11 Nov 1994); *Heir* s, Hon John Frederick Strutt, b 29 March 1993; *Career* Lt Welsh Guards (ret); chm Lord Rayleigh's Farms Inc; Liveryman: Worshipful Co of Grocers, Worshipful Co of Farmers; *Style*— The Rt Hon the Lord Rayleigh; ✉ Terling Place, Chelmsford, Essex CM3 2PJ

RAYMOND, Diana Joan; da of Lt William Thomas Young, RA (d 1917), and Hilda Joan Drummond, *née* Black (d 1952); *b* 25 April 1916; *Educ* Cheltenham Ladies' Coll; *m* 12 Aug 1940, Ernest Raymond, s of Maj-Gen George Frederic Blake, RM (d 1904); 1 s (Peter John Francis b 1 June 1941); *Career* author; *Books* Joanna Linden (1952), The Small Rain (1954), Between the Stirrup and the Ground (1956), Strangers' Gallery (1958), The Five Days (1959), Guest of Honour (1960), The Climb (1962), People in the House (1967), Are You Travelling Alone? (1969), The Best of the Day (1972), Incident on a Summer's Day (1974), Horseman Pass By (1977), The Dark Journey (1978), Emma Pride (1981), The Dancers All Are Gone (1983), House of the Dolphin (1985), Lily's Daughter (1988), Roundabout (1995); *Recreations* reading, travel, walking; *Style*— Mrs Diana Raymond; ✉ 22 Pryors, East Heath Rd, London NW3 1BS (☎ 0171 435 3716)

RAYMOND, Paul; *b* 15 Nov 1925; *Educ* St Francis Xaviers Coll Liverpool, Glossop GS Glossop Derbyshire; *children* 1 s (Howard b 23 Nov 1959), 1 da (Deborah b 28 Jan 1956 d 1992); *Career* RAF 1944–47; musician, music hall artiste, impresario, night club proprietor, publisher, West End property owner; memb Grand Order of Water Rats; *Style*— Paul Raymond, Esq; ✉ Arlington St, London SW1; Paul Raymond Organisation Ltd, 2 Archer St, London W1V 7HF (☎ 0171 734 9191, fax 0171 734 5030)

RAYMOND, Peter James; s of George Arthur Raymond (d 1986), of Tunbridge Wells, and Joyce, *née* Goodwin; *b* 16 Feb 1947; *Educ* Tonbridge Sch; *m* (sep); 1 s (Tom b 26 June 1974), 1 da (Anna b 16 Feb 1978); *Career* Cripps Harries Hall: joined 1967, admitted slr 1969, ptnr 1972–, head Private Client Dept 1990–96; memb Cncl Law Soc 1996–; pres Tonbridge and Dist Law Soc 1989 (former sec); memb Cncl South of Eng Agric Soc 1971–86, memb Tunbridge Wells AHA, vice-pres Cncl League of Friends Pembury Hosp (former chm), hon slr Crowborough Citizens' Advice Bureau; *Style*— Peter Raymond, Esq; ✉ Cripps Harries Hall, Croham House, Croham Road, Crowborough, East Sussex TN6 2RL (☎ 01892 662233, fax 01892 601010)

RAYMOND, William Francis (Frank); CBE (1978); s of Capt Leonard William Raymond, ISO (d 1973), of Maidenhead, Berks, and May Raymond, MBE, *née* Bennett (d 1973); *b* 25 Feb 1922; *Educ* Bristol GS, Queen's Coll Oxford (BA, MA); *m* 13 Aug 1949, Amy Elizabeth (Betty), da of Maj Charles Kingston Kelk (d 1993); 3 s (Christopher b 1950, Robin b 1954, Charles b 1959), 1 da (Karen b 1952); *Career* res scientist: MRC 1943–45, Grassland Res Inst 1945–72 (asst dir 1962–72); chief scientist MAFF London 1980–82 (dep chief scientist 1972–80); agric sci conslt: EEC, FAO, World Bank; visiting prof of agric Wye Coll London 1978–83, chm Int Review of Danish Agric Res 1992, memb Int Review of Agric Res Centre of Finland 1996; hon treas Soc for the Responsible Use of Resources in Agric and on the Land (Rural); memb Policy Ctee Cncl for the Protection of Rural England (CPRE) 1993–96, chm Stapledon Meml Tst 1982–92; FRSC, CChem 1962; *Books* Forage Conservation and Feeding (with Waltham, 5 edn 1996); *Recreations* gardening; *Clubs* Farmers'; *Style*— Frank Raymond, Esq, CBE; ✉ Periwinkle Cottage, Christmas Common, Watlington, Oxon OX9 5HR (☎ 01491 612942)

RAYNE, Baron (Life Peer UK 1976), of Prince's Meadow in Greater London; Max Rayne; kt (1969); er s of Phillip and Deborah Rayne; *b* 8 Feb 1918; *Educ* Central Fndn Sch, UCL; *m* 1, 1941 (m dis 1960), Margaret, da of Louis Marco; 1 s (Hon Robert Anthony b 1949), 2 da (Hon Madeleine Barbara (Hon Mrs Rayner) b 1943, Hon Susan Ann (Hon Mrs Rubin) b 1945); m 2, 1965, Lady Jane Antonia Frances Vane-Tempest-Stewart, da of 8 Marquess of Londonderry, JP, DL; 2 s (Hon Nicholas Alexander b 1969, Hon Alexander Philip b 1973), 2 da (Hon Natasha Deborah b 1966, Hon Tamara Annabel b 1970); *Career* served WWII RAF; chm: London Merchant Securities plc 1960–, Westpool Investment Trust plc 1980–; non-exec dir First Leisure Corporation plc 1995– (dep chm 1984–92, chm 1992–95); dep chm British Lion Films 1967–72, dir Housing Corp (1974) Ltd 1974–78; chm: London Festival Ballet Trust 1967–75, Nat Theatre Bd 1971–88; govr: St Thomas' Hosp 1962–74 (special tstee 1974–92), Royal Ballet Sch 1966–79, Yehudi Menuhin Sch 1966–87 (vice pres 1987–), Malvern Coll 1966–, Centre for Environmental Studies 1967–73; memb: Gen Cncl King Edward VII's Hosp Fund for London 1966–96, Cncl RADA 1973–, South Bank Bd 1986–92, Cncl of Govrs United Medical Sch of Guy's and St Thomas' Hosps 1982–89; fndr patron Rayne Fndn 1962–, hon vice-pres Jewish Care (formerly Jewish Welfare Bd) 1966–, life vice pres Motability 1996– (fndr memb 1977–96); hon fellow: Darwin Coll Cambridge 1966, UCL 1966, LSE 1974, King's Coll Hosp Med Sch 1980, Univ Coll Oxford 1982, King's Coll London 1983, Westminster Sch 1989, RCP 1992, UMDS Guy's and St Thomas's Hosps 1992; Hon FRCPsych 1977, Hon LLD Univ of London 1968; Officier Légion d'Honneur 1987 (Chevalier 1973); *Style*— The Rt Hon the Lord Rayne; ✉ 33 Robert Adam St, London W1M 5AH (☎ 0171 935 3555)

RAYNE, Hon Robert Anthony; s of Baron Rayne by his 1 w, Margaret; *b* 1949; *m* Jane, da of late Robert Blackburn, the aviation pioneer; 1 s; *Career* dir: London Merchant Securities Plc 1983–, First Leisure Corporation plc 1983–, Westpool Investment Trust plc 1984–, Ballet Rambert Ltd 1991–; chm: Cullens Holdings plc, Golden Rose Communications 1993–; govr Eastman Dental Hosp Special Health Authy 1990–96; *Recreations* art, cycling; *Style*— The Hon Robert A Rayne; ✉ London Merchant Securities plc, Carlton House, 33 Robert Adam Street, London W1M 5AH (☎ 0171 935 3555, fax 0171 935 3737)

RAYNER, Prof Anthony John; s of Cyril Spencer Rayner, of E Markham, Newark, Notts, and Lucy Mary, *née* Boothroyd; *b* 27 Aug 1943; *Educ* King Edward VI GS Retford, Univ of Cambridge (BA, MA), Univ of Manchester (PhD); *m* 1 July 1967, Patricia Florence, da of James Leonard Kester, of Radcliffe-on-Trent, Notts; 1 s (John b 1977), 2 da (Catherine b 1971, Clare b 1973); *Career* lectr Univ of Manchester 1969–73 (asst lectr 1967–69), prof Univ of Nottingham 1980– (reader 1973–80); author of numerous scientific papers; memb AES; *Books* contrib: Resource Structure of Agriculture - An Economic Analysis (1970), The Demand for Food - An Exercise in Household Budget Analysis (1972), Agricultural Marketing Boards - An International Perspective (1979), Forecasting Milk Supply (1982), Price and Market Policies in European Agriculture (1984), Current Issues in Development Economics (1991), Case Studies in Economic Development - Policy Adjustments in Africa (1991), Current Issues in Agricultural Economics (1993), Agriculture in the Uruguay Round (1994); *Recreations* cricket, badminton, gardening; *Style*— Prof Anthony Rayner; ✉ Department of Economics, The University of Nottingham, University Park, Nottingham NG7 2RD (☎ 0115 951 5462)

RAYNER, Claire Berenice; OBE (1996); *b* 22 Jan 1931; *Educ* City of London Sch for Girls, Royal Northern Hosp Sch of Nursing (SRN, awarded Hosp Gold medal for outstanding achievement), Guy's Hosp; *m* 1958, Desmond Rayner; 2 s (Adam, Jay), 1 da (Amanda); *Career* sister Paediatric Dept Whittington Hosp; writer, broadcaster and public speaker; Woman's Own: as Ruth Martin 1966–75, own by-line 1975–88; Woman Magazine 1988–; radio appearances incl: Woman's Hour, Schools, Today, Contact (BBC Wales), Mike Aspel Show (Capital Radio London) 1982–85, Claire Rayner Living With....., Myself When Young (BBC Radio 2) 1990–; TV appearances incl: Pebble Mill at One, Kitchen Garden, Claire Rayner's Casebook (BBC) 1980–84, TV-am 1986–92, Sky TV 1989–90; former advice columnist: Petticoat, The Sun 1972–80, Today 1988–92, The Sunday Mirror 1980–88; awarded Best Specialist Columnist Publisher Magazine 1988; hon fell Univ of North London 1988; Freeman City of London 1981; *Books* Over 90 (some under the pseudonyms of Sheila Brandon and Ann Lynton) incl: The Meddlers, A Time to Heal, The Running Years, Clinical Judgements, The Performers (12 vol family sequence, translated into several languages), The Poppy Chronicles (6 vol sequence), The George Barnabas novels; contrib: Design magazine (the journal of the Design Council), The Lancet, Medical World, Nursing Times, Nursing Mirror, UK national newspapers and leading magazines; *Clubs* Royal Soc of Medicine, Royal Soc of Arts; *Style*— Mrs Claire Rayner, OBE; ✉ PO Box 125, Harrow, Middx HA1 3XE

RAYNER, Colin Robert; s of Charles Wilfred Rayner, of Brighton, and Helen Patricia, *née* Rolling; *b* 28 Oct 1938; *Educ* St George's Coll Weybridge Surrey, Middx Hosp Univ of London (MB BS, MS); *m* 1 Jan 1966, Margaret Mary, da of Harold Salt (d 1973), of Cheltenham; 1 s (Dominic James b 5 Feb 1969), 2 da (Clare Rachel b 9 Nov 1967, Suzannah Louise b 15 March 1971); *Career* Ethicon res fell 1974, John Lawson fell Westminster Hosp 1975, conslt plastic surgn Aberdeen Royal Infirmary and Royal Aberdeen Children's Hosp 1978–91; dir of clinical burns res and conslt plastic surgeon Birmingham Accident Hosp and Selly Oak Hosp Birmingham Dec 1991–June 1992, dir of burns and plastic surgery S Birmingham Health Authy July 1992–95, dir of plastic surgery University Hosp Birmingham 1995–; over 40 scientific pubns; Pulvertaft prize (hand surgery) 1976, Assoc of Surgns special educnl award 1981; chm Ethical Ctee and memb Nat Disaster Planning Ctee Br Assoc of Plastic Surgns, advsr to Soviet Govt at time of train disaster 1989; memb: Br Soc Surgery of Hand, Br Assoc Head and Neck Oncologists, Br Assoc Plastic Surgns; FRCS 1969, FRCSEd 1980; *Recreations* skiing, opera, developing international medical relationships; *Style*— Colin Rayner, Esq; ✉ University Hospital, Raddlebarn Road, Selly Oak, Birmingham B29 6JD (☎ 0121 627 1627, fax 0121 627 8794)

RAYNER, Baron (Life Peer UK 1983), of Crowborough in Co of East Sussex; Derek George Rayner; kt (1973); s of George William Rayner; *b* 30 March 1926; *Educ* City Coll Norwich, Selwyn Cambridge; *Career* Marks & Spencer: joined 1953, dir 1967–, jt md 1973–91, jt vice chm 1982, chief exec 1983–88, chm 1984–91; special advsr to Govt 1970, chief exec Procurement Exec Mgmnt Bd MOD 1971–72, memb UK Permanent Security Cmmn 1977–80, dep chm Civil Service Pay Board 1978–80, adviser to PM on improving efficiency in Civil Service 1979–82; former memb: Design Cncl, Cncl of Royal Coll of Art; pres The Med Coll St Bartholomew's Hosp London 1988–93, tstee Royal Botanic Gardens Kew Fndn 1992–94; Liveryman Worshipful Co of Fruiterers; hon fell: Selwyn Coll Cambridge, Shenkar Coll Israel; Hon DPhil Bar Ilan Univ Israel, Hon DUniv Surrey; *Clubs* Athenaeum; *Style*— The Rt Hon the Lord Rayner; ✉ c/o Marks & Spencer, Michael House, Baker St, London W1

RAYNER JAMES, Jonathan Elwyn; QC (1988); s of Basil James, and Moira Holding, *née* Rayner; *b* 25 July 1950; *Educ* King's Coll Sch Wimbledon, Christ's Coll Cambridge (MA, LLB), Univ of Brussels (grad course Licencie Special en Droit Europeen (Grande Distinction)); *m* 3 Jan 1981, Anne James, *née* McRae; 1 s (Daniel Charles b 23 Dec 1981); *Career* called to the Bar Lincoln's Inn 1971 (Hardwick entrance scholar, Eastham (Maj) scholar), in practice specialising in intellectual property Chancery Bar 1975–, Bencher Lincoln's Inn 1994, asst recorder of the Crown Court 1994–; memb Editorial Bd Entertainment Law Review 1990–; memb: Chancery Bar Assoc 1975, Patent Bar Assoc and Centrebar 1975; *Books* EEC Anti-Trust Law (co-author, 1975), Executors and Administrators, Halsbury Laws (co-ed 4 edn vol 17, 1976), Copinger and Skone James on Copyright (co-ed 12 edn, 1980 and 13 edn, 1991), The Encyclopaedia of Forms and Precedents (jt consltg ed for Intellectual Property matters vol 15, 1989); *Recreations* France; *Clubs* RAC; *Style*— Jonathan Rayner James, Esq, QC; ✉ 5 New Square, First Floor, Lincoln's Inn, London WC2A 3RJ (☎ 0171 404 0404, fax 0171 831 6016)

RAYNES, Prof (Edward) Peter; s of Edward Gordon Raynes (d 1995), and Ethel Mary, *née* Wood (d 1994); *b* 4 July 1945; *Educ* St Peter's York, Gonville and Caius Coll Cambridge (MA, PhD); *m* 19 Sept 1970, Madeline, da of Cecil Ord (d 1967); 2 s (Michael b 1974, Andrew b 1977); *Career* dep chief scientific offr Royal Signals and Radar Establishment Malvern until 1992 (joined 1971), dir of research Sharp Laboratories of Europe Ltd 1995– (chief scientist 1992–95); hon prof Sch of Chem Univ of Hull 1990–; FRS 1987, FInstP; *Books* Liquid Crystals: Their Physics, Chemistry and Applications (with C Hilsum 1983); *Recreations* choral and solo singing; *Style*— Prof Peter Raynes, FRS; ✉ 23 Leadon Rd, Malvern, Worcs WR14 2XF (☎ 01684 565497); Sharp Laboratories of Europe Ltd, Edmund Halley Road, Oxford Science Park, Oxford OX4 4GA (☎ 01865 747711, fax 01865 747717)

RAYNHAM, Viscount; Charles George Townshend; s and h of 7 Marquess Townshend, *qv*; *b* 26 Sept 1945; *Educ* Eton, Royal Agricultural College Cirencester; *m* 1, 1975, Hermione (d 1985), da of Lt-Cdr Robert Martin Dominic Ponsonby; 1 s, 1 da (Hon Louise b 1979); m 2, 6 Dec 1990, Mrs Alison Marshall, yr da of Sir Willis Ide Combs, KCVO, CMG (d 1994); *Heir* s, Hon Thomas Charles Townshend b 2 Nov 1977; *Career* dir Pera International 1986–96 (chm 1992–94), md The Raynham Workshops Ltd 1984–93, gen cmmr for Income Tax Norwich 1986–95; memb Cncl Royal Agricultural Soc of England; *Style*— Viscount Raynham; ✉ 22 Ebury Street, London SW1W 0LU

RAYNOR, Philip Ronald; QC (1994); s of Wilfred Raynor, of Leeds, and Sheila, *née* Zermansky; *b* 20 Jan 1950; *Educ* Roundhay Sch Leeds, Christ's Coll Cambridge (scholar, MA); *m* 20 Oct 1974, Judith Marion, da of late Gustav Braunsberg; 1 da (Michelle Stephanie b 10 Jan 1979), 1 s (Jonathan Mark b 12 Jan 1984); *Career* lectr in law Univ of Manchester 1971–74, called to the Bar Inner Temple 1973, in practice Northern Circuit, recorder of the Crown Court 1993– (asst recorder 1988–93); *Recreations* travel, music, dining out; *Style*— Philip Raynor, Esq, QC; ✉ 40 King Street, Manchester M2 6BA (☎ 0161 832 9082, fax 0161 835 2139); Hardwicke Building, New Square, Lincoln's Inn, London WC2A 3SB (☎ 0171 242 2523, fax 0171 831 6968)

RAYNSFORD, Hon Mrs (Joan Rosemary); *née* Wakefield; OBE (1981); eldest da of 1 and last Baron Wakefield of Kendal (d 1983), and Rowena Doris, *née* Lewis (d 1981); the Wakefield family can trace its lineage to Roger Wakefield, of Challon Hall, near Kendal, Westmorland, *temp* Elizabeth I. The family is recorded in the first generation of Kendal money men and was contemporary with London Bankers listed in the first London Directory of 1677. Wakefield's Bank was established in 1788 in the Old House, Kendal, which the family still occupies, and subsequently became the Kendal Bank. This was taken over by the Bank of Liverpool in 1893 which amalgamated with Martins Bank in 1918 and is now Barclays Bank; *b* 18 Nov 1920; *Educ* Francis Holland Sch London, Downe House Newbury, Univ of Berlin; *m* 18 March 1944, Capt Antony Edward Montague Raynsford, DL, RN (ret) (d 1993, sr descendant of Henry Rainsford, of Rainford Hall, Lancs, and of the Manor of Great Tew, Oxon (d ca 1430)), er s of Lt-Col Richard M Raynsford, DSO, JP, DL (d 1965); 1 s (Richard), 1 da (Julia (Lady Boyd)); *Career* chm: Battlefields (Holdings) Ltd, Shapland & Petter Holdings Ltd 1983–92, Lake District Estates Co Ltd, Ullswater Navigation & Transit Co Ltd, Ravenglass & Eskdale Railway Co Ltd; vice-chm Cons National Women's Ctee 1971–72 (chm Gtr London Women's Ctee 1968–71); memb Int Exec Ctee European Union of Women 1979–81; vice-pres British Ski Fedn 1966–69; *Recreations* skiing, walking in mountains; *Clubs* Lansdowne, Ski Club of GB (chm 1972–75, pres 1981–91), Kandahar Ski (chm 1977–82); *Style*— The Hon Mrs Raynsford, OBE; ✉ Milton Malsor Manor, Northampton NN7 3AR (☎ 01604 858251); The Old House, Kendal, Cumbria LA9 4QG (☎ 01539 720861)

RAYNSFORD, Wyvill Richard Nicolls (Nick); MP (Lab) Greenwich (majority 1,357); s of Wyvill John Macdonald Raynsford (Capt Northants Yeo, ka 1944), and Patricia Howell, *née* Dunn (d 1956); *b* 28 Jan 1945; *Educ* Repton, Sidney Sussex Coll Cambridge (MA), Chelsea Sch of Art (Dip Art and Design); *m* 30 Aug 1968, Anne Elizabeth, da of Col Marcus Jelley, of Northampton; 3 da; *Career* market res A C Neilsen Co Ltd 1966–68, Student Co-operative Dwellings 1972–73, SHAC (London Housing Aid Centre) 1973–86 (dir 1976–86), dir Raynsford Dallison Associates Ltd (housing conslts) 1987–93; cncllr London Borough of Hammersmith and Fulham 1971–75, MP (Lab) Fulham 1986–87, MP (Lab) Greenwich 1992–; front bench spokesman for London 1993–94, shadow housing and construction min and spokesman for London 1994–; memb Inst of Housing 1978; *Books* A Guide to Housing Benefit (1982); *Style*— Nick Raynsford, MP; ✉ House of Commons, London SW1A 0AA (☎ 0171 219 2773, fax 0171 219 2619)

RAZ, Prof Joseph; s of Shmuel Zaltsman, and Sonya, *née* Alterkovski; *b* 21 March 1939; *Educ* Hebrew Univ Jerusalem (MJuris), Univ of Oxford (DPhil); *m* 8 Sept 1963 (m dis 1979), Yael; 1 s (Noam b 1969); *Career* lectr then sr lectr in Hebrew Univ of Jerusalem 1967–72; Balliol Coll Oxford: fell and tutor in jurisprudence 1972–85, prof of philosophy of law 1985–; visiting prof Columbia Univ NY 1995–; hon foreign memb American Acad of Arts and Sciences 1992; Hon Dr Catholic Univ Brussels 1993; FBA 1987; *Books* The Concept of a Legal System (1970, 1980), Practical Reason and Norms (1975, 1990), The Authority of Law (1979), The Morality of Freedom (1986), Ethics in the Public Domain (1994); *Style*— Prof Joseph Raz, FBA; ✉ Balliol College, Oxford OX1 3BJ (☎ 01865 277721, fax 01865 277803)

RAZZALL, (Edward) Timothy; CBE (1993); s of Leonard Humphrey Razzall, of Barnes, London, a Master of the Supreme Court 1954–81, and Muriel, *née* Knowles (d 1968); *b* 12 June 1943; *Educ* St Paul's, Worcester Coll Oxford (BA); *m* 1 (m dis); 1 s (James Timothy b 8 Nov 1972), 1 da (Katharine Mary b 31 Oct 1970); m 2, 30 Sept 1982, Deirdre Bourke, da of Duncan Taylor-Smith (d 1985); *Career* admitted slr 1969; ptnr Frere Cholmeley (now Frere Cholmeley Bischoff) 1973–95; ptnr Argonaut Associates 1995–; dir: Cala plc 1973–, Speciality Shops plc Collins and Brown Ltd, Star Mining Corp NL 1993–; London Borough of Richmond upon Thames: cncllr 1974–, chm Policy and Resources Ctee and dep ldr 1983–; treas: Lib Pty 1987–88, Lib Democrats 1988–; *Recreations* all sports; *Clubs* Nat Lib, MCC; *Style*— Timothy Razzall, Esq, CBE; ✉ Argonaut Associates, 17 Exeter Street, London WC2E 7DU (☎ 0171 629 3545, fax 0171 629 2230)

REA, Christopher William Wallace (Chris); s of William Wallace Rea, TD, DL, of Meigle Perthshire, and Helen Chalmers, *née* Bissett; *Educ* HS of Dundee, Univ of St Andrews (MA); *m* 18 Sept 1974, Daphne Theresa (Terri), da of George James Manning (d 1973); 1 da (Alison Jane b 2 July 1981); *Career* rugby union footballer and broadcaster; 13 caps for Scotland 1968–71; memb: Br Lions tour party to NZ 1971, 4 major overseas tours; played for Barbarians RFC; BBC: joined admin 1970, rugby corr Radio Sports Dept 1972, presenter TV's Rugby Special 1988–94, radio golf commentator 1985; asst sec MCC 1995–; rugby and golf corr The Scotsman, ed Rugby News, rugby corr Independent on Sunday 1990–; *Books* Illustrated History of Rugby Union (1977), Injured Pride (1980), Scotland's Grand Slam (1984); *Recreations* golf, walking; *Clubs* Luffenham Heath Golf, MCC; *Style*— Chris Rea, Esq; ✉ c/o MCC, Lord's Cricket Ground, St John's Wood Road, London NW8 8QN

REA, Rev Ernest; s of Ernest Rea (d 1975), of Belfast, NI, and Mary Wylie, *née* Blue (d 1973); *b* 6 Sept 1945; *Educ* Methodist Coll Belfast, Queen's Univ Belfast (BA, BD), Union Theol Coll Belfast; *m* 1, 13 Sept 1973 (m dis 1994), Kathleen (Kay), da of Robert Kilpatrick (d 1987), of Belfast, NI; 2 s (Stephen Ernest b 28 April 1975, Jonathan Robert b 17 April 1978); m 2, 1 July 1995, Gaynor Vaughan, da of David and Leah Jones, of Tamworth, Staffs; *Career* asst minister Woodvale Park Presbyterian Church Belfast 1971–74, minister Bannside Presbyterian Church Banbridge Co Down 1974–79; prodr religious progs BBC NI 1979–84, sr prodr religious progs BBC South and West 1984–88, editor Network Radio 1988–89, head of religious bdcasting BBC 1989–; *Recreations* theatre, reading, playing tennis and golf, music, good company; *Style*— The Rev Ernest Rea; ✉ BBC, New Broadcasting House, Oxford Road, Manchester (☎ 0161 955 3672)

REA, Hon Matthew James; s and h of 3 Baron Rea, *qv*; *b* 28 March 1956; *Educ* William Ellis Sch, Univ of Sheffield; 1 da (Ellis Kelsey Haslam Rea b 2 Feb 1989), 1 s (Ivan Rea b Nov 1992); *Style*— The Hon Matthew Rea; ✉ 12 St Leonards Bank, Edinburgh

REA, 3 Baron (UK 1937); Sir (John) Nicolas Rea; 3 Bt (UK 1935); s of Hon James Rea (d 1954; 2 s of 1 Baron Rea), by his 1 w, Betty, *née* Bevan (d 1965); suc unc, 2 Baron, 1981; *b* 6 June 1928; *Educ* Dartington Hall, Belmont Hall Sch Mass USA, Dauntsey's Sch, Christ's Coll Cambridge (MA, MD), Univ Coll Hosp Med Sch London; *m* 1, 1951 (m dis 1991), Elizabeth Anne, da of William Hensman Robinson (d 1944), of Woking; 4 s (Matthew, Daniel, Quentin, Nathaniel), 2 da (Bess, Rosy); m 2, 1991, Judith Mary, da of Norman Powell (d 1989), of Lytham St Anne's, Lancs; *Heir* s, Hon Matthew Rea; *Career* Nat Serv Actg Sergeant Suffolk Regt; sits as Labour peer in House of Lords, spokesman on health and overseas devpt; research fellow Paediatrics Ibadan Univ Nigeria 1962–65, lectr in Social Medicine St Thomas's Hosp Med Sch 1966–68, medical practitioner in NHS general practice (Kentish Town Health Centre), ret 1993; vice chm Nat Heart Forum 1985–95; chm: Appropriate Health Resources and Technology Action Gp (AHRTAG) 1992–, All Party Food and Health Forum 1992–; memb Cncl Outward Bound Tst 1988–95; DPH, DCH, DObst; FRCGP, FRSocMed (pres Section of Gen Practice 1985–86); *Recreations* music (bassoon), travel, restoring and improving old buildings, gardening; *Clubs* Royal Soc of Medicine; *Style*— The Rt Hon the Lord Rea; ✉ House of Lords, London SW1A 0PW (☎ and fax 0171 607 0546)

REA PRICE, (William) John; OBE (1991); s of late John Caxton Rea Price, and Mary Hilda Rea Price; *b* 15 March 1937; *Educ* Univ Coll Sch, Corpus Christi Coll Cambridge (MA), LSE (DSA); *m* 1962, Maryrose Wingate, *née* Miller; 2 s, 1 da; *Career* London Probation Service 1962–65, Children's Dept London Borough of Islington 1965–68, Nat Inst for Social Work 1968–69, Community Devpt Project Home Office 1969–72, dir of social servs London Borough of Islington 1972–90, dir National Children's Bureau 1991–;

pres Assoc of Dirs of Social Services 1989–90; *Style—* John Rea Price, Esq, OBE; ✉ National Children's Bureau, 8 Wakley Street, London EC1V 7QE (☎ 0171 843 6011)

REACHER, Fred; s of Arthur Reacher (d 1986), of Nottingham, and Mabel, *née* Fox (d 1958); *b* 5 July 1932; *Educ* Mundella GS Nottingham; *m* 14 Feb 1957, Ida Margaret, da of John Andrew Pike (d 1967); 1 s (Michael Arthur b 5 June 1958), 1 da (Sally Jane b 17 March 1960); *Career* industl chemist Beardalls Ltd Nottingham 1948–53, Nottingham City Police Force (Foot Div, Mechanised Div, CID) 1953–67, licensed victualler and property developer 1967–90; Nottingham Forest FC: memb Ctee 1974–, vice chm 1980–83, chm 1992–; *Recreations* golf, horse racing (registered owner); *Clubs* Radcliffe-on-Trent Golf, Mapperley Golf; *Style—* Fred Reacher, Esq; ✉ Ifonly, 25 Main St, Woodborough, Notts NG14 6EA (☎ 0115 982 0840); Nottingham Forest FC Ltd, City Ground, Trent Bridge, Nottingham NG2 5FJ

READ, Bryan Colman; CBE (1984), JP (1965), DL (1986); s of L Hector Read (d 1963), of Norwich, and Ena P Read (d 1985); *b* 1 Oct 1925; *Educ* Bishop's Stortford Coll, St John's Coll Cambridge (MA); *m* 1949, Sheila Mary, da of Frank Oliver Winter, of Norwich; 1 s (James b 1953), 3 da (Joanna b 1950, Susan b 1950, Rebecca b 1960); *Career* flour miller; R J Read (Holdings) Ltd 1954–87, Pasta Foods Ltd 1955–85; pres Nat Assoc of Br and Irish Flour Millers 1968 and 1983; chm: Nat Inst of Agricultural Botany 1976–78, Cncl Flour Milling and Baking Res Assoc 1989–94; memb: Home Grown Cereals Authy 1966–91, AFRC 1983–88; chm: Norfolk and Norwich Festival 1982–, Broads Authy 1988–93, Norfolk Heritage Fleet Tst 1995–; pres Broads Soc 1994–; Hon Dr of Civil Law Univ of East Anglia 1996; *Recreations* sailing, music; *Clubs* Farmers'; *Style—* Bryan Read, Esq, CBE, JP, DL; ✉ 21 Upton Close, Norwich NR4 7PD (☎ 01603 454281, fax 01603 507048)

READ, Prof Frank Henry; s of Frank Charles Read (d 1976), and Florence Louisa, *née* Wright; *b* 6 Oct 1934; *Educ* Haberdashers' Aske's, Univ of London (ARCS, BSc), Univ of Manchester (PhD, DSc); *m* 16 Dec 1961, Anne Stuart, da of Neil Stuart Wallace; 2 s (Jonathon Hugh Tobias b 16 June 1965, Sebastian Timothy James b 18 Aug 1970), 2 da (Kirsten Victoria b 17 Oct 1962, Nichola Anne b 12 Feb 1964); *Career* Univ of Manchester: lectr 1959–68, sr lectr 1968–74, reader 1974–75, prof of physics 1975–, res dean of Faculty of Science 1993–95; vice pres Inst of Physics 1984–89; memb: Cncl of Royal Soc 1987–89, Sci Bd Sci and Engrg Res Cncl (SERC) 1987–90; FRS 1984, FInstP 1973; *Books* Electrostatic Lenses (1976), Electromagnetic Radiation (1980); *Recreations* farming, stone-masonry, landscaping; *Style—* Prof Frank Read, FRS; ✉ Hardingland Farm, Macclesfield Forest, Cheshire SK11 0ND (☎ 01625 425759); Department of Physics and Astronomy, University of Manchester, Manchester M13 9PL (☎ 0161 275 4141, fax 0161 275 4259)

READ, Dr Graham; *b* 16 Jan 1947; *Educ* Queen Elizabeth's GS Barnet, Fitzwilliam Coll Cambridge (open exhibitioner in natural scis, MA, MB BChir, college prize, MRCP), Univ of Manchester Med Sch (surgical prize); *m* 13 April 1974, Joan Elizabeth, *née* Hughes; 2 s (Philip Alexander b 17 March 1976, Stuart Noel b 17 April 1979), 1 da (Helena Magdalen b 1 Aug 1977); *Career* jr posts in med Manchester Royal Infirmary and Crumpsall Hosp Manchester, registrar then sr registrar in radiotherapy Christie Hosp Manchester; currently: conslt in radiotherapy and oncology Christie Hosp Manchester and hon assoc lectr in radiotherapy Univ of Manchester, dir of cancer servs Royal Preston Hosp; memb: MRC Working Pty on Testicular Tumours 1979–, Cancer Statistics Gp Cancer Research Campaign 1982, MRC Working Pty on Advanced Bladder Cancer 1983–, NW Regnl Med Ctee 1988–92, Clinical Oncology Casemix Gps Devpt Project, Integrated Clinical Workstation Project, Cncl RCR (memb Faculty Bd of Clinical Oncology 1988–94); chm Clinical Oncology Speciality Working Gp NHSME Clinical Terms Project; memb: Br Assoc for Cancer Research, Br Inst of Radiology, Br Oncological Assoc, American Soc of Clinical Oncology; FRCR 1978; *Publications* author of numerous articles in the fields of testicular and bladder cancer and gen oncology, also author of book chapers; *Style—* Dr Graham Read; ✉ Department of Radiotherarpy, Christie Hospital, Wilmslow Road, Manchester M20 4BX (☎ 0161 446 3000, fax 0161 446 3352); Director of Cancer Services, Royal Preston Hospital, Sharoe Green Lane North, Fulwood, Preston PR2 9HT (☎ 01772 716565, fax 01772 710089)

READ, Imelda Mary (Mel); MEP (Lab) Nottingham and Leicestershire North West (majority 39,668); da of Robert Alan Hocking, and Teresa Mary Hocking; *b* 8 Jan 1939; *Educ* Bishopshalt Sch Hillingdon, Univ of Nottingham (BA); *m* Aug 1991, Michael Thomas Tengue; 1 s, 1 da, 1 step s; *Career* laboratory technician Plessey 1963–74; teacher 1977–84: Trent Poly, Leicester Poly, WEA, Beeston Coll of Further Educn, Clarendon Coll of Further Educn; employment worker Community Relations Council Nottingham 1984–89; MEP (Lab): Leicester 1989–94, Nottingham and Leics NW 1994–; chair Euro Parly Lab Party 1990–91; memb: Econ, Monetary & Industry Ctee, Agric Budget's Ctee, Women's Ctee, South Asia Delgn; Parly candidate (Lab): Melton 1979, NW Leics 1983; memb: MSF (elected NEC 1975–90), Child Poverty Action Gp, Rural Revival, Cradock No 1 Allotment Soc; former chair: Notts Area Manpower Bd, TVC Regnl Women's Ctee; *Recreations* bee-keeping, gardening; *Style—* Ms Mel Read, MEP; ✉ Labour European Office, Marlene Reid Centre, 85 Belvoir Road, Coalville, Leics LE67 3PH (☎ 01530 830780)

READ, Gen Sir John Antony Jervis; GCB (1972, KCB 1967, CB 1965), CBE (1959, OBE 1957), DSO (1945), MC (1941); s of John Dale Read, of Heathfield, Sussex (d 1940), and Evelyn Constance Bowen; *b* 10 Sept 1913; *Educ* Winchester, RMC Sandhurst; *m* 14 June 1947, Sheila, da of Frederick G C Morris, of London NW8; 3 da; *Career* 2 Lt Oxford and Bucks LI 1934, served Africa and Burma WWII, dep asst mil sec WO 1947–49, Co Cdr Sandhurst 1949–52, AA & QMG 11 Amd Div 1952–54, Lt-Col 1952, cdm 1 Oxford Bucks LI 1954–57, Temp Brig 1957, cmd 3 Inf Bde 1957–59, Cmdt Sch of Inf Warminster 1959–62, Brig 1961, GOC 50 Inf Div TA and Northumbrian Dist 1962–64, Maj-Gen 1962, Vice QMG 1964–66, Lt-Gen 1966, GOC-in-C Western Cmd 1966–69, Gen 1969, QMG 1969–72, ADC (Gen) to HM The Queen 1971–73, Cmdt RCDS 1973–74; Col Cmdt: Army Catering Corps 1966–76, Light Div 1968–73, Small Arms Sch Corps 1970–75; special cmmr Duke of York's Royal Mil Sch 1974–90; pres: Ex-Services Fellowship Centre 1974–91, TA Rifle Assoc 1974–90; chm: Army Cadet Force Assoc 1973–82 (pres 1982–92), Royal Sch for Daughters of Offrs 1975–82 (govr 1966); govr: St Edward's Sch Oxford 1972–87, Royal Hosp Chelsea 1975–81; *Clubs* Army & Navy; *Style—* Gen Sir Antony Read, GCB, CBE, DSO, MC; ✉ Brackles, Little Chesterton, nr Bicester, Oxon OX6 8PD (☎ 01869 252189)

READ, Sir John Emms; kt (1976); s of William Emms Read, of Brighton (d 1952); *b* 29 March 1918; *Educ* Brighton Hove and Sussex GS, Admin Staff Coll Henley; *m* 1942, Dorothy Millicent, da of Thomas Alfred Berry; 2 s; *Career* Cdr (S) RN 1939–46; qualified CA; Ford Motor Co Ltd 1946–64 (dir of sales 1961–64), dir EMI Ltd 1965–87; EMI Group: jt md 1967, chief exec 1969–79, dep chm 1973–74, chm 1974–79; dep chm: Thorn-EMI 1979–81 (dir 1981–87), Thames TV 1981–88 (dir 1973–88); dir Capital Industries-EMI Inc 1970–83; chm: TSB Holdings Ltd 1980–88, Central Bd TSB Ltd 1980–88, TSB Group plc 1986–88, United Dominions Trust 1981–85; dir: Wonder World plc 1983–, FI Group plc 1989–93, Cafman Ltd 1991–, NCVO Ltd 1991–94; ptnr Cadmus Investment Management 1993–; memb Cncl CBI 1977–90 (chm Fin & Gen Purposes Ctee 1978–84); chm: Cncl of Mgmnt Inst of Neurology 1982–, Brain Research Tst 1986– (tstee 1982–); dep chm Governing Body Br Post Grad Med Fedn Univ of London 1987–96 (memb 1982–); tstee: Westminster Abbey Tst 1979–86, Community Action Tst (now Crimewatch Tst) 1985–, United Westminster Almshouses 1985–, Brighton Festival Tst 1975–92, LSO Tst 1985–91, Eyeless Tst; pres: Sussex Assoc of Boys' Clubs 1982–, Charities Aid Fndn 1994– (tstee 1985–90, chm 1990–94); govr Henley Mgmnt Coll 1974–92 (hon fell 1993), memb Ct Univ of Surrey 1986–; Hon DUniv Surrey 1987; FCA, CIMgt, FIB; *Recreations* music; *Clubs* MCC, Royal Over-Seas League; *Style—* Sir John Read; ✉ Muster House, 12 Muster Green, Haywards Heath, W Sussex RH16 4AG; 41 Portman Square, London W1H 9FH (☎ 0171 935 7888)

READ, Katharine (Kathy); da of Percy Read, and Eileen Read; *b* 30 June 1969; *Educ* Oriel HS, East Norfolk Sixth Form Coll; *m* 31 Oct 1992, Michael Osher; *Career* swimmer; memb: Barnet Copthall Club until 1995, Ealing Swim Club 1995–, England youth squad 1982–84 (competed in Euro Youth Championships Austria 1982), Br sr team 1983–95, England sr team 1984–96; achievements incl: nat ASA 400m champion 1985/86, nat ASA 200m backstroke champion 1984–87, 1989, 1991, 1992, 1993, 1994 and 1995/96, nat ASA 100m backstroke champion 1984–89, 1991, 1992, 1993 and 1996 (only person to hold a title for 6 consecutive years), nat ASA 50m backstroke champion 1991, 1992, 1993 and 1994, Silver medal 200m backstroke Cwlth Games Edinburgh 1986, Bronze medal 4 x 100m medley relay European Championships Sheffield 1993, 6th place 100m and 200m backstroke European Championships Sheffield 1993, Silver medal 4 x 100m medley relay Cwlth Games Victoria 1994, Bronze medal 100m backstroke Cwlth Games 1994, competed in European Championships 1985, 1987, 1989, 1991, 1993 and 1995; holder of 39 nat ASA sr titles, also competed in Olympic Games 1984, 1988 and 1992; jr records: Br/Eng 200m long course backstroke (2:16:00) 1984, Br/Eng short course backstroke (2:15:19) 1986; Br sr long course records: 50m backstroke (30:06) 1992, 100m backstroke (1:03:27) 1994, 200m backstroke (2:14:07) 1992; only person to hold 11 individual sr titles (200m backstroke) 1996, only person to hold 42 ASA nat titles 1984–96; GB Sports Writers swimming award 1985, 1986 and 1992; *Recreations* all aspects of fitness, fitness promotions, antiques; *Style—* Miss Kathy Read; ✉ 49 Manor Court, York Way, Whetstone, London N20 0DR (☎ 0181 361 7679)

READ, Leonard Ernest (Nipper); QPM (1976); s of late Leonard Read, of Nottingham, and Ida, *née* Morris (d 1929); *b* 31 March 1925; *Educ* Bramshill Nat Police Coll; *m* 1, 4 June 1951 (m dis 1979), Marion, *née* Millar; 1 da (Maralyn b 1953); m 2, 3 April 1980, Patricia Margaret, *née* Allen; *Career* WWII petty offr RN 1943–46; Met Police 1947–70: served every rank CID to Detective Chief Supt Murder Squad, seconded to Bucks Constabulary 1963 to assist investigation of Gt Train Robbery, formed squad to enquire into activities of Kray Bros 1968 (Kray twins convicted of murder 1969); appt Asst Chief Constable Notts 1970, appt nat co-ordinator Regnl Crime Squads England and Wales 1972, ret 1976; nat security advsr Museums and Galleries Commission 1976–86; vice pres World Boxing Assoc, vice pres and chm Br Boxing Bd of Control; Freeman City of London 1983; *Books* Nipper (with James Morton); *Recreations* swimming, keyboard playing, computers; *Clubs* Anglo American Sporting, Our Society; *Style—* Nipper Read, Esq, QPM; ✉ 23 North Barn, Broxbourne, Herts EN10 6RR (☎ and fax 01992 440902); British Boxing Board of Control, Jack Petersen House, 52A Borough High Street, London SE1 1XW (☎ 0171 403 5879, fax 0171 378 6670)

READ, Lionel Frank; QC (1973); s of Frank William Charles Read (d 1966), and Lillian Alberta Victoria, *née* Chatwin (d 1984); *b* 7 Sept 1929; *Educ* Oundle, St John's Coll Cambridge (MA); *m* 24 Aug 1956, Shirley, *née* Greenhalgh; 2 s (Nigel Peter Lionel b 25 Jan 1959, David William Charles b 2 June 1962), 1 da (Alexandra Barbara b 24 May 1967); *Career* MOCS (Stick of Honour) 1949, cmmnd 4 RHA 1949; called to the Bar Gray's Inn 1954 (bencher 1981), recorder of the Crown Ct 1974–, dep judge of the High Ct 1989; memb Senate Inns of Ct and Bar 1974–77, gen cmmr of income tax (Gray's Inn Div) 1986–90, chm Local Govt & Planning Bar Assoc 1990–94 (vice chm 1986–90), memb Cncl on Tbnls 1990–96; memb: Western Circuit, Planning & Environmental Bar Assoc, Administrative Law Bar Assoc; *Recreations* golf; *Clubs* Garrick, Hawks' (Cambridge); *Style—* Lionel Read, Esq, QC; ✉ 1 Serjeants' Inn, Fourth Floor, London EC4Y 1NH (☎ 0171 583 1355, fax 0171 583 1672)

READ, Martin; s of Charles Enderby Read, of Nine Acres, Ulceby, Alford, Lincs, and Lillian Clara, *née* Chambers; *b* 24 July 1938; *Educ* Queen Elizabeth's GS Alford, Wadham Coll Oxford (MA); *m* 27 April 1963, Laurette, da of J T Goldsmith (d 1960), of Green Walk, Hendon, London; 2 da (Robyn Lisa b 7 Sept 1966, Abigail Kim b 14 May 1970); *Career* articled clerk Hammond Suddards Bradford 1959–62; Slaughter and May: asst slr 1963–70, ptnr 1971–95, conslt 1995–; past vice chm Law Soc Standing Ctee on Company Law, past chm Company Law Sub Ctee City of London Law Soc; memb Law Soc 1963; *Recreations* theatre, literature, golf, cricket, tennis; *Clubs* MCC, Royal St George's; *Style—* Martin Read, Esq; ✉ Michaelmas House, Bois Avenue, Chesham Bois, Amersham, Bucks HP6 5NS; Slaughter and May, 35 Basinghall St, London EC2V 5DB (☎ 0171 600 1200, fax 0171 726 0038, 0171 600 0289, telex 883486, 8888926)

READ, District Judge Maureen Antonia; da of Marcel Meisl (d 1991), of Senica, Slovakia, and Gertrude, *née* Schwarz (d 1955), of Vienna; *b* 19 June 1945; *Educ* Queenswood Sch Herts, Kingston Poly (BA); *m* 29 June 1968, Derek Alan Read; 1 da (Charlotte Helen b 23 May 1970), 1 s (Marcel James b 6 July 1971); *Career* justice clerks asst Malden and Surbiton Magistrates Ct 1967–70, articles 1976–79, admitted as slr 1979, dep co ct and district registrar Western Circuit 1988–92, district judge Bow Co Ct 1992–, asst recorder 1996–; memb Law Soc; *Recreations* theatre, swimming; *Style—* District Judge Maureen Read; ✉ Bow County Court, 96 Romford Road, Stratford, London E15 4EG

READ, Prof Nicholas Wallace; s of Wallace Frederick Read, of Restharrow, Blagdon Hill, Taunton, Somerset, and Doris Vera, *née* Scriven; *b* 7 July 1945; *m* 27 Nov 1976, Maria Grazyna, da of Capt Alexander Zaga-Pietkiewicz (d 1959), of London; 1 s (Alexander b 1980), 4 da (Esther b 1973, Katherine b 1978, Emily b 1982, Diane b 1986); *Career* conslt gastroenterologist Trent RHA Sheffield 1981, prof of gastrointestinal physiology and nutrition Univ of Sheffield 1988, dir Centre for Human Nutrition 1988; trainee analytical psychotherapist 1994–; memb: Br Soc of Gastroenterology 1979, Physiological Soc 1980, Nutrition Soc 1986; FRCP 1987; *Books* Irritable Bowel Syndrome (1984, 2 edn 1990), BDS Textbook of Physiology (1988), Gastrointestinal Motility, Which Test (1989); *Recreations* hill walking, cycling, writing; *Style—* Prof Nick Read; ✉ 74 Nairn Street, Crookes, Sheffield S10 1UN (☎ 0114 267 8633); Centre for Human Nutrition, Northern General Hospital, Sheffield S5 7AU (☎ 0114 242 1528, fax 0114 261 0112)

READ, (Charles) Patrick Wilson; s of Sir Charles David Read (d 1957), of London, and Frances Edna, *née* Wilson; *b* 17 March 1942; *Educ* Harrow; *m* 1966, Susan Viner, da of Brian Viner Edsall, of Wisborough Green, W Sussex; 1 s (Jason b 1968); *Career* md Young & Co's Brewery plc 1976–; Liveryman Worshipful Co of Brewers; *Recreations* shooting, fishing; *Style—* Patrick Read, Esq; ✉ Malthouse Cottage, Little Bognor, nr Fittleworth, Pulborough, W Sussex (☎ 01798 865260); Young & Co's Brewery plc, Ram Brewery, Wandsworth, London SW18 (☎ 0181 875 7000, fax 0181 870 9444, telex 8814530)

READ, Piers Paul; s of Sir Herbert Edward Read, DSO, MC (d 1968), and Margaret, *née* Ludwig (d 1996); *b* 7 March 1941; *Educ* Ampleforth, St John's Coll Cambridge (BA, MA); *m* 29 July 1967, Emily Albertine, da of (Evelyn) Basil Boothby, CMG, of London; 2 s (Albert b 1970, William b 1978), 2 da (Martha b 1972, Beatrice b 1981); *Career* author; artist in residence Ford Fndn Berlin 1963–64, sub ed Times Literary Supplement London 1965, Harkness fell Cwlth Fund NY 1967–68, adjunct prof of writing Univ of Columbia 1980; memb: Ctee of Mgmnt Soc of Authors 1973–76, Literature Panel Arts Cncl London 1975–77; chm Catholic Writers' Guild 1992–97, govr Cardinal Manning

Boys' Sch London 1985–90; FRSL 1972; *Books* Games in Heaven with Tussy Marx (1966), The Junkers (1968), Monk Dawson (1969), The Professor's Daughter (1971), The Upstart (1973), Alive: the story of the Andes Survivors (1974), Polonaise (1976), The Train Robbers (1978), A Married Man (1979), The Villa Golitsyn (1981), The Free Frenchman (1986), A Season in The West (1988), On the Third Day (1990), Ablaze, The Story of Chernobyl (1993), A Patriot in Berlin (1995), Knights of the Cross (1997); *Style—* Piers Paul Read, Esq, FRSL; ✉ 50 Portland Rd, London W11 4LG (☎ 0171 727 5719, fax 0171 727 4683)

READ, Richard Michael Hodgson; s of Lt Richard Hodgson Read (d 1936), of Eastbrook Hall, Dinas Powis, and Dorothy Jessie, *née* Penwarden (d 1985); *b* 24 Dec 1936; *Educ* Clifton Coll, St James' Sch Maryland USA, Univ of London (BSc); *m* 1, 21 July 1964 (m dis 1969), Jennifer Diane, da of Marcus Leaver (d 1966), of Mill Hill; m 2, 29 Oct 1993, Susan Anne Icke; *Career* CA; R H March Son & Co and Mann Judd & Co 1962–79, ptnr Touche Ross & Co 1979–81, dir various cos affiliated to Lloyd's 1981–90; chm: D G Durham Group plc 1988–93, Culver Holdings plc 1991–; underwriting memb Lloyd's; memb CBI: Smaller Firms Cncl 1973–79, Cncl 1978–79, Welsh Cncl; FCA; *Recreations* skiing, tennis, swimming; *Clubs* Cardiff & County; *Style—* Richard Read, Esq; ✉ Llanmaes, St Fagans, Cardiff CF5 6DV (☎ 01222 675100)

READ, Thomas Bonamy; s of Sir Herbert Edward Read, DSO, MC (d 1968), and Margaret, *née* Ludwig (d 1996); *b* 21 Dec 1937; *Educ* Ampleforth, Univ of Leeds (BA); *m* Celia Mary, da of Charles Guy Vaughan-Lee, DSC (d 1984); 3 s (Alexander Paul b 26 April 1968, James Herbert b 6 Dec 1969, Matthew Charles b 16 April 1974); *Career* reporter and educn correspondent Daily Mirror 1962–67, BBC Radio 1967–; prodr Reith Lectures 1981, ed Analysis Radio 4 1982–84; World Serv 1984–96: head of Central Talks and Features 1987, acting ed World Serv in English 1989, dir BBC Monitoring 1991–96; winner Sony Award for best documentary 1984; RIIA; *Recreations* travel; *Style—* Thomas Read, Esq; ✉ 31 St Albans Road, London NW5 1RG (☎ 0171 485 0256)

READING, Anthony John; MBE (1978); *b* 8 Aug 1943; *Educ* Brighton Coll Sussex; *m* 1966; 1 s; *Career* articled clerk Spain Bros Dalling and Co Brighton 1962–66, audit sr and asst mangr Whinney Murray Ernst and Ernst Brussels 1966–70, md Donaldson Europe Belgium 1978–80 (dir of fin 1970–76, dir of mfrg 1976–77), gp exec Thomas Tilling plc London 1980–83, divnl gp chief exec BTR plc 1983–87, gp md Polly Peck International plc 1987–89, gp md Pepe Group plc 1989–90; Tomkins plc: divnl dir 1990–92, chief operating offr North America 1992–95, jt md Operations 1995–96, chm Tomkins Corp USA 1996–; FCA 1966, FIMgt 1989; *Recreations* family, music, golf, watersports; *Clubs* Naval and Mil; *Style—* Anthony Reading, Esq, MBE; ✉ Tomkins plc, East Putney House, 84 Upper Richmond Rd, London SW15 2ST (☎ 0181 871 4544, fax 0181 877 5113)

READING, Dowager, Marchioness of; Margot Irene; da of Percival Augustus Duke, CBE, of Walton-on-the-Hill, and Violet Maud, *née* Mappin; *b* 11 Jan 1919; *Educ* Benenden; *m* 7 June 1941, 3 Marquess of Reading, MBE, MC (d 1980); 3 s (4 Marquess, Lord Anthony Rufus-Isaacs, Lord Alexander Rufus-Isaacs), 1 da (Lady Jacqueline Thomson); *Style—* The Most Hon the Dowager Marchioness of Reading; ✉ Glebe Farm House, Cornwell, nr Chipping Norton, Oxon (☎ 01608 658523)

READING, Peter; s of Wilfred Gray Reading, of Liverpool, and Ethel Mary, *née* Catt; *b* 27 July 1946; *Educ* Liverpool Coll of Art (BA); *m* 5 Oct 1968 (m dis 1996), Diana Joy, da of Edward Thomas Gilbert; 1 da (Angela b 14 April 1977); *partner* since 1993, Deborah Jackson; *Career* poet; schoolteacher 1967–68, lectr in art history Liverpool Coll of Art 1968–70; writer in residence Sunderland Poly 1980–82; Cholmondeley Award for Poetry 1978, Dylan Thomas Award 1983, Whitbread Award (Poetry Category) 1986, literary fellowship award Lannan Fndn USA 1990; FRSL 1988; *Poetry* Water and Waste (1970), For the Municipality's Elderly (1974), The Prison Cell & Barrel Mystery (1976), Nothing for Anyone (1977), Fiction (1979), Tom O'Bedlam's Beauties (1981), Diplopic (1983), 5 x 5 x 5 x 5 x 5 (1983), C (1984), Ukulele Music (1985), Stet (1986), Essential Reading (1986), Final Demands (1988), Perduta Gente (1989), Shitheads (1989), Evagatory (1992), 3 in 1 (1992), Last Poems (1994), Collected Poems (2 Vols, 1995 and 1996); *Style—* Peter Reading; ✉ 9 Havelock Road, Belle Vue, Shrewsbury SY3 7ND

READING, 4 Marquess of (UK 1926); Simon Charles Henry Rufus Isaacs; also Baron Reading (UK 1914), Viscount Reading (UK 1916), Earl of Reading and Viscount Erleigh (both UK 1917); s of 3 Marquess of Reading, MBE, MC (d 1980); *b* 18 May 1942; *Educ* Eton, Univ of Tours; *m* 1979, Melinda, yr da of Richard Dewar; 1 s, 2 da (Lady Sybilla b 3 Nov 1980, Lady Natasha b 24 April 1983); *Heir* s, Julian Michael Rufus, Viscount Erleigh b 26 May 1986; *Career* Lt 1st Queen's Dragoon Gds 1961–64; heritage dir Open World, pres House of Windsor Inc, dir Heirloom (US) Inc; pres Dean Close Sch; Hon PhD Soka Univ of Tokyo; *Clubs* Cavalry and Guards', MCC, All England Lawn Tennis, White's; *Style—* The Most Hon the Marquess of Reading; ✉ Jayne's Court, Bisley, Glos GL6 7BE

READY, Nigel Peter; s of Colin Peter Ready (d 1986), and Monica Isabel Elms, *née* Tapper; *b* 13 July 1952; *Educ* Wycliffe Coll, Jesus Coll Cambridge (MA); *m* 29 Dec 1973, Marisa, da of Germano Brignolo, of Asti, Italy; 2 s (Oliver James b 1976, Thomas Nigel b 1985), 1 da (Natasha Isabella b 1975); *Career* ptnr Cheeswrights 1981–, Notary Public 1980; hon sec Soc of Public Notaries of London 1988–, Dep Cmmr of Maritime Affrs Repub of Vanuatu 1995–; vice pres Fédération des Associations de Notaires Européens 1991–; memb Editorial Bd International Maritime Law; assoc memb American Bar Assoc; Freeman City of London, asst Worshipful Co of Scriveners; memb Baltic Exchange; *Books* The Greek Code of Private Maritime Law (jtly, 1982), Brooke's Notary (10 edn, 1988, Supplement 1991, 11 edn 1992, Supplement 1994), Ship Registration (1991, 2 edn 1994); *Recreations* wine, opera, reading; *Style—* Nigel Ready, Esq; ✉ 206 Denmark Hill, London SE5 8DX; Old Point House, 4 Old Point, Middleton-on-Sea, West Sussex PO22 7RY; c/o Cheeswrights, 10 Philpot Lane, London EC3M 8AA (☎ 0171 623 9477, fax 0171 623 5428, telex 883806)

REAMSBOTTOM, Barry Arthur; s of Agnes Mulholland; *b* 4 April 1949; *Educ* St Peter's RC Secondary Sch Aberdeen, Aberdeen Acad; *Career* trade union leader; scientific asst Isaac Spencer & Co Aberdeen 1966–69, social security offr DHSS Aberdeen 1969–76, area offr NUPE Edinburgh 1976–79; Civil and Public Servs Assoc: head of Educn Dept 1979–87, ed Red Tape (CPSA official jl) and press offr 1987–92, gen sec 1992–; memb NUJ 1987–; fell Centre for American Studies Salzburg; *Recreations* golf, books, music, art appreciation; *Style—* Barry Reamsbottom, Esq; ✉ Civil and Public Services Association, 160 Falcon Road, London SW11 2LN (☎ 0171 924 2727, fax 0171 924 1847)

REARDON, John Michael; s of J F J Reardon (d 1987), of Greenford, Middx, and Geerdina, *née* Theodore; *b* 8 July 1938; *Educ* Salvatorian Coll Harrow; *m* April Anne; 2 s (Paul Philip, Michael John); *Career* director; Nat Serv; gen trainee then trainee TV cameraman Associated Rediffusion 1955–68, joined LWT 1968, subsequently became TV dir; memb Dirs' Guild of GB; *Television* credits incl: Whoops Apocalypse, Agony, Two's Company, Me & My Girl, Drummonds, Bust, Re-Joyce (starring Maureen Lipman, BBC), London's Burning (7th series), Jeeves & Wooster (with Stephen Fry and Hugh Laurie), Elidor (BBC), Independent Man (with George Cole); *Awards* BAFTA nominations for Two's Company and Agony; *Style—* John Reardon, Esq

REARDON, Rev John Patrick; s of John Samuel Reardon (d 1978), of Gravesend, Kent, and Ivy Hilda, *née* Coombs (d 1990); *b* 15 June 1933; *Educ* Gravesend Co GS for Boys, UCL (BA), King's Coll London (Postgrad CertEd); *m* 24 Aug 1957, Molly Pamela, da of Norman Henry Young (d 1976), of Sudbury, Suffolk; 4 s (Mark Andrew b 1960, Simon John b 1962, David Philip b 1964, Thomas Paul b 1968), 1 da (Sarah Catherine b 1965); *Career* Nat Serv RA 1951–53; min: Horsham Congregational Church 1961–68, Trinity Congregational Church St Albans 1968–72; dep gen sec United Reformed Church 1983–90 (sec Church and Society Dept 1972–90), gen sec Cncl of Churches for Britain and Ireland 1990–, moderator United Reformed Church 1995–96; memb: Cncl World Devpt Movement 1975–88, Bd Christian Aid; chm: Sussex Congregational Union 1967, Herts Congregational Union 1971; *Books* Leaves from the Tree of Peace (ed, 1986), Threads of Creation (ed, 1989), More Everyday Prayers (contrib); *Recreations* photography, modern literature, travel; *Style—* The Rev John Reardon; ✉ 27 Vanda Crescent, St Albans, Herts AL1 5EX (☎ 01727 852921); Inter-Church House, 35–41 Lower Marsh, London SE1 7RL (☎ 0171 620 4444)

REARDON, Rev Canon Martin Alan; s of Ernest William Reardon, CBE (d 1981), and Gertrude Mary, *née* Pyne (d 1991); *b* 3 Oct 1932; *Educ* St Edward's Sch Oxford, Selwyn Coll Cambridge (BA, MA), Cuddesdon Coll; *m* 22 July 1964, Ruth Maxim, da of (Henry) George Slade; 1 s (John Paul b 1970), 1 da (Sarah Mary b 1972); *Career* ordained: deacon 1958, priest 1959; curate: Rugby St Andrew Coventry 1958–62, Wicker with Neepsend Sheffield 1962–65; sec Sheffield Cncl of Churches 1962–71, sub warden Lincoln Theol Coll 1971–78, sec Gen Synod Bd for Mission and Unity C of E 1978–89, canon and prebendary Lincoln Cathedral 1979, rector Plumpton Dio of Chichester 1989–90, gen sec Churches Together in England 1990–; *Books* Christian Unity in Sheffield (1967), Social Questions (with Kenneth Greet, 1964), What on Earth is the Church For? (1985), Christian Initiation - A Policy for the Church of England (1991); *Style—* The Rev Canon Martin Reardon; ✉ Inter-Church House, 35–41 Lower Marsh, London SE1 7RL

REARDON SMITH, Sir William Antony John; 4 Bt (UK 1920), of Appledore, Co Devon; s of Sir William Reardon Reardon Smith, 3 Bt (d 1995), and his 1 w, Nesta, *née* Phillips (d 1959); *b* 20 June 1937; *Educ* Wycliffe Coll Gloucester; *m* 1962, Susan Wight, da of Henry Wight Gibson, of Cardiff; 3 s ((William) Nicolas Henry b 1963, Giles Antony James b 1968, Harry Alexander b 1979), 1 da (Henrietta Nesta b 1965); *Heir* s, (William) Nicolas Henry Reardon Smith b 10 June 1963; *Career* dir Reardon Smith Line plc 1959–85, dir World Trade Centre 1986–87, tstee and chm Joseph Strong Frazer Trust; chm North Eastern Rubber Co Ltd; tstee and vice-pres Royal Merchant Navy Sch Fndn and Bearwood Coll; memb Milford Haven Port Authority, dir Milford Dock Co and Marine and Port Services; Liveryman Worshipful Co of Shipwrights and Worshipful Co of Poulters; *Recreations* golf, shooting, walking; *Clubs* Royal Porthcawl, Cardiff & County; *Style—* Sir William Reardon Smith, Bt; ✉ 26 Merrick Square, London SE1 4JB (☎ 0171 403 5723, fax 0171 378 7012)

REAVILLE, Richard Maxwell; s of Jack Reaville, and Pauline Elizabeth, *née* Sharp; *b* 4 June 1954; *Educ* Claremont Sch Nottingham, Clarendon Coll of FE, RNCM; *Career* tenor; business career 1975–82, studied at RNCM with John Cameron 1982–86; professional debut as Don Jose in Carmen (WNO) 1985, solo debut in L'Incoronazione di Poppea (Glyndebourne) 1986; *Performances* operas incl: Billy Budd (ENO), Tamino in The Magic Flute (London Chamber Opera), Ferrando in Cosi fan Tutte (Holland Park Festival), Lord Puff in The English Cat (Henze Biennial Festival Gütersloh and Berlin) 1989, Ernesto in Don Pasquale (tour of Far E), Simon Boccanegra (concert performance at Tivoli Festival Copenhagen) 1992, Eisenstein in Die Fledermaus (Mid Wales Opera) 1992, Hoffmann in Les Contes d'Hoffman (Bristol) 1993, Don Jose in Carmen (European Chamber Opera) 1996; concert and recital performances incl: Mendelssohn Paulus (Staatskapelle Weimar), Verdi Requiem (with Orchestre Philharmonique de Loraine), Beethoven Ninth Symphony (with Odense Symphony Orch Denmark 1990, also Brussels, Namur and Dinant 1992, Brugge, Antwerp and Ninoue with Belgium Nat Orch 1995), Mozart Requiem and Bach Johannes Passion (with Århus Chamber Orch Denmark, Randers Byorkester) Messiah, Dvorak Stabat Mater and Mahler Das Lieb Von Der Erde (with Esbjerg Chamber Orch in tour of Denmark), J S Mayr Requiem (UK première at St John's Smith Square) 1992, Verdi Requiem (Köln, Düsseldorf and St Malo) 1993, Mozart Requiem (with Orchestre de Chambre de Wallonie at Knokke-Heist Concert Rossini Petite Messe Solonelle (with Copenhagen Boys' Choir), Bach St John Passion arias (with Sönerjuland Orch Denmark under Nicholas Cleobury) 1995, Rossini Stabat Mater (Finland) 1995, Festival Belgium) 1994, Bach St Matthew Passion (with Juaskyla Orch Finland) 1996, various other concert engagements with orchs incl BBC Philharmonic and English String Orch; *Recordings* incl: Billy Budd (ENO), The Love for Three Oranges (with Lyon Opera Orch, finest classical music recording award 1989), Puccini's Messe di Gloria (with Ostrava Choir and Orch of Czech Republic) 1995; *Recreations* politics, golf; *Style—* Richard Reaville, Esq; ✉ c/o Cathy Scott, Concert Directory International, Lyndhurst, Denton Rd, Ben Rhydding, Ilkley, W Yorks LS29 8QR (☎ 01943 607821, fax 01943 817063)

REAY, Master of; Hon Aeneas Simon Mackay; also Baron Aeneas Mackay; s and h of 14 Lord Reay (and h to S Btcy, Netherland Baronies and Jonkheership), and his 1 w, Hon Annabel Thérèse Fraser, da of 15 Lord Lovat, DSO, MC, TD (d 1995); *b* 20 March 1965; *Educ* Westminster Sch, Brown Univ USA; *Style—* The Master of Reay

REAY, Lt-Gen Sir (Hubert) Alan John; KBE (1981); s of Rev John Reay; *b* 19 March 1925; *Educ* Lancing, Edinburgh Univ; *m* 1960, Ferelith Haslewood Deane; 2 s (and 1 s decd), 2 da; *Career* formerly postgraduate dean Royal Army Med Coll, dir Medical Services HQ BAOR 1979–81, dir-gen Army Medical Services 1981–85; chief hon steward Westminster Abbey 1985–, govr and chm Med Ctee Royal Star and Garter Home Richmond 1986–92, chm West Lambeth Community Care NHS Tst 1991–, pres Friends of St Thomas' Hosp 1993–, vice chm Thames Reach Homelessness Project 1992–94, tstee The Buttle Tst 1991–; Liveryman Worshipful Soc of Apothecaries; QHP, FRCP, FRCPE; *Style—* Lt-Gen Sir Alan Reay, KBE; ✉ c/o National Westminster Bank, 27–29 Horseferry Road, London SW1P 2AZ

REAY, 14 Lord (S 1628); Sir Hugh William Mackay; 14 Bt (NS 1627); also Chief of Clan Mackay, Jonkheer Mackay (Netherlands 1816), Baron Mackay van Ophemert (Netherlands 1822), and Baron Mackay (Netherlands 1858); s of 13 Lord Reay (d 1963, having been naturalised a British subject 1938), by Charlotte, da of William Younger (bro of 1 Viscount Younger of Leckie); *b* 19 July 1937; *Educ* Eton, Ch Ch Oxford; *m* 1, 1964 (m dis 1978), Hon Annabel Thérèse Fraser, da of 15 Lord Lovat, DSO, MC, TD (d 1995); 2 s (Master of Reay b 1965, Hon Edward Andrew b 1974), 1 da (Hon Laura Elizabeth b 1966); m 2, 1980, Hon Victoria Isabella Anne, *née* Warrender, da of 1 Baron Bruntisfield, MC (d 1993); 2 da (Hon Antonia Alexandra b 1981, Hon Isabel Violet Grace b 1985); *Heir* s, Hon Aeneas Simon Mackay, Master of Reay b 20 March 1965; *Career* MEP 1973–79; vice-chm Cons Gp European Parl; delegate to Cncl of Europe and WEU 1979–85; sits as Conservative in House of Lords; a Lord in Waiting 1989–91; Parly under-sec of state DTI 1991–92; *Clubs* Pratt's, White's; *Style—* The Rt Hon the Lord Reay; ✉ Kasteel Ophemert, Ophemert in Gelderland, The Netherlands; House of Lords, London SW1

REAY, William Robert; s of Michael Errington Reay (d 1979), and Agnes Clara, *née* Heslop; *b* 15 March 1925; *Educ* Heaton GS Newcastle Upon Tyne; *m* 20 Sept 1952, Mary Alison, da of Charles Lane (d 1928); 1 da (Susan Margaret b 1956); *Career* Sub Lt RNVR 1943–46 (combined ops and minesweeping); Joseph Miller and Co CAs: ptnr 1952–73, sr ptnr 1973–87, conslt 1987–; FCA 1957 (ACA 1952); *Recreations* painting, music, caravanning; *Clubs* Pen & Palette (Newcastle); *Style—* William Reay, Esq; ✉ 5

Grasmere Crescent, Monkseaton, Whitley Bay NE26 3TB (☎ 0191 252 4265); Joseph Miller & Co, 31 Mosley St, Newcastle upon Tyne (☎ 0191 232 8065, fax 0191 222 1554)

REBELLO, Jason Matthew; s of Patrick Arnold Rebello, and Mary Elizabeth, *née* Thurley; *b* 29 March 1969; *Educ* John Griffiths Secdy Sch, Guildhall Sch of Music & Drama (GGSM); *Career* jazz pianist; began learning piano aged 8, formed first jazz group aged 15; debut album A Clearer View 1990 (nat tour, no 1 Jazz FM chart); presenter Artrageous (youth TV prog) 1992–; numerous TV appearances incl: South Bank Show, Late Show, This Morning; *Awards* Wire magazine Most Promising Newcomer 1988, Pat Smythe Award 1988, Wire magazine Best Instrumentalist Award 1991, Perrier Br Jazz Award 1991; *Style*— Jason Rebello, Esq

REBUCK, Gail Ruth; da of Gordon Woolfe Rebuck, and Mavis, *née* Joseph; *b* 10 Feb 1952; *Educ* Lycée Français de Londres, Univ of Sussex (BA); *m* 1 April 1985, Philip Gould; 2 da (Georgia Anne Rebuck Gould 18 May 1986, Grace Atalanta Rebuck Gould b 6 June 1989); *Career* prodn asst Grisewood & Dempsey 1975, ed then publisher Robert Nicholson Pubns 1976–79, publisher Hamlyn Paperbacks 1979–82, fndr ptnr and publishing dir non-fiction Century Publishing Co Ltd 1982–85, publisher Century Hutchinson 1985–89, chm Random House Div Random Century (Century Hutchinson bought by Random House Inc) 1989–91, chm and chief exec Random House UK Ltd 1991–; *Recreations* reading, travel; *Style*— Ms Gail Rebuck; ✉ Random House UK Ltd, 20 Vauxhall Bridge Road, London SW1V 2SA (☎ 0171 973 9000, fax 0171 233 6120)

RECORD, Norman John Ronald; s of George Ronald Record (d 1967), of Newton Abbot, Devon, and Dorothy Millie Rowland; *b* 19 May 1934; *Educ* Wembley Co GS, UCL (BSc); *m* 1 April 1961, Susan Mary, da of Ernest Samuel Weatherhead (d 1969), of Paignton, Devon; 2 s (Guy b 1964, Justin b 1966); *Career* 2 Lt RAOC 1955–57; economist; formerly held planning and mktg posts in C & J Clark Ltd from 1964, and Perkins Engines Ltd 1957–64, corp planning dir C & J Clark Ltd 1980–91, sr ptnr Business Economics Management Consultants 1991–; memb Cncl CBI 1982–93; memb: The Strategic Planning Soc, The Lab Fin and Indust Gp; author of papers on Macro-Economics; originator of The Theory of The Output Gap in the Control of The Economy; fell Soc Business Economists; FIMgt; *Recreations* current affrs, theatre, local history, swimming; *Clubs* Royal Over-Seas League; *Style*— Norman Record, Esq; ✉ The Old Vicarage, Wedmore, Somerset BS28 4AA (☎ 01934 713123, fax 01934 712326)

REDDAWAY, Prof (William) Brian; CBE (1971); s of William Fiddian Reddaway (d 1949), of Cambridge, and Kate Waterland, *née* Sills (d 1966); *b* 8 Jan 1913; *Educ* King's Coll Sch Cambridge, Lydgate House Hunstanton, Oundle, King's Coll Cambridge (BA, MA); *m* 17 Sept 1938, Barbara Augusta (d 1996), da of Edward Bennett (d 1916), of Lydbrook, Glos; 3 s (Peter b 1939, Stewart b 1941, Lawrence b 1943), 1 da (Jacqueline b 1947); *Career* asst Bank of England 1934–35, res fell Univ of Melbourne 1936–37, fell Clare Coll Cambridge 1938–, statistician Bd of Trade 1940–47, economics dir Orgn for Euro Econ Co-operation Paris 1951–52; Univ of Cambridge: lectr 1939–55, dir Dept of Applied Economics 1955–70, prof of political economy 1969–80, prof emeritus 1980–; memb: Royal Cmmn on the Press 1961–62, Nat Bd for Prices and Incomes 1967–71; conslt World Bank 1967–87; ed Economic Jl 1970–76; FBA 1967; *Books* Russian Financial System (1935), Economics of a Declining Population (1939), Measurement of Production Movements (1948), Development of the Indian Economy (1962), Effects of UK Direct Investment Overseas (1968), Effects of the Selective Employment Tax (1973), Some Key Issues for the Development of the Economy of Papua New Guinea (1986); *Recreations* chess, skating, swimming, walking; *Style*— Prof Brian Reddaway, CBE, FBA; ✉ 12 Manor Court, Grange Rd, Cambridge CB3 9BE (☎ 01223 350041); Economics Faculty, Sidgwick Ave, Cambridge CB3 9DD (☎ 01223 335228); Clare Coll, Cambridge (☎ 01223 333200)

REDDAWAY, David Norman; CMG (1993), MBE (1980); s of (George Frank) Norman Reddaway, CBE, *qv*, and Jean Muriel, *née* Brett, OBE; *b* 26 April 1953; *Educ* King's Coll Sch Cambridge, Oundle, Fitzwilliam Coll Cambridge (exhibitioner, MA); *m* 1981, Roshan Taliyeh, da of late Narcy Mirza Firouz, and Louise Laylin Firouz; 2 s (Alexander Bahram b 1983, Milo Firouz b 1996), 1 da (Nicola Touran b 1987); *Career* joined FCO 1975, language trg SOAS 1976, language trg Iran 1977, third then second sec (Commercial) Tehran 1978–79, second then first sec (Chancery) Tehran 1979–80, first sec Madrid 1980–84, first sec FCO 1985–86, private sec to Min of State FCO 1986–88, first sec (External Political) New Delhi 1988–90, chargé d'Affaires Tehran 1990–93 (cnsllr 1991), minister Buenos Aires 1993–; *Recreations* skiing, tennis, Persian carpets and art; *Clubs* Royal Commonwealth Soc, Hawks', Leander, Hurlingham (Buenos Aires); *Style*— David Reddaway, Esq, CMG, MBE; ✉ c/o FCO (Buenos Aires), King Charles Street, London SW1A 2AH

REDDAWAY, (George Frank) Norman; CBE (1965, MBE (Mil) 1946); s of William Fiddian Reddaway (d 1949), of King's College, Cambridge, and Kate Waterland, *née* Sills (d 1966); *b* 2 May 1918; *Educ* Oundle, King's Coll Cambridge (MA), Staff Coll Camberley, IDC; *m* 19 Feb 1944, Jean Muriel, OBE, da of (William) Harold Brett (d 1981), of Southport; 2 s (John b 1946, David b 1953, *qv*), 3 da (Helen b 1948, Catharine b 1951, m Sir Stephen Wall, *qv*, Lucy b 1960); *Career* Lance-Corpl Suffolk Regt 1939, 2 Lt No 3 Mil & Air Mission 1940, Capt GHQ Liaison Regt (Phantom) 1941–44, Maj Military Govt 1944, Maj/actg Lt-Col Greater Berlin Mil Govt 1945–46; FO: German Dept 1946, private sec to Parly under-sec 1947–49, HM Embassy Rome 1949–52, UK High Cmmn Ottawa 1952–55, Info Res Dept FO 1955–59, IDC 1960, regnl info offr HM Embassy Beirut 1961–65, Singapore 1965–66, Khartoum 1967–69, asst under-sec FCO 1970–74, HM ambass Warsaw 1974–78; chm International House 1978–, dir Stearns Catalytic International Ltd 1978–89 (now Raytheon Engineers & Constructors, to which currently pt/t conslt), tstee Thomson Fndn; Cdr Order of Merit (Polish People's Republic) 1985; *Recreations* int affairs, gardening, family history; *Clubs* Athenaeum, Oxford and Cambridge, Royal Cwlth Soc; *Style*— Norman Reddaway, Esq, CBE; ✉ 51 Carlton Hill, London NW8 (☎ 0171 624 9238)

REDDIHOUGH, John Hargreaves; s of Frank Hargreaves Reddihough, of Manchester, and Mabel Grace, *née* Warner; *b* 6 Dec 1947; *Educ* Manchester GS, Univ of Birmingham (LLB); *m* 26 June 1981, Sally Margaret, da of Bert Fryer, of Crawley, 1 s (Alex b 1984), 1 da (Gayle b 1981); *Career* called to the Bar Gray's Inn 1969, currently recorder; *Recreations* skiing, running, gardening, music, reading; *Style*— John Reddihough, Esq; ✉ Clyde House, Coley Avenue, Woking, Surrey GU22 7BT (☎ 0171 353 5371, fax 0171 353 1344)

REDDINGTON, John; CBE (1995), QPM (1985); s of John Patrick Reddington, and Margaret, *née* Boardman; *b* 19 Aug 1932; *Educ* St Paul's Church Sch, Liverpool Tech Coll; *m* 1, 29 Aug 1953 (m dis); 1 da (Janice Patricia b 5 April 1958); m 2, 17 April 1963, Sylvia Margaret, da of Sidney Rupert Corkhill; 1 da (Sarah Catherine Corkhill b 2 March 1969), 1 s (Jonathan Mark b 9 Jan 1973); *Career* early career in music co; served Army, Sgt Explosive Disposal Unit; beat duty Liverpool City Police 1954–57, joined CID 1957, detective until 1978 (divnl work, Flying Squad, Criminal Intelligence, Trg, also commanded Murder and Fraud Squads), completed Jr, Intermediate and Sr Cmd Courses Police Staff Coll Bramshill; successively: Sub-Divnl then Divnl Cdr Merseyside until 1980, Asst Chief Constable (Crime) Thames Valley Police, asst sec ACPO (involved in drafting of PACE Act), seconded as asst dir to Sr Command Course Police Staff Coll 1982, Asst Chief Constable (Support) Thames Valley Police, Dep Chief Constable Avon and Somerset Constabulary until 1985; Chief Constable: UKAEA Constabulary 1985–89, MOD Police 1990– (Chief Constable designate 1989–90); 17 commendations for crime detection; county cdr St John Ambulance Oxon 1995; CIMgt 1995; *Recreations* archaeology, history, gardening, cricket; *Style*— J Reddington, Esq, CBE, QPM; ✉ Chief Constable, MOD Police, Empress State Building, Lillie Road, London SW6 1TR (☎ 0171 824 4053)

REDDISH, John Wilson; s of Frank Reddish, of Middleton, Gtr Manchester, and Elizabeth, *née* Hall; *b* 19 Jan 1950; *Educ* Manchester GS, Lincoln Coll Oxford (MA); *m* 20 May 1978, Dawn Marian, da of Edward Henry John McKenzie Russell (d 1963); 1 da (Helena b 1987); *Career* teaching assoc NorthWestern Sch of Law Chicago 1971–72, called to the Bar Middle Temple 1973, in practice 1974–, pt/t chm Special Educnl Needs Tbnl 1994–; memb: Family Law Bar Assoc, London Commercial and Common Law Bar Assoc; *Recreations* cricket, squash; *Clubs* Dulwich Sports; *Style*— John Reddish, Esq; ✉ 1 King's Bench Walk, Temple, London EC4Y 7DB (☎ 0171 583 6266, fax 0171 583 2068)

REDDY, Joanne Elizabeth; da of John William Thomas Staley, of Norton, nr Evesham, Worcs, and Jean Elizabeth, *née* Heighway; *b* 19 Feb 1969; *Educ* Prince Henry's HS Evesham Worcs; *m* 25 Aug 1990, (Vuchuru) Sadhana Reddy, s of Drs V V and V K Reddy; 1 s (Jay b 21 Sept 1996); *Career* hockey player; memb: Evesham Ladies Hockey Club 1983–88, Olton and West Warwicks Hockey Club 1988– (capt 1992–); rep: Worcs under 21 1983–89 (capt 1989), Worcs Srs 1983–93, Midlands Srs 1990–92 (under 18 1987, under 21 1987–90); England under 21 appearances 1989–90 (vice capt 1990): Holland BMW Four Nations Tournament 1989, Home Countries Tournament Nottingham 1989, Under 21 Jr World Cup Ottawa Canada 1989, Home Countries Tournament Ireland 1990; memb: England Sr Training Squad 1990–91, England Mixed Hockey Squad 1991–94; athletics: formerly Worcs Schs co javelin champion, Worcs capt Nat Schs Athletics Championships 1983–86; trainee accountant HDA Forgings Redditch 1989–91, mgmnt accountant GKN Axles Birmingham 1991–92, information analyst TSB Bank plc Birmingham 1992–95; CIMA (Stages 1, 2 & 3); *Style*— Mrs Joanne Reddy; ✉ 60 Lady Byron Lane, Knowle, Solihull, West Midlands B93 9AY (☎ 01564 777146)

REDDY, Thomas; s of Thomas Reddy (d 1973), of Poulton-le-Fylde, and Charlotte Winifred Teresa, *née* Hickey (d 1987); *b* 6 Dec 1941; *Educ* Baines's Sch Poulton; *m* 30 Aug 1969, Phyllis Wendy, da of Stanley Smith (d 1969), of Manchester and Lytham St Anne's; 1 s (Christian b 1973), 1 da (Verity b 1971); *Career* journalist 1968–70, dir and exec creative dir Royds McCann 1970–87, chief exec Tom Reddy Advertising 1987–; broadcaster on advertising TV and radio; guest lectr in advertising UMIST; memb: IPA, Manchester Publicity Assoc; *Recreations* book collecting; *Clubs* Manchester Tennis and Racquets, St James's (Manchester); *Style*— Thomas Reddy, Esq; ✉ Byeways, White House Lane, Great Eccleston, Lancs; Tom Reddy Advertising, Old Colony House, 6 South King St, Manchester (☎ 0161 832 0182)

REDER, Dr Peter; s of Jack Mannie Reder, of London, and Beatrice, *née* Kantor; *b* 29 June 1946; *Educ* Kilburn GS, Birmingham Univ Med Sch (MB, ChB); *m* 15 Aug 1979, Dr Geraldine Sarah Mary, *née* Fitzpatrick; 1 s (Nicholas b 17 Jan 1984); *Career* conslt child psychiatrist Wolverton Gdns Child and Family Consultation Centre Riverside Mental Health Tst 1985–; hon sr lectr Charing Cross and Westminster Med Sch 1990–, lead clinician Riverside Mental Health Tst Child and Adolescent Servs 1991–, dir Wolverton Gdns Centre for Relationship Studies 1993–; DPM, DCH, DObstRCOG, FRCPsych 1993 (MRCPsych 1975); *Books* Beyond Blame: Child Abuse Tragedies Revisited (Routledge, jtly, 1993), Assessment of Parenting (Routlege, jtly, 1995); author of pubns on psychotherapy, family therapy, child psychiatry and child abuse; *Clubs* Roehampton; *Style*— Dr Peter Reder; ✉ Wolverton Gardens, Child and Family Consultation Centre, 1 Wolverton Gardens, London W6 7DQ (☎ 0181 846 7806/7)

REDESDALE, 6 Baron (UK 1902), of Redesdale, Co Northumberland; Rupert Bertram Mitford; o s of 5 Baron Redesdale (d 1991), and Sarah Georgina Cranstoun, *née* Todd; *b* 18 July 1967; *Educ* Milton Abbey, Highgate, Univ of Newcastle (BA); *Heir* none; *Career* overseas devpt spokesman for Liberal Democrats 1993–; memb cncl Inst Advanced Motorists; *Style*— The Rt Hon Lord Redesdale; ✉ The School House, Rochester, Newcastle upon Tyne NE19 1RH; 2 St Mark's Square, London NW1 7TP

REDFARN, Stephen Charles; s of Dr Cyril Aubrey Redfarn (d 1988), of London, and Isabel Mary, *née* Williams (d 1987); *b* 7 May 1943; *Educ* Westminster, King's Coll London (BSc), London Mgmnt Centre (Dip in Business Admin); *m* 1990, Frances Yin Hong; 1 s (James Yin Aubrey b 26 Oct 1995); *Career* with Hill Samuel & Co Ltd 1966–68, dir Dawnay Day & Co Ltd investmt bankers 1968–78, head of corp fin Henry Ansbacher & Co 1978–83, conslt Touche Ross 1983–87, head of capital markets AIB London 1987–90, chief exec Westcountry Television Ltd 1990–; external examiner in accounting CNAA 1986; chm Business Graduates Assoc 1981; Freeman City of London, Liveryman Worshipful Co of Tallow Chandlers; *Recreations* fly fishing, collecting 18th century glass, opera; *Clubs* Reform, City of London; *Style*— Stephen Redfarn, Esq; ✉ Westcountry Television Ltd, Langage Science Park, Plymouth, Devon PL7 5BG (☎ 01752 333333, fax 01752 333444)

REDFERN, (David) Alan; s of Thomas Leonard Redfern (d 1991), and Gladys, *née* George (d 1974); *b* 23 Nov 1932; *Educ* Wyggeston Sch Leicester, Sidney Sussex Coll Cambridge (exhibitioner, MA); *m* 1, 1958, Edith Marie Allamand (d 1980); 1 s (Charles b Feb 1964), 1 da (Isabelle b Sept 1961); m 2, 1983, Marie-Louise Montmasson; 1 s (Alexander b Dec 1980), 1 da (Céline b Aug 1984); *Career* admitted slr 1958; ptnr specialising in int commercial arbitration and construction law Freshfields 1963–95 (formerly articled clerk); called to the Bar Middle Temple 1995; memb Chambers at 1 Essex Court Temple 1995–; memb Int Bar Assoc; FCIArb; *Books* Law & Practice of International Commercial Arbitration (2 edn, 1991); *Recreations* literature, art, windsurfing, walking; *Clubs* Royal Thames Yacht, Roehampton; *Style*— Alan Redfern, Esq; ✉ 1 Essex Court, Temple, London EC4Y 9AF (☎ 0171 583 2000, fax 0171 583 0118)

REDFERN, (Margaret) June; da of John Towers Redfern, of West Ferry, Dundee, and Margaret, *née* Campbell (d 1979); *b* 16 June 1951; *Educ* Edinburgh Coll of Art; *Career* artist; pt/t tutor (fine art) Preston Poly 1982–83, jr fell (fine art) Cardiff Coll of Art 1983, artist in residence Nat Gallery London 1985; guest artist: Univ of Minnesota USA 1986, Kunstacademie I Trondheim Norway 1992; recipient: Andrew Grant scholarship 1972–73, First Prize Scottish Young Contemporaries 1972, Scottish Arts Cncl Award 1982; patron Child Pyschotherapy Tst Scotland 1992–; *Solo Exhibitions* Scottish Arts Cncl Edinburgh 1976, Third Eye Centre Glasgow 1977, Leeds Educn Authy 1977, Women's Arts Alliance London 1978, Henderson Gallery Edinburgh 1978 (drawings 1980), 369 Gallery Edinburgh 1981, Air Gallery London 1984, Third Eye Centre Glasgow 1985, Marianne Deson Gallery Chicago 1985, Nat Gallery London 1986, Mercury Gallery Edinburgh 1987, Bradford Art Galleries and Museums 1987, Aberdeen Art Galleries and Museums 1988, Towner Art Gallery Eastbourne 1988, Mercury Gallery London 1988, Trinity Gallery London 1990, Compass Gallery Glasgow 1991, Bohun Gallery Henley 1992 and 1994, Wrexham Arts Centre 1992, Maclaurin Art Gallery Ayr 1992, Wrexham Library Arts Centre 1992 (touring Maclaurin Art Gallery and Museum Ayr 1992), MAC Birmingham 1993, Oriel 31 Davies Meml Gallery Newtown 1993, Portal Gallery Bremen 1994, Bohun Gallery 1994, Scottish Gallery 1996, Boundary Gallery London 1996; *Public Collections* incl: Nat Gallery London, BBC TV, Robert Fleming plc, Hiscox Holdings, Charlotte Englehart Fndn Boston, Texaco, Albertina Museum Vienna, Proctor and Gamble, Glasgow Art Galleries and Museums, LIllie Art Gallery Glasgow, Lithoprint UK; *Television* incl: The Bigger Picture (BBC 2) 1994, Edinburgh Nights (The

Late Show, BBC 2) 1994, Weathering the Storm (BBC Scotland and BBC 2); *Style*— Ms June Redfern; ✉ 12 Lawley St, London E5 0RJ (☎ 0181 985 1426)

REDFERN, Prof Walter David; s of Walter Barton Redfern (d 1968), of Liverpool, and Charlotte, *née* Jones (d 1986); *b* 22 Feb 1936; *Educ* Bootle GS, Univ of Cambridge (MA, PhD); *m* 30 March 1963, Angela, da of John Robert Kirkup (d 1978), of Chester-Le-Street, Co Durham; 1 s (Sam b 9 Dec 1970), 1 da (Kate b 20 Sept 1968); *Career* prof of French Univ of Reading 1980– (lectr 1963, reader 1972); visiting prof Univ of Illinois 1981–82; memb Assoc For French Studies; FRSA 1991; *Books* Private World of Jean Giono (1968), Paul Nizan (1972), Queneau: Zazie Dans le Métro (1980), Puns (1984), Georges Darien (1985), A Calm Estate (1986), Clichés and Coinages (1989), Feet First: Jules Vallès (1992); *Recreations* jazz, cinema, writing; *Style*— Prof Walter Redfern; ✉ 8 Northcourt Ave, Reading RG2 7HA (☎ 0118 987 1083); French Department, University of Reading, Whiteknights, Reading RG6 2AA (☎ 0118 987 5123 ext 7323)

REDFORD, Donald Kirkman; CBE (1980), DL (Lancs 1983); s of Thomas Johnson Redford (d 1965), of Whetstone, London; *b* 18 Feb 1919; *Educ* Culford Sch, King's Coll London (LLB); *m* 1942, Mabel, second da of Wilfrid Wilkinson, of Humberston, Lincs; 1 s, 1 da; *Career* Wing Cdr RAFVR; called to the Bar, practising barr until 1946; Manchester Ship Canal Co: joined 1946, md 1970, chm 1972–86; chm: Nat Assoc of Port Employers 1972–74, British Ports Assoc 1974–78; memb Ctee of Mgmnt RNLI 1977–94; Univ of Manchester Court: dep treas 1980–82, treas 1982–83, chm of Cncl 1983–87; *Clubs* Oriental; *Style*— Donald Redford, Esq, CBE, DL; ✉ 8 Harrod Drive, Birkdale, Southport, Lancs PR8 2HA

REDGRAVE, Adrian Robert Frank; QC (1992); s of Cecil Frank Redgrave, and Doris Edith, *née* Goss; *b* 1 Sept 1944; *Educ* Abingdon Sch, Univ of Exeter (LLB); *m* 7 Oct 1967, Ann, da of late Jack Bryan Cooper; 2 s (William Alexander Frank b 6 April 1971, Matthew Robert Charles b 23 May 1977), 1 da (Lucy Rebecca Jane b 28 Sept 1972); *Career* called to the Bar Inner Temple 1968, recorder 1985–; *Recreations* tennis, wine, garden, France, Bangalore Phall; *Style*— Adrian Redgrave, Esq, QC; ✉ 1 Serjeants' Inn, Fleet Street, London EC4Y 1LL (☎ 0171 353 9901)

REDGRAVE, Lynn; da of Sir Michael Redgrave (d 1985), and Lady Redgrave (Rachel Kempson); sis of Vanessa Redgrave, *qv*; *b* 8 March 1943; *Educ* Queensgate Sch, Central Sch of Speech and Drama; *m* 2 April 1967, John Clark; 1 s (Benjamin b 7 May 1968), 2 da (Kelly b 26 Feb 1970, Annabel b 5 July 1981); *Career* actress and playwright; *Theatre* professional debut in A Midsummer Night's Dream (Royal Court) 1962; Nat Theatre 1963–66 (fndr memb): Hamlet, The Recruiting Officer, Much Ado About Nothing, Hay Fever, Andorra, Mother Courage, Love for Love (tour Moscow and Berlin); West End roles 1968–71 incl: The Tulip Tree, Slag, Born Yesterday, The Two of Us; A Better Place (Gate Theatre Dublin) 1972; Broadway roles incl: debut Black Comedy 1967, My Fat Friend, Knock Knock, Mrs Warren's Profession (Tony nomination), Saint Joan, Sister Mary Ignatius Explains It All For You, Aren't We All? (Drama Desk nomination) 1985–86, Sweet Sue 1987, Love Letters 1989, Shakespeare For My Father (Tony nomination) 1993, The Master Builder 1993, Moon Over Buffalo 1996; US tours 1976–77: California Suite, The Two of Us, Saint Joan, Thursday's Girls, Hellzapoppin; other plays: Misalliance (Chicago, Sarah Siddons and Jefferson Awards), Twelfth Night (American Shakespeare Festival Conn) 1978, The King and I (tour) 1982, Les Liaisons Dangereuses (Ahmanson Theatre LA) 1988–89, The Cherry Orchard (La Jolla Playhouse San Diego) 1990, Three Sisters (London) 1990, Don Juan in Hell (Hollywood) 1991, The Notebook of Trigorin 1996; *Television* in UK: A Midsummer Night's Dream, Pygmalion, Vienna 1900, Egg on the Face of the Tiger, Pretty Polly, A Woman Alone (BBC) 1988, Death of a Son (Best TV Actress) 1989, Fighting Back 1992, Calling the Shots 1994; in US: Love Boat, Fantasy Island, Hotel, House Calls (CBS, Golden Globe nomination), Teachers Only (NBC), Chicken Soup (ABC), Gauguin the Savage (CBS), Rehearsal for Murder (CBS), The Shooting (CBS, Emmy nomination), The Bad Seed (ABC), Walking on Air (PBS), The Old Reliable (PBS) 1988, Jury Duty (ABC) 1990, Whatever Happened to Baby Jane (ABC) 1991; host: Not for Women Only, AM America, The Weight Watchers Magazine Show, One Second Before Sunrise, In Performance at the White House (PBS) 1989; *Radio* As You Like It (BBC), Three Sisters (BBC), Vile Bodies (BBC), Artist Descending a Staircase (Irish Radio), Tales for Halloween (US); *Films incl* Tom Jones, Girl With Green Eyes, Georgy Girl (Best Actress NY Film Critics, Golden Globe Award, Academy nomination Best Actress 1967), The Deadly Affair, Smashing Time, The Virgin Soldiers, The Last of the Mobile Hotshots, Don't Turn the Other Cheek, The National Health, Every Little Crook and Nanny, Everything You Always Wanted to Know About Sex, The Happy Hooker, The Big Bus, Sunday Lovers, Morgan Stewart's Coming Home, Getting It Right 1989, Midnight 1990, Shine 1996; *Books* This is Living (1991), Named Presidents of the Players (1994); *Recreations* cooking, gardening, horse riding; *Style*— Ms Lynn Redgrave; ✉ c/o John Clark, PO Box 1207, Topanga Canyon, California 90290, USA (☎ 00 1 310 455 1334, fax 00 1 310 455 1032)

REDGRAVE, Maj-Gen Sir Roy Michael Frederick; KBE (1979), MC (1945); s of Robin Roy Redgrave (d 1972), of Rye, Sussex, and Jean Micheline, *née* Capsa (d 1977); *b* 16 Sept 1925; *Educ* Sherborne, Staff Coll Canada; *m* 1953, Valerie, da of Maj (Richard) Arthur Colley Wellesley (d 1984); 2 s (Alexander, Robin); *Career* Trooper RHG 1943, cmd Household Cavalry Regt 1962–64, cmd RHG 1964–67; Nat Def Coll Canada 1973, Cmdt RAC Centre 1974–75, British Cmdt Berlin 1975–78, Cdr British Forces Hong Kong and Maj-Gen Bde of Gurkhas 1978–80, Hon Col 31 Signal Regt Volunteers 1982–86; DG Winston Churchill Meml Tst 1980–82; chm: Hammersmith and Fulham Dist Health Authy 1981–85, Cncl Victoria League for Cwlth Friendship 1981–92; currently: chm of special tstees Charing Cross W London Hosps, memb Cncl Charing Cross & Westminster Med Sch, tstee Chelsea and Westminster Hosp, memb Cncl Br Nepal Soc, memb Cncl Br Romanian Assoc, govr Cwlth Tst; Grand Prior Knights Templar Grand Priory of England; FRGS; *Recreations* archaeology, travel, philately; *Clubs* Cavalry and Guards'; *Style*— Maj-Gen Sir Roy Redgrave, KBE, MC; ✉ 44 Slaidburn Street, Chelsea, London SW10 0JW (fax 0171 351 4835)

REDGRAVE, Steven Geoffrey; CBE (1997, MBE 1986); s of Geoffrey Edward Redgrave, of Marlow Bottom, Bucks, and Sheila Marion, *née* Stevenson; *b* 23 March 1962; *Educ* Marlow C of E First Sch, Holy Trinity Sch Marlow, Burford Sch Marlow Bottom, Great Marlow Sch; *m* 12 March 1988, (Elizabeth) Ann, da of Brian John Callaway, of Cyprus; 2 da (Natalie b 1991, Sophie b 1994); *Career* sports conslt and amateur rower; notable achievements incl: runner-up double sculls Jr World Championships 1980, 15 wins Henley Royal Regatta 1981–, Gold medal coxed fours Olympic Games 1984, Wingfield Sculls champion 1985–89, Gold medal coxless pairs World Championships 1986 and 1987 (Silver medal coxed pairs 1987), 3 Gold medals Cwlth Games 1986 (single sculls, coxed fours, coxless pairs), Gold medal coxless pairs Olympic Games 1988 (Bronze medal coxed pairs), indoor world rowing champion 1991, world champion coxless pairs 1991, world record holder coxless pairs 1994, Gold medal coxless pairs Olympic Games 1992, world champion coxless pairs 1993, 1994 and 1995, Gold medal coxless pairs Olympic Games Atlanta 1996; winner Team of the Year (with M Pinsent) BBC Sports Personality of the Year Awards 1996; *Clubs* Marlow Rowing, Leander; *Style*— Steven G Redgrave, Esq, CBE; ✉ c/o British Olympic Assoc, 1 Wandsworth Plain, London SW18 1EH

REDGRAVE, Vanessa; CBE (1967); da of Sir Michael Redgrave (d 1985), and Lady Redgrave (Rachel Kempson); sis of Corin Redgrave, the actor, and Lynn Redgrave, the actress; *b* 30 Jan 1937; *Educ* Queensgate Sch, Central Sch of Speech and Drama; *m* 1962 (m dis 1967), Tony Richardson (d 1991), s of Clarence Albert Richardson (d 1969); 2 da (Natasha Richardson, Joely Richardson, the actresses); *Career* actress, numerous stage and film performances; *Theatre* Touch of the Sun (Saville) 1958, A Midsummer Night's Dream (Stratford) 1959, Look on Tempests 1960, The Tiger and the Horse 1960, Lady from the Sea 1960; with Royal Shakespeare Theatre Co: As You Like It 1961, Taming of the Shrew 1961, Cymbeline 1962; The Seagull 1964, The Prime of Miss Jean Brodie (Wyndham's) 1966, Daniel Deronda 1969, Cato Street 1971, The Threepenny Opera (Prince of Wales) 1972, Twelfth Night (Shaw Theatre) 1972, Antony and Cleopatra (Bankside Globe) 1973, Design for Living (Phoenix) 1973, Macbeth (LA) 1974, Lady from the Sea (NY) 1976, Roundhouse 1979, The Aspern Papers (Haymarket) 1984, The Seagull (Queen's) 1985, Chekov's Women (Lyric) 1985, The Taming of the Shrew and Antony and Cleopatra (Haymarket) 1986, Ghosts (Young Vic, transferred to Wyndham's) 1986, Touch of the Poet (Young Vic, transferred to Comedy) 1988, Orpheus Descending (Haymarket) 1988 and (NY) 1989, A Madhouse in Goa (Lyric Hammersmith) 1989, When She Danced (Globe, Best Actress Evening Standard Drama Awards) 1991, Heartbreak House (Yvonne Arnaud Guildford and Haymarket) 1992, Maybe (Royal Exchange) 1993, John Gabriel Borkman (RNT) 1996; theatrical debut as director: Antony and Cleopatra (Riverside Studios) 1995; *Films* A Suitable Case for Treatment 1966 (Cannes Festival Best Actress Award 1966), The Sailor from Gibraltar 1967, Blow-Up 1967, Camelot 1967, Red White and Zero 1967, Charge of the Light Brigade 1968, Isadora 1968, A Quiet Place in the Country 1968, The Seagull 1969, Drop-Out 1970, La Vacanza 1970, The Trojan Women 1971, The Devils 1971, Mary Queen of Scots 1972, Murder on the Orient Express 1974, Out of Season 1975, Seven Per Cent Solution 1975, Julia 1976 (Academy Award 1977, Golden Globe Award), Agatha 1978, Yanks 1978, Bear Island 1978, Playing for Time 1980, My Body My Child 1981, Wagner 1983, The Bostonians 1984, Wetherby 1985, Steaming 1985, Comrades 1987, Prick Up Yours Ears 1987, Consuming Passions 1988, A Man for All Seasons 1988, Orpheus Descending 1990, Young Catherine 1990, Howards End (1992, best supporting actress Oscar nomination 1993), The Wall 1992, Great Moments in Aviation 1993, Mother's Boy 1993, The House of the Spirits 1993, Crime & Punishment 1993, They 1993, Little Odessa 1994, A Month by the Lake 1996, Deja Vu 1996; *Publications* Pussies and Tigers (1963), Vanessa - An Autobiography (1992); *Style*— Miss Vanessa Redgrave, CBE; ✉ c/o James Sharkey Associates Ltd, 21 Golden Square, London W1R 3PA (☎ 0171 434 3801, fax 0171 494 1547)

REDGROVE, Peter William; s of late Gordon James Redgrove, and late Nancy Lena, *née* Cestrilli-Bell; *b* 2 Jan 1932; *Educ* Taunton Sch Somerset, Queens' Coll Cambridge; *m* 2, Penelope Shuttle, *qv*; *Career* scientific journalist and ed 1954–61, won Fulbright Award to travel to US as visiting poet to Univ of Buffalo NY 1961, Gregory fell in poetry Univ of Leeds 1962–65, resident author and sr lectr in complementary studies Falmouth Sch of Art Cornwall 1966–83, O'Connor prof of lit Colgate Univ NY 1974–75; freelance writer, poet, analytical psychologist; broadcaster BBC 1956–, reviewer Guardian 1975–, numerous prose articles for other jls; contrib: TLS, Spectator, New Statesman, Observer, Listener; writer of radio and TV drama (Imperial Tobacco prize for Radio Drama 1978, Giles Cooper Award for Radio Drama 1981, Prix Italia 1982); Queen's Gold Medal for Poetry 1996; FRSL; *Books* playbooks incl: Miss Carstairs Dressed for Blooding and other plays (1976), In the Country of the Skin (1973); psychology and sociology: The Wise Wound (with Penelope Shuttle, 1978), The Black Goddess and the Sixth Sense (1987), Alchemy for Women (with Penelope Shuttle, 1995); prose fiction incl: The Beekeepers (1980), The Facilitators (1982), The One Who Set Out to Study Fear (1989), The Cyclopean Mistress: Selected Short Fiction 1960–90 (1992); poetry incl: The Collector and Other Poems (1960), Penguin Modern Poets II (1968), Dr Faust's Sea-Spiral Spirit and Other Poems (1972), The Apple-Broadcast and Other New Poems (1981), The Working of Water (1984), The Mudlark Poems and Grand Buveur (1986), The Moon Disposes: Poems 1954–87, In the Hall of the Saurians (1987), The First Earthquake (1989), Poems 1954–87 (1989), Dressed as For a Tarot Pack (1990), Under the Reservoir (1992), The Cyclopean Mistress (1993), The Laborators (1993), My Father's Trapdoors (1994), Abyssophone (1995), Assembling a Ghost (1996); anthologies incl: Poets' Playground (1963), Lamb and Thundercloud (1975); *Recreations* work, photography, yoga; *Style*— Peter Redgrove, Esq; ✉ c/o David Higham Associates, 5–8 Lower John St, Golden Square, London W1R 4HA

REDHEAD, Prof Michael Logan Gonne; s of Robert Arthur Redhead (d 1992), and Christabel Lucy Gonne, *née* Browning (d 1966); *b* 30 Dec 1929; *Educ* Westminster, UCL (BSc, PhD); *m* 3 Oct 1964, Jennifer Anne, da of Montague Arthur Hill; 3 s (Alexander b 1965, Julian b 1968, Roland b 1974); *Career* dir Redhead Properties Ltd 1962, ptnr Galveston Estates 1970; prof: philosophy of physics Chelsea Coll London 1984–85, philosophy of physics King's Coll London 1985–87, history and philosophy of sci Univ of Cambridge 1987–; vice-pres Wolfson Coll Cambridge 1992–96 (fell 1988), Tarner lectr Trinity Coll Cambridge 1991; visiting fell All Souls Coll Oxford 1995; pres Br Soc for the Philosophy of Sci 1989; Lakatos award 1988; FInstP, FBA; *Books* Incompleteness Nonlocality and Realism (1987), From Physics to Metaphysics (1995); *Recreations* tennis, music, poetry; *Clubs* Athenaeum, Hurlingham, Queen's; *Style*— Prof Michael Redhead, FBA; ✉ 34 Coniger Rd, London SW6 (☎ 0171 736 6767); Department of History and Philosophy of Science, University of Cambridge, Free Sch Lane, Cambridge (☎ 01223 334540, car 0865 263199)

REDINGTON, (John) Michael; s of John William Clarence Redington (d 1932), and Kathleen, *née* Mawby (d 1944); *b* 18 May 1927; *Educ* Royal Wanstead Sch Essex; *m* Ann, da of John Clifford Connell (d 1974); 1 s (Simon John b 28 Sept 1958), 1 da (Amanda Jane (Mrs Stewart) b 20 Aug 1956); *Career* theatrical prodr; first prodn Theatre Royal Leicester 1942, toured with Old Vic Co Aust and NZ 1948 and USA 1953, with Associated Television Ltd 1954–64, ABC TV 1964–79, theatrical prodr 1979–; W End prodns incl: 84 Charing Cross Road (also on Broadway), Pack of Lies (also on Broadway), Mr and Mrs Nobody, Breaking the Code (also on Broadway), The Best of Friends, Jeffrey Bernard is Unwell, Bookends, It's Ralph, Our Song, Peace in Our Time, Sylvia; Soc of Film and TV Arts (now BAFTA) factual progs award 1960, Leonard Brett award 1960, Eisenhower Exchange fellowship 1964; *Books* About Religion (ed); *Clubs* Garrick; *Style*— Michael Redington, Esq; ✉ 10 Maunsel Street, Westminster, London SW1P 2QL (☎ 0171 834 5119, fax 0171 828 6947)

REDMAN, Prof Christopher Willard George; s of Prof Roderick Oliver Redman (d 1975), and (Annie) Kathleen Redman (d 1996); *b* 30 Nov 1941; *Educ* Perse Sch Cambridge, Univ of Cambridge (MA, MB BChir); *m* 8 Aug 1964, Corinna Susan, da of Prof Sir Denys Lionel Page, KBE (d 1978); 4 s (Paul b 1967, Andrew b 1969, George b 1972, Oliver b 1982), 1 da (Sophie b 1972); *Career* intern and resident dept of pathology Johns Hopkins Hosp Baltimore USA 1967, house offr Children's Hosp Sheffield 1969, sr house offr Jessop Hosp Sheffield 1969, lectr regius Dept of Med Radcliffe Infirmary Oxford 1970 (house offr 1968), prof Nuffield Dept of Obstetrics John Radcliffe Hosp Oxford 1993– (univ lectr 1976, clinical reader 1988, clinical prof 1992); FRCP 1982, FRCOG as eundum 1993; *Recreations* walking; *Style*— Prof Christopher Redman; ✉ Nuffield Department of Obstetrics and Gynaecology, John Radcliffe Hospital, Oxford OX3 9DU (☎ 01865 221009)

REDMAN, Creighton Thomas; s of Thomas Henry Redman (d 1986), of Towcester, Northants, and Nelsy Jennetta, *née* Bragg; *b* 24 Sept 1933; *Educ* Tiffin Boys' Sch Kingston Surrey; *m* 1, 2 Sept 1961 (m dis 1973), Diane Mary, da of Harold Hewitt, of

Blackpool; 2 da (Denise Helen b 1965, Fiona Jane b 1967); m 2, 1974, Josephine Willmott, *née* Russell; *Career* National Westminster Bank plc: joined 1948, commodities mangr Mincing Lane Branch London, chief mangr Lothbury Office, dep chm County NatWest Ltd; ret 1993; chm Westerly Yacht Construction Ltd 1991–94, currently dir Versailles Group plc; Gold medal rowing coxless IVs Commonwealth Games 1958, rep GB rowing coxless IVs World Championships 1957 and 1958; dep chm of Govrs Surrey Inst of Art & Design, memb Cncl Shaftesbury Homes & Arethusa, past pres Nat West Bank Rowing Club; memb Court of Assts Worshipful Co of Farmers, Freeman City of London; MInstD, MIOB; *Recreations* sailing, opera, rowing, shooting; *Clubs* Leander, Farmers', Royal Lymington Sailing; *Style*— Creighton Redman, Esq; ✉ Woodside Cottage, High Street Green, Chiddingfold, Surrey GU8 4XY (☎ and fax 01483 200241)

REDMAN, Timothy Stewart; s of Dudley Stewart Redman (d 1960), and Josephine Mary, *née* Baker (d 1952); *b* 4 June 1940; *Educ* Cheltenham Coll; *m* 23 May 1964, Gillian Judith, da of John Pillar (d 1974); 2 s (Jonathan Stewart b 1967, Nicholas Timothy b 1970); *Career* brewer; dir Greene King plc 1975–; *Recreations* gardening, fishing, shooting; *Style*— Timothy Redman, Esq; ✉ Orchard House, Comberton, Cambridge CB3 7EE; Chalet le Caribou, Les Carroz d'Araches, France; Greene King plc, Westgate Brewery, Bury St Edmunds, Suffolk IP33 1QT (☎ 01284 763222, fax 01284 706502)

REDMAN-BROWN, Geoffrey Michael; s of Arthur Henry Brown, of Newport, Gwent, and Marjorie Frances Joan, *née* Redman (d 1969); assumed by Deed Poll the additional surname of Redman before his patronymic 1960; *b* 30 March 1937; *Educ* Newport HS, Balliol Coll Oxford (MA); *m* 23 Feb 1988, Mrs Jean Wadlow, da of Leslie James Wilkinson (d 1986), of Essex; *Career* Nat Serv RAF 1956–58; Phillips & Drew (now UBS Ltd): joined 1961, ptnr 1970–86, dir 1986–90, ret 1990; dir: Wadlow Grosvenor Ltd 1990–93, Jean Wadlow Associates Ltd 1991– (chm 1994–); endowment fund tstee Balliol Coll Oxford 1988–, chm Balliol Coll Old Membs' Ctee 1991–; Prov Grand Master for Oxfordshire: United Grand Lodge of England 1985–, Grand Lodge of Mark Master Masons 1994–; tstee New Masonic Samaritan Fund 1991–; hon treas The League of Remembrance 1990–; Freeman City of London, Liveryman Worshipful Co of Broderers 1977; MSI (memb Stock Exchange 1967), AIIMR (AMSIA 1972); *Recreations* swimming, gardening, travel; *Clubs* Athenaeum, City of London, RAC; *Style*— Geoffrey Redman-Brown, Esq; ✉ 5 Three Kings Yard, Mayfair, London W1Y 1FL (☎ 0171 629 2638, fax 0171 495 6682); Priestfield, Hook Norton, Banbury, Oxon OX15 5NH (☎ 01608 737738, fax 01608 737648)

REDMAYNE, Clive; s of Procter Hubert Redmayne (d 1965), of Stockport, Cheshire, and Emma, *née* Torkington (d 1976); *b* 27 July 1927; *Educ* Stockport Sch, Univ of London (BSc); *m* 19 July 1952, Vera Muriel, da of Wilfred Toplis, MM (d 1983), of Stockport, Cheshire; 1 s (John Clive James b 27 July 1959), 1 da (Jane Susan (Mrs Goodwin) b 6 April 1956); *Career* stress offr: Fairey Aviation Co Stockport 1948–50 (apprentice 1944–48), English Electric Co Warton 1950–51, A V Roe & Co Chadderton 1951–55; head of structural analysis Weapons Div Woodford 1955–62, Structures Dept Royal Aircraft Estab Farnborough 1962–67, asst dir Project Time and Cost Analysis Miny of Technol 1967–70; MOD(PE): asst dir/MRCA 1970–74, dir Harrier 1978–80, dir gen Future Projects 1980–81, dir gen Aircraft 3 1981–84; div ldr systems engrg Namma Munich 1974–76, chief supt A & AEE Boscombe Down 1976–78, conslt aeronautical engr 1985–; MIMechE 1956, CEng 1970, FRAeS 1981; *Recreations* caravanning, walking, skiing, chess, bridge, reading; *Clubs* Caravan; *Style*— Clive Redmayne, Esq; ✉ Bowstones, 5 Westbrook View, Stottingway St, Upwey, Weymouth, Dorset (☎ 01305 814691)

REDMAYNE, Hon Sir Nicholas John; 2 Bt (UK 1964), of Rushcliffe, Nottingham; s of Baron Redmayne, DSO, TD, PC, DL (Life Peer and 1 Bt, d 1983); *b* 1 Feb 1938; *Educ* Radley, RMA Sandhurst; *m* 1, 7 Sept 1963 (m dis 1976), Ann (d 1985), da of Frank Birch Saunders, of Kineton, Warwicks; 1 s, 1 da; m 2, 1978, Mrs Christine Diane Wood Hewitt, da of late Thomas Wood Fazakerley; 2 step s; *Heir* s, Giles Martin Redmayne b 1 Dec 1968; *Career* cmmnd Grenadier Gds 1958–62; stockbroker; chm: Kleinwort Benson Securities, Kleinwort Benson Investment Management; dep chm Kleinwort Benson Group plc; *Recreations* shooting, tennis, skiing; *Style*— The Hon Sir Nicholas Redmayne, Bt; ✉ Walcote Lodge, Walcote, Lutterworth, Leics LE17 4JR (☎ 01455 55 2637, business 0171 623 8000)

REDMOND, Dr Aileen Oonagh Beatrice; da of Dr William Alexander Redmond (d 1948), of Ballyward, Co Down, NI, and Sheila Arabella, *née* Badger (d 1986); *b* 17 Oct 1936; *Educ* Alexandra Coll Dublin, Rainey Endowed Sch, Magherafelt Co Derry, Univ Trinity Coll Dublin (MB BCh, BAO, BA); *Career* assoc chief res Hosp for Sick Children Toronto 1966–67, clinical fell Harvard Med Sch Boston Mass 1967–68, clinical res fell Nutrition Unit Red Cross Childrens Hosp Capetown SA 1970–71, conslt paediatrician Royal Belfast Hosp for Sick Children and Belfast City Hosp 1971–; hon med advsr Cystic Fibrosis Res Tst NI Regn, memb Children in Need Appeals Ctee and NI Appeals Advsy Ctee BBC; memb Br Paediatric Assoc; *Recreations* gardening, travel; *Style*— Dr Aileen Redmond; ✉ 4 Rosevale Close, Drumbeg, Dunmurray, Belfast BT17 9LQ (☎ 01232 612024); Royal Belfast Hospital for Sick Children, Belfast (☎ 01232 240503)

REDMOND, Prof Anthony Damien; OBE (1994); s of Gerard Redmond (d 1976), and Kathleen, *née* Bates; *b* 18 Nov 1951; *Educ* Cardinal Langley Sch, Univ of Manchester (MB ChB, MD); *m* 22 Dec 1972, Caroline Ann, da of Dr John Arthur Howarth, of Devon; 3 da (Katherine Mary b 12 Dec 1978, Sarah Michelle b 15 Sept 1980, Helen Margaret b 24 April 1982); *Career* dir S Manchester Accident Rescue Team 1987–92 (attended Armemian Earthquake 1988, Lockerbie Air Crash 1988, Iranian Earthquake 1990, Kurdish refugees 1991, Ex-Yugoslavia 1992), conslt in emergency med N Staffs Trauma Centre 1991–, prof of emergency med Keele Univ 1995– (sr lectr 1992–95); chief exec UK-Med 1993–; dir Operation Phoenix Sarajevo 1994– (ldr ODA med team Sarajevo 1993); WHO conslt Ex-Yugoslavia 1992–93, memb UN Disaster Assessment and Co-ordination Team; fndr ed Archives of Emergency Med 1984–93; memb: Resuscitation Cncl UK, Fontmell Gp for Disaster Relief; Soviet Order for Personal Courage 1989 (for work in Armenian Earthquake), Mancunian of the Yr 1992; fell Royal Soc of Med; MRCP UK 1981, FRCSEd 1982, MIMgt 1985, FRCP (Glas) 1991; *Books* Lecture Notes on Accident and Emergency Medicine (1984), Accident and Emergency Medicine (jtly 1989), The Management of Major Trauma (1991); *Recreations* music; *Style*— Prof Anthony D Redmond, OBE; ✉ 27 Byrom St, Manchester M3 4PF; North Staffordshire Trauma Centre, Stoke-on-Trent, Staffs

REDMOND, Derek Anthony; s of Jim Redmond, and Jenny, *née* Howard; *b* 3 Sept 1965; *Educ* Roade Sch, Neane Coll; *m* Sharron Davies, *qv*; 1 s (Elliott Anthony Mark b 4 Nov 1993); *Career* athlete; full UK int 1985–; achievements at 400m: fourth Euro Championships 1986, fifth World Championships 1987; Br record holder; achievements in 4 x 400m relay: Gold Euro Championships 1986 and 1991 (Br, Euro and Commonwealth record), Gold World Championships 1991; *Recreations* golf (handicap 24); *Style*— Derek Redmond, Esq; ✉ c/o British Athletic Federation, 225a Bristol Road, Edgbaston, Birmingham B5 7UB

REDMOND, Geraldine Melaine; da of Jerome Anthony Wilson, of Liverpool, and Dorothy Kathleen, *née* Hoult; *b* 20 Jan 1953; *Educ* Notre Dame Convent Woolton, Upton RC Convent Wirral, Cygnets House London; *m* (m dis); 2 da (Melaine Francesca, Philippa Frances Kathleen); *Career* md Famous Army Stores (Holdings) Ltd; *Recreations* cookery, swimming, classic vintage car driving; *Style*— Mrs G M Redmond; ✉ Sunbeam House, Woolton Rd, Garston, Liverpool L19 5PH (☎ 0151 427 5151, fax 0151 427 3918)

REDMOND, Sir James; kt (1979); s of Patrick and Marion Redmond; *b* 8 Nov 1918; *Educ* Graeme HS Falkirk; *m* 1942, Joan Morris; 1 s, 1 da; *Career* radio offr Merchant Navy 1937–38 and 1939–45; BBC Television Alexandra Palace 1937–39; BBC: installation engr 1949, supt engr Television Recording 1960, sr supt engr TV 1963, asst dir of engrg 1967, dir of engrg 1968–78; pres IEE 1978–79; memb: Cncl Brunel Univ 1980–88, Cncl Open Univ 1981–95, Bd Services Sound & Vision Corp 1983–90; Hon DTech Brunel Univ 1991, Hon DUniv Open Univ 1995; FEng 1978, Hon FIEE; *Clubs* Athenaeum; *Style*— Sir James Redmond, FEng; ✉ 43 Cholmeley Crescent, Highgate, London N6 5EX (☎ 0181 340 1611)

REDMOND, John Vincent; s of Maj Robert Spencer Redmond, TD, of Knutsford, Cheshire, and Marjorie Helen, *née* Heyes; *b* 10 April 1952; *Educ* Wrekin Coll, Western Reserve Acad Ohio USA, Univ of Kent at Canterbury (BA); *m* 21 May 1977, Tryphena Lloyd (Nina), da of Jenkin John Lloyd Powell, of Carmarthen, Dyfed; 2 s (William b 1981, Samuel b 1985); *Career* admitted slr 1976; Cobbetts Manchester 1974–75, Clyde & Co Guildford and London 1975–78, Laytons Bristol and London 1978– (currently ptnr and head of construction law); chm Soc of Construction Law, Law Soc 1976; FCIArb; *Recreations* mountains, sailing; *Style*— John Redmond, Esq; ✉ Hafod, Scot Lane, Chew Stoke, Bristol BS18 8UW (☎ 01275 333181); Laytons, St Bartholomews, Lewins Mead, Bristol BS1 2NH (☎ 0117 929 1626, fax 0117 929 3369)

REDMOND, Martin; MP (Lab) Don Valley (majority 13,534); *b* 15 Aug 1935; *Educ* Woodlands RC Sch, Univ of Sheffield; *Career* memb Doncaster BC 1975– (chm Lab Gp and ldr Cncl 1982–), vice chm Doncaster AHA, MP (Lab) Don Valley 1983– (NUM. sponsored), memb Cncl of Europe 1987–; *Style*— Martin Redmond, Esq, MP; ✉ House of Commons, London SW1A 0AA

REDPATH, Bryan William; s of Andrew Redpath, of Charlesfield, St Boswells, and Margarette Riddle, *née* Craig; *b* 2 July 1971; *Educ* Kelso HS; *m* 11 Aug 1995, Gillian; *Career* rugby union scrum-half; debut Melrose RFC 1989; 5 full Scottish caps (debut v New Zealand 1993), memb World Cup squad 1995; joiner 1988–; *Recreations* golf; *Style*— Bryan Redpath, Esq; ✉ c/o Ian McLauchlan Associates, 35 Chester Street, Edinburgh EH3 7EN (☎ 0131 226 2277); c/o Melrose Rugby Club, Greenyards, Melrose (☎ 01896 822993)

REDWOOD, Dr David Robert; s of Edward James Redwood (d 1967), and Florence Maude Elizabeth, *née* Harper; *b* 4 Nov 1935; *Educ* King's Sch Worcester, Jesus Coll Cambridge (MA, MB BChir); *m* 1, 1960, Mehranguise (d 1980); 3 s (Michael b 1961, Simon b 1963, David b 1970); m 2, 1 May 1982, Janet Elizabeth, da of George Young, CBE; 1 s (Jamie b 1987), 1 da (Katherine b 1984); *Career* head of cardiovascular diagnosis Nat Inst of Health Bethesda Maryland USA 1973–76 (visiting scientist 1968–76), head of cardiology Cedars of Lebanon Hosp Miami Florida USA 1976–77; conslt cardiologist: St George's Hosp London, Harley St, St Anthony's Hosp Cheam Surrey 1977–; author of chapters in cardiology textbooks and numerous papers in scientific jls; FRCP; *Recreations* sailing, walking, photography, golf; *Style*— Dr David Redwood; ✉ St Anthony's Hospital, London Rd, Cheam, Surrey SM3 9DW (☎ 0181 337 6691)

REDWOOD, Rt Hon John Alan; MP (C) Wokingham (majority 25,709), PC (1993); s of William Charles Redwood, of Kent, and Amy Emma, *née* Champion; *b* 15 June 1951; *Educ* Kent Coll Canterbury, Magdalen Coll Oxford (BA), St Antony's Coll (DPhil, MA); *m* 1974, Gail Felicity, da of Robert Stanley Chippington; 1 s (Richard b 1982), 1 da (Catherine b 1978); *Career* fell All Souls Coll Oxford 1972–87; investmt analyst Robert Fleming & Co 1974–77, clerk, mangr then dir NM Rothschild Asset Mgmnt 1977–83, advsr to Treasy and Civil Service Select Ctee 1981, head Prime Minister's Policy Unit 1983–85, dir (Overseas Corporate Finance) NM Rothschilds 1986–87, non-exec dir Norcros plc 1986–89 (chm 1987–89); MP (C) Wokingham 1987–, Parly under-sec of state for corporate affrs DTI 1989–90, min of state for corporate affairs, fin servs and telecommunications 1990–92, min of state for local govt and inner cities DOE 1992–93, sec of state for Wales 1993–95 (resigned to contest Cons leadership); cncllr Oxfordshire CC 1973–77; *Books* Reason, Ridicule and Religion: The Age of Enlightenment in England 1660–1750 (first published 1976, reissued 1996); *Recreations* village cricket, water sports; *Style*— The Rt Hon John Redwood, MP; ✉ House of Commons, London SW1A 0AA (☎ 0171 219 4205, constituency 0118 978 4464)

REDWOOD, Sir Peter Boverton; 3 Bt (UK 1911), of Avenue Road, St Marylebone; s of Sir Thomas Boverton Redwood, 2 Bt (d 1974), and his 1 w, Ruth Mary, *née* Creighton (d 1989); *b* 1 Dec 1937; *Educ* Gordonstoun; *m* 22 Aug 1964, Gilian Waddington, o da of John Lee Waddington Wood, of Limuru, Kenya; 3 da (Anna Kathryn (Mrs Patrick Thomson) b 1967, Colina Margaret Charlotte b 1969, Gaynor Elizabeth b 1972); *Heir* half-bro, Robert Boverton Redwood b 24 June 1953; *Career* Nat Serv 1956–58, cmmnd Seaforth Highlanders (Reg Cmmn) 1959, KOSB served in UK (despatches), BAOR, Netherlands, ME, Africa and Far East, Staff Coll Camberley 1970, Nat Def Coll Latimer 1978–79, Col KOSB, ret 1987; memb Queen's Body Guard for Scotland (Royal Co of Archers); Liveryman Worshipful Co of Goldsmiths; *Recreations* shooting, silversmithing; *Clubs* Army and Navy; *Style*— Sir Peter Redwood, Bt; ✉ c/o National Westminster Bank, 80 Market Place, Warminster, Wiltshire BA12 9AW

REDWOOD, Robert Boverton; s of Sir Thomas Boverton Redwood, 2 Bt (d 1974); hp of half-bro, Sir Peter Redwood, 3 Bt; *b* 24 June 1953; *Educ* Truro Cathedral Sch; *m* 1978, Mary Elizabeth Wright; 1 s (James Boverton b 2 Oct 1985), 1 da (Morwenna Anne Carlile b 1982); *Career* police offr; *Style*— Robert Redwood, Esq

REECE, Sir Charles Hugh; kt (1988); s of Charles Reece (d 1962), and Helen Yuille Reece; *b* 2 Jan 1927; *Educ* Pocklington Sch, Huddersfield Coll, Univ of Leeds (BSc, PhD); *m* 1951, Betty, *née* Linford; 2 da (Ann Heather b 1954, Pamela Janet b 1957); *Career* ICI plc (formerly ICI Ltd): res chemist 1949–69, res dir Mond Div 1969–72, dep chm Mond Div 1972–75, chm Plant Protection Div 1975–79, res and technol dir 1979–89; dir Finnish Chemicals Oy 1971–75, chm Teijin Agricultural Chemicals Ltd 1975–78, chm Robens Inst of Industl and Environmental Health 1984–93; non-exec dir: APV plc 1984–96, British Biotechnology plc 1989–95; memb: ACOST 1983–89, SERC 1984–89, Advsy Bd of Res Cncls 1989–92, Univs Funding Cncl 1989–93, Ctee for the Euro Devpt of Sci and Technol 1989–93; Hon DSc: Univ of St Andrews, Queen's Univ Belfast, Univ of Bristol, Univ of Surrey, Univ of Plymouth; FRSC; *Recreations* sailing, gardening; *Style*— Sir Charles Reece; ✉ Heath Ridge, Graffham, Petworth, W Sussex (☎ 01798 876274)

REECE, His Hon Judge; (Edward Vans) Paynter; s of Clifford Mansel Reece, QC (d 1973), and Catherine Barbara, *née* Hathorn (d 1974); *b* 17 May 1936; *Educ* Blundell's, Magdalene Coll Cambridge (MA); *m* 23 Sept 1967, Rosamund Mary, da of Thomas Vaughan Roberts; 3 s (Rupert Vaughan Paynter b 6 July 1968, William Hugh Hathorn b 11 April 1970, Henry John Mansel b 25 March 1975), 1 da (Alexandra Catherine b 2 July 1973); *Career* RA 1954–56 (2 Lt 1955); called to the Bar Inner Temple 1960, recorder of the Crown Court S Eastern Circuit 1980–82, circuit judge (SE Circuit) 1982–; *Recreations* fishing, golf; *Clubs* Garrick, New Zealand Golf; *Style*— His Hon Judge Reece; ✉ Romford County Court, 2a Oaklands Avenue, Romford, Essex RM1 4DP

REED, Alec Edward; CBE (1994); s of Leonard Reed (d 1953), of London, and Anne, *née* Underwood (d 1983); *b* 16 Feb 1934; *m* 16 Sept 1961, Adrianne Mary, da of Harry Eyre (d 1943); 2 s (James b 12 April 1963, Richard b 27 March 1965), 1 da (Alexandra b 22 Jan 1971); *Career* fndr chm: Reed Executive plc 1960–, Inter-Co Comparisons Ltd 1969–70, Reed Coll of Accountancy 1971, Medicare Ltd 1975–86; hon chm and chief exec Andrews and Ptnrs Ltd 1985–89; pres: Inst of Employment Consits 1974–78, Int Confedn of Private Employment Agencies Assoc 1978–81; chm Employment Think

Tank 1979; memb: Helpage Exec Ctee 1983–88, Oxfam Fundraising Ctee 1989–92, Cncl CIMA 1991–95; fndr: Womankind Worldwide 1988, Ethiopiaid 1989–; prof of enterprise and innovation Royal Holloway Univ of London 1993–; elected hon fell Royal Holloway 1988; FCMA, FIPD; *Books* Returning to Work (1989), Reed My Lips (1990); *Recreations* family, theatre, cinema, tennis, riding; *Clubs* Royal Over-Seas League; *Style*— Alec Reed, Esq, CBE; ✉ Reed Executive plc, Bedford House, Madeira Walk, Windsor, Berks SL4 1EU (☎ 01753 850441, fax 01753 841688)

REED, Air Cdre April Anne; RRC (1981); da of Capt Basil Duck Reed, RN (d 1969), and Mignon Ethel Nancy, *née* Neame (d 1976); *b* 25 Jan 1930; *Educ* Sherborne House Chandlers Ford, Channing Sch Highgate, Middx Hosp London, Royal Maternity Hosp Belfast; *Career* Princess Mary's RAF Nursing Serv: joined as Flying Offr 1954, Flt Offr 1958, Sqdn Ldr dep matron 1970, Wing Cdr sr matron 1976, Gp Capt princ matron 1980, Air Cdre dir nursing servs 1984; ret due to serv reorganistaion 1985; memb charity exec RAF Benevolent Fund 1985–89; *Recreations* gardening, wildlife, hill walking, antiques, oriental rugs; *Clubs* RAF; *Style*— Air Cdre April Reed, RRC; ✉ 3 Garners Row, Burnham Thorpe, Norfolk (☎ 01328 730486); 2 Murlaggan, Roy Bridge, By Fort William, Inverness-shire (☎ 01397 732225)

REED, Gavin Barras; s of Lt-Col Edward Reed (d 1953), and Greta Milburn, *née* Pybus (d 1964); *b* 13 Nov 1934; *Educ* Eton, Trinity Coll Cambridge (BA); *m* 28 June 1957, Muriel Joyce, da of Humphrey Vaughan Rowlands (d 1985), and Edna Muriel, *née* Foster (d 1990); 1 s (Christopher b 1964), 3 da (Fiona b 1958, Joanna b 1960, Lucinda b 1962); *Career* Nat Serv Pilot Fleet Air Arm; vice chm Scottish & Newcastle plc until 1994; directorships incl: Wainhomes plc (chm), John Menzies Plc, Burtonwood Brewery PLC, Ivory & Sime Enterprise Capital plc, Ivory & Sime Trustlink Ltd (chm), Milburn Estates Ltd (chm); Liveryman Worshipful Co of Brewers; *Recreations* shooting, tennis; *Clubs* Naval, New (Edinburgh); *Style*— Gavin Reed, Esq; ✉ Whitehill, Aberdour, Burntisland, Fife KY3 0RW; Broadgate, West Woodburn, Northumberland NE48 2RN

REED, Glenn Maximillian; s of John Wilfred James Reed, of Westbury-on-Trym, Bristol, and Jean, *née* Arnold; *b* 25 Dec 1955; *Educ* Henbury Sch, S Bristol Tech Coll, Univ of Southampton (LLB); *m* 31 July 1985, Dr Deborah Lyn Reed, da of Denis Raymond, of Knowle, Bristol; 1 s (Alexander Timothy Maximillian b 26 April 1992); *Career* called to the Bar Michaelmas 1982, admitted slr 1993; ptnr Messrs Longrigg Harris, princ dir Serious Crime Div, Higher Ct advocate (all proceedings); former memb Hon Soc of the Inner Temple (Duke of Edinburgh scholar) 1978; *Recreations* cooking, reading, ancient history, horse riding; *Style*— Glenn Maximillian Reed, Esq; ✉ Longrigg Harris, Trafalgar House, Nelson Street, Bristol BS1 2JT (☎ 0117 929 7972, fax 0117 929 7088)

REED, Jane Barbara; da of William Charles Reed, and Gwendoline Laura, *née* Plaskett; *b* 31 March 1940; *Educ* Royal Masonic Sch for Girls; *Career* ed Woman's Own 1969–79, publisher Quality Monthly Gp IPC 1979–81, ed-in-chief Woman 1981–83, md Holborn Publishing Gp IPC 1983–85, managing ed (features) Today Newspaper 1985–86, managing ed News UK Ltd 1986–89, dir of corporate affairs News International 1989–; memb Cncl Literacy Tst, tstee St Katharine & Shadwell Tst; chm Media Soc; *Books* Girl about Town (1964), Kitchen Sink or Swim (with Deirdre Saunders, 1981); *Recreations* music, writing, work, family; *Clubs* Groucho, Reform; *Style*— Miss Jane Reed; ✉ News International, 1 Virginia Street, London E1 9XY

REED, Dr John Langdale; CB (1993); s of John Thompson Reed (d 1966), of Northampton, and Elsie May, *née* Abbott (d 1962); *b* 16 Sept 1931; *Educ* Oundle, Cambridge Univ (MA, MB BChir), Guy's Hosp; FRCP 1974, FRCPsych 1974 (Hon FRCPsych 1994); *m* 7 Jan 1959, Hilary, da of Lt-Col John Freeman Allin, MC (d 1976), of Kings Norton; 1 s (John Richard b 1967), 1 da (Alison b 1960); *Career* Nat Serv RAMC 1958–60; conslt psychiatrist Bart's London 1967–96, sr lectr Bart's Med Coll 1967–96; dir Community Psychiatry Res Unit 1979–86, chm Vanguard Housing 1981–86, sr princ med offr Health Care Div (Med) Dept of Health London 1986–93, special advsr in forensic psychiatry Dept of Health 1993–96, med inspr HM Inspectorate of Prisons 1996–; chm: Dept of Health/Home Office Review of servs for Mentally Disordered Offenders 1990–92, Dept of Health/Home Office Working Gp on High Security Psychiatry Care 1992–93, Dept of Health/Home Office Working Gp on Psychopathic Disorder 1992–93, Advsy Ctee on Mentally Disordered Offenders 1993–96; *Books* Psychiatric Services in the Community (jtly 1984); *Recreations* genealogy, bridge, walking; *Style*— Dr John Reed, CB; ✉ Willow Tree House, Westleigh Drive, Bromley, Kent BR1 2PN (☎ 0181 467 1452, fax 0181 249 4940)

REED, Malcolm Edward; s of Colin Reed, of Barnsley, Yorks, and Lilian, *née* Dixon; *b* 5 May 1947; *Educ* Penistone GS, Hollings Coll Manchester (HND), Univ of Durham (MSc); *Career* joined Trust House Hotels 1966; trained in Weston-super-Mare, Nice and Edinburgh; mangr: George Hotel Huddersfield 1971, Tyneside Post House 1973, Randolph Hotel Oxford 1976; dir Swallow Hotels 1982–96 (resigned, joined 1978); lay reader C of E 1976; Freeman City of London 1978; memb Assoc of MBAs 1966, FHCIMA 1979; *Recreations* church music, opera, walking, cooking; *Clubs* Wig & Pen; *Style*— Malcolm Reed, Esq; ✉ Clough Cottage, Cathill, nr Sheffield, Yorkshire S30 6JB (☎ 01226 767328)

REED, Paul; s of Donald Henry Reed, of 2 Mercer Court, Exeter, Devon, and Irene, *née* Vanstone; *b* 18 Aug 1956; *Educ* Ladysmith Secdy Modern Sch, Exeter Coll Catering Dept; *m* Sheridan Elizabeth, da of Alan Woodman; 2 da (Harriet b 6 April 1987, Emily 20 October 1990); *Career* commis chef rising to head chef Buckerell Lodge Hotel 1974–79, commis chef rising to sous chef Hilton Hotel Park Lane London 1979–82, sr chef de partie Dorchester Hotel Park Lane London 1982–83, chef and owner London House Restaurant Broad Clyst Devon 1983–84, head chef Copper Inn Pangbourne Berks 1984–85, sr sous chef The Dorchester Hotel Park Lane London 1985–86, exec chef The Chester Grosvenor Hotel Chester 1986–; Gold medallist Culinary World Cup 1986, Northern Chef of the Year Life Mgazines; memb Academie Culinaire de France; *Recreations* golf; *Clubs* Upton by Chester Golf; *Style*— Paul Reed, Esq; ✉ 4 Westway, Trevalyn Estate, Rossett, Clwyd LL12 0DX (☎ 01244 571149); Chester Grosvenor Hotel, Eastgate St, Chester, Cheshire CH1 1LT (☎ 01244 324024, fax 01244 313246)

REED, Dr William Leonard; s of William Alfred Reed (d 1949), of Dulwich, and Alice Kate, *née* Bloxam (d 1964); *b* 16 Oct 1910; *Educ* Dulwich Coll, Guildhall Sch of Music, Jesus Coll Oxford (MA, DMus, DipEd), RCM; *Career* Nat Fire Serv 1941–44; music lectr Br Cncl in Scandinavia, Baltic States and Finland 1937–39, music master Sloane Sch Chelsea 1945, tutor adult educn classes in music appreciation for Oxford Delegacy for Extra Mural Studies ILEA and WEA 1962–, dir music Westminster Theatre Arts Centre 1967–80; Freeman Worshipful Co of Musicians 1944; memb: Sullivan Soc, Grainger Soc, Howells Soc, PRS; *Compositions* Variations on 'On Ilkley Moor baht 'At' for Piano Duet (1933), Fantasy for Flute, Viola and Harp (1934), Sonata for Violin and Piano (1934), Recitative and Dance for Orchestra (1935), Concert Piece for Two Clarinets and Piano (1936), Suite for Organ (1936), Triumphal March for Organ (1936), Idyll for Small Orchestra (first bdcast 1936), Saraband for Orchestra (first bdcast 1936), Pavane Caprice and Child Portrait for Orchestra (1937), Two Short Pieces for Orchestra (1937), Hornpipe for Orchestra (first bdcast 1938), Two Short Pieces for Orchestra (first bdcast 1938), Song of the Countrywomen (1939), Six Facets for Orchestra (first bdcast 1939), Lady Nevell Suite for String Orchestra (first bdcast 1939), Fantasy for Piano Quartet (first bdcast 1940), Suite for Clarinet and Strings (1942), Toccata for Two Pianos (1942), Theme and Variations for Two Pianos (1942), Four Child Portraits for Piano (1943–49), Dr Johnson's Suite for String Quartet (1944), Country Piece and Scherzo for String Quartet (1944), Clive's House for Piano (1944), Waltz for Two Pianos (1945), Peter's Prelude and Anne's Gavotte for Piano (1945), Fantasia on 'Bridgebuilders' for Organ (1946), Interlude on 'Solemn Melody' for Organ (1946), Suite ('The Top Flat') for Viola and Piano (1947), Suite ('On the Road') for Violin and Piano (1947–48), Penelope's Pavane (Pavane Caprice) for Flute and Piano (1948), Mountain House Suite for Orchestra (1949), Waltz Fantasy for Orchestra (first bdcast 1949), Rhapsody on Christmas Carols for Violin and Piano (1951), Two Pieces for String Quartet (1957), Easter Morning for Mezzo-Soprano, Chorus and Piano (1959), A Reflection for Small Orchestra (first bdcast 1969), Scherzo for Orchestra (first bdcast 1970), Forty Personal Pieces for Piano (1970–91), Festive March for Orchestra (1978), Four Airs for Basset Horn and Piano (1979), Christmas Piece for Reciter, Chorus and Orchestra (1981), Concert Overture for Orchestra (first bdcast 1981), Five Spiritual Songs for Baritone and Piano (first bdcast 1981), Fantasy for String Quartet (first bdcast 1985), Three Surrey Impressions for Two Pianos (first bdcast 1985), Dr Johnson's House for String Orchestra (first bdcast 1986), Concert Suite - Prelude, Nocturne and Rhapsody for Piano (first bdcast 1988), Piano Trio (first bdcast 1990), Child Portraits for Piano (first bdcast 1990), Concert Waltz for Piano (first bdcast 1991), over 80 songs (mostly choral); *Arrangements* for string orchestra incl: Two German Suites (1936), Two Italian Suites (1936), Three Flemish Pieces (1936), Corelli Suite (1937), Thomas Arne Suite (with optional Wind) (1938), Purcell - Two Suites from 'The Faery Queen' (1939); others incl: Petrocokino - Tercentenary Suite for Piano (Homage to Handel and Bach) arranged for Orchestra (1979–82), Penelope Thwaites - A Lambeth Garland for Vocal Quartet and Piano Duet arranged for Two Pianos without voices (1987); *Musicals* Annie (1967), Love All (1978); collaborations with other composers: The Vanishing Island (1955), The Crowning Experience (1958), High Diplomacy (1969); *Books* ed: The Treasury of Christmas Music (1950), Music of Britain (1952), The Treasury of Easter Music (1963), The Second Treasury of Christmas Music (1967); jt ed: The Treasury of English Church Music (1965), The Treasury of Vocal Music (1969), National Anthems of the World (with M J Bristow, 1985, 1987, 1993 and 1997); *Recreations* photography; *Style*— Dr William L Reed; ✉ Upper Suite No 7, The Quadrangle, Morden College, London SE3 OPW (☎ 0181 305 0380)

REED-PURVIS, Air Vice-Marshal Henry; CB (1982), OBE (1972); *b* 1 July 1928; *Educ* King James I Sch, Univ of Durham (BSc); *m* 1951, Isabel Price; 3 da (Jane, Sara, Shona); *Career* served RAF Regt in: Iraq, Persian Gulf, Oman, Malaya, Borneo, Europe, N America; dir RAF Regt 1976–79, Cmdt-Gen RAF Regt and Dir-Gen Security (RAF) 1979–83, ret; mktg and sales dir Br Aerospace Dynamics 1983–91; vice pres Cncl for Cadet Rifle Shooting; dir and tstee SAAFA Forces Help; *Recreations* golf, archaeology, bridge; *Clubs* RAF; *Style*— Air Vice-Marshal Henry Reed-Purvis, CB, OBE; ✉ Little Lem Hill Farm, Nr Lechlade, Gloucestershire GL7 3EB

REEDAY, (Thomas) Geoffrey; s of Thomas Cockcroft Reeday (d 1947), and Marion, *née* Johnson (d 1975); *b* 20 July 1924; *Educ* Queen Elizabeth GS Wakefield, Univ of London (LLB); *Career* Nat Serv WWII Army 1943–47, NW Europe RASC 1944–47; banker, lawyer, lectr; called to the Bar Lincoln's Inn 1954; head Dept of Law Poly of Central London (now Univ of Westminster) 1977–85, chief examiner in law relating to banking Inst of Bankers 1973–86; hon pres Keighley Charity Gala Ctee 1993; Freeman City of London 1977, Liveryman Worshipful Co of Chartered Secs and Administrators 1978; FCIS 1978, Hon FCIB 1989; *Books* Law Relating to Banking (5 edn, 1985), Legal Decisions Affecting Bankers (co-ed vols 9, 10 and 11, 1991); *Recreations* railway preservation; *Style*— Geoffrey Reeday, Esq; ✉ 66 Lamorna Grove, Stanmore, Middx HA7 1PG (☎ 0181 952 4591)

REEKIE, Jonathan; s of Dr Andrew Reekie, of New Delhi, and Virginia, *née* Cadbury; *b* 2 Sept 1964; *Educ* Marlborough, Bristol Business Sch; *m* 18 June 1993, Caroline, *née* Gibbs; 2 da (Honor b 25 May 1994, Rose b 17 Sept 1995); *Career* co mangr Musica Nel Chiostro Batignano Italy 1984–88 (dir 1989–), co co-ordinator Glyndebourne Festival Opera 1987–91, dir Almeida Opera and gen mangr Almeida Theatre 1991–; vice chair Opera Music Theatre Forum; *Style*— Jonathan Reekie, Esq; ✉ Almeida Theatre, Almeida Street, London N1 1TA (☎ 0171 226 7432, fax 0171 704 9581)

REEN, Rob; s of William John Reen, of Swansea, and Olwen Beryl, *née* Kimmings; *b* 31 July 1951; *Educ* Penlan Sch Swansea, Cheltenham Coll of HE (BA), Univ of Wales Cardiff (PGCE); *m* Joan, da of Bob Kerfoot; 1 step s (Christopher), 1 step da (Kirsty); *Career* hotelier and painter; teacher in art and design Mayfield GS 1974–76, head Art and Design Sir Henry Floyd GS 1976–89; proprietor Ynyshir Hall 1989–; numerous exhbns and one-man shows, work in int collections; memb: Pride of Britain consortium, Welsh Rarebits consortium; *Awards* Welsh Tourist Bd De Luxe Award 1992–96, RAC Blue Ribbon Award 1993–96, AA Courtesy and Care Award 1994, AA 3 Red Star Status 1995–96; *Recreations* golf; *Clubs* Aberdovey Golf, Machynlleth Golf; *Style*— Rob Reen, Esq; ✉ Ynyshir Hall, Eglwysfach, Nr Machynlleth, Powys SY20 8TA (☎ 01654 781209, fax 01654 781366)

REES, Allen Brynmor; s of Allen Brynmor Rees, of Penarth, S Glamorgan (d 1941), and Elsie Louise, *née* Hitchcock (d 1958); *b* 11 May 1936; *Educ* Monmouth Sch, Univ of Wales Aberystwyth (LLB); *m* 26 Aug 1961, Nerys Eleanor, da of Wynne Evans (d 1977), of Upper Maen, Meifod, Powys; 2 da (Meriel Anne Brynmor b 7 Oct 1968, Eleanor Haf Brynmor b 22 Aug 1975); *Career* former sr ptnr Rees Page Slrs (incorporating Darbey-Scott-Rees and Pages and Skidmore Hares & Co); chm W Mids Rent Assessment Panel 1968–93, princ slr to Birmingham Midshires Building Society 1976–92; pt/t chm Social Security Tbnls 1980–92, regnl chm Industl Tbnls 1993–; author of The Solicitors Notebook for the Slrs Jl 1968–91, chm Bilston Round Table 1974 (memb 1966–77), memb Legal Aid Bd Ctee 1975–92, pres Exec Ctee Old Monmothians 1977 (memb 1966–92), Negligence Panel rep for Wolverhampton Area of Law Soc 1982–92, pres Bilston Rotary Club 1984 and 1985 (memb 1974–93); memb Law Soc 1962; *Recreations* squash, canoeing, shooting, skiing, gardening; *Style*— Allen Rees, Esq; ✉ Rossleigh, Shaw Lane, Albrighton, Wolverhampton WV7 3DS; Yr Hen Ystabl, Meifod, Powys (☎ 01902 372423)

REES, Andrew Merfyn; s of Peter Donald Rees, and Rita Clarice, *née* Coleshaw; *b* 20 July 1954; *Educ* Culford Sch, FitzWilliam Coll Cambridge (MA); *m* 11 Sept 1981, Monica, da of Rosman Gordon; 2 s (Richard b 1983, Charles b 1987); *Career* admitted slr 1981; ptnr Eversheds 1985–94; dir AMG Industries Corporation 1994–; *Recreations* shooting, travel, tennis; *Style*— A M Rees, Esq; ✉ AMG Industries Corporation, Harborne House, 70 High Street, Harborne, Birmingham B17 9NJ (☎ 0121 427 7272, fax 0121 427 2404)

REES, Angharad Mary; da of Prof Linford Rees, CBE, *qv*, and Catherine Magdalen, *née* Thomas (d 1993); *b* 16 July 1949; *Educ* Commonwealth Lodge Surrey, Sorbonne Paris, Rose Bruford Drama Coll, Univ of Madrid; *m* 12 Sept 1973, Christopher de Lerisson Cazenove, *qv*, the actor; 2 s (Linford James de Lerrison b 20 July 1974, Rhys William de Lerrison b 12 Dec 1976); *Career* actress; nominated Best Newcomer (Film) award for Moments, nominated Best Actress (Radio) award 1985; *Theatre* incl: A Winter's Tale (Young Vic), Gulliver's Travels (Mermaid), It's a Two Foot Six Inch Above the Ground Word (Wyndhams), John Osborne's A Picture of Dorian Gray (Greenwich), The Millionairess (Haymarket), A Handful of Dust (Lyric Hammersmith), Romeo and Juliet (Watford), Hamlet (Welsh Nat Theatre), Richard II (Redgrave Theatre), An Ideal Husband (Peter Hall Prodn); *Television* for BBC incl: As You Like It, Dennis Potter's Joe's Ark, Dear Brutus, Gathering Storm, Anthony Trollope's The Way We Live Now (series), Poldark (series), Brian Moore's The Temptation of Eileen Hughes, Trainer (series); other credits incl: The Piano Player (YTV), Forgotten Story (series, HTV), Master of the Game (CBS), Close to Home (2 series, LWT); *Films* incl: Under Milk Wood, Moments, the Girl in Blue Velvet, The Love Bug; *Style*— Ms Angharad Rees; ✉ c/o James Sharkey Associates Ltd, Third Floor Suite, 15 Golden Square, London W1R 3AG (☎ 0171 434 3801, fax 0171 494 1547)

REES, Arthur Morgan; OBE (1963, CBE 1970), QPM (1970), DL (Staffs 1967); s of Thomas Rees, of S Wales; *b* 20 Nov 1912; *Educ* Llandovery Coll, St Catharine's Coll Cambridge (BA, MA, Rugby blue); *m* 1943, Dorothy, *née* Webb (d 1988); 1 da (Rosemary); *Career* RAF Pilot 1941–46, Substantive Sqdn Ldr and Actg Wing Cdr; Chief Constable: Denbighshire Constabulary 1956–64, Staffordshire & Stoke on Trent Police 1964–77; conslt dir: Wedgwood 1977–80, Royal Doulton 1980–83, Armitage Shanks 1980–83, Wales Britannia Building Soc 1983–87, Inter Globe Security Servs Ltd 1985–; chm: Midlands Sport Cncl 1967–77 (life memb Midlands Sports Advsy Cncl), Staffs St John Cncl 1967–88, Queen's Silver Jubilee Appeal Sports Ctee, Prince's Tst 1974–88, English Karate Bd, Br Karate Bd, Hawks Dinner Ctee 1986; dep pres Staffs Boys' Club 1970–; pres: (fndr) Ex Police in Indust and Commerce Soc, Eccleshall RFC 1979–, Staffs Playing Fields Assoc 1986, Crawshays RFC 1992– (chm 1962–92); former Wales Rugby Union Int rugby referee for London Soc; KStJ; *Recreations* rugby, karate, hockey; *Clubs* RAF, Hawks (Cambridge); *Style*— Arthur Rees, Esq, CBE, QPM, DL; ✉ 18 Broom Hall, Oxshott, Surrey KT22 OJ2 (☎ 0137 284 3500)

REES, Brian; s of Frederick Thomas Rees (d 1966), of Sunderland, and Anne, *née* Keedy (d 1976); *b* 20 Aug 1929; *Educ* Bede GS Sunderland, Trinity Coll Cambridge; *m* 1, 17 Dec 1959, Julia (d 1978), da of Sir Robert Birley, KCMG, FSA (d 1983), of Somerton, Somerset; 2 s (Robert Hugh Corrie b 13 April 1961, Philip Timothy b 28 Aug 1964), 3 da (Jessica Margaret Anne b 19 April 1963, Natalia Rachel b 24 Jan 1966, Camilla Marion b 2 April 1969); m 2, 3 Jan 1987, Juliet Mary Akehurst, da of C D'O Gowan (d 1996); *Career* Nat Serv RASC 1948–49; housemaster Eton 1963–65 (asst master 1952–63); headmaster: Merchant Taylors' 1965–73, Charterhouse 1973–81, Rugby 1981–84; dir Argentine-Br Conf 1989–91, res asst House of Commons 1991–92; chm ISIS 1982–83, patron Conf for Ind Educ 1983– (former pres); Liveryman Worshipful Co of Merchant Taylors; *Books* A Musical Peacemaker (Biography of Sir Edward German, 1987), History of Idealism: Essays and Addresses of Sir Robert Birley (ed, 1990); *Recreations* music, painting, travel; *Style*— Brian Rees, Esq; ✉ 52 Spring Lane, Flore, Northants NN7 4LS (☎ 01327 340621)

REES, Prof Brinley Roderick; s of John David Rees (d 1947), of Port Talbot, W Glamorgan, and Mary Ann, *née* Roderick (d 1976); *b* 27 Dec 1919; *Educ* Christ Coll Brecon, Merton Coll Oxford (MA), Univ of Wales (PhD); *m* 23 Aug 1951, Zena Muriel Stella, da of Alfred Reginald Mayall, of Leominster; 2 s ((Idris John) Mark b 1954, (Alan) Hugh b 1957); *Career* Welch Regt 1940–45, Capt 4 Welch Regt 1943, Capt/Adj 15 Welch Regt 1945; Univ Coll Cardiff: prof of Greek 1958–70, dean of arts 1963–65, dean of students 1968–69, hon lectr 1980–88, emeritus prof 1981, vice pres 1986–88; Univ of Birmingham: prof of Greek 1970–75, dean of arts 1973–75, life memb Univ Ct 1982–; princ St David's Univ Coll Lampeter 1975–80, pres Classical Assoc 1978–79; Rotarian 1966–75, Hon Rotarian 1975–; Hon LLD Univ of Wales 1981, Leverhulme emeritus fell 1984–86; *Books* The Merton Papyri, II (with Bell and Barns, 1959), Papyri from Hermopolis and Elsewhere (1964), Lampas (with Jervis, 1970), Classics for the Intending Student (ed, 1970), Pelagius - A Reluctant Heretic (1988), The Letters of Pelagius and his Followers (1991); *Recreations* writing, reading; *Style*— Prof Brinley Rees; ✉ 31 Stephenson Ct, Wordsworth Ave, Cardiff, S Glam CF2 1AX (☎ 01222 472058)

REES, Prof Charles Wayne; CBE (1995); s of Percival Charles Rees (d 1963), and Daisy Alice, *née* Beck (d 1941); *b* 15 Oct 1927; *Educ* Farnham GS, Univ Coll Southampton, Univ of London (BSc, PhD, DSc); *m* 19 Dec 1953, Patricia Mary, da of George Walter Francis; 3 s (David Charles b 1958, George Wayne b 1959, Michael Francis b 1961); *Career* lectr in organic chemistry: Birkbeck Coll London 1955–57, King's Coll London 1957–63 (reader 1963–65); prof of organic chemistry: Univ of Leicester 1965–69, Univ of Liverpool 1969–78 (Heath Harrison prof 1977–78); Hofmann prof of organic chemistry Imperial Coll London 1978–93 (emeritus prof 1993–); visiting prof Univ of Würzburg 1968; has lectured widely in Australia, China, Japan and USA; Royal Soc of Chemistry: Tilden lectr 1973–74, Pedler lectr 1984–85, Award in Heterocyclic Chemistry 1980, Int Award in Heterocyclic Chemistry 1995; Andrews lectr Univ NSW 1988; pres: Chemistry Section Br Assoc for the Advancement of Sci 1984, Royal Soc of Chemistry 1992–94 (pres Perkin Div 1981–83); Hon DSc Univ of Leicester 1994; has written/edited approx 30 books and 350 res papers on organic chemistry; FRSC 1966, FRS 1974; *Recreations* food and wine, music, London; *Style*— Prof Charles Rees, CBE, FRS; ✉ 67 Hillgate Place, London W8 7SS (☎ 0171 229 5507); Chemistry Department, Imperial College, London SW7 2AY (☎ 0171 594 5768, fax 0171 594 5800)

REES, Sir David Allan (Dai); kt (1993); *b* 28 April 1936, Silloth, Cumbria; *Educ* UCNW Bangor (BSc, PhD), Univ of Edinburgh (DSc), Sloan Sch of Industl Mgmnt (graduate Sr Execs Prog 1977); *m* 1959, Myfanwy Margaret, *née* Parry Owen; 2 s, 1 da; *Career* lectr in chemistry Univ of Edinburgh 1960–70, visiting prof of biochemistry Univ of Wales Cardiff 1972–77, various positions rising to princ scientist and sci policy exec Unilever Research Colworth Lab Sharnbrook Bedford 1970–82, pt/t dir MRC Cell Biophysics Unit KCL 1980–82, dir Nat Inst for Med Res 1982–87, chief exec MRC 1987–96 (memb Cncl 1983–96, fndr dir MRC Collaborative Centre Mill Hill 1983–86); memb: LINK Steering Gp 1987–89, Advsy Bd for Res Cncls 1987–93, Ctee for the Euro Devpt of Sci and Technol (CODEST) 1991–94, Advsy Bd Forensic Scis Serv Agency 1992–, Euro Sci and Technol Assembly (ESTA) and Bureau 1994–; chm Euro Med Res Cncls 1990–94, vice pres Fondation Louis Jeantet de Medicine 1991–, pres Euro Sci Fndn 1994–; Carbohydrate Chemistry Award Chemical Soc 1970, Colworth Medal Biochemical Soc 1970; Hon DSc: Edinburgh 1989, Wales 1991; FRSC 1975, FRS 1981 (Philips lecture 1984, memb Cncl 1985–87), FIBiol 1983; Hon FRCP 1986, hon fell UCNW 1988, FKC 1989, FRCPath 1992; *Publications* numerous res pubns in learned jls on polysaccharide biochemistry and biophysics, cell surface interactions and on sci policy; *Style*— Sir Dai Rees, FRS

REES, Gareth Mervyn; s of Joseph Rees (d 1981), of Llangadog, Wales, and Gwen Rees (d 1988); *b* 30 Sept 1935; *Educ* Llandovery HS, St Mary's Hosp Univ of London (MB BS, MS); *m* 1, 1962 (m dis 1968), Anne Frisby Richards; 1 s (Philip b 1964); m 2, 21 Dec 1969, Prof Lesley Rees, *qv*, da of Howard Leslie Davis (d 1942); *Career* house surgn and house physician St Mary's Hosp 1960, int res fell Dept of Heart Surgery Univ of Oregon Portland USA 1970, conslt i/c Dept of Cardio-thoracic Surgery St Bartholomew's Hosp London 1984– (conslt heart surgn 1973–), sr surgeon St Bartholomew's Hosp 1996–; memb: Cardiac Soc, Int Coll of Surgns, Assoc of Thoracic Surgns UK; FRCS 1966, FRCP 1983; *Recreations* fishing, skiing, rugby football; *Clubs* Garrick, RAC; *Style*— Gareth Rees, Esq; ✉ 10 Upper Wimpole St, London W1 (☎ 0171 487 3598)

REES, Geoffrey; s of Sidney Rees, of Neath, W Glam, and Mary, *née* Thomas (d 1981); *b* 28 Feb 1946; *Educ* Neath Boys' GS, St Luke's Coll Univ of Exeter (RFC, Devon RFC, Neath RFC), Emmanuel Coll Cambridge (Rugby blue, capt CURUFC, London Welsh RFC, Middx RFC); *m* June 1974, Diana Jane, da of Peter Wride; 1 da (Rebecca Jane b Aug 1976), 1 s (Gareth Thomas b Jan 1978); *Career* asst history master Shene Boys' Sch Richmond 1969–71, history master and house tutor Eastbourne Coll Sussex 1974–76, head of humanities and head of sixth form Billericay Sch Essex 1976–79, dir of studies Coombe Dean Sch Plymouth 1979–82, dep princ Bideford Community Coll Devon 1982–85, headmaster Burrington Sch Plymouth 1985–87, princ Ivybridge Community Coll 1987–; chm Devon Science and Technol Regnl Orgn 1988–90; educn liaison offr IOD 1991–; chm Devon Assoc of Secdy Heads 1992–94, vice chm Devon Educn Business Ptnrship Cncl 1992–93, memb Devon and Cornwall TEC Strategic Educn Forum 1993–; memb NAHT 1988–; FRSA 1994; *Recreations* rugby, sailing, surfing, theatre, travel; *Clubs* Welsh Academicals RFC, London Welsh RFC, Hawks (Cambridge); *Style*— Geoffrey Rees, Esq; ✉ Ivybridge Community College, Harford Road, Ivybridge, Devon PL21 0JA (☎ 01752 691000/896662, fax 01752 691247)

REES, (Thomas Morgan) Haydn; CBE (1975), DL (Flints 1969, Clwyd 1974); s of late Thomas Rees, of Gorseinon, Swansea, and Mary, *née* Bowen; *b* 22 May 1915; *Educ* Swansea Business Coll; *m* 12 July 1941, Marion, da of A B Beer, of Mumbles, Swansea; 1 da ((Elizabeth) Maryon Haydn (Mrs Hughes)); *Career* serv WWII 1939–45; slr 1946, sr asst slr Caernarvonshire CC 1947; Flints CC 1948–74: dep clerk until 1965, chief exec 1966–74, clerk of the peace (until office abolished 1971, formerly dep clerk), clerk Police Authy (until merger with N Wales Police Authy 1967, formerly dep clerk), clerk Magistrates Cts Ctee (formerly dep clerk), clerk Probation Ctee (formerly dep clerk), clerk Justices Advsy Ctee, Clerk to Lieutenancy; Clwyd CC 1974–77: chief exec, clerk Magistrates Cts Ctee, clerk Justice Advsy Ctee, Clerk to Lieutenancy; clerk N Wales Police Authy 1967–77, sec Welsh Counties Ctee 1968–77, asst cmmr Royal Cmmn on Constitution 1969–73; memb: Welsh Cncl 1968–79, Welsh Arts Cncl 1968–77 (memb Regnl Ctee 1981–93), Lord Chllr's Ctee for Wales and Chester circuit 1972–77, Prince of Wales Ctee 1976–79, Gorsedd Royal National Eisteddfod of Wales, Nat Water Cncl 1977–82, Water Space Amenity Cmmn 1977–82, Severn Bridge Ctee 1978–81, Theatre Clwyd Govrs 1983– (clerk 1974–77), North Wales Music Festival 1983–; pt/t memb Bd BSC (Indust) Ltd 1979–83; chm: Govt Quality of Life Experiment in Clwyd 1974–76, Welsh Water Authy 1977–82, New Jobs Team Shotton Steelworks 1977–82, N Wales Arts Assoc 1981–93, Deeside Enterprise Tst Ltd 1982–89, Mold Mags 1985 (vice chm 1978–84); pres: Clwyd Voluntary Servs Cncl 1980–, Mold Cancer Research Ctee 1982–, Clwyd Pre-Retirement Assoc 1986–91; JP Mold 1977; *Recreations* the arts; *Style*— Haydn Rees, Esq, CBE, DL; ✉ Cefn Bryn, Gwernaffield Rd, Mold, Clwyd CH7 1RQ (☎ 01352 752421)

REES, Dr Helene Ceredwyn; da of Delwyn Garland Rees, of South Yarra, Victoria, Aust, and Jean Helene, *née* Höette; *b* 8 April 1948; *Educ* Presbyterian Ladies Coll Melbourne Aust, Univ of Melbourne (MB BS), LLB 1996; *m* 1, 17 Dec 1971 (m dis 1984), David Alan McDonald, s of Alan McDonald; 2 s (Lachlan James b 11 March 1974, Alexander Rhys b 25 April 1980), 1 da (Kate Helene b 17 July 1975); m 2, 4 May 1991, Dr Christopher Daking Macfarlane Drew, s of late Sir Robert Drew, KCB, CBE; *Career* annual appts in gen med and surgery in maj teaching hosps in Melbourne 1972–73, in trg in pathology Melbourne Aust 1973–81 (The Royal Children's Hosp, Fairfield Infectious Diseases Hosp, Alfred Hosp, Prince Henry's Hosp), sr registrar in histopathology Hammersmith Hosp 1984–86 (registrar 1981–84), sr lectr and hon conslt in histopathology St Bartholomew's Hosp Med Coll 1986–94, pathologist Farrer-Brown Histopathology 1994–; memb: Kew Soc, Aust and NZ Med and Dental Assoc 1984, Hunterian Soc 1984, Graduate Union of Univ of Melbourne 1980, Soc of Doctors in Law 1993; vice pres Med Soc of London 1990–91 (fell 1984); Freeman City of London 1986, Liveryman Worshipful Soc of Apothecaries 1989 (Yeoman 1985); FRCPA (Aust) 1980, FRCPath 1996 (MRCPath 1984); *Recreations* gymnastics, golf, classical music; *Clubs* Hogarth, Meon Valley Country, Overstone Golf; *Style*— Dr Helene Rees; ✉ c/o Farrer-Brown Histopathology, Bewlay House, 32 Jamestown Road, London NW1 7BY

REES, (William) Howard Guest; CB (1988); s of Walter Guest Rees (d 1967), of S Wales, and Margaret Elizabeth, *née* Harries (d 1978); *b* 21 May 1928; *Educ* Llanelli GS, Royal Veterinary Coll London (BSc, MRCVS, DVSM); *m* 1952, Charlotte Mollie, da of Enoch Collins (d 1979), of S Wales; 3 s (Michael, Nicholas, Alan), 1 da (Amanda); *Career* vet surgn; chief vet offr MAFF 1980–88 (joined 1953); memb Cncl RVC 1989–, pres Int Animal Health Code Cmmn OIE Paris 1988–, vice pres Br Veterinary Assoc 1994–96, vice chm Soc for the Protection of Animals Abroad 1992–95; Hon FRASE 1988; *Recreations* golf; *Clubs* Pennard Golf (S Wales), Tyrrells Wood (Leatherhead); *Style*— Howard Rees, Esq, CB; ✉ Taliesin, Paddocks Way, Ashtead, Surrey KT21 2QY

REES, Prof Hubert; DFC (1944); s of Owen Rees (d 1970), and Evelyn Tugela, *née* Bowen; *b* 2 Oct 1923; *Educ* Llanelli Co and Llandovery Co Sch, Univ Coll Wales (BSc), Univ of Birmingham (PhD, DSc); *m* 26 Dec 1946, Mavis Rosalind, da of Roland Hill; 2 s (Wynne d 1977, Hubert), 2 da (Gwyneth, Judith); *Career* RAFVR 1942–46; lectr Genetics Dept Univ of Birmingham 1950–59; Dept of Agric Botany University College of Wales: sr lectr 1959, reader 1966, prof 1967–91; FRS 1976; *Recreations* fishing; *Style*— Prof Hubert Rees, DFC, FRS; ✉ Irfon, Llanbadarn Rd, Aberystwyth SY23 1EY (☎ 01970 623 668)

REES, Rt Rev (John) Ivor; s of David Morgan Rees (d 1928), and Cecilia Maria Perrott, *née* Evans (d 1955); *b* 19 Feb 1926; *Educ* Llanelli GS, Univ Coll of Wales (BA), Westcott House Cambridge; *m* 5 Aug 1954, Beverley, da of Henry Albert Richards (Co Sergeant-Major, d 1946); 3 s ((Christopher) Meirion b 1956, (David) Mark b 1958, Stephen (Wynne) b 1963); *Career* Coastal forces and Pacific fleet RN 1943–47; curate: Fishguard 1952–55, Llangathen 1955–57; vicar: Slebech & Uzmaston 1957–65 (priest in charge 1957–59), Llangollen 1965–74; rector Wrexham 1974–76, canon St Asaph 1975–76, dean of Bangor Cathedral 1976–88, vicar of the cathedral parish of Bangor 1979–88, archdeacon of St Davids 1988–91, bishop of St Davids 1991–Oct 1995 (asst bishop 1988–91), ret; OStJ 1981, sub-prelate Order of St John 1993; *Books* The Parish of Llangollen and its Churches (1971), Keeping Forty Days - Addresses for Lent (1989); *Recreations* good music, light reading; *Style*— The Rt Rev Ivor Rees; ✉ Llys Dewi, 45 Clover Park, Uzmaston Road, Haverfordwest, Dyfed SA61 1UE (☎ 01437 764846)

REES, John Charles; QC (1991); s of Ronald Leslie Rees (d 1985), of Cardiff, and Martha Terese, *née* Poole; *b* 22 May 1949; *Educ* St Joseph's Sch Cardiff, St Illtyd's Coll Cardiff, Jesus Coll Cambridge (McNair scholar, LLB, Russell Vick prize, boxing blue); *m* 30 July 1970, Dianne Elizabeth, da of William Kirby, of Cardiff; 3 s (Christopher Lloyd b 26 Nov 1973, Jonathan Elystan b 27 Feb 1977, William Ronald b 7 Nov 1987), 1 da (Felicity Ann Rose b 21 Aug 1980); *Career* called to the Bar Lincoln's Inn 1972, currently asst recorder of the Crown Court; steward Br Boxing Bd of Control (chm Welsh Area Cncl); tstee and govr St John's Coll Cardiff; *Recreations* reading, music, sport (especially football and boxing); *Clubs* Hawks' (Cambridge); *Style*— John Rees, Esq, QC; ✉ Marleigh Lodge, Druidstone Road, Old St Mellons, Cardiff, South Glamorgan CF3 9XD (☎ 01222 794918); 33 Park Place, Cardiff, South Glamorgan CF1 3BA (☎ 01222 233313)

REES, Jonathan Michael; s of Robert Bruce Rees (d 1981), and Evelyn Foy, *née* Puckey; *b* 25 Feb 1965; *Educ* Edgbarrow Sch Crowthorne, Univ of Southampton (BSc); *Career* hockey player; capt Wales Hockey Team 1989– (rep 1986–), rep GB 1988, memb GB Olympic Trg Squad 1991–92; *Recreations* wine tasting, films, music, books; *Clubs* Hounslow Hockey; *Style*— Jonathan Rees, Esq; ✉ Ormandine, 10 Hurst Close, Hook Heath, Woking, Surrey GU22 0DU (☎ 01483 723518); Andersen Consulting, 2 Arundel St, London WC2R 3LT (☎ 0171 438 5000)

REES, Prof Lesley Howard; da of Howard Leslie Davis (d 1942), and Charlotte Patricia Siegrid, *née* Young (d 1960); *b* 17 Nov 1942; *Educ* Pates Girls' GS Cheltenham, Malvern Girls' Coll, Bart's Med Coll Univ of London (MB BS, MD, DSc); *m* 21 Dec 1969, Gareth Mervyn Rees, *qv*, s of Joseph Philip Rees; *Career* ed Clinical Endocrinology 1979–84, public orator Univ of London 1984–86, sub dean Bart's Med Coll 1983–87, chm Soc for Endocrinology 1984–87, sec gen Int Soc for Endocrinology 1984–, prof of chem endocrinology Bart's Med Coll, dean Bart's Med Coll 1989–95; FRCP 1979, FRCPath 1988; *Books* author numerous papers on endocrinology; *Recreations* reading, music, art, skiing, cooking; *Style*— Prof Lesley Rees; ✉ 23 Church Row, Hampstead, London NE3 6UP (☎ 0171 794 4936); Medical College of St Bartholomew's Hospital, West Smithfield, London EC1A 7BE (☎ 0171 601 7437, 0171 600 7522)

REES, Prof (William) Linford Llewelyn; CBE (1977); s of Edward Parry Rees (d 1947), and Mary Rees (d 1952); *b* 24 Oct 1914; *Educ* Llanelli GS, Univ Coll Cardiff (BSc), WNSM (MB BCh, MD), Univ of London (DSc); *m* 1940, Catherine Magdalen (d 1993), da of David Thomas, of Alltwen (d 1941); 2 s, 3 da (incl Angharad Rees, *qv*); *Career* emeritus prof Univ of London; conslt physician Bart's 1980–, civilian conslt in psychiatry to RAF until 1983; treas World Psychiatric Assoc 1966–78, pres Psychiatric Rehabilitation Assoc 1995 (former vice chm), pres RCPsych 1975–78, pres BMA 1978–79, chm Stress Fndn (vice pres) and Medico-Pharmaceutical Forum 1980, psychiatrist in chief and exec med dir Charter Medical 1984–89, dir and med advsr Huntercombe Manor Hosp and Rehabilitation Group Ltd 1989– (pres 1992–); Liveryman: Worshipful Co of Barber Surgns, Worshipful Soc of Apothecaries; Hon LLD Univ of Wales; distinguished fell American Psychiatric Assoc 1968, hon FRCPsych, hon fell American Coll of Psychiatrists 1977; FRCP; *Recreations* photography, entertaining grandchildren, gardening, swimming; *Clubs* Athenaeum; *Style*— Prof Linford Rees, CBE; ✉ 62 Oakwood Ave, Purley, Surrey; 27 Speed House, Barbican, London EC1 (☎ 0171 588 4881)

REES, Rt Rev (Leslie) Lloyd; s of Rees Thomas Rees (d 1939), of Trebanos, Swansea, Glam, and Elizabeth Rees (d 1965); *b* 14 April 1919; *Educ* Pontardawe GS, Kelham Theol Coll; *m* 5 Feb 1944, Rosamond (d 1989), da of Thomas Smith (d 1960); 2 s (Christopher Michael b 1946, Gerald Hugh b 1948); *Career* curate St Saviour's Roath Cardiff and asst chaplain HM Prison Cardiff 1942–45; chaplain: HM Prison Durham 1945–48, HM Prison Dartmoor (and vicar of Princetown) 1948–55, HM Prison Winchester 1955–62; chaplain gen of prisons 1962–80, hon canon of Canterbury 1966–80, chaplain to HM The Queen 1971–80, bishop of Shrewsbury 1980–86, hon canon Lichfield 1980–86, asst bishop Diocese of Winchester 1986–; memb Parole Bd 1987–90; ChStJ; Freeman of the City of London; *Recreations* music; *Style*— The Rt Rev L Lloyd Rees; ✉ Kingfisher Lodge, 20 Arle Gardens, Alresford, Hants SO24 9BA (☎ 01962 734619)

REES, Prof Lovat Victor Charles; s of Sqdn Ldr Daniel George Rees (d 1960), of Nairn, Scotland, and Margaret Jane, *née* Urquhart Stephen (d 1967); *b* 7 Nov 1927; *Educ* Robert Gordon's Coll Aberdeen, Univ of Aberdeen (BSc, PhD, DSc); *m* 12 Aug 1953, Elizabeth Margaret, da of Joseph Main (d 1989), of Stonehaven, Scotland; 1 s (Lovat Michael Graham b 1959), 3 da (Lesley Elizabeth b 1957, Shauna b 1961, Gillian Main b 1963); *Career* asst lectr Univ of Aberdeen 1952–53, sr scientific offr AWRE Aldermaston 1953–57, prof Imperial Coll London 1958–93 (prof emeritus 1993–); hon fell Univ of Edinburgh 1993–; FRSC, CChem 1984, FRSE 1996; *Recreations* rifle shooting, golf; *Clubs* St Nicholas Rifle & Pistol, Chislehurst Brechin Golf; *Style*— Prof Lovat Rees, FRSE; ✉ 12 Netherbank View, Edinburgh EH16 6YY (☎ 0131 658 1670); University of Edinburgh, Chemistry Department, West Mains Road, Edinburgh EH9 3JJ (☎ 0131 650 4766, fax 0131 650 6472, telex 727442 (UNIVED G), e-mail lvcr01@tattoo.ed.ac.uk)

REES, Prof Sir Martin John; kt (1992); s of Reginald Jackson Rees (d 1994), and (Harriette) Joan, *née* Bett (d 1985); *b* 23 June 1942; *Educ* Shrewsbury, Trinity Coll Cambridge (MA, PhD); *Career* prof Univ of Sussex 1972–73, Plumian Prof of astronomy and experimental philosophy Univ of Cambridge 1973–91, dir Cambridge Inst of Astronomy 1977–91, Royal Soc res prof 1992–; Astronomer Royal 1995–; Regents fell Smithsonian Inst Washington 1984–88, visiting prof Harvard Univ, foreign assoc US Nat Acad Sci; pres: Royal Astronomical Soc 1992–94, British Assoc for Advanced Science 1994–95; tstee of the British Museum 1996–; fell King's Coll Cambridge 1969–, foreign hon memb American Acad of Arts and Scis, memb Pontifical Acad of Scis, memb Academia Europaea; foreign memb: Royal Swedish Acad of Science, Accademia Lincei (Rome), Norwegian Acad of Sciences; hon memb: American Philosophical Soc, Russian Acad of Science; hon fell Trinity Coll Cambridge 1995–, hon fell Jesus Coll Cambridge 1996–; hon fell Indian Acad of Scis, officier dans l'Ordre des Arts et des Lettres 1991; FRS; *Recreations* rural pursuits; *Style*— Prof Sir Martin Rees, FRS; ✉ West Farm House, Orwell, Royston, Herts SG8 5QN; c/o King's College, Cambridge CB2 1ST

REES, Rev Canon (Richard) Michael; s of Rev Richard Rees (d 1975), of Bedford, and Margaret Patricia, *née* Head; *b* 31 July 1935; *Educ* Brighton Coll, St Peter's Coll Oxford (MA), Tyndale Hall Bristol; *m* 6 Sept 1958, Yoma Patricia, da of Maj the Rev Cyril Herbert Hampton (d 1995); 1 s (Timothy b 1960), 1 da (Killadeas b 1961); *Career* ed Missionary Mandate 1956–69; curate: All Saints Crowborough Sussex 1959–62, Christ Church with Emmanuel Clifton Bristol 1962–64; chaplain Bristol ATC 1963–64, vicar Christ Church Clevedon Avon 1964–72, chaplain Clevedon Maternity Hosp, vicar Holy Trinity Church Cambridge 1972–84, chm Cambridge Cncl of Churches, Br Cncl of Churches 1983–90, chief sec Church Army 1984–90, canon missioner Chester Dio 1990–, canon residentiary Chester Cathedral 1990– (vice-dean 1993–), county ecumenical offr 1991–; tstee: Disabled Christians Fellowship 1962–96 (chm 1962–72), Cambridge Work Relations Gp 1984–90, Simeon's Tstees 1969– (chm 1983–); govr St Brandon's Sch Clevedon 1969–87; *Recreations* photography, tropical fish, classical music; *Style*— The Rev Canon Michael Rees; ✉ 5 Abbey Green, Chester CH1 2JH (☎ and fax 01244 347500)

REES, Prof Michael Ralph; *b* 19 April 1950; *Educ* Shene GS, Univ of E Anglia (BSc), Univ of Sheffield (MB ChB, Herbert Price Prize (jtly)), MRCP (UK), DMRD, FRCR; *m*; 2 c; *Career* jr hosp appts Royal Infirmary and Royal Hallamshire and Northern Gen Hosps Sheffield 1976–79, sr registrar in radiology Sheffield Area and Trent Regnl Trg Scheme 1981–83 (registrar 1979–81), sr registrar in cardiac radiology Northern Gen Hosp Sheffield 1983–84, conslt cardiac radiologist Killingbeck Regnl Cario-thoracic Unit and St James Univ Hosp Leeds 1984–93, prof of radiological sci Univ of Keele Sch of Postgrad Med and conslt in cardiovascular intervention North Staffordshire Hosp Stoke-on-Trent 1993–95, prof of clinical radiology Univ of Bristol 1995–; res fell/assoc Dept of Radiology and Cardiology Univ of Iowa USA June 1984–April 1985, research assoc in cardiac imaging Deborah Heart & Lung Centre New Jersey USA May-Sept 1985, prof of radiology and med (cardiology) Stanford Univ Palo Alto Calif USA June 1992–Jan 1993; visiting prof Univ of Ioannina Greece 1996–; chm: Nat Hosp Jr Staff Ctee 1979–84, Jr Membs Forum BMA 1982–83, Non Trust Hosps Gp Med Ctee 1991–93; elected memb GMC 1984–89; BMA: memb 1976, memb Cncl 1979–84, memb Leeds Exec Ctee 1986–88, memb Med Academic Staff Ctee 1995–, memb Central Conslts Staff Ctee 1996–, memb Negotiating Sub-ctee 1996–; memb: American Med Assoc 1985–86, Radiological Soc of N America 1985, Br Cardiac Soc 1986, Br Cardiovascular Intervention Soc 1987 (memb Cncl 1992–), Br Interventional Radiology Soc 1988, Cardiovascular Cncl American Heart Assoc 1988, Br Med Laser Assoc 1989 (memb Cncl 1990–), Cardiovascular and Interventional Radiology Soc of Europe 1990 (memb Membership Ctee 1993–), Euro Med Laser Assoc 1992, Int Soc of Endovascular Surgery 1993, RSM 1993, Forum on Angiology 1993; fell: Int Coll of Angiology 1988, American Coll of Angiology 1992; *Books* A Colour Atlas of Interventions in Cardiovascular Disease (in preparation), Interventional Cardiovascular Disease (in preparation); author of various book chapters and numerous articles in academic jls; *Style*— Prof Michael Rees; ✉ University of Bristol, Department of Clinical Radiology, Bristol Royal Infirmary, Marlborough Street, Bristol BS2 8HW (☎ 0117 928 2731, fax 0117 928 2319, e-mail m.rees@bris.ac.uk)

REES, Nigel Thomas; s of (John Cedric) Stewart Rees (d 1989), and Frances Adeline, *née* Gleave (d 1982); *b* 5 June 1944; *Educ* Merchant Taylors', New Coll Oxford (MA); *m* 6 May 1978, Susan Mary, da of Raymond Bates (d 1962); *Career* radio and TV presenter, author; BBC Radio 4: Today 1976–78, Quote...Unquote 1976–, Stop Press 1984–86; ITV: Amoebas to Zebras 1985–87, Challenge of the South 1987–88; *Books* Quote...Unquote (3 vols 1978–83), Graffiti (5 vols 1978–86), Why do We Say...? (1987), The Newsmakers (1987), Talent (1988), A Family Matter (1989), Dictionary of Popular Phrases (1990), Dictionary of Phrase and Allusion (1991), Best Behaviour (1992), Politically Correct Phrasebook (1993), Epitaphs (1993), Chambers Dictionary of Modern Quotations (1993), Letter Writing (1994), Brewer's Quotations (1994), Guinness Book of Humorous Anecdotes (1994), As We Say In Our House (1994), Guinness Dictionary of Jokes (1995), Phrases and Sayings (1995), Cassell Dictionary of Clichés (1996); *Recreations* listening to music, swimming; *Style*— Nigel Rees, Esq; ✉ 24 Horbury Crescent, London W11 3NF (fax 0171 727 8535)

REES, Owen; CB (1991); s of John Trevor Rees (d 1970), of Trimsaran, Dyfed, and Esther (d 1977), *née* Phillips; *b* 26 Dec 1934; *Educ* Llanelli GS, Univ of Manchester (BA); *m* 17 May 1958, Elizabeth (d 1991), da of Harold Frank Gosby (d 1955), of Henley-on-Thames and Trimsaran; 1 s (David), 2 da (Philippa, Helen); *Career* Civil Serv; Bd of Trade 1959–69, Cabinet Office 1969–71, Welsh Office 1971–, head Euro Div Welsh Office 1972–75, sec for Welsh Educn 1977–78, head Educn Dept 1978–80, dir Indust Dept 1980–85, head Econ and Regnl Policy Gp 1985–89, head Agriculture Dept 1990–94; *Style*— Owen Rees, Esq, CB; ✉ 4 Llandennis Green, Cyncoed, Cardiff CF2 6JX

REES, Peter John; s of Leslie Marchant Rees, of St Florence, nr Tenby, Dyfed, and Betty, *née* Bass; *b* 21 April 1957; *Educ* Baines Sch Poulton-le-Fylde Lancashire, Downing Coll Cambridge (MA); *m* 15 Aug 1981, Allison Mary, da of Patrick John Williams, of Wallingford, Oxon; 1 da (Megan b 7 May 1988); *Career* admitted slr 1981; ptnr Norton Rose 1987–; memb IBA (vice-chm Int Construction Projects Ctee), sec Official Referees Slrs Assoc; Freeman Worshipful Co of Slrs (memb Insurance Sub Ctee); memb: RHS, Law Soc; hon memb Assoc of Fells and Legal Scholars Center and hon memb Bd of Advsrs for Int Legal Studies; ACIArb; *Books* Norton Rose on Jurisdiction and Judgments (1993); *Recreations* rugby football, association football, golf, scuba diving, theatre, gardening; *Clubs* Hawks, Stapleford Abbots Golf, Brentwood RUFC; *Style*— Peter Rees, Esq; ✉ Norton Rose, Kempson House, Camomile Street, London EC3 (☎ 0171 283 6000, fax 0171 283 6500)

REES, Baron (Life Peer UK 1987), of Goytre, Co Gwent; Peter Wynford Innes Rees; PC (1983), QC (1969); s of Maj-Gen Thomas Wynford Rees, CB, CIE, DSO, MC, Indian Army (d 1959), of Goytre Hall, Abergavenny, and Rosalie, da of Sir Charles Alexander Innes, KCSI, CIE (d 1959); *b* 9 Dec 1926; *Educ* Stowe, ChCh Oxford; *m* 1969, Mrs Anthea Peronelle Wendell, da of late Maj Hugh John Maxwell Hyslop, Argyll & Sutherland Highlanders; *Career* served Scots Gds 1945–48; barr 1953, practised Oxford circuit; contested (C): Abertillery 1964 and 1965, Liverpool, West Derby, 1966; MP (C): Dover 1970–74, Dover and Deal 1974–83, Dover 1983–87; PPS to Solicitor-Gen 1972; min of state HM Treasury 1979–81; min for Trade 1981–83, chief sec to Treasury and memb Cabinet 1983–85; memb: Ct and Cncl Museum of Wales, Museum and Galleries Cmmn; chm CLM plc and various other companies, dep chm Leopold Joseph plc, chm and dir of various other companies; Liveryman Worshipful Co of Clockmakers; *Clubs* Boodle's, Beefsteak, White's, Pratt's; *Style*— The Rt Hon Lord Rees, PC, QC; ✉ Goytre Hall, Abergavenny, Gwent; 39 Headfort Place, London SW1X 7DE

REES, Peter Wynne; s of Gwynne Rees, of Virginia Water, Surrey, and late Elizabeth Rodda, *née* Hynam; *b* 26 Sept 1948; *Educ* Pontardawe GS, Whitchurch GS, Bartlett Sch of Architecture, UCL (BSc), Welsh Sch of Architecture, Univ of Wales (BArch), Poly of the South Bank (BTP); *Career* architectural asst Historic Buildings Div GLC 1971–72, asst to Gordon Cullen CBE 1973–75, architect Historic Areas Conservation Div DOE 1975–79, asst chief planning offr Borough of Lambeth 1979–85; Corp of London: controller of planning 1985–87, city planning offr 1987–; tstee Bldg Conservation Tst 1987–91, fndr memb and dir Br Cncl for Offices; life memb: SPAB, Nat Tst; Freeman City of London 1985; memb: RIBA 1975, FRTPI 1982, FRSA 1988; *Recreations* swimming, Nordic skiing, playing the viola, music and tidying; *Style*— Peter Wynne Rees, Esq; ✉ City Planning Officer, Corporation of London, PO Box 270, Guildhall, London EC2P 2EJ (☎ 0171 332 1700, fax 0171 332 1806)

REES, Philip; s of John Trevor Rees, of Ebbw Vale, Gwent, and Olwen Muriel, *née* Jones (d 1982); *b* 1 Dec 1941; *Educ* Monmouth Sch, Univ of Bristol (LLB); *m* 6 Aug 1969, Catherine, da of Joseph Stephen Good, of Cardiff; 1 s (David Stephen b 27 Aug 1970), 1 da (Siân Catrin b 1 Oct 1973); *Career* called to the Bar 1965, recorder of the Crown Ct 1983–, head of chambers; *Recreations* music, sport; *Clubs* Cardiff and County; *Style*— Philip Rees, Esq; ✉ 35 South Rise, Llanishen, Cardiff CF4 5RF (☎ 01222 754364); 34 Park Place, Cardiff CF1 3TN (☎ 01222 382731, fax 01222 22542)

REES, Dr Richard John William (Dick); CMG (1979); s of William Rees, MVO (d 1952), of London, and Gertrude Ethel, *née* Smith (d 1959); *b* 11 Aug 1917; *Educ* E Sheen County Sch, Univ of London, Guy's Hosp Med Sch (BSc, MB BS, FRCPath, FRCP); *m* 1942, Kathleen, da of Joseph Harris, MVO (d 1967), of Yorks; 3 da (Lorna, Hazel, Diana); *Career* Capt RAMC Army Blood Transfusion Service, served in N Africa and Italy campaigns 1942–46; asst clinical pathologist Guy's Hosp 1946–49, memb Scientific Staff Nat Inst for Med Res London 1949–69, head of Laboratory for Leprosy and Mycobacterial Res Nat Inst for Med Res 1969–82; chm Lepra Med Advsy Bd 1963–87, pres Section of Comparative Med Royal Soc of Med 1975, memb Lepra Exec Ctee 1964–87; vice pres: Lepra 1987–, Int Leprosy Assoc 1988–94; memb: MRC Tropical Med Res Bd 1968–72, WHO Advsy Panel on Leprosy 1969–94, Editorial Bd Leprosy Review 1960–95; hon memb Section of Comparative Med RSM; Royal Soc of Tropical Med and Hygiene Manson medal 1980; *Publications* more than 200 Scientific papers on basic and applied studies on animals and man relevant to pathology, immunology and chemotherapy of leprosy and tuberculosis; *Recreations* theatre, gardening; *Style*— Dr Dick Rees, CMG; ✉ 10 Home Farm Court, Greenway Lane, Charlton Kings, Cheltenham, Glos GL52 6LA (☎ 01242 574953)

REES, Roger Thomas; s of Aerwyn Howell Rees, of Capel Hendre, Ammanford, Dyfed, S Wales, and Llowella Francis, *née* Roberts; *b* 16 Oct 1943; *Educ* Mercer's Sch, Colfe's GS, Royal Dental Hosp, St Bartholomew's Med Coll Univ of London (MB BS, BDS); *m* 10 Aug 1969, Sandra Jones, da of David Williams, of Cross Hands, Dyfed, S Wales; 1 s (Richard Hywell b 9 Dec 1973), 1 da (Sara Jane b 22 June 1977); *Career* sr registrar King's Coll Hosp London and Queen Victoria Hosp E Grinstead 1974–79, tech advsr to Nigerian Mil Govt in maxillo-facial surgery (seconded by Dept of Overseas Admin) 1976; conslt oral and maxillo-facial surgn: Norfolk and Norwich NHS Tst, James Paget Hosp NHS Tst 1979–; chm Dist Dental Ctee, co-ordinator Regnl Audit Dental Specialties E Anglian RHA 1991–95; memb: Br Dental Assoc, Br Med Assoc; Freeman City of London 1968; fell Br Assoc of Oral and Maxillo-Facial Surgns 1979; FDSRCS; *Style*— Roger Rees, Esq; ✉ Norfolk & Norwich Hospital, Brunswick Road, Norwich, Norfolk NR1 3SR (☎ 01603 286286)

REES, Simon John; s of Dan Rees, of New Malden, Surrey, and Margaret May Rose, *née* Stephenson; *b* 7 July 1960; *Educ* Kingston GS (schoolboy hockey int England); *m* 18

Aug 1984, Gillian Gaye, da of Kenneth Horne; 1 s (Jonathan Charles b 24 Nov 1987), 1 da (Charlotte Emma b 2 Oct 1989); *Career* media asst rising to TV buyer D'Arcy McManus & Masius 1978–81, sr planner/buyer Colman and Partners 1982–86 (TV buyer 1981–82); TMD Carat Advertising: sr TV buyer 1986–88, TV mangr then assoc dir 1988, bd memb and bdcast dir 1989, head of Carat TV (UK) 1990–, dep md 1995–; MIPA, FRGS; *Sporting Achievements* schoolboy hockey int (England) 1976–78, 96 full int caps hockey (indoor and field) Wales 1979–90; *Recreations* running, cycling, swimming, mountaineering, walking, golf; *Clubs* Southgate Hockey (various League and Cup Winner medals), Berkshire Triathlon Squad; *Style—* Simon Rees, Esq; ✉ TMD Carat Advertising Ltd, 172 Drury Lane, London WC2B 5QR (☎ 0171 611 8000)

REES, Dr (Robert) Simon Owen; s of Edward Bertram Rees (d 1985), of Carmarthen, Dyfed, and Dorothy, *née* Owen; *b* 24 May 1933; *Educ* Harrow, Gonville and Caius Coll Cambridge (MA), Westminster Med Sch Univ of London (MB BChir); *m* 13 Dec 1958, Dr Jacqueline Jane Rees, da of James Layton (d 1992), of Hampstead, London; 3 s (Rupert b 18 Aug 1962, Jasper b 7 Dec 1964, Sheridan b 13 March 1967); *Career* conslt radiologist: Nat Heart Hosp London 1966–90, St Bartholomew's Hosp London 1967–88; dean Inst of Cardiology Univ of London 1969–72, dir of imaging Royal Brompton Hosp London 1988–92; Liveryman Worshipful Soc of Apothecaries 1964; FRCP, FRCR, FRSM; *Books* Clinical Cardiac Radiology (1973, 2 ed 1980); *Recreations* hunting, driving, real tennis, choral singing, skiing; *Clubs* Boodle's, Charlton Hunt (chm); *Style—* Dr Simon Rees; ✉ Rubbin Cottage, Treyford, Midhurst, West Sussex GU29 0LD (☎ 01730 825444)

REES, Sir (Charles William) Stanley; kt (1962), TD (1950), QC (1957), DL (Sussex 1968); s of Dr David Charles Rees (d 1917), first supt and med tutor to London Sch of Tropical Medicine (went to SA in 1901 at invitation of Cape Govt to deal with outbreak of bubonic plague, where he remained until his death from typhus), and Myrtle May, *née* Dolley (d 1950); *b* 30 Nov 1907; *Educ* St Andrew's Coll Grahamstown SA, Univ Coll Oxford (BA, BCL); *m* 1934, Jean Isabel (d 1985), da of Laurence Henry Munro (d 1906), of Melbourne, Aust; 1 s; *Career* 2 Lt 99 Anti-Aircraft RA Regt (London Welsh) 1939, Capt 1940, JAG's Office in Home Cmd 1940–43, Lt-Col 1943, i/c JAG's branch HQ Palestine Cmd 1944–45, ret as Hon Lt-Col 1945; called to the Bar Inner Temple 1931, rec Croydon 1961–62, bencher 1962, Judge of the High Ct of Justice Family Div (formerly Probate Divorce and Admty Div) 1962–77, chm E Sussex QS 1964–70 (dep chm 1959–64), pt/t memb Ct of Appeal 1979–82; vice patron Brighton Coll 1983– (govr 1954–83, pres 1974–83), chm Statutory Ctee Pharmaceutical Soc of GB 1980–81; *Recreations* walking, gardening; *Clubs* United Oxford and Cambridge, Sussex; *Style—* Sir Stanley Rees, TD, DL; ✉ Lark Rise, Lyoth Lane, Lindfield, Haywards Heath, W Sussex RH16 2QA (☎ 01444 482049)

REES-JONES, Elizabeth Helen; da of William Jones (d 1980), of Goring on Thames, Oxon, and Elizabeth, *née* Thomas; *b* 9 Sept 1944; *Educ* The Alice Ottley Sch Worcester, Trinity Coll Dublin (BA); *m* 1975 (m dis 1992), George Cambitzi, s of Anthony G Cambitzi; 1 s (Alexander b 1977), 1 da (Anastasia b 1982); *Career* promotions ed Harpers' Bazaar 1967–71, promotions conslt National Magazine Co 1975–87 (promotions dir 1971–75), md Elle 1987–88, jt chm News International/Hachette 1987–91, md Murdoch Magazines 1987–91, exec dir EMAP Consumer Magazines 1991–92, md Presse Publishing Ltd 1992–; memb: Appeals Ctee Birthright, Cncl ICA; assoc Women of the Year Luncheon; *Recreations* travel, spectator sports; *Style—* Ms Elizabeth Rees-Jones; ✉ Presse Publishing Ltd, 17 Radley Mews, Kensington, London W8 6JP (☎ 0171 938 3033, fax 0171 938 5464)

REES-MOGG, Baron (Life Peer UK 1988), of Hinton Blewitt, Co Avon; William Rees-Mogg; kt (1981); s of late Edmund Fletcher Rees-Mogg, JP, of Cholwell House, Somerset, and Beatrice, da of Daniel Warren, of New York State, USA; *b* 14 July 1928; *Educ* Charterhouse, Balliol Coll Oxford (MA); *m* 1962, Gillian Shakespeare, yr da of Thomas Richard Morris, JP, Mayor of St Pancras 1962; 2 s (Hon Thomas Fletcher b 1966, Hon Jacob William b 1969), 3 da (Hon Emma Beatrice b 1962, Hon Charlotte Louise b 1964, Hon Annunziata Mary b 1979); *Career* pres Oxford Union 1951; Financial Times 1952–60: chief ldr writer 1955–60, asst ed 1957–60; Sunday Times 1960–67: city ed 1960–61, political and economic ed 1961–63, dep ed 1964–67; ed The Times 1967–81; memb Exec Bd Times Newspapers Ltd 1968–81; dir: The Times 1968–81, Times Newspapers Ltd 1978–81; chm: Pickering & Chatto (Publishers) Ltd 1983–, Sidgwick & Jackson 1985–88, Sinclair-Stevenson Ltd 1989–92, IBC Group plc 1993–, Fleet Street Publications Ltd 1995–; dir: GEC plc 1981–, M&G Group 1986–94, The Private Bank and Trust Co, Value Realisation Trust plc; vice chm Bd of Govrs BBC 1981–86; chm: Arts Cncl of GB 1982–88, Broadcasting Standards Cncl 1988–93; pres: Inst of Journalists 1963–64, English Assoc 1983–84, Thorney Island Soc 1996–97; High Sheriff Somerset 1978; *Books* An Humbler Heaven (1977), The Reigning Error: The Crisis of World Inflation (1974), Blood in the Streets (1987), The Great Reckoning (1991), Picnics on Vesuvius (1992); *Clubs* Garrick; *Style—* The Rt Hon Lord Rees-Mogg; ✉ 17 Pall Mall, London SW1Y 5NB (☎ 0171 930 3088, fax 0171 839 4509)

REES ROBERTS, Tristan William Otway; s of Peter William Rees Roberts, of Hants, and Ursula Vivien, *née* McCannell; *b* 11 April 1948; *Educ* Frensham Heights, Farnham GS, Trinity Hall Cambridge (MA, BArch, DipArch); *m* 21 March 1970, Anna Ingelin, da of Edmund George Noel Greaves, of Cambridge; 1 s (Marcus Lucien Branch b 1975), 2 da (Saria Mona Natascha b 1973, Ariana Lucia Katrina b 1979); *Career* architect in private practice with Henry Freeland and Jeremy Lander 1980–; most important cmmns: King's Coll and other Cambridge Colls, Temple Bar, Thorpe Hall, Bishop's Palace Ely, Univ of Cambridge; Freeman City of London 1986; *Recreations* painting, massage therapist, hill walking; *Style—* Tristan Rees Roberts, Esq; ✉ 13 Caius Terrace, Glisson Rd, Cambridge CB1 2HJ (☎ 01223 368101); Freeland Rees Roberts Architects, 25 City Rd, Cambridge (☎ 01223 366555)

REES-WILLIAMS, Jonathan; s of Ivor Rees-Williams (d 1990), and Barbara, *née* Stone, of Penrith; *b* 10 Feb 1949; *Educ* Kilburn GS, RAM (LRAM, Dip RAM, Hubert Kiver Prize for organ playing, aural-trg prize), New Coll Oxford (organ scholar, MA); *m* 25 May 1985, Helen Patricia Harling; 2 da (Caroline b 4 June 1986, Rosemary b 20 Feb 1990), 1 s (Richard b 31 Aug 1987); *Career* organist and choirmaster: St Edmund the King Yeading 1967–68, Church of the Ascension Wembley 1968–69; acting organist New Coll Oxford 1972, asst organist Hampstead PC and St Clement Danes London 1972–74, asst organist Salisbury Cathedral 1974–78 (dir of music 1974–78), organist and master of the choristers Lichfield Cathedral 1978–91 (conductor special choir 1978–91), organist and master of the choristers St George's Chapel Windsor Castle 1991–; chorusmaster Portsmouth Festival Choir 1974–78; recitals incl: Southern Cathedrals Festival, Lichfield Festival, Windsor Festival, London Handel Festival, Hambleden Festival, 70 Birthday Concert for HM Queen Elizabeth, farewell concert for Sir David Lumsden (princ RAM) 1993; numerous tv and radio broadcasts incl N German Radio Choir Hamburg; numerous recordings as conductor and organist; tours incl: USA, Italy, Germany, Holland; memb Cathedral Organists' Assoc 1978, hon ARAM 1984; FRCO 1968 (ARCO 1965); *Recreations* cycling, model railways, wine; *Style—* Jonathan Rees-Williams, Esq; ✉ Organist and Master of the Choristers, St George's Chapel, Windsor Castle, Berkshire (☎ 01753 864529, fax 01753 620165)

REESE, Dr Alan John Morris; TD (1958, clasps 1964, 1970 and 1976), JP (Middx 1974); s of Joseph Reese (d 1968), of Plymouth, Devon, and Emily, *née* Brand (d 1984); *b* 26 Aug 1920; *Educ* Plymouth Coll, Bart's Med Coll Univ of London (MB BS, MD); *m* 24 Jan 1959, Margaret Denise, da of Ernest George Turner (d 1969), of Battersea, London; 1 s (Charles b 1962), 1 da (Victoria b 1960); *Career* emergency cmmn RAMC 1945; served: Egypt, Palestine, Cyrenaica, Malta; war substantive Capt 1946, released 1948; TA: Capt 1948, Maj 1953, Lt Col 1966; TAVR 1967, Lt-Col RARO; sr registrar in pathology St George's Hosp London 1950–54, lectr in pathology Univ of Bristol 1954–56, sr lectr in pathology Inst of Basic Med Scis Univ of London RCS 1956–82, WHO prof of pathology Univ of Mandalay Burma 1963–64, hon conslt in morbid anatomy Whittington Hosp 1966–82; memb Senate Univ of London 1974–83; examiner in pathology: RCS 1973–79, RCSEd 1978–92; called to the Bar Middle Temple 1955; memb Islington Cons Assoc 1960–, contested seats on Islington Borough Cncl, vice pres Islington S and Finsbury Cons Assoc 1987–, contested Lewisham W on ILEA 1986, Cons cncllr and chm Health Ctee Met Borough of St Pancras 1959–62; govr Godolphin and Latymer Sch 1976–85; OStJ 1974; Freeman City of London 1944, Liveryman Worshipful Soc of Apothecaries 1948 (Yeoman 1943–48); MRCPath 1963, FRCPath 1968, LMSSA 1943; *Books* The Principles of Pathology (2 edn, 1981); *Recreations* fishing; *Clubs* Army and Navy; *Style—* Dr Alan Reese, TD, JP; ✉ 9 Hopping Lane, Canonbury, London N1 2NU (☎ 0171 226 2088); 14 Herd St, Marlborough, Wilts SN8 1DF (☎ 01672 512339)

REESE, Prof Colin Bernard; s of Joseph Reese (d 1968), of London, and Emily Reese (d 1984); *b* 29 July 1930; *Educ* Dartington Hall Sch, Clare Coll Cambridge (BA, PhD, MA, ScD); *m* 29 June 1968, Susanne Leslie, da of Joseph Charles Henry Bird (d 1985); 1 s (William Thomas b 11 July 1972), 1 da (Lucy b 13 Aug 1970); *Career* res fell Harvard Univ 1957–58; Univ of Cambridge: res fell Clare Coll 1956–59, univ demonstrator in chemistry 1959–63, official fell and dir of studies in chemistry Clare Coll 1959–73, asst dir of res 1963–64, lectr in chemistry 1964–73; King's Coll London: Daniell prof of chemistry 1973–; FRS 1981, FKC 1989; *Style—* Prof Colin Reese, FRS; ✉ 21 Rozel Rd, London SW4 0EY (☎ 0171 498 0230); Department of Chemistry, King's Coll London, Strand, London WC2R 2LS (☎ 0171 873 2260, fax 0171 873 2899)

REEVE, Sir Anthony; KCMG (1992, CMG 1986), KCVO (1995); s of Sidney Reeve, of Cheltenham, Glos, and Dorothy, *née* Mitchell; *b* 20 Oct 1938; *Educ* Queen Elizabeth GS Wakefield, Marling Sch Stroud, Merton Coll Oxford (MA); *m* 1 Feb 1964 (m dis 1988), Pamela Margaret Angus; 1 s (James b 1968), 2 da (Emily b 1972, Anna b 1977); *Career* Lever Brothers and Associates 1962–65; HM Dip Serv: entered 1965, MECAS 1966–68, asst political agent Abu Dhabi 1968–70, FCO 1970–73, first sec (later cnsllr) Washington 1973–78, cnsllr FCO 1978–81, cnsllr Cairo 1981–84, cnsllr then asst under sec of state FCO 1984–88, HM ambass to the Hashemite Kingdom of Jordan 1988–91, HM ambass then high cmmr to S Africa 1991–Oct 1996, ret; *Recreations* writing, music; *Clubs* United Oxford and Cambridge Univ, Leander, Minchinhampton Golf; *Style—* Sir Anthony Reeve, KCMG, KCVO; ✉ Box Cottage, Horslet, Stroud, Glos GL6 0QB

REEVE, Dermot Alexander; OBE (1996); s of Alexander James Reeve, and Monica, *née* Reagan; *b* 2 April 1963; *Educ* King George V Sch Kowloon Hong Kong; *m* 20 Dec 1986, Julie Lynne, da of Keith Chester; 1 da (Emily Kaye b 14 Sept 1988); *Career* professional cricketer; Sussex CCC 1983–87 (awarded county cap 1986); Warwickshire CCC: joined 1988, awarded county cap 1989, vice capt 1990–, best bowling 7–37 v Lancs 1987, best batting 202 not out v Northants 1990; played 9 off-seasons in Perth WA; England: memb tour NZ 1992, memb World Cup squad Aust 1992, memb tour to India and Sri Lanka 1992/93, one day ints debut v W Indies 1991, memb squad 7 match one-day int series S Africa 1996; honours: Hong Kong Cricketer of the Year 1980, Hong Kong Sports Personality of the Year 1980, NatWest Trophy winners Sussex 1986 (Man of the Match award) and Warwicks 1990 (Man of the Match award, only player to achieve award for different counties in finals), twice W Australian Pennent Cricketer of the Year, League Premiers with Mount Lawley CC 1987 and Claremont Nedlands CC 1990, Benson & Hedges Cup winners Warwickshire 1994 and 1995, Britannic Assurance County Championship winners Warwickshire 1994 and 1995, winners NatWest Trophy Warwickshire 1995 (runners-up 1994), Axa Equity & Law League Champions Warwickshire 1994; mktg appt Warwick Group Birmingham off-season 1991–92; Hon DSc Univ of Birmingham 1996; *Recreations* after-dinner speaking, enjoying food and having to regularly visit a health club; *Style—* Dermot Reeve, Esq, OBE; ✉ c/o Warwickshire County Cricket Club, County Ground, Edgbaston, Birmingham B5 7QU

REEVE, James Ernest; CMG (1982); s of Ernest Stanley Reeve (d 1970), of Surrey, and Margaret Anthea, *née* James (d 1939); *b* 8 June 1926; *Educ* Bishop's Stortford Coll Herts; *m* 20 Aug 1947, Lillian Irene, da of Capt Albert Edward Watkins, OBE, of Epsom, Surrey; 1 s (Christopher b 30 April 1953), 1 da (Sandra b 8 Oct 1955); *Career* HM Dip Serv 1949–83: HM vice consul Ahwaz and Khorramshahr Iran 1949–51, UN Gen Assembly Paris 1951, private sec to Rt Hon Selwyn Lloyd FO 1951–53, HM Embassy Washington 1953–57, HM Embassy Bangkok 1957–59, Northern Dept FO 1959–61, HM consul Frankfurt W Germany 1961–65, first sec HM Embassy Libya 1965–69, first sec HM Embassy Budapest 1970–72, chargé d'affaires and cnsllr for estab of first Br Embassy to GDR E Berlin 1973–75, HM consul gen Zurich and Liechtenstein 1975–80, HM min and consul gen Milan 1980–83; dir Sprester Investments Ltd 1983–91, delegate UNCTAD Geneva 1991, conslt Business Week 1991, int mgmnt conslt 1993–; memb Int Aluminium Inst London 1983–93; *Recreations* theatre, tennis, skiing, travel; *Clubs* RAC, East Gloucester; *Style—* James Reeve, Esq, CMG; ✉ 19 Montpellier Apartments, Montpellier Spa Road, Cheltenham, Glos GL50 1UL; (☎ and fax 01242 578033)

REEVE, John; s of Clifford Alfred Reeve, and Irene Mary Turnidge Osborne; *b* 13 July 1944; *Educ* Westcliff HS Essex; *m* 2, 21 Dec 1974, Sally Diane, da of Eric Welton; 1 da (Emily Virginia Welton b 27 Jan 1979); *Career* Corporation of Lloyd's 1960–62, Selby Smith & Earle 1962–67, Peat Marwick Mitchell & Co 1967–68, Roneo Vickers Office Equipment Group 1968–76, Wilkinson Match Ltd 1976–77, Amalgamated Metal Corporation Ltd 1977–80, dir of finance British Aluminium Co plc 1980–83, dir of finance Mercantile House Holdings plc 1983–87; Sun Life Corporation plc: joined as dep gp md Sun Life Assurance Society plc 1988, gp md 1989–95, non-exec dir 1995–96; exec chm Willis Corroon Group plc 1995–; chm The English Concert 1987–; non-exec dir: HMC Group plc 1988–94, Temple Bar Investment Trust PLC 1992–; govr Research into Ageing 1991–95; pres Inst of Business Ethics 1997– (dep pres 1991–96); chm East London Partnership 1996– (memb Bd 1991–96); memb: Cncl Business in the Community, Bd ABI 1993–95, Bd and Exec Ctee Int Insurance Soc; govr NIESR; FCA 1977 (ACA 1967), CIMgt 1990; *Recreations* yachting, music, theatre; *Clubs* National Liberal, Essex Yacht; *Style—* John Reeve, Esq; ✉ Cliff Dene, 24 Cliff Parade, Leigh-on-Sea, Essex SS9 1BB (☎ 01702 77563); Willis Corroon Group plc, Ten Trinity Square, London EC3P 3AX (☎ 0171 488 8299, fax 0171 488 8085)

REEVE, Kathryn May; da of Frank Evelyn Heppenstall (d 1992), and Doris May, *née* Davison; *b* 22 July 1948; *Educ* Sutton HS GPDST, New Hall Cambridge (MA); *m* 14 April 1971, Peter Joseph Reeve, s of late Joseph Reeve, of Leamington Spa, Warwickshire; *Career* admitted slr 1973; ptnr Shoosmiths & Harrison 1989–; former treas Leamington Hastings Parochial Church Cncl, assoc Royal Photographic Soc, former pres Dunchurch Photographic Soc, govr Rugby Coll of Further Educn; memb Law Soc; *Recreations* natural history, photography, tennis; *Style—* Mrs Kathryn Reeve; ✉ Bloxam Court, Corporation Street, Rugby, Warwickshire CV21 2DU (☎ 01788 573111, telex 265871, fax 01788 536651)

REEVE, Michael Arthur Ferard; s of Maj Wilfrid Norman Reeve, OBE, MC (d 1976), of London, and Agnes Bourdon, *née* Ferard; *b* 7 Jan 1937; *Educ* Eton, Univ Coll Oxford (MA); *m* 30 Dec 1970, Charmian Gay, da of David Royden Rooper, of London; 2 s (Hugo b 10 Dec 1973, Luke b 15 Sept 1977); *Career* dir: Elliott Group of Peterborough 1969–83, Charterhouse Bank 1965–74, Rea Bros 1977–80, Collins Collins & Rawlence (Hamptons estate agents) 1982–85, The Tregeare Company Ltd 1981–, Finsbury Trust plc 1990–, Finsbury Growth Trust plc 1991– (chm); md Copley & Bank 1974–80, Greyhound Bank 1981–87; memb: Royal Inst of Int Affrs, The Pilgrims; FCA 1964; *Recreations* horses, gardening, reading; *Clubs* Institute of Directors, Royal Over-Seas League; *Style*— Michael Reeve, Esq; ✉ 138 Oakwood Court, London W14 8JL (☎ 0171 602 2624)

REEVE, Nigel John; s of George Edward Reeve, of Bramford, Ipswich, Suffolk, and Edna May, *née* Chennary; *b* 19 Aug 1952; *Educ* Everton House Sch Ipswich; *m* 1, 1982 (m dis 1988), Maritje Geertruida, *née* Lamberts, of Haarlem, Holland; m 2, 7 Oct 1988, Lindsay Marion, da of Capt Trevor Maldwyn Jones (d 1973); *Career* admin Eastern Counties Newspapers 1969–76, sales Radio Orwell Ipswich 1976–81, sales mangr Two Counties Radio Bournemouth 1981–83, sales dir County Sound Guildford 1983–85; Invicta Sound: sales dir 1985–87, dep md 1985–88, md 1988–91; conslt Essex Radio 1991–92, sales dir Classic FM 1992–; dir: Mellow 1557 Ltd Colchester Essex until 1991, Invicta Continental SARL France until 1991, Radio Advertising Bureau 1994–; dir and tstee Invicta Charity for the Disabled of Kent until 1991; chm commercial Radio Creative Awards until 1994, chm Ind Radio Conf Ctee until 1994; memb: The Marketing Soc 1994–, Ctee The Radio Festival 1995–; *Recreations* golf, soccer (Ipswich Town FC); *Clubs* Chart Hills Golf; *Style*— Nigel Reeve, Esq; ✉ Little Bletchenden, Bletchenden, Headcorn, Kent TN27 9JB (☎ 01622 890343, fax 01622 891680); c/o Classic FM, Academic House, 24–28 Oval Road, London NW1 7QD (☎ 0171 284 3000)

REEVE, Robin Martin; s of Percy Martin Reeve, of Lancing, W Sussex, and Cicely Nora, *née* Parker; *b* 22 Nov 1934; *Educ* Hampton Sch, Gonville and Caius Coll Cambridge (BA, MA), Univ of Bristol (PGCE); *m* 25 July 1959, Brianne Ruth, da of Leonard Stephen Hall (d 1953), of Ashford, Middx; *Career* Lancing Coll: head of History Dept 1962–80, dir of studies 1975, asst master 1962–80; head master King's Coll Sch Wimbledon 1980– (asst master 1958–62); memb: HMC 1980–, SHA; *Recreations* gardening, architecture, reading; *Clubs* East India Public Schs; *Style*— Robin Reeve, Esq; ✉ Rushmere, Wimbledon Common, London SW19 4TL; King's College School, Southside, Wimbledon Common, London SW19 4TT (☎ 0181 225 5300)

REEVE, HE Roy Stephen; s of Ernest Arthur Reeve, of London, and Joan, *née* Thomas; *b* 20 Aug 1941; *Educ* Dulwich, LSE (BScEcon, MScEcon), Chartered Inst of Secs (postgrad scholar); *m* 6 June 1964, Gill, da of Leslie Lee (d 1993); 2 da (Kirsti Jane b 3 March 1969, Sally Elizabeth b 1 Aug 1971); *Career* HM Customs and Excise 1961–62; HM Dip Serv: joined FCO 1966, third sec Moscow 1968–71, first sec FCO 1973–78, first sec (commercial) Moscow 1978–80, FCO 1980–83, cnsllr on loan to Home Civil Serv 1983–85, dep consul-gen Johannesburg 1985–88, head of Commercial Mgmnt and Export Dept FCO 1988–91, consul-gen Sydney 1991–95, HM ambass Ukraine 1995–; *Recreations* motorcycling, scuba diving; *Clubs* Union (Sydney); *Style*— HE Mr Roy Reeve; ✉ c/o Foreign & Commonwealth Office (Kiev), King Charles Street, London SW1A 2AH

REEVE, Tessa; da of Bernard Dixon (d 1983), of Pampisford, Cambridge, and Olive Marie, *née* Watts; *b* 23 July 1937; *Educ* Chatelard Sch Les Avants Montreux Switzerland; *m* 1, 26 July 1958 (m dis 1979), James Anthony Gerard Malcolm-Brown, s of William Isbister Malcolm-Brown, of Harpenden; 3 s (Charles Barry b 13 Dec 1961, Guy James b 15 Nov 1963 (decd), Mark b 19 May 1965); m 2, 29 Oct 1994, William Ernest Reeve; *Career* chm and md since 1984: Dixon International Group Ltd, Dixon International Ltd (dir 1979–), Sealmaster Ltd (dir 1968–), SK Bearings Ltd (dir 1979–), The Dixon Malt Co Ltd (dir 1979–), Intumescent Seals Ltd (dir 1980–); MInstPI; *Recreations* breeding Morgan horses, carriage driving, piano; *Clubs* Br Driving Soc (horse carriages), Morgan Horse Assoc (UK), American Morgan Horse Assoc; *Style*— Mrs Tessa Reeve; ✉ Wells Park Farm, Whittlesford, Cambridge CB2 4PG (☎ 01223 832851, telex 81664 Dixon G, fax 01223 837215)

REEVES, Anthony Alan; s of Allen Joseph Reeves, MBE (d 1976), and Alice Turner, *née* Pointon (d 1966); *b* 5 March 1943; *Educ* Hanley HS, Coll of Law; *m* 19 Aug 1967, Jane, da of William Thowless (d 1942); 1 s (Max b 1972), 2 da (Rachel b 1969, Ruth b 1974); *Career* admitted slr 1965; sr ptnr Kent Jones and Done Slrs 1978–; non-exec dir: Steelite International plc 1983–, Bullers plc 1984–86, Stoke City FC 1984–85, Butler Woodhouse Ltd 1987–94; chm The CAS Group plc 1985–90, chm Daniel Platt (Holdings) Ltd 1992–; sr tstee The Beth Johnson Fndn 1972–, Univ of Keele Devpt Tst 1993–, memb N Staffs Med Inst Cncl 1979–82; chm Law Soc Sub Ctee on Coal Mining Subsidence 1985–; memb Law Soc; *Recreations* fishing, shooting, supporting ballet, contemporary art; *Style*— Anthony Reeves, Esq; ✉ Churchill House, 47 Regent Rd, Hanley, Stoke on Trent ST1 3RQ (☎ 01782 202020, fax 01782 266060)

REEVES, Anthony Henry; s of Herbert Henry Reeves, of Limpsfield Chart, Surrey, and Kathleen Norah Reeves (d 1963); *b* 8 Sept 1940; *Educ* Sir Walter St Johns; *m* 1972, Jacqueline, da of Herbert Mitchell Newton-Clare, of Edgeworth, Cirencester; 4 s, 2 da; *Career* former dir Alfred Marks Bureau Ltd, chm and chief exec Lifetime Corp USA (acquired HCC 1986) 1986–93, chm Medic International 1993–96, chm and chief exec Delphi Group plc (formerly Computer People Group plc) 1994–; *Recreations* golf, running, squash; *Clubs* Royal Automobile, Royal Wimbledon Golf, Reform, Royal Mid-Surrey Golf; *Style*— Anthony H Reeves, Esq; ✉ Spur Lodge, 142 Upper Richmond Road West, London SW14 8DS (☎ 0181 878 4738); Delphi Group plc, Piccadilly House, 33 Regent Street, London SW1Y 4NB (☎ 0171 440 2000, fax 0171 440 2012)

REEVES, Christopher Reginald; s of Reginald Raymond Reeves (d 1989), and Dora Grace, *née* Tucker (d 1962); *b* 14 Jan 1936; *Educ* Malvern; *m* June 1965, Stella Jane, da of Cdr Patrick Whinney, of Guernsey; 3 s; *Career* Nat Serv cmmnd Rifle Bde (served Kenya and Malaya) 1955–58; merchant banker; Bank of England 1958–63, Hill Samuel Ltd 1963–67; Morgan Grenfell & Co Ltd: joined 1968, dir 1970, head Banking Div 1972, dep chm and dep chief exec 1975, gp chief exec 1980, jt chm 1984; dep chm and gp chief exec Morgan Grenfell Group plc (formerly Morgan Grenfell Holdings Ltd) 1985–87; Merrill Lynch: sr advsr to pres of Merrill Lynch Capital Markets 1988, vice chm Merrill Lynch International Ltd 1989–93, chm 1993–, chm Merrill Lynch Europe/ME 1993; dir: India Fund, India Growth Fund, Latin America Capital Partners Ltd; non-exec dir: BICC plc 1982–, Allianz Cornhill International Insurance Co Ltd 1983–93, Cornhill Insurance 1993–, Oman International Bank 1984–, International Freehold Properties (Supervisory Bd) 1988–96; govr Dulwich Coll Prep Sch, treas City Univ; CIMgt; *Recreations* sailing, shooting, skiing; *Clubs* Boodle's, Royal Southern Yacht, Itchenor Sailing; *Style*— Christopher Reeves, Esq; ✉ 64 Flood St, London SW3 5TE

REEVES, Colin Leslie; s of Leslie Reeves, of Warwicks, and Isabelle; *b* 4 April 1949; *Educ* Birkenhead Sch, Clare Coll Cambridge (MA), UCNW (MSc, PhD), John Moores Univ (IPFA), Cornell Univ (Dip in Business Admin); *m* Christine, *née* Lloyd; 2 da (Helen Madeleine b 12 Aug 1981, Caroline Georgina b 11 Jan 1984); m; 2 da; *Career* lectr UCNW 1971–73, accountancy and audit asst Warrington Co Borough 1973–75, asst treas Ellesmere Port and Neston Borough Cncl 1975–80, dep dir of fin Stratford on Avon DC 1980–84, dep dir of fin NW Thames RHA 1984–85, dir of fin Paddington and N Kensington DHA 1985–86, regnl dir of fin NW Thames RHA 1986–94, national dir of fin NHS Executive 1994–; memb: National Steering Gp on Capitation 1995–, National Steering Gp on Capital 1995–, Research and Devpt Task Force 1995–, Advsy Ctee on Mentally Disordered Offenders Dept of Health/Home Office 1995–, National Private Finance Panel 1995–, Nat Breast Screening Ctee 1996–; *Books* The Applicability of the Monetary Base Hypothesis to the UK, the USA, France and West Germany (1974); regular contrib to various professional jls; *Recreations* sport (especially cricket and golf), history of test match cricket, former regnl int and county player at hockey; *Clubs* Royal Automobile, Goring and Streatley Golf, Mapledurham Golf; *Style*— Colin L Reeves, Esq; ✉ NHS Executive, Department of Health, Quarry House, Quarry Hill, Leeds, W Yorks LS2 7UE (☎ 01132 545527)

REEVES, Rev Donald St John; s of Henry St John Reeves (d 1984), and Barbara Eugn, *née* Rusbridger (d 1967); *b* 18 May 1934; *Educ* Sherborne, Queens' Coll Cambridge; *Career* lectr British Cncl 1957–60, curate All Saints Maidstone 1963–65, domestic chaplain to Bishop of Southwark 1965–68, vicar St Peter's St Helier 1968–80, rector St James's Piccadilly 1980–; *Books* Church and State (ed, 1984), For God's Sake (1988), Making Sense of Religion (1989), Down to Earth (1996); *Recreations* playing the organ, gardening, bee-keeping, watching TV soap operas; *Clubs* Arts, RAC; *Style*— Rev Donald Reeves; ✉ St James's Church, 197 Piccadilly, London W1V 9LF (☎ 0171 734 4511)

REEVES, Helen May; OBE (1986); da of Leslie Percival William Reeves (d 1967), and Helen Edith, *née* Brown; *b* 22 Aug 1945; *Educ* Dartford Girls' GS, Univ of Nottingham; *Career* probation offr then sr probation offr Inner London Probation Serv 1967–79, dir Nat Assoc of Victims Support Schemes 1980–; currently: vice pres World Soc of Victimology, sec Euro Forum for Victim Servs; memb: Nat Bd for Crime Prevention 1993–95, Cncl Kidscape 1993–; FRSA 1991; *Recreations* gardening, food, architecture; *Style*— Ms Helen Reeves, OBE; ✉ Victim Support, Cranmer House, 39 Brixton Rd, London SW9 6DZ (☎ 0171 735 9166, fax 0171 582 5712)

REEVES, Jonathan Harvey William; s of Lt-Col William Robert Reeves, DSO, of Whitegate, Cheshire, and Joan Riddell Scudamore, *née* Jarvis; *b* 9 Aug 1937; *Educ* Monkton Combe, RAC Cirencester; *m* 1, 29 July 1961, Daphne Susan, da of Col Brian Pierson Doughty-Wylie, MC (d 1981); 1 s (Thomas b 1969), 2 da (Emma (Mrs Farquhar) b 1963, Katherine (Mrs Morlock) b 1966); m 2, 14 Sept 1974, Susan Elizabeth, da of Maj John Frederick Michael Mowat (d 1988); *Career* served RWF 1960–70, Queen's Own Mercian Yeo 1971–74; ptnr Fisher Hoggarth land agents and chartered surveyors 1983–, surveyor to Diocese of Worcester 1986–; FRICS 1984; *Recreations* shooting, fishing, skiing, gardening; *Clubs* Army and Navy; *Style*— Jonathan Reeves, Esq; ✉ The Old Rectory, Aston Somerville, nr Broadway, Worcestershire (☎ 01386 852466); Fisher Hoggarth, The Estate Office, Dumbleton, Evesham, Worcestershire (☎ 01386 881214)

REEVES, Dr Marjorie Ethel; CBE (1996); da of Robert John Ward Reeves (d 1935), and Edith Saffery, *née* Whitaker (d 1980); *b* 17 July 1905; *Educ* Trowbridge Girls HS Wilts, St Hugh's Coll Oxford (BA, MA, DLitt), Westfield Coll London (PhD); *Career* history teacher Roan Sch Greenwich 1927–29, lectr St Gabriel's Coll of Educn London 1932–38, vice princ St Anne's Coll Oxford 1938–72 (former tutor and fell); hon warden House of St Gregory & St Macrina Oxford, memb Dante Soc, corresponding fell Medieval Acad of America; former memb: Central Advsy Cncl for Educn, Academic Planning Bds Univ of Kent and Univ of Surrey, Br Cncl of Churches; former chm Higher Educn Gp, vice pres Higher Educn Fndn; church warden Univ Church Oxford, hon fell: St Anne's Coll Oxford, St Hugh's Coll Oxford; Hon DLitt Univ of Bath; FRHistS 1945, FBA 1972; *Books* The Influence of Prophecy in the Later Middle Ages (1969), The Figurae of Joachim of Fiore (1972), Then and Then Series (gen ed), Why History? (1980), The Myth of the Eternal Evangel in the Nineteenth Century (1987), The Crisis in Higher Education (1988), The Diaries of Jeffrey Whitaker (1989), Prophetic Rome in the High Renaissance Period (ed and contrib, 1992); *Recreations* gardening, music; *Clubs* Univ Women's; *Style*— Dr Marjorie Reeves, CBE, FBA; ✉ 38 Norham Rd, Oxford OX2 6SQ (☎ 01865 557039)

REEVES, Prof Nigel Barrie Reginald; OBE (1987); s of Capt Reginald Arthur Reeves (d 1994), of Battle, E Sussex, and Marjorie Joyce, *née* Pettifer (d 1993); *b* 9 Nov 1939; *Educ* Merchant Taylors', Worcester Coll Oxford (BA), St John's Coll Oxford (DPhil); *m* 1, 1964 (m dis 1976), Ingrid, *née* Söderberg; 1 s (Dominic Hans Adam b 1968), 1 da (Anna b 1973); m 2, 3 April 1982, Minou, da of Sadegh Samimi (d 1978); *Career* lectr in English Univ of Lund 1964–66, lectr in German Univ of Reading 1968–74, Alexander von Humboldt fell Univ of Tübingen 1974–75, Univ of Hamburg 1986; Univ of Surrey: prof of German 1975–90, head Linguistic and Int Studies Dept 1979–89, dean Faculty of Human Studies 1986–90, dir Surrey Euro Mgmnt Sch 1989–90; Univ of Aston: prof of German and head of Languages and Euro Studies Dept 1990–96, pro-vice-chllr 1996–; visiting prof and cncl memb Euro Business Sch London 1983–90; chm Inst of Linguists 1985–88 (vice pres 1989–); pres: Nat Assoc of Language Advsrs 1986–90, Assoc of Teachers of German 1987–89; chm Nat Congress on Languages in Educn 1986–90, vice-pres Conference of Univ Teachers of German 1995–(exec vice-pres 1988–91); memb: Governing Bd Inst of Germanic Studies Univ of London 1989–94, Academic Advsy Cncl Linguaphone Inst 1989–, Steering Ctee Centre for Modern Languages Open Univ 1991–, Academic Advsy Cncl Univ of Buckingham 1991–, Educn Ctee London C of C and Indust Examinations Bd 1993–; FIL 1981, FRSA 1986, CIEX 1986; Goethe Medaille (Goethe Inst Munich) 1989, medal Euro Fndn for Quality Mgmnt 1996; *Books* Heinrich Heine, Poetry and Politics (1974, 2 edn 1994), Friedrich Schiller, Medicine, Psychology and Literature (with K Dewhurst, 1978), The Marquise of O and Other Short Stories by Heinr Kleist (with F D Luke, 1978), Business Studies, Languages and Overseas Trade (with D Liston, 1985), The Invisible Economy, A Profile of Britain's Invisible Exports (with D Liston, 1988), Making Your Mark, Effective Business Communication in Germany (with D Liston, M Howarth and M Woodhall, 1988), Franc Exchange, Effective Business Communication in France (with C Sanders, Y Gladkow and C Gordon, 1991), Spanish Venture. Basic Business Communication in Spanish (with B Gould, L Nogueira-Pache and K Bruton, 1992), Linguistic Auditing, Corporate Foreign Language Communication (with C Wright, 1996); *Recreations* gardening, walking; *Style*— Prof Nigel Reeves, OBE; ✉ Pro-Vice-Chancellor's Office, Aston University, Birmingham B4 7ET (☎ 0121 359 3611 ext 4214, fax 0121 359 2792, e-mail N.B.R.Reeves@aston.ac.uk)

REEVES, Philip Thomas Langford; s of Herbert John Reeves (d 1983), of Cheltenham, and Lilian, *née* Langford (d 1963); *b* 7 July 1931; *Educ* Naunton Park Secdy, Cheltenham Sch of Art, RCA; *m* 1961, Christina Donaldina, *née* MacLaren (d 1994); 1 da; *Career* artist; head of printmaking Glasgow Sch of Art 1972–91 (lectr in graphic design 1954–70); *Exhibitions* Compass Gall 1974, 1977 and 1990, Edinburgh Printmaker's Workshop (retrospective) 1981, New 57 Gall (retrospective) 1982, Mercury Gall 1987, Cyril Gerber Fine Art 1993, Paintings and Prints 1983–93 (Lillie Art Gall) 1993, Fine Art Soc 1994, Dick Inst 1994; fndr memb: Edinburgh Printmaker's Workshop 1963, Glasgow Print Studio 1972; winner Glasgow Herald Art Exhbn 1980; memb: SSA 1965, Royal Glasgow Inst of the Fine Arts 1981; fell Royal Soc of Painter Etchers 1963; RSW 1959, RSA 1976 (ARSA 1972); *Recreations* table tennis, snooker; *Style*— Philip Reeves, Esq, RSA; ✉ 13 Hamilton Drive, Glasgow G12 8DN (☎ 0141 339 0720)

REEVES, Vic; *né* (Roderick) James (Jim) Moir; *b* 24 Jan 1959; *Career* comedian, part of comedy duo with Bob Mortimer, *qv*; *Television* incl: Vic Reeves Big Night Out (Channel 4) 1990 and 1991, Weekenders (Channel 4) 1992, The Smell of Reeves and Mortimer (2 series, BBC) 1993 and 1995, A Night in with Vic and Bob (Boxing Day special) 1993, Shooting Stars 1995 and 1996, A Nose Through Nature 1995; *Tours* Vic Reeves Big Night Out 1990 and 1991, The Smell of Reeves and Mortimer 1994 and The Weathercock Tour 1995; *Awards* BAFTA Award for Originality 1991, Best Live Performance British Comedy Awards 1992, Best Comedy Series British Comedy Awards 1993; *Recordings* Dizzy (single, UK no 1), I Will Cure You (album), I'm A Believer (EMF) 1995; *Books* Big Night In (1991), Smell of Reeves and Mortimer (1993); *Style*— Vic Reeves; ✉ c/o

PBJ Management Ltd, 5 Soho Square, London W1V 5DE (☎ 0171 287 1112, fax 0171 287 1448)

REEVES-SMITH, Leonard Edward; OBE (1977); s of Edward Kitchener Reeves-Smith (d 1975), of Mitcham, and Rose, *née* Reeves (d 1979); *Educ* Hampton GS; *m* 6 Feb 1952, Jeannette Avril, da of Henri Askew (d 1981); 1 s (Gary b 22 Feb 1953); *Career* WWII enlisted RAC 1944, served Italy, demobbed Capt 1948; buyer and gen mangr family retail grocery business 1948–62; chief exec Nat Grocers Fedn 1965 (exec asst 1962, nat sec 1963) and chm Nat Grocers Benevolent Fund 1980–95 (dir gen 1980–93), chm Nat Grocers Benevolent Fund (Properties) Trust Ltd 1995– (former dir); gen sec: Grocers Fedn Benevolent Fund, London Grocers and Tea Dealers Benevolent Soc, Grocery Employees Nat Benefits Soc; JP 1970–92, formerly dep chm Farnham Petty Sessional Div and of Juvenile and Domestic Panels; Freeman City of London 1978, Liveryman Worshipful Co of Chartered Secs and Admins 1978; MIGD 1963, FCIS 1970, FRSA 1970, MIMgt 1970; *Recreations* walking, bird watching, conservation; *Style*— Leonard Reeves-Smith, Esq, OBE, JP; ✉ Marralomeda, 25 Mount Pleasant Close, Lightwater, Surrey; c/o National Grocers Benevolent Fund, 17 Farnborough St, Farnborough, Hants (☎ 01252 515946)

REFFELL, Sir Derek Roy; KCB (1984); s of Edward Pomeroy Reffell (d 1974), and Murielle Frances Reffell (d 1975); *b* 6 Oct 1928; *Educ* Culford Sch, RNC Dartmouth; *m* 1956, Janne Marilyn Gronow, da of Capt William Gronow Davis, DSC, RN (d 1946); 1 s (David b 1960), 1 da (Jane b 1962); *Career* Capt HMS Hermes 1974–76, Rear Adm 1980, Asst Chief Naval Staff (Policy) 1980–81, Flag Offr Third Flotilla (Cdr Naval Task Gp South Atlantic July-Oct 1982) 1982–83, Flag Offr Naval Air Cmd 1983–84, Controller of the Navy 1984–89, Adm 1988, Govr and C-in-C Gibraltar 1989–93; chm Friends of Gibraltar Heritage Soc 1994–, govr Royal Sch Hindhead; Renter Warden Worshipful Co of Coachmakers and Coach Harness Makers; KStJ 1989, FNI, CIMgt; *Recreations* painting, golf, wine making; *Style*— Sir Derek Reffell, KCB

REGAN, Rt Rev Edwin; *see:* Wrexham, Bishop of (RC)

REGAN, Michael Denis; s of Denis Charles Regan (d 1965), of Westcliff-on-Sea, Essex, and Selina, *née* Webb; *b* 4 Oct 1955; *Educ* Westcliff HS for Boys, Pembroke Coll Oxford (MA); *m* 20 Feb 1987, Henrietta, da of Henry George Richard Falconar (d 1981), of Horsham, W Sussex; 1 s (George b 1987), 1 da (Grace b 1990); *Career* admitted slr 1980; Rowe and Maw: articled clerk 1978–80, asst slr 1980–85, ptnr 1985–, ptnr i/c Lloyd's office 1988–92, ptnr in insurance and construction law at Lloyd's office 1994– (main office 1992–94); ACIArb 1984; *Books* JCT Management Contract (jtly); *Recreations* watching cricket; *Style*— Michael Regan, Esq; ✉ Rowe & Maw, Room 892/894 The Lloyd's Building, 1 Lime Street, London EC3M 7DQ (☎ 0171 327 4144, fax 0171 623 7965)

REGER, Janet; da of Hyman Phillips (d 1981), of Reading, Berks, and Rachel, *née* Leven (d 1992); *b* 30 Sept 1937; *Educ* Kendrick Sch Reading, Leicester Coll of Arts and Technol (Dip); *m* 1 Jan 1961, Peter Reger (d 1985), s of Josef Reger (d 1955), of Munich; 1 da (Aliza b 1961); *Career* freelance designer Zurich 1960–67, fndr Janet Reger exclusive designer lingerie and nightwear 1967–, own boutique Beauchamp Place Knightsbridge 1974–; *Style*— Mrs Janet Reger; ✉ 2 Beauchamp Place, London SW3 1NG (☎ 0171 584 9360)

REGESTER, Michael; s of Hugh Adair Regester (d 1994), of Royston, Herts, and Monique, *née* Levrey; *b* 8 April 1947; *Educ* St Peter's Sch Guildford Surrey, Newport GS Newport Essex; *m* 1, (m dis 1993), Christine Mary, da of Denis Harrison; 2 da (Lucinda Jane b 12 April 1971, Alice Mary b 8 Aug 1975); m 2, 1994, Leanne Tara, da of Margaret Moscardi; 1 s (Daniel b 13 Feb 1995), 1 da (Kimberley (twin)); *Career* mangr of public affrs (Euro, W Africa, ME) Gulf Oil Corporation 1975–80, jt md Traverse-Healy & Regester Ltd 1980–87, dir Charles Barker Public Relations 1987–90, md Regester plc 1990–94, ptnr Regester & Larkin Ltd 1994–; memb Bd Int PR Assoc 1988, FIPR 1990, MInstPet 1990; *Books* Crisis Management (1987), Investor Relations (with Neil Ryder, 1990); *Recreations* sailing, opera, cooking; *Clubs* Wig and Pen; *Style*— Michael Regester, Esq; ✉ Regester & Larkin Ltd, 505 Coppergate House, 16 Brune Street, London E1 7NS (☎ 0171 721 7395, fax 0171 721 7810)

REGIS, John Paul Lyndon; s of Tony Regis, and Agnes Regis; *b* 13 Oct 1966; *Educ* St Austin's RC Boys' Sch; *Career* athlete; Bronze medal 100m and Gold medal 4 x 100m Euro Jr Championships 1985, Bronze medal 200m Euro Indoor Championships (Br record) 1986, Bronze medal 200m World Championships 1987, Silver medal 4 x 100m (Br record) Olympic Games Seoul 1988, Gold medal 200m World Indoor Championships 1989; Euro Championships 1990: Bronze medal 100m, Gold medal 200m, Silver medal 4 x 100m, Gold medal 4 x 400m; Gold medal 4 x 400m World Championships Tokyo 1991, Bronze medal 4 x 400m Olympic Games Barcelona 1992, Gold medal 200m and 4 x 400m relay Euro Cup 1993, Silver medal 200m World Championships (Silver 4 x 100m), Gold medal World Cup 1994, memb Br team Olympic Games Atlanta 1996; Cwlth record holder 4 x 200m indoor relay; *Recreations* golf, tennis; *Clubs* Queen's Tennis, Sundridge Park Golf; *Style*— John Regis, Esq; ✉ Belgrave Harriers AC, Barley Croft, 58 Harvest Road, Englefield Green, Surrey (☎ 01784 431012)

REGO, Paula; da of José Fernandes Figueiroa Rego (d 1966), of Portugal, and Maria Des José Paiva; *b* 26 Jan 1935; *Educ* St Julian's Sch Carcavelos Portugal, Slade Sch of Fine Art UCL; *m* 1959, Victor Willing, s of George Willing; 1 s (Nicholas Juvenal b 1961), 2 da (Caroline b 1956, Victoria Camilla b 1959); *Career* artist; pt/t lectr Slade Sch of Fine Art 1983–90, assoc artist Nat Gallery London 1990, Gulbenkian Fndn bursary 1962–63; sr fell RCA; subject of book Paula Rego (by John McEwen, 1992); *Solo Exhibitions* SNBA Lisbon 1965, Galeria S Mamede Lisbon 1971, Galeria da Emenda Lisbon 1974, Galeria Modulo Oporto 1977, Galeria III Lisbon 1978, Air Gallery London 1981, Edward Totah Gallery London 1982, 1984, 1985 and 1987, Arnolfini Bristol 1983, Gallery Espace Amsterdam 1983, Midland Group 1984, The Art Palace NY 1985, Travelling Show 1987, Retrospective Exhibition (Gulbenkian Fndn Lisbon and Serpentine Gallery London) 1988, Nursery Rhymes (Marlborough Graphics, travelling exhbn Plymouth, Manchester and elsewhere, Nat Gallery 1991, South Bank Centre) 1991–96, Peter Pan and Other Stories (Marlborough Fine Art) 1992, Peter Scott Gallery Univ of Lancaster 1993, Dog Woman (Marlborough Fine Art) 1994; *Group Exhibitions* incl: S Paulo Biennale 1969 and 1985, Br Art Show 1985, Cries and Whispers (Br Cncl) 1988, Br Art (Japan) 1990, Innocence and Experience (Manchester City Art Gallery and touring) 1992, British Figurative Art in the 20th Century (British Arts Cncl and the Israel Museum Jerusalem) 1993, Unbound (Hayward Gallery) 1994, Saatchi Gallery 1994, Spellbound (Hayward Gallery) 1996; *Books* Peter Pan (Folio), Nursery Rhymes (Folio Society, together with Thames and Hudson); *Style*— Ms Paula Rego; ✉ Marlborough Fine Art, 6 Albemarle St, London W1X 4BY (☎ 0171 629 5161, fax 0171 629 6338)

REHDER, Frank Ernest; CVO (1976); s of Ernest A Rehder (d 1955), of Dulwich, London, and Julia Clara Dorothea, *née* Lienau (d 1959); *b* 4 Aug 1918; *Educ* Charterhouse, CCC Oxford (MA); *Career* WWII Capt RA 1940–45, Capt Royal Northumberland Fus 1945–46; admitted slr 1948, ptnr Sinclair Roche & Temperley London 1953–83 (conslt 1984–96), maritime and commercial arbitrator 1975–; memb and hon slr London Maritime Arbitrators Assoc 1960–90 (hon memb 1977–), dir London Ct of Int Arbitration 1985–92; vice-pres emeritus CIArb 1993– (chm 1984–86); chm Dulwich Cons Assoc 1963–67; cncllr Camberwell Borough Cncl 1960–65; Freeman City of London; Liveryman: Haberdashers Co, City of London Solicitors Co, Worshipful Co of Arbitrators (Master 1985–86); FCIArb 1972; *Recreations* gardening, walking; *Style*— Frank E Rehder, Esq, CVO; ✉ Rooks' Hill, Mid-Lavant, Chichester PO18 0BQ (☎ 01243 528400, fax 01243 531971)

REICH, Steve; s of Leonard J Reich (d 1991), of New York, and June, *née* Sillman, of Los Angeles; *b* 3 Oct 1936; *Educ* Cornell Univ, Juilliard Sch of Music, Mills Coll (MA); *m* 30 June 1976, Beryl, *née* Korot; 1 s (Ezra b 13 Aug 1978); *Career* composer; studied under Darius Milhaud and Luciano Berio; fndr Steve Reich and Musicians 1966; works incl: The Plastic Haircut 1963, Music for 3 or more pianos 1964, Oh Dem Watermelons 1965, Violin Phase 1967, Pendulum Music 1968, Four Log Drums 1969, Phase Patterns (for four electric organs) 1970, Clapping Music 1972, Music for Eighteen Musicians 1976, Variations for Winds, Strings, and Keyboards 1979, Tehillim 1981, Vermont Counterpoint 1982, Eight Lines 1983, The Desert Music 1984, New York Counterpoint 1985, Six Marimbas 1986, The Four Sections 1987, Electric Counterpoint 1987, Different Trains 1988 (winner Grammy Award for Best Contemporary Composition 1990), Typing Music 1 (from The Cave) 1989, The Cave 1993, Nagoya Marimbas 1994, Duet 1994, City Life 1995 (premiered at Queen Elizabeth Hall), Proverb 1995 (cmmnd for BBC Proms); dance music: Fase 1983, Falling Angels, Eight Lines, Sextet, Impact (winner of Bessie Award 1986); all major works recorded on: Nonesuch label, RCA Victor, ECM, Deutsche Grammophon, Angel, Disques Shandar, Columbia, CBS Odyssey; cmmns for: Holland Festival, San Francisco Symphony Orch, Rothko Chapel, Ransom Wilson, Brooklyn Academy of Music (for Pat Metheny), WDR Cologne, Saint Louis Symphony Orch, Kronos Quartet, London Sinfonietta, South Bank Centre/Serious Speakout; elected to: American Acad of Arts and Letters 1994, Bavarian Academy of Arts; *Awards* study grants incl: Univ of Ghana, American Soc for Eastern Arts California, Jerusalem New York State Cncl on the Arts 1974, DAAD Artists in Residence Award Berlin 1974, Rockefeller Foundation Grants 1975, 1978, 1981 and 1990, National Endowment for the Arts Grants 1974 and 1976, Guggenheim Fellowship 1978, Koussevitzky Foundation Award 1981; *Style*— Steve Reich, Esq; ✉ c/o Andrew Rosner, Allied Artists Agency, 42 Montpelier Square, London SW7 1JZ (☎ 0171 589 6243, fax 0171 581 5269)

REID, (Philip) Alan; s of Philip Reid (d 1981), of Glasgow, and Margaret, *née* McKerracher (d 1976); *b* 18 Jan 1947; *Educ* Fettes, Univ of St Andrews (LLB); *m* 14 July 1971, Maureen Anne Reid, da of Alexander Petrie, of Cupar, Fife, Scotland; 1 s (Richard b 1984), 1 da (Caroline b 1981); *Career* exec chm KPMG Management Consultancy Europe and head UK Management Consultancy KPMG 1994–; pres Management Consultancies Assoc; chm Int Tax Ctee Inst of CAs of Scot 1982–93; memb: Tax Steering Ctee Consultative Ctee of Accountancy Bodies 1982–85, Tax Practices Ctee Inst of CAs of Scot 1982–94; CA 1973, FTII 1981, FRSA 1993; *Recreations* family, skiing, theatre, golf; *Clubs* RAC; *Style*— Alan Reid, Esq; ✉ KPMG, 8 Salisbury Square, London EC4Y 8BB (☎ 0171 311 8934, 0171 311 8499, telex 8811541)

REID, Sir Alexander James; 3 Bt (UK 1897), of Ellon, Aberdeenshire; JP (Cambs and Isle of Ely 1971), DL (1973); s of Sir Edward James Reid, 2 Bt, KBE (d 1972), and Tatiana (Tania), *née* Fenoult (d 1992); *b* 6 Dec 1932; *Educ* Eton, Magdalene Coll Cambridge; *m* 1955, Michaela Ann, da of late Olaf Kier, CBE, of Royston, Herts; 1 s Charles Edward James b 1956), 3 da (Christina b 1958, Jennifer (Mrs Rory Collins) b 1959, Alexandra Catherine (Mrs Charles Lloyd) b 1965); *Heir* s, Charles Edward James Reid, *qv*; *Career* 2 Lt 1 Bn Gordon Highlanders 1951, served Malaya; Capt 3 Bn Gordon Highlanders TA, ret 1964; chm: Ellon Castle Estates Co Ltd 1965–96, Cristina Securities Ltd 1970–, Cytozyme (UK) Ltd 1985–92; govr Heath Mount Prep Sch 1970–92 (chm 1976–92), chm Clan Donnachaidh Soc 1994–; Liveryman Worshipful Co of Farmers; High Sheriff of Cambridge 1987–88; *Recreations* shooting, all country pursuits; *Clubs* Caledonian, New (Edinburgh); *Style*— Sir Alexander Reid, Bt, JP, DL; ✉ Lanton Tower, Jedburgh, Roxburghshire TD8 6SU (☎ 01835 863443, fax 01835 864636)

REID, Andrew Milton; s of late Rev A R R Reid, DD; *b* 21 July 1929; *Educ* Glasgow Acad, Jesus Coll Oxford; *m* 1, 1953, Norma MacKenzie (d 1993), da of late Norman Davidson; 2 s (Ian, Roderick); m 2, 1995, Audrey Bruell; *Career* asst md John Player Sons 1975–77, dir Imperial Group Ltd 1978–89, chm Imperial Tobacco Ltd 1979–86 (full-time chm and chief exec 1983), dep chm Imperial Group Ltd 1986; dir: Trade Indemnity plc 1982–96 (dep chm 1993), Renold plc 1983–96; memb: Cncl Royal Sch of Church Music 1986–91, Tobacco Advsy Cncl 1977–87, Bristol Devpt Corp until 1996 (dep chm 1993), Cncl Univ of Bristol; High Sheriff of Avon 1991; Master Soc of Merchant Venturers of Bristol 1991, Liveryman Worshipful Co of Tobacco Pipe Makers & Tobacco Blenders; *Recreations* fishing, golf, sailing; *Clubs* United Oxford and Cambridge; *Style*— Andrew Reid, Esq; ✉ Parsonage Farm, Publow, Pensford, nr Bristol

REID, Charles Edward James; s and h of Sir Alexander Reid, 3 Bt, *qv*; *b* 24 June 1956; *Educ* Rannoch Sch, RAC Cirencester; *Recreations* shooting, fishing; *Clubs* Clifton, Caledonian; *Style*— Charles Reid, Esq

REID, Prof Daniel; OBE (1989); s of John Dinsmore Reid (d 1972), of Glasgow, and Ethel, *née* Cheyne (d 1978); *b* 5 Feb 1935; *Educ* Allan Glen's Sch Glasgow, Univ of Glasgow (MB ChB, MD), Royal Inst of Public Health and Hygiene (DPH); *m* 3 Aug 1963, Eileen (d 1991), da of William James Simpson (d 1939), of Greenock, Renfrewshire; 2 da (Anne Cheyne b 21 April 1965, Jane Anderson b 25 July 1967); *Career* Nat Serv Capt RAMC 1960–62, attached Royal Northumberland Fus Hong Kong; registrar Univ Dept of Infectious Diseases Ruchill Hosp Glasgow 1963–65, sr registrar epidemiological res laboratory Central Public Health Laboratory London 1965–69, dir Scottish Centre for Infection and Environmental Health Ruchill Hosp Glasgow 1969–; hon prof Univ of Glasgow 1994–; hon sr lectr: Dept of Infectious Diseases Univ of Glasgow 1969–, Univ of Edinburgh 1991–; visiting prof Univ of Strathclyde 1989–; chm: Advsy Gp on Infection Scottish Health Servs Planning Cncl 1983–, Glasgow Assoc for the Welfare of the Disabled 1983–87; FFPHM 1977, FRSH 1976, FRCPG 1983, FRCPEd 1994; Encomienda con placa de la Orden Civil de Sanidad Spain 1975; *Books* Infections in Current Medical Practice (jt ed, 1986); *Style*— Prof Daniel Reid, OBE; ✉ Scottish Centre for Infection and Environmental Health, Ruchill Hospital, Glasgow G20 9NB (☎ 0141 946 7120, fax 0141 946 4359, telex 776373)

REID, David Ronald; s of David Ronald Reid (d 1957), and Martha, *née* Laurie (d 1986); *b* 23 June 1937; *Educ* Daniel Stewart's Coll Edinburgh, Univ of Edinburgh (MA Classics, LLB); *m* 23 Dec 1980, Ruth Edith; 1 da (Pamela Jane b 20 May 1967); *Career* Slaughter & May London; W & J Burness: apprentice, ptnr 1965, partnership chm 1992–; sometime conveyancing tutor Univ of Edinburgh and former memb Cncl WS Soc; dir Edinburgh Assured Properties plc; advsr Cancer Relief Macmillan Fund; memb WS Soc; *Recreations* golf, hill-walking, music, swimming; *Style*— David Reid, Esq; ✉ W & J Burness, 16 Hope Street, Charlotte Square, Edinburgh EH2 4DD (☎ 0131 226 2561, fax 0131 225 5075)

REID, Derek D; *Educ* Inverurie Acad, Univ of Aberdeen, Robert Gordon Univ; m; 2 c; *Career* Cadbury-Schweppes: joined 1968, variously dir foods business then tea business until 1986; involved with MBO of Cadbury-Schweppes to form Premier Brands plc 1986, left following takeover by Hillsdown Holdings plc 1990; currently proprietor Farleyer House Hotel, dir various small cos; chief exec Scottish Tourist Bd 1994–96; Hon DBA Robert Gordon Univ 1995; *Recreations* Scottish contemporary art, classical music, cricket, golf, fishing; *Style*— Derek Reid, Esq; ✉ Bon Hard House, Scone, Perth PH2 7PQ (☎ 01738 552471, fax 01738 553911)

REID, Rt Rev Gavin Hunter; *see:* Maidstone, Bishop of

REID, George Newlands; s of George Reid (d 1978), and Margaret Forsyth (d 1969); *b* 4 June 1939; *Educ* Dollar Acad, Univ of St Andrews (MA, Gold Medal in history, pres

Students' Rep Cncl); *m* 1, 11 April 1964 (m dis), Catherine Stott; 1 da (Caroline Lucinda b 20 June 1965); m 2, 4 July 1968, Daphne Ann, da of Calum McColl; 1 da (Morag Marsaili); *Career* reporter: Daily Express 1961–62, political correspondent Scottish TV 1962–64; prodr Granada TV 1964–68, head of News and Current Affrs Scottish TV 1968–74, MP (SNP) Clackmannan and E Stirlingshire 1974–79 (memb Assembly of Cncl of Europe 1976–79 and Assembly of Western Europe Union 1976–79), freelance broadcaster and journalist (BBC TV and Radio and various newspapers) 1979–84, dir Public Affrs League of Red Cross and Red Crescent Socs Geneva 1985–90 (head of information 1984–90), dir Int Red Cross Promotion Bureau 1990–; dir Scottish Cncl Res Inst 1978–81; Pirogov Gold Medal (for work as chief Red Cross Del in Armenian Earthquake) USSR 1989 and 1990; *Books* Red Cross, Red Crescent (ed, 1989), Casualties of Conflict (ed, 1990); *Recreations* gardening, hill walking, cross-country skiing; *Style—* George Reid, Esq; ✉ Villa Rosemont, 23 Avenue du Bouchet, Petit Saconnex 1209, Geneva, Switzerland (☎ 00 41 22 734 6705)

REID, (James) Gordon; QC (Scot 1993); s of James Rae Reid (d 1977), of Edinburgh, and Constance May, *née* Lawrie; *b* 24 July 1952; *Educ* Melville Coll Edinburgh, Univ of Edinburgh (LLB Hons); *m* 12 Sept 1984, Hannah Hogg, da of William Hopkins; 3 s (William Lawrie b 21 July 1987, James Hogg (twin), Jonathan Rae b 10 Dec 1989), 1 da (Joanna Margaret Grant b 26 Oct 1991); *Career* slr in Scot 1976–80 (apprentice slr 1974–76), admitted Faculty of Advocates 1980, standing jr counsel to Scot Office Environment Dept 1986–93; called to the English Bar Inner Temple 1991; memb: Soc of Construction Law 1990, Agric Law Assoc 1990; FCIArb 1994; *Recreations* music, MIDI sequencing, computers and music, general fitness; *Style—* J Gordon Reid, Esq, QC; ✉ Blebo House, By St Andrews, Fife KY15 5TZ (☎ 01334 655775, fax 01334 656765); Advocates' Library, Parliament House, Edinburgh EH1 1RF (clerk ☎ 0131 260 5615, fax 0131 225 3662); Atkin Chambers, 1 Atkin Building, Gray's Inn, London WC1R 5BQ (☎ 0171 404 0102)

REID, Graham Charles; s of Charles Anderson Reid (d 1984), of Stoke D'Abernon, Surrey, and Mona Ethel, *née* Hinton (d 1993); *b* 29 Aug 1945; *Educ* King's Coll Sch Wimbledon (scholarship), King's Coll Univ of London; *m* 22 Aug 1970, Gaye, da of Leonard Frank Peskett; 1 s (Stephen James b 27 May 1974); *Career* articled clerk Legg London & Co 1965–68; Grant Thornton (formerly Thornton Baker): rose to mangr London office 1969–77, estab Ipswich office 1977–, ptnr 1979–; treas Suffolk Branch IOD 1990–, memb Area Bd for Suffolk PYBT 1991– (vice chm 1993–95, chm 1995–), memb Steering Ctee Suffolk Small Business Initiative 1995–; FCA 1979 (ACA 1970); *Recreations* music, wine, sport, walking; *Style—* Graham Reid, Esq; ✉ Mitchery Farmhouse, Rattlesden, nr Bury St Edmunds, Suffolk IP30 0SS (☎ 01449 736259); Grant Thornton, Crown House, Crown St, Ipswich, Suffolk IP1 3HS (☎ 01473 221491, fax 01473 230304)

REID, Harry; *b* Scotland; *m*; 2 s; *Career* Ogilvy & Mather advtg: joined early '70s, regional dir Asia (Hong Kong) 1986–91, chm and regional dir for Europe and ME (London) 1991–94, chief operating offr worldwide 1994–95; pres FCB International 1995–; *Recreations* cricket, Asian antiques, recently golf; *Style—* Harry Reid, Esq; ✉ President, FCB International, 110 St Martin's Lane, London WC2N 4DY (☎ 0171 240 7100, fax 0171 240 5500)

REID, Sir Hugh; 3 Bt (UK 1922), of Springburn, Co of City of Glasgow, and of Kilmaurs, Co Ayr; s of Sir Douglas Neilson Reid, 2 Bt (d 1971), and Margaret Brighton Young, *née* Maxtone (d 1992); *b* 27 Nov 1933; *Educ* Loretto; *Heir* none; *Career* RAF 1952–56, served Egypt and Cyprus, RAF (VRT) 1963–75, Flying Offr; self-employed travel conslt 1961–; *Recreations* travel, skiing, aviation, cooking; *Style—* Sir Hugh Reid, Bt; ✉ Caheronaun Park, Loughrea, Co Galway, Ireland

REID, Dr (Richard) Ian; s of Richard Morton Reid (d 1971), of Coatbridge, Scot, and Margaret Mackay, *née* McCaul; *b* 12 May 1951; *Educ* Coatbridge HS, Univ of Glasgow (MB ChB); *m* 1, 2 Sept 1975 (m dis 1980), Carole Jane Westley; m 2, 28 March 1981, Amanda Jane, da of Maj Peter Munden, of Andover, Hants; 2 da (Jeannie Isabel b 1982, Eleanor Susan b 1984); *Career* conslt in geriatric med Southampton Community Health Servs NHS Tst; hon clinical teacher Univ of Southampton 1982; pres Ashton Club Moorgreen Hosp Southampton, memb Br Geriatrics Soc 1979; FRCP (Glas), FRCP; *Recreations* windsurfing, walking, swimming, railway modelling; *Style—* Dr Ian Reid; ✉ Department of Geriatric Medicine, Glevel, West Wing, Southampton General Hospital, Southampton, Hants SO9 4XY (☎ 01703 796805/794656)

REID, Dr John; MP (Lab) Motherwell North (majority 18,910); *b* 8 May 1947; *m* Cathie; 2 s (Kevin, Mark); *Career* res Lab Pty in Sco 1979–83, advsr to Rt Hon Neil Kinnock MP 1983–86, Scot organiser Trade Unionists for Labour 1986–87; MP (Lab) Motherwell N 1987–, front bench dep spokesman on children 1989–90, front bench spokesman on armed forces 1990–; *Style—* Dr John Reid, MP; ✉ (home ☎ 01698 861817); House of Commons, London SW1A 0AA (☎ 0171 219 3000)

REID, Rev Prof John Kelman Sutherland; CBE (1970), TD (1961); s of David Reid (d 1933), of Edinburgh, and Georgina Thomson, *née* Stuart (d 1946); *b* 31 March 1910; *Educ* George Watson's Boys' Coll Edinburgh, Univ of Edinburgh (MA, BD); *m* 3 Jan 1950, Margaret Winifrid, da of Rev W S Brookes (d 1958), of Corrie, Isle of Arran; *Career* Royal Army Chaplains Dept, Chaplain Class 4 Royal Signals 1942–43, Parachute Regt 1943–46, TA 1946–62; prof of philosophy Univ of Calcutta 1936–38, min of religion Craigmillar Park Church Edinburgh, prof of theology Univ of Leeds 1952–61, prof of systematic theology Univ of Aberdeen 1961–76; ed (now emeritus) Scottish Jl of Theology 1948–, sec New English Bible 1949–82; memb: World Cncl of Churches Faith and Order Cmmn 1961–82, Br Cncl of Churches 1961–68, Soc for Study of Theology, Societas NT Studiorum, Scottish Church Theology Soc, Church Serv Soc, Scottish Church Soc; Hon DD Edinburgh Univ 1957; *Books* The Authority of Scripture (third edn 1981), Presbyterians and Unity (1962), Life in Christ (1963), Christian Apologetics (1969), Calvin's Concerning the Eternal Predestination of God (trans, second edn 1982), Oscar Cullmann: Baptism in the New Testament (trans 1950); *Style—* The Rev Prof John K S Reid, CBE, TD; ✉ 8 Abbotsford Court, 18 Colinton Road, Edinburgh EH10 5EH (☎ 0131 447 6855)

REID, Prof John Low; s of James Reid (d 1961), of Glasgow, and Irene Margaret; *b* 1 Oct 1943; *Educ* Kelvinside Acad Glasgow, Fettes, Univ of Oxford (MA, BM, BCh, DM); *m* 2 May 1964, Randa, da of Naguib Aref Pharaon (d 1987), of London; 1 s (James b 1965), 1 da (Rebecca b 1967); *Career* house offr Radcliffe Infirmary Oxford and Brompton Hosp London 1968–70, res fell, sr lectr then reader Royal Postgrad Med Sch London 1970–78, visiting scientist Nat Inst of Health Bethesda Maryland USA 1973–75; Univ of Glasgow: regius prof materia medica 1978–89, regius prof of med and therapeutics 1989–; ed: Clinical Science 1982–84, Journal of Hypertension 1987–94; FRCPGlas 1979, FRCP 1987, FRSE 1995; *Books* Handbook of Hypertension (1981), Lecture Notes on Clinical Pharmacology (1981); *Recreations* gardening, books, outdoors; *Style—* Prof John Reid; ✉ Dhubaniel, Gartocharn, Dunbartonshire G83 8NJ (☎ 01389 830315); Western Infirmary, Glasgow (☎ 0141 211 2884, fax 0141 339 2800)

REID, Dr Mark McClean; s of E Mayne Reid, CBE (d 1985), and Meta, *née* Hopkins (d 1990); *b* 27 Dec 1937; *Educ* Bangor GS, Queen's Univ Belfast (MB BChir); *m* 10 July 1964, Barbara, da of James Cupples (d 1986); 1 s (Alistair b 18 Aug 1966), 2 da (Fiona b 1 Nov 1968, Claire b 20 July 1973); *Career* conslt paediatrician with special interest in new-born Royal Maternity Hosp Belfast 1978–; pres: Irish Perinatal Soc 1979–80, Ulster Paediatric Soc 1987–88; chm NI Postgrad Paediatric Cmmn 1985–; memb: BMA, Br Paediatric Assoc (memb Cncl 1981–84), Ulster Med Soc, Ulster Paediatric Soc, Irish Perinatal Soc, Ulster Obstetric and Gynaecological Soc, Cncl RCPI 1994–96; FRCPGlas, FRCPI, FRCPEd; *Books* Handbook Neonatal Intensive Care (jtly, first and second edns), various pubns on perinatal or neonatal field in Br Euro and N American jls 1967–; *Recreations* mountain climbing, travel, Alpine gardening, photography; *Style—* Dr Mark Reid; ✉ 10 Kensington Gardens, Hillsborough, Co Down BT26 6HP (☎ 01232 682267); Regional Neonatal Intensive Care Unit, Royal Maternity Hospital, Belfast B12 6BA (☎ 01232 240503)

REID, Sir (Harold) Martin (Smith); KBE (1987), CMG (1978); s of Marcus Reid (d 1948), and Winifred Mary Reid, *née* Stephens (d 1969); *b* 27 Aug 1928; *Educ* Merchant Taylors' Sch, BNC Oxford (MA); *m* 1956, Jane Elizabeth, da of Frank Lester Harwood (d 1975), of Hants; 1 s (Thomas), 3 da (Philippa, Emily, Alice); *Career* RN 1947–49; entered Foreign Serv 1953; served: London, Paris, Rangoon, London; political advsr to Govr Br Guyana 1965–66, dep high cmmnr Guyana 1966–68, no 2 in Bucharest and Blantyre Malawi 1968–73, princ private sec to successive Secs of State for NI 1973–74, head Central and S African Dept FCO 1974–78, min Pretoria 1979–82, seconded as dip serv res chm Civil Serv Selection Bd 1983, Br high cmmr Kingston and concurrently ambass (non res) Port au Prince 1984–87, special res advsr FCO 1987–88, ret 1988; *Books* Camille Pissarro (1993); *Recreations* painting (sixth one-man exhibition 1994, several works in the Jamaican nat collection); *Style—* Sir Martin Reid, KBE, CMG; ✉ 43 Carson Road, London SE21 8HT (☎ 0181 670 6151)

REID, Michael William Peter Cameron; s of late William Arthur Reid, colonial offr, and Judy, *née* McNally (civil servant); *b* 25 April 1946; *Educ* Gordonstoun, City of London Coll; *m* 22 April 1970, Margaret Wendy, *née* Aikman; 2 s (James Cameron b 24 Sept 1973, Alexander Cameron b 21 July 1978), 1 da (Victoria Sarah Cameron b 21 Feb 1975); *Career* chief exec Titmuss Sainer Dechert Slrs 1987–95, chief exec Watson, Farley and Williams Slrs 1995–; FCCA 1980 (ACCA 1973); *Recreations* shooting, mountain walking, flying; *Clubs* East India; *Style—* Michael Reid; ✉ Biggin Lodge, Yardley Hastings, Northants NN7 1HN; Watson, Farley and Williams, 15 Appold Street, London EC2A 2HB (☎ 0171 814 8000, fax 0171 814 8141)

REID, Mike; *b* 19 Jan 1940; *Educ* Roland Hill Sch for Boys Tottenham; *m* Shirley; *Career* actor and comedian; stuntman for The Saint and The Baron TV series; TV: The Comedians (26 shows), numerous variety shows (BBC and ITV), Runaround (ITV), starred in Yus My Dear (4 series), starred in six Mike Reid TV specials (BBC) from 1977, Big Deal (BBC) 1986, Frank Butcher in EastEnders (BBC) 1987–94 and 1996; theatre: nationwide tour with The Comedians, numerous performances nationwide of his own adult comedy show; video: Mike Reid, Live and Uncensored 1992, Mike Reid, Live and Uncensored II 1993, Live at the Palladium 1995; album Mike Reid Sings... (1993); *Recreations* golf; *Style—* Mike Reid, Esq; ✉ c/o Tony Lewis Entertainments, 235–241 Regent Street, London W1R 8TL

REID, Sir Norman Robert; kt (1970); s of Edward Daniel Reid (d 1956); *b* 27 Dec 1915; *Educ* Wilson's GS Camberwell, Edinburgh Coll of Art, Univ of Edinburgh (DA); *m* 1941, Jean Lindsay, da of Alexander Taylor Bertram, of Brechin; 1 s, 1 da; *Career* served A&SH WWII, Maj 1946; Tate Gallery: joined 1946, dep dir 1954, keeper 1959, dir 1964–79; memb: Cncl Friends of the Tate Gallery 1958–79, Arts Cncl Panel 1964–74, Advsy Panel ICA 1965, Advsy Ctee Paintings in Hosps 1965–69, Br Cncl Fine Arts Ctee 1965–77 (chm 1968–75), Cultural Advsy Ctee UK Nat Cmmn for UNESCO 1966–70, Studies in History of Art Bd London Univ 1968, The Rome Centre 1969–77 (pres 1975–77), Burlington Magazine Bd 1971–75, Advsy Cncl Paul Mellon Centre 1971–78, Cncl of Mgmnt Inst of Contemporary Prints 1972–78, Contemporary Arts Soc Ctee 1973–77 (and 1965–72), Cncl RCA 1974–77; pres Penworth Soc of Arts, tstee Graham and Kathleen Sutherland Fndn 1980–86; paintings in the Tate Gallery and in the Scottish Nat Collection of Modern Art Edinburgh; Hon DLitt UEA; FMA, FIIC; Offr of the Mexican Order of the Aztec Eagle; *Clubs* Arts; *Style—* Sir Norman Reid; ✉ 50 Brabourne Rise, Park Langley, Beckenham, Kent BR3 6SH

REID, (James) Robert; QC (1980); s of His Hon Judge John Alexander Reid, MC (d 1969), and Jean Ethel, *née* Ashworth (d 1991); *b* 23 Jan 1943; *Educ* Marlborough, New Coll Oxford, (MA); *m* 25 May 1974, Anne Prudence, da of John Arkell Wakefield; 2 s (Edward b 1976, David b 1978), 1 da (Sarah b 1980); *Career* called to the Bar Lincoln's Inn 1965, recorder of the Crown Court 1985–, bencher 1988, head of chambers; Barristers' Benevolent Assoc: jt treas 1986–91, dep chm 1991–95, chm 1995–; FCIArb; *Style—* Robert Reid, Esq, QC; ✉ 9 Old Square, Lincoln's Inn, London WC2A 3SR

REID, Sir Robert Paul (Bob); kt (1990); *b* 1 May 1934; *Educ* Univ of St Andrews (MA); *m* 1958, Joan Mary; 3 s; *Career* Shell International Petroleum Co Ltd: Sarawak Oilfields and Brunei 1956–59, Nigeria 1959–67, Africa and S Asia Regnl Orgn 1967–68, PA and planning advsr to Chm Shell & BP Services Kenya 1968–70, md Nigeria 1970–74, md Thailand 1974–78, vice pres int aviation and products trading 1978–80, exec dir downstream oil Shell Co of Australia 1980–83, co-ordinator supply and mktg London 1983, dir 1984–90, chm and chief exec Shell UK Ltd 1985–90; chm: British Rail 1990–95, British-Borneo 1995–, Rosyth 2000 1995–; non-exec chm London Electricity plc 1994– (non-exec dir 1993–), non-exec chm Sears plc 1995–; non-exec dir Bank of Scotland; memb President's Ctee CBI; chm: Nat Forum for Mgmnt Educn and Devpt 1986–95, BIM 1988–89, Fndn Mgmnt Educn, Robert Gordon Univ; pres Assoc Project Mangrs 1995–; tstee Sci Museum 1987–92; Hon LLD: Univ of St Andrews 1987, Univ of Aberdeen 1988; Hon DSc Univ of Salford 1990; *Recreations* golf, sailing; *Clubs* MCC, R & A, Royal Melbourne (Melbourne), Frilford Heath Golf; *Style—* Sir Bob Reid; ✉ Sears plc, 40 Duke Street, London W1A 2HP (☎ 0171 408 1180)

REID, (William) Russell; s of William Livingstone Reid (d 1973), and Louise Margaret, *née* Kidd; *b* 27 Jan 1936; *Educ* Harris Acad Dundee, Arbroath HS; *m* 1964, Patricia Anne, da of late John G Rutherford; 2 da (Jacqueline Anne b 1966, Susan Elizabeth b 1969); *Career* reporter on Courier and Evening Telegraph (D C Thomson & Co Ltd) 1953–57; Sunday Post: reporter and feature writer 1957–83, dep ed 1983–89, ed 1989–; vice chm Eds' Ctee Scottish Daily Newspaper Soc 1996– (memb 1989–); memb Code Ctee PCC 1994–; hon pres Univ of Dundee Music Soc 1982–, hon vice-pres Univ of Dundee Operatic Soc 1986–; *Recreations* music, walking, reading, talking; *Style—* Russell Reid, Esq; ✉ The Sunday Post, 2 Albert Square, Dundee DD1 9QJ (☎ 01382 223131, fax 01382 201064)

REID, Prof Stephen Robert; s of Stephen Robert Reid (d 1978), of Manchester, and Mary, *née* Beresford (d 1976); *b* 13 May 1945; *Educ* Chorlton GS Manchester, Univ of Manchester (BSc, PhD), Univ of Cambridge (MA, ScD), winner Safety Award in Mech Engrg (IMechE); *m* 30 Aug 1969, Susan, da of Geoffrey Bottomley; 3 s (Andrew b 25 June 1971, David b 24 April 1974, Alistair 10 Oct 1980); *Career* research offr CEGB 1969–70; lectr: Dept of Engrg UMIST 1970–76, Dept of Engrg Univ of Cambridge 1976–80; Jackson prof of engrg sci Univ of Aberdeen 1980–84, Conoco prof of mech engrg UMIST 1985– (pro vice-chllr for academic devpt 1992–95); ed-in-chief Int Jl of Mechanical Sciences 1987–; author of over 100 tech papers; fell Clare Coll Cambridge 1977–80; FIMA 1982, FIMechE 1984, FASME 1992, FEng 1993; *Recreations* Poynton Baptist Church (elder); *Style—* Prof Stephen Reid, FEng; ✉ 2 Waters Reach, Poynton, Stockport, Cheshire SK12 1XT (☎ 01625 872842); Department of Mechanical Engineering, UMIST, PO Box 88, Sackville Street, Manchester M60 1QD (☎ 0161 200 3848, fax 0161 200 3849)

REID, Flt Lt William; VC (1943); s of William Reid (d 1941), and Helena, *née* Murdoch (d 1972); *b* 21 Dec 1921; *Educ* Baillieston Sch, Coatbridge Secdy Sch, W of Scot Agric Coll, Univ of Glasgow (BSc(Agric)); *m* 28 March 1952, Violet Campbell, da of William George Gallagher (d 1976); 1 s (William Graeme b 1961), 1 da (Susan May b 1963); *Career* RAFVR Bomber Cmd 1941–46: 61 Sqdn 1943, 617 sqdn 1944 (POW 1944), demobbed 1946; farms mangr Macrobert Farms Douneside Ltd 1950–59, nat cattle and sheep advsr Spillers Ltd 1959–81; pres Br Legion (Crieff), pres Strathallan Aircraft Assoc, hon life pres Air Crew Assoc (chm Saltire branch); Freeman City of London 1988; *Recreations* golf, fishing, shooting; *Clubs* RAF; *Style*— Flt Lt William Reid, VC; ✉ Cranford, Ferntower Place, Crieff, Perthshire, Scotland PH7 3DD (☎ 01764 652462)

REID, William; CBE (1987); *b* 8 Nov 1926; *Educ* Eastwood Secdy Sch Glasgow, Univs of Glasgow and Oxford; *m* 1958, Nina Frances Brigden; *Career* RAF 1945–48 (cmmnd 1946); asst keeper The Armouries HM Tower of London 1956–70, dir Army Nat Museum 1970–88, consultative dir The Heralds' Museum 1988–92; memb Br Nat Ctee ICOM 1973–88; hon memb: The American Soc of Arms Collectors 1975, The Indian Army Assoc 1981; hon life pres Int Assoc of Museums of Arms and Military History 1987, hon life memb Friends of the Nat Army Museum 1987; tstee: Florence Nightingale Museum, Museum of Richmond, Museum of the Royal Army Educational Corps, Museum of the Royal Hampshire Regt, Lord Brock Meml Tst; memb: Founding Cncl The Army Records Soc, Cons Ctee for the Arts and Heritage 1987–; The North Parish Washing Green Soc (Glasgow) 1988; Liveryman Worshipful Co of Scriveners, Freeman City of London; FSA 1965, FMA 1974–88 (resigned); *Books* European Armour in the Tower of London (with A R Dufty, 1968), The Lore of Arms (1976); *Recreations* music, bird watching, the study of armour and arms; *Clubs* The Athenaeum; *Style*— William Reid, Esq, CBE, FSA; ✉ 66 Ennerdale Rd, Richmond, Surrey TW9 2DL (☎ 0181 940 0904)

REID, Sir William Kennedy; KCB (1996, CB 1981); s of late James Reid, and late Elspet Stewart; *b* 15 Feb 1931; *Educ* Robert Gordon's Coll Aberdeen, George Watson's Coll Edinburgh, Univ of Edinburgh (MA), Trinity Coll Cambridge (maj scholar, MA); *m* 1959, Ann, da of Lt-Col The Rev Donald Campbell; 2 s, 1 da; *Career* Miny of Educn 1956, Cabinet Office 1964–67, DES 1967–78, dep sec Scot Office 1978–84, sec Scot Home and Health Dept 1984–89; chm: Govrs Scot Police Coll 1984–89, Tstees James Smart Lecture Fund 1984–89; Parly cmmr for Admin and Health Service Cmmrs for Eng, Scot and Wales 1990–97; Sydenham lectr Soc of Apothecaries 1994, Crookshank lectr RCR 1994, Hunt lectr RCGP 1996; memb: Cncl on Tbnls, Cmmns for Local Admin in England and in Wales 1990–97; Hon LLD Univ of Aberdeen 1996; *Books* Outlook (contrib 1963); *Recreations* hill walking, verse; *Clubs* New (Edinburgh); *Style*— Sir William Reid, KCB; ✉ 11 Inverleith Terrace, Edinburgh EH3 (☎ 0131 556 1089)

REID ENTWISTLE, Dr Ian; s of John Morton Entwistle, and Mary, *née* Reid; *b* 29 Sept 1931; *Educ* Rivington and Blackrod Sch, Univ of Liverpool Med Sch (MB ChB, FRCGP, FFOM (I), FFOM, DFFP, Cert GAM); *m* 1, 15 May 1969, Anthea Margaret (d 1979), da of Kenneth Evans, of West Kirby, Wirral; 2 s (John b 1972, Alexander b 1973); m 2, Rosemary Elizabeth, *née* Harrison; *Career* Surgn Lt HMS Eaglet RNR 1962–65; specialist (EC accredited) in occupational med Royal Coll of Physicians London; princ med offr RMS Queen Mary, Queen Elizabeth and Queen Elizabeth II 1961–; casualty offr David Lewis Northern Hosp Liverpool 1957, house physician to prof of child health Royal Liverpool Children's Hosp 1957, princ in private and NHS practice 1958–, med supt Cunard PLC 1966–; conslt in occupational med to Nuffield Hosps 1993–95; sr med conslt BHS plc; pt/t med conslt: Spillers Foods Ltd, Bass Taverns 1993–95, American Colloid Co 1989–95; pt/t authorised assessor and examiner: Civil Aviation Authy, Dept of Tport; conslt Pre-Retirement Assoc; chm Benefits Agency Medical Service; med dir Barkley St Travel Clinic 1996–, conslt occupational physician Sedgwick Noble Lounds 1996–; formerly med conslt Br Eagle Int Airlines 1966–68, sr gp med conslt Utd Gas Industs 1971–80; treas and sec Merseyside and N Wales RCGP 1973–80 (bd memb 1963–89), jt treas and sec Soc of Occupational Med (Merseyside) 1961–67, chm Brewing Indust Med Advsrs 1987–, memb Cncl Birkenhead Med Soc 1995–; memb: Aerospace Physiology and Med Working Pty Cncl of Europe 1974–, NASA 1969–; med advsr West Kirby Swimming Club for Disabled; underwriting memb Lloyd's 1978–, assoc fell Aerospace Med Assoc USA 1973–; memb: RAeS, Assur Med Assoc; MRAeS, FIMgt 1988; *Books* Exacta Medica (12 edn, 1994, Spanish, Polish, Italian 3 edn 1996), Exacta Mecanix (5 edn, 1988), Exacta Paediatrica (2 edn, 1996, Spanish edn 1996, Polish edn 1996, Italian edn 1996); *Recreations* motor racing, horticulture, sailing, horology, photography, railway modelling; *Clubs* Mid Cheshire Pitt, Manchester Naval Offrs Assoc, The Twenty Club; *Style*— Dr Ian Reid Entwistle; ✉ Knollwood, Well Lane, Gayton, Wirral L60 8NG (☎ 0151 342 2332); consultation suite, 27 Banks Rd, West Kirby, Wirral L48 0RA (☎ 0151 625 6600, fax 0151 625 3393); Fitzroy Nuffield Hospital, Bryanston Square, London W1H 8BB (☎ 0171 723 1288, fax 0171 262 6357)

REID SCOTT, David Alexander Carroll; s of Maj Alexander Reid Scott, MC (d 1960), and Ann, *née* Mitchell (d 1953); *b* 5 June 1947; *Educ* Eton, Lincoln Coll Oxford (MA); *m* 1, 23 April 1972, Anne (d 1988), da of Phillipe Clouet des Pesruches (d 1977); 3 da (Iona b 1975, Camilla b 1976, Serena b 1979); m 2, 7 July 1990, Elizabeth, da of John Latshaw; *Career* 1 vice pres White Weld & Co 1969–77, seconded sr advsr Saudi Arabian Monetary Agency 1978–83, md Merrill Lynch & Co 1983–84, md Phoenix Securities Ltd 1984–; *Recreations* Irish country life, farming, arts, antiques; *Clubs* White's, Turf, Kildare St, Coningsby; *Style*— David Reid Scott, Esq; ✉ 33 Argyll Road, London W8 7DA (☎ 0171 938 1831); Ballynure, Grange Con, Co Wicklow, Ireland (☎ 00 353 45 403162, fax 00 353 45 403329); Phoenix Securities Ltd, 1 Laurence Pountney Hill, London EC4 0EU (☎ 0171 638 2191, fax 0171 638 0707)

REIDHAVEN, Viscount; James Andrew Ogilvie-Grant; also Master of Seafield; er s and h of 13 Earl of Seafield; *b* 30 Nov 1963; *Educ* Harrow; *Style*— Viscount Reidhaven

REIDY, Dr John Francis; s of Frederick Cyril Reidy (d 1957), and Marie Isobel, *née* Smith; *b* 25 Aug 1944; *Educ* Stonyhurst, St George's Hosp Med Sch and King's Coll London (MB BS, MRCS, LRCP 1967, MRCP 1970); *m* 25 Nov 1978, Dianne Patricia, da of Gerald Eugene Murphy, of Launceston, Tasmania, Australia; 1 s (Thomas Edward b 19 Nov 1980), 1 da (Laura Eugenie b 1 June 1982); *Career* conslt radiologist Guy's Hosp 1980–; Liveryman Worshipful Soc of Apothecaries; FRCR 1975, FRCP 1988; *Books* numerous pubns on cardiovascular and interventional radiology; *Style*— Dr John Reidy; ✉ 19 Cumberland St, London SW1V 4LS (☎ 0171 834 3021); Radiology Dept, Guy's Hosp, London SE1 (☎ 0171 955 4117)

REIF, Dr Stefan Clive; s of Peter Reif (d 1989), and Annie, *née* Rapstoff; *b* 21 Jan 1944; *Educ* Boroughmuir Sch Edinburgh, Univ of London (BA, William Lincoln Shelley studentship, PhD), Univ of Cambridge (MA); *m* 1967, Shulamit, da of Edmund (d 1995) and Ella Stekel (d 1992); 1 da (Tanya b 25 Dec 1968), 1 s (Aryeh b 30 Jan 1970); *Career* lectr in Hebrew and Semitic languages Univ of Glasgow 1968–72, asst prof of Hebrew language and literature Dropsie Coll Philadelphia 1972–73; Univ of Cambridge: dir Genizah Res Unit and teacher of Hebrew and Jewish studies 1973–, head Oriental Div Univ Library 1983–; visiting prof Hebrew Univ of Jerusalem 1989 and 1996–97; memb Br Assoc for Jewish Studies (pres 1992), memb Jewish Historical Soc of England (pres 1991–92); FRAS 1980; *Books* Shabbethai Sofer and his Prayer-Book (1979), Interpreting the Hebrew Bible (1982), Published Material from the Cambridge Genizah Collections (1988), Genizah Research After Ninety Years (1992), Judaism and Hebrew Prayer (1993), Hebrew Manuscripts at Cambridge University Library (1996); *Recreations* squash, cricket and football; *Style*— Dr Stefan Reif; ✉ Genizah Research Unit, Cambridge University Library, West Road, Cambridge CB3 9DR (☎ 01223 333000/333129, fax 01223 333160)

REIGATE, Archdeacon of; *see:* Baddeley, Ven Martin James

REILLY, Lt-Gen Sir Jeremy Calcott; KCB (1987), DSO (1973); s of Lt-Col Julius Frank Calcott Reilly (d 1984), of Chilbolton, Hants, and Eileen Norah, *née* Moreton; *b* 7 April 1934; *Educ* Uppingham, RMA Sandhurst; *m* 12 Nov 1960, Julia Elizabeth, da of William Forrester (d 1984), of Weymouth, Dorset; 3 da (Katherine b 1961, Penelope b and d 1964, Brigid b 1965); *Career* cmmnd Royal Warwicks Regt 1954, CO 2 Bn Royal Regt of Fusiliers 1971–73, instr Staff Coll 1974–75, Col GS MOD 1975–77, PSO to FM Lord Carver and attached to FCO (Rhodesia) 1977–79, Brig 1979, Cdr 6 Field Force and UK Mobile Force 1979–81, Maj-Gen 1981, GOC 4 Armd Div BAOR 1981–83, Dep Col Royal Regt Fusiliers 1981–86, DBD MOD 1983–84, ACDS MOD 1985–86, Col Royal Regt Fusiliers 1986–, Lt-Gen 1986, CTAD 1986–89, Col Cmdt Queen's Div 1988–90, ret 1989; *Style*— Lt-Gen Sir Jeremy Reilly, KCB, DSO; ✉ c/o Royal Regt Fusiliers, HM Tower of London, London EC3N 4AB

REILLY, Malcolm John; OBE (1991); s of Robert Reilly, of Kippax, nr Leeds, and Annie, *née* Wood; *b* 19 Jan 1948; *Educ* Ashton Rd Secdy Sch Castleford, Whitwood Tech Coll Castleford; *m* 19 Nov 1972, Susan, da of Harold Leonard Sault (d 1982); 1 s (Glen Robert b 26 Jan 1974), 1 da (Lyndsey Clare b 24 May 1978); *Career* rugby league coach; former amateur footballer Kippax Welfare, switched to rugby league with Kippax Amateur Club 1967; professional Castleford 1967–71 and 1975–87 (player-coach then coach), total 330 appearances; transferred for a fee of £15,000 to Manly Warringah Aust 1971–75 (87 appearances); 3 England caps, 9 GB caps incl tour Aust and NZ 1970; coach GB 1987–94: 40 matches, 30 wins, won series v NZ 1989, 1990 and 1993; also coach Halifax RLFC 1992–94, coach Newcastle Knights (Aust) 1994–; honours as player Castleford: Challenge Cup 1969 (awarded Lance Todd Trophy) and 1970, Grand Final winners 1972 and 1973, try of the year 1972; honours as coach Castleford: John Player Final winners 1976 and 1977, Yorkshire Cup winners 3 times, Challenge Cup 1986; honours as coach Newcastle Knights: winners Coca Cola World Sevens 1996; mechanic 1963–70, area sales mangr Aust 1970–75, area sales rep Rocol Ltd 1975–80, publican 1980–82, account mangr John Smiths Free Trade 1982–90; *Recreations* keeping fit, jogging, strength training, cooking, eating, athletics, nature, sub-aqua diving; *Style*— Malcolm Reilly, Esq, OBE; ✉ 5 Warialda Close, Belmont North, Newcastle, NSW 2300, Australia

REILLY, Mary Margaret; da of John Patrick Reilly (d 1987), of Ireland, and Helena, *née* MacAndrew; *b* 22 May 1953; *Educ* Notre Dame, UCL (BA); *m* 17 March 1979, Mark Richard Charles Corby, s of Peter John Siddons Corby; 1 da (b 1981), 1 s (b 1986); *Career* ptnr Binder Hamlyn 1987–; FCA 1989 (ACA 1978), FRSA 1989; *Recreations* country pursuits, skiing, opera, theatre; *Style*— Ms Mary Reilly; ✉ Binder Hamlyn, 20 Old Bailey, London EC4M 7BH (☎ 0171 489 6224, fax 0171 489 6293)

REILLY, (David) Nicholas (Nick); s of John Reilly (d 1981), of Anglesey, and Mona, *née* Glynne Jones; *b* 17 Dec 1949; *Educ* Harrow, St Catharine's Coll Cambridge (MA (Econ)); *m* Susan, *née* Haig; 2 da (Natasha b 1978, Jessica b 1981), 1 s (George b 1979); *Career* investment analyst 1971–74; General Motors: joined 1974, finance dir Moto Diesel Mexicana Mexico 1980–83, supply dir Vauxhall Motors 1984–87, vice pres IBC 1987–90, mfrg dir Vauxhall Ellesmere Port 1990–94, vice pres Quality General Motors Europe 1994–96, chm and md Vauxhall Motors 1996–; chm IBC Vehicles 1996–, memb Bd Saab GB 1996–; chm Chester, Ellesmere, Wirral TEC (CEWTEC) 1990–94; FIMI 1990 (vice pres 1996); *Recreations* tennis, swimming, sailing, golf, watching rugby and other sports, music, opera, theatre; *Clubs* Oundle Rugby (founding memb), Luton Rugby; *Style*— Nick Reilly, Esq; ✉ Vauxhall Motors, Griffin House, Osborne Road, PO Box 3, Luton, Bedfordshire LU1 3YT (☎ 01582 427578)

REILLY, Sir (D'Arcy) Patrick; GCMG (1968), OBE (1942); s of Sir D'Arcy Reilly (d 1948), and Margaret Florence, *née* Wilkinson; *b* 17 March 1909; *Educ* Winchester, New Coll Oxford (MA); *m* 1, 27 July 1938, Rachel Mary (d 1984), da of Brig-Gen Sir Percy Sykes, KCIE, CB, CMG; 2 da (Jane b 1939, Sarah b 1941); m 2, 23 Oct 1987, Ruth Margaret, wid of Sir Arthur Norrington; *Career* joined Dip Serv 1933; third sec Tehran 1935, second sec FO 1938, Miny Econ Warfare 1939–42, first sec Algiers 1943 and Paris 1944, cnsllr Athens 1947, Imperial Def Coll 1949, asst under sec 1950–53, min Paris 1953–56, dep under sec FO 1956, ambass to USSR 1957–60, dep under sec FO 1960–64, ambass to France 1965–68; chm: Banque Nationale de Paris plc 1969–80, United Bank for Africa (Nigeria) 1969–74, pres London Chamber of Commerce and Indust 1972–75; chm: Cncl Bedford Coll Univ of London 1970–75, N Kensington Amenity Tst 1971–74; fell All Souls Coll Oxford 1932–39 and 1969–, hon fell New Coll Oxford 1972; Hon LittD Univ of Bath 1982; Commandeur Légion d'Honneur France 1979; *Recreations* gardening, travel; *Clubs* Athenaeum; *Style*— Sir Patrick Reilly, GCMG, OBE; ✉ 75 Warrington Crescent, London W9 1EH (☎ 0171 289 5384)

REILLY, Wyn Anthony Prowse; s of Dr Noel Marcus Prowse Reilly, CMG (d 1991), of N Sandwich, USA, and Dolores Albra Thompson, *née* Pratten (d 1982); *b* 17 March 1930; *Educ* Leighton Park Sch, Trinity Hall Cambridge (MA), Univ Coll Oxford; *m* 4 Sept 1965, Annuschka Maria, da of Capt Peterpaul Maria Pilarski (d 1970); 2 s (J Alyosha J b 1968, P M Julian P b 1971), 1 da (S Natasha S b 1972); *Career* ADC and private sec to HE Govr The Gambia 1953–54, admin offr Tanganyika HMOCS 1956–62; sr lectr in public admin Univ of Manchester 1962–95; on secondment from Univ of Manchester: prof of admin Univ of Mauritius 1969–71, princ Admin Coll of Papua New Guinea 1973–75, sr planning offr Local Govt Botswana 1978–79, dir gen Mgmnt Devpt Inst The Gambia 1984–85, dir Cyprus Acad of Public Admin 1991–94; private mgmnt conslt 1995–; FIPD 1993; *Recreations* sailing, skiing, walking, music; *Style*— Wyn Reilly, Esq; ✉ West Cottage, Birtles Rd, Macclesfield, Cheshire SK10 3JG (☎ and fax 01625 431114)

REINHARDT, Max; s of Ernest Reinhardt (d 1942), of Istanbul, Turkey, and Frieda *née* Darr (d 1960); *b* 30 Nov 1915; *Educ* English HS Istanbul, Ecole Des Hautes Etudes Commerciales Paris, LSE; *m* 1957, Joan Dorothy, da of Carlisle MacDonald (d 1972), of NY, USA; 2 da (Alexandra, Veronica); *Career* book publisher; chm and md Bodley Head 1957–87, jt chm Bodley Head Chatto and Jonathan Cape 1973–87; chm: Reinhardt Books Ltd, The Nonesuch Press Ltd; memb Cncl: RADA, The Pilgrims 1966–, RSA 1958–; *Recreations* swimming, bridge, reading for pleasure; *Clubs* Garrick, Beefsteak, RAC; *Style*— Max Reinhardt, Esq; ✉ Flat 2, 43 Onslow Square, London SW7 3LR (☎ 0171 589 5527)

REISS, Charles Alexander; s of Dr J C Reiss, (d 1979), of London; *b* 23 March 1942; *Educ* Bryanston; *m* 1978, Susan, da of Sir John Newson-Smith; 3 da (Rowan b 10 Sept 1978, Holly b 1 Sept 1980, Bryony b 22 Aug 1986); *Career* political corr and chief leader writer Evening News 1975–80, political editor Evening Standard 1985– (political corr and leader writer 1980–85); *Clubs* RAC; *Style*— Charles Reiss, Esq; ✉ Evening Standard, Northcliffe House, 2 Derry St, London W8 5EE

REISS, Ven Robert Paul; s of Paul Reiss (d 1986), and Beryl Reiss (d 1995); *b* 20 Jan 1943; *Educ* Haberdashers' Aske's Sch Hampstead, Trinity Coll Cambridge (MA), Westcott House Cambridge; *m* 7 Nov 1985, Dixie, *née* Nichols; 1 da (Anya b 27 Nov 1991); *Career* ordained deacon 1969, priest 1970; curate St John's Wood Dio of London 1969–73, asst missioner Rajshahi Mission Dio of Dacca Bangladesh May-Sept 1973, chaplain Trinity Coll Cambridge 1973–78, selection sec Advsy Cncl for the Church's Miny 1978–85 (sr selection sec 1983–85), team rector Grantham Dio of Lincoln 1986–96, archdeacon of Surrey 1996–; chm Further and Higher Educn Ctee Gen Synod's Bd of

Educn; *Publications* Say One For Me (contrib, 1992); *Recreations* cricket, golf; *Clubs* United Oxford and Cambridge, MCC, Worplesdon Golf; *Style—* The Ven the Archdeacon of Surrey; ✉ Archdeacon's House, New Road, Wormley, Surrey GU8 5SU (☎ 01428 682563, fax 01428 682993)

REISS, Stephen Charles; OBE (1973); s of Richard Leopold (Dick) Reiss (d 1959), and Celia, *née* Butts; *b* 7 Aug 1918; *Educ* Gresham's Sch, Balliol Coll Oxford, Chelsea Sch of Art; *m* 17 Jan 1942, Elizabeth Ruth (Beth) (d 1995), da of George Moore Gladden (d 1984), of Brunstead, Norfolk; 1 s (Nicholas b 6 May 1943 d 1994), 1 da (Bridget b 14 April 1946); *Career* Capt Bedfordshire and Hertfordshire Regt 1939–45; gen mangr Aldeburgh Festival of Music and the Arts 1955–71, dir Fanfare For Europe 1972–73, arranged Aelbert Cuyp in Br Collections Exhibition Nat Gallery 1973, admin LSO 1974–75, md Curwen Prints 1975–80, fndr and md Business Art Galleries 1978–85, md Stephen Reiss Fine Art 1985–93; *Books* Aelbert Cuyp (1975), The Child Art of Peggy Somerville (1990); *Style—* Stephen Reiss, Esq, OBE; ✉ 15 Lee Road, Aldeburgh, Suffolk IP15 5HG (☎ 01728 452499)

REITH, Robert Davidson; s of Alexander Davidson Reith (d 1974), and Margaret, *née* Hunter (d 1979); *b* 25 July 1938; *Educ* Dulwich; *m* 30 Sept 1961, Stella Ann, da of Francis Joseph Lewis (d 1984); 1 s (Martin Robert Davidson b 1965), 1 da (Catherine Ann b 1963); *Career* formerly: md Oscar Faber Consulting Engineers Ltd, dir Oscar Faber plc (currently conslt); chm: Assoc of Consltg Engrs, CIC Consltts' Forum; past pres Euro Fedn of Engrg Consultancy Assoc; former memb Watford BC; memb Worshipful Co of Engrs; CEng, FICE, FIStructE, MConsE; *Recreations* golf, tennis, private flying; *Clubs* Caledonian; *Style—* Robert Reith, Esq; ✉ Loomwood, 35 Loom Lane, Radlett, Herts AL1 3UT (☎ 01923 469260)

REITH, Dr William (Bill); s of Andrew Christie Millar Reith, of N Berwick, and Catherine Mathieson, *née* Wishart; *b* 17 Aug 1950; *Educ* N Berwick HS, Univ of Edinburgh (BSc, MB ChB, Judo blue); *m* Gillian, da of John Brown; 2 da (Jane Susan b 27 March 1980, Sally Fiona b 7 May 1982); *Career* trainee Aberdeen Vocational Training Scheme for General Practice 1975–78, princ in general practice Westburn Medical Group Foresterhill Health Centre Aberdeen 1978–; regnl advsr in general practice Grampian Health Bd 1986– (assoc advsr 1983–86); RCGP: chm NE Scotland Faculty Bd 1986–89 (treas 1983–86, vice chm 1985–86), faculty rep UK Cncl 1990–, chm Educn Network 1993–94, hon sec of Cncl 1994–; memb: Euro Acad of Teachers in General Practice 1992–, Jt Ctee on Postgrad Trg for General Practice 1992–, Clinical Res and Audit Gp Health Dept Scottish Office 1993–; hon sr lectr Dept of General Practice Univ of Aberdeen 1993– (hon clinical lectr 1983–93); FRCGP 1991 (MRCGP 1978), FRCPEd 1994; *Recreations* food and wine, hill walking; *Style—* Dr Bill Reith; ✉ 54 Gray Street, Aberdeen AB1 6JE (☎ 01224 326380); Royal College of General Practitioners, 14 Prince's Gate, Hyde Park, London SW7 1PU (☎ 0171 581 3232, fax 0171 589 3145)

RELLIE, Alastair James Carl Euan; CMG (1987); s of Lt Cdr William Rellie (d 1943), and Lucy Rellie, *née* Modin (d 1974); *b* 5 April 1935; *Educ* Michaelhouse S Africa, Harvard (BA); *m* 1961, Annalisa, da of Maj Clive Modin (d 1944), and late Mary, *née* Ledingham; 1 s (Euan b 1968), 2 da (Jemima b 1970, Lucasta b 1972); *Career* Lt Rifle Bde 1958–60; second sec FCO 1963–64, vice consul Geneva 1964–67, first sec FCO 1967–68, (commercial) Cairo 1968–70, Kinshasa 1970–72, FCO 1972–74; cnsllr: UK Mission to UN, NY 1974–79, FCO 1979–92; vice pres market relations British Aerospace Defence 1993–; *Clubs* Brooks's, Greenjackets; *Style—* Alastair Rellie, CMG; ✉ 50 Smith St, London SW3 4EP (☎ 0171 352 5734)

RELPH, Michael Leighton George; s of George Relph, CBE, and Deborah Caroline, *née* Nanson; *Educ* Bembridge Sch Isle of Wight; *m* 1, 1940 (m dis 1948), Doris, *née* Ringwood; 1 s (Simon); m 2, 1950, Maria Rose, *née* Barry; 1 da (Emma); *Career* stage designer West End 1940–50, asst art dir (originally apprentice) Gaumont Br Studios, art dir: Warner Bros Studios, Ealing Studios 1942; assoc prodr to Michael Balcon 1945, prodr-writer in partnership with Basil Dearden (dir) until his death in 1972; Ealing prodns incl: The Captive Heart, Kind Hearts and Coronets, The Blue Lamp (Best Film Award Br Film Acad), Saraband for Dead Lovers (nominated Oscar for Prodn and Design); also produced and/or wrote, directed for: Ealing MGM, Rank Orgn (Best British Film Award Br Film Acad for Sapphire), Br Lion, United Artists, Paramount, EMI; fndr dir Allied Film Makers produced: League of Gentlemen, Victim, Man in the Moon; independent prodr Heavenly Pursuits (Channel 4), prodn conslt The Torrents of Spring; screenplay: Seven Against the West; chm Film Prodn Assoc of GB 1971–76, memb Cinematograph Films Cncl 1971–76, govr Br Film Inst (chm Prodn Bd) 1971–78; *Style—* Michael Relph, Esq; ✉ The Lodge, Primrose Hill Studios, Fitzroy Rd, London NW1 (☎ 0171 586 0249)

RELPH, Simon George Michael; s of Michael George Leighton Relph, and Doris, *née* Ringwood (d 1978); *b* 13 April 1940; *Educ* Bryanston, King's Coll Cambridge (MA); *m* 14 Dec 1963, Amanda Jane, da of Col Anthony Grinling, MC (d 1981), of Dyrham Park, Avon, Wilts; 1 s (Alexander James b 16 June 1967), 1 da (Arabella Kate b 17 Sept 1975); *Career* film producer; asst dir feature films 1961–73, prodn admin Nat Theatre 1974–78, prodn supervisor Yanks 1978, exec prodr Reds 1979–80; prodr and co-prodr 1981–85: The Return of the Soldier, Privates on Parade, The Ploughman's Lunch, Secret Places, Wetherby, Comrades; chief exec Br Screen Finance Ltd 1986–90, exec-prodr Enchanted April 1991, co-prodr Damage 1992; prodr: Secret Rapture 1992, Camilla 1993, Look me in the Eye (1994), Blue Juice (1994); vice chm (Film) BAFTA, memb Cncl RCA, exec memb Producers' Assoc for Cinema and Television, govr British Film Inst; Chevalier des Arts et des Lettres; *Recreations* golf, photography, fishing; *Style—* Simon Relph, Esq; ✉ Skreba Creon Films, 5A Noel Street, London W1V 3RB (☎ 0171 437 6492, fax 0171 437 0644)

REMFRY, David Rupert; s of Geoffrey Rupert Remfry, of Worthing, Sussex, and Barbara, *née* Ede; *b* 30 July 1942; *Educ* Hull Coll of Art; *m* 1, 1963 (m dis 1971), Jacqueline Wayne Alwyn; 2 s (Jacob Rupert b 1967, Samuel b 1968); m 2, 1976 (m dis 1994), Jacqueline Ruby Crisp; 1 step s (Joe b 1966), 1 s (Gideon Jethro b 1970); *Career* artist; elected memb Royal Watercolour Soc 1987; *Solo Exhibitions* incl: New Grafton Gallery 1973, Editions Graphiques 1974, Ferens Gallery Hull 1975, Folkestone Art Gallery 1976, Mercury Gallery London (biennially) 1978–94, Bohun Gallery Henley-on-Thames 1978, 1981, 1983, 1985, 1987, 1991, 1993 and 1996, Galerie de Beerenburght Holland 1979, 1980, 1982 and 1983, Ankrum Gallery Los Angeles 1980, 1983, 1985 and 1987, Middlesbrough Art Gallery 1981, Zack Schuster Gallery Boca Raton 1986, 1988 and 1990, Margaret Lipworth Fine Art Boca Raton 1992, 1994 and 1997, Nat Portrait Gallery 1992, Portal Gallery Bremen Germany 1993 and 1995, Tatistcheff Gallery NY 1996; *Work in Collections* Nat Portrait Gallery, V & A Museum, Middlesbrough Art Gallery, Swathmore Coll Pa, Museo Rayo Columbia, Minneapolis Museum of Art USA; *Recreations* opera and music generally, theatre, reading, dancing; *Clubs* Chelsea, Colony, Greens, Groucho's; *Style—* David Remfry, Esq; ✉ 19 Palace Gate, London W8 5LS (☎ 0171 584 0227)

REMINGTON, (James) Stephen Steel; s of Douglas Gordon Remington (d 1983), and Marjorie, *née* Steel (d 1983); *b* 19 March 1947; *Educ* Wellington Coll, Trinity Coll Dublin (BA); *Career* theatre mangr Nottingham Playhouse 1971–72, drama offr Eastern Arts Association 1972–74, dir The Playhouse Harlow 1974–79, chief exec Sadler's Wells London 1979–94 (joined as dir), chief exec Action for Blind People 1994–; Chevalier dans l'Ordre des arts et des lettres 1991; *Recreations* windsurfing, gym, walking; *Clubs* Garrick; *Style—* Stephen Remington; ✉ Action for Blind People, 14–16 Verney Road, London SE16 3DZ (☎ 0171 732 8771, fax 0171 639 0948)

REMINGTON-HOBBS, Col Edward; DSO (1945), OBE (1947); s of A Remington-Hobbs, MD (d 1933), and gs of Sir Joseph Wilkinson (d 1902); *b* 7 Feb 1916; *Educ* Westminster, RMC Sandhurst; *m* 1, 1950, Angela Susan (k in air crash 1953), only da of Capt Marshall Owen Roberts (d 1931), of Grosvenor Sq, London; 1 da (Julie Marguerite b 1951); m 2, 1957 (m dis 1967), Ann; m 3, 1972, Susan Mary Sheila, da of Hon Charles Winn; *Career* Argyll and Sutherland Highlanders serv WWII: UK, BNAF, NW Europe (wounded), SEAC; instr Staff Coll Camberley 1944, ret 1950; gold staff offr Coronation of HM The Queen 1953, silver staff offr Jubilee Thanksgiving Serv 1977; underwriting memb of Lloyd's 1959–90; chm and md: Polyseal Ltd 1960–75, Bellfax International Ltd 1975–84, Snuffers Ltd 1984–; Order of St John: memb Cncl for Sussex 1965–69, Order Cross Bearer 1966–90, memb Chapter Gen 1972–94; Freeman City of London 1960, memb The Pilgrims 1971, Guild of Freemen 1987, Liveryman Worshipful Co of Gunmakers 1988; KStJ 1976; *Recreations* cricket, shooting, golf; *Clubs* Boodle's, Pratt's, MCC, I Zingari, Free Foresters, Butterflies, Swinley Forest; *Style—* Colonel E Remington-Hobbs, DSO, OBE; ✉ The Maidens' Tower, Leeds Castle, Maidstone, Kent ME17 1PL (☎ 01622 880272); 3 Lyall Mews, London SW1X 8DJ (☎ 0171 235 0930); 117 Newgate St, London EC1A 7AE (☎ 0171 796 3056, fax 0171 600 1149)

REMNANT, 3 Baron (UK 1928); Sir James Wogan Remnant; 3 Bt (UK 1917), CVO (1979); o s of 2 Baron Remnant, MBE (d 1967), and Norah Susan, *née* Wogan-Browne (d 1990); *b* 23 Oct 1930; *Educ* Eton; *m* 24 June 1953, Serena Jane, o da of Cdr Sir Clive Loehnis, KCMG, RN (ret), and his w, Rosemary Beryl, o da of Maj Hon Robert Dudley Ryder, 4 s of 4 Earl of Harrowby; 3 s, 1 da; *Heir* s, Hon Philip John Remnant, *qv*; *Career* Nat Serv Lt Coldstream Guards 1948–50; ptnr Touche Ross & Co 1958–70; dir: Australian Mercantile Land and Finance 1957–69, Australia & NZ Banking Group 1965–81; chm: Touche Remnant & Co 1980–89 (md 1970–80), TR City of London Trust 1978–90 (dir 1973–90), TR Pacific Investment Trust 1987–94, National Provident Institution (now NPI) 1990–95 (dir 1963–95); dir: Union Discount Co of London 1969–92 (dep chm 1970–86), Ultramar plc 1970–91 (dep chm 1981–91), TR Technology 1988–, Bank of Scotland 1989–96 (chm London Bd 1979–91), London Merchant Securities 1994–, various other cos; pres: Nat Cncl of YMCAs 1983–96 (previously govr and pres London Central YMCA), Florence Nightingale Fndn; tstee: The Royal Jubilee Trusts 1989– (chm 1980–88, hon treas 1972–80); chm Learning Through Landscapes Trust 1989–; chm Assoc of Investmt Tst Cos 1977–79; church cmmr 1976–84; Liveryman Worshipful Co of Salters (Master 1995–96), Liveryman Worshipful Co of Chartered Accountants; Bailiff of Egle OStJ 1993–, GCStJ; FCA; *Style—* The Rt Hon the Lord Remnant, CVO; ✉ Bear Ash, Hare Hatch, Reading, Berks RG10 9XR (☎ 0118 940 2639)

REMNANT, Hon Philip John; s and h of 3 Baron Remnant, CVO; *b* 20 Dec 1954; *Educ* Eton, New Coll Oxford (MA); *m* 1977, Caroline, da of Capt Godfrey Cavendish; 1 s (Edward b 1981), 2 da (Eleanor b 1983, Sophie b 1986); *Career* Peat Marwick Mitchell and Co 1976–82, Kleinwort Benson Limited 1982–90 (dir 1988–90); Barclays de Zoete Wedd Limited: dir 1990–, md corp fin 1992–, jt head UK corp fin 1993–94, head UK corp fin 1994–95, dep chief exec corp fin 1995–; ACA, MSI; *Style—* The Hon Philip Remnant; ✉ Barclays de Zoete Wedd Ltd, Ebbgate House, 2 Swan Lane, London EC4R 3TS (☎ 0171 623 2323, fax 0171 623 6075)

RENALS, Sir Stanley; 4 Bt (UK 1895); s of Sir James Herbert Renals, 2 Bt (d 1927), and Susan Emma, *née* Crafter (d 1957); suc bro, Sir Herbert Renals, 3 Bt (d 1961); *b* 20 May 1923; *Educ* City of London Freemen's Sch; *m* 2 Jan 1957, Maria Dolores Rodriguez Pinto, da of José Rodriguez Ruiz (d 1948); 1 s; *Heir* s, Stanley Michael Renals, *qv*; *Career* serv Merchant Navy 1939–62, entered as apprentice and ret with Master Mariner (FG) Certificate World Wide; *Style—* Sir Stanley Renals, Bt; ✉ 52 North Lane, Portslade, East Sussex BN4 2HG

RENALS, Eur Ing Stanley Michael; s and h of Sir Stanley Renals, 4 Bt, *qv*, of Portslade, Sussex, and Maria Dolores Rodriguez, *née* Pinto; *b* 14 Jan 1958; *Educ* Falmer HS, Brighton Univ (BSc); *m* 28 Aug 1982, Jacqueline Ann, da of Roy Denis Riley, of Hollingdean, Brighton, Sussex; 1 s (Lloyd James b 17 May 1985), 1 da (Frances Emma b 20 Dec 1986); *Career* design engr Kulicke & Soffa 1983–85; Alpha Metals: area mangr 1985–88, sales and marketing mangr 1988–91, gen mangr Alpha Metals Singapore 1991–95; vice-pres and gen mangr Arconium/Oster Alloys Providence USA 1995–; CEng, MIElecE, MIMfgE; *Recreations* golf, squash; *Clubs* RAC, Epsom; *Style—* Eur Ing Stanley Renals; ✉ 80 Falcon Circle, East Greenwich, RI 02818, USA; Arconium, 50 Sims Avenue, Providence RI 02909, USA (☎ 00 1 401 456800, fax 00 1 401 421 2419)

RENCHER, Derek; s of Walter Samuel Rencher (d 1974), of Birmingham, and Alice Gertrude, *née* Houlton (d 1960); *b* 6 June 1932; *Educ* Handsworth GS, Janet Cranmore Sch of Ballet Birmingham, Bourneville Sch of Arts and Crafts Birmingham, RCA, Barbara Vernon Sch of Russian Ballet, Royal Ballet Sch; *Career* Royal Ballet performances: King of the East and Pas de Six in Prince of the Pagodas, Demophoon in Persephone, Haeman in Antigone, Grey Prince in Lady and the Fool, Lysander in A Midsummer Night's Dream, White Boy in Patineurs, Paris and Lord Capulet in Romeo and Juliet, Elgar in Enigma Variations, Czar Nicholas in Anastasia, Rothbart in Swan Lake, Duke in Giselle, Prince and King in Beauty, Paris Singer in Isadora, Rakitin in Month in the Country, Ancestor in Shadow Play, Emperor Franz Josef in Mayerling, Mons G M in Manon, Zeus in Creatures of Prometheus, Brahmin in La Bayadere, Doctor in Winter Dreams, Don Quixote in Don Quixote, Carrabosse in Sleeping Beauty; designer of: Swanlake Act III (Philadelphia Ballet), One in Five (Canadian National and Australian Ballet), Lament of the Waves and Siesta (Royal Opera House); *Recreations* gardening, painting, needlework, cooking, swimming, walking; *Style—* Derek Rencher, Esq; ✉ The Royal Opera House, Covent Garden, London WC2 (☎ 0171 240 1200)

RENDALL, Max; s of Richard Antony Rendall, CBE (d 1957), of Park Square East, London NW1, and Anne, *née* Moinet (d 1960); *b* 2 April 1934; *Educ* Winchester, Trinity Coll Cambridge (MA), Middx Hosp Med Sch (MB BChir); *m* 2 Oct 1963, Mary, da of George Douglass Debevoise (d 1980), of Brookville, Long Island, NY, USA; 1 s (Julian Douglass b 1969); *Career* Guy's Hosp: conslt surgn 1969, clinical supt 1981, ret 1994; seconded to King Fahd Armed Forces Hosp Jeddah 1991–94; FRCS 1964; *Recreations* woodwork, walking, wine; *Style—* Max Rendall, Esq; ✉ 4 Ladbroke Square, London W11 3LX (☎ 0171 221 4847)

RENDEL, Christopher; s of Peter Leland Fitzgerald Rendel, of Hourne Farm, Crowborough, E Sussex, and Mona Catherine, *née* Milligan, of Hammersmith, London; *b* 1 Feb 1955; *Educ* Bryanston, Univ of Bristol; *m* Patricia Mary; 2 s (George Oliver b 1983, Charles William b 1988); *Career* advtg exec; account mangr Mathers & Bensons 1974–80, account dir Abbott Mead Vickers 1981–87, dir FCO 1987–90, gp dir Ogilvy & Mather 1990–95, md Foote Cone & Belding 1995–; dir Ambache Chamber Orch 1994–; MIPA; *Recreations* music, antiques, classic cars, tennis and (watching) football; *Style—* Christopher Rendel, Esq; ✉ Foote Cone & Belding Ltd, 110 St Martin's Lane, London WC2N 4DY (☎ 0171 240 7100, fax 0171 240 5500)

RENDEL, David; MP (Lib Dem) Newbury (majority 22,055); *b* 15 April 1949; *Educ* Eton, Univ of Oxford (BA, rowing blue 1974); *m*; 3 s; *Career* vol teacher VSO Cameroon and Uganda, computing and fin mgmnt with Shell International, British Gas and Esso until 1990; Parly candidate (Lib Dem): Fulham 1979 and 1983, Newbury 1987 and 1992; MP (Lib Dem) Newbury 1993–, spokesman (Lib Dem) Local Govt 1993–; cncllr Newbury DC 1987–95 (chm Fin Sub-Ctee 1991–92, chm Recreation Ctee 1992–93); *Recreations* sport, travel, walking; *Style*— David Rendel, Esq, MP; ✉ House of Commons, London SW1A 0AA (☎ 0171 219 3000)

RENDELL, John Jeremy (Jerry); s of George Arthur Rendell (d 1975), and Elizabeth Joyce, *née* Smith; *b* 28 Sept 1938; *Educ* Guildford GS W Aust, Univ of Bristol (BSc(Eng)); *m* 14 Sept 1963, Anne, *née* Gabe; *Career* engr Binnie & Partners 1964–67 (trainee 1961–64), sr tech offr British Standards Institution 1967–69, princ Miny of Public Building and Works 1970–72, asst sec DOE 1976–92 (princ 1972–76), chief exec UK Ecolabelling Board 1992–; *Style*— Jerry Rendell, Esq; ✉ UK Ecolabelling Board, 7th Floor, Eastbury House, 30–34 Albert Embankment, London SE1 7TL (☎ 0171 820 1199)

RENDELL, Ruth Barbara; CBE (1996); da of Arthur Grasemann (d 1973), and Ebba Elise Grasemann, *née* Kruse (d 1963); *b* 17 Feb 1930; *m* 1950 (re-married 1977), Donald John Rendell; 1 s (Simon b 1953); *Career* writer; FRSL; *Awards* incl: Arts Cncl Nat Book Award Genre Fiction 1981, CWA 4 Gold Dagger Awards 1976/87/88/90, 1 Silver Dagger 1984, Mystery Writers of America 3 Edgar Allen Poe Awards 1974, 1984 and 1987, Sunday Times Award for Literary Excellence 1990, Cartier-CWA Diamond Dagger Award 1991; *Books* From Doon with Death (1964), The Face of Trespass (1971), A Judgement in Stone (1976), Master of the Moor (1982), The Killing Doll (1984), An Unkindness of Ravens (1985), The New Girlfriend (1985), Live Flesh (1986), Talking to Strange Men (1987), The Veiled One (1988), The Bridesmaid (1989), Going Wrong (1990), Kissing the Gunner's Daughter (Hutchinson, 1991), The Crocodile Bird (1993), Simisola (1994), Blood Lines (1995), The Keys to the Street (1996); under pseudonym Barbara Vine: A Dark-Adapted Eye (1986), A Fatal Inversion (1987), House of Stairs (1989), Gallowglass (1990), King Solomon's Carpet (1991), Asta's Book (1992), No Night Is Too Long (1994), The Brimstone Wedding (1996); *Recreations* reading, walking, opera; *Clubs* Groucho's, Detection; *Style*— Mrs Ruth Rendell, CBE; ✉ Nussteads, Polstead, Suffolk; 26 Cornwall Terrace Mews, London NW1

RENDER, Phillip Stanley; s of Stanley Render, of Bransholme, Hull, and Bessie, *née* Bestwick; *b* 15 Jan 1944; *Educ* Malet Lambet HS Hull; *m* 21 Oct 1967, Patricia Mary, da of Alfred Bernard Rooms, of Parkstone Rd, Hull; 2 s (Adrian b 1973, Andrew b 1978), 1 da (Suzanne b 1982); *Career* chartered surveyor in sole practice 1982–, dir Beverley Building Society 1986–; surveyor to Tstees Beverley Consolidated Charity 1973–; memb: Sub Ctee Northern Assoc of Surveyors 1988–, Exec Ctee E Yorks Branch Salmon and Trout Assoc; FRICS 1968; *Recreations* salmon and trout fishing, badminton; *Clubs* Hull and East Riding Sports, S Hunsley Fly Fishing; *Style*— Phillip Render, Esq; ✉ Virginia House, 245 Northgate, Cottingham, N Humberside (☎ 01482 848327); Render Richardson & Co, 7 North Bar Within, Beverley, N Humberside (☎ 01482 860169, fax 01482 872340)

RENDLE, Michael Russel; s of late H C R Rendle, and Valerie Patricia, *née* Gleeson; *b* 20 Feb 1931; *Educ* Marlborough, New Coll Oxford (MA); *m* 1957, Elizabeth Heather, da of J W J Rinkel; 2 s, 2 da; *Career* joined Anglo-Iranian Oil Co (now BP) 1954; md: BP Trinidad 1967–70, BP Australia Ltd 1974–78, BP Trading Ltd 1978–81, BP Co plc 1981–86; chm: BP Chemicals International Ltd 1981–83, BP Nutrition 1981–86, BP Coal Ltd 1983–86; chm: FIM Ltd 1988–, TBI plc (formerly Markheath plc) 1991–95, OIS International Inspection plc 1995–96 (dir 1993–), Campbell & Armstrong plc 1996– (dep chm 1992–96); dep chm: IC Gas Association 1986–87, British Borneo Petroleum Syndicate plc 1986–, Tace plc 1991; dir: Willis Corroon plc (formerly Willis Faber plc) 1985–, Petrofina SA 1986–87; chm: European Trade Ctee 1982–86, INSEAD Int Cncl and UK Advsy Bd 1984–86; pres Social Affairs Ctee UNICE 1984–87; memb: London Advsy Bd Westpac Banking Corporation (Aust) 1978–89, BOTB 1982–86, Cncl Marlborough Coll 1987–95; *Recreations* golf, music, outdoor sports, gardening; *Clubs* Vincent's (Oxford), Australian (Melbourne), Royal Melbourne Golf; *Style*— Michael Rendle, Esq; ✉ c/o Willis Corroon Group plc, 10 Trinity Square, London EC3P 3AX (☎ 0171 481 7152)

RENDLE, Sharon Susan; MBE (1993); da of John Michael Rendle, of Hull, and Brenda Susan, *née* Denman (d 1983); *b* 18 June 1966; *Educ* Villa Place Junior HS Hull, Kingston HS Hull; *Career* judoist; memb Grimsby Judo Club; achievements: 7 times Br Open champion, Commonwealth Games champion Edinburgh 1986 and Auckland NZ 1990, World champion Essen 1987 and Dubrovnik 1989, Olympic champion Seoul (Bronze medal Barcelona 1992) 1988, Bronze medal Tournoi de Paris 1995; *Recreations* reading, watching old Bette Davis films, night clubbing; *Style*— Ms Sharon Rendle, MBE; ✉ 17 Lawson Avenue, Grimsby, South Humberside DN31 2EN (☎ 01472 348837)

RENDLESHAM, 8 Baron (I 1806); Charles Anthony Hugh Thellusson; s of Lt-Col Hon Hugh Thellusson, DSO, 3 s of 5 Baron Rendlesham, JP, DL, by his w Lady Egidia Montgomerie (da of 13 Earl of Eglinton and Winton, KT); Hugh was bro of 6 and 7 Barons Rendlesham and m Gwynnydd, da of Brig-Gen Sir Robert Colleton, 1 and last Bt, CB; suc unc 1943; the Thellussons descend from an eighteenth century Swiss Ambass to the court of Louis XV of France, one Isaac de Thellusson; *b* 15 March 1915; *Educ* Eton; *m* 1, 1940 (m dis 1947), Margaret, da of Lt-Col Robin Rome, MC; 1 da (Hon Lady Goring); m 2, 1947, Clare (d 1987), da of Lt-Col Douglas McCririck, of Wiveliscombe, Somerset; 1 s, 3 da; *Heir* s, Hon Charles Thellusson; *Career* late Royal Corps of Signals, Capt, served WWII; *Style*— The Rt Hon The Lord Rendlesham

RENFREW OF KAIMSTHORN, Baron (Life Peer UK 1991), of Hurlet in the District of Renfrew; (Andrew) Colin Renfrew; s of Archibald Renfrew (d 1978), of Giffnock, Glasgow, and Helena Douglas, *née* Savage (d 1994); *b* 25 July 1937; *Educ* St Albans Sch, St John's Coll Cambridge (BA, PhD, ScD); *m* 21 April 1965, Jane Margaret, da of Ven Walter Frederick Ewbank, Archdeacon Emeritus and Canon Emeritus of Carlisle Cathedral; 2 s (Hon Alban b 24 June 1970, Hon Magnus b 5 Nov 1975), 1 da (Hon Helena (Hon Mrs Knight) b 23 Feb 1968); *Career* Nat Serv Flying Offr (Signals) RAF 1956–58; reader in prehistory & archaeology Univ of Sheffield 1965–72 (formerly lectr and sr lectr), res fell St John's Coll Cambridge 1965–68, Bulgarian Govt scholarship 1966, visiting lectr Univ of California (Los Angeles) 1967, prof of archaeology and head of dept Univ of Southampton 1972–81, Disney prof of archaeology 1981– and head of dept Univ of Cambridge 1981–92, dir McDonald Inst for Archaeological Res 1992–; fell St John's Coll Cambridge 1981–86, master Jesus Coll Cambridge 1986–; memb: Royal Cmmn for Historic Monuments of England 1977–87, Ancient Monuments Advsy Bd 1983–, Historic Bldgs & Monuments Cmmn 1984–86 (chm Sci Panel 1983–89); chm Nat Curriculum Art Working Gp 1990–91; Freeman City of London; Hon DLitt: Univ of Sheffield 1987, Univ of Southampton 1995; Dr (hc) Athens Univ 1991; FSA 1968, FSA Scot 1970, FBA 1980; *Books* The Explanation of Culture Change: Models in Prehistory (ed, 1973), British Prehistory, a New Outline (ed, 1977), Problems in European Prehistory (1979), Approaches to Social Archaeology (1984), The Archaeology of Cult: The Sanctuary at Phylakopi (1985), Archaeology and Language: The Puzzle of Indo-European Origins (1987), The Cycladic Spirit (1991); *Recreations* modern art, numismatics, travel; *Clubs* Athenaeum, United Oxford and Cambridge Univ; *Style*— The Rt Hon Lord Renfrew of Kaimsthorn, FBA, FSA; ✉ The Master's Lodge, Jesus College, Cambridge CB5 8BL (☎ 01223 323 934); University of Cambridge, Department of Archaeology, Downing Street, Cambridge CB2 3DZ (☎ 01223 333 521)

RENNELL, 3 Baron (UK 1933); (John Adrian) Tremayne Rodd; 2 but only surviving s of Cdr Hon Gustaf Rodd (bro of: (1) 2 Baron Rennell, KBE, CB, JP, DL, who d 1978, (2) Hon Peter Rodd, who d 1968, husb of late Nancy Mitford and allegedly the model for Evelyn Waugh's character Basil Seal, (3) late Baroness Emmet of Amberley, and (4) late Hon Mrs (Lt-Col Simon) Elwes, wife of the former Official War Artist); *b* 28 June 1935; *Educ* Downside, RNC Dartmouth; *m* 1977, Phyllis Caroline, da of Thomas David Neill, of Portadown, Co Armagh; 1 s, 3 da (Hon Sophie Mary Jane b 1981, Hon Rachel b 1987, Hon Lilias b 1989); *Heir* s, Hon James Roderick David Tremayne Rodd b 9 March 1978; *Career* served RN 1952–62; Morgan Grenfell & Co 1963–66, former freelance journalist & Scottish Rugby International; dir Tremayne Ltd 1980–; *Clubs* White's, Brooks's, Portland, Queens, Sunningdale; *Style*— The Rt Hon Lord Rennell; ✉ c/o House of Lords, Westminster, London SW1

RENNELLS, William John (Bill); s of Albert Edward Rennells (d 1975), of Canterbury, and Alice Emily, *née* Gambrell (d 1970); *b* 25 July 1931; *Educ* Bridge Sch nr Canterbury; *m* 1, 19 June 1954 (m dis 1988), Lois Brunger; 2 da (Susan b 20 July 1963, Jane b 23 May 1965); m 2, 21 May 1988, Mrs Angela Valera Griffiths, *née* Minchin; 1 step s (Marcus John b 4 July 1971), 1 step da (Sarah Louise b 4 April 1969); *Career* Nat Serv Pay Corps 1949–51; chief reporter Eastbourne Gazette 1957–61, asst dist news ed Oxford Mail 1961–70, prodr BBC Radio Oxford 1970–78, announcer and presenter BBC Radio 2 1978–96; presenter: Test Match Special Radio 3 1985–, Sounds of Jazz Radio 1; has deputised for Jimmy Young, Ray Moore, Gloria Hunniford and John Dunn on Radio 2, freelance presenter BBC Radio Oxford and Melody Radio 1992–, presenter BBC Thames Valley FM 1996–; life pres Abingdon Keyboard Club, patron Abingdon Operatic Soc; memb: Inst of Journalists 1955–70, Equity; *Recreations* walking, watching cricket, reading, visiting jazz clubs; *Clubs* Forty; *Style*— Bill Rennells, Esq; ✉ The Arbour, 41 Foster Road, Abingdon, Oxon OX14 1YW (☎ 01235 553436)

RENNERT, Jonathan; s of Sidney Rennert, of London, and Patricia, *née* Clack; *b* 17 March 1952; *Educ* St Paul's, RCM (fndn scholar), St John's Coll Cambridge (organ scholar, MA); *m* 10 April 1992, Sheralyn, *née* Ivil; 1 da (Imogen b 7 Jan 1996); *Career* dir of music and organist: St Jude's Church London SW5 1975–76, St Matthew's Ottawa Canada 1976–78, St Michael's Cornhill City of London 1979–, St Mary-at-Hill City of London 1996–; organ recitalist, choral conductor and lectr on four continents; musician-in-residence Grace Cathedral San Francisco 1982; made various CD and LP recordings, radio and TV broadcasts as conductor, solo organist, organ accompanist, harpsichord continuo player; conductor: Cambridge Opera 1972–74, St Michael's Singers 1979–, The Elizabethan Singers 1983–88, English Harmony 1988–, St Mary-at-Hill Baroque Players & Soloists 1996–; fndr and dir Cornhill Festival of Br Music; moderating and trg examiner and professional devpt mentor Assoc Bd of the Royal Schs of Music; examiner Royal Coll of Organists; course dir and chm Central London District Ctee Royal Sch of Church Music; admin and chm Exec Ctee Int Congress of Organists 1987; hon sec to the tstees Sir George Thalben-Ball Meml Tst; memb Cncl Royal Coll of Organists and Organists' Benevolent League; past pres The Organ Club; hon fell Royal Canadian Coll of Organists 1987; Ct Asst and pres Livery Club Worshipful Co of Musicians; memb Performers' & Composers' Section Ctee Inc Soc of Musicians; FRCO 1970, ARCM 1970, LRAM 1970; *Books* William Crotch 1775–1847 Composer Artist Teacher (1975), George Thalben-Ball (1979); *Style*— Jonathan Rennert, Esq; ✉ 57b Wickham Road, Beckenham, Kent BR3 6QJ (☎ and fax 0181 658 9428)

RENNIE, Archibald Louden; CB (1980); s of John Rennie (d 1974), of Lindores, Fife, and Isabella Mitchell, *née* Louden (d 1979); *b* 4 June 1924; *Educ* Madras Coll St Andrews, Univ of St Andrews (BSc); *m* 14 Sept 1950, Kathleen, da of John James Harkess (d 1955), of Chingford, Essex; 4 s (Adam b 1951, John b 1953, David b 1956, Simon b 1959); *Career* temp experimental offr Mine Design Dept Minesweeping Res Div Admty 1944–47; Dept of Health for Scotland 1947–62, private sec to Sec of State for Scotland 1962–63, asst sec Scottish Home and Health Dept 1963–69, registrar gen for Scotland 1969–73, under sec Scottish Econ Planning Dept 1973–77, sec Scottish Home and Health Dept 1977–84, ret 1984; vice chm NHS Advsy Ctee on Distinction Awards 1985–94; assessor Ct St Andrews Univ 1984–89 (chllr's assessor 1986–89); memb: Scottish Records Advsy Cncl 1985–93, Cncl on Tbnls (and Scottish Ctee) 1987–88; chm Hong Kong Disciplined Servs Pay Review Ctee 1988; chm Blacket Assoc (local conservation soc) 1970–73, tstee Lockerbie Air Disaster Tst 1988–91, Cdre Elie and Earlsferry SC 1991–93, chm Elie Harbour Tst 1993–, memb Bd Madras Coll Sch 1994–; Hon LLD Univ of St ndrews 1990; FDSRCS 1995; *Recreations* sailing, sea-fishing, scenery, Scottish literature; *Clubs* Scottish Arts (Edinburgh); *Style*— Archibald Rennie, Esq, CB; ✉ Well Wynd House, South St, Elie, Fife KY9 1DN (☎ 01333 330741)

RENNIE, Prof Ian George; s of Peter Bruce Rennie, of Whirlowdale, Sheffield, Yorkshire, and Vera Margaret, *née* Haworth; *b* 10 Nov 1952; *Educ* Prescott GS, Univ of Sheffield (MB ChB); *m* 1, 28 Aug 1976 (m dis 1986), Janet Mary Rennie; m 2, 19 July 1986, Sharon, da of Stanley Herbert Markland, of Waterloo, Liverpool; 1 s (James Peter b 1987), 1 da (Rachel Anne b 1988); *Career* lectr Dept of Ophthalmology Univ of Liverpool 1982–85, prof Dept of Ophthalmology and Orthoptics Univ of Sheffield 1995– (sr lectr 1985–95); non-exec dir Central Sheffield Univ Hosps Tst 1991–; hon conslt ophthalmic surgn Royal Hallamshire Hosp 1985–; ed Eye 1995–; memb RSM, FRCSEd 1981, FRCOphth 1989 (memb Cncl 1995–); *Recreations* astronomy, windsurfing; *Style*— Prof Ian Rennie; ✉ Church Lane House, Litton, nr Buxton, Derbyshire SK17 8QU (☎ 01298 871586); Department of Ophthalmology and Orthoptics, University of Sheffield, Royal Hallamshire Hospital, Sheffield (☎ 0114 276 2902, fax 0114 276 6381)

RENNIE, Dr James Stark; s of Gavin Gordon Rennie (d 1988), of Elie, Fife, and Euphemia Mourning, *née* Agnew (d 1985); *b* 22 May 1949; *Educ* Coatbridge HS, Univ of Glasgow (BDS, PhD, FDS RCPSGlas, FRCPath); *m* 1976, Ann Maris, da of Dr Douglas Campbell; 2 s (Gavin Alistair Gordon b 23 Jan 1979, David Anthony Cameron b 26 Aug 1980); *Career* house offr Glasgow Dental Hosp 1973–74, MRC research fell Glasgow Dental Hosp and Dept of Pathology Glasgow Royal Infirmary 1974–77, research fell Dept of Dental Med and Surgery Univ of Melbourne 1980–82, hon conslt in oral pathology Gtr Glasgow Health Bd 1983–; Univ of Glasgow: lectr Dept of Oral Med and Pathology 1977–84, sr lectr Dept of Oral Scis 1984–, memb Faculty of Med 1984–87, memb Senate 1985–88, memb Admissions Ctee 1987–90, memb Dental Sch Academic Bd 1991–; W of Scotland postgraduate advsr in dentistry 1990–94; Scottish Cncl for Postgraduate Med and Dental Educn: dental co-ordinator 1993–94, dir of postgraduate dental educn 1994–; visiting lectr Dept of Oral Surgery Univ of Cork 1991–93; speaker at many nat and int research meetings and invited participant at meetings of Int Assoc of Oral Pathologists and American Acad of Oral Pathology; exec offr: Dental Ctee Scottish Cncl for Postgraduate Med and Dental Educn 1993– (vice chm 1991–94), Scottish Dental Vocational Trg Ctee 1993–; memb: Chief Med Offr's Advsy Gp on Postgraduate Med and Dental Educn 1990–91, Exec Ctee Conf of UK Postgraduate Dental Deans 1991–, Exec Gp Scottish Cncl for Postgraduate Med and Dental Educn 1993–, GDC 1994–; Royal Coll of Physicians and Surgeons Glasgow: memb Dental Cncl 1990–94, sec Dental Cncl 1992–94, memb Overseas Ctee 1992–, memb Educn and Symposium Ctees 1992–94; author of numerous scientific pubns in academic jls; tstee: Yorkhill Children's Tst 1988–90, Dental Educnl Tst 1990–94; deacon Incorporation of Skinners and Glovers of Glasgow 1986–87; memb: Int Assoc of Dental Research, Br Soc for Dental Research, Int Assoc of Oral Pathologists, Pathological Soc of GB and NI, Glasgow Odontological Soc, Assoc of Clinical Pathologists, Br Soc for Oral Pathology; *Recreations* golf (handicap 7), salmon fishing; *Clubs* RSM; *Style*— Dr James Rennie; ✉ Scottish Council for Postgraduate Medical and Dental Education, 12 Queen Street, Edinburgh EH2 1JE (☎ 0131 225 4365, fax 0131 225 5891, mobile 0831 222406)

RENNIE, Dr Janet Mary; da of Arthur Ball (d 1965), of Liverpool, and Marjorie Kennerley, *née* Jones; *b* 2 Dec 1954; *Educ* Belvedere Sch GPDST Liverpool, Univ of Sheffield (MA, MB ChB, MD, FRCP, DCH); *m* 1, 28 Aug 1976 (m dis 1986), Ian George

Rennie, s of Peter Bruce Rennie; m 2, 28 Aug 1992, Ian Roscoe Watts, s of William Watts; *Career* jr hosp posts 1978–85, sr res asst Univ of Liverpool 1983–85, lectr in paediatrics Univ of Cambridge 1985–88, conslt neonatal med Rosie Maternity Hosp Cambridge 1988–95, conslt and sr lectr in neonatal med King's Coll Hosp London 1995–; dir of med studies Girton Coll Cambridge 1991–95; memb: Changing Childbirth Implementation Gp Scientific Advsy Ctee Fndn for the Study of Infant Deaths, Paediatric Assoc, Royal Soc of Med, Paediatric Res Assoc; memb Ctee: Br Assoc of Perinatal Medicine, Neonatal Soc; *Books* Neonatal Cranial Ultrasound, Textbook of Neonatology; Chapter in Fetal and Neonatal Neurology and Neurosurgery; *Recreations* piano, cooking; *Style*— Dr Janet Rennie; ✉ NICU, King's College Hospital, Denmark Hill, London SE5 9RS (☎ 0171 346 3574)

RENNIE, John Aubery; s of James Rennie (d 1987), and Ethel May Aubrey, *née* Byford; *b* 19 Jan 1947; *Educ* Kings Coll Sch Wimbledon, St Bartholomew's Med Sch London; *m* 12 Aug 1972, Sheelagh Ruth, da of John Robert Winter, of White Cottage, Harmans Cross, Dorset; 1 s (Alexander John b 1982), 3 da (Natasha Louise b 1973, Sara Rosalind b 1976, Rachel Suzannah b 1979); *Career* lectr in surgery Charing Cross Hosp London, resident surgical offr St Mark's Hosp London, sr lectr and conslt King's Coll Hosp London (formerly sr registrar); fndr memb Bureau of Overseas Med Servs; FRSM, FRCS; *Style*— John Rennie, Esq; ✉ 94 Burbage Road, Dulwich, London SE24 9HE (☎ 0171 274 0233); Department of Surgery, King's College Hospital, London SE5 (☎ 0171 346 3017, fax 0171 346 3438)

RENNIE, Sir John Shaw; GCMG (1968, KCMG 1962, CMG 1958), OBE 1955; s of late John Shaw Rennie, of Saskatoon, Saskatchewan, Canada; *b* 12 Jan 1917; *Educ* Hillhead HS Glasgow, Univ of Glasgow, Balliol Coll Oxford; *m* 1946, Mary Winifred Macalpine, da of James Bryson Robertson, of Hillhead, Glasgow; 1 s; *Career* entered Colonial Administrative Serv Tanganyika 1940: asst dist offr 1942, dist offr 1949, dep colonial sec Mauritius 1951, Br res cmmr New Hebrides 1955–62, govr and CIC Mauritius 1962–68, govr-gen 1968, dep cmmr gen UN Relief and Works Agency for Palestine Refugees 1968–71, cmmr gen 1971–77; Hon LLD Univ of Glasgow; *Clubs* Royal Cwlth Soc; *Style*— Sir John Rennie, GCMG, OBE; ✉ 26 College Cross, London N1 1PR; Via Roma 37, 06050 Collazzone (PG), Italy

RENNIE, Michael Christopher Gibson; s of Thomas Gibson Rennie (d 1970), of Glasgow, and Elizabeth Livingstone, *née* McCorquodale (d 1962); *b* 6 June 1933; *Educ* Fettes, Univ of Glasgow (MB ChB); *Career* Nat Serv RAF 1958–60; med practitioner, princ in gen practice 1968, med advsr and examiner in occupational health and life assurance med 1968; memb: Assurance Med Soc 1960, Scottish Soc of the History of Med 1975, Nat Exec Epilepsy Assoc of Scotland 1983–91; chm The St Andrew Soc Glasgow 1992–; Deacon Incorporation of Hammermen of Glasgow 1983–84; FInstPet 1978; *Recreations* hillwalking; *Style*— Michael Rennie, Esq

RENNOCKS, John Leonard; s of Leonard Joseph Thomas Rennocks, of Broxbourne, Herts; *b* 27 June 1945; *m*; 4 c; *Career* articled clerk Tayler Hounsfield & Co then Allfields 1962–67, CA, audit sr Harmood Banner & Co 1967–69, with Arthur Woods & Co stockbrokers 1969–70, gp accountant/gp planning mangr Charrington Gardner Locket & Co Ltd 1970–74; Smith & Nephew plc: gp accountant 1974–77, gp financial controller 1977–81, gp fin dir/co sec 1981–89; fin dir PowerGen plc 1989–96, fin dir British Steel plc 1996–; chm PowerGen Pension Fund Tstees until 1996; non-exec dir: Kleinwort European Privatisation Investment Trust plc 1993–, Biocompatibles International plc 1995–, Nynex Cablecomms Group PLC 1995–, Nynex Cablecomms Group Inc 1995–, Avesta Sheffield ab 1996–; *Recreations* watching cricket, rugby and golf, fly fishing; *Style*— John Rennocks, Esq; ✉ British Steel plc, 9 Albert Embankment, London SE1 7SN (☎ 0171 820 7385, fax 0171 582 1716)

RENOUF, Sir Francis Henry; kt (1987); s of Francis Charles Renouf (d 1983), of NZ, and Mary Ellen, *née* Avery (d 1973); *b* 31 July 1918, Wellington, NZ; *Educ* Wellington Coll, Victoria Univ Coll Wellington (MCom (NZ)); *m* 1, 1954 (m dis 1985), Ann Marie Harkin; 4 c (Paula J b 1955, Frances G b 1957, Catherine M b 1957, John Philip b 1962); m 2, 1985 (m dis 1989); m 3, 1991 (m dis); *Career* company chairman; Renouf Underwriters Pty Limited Sydney, Renouf Corporation Ltd, Renouf Asset Management Ltd, New Merchant Bank, Funds Management; Offr's Cross of the Order of Merit (FRG) 1986; military service 2 NZEF 1940–46, Capt; represented NZ Univs 1938–40, Oxford Univ 1948 and 1949 at tennis, Oxford blue 1948–49; pres NZ Lawn Tennis Assoc 1985 and 1986; *Recreations* lawn tennis; *Clubs* Cavalry and Guards'; *Style*— Sir Francis Renouf; ✉ 11 Wharemauku Road, Paraparaumu, New Zealand

RENOWDEN, Ven Glyndwr Rhys; CB (1987); s of Rev Canon Charles Renowden (d 1964), and Mary Elizabeth, *née* Williams (d 1974); *b* 13 Aug 1929; *Educ* Llanelli GS, Univ of Wales Lampeter (BA, LTh); *m* 1956, Mary Kinsey-Jones; 1 da; *Career* Chaplain in Chief RAF 1983–88, QHC 1980–88; *Style*— The Venerable Glyndwr R Renowden, CB; ✉ Red Cedars, Kenystyle, Penally, nr Tenby, Pembrokeshire SA70 7PJ

RENSHALL, (James) Michael; CBE (1991, OBE 1977); s of Arthur Renshall (d 1973), and Ethel, *née* Gardner (d 1970); *b* 27 July 1930; *Educ* Rydal Sch, Clare Coll Cambridge (MA); *m* Aug 1960, Kathleen Valerie, da of Harold Tyson, of Liverpool; 1 da (Susan b 1961); *Career* CA; ptnr KPMG Peat Marwick 1977–92; ICAEW: tech dir 1970–77, memb Cncl 1986–90, chm Accounting Standards Ctee 1986–90, dep chm Fin Reporting Review Panel 1991–96; dir Centre for Dispute Resolution 1990–, govr Expert Witness Inst 1996–; Master Worshipful Co of Chartered Accountants 1995–96; FCA, MSI; *Recreations* theatre, art, economic and military history, gardens; *Clubs* Utd Oxford and Cambridge Univ; *Style*— Michael Renshall, Esq, CBE; ✉ New House, Staunton-on-Wye, Herefordshire HR4 7LW (☎ 01981 500624)

RENSHAW, (John) David; s and h of Sir (Charles) Maurice Bine Renshaw, 3 Bt, *qv*, and Isabel Bassett Popkin (now Mrs L E S Cox); *b* 9 Oct 1945; *Educ* Ashmole Sch Southgate; *m* 1970 (m dis 1988), Jennifer, da of late Gp Capt Fredrick Murray, RAF; 1 s (Thomas b 1976), 2 da (Joanna b 1973, Catherine b 1978); *Career* served Army 1960–69, Corpl; fatstock offr Meat and Livestock Cmmn 1974–88, self-employed furniture maker; *Recreations* skiing, narrowboating; *Style*— David Renshaw, Esq; ✉ c/o 8 Graham House, Birdcage Walk, Newmarket, Suffolk CB8 0NE (☎ 01638 667341)

RENSHAW, Sir (Charles) Maurice Bine; 3 Bt (UK 1903), of Coldharbour, Wivelsfield, Sussex; s of Capt Sir (Charles) Stephen Bine Renshaw, 2 Bt (d 1976), and (Edith) Mary (d 1976), 4 da of Rear-Adm Sir Edward Chichester, 9 Bt, CB, CMG; *b* 7 Oct 1912; *Educ* Eton; *m* 1, 1942 (m dis 1947), Isabel Bassett, da of late Rev John L T Popkin; 1 s (and 1 s decd), 1 da; m 2, Winifred May, da of H F Gliddon, and formerly w of James H T Sheldon; 3 s, 3 da; *Heir* s, (John) David Renshaw, *qv*; *Career* late Flying Offr RAF; *Style*— Sir Maurice Renshaw, Bt; ✉ Tom-na-Margaidh, Balquhidder, Perthshire; Linwood, Instow, N Devon

RENSHAW, Peter Bernard Appleton; s of Bernard Artoune Renshaw (d 1991), of Sale, Cheshire, and Elsie Renshaw, *née* Appleton (d 1954); *b* 23 July 1954; *Educ* Charterhouse, Selwyn Coll Cambridge; *m* 16 Oct 1982, Patricia Ann, da of Robert Vernon Caffrey, of Sale; 1 s (Thomas Peter b 1987); *Career* ptnr Slater Heelis Slrs Manchester 1982– (articled clerk 1977–79, slr 1979–82); Notary Public 1988; memb Law Soc; *Recreations* walking, gardening, DIY; *Style*— Peter Renshaw, Esq; ✉ Slater Heelis, 71 Princess St, Manchester, Greater Manchester M2 4HL (☎ 0161 228 3781, fax 0161 236 5282, e-mail 101642.1315@Compuserve.com)

RENTON, Dr Andrew; s of Michael Paul Renton, of London, and Yvonne Renee, *née* Labaton; *b* 8 Feb 1963; *Educ* Manchester GS, Univ of Nottingham (BA), Univ of Reading (PhD); *Career* fndr and artistic dir Quiet Theatre 1985–88, fndr memb Thin Men Performance Ensemble 1985–89, art critic Blitz magazine 1988–91, Br corr Flash Art magazine 1989, dir Cleveland Project Space and Imprint London 1996–; exhibitions curated: The Times London's Young Artists (Olympia London) 1991, Show Hide Show (Anderson O'Day London) 1991, Confrontaciones (Palacio di Velázquez Madrid) 1991–92, Molteplici Culture (Museo del Folklore Rome) 1992, Barcelona Abroad (Euro Visual Arts Centre Ipswich) 1992, Nothing is Hidden (London) 1992, Walter Benjamin's Briefcase (Oporto) 1993, Manifesta I (Rotterdam) 1996; *Books* Technique Anglaise: current trends in British art (ed jtly, 1991); *Recreations* sleep; *Style*— Dr Andrew Renton; ✉ 2 Grove End Gardens, Grove End Road, London NW8 9LL (☎ 0171 289 6868, fax 0171 286 8487, e-mail andren@easynet.co.uk)

RENTON, Baron (Life Peer UK 1979), of Huntingdon in Co Cambs; David Lockhart-Mure Renton; KBE (1964), TD, QC (1954), PC (1962), DL (Hunts 1962, Huntingdon & Peterborough 1964, Cambs 1974); s of Dr Maurice Waugh Renton; *b* 12 Aug 1908; *Educ* Oundle, Univ Coll Oxford (MA, BCL); *m* 1947, Claire Cicely (d 1986), yst da of late Walter Atholl Duncan; 3 da (Hon Caroline Mary (Hon Mrs Parr) b 1948, Hon Clare Olivia (Hon Mrs Scott) b 1950, Hon Davina Kathleen b 1954); *Career* Maj RA, served in S England 1939–42, Egypt and Libya 1942–45; barr 1933; sits as Cons peer in House of Lords; MP Huntingdonshire 1945–79: Nat Lib 1945–50, Nat Lib & Cons 1950–68, Cons 1968–79; min of state Home Office 1961–62; memb Cmmn on the Constitution 1971–74, chm Ctee on Preparation of Legislation 1973–75; pres: Conservation Soc 1971–72, Statute Law Soc 1980–, Nat Cncl for Civil Protection 1980–91, Nat Soc of Mentally Handicapped Children 1982–88 (chm 1978–82), All Pty Arts and Heritage Gp 1992–; dep speaker House of Lords 1982–88, bencher Lincoln's Inn 1963– (treas 1979); patron: Hunts Cons Assoc, Nat Law Library, Ravenswood Fndn, Design and Mfr for Disability (DEMAND), Greater London Assoc for the Disabled; hon fell Univ Coll Oxford; *Recreations* shooting, tennis, gardening; *Clubs* Carlton, Pratt's; *Style*— The Rt Hon Lord Renton, KBE, TD, QC, DL; ✉ Moat House, Abbots Ripton, Huntingdon, Cambs PE17 2PE (☎ 01487 3227); 16 Old Buildings, Lincoln's Inn, London WC2A 3TL (☎ 0171 242 8986)

RENTON, Rt Hon Ronald Timothy (Tim); PC (1989), MP (C) Sussex Mid (majority 20,528); yr s of Ronald Kenneth Duncan Renton, CBE (d 1980), by his 2 w Eileen, MBE, yst da of Herbert James Torr, of Morton Hall, Lincs, and gda of John Torr, MP for Liverpool 1873–80; *b* 28 May 1932; *Educ* Eton, Magdalen Coll Oxford (MA); *m* 1960, Alice Blanche Helen, da of Sir James Fergusson of Kilkerran, 8 Bt (d 1943); 2 s (Alexander James Torre b 1961, Daniel Charles Antony b 1965), 3 da (Christian Louise b 1963, (Katherine) Chelsea (twin) b 1965, Penelope Sally Rosita b 1970); *Career* dir: Silvermines Ltd 1967–84, ANZ Banking Gp 1968–75; former md Tennant Trading; Parly candidate (C) Sheffield Park 1970, MP (C) Sussex Mid 1974–, chm Cons Employment Ctee, PPS to John Biffen (as chief sec to Treasy) 1979–81, pres Cons Trade Unionists 1980–84 (vice pres 1978–80), PPS to Sir Geoffrey Howe (as chllr and foreign sec) 1983–84, Parly under sec FCO 1984, min of state FCO 1984–87, min of state Home Office 1987–89, govt chief whip 1989–90, min for the Arts 1990–92, memb Select Ctee on Nat Heritage 1995–; chm Br Hong Kong Parly Gp 1992–, memb Advsy Bd Know-How Fund for Central and Eastern Europe FCO (assistance to Russia, Central and Eastern Europe) 1992–, vice chm Br Cncl 1992–; Parly conslt to Robert Fleming & Co, dir Fleming Continental Euro Investment Trust plc and other cos 1992–; fndr pres Nat Music Day (with Mick Jagger) 1992; memb: Advsy Cncl BBC 1982–84, Governing Cncl Roedean Sch 1982–, Devpt Cncl Parnham Tst 1992–, Criterion Theatre Tst 1992–; chm Cons Foreign and Cwlth Cncl 1983–84, tstee Mental Health Fndn 1985–89; *Publications* The Dangerous Edge (1994); *Recreations* writing, gardening, mucking about in boats, listening to opera; *Clubs* Garrick; *Style*— The Rt Hon Tim Renton, MP; ✉ c/o House of Commons, London SW1A 0AA

RENTOUL, James Alexander (Alex); s of Francis Rentoul, of Chiswick, London, and Sylvia Christian Rentoul; *b* 23 June 1952; *Educ* Westminster, Worcester Coll Oxford (MA); *m* 25 June 1983, Tessa Caroline Anna, da of Jeremy Stuart Latham; 3 da (Rebecca Katherine b 20 March 1990, Olivia Caroline Anna b 7 Dec 1991, Hannah Clementine Poppy b 6 March 1995); *Career* chartered accountant: KPMG Peat Marwick London 1975–79, Arthur D Little Inc London 1980–84, assoc dir corp devpt Martin Bierbaum PLC 1984–85; sr planning mangr Imperial Group PLC 1985, princ Fin Servs & Strategy Practice Booz Allen & Hamilton Inc London 1985–87, dir Sandler Rentoul Associates Ltd 1987–93, gp commercial dir Nurdin & Peacock PLC 1993–96; ACA 1979; *Style*— Alex Rentoul, Esq; ✉ Dartmouth House, Dartmouth Place, London W4 2RH (☎ 0181 987 9777, fax 0181 987 9747)

RENWICK, David; *Career* comedy screenwriter; Writers' Guild Award for Best Comedy Writer 1992; *Work* with Andrew Marshall, *qv*, for LWT: End of Part One (Harlequin Award), Whoops Apocalypse (NY International Film and TV Festival Award, RTS Award 1981), Hot Metal (Emmy nomination); for BBC TV: Alexei Sayle's Stuff 1989–91 (International Emmy, BPG Award, RTS Award), If You See God, Tell Him 1993; others incl: The Burkiss Way (BBC Radio 4), The Steam Video Company (Thames), Whoops Apocalypse (film, ITC), Wilt (film, Rank/LWT); as solo writer: One Foot in the Grave (BBC 1) 1989– (Br Comedy Award 1991, 1992, 1993 and 1994, RTS Awards 1992, 1993 and 1994, Br Academy Award 1992, TV and Radio Club Industries Award 1995), four episodes of Agatha Christie's Poirot (LWT) 1990–91, Angry Old Men (stage play and Radio 4) 1996, Jonathan Creek (BBC) 1997; *Style*— David Renwick, Esq; ✉ c/o Roger Hancock Ltd, 4 Water Lane, London NW1 8NZ (☎ 0171 267 4418)

RENWICK, George Frederick; s of George Russell Renwick (d 1984), of The Old Parsonage, Sidlesham, Sussex, and Isabella Alice, *née* Watkins; *b* 27 July 1938; *Educ* Charterhouse, New Coll Oxford (MA); *m* 16 March 1974, Elizabeth Zoe, da of Strathearn Gordon, CBE (d 1983); 1 da (Helen b 1978); *Career* Nat Serv Lt RA 1957–59; teaching assoc Northwestern Univ Sch of Law Chicago 1962–63; admitted slr 1966; ptnr Slaughter and May 1970–96 (joined 1963); memb: Addington Soc (chm 1990–91), Law Soc, Int Bar Assoc; slr Worshipful Co of Fishmongers 1986–96, chm Railway Industry Dispute Resolution Ctee 1996–; *Clubs* Athenaeum, MCC; *Style*— George Renwick, Esq; ✉ 33 Dovehouse Street, London SW3 6JY (☎ 0171 352 7895)

RENWICK, 2 Baron (UK 1964), of Coombe, Co Surrey; Sir Harry Andrew Renwick; 3 Bt (UK 1927); s of 1 Baron Renwick, KBE (d 1973), by his 1 w, Dorothy, *née* Parkes; *b* 10 Oct 1935; *Educ* Eton; *m* 1, 1965 (m dis 1989), Susan, da of Capt Kenneth Lucking (decd), and Mrs M Stormonth Darling; 2 s (Hon Robert b 19 Aug 1966, Hon Michael b 26 July 1968); m 2, 1989, Mrs Homayoun Mazandi, da of late Col Mahmoud Yasdanparst (Pakzad); *Heir* s, Hon Robert James Renwick b 19 Aug 1966; *Career* dir Gen Technology Systems 1975–93, chm EURIM (European Informatics Market) 1993–; ptnr W Greenwell and Co 1963–80; vice pres Br Dyslexia Assoc 1982– (chm 1977–82), chm Dyslexia Educnl Tst 1986–; memb House of Lords Select Ctee: on the Euro Communities 1988–92 and of Sub-ctee B (energy tport and technol) 1987–92, on Sci and Technol 1992–96; memb Cncl Nat Cncl of Educnl Technol 1994–, hon sec Parly Information Technol Ctee 1992, hon treas Parly Space Ctee 1995–; *Clubs* White's, Turf; *Style*— The Rt Hon Lord Renwick; ✉ House of Lords, Westminster SW1A 0PW (☎ 0171 219 6961, fax 0171 219 2333)

RENWICK, Sir Richard Eustace; 4 Bt (UK 1921), of Newminster Abbey, Morpeth, Northumberland; s of Sir Eustace Deuchar Renwick, 3 Bt (d 1973), and Diana Mary, *née* Cruddas; *b* 13 Jan 1938; *Educ* Eton; *m* 1966, Caroline Anne, da of late Maj Rupert

Leonard Eversley Milburn, JP (2 s of Sir Leonard Milburn, 3 Bt, JP), and late Anne, da of Maj Austin Scott Murray, MC; 3 s (Capt Charles Richard b 1967, Harry Timothy b 1968, Rory Eustace Deuchar b 1975); *Heir* s, Charles Richard Renwick b 10 April 1967; *Career* late Capt Northumberland Hussars; md and proprietor Master Saddlers Co; *Recreations* tennis, hunting, point-to-pointing; *Clubs* Northern Counties (Newcastle); *Style*— Sir Richard Renwick, Bt; ✉ Whalton House, Whalton, Morpeth, Northumberland (☎ 01670 775383)

RENWICK, Sir Robin William; KCMG (1989, CMG 1980); s of Richard Renwick, of Edinburgh, and late Clarice, *née* Henderson; *b* 13 Dec 1937; *Educ* St Paul's, Jesus Coll Cambridge (hon fell 1992), Univ of Paris (Sorbonne); *m* 1965, Annie Colette, *née* Giudicelli; 1 s (John), 1 da (Marie-France); *Career* Nat Serv Army 1956–58; entered Foreign Service 1963, Dakar 1963–64, FO 1964–66, New Delhi 1966–69, private sec to Min of State FCO 1970–72, first sec Paris 1972–76, cnsllr Cabinet Office 1976–78, head Rhodesia Dept FCO 1978–80, political advsr to Lord Soames as Govr of Rhodesia 1980, visiting fellow Center for Int Affairs Harvard 1980–81, head of chancery Washington 1981–84, asst under sec of state FCO 1984–87; HM ambass: to South Africa 1987–91, to Washington 1991–95, ret; dir: Robert Fleming (Holdings) Ltd 1995–, Richemont 1995–, Liberty International; chm: Save and Prosper, Fluor Daneil (UK); tstee The Economist; Hon LLD Wits Univ Johannesburg, Hon DLitt Coll of William and Mary Williamsburg Va; FRSA; *Books* Economic Sanctions (Harvard 1981), Fighting with Allies (1996), Unconventional Diplomacy (1997); *Recreations* tennis, trout fishing; *Clubs* Hurlingham, Travellers', Brooks's; *Style*— Sir Robin Renwick, KCMG; ✉ c/o Robert Fleming & Co Ltd, 25 Copthall Avenue, London EC2R 7DR

REPIN, Vadim Victorovich; s of Victor Repin, of Novosibirsk, Russia, and Galina Karpova Repin; *b* 31 Aug 1971; *Educ* Novosibirsk Conservatory; *m* Natalia Gabounia; *Career* violinist; first prize Wieniawski Int Competition (aged eleven), winner Reine Elisabeth Concours; appeared with numerous orchs incl: Concertgebouw Orch, Berlin Symphony, NHK of Japan, Kirov Orch, San Francisco Symphony Orch, RPO, Chicago Symphony Orch, Montreal Symphony Orch, Orchestre de la Suisse Romande, Detroit Symphony, Tonhalle Zürich Orch, Sydney Symphony Orch (BBC Proms), Hallé Orch, Los Angeles Philharmonic, Orchestre National de France; recent recitals incl: La Scala, Miami, Seattle Int Music Festival, Teatro Manzoni, Tokyo, Valencia; *Recordings* on Erato Disques: Shostakovich Violin Concerto Op 99 No 1 and Prokofiev Violin Concerto Op 63 No 2 (with Hallé Orch under Kent Nagano) 1995, Prokofiev Violin Sonata Op 80 No 1 and Op 94 No 2 (with pianist Boris Beresovsky) 1995, Tchaikovsky Violin Concerto and Sibelius Violin Concerto (with LSO under Emmanuel Krivine) 1996; *Recreations* motoring; *Style*— Vadim Repin, Esq; ✉ c/o Eleanor Hope, SYM Music Co Ltd, 9 Southwood Hall, Wood Lane, London N6 5UF (☎ 0181 883 1896, fax 0181 883 6495)

REPTON, Bishop of 1986–; Rt Rev (Francis) Henry Arthur Richmond; s of Francis Richmond (d 1985), of Newtownbutler, Co Fermanagh, N Ireland, and Lena, *née* Crawford (d 1994); *b* 6 Jan 1936; *Educ* Portora Royal Sch Enniskillen, Trinity Coll Dublin (BA, MA), Strasbourg Univ, Linacre Coll Oxford (MLitt), Wycliffe Hall Oxford; *m* 10 Sept 1966, Caroline Mary, da of Herbert Siegmund Berent (d 1988), and Daphne Mary Berent, of Blechingley, Surrey; 2 s (Patrick b 1969, Gerald b 1971), 1 da (Harriet b 1974); *Career* curate All Saints Woodlands Doncaster 1963–66, Sir Henry Stephenson res fell and hon lectr Dept of Biblical Studies Univ of Sheffield 1966–69, vicar of St George's Sheffield 1969–77, hon lectr on New Testament Dept of Biblical Studies Univ of Sheffield 1969–77, anglican chaplain Univ of Sheffield 1974–77, warden Lincoln Theol Coll 1977–85, canon Lincoln Cathedral 1977–85, proctor in convocation 1980–85, Archbishop's representative for rels with the Old Catholic Churches 1991–; *Recreations* music, gardening, walking; *Style*— The Rt Rev the Bishop of Repton; ✉ Repton House, Lea, Matlock, Derbyshire DE4 5JP (☎ 01629 534644, fax 01629 534003)

RETALLACK, James Keith; s of Capt Keith Retallack (d 1975), of Birmingham, and Betty Margery, *née* Heaps (d 1978); *b* 8 July 1957; *Educ* Malvern, Univ of Manchester (LLB); *m* 11 Nov 1989, Carol Krystal, da of Charles Henry Mosley (d 1987), of Birmingham; *Career* articled clerk Lee Crowder & Co 1979–81, admitted slr 1981; Edge & Ellison: asst slr 1981–84, assoc 1984–88, ptnr 1988–, head Employment Unit 1990–, memb Bd of Mgmnt; memb: Law Soc, Birmingham Law Soc, Employment Lawyers Assoc; *Recreations* music, reading, gardening, skiing, travel; *Style*— James Retallack, Esq; ✉ Edge & Ellison, Rutland House, 148 Edmund St, Birmingham B3 2JR (☎ 0121 200 2001, fax 0121 200 1991)

RETTIE, (James) Philip; CBE (1987), TD (1964); s of James Low Rettie (d 1962), of Balcairn, Dundee, and Josephine Rachel, *née* Buist (d 1989); *b* 7 Dec 1926; *Educ* Trinity Coll Glenalmond, Univ of Manchester; *m* 1, 1955 Helen Grant; 2 s (Andrew, Simon), 1 da (Sarah); m 2, 1980, Diana Mary, da of Col Colin John Ballantyne, TD, DL (d 1981); *Career* RE 1945–48, Maj RETA 1949–65; William Low & Co plc 1948–85 (chm 1980–85); farmer 1964–; chm Sea Fish Indust Authy 1981–87; tstee: TSB 1967–88, Scottish Civic Tst 1983–; dir: Edinburgh & Glasgow Investment Co 1989–, Rettie & Co 1993–; chm Scottish Soc for Employment of Ex Regular Soldiers, Sailors and Airman; memb Highland TA Assoc 1975–93; Hon Col 117 Field Sqdn RETA 1982–87, Hon Col 277 Field Sqdn RETA 1983–89; *Recreations* shooting, hill walking; *Style*— Philip Rettie, Esq, CBE, TD; ✉ Hill House, Ballindean, Inchture, Perthshire PH14 9QS (☎ 01828 686337)

REUPKE, Michael; s of Dr Willm Reupke (d 1968), and Frances Graham, *née* Kinnear; *b* 20 Nov 1936; *Educ* Latymer Upper Sch, Jesus Coll Cambridge (MA), Coll of Europe Bruges (Dip Euro Studies); *m* (Helen) Elizabeth, da of Edward Restrick (d 1988); 1 s (Peter b 1965), 2 da (Alison b 1968, Rachel b 1971); *Career* Reuters 1962–89: trainee journalist 1962, journalist (Geneva, London, Conakry, Paris, Bonn) 1962–69, Euro mgmnt 1970–73, chief rep W Germany 1973–74, mangr Latin America 1975–77, ed-in-chief 1978–89, gen mangr 1989; conslt 1990–; dir: Visnews Ltd 1985–89, International Business Information Services SA France 1991–93, Company Information Exchange (COMPEX) Ltd 1992–, Staria Ltd 1993–94, Radio Acad 1994–; tstee Reuter Fndn 1984–89; memb: Int Inst of Communications, Media Law Gp, Int Press Inst; *Recreations* walking, sailing; *Clubs* Leander, Royal Automobile; *Style*— Michael Reupke; ✉ Tippings, The Common, Stokenchurch, Bucks HP14 3UD (☎ 01494 482341, office ☎ 01494 483310, fax 01494 485633)

REVELEY, Mary; da of Henry Allison (d 1956), and Mary, *née* Myers (d 1968); *b* 22 Sept 1940; *Educ* The Towers Saltburn; *m* 11 June 1960, George Reginald Reveley, s of Thomas Reginald Reveley; 2 s (Keith George b 14 April 1963, Andrew John b 11 May 1968); *Career* horse-racing trainer; *Style*— Mrs M C Reveley; ✉ Groundhill Farm, Lingdale, Saltburn, Cleveland TS12 3HD (☎ 01287 650456, fax 01287 653095)

REVELL, Surgn Vice-Adm Anthony Leslie (Tony); CB (1997), QHS (1989); s of Leslie Frederick Revell (d 1982), of Eastbourne, E Sussex, and Florence Mabel, *née* Styles; *b* 26 April 1935; *Educ* King's Coll Sch Wimbledon, Ashford and Eastbourne Grammar Schs, Univ of Birmingham Med Sch (MB ChB); *Career* RN 1960–; HMS Troubridge 1960–62, HMS Dampier 1962, HMS Loch Fada and 5 Frigate Sqdn 1963, anaesthetist RN Hosp Plymouth 1964–65, HMS Eagle 1965–67, clinical asst Radcliffe Infirmary Oxford, Alder Hey Children's Hosp Liverpool and various courses 1967–69, anaesthetist RN Hosp Plymouth 1969–70, RAF Hosps Nocton Hall and Akrotiri Cyprus 1970–72, ANZUK Mil Hosp Singapore 1972–74, conslt anaesthetist RN Hosp Haslar 1974–79, Nat Def Coll Latimer 1979–80, recruiter MoD 1980, dir of studies Inst of Naval Med 1980–82, on staff Surgn Rear Adm (Naval Hosps) 1982–84, dir of med personnel 1984–86, RCDS 1986, med offr i/c RN Hosp Plymouth 1987–88, on staff CINCFLEET 1988–89, dir of clinical servs Def Med Directorate 1990–91, Surgn Rear Adm Operational Med Servs 1991–92, CSO (Med and Dental) to CINCFLEET 1992–93, Med Dir-Gen (Navy) 1993–94, Surgn Gen MoD 1994–; Hon MD Univ of Birmingham 1995; CStJ 1994 (OStJ 1984); DA 1968, FRCA 1969, FRSM 1970; *Publications* Haslar, The Royal Hospital (1979); *Recreations* choral music, gardening, travelling; *Clubs* Naval & Military; *Style*— Surgn Vice-Adm Tony Revell, CB, QHS; ✉ 29 Little Green, Alverstoke, Gosport, Hants PO12 2EX (☎ and fax 01705 588296); Ministry of Defence, Lacon House, Theobalds Road, London WC1X 8RY (☎ 0171 305 5418, fax 0171 305 5486, mobile 0374 682682)

REVELL, John; s of Charles Revell, and Christine, *née* Neal; *b* 4 Jan 1959; *Educ* Thomas Calton Comp London; *m* 16 June 1984, Deborah, da of John Shackleton; 2 s (Joe b 16 Feb 1986, Max b 1 Oct 1989); *Career* prog asst BBC Radio N Yorks 1984–86, prodr Virgin Broadcast 1986–89, prodr BBC GLR 1989–92, jt prog dir Virgin Radio 1992–94, dir of devpt Virgin Radio 1994–95, md Ginger Television and Radio 1995–; exec prodr Ginger prodns: Chris Evans breakfast show BBC Radio One FM 1995–, TFI Friday (Channel Four) 1996–; chief exec Ginger Roots Ltd (Ginger Group of Cos) 1996–; *Recreations* skiing, music, reading; *Style*— John Revell, Esq; ✉ c/o BBC Radio One FM, Broadcasting House, Portland Place, London W1A 1AA (☎ 0171 580 4468)

REVELL, Prof Peter Allen; s of William Allen Revell, of Leicester, and Edith Emma, *née* Pitts; *b* 1 Jan 1943; *Educ* Wyggeston GS Leicester, Univ of London (BSc, MB BS, PhD); *m* 11 Nov 1967, Margaret Ruth, da of John Sharples (d 1982), of Exeter; 2 s (Matthew Peter b 14 Jan 1969, David John b 25 Sept 1977), 1 da (Elizabeth Ruth b 23 March 1971); *Career* res fell MRC; presently prof and conslt pathologist Dept of Histiopathology Royal Free Hosp Sch of Med; formerly lectr, sr lectr then reader Inst of Pathology The London Hosp Med Coll; visiting prof Queen's Univ Kingston Ontario; FRCPath 1988 (MRCPath 1976); memb: Int Skeletal Soc, Euro Soc of Biomaterials, various scientific socs in pathology and orthopaedics; *Books* Pathology of Bone (1986), contrib chapters in various other books, many papers in med jls; *Recreations* choral singing and music, walking, swimming, photography; *Style*— Prof Peter Revell; ✉ The Royal Free Hospital School of Medicine, Hampstead, London NW3 2RF (☎ 0171 794 0500, direct line 0171 830 2227, fax 0171 455 3283)

REVELL, Stephen Michael; s of Alfred Vincent Revell, of Beardwood Meadow, Blackburn, Lancs, and Doris, *née* Peaty (d 1985); *b* 20 Dec 1956; *Educ* St Mary Coll Blackburn, Christ's Coll Cambridge (MA); *m* 10 Nov 1979, Anne Marie, da of Brian Higgins, of Whitefield, Greater Manchester; *Career* ptnr Freshfields 1987– (asst slr 1979–87); Freeman Worshipful Co of Slrs 1988; memb: Int Bar Assoc, American Bar Assoc, Law Soc; Freeman City of London 1995; *Recreations* skiing, fell walking, sugar lump collecting, travelling; *Style*— Stephen Revell, Esq; ✉ 42 Canonbury Park South, London N1; Freshfields, Whitefriars, 65 Fleet Street, London EC4Y 1HS (☎ 0171 936 4000, fax 0171 832 7001, telex 889292)

REVELSTOKE, 5 Baron (UK 1885), of Membland, Co Devon; John Baring; er s 4 Baron Revelstoke (d 1994), and Hon Florence (Flora) Fermor- Hesketh (d 1971), da of 1 Baron Hesketh; *b* 2 Dec 1934; *Educ* Eton; *Heir* bro, Hon James Cecil Baring b 16 Aug 1938; *Style*— The Rt Hon Lord Revelstoke; ✉ Lambay Island, Rush, Co Dublin, Republic of Ireland

REWSE-DAVIES, Jeremy Vyvyan; *b* 24 Nov 1939; *m* 1, 1961 (m dis) Teri Donn; 1 s (Jason Saul b 1968), 1 da (Jessica Lucy b 1968); m 2, 1975 (m dis), Kezia de Winne; m 3, 1981, Iga Przedrzymirska; 1 s (Alexander Henry Thomas b 1985); *Career* prodn designer BBC TV 1964–74 (jtly designed Dr Who Daleks), freelance interior and TV designer 1974–76; Office Planning Consultants: sr designer 1976–79, design dir 1979–81, md 1981–86; design dir and dep chm Business Design Group 1986–88, dir of design London Transport 1988–; pres Chartered Soc of Designers 1992–93; FCSD 1978 (MCSD 1964), FRSA 1980; *Books* Designed for London (jtly, 1995); *Recreations* birdwatching, gardening and trips to Africa; *Clubs* The Arts, Reform; *Style*— Jeremy Rewse-Davies, Esq; ✉ The Manor, Steeple Ashton, nr Trowbridge, Wiltshire (☎ 01380 870776); London Transport, 55 Broadway, London SW1 (☎ 0171 227 3611)

REX, Prof John Arderne; s of Frederick Edward George Rex, and Winifred Natalie, *née* Arderne; *b* 5 March 1925; *Educ* Grey HS Port Elizabeth SA, Rhodes Univ Grahamstown SA (BA), Univ of Leeds (PhD); *m* 1, 6 July 1949 (m dis 1964), Pamela Margaret Rex; 2 da (Catherine b 1952, Helen b 1955); m 2, 5 June 1965, Margaret Ellen, da of Frank Biggs (d 1977); 2 s (Frederick b 1966, David b 1968); *Career* able seaman SA Naval Forces, seconded to RN 1943–45; lectr: Univ of Leeds 1949–62, Univ of Birmingham 1962–64; prof of social theory and instns Univ of Durham 1964–70, prof of sociology Univ of Warwick 1970–79 (emeritus prof 1990–); dir: Res Unit on Ethnic Rels Aston Univ 1979–84, Centre for Res in Ethnic Rels Univ of Warwick 1984–90; chm Br Sociological Assoc 1969–71; *Books* Key Problems of Sociological Theory (1961), Race Relations in Sociological Theory (1970), Sociology and the Demystification of the Modern World (1973), Colonial Immigrants in a British City (1979), Race and Ethnicity (1985), The Ghetto and the Underclass (1986), Ethnic Identity and Ethnic Mobilisation in Great Britain (1989), Ethnic Mobilisation in a Multi-Cultural Europe (1994), Ethnic Minorities in the Modern State (1995); *Recreations* spectator football; *Clubs* Coventry City FC; *Style*— Prof John Rex; ✉ 33 Arlington Ave, Leamington Spa, Coventry CV32 5UD (☎ 01926 425781); University of Warwick, Centre for Research in Ethnic Relations, Coventry CV4 7AZ (☎ 01203 523523, fax 01203 524324)

REX-TAYLOR, David; s of William Walter Taylor (d 1953); *b* 25 Jan 1947; *Educ* Jt Servs Sch Linguists, Birkbeck Coll London; *Career* asst mangr (Russia) BEA 1969–71, regnl organiser (London) Nat Fund for Res into Crippling Diseases 1971–72; fndr: Bibliagora Publishers and International Book Mail Order Co 1973, Bridge Book Club and Lineage Res Unit, Evening Standard Bridge Congress; exec ed Int Bridge Press Assoc (md USA); discovered origin of word Bridge from obsolete Russian word Biritch meaning 'Declarer'; FInstSMM; *Recreations* snooker (official referee and player), bridge; *Style*— David Rex-Taylor, Esq; ✉ PO Box 77, Feltham TW14 8JF (☎ 0181 898 1234, e-mail 100525.1225@compuserve.com, fax 0181 844 1777)

REYNIERS, Paul Jonathan; *b* 19 April 1951; *Educ* The John Lyon Sch Harrow, BA(Econ), MBA; *m* 1973, Lindsay Susan, *née* Hurst; *Career* asst to Dep Chm then corp fin mangr Anglo-American Corporation 1973–79; Price Waterhouse 1979–91: successively mangr, ptnr i/c Financial Markets Div, then managing ptnr Global Capital Markets; ptnr i/c Global Risk Management Practice Coopers & Lybrand 1991–; FCMA, FCT; *Books* International Treasury Management - Euromoney, Strategic Risk Management, Economist Intelligence Unit; *Recreations* swimming, the arts, classic cars; *Clubs* Carlton, Annabel's; *Style*— Paul J Reyniers, Esq; ✉ Coopers and Lybrand, 1 Embankment Place, London WC2N 6NN (☎ 0171 212 4727)

REYNOLDS, Prof Alan James; s of Russell Hogarth Reynolds (d 1972), of Toronto, Canada, and Edith Emily, *née* Brownlow; *b* 8 Sept 1934; *Educ* Univ of Toronto (BASc), Univ of London (PhD); *m* 31 July 1962, Caroline Mary, da of Albert William Edwin Bury (d 1985), of Billericay, Essex; 2 s (Andrew Hogarth b 1963, James Haldane b 1967); *Career* res fell Cavendish Laboratory Univ of Cambridge 1960–62, assoc prof Dept of Civil Engrg and Applied Mechanics McGill Univ Montreal Canada 1962–66; Brunel Univ: reader 1966–82, prof 1982–, head Dept of Mechanical Engrg 1983–94, pro vice chllr 1991–96; dir of research Buckinghamshire Coll 1995–; memb CVCP Academic Audit Unit 1992–94, memb Cncl Inst of Mechanical Engrs (chm Gtr London Branch) 1990–92; FIMechE 1980, FRSA 1983; *Books* Thermofluid Dynamics (1970), Turbulent

Flows in Engineering (1974, Russian edn 1976, Romanian edn 1980), The Finances of Engineering Companies (1992); *Style—* Prof Alan Reynolds; ✉ Department of Mechanical Engineering, Brunel University, Kingston Lane, Uxbridge, Middx UB8 3PH (☎ 01895 203339)

REYNOLDS, Alan Munro; *b* 27 April 1926; *Educ* Woolwich Poly Sch of Art, RCA; *m* 1951, Vona; *Career* teacher Central Sch of Arts and Crafts London 1954–61, sr lectr St Martin's Sch of Art London 1985– (teacher 1954–85); *Solo Exhibitions* Redfern Gallery London 1952, 1960 and 1972, Durlacher Gallery New York 1954, Leicester Galleries London 1958, Annely Juda Fine Art London 1978, Gallerie Rénee Ziegler Zurich 1980 (with Malcom Hughes and Peter Lowe), Juda Rowan Gallery London 1982 and 1986, Galerie Wack Kaiserslauten 1986 and 1990, Repères A la Galerie Lahumière Paris; *Gp Exhibitions* incl: London Gp Exhibition 1950, British Contemporary Painting (British Cncl Exhibition Olso and Coppenhagen) 1955, British Painting 1952–77 (Royal Acad London) 1977, Creation Modern Art and Nature (Scottish National Gallery of Modern Art Edinburgh) 1984, Systematic Constructive Drawings (Univ of York) 1986, Non-Objective World Revisited (Annely Juda Fine Art London) 1988, 1959–1989 30 years (Galerie Renée Ziegler Zurich) 1989; One Man Exhibition Annely Juda Fine Art London 1991, One Man Exhibition Galerie Art Nürnberg 1992; *Selected Public Collections* Walker Art Gallery Liverpool, Tate Gallery London, Victoria and Albert Museum London, Nat Gallery of Victoria Melbourne, Cincinnati Art Museum Ohio, Nat Gallery of Canada Ottawa, Bibliothèque Paris; Arts Cncl Purchase Award 1967; *Style—* Alan Reynolds, Esq

REYNOLDS, Antony James (Tony); s of C V Reynolds, of Hertford, Herts, and Mildred Vera Reynolds; *b* 21 April 1936; *Educ* Westminster; *m* 14 June 1955, Grace; 2 da (Kim Laura b 1959, Briony Jane b 1963), 1 s (Kevin Antony b 1961); *Career* Proctor & Gamble 1960–65, vice pres sales and mktg Tenco Div Coca Cola Foods 1965–83, fndr own business (UB Group) 1983; currently gp md: United Beverages Ltd, Master Brew Ltd, Boston Foods Ltd, South West Coffee Co Ltd; lectr on franchising; FCIM; *Recreations* water skiing, windsurfing, swimming; *Clubs* Rotary; *Style—* Tony Reynolds, Esq; ✉ Master Brew, Beverages House, 7 Ember Centre, Hersham Trading Estate, Hersham, Surrey KT12 3PT (☎ 01932 253787, fax 01932 253520)

REYNOLDS, Dr (Eva Mary) Barbara; da of Alfred Charles Reynolds (d 1969), and Barbara, *née* Florac (d 1977); *b* 13 June 1914; *Educ* St Paul's Girls' Sch, UCL (BA, PhD), Univ of Cambridge (MA); *m* 1, 5 Sept 1939, Lewis Guy Melville Thorpe (d 1977); 1 s (Adrian Charles b 1942), 1 da (Kerstin b 1949); m 2, 30 Oct 1982, Kenneth Robert Imeson (d 1994); *Career* asst lectr in Italian LSE 1937–40, lectr in Italian Univ of Cambridge 1940–62, reader in Italian Univ of Nottingham 1966–78 (warden of Willoughby Hall 1963–69); visiting prof in Italian: Univ of Calif Berkeley 1974–75, Wheaton Coll Illinois 1977–78, Trinity Coll Dublin 1980 and 1981, Hope Coll Michigan 1982; hon reader Univ of Warwick 1975–80; managing ed Seven (an Anglo-American literary review) 1980–88 and 1993–; chm: Univ Women's Club 1988–90, Dorothy L Sayers Soc 1983–94 (pres 1994–); Hon DLitt: Wheaton Coll Illinois 1979, Hope Coll Michigan 1982, Univ of Durham 1995; Silver medal for servs to Italian culture 1964, Silver medal for servs to Anglo-Veneto cultural rels 1971, Cavaliere Ufficiale al Merito della Repubblica Italiana 1978; *Books* The Linguistic Writings of Alessandro Manzoni (1952), The Cambridge Italian Dictionary (gen ed Vol I 1962, Vol II 1981), Dante: Paradise (trans with Dorothy L Sayers, 1962), Guido Farina, Painter of Verona (with Lewis Thorpe, 1967), Dante: Poems of Youth (trans, 1969), Concise Cambridge Italian Dictionary (1975), Ariosto: Orlando Furioso (trans Vol I 1975, Vol II 1977), Dizionario Italiano-Inglese, Inglese-Italiano (Signorelli-CUP, 1985), The Translators Art (ed with William Radice, 1987), The Passionate Intellect: Dorothy L Sayers' Encounter with Dante (1989), Dorothy L Sayers: Her Life and Soul (1993), The Letters of Dorothy L Sayers: 1899–1936, The Making of a Detective Novelist (ed, 1995); *Recreations* travel; *Clubs* University Women's, Authors', RAF; *Style—* Dr Barbara Reynolds; ✉ 220 Milton Rd, Cambridge CB4 1LQ (☎ 01223 565380, fax 01223 424894)

REYNOLDS, Brian James; s of Thomas Reynolds, of 19 Ferndale Lodge, Eastbourne, and Beatrice, *née* Rutherford; *b* 22 April 1938; *Educ* Downhills Sch Tottenham; *m* 1, 19 Sept 1959 (m dis 1977), Janet, *née* Gallagher; 1 s (Andrew), 1 da (Suzanne); m 2, 1982, Patricia Ann, da of George McIntyre; *Career* slr's clerk and litigation clerk 1953–59, fin journalist, dir and co sec Financial Information Co 1959–81, Daily Express 1981–85; dir: Money Marketing (Design) Public Relations Ltd 1985–86, Streets Communications Ltd 1986–92, Paternoster Partnership Ltd; *Recreations* lifetime supporter Tottenham Hotspur FC; *Style—* Brian Reynolds, Esq; ✉ Paternoster Partnership Ltd, 99 Charterhouse Street, London EC1M 6HR (☎ 0171 336 7776, fax 0171 336 7736)

REYNOLDS, David Alan Clifton; s of Clifton George Reynolds (d 1969), of Beaconsfield, Bucks, and Mary Lois, *née* Miller (d 1994); *b* 13 Oct 1948; *Educ* Radley Coll, LSE (BSc(Econ)); *m* 1, 1 May 1976, Philippa, *née* Preston; 3 da (Martha b 18 June 1977, Grace b 22 Oct 1980, Rose b 9 Feb 1984); m 2, 27 June 1992, Penny, *née* Phillips; *Career* trainee ed Oz Magazine 1967–68, ed The Freethinker 1968–70, undergraduate LSE 1970–73, ed with Reader's Digest 1973–75, ed with Dorling Kindersley 1975–78, fndr dir Shuckburgh Reynolds Ltd 1978–86, fndr dir and dep managing dir Bloomsbury Publishing Plc 1986–; *Recreations* walking, Brookside; *Style—* David Reynolds, Esq; ✉ Bloomsbury Publishing Plc, 2 Soho Square, London W1V 5DE (☎ 0171 494 2111)

REYNOLDS, David Geoffrey; s of William Oliver Reynolds, OBE, of Follifoot, nr Harrogate, and Eleanor, *née* Gill; *b* 11 June 1948; *Educ* Bedford Sch, LAMDA; *m* 5 Sept 1970, Valerie, *née* Wells; 2 da (Emma b 5 Oct 1973, Tessa b 7 July 1976); *Career* dep stage mangr Spa Theatre Whitby 1967, stage mangr Sheffield Playhouse 1967–68, dir Yorkshire Television 1973–79 (floor mangr 1968–73), freelance dir 1979–86, controller of entertainment Yorkshire Television 1993–95 (dep controller of entertainment 1986–92), gp controller of entertainment Yorkshire Tyne-Tees Television plc 1995–; TV work incl: Emmerdale, Hadleigh, The Sandbaggers, The Onedin Line, When The Boat Comes In, Juliet Bravo, Give Us a Break, Big Deal, Bergerac, Lovejoy, The Beiderbecke Affair, Room At The Bottom (Int Emmy nomination and Best Comedy award Banff Festival), prodr The New Statesman (Int Emmy winner, BAFTA award), prodr and dir Home to Roost (Int Emmy nomination), prodr and co-dir A Bit of a Do (TRIC award for Best Sitcom, Broadcasting Press and Guild award for Best Entertainment Series, RTS award Best Drama Series and Br Comedy awards Best ITV and Channel 4 Sitcom and Best Br TV Comedy), prodr and dir Stay Lucky, prodr and dir Rich Tea and Sympathy, dir A Touch of Frost; *Recreations* boating, theatre, photography, films, travel; *Style—* David Reynolds, Esq; ✉ Pencob House, Scotton, Knaresborough, North Yorkshire HG5 9HZ (☎ 01423 862854); Yorkshire-Tyne Tees Television, The Television Centre, Leeds LS3 1JS (☎ 0113 243 8283, fax 0113 244 5107)

REYNOLDS, Sir David James; 3 Bt (UK 1923), of Woolton, Co Lancaster; s of Lt-Col Sir John Francis Roskell Reynolds, 2 Bt, MBE (d 1956), and Millicent Orr-Ewing (d 1932); gda of 7 Duke of Roxburgh, and ggda of 7 Duke of Marlborough; *b* 26 Jan 1924; *Educ* Downside; *m* 1966, Charlotte Baumgartner; 1 s (James Francis), 2 da (Lara Mary b 1 March 1967, Sofie Josefine b 5 May 1968); *Heir* s, James Reynolds b 10 July 1971; *Career* serv WWII Capt 15/19 Hussars Italy; *Style—* Sir David Reynolds, Bt; ✉ Blanchepierre House, rue de la Blanchepierre, St Lawrence, Jersey, CI

REYNOLDS, Dr Edward Henry; s of William Henry Reynolds, of Broad Towers, Caerleon, Gwent, and (Mary) Angela, *née* Keane (d 1989); *b* 13 Oct 1935; *Educ* The Oratory, The Welsh Nat Sch of Med Cardiff (MB BCh, MD); *m* 20 July 1968, Angela Pauline, da of John Martin Anthony Sheehan (d 1960), of 28 Manor Rd, Cheam, Surrey; 1 da (Catherine b 1974); *Career* visiting asst prof of neurology Yale Univ Med Sch 1970, conslt neurologist Maudsley and King's Coll Hosps London 1974–, chm The Centre for Epilepsy Maudsley Hosp 1993–, dir Inst of Epileptology King's Coll 1994–; sec MRC Coordinating Gp for Epilepsy 1978–83, memb Ctee Br Neuropsychiatry Assoc 1987–93, pres Int League Against Epilepsy 1993– (pres Br branch 1993– (sec 1979–84), vice pres 1983–93); memb BMA, FRCP 1980, FRCPsych 1985; *Books* incl: Folic Acid in Neurology, Psychiatry and Internal Medicine (ed with M I Botez, 1979), Epilepsy and Psychiatry (ed with M R Trimble, 1981), Paediatric Perspectives on Epilepsy (ed with E Ross, 1985), The Bridge Between Neurology and Psychiatry (ed with M R Trimble, 1989); *Recreations* golf, tennis; *Clubs* RAC; *Style—* Dr Edward Reynolds; ✉ Dept of Neurology, King's College Hospital, London SE5 (fax 0171 346 3130); Centre for Epilepsy (☎ 0171 277 1985)

REYNOLDS, Fiona Claire; da of Dr Jeffrey Alan Reynolds, of Sheffield, and Margaret Mary, *née* Watson; *b* 29 March 1958; *Educ* Rugby HS for Girls, Newnham Coll Cambridge (MPhil); *m* 23 May 1981, Robert William Tinsley Merrill; 3 da (Alice Kezia b 12 Nov 1990, Margaret Rose b 28 March 1992, Olivia Jane b 13 June 1995); *Career* sec Council for National Parks 1980–87, dir Council for the Protection of Rural England 1992– (asst dir (Policy) 1987–92); *Awards* Global 500 UN Environment Prog 1990; *Recreations* walking, cycling, reading, classical music; *Style—* Ms Fiona Reynolds; ✉ 13 Ferntower Road, Highbury, London N5 2JE; Council for the Protection of Rural England, Warwick House, 25 Buckingham Palace Road, London SW1W 0PP (☎ 0171 976 6433, fax 0171 976 6373)

REYNOLDS, Prof Francis Martin Baillie; Hon QC (1993); s of Eustace Baillie Reynolds (d 1948), and Emma Margaret Hanby, *née* Holmes (d 1933); *b* 11 Nov 1932; *Educ* Winchester, Worcester Coll Oxford (scholar, MA, DCL); *m* 1965, Susan Claire, da of Hugh William Shillito; 2 s (Barnabas William Baillie b 1967, Martin Alexander Baillie b 1969), 1 da (Sophie Francesca b 1973); *Career* Bigelow teaching fell Univ of Chicago 1957–58, fell Worcester Coll Oxford 1960– (lectr 1958–60); called to the Bar Inner Temple 1961; prof of law Univ of Oxford 1992– (reader 1977–92); visiting lectr Univ of Auckland 1971 and 1977; Arthur Robinson & Hedderwicks visiting fell: Univ of Melbourne, Monash Univ 1989; Ebsworth & Ebsworth visiting prof Univ of Sydney 1993, Simpson Grierson visiting prof Univ of Auckland 1995; visiting prof: Nat Univ of Singapore 1984, 1986, 1988, 1990–92, 1994 and 1996, UCL 1986–89, Univ of Otago 1993; ed: Lloyd's Maritime and Commercial Law Quarterly 1983–87, The Law Quarterly Review 1987–; hon bencher Inner Temple 1979; FBA 1988; *Books* Bowstead and Reynolds On Agency (co-ed 13 and 14 edns, ed 15 and 16 edns), Chitty On Contract (co-ed 24–27 edns), Benjamin's Sale of Goods (co-ed 1–4 edns); *Recreations* music, walking, travel; *Style—* Prof Francis Reynolds, QC, FBA; ✉ Worcester College, Oxford OX1 2HB (☎ 01865 278300, fax 01865 278387)

REYNOLDS, Gillian; da of Charles Beresford Morton (d 1970), of Liverpool, and Ada Kelly (d 1962); *b* 15 Nov 1935; *Educ* Liverpool Inst HS for Girls, St Anne's Coll Oxford (BA), Mount Holyoke Coll South Hadley Mass; *m* 23 Sept 1958 (m dis 1983), Stanley Ambrose Reynolds, s of Ambrose Harrington Reynolds (d 1970), of Holyoke, USA; 3 s (Ambrose Kelly b 12 June 1960, Alexander Charles b 3 Jan 1970, Abel Stanley b 5 Sept 1971); *Career* TV and radio broadcaster 1964–; radio critic: The Guardian 1967–74, The Daily Telegraph 1975–; prog controller Radio City Liverpool 1974–75; pres Sr Assoc Ctee St Anne's Coll Oxford 1990–; memb Mount Holyoke Coll Alumnae Assoc; first fell Radio Acad 1990, FRSA, FRTS; *Recreations* listening to the radio, the company of friends; *Clubs* Royal Society of Arts; *Style—* Ms Gillian Reynolds; ✉ Flat 3, 1 Linden Gardens, London W2 4HA (☎ 0171 229 1893, fax 0171 243 2621)

REYNOLDS, Graham; OBE (1984); s of the late Arthur Thomas Reynolds, and Eva Mullins; *b* 10 Jan 1914; *Educ* Highgate Sch, Queens' Coll Cambridge (BA); *m* 6 Feb 1943, Daphne, da of Thomas Dent, of Huddersfield; *Career* asst keeper V & A Museum 1937, seconded to Miny of Home Security 1939, princ 1942, dep keeper V & A (Dept of Paintings) 1947–58, keeper V & A (Dept of Prints, Drawings and Paintings) 1959–74; tstee William Morris Gallery Walthamstow 1972–75, chm Gainsborough's House Soc Sudbury 1977–79, memb Reviewing Ctee on Export of Works of Art 1984–90; Leverhulme emeritus fellowship 1980–81; FBA 1993; *Publications incl* Nicholas Hilliard and Isaac Oliver (1947, 1971), English Watercolours (1959, revised 1988), English Portrait Miniatures (1952, revised 1988), Painters of the Victorian Scene (1953), Constable the Natural Painter (1965), Victorian Paintings (1966, 1987), Turner (1969), Catalogue of the Constable Collection V & A Museum (1960, revised 1973), Concise History of Watercolour Painting (1972), Catalogue of Portrait Miniatures Wallace Collection (1980), Constable's England (1983), The Later Paintings and Drawings of John Constable (1984, awarded Mitchell Prize 1984), The Earlier Paintings and Drawings of John Constable (1996), European Miniatures in the Metropolitan Museum of Art (jtly, 1996), Catalogue of Tudor and Stuart Miniatures in the Royal Collection (1998); *Clubs* Athenaeum; *Style—* Graham Reynolds, Esq, OBE, FBA; ✉ The Old Manse, Bradfield St George, Bury St Edmunds, Suffolk IP30 0AZ (☎ 01284 386610)

REYNOLDS, Ian Tewson; s of Eric Tewson Reynolds (d 1968), of Radlett, Herts, and Joyce, *née* Holt; *b* 3 Dec 1943; *Educ* Watford GS, LSE (BSc Econ); *m* 20 Dec 1980, Gillian Eadie, da of Thomas Noel Castree Prosser (d 1994); 2 da (Christina Louise b 12 Oct 1982, Frances Emilie b 3 Feb 1986); *Career* sales rep Shell Mex and BP 1965–67, sales exec Haymarket Press 1967–68; IBM UK Ltd: sales rep London 1968–73, mktg mangr Birmingham 1974–75, mangr W Mids Branch 1976–77, mangr Central & Northern Region Manchester 1977–81, gp dir of admin Paris 1982–83, dir of Info Systems Mktg Basingstoke 1983–85, dir of Business Devpt London 1986, area gen mangr Paris 1986–87, dir of Mktg and Servs Basingstoke 1987–90, vice pres of Communications Paris 1991–92, dir of Personnel and Corp Affrs Portsmouth 1992–94; chief exec ABTA Ltd 1994–; non-exec dir St Mary's NHS Tst 1995–; fell Indust and Parliament Tst 1993; MBCS 1973, CIMgt 1990, FInstD 1992, FRSA 1992; *Recreations* golf, tennis, skiing, sailing; *Clubs* Hurlingham; *Style—* Ian Reynolds, Esq; ✉ Murray Cross, 4 Murray Road, Wimbledon, London SW19 4PB (☎ 0181 946 7978); Chief Executive, ABTA, 55–57 Newman Street, London W1P 4AH (☎ 0171 307 1914, fax 0171 636 4642)

REYNOLDS, Jane Caroline Margaret; JP (1991); da of Maj Thomas Reynolds, MC (d 1981), of Richmond, N Yorks, and Cynthia Myrtle Margaret, *née* Eden (later Mrs Witt, d 1982); *b* 4 March 1953; *Educ* Winchester Co HS for Girls, Brighton Poly, Lincoln Meml Clinic for Psychotherapy; *Career* student teacher St Mary's Wrestwood Educnl Tst Ltd 1970–72, offr i/c Gary Richard Homes Ltd 1972–76, matron Alison House (St John's Wood) Ltd 1976–81, dir The Westminster Soc for Mentally Handicapped Children and Adults 1983–87 (devpt offr 1981–83), hosp mangr Leavesden Hosp 1987–91, chief exec The Royal Masonic Benevolent Instn 1991–, sec The Masonic Fndn for the Aged and the Sick 1992–; memb Registered Homes Act (1984) Tbnl Panel 1990–; chm Life Opportunities Tst 1990–; Freeman City of London 1993, Liveryman Worshipful Co of Glass-sellers 1994; FIMgt 1988 (MBIM 1977); *Recreations* travelling, the arts, seizing opportunities; *Style—* Ms Jane Reynolds, JP; ✉ The Royal Masonic Benevolent Institution, 20 Great Queen Street, London WC2B 5BG (☎ 0171 405 8341, fax 0171 404 0724)

REYNOLDS, John Roderick; s of David Reynolds (d 1988), of Peterborough, and Gwen Reynolds, *née* Roderick; *b* 11 Oct 1948; *Educ* Laxton Sch, Oundle, Imperial Coll London (BSc); *m* 7 Sept 1974, Jane Elizabeth, da of David Berridge, of Cambridgeshire; 2 s (Henry b 1980, Guy b 1982), 1 da (Daisy b 1985); *Career* Price Waterhouse 1970–76, dir J Henry Schroder & Co Ltd 1976–; FCA; *Recreations* riding, skiing, tennis, opera, bridge; *Clubs* Boodle's, Annabel's, Hurlingham, Groucho, Bath Racquets; *Style—* John Reynolds, Esq; ✉ The Manor House, Weston-sub-Edge, Chipping Campden, Glos; 32 Winchendon Road, London SW6; J Henry Schroder & Co, 120 Cheapside, London EC2 (☎ 0171 382 6000, fax 0171 382 3881)

REYNOLDS, (James) Kirk; QC (1993); s of The Hon Mr Justice James Reynolds, of Helen's Bay, Co Down, N Ireland, and Alexandra Mary Erskine, *née* Strain; *b* 24 March 1951; *Educ* Campbell Coll Belfast, Peterhouse Cambridge (MA); *Career* called to the Bar Middle Temple 1974; *Books* Handbook of Rent Review (1981), Dilapidations: the Modern Law and Practice (1994), Essentials of Rent Review (1995), Renewal of Business Tenancies (1997); *Style—* Kirk Reynolds, Esq, QC; ✉ Falcon Chambers, Falcon Court, London EC4Y 1AA

REYNOLDS, His Hon Judge; Martin Paul; s of Cedric Hinton Fleetwood Reynolds (d 1993), of London, and Doris Margaret, *née* Bryan (d 1982); *b* 25 Dec 1936; *Educ* Univ Coll Sch, St Edmund Hall Oxford (MA); *m* 17 June 1961, Gaynor Margaret, da of Stuart Morgan Phillips (d 1957); 3 s (Simon Stuart Hinton b 1964, Peter Bryan b 1966, Thomas Edward Barnsbury b 1969); *Career* qualified teacher 1961; called to the Bar Inner Temple 1962, recorder of the Crown Court 1993–95, circuit judge (SE Circuit) 1995–; cncllr London Borough of Islington 1968–71 and 1973–82; Parly candidate Harrow W Oct 1974; ACIArb 1985; *Books* Negotiable Instruments for Students (1964); *Recreations* sailing, travel in France, music; *Clubs* Savage; *Style—* His Hon Judge Reynolds; ✉ c/o South Eastern Circuit Office, New Cavendish House, 18 Maltravers Street, London WC2R 3EU (☎ 0171 936 7235); The Crown Court at Snaresbrook, 75 Hollybush Hill, Snaresbrook, London E11 1QW (☎ 0181 982 5500)

REYNOLDS, Dr Mary Angela; OBE (1991); da of Dr William Henry Reynolds, of Mill Hill, London NW7, and Mary Angela, *née* Keane (d 1989); *Educ* St Mary's Convent Shaftesbury Dorset, Charing Cross Hosp Med Sch (MB BS); *Career* MO to US Public Health Serv American Embassy 1967–68, asst gen mangr chief underwriter and chief med offr Canada Life Assur Co (UK and Ireland) 1978–92; first lady pres Assur Med Soc 1989, chm Med Affrs Ctee Assoc of Br Insurers, vice-pres London Insur Inst (former cncl memb), dep chm Life Underwriters Club 1988–; memb: Steering Ctee Women in Mgmnt Insur Project MSC and Industl Soc, Gen Ctee Insur Benevolent Fund (dir Insur Orphans Fund), Perm Health Insur Club; Assur Med Soc: memb working pty for Chartered Insur Insts Underwriting Dip, first ed bulletin; Freeman City of London 1983, Liveryman Worshipful Co of Insurers 1983; FIMgt 1980, FAMS; *Books* Your Health is Your Wealth (1978), Ethics of Modern Life Underwriting (1978); *Recreations* opera, tennis; *Style—* Dr Mary Reynolds, OBE

REYNOLDS, (Thomas James) Michael; s of George Thomas Reynolds (d 1943), and Millicent Theresa, *née* Frayne (d 1993); *b* 30 Aug 1933; *Educ* Varndean GS, Brighton Coll of Art (NDD, ATD); *m* 1955, Rosemary Elizabeth (d 1991), da of Kenneth Albert Hill; *Career* artist; former teacher: Raine's Fndn Grammar 1959–61, Birmingham Sch of Art 1961–62, Stourbridge Coll of Art 1962, Beckenham Adult Centre 1965–72 (vice princ 1969–72); portraits incl: Cardinal Heenan 1965, Lady Zuckerman 1974, Lady Margaret Douglas-Home 1976, Cyril Cusack 1986, J P Donleavy 1986, Paul Eddington 1989, Michael Shea 1994, Mrs Michael Shea 1996; other works incl: etched wall decoration FAO Building Rome 1964, mosaic Southgate House Stevenage 1966, doors of Midland Bank King's Lynn 1973; Rome scholar in engraving 1962–64, Hunting Gp Public Prize 1985, Singer & Friedlander Prize 1994, 1995 and 1996; RP 1977, RBA 1989; *Recreations* music, reading, cooking, table games, wine; *Clubs* Arts; *Style—* Michael Reynolds, Esq, RP; ✉ c/o Royal Society of Portrait Painters, 17 Carlton House Terrace, London SW1Y 5BD (☎ 0171 930 6844, fax 0171 839 7830)

REYNOLDS, Michael Arthur; s of William Arthur Reynolds (d 1981), of Hakin, Milford Haven, Dyfed, and Violet Elsie, *née* Giddings (d 1978); *b* 28 Aug 1943; *Educ* Milford Haven GS, Cardiff Coll of Art (DipAD); *m* 1 (m dis 1971), Patricia; 1 s (Joseph Michael b 1970); m 2 (m dis 1974), Judith; m 3 (m dis 1995), Jill Caroline; partner Gill Debell; 1 s (Oliver Michael b 1992); *Career* creative dir KPS Ltd Nairobi 1968, copywriter J Walter Thompson 1971, gp head Benton & Bowles 1973; creative dir; ABM 1975, McCann Erickson 1979, Interlink 1981, MWK (and shareholder) 1983, Pearson Partnership 1987; film dir Good Film Co 1991–; gp creative dir Osprey Communications plc; MIPA; *Recreations* gardening, archery, rare books; *Clubs* Chelsea Arts; *Style—* Michael Reynolds, Esq; ✉ Beeholm, Howlett End, Wimbish, nr Saffron Walden, Essex CB10 2XW (☎ 01799 599247); Osprey Communications plc, 10 Little Portland Street, London W1N 5DF (☎ 0171 637 8575, fax 0171 637 1432)

REYNOLDS, Michael John; s of William James Reynolds (d 1981), and Audrey, *née* Turpitt; *b* 8 Oct 1950; *Educ* Felsted Sch, Univ of Keele, Strasbourg Univ (Droit Compare); *Career* Allen & Overy: articled clerk 1974–76, asst slr 1976–81, seconded to EC 1978, ptnr and head EC Law Dept 1981–; visiting prof of Euro competition law Univ of Durham; chm Anti Trust Ctee Int Bar Assoc; memb Euro Ctee British Invisibles; *Recreations* boats, learning languages, travel; *Clubs* Travellers, Cercle Gaulois (Brussels), Warande (Brussels); *Style—* Michael Reynolds, Esq; ✉ Allen & Overy, One New Change, London EC4 (☎ 0171 330 3000, fax 0171 330 9999)

REYNOLDS, (Arthur) Paul; s of Capt A C J Reynolds (d 1954), of Cornwall, and Violet Emma, *née* Tuttle (d 1966); *b* 1 May 1917; *Educ* St Austell GS Cornwall, Coll of Estate Mgmnt London; *m* 1, 1945, Joyce (d 1979), da of Flt Lt Harold Arthur Rolls, of Leighton Buzzard (d 1980); 1 s (Christopher b 1946), 1 da (Elizabeth b 1950); m 2, 1981, Diana, da of Edward John Pyman (d 1985), of Leighton Buzzard; *Career* Capt RA 1940–46, attached to Indian Artillery; former ptnr H A Rolls & Ptnrs, specialist in the care and restoration of churches (St Albans and Oxford Dioceses), ret; former surveyor to the fabric of All Saints Church Leighton Buzzard; pres Leighton Buzzard Festival Singers; FRICS, EASA; *Recreations* music - choral singing, oil painting, golf, cricket, swimming; *Style—* Paul Reynolds, Esq; ✉ Sandy Mount, Plantation Road, Leighton Buzzard, Beds LU7 7HR (☎ 01525 373307)

REYNOLDS, (Christopher) Paul Michel; s of Christopher John Loughborough Reynolds, of Salter's Green, Lymington, Hants, and Elisabeth, *née* Ewart-James; *b* 23 Feb 1946; *Educ* Ardingly Coll, Worcester Coll Oxford (BA); *m* 25 July 1950, Louise, da of Bishop Eric William Bradley Cordingly (d 1976); 1 s (James Edward b 1974), 1 da (Alice Elizabeth b 1976); *Career* joined BBC Norwich 1968, BBC Radio London 1970–78; BBC corr: NY 1978–82, Brussels 1982–85, Jerusalem 1985–87; diplomatic and court corr BBC News & Current Affrs Radio 1987–; *Recreations* birdwatching, archaeology; *Style—* Paul Reynolds, Esq; ✉ c/o Foreign Affairs Unit, BBC Broadcasting House, London W1A 1AA (☎ 0171 927 4547)

REYNOLDS, Sir Peter William John; kt (1985), CBE; s of late Harry Reynolds, of Amersham, and Gladys Victoria French; *b* 10 Sept 1929; *Educ* Haileybury; *m* 1955, Barbara Anne, da of Vincent Kenneth Johnson, OBE; 2 s (Mark, Adam); *Career* Nat Serv 2 Lt RA 1948–50; Unilever Ltd 1950–70 (trainee, md then chm Walls (Meat & Handy Foods) Ltd); Rank Hovis McDougall plc: asst gp md 1971, gp md 1972–81, chm 1981–89, dep chm 1989–93; chm Pioneer Concrete (Holdings) plc 1992–; dir 1981–93: Ranks Pension Ltd, RHM Overseas Ltd, RHM Research Ltd, RHM Overseas Finance BV (Holland), RHM International Finance NV, RHM Holdings (USA) Inc, Purchase Finance Co Ltd, RHM Operatives Pensions Ltd; dir: Avis Europe Ltd, Cilva Holdings plc, The Boots Co plc 1986–, Guardian Royal Exchange plc; dir Nationwide Anglia Building Society 1990–92; memb Consultative Bd for Resources Devpt in Agric 1982–84, chm Resources Ctee Food & Drink Fedn 1983–86 (fndr memb of Ctee 1974–), memb EDC for Food and Drink Mfrg Indust 1982–87, memb Covent Garden Market Authy; dir Industl Devpt Bd for NI 1982–89, memb Peacock Ctee on Financing the BBC 1985–86, govr Berkhamsted Schs 1985–, life govr Haileybury Coll 1985–, dir Fremantle Housing Tst 1992–; High Sheriff Bucks 1990–91; *Recreations* gardening; *Clubs* Naval Club; *Style—* Sir Peter Reynolds, CBE

REYNOLDS, Richard Christopher; s of Stanley Reynolds (d 1960), and Christine, *née* Barrow; *b* 2 June 1945; *Educ* Peter Simmons Sch Winchester, Croydon Tech Sch, Croydon Tech Coll; *m* 2 March 1968, Sharon, da of Peter Bragg, of Great Bookham, Surrey; 1 s (Paul), 1 da (Julia); *Career* md Barratt London 1983–; dir: Barratt Southern 1983–, Stratford Development Partnership Ltd 1993–; FCIM, FCIH, FCIOB, FIMgt, FASI, FInstD; *Recreations* clay pigeon shooting, scuba diving, cycling; *Style—* Richard Reynolds, Esq; ✉ Barratt London, Warton House, 150 High St, Stratford E15 2NE (☎ 0181 555 3242, fax 0181 519 5536, dx 5408)

REYNOLDS, Ruth Evelyn Millicent; da of Lt-Col Charles Ernest White-Spunner Fawcett, RAMC (d 1944), of Littlewood, Ganghill, Guildford, and Millicent Aphrasia, *née* Sullivan (d 1971); *b* 4 Oct 1915; *Educ* Conamur Sandgate Kent, Guildford Sch of Art, Wycombe Coll of Art; *m* 4 Nov 1939, Lt-Col Dudley Lancelot Collis Reynolds, OBE, s of Maj James Christopher Reynolds (d 1923), of The Lawns, Alveston, Glos; 1 s (John b 1950), 2 da (Jenny b 1941, Diana b 1946); *Career* J Stanley Beard & Bennett Architects 1934–37, BBC Admin Dept 1937–39 (six months in News Talks run by Richard Dimbleby, later Talks Dept and Features and Drama); served WWII WAAF Bomber Cmd HQ Langley Bucks; sculptor and artist in oil and watercolour; *Solo Exhibitions* incl: Halifax House, Univ of Oxford Graduate Centre 1965, ESU Oxford 1967, Co Museum Aylesbury 1976, Loggia Gallery London 1982, Century Galleries Henley-on-Thames 1986, Fawley Court Henley-on-Thames 1991; *Group Exhibitions* incl: Loggia Gallery, Amnesty Int Sculpture Exhibition Bristol and London 1979, Mall Galleries, Art for Winchester (Angelus Gallery Winchester) 1992; *Work in Private Collections* incl: Anne Duchess of Westminster's Arkle Collection, Guinness Ltd (Park Royal), RAF Halton Bucks, Welch Regt Museum, Cardiff Castle, Lambeth Palace; fndr memb Aylesbury Decorative and Fine Arts Soc, former tutor Duke of Edinburgh's Gold Award in Art, memb Buckinghamshire Art Soc; asst organizer Millenium Art Exhibition (St Dunstan's Church Monks Risborough Aylesbury) 1988; former memb: FPS, AFAS; FRSA 1980; *Recreations* sketching, dog-walks in Chilterns, travel; *Clubs* Int Lyceum Club of London; *Style—* Mrs Ruth Reynolds

REYNOLDS, Simon Anthony; s of Maj James Reynolds (d 1982), of Leighton Hall, Carnforth, Lancs, and Helen Reynolds (d 1977); *b* 20 Jan 1939; *Educ* Ampleforth, Heidelberg Univ; *m* 1970, Beata Cornelia, da of late Baron Siegfried von Heyl zu Herrnsheim (d 1982), of Schlosschen, Worms, Germany; 2 s, 2 da; *Career* dealer in fine art; *Books* The Vision of Simeon Solomon (1984), Hymns to Night...and the Poets of Pessimism (1994), Sir William Blake Richmond RA (biography, 1995); *Recreations* writing, collecting fine art, travelling; *Style—* Simon Reynolds, Esq; ✉ 64 Lonsdale Rd, Barnes, London SW13 (☎ 0181 748 3506)

REYNOLDS, (Thomas) Watson; s of Capt Thomas Reynolds (d 1933), of Cambridge, and Winifred Jessie, *née* Wells (d 1988); *b* 26 April 1924; *Educ* Harrow, Peterhouse Cambridge; *m* 17 July 1948, Gabrielle Ann, da of Lt-Col Jonathan Richard Greenbank (d 1964), of Galphay, Ripon, N Yorks; 2 s (Thomas, John); *Career* RAFVR 1942–46 (despatches 1945), 37 Sqdn CMF Italy 1944, pilot, shot down 13 June 1944, evaded capture, returned allied lines 8 Nov 1944, 7 Sqdn Bomber Cmd 1945–46; farmer and landowner 1948–; chm: Fen Centre Nat Ice Skating Assoc 1948–, Waterbeach Level Internal Drainage Bd 1977– (cmmr 1948–, vice chm 1966–77); Liveryman Worshipful Co of Curriers 1982, Freeman City of London 1982; *Recreations* outdoor ice speed skating, shooting; *Clubs* RAF; *Style—* Watson Reynolds, Esq; ✉ Waterbeach Hall, Waterbeach, Cambridgeshire (☎ 01223 860216); Bank Farm, Waterbeach, Cambridgeshire (☎ 01223 860250, fax 01223 441868)

REYNTIENS, (Nicholas) Patrick; OBE (1976); s of Nicholas Serge Reyntiens, OBE (d 1951), and Janet Isabel, *née* MacRae (d 1975); *b* 11 Dec 1925; *Educ* Ampleforth, Regent St Poly, Edinburgh Coll of Art (DA); *m* 8 Sept 1953, Anne Mary, da of Brig-Gen Ian Bruce, DSO, MBE (d 1956); 2 s (Dominick Ian, John Patrick), 2 da (Edith Mary, Lucy Anne); *Career* WWII Lt 2 Bn Scots Guards 1943–47; artist specialising in stained glass; work includes: Coventry Cathedral, Liverpool Met Cathedral, Derby Cathedral, Eton Chapel, Great Hall Christ Church Oxford, Washington DC Episcopalian Cathedral; other works included in private collections; co-fndr Burleighfield and Reyntiens Trust 1967–76; lectured world-wide incl: Canada, USA, Mexico, Paris, Ghent, Calcutta, Delhi, Bombay; memb Panel of Architectural Advsrs to: Westminster Abbey until 1996, Westminster Cathedral, Brompton Oratory; fell Br Soc of Master Glass Painters; *Books* The Beauty of Stained Glass (1990), The Technique of Stained Glass (4 edn 1991); *Style—* Patrick Reyntiens, Esq, OBE; ✉ Ilford Bridges Farm, Close Stocklinch, Ilminster, Somerset (☎ 01460 52241)

RHEAD, David Michael; s of late Harry Bernard Rhead, JP; *b* 12 Feb 1936; *Educ* St Philip's GS Edgbaston; *m* 1958, Rosaleen Loretto, *née* Finnegan; 4 da; *Career* chm LCP Holdings plc 1975–87 (fin dir 1968, dep chm 1973), chm Capital Industries PLC 1991–, chm Benson Group plc 1995–; non-exec dir Brintons Ltd 1995–; chm W Midlands Ambulance NHS Tst 1995–; Freeman: City of London, Worshipful Co of CAs; FCA, CIMgt, FRSA; *Recreations* fishing, golf; *Style—* David Rhead, Esq; ✉ Cherry Trees, 62 Little Sutton Lane, Sutton Coldfield, W Midlands B75 6PE (☎ 0121 308 4762)

RHIND, Prof David William; s of William Rhind (d 1976), and Christina, *née* Abercombie; *b* 29 Nov 1943; *Educ* Berwick GS, Univ of Bristol (BSc), Univ of Edinburgh (PhD), Univ of London (DSc); *m* 27 Aug 1966, Christine, da of William Frank Young, of Berwick-upon-Tweed; 1 s (Jonathan b 1969), 2 da (Samantha b 1972, Zoe b 1979); *Career* res offr Univ of Edinburgh 1968–69, res fell RCA 1969–73, reader (former lectr) Univ of Durham 1973–81, prof of geography Birkbeck Coll Univ of London 1982–91, dir gen and chief exec Ordnance Survey 1992–; visiting fell: Int Trg Centre Netherlands 1975, Aust Nat Univ 1979; author of over 100 tech papers; govr Bournemouth Univ 1995–; hon sec RGS 1988–91, vice pres Int Cartographic Assoc 1984–91; advsr House of Lords Select Ctee Sci of Technol 1984–85, memb Govt Ctee of Enquiry on Handling of Geographic Info 1985–87; Hon DSc: Univ of Bristol 1993, Univ of Loughborough 1996; MIBG, FRGS 1970, FRICS 1991; *Books* Land Use (with R Hudson, 1980), A Census User's Handbook (1983), An Atlas of EEC Affairs (with R Hudson and H Mounsey, 1984), Geographical Information Systems (ed, with D Maguire and M Goodchild, 1991), The New Geography (with J Roper and J Shepherd, 1992); *Style—* Prof David Rhind; ✉ Ordnance Survey, Romsey Road, Maybush, Southampton SO16 4GU (☎ 01703 792000, fax 01703 792660)

RHODES, Anthony John David; s of John Percy Rhodes (d 1985), of Leigh-on-Sea, Essex, and Eileen Daisy, *née* Frith (d 1984); *b* 22 Feb 1948; *Educ* Westcliff GS, Corpus Christi Coll Cambridge (MA); *m* 14 Dec 1974, Elisabeth Marie Agnes Raymonde, da of Lt-Col Pierre Fronteau (ret French Army), of Lisieux, France; 1 s (Christophe b 1978), 1 da (Sophie b 1984); *Career* project mangr Shell International Petroleum Co 1969–73, dep treas Ocean Transport & Trading Ltd 1975–80, md Bank of America International Ltd 1980–95, head syndicated finance Credit Suisse 1995–; *Recreations* opera, classical music, golf, hill walking, philately; *Style—* Anthony Rhodes, Esq; ✉ Credit Suisse, 5

Cabot Square, Canary Wharf, London E14 4QR (☎ 0171 888 8354, fax 888 8391, telex 887322)

RHODES, Sir Basil Edward; CBE (1981, OBE (mil) 1945, MBE (mil) 1944), TD, DL (S Yorks 1975); s of Col Harry Rhodes, TD, of Lane End House, Rotherham, S Yorks, and Astri Alexandra, *née* Natvig (d 1969); *b* 8 Dec 1915; *Educ* St Edward's Sch Oxford; *m* 21 Sept 1962, Joëlle, da of Robert Vilgard; 1 s (Charles Edward Robert Christian); *Career* served WWII: Western Desert, Greece, Crete, Burma (wounded and mentioned in despatches); York and Lancaster Regt Yorks Dragoons and Queen's Own Yeo (Hon Col 1973–81) TA; admitted slr 1946, ptnr Gichard & Co Rotherham 1946–; dir: Carlton Main Brickworks Ltd, Wessex Fare Ltd; pres Sheffield & Dist Law Soc 1983–84; pres Rotherham Cons Assoc, Cons Pty area treas for Yorks 1983–88; Mayor of Rotherham 1970–71, High Sheriff S Yorks 1982–83; *Recreations* field-sports, skiing, gardening; *Clubs* Cavalry and Guards', Sheffield; *Style*— Sir Basil Rhodes, CBE, TD, DL; ✉ Bubnell Hall, Baslow, Derbys (☎ 01246 583266); Gichard & Co, 31/33 Doncaster Gate, Rotherham S65 1DF (☎ 01709 365 531, fax 01709 829 752)

RHODES, Benjamin; s of Dr Brian William Rhodes (d 1994), and Joan, *née* Martin (d 1972); *b* 12 Nov 1952; *Educ* Oundle, Univ of Manchester; *m* 1977, Carol, da of Dr Falk Heinz Kroch (d 1983); 2 s; *Career* opened Benjamin Rhodes Gallery (in partnership with Carol Kroch-Rhodes) July 1985–Aug 1994, opened Jason & Rhodes (with Gillian Jason) 1994–; *Style*— Benjamin Rhodes, Esq; ✉ Jason & Rhodes, 4 New Burlington Place, London W1X 1FB (☎ 0171 434 1768, fax 0171 287 8841)

RHODES, Elvi Yvonne; da of late Thomas Holliday, of Bradford, and Emily Irene, *née* Goldsborough (d 1968); *Educ* Bradford Girls' GS; *m* Harry Rhodes (decd), s of Freddie Rhodes; 2 s (Stephen, Anthony (decd)); *Career* author; admin to Agric Res Unit Univ of Sussex 1967–76, full-time writer 1976–; memb: Soc of Authors 1985, Romantic Novelists Assoc 1986; *Books* Opal, Doctor Rose, Ruth Appleby, Golden Girls, Madeleine (short-listed for Romantic Novel of the Year 1990), House of Bonneau, Cara's Land, Summer Promise, The Rainbow Through The Rain, The Bright One, The Mountain, Church and Village Guide to Rottingdean East Sussex; also author of numerous short stories and articles; *Recreations* reading, listening to music, gardening, travel, dogs; *Clubs* Royal Over-Seas League; *Style*— Mrs Elvi Rhodes; ✉ c/o Mary Irvine, 11 Upland Park Rd, Oxford OX2 7RU (☎ 01865 513570)

RHODES, Gary; step s of John Smellie, of London, and Jean, *née* Ferris; *b* 22 April 1960; *Educ* Howard Sch Gillingham Kent, Thanet Tech Coll (City and Guilds, Chef of the Year, Student of the Year); *m* 7 January 1989, Yolanda Jennifer, da of Harvey Charles Adkins; 2 s (Samuel James b 24 Sept 1988, George Adam b 17 May 1990); *Career* Amsterdam Hilton Hotel 1979–81 (commis de cuisine, chef de partie), sous chef Reform Club Pall Mall 1982–83, head chef Winstons Eating House Feb-Oct 1983, sr sous chef Capital Hotel Knightsbridge 1983–85; head chef: Whitehall Restaurant Essex 1985–86, Castle Hotel Taunton 1986–90, Greenhouse Restaurant Mayfair 1990–96; Gardner Merchant 1996–; temp appts: Lameloise and La Cote St Jacques (Michelin starred restaurants in France); TV work: series BSB 1990, Hot Chefs series (BBC) 1991, Food Wise christmas special 1991, Rhodes Around Britain (series, BBC) 1994, More Rhodes Around Britain (BBC) 1995; runner up: Mumm Champagne Chef of Tomorrow 1978, William Hepinstall award 1979; Michelin star Castle Hotel 1986, finalist Meilleur Ouvrier de Grande Bretagne competition 1987, 30 under 30 award 1988, rep GB at a cooking festival Singapore Hilton Hotel 1989, Michelin star The Greenhouse 1996, Special Award Catey Awards 1996; *Style*— Gary Rhodes, Esq; ✉ c/o Gardner Merchant, Merchant Centre, New Street Square, London EC4 (☎ 0171 353 6211)

RHODES, Sir John Christopher Douglas; 4 Bt (UK 1919), of Hollingworth, Co Palatine of Chester; s of Lt-Col Sir Christopher George Rhodes, 3 Bt (d 1964); *b* 24 May 1946; *Heir* bro, Michael Philip James Rhodes, *qv*; *Style*— Sir John Rhodes, Bt

RHODES, Prof John David; OBE (1992); *b* 9 Oct 1943; *Educ* Univ of Leeds (BSc, PhD, DSc), Univ of Bradford (DEng); *Career* Dept of Electrical and Electronic Engrg Univ of Leeds: res fell 1966–67, lectr 1969–72, reader 1972–75, prof 1975–81, industl prof 1981–; fndr, chm and tech dir Filtronic Components Ltd 1977–; awards incl: Microwave Prize (USA) 1969, Browder J Thompson Award (USA) 1970, Queen's Award for Technological Achievement (UK) 1985, Queen's Award for Export Achievement (UK) 1988; FIEEE 1980, FIEE 1984, FEng 1987; *Publications* Theory of Electrical Filters (1976), author of numerous technical papers; *Style*— Prof John Rhodes, OBE, FEng; ✉ Boodles, Thorpe Lane, Tranmere Park, Guiseley, Leeds LS20 8JH; Department of Electrical and Electronic Engineering, University of Leeds, Leeds LS2 9JT (☎ 0113 243 1751, fax 0113 283 4122)

RHODES, John David McKinnon; s of John I M Rhodes, CMG, of West Sussex, and late Eden Annetta Rhodes; *b* 20 Aug 1950; *Educ* Dulwich Coll, Univ of Sussex (BA), London Business Sch (Sloan prog 1983–84); *m* Sarah Elizabeth; 3 c; *Career* Lithotype Inc 1971–72; DTI: joined 1972, princ private sec to Sec of State for Trade 1981–83, Projects and Exports Policy Div 1984–86, dir Br Trade & Investment Office NY 1987–90, Euro Community and Trade Relations Div (EC single market policy) 1991–94, Electricity and Nuclear Fuels Div 1994–; *Recreations* family, cooking; *Style*— John Rhodes, Esq; ✉ Department of Trade & Industry, 1 Victoria Street, London SW1H 0ET (☎ 0171 215 2890, fax 0171 215 2843)

RHODES, John Guy; s of Canon Cecil Rhodes, of Bury St Edmunds, and Gladys, *née* Farlie; *b* 16 Feb 1945; *Educ* King Edward VI Birmingham, Jesus Coll Cambridge (MA); *m* 11 June 1977, Christie Joan, da of Peter Dorrington Batt, MC, of Bury St Edmunds; 2 s (Alexander Luke b 1979, Nicholas Hugh b 1981); *Career* articled clerk Macfarlanes 1968; admitted slr 1970, ptnr Macfarlanes 1975– (trusts and tax for private clients, both UK and international); *Recreations* woodlands, tennis, skiing; *Clubs* City; *Style*— John Rhodes, Esq; ✉ Macfarlanes, 10 Norwich St, London EC4A 1BD (☎ 0171 831 9222, fax 0171 831 9607)

RHODES, Hon Mrs (Margaret); *née* Elphinstone; da of late 16 Lord Elphinstone, KT, and Lady Mary Bowes-Lyon, DCVO, da of 14 Earl of Strathmore, whereby Mrs Rhodes is first cous of HM The Queen (at whose wedding Mrs Rhodes was a bridesmaid); *b* 9 June 1925; *m* 1950, Denys Gravenor Rhodes (d 1981), er s of Maj Tahu Rhodes, Gren Gds, and Hon Helen (eldest da of 5 Baron Plunket); 2 s, 2 da; *Career* Lady-in-Waiting to Queen Elizabeth The Queen Mother 1991–; *Style*— The Hon Mrs Rhodes; ✉ The Garden House, Windsor Great Park, Windsor, Berks (☎ 01784 434617)

RHODES, Michael Philip James; s of late Lt-Col Sir Christopher Rhodes, 3 Bt (d 1964); hp of bro, Sir John Rhodes, 4 Bt, *qv*; *b* 3 April 1948; *m* 1973, Susan Elizabeth, 2 da of Richard Patrick Roney-Dougal, of South Lodge, Norton, Shifnal, Shropshire; 1 da (Louise b 1974); *Style*— Michael Rhodes Esq; ✉ Southdown, Blakeney, Holt, Norfolk

RHODES, Sir Peregrine Alexander; KCMG (1984, CMG 1976); s of Cyril Edmunds Rhodes (d 1966), and Elizabeth Frances (d 1962); *b* 14 May 1925; *Educ* Winchester, New Coll Oxford (BA); *m* 1, 1951 (m dis), Jane Hassell; 2 s, 1 da; m 2, 1969, Margaret Rosemary, da of Eric Page (d 1979); *Career* Coldstream Gds 1944–47; HM Dip Serv 1950–85: served Rangoon, Vienna, Helsinki and Rome, seconded to Inst for Study of Int Orgn Univ of Sussex 1968–69, chargé d'affaires E Berlin (opening Embassy) 1973–75, under sec Cabinet Office 1975–78, high cmmr Cyprus 1979–82, ambass Greece 1982–85; dir gen Br Property Fedn 1986–93, dir Henry Sotheran Ltd 1994–; chm Anglo Hellenic League 1986–90, vice pres Br Sch Athens 1986–; Liveryman Worshipful Co of Glaziers 1986–; FRSA 1988; *Recreations* photography, reading; *Clubs* Travellers'; *Style*— Sir Peregrine Rhodes, KCMG; ✉ Pond House, Thorpe Morieux, Bury St Edmunds, Suffolk IP30 0NW

RHODES, Prof Peter John; s of George Thomas Rhodes (d 1969), and Elsie Leonora, *née* Pugh; *b* 10 Aug 1940; *Educ* Queen Elizabeth's GS Barnet Herts, Wadham Coll Oxford (minor scholar, MA), Merton Coll Oxford (Harmsworth sr scholar, Craven fell, DPhil); *m* 1971, Jan Teresa, da of John Mervyn Adamson; *Career* Univ of Durham: lectr in classics and ancient history 1965–77, sr lectr 1977–83, prof of ancient history 1983–; jr fell Center for Hellenic Studies Washington DC 1978–79, visiting fell Wolfson Coll Oxford 1984, visiting research fell Univ of New England NSW Australia 1988, memb Inst for Advanced Study Princeton NJ 1988–89; visiting fell Corpus Christi Coll Oxford 1993, Leverhulme research fell 1994–95; FBA 1987; *Books* The Athenian Boule (1972), Commentary on the Aristotelian Athenaion Politeia (1981), Aristotle: The Athenian Constitution (1984), The Greek City States (1986), Thucydides II (1988), Thucydides III (1994); also author of various articles and reviews in learned jls; *Recreations* music, travel, typography; *Style*— Prof P J Rhodes; ✉ Department of Classics, University of Durham, 38 North Bailey, Durham DH1 3EU (☎ 0191 374 2073, fax 0191 374 7338)

RHODES, Prof Philip; s of Sydney Rhodes (d 1962), of Sheffield, and Harriett May, *née* Denniff (d 1981); *b* 2 May 1922; *Educ* King Edward VII Sch Sheffield, Clare Coll Cambridge (BA, MA), St Thomas' Hosp Med Sch (MB BChir); *m* 26 Oct 1946, Mary Elizabeth, da of Rev John Kenneth Worley, MC (d 1957), of Barrowden, Rutland; 3 s (Richard, David, Kenneth), 2 da (Susan (Mrs Lutwyche), Frances (Mrs Marshall)); *Career* Maj RAMC 1949–51; St Thomas' Hosp: obstetric physician 1958–64, prof of gynaecology 1964–74, dean Med Sch 1968–74; dean Faculty of Med Univ of Adelaide S Aust 1974–77, postgrad dean of med Univ of Newcastle upon Tyne 1977–80, postgrad dean and prof of postgrad med educn Univ of Southampton 1980–87; Brontë Soc prize 1972; chm Educn Ctee King Edward's Hosp Fund for London, memb Gen Med Cncl 1979–89; FRCS, FRCOG, FRACMA, FFOM, FRSA; *Books* Fluid Balance in Obstetrics (1960), An Introduction to Gynaecology and Obstetrics (1967), Woman: A Biological Study (1969), Reproductive Physiology for Medical Students (1969), The Value of Medicine (1976), Doctor John Leake's Hospital (1977), Letters to a Young Doctor (1983), An Outline History of Medicine (1985), Wakerley: A Village in E Northamptonshire (1994), A Short History of Clinical Midwifery (1995), Gynaecology for Everywoman (1996); *Recreations* writing, reading; *Style*— Prof Philip Rhodes; ✉ 1 Wakerley Court, Wakerley, Oakham, Leicester, LE15 8PA (☎ 01572 747871)

RHODES, Philip John; s of late (Osmond) Cyril Rhodes, of Lincoln, and Dorothy, *née* Ibbetson; *b* 23 Aug 1937; *Educ* City Sch Lincoln; *m* 11 Sept 1965, Madeleine Ann, da of Samuel Edward Blaza, of Waltham, Lincs; 2 da (Jane b 1966, Judith b 1969); *Career* Nat Serv Sherwood Foresters 1956, Intelligence Corps 1957; dep gen mangr General Accident plc 1991–; pres: Perth C of C 1982–83, The Insurance Inst of London 1992, The Chartered Insurance Inst 1995; Freeman City of London, Liveryman Worshipful Co of Insurers 1988; ACII; *Recreations* music, flying, golf, tennis; *Clubs* Royal Cwlth Soc; *Style*— Philip Rhodes, Esq; ✉ General Accident plc, Becket House, 87 Cheapside, London EC2V 6AY (☎ 0171 606 1030, fax 0171 726 2884)

RHODES, Richard David Walton; JP (Fylde 1978); s of Harry Walton Rhodes (d 1966), of Preston, Lancs, and Dorothy Fairhurst (d 1986); *b* 20 April 1942; *Educ* Rossall Sch Fleetwood, St John's Coll Durham (BA), Hertford Coll (Dip Ed); *m* 11 Aug 1966, Stephanie, da of Frederic William Heyes (d 1978), of Preston, Lancs; 2 da (Deborah b 1968, Victoria b 1971); *Career* asst master St John's Sch Leatherhead 1964–75; headmaster: Arnold Sch Blackpool 1979–87 (dep headmaster 1975–79), Rossall Sch Fleetwood 1987–; chm: NW Div HMC 1987, Northern ISIS 1993–95; memb: Social Services Advsy Ctee Lancs CC 1992–, Lancs Magistrates' Courts Ctee 1993–95; govr Terra Nova Sch Jodrell Bank 1989–; *Recreations* sports, photography, public speaking, gardening; *Clubs* East India, Devonshire, Sports and Public Schs; *Style*— Richard Rhodes, Esq; ✉ The Hall, Rossall Sch, Fleetwood, Lancs FY7 8JW (☎ 01253 774201, fax 01253 772052)

RHODES, Robert Elliott; QC (1989); s of Gilbert Gedalia Rhodes (d 1970), of London, and Elly Brook; *b* 2 Aug 1945; *Educ* St Paul's, Pembroke Coll Oxford (MA); *m* 16 March 1971 (m dis 1996), Georgina Caroline, da of Jack Gerald Clarfelt, of Timsbury, Hants; 2 s (Matthew b 1973, James b 1975), 1 da (Emily b 1983); *Career* called to Bar Inner Temple 1968; first prosecuting counsel to Inland Revenue at Central Criminal Ct and Inner London Crown Cts 1981 (second prosecuting counsel 1979), recorder of the Crown Ct 1987, dep chm IMRO Membership Tbnl Panel 1992; *Recreations* reading, listening to opera, watching cricket, playing real tennis; *Clubs* MCC, Épée, Annabel's; *Style*— Robert Rhodes, Esq, QC; ✉ Littleton Buildings, 3 King's Bench Walk North, Temple, London EC4Y 7HR (☎ 0171 797 8600, fax 0171 797 8699)

RHODES, Prof Roderick Arthur William; s of Keith Firth Rhodes, and Irene, *née* Clegg; *b* 15 Aug 1944; *Educ* Fulneck Boys' Sch, Univ of Bradford (BSc), St Catherine's Coll Oxford (BLitt), Univ of Essex (PhD); *m* 2 Dec 1978, Cynthia Margaret, da of John Marshall; 1 s (Edward Roderick b 25 June 1979), 1 da (Bethan Margaret b 30 Oct 1981); *Career* Univ of Birmingham 1970–76, Univ of Strathclyde 1976–79, Univ of Essex 1979–89, prof of politics and head of Dept Univ of York 1989–94, prof of politics Univ of Newcastle upon Tyne 1994–; chm Public Admin Ctee Jt Univ Cncl for Social and Public Admin; memb Political Studies Assoc of UK, res dir ESRC Whitehall Res Prog, chair Local Governance Steering Ctee of ESRC; *Books* Control and Power in Central-Local Government Relations (1979), The National World of Local Government (1986), Beyond Westminster and Whitehall (1988), Policy Networks in British Government (ed with D Marsh, 1992), Prime Minister, Cabinet and Core Executive (ed with P Dunleavy, 1995), Understanding Governance (1996); ed Public Admin 1986–; *Style*— Prof Roderick Rhodes; ✉ Department of Politics, University of Newcastle, Newcastle upon Tyne NE1 7RU (☎ 0191 222 8823, fax 0191 222 5069)

RHODES, Steven John; s of William Rhodes, and Norma, *née* Roberts; *b* 17 June 1964; *Educ* Carlton-Bolling Comp Sch Bradford; *m* 1993, Judy March; 2 da (Holly Jade, Lily Amber), 1 s (George Harry); *Career* professional cricketer; Yorkshire CCC 1981–84; Worcestershire CCC: debut 1985, awarded county cap 1986, currently vice capt, winners NatWest Trophy 1994; England: 6 one day ints, memb A tours to Sri Lanka 1986, Zimbabwe 1989–90, Pakistan 1990–91 and W Indies 1992, selected for cancelled full tour to India 1988–89, A tour to S Africa 1993–94, Ashes tour Australia 1994; holds record for dismissals (29) in Sunday League season; columnist Birmingham Sporting Argus 1989–; *Recreations* tropical fish, golf, rugby league; *Style*— Steven Rhodes, Esq; ✉ Worcestershire CCC, County Ground, New Rd, Worcester WR2 4QQ (☎ 01905 422694)

RHODES, Zandra Lindsey; da of Albert James Rhodes (d 1988), of Chatham, Kent, and Beatrice Ellen, *née* Twigg (d 1968), fitter at Worth, Paris; *b* 19 Sept 1940; *Educ* Medway Technical Sch for Girls Chatham, Medway Coll of Art Rochester Kent, Royal Coll of Art (DesRCA); *Career* started career as textile designer 1964, set up print factory and studio with Alexander McIntyre 1965, transferred to fashion indust 1966, ptnrship with Sylvia Ayton producing dresses using own prints, opened Fulham Rd clothes shop (fndr ptnr and designer) 1967–68, first solo collection US 1969 (met with phenomenal response from Vogue and Women's Wear Daily), thereafter established as foremost influential designer (developed unique use of printed fabrics and treatment of jersey), prodr annual spectacular fantasy shows USA; fndr (with Anne Knight and Ronnie Stirling): Zandra Rhodes (UK) Ltd, Zandra Rhodes Shops 1975–86; md ZLR Ltd (formerly Zandra Rhodes Shops); first shop London 1975 (others opened in Bloomingdales NY and Marshall Field Chicago), shops and licencees now worldwide;

Zandra Rhodes designs currently incl: interior furnishing, sheets and pillowcases, sarees, jewellry, rugs, kitchen accessories, fine china figurines; launched fine arts and prints collections Dyanssen Galleries USA 1989; solo exhibitions incl: Texas Gallery Houston 1981, La Jolla Museum of Contemporary Art San Diego 1982, Barbican Centre 1982, Parson's Sch of Design NY 1982, Art Museum of Santa Cruz Co California 1983; work represented in numerous permanent costume collections incl: V & A, City Museum & Art Gallery Stoke-on-Trent, Royal Pavilion Brighton Museum, City Art Gallery Leeds, Met Museum NY, Museum of Applied Arts & Scis Sydney, Nat Museum of Victoria Melbourne; acknowledged spokeswoman and personality of 60s and 70s (famous for green and later pink coloured hair), frequent speaker on fashion and design, subject of numerous documentaries and films; Designer of the Year English Fashion Trade UK 1972, Emmy Award for Best Costume Design Romeo and Juliet on Ice CBS TV 1984, Best Show of the Year New Orleans 1985, Woman of Distinction Award Northwood Inst Dallas Texas 1986, Lifetime Achievement Award (Hall of Fame) Br Fashion Awards 1995; key to City of Miami and City of California; Hon DFA Int Fine Arts Coll Miami, Hon Dr RCA, Hon DD Cncl for Nat Acad Awards 1987; RDI 1977, FSIAD 1982; *Books* The Art of Zandra Rhodes (1984, US edn 1985); *Recreations* gardening, travelling, drawing, watercolours; *Style—* Miss Zandra Rhodes; ✉ 85 Richford Street, London W6 7HJ (☎ 0181 749 3216)

RHODES JAMES, Sir Robert Vidal; kt (1991), DL (1993 Cambs); s of Col William Rhodes James, OBE, MC (d 1972), Indian Army; *b* 10 April 1933; *Educ* Sedbergh, Worcester Coll Oxford; *m* 1956, Angela Margaret, eld da of late Ronald Robertson; 4 da; *Career* clerk House of Commons 1955–64, fell All Souls Coll Oxford 1964–68, dir Inst for Study of Int Orgn Univ of Sussex 1968–73, PA to UN Sec-Gen 1973–76; MP (C) Cambridge 1976–92; PPS FCO 1979–82, Cons liaison offr for Higher Educn 1979–87, vice chm Home Affrs and Constitutional Ctees; chm History of Parliament Tst 1983–93, memb Chairman's Panel of House of Commons 1987–92, pres Cons Friends of Israel 1995– (chm 1988–95); Hon DLitt Westminster Coll Fulton Missouri 1986, Hon MA Univ of Cambridge 1994; FRSL, FRHistS; *Books* Lord Randolph Churchill (1959), An Introduction to the House of Commons (1961), Rosebery (1963), Gallipoli (1965), Chips: The Diaries of Sir Henry Channon (1967), JCC Davidson: Memoirs of a Conservative (1968), Churchill, A Study in Failure 1900–1939 (1970), Ambitions and Realities (1972), The Complete Speeches of Sir Winston Churchill (eight volumes, 1974), Victor Cazalet, A Portrait (1975), The British Revolution 1880–1939 (two volumes, 1976, 1977), Albert, Prince Consort (1983), Anthony Eden (1986), Bob Boothby, A Portrait (1991), Henry Wellcome - A Biography (1994); *Recreations* sailing; *Clubs* Travellers, Grillions; *Style—* Sir Robert Rhodes James, DL, FRSL; ✉ The Stone House, Great Gransden, nr Sandy, Beds SG19 3AF

RHYS, Lady Anne Maud; *née* Wellesley; da of 5 Duke of Wellington, and Hon Lilian Coats, da of 1 Baron Glentanar; *b* 2 Feb 1910; *m* 1933 (m dis 1963), Hon David Reginald Rhys (d 1991), 3 s of 7 Baron Dynevor; 1 s, 1 da; *Career* inherited Duchy (Sp) of Ciudad Rodrigo and Grandeeship of 1 Class on death of her bro, 6 Duke, 1943, but ceded them to unc, 7 Duke, 1949; *Style—* The Lady Anne Rhys; ✉ Le Bourg, Rue de Tertrie, Castel Parish, Guernsey

RHYS, Prof (David) Garel; OBE (1989); s of Emyr Lewys Rhys, and Edith Phyllis, *née* Williams; *b* 28 Feb 1940; *Educ* Ystalyfera GS, Univ of Swansea (BA), Univ of Birmingham (MCom); *m* (Charlotte) Mavis, da of Edward Colston Walters; 1 s (Jeremy Charles), 2 da (Angela Jayne, Gillian Mary); *Career* lectr Univ of Hull 1967–70 (asst lectr 1965–67); Univ Coll Cardiff 1970–87: lectr, sr lectr, prof; prof Cardiff Business Sch Univ of Wales 1987–; advsr to: select ctees House of Commons, Nat Audit Office; conslt to govt depts; memb Bd Welsh Devpt Agency 1994–; FITA 1987, FIMI 1989; *Books* The Motor Industry: An Economic Survey (1971), The Motor Industry in the European Community (1989); *Recreations* walking, gardening,; *Clubs* RAC; *Style—* Prof Garel Rhys, OBE; ✉ Cardiff Business School, University of Wales, Aberconway Building, Colum Drive, Cardiff CF1 3EU (☎ 01222 874281, fax 01222 874419)

RHYS, (William Joseph) St Ervyl-Glyndwr; s of Edward John Rhys (d 1955), and Rachel, *née* Thomas (d 1986); *b* 6 July 1924; *Educ* Newport HS, Univ of Wales, Guy's Hosp Univ of London, St John's Coll Cambridge (MA, MB BS); *m* 1961, Dr Ann Rees; 6 da (Rhian b 1962, Catrin b 1964, Mared b 1966, Ceril b 1969, Ffion b 1973, Mirain b 1980), 1 s (Rob b 1981); *Career* Nat Serv Sqdn Ldr RAF Inst Aviation Med & Empire Test Pilot Sch; house surgn and registrar appts: Guy's Hosp 1948, Addenbrooke's Hosp 1949, Royal Postgraduate Med Sch Univ of London 1953, Univ of Wales Coll of Med 1956; conslt gynaecologist Welsh Hosp Bd 1962, MOH Cardiganshire 1966–74, conslt physician in community med Dyfed 1974–82, hon med advsr Welsh Nat Water Devpt Authy 1966–82, hon chm f med servs Royal Nat Eisteddfod of Wales 1976, 1984 and 1992, Univ of Camb rep on Cncl and Ct of Govrs Univ Coll Wales 1979–86, chm of tstees St John's Coll Dyfed 1987–96 (memb 1979–); High Sheriff Co of Dyfed 1979–80; cmmr St John Ambulance Bde Ceredigion 1982–89, pres Scout Assoc Ceredigion 1983–, chm Hospitallers' Club Dyfed 1983–; memb: Exec Ctee Assoc of Friends of Nat Library of Wales 1984–, Governing Body Ceredigion Schs memb 1985– (chm 1987–91); tstee The Two Red Dragons Educn Tst (promotes Japan studies in Europe) 1988–; hon memb (White Robe) Gorsedd of Bards of Wales; Lord of the Barony of Llawhaden, Lord of the Manor of Llanfynydd (Celtic, pre-Norman), Freeman City of London, Liveryman Worshipful Soc of Apothecaries; MRCOG, MFCM; CStJ; *Recreations* medical history, genealogical research, local history, walking; *Clubs* RAF; *Style—* St Ervyl-Glyndwr Rhys, Esq; ✉ Plas Bronmeurig, Ystrad Meurig, Ceredigion (☎ 01974 831650); Minffordd, Llangadog, Dyfed

RHYS EVANS, Peter Howell; s of Gwilym Rhys Evans, MC, of Rickledown, Durham, and Jean Marjorie, *née* Foord; *b* 17 May 1948; *Educ* Ampleforth, Bart's (MB BS, Cricket and Rugby colours), Univ of Paris, Gustave-Roussy Inst (DCC); *m* 6 Jan 1973 (m dis), Irene Mossop; 2 s (Matthew b 1 Feb 1976, Marc b 2 May 1980), 1 da (Melissa b 2 March 1984); m 2, 30 Sept 1994, Frances Knight; 1 da (Olivia Frances b 5 April 1996); *Career* qualified Bart's 1971, sr house offr plastic surgery Hull Royal Infirmary 1975, The Royal Nat Throat Nose and Ear Hosp London 1975–79, sr ENT registrar Queen Elizabeth Hosp Birmingham 1979–80, conslt and sr lectr ENT surgery Univ of Birmingham 1981–84, conslt ENT surgn Queen Elizabeth Hosp Birmingham 1984–86, conslt ENT and head neck surgn The Royal Marsden Hosp 1986–; hon civilian conslt ENT surgn to the RN 1991–; visiting conslt ENT surgn St Bernard's Hosp Gibraltar; examiner RCS 1986–, fndr memb Euro Acad of Facial Surgeons 1978 (vice pres 1987), memb Nat Cncl Otolaryngological Res Soc 1984–88, memb Cncl RSM 1991–; asst ed Journal of Laryngology & Otology 1986–; Freeman City of London 1990, Freeman Worshipful Soc of Apothecaries; hon ENT surgn: St Mary's Hosp, King Edward VII Hosp for Officers; hon sr lectr Univ of London; MRCS 1971, LRCP, FRSM, FRCS 1978, memb BMA; *Publications* Cancer of Head and Neck (ed, 1983), Face and Neck Surgical Techniques - Problems and Limitations (ed, 1983), Facial Plastic Surgery - Otoplasty (guest ed, 1985), contrib to med jls and books on head and neck cancer and aquatic ape theory; *Recreations* skiing, golf, tennis, anthropology; *Style—* Peter Rhys Evans, Esq; ✉ 44 Settrington Road, London SW6 3BA (☎ 0171 731 8115); 106 Harley St, London W1N 1AF; The Royal Marsden Hospital, Fulham Rd, London SW3 6JJ (☎ 0171 935 3525, 0171 352 8171 ext 2730 and 2731, fax 0171 351 3785)

RHYS JONES, Griffith (Griff); s of Elwyn Rhys Jones, and Gwyneth Margaret Jones; *b* 16 Nov 1953; *Educ* Brentwood Sch, Emmanuel Coll Cambridge (MA); *m* 21 Nov 1981, Joanna Frances, da of Alexander James Harris; 1 s (George Alexander b 1985), 1 da (Catherine Louisa b 1987); *Career* actor and writer; BBC radio prodr 1976–79; columnist for The Times 1989–90; dir: Talkback, Smith Jones Brown & Cassie; *Theatre* Charley's Aunt 1983, Trumpets and Raspberries 1985, The Alchemist 1986, Arturo Ui 1987, Thark 1989–90, Wind in the Willows 1990–91, The Revengers' Comedies 1991, An Absolute Turkey 1994; dir Twelfth Night RSC 1989; *Opera* Die Fledermaus 1989; *Television* comedy series incl: Not The Nine O'Clock News 1979–82, Alas Smith and Jones 1984–, The World According to Smith and Jones 1986–87, Small Doses 1989, Smith and Jones 1991–; co-presenter Comic Relief (BBC), presenter Bookworm; plays incl: A View of Harry Clarke 1989, Ex (Screen One) 1991, Demob 1993; *Films* Morons From Outer Space 1985, Wilt 1989; *Records* Bitter & Twisted, Scratch 'n' sniff, Alas Smith & Jones, Not the Nine O'Clock News; *Awards* Emmy Award for Alas Smith & Jones, Br Comedy Top Entertainment Series Award for Smith & Jones 1991, Br Comedy Top Entertainment Performer (with Mel Smith) for Smith & Jones 1991, Olivier Award for Best Comedy Performance for Absolute Turkey 1994; *Books* The Lavishly Tooled Smith and Jones (1986), Janet Lives with Mel and Griff (1988), Smith and Jones Head to Head (1992); *Clubs* Groucho; *Style—* Griff Rhys Jones, Esq; ✉ Talkback, 36 Percy Street, London W1P 0LN (☎ 0171 631 3940, fax 0171 637 5105)

RHYS WILLIAMS, Sir (Arthur) Gareth Ludovic Emrys; 3 Bt (UK 1918), of Miskin, Parish of Llantrisant, Co Glamorgan; s of Sir Brandon Rhys Williams, 2 Bt, MP (d 1988), and Caroline Susan, eldest da of Ludovic Anthony Foster (d 1990), of Greatham Manor, Pulborough, Sussex; *b* 9 Nov 1961; *Educ* Eton, Univ of Durham, INSEAD; *m* 14 Sept 1996, Harriet, da of Maj Tom Codnor, of Glos; *Heir* none; *Career* md: NFI Electronics Isle of Wight 1990–93, Rexam 1992–93, Rexam Custom Europe 1994–; CEng, MIEE, MIMechE; *Recreations* Bow Group, target shooting, TA, conjuring, travel; *Clubs* Brooks's, Garrick; *Style—* Sir Gareth Rhys Williams, Bt; ✉ Gadairwen, Groes Faen, Mid Glamorgan; 32 Rawlings St, London SW3 2LT (☎ 0171 584 0636)

RIBBANDS, Mark Jonathan; s of Henry Stephen Ribbands, of Hornchurch, and Christina Ivy, *née* Saggers (d 1984); *b* 6 Jan 1959; *Educ* Forest Sch Snaresbrook, NE London Poly (BSc); *m* 30 May 1987, Maya, da of Flt Offr Wassoudeve Goriah, DFC (d 1969); 1 s (Adam b 27 Sept 1993); *Career* md Ribbands Explosives Ltd 1982–; involved with: explosives disposal, demolition, dealing in arms, ammunition and explosives, supply of explosive ordnance disposal personnel worldwide; memb Cncl Inst of Explosives Engrs 1988 and 1992–; FGS 1983, FRGS 1983, MIExpE 1985; *Recreations* scuba diving, flying (helicopters), motorcycling, shooting, playing with fire; *Style—* Mark Ribbands, Esq; ✉ Dyson's Farm, Long Row, Tibenham, Norfolk NR16 1PD (☎ 01379 674444, fax 01379 674213, e-mail 100437.3132@compuserve.com, internet http://www.ribbands.co.uk)

RIBBANS, William; s of Maurice Arthur Ribbans, MBE, of Alcester, Warwickshire, and Sheila Beryl, *née* Brightwell; *b* 28 Nov 1954; *Educ* Northampon GS for Boys, Royal Free Hosp Sch of Med, Univ of London (BSc, MB BS), Univ of Liverpool (MChOrth); *m* 10 Sept 1983, Siân Elizabeth, da of Phillip Noel Williams; 3 da (Rebecca Elizabeth b 3 Feb 1985, Hannah Alexandra b 31 Dec 1988, Abigail Victoria b 4 May 1992); *Career* house surgn and physician Royal Free Hosp London 1980–81; SHO: in orthopaedics and casualty Luton and Dunstable Hosp 1981–82, in gen surgery Northwick Park Hosp Harrow 1982–84; radiology registrar St Mary's Paddington 1984–85; orthopaedic registrar: Wexham Park Slough 1985–86, Northwick Park Hosp Harrow 1986–87; orthopaedic clinical fell Harvard Univ 1987–88; orthopaedic sr registrar: Central Middx Hosp 1988–89, Middx and UC Hosps 1989–90; orthopaedic fell Sheffield Children's Hosp 1990, conslt in orthopaedic surgery (with special interests in sports injuries, post-traumatic limb reconstruction and surgery for the haemophilic patient) Royal Free Hosp, reader in surgery Univ of London 1991–95 and Northampton General Hosp 1996–; FRCSEd 1985, FRCSOrth 1990, FBOA 1991; *Recreations* sports (especially rugby and athletics), antiques, philately; *Clubs* Old Northamptonians RFC; *Style—* William J Ribbans, Esq; ✉ Chartlands, Cherry Tree Lane, Great Houghton, Northants NN4 7AT; Department of Orthopaedic Surgery, Northampton General Hospital, Cliftonville, Northampton NN1 5BD (☎ 01604 235943)

RICE, Anneka; da of John Rice; *b* 4 Oct 1958; *Educ* St Michael's Sch Limpsfield Surrey, Croydon HS for Girls; *m* 5 Aug 1988, Nicholas David Allott, s of Brig David Allott (d 1969); 2 s (Thomas Alexander David b 17 Jan 1989, Joshua James b 20 June 1990); *Career* journalist and broadcaster; principal series: CBTV 1982–85, Treasure Hunt 1983–88, Wish You Were Here 1984–91, TV-am 1985–86, Sporting Chance 1984–85, Challenge Anneka 1989–94, Holiday '92, Play it Safe, Passport 1992–93, Capital Woman (Carlton) 1993–94; numerous guest appearances on radio and TV; patron Romanian Challenge Appeal; Cncl memb: WWF, Nat Cncl of Women, Parents for Safe Food, Nat Playbus Assoc; pres Cowbridge Male Voice Choir; *Books* The Adventure Series: Scuba-Diving, Skiing, Sailing; *Recreations* tennis, swimming; *Style—* Miss Anneka Rice; ✉ c/o Run Riot Ltd, 140 Wardour Street, London W1V 4LJ (☎ 0171 734 8002, fax 0171 734 2414)

RICE, Maj-Gen Sir Desmond Hind Garrett; KCVO (1989, CVO 1985), CBE (1976, OBE 1970); s of Arthur Garrett Rice (d 1948), of Battle, Sussex; *b* 1 Dec 1924; *Educ* Marlborough; *m* 1954, Denise Anne, da of Stanley Ravenscroft (d 1956), of Budleigh Salterton, Devon; 1 da; *Career* served in: Italy, Egypt, Libya, Germany, W Berlin; Vice Adj Gen 1978–79, Maj-Gen, Col 1 The Queen's Dragoon Gds 1980–86; Extra Gentleman Usher to Hm the Queen 1989–; sec The Central Chancery of The Orders of Knighthood 1980–89; *Recreations* field sports, gardening; *Clubs* Cavalry and Guards'; *Style—* Maj-Gen Sir Desmond Rice, KCVO, CBE; ✉ Fairway, Malacca Farm, W Clandon, Guildford, Surrey GU4 7UQ (☎ 01483 222677)

RICE, His Hon Judge Gordon Kenneth; s of Victor Rice (d 1947); *b* 16 April 1927; *Educ* BNC Oxford; *m* 1967, Patricia Margaret; *Career* called to the Bar Middle Temple 1957, circuit judge (SE Circuit) 1980–; *Style—* His Hon Judge Gordon Rice; ✉ 83 Beach Ave, Leigh-On-Sea, Essex (☎ 01702 73485); Southend County Court, Tylers House, Tylers Avenue, Southend-on-Sea, Essex SS1 2AW

RICE, Janet; da of George Robert Whinham (d 1992), of Amble, Northumberland, and Ella, *née* Grey (d 1972); *b* 14 Dec 1949; *Educ* Duchess's County GS for Girls Alnwick Northumberland, City of Leeds & Carnegie Coll of Educn (Cert Ed); *m* 7 Aug 1971, Martin Graham Rice, s of Alfred Victor Rice; *Career* pensions asst Clarke Chapman-John Thompson Ltd 1972–74, clerical offr DHSS 1974; British Gas: pensions asst northern region 1974–78, pensions offr HQ 1978–85, asst pensions admin mangr 1985–86, pensions admin mangr 1986–89, mangr Pensions and Int Benefits 1989–96, head of pensions 1996–; fell Pensions Management Inst 1993 (assoc 1979), memb Int Employee Benefits Assoc 1994; *Recreations* walking, gardening, reading, music; *Style—* Mrs Janet Rice; ✉ British Gas plc, Rivermill House, 152 Grosvenor Rd, London SW1V 3JL (☎ 0171 611 2355, fax 0171 611 2591)

RICE, Ladislas Oscar; *b* 20 Jan 1926; *Educ* Reading Sch, LSE (BSc), Harvard Grad Sch of Business Admin (MBA); *children* 1 s (Sebastian b 1970), 1 da (Valentina b 1973); *Career* W H Smith & Son Ltd 1951–53, sr ptnr Urwick Orr & Partners 1953–66, md Minerals Separation 1966–69, chm Burton Group plc 1969–80 (dep chm 1980–93); current directorships incl: Huntingdon International Holdings plc, Stanley Gibbons Holdings plc, Fndn for Mgmnt Educn, Sovereign High Yield Investment Co NV, Scudder New Europe Fund Inc, Venezuela High Income Fund NV; memb Cncl: CBI 1972–79, RSA 1977–82; memb Fin Ctee Nat Tst 1980–88; vice chm E Anglian RHA 1987–93, dir

Whittington Hosp NHS Tst; CIMgt, FIMC; *Recreations* travel, books, pictures; *Clubs* Brooks's, Harvard (New York City); *Style*— Ladislas Rice, Esq; ✉ 19 Redington Rd, London NW3 (☎ 0171 435 8095); La Casa di Cacchiano, Monti in Chianti, Siena, Italy

RICE, Michael Penarthur Merrick; s of Arthur Vincent Rice (d 1969), of Penarth, Glam, and Dora Kathleen, *née* Blacklock (d 1980); *b* 21 May 1928; *Educ* Challoner Sch; *Career* Nat Serv Royal Norfolk Regt 1946–48; chm Michael Rice Group Ltd 1955–, dir Eastern England TV Ltd 1969–83; hon sec The Bahrain-Br Fndn 1990–; conslt: Govts of Egypt, Jamaica, and Oman, and also Carreras-Rothmans Ltd 1956–75, Govt of Bahrain 1963–, Saudi Arabia 1974–: chm The PR Consultants' Assoc 1978–81; The Aga Khan Award for Architecture 1980; museum planning and design for: Qatar Nat Museum, The Museum of Archaeology and Ethnography Riyadh Saudi Arabia, 6 prov museums in Saudi Arabia, Oman National Museum, The Museum of the Sultan's Armed Forces Oman, Qasr al-Masmak Riyadh Saudi Arabia; co-fndr The PR Conslts' Assoc (hon memb 1985), tstee The Soc for Arabian Studies; memb Advsy Bd The Inst of Archaeology; FIPR 1975, FRSA 1987; *Books* Dilmun Discovered The First Hundred Years of the Archaeology of Bahrain (1984), The Temple Complex at Barbar Bahrain (1983), Search for the Paradise Land: the Archaeology of Bahrain and the Arabian Gulf (1985), Bahrain Through the Ages: The Archaeology (ed, 1985), The Excavations at Al-Hajjar Bahrain (1988), Egypt's Making (1990), The Archaeology of the Arabian Gulf (1993), Bahrain Through The Ages: The History (ed, 1993), False Inheritance - Israel in Palestine (1994), The Power of the Bull, Egypt's Legacy - The Archetypes of Western Civilisation; *Recreations* collecting English watercolours, antiquarian books and early Egyptian artefacts, embellishing a garden, the opera and listening to music; *Clubs* Athenaeum; *Style*— Michael Rice, Esq; ✉ Odsey House, Odsey, nr Baldock, Herts SG7 6SD (☎ 01462 742706, fax 01462 742395); The Glassmill, 1 Battersea Bridge Rd, London SW11 3BG (☎ 0171 223 3431, fax 0171 228 4229)

RICE, Olwen Mary; da of James Anthony Rice, of Rugeley, Staffs, and Mary, *née* Wood; *b* 2 Aug 1960; *Educ* Hagley Park Sch Rugeley Staffs, London Coll of Printing (HND, NCTJDip); *m* 16 Nov 1990, Andrew Tilley, s of Raymond Tilley, of Tettenhall, Wolverhampton; 1 da (Grace b 27 June 1995); *Career* rep Oxford Mail 1980–84, news ed Fitness Magazine 1984–85, health and beauty ed Chat Magazine 1985–87, dep ed Best Magazine 1987–88, ed Living Magazine 1988–93, ed Woman's Weekly 1993–; *Recreations* sport, reading, writing; *Style*— Ms Olwen Rice; ✉ Woman's Weekly, Kings Reach Tower, Stamford Street, London SE1

RICE, Peter Anthony; s of John Daniel Rice (d 1981), of Newry, Co Down, NI, and Brigid Tina, *née* McVerry (d 1990); *b* 25 June 1950; *Educ* Abbey GS Newry, Univ of Lancaster (BA); *Career* ptnr Wood Mackenzie & Co 1981– (joined 1974), dir Hill Samuel & Co 1986–87, gp corp fin and planning mangr Commercial Union Assurance plc 1988–92, UK divnl dir Commercial Union 1992–; non-exec dir Lloyd Thompson plc 1990–94; chm Edinburgh Central Cons Assoc 1977–79, fndr chm Scot Bow Group 1980–82; MSI (memb Stock Exchange 1981), FIA 1974; *Style*— Peter Rice, Esq; ✉ The Old Rectory, 6 Redington Rd, Hampstead, London NW3 7RG (☎ 0171 431 3176); Commercial Union, St Helens, Undershaft, London EC3P 2DQ (☎ 0171 283 7500)

RICE, Sir Timothy Miles Bindon (Tim); kt (1994); s of Hugh Gordon Rice (d 1988), and Joan Odette, *née* Bawden; *b* 10 Nov 1944; *Educ* Lancing, La Sorbonne; *m* 1974, Jane, da of Col A H McIntosh, OBE (d 1979); 1 da (Eva Jane Florence), 1 s (Donald Alexander Hugh); *Career* writer and broadcaster; lyricist for stage shows: Joseph and the Amazing Technicolour Dreamcoat (music by Andrew Lloyd Webber) 1968, Jesus Christ Superstar (music by ALW) 1970, Evita (music by ALW) 1976, Blondel (music by Stephen Oliver) 1983, Chess (music by Bjorn Ulvaeus and Benny Andersson) 1984, Cricket (music by ALW) 1986, Starmania/Tycoon (music by Michel Berger) 1991, some lyrics for Beauty and the Beast (music by Alan Menken) 1994, Heathcliff (music by John Farrar) 1996, King David (music by Alan Menken) 1997; lyrics for Disney animated film musicals: Aladdin (music by Alan Menken) 1992, The Lion King (music by Elton John) 1993; major songs incl: Don't Cry For Me Argentina, A Whole New World, The World is Stone, One Night in Bangkok, I Know Him So Well, Superstar, Any Dream Will Do, I Don't Know How To Love Him, Can You Feel The Love Tonight?, Circle of Life, All Time High; awarded many gold and platinum discs, 11 Ivor Novello awards, 2 Tony awards, 5 Grammys, Golden Globe and Oscar for A Whole New World (from Aladdin) 1993, Golden Globe and Oscar for Can You Feel The Love Tonight? (from The Lion King) 1995; co-fndr: Pavilion Books, GRRR Books; chm Stars Organisation for Spastics 1983–85, pres Lord's Taverners 1988–90, chm Fndn for Sport and the Arts 1991–; *Publications incl* Guinness Book of British Hit Singles (10 vols) and many related books, Evita (1978), Treasures of Lord's (1989); *Recreations* cricket, history of popular music; *Clubs* MCC (memb Ctee 1991–94 and 1995–), Garrick, Saints & Sinners (chm 1990–91), Groucho, Dramatists', Fonograf (Budapest); *Style*— Sir Tim Rice

RICE EDWARDS, (John) Martin; s of James Trevor Rice Edwards (d 1984), and Edith Anne, *née* Gower (d 1990); *b* 25 Feb 1934; *Educ* Charterhouse, Wadham Coll Oxford (MA), Radcliffe Infirmary Oxford (BM BCh); *m* Minette, da of Reginald Harding; 3 s (Sam b 1975, Sebastian b 1977, Hallam b 1981); *Career* Radcliffe Infirmary Oxford: house surgn and house physician 1960, sr house offr then registrar Dept of Neurosurgery 1965; sr registrar in neurosurgery Nat Hosp for Nervous Diseases currently conslt neurosurgeon Chelsea and Westminster Hosp and NW Thames Regnl Neurosciences Centre Charing Cross Hosp London; memb Cncl Soc of Br Neurosurgeons; memb: Royal Med Soc, Georgian Gp; FRCS; *Books* Topical Reviews in Neurosurgery (1985); *Recreations* architecture, fine arts, opera; *Style*— Martin Rice Edwards, Esq; ✉ Ham House Stables, Ham, Richmond, Surrey TW10 7RS (☎ 0181 940 6605); Regional Neurosciences Centre, Charing Cross Hospital, Fulham Palace Rd, London W6 8RF (☎ 0181 846 1182, fax 0181 846 1195)

RICE-OXLEY, James Keith; CBE (1981); s of Montague Keith Rice-Oxley (d 1956), and Marjorie, *née* Burrell (d 1929); *b* 15 Aug 1920; *Educ* Marlborough, Trinity Coll Oxford (MA); *m* 1949, Barbara Mary Joan, da of Frederick Parsons (d 1957), of Bull Lane, Gerrards Cross; 2 da; *Career* Maj (despatches) 1944; chm: Nat Sea Trg Tst 1965–80, Shipowners Gp ILO 1969–80; dir: Gen Cncl of Br Shipping 1965–80, Int Shipping Fedn 1969–80; chm MN Trg Bd 1981–, UK govr World Maritime Univ 1983–89; memb: Cncl Barnardo's 1981–95 (vice chm 1988 and 1994), Industl Tribunals of Eng and Wales 1981–88, Engrg Bd Business and Technician Educn Cncl 1983–87; Gen Cmmr of Income Tax 1986–95; *Recreations* ceramics, squash; *Style*— James Rice-Oxley, Esq, CBE; ✉ Ox House, Bimport, Shaftesbury, Dorset SP7 8AX (☎ 01747 852741)

RICH, Allan Jeffrey; s of Norman Rich, and Tessa, *née* Sawyer; *b* 9 Oct 1942; *m* 5 June 1966, Vivienne, da of Fred Ostro; 1 s (Jason b 8 May 1970), 2 da (Michaela b 6 May 1968, Natalie b 13 May 1972); *Career* TV buyer Masius Wynne Williams 1959–65, co fndr and media dir Davidson Pearce Berry & Spottiswoode 1965–74, fndr, chm and chief exec The Media Business (now The Media Business Group plc) 1975–; MAA 1966, MIPA 1966; *Recreations* tennis, football, cricket, golf; *Style*— Allan Rich, Esq; ✉ The Media Business Group plc, 70 North Row, Park Lane, London W1R 1DE (☎ 0171 408 4400, fax 0171 499 7279)

RICH, Josef Lionel (Joe); OBE (1997); s of Morris Rich (d 1990), of Manchester, and Sarah, *née* Cohen (d 1995); *b* 13 Aug 1938; *Educ* Stand GS for Boys, Univ of Edinburgh (BDS), Faculty of General Dental Practitioners RCS England (DGDP UK); *m* 1, 1962 (m dis 1980), Jennifer, da of George Brown; 2 da (Deborah b 1968, Katherine b 1973), 1 s (Daniel b 1969); m 2, 1984, Jacqueline, da of Edward Tawil; 1 da (Sylvia b 1985), 1 s (Charles b 1986); *Career* assoc gen dental practitioner 1962–65, in own dental practice Eccles Manchester 1966–; pt/t dental surgn Hope Hosp Salford 1968–74, pt/t lectr Oral Surgery Dept Dental Sch Univ of Manchester 1976–81; postgraduate dental tutor Salford and Trafford HAs, dental practice advsr Manchester FHSA 1988–91; elected memb GDC 1996–, memb Representative Bd BDA 1996–; chm: Salford Local Dental Ctee 1977–87, Fedn of NW Local Dental Ctees 1980–87, Gen Dental Servs Ctee BDA 1991–97 (ex officio memb Representation Bd, Cncl and Cncl Exec), Central Assessment Panel (Peer Review) 1991–95, Central Audit and Peer Review Panel 1995–; memb Bd of Mgmnt Br Dental Guild 1989–; past pres Manchester Edinburgh Univ Club, pres Odontology Section Manchester Med Soc 1979; fndr, past warden and life memb Cncl Hale and Dist Hebrew Congregation; memb: RSM, Br Endodontic Soc, Edinburgh Dental Alumni Soc, Faculty of Gen Dental Practitioners RCS, BDA; *Recreations* salmon fishing (memb Salmon and Trout Assoc), bridge, food and wine, watching Manchester City FC; *Style*— Joe Rich, Esq, OBE; ✉ 1 Stanhope Road, Bowdon, Altrincham, Cheshire WA14 3LB (☎ 0161 926 8115); Rich & King Dental Practice, 6 Regent Street, Eccles, Manchester M30 0AP (☎ 0161 788 9815, mobile 0973 502068)

RICH, His Hon Judge; Michael Samuel; QC (1980); s of Sidney Frank Rich, OBE, JP (d 1985), of Streatham, and Erna Babette, *née* Schlesinger (d 1988); *b* 18 Aug 1933; *Educ* Dulwich, Wadham Coll Oxford (MA); *m* 31 July 1983, Janice Sarita, da of Henry Jules Benedictus; 3 s (Benedict b 1966, Jonathan b 1969, Edmund b 1970), 1 da (Sara b 1964); *Career* Lt RASC 1954; called to the Bar Middle Temple 1959, bencher 1985, recorder 1986–91, circuit judge (SE Circuit) 1991–; pt/t memb Lands Tbnl 1993–; memb Hong Kong Bar; tstee S London Liberal Synagogue; *Books* Hills Law of Town and Country Planning (1968); *Clubs* Garrick; *Style*— His Hon Judge Rich, QC; ✉ 18 Dulwich Village, London SE21 7AL (☎ 0181 693 1957); Central London County Court, 13–14 Park Crescent, London W1N 3PD

RICH, Timothy James; s of Kenneth Rich, of Rotherfield, E Sussex, and Maureen, *née* Dunne (now Mrs Pope); *b* 12 Jan 1967; *Educ* Mayfield Sch, Heathfield Sch, Univ of E Anglia (BA, ed univ magazine); *Career* exhbns asst: Nat Portrait Gallery London 1985, Royal Acad London 1986; Hotshoe International: reporter 1989–90, features 1991–92, ed 1992–95; Graphics International and ads international: sr features writer 1990–91, features ed 1991–92; ed Graphics International 1992–; London corr: Blad Magazine (Amsterdam) 1992–, Print Magazine (NY) 1995–; contrib writer Photo District News (NY) 1995–; judge: Typographers Int Assoc Awards 1993, Assoc of Photographers 11th Awards 1994, Print European Designs Annual 1995 and 1996; *Recreations* playing the piano, collecting art, reading modern fiction, playing football and squash, watching Chelsea FC; *Style*— Timothy Rich, Esq; ✉ 61 Messina Avenue, West Hampstead, London NW6 4LG (☎ 0171 328 9622); Creative Magazines Ltd, 35 Britannia Row, London N1 8QH (☎ 0171 226 1739, fax 0171 226 1540)

RICHARD, Sir Cliff, *né* Harry Rodger Webb; kt (1995), OBE (1980); s of Rodger Oscar Webb (d 1961), and Dorothy Marie Bodkin (formerly Webb), *née* Beazley; *b* 14 Oct 1940; *Educ* Riversmead Sch Cheshunt; *Career* singer and actor; first hit record Move It 1958, own series on BBC and ITV, various repertory and variety seasons; 14 gold records, 35 silver records; films: Serious Charge 1959, Expresso Bongo 1960, The Young Ones 1961, Summer Holiday 1962, Wonderful Life 1964, Finders Keepers 1966, Two a Penny 1968, His Land 1970, Take Me High 1973; musical: Heathcliff (title role) 1996; vice pres: PHAB, Tear Fund, Princess Alice Hospice Tst, various other charitable orgns; Bernard Delfont Award for outstanding contribution to showbusiness 1995; *Books* Which One's Cliff (1977), Happy Christmas from Cliff (1980), You, Me and Jesus (1983), Jesus, Me and You (1985), Single-Minded (1988); *Recreations* tennis; *Style*— Sir Cliff Richard, OBE; ✉ PO Box 46C, Esher, Surrey KT10 0RB (☎ 01372 467752, fax 01372 462352)

RICHARD, Baron (Life Peer UK 1990), of Ammanford in the County of Dyfed; Ivor Seward Richard; PC (1993), QC (1971); s of Seward Thomas Richard, of 30 Heol Nant Castan, Rhiwbina, Cardiff, and Isabella Irene Richard; *b* 30 May 1932; *Educ* St Michael's Sch Llanelly, Cheltenham, Pembroke Coll Oxford (BA 1953, MA 1970); *m* 1, 1956 (m dis 1962), Geraldine Maude, da of Alfred Moore, of Hartlepool, Co Durham; 1 s (Hon David Seward b 1959); m 2, 1962 (m dis 1985), Alison Mary, da of Joseph Imrie, of Alverstoke, Hants; 1 s (Hon Alun Seward b 1963), 1 da (Hon Isabel Margaret Katherine b 1966); m 3, 1989, Janet, da of John Jones, of Oxford; 1 s (Hon William John b 1990); *Career* called to the Bar Inner Temple 1955, Parly candidate (Lab) S Kensington Gen Election 1959 and LCC Election 1961, MP (Lab) Barons Court 1964–74, PPS to Sec of State for Def 1966–69, Parly under-sec of state for Def (Army) 1969–70, oppn spokesman Posts and Telecommunications 1970–71, dep oppn spokesman for Foreign Affrs 1971–74, UK perm rep at the UN 1974–79, chm Rhodesia Conf Geneva 1976; UK cmmr to the Cmmn of the European Communities 1981–85 responsible for: employment, social affrs, educn and vocational trg; leader of the Opposition in House of Lords 1992–; memb: Fabian Soc, Lab Lawyers; *Style*— The Rt Hon Lord Richard, PC, QC; ✉ 2 Paper Buildings, Temple, London EC4

RICHARD, John Walter Maxwell Miller; s of Col J E M Richard, OBE, of Kiakzie, Peebles, and Gaynor Richard (d 1933); *b* 19 April 1933; *Educ* Cargilfield, Eton, Trinity Coll Cambridge (BA); *m* 1977, Christine Margaret, da of Ludwig Christian Saam (d 1954); 1 s, 3 da; *Career* ptnr Bell Lawrie Macgregor & Co (now Bell Lawrie White & Co Ltd); memb Stock Exchange 1959 (memb Cncl, former memb Cncl's Markets Ctee); chm and chief exec offr Monktonhall Mineworkers Ltd; *Style*— John Richard Esq; ✉ 8 Braid Hills Approach, Edinburgh EH10 6JY (☎ 0131 447 9313); Bell Lawrie White & Co Ltd, 7 Drumsheugh Gardens, Edinburgh EH3 7QJ (☎ 0131 225 2566)

RICHARD, Wendy; da of Henry William Emerton (d 1954), of St Albans, and Beatrice Reay, *née* Cutter (d 1972); *Educ* Royal Masonic Sch Rickmansworth, Italia Conti Drama Sch; *m* 17 March 1990, Paul Peter Anthony Glorney; *Career* actress; *Theatre* incl: Blithe Spirit, Cinderella, No Sex Please We're British, Are You Being Served?, Let's Go Camping; *Television* roles and appearances incl: Harpers - West One, Arthur Haynes Show, Dixon of Dock Green, Dad's Army, Z Cars, West Country Tales, various TV plays, Are You Being Served?, Eastenders, Grace and Favour, Up Pompeii, Spooner's Patch, Little and Large, Blankety Blank, Punchlines, Pyramid Game, Not on Your Nellie, On the Buses, Fenn Street Gang, Please Sir, Hugh and I, Hogg's Back, Rainbow, No Hiding Place, Both Ends Meet, Newcomers, Give us a Clue, Celebrity Squares, We Love TV, All Star Secrets, Crackerjack, Secrets Out, Music Game, Zodiac Game, Wogan, 3–2–1, TV-am, Breakfast TV, Nationwide, Thank Your Lucky Stars, Dad You're A Square, Vintage Quiz, Kelly Monteith, Dick Emery, Telly Addicts, Danger Man; *Radio* incl: Just a Minute, Film Quiz, The Law Game; *Films* incl: Bless This House, No Blade of Grass, Carry on Matron, Carry on Girls, Are You Being Served?, Gumshoe, Don't I Look Like the Lord's Son, Doctor in Clover; *Awards* Northern TV Personality of the Year 1989; *Recreations* embroidery work, gardening, cooking; *Style*— Ms Wendy Richard; ✉ BBC TV, Elstree Studios, Elstree, Herts

RICHARDS, (Joseph) Alan; s of Albert John Knight-Richards (d 1967), of Dudley, Worcs, and Sarah, *née* Jones (d 1968); *b* 23 March 1930; *Educ* Dudley GS, Birmingham Sch of Architecture (DipArch); *m* 20 Dec 1952, Tess, da of Frederic Dutton Griffiths (d 1981), of Dudley, Worcs; 2 da (Julia, Wendy); *Career* princ asst architect Co Borough of Wolverhampton 1952–58, co fndr and jt sr ptnr Mason Richards Partnership 1958– (fndr consultancy serv for expert witness 1977–); Freeman City of London 1983; Liveryman: Worshipful Co of Arbitrators 1983, Worshipful Co of Architects 1988; RIBA

1952, FCIArb 1979, FBAE 1989; *Recreations* power boating, cruising, travel; *Clubs* City Livery, RYA; *Style*— J Alan Richards, Esq; ✉ Salisbury House, Tettenhall Rd, Wolverhampton WV1 4SG (☎ 01902 771331, fax 01902 21914)

RICHARDS, Sir (Francis) Brooks; KCMG (1976, CMG 1963), DSC (and Bar 1943); s of Francis Bartlett Richards (d 1955), of Cobham, Surrey, and Mary Bertha, *née* Street (d 1974); *b* 18 July 1918; *Educ* Stowe, Magdalene Coll Cambridge (MA); *m* 1941, Hazel Myfanwy, da of Lt-Col Stanley Price Williams, CIE, of London (d 1977); 1 s (Francis Neville, *qv*), 1 da; *Career* served WWII RN (Lt-Cdr RNVR), Br Embassy Paris 1944–48; Foreign Serv: joined 1946, German Political Dept FO 1948–52, first sec Athens 1952–54, Political Residency Bahrain 1954–57, asst private sec to Foreign Sec 1958–59, cnsllr Paris 1959–64, head of Info Policy Dept FCO/CRO 1964, seconded to Cabinet Office 1966, HM min Bonn 1969–71; ambass: Vietnam 1972–74, Greece 1974–78; dep sec Cabinet Office 1978–80, security co-ordinator NI 1980–81; vice pres Friends of The Imperial War Museum, pres Farnham Soc; chm: Ctee of Mgmnt Br Inst Paris 1979–88, CSM Parly Conslts 1983–96, Gerry Holdsworth Special Forces Club Charitable Tst, Paintings in Hosps until 1996; Chevalier de la Légion d'Honneur, Croix de Guerre; *Recreations* gardening, drawing, collecting; *Clubs* Travellers', Special Forces (chm 1983–86, pres 1986–89); *Style*— Sir Brooks Richards, KCMG, DSC; ✉ Folly Barn, Norton Lane, Durweston, Blandford Forum, Dorset DT11 0QP (☎ 01258 452588)

RICHARDS, (William Samuel) Clive; *b* 1 Sept 1937; *Educ* Bishop Vesey GS Sutton Coldfield; *m*; 3 c; *Career* articled clerk Peat Marwick Mitchell & Co Birmingham Office 1959–60, investment analyst rising to managing ptnr Wedd Durlacher & Co 1960–70, chief exec Rothschild Investment Trust 1970–75, gp fin dir N M Rothschild & Sons Ltd 1974–76, fndr Clive Richards & Co (investment and fin servs co, specialising in venture capital) 1976–; fndr Micro Business Systems plc 1978 (floated 1982, now taken over); chm: Steel Burrill Jones Group PLC, Telephone Information Services PLC; non-exec dir: Minerva plc, Dalkeith Holdings PLC, Tetra Holdings Ltd, Bankside Members Agency Ltd, various other private cos; commercial farm owner (2,300 acres) Herefordshire; pres Hereford Fedn of Young Farmers' Clubs, memb Bd of Mgmnt Nat Fedn of Young Farmers' Clubs; memb Cncl (representing Herefordshire) Royal Agric Soc of England 1995–; memb Cncl ICAEW 1995–; fndr Clive Richards Charity 1987, vice pres Shaw Tst, memb Ctee Lord Mayor of London's Charity 1996–97; govr: Bishop Vesey GS, Hereford Cathedral Sch; chm Malvern Festival Theatre Tst; former treas and memb Ctee London Welsh RFC, patron and chm Bromyard Sports Assoc; High Sheriff Gtr London 1991–92; memb Ct Worshipful Co of Chartered Accountants (Master 1996–97); FIMgt, FCMA 1960, FCA 1960; *Recreations* rugby, cricket, shooting, gardening, art, Nelsonia, breeding Hereford cattle; *Style*— Clive Richards, Esq; ✉ Clive Richards & Co, Avalon House, 57–63 Scrutton Street, London EC2A 4PJ (☎ 0171 739 6360, fax 0171 729 9841)

RICHARDS, David Anthony Stewart; QC (1992); s of Kenneth Richards, of Heswall, Wirral, and Winifred Edith, *née* Purdoe; *b* 9 June 1951; *Educ* Oundle, Trinity Coll Cambridge (MA); *m* 28 April 1979, Gilliam Moira, da of Lt-Col W A Taylor; 1 s (Mark b 16 Oct 1981), 2 da (Sarah b 13 Jan 1985, Charlotte b 13 Jan 1985); *Career* called to the Bar Inner Temple 1974, jr counsel (Chancery) to DTI 1989–92; *Style*— David Richards, Esq, QC; ✉ Erskine Chambers, 30 Lincoln's Inn Fields, London WC2A 3PF (☎ 0171 242 5532, fax 0171 831 0125)

RICHARDS, David Gordon; CBE (1989); s of Gordon Charles Richards (d 1956), and Vera Amy, *née* Barrow (d 1962); *b* 25 Aug 1928; *Educ* Highgate Sch; *m* 1960, Catherine Stephanie, da of Edward Gilbert Woodward (d 1949); 1 s (Edwin), 2 da (Victoria, Katharine); *Career* 8 RTR 1947–49; CA; ptnr: Harmood Banner & Co 1955–74, Deloitte Haskins & Sells 1974–84; non-exec chm: Walker Greenbank plc, Discretionary Unit Fund Managers Ltd; ICEAW: cncl memb 1970–87, vice pres 1977–78, dep pres 1978–79, centenary pres 1979–80, memb Gen Purposes and Fin Ctee 1977–83, chm Int Affrs Ctee 1980–83; chm Cncl of Accountancy Bodies 1979–80, dep chm Monopolies and Mergers Cmmn 1983–90; memb: Ctee London Soc of CAs 1966–70 and 1981–82 (chm 1969–70), Ctees of Investigations under Agric Mktg Act 1972–88, Cncl for Securities Indust 1979–80, Panel on Take Overs and Mergers 1979–80, Review Body of Doctors' and Dentists' Remuneration 1984–90, UK and Ireland Rep Cncl Int Fedn of Accountants 1981–83, Disciplinary Bd Inst of Actuaries 1986–; chm Disciplinary Bd Br Psychological Soc 1988–95; govr Highgate Sch 1982– (chm 1983–); tstee: Bob Champion Cancer Tst 1983–94, Prince's Youth Business Tst 1986–93, Royal Acad of Music Fndn 1985–; govr Assoc Bd Royal Schs of Music 1987–; Worshipful Co of CAs: Jr Warden 1984–85, Sr Warden 1985–86, Master 1986–87, currently Hon Memb of Ct; Hon FRAM 1994; FCA (ACA 1951); *Recreations* gardening, silviculture, tennis, golf, shooting; *Style*— David Richards, Esq, CBE; ✉ Eastleach House, Eastleach, Glos GL7 3NW (☎ 01367 850416)

RICHARDS, Dean; MBE (1996); s of Brian Richards, of Hinckley, Leics, and Marion, *née* Green; *b* 11 July 1963; *Educ* St Martins HS, John Cleveland Coll; *m* 2 Aug 1986, Nicola Anne, da of Kenneth Milbank Stephenson; 1 da (Jessica b 6 April 1993); *Career* rugby union player (number 8); former club Roanne France, with Leicester RFC 1982– (over 250 appearances, currently capt), winners Courage Clubs' Championship 1994/95 season; England: former schs and under 21 rep, full debut v Ireland 1986 (scoring 2 tries), 48 full caps, memb World Cup squads 1987, 1991 (runners-up) and 1995 (4th place), memb Grand Slam winning squads 1991 and 1992; memb Br Lions tour to Aust 1989 (3 test appearances), memb Br Lions tour to NZ 1993 (3 test appearances); also rep Leics and Midlands Div; Whitbread/Rugby World Player of the Year 1991; constable Leics Constabulary 1982–; *Recreations* shooting, anything sport related except ultra distance running; *Style*— Dean Richards, Esq, MBE; ✉ Leicester Rugby Football Club, Aylestone Road, Leicester LE2 7LF (☎ 01533 540276)

RICHARDS, Derek James; s of late William Richards, of Kenmore, Cricket Lane, Lichfield, Staffs, and Grace Winifred, *née* Funnell; *b* 12 Nov 1934; *Educ* King Edward VI Sch Lichfield, Jesus Coll Cambridge (BA, MA), Guy's Med Sch (MB BChir, LRCP); *m* 22 Sept 1962, Angela, da of late William Hugh Maton; 2 s (Michael John b 29 July 1964, Simon William b 11 Jan 1969), 2 da (Elizabeth Jane b 21 April 1966, Alice Louise b 16 April 1978); *Career* house offr and registrar Guy's, sr house offr Bristol Royal Infirmary, sr registrar UCH, conslt surgn emeritus Eastbourne Health Authy; memb Ctee of Mgmnt Horder Centre Crowborough E Sussex, pres League of Friends Uckfield Hosp Uckfield E Sussex; memb BMA, FBOA, FRCS 1964; *Recreations* golf, shooting, following Grand Prix racing; *Style*— Derek Richards, Esq; ✉ Clare Glen, High Hurstwood, nr Uckfield, East Sussex TN22 4BN (☎ 0182 585 73306); 28 Lushington Rd, Eastbourne BN21 4LL (☎ 01323 34030)

RICHARDS, Derek William; s of William Albert Richards (d 1985), of Croydon, Surrey, and Mary Ann Ruby, *née* Bissell (d 1985); *b* 6 Dec 1943; *Educ* Wandsworth GS, Regent Street Poly Sch of Photography (Kodak scholarship, Dip in Advtg Photography); *m* 10 June 1972, Rosemary Pauline, da of Reginald Arthur Sturman; *Career* photographer (specialising in people, travel and locations); initially asst to David Swann and Norman Parkinson, freelance advtg photographer 1967–, fndr Derek Richard Studios Ltd 1972, San Francisco 1982–84; numerous assignments for leading UK and USA based advtg agencies and design gps; memb Assoc of Photographers 1972 (memb Ctee 1973–75), fndr memb British Decoy and Wildfowl Carvers' Assoc (award-winner 1989, 1991, 1992, 1993, 1994, 1995 and 1996); *Recreations* restoring and 'trialing' vintage sports cars, decoy carving, film, theatre, walking, birdwatching; *Clubs* Vintage Sports Car; *Style*— Derek Richards, Esq; ✉ 11 Napier Road, London W14 8LQ (☎ 0171 603 8019); Hardy's Cottage, Purse Caundle, Dorset DT9 5QZ; Derek Richards Studio Ltd, 1 Alma Studios, 32 Stratford Road, London W8 6QF (☎ 0171 937 7533, fax 0171 937 8285)

RICHARDS, Francis Neville; CMG (1994), CVO (1991); o s of Sir (Francis) Brooks Richards, KCMG, DSC, *qv*; *b* 18 Nov 1945; *Educ* Eton, King's Coll Cambridge (MA); *m* 16 Jan 1971, Gillian Bruce, da of I S Nevill, MC (d 1948); 1 s (James b 1975), 1 da (Joanna b 1977); *Career* Royal Green Jackets 1967–69; HM Dip Serv; third sec to Second Sec Br Embassy Moscow 1971–73; second sec to First Sec UK Delgn to MBFR talks Vienna 1973–76, FCO 1976–85, asst private sec to Sec of State 1980–82, cnsllr (econ and commercial) Br High Cmmn New Delhi 1985–88, head of S Asian Dept FCO 1988–90, Br high cmmr Namibia 1990–92, min Br Embassy Moscow 1992–95, asst under sec of state Central and Eastern Europe FCO 1995–96, dir Europe FCO 1996–; *Recreations* riding, walking, travel; *Clubs* Travellers', President's Estate Polo (New Delhi); *Style*— Francis Richards, Esq, CMG, CVO; ✉ c/o Foreign and Commonwealth Office, London SW1

RICHARDS, Gordon W; *b* 7 Sept 1930; *m* 18 June 1980, Joan Dacre, da of late Lt-Col Henry Anthony Camillo Howard, CMG, yst s of 1 Baron Howard of Penrith; 2 c from previous m (Nicholas Gordon, Joanna); *Career* national hunt trainer; first ride as jockey 1943, trainer 1964–; major races won: Grand Nat twice, Scot Nat twice, Great Yorks Chase, Mackeson Gold Cup, A F Budge Gold Cup, Whitbread Gold Cup, King George VI Chase, Stones Ginger Wine Chase, Greenall Witney Gold Cup (twice), Newton Chase, Hennessy Cognac Gold Cup; horses trained incl: Playlord, Titus Oats, Lucius, Sea Pigeon, Noddys Ryde, Hallo Dandy, Dark Ivy, Little Bay, Twinoaks, Four Trix, Clever Folly; *Recreations* tennis, swimming; *Style*— Gordon Richards, Esq; ✉ The Old Rectory, Greystoke, Penrith, Cumbria CA11 0UJ (fax 017684 83933)

RICHARDS, Prof Ivor James; s of Philip James Richards (d 1981), of Newmarket, Suffolk, and Ivy Gwenllian, *née* Kimber (d 1995); *b* 1 May 1943; *Educ* Newmarket GS, Univ of Wales (MA); *m* 5 June 1976 (m dis 1995), Anne Rostas; 1 s (Owen James b 30 Dec 1984), 1 da (Sarah Elizabeth b 13 March 1983); *Career* assoc architect Sir Leslie Martin Architects Cambridge 1969–87; works incl: Faculty of Music Univ of Cambridge 1975–85, Royal Concert Hall Glasgow 1978–90, Royal Scottish Acad of Music and Drama Glasgow 1988, Centro de Arte Moderna Gulbenkian Fndn Lisbon 1980–84, Masters' Houses Stowe Sch Buckingham 1993–, Ecumenical Church Cambridge 1991–; prof of architecture Sch of Architecture: Univ of Wales Cardiff until 1995, Univ of Newcastle upon Tyne 1995–; external examiner: Sch of Architecture Univ of Newcastle upon Tyne, Sch of Architecture Univ of Nottingham, Sch of Architecture Univ of Central England; memb ARCUK, ARIBA; *Recreations* writing, walking, cities and architecture; *Style*— Prof Ivor Richards; ✉ 6 Buston Terrace, Jesmond, Newcastle upon Tyne NE2 2JL (☎ 0191 281 2610); School of Architecture, The Quadrangle, University of Newcastle upon Tyne, Newcastle NE1 7RU (☎ 0191 222 6015, fax 0191 222 6115)

RICHARDS, Rt Rev John; *see:* Ebbsfleet, Bishop of

RICHARDS, Lt-Gen Sir John Charles Chisholm; KCB (1980), KCVO (1990); s of Charles Richards, and Alice Milner; *b* 21 Feb 1927; *Educ* Worksop Coll Notts; *m* 1953, Audrey Hidson; 2 s, 1 da; *Career* joined Royal Marines 1945, served in HM Ships and Commando Units worldwide, Jt Warfare Attaché Washington DC and memb UN Mil Staff Ctee 1972–74, Brig cmdg 3 Commando Brigade 1975–76, Cmdt Gen RM 1977–81; HM Marshal of the Dip Corps 1982–92, Rep Col Cmdt RM 1989–90; non-exec dir: DSC Communications (Europe) Ltd 1985–92, Andrew Ltd 1986–94; Extra Equerry to HM The Queen 1992–; Freeman City of London 1982; CIMgt 1980; *Recreations* golf, gardening, swimming; *Clubs* Army and Navy; *Style*— Lt-Gen Sir John Richards, KCB, KCVO; ✉ c/o NatWest Bank plc, 36 St James's Street, London SW1A 1JF

RICHARDS, John Deacon; CBE (1978); s of William John Richards (d 1985), and Ethel, *née* Waggott (d 1971); *b* 7 May 1931; *Educ* Geelong GS Aust, Cranleigh Sch, Architectural Assoc Sch of Architecture (AADipl); *m* 1958, Margaret, da of William Brown (d 1983); 1 s (Alan), 3 da (Kathleen, Lucy, Jessica); *Career* architect; past chm Robert Matthew, Johnson-Marshall and Ptnrs (architect and planner of Univ of Stirling), currently princ John Richards Assocs, Housing Assoc Ombudsman for Scotland; past bd memb and dep chm Scottish Homes 1988–93; *Recreations* country life; *Clubs* Athenaeum; *Style*— John Richards, Esq, CBE; ✉ Lady's Field, Whitekirk, Dunbar, East Lothian (☎ 01620 870206)

RICHARDS, John Parry; s of Ellis Parry Richards (d 1985), of Rhiwbina, Cardiff, and Gwyneth, *née* Prosser; *b* 16 Aug 1947; *Educ* Highgate Sch; *m* 31 Dec 1976, Elizabeth Wendy Strachan (d 1995), da of James Douglas Moore Mather; 2 s (Robert James b 1 Nov 1978, Alastair John b 16 Sept 1981); *Career* articled clerk Barton Mayhew & Co (now part of Ernst & Young) 1967; specialist in insolvency and rescue work 1975–; ptnr Deloitte & Touche 1983– (joined 1979); memb: London Region and Membership Ctees Soc of Practitioners of Insolvency, Inst of Credit Mgmnt 1987, Soc of Practitioners of Insolvency 1990; FCA 1979 (ACA 1971), FIPA 1986 (MIPA 1982); *Recreations* golf, classic cars, gardening, watching cricket and rugby, opera and ballet; *Clubs* Old Cholmeleian Soc, Hever Golf, Queenhithe Ward; *Style*— John Richards, Esq; ✉ Deloitte & Touche, PO Box 810, Hill House, 1 Little New Street, London EC4A 3TR (☎ 0171 936 3000, fax 0171 480 6881)

RICHARDS, Keith; *b* 18 Dec 1943; *Educ* Sidcup Art Sch; *partner* (sep) Anita Pallenberg; 2 s (Marlon b 10 Aug 1969, Tara b 26 March 1976 d 4 June 1976), 1 da (Dandelion b 17 April 1972); m 1, 18 Dec 1983, Patti, *née* Hansen; *Career* guitarist and songwriter; Rolling Stones formed London 1962; signed recording contracts with: Impact Records/Decca 1963, London Records/Decca 1965, CBS 1983, Virgin 1992; has worked with Chuck Berry, Buddy Guy, Muddy Waters, Eric Clapton, Johnnie Johnson, John Lee Hooker and others; albums with Rolling Stones: The Rolling Stones (1964, reached UK no 1), The Rolling Stones No 2 (1965, UK no 1), Out Of Our Heads (1965, UK no 2), Aftermath (1966, UK no 1), Big Hits: High Tide and Green Grass (compilation, 1966, UK no 4), got LIVE if you want it! (live, 1967), Between The Buttons (1967, UK no 3), Flowers (US compilation, 1967, US no 3), Their Satanic Majesties Request (1967, UK no 3), Beggars Banquet (1968, UK no 3), Through The Past Darkly: Big Hits Vol 2 (compilation, 1969, UK no 2), Let It Bleed (1969, UK no 1), Get Yer Ya-Ya's Out! (live, 1970, UK no 1), Stone Age (compilation, 1971, UK no 4), Sticky Fingers (1971, UK no 1), Hot Rocks 1964–71 (US compilation, 1972, US no 4), Exile On Main Street (1972, UK no 1), More Hot Rocks (US compilation, 1973, US no 9), Goat's Head Soup (1973, UK no 1), It's Only Rock'n'Roll (1974, UK no 2), Made In The Shade (compilation, 1975, UK no 14), Rolled Gold - The Very Best of The Rolling Stones (compilation, 1975, UK no 7), Black and Blue (1976, UK no 2), Love You Live (live, 1977, UK no 3), Some Girls (1978, UK no 2), Emotional Rescue (1980, UK no 1), Tattoo You (1981, UK no 2), Still Life: American Concert 1981 (live, 1981, UK no 4), Undercover (1983, UK no 3), Rewind 1971–1984 (compilation, 1984, UK no 23), Dirty Work (1986, UK no 4), Steel Wheels (1989, UK no 2), Flashpoint (live, 1991, UK no 6), Voodoo Lounge (1994), Stripped (1995); solo albums: Talk Is Cheap (1988, UK no 37), Main Offender (1992); concert films: Sympathy For The Devil (dir Jean Luc Godard) 1969, Gimme Shelter 1970, Ladies and Gentlemen, The Rolling Stones 1977, Let's Spend The Night Together (dir Hal Ashby) 1983, Hail, Hail, Rock'n'Roll (with Chuck Berry) 1986, Flashpoint (film of 1990 Steel Wheels World Tour) 1991; feature film: Michael Kohlhgaas 1969; *Style*— Keith Richards, Esq; ✉ c/o Munro Sounds, 5 Church Row, Wandsworth Plain, London SW18 1ES

RICHARDS, Martin Edgar; s of Edgar Lynton (Tony) Richards, CBE, MC, TD (d 1983), and Barbara, *née* Lebus (d 1993); *b* 27 Feb 1943; *Educ* Harrow; *m* 30 Jan 1969, Caroline, da of Edwin Billing Lewis (d 1948); 1 s (Charles b 1975), 1 da (Catherine b 1972); *Career* admitted slr 1968; ptnr Clifford Chance (formerly Clifford-Turner) 1973–; *Style*— Martin E Richards, Esq; ✉ Clifford Chance, 200 Aldersgate Street, London EC1A 4JJ (☎ 0171 600 1000, fax 0171 600 5555)

RICHARDS, Hon Michael Hugh; s of 1 Baron Milverton, GCMG (d 1978); hp of bro, 2 Baron Milverton; *b* 1 Aug 1936; *Educ* Ridley Coll Ontario, Clifton; *m* 1960, Edna Leonie B, da of Col Leo Steveni, OBE, MC, IA (ret); 1 s (Arthur Hugh b 10 Jan 1963); *Career* Capt (ret) Rifle Bde; Malaya 1957 (despatches); attached Royal Nigerian Army 1962, memb UN Congo Force, 1963–65; md Philip Morris Nigeria Ltd 1972–, dir Africa Carreras-Rothmans Ltd 1978–82, md Murray Son & Co, dir personnel Rothmans International Tobacco, md Rothmans of Pall Mall (New Zealand) Ltd; memb Ct of Assts Worshipful Co of Tobacco Pipe Makers & Tobacco Blenders; *Clubs* Cavalry and Guards'; *Style*— The Hon Michael Richards; ✉ Lovelynch House, Middleton Stoney Rd, Bicester, Oxon

RICHARDS, Maj Gen Nigel William Fairbairn; OBE (1987); s of Lt-Col William Fairbairn Richards, TD (d 1987), of Eastbourne, and Marjorie May, *née* Salter; *b* 15 Aug 1945; *Educ* Eastbourne Coll, Peterhouse Cambridge; *m* 27 July 1968, Christine Anne Helen, da of Maj-Gen Charles William Woods, CB, MBE, MC; 2 s (Charles b 1972, Peter b 1976), 1 da (Helen b 1971); *Career* cmmnd RA 1965, RN Staff Coll 1976, CO 7 Regt RHA 1983–86, cmd 5 Airborne Bde 1989–90, Dir Army Staff Duties MOD 1991–93, chief of Combat Support HQ ACE Rapid Reaction Corps 1994–96, GOC 4 Div 1996–; *Recreations* tennis, cricket, skiing, golf, history; *Clubs* Army and Navy; *Style*— Maj Gen Nigel Richards, OBE

RICHARDS, Prof Peter; s of Dr William Richards (d 1981), and Barbara Ashton, *née* Taylor (d 1971); *b* 25 May 1936; *Educ* Monkton Combe Sch, Emmanuel Coll Cambridge (MA, MB BCh, MD), St George's Hosp Med Sch, RPMS London (PhD); *m* 1, 6 July 1959 (m dis 1986), Anne Marie, da of Svend Larsen (d 1964), of Odense, Denmark; 1 s (Allan), 3 da (Marianne, Annette, Christina); m 2, 26 July 1987, Dr Carol Anne, da of Dr Raymond Seymour, of Wendlebury; *Career* hon sr lectr St Mary's Hosp Med Sch (lectr in med 1967–70) and conslt physician St Peter's Hosp Chertsey 1970–73, sr lectr and conslt physician St George's Hosp and Med Sch 1973–79, dean, prof of med and hon conslt physician St Mary's Hosp Med Sch 1979–95, pro rector med educn Imperial Coll of Sci Technol and Med 1988–95, med dir and conslt physician Northwick Park Hosp 1995–; chm Cncl of Deans of UK Medical Schs and Faculties 1994–95; RCP: chm Educn Ctee 1992–95, memb Cncl 1994–95; memb GMC 1994–; memb Cncl Anglo-Finnish Soc; Liveryman Worshipful Soc of Apothecaries 1984, Freeman City of London 1985; FRCP 1976; *Books* The Medieval Leper and His Northern Heirs (1977), Understanding Water, Electrolyte and Acid Base Metabolism (jtly, 1983), Wasser-und Elektrolythaushalt: Diagnostik und Therapie (jtly, 1985), Living Medicine (1990), Learning Medicine (13 edn, 1996), Entry to Medicine (1996); *Recreations* social history, walking, listening to music, Finland; *Clubs* Garrick; *Style*— Prof Peter Richards; ✉ Northwick Park Hospital, Watford Road, Harrow, Middx HA1 3UJ (☎ 0181 869 2609, fax 0181 869 2014)

RICHARDS, Peter; s of Alfred James Clifford Richards (d 1969), of Stoke-sub-Hamdon, Somerset, and Eileen Mary Richards; *b* 10 Dec 1954; *Educ* Yeovil GS, Plymouth Poly, Canterbury Sch of Architecture (DipArch), Univ of Reading (MSc); *m* 1, 1983 (m dis 1986), Elizabeth, *née* Wilmott; m 2, 1988, Isabel, *née* Miles; *Career* DOE PSA 1980–83; HOK Cecil Denny Highton 1983–: project architect 1983–88, assoc 1988–90, ptnr 1990–95, dir (i/c Museums and Educnl Projects) 1996–; Conservation Award for works to the Alfred Waterhouse bldg Royal Borough of Kensington and Chelsea; RIBA, memb Assoc of Project Mangrs (MAPM); *Recreations* conservation, art and participation in university research; *Style*— Peter Richards, Esq; ✉ HOK Cecil Denny Highton, Axtell House, 23–24 Warwick Street, London W1R 6DH (☎ 0171 734 6831, fax 0171 734 0508)

RICHARDS, Gp Capt Peter Bruce Mansell; s of Frank Mansell Richards (ka 1943), and Eileen Elizabeth, *née* Shaw; *b* 27 April 1942; *Educ* St Columba's Coll Dublin, RAF Coll Cranwell; *m* 24 June 1967, Marion Lesley, da of Leslie William Bass, of Ninfield, Sussex; 1 s (Robin b 1 Oct 1971), 1 da (Emma b 6 Feb 1970); *Career* stock control offr RAF Honington 1964–66, air transportation offr RAF Wildenrath, West Germany 1966–69, systems analyst RAF Hendon 1969–73, supply advsr to chief scientist (RAF) MOD London 1973, movement planning HQ RAF Germany, Rheindahlen 1974–78, cmd Supply and Movements sqdn RAF Coningsby 1978–79, freight movement policy MOD London 1979–83, Armed Forces Staff Coll Norfolk Virginia 1983, plans and progs HQ USAF, Pentagon, Washington DC 1984–86, ground supply support HQ Strike Command High Wycombe 1986–87, dir of defence logistics (NATO, UK) MOD London 1987–90, dep dir supply policy (RAF) MOD London 1991–93, gp capt Logistics Saudi Arabia 1994–; cncl memb IMPACT (charity to combat disability); *Recreations* travelling, theatre, skiing, countryside; *Clubs* RAF; *Style*— Gp Capt Peter Richards; ✉ UKMOD (Air) Team, Riyadh

RICHARDS, Philip Brian; s of Glyn Bevan Richards (d 1976), of Ynysybwl, and Nancy Gwenhwyfar, *née* Evans of Bargoed (d 1992); *b* 3 Aug 1946; *Educ* Cardiff HS, Univ of Bristol (LLB); *m* 1, 17 July 1971 (m dis 1988), Dorothy Louise, da of Victor George, of Ystrad Mynach; 2 da (Rhuanedd b 1974, Lowri b 1978); m 2, 26 March 1994, Julia, da of Roy Jones, of Tylorstown; 1 step s (David b 1980), 1 da (Megan b 1995); *Career* called to Bar Inner Temple 1969; in practice 1969–; circuit jr Wales and Chester Circuit 1994, head of chambers 30 Park Place Cardiff 1994–, asst recorder of the Crown Court 1995–; Parly candidate (Plaid Cymru) 1974 and 1979; chm Parliament for Wales Campaign; vice pres: Mountain Ash RFC, Neyland RFC; tstee Welsh Writers' Tst, chm Bd of Govrs Ysgol Gyfun Rhydfelen 1988–95; *Recreations* music, sport, literature, walking; *Clubs* Cardiff and County; *Style*— Philip Richards, Esq; ✉ Cwm Pandy, Llanwynno Road, Cwmaman, Aberdare CF44 6PG (☎ 01685 870864); 30 Park Place, Cardiff CF1 3BA (☎ 01222 398421, fax 01222 398725)

RICHARDS, Sir Rex Edward; kt (1977); s of late Harold William Richards, of Colyton, Devon; *b* 28 Oct 1922; *Educ* Colyton GS Devon, St John's Coll Oxford (DSc); *m* 1948, Eva Edith, da of Paul Vago, of London (d 1948); 2 da; *Career* Univ of Oxford: fell and tutor Lincoln Coll 1947–64, Dr Lee's prof of chemistry and fell Exeter Coll 1964–69, warden Merton Coll 1969–84, vice chllr Univ of Oxford 1977–81; dir Leverhulme Trust 1985–93; non-exec dir: IBM-UK 1978–83, Oxford Instruments Group 1982–91; chllr Univ of Exeter 1981–; chm Oxford Enzyme Group 1969–83; memb: Scientific Advsy Ctee Nat Gallery 1978–, Advsy Bd Research Cncls 1980–83, Advsy Cncl for Applied Res and Devpt 1984–87; tstee: CIBA Fndn 1978–, Nat Heritage Meml Fund 1980–84, Tate Gallery 1982–88 and 1991–93, Nat Gallery 1982–89 and 1990–94, Henry Moore Fndn 1990 (chm 1994–); cmmr Royal Cmmn for Exhbn of 1851 1984–; pres RSC 1990–92, chm Br Postgrad Med Fedn 1986–93; Tilden lectr Chemical Soc 1962; Corday-Morgan Medal (Chemical Soc) 1954, Davy Medal (Royal Soc) 1976, Award for Theoretical Chemistry & Spectroscopy (Chemical Soc) 1977, EPIC Award (DTI) 1982, Royal Medal (Royal Soc) 1986, Medal of Honour Rheinische Friedrich Wilhelm Univ Bonn 1983, President's Medal (Soc of Chemical Indust) 1991; Associé Étranger Académie des Sciences Institut de France; Hon DSc: UEA, Univ of Exeter, Univ of Leicester, Univ of Salford, Univ of Edinburgh, Univ of Leeds, Univ of Kent, Univ of Birmingham, Univ of London; Hon ScD Univ of Cambridge, Hon LLD Univ of Dundee; Centenary Fell Univ of Greenwich; hon FRCP, hon FBA, hon FRAM, FRS, FRSC; *Recreations* twentieth century painting and sculpture; *Clubs* Royal Soc; *Style*— Sir Rex Richards, FRS; ✉ 13 Woodstock Close, Oxford OX2 8DB (☎ 01865 513621, fax 01865 513621, e-mail rex.richards@merton.ox.ac.uk)

RICHARDS, Roderick (Rod); MP (C) Clwyd North West (majority 6,050); s of late Ivor Richards, and Lizzie Richards; *b* 12 March 1947; *Educ* Llandovery Coll, UC Swansea (BSc(Econ)); *m* 6 Sept 1975, Elizabeth, *née* Knight; 2 s, 1 da; *Career* short serv cmmn Royal Marines 1969–71; econ forecaster 1975–77, civil servant Defence Intelligence Staff MOD 1977–83, bdcaster and journalist BBC News and Current Affrs 1983–86 and 1988–89, dir CSD Ltd 1986–87 and 1989–90, political advsr to Rt Hon David Hunt as Sec of State for Wales 1990; Parly candidate (C): Carmarthen 1987, Vale of Glamorgan 1989; MP (C) Clwyd NW 1992–, memb House of Commons Welsh Affrs Select Ctee 1992–94, PPS Foreign Office 1993–94, Parly under sec of state Welsh Office 1994–96 (resigned); memb: Welsh Consumer Cncl 1986–89, Devpt Bd for Rural Wales 1987–89; *Recreations* rugby, cricket, family; *Clubs* Special Forces; *Style*— Rod Richards, Esq, MP; ✉ House of Commons, London SW1A 0AA (☎ 0171 219 6253/5092; constituency office ☎ 01492 530505)

RICHARDS, Stephen Price; s of Richard Alun Richards, of Llandre, Aberystwyth, Dyfed, and late Ann Elonwy Mary, *née* Price; *b* 8 Dec 1950; *Educ* King's Coll Wimbledon, St John's Coll Oxford (MA); *m* 29 May 1976, Lucy Elizabeth, da of Dr Frank Henry Stubbings, of Cambridge; 2 s (Matthew b 1979, Thomas b 1981), 1 da (Emily b 1984); *Career* called to the Bar Gray's Inn 1975, bencher 1992; standing counsel to Dir Gen of Fair Trading 1989–91 (second jr counsel to DG 1987–89), a jr counsel to The Crown common law 1990–91, first jr Treasy counsel common law 1992–; recorder of the Crown Court 1996– (asst recorder 1992); *Books* Chitty on Contracts (co ed 25 and 26 edns); *Recreations* the Welsh hills; *Style*— Stephen Richards, Esq; ✉ 4 Raymond Buildings, Gray's Inn, London WC1R 5BP (☎ 0171 405 7211, fax 0171 405 2084)

RICHARDS, Prof Thomas Harford Evans; s of (David) Brinley Richards, MBE, BEM, of Cwmbran, Gwent, and (Lizzie) Mary Evans (d 1988); *b* 21 Feb 1931; *Educ* Jones West Monmouth Sch, Univ of Birmingham (BSc, MSc), Univ of Aston (DSc); *m* 20 April 1957, Frances Jean, da of George Ewart Holden (d 1982); 2 s (Mark b 1959, David b 1968), 1 da (Louise b 1961); *Career* lectr in civil engrg Univ of Birmingham 1957–62, mechanical design conslt Lucas Gte Ltd 1961–62, sr lectr Birmingham CAT 1962–66; Aston Univ: sr lectr 1966–78, reader 1978–89, head Mechanical Engrg Div 1983–86, sub dean of engrg 1984–86, dean of engrg 1986–90, prof of mechanical engrg 1989–94 (emeritus prof 1994), sr pro-vice chllr 1990–94; FIMechE 1979, FIMA 1978; *Books* Stress, Vibration and Noise Analysis in Vehicles (with H G Gibbs, 1975), Energy Methods in Stress Analysis (1977), Stability Problems in Engineering Structures (with P Stanley, 1979); *Recreations* gardening, DIY, school governor; *Style*— Prof T H E Richards; ✉ Aston University, Aston Triangle, Birmingham B4 7ET (☎ 0121 359 3611, fax 0121 359 6470, telex 336997 UNIAST G)

RICHARDS, (David) Wyn; s of Evan Gwylfa Richards (d 1987), of Llanelli, and Florence Margretta, *née* Evans (d 1988); *b* 22 Sept 1943; *Educ* Gwendraeth GS, Llanelli GS, Trinity Hall Cambridge; *m* 23 Dec 1972, Thelma Frances, *née* Hall; 5 s (Mark b 1974, Cennydd b 1976, Hywel b 1977, Daniel Owen b 1981, Aled Wyn b 1988); *Career* called to the Bar Inner Temple 1968, recorder of the Crown Court 1985–, asst cmmr Boundary Cmmn Wales; *Style*— Wyn Richards, Esq; ✉ 2 Queens Rd, Sketty, Swansea, W Glamorgan SA2 0SD (☎ 01792 202 462); Iscoed Chambers, 86 St Helen's Rd, Swansea, W Glamorgan SA1 4BQ (☎ 01792 6529 88, fax 01792 458 089)

RICHARDSON, *see:* Stewart-Richardson

RICHARDSON, Prof Andrew; s of Andrew Phillips Harley Richardson (d 1977), and Williamina, *née* Mitchell; *b* 23 Jan 1933; *Educ* Grove Acad Broughty Ferry, Univ of St Andrews; *m* Margaret Elizabeth, da of George Dean Sweeney (d 1987), of Brazeel, Barnetts Rd, Belfast; 1 s (Mark Andrew b 1967, d 1985), 1 da (Lindsay Jane b 1966); *Career* Lt RADC 1956, Capt RWAFF 1956–59; Queen's Univ Belfast 1961–: tutor/registrar 1961–64, lectr/sr hosp dental offr 1964–68, sr lectr/conslt 1968–73, reader/conslt 1973–85, prof/conslt 1985–; pres: Br Dental Students' Assoc 1955–56, Br Dental Assoc NI Branch 1982; memb: BDA, BSSO; *Books* Interceptive Orthodontics in General Dental Practice (1984), Interceptive Orthodontics (1989); *Recreations* restoration of classic cars; *Style*— Prof Andrew Richardson; ✉ 33 Cherryvalley Park, Belfast, N Ireland BT5 6PN (☎ 01232 796548); The Cottage, Dooey, Glencolumcille, Eire; Orthodontic Department, School of Dentistry, Royal Victoria Hospital, Belfast BT12 6BP (☎ 01232 240503, fax 01232 438861)

RICHARDSON, (Henry) Anthony; s of Thomas Ewan Richardson (d 1974), of Batley, W Yorks, and Jessie, *née* Preston (d 1986); *b* 28 Dec 1925; *Educ* Giggleswick Sch, Univ of Leeds (LLB 1950, LLM 1956); *m* 8 May 1954, Georgina, *née* Lawford, step da of Gp Capt George Richard Bedford, RAF (ret), of Wetherby, W Yorks; *Career* called to the Bar Lincoln's Inn 1951; NE Circuit: dep circuit judge 1972–78, recorder of the Crown Ct 1978–96, ret; dep traffic cmmr and dep licensing authy N-Eastern Traffic Area 1989–93; *Recreations* walking, gardening, listening to music; *Style*— Anthony Richardson, Esq; ✉ Grey Thatch, Wetherby Rd, Scarcroft, Leeds LS14 3BB (☎ 0113 289 2555); 37 Park Square, Leeds LS1 2PA (☎ 0113 243 9422)

RICHARDSON, Sir Anthony Lewis; 3 Bt (UK 1924), of Yellow Woods, Province of Cape of Good Hope, South Africa; s of Sir Leslie Lewis Richardson, 2 Bt (d 1985), of Constantia Village, Cape Town, SA, and Joy Patricia, *née* Rillstone; *b* 5 Aug 1950; *Educ* Diocesan Coll Cape Town SA; *m* 1985, (Honor) Gillian, da of Robert Anthony Dauney, of Paddington, Sydney, Australia; 1 s (William Lewis b 15 Oct 1992), 1 da ((Honor) Olivia Phoebe b 9 Sept 1990); *Heir* s, William Lewis Richardson b 15 Oct 1992; *Career* stockbroker L Messel & Co London 1973–75, insurance broker C T Bowring London and Johannesburg 1975–76; stockbroker: Fergusson Bros Hall Stewart & Co Johannesburg and Cape Town 1976–78, W Greenwell & Co London 1979–81; dir S G Warburg Securities London 1986–95 (joined 1981), exec dir SBC Warburg London 1995–; seconded to: S G Warburg Securities/Potter Partners Australia 1986–89, SBC Warburg SA 1996–; memb London Stock Exchange; *Recreations* various sports, photography; *Clubs* Boodle's, Hurlingham, Annabel's; *Style*— Sir Anthony Richardson, Bt; ✉ 128 Trafalgar Place, Sandhurst 2196, Johannesburg, South Africa; SBC Warburg, PO Box 61028, Marshaltown 2107, South Africa (☎ 00 27 11 836 2601, fax 00 27 11 836 2609)

RICHARDSON, David; s of Harold George Richardson (d 1986), of Ewell, Surrey, and Madeleine Raphaële, *née* Lebret (d 1993); *b* 24 April 1928; *Educ* Wimbledon Coll, King's Coll London (BA); *m* 14 Feb 1951, (Frances) Jean, da of Ernest Pendrell Pring (d 1971), of Looe, Cornwall; 3 s (Stephen Michael b Dec 1951, Nicholas Henry b April 1954, Benedict Hugh b Sept 1965), 1 da (Catherine Anne b March 1957); *Career* RAF 1949–51: PO 1949, Flying Offr 1950; RAF Res 1951–56; HM Inspr of Taxes 1953–55; Miny of Lab (later Dept of Employment) 1956–82: chief exec Construction Indust Trg Bd 1964–66, chm Central Youth Employment Exec 1969–71, under sec industl rels 1972–75, dir of safety policy Health and Safety Exec 1975–77, dir ACAS 1977–82; dir: ILO (London) 1982–91, Tablet Publishing Co Ltd 1985–, Industrial Training Service Ltd 1986–92; govr Br Inst of Human Rights 1987–91; FIPM; *Recreations* music, landscape gardening, ceramic sculpture; *Style*— David Richardson, Esq; ✉ 183 Banstead Rd, Carshalton, Surrey SM5 4DP (☎ 0181 241 4614)

RICHARDSON, Sir (John) Eric; kt (1967), CBE (1962); s of William Richardson, of Birkenhead (d 1952); *b* 30 June 1905; *Educ* Higher Elementary Sch Birkenhead, Univ of Liverpool (BEng, PhD); *m* 1941, Alice May, da of Hugh Munro Wilson, of Hull (d 1979);

1 s, 2 da (and 1 da decd); *Career* engr and educationalist; head of Engrg Dept Hull Municipal Tech Coll 1937–41; princ: Oldham Municipal Tech Coll 1942–44, Royal Tech Coll Salford 1944–47, Northampton Poly (now City Univ London) 1947–56; dir Poly of Central London (now Univ of Westminster) 1957–70; Hon DSc City Univ London 1979; FIEE, MIMechE, FBHI, FBOA, FPS, FRSA, FCGI; *Recreations* photography, gardening; *Style—* Sir Eric Richardson, CBE; ✉ 73 Delamere Rd, Ealing, London W5 3JP (☎ 0181 567 1588)

RICHARDSON, Frank Anthony; s of Albert Edward Richardson, and Eileen, *née* Roberts; *b* 20 March 1933; *Educ* Leeds Central HS; *m* 6 Sept 1958, Patricia Elsie, da of Robert Stevenson Taylor; *Career* agent and organiser Cons Party 1956–73, sec Nat Union of Cons Agents 1971–73; assoc dir: John Addey Assocs 1973–77, Charles Barker Watney & Powell 1978–83; dir: Charles Barker Watney & Powell 1983, Shandwick Public Affairs 1990–94; sr ptnr Richardson Consultants 1994–; admin sec: Parly Info Tech Ctee 1985–, Parly Space Ctee 1989–, Parly Roads Study Gp 1987–; vice pres Cons Group for Europe 1992–95; Freeman City of London 1993; memb Yorks Athletics Team 1958; MIPR; *Recreations* tennis, swimming, travel; *Style—* Frank Richardson, Esq; ✉ 22 Gloucester Place Mews, London W1 (☎ 0171 487 4872)

RICHARDSON, Dr George Barclay; CBE (1978); s of George Richardson (d 1970), and Christina Richardson (d 1975); *b* 19 Sept 1924; *Educ* Aberdeen Central Secdy Sch, Univ of Aberdeen (BSc), Univ of Oxford (MA); *m* 21 Sept 1957, Isabel Alison, da of Laurence Chalk (d 1979); 2 s (Graham b 25 April 1960, Andrew b 25 July 1962); *Career* Lt RNVR 1945–46; third sec Dip Serv 1949–50; Univ of Oxford: fell St John's Coll 1951–88, reader in economics 1959–74, chief exec and sec to the delegates OUP 1974–88, pro vice chllr 1988–94, vice pres Oxford Univ Appeal Campaign 1988–89, warden Keble Coll 1989–94; econ advsr UKAEA 1968–74; memb: Econ Devpt Ctee For Electrical Engrg Ctee 1964–73, Monopolies Cmmn 1969–74, Royal Cmmn on Enviromental Pollution 1973–74; hon fell CCC Oxford 1987, Hon DCL Oxford 1988, hon fell St John's Coll Oxford 1989, hon fell Keble Coll Oxford 1994, Hon LLD Aberdeen; *Books* Information and Investment (1960, re-issued 1990), Economic Theory (1964); *Recreations* reading, music, swimming; *Style—* Dr George Richardson, CBE; ✉ 33 Belsyre Court, Observatory Street, Oxford OX2 6HU (☎ and fax 01865 510113)

RICHARDSON, Ian William; CBE (1989); s of John Richardson, and Margaret, *née* Drummond; *b* 7 April 1934; *Educ* Tynecastle Edinburgh, Royal Scottish Acad of Music and Drama; *m* 2 Feb 1961, Maroussia, da of Alexei Simeonitch Frank (d 1967); 2 s (Jeremy b 24 Dec 1961, Miles b 15 July 1963); *Career* actor; FRSAMD 1971; *Theatre* joined Birmingham Repertory Co 1958, played Hamlet 1959; roles with RSC 1960–75: Aragon in Merchant of Venice, Malateste in Duchess of Malfi 1960, Oberon in A Midsummer Night's Dream 1961, Edmund in King Lear 1964, Herald and Marat in Marat/Sade 1964–65, Vendice in Revenger's Tragedy 1965 and 1969, Coriolanus 1966, Bertram in All's Well That Ends Well 1966, Cassius in Julius Caesar 1968, Pericles 1969, Angelo in Measure For Measure 1970, Prospero in The Tempest 1970, Richard II and Bolingbroke 1973, Berowne in Love's Labours Lost 1973, Ford in The Merry Wives of Windsor 1975, Richard III 1975; other roles incl: Professor Higgins in My Fair Lady (NY, Drama Desk Award) 1976–77, Man and Superman (Shaw Festival Ontario) 1977, Lolita (Broadway) 1981, The Miser (Chichester) 1995; *Television* series incl: Tinker Tailor Soldier Spy 1979, Private Schulz 1981, The Woman in White 1982, The Master of Ballantrae 1984, Mistral's Daughter 1985, Porterhouse Blue 1987, Troubles 1988, The Gravy Train 1989, House of Cards 1990, The Gravy Train Goes East 1991, To Play The King 1993, Catherine the Great 1994, The Final Cut; TV plays incl: Danton's Death 1978, Monsignor Quixote 1985, Blunt 1987, An Ungentlemanly Act 1992; *Films* incl: Man of La Mancha 1972, Sherlock Holmes in The Sign of Four and The Hound of the Baskervilles 1982, Brazil 1984, Whoops Apocalypse 1987, The Fourth Protocol 1987, Rosencrantz and Guildenstern Are Dead 1990, The Year of the Comet 1991, BAPS 1996, The Fifth Province 1996; *Awards* RTS Award 1982, American Arts Club Gold Medal 1988, BAFTA Award 1990, RTS Award 1990, Br Press Guild Award 1990; *Publications* prefaces to: Cymbeline, Richard II, The Merry Wives of Windsor; *Recreations* history, music, reading; *Clubs* Garrick; *Style—* Ian Richardson, Esq, CBE; ✉ c/o London Management, 2–4 Noel Street, London W1V 3RB (☎ 0171 287 9000, fax 0171 287 3036)

RICHARDSON, Rev Canon James John (Jim); s of James John Richardson (d 1957), of London, and Gladys May, *née* Evans; *b* 28 March 1941; *Educ* Catford Sch London, Univ of Hull (BA), Univ of Sheffield (DipEd), Cuddesdon Coll Oxford; *m* 30 July 1966, Janet Rosemary, da of Harold Welstand; 2 s (Mark b 1968, Ben b 1974), 1 da (Anna b 1970); *Career* asst master Westfield Comp Sch Sheffield 1964–66, curate St Peter's Collegiate Church Wolverhampton 1969–72, priest-in-charge All Saints Hanley Stoke-on-Trent 1972–75, rector Nantwich 1975–82, vicar Leeds 1982–88, hon canon Ripon Cathedral 1982–88 (canon emeritus 1988–), exec dir The Cncl of Christians and Jews 1988–92, priest-in-charge: Great Brington, Whilton and Norton (Northampton) Dio of Peterborough 1993–96, Chapel Brampton, East Haddon with Holdenby, and Harlestone 1994–96; team rector Bournemouth Town Centre Parish 1996–; town cncllr Nantwich 1977–79; chm Racial Harrassment Cmmn Leeds 1986–87, N of Eng vice pres UN Year of Peace 1986–87, memb Court Univ of Leeds 1986–88; chm of Govrs: Leeds GS 1983–88, Abbey Grange HS Leeds 1982–86; govr Leeds Girl's HS 1982–88; contrib to: Yorkshire Post 1982–89, Four Score Years Lord Coggans 80th Birthday Tribute by his Friends; Hon MA Univ of Leicester 1995; author of articles on interfaith subjects; FRSA 1991; *Recreations* leading pilgrimages, biography (especially First World War poets); *Style—* The Rev Canon Jim Richardson; ✉ Bournemouth Town Centre Parish, St Peter's Rectory, 18 Wimborne Road, Bournemouth, Dorset BH2 6NT (☎ 01202 554058)

RICHARDSON, Jeremy William; s of Thomas William Sydney Raymond Richardson, of Retford, Nottinghamshire, and Jean Mary, *née* Revill; *b* 3 April 1958; *Educ* Forest Sch, QMC (LLB); *Career* called to the Bar Inner Temple 1980; memb: North Eastern Circuit 1982– (sec 1991–96), Gen Cncl of the Bar 1992–94; cncllr Sheffield City Cncl 1983–87; *Style—* Jeremy Richardson, Esq; ✉ 36 St Paul's Square, York YO2 4BD (☎ and fax 01904 627490); 11 King's Bench Walk, Temple, London EC4Y 7EQ (☎ 0171 353 3337, fax 0171 583 2190, car 0860 650371); Third Floor, Goodbard House, Infirmary Street, Leeds LS1 2JS (☎ 0113 245 1156, fax 0113 244 5564)

RICHARDSON, Joanna; da of Capt Frederick Richardson, Intelligence Corps (d 1978), and Charlotte Elsa, *née* Benjamin (d 1978); *Educ* The Downs Sch Seaford, St Anne's Coll Oxford (MA); *Career* author; FRSL 1959 (memb Cncl 1961–86); Chev de l'Ordre des Arts et des Lettres (France) 1987; *Books* Fanny Brawne: A Biography (1952), Théophile Gautier: His Life and Times (1958), Edward FitzGerald (1960), FitzGerald: Selected Works (ed, 1962), The Pre-Eminent Victorian: A Study of Tennyson (1962), The Everlasting Spell: A Study of Keats and His Friends (1963), Essays by Divers Hands (ed, 1963), Edward Lear (1965), George IV: A Portrait (1966), Creevey and Greville (1967), Princess Mathilde (1969), Verlaine (1971), Enid Starkie (1973), Verlaine, Poems (ed and translator, 1974), Stendhal: A Critical Biography (1974), Baudelaire, Poems (ed and translator, 1975), Victor Hugo (1976), Zola (1978), Keats and His Circle: An Album of Portraits (1980), Gautier, Mademoiselle de Maupin (translator, 1981), The Life and Letters of John Keats (1981), Letters From Lambeth: the Correspondence of the Reynolds Family with John Freeman Milward Dovaston 1808–1815 (1981), Colette (1983), Judith Gautier (1986, French edn 1989, awarded Prix Goncourt de la biographie, first time to a non-French writer), Portrait of a Bonaparte: the Life and Times of Joseph-Napoleon Primoli 1851–1927 (1987), Baudelaire (1994); *Style—* Miss Joanna Richardson; ✉ c/o Curtis Brown Ltd, 4th Floor, Haymarket House, 28–29 Haymarket, London SW1Y 4SP (☎ 0171 396 6600)

RICHARDSON, Rt Rev John Henry; *see:* Bedford, Bishop of

RICHARDSON, Baron (Life Peer UK 1979), of Lee, Co Devon; Sir John Samuel Richardson; 1, kt (1960), Bt (UK 1963), LVO (1943); s of Maj John Watson Richardson (ka 1917, formerly solicitor), of Sheffield, and Elizabeth Blakeney, da of Rt Hon Sir Samuel Roberts, 1 Bt, JP, DL; *b* 16 June 1910; *Educ* Charterhouse, Trinity Coll Cambridge (MA, MD); *m* 6 June 1933, Sybil Angela Stephanie (d 1991), 3 da of Arthur Ronald Trist (d 1971), of Stanmore; 2 da (Hon Elizabeth-Ann (Hon Mrs Stafford) b 1937, Hon Susan Clare (Hon Mrs Wales) b 1940); *Heir* to Btcy, none; *Career* sits as independent peer in House of Lords; medical specialist RAMC 1939–45, Lt-Col; conslt physician St Thomas's Hosp 1947–75 and to Metropolitan Police 1957–80; hon conslt physician to Army 1963–75, emeritus 1976–; pres: Royal Soc of Med 1969–71, BMA 1970–71, Gen Medical Cncl 1973–80; Master of Apothecaries Soc 1971–72 (asst emeritus), Liveryman Worshipful Co of Cutlers; Hon DSc: Nat University of Ireland 1975, Hull 1981; Hon DCL Newcastle 1980; Hon LLD: Nottingham 1981, Liverpool 1983; hon fell Trinity Coll Cambridge 1979; Hon FRCS, FRCP, FRCGP, FFCM, FRPharmS, Hon FRCP Glasgow and I, Hon FRCPE; hon bencher Gray's Inn; CStJ; *Style—* The Rt Hon the Lord Richardson, LVO; ✉ Windcutter, Lee, Ilfracombe, Devon (☎ 01271 63198)

RICHARDSON, Very Rev John Stephen; s of James Geoffrey Richardson, of Rossendale, Lancs, and Myra, *née* Greenwood; *b* 2 April 1950; *Educ* Haslingden GS, Univ of Southampton (BA), St John's Coll Nottingham; *m* 29 July 1972, Elizabeth Susan (Sue), da of James Anness Wiltshire (d 1986), of Calne, Wilts; 2 s (Benjamin Stephen b and d 1981, Thomas Samuel John b 1982), 2 da (Sarah Elizabeth b 1975, Ruth Mary b 1977); *Career* various appts Cadbury Schweppes Bristol; asst curate St Michael and All Angels Bramcote Nottingham 1974–77, priest-in-charge Emmanuel Church Southill and curate Radipole and Melcombe Regis Team Miny 1977–80, asst missioner and lay trg advsr Diocese of Salisbury and priest-in-charge Winterborne Monkton with Winterborne Came and Whitcombe with Stinsford 1980–83, vicar Christ Church Nailsea 1983–90, advsr in evangelism Diocese of Bath and Wells 1986–90, provost and vicar of the Cathedral Church of St Peter Bradford 1990–; memb: Cncl St John's Theological Coll Nottingham 1988–94, General Synod 1993–, Cncl Evangelical Alliance 1994–, Cncl Church's Ministry to the Jews 1994–, Bd of Mission of the Gen Synod 1995–; govr: Bradford GS 1990–, Giggleswick Sch 1993–; tstee: Acorn Christian Healing Tst 1990–, Spennithorne House of Healing 1990–; involved with local radio stations 1985–, memb Radio Leeds Local Broadcasting Cncl 1991–95; dir Bradford Breakthrough 1992–; MInstD 1994; *Books* Ten Rural Churches (1988); *Recreations* football, cricket, spotting 1950's and 1960's municipal bus fleets; *Clubs* Bradford, Nat Liberal; *Style—* The Very Rev the Provost of Bradford; ✉ The Provost's House, 1 Cathedral Close, Bradford BD1 4EG (☎ 01274 777722, fax 01274 777730)

RICHARDSON, Rev Prof John Stuart; s of Ronald Hugo Richardson (d 1975), and Enid Stuart, *née* Stephens (d 1980); *b* 4 Feb 1946; *Educ* Berkhamsted Sch, Trinity Coll Oxford (MA, DPhil); *m* 12 April 1969, Patricia Helen, da of Ralph Edward Robotham; 2 s (Thomas b 1971, Martin b 1974); *Career* lectr in ancient history: Exeter Coll Oxford 1969–72, Univ of St Andrews 1972–87; Univ of Edinburgh: prof of classics 1987–, dean Faculty of Arts and provost Faculty Gp of Arts, Divinity and Music 1992–; ordained deacon Scot Episcopal Church 1979, priest 1980, Anglican chaplain Univ of St Andrews 1980–87, team priest St Columba's Edinburgh 1987–, convener SEC Ctee on Canons 1994–; FRSE 1996; *Books* Roman Provincial Administration (1976), Hispaniae (1986), The Romans in Spain (1996); *Recreations* choral singing; *Style—* The Rev Prof John Richardson, FRSE; ✉ 29 Merchiston Ave, Edinburgh EH10 4PH (☎ 0131 228 3094); Faculty of Arts, Univ of Edinburgh, David Hume Tower, George Square, Edinburgh EH8 9JX (☎ 0131 650 3571)

RICHARDSON, (William) Kenneth; s of James McNaughton Richardson, of Stirling, and Jane Ann McKay, *née* Monteith; *b* 16 Nov 1956; *Educ* High Sch of Stirling, Univ of St Andrews (MA); *Career* mgmnt trainee: United Biscuits, Sue Ryder Fndn; planning asst Scot Opera 1983–87; Royal Opera: co-mangr 1987–90, gen mangr 1990–94, admin Royal Opera House Garden Venture 1987–91; artistic dir Dublin Grand Opera Soc 1990–91; arts dir Barbican Centre 1994, independent opera conslt 1995–; dir BOC Covent Garden Festival 1996–; *Clubs* Peg's; *Style—* Kenneth Richardson, Esq; fax 0171 609 3910, e-mail howrich@mail.bogo.co.uk

RICHARDSON, Mark Ashton; s of Ashton Cuthbert Richardson, of Maidenhead, Berks, and Lorna, *née* Barry; *b* 26 July 1972; *Educ* Claires Court Sch, Desborough Comp, Windsor and Maidenhead Coll, Loughborough Univ; *Career* athlete; achievements at 400m: first English Schs Championships 1989, third World Jr Championships 1990 (fourth 1988), third UK Sr Championships 1990, second Euro Jr Championships 1991, second AAA Championships 1991, second World Cup 1992, second UK Championships 1992 (third 1991); achievements at 4 x 400m: second World Jr Championships 1990, first Euro Jr Championships 1991, Gold medal World Championships 1991, third World Cup 1992, Silver medal Olympic Games Barcelona 1992, first Euro Under 23 Cup 1992, Silver medal Olympic Games Atlanta 1996; Rotary Jr Athlete of the Month July 1988, Dairy Crest Jr Athlete of the Month July 1990, AAA Jr Athlete of the Year 1988; *Recreations* reading science fiction novels; *Style—* Mark Richardson, Esq

RICHARDSON, Mark Rushcliffe; s of late Brig Charles Walter Philipps Richardson, DSO, and Hon Averil Diana Richardson, of Headbourne Worthy, Winchester, Hants; *b* 17 Sept 1947; *Educ* Wellington, ChCh Oxford (BA); *m* 29 Sept 1983, Cherry Victoria, da of Sidney Wallace Smart, of Woolstone Manor, Faringdon, Oxon; 1 s (Hugo b 24 Nov 1981), 2 da (Melanie b 13 Nov 1974 d 1994, Davina b 19 Jan 1976); *Career* dir Lazard Bros & Co Ltd 1986–90, chief investment offr Chase Manhattan Private Bank 1992–95, chief exec offr and chief investment offr Chase Asset Management 1996–; hon treas Riding for the Disabled Assoc 1985–92, memb Fin Ctee Br Red Cross Soc 1988–92; *Recreations* country pursuits, skiing; *Clubs* Pratt's, Boodle's, Piping Rock; *Style—* Mark Richardson, Esq; ✉ Priors Court, West Hanney, Wantage, Oxon (☎ 01235 868210); 175 East 62nd Street, New York (☎ 00 1 212 838 4288)

RICHARDSON, Michael John; s of George Frederick Richardson (d 1979), and Mabel Alice, *née* Cox; *b* 28 March 1935; *Educ* Epsom Coll; *m* 22 Aug 1959, Helen Patricia, da of Percival Bluett Bray (d 1942); 1 s (David b 16 Jan 1962), 1 da (Susan b 2 Jan 1965); *Career* CA; FW Smith Riches 1952–60, Price Waterhouse 1960–63, dir 3i Group (3i Corporate Finance Ltd) 1963–80, fin dir Shandwick Group 1980–81, dir West Merchant Bank Ltd (formerly Standard Chartered Merchant Bank Ltd) 1986–93 (joined 1981, sr vice pres 1993–); steward Sevenoaks Methodist Church; Freeman City of London, Liveryman Worshipful Co of CAs; FCA; *Books* Going Public (1973); *Recreations* singing, swimming, gardening; *Style—* Michael Richardson, Esq; ✉ 19 Mount Harry Rd, Sevenoaks, Kent TN13 3JJ (☎ 01732 453839); West Merchant Bank Ltd, 33–36 Gracechurch St, London EC3V 0AX (☎ 0171 623 8711, fax 0171 626 1610, telex 884689)

RICHARDSON, Sir Michael John de Rougemont; kt (1990); s of Sir Arthur Wray Richardson, of Hove, Sussex, and Audrey, *née* de Rougemont (d 1994); *b* 9 April 1925; *Educ* Harrow, RMC Sandhurst; *m* 16 July 1949, Octavia, yr da of Arthur Joyce Mayhew (Capt Denbighshire Hussars); 1 s, 2 da; *Career* Capt Irish Gds 1943–47; Drayton Group 1947–52; chm: Invesco English & International Trust plc 1961–, Derby Trust plc 1981–95, Mithras Investment Trust plc 1990–, Smith New Court plc (non-exec) 1990–94,

Moorgate Smaller Companies Incomes Trust plc 1991–96, Surgicraft Ltd 1994–; partner: Panmure Gordon & Co 1952–70, Cazenove & Co 1970–80; md N M Rothschild & Sons Ltd 1981–90; vice chm: N M Rothschild & Sons Ltd 1990–95, J O Hambro Magan & Co 1995–; dir: Drayton Far Eastern plc 1964–95, Anglo-Scottish Amalgamated Corporation Ltd 1972–89, The Savoy Hotel plc 1979–96, The Rank Foundation 1983–, Rothschild North America Inc 1983–94, Sedgwick Group plc 1984–96, N M Rothschild & Sons (Wales) Ltd 1988–95, Rothschild Continuation Ltd 1989–93, Invesco Asia Trust plc 1995–, Invesco Tokyo Trust plc 1995–, Norman Broadbent International Ltd 1995–; managing tstee Inst of Economic Affairs 1991–, tstee Fndn for Mfrg and Industry 1993–; Liveryman Worshipful Co of Gunmakers; *Recreations* sailing, foxhunting; *Style*— Sir Michael Richardson; ✉ J O Hambro Magan & Co, 32 Queen Anne's Gate, London SW1H 9AB (☎ 0171 233 1400, fax 0171 222 4978)

RICHARDSON, Michael (Mike); s of (James) Brian Richardson; *b* 20 Sept 1954; *Educ* Henley GS, Univ of Bradford Mgmnt Centre (BSc); *children* 2 s (Thomas James b 9 April 1986, Alexander Fraser b 4 July 1989); *Career* brand mgmnt John Player & Sons Nottingham 1976–79, Quaker Oats Ltd Southall 1979–86 (brand mgmnt, trade mktg, new prod devpt), mktg mangr Chessington Tussauds Group London 1986–87, dir of mktg English Tourist Board 1990–94 (asst dir 1987–90), dir of mktg and client servs COI 1994–; fell Tourism Soc, memb Mktg Soc; *Style*— Mike Richardson, Esq; ✉ COI, Hercules Road, London SE1 7DU (☎ 0171 261 8537)

RICHARDSON, Michael Norman; s of Norman Richardson (d 1965), and Ethel, *née* Spittle (d 1978); *b* 23 Feb 1935; *Educ* Dulwich; *m* 13 April 1976, Rosemarie Christina, da of Emmerich von Moers (d 1946); 4 da (Penelope, Theresa, Christina, Alexandra); *Career* RAF 1958–60, Flying Offr in Directorate of Legal Servs Far E Air Force; admitted slr 1958; asst slr Coward Chance & Co 1960–63; ptnr: Jaques & Co 1963–73, Richardson & Oakley 1977–85, Lawrence Graham (specialising Int Corporate Fin) 1985–; dep chm Henry Ansbacher & Co Ltd 1970–77; memb Law Soc 1958, FInstD 1987; *Recreations* all sports, gardening, art; *Clubs* Oriental, MCC; *Style*— Michael Richardson, Esq; ✉ Fernhill Cottage, Hatchet Lane, Windsor Forest, Berks SL4 2DZ (☎ 01344 882 635); Lawrence Graham, 190 Strand, London WC2R 1JN (☎ 0171 379 0000, fax 0171 379 6854, telex 22673)

RICHARDSON, Natasha Jane; da of Tony Richardson (d 1991), and Vanessa Redgrave, *qv*; *b* 11 May 1963; *Educ* Central Sch of Speech and Drama; *m* 1, 1990 (m dis), Robert Michael John Fox; m 2, 1994, Liam Neeson; *Career* actress; *Theatre* season at Leeds Playhouse, A Midsummer Night's Dream (New Shakespeare Co), Hamlet (Young Vic), The Seagull (Lyric Hammersmith, tour and Queen's Theatre) 1985, China (Bush Theatre), High Society (Haymarket and Victoria Palace) 1986, Anna Christie (Young Vic 1990, Broadway 1993); *Television* In A Secret State (BBC) 1985, Ghosts (BBC) 1986, Hostages (Granada) 1992, Suddenly Last Summer (BBC) 1993, Zelda (TNT) 1993, *Films* Every Picture Tells A Story 1985, Gothic 1987, A Month In The Country 1987, Patty Hearst 1988, Fat Man and Little Boy 1989, The Handmaid's Tale 1990, The Comfort of Strangers 1990, The Favor, the Watch and the Very Big Fish 1991, Past Midnight 1991, Sins of the Flesh 1992, Widow's Peak 1994, Nell 1994; *Awards* Most Promising Newcomer Plays and Players 1986; Best Actress: London Theatre Critics 1990, Plays and Players 1990, Evening Standard Film Awards 1990, Prague Film Festival 1994; for Anna Christie: Outer Critics' Circle Award for Best Actress, Tony Award nomination, Drama Desk Award for Best Actress; *Style*— Miss Natasha Richardson; ✉ c/o Hutton Management Ltd, 200 Fulham Road, London SW10 9PN (☎ 0171 352 4825, fax 0171 352 8579)

RICHARDSON, (William) Norman Ballantyne; DL (Greater London 1985); s of Robert Richardson (d 1974), of Wishaw, Lanarkshire, and Sarah Maddick, *née* Shields; *b* 8 Oct 1947; *Educ* King Edward VI GS Birmingham, Goldsmiths' Coll Univ of London (CertEd); *Career* dep head Emmanuel C of E Sch London NW6 1979–81; headmaster: All Saints' C of E Sch London SW6 1981–85, Christ Church C of E Sch London SW3 1985–92, St Michael's C of E Sch London N6 1992–96; chm: ILEA Divnl Consultative Ctee of Headteachers 1985–86 and 1989–90 (memb 1981–90), Local Advsy Ctee on Primary/Secondary Transfer 1987–88, ILEA Central Consultative Ctee of Headteachers 1989–90 (memb 1982–90), Consultative Ctee of Heads and Deputies in the Royal Borough of Kensington and Chelsea 1989–90, London Headteachers' Assoc (Kensington and Chelsea) 1990–91, London Diocesan Headteachers' Cncl 1991–92, 1993–94 and 1995–96 (memb 1984–96); memb: Colne/East Gade Advsy Ctee on Educn 1977–81, ILEA Standing Advsy Cncl on Religious Educn 1985–90, Royal Borough of Kensington and Chelsea Standing Advsy Cncl on Religions Educn 1989–92, London Borough of Haringey Standing Advsy Cncl on Religious Educn 1992–94; govr: Leavesden Green Infant Sch 1977–81, Leavesden Green Junior Sch 1977–81; chm London (South) Ctee: Royal Jubilee and Prince's Tsts 1984–90, The Prince's Tst 1990–95; sec: London Youth Involvement Ctee Queen's Silver Jubilee Tst 1981–83, Greater London Ctee Royal Jubilee and Prince's Tsts 1983–84; FRGS 1969, FRSA 1974, MCollP 1985, MIMgt 1986, FCP 1989, MInstAM 1990, MIIM 1990, MISM 1990, MInstFM 1990; *Recreations* reading biographies, travel and generally recharging the batteries; *Clubs* Royal Commonwealth Society, Civil Serv, Royal Over-Seas League, The Pilgrims, RSA; *Style*— W N B Richardson, Esq, DL; ✉ 6 The Hedgerows, Chells Manor Village, Stevenage, Hertfordshire SG2 7BW

RICHARDSON, Paul Michael; JP (Nottingham 1978); s of George Herbert Richardson, of Ravenshead, Nottingham, and Evelyn, *née* O'Neil; *b* 4 Jan 1941; *Educ* West Bridgford HS, Alfreton HS; *m* 14 Nov 1970, Jacqueline Margaret, da of John Sydney Edwards, of Aspley, Nottingham, and Sarah, *née* Shaw; 2 s (Michael b 10 Nov 1972, William b 22 July 1975), 1 da (Joanne b 16 Aug 1971); *Career* md FW Buck and Sons Ltd 1977–92, dir Long Eaton Advertiser Co Ltd 1980–92, head weekly publications T Bailey Forman Ltd 1982–92, jt md Business Magazine Group Ltd 1992–; memb Rotary Club Sutton-in-Ashfield 1977–; cncllr (Lib) Sutton-in-Ashfield Urban 1967–70; *Recreations* sports enthusiast; *Style*— Paul Richardson, Esq, JP; ✉ Business Magazine Group Ltd, Briarwood House, St John Street, Mansfield, Notts NG18 1QH (☎ 01623 655933)

RICHARDSON, Peter Edward Hugh; s of Edward William Moreton Richardson, of Malvern, Worcs, and Pamela Merle, *née* Case-Morris; *b* 12 April 1955; *Educ* Malvern Coll, The Queen's Coll Oxford (MA); *m* 22 Sept 1984, Miriam Elizabeth, da of Dennis Brian Chance, of Chesham, Bucks; 1 s (Michael William b 1 Nov 1987), 1 da (Heather Caroline b 9 April 1990); *Career* trainee CA Price Waterhouse & Co 1976–77; Butterworth & Co (Publishers) Ltd: commissioning ed 1977–82, sr commissioning ed 1982–84, managing ed 1984–85; Churchill Livingstone (medical div of Pearson Professional): publisher 1985–87, publishing mangr 1987–90, publishing dir 1990–94, dir healthcare info and mgmnt 1994–; chm Exec Medical Gp of the Publishers Assoc 1993–; *Recreations* music, dealing with small children; *Style*— Peter Richardson, Esq; ✉ 3 Butlers Close, Amersham, Bucks HP6 5PY (☎ 01494 722017); Churchill Livingstone, 102–108 Clerkenwell Road, London EC1M 5SA (☎ 0171 282 8301, fax 0171 282 8311)

RICHARDSON, Philip Edward; s of Wilfrid Laurence Richardson (d 1983), of Solihull, and Nellie Elizabeth, *née* Hands (d 1966); *b* 6 Oct 1945; *Educ* Tudor Grange GS Solihull, Coll of Law; *m* 26 May 1969, Corrinne Mary, da of John Woodall (d 1983), of Flyford Flavell; 2 s (Toby b 1972, Tom b 1977), 2 da (Polly b 1975, Prue b 1980); *Career* slr; ptnr Dawkins and Grey 1971–, dir English String Orch Ltd 1984–; chm of govrs Pershore HS 1988–, pres Birmingham Consular Assoc 1987–89, vice chm Hill and Moor PC 1987–89, hon consul: The Netherlands 1982–, Belgium 1984–; Chevalier of the Order of Orange Nassau (Netherlands); memb: Law Soc 1970, Birmingham Law Soc 1970 (jt hon sec 1980–89, PR offr 1987, vice pres 1989–90, pres 1990–91); tstee The Housing Assoc Charitable Tst 1995; *Recreations* music, railways; *Clubs* The Birmingham; *Style*— Philip Richardson, Esq; ✉ Bluebell Cottage, Hill, Pershore, Worcs (☎ 01386 860664); Dawkins and Grey, 40 Great Charles St, Queensway, Birmingham B3 2AR (☎ 0121 233 1021, fax 0121 200 1548, car 0860 202994)

RICHARDSON, Ray; *b* 3 Nov 1964; *Educ* John Road Sch, St Martin's Sch of Art, Goldsmiths Coll (degree); *m* 1989; 2 s; *Career* artist; *Solo Exhibitions* Greenwich Theatre Gallery 1985, Boycott Gallery Brussels 1989, Backhanders (Woodlands Art Gallery London) 1990, Gallery 31 Lille 1990, Beaux Arts Bath 1991, 1992 and 1993, ART/LA91 (Beaux Arts LA) 1991, ART92 (Beaux Arts London) 1992, LINEART 92 (Beaux Arts Ghent) 1992, ART/LA92 (Beaux Arts LA) 1992, ART93 (Beaux Arts London) 1993, Beaux Arts London 1994, Galerie Alain Blondel Paris 1994, Boycott Gallery Brussels 1995; *Group Exhibitions* Greenwich Open Woodlands Art Gallery 1983 and 1985, True to Form - Twenty Emerging British Artists (The Orangery London) 1987, John Player Portrait Award (Nat Portrait Gallery) 1988, Lineart '90 (Ghent) 1990, BP Portrait Award (Nat Portrait Gallery) 1990; Br Cncl award 1989, special commendation BP Portrait award 1990; *Recreations* football; *Clubs* King Vic Football, The Royal Brussels British Football; *Style*— Ray Richardson, Esq; ✉ c/o The Beaux Arts Gallery, 22 Cork Street, London W1X 1HB (☎ 0171 437 5799, fax 0171 437 5798); The Beaux Arts Gallery, 12/13 York Street, Bath BA1 1NG (☎ 01225 464850, fax 01225 422256)

RICHARDSON, Lt-Gen Sir Robert Francis; KCB (1982), CVO (1978), CBE (1975, OBE 1971, MBE 1965); s of Robert Buchan Richardson; *b* 2 March 1929; *Educ* George Heriot's Sch Edinburgh, RMA Sandhurst; *m* 1, 1956, Maureen Robinson (d 1986); 3 s, 1 da; m 2, 7 May 1988, Mrs Alexandra Inglis, *née* Bomford; 2 stepsons; *Career* GSO2 MO4 MOD 1961–64, Bde Maj Aden Bde 1967 (despatches), GSO 2 asst chief Def Staff Ops MOD 1968–69, CO 1 Bn Royal Scots 1969–71, Col Gen Staff Staff Coll Camberley 1971–74, Cdr 39 Inf Bde NI 1974–75, Dep Adj-Gen HQ BAOR 1975–78, GOC Berlin 1978–80, V-Adj Gen/Dir Manning (Army) MOD 1980–82, Col The Royal Scots (The Royal Regt) 1980–90 (cmmnd 1949), GOC NI 1982–85; admin The MacRobert Tsts 1985–95; Lt of the Tower of London 1992–95; *Recreations* golf, shooting, gardening; *Clubs* Royal Scots, Hon Co of Edinburgh Golfers (Muirfield); *Style*— Lt-Gen Sir Robert Richardson, KCB, CVO, CBE; ✉ c/o Bank of Scotland, 38 Threadneedle Street, London EC2P 2EH

RICHARDSON, Robert Oliver; s of Robert Frederick Oliver (d 1987), and Marie, *née* Richardson; *b* 26 Sept 1940; *Educ* Stretford GS; *m* 1, 1968 (m dis), Gwyneth Marilyn, *née* Hunt; m 2, 24 Aug 1974, Sheila Muriel Boustead, da of Cecil John Norman Miller, MBE; 1 s (James Malcolm b 8 April 1977), 1 step s (Michael John b 6 Oct 1961); *Career* journalist Daily Mail 1965–67 and 1968–72, ed Welwyn and Hatfield Times 1973–81, ed Herts Advertiser 1981–87, freelance journalist 1987–92 (contracted to The Independent 1990–92), staff journalist The Independent 1992–94, freelance journalist 1994–; memb Crime Writers' Assoc 1985– (vice chm 1992–93, chm 1993–94); *Books* The Book of Hatfield (1977), The Latimer Mercy (1985, John Creasey Meml Award for best first crime novel), Bellringer Street (1988), The Book of the Dead (1989), The Dying of the Light (1990), Sleeping in the Blood (1991), The Lazarus Tree (1992), The Hand of Strange Children (1993), Significant Others (1995); *Recreations* reading, walking, history, crosswords; *Style*— Robert Richardson, Esq; ✉ c/o Gregory and Radice, 3 Barb Mews, London W6 7PA (☎ 0171 610 4676, fax 0171 610 4686)

RICHARDSON, Roger Hart; RD (1965); s of Justin Richardson, of Headley, Surrey (d 1975), and Margery, *née* Wolfe (d 1996); *b* 13 Aug 1931; *Educ* Rugby, Christ's Coll Cambridge (MA); *m* 25 Oct 1967, Evelyn Louise, da of Dr Paul Kane, MD (d 1994); 1 s (Matthew b 1969), 1 da (Lydia b 1970); *Career* Lt Cdr RNR 1949–70; chm and md Beaver & Tapley Ltd (furniture mfrs) Southall Middx 1975–; Master Worshipful Co of Furniture Makers 1988 (Liveryman 1961, memb Ct of Assts 1974, Jr Warden 1987, Sr Warden 1987); FRSA 1992; *Recreations* sailing, music, bird-watching, wine; *Clubs* RNSA; *Style*— Roger Richardson, Esq, RD; ✉ 11 Broom Water, Teddington, Middx TW11 9QJ (☎ 0181 977 7921, fax 0181 255 6494); Beaver & Tapley Ltd, Scotts Rd, Southall, Middx UB2 5DJ (☎ 0181 574 4311)

RICHARDSON, Stephen Laurence; s of Laurence Richardson, of St Davids, Dyfed, and Rosalae, *née* Reilly; *b* 20 June 1959; *Educ* Maghull GS Liverpool, Ysgol Dewi Sant St Davids, Faculty of Music Univ of Manchester, RNCM (Countess of Munster Award, Moores Fndn Award, Kay Opera Prize); *m* 19 July 1986, Colleen Delores, *née* Barsley; 2 da (Elise Delores b 3 Dec 1990, Abigail Rosina b 27 Sep 1992); *Career* bass; performed with orchs incl: LSO, City of Birmingham Symphony, Montreal Philharmonic, London Philharmonic, Hallé, Scottish National, London Sinfonietta, LSO, English String Orch, BBC Philharmonic, English Concert, Prague Symphony, BBC National Orch of Wales; worked with conductors incl: Sir John Pritchard, Neeme Jarvi, Oliver Knussen, Trevor Pinnock, Sir Simon Rattle, Andrew Parrott, Jiri Belohlavec, Richard Hickox; appeared at festivals incl: Aldeburgh, Edinburgh, Frankfurt, Singapore, Brussels, Turin, Boston, Tanglewood, Hong Kong; *Performances* over 70 operatic roles incl: The King in Aida (ENO, Opera North), Colline in La Boheme (WNO), Priam in The Trojans (WNO), Da Silva in Ernani (WNO), Don Ferrando in Il Trovatore (Scottish Opera), Private Willis in Iolanthe (Scottish Opera), Ratcliffe in Billy Budd (Scottish Opera), Johann in Werther (Scottish Opera), Sarastro in The Magic Flute (Opera North), He-Ancient in A Midsummer Marriage (Opera North), Father in The Jewel Box (Opera North), Mongolian Soldier in Judith Weir's A Night at the Chinese Opera (Kent Opera), 150 anniversary performance of Mendelssohn's Elijah (BBC Proms) 1996; world premieres incl: Sir Joshua Cramer in Gerald Barry's The Intelligence Park, Where the Wild Things Are (Glyndebourne Festival Opera), Higglety Pigglety Pop (Glyndebourne Festival Opera), John Taverner's Eis Thanaton and Resurrection, Benedict Mason's Music for Three Charlie Chaplin Films; given recitals in Wigmore Hall London, Frankfurt, Prague, Berlin and Cologne; *Recordings* incl: Where the Wild Things Are, Goehr's The Death of Moses, Purcell's Ode for the Birthday of Queen Mary 1694, Mozart's Requiem, Macmillan's Vistitatio Sepulchri; *Recreations* sailing, fishing, painting, family life; *Style*— Stephen Richardson, Esq; ✉ Harrison/Parrott Ltd, 12 Penzance Place, London W11 4PA (☎ 0171 228 9166, fax 0171 221 5042)

RICHARDSON, Prof Stephen Michael; s of David Richardson, of Carshalton, Surrey, and Frances Joan, *née* Pring; *b* 8 Dec 1951; *Educ* Wimbledon Coll, Imperial Coll London (BSc(Eng), PhD, Hinchley Medal IChemE); *m* 5 June 1976, Hilary Joy, da of Malcolm Graham Burgess; 2 da (Helen Alice b 23 Feb 1979, Susan Margaret Clare b 7 June 1984), 1 s (Martin David b 4 Oct 1980); *Career* Univ of Cambridge: Rolls-Royce research asst 1975–76, 1851 research fell 1976–77; Dept of Chemical Engrg Imperial Coll London: lectr 1978–87, Nuffield research fell 1984–85, sr lectr 1987–92, reader 1992–94, prof 1994–; visiting prof Univ of Loughborough 1995–98; vice chm Subject Gp on Oil & Natural Gas Production IChemE; CEng 1988, FIChemE 1990 (MIChemE 1988), FEng 1996; *Publications include* Fluid Mechanics (Hemisphere NY, 1989), Blowdown of Pressure Vessels (Trans IChemE, 1992), Piper Alpha (Loss Prevention Bulletin, 1995); *Recreations* music, gardening, walking; *Style*— Prof Stephen Richardson, FEng; ✉ Department of Chemical Engineering, Imperial College, London SW7 2AZ (☎ and fax 0171 594 5589, e-mail s.m.richardson@ic.ac.uk)

RICHARDSON, Maj-Gen Thomas Anthony (Tony); CB (1974), MBE (1960); s of Maj-Gen Thomas William Richardson, OBE, of Norfolk (d 1968), and Josephine Mary

Herbert Wickham Clarke (d 1973); *b* 9 Aug 1922; *Educ* Wellington, Military Coll of Science; *m* 1, 1945, Katharine Joanna Ruxton (d 1988), da of Maj Charles Minto Roberts (d 1956), of Somerset; 1 s (Christopher), 1 da (Charlotte); m 2, 1991, Anthea Rachel, da of Prof Dennis Butler Fry (d 1973), of Wimbledon; *Career* CO 7 RHA 1964–67, Cdr RA 2 Div (Brig) 1967–69, Dir of Operational Requirements (Brig) 1970–71, Dir of Army Aviation (Maj-Gen) 1971–74, Head Br Defence Liaison Staff India (Maj-Gen) 1974–77; sec: Timber Growers Eng and Wales 1978–84, Br Christmas Tree Growers' Assoc 1980–, Christmas Tree Growers' Assoc of Western Europe 1989–; vice chm Br Home and Hosp for Incurables 1995– (chm Gen Purposes Ctee 1988–); chm: Tree Cncl 1986, Army Aviation Assoc, Army Gliding Assoc, RA Rugby Club, Rhine Army Free Fall Parachute Club, 2nd Div Ski Ctee; Cdre Army Sailing Assoc; vice cdre: RA Yacht Club, (and chm) RAYC Germany; hon sec RA Garrison Shoot Larkhill; tstee Queen Mary's Roehampton Tst 1985–, pres Essex Yeo Assoc 1981–; *Recreations* fishing, skiing, sailing, travelling; *Clubs* Army and Navy; *Style*— Maj-Gen Tony Richardson, CB, MBE; ✉ 12 Lauriston Rd, Wimbledon, London SW19 4TQ (☎ 0181 946 2695, fax 0181 947 0211)

RICHARDSON, HE Thomas Legh; CMG (1991); s of Arthur Legh Turnour Richardson (d 1984), and Penelope Margaret, *née* Waithman; *b* 6 Feb 1941; *Educ* Westminster, Ch Ch Oxford (MA); *m* 10 Feb 1979, Alexandra Frazier Wasiqullah, da of John D Ratcliff (d 1974), of New York; *Career* joined FCO 1962; serv in: Accra, Dar Es Salaam, Milan, New York, Rome; dep perm rep UK Mission to UN with personal rank of Ambass 1989–94, asst under-sec of state Western Europe FCO 1994–96, ambass to Italy 1996–; *Recreations* reading, walking, music; *Style*— HE Mr Thomas Richardson, CMG; ✉ c/o Foreign & Commonwealth Office (Rome), King Charles Street, London SW1A 2AH

RICHARDSON, William; CBE (1981), DL (Cumbria 1982); s of Edwin Richardson; *b* 15 Aug 1916; *Educ* Jr Tech Coll, Tech Colls Barrow-in-Furness; *m* 1941, Beatrice Marjorie Iliffe; 1 s, 1 da; *Career* chm: Vickers Shipbuilding & Engineering 1976–83 (md 1969–76), Vosper Thornycroft UK 1978–83, Barclay Curle 1978–83, Brooke Marine 1981–83; dep chm British Shipbuilders 1981–83 (memb Bd 1977–83); dir Vickers Cockatoo Dockyard Pty (Australia) 1977–84, Vosper Shiprepairers 1979–82; memb Res Cncl and office bearer Br Ship Res Assoc 1976–78, chm Mgmnt Bd Shipbuilders and Repairers Nat Assoc 1976–78 (memb Exec Cncl 1969–77), pres Br Productivity Cncl Area Assoc 1969–72, shipbuilding indust rep on Def Industs Quality Assur Panel 1972–82; memb: Shipbuilding Indust Trg Bd 1979–82, NE Coast Inst of Engrs and Shipbuilders 1967–; author of papers on various aspects of UK shipbuilding indust, contrib to tech journals; Silver Jubilee medal (1977); Liveryman Worshipful Co of Shipwrights 1978; CEng, FRINA 1970 (assoc memb 1950, memb 1955), FInstD, CIMgt (fell 1977); *Recreations* sailing, small-bore shooting, golf, fishing; *Clubs* National Small-Bore Rifle Assoc; *Style*— William Richardson, Esq, CBE, DL; ✉ Sequoia, Sunbrick Lane, Baycliff, Ulverston, Cumbria LA12 9RQ (☎ 01229 869434)

RICHARDSON-BUNBURY, Lt Cdr Sir (Richard David) Michael; 5 Bt (I 1787), of Augher, Co Tyrone; eldest s of Richard Richardson-Bunbury (d 1951; ggs of Sir James Richardson-Bunbury, 2 Bt), and Florence Margaret Gordon (d 1993), da of Col Roger Gordon Thomson; suc kinsman, Sir Mervyn Richardson-Bunbury, 4 Bt (d 1953); *b* 27 Oct 1927; *Educ* RNC Dartmouth; *m* 15 July 1961, Jane Louise, da of Col Alfred William Pulverman, IA (d 1938); 2 s (Roger Michael b 1962, d 1994, Thomas William b 1965); *Heir* s,Thomas William Richardson-Bunbury b 4 Aug 1965; *Career* Midshipman (S) RN 1945, Sub Lt (S) 1947, Lt (S) 1948, Lt Cdr 1956, sec to Head of UK Serv Liaison Staff Australia 1956–58, RN Staff Coll, Greenwich 1960–61, Capt's sec HMS Ark Royal 1961–64, sec to Flag Offr Naval Flying Trg 1964–67, ret 1967; entered computer servs indust 1967, ret 1987; dir Sandy Laird Ltd 1988; pres HMS Sussex Assoc 1991; *Recreations* woodwork, gardening, reading, travel; *Style*— Lt Cdr Sir Michael Richardson-Bunbury, Bt, RN; ✉ Upper House, Crowcombe, Taunton, Somerset TA4 4AG (☎ 01984 618223)

RICHARDSON OF DUNTISBOURNE, Baron (Life Peer UK 1983), of Duntisbourne in the Co of Gloucestershire; Gordon William Humphreys Richardson; KG (1983), MBE (1944), TD (1979), PC (1976); s of John Robert and Nellie Richardson; *b* 25 Nov 1915; *Educ* Nottingham HS, Gonville and Caius Coll Cambridge (MA, LLB); *m* 1941, Margaret Alison, er da of late Very Rev Hugh Richard Lawrie Sheppard, Canon and Precentor of St Paul's Cathedral; 1 s (Hon Simon Bruce Sheppard b 1944), 1 da (Hon Sarah (Hon Lady Riddell) b 1942); *Career* govr Bank of England 1973–83 (memb Ct 1967–83), serv WWII S Notts Hussars Yeo, Staff Coll Camberley and War Office; barr 1946–55, memb Bar Cncl 1951–55, hon bencher Gray's Inn 1973; with ICFC 1955–57; former chm: J Henry Schroder Wagg, Schroders Ltd, Schroders Inc; former chm Industl Devpt Advsy Bd, former chm Ctee on Turnover Taxation 1963–64; memb NEDC 1980–83 (and 1971–73); one of HM Lts City of London 1974–; former memb Ct London Univ, former tstee Nat Gallery, dep high steward Cambridge Univ 1982–; dir: Glyndebourne Arts Tst 1980–88, Royal Opera House 1983–88; Hon DSc: City Univ 1976, Univ of Aston 1979; Hon LLD Univ of Cambridge 1979, Hon DCL Univ of E Anglia 1984; Liveryman Worshipful Co of Mercers; *Clubs* Athenaeum, Brooks's, Pratt's; *Style*— The Rt Hon the Lord Richardson of Duntisbourne, KG, MBE, TD, PC; ✉ c/o Morgan Stanley UK Group, 25 Cabot Square, Canary Wharf, London E14 4QA

RICHBOROUGH, Bishop of 1995–; Rt Rev Edwin Barnes; s of Edwin Barnes (d 1970), of Yeovil, Somerset, and Dorothy Barnes; *b* 6 Feb 1935; *Educ* Plymouth Coll, Pembroke Coll Oxford (open history scholar, MA), Cuddesdon Theol Coll; *m* 1 Aug 1963, June Elizabeth, da of Norman Green; 1 da (Nicola b 28 Sept 1967), 1 s (Matthew James b 21 Sept 1969); *Career* Nat Serv RAF 1953–55, Pilot Offr (Fighter Control) 1954; asst curate: St Mark's N End Portsmouth 1960–64, All Saints Woodham (Guildford Dio) 1964–67; rector St John's Farncombe 1967–78, vicar All Saints Hessle (York Dio) 1978–87, princ St Stephen's House Oxford 1987–95, hon canon of Christ Church Oxford 1994–95, provincial episcopal visitor Canterbury 1995–; memb Gen Synod 1975–78, 1985–87 and 1990–95 (memb Standing Ctee 1994–95), C of E rep CCBI and CTE 1994–95; *Style*— The Rt Rev the Bishop of Richborough

RICHES, Sir Derek Martin Hurry; KCMG (1963, CMG 1958); s of Claude W H Riches, of Cardiff (d 1947), and bro of Gen Sir Ian Riches, KCB, DSO (d 1996); *b* 26 July 1912; *Educ* Univ Coll Sch, Univ Coll London; *m* 1942, Helen (d 1989), da of George Washburn Hayes, of Poughkeepsie, NY, USA; 1 da; *Career* entered Foreign Service 1934, chargé d'affaires Jedda 1952, cnsllr and head of Eastern Dept Foreign Office 1955–59; ambass to: Libya 1959–61, Republic of Congo 1961–63, Lebanon 1963–67, ret; *Style*— Sir Derek Riches, KCMG; ✉ 48 The Ave, Kew Gardens, Surrey

RICHMOND, Sir Alan James; kt (1969); *b* 12 Oct 1919; *Educ* Berlin, Les Rayons Switzerland, Univ of London (BSc, PhD); *m* 1951, Sally; 1 step s, 1 step da; *Career* engrg industry 1938–45; chartered mech engr; lectr Battersea Poly 1946–55, head Dept of Mech Engrg Welsh Coll of Advanced Technol 1955–58, princ Lanchester Coll of Technol Coventry 1958–70, dir Lanchester Poly Coventry 1970–72, princ Strode Coll Street Somerset 1972–81, conslt, expert witness and commercial arbitrator 1982–; Hon DSc CNAA; CEng, FIMechE, FCIArb; *Recreations* law, gardening, reading; *Clubs* Royal Cwlth Soc; *Style*— Sir Alan Richmond; ✉ 5 The Orchard, Westfield Park South, Bath BA1 3HT (☎ 01225 333393)

RICHMOND, Rear-Adm Andrew John; CB (1987); s of Albert George Richmond (d 1976), and Emily Margaret, *née* Denbee; *b* 5 Nov 1931; *Educ* King's Sch Bruton, Pangbourne Coll; *m* 1 June 1957, Jane Annette (Toni), da of Lionel Ley, of New Zealand (d 1991); 1 s (Julian Andrew b 28 Nov 1958), 2 da (Alison Anna Claire b 18 Sept 1960, Carolyn Jane Louise b 21 Feb 1962); *Career* RN: joined 1950, staff of C-in-C East Indies 1953, flying training 1955, Cyprus 847 Sqdn 1956, HMS Victorious 824 Sqdn 1958, staff of Flag Offr Arabian Sea 1960, BRNC Dartmouth 1963, sec to Flag Offr Carriers and Amphibious Ships 1968, Supply Sch HMS Pembroke 1970, Supply Offr HMS Bulwark 1972, Fleet Supply Offr 1974, asst dir Naval Manpower 1976, sec to C-in-C Naval Home Command 1977, Capt HMS Cochrane 1979, dir Naval Logistic Planning 1982, ADC 1984, asst chief of Defence Staff (Logistics) 1985, Chief Naval Supply & Secretariat Offr 1986; chief exec RSPCA 1987–91; *Recreations* golf, gardening, countryside; *Clubs* Goodwood Golf; *Style*— Rear Adm Andrew Richmond, CB; ✉ c/o Royal Bank of Scotland, Chichester, W Sussex PO19 1DS

RICHMOND, Anthony John (Tony); s of Arthur Geoffrey Richmond (d 1981), of Parkstone, Poole, Dorset, and Hilda Mary, *née* Pumphrey (d 1986); *b* 11 April 1938; *Educ* Wychwood Sch Bournemouth, Leighton Park Sch Reading, Brasenose Coll Oxford; *m* 1, 1965 (m dis), Elizabeth Ann, da of Peter Marshall; 2 s (Mark Benjamin b 1968, Peter Spencer b 1971); m 2, 1983, Julia Ruth, da of Donald Diggles; *Career* articled clerk Edwin G Pulsford & Co Chartered Accountants Poole Dorset 1961–65; KPMG: joined 1965, ptnr Sheffield 1971, NE Region Corp Recovery ptnr Leeds 1980– (provisional liquidator Middlesbrough FC 1986, first High Court admin Charnley Davies Group 1987, jt admin James Ferguson Holdings plc 1988, receiver Burrells Wharf Development Kentish Homes Ltd 1989, jt admin receiver Capital Airlines Ltd 1990–); memb Insolvency Courses Ctee ICAEW 1973–79; FCA (ACA 1965); memb: Insolvency Practitioners' Assoc 1977, Soc of Insolvency Practitioners 1990; Dorset Co Golf Champion 1962 and 1964; *Recreations* golf, windsurfing, skiing; *Clubs* Lindrick Golf, Oxford & Cambridge Golfing Soc; *Style*— Tony Richmond, Esq; ✉ KPMG, 1 The Embankment, Neville St, Leeds LS1 4DW (☎ 0113 231 3000, fax 0113 231 3200)

RICHMOND, Archdeacon of; *see:* Good, Ven Kenneth Roy

RICHMOND, Dr David John Hamilton; s of Dr Jack Hamilton Richmond (Maj RAMC, d 1969), and Gwendoline Mabel, *née* Thompson; *b* 18 Oct 1936; *Educ* Leighton Park Sch Reading, Pembroke Coll Cambridge, Guy's Hosp (MA, MB BChir, DObst RCOG, FRCA); *m* 14 Feb 1975, Susan Elizabeth Helen, da of Charles W Malcolm, of Kepa Rd, Auckland, New Zealand; 1 s (William b 11 March 1979), 2 da (Felicity b 4 Oct 1977, Amanda b 11 Feb 1982); *Career* Nat Serv, PO navigator RAF 1955–57; formerly: registrar St George's Hosp, registrar Bart's, sr registrar Queen Elizabeth Hosp Birmingham; conslt anaesthetist Royal Wolverhampton Hosps NHS Trust 1971–; memb: Obstetric Anaesthetist Assoc, Assoc of Anaesthetists of GB; *Recreations* golf, tennis, bridge; *Clubs* South Staffordshire Golf, Wolverhampton Lawn Tennis & Squash; *Style*— Dr David Richmond; ✉ Greenways, Stockwell End, Tettenhall, Wolverhampton WV6 9PH (☎ 01902 751448); New Cross Hospital, Wolverhampton WV10 0QP (☎ 01902 307999)

RICHMOND, Eric; s of Edwin Richmond, of Lofting Road, London, and Patricia Cooper; *b* 6 March 1954; *Educ* St Stephen's Sch Rome, The Forum Sch Rome, Columbia Univ NYC, Art Center Coll of Design LA; *m* 8 Aug 1984, Alison, da of Ronald Dick; 1 step s (Taylor b 8 Oct 1970); *Career* freelance portrait photographer 1984– (magazine, corp brochure and advtg cmmns); documented Northern Telecom's Arts Europe grant initiative for book and exhbn 1993–95; one-man exhbns: Assembly Rooms Edinburgh Festival 1991, First Light Gallery Brighton 1994; memb AFAEP; *Style*— Eric Richmond, Esq; ✉ 15a Pembridge Crescent, London W11 3DX (☎ 0171 727 6257)

RICHMOND, Rt Rev (Francis) Henry Arthur; *see:* Repton, Bishop of

RICHMOND, Prof John; CBE (1993); s of Hugh Richmond (d 1952), and Janet Hyslop, *née* Brown (d 1985); *b* 30 May 1926; *Educ* Doncaster GS, Univ of Edinburgh (MB ChB, MD); *m* 29 Sept 1951, Jenny, da of Thomas Nicol (d 1977); 2 s (David b 1953, Michael b 1956), 1 da (Virginia b 1961); *Career* RAMC 1949–50; served: Ethiopia, Kenya, N Rhodesia (MO 1 Bn KAR); jr hosp appts Edinburgh 1948–49, GP Galloway 1950–52, hosp appts Northants 1952–54, res fell N Gen Hosp Edinburgh 1955, lectr (later sr lectr and reader) Univ of Edinburgh 1956–73 (secondments: res fell Meml Sloan Kettering Cancer Center NY 1958–59, Makerere Univ Med Sch Uganda 1965); prof of med Univ of Sheffield 1973–89 (dean Med Sch 1985–88); pres RCPEd 1988–91, chm UK MRCP Examining Bd 1985–89, sr censor and sr vice pres RCP London 1984–85; memb: Sheffield Health Authy 1981–84, High Constables of Edinburgh 1962–71, Bd of Advsrs Univ of London 1984–93, Cncl of Mgmnt Yorks Cancer Res Campaign 1989–93; external advsr Chinese Univ Hong Kong 1982–; memb: Dept of Health Clinical Standards Advsy Gp 1991–94, Scottish Advsy Bd Br Cncl 1991–, Scottish Ctee Marie Curie Meml Fndn 1992–; memb Assoc of Physicians of GB and I; Hon MD Univ of Sheffield; FRCP, FRCPE, FRCPSG, FRCPI, FRCSE, FRSE; Hon: FFPHM, FFPM, FACP, FRACP, FCPS (Pakistan), FCP (SA); *Style*— Prof John Richmond, CBE; ✉ 15 Church Hill, Edinburgh EH10 4BG (☎ 0131 447 2760)

RICHMOND, John; *b* 1960; *Educ* Kingston Poly (BA); *m* Angie Hill; *Career* fashion designer; began career in own co producing John Richmond collection, simultaneously worked freelance for Emporia Armani, Fiorucci, Joseph Tricot and 'Pin-Up' for Deni Cler, ptnr with Maria Cornejo producing Richmond/Cornejo label 1984–87 (shops in London and 16 in Japan), solo 1987–; int catwalk shows from 1991: The International Palace of Destroy, Dinner with Dali March 1992; recently estab diffusion range 'Destroy', clients incl Elton John, George Michael, Madonna and Prince; *Style*— John Richmond, Esq; ✉ World Clothes Inc, 25 Battersea Bridge Road, London SW11 3BA (☎ 0171 978 5278, fax 0171 978 4068)

RICHMOND, Kevin Charles; s of Eric Charles Richmond, of Nottingham, and Loraine Christine, *née* Turner; *Educ* Padstow Comp, Nottingham Acad of Speech Dance and Drama; *partner* Angela Demello; *Career* ballet dancer; child actor Nottingham Playhouse Rep 1971 (also appeared in film The Ragman's Daughter), with touring co Dance for Everyone (Theatre in Education) 1976–77, with London Festival Ballet/English Nat Ballet 1977–; *Roles* danced in all Christopher Bruce prodns for English Nat Ballet incl: The Dream is Over, The World Again (cr role), Land (cr role), Cruel Garden, Symphony in Three Movements (cr role), Swansong (SWET Award nomination 1988, also produced for TV); other Eng Nat Ballet roles incl: Furbo in Tetley's Pulcinella, Jester and an Ugly Sister in Stevenson's Cinderella, Hilarion in Skeaping's Giselle, Headmistress in Lichine's Graduation Ball (also produced for TV), Dr Coppélius in Hynd's Coppélia, Tybalt in Sir Frederick Ashton's Romeo and Juliet, Lead Bandit in Petit's Carmen, Lead Boy in Ailey's Night Creature, Chief Eunuch in Schéhérazade, Tchaikovsky/Drosselmeyer in Schaufuss' The Nutcracker, Hortensio in John Cranko's The Taming of the Shrew, The Gopak and Chinese Dance in Ben Stevenson's The Nutcracker, Fate in Robert North's A Stranger I Came (cr role), Young Man in Brandstrup's White Nights (cr role); also appeared in film Nijinsky; *Recreations* enjoying life to the full, water skiing, writing; *Style*— Kevin Richmond, Esq; ✉ English National Ballet, 39 Jay Mews, London SW7 2ES (☎ 0171 581 1245)

RICHMOND, Sir Mark Henry; kt (1986); s of Harold Sylvestor Richmond (d 1952), and Dorothy Plaistowe (d 1976); *b* 1 Feb 1931; *Educ* Epsom Coll, Clare Coll Cambridge (BA, PhD, ScD); *m* 1958, Shirley Jean, da of Dr Vincent Townrow (d 1982); 1 s (Paul b 1964), 2 da (Clare b 1959, Jane b 1962, d 1987); *Career* scientific staff Med Res Cncl 1958–65; reader in molecular biology Univ of Edinburgh 1965–68, prof of bacteriology Univ of Bristol 1968–81, vice chllr Univ of Manchester 1981–90, chm SERC 1990–94, gp head of research Glaxo 1993–95; pres Epsom Coll 1992–; chm Ctee of Vice Chllrs and Princs 1987–89; tstee: Nat Gallery 1993–, Tate Gallery 1995–; FRS 1980; *Recreations* walking, gardening; *Clubs* Athenaeum; *Style*— Sir Mark Richmond, FRS; ✉ Glaxo

Wellcome plc, Landsdowne House, Berkeley Square, London W1X 6BQ (☎ 0171 408 8704, fax 0171 408 0228)

RICHMOND, William John (Bill); s of Alfred Richmond (d 1992), of Derby, and Muriel Harland, *née* Woodruff (d 1984); *b* 2 Aug 1947; *Educ* Bemrose GS, Derby Poly, Middx Univ (PGCE), BSc; *m* 21 Aug 1970, Ann, da of Bert Collis; 1 s (Andrew Peter b 7 Feb 1978), 1 da (Jill Laura b 23 May 1981); *Career* photographer's asst 1967–71 (Zoe Dominic theatrical work, Norman Gold advertising work), photographer Advertising and Design Dept Wiggins Teape Paper 1971–73, ind photographer 1973– (latterly specialising in still life, food and roomset work), proprietor studio practice 1977; external assessor and moderator: CNAA degree course Manchester Poly (former memb Validation Panel), BTech course Gloucester and Derby Colls until 1989; currently teacher in design Haydon GM Sch Northwood Hills; FBIPP 1974 (former memb Admissions Panel); *Recreations* 400 and 800 metre track athletics; *Clubs* Thames Valley Harriers Athletic; *Style*— William Richmond, Esq; ✉ 38 Normandy Ave, Barnet, Herts EN5 2JA (☎ 0181 440 0822); BMR Studios, 51–55 Stirling Road, London W3 8DJ (fax 0181 993 7589, mobile 0836 674730)

RICHMOND, LENNOX AND GORDON, 10 (and 5 respectively) Duke of (E 1675, UK 1876); Charles Henry Gordon Lennox; also Earl of March, Baron Settrington (both E 1675), Earl of Darnley, Lord Torbolton (all S 1675), Duc d'Aubigny (Fr 1684), Earl of Kinrara (UK 1876), and Hereditary Constable of Inverness Castle; s of 9 Duke of Richmond and (4 of) Gordon (d 1989), and Elizabeth Grace, *née* Hudson (✝ 1992); descended from King Charles II and Louise Renée de Penançoët de Kéroualle, who was cr Baroness Petersfield, Countess of Fareham and Duchess of Portsmouth for life by King Charles II and Duchesse d'Aubigny by King Louis XIV of France; *b* 19 Sept 1929; *Educ* Eton, William Temple Coll Rugby; *m* 26 May 1951, Susan Monica, o da of Col Cecil Everard Grenville-Grey, CBE, of Hall Barn, Blewbury, Berks, by his w, Louise Monica, eldest da of Lt-Col Ernest Fitzroy Morrison-Bell, OBE, JP, DL; 1 s (Earl of March and Kinrara), 2 da (Lady Ellinor Caroline b 1952, Lady Louisa Elizabeth b 1967), and 2 adopted da (Maria b 1959, Naomi b 1962); *Heir* s, Earl of March and Kinrara, *qv*; *Career* late 2 Lt KRRC; FCA 1956–; chm: Dexam International (Holdings) Ltd 1956–, Goodwood Group of Cos 1969–; chm John Wiley & Sons Ltd 1991– (previosly vice chm and dir); dir Country Gentlemen's Assoc Ltd 1975–89; memb: House of Laity Gen Synod 1960–80, Central and Exec Ctee World Cncl Churches 1968–75; church cmmr 1962–75; chm: Bd for Mission and Unity Gen Synod 1968–77, House of Laity Chichester Dio 1976–79, Chichester Cathedral Tst 1985–91; vice chm Archbishops' Cmmn on Church and State 1966–70, memb W Midlands Regnl Econ Planning Cncl 1965–68; pres: Sussex Rural Community Cncl 1973–, SE England Tourist Bd 1990– (vice pres 1974–90), Sussex CCC 1991–; chm: Rugby Cncl of Social Serv 1961–68, Dunford Coll (YMCA) 1969–82, Tstees Sussex Heritage Tst 1978–; Chllr Univ of Sussex 1985– (treas 1979–82); Lord Lt of West Sussex 1990–94 (DL 1975–90); hon treas and dep pres Historic Houses Assoc 1975–86; chm: Christian Orgns Res and Advsy Tst (CORAT) 1970–87, Assoc of Int Dressage Event Organisers 1987–94; pres: S of England Agric Soc 1981–82, Br Horse Soc 1976–78, Planning for Economic Prosperity in Chichester and Arun Dists 1989– (chm 1985–89); Hon LLD Sussex 1987; Medal of Honour Br Equestrian Fedn 1983; CIMgt 1982; *Style*— His Grace the Duke of Richmond, Lennox and Gordon; ✉ Molecomb, Goodwood, Chichester W Sussex PO18 OPZ (☎ 01243 532815; office: 01243 774107, fax 01243 774313)

RICHMOND-WATSON, Anthony Euan; s of Euan Owens Richmond-Watson (d 1954), and Hon Gladys Gordon, *née* Catto (d 1967); *b* 8 April 1941; *Educ* Westminster, Edinburgh Univ (BCom); *m* 1, 1966, Angela, da of John Broadley, of Somerset (d 1979); 1 s (Luke b 1971), 1 da (Tamsin b 1967); m 2, 1976, Geraldine Ruth Helen, da of Charles Barrington, of Cornwall (d 1966); 1 da (Alice b 1976); *Career* merchant banker; dir Morgan Grenfell & Co Ltd 1975– (joined 1968), dir and dep chm Morgan Grenfell Group plc 1989–; non-exec dir Yule Catto and Co plc 1978–, chm Norfolk Capital Gp plc 1986–90 (dir 1985–90); MICAS; *Style*— Anthony Richmond-Watson, Esq; ✉ Morgan Grenfell Group plc, 23 Great Winchester Street, London EC2P 2AX (☎ 0171 588 4545, fax 0171 826 6155)

RICKARD, Dr John Hellyar; s of Peter John Rickard, of Devon, and Irene Eleanor, *née* Hales; *b* 27 Jan 1940; *Educ* Ilford Co HS, Univ of Oxford (MA, DPhil), Univ of Aston (MSc); *m* 6 April 1963, Christine Dorothy, da of Claude Hudson (d 1963), of Essex; 1 s (Robin b 1965), 2 da (Rosemary b 1964, Wendy b 1967); *Career* former res fell Univ of Oxford; sr econ advsr: Dept of Prices and Consumer Protection 1976–78, central policy review staff Cabinet Office 1978–82, HM Treasy 1982–84; the econ advsr State of Bahrain 1984–87, chief econ advsr Dept of Tport 1987–91, under sec economics HM Treasy 1991–94, chief econ advsr Dept of Tport 1994, IMF fiscal advsr Miny of Finance Moldova 1995, conslt economist 1995–; MCIT; *Books* Macro-Economics (with D Aston, 1970); *Recreations* sailing, music; *Clubs* Civil Service Sailing, Royal Solent Yacht; *Style*— Dr John Rickard; ✉ Bay House, Lanes End, Totland Bay, Isle of Wight PO39 0BE (☎ and fax 01983 754669)

RICKARDS, Dr Anthony Francis; s of Anthony Gerard Rickards (d 1984), of Chettle, Dorset, and Eileen Mary, *née* O'Hara; *b* 17 Feb 1945; *Educ* Stonyhurst, Université de Grenoble, Middx Hosp Med Coll (MB BS, MRCP); *m* 13 June 1970, Trisha Lesley, da of Henry Weeks (d 1972); 2 da (Antonia Jane and Sophie Anne (twins) b 25 Sept 1978); *Career* house surgn Dept of Thoracic Surgery Middx Hosp then house physician Central Middx Hosp 1968–69, resident MO Nat Heart Hosp 1969–70, house physician Professorial Med Unit Brompton Hosp 1970–71, registrar Dept of Cardiology London Chest Hosp 1971–73, clinical lectr Professorial Dept of Cardiac Med Cardiothoracic Inst Univ of London 1973–74, sr registrar Nat Heart Hosp 1974, Wellcome sr fell in clinical sci, lectr and hon sr regisrar Cardiothoracic Inst and Nat Heart Hosp 1974–75; Royal Brompton and Nat Heart and Chest Hosps: conslt cardiologist 1975–, dir of info 1992–; vice dean Cardiotharcic Inst 1977–81, hon sec Br Cardiac Soc 1978–82, pres Soc of Cardiological Technicians 1979–83, fndr memb, treas and memb Cncl Br Pacing Group; Euro Soc of Cardiology: chm Working Pty on LV Function 1980–84, chm Euro Working Gp on Cardiac Pacing 1989–; memb: Scientific Advsy Bd Br Heart Fndn 1979–83, Ctee on Cardiology RCP 1982; asst ed Euro Heart Jl 1983–89; memb Editorial Bd: Cardiostim 1984–, Jl of Interventional Cardiology 1988–; memb EEC Specialist Cmmn on Implantable Device Regulation 1984–, Sec of State's Med Advsy Ctee memb on Med Aspects of Fitness to Drive 1985–; one of four finalists Euro Soc of Cardiology Young Res Workers prize 1980, Gold Medal for scientific contributions to pacing Cardiostim 94 1994; author of over 300 pubns; FACC 1982, FRCP 1983, FESC 1988; *Recreations* sailing, skiing, diving, golf; *Clubs* Royal Lymington Yacht, Royal Welsh Yacht, S Caernarvonshire Yacht, Bramshaw Golf; *Style*— Dr Anthony Rickards; ✉ 47 Wimpole Street, London W1M 7DG (☎ 0171 573 8899, fax 0171 573 8898)

RICKAYZEN, Prof Gerald; s of Solomon Rickayzen (d 1969), of London, and Jane Culank (d 1975); *b* 16 Oct 1929; *Educ* Teignmouth GS, Central Fndn Boys' Sch, QMC London (BSc), Christ's Coll Cambridge (PhD); *m* 20 Dec 1953, Gillian Thelma, da of Maurice Lewin (d 1972), of Dunstable, Beds; 3 s (Alan Michael b 15 Jan 1957, (Martin) Asher b 28 Dec 1960, Benjamin David b 1 June 1963), 1 da (Sonia Ruth (Mrs Joseph) b 29 Nov 1958); *Career* jr res fell Services Electronics Research Laboratory Baldock Herts 1954–57, res assoc Univ of Illinois USA 1957–59, lectr in physics Univ of Liverpool 1959–65; Univ of Kent: reader in theoretical physics 1965–66, prof of theoretical physics 1966–, dean of Faculty of Natural Sciences 1977–82, pro vice-chllr 1982–90, dep vice-chllr 1984–90; govr: Simon Langton Girls' Sch Canterbury (chm 1985–93) 1975–, Simon Langton Boys' Sch 1975–94; memb American Physical Soc 1958, fell Former Physical Soc 1957, FInstP 1982, CPhys 1985; *Books* Theory of Superconductivity (1965), Green's Functions and Condensed Matter (1980, reprinted in paperback 1984); *Recreations* playing the cello, tennis; *Style*— Prof Gerald Rickayzen; ✉ The Physics Laboratory, The University, Canterbury, Kent CT2 7NR (☎ 01227 764000, fax 01227 827558, telex 965449, e-mail g.rickayzen@ukc.ac.uk)

RICKETT, Sir Denis Hubert Fletcher; KCMG (1956, CMG 1947), CB (1951); s of Hubert Cecil Rickett, OBE, JP (d 1950), and Mabel Fletcher (d 1969); *b* 27 July 1907; *Educ* Rugby, Balliol Coll Oxford (scholar, Jenkyns exhibitioner, MA); *m* 1946, Ruth Pauline, da of late William Anderson Armstrong, JP; 2 s, 1 da; *Career* fell All Souls Coll Oxford 1929–49, joined staff of Economic Advsy Cncl 1931, Offices of War Cabinet 1939, PPS to Rt Hon Oliver Lyttelton (later Viscount Chandos) as min of prodn 1943–45, PA (for work on atomic energy) to Rt Hon Sir John Anderson (later Viscount Waverley) as Chllr of the Exchequer 1945, PPS to Rt Hon Clement Attlee (later 1 Earl Attlee) as Prime Minister 1950–51, economic min Br Embassy Washington and head of UK Treasy and Supply Delegation 1951–54, second sec HM Treasy 1960–68 (third sec 1955–60); vice pres World Bank 1968–74; dir Schroder International and advsr J Henry Schroder Wagg & Co 1974–79, dir De La Rue Co plc 1974–77; *Recreations* music; *Clubs* Brooks's, Athenaeum; *Style*— Sir Denis Rickett, KCMG, CB; ✉ 9 The Close, Salisbury, Wiltshire SP1 2EB

RICKETT, Brig Johnny Francis; CBE (1990, OBE 1982, MBE 1967); s of Francis William Rickett (d 1981), and Lettice Anne, *née* Elliot (d 1985); *b* 7 Sept 1939; *Educ* Eton, RMCS Def Servs Staff Coll India, Royal Coll of Defence Studies; *m* June 1964, Frances Seton (Fanny), da of Charles Francis Seton de Winton, CBE, of Burford, Oxon; 1 s (Charles Edward Francis (Charlie) b 1975), 2 da (Sophy Frances b 1965 d 1970, Emily Frances b 1974); *Career* Welsh Guards Nat Serv Offr 1959, 1st Bn UK and BAOR, seconded for loan serv Fed Reg Army S Arab Emirates 1963–65; 1 Bn Welsh Guards: Aden 1965–67 (Political Offr for some of period), Adj 1968–70, served Hong Kong, Kenya, Germany, USA, NI, MOD 1977–80, CO 1980–82 (incl Falklands conflict); leader Falklands Presentation Team 1982, MOD 1983, cmd 19 Inf Brigade and Colchester Garrison 1984–86, Dep Cdr and Chief of Staff HQ SE Dist Aldershot 1987–90, Mil Attaché Paris 1991–94, Regtl Lt-Col Welsh Guards 1989–94, Comptroller Union Jack Club 1995–; ADC to HM The Queen 1993; author of articles in jls and magazines; govr of boys prep sch, memb Exec Cncl Ex-Service Fellowship Centres, tstee Old Etonian Assoc, pres Welsh Guards Regtl Assoc; Queen's Commendation for Brave Conduct 1964, mentioned in despatches 1974, Chevalier of the Order of Danneborg Denmark 1975, Cdr Order of Merit France 1992; FIMgt 1990, MInstD 1996; *Recreations* country sports, riding, polo, rowing, parachuting, running; *Clubs* Cavalry and Guards', Interalliée Paris; *Style*— Brig Johnny Rickett, CBE; ✉ Union Jack Club, Sandell Street, Waterloo, London SE1 8UJ (☎ 0171 928 6401, fax 0171 620 0565)

RICKETT, William Francis Sebastian; s of Sir Denis Hubert Fletcher Rickett, KCMG, CB, *qv*, of Salisbury, and Ruth Pauline, *née* Armstrong; *b* 23 Feb 1953; *Educ* Eton (Oppidan scholar), Trinity Coll Cambridge (MA); *m* 16 June 1979, Lucy Caroline, da of J H Clark; 1 s ((Oliver Patrick) Oscar b 20 June 1983), 1 da (Rosanna Madeleine b 14 March 1986); *Career* Department of Energy: joined 1975, private sec to Perm Sec 1977–78, princ 1978–81, private sec to Prime Minister 1981–83, seconded to Kleinwort Benson Ltd 1983–85, asst sec Electricity Privatisation 1987–90 (Oil Div 1985–87), under sec Energy Efficiency Office 1990–93; dir of fin DOE 1993–; non-exec dir Redland Roof Tiles 1994–; FRSA; *Recreations* sport, painting, family; *Style*— William Rickett, Esq; ✉ Department of the Environment, 2 Marsham Street, London SW1

RICKETTS, Prof Martin John; s of Leonard Alfred Ricketts, and Gertrude Dorothy, *née* Elgar; *b* 10 May 1948; *Educ* City of Bath Boys' Sch, Univ of Newcastle (BA), Univ of York (DPhil); *m* 1975, Diana Barbara, *née* Greenwood; 1 s, 1 da; *Career* econ asst Industl Policy Gp 1970–72, research fell Inst of Econ and Social Research Univ of York 1975–77, Univ of Buckingham (formerly Univ Coll at Buckingham): lectr in econs 1977–82, sr lectr 1982–85, reader 1985–87, prof of econ orgn 1987–, dean Sch of Accountancy, Business and Econs 1993–, pro-vice chllr 1993; econ dir NEDO 1991–92; visiting prof Virginia Poly, Inst and State Univ 1984; tstee Inst of Econ Affrs 1992–; *Books* The Economics of Energy (with M G Webb, 1980), The Economics of Business Enterprise: new appproaches to the firm (1987, 2 edn 1994); also author of numerous papers on public finance, public choice, housing economics and economic organisation; *Recreations* music (especially playing piano and oboe); *Style*— Prof Martin Ricketts; ✉ School of Business, University of Buckingham, Hunter Street, Buckingham MK18 1EG (☎ 01280 814080, fax 01280 822245)

RICKETTS, Peter Forbes; s of Maurice Alan Ricketts, of Lechlade, and Dilys, *née* Davies; *b* 30 Sept 1952; *Educ* Bishop Vesey's GS Sutton Coldfield, Pembroke Coll Oxford (BA); *m* 13 Sept 1980, Suzanne Julia, da of Ivor Horlington; 1 s (Edward b 1982), 1 da (Caroline b 1987); *Career* FCO: joined UK Mission to the UN 1974, third sec Singapore 1975–78, second sec UK Delgn to NATO 1978–81, first sec 1981–83, asst private sec to Foreign Sec 1983–85, first sec Washington 1986–89, dep head of Security Policy Dept 1989–91, head of Hong Kong Dept 1991–94, cnsllr (Financial and Euro Affairs) Paris 1994–; *Recreations* reading, Victorian art, Chinese porcelain; *Style*— Peter Ricketts, Esq; ✉ c/o FCO (Paris), King Charles Street, London SW1A 2AH (☎ 0171 270 2533)

RICKETTS, Prof Peter Thomas; s of Thomas Edward Ricketts (d 1977), of Birmingham, and Rose Ellen, *née* Pennell (d 1988); *b* 14 Dec 1933; *Educ* King Edward VI GS Birmingham, Univ of Birmingham (BA, PhD); *m* 23 July 1960, Monica Ann, da of Frederick George Bishop (d 1977), of Broadstairs; 1 s (David), 1 da (Jane); *Career* Nat Serv Sgt Instr RAEC 1959–61; asst d'anglais Lycée des Garçons Nimes France 1954–55, lecteur d'anglais Université de Montpellier 1957–58; Dept of French Victoria Coll Univ of Toronto: temp lectr 1958–59, lectr and asst prof 1961–64; Univ of Birmingham: lectr in romance philology Dept of Latin 1964–68, sr lectr in romance philology 1968–78, reader in romance linguistics 1978–80; visiting prof Dept of French Univ of Br Columbia Vancouver Canada 1967–68, James Barrow prof of French Univ of Liverpool 1980–83, prof of romance philology Queen Mary and Westfield Coll Univ of London (formerly Westfield Coll) 1983–91, dean Westfield Coll Univ of London 1986–89 (dep dean 1984–86), dep dean Queen Mary and Westfield Coll 1989–91, prof emeritus Univ of London, hon fell Inst for Advanced Research in the Humanities Univ of Birmingham 1994–, hon sr lectr Dept of French Univ of Birmingham 1995–, fell Queen Mary and Westfield Coll; author of numerous articles in learned jls; memb Advsy Ctee Br Branch Int Courtly Lit Soc, memb Medieval Acad of America; Association Internationale d'Etudes Occitanes: fndr pres 1981–90, gen ed 1981–90, memb Cncl 1996–; created Sòci of the Felibrige 1982, memb Comité d'honneur Revue des Langues Romanes 1982; Chevalier dans l'order des Palmes Académiques 1995; *Books* incl: Introduction à l'étude de l'ancien provençal (with F Hamlin and J Hathaway, 1967), Le Breviari d'Amor de Matfre Ermengaud, tome V (1976), Fouke le Fitz Waryn (with J Hathaway C Robson and A Wilshere, 1976), Proceedings of the First Conference on Medieval Occitan Language and Literature (ed, 1979), Actes du premier congrès international de l'Association Internationale d'Etudes Occitanes (ed 1987), Le Breviari d'Amor de Matfre Ermengaud, tome II (1989); *Recreations* theatre; *Style*— Prof Peter Ricketts; ✉ 89 Reddings Rd, Moseley, Birmingham B13 8LP

RICKETTS, Sir Robert Cornwallis Gerald St Leger; 7 Bt (UK 1828), of The Elms, Gloucestershire, and Beaumont Leys, Leicestershire; s of Sir Claude Ricketts, 6 Bt (d 1937); *b* 8 Nov 1917; *Educ* Haileybury, Magdalene Coll Cambridge (MA); *m* 1945, (Anne) Theresa (*see* Lady Ricketts, CBE); 2 s, 2 da (*see* His Hon Peter Mason, QC); *Heir* s, (Robert) Tristram Ricketts, *qv*, b 17 April 1946; *Career* slr 1949, formerly ptnr Wellington and Clifford; PA to COS Gibraltar 1942–45 and ADC to Lt-Govr of Jersey 1945–46; hon citizen of Mobile Alabama USA; FRSA; *Recreations* books, history; *Style—* Sir Robert Ricketts, Bt; ✉ Forwood House, Minchinhampton, Stroud, Glos GL6 9AB (☎ 01453 882160)

RICKETTS, Lady; (Anne) Theresa; CBE (1983); da of late Rt Hon Sir Stafford Cripps, CH, PC, QC (chllr of the Exchequer in Attlee's Govt and 4 s of Baron Parmoor, KCVO, PC, JP); *b* 12 April 1919; *m* 1945, Sir Robert Ricketts, 7 Bt, *qv*; 2 s, 2 da (*see* His Hon Peter Mason, QC); *Career* chm Nat Assoc of Citizens' Advice Bureaux 1979–84; memb Electricity Consumers' Cncl 1978–90; memb Direct Mail Services Standards Bd 1985–92; *Style—* Lady Ricketts, CBE; ✉ Forwood House, Minchinhampton, Stroud, Glos GL6 9AB (☎ 01453 882160)

RICKETTS, (Robert) Tristram; s and h of Sir Robert Ricketts, 7 Bt, *qv*, of Forwood House, Minchinhampton, Glos, and Anne Theresa, *née* Cripps (*see* Lady Ricketts, CBE); *b* 17 April 1946; *Educ* Winchester, Magdalene Coll Cambridge (MA); *m* 1969, Ann, yr da of Eric William Charles Lewis, CB (d 1981), of London; 1 s, 1 da; *Career* chief exec: Horserace Betting Levy Bd 1980–93 (memb 1993–), British Horseracing Bd 1993–; dir: Racecourse Technical Services Ltd 1980–93 and 1994–, Horseracing Forensic Laboratory Ltd 1986–93; *Clubs* Athenaeum; *Style—* Tristram Ricketts, Esq; ✉ 47 Lancaster Ave, London SE27 9EL (☎ 0181 670 8422); office: 42 Portman Square, London W1H 0EN (☎ 0171 343 3304, fax 0171 935 3626)

RICKFORD, Jonathan Braithwaite Keevil; s of Richard Braithwaite Keevil Rickford (d 1990), and Dorothy Margaret, *née* Latham; *b* 7 Dec 1944; *Educ* Sherborne, Magdalen Coll Oxford (BA, BCL, Gibbs prize in law); *m* 20 July 1968, Dora Rose, da of Rt Rev Norman Sargant (d 1985); 1 s (Richard b 7 July 1971), 2 da (Margaret b 10 Dec 1973, Alice b 24 March 1975); *Career* barr 1970–85, slr 1985–; teaching assoc in law Univ of California Sch of Law 1968–69, lectr in law LSE 1969–72, sr legal asst Dept of Trade 1974 (asst 1972), Law Offrs Dept AG's Chambers 1976–79; DTI (formerly Dept of Trade): asst slr (co law) 1979–82, under sec (legal) 1982–84, the Slr 1984–87; British Telecommunications plc: slr and chief legal offr 1987–89, dir of govt rels 1989–93, dir of corp strategy 1993–96; sr fell Br Inst of Int and Comparative Law 1996–; FRSA 1991; *Recreations* sailing; *Clubs* Reform; *Style—* Jonathan Rickford, Esq; ✉ British Institute of International and Comparative Law, Charles Clore House, 17 Russell Square, London WC1B 5DR (☎ 0171 636 5802)

RICKFORD, Dr William Jeremy Keevil; s of Richard Braithwaite Keevil Rickford (d 1990), of Dartmouth, Devon, and Dorothy Margaret Hart, *née* Latham; *b* 4 Dec 1949; *Educ* Sherborne, St Thomas' Hosp Med Sch London (MB BS); *m* 9 Oct 1982, Jacqueline Ann, da of Kenneth Cooke Burrow, MBE, of Sandgate, Folkestone, Kent; 1 s (Thomas b 7 Jan 1986), 1 da (Emma b 15 Dec 1983); *Career* asst prof Dept of Anaesthesiology Univ of Maryland Baltimore USA 1986–88, conslt anaesthetist N Hertfordshire Health Tst 1988–; FRCA, FFARCSI; *Recreations* skiing, sailing; *Clubs* Ski Club of GB, Royal Dart Yacht; *Style—* Dr W J K Rickford; ✉ Rushcroft, Green End, Weston, nr Hitchin, Herts SG4 7AL (☎ 01462 790323); Department of Anaesthetics, Lister Hospital, Corey's Mill, Stevenage, Herts SG1 4AB (☎ 01438 314333)

RICKMAN, Alan; *Educ* Latymer Upper Sch, Chelsea Sch of Art, RCA, RADA; *Career* actor and director; seasons at Library Theatre Manchester, Haymarket and Phoenix Theatre Leicester, Crucible Theatre Sheffield, Birmingham Rep Theatre and Bristol Old Vic; *Theatre* incl: The Devil is an Ass and Measure for Measure (Birmingham, Edinburgh Festival and NT) 1976–77, The Tempest, Captain Swing, Love's Labours Lost and Antony and Cleopatra (RSC) 1978–79, Antonio (Nottingham Playhouse) 1979, Fears and Miseries of the Third Reich (Glasgow Citizens' Theatre) 1979–80, The Summer Party (Crucible Sheffield) 1980, The Devil Himself (Lyric Studio) 1980, Commitments (Bush Theatre) 1980, Philadelphia Story (Oxford Playhouse) 1981, The Seagull (Royal Court) 1981, Brothers Karamazov (Edinburgh Festival and USSR) 1981, The Last Elephant (Bush Theatre) 1981, Bad Language (Hampstead Theatre Club) 1983, The Grass Widow (Royal Court) 1983, The Lucky Chance (Royal Court) 1984, As You Like It, Troilus and Cressida, Les Liaisons Dangereuses and Mephisto (RSC) 1985–86, Les Liaisons Dangereuses (West End and Broadway) 1986–87, Tango at the End of Winter (Edinburgh and West End) 1991, Hamlet (Riverside Studios and Br tour) 1992; as director prodns incl: Desperately Yours (New York) 1980, Other Worlds (asst dir, Royal Court) 1983, Live Wax (Edinburgh Festival) 1986, Wax Acts (West End and tour) 1992, The Winter Guest (Yorkshire Playhouse and Almeida) 1995; *Television* incl: Romeo and Juliet 1978, Therese Raquin 1979, Barchester Chronicles 1982, Busted 1982, Pity in History 1984, Benefactors 1989, Revolutionary Witness 1989, Spirit of Man 1989; *Radio* incl: The Dutch Courtesan, Polly, Rope, Manchester Enthusiasts, Gridlock, Trick to Catch the Old One, A Good Man in Africa, That Man Bracken, Blood Wedding, The Seagull, The Magic of my Youth; *Films* incl: Die Hard 1988, The January Man 1989, Quigley Down Under 1990, Truly, Madly, Deeply 1991, Closetland 1991, Close My Eyes 1991, Robin Hood, Prince of Thieves 1991, Bob Roberts 1992, Fallen Angels 1993, Mesmer 1993, An Awfully Big Adventure 1994, Sense and Sensibility 1995, Michael Collins 1995, Rasputin 1995; *Awards* Bancroft Gold Medal RADA 1974, Tony Nomination for Les Liaisons Dangereuses 1988, Time Out Award for Tango at the End of Winter 1992, Best Actor Evening Standard Film Awards (for Robin Hood, Prince of Thieves, Close My Eyes and Truly, Madly, Deeply) 1991, Best Supporting Actor BAFTA Film Awards for Robin Hood, Prince of Thieves 1992, Best Actor for Mesmer Montreal Film Festival 1994, Emmy Award for Rasputin 1996, BAFTA nomination for Sense and Sensibility 1996; *Style—* Alan Rickman; ✉ c/o ICM Ltd, Oxford House, 76 Oxford Street, London W1N 0AX (☎ 0171 636 6565, fax 0171 323 0101)

RICKMAN, Prof Geoffrey Edwin; *b* 9 Oct 1932; *Educ* Peter Symonds Sch Winchester, Brasenose Coll Oxford (MA, DPhil); *m* 18 April 1959, Anna Rosemary, *née* Wilson; 1 s (David Edwin b 1964), 1 da (Elizabeth Jane b 1962); *Career* jr res fell The Queen's Coll Oxford 1959–62; Univ of St Andrews: lectr in ancient history 1962–, sr lectr 1968–, prof 1981–, Master Utd Coll of St Salvator and St Leonard 1992–96, pro-vice-chllr 1996–; FSA 1963, FBA 1989; *Books* Roman Granaries and Storebuildings (1971), The Corn Supply of Ancient Rome (1980); *Recreations* swimming, listening to opera; *Style—* Prof Geoffrey Rickman, FSA, FBA; ✉ 56 Hepburn Gardens, St Andrews, Fife, Scotland KY16 9DG (☎ 01334 472063); Department of Ancient History, St Salvator's College, The University, St Andrews, Fife, Scotland (☎ 01334 476161)

RICKMAN, John Eric Carter; s of Maj Eric Roper Rickman (d 1976), of Regents Park, London, and Catherine Mary, *née* Carter (d 1964); *b* 28 May 1913; *Educ* Feltonfleet, Haileybury, Fleet St, Army; *m* 29 April 1939, Margaret Wood, da of Robert Oswald Law (d 1954), of Princes Gate, London; 1 s (Robin b 1942), 2 da (Jill b 1940, Rosemary b 1945); *Career* serv TA Cmmn, Glos and Reconaissance Regts 1931–46, serv WWII in NW Europe, 1 Canadian Air Staff, 84 Gp TAF (Maj) 1943–45; reporter: Bristol Evening World 1931, Glos Echo 1932, Daily Mail 1934 (reporter and zoo correspondent), succeeded from Robin Goodfellow, chief horse racing corr Daily Mail 1949, 'Gimcrack' Daily Sketch 1961–71, returned to Daily Mail 1971–78, ITV horse racing commentator (front man famous for hat raising welcome to viewers) 1955–78; winner of showing awards with home bred Welsh Cobs and Faverolles poultry; *Books* Homes of Sport: Horse Racing (1952), Eight Flat Racing Stables (1979), Old Tom and Young John (1990), Laird of The Light Houses (1994); *Recreations* golf, writing, Euro travel, sailing, country pursuits; *Clubs* Kennel, Twelve, Liphook Golf, Bosham Sailing; *Style—* John Rickman, Esq; ✉ Pheasants Walk, Copyhold Lane, Fernhurst, Haslemere, Surrey GU27 3DZ (☎ and fax 01428 643197)

RICKS, David Trulock; CMG (1997), OBE (1981); s of Percival Trulock Ricks (d 1983), of Bromham, Beds, and Annetta Helen, *née* Hood (d 1967); *b* 28 June 1936; *Educ* Kilburn GS, RAM, Merton Coll Oxford (MA), Univ of London Inst of Educn, Univ of Lille (Licence-en-Lettres); *m* 1 Aug 1960, Nicole Estelle Aimée, da of André Armand Chupeau (d 1973), of Marans, France; 2 s (Ralph Antoine b 1964, Quentin Nicholas b 1969); *Career* teacher and lectr in London 1960–67; Br Cncl 1967–: dir of studies Morocco 1967–70, Univ of Essex 1970–71, dir State Inst of Language Studies Jaipur India 1971–74, dep dir Tanzania 1974–76, dep dir Iran 1976–79, dir Iran and cultural attaché HM Embassy Tehran 1979–80, dir Serv Conditions Dept London 1980–85, dir Italy and cultural cnsllr HM Embassy Rome 1985–90, dir France and cultural cnsllr HM Embassy Paris 1990–96; govr Br Inst in Florence 1985–90; memb Rome Ctee Keats-Shelley Meml House Rome 1985–90; *Books* Penguin French Reader (jt ed, 1967), New Penguin French Reader (jt ed, 1992); *Recreations* playing the piano, music, skiing; *Clubs* United Oxford and Cambridge; *Style—* David Ricks, Esq, CMG, OBE; ✉ c/o The British Council, 10 Spring Gardens, London SW1

RICKS, Robert Neville; s of Sir John Plowman Ricks (d 1991), of 8 Sunset View, Barnet, Herts, and his 1 w, May Celia, *née* Chubb (d 1975); *b* 29 June 1942; *Educ* Highgate Sch, Worcester Coll Oxford (MA); *Career* admitted slr 1967; Treasy Slr's Dept: legal asst 1969–73, sr legal 1973–81, asst slr 1981–86, princ asst slr 1986; legal advsr Dept for Education 1990–95 (Dept for Education and Employment 1995–); memb Gen Synod C of E 1980–85, chair of tstees Othona Community; *Recreations* wine, collecting original cartoons; *Clubs* United Oxford and Cambridge Univ; *Style—* Robert Ricks, Esq; ✉ 2 Eaton Terrace, Aberavon Road, London E3 5AJ (☎ 0171 981 3722)

RIDD, Prof John Howard; s of Herbert William Ridd (d 1971), of Ashtead, Surrey, and Emma Roadley, *née* Elmes (d 1977); *b* 7 Oct 1927; *Educ* Epsom GS, UCL (BSc, PhD, DSc); *m* 31 Dec 1955, Freda Marie, da of Harold George Williams (d 1956), of Mountain Ash, Glamorgan; 1 s (David b 1957), 1 da (Margaret (Mrs Bale) b 1959); *Career* res fell Harvard Univ 1951–52, emeritus prof of chemistry UCL 1993– (asst lectr 1952–55, lectr 1955–65, reader 1965–71, prof 1971–93); chm Bd of Studies in Chemistry Univ of London 1983–85; fell UCL 1995; FRSC 1971; *Awards* Ramsay Medal 1950, Organic Reaction Mechanisms Royal Soc of Chemistry 1984; *Books* Aromatic Substitution (with P B D De La Mare, 1959); *Recreations* photography; *Style—* Prof John Ridd; ✉ Chemistry Department, University College, 20 Gordon Street, London WC1H 0AJ (☎ 0171 387 7050 ext 4701, fax 0171 380 7463)

RIDDELL, Dr (John) Alistair; OBE (1988); s of Alexander Riddell (d 1954), and Mary McFarlane, *née* Mackintosh (d 1946); *b* 11 Feb 1930; *Educ* Glasgow Acad, Univ of Glasgow (MB ChB); *m* 23 March 1956, Elizabeth Park McDonald, da of Alexander Davidson; 1 s (Alexander Davidson b 10 June 1957), 3 da (Frances Anne Mackintosh b 23 Jan 1960, Aileen McDonald b 7 May 1962, Valerie Elizabeth b 21 April 1968); *Career* house offr (med and surgery) Hairmyres Hosp Lanarkshire 1953–54, SHO (obstetrics) Bellshill Hosp Lanarkshire 1954–55, trainee GP Glasgow 1955, princ in gen practice East End Glasgow 1956–95, estab gp practice Easterhouse Glasgow 1958, pt/t clinical asst (geriatrics) Lightburn Hosp 1968–78; memb: Glasgow Local Med Ctee 1964–95 (treas 1972–78, sec 1978–91), Glasgow Area Med Ctee 1974–94, Bd CAB Easterhouse 1978–82, Bd of Gen Practice Fin Corp 1975–90 (vice chm 1989–90); BMA: memb Gen Med Servs Ctee 1972–96 (negotiator 1982–87, vice chm 1984–87), memb Cncl 1983–, chm Scottish Gen Med Servs Ctee 1984–87, treas 1987–96, memb Bd BMA Services Ltd 1987–, chm Community Care Ctee 1991–94, BMA Professional Services 1996; treas Cwlth Med Assoc 1988–, chm Jt Professional Bd of Mgmnt Healthcall 1994–96, memb GMC 1994–; elder Church of Scotland; Freeman Citizen of Glasgow 1961, memb Incorporation of Bonnetmakers and Dyers 1961; memb: Grand Antiquity 1967, N Parish Washing Green Soc 1967; FRCGP 1983 (MRCGP 1966); *Recreations* golf, skiing, hill walking; *Clubs* RSM; *Style—* Dr Alistair Riddell, OBE; ✉ 4 Easter Drumlins, 47 Partickhill Road, Glasgow G11 5AB (☎ 0141 337 3304)

RIDDELL, Sir John Charles Buchanan; 13 Bt (NS 1628), of Riddell, Roxburghshire, CVO (1990), DL (Northumberland 1990); s of Sir Walter Riddell, 12 Bt (d 1934), and Hon Rachel Lyttelton, JP (d 1965) (yst da of 8 Viscount Cobham, JP, DL, and Hon Mary Cavendish, da of 2 Baron Chesham); *b* 3 Jan 1934; *Educ* Eton, ChCh Oxford (BA, MA); *m* 1969, Hon Sarah, LVO (1993), da of Baron Richardson of Duntisbourne, KG, MBE, TD, PC, *qv*, sometime govr of Bank of England; 3 s (Walter John b 1974, Hugh Gordon b 1976, Robert Henry b 1982); *Heir* s, Walter John Riddell b 10 June 1974; *Career* 2 Lt 2 KRRC; CA; banker; contested (C): Durham NW Feb 1974, Sunderland S Oct 1974; dir: UK Provident 1975–85, First Boston (Europe) Ltd 1975–78, Northumbrian Water Group plc 1992–; chm Govett Strategic Investment Trust 1995–; dep chm: IBA 1981–85, Credit Suisse First Boston 1990–95 (dir 1978–85), Northern Rock Building Soc 1992– (dir 1981–85 and 1990–), Alpha Bank London Ltd 1995–; exec dir: MC BBL Securities Ltd 1995–; private sec and treas to TRH The Prince and Princess of Wales 1985–90, memb Prince's Cncl 1985–90, chm Northumbria Ctee National Trust 1995–; FRSA 1989; *Clubs* Garrick, Northern Countries; *Style—* Sir John Riddell, Bt, CVO, DL; ✉ Hepple, Morpeth, Northumberland; 49 Campden Hill Square, London W8 7JR

RIDDELL, Norman Malcolm Marshall; *b* 30 June 1947; *m*; 3 s; *Career* Royal Bank of Scotland plc: commercial banking 1965–69, res analyst 1969–73, investmt analyst 1973–74, head of Investmt Res Dept and i/c holdings in US 1974–79; dir Britannia Group of Unit Trusts Ltd 1980–85 (sr investmt mangr 1979–80), md Britannia Unit Trust Managers Ltd 1985–86, chief investmt dir then md Britannia Group of Investment Companies 1982–86, chief exec Capital House Investment Management Ltd 1986–93, chief exec INVESCO Europe Ltd and chm INVESCO Asset Management Ltd 1993– late 96; MCIBS, AIIMR (AMSIA 1974); *Recreations* sports, travel, plate collecting; *Clubs* Hanbury Manor; *Style—* Norman Riddell, Esq; ✉ c/o INVESCO Group Ltd, 11 Devonshire Square, London EC2M 4YR (☎ 0171 626 3434)

RIDDELL, Peter John Robert; s of Kenneth Robert Riddell (d 1964), and Freda Riddell; *b* 14 Oct 1948; *Educ* Dulwich Coll, Sidney Sussex Coll Cambridge (MA); *m* 23 July 1994, Avril, da of late Richard Hillier Walker; 1 da (Emily b 16 July 1996); *Career* Financial Times: city staff 1970–72, property corr 1972–74, Lex columnist 1975–76, econ corr 1976–81, political ed 1981–88, US ed 1989–91; The Times: political columnist and commentator 1991–, political ed 1992–93, asst ed (politics) 1993–; Econ and Fin Journalist of the Year Wincott Awards 1981, Political Journalist of the Year 1985; regular appearances on radio and TV current affairs progs such as Week in Westminster; memb Cncl Hansard Soc for Parly Govt; *Books* The Thatcher Government (1983, 2 edn 1985), The Thatcher Decade (1989, 2 edn as The Thatcher Era and Its Legacy, 1991), Honest Opportunism - the rise of the career politician (1993, 2 edn 1996); *Recreations* opera, theatre, watching cricket and baseball, reading; *Clubs* Garrick, Surrey CC, MCC; *Style—* Peter Riddell, Esq; ✉ The Times, 1 Pennington Street, London E1 9XN (☎ 0171 782 5578)

RIDDELL-CARRE, Ralph John; s of Gervase Robert Riddell-Carre (d 1989), and Eileen Inez, *née* Tweedie (d 1993); *b* 8 Oct 1941; *Educ* Harrow; *m* 1972, Valerie Caroline, da of late Walter Thomas Wells Tickler; 3 s (John Timothy b 1976, Peter Thomas b 1979, David Alexander b 1983); *Career* Lindsay Jamieson & Haldane Edinburgh 1960–65, Ernst & Young (formerly Arthur Young, Arthur Young McClelland Moores & Co, McClelland Moores & Co) 1965– (ptnr 1974–); MICAS 1965; *Recreations* golf; *Style*— Ralph Riddell-Carre, Esq; ✉ Ernst & Young, Rolls House, 7 Rolls Buildings, Fetter Lane, London EC4A 1NH (☎ 0171 928 2000, fax 0171 405 2147)

RIDDELL-CARRE, Walter Gervase; s of Gervase Robert Riddell-Carre (d 1989), and Eileen Inez, *née* Tweedie (d 1993); *b* 10 Jan 1944; *Educ* Harrow; *m* 1975, Carolyn Anne, da of Maj Antony Ricketts, of Nigg, Ross-shire; 2 s (Andrew Gervase b 6 Feb 1979, James Walter b 31 March 1981); *Career* apprentice chartered accountant Lindsay Jamieson & Haldane Edinburgh 1962–67, investment mangr Kleinwort Benson Ltd London 1968–72, dir Edinburgh Fund Managers plc 1988–96 (investment mangr 1972–96); dir Edinburgh Japan Trust plc 1992–; memb Queen's Body Guard for Scotland (Royal Co of Archers) 1985; elder Church of Scotland; MICAS 1967; *Recreations* golf, archery, shooting; *Clubs* New (Edinburgh), Hon Co of Edinburgh Golfers; *Style*— Walter Riddell-Carre, Esq; ✉ Cavers Carre, Melrose, Roxburghshire TD6 9EJ (☎ 01835 870284)

RIDDELL-WEBSTER, John Alexander; MC (1943); s of Gen Sir Thomas Sheridan Riddell-Webster, GCB, DSO, DL (d 1974), of Lintrose, Coupar Angus, and Harriet Hill, *née* Sprot (d 1977); *b* 17 July 1921; *Educ* Harrow, Pembroke Coll Cambridge; *m* 16 Jan 1960, Ruth, da of (Samuel Plenderleith) Laurence Lithgow (d 1972), of Great Barton, Suffolk; 2 s (Michael b 1960, Thomas b 1962), 1 da (Caroline b 1964); *Career* served Seaforth Highlanders 1940–46: UK, Madagascar, India, Paiforce, Syria, Sicily (wounded, MC), WO 1944–45, Staff Capt and DAQMG, BAOR 1945–46; Anglo-Iranian Oil Co (later BP): joined 1946, served Iran, Iraq, Bahrain and London 1946–54, Aden and Basrah 1954–55, London 1954–56, Canada 1956–63 (vice pres mktg BP Canada 1959–63), London 1963–80 (dir Shell Mex and BP 1965, md mktg 1971–75, md mktg BP Oil Ltd 1976–80), ret 1980; dir of Scot affairs BP Edinburgh 1980–82; farmer 1982–; memb Cncl: Incorporated Soc of Br Advertisers 1967–80, Advtg Assoc 1973–80, British Roads Fedn 1975–80, Royal Warrant Holders' Assoc 1967 (pres 1980); memb Automobile Assoc Ctee 1980–90, pres Oil Industries Club 1977–78, chm Transport Action Scotland 1982; regnl cncllr Tayside 1986–94; CIMgt, FInstPet; *Recreations* shooting, fishing, gardening; *Clubs* New (Edinburgh), Royal Perth Golfing Soc; *Style*— John Riddell-Webster, Esq; ✉ Lintrose, Coupar Angus, Perthshire PH13 9JQ (☎ 01828 627472)

RIDDELSDELL, Dame Mildred; DCB (1972), CBE (1958); da of Rev H J Riddelsdell; *b* 1 Dec 1913; *Educ* St Mary's Hall Brighton, Bedford Coll London; *Career* asst sec Min of Nat Insur 1945, under sec 1950, loaned to UN 1953–56, sec Nat Incomes Cmmn 1962–65, second perm sec DHSS 1971–73, chm CS Retirement Fellowship 1974–77; *Style*— Dame Mildred Riddelsdell, DCB, CBE; ✉ 26A New Yatt Rd, Witney, Oxon OX8 6NZ

RIDDICK, Graham Edward Galloway; MP (C) Colne Valley (majority 7,225); s of John Julian Riddick, and late Cecilia Margaret, da of Sir Edward Ruggles-Brise, 1 Bt, MC, TD, MP for Maldon (Essex) 1922–42 (d 1942); *b* 26 Aug 1955; *Educ* Stowe, Univ of Warwick; *m* 1988, Sarah Northcroft; 1 s (George John Galloway b 5 Jan 1991), 2 da (Rosannah Cecilia Mary b 10 April 1993, Charlotte Louise b 3 Jan 1996); *Career* MP (C) Colne Valley 1987–, PPS to Hon Francis Maude as Fin Sec to the Treasy 1990–92, PPS to John MacGregor as Sec of State for Tport 1992–94; memb: Educn Select Ctee 1994–95, Deregulation Select Ctee 1995–, Educn and Employment Select Ctee 1996–; former chm Angola Study Gp, former vice chm Cons Back Bench Employment Ctee; sec: All Pty Wool Textile Parly Gp, Cons Back Bench Trade and Industry Ctee; memb Freedom Assoc Nat Cncl; *Recreations* shooting, fishing, tennis, squash, bridge, photography; *Style*— Graham Riddick, Esq, MP; ✉ c/o House of Commons, London SW1A 0AA (☎ 0171 219 6285)

RIDDLE, Howard Charles Frazer; s of Cecil Riddle (d 1987), of Sevenoaks, Kent, and Eithne, *née* McKenna; *b* 13 Aug 1947; *Educ* Judd Sch Tonbridge, LSE (LLB); *m* 31 Aug 1974, (Susan) Hilary, da of Dr André Hurst (d 1992), of Ottawa, Canada; 2 da (Stephanie b 1979, Poppy b 1984); *Career* SSRC Canada 1971–76, sr ptnr Edward Fail Bradshaw & Waterson 1985–95; met stipendiary magistrate 1995– (acting met stipendiary magistrate 1993–95); vice-chm London Area Ctee Legal Aid Bd 1993–95; memb Law Soc 1969; *Recreations* rugby football, walking, tennis, cycling; *Clubs* Druidstone; *Style*— Howard Riddle, Esq; ✉ Greenwich Magistrates Court, 9 Blackheath Road, London SE18 8PG (☎ 0181 694 0033); Woolwich Magistrates Court, Market Street, London SE18 6QY (☎ 0181 855 8518)

RIDEL, David William; s of Maurice William Ridel, of Wimborne, Dorset, and Violet Georgina, *née* Tull (d 1983); *b* 20 Dec 1947; *Educ* Forest GS Wokingham Berks, Univ of Bristol (BA, BArch); *m* 23 Nov 1971, Felicity Laura, da of Rev Thomas Herbert Lewis; 2 s (Thomas William b 6 Jan 1976, Jack William b 7 Feb 1983), 1 da (Gemma Laura b 31 July 1977); *Career* architectural asst Marshall Macklin Monaghan Toronto Canada 1969–70, assoc architect Richard Lee Architect Bristol 1972–75, chief architect Community Housing Architects Team London 1975–79, chief exec Community Housing Assoc London 1979, sr architect YRM Architects London 1979–86, ptnr Building Design Partnership 1986–92, ptnr Lambert Scott & Innes Norwich 1992–; corp memb RIBA 1974; govr Norwich Sch of Art & Design 1993–; *Recreations* skiing, jogging, windsurfing, ballet, opera, theatre; *Style*— David Ridel, Esq; ✉ Lambert Scott & Innes, The Old Drill Hall, 23A Cattle Market Street, Norwich NR1 3DY (☎ 01603 660711, fax 01603 623213)

RIDEOUT, Paul David; s of David Julian Rideout, of Swindon, Wilts, and Glenys, *née* Jefferies; *b* 14 Aug 1964; *Educ* Kingsdown Sch Swindon; *m* 15 July 1988, Carolyn, da of Raymond Edward Whatley; 2 s (Benjamin Paul b 19 Oct 1988, Jordan David b 26 Feb 1993); *Career* professional footballer; Swindon Town 1981–83 (95 appearances), Aston Villa 1983–85 (60 appearances), Bari Italy 1985–88 (120 appearances), Southampton 1988–91 (over 80 appearances), Notts County 1991–92, Glasgow Rangers 1992; Everton FC: joined 1992–, winners FA Cup 1995 (scorer of winning goal); England: 14 schoolboy under 15 caps (scored on each appearance at Wembley incl hat-trick v Scotland), 12 youth caps, 6 under 21 caps; *Recreations* golf, snooker, tennis; *Style*— Paul Rideout, Esq; ✉ Everton FC, Goodison Park, Liverpool L4 4EL (☎ 0151 521 2020)

RIDEOUT, Prof Roger William; s of Sidney Rideout (d 1949), of Bromham, Bedfordshire, and Hilda Rose, *née* Davies (d 1985); *b* 9 Jan 1935; *Educ* UCL (LLB, PhD); *m* 1, 30 July 1960 (m dis 1976), Marjorie Roberts, da of Albert Roberts of Bedford; 1 da (Tania Mary b 1965); m 2, 24 Aug 1977, Gillian Margaret, *née* Lynch; *Career* Nat Serv Lt RAEC 1958–60; lectr: Univ of Sheffield 1960–63, Univ of Bristol 1963–64; called to the Bar Gray's Inn 1964; UCL: sr lectr 1964–65, reader in Eng law 1965–73, prof of lab law 1973–, dean of faculty 1975–77, vice dean and dep head Dept of Law 1982–89, dir of res studies 1993–; memb Phelps-Brown Ctee 1967–68, chm Industl Law Soc 1977–80 (vice pres 1983–), pt/t chm Indust Tbnls 1983–, dep chm Central Arbitration Ctee 1978–; ILO Missions to: Gambia 1981–83, Somalia 1990–91, Egypt 1992–94; ed Longmans Law Series; *Books* Principles of Labour Law (5 edn, 1989), Trade Unions and the Law (1973), Industrial Tribunal Law (1980); *Recreations* local history; *Clubs* MCC; *Style*— Prof Roger Rideout; ✉ 255 Chipstead Way, Woodmansterne, Surrey SM7 3JW (☎ 01737 552033); Faculty of Laws, University College London, Bentham House, Endsleigh Gardens, London WC1H OEG (☎ 0171 391 1449, fax 0171 209 3470)

RIDGE, Rupert Leander Pattle; s of Maj Robert Vaughan Ridge (d 1987), of Brockley and Lacock, and Marian Ivy Edith, *née* Pattle (d 1977); *b* 18 May 1947; *Educ* King's Coll Taunton; *m* 1971, Mary Blanche, da of Maj Martin Gibbs (d 1994), of Chippenham, and Elsie Margaret Mary, *née* Hamilton Dalrymple; 4 c (Thomas Leander Pattle b 1972, Marian Sophia b 1973, Edward Francis b 1976, Adeline Dyce Albinia Rose b 1979); *Career* offr Light Infantry 1968–73; with British Aerospace Defence (formerly British Aircraft Corporation) 1973–94 (numerous roles mostly as commercial exec); int dir The Leonard Cheshire Fndn 1994–; former chm St Michael's Cheshire Home Axbridge, tstee Action around Bethlehem Children with Disability (ABCD) 1994–; *Recreations* gardening and smallholding mgmnt; *Clubs* Army and Navy; *Style*— Rupert Ridge, Esq; ✉ Leonard Cheshire Foundation International, 26–29 Maunsel Street, London SW1P 2QN (☎ 0171 828 1822, fax 0171 828 0699)

RIDGEON, David Cyril Elliot; s of Cyril Elliot Ridgeon (d 1973), and Kathleen Joan, *née* Miller; *b* 6 May 1935; *Educ* Monkton Combe Sch Bath; *m* 30 Sept 1961, Jill Elizabeth, da of Lewis Starling (d 1966); 2 da (Rachel b 1962, Anne b 1966); *Career* builders merchant and timber importer; dir: Ridgeons Ltd (joined 1960), CRS (Wholesale) Ltd 1976–, National Home Improvements Cncl 1991–; pres Builders Merchant Fedn 1989–90; sch govr Hills Road 6th Form Coll; Liveryman and memb Ct of Assts Worshipful Co of Builders Merchants; *Recreations* tennis; *Clubs* Rotary; *Style*— David Ridgeon, Esq; ✉ Rectory Farm, Madingley Rd, Coton, Cambridge CB3 7PG; Tenison Rd, Cambridge (☎ 01223 467467)

RIDGEON, Jonathan Peter (Jon); s of Peter James Ridgeon, of Cambridge, and Margaret Anne, *née* Allum; *b* 14 Feb 1967; *Educ* Newmarket Upper Sch, Magdalene Coll Cambridge; *Career* former athlete; achievements at 110m hurdles: Euro jr champion 1985, runner-up World Jr Championships 1986, runner-up World Championships 1987 (Br record time), AAA champion 1987, World Student Games champion 1987, fifth place Olympic Games Seoul 1988; achievements at 60m hurdles: runner-up World Indoor Championships 1985, runner-up Euro Indoor Championships 1988, AAA champion 1985, 1987 and 1988; 2nd at World Cup in 400m hurdles 1992, semi finalist 400m hurdles Olympic Games Atlanta 1996; currently tv & radio presenter (BSkyB, ITV, BBC Radio 5 Live), sponsorship conslt APi; *Recreations* tennis; *Clubs* Hawks', Achilles Athletics; *Style*— Jonathan Ridgeon, Esq; ✉ 60 Spring Close, Burwell, Cambridge

RIDGWAY, George; s of John George Ridgway (d 1988), of Leicester, and Constance Winifred, *née* Bruce (d 1980); *b* 16 Oct 1945; *Educ* Wyggeston Sch, Leicester Poly; *m* 20 June 1970, Mary Chamberlain, da of John Chamberlain; 2 c (Imogen Kate b 6 Nov 1973, Julian George b 14 March 1978); *Career* chartered accountant in public practice; currently sr ptnr Pole Arnold Leics and fin dir Ridgway & Co (Leicester) Ltd (machine tool manufacturers); pres Leics and Northants Soc of CAs 1990–91, memb Cncl ICAEW 1994–; former capt, chm and pres Aylestone St James RFC (503 1st XV appearances), various Rugby Union chairmanships until 1988; FCA (ACA 1972), FInstD 1980; *Style*— George Ridgway, Esq; ✉ 449 London Road, Leicester LE2 3JW (☎ 0116 270 5203); Pole Arnold, Chartered Accountants, Stoughton House, Harborough Rd, Oadby, Leicester LE2 4LP (☎ 0116 271 7551, fax 0116 271 0597)

RIDGWAY, Judith Anne (Judy); da of Dr Leslie Randal Ridgway, of Eastbourne, and Lavinia, *née* Bottomley; *Educ* St Christopher Sch Letchworth Garden City, Univ of Keele; *Career* former assoc dir Welbeck PR; cookery ed Woman's World Magazine 1984–90; freelance writer on: food, wine, cookery, catering, travel; memb: Guild of Food Writers, Circle of Wine Writers, Soc of Authors; Companion Guilde de Fromagers, Confrerie de St Uguzon 1990; *Books* Adult Cookery: The Vegetarian Gourmet (1979), Salad Days (1979), Home Preserving (1980), The Seafood Kitchen (1980), The Colour Book of Chocolate Cookery (1981), Mixer, Blender, Processor Cookery (1981), The Breville Book of Toasted Sandwiches (1982), Waitrose Book of Pasta, Rice and Pulses (1982), Making the Most of: Rice, Pasta, Potatoes, Bread, Cheese, Eggs (1983), The Little Lemon Book, The Little Rice Book, The Little Bean Book (1983), Barbecues (1983), Cooking with German Food (1983), Frying Tonight (1984), Sprouting Beans and Seeds (1984), Man in the Kitchen (jtly, 1984), Nuts and Cereals (1985), The Vegetable Year (1985), Wining and Dining at Home (1985), Wheat and Gluten-Free Cookery (1986), Vegetarian Wok Cookery (1986), Cheese and Cheese Cookery (1986), 101 Ways with Chicken Pieces (1987), Pocket Book of Oils, Vinegars and Seasonings (jtly, 1989), Carr's Connoisseurs Cheese Guide (1989), The Vitamin and Mineral Diet Cookbook (1990), Catering for a Wedding (1991), The Vegetarian Delights (1992), The Quick After Work Pasta Cookbook (1993), Food for Sport (1994), Quick After-Work Vegetarian Cookbook (1994), The Noodle Cookbook (1994), Clearly Delicious (jtly, 1994), Quick After Work Winter Vegetarian Cookbook (1996), The Olive Oil Companion (1997); Wine: The Wine Lover's Record Book (1988), The Little Red Wine Book (1989), The Little White Wine Book (1989), Best Wine Buys in the High Street (1996), The Wine Tasting Class (1996); Children's Cookery: 101 Fun Foods to Make (1982), Cooking Round the World (1983), Festive Occasions (1986), Food and Cooking Round the World (jtly, 1986), Healthy Eating (jtly, 1990); How to Books: Home Cooking for Money (1983), Running Your Own Wine Bar (1984), Successful Media Relations (1984), Running Your Own Catering Business (1993), Catering Management Handbook (jtly, 1994); *Recreations* opera, bridge, walking, cycling; *Style*— Ms Judy Ridgway; ✉ 46 Gloucester Square, London W2 2TQ (☎ 0171 706 3286)

RIDGWELL, Patrick John; s of Joseph Thomas Ridgwell (d 1969), and Ida May Mann (d 1988); *b* 15 March 1930; *Educ* St David's Coll Lampeter, Corpus Christi Coll Cambridge (MA); *m* 1965, Maryla, da of Capt Maximillian Statter (d 1947); 1 s (Jolyon b 1967), 1 da (Caroline b 1965); *Career* md Anthony Wieler & Co Ltd 1972–89; dir: Anthony Wieler Unit Tst Mgmnt 1973–89, Arbuthnot Unit Tst Mgmnt 1989–; chm The Assoc of Ind Investmt Mangrs 1976–88, pres Exec Int Investors 1978–83; AIIMR; *Recreations* choral singing, mountain walking, architecture; *Clubs* United Oxford and Cambridge Univ; *Style*— Patrick Ridgwell, Esq; ✉ Hambutts House, Painswick, Gloucestershire GL6 6UP (☎ 01452 813230)

RIDING, Joanna; da of Alan Riding, of Longridge, Lancs, and Glenys Pauline, *née* Duxbury; *b* 9 Nov 1967; *Educ* Penwortham Girls HS, Blackpool & Fylde Coll of FE, Bristol Old Vic Theatre Sch; *Career* actress; spent 3 yrs whilst a student as solo and band vocalist; advanced stage combat certificate 1989; *Theatre* for Bristol Old Vic 1986–89 incl: Jane in Salad Days, Celia in As You Like It, Polly Peachum in The Beggar's Opera, Constance in She Stoops to Conquer; for Chichester incl: Dorothy in The Wizard of Oz, Anne in The Merry Wives of Windsor, Rosie in My Mother Said I Never Should; for RNT incl: Julie Jordan in Carousel, Anne Egerman in A Little Night Music, most recently Sarah Brown in Guys and Dolls; other credits incl: Happy as a Sandbag (Swan Worcester), Around the World in Eighty Days (Liverpool), Sally in Me and My Girl (Adelphi), Susie in Lady Be Good (Regents Park), The Picture of Dorian Day (Lyric Hammersmith and tour); *Television* incl: Sean's Show (Channel X), The Brian Conley Show (LWT), Casualty (BBC), Strike Command (YTV); *Awards* Olivier Award for Best Actress in a Musical for Carousel 1993; *Recreations* music, reading, crosswords, running, Manchester United FC; *Style*— Ms Joanna Riding; ✉ c/o Scott Marshall Personal Management, 44 Perryn Road, London W3 7NA (☎ 0181 749 7692, fax 0181 743 1669)

RIDING, (Frederick) Michael Peter; s of Frederick N Riding, of Alton, Hants, and Elizabeth, *née* Lockwood; *Educ* Barnard Castle Sch, Univ of Leeds (BA); *m* 21 March 1967, Vivian Ann, da of late Joseph M Dodds; 1 da (Victoria b 10 Jan 1970), 2 s (George b 20 Dec 1971, Samuel b 21 Feb 1973); *Career* sr vice pres Asia Chemical Bank NY 1980–83; Lloyds Bank plc: princ mangr Far E Div Lloyds Bank International Ltd 1984–85, gen mangr Asia 1985–87, gen mangr trade finance 1987–89, gen mangr UK retail banking 1989–91, gen mangr commercial banking 1991–95, dir of commercial banking 1996–; FCIB 1991; *Recreations* golf, theatre, art, opera; *Clubs* Royal Lytham St Anne's Golf, Weston-Super-Mare Golf; *Style*— Michael Riding, Esq; ✉ Lloyds Bank plc, Canons House, Bristol BS99 7LB (☎ 0117 943 3687, fax 0117 943 3096)

RIDING, Peter Anthony; s of William Riding (d 1990), and Ina, *née* Bunnell; *b* 3 Nov 1941; *Educ* St Paul's Sch Sao Paulo Brazil, Rossall Sch, Imperial Coll London (BSc); *m* 1 (m dis); 1 s (Dominic William b 27 Nov 1972); m 2, 27 July 1990, Marylyn Susan (Lyn) (d 1992); *Career* BBC TV: researcher 1966–67, prodn asst 1967–68, asst prodr 1969–70, prodr 1970–74, sr prodr 1974–79, exec prodr 1980–91, dep head Continuing Educn and Training Television 1991–93; media conslt 1994–; dir Webserve Ltd 1995–; ARCS; *Recreations* tennis, photography, yoga, DIY; *Style*— Peter Riding, Esq; ✉ 15a Fitzjohn's Avenue, London NW3 5JY

RIDING, Robert Furniss; s of William Furniss Riding, FCA (d 1985), of Manchester, and Winifred, *née* Coupe (d 1993); *b* 5 May 1940; *Educ* Stockport GS, ChCh Oxford (MA); *Career* dir and later chm National Commercial Development Capital Ltd 1980–85, gen mangr Williams & Glyn's Bank plc 1982–85, treas and gen mangr The Royal Bank of Scotland plc 1985–86, dep chm and chief exec RoyScot Finance Group plc 1986–90; chm: RoyScot Trust plc 1984–90, Royal Bank Leasing Ltd 1986–90, RoyScot Vehicle Contracts Ltd 1986–90, RoyScot Factors Ltd 1986–90, RoyScot Finance Services Ltd 1988–90, Conister Trust PLC (Isle of Man) 1992– (dir 1991–); non-exec dir: International Commodities Clearing House Ltd 1985–86, Royal Bank of Scotland AG (Switzerland) 1985–86, Direct Line Insurance plc 1986–88, Royal Bank Group Services Ltd 1987–90, A T Mays Group plc 1988–90, Commercial Finance Ltd (Isle of Man) 1992–, Rycroft Finance & Leasing Ltd (Isle of Man) 1996–, The With Profits Plus Fund PLC (Isle of Man) 1996–; memb: Exec Ctee Assoc of Manx Bankers 1993– (vice pres 1995–), Exec Ctee IOM Centre IOD 1994– (vice chm 1995–); tstee and former chm Assoc of Sea Trg Orgns, tstee Seamanship Foundation 1990–96; The Royal Yachting Assoc: memb Cncl 1983–, chm of trg 1984–89, hon treas 1994–; memb St Johns PCC 1993–; chm Friends of St German's Cathedral 1996–; FCIB 1976; *Recreations* sailing, motoring; *Clubs* Island Cruising (vice pres, cdre 1988–90), Cruising Assoc, Manx Motor Racing, Manx Classic Car, Rolls-Royce Enthusiasts', Westfield Sports Car, IOD; *Style*— Robert Riding, Esq; ✉ Allo, Balladoyne, St Johns, Isle of Man IM4 3LX (☎ 01624 801410); Middlewood, Old Banwell Road, Locking BS24 8BT (☎ 01934 822587); 2 Garden Close, Salcombe, S Devon TQ8 8HF

RIDLER, Anne Barbara; da of Henry Christopher Bradby (d 1947), and Violet Alice, *née* Milford (d 1956); *b* 30 July 1912; *Educ* Downe House Sch, King's Coll London; *m* 2 July 1938, Vivian Hughes Ridler, s of Bertram Hughes Ridler (d 1934); 2 s (Benedict b 1947, Colin b 1952), 2 da (Jane b 1941, Kate b 1943); *Career* sec and asst ed to T S Eliot Faber and Faber (publishers of The Criterion quarterly); memb Literary Panel for New English Bible Old Testament; *Books* New and Selected Poems (1988), Collected Poems (1994); verse plays incl: The Trial of Thomas Cranmer (1956), The Jesse Tree (1972); many trans of Italian opera libretti (incl Monteverdi, Mozart); ed: Image of the City, essays of Charles Williams (1958), Poems of James Thomson (1963), Poems of Thomas Traherne (1966), Poems of George Darley (1979), A Victorian Family Postbag (1988); criticism: Profitable Wonders: aspects of Traherne (jtly, 1989), A Measure of English Poetry (1991); *Style*— Mrs Anne Ridler

RIDLEY, Sir Adam Nicholas; kt (1985); s of Jasper Ridley (s of Maj Hon Sir Jasper Ridley, KCVO, OBE, 2 s of 1 Viscount Ridley, by the Maj's w Countess Nathalie, da of Count Benckendorff, sometime Russian ambass in London) and Cressida Bonham Carter (da of Baroness Asquith of Yarnbury and gda of H H Asquith the Lib PM); nephew by marriage of Baron Grimond, TD, PC, of Firth, Co Orkney; *b* 14 May 1942; *Educ* Eton, Balliol Coll Oxford, Univ of California Berkeley; *m* 1, 1970 (m dis), Lady Katharine Rose Celestine Asquith, 2 da of 2 Earl of Oxford and Asquith; m 2, 1981, Margaret Anne (Biddy), da of Frederic Passmore, of Virginia Water, Surrey; 3 s (Jasper b 29 May 1987, Luke (twin) b 29 May 1987, Jo b 16 Aug 1988); *Career* Dept of Economic Affairs 1965–69, HM Treasy 1970–71, Central Policy Review Staff 1971–74; former econ advsr and asst dir CRD, dir CRD 1979 election campaign; special advsr to the Chllr of the Exchequer 1979–84, to Chllr of the Duchy of Lancaster; min in charge of the Office of Arts and Libraries (also mangr Personnel Office) 1985; exec dir Hambros Bank Ltd and Hambros plc 1985–; dep chm Nat Lottery Charities Bd 1995–; chm Names Ctee Lloyds of Londons 1994–95, dep chm Assoc of Lloyds Membs 1995– (memb Ctee 1990–); *Style*— Sir Adam Ridley; ✉ c/o Hambros plc, 41 Tower Hill, London EC3N 4HA (☎ 0171 480 5000)

RIDLEY, Viscountess; Lady Anne Katharine; *née* Lumley; da of late 11 Earl of Scarbrough, KG, GCSI, GCIE, GCVO, TD, PC, and Katharine, *née* McEwen, DCVO; *b* 16 Nov 1928; *m* 3 Jan 1953, 4 Viscount Ridley, *qv*; *Style*— The Rt Hon the Viscountess Ridley; ✉ Blagdon, Seaton Burn, Northumberland

RIDLEY, Dame (Mildred) Betty; DBE (1975); da of Rt Rev Henry Mosley (d 1948), sometime Bishop of Southwell, and Mildred, *née* Willis (d 1963); *b* 10 Sept 1909; *Educ* North London Collegiate Sch, Cheltenham Ladies' Coll; *m* 3 Sept 1929, Rev Michael Ridley (d 1953), Rector of Finchley, s of Samuel Forde Ridley (d 1942); 3 s (Simon b 1933, Adam b 1937, Giles b 1946), 1 da (Clare (Mrs West) b 1930); *Career* vice pres Br Cncl of Churches 1954–56, church cmmr 1958–81, memb Gen Synod of C of E 1970–81, Third Church Estates cmmr 1972–81; MA Lambeth 1958, Hon DSc Univ of Southampton 1993; *Recreations* making and listening to music; *Clubs* Reform; *Style*— Dame Betty Ridley, DBE; ✉ 6 Lions Hall, St Swithun St, Winchester SO23 9HW (☎ 01962 855009)

RIDLEY, Prof Brian Kidd; s of Oliver Archbold Ridley (d 1990), and Lillian Beatrice, *née* Dunn (d 1965); *b* 2 March 1931; *Educ* Yorebridge GS, Gateshead GS, Univ of Durham (BSc, PhD); *m* 16 May 1959, Sylvia Jean, da of Walter Reginald Nicholls; 1 s (Aaron Max b 31 July 1962), 1 da (Melissa Sophie b 3 Sept 1965); *Career* research appt Mullard Research Lab Redhill 1956–64; Dept of Physics Univ of Essex: lectr 1964–67, sr lectr 1967–71, reader 1971–84, prof 1984–90, research prof 1990–; visiting appt RRE Malvern 1966; distinguished visiting prof Cornell Univ 1967; visiting prof: Stanford Univ 1967, Danish Tech Univ 1969, Princeton Univ 1973, Cornell Univ 1976, Univ of Lund 1977, Univ of Santa Barbara 1981, Eindoven Tech Univ 1983, Cornell Univ 1990–; various consultancy appts; memb American Physical Soc 1992; FInstP 1972, FRS 1994; *Books* The Physical Environment (1979), Quantum Processes in Semiconductors (3 edn, 1993), Time, Space and Things (3 edn, 1995), Electrons and Phonons in Semiconductor Multilayers (1996); *Recreations* piano, tennis; *Style*— Prof Brian Ridley, FRS; ✉ Department of Physics, University of Essex, Colchester, Essex CO4 3SQ (☎ 01206 873333)

RIDLEY, David; s of George Kershaw Ridley, of Eccleston, Chester, and Mary, *née* Partington; *b* 25 May 1941; *Educ* Stowe, Trinity Coll Dublin (BA, BComm); *m* 9 Aug 1968, Caroline, da of Kenneth Seton-Karr; 3 s (William Luke Seton b 18 Sept 1969, George Benjamin Karr b 2 March 1972, Simon Charles Schwalm b 10 Aug 1976); *Career* Grenfell & Co stockbrokers 1964–66; Williams de Broë stockbrokers 1966–91: mining analyst, mining salesman, dealing ptnr, compliance dir; conslt Ermitage 1993–, fndr and princ Goliath 1993–; author of S African Reviews, lectr on S African affrs ABIN Bad Homburg Frankfurt 1988–; lay chm Chelsea Deanery Synod 1984–90; MSI; *Recreations* cycling to the City; *Clubs* City University (chm 1990–94); *Style*— David Ridley, Esq; ✉ 47 Boscobel Place, Eaton Square, London SW1 (☎ 0171 235 2120)

RIDLEY, Lt Cdr (Charles) David Matthew; DL (Northumberland 1992); s of Arthur Hilton Ridley, CBE (d 1974), of Park End, Simonburn, Hexham, and Kathleen Thelma (d 1982); *b* 27 June 1928; *Educ* RNC Dartmouth; *m* 1960, Alison Hay (d 1989), da of Major David Hay Thorburn (d 1963), of Burnside, Fairlie, Ayrshire; 1 s; *Career* Lt Cdr RN on staff of SNO W Indies 1958–60, FOST 1960–62, HMS Ganges 1962–64, CINC S Atlantic 1964–66; farmer 1966–; chm Hexham Constituency Cons Assoc 1985–88 (pres 1988–91); High Sheriff Northumberland 1981; *Recreations* gardening, shooting; *Style*— Lt Cdr David Ridley, DL; ✉ Little Park End, Simonburn, Hexham, Northumberland NE48 3AE (☎ 01434 681497)

RIDLEY, Prof Frederick Fernand; OBE (1978); *b* 11 Aug 1928; *Educ* The Hall Hampstead, Highgate Sch, LSE (BSc, PhD), Univ of Paris, Univ of Berlin; *m* 1967, Paula Frances Cooper Ridley, OBE, JP, DL, *qv*; 2 s, 1 da; *Career* Univ of Liverpool: lectr 1958–65, prof of political theory and instns 1965–95, sr fell Inst of Public Admin & Mgmnt 1995–; visiting prof: Graduate Sch of Public Affairs Univ of Pittsburgh 1968, Coll of Europe Bruges 1975–83; chm: Job Creation Prog Manpower Servs Cmmn Merseyside 1975–77, Area Manpower Bd 1987–88 (vice chm 1978–87); memb: Jt Univ Cncl for Social and Public Admin 1964– (chm 1972–74), Exec Political Studies Assoc 1967–75 (hon vice pres 1995–), Cncl Hansard Soc 1970–94, Political Sci Ctee SSRC 1972–76, Ctee Euro Gp on Public Admin 1973–92, Public and Social Admin Bd CNAA 1975–82, Res Advsy Gp Arts Cncl 1979–82, Exec Merseyside Arts (Regnl Arts Assoc) 1979–84, Social Studies Res Ctee CNAA 1980–83 (chm), Advsy Cncl Granada Fndn 1984–, Academic Ctee Assoc Int de la Fonction Publique 1988–92; vice pres: Rencontres Européennes des Fonctions Publiques 1990–, Acad Cncl Forschungsinstitut für Verwaltungswissenschaft Speyer 1992–; tstee Friends of Merseyside Museums and Galleries 1977–85; hon pres Politics Assoc 1976–81 (hon fell 1995–); ed: Political Studies 1969–75, Parliamentary Affairs 1975–; *publications* numerous books and articles on political science and public admin; *Style*— Prof Frederick Ridley, OBE; ✉ Riversdale House, Grassendale Park, Liverpool L19 0LR (☎ 0151 427 1630, fax 0151 794 3948)

RIDLEY, (Nicholas) Harold (Lloyd); s of late N C Ridley, FRCS, RN, of Leicester; *b* 10 July 1906; *Educ* Charterhouse, Pembroke Coll Cambridge (MA, MD), St Thomas' Hosp London; *m* 1941, Elisabeth Jane, da of late H B Wetherill, CIE; 2 s, 1 da; *Career* temp Maj RAMC; originator of intraocular implants 1949, former hon ophthalmic surgn Royal Buckinghamshire Hosp, hon conslt in ophthalmology MOD (Army) 1964–71; hon conslt surgn Moorfields Eye Hosp 1938–48 and 1971 (surgn 1938–71, conslt surgn 1948–71), Ophthalmic Dep St Thomas' Hosp 1971 (ophthalmic surgn 1946–71); numerous contribs in textbooks and med jls on intraocular implant surgery, tropical ophthalmology and other subjects; hon memb Oxford Ophthalmological Congress, former vice pres Ophthalmological Soc UK, hon fell Int Coll of Surgns Chicago 1952; hon memb: Peruvian Ophthalmic Soc 1957, Ophthalmological Soc Aust 1963, Aust Coll of Ophthalmologist; memb Advsy Panel Parasitology WHO 1966–71, life pres Int Intraocular Implant Club 1972; memb: Irish Ophthalmological Soc, American Soc of Cataract and Refractive Surgery (formerly American Intraocular Implants Soc) 1974–, Euro Intraocular Implantlens Cncl 1983, Ophthalmological Soc UK 1984; Hon LHD Med Univ of S Carolina 1989, Hon DSc City Univ 1990; Galen Medal Apothecaries Soc 1986, Lord Crook Gold Medal Spectacle Makers' Co 1987; medals: Euro Implantlens Cncl 1979, UK Intraocular Lens Soc 1984, Swedish Med Assoc 1989, Congress d'Association Francaise des Implants Intraoculan 1979, Gullstrand Medal 1992, Jules Gonin medal Swiss Ophthalmological Soc and Int Congress of Opthalmology 1994; FRCS 1932 (Hon FRCS 1986), FRS 1986, FRCOphth 1988 (Hon FCOphth 1990), Hon FRCOpath 1993; *Books* Monograph on Ocular Onchocerciasis; *Recreations* fly-fishing; *Clubs* Flyfishers'; *Style*— Harold Ridley, Esq, FRS; ✉ Keeper's Cottage, Stapleford, Salisbury, Wilts SP3 4LT (☎ 01722 790209)

RIDLEY, Ian Robert; s of Robert Edwin Ridley, of Weymouth, Dorset, and Barbara, *née* Fullbrook; *b* 23 Jan 1955; *Educ* Hardye's Sch Dorchester Dorset, Bedford Coll London (BA); *m* 22 Oct 1977, Josephine Anne, da of Gerald Leighton; 1 s (Jack William b 6 April 1990), 1 da (Alexandra Judith b 12 Feb 1986); *Career* editorial asst Building Magazine 1976, sports ed Worksop Guardian 1977–79, sports sub ed and reporter Evening Post Echo Hemel Hempstead 1979–80; The Guardian: sports sub ed 1980–85, asst sports ed 1985–87, dep sports ed 1987–88, sports writer 1988–90; sports feature writer The Daily Telegraph 1990–93, freelance writer and journalist 1993–94, football corr The Independent on Sunday 1994–; memb: NUJ, Football Writers' Assoc, SWA, Assoc Internationale de Presse Sportive; *Books* Season in the Cold, a journey through English football (Kingswood Press), Cantona - The Red and the Black (Victor Gollancz); *Style*— Ian Ridley, Esq; (☎ 01727 839489)

RIDLEY, Jasper Godwin; s of Geoffrey William Ridley, OBE (d 1957), of W Hoathly, Sussex, and Ursula Mary, *née* King; *b* 25 May 1920; *Educ* Felcourt Sch E Grinstead, Sorbonne, Magdalen Coll Oxford; *m* 1 Oct 1949, Vera, da of Emil Pollak (d 1974), of Prague, Czechoslovakia; 2 s (Benjamin b 1952, John b 1956), 1 da (Barbara b 1950); *Career* called to the Bar Inner Temple 1945, in practice 1946–52; cncllr St Pancras Borough Cncl 1945–49; memb Ct of Assts Worshipful Co of Carpenters (Liveryman 1943, Warden 1985, Master 1988 and 1990); FRSL 1963, vice pres English Section Int PEN 1985; *Books* Nicholas Ridley (1957), The Law of Carriage of Goods (1957), Thomas Cranmer (1962), John Knox (1968), Lord Palmerston (1970, James Tait Black Memorial prize), Mary Tudor (1973), Garibaldi (1974), The Roundheads (1976), Napoleon III and Eugénie (1979), The History of England (1981), The Statesman and the Fanatic (1982), Henry VIII (1984), Elizabeth I (1987), The Tudor Age (1988), The Love Letters of Henry VIII (1988), Maximilian and Juárez (1992), Tito (1994), The History of the Carpenters' Company (1995); *Recreations* chess, walking; *Style*— Jasper Ridley, Esq; ✉ 6 Oakdale Rd, Tunbridge Wells, Kent (☎ 01892 522460)

RIDLEY, Malcolm James; s of Eric Malcolm Thomas Ridley (d 1972), and Pauline Esther (d 1972); *b* 10 March 1941; *Educ* Trinity Sch Croydon, Univ of Bristol (LLB); *m* 1, 14 July 1962 (m dis 1976), Joan Margaret, da of Stanley Charles Martin, of Alfriston, Sussex; 2 da (Camilla b 1970, Estelle b 1972); m 2, 9 April 1977, Bridget Mina, da of Dr Charles Edward O'Keeffe (d 1963); 1 s (John b 1979), 1 da (Susannah b 1977); *Career* CA; Price Waterhouse Vancouver 1962–68, Price Waterhouse London 1974–79, ptnr Coopers & Lybrand London 1981–96 (joined 1979), sole practitioner 1996–; CA Canada 1966, FCA 1980, ATII 1974; *Recreations* cricket, golf, tennis, bridge, theatre, opera; *Clubs* RAC, MCC; *Style*— Malcolm Ridley, Esq; ✉ Moor Lodge, South Holmwood, Dorking, Surrey RH5 4NA (☎ 01306 889594); office (☎ 01306 741457, fax 01306 741458)

RIDLEY, Dr Matthew White (Matt); s and h of 4 Viscount Ridley, KG, GCVO, *qv*; *b* 7 Feb 1958; *Educ* Eton, Magdalen Coll, Oxford (DPhil); *m* 16 Dec 1989, Dr Anya Christine Hurlbert, da of Dr Robert Hurlbert, of Houston, Texas, USA; 1 s (Matthew White b 27 Sept 1993); *Career* author and journalist; The Economist: sci ed 1984–87, Washington corr 1987–89, American ed 1990–92; dir Northern Rock Building Soc 1995–; *Books* Warts and All - The Men Who Would Be Bush (1989), The Red Queen - Sex and the Evolution of Human Nature (1993), The Origins of Virtue (1996); *Style*— Dr Matt Ridley; ✉ Boston House, Blagdon, Seaton Burn, Newcastle upon Tyne NE13 6DB

RIDLEY, 4 Viscount (UK 1900); Sir Matthew White Ridley; 8 Bt (GB 1756), KG (1992), GCVO (1994), TD, JP (1957); also Baron Wensleydale (UK 1900); s of 3 Viscount Ridley, CBE (d 1964), and Ursula, OBE, 2 da of Sir Edwin Lutyens, OM, KCIE, the architect, by Sir Edwin's w Lady Emily Lytton (da of 1 Earl of Lytton, GCB, GCSI, CIE, PC, sometime Viceroy of India and s of the novelist Bulwer Lytton, cr Baron Lytton);

b 29 July 1925; *Educ* Eton, Balliol Coll Oxford (BA); *m* 3 Jan 1953, Lady Anne Lumley, da of 11 Earl of Scarbrough, KG, GCSI, GCIE, GCVO, PC; 1 s, 3 da; *Heir* s, (Hon) Dr Matt Ridley, *qv*; *Career* served Coldstream Gds (NW Europe) 1943–46, served Northumberland Hussars 1947–64, Lt-Col TA, Bt-Col, Hon Col Northumberland Hussars Sqdn Queen's Own Yeo RAC TA, Col Cmdt Yeo RAC TA 1982–86; chm Northumberland CC 1967–79, pres Assoc of CCs 1979–84, chllr Newcastle Univ 1989; Lord Steward of HM's Household 1989–; dir Northern Rock Building Society; chm: College Valley Estates, Samares Investments; memb Layfield Ctee 1974–76; Lord-Lt for Northumberland 1984– (DL 1968); chm N of England TA&VRA 1980–84; pres Cncl of TAVRAS 1984–; Hon DCL Newcastle 1989; hon fell: ARICS, Newcastle Poly; OM (W Germany), KStJ 1984; *Recreations* dendrology, shooting, fishing; *Clubs* Boodle's, Pratt's; *Style*— Col the Rt Hon the Viscount Ridley, KG, GCVO, TD, JP; ✉ Blagdon, Seaton Burn, Newcastle on Tyne NE13 6DD (☎ 01670 789236, fax 01670 789560)

RIDLEY, Michael Kershaw; CVO (1992); s of George K Ridley, of Eccleston, Chester (d 1995), and Mary, *née* Partington; *b* 7 Dec 1937; *Educ* Stowe, Magdalene Coll Cambridge (MA); *m* 1968, Diana Loraine, da of Roy A McLernon, of Knowlton PQ, Canada; *Career* Grosvenor Estate: Canada and US 1965–68, London 1969–72; property mangr British and Commonwealth Shipping Co 1972–81, clerk of the Cncl Duchy of Lancaster 1981–; memb Advsy Panel Greenwich Hosp 1978–; FRICS; *Recreations* reading, golf, walking; *Clubs* Brooks's, Garrick, Royal Mid-Surrey (Golf); *Style*— Michael K Ridley, Esq, CVO; ✉ 37 Chester Row, London SW1W 9JE

RIDLEY, Brig Nicholas John; OBE (1983, MBE 1979); s of Col C W Ridley, OBE, DL, of The Glebe House, Shrawadine, nr Shrewsbury, and late Heather Cameron, *née* Christison; *b* 25 March 1941; *Educ* Shrewsbury, RMA Sandhurst; *m* 25 June 1966, (Isabel) Susan, da of late (Robert) Frank Spencer-Nairn, of Castle Carey, Guernsey, Channel Islands; 1 s (Nicholas Charles Philip Christison), 2 da (Alexia Kathleen d 1992, Susanna Mary); *Career* enlisted Queen's Own Cameron Highlanders 1959; Queen's Own Highlanders: 2 Lt 1962, active serv Brunei, Borneo and Sarawak 1962–63, Staff Coll 1971–72, Lt-Col 1980, CO 1 Bn 1982–84, Col 1984; mil dir of studies RMCS Shrivenham 1984–87, procurement exec project mangr 1987–88, Brig and cmd 54 Inf Bde 1988–91, Dep Cmdt RMCS Shrivenham 1992; chief exec Faculty of Advocates Edinburgh 1993–94; currently: appeals dir Guy's and St Thomas' NHS Tst, dir M A Associates; *Recreations* field sports, music and cabinet making; *Clubs* New (Edinburgh); *Style*— Brig Nicholas Ridley, OBE; ✉ c/o New Club, 86 Princes Street, Edinburgh (☎ 0131 447 6689)

RIDLEY, Paula Frances Cooper; OBE (1996), JP (Liverpool City 1977), DL (Merseyside 1989); da of Ondrej Clyne, and Ellen, *née* Cooper; *b* 27 Sept 1944; *Educ* Greenhead HS Huddersfield, Kendal HS Westmorland, Univ of Liverpool (BA, MA); *m* 21 Jan 1967, Prof Frederick Fernand Ridley, OBE, *qv*; 2 s (Joseph Francis b 12 July 1970, Dominic Andrew b 29 Sept 1974), 1 da (Caroline Rachel b 3 April 1976); *Career* lectr in politics and public admin Liverpool Poly 1966–72; project coordinator Regeneration Projects Ltd 1981–84, conslt BAT Industries Small Business 1983–95, dir Community Initiatives Res Tst 1983–90, memb Bd Brunswick Small Business Centre Ltd 1984–95, assoc CEI Consultants 1984–88, presenter and assoc ed Helpful Productions ind TV prodn co 1989–92; chm Liverpool Housing Action Tst 1992–; memb Bd: Merseyside Development Corp 1991–, IBA 1982–88; tstee: Tate Gallery 1988– (chm Tate Gallery Liverpool 1988–), Granada TV Tst 1988–94, National Gallery 1995–; memb Ct Univ of Liverpool 1972–, chm Merseyside Civic Soc 1986–91, life govr Liverpool and Huyton Colls 1979–94; FRSA; author of articles in various professional jls; *Recreations* art, architecture and heritage; *Style*— Mrs Paula Ridley, OBE, JP, DL; ✉ 24 North Road, Grassendale Park, Liverpool L19 0LR (☎ 0151 427 1630); Liverpool Housing Action Trust, Cunard Building, Water Street, Liverpool L3 1EG (☎ 0151 227 1099, fax 0151 236 3360)

RIDLEY, Capt Peter William Wake; s of Rear Adm William Terence Colbourne Ridley, CB, OBE, of Bath, and Barbara Ridley; *b* 27 Nov 1939; *Educ* Marlborough, RNC Dartmouth, RNEC Manadon (BSc London); *m* 14 Aug 1965, Jenifer Gaye, da of Capt William Jaspar MacDonald Teale, of Chicester; 2 s (Timothy b 1967, Nicolas b 1971); *Career* RNC Dartmouth 1958, HMS Belfast 1960, RNEC Manadon 1961, HMS Hermes 1965, RNC Greenwich 1968, HMS Andromeda 1969, Aux Machinery Engrg Estab Hasler 1970, marine engrg offr HMS Ashanti 1973, dir gen ships in Forward Design Gp 1975, MEO during building of HMS Invincible 1978, dir gen ships as asst dir marine gas turbines 1981, CO Naval Party 2010 1985, head of prog co-ordination in Chief Strategic Systems Exec 1986, RN job evaluation judge 1990, ret 1994; currently proprietor VideoScope Productions; MIMechE 1970; *Recreations* music (esp opera), theatre, cricket, golf; *Style*— Capt Peter Ridley, RN; ✉ 24 Entry Hill Park, Bath BA2 5ND

RIDLEY, Rear Adm (William) Terence Colborne; CB (1968), OBE (1954); s of late W H W Ridley; *b* 9 March 1915; *Educ* RNC Dartmouth, RNEC Keyham; *m* 1, 1938, Barbara, *née* Allen (d 1989); 1 s; m 2, 1993, Joan Elaine, da of E S Dowding, and wid of Rev John Norman; *Career* serv RN: Atlantic, Mediterranean and Pacific, Capt RNEC 1962–64, Rear Adm 1966, Adm Superintendent HM Dockyard Rosyth 1966–71, Port Adm Rosyth 1971–72; chm Ex Serv Mental Welfare Soc 1973–83; *Recreations* gardening; *Style*— Rear Adm Terence Ridley, CB, OBE; ✉ 4 Hill View Road, Bath BA1 6NX (☎ 01225 333584)

RIDLEY, Prof Tony Melville; CBE (1986); s of John Edward Ridley (d 1982), and Olive, *née* Armstrong; *b* 10 Nov 1933; *Educ* Durham Sch, King's Coll Univ of Durham (BSc), Northwestern Univ Illinois (MS), Univ of California Berkeley (PhD); *m* 20 June 1959, Jane, da of John William Dickinson (d 1984); 2 s (Jonathan b 1963, Michael b 1966), 1 da (Sarah b 1962); *Career* Nuclear Power Gp 1957–62, GLC 1965–69, DG Tyne & Wear Passenger Tport Exec 1969–75, md Hong Kong Mass Transit Railway Corporation 1975–80, memb Bd London Regnl Tport (formerly London Tport Exec) 1980–88 (md Railways 1980–85), chm London Underground Ltd 1985–88; dir: Docklands Light Railway 1982–88 (chm 1987–88), London Transport International 1981–88 (chm 1982–87); md Eurotunnel 1989–90 (non-exec dir 1987–90), dir Halcrow Fox & Associates 1980–; prof of tport engrg Imperial Coll London 1991– (Rees Jeffreys prof of tport engrg 1991–95), dir Univ of London Centre for Tport Studies 1994–95; pres Light Rail Transit Assoc 1974–92; memb Res Cncl Euro Centre for Infrastructure Studies; first recipient of Highways award of Inst of Highways and Transportation 1988; Freeman City of London 1982, Liveryman Worshipful Co of Carmen 1982; Hon DTech Napier Univ 1996; FICE (pres 1995–96), FCIT, FIHT, fell Hong Kong Inst of Engineers, fell Inst of Transportation Engrs, FRSA, FEng 1992, FCGI 1995, FAPM 1996; *Publications* articles in transport, engineering and other journals; *Recreations* theatre, music, international affairs, rejuvenation of Britain; *Clubs* Hong Kong, Hong Kong Jockey; *Style*— Prof Tony M Ridley, CBE, FEng; ✉ 77 Church Rd, Richmond, Surrey TW10 6LX (☎ 0181 948 3898); Imperial College, Department of Civil Engineering, London SW7 2BU (☎ 0171 594 6097, fax 0171 594 6102)

RIDLEY-THOMAS, Roger; s of John Montague Ridley-Thomas (d 1973), of Norwich, and Christina Anne, *née* Seex (d 1976); *b* 14 July 1939; *Educ* Greshams Sch; *m* 1962, Sandra Grace McBeth, da of William Morrison Young, OBE, of Gt Glen, Leics; 2 s (Christopher b 1964, Simon b 1966), 2 da (Philippa b 1970, Sarah b 1972); *Career* Royal Norfolk Regt 1958–60; newspaper publishing; Eastern Counties Newspapers Ltd 1960–65; advertisement mgmnt: Middlesbrough Evening Gazette 1965–67, Western Mail and Echo Ltd 1968–70, Newcastle Chronicle and Journal Ltd 1970–72; asst md The Scotsman Publications Ltd 1972–80, md Aberdeen Journals Ltd 1980–84, md The Scotsman Publications Ltd 1984–89, md Thomson Regnl Newspapers Ltd 1989–94, chm and dir Thomson Free Newspapers Ltd 1989–94; dir: Radio Forth Ltd 1978–81, Aberdeen Journals Ltd 1980–84 and 1990–94, Aberdeen C of C 1981–84, Scottish Business in the Community 1984–90, The Scotsman Publications Ltd 1984–94, The Scotsman Communications Ltd 1984–94, Thomson Regional Newspapers Ltd 1985–94, Scottish Business Achievement Award Tst Ltd 1985–, Edinburgh C of C and Mfrs 1985–88, Regnl Daily Advertising Cncl 1989–93, Belfast Telegraph Newspapers Ltd 1990–94, Western Mail & Echo Ltd 1990–94, Chester Chronicle Ltd 1990–94, Newcastle Chronicle & Journal Ltd 1990–94, Thames Valley Newspapers Ltd 1990–94, Cardrona Ltd 1995–, Milex Ltd 1996–, Norcor Holdings plc 1996–; chm Anglia FM Ltd 1996–; pres Scottish Daily Newspaper Soc 1983–85; cncl memb: CBI 1983–86, Scottish Wildlife Appeal Ctee 1985–88; *Recreations* vegetable growing, shooting, fishing, golf, tennis, travel; *Clubs* New (Edinburgh), Caledonian; *Style*— Roger Ridley-Thomas, Esq; ✉ Booton Manor, Booton, Reepham, Norfolk NR10 4NZ

RIDPATH, Michael William Gerrans; s of Andrew Ridpath, of Bircham, Norfolk, and Elizabeth, *née* Hinds Howell; *b* 7 March 1961; *Educ* Millfield, Merton Coll Oxford (exhibitioner, BA); *m* 1, 1985, Candy Ann Helman (d 1992); 2 da (Julia b 17 Feb 1990, Laura b 30 Dec 1992); m 2, 1994, Barbara Ann, da of James P Nunemaker; *Career* writer; trader Saudi Int Bank 1982–91, venture capitalist Apax Partners & Co 1991–94; author 1994–; memb: Soc of Authors 1995, Crime Writers' Assoc 1995; *Books* Free to Trade (1995), Trading Reality (1996); *Style*— Michael Ridpath, Esq; ✉ c/o Carole Blake, Blake Friedman Literary Agency Ltd, 37–41 Gower Street, London WC1E 6HH (☎ 0171 872 6417, fax 0171 872 6405)

RIDSDALE, Sir Julian Errington; kt (1981), CBE (1977); s of Julian Ridsdale, of Rottingdean, Sussex; *b* 8 June 1915; *Educ* Tonbridge, RMC Sandhurst, Oriental Sch of Languages London; *m* 1942, Victoire Evelyn Patricia, DBE, da of Col J Bennett, of Kensington; 1 da; *Career* served WWII Royal Norfolk Regt, Royal Scots and Somerset LI, ret as Maj 1946; Parly candidate (C): SW Islington 1949, Paddington 1951; MP (C) Harwich 1954–92; Parly under sec of state Air Miny and vice-pres Air Cncl 1962–64, Parly under sec RAF MOD 1964, chm Br Japanese Parly Gp 1961–92, vice chm UN Parly Assoc 1966–82, ldr Parly Delgns to Japan 1973, 1975 and 1977–83; memb: Trilateral Cmmn EEC, USA and Japan 1973–93, N Atlantic Assembly 1979–92; dep chm Int Triangle USA, Japan and Europe 1981–86; vice pres Political Ctee N Atlantic Assembly 1983–87; chm All Party Gp on Engineering Devpt 1985–92; Br Cmmr Gen Expo 90 Osaka Japan 1990; hon fell Univ Coll London 1991; memb Ct of Assts Worshipful Co of Skinners; Grand Cordon Order of the Sacred Treasure (Japan) 1990, Commandeur d'Honneur de Commanderie du Bon Temps de Medoc et des Graves 1996; *Style*— Sir Julian Ridsdale, CBE; ✉ 12 The Boltons, London SW10 (☎ and fax 0171 373 6159)

RIDSDALE, (Robert) Peter; s of Arthur Ridsdale (d 1985), and Audrey Gwendoline, *née* Oakley (d 1974); *b* 11 March 1952; *Educ* Leeds Modern GS; *m* 1 (m dis), Shirley Ruth; 2 s (Simon Nicholas b 5 Sept 1976, Paul Anthony b 30 Jan 1979); m 2 (m dis), Jacqueline; 2 s (Matthew Peter b 30 Jan 1985, Joseph Michael b 23 May 1988); m 3, 22 April 1995, Sophie Victoria, *née* Hobhouse; 1 da (Charlotte Louise b 13 May 1996); *Career* personnel offr Appleyard of Leeds 1969–72, personnel mangr Baker Perkins 1972–78, industl relations mangr ICL 1978–81, vice pres human resources International Div Schering Plough Corp 1981–85, md Top Man then md Evans Ltd Burton Group plc 1985–91, jt chief operating offr Alexon Group plc 1991–93, chief exec QVC - The Shopping Channel 1993–94, gp md then chief exec The Tulchan Group Ltd 1994–; dir Leeds United FC; FInstD, memb Mktg Soc; *Style*— Peter Ridsdale, Esq

RIEDL, Martin Paul; s of Kurt Riedl, and Ruth, *née* Schechner; *b* 12 Sept 1949; *Educ* Sutton Valence, Ealing Sch of Photography (Dip in Photography); *m* 18 April 1980 (m dis 1990), Patricia Kilbourn, *née* Dumond; 2 s (Alexander David b 17 Nov 1981, Arthur Jonathan b 15 June 1983); *partner* Annie Bronwen, da of Edward Augustus Williams; 1 s (Harry Edward b 11 Sept 1990); *Career* photographer; asst to: Robert Dowling 1973–75, Derek Coutts 1975–77; freelance photographer 1978–, opened own studio 1979–; awarded two merits and two silvers Assoc of Photographers, D & AD silver nomination, second place Polaroid European Final Art Awards; memb Assoc of Photographers 1976; *Recreations* sculpture, skiing, badminton, tennis; *Clubs* Chelsea Arts; *Style*— Martin Riedl, Esq; ✉ Martin Riedl Photography, 3 Water Lane, London NW1 8NZ (☎ 0171 428 9262, fax 0171 482 1822, e-mail shelpost@mail.bogo.co.uk)

RIFKIND, Rt Hon Malcolm Leslie; PC (1986), QC (Scot 1985), MP (C) Edinburgh Pentlands (majority 4,290); s of Elijah Rifkind, of Edinburgh; *b* 21 June 1946; *Educ* George Watson's Coll Edinburgh, Univ of Edinburgh (LLB, MSc); *m* 1970, Edith Amalia, *née* Steinberg; 1 s, 1 da; *Career* advocate, called to the Bar Edinburgh 1970; Parly candidate Edinburgh Central 1970, MP (C) Edinburgh Pentlands Feb 1974–, memb Select Ctee Euro Secdy Legislation 1975–76, oppn front bench spokesman on Scottish affrs 1975–76, jt sec Cons Foreign and Cwlth Affrs Ctee 1978, memb Select Ctee on Overseas Devpt 1978–79; Parly under sec of state: Scottish Office 1979–82, FCO 1982–83; min of state FCO 1983–86, sec of state for Scotland 1986–90, sec of state for transport 1990–92, sec of state for defence 1992–95, sec of state for foreign and Cwlth affrs 1995–; memb Queen's Body Guard for Scotland (Royal Co of Archers) 1993–; Hon Col 162 Movement Control Regt Royal Logistics Corps 1996–; *Recreations* walking, reading, field sports; *Style*— Rt Hon Malcolm Rifkind, QC, MP; ✉ House of Commons, London SW1A 0AA

RIGBY, Alfred; s of Robert Marsden Rigby (d 1984), of Freckleton, Lancs, and Betsy Alice, *née* Bownass (d 1980); *b* 18 June 1934; *Educ* Kirkham GS, Univ of Manchester (BA, MA), Univ of London (DipTP), British Sch Rome (RS); *m* 4 Sept 1958, Ann Patricia, da of Maj George Flynn, MBE, MC (d 1978), of Berkhamsted, Bucks; 1 s (Christopher Simon b 1961), 1 da (Susan Elizabeth b 1964); *Career* dep regnl architect NW Metropolitan RHB 1960–64, chief architect City of Westminister 1964–73 (2 Civic Tst awards), dir of architecture London Borough of Camden 1973–79 (3 Civic Tst awards), sr ptnr John R Harris Partnership (conversion of Dorchester Hotel, rehabilitation of HM Prison Strangeways) 1986–93, Rigby Culpin Partnership 1993–; chm Cmmn for Fine Arts Br Acad Rome, chm Shenley Cricket Centre, patron Bath FC (RFU); memb Cons Pty; FRIBA, FIMgt, FRSA, RTPI; *Books* Sir Banister Fletcher: A History of Architecture on the Comparative Method (contrib 1963 edn); *Recreations* painting, cricket, rugby, opera, theatre; *Clubs* MCC, Athenaeum; *Style*— Alfred Rigby, Esq; ✉ Meadlands, 3 Pickwick, Corsham, Wilts SN13 0JD (☎ 01249 713 228); East Leigh, West Scrafton, Middleham, Leyburn, North Yorks (☎ 01969 40672)

RIGBY, Anthony John; s and h of Sir John Rigby, 2nd Bt, ERD; *b* 3 Oct 1946; *Educ* Rugby; *m* 1978, Mary, da of Robert Oliver, of Cheshire; 3 s, 1 da; *Career* sch teacher; *Style*— Anthony Rigby, Esq; ✉ Honeysuckle Cottage, Haughton, West Felton, Oswestry (☎ 01691 610573)

RIGBY, Bryan; s of William George Rigby (d 1971), and Lily Rigby; *b* 9 Jan 1933; *Educ* Wigan GS, King's Coll London (BSc DipChemEng); *m* 1978, Marian Rosamund, da of David Ellis (d 1979); 1 s, 1 da; 1 step s, 1 step da; *Career* UKAEA Industl Gp Capenhurst 1955–60, Beecham Gp London and Amsterdam 1960–64, mktg dir Laporte Industs 1964–78, dep dir gen CBI 1978–Jan 1984, md BASF UK Ltd 1984–86, regnl md BASF AG 1987–93, dir MEDEVA plc 1993–, chm Streamline Holding Ltd 1994–; vice-pres British Assoc for the Advancement of Science 1993–; memb Social Security Advsy Ctee 1994–, tstee Anglo-German Fndn 1992–, govr Henley Mgmnt Coll 1993–, chm Review Body for Nursing Staff, Midwives, Health Visitors and Professions Allied to Med 1995–;

CEng, FIChemE, FRSA, CIMgt, MInstM; *Recreations* music, golf, gardening; *Clubs* Reform; *Style—* Bryan Rigby, Esq; ✉ Cluny, 61 Penn Road, Beaconsfield, Bucks (☎ and fax 01494 673206)

RIGBY, Jean Prescott; da of Thomas Boulton Rigby (d 1987), and Margaret Annie, *née* Whiteside; *Educ* Elmslie Girls' Sch Blackpool, Birmingham Sch of Music, RAM (Principal's prize), RSA (Peter Stuyvesant scholarships), Nat Opera Studio (Leverhulme & Munster scholar); *m* 21 Nov 1987, Jamie Hayes; 3 s (Daniel Thomas b 7 March 1989, Oliver James b 27 Nov 1990, Matthew Peter b 25 Sept 1992); *Career* opera singer (mezzo soprano); princ mezzo soprano ENO 1982–90; Royal Opera House debut 1983, Glyndebourne debut 1984; roles incl: title role in Carmen, Octavian in Der Rosenkavalier, Lucretia in The Rape of Lucretia, Penelope in Il Ritorno d'Ulisse in Patria, Magdalena in Die Meistersinger, Maddalena in Rigoletto, Dorabella in Cosi fan Tutte, Jocasta in Oedipus Rex, Nicklaus in Les Contes d'Hoffman, Isabella in L'Italliana in Algeri, Charlotte in Werther, Helen in King Priam, Rosina in The Barber of Seville, 150 anniversary performance of Mendelssohn's Elijah (BBC Proms) 1996; numerous TV appearances and recordings; winner: bursary Royal Opera House, Royal Overseas League competition, ENO Young Artists competition, Silver medal Worshipful Co of Musicians; Hon ARAM 1984, Hon FRAM 1989, ARCM, ABSM; *Recreations* sport, cooking, British heritage; *Style—* Ms Jean Rigby; ✉ Harold Holt Ltd, 31 Sinclair Road, London W14 0NS

RIGBY, Lt-Col Sir (Hugh) John Macbeth; 2 Bt (UK 1929), of Long Durford, Rogate, Co Sussex; ERD and two clasps; s of Sir Hugh Rigby, 1 Bt, KCVO (d 1944); *b* 1 Sept 1914; *Educ* Rugby, Magdalene Coll Cambridge (MA); *m* 1946, Mary Patricia Erskine (d 1988), da of Edmund Erskine Leacock; 4 s; *Heir* s, Anthony John Rigby b 3 Oct 1946; *Career* Lt-Col (ret) RCT, serv UK and SEAC; dir Executors of James Mills Ltd to 1977; *Style—* Lt-Col Sir John Rigby, Bt, ERD; ✉ Casa das Palmeiras, Armação de Pêra, Algarve, Portugal (☎ 00 351 82 312548); 5 Park St, Macclesfield, Cheshire (☎ 01625 613959)

RIGBY, Dr Michael Laurence; s of Thomas Rigby, of Burnley, and Kathleen, *née* Barker; *b* 19 March 1947; *Educ* Colne GS, Univ of Leeds Med Sch (MB ChB, FRCP, MD); *m* 1976, Joanne, da of Roland Ireland; 3 da (Jessica Clair Louise b 27 March 1981, Olivia Jane b 21 Oct 1982, Claudia Anne b 19 April 1985); *Career* registrar Gen Infirmary Leeds 1974–75, res registrar Children's Hosp Birmingham 1975–77, Canadian Heart fndn fell Hosp for Sick Children Toronto Canada 1978–79, conslt paediatric cardiologist Brompton Hosp london 1983–90 (sr registrar 1979–83), dir Paediatrics and conslt paediatric cardiologist Royal Brompton and Nat Heart Hosp London 1990–, sr lectr in paediatics Nat Heart and Lung Inst London 1990–; memb: Paediatric Res Soc 1978, Br Paediatric Assoc 1983, Br Cardiac Soc 1990; FRCP 1988; *Books* The Morphology of Congenital Heart Disease (1983), The Diagnosis of Congenital Heart Disease (1986); *Recreations* athletics, the study of terrapins; *Style—* Dr Michael Rigby; ✉ Royal Brompton National Heart and Lung Hosp, Sydney St, London SW3 6NP (☎ 0171 351 8542/352 8121, fax 0171 352 8547)

RIGBY, Peter Philip; CBE (1990), JP; s of Philip James Rigby (d 1985), of Kingston, and Edith, *née* O'Donoghue (d 1969); *b* 12 Aug 1929; *Educ* Ampleforth; *m* 3 April 1959, Jean Rosalie, da of Capt James Wilson Wilson (d 1958), of London; 3 s (Philip James Luke b 26 Feb 1960, Robert Charles b 19 April 1961, Richard Peter b 1 April 1965); *Career* chm and md Philip Rigby and Sons Ltd; cncllr Middx CC 1961, mayor Hornsey Borough Cncl 1963 (elected 1953), fndr and chm Hornsey Centre for Handicapped Children 1963–, ldr London Borough of Haringey 1968–71 (elected 1964); memb: BBFC 1975–, Spastics Soc (now Scope) Exec 1975–83, EITB 1976–84; Corp of London: elected 1972, chm Policy and Resources Ctee Ct of Common Cncl 1984–91, chief commoner 1992; chm: Habinteg Housing Assoc 1989–94 (fndr 1969), London Drug Policy Forum 1990–; dep govr The Hon Irish Soc 1996; Liveryman Worshipful Co of Fletchers (Master 1989–90); FRSA 1979; Knight Cdr of the Holy Sepulchre 1964, KCSG 1995 (KSG 1973); *Recreations* golf, reading; *Clubs* Royal Over-Seas League, City Livery; *Style—* Peter Rigby, Esq, CBE, JP; ✉ 14 Creighton Avenue, Muswell Hill, London N10 1NU (☎ 0181 883 3703, fax 0181 444 3620)

RIGBY, Peter Stephen; *b* 30 July 1955; *Educ* King George V GS Southport, Univ of Manchester (BA); *m* 25 Aug 1979, Stasia Teresa; 1 s (Nicholas Ian b 1981); *Career* asst factory accountant Metal Box 1978–80 (trainee accountant 1976–78), fin accountant Book Club Associates 1980–83; IBC (Holdings) plc (formerly Stonehart Publications): joined 1984, gp accountant, fin dir 1987, dep chief exec 1988, chief exec 1989; formerly dir: Teacher Marks Deal Holdings plc (resigned 1989), Nicholas Stracey (UK) Ltd (resigned 1989), RST Printers Ltd (resigned 1987); chief exec International Business Communications (Holdings) plc 1989–; currently dir: Barham Group plc, A L Bawtree Limited, Barham Limited, Cocks Williamson Associates Limited, Fleet Street Publications Limited, IBC Magazines Limited, Stonehart Leisure Magazines Ltd (resigned 1986, subsequently rejoined and again resigned 1993); ACMA 1980; *Recreations* golfing, jogging, squash, weight training, soccer, rugby, reading, theatre, music; *Style—* Peter Rigby, Esq; ✉ IBC Group plc, 57/61 Mortimer St, London W1N 7TD (☎ 0171 637 4383, fax 0171 631 3214, telex 8956007)

RIGGS, David George; s of George Fletcher Riggs (d 1967), and Ada, *née* Lloyd (d 1985); *b* 6 May 1942; *Educ* Bury GS, Univ of Manchester (BA); *Career* Bury County Borough Council: trainee accountant 1958–63, sr accountant 1963–66, chief internal auditor 1966–67, chief tech asst 1967–68; Greater London Council: worked in Econ Efficiency Unit 1968–71, head of public servs fin 1971–75, asst comptroller of fin 1975–82; dir of fin Inner London Education Authority 1982–90, acting dir London Borough of Hammersmith and Fulham 1990–91, fin dir Benefits Agency 1991–; CIPFA 1963; *Recreations* singing, family, swimming; *Style—* David Riggs, Esq; ✉ Benefits Agency, Room 8E07, Quarry House, Quarry Hill, Leeds LS2 7UA (☎ 0113 2324229, fax 0113 2324235)

RILEY, Dr Alan John; s of Arthur Joseph Riley (d 1993), of Chestfield, Kent, and Edith Ada, *née* Rashbrook; *b* 16 July 1943; *Educ* Bexley GS, Univ of London, Charing Cross Hosp Med Sch London Univ (MB BS), Univ of Manchester (MSc); *m* 1, 14 Nov 1964 (m dis 1976), Pamela Margaret, da of Leonard George Allum, of London; 1 s (John b 1971), 1 da (Veronica b 1968), 2 adopted s (Grant b 1968, Robert b 1970); m 2, 11 Dec 1976, Elizabeth Jane, da of Capt Arthur Norman Robertson (d 1959); *Career* GP Bideford Devon 1970–76, specialist in sexual med 1972–; sr lectr and hon conslt in human sexuality St George's Hosp Med Sch 1995–; dir: MAP Publishing Ltd 1991–95, Sexual Problems Services St George's Hosp London 1995–; ptnr: SMC Developments 1986–, SMC Research 1985–; ed: British Journal of Sexual Medicine 1983–91, Sexual and Marital Therapy 1986–, The Journal of Sexual Health 1991–96; author of over 100 pubns on aspects of sexual and reproductive med; dep co surgn St John Ambulance Bde (ret 1988); LRCP 1967, MRCS 1967, DObstRCOG 1969, FZS 1977, FFPM RCP 1992 (MFPM RCP 1989); accredited memb: Assoc of Sexual and Marital Therapists 1979, RSM, BMA; OStJ 1983; *Recreations* woodwork, photography, boating, natural history; *Style—* Dr Alan Riley; ✉ Field Place, Dunsmore, Bucks HP22 6QH (☎ and fax 01296 622070, car 0831 882481)

RILEY, Barry John; s of Peter Riley (d 1978), and Barbara, *née* Pitt; *b* 13 July 1942; *Educ* Jesus Coll Cambridge (BA); *m* 16 Aug 1969, Anne Geraldine; 2 s (Paul b 20 April 1971, Timothy b 16 April 1976), 1 da (Martha b 4 Nov 1972); *Career* ed asst Investors Chronicle 1964, dep city ed Morning Telegraph Sheffield 1966; Financial Times 1967–: ed Lex column 1978 (asst 1968, jt ed 1974), fin ed 1981, investmt ed and columnist 1987–; memb Bd of Tstees Pearson Group Pension Plan 1993–; *Style—* Barry Riley, Esq; ✉ 17 Mount Pleasant Rd, London W5 1SG (☎ 0181 998 5829); The Financial Times, 1 Southwark Bridge, London SE1 9HL (☎ 0171 873 3000)

RILEY, Bridget; CBE (1972); da of John Fisher Riley (d 1991), of Cornwall and, Bessie Louise, *née* Gladstone (d 1975); *b* 24 April 1931; *Educ* Cheltenham Ladies' Coll, Goldsmiths' Coll of Art, RCA; *Career* artist; AICA critics' prize 1963, John Moores Exhibition prize Liverpool 1963, Peter Stuyvesant Fndn travel bursary to USA 1964, int prize XXXIV Venice Biennale 1968, int prize Ohara Museum 8 Int Print Biennale Tokyo 1972; colour projects for: Royal Liverpool Hosp 1980–83, St Mary's Hosp Paddington 1987–88; designed Colour Moves (Ballet Rambert) 1983; tstee Nat Gallery 1981–88, represented in major museums and art collections worldwide; Hon DLitt: Univ of Manchester 1976, Univ of Ulster 1986, Univ of Oxford 1993, Univ of Cambridge 1995, De Montfort Univ 1996; *Exhibitions* int retrospective museum touring exhibitions (Arts Cncl 1970–71, Br Cncl 1978–81), Bridget Riley - According to Sensation 1982–1992 (Hayward Gallery 1992, Ikon Gallery Birmingham 1993), Six Paintings from the Collection (Tate Gallery London 1994), Kettles Yard Cambridge 1995, Spacex Gallery Exeter 1995, Museum Moderner Kunst Laudkreis Otterdoff Germany 1996, British Sch of Rome 1996, City Art Gallery Leeds 1996; *Style—* Miss Bridget Riley, CBE; ✉ c/o Karsten Schubert Contemporary Art Ltd, 41/42 Foley Street, London WI (☎ 0171 631 0031, fax 0171 436 9255)

RILEY, Christopher John (Chris); s of Bernard Francis Riley (d 1981), of Nottingham, and Phyllis Wigley (d 1954); *b* 20 Jan 1947; *Educ* Ratcliffe Coll, Wadham Coll Oxford (MA), Univ of East Anglia (MA); *m* 24 Sept 1982, Helen Marion, da of Ernest Amos Arthur Mynett, of Sidcup, Kent; 2 s (Timothy James b 1983, Mark Edward b 1985); *Career* HM Treasury: econ asst 1969–72, sr econ asst 1972–74, econ advsr 1974–79, sr econ advsr 1979–88, under sec 1988–95; chief economist DOE 1995–; Gwilym Gibbon res fell Nuffield Coll Oxford 1977–78; *Recreations* music, especially choral singing; *Style—* Chris Riley; ✉ Department of the Environment, Eland House, Stag Place, London SW1E 5DU (☎ 0171 890 4460, fax 0171 890 4509)

RILEY, Very Rev Kenneth Joseph; s of Arthur Riley (d 1954), of Flint, and Mary Josephine, *née* Birks (d 1975); *b* 25 June 1940; *Educ* Holywell GS, UCW Aberystwyth (Robert Bryan music scholar, BA), Linacre House Oxford (MA), Wycliffe Hall Oxford; *m* 4 Jan 1968, Margaret, da of Aubrey Deninson; 2 da (Jane b 27 Jan 1969, Kay b 17 May 1972); *Career* ordained: deacon 1964, priest 1965; asst curate Emmanuel Fazakerley Liverpool 1964–66; chaplain: Brasted Place Coll 1966–69, Oundle Sch 1969–75, Univ of Liverpool 1975–83; vicar Mossley Hill Liverpool 1975–83, warden of readers Liverpool 1979–83, rural dean Childwall 1982–83, canon residentiary Liverpool Cathedral 1983–93, dean of Manchester 1993–; *Books* Liverpool Cathedral (1987); *Recreations* music, drama, films; *Clubs* St James' (Manchester); *Style—* The Very Rev Kenneth Riley; ✉ The Deanery, 44 Shrewsbury Road, Prestwich, Manchester M25 9GQ (☎ 0161 773 2959); Manchester Cathedral, Manchester M3 1SX (☎ 0161 833 2220)

RILEY, (John) Martin; s of Rev Lambert Riley (d 1948), of Roehampton, London, and Marjorie Grace, *née* Maton (d 1973); *b* 15 Nov 1931; *Educ* Bradfield, Queens' Coll Cambridge (MA); *m* 1, 5 Oct 1963 (m dis 1991), Alison Rosemary, *née* Dewar; 2 s (Charles b 1965, Hugh b 1968), 1 da (Philippa b 1970); m 2, 4 June 1992, Angela Margaret, er da of Frank Wright, of Brightwell Park, Brightwell Baldwin, Oxon; *Career* admitted slr 1963, sr ptnr Mercers of Henley-on-Thames 1977–93 (ptnr and conslt 1964–); chm Turners Ct Boys' Home 1976–92; cncllr Oxfordshire CC 1970–81; *Style—* Martin Riley, Esq; ✉ The Dower House, Brightwell Park, Brightwell Baldwin, Oxon OX9 5NS

RILEY, Norman; s of Herman Riley (d 1975), and Ada Riley (d 1986); *b* 1 May 1926; *Educ* Univ of Sheffield (DipArch); *m* 31 July 1954, Madeleine, da of James Smith; 4 s (Andrew b 1955, Michael b 1958, Duncan b 1960, Lawrence b 1962), 1 da (Catherine b 1956); *Career* dep surveyor Univ of Oxford 1955–63, estates bursar Univ of Warwick 1963–67, dep divisional architect GLC 1970–75, official architect to the Church Commissioners 1976–81, conservation architect and expert witness Bickerdike Allen Partners 1981–87, Brock Riley Partners Architects 1987–; assessor for Civic Tst 1966–75, pres Ecclesiastical Architects' and Surveyors' Assoc 1985, ed Advsy Ctee Church Building 1986–, memb Advsy Ctee St Albans Diocese 1989–90; RIBA 1954; *Recreations* foreign travel; *Style—* Norman Riley, Esq; ✉ The Manor House, Main Street, Wolston, Warwickshire CV8 3HH; Brock Riley Partners, Architects, 10 Albert St, London NW1 7NZ (☎ 0171 387 2077)

RILEY, Prof Norman; s of Willie Riley, of Hebden Bridge, West Yorkshire, and Minnie, *née* Parker; *Educ* Calder HS West Yorks, Univ of Manchester (BSc, PhD); *m* 5 Sept 1959, Mary Ann, da of Michael Mansfield, of Manchester; 1 s (Stephen b 1961), 1 da (Susan b 1964); *Career* asst lectr in mathematics Univ of Manchester 1959–60, lectr in mathematics Univ of Durham 1960–64; UEA: sr lectr in mathematics 1964–66, reader in mathematics 1966–71, prof of applied mathematics 1971–; FIMA 1964; *Recreations* music, photography, travel; *Style—* Prof Norman Riley; ✉ School of Mathematics, Univ of East Anglia, Norwich, Norfolk NR4 7TJ (☎ 01603 592586)

RILEY, Prof Patrick Anthony; s of Bertram Hurrell Riley (d 1961), and Olive, *née* Stephenson (d 1987); *b* 22 March 1935; *Educ* Manegg Sch Zurich, King Edward VII Sch King's Lynn, UCL, UCH Med Sch London (MB BS, PhD, DSc); *m* 5 July 1958, Christine Elizabeth, da of Dr Islwyn Morris (d 1972), of Treorchy, Rhondda, Glam; 1 s (Benjamin b 20 Feb 1968), 2 da (Sian b 12 Feb 1962, Caroline b 25 June 1963); *Career* Rockefeller res scholar 1962–63, MRC jr clinical res fell 1963–66, Beit Meml res fell 1966–68, Wellcome res fell 1968–70, sr lectr in biochemical pathology UCH Med Sch 1974–76 (lectr 1970–73), prof of cell pathology UCL 1984– (reader 1976–84); memb Cncl Euro Soc of Pigment Cell Res, vice pres Int Fedn of Pigment Cell Socs, memb Cncl NCUP; FIBiol 1976, FRCPath 1985; *Books* Faber Pocket Medical Dictionary (with P J Cunningham, first edn 1966), Hydroxyanisole: Recent Advances in Anti-Melanoma Therapy (1984); *Recreations* music, painting, stereo photography; *Clubs* Athenaeum, Linnean; *Style—* Prof Patrick Riley; ✉ 2 The Grange, Grange Avenue, London N20 8AB (☎ 0181 445 5687); Department of Molecular Pathology, University College Medical School, London W1P 6DB (☎ 0171 380 9323, fax 0171 637 4436, e-mail REBC900@UCL.AC.UK)

RILEY, Peter Lawrence; s of Lawrence Joseph Riley (d 1957), and Freda, *née* Cronshaw (d 1985); *b* 10 May 1947; *Educ* St Joseph's GS Blackpool; *m* 16 Oct 1971, Sandra Carol, da of Tom Gartside (d 1974); 1 s (Peter Mark b 2 July 1974), 1 da (Caroline Louise b 6 June 1977); *Career* CA; ptnr Condy & Co 1973–80, dir numerous Cos 1974–87, dir Plymouth Argyle Football Co Ltd 1977–81, sr ptnr Riley 1981–; FCA 1970; *Recreations* yachting, flying, travel, squash; *Clubs* Royal Western YC, St Mellion Golf And Country, Yealm YC; *Style—* Peter Riley, Esq; ✉ Britannic House, 51 North Hill, Plymouth PL4 8HZ (☎ 01752 203640, fax 01752 203641)

RILEY, Sir Ralph; kt (1984); s of late Ralph Riley, and late Clara Riley; *b* 23 Oct 1924; *Educ* Audenshaw GS, Univ of Sheffield (BSc, PhD, DSc); *m* 1949, Joan Elizabeth Norrington; 2 da (Susan, Jennifer); *Career* serv WWII Capt 6 KOSB and 1 S Lancs Regt 1943–47, W Europe and Palestine; Cambridge Plant Breeding Inst: res worker 1952–78, head of Cytogenetics Dept 1954–72 (dir 1971–78); dep chm and sec Agric and Food Res Cncl 1978–85, chm Rothamsted Experimental Station 1990–; memb Bd BTG Ltd 1984–, memb Tech Advsy Ctee Cons Gp Int Agric Research 1993–; emeritus fell Wolfson Coll Cambridge; Royal Soc Royal medal 1981, Wolf prize in Agric 1986, William Bate Hardy prize; foreign memb: Indian Nat Sci Acad, Nat Acad Sci USA, Acad Agric France, Indian Acad of Agric Sci; Hon DSc: Edinburgh 1976, Hull 1982, Cranfield 1985; Hon LLD Sheffield 1984; Hon FRASE 1980; FRS 1967; *Clubs* Athenaeum; *Style—* Sir Ralph Riley, FRS; ✉ 16 Gog Magog Way, Stapleford, Cambridge CB2 5BQ (☎ 01223 843845, fax 01223 845825, e-mail R.RILEY@CGNET.COM)

RILEY, Simon James Blair; s of James Riley (d 1985), and Joanna, *née* Walker; *b* 27 Feb 1946; *Educ* Gordonstoun; *m* 1, 7 April 1973 (m dis 1984), Jacqueline Lila (Jackie), da of Col Henry Lancelot (Harry) Gullidge, of Taunton, Somerset; 2 da (Claire-Louise b 6 Sept 1975, Victoria b 19 Aug 1980); m 2, 29 Oct 1988, Estaire Joyce Danielle, da of Prof Johan De Vree; *Career* surveyor; Kirk & Kirk 1964–67, Grant Wilkinson & Co 1967–73 (dir 1970), dir James Riley & Associates 1973–83, conslt in Spain 1983–88, specialist with Secure Storage 1989–; memb Ctee Br Automobile Racing Club; MNAEA 1965; *Recreations* racing motor cars, reading, collecting; *Clubs* Lighthouse, British Automobile Racing; *Style—* Simon Riley, Esq; ✉ 23 Rossetti Garden Mansions, Flood Street, Chelsea, London SW3 5QX (☎ 0171 351 0248, fax 0171 627 8326)

RILEY-SMITH, Prof Jonathan Simon Christopher; s of Maj (William Henry) Douglas Riley-Smith (d 1981), of Tadcaster, N Yorks and Brewhurst, Loxwood, W Sussex, and Elspeth Agnes Mary, *née* Craik Henderson (d 1990); *b* 27 June 1938; *Educ* Eton, Trinity Coll Cambridge (BA, MA, PhD); *m* 27 July 1968, Marie-Louise Jeannetta, da of Wilfred John Sutcliffe Field, of Norwich, Norfolk; 1 s (Tobias Augustine William b 19 Oct 1969), 2 da (Tamsin Elspeth Hermione b 10 Sept 1971, Hippolyta Clemency Magdalen b 10 Nov 1975); *Career* lectr in medieval history Univ of St Andrews 1966–72 (asst lectr 1964–65); Univ of Cambridge: asst lectr 1972–75, lectr 1975–78, fell Queen's Coll 1972–78, dir of studies in history 1972–78, praelector 1973–75, librarian 1973 and 1977–78; prof of history Royal Holloway and Bedford New Coll Univ of London 1978–94 (head Dept of History 1984–90); Dixie prof of ecclesiastical history Univ of Cambridge 1994–, fell Emmanuel Coll Cambridge 1994–; librarian Priory of Scotland Most Ven Order of St John 1966–78, Grand Priory 1982–; KStJ 1969, CStJ 1966; FRHistS 1971; Knight of Magistral Grace SMOM 1971 (Officer of Merit Pro Merito Melitensi 1985); *Books* The Knights of St John in Jerusalem and Cyprus (1967), Ayyubids, Mamlukes and Crusaders (with U and M C Lyons, 1971), The Feudal Nobility and The Kingdom of Jerusalem (1973), What Were The Crusades? (1977, 2nd ed 1992), The Crusades Idea and Reality (with L Riley-Smith, 1981), The First Crusade and The Idea of Crusading (1986), The Crusades: A Short History (1987), Les Croisades (translation, 1990), Breve storia della Crociate (trans, 1994), The Atlas of the Crusades (ed, 1991), Grosser Bildatlas der Kreuzzüge (translation, 1992), The Oxford Illustrated History of the Crusades (ed, 1995); *Recreations* the past and present of own family; *Style—* Prof Jonathan Riley-Smith; ✉ Emmanuel College, Cambridge CB2 3AP (☎ 01223 330196)

RIMER, Hon Mr Justice; Hon Sir Colin Percy Farquharson; kt (1994); s of Kenneth Rowland Rimer, of Beckenham, Kent, and Maria Eugenia, *née* Farquharson; *b* 30 Jan 1944; *Educ* Dulwich, Trinity Hall Cambridge (MA, LLB); *m* 3 Jan 1970, Penelope Ann, da of late Alfred William Gibbs; 2 s (David b 1972, Michael b 1974), 1 da (Catherine b 1971); *Career* res asst Inst of Comparative Law Paris 1967–68, called to the Bar Lincoln's Inn 1968 (bencher 1994), in practice 1969–94, QC 1988, judge of the High Court (Chancery Div) 1994–; *Recreations* music, photography, novels, sailing, walking; *Style—* The Hon Mr Justice Rimer; ✉ Royal Courts of Justice, Strand, London WC2A 2LL

RIMINGTON, John David; CB (1987); s of John William Rimington, MBE (d 1996), of Eastbourne, and Mabel, *née* Dorrington; *b* 27 June 1935; *Educ* Nottingham HS, Jesus Coll Cambridge (MA); *m* 16 March 1963, Dame Stella Rimington, DCB, *qv*, da of David Whitehouse, of Newstead; 2 da; *Career* Nat Serv Lt RA 1954–56; asst princ Bd of Trade and Treasy 1959–63, princ Tariff Div BOT 1963, first sec (econ) New Delhi 1965, asst sec (unemployment) Dept of Employment 1972, cnsllr UK representation to the EC Brussels 1974, under sec Trg Div MSC 1977, dir gen HSE 1984 (dir safety policy 1981), advanced to perm sec rank on personal merit 1992, ret 1995; non-exec dir Magnox Electric plc; memb Cncl Consumers' Assoc; Hon DSc Univ of Sheffield; CIMgt; *Recreations* cricket, walking; *Clubs* Athenaeum; *Style—* John Rimington, Esq, CB; ✉ 9 Highbury Hill, London N5 1SU (☎ 0171 354 5379)

RIMINGTON, Dame Stella; DCB (1996); da of David Whitehouse, of Newstead; *b* 1935; *Educ* Nottingham HS for Girls, Univ of Edinburgh (MA); *m* 16 March 1963, John David Rimington, CB, *qv*, s of John William Rimington, MBE (d 1996), of Eastbourne; 2 da; *Career* dir gen Security Service 1992–96 (joined 1969); non-exec dir Marks & Spencer plc 1997–; *Clubs* Reform; *Style—* Dame Stella Rimington, DCB

RING, Malcolm Spencer Humbert; TD; s of Gp Capt Spencer Leonard Ring, CBE, DFC (d 1980), and Jessie Margaret Ring; *b* 25 Feb 1944; *Educ* Haileybury; *m* 17 Aug 1978, Elizabeth Anne Ring, da of Michael Henman; 3 s (Jonathan b 1980, Charles b 1982, Thomas b 1985), 1 da (Emma b 1987); *Career* Regtl Col TA HAC 1989–90 (joined 1969, CO Lt-Col 1986–88); admitted slr 1969; ptnr: Taylor & Humbert 1973–82, Taylor Garrett (now Taylor Joynson Garrett) 1982– (managing ptnr 1989–90); memb Law Soc; *Recreations* fishing, cricket, hockey, gardening; *Clubs* Oriental, HAC; *Style—* Malcolm Ring, Esq, TD; ✉ Carmelite, 50 Victoria Embankment, Blackfriars, London EC4Y 0DX (☎ 0171 353 1234, fax 0171 936 2666, telex 268014)

RINK, John Stuart; s of Paul Lothar Max Rink (d 1977), and Mary Ida McCall, *née* Moore; *b* 25 Oct 1946; *Educ* Sedbergh, Bristol Poly (LLB); *m* 22 May 1971, Elizabeth Mary, da of Thomas Edgar Pitkethly; 1 s (Max Edgar b 2 Feb 1973), 1 da (Lucinda Mary b 1 Jan 1975); *Career* Allen & Overy: trainee slr 1970–72, asst slr 1972–77, ptnr 1977–, managing ptnr Litigation Dept 1989, managing ptnr Allen & Overy 1994–; legal dir British Aerospace plc 1994–95; memb Law Soc; *Recreations* golf, rugby, walking, opera; *Clubs* City Law, Royal Wimbledon Golf, Royal West Norfolk Golf, Windermere Motor Boat Racing; *Style—* John Rink, Esq; ✉ Managing Partner, Allen & Overy, One New Change, London EC4M 9QQ (☎ 0171 330 3000, fax 0171 330 9999)

RIORDAN, Prof James William; s of William James Riordan (d 1979), of Portsmouth, and Kathleen May, *née* Smith (d 1985); *b* 10 Oct 1936; *Educ* Portsmouth Southern GS, Univ of Birmingham (BSocSc, PhD), Univ of London (PGCE), Univ of Moscow (DipPolSc); *m* 1, 1 May 1961 (m dis 1965), Annick, da of Heron Vercaigne, of Clastres, France; 2 da (Tanya Marie b 1962, Nadine b 1963); m 2, 19 May 1965, Rashida, da of Gabdul Davletshin (d 1969), of Bashkiria, USSR; 1 s (Sean Stephen b 1966), 2 da (Nathalie Anara b 1969, Catherine Bella b 1976); *Career* Nat Serv RAF 1955–57; sr translator Progress Publishers Moscow 1963–65, lectr in liberal studies Portsmouth Poly 1965–69, sr res fell Centre for Russian and East European Studies Univ of Birmingham 1969–71, Russian Studies Dept Univ of Bradford 1971–88 (lectr, sr lectr, reader, prof), prof of Russian studies and head Linguistic & Int Studies Dept Univ of Surrey 1989–; vice pres: Soc for Cultural Relations with the USSR, Int Sport History Assoc; memb Ethics Cmmn IOC; USSR Peace prize for contribution to Russian folklore 1982; Hon Doctorate Stendhal Univ Grenoble; FRSA 1991; *Books* Sport in Soviet Society (1977), A World of Folk Tales (1979), Tales of King Arthur (1982), Russian Gypsy Tales (1986), Soviet Union - The Land and its People (1986), Soviet Youth Culture (1990), Korean Folktales (1994); *Recreations* swimming, snooker, music; *Clubs* St George's Day, Portsmouth FC; *Style—* Prof James Riordan; ✉ Department of Linguistic & International Studies, University of Surrey, Guildford, Surrey GU2 5XH (☎ and fax 01483 300803)

RIORDAN, Stephen Vaughan; QC (1992); s of Charles Maurice Riordan, and Betty Morfydd, *née* Harries (d 1983); *b* 18 Feb 1950; *Educ* Wimbledon Coll, Univ of Liverpool (LLB); *m* 19 Feb 1983, Jane Elizabeth, da of Ernest Victor Thomas; 2 da (Alexandra Jane b 24 Aug 1983, Charlotte Ann b 2 March 1985); *Career* called to the Bar Inner Temple 1972, recorder of the Crown Court 1990– (asst recorder 1986–90), head of chambers; *Recreations* singing; *Style—* Stephen Riordan, Esq, QC; ✉ 19 Gwydrin Road, Liverpool L18 3HA (☎ 0151 722 1726); 1st Floor, 25–27 Castle Street, Liverpool, Merseyside L2 4TA (☎ 0151 236 5072)

RIPLEY, Prof Brian David; s of Eric Lewis Ripley, of Farnborough, Hants, and Sylvia May, *née* Gould; *b* 29 April 1952; *Educ* Farnborough GS, Churchill Coll Cambridge (MA, Smith's Prize, PhD); *m* 1973, Ruth Mary, *née* Appleton; *Career* Univ of London: lectr in statistics Imperial Coll 1976–80, reader in statistics 1980–83; prof of statistics Univ of Strathclyde 1983–90, prof of applied statistics Univ of Oxford 1990–, professorial fell St Peter's Coll Oxford 1990–; Adams Prize Univ of Cambridge 1987; memb Int Statistical Inst 1982, fell Inst of Mathematical Statistics 1987, FRSE 1990; *Books* Spatial Statistics (1981), Stochastic Simulation (1987), Statistical Inference for Spatial Processes (1988), Modern Applied Statistics with S-Plus (with W N Venables, 1994), Pattern Recognition and Neural Networks (1996); *Recreations* natural history; *Style—* Prof Brian Ripley, FRSE; ✉ Department of Statistics, University of Oxford, 1 South Parks Road, Oxford OX1 3TG (☎ 01865 272861, fax 01865 272595)

RIPLEY, David; s of Arthur Ripley, of Leeds, and Brenda, *née* Battey; *b* 13 Sept 1966; *Educ* Royds Sch Leeds; *m* 24 Sept 1988, Jackie Louise, da of Ronald Marsh; 2 s (Joe David b 10 Oct 1989, George William b 5 March 1994); *Career* professional cricketer; Northamptonshire CCC: debut 1984, awarded county cap 1987, NatWest Trophy winners 1992; rep Young England on tour W Indies 1985 and v Sri Lanka 1986; highest number of dismissals by a wicket keeper 1988 and 1992; *Recreations* Leeds Utd FC, golf; *Style—* David Ripley, Esq; ✉ Northamptonshire CCC, County Ground, Wantage Rd, Northampton NN1 4TV (☎ 01604 32917)

RIPLEY, Sir Hugh; 4 Bt (UK 1880), of Rawdon, Yorks; s of Sir Henry Ripley, 3 Bt, JP (d 1956), and Dorothy, *née* Harley (d 1964); *b* 26 May 1916; *Educ* Eton; *m* 1, 1946 (m dis 1971), Dorothy Mary Dunlop, yr da of John Cumming Bruce-Jones, and Dorothy Euphemia Mitchell, da of Sir Thomas Dunlop, 1 Bt, GBE, JP, DL; 1 s, 1 da; m 2, 1972, Susan, da of William Parker, of Keythorpe Grange, E Norton, Leics; 1 da; *Heir* s, William, b 13 April 1950; *Career* former Maj King's Shropshire LI, served WW II N Africa, Italy; dir John Walker & Sons 1956–81; Liveryman Worshipful Co of Distillers; *Recreations* fishing, shooting; *Clubs* Boodle's; *Style—* Sir Hugh Ripley, Bt; ✉ The Oak, Bedstone, Bucknell, Salop; 20 Abingdon Villas, London W8

RIPLEY, Stuart; *b* 20 Nov 1967; *Career* professional footballer; over 200 appearances Middlesbrough 1984–92, 5 appearances Bolton Wanderers 1985–86; Blackburn Rovers FC: joined 1992–, winners FA Premier League 1994/95; first cap (v San Marino) England 1993; *Style—* Stuart Ripley, Esq; ✉ Blackburn Rovers FC, Ewood Park, Nuttall Street, Blackburn BB2 4JF (☎ 01254 673525)

RIPLEY, William Hugh; s and h of Sir Hugh Ripley, 4 Bt; *b* 13 April 1950; *Educ* Eton, McGill Univ Canada (BA); *Recreations* rare books, writing, the Welsh borderland; *Style—* William Ripley, Esq; ✉ Dove Cottage, Bedstone, Bucknell, Salop

RIPON, 11 Bishop of 1977–; Rt Rev David Nigel de Lorentz Young; see founded AD 678 but merged in York till reconstituted 1836; patron of 38 livings and 20 alternately with others, all the Canonries in the Cathedral, the Archdeaconries of Richmond and Leeds and the chancellorship of the diocese; s of Brig Keith Young, CIE, MC, and Ada Lilian, *née* Tollinton; *b* 2 Sept 1931; *Educ* Wellington, Balliol Coll Oxford (MA); *m* 1, 1962, Rachel (d 1966), da of Jack Lewis, of Liverpool; 1 s (Mark b 1965), 1 da (Kate b 1963); m 2, 17 June 1967, Jane, da of Lewis Herbert Collison, TD, JP (d 1988); 3 s (James b 1968, Peter b 1968, Thomas b 1981); *Career* RE 1950–51, 2 Lt Troop Cdr Sch of Mil Survey 1951; research mathematician Plessey Co 1955–59; ordained: deacon 1959, priest 1960; curate All Hallows Allerton Liverpool 1959–62, Church Missionary Soc missionary Sri Lanka 1962–67, lectr in Buddhist studies Univ of Manchester 1967–70, vicar Burwell Cambridge 1970–75, archdeacon Huntingdon and hon canon Ely Cathedral 1975–77; chm: Governing Body SPCK 1978–87, Partnership World Mission 1978–85, C of E Bd of Educn 1994–, Nat Soc for Promoting Religious Educn 1994–; memb Doctrine Cmmn 1978–81; *Recreations* fell walking, sailing; *Clubs* Army & Navy; *Style—* The Rt Rev the Bishop of Ripon; ✉ Bishop Mount, Ripon, N Yorks HG4 5DP (☎ 01765 602045)

RIPON, Dean of; *see:* Methuen, Very Rev John Alan Robert

RIPPENGAL, Derek; CB (1982), QC (1980); s of William Thomas Rippengal (d 1972), of Middlesex, and Margaret Mary, *née* Parry (d 1982); *b* 8 Sept 1928; *Educ* Hampton Sch, St Catharine's Coll Cambridge (MA); *m* 1963, Elizabeth (d 1973), da of Charles Gordon Melrose (d 1985), of East Lothian; 1 s (Robert b 1966), 1 da (Emma b 1970); *Career* called to the Bar Middle Temple 1953; Chancery Bar and univ posts 1953–58, Treasy Slr's Office 1958–72 (princ asst treasy slr 1971), slr and legal advsr to DTI 1972–73, dep Parly counsel Law Cmmn 1973–74, Parly counsel 1974–76, counsel to chm of Ctees of House of Lords 1977–; *Recreations* music, fishing; *Clubs* Athenaeum; *Style—* Derek Rippengal, Esq, CB, QC; ✉ Wychwood, Bell Lane, Little Chalfont, Bucks HP6 6PF

RIPPON OF HEXHAM, Baron (Life Peer UK 1987), of Hesleyside, Co Northumberland; (Aubrey) Geoffrey Frederick Rippon; PC (1962), QC (1964); o s of Arthur Ernest Sydney Rippon (d 1966), of Surbiton, Surrey; *b* 28 May 1924; *Educ* King's Coll Taunton, BNC Oxford (MA); *m* 1946, Ann Leyland, OBE, da of Donald Yorke, MC, of Birkenhead; 1 s (Hon Anthony Simon Yorke b 4 Oct 1959), 3 da (Hon Fiona Carolyn b 28 June 1947, Hon Sarah Lovell (*see* Hon Mrs Sarah Taylor), Hon Penelope Ann); *Career* called to the Bar 1948; Mayor of Surbiton 1951–52, ldr Cons Gp LCC 1957–59 (memb LCC (Chelsea) 1952–61); Parly candidate (C): Shoreditch 1950, Finsbury 1951; MP (C): Norwich S 1955–64, Hexham 1966–87; PPS to: Min of Housing and Local Govt 1956–57, Min of Defence 1957–59; parly sec Miny of Aviation 1959–61, jt parly sec Miny of Housing and Local Govt 1961–62, min of public bldgs and works 1962–64 (with seat in Cabinet 1963–64); chief oppn spokesman on: housing, local govt and land 1966–68, defence 1968–70; min of technol 1970, chllr Duchy of Lancaster 1970–72, sec of state for the environment 1972–74, chief oppn spokesman on foreign and cwlth affrs 1974–75, chm Cons Foreign Affrs Ctee 1979–81; chm House of Lords Ctee on the Scrutiny of Legislation 1992–95; ldr: Cons Delgn to Cncl Europe and WEU 1967–70, Cons Gp Euro Parl 1977–79; pres Br Section Euro League for Economic Cooperation 1992– (chm 1977–92); chm: Dun & Bradstreet 1976–96, Britannia Arrow Holdings (now INVESCO plc) 1977–89 (pres 1989–93), Brassey's Defence Publishers 1977–96 (pres 1997–), Michael Page Group 1989–95, UniChem plc 1990–; former chm: Holland Hannen & Cubitts, Singer & Friedlander Holdings; Univ of London: memb Court (now Cncl) 1958–, chm Ct 1991–94, first chm Cncl and pro-chllr 1994–; pres: Assoc of Dist Cncls 1987–95, Town & Country Planning Assoc 1988–95, Inst of Credit Mgmnt 1992–95; hon fell BNC Oxford, Hon LLD Univ of London; Grand Cross Order of Merit (Liechtenstein) 1967, Knight Grand Cross Royal Order of North Star (Sweden) 1982; *Clubs* White's, Pratt's, MCC; *Style—* The Rt Hon the Lord Rippon of Hexham, PC, QC; ✉ The Old Vicarage, Broomfield, Bridgwater, Somerset TA5 2EQ; office: 4 Breams Buildings, London EC4A 1AQ (☎ 0171 353 5835)

RISDON, Prof (Rupert) Anthony; s of Capt Dennis Stanley Risdon (d 1986), and Olga Caris Argent, *née* Davis; *b* 5 March 1939; *Educ* Charing Cross Hosp Med Sch (MB BS, MD); *m* 15 April 1961, Phyllis Mary, da of Frederick Hough, of IOM; 2 s ((James) Mark b 1964, Simon Paul b 1967); *Career* lectr in histopathology Charing Cross Hosp Med Sch 1966–68, conslt pathologist Addenbrooke's Hosp Cambridge 1975–76, reader in morbid anatomy London Hosp Med Coll 1976–85, head Histopathology Dept Great Ormond St Hosp for Sick Children 1985–; memb: Pathology Soc of GB and I, Int Acad Pathology, Assoc of Clinical Pathologists; FRCPath; *Recreations* walking, swimming; *Style*— Prof Anthony Risdon; ✉ The Hospital for Sick Children, Department of Histopathology, Great Ormond St, London WC1N 3JH (☎ 0171 405 9200 ext 5463)

RISK, Sheriff Douglas James; QC (Scot 1992); s of James Risk (slr), of Glasgow, and Isobel Katherine Taylor, *née* Dow; *b* 23 Jan 1941; *Educ* Glasgow Acad, Gonville and Caius Coll Cambridge (MA), Univ of Glasgow (LLB); *m* 4 Aug 1967, Jennifer Hood, da of John Howat Davidson (d 1985, schoolmaster), of Glasgow; 3 s (Kenneth b 1968, Malcolm b 1972, Colin b 1974), 1 da (Helen b 1970); *Career* admitted to Faculty of Advocates 1966; standing jr counsel Scottish Educn Dept 1975; Sheriff of: Lothian and Borders at Edinburgh 1977–79, Grampian Highland and Islands at Aberdeen 1979–93; Sheriff Princ of Grampian Highland and Islands 1993–; temporary Judge of the Ct of Session and High Ct of Justiciary 1992–93; hon prof Faculty of Law Univ of Aberdeen 1994– (hon lectr 1981–94); *Clubs* Royal Northern and Univ (Aberdeen); *Style*— Sheriff Douglas Risk, QC; ✉ Sheriffs Chambers, Sheriff Court House, Castle Street, Aberdeen AB10 1WP (☎ 01224 648316)

RISK, Sir Thomas Neilson; kt (1984); s of late Ralph Risk, CBE, MC; *b* 13 Sept 1922; *Educ* Kelvinside Acad, Univ of Glasgow (BL, LLD); *m* 1949, Suzanne Eiloart; 4 s (1 decd); *Career* served WWII RAF; ptnr Maclay Murray & Spens slrs 1950–81, chm Standard Life Assurance Co 1969–77 (dir 1965–88); govr: British Linen Bank 1977–86, Bank of Scotland 1981–91 (dep govr 1977–81, dir 1971–91); dir: Shell UK Ltd 1982–93, Barclays Bank 1983–85, Bank of Wales 1986–91; chm Scottish Financial Enterprise 1986–89; dir: Howden Group 1971–87, Merchants Trust 1973–94, MSA (Britain) Ltd 1958–; memb: Scottish Industl Devpt Bd 1972–75, Scottish Econ Cncl 1983–91, NEDC 1987–91; FRSE 1988; *Style*— Sir Thomas Risk, FRSE; ✉ 10 Belford Place, Edinburgh EH4 3DH (☎ 0131 332 9425)

RISLEY, George Francis; s of Thomas Risley (d 1971); *b* 23 Dec 1929; *Educ* Doncaster GS, Coll of Technol Liverpool, IMEDE Lausanne Switzerland; *m* 1; 2 s, 1 da; m 2, 1975, Rosemary Wendy Pamela, da of Cecil Lionel Bell; 1 s, 1 da; *Career* sales and mktg dir Hazlewood Foods plc; dir: Hazlewood International BV, Sandyford Meats Ltd, Campsie Springs (Scotland) Ltd; formerly: sales and marketing dir Findus Ltd, gp md Brekkes Foods Ltd; exec memb Cncl of Inst of Grocery Distribution; *Recreations* golf; *Clubs* RAC, Breadsall Priory Golf; *Style*— George Risley, Esq; ✉ Hazlewood Foods plc, Rowditch, Derby DE1 1NB (☎ 01332 295295, fax 01332 292300, telex 377872)

RISNESS, Dr Eric John; CBE (1982); s of Kristen Riisnaes *(sic)* (d 1981), and Ethel Agnes, *née* Weeks, of Bedford; *b* 27 July 1927; *Educ* Stratford GS, Univ of Cambridge (MA, PhD); *m* 26 July 1952, Colleen Edwina, da of Reginald Edwin Armstrong (d 1975); 2 s (Michael b 1958, Stephen b 1972), 2 da (Susan b 1953, Julia b 1968); *Career* joined MOD 1954; various posts in res and devpt of naval equipment incl: dir of res (Undersea Warfare) 1975–76, project mangr (Sting Ray torpedo) 1976–78, dir of naval analysis 1982–83, DG surface weapons 1983–84, dep dir and md Admty Res Estab Portland 1984–87; md STC Technology Ltd 1987–90; FIEE 1963, FEng 1990; *Recreations* genealogy, music, golf; *Clubs* Bramley Golf; *Style*— Dr Eric Risness, CBE, FEng; ✉ 8 Orchard Rd, Shalford, Guildford, Surrey GU4 8ER (☎ 01483 34581)

RITBLAT, Jillian Rosemary (Jill); da of Max Leonard Slotover, FRCS, of Monte Carlo, Monaco, and Peggy Cherna, *née* Cohen; *b* 14 Dec 1942; *Educ* Newcastle upon Tyne Church HS, Roedean, Westfield Coll London (BA); *m* 1, 21 April 1966 (m dis 1981), Elie Zilkha; 1 s, 1 da; m 2, 27 Feb 1986, John Ritblat, *qv*; *Career* called to the Bar Gray's Inn 1964; pupillage to Robin Simpson (now QC) Victor Durand & Jeremy Hutchinson's Chambers 1964–65; alternate delegate for Int Cncl of Jewish Women UN Geneva 1977–79; Patrons of New Art Tate Gallery: events organiser 1984–87 chm 1987–90, memb Acquisitions Sub-Ctee 1992–93; memb Int Cncl Tate Gallery 1995– (vice chm 1996–); co-curator: The Curator's Egg Anthony Reynolds Gallery 1994, When Logics Die, British Art Show; exec prodr Normal Conservative Rebels: Gilbert & George in China; memb: Assoc of Museum of Modern Art Oxford 1986– (memb Cncl 1993–), Int Cncl Jerusalem Museum 1987–, Advsy Cncl Friends of the Tate Gallery 1990–, Nat Art Collections Fund Special Events Ctee 1991–92, William Townsend Meml Lectureship Ctee 1991–, Bd British Telecom New Contemporaries 1991– (vice chm 1992–), Bd Jerusalem Music Centre 1991–, Arts Cncl Appraisal for W Midlands Arts 1994; patron Nat Alliance for Art, Architecture and Design 1994–; memb Jury: Painting in the Eighties 1987, Turner Prize 1988, British Airways New Artist Award 1990, Swiss Bank Corporation Euro Art Competition 1994 and 1995, NatWest 90's Prize for Art 1994 and 1995; *Recreations* art, opera, travelling, skiing, food, people; *Style*— Mrs John Ritblat; ✉ 10 Cornwall Terrace, London NW1 4QP

RITBLAT, John Henry; s of Montie Ritblat (d 1984), and Muriel, *née* Glaskie; *b* 3 Oct 1935; *Educ* Dulwich, Univ of London, Coll of Estate Management; *m* 1, 1960, Isabel Paja Steinberg (d 1979); 2 s (Nicholas b 19 Aug 1961, James b 18 Feb 1967), 1 da (Suzanne b 15 Sept 1962); m 2, 27 Feb 1986, Jill Ritblat, *qv*, *née* Zilkha; *Career* articles West End firm of surveyors and valuers 1952–58, fndr ptnr and chm Conrad Ritblat and Co (conslt surveyors and valuers) 1958, md Union Property Holdings (London) Ltd 1969, chm and md The British Land Company PLC 1970–; cmmr Crown Estate Paving Cmmn 1969, memb Bd of Govrs The Weizmann Inst 1991, sole sponsor British Nat Ski Championships 1978–96, hon surveyor King George's Fund for Sailors 1979, memb Cncl RGS 1984 (life memb 1982), pres British Ski Fedn 1994– (vice pres 1984–89); memb: Prince of Wales' Royal Parks Tree Appeal Ctee, Fin Devpt Bd NSPCC, British Library Bd 1995; dep chm and govr Hall Sch, govr London Business Sch; FSVA 1968, CIMgt; hon life FRSA; *Recreations* antiquarian books, old buildings, squash, golf, skiing, real tennis; *Clubs* RAC, MCC, Carlton, Cresta (St Moritz), Queen's; *Style*— John Ritblat, Esq; ✉ The British Land Company PLC, 10 Cornwall Terrace, Regent's Park, London NW1 4QP (☎ 0171 486 4466, fax 0171 935 5552)

RITCHIE, Alasdair William; s of James Martin Ritchie (d 1993), of Tilehouse, Beaconsfield, and Noreen Mary Louise, *née* Johnston; bro of Hamish Martin Johnston Ritchie, *qv*; *b* 10 March 1946; *Educ* Loretto; *m* 4 April 1970, Fiona Margaret, da of James Barr Richardson; 1 s (Cameron Glen b 28 April 1976), 1 da (Sally Ann b 2 June 1973); *Career* trainee Trumans Brewery 1964–66, mktg exec Scott Paper USA 1966–68, dir Lonsdale Crowther UK 1971–73 (dep md 1973–76), dir Grey Advertising UK 1976–79, fndr Holmes Knight Ritchie (md 1979–90); TBWA: UK chm 1990–96, UK chief exec 1990–, pres Europe 1996–; MIPA; *Recreations* shooting, fishing, golf; *Clubs* Denham Golf, Mosimans; *Style*— Alasdair Ritchie, Esq; ✉ Oakendell, Wilton Lane, Jordans, Bucks HP9 2RF (☎ 012407 3119); TBWA, 8 Crinan Street, London N1 9UF (☎ 0171 833 5544)

RITCHIE, Dr Anthony Elliot; CBE (1978); s of Prof James Ritchie, CBE (d 1958), and Jessie Jane, *née* Elliot (d 1933); *b* 30 March 1915; *Educ* Edinburgh Acad, Univ of Aberdeen (MA, BSc), Univ of Edinburgh (MB ChB, MD); *m* 18 July 1941, Elizabeth Lambie, da of John Knox (d 1956), of Dunfermline; 1 s (James Knox b 1949), 3 da (Innes Elizabeth b 1945, Margaret b 1950, Alison b 1958); *Career* Carnegie res scholar and lectr Physiology Dept Univ of Edinburgh 1941–48, prof of physiology Univ of St Andrews 1948–69, sec and treas Carnegie Tst for Univs of Scotland 1969–86; chm numerous Govt educn and sci ctees, memb Advsy Ctee on Med Res 1960–69, sci advsr civil defence 1961–80, memb Br Library Bd 1973–80; tstee: Nat Library of Scotland 1975–86, Carnegie Tst 1986–; Hon DSc St Andrews 1972, Hon LLD Strathclyde 1985; Hon FCSP 1970, Hon FRCPEd 1986, FRSE 1951 (memb Cncl 1957–80, gen sec 1966–76, bicentenary gold medal 1983); *Books* Clinical Electromyography (with Dr Jar Lenman, 4 edn 1986); *Recreations* reading, hill-walking, motor cars, electronics; *Clubs* New (Edinburgh), Caledonian; *Style*— Dr Anthony Ritchie, CBE, FRSE; ✉ 12 Ravelston Park, Edinburgh EH4 3DX (☎ 0131 332 6560)

RITCHIE, David Robert; s of late James Ritchie, and Edith, *née* Watts; *b* 10 March 1948; *Educ* Manchester GS, St John's Coll Cambridge (BA, MA); *m* 1989, Joan Gibbons; *Career* Miny of Tport 1970; DOE: joined 1970, chm Regnl Bd and regnl dir West Midlands Regnl Office Depts of the Environment and Tport 1989–94; regnl dir Govt Office for the West Midlands 1994–; *Recreations* fell-walking, cooking; *Style*— David Ritchie, Esq; ✉ 77 Paradise Circus, Queensway, Birmingham B1 2DT (☎ 0121 212 5155, fax 0121 212 5132)

RITCHIE, Prof Donald Andrew; s of Andrew Ritchie (d 1985), of Falkirk, and Winifred Laura, *née* Parkinson; *b* 9 July 1938; *Educ* Latymer's Sch London, Univ of Leicester (BSc), Postgrad Med Sch Univ of London (PhD); *m* 22 Aug 1962, (Margaret) Jeanne, da of Henry Eden Collister, of Port St Mary, IOM; 1 s (Charles b 1969), 1 da (Sarah b 1967); *Career* res assoc Biophysics Dept Johns Hopkins Univ Baltimore USA 1964–66, sr lectr Dept of Virology Univ of Glasgow 1972–78 (lectr 1966–72), prof of genetics Univ of Liverpool 1978– (head Dept of Genetics 1978–88, head Dept of Genetics and Microbiology 1988–91); Royal Soc Leverhulme Tst sr res fell 1991–92; pro vice-chllr Univ of Liverpool 1992–95; chm Terrestrial and Freshwater Science and Technol Bd NERC 1994–95 (memb 1990–94); chm Merseyside National Art Collections Fund 1996–; memb: Science Bd SERC 1988–91, DTI Biotechnol Jt Advsy Bd 1991–94, Cncl NERC 1990–95, Food Res Ctee AFRC 1991–94, Cncl Marine Biological Assoc 1991–94, Br Legion Liverpool City Club 1989–, Cncl Liverpool Sch of Tropical Med 1993–, Exec Ctee Cncl of Military Educn Ctees 1994–, TAVRA NW England and IOM 1995–, Fin and Environment Ctees Inst of Biology 1996–; govr Merseyside Open Coll Fedn 1995–; FIBiol 1978, FRSE 1979, FRSA 1983, CBiol 1985; *Books* Molecular Virology (with T H Pennington, 1975), Introduction to Virology (with K M Smith FRS, 1980); *Recreations* painting, gardening, walking; *Clubs* Athenaeum (Liverpool); *Style*— Prof Donald Ritchie, FRSE; ✉ Glenfinnan, 19 Bertram Drive, Meols, Wirral L47 OLG (☎ 0151 632 1985); University of Liverpool, School of Biological Sciences, Donnan Laboratories, Liverpool L69 3BX (☎ 0151 794 3624, fax 0151 794 3655, telex 627095)

RITCHIE, Hamish Martin Johnston; s of James Martin Ritchie (d 1993), of Tilehurst, Beaconsfield, Bucks, and Noreen Mary Louise, *née* Johnston; bro of Alasdair William Ritchie, *qv*; *b* 22 Feb 1942; *Educ* Loretto, ChCh Oxford (MA); *m* 20 Sept 1967, (Judith) Carol, da of Frank Knight Young (d 1992), of Bearsden, Scotland; 1 s (Stuart b 1970), 1 da (Susan b 1972); *Career* md Hogg Robinson UK Ltd 1980–81 (dir 1974–80); chm: Bowring London Ltd 1981–, The Bowring Group 1983–, C T Bowring (Charities Fund) Ltd 1983–, Bowring Marsh & McLennan Ltd 1985–; dir The Royal Automobile Club 1990–; chm of govrs Caldicott Sch; CIMgt; *Recreations* music and all sport (especially golf); *Clubs* MCC, RAC, R & A, Denham Golf; *Style*— Hamish Ritchie, Esq; ✉ Oldhurst, Bulstrode Way, Gerrards Cross, Bucks SL9 7QT (☎ 01753 883262); The Bowring Group, The Bowring Building, Tower Place, London EC3P 3BE (☎ 0171 357 3030, fax 0171 357 3038, telex 882191)

RITCHIE, Ian Carl; s of Christopher Charles Ritchie (d 1959), and Mabel Berenice, *née* Long (d 1981); *b* 24 June 1947; *Educ* Varndean-Brighton Liverpool, Sch of Architecture Central London Poly (DipArch); *m* Jocelyne Van den Bossche; 1 s (Inti Timote Hugo b 1983); *Career* architect; ptnr Chrysalis Architects 1979–81, princ Ian Ritchie Architects 1981–, dir Rice Francis Ritchie (RFR) Paris (engrg design) 1981–86; projects incl: Fluy House Picardy France 1976–77, Eagle Rock House Sussex 1980–82, Law Villette Science City (with A Fainsilber) Paris 1981–86, The Louvre (sculpture courts and pyramids with I M Pei) Paris 1985–93, Royal Square Housing Limehouse 1986–88, The Ecology Gallery at The Natural History Museum 1989–90, Reina Sofia Museum of Modern Art Madrid 1989–91, offices at Stockley Park London 1989–91, Albert Cultural Centre Somme France 1991–93, Terrasson Cultural Greenhouse France 1992–94, new Leipzig Messe Central Glass Hall Germany 1992–96, int competition winning design for new HY Pylons for Electricité de France 1995; designs exhibited at: ICA, Biennale de Paris, Centre Pompidou Paris, Br Architects Moscow, Tokyo, Salon International d'Architecture Paris, Milan, Grassi Museum Leipzig; work published in architectural books and magazines in UK, Europe, USA and Asia; has taught at: Oita Univ Japan 1970, Planning Sch PCL London 1972, Architectural Assoc 1979–82; visiting prof TU Vienna 1994–95; advsr Nat History Museum 1991–95, cmmr Fine Art Cmmn 1995–, DTI IBIS Project gatekeeper 1996–, chm European UK 1996; memb: Research Advsy Ctee Nat Maritime Museum, Cncl UK Steel Construction Inst, Urban Design Advsy Gp LDDC 1990–, Editorial Bd CITY jl 1994–, UK Govt Technol Foresight Construction Panel 1996–; RIBA: external examiner 1983–, Pres's Medal assessor 1987, nat chm of awards 1988, Civic Tst assessor; Tableau de L'Ordre des Architectes Francais 1982, Silver Medal Architectural Design 1982, Plus Beaux Ouvrages de Construction Metallique France 1986 and 1988, IRITECNA Prize for Europe 1991, Eric Lyons Meml Award 1992, Robert Matthew Award for innovation and advancement of architecture Commonwealth Assoc of Architects 1994; RIBA, MCSD, FRSA; registered German architect 1993; *Books* (Well)Connected Architecture (1994); *Recreations* art, swimming, reading, writing; *Clubs* Architecture; *Style*— Ian C Ritchie, Esq; (☎ 0171 481 4427, fax 0171 481 8200)

RITCHIE, Ian Russell; s of Hugh Russell Ritchie (d 1985), of Leeds, and Sheelah, *née* Mathews; *b* 27 Nov 1953; *Educ* Leeds GS, Trinity Coll Oxford (MA); *m* 10 June 1982, Jill Evelyn, da of Douglas Middleton-Walker, of Thorpe Arch, Boston Spa, W Yorks; 2 s (Andrew Russell b 13 Jan 1987, Bruce Douglas b 6 March 1990); *Career* called to the Bar Middle Temple 1976 (Astbury law scholar), in practice 1976–78; industl rels advsr Engrg Employers' Assoc Yorks 1978–80, various posts rising to head of prodn servs Granada Television Manchester 1980–88; Tyne Tees Television: dir of resources 1988–91, md 1991–93, gp dep chief exec Yorkshire Tyne Tees Television Holdings plc (following merger) 1992–93 (resigned 1993); md The Television House 1993–94, md London News Network 1994–95, chief exec Channel 5 Broadcasting 1996–; formerly: chm Newcastle Common Purpose, dir The Wearside Opportunity, govr Univ of Northumbria at Newcastle (formerly Newcastle Poly); FRSA; *Recreations* golf, tennis, theatre; *Clubs* Vincent's (Oxford); *Style*— Ian Ritchie, Esq; ✉ Channel 5 Broadcasting Ltd, 22 Long Acre, London WC2E 9LY (☎ 0171 911 0055)

RITCHIE, James Walter; MC; s of Sir Adam Ritchie (d 1957), and Vivienne, *née* Lentaigne; *b* 12 Jan 1920; *Educ* Ampleforth, Clare Coll Cambridge; *m* 10 March 1951, Penelope June, da of late Thomas Lawrence Forbes, of Chilbolton; 2 s (Michael b 3 Aug 1953, Peter b 21 Sept 1958), 2 da (Jennifer (Mrs Corry) b 3 March 1952, Vivienne (Mrs Brann) b 20 Sept 1956); *Career* 2 Lt to Capt (Res) Adj 5/7 and 1 Bn Gordon Highlanders 1942–46; Smith Mackenzie & Co Ltd: Tanzania Uganda Kenya 1946–61, chm Nairobi 1970; md Inchcape plc 1976–84; jt master Tedworth Hunt 1986–90; *Recreations* hunting, fishing, golf; *Clubs* Oriental; *Style*— James Ritchie, Esq, MC; ✉ Lockeridge Down, Marlborough, Wilts SN8 4EL (☎ 01672 861244)

RITCHIE, Jean Harris; QC (1992); da of Walter Weir Ritchie (d 1979), and Lily, *née* Goodwin; *b* 6 April 1947; *Educ* St Martin's Sch Solihull (scholar), King's Coll London (LLB, AKC), McGill Univ Montreal (LLM); *m* Guy Thomas Knowles Boney, QC, *qv*, s of Dr Knowles Boney, MD; 2 s (R Oliver C b 21 Jan 1979, Christian V K b 29 March 1981); *Career* called to the Bar Gray's Inn 1970 (Churchill scholarship, Lord Justice Holker sr exhbn), recorder W Circuit 1993–; memb Supreme Ct Rule Ctee 1993–; chm of the inquiry into the care and treatment of Christopher Clunis 1993–94; *Recreations* family; *Style*— Miss Jean Ritchie, QC; ✉ 4 Paper Buildings, Temple, London EC4Y 7EX (☎ 0171 353 3366, fax 0171 353 5778)

RITCHIE, Dr John Hindle; MBE (1985); s of Charles Ritchie, of Wylam, Northumberland (d 1983), and Bertha, *née* Hindle (d 1972); *b* 4 June 1937; *Educ* Royal GS Newcastle upon Tyne, Univ of Liverpool (BArch), Univ of Sheffield (PhD); *m* 24 August 1963, Anne, da of John Leyland, of Upton Wirral; 2 da (Jane b 1968, Nicola b 1971); *Career* SRC 1963–66, Liverpool City Cncl 1966–69, Rowntree Housing Trust 1969–72, Cheshire CC 1972–74, Merseyside CC 1974–80, chief exec and memb Bd Merseyside Development Corporation 1985–91 (dir of devpt 1981–85), devpt mgmnt conslt 1991–; memb Lord Chllr's Panel of Ind Insprs 1993–, chm Merseyside Sculptors Guild 1993–; dir: Wirral Community Healthcare Tst 1993–, Liverpool Community Coll 1995–, The Landscape Tst 1996–; CIMgt; *Style*— Dr John Ritchie, MBE; ✉ The Mount, Heswall, Wirral L60 4RD

RITCHIE, John Vivian; s of Maj John Stewart Ritchie (ka 1940), and Doris Ritchie (d 1934); *b* 30 Oct 1928; *Educ* Clifton Coll Bristol, RMA Sandhurst; *m* 1 (m dis); 1 s (Guy b 1968), 1 da (Tabitha b 1966); m 2, Shireen, *née* Folkard; 1 step s (Oliver Williams b 1979); *Career* Army: private Seaforth Highlanders 1947–48, cadet RMA Sandhurst 1948–50, offr Seaforth Highlanders served Malaya 1950–53 and Germany 1953–56 (ret as Capt); advtg exec C J Lytle Advertising 1956–60, account exec Smith Warden 1960–62, TV prodr Grants Advertising 1962–63, Collett Dickenson Pearce 1963–64, mktg mangr John Player & Sons 1965–68; Collett Dickenson Pearce: account dir 1968–79, dep chm 1979–94, ret; non-exec dir ARM (Advertising Research Marketing Ltd) 1995–; chm Advtg Ctee (Brussels) European Assoc of Advertising Agencies; MCIM, FIPA; *Recreations* tennis, sailing; *Style*— John Ritchie, Esq

RITCHIE, Kirk; *Career* hotelier; md and gen mangr The Lygon Arms Worcestershire (joined 1975, Queen's Award to Industry 1985); former memb Advsy Panel BHRCA, former chm Broadway and Dist Ctee Cancer Relief Macmillan Fund, hon fell Cheltenham and Gloucester Univ; memb: Br Hospitality Assoc (chm Divnl Ctee), IHA, Savoy Gastronomes; Freeman City of London, Liveryman Worshipful Co of Distillers; FHCIMA, Master Innholder; *Style*— Kirk Ritchie, Esq; ✉ Managing Director and General Manager, The Lygon Arms, Broadway, Worcestershire WR12 7DU (☎ 01386 852255, fax 01386 858611)

RITCHIE, Prof Lewis Duthie; s of Lewis Duthie Ritchie, of Fraserburgh, and Sheila Gladys, *née* Noble; *b* 26 June 1952; *Educ* Fraserburgh Acad, Univ of Aberdeen (Collie bursar, BSc, MB ChB, MD, John Watt prize, Munday and Venn prize, RCGP Aberdeen and Kincardine prize), Univ of Edinburgh (MSc); *m* 8 July 1978, Heather, da of Arthur William Skelton; *Career* MO Aberdeen Hosps 1978–81, trainee in community med 1981–84, princ GP Peterhead Health Centre 1984–, hon conslt in public health med Grampian Health Bd 1993– (conslt in public health med 1987–92), Sir James Mackenzie prof of gen practice Univ of Aberdeen 1993– (lectr in gen practice 1984–92); John Perry Prize (Primary Health Care Gp Br Computer Soc) 1991, Ian Stokoe Meml Award (RCGP) 1992; MBCS 1985, chartered computer engr 1993; FRSM 1985, FFPHM 1993 (MFPHM 1983), FRCGP 1994 (MRCGP 1982), FRCPE 1995; *Books* Computers in Primary Care (1984, 2 edn 1986, Spanish edn 1991); *Recreations* church work, dog walking, swimming, scuba diving, stock market analysis, reading naval history and analytical chemistry, classical music, art appreciation; *Style*— Prof Lewis Ritchie; ✉ Cramond, 79 Strichen Road, Fraserburgh, Aberdeenshire AB43 5QJ (☎ 01346 510191, fax 01346 515598); Department of General Practice, University of Aberdeen, Foresterhill Health Centre, Westburn Road, Aberdeen AB9 2AY (☎ 01224 663131 ext 53993, fax 01224 840683)

RITCHIE, Margaret Claire; JP (1991); da of Roderick Macintosh Ritchie (d 1975), of Edinburgh, and Ida, *née* Neal; *b* 18 Sept 1937; *Educ* Central Newcastle HS, Leeds Girls' HS, Univ of Leeds (BSc), Univ of London (PGCE); *Career* asst sci teacher St Leonard's Sch St Andrews 1960–64, head of sci dept Wycombe Abbey Sch 1964–71, headmistress Queenswood Sch Hatfield 1971–81, headmistress Queen Mary Sch Lytham 1981–; memb: SHA, GSA; *Style*— Miss Margaret Ritchie, JP; ✉ Queen Mary School, Lytham, Lancs FY8 1DS (☎ 01253 723246)

RITCHIE, Richard Bulkeley; s of W Ritchie (d 1984), of Dublin, and Ruth Mary, *née* Bulkeley; *b* 6 Sept 1952; *Educ* Shrewsbury, St Catherine's Coll Oxford (BA); *m* 28 Sept 1985, Dr Susan Rosemary Foister, da of Philip Foister, Hastings; 2 s (Felix b 1986, Joshua b 1992), 1 da (Isabella b 1988); *Career* called to the Bar Middle Temple 1978, standing counsel to the DTI in insolvency matters 1989, jr cncl to the Crown (Chancery) 1994; *Style*— Richard Ritchie, Esq; ✉ 24 Old Buildings, Lincoln's Inn, London WC2A 3UJ (☎ 0171 404 0946, fax 0171 405 1360)

RITCHIE, Hon (Charles) Rupert Rendall; s and h of 5 Baron Ritchie of Dundee, *qv*; *b* 15 March 1958; *m* 1984 (m dis 1990), Tara, da of Howard J Koch, Jr, of USA; *Style*— The Hon Rupert Ritchie

RITCHIE, Her Hon Judge; Shirley Anne; QC (1979); da of James Ritchie (d 1991), of Johannesburg, SA, and Helen Sutherland, *née* Peters; *b* 10 Dec 1940; *Educ* St Mary's Diocesan Sch Pretoria, Rhodes Univ (BA, LLB); *m* 23 May 1969, Robin Hamilton Corson Anwyl, s of Douglas Fraser Corson (d 1978); 2 s (Jonathan b 1973, James b 1975); *Career* called to S African Bar 1963 and Inner Temple 1966; recorder of the Crown Court 1981–95, circuit judge (SE Circuit) 1995–; memb: Senate of Inns of Court and Bar 1978–81, Gen Cncl of the Bar 1987, Criminal Injuries Compensation Bd 1980–, Mental Health Review Tbnl 1983–; chm Barristers' Benevolent Assoc 1989–; Master of the Bench of the Inner Temple 1985; FRSA; *Recreations* theatre, music, sailing; *Clubs* Guild of Freemen of the City of London, The Acad; *Style*— Her Hon Judge Ritchie, QC; ✉ c/o 4 Paper Buildings, Ground Floor, Temple, London EC4Y 7EX (☎ 0171 353 1131, fax 0171 353 4979)

RITCHIE, Prof William; OBE (1994); s of Alexander Ritchie, and Rebecca Smith, *née* Caldwell; *b* 22 March 1940; *Educ* Wishaw High Sr Secdy Sch, Univ of Glasgow (BSc, PhD); *m* 29 March 1965, Elizabeth Armstrong Bell; 2 s (Derek Alexander b 26 June 1967, Craig William b 11 Dec 1968), 1 da (Lynne Elspeth b 10 Feb 1978); *Career* res asst Univ of Glasgow 1963; Univ of Aberdeen: asst lectr 1964–66, lectr 1966–72, sr lectr 1972–79, prof 1979–95, dean of Faculty of Arts and Social Sciences 1988–89, vice princ 1990–95; vice-chllr Univ of Lancaster 1995–; hon prof Louisiana State Univ; sometime memb: Scot Examination Bd, Scot Univs Cncl of Entrance, Nature Conservancy Cncl (Scot); formerly chm Aberdeen Branch Royal Scottish Geographical Soc, formerly recorder and pres Section E Br Assoc for Advancement of Sci, cncl memb RSE; formerly: chm Scottish Office Ecological Steering Gps for the oil spill in Shetland, chm Sec of State for Scotland's Advsy Ctee on Sustainable Devpt, vice chm Sullom Voe Oil Terminal Environmental Advsy Gp, chm St Fergus Dunes Tech Mgmnt Ctee, convenor SCOVACT, memb Fulbright Cmmn, memb Environmental Ctee American Assoc of Petroleum Geologists; FRSGS 1980 (vice pres), FRSE 1982, FRICS 1989; *Books* Mapping for Field Scientists (1977), Beaches of Highlands and Islands of Scotland (1978), Beaches of Scotland (1984), Surveying and Mapping for Field Scientists (1988), The Coastal Sand Dunes of Louisiana (Volume 1 Isles Dernieres (1989), Volume 2 Plaquemines (1990), Volume 3 Chandeleurs (1992)), Bayou Lafourche Coastline (1995); *Style*— Prof William Ritchie, OBE, FRSE; ✉ Office of the Vice-Chancellor, University of Lancaster, Lancaster LA1 4YW (☎ 01524 592000, fax 01524 36841)

RITCHIE OF DUNDEE, 5 Baron (UK 1905); (Harold) Malcolm Ritchie; s of 2 Baron Ritchie of Dundee (d 1948), and Sarah Ruth, da of Louis Jennings, MP; suc bro, 4 Baron 1978; *b* 29 Aug 1919; *Educ* Stowe, Trinity Coll Oxford (MA); *m* 1948, Anne, da of Col Charles G Johnstone, MC, of Durban, S Africa; 1 s (Hon (Charles) Rupert Rendall b 1958), 1 da (Hon Philippa Jane b 1954); *Heir* s, Hon (Charles) Rupert Rendall Ritchie; *Career* Capt KRRC WWII, served ME, Greece and Italy; headmaster Brickwall House Sch 1965–72 (asst headmaster 1952–65), Eng and drama teacher Bedgebury Sch Kent until 1984; Lib Dem educn spokesman in House of Lords 1985–93; *Recreations* the arts, gardening, walking; *Style*— Rt Hon Lord Ritchie of Dundee; ✉ The Roundel, Springsteps, Winchelsea, E Sussex (☎ 01797 226440)

RITCHLEY, Martin Howard; s of Robert William Ritchley (d 1964), of Orpington, Kent, and Bertha Amy, *née* Jones; *b* 1 July 1946; *Educ* City of London Sch; *m* 3 July 1970, (Mary) Elizabeth, da of Albert William Burns (d 1969), of Stevenage; 1 s (David b 1975), 2 da (Catherine b 1971, Anna b 1980); *Career* articled to Barton Mayhew & Co CAs 1964–70; Coventry Economic Building Society: chief accountant 1970–76, sec 1976–83; Coventry Building Society: sec 1983–89, dir 1985–, dep chief exec 1989–90, chief exec 1990–; govr Coventry Univ 1993–; dir Coventry & Warwickshire Partnership Ltd 1995–, dir Coventry Housing Action Partnership Ltd 1995–; FCA 1979 (ACA 1969); *Recreations* golf; *Clubs* Coventry Golf; *Style*— Martin Ritchley, Esq; ✉ 6 Cannon Hill Rd, Coventry CV4 7AZ (☎ 01203 418148); Coventry Building Society, Oakfield House, PO Box 600, Birley Business Park, Coventry CB3 2TQ (☎ 01203 653513, fax 01203 653576)

RITSON, Dr (Edward) Bruce; s of Maj Harold Ritson (d 1979), of Edinburgh, and Ivy, *née* Catherall (d 1972); *b* 20 March 1937; *Educ* Edinburgh Acad, Univ of Edinburgh, Harvard Univ (MD, MB ChB, DPM); *m* 25 Sept 1965, Eileen Teresa, da of Leonard Carey, of Dublin; 1 s (Gavin b 1970), 1 da (Fenella b 1968); *Career* dir Sheffield Region Addiction Unit 1968–71, conslt and clinical dir Royal Edinburgh Hosp 1971–, sr lectr in psychiatry Univ of Edinburgh 1971–; advsr WHO 1977–, conslt W Australia Alcohol and Drug Authy 1983; chm: Howard League (Scotland), Med Cncl on Alcoholism, Professional Advsy Ctee Scottish on Alcohol; chm Substance Misuse Section RCPsych; FRCPsych 1979, FRCP (Edinburgh) 1987; *Books* The Management of Alcoholism (with C Hassall, 1970), Alcohol: The Prevention Debate (with M Grant, 1983), Alcohol Our Favourite Drug (1986); *Recreations* theatre, travel, squash; *Clubs* Edinburgh Univ; *Style*— Dr Bruce Ritson; ✉ 4 McLaren Rd, Edinburgh, Scotland EH9 2BH (☎ 0131 667 1735); Royal Edinburgh Hospital, Morningside Park, Edinburgh (☎ 0131 537 6000)

RITTERMAN, Dr Janet Elizabeth; da of Charles Eric Palmer, of Sydney, and Laurie Helen, *née* Fuller; *b* 1 Dec 1941; *Educ* North Sydney Girls' HS, NSW State Conservatorium of Music (Frank Shirley Prize, Shadforth Hooper Prize, DSCM), Sydney Teachers' Coll Univ of Sydney (DipEd), Univ of Durham (BMus), Univ of London (Hilda Margaret Watts Prize for Musicology, MMus, PhD); *m* 19 Dec 1970, Gerrard Peter Ritterman; *Career* teacher: Strathfield Girls' HS Sydney 1963–66, Swaffield JMI Sch London 1967–68, Cheltenham Girls' HS Sydney 1968–69, Watford GS for Girls 1969–74; sr lectr in music: Middx Poly 1975–79, Goldsmiths' Coll Univ of London 1980–87; recognised teacher Univ of London 1984; Dartington Coll of Arts: head of music 1987–90, dean 1988–90, princ 1990–93; dir Royal Coll of Music 1993–; visiting prof in music educn Univ of Plymouth 1993–; external examiner: BA Kingston Poly 1987–90, Univ of Glasgow 1991–95, KCL 1995–; chief external examiner: PGCE Bradford and Ilkley Community Coll 1987–91, Welsh Coll of Music and Drama 1990–93, Manchester Metropolitan Univ 1991–93; chair: Arts Cncl Review of Training of Opera Singers 1992–93, ABRSM (Publishing) Ltd 1993–, Arts Cncl of England and BBC Nat Review of Orchestral Provision 1994–95, Subject Panel in Music Univ of London 1994–, The Mendelssohn and Boise Fndns 1996–; memb: Music Ctee Schools Examination and Assessment Cncl 1989–92, Exec Bd SW Arts 1991–93, Music Panel Arts Cncl of GB 1992–, RMA Cncl 1994–, Bd ENO 1996–, Exec Ctee ISM 1996–; conslt Govrs' Music Ctee Bd of Govrs of Wells Cathedral Sch 1993–; tstee 1993–: Prince Consort Fndn, The Martin Trust, The Countess of Munster Musical Trust; memb: ISM, RMA, RSM, Soc for Research in the Psychology of Music and Music Educn; DUniv Univ of Central England Birmingham 1996; Hon RAM 1995; FRSA; *Conference papers* incl: A Nineteenth Century Phoenix: the Concert Spirituel in Paris 1800–1830 (1986), Educating Tomorrow's Musicians (1988), Music History: its role in Higher Education Music (1989), Principle and Practice: the future of higher education in music (1991), First Impressions, Second Thoughts: Composers and their Reworkings (1993), Tradition and the individual talent: a musical perspective (1993), The Conservatoire within the Community: Challenging the Values (1994), Music Education National Debate' Performing Music, Knowing Music' (1995); *Publications* Training the Specialist Class Music Teacher of the Future (Music for a Small Planet, Int Soc for Music Educn Yearbook 1984), Les concerts spirituels à Paris au début du XIXe siècle (Revue internationale de musique française 1985), Questions unanswered or unasked?: Thoughts on teacher-student interaction in music education (Int Jl of Music Educn 1987), Music plus?: a recipe for success (Music Teacher 1989), Music History - on the decline? (Br Jl of Music Educn 1990), Piano Music and the Public Concert (Chopin Studies ed J Samson 1992), Craft for Art's Sake: Variations on a Traditional Theme (1995); *Reports* National Review of Opera Training (Arts Cncl of GB 1993), ACE and BBC Review of National Orchestral Provision - Consultation Document (Arts Cncl 1995); *Recreations* theatre, reading, country walking; *Style*— Dr Janet Ritterman; ✉ Royal College of Music, Prince Consort Road, London SW7 2BS (☎ 0171 589 3643, fax 0171 589 7740)

RITTNER, Luke Philip Hardwick; *b* 24 May 1947; *Educ* Blackfriars Sch Northants, City of Bath Tech Coll, Dartington Coll of Arts, LAMDA; *m* 1974, Corinna Frances Edholm; 1 da; *Career* asst admin Bath Festival 1968, admin dir Bath Festival 1974–76, dir and fndr Assoc for Business Sponsorship of the Arts 1976–83, sec-gen Arts Council 1983–90, British cultural dir Expo '92 Seville, communications dir Sotheby's 1992–; non-exec dir Carlton Television 1990–93; judge Olivier Awards 1992–94; chm: English Shakespeare Co 1990–94, memb Exec Bd London Acad of Music and Dramatic Art 1994–, London Choral Soc 1994–; *Clubs* Garrick; *Style*— Luke Rittner, Esq; ✉ 29 Kelso Place, London W8 5QG

RIVERDALE, 2 Baron (UK 1935); Sir Robert Arthur Balfour; 2 Bt (UK 1929), DL (S Yorks 1959); s of 1 Baron Riverdale, GBE (d 1957); *b* 1 Sept 1901; *Educ* Oundle; *m* 1, 1926, Nancy Marguerite (d 1928), da of Engr Rear Adm Mark Rundle, DSO; 1 s (Hon Mark Robin b 1927, d 1995); m 2, 1933, Christian Mary (d 1991), da of Maj Arthur Rowland Hill (ka 1915, ggggs of Sir Rowland Hill, 1 Bt); 1 s (Hon David Rowland b 1938), 1 da (Hon Frances Christian b 1946); *Heir* gs, Anthony Robert Balfour b 1960; *Career* Arthur Balfour & Co Ltd: joined 1918, dir 1924, asst md 1934, md 1949, chm and md 1957–61, exec chm 1950–66; dir various cos 1936–; dir Eastern Region Bd Nat Westminster Bank Ltd 1969–71, dir Yorkshire Television Ltd 1967–73; patron Sheffield Savings Bank 1958– (govr 1948–58); pres Br Assoc of Chambers of Commerce 1954–56; town tstee Sheffield Town Tst 1958–; JP Sheffield 1950–66; memb: Royal Yachting Assoc 1960–, Royal Naval Sailing Assoc 1960–; pres: Amateur Yacht Research Assoc 1966, Derwent Fly Fishing Club 1974; Chevalier Order of the Crown of Belgium 1956, La Medaille Civique de premiere classe, Offr de l'Ordre de Leopold II 1971, Acclaim Award Cutlers' Co Sheffield 1991; *Books* Squeeze The Trigger Gently (1991), A Life, A

Sail, A Changing Sea (1995); *Recreations* yachting, shooting, stalking, fishing; *Clubs* Sheffield, Bath, Royal Cruising; *Style—* Rt Hon Lord Riverdale, DL; ✉ Ropes, Grindleford, via Sheffield S30 1HX (☎ 01433 630408)

RIVETT-CARNAC, Cdr Miles James; DL (Hampshire 1996); s of Vice Adm James Rivett-Carnac (d 1970), and Isla Nesta, *née* Blackwood (d 1973); hp of bro, Rev Canon Sir (Thomas) Nicholas Rivett-Carnac, 8 Bt, *qv*; *b* 7 Feb 1933; *Educ* RNC Dartmouth; *m* 11 Oct 1958, April Sally, da of Maj Arthur Andrew Sidney Villar (d 1966), of London SW1; 2 s (Jonathan James b 1962, Simon Miles b 1966), 1 da (Lucinda Jane Guinness, *qv*, b 1960); *Career* Cdr RN 1965, cmd HMS Woolaston 1963–65 (despatches), Armed Forces Staff Coll Norfolk Virginia USA 1965, cmd HMS Dainty 1966–68, MOD 1968–70, ret 1970; joined Baring Bros & Co Ltd 1970 (dir 1975), md Outwich Ltd Johannesburg 1976–78, pres Baring Bros Inc 1978–81; memb Exec Ctee Baring Bros & Co 1981, dir Barings plc 1986–94, chief exec Baring Asset Management Ltd 1986–92, chm Baring Securities 1993–94; chm Tribune Investment Trust 1985–; dir: London Stock Exchange 1992–95, Allied Domecq plc (Allied-Lyons plc until 1994) 1992–; chm Hampshire and IOW Boys' Clubs, memb Exec Ctee King Edward VII Hosp, memb Cncl King George V Fund for Sailors; High Sheriff for Co of Hampshire 1995; Elder Brother Trinity House 1992; *Recreations* golf, tennis, stamps, racing; *Clubs* White's, Links (NY); *Style—* Cdr Miles Rivett-Carnac, RN, DL; ✉ Martyr Worthy Manor, nr Winchester, Hants SO12 1DY (☎ 0196 278 311); ING Barings, 60 London Wall, London EC2M 5TQ (☎ 0171 767 1000)

RIVETT-CARNAC, Rev Canon Sir (Thomas) Nicholas; 8 Bt (UK 1836), of Derby; s of Vice Adm James William Rivett-Carnac, CB, CBE, DSC (d 1970; 2 s of 6 Bt), and Isla Nesta, *née* Blackwood (d 1974); suc unc Sir Henry George Crabbe Rivett-Carnac, 7 Bt 1972; *b* 3 June 1927; *Educ* Marlborough; *m* 1977, Susan Marigold MacTier, yr da of late C Harold Copeland; *Heir* bro, Miles James Rivett-Carnac, *qv*, b 7 Feb 1933; *Career* served Scots Gds 1945–55; ordained 1962, curate Holy Trinity Rotherhithe 1964–68, curate Holy Trinity Brompton 1968–72, priest i/c St Mark's Kennington Oval 1972–89, rural dean of Lambeth 1978–82, hon canon Southwark Cathedral 1980–; memb London Probation Serv 1958–60, pastor Kingdom Faith Ministries Roffey Place Horsham W Sussex 1989–93, pastor Ashburnham Christian Tst; *Style—* The Rev Canon Sir Nicholas Rivett-Carnac, Bt; ✉ Ashburnham Christian Trust, 1 The Stable, Ashburnham Place, Battle, E Sussex TN33 9NF

RIVETT-DRAKE, Brig Dame Jean Elizabeth Rivett; DBE (1964, MBE 1947), JP (1965), DL (E Sussex 1983); da of Cdr Bertram Gregory Drake, and Dora Rivett-Drake; *b* 13 July 1909; *Educ* St Mary's Hall Brighton, Paris, RAM (LRAM piano); *Career* served WWII, driver 1 London Motor Transport Co, Women's Tport Serv (FANY) 1940, cmmnd ATS 1942, served with Br Liberation Army 1945–47 (despatches 1946), Lt-Col WRAC 1948–56, dep pres Regular Cmmns Bd 1948–49, London Dist 1952–54, asst dep dir FARELF 1954–56, dep dir War Office 1957–60, Eastern Cmd 1960–61, Col 1957–61, Brig 1961–64, ADC (Hon) to HM The Queen 1961–64; memb Hove Borough Cncl 1966–83, lay memb Press Cncl 1973–78, memb E Sussex CC 1973–77, mayor of Hove 1977–78; *Clubs* English Speaking Union; *Style—* Brig Dame Jean Rivett-Drake, DBE, JP, DL; ✉ c/o Barclays Bank, Hove Branch, South Coast Group of Branches, PO Box 358, Brighton BN1 1SF

RIVIÈRE, William D'Oyly; s of Michael Valentine Briton Rivière, of Dilham Grange, North Walsham, Norfolk, and Bridget D'Oyly, *née* D'Oyly-Hughes; *b* 15 May 1954; *Educ* Summerfields, Bradfield, King's Coll Cambridge (MA); *m* 29 Aug 1992, Isabelle Sarah, *née* Corbett; 1 s from previous partner (Leo Forte b 27 June 1975); *Career* lectr: Univ of Verona Italy 1980–84, Osaka Gakuin Univ Japan 1985–89, Univ of Urbino Italy 1990–; author; memb Royal Soc of Asian Affairs 1990–; runner-up Trask Awards Royal Soc of Lit 1989; Freeman Worshipful Co of Goldsmiths 1990; *Books* Watercolour Sky (1990), A Venetian Theory of Heaven (1992), Eros and Psyche (1994), Borneo Fire (1995); *Recreations* travelling, sailing and planting trees; *Clubs* Travellers'; *Style—* William Rivière, Esq; ✉ Dilham Grange, North Walsham, Norfolk NR28 9PZ (☎ 01692 536258); Peters Fraser & Dunlop Ltd, 503 The Chambers, Chelsea Harbour, Lots Road, London SW10 0XF (☎ 0171 376 7676, fax 0171 352 7356)

RIVINGTON, James Maitland Hansard; s of Herbert Lawrence Rivington, of London, and Catherine Sybil, *née* Cooke; *b* 21 Oct 1959; *Educ* St Paul's Sch London (Fndn Scholar), Magdalen Coll Oxford (exhibitioner, BA), Oxford Poly; *partner* Hon Emma Lucia Lawson; *Career* Blackwell Scientific Publications London and Oxford 1982–86, publications offr The British Academy 1986–; Liveryman Worshipful Co of Stationers & Newspaper Makers 1984; Freeman City of London 1982; *Recreations* playing cricket in the summer, supporting Brentford FC in the winter; *Style—* James Rivington, Esq; ✉ 43 Woodfield Road, Ealing, London W5 1SL (☎ 0181 998 9291); The British Academy, 20–21 Cornwall Terrace, London NW1 4QP (☎ 0171 487 5966, fax 0171 224 3807)

RIVLIN, His Hon Judge; Geoffrey; QC (1979); s of Allenby Rivlin (d 1973), and May Rivlin (d 1980); *b* 28 Nov 1940; *Educ* Bootham Sch York, Univ of Leeds (LLB); *m* 1974, Maureen Smith, Hon ARAM, violinist; 2 da (Emma b 30 Aug 1977, Sophie b 29 Nov 1981); *Career* called to the Bar Middle Temple 1963 (Colombus Prize of Int Law), in practice NE Circuit 1963–89, jr of NE Circuit 1967–78, recorder of the Crown Court 1978–89, bencher Middle Temple 1987, circuit judge (SE Circuit) 1989–; chm Advsy Bd Computer Related Crime Research Centre Queen Mary & Westfield Coll London 1996–; govr: St Christopher's Sch Hampstead 1990–, North London Collegiate Sch Edgware 1992–; *Style—* His Hon Judge Rivlin, QC; ✉ Southwark Crown Court, 1 English Grounds, off Battlebridge Lane, London SE1 2HU

RIX, Hon Mr Justice; Hon Sir Bernard Anthony; kt (1993); s of Otto Rix (d 1982), of London, and Sadie, *née* Silverberg (d 1996); *b* 8 Dec 1944; *Educ* St Paul's, New Coll Oxford (MA), Harvard Law Sch (Kennedy Scholar, LLM); *m* 1983, Hon Karen Debra Young, er da of Baron Young of Graffham, PC, *qv*; 3 s (Jacob, Gideon, Jonathan), 2 da (Hannah, Rachel); *Career* called to the Bar Inner Temple 1970, QC 1981; memb Senate of the Inns of Ct and Bar 1981–83, bencher Inner Temple 1990, recorder of the Crown Court 1990–93, judge of the High Court of Justice (Queen's Bench Div) 1993–; dir London Philharmonic Orch 1986–; chm British Friends of Bar Ilan Univ 1987–, memb Bd of Tstees of Bar Ilan Univ 1988–; chm Commercial Bar Assoc 1992–93, vice-chm Central Cncl for Jewish Community Servs 1993–96; dir The Spiro Inst 1995–; *Publications* author report on Jewish Youth Services and Organisations 1994; *Recreations* music, opera, Italy; *Style—* The Hon Mr Justice Rix; ✉ Royal Courts of Justice, Strand, London WC2R 2LL (☎ 0171 936 6000)

RIX, Baron (Life Peer UK 1992), of Whitehall in the City of Westminster and of Hornsea in Yorkshire; Sir Brian Norman Roger Rix; kt (1986), CBE (1977), DL (Greater London 1987); s of Herbert Dobson Rix (d 1966), of E Yorks, and Fanny, *née* Nicholson (d 1976); *b* 27 Jan 1924; *Educ* Bootham Sch York; *m* 1949, Elspet Jeans (the actress Elspet Gray), da of James MacGregor-Gray (d 1954), of Surrey; 2 s (Hon Jamie MacGregor b 1958, Hon Jonathan Robert MacGregor b 1960), 2 da (Hon (Elspet) Shelley b 1951, Hon Louisa (Louisa MacGregor Rix, *qv*) b 1955); *Career* WWII RAF and Bevin Boy; actor-manager 1948–77; ran repertory cos at Ilkley, Bridlington and Margate 1948–50, toured Reluctant Heroes and brought to Whitehall Theatre 1950–54, Dry Rot 1954–58, Simple Spymen 1958–61, One for the Pot 1961–64, Chase Me Comrade 1964–66, Stand By Your Bedouin, Uproar in the House and Let Sleeping Wives Lie Garrick Theatre 1967–69, She's Done It Again 1969–70, Don't Just Lie There, Say Something! 1971–73 (filmed 1973), Robinson Crusoe 1973, A Bit Between the Teeth 1974–75, Fringe Benefits 1976–77; entered films 1951 and subsequently made 13 films incl Reluctant Heroes 1951 and Dry Rot 1956; BBC TV contract to present farces on TV 1956–72, first ITV series Men of Affairs 1973, A Roof Over My Head (BBC) 1977; presenter: Let's Go (BBC TV series, first ever for people with a mental handicap) 1978–83, BBC Radio 2 Series 1978–80; dir and theatre controller Cooney-Marsh Group 1977–80, chm Playhouse (Whitehall) Ltd 1992–93; memb Arts Cncl 1986–93 (chm Drama Panel); chm: Ind Devpt Cncl for People with Mental Handicap 1981–88, Arts and Disability Monitoring Ctee 1986–93, Friends of Normansfield 1976–, Libertas 1987–, MENCAP 1988– (sec gen 1980–87); tstee Theatre of Comedy 1983–93, hon vice pres Radio Soc of GB; fell Humberside Univ 1984; Hon MA Hull 1981, Hon MA Open Univ 1983, Hon DSc Nottingham, Hon DUniv Essex 1984; Hon LLD: Manchester 1986, Dundee 1994; Vice Lord-Lt Greater London 1988–; *Books* My Farce from My Elbow (autobiography, 1975), Farce about Face - A Further Autobiography (1989), Tour de Farce (Touring Theatres and Strolling Players, 1992), Life in the Farce Lane (1995), Gullible's Travails (ed and contrib, 1996); *Recreations* cricket, gardening, amateur radio; *Clubs* Garrick, MCC, Lord's Taverners (past pres), Yorkshire CCC; *Style—* The Rt Hon Lord Rix, CBE, DL; ✉ House of Lords, London SW1A 0PW

RIX, Gerald George; TD (and Clasp); s of Frederick Thomas Rix, DFC (d 1996), of Herts, and Olive Louise, *née* Sharp; *b* 19 Nov 1934; *Educ* East Barnet GS, Univ of Dundee (MA), DipCAM; *m* 1, Nov 1957 (m dis 1973), Patricia Dyer; 2 s (Jonothan b 1961, Matthew Gerald b 1963), 1 da (Charlotte Emma b 1960); m 2, Dec 1975, Isla, da of Thomas McLauchlan (d 1967), of Clunes, Perthshire; *Career* RAF 1953–55; TA 1959–86, various Logistic, Engr and Reconnaissance Units, UK and NATO staff appts, Maj 1976; PR Div and Marine Fuel Mktg Div Shell International Petroleum Company Ltd 1955–61; Foote, Cone & Belding Group: joined PR Div 1961, fndr dir Welbeck PR 1967 (later concurrently md Welbeck City); Carl Byoir & Associates: dep chm 1984–86, chm 1986–87; gp md Hill and Knowlton London 1986– (gp dep chm 1987); fndr Minerva Communications Services 1987–92, dir Hallmark Marketing Communications Winchester 1987–92; memb Educn Ctee IPR 1972 and 1978, diploma examiner, chief examiner and moderator CAM Fndn 1974–79 (visiting lectr to Athens 1976), memb Nat Speakers' Panel Advertising Assoc 1976–93, educn convenor Int PR Assoc World Congress London 1979, PR moderator Centre for Business Studies 1981–85, memb Mgmnt Ctee Assoc for Business Sponsorship of the Arts 1983–85, chm Diploma Working Party IPR 1985–86, memb Consultancy Mgmnt Ctee PRCA 1987–88, personal tutor Univ of Stirling 1990–94; double Abertay Soc prizewinner 1993; FIPR 1987 (MIPR 1962), MIPA 1971, memb Int PR Assoc 1979; *Recreations* fly fishing, shooting, archaeology; *Clubs* Special Forces; *Style—* Gerald Rix, Esq, TD; ✉ Montchanin, 71250 Bergesserin, France (☎ and fax 00 33 85 50 83 92)

RIX, Sir John; kt (1977), MBE (1955), DL (Hants 1985); s of Reginald Arthur Rix (d 1948), of Burnham, Bucks; *b* 30 Jan 1917; *Educ* ISC Haileybury, Univ of Southampton; *m* 1953, Sylvia Gene, da of Capt Cecil Lewis Howe (d 1979); 2 s, 1 da; *Career* Vosper plc: joined 1937, gen mangr 1955, dir 1958, md 1963–78, chm and chief exec 1978–82, chm 1982–85; dir Vosper Private Ltd 1966–85, chm and chief exec Vosper Thornycroft (UK) Ltd 1970–77 (md 1966–70), dir Charismarine Ltd 1976–88; chm: Vosper Ship Repairs Ltd 1977–78, Vosper Hovermarine Ltd 1980–85, Mainwork Ltd 1980–85, David Brown Gear Industries Ltd 1980–85, Southampton Cable Ltd 1985–87, Chilworth Centre Ltd 1985–94, Seahorse Int Ltd 1986–90; dep chm Victorian Cruise Line Ltd 1988–96; Liveryman Worshipful Co of Shipwrights; FEng 1979; *Recreations* sailing, tennis, walking, golf; *Clubs* Royal Thames Yacht, Hockley Golf; *Style—* Sir John Rix, MBE, DL, FEng; ✉ Lower Baybridge House, Owslebury, Winchester, Hants (☎ 01962 777306)

RIX, Dr Keith John Barkclay; s of Sgt Kenneth Benjamin Rix, of Wisbech, and Phyllis Irene, *née* Cousins (d 1984); *b* 21 April 1950; *Educ* Wisbech GS, Univ of Aberdeen (BMedBiol, MB ChB, MD), Univ of Edinburgh (MPhil); *m* 31 Jan 1976, Elizabeth Murray, da of Robert Lumsden (d 1993), of Tullibody, Clackmannanshire; 3 da (Virginia b 1977, Marianne b 1981, Rowena b 1982); *Career* visiting res scientist Res Inst on Alcoholism NY State Dept of Mental Hygiene 1973, res fell Dept of Physiology Univ of Aberdeen 1975–76, registrar in psychiatry Royal Edinburgh Hosp 1976–79, visiting lectr Alcohol Studies Centre Univ of Paisley 1979–, lectr in psychiatry Univ of Manchester 1979–83, sr lectr in psychiatry Univ of Leeds 1983–, unit med advsr and conslt psychiatrist St James's Univ Hosp Leeds 1983–94, visiting conslt psychiatrist HM Prison Leeds 1983–, conslt psychiatrist Leeds Community and Mental Health Servs Teaching NHS Tst 1994–; fndr Aberdeen Cncl on Alcohol Problems, fndr memb Scottish Cncl on Alcohol Problems; past chm Ctee of Leeds Conslt Psychiatrists; memb: RCPsych MCQ Examination Ctee and Panel of Observers, Assoc of Police Surgns, British Acad of Forensic Scis; MIBiol, CBiol 1985, FRCPsych 1992 (MRCPsych 1979), MAE 1995; *Books* Alcohol and Alcoholism (1977), Alcohol Problems (with Elizabeth Lumsden Rix, 1983), A Handbook for Trainee Psychiatrists (1987); *Recreations* bird watching, jazz, theatre; *Clubs* Parkway Health, RSM; *Style—* Dr Keith Rix; ✉ High Royds Hospital, Menston, Ilkley, West Yorkshire LS29 6AQ (01943 876151, fax 01943 870471)

RIX, Louisa MacGregor; da of Baron Rix, CBE, DL (Life Peer), *qv*, and Elspet Jeans, *née* MacGregor-Gray (the actress Elspet Gray); *b* 2 Feb 1955; *Educ* Ibstock Place Roehampton, Queensgate Girls' Sch Kensington, Twickenham Tech Coll, LAMDA; *m* 12 April 1981 (m dis 1992), Jonathan Coy; 1 s (Jolyon b 9 Sept 1985), 1 da (Charlotte b 16 May 1983); *Career* actress; *Theatre* Nurse Sadler in Whose Life Is It Anyway? (Savoy) 1979, Margaret in Much Ado About Nothing and Charlotte in Don Juan (NT) 1981–82, Kitty in Charley's Aunt (Chichester Festival Theatre) 1979–80, Hazel in Time and the Conways (Greenwich) 1980, Lucy Fairweather in The Streets of London (Stratford) 1980, Theresa in How the Other Half Loves (Greenwich 1987 and Duke of York's 1988), Marion in Valued Friends (Hampstead) 1989–90, Jill Rillington in Man of the Moment (Globe) 1990, Phyllida Brewster in The Pocket Dream (Nottingham Playhouse 1991 and Albery 1992); *Television* Breakaway Girls (BBC) 1977, Danger UXB (Euston Films), Colin's Sandwich (BBC), Made in Heaven (Granada), Side By Side (BBC); *Recreations* painting, reading, holidays; *Clubs* 2 Brydges Place; *Style—* Miss Louisa Rix; ✉ c/o Peters Fraser & Dunlop Ltd, 5th Floor, The Chambers, Chelsea Harbour, Lots Rd, London SW10 0XF (☎ 0171 376 7676, fax 0171 352 7356)

RIX, Timothy John; CBE (1997); s of Howard Terrell Rix (d 1979), and Marguerite Selman, *née* Helps (d 1996); *b* 4 Jan 1934; *Career* Sub Lt RNVR 1952–54; Mellon Fell Yale 1957–58; Longmans Green & Co Ltd: joined 1958, overseas educnl publisher 1958–61, publishing mangr Far E and SE Asia 1961–63, head of English language teaching publishing 1964–68, divnl md 1968–72, jt md 1972–76, chief exec 1976, chm 1984; chm and chief exec: Longman Group Ltd 1984–90, Addison-Wesley-Longman Group Ltd 1988–89; dir: Pearson Longman Ltd 1979–83, Goldcrest TV 1982–83, Yale University Press 1984–, ECIC (Management) Ltd 1990–92, Blackie and Son Ltd 1990–95, Blackwell Ltd 1991–95; chm Book Marketing Ltd 1990–, sr conslt The Pofcher Co 1990–; pres Publishers Assoc 1982–84, dep chm Nat Book League 1985–86; chm: Book Tst 1986–88, Book House Training Centre 1986–89, Br Library Centre for the Book 1990–95, Soc of Bookmen 1990–92, British Library Publishing 1991–, Book Aid Int 1994–, Bell Educnl Tst 1994– (govr 1990–94), Nat Book Ctee 1996–; memb: Br Cncl Publisher Advsy Ctee 1978– (chm 1993–), Br Cncl Bd 1988–, Arts Cncl Lit Panel 1983–87, Br Library Advsy Cncl 1982–86, Br Library Bd 1986–96, Devpt Ctee Oxford Poly (now Oxford Brookes Univ) 1991–, Cncl Ranfurly Library Servs 1991–94, Fin Ctee of Delegacy Oxford

University Press 1992–, Health Educn Authy Bd 1995–; hon pres Ind Publishers Guild 1993–; Liveryman Worshipful Co of Stationers & Newspaper Makers; CIMgt, FRSA; *Recreations* reading, landscape, wine; *Clubs* Garrick; *Style*— Timothy Rix, Esq, CBE; ✉ 27 Wolseley Rd, London N8 8RS (☎ 0181 341 4160)

RIZA, Alper; QC (1991); s of Ali Riza (d 1985), and Elli, *née* Liasides; *b* 16 March 1948; *Educ* American Acad Larnaca Cyprus, English Sch Nicosia Cyprus; *m* 14 Aug 1981, Vanessa, da of Dr Patrick Hall-Smith, of Brighton; 2 da (Lily b 27 Dec 1981, Isabella b 20 July 1989); *Career* called to the Bar Gray's Inn 1973, asst recorder 1992–; *Recreations* music; *Style*— Alper Riza, Esq, QC; ✉ 10 King's Bench Walk, Temple EC4Y 1EB (☎ 0171 353 2501, fax 0171 353 0658, DX LDE 294 Chancery Lane)

RIZK, Dr Waheeb; CBE (1984, OBE 1977); s of Dr I Rizk, MD (d 1963), and Emily, *née* Elias (d 1935); *b* 11 Nov 1921; *Educ* EMC Cairo Egypt, Emmanuel Coll Cambridge (MA, PhD); *m* 5 April 1952, Vivien, da of Samuel Henry Leonard Moyle (d 1972), of Norwich, Norfolk; 1 s (Martin b 1959), 2 da (Imogen b 1953 d 1982, Meri b 1955); *Career* English Electric Research Laboratories: dept head 1954, chief engr Gas Turbine Dept 1957, gen mangr Gas and Industl Steam Turbine Div 1967; chm: Gas Turbines Ltd 1983–86 (md 1971), Ruston Diesels Ltd 1983–86; sr conslt W R Associates 1986–; winner American Soc Mech Engrs RT Sawyer award 1974, CIMAC Gold medal 1983; pres: Int Cncl of Combustion Engines CIMAC 1973–77, IMechE 1984–85 (memb Cncl 1978–89); chm Bd BSI 1982–85, chm Smallpeice Tst 1991–, memb Cncl Cranfield Univ 1986–94, memb Ct Brunel Univ; Freeman City of London 1983; FIMechE 1973, FEng 1979; *Clubs* Athenaeum; *Style*— Dr Waheeb Rizk, CBE, FEng; ✉ W R Associates, 231 Hillmorton Road, Rugby, Warwickshire CV22 5BD (☎ 01788 565093)

RIZZELLO, Michael Gaspard; OBE (1977); *b* 1926; *Educ* RCA (drawing prize, maj travelling scholarship); *Career* sculptor; served WWII cmmnd Royal Fus, seconded 8 Punjab Regt India and Far East 1944–47; produced busts of heads of state and coin designs for over 100 countries; recent work incl: eleven foot statue and Beaver fountain for New Brunswick Canada, bust of Lord Stevens of Ludgate at Ludgate House, sculpture at Stave Hill, over life-size portrait of James Walker (civil engr) at Brunswick Quay London Docklands, heroic bust of Nelson Mandela (exhibited Royal Acad 1990), bronze fountain sculptures Hemel Hempstead, Conspicuous Gallantry Cross and UN coins 1995; pres: Royal Soc of Br Sculptors 1976–86, Soc of Portrait Sculptors 1968–73; Queen's Silver Jubilee Medal 1977; *Awards* Prix de Rome for sculpture 1951, Sir Otto Beit Silver Medal for Sculpture 1961; *Style*— Michael Rizzello, Esq, OBE; ✉ Melrose Studio, 7 Melrose Road, London SW18 1ND (☎ 0181 870 8561, fax 0181 877 9842)

RIZZI, Carlo; *Educ* Milan Conservatoire (studied with Maestro Rosada), Bologna (studied with Vladimir Delman), Academia Chigiana (studied with Franco Ferrara, awarded Dip of Merit); *Career* conductor; currently music dir Welsh Nat Opera; debut 1982 conducting Donizetti's L'Ajo nell'imbarrazzo (Angelicum, Milan); works conducted incl: Rigoletto, La Traviata, Tancredi (Rossini), Torquato Tasso (Donizetti), Beatrice di Tenda (Bellini), La Voix Humaine (Poulenc), Don Giovanni, L'Italiana in Algeri, Falstaff (Salieri's as well as Verdi's), Cavalleria rusticana, Paliacci; has worked with orchs in Milan, Bologna, Rome, London, Tel Aviv, Paris, and at the Ravinia and Edinburgh Festivals; debuts: Britain, Australian Opera Co in Sydney 1989 (Il Barbiere di Siviglia), Netherlands Opera Amsterdam 1989 (Don Pasquale), Royal Opera House Covent Garden 1990 (La Cenerentola), Berlin 1992 (L'Ittaliana in Algeri), Cologne 1992 (La Scala di Seta and l'Occasione fa il ladro), with Israel Philharmonic 1993 (Rossini's Mosé), Metropolitan Opera NY 1993 (La Boheme and Il Barbiere di Siviglia); *Recordings* incl: L'Italiana in Londra (Cimarosa), Il Furioso sull'Isola di San Domingo (Donizetti), Ciro in Babilonia (Rossini), La Scuffiara (Paisiello), La Pescatrice (Piccinni), La Traviata (Verdi), Faust (Gounod), Rigoletto (operatic arias with Thomas Hampson and Jerry Hadley), Verdi Choruses with the Accademia di Santa Cecilia, Resphighi Tone Poems with the London Philarmonic; *Awards* second prize Besancon Conductor's Competition 1983, first prize Toscanini Conductors' Competition in Parma 1985, Italian Critics' Prize (for L'Italiana in Londra); *Style*— Carlo Rizzi, Esq; ✉ Allied Artists Agency, 42 Montpelier Square, London SW7 1JZ (☎ 0171 589 6243, fax 0171 581 5269)

ROACH, Prof Gary Francis; s of John Francis Roach (d 1982), and Bertha Mary Ann, *née* Walters (d 1975); *b* 8 Oct 1933; *Educ* Univ Coll of S Wales and Monmouthshire (BSc), Univ of London (MSc), Univ of Manchester (PhD, DSc), Technical Univ of Lodz (ScD); *m* 3 Sept 1960, Isabella Grace Willins Nicol; *Career* Flying Offr Educn Branch RAF 1955–58; res mathematician BP 1958–61, lectr UMIST 1961–66, visiting prof Univ of Br Columbia 1966–67; Univ of Strathclyde: lectr 1967–70, sr lectr 1970–71, reader 1971–79, prof 1979–, dean Faculty of Sci 1982–85; Incorporation of Bonnetmakers & Dyers Glasgow 1981; FRAS 1964, FIMA 1967, FRSE 1975, FRSA 1991; *Books* Green's Functions (2 edn, 1982); *Recreations* mountaineering, photography, philately, gardening, music; *Style*— Prof Gary Roach, FRSE; ✉ 11 Menzies Ave, Fintry, Glasgow G63 0YE (☎ 01360 860335); Dept of Mathematics, Univ of Strathclyde, Livingstone Tower, 26 Richmond St, Glasgow G1 1XH (☎ 0141 552 4400, ext 3800)

ROACHE, Linus William; s of William Patrick (Bill) Roache, *qv*, of Manchester, and Anna, *née* Cropper; *b* 1 Feb 1964; *Educ* Bishop Luffa Comp Sch Chichester, Rydal Sch N Wales, Central Sch of Speech and Drama; *Career* actor; *Theatre* Clive in Five Finger Exercise (Cambridge Theatre Co), Pavel in the Mother (Contact Theatre Manchester), Billy in a Colder Climate (Royal Court), Geoff in A Taste of Honey (Theatre Royal Nottingham), Tom in Keeping Tom Nice (Almeida Theatre), Eric Blair in Divine Gossip; RSC Stratford/Barbican season 1987–88: Martius in Titus Andronicus, William in Indigo, Sacha in A Question of Geography, Mark Antony in Julius Caesar; Johnny Boyle in Juno and the Paycock (RNT), Tom in The Glass Menagerie (Royal Exchange Manchester); RSC season 1990–91: Aumerle in Richard II, Edgar in King Lear, Don Juan in The Last Days of Don Juan, Berowne in Love's Labours Lost (Royal Exchange Manchester) 1992; *Television* work incl: Peter Davison in A Sort of Innocence (BBC) 1986, Danny in Saracen (Central) 1989, Vincent in Vincent Van Gogh (Omnibus, BBC) 1990, Tom in Keeping Tom Nice (BBC) 1990, DS Tait in G F Newman's Black and Blue (BBC) 1992; *Films* lead role in Priest (BBC/Miramax, dir Antonia Bird) 1994; *Awards* Manchester Evening News Awards nominations: Best Supporting Actor (for Pavel in The Mother) 1986, Best Actor (for Tom in The Glass Menagerie) 1990; *Recreations* golf, walking and exploring Great Britain; *Style*— Linus Roache, Esq; ✉ Kate Feast Management, 10 Primrose Hill Studios, Fitzroy Road, London NW1 8TR (☎ 0171 586 5502, fax 0171 586 9817)

ROACHE, William Patrick (Bill); s of Dr William Vincent Roache (d 1982), and Hester Vera, *née* Waddicor; *b* 25 April 1932; *Educ* Rydal Sch Colwyn Bay N Wales; *m* 1978, Sara McEwan, da of Sidney Mottram; 1 s (William James b 1986), 2 da (Verity Elizabeth b 1981, Edwina b 1982, d 1984); 2 c from previous m (of whom Linus William Roache, *qv*); *Career* army serv: joined RWF 1951, cmmnd 1952, served W Indies and Germany, seconded Trucial Oman Scouts, Capt Gulf 1955–56; actor in repertory film and TV; role of Ken Barlow in Coronation St 1960–; chm Mambi Games Ltd; vice pres E Cheshire Hospice; *Recreations* golf, tennis; *Clubs* Wilmslow Golf; *Style*— William Roache, Esq; ✉ Granada TV, Quay St, Manchester M60 9EA (☎ 0161 832 7211)

ROAD, Christopher John; s of Alfred Sinclair Road, OBE, and Eve Helen, *née* Adlerova; *b* 7 May 1948; *Educ* St Paul's, Trinity Hall Cambridge (MA); *m* 5 June 1971, Zofia Alicja, da of Piotr Jan Pialucha (d 1972); 1 s (Thomas b 1980), 1 da (Katharine b 1974); *Career* gen serv offr Br Cncl 1971–78, ptnr Macfarlanes Slrs 1983– (joined 1979); memb: City of London Slrs Co, Law Soc; *Style*— Christopher Road, Esq; ✉ 50 Coalecroft Rd, London SW15 6LP (☎ 0181 788 5601); 10 Norwich St, London EC4A 1BD (☎ 0171 831 9222, fax 0171 831 9607, telex 296381 MACFAR G)

ROADS, Dr Christopher Herbert; s of Herbert Clifford Roads (d 1963), of Kneesworth, Cambs, and Vera Iris, *née* Clark (d 1986); *b* 3 Jan 1934; *Educ* Cambridge & County Sch, Trinity Hall Cambridge (open scholar, BA, MA, PhD); *m* 24 April 1976 (m dis 1996), Charlotte Alicia Dorothy Mary, da of Neil Lothian (d 1996), of Minterne House, Minterne Magna, Dorchester, Dorset; 1 da (Cecilia Iris Muriel Lothian b 1981); *Career* Lt RA Egypt 1952–54; advsr to War Office on Disposal of Amnesty Arms 1961–62, keeper Dept of Records Imperial War Museum 1962–70 (dep DG 1964–79); fndr and dir: Cambridge Coral Starfish Res Gp 1968–, Duxford Aviation Museum (IWM) 1971–79; tstee later dir HMS Belfast Pool of London 1970–79; UNESCO conslt in design and operation of audiovisual archives and museums in general 1976–; dir: Nat Sound Archive 1983–92, Historic Cable Ship John W Mackay 1986–; dir: Museums and Archives Development Associates Ltd 1977–85, Cedar Audio Ltd 1986–92, AVT Communications Ltd 1986–92, National Discography Ltd 1986–92, Symcom Ltd 1994–95; assoc dir (consultancy) R & D Dept British Library 1992–94, advsr and dir-elect Jet Heritage Museum Hurn 1995–; hon pres World Expeditionary Assoc 1971–; vice pres: Duxford Aviation Soc 1974–, English Eight 1980–; pres: Cambridge Numismatic Soc 1964–66, Archive and Cataloguing Commission of Int Film and TV Cncl (UNESCO category A) 1970–, Int Film and TV Cncl 1990–92; memb Cncl of Scientific Exploration Soc 1971–82; pres Historical Breech Loading Small Arms Assoc 1973–, hon sec Cambridge Univ Long Range Rifle Club 1979–, vice pres Cambridge Univ Rifle Assoc 1987– (memb 1955–87); Churchill fellowship 1971, visiting fell Centre of Int Studies Univ of Cambridge 1983–84; Silver Jubilee medal 1977; Order of Independence 2 class (Jordan) 1977; Freeman City of London 1996, Liveryman Worshipful Co of Gunmakers 1996; FRGS; *Recreations* rifle shooting (winner of various competitions incl Nat Match Rifle Championship Hopton 5 times), flying, marine and submarine exploration, wind surfing, cine & still photography; *Clubs* Hawks' (Cambridge), United Oxford and Cambridge Univ; *Style*— Dr Christopher Roads; ✉ The White House, 90 High Street, Melbourn, nr Royston, Herts SG8 6AL (☎ 01763 260866, fax 01763 262521, mobile 0802 403164); DX 12, Bahia Dorada, 29693 Estepona, Malaga, Spain (☎ and fax 00 34 52 76 9407)

ROADS, Elizabeth Ann; MVO (1990); da of Lt-Col James Bruce, MC (d 1973), and Mary Hope, *née* Sinclair (d 1993); *b* 5 July 1951; *Educ* Lansdowne House Edinburgh, Cambridgeshire Coll of Technol, Study Centre for Fine Art London; *m* 23 April 1983, Christopher George William Roads, s of Dr Peter George Roads; 2 s (Timothy George Sinclair b 7 Sept 1986, William Peter Alexander b 22 Sept 1988), 1 da (Emily Ann Hope Clara b 3 Oct 1994); *Career* Inst of Educn Univ of London 1970, Christie's London 1970–74, Ct of The Lord Lyon 1975–, Lyon Clerk and Keeper of the Records 1986–, temp Linlithgow Pursuivant of Arms Extraordinary 1987, Carrick Pursuivant of Arms 1992–; fell Heraldry Soc of Scotland (memb 1977, ctee memb 1992–95 and 1996–); chm Heraldic Exhbn 1995; articles in heraldic and genealogical jls; Queen's Silver Jubilee medal 1977; FSA (Scot) 1986; *Recreations* history, reading, country pursuits, the family; *Style*— Mrs C G W Roads, MVO; ✉ 9 Denham Green Place, Edinburgh EH5 3PA; Court of The Lord Lyon, HM New Register House, Edinburgh EH1 3YT (☎ 0131 556 7255, fax 0131 557 2148)

ROBARDS, Prof Anthony William; s of Albert Charles Robards, of Lamberhurst, Tunbridge Wells, and Kathleen Emily Robards; *b* 9 April 1940; *Educ* The Skinners' Sch, UCL (BSc, PhD, DSc); *m* 1, 1962 (m dis 1985), Ruth, *née* Bulpett; 1 s (Martin David b 1967), 1 da (Helen Elizabeth b 1970); m 2, 30 March 1987, Eva Christina, da of Bo Knutson-Ek, of Lidingo, Sweden; *Career* currently prof and dir Industl Devpt and pro-vice-chllr Univ of York; visiting res fell: Australian Nat Univ 1975, Univ of Stockholm 1986; chm York Science Park Innovation Centre Ltd; pres: Royal Microscopical Soc 1982–84, York & N Yorks C of C; memb Co of Merchant Adventurers of the City of York; FIBiol, DipRMS; *Books* Low Temperature Methods in Biological Electron Microscopy (with U B Sleytr, 1985); *Recreations* horse-riding, horology; *Style*— Prof Anthony Robards; ✉ Shrubbery Cottage, Nun Monkton, Yorks YO5 8EW (☎ 01423 331023); The Innovation Centre, York Science Park, York YO1 5DG (☎ 01904 435104, fax 01904 435135, e-mail AWR1@YORK.AC.UK)

ROBARTS, (Anthony) Julian; s of Lt-Col Anthony Vere Cyprian Robarts (d 1982); *b* 6 May 1937; *Educ* Eton; *m* 1961, Edwina Beryl, da of the Rt Hon John Gardiner Sumner Hobson, OBE, TD, QC, MP (d 1967); 2 s, 1 da; *Career* banker; dir then md Coutts & Co 1963–91, dir Coutts Fin Co 1967–91, regnl dir NatWest Bank 1971–92; dir: The Int Fund for Insts Inc (USA) 1983–92, The F Bolton Group Ltd 1970–, Hill Martin 1992– (chm 1993–); chief exec The Iveagh Trustees Ltd 1993–; *Recreations* shooting, gardening, opera; *Clubs* Pratt's, MCC, Brooks's; *Style*— Julian Robarts, Esq; ✉ Bromley Hall, Standon, Ware, Herts SG11 1NY (☎ 01279 842422)

ROBATHAN, Andrew Robert George; MP (C) Blaby (majority 25,347); s of Douglas Robathan, and Sheena, *née* Gimson; *b* 17 July 1951; *Educ* Merchant Taylors' Sch Northwood, Oriel Coll Oxford; *m* 20 Dec 1991, Rachael, *née* Maunder; 1 s (Christopher Nicholas Andrew b 6 Dec 1996); *Career* offr Coldstream Gds 1974–89, rejoined for Gulf War 1991; cncllr London Borough of Hammersmith and Fulham 1990–92, MP (C) Blaby 1992–, PPS to Iain Sproat as Min of State Dept of Nat Heritage 1995–; chm Cons Backbench Defence Ctee 1994–95, vice-chm Cons Backbench NI Ctee 1994–95, chm All Party Cycling Gp; *Recreations* mountain walking, tennis, skiing, wildlife, shooting; *Style*— Andrew Robathan, Esq, MP; ✉ House of Commons, London SW1A 0AA

ROBB, Prof Alan Macfarlane; s of Alexander Robb (d 1982), of Aberdeen, and Jane Margaret; *b* 24 Feb 1946; *Educ* Robert Gordon's Coll Aberdeen, Gray's Sch of Art, RCA (MA); *m* 1969, Cynthia Jane, da of John Neilson, of Glasgow; 1 s (Daniel Alexander John b 1971), 1 da (Annabel Ellen Jane b 1974); *Career* artist and teacher; art master Oundle Sch Peterborough 1972–75; Crawford Sch of Art Cork Ireland: lectr in painting 1975–78, head of painting 1978–80, head of fine art 1980–82; head Sch of Fine Art Duncan Jordanstone Coll of Art Dundee 1983– (prof 1990–); speaker Context and Collaboration Int Public Art Symposium Birmingham 1990; CNAA: memb Fine Art Bd, specialist advsr in fine art 1987–; chief examiner in fine art NCEA Ireland, external examiner in painting and printmaking Sheffield Poly 1987–90; memb: Steering Gp Nat Assoc for Fine Art Educn 1988–, Chief Exec's Res Advsy Gp Ctee Scottish Higher Educn Funding Cncl; lead assessor (quality assessment) in fine art SHEFC; dir: Art in Partnership 1986–91, Workshop and Studio Provision for Artists Scotland (WASPS) 1984–94, Br Health Care Arts 1989–93; work in various private and public collections; *Exhibitions* regularly exhbns since 1968 at: Aberdeen Artists, Scot Soc of Artists, Royal Scot Acad, Royal Glasgow Inst, Royal Scottish Soc Watercolourists; solo incl: The New 57 Gallery Edinburgh 1972, Cork Art Soc 1976, Scot Arts Cncl touring exhibition 1978–79, Triskel Art Centre Cork 1979, Gallery 22 Cupar 1986, Francis Cooper Gallery DJCA Dundee 1991, Seagate Gallery 1996; group incl: Scot Young Contemporaries 1967–68, Univ of York 1970, RCA 1971, Architectural Assoc 1971, Napier Ct Trinity Coll Cambridge 1971, Eduardo Paolozzi's choice of the London postgrad sch shows 1972, Royal Acad 1972, E Midlands Arts 1973, EVA Limerick 1977–81, Clare Morris Open 1980 and 1982, Cork Art Soc 1978 and 1980, Peacock Printmakers touring exhibition The Art of Thinking 1985, 'Allegories of Desire' Small Mansion House London 1992, 'Five Scottish Artists' Centre D'Art En I'lle Geneva 1994, Allan Stone Gallery NY 1996, Bruton St Gallery London 1996; *Awards* (painting) Arbroath Open 1968, (painting) Irish Open Exhibition of Visual Art Limerick 1977, (painting) Clare Morris Open 1982, Aberdeen Artists 1989; *Publications* Irish Contemporary Art (1982), In the Minds Eye (Ewan McArthur, 1996); *Style*— Prof Alan Robb; ✉ Head of School of Fine Art, Duncan of Jordanstone College of Art, University of Dundee, Perth Rd, Dundee (☎ 01382 345226, fax 01382 200983)

ROBB, Andrew MacKenzie; s of William MacKenzie Robb (d 1983), and Kathleen Rhona Harvey, *née* Gibbs (d 1990); *b* 2 Sept 1942; *Educ* Rugby; *m* 19 June 1965, Barbara Karin Erika, da of Ronald Hamm, of Cheltenham; 2 da (Fiona b 1967, Erica b 1969); *Career* accountant T Wall & Sons Ltd 1961–69, gp accountant Hoskyns Gp Ltd 1969–71, gp fin dir P & O 1983–89 (fin controller Bulk Shipping Div 1971–75, gp fin controller 1975–83), exec dir Pilkington plc 1989–, non-exec dir Alfred McAlpine plc 1993–; memb Urgent Issues Task Force Accounting Standards Bd 1992–; memb 100 Gp; JDipMA 1973; FCMA 1968, FCT 1992; *Recreations* golf, gardening, bridge, reading; *Style*— Andrew Robb, Esq; ✉ Pilkington plc, Prescot Rd, St Helens WA10 3TT (☎ 01744 692786, fax 01744 20038, telex 627441)

ROBB, Curtis Alexander; s of Alexander Robb, of Woolton, Liverpool, and Sylvia, *née* Hoogensen; *b* 7 June 1972; *Educ* Liverpool Coll; *Career* athlete (middle distance runner); achievements incl: Gold medal 800m Euro Jr Championships 1991, AAA jr 1500m champion 1990 and 1991, AAA indoor jr 1500m champion 1991, English schs 1500m champion 1989 and 1990, Silver medal 800m World Student Games 1991, UK and AAA sr 800m champion 1992, Gold medal 800m Under 23 Euro Cup 1992, sixth 800m Olympic Games 1992, fourth 800m World Championships Stuttgart 1993, AAA 800m champion 1995 and 1996, semi-finalist Olympic Games Atlanta 1996; currently med student Sheffield; *Style*— Curtis Robb, Esq; ✉ c/o Liverpool Harriers, Wavertree Athletics Centre, Liverpool

ROBB, George Alan; WS (1968); s of George Robb (d 1969), of Inverdee, Cults, Aberdeen, and Phyllis Mary, *née* Allan (d 1966); *b* 20 May 1942; *Educ* Aberdeen GS 1946–60, Univ of Aberdeen (MA), Univ of Edinburgh (LLB); *m* 3 Aug 1973, Moira Ann, da of Sidney Milne Clark, of Bieldside, Aberdeen; 3 s (Andrew George b 19 Oct 1976, Michael Nicholas b 22 Dec 1984, Jonathan Alexander b 17 Mar 1991), 1 da (Judith Olivia b 30 May 1978); *Career* law apprentice Davidson and Syme WS Edinburgh 1966–68; asst: Davidson and Syme WS 1968–69, Edmonds and Ledingham Aberdeen 1969–71, Brander and Cruickshank Advocates Aberdeen 1971–73 (ptnr 1973–83); dir: Aberdeen Trust PLC 1983–91 (chm 1991–92), Aberdeen Petroleum plc 1982 (chm 1992–93), Abtrust Scotland Investment Co plc 1986, Radiotrust plc 1989, Abtrust New European Investment Trust plc 1990, Grampian Healthcare NHS Tst 1993, Asset Management Investment Company plc 1994 (md); memb: Law Soc of Scot 1966, WS Soc 1968, IOD 1984 (memb Aberdeen Ctee 1984–88); FInstPet 1983; *Recreations* shooting, gardening, family; *Clubs* Aberdeen Petroleum, Aberdeen; *Style*— George A Robb, Esq, WS; ✉ Birchwood, 6 Hillhead Rd, Bieldside, Aberdeen AB15 9EJ (☎ 01224 869043, fax 01224 869044)

ROBBÉ, Dr Iain J; s of Jack Robert Robbé, and (Annette) Yvonne, *née* Conners; *b* 3 Nov 1955; *Educ* Charterhouse, KCL (BSc), Westminster Med Sch (MB BS, MRCS, LRCP), Univ of London (MSc); *m* 1984, Gillian Nancy, da of Brig P Douglas Wickenden, RAMC (ret); *Career* jr hosp doctor 1980–84, specialist trg in public health med 1984–88, dir of public health and planning Worthing Health Authy 1988–91, dir of public health med Gwent Health Authy 1991–93, sr lectr in public health med Univ of Wales Coll of Med 1993–; MFPHM 1987; *Recreations* wildlife and environmental protection, wine tasting, gardening; *Style*— Dr Iain Robbe; ✉ Whips Cottage, Dawn of Day, Grosmont, Abergavenny, Gwent NP7 8LT; Centre for Applied Public Health Medicine, University of Wales College of Medicine, Temple of Peace and Health, Cathays Park, Cardiff CF1 3NW (☎ 01222 231021, fax 01222 238606)

ROBBIE, Victor Allan Cumming; s of W Allan Robbie (d 1995), of Aberdeen, and Mae, *née* Milne; *b* 22 March 1945; *Educ* Dumbarton Acad, Shawlands Acad; *m* 20 Jan 1968, Christine Elisabeth, da of Harold Featherby Jaggard (d 1987); 2 da (Gabrielle Sara b 3 Sept 1971, Kirsten Nicola b 7 May 74), 1 s (Nicholas Allan Graham b 13 June 1978); *Career* Sunday Post and Weekly News 1963–65, Scottish Daily Mail 1965–66, Daily Telegraph 1967–68, Daily and Sunday Telegraph (Sydney) 1969–71, Evening Standard 1971–73, athletics corr Daily Mirror 1980–86 (joined 1973), The Independent 1986–87, sports ed Scotland on Sunday 1988–89, sports ed The Independent 1989–91, asst ed and head of sport Daily Mail 1991–; memb Athletics Writers' Assoc; *Books* Athletics Yearbook (1987); *Recreations* archaeology, travel, golf, watching my wife garden, Usquebaugh; *Clubs* Sloane, Harris Golf, Hartley Wintney Golf; *Style*— Victor Robbie, Esq; ✉ The Daily Mail, Northcliffe House, 2 Derry Street, Kensington, London W8 5TT (☎ 0171 938 6200)

ROBBINS, James; s of (Richard) Michael Robbins, of London, and Elspeth, *née* Bannatyne; *b* 19 Jan 1954; *Educ* Westminster, ChCh Oxford (BA, ed Isis); *m* 30 Oct 1981, Gillian Elizabeth Cameron, da of Dr Brian C Gee, of Portadown; 1 da (Emily Maeve Cameron b 23 March 1991); *Career* BBC: news trainee 1977, Belfast newsroom 1979–83, reporter TV news (based London) 1983–87, Southern Africa corr (based Johannesburg) 1987–91, Europe corr (based Brussels) 1992–; major assignments incl: Bangladesh floods, famine in Sudan, pro-democracy riots S Korea, hunger strikes Maze Prison, UK miners' strike, resignation of Pres P W Botha, rise of F W De Klerk, release of Nelson Mandela, political reforms and violence S Africa, independence process in Namibia, aftermath of Maastricht Summit, future of the Euro Union, conclusion of GATT world trade deal; *Recreations* family, reading, walking, music, eating, tennis; *Style*— James Robbins; ✉ BBC, International Press Centre, Boulevard Charlemagne 1, B-1040 Brussels, Belgium (☎ 00 32 2 230 2120, fax 00 32 2 230 2688)

ROBBINS, John; s of Frederick Ernest Robbins (d 1992), and Dora Elizabeth Crump (d 1985); *b* 5 May 1933; *Educ* Wolverhampton GS, Univ of Birmingham (LLB); *m* 4 Sept 1963, Maria Krystina, da of Frank Grzymek, of Wolverhampton; 1 s (Robert b 1966), 2 da (Lucy b 1970, Annalisa b 1975); *Career* admitted slr 1957; sr ptnr Woolley Beavon Slrs Wolverhampton; pres Wolverhampton Law Soc 1985; memb Law Soc; *Recreations* cricket, music, local history; *Clubs* Wig and Pen, Old Wulfrunians; *Style*— John Robbins, Esq; ✉ George House, St John's Sq, Wolverhampton, West Midlands WV2 4BZ (☎ 01902 25733, fax 01902 311886)

ROBBINS, Prof Keith Gilbert; s of Gilbert Henry John Robbins, and Edith Mary, *née* Carpenter; *b* 9 April 1940; *Educ* Bristol GS, Magdalen and St Antony's Colls Oxford (MA, DPhil), Univ of Glasgow (DLitt); *m* 24 Aug 1963, Janet Carey, da of John Thomson, of Fulbrook, Oxon; 3 s (Paul b 1965, Daniel b 1967, Adam b 1972), 1 da (Lucy b 1970); *Career* lectr Univ of York 1963–71, dean of Faculty of Arts UCNW Bangor 1977–79 (prof of history 1971–79), prof of modern history Univ of Glasgow 1980–91, vice chllr Univ of Wales Lampeter 1992–, sr vice-chllr Univ of Wales 1995–; vice pres RHS 1984–88; pres: Historical Assoc 1988–91, Ecclesiastical History Soc 1980–81; Raleigh lectr Br Acad 1984, Ford lectr Oxford 1987, Winston Churchill travelling fell 1990; memb Humanities Res Bd Br Acad 1994–; ed History 1977–86; FRHistS 1970; FRSE 1991; *Books* Munich 1938 (1968), Sir Edward Grey (1971), The Abolition of War (1976), John Bright (1979), The Eclipse of a Great Power: Modern Britain 1870–1975 ((1983), 2 edn 1870–1992 (1994)), The First World War (1984), Nineteenth Century Britain: Integration and Diversity (1988), Appeasement (1988), Churchill (1992), History, Religion and Identity in Modern Britain (1993), Politicians, Diplomacy and War in Modern British History (1994), Bibliography of British History 1914–89 (1996); *Recreations* music; *Style*— Prof Keith Robbins, FRSE; ✉ Rhydyfran, Cribyn, Lampeter, Ceredigion SA48 7NH; University of Wales, Lampeter, Ceredigion SA48 7ED (☎ 01570 423498, fax 01570 423423)

ROBBINS, Dr (Raymond Frank) Michael; CBE (1987); s of Harold Robbins (d 1982), of Wrexham, Clwyd, and Elsie, *née* Croft (d 1975); *b* 15 Feb 1928; *Educ* Grove Park GS, Univ of Wales Aberystwyth (BSc, PhD, Monsanto fell); *m* Ann Eirian Meredith, da of John Meredith Edwards (d 1970), of Bow St, Dyfed; 2 da (Rhian Mair b 1960, Sian Eryl b 1964); *Career* RAF 1946–48; res chemist Monsanto Chemicals 1954–55, Med Res Cncl fell Univ of Exeter 1955–56, lectr in organic chemistry Nottingham Poly 1956–59, head Chemistry and Biology Dept Hatfield Poly 1961–70 (sr lectr in organic chemistry 1960), dir Poly South West (formerly Plymouth Poly) 1974–89 (dep dir 1970–74); chm Sci Prog Advsy Gp Polytechnics and Colleges Funding Cncl 1989–92; hon fell Poly South West 1989; *Recreations* hill walking, gardening; *Style*— Dr Michael Robbins, CBE

ROBBINS, Dr (Richard) Michael; CBE (1976); s of (Alfred) Gordon Robbins (d 1944), of Cherry Wood, Woldingham, Surrey, and Josephine, *née* Capell (d 1987); *b* 7 Sept 1915; *Educ* Westminster, Ch Ch Oxford (MA), Univ of Vienna; *m* 21 Oct 1939, (Rose Margaret) Elspeth (d 1993), da of Sir Robert Reid Bannatyne, CB (d 1956), of Lindfield, Sussex; 1 s ((Michael) James Gordon b 19 Jan 1954), 2 da ((Helen) Caroline (Mrs Shaw) b 10 Feb 1941, Celia Margaret (Mrs Morley) b 2 April 1948); *Career* RE (Transportation) 1939–46, 2 Lt 1940, Capt 1942, Maj 1944; memb London Tport Bd/London Tport Exec 1965–80 (joined 1939, rejoined 1946, sec to Exec 1950, sec and chief PR offr 1955, chief commercial and PR offr 1960, md railways 1971–78); chm Museum of London 1979–90; Hon DLitt City Univ 1987; FCIT 1954 (pres 1975–76), FRSA 1976, FSA 1957 (treas 1971–87, pres 1987–91); *Books* The North London Railway (1937), 190 in Persia (1951), The Isle of Wight Railways (1953), Middlesex (1953), Middlesex Parish Churches (ed, 1955), The Railway Age (1962), History of London Transport (with T C Barker, vol I 1963, vol II 1974), George and Robert Stephenson (1966), Points and Signals (1967), A Public Transport Century (1985), Journal of Transport History (jt ed, 1953–65); *Clubs* Athenaeum; *Style*— Dr Michael Robbins, CBE, FSA; ✉ 7 Courthope Villas, London SW19 4EH (☎ 0181 946 7308)

ROBBINS, His Hon Judge Stephen Dennis; s of Lt-Col J Dennis Robbins, OBE, TD (d 1986), of Essex, and Joan, *née* Mason; *b* 11 Jan 1948; *Educ* Marlborough, Coll of Europe Bruges; *m* 28 Sept 1974, Amanda Robbins, JP, da of J Michael Smith, of Macclesfield, Cheshire; 3 da (Harriet b 1976, Victoria b 1979, Camilla (twin) b 1979); *Career* called to the Bar Gray's Inn 1969; in practice SE Circuit 1972–94, recorder Crown Court 1987–94, circuit judge (SE Circuit) 1994–; London Common Law Bar Assoc and Senate Overseas Rels; chm: Disciplinary Ctee Potato Mktg Bd 1988–94, Mental Health Review Tbnls 1994–; *Recreations* Scottish hill walking, fishing, swimming, shooting, cross country skiing, music, collecting ephemera; *Style*— His Hon Judge Robbins; ✉ Hillcrest Farm, Sevington, nr Ashford, Kent (☎ 01233 502732); 2 The Studios, Edge St, London W8 (☎ 0171 727 7216); Snaresbrook Crown Court, Hollybush Hill, London E11 1QW

ROBENS OF WOLDINGHAM, Baron (Life Peer UK 1961), of Woldingham, Co Surrey; Alfred Robens; PC (1951); s of George Robens, of Manchester, and Edith Robens, of Manchester; *b* 18 Dec 1910; *Educ* Manchester Secdy Sch, DCL, LLD; *m* 1937, Eva, da of Fred Powell, of Manchester; 1 adopted s; *Career* MP (Lab): Northumberland Wansbeck 1945–50, Blyth 1950–60; PPS to Min of Tport 1945–47, parly sec Miny of Fuel and Power 1947–50, min Labour and Nat Service 1951; chm: NCB 1960–71, MLH Consultants 1971–83, Johnson Matthey & Co (precious metal refiners, traders and bankers) 1971–85, Vickers Plc 1971–81, St Regis Newspapers Bolton 1975–80, St Regis International 1976–80, Snamprogetti 1980–; dir: Bank of England 1966–80, Times Newspapers Holdings 1980–83, British Fuel Co 1967–85, AAH 1971–88, St Regis Paper Co (NY) 1976–80, THF 1971–86, AMI Europe Ltd 1980–89; memb Royal Cmmn on Trade Unions and Employers' Assocs 1965–68; chm: Ctee of Inquiry on Safety and Health at Work 1970–72, Engrg Industs Cncl 1976–80, Guy's Hosp Med and Dental Sch 1974–; *Style*— The Rt Hon the Lord Robens of Woldingham, PC; ✉ House of Lords, London SW1A 0PW

ROBERSON, Sidney (Sid); s of Percy Harold Roberson, of Worthing, and Ivy Ethel Hannah, *née* Holliwell (d 1970); *b* 15 March 1937; *Educ* Enfield GS; *m* 1, 1961, Brenda, da of Harold Milverton; 1 da (Hannah b 1967); m 2, 1990, Suzi Staniland; 2 s (Charlie b 1984, Nathaniel b 1991), 1 da (Florence Ivy b 1988); *Career* began career as runner in art studio, resident in USA 1961–64, subsequently art dir then copywriter various advtg agencies; int photographer 1968–, commercial dir 1971– (own co 1973–92, with Fat Fish Films then Mendoza Productions 1992–96, own co 1996–); freelance dir (progs incl The Sweeney, Robin of Sherwood, Lab Pty Political Broadcasts 1988 and 1989); *Awards* over fifty int awards for commercials incl: two Gold Lions at Cannes, two Gold Arrows Br TV Advtg awards, Silver award D & AD; 3rd place Mr Universe; *Recreations* gym, tennis, children, travel; *Style*— Sid Roberson, Esq; ✉ Roberson Films, 13 Orme Square, London W2 4RS (☎ 0171 221 4924, fax 0171 792 2134)

ROBERTON OF LAUCHOPE, Dr Norman Reid Clifford (Cliff); s of Norman McCulloch Roberton of Lauchope (d 1981), of Hillcourt, Lockerbie, Dumfriesshire, and Nora Helen McCulloch, *née* Holden (d 1990); *b* 3 Sept 1939; *Educ* Accrington GS, Downing Coll Cambridge (BA, MB BChir, MA, MRCP), UCH; *m* 1, 6 Sept 1964 (m dis 1978), Mary, da of Frank Lloyd, of Penmaenmawr, Dyfed; 2 s (David Hugh Gershom b 7 Sept 1966, Gareth Iain McCulloch b 4 Oct 1970), 1 da (Fiona Mairi b 6 July 1972); m 2, 26 Jan 1980, Patricia Marshall, da of Thos Alfred Parker, of Bottisham, Cambs; *Career* clinical reader in paediatrics Univ of Oxford 1973–74, conslt paediatrician Cambridge Health Authy 1974–93, head of paediatrics Riyadh Armed Forces Hosp Saudi Arabia 1987–89; Fitzwilliam Coll Cambridge: fell 1979–93, dean 1980–87, dir studies in med 1983–93, graduate tutor 1989–93; memb Ctee Paediatric Section RSM 1980–87 and 1990–95 (sec 1982–84, pres 1991–92); memb: Neonatal Soc 1968 (memb Ctee 1974–78, sec 1983–87), Br Assoc of Perinatal Med 1976 (pres 1985–87), Sci and Pathology Advsy Ctee RCOG 1978–81, Paediatric Ctee RCP 1980–87, Res Advsy Ctee Birthright 1980–83, Cncl Baby Life Support Systems 1983–93, Br Paediatric Assoc, Euro Soc of Paediatric Res; Freeman City of London 1968, Liveryman Worshipful Soc of Apothecaries 1970 (memb Livery Ctee 1983–85); FRCP 1979; *Books* Separation and Special Care Baby Units (1978), Manual of Neonatal Intensive Care (1981, 3 edn 1993), Paediatrics (1981), Parent Baby Attachment in Premature Infants (1983), Textbook of Neonatology (1986, 2 edn 1992), Lecture Notes in Neonatology (1987), Manual of Normal Neonatal Care (1988, 2nd edn 1996), Lung Disease in the Newborn (1995); *Recreations* golf, Scottish history and archaeology, wildlife; *Style*— Dr Cliff Roberton of Lauchope; ✉ Sea Cottage, Lower Harrapool, Broadford, Isle of Skye IV49 9AQ (☎ 01471 822467)

ROBERTS, *see also:* Hardy-Roberts

ROBERTS, Prof (Edward) Adam; s of Michael Roberts (d 1948), of London, and Janet, *née* Adam-Smith; *b* 29 Aug 1940; *Educ* Westminster, Magdalen Coll Oxford (BA); *m* 16 Sept 1966, Frances Primrose, da of Raymond Horace Albany Dunn (d 1951), of Ludham, Norfolk; 1 da (Hannah b 1970), 1 s (Bayard b 1972); *Career* asst ed Peace News 1962–65, lectr int rels LSE 1968–81 (Noel Buxton student 1965–68); Univ of Oxford: Alastair Buchan reader in int rels 1981–86, professorial fell St Antony's Coll 1981–86, Montague Burton prof of international relations 1986–, fell Balliol Coll 1986–; chm of govrs William Tyndale Sch 1976–78; FBA 1990; *Books* The Strategy of Civilian Defence: Non-violent Resistance to Aggression (ed, 1967), Nations in Arms: The Theory and Practice of Territorial Defence (2 edn, 1986), Documents on the Laws of War (with Richard Guelff 2 edn, 1989), United Nations, Divided World: The UN's Roles in

International Relations (ed with Benedict Kingsbury, 2 edn 1993), Hugo Grotius and International Relations (ed with Hedley Bull and Benedict Kingsbury, 1990); *Recreations* rock-climbing, mountaineering; *Clubs* Alpine; *Style—* Prof Adam Roberts, FBA; ✉ Balliol College, Oxford OX1 3BJ (☎ 01865 277777, fax 01865 277803)

ROBERTS, Col Alan Clive; MBE (1982), TD (1969), JP (1977), DL (W Yorks 1982); s of late Maj William Roberts, MBE, RA, and Kathleen Roberts; *b* 28 April 1934; *Educ* Askham House Sch Taunton, Rutherford Coll Newcastle, Manchester Poly (MPhil), Univ of Bradford (PhD); *m* 1956, Margaret Mary, *née* Shaw; 2 s; *Career* Nat Serv 1954–56; Territorial Army: Lt 269 (W Riding) Field Regt RA 1956, Capt 1962, Maj 1968, Lt-Col cmdg Univ of Leeds OTC 1972–79, Col and Dep Cdr TA NE Dist 1980–, TA advsr to GOC NE Dist 1980–, Regtl Col Univ of Leeds OTC 1980–90; ADC 1980–84; Hon Col: 269 (W Riding) Battery 19 Field Regt RA 1983–, Univ of Leeds OTC 1990–, Yorks ACF (N & W) 1993–; Hon Col Commandant RA 1996; head of Biomaterials Lab Dept of Plastic & Maxillo-Facial Surgery St Lukes Hosp Bradford 1960–; Bradford Hosps NHS Tst and predecessors: conslt clinical scientist 1970–, dir of R&D 1992–; Univ of Leeds: Crown rep Cncl 1985, pro-chllr 1986–, chm Ct and Cncl 1986–, dir Univ of Leeds Fndn 1986–, chm Advsy Bd Inst of Nursing 1994–96; Univ of Bradford: visiting sr research fell Plastic & Burns Research Unit 1988–, dir Biomaterials Research Unit 1990–, memb Advsy Ctee Dept of Biomedical Sciences 1992; Cncl of Europe fell Univs of Gothenburg, Malmö and Stockholm 1968, prof of biomaterials in surgery Academic Surgical Unit Univ of Hull 1994; visiting prof/lectr: Univ of Indiana 1968, Univ of Texas 1968, 1974 and 1985, Dept of Polymer Technol Manchester Poly 1970–80, Stomatology Inst Univ of Bordeaux 1971, Plastic Surgery Inst Univ of Utrecht 1972, Univ of Pennsylvania 1975, Twente Univ of Technol Netherlands 1976, Univ of São Paulo 1976, Univ of Jakarta 1986, Trinity Coll Dublin 1987, Univ of Tokyo 1987, Univ of Moscow 1987, Univ of Malaysia 1988; guest lectr: Faculty of Dental Surgery RCS England 1969 and 1980, Faculty of Plastic Surgery RCS England 1976; dean's research lectr RMCS 1977; numerous research and consultancy appts in the field of biomaterials and adhesives for plastic/reconstructive surgery; memb Br Standards Ctees on Cardio-Vascular Materials and Toxicology of Med Polymers; vice chm Co of W Yorks Jt Emergency Exec Ctee 1983–, chm Quality of Life Gp and memb Head and Neck Working Gp Yorks Regnl Cancer Orgn 1993–, vice chm Expert Working Gp Regnl R&D Ctee Yorks RHA 1994–95, memb Health Servs Res Gp Northern & Yorks RHA 1995–; ed Jl of the Inst of Br Surgical Technol 1965–69, assessor Jl of Biomedical Engrg 1979; chief examiner in maxillo-facial technol CGLI 1968–, moderator BTech higher technol courses 1985–97, examiner Univ of Sheffield Sch of Clinical Dentistry 1995–; chm Cncl of Mil Educn Ctees UK Univs 1990–96, vice chm Sr Awards Ctee CGLI 1991–, dep chm Ctee of Chairmen of Univ Cncls 1993–, memb Int Advsy Bd Med Sch Universiti Malaysia Sarawak 1993–; vice pres Leeds Boys' Bde 1972–, chm Tstees W Riding Artillery Tst 1983–, chm Co of W Yorks SSAFA 1985–, vice chm Yorks & Humberside TAVRA 1987–89 and 1993–; dir Weetwood Hall Ltd 1992–, govr Gateways Sch 1992–; tstee: Edward Boyle Meml Tst 1986–, W Yorks Sculpture Park 1995–; patron: Crime Stoppers 1995–, Age Concern 1995–; memb Cncl Br Red Cross Soc 1995–; Denney Award for Innovation in Surgical Technol Inst of Surgical Technol 1960, Insignia Award in Technol CGLI 1969 and 1976, Prince Philip Medal for outstanding achievements in Sci and Technol 1970, Merit and Achievement Award for Medical Materials Devpt Inst of Sci and Technol 1972, Red Cross Badge of Honour 1992; hon sec: Fellowship of Prince Philip Medallists 1993–, Bradford Medico-Chirurgical Soc; hon life memb: US Army Med Research Soc 1971, CGLI 1978; memb: Medical Protection Soc, Biological Engrg Soc (also memb Artificial Organs Gp), Assoc of Clinical Biochemists, W Riding Medico Legal Soc; AIMechE 1967, CBiol 1971, FIBiol 1987 (MIBiol 1970), memb NY Acad of Sciences 1987, FCGI 1990, FRSM 1993, CIMechE 1996; OStJ 1994; *Books* Obturators and Prosthesis for Cleft Palate (1965), Facial Prosthesis: The Restoration of Facial Defects by Prosthetic Means (1972), Maxillo-Facial Prosthetics: A Multidisciplinary Practice (jtly, 1972), Adhesives in Surgery: How it Works Encyclopaedia (jtly, 1988), A Text and Colour Atlas of Head and Neck Prosthetics (1994); also author of numerous papers in med and scientific jls; *Recreations* silver, sculpture, music; *Style—* Col Alan Roberts, MBE, TD, JP, DL; ✉ The Grange, Rein Road, Morley, Leeds, W Yorkshire LS27 0HZ; University of Leeds, Leeds LS2 9JT (☎ 0113 233 5000, fax 0113 233 3988)

ROBERTS, Dr Alan Frederick; CBE (1996); s of Harry Frederick Roberts (d 1982), of Sussex, and Edith Clara, *née* Reid; *b* 13 Oct 1935; *Educ* Whitgift Sch Croydon, Imperial Coll London (BSc, PhD, DSc, ACGI, DIC); *m* 12 March 1960, Kathleen Joan, da of Owen Leonard Wallis; 2 s (David Alan b 1963, Patrick James b 1965); *Career* post-doctoral fell Imperial Coll 1959–60; Safety in Mines Research Estab: jr res fell 1960–62, sr sci offr 1962–67, princ sci offr 1967–75; Health and Safety Exec: head Res Planning Gp 1975–77, dep dir Safety Engrg Lab 1977–78, dir Explosion and Flame Lab 1981–89 (dep dir 1978–81), dir Nuclear Safety Res Mgmnt Unit 1989–92, dir Res and Lab Servs Div 1992–94, chief exec Health and Safety Laboratory 1994–95, conslt 1995–; FIChemE 1978, FEng 1993 (CEng 1967); *Books* The Coal Mines of Buxton (1985), Turnpike Roads around Buxton (1993); *Recreations* walking, local history; *Style—* Dr Alan Roberts, CBE, FEng; ✉ 18 Dovedale Crescent, Buxton, Derbyshire SK17 9BJ (☎ 01298 24952)

ROBERTS, Allan Deverell; s of Irfon Roberts, of Priory Wall House, Lewes, E Sussex, and Patricia Mary, *née* Allan; *b* 14 July 1950; *Educ* Eton, Magdalen Coll Oxford (MA); *m* 7 Dec 1991, Dr Irene Anne Graham Reilly; 2 s (Hugh b 14 Feb 1993, Duncan b 26 April 1995); *Career* slr in private practice 1974–76; Govt Legal Serv: legal asst 1976–78, sr legal asst 1978–84, asst slr 1984–89, under sec 1989–; memb Law Soc; *Recreations* walking, music, football; *Style—* Allan Roberts, Esq; ✉ Solicitor's Office, Depts of Health and Social Security, New Court, Carey St, London WC2 (☎ 0171 412 1465)

ROBERTS, Alwyn; s of Rev Howell Roberts and Buddug, *née* Jones; *b* 26 Aug 1933; *Educ* Penygroes GS, Univ Coll of Wales Aberystwyth (LLB), Univ Coll of North Wales Bangor (BA), Univ of Cambridge (MA); *m* 28 July 1960, Mair Rowlands, da of W R Williams; 1 s (Hywel Glyn b 9 June 1962); *Career* princ PM Govt Coll Aizawl Assam India 1960–67, lectr Univ Coll Swansea 1967–70; Univ Coll North Wales Bangor: lectr and sr lectr 1970–79, dir Extra Mural Studies 1979–95, vice princ 1985–94, pro-vice-chllr 1994–; memb: Gwynedd CC 1973–81, Gwynedd Health Authy 1973–80, Royal Cmmn on Legal Servs 1976–79, Welsh Fourth Channel Authy 1981–86, Parole Bd 1987–90; Welsh Nat govr of BBC 1979–86, pres Royal Nat Eisteddfod of Wales 1993–96 (chm 1989–92), chm N Wales Arts Assoc 1993–94; vice chm Arts Cncl of Wales 1994–; *Style—* Alwyn Roberts, Esq; ✉ Brithdir, 43 Talycae, Tregarth, Gwynedd (☎ 01248 600007); University Wales, Bangor, Gwynedd (☎ 01248 352045, fax 01248 383876)

ROBERTS, Air Vice-Marshal Andrew Lyle; CB (1992), CBE (1983), AFC (1969); s of Ronald Lyle Roberts, Ferndown, Wimborne, Dorset, and Nora, *née* Poole; *b* 19 May 1938; *Educ* Cranbook Sch, RAF Coll Cranwell; *m* 18 Aug 1962, Marcia Isabella, da of Lt-Col Christopher Lane Cecil Ward, of Bridge House, Buckland Newton, Dorchester, Dorset; 3 da (Katherine Lucy b 1963, Penelope Susan b 1965, Sarah Jane b 1968); *Career* RAF Coll Cranwell 1956–58, PO 1958, 38 Sqdn RAF Luqa Malta 1959–61, Flying Offr 1960, Flt Lt 1961, Instr RAF Coll Cranwell 1962–64, ADC AOC 18 Gp RAF Pitreavie Castle 1965–66, Flt Cdr 201 Sqdn 1967–68, Sqdn Ldr 1967, student RN Staff Coll 1969, personal air sec to Under Sec of State RAF 1970–71, Wing Cdr OC 236 Operational Conversion Unit RAF St Mawgan 1972–73, US Armed Forces Staff Coll 1974, HQ SACLANT 1975–77, Gp Capt Station Cdr RAF Kinloss 1977–79, Gp Capt Ops HQ Strike Cmd 1980–82, student Royal Coll of Def Studies 1983, Air Cdre Dir Air Force Plans and Progs MOD 1984–86, Air Vice-Marshal COS HQ 18 Gp 1987–89, ACDS (concepts) MOD 1989–92, RAF Manpower Structure Study 1992–94 (ret RAF 1994); memb Lord Chllr's Panel of Independent Inspectors 1994–; MIMgt 1969, FRAeS 1994; *Recreations* walking, natural history, music (church organ and choral singing) off-shore sailing; *Clubs* RAF; *Style—* Air Vice-Marshal Andrew Roberts, CB, CBE, AFC; ✉ c/o Midland Bank, 61 High St, Staines, Middx TW18 4QW

ROBERTS, Anne Clark; da of William Cunningham (d 1972), of Scotland, and Ann Simpson Lyon, *née* Clark; *b* 11 Jan 1961; *Educ* Larbert HS, Univ of Aberdeen (MA); *m* 13 Aug 1988, Thomas John Blackburn Roberts, s of Thomas Blackburn Roberts, CBE, TD, DL (d 1979), of Waterwynch, Park Drive, Blundellsands, Liverpool; 1 da (Verity Anne b 15 Jan 1992), 1 s (William John Blackburn b 1 March 1995); *Career* with Next plc 1984–88, md The National Trust (Enterprises) Ltd 1988–94; non-exec dir Remploy Ltd 1993–; memb Inland Waterways Amenity Advsy Cncl 1993–95; winner: Nat Training Award 1987, Cosmopolitan Woman of Tomorrow Award (Indust and Commerce) 1989; *Recreations* antique collecting, conservation; *Style—* Mrs Anne C Roberts; ✉ Southwick Court, Southwick, Wilts BA14 9QB

ROBERTS, Anthony Howard Norman; s of Kenneth Arthur Norman Roberts (d 1982), and Ivy Beatrice Maude Roberts (d 1970); *b* 15 Nov 1938; *Educ* Bancroft's Sch, Univ of Leeds (BSc), Univ of Cambridge (BA, MA), Univ of Oxford (BA, MA, BM BCh); *m* 24 March 1972, Dr (Fiona Edith) Vivian, da of Prof Richard Broxton Onians (d 1986); 2 da (Clare b 1974, Natasha b 1976); *Career* lectr in chemical engrg Univ of Surrey 1961–64; hon lectr Dept of Biomedical Scis Univ of Bradford 1984–, conslt plastic surgn Stoke Mandeville Hosp and dir Oxford Region Burn Unit 1985–, surgical tutor 1989–94, regnl advsr in plastic surgery 1996–; visiting prof Chinese Univ of Hong Kong 1990– (C C Wu prof 1996); visiting lectr/prof: Southern Africa 1988 and 1995, Australia 1990 and 1993, India 1990 and 1993, Israel 1992, Papua New Guinea 1993, Egypt 1995, Bosnia 1996; admin Stoke Mandeville Burns and Reconstructive Surgery Res Tst; author of articles in med and surgical jls; second in command surgical team the Bradford disaster 1985; ldr disaster relief team: Athens Refinery Fire 1992, 'Operation Phoenix' Bosnia 1994; memb: Br Burns Assoc 1976–, Br Assoc of Plastic Surgns 1986–, Br Soc for Surgery of the Hand 1986–, Int Soc for Burn Injuries 1990– (memb Disaster Planning Ctee); FRCS 1976; *Books* contrib Bander's Aid (A Guide to the Australian Bird in the Hand) (3 edn, 1994); *Recreations* ornithology, sport; *Clubs* Hawks, British Ornithological Union, Cambridge Univ Cruising; *Style—* Mr Anthony Roberts; ✉ The Old House, Whitchurch, Bucks HP22 4JX (☎ 01296 641232, fax 01296 641820); Stoke Mandeville Hospital, Aylesbury, Bucks HP21 8AL (☎ 01296 315116)

ROBERTS, Antony Mabon (Tony); s of Lt Hylton Mabon Roberts (d 1987), and Phyllis Mary, *née* Dickinson; *b* 9 July 1939; *Educ* Birkenhead Sch, Univ of Hamburg, Univ of Cambridge (MA), Yale Univ (MA); *m* 7 Aug 1965, Angela Dale, da of Maj Eric William Huggins, of Southwold, Suffolk; 1 s (Benjamin Mabon b 1969), 1 da (Clare Joy b 1972); *Career* sr prodr BBC TV 1976–; prodns incl: English Law 1968, Avventura 1971, Ensemble 1975, The Living City 1977, Wainwright's Law 1980, Whatever Happened to Britain 1982, Honourable Members 1983, Politics of Pressure 1985, Téléjournal 1983, Heute Direkt 1984, Issues of Law 1986, Person to Person 1988, Give and Take 1989, When In Germany 1991; ptnr Gratus and Roberts Productions 1991–; memb HAC; *Recreations* cricket, tennis, golf; *Clubs* MCC; *Style—* Tony Roberts, Esq; ✉ 59 Breamwater Gardens, Ham, Richmond, Surrey (☎ 0181 940 9631)

ROBERTS, Bernard; s of William Wright Roberts (d 1960), and Elsie Alberta, *née* Ingham (d 1976); *b* 23 July 1933; *Educ* William Hulme's GS Manchester, RCM (scholar); *m* 1, 1955 (m dis 1987), Patricia May, da of Victor George Russell (d 1987); 2 s (Andrew John b 1958, Nicholas Keith b 1960); m 2, 1992, Caroline Ireland; *Career* solo pianist; debut Wigmore Hall 1957, numerous solo performances nationally and internationally, Henry Wood Promenade Concerts 1979, prof RCM 1962–80 and 1992–; played in numerous chamber groups (including Parikian Fleming Roberts Trio) 1975–84; Nimbus Records 1982–85: Complete Beethoven Piano Sonatas, Eroica and Diabelli Variations; Hon DUniv Brunel 1989; FRCM 1981; *Recreations* reading, philosophy, religion, model railway; *Style—* Bernard Roberts, Esq; ✉ Uwchlaw'r Coed, Llanbedr, Gwynedd LL45 2NA (☎ and fax 01341 241532)

ROBERTS, Dr Bryon Edward; s of Albert Roberts, JP, DL (former MP Normanton), of Oulton, nr Leeds, and Alice Ashton (d 1989); *b* 17 Feb 1933; *Educ* Rothwell GS, Univ of Leeds (MB ChB, MD); *m* 17 Aug 1957, Audrey Jeanette, da of Herbert Knee (d 1964); 1 s (David b 27 Sept 1958); *Career* registrar Royal Postgrad Med Sch 1962–63, lectr Dept of Pathology Univ of Leeds 1963–70, conslt haematologist Leeds Western Health Authy 1970–92, dir of pathology Utd Leeds Teaching Hosp Tst 1992–; pres Br Soc for Haematology 1993–94, regnl advsr RCPath 1983–94; FRCPath 1965, FRCPE 1990; *Recreations* gardening, running, watching football, golf; *Style—* Dr Bryon Roberts; ✉ 9 Ladywood Mead, Leeds LS8 2LZ (☎ 0113 293 3193); Dept of Haematology, Leeds General Infirmary, Leeds LS1 3EX (☎ 0113 292 6643, fax 0113 242 0881)

ROBERTS, Christopher Keepfer; s of John Anthony Roberts, and Pauline Isobel, *née* Keepfer; *b* 26 March 1956; *Educ* Denbigh HS, Jesus Coll Cambridge (MA); *Career* ptnr Allen & Overy 1985– (asst 1978–85); memb Law Soc; *Recreations* sailing, squash; *Clubs* Royal Automobile, Little Ship; *Style—* Christopher Roberts, Esq; ✉ Allen & Overy, One New Change, London EC4M 9QQ (☎ 0171 330 3000, fax 0171 330 9999)

ROBERTS, Dr Clive John Charlton; s of Capt John Charlton Roberts (d 1982), of Taunton, and Monica, *née* Cousins; *b* 27 May 1946; *Educ* Taunton Sch, King's Coll Med Sch London (MB BS), Univ of Bristol (MD); *m* 6 April 1968, Ruth Diane, da of Charles Henry Sandham, of Wigan; 2 s (Daniel John Charlton b 1975, Samuel James b 1982), 2 da (Sally Kathryn b 1973, Rebecca b and d 1972); *Career* registrar in med Plymouth Gen Hosp 1972–74, conslt sr lectr in clinical pharmacology and med Bristol Royal Infirmary and Univ of Bristol 1981–, chm Div of Med Bristol Royal Infirmary 1993–95; chief med offr Sun Life Assurance Soc PLC 1993–; author of papers and ed of books on clinical pharmacology; vice chm Backwell PC 1987–95, memb Acad Med Gp at RCP; chm: Standing Ctee Membs of RCP 1986, Backwell Residents' Assoc 1990–95; regnl advsr Royal Coll of Physicians 1994–96; memb Br Pharmacological Soc, FRCP 1987; *Books* Treatment in Clinical Medicine, Gastro Intestinal Disease (1983); *Recreations* local and family history, cycling, running; *Clubs* W Country Physicians; *Style—* Dr Clive Roberts; ✉ 52 Church Lane, Backwell, Bristol BS19 3PQ (☎ 01275 463100); Bristol Royal Infirmary, Dept of Medicine, Bristol BS2 8HW (☎ 0117 9 230 000, fax 0117 928 2254)

ROBERTS, Prof (Victor) Colin; s of Ernest Roberts (d 1993), and Marjorie Frances, *née* Edwards (d 1987); *b* 11 Feb 1943; *Educ* Christ's Hosp Horsham, KCL (BSc(Eng), AKC), Univ of Surrey (MSc, PhD); *m* 27 July 1968, Christine Joan, da of Walter Clifford Lake; 2 da (Tara Jane b 27 June 1972, Catherine Elizabeth b 30 Nov 1973); *Career* apprentice Associated Electrical Industries Rugby 1961, engr Associated Electrical Industries Manchester then Compagnie Francaise Thomson-Houston Paris until 1967; King's Coll Hosp Med Sch London: research asst 1967–71, lectr in biomedical engrg 1971–75, sr lectr 1975–83, prof of biomedical engrg 1983–90; fndn prof of med engrg and physics King's Coll Sch of Med and Dentistry London 1990–, dir of med engrg King's Healthcare Tst 1990–, dir Nat Centre of Rehabilitation Engrg 1991–; ed: Medical and Biological Engineering and Computing 1985–92, Medical Engineering and Physics 1993–; memb: Bd of Surgical Specialties RCS 1977–82, Med Engrg and Sensors Ctee SERC 1984–87 and 1991–94, Admin Cncl Int Fedn for Med and Biological Engrg 1991–,

Med Engrg Coll Engrg and Physical Sci Research Cncl 1995–; chm: Professional Ctee on Med Electronics IEE 1976–77, Br Design Awards Panel for Med Equipment Design Cncl 1979–81, Working Gp on Clinical Engrg Int Fedn for Med and Biological Engrg 1982–85; Pres's Prize Biological Engrg Soc 1980, distinguished overseas lectr Instn of Engrs Aust 1987; hon memb: Instn of Biomedical Engrs of Aust 1987, Romanian Soc for Clinical Engrg 1991; FRSM 1973, FIEE 1981, FInstP 1981, FSIAD 1981, fell Biological Engrg Soc 1993 (pres 1976–78), founder fell Instn of Physics and Engrg in Med and Biology 1995; *Books* Blood Flow Measurement (1972), Doulton Ink Wares (1993), Amputee Management (1995), Medical Radiation Physics (1995); *Recreations* playing violin, classical music, opera, windsurfing, antique restoration; *Clubs* Christ's Hosp; *Style—* Prof Colin Roberts; ✉ 39 Half Moon Lane, London SE24 9JX; Department of Medical Engineering and Physics, King's College School of Medicine and Dentistry, Denmark Hill, London SE5 8RS (☎ 0171 346 3491, fax 0171 346 3314)

ROBERTS, Prof Colin; s of Theophilus Roberts (d 1991), of Wrexham, and Daisy, *née* Roberts (d 1989); *b* 25 Jan 1937; *Educ* Univ of Liverpool (Med Students undergrad scholar, BSc, MB ChB, MD), Univ of Manchester (DipBact); *m* 8 July 1961, Marjorie Frances, da of James Conway; 2 s (David Colin b 15 Oct 1962, Philip John b 10 Oct 1967); *Career* registrar in pathology Sefton Gen Hosp Liverpool 1964–66 (house physician and house surgn 1963–64), hon sr registrar United Liverpool Hospitals 1966–70, lectr in med microbiology Univ of Liverpool 1969–70 (lectr in pathology 1966–69); Regnl Public Health Lab Fazakerley Hosp Liverpool: asst microbiologist (sr registrar) 1970–73, sr microbiologist 1973–75, conslt med microbiologist 1975–87, dep dir 1977–87; Public Health Lab Serv: conslt med microbiologist 1987–, dep dir 1987–93, med and scientific postgrad dean 1993–; hon conslt med microbiologist Mersey RHA 1975–87; hon lectr in infectious diseases Univ of Liverpool 1975–87, hon lectr Sch of Tropical Med and Infectious Diseases Univ of Liverpool 1985–87, visiting prof Environmental Health Div Univ of Strathclyde 1993–; memb Cncl: Assoc of Clinical Pathologists (asst sec 1990–92), Assoc of Med Microbiologists (pres 1994–95), Royal Coll of Pathologists (asst registrar 1990–92, registrar 1992–96, vice pres 1996–), Royal Inst of Public Health and Hygiene; chm Med Microbiol Scientific Advsy Ctee Clinical Pathology Accreditation (UK) 1996–; hon life memb Central Sterlising Club 1996 (chm 1992–96); memb numerous professional socs incl: Br Soc for the Study of Infection, Pathological Soc of GB and I; FRCPath 1986, FRIPHH 1992, Hon FRCPCH 1996, MRCP 1996; *Publications* contrib chapters/ed various books and proceedings incl: Infectious and Communicable Diseases in England and Wales (contrib, 1990), Quality Control: Principles and Practice in the Microbiology Laboratory (jt ed, 1991, 2 edn 1997), A Supervisor's Handbook of Food Hygiene and Safety (1995); also author of numerous pubns in academic jls; memb Editorial Bd Jl of Clinical Pathology; *Recreations* theatre, music, art, literature, sport (rep Wales at schoolboy and youth level in soccer); *Clubs* Athenaeum, Savage, Royal Society of Medicine; *Style—* Prof Colin Roberts; ✉ Public Health Laboratory Service, 61 Colindale Avenue, London NW9 5DF (☎ 0181 200 1295, fax 0181 200 8130)

ROBERTS, Dr Dafydd Llewellyn Lloyd; s of Capt William Jones Roberts (d 1981), of Holyhead, Gwynedd, and Kate, *née* Griffiths (d 1991); *b* 6 Jan 1949; *Educ* Holyhead Comp Sch, Univ of London (MB BS, MRCP); *m* Mary Josephine, da of Richard Joseph Farrell; 1 da (Catherine Mary Lloyd b 17 Sept 1977), 1 s (Daniel William Lloyd b 12 Dec 1984); *Career* jr hosp appointments Royal London Hosp, Harold Wood Hosp Essex, Chase Farm Hosp Middx and Univ Hosp of Wales Cardiff 1972–75, med offr and GP 1975, dermatology trg posts Univ Hosp of Wales and N Staffs Hosps 1976–81, conslt dermatologist West Glamorgan Health Authy 1981, currently conslt dermatologist Swansea NHS Tst; sec Med Staff Ctee Swansea Hosps, memb W Glamorgan District Med Ctee, memb Welsh Med Ctee; chm: Welsh Sub-Ctee of Dermatology, Welsh Audit Gp (Dermatology); author of various pubns relating to clinical dermatology especially on malignant melanoma and skin cancers; memb: BMA, Br Assoc of Dermatologists (hon treas); fell American Acad of Dermatology, FRSM, FRCP 1994; *Style—* Dr Dafydd Roberts; ✉ 49 Higher Lane, Langland, Swansea SA3 4NT (☎ 01792 369919); Singleton Hospital, Sketty, Swansea SA22 8QA (☎ 01792 205666, fax 01792 208647)

ROBERTS, His Hon; David Ewart; s of John Hobson Roberts (d 1969), of Birmingham, and Dorothy, *née* Rolason (d 1979); *b* 18 Feb 1921; *Educ* Abingdon Sch, St John's Coll Cambridge (MA, LLB); *Career* Nat Serv WWII 1941–46, cmmnd RA; served: Egypt, N Africa, Italy, Yugoslavia, Germany; called to the Bar Middle Temple; in practice Midland Circuit 1948, asst recorder Coventry QS 1966–71, recorder Crown Ct Midland & Oxford Circuit 1978–82, circuit judge 1982–93; *Recreations* travel, photography; *Style—* His Hon David Roberts; ✉ 4 Greville Dr, Birmingham B15 2UU (☎ 0121 440 3231)

ROBERTS, David Francis; s of Arthur Roberts; of Plealey, Shropshire, and Mary Kathleen, *née* Maddox; *b* 28 Aug 1941; *Educ* Priory GS Shrewsbury, Worcester Coll Oxford (MA); *m* 3 July 1974, Astrid Suhr, da of Ernest Suhr Henriksen, of Vancouver, Canada; 2 s (Peter b 21 July 1978, Mark b 24 July 1981), 1 da (Rachel b 1 July 1975); *Career* MAFF: asst princ 1964, private sec to Parly Sec (John Mackie, MP) 1967–69, princ 1969, head of branch Tropical Foods Div 1969–70, seconded as first sec (Agric) FCO Copenhagen 1971–74, private sec to Min of Agric (Fred Peart, MP) 1975–76, head of Euro Community Div 1976–78, seconded as head of Agric Div HM Treasy 1979–80, head of Sugar Oils and Fats Div 1980–84, under sec 1985, seconded as min (Agric) UK Representation to Euro Community 1985–90; dep dir gen (Agric) Euro Commission 1990–; *Recreations* rowing, squash, sailing; *Style—* David Roberts, Esq; ✉ Commission of the European Communities, Rue de la Loi 120, 1040 Brussels

ROBERTS, David John Marling; MC (1965); s of John Edmund Marling Roberts (d 1980), of Checkendon, Oxfordshire, and Jean, *née* Wheelock (d 1988); *b* 6 Feb 1943; *Educ* Marlborough, RMA Sandhurst, Manchester Business Sch; *m* 16 Dec 1967, Nicola Chamberlin; 2 da (Kate (Mrs Harries), Harriet d 1996), 1 s (Mark); *Career* served Army (Green Jackets) 1961–71 (ret as Capt); W H Smith plc: graduate trainee and various positions in gen mgmnt 1971–80, md Wholesale Div 1980–85, md Retail 1985–91 (Main Bd 1988), dep gp md 1991–94, gp md (responsible for distribution and servs) 1994–96; non-exec chm NAAFI 1996– (dir 1993–); non-exec dir: NPI 1993– (chm Remuneration Ctee and memb Audit Ctee 1995–), Stephens Inc Ltd; ind dir W H Smith Pension Trustees Ltd; memb: Exec Cncl Army Benevolent Fund 1988–, Br Retailers' Assoc 1986–91; JP (Berks) 1978–87; CIMgt; *Recreations* country activities, tennis, golf, restoring old houses; *Clubs* Army & Navy, MCC; *Style—* David Roberts, Esq, MC; ✉ NAAFI, London Road, Amesbury, Wilts (☎ 01488 685439, fax 01488 681115)

ROBERTS, Maj-Gen David Michael; s of James Henry Roberts (d 1983), of London, and Agnes Louise Roberts; *b* 9 Sept 1931; *Educ* Emanuel Sch, Royal Free Hosp Sch of Medicine (MB BS, MD); *m* 1964, Angela Louise, da of Capt James Henry Squire, of Herefordshire; 1 s (Justin b 1965), 2 da (Katie b 1966, Eleanor b 1970); *Career* cmmnd RAMC 1955, BAOR 1955–89, hon registrar in med Radcliffe Infirmary Oxford 1960, various med appts in mil hosps 1960–75, graded conslt physician 1968, jt prof of mil med Royal Army Med Coll and Royal Coll of Physicians 1975–81, cmd conslt physician BAOR 1981–84, Dir Army Med and Conslt Physician to the Army 1984–88, MO (Research) MOD 1988–90; lectr in tropical med Middx Hosp Med Sch 1976–81, conslting physician Royal Hosp Chelsea 1984–88; examiner in tropical med RCP 1981–88; QHP 1984–88; published many papers in gastroenterology; Jubilee Medal; FRCP, FRCPE; *Recreations* equestrianism; *Style—* Maj-Gen David Roberts; ✉ Larmer Tree Cottage, Elham Court, Farnham, Dorset

ROBERTS, Denis Edwin; CBE (1974, MBE (Mil) 1945); s of Edwin Roberts (d 1964), of Bromley, Kent, and Alice Gertrude, *née* West (d 1982); *b* 6 Jan 1917; *Educ* Holgate GS Barnsley; *m* 19 Oct 1940, Edith, da of Harry Whitehead (d 1946), of Barnsley Yorks; 2 s (David Harry b 1947, Andrew John b 1950); *Career* Nat Serv WWII Royal Signals 1939–46: France, N Africa, Italy, Austria; PO 1933–80: dir of ops 1971–75, sr dir Postal Servs 1975–77, md posts 1977–80; chm Br Philatelic Tst 1981–85, memb Industl Tbnl 1982–86; Freeman City of London 1978, Liveryman Worshipful Co of Gardeners; *Clubs* City of London, City Livery; *Style—* Denis E Roberts, Esq, CBE; ✉ 302 Gilbert House, Barbican, London EC2Y 8BD (☎ 0171 638 0881)

ROBERTS, Dennis Laurie Harold; s of William Harold Roberts, of Meopham, Kent, and Gwendoline Vera, *née* Edwards; *b* 24 Jan 1949; *Educ* Univ of Sheffield (BA, MSc); *m* 1980, Anne Mary, *née* Hillhouse; 1 s (Edward William b 31 Dec 1985); *Career* civil servant; CSO 1972–76, DOE 1976–83, MOD 1983–85; DOE: head Local Govt Fin Div 1985–89, head Water Environment Div 1989–92, head Fin Div 1992–94; dir of statistics Office of Population Censuses and Surveys 1994–96, gp dir Socio-Economic Statistics Office for Nat Statistics 1996–; memb RSS 1975; *Recreations* walking, reading, watching football; *Style—* Dennis Roberts, Esq; ✉ Office for National Statistics, 1 Drummond Gate (B.3.2), London SW1V 2QQ (☎ 0171 533 6155)

ROBERTS, Hon Mr Justice; Hon Sir Denys Tudor Emil; KBE (1975, CBE 1970, OBE 1960); s of William David Roberts (d 1954), of St Albans; *b* 19 Jan 1923; *Educ* Aldenham, Wadham Coll Oxford (MA, BCL); *m* 1, 1949 (m dis 1973), Brenda Dorothy, da of L Marsh; 1 s, 1 da; m 2, 1985, Anna Fiona Dollar, da of N G A Alexander; 1 s; *Career* WWII serv RA; called to the Bar Lincoln's Inn 1950; barr London 1950–53, crown counsel Nyasaland 1953–59; Gibraltar: QC 1960, attorney-gen 1960–62; Hong Kong: slr-gen 1962–66, QC 1964, attorney-gen 1966–73, chief sec 1973–78, chief justice 1979–88; chief justice Brunei 1979–; memb and pres Ct of Appeal for Bermuda 1988–94; hon bencher Lincoln's Inn 1978, hon fell Wadham Coll 1984; SPMB (Brunei) 1984; pres MCC 1989–90; *Books* Smuggler's Circuit (1954), Beds and Roses (1956), The Elwood Wager (1958), The Bones of the Wajingas (1960), How to Dispense with Lawyers (1964), I'll Do Better Next Time (1995); *Recreations* cricket, tennis, writing, walking; *Clubs* MCC, Hong Kong, Garrick, Royal Commonwealth Soc; *Style—* The Hon Mr Justice Roberts, KBE; ✉ The Supreme Court, Bandar, Seri Begawan, Brunei, Darussalam; 2 Knightsbridge Court, 12 Sloane Street, London SW1X 9LQ

ROBERTS, Prof Derek Frank Bruce; s of Lt-Col Percy Frank Roberts, of St Margarets at Cliffe, and Winifred Caroline, *née* Bromwich; *b* 20 July 1925; *Educ* St Catharine's Coll Cambridge (ScD, MA, Dip), Worcester Coll Oxford (DPhil); *m* Mary Josephine; 4 s (Ralph b 1951, Malcolm b 1954, Vaughan b 1958, Clive b 1961), 2 da (Honor b 1956, Caroline b 1963); *Career* cmmnd Lincolnshire Regt 1943–46; demonstrator Dept of Human Anatomy Oxford 1949–63, prof Univ of Washington Seattle 1963–64, MRC Population Genetics Unit Oxford 1964–65, prof of human genetics Univ of Newcastle upon Tyne and hon conslt to Royal Victoria Infirmary 1965–90 (emeritus prof 1990–); pres Clinical Genetics Soc 1976–78, ed Jl of Biosocial Science 1978–90, pres Euro Anthropological Assoc 1990–93; hon sec: Galton Inst 1974–93, Int Assoc Human Biologists 1980–92; hon treas Int Union of Biological Scis 1985–94; corresponding memb Med Acad of Croatia 1990, hon fell Hungarian Acad of Scis 1993; CBiol, FRSE 1985; *Books* Genetic Variation in Britain (1973), Biology of Human Fetal Growth (1976), Climate and Human Variability (1978), Changing Patterns of Conception and Fertility (1981), Genetic Variation and its Maintenance (1986), Capacity for Work in the Tropics (1988), Molecular Genetics in Medicine - Advances, Applications and Ethical Implications (1991), Minority Populations - Genetics, Demography and Health (1992), Isolation, Migration and Health (1992), Issues in Fetal Medicine (1995); *Recreations* travel, walking; *Style—* Prof Derek Roberts, FRSE; ✉ 17 Montagu Court, Gosforth, Newcastle upon Tyne NE3 4JL (☎ 0191 284 6832, fax 0191 213 1378)

ROBERTS, Derek Franklyn; s of Frank Roberts, MBE (d 1981), of Wirral, Cheshire, and May Evelyn Roberts (d 1991); *b* 16 Oct 1942; *Educ* Park High GS Birkenhead, Liverpool Coll of Commerce, Harvard Business Sch (AMP); *m* 6 Sept 1969, Jacqueline, da of Sylvio Velho; 2 s (Maxwell Franklyn b 9 March 1971, Daniel Downes b 29 Dec 1972), 1 da (Katie Jane b 3 Sept 1976); *Career* Royal Insurance Co Ltd 1961–72; Huddersfield Building Society: insur servs mangr 1972, business devpt mangr 1975, devpt mangr 1979, asst gen mangr (mktg) upon formation of Yorkshire Building Society 1982; Yorkshire Building Society: dir and chief exec 1987–96, chm (designate) 1996–; non-exec dir Yorkshire Water Plc 1996–; FCII, FCIB, CIMgt; *Recreations* golf, gardening, skiing; *Clubs* Royal Liverpool Golf, Huddersfield Golf, Huddersfield RUFC; *Style—* Derek Roberts, Esq; ✉ Yorkshire Building Society, Yorkshire Drive, Bradford, West Yorks (☎ 01274 740740, fax 01274 726366)

ROBERTS, Sir Derek Harry; kt (1995), CBE (1983); s of Harry Roberts (d 1963), of Manchester, and Alice, *née* Storey (d 1973); *b* 28 March 1932; *Educ* Manchester Central HS, Univ of Manchester (BSc); *m* 2 Aug 1958, Winifred, da of James Short (d 1954), of Sheffield; 1 s (Simon b 1964), 1 da (Helen b 1966); *Career* with Plessey Co plc 1953–79; General Electric Co plc: joined as dir of research 1979, main bd dir 1983–93, tech dir 1983–85, jt dep md (tech) 1985–88, non-exec dir 1988–93; non-exec dir Great Universal Stores PLC 1993–; provost UCL 1989–; Freeman Worshipful Co of Goldsmiths 1983; Hon DSc: Univ of Bath 1982, Open Univ 1984, Loughborough Univ of Technol 1984, City Univ 1984, Univ of Lancaster 1986, Univ of Manchester 1987, Univ of Salford 1988, Univ of Essex 1988, Univ of London 1988, Queen's Univ of Belfast 1990; FRS 1980, FEng 1980 (memb Cncl until 1994); *Style—* Sir Derek Roberts, CBE, FRS, FEng; ✉ The Provost, University College London, Gower St, London WC1E 6BT (☎ 0171 380 7234, fax 0171 388 5412)

ROBERTS, Dorothy Elizabeth (Mrs Glen-Doepel); da of Noel Lee Roberts (d 1969), of Sydney, and Myrtle Winifred, *née* Reid (d 1969); *Educ* Methodist Ladies Coll Sydney, Sydney Conservatorium; *m* 1957 (m dis 1969), William Glen-Doepel, s of Otto Glen-Doepel; 1 s (Peter Lee b 1969); *Career* concert pianist; appeared as soloist at venues incl Royal Albert Hall, worked with orchs incl Hallé and Northern Sinfonia, given recitals in London and provinces, Australia, Amsterdam, Paris, Schloss Leitheim Concert Series Germany; known as performer of Clara Schumann tradition; protegée of: Sir John Barbirolli, Sir Malcolm Sargent, Sir Eugene Goossens, Adelina de Lara, OBE; last surviving pupil of Clara Schumann; sold own abstract paintings signed Dorothy Lee Roberts as professional painter to London, NY and provincial galleries; winner Top 70 Art 95 NY (Manhattan Winter); Hon AMusA 1945, Hon LMus 1947; Hon DLitt Univ of Bradford 1995; memb: Friends of Usher Gallery Lincoln, Lincoln Soc, Nat Arts Collection Fund; *Recreations* travel, reading; *Clubs* Royal Over-Seas League; *Style—* Ms Dorothy Roberts; ✉ Alveley House, 17 Lindum Rd, Lincoln LN2 1NS (☎ 01522 520942); Lincoln Fine Art, 33 The Strait, Lincoln LN2 1JD (☎ 01522 533029)

ROBERTS, His Hon Judge (Hugh) Eifion Pritchard; QC (1971), DL (Clwyd 1988); s of Rev Evan Pritchard Roberts, of Anglesey, and Margaret Ann, *née* Jones; *b* 22 Nov 1927; *Educ* Beaumaris GS, UCW Aberystwyth (LLB), Exeter Coll Oxford (BCL); *m* 14 Aug 1958, Buddug, da of Griffith John William; 1 s (Huw b 5 May 1971), 2 da (Siân b 13 March 1967, Rhian b 18 Aug 1969); *Career* flying Offr RAF 1948–50; called to the Bar Gray's Inn 1953, jr barr on Wales and Chester Circuit practising from Chester 1953–71, appointed QC 1971, recorder of the Crown Ct 1971–77, circuit judge (Wales and Chester Circuit) 1977, liaison judge for Clwyd; asst Parly boundary cmmnr for Wales 1967–68, memb Crawford Ctee on Broadcasting Coverage 1973–74, vice pres

UCW Bangor 1991–; *Recreations* gardening, cycling, walking; *Style*— His Hon Judge Eifion Roberts, QC, DL; ✉ Maes-y-Rhedyn, Gresford Rd, Llay, Wrexham, Clwyd (☎ 0197 885 2292)

ROBERTS, Elizabeth Jane (Liz); da of Martin Gwylfa Roberts, of Timperly, Cheshire, and Hilda Elizabeth, *née* Gilbert; *b* 10 June 1960; *Educ* Sale GS for Girls, Univ of Sussex; 1 da (Eve b Nov 1992); *Career* ed asst Phaidon Press 1982–83, Building Magazine 1984–86 (sub editor, chief sub editor); Media Week: broadcast reporter 1986–87, broadcast ed 1987–88, news ed 1988–89, dep ed 1989–90, ed 1990–92; freelance journalist 1993–96: The Guardian, Sunday Telegraph, Esquire, She; features ed Nursery World 1996–; *Recreations* rock climbing, walking, travel, cinema, literature; *Style*— Ms Liz Roberts

ROBERTS, Prof Eric Hywel; s of John Hywel Roberts (d 1942), and Elizabeth Mildred, *née* Ryle; *b* 27 Jan 1930; *Educ* Lucton Sch Herefordshire, Univ of Manchester (BSc, PhD, DSc), Univ of Cambridge; *m* Dorothy Laura, *née* Mollart; 2 s (Peter b 15 March 1961, Ian b 9 Dec 1963); *Career* sr scientific offr W African Rice Res Station Sierra Leone 1955–63, lectr in horticulture Univ of Manchester 1963–68; Univ of Reading: prof of crop prodn 1968–95 (emeritus prof 1996–), head Dept of Agric 1971–75, dean Faculty of Agric and Food 1989–92 (1977–80), pro-vice-chllr 1982–86; author of numerous scientific papers on seeds and plant physiology; FIBiol 1973, FIHort 1987; *Books* Viability of Seeds (1972), Food Production and Consumption (with A N Duckham and J G W Jones, 1976), Recalcitrant Crop Seeds (with H F Chin, 1980), Grain Legume Crops (with R J Summerfield, 1985); *Recreations* sailing; *Style*— Prof Eric Roberts; ✉ c/o Department of Agriculture, University of Reading, PO Box 236, Earley Gate, Reading RG6 6AT (☎ 0118 931 8475, telex 847813)

ROBERTS, Sir Frank Kenyon; GCMG (1963, KCMG 1953, CMG 1946), GCVO (1965); s of Henry George Roberts, of Preston, and Gertrude, *née* Kenyon; *b* 27 Oct 1907, Buenos Aires; *Educ* Bedales, Rugby, Trinity Coll Cambridge; *m* 1937, Celeste Leila (Cella) Beatrix (d 1990), da of Sir Said Shoucair Pasha, of Cairo, sometime financial advsr to Sudan Govt; *Career* entered FO 1930, serv Paris, Cairo, and as Br min Moscow 1945–47, princ private sec to Foreign Sec 1947–49, dep high cmmr India 1949–51, dep under sec FO 1951–54, ambass Yugoslavia 1954–57, UK perm rep N Atlantic Cncl 1957–60; ambass: USSR 1960–62, W Germany 1963–68; dir: Hoechst UK, Daimler-Benz, Amalgamated Metal Corp until 1990; vice pres Br-Atlantic Ctee (pres 1968–81), vice pres Euro-Atlantic Group (formerly president and chm), patron Atlantic Treaty Assoc (pres 1969–73), pres Anglo-German Assoc; vice pres: Britain-Russia Centre, British-German Chamber of Commerce UK (formerly pres); German Order of Merit 1965; Hon LLD Manchester 1991; *Clubs* Brooks', RAC; *Style*— Sir Frank Roberts, GCMG, GCVO; ✉ 25 Kensington Court Gardens, London W8 5QF (☎ 0171 937 1140)

ROBERTS, Prof Gareth Gwyn; s of Edwin Roberts (d 1974), of Penmaenmawr, N Wales, and Meri, *née* Jones (d 1959); *b* 16 May 1940; *Educ* John Bright GS Llandudno, Univ Coll of N Wales Bangor (BSc, PhD, DSc); *m* 1, (m dis); 2 s (Peris, Daron), 1 da (Bronwen); m 2, Feb 1994, Carolyn Mary, *née* Butler; *Career* lectr Univ Coll of N Wales 1963–66, res scientist Xerox Corp Rochester NY 1966–68, prof of physics New Univ of Ulster Coleraine 1968–76, prof of applied physics Univ of Durham 1976–85, fell Brasenose Coll and visiting prof of electronic engrg Univ of Oxford 1985–, dir of res Thorn EMI plc 1985–90, vice chancellor Univ of Sheffield 1991–, chm Defence Scientific Advisory Cncl 1993–; Holweck Gold Medal and Prize 1986, Royal Inst/BBC Christmas Lectures 1988; author of 200 articles and patents; ed Jl of Molecular Electronics; memb: Univ Funding Cncl 1989–91, SERC Ctees, Royal Soc Ctees, Bd Sheffield Devpt Corp 1992–, Bd Defence Evaluation and Research Agency (DERA) 1995–; chm CVCP 1995–; govr Wellington Coll 1993–; Hon MA Oxford 1987, Hon LLD Univ of Wales 1990; FRS 1984, FInstP 1972, FIEE 1974; *Books* Insulating Films on Semiconductors (1979), Langmuir - Blodgett Films (1990); *Recreations* soccer, duplicate bridge, classical music; *Style*— Prof Gareth Roberts, FRS; ✉ The University of Sheffield, PO Box 594, Firth Court, Western Bank, Sheffield S10 2UH (☎ 0114 276 8555, fax 0114 272 7407)

ROBERTS, Prof Geoffrey Frank Ingleson; CBE (1978); s of Arthur Reginald Wilfred Roberts (d 1959), of Venns Lane, Hereford, and Laura, *née* Ingleson (d 1971); *b* 9 May 1926; *Educ* Hereford Cathedral Sch, HS for Boys Hereford, Univ of Leeds (BSc); *m* 14 Sept 1949, Veronica (d 1993), da of Capt John Busby, MN (d 1952); 2 da (Lesley Jane b 1952, Ellice Catherine b 1955); m 2, 19 May 1995, Patricia, wid of Neville Johnson; *Career* dep dir (ops) Gas Cncl 1968–71; Gas Cncl and Br Gas Corpn: memb prodn and supply 1972–78, memb external affrs 1979–81, ret 1988; chm Br Pipe Coaters, conslt prof of gas engrg Univ of Salford 1983–91; FEng 1978; *Recreations* reading, DIY, gardening, caravan touring; *Style*— Prof Geoffrey Roberts, CBE, FEng; ✉ 2 Birchwood Court, South Parade, Ilkley, West Yorkshire LS29 9AW (☎ 01943 601671)

ROBERTS, Sir Gilbert Howland Rookehurst; 7 Bt (UK 1809), of Glassenbury, Kent, of Brightfieldstown, Co Cork and of the City of Cork; s of Col Sir Thomas Langdon Howland Roberts, CBE, 6 Bt (d 1979), and (Evelyn) Margaret, *née* Fielding-Hall (d 1992); *b* 31 May 1934; *Educ* Rugby, Gonville and Caius Coll Cambridge (BA); *m* 1958, Ines Eleonore, o da of late Alfons Leo Labunski, of Danzig; 1 s, 1 da; *Heir* s, Howland Langdon Roberts b 19 Aug 1961; *Career* serv Kenya with RE (E African GS medal); MIMechE; *Style*— Sir Gilbert Roberts, Bt; ✉ 3340 Cliff Drive, Santa Barbara, Calif 93109–1079, USA

ROBERTS, (David Edward) Glyn; s of David Emlyn Roberts (d 1975), and Henrietta Liston, *née* Griffiths; *b* 29 Feb 1932; *Educ* Calday Grange GS; *m* 1, 13 Oct 1955, Beryl Shelia Price (d 1968); 3 da (Deborah Mary, Angela Margeret, Ruth Alexandra); m 2, 11 Aug 1972, Elizabeth Mary, *née* Grimwade; 2 step s (Adrian Edward Ainsworth Thorn, Richard Charles Ainsworth), 1 da (Patricia); *Career* Nat Serv 2 Lt RA 1955–57; actuary Royal Insur Co 1949–61; stockbroker: Tilney and Co 1961–74, Roberts and Huish 1974–85, Ashton Tod McLaren 1985–88; md Quilter Goodison 1988–92 (dep chm 1992–96); FIA 1955, FCII 1959, memb Stock Exchange; *Style*— Glyn Roberts, Esq; ✉ Breiry Mount, Briery Close, Holbeck Lane, Windermere, Cumbria LA23 1NB (☎ 01539 432047)

ROBERTS, Sir Gordon James; kt (1984), CBE (1975), JP (Northants 1952), DL (Northants 1984); s of Archie Roberts (d 1963), of Deanshanger, Milton Keynes, and Lily, *née* Maycock (d 1979); *b* 30 Jan 1921; *Educ* Deanshanger Sch Northants; *m* 1944, Barbara, da of Geoffrey Leach (d 1961), of Haversham, Milton Keynes; 1 s (Adrian), 1 da (Diane); *Career* ldr Northants CC 1974–77, dep chm Cmmn for the New Towns 1978–82 (memb Bd 1978–90); chm: Northants AHA 1973–78, Oxford RHA 1978–90, RHA Chairmen 1982–84, Computer Policy Ctee NHS 1981–84, Supervisory Bd Mgmnt Advsy Serv NHS 1982–86; High Sheriff Northamptonshire 1989–90, pres Br Red Cross (Northants Branch) 1990–92; memb Ct of Govrs Nene Coll Northampton 1995–; FRSA; *Recreations* local history, reading, walking; *Style*— Sir Gordon Roberts, CBE, JP, DL; ✉ 114 Ridgmont, Deanshanger, Milton Keynes, Bucks MK19 6JG (☎ 01908 562605)

ROBERTS, (David) Gwilym Morris; CBE (1987); s of Edward Humphrey Roberts (d 1949), of Crosby, Merseyside, and Edith, *née* Roberts (d 1983); *b* 24 July 1925; *Educ* Merchant Taylors' Crosby, Sidney Sussex Coll Cambridge (BA, MA); *m* 1, 16 Oct 1960, Rosemary Elizabeth Emily (d 1973), da of John Edmund Giles (d 1971), of Tavistock, Devon; 1 s ((Edward) Matthew Giles b 1963), 1 da (Annabel Elizabeth Giles b 1967); m 2, 14 Oct 1978, Wendy Ann, da of Dr John King Moore (d 1975), of Beckenham, Kent; *Career* Lt Cdr RNR, ret 1961; chartered civil engr; sr ptnr John Taylor and Sons 1981–90 (ptnr 1956–90), dir Thomas Telford Ltd 1983–89; chm: Acer Group Ltd 1987–92, Prog Bd BGS 1989–93, Football Stadia Advsy Design Cncl 1990–93, Westmeston Parish Cncl 1990– (memb 1983–), Second Severn Crossing Tech Adjudication Panel 1992–; visiting prof Loughborough Univ of Technol 1991–95; hon fell Sidney Sussex Coll Cambridge 1994–, pres ICE 1986–87; memb Cncl: NERC 1987–93, Brighton Poly 1983–86; govr: Chailey Sch 1987–92, Roedean Sch 1987–93; Liveryman: Worshipful Co of Engrs, Worshipful Co of Constructors, Co of Water Conservators; Freeman City of London; FEng 1986; *Recreations* tennis, golf, local history; *Clubs* United Oxford and Cambridge Univ, MCC, Piltdown Golf; *Style*— Gwilym Roberts, Esq, CBE, FEng; ✉ North America Farm, Hundred Acre Lane, Westmeston, Hassocks, Sussex BN6 8SH (☎ 01273 890010, fax 01273 890991)

ROBERTS, Dr Howard Frederick; s of William Frederick John Roberts (d 1985), of Wallington, Surrey, and Hilda Gertrude, *née* Ward; *b* 7 Jan 1937; *Educ* Univ of London (MB BS, MPhil, MRCP); *m* 22 Aug 1981, Judith Margaret, da of William Bertram Wilson (d 1994), of Rowledge, Surrey; 3 da (Henrietta b 1983, Lucinda b 1985, Georgina b 1987); *Career* conslt child and adolescent psychiatrist St Thomas' Hosp; assoc memb Br Psycho Analytical Soc 1985; MRCPsych 1974; *Style*— Dr Howard Roberts; ✉ 73 Onslow Gardens, London N10 3JY (☎ 0181 883 7473); St Thomas' Hospital, London SE1 (☎ 0171 793 7113)

ROBERTS, Howland Langdon; s and h of Sir Gilbert Roberts, 7 Bt, *qv*; *b* 19 Aug 1961; *Style*— Howland Roberts, Esq; ✉ Dooish, Ballybofey, Co Donegal, Ireland (☎ 011 44 74 32596)

ROBERTS, Hugh Ashley; LVO (1995); s of Rt Rev Dr Edward Roberts, and Dorothy Frances, *née* Bowser (d 1982); *b* 20 April 1948; *Educ* Winchester, Corpus Christi Coll Cambridge (MA); *m* 13 Dec 1975, Hon (Priscilla) Jane Stephanie Low, see Hon Mrs Roberts, LVO, er da of 1 Baron Aldington, KCMG, CBE, DSO, TD, PC, DL, *qv*; 2 da (Sophie b 1978, Amelia b 1982); *Career* Christie Manson & Woods Ltd 1970–87 (dir 1978–87); dep surveyor of The Queen's Works of Art 1988–96, dir of the Royal Collection and Surveyor of The Queen's Works of Art 1996–; FSA; *Recreations* gardening; *Style*— Hugh Roberts, Esq, LVO, FSA; ✉ Adelaide Cottage, Home Park, Windsor, Berks (☎ 01753 855581)

ROBERTS, Humphrey Richard Medwyn; s of Hugh Medwyn Roberts (d 1961), of Southport, Lancs, and Enid Marjorie, *née* Pochin (d 1987); *b* 29 May 1931; *Educ* Leas Sch Hoylake, Aldenham Sch, King's Coll Cambridge (BA, MA), Westminster Med Sch (MB BChir, Bulkeley medal, Arthur Evans prize); *m* 21 March 1964, Pamela Ruth, da of Robert Barker; 1 s (James Hugh Medwyn b 28 June 1969), 2 da (Caroline Jane Medwyn b 1 Aug 1965, Katharine Lucy Medwyn b 29 June 1967); *Career* sr house offr Chelsea Hosp for Women 1963–64, res obstetrician Queen Charlotte's Hosp 1966–67, conslt obstetrician and gynaecologist Queen Mary's Hosp Roehampton 1968–79; Westminster Hosp: house surgn 1957–58, res obstetric asst 1958, registrar in obstetrics and gynaecology 1964–66, conslt obstetrician and gynaecologist 1968–91; hon conslt gynaecologist: Hosp of St John and Elizabeth 1971–80, St Luke's Hosp for Clergy 1986–96; examiner: obstetrics and gynaecology Univs of Cambridge and London, diploma and membership RCOG, Central Midwives Bd; memb: BMA 1957, Medical Def Union 1957, Hospital Conslt and Staff Assoc 1982, Chelsea Clinical Soc 1979 (pres 1993–94); FRCS (Eng) 1961, FRCOG 1978 (MRCOG 1965); *Recreations* Sherlock Holmes, birdwatching, gardening; *Style*— Humphrey Roberts, Esq; ✉ 64 Chartfield Avenue, London SW15 6HQ (☎ 0181 789 1758)

ROBERTS, (Thomas) Ian; s of Thomas Ormerod Roberts, of Settle, N Yorks, and Joan, *née* Bilsborough; *b* 8 Nov 1956; *Educ* Giggleswick, The Queen's Coll Oxford (BA, MA); *Career* admitted slr 1982; ptnr Booth & Co 1988–92 (joined 1982, assoc 1986), ptnr Irwin Mitchell 1992–; sec: Yorkshire Glass Manufacturers' Assoc 1983–88, Yorkshire Young Slrs Gp 1982–88 (memb Ctee 1985–88); memb: Law Soc, Sheffield Law Soc; north area rep Legal Educn and Trg Gp 1993–93, business govr The Sheffield Coll 1993–; dir Kaye & Co (Huddersfield) Ltd 1989–; hon sec Old Giggleswickians' Club 1995–; life memb Nat Tst and English Heritage; *Books* A Walk Round Stackhouse (1979); *Recreations* genealogy, local history, long case clocks, fives; *Clubs* Jesters, Rugby Fives Association; *Style*— Ian Roberts, Esq; ✉ Irwin Mitchell, St Peter's House, Hartshead, Sheffield S1 2EL (☎ 0114 276 7777, fax 0114 275 3306)

ROBERTS, HE Ivor Anthony; s of Leonard Moore Roberts (d 1981), and Rosa Maria, *née* Fusco; *b* 24 Sept 1946; *Educ* St Mary's Coll Crosby, Keble Coll Oxford (Gomm scholar, BA, MA); *m* 4 May 1974, Elizabeth Bray, da of Norman Douglas Bernard Smith, of Stanstead Hall, Halstead, Essex; 2 s (Huw Benedict Bernard b 1976, David Daniel Rowland b 1979), 1 da (Hannah Rebecca Louise b 1982); *Career* HM Dip Serv: joined 1968, ME Centre for Arabic Studies 1969, third then second sec Paris 1970–73, second then first sec FCO 1973–78, first sec Canberra 1978–82, dep head News Dept FCO 1982–86, head Security Co-ordination Dept FCO 1986–88, minister Br Embassy Madrid 1989–93, HM ambass Br Embassy Belgrade 1996– (chargé d'affaires 1994–96); fell Inst of Linguists; *Recreations* opera, skiing, golf; *Clubs* United Oxford & Cambridge University, Downhill Only Club Wengen; *Style*— HE Mr Ivor Anthony Roberts, CMG; ✉ c/o British Embassy, Belgrade (☎ 00 381 11 645 055, fax 00 381 11 659 651); c/o Foreign & Commonwealth Office (Belgrade), King Charles Street, London SW1A 2AH (☎ 0171 270 2063, fax 0171 839 2417)

ROBERTS, Hon Mrs (Priscilla) Jane Stephanie; *née* Low; LVO (1995, MVO 1985); da of 1 Baron Aldington, KCMG, CBE, DSO, TD, PC, DL, *qv*, and Araminta, *née* MacMichael; sis of Hon Charles Low, *qv*; *b* 4 Sept 1949; *Educ* Cranborne Chase, Westfield Coll London, Courtauld Inst of Art London; *m* 1975, Hugh Ashley Roberts, LVO, FSA, *qv*, s of Rt Rev Dr Edward Roberts, sometime Bishop of Ely; 2 da (Sophie Jane Cecilia b 28 March 1978, Amelia Frances Albinia b 8 Feb 1982); *Career* curator of the Print Room Royal Library Windsor Castle 1975–; *Books* Holbein (1979), Royal Artists (1987); *Exhibition Catalogues* Master Drawings in the Royal Collection (1985), Leonardo Da Vinci (1989), A King's Purchase (1993), Holbein and the Court of Henry VIII (1993), Views of Windsor: Watercolours by Thomas and Paul Sandby (1995); *Recreations* piano playing, singing, sewing; *Style*— The Hon Mrs Roberts, LVO; ✉ Adelaide Cottage, Home Park, Windsor, Berkshire SL4 2JQ (☎ 01753 855581); Royal Library, Windsor Castle, Windsor, Berkshire SL4 1NJ (☎ 01753 868286, fax 01753 854910)

ROBERTS, Jeremy Michael Graham; QC (1982); s of Lt-Col John Michael Harold Roberts (d 1954), and Eileen Dora, *née* Chaplin; *b* 26 April 1941; *Educ* Winchester, Brasenose Coll Oxford (BA); *m* 25 July 1964, Sally Priscilla, da of Col Frederick Peter Johnson, OBE, of Hants; *Career* called to the Bar Inner Temple 1965, recorder of the Crown Court 1981–; bencher 1992; *Recreations* theatre, opera, reading, horse and dog racing, canals; *Style*— Jeremy Roberts, Esq, QC; ✉ 9 Gough Square, London EC4A 3DE (☎ 0171 353 5371, fax 0171 353 1344)

ROBERTS, (Anthony) John; CBE (1991); s of Leonard Douglas Treeweek Roberts, of Tavistock, Devon, and Margaret, *née* Long; *b* 26 Aug 1944; *Educ* Hampton Sch, Univ of Exeter (BA); *m* 3 Oct 1970, Diana June, da of Norman George Lamdin, of Bexhill-on-Sea, Sussex; 2 s (Ian, Neil); *Career* The Post Office: various posts incl PA to chief exec 1967–74, regnl memb Bd for Personnel & Fin 1974–76, dir Chm's Office 1976–80, sec of the PO 1980–82, dir Counter Services 1982–85, md Post Office Counters Ltd 1985–93 (chm 1993–), chm Post Office Finance Ltd 1990–, chm Subscription Services Ltd 1993–, md gp services 1993–95, chief exec 1995–; memb: Govt Assessors' Ctee on TECs 1993–, Cncl Inst of Employment Studies 1995–, Bd Br Quality Fndn 1996–; govr Henley Mgmnt Coll 1996–; Freeman City of London 1982; CIMgt 1986; *Recreations* watching rugby, squash, reading, music; *Clubs* Betchworth Park Golf, Oxshott Squash; *Style*— John Roberts, Esq, CBE; ✉ The Post Office, 148 Old Street, London EC1V 9HQ (☎ 0171 250 2500)

ROBERTS, John Anthony; s of Walter Ben Roberts (d 1978), of Kirk Hammerton, Yorks, and Betty Joyce, *née* England; *b* 3 Dec 1940; *Educ* Harrow; *m* 9 Sept 1972, Margaret Mary, da of Maurice Houdmont, of Sheffield; 1 s (Piers b 1980), 2 da (Tabitha b 1973, Alexandra b 1975); *Career* HAC 1961–64; CA; articled clerk Mellors Basden & Co 1959–64; ptnr Coopers & Lybrand 1964–; memb: Trent Business Sch Advsy Ctee, Notts & Derby Inst of Dirs' Ctee, Bd Prince's Youth Business Tst (Nottingham area); pres: Notts Soc of CAs 1983–84, Farnsfield Horticultural Soc 1987–88; chm Friends of the Turf 1994–95; FCA 1964; *Recreations* wine, food, travel, music; *Clubs* Nottinghamshire United Services; *Style*— John Roberts, Esq; ✉ The Old Vicarage, Farnsfield, Nottinghamshire (☎ 01623 882 835); Coopers & Lybrand, Cumberland House, 35 Park Row, Nottingham NG1 6FY (☎ 0115 950 3500, fax 0115 947 0862)

ROBERTS, John Anthony; s of John Owen Roberts (d 1985), and Elsie Edna May, *née* Leese (d 1994); *b* 12 Feb 1941; *Educ* Avondale Secdy Sch Stockport, Stockport Jr Commercial Sch; *m* 2 Sept 1967, Philomena Mary Therese, da of Christopher Thomas Coyne; 2 s (Christopher b 26 Oct 1971, Gerard b 30 Aug 1978), 1 da (Leanne b 5 Sept 1974); *Career* reporter Stockport Express 1958–62 (sports ed 1960–62); sports reporter: The Daily Express Manchester 1965–78 (sports sub-ed 1962–65), The Guardian 1978–80; sports feature writer The Daily Mail 1981–86, tennis corr and dep chief sports writer The Independent 1986– (football corr 1991); NW Sports Journalist of the Year 1987; memb: Football Writers' Assoc, Lawn Tennis Writers' Assoc; *Books* George Best - Fall of a Superstar (1973), The Team That Wouldn't Die (The Story of the Busby Babes) (1975), Official Centenary History of Everton (1978); ghosted autobiographies: Bill Shankly (1976), Kevin Keegan (1977); *Style*— John Roberts, Esq; ✉ 1 Bath Crescent, Cheadle Hulme, Cheshire SK8 7QU (fax 0161 439 3097); The Independent, 1 Canada Square, Canary Wharf, London E14 5DL (☎ 0171 293 2000, fax 0171 293 2435)

ROBERTS, John Charles Quentin; s of late Hubert C Roberts, of Binsted, Sussex; *b* 4 April 1933; *Educ* King Coll Taunton, Univ of London (CSC Interpretership), Merton Coll Oxford (MA); *m* 1, 1959 (m dis 1979), Dinah, da of late Maj Trevor Webster-Williams, TD (d 1987), of Cheltenham; 1 da (Gwen b 1960), 1 s (Stephen b 1963); m 2, 1982, Elizabeth, *née* Gough-Cooper; 2 step da (Abigail b 1970, Eloise b 1971); *Career* Nat Serv Intelligence Offr RAF 1951–53; Shell International Petroleum Co (various mgmnt posts in Europe and Africa) 1956–61, asst master Marlborough 1963–73, dir The Britain-Russia Centre (formerly The Great Britain-USSR Assoc) 1974–93; memb: Cncl Sch of Slavonic and E Euro Studies Univ of London 1981–92, chm of tstees State Library for Foreign Lit Moscow 1994–; *Recreations* music, family, gardening; *Clubs* Athenaeum, Special Forces; *Style*— John Roberts, Esq; ✉ 52 Paultons Square, London SW3 5DT (☎ 0171 352 3882); Croodedstane Rig, Elvanfoot, Biggar, Lanarkshire ML12 6TJ (☎ 01864 505233)

ROBERTS, John Frederick; *b* 30 March 1946; *Educ* Bristol GS, Univ of Bristol (BDS), Eastman Dental Center Rochester NY (Cert in Paedodontics); *m* Gabriele Elizabeth; 2 s (Alexander John b 14 Oct 1979, Sebastian Frederick b 24 March 1983); *Career* house offr Bristol Dental Hosp 1971, assoc in gen dental practice Bristol 1972–74, princ in gen dental practice Johannesburg 1974–76, sr ptnr private paedodontic practice London 1978–, sr demonstrator Dept of Orthodontics and Dentistry for Children UMDS Guy's Hosp; recognized teacher status in paediatrics Univ of London Faculty of Med and Dentistry 1990–; numerous invited lectures and courses UK and abroad; memb: BDA, Br Soc of Paediatric Dentistry, American Acad of Paedodontics, American Soc of Dentistry for Children, American Dental Soc of London, American Bd of Paedodontics, Euro Acad of Paediatric Dentistry; *Publications* Kennedy's Paediatric Dentistry (co-author); author of various articles in Br Dental Jl; *Style*— John Roberts, Esq; ✉ 74 Bois Lane, Amersham, Bucks HP6 6BX (☎ 01494 725685); 33 Weymouth St, London W1N 3FL (☎ 0171 580 5370, fax 0171 636 3094)

ROBERTS, His Hon Judge John Houghton; s of John Noel Roberts, and Ida, *née* Houghton; *b* 14 Dec 1947; *Educ* Calday Grange GS, Trinity Hall Cambridge (MA); *m* 1, 1972 (m dis 1990), Anna Elizabeth, da of Peter Tooke Sheppard, of Essex; 3 s (James b 1974, Edward b 1976, William b 1978); m 2, 20 April 1991, Janice Mary, da of Frederick Wilkinson, of Blundellsands; *Career* called to the Bar Middle Temple 1970; recorder of the Crown Ct 1988–93, circuit judge (Northern Circuit) 1993–; *Recreations* golf, rugby football, music; *Clubs* Athenaeum (Liverpool), Heswall Golf, Birkenhead Park FC; *Style*— His Hon Judge John Roberts; ✉ Manchester Crown Court, Crown Square, Manchester

ROBERTS, John Leonard; s of Maj Robert Edward Roberts, and Dorothea, *née* Goodchild; *b* 19 Jan 1939; *m* 22 Oct 1963, Gillian Lesley, da of Leslie Low; 1 s (Alexander b 12 Dec 1972); *Career* reporter; sub ed and dir City Press 1957–63, fin ed Thomson Newspapers 1963–67, exec Minster Tst 1967–68, asst ed Investors' Chronicle 1968–73, City ed Daily Express 1974–76, freelance business journalist and broadcaster BBC Radio 4 and World Serv 1976–91; ed The International Broker 1992; chm Capital Counsel; vice-pres Citibank; award for business journalism for Men in the Middle 1977; *Books* Megalomania, Managers and Mergers (1987), $1,000 Billion a Day (1995); *Recreations* gardening; *Style*— John Roberts, Esq; ✉ Old Bartholmy Brooms, Sundridge, Kent TN14 6AR (☎ 01959 563677, fax 01959 561805)

ROBERTS, John Lewis; CMG (1987); s of Thomas Hubert Roberts (d 1971), of Danygraig, Ynysmeudwy, Pontardawe, Swansea, and Hannah Meudwen, *née* Lewis (d 1968); *b* 21 April 1928; *Educ* Pontardawe GS, Trinity Hall Cambridge (BA); *m* 5 Dec 1952, Maureen Jocelyn, da of Lt-Col Denis Moriarty, IA (d 1985), of Eastbourne, Sussex; 2 s (Patrick Gereint b 4 Sept 1954, David Gareth b 31 Oct 1957); *Career* 2 Lt RA 1948–50; joined Miny of Civil Aviation 1950, private sec to Parly sec for Civil Aviation 1954–56, civil air attaché Br Embassy Bonn 1959–62, def supply cnsllr Br Embassy Paris 1966–69; asst under sec of state for: Def Sales 1975–77, Air Dept (Personnel) 1977–79, Industl and Int Policy 1982–88; memb Electronics Indust NEDC 1982–84; memb: Richmond Soc, Richmond Hist Soc, Richmond Archeological Soc; FRSA 1988; *Recreations* sailing, fly fishing, gardening; *Clubs* Piscatorial Soc; *Style*— John Roberts, Esq, CMG

ROBERTS, Dr John Morris; CBE (1996); s of Edward Henry Roberts (d 1969), and Dorothy Julia Roberts (d 1963); *b* 14 April 1928; *Educ* Taunton Sch, Keble Coll Oxford (BA, MA, DPhil); *m* 29 Aug 1964, Judith Cecilia Mary, da of late Rev James Armitage; *Career* Nat Serv 1949–50; prize fell Magdalen Coll Oxford 1951–53, Cwlth Fund fell Princeton and Yale 1953–54, ed English History Review 1967–77, vice chllr Univ of Southampton 1979–85, warden Merton Coll Oxford 1984–94 (fell and tutor 1953–79, hon fell 1980), presenter TV series The Triumph of The West 1985, gov BBC 1988–93; sec Harmsworth Tst 1962–68, memb Gen Ctee Royal Literary Fund 1975–, cncl pres Taunton Sch 1978–88, cncl memb Euro Univ Inst 1980–88, memb US and UK Educn Cmmn 1981–88, tstee Nat Portrait Gallery 1984–, Rhodes tstee 1988–95, memb Bd of Br Cncl 1991–; Hon DLitt Southampton 1987; FRHistS; *Books* French Revolution Documents (1966), Europe 1880–1945 (1967, new edn 1992), The Mythology of the Secret Societies (1972), The Paris Commune from the Right (1974), The Age of Revolution and Improvement (1975), History of the World (1976, 3rd edn 1993), The French Revolution (1978), Illustrated History of the World (1980), The Triumph of the West (1985), Shorter Illustrated History of the World (1993), A History of Europe (1996); numerous articles in academic jls; *Recreations* music; *Clubs* Groucho, Reform, United Oxford & Cambridge Univ; *Style*— Dr John Roberts, CBE; ✉ c/o Merton College, Oxford, OX1 4JD

ROBERTS, (Richard) Julian; s of Albert Reginald Roberts (d 1970), of Birmingham, and Kate Marjorie Scudamore-Roberts (d 1976); *b* 18 May 1930; *Educ* King Edward's Sch Birmingham, Magdalen Coll Oxford (MA); *m* 27 April 1957, Anne, da of Henry Bedford Ducé (d 1968), of Cardiff; 1 s (Alun b 1965), 1 da (Hilary b 1962); *Career* asst keeper Br Museum 1958–74, dep librarian Bodleian Library Oxford 1985– (keeper of printed books 1974–); fell Wolfson Coll Oxford 1975 (vicegerent 1983–85), Regents' prof Univ of Calif Los Angeles 1991; pres Bibliographical Soc 1986–88 (sec 1961–81), associate of Library Assoc; FSA; *Books* Beauty in Raggs: Poems by Cardell Goodman (ed, 1958), John Dee's Library Catalogue (with A G Watson, 1990); *Recreations* antiquarianism, natural history, fell walking; *Style*— Julian Roberts, Esq, FSA; ✉ St John's Farm House, Tackley, Oxford OX5 3AT (☎ 01865 277021, fax 01865 277182)

ROBERTS, Keith John Kingston; *b* 20 Sept 1935; *Educ* Kettering GS, Northampton Sch of Art (NDD); *Career* writer; gen work in advtg 1960–64, freelance assoc with Science Fantasy Magazine 1964–66, asst ed then gen ed SF Impulse 1966; *Books* The Chalk Giants (1974), Molly Zero (1980), Kiteworld (1985), Kaeti & Company (1985, best short story Br Sci Fiction Assoc 1986, year's best artwork BSFA 1986), Grainne (1987, year's best novel BSFA), The Road to Paradise, Winterwood and Other Hauntings, Kaeti on Tour (1992); *Style*— Keith Roberts, Esq; ✉ 25 Essex Square, West Harnham, Salisbury, Wiltshire SP2 8JA (☎ 01722 324134); George H Scithers, Owlswick Literary Agency, 113 Deepdale Road, Strafford PA 19087, USA (☎ 00 1 215 275 4463, fax 00 1 215 688 2887)

ROBERTS, Prof Kenneth; s of Ernest William Roberts, and Nancy, *née* Williams; *b* 24 Sept 1940; *Educ* Stockport Sch, LSE (BSc, MSc); *m* 8 Aug 1964, Patricia, da of Frank Newton, of Macclesfield; 1 s (Gavin Paul b 19 Feb 1968), 2 da (Susan Alexis b 18 Dec 1970, Vanessa Jane (twin) b 19 Dec 1970); *Career* successively asst lectr, sr lectr, reader then prof Univ of Liverpool 1966–; memb: Br Sociological Assoc, Int Sociological Assoc, Euro Sociological Assoc, Leisure Studies Assoc, Inst of Careers Guidance; *Books* Youth and Leisure (1983), The Changing Structure of Youth Labour Markets (1987), Leisure and Lifestyle (1989), Youth and Work (1991), Careers and Identities (1992), Youth and Employment in Modern Britain (1995), Poland's First Post-Communist Generation (1995); *Style*— Prof Kenneth Roberts; ✉ 2 County Rd, Ormskirk, Lancs L39 1QQ (☎ 01695 574962); Sociology Dept, Univ of Liverpool, PO Box 147, Liverpool L79 3BX (☎ 0151 794 2971)

ROBERTS, Malcolm John Binyon; s of Sqdn Ldr Kenneth Arthur Norman Roberts (d 1973), and Greta Kathleen, *née* Cooper; *b* 3 July 1951; *Educ* St Edmund's Sch Canterbury; *m* 28 April 1984, Caroline Mary, da of John Harry Scrutton; 2 s (Frederick, Charles), 1 da (Iona); *Career* ptnr Montagu Loebl Stanley 1979–86, dir Fleming Private Asset Management 1986–; memb Stock Exchange 1978; govr Granville Sch Sevenoaks 1986–, tstee Moorfields Eye Hosp 1996–; Liveryman Worshipful Co of Barbers; *Recreations* tennis, golf, planting trees; *Clubs* City; *Style*— Malcolm Roberts, Esq; ✉ Hillsmead, Godden Green, Sevenoaks, Kent TN15 0JR; Fleming Private Asset Management, 20 Finsbury Street, London EC2Y 9AQ (☎ 0171 814 2814)

ROBERTS, Martin Charles; s of Denis Walter Wakem Roberts (d 1988), of Epsom, Surrey, and Joan Mary, *née* Saunders; *b* 11 April 1955; *Educ* City of London Freemen's, Univ of Kingston upon Thames (BA), Guildford Law Sch; *m* 3 Sept 1988, Jane Rosalind, da of John Henderson; 1 s (James William b 27 Sept 1992), 1 da (Georgina Rosalind b 5 Sept 1994); *Career* Masons: articled clerk 1977–79, asst slr 1979–83, ptnr 1983–, memb Partnership Bd 1992–, dep head Construction and Engineering Law Dept 1994–; Freeman City of London 1975, Liveryman City of London Slrs' Co 1985; memb: Law Soc 1977, City of London Law Soc 1985 (ctee memb Litigation Sub Ctee 1991–); *Recreations* tennis, swimming, music, theatre, cinema; *Clubs* RAC, Harlequins RFC; *Style*— Martin Roberts, Esq; ✉ Masons, 30 Aylesbury Street, London EC1R 0ER (☎ 0171 490 4000, fax 0171 490 2545)

ROBERTS, Martin John Dickin; s of John Kenneth Dickin Roberts (d 1990), of Chester, and Iris Ruth, *née* Bond (d 1970); *Educ* Shrewsbury, Trinity Hall Cambridge (MA); *m* 26 Sept 1970, Ruth, da of Frank Packard (d 1982); 3 da (Anne b 1972, Sarah b 1975, Catheryn b 1985); *Career* admitted slr 1969; ptnr Slaughter and May 1975–; Freeman Worshipful Co of Slrs; memb Law Soc; *Recreations* spectator sports, boating, golf, reading; *Clubs* RAC; *Style*— Martin Roberts, Esq; ✉ Arbourne, Copsem Lane, Esher, Surrey KT10 9HE (☎ 01372 465252); Slaughter & May, 35 Basinghall Street, London EC2V 5DB (☎ 0171 600 1200)

ROBERTS, Rev Michael Graham Vernon; s of Walter Graham Southall Roberts (d 1960), and Pamela Middleton, *née* Abel; *b* 4 Aug 1943; *Educ* Eton, Keble Coll Oxford (MA), Cuddesdon Coll Oxford, Church Divinity Sch of the Pacific Berkeley Calif (BD); *m* 1 Aug 1970, Susan Elizabeth, da of Stanley Marcus Merry; 1 s (Benjamin b 1 Jan 1972), 2 da (Kate b 13 June 1973, Rebecca b 16 June 1974); *Career* curate Exmouth-cum-Littleham 1967–70, chaplain Clare Coll Cambridge 1970–74, vicar St Mark Bromley Kent 1974–79, tutor Queen's Coll Birmingham 1979–85, team rector High Wycombe 1985–90, princ Westcott House Cambridge 1994– (vice princ and dir of pastoral studies 1990–93); *Style*— The Rev Michael Roberts; ✉ Principal's Lodge, Westcott House, Jesus Lane, Cambridge CB5 8BP (☎ 01223 321475, fax 01223 301512, office 01223 350074)

ROBERTS, Michael Victor; s of Ernest Alfred Roberts (d 1990), of Waltham Abbey, Essex, and Lilian May, *née* Piper (d 1979); *b* 23 Sept 1941; *Educ* Cheshunt GS, Clare Coll Cambridge (BA, MA), Loughborough Tech Coll; *m* 6 July 1972, Jane Margaret (d 1991), da of Francis Huddleston (d 1986); 1 s (Alfred b 1973), 1 da (Mary b 1975); *Career* asst librarian Loughborough Tech Coll 1964–66, asst cataloguer Leeds City Libraries 1966–68, dep bibliographical servs librarian City of London Libraries 1968–70; Guildhall Library: princ cataloguer 1970–73, keeper of Enquiry Servs 1973–82; dep dir City of London Libraries and Art Galleries 1982–95; ed Guildhall Studies in London History 1973–81; chm and ed Library Assoc Local Studies Gp London and Home Counties Branch, ctee memb Library Assoc London and Home Counties Branch, memb Cncl Br Records Assoc; govr Bishopsgate Fndn, tstee and treas Framlington Lanman Museum; Freeman City of London 1983, Liveryman Worshipful Co of Fletchers 1984; ALA 1967; *Recreations* fishing, walking, local history; *Clubs* Harwich and Dovercourt Sailing; *Style*— Michael Roberts, Esq; ✉ 43 College Road, Framlingham, Suffolk IP13 9ER

ROBERTS, Michèle Brigitte; da of Reginald George Roberts, of Felton, nr Bristol, and Monique Pauline Joseph, *née* Caulle; *b* 20 May 1949; *Educ* St Mary's Abbey London, St Michael's Convent London, Univ of Oxford (MA), Univ Coll London (ALA); *Career* author and poet; formerly: p/t journalist, p/t teacher, pregnancy tester, cnsllr, res asst, book reviewer; librarian British Council Bangkok (responsible for S Vietnam and Cambodia) 1972–73; poetry ed: Spare Rib 1974–76, City Limits 1981–83; various Arts Council fellowships; visiting fell Nottingham Trent 1995–96, visiting prof Nottingham Trent Univ 1996–; univ writer in residence: Univ of Essex 1987–88, UEA 1992; Gay News Literary Award 1978, Arts Council Grant 1978, W H Smith Literary Award 1993; involved in Int Women's Liberation Movement 1970–; *Novels* A Piece of the Night (1978), The Visitation (1983), The Wild Girl (1984), The Book of Mrs Noah (1987), In The Red Kitchen (1990), Daughters of the House (1992, shortlisted Booker Prize 1992, W H Smith Literary Award 1993), Flesh and Blood (1994), Impossible Saints (1997); *Poetry* The Mirror of the Mother (1986), Psyche And the Hurricane (1991), All the Selves I Was

(1995); *Short stories* During Mother's Absence (1993); *Other works* contrib numerous stories and essays to anthologies, co-author numerous books of poetry and short stories, première of play The Journeywoman Colchester 1988, recent film script The Heavenly Twins (French TV and Channel 4); *Recreations* food, sex, foreign travel, gardening, reading; *Style*— Ms Michèle Roberts; ✉ c/o Aitken & Stone Ltd, 29 Fernshaw Road, London SW10 0TG (☎ 0171 351 7561, fax 0171 376 3594)

ROBERTS, Paul Bartholemew; s of Joseph Roberts (d 1984), of London, and Angela, *née* Coletta; *b* 4 Sept 1941; *Educ* St Michael's Convent Finchley, St Aloysius Coll Highgate; *m* 1, 15 July 1972, Clare Celia Fay, da of Cochrane H Campbell, CBE, of Helensborough, Scotland; m 2, 10 Dec 1983 (m dis 1988), Nicola Anne, da of Dr Peter Stuart; 1 da (Lucy b 22 June 1984); *Career* dir John Rigby and Co Gunmakers 1984– (Royal Warrant of Appointment as Rifle and Cartridge Makers 1994); chm Gun Trade Assoc 1986–89, memb Home Office Firearms Consultative Ctee 1989–92; Freeman: Worshipful Co of Gunmakers 1980, City of London 1980; *Recreations* shooting, big game hunting, polo; *Clubs* Cowdray Park Polo, Shikar; *Style*— Paul Roberts, Esq; ✉ Beeches, Loxwood, W Sussex; 66 Great Suffolk St London SE1 OBU (☎ 0171 620 0690, fax 0171 928 9205)

ROBERTS, Prof Paul Harry; s of Percy Harry Roberts (d 1969), and Ethel Francis, *née* Mann; *b* 13 Sept 1929; *Educ* Ardwyn Sch Aberystwyth, UCW Aberystwyth (David Davies scholar), Gonville & Caius Coll Cambridge (minor scholar, BA, MA, PhD, ScD, George Green student, Smith Prize); *m* 16 Dec 1989, Mary Francis, *née* Tabrett; *Career* res assoc Univ of Chicago 1954–55, scientific offr AWRE Aldermaston 1955–56; ICI fell Univ of Durham 1956–59, lectr in physics King's Coll Univ of Durham 1959–61, assoc prof Yerkes Observatory Univ of Chicago 1961–63, prof of applied mathematics Univ of Newcastle upon Tyne 1963–86, prof of mathematics and geophysical sciences UCLA Los Angeles 1986–; FRAS 1955, FRS 1979; *Recreations* chess, playing bassoon; *Style*— Prof Paul Roberts, FRS; ✉ Department of Mathematics, UCLA, Los Angeles, CA 90024, USA (☎ 310 206 2707, fax 310 206 6673, telex 3716012)

ROBERTS, Peter David Thatcher; s of Leonard Charles Roberts (d 1978); *b* 1 March 1934; *Educ* Alleyns Sch Dulwich, Sir John Cass Coll Univ of London; *m* 1959, Elizabeth June Dodds; 1 s, 2 da; *Career* MN 1951–59, Lt RNR; Leinster/Hispania Maritime Ltd: joined 1960, dir 1963, md 1965; dir Hays plc 1983–93 (joined 1969); chm: Shipowners P & I Assoc Ltd, Spandilux SA; dir Minories Holdings Ltd; memb Gen Ctee Lloyd's Register of Shipping; Master The Co of Watermen and Lightermen of River Thames 1993–94, asst Court of Worshipful Co of Shipwrights; MICS 1962, FIMgt 1981; *Recreations* offshore sailing, golf; *Clubs* Royal Ocean Racing, RAC, Wildernesse Golf; *Style*— Peter Roberts, Esq; ✉ Callenders Cottage, Bidborough, nr Tunbridge Wells, Kent TN3 0XJ (☎ 01892 529053, fax 01892 535339)

ROBERTS, Peter John; s of Reginald Sidney Roberts (d 1992), of Horsham, West Sussex, and Evelyn Isobel, *née* Turner; *b* 27 Nov 1938; *Educ* St Dunstan's Coll, Trinity Coll Cambridge (MA); *m* 1, 9 July 1960, Ann Belinda Le Grys (d 1990), da of Albert Kenneth Rice (d 1969); 2 s (Simon b 1963, Ben b 1965), 2 da (Rachel b 1961, Hannah b 1966); m 2, 19 July 1991, Anne Veronica, da of Patrick Joseph Dillon; *Career* C & J Clark Ltd 1960–93: md Neptune Shoes Ltd 1972–80, head of corp planning Clarks Shoes 1980–85, mktg and prodn servs dir Clarks Shoes 1985–86, md Torlink Ltd 1987–93, franchise dir C & J Clark International 1992–93; chief exec DGAA Homelife (formerly Distressed Gentlefolks' Aid Association) 1993–; chm of Govrs: Crispin Sch 1978–89, Strode Coll 1989–93; chm Somerset Relate Marriage Guidance 1979–82 and 1987–90, memb Nat Cncl of RELATE 1979–, tstee Bishop Simeon Tst for Educn & Welfare of S African Students; *Recreations* gardening, travel, music, skiing; *Clubs* Reform; *Style*— Peter Roberts, Esq; ✉ Chief Executive, DGAA Homelife, 1 Derry Street, Kensington, London W8 5HY (☎ 0171 396 6700, fax 0171 396 6734)

ROBERTS, Dr Philippa Mary Elizabeth; MBE (1993); da of Dr James Roberts, of Manchester, and Dr Raine Emily Ireland Roberts, MBE; *b* 11 April 1960; *Educ* Withington Girls' Sch Manchester, Charing Cross Hosp Med (MB BS); *Career* joined Br waterskiing team 1974, nat champion 1977, 1982 and 1985–96, Euro overall champion 1986 and 1990, Euro slalom champion 1991 and 1994, World Games champion 1989 and 1993; *Recreations* waterskiing; *Clubs* Princes; *Style*— Dr Philippa Roberts, MBE; ✉ 20 Gregory Drive, Old Windsor, Berkshire SL4 2RG

ROBERTS, Ven Raymond Harcourt; CB (1984); s of Thomas Roberts (d 1981), and Caroline Maud, *née* Braine (d 1988); *b* 14 April 1931; *Educ* Pontywaun GS Gwent, St Edmund Hall Oxford (MA), St Michael's Coll Llandaff; *Career* ordained Diocese of Monmouth, deacon 1956, priest 1957, curate of Bassaleg 1956–59, Chaplain RNVR 1958–59, Chaplain RN 1959–84, Chaplain of the Fleet and Archdeacon for the RN 1980–84; QHC 1980–84, hon canon of Gibraltar 1980–84, archdeacon emeritus 1985; gen sec Jerusalem and Middle East Church Assoc 1985–89, hon chaplain Llandaff Cathedral 1990; chm Office of Water Services Customer Service Ctee for Wales 1990; pres Llandaff North Div St John Ambulance Brigade; govr Rougemont Sch Gwent 1993; chaplain and Liveryman Welsh Livery Guild 1993, chaplain Worshipful Co of Drapers 1996; *Recreations* listening to Mozart, cooking, owning and driving reasonably fast cars; *Clubs* Naval; *Style*— The Ven Raymond H Roberts, CB; ✉ 8 Baynton Close, Llandaff, Cardiff CF5 2NZ (☎ 01222 578044)

ROBERTS, Prof Richard Henry; *b* 6 March 1946; *Educ* William Hulme's GS Manchester, Univ of Lancaster (BA), Univ of Cambridge (MA, BD), Univ of Edinburgh (PhD); *m* 7 Sept 1968, Audrey, *née* Butterfield; 1 s (Anthony James b 10 Aug 1982); *Career* temp lectr in theology and religious studies Univ of Leeds 1975–76, lectr in systematic theology Univ of Durham 1976–89, Maurice B Reckitt res fell Dept of Religious Studies Univ of Lancaster 1988–91, prof of divinity Univ of St Andrews 1991–95, prof of religious studies Univ of Lancaster 1995–; founding dir: Centre for the History of the Human Sciences Univ of Durham 1988–91, Inst for Religion and the Human Scis Univ of St Andrews 1991–95; sr hon res fell Dept of Religious Studies Univ of Lancaster 1994–95; memb: Int Advsy Bd Cncl for Ethics in Economics Ohio 1991–, Religion et Economie and Centre euro-mediterranean de sciences sociales des religions CNRS, Sociology of Religion Advsy Bd Int Theological Jl Concilium 1992–93; founding memb Scientific Ctee Assoc for Rhetoric and Communication in S Africa; rapporteur res projects in sociology of religion ESRC 1993–; memb ed bd: Literature and Theology 1988–, Jl of Contemporary Religion 1994–: memb: Soc for the Study of Theology 1975–, Ecclesiastical History Soc 1979–92, Assoc for the Sociology of Religion USA 1986–, Centre for the History of the Human Scis Univ of Durham 1985–, Br/Int Comparative Literature Assoc 1987–, Int Sociological Assoc 1995–, Societé Internationale des Religions 1988–, Centre for the Study of Cultural Values Univ of Lancaster 1989–91, Cncl for Academic Autonomy 1988–, Br/Int Assoc for the History of Religion 1991–, Assoc Française de Sociologie Religieuse, Br Sociological Assoc 1988–, Soc for Christian Ethics 1993–, Cheiron Euro 1992–; *Books* Hope and its Hieroglyph: a critical decipherment of Ernst Bloch's' Principle of Hope' (1990), A Theology on Its Way: Essays on Karl Barth (1992), The Recovery of Rhetoric: persuasive discourse and disciplinarity in the human sciences (co-ed with J M M Good, 1993), Religion and the Transformations of Capitalism: Comparative Approaches (1995); *Recreations* Shotakan karate, hill-walking, music; *Style*— Prof Richard H Roberts; ✉ Department of Religious Studies, University of Lancaster, Lancaster LA1 4YG (☎ 01524 592423, fax 01524 847039, e-mail R.Roberts@lancaster.ac.uk)

ROBERTS, Dr Richard John; s of John Walter, and Edna Wilhelmina, Roberts, of Saltford, Bristol; *b* 6 Sept 1943; *Educ* City of Bath Boys' Sch, Univ of Sheffield (BSc, PhD); *m* 1, 1965, Elizabeth, *née* Dyson; 1 da (Alison Elizabeth b 11 April 1967), 1 s ((Richard) Andrew b 30 April 1968); m 2, 1986, Jean Elizabeth Tagliabue; 1 s (Christopher John b 25 Jan 1987), 1 da (Amanda Rae b 10 Aug 1989); *Career* res assoc in biochemistry Harvard Univ 1971–72 (res fell 1969–70), asst dir for res Cold Spring Harbor Lab 1986–92 (sr staff investigator 1972–86), res dir New England Biolabs 1992–; conslt and chm Scientific Advsy Bd New England Biolabs 1974–92, chm Nat Advsy Ctee BIONET 1987–90 (memb 1984–86), exec ed Nucleic Acids Res 1987–; memb: Scientific Advsy Bd Genex Corp 1977–85, Editorial Bd Nucleic Acids Research 1977–87, Editorial Bd Jl of Biological Chemistry 1979–84, Nat Advsy Ctee GENBANK 1982–89, panel NIH Study Section in Biochemistry 1985–88, Editorial Bd CABIOS (Computer Applications in the Biosciences) 1985–, panel NCI Cancer Centers Support Grant Review Ctee 1990–; memb: American Soc of Biological Chemistry, American Chemical Soc, American Soc for Microbiology, American Assoc for the Advancement of Science; Hon MD: Univ of Uppsala 1992, Univ of Bath 1994; Hon DSc: Univ of Sheffield 1994, Univ of Derby 1995; FRS 1995; *Awards* John Simon Guggenheim fell 1979–80, ASM Fndn lectr 1988–89, Miller prof Univ of Calif at Berkeley 1991, Nobel Prize for Physiology or Med 1993; *Style*— Dr Richard Roberts; ✉ New England Biolabs, 32 Tozer Road, Beverly, MA 01915, USA (☎ 00 1 508 927 3382, fax 00 1 508 921 1527)

ROBERTS, Prof Ronald John; *b* 28 March 1941; *Educ* The GS Campbeltown, Univ of Glasgow (BVMS, PhD); m; 2 s; *Career* lectr in veterinary pathology Univ of Glasgow 1966–71 (asst in microbiology 1964–66); Univ of Stirling: sr lectr in biology and dir Aquatic Pathobiology Unit 1972–76, reader in aquatic pathobiology 1976–79, prof and dir Inst of Aquaculture 1979–; advsr on fish pathology: Miny of Overseas Devpt UK 1973–, FAO 1974–; dir: Heron Associates, Stirling Aquaculture, Campbeltown and Kintyre Enterprise; memb: Animals Ctee AFRC 1989–92, Fisheries Strategy Advsy Ctee ODA 1989–, Scientific Advsy Ctee Cabinet Office 1994–95; chm Argyll and Bute Countryside Tst; ed: Jl of Fish Diseases 1977–, Aquaculture Research 1985–; Buckland Gold Medal 1985, Crookes Veterinary Award for res BVA 1989, Dalrymple-Champneys Cup and Medal 1990; cdr Most Noble Order of the Crown (Thailand) 1992; FRSE 1978 (memb Cncl 1980–83), FIBiol 1980, FRCPath 1985 (MRCPath 1974), FRCVS 1991 (MRCVS 1964); *Books* Fish Pathology (1978); author of numerous scientific papers; *Style*— Prof Ronald Roberts, FRSE; ✉ Institute of Aquaculture, University of Stirling, Pathfoot Building, Stirling FK9 4LA

ROBERTS, Sir Samuel; 4 Bt (UK 1919), of Ecclesall and Queen's Tower, City of Sheffield, and West Riding of Yorkshire; s of Sir Peter Roberts, 3 Bt (d 1985), and Judith Randall, *née* Hempson; *b* 16 April 1948; *Educ* Harrow, Univ of Sheffield (LLB), Manchester Business Sch (MBA); *m* 1977, Georgina Ann, yr da of David Cory, of Bluetts, Peterston-super-Ely, nr Cardiff, S Glam; 1 s (Samuel b 1989), 3 da (Eleanor Judith b 1979, Olivia b 1982, Amelia b 1985); *Heir* s, Samuel Roberts b 1989; *Career* called to the Bar Inner Temple 1972; chm: Curzon Steels Ltd 1980–84, Cleyfield Properties Ltd, Angerman Godard & Loyd Ltd; dir Wiltshire & Co Ltd (insurance brokers); *Style*— Sir Samuel Roberts, Bt; ✉ 6 Caversham Street, London SW3 4AH (☎ 0171 351 5663)

ROBERTS, Stephen Cheveley; s of Dr David Cheveley Roberts (d 1993), of Mill Hill, London, and Elizabeth, *née* Thornborough (d 1990); *b* 23 Aug 1956; *Educ* Mill Hill Sch, Univ Coll Oxford (MA, PGCE); *m* March 1985, Joanna Meryl, da of John Andrew Cunnison; 2 s (Matthew Timothy b 6 March 1986, Douglas Mark b 27 Sept 1987); *Career* credit analyst Orion Bank 1980–81, asst master Christ's Hosp Sch Horsham 1981–85, head of physics and housemaster Oundle Sch 1985–93, headmaster Felsted Sch 1993–; memb: HMC 1993, Secdy Heads Assoc 1993; *Recreations* golf, walking, reading; *Clubs* Vincents; *Style*— Stephen Roberts, Esq; ✉ Headmaster's House, Felsted School, Felsted, Dunmow, Essex CM6 3LL (☎ 01371 820258, fax 01371 821232)

ROBERTS, Sir Stephen James Leake; kt (1980); s of Frank Roberts (d 1964), of Shropshire, and Annie Leake (d 1933); *b* 13 April 1915; *Educ* Wellington GS; *m* 1940, Muriel, da of James Hobbins, of Rosedene, Lawley Bank, Shropshire; 2 s, 2 da; *Career* chm: Milk Marketing Board 1977–87 (W Midland regnl memb 1966–87), Littleworth Enterprises Ltd; farmer (Salop delegate to NFU Cncl 1962–70); *Recreations* football; *Clubs* Farmers; *Style*— Sir Stephen Roberts; ✉ Littleworth Enterprises Ltd, Lydebrook House, Coalmoor Road, Little Wenlock, Telford, Shropshire TF6 5AS (☎ 01952 504569, fax 01952 505814)

ROBERTS, Stephen Pritchard; s of Edward Henry Roberts (d 1987), and Violet, *née* Pritchard; *b* 8 Feb 1949; *Educ* RCM (ARCM 1969, GRSM 1971); *Career* professional singer (concert, oratorio and opera), baritone; regular performances Europe, tours to Far East, USA, Canada, S America, BBC recordings for radio and TV (Prom appearances); commercial recordings (Decca, EMI, Virgin) incl: St Matthew Passion, Carmina Burana, Sea Symphony, Elgar's The Apostles, Penderecki's St Luke Passion; opera repertoire incl: Marriage of Figaro and Die Fledermaus (Opera North), Gluck's Armide, Ravel's L'Heure Espagnol; opera recordings incl: Tippett's King Priam and Birtwistle's Punch and Judy; *Style*— Stephen Roberts, Esq; ✉ 144 Gleneagle Rd, London SW16 6BA (☎ 0181 769 1512, fax 0181 769 1512, compuserve 101666, 2164)

ROBERTS, Trevor John; s of Howard William Roberts (d 1982), of Wolverhampton, and Melba Lewis, *née* Bushell; *b* 22 April 1940; *Educ* King Edward GS Stafford, Wolverhampton Poly; *m* 30 March 1970, Judith, da of William Samuel Wiggin, of Cannock, Staffs; 1 s (James b 1980), 1 da (Andrea b 1978); *Career* mangr of manufacturing depts Charles Richards & Sons Ltd 1969–74, tech mktg mangr Charles Richards Fasteners Ltd 1978–80 (prodn mangr 1974–78); jt owner and md: Doran Engineering Co Ltd 1982– (manufacturing dir 1980–82), Doran Engineering Holdings Ltd 1983–; dir: Village Engineering Co Ltd 1983–, Petrospec Bolting Ltd 1990; Inst of Industl Mangrs: former memb Nat Cncl, former memb Nat Membership Exec, former chm and pres Wolverhampton Branch; pres Willenhall Rotary Club 1991–92; CEng, FIEE, FIMgt 1987, FIIM 1987, FIProdE 1988; *Recreations* swimming, reading, photography; *Style*— Trevor Roberts, Esq; ✉ Ashley Croft, Church Eaton, Stafford ST20 0BJ (☎ 01785 823624); Doran Engineering (Holdings) Ltd, Planetary Rd, Willenhall, W Midlands WV13 3XW (☎ 01902 732691, fax 01902 864663)

ROBERTS, Sir William James Denby; 3 Bt (UK 1909), of Milner Field, Bingley, W Riding of Yorkshire; s of Sir James Denby Roberts, OBE, 2 Bt (d 1973); *b* 10 Aug 1936; *Educ* Rugby, RAC Cirencester; *Heir* nephew, James Elton Denby Roberts-Buchanan b 12 July 1966; *Career* collector of vintage aircraft; fndr and former owner Strathallan Aircraft Collection; *Style*— Sir William Roberts, Bt; ✉ Strathallan Castle, Auchterarder, Perthshire; Combwell Priory, Flimwell, Wadhurst, Sussex

ROBERTS, William Morys; s of Gwilym James Roberts, MD (Maj Royal Army Med Corps 1945–46, d 1990), of Penarth, South Glamorgan, and Eileen Burford, *née* Chivers (d 1995); *b* 8 Dec 1934; *Educ* Kingswood Sch Bath Avon, Gonville and Caius Coll Cambridge (MA); *m* 29 July 1967, Patricia Anne, da of John Stratford Bettinson, of Ickleton, Cambridgeshire; 1 s (Simon b 1972), 2 da (Sarah b 1969, Alice b 1974); *Career* RA 1953–54, Intelligence Corps 1954–55, 2 Lt (later Lt RARO) 1955–67; Turquand, Youngs and Co 1958–61; WM Brandt's Sons & Co Ltd 1961–73: chief accountant 1965, sec 1970, dir 1971–73; dir Edward Bates and Sons Ltd 1973–75; Ernst & Young: ptnr 1976–94, head of London Insolvency Servs 1987–89, head of Corp Advsy Servs London 1989–92 and National 1991–94; Soc of Practitioners of Insolvency: memb Insolvency Rules Advsy Ctee 1984–92, memb Tech Ctee 1990– (chm 1995–), dir of tech servs 1990–;

memb: Insolvency Practitioners Tbnl 1996–, Saffron Walden Deanery Synod 1996–; churchwarden All Saint's Church Great Chesterford 1976–93; FCA 1971 (ACA 1961); *Books* Insolvency Law and Practice (with J S H Gillies, 1988); *Recreations* gardening; *Clubs* IOD, Sea View Yacht; *Style*— W M Roberts, Esq; ✉ Brock House, Great Chesterford, Saffron Walden, Essex CB10 1PJ (☎ and fax 01799 30470); 1 Elgin House, Ryde Rd, Seaview, IOW; c/o Society of Practitioners of Insolvency, 18–19 Long Lane, London EC1A 9HE (☎ 0171 600 3375, fax 0171 600 3602)

ROBERTS, Prof (Meirion) Wyn; s of Tom Roberts, OBE (d 1979), of Ammaford, Dyfed, and Mary, *née* Williams (d 1968); *b* 1 Feb 1931; *Educ* Amman Valley GS Ammanford, Univ of Swansea, Univ of Wales (BSc, PhD, DSc); *m* 23 March 1957, Catherine Angharad, da of John Lewis, of Ammanford, Dyfed; 1 s (Mark b 6 March 1964), 1 da (Karen b 26 May 1961); *Career* Imperial Coll of Sci London 1955–57, sr scientific offr Nat Chem Laboratory 1957–59, lectr Queen's Univ of Belfast 1959–66, chair of physical chem Univ of Bradford 1966–79, head Dept of Physical Chem Univ Coll Cardiff 1986–88 (chair 1978–86), dep princ Univ of Wales Coll of Cardiff 1989–92, head of Sch of Chemistry 1988–; visiting prof: Univ of Xiamen China 1985–, Univ of California Berkeley 1984; centenary lectr Indian Acad of Sciences 1984; chm Tstees of the Wool Fndn 1981–; memb: SERC Chem Ctee 1972–78, Univ Grants Physical Scis Ctee 1982–88, Cncl for Nat Academic Awards 1989; hon fell Univ Coll of Swansea 1987, Tilden Medal and Prize Royal Soc of Chem 1976, Royal Soc of Chem Award in Surface Chem 1987; FRSC 1966; *Books* Reactivity of Solids (ed, 1972), The Chemical Physics of Solids and their Surfaces (Chemical Soc Reports, 1972–79), Chemistry of the Metal Gas Interface (jtly, 1978); *Recreations* rugby football; *Style*— Prof Wyn Roberts; ✉ 37 Heol-Y-Delyn, Lisvane, Cardiff CF4 5SR (☎ 01222 752452); University of Wales, Cardiff, Department of Chemistry, PO Box 912, Cardiff CF1 3TB (☎ 01222 874805, fax 01222 874030, telex 498635)

ROBERTS, Rt Hon Sir (Ieuan) Wyn Pritchard; kt (1990), PC (1991), MP (C) Conwy (majority 995); s of Rev E P Roberts, of Anglesey; *b* 10 July 1930; *Educ* Harrow, Univ of Oxford; *m* 1956, Enid Grace, da of W Williams, of Anglesey; 3 s; *Career* formerly journalist with The Liverpool Post and news asst with the BBC, Welsh controller and exec prodr TWW 1959–68, programme exec Harlech TV 1969; MP (C) Conwy 1970–, PPS to Sec of State for Wales 1970–74, oppn front bench spokesman on Welsh affrs 1974–79, Parly under sec Welsh Office 1979–87, min of state for Wales 1987–94; memb Gorsedd Royal National Eisteddfod 1966; *Style*— The Rt Hon Sir Wyn Roberts, MP; ✉ Tan y Gwalia, Conway, Gwynedd

ROBERTS-CAIRNS, Patricia Rose Marie (Pat); da of Maj William Roberts, MBE, RA (d 1966), and Catherine, *née* Slawson (d 1983); *b* 27 Nov 1947; *Educ* St Barnabas Sch Woodford Green Essex; *m* Dr D A O Cairns, MRCGP; *Career* reporter Independent Newspapers Essex 1965–68, features writer IPC Magazines 1968–72, fndr ed Girl About Town (London's first free magazine) 1972–80, feature writer 'Femail' Daily Mail 1980–82, assoc ed Family Circle Magazine 1982–84, ed Over 21 Magazine 1984–89, fndr ed House Beautiful Magazine 1989–95, ed Good Housekeeping 1995–; Launch Ed of the Year Br Soc of Magazine Eds 1990, Ed of the Year Periodical Publishers Assoc 1992; memb: Editorial Ctee Periodical Trg Cncl, Women of the Year Ctee, British Soc of Magazine Eds Ctee, Periodical Publishers Assoc Editorial Public Affairs Ctee; *Books* Living Images - Styling Yourself for Success (1990), House Beautiful Home Handbook (1992); *Style*— Ms Pat Roberts-Cairns; ✉ National Magazine Company, National Magazine House, 72 Broadwick Street, London W1V 2BP (☎ 0171 439 5000, fax 0171 439 5595)

ROBERTSHAW, His Hon Judge; Patrick Edward; s of George Edward Robertshaw, and late May, *née* Tallis; *b* 7 July 1945; *m* 1972, Sally Christine Greenburgh, *née* Searle; 2 s, 2 da; *Career* called to the Bar Inner Temple 1968, recorder Crown and County Cts 1989–94, circuit judge (NE Circuit) 1994–; *Recreations* travel, reading; *Style*— His Hon Judge Robertshaw; ✉ Sheffield Combined Court Centre, 50 West Bar, Sheffield S3 8PH (☎ 0114 281 2400)

ROBERTSON, Anderson Bain; s of Mungo Manderson Robertson (d 1932), of Bristol, and Minnie McAllister Bain, *née* Anderson (d 1987); *b* 22 Oct 1929; *Educ* Ardrossan Acad Ayrshire, Gray's Sch of Art, Aberdeen and Glasgow Sch of Art (DA, BA); *m* 13 July 1955, Mary Margaret Moffat, da of Alexander Stewart Christie (d 1979), of Wishaw; 2 s (Maxwell Stewart b 1959, Paul Noel b 1961); *Career* RAOC 1948–50; head Dept of Art Nicolson Inst Stornoway 1969–79, govr Aberdeen Coll of Educn 1974–78, convener Central Advsy Ctee of Art EIS 1977–81, assessor Certificate of Sixth Year Studies in Art and Design 1977–89; artist; exhibitions at: Royal Scot Acad, Royal Glasgow Inst of Fine Arts, Royal Scot Soc of Painters in Water Colours, Royal Soc of Portrait Painters, Soc Artists and Artist Craftsmen; private collections in GB and USA; professional memb Soc Artists and Artist Craftsmen (SAAC) 1996; *Recreations* sailing; *Clubs* Glasgow Art; *Style*— Anderson B Robertson, Esq; ✉ Window Rock, Innellan, Dunoon, Argyll PA23 7TR (☎ and fax 01369 830755)

ROBERTSON, Andrew John; s of John Hector Robertson, and Jennifer Mary, *née* Cullen; *b* 17 Nov 1960; *Educ* Michaelhouse Balgowan Natal SA, City of London Poly, City Univ (BSc); *m* 13 Feb 1987, Susan Louise, da of Michael John Bayliss; 2 da (Amy Louise b 13 Aug 1988, Louisa Jane b 25 July 1991); *Career* Ogilvy & Mather: trainee media planner 1982, account dir 1986, memb Bd of Dirs 1987, mgmnt supervisor and new business dir 1988–89; gp dir J Walter Thompson Co 1989, chief exec WCRS 1990–95, md Abbott Mead Vickers BBDO Ltd 1995–; FIPA 1987; *Recreations* tennis, squash, opera, ballet; *Style*— Andrew Robertson, Esq; ✉ Abbott Mead Vickers BBDO Ltd, 191 Old Marylebone Road, London NW1 5DW (☎ 0171 402 4100)

ROBERTSON, Andrew Ogilvie; OBE (1994); s of Alexander McArthur Ogilvie Robertson (d 1971), and Charlotte Rachel, *née* Cuthbert (d 1989); *b* 30 June 1943; *Educ* Glasgow Acad, Sedbergh, Univ of Edinburgh (LLB); *m* 4 July 1974, Sheila, da of Philip Sturton; 2 s (James Mungo Ogilvie b 9 Nov 1975, Alexander Philip Ogilvie b 11 Aug 1977); *Career* apprentice slr Maclay Murray Spens Glasgow 1964–67, currently sr ptnr T C Young & Son (joined 1967, ptnr 1968); sec Erskine Hosp Bishopston 1976–, sec and treas Clydeside Fedn of Community Based Housing Assocs 1978–93, sec The Briggait Co Ltd 1983–88, founding sec and legal advsr The Princess Royal Tst for Carers 1990–; chm: Post Office Users' Cncl for Scotland 1988–, Scottish Housing Assocs Charitable Tst 1990–, Gtr Glasgow Community & Mental Health Servs NHS Tst 1994–; dir: The Merchants House of Glasgow 1980–, Glasgow C of C 1981–94; *Recreations* mountaineering, sailing, swimming, reading; *Clubs* Western (Glasgow); *Style*— Andrew Robertson, Esq, OBE; ✉ T C Young & Son, 30 George Square, Glasgow G2 1LH (☎ 0141 221 5562, fax 0141 221 5024)

ROBERTSON, Angus Frederick; s of Eric Desmond Robertson, OBE (d 1987), and Aileen Margaret, *née* Broadhead; *b* 4 Nov 1954; *Educ* Westminster, Univ of Stirling (BA); *m* (m dis), Frances Ellen, da of Patrick Carroll Macnamara, of Ardgay, Sutherland; *Career* called to the Bar Middle Temple 1978; *Style*— Angus Robertson, Esq; ✉ 44 Rawlings St, London SW3 2LS (☎ 0171 581 2719); 10 King's Bench Walk, Temple, London EC4Y 7EB (☎ 0171 353 7742, fax 0171 583 0579, telex 8811 61210 KBW G)

ROBERTSON, (James) Campbell; s of Surgn Lt James Robertson (ka 1942), of Edinburgh, and Mathilda Mary, *née* Campbell; *b* 15 Oct 1941; *Educ* Epsom Coll, Guy's Hosp, Univ of London (MB BS); *m* 2 May 1970, Dr Margaret Elizabeth Robertson, da of late Charles Edwin Kirkwood, of Salisbury, Wilts; 3 s (Charles James b 1971 d 1995, Andrew b 1973, Alistair b 1974); *Career* conslt physician in rheumatology and rehabilitation Salisbury and Southampton DHAs and Wessex Regnl Rehabilitation Unit 1974–; dir Wessex Regnl Rehabilitation Unit 1980–90, med dir Preventative Rheumatology Unit; fndr ed Care Science and Practice (now Jl of Tissue Viability); author of papers on prevention of neck and back pain, osteoporosis, measurement of physical signs, patient support systems, bandaging and interface pressure mgmnt and burns scarring; former chm and fndr memb Soc for Tissue Viability, memb Wessex Rehabilitation Assoc; chm Chronic Pain Forum; memb: BMA, Br Soc of Rheumatology, Ergnomics Soc, Back Pain Soc, Soc for Res in Rehabilitation (former sec), Workfit Tst; LRCP, FRCP, MRCS; *Books* Blueprint for a Clinical Grip Strength Monitor and Limb Strength Measurement System (1986); *Recreations* windsurfing, sailing, DIY, medical journalism; *Clubs* S Wales and S W Wessex Rheumatology; *Style*— Dr James Robertson; ✉ Wessex Regional Rehabilitation Unit, Salisbury District Hospital, Salisbury, Wilts (☎ 01722 336262)

ROBERTSON, Rev Charles; JP (City of Edinburgh 1980); s of Thomas Robertson (d 1941), of Glasgow, and Elizabeth, *née* Halley (d 1942); *b* 22 Oct 1940; *Educ* Camphill Sch Paisley, Univ of Edinburgh, New Coll Edinburgh; *m* 30 July 1965, Alison Margaret, da of the Rev John Strachan Malloch, MBE, of Aberdeen; 1 s (Duncan John b 6 June 1967), 2 da (Mary Blackadder b 29 Dec 1968, Margaret Isobel b 5 Feb 1976); *Career* asst minister N Morningside Church Edinburgh 1964–65; parish minister: Kiltearn Ross-shire 1965–78, Canongate Kirk (The Kirk of Holyroodhouse) Edinburgh 1978–; chaplain: to HM the Queen in Scotland 1991–, to the Lord High Cmmr to the Gen Assembly of the Church of Scotland 1990 and 1991, to the High Constables and Guard of Honour of Holyroodhouse 1993–; convenor Gen Assembly's Panel on Worship 1995– (sec 1982–95); Church of Scotland rep Jt Liturgical Gp 1984– (chm 1994–), tstee Church Hymnary Tst 1987–, pres Church Service Soc 1988–91 (hon pres 1991–); chaplain: Clan Donnachaidh Soc 1981–, Elsie Inglis Maternity Hosp 1982–87, New Club Edinburgh 1986–, Moray House Coll of Educn 1986–, No 2 (City of Edinburgh) Maritime HQ Unit RAAF 1987–; lectr in church praise St Colm's Coll Edinburgh 1980–93; tstee: Edinburgh Old Town Tst 1987–91, Edinburgh Old Town Charitable Tst 1991–; govr St Columba's Hospice 1986–; Queensberry House Hosp: dir 1978–, vice chm 1985–89, chm 1989–; memb: Exec Ctee Scot Veterans' Residences 1978–, Bdcasting Standards Cncl 1988–91 and 1992–94, Historic Bldgs Cncl for Scotland 1990–93 and 1993–; *Books* Singing the Faith (ed, 1990), Common Order (1994), St Margaret Queen of Scotland and Her Chapel (ed, 1994); *Recreations* Scottish and Edinburgh history, hymnody, collecting Canongate miscellanea; *Clubs* Athenaeum, New (Edinburgh); *Style*— The Rev Charles Robertson, JP; ✉ Manse of Canongate, Edinburgh EH8 8BR (☎ 0131 556 3515)

ROBERTSON, Brig Clive Henderson; CVO (1991), DL (Dorset 1984); s of Lt-Col William Henderson Robertson, MC (d 1976), and Alice Maud, *née* Jackaman (d 1974); *b* 21 Aug 1927; *Educ* Radley; *m* 5 Sept 1959, Fiona Ann, da of Col Ronald Scott-Dempster; 1 s (Andrew b 19 May 1962), 1 da (Caroline b 22 June 1960); *Career* cmmnd 11 Hussars (PAO) 1947, ADC to GOC 7 Armd Div 1952–53 (despatches Malaya 1955 and 1956), Staff Coll Camberley 1960, JSSC 1964, CO 11 Hussars 1968–69, CO Royal Hussars (PWO) 1969–71, mil asst to Mil Sec 1971–72, Col Gen Staff MOD 1972–74, Cmdt RAC Gunnery Sch 1974–75, Cdr RAC Centre Bovington 1975–78, vice pres Reg Cmmns Bd 1978–80; extra equerry to HRH The Duke of Edinburgh 1992– (asst private sec 1984–91); chm: Govrs Hardy's Sch 1982–83, Army Benevolent Fund Dorset 1983–95; *Recreations* skiing, gardening, theatre; *Clubs* Cavalry & Guards'; *Style*— Brig Clive Robertson, CVO, DL

ROBERTSON, Sheriff Daphne Jean Black; WS (1977); da of Rev Robert Black Kincaid (d 1980), and Ann Parker Collins; *b* 31 March 1937; *Educ* Hillhead HS, Greenock Acad, Univ of Edinburgh (MA), Univ of Glasgow (LLB); *m* 1965, Donald Buchanan, s of Donald Robertson (d 1948), of Argyll; *Career* admitted slr 1961; Sheriff of: Glasgow and Strathkelvin 1979–96, Lothian & Borders at Edinburgh 1996–; *Style*— Sheriff Daphne Robertson, WS; ✉ Sheriff Court House, 27 Chambers Street, Edinburgh EH1 1LB (☎ 0131 225 2525)

ROBERTSON, Douglas Laurence; s of Ronald John Robertson, of Milton Keynes, and Agnes McKay (Nanette), *née* Reid; *b* 12 June 1952; *Educ* Dalkeith HS, Langley Park Sch for Boys, St Edmund Hall Oxford (MA); *m* 1 Nov 1975, Susan Winifred, da of John St Clair (d 1989), of Marden, Herefordshire; 1 s (Iain b 1979), 1 da (Carolyn b 1982); *Career* admitted slr 1977; ptnr: Kenneth Brown Baker Baker 1981, Turner Kenneth Brown 1983, Memery Crystal 1992–; Freeman City of London 1986; *Recreations* rugby and football, church activities; *Clubs* Vincent's; *Style*— Douglas L Robertson, Esq; ✉ Memery Crystal, 31 Southampton Row, London WC1B 5HT (☎ 0171 242 5905, fax 0171 242 2058)

ROBERTSON, (James) Douglas Moir; CBE (1992), DL (Surrey 1988); s of George Robertson (d 1984), and Jessie Barrie, *née* Brough (d 1993); *b* 15 Nov 1938; *Educ* Trinity Acad Edinburgh, Heriot-Watt Univ Edinburgh; *m* 29 June 1963, Caroline Blanche, da of David Stephen Adams (d 1994), of Edinburgh; 2 s (Graham b 1965, Brian b 1977), 1 da (Alison b 1970); *Career* princ Surveyors Collaborative 1969–; dir: Building Cost Information Service Ltd RICS 1962–95, Bobbett and Robertson 1994–, Research Park Developments Ltd; chm: Airports Policy Consortium 1984–93, Building Data Banks Ltd 1985–95; ldr Surrey CC 1990–93 (chm 1987–90); chm Environment Ctee Assoc of CCs 1990–92; chm Cncl Univ of Surrey 1992–; FRICS 1969, FIMgt 1971, FRSA 1989; *Recreations* golf; *Clubs* RAC, Burhill; *Style*— Douglas Robertson, Esq, CBE, DL; ✉ 16 Homewaters Avenue, Sunbury-on-Thames, Middlesex TW16 6NS (☎ 01932 786624, fax 01932 786190)

ROBERTSON, Dr Elizabeth Margaret; da of Alastair Robertson, of Aberdeen, and Dorothy Elizabeth, *née* Barron; *b* 7 Oct 1951; *Educ* St Margaret's Sch for Girls Aberdeen, Univ of Aberdeen (MB ChB, DMRD); *Career* clinical dir of radiology Aberdeen Royal Hosps NHS Tst, hon clinical sr lectr in radiology Univ of Aberdeen; memb: BMA, BIR, RSM; FRCR; *Style*— Dr Elizabeth Robertson; ✉ 95 King's Gate, Aberdeen AB15 4EN (☎ 01224 313111); In Patient X-Ray Dept, Aberdeen Royal Infirmary, Foresterhill, Aberdeen (☎ 01224 681818 ext 52176)

ROBERTSON, Geoffrey Ronald; QC (1988); s of Francis Albert Robertson, of Longueville, Sydney, Australia, and Bernice Joy, *née* Beattie; *b* 30 Sept 1946; *Educ* Epping Boys HS, Sydney Univ (BA, LLB), Univ of Oxford (Rhodes scholar, BCL); *m* Kathy Lette; 1 s (Julius Blake), 1 da (Georgina Blaise); *Career* called to the Bar Middle Temple 1973, head of Doughty St Chambers 1990–, asst recorder 1993–; visiting fell: Univ of NSW Australia 1977, Univ of Warwick 1980–81; memb Exec Cncl ICA, exec memb Freedom of Info Campaign, cncl memb JUSTICE, tstee Parents For Safe Food; *Books* Reluctant Judas (1976), Obscenity (1979), People Against the Press (1983), Media Law (1984, 3 edn 1992), Hypotheticals (1986), Does Dracula Have Aids? (1987), Freedom, The Individual and the Law (1989, 2nd edn 1993); *Plays* The Trials of Oz (BBC TV, 1991); *Recreations* tennis, opera, fishing; *Style*— Geoffrey Robertson, Esq, QC; ✉ 11 Doughty Street, London WC1N 2PG (☎ 0171 404 1313, fax 0171 404 2283)

ROBERTSON, George Islay MacNeill; MP (Lab) Hamilton (majority 16,603); s of George P Robertson, of Dunoon, Argyll, and Marion I, *née* MacNeill; *b* 12 April 1946; *Educ* Dunoon GS, Univ of Dundee (MA); *m* 1 June 1970, Sandra, da of late James U Wallace, of Dundee; 2 s (Malcolm b 1972, Martin b 1975), 1 da (Rachael b 1980); *Career* res asst Econs Gp Tayside Study 1968–69, Scottish organiser GMWU (now GMB) 1969–78; MP (Lab) Hamilton 1978–, PPS to Sec of State for Social Servs 1979; oppn spokesman on: Scotland 1979–80, Defence 1980–88, Foreign and Cwlth Affrs 1981–93 (dep FCO spokesman 1983, princ spokesman on Europe 1986–93); memb Shadow Cabinet, chief oppn spokesman on Scotland 1993–; memb Steering Ctee: Konigswinter (Br-German) Conf 1983–92, Atlantic Conf 1988–; vice-chm Br-German Parly Gp 1983– (chm 1992–93), co-chm Br Parly Lighting Gp 1983–94, chm Scottish Lab Pty 1977–78; vice-chm: Bd of Br Cncl 1985–94, Advsy Bd Know How Funds for Eastern Europe 1989–93, Westminster Fndn for Democracy 1992–94, Parly Photographic Gp; memb: Bd Scottish Devpt Agency 1975–78, Bd of Govrs Scottish Police Coll 1975–78, Br Exec Serv Overseas 1991–; memb Advsy Bd: European Business Journal, House Magazine, Br American Successor Generation Conf; tstee 21st Century Tst, govr Ditchley Fndn 1988–, hon vice pres Operation Raleigh; Commander's Cross Order of Merit (Federal Republic of Germany) 1991; *Recreations* photography, golf; *Style*— George Robertson, Esq, MP; ✉ c/o House of Commons, London SW1A OAA (☎ 0171 219 4005, fax 0171 219 4921)

ROBERTSON, Dr George Slessor; s of John Bruce Robertson (d 1971), of Aberdeenshire, and Alice Jane Slessor Clyne (d 1980); *b* 30 Dec 1933; *Educ* Peterhead Acad, Univ of Aberdeen (MB ChB, MD); *m* 21 Sept 1960, Audrey Esslemont, da of Hector McDonald (d 1955), of Aberdeen; 1 s (Neil b 1961), 2 da (Denise b 1963, Judith b 1966); *Career* res asst in anaesthetics Aberdeen Royal Infirmary 1964–65, asst anaesthetist Winnipeg Gen Hosp Canada 1967–68, conslt anaesthetist Aberdeen Royal Infirmary 1969–96, hon sr lectr in anaesthetics Univ of Aberdeen 1969–96; SBStJ 1985; memb: Scottish Soc of Anaesthetists, NE of Scotland Soc of Anaesthetists (pres 1973–74); FFARCS 1964; *Books* The Living Will (1988), author of numerous scientific and medical ethics papers incl jt author The Appleton Concensus on Decisions to Forgo Medical Treatment; *Recreations* golf, hill-walking, painting; *Clubs* Royal Aberdeen Golf; *Style*— Dr George Robertson; ✉ Hazelwood, 12 Queen's Den, Woodend, Aberdeen AB15 8BW (☎ 01224 311903); Department of Anaesthetics, Aberdeen Royal Infirmary, Foresterhill, Aberdeen AB9 2ZB

ROBERTSON, Dr (Andrew) Gerard; s of Henry Robertson, OBE (d 1974), of Lagos, Nigeria and Edinburgh, and Helen, *née* Flynn; *b* 14 Jan 1945; *Educ* St Joseph's Coll Dumfries, Univ of Glasgow (BSc, PhD, MB ChB); *m* 2 April 1970, Margaret Mary Dorothy, da of John Joseph McKee, KSG, of Glasgow; 5 s (John b 1977, Andrew b 1980, Francis b 1984, Gregory b 1986, Bernard b 1986); *Career* sr registrar in radiotherapy and oncology Christie Hosp Manchester 1981, conslt in radiotherapy and oncology Western Infirmary Glasgow 1982– (formerly registrar); treas Assoc of Head and Neck Oncologists of GB, memb Catholic Union of GB, FRCR 1980, FRCPG 1988; *Recreations* golf; *Clubs* East Renfrewshire Golf; *Style*— Dr Gerard Robertson; ✉ Western Infirmary, Beatson Oncology Centre, Glasgow G11 6NT (☎ 0141 211 2000)

ROBERTSON, Grace; da of James Fyfe Robertson (d 1987), and Elizabeth, *née* Muir (d 1973); *b* 13 July 1930; *Educ* Kendal HS for Girls, Eothen Sch Caterham, Maria Grey Teacher Trg Coll Twickenham; *m* 16 Dec 1954, (Godfrey) Thurston Hopkins, s of Robert Thurston Hopkins (d 1958); 1 da (Joanna b 15 Jan 1960), 1 s (Robert James b 27 Oct 1961); *Career* photographer, lectr and broadcaster; photojournalist Picture Post 1949–57, freelance 1957–60, teacher 1965–78, Hon DLitt Univ of Brighton 1995, Hon FRPS 1996; *Exhibitions* Nat Museum of Photography, Film and TV 1986, Photographers Gallery 1987, Zelda Cheatle Gallery London 1989, Nat Museum of Wales Cardiff 1989, Gardner Centre Univ of Sussex 1990, Cathleen Ewing Gallery Washington DC 1992, Royal National Theatre (restrospective exhbn) 1993, Watershed Bristol 1993, Univ of Brighton Sussex 1994, Towner Gallery (Leaving Their Mark - sixteen achieving Women of Eastbourne) 1995; *Photographic Work in Collections incl* V&A Museum London, Nat Museum of Photography, Film and TV Bradford, Helmut Gernsheim Collection Switzerland, Nat Gallery of Aust, Hulton Deutsch Collection (now Hulton Getty) London; subject of Channel 4 documentary 1986, monograph Grace Robertson, Photojournalist of the 50's (Virago pubn) 1989, subject of Master Photographers (BBC Radio 3 series) 1991, pubn The Nineties (BBC 2 prodn) 1993; *Awards* Distinguished Photographers' Award (American Women in Photography Int) 1992; *Recreations* painting, reading, walking, listening to music; *Style*— Ms Grace Robertson; ✉ c/o The Photographers Gallery, Halina House, 5 Great Newport Street, London WC2H 7HY (☎ 0171 831 1772); c/o The Zelda Cheatle Gallery, 8 Cecil Court, London WC2N 4HE (☎ 0171 836 0506)

ROBERTSON, Air Vice-Marshal Graeme Alan; CBE (1988, OBE 1985); s of Ronald James Harold Robertson, DFC, of Walton on the Naze, Essex, and Constance Rosemary, *née* Freeman; *b* 22 Feb 1945; *Educ* Bancroft's Sch, RAF Coll Cranwell (Sir Philip Sassoon Meml Prize), Open Univ (BA); *m* Barbara Ellen, da of Frederick William Mardon (d 1975); 1 da (Nicole Jane b 17 Dec 1975); *Career* pilot No 8 Sqdn (Hunters) Bahrain 1968–69, pilot/weapons instr No 6 Sqdn RAF Coningsby (Phantoms) 1970–72, instr pilot 288 Operational Conversion Unit RAF Coningsby (Phantoms) 1972–73, instr pilot/Flt Cdr 550th Tactical Fighter Trg Sqdn Luke AFB Arizona (Phantoms) 1973–75, Flt Cdr No 56 Sqdn RAF Wattisham (Phantoms) 1975–77, RAF Staff Coll 1977–78, Operational Requirements/Plans Staff MOD 1978–82, CO No 92 Sqdn RAF Wildenrath Germany (Phantoms) 1982–84, CO No 23 Sqdn RAF Stanley Falkland Is (Phantoms) 1984–85, CO RAF Wattisham 1985–87, Dir of Air Staff Briefing and Co-ordination MOD 1987–88, RCDS 1989, Dir of Defence Progs MOD 1990–91, Dep Cdr RAF Germany 1991–93, AOC No 2 Group 1993–94, ACDS (Programmes) MOD 1994–96, Chief of Staff and Dep C-in-C Strike Command 1996–; Hon ADC to HM the Queen 1986–87; QCVSA 1973; *Recreations* shooting, golf, sailing, winter sports; *Clubs* MCC, St Moritz Toboganning, RAF; *Style*— Air Marshal Graeme Robertson, CBE; ✉ Chief of Staff and Deputy Commander-in-Chief, HQ Strike Command, RAF High Wycombe, Bucks HP14 4XW (☎ 01494 497605, fax 01494 497112)

ROBERTSON, Iain Alasdair; CBE (1995); s of Rev R Robertson, of Scone, Perthshire; *b* 1949; *Educ* Perth Acad, Univ of Aberdeen (LLB); *m* Judith; 2 s (Niall b 1980, Calum b 1982), 1 da (Johanna b 1983); *Career* dir Acquisitions and Divestitures BP America until 1990 (joined North Sea ops 1975), chief exec Highlands and Islands Enterprise 1990–; non-exec dir Scottish Tourist Bd 1993–95; *Recreations* skiing, siling, reading, music; *Style*— Iain Robertson, Esq, CBE; ✉ 37 Southside Rd, Inverness, IV2 4XA; Chief Executive, Highlands and Islands Enterprise, Bridge House, 20 Bridge Street, Inverness IV1 1QR (☎ 01463 244204, fax 01463 224201)

ROBERTSON, Maj-Gen Ian Argyll; CB (1968), MBE (1947); s of John Argyll Robertson (d 1943), and Sarah Lilian Pitt Healing (d 1962); *b* 17 July 1913; *Educ* Winchester, Trinity Coll Oxford; *m* 1939, Marjorie Violet Isobel, da of Maj Malcolm Bedford Duncan (d 1956); 2 da; *Career* cmmnd Seaforth Highlanders 1934, cmd 1 Bn Seaforth Highlanders 1954–57, cmd Sch Inf 1963–64, cmd 51 Inf Div 1964–66 (ret 1968); DL (Nairn 1973–88); HM Vice Lord Lt Highland Region 1973–88; *Recreations* gardening, golf; *Clubs* Army and Navy, MCC, Vincent's (Oxford); *Style*— Maj-Gen Ian Robertson, CB, MBE; ✉ Gardener's Cottage, Brackla, Nairn IV12 5QY (☎ 01667 404220)

ROBERTSON, Dr James Andrew Stainton; s of James Robertson, and Margaret Elodie, *née* Stainton; *b* 23 April 1949; *Educ* Highgate Sch, Univ of Essex (BA), LSE (MSc (Econ), PhD); *m* 1979, Ann Elizabeth Leatherbarrow; 1 da (Elodie b 1982), 1 s (Andrew b 1987); *Career* civil servant; sr econ asst and econ advsr Dept of Employment 1975–82, econ advsr Dept of Energy 1982–86, sr econ advsr DTI 1986–89, Dept of Tport 1989–90, head Industl and Regnl Economics DTI 1990–93, chief econ advsr Dept of Employment 1993–95, dir Nat Audit Office 1995–; contrib various learned jls; *Recreations* family, D-I-Y, recreational computing; *Style*— Dr James Robertson; ✉ National Audit Office, 157–197 Buckingham Palace Road, London SW1W 9SP

ROBERTSON, James D; *b* 1931; *Educ* Glasgow Sch of Art; *Career* artist; Glasgow Sch of Art: pt/t lectr 1959, lectr 1967, sr lectr in drawing and painting 1975–96, artist in residence 1996–; visiting lectr: Michaelis Sch of Fine Art Cape Town 1970, Gray's Sch of Art 1986, Duncan of Jordanstone Coll of Art 1986, Newcastle Poly 1986, Millersville Univ 1987; memb RGI 1980; RSW 1962, RSA 1989 (ARSA 1974); *Solo Exhibitions* Douglas & Foulis Gall 1961, Forum Gall 1963, Loomshop Gall 1972, Art Space Gall 1980, Gallery 10 1982, Christopher Hull Gall 1984, 1987 and 1989, Washington Gall 1986, Ganser Gall 1987, Ancrum Gall 1989, 1991 and 1992, Blythswood Gall 1989 and 1993, Lynne Stern Gall 1990, Glasgow Art Club 1990, Portland Gall 1992, William Hardie Gall 1993, Jorgenson Fine Art Dublin 1995; *Group Exhibitions* incl: Richard De Marco Gall, Five Glasgow Artists (Edinburgh Arts Centre), Contemporary Art from Scotland (Scottish Arts Cncl tour), Fine Art Soc, Compass Gall, J D Kelly Gall, Parkin Gall, Gallery 10 1986, Interior (RA) 1986, Nine Glasgow Painters (Washington Gall) 1987, Chicago Art Fair 1987, Bath Festival 1987, Hambledon Gall 1987, Mayfair Gall 1990 and 1993, Beaux Arts Gall 1990, Macaulay Gall 1990, Lynne Stern Gall 1991, RSA 1991, RSW 1991, New Acad Gall 1991 and 1992, Blythswood Gall 1993, Christopher Hull Gall 1993, N S Gall 1994; *Work in Public Collections* Br Contemporary Arts Soc, Hunterian Museum, Scottish Arts Cncl, Glasgow Art Galls and Museums, RSA; *Awards* Cargill award RGI 1971 and 1982, May Marshall Brown award RSW 1976, Sir William Gillies award RSW 1981, Shell Expro award 1985, Graham Munro award RSW 1987, Scottish Amicable award 1989, Scottish Post Office award RSA 1993; *Style*— James D Robertson, Esq, RSA

ROBERTSON, James Ian Alexander (Nander); s of Capt Ian Greig Robertson, DSO, DSC (d 1987), of Mallorca, and Elizabeth Marion, *née* Aitken (d 1982); *b* 7 Feb 1943; *Educ* Ampleforth; *m* 1, 9 Sept 1966, Lucy (d 1987), da of 3 Baron Maclay, *qv*; 3 s (Hugh Sebastion b 4 Sept 1967, David Ian b 31 Dec 1969, Dominic James b 25 June 1973), 1 da (Anna Marcelle b 23 April 1971); m 2, 31 Aug 1990, Fiona, da of Jock Hunter, wid of Prof Patrick Hamilton (d 1988); 1 step s (John Paul b 16 June 1973), 1 step da (Elizabeth Lilias b 4 Jan 1977); *Career* shipping Glasgow 1961–68, forestry engr 1968–82, organic farmer 1968–, md Glenside Organics 1982–; chm Organic Farmers and Growers Scot, memb Bd UK Register of Organic Food Standards 1987–93, vice chm Scot Organic Prodrs' Assoc; FICS 1965; *Recreations* shooting, sailing, planting trees; *Clubs* Lansdowne; *Style*— Nander Robertson, Esq

ROBERTSON, John; s of Joseph Robertson, of Warwickshire, and Romaine, *née* Howell; *b* 3 May 1957; *Educ* Alcester GS, West Bromwich Coll of Commerce and Technol, London Coll of Printing (NCTJ proficiency certificate); *m* 3 May 1980, Susan Margaret, *née* Field; 1 da (Sarah Louise b 24 May 1984); *Career* photographer: Stratford-upon-Avon Herald 1974–75, Wellingborough News Echo 1975–77, Northants Evening Telegraph 1977–93; freelance photographer: The Guardian 1993– (part time 1989–93), The Sunday Telegraph 1993– (part time 1992–93); *Awards* News Photographer of the Year E Midlands Allied Press 1985 and 1986, Press Photographer of the Year UK Press Gazette 1989, British Regnl Press Photographer of the Year 1989, News Photographer of the Year Birmingham Press Club 1989, winner Ilford Nat Photo of the Month Aug 1991, winner (Features) Ilford Nat Awards 1991; ARPS; *Recreations* cinema, theatre, reading, swimming, ice-skating; *Style*— John Robertson, Esq; ✉ 1 Nansen Close, Rothwell, nr Kettering, Northants NN14 6TZ (☎ 0850 931219); Picture Desk, The Guardian, 119 Farringdon Road, London EC1R 3ER

ROBERTSON, John Davie Manson; CBE (1993, OBE 1978); s of John Robertson (d 1972), and Margaret Gibson Wright (d 1987); *b* 6 Nov 1929; *Educ* Kirkwall GS, Univ of Edinburgh (BL); *m* 25 Feb 1959, Elizabeth Amelia, da of Donald William Macpherson (d 1987); 2 s (John b 1961, Sinclair b 1967), 2 da (Susan b 1959, Fiona b 1965); *Career* Anglo Iranian Oil Co (later BP) UK and ME 1953, chm S & J D Robertson Group Ltd 1980– (joined 1958), dir Stanley Services Ltd 1987–; chm North of Scotland Water Authority 1995–; memb Bd of Mgmnt Orkney Hosps 1970–74; chm: Orkney Health Bd 1983–91 (memb 1974–79, vice chm 1979–83), Highland Health Bd 1991–; chm Scot Health Mgmnt Efficiency Gp (SCOTMEG) 1985–95; memb: Highlands and Islands Devpt Consultative Cncl 1988–91, Bd Highlands and Islands Enterprise 1990–95; tstee TSB Scotland Fndn 1989–; chm Children's Panel Orkney 1971–76 (chm Advsy Ctee 1977–82); chm: Orkney Savings Ctee 1974–78, Highland and Islands Savings Ctee 1975–78; memb Nat Savings Ctee for Scot 1975–78; hon vice consul Denmark 1972–, hon consul Germany 1976–, Hon Sheriff Grampian Highland and Islands 1977–; Royal Order of Knight of Dannebrog (Denmark) 1982, The Cavalier's Cross of the Order of Merit (Germany) 1986; *Books* Uppies & Doonies (1967), An Orkney Anthology (1991); *Recreations* rough shooting, fishing; *Clubs* New (Edinburgh); *Style*— John D M Robertson, Esq, CBE; ✉ Spinningdale House, Sutherland; S & J D Robertson Group Ltd, Shore St, Kirkwall, Orkney (☎ 01856 872961, fax 01856 875043)

ROBERTSON, John William; s of Ian Middleton Strachen Robertson, of Broughty Ferry, Dundee, and Agnes Ramsey Seaton, *née* Findlay; *b* 27 Aug 1956; *Educ* The HS of Dundee, Univ of Dundee (BSc, Zinn Hunter Award, Henry Dickson Prize, Gordon Mathewson Award), Univ of Liverpool (BArch); *m* 27 July 1984, Judy Ann, da of Thomas Gordon John Peacock; 2 da (Charlotte Elizabeth b 21 April 1986, Georgina Emily b 10 Feb 1988); 1 s (Edward Jams b 4 June 1990); *Career* architect; formerly Fitzroy Robinson Partnership: employed during intercalary year of trg 1976–77 and 1979–80, qualified architect 1980, assoc 1983, ptnr 1985; formed Hurley, Robertson & Associates 1993–, currently specialises in interior architectural projects and the design and construction of well known architectural projects in the Cities of London and Westminster; commendation for high standard of design achieved in the Structural Steel Awards for Aviation House Gatwick Airport 1989; Freeman City of London 1986; memb: City Architecture Forum, City Property Assoc; RIBA 1981; *Recreations* golf, sailing, skiing; *Clubs* Berkshire Golf (Ascot), RAC, Blairgowrie Golf (Rosemount Scotland); *Style*— John Robertson, Esq; ✉ Hurley, Robertson & Associates, 146 Grosvenor Road, London SW1V 3JY (☎ 0171 932 0599); Westcroft, 16 Clare Hill, Esher, Surrey (☎ 01372 466834)

ROBERTSON, John Windeler; s of Maj John Bruce Robertson (d 1973); *b* 9 May 1934; *Educ* Winchester; *m* 1959 (m dis 1984), Jennifer-Ann, da of Gontran Gourdou, of Switzerland; 1 s, 1 da; m 2, 1987, Rosemary Helen Jane Banks; *Career* dep chm Stock Exchange 1976–79 (memb 1956–89, memb Cncl 1966–86), sr ptnr Wedd Durlacher Mordaunt & Co 1979–86, dep chm Barclays de Zoete Wedd Securities Ltd (BZW) 1986–88; dir The Securities Assoc 1986–88; chm Guide Dogs for the Blind Assoc 1993– (memb Cncl 1989–); tstee TSB Fndn for Eng and Wales 1991–; *Recreations* 17th and 18th century marine art, deer stalking, golf, powerboating; *Clubs* City of London; *Style*— John Robertson, Esq; ✉ Eckensfield Barn, Compton, nr Chichester, West Sussex PO18 9NT (☎ 0170563 1239)

ROBERTSON, Julia Anne; da of Alan James Robertson, of Welwyn, Herts, and Pearl Anita, *née* Perrett; *b* 14 Feb 1970; *Educ* Sir Frederic Osborn Sch Welwyn Garden City, Univ of Hertfordshire; *Career* hockey player; memb: Welwyn Garden City Ladies Hockey Club 1985–90, Ealing Ladies Hockey Club 1990–92, Slough Ladies Hockey Club 1992–; England: under 18 debut 1988 (7 caps), under 21 debut 1989 (27 outdoor and 3 indoor caps), sr debut 1990 (5 caps); Silver medal Euro Indoor Under 21 Championships Vienna 1991, GB students debut 1990 (13 caps, played in World Student Games Sheffield 1991); also long jumper: represented GB jrs 1987, English Schs Athletics Championships 1984–88; currently sports devpt offr Ealing Sports Devpt Team; *Recreations* jigsaw puzzles, theatre, reading; *Style*— Miss Julia Robertson; ✉ c/o All England Women's

Hockey Association, The Stadium, Silbury Boulevard, Milton Keynes, Bucks MK9 1HA (☎ 01908 689290)

ROBERTSON, Katharine Eleanor Hannah Maria (Kate); da of William Anthony Archibald Godfrey, of Hadleigh, Suffolk, and Eleanor Bedford, *née* Wilson; *b* 10 Oct 1955; *Educ* St John's Coll Houghton Johannesburg, Univ of Cape Town (BA, LLB); *m* 23 June 1990, Bruce Michael Edwin Granville Robertson, s of Kenneth Robertson; 1 da (Ella Katharine Marjorie b 27 Nov 1991); *Career* advtg exec; J Walter Thompson Johannesburg SA: account supr 1982–83, account dir 1983–84, client servs dir 1984–86; J Walter Thompson Europe: Euro account dir 1987–91, regional dir-in-charge 1992–94; dir and head of Euro new business Bates Europe 1995–; *Style*— Ms Kate Robertson; ✉ Bates Europe, 121–141 Westbourne Terrace, London W2 6JR (☎ 0171 262 5077, fax 0171 706 3159)

ROBERTSON, Dr Kevin William; s of James Alexander Robertson, of Thurso, Caithness, and Elizabeth Margaret, *née* Grant; *b* 22 Aug 1965; *Educ* Thurso HS, Univ of Glasgow (MB ChB, Livingstone prize for physiology); *Career* jr house offr Univ Dept of Surgery then Univ Dept of Med Glasgow Royal Infirmary 1988–89, SHO Western Infirmary surgical specialities rotation Glasgow 1989–91, SHO W of Scotland rotation in surgery in gen 1991–93, SHO Dept of Vascular Surgery Glasgow Royal Infirmary 1993–94, SHERT (Scottish Hosps Endowment Research Tst) research fell and hon SHO Univ Dept of Surgery Glasgow Royal Infirmary and Beatson Inst for Cancer Research 1994–96, W of Scotland Higher Surgical trainee 1996–; FRCSGlas 1992 (memb Cncl and Jr Advsy Ctee 1993–); *Recreations* swimming, football, travel; *Clubs* Western Baths Swimming; *Style*— Dr Kevin Robertson; ✉ University Department of Surgery, Queen Elizabeth Building, Glasgow Royal Infirmary, Glasgow G31 2ER (☎ 0141 522 3535)

ROBERTSON, Sir Lewis; kt (1991), CBE (1969); s of John Robertson (d 1976); *b* 28 Nov 1922; *Educ* Trinity Coll Glenalmond; *m* 1950, Elspeth, *née* Badenoch; 2 s, 1 da (and 1 s decd); *Career* served RAF; accountant, industrialist, administrator; dep chm and chief exec: Grampian Holdings Ltd 1971–76, Scottish Devpt Agency 1976–81; chm: F H Lloyd Holdings 1982–87, Triplex Foundries Group 1983–90 (now Triplex Lloyd plc), Girobank Scotland 1984–90, Borthwicks 1985–89, Lilley plc 1986–93, Havelock Europa plc 1989–92, Stakis plc 1991–95, Postern Ltd 1991–96; dir: Scottish & Newcastle Breweries 1975–87, Whitman International SA Geneva 1987–90, EFM Income Trust 1991–, Bank of Edinburgh plc 1990–94, Scottish Financial Enterprise 1990–93, The Berkeley Hotel Co 1995–, Advanced Management Programme Scotland Ltd 1996–; chm: Carnegie Tst for Univs of Scotland 1990– (tstee and memb Exec Ctee 1963–); memb: Monopolies Cmmn 1969–76, Restrictive Practices Court 1983–; FRSE 1978; *Recreations* work, reading, classical music, things Italian, listmaking; *Clubs* Athenaeum, New (Edinburgh); *Style*— Sir Lewis Robertson, CBE, FRSE; ✉ 32 Saxe-Coburg Place, Edinburgh EH3 5BP (☎ 0131 332 5221)

ROBERTSON, Liz; *partner* Patrick Deuchar, *qv*; 1 da (Briony Elizabeth b 4 July 1991); *Career* actress, singer and dancer; professional debut with dance gp The Go-Jos, formerly lead singer and dancer The Young Generation; theatre incl: Side By Side By Sondheim (Toronto), I Love My Wife (West End) 1977–78, Eliza Doolittle in My Fair Lady (tour then West End, Most Promising Actress Variety Club) 1979, Jessica Mitford in The Mitford Girls (Chichester Festival) 1980, one-woman show West End (later on TV), Dance A Little Closer (Broadway), Song and Dance (West End), Kern Goes to Hollywood (Donmar Warehouse then Broadway) 1985, Killing Jessica (Richmond then West End) 1986, Canaries Sometimes Sing (West End) 1987, A Touch of Danger (tour) 1987, Bella Moriarty in Sherlock Holmes - The Musical (Exeter then West End) 1988/89, Anna in The King and I (US tour, Best Actress Award Miami) 1989/90, Maria in The Sound of Music (tour then Sadler's Wells and continued tour) 1991–93, Lets Do It (musical revue, Oxford and Chichester) 1994, Anna in The King and I (Covent Garden Festival) 1995, Marion in The Music Man (Regents Park) 1995, Olivia in Twelfth Night (Holders Festival Barbados) 1996, Jessica Fauldegate in Beethoven's Tenth (Chichester) 1996; appeared in 4 Royal Variety Performances, VE Day celebrations Hyde Park; Enchanted Evenings with Liz Robertson (Radio 2) 1995–96; recorded albums: Somebody's Girl 1984, The Sound of Music 1993, My Fair Lady 1993; *Style*— Ms Liz Robertson; ✉ c/o Jonathan Altaras Associates Ltd, 27 Floral Street, London WC2E 9DP (☎ 0171 836 8722, fax 0171 836 6066)

ROBERTSON, Maximilian (Max); s of Cdr Craig Alexander Robertson, RN (ret), of Langport, Somerset, and Patricia Mary, *née* Goddard; *b* 27 Dec 1963; *Educ* Shaftesbury GS, Crewe & Alsager Coll of Further Educn; *m* 26 Sept 1987 (m dis 1992), Lesley Alison, da of Maj John Skinner; *Career* athlete; memb Belgrave Harriers; represented: England Schs 1980, England 1982–, UK 1985–; achievements at 400m hurdles: AAA champion 1986–89 and 1991, UK champion 1986, 1987, 1989 and 1991, Silver medal Cwlth Games Edinburgh 1986, semi-finalist Euro Championships Stuttgart 1986 and Split 1990, semi-finalist World Championships Rome 1987, injured Tokyo 1991, Silver medal Euro Cup Prague 1987, competed Olympic Games Seoul 1988, Barcelona 1992; athletics devpt offr Wigan Met Borough Cncl 1986–88, sports mangr Wrightington Country Club 1988–89, athletics devpt offr and track supervisor Bury Met Borough Cncl 1989–90, athletics coach Millfield Sch Somerset 1990–92, owner health and fitness club since 1993; qualified club coach BAAB; *Recreations* history, art, reading, motorsports, music, house restoration; *Style*— Max Robertson, Esq; ✉ c/o British Athletic Federation, Edgbaston House, 3 Duchess Place, off Hagley Road, Edgbaston, Birmingham B16 8NM (☎ 0121 456 4050, fax 0121 456 4061)

ROBERTSON, Cmdt Dame Nancy Margaret; DBE (1957, CBE 1953, OBE 1946); da of Rev William Cowper Robertson, and Jessie, *née* McGregor; *b* 1 March 1909; *Educ* Esdaile Sch Edinburgh, Paris; *Career* secretarial work in London and Paris 1928–39; WRNS 1939, dir of WRNS 1954–58, now retired; *Recreations* needlework, bridge; *Style*— Cmdt Dame Nancy Robertson, DBE; ✉ 10 Park View Court, Park View Road, Berkhamstead, Herts HP4 3ES (☎ 01442 879109)

ROBERTSON, Prof Norman Robert Ean; CBE (1991); s of Robert Robertson (d 1980), and Jean Thompson Robertson (d 1994); *b* 13 March 1931; *Educ* Hamilton Acad, Univ of Glasgow (BDS), Univ of Manchester (MDS, DDS); *m* 14 Aug 1954, Morag Wyllie, da of George McNicol (d 1936); 3 s (Stephen b 1955, Peter b 1960, Nigel b 1963), 2 da (Lois b 1958, Mary b 1966); *Career* Nat Serv RAF 1954–56; sr lectr in orthodontics Univ of Manchester 1963–70; hon conslt in orthodontics: United Manchester Hosps, Manchester Regnl Hosp Bd 1965–70, S Glamorgan and Gwent Health Authy 1970–92; Univ of Wales Coll of Med Cardiff: prof and head of Dept of Orthodontics 1970–85, prof and head of Dept of Child Dental Health 1985–92, dean of Dental Sch 1985–92; memb: UGC Dental Review Working Pty (co-author of its report 1988), S Glamorgan Health Authy 1976–92, Gen Dental Cncl and Dental Educn Advsy Cncl 1985–93, Cncl Univ of Wales Coll of Med 1985–92, Conslt Orthodontists Gp 1988–92, Standing Dental Advsy Ctee 1988–92, Welsh Cncl Postgrad Med and Dental Educn 1989–92; memb: BDA, COG, BSSO, BAO; *Books* Oral Orthopaedics and Orthodontics for Cleft Lip and Palate: A Structured Approach (1983); *Recreations* sailing, watercolour painting; *Style*— Prof Norman Robertson, CBE; ✉ 26 Heol Tyn y Cae, Rhiwbina, Cardiff CF4 6DJ (☎ 01222 613439)

ROBERTSON, Prof Paul; *Career* violinist; leader Medici String Quartet; Medici String Quartet: formed 1971, artists in residence and fells of Univ of Lancaster, currently artists in residence Univ of Surrey, launched own record label Whitehall 1992; currently visiting prof of music and psychiatry Kingston Univ; recent guest lectures incl: City Univ, Medical Soc of London, The Study Soc, Coll of Psychic Studies, Music and The Young Mind Conference New Coll Sch Oxford, Brain, Art, Mind, Music Conference Univ of Bath, Music, Brain Function, SEAL Conference Budapest, Brain Function and The Mind Conference (with concert by Medici Quartet) Geneva Cantonal Hosp, Holburne Museum (Bath Festival), The Art and Music of Business (with concert by Medici String Quartet) Roffey Park Mgmnt Inst; broadcasts incl: interview with Margaret Howard (Classic FM, nominated for Prix Italia 1993), The Mind of Music (series of six dialogues and concerts for Classic FM) 1995, Music & The Mind (Channel 4 Television) 1995; 1995–96 tours: Italy, Bulgaria, Germany, The Netherlands, Scandinavia, Spain; 1994–95 festival appearances incl: Bath, Lichfield, Salisbury, Three Choirs; BBC Lunchtime Recital St John's Smith Square, Glories of the String Quartet (series of 6 concerts) Braithwaite Hall Croydon Clocktower; *Recordings* with Medici String Quartet incl: Beethoven The Complete String Quartets Cycle, Alan Bush Dialectic Quartet Op 15, Elgar String Quartet, Franck Piano Quintet in F minor (with John Bingham), Janacek The Kreutzer Sonata and Intimate Letters, Mendelssohn String Quartet Op 13, Shostakovich Two Pieces for Octet (with Alberni String Quartet), Ravel String Quartet, Smetana From My Life, Vaughan Williams Phantasy Quintet (with Simon Rowland-Jones), Music and the Mind - Musical Illustrations from Channel 4 series, double CD of selected works; recordings on own label incl: Brahms Piano Quintet in F minor Op 13 (with John Lill), Delius A Song before Sunrise, Haydn Six String Quartets Op 20, Mozart's Journey to Prague (with Dorothy Tutin and Richard McCabe), Mozart Clarinet Quintet in A major K 581 (with Jack Brymer), Schubert Death and the Maiden, Dvorak String Quartet in F major Op 96 American; *Style*— Prof Paul Robertson; ✉ c/o Georgina Ivor Associates, 66 Alderbrook Road, London SW12 8AB (☎ 0181 673 7179, fax 0181 675 8058)

ROBERTSON, Peter Duncan Neil; s of Laurence Neil Robertson, Flt Lt RAF (despatches, d 1961), and Edith Pamela, *née* Moorhouse; *b* 23 May 1940; *Educ* Sandroyd Sch, Harrow; *m* 13 July 1962, Diana Helen, da of Dr R C Barbor (d 1989), of Rosefield Peldon, nr Colchester, Essex; 1 s (Toby Neil b 1970), 1 da (Tania Gay b 1967); *Career* trainee R C Greig and Co 1958–61, Philip Hill Higginson Private Client and Pension Fund Management 1961–64, M&G Group plc 1965–95 (Far East investment dir M&G Investment Management 1971–95); dir: Invesco Asia plc 1980–, China Assets (HK) Ltd 1991–, China North Industries Investment Ltd 1995–, Govett Smaller Companies Investment Trust Ltd 1996–; *Recreations* shooting, golf, falconry, cooking, racing; *Clubs* Turf; *Style*— Peter Robertson, Esq; ✉ 12 Ropers Orchard, Danvers Street, London SW3 5AX (☎ 0171 352 5759, fax 0171 351 4639)

ROBERTSON, Peter McKellar; OBE (1987), JP (Ayrshire 1976), DL (1960); s of John McKellar Robertson, CBE (d 1939); *b* 5 June 1923; *Educ* Marlborough, Royal Tech Coll Glasgow (BSc); *m* 1951, Elspeth Marion, da of late James Charles Hunter, of Glentyan, Kilbarchan, Renfrewshire; 1 s (John), 2 da (Jane, Angela); *Career* RN VR 1944–46; landowner; memb Ayrshire CC 1949–75; pres Assoc of CCs in Scotland 1974–75, memb Local Authy Accounts Cmmn Scotland 1974–87 (vice chm 1983–87); *Recreations* music; *Clubs* Western (Glasgow); *Style*— Peter M Robertson, Esq, OBE, JP, DL; ✉ Noddsdale, Largs, Ayrshire KA30 8SL (☎ 01475 672382)

ROBERTSON, (David) Ranald Craig; s of David Stanley Robertson (d 1989), and Olive Mary, *née* Svendsen; *b* 23 April 1948; *Educ* Pukekohe HS NZ, Univ of Auckland (LLB); *m* 10 Sept 1977, Gillian Susan, da of Reginald Berwick; 1 s (Andrew), 1 da (Rhiannon); *Career* Lt 4 Medium Battery Royal NZ Artillery 1971–76, attachment to 200 Sussex Yeomanry Medium Battery RA(V) 1974–76; admitted barrister and slr of Supreme Court of NZ 1973; EMI Music London 1974–80: business affrs exec, business affrs mangr (also of Liberty United Records); legal servs mangr CAP Gp plc 1980–87, admitted slr of Supreme Court of England 1980; ptnr: Stephenson Harwood 1987–93, Field Fisher Waterhouse 1993–96, Taylor Joynson Garrett 1996–; fndr chm Legal Affrs Gp Computing Servs Assoc 1982–87, chm Fedn Against Software Theft 1985–86 (fndr and dir); dir Computer Law Assoc Inc memb: Worshipful Co of Information Technologists, City of London Solicitors Co; memb Law Soc; *Books* Legal Protection of Computer Software, Encyclopaedia of Information Technology (contrib), Butterworths Encyclopaedia of Forms and Precedents (contrib), European Computer Law (contrib); *Style*— Ranald Robertson, Esq; ✉ Taylor Joynson Garrett, Carmelite, 50 Victoria Embankment, London EC4Y 0DX (☎ 0171 353 1234, fax 0171 936 2666)

ROBERTSON, Raymond S; MP (C) Aberdeen South (majority 1,517); s of James Robertson, and Marion Robertson; *b* 11 Dec 1959; *Educ* Garrion Acad Wishaw, Univ of Glasgow; *Career* former teacher Dumbarton Acad; nat chm Scottish Young Conservatives 1982–84, officer Scottish Cons and Unionist Assoc 1982–84 (memb Exec Ctee 1987–), chm Scottish Soc of Cons Teachers 1985–87, Parly candidate (C) Clydesdale 1987, chm Scottish Cons Parly Candidates' Assoc 1988–89, North East political v[illegible] Scottish Cons Pty 1989–92, MP (C) Aberdeen S 1992–, vice-chm Scottish Cons P[illegible] 1993–95, PPS to Michael Ancram as Min of State Northern Ireland Office 1994–9[illegible] Parly under-sec of state Scottish Office with responsibility for educn, housing, fisheries and sport 1995–; *Recreations* reading; *Style*— Raymond S Robertson, Esq, MP; ✉ House of Commons, London SW1A 0AA

ROBERTSON, Robert; CBE (1967), JP (1958); s of Rev William Robertson, HCF (d 1950), and Jessie Douglas (d 1961, authoress of Patchwork Quilt); *b* 15 Aug 1909; *Educ* Forres Acad, Royal Tech Coll Glasgow, Univ of Strathclyde; *m* 1938, Jean, da of James Moffatt (d 1931), of Glasgow; 1 s (Struan), 1 da (Margaret); *Career* Nat Serv WWII with jt responsibility for safe passage of special trains for important persons such as Churchill (code Rapier), Eisenhower (code Cutlass) and royalty (code Grove); ambulance trains for D day landings; civil engr; govr Jordanhill Coll of Educn 1960–83; memb: Scot Cncl for Res in Educn, Scot Cncl for Commercial Admin and Professional Educn 1962–68; chm: Renfrewshire Educn Ctee 1960–72, Sec of State for Scotland's Standing Ctee on Supply and Trg of Teachers for Further Educn 1963–72, Nat Ctee for In-service Trg of Teachers (Scotland) 1966–70; convener Renfrewshire CC 1972–75; govr Jordanhill Sch of Further Educn 1968–83, chm E Renfrewshire Cons Assoc 1971–74; memb Strathclyde Regnl Cncl 1974–86; memb Cncl: Glasgow Coll of Bldg and Printing, Langside Coll, Reid Kerr Coll 1974–86; FEIS Univ of Stirling 1973; *Publications* Robertson Report on Supply and Training of Teachers in Scotland (HMSO, 1965); *Recreations* painting, fishing; *Style*— Robert Robertson, Esq, CBE, JP; ✉ 24 Broadwood Park, Alloway, Ayrshire (☎ 01292 443820); Castlehill, nr Maybole, Ayrshire (☎ 01292 50337)

ROBERTSON, Shirley Ann; da of Iain Robertson, of Dundee, and Elizabeth Ann, *née* Burnett; *b* 15 July 1968; *Educ* Alva Acad, Moray House Coll of Educn (BA Hons); *Career* yachtswoman; competitive laser sailing 1983–88; memb Scottish squads: second Euro Championships 1986, third Euro Championships 1988, eighth World Championships 1988; transferred to Europe class 1988–, winner Br Olympic Trials 1992, ninth Olympic Games Barcelona 1992, second World Championships 1993, ranked World and European number one 1993–; selected memb Br Olympic Team Atlanta 1996 (fourth place) memb Br Sailing Team 1986–; winner Skol sports awards 1986 and 1988; runner-up: Sunday Times Sportswoman of the Yr 1993, Yachtsman of the Yr 1993; *Style*— Miss Shirley Robertson; ✉ 31 Lipney, Menstrie, Clackmannanshire (☎ 01259 761638); 91 Desborough Rd, Eastleigh, Hants (☎ 01703 610229, fax 01703 650595)

ROBERTSON, Brig Sidney Park; MBE (1962), TD (1967), JP (1968), DL (1968); s of John Davie Manson Robertson (d 1934), and Elizabeth Park, *née* Sinclair; *b* 12 March 1914; *Educ* Kirkwall GS, Univ of Edinburgh (BCom), MIBS; *m* 1940, Elsa Miller, da of James Miller Croy (d 1943); 1 s, 1 da; *Career* served WWII, cmmnd RA 1940 (despatches

NW Europe 1945); Maj cmdg 861 (independent) Light Anti-Aircraft Battery RA (Orkney and Zetland) TA 1956–61, Lt-Col cmd Lovat Scouts TA 1962–65, Brig CRA 51 Highland Div TA 1966–67, Hon Col 102 (Ulster and Scot) Light Air Def Regt RA (TA) 1975–80, Hon Col Cmdt RA 1977–80; managerial posts: Anglo-Iranian Oil Co ME 1946–51, mangr operations/sales Southern Div Shell-Mex and BP 1951–54, fndr Robertson firm 1954; chm Orkney Hosps Bd of Mgmnt and Orkney Health Bd 1965–79, chm RA Cncl of Scotland 1980–84; Royal Br Legion Scotland: pres Kirkwall Branch, hon vice-pres Highlands and Islands Area; vice-pres Nat Artillery Assoc 1977–, hon pres Orkney Bn Boys' Brigade, vice-pres RNLI Inst 1985–; hon pres Soc of Friends of St Magnus Cathedral; Hon Sheriff Grampian Highlands and Islands 1969–, Vice Lord-Lt for the Islands Area of Orkney 1987–90; Freedom of Orkney 1990; hon fell Univ of Edinburgh 1996; *Recreations* travel, hill walking, angling; *Clubs* Army and Navy, Caledonian, New (Edinburgh); *Style*— Brig Sidney Robertson, MBE, TD, JP, DL; ✉ Daisybank, Kirkwall, Orkney KW15 1LQ (☎ 01856 872085)

ROBERTSON, Simon Manwaring; s of David Lars Manwaring Robertson, of Ketches, Newick, Sussex, and Pamela Lauderdale Manwaring, *née* Meares; *b* 4 March 1941; *Educ* Cothill Sch, Eton; *m* 26 June 1965, Virginia Stewart, da of Mark Richard Norman (d 1994), of Garden House, Much Hadham, Herts; 1 s (Edward Manwaring b 1968), 2 da (Selina Manwaring b 1969, Lorna Manwaring b 1973); *Career* dir: Kleinwort Benson Ltd 1977–; Kleinwort Benson Group plc: dir 1988–, dep chm 1991–96, chm 1996–; non-exec dir: John Mowlem Group plc 1987–, Inchcape plc 1996–; *Recreations* being in the Prättigau, tennis; *Clubs* Boodle's, Marks, Racquet (New York); *Style*— Simon M Robertson, Esq; ✉ Kleinwort Benson Group plc, 20 Fenchurch St, London EC3P 3DB (☎ 0171 623 8000, fax 0171 956 5391)

ROBERTSON, Stanley Stewart John; s of Jock Stanley Robertson, and Florence Kathleen, *née* Carpenter; *b* 14 July 1938; *Educ* Liverpool Poly (DipEE); *m* 1961, Valerie, *née* Housley; 2 s, 2 da; *Career* student engrg apprentice UKAEA 1956–62, asst electrical engr CEGB 1961–67, electrical engrg mangr Shell Chemicals UK 1967–74; Health and Safety Exec: sr electrical inspr 1974–77, superintending inspr 1980–91 (dep superintending inspr 1977–80), dep chief inspr and regnl dir 1991–93, chief inspecting offr Railways 1993–; non-exec dir NQA Ltd 1993–; chm: Railway Industry Advsy Ctee Health and Safety Cmmn 1993–, Nat Inspection Cncl for Electrical Installation Contracting 1993–95; author of various pubns and tech papers on electrical safety matters; FIEE 1987 (MIEE 1973), MCIT 1994; *Recreations* listening to music, gardening; *Style*— Stanley Robertson, Esq; ✉ HM Railway Inspectorate, Rose Court, 2 Southwark Bridge, London SE1 9HS (☎ 0171 717 6501)

ROBERTSON, Prof Stephen Edward; s of Prof Charles Martin Robertson, and Theodosia Cecil, *née* Spring Rice (d 1984); *b* 4 April 1946; *Educ* Westminster, Trinity Coll Cambridge (BA, MA), City Univ (MSc), UCL (PhD); *m* 25 June 1966, Judith Anne, da of Edwin Donald Kirk (d 1943); 1 s (Colin b 1979), 1 da (Magdalene b 1977); *Career* Royal Soc Scientific Info Res Fell UCL 1973–78, Fulbright scholar Univ of Calif at Berkeley 1981, prof of info systems City Univ 1988–; memb Universities' Research Assessment Panel for Library and Information Management 1996; memb Local Ctee Nat Schizophrenia Fellowship; fell Inst of Info Sci, MBCS; *Style*— Prof Stephen Robertson; ✉ Department of Information Science, City University, Northampton Square, London EC1V OHB (☎ 0171 477 8380, fax 0171 477 8584)

ROBERTSON, Stephen Peter; *b* 17 Nov 1954; *Educ* Shenfield Sch, Univ of Nottingham (BSc Chemistry); *Career* mktg asst Dunlop Consumer Products 1976–79, gp product mangr Ashe Consumer (now Sara Lee) 1979–81, sr brands mangr Brooke Bond Oxo Foods (Unilever) 1981–85, mktg devpt mangr Alberto-Culver Co Ltd 1985–86, Euro mktg mangr Mars Inc Drinks Gp Europe 1986–92, mktg dir UK and Ireland Mattel Toys Ltd 1992–93, dir of mktg B & Q plc (subsid of Kingfisher plc) 1993–; memb Mktg Soc 1991 (memb Mgmnt Team and dir of Soc 1994); *Style*— Stephen Robertson, Esq; ✉ B & Q plc, Portswood House, 1 Corporate Park, Chandlers Ford, Hampshire SO53 3YX (☎ 01703 256256, fax 01703 257481, mobile 0374 219745)

ROBERTSON, Sue; *b* 17 Aug 1952; *Educ* Midhurst GS Sussex, Univ of York (BA), Univ of Nottingham (PGCE), City Univ London (arts admin dipl); *Career* English and drama teacher Brakenhale Sch Bracknell Berks 1975–79, sr educn offr Arts Cncl of GB 1983–86 (asst educn offr 1980–82), dir educn programmes South Bank Centre 1986–92, exec dir Southern Arts Bd 1993–96, chief exec London Arts Bd 1996–; *Style*— Ms Sue Robertson; ✉ London Arts Board, Elme House, 133 Long Acre, Covent Garden, London WC2E 9AF (☎ 0171 240 1313, fax 0171 240 4580)

ROBERTSON, Timothy Kenneth Hickman; s of Roy Hickman Robertson (d 1981), of Standish, Glos, and Kathleen Hilda Alice, *née* Barford (d 1988); *b* 10 Feb 1937; *Educ* Shrewsbury, Trinity Hall Cambridge (BA); *m* 5 Sept 1969, Bridget Sara, da of Edward Noel Riddihough Hewitt (d 1974), of Addingham, Yorks; 2 s (James b 1972, Mark b 1974); *Career* Nat Serv; admitted slr 1963; ptnr Rubinstein Callingham 1968–94, conslt Manches & Co 1994–; tstee The Buttle Tst for Children; memb Law Soc; vice-chm British-Albanian Legal Assoc; *Style*— Timothy Robertson, Esq; ✉ The Fobury, Hertingfordbury, Hertford, Herts SG14 2LD (☎ 01992 584022); Manches & Co, Aldwych House, 81 Aldwych, London WC2B 4RP

ROBERTSON, (Sholto David Maurice) Toby; OBE (1978); s of late Cdr David Lambert Robertson, RN, and Felicity Douglas, *née* Tomlin; *b* 29 Nov 1928; *Educ* Stowe, Trinity Coll Cambridge (BA, MA); *m* 1963 (m dis 1981), (Teresa) Jane, *née* McCulloch; 2 s (Sebastian James Lambert b 1964, Joshua David Nathaniel b 1969), 2 da (Francesca Kate Tomlin b 1965, Sasha Corinna Jane b 1967); *Career* director; first professional prodn The Iceman Cometh (New Shakespeare, Liverpool) 1958; dir Prospect Theatre Co 1966–78, Old Vic Theatre (Old Vic Co 1979–80) 1977–80; artistic dir Theatr Clwyd 1985–92; hon fell Univ Coll of North Wales 1996; *Theatre* over 40 prodns incl: The Soldier's Fortune 1964, The Confederacy 1964, The Importance of Being Earnest 1964, The Man of Mode 1965, Macbeth 1966, The Tempest 1966, A Murder of No Importance 1967, A Room with a View 1967, Twelfth Night 1968 & 1973–78, No Man's Land 1968, The Beggar's Opera (also for Phoenix Opera 1972) 1968, The Servant of Two Masters 1968, Edward II 1969, Boswell's Life of Johnson 1969, King Lear 1971 & 1978, Loves Labour's Lost 1971, Richard III 1972, Ivanov 1972 & 1978, Pencles Royal Hour of the Sun 1973, The Pilgrims Progress 1974 & 1977, Hamlet 1974 & 1979 (Ohio USA 1996), War Music 1974, Antony and Cleopatra 1974, Smith of Smiths 1974, 1978 & 1979, Buster 1974, The Lunatic 1978, The Lover and the Poet 1978 & 1979, Romeo and Juliet 1979, The Government Inspector 1979, Next Time I'll Sing to You 1980, Pericles 1980 (NY, OBIE Award for outstanding dir 1981), Measure for Measure 1981 (People's Arts Theatre, Peking), The Revenger's Tragedy 1981 (NY, Villager Award for Outstanding Treatment of Classical Text 1982), Richard II (Washington DC) 1988, York Cycle of Mystery Plays (York Festival) 1984, A Midsummer Night's Dream 1985, Medea (Young Vic 1986, California Shakespeare Festival San Francisco 1996), Taming of the Shrew 1986, You Never Can Tell (Theatre Royal Haymarket) 1987, Captain Carvallo 1988, The Glorious Years 1988, Kingsley Amis' The Old Devils (adapted Robin Hawdon) 1989, Othello 1989, Barnaby and the Old Boys (Vaudeville Theatre), Enemy of the People (Lyric Hammersmith), The Cherry Orchard, Hamlet, Marching Song, The Seagull, Trelawnay of the Wells (Comedy Theatre) 1992, The Old Devils (Philadelphia) 1993, The Taming of the Shrew (Regent's Park) 1993, Macbeth (Habimah Theatre Israel) 1994, Loot (Theatr Clywd) 1995; *Opera* incl: Marriage of Figaro 1977, Elisir d'Amore (Opera Co of Philadelphia), Oedipus Rex 1982, Dido and Aeneas; *Television* various TV plays 1959–63 (over 25 TV prodns); *Films* asst dir Lord of the Flies 1961; *Awards* TMA/Martini Rossi Award for Outstanding Contribution to Theatrical Life 1991; *Recreations* painting, sailing; *Clubs* Garrick; *Style*— Toby Robertson, Esq, OBE; ✉ 210 Brixton Road, London SW9 6AP

ROBERTSON-GLASGOW, Robert Foxcroft; s of Robert Wilson Robertson-Glasgow (d 1977), of Hinton House, Hinton Charterhouse, Bath, and Phyllis Mary Helen (d 1971), whose ggf Thomas Jones (d 1848) suc to Hinton in 1846 and was s of Thomas Jones, of Stapleton House, Glos, and Frances Foxcroft (*see* Burke's Landed Gentry, 18 ed, vol II, 1969); *b* 11 Sept 1935; *Educ* Radley, Lincoln Coll Oxford, RAC Cirencester; *m* 10 Sept 1983, Patricia Coleridge, da of Thomas Patrick Shevlin (d 1950), of Wallsend on Tyne; *Career* Lt The Royal Scots (The Royal Regt) 1955–56; past memb: Somerset CC, London Delgn of Somerset and S Avon branch Nat Farmers' Union; currently gen cmmr of taxes; High Sheriff of Avon 1990–91; *Recreations* shooting, gardening, art history; *Clubs* Army & Navy; *Style*— R F Robertson-Glasgow, Esq; ✉ 19 Green Lane, Hinton Charterhouse, Bath BA3 6BL (☎ 01225 723230)

ROBERTSON-MacLEOD, (Roderick) James Andrew; s of Roderick Cameron Robertson-MacLeod (d 1991), and Daphne Mary, *née* Bick; *b* 5 March 1951; *Educ* St Aubyn's Rottingdean Sussex, Milton Abbey Sch Blandford Dorset; *m* July 1991, Karen Theodora, da of Petre Barclay; 2 da (Katrina Rose b 2 Jan 1992, Louisa Iona b 15 Dec 1995), 1 s (Jack Alexander b 30 Sept 1993); *Career* joined Royal Green Jackets HM Forces 1970, UN Forces Cyprus 1971, Regtl Serv 1971–74, served NI 1975–76, ADC to GOC NI 1976–78, Adj 4 Royal Green Jackets, ADC to Prince and Princess of Monaco 1980–83; dir sports sponsorship co (pt of Markham Gp) 1983–89, commercial dir Operation Raleigh 1990–92, chief exec Raleigh International 1992–; *Recreations* tennis, skiing, running, politics; *Style*— James Robertson-MacLeod, Esq; ✉ Chief Executive, Raleigh International, Raleigh House, 27 Parsons Green Lane, London SW6 4HS (☎ 0171 371 8585, fax 0171 371 5116)

ROBERTSON OF OAKRIDGE, 2 Baron (UK 1961); Sir William Ronald Robertson; 3 Bt (UK 1919); s of Gen 1 Baron Robertson of Oakridge, GCB, GBE, KCMG, KCVO, DSO, MC (d 1974); *b* 8 Dec 1930; *Educ* Charterhouse; *m* 1972, Celia, da of William Elworthy; 1 s; *Heir* s, Hon William Brian Elworthy Robertson b 15 Nov 1975; *Career* sits as Independent peer in House of Lords; memb London Stock Exchange 1973–95, late Maj Royal Scots Greys; memb Ct of Assts Worshipful Co of Salters (master 1985–86); *Style*— Lord Robertson of Oakridge; ✉ House of Lords, London SW1A 0PW

ROBERTSON-PEARCE, Dr Anthony Brian; s of John Gilbert Robertson-Pearce (d 1967), of Testwood House, Lyndhurst, Hants, and Damaris Aubrey, *née* Wilce (d 1946); *b* 3 April 1932; *Educ* Chideock Manor Sch, Christ's Coll Cambridge (BA), Univ of Stockholm (Dip in Archaeological Photography), Alliance Française Paris (Dip in French); *m* 1, 18 May 1956 (m dis 1973), (Ingrid) Christina, da of Erik Nystrom (d 1957), of Stockholm, Sweden; 1 s (Michael b 3 Aug 1960), 2 da (Pamela b 22 April 1957, Penelope b 3 Oct 1965); m 2, 7 June 1974 (m dis 1980), Catharina Carlsdotter, da of Capt Soldan Carl Fredrik Henningsson Ridderstad (d 1973), of Linkoping, Sweden; *Career* supervisor and photographer excavations Motya Sicily 1965, Br Sch of Archaeology Baghdad 1966, supervisor and MO Tell-A-Rimah N Iraq 1967, photographer and MO Br Excavations Tawilan Jordan 1968; Central Bd of Nat Antiquities (Riksantikvarieambetet) Stockholm: field archaeological photographer 1969, joined Publishing Dept 1972, subsequently head of publishing; Swedish TV film debut The Inquiry 1990 as Cdre in Royal Swedish Navy; PRO Sollentuna Kommun Stockholm 1983–88; dep govr Bd of Govrs American Biographical Inst Res Assoc, dep dir gen (Europe) Int Biographical Centre Cambridge, memb Swedish Nat Ctee ICOMOS, dep memb Assembly (Region R33) UN Int Parliament for Safety and Peace 1991–; Duine Uasal of the Clan Dhonnachaidh (Scotland); awarded Int Order of Merit (IOM) by The Int Biographical Centre Cambridge for Services to Science 1990, Hon DH London 1991; FRAI, FIBA; *Books* Dr James Robertson 1566–1652 (1972), The Prehistoric Enclosure of Ekornavallen Sweden (1974), The Ruins of Kronoberg Castle (1974), Kaseberg Ship-setting (1975), The Battle of Rotebro 1497 (1986), Klasroskolan 1804–1881 (1987); *Recreations* riding, golf, painting watercolours; *Clubs* Naval, Sallskapet Stockholm; *Style*— Dr Anthony B Robertson-Pearce; ✉ IPSP, Nybrogatan 54, S-11440 Stockholm, Sweden (☎ 00 46 8 661 02 68); Film Lance International AB, Box 27156, S-10252, Stockholm, Sweden (fax 00 46 8 662 04 44)

ROBIN, Sister (Mary) Gabriel; da of Clement Ernest Robin (d 1992), and Agnes Gertrude, *née* Appleton, of Harborne, Birmingham; *b* 27 Dec 1935; *Educ* St Paul's GS Edgbaston, Girton Coll Cambridge (MA), Inst of Educn London (Dip in Religious Educn); *Career* headmistress Les Oiseaux Sch Westgate-on-Sea Kent 1965–72 (asst mistress 1957–65); memb Int Gen Cncl Canonesses of St Augustine Congregation of Our Lady 1972–81 and 1990–96, provincial superior Br Province 1981–90, gen sec Conf of Religious in England and Wales 1989–; *Style*— Sister Gabriel Robin, CSA; ✉ Conference of Religious Secretariat, 114 Mount Street, London W1Y 6DQ (☎ 0171 493 1817, fax 0171 409 2321)

ROBIN, Ian Gibson; s of Dr Arthur Robin (d 1956), of Edinburgh, and Elizabeth Parker, *née* Arnold (d 1953); *b* 22 May 1909; *Educ* Merchiston Castle Sch Edinburgh, Clare Coll Cambridge (MA, MB BCh); *m* 19 July 1939, Shelagh Marian, da of Cyril Merton Croft (d 1951), of Wimbledon; 1 s (Graham Luke), 2 da (Shirley, Wendy); m 2, 21 May 1994, Patricia Lawrence; *Career* RNVR 1939 (invalided out); registrar and chief clinical asst Guy's Hosp 1935–36, private practice Harley St 1937–94, ret, conslt ENT surgn Royal Northern Hosp 1937–74, surgn EMS Sector 3 London Area 1939–45; conslt ENT surgn: St Mary's Hosp 1948–74, Princess Louise Hosp for Children 1948–68, Paddington Green Children's Hosp 1968–74; formerly: vice chm Nat Inst for the Deaf, pres Br Assoc of Otolaryngologists, pres Laryngology Section and vice pres Otological Section RSM, hon memb Br Soc of Audiology, memb Cncl Nat Deaf Children's Soc; memb: Med Soc of London 1947–67, Hunterian Soc 1948–; FRCS 1935; *Books* Diseases of Ear Nose and Throat (2 edn, 1961); *Recreations* golf, gardening, sketching; *Clubs* Hawks' (Cambridge), Achilles, Hampstead Golf; *Style*— Ian Robin, Esq; ✉ Merchiston, 4 Lodge Gardens, Oakham, Rutland LE15 6EP

ROBINS, Prof David John; s of Ernest Arthur Robins (d 1974), of Coulsdon, Surrey, and Edith Mabel, *née* Reynolds (d 1987); *b* 12 Aug 1945; *Educ* Purley GS, Univ of Exeter (BSc, PhD), Univ of Glasgow (DSc); *m* 12 April 1969, Helen Dorothy, da of Eric Alfred George Skinner; 1 da (Linda Sarah b 16 June 1976), 1 s (Stephen David b 6 Dec 1977); *Career* NIH postdoctoral fell Dept of Biochemistry Univ of Pittsburgh USA 1969–71, SRC fell Dept of Chemistry Univ of Surrey 1971–72, tutorial fell Univ of Reading 1972–73; Univ of Glasgow: lectr in organic chemistry 1974–87, sr lectr 1987–88, reader 1988–90, prof of bio-organic chemistry 1990–; FRSC 1987, FRSE 1994; *Publications* author of over 170 articles in scientific jls; *Style*— Prof David Robins, FRSE; ✉ Department of Chemistry, University of Glasgow, Glasgow G12 8QQ (☎ 0141 330 4378, fax 0141 330 4888)

ROBINS, Hon Mrs (Elizabeth Mary Gerran); *née* Lloyd; JP (SW London 1989); er da of Baron Lloyd of Kilgerran, CBE, QC, JP (Life Peer, d 1991), and Phyllis Mary, *née* Shepherd; *b* 1944; *m* 25 May 1968, Daniel Gerard Robins, QC (d 1989), s of William Albert Robins (d 1991); 3 da (Charlotte b 1971, Sophie b 1974, Anneli b 1976); *Career* tstee Brantwood Tst 1989–, chm Education Trust Ltd 1991–, memb Bd Royal Hosp for Neuro-disability Putney 1990–, govr Dulwich Coll Prep Sch 1992–, tstee Ruskin Fndn 1993–, govr Ryde Sch 1995–; *Clubs* Royal Commonwealth Society, Royal Wimbledon

Golf, The Roehampton; *Style—* The Hon Mrs Robins, JP; ✉ 66 Church Rd, Wimbledon, London SW19 5AA

ROBINS, Grant Alan; s of Brian John Robins, of Portsmouth, and Maureen Betty Robins; *b* 21 May 1969; *Educ* Portsmouth Boys' Sch, Portsmouth Sixth Form Coll; *Career* swimmer; England: 50 caps (jr and sr) 1983–94, capt Br team 1990–94; British record holder: 100m and 200m backstroke short course, 200m and 400m individual medley short course, 200m backstroke long course; memb Channel Relay team; commentator Sky TV; *Recreations* triathlon, my car, wine, food; *Style—* Grant Robins, Esq; ✉ 17 Inverewe Way, Newton Mearns, Scotland G77 6XH (☎ 01505 331954)

ROBINS, John Elgar; s of Herbert William Henry Robins (d 1951), of Bromley, and Anna Marie Angela, *née* Foley (d 1948); *b* 18 July 1926; *Educ* Hurstpierpoint Coll Sussex, St John's Coll Oxford (MA); *m* 4 Aug 1956, Hazel Margaret Rachel, da of John Archibald Robert Snape (d 1962), of 77 Cowbridge Rd, Bridgend, Glamorgan; 1 s (Timothy John b 1 Sept 1965), 1 da (Carol Hazel b 19 Aug 1958); *Career* RAF 1945–48; admitted slr 1953; conslt Trowers and Hamlins 1989–96 (slr 1953–58, ptnr 1958–89); former memb Legal Aid: Certifying Ctee, Area Ctee, panel chm Gen Ctee; memb Law Soc; former local dir Guardian Royal Exchange Assurance; chm Examinations Bd (for Cert in Residential Estate Agency) Coll of Estate Mgmnt 1983–; *Recreations* travel and military history; *Style—* John Robins, Esq; ✉ Elmroyd, 60 Widmore Rd, Bromley BR1 3BD (☎ 0181 460 2107)

ROBINS, John Vernon Harry; s of Col W V H Robins, DSO (d 1990), and Charlotte Mary, *née* Grier (d 1979); *b* 21 Feb 1939; *Educ* Winchester, Stanford Univ USA (SEP); *m* 11 Aug 1962, Elizabeth Mary, da of Alex Banister, OBE, of Sussex; 2 s (Nicholas Vivian James b 1963, Michael Victor Andrew b 1973), 1 da (Tessa Vivienne Mary b 1965); *Career* Nat Serv 2 Lt 2/10 PMO Gurkha Rifles 1959–61; md SNS Communications Ltd 1966–74, chief exec Bally Group (UK) Ltd 1974–79, gp fin dir Fitch Lovell plc 1979–84, dir fin and mgmnt servs Willis Faber plc 1984–89, gp fin dir Willis Corroon Group plc 1990–94, gp chief exec Guardian Royal Exchange plc 1994–; non-exec dir: Church & Co PLC 1993–96, Yorkshire Electricity Group plc 1996–; formerly chm Assoc of Corporate Treasurers; Past Warden Worshipful Co of Glovers; FCT 1979; *Recreations* clocks, music; *Clubs* Brooks's; *Style—* John Robins, Esq; ✉ Guardian Royal Exchange, Royal Exchange, London EC3V 3LS (☎ 0171 696 5331)

ROBINS, Peter Marshall; OBE (1981); s of Henry Joseph Robins (d 1951), of Newent, and Maudie Theresa, *née* White; *b* 3 July 1932; *Educ* Newent GS; *m* 20 Sept 1958, Iona Naomi Irene Juliana, da of Edwin Jack Hill (d 1987); 2 s (Adrian Peter b 1963 d 1995, Arlene b 1966); *Career* slr; dir Bentham Properties Ltd 1966; farmer; Mayor City of Gloucester 1975–76, memb Gloucester City Cncl 1974–82 (chm 1973–74, ldr 1973–82), dep Mayor 1976–82; memb: Gloucester Co Borough Cncl 1965–74, Gloucester CC 1973–85; *Recreations* golf; *Style—* Peter Robins, Esq, OBE; ✉ Robins Farm, Matson Lane, Gloucester GL4 6DZ (☎ 01452 529681); Rowan House, Barnett Way, Gloucester GL4 7RT (☎ 01452 612345, fax 01452 611922)

ROBINS, Sir Ralph Harry; s of Leonard Haddon Robins, and Maud Lillian Robins; *b* 16 June 1932; *Educ* Imperial Coll London (BSc, ACGI); *m* 1962, Patricia Maureen, *née* Grimes; 2 da; *Career* devpt engr Rolls-Royce Derby 1955–56, exec vice pres Rolls-Royce Inc 1971, md RR Indust & Marine Div 1973, chm International Aero Engines AG 1983–84; Rolls-Royce plc: md 1984, dep chm 1989, exec chm 1992–; non-exec dir: Marks & Spencer plc 1992–, Standard Chartered plc 1988–, Schroders plc 1990–, Cable and Wireless plc 1994–; chm Defence Industries Cncl 1986–, pres Soc of Br Aerospace Cos 1986–87; fell Imperial Coll 1993; FEng 1988, Hon FIMechE; *Style—* Sir Ralph Robins, FEng; ✉ Rolls-Royce plc, 65 Buckingham Gate, London SW1E 6AT (☎ 0171 222 9020)

ROBINS, Prof Robert Henry; s of Dr J N Robins (d 1958), of Folkestone, Kent, and Muriel Winifred, *née* Porter (d 1960); *b* 1 July 1921; *Educ* Tonbridge, New Coll Oxford (BA, MA); *m* 29 Aug 1953, Sheila Marie (d 1983), da of Arthur Fynn (d 1944), of Norwood; *Career* WWII Flt Lt RAFVR 1942–45; lectr in linguistics Sch of Oriental and African Studies Univ of London 1948–55, prof of gen linguistics Univ of London 1966–86 (reader 1965–65), emeritus prof 1986; pres Int Ctee of Linguists 1977–97, Philological Soc 1988–92; rep Tport Users' Consultative Ctee Caterham Residents' Assoc 1983–; DLit Univ of London; FBA; hon memb Linguistic Soc of America, memb Academia Europaea 1991; *Books* Ancient and Medieval Grammatical Theory in Europe (1951), The Yurok Language (1958), General Linguistics: an Introductory Survey (1964, 1989), A Short History of Linguistics (1967, 1990), The Byzantine Grammarians: Their Place in History (1993); *Recreations* gardening, travel; *Clubs* Royal Cwlth Soc, Athenaeum; *Style—* Prof R H Robins, FBA; ✉ 65 Dome Hill, Caterham, Surrey CR3 6EF (☎ 01883 343778); School of Oriental and African Studies, University of London, London WC1H 0XG (☎ 0171 637 2388)

ROBINS, Maj-Gen William J P; OBE; *Educ* BSc(Eng), MPhil; *Career* cmmnd Royal Corps of Signals; Dir of Cmd Control Communications and Info Systems (Army) until 1993, Maj-Gen 1993, Asst Chief of Defence Staff (CIS) 1993–95, Dir Gen Information and Communication Services 1995–; Col Commandant Royal Signals; CEng, FIEE, FBCS; *Style—* Maj-Gen W J P Robins, OBE; ✉ Ministry of Defence, Main Building, Whitehall, London SW1A 2HB (☎ 0171 218 7445, e-mail wrobins@dgics.mod.uk)

ROBINSON, *see:* Lynch-Robinson

ROBINSON, (George) Adrian; s of Thomas Gerard Robinson, BEM (d 1994), of Preston, Lancs, and Elizabeth, *née* Gillow; *b* 3 Nov 1949; *Educ* Preston Catholic Coll, Pembroke Coll Oxford (MA, cricket blue); *m* 6 April 1974, Susan Margaret, da of James Hopwood Edmondson (d 1995), of Accrington, Lancs; 2 s (Philip Adrian b 9 Sept 1984, Andrew James b 3 May 1987); *Career* various appts Midland Bank Ltd 1971–80; Airbus Industrie: sales fin mangr 1980–82, dep sales fin dir 1982–84, sales fin dir 1984; corporate fin dir Midland Bank plc 1985; md special fin gp Chemical Bank 1987–89 (dir Aerospace 1986–87), dep gen mangr The Nippon Credit Bank 1990–92; aerospace conslt 1992–; dir: Aircraft Lease Portfolio Securitization 94–1 Limited, ALPS 94–1 (France) SARL, ALPS 94–1 (Belgium) NV, Pergola Limited, Aircraft Lease Portfolio Securitization 92–1 Limited; ACIB 1973; *Recreations* golf, tennis, shooting; *Clubs* Oxford University Cricket, Bearsted Golf; *Style—* Adrian Robinson, Esq

ROBINSON, (Francis) Alastair Lavie; s of late Mr and Mrs Stephen Robinson; *b* 19 Sept 1937; *Educ* Eton; *m* 29 April 1961, Lavinia Elizabeth Napier, da of late Cdr Trevylyan Napier, DSC (d 1940), and Mrs T Napier; 2 da (Camilla (Mrs Adam Fox) b 1967, Zoe b 1970); *Career* 2 Lt 4/7 Royal Dragoon Guards 1956–68; dir Mercantile Credit Co Ltd 1978–81 (joined 1959, gen mangr 1971–78); Barclays plc: chief exec pres Barclays American Corpn NC USA 1981–84, regnl gen mangr Barclays Bank International 1984–87, dir personnel Barclays Bank plc 1987–90, exec dir Barclays plc 1990–96, vice chm 1992–96, chm UK Banking Services Barclays plc 1994–96; non-exec dir: London Goodenough Trust for Overseas Students, RMC Group plc 1996–, Marshall of Cambridge (Holdings) Ltd; *Recreations* music, country pursuits, golf; *Style—* Alastair Robinson, Esq; ✉ Ousden House, Ousden, Suffolk CB8 8EN

ROBINSON, (Richard) Andrew; s of Raymond Thomas Robinson, of Taunton, and Patricia Mary, *née* Beckett; *b* 3 April 1964; *Educ* Richard Huish Coll, Loughborough Univ; *m* Samantha Elizabeth, da of John Andrew Morrison; 3 s (Oliver James b 21 July 1991, Edward George b 1 Feb 1993, Henry John b 12 Aug 1995); *Career* rugby union player (flanker); clubs: Taunton 1981–83, Loughborough Univ 1982–86 (capt 1986), Bath 1986– (capt 1991–93, currently full time professional); most recent honours with Bath: Courage League Champions 1996, winners Pilkington Cup 1996; England: 8 caps, debut v Aust 1988, five nations debut v Scotland 1989, asst coach U21 1996–; 6 appearances Br Lions tour Aust 1989; physical educn and maths teacher: Writhlington Sch 1986–89, King Edward Sch Bath 1989–94; sports dir Colstons Collegiate Sch 1994–96; Player of the Year Five Nations Championship 1989; *Recreations* all sports (especially golf and cricket), gambling; *Style—* Andrew Robinson, Esq; ✉ c/o Bath RFC, Recreation Ground, Bath (☎ 01225 425192)

ROBINSON, Andrew William Stewart; s of Douglass Robinson (d 1981), of Halifax, Yorks, and Nell Summerton Bywater; *b* 26 Nov 1937; *Educ* Repton Sch, Oriel Coll Oxford (MA, soccer blue 1961 and 1962); *m* April 1964, Rachel Patricia, da of Gilbert Charles Dare and Nora Tempest Gray; 2 s (Mark William b 4 April 1965, James Stewart b 3 April 1967); *Career* asst master Temple Grove Prep Sch 1963–67; headmaster: Brocksford Hall Prep Sch 1967–83, Walhampton Prep Sch 1983–; memb Inc Assoc of Prep Schs 1968–; *Recreations* cricket, golf, ornithology, photography, walking; *Clubs* Vincent's (Oxford); *Style—* Andrew Robinson, Esq; ✉ The Headmaster's House, Walhampton School, Lymington, Hants SO41 5ZG (☎ 01590 676270)

ROBINSON, Dr (Elizabeth) Angela Eleanor; da of Harold Jeffs (d 1990), and Phyllis, *née* Field, of Bedford; *b* 27 Dec 1942; *Educ* The Dame Alice Harpur Sch for Girls Bedford, St Mary's Hosp Med Sch London (Max Bonn Pathology Prize); *m* 1, 1965 (m dis 1994); 2 da (Amy b 1972, Isobel b 1979), 1 s (Alexander b 1975); *partner* G A Milnes; *Career* house physician then house surgn St Mary's Hosp London 1967–68, SHO, registrar then sr registrar in clinical haematology and blood transfusion Yorks Regnl Haematology Rotational Trg Scheme 1968–76, conslt in clinical haematology and blood transfusion Yorks Regnl Blood Transfusion Serv and in paediatric haematology and oncology Seacroft Hosp 1976– (memb Bone Marrow Transplant Team 1982–), opened first vol donor automated plasmapheresis unit in Europe (Bradford) 1982, hon sr clinical lectr Dept of Med Univ of Leeds 1987–, chief exec/med dir Yorks Regnl Blood Transfusion Serv 1988–94, nat med dir Nat Blood Authy 1994–; tstee Candlelighters (childhood cancer charity) 1979–92, vice pres World Apheresis Assoc 1994–; memb Cncl: Euro Soc of Haemaphersis 1990–, Royal Coll of Pathologists 1995–; FRCPath 1986 (MRCPath 1973); *Publications* Pilot Sutdy for Large-Scale Plasma Procurement Using Automated Plasmopheresis (1983), Plasma Exchange for Rhesis Haemolytic Disease (1986), Prognastic Factors in Juvenile Chronic Granulocytic Leukaemia (1992), Donor and Therapeutic Apheresis (1994); *Recreations* singing (memb Chamber Choir), flautist, horse riding; *Clubs* Mid Yorks Riding; *Style—* Dr Angela Robinson; ✉ National Blood Authority, Oak House, Reeds Crescent, Watford, Herts WD1 1QH (☎ 01923 212121, fax 01923 211031)

ROBINSON, Dr Ann; da of Edwin James and Dora, *née* Thorne; *b* 28 Jan 1937; *Educ* St Anne's Coll Oxford (MA), McGill Univ Montreal (MA, PhD); *m* 1961, Michael Robinson; 2 s; *Career* fin journalist Beaverbrook Newspapers 1959–61; sometime lectr at Univs of: Durham, Bristol, Bath, Univ of Wales Coll of Cardiff (sr lectr in politics 1987–89); head of Policy Unit Inst of Directors 1989–95, DG Nat Assoc of Pension Funds 1995–; memb: Cncl RIIA 1991–, MMC 1993–; Euro Parly candidate (Cons) SE Wales 1979; memb: Equal Opportunities Cmmn 1980–85, Economic and Social Ctee EC 1986–93 (chm Industry Section 1990–92), Welsh Arts Cncl 1991–93, HEFC for Wales 1993–; memb: Bd of Academic Govrs Richmond Coll London 1992–, Bd of Govrs Commonwealth Inst 1992–; dir WNO 1993–94; *Publications* Parliament and Public Spending (1978), Tax Policy Making in the UK (with Prof C T Sandford, 1984), also author of numerous articles and chapters on public expenditure, House of Commons select ctees, taxation policy and EC matters; IoD publications: Business Leaders' Manifesto for the European Election (1989 and 1994), European Political Union (1990), A Currency for the Single Market (1990), Continuing Tax Reform (1990), Forward to Prosperity: A Business Leaders' Manifesto for the Next Government (1992); *Style—* Dr Ann Robinson; ✉ National Association of Pension Funds, 12–18 Grosvenor Gardens, London SW1W 0DH (☎ 0171 730 0585, fax 0171 730 2595)

ROBINSON, Anne; da of late Bernard Robinson, and late Anne, *née* Wilson; *b* 26 Sept 1944; *Educ* Farnborough Hill Convent, Les Ambassadrices Paris XVI; *m* 1, 1968 (m dis 1973), Charles Martin Wilson, *qv*; 1 da (Emma Alexandra Wilson b 18 July 1970); m 2, 1980, John Penrose; *Career* Daily Mail 1966–67, Sunday Times 1968–77; columnist: Daily Mirror 1980–93, Today 1993–95, Times 1994–95, The Sun 1995–; presenter: Points of View (BBC TV) 1988–, Watchdog (BBC TV) 1993–; hon fell Liverpool John Moores Univ 1996; *Recreations* reading, television, dogs, having opinions; *Clubs* Bibury Cricket (vice pres), Bibury Tennis (pres); *Style—* Ms Anne Robinson; ✉ c/o Penrose Media, 19 Victoria Grove, London W8 5RW (☎ 0171 584 2969, fax 0171 589 8101)

ROBINSON, Anthony Edward (Tony); s of Flt Lt Robbie Robinson, of St Albans, and Margaret Susan, *née* Harris; *b* 4 Oct 1943; *Educ* St Albans Sch, UCL, Univ of London (BSc); *m* 1, 12 Aug 1969, Margaret Janet (d 1983), da of Alexander Buchanan (d 1967); 1 s (James Alexander b 26 March 1975); m 2, 15 Oct 1991, Katherine Charlotte, da of Peter Leslie Andre Selby; 1 da (Victoria Charlotte b 14 April 1993); *Career* product mangr May & Baker Ltd 1969–73, dir ADA-P 1973–77; md: Pharmatek 1977–82, The PTK Partnership 1983–; vice-pres OARFC; MRSC 1975, MInstM 1975; *Clubs* Old Albanian; *Style—* Tony Robinson, Esq; ✉ 1 Ash Grove, Wheathampstead, St Albans AL4 8DF (☎ 01582 832735); The PTK Partnership, 81 Gower St, London WC1E 6HJ (☎ 0171 636 7436, fax 0171 255 3152)

ROBINSON, Antony John (Tony); s of Frederick William John Robinson, TD (d 1980), and Eunice Cherry Robinson, of Kingswood, Surrey; *b* 11 Dec 1947; *Educ* Cranbrook Sch Kent; *m* 20 Nov 1971, Lesley Anne, da of Victor Lewis Waller, of Mallorca; 4 s (David Andrew b 12 July 1973, Mark Daniel b 15 July 1977, James Antony, Matthew John (twins) b 4 May 1983), 1 da (Natasha Louise b 17 Oct 1974); *Career* trained clerk Harmood Banner Cash Stone & Mouncey (merged with Deloittes 1973) 1966–71, mangr Tax Dept Deloittes 1973–75; Binder Hamlyn: joined 1976, tax ptnr London office 1980, dep head Tax Dept 1987–89, head Tax Dept Leeds and sr tax ptnr Yorkshire Region 1989–95; currently specialist in int and large corp tax planning; memb: Int Fiscal Assoc (repesenting BDO from UK), Taxation Events Working Party ICAEW 1984–87; FCA (ACA 1971); *Recreations* golf, angling, boating, snooker; *Clubs* Franco British Business (Yorkshire Region); *Style—* Tony Robinson, Esq; ✉ 22 Swan Road, Harrogate, North Yorkshire HG1 2SA (☎ 01423 563621)

ROBINSON, Arthur Geoffrey; CBE (1978); s of Arthur Robinson (d 1987), and Frances May Mason (d 1970); *b* 22 Aug 1917; *Educ* Lincoln Sch, Jesus Coll Cambridge (MA), SOAS Univ of London; *m* 1, 1943, Patricia (d 1971), da of William MacAllister (d 1922), of Wetherby; 3 s (Matthew b 1944, Thomas b 1950, George b 1961), 1 da (Sophy b 1955); m 2, 1973, Gai Rencie, wid of Martin Treves and da of Baron Salmon of Sandwich; *Career* served RA 1939–46; admitted slr 1948; Treasy Slrs Dept 1954–62, PLA 1962–66, md Tees and Hartlepool Port Authy 1966–77; chm: English Industl Estates Corp 1974–84, Medway Ports 1978–87; memb Nat Ports Cncl 1980–81, chm Br Ports Assoc 1983–85; *Books* Hedingham Harvest (1977); *Recreations* music; *Clubs* United Oxford and Cambridge Univ; *Style—* A G Robinson, Esq, CBE; ✉ 6 Archery Square, Deal, Kent CT14 7HP; La Baume, Uzes 30700, Gard, France

ROBINSON, Barry John; s of Alfred Henry Robinson, of Rayleigh, Essex, and Amy Alice, *née* Cheverals; *b* 27 May 1946; *Educ* Southend Sch of Art, London Coll of Printing; *m* 24 Aug 1968, Caroline Erica, da of Eric John Field; 1 s (Barnaby James b 1973), 1 da (Kirsten Jane b 1971); *Career* freelance designer 1966–68; design mangr: BOC (British Oxygen Co) 1968–70, ICL (Int Computers) 1970–72, Bovis and P & O 1972–77; design advsr to The Post Office and dir of design Royal Mail National 1977–; external assessor: Camberwell Sch of Art 1985–89, Exeter Sch of Art 1990–96, Croydon Sch of Art 1994–; FCSD 1996, FRSA 1983, hon fell RCA 1991; *Awards* Design Cncl awards 1973 and 1981, Il Gran Premio Dell'arte Filatelica Italy 1983 and 1985, The Most Beautiful Stamp in the World Il Francobollo d'Oro Italy 1983, 1984, 1985 and 1990, Award of Excellence Communication Arts Magazine USA 1989, The Reginald Phillips Gold Medal for Stamp Design 1989, Graphics Section BBC Design Awards 1987 and 1990, The Art Directors' Club of New York Gold Award 1991; D&AD annual awards: Silver 1984, 1986 and 1990, Gold and Silver 1985; *Style*— Barry Robinson, Esq; ✉ 11 Fitzjames Avenue, Croydon, Surrey CR0 5DL; Royal Mail National, 22 Finsbury Square, London EC2A 1NL (☎ 0171 614 7200, fax 0171 614 7209)

ROBINSON, Dr Bill; s of Harold Desmond Robinson (d 1988), and Joyce Grover, *née* Liddington; *b* 6 Jan 1943; *Educ* Bryanston, Univ of Oxford (BA), Univ of Sussex (DPhil), LSE (MSc); *m* 19 Aug 1966, Heather Mary, da of James Albert Jackson; 2 s (Nicholas, Matthew), 1 da (Rosemary); *Career* systems analyst IBM 1968–69, econ asst Cabinet Office 1969–70, econ advsr HM Treasy 1971–74, head of div Euro Cmmn 1974–78, ed Econ Outlook London Business Sch 1978–86, dir Inst of Fiscal Studies 1986–91; advsr Treasy Ctee House of Commons 1981–86, memb Retail Prices Advsy Ctee 1988–90; econ columnist The Independent 1989–91, special advsr to Chllr of Exchequer 1991–93, dir London Economics 1993–; *Books* Medium Term Exchange Rate Guidelines for Business Planning (1983), Britain's Borrowing Problem (1993); *Recreations* the bassoon, skiing, opera, bridge, windsurfing; *Style*— Dr Bill Robinson; ✉ London Economics, 66 Chiltern Street, London W1M 7PR (☎ 0171 446 8493)

ROBINSON, (Francis) Brian; s of Thomas Robert Robinson, and Hannah Margaret Ruth, *née* Ligget; *b* 20 March 1966; *Educ* Cambridge House Boys' GS Ballymena, Univ of Ulster, Loughborough Univ (MSc Sports Sci); *Career* rugby union player; rep: Ballymena under 20's 1986 (capt), Combined Provinces under 21's 1986, Ulster under 20's (interprovincial champions) 1986, Ulster tour Zimbabwe 1987, Ballymena 1st XV 1989–92 and 1993–, Ulster XV 1989–90, Irish Wolfhounds 1990, Calgary Irish XV 1990, Northern Hemisphere XV 1991, London Irish 1992–; Ireland: B debut 1989, under 25 debut 1990, full debut 1991, memb tours Namibia 1991 and NZ 1992, 3 appearances World Cup 1991, 18 full caps; holder Irish record for number of tries in a match (4 v Zimbabwe 1991); *Recreations* fitness and conditioning, reading, photography, most sports; *Style*— Brian Robinson, Esq

ROBINSON, Brian Graham; s of Albert Robinson (d 1985), of Leigh-on-Sea, and Lilian Robinson (d 1978); *b* 27 March 1940; *Educ* Heversham GS, Burnley GS, LSE (LLB, LLM); *m* 29 Feb 1964, Jennifer Elizabeth, da of Herbert Jones; 1 s (Graham David b 25 Aug 1968), 1 da (Helen Susan b 27 Feb 1971); *Career* articled clerk then asst slr Finch Turner & Taylor (later Peacock Fisher & Finch) 1960–64, lectr Victoria Univ of Wellington NZ 1964–65, ptnr Holman Fenwick & Willan 1969– (asst slr 1966–68); tstee Sir John Fisher Fndn; Liveryman Worshipful Co of Shipwrights; memb Law Soc 1964; *Recreations* golf, theatre, music; *Clubs* Malden Golf; *Style*— Brian Robinson, Esq; ✉ Holman, Fenwick & Willan, Marlow House, Lloyds Avenue, London EC3N 3AL (☎ 0171 488 2300, fax 0171 481 0316)

ROBINSON, Air Vice-Marshal Brian Lewis (Boz); s of Frederick Lewis Robinson (d 1993), of Bradford, and Ida, *née* Croft (d 1984); *b* 2 July 1936; *Educ* Bradford GS; *m* 21 April 1961, Ann, da of Albert Thomas Faithfull (d 1956), of Bristol; 1 s (Symon Andrew b 1964), 1 da (Sarah Ann b 1962); *Career* RAF: No 74 (Fighter) Sqdn 1956–59, Oxford Univ Air Sqdn 1959–62, No 73 Sqdn 1963–65, Canberra Trials and Taceval Unit 1966, Directorate of Flight Safety 1967–69, 60 Course RAF Staff Coll Bracknell 1970, OC 1 Sqdn 4 Flying Training Sch 1971–73, SO Second Allied Tactical Air Force 1973–74, memb Directing Staff Canadian Forces Command and Staff College Toronto 1974–76, chief instr 4 Flying Training Sch 1976–78, OC RAF Valley 1978–80, memb Int Military Staff NATO Brussels 1980–82, defence and air attaché Moscow 1983–86, dir orgn MOD 1986–88, Air OC Directly Administered Units and Air Offr i/c admin Strike Command 1989–91 (ret 1991); sr ptnr Belmont (Aviation) Consultants 1991–, md Westavia Ltd 1996–, ptnr Brimpex 1996–; qualified flying instructor 1959, pilot attack instructor 1962, qualified USA airline tport pilot 1995; aerobatic display pilot for Butane Buzzard Aviation Corp 1992; memb: RAF Bobsleigh Team 1965–74, Br Bobsleigh Team 1967, 1969 and 1972; pres No 74 (Tiger) Sqdn Assoc; FIMgt; *Recreations* aerobatics, travel; *Style*— Air Vice-Marshal Boz Robinson; ✉ Cheldon House, Cheldon, Chulmleigh, Devon EX18 7JB (☎ 01769 580117, fax 01275 874434)

ROBINSON, Maj (Alfred) Christopher; s of Col Annesley Robinson, DSO (d 1976), of Long Melford, Suffolk, and Doris Lilian, *née* Barrett (d 1988); *b* 18 Nov 1930; *Educ* Wellington, RMA Sandhurst; *m* 1, 17 Aug 1957 (m dis 1961), Caroline Stafford, da of Maj Christopher Scott-Nicholson (ka 1945), of Ruthwell, Dumfriesshire; m 2, 31 March 1962 (m dis 1978), Amanda, da of Paul Boggis-Rolfe (d 1988), of Bampton, Oxon; 2 s (Charles b 1964, Barnaby b 1970), 2 da (Nicola b 1963, Polly b 1964); *Career* 16/5 The Queen's Royal Lancers 1951–65; Trade Imdemnity Co Ltd 1966–70, Glanvill Enthoven & Co Ltd 1970–73, The Spastics Soc (now Scope) 1973–91; tstee: The Little Fndn, The Mother and Child Fndn; chm Ferriers Barn Disabled Centre; chm W Suffolk Red Cross Fundraising Ctee, vice chm Colne Stour Countryside Assoc; memb: Sudbury Deanery Synod, St Edmondsbury and Ipswich Diocesan Synod; memb ICFM 1986; *Recreations* country pursuits, travel, wine appreciation; *Clubs* Essex; *Style*— Maj Christopher Robinson; ✉ Water Lane Cottage, Bures, Suffolk CO8 5DE (☎ 01787 227179); The Little Foundation, 12 Park Crescent, London W1N 4EQ (☎ 0171 636 5020, fax 0171 436 2601)

ROBINSON, Christopher John; CVO (1992, LVO 1986); s of Rev Preb John Robinson (d 1974), of W Malvern, and Esther Hilda, *née* Lane (d 1983); *b* 20 April 1936; *Educ* Rugby, ChCh Oxford (MA, BMus), Univ of Birmingham (CertEd); *m* 6 Aug 1962, Shirley Ann, da of Harry Frederick Churchman (d 1991); 1 s (Nicholas b 3 June 1970), 1 da (Elizabeth b 26 Sept 1968); *Career* asst organist: ChCh Oxford 1955–58, New Coll Oxford 1957–58; music master Oundle Sch 1959–62; organist: Worcester Cathedral 1963–74 (asst organist 1962–63), St George's Chapel Windsor Castle 1975–91; organist and dir of music St John's Coll Cambridge 1991–; conductor: City of Birmingham Choir 1964– (princ conductor Three Choirs Festivals 1966, 1969 and 1972), Leith Hill Festival 1977–80, Oxford Bach Choir 1977–97; pres RCO 1982–84, chm Elgar Soc 1988–92; hon memb: RAM 1980, MMus Univ of Birmingham 1987; hon fell Univ of Central England 1990; FRCO 1954; *Recreations* cricket, foreign travel; *Clubs* MCC; *Style*— Christopher Robinson, Esq, CVO; ✉ Manor Farmhouse, 51 Church Rd, Hauxton, Cambs CB2 5HS (☎ 01223 871911)

ROBINSON, Sir Christopher Philipse; 8 Bt (UK 1854), of Toronto, Canada; s of Christopher Robinson, QC (d 1974); suc kinsman, Sir John Robinson, 7 Bt (d 1988); *b* 10 Nov 1938; *m* 1962, Barbara Judith, da of Richard Duncan, of Ottawa; 2 s (Peter Duncan b 1967, Jonathan Richard b 1969); *Heir* s, Peter Duncan Robinson b 31 July 1967; *Style*— Sir Christopher Robinson, Bt; ✉ 460 RR1, Chelsea, PQ, J0X 1N0, Canada

ROBINSON, Prof Colin; s of James Robinson (d 1937), of Stretford, Lancs, and Elsie, *née* Brownhill (d 1959); *b* 7 Sept 1932; *Educ* Stretford GS, Univ of Manchester (BA); *m* 1, 13 July 1957 (m dis 1983), Olga, da of Harry West; 2 s (Julian b 1961, Stewart b 1964); m 2, 18 June 1983, Eileen Catherine, *née* Marshall; 2 s (Richard b 1966, Christopher b 1971), 2 da (Louise b 1967, Elaine b 1969); *Career* RAF 1950–53; head Economics Div Corp Planning Dept Esso Petroleum 1960–66, econ advsr natural gas Esso Euro 1966–68, prof of economics Univ of Surrey 1968–; editorial dir Inst of Econ Affrs 1992–; Br Inst of Energy Economists' Economist of the Yr 1992; memb Monopolies and Mergers Cmmn; tstee Wincott Fndn; FSS 1969, FInstPet 1979; *Books* Business Forecasting (1970), North Sea Oil in the Future (1977), The Economics of Energy Self Sufficiency (1984), Can Coal Be Saved? (1985), Energy Policy: Energy, Illusions and Market Realities (1993); *Recreations* walking, music, home improvements; *Style*— Prof Colin Robinson; ✉ Department of Economics, University of Surrey, Guildford, Surrey GU2 5XH (☎ 01483 259171)

ROBINSON, Ven (William) David; s of William Robinson (d 1969), of Blackburn, and Margaret, *née* Bolton (d 1982); *b* 15 March 1931; *Educ* Queen Elizabeth GS Blackburn, Univ of Durham (BA, DipTheol, MA); *m* 30 Jul 1955, Carol Averil Roma, da of Norman William Edward Hamm, of Blackburn; 1 s (Christopher b 1956), 1 da (Catherine b 1960); *Career* pilot offr RAF 1949–51; curate St Wilfrid Standish 1958–61, sr curate Lancaster Priory (priest i/c St George) 1961–63, vicar St James Blackburn 1963–73, diocesan stewardship advsr and priest i/c St James Shireshead 1973–86, hon canon Blackburn Cathedral 1975–86, vicar of Balderstone 1986–87, archdeacon of Blackburn 1986–96, ret; *Recreations* fell walking; *Style*— The Ven David Robinson; ✉ 21 Westbourne Road, Warton, Carnforth, Lancs LA5 9NP (☎ 01524 720591)

ROBINSON, David Foster; s of Arthur Robinson, of Witney, Oxon, and Ellen Robinson, *née* Jackson (d 1989); *b* 29 May 1936; *Educ* King's Sch Macclesfield, Univ of Manchester (BA); *m* 5 Nov 1966, Hannah, da of Roger Alan Watson (d 1979), of Edinburgh; 2 s (William b 1968, Edward b 1970), 1 da (Caroline b 1971); *Career* Nat Serv 2 Lt RAPC 1960–62; ptnr Spicer & Oppenheim (formerly Spicer & Pegler) 1974–90 (joined 1962); chm: M M & K Ltd 1991–94, Interscene Ltd 1991–95, Oldham Lighting Ltd 1993–; dir: The Ratcliff Group Ltd 1992–, Identica Ltd 1992–, Exxtor Group (Holdings) Ltd 1994–; chm Langford & Ulting PC 1978–, chm Plume Housing Assoc 1994–, vice chm Moat Housing Group 1996–; FCA, FIMC; *Books* Human Asset Accounting (1972), Key Definitions in Finance (1980), Managing People (1984), Getting the Best out of People (1988), The Naked Entrepreneur (1990), Business Etiquette (1994); *Recreations* gardening, walking, tennis; *Clubs* City of London, IOD; *Style*— David Robinson, Esq; ✉ Luards, Langford, Maldon, Essex CM9 6QB (☎ and fax 01621 859707); 35 Taeping St London E14

ROBINSON, David James Roper; s of Andrew Thomas Roper, of Dulwich, London, and Barbara Anne, *née* Black; *b* 19 July 1955; *Educ* Westminster Sch (Queen's scholar), Pembroke Coll Cambridge (fndn exhibitioner, MA); *m* 15 June 1996, Jennifer Jane, da of (Charles) Alan McLintock, *qv*; *Career* articled Bennett Welch & Co 1979–81, asst slr Glover & Co 1981–85, ptnr Frere Cholmeley 1989– (joined 1985), head Private Client Dept Frere Cholmeley Bischoff 1994–; *Recreations* music, art, collecting books, travel; *Style*— David Robinson, Esq; ✉ Frere Cholmeley Bischoff, 4 John Carpenter Street, London EC4Y 0NH (☎ 0171 615 8000, fax 0171 615 8080)

ROBINSON, Derek; CBE (1979); of Benjamin Robinson (d 1981), of Barnsley, S Yorkshire, and Gertrude Mary, *née* Wade; *b* 9 Feb 1932; *Educ* Barnsley Holgate GS, Ruskin Coll Oxford (Dip), Lincoln Coll Oxford (MA); *m* 6 Oct 1956, Jean Evelyn, da of Charles Lynch (d 1957); 1 s (Tobias Edward b 1964), 1 da (Lucy Matilda b 1969); *Career* Nat Serv Corpl RASC 1950–52; sr res offr Oxford Univ Inst of Economics and Statistics 1961–, fell Magdalen Coll Oxford 1969–; econ advsr NBPI 1965–67, sr econ advsr Dept of Employment and Productivity 1968–70, dep chm Pay Bd 1973–74, chm SSRC 1975–78, chm Ctee of Inquiry into the System of Remuneration of Membs of Local Authorities 1977, bd memb Br Library Bd 1979–82; *Books* Monetarism and the Labour Market (1986), Civil Service Pay in Africa (1990); *Recreations* music; *Clubs* Reform; *Style*— Derek Robinson, Esq, CBE; ✉ 56 Lonsdale Road, Oxford OX2 7EP (☎ 01865 552276); Institute of Economics and Statistics, St Cross Building, Manor Rd, Oxford OX1 3UL (☎ 01895 271064, fax 01865 271094)

ROBINSON, Derek; s of Alexander Smith Robinson (d 1957), of Bristol, and Margaret Low, *née* MacAskill (d 1993); *b* 12 April 1932; *Educ* Cotham GS Bristol, Downing Coll Cambridge (MA); *m* 1968, Sheila, *née* Collins; *Career* copywriter: McCann Erickson Advertising London 1956–60, BBDO Advertising NY 1960–66; author and freelance writer; *Novels* Goshawk Squadron (1971, short-listed Booker prize), Rotten with Honour 1973, Kramer's War 1977, The Eldorado Network 1979, Piece of Cake (1983, televised, Book of the Month Club Choice), War Story 1987, Artillery of Lies 1991, A Good Clean Fight 1993; *Non-Fiction* Just Testing 1985, Run With The Ball! 1984, The Laws in Plain English (1994, awarded Crystal Mark of the Plain English Campaign), Rugby: a player's guide to the laws (1995); *Recreations* squash, rugby union referee, trout fishing; *Style*— Derek Robinson, Esq; ✉ Shapland House, Somerset St, Kingsdown, Bristol BS2 8LZ (☎ and fax 0117 924 1057); Curtis Brown Farquharson, Haymarket House, 28–29 Haymarket, London SW1Y 4SP (☎ 0171 396 6600)

ROBINSON, Derek Hugh; s of Cyril Thomas John Robinson (d 1967), of Derby, and Doris Isabel, *née* Garrett (d 1960); *b* 5 June 1929; *Educ* Bemrose Sch Derby, Tech Coll Derby, Univ of Southampton, UCL (BSc); *m* 15 Dec 1958, Heather Margaret Anne, da of Reginald Walter Merrick (d 1962), of Midsomer Norton, Somerset; 2 s (Ian, Edward d 1993), 1 da (Fiona); *Career* engr: John Laing & Son Ltd 1950–52, Ontario Dept of Highways Toronto 1952–54; offr US Army Corps of Engrs Labrador 1954; engr: Turriff Construction Corporation Warwick 1954–55, E W H Gifford & Partners Southampton 1957–63; consulting engr: D H Robinson Associates Winchester 1963–87, Allott & Lomax Winchester 1987–95; CEng, FICE, FIStructE, MConsE; *Recreations* walking, photography, nature study, family life, motoring, travel; *Style*— Derek H Robinson, Esq; ✉ 6 Palmerston Court, Barnes Close, Winchester, Hants (☎ 01962 854905)

ROBINSON, Prof (David) Duncan; s of Tom Robinson (ka 1944), and Ann Elizabeth, *née* Clarke; *b* 27 June 1943; *Educ* King Edward VI Sch Macclesfield, Clare Coll Cambridge (scholar, BA, MA), Yale Univ (Mellon fellowship, MA); *m* 7 Jan 1967, Elizabeth Anne (Lisa), da of Frederick Totten Sutton (d 1979), of Fairfield, Conn, USA; 1 s (Thomas Edward b 1975), 2 da (Amanda Jane b 1971, Charlotte Elizabeth b 1989); *Career* keeper of paintings and drawings Fitzwilliam Museum Cambridge 1976–81 (asst keeper 1970–76), fell and coll lectr Clare Coll Cambridge 1975–81; dir of studies in history of art Univ of Cambridge until 1981: Churchill, Clare, Lucy Cavendish, Queens' and Sidney Sussex Colls and New Hall; dir Yale Center for British Art New Haven 1981–95, chief exec offr Paul Mellon Centre for Studies in British Art London, adj prof of history of art Yale Univ 1981–95, fell Berkeley Coll Yale Univ 1981–95, fell Clare Coll Cambridge 1995–; dir Fitzwilliam Museum Cambridge 1995–; memb: Ctee of Mgmnt Kettle's Yard Univ of Cambridge 1970–81 (and chm Exhibitions Ctee 1995–), Ct RCA 1975–78, Art Advsy Panel Arts Council of GB 1978–81 (memb Exhibitions Sub Ctee 1978–79, memb Art Fin Ctee 1979–80, memb Cncl and vice chm Art Panel 1981), Assoc of Art Museum Dirs 1983–88; elector to Slade Professorship of Fine Art Univ of Cambridge 1978–81, govr Yale Univ Press 1987–95; memb: Art and Artefacts Indemnity Advsy Panel to Fed Cncl on the Arts and the Humanities 1991–94 (chm 1992–94), Museums and Collections Advsy Ctee English Heritage, Fitzwilliam Museum Trust; tstee: Yale Univ Press London 1990–, Charleston Tst (USA) 1990–92, American Friends of the Georgian Gp 1992–94; public, visiting and pt/t lectr UK and USA; FRSA 1990, memb Conn Acad of Arts & Scis 1991; *Publications* numerous catalogues, articles and reviews; author of: A Companion Volume to the Kelmscott Chaucer (1975, re-issued as Morris, Burne-Jones and the Kelmscott Chaucer, 1982), Stanley Spencer (1979, revised edn 1990); *Clubs* Athenaeum (London), Knickerbocker (New York); *Style*— Duncan Robinson, Esq; ✉ Grove Lodge, Trumpington Street, Cambridge CB2 1QG; Hall's Farm, South

Windham, Vermont 05359, USA; The Fitzwilliam Museum, Trumpington Street, Cambridge CB2 1RB (☎ 01223 332925, fax 01223 332923)

ROBINSON, Geoffrey; MP (Lab) Coventry North West (majority 6,432); s of Robert Robinson; *b* 25 May 1938; *Educ* Emanuel Sch, Univ of Cambridge, Yale Univ; *m* 1967, Marie Elena Giorgio; 1 da, 1 s; *Career* Lab Pty res asst 1965–68, sr exec Industl Reorganisation Corpn 1968–70, fin controller BL 1971–72, md Leyland Innocenti Milan 1972–73; chief exec: Jaguar Motor Cars Coventry 1973–75, Meriden Co-Op 1979–80; MP (Lab) Coventry NW 1976–; oppn spokesman: Regnl Affairs 1983–84, Indust 1984–86; chm TransTec plc 1994–; *Style—* Geoffrey Robinson, Esq, MP; ✉ House of Commons, London SW1A 0AA

ROBINSON, Dr Geoffrey Walter; s of George Robinson (d 1987), of Loughborough, Leics, and Edith Margaret, *née* Wilson (d 1988); *b* 9 Nov 1945; *Educ* Aireborough GS Leeds, Univ of Nottingham (BSc, PhD); *m* 12 Aug 1967, Edwina, da of Thomas Ernest Jones; 1 s (Richard Antony b 13 Oct 1970), 1 da (Catherine Louise b 29 April 1972); *Career* IBM: UK Laboratories 1969–82, scientific centre mangr 1982–84, tech programmes mangr 1984–85, UK tech dir 1985–86, dir of software devpt 1986–88, dir Hursley Laboratory 1988–92 and 1994–96, dir of technol 1996–; chief advsr on sci and technol DTI 1992–94; memb: Ordnance Survey Scientific Advsy Ctee 1986–89, Centre for Exploitation of Sci and Technol 1986–92, Natural Environment Res Cncl 1992–94, SERC 1992–94, Particle Physics & Astronomy Res Cncl 1994–, Innovative Mfrg Initiative Mgmnt Ctee 1994–, Cncl for the Central Lab of the Res Cncls 1995–; chm ESRC: Innovation Res Prog 1994–, Intellectual Property Res Prog 1995–; pres Br Computer Soc 1995–96 (dep pres 1994); memb Worshipful Co of Info Technologists 1988, Freeman City of London 1989, memb Worshipful Co of Scientific Instrument Makers 1996; Hon DTech King Alfred's Coll Winchester (CNAA) 1992; FRSA 1992, FIEE 1993, FEng 1994, FBCS 1994 (MBCS 1988); *Recreations* music; *Clubs* Athenaeum; *Style—* Dr Geoffrey Robinson, FEng; ✉ Fardale, Hookwood Lane, Ampfield, Romsey, Hants SO51 9BZ (☎ 01703 261837, fax 01703 271926); IBM UK, Hursley Park, Winchester, Hants SO21 2JN (☎ 01962 816372, fax 01962 818309)

ROBINSON, Gerrard Jude (Gerry); s of Anthony Robinson (d 1990), and Elizabeth Ann, *née* Stuart; *b* 23 Oct 1948; *Educ* St Mary's Coll Castle Head; *m* 1, 1969 (m dis 1990), Maria Ann, *née* Borg; 1 da (Samantha Erica b 22 April 1975), 1 s (Richard Steven b 30 Dec 1977); m 2, 1990, Heather Peta, da of Kenneth Arthur Leaman; 1 da (April Heather b 4 May 1991), 1 s (Timothy Gerrard b 23 April 1994); *Career* works accountant Lesney Products Ltd 1965–74, fin controller Lex Industrial Distribution and Hire 1974–80; Coca Cola: fin dir 1980–81, sales and mktg dir 1981–83, md 1983–84; md Grand Metropolitan Contract Services 1984–87, chief exec Compass Group plc (following buyout from GrandMet) 1987–91; Granada Group plc: chief exec 1991–96, chm 1996–; chm: Independent Television News Ltd (ITN) 1995–, BSkyB PLC 1995–; FCMA; *Recreations* golf, opera, chess, skiing, reading, music; *Clubs* Roehampton, Wisley; *Style—* Gerry Robinson, Esq; ✉ Granada Group plc, Stornoway House, 13 Cleveland Row, London SW1A 1GG (☎ 0171 451 3000)

ROBINSON, Helen; OBE; *Educ* Roedean; *m* Desmond Preston (decd); 2 c, 4 step c; *Career* fashion asst, fashion ed and latterly exec ed Vogue Magazine London and New York 1952–75; Debenhams plc: joined 1975, dir Dept Store, mktg and design mgmnt dir (Main Bd) 1981–86; mktg dir Conde Nast Publications Ltd 1986–88, gp md Thomas Goode & Co Ltd 1988–93 (resigned upon sale of co); non-exec dir: British Airports Authy 1978–84 (memb Chm's Design Ctee 1988–95), London Transport 1984–95, London Electricity 1989–94, Churchill China plc 1995–; special projects and mktg Asprey plc 1995–; vice chm Cncl (and chm Staff Ctee) Royal Coll of Art 1982–, tstee WWF (and chm WWF UK Ltd) 1988–95, memb Design Mgmnt Advsy Gp London Business Sch 1985–, govr Cwlth Inst 1994–, memb Cncl The Cottage Homes (retail trade charity) 1995–96; Hon FRCA, Hon FCSD, FRSA; *Style—* Mrs Helen Robinson, OBE; ✉ 18 Doria Road, London SW6 4UG (☎ 0171 736 8814, fax 0171 731 2165)

ROBINSON, Hilary Frances; da of Ivor Robinson, of Oxford, and Olive, *née* Trask; *b* 25 June 1956; *Educ* John Mason HS Abingdon Oxon, Univ of Newcastle upon Tyne (BA), RCA (MA, Allen Lane/Penguin Books award); *m* 1995, Alastair MacLennan; *Career* painted and exhibited 1979–85; freelance writer; tutor Glasgow Sch of Art 1987–92, ed Alba (Scot visual art magazine) 1990–92, lectr in fine art Univ of Ulster at Belfast 1992–; author of numerous pubns on feminist art; memb: Assoc of Art Historians 1988, Coll Art Assoc USA 1993; *Books* Visibly Female (ed, 1987), The Rough Guide to Venice (co-author, 1989, 2nd edn 1993); *Style—* Ms Hilary Robinson; ✉ School of Fine and Applied Art, University of Ulster at Belfast, York Street, Belfast BT15 1ED (☎ 01232 328515, fax 01232 267356)

ROBINSON, Ian; s of Thomas Mottram Robinson (d 1972), and Eva Iris, *née* Bird (d 1984); *b* 3 May 1942; *Educ* Univ of Leeds (BSc), Harvard (SMP); *m* 28 Oct 1967, Kathleen Crawford, da of James Leay, of Edinburgh; 1 s (Andrew John b 1977), 1 da (Caroline Anne b 1973); *Career* Ralph M Parsons Co Ltd: dir of ops 1979, vice pres (USA) 1983, md 1985; md John Brown Engineering Constructors Ltd 1986–, chief exec John Brown Engineers & Constructors 1990–92; chm and chief exec John Brown plc 1992–95, chm Davy Corporation 1992–, chm Engrg Div and main bd dir Trafalgar House plc 1992–95, chief exec Scottish Power plc 1995–, chm Manwels 1995–, chm Southern Water 1996–; non-exec dir: Lloyd's Register of Shipping, Scottish Enterprise; memb Senate Engrg Cncl; FIChemE, FEng 1994; *Recreations* gardening, golf; *Clubs* RAC; *Style—* Ian Robinson, Esq, FEng; ✉ Scottish Power plc, 1 Atlantic Quay, Glasgow G2 8SP (☎ 0141 248 8200, fax 0141 248 8300)

ROBINSON, Jancis Mary (Mrs N L Lander); da of Thomas Edward Robinson, of Eden House, Kirkandrews-on-Eden, Cumbria, and Ann, *née* Conacher; *b* 22 April 1950; *Educ* Carlisle HS, St Anne's Coll Oxford (MA); *m* 22 Oct 1981, Nicholas Laurence Lander, s of Israel Lennard Lander; 1 s (William Isaac b 5 Sept 1984), 2 da (Julia Margaux b 10 July 1982, Rose Ellen b 6 March 1991); *Career* early career experience: mktg and producing skiing holidays for Thomson Holidays 1971–74, undertaking odd jobs while writing for Good Food Guide 1975; asst ed then ed Wine and Spirit 1975–80, fndr Drinker's Digest 1977 (became Which? Wine Monthly 1980), ed Which? Wine Monthly and Which? Wine Annual Guide 1980–82, Sunday Times 1980–86 (wine corr, food corr, gen features); wine corr: The Evening Standard 1987–88, Financial Times 1989–; presenter and writer The Wine Programme (1983, 1985 and 1987), presenter Jancis Robinson's Christmas Wine List 1985, presenter BBC Design Awards 1986–87, narrator Design Classics 1987; presenter and writer: Jancis Robinson Meets 1987, Matters of Taste 1989 and 1991, Vintners' Tales 1993, Grape Expectations (US) 1994 and 1995, Jancis Robinson's Wine Course 1995, The Food Chain 1996; dir Eden Productions Ltd; wine conslt British Airways; Glenfiddich Awards: Best Book on Wine (The Great Wine Book) 1983, Broadcaster of the Year and Glenfiddich Trophy 1984, Wine Writer 1986, Food Writer 1986, Best Book on Wine (The Oxford Companion to Wine) 1995, Drink Writer of the Year and Glenfiddich Trophy 1996; winner: Marques de Caceres Award 1985, Wine Guild of UK Premier Award 1986 and 1996, André Simon Meml Award 1987 and 1995, Wine Guild Award for Reference Book 1987, Clicquot Book of the Year (Vines, Grapes and Wines) 1987 and (The Oxford Companion to Wine) 1995, Silver Medal German Academy of Gastronomy 1988 and Gold Medal 1996; memb Inst of Masters of Wine 1984; Jurade de St Emilion, Commanderie de Bontemps de Médoc et Graves; *Books* The Wine Book (1979), The Great Wine Book (1982), Masterglass (1983), How to Choose and Enjoy Wine (1984), Vines, Grapes and Wines (1986), Jancis Robinson's Food and Wine Adventures (1987), Jancis Robinson on The Demon Drink (1988), Vintage Timecharts (1989), The Oxford Companion to Wine (ed, 1994), Jancis Robinson's Wine Course (1995), Jancis Robinson's Guide to Wine Grapes (1996); *Style—* Ms Jancis Robinson

ROBINSON, Prof (Jenifer Ann) Jane; da of Reginald Milton London (d 1965), of Birmingham, and Flornce, *née* Troop (d 1946); *b* 6 Nov 1935; *Educ* King Edward VI HS for Girls, Univ of Keele (RHV, MA, PhD), N Staffs Poly (IPM), Wolverhampton Poly (CertEd HVT); *m* 6 Feb 1959, Anthony David Robinson, s of Alfred Anthony Robinson; 3 da (Ann Louise (Mrs Sutcliffe) b 3 Dec 1959, Felicity Jane (Mrs Wood) b 26 March 1962, Kathryn Mary (Mrs Roodner) b 21 April 1964); *Career* nursing educn and trg: The Royal Orthopaedic Hosp Birmingham (ONC) and The Queen Elizabeth Hosp Birmingham (RGN) 1952–57, Southmead Hosp Bristol (CMB Part 1) 1958–59; theatre sister Winford Orthopaedic Hosp Bristol 1957–58; staff nurse: Bristol Homeopathic Hosp 1959, North Staffs Royal Infirmary 1968–69; health visitor/school nurse: Staffs CC 1970–74, Staffs Area Health Authy 1977–80 (nursing offr 1974–77); lectr in health visiting Wolverhampton Poly 1980–81, res offr Med Dept Sandwell Health Authy 1981–83, lectr in health visiting Wolverhampton Poly 1983–84, dir Nursing Policy Studies Centre Univ of Warwick 1985–89, prof and head Dept of Nursing and Midwifery Studies Univ of Nottingham 1989–; advsr to WHO 1985–; Fulbright sr research scholarship 1996; chair: Nursing Research Ctee Trent Regnl Health Authy 1989–92, Women's Issues Sub-ctee RCN 1995– (memb Health and Social Policy Ctee 1991–92); Sec of State's appt United Kingdom Central Cncl for Nursing Midwifery and Health Visiting 1993–96; MIPD 1988, FRCN 1994; *Publications* An Evaluation of Health Visiting (1982), The NHS Under New Management (1990), Policy Issues in Nursing (1992), Nursing Beyond 2000 (contrib, 1994), Nurses Manage (1995), Health Needs Assessment (1996); author of numerous articles and chapters in medical books; *Recreations* being warden of Nightingale Hall, family pursuits with five grand-daughters, travel; *Clubs* Univ Women's; *Style—* Prof Jane Robinson; ✉ Department of Nursing and Midwifery Studies, Medical School, Nottingham NG7 2UH (☎ 0115 970 9265)

ROBINSON, Prof John; s of William Clifford Robinson (d 1982), and Annie, *née* Banks; *b* 11 July 1933; *Educ* Little Lever Secondary Sch, Radcliffe Jr Tech Coll, Salford Tech Coll (HND), Cranfield Inst of Technol (MSc), Inst of Sound and Vibration Res Univ of Southampton (PhD); *m* 1, 3 Aug 1957 (m dis 1980), Cynthia, da of late Eric Nicholls; 2 s (Gary Edward b 16 Aug 1958, Lee John b 16 May 1961); m 2, 12 Sept 1984, Shirley Ann, da of Roland Walter Bradley, of Bidford-on-Avon, Warwicks; *Career* Br and USA Aerospace Indust 1949–71, head Robinson and Associates 1971–; conslt organiser World Congress and Exhibition on Finite Element Methods 1975– (ed and publisher World Congress Proceedings 1975–), ed and publisher Finite Element News 1976–, lectr of worldwide courses on Understanding Finite Element Stress Analysis 1980–, fndr and memb Steering Ctee Nat Agency for Finite Element Methods and Standards 1983–, dir Robinson FEMInst 1986–, industl res prof Univ of Exeter 1986–; MRAeS 1962, MIMechE 1964, CEng; *Books* Structural Matrix Analysis for the Engineer (1966), Integrated Theory of Finite Element Methods (1973), Understanding Finite Element Stress Analysis (1981), Early FEM Pioneers (1985), articles; *Style—* Prof John Robinson

ROBINSON, John Harris; *b* 22 Dec 1940; *Educ* Woodhouse Grove Sch, Univ of Birmingham (BSc); *m* 2 March 1963, Doreen Alice; 1 s (Mark John b 9 March 1965), 1 da (Karen Claire b 1 Nov 1968); *Career* ICI 1962–65, Fisons 1965–70, sr conslt PA Consulting Group 1970–75, chief exec Woodhouse & Rixon (Holdings) 1975–79; Smith & Nephew plc: md Smith & Nephew Medical 1979–85, gp dir UK and Europe 1985–90, gp chief exec 1990–, dep chm 1996–; non-exec dir: Delta plc 1993–, Low & Bonar plc 1996–; memb Advsy Bd Univ of Birmingham Business Sch 1993–, govr Hymers Coll Hull 1984–, memb Ct Univ of York 1994–; CEng, FIChemE, CIMgt; *Recreations* golf, cricket, walking; *Clubs* Athenaeum; *Style—* John Robinson, Esq; ✉ 35 Marsham Court, Marsham Street, London SW1 4JY

ROBINSON, Sir John James Michael Laud; 11 Bt (E 1660), of London, DL (Northants); s of Michael Frederick Laud-Robinson (d 1971), and Elisabeth Bridge (d 1977); suc gf, Maj Sir Frederick Robinson, 10 Bt, MC (d 1975, descended from Sir John Robinson, 1 Bt, Lord Mayor of London 1662–63 and s of Ven William Robinson, sometime Archdeacon of Nottingham and half-bro of Archbishop Laud); *b* 19 Jan 1943; *Educ* Eton, Trinity Coll Dublin (MA); *m* 1968, (Kathryn) Gayle Elizabeth, da of Stuart Nelson Keyes, of Orillia, Ontario; 2 s, 1 da; *Heir* s, Mark Christopher Michael Villiers Robinson b 23 April 1972; *Career* chartered fin analyst; landowner; chm: St Andrew's Hosp Northampton 1982–93, Northampton Gen Hosp NHS Tst; *Style—* Sir John Robinson, Bt, DL; ✉ Cranford Hall, Cranford, Kettering, Northants NN14 4AD (☎ 0153 678 248)

ROBINSON, Dr John Joseph; s of James Reid Robinson (d 1983), and Elizabeth Mary, *née* Ennis (d 1985); *b* 11 June 1940; *Educ* Down HS Downpatrick, Queen's Univ Belfast (BAgr, PhD); *m* 26 Sept 1967, Margaret, da of Samuel James Magill; 1 s (Andrew James b 11 July 1974), 1 da (Lyn Elizabeth b 29 Dec 1972); *Career* post-doctoral research fell Queen's Univ Belfast 1966–67, ARC post-doctoral researcher Wye Coll Univ of London 1967–68; Rowett Research Inst Bucksburn Aberdeen: sr scientific offr 1968–73, principal scientific offr 1973–83, sr principal scientific offr (individual merit) 1983–94; sr scientist in animal reproduction Scottish Agricultural Coll Aberdeen 1994–; pres British Soc of Animal Science 1993–94; Fish Meal Manufacturers' Annual Research Award 1979, Research Medal RASE 1982, Sir John Hammond Meml Prize British Soc of Animal Production 1984, Sir William Young Award Royal Highland Agricultural Soc of Scotland 1989, George Hedley Meml Award Nat Sheep Assoc 1991; FRSE 1996; *Publications* author and co-author of over 250 publications incl refereed scientific papers, invited scientific reviews, book chapters and technical bulletins; *Recreations* gardening, club rambling; *Style—* Dr John Robinson, FRSE; ✉ 4 Hopecroft Terrace, Bucksburn, Aberdeen, Grampian AB21 9RL; Scottish Agricultural College, The Ferguson Building, Craibstone Estate, Bucksburn, Aberdeen AB21 9YA (☎ 01224 711052, fax 01224 711292)

ROBINSON, John Martin; s of John Cotton Robinson, and Ellen Anne Cecilia, eld da of George Adams, of Cape Town, S Africa; *b* 10 Sept 1948; *Educ* Fort Augustus Abbey, St Andrews, Oriel Coll Oxford (MA, DPhil); *Career* librarian to Duke of Norfolk 1978–; ptnr Historic Bldgs Conslts; vice chm Georgian Gp; Donat of SMO Malta; Maltravers Herald of Arms Extraordinary 1989–; memb NW Regnl Ctee Nat Tst, tstee Abbot Hall Art Gallery 1993–; FSA; *Books* The Wyatts (1980), Dukes of Norfolk (1983, 2 edn 1995), Georgian Model Farms (1983), Latest Country Houses (1984), Cardinal Consalvi (1987), Oxford Guide to Heraldry (jtly with Thomas Woodcock, 1988), Temples of Delight (1990), Country Houses of the North West (1991), Treasures of The English Churches (1995), Windsor Castle (1996); *Clubs* Travellers; *Style—* John Robinson, Esq, FSA, Maltravers Herald of Arms Extraordinary; ✉ Beckside House, Barbon, via Carnforth, Lancs (☎ 01524 276300; fax 0171 831 8831)

ROBINSON, Rev Canon Joseph; s of Thomas Robinson (d 1967), of Wigan, Lancs, and Maggie, *née* Wright (d 1981); *b* 23 Feb 1927; *Educ* Upholland GS, King's Coll London (BD, MTh); *m* 5 Sept 1953, Anne, da of James Antrobus (d 1978), of Wigan, Lancs; 2 s (Michael Francis b 1954, Christopher John b 1959), 2 da (Gillian Elizabeth b 1956, Katherine Mary b 1961); *Career* ordained: deacon 1952, priest 1953; curate Tottenham 1952–55, minor canon St Paul's Cathedral 1955–68, lectr in Old Testament studies King's Coll London 1959–68, canon of Canterbury 1968–80, master of the Temple 1980–; hon bencher Inner Temple 1994–; govr: Sons of the Clergy, Hurstpierpoint Coll; fell

Woodward Fndn; Liveryman Worshipful Co of Wax Chandlers, Chaplain Worshipful Co of Cutlers, former Master Worshipful Co of Parish Clerks; Hon LLD Simon Greenleafe Law Sch Anaheim California; FKC; *Books* Cambridge Bible Commentary on 1 Kings (1972), Cambridge Bible Commentary on 2 Kings (1976); *Recreations* reading, gardening; *Clubs* Athenaeum; *Style*— The Rev Canon Joseph Robinson; ✉ The Master's House, Temple, London EC4Y 7BB (☎ 0171 353 8559)

ROBINSON, (Leonard) Keith; CBE (1981), DL (Hampshire 1985); *b* 2 July 1920; *Educ* Queen Elizabeth's GS Blackburn, Victoria Univ Manchester (LLB); *m* 1948, Susan May, da of the late Vice-Adm W Tomkinson; 2 s, 2 da; *Career* WWII RAFVR Sqdn Ldr Coastal Cmd 1940–46; slr Bristol 1948–55; dep town clerk Birkenhead Co Borough Cncl 1955–65, town clerk Stoke on Trent City Cncl 1966–73, co chief exec Hants CC 1973–85; chm Assoc of Co Chief Execs 1975–77, a princ advsr to Assoc of CCs 1974–85, memb W Midlands Econ Planning Cncl 1967–73, former memb Central Ctee for Reclamation of Derelict Land, memb Advsy Cncl for Energy Conservation 1982–84; mgmnt conslt 1985–87; dir Salisbury Playhouse Bd 1978–93; vice chm: Nuffield Theatre 1985–95, Southern Arts Mgmnt Cncl 1985–91; asst cmmr Local Govt Boundary Cmmn 1987–91; pres: The Castle CC Winchester 1977–92, Winchester Dramatic Soc 1984–95; memb Mgmnt Ctee: Hants Gdn Tst 1984–, Hillier Arboretum 1985–, Hants Devpt Assoc 1985–91; *Recreations* theatre, fly-fishing, gardening, cricket, travel; *Clubs* MCC; *Style*— Keith Robinson Esq, CBE, DL; ✉ Bransbury Mill Cottage, Bransbury, Barton Stacey, Winchester, Hants S021 3QJ (☎ 01962 760124)

ROBINSON, Prof Kenneth Ernest; CBE (1971); s of Ernest Robinson (d 1917), of Plumstead, Kent, and Isabel May, *née* Chadk (d 1954); *b* 9 March 1914; *Educ* Sir George Monoux GS London, Hertford Coll Oxford (BA, MA), LSE; *m* 4 Nov 1938, Stephanie Christine Sara (d 1994), da of William Wilson (d 1951), of Westminster; 1 s (Julian b 1944), 1 da (Miranda b 1947); *Career* Home Civil Serv Admin Class: asst princ Colonial Office 1936, princ 1942, asst sec 1946, resigned 1948; official fell Nuffield Coll Oxford 1948–57 (hon fell 1984), reader in cwlth govt Univ of Oxford 1948–57; Univ of London: dir of Inst of Cwlth Studies, prof of cwlth affrs 1957–65 (hon life memb 1979–); Reid lectr Acadia Univ Canada 1963, vice-chllr Univ of Hong Kong 1965–72, Hallsworth fell Univ of Manchester 1972–74, Callander lectr Univ of Aberdeen 1979; hon vice-pres Royal Cwlth Soc 1995, pres Royal African Soc 1987–96; govr LSE 1959–65; JP Hong Kong 1967–72; Hon LLD Chinese Univ of Hong Kong 1968, Hon DLitt Univ of Hong Kong 1972, Hon Dr Open Univ 1978, corresponding memb Academie des Sciences D'Outre-Mer Paris 1959–; FRHistS 1959; *Books* Five Elections in Africa (with W J M McKenzie, 1960), Essays in Imperial Government (with A F Madden, 1963), The Dilemmas of Trusteeship (1965), Imperialism - The State and the Third World (festschrift, ed M Twaddle, 1992), Decolonisation and the International Community (festschrift, 1993); *Clubs* Royal Commonwealth Soc, Lansdowne, Hong Kong; *Style*— Prof Kenneth Robinson, CBE; ✉ 52 The Cloisters, Pegasus Grange, Whitehouse Road, Oxford OX1 4QQ (☎ 01865 725517)

ROBINSON, Prof Kenneth (Ken); s of James Robinson (d 1977), of Liverpool, and Ethel, *née* Allen; *b* 4 March 1950; *Educ* Liverpool Collegiate GS, Wade Deacon GS, Bretton Hall Coll, Univ of Leeds (BED), Univ of London (PhD); *m* 30 Jan 1982, Marie-Thérèse, da of Frederick George Watts, of Liverpool; 1 s (James b 11 Oct 1984), 1 da (Katherine Marie b 4 May 1989); *Career* educationist; dir Nat Curriculum Cncl Arts in Schools project 1985–89, chm Artswork 1987–, prof of arts educn Univ of Warwick 1989–; FRSA; *Books* Learning Through Drama (1977), Exploring Theatre and Education (ed 1980), The Arts in Schools (princ author, 1982), The Arts and Higher Education (ed 1983), The Arts 5–16 (1990); *Recreations* theatre, music, cinema; *Style*— Prof Ken Robinson; ✉ University of Warwick, Westwood, Coventry CV4 7AL (☎ 01203 524152)

ROBINSON, Kent Seafield; s of Maj Geoffrey Seafield Robinson, (d 1974), of E Grinstead, Sussex, and Irene Marian, *née* Valpy; *b* 1 May 1938; *Educ* King's Sch Canterbury, RMA Sandhurst; *m* 1, 12 March 1960 (m dis 1985), Cicelie Amanda Stewart, da of Sqdn Ldr Ronald Ernest Cheesman, of Hartley Wintney, Hants; 2 s (Mark b 1961, Andrew b 1963); m 2, 20 June 1985, Carol Patricia Palmer, da of Eric Dean, CB, CBE, of Hove, Sussex; *Career* RASC 1958–65; capt Army Cross Country Driving Champion Team 1963, Far E Army Rally Champion 1964, medically ret 1965; int money broker 1969–79; opened offices: Jersey 1972, Kuwait 1976, Tokyo 1978; chm Lionel Robinson & Co Ltd (electrical wholesalers and distributors) 1974–94; chm Basingstoke IOD 1984–87, pres Electrical Wholesalers Fedn 1989–90, memb Cncl CBI 1992–95; FInstD 1974; *Recreations* vintage motor cars, continental tours; *Style*— Kent Robinson, Esq; ✉ Wedmans Farm, Rotherwick, Hook, Hants RG27 9BX (☎ and fax 01256 763285)

ROBINSON, Gp Capt Marcus; CB (1956), AFC (1941, and Bar 1944), AE (1942), DL (1953); s of Wilson Robinson (d 1953), of Glasgow, and Eileen Charlotte, *née* Colvil (d 1959); *b* 27 May 1912; *Educ* Rossall; *m* 1, 4 April 1941 (m dis 1950), Mary Playfair; 1 s (Ainslie b 18 April 1942), 1 da (Elaine b 26 Nov 1944); m 2, 25 Sept 1953, Joan Elizabeth Weatherlake, da of O C Carter (d 1964), of Bournemouth; *Career* cmmnd 602 Sqdn Aux Air Force 1934, Flt Cdr 1938–40, Sqdn Ldr i/c 616 Sqdn 1940, Sqdn Ldr flying instr 1940, Wing Cdr 1942, chief instr 15 Pilot Advanced Flying Unit, Gp Capt 1945, i/c 20 and 21 Flying Trg Schs 1945, Sr Air SO 23 Gp RAF, demobbed 1946, reformed 602 City of Glasgow Fighter Sqdn 1946–51; memb Air Advsy Cncl Air Min 1952–56, chm Glasgow Territorial and Aux Forces Assoc 1952–56; Robinson Dunn & Co Ltd: dir 1939–66, chm and md 1966–77, ret 1977; chm: Glasgow Rating and Valuation Appeals Ctee 1963–77 (dep chm 1958–63), Earl Haig Fund Scotland 1974–78 (vice pres 1978); awarded Silver Jubilee medal 1977; *Recreations* skiing, sailing, golf; *Clubs* Royal Northern and Clyde Yacht; *Style*— Gp Capt Marcus Robinson, CB, AFC, AE, DL; ✉ Rockfort, Helensburgh, Strathclyde G84 7BA (☎ 01436 672097)

ROBINSON, Mark Nicholas; s of Eric Robinson, of Leigh on Sea, Essex, and Kate Emily Robinson; *b* 24 Jan 1952; *Educ* Westcliff GS for Boys, Univ of Dundee (MA, vice pres Students' Union); *m* 4 June 1976, Patricia Margaret, da of John Malone; 2 s (Matthew John b 31 July 1981, Rory Patrick b 20 Aug 1985), 1 da (Chloe Elizabeth b 16 Nov 1983); *Career* salesman Thomson Regional Newspapers 1975–76, Allardyce Advertising 1976–77, account exec Manton Woodyer Ketley 1977–78, account dir CDP/Aspect Advertising 1981–85 (account mangr 1978–81), dir Ted Bates 1985–87; business devpt dir: Dorland Advertising 1987–88, Horner Collis & Kirvan 1988–92, GGK 1992–93, Publicis 1993–97; mktg dir J Walter Thompson 1997–; fndr and dir Radio Feltham 1994–; IPA: chm IPA Soc 1987–88, memb various ctees incl Effectiveness Awards Ctee, chm Media Ctee 1994–; memb Gen Mgmnt Ctee Nat Advertising Benevolent Soc; FIPA 1991; *Recreations* tennis, cycling; *Style*— Mark Robinson, Esq; ✉ J Walter Thompson Company Ltd, 40 Berkeley Square, London W1X 6AD (☎ 0171 499 4040)

ROBINSON, Mark Noel Foster; MP (C) Somerton and Frome (majority 4,341); s of John Foster Robinson, CBE, DL (d 1988), and Margaret Eva Hannah, *née* Paterson (d 1977); *b* 26 Dec 1946; *Educ* Harrow, ChCh Oxford (MA); *m* 1982, Vivien Radclyffe, da of Alan Roger Douglas Pilkington (d 1968); 1 s (James b 1986), 1 da (Alice b 1983); *Career* called to the Bar Middle Temple; UN Office 1972–77, exec office of UN Sec Gen as second offr 1975–77, asst dir Dip Staff Cwlth Secretariat 1977–83; MP (C): Newport W 1983–87, Somerton and Frome 1992–; PPS to Rt Hon Nicholas Edwards as Sec of State for Wales 1984–85, Parly under sec of state Welsh Office 1985–87, PPS to Rt Hon Baroness Chalker as Min for Overseas Devpt FCO and to Parly Under Sec of State FCO 1992–94, PPS to Rt Hon Douglas Hurd as Sec of State for Foreign and Commonwealth Affairs 1994–95, currently PPS to Rt Hon William Waldegrave as Chief Sec to the Treasy; dir: Leopold Joseph & Sons Ltd 1988–91 (non-exec 1991–94), Leopold Joseph Holdings PLC 1994–95; memb Bd Cwlth Devpt Corp 1988–92; fell Indust and Parl Tst; cncl memb Winstn Churchill Meml Tst 1993; memb: RIIA, RUSI; FIMgt, FRSA; *Recreations* fishing, country pursuits; *Clubs* Travellers', Pratt's, Brooks's; *Style*— Mark Robinson, Esq, MP; ✉ House of Commons, London SW1A 0AA (☎ 0171 219 3000)

ROBINSON, Air Vice-Marshal Michael Maurice Jeffries; CB (1982); s of Dr Maurice Robinson (d 1983), and Muriel Maud, *née* Jeffries (d 1981); *b* 11 Feb 1927; *Educ* King's Sch Bruton, Queen's Coll Oxford, RAF Coll Cranwell, Univ of the W of England (MA 1994); *m* 19 April 1952, Drusilla Dallas, da of Dr Harry Julius Bush (d 1962); 1 s (Ian), 2 da (Jennie, Sarah); *Career* Cdr RAF Lossiemouth 1972–74, Asst Cmdt RAF Coll Cranwell 1974–77, sr air SO HQ No 1 Gp 1977–79, dir gen Orgn (RAF) MOD (Air) 1979–82; govr: King's Sch Bruton, Duke of Kent Sch (RAF Benevolent Fund) Ewhurst; *Recreations* golf, gardening, going to the opera; *Clubs* RAF; *Style*— Air Vice-Marshal Michael Robinson, CB

ROBINSON, Ven Neil; s of James Neesom Robinson (d 1972), and Alice Carter, *née* Harness (d 1976); *b* 28 Feb 1929; *Educ* Penistone GS, St John's Coll Durham (BA, Dip Theol); *m* 3 April 1956, Kathlyn, da of Thomas Williams (d 1951); 2 s (Peter b 1957, John b 1965), 2 da (Anne b 1958, Susan b 1962); *Career* Nat Serv RA 1947–49; curate and precentor of Holy Trinity Hull 1954– 58, vicar of Glen Parva with S Wigston Leicester 1958–69, hon canon of Leicester Cathedral 1968–83, rector and rural dean Market Bosworth 1969–83, residentiary canon of Worcester Cathedral 1983–87, archdeacon of Suffolk 1987–94; *Recreations* hill walking; *Style*— The Ven Neil Robinson; ✉ Skell Green, 32 Mallorie Park Drive, Ripon, N Yorkshire HG4 2QF (☎ 01765 603075)

ROBINSON, Nicholas; s of Samuel Robinson (d 1987), and Sarah, *née* McCloy; *b* 7 Nov 1948; *Educ* The HS Greenock, Univ of Glasgow; *m* 15 April 1971, Elizabeth, da of Donald Campbell Service; 3 s (Gary b 16 Sept 1971, Graeme Campbell b 21 March 1974, Gordon Douglas b 15 July 1976); *Career* apprentice CA Wylie & Bisset CA's 1967–73, accountant then fin dir TAB Ltd 1973–76, accountant Fleming & Wilson CA's 1976–78, British National Oil Corporation 1978–79, fndr own practice 1979 (merged with Kidsons Impey 1982), currently dir of business devpt and Central region managing ptnr Kidsons Impey; regular contrib to Business Press; MICAS 1973; *Recreations* motor cruising, golf, music; *Clubs* St James' (Manchester); *Style*— Nicholas Robinson, Esq; ✉ Kidsons Impey, Devonshire House, 36 George Street, Manchester M1 4HA (☎ 0161 236 7733)

ROBINSON, Nicholas Ambrose Eldred; s of late Gerard Robinson; *b* 26 July 1941; *Educ* Birkenhead Sch; *m* 1977, Annie Georgette Gabrielle, *née* Barada; 2 s, 2 da; *Career* chartered surveyor; princ Eddisons (Leeds), dir Bradford Property Trust plc; FRICS, ACIArb; *Recreations* sailing; *Clubs* Bradford; *Style*— Nicholas Robinson, Esq; ✉ 6 Strayside Mews, 2 Leeds Rd, Harrogate HG2 8AA (☎ 01423 502 530)

ROBINSON, Nicholas Ridley; s of late Capt Leslie Jack Robinson, JP, of College Rd, Dulwich, and Eileen Mary, *née* Phillips; *b* 2 Sept 1952; *Educ* Dulwich; *m* 1, 26 May 1976 (m dis 1980), Vivienne; m 2, 13 Sept 1980, Joanna Mary, da of Wilford Henry Gibson, CBE, of Sanderstead, Surrey; 2 s (Stuart Laurence Ridley b 9 May 1984, Duncan Henry b 18 Aug 1987), 1 da (Felicity Mary b 1 April 1990); *Career* admitted slr 1977; sr ptnr Sandoms 1988 (ptnr 1978); hon sec ICIS Football League; co sec The Isthmian Football League Ltd; dir Dulwich Coll Mission, memb Bd Br Home and Hosp for Incurables 1996–; Freeman: City of London, Worshipful Co of Slrs, Worshipful Co of Farriers; memb Law Soc 1977; FCIArb 1993; *Recreations* horse racing, football; *Clubs* RAC; *Style*— Nicholas Robinson, Esq; ✉ 226 Rye Lane, Peckham, London SE15 4NL (☎ 0171 639 5726, fax 0171 277 6061, home fax 0181 653 4344, car 0836 241666)

ROBINSON, Nick; s of John Robinson, and Barbara Robinson; *b* 7 April 1947; *Educ* Wadham Coll Oxford (open scholar, MA); *m* 1985, Janice; 1 da (Elisabeth b 23 Nov 1988); *Career* dir Hicks Oubridge Public Affairs Ltd 1970–72, PR mangr Cooperative Wholesale Society 1972–74, PR mangr Manpower Ltd 1974–79, chm Datanews Ltd 1979–90, chm The Marketing Guild 1990–; hon ed Strategic Marketing magazine, fndr faculty dir in PR Inst of Mktg 1982–84; memb Br Assoc of Industl Editors 1976, MIPR 1984; *Books* The Marketing Toolkit (1988), Persuasive Business Presentations (1989), Strategic Customer Care (1991); *Style*— Nick Robinson, Esq; ✉ The Marketing Guild Ltd, 1 Houghton Court, Houghton Regis, Bedfordshire LU5 5DY (☎ 01582 861556)

ROBINSON, Paul; s of Harold George Robert Robinson (d 1995), and Sonja Diana, *née* Lapthorn, of Camberley, Surrey; *b* 31 Dec 1956; *Educ* Camberley GS, Magdalene Coll Cambridge, Univ of Manchester (BSc), MBA (Bradford) 1996; *m* 11 June 1983, Gillian, *née* Whitton; 2 s (Mathew Joseph b 22 May 1987, Joshua James b 2 Jan 1995); *Career* presenter ILR 1970s, gp prog dir Chiltern Radio Network 1980s (successfully relaunched Galaxy as a dance station); BBC Radio 1991–96: managing ed (latterly md and dep controller) Radio 1 1991–95, head of strategy and devpt responsible for new product devpt of Radios 1, 2, 3, 4 and 5 Live 1995–96; gen mangr Talk Radio 1996–; pioneered introduction of the selector computer music scheduling system into the BBC; vice pres Macmillan Nurses, sch govr Kempston Rural; MIMgt 1985, memb Radio Acad 1986; *Recreations* swimming, walking, gardening; *Style*— Paul Robinson, Esq; ✉ Talk Radio, PO Box 1089, London W1A 1PP (☎ 0171 636 1089, fax 0171 636 1053)

ROBINSON, Dr Paul Hyman; s of Maurice Isaac Robinson, of Finchley, London, and Stella Robinson, *née* Hymanson; *b* 14 Feb 1958; *Educ* Haberdashers' Aske's, Univ Coll Hosp Med Sch (BSc, MB, BS); *m* 29 July 1974 (m dis 1992), Susan Deborah, da of Joseph Saffer, of Bournemouth, Hants; 2 s (Matthew b 1981, Daniel b 1986), 2 da (Jessica b 1979, Zoë b 1988); *Career* jr hosp doctor at UCH, Whittington Hosp, Nat Hosp Queen Square 1975–80, trainee psychiatrist Bethlem Royal and Maudsley Hosps 1980–86, sr lectr and conslt psychiatrist King's Coll Hosp and Maudsley Hosp 1986–90, conslt psychiatrist Gordon and Westminster Hosps and head Eating Disorders Unit Gordon Hosp 1990–96; numerous pubns on anorexia nervosa, bulimia nervosa, gastric function and biology of cholecystokinin; MRCP 1977, MRCPsych 1982, FRSM 1983; *Style*— Dr Paul Robinson; ✉ 75 Hillfield Park, Muswell Hill, London N10 3QU (☎ 0181 444 5228)

ROBINSON, Prof (William) Peter; s of John Robinson (d 1955), of Chichester, Sussex, and Winifred Jenny, *née* Napper (d 1975); *b* 8 May 1933; *Educ* Christ's Hosp, BNC Oxford (MA, DPhil); *m* 21 Sept 1973, Elizabeth Joan, da of Peter Peill (d 1973), of Duffield, Derbyshire; 2 da (Katherine b 1975, Clare b 1977); *Career* Intelligence Corps 1 Lt 1952–54; lectr in psychology Univ of Hull 1961–65, sr res offr Inst of Educn London 1965–66, reader in psychology Univ of Southampton 1966–73, prof of educn Macquarie Univ Aust 1974–77, prof of social psychology Univ of Bristol 1988– (prof of educn, dir Overseas Studies Centre, and dean of faculty 1977–88); former memb: Econ and Social Res Cncl, Psychology Ctee Educn and Human Devpt Ctee; former tstee Coll of St Paul and St Mary Cheltenham, vice chm Redmaids Sch Bristol, tstee Bristol Municipal Charities, chm Deaf Studies Tst Bristol; hon prof Inst Superior de Psicologia Aplicada Lisbon; fell Br Psychological Soc 1972–, Aust Psychological Soc 1975–81; FBPsS; *Books* Language and Social Behaviour (1972), A Question of Answers (1972), Language Management in Education (1978), Communication in Development (1981), Handbook of Language and Social Psychology (1990), Deception, Delusion and Detection (1996); *Recreations* squash, badminton, travel; *Style*— Prof Peter Robinson; ✉ Department of Psychology, University of Bristol, Bristol BS8 1TN (☎ 0117 928 8451, telex 445938, fax 0117 928 8588)

ROBINSON, Peter Damian; CB (1983); s of John Robinson (d 1957), and Florence Eleanor, *née* Easten (later Mrs Clegg, d 1972); *b* 11 July 1926; *Educ* Corby Sch Sunderland, Lincoln Coll Oxford (MA); *m* 1, 1956, Mary Katinka (d 1978), da of Dr

William Percy Bonner (d 1960), of Peterborough; 2 da; m 2, 1985, Sheila Suzanne Gibbins, da of Charles Gorguet Guille (d 1966), of Finchley, London; *Career* RM Commandos 1944–46; called to the Bar Middle Temple 1951, Common Law Bar 1952–59, clerk of Assize NE circuit 1959–70, admin NE circuit 1970–74, SE circuit 1974–81, dep sec Lord Chllr's Dept 1981–86, dep clerk of the Crown in Chancery 1982–86, advsr on Hong Kong Judiciary 1986–87, ret 1987; *Recreations* books, walking, theatre, antiques, travel; *Clubs* Mensa; *Style*— Peter Robinson, Esq, CB; ✉ 15 Birklands Park, St Albans, Herts AL1 1TS (☎ 01727 843060)

ROBINSON, Peter David; MP (UDUP) Belfast East (majority 7,787); s of David and Sheliah Robinson; *b* 29 Dec 1948; *Educ* Annadale GS, Castlereagh Coll of Further Educn; *m* 1970, Iris Collins; 2 s, 1 da; *Career* MP (UDUP) Belfast E 1979–, memb NI Assembly 1982–86; gen sec DUP 1975–79, dep ldr DUP 1980– (resigned 1987, re-elected 1988); alderman Castlereagh Boro Cncl 1977–; *Style*— Peter Robinson Esq, MP; ✉ 51 Gransha Rd, Dundonald, Belfast (☎ 01232 473111)

ROBINSON, Peter Frank; s and h of Sir Wilfred Robinson, 3rd Bt, *qv*; *b* 23 June 1949; *m* 1988, Alison Jane, eldest da of D Bradley, of Rochester, Kent; *Style*— Peter Robinson, Esq; ✉ 14 Wellgarth Road, London NW11 7HS

ROBINSON, Peter James; s of Percival Albert Robinson, and Lillian Caroline Robinson; *b* 28 April 1941; *Educ* Erith County GS, City of London Coll; *m* Janice Helen; *Career* gp chief exec Woolwich Building Society 1995–96 (joined 1963), conslt Direct Line Insurance 1996–; pres Kent Cricket League; Freeman: City of London, Worshipful Co of Chartered Secretaries & Administrators; FCIS, FCIB, CIMgt; *Recreations* cricket, golf, gardening; *Clubs* MCC, RAC, West Kent Golf, Littlestone Golf, Bromley Cricket; *Style*— Peter Robinson, Esq

ROBINSON, Prof Peter Michael; s of Maurice Allan Robinson, and Brenda Margaret, *née* Ponsford; *b* 20 April 1947; *Educ* Brockenhurst GS, UCL (BSc), LSE (MSc), Australian Nat Univ (PhD); *m* 27 Feb 1981, Wendy Rhea, da of Morris Brandmark; 1 da; *Career* lectr LSE 1969–70; assoc prof: Harvard Univ 1977–79 (asst prof 1973–77), Univ of Br Columbia 1979–80; prof Univ of Surrey 1980–84, prof of econometrics LSE 1984–95, Tooke prof of economic science and statistics LSE 1995–; author of numerous articles in learned jls and books; co ed: Econometric Theory 1989–91, Econometrica 1991–96; memb Editorial Bds of various jls; fell Econometric Soc; *Recreations* walking; *Style*— Prof Peter M Robinson; ✉ Department of Economics, London School of Economics, Houghton Street, London WC2A 2AE (☎ 0171 955 7516)

ROBINSON, Philip; s of Sydney Albert Robinson (d 1971), of Hackney, London, and Myra Isabel, *née* Kelly (d 1981); *b* 8 May 1954; *Educ* Hackney Downs GS; *m* 2 July 1984, Charman, da of Percival Leonard Davis; 1 da (Olivia b 19 Nov 1985), 1 s (James b 10 Oct 1987); *Career* sr contract auditor Philips Petroleum Co Europe Africa 1972–76, articled clerk then audit mangr with John Burnett & Co, Saffery Champness then Fraser Littlejohn 1976–83, financial controller Holco Trading Co Ltd commodities traders 1983–86, gen mangr London Metal Exchange servs International Commodities Clearing House 1986–87, fin dir Metallgesellschaft Ltd 1987–90, dir of fin Assoc of Futures Brokers and Dealers 1990–91, sr staff dir fin and admin Securities and Futures Authy (following merger) 1991–93, dir of planning and fin then chief operating offr Investmt Mgmnt Regulatory Orgn (IMRO) 1993–; memb Cncl ACCA 1993–; FCCA 1985 (ACCA 1981, first prize PE1), MSI 1992; *Recreations* sailing, Christianity; *Style*— Philip Robinson, Esq; ✉ The Investment Management Regulatory Organisation Ltd, Lloyds Chambers, Portsoken Street, London E1 8BT (☎ 0171 390 5600)

ROBINSON, (Henry) Richard Gwynne; OBE (1994); s of Dr Henry Robinson, JP, DL (d 1960), and Margaret, *née* Barnes (d 1963); *b* 25 Oct 1916; *Educ* Radley; *m* 10 Jan 1959, Rose Mary, da of Col Leslie Herbert Queripel, CMG, DSO (d 1962), of Tunbridge Wells; 2 s (David b 1964, Philip b 1965); *Career* Gunner HAC TA 1939, HAC and RA 1939–46, Maj 1945, IG; Prudential Assurance Co Ltd 1934–67; Lawn Tennis Assoc: memb Cncl 1954, chm 1973, vice pres 1974, hon life vice pres 1987; memb Sports Cncl 1979–88; Central Cncl of Physical Recreation: rep memb 1973, memb Exec Ctee 1979–, chm Major Spectator Sports Div 1983–95; memb Ctee: Wimbledon Championships 1972–87, Wimbledon Lawn Tennis Museum 1975–; Kent Co Lawn Tennis Assoc: memb Cncl 1950, hon sec 1953, jt hon sec 1967, vice pres 1977–89, life vice pres 1990–; memb Ctee: Tunbridge Wells Lawn Tennis Club 1947–65 (chm 1962–65), Tunbridge Wells Lawn Tennis Tournament 1948–85 (chm 1956–59 and 1967–85); memb HAC 1939, Freeman City of London 1946, Liveryman Worshipful Co of Skinners 1946; FCII 1950; *Recreations* lawn tennis, squash rackets, shooting, sports administration; *Clubs* All England Lawn Tennis & Croquet; *Style*— Richard Robinson, Esq, OBE; ✉ Long View, Limes Lane, Buxted, nr Uckfield, E Sussex TN22 4PB (☎ 01825 732551)

ROBINSON, Robert Henry; s of Ernest Redfern Robinson (d 1962), and Johanna Hogan (d 1978); *b* 17 Dec 1927; *Educ* Raynes Park GS, Exeter Coll Oxford (MA); *m* 1958, Josephine Mary, da of Paul Richard; 1 s (Nicholas), 2 da (Lucy, Suzy); *Career* writer and broadcaster; *Books* Landscape with Dead Dons (1956), Inside Robert Robinson (1965), The Conspiracy (1968), The Dog Chairman (1982), The Everyman Book of Light Verse (1984), Bad Dreams (1989), Prescriptions of a Pox Doctor's Clerk (1990), Skip all That (memoirs, 1996); *Clubs* Garrick; *Style*— Robert Robinson, Esq; ✉ 16 Cheyne Row, London SW3; Laurel Cottage, Buckland St Mary, Somerset

ROBINSON, Prof Roger James; s of Albert Edward Robinson, of Axmouth, Devon, and Leonora Sarah, *née* Potts; *b* 17 May 1932; *Educ* Poole GS, Balliol Coll Oxford (BA, MA, DPhil, BM, BCh); *m* 1962, Jane Hippisley, da of John Douglas Packham (d 1941); 2 s (Andrew b 1964, James b 1971), 1 da (Sarah b 1965); *Career* lectr ChCh Oxford 1953–56; med appts 1960–67: Radcliffe Infirmary, Hammersmith Hosp, Nat Hosp Queen Square; sr lectr Inst of Child Health 1967–71, conslt paediatrician Guy's Hosp 1971–75, Ferdinand James de Rothschild prof of paediatrics Guy's Hosp Med Sch (now Guy's and St Thomas's) 1975–90, emeritus prof of paediatrics Univ of London 1990–, assoc ed BMJ 1990–; hon fell English Dept Univ of Aberdeen 1996–; FRCP 1975; *Books* Medical Care of Newborn Babies (jtly, 1972), The Works of James Beattie (1996); *Recreations* walking, canoeing, eighteenth-century literature; *Style*— Prof Roger Robinson; ✉ 60 Madeley Road, Ealing, London W5 2LU

ROBINSON, Prof Ronald Edward; CBE (1971), DFC (1944); s of William Edward Robinson (d 1964), and Ada Theresa, *née* Goldsmith; *b* 3 Sept 1920; *Educ* Battersea GS, St John's Coll Cambridge (BA, MA, PhD); *m* 12 Aug 1948, Alice Josephine, da of Ludwell Howard Denny (d 1970), of Washington DC; 2 s (Peter Denny b 1950, Mark David Ludwell b 1961), 2 da (Alice Star Theresa b 1951, Kristin Day b 1955); *Career* served RAF 1941–45, Bomber Pilot 58 Sqdn; res offr African Div Colonial Office 1947–49, fell St John's Coll Cambridge 1948–71 (res fell 1949–51); Univ of Cambridge: lectr in history 1951–66, Smuts reader in Cwlth studies 1966–71; visiting fell Inst of Advanced Studies Princeton 1959–61, Beit prof of history of Br Empire and Cwlth Univ of Oxford 1971–87, emeritus prof and fell Balliol Coll Oxford 1987; visiting prof Univ of S Carolina 1988, visiting Cline prof of Br history Texas 1990; FRCS; *Books* Developing The Third World (1971), Africa and The Victorians (2 edn, 1981) Bismarck, Europe and Africa (1988), Railway Imperialism (1991); *Recreations* room cricket; *Clubs* Hawks, Gridiron; *Style*— Prof Ronald Robinson, CBE, DFC; ✉ 79 Mill Road, Cambridge (☎ 01223 357063)

ROBINSON, Sheriff Stanley Scott; MBE (1944), TD (1953); s of William Scott Robinson (d 1962), of Edinburgh, and Christina Douglas, *née* Wallace (d 1989); *b* 27 March 1913; *Educ* Boroughmuir Sch Edinburgh, Univ of Edinburgh (BL); *m* 14 April 1937, Helen Annan, da of late John Hardie, of Edinburgh; 3 s (Derek John Scott b 1938, Alastair Stanley Scott b 1942, Ian George Scott b 1951); *Career* RA (TA): cmmnd 2 Lt 1935, Lt-Col 1945, ret 1953; served WWII: France 1939–40, France and Germany 1944–45 (despatches twice); admitted slr 1935, slr Supreme Cts 1962; Sheriff of Grampian Highlands and Is 1972 (ret 1985), Hon Sheriff of Inverness 1985–; Hon Sheriff of Forfarshire, vice pres Law Soc Scot 1969–72, former dean Faculty of Slrs Slrs of Forfarshire (now Angus); formerly chm Regnl Advsy Ctee Forestry Cmmn (Highland); memb Soc of Slrs in Supreme Ct 1962; *Books* The Law of Interdict in Scotland (1987), Stair Encyclopedia of Laws of Scotland (contrib on law of crofting, law of railways and canals, law of game, 1987), Law of Game, Salmon and Freshwater Fishing (1990); *Recreations* bowling, caravanning; *Clubs* Highland (Inverness); *Style*— Sheriff Stanley Scott Robinson, MBE, TD; ✉ Drumalin House, 16 Drummond Rd, Inverness IV2 4NB (☎ 01463 233488)

ROBINSON, Stephen Joseph; OBE (1971); s of Joseph Alan Robinson, of Leicester, and Ethel Bunting (d 1962); *b* 6 Aug 1931; *Educ* Sebright Sch, Univ of Cambridge (MA), Harvard Business Sch; *m* 13 April 1957 (m dis 1994), Monica Mabs, da of John Scott (d 1986); 1 da (Marion Jean b 1961), 1 s (Peter Joseph b 1962); *Career* Pilot Offr RAF 1950; Mullard Research Lab 1954–71, MEL Equipment Ltd 1971–79, product dir MEL Bd 1973, md Pye TVT Ltd 1980–84, dir Royal Signals and Radar Establishment MOD 1989–91; S G Brown Medal 1972; FRS, FEng 1979, FIEE, FInstP; *Recreations* saling, skiing, walking; *Style*— Stephen Robinson, Esq, OBE, FRS, FEng; ✉ 140 The Street, Kirtling, Newmarket, Suffolk CB8 9PD (☎ 01368 730104)

ROBINSON, Stephen Julian Roper; s of Andrew Thomas Roper Robinson, of London, and Barbara Anne, *née* Black; *b* 28 Sept 1961; *Educ* Westminster, Queen's Coll Oxford (scholar, BA); *Career* reporter Natal Witness SA 1983–85, freelance writer Cape Town SA 1985–86; The Daily Telegraph: joined 1986, Belfast corr 1987, Johannesburg corr 1987–90, Washington corr 1990–; contrib Spectator 1985–; winner T E Utley Meml Prize 1990; *Recreations* tennis, reading; *Style*— Stephen Robinson, Esq; ✉ 1321 35th Street NW, Washington DC 20007, USA (☎ 00 1 202 965 3482); The Daily Telegraph, Suite 904, 1331 Pennsylvania Avenue NW, Washington DC 20004, USA (☎ 00 1 202 393 5195, fax 00 1 202 393 1335)

ROBINSON, Stuart Jackson; *b* 21 Sept 1948; *Educ* Monks Park Comp Sch Bristol, Univ of Newcastle upon Tyne (BA), Dept of Educn Univ of Bristol (PGCE); *Career* Colston's Sch Bristol: head Econ Dept 1971–79, asst housemaster 1972–75, sixth form housemaster (boarding) 1975–79; head of Upper Sch Cheadle Hulme HS 1979–82; Southway Sch Plymouth: dep head 1982–87, acting head teacher 1987; head teacher: The John Bentley Sch 1987–94, St Bartholomew's Sch 1994–; chair: Assoc of Secdy Heads in Wilts 1991–92, treas Calne Project Devpt Ctee 1990–94; memb: Exec Bd Wilts Educn Business Ptnrship 1992–94, Sports Centre Mgmnt Ctee 1987–94, Calne Business Assoc, Mgmnt Ctee Further Educn Centre; contrib Wilts Govr Trg Prog; tstee West Berkshire Education Business Partnership 1995–; MCC coach, Hockey Assoc coach; FRSA; *Recreations* squash, village cricket, staff soccer; *Style*— Stuart Robinson, Esq; ✉ St Bartholomew's School, Andover Road, Newbury, Berks RG14 6JP (☎ 01635 521255, fax 01635 516420)

ROBINSON, Rev Thomas Hugh (Tom); CBE (1989); s of Lt-Col James Arthur Robinson, OBE (d 1944), and Maud Loney, *née* Trayer (d 1980); *b* 11 June 1934; *Educ* Bishop Foy Sch Waterford, Trinity Coll Dublin (BA, MA); *m* 9 July 1959, Mary Elizabeth Doreen, da of Richard Edmund Clingan (d 1988), of Portadown; 2 s (Peter b 1962, Keith b 1964), 1 da (Kathryn b 1967); *Career* ordained: deacon 1957, priest 1958; curate asst St Clements Belfast 1957–60, chaplain Missions to Seamen Mombasa 1961–64, rector St Mary's Youghal Co Cork 1964–66; cmmnd Royal Army Chaplains Dept 1966, dep asst chaplain gen 2 Armd Div 1977–80, chaplain RMCS 1980–82; sr chaplain: Eastern Dist 1982–84, 1 Br Corps 1984–85, BAOR 1985–86; dep chaplain gen 1986–89; team rector Cleethorpes 1990–; *Recreations* travel, photography; *Style*— The Rev Tom Robinson, CBE; ✉ St Peter's Rectory, 42 Queen's Parade, Cleethorpes, N E Lincolnshire DN35 0DG (☎ 01472 693234)

ROBINSON, Tony; *Educ* Central Sch of Speech and Drama; *children* 1 s (Luke), 1 da (Laura); *Career* actor and writer; *Theatre* numerous appearances as child actor incl original version of stage musical Oliver!, several years in rep theatre, theatre dir for 2 years, then successively with Chichester Festival Theatre, RSC and NT; *Television* incl: Ernie Roberts in Horizon documentary Joey, Baldrick in Black Adder (4 series, BBC), Sheriff of Nottingham in Maid Marian and Her Merry Men (also writer, 4 series); as presenter: Points of View, Stay Tooned, three African documentary features for Comic Relief, Time Team (archaeology series, Channel 4), Great Journey to the Caribbean, Hospital Watch (BBC) 1995; as writer: Fat Tulip's Garden (30 episodes, Central), Odysseus - the Greatest Hero of Them All (13–part series, BBC), Blood and Honey (26 episodes, BBC); *Awards* for writing: 2 RTS, BAFTA, Int Prix Jeunesse; *Publications* 16 children's books incl 8 Maid Marian comic books; *Style*— Tony Robinson, Esq; ✉ c/o Kate Feast Management, 10 Primrose Hill Studios, Fitzroy Road, London NW1 8TR (☎ 0171 586 5502, fax 0171 586 9817)

ROBINSON, (Walter) Trevor; TD (1956); s of Joseph Robinson (d 1969), of Sheffield, and Nellie, *née* Briggs (d 1977); *b* 2 Sept 1925; *Educ* City GS Sheffield; *m* 6 Sept 1947, Olive, da of Frederick Richer (d 1942), of Sheffield; 2 s (Michael b 1950, Anthony b 1954); *Career* Capt York and Lancaster Regt 1943–47; gen mangr Nat West Bank (formerly Westminster Bank) 1969–73 (joined 1941), chief exec Texas Commerce Bank International 1973–75, gen mangr Midland and International Banks Ltd 1975–78, exec vice pres Manufacturers Hanover Tst Co 1978–86, dir TSB Bank plc 1986–90, chm Five Oaks Investments plc 1987–95; dir: National Grid Co plc 1989–95, National Grid Group plc 1995–, Republic Nat Bank of New York (gen mangr 1986–); Freeman City of London 1974; FCIB; *Recreations* banking; *Style*— Trevor Robinson, Esq, TD; ✉ 30 Monument Street, London EC3R 8NB (☎ 0171 409 2426, fax 0171 860 3178, telex 889 217, car 0385 245220)

ROBINSON, Dr Trevor Walter Ernest; s of Sir Harold Ernest Robinson (d 1979), of Trinidad, W Indies, and Lady Clarice Graeme Robinson, *née* Yearwood (d 1989); *b* 9 Jan 1932; *Educ* Lodge Sch Barbados, Stowe, Univ of Cambridge (MA, MB BChir, MRCP); *m* 1, 27 April 1963 (m dis 1975), Jean Ewen, da of George Barbour, of India; 1 da (Karen b 19 Aug 1967); m 2, Angela Judith Keeble, *née* Hole; 1 da (Kate b 25 Feb 1985); *Career* RMO and SHO Inst of Dermatology London 1960–61, sr dermatological registrar St Bartholomew's Hosp 1962–67 (registrar), res fell in dermatology Scripps Clinic and Res Fndn La Jolla California USA 1968–69, conslt dermatologist Univ Coll London Hosps 1969–94 (lectr 1969–94), conslt Edgware General Hosp 1971–96; memb Dowling Club, fell and pres St John's Dermatological Soc 1988–89; FRSM, FRCP 1975; *Books* Virus Diseases and the Skin (1983), Herpes Simplex in Practical Management of the Dermatologic Patient (1986); *Recreations* gardening, deep sea fishing, poetry, painting; *Clubs* RSM; *Style*— Dr Trevor Robinson; ✉ Flat 3, 51 Harley Street, London W1M 1DD (☎ 0171 387 2160, 0171 637 7325, fax 0171 637 5383)

ROBINSON, Victor Philip; s of Francis Herbert Robinson (d 1962), and Constance Harriet, *née* Phillips (d 1975); *b* 26 Nov 1943; *Educ* Cranleigh Sch Surrey, St Mary's Hosp Med Sch (MB BS); *m* 30 Oct 1965, Elizabeth Margaret, da of Lt Cdr Kenneth Thomas Basset, of Hareston Manor, Brixton, Devon (d 1989); 4 da ((Anne) Michelle b 30 Aug 1966, Louise Frances b 27 Aug 1969, Charlotte Faye b 31 Jan 1972, Victoria Jane b 29 Aug 1974); *Career* conslt obstetrician and gynaecologist: Queen Charlotte's Maternity Hosp, St George's Hosp Med Sch, Hillingdon and Mount Vernon Hosps, Hillingdon

Health Authy, Harefield Hosp 1982–; obstetrician reponsible for the care of first known pregnancies following heart and lung transplantations (presentation to World Congress); memb Sailing Tst; memb: RSM, BMA, BFS, RCOG; *Clubs* Ocean Youth; *Style—* Victor Robinson, Esq; ✉ Hillingdon Hospital, Uxbridge, Middx UB8 3NN

ROBINSON, Vivian; QC (1986); s of William Robinson (d 1986), of Wakefield, and Ann, *née* Kidd; *b* 29 July 1944; *Educ* Queen Elizabeth GS Wakefield, The Leys Sch Cambridge, Sidney Sussex Coll Cambridge (BA); *m* 19 April 1975, (Nora) Louise, da of Maj Peter Duncan Marriner, TD (d 1988), of Rayleigh; 1 s (Edward Duncan b 30 Jan 1980), 2 da (Katherine Anne b 12 Sept 1977, Anna Ruth b 12 July 1981); *Career* called to the Bar Inner Temple 1967, Master of the Bench Inner Temple 1991; recorder of the Crown Court 1986–; Liveryman and memb Ct of Assts Worshipful Co of Gardeners; *Recreations* gardening, reading; *Clubs* Garrick, RAC, MCC; *Style—* Vivian Robinson, Esq, QC; ✉ Queen Elizabeth Building, Temple, London EC4Y 9BS (☎ 0171 583 5766, fax 0171 353 0339)

ROBINSON, Sir Wilfred Henry Frederick; 3 Bt (UK 1908), of Hawthornden, Wynberg, Cape Province, S Africa, and Dudley House, City of Westminster; s of late Wilfred Henry Robinson (3 s of 1 Bt), and late Eileen, *née* St Leger; suc unc, Sir Joseph Benjamin Robinson 1954; *b* 24 Dec 1917; *Educ* Diocesan Coll Rondebosch, St John's Coll Cambridge; *m* 1946, Margaret Alison Kathleen, da of late Frank Mellish, MC, of Rondebosch, Cape, S Africa; 1 s, 2 da; *Heir* s, Peter Frank Robinson b 23 June 1949; *Career* former Maj Para Regt; vice-princ of Diocesan Coll Sch Rondebosch Cape S Africa 1969–77; fin offr Soc of Genealogists 1980–92; *Style—* Sir Wilfred Robinson, Bt; ✉ 37 Riverview Drive, Barnes, London SW13 9QJ

ROBLIN, Ven Graham Henry; OBE (1984); s of Ewart Roblin, of Cardiff, and Marjorie, *née* Taylor; *b* 18 Aug 1937; *Educ* The Choristers Sch Exeter, King's Coll Taunton, King's Coll London (AKC); *m* Penelope Ann, da of Brig J G Cumberlege, OBE, TD, of Uplyme, Devon; 1 s (David John Henry b 1967), 1 da (Catherine Clare b 1965); *Career* ordained Southwark Cathedral 1962, chaplain to the Forces 1966–, dep asst chaplain gen 1979, warden Bagshot Park 1983–86, asst chaplain gen 1986–89, dep chaplain gen 1989–92, archdeacon of the Army 1990–92; hon chaplain to HM the Queen 1988, vicar Bere Regis Dorset 1993–; *Style—* The Ven Graham Roblin, OBE

ROBOROUGH, 3 Baron (UK 1938); Sir Henry Massey Lopes; 6 Bt (UK 1805); s of 2 Baron Roborough (d 1992), and Helen, *née* Dawson; *b* 2 Feb 1940; *Educ* Eton; *m* 1, 1968 (m dis 1986), Robyn Zenda Carol, da of John Bromwich, of Point Lonsdale, Victoria, Aust; 2 s (Hon Massey John Henry b 1969, Hon Andrew James b 1971), 2 da (Hon Katie Victoria b 1976, Hon Melinda Claire b 1978); m 2, 1986, Sarah Anne Pipon, 2 da of Colin Baker, of Peter Tavy, Devon; 2 da (Hon Emily Jane b 1987, Hon Louisa Constance b 1989); *Heir* s, Hon Massey John Henry Lopes b 22 Dec 1969; *Career* late Lt Coldstream Guards; landowner; *Style—* The Rt Hon the Lord Roborough; ✉ Briscoe House, Ford Street, nr Wellington, Somerset (☎ 01823 660730)

ROBOTHAM, (John) Michael; s of Alpheus John Robotham, OBE, JP, DL (d 1994), of Quarndon, Derby, and Gwendolyn Constance, *née* Bromet; *b* 27 March 1933; *Educ* Clifton Coll; *m* 29 June 1963 (m dis 1989), Diana Elizabeth, da of Alfred Thomas Webb (d 1967); 2 s (Guy Thomas Blews b 1967, Adam John Blews b 1971 d 1982); m 2, 1990, Victoria Mary Cronjé, da of Victor St Clair Yates; *Career* 2 Lt 12 Royal Lancers 1957–59; memb Stock Exchange 1963, assoc J M Finn & Co (membs of SFA) 1980–; dir: Western Selection plc 1971–, Burlington Group plc 1984–, London Finance & Investment Group plc 1984–; chm Monteagle SA 1996–; chm: Mile-Posts Publications 1975–, Inst of Advanced Motorists 1989–; FCA, FIMBRA; *Recreations* tennis, shooting, skiing, gardening; *Clubs* Cavalry and Guards', HAC, City of London; *Style—* Michael Robotham, Esq; ✉ Brickwall Farm House, Clophill, Bedford MK45 4DA (☎ 01525 861333); J M Finn & Co, Salisbury House, London Wall, London EC2M 5TA (☎ 0171 628 9688, fax 0171 628 7314); City Group Ltd, 25 City Rd, London EC1Y 1BQ (☎ 0171 628 9371, fax 0171 638 9426, mobile 0468 291500)

ROBOZ, Zsuzsi; da of Imre Roboz (d 1945), and Edith, *née* Grosz (d 1976); *b* 15 Aug 1939; *Educ* Royal Acad of Arts London; *m* 22 Jan 1964, (Alfred) Teddy Smith; *Career* artist; solo exhibitions incl: Hong Kong Arts Festival 1976, Revudeville (V&A) 1978, Drawn to Ballet (Royal Festival Hall) 1983, Budapest Spring Festival 1985 and 1988, Music Makers (Royal Festival Hall) 1987, Lincoln Center New York 1989, British Art Now - a personal view (ART 93, Business Design Centre) 1993, The Creators (Roy Miles Gallery London) 1994, The Spirit of Nature (David Messum Fine Art London) 1995; portraits incl: Lord Olivier in the Theatre Museum, Dame Ninette de Valois in Nat Portrait Gallery, Sir George Solti, Sir John Gielgud, Prince William of Gloucester in Barnwell Church; permanent collections incl: Tate Gallery London, Theatre Museum, V&A, Museum of Fine Arts Budapest, Pablo Casals Museum Puerto Rico, St John's Coll Cambridge, Royal Festival Hall London; memb Pastel Soc, FRSA; *Books* Women & Men's Daughters (1970), Chichester Ten, Portrait of a Decade (1975), British Ballet To-day (1980), British Art Now - a personal view (text by Edward Lucie-Smith, 1993); *Recreations* music, swimming, reading; *Style—* Ms Zsuzsi Roboz; ✉ The Studio, 76 Eccleston Square Mews, London SW1 (☎ 0171 834 4617)

ROBSON, Andrew Maxwell; s of Harry Robson (d 1977), and Maria Jenny Robson; *b* 11 April 1942; *Educ* St Peter's Sch York, Univ of Leeds (BSc); *m* 1 April 1967, Susan Jennifer, da of Guy Garside Davies, of Wybunbury, Nantwich, Cheshire; 2 s (Michael J b 1969, Guy A b 1972); *Career* Taylor Woodrow construction 1964–67, Ove Arup & Ptnrs (conslts) 1967–69, Dow Mac Concrete (precast concrete) 1969–72, chief engr Crendon Structures 1972–76; Turner Wright & Partners (UK) Ltd: chief designer 1976–81, assoc ptnr 1981–87, dir 1987–88, chm and md 1988–; memb Soc of American Mil Engrs 1981, MInstD 1984 (branch sec 1982–84); MICE 1973; *Recreations* golf, bridge; *Clubs* Henley Golf; *Style—* Andrew Robson, Esq; ✉ Turner Wright & Partners (UK) Ltd, 164 West Wycombe Road, High Wycombe, Bucks HP12 3EA (☎ 01494 448824, fax 01494 448830)

ROBSON, Brian; s of Gilbert Brown Robson (d 1972), of Hexham, Northumberland, and Lily, *née* Robinson; *b* 3 Feb 1936; *Educ* Hexham Queen Elizabeth GS; *m* 1, 8 Aug 1959 (m dis 1980), Christine Angela; 1 s (Dean Anthony b 5 April 1965), 1 da (Penelope Ann b 13 Jan 1963); m 2, 5 Dec 1981 (m dis 1994), Esther; *Career* cricket administrator; sec Nottinghamshire CCC 1982– (asst sec 1979–82); ACIS; *Recreations* gardening, golf; *Style—* Brian Robson, Esq; ✉ 18 Marl Rd, Radcliffe-on-Trent, Nottingham (☎ 0115 933 5807); Nottinghamshire CCC, Trent Bridge, Nottingham (☎ 0115 982 1525)

ROBSON, Prof Brian Turnbull; s of Oswell Robson (d 1973), and Doris Lowes, *née* Ayre (d 1984); *b* 23 Feb 1939; *Educ* RGS Newcastle, St Catharine's Coll Cambridge (MA, PhD); *m* 21 Dec 1973, Glenna, da of Jack Leslie Ransom, MBE, DCM, Croix de Guerre (d 1974); *Career* lectr Univ Coll of Wales Aberystwyth 1964–67, Harkness fellowship Univ of Chicago 1967–68, lectr Univ of Cambridge 1968–77, fell Fitzwilliam Coll Cambridge 1968–77; Univ of Manchester: prof of geography 1977–, dean Faculty of Arts 1988–90, pro-vice-chllr 1993–; chm Manchester Cncl for Voluntary Servs 1983–91, pres Inst of Br Geographers 1992–93, pres Manchester Statistical Soc 1995–; FRGS 1973; *Books* Urban Analysis (1969), Urban Growth (1973), Urban Social Areas (1975), Managing The City (1987), Those Inner Cities (1988), Assessing the Impact of Urban Policy (1994), Index of Local Conditions (1995); *Recreations* theatre, watercolour painting, gardening; *Style—* Prof Brian Robson; ✉ 32 Oaker Avenue, West Didsbury, Manchester M20 2XH (☎ 0161 445 2036); La Ratière, 82110 Lauzerte, Tarn et Garonne, France; Department of Geography, University of Manchester, Manchester M13 9PL (☎ 0161 275 3639, fax 0161 273 4407)

ROBSON, Bryan; OBE; s of Brian Jackson Robson, of S Pelaw, Chester-Le-Street, Co Durham, and Maureen, *née* Lowther; *b* 11 Jan 1957; *Educ* Birtley Lord Lawson Comp; *m* 2 June 1979, Denise Kathleen, da of George Brindley, of Gt Barr, Birmingham; 1 s (Ben b 2 Sept 1988), 2 da (Claire b 17 Sept 1980, Charlotte b 17 June 1982); *Career* professional footballer/manager; West Bromwich Albion 1974–81, Manchester Utd 1981–94: 359 appearances and 99 goals, capt until 1994; honours with Manchester Utd: FA Cup winners 1983, 1985 and 1990, Charity Shield winners 1983 and 1993, winners Euro Cup Winners' Cup 1991, Rumbelows Cup winners 1992, Charity Shield 1992, winners inaugural FA Premier League Championship 1992/93 and 1993/94; 90 England caps (26 goals); asst coach English Nat Team 1994–; player/manager Middlesbrough FC 1994–; charity work incl: Wallness Hurdles and Adventure Farm, Bryan Robson Scanner Appeal; Hon MA: Univ of Manchester 1992, Univ of Salford 1992; *Books* United I Stand (1984); *Style—* Bryan Robson, Esq, OBE; ✉ Middlesbrough FC, Cellnet Riverside Stadium, Middlesbrough, Cleveland TS3 6RS (☎ 01642 227227)

ROBSON, Christopher; s of John Thomas Robson, and Eva Elizabeth, *née* Leatham; *b* 9 Dec 1953; *Educ* Cambridge Coll of Arts & Technol, Trinity Coll of Music London; *m* 1974 (m dis 1983), Laura Carin, da of Leonard Snelling, of Blackheath; *Career* counter-tenor; studied with: Nigel Wickens, James Gaddarn, Paul Esswood, Helga Mott, Geoffrey Parsons, Sir Peter Pears, Laura Sarti, Thomas Helmsley, John Shirley Quirke; concert debut Queen Elizabeth Hall with London Orpheus Choir and Orch 1976, operatic debut as Argones in Sosarme with Barber Opera Birmingham 1979; memb: London Oratory Choir 1974–81, Monteverdi Choir 1974–85, King's Consort 1979–86, Westminster Cathedral Choir 1981–84, ENO 1981–, New London Consort 1985–; roles with ENO incl: Shepherd in Monteverdi's Orfeo (ENO debut) 1981, title role in Akhnaten (UK première), Edgar/Mad Tom in Lear (UK première), Arsamenes in Xerxes, title role in Julius Caesar, Polinesso in Ariodante 1993 and 1996, Oberon in Midsummer Night's Dream 1995; has also performed princ roles with opera cos incl: Royal Opera Co Covent Garden, Houston Grand Opera, NY City Opera, Northern Stage, Covent Garden Opera Festival, Opera Factory London, Opera Factory Zurich, Nancy Opera, Frankfurt Opera, Scottish Opera, Berlin Kammeroper, Bavarian State Opera, Sao Paulo Opera, Innsbruck Landestheater, Badisches Staatstheater Karlsruhe, Pfalzbautheater Ludwigshafen, Bayerisches Staatsoper Munich, Opera North, Chicago Lyric Opera, Flanders Opera, Glyndebourne Touring Opera; has performed with orchs incl: Royal Philharmonic, English Chamber Orch, London Sinfonietta, London Bach Orch, BBC Philharmonic, Northern Sinfonia, Bournemouth Sinfonietta, London Baroque Orch, European Baroque Orch, Hanover Band, Concentus Musicus Vienna, Tonhalle Orch Zurich, Vienna Symphony, City of London Sinfonia, Rochester Symphony Orch USA, Sharoun Ensemble Berlin; worked with conductors incl: Sir Charles Mackerras, Walter Weller, Claudio Abbado, Gustav Leonhardt, Roy Goodman, Niklaus Harnoncourt, Richard Hickox, Mark Elder, Paul Daniel, Ton Koopman, Rene Jacobs, Howard Arman, David Atherton, Noel Davies, Sir Peter Maxwell Davies, John de Main, Christopher Keene, Peter Neumann, Brenton Langbein; performed at festivals incl: BBC Proms, Chichester, Three Choirs, Greenwich, Camden, Almeida (world première of Casken's Golem), Huddersfield Contemporary Music, Aix en Provence, Montpelier, Stuttgart, Den Haag, Bruges, Barcelona, San Sebastian, Zurich, Wiener Moderne, Warsaw; gala performances incl: Royal Opera House Covent Garden 1986, ENO 1987, Sadler's Wells 1991; *Recordings* Valls' Missa Scala Aretina (with Thames Chamber Orch), Vivaldi's Nisi Dominus (with Kings Consort), Biber's Marienvespers (with Salzburg Bachchor) and Requiem (with New London eonsort), The Delights of Posilipo (with New London Consort), Monteverdi's 1610 Vespers (with New London Consort), Monteverdi's Orfeo (with New London Consort), Blow's Venus and Adonis (with New London Consort), Heinrich Schütz Auferstehungs and Weinacht Historias, Tippett's The Ice Break (with London Sinfonietta), Maxwell-Davies' Resurrection (with BBC Philharmonic), Handel's Messiah (with Collegium Musicum 90), Purcell Songs (Cambridge Musick), Casken's Golem (with Music Projects London), Locke's Psyche and Bach Magnificat (with New London Consort), Purcell's Odes (with the Orch of the Age of Enlightenment); *TV/Video* Xerxes (ENO), Ariodante (ENO), Orontea (Innsbruck Festival), Hail Bright Cecilia (Norrington); *Awards* finalist Kathleen Ferrier Award 1978, winner GLAA Young Musician Award 1979, winner Wroclawskiego Szermierza Statuette Wroclaw Int Music Festival 1991; *Recreations* films, theatre, food and wine, driving; *Style—* Christopher Robson, Esq; ✉ c/o Music International, 13 Ardilaun Road, London N5 2QR (☎ 0171 359 5183, fax 0171 226 9792)

ROBSON, Christopher William; s of Leonard Robson (d 1970), of Egglescliffe, Stockton-on-Tees, and Irene Beatrice, *née* Punch (d 1984); *b* 13 Aug 1936; *Educ* Rugby; *m* 17 July 1965, Susan Jane, da of Maj John Davey Cooke-Hurle (d 1979), of Co Durham; 1 s (Andrew Leonard Feilding b 1973), 2 da (Sarah Louise b 1966, Lydia Katharine b 1969); *Career* Nat Serv Lt RASC 1955–57; admitted slr 1962, sr ptnr Punch Robson (formerly JWR Punch and Robson) 1971–95; fell Woodard Schs (Northern Div) Ltd 1974–85; memb: Law Soc, Br Astronomical Soc; *Recreations* astronomy, skiing, shooting, walking; *Style—* Christopher Robson, Esq; ✉ Rudd Hall, E Appleton, Richmond, N Yorks DL10 7QD (☎ 01748 811339)

ROBSON, (William) David; s of (William) Michael Robson, of Haslemere, Surrey, and Audrey Isobel Wales, *née* Dick (d 1964); *b* 28 Jan 1944; *Educ* Eton; *m* 27 Sept 1975, (Anne) Helen, da of Cecil Henry Gosling (d 1974); 1 s ((William) Henry b 1979), 1 da (Emma Lucy b 1977); *Career* Lloyd's member agent; chm Anton Jardine Members Agency Ltd 1991–; Freeman City of London, Liveryman Worshipful Co of Vintners; *Recreations* golf, opera; *Clubs* White's, Pratt's; *Style—* David Robson, Esq; ✉ The Woods, Hatfield Broad Oak, Bishop's Stortford, Herts CM22 7BU (☎ 012797 18452); Anton Jardine Members Agency Ltd, Latham House, 16 Minories, London EC3N 1EX (☎ 0171 702 1234, fax 0171 702 4062)

ROBSON, David Ernest Henry; QC (1980); s of Joseph Robson (d 1979), and Caroline, *née* Bowmaker; *b* 1 March 1940; *Educ* Robert Richardson GS Ryhope, ChCh Oxford (MA); *Career* called to the Bar Inner Temple 1965, memb NE circuit 1965, recorder Crown Ct (NE circuit) 1979–, bencher Inner Temple 1988, head of chambers; pres Herrington Burn (Sunderland) YMCA 1986–, artistic dir Royalty Studio Theatre Sunderland 1986–88; *Recreations* acting, Italy; *Clubs* County Durham; *Style—* David Robson, Esq, QC; ✉ Whitton Grange, Rothbury, Northumberland NE65 7RL (☎ 01669 620929); 3 Broad Chare, Quayside, Newcastle upon Tyne NE1 3DQ (☎ 0191 232 2392)

ROBSON, Dr David John; s of Alan Victor Robson, TD, LDS, RCS (Edin), and Joan Dales, *née* Hawkins; *b* 23 Feb 1944; *Educ* Repton Sch, Middx Hosp Univ of London (MB BS); *Career* conslt physician Greenwich Health Authy 1978–, dir Greenwich Health Authy HISS Project 1990–93; dir Greenwich Healthcare: med 1993–96, information 1996–; FRCP 1986; *Style—* Dr David Robson; ✉ Greenwich District Hospital, Vanbrugh Hill, London SE10 9HE (☎ 0181 858 8141, fax 0181 293 4030)

ROBSON, (William) Frank; s of John William Robson (d 1956), and Mary, *née* Bradley (d 1981); *b* 27 Oct 1928; *Educ* St Aloysius Sch Newcastle upon Tyne; *m* 21 Sept 1957, Barbara Mary Hallwood; 3 da (Angela Mary b 28 July 1960, Susan Jennifer (twin) b 28 July 1960, Julia Charlotte b 19 June 1964); *Career* journalist; Nat Serv, able seaman RN 1947–49; reporter Morpeth Herald 1949–51, reporter and sub-ed Newcastle Evening Chronicle and Jl 1951–54, Sunderland Echo 1954–56; air corr Daily Express 1973–86 (joined 1956, dep def corr 1968–86), estab Aeronews London 1986, corr covering flight-testing of Concorde 001 prototype 1971, only newsman to accompany 002 prototype on world premiere demonstration tour 1972, author of Sunday Express Red Arrows special souvenir edn 1989, author of Sunday Express and Daily Express Fighter Meet '90 and Fighter Meet '91 special souvenir edns; ARAeS 1986; *Clubs* Canterbury RFC, Aviation Club of GB; *Style—* Frank Robson, Esq; ✉ 12 Birchmead Avenue, Pinner, Middlesex HA5 2BG (☎ and fax 0181 866 4930, telex 94018381 AERO G, Mercury Link 7500 mailbox 19041815)

ROBSON, Dr Frank Elms; OBE (1991); s of Joseph Aisbitt Robson (d 1961), of Newbiggin-by-the-Sea, Northumberland, and Barbara, *née* Waters (d 1993); *b* 14 Dec 1931; *Educ* King Edward VI GS Morpeth, Selwyn Coll Cambridge (MA), DCL (Lambeth) 1991; *m* 25 July 1958, Helen, da of Edward Challoner Jackson (d 1950), of Morpeth, Northumberland; 4 s (Aidan b 1960, Martin b 1963, Stephen b 1965, Jonathan b 1967), 1 da (Lorna b 1959); *Career* ptnr Winckworth & Pemberton 1960– (sr ptnr 1990–94); registrar: Diocese of Oxford 1970, Province of Canterbury 1982; memb: Church Assembly 1960–70, Gen Synod 1970–75; vice chm Legal Advsy Cmmn of the Gen Synod, chm Ecclesiastical Law Soc; *Recreations* supporting Oxford United, walking; *Style—* Dr Frank Robson, OBE; ✉ 2 Simms Close, Stanton St John, Oxford OX33 1HB (☎ 01865 351393); 16 Beaumont St, Oxford OX1 2LZ (☎ 01865 241974)

ROBSON, Prof Sir (James) Gordon; kt (1982), CBE (1977); s of James Robson; *b* 18 March 1921; *Educ* Stirling HS, Univ of Glasgow (MB ChB); *m* 1, 1945, Dr Martha Kennedy (d 1975); 1 s; m 2, 1984, Jennifer Kilpatrick; *Career* Wellcome research prof of anaesthetics McGill Univ 1956–64, prof of anaesthetics Royal Postgrad Med Sch Univ of London 1964–86, ret; hon conslt Hammersmith Hosp 1964–86, conslt advsr anaesthetics DHSS 1975–84; currently: conslt med advsr International Hospitals Gp, chm Med Advsy Gp Q R M Healthcare Ltd; hon memb USA Assoc Univ Anaesthetists; memb: Physiological Soc, Cncl Assoc of Anaesthetists of GB and Ireland 1973–84, Editorial Bd and consulting ed British Journal of Anaesthesia 1965–85; hon sec Conf of Med Royal Colls and Their Faculties in UK 1976–82; master Hunterian Inst RCS 1982–88, hon conslt in anaesthetics to the Army 1983–87, chm Advsy Ctee on Distinction Awards 1984–94; pres: Scottish Soc of Anaesthetists 1985–86, Royal Soc of Medicine 1986–88; memb Ctee of Automobile Assoc 1979–90; RNLI: memb Ctee of Mgmnt 1988–, chm Med and Survival Ctee 1988–91 (memb 1981), vice pres 1992; Hon DSc: McGill Univ Canada 1984, Univ of Glasgow 1991; hon fell: Royal Coll of Physicians and Surgeons of Canada 1987, Royal Med Soc (Edinburgh) 1987; FRCS (Eng), Hon FRCA, Hon FANZCA, Hon FFARCSI, Hon FDSRCS, Hon FRCPS(Glas) 1993; *Recreations* golf, wet fly-fishing; *Style—* Prof Sir Gordon Robson, CBE; ✉ Brendon, Lyndale, London NW2 2NY

ROBSON, Ian; s of Edward Robson, of Langport, Somerset, and Lucy, *née* Greatorex; *b* 21 July 1950; *Educ* Consett GS Co Durham, Bath Acad of Art (BA), Brighton Poly (Postgrad Dip); *m* 1, 1974, Julia Mary, da of Thomas William Manning; 2 da (Sarah Rose b 4 June 1978, Tessa Imogen Eva b 10 April 1980); m 2, 1987, Ellen Alunwen Frances, da of Alun Williams; 3 da (Lois Amy b 2 Nov 1988, Miranda Lucy b 5 March 1991, Sophie Frances (twin) b 5 March 1991); *Career* princ Robson Design Associates graphic design consultancy 1976–; pt/t lectr in printmaking Brighton Poly 1975, visiting lectr in graphic design Fndn Studies Dept Winchester Sch of Art 1975–79, pt/t lectr in graphic design Somerset Coll of Arts and Technol 1984–86, memb DBA Trg Task Gp 1988–89, advsy memb Yeovil Coll of Art Advsy Panel 1989, indust rep govr Somerset Coll of Arts and Technol (memb Art and Design Advsy and Liaison Ctees) 1990; CSD: area rep and memb Cncl SW Region 1984–91, hon treas SW Region 1985–89, educn rep to Bath Coll of HE 1987–88, memb Cncl 1993–; MSCD (MSIAD 1982); *Awards and Exhibitions* Gane Meml travelling scholar (Italy, Germany and Switzerland) 1972, open field print exhbn (UK tour) 1974, print graphic exhbn (Thumb Gallery London) 1975, Bull Meml scholar 1976, SW Arts Award for Photography 1979, design work selected for Graphics UK London 1983/for London and overseas 1984, report and accounts work selected for exhbn at World Trade Centre 1987 and 1988, finalist Rank Xerox DTP Document of the Yr Award 1989, Creative Contact Award for Promotional Lit 1991; *Recreations* family and home, the development of the design industry (art, architecture and design generally), gardening (practical as well as the history of gardens), photography (particularly rural and urban landscape), travelling in the UK and overseas, walking rural and coastline areas (with a particular interest in islands), skiing, tennis (club member), films and reading; *Style—* Ian Robson, Esq; ✉ Robson Design Associates Ltd, 69 Princess Victoria Street, Clifton, Bristol BS8 4DD (☎ 0117 946 6669, fax 0117 946 6978)

ROBSON, Prof James Scott; s of William Scott Robson (d 1950), of Hawick, and Elizabeth Hannah, *née* Watt (d 1974); *b* 19 May 1921; *Educ* Hawick HS, Univ of Edinburgh (MB ChB, MD), New York Univ; *m* 2 March 1948, Mary Kynoch, da of Alexander Knight MacDonald (d 1960), of Perth; 2 s (Michael Knight b 1952, Christopher James b 1957); *Career* RAMC: Lt India 1945, Capt Palestine 1946, Egypt 1947–48, MO i/c Med Div BMH Suez; Rockefeller studentship NY 1942–44, Rockefeller res fell Harvard 1949–50; Univ of Edinburgh: sr lectr in therapeutics 1959–60, reader in therapeutics 1959–60 and 1961–68, reader in med 1968–76, prof of med 1977–86; contrib to numerous medical pubns; hon assoc prof of med Harvard Univ 1962, visiting prof Merck Sharp & Dome Australia 1968; pres Renal Assoc London 1977–80, memb Biomedical Res Ctee SH & H Dept, chm Nat Med Consultative Ctee in Med, memb Editorial Bd and dep editorial chm Clinical Science; FRCPE 1948, hon memb Australasian Renal Assoc 1969, FRCP 1977; *Books* Companion to Medical Studies (co-ed, 1968–88); *Recreations* gardening, theatre, travel, contemporary art, reading; *Clubs* New (Edinburgh); *Style—* Prof James Robson; ✉ 1 Grant Ave, Edinburgh EH13 0DS (☎ 0131 441 3508)

ROBSON, John Malcolm; s of Edward Stephen Robson (d 1989), and Joan Barbara, *née* Burchett; *b* 16 March 1952; *Educ* King's Coll Sch Wimbledon, Univ of London (LLB); *m* 30 Aug 1991, Jennifer Lillias, da of Bernard Seed, of Sutton, Surrey; 2 s (David, Aidan), 1 da (Lillias); *Career* called to the Bar Inner Temple 1974, pt/t chm Ind Tbnl Serv; FCIArb; *Recreations* swimming, ceramics, wines; *Clubs* RAC; *Style—* John Robson, Esq; ✉ 265 Fir Tree Road, Epsom Downs, Surrey (☎ 01737 353834); 2 Gray's Inn Square, Gray's Inn, London WC1R 5AA (☎ 0171 405 1317, fax 0171 405 3082)

ROBSON, Rev John Phillips; s of Thomas Herbert Robson (d 1965), of Shenfield, Essex, and Nellie Julia, *née* Hilling (d 1984); *b* 22 July 1932; *Educ* Hele's Sch Exeter, Brentwood Sch Essex, St Edmund Hall Oxford (Liddon exhibitioner), King's Coll London (AKC); *Career* Nat Serv Br Mil Hosp Münster 1952–54; laboratory technician and med student Guy's Hosp London 1949–52; ordained priest Wakefield Cathedral 1960 (ordained deacon 1959), curate Huddersfield Parish Church 1959–62, asst chaplain and jr housemaster Christ's Hosp Horsham Sussex 1962–65 (sr chaplain, head of divinity and biology teacher 1965–80), sr chaplain Wellington Coll Berkshire 1980–89; chaplain: Queen's Chapel of the Savoy 1989–, Royal Victorian Order 1989–, Instn of Electrical Engineers, The Savoy Hotel, Actors' Church Union Savoy Theatre, Vaudeville Theatre; memb West End/Central Police Community Consultative Group; chaplain to HM The Queen 1993–; work with various orgns for young homeless; *Recreations* golf, theatre, cinema, reading; *Clubs* Garrick; *Style—* The Rev John Robson; ✉ The Queen's Chapel of the Savoy, Savoy Hill, Strand, London WC2R 0DA (☎ 0171 379 8088)

ROBSON, John Robert; s of Maj William Michael Robson, of Tenterden, Kent, and Audrey Isabel, *née* Dick (d 1962); *b* 12 Jan 1947; *Educ* Eton; *m* 21 Jan 1969, Tessa Diana, da of Capt William J Straker-Smith, of Cornhill on Tweed, Northumberland; 1 s (James b 30 Oct 1975), 1 da (Claire b 2 Jan 1972); *Career* md Anton Members Agency Ltd; underwriting memb Lloyd's 1969, govr Wellesley House and St Peter's Ct Sch; Freeman City of London 1977, Liveryman Worshipful Co of Vintners 1982; FRPS; *Recreations* sailing, golf, Zululand, philately; *Clubs* Pratt's, Honourable Company of Edinburgh Golfers, Rye Golf; *Style—* John Robson, Esq; ✉ Latham House, 16 Minories, London EC3N 1EX (☎ 0171 702 1234, fax 0171 702 4062, car 0831 474023)

ROBSON, Hon (Erik) Maurice William; s of Sir Lawrence William Robson (d 1982), and Baroness Robson of Kiddington (Life Peeress), *qv*; *b* 20 Dec 1943; *Educ* Eton, Ch Ch Oxford; *m* 7 Sept 1985, Chloë Annabel, elder da of Richard Arthur Edwards, and Eileen Daphne, *née* Joliffe; 1 s (James (Jamie) Patrick b 27 Sept 1990), 1 da (Natasha Lilly b 17 March 1993); *Career* chartered accountant; articled clerk Deloitte Plender, Griffiths & Co 1965–68, salesman IBM 1968–72; Robson Rhodes: mangr 1973, ptnr 1974–89; currently: chm Brackley Sawmills Ltd, dir National Liberal Club Ltd, chm Game Fair 1994; farmer and landowner; former hon treas Highland Soc of London and Anglo Swedish Soc, memb Lloyd's of London, memb Cncl CLA; Renter Warden Worshipful Co of Painter Stainers 1992–93; FCA; *Recreations* music, sailing, skiing, stalking, fishing, shooting, hunting; *Clubs* Leander, Boodle's, National Liberal, Royal Lymington Yacht; *Style—* The Hon Maurice Robson

ROBSON, Michael Anthony; s of Thomas Chester Robson, MM, CDM (d 1984), of Sunderland, and Gertrude Edith, *née* Thomas (d 1975); *b* 29 Nov 1931; *Educ* W Hartlepool GS, St Edmund Hall Oxford (MA); *m* 1, 6 Dec 1952, Cicely, da of James Frederick Bray (d 1934), of Hull; 1 s (Jake b 1957), 1 da (Zuleika b 1953); m 2, 11 Feb 1977, Judith, da of James Francis Smithies (d 1979), of Woolpit, Suffolk; *Career* RAF 1950–51; teacher Norfolk 1954–63; writer and film dir: Anglia TV 1963–69, BBC2 1970; freelance; memb Bdcasting Ctee Soc of Authors 1991–94; Liveryman Worshipful Co of Bowyers 1980; life memb John Buchan Soc; *Books* incl: The Beargarden (1958), Time After Rain (1962), On Giant's Shoulders (jtly, 1976), Opium: The Poisoned Poppy (1992), Theatre: Buy Your Clichés Here (1992), The Girl from Arles (1994); *Radio Plays* incl: Landscape with Lies (1974), Weekend at Montacute (1976), Welcome, These Pleasant Days! (1981), Intent to Deceive (1988), A Cambridge Mystery (1992), Obsession (1993), Jack's Back! (1994), Full Fathom Five (1995); *TV Plays* incl: An Adventure in Bed (1975), No Name, No Packdrill (1977), Heart to Heart (1979), Swallows and Amazons Forever! (1984), This Lightning Strikes Twice (1985), Hannay (series 1988–89), Handles (1989), An Ideal Husband (1990), The House of Eliott (1991), The Letter Killeth (1995), William Tell (1997); *Feature Films* incl: Got it Made (1974), The Water Babies (1978), Holocaust 2000 (jtly, 1978), The Thirty-Nine Steps (1979), The Ballad of the Lost Valley (1990), In Silver Mist (1991); *Recreations* riding, reading, music, politics; *Clubs* Oxford and Cambridge; *Style—* Michael Robson, Esq; ✉ Baker's Arch, Hindon, Salisbury, Wiltshire SP3 6DR (☎ 01747 820277, fax 01747 820779)

ROBSON, Peter Gordon; s of Donald Robson (d 1981), and Lette, *née* Brewer (d 1996); *b* 5 Nov 1937; *Educ* Scarborough HS; *Career* asst master Marton Hall Bridlington 1962–70, head of maths Cundall Manor York 1972–89 (sr master 1973–76), fndr Newby Books publishers 1990; *Books* Between the Laughing Fields (poems, 1966), Maths Dictionary (1979), Maths for Practice and Revision (5 vols, 1982–90), Fountains Abbey - a Cistercian Monastery (1983), The Fishing Robsons (1991), Everyday Graphs (1993), Coordinate Graphs (1993), Science Dictionary (1994); *Recreations* music, genealogy, heraldry, photography; *Style—* Peter Robson, Esq; ✉ 31 Red Scar Lane, Scarborough, N Yorks YO12 5RH; Newby Books, PO Box 40, Scarborough, N Yorks YO12 5TW

ROBSON, Prof Peter Neville; OBE (1983); s of Thomas Murton Robson (d 1956), of Bolton, Lancs, and Edith, *née* Gresty (d 1980); *b* 23 Nov 1930; *Educ* Bolton Sch, Univ of Cambridge (BA), Univ of Sheffield (PhD); *m* 4 May 1957, Anne Ross, da of William Semple (d 1964), of Glasgow; 1 da (Fiona Susan b 1963); *Career* res engr Metropolitan Vickers Electrical Co Ltd Manchester 1954–57; Univ of Sheffield: successively lectr, sr lectr then reader 1957–68, prof of electronic and electrical engrg 1968–96, emeritus prof 1996–; FIEE, FEng 1983, FRS 1987; *Style—* Prof P N Robson, OBE, FRS, FEng; ✉ 46 Canterbury Ave, Sheffield S10 3RU; Department of Electronic and Electrical Engineering, University of Sheffield, Sheffield S1 3JD (☎ 0114 282 5131, fax 0114 272 6391, telex 547216 UGSHEF G)

ROBSON, Rev Richard Arnold (Stephen); s of Sydney Arnold Robson (d 1996), of York, and Laura, *née* Patterson (d 1972); *b* 4 Aug 1946; *Educ* Wennington Sch, York Coll of Art, Guildhall Sch of Music and Drama; *Career* teacher Suffolk 1966–67, curator of Costume Galleries Castle Howard York 1974–94 (asst curator 1967–74), furnishing offr Archdiocese of York 1978–81; lectures and exhibitions in UK, Japan, USA and Sweden; subjects incl: Castle Howard, social history, costume and textiles, vestments in the Western church, Christian art, the Crown Jewels; Costume Soc: memb, prog co-ordinator 1988–91, memb Ctee 1980, memb Prog Sub Ctee 1981, chm Prog Sub Ctee 1985; vice chm Northern Soc of Costume and Textiles 1990 (fndr chm 1977, former chm and ctee memb); ordained as Father Stephen in the British Diocese of the Coptic Orthodox Patriarchate of Alexandria 1991, priest at St Mark and St Hubert's Church Cusworth Doncaster 1993–95, pastoral responsibility for the City of York and N Yorks 1993–, raised to hegoumenos 1994, hegoumenos i/c St Constantine's Orthodox Church in York 1995–, priest of St Anne's Chapel York 1995–; gen sec Br Orthodox Soc 1992–; BD St Justin's Theological Seminary California USA; Vigneron D'Honneur de Saint Emilion 1987; *Style—* The Rev Father Stephen Robson; ✉ Saint Anne's House, 33 Brownlow Street, York YO3 7LW (☎ and fax 01904 626599)

ROBSON, Air Vice-Marshal Robert Michael (Bobby); OBE (1971); s of Dr John Alexander Robson (d 1988), of Dorset, and Edith, *née* Knape (d 1992); *b* 22 April 1935; *Educ* Sherborne, RMA Sandhurst; *m* 4 April 1959, Brenda Margaret, da of Leslie Clifford Croysdill, MBE (d 1970), of Dorset; *Career* cmmnd 1955, RAF Regt 1958, navigator trg 1959, strike sqdns 1965, sqdn cdr RAF Coll 1968, def advsr Br High Cmmr Sri Lanka 1972, Nat Def Coll 1973, CO 27 Sqdn 1974–75, staff duties MOD 1978, CO RAF Gatow 1978–80, RCDS 1981, dir of initial offr trg RAF Coll 1982–84, dir of PR (RAF) 1985–87, head of study into offrs' terms of service 1987; ADC to the Queen 1979–80; ret 1987; sheep farmer 1987–; dir Advanced Technology Industries Ltd 1993; chm: Prince's Tst Lincolnshire, Governors Witham Hall Prep Sch 1995 (govr 1987–), Fuel Mechanics Ltd 1995, Turbo UK Ltd 1994; FIMgt 1983; *Recreations* reading, opera, fishing; *Clubs* RAF; *Style—* Air Vice-Marshal Bobby Robson, OBE; ✉ Long Row Cottage, N Rauceby, Sleaford, Lincolnshire NG34 8QP (☎ 01529 488631)

ROBSON, Robert William (Bobby); CBE (1991); s of Philip Robson, of Langley Park, Co Durham, and Lilian, *née* Watt; *b* 18 Feb 1933; *Educ* Waterhouses Secdy Modern Sch Co Durham; *m* 25 June 1955, Elsie Mary, da of Jack Wilfred Gray (d 1980); 3 s (Paul Martin b 24 June 1957, Andrew Peter b 28 March 1959, Robert Mark b 9 April 1963); *Career* professional footballer: Fulham FC 1950–56, West Bromwich Albion FC 1956–62, Fulham FC 1962–67; England international 1957–62: 20 full caps, under 23 and B caps, appeared in World Cup Sweden (1958) and Chile (1962); mangr: Vancouver Royals 1967–68 (also coach), Fulham FC Jan-Nov 1968, Ipswich Town FC 1969–82 (FA Cup winners 1978, UEFA Cup winners 1981), England Football Team 1982–90 (fourth place World Cup Italy 1990), PSV Eindhoven 1990–92 (Dutch League winners 1991 and 1992), Sporting Lisbon 1992–93; head coach FC Porto 1994–96 (Portuguese Cup winners 1993/94, Portuguese Super Cup winners 1993/94 and 1994/95, Portuguese League winners 1994/95 and 1995/96), head coach Barcelona FC 1996– (Spanish Super Cup winners 1996); *Books* Time on the Grass (autobiography, 1982), So Near Yet So Far: Bobby Robson World Cup Diary (with Bob Harris, 1986), Against the Odds (with Bob Harris, 1990); *Recreations* golf, gardening, skiing, reading, music; *Style*— Bobby Robson, Esq, CBE

ROBSON, Stephen Arthur; CB (1997); s of Arthur Cyril Robson, ISO, of Scruton, N Yorks, and Lilian Marianne, *née* Peabody (d 1972); *b* 30 Sept 1943; *Educ* Pocklington Sch Yorks, St John's Coll Cambridge (BA, MA, PhD), Stanford Univ California (MA); *m* 14 Dec 1974, Meredith Hilary, da of Ernest Lancashire (d 1982); 2 s (David Robert b 1 March 1978, Andrew Luke b 8 Sept 1979); *Career* deputy sec HM Treasy, currently fir Fin, Regulation and Indust Directorate HM Treasy; *Recreations* sailing; *Clubs* Bosham Sailing; *Style*— Stephen Robson, Esq, CB; ✉ HM Treasury, Parliament Street, London SW1P 3AG (☎ 0171 270 4440)

ROBSON OF KIDDINGTON, Baroness (Life Peeress UK 1974), of Kiddington in Oxfordshire; Inga-Stina Robson; JP (Oxon 1955); da of Erik R Arvidsson, of Stockholm; *b* 20 Aug 1919; *Educ* Stockholm; *m* 1940, Sir Lawrence William Robson (d 1982), sometime sr ptnr Robson Rhodes & Co (accountants); 1 s (Hon (Erik) Maurice William b 1943), 2 da (Hon Kristina Elizabeth (Hon Mrs Mason) b 1946, Hon Vanessa Jane (Hon Mrs Potter) b 1949); *Career* sits as Lib in House of Lords; chm: SW Thames RHA 1974–82, Bd Govrs Queen Charlotte's and Chelsea Hosps 1970–84; Swedish Foreign Office 1939–40, min of info 1942–43; Party candidate (Lib): Eye 1955 and 1959, Gloucester 1964 and 1966; pres Lib Pty Orgn 1970–71; chm: Anglo-Swedish Soc 1982–92, Nat Assoc of Leagues of Hosp Friends 1986–94; *Recreations* skiing, sailing, fishing; *Clubs* Nat Lib; *Style*— The Rt Hon Baroness Robson of Kiddington, JP; ✉ The Dower House, Kiddington, Woodstock, Oxford OX20 1BU

ROCH, Rt Hon Lord Justice; Rt Hon Sir John Ormond; kt (1985), PC (1993); s of Frederick Ormond Roch (d 1973), and Vera Elizabeth Roch, *née* Chamberlain; *b* 19 April 1934; *Educ* Wrekin Coll, Clare Coll Cambridge (BA, LLB); *m* 1, 1967, Anne Elizabeth (d 1994), da of Dr Willoughby Hugh Greany, MC; 3 da (Joanna b 1968, Lucinda Jane (Mrs Nicolas Roach) b 1970, Charlotte b 1972); m 2, 1996, Susan Angela Parry, *née* Nicholls; *Career* recorder of the Crown Court 1968–85, QC 1976, bencher Gray's Inn, judge of the High Court (Queen's Bench Div) 1985–93, a Lord Justice of Appeal 1993–; treas Wales and Chester Circuit 1980–84, memb Mgmnt Ctee RNLI 1996; *Recreations* music, reading, sailing (Cantabile of Dale); *Clubs* Dale Yacht; *Style*— The Rt Hon Lord Justice Roch; ✉ Royal Courts of Justice, Strand, London WC2A 2LL

ROCHA, John; *b* 23 Aug 1953, Hong Kong; *Educ* Croydon Art Coll; *m* 2, Odette Gleeson; 3 c; *Career* fashion designer; encouraged by Irish Export Council estab career in Dublin late 1970s, worked in Milan 1988–90, subsequently estab John Rocha/Chinatown label backed by Brown Thomas Group, introduced first menswear collection Autumn 1991, currently shows biannually in Milan, Paris, London, Amsterdam and Dusseldorf with over 400 retail outlets in 21 countries worldwide; British Fashion Designer of the Year 1993; *Style*— Mr John Rocha; ✉ 12–13 Temple Lane, Temple Bar, Dublin 2, Eire (☎ 00 353 1 677 2011)

ROCHDALE, Archdeacon of; *see:* Dalby, Ven (John) Mark Meredith

ROCHDALE, 2 Viscount (UK 1960); St John Durival Kemp; also Baron Rochdale (UK 1913); s of 1 Viscount Rochdale, OBE, TD, DL (d 1993), and Elinor Dorothea, CBE, JP, *née* Pease (d 1997); *b* 15 Jan 1938; *Educ* Eton; *m* 1, 5 Jan 1960 (m dis 1974), Serena Jane, da of Michael Clark-Hall, of Wissenden, Bethersden, Kent; 2 s (Hon Jonathan Hugo b 1961, Hon Christopher George b 1969), 2 da (Hon Joanna Victoria b 1964, Hon Susanna Jane b 1965); m 2, 1976, Mrs Elizabeth Anderton, da of Robert Norman Rossiter Boldon; *Heir* s, Hon Jonathan Hugo Durival Kemp b 10 June 1961; *Style*— The Rt Hon Viscount Rochdale; ✉ Lingholm, Portinscale, Keswick, Cumbria CA12 5TZ

ROCHE, Barbara; MP (Lab) Hornsey and Wood Green (majority 5,177); da of Barnet Margolis, and Hannah Margolis; *b* 13 April 1954; *Educ* Lady Margaret Hall Oxford; *m* 1 Aug 1977, Patrick Roche; 1 da; *Career* called to the Bar 1977, local authy crime prevention conslt; MP (Lab) Hornsey and Wood Green 1992– (also contested 1987); memb Commons Select Ctee on Home Affrs 1992–94, oppn whip 1994–95, shadow Trade and Industry min 1995–; memb: Standing Ctee on Finance Bill 1992, Standing Ctee on Asylum and Immigration Appeals Bill 1992; vice chair PLP Treasy Ctee 1992–94; former exec memb NCCL, chair Battersea Lab Pty 1981–85; memb: Lab Co-ordinating Ctee, Soc of Lab Lawyers, Unison; *Recreations* theatre, family; *Style*— Ms Barbara Roche, MP; ✉ House of Commons, London SW1A 0AA

ROCHE, Sir David O'Grady; 5 Bt (UK 1838), of Carass, Limerick; s of Lt-Cdr Sir Standish O'Grady Roche, 4 Bt, DSO, RN (d 1977), and Evelyn Laura, only da of late Maj William Andon, of Jersey; *b* 21 Sept 1947; *Educ* Wellington Coll, Trinity Coll Dublin; *m* 1971, Hon (Helen) Alexandra Briscoe Gully, JP, da of late 3 Viscount Selby (d 1959), and formerly w of Roger Moreton Frewen (d 1972); 2 s (David b 1976, 1 s decd), 1 da (Cecilia Evelyn Jonnë b 1979); *Heir* s, David Alexander O'Grady Roche b 28 Jan 1976; *Career* CA, formerly with Peat Marwick Mitchell & Co; mangr Samuel Montagu Ltd; chm: Carlton Real Estates plc 1978–82, Echo Hotel 1986–94, Roche & Co Ltd; cncllr London Borough of Hammersmith and Fulham 1978–82; Liveryman Worshipful Co of Saddlers; FCA; *Recreations* shooting, sailing (yacht 'Lady Nicola'); *Clubs* Buck's, Kildare St, University (Dublin), Royal Yacht Squadron; *Style*— Sir David Roche, Bt; ✉ Norris Castle Farm, IOW PO32 6AZ (☎ 01983 299126); Bridge House, Starbotton, Skipton, N Yorks (☎ 0175 676 0863); 36 Coniger Rd, London SW6 (☎ 0171 736 0382, fax 0171 371 5512)

ROCHE, Dr Denis Arthur; s of Dr Augustine Kevin Roche (d 1929), and Dorothy Mabel, *née* Colmer (d 1993); *b* 3 April 1929; *Educ* Epsom Coll; *m* 27 Sept 1958, Ann Denise, da of John Rupert Wilson; 4 da (Sarah b 21 July 1959, Elaine (Mrs Evans) b 3 Nov 1960, Jeanette (Mrs Happ) b 5 March 1962, Patsy (Mrs Earl) b 7 Nov 1964); *Career* Nat Serv Capt RAMC 1952–54; med supt United Mission Hosp Bhaktapur and Tansen Hosp Nepal 1960–78, occupational physician Worcester and Dist Health Authy 1979–90, med advsr Int Office InterServe 1990–94; memb Droitwich Churches Together; *Style*— Dr Denis Roche; ✉ 44 Corbett Avenue, Droitwich, Worcestershire WR9 7BE (☎ 01905 773956)

ROCHE, Prof Laurence Anthony; s of William Roche (d 1963), of Wexford, Ireland, and Brigitte, *née* Banville, of Wexford, Ireland; *b* 20 Oct 1927; *Educ* CBS Wexford Ireland, Trinity Coll Dublin (B Agric, MA), Univ of Br Columbia (MF, PhD); *m* 20 Oct 1962, Felicity Eleanor Anne, da of F A Bawtree, of Murroe, Co Limerick, Ireland; 1 s (Christopher b 5 June 1967), 2 da (Nicola b 4 Aug 1963, Patricia b 15 June 1968); *Career* merchant marine 1945–52; res offr Br Columbia Forest Serv 1961–66, res scientist and res mangr Canadian Forestry Serv 1966–72, prof of forestry Univ of Ibadan Nigeria 1972–75, head Sch of Agric and Forest Scis Univ of Wales Bangor 1987–90 (head Dept of Forestry and Wood Scis 1975–87, prof of forestry 1975), prof emeritus Univ of Wales; pres Int Union of Forestry Socs 1979–84, vice chm Bd of Tstees Int Cncl for Res in Agroforestry 1983–87, fndr and ed Int Jl of Forest Ecology and Mgmnt, memb Ctee for Int Cooperation in Higher Educn Br Cncl; memb: Univ Funding Agric Panel, Governing Cncl Cwlth Forestry Assoc; Chevalier de L'Ordre du Mérite Agricole; hon fell Trinity Coll Dublin, fell Inst of Chartered Foresters; *Books* The Genetics of Forest Ecosystems (jtly, 1976); *Recreations* English literature, sailing, fishing; *Clubs* Savile, Kildare Street Univ; *Style*— Prof Laurence Roche; ✉ Madaboy House, Murroe, Co Limerick, Ireland (☎ 00 353 61 386435)

ROCHE, Peter Charles Kenneth; s of Dr (George) Kenneth Trevor Roche (d 1989), and Margaret Bridget, *née* Tyrrell; *b* 27 Jan 1947; *Educ* Stonyhurst; *m* 24 April 1971, Gloria Evelyn Margarita, da of John Hugh Cogswell Hicks MBE; 2 s (Daniel Peter James b 19 May 1977, Simon Matthew John b 5 Nov 1981), 1 da (Lucy Georgina 16 Feb 1979); *Career* articled clerk then audit sr Barton Mayhew & Co 1965–71, audit supervisor Deloitte & Co Nairobi 1971–73, chief accountant then gen mangr East African Fine Spinners Nairobi 1973–75, fin dir then dep md Futura Publications Ltd London 1975–80, fin and admin dir MacDonald Futura Publishers Ltd 1980–81, fin dir MacDonald & Co 1981–82, co-fndr, fin dir and dep md Century Publishing Co Ltd 1982–85, fin dir and dep md Century Hutchinson Ltd 1985–89, fin dir then gp md Random Century Group Ltd (Century Hutchinson bought by Random House Inc) 1989–92, gp md The Orion Publishing Group Ltd 1992–; non exec chm Boxtree Ltd 1989–; FCA 1976 (ACA 1971); *Recreations* cricket, rugby, tennis, books and newspapers; *Clubs* Kongonis Cricket; *Style*— Peter Roche, Esq; ✉ Field House, 20 Leigh Hill Road, Cobham, Surrey KT11 2HX (☎ 01932 862713); The Orion Publishing Group Ltd, Orion House, 5 Upper St Martin's Lane, London WC2H 9EA (☎ 0171 240 3444, fax 0171 240 4822)

ROCHESTER, Prof Colin Herbert; s of Herbert Rochester (d 1973), and Doris, *née* Wilson (d 1992); *b* 20 March 1937; *Educ* Hymers Coll Hull, Royal Liberty Sch Romford, King's Coll London (BSc, PhD, DSc); *m* 24 Oct 1959, Jennifer Mary, da of Capt William Orrell (d 1982); 2 s (Christopher b 1960, John b 1963), 2 da (Elizabeth b 1965, Lynda b 1968); *Career* reader in chemistry Univ of Nottingham 1973–80 (lectr 1962–73), Baxter prof of chemistry Univ of Dundee 1980–; author of 247 scientific papers; FRSC 1973, FRSE 1985; *Books* Acidity Functions (1970); *Recreations* fossil collecting, swimming; *Style*— Prof Colin Rochester, FRSE; ✉ 18 Greystane Road, Invergowrie, Dundee DD2 5JQ (☎ 01382 562614); Department of Chemistry, The University, Dundee DD1 4HN (☎ 01382 344327)

ROCHESTER, David John; s of Edward Rochester (d 1983), and Anne Edna, *née* Raine; *b* 29 Oct 1939; *Educ* The GS Reigate, Sorbonne; *m* 1, 2 Sept 1961 (m dis 1977), Anne, da of Joseph Ganter, of Morden, Surrey; 2 da (Lisa b 1966, Susan b 1968); m 2, 31 Dec 1977, Shannon Marie, da of Joseph Clements, of Twin Falls, Idaho, USA; 2 da (Raine b 1981, Hailey b 1984); *Career* ptnr Cazenove & Co 1961–81, pres Wedd Durlacher Mordaunt Inc 1981–83, md Merrill Lynch Ltd 1983–89, dir Private Fund Managers Ltd 1990–94, pres Private Fund Managers Inc 1992–94, sr vice pres Bream Murray, Foster Securities Inc 1994–; *Recreations* shooting, tennis, fishing, golf; *Style*— David Rochester, Esq; ✉ 41 Beechcroft Road, Greenwich, CT-06830, USA; Bream Murray, Foster Securities Inc, 570 Lexington Avenue, New York, NY 10017, USA

ROCHESTER, Dean of; *see:* Shotter, Very Rev Edward Frank

ROCHESTER, 2 Baron (UK 1931); Foster Charles Lowry Lamb; s of 1 Baron Rochester, CMG, JP, sometime MP Rochester and paymaster-gen in 1931 Nat Govt (d 1955); *b* 7 June 1916; *Educ* Mill Hill, Jesus Coll Cambridge (MA); *m* 12 Dec 1942, Mary, da of Thomas Benjamin Wheeler, CBE (d 1981); 2 s, 1 da (and 1 da decd); *Heir* s, Hon David Lamb; *Career* sits as Lib Democrat in House of Lords; former Capt 23 Hussars WWII; personnel mangr Mond ICI 1964–72; pro-chllr Univ of Keele 1976–86; DL (Cheshire) 1979; Hon D Univ Keele 1986; *Clubs* Reform; *Style*— The Lord Rochester; ✉ The Hollies, Hartford, Cheshire (☎ 01606 74733)

ROCHESTER, Bishop of 1994–; Rt Rev Dr Michael James Nazir-Ali; *b* 19 Aug 1949; *Educ* Univ of Karachi (BA), Fitzwilliam Coll and Ridley Hall Cambridge, St Edmund Hall Oxford (BLitt, Oxford Soc graduate award), Univ of Cambridge (Burney and Langham student, MLitt), Aust Coll of Theol Univ of NSW with Centre for World Religions Harvard (PhD); *m* 1972, Valerie Cree; 2 s (Shamaoun b 1975, Ross b 1979); *Career* ordained: deacon 1974, priest 1976; asst curate Holy Sepulchre Cambridge 1974–76, tutorial supervisor in theology Univ of Cambridge 1974–76 (Burnely lectr in Islam 1973–74), tutor then sr tutor Karachi Theol Coll 1976–81, assoc presbyter Holy Trinity Cathedral Karachi 1976–79, priest-in-charge St Andrew's Akhtar Colony Karachi 1979–81, provost Lahore Cathedral 1981–84, bishop of Raiwind 1984–86, asst to Archbishop of Canterbury and dir in residence Oxford Centre for Mission Studies 1986–89, asst bishop and hon curate Limpsfield and Titsey Diocese of Southwark and gen sec Church Missionary Society 1989–94; sec Archbishop's Cmmn on Communion and Women in the Episcopate (Eames Cmmn) 1988–, Archbishop's nominee Cncl of Churches for Britain and Ireland 1990–95, memb Anglican-RC Int Cmmn 1991–, canon theologian Leicester Cathedral 1992–94, memb Bd of Mission Gen Synod C of E 1992–95 and 1996–, chm Mission Theological Advsy Gp 1992–; dir Christian Aid 1992–, tstee Traidcraft 1987–89; visiting lectr Selly Oak Colls Birmingham 1986–, tutor and examiner in postgraduate studies CNAA and Open Univ 1987–; Charles Sadleir lectr Wycliffe and Trinity Colls Toronto 1987, lectr on church and state rels Univ of Cambridge 1988, Church of Ireland lectr Queen's Univ Belfast 1989, Henry Martyn lectr Univ of Cambridge 1990, select preacher Univ of Oxford 1992, Selwyn lectr St John's Coll Aukland 1993, visiting prof in theology and religious studies Univ of Greenwich 1996–; *Books* Islam - A Christian Perspective (1982), Frontiers in Christian-Muslim Encounter (1987), Martyrs and Magistrates: Toleration and Trial in Islam (1989), From Everywhere to Everywhere: a World-View of Christian Mission (1990), The Roots of Islamic Tolerance: Origin and Development (1990), Mission and Dialogue (1995), The Mystery of Faith (1995); author of numerous articles, ed various papers and reports incl Report of the Lambeth Conf 1988; *Recreations* cricket, hockey, table tennis, scrabble, listening to music and watching TV, reading humour and detective fiction, writing poetry (in English and Persian); *Style*— The Rt Rev the Bishop of Rochester; ✉ Bishopscourt, Rochester, Kent ME1 1TS (☎ 01634 842721)

ROCK, Angus James; s of Ian George Rock, and Anne Elizabeth, *née* Lyons; *b* 16 Sept 1964; *Educ* Cooper Sch Bicester Oxfordshire, Gosford Hill Sch Kidlington Oxfordshire; *Career* designer Cherwell Laboratories 1983–86, proprietor A J R Marketing (design and mktg an electronic instrumentation range for motorsport) 1986–88, sales and mktg mangr Stack Ltd 1988–91; ptnr: Design Graphique 1991–, Head to Toe 1993–; winner Br Design Award 1990; *Recreations* squash, tennis, skiing, music,golf, classic cars; *Style*— Angus J Rock, Esq; ✉ Design Graphique/Head to Toe, 6 Cumnor Rd, Wootton, Boars Hill, Oxford OX1 5JP (☎ and fax 01865 326600)

ROCK, David Annison; s of Thomas Henry Rock (d 1964), of Sunderland, Co Durham, and Muriel Rock, *née* Barton (d 1964); *b* 27 May 1929; *Educ* Bede GS Sunderland, Univ of Durham (BArch); *m* 18 Dec 1954 (m dis 1985), Daphne Elizabeth Richards; 3 s (Adam b 1960, Jacob b 1961, Mark b 1963), 2 da (Felicity b 1957, Alice b 1963); m 2, 1989, Lesley Patricia, *née* Murray; *Career* 2 Lt BAOR RE 1953–55; sr architect Sir Basil Spence 1952–53 and 1955–58, ptnr and fndr London Group Building Design Partnership 1959–71, fndr ptnr and chm Rock Townsend 1971–92, co fndr Workspace Business Centre concept in UK 1971, fndr dir Barley Mow Workspace 1974–93, fndr chm Dryden Street Collective 1971–78, fndr ptnr Camp 5 1992–; conslt architect Arts Cncl of England Lottery Bd 1995–; memb Sports Cncl Lottery Awards Panel 1995–; Graham Willis visiting prof Univ of Sheffield 1990–92; vice pres RIBA 1987–88 and 1995– (memb Cncl 1970–76, 1986–88 and 1995–, pres-elect 1997–), chm Soc of Architect Artists 1986–92; memb CNAA, specialist assessor Higher Educn Funding Cncl England 1993–; personal awards: Soane Medallion, Owen Jones Studentship, H B Saint Award, RIBA Building Industry Tst Fellowship, Crown Prize, Glover Medal; FRIBA 1953, FCSD, FRSA; *Books* Vivat Ware! Strategies to Enhance an Historic Town (1974), The Grassroot Developers

(1980); *Recreations* painting, illustration, work; *Style—* David Rock, Esq; ✉ 13 London Road, Harleston, Norfolk IP20 9BH (☎ 01379 852624; Camp 5 ☎ and fax 01379 854897)

ROCK, Prof Paul Elliot; s of Ashley Rock, of London, and Charlotte, *née* Dickson (d 1969); *b* 4 Aug 1943; *Educ* William Ellis GS, LSE (BSc), Nuffield Coll Oxford (DPhil); *m* 25 Sept 1965, Barbara, da of Hayman Ravid (d 1989); 2 s (Matthew Charles b 1970, Oliver James b 1974); *Career* visiting prof Princeton Univ USA 1974–75, visiting scholar Miny of the Slr Gen of Canada; LSE: asst lectr 1967–70, lectr 1970–76, prof of sociology 1986–95, prof of social instns 1995–; fell Center for Advanced Studies in Behavioral Sciences Stanford California 1996; dir The Mannheim Centre 1992–95; memb: Sociology and Social Admin Ctee SSRC 1976–80, Exec Ctee Br Sociological Assoc 1978–79, Parole Bd 1986–89; ed The British Journal of Sociology 1988–95; *Books* Making People Pay (1973), The Making of Symbolic Interactionism (1979), Understanding Deviance (jtly, 1982–88), A View From The Shadows (1987), Helping Victims of Crime (1990), The Social World of an English Crown Court (1993), Reconstructing a Women's Prison (1996); *Style—* Prof Paul Rock; ✉ London School of Economics, Houghton Street, Aldwych, London WC2A 2AE (☎ 0171 955 7296, fax 0171 955 7405)

ROCK, Stuart Peter; s of Peter Illsley Rock, of 10 Marlborough Place, Wimborne Minster, Dorset, and Wendy Julie, *née* Ives; *b* 23 Sept 1960; *Educ* Malvern, Magdalen Coll Oxford (BA); *Career* PR exec Sabatini Taylor & Associates 1983–85, freelance writer 1985–87, ed Director Publications 1989– (joined 1987); *Books* Family Firms (1991); *Recreations* architecture, photography, beer, reading, would like to improve cooking; *Style—* Stuart Rock, Esq; ✉ Director Publications Ltd, Mountbarrow House, 12–20 Elizabeth St, London SW1W 9RB (☎ 0171 730 8320, fax 0171 235 5627)

ROCKER, David; s of Richard Frederick Rocker (d 1984), of Hatfield Peverel, Essex, and Elizabeth Ellen, *née* Lewis; *b* 9 June 1944; *Educ* King Edward VI Sch Chelmsford; *m* 1972 (m dis 1992), Jacolyn Jane, da of John Geoffry Matthews, of Finchingfield, Essex; *Career* admitted slr; ptnr Leonard Gray & Co 1968–71; legal advsr: Hawker Siddeley Group Ltd 1971–73, Trident TV 1973–79; dir of legal affrs Guinness plc 1982–86; chm: Guinness Superlatives Ltd 1984–85, Guinness Overseas Ltd 1985–86; sr ptnr David Rocker & Co 1986–, chm Rocker Ltd 1989–, dir Luminar plc; *Recreations* motor-racing, riding, bridge; *Style—* David Rocker, Esq; ✉ The Maltings, 21 The Green, Writtle, Essex (☎ 01245 420141)

ROCKLEY, Edward George (Ted); s of George Alfred Rockley (d 1982), and Catherine Rockley; *b* 27 April 1952; *Educ* Quintin Kynaston, Hornsey Sch of Art, Middlesex Poly (DipAD); *m* 1983, Lyn Michelle Joniel, da of Colin Wakeley; 1 s (Joshua b 17 March 1987), 2 da (Camilla b 14 Sept 1984, Roseanna b 26 Nov 1992); *Career* animator and designer BBC Adult Literacy Project 1974–77, freelance animator 1977–81, co-dir Klactoveesedstene Animations Ltd 1981–; *Style—* Ted Rockley, Esq; ✉ Klactoveesedstene Animations Ltd, 49–50 Great Marlborough Street, London W1V 1DB (☎ 0171 439 1420, fax 0171 434 0410)

ROCKLEY, 3 Baron (UK 1934); James Hugh Cecil; s of 2 Baron Rockley (d 1976, whose f, 1 Baron, was er s of Lord Eustace Cecil, 3 s of 2 Marquess of Salisbury by his 1 w, Frances, the Gascoyne heiress), and Anne, da of Adm Hon Sir Herbert Meade-Fetherstonhaugh, GCVO, CB, DSO, yr bro of 5 Earl of Clanwilliam; *b* 5 April 1934; *Educ* Eton, New Coll Oxford; *m* 1958, Lady Sarah Primrose Cadogan, eldest da of 7 Earl Cadogan, MC, DL; 1 s, 2 da; *Heir* s, Hon Anthony Robert Cecil, *qv*; *Career* chm Kleinwort Benson Group plc 1993–96; dir: Kleinwort Benson Ltd 1970–, Equity & Law plc 1980–91, Christies International plc 1989–, Cobham plc 1989–, Abbey National plc 1990–, The Foreign and Colonial Investment Trust plc 1991–, Cadogan Group Ltd 1996–; chm: Kleinwort Development Fund plc 1990–93, Dartford River Crossing 1988–93, Midland Expressway 1992–93; tstee Nat Portrait Gallery 1981–88; chm Issuing Houses Assoc 1987–89; memb Design Cncl 1988–94; Second Warden Worshipful Co of Salters; *Style—* The Rt Hon the Lord Rockley; ✉ Lytchett Heath, Poole, Dorset (☎ 01202 622228); Cadogan Oakley Ltd, 136 Sloane Street, London SW1X 9AY (☎ 0171 730 5800)

RODBER, Timothy Andrew Keith (Tim); s of Keith Rodber, of Cheriton, Hampshire, and Sue, *née* Bates; *b* 12 July 1969; *Educ* Churcher's Coll Petersfield Hants, Oxford Poly, RMA Sandhurst; *Career* Rugby Union No 8 England, Northampton FC and Army; clubs: Petersfield RFC 1987, Oxford Old Boys RFC 1987–88, Oxford Poly RFC 1988–91, Northampton RFC 1989–, Army RFC 1989–; rep: Eng U18 trialist 1986 and 1987, Oxfordshire RFC 1988, Br Polys 1988, Combined Servs RFC 1989–, Midlands Div 1989–; Eng U21 1989 (v Romania), Eng B (debut v France) 1990, Eng 7s squad; England: tour Argentina 1990, tour to S Africa 1994, 4th place World Cup S Africa 1995, over 25 full caps; Army Cadet 1988, cmmnd as 2 Lt Green Howards 1992, Capt 1995; *Recreations* music, films, exercise (gen sport); *Style—* Capt Tim Rodber; ✉ c/o Northampton FC, Franklin Gardens, Weedon Rd, Northampton (☎ 01604 751543)

RODD, Michael Philip; s of Howard Philip Rodd, of San Jose, Ibiza, and Jean Dunn, *née* Allon; *b* 29 Nov 1943; *Educ* Trinity Coll Glenalmond, Univ of Newcastle upon Tyne (LLB); *m* 1966, Nita Elizabeth, da of Dr Donald Robert Cubey, of Whitley Bay, Tyne and Wear; 3 s (Benjamin b 1968, Jonathan b 1971, Owen b 1978); *Career* prodr: Border TV 1965–67, BBC Newcastle 1967–71, BBC London 1971–81; sometime presenter: Tomorrow's World (BBC), The Risk Business (BBC); fndr Blackrod and dir of communication servs First Information Group plc (leading prodrs of audio, video and multimedia communications prodns for business and indust); Industrial Broadcaster of the Year (Br Inst of Mgmnt) 1980; *Recreations* music, home decorating; *Style—* Michael Rodd, Esq; ✉ First Information Group plc, Knightsbridge House, 197 Knightsbridge, London SW7 1RB (☎ 0171 393 3000, fax 0171 393 3033)

RODDA, James (Jim); s of Alfred George Rodda, and Constance Ruby, *née* Thompson; *b* 16 Aug 1945; *Educ* Maldon GS, Univ of Reading (BA), Univ of Leicester; *m* July 1967, Angela Faith Hopkinson; 2 da, 1 s; *Career* successive appts at: Chamberlain Turton & Dunn Nottingham, Coopers & Lybrand London & Brussels, Thomas Cook Peterborough and New York, Lonconex London, Dial Contracts London, London Commodity Exchange; former dir of fin and admin House of Commons, currently fin dir Nat Film and Television Sch; memb ICAEW; *Recreations* music, rambling; *Style—* Jim Rodda, Esq; ✉ NFTS, Beaconsfield Studios, Station Road, Beaconsfield, Bucks HP9 1LG

RODDAN, Ronald (Ron); s of Sidney Roddan (d 1976), of Crewe, Cheshire, and Constance Ada, *née* Cooke (d 1982); *b* 8 May 1931; *Educ* Acton Wells Sch, Acton Central Sch; *Career* athletics coach; joined Thames Valley Harriers 1947, competed until 1962–63 season first as 800–1500m runner then as sprinter, finally as 400m runner (best time 50.3); athletes coached incl: Linford Christie, Jason Livingston, Ade Mafe, Beverly Kinch, Simmone Jacobs, K Bentham, Adrian Patrick; BANC Coach of Year 1989, Barclaycard Coach of Year 1989, Nat Mastercoach 1990, Post Office Counters Coach of the Year 1992; engineer; *Recreations* coaching athletics; *Style—* Ron Roddan, Esq; ✉ 6B Victoria Terrace, London NW10 6EG (☎ 0181 961 3967); Thames Valley Harriers, Linford Christie Stadium, off Ducane Rd, Hammersmith, London

RODDICK, Anita Lucia; OBE (1988); da of Henry Perilli (d 1952), and Gilda, *née* de Vita; *b* 23 Oct 1942; *Educ* Maude Allen Secdy Modern Sch for Girls, Newton Park Coll of Educn Bath; *m* 1970, Thomas Gordon Roddick; 2 da (Justine b 1969, Samantha b 1971); *Career* Library of International Herald Tribune Paris; subsequently: teacher of English and history, researcher Women's Rights Dept ILO Geneva, owner and mangr of hotel and restaurant; The Body Shop International plc: opened first branch Brighton 1976, Stock Market flotation 1984, md 1976–94, chief exec 1994–; tstee: The Body Shop Fndn 1989–, New Acad of Business 1996–; hon dip fell City & Guilds of London Inst 1991, hon fell Bath Coll of HE 1994; Hon LLD: Univ of Sussex 1988, Univ of Nottingham 1990, Univ of Portsmouth 1994; Hon Dr New England Coll Sussex 1991, Hon DSc Univ of Victoria (Canada) 1995, Hon DUniv Open Univ 1995, Hon DBA Kingston Univ 1996; *Style—* Anita Roddick, OBE; ✉ The Body Shop International plc, Watersmead, Littlehampton, West Sussex BN17 6LS (☎ 01903 731500, fax 01903 726250, telex 877055, web http://www.the-body-shop.com, e-mail info@bodyshop.co.uk)

RODDICK, (Thomas) Gordon; *m* 1970, Anita Roddick, *qv*; 2 da (Justine b 1969, Samantha b 1971); *Career* chm The Body Shop International 1976–; *Style—* Gordon Roddick, Esq; ✉ The Body Shop International plc, Watersmead, Littlehampton, West Sussex BN17 6LS (☎ 01903 731500, fax 01903 726250, telex 877055)

RODDICK, (George) Winston; QC (1986); s of William Daniel Roddick (d 1977), of Caernarfon, and Aelwen, *née* Hughes (d 1992); *b* 2 Oct 1940; *Educ* Caernarfon GS, Tal-Handak Malta, UCL; *m* 24 Sept 1966, Cennin, da of James Parry, BEM (d 1986), of Caernarfon; 1 s (Daniel b 1977), 1 da (Helen b 1979); *Career* called to the Bar Gray's Inn 1968, recorder 1986–; memb Welsh Language Bd 1986–92; *Recreations* walking the countryside, fishing; *Clubs* Cardiff & County, Caernarfon Sailing; *Style—* Winston Roddick, Esq, QC; ✉ 17 Llandennis Avenue, Cyncoed, Cardiff CF2 6JD; 10 King's Bench Walk, Temple, London EC4Y 7EB (☎ 0171 353 2501)

RODDIE, Prof Ian Campbell; CBE (1987), TD (1967); s of Rev John Richard Wesley Roddie (d 1953), of Belfast, NI, and Mary Hill, *née* Wilson (d 1973); *b* 1 Dec 1928; *Educ* Methodist Coll Belfast, Queen's Univ of Belfast (BSc, MB BCh, BAO, MD, DSc); *m* 1, 14 Feb 1958, Elizabeth (Betty) Ann Gillon (d 1974), da of Thomas Honeyman, of Cheltenham, Glos; 1 s (Patrick b 1965), 3 da (Mary b 1960, Catherine b 1962, Sarah b 1963); m 2, 29 Nov 1974 (m dis 1983), Katherine Anne, da of Edward O'Hara, of Belfast, NI; 1 s (David b 1977), 1 da (Claire b 1975); m 3, 14 Nov 1987, Janet Doreen, da of Thomas Russell Lennon (d 1978), of Larne, NI; *Career* RAMC and T & AVR 1951–68, Queen's Univ Belfast OC Med Sub-Unit, ret Maj 1968; res med offr Royal Victoria Hosp Belfast 1953–54; Queen's Univ Belfast: lectr, sr lectr and reader in physiology 1954–64, Dunville prof of physiology 1964–87, dean Faculty of Med 1976–81, pro vice chllr 1984–87, prof emeritus 1988–; Harkness fell Univ of Washington Seattle USA 1960–61; staff conslt: Asian Development Bank Manila 1978–88, International Finance Corporation/World Bank Washington 1989–; visiting prof: Univ of NSW Sydney Aust 1983–84, Shinshu Univ Matsumoto Japan 1984, The Chinese Univ of Hong Kong 1988–90; conslt physiologist Eastern Health and Social Servs Bd NI 1957–88 (memb Bd 1976–81), dep med dir and dir of med educn King Khalid Nat Gd Hosp Jeddah Saudi Arabia 1990–94; pres: Belfast Assoc of Univ Teachers 1974–76, Ulster Biomedical Engrg Soc 1979–81, Belfast Med Students Assoc 1982–83; memb: Physiological Systems Bd MRC 1974–76, NI Postgraduate Med Cncl 1976–81, Med Advsy Ctee CVCP 1976–81, Home Def Scientific Advsy Ctee (chief regnl scientific advsr) 1977–88, Gen Dental Cncl 1978–81, Royal Irish Acad 1978–, GMC 1979–81; pres Royal Acad of Medicine in Ireland 1985–87, chm Ctee The Physiological Soc (UK) 1986–88; memb Physiological Soc 1956 (hon memb 1988), MRCPI 1957, FRCPI 1965, MRIA 1978, emeritus memb Int Soc of Lymphology 1995; *Books* Physiology for Practitioners (2 edn, 1975), The Physiology of Disease (1975), Multiple Choice Questions in Human Physiology (5 edn, 1996); *Recreations* reading, writing, travel; *Style—* Prof Ian Roddie, CBE, TD; ✉ Calle San Bernabe 3, Lomas Club-Pueblo, 29600 Marbella, Malaga, Spain (☎ 00 34 5 277 2596, fax 00 34 5 277 8641)

RODDIS, Peter; s of John Roddis (d 1964), of Northampton, and Kathleen Maude, *née* Foster (d 1980); *b* 10 Dec 1937; *Educ* Kettering GS; *children*: 3 da (Sarah b 1965, Johanna b 1967, Petra b 1970); *Career* RAF 1956–59, PO 1958; chm PRP Communication Gp, md Cinesound International Group, dir MCA Records, dir artistes and repertoire RCA Records; chm: BBC Local Radio Advsy Cncl Cambridge, BBC TV E Advsy Ctee; vice chm BBC S and E Regnl Advsy Cncl 1987–92; tstee Huntingdonshire Royal Coll 1992–94; ed Brooklands Soc Gazette 1978–82, currently ed in chief Active Risk Management Journal; MIPR 1985, FInstSMM 1986; *Books* Brooklands The 40 Acres (1978), The Advanced Training Technique (1994), Managing Small Business (1994), Team Centred Management (1995); *Style—* Peter Roddis, Esq; ✉ Editor-in-Chief, Active Risk Management Journal, 28 Rookery Place, Fenstanton, Huntingdon RE18 9LZ (☎ and fax 01480 467072)

RODEN, Countess of; Ann Margareta Maria Henning Jocelyn; da of Dr Gunnar Henning (d 1948), and Mrs Kerstin Magnusson; *b* 5 Aug 1948; *Educ* Lund Univ Sweden (BA); *m* 13 Feb 1986, as his 2 w, 10 Earl of Roden; 1 s (Viscount Jocelyn b 1989); *Career* author and literary translator (Swedish/English); memb: Soc of Authors, Irish Writers' Union, Soc of Irish Playwrights; *Books* (as Ann Henning) Modern Astrology (1984), The Connemara Whirlwind (1990), The Connemara Stallion (1991), The Connemara Champion (1994), Honeylove (1995), The Cosmos and You (1995); *Style—* The Rt Hon the Countess of Roden; ✉ 4 The Boltons, London SW10 9TB

RODEN, 10 Earl of (I 1771); Sir Robert John Jocelyn; 14 Bt (E 1665); also Baron Newport (I 1743) and Viscount Jocelyn (I 1755); s of 9 Earl of Roden (d 1993), and Clodagh Rose, *née* Kennedy (d 1989); *b* 25 Aug 1938; *Educ* Stowe; *m* 1, 1970 (m dis 1982), Sara Cecilia, da of late Brig Andrew Dunlop; 1 da (Lady Cecilia Rose b 1976); m 2, 13 Feb 1986, Ann Margareta Maria, da of late Dr Gunnar Henning (d 1948); 1 s (Viscount Jocelyn b 1989); *Heir* s, Shane Robert Henning, Viscount Jocelyn b 9 Dec 1989; *Style—* The Rt Hon the Earl of Roden; ✉ 4 The Boltons, London SW10 9TB

RODENBURG, Patsy; da of Marius Rodenburg, of London, and Margaret Edna, *née* Moody; *b* 2 Sept 1953; *Educ* St Christopher's Sch Beckenham, Central Sch of Speech and Drama London; *Career* voice coach RSC 1981–90; formed The Voice and Speech Centre 1988; head of voice: Guildhall Sch of Music and Drama 1981–, RNT 1990–; LGSM (The City of London) 1982, distinguished visiting prof Southern Methodist Univ Dallas 1989, hon memb VASTA 1995; works extensively in Theatre, Film, TV, Opera incl: Europe, USA, Canada, Asia and Aust; coached many leading theatre and opera cos incl: Stratford Festival Theatre Canada, Kabuki Theatre Japan, NT of Greece, Lithuania, Norway, NT Sch of India, The Market Theatre Johannesburg, Peking Opera, Ex Machina (Robert Lepage); for GB: Royal Opera, ENO, Opera North, English Shakespeare Co, Cheek by Jowl, Theatre de Complicité, Method and Madness; recent RNT prodns incl: Richard II, Volpone, Wild Oats, The Way of the World, Rosencrantz and Guildenstern are Dead, Blue Remembered Hills, Death of a Salesman, Oedipus; *Publications* The Right to Speak (Methuen, 1992), The Need for Words (Methuen, 1993), A Voice of your Own (video, 1995), The Actor Speaks (Methuen, 1996); *Recreations* reading, travelling, tae kwondo; *Style—* Ms Patsy Rodenburg; ✉ c/o Royal National Theatre, Upper Ground, South Bank, London SE1 9PX (☎ 0171 928 2033)

RODENHURST, John Emberton; s of Jeffrey Royle Rodenhurst (d 1964), of Brook Mill Farm, Ellesmere, Shropshire, and Margaret Elizabeth, *née* Emberton, of Wackley, Cockshutt, Shrewsbury; *b* 9 Aug 1941; *Educ* Oswestry HS for Boys; *m* 26 April 1967, Rosemary Barbara, da of Horace Harrison, of Church Farm, Moreton Say, Market Drayton; 1 s (Simon John b 29 Dec 1967), 1 da (Penelope-Jane b 30 Jan 1970); *Career* hotelier; proprietor Soughton Hall Hotel 1986–; *Recreations* shooting and country pursuits, good food and wine, a little golf, widespread travel, horse racing; *Style—* John Rodenhurst, Esq; ✉ Soughton Hall, Northop, Mold, Clwyd CH7 6AB (☎ 01352 840 811, fax 01352 840 382)

RODGER, Nicholas Andrew Martin; s of Lt Cdr Ian Alexander Rodger, RN, of Arundel, Sussex, and Sara Mary, *née* Perceval; *b* 12 Nov 1949; *Educ* Ampleforth, Univ

Coll Oxford (BA, MA, DPhil); *m* 28 Aug 1982, Susan Eleanor, da of Henry Meigs Farwell, of Ickenham, Middx; 2 s (Christopher b 1987, Alexander b 1989), 1 da (Ellen b 1984); *Career* asst keeper of Public Records 1974–91; Anderson fell National Maritime Museum Greenwich 1992–; hon sec Navy Records Soc 1976–90; FSA, FRHistS; *Books* The Admiralty (1979), The Wooden World, An Anatomy of the Georgian Navy (1986), The Insatiable Earl: A Life of John Montagu, Fourth Earl of Sandwich 1718–1792 (1993); *Recreations* hill walking, hagiology, music, history of weights and measures; *Style*— N A M Rodger, Esq, FSA; ✉ c/o National Maritime Museum, Greenwich, London SE10 9NF

RODGER, Rt Rev Patrick Campbell; s of Patrick Wylie Rodger; *b* 28 Nov 1920; *Educ* Rugby, Ch Ch Oxford; *m* 1952, Margaret, da of Dr William Menzies Menzies, of Edinburgh (d 1989); 1 s (and 1 s decd); *Career* served WWII; ordained 1949, rector St Fillan's Kilmacolm with St Mary's Bridge of Weir 1958–61, exec sec Faith and Order in World Cncl of Churches 1961–66, provost St Mary's Cathedral Edinburgh 1967–70 (vice provost 1966–67); 8 bishop of Manchester 1970–78, 40 bishop of Oxford 1978–86, asst bishop Diocese of Edinburgh 1986–; memb: House of Lords 1974–86, Praesidium Conf of Euro Churches 1974–86; hon student Christ Church Oxford 1989; *Style*— The Rt Rev Patrick Rodger; ✉ 12 Warrender Park Terrace, Edinburgh EH9 1EG (☎ 0131 229 5075)

RODGER OF EARLSFERRY, Baron (Life Peer UK 1992), of Earlsferry in the District of North East Fife; Alan Ferguson Rodger; PC (1992); s of Prof Thomas Ferguson Rodger, CBE (d 1978), of Glasgow, and Jean Margaret Smith, *née* Chalmers (d 1981); *b* 18 Sept 1944; *Educ* Kelvinside Acad Glasgow, Univ of Glasgow (MA, LLB), New Coll Oxford (DCL, MA, DPhil); *Career* jr res fell Balliol Coll 1969–70, fell and tutor in law New Coll Oxford 1970–72, memb Faculty of Advocates 1974 (clerk 1976–79), standing jr counsel (Scotland) to Dept of Trade 1979, advocate depute 1985–88, QC (Scot) 1985, home advocate depute 1986–88, SG Scotland 1989–92, Lord Advocate 1992–96, Lord Justice-Gen and Lord Pres of the Court of Session 1996–; memb Mental Welfare Cmmn for Scotland 1982–85; Maccabaean lectr British Acad 1991; FBA 1991; hon bencher Lincoln's Inn 1992, hon memb Soc of Public Teachers of Law 1992; Hon LLD Univ of Glasgow 1995; FRSE 1992; *Books* Owners and Neighbours in Roman Law (1972), Gloag and Henderson's Introduction to the Law of Scotland (asst ed, tenth edn, 1995); *Recreations* writing, walking; *Clubs* Athenaeum; *Style*— The Rt Hon Lord Rodger of Earlsferry, PC, FBA, FRSE; ✉ Parliament House, Edinburgh EH1 1RF (☎ 0131 225 2595, fax 0131 226 3730)

RODGERS, David Ernest; s of late Ernest Rodgers, of Sutton, nr Peterborough, and Pamela Anne, *née* Wilkins; *b* 1 Feb 1942; *Educ* King Edward VII Sch Sheffield, St John's Coll Cambridge (BA, MA); *Career* art asst York City Art Gallery 1963–65, dep dir Sheffield City Art Galleries 1965–68; curator: Old Battersea House 1968–69, Wolverhampton Art Gallery and Museums 1969–81; dir: Exeter Museums 1981–86, Geffrye Museum 1986–90; curator William Morris Soc 1990–; memb Bd of Mgmnt Ikon Gallery Birmingham 1976–81 (vice chm 1979–81), external assessor in history of art NCAA 1977–79, govr Wolverhampton Poly 1978–81, hon sec Exeter Festival Ctee 1981–86, tstee James Henry Green Charitable Tst 1991–, area ed Oxford Companion to Western Art 1994–; *Books* Coronation Souvenirs and Commemoratives (1976), A Victorian Schoolboy in London (ed, 1989), William Morris at Home (1996), Rossetti (1996); *Recreations* collecting, cooking, gardening; *Style*— David Rodgers, Esq; ✉ Clevedon Lodge, 15C Stockwell Park Rd, London SW9 0AP; William Morris Society, Kelmscott House, 27 Upper Mall, London W6

RODGERS, Ian Louis; s of Charles Augustus Rodgers (ka 1942), and Doris, *née* Hanneman; *b* 12 Jan 1943; *Educ* Christ's Hospital; *m* 3 June 1967, Susanna, da of Rev Stanley James Pert (d 1974); 2 s (Mark b 1969, Paul b 1971); *Career* with Laurence Keen & Gardner 1959–71, ptnr Laurence Prust 1977–86 (joined 1971); dir: Framlington Asset Management Ltd 1986–89, Framlington Investment Management Ltd 1986–89, Framlington Investment Trust Services 1986–89; partnership dir Christ's Hosp 1989–91, One ACT (Consultancy) 1991–; dir and memb Gen Cncl S American Missionary Soc 1986– (treas 1994–), memb Investment Ctee The Girls Bde, donation govr Christ's Hosp, fndr The Christ's Hosp Partnership; Freeman City of London 1978, Liveryman Worshipful Co of Poulters 1979; memb Stock Exchange 1973–86, MInstD 1989, MICFM 1989, MSI 1993; *Recreations* fly fishing, music, theatre, photography; *Clubs* City Livery; *Style*— Ian Rodgers, Esq; (☎ 0181 460 4280, fax 0181 313 3280)

RODGERS, Joan; da of Thomas Rodgers (d 1971), and Julia Rodgers; *b* 4 Nov 1956; *Educ* Whitehaven GS, Univ of Liverpool (BA), RNCM Manchester; *m* 1988, Paul Daniel, *qv*; 2 da (Eleanor b 4 Sept 1990, Rose b 14 May 1993); *Career* soprano; debut as Pamina in Die Zauberflöte at the Aix-en-Provence Festival; major roles incl: Zerlina in Don Giovanni (Royal Opera House Covent Garden, Paris), Pamina (Covent Garden, ENO, Paris Opera), Gilda in Rigoletto (ENO), Nannetta (ENO), Countess Almaviva in The Marriage of Figaro/Le Nozze di Figaro (ENO, Netherlands Opera Amsterdam), Susanna in Le Nozze di Figaro (Glyndebourne, Paris), Cleopatra in Giulio Cesare (Scottish Opera), Yolande (Edinburgh Festival), Despina in Cosi fan Tutte (Paris), Br premiere of Chabrier's Briséis (Edinburgh Festival), Fiordiligi in Cosi fan Tutte (Theatre de la Monnaie Brussels), Donna Elvira in Don Giovanni (Scottish Opera 1995, Paris 1996), Pamina in Die Zauberflöte (Met Opera NY 1995, Berlin 1996), Ginerva in Ariodante (ENO) 1996, Hero in Beatrice et Benedict (Brussels Opera), Blanche in Les Dialogues des Carmelites (Amsterdam), Governess in Britten's Turn of the Screw (Royal Opera House); appeared at other operatic venues incl: Opera Bastille Paris, Zurich, Munich; given concerts in: London, Vienna, Madrid, Copenhagen, Salzburg, Paris, Lisbon; ABC tour of Australia 1995, BBC Proms 1996; worked with conductors incl: Sir Colin Davis, Sir George Solti, Andrew Davis, Daniel Barenboim, Jeffrey Tate, Sir Simon Rattle, Zubin Mehta; winner Kathleen Ferrier Meml Scholarship 1981; *Recordings* incl: solo recital of Tchaikovsky Songs, Mozart C minor Mass (under Harnoncourt), Mozart Da Ponte Operas (with the Berlin Philharmonic under Barenboim), Vaughan Williams Sea Symphony (with the Royal Liverpool Philharmonic under Vernon Handley), Beethoven 9th Symphony (with the Royal Liverpool Philharmonic under Charles Mackerras), Handel Messiah (under Richard Hickox), Creation (with Frans Brüggen), Rachmaninov Songs (with Howard Shelley); *Recreations* walking, cooking, playing with my children; *Style*— Ms Joan Rodgers; ✉ Ingpen & Williams Ltd, 14 Kensington Court, London W8 5DN (☎ 0171 937 5158, fax 0171 938 4175)

RODGERS, Worshipful (Doris) June (Mrs Roger Evans); da of James Alfred Rodgers, JP, of Craigavad, Co Down, Northern Ireland, and Margaret Doris, *née* Press; *b* 10 June 1945; *Educ* Victoria Coll Belfast, Trinity Coll Dublin (MA), Lady Margaret Hall Oxford (MA); *m* 6 Oct 1973, Roger Kenneth Evans, MP, *qv*, s of Gerald Raymond Evans of Mere, Wilts; 2 s (Edward Arthur b 13 May 1981, Henry William b 8 Feb 1983); *Career* called to the Bar Middle Temple 1971, recorder of the Crown Ct 1993–; chllr of the Dio of Gloucester 1990–; memb Ct of Common Cncl City of London Ward Farringdon Without 1975–, former memb City & East London Area Health Authy; Freeman City of London 1975; memb: Hon Soc of Middle Temple, Ecclesiastical Law Soc; *Recreations* architectural history, Anglo-Normandy; *Clubs* United Oxford & Cambridge Univ; *Style*— The Worshipful Miss June Rodgers; ✉ 2 Harcourt Buildings, The Temple, London EC4Y 9DB (☎ 0171 353 6961, fax 0171 353 6968)

RODGERS, Peter David; s of late Francis Norman Rodgers, of Glemsford, Suffolk, and Margaret Elizabeth, *née* Harte; *b* 8 Oct 1943; *Educ* Finchley Catholic GS, Trinity Coll Cambridge (MA); *m* 14 Sept 1968, Christine Mary Agnes, da of late Dr Duncan Primrose Wilkie, OBE, of Epping, Essex; 2 s (Benedict b 4 Nov 1980, William b 18 Jan 1982), 2 da (Susannah b 29 May 1974, Georgia b 17 Oct 1985); *Career* trainee Oxford Mail 1966–67, regions ed Industry Week 1967–69, industl corr The Guardian 1973–76 (technol corr 1970–73), energy ed The Sunday Times 1976–81; The Guardian: fin corr 1981–84, city ed 1984–90; fin ed The Independent 1990–; *Books* The Work of Art (1989); *Recreations* offshore cruising and racing, gardening, theatre, music; *Style*— Peter Rodgers, Esq; ✉ The Independent, 1 Canada Square, Canary Wharf, London E14 5DL (☎ 0171 293 2059, fax 0171 293 2098/6); home (☎ 0171 278 5628)

RODGERS, (Andrew) Piers Wingate; yr s of Sir John Charles Rodgers, 1 Bt, DL (d 1993), and Betsy, *née* Aikin-Sneath; hp of bro, Sir Tobias Rodgers, 2 Bt; *b* 24 Oct 1944; *Educ* Eton, Merton Coll Oxford (BA); *m* 9 Sept 1979, Marie-Agathe, da of Charles-Albert Houette, Croix de Guerre (d 1989), of Bléneau, France; 2 s (Thomas b 1979, Augustus b 1983); *Career* with J Henry Schroder Wagg & Co Ltd 1967–73 (PA to chm 1970–73), dir Int Cncl on Monuments & Sites (ICOMOS) Paris 1973–79 (sec UK Ctee 1981), UNESCO expert (Implementation of World Cultural Heritage Convention) 1979–80, sec of Royal Academy of Arts London (also sec of Chantrey Bequest and British Inst Fund) 1981–96, dir Burlington Gardens Project Royal Acad of Arts 1996–; memb Bd Warburg Inst Univ of London 1993–; Freeman City of London, Hon Court Memb Worshipful Co of Masons; memb Co of Merchant Adventurers of City of York; FRSA; Chevalier de l'Ordre des Arts et des Lettres (France) 1987, Ordre National du Mérite (France) 1991, Cavaliere Ufficiale Ordine al Merito della Repubblica Italiana 1992; *Clubs* Brooks's, Pratt's, MCC; *Style*— Piers Rodgers, Esq; ✉ Peverell House, Bradford Peverell, Dorset

RODGERS, Walter Shaw; s of Booth Rodgers, JP (d 1961), of Netherthong, Yorks, and Beatrice, *née* Lockwood (d 1948); *b* 20 Jan 1922; *Educ* Holme Valley GS, Univ of Leeds (BCom, MCom); *m* 31 Aug 1957, Phyllis, da of Ernest Kenworthy (d 1971), of Totties, Holmfirth; 2 s (Martin Lockwood b 14 Jan 1959, Philip Nicholas (twin) b 14 Jan 1959), 1 da (Janet Christine b 20 March 1962); *Career* WWII 1942–47, Flt Sgt radar operator, educn instr SEAAF; cost accountant Dyestuffs Div ICI 1952–64, mgmnt accountant Organics Div ICI 1964–76; dir ICI subsidiaries: Armalux Flooring Ltd 1969–76, Bibby Chemicals Ltd 1971; business controller Vulnax International Group St Cloud Paris 1976–79, fin controller and company sec Pennine Fibres Gp (now part of British Vita plc) 1979–87; dir: Pennine Fibre Industries Ltd, Package Recovery Services Ltd 1987–88; visiting lectr in ind organisation and mgmnt Huddersfield Poly 1951–60, chm New Mill Probus Club 1993–94 (vice chm 1992–93, treas 1988–92), ctee memb Huddersfield Family History Soc 1988–; memb: Yorks Archaeological Soc, Royal Economic Soc, Richard III Soc; govr Shepley First Sch 1989–93; FCCA 1964 (ACCA 1957); *Recreations* travel, art & architecture, history, photography, swimming, gardening, genealogy; *Clubs* ICI Woodlands, Manchester; *Style*— Walter Rodgers, Esq; ✉ Shaldon, 80 Marsh Lane, Shepley, Huddersfield HD8 8AS (☎ 01484 602945)

RODGERS OF QUARRY BANK, Baron (Life Peer UK 1992), of Kentish Town in the London Borough of Camden; William Thomas Rodgers; PC (1975); s of William Arthur Rodgers and Gertrude Helen Rodgers; *b* 28 Oct 1928; *Educ* Quarry Bank HS Liverpool, Magdalen Coll Oxford; *m* 1955, Silvia, da of Hirsch Szulman; 3 da; *Career* MP (Lab until 1981, thereafter SDP) Teesside Stockton 1962–79, Stockton N 1979–83, Parly candidate Bristol W March 1957; in Lab Govts: parly under sec DEA 1964–67, FO 1967–68, min of state BOT 1968–69, min state Treasy 1969–70, MOD 1974–76, tport sec 1976–79; gen sec Fabian Soc 1953–60 (remained memb until 1981), ldr UK Delgn Cncl Europe & WEU 1967–68, chm Expenditure Ctee Trade & Industry 1971–74; dir gen RIBA 1987–94, chm Advertising Standards Authy 1995–; Hon FRIBA, Hon FIStructE; *Books* Hugh Gaitskell (1963), The People into Parliament (1966), The Politics of Change (1982), Government and Industry (1986); *Style*— The Rt Hon Lord Rodgers of Quarry Bank, PC; ✉ 43 North Road, London N6 4BE

RODIN, Jack; CBE (1992); s of Mark Rodin (d 1966), of London, and Sarah, *née* Zeff (d 1960); *b* 2 Jan 1926; *Educ* Raines Fndn London, Univ of London (BSc); *m* 14 Feb 1964, (Marie) Elizabeth, da of Charles Paddison, of Newtown, Llantwit, S Glam; 1 s (Jonathan), 2 da (Penelope, Sarah); *Career* engr; Sir Alexander Gibb and Ptnrs Consulting Engrs 1947–54, sr engr specialist conslts (chief engr, dir) 1954–60, jt fndr Lowe and Rodin Consulting Engrs 1960 (merged with Bldg Design Ptnrship 1970), chief exec Bldg Design Partnership 1984–88; pres Concrete Soc 1988–; MConsE 1964, FICE 1968, FIStructE 1974; *Recreations* music, art, golf, tennis; *Clubs* Arts; *Style*— Jack Rodin, Esq, CBE; ✉ 109 Blackheath Park, Blackheath, London SE3 0EY (☎ 0181 852 8048)

RODNEY, 10 Baron (GB 1782); Sir George Brydges Rodney; 10 Bt (GB 1764); s of 9 Baron Rodney (d 1992), and Régine Elisabeth Lucienne Thérèse Marie Ghislaine, *née* Pangaert d'Opdorp; *b* 3 Jan 1953; *Educ* Eton; *m* 20 Aug 1996, Jane, da of Rowan Blakeney, of The Old Rectory, Hatherop, Glos; *Heir* kinsman, Nicholas Simon Harley Rodney b 1947; *Style*— The Rt Hon the Lord Rodney; ✉ House of Lords, London SW1A 0PW

RODNEY BENNETT, *see:* Bennett

RODRIGUE, Claude; s of Ezra Rodrigue (d 1946), of Cairo, and Bella, *née* Semah; *b* 17 April 1930; *Educ* English Sch Cairo, Imperial Coll London (SIMechE); *m* 17 Oct 1958, Ann, da of Lt-Col Sir John Rhodes, Bt, DSO (d 1954), of London; 2 s (Philip b 24 March 1960, Michael b 16 Oct 1966), 1 da (Carolyn b 10 Oct 1962); *Career* Dunkley Marshall and Co 1960–81 (ptnr 1975–81), Strauss Turnbull and Co Ltd 1981–88, Townsley and Co 1988–92, Durlacher & Co 1992–; memb Br Bridge Team 1960–82, Euro Champion 1960, World Olympic par point Champion, 3 Olympic Championship 1976, multi-winner Camrose Trophy; invited commentator to first bridge match between nationalist and socialist China (Hong Kong) 1982; Freeman of the City of London 1977; memb IBPA, MSI (memb Stock Exchange 1966); *Recreations* good food and wine, bridge, opera; *Clubs* TGR Bridge; *Style*— Claude Rodrigue, Esq; ✉ Flat 1, 18 Hyde Park Gate, London SW7 5DH (☎ 0171 225 2252); Durlacher & Co, 10 Throgmorton Avenue, London EC2N 2DL (☎ 0171 628 4306, fax 0171 638 8848)

RODRIGUES, Sir Alberto Maria; kt (1966), CBE (1964, OBE 1960, MBE 1948), ED; s of late Luiz Gonzaga Rodrigues; *b* 5 Nov 1911; *Educ* St Joseph's Coll, Univ of Hong Kong (MB BS); *m* 1940, Cynthia Maria de Silva; 1 s, 2 da; *Career* Med Offr Hong Kong Defence Force (POW 1940–45); general medical practitioner 1953–; memb Legislative Cncl Hong Kong 1953–60, memb Exec Cncl Hong Kong 1960–74 (sr unofficial memb 1964–74); pro-chancellor Hong Kong Univ 1968–; dir: Hong Kong & Shanghai Hotels 1969–, Lap Heng Co 1970–, Peak Tramways Co 1971–, Computer Data (Hill) 1973–, Hong Kong Commercial Broadcasting Co 1974–; *Style*— Sir Alberto Rodrigues, CBE, ED; ✉ St Paul's Hospital, Medical Superintendent, Causeway Bay, Hong Kong (☎ 00 852 2890 6008)

RODRIGUES, Christopher John; s of Alfred John Rodrigues, of London, and Joyce Margaret, *née* Farron-Smith; *b* 24 Oct 1949; *Educ* Univ Coll Sch, Jesus Coll Cambridge (BA, rowing blue, pres Univ Boat Club), Harvard Business Sch (Baker scholar, MBA); *m* Priscilla Purcell Young; 1 s, 1 da; *Career* with Spillers Foods London 1971–72, Foster, Turner & Benson London 1972–74, MBA Harvard 1974–76, McKinsey & Co London 1976–79, American Express NY and London 1979–88; Thomas Cook Group Ltd: chief operating offr 1988–90, gp md 1990–92, gp chief exec 1992–95; chief exec Bradford & Bingley Building Society 1996–; FRSA; *Recreations* cooking, skiing, rowing, shooting, opera, ballet; *Clubs* Leander (chm), Hawks', Century (Harvard); *Style*— Christopher

Rodrigues, Esq; ✉ Bradford & Bingley Building Society, Crossflatts, Bingley, West Yorkshire BD16 2UA (☎ 01274 555555)

RODWAY, Simon Richard Noel; s of Flt Lt Ernest Allan Rodway (d 1991), and Emily Alice, *née* Nutt (d 1994); *b* 14 July 1932; *Educ* Westminster, Keble Coll Oxford, LSE (Dip in Social Science and Public Admin, Dip in Mental Health, Certificate in Child Care); *Career* sr house master The Caldecott Community 1958–63, sr child care offr Royal Borough of Kensington and Chelsea 1964–68, lectr in child care NW Poly 1968–70, asst dir of social servs London Borough of Barnet 1971–76 (dep childrens offr 1970–71), dir of social servs London Borough of Merton 1976–85, chief social servs advsr Br Red Cross 1986–; memb Inquiry Panel into Nye Bevan Lodge London Borough of Southwark 1986–87; chm: Caldecott Community Ashford Kent 1970–; tstee: Disabled Living Fndn 1980–94, John Hunt Tst 1985–; vice pres Assoc Workers with Maladjusted Children 1978–; chm: Charterhouse Gp of Therapeutic Communites 1987–, Tylehurst Sch Tst 1960–95, Caldecott Coll 1994–96; memb Br Assoc of Psychotherapists 1977, dep pres Merton Voluntary Assoc for Welfare of the Blind 1985, fell Royal Inst of Public Health and Hygiene 1988; *Recreations* theatre, travelling, walking, swimming; *Style—* Simon Rodway, Esq; ✉ 6 Cornwall Grove, London W4 2LB (☎ 0181 994 7461); British Red Cross, 9 Grosvenor Cresent, London SW1X 7EJ (☎ 0171 235 5454)

RODWELL, Andrew John Hunter; er s of Col Evelyn John Clive Hunter Rodwell, MC, TD, JP (d 1981), of Woodlands, Holbrook, Suffolk, and Martha, *née* Girdlestone (d 1996); the Rodwells have lived in Suffolk since the early 18 century and acquired Woodlands in 1840 (*see* Burke's Landed Gentry, 18 edn, vol II, 1969); *b* 23 Dec 1938; *Educ* Eton; *m* 20 July 1963, Susan Eleanor, da of Peter Comley Pitt (d 1995), of Cranbrook, Kent; 3 da (Camilla Eleanor Hunter b 21 July 1964, Miranda Harriet Hunter (Mrs Damian Kwiatkowski) b 29 May 1967, Patricia Louise Hunter b 17 May 1971); *Career* short service cmmn with RWAFF 1957–60; farmer; md SCH (Supplies) Ltd; *Recreations* country pursuits; *Style—* Andrew Rodwell, Esq; ✉ Woodlands, Holbrook, Suffolk (☎ 01473 328800/328272)

RODWELL, Crispin Richard; s of Robert Richard Rodwell, of Ballyhalbert, Co Down, and Hilary Cecelia Rosemary Ann, *née* Harbord; *b* 10 Dec 1961; *Educ* Royal Belfast Academical Inst, Grosvenor HS; *m* 1983, Heather, da of late Lewis Reford Lee; 1 da (Emma Lee b 16 July 1984), 2 s (Jason Richard b 25 Aug 1987, Ryan Peter b 5 April 1991); *Career* news and feature photographer; Keystone Press Agency London 1981, freelance photographer based Belfast 1981–87; contract photographer: The Sunday Times (Ireland photographer) 1987–, Reuters 1993–; reg cmmns for nat newspapers, magazines and books in Europe and USA; memb: NI Press Photographers' Assoc, Press Photographers' Assoc of Ireland; *Awards* NI Press Photographer of the Yr 1992 and 1994, Irish Press Photographer of the Yr 1994, Nikon Regnl Photographer of the Yr 1994, numerous other awards for news and feature photography 1991, 1992 and 1994; *Recreations* salmon fishing and salmon fly dressing, restoring 200–year-old farmhouse; *Style—* Crispin Rodwell, Esq

RODWELL, His Hon Judge; Daniel Alfred Hunter; QC (1982); s of Brig Reginald Mandeville Rodwell, AFC (d 1974), and Nellie Barbara, *née* D'Costa (d 1967); *b* 3 Jan 1936; *Educ* Munro Coll Jamaica, Worcester Coll Oxford (BA); *m* 1967, Veronica Frances Ann, da of late Robin Cecil, CMG, of Hants; 2 s (William b 1967, Thomas b 1970), 1 da (Lucy b 1974); *Career* Nat Serv in W Yorks Regt, 2 Lt, TA (Capt); barr, recorder Crown Ct 1980–86, circuit judge 1986–; *Recreations* hunting, sailing (Emrys), gardening; *Clubs* Pegasus, Bar Yacht; *Style—* His Hon Judge Rodwell, QC; ✉ Luton Crown Court, 7 George Street, Luton, Beds LU1 2AA

RODWELL, Dennis Graham; s of Albert James Rodwell, MBE (d 1991), and Constance Edith, *née* Scaddan; *b* 24 Jan 1948; *Educ* Kingswood Sch Bath, Clare Coll Cambridge (MA, DipArch); *m* 10 May 1975, Rosemary Ann, *née* Rimmer; 2 s (Nicholas b 1978, Christopher b 1979), 1 da (Melanie b 1982); *Career* architect, author and lectr; in practice Dennis Rodwell Architects 1975–; works incl: historic building restorations, urban conservation and regeneration, heritage presentation, the promotion of long-term conservation strategies for the protection and devpt of historic towns and cities, restoration of Melrose Station and its mgmnt as a Crafts and Heritage Centre 1985–90; awards and commendations incl: Assoc for the Protection of Rural Scotland 1985, Edinburgh Architectural Assoc 1987, RICS/The Times Conservation 1989, The Ian Allan Railway Heritage 1989, The Sunday Times Scotland/Morton Fraser Milligan Heritage 1990, Borders Regnl Cncl 1990, British Tourist Authy 1990, Europa Nostra/IBI 1991; memb The Edinburgh New Town Conservation Ctee 1981–84 and 1987–90, tstee The Trimontium Tst 1988– (chm 1988–90); served ctees: The Scottish Georgian Soc, The Borders Architects Gp, The Cncls of the Royal Incorpn of Architects in Scotland, The Edinburgh Architectural Assoc; lecturing incl Euro Urban Conservation course Univ of Dundee 1991–93, speaking incl at int conservation confs 1975–; RIBA 1973, FRIAS 1982, FSA Scot 1990, FRSA 1991; *Publications* articles in jls and books upon historical, travel and architectural conservation subjects incl: European Heritage (1975), Architectural Conservation in Europe (1975), Civilising the City (1991), Stone Cleaning (1992); *Recreations* travel, walking, reading, photography, gardening; *Style—* Dennis Rodwell, Esq; ✉ Greenside Park, St Boswells, Melrose, Roxburghshire TD6 0AH (☎ 01835 823289, fax 01896 823809)

RODWELL, John Francis Meadows; s of Maj Percival Francis (Jim) Rodwell, MBE, TD, of Halesworth, Suffolk; *b* 11 July 1946; *m* 9 March 1974, Rosie, da of John Trevor Munden Brook (d 1981), of Meole Brace, Shrewsbury; *Career* joined Cambs and Suffolk Regt 1965, Mons OCS 1965, Grenadier Gds 1968, psc 1979, ret Army 1983; S G Warburg Group plc: joined 1983, corp and community affrs dir Mercury Asset Management 1996– (admin dir 1989–96); tstee and dir Hedley Foundation, dir various property cos, memb Cncl Action on Addiction, memb Devpt Cncl Shakespeare's Globe; *Recreations* skiing, golf, wine; *Clubs* Cavalry and Guards' (chm 1996–), Hunstanton Golf; *Style—* John Rodwell, Esq; ✉ 1 Palmerston House, 60 Kensington Place, London W8 7PU; Bunkles, Church Street, Thornham, Norfolk PE36 6NJ

ROE, (Eileen) Betty; da of Reginald William Roe (d 1977), and Elsie Maud Roe (d 1988); *b* 30 July 1930; *Educ* Burlington GS, Royal Acad of Music; *m* 1954, John Bishop; 2 da (twins b 7 May 1958), 1 s (b 28 May 1961); *Career* choir trainer and organist: St George's Bloomsbury 1947, St James's Norlands 1949, St Helen's Kensington 1958–68 and 1977–86; London Opera Chorus, John Alldis Singers, St Clement Dane Chorale 1961–82, dir of music London Acad of Music and Dramatic Art 1968–78; composer of numerous works; currently gen music adjudicator, examiner and composer, dir of music with Northken Concerts; ARAM 1990, LRAM, ARCM, FTCL; *Style—* Ms Betty Roe; ✉ 14 Barlby Road, N Kensington, London W10 6AR (☎ 0181 969 3579)

ROE, Geoffrey Eric; s of Herbert William Roe, of Cowes, IOW, and Florence, *née* Gordon; *b* 20 July 1944; *Educ* Tottenham GS; *m* 4 Oct 1968, Elizabeth Anne, da of Alfred George Ponton; 1 da (Alison b 2 Dec 1981), 1 s (David b 28 July 1985); *Career* Miny of Aviation 1963–67, asst private sec to Sir Ronald Melville 1967–69, Exports and Int Div Miny of Technol 1969–74, Army Guided Weapons Contracts Branch 1974–76, seconded to British Aerospace 1976–78; MOD: sec Rocket Motor Executive 1978–81, asst dir Contracts (Air) 1981–86, dir Contracts (Underwater Weapons) 1986–89, head Material Co-ordinations (Navy) 1989–90, princ dir Navy and Nuclear Contracts 1990–91, DG Def Contracts 1991–95, DG Aircraft Systems 2 1995–; MCIPS 1993; *Recreations* skiing, sailing, fell-walking, private flying; *Clubs* Wiltshire Aero, Ski Club of Great Britain; *Style—* Geoffrey Roe, Esq; ✉ Procurement Executive, Walnut 1c, MOD Abbey Wood No 69, PO Box 702, Bristol BS12 DY (☎ 0117 913 4500, fax 0117 913 4950)

ROE, Rt Rev Dr (William) Gordon; s of William Henry Roe (d 1965), and Dorothy Myrtle, *née* Hayman (d 1975); *b* 5 Jan 1932; *Educ* Bournemouth Sch, Jesus Coll Oxford, St Stephen's House Oxford (MA, DPhil, DipTheol); *m* 1953, Mary Primrose, da of Nils Arthur Efram Andreén (d 1973); 2 s (Patrick b 1957, Michael b 1964), 2 da (Helen b 1955, Rachel b 1959); *Career* RAEC Sgt Instr; asst curate St Peter's Bournemouth 1958–61, priest i/c St Michael's Abingdon 1961–69, vice princ St Chad's Coll Durham 1969–74, vicar St Oswald's Durham and rural dean Durham 1974–80, hon canon Durham 1979–80, bishop of Huntingdon 1980–97; co-chm Meissen Cmmn 1991–96; Hon DUniv Oxford; *Books* Lamennais and England (1966), J B Dykes, Priest and Musician (with Arthur Hutchings, 1976); *Recreations* French literature, painting; *Style—* The Rt Rev Dr W G Roe; ✉ 8 Eldon Road, Bournemouth, Dorset BH9 2RT (☎ 01202 535127)

ROE, (Colin) Graeme Algernon Maitland; s of late Colin Drummond Roe, and late Irene Jesse; *b* 15 Aug 1935; *Educ* Hampton GS, Univ of Nottingham; *m* 15 Sept 1967, Jean, da of John Mcgregor (d 1987), of Minchinhampton, Glos; 1 da (Jessica b 29 May 1969); *Career* Nat Serv Flt Lt RAF 1956–58; account dir Garland Compton 1958–61, Euro marketing dir Alberto-Culver 1961–63, marketing dir Philip Morris and Ever-Ready Personna 1963–68, chm Roe Downton and dir Saatchi and Saatchi 1968–78, vice chm McCann Erickson 1978–82; chm: Roe Byfield 1982–, Roe Racing 1984–, Greenaway Burdett Martin 1987–89; as racehorse trainer winners incl: All Bright, Dom Perignon, Nippy Chippy, We're in the Money, Kitty Wren, Le Grand Maitre; English Amateur Athletic Assoc 440 yards hurdles, amateur steeplechase jockey 1975–85; FIPA 1977; *Books* Profitable Marketing for the Smaller Company (1969), Changing Role of the Chief Executive (1977); *Recreations* reading, riding, theatre, writing; *Clubs* Turf, RAF; *Style—* Graeme Roe, Esq; ✉ Hyde Park Farm, Lower Hyde, Chalford, nr Stroud, Gloucestershire (☎ 01453 885487, fax 01453 885204, telex 437105, car 0374 725044)

ROE, James Kenneth; s of Kenneth Alfred Roe (d 1988), of Devon, and Zirphie Norah, *née* Luke (d 1940); *b* 28 Feb 1935; *Educ* King's Sch Bruton; *m* 15 March 1958, Marion Audrey Roe, MP, *qv*, da of William Keyte (d 1977), of Chagford, Devon; 1 s (William b 1969), 2 da (Philippa b 1962, Jane b 1965); *Career* Nat Serv cmmnd RN; banker; dir: NM Rothschild & Sons Ltd 1970–92, Rothschild Tst Corp 1970–95, Tokyo Pacific Holdings NV 1969–92, GAM Selection Inc 1992–, Microvite PLC 1993–, Jupiter International Group PLC 1993–; chm: Equity Consort Investment Trust plc 1973–95 (dir 1967–95), China Investment Trust PLC 1993–, Ronson plc 1993–; dep chm Innovations Group plc 1985–96, dir: Jupiter European Investment Trust plc 1990–, The Fleming Capital and Income Trust plc 1995–; FInstD, FRSA; *Clubs* Brooks's, Carlton, MCC; *Style—* James Roe, Esq; ✉ Petleys, Downe, Kent BR6 7JS (☎ 01689 854901); c/o Jupiter International Group PLC, 197 Knightsbridge, London SW7 1RB (☎ 0171 412 0703)

ROE, Marion Audrey; MP (C) Broxbourne (majority 23,970); da of William Keyte (d 1977), and Grace Mary, *née* Bocking (d 1983); *b* 15 July 1936; *Educ* Bromley HS, Croydon HS (both GPDST), English Sch of Languages Vevey Switzerland; *m* 1958, James Roe, *qv*, s of Kenneth Roe; 1 s (William b 1969), 2 da (Philippa b 1962, Jane b 1965); *Career* Parly candidate (C) Barking 1979, MP (C) Broxbourne 1983–; PPS to Rt Hon John Moore as Sec of State for Tport 1986–87 (PPS to jr tport mins 1985–86), Parly under sec of state Dept of the Environment 1987–88; chm Commons Select Ctee on Health 1992–; memb Commons Select Ctees on: Agriculture 1983–85, Social Servs 1988–89, Commons Procedure 1990–92, Sittings of the House 1991–92, Commons Liaison 1992–; managing tstee Parly Contributory Pension Fund 1990–, memb House of Commons Admin Ctee 1991–; jt sec Cons Pty Orgn 1985, memb Exec 1922 Ctee 1992–; chm Cons Pty Parly Ctees on: Horticulture and Markets 1989– (sec 1983–85), Social Security Ctee 1990– (vice chm 1988–90); vice chm Cons Pty Parly Environment Ctee 1990–; sec All Pty Br-Canadian Parly Gp 1991–, chm All Pty Hospices Gp 1992– (sec 1990–92); vice chm: All Pty Fairs and Showgrounds Gp 1992– (jt chm 1989–92), All Pty Parly Garden Club 1995–; memb Dept of the Environment Advsy Ctee on Women's Employment 1989–92, substitute memb UK Delgn to Cncl of Europe and WEU 1989–92, UK rep on Cwlth Observer Gp monitoring elections in the Seychelles 1992; successfully sponsored Prohibition of Female Circumcision Act 1985 (Private Member's Bill); Parly conslt to Horticultural Trades Assoc 1990–95; cncllr: London Borough of Bromley 1975–78, GLC (Ilford North Div) 1977–86; GLC: vice chm Historic Bldgs Ctee 1977–78, whip for Planning and Communications Gp 1977–78, Cons dep chief whip 1978 82, vice chm Gen Mgmnt Ctee 1978–81, leading Cons spokesman Police Ctee 1982–83, memb Cons Ldr's Ctee 1982–83, memb various other GLC ctees 1978–82; GLC rep on Gen Servs Ctee of AMA 1978–81, UK rep Conf of Local and Regnl Authorities of Europe 1981; memb Gen Advsy Cncl BBC 1986–87, govr Research into Ageing Tst 1988–, memb International Women's Forum 1992–, hon regnl vice pres Eastern Region Housebuilders Fedn 1993–, memb Euro Research Gp 1994–; pres: Broxbourne Orgn for the Disabled (co-pres) 1991–, Save Temple Bar Campaign 1991–, Lea Valley Arthritis Care 1993–; vice pres: Women's Nat Cancer Control Campaign 1985–87 and 1988–, Herts Chamber of Trade & Commerce 1983–87 and 1988–, E Herts Operatic Soc 1986–, Herts Alcohol Problems Advsy Serv 1991–, Herts Assoc of Local Cncls 1991–, Capel Manor Horticultural and Environmental Centre Tst Fund 1994– (chm 1989–94), Assoc of Dist Cncls 1994–, Herts Cons Soc 1995–; patron: Herts St John Ambulance Appeal 1989, E Hertfordshire Hospice Care Serv 1994–, Oxford Int Centre for Palliative Care 1994–, Herts Co Youth Orchestras and Choirs 1995–; Freeman City of London, Liveryman Worshipful Co of Gardeners 1993 (Freeman 1989); fell Indust and Parl Tst 1990, FRSA 1990, Hon MIHort 1993, Hon Fellowship of Professional Business and Tech Mgmnt 1995; *Publications* The Labour Left in London - A Blueprint for a Socialist Britain (CPC pamphlet, 1985); *Recreations* opera, ballet, theatre; *Style—* Mrs Marion Roe, MP; ✉ House of Commons, London SW1A 0AA (☎ 0171 219 3528)

ROE, Mark Adrian; s of Gordon Arthur Roe, and Phyllis, *née* Flowers; *b* 20 Feb 1963; *Educ* Henry Fanshaw GS; *m* 12 Nov 1988 (m dis 1995), Jane Patricia, da of Kenneth Gill; *Career* former springboard and highboard diving champion of Derbyshire, junior int golfer GB & I and Eng 1980, professional golfer 1981–, joined EuroTour 1985, Catalan Open Champion 1989, Lancome Trophy Champion 1992, French Open Champion 1994; team memb Eng: World Cup 1989, 1994 and 1995, Alfred Dunhill Cup 1994; *Recreations* snooker, history of golf, antiques; *Clubs* The Hallowes Golf; *Style—* Mark Roe, Esq; ✉ PGA European Tour, Wentworth Drive, Virginia Water, Surrey (☎ 019904 2881)

ROE, Air Chief Marshal Sir Rex David; GCB (1981, KCB 1977, CB 1974), AFC; *b* 1925; *Educ* City of London Sch, Univ of London; *m* 1948, Helen, *née* Nairn (d 1981); 1 s, 2 da; *Career* joined RAF 1943; cmd RNZAF Centl Flying Sch 1956–58, RCDS 1971; SASO HQ Near East AF 1974–76; AOC-in-C: Support Cmd 1977–78, Trg Cmd 1976–77; Air Memb Supply & Orgn 1978–81, ret; *Style—* Air Chief Marshal Sir Rex Roe, GCB, AFC; ✉ c/o Lloyds Bank, 7 Pall Mall, London SW1

ROEBUCK, Christina Rowena Margaret; da of Rev Eric Stopford, of Pewsey, Wiltshire, and Christina Heather Liddle, *née* Muir; *b* 28 Feb 1943; *Educ* Orme Girls' GS Staffs, Harper Adams Agric Coll (Nat Dip in Poultry Husbandry); *m* 1, 1968 (m dis 1985), Ian Patrick, s of late Edward Caudwell, of Culter, Kincardineshire; 2 da (Charlotte b 1971, Rosalind b 1973); m 2, 1986, Simon John, s of John Frederick Roebuck, of Walton, Derbys; 1 s (Harry b 1987); *Career* farmer; agric advsr Br Egg Mktg Bd 1962–68; co-ordinator World Arabian Horse Orgn Conf London 1988; Arab Horse Soc: memb Int

Judges' Panel, memb Cncl, chm Scottish Regional Gp 1996; *Recreations* breeding arabian horses, shooting, gardening; *Style*— Mrs Christina R M Roebuck; ✉ Lendrum Farm, Turriff, Aberdeenshire AB53 8HA (☎ 01888 544285)

ROEBUCK, John Stanley; *b* 26 Feb 1953; *Educ* Chetham's Hosp Sch Manchester, Manchester Poly (hotel and catering admin), Ashridge Mgmnt Coll (exec devpt prog); *m* Susan Roebuck, *qv*; 1 da; *Career* hotelier; Trust House Forte (now Forte plc): grad mgmnt trainee THF Leisure Ltd 1967–77 (gen asst mangr Greenriggs Country House Hotel Kendal 1974–75, asst mangr rising to dep mangr Cresta Court Hotel Altrincham 1975–77), Trust House Forte 1977–78, area trg offr THF Popular Catering Ltd 1978, regnl mangr Little Chef 1979, dep regnl dir Little Chef North East 1979–81, regnl dir Little Chef North East 1981–83, gen mangr Little Chef North 1984, ops dir Little Chef THF Catering Div 1984–86, exec dir Happy Eater Restaurants THF Roadside Catering Div 1986–89; md Etrop Grange Ltd and Etrop Restaurants Ltd 1989– (5 crowns classification English Tourist Bd, County Hotel of the Year Good Food Guide 1993); *Style*— John Roebuck, Esq; ✉ Etrop Grange, Outwood Lane, Manchester Airport, Manchester M22 5NR (☎ 0161 499 0500)

ROEBUCK, Roy Delville; *b* 25 Sept 1929; *m* 1957, Dr Mary Ogilvy, *née* Adams (d 1995); 1 s (Gavin Macgregor b 1957); *Career* Nat Serv RAF FEAF 1947–50; journalist Stockport Advertiser, Northern Daily Telegraph, Yorkshire Evening News, News Chronicle, Daily Express, Manchester Evening Chronicle and Daily Herald 1950–66; contested (Lab) Altrincham and Sale gen election 1964 and by-election 1965, MP (Lab) Harrow E 1966–70, contested (Lab) Leek gen election 1974; sometime asst ed Forward, columnist London Evening News 1968–70; PA to Col George Wigg as Paymaster-Gen 1966–67, called to the Bar Gray's Inn 1974, advsr to Lord Wigg as Pres Betting Office Licensees Assoc 1975–83; fell Atlantic Cncl 1993–; govr Moorfields Eye Hosp 1984–88, memb Islington Community Health Cncl 1988–92; *Recreations* reading Hansard, music, tennis, walking, watching Coronation Street on Mondays, Wednesdays and Fridays; *Clubs* RAC; *Style*— Roy Roebuck, Esq; ✉ 12 Brooksby Street, London N1 1HA (☎ 0171 607 7057); Bell Yard Chambers, 116–118 Chancery Lane, London WC2A 1PP (☎ 0171 306 9292, fax 0171 404 5143)

ROEBUCK, Susan; *b* 15 Nov 1953; *Educ* Cheadle GS for Girls, Bramhall County HS, Manchester Poly (HND institutional mgmnt); *m* John Stanley Roebuck, *qv*; 1 da; *Career* hotelier; early career experience as asst manageress Pownall Arms Hotel Bramhall and trainee asst mangr with Stanneylands Group working at Old Trafford Cricket Club (Banqueting Op) and Mottram Hall Hotel Prestbury; subsequently: asst mangr Mottram Hall, mangr Glengarry Hotel Manchester, sales experience Trusthouse Forte Leisure Group and York House Ashton; freelance conslt (Bredbury Hall Hotel Stockport/Ring and Brymer) and mangr own outside catering business 1981–, co-proprietor Etrop Grange Hotel 1986– (5 crowns classification English Tourist Bd, County Hotel of the Year Good Food Guide 1993); *Style*— Mrs Susan Roebuck; ✉ Etrop Grange, Outwood Lane, Manchester Airport, Manchester M22 5NR (☎ 0161 499 0500, fax 0161 499 0790)

ROEDY, William H (Bill); *b* 13 June 1948; *Educ* West Point, Harvard Univ (MBA); *Career* served US Military 10 years (incl as pilot and as Cdr NATO Missile Base); sometime vice pres Nat Accounts LA, joined Home Box Office Cable TV and Cinemax 1979, various mktg appts and mgmnt conslt for TV stations in Boston Mass 1979–89, md and chief exec MTV Europe 1989–94, pres MTV Networks International 1994–; memb CCTA; *Style*— Bill Roedy, Esq; ✉ MTV Networks International, Hawley Crescent, London NW1 8TT (☎ 0171 284 7777, fax 0171 284 7788)

ROEG, Nicolas Jack; CBE (1996); s of Jack Nicolas Roeg (d 1952), and Mabel Gertrude Silk (d 1985); *b* 15 Aug 1928; *Educ* Mercers Sch; *m* 1, 1957, Susan Rennie, da of Maj F W Stephen MC; 4 s (Joscelin, Nicolas, Lucien, Sholto); m 2, 1986, Theresa Russell; 2 s (Statten Jack, Maxmilian Nicolas Sextus); *Career* film director; *Films* credits incl: Performance, Walkabout, Don't Look Now, The Man Who Fell to Earth, Bad Timing, Eureka, Insignificance, Castaway, Track 29, Sweet Bird of Youth, Without You I'm Nothing (exec prodr), Cold Heaven, Young Indy, Cold Heaven, The Witches, Heart of Darkness, Two Deaths, Full Body Massage, Hotel Paradise, Samson and Delilah; *Style*— Nicolas Roeg, Esq, CBE; ✉ c/o ICM Ltd, Oxford House, 76 Oxford Street, London W1N 0AX (☎ 0171 636 6565, fax 0171 323 0101)

ROFE, Prof Brian Henry; s of Henry Alexander Rofe (d 1979), and Marguerite, *née* Browne; *b* 7 Jan 1934; *Educ* Shrewsbury, St John's Coll Cambridge (BA, MA); *m* 26 May 1962, (Margaret) Anne, da of Rev Phillip R Shepherd; 2 s (Christopher Henry b 16 Jan 1965, Andrew John b 1 April 1968), 1 da (Katharine (Mrs Johns) b 1 July 1963); *Career* Nat Serv RA 1952–54, 2 Lt 1953, Actg Lt TA 1955; chartered engr, asst civil engr John Laing Construction 1957–63, asst/sr engr Rofe and Raffety 1963–69, res engr Draycote Reservoir 1967–69, sr ptnr Rofe Kennard and Lapworth (consulting water engrs) 1992– (ptnr 1970), prof of engrg design Univ of Hertford 1995–; contracts incl: Thames Groundwater Scheme 1971–76, Malaysia Lower Perak Scheme 1979–85, Ashford Flood Alleviation Scheme 1985–91, Blashford and Testwood Lakes Schemes 1986–96; All Reservoirs Panel engr 1985–; Freeman: City of London, Worshipful Co of Grocers; FCIWEM (pres 1990–91), FICE 1972 (memb Cncl 1993–96), MConsE 1972, FEng 1993; *Books* Kempe's Engineers Year Book (Water Supply Chapter 1970–), Civil Engineering Reference Book (Water Supply Section); *Recreations* bridge, sailing, painting; *Clubs* Royal Cwlth Soc; *Style*— Prof Brian Rofe, FEng; ✉ Laleham Cottage, 40 Churchfield Rd, Walton-on-Thames, Surrey KT12 2SY (☎ 01932 223147); Rofe Kennard & Lapworth, Raffety House, 2 Sutton Court Road, Sutton SM1 4SS (☎ 0181 643 8201, fax 0181 642 8469)

ROFFE, Clive Brian; JP (1987); s of Philip Roffe (d 1961); *b* 4 June 1935; *Educ* Brighton Coll; *m* 1966, Jacqueline Carole, *née* Branston; 2 da (Danielle Philippa Geraldine b 1970, Natasha Nicole b 1974); *Career* Lloyd's underwriter 1966, fin conslt; chm: Melbo Petroleum Ltd 1970, Edinburgh Insurance Services 1971, Offshore Investments Ltd 1968, Gemini Business Centre 1992; co dir; Freeman City of London; Liveryman Worshipful Co of Bakers, memb Ct of Assts Worshipful Co of Upholders; *Recreations* organ, philately, jogging; *Clubs* RAC, Guards Polo, City Livery, Lloyd's Yacht; *Style*— Clive Roffe, Esq, JP; ✉ 50 Kingsway Court, Hove, Sussex (☎ 01273 737 044)

ROGER, David Bernard; s of John Grant Roger, of Newstead, Scotland, and Margaret Jean, *née* Dymock; *b* 23 Feb 1951; *Educ* Melville Coll Edinburgh, Univ of Newcastle upon Tyne (BA), Univ of Bristol (MA), Univ of Paris (Scenographic Diploma), ENO theatre design course; *Career* theatre designer; designs incl: La Mort de Zarathustra (Lucernaire Paris) 1979–80, The Mission (Soho Poly) 1982, The Knot Garden (Opera Factory) 1984, Akhnaten (ENO) 1985, La Boheme (Opera North) 1986, Temptation (RSC The Other Place) 1987, Faust parts 1 and 2 (Lyric Hammersmith) 1988, Simplicius Simplicissimus 1989, Cosi Fan Tutte (TV version Channel 4) 1989, Figaro (Opera Factory Zurich) 1990, Morte d'Arthur (Lyric Hammersmith) 1990, Manon Lescaut (Opera Comique Paris) 1990, Don Giovanni (TV version Channel 4) 1990, The Fiery Angel (Kirov St Petersburg, Royal Opera House and NY Met Opera) 1991–92, The Return of Ulysses (ENO) 1992, The Coronation of Poppea (Opera Factory) 1992, The Bacchae (Opera Factory) 1993; memb Soc of Br Theatre Designers; *Clubs* 2 Brydges Place; *Style*— David Roger, Esq; ✉ Garricks Management, 7 Garrick Street, London WC2E 9AR (☎ 0171 240 0660, fax 0171 497 9242)

ROGER, Peter Charles Marshall; s of Matthew McCargo Roger (d 1977), and Muriel Ethel, *née* Morrison (d 1993); *b* 11 April 1942; *Educ* Glasgow HS; *m* 21 April 1972, Fiona Ann, da of James Murray (d 1986); 2 s (Kenneth b 1975, Andrew b 1979), 1 da (Alison b 1982); *Career* CA, Thomson McLintock & Co 1964–71, Speirs & Jeffrey 1971–, chm Stock Exchange Scot Unit 1989–91; MICAS 1964; *Recreations* golf; *Clubs* Prestwick, Pollok, Boat of Garten; *Style*— Peter Roger, Esq; ✉ 36 Renfield St, Glasgow G2 1NA (☎ 0141 248 4311, fax 0141 221 4764)

ROGERS, Allan Ralph; MP (Lab) Rhondda (majority 28,816); s of John and Madeleine Rogers; *b* 24 Oct 1932; *Educ* University Coll of Swansea; *m* 1955, Ceridwen James; 1 s, 3 d; *Career* sometime geologist, teacher, visiting prof Univ of Glamorgan; MEP (Lab) SE Wales 1979–84, vice pres Euro Parl 1979–82; MP (Lab) Rhondda 1983–; oppn spokesman on: defence 1987–92, foreign affrs 1992–; memb Intelligence and Security Ctee; *Style*— Allan Rogers Esq, MP; ✉ House of Commons, London SW1A 0AA (☎ 0171 219 3560, fax 0171 219 5909)

ROGERS, Prof (Claude) Ambrose; s of Sir Leonard Rogers, KCSI, CIE, FRS (d 1962), and Una Elsie North (d 1951); *b* 1 Nov 1920; *Educ* Berkhamsted Sch, UCL, Birkbeck Coll London (BSc, PhD, DSc); *m* 1952, Joan Marian, wid of W G Gordon and da of F North; 2 da; *Career* experimental offr Miny of Supply 1940–45; lectr and reader UCL 1946–54, prof of pure mathematics Univ of Birmingham 1954–58, Astor prof of mathematics UCL 1958–86; pres London Mathematical Soc 1970–72; chm Jt Mathematical Cncl 1981–84; prof emeritus Univ of London 1986; FRS 1959; *Books* Packing and Covering (1964), Hausdorff Measures (1970), Analytic Sets (1980); *Style*— Prof Ambrose Rogers, FRS; ✉ 8 Grey Close, London NW11 6QG (☎ 0181 455 8027)

ROGERS, Anthony Crawford Nugent; s of (Sidney) Crawford Rogers (d 1964), of Bardowie, and Joan Diane, *née* Nugent; *b* 22 July 1938; *Educ* Larchfield Sch Helensburgh, Second Glasgow Acad, Univ of Glasgow (MB ChB, FRCS, FRCPS); *m* 4 June 1964, Teresa Rhind (Terri), da of Lt Cdr Eric Patrick (d 1944), of Glasgow; 3 da (Sarah Jane b 1965, Jennifer Diane b 1966, Gillian Victoria b 1970); *Career* registrar in surgery Glasgow 1966–68, registrar in urology Newcastle upon Tyne 1968–72, sr registrar urology Aberdeen 1972–76, conslt urologist Stirling and Falkirk 1976–, dir of surgical specialities 1993–; sr coach Jumps; memb: BMA, BAUS; *Recreations* athletics coaching; *Clubs* Central Region Athletic; *Style*— Anthony Rogers, Esq; ✉ Stirling Royal Infirmary NHS Trust, Livilands, Stirling FK8 2AU (☎ 01786 434000)

ROGERS, Maj Gen Anthony Peter Vernon (Tony); OBE (1985); s of Kenneth David Rogers (d 1983), and Eileen, *née* Emmott; *b* 10 July 1942; *Educ* Highgate Sch, Coll of Law, Univ of Liverpool (LLM); *m* 31 July 1965, Anne-Katrin Margarethe, da of Dr Ewald Lembke; 2 da (Denise Claudia b 25 Aug 1966, Julia Simone b 12 July 1969); *Career* articled clerk London 1959–64, admitted slr 1965; cmmnd Army Legal Servs 1968, Capt 1968–73, Maj 1973–81, Lt Col 1981–89, Col 1989–92, Brig 1992–94, Maj Gen 1994–, currently dir Army Legal Servs; vice-pres Int Soc for Mil Law and the Law of War 1994– (memb 1979–); memb: Law Soc 1965, Int Inst of Humanitarian Law 1993 (chm Ctee for Mil Instruction 1993–); FRSA 1995; *Books* Law on the Battlefield (1995); *Recreations* music and the Arts, playing the piano (especially as an accompanist), walking (preferably in mountains), cricket; *Style*— Maj Gen Tony Rogers, OBE; ✉ Army Legal Services, Ministry of Defence, Trenchard Lines, Upavon, Pewsey, Wilts SN9 6BE (☎ 01980 615966, fax 01980 615978)

ROGERS, Prof Colin; s of William Joseph Rogers (d 1952), and Margaret Anne Gwendoline, *née* Goodgame (d 1971); *b* 1 Dec 1940; *Educ* Magdalen Coll Sch Oxford, Univ of Oxford (BA), Univ of Toronto (MEd), Univ of Nottingham (MSc, PhD, DSc); *Career* lectr Univ of Nottingham 1968–71; assoc prof: Old Dominion Univ Virginia USA 1973–74, Univ of W Ontario Canada 1974–78 (asst prof 1971–73); visiting prof Univ of Adelaide Aust 1975, sr visitor Dept of Applied Mathematics and Theoretical Physics Univ of Cambridge 1979, prof Univ of Waterloo Canada 1981–88 (assoc prof 1978–81), visiting prof Georgia Inst of Technol USA 1982 and 1984, chair mathematical engrg Loughborough Univ of Technology 1988–92, chair applied mathematics Univ of New South Wales 1992–; adjunct princ res scientist Georgia Inst Technol 1989–; FInstP; *Books* Bäcklund Transformations and Their Applications (with W F Shadwick, 1982), Wave Phenomena: Modern Theory and Applications (ed with T B Moodie, 1986), Nonlinear Boundary Value Problems in Science and Engineering (with W F Ames, 1989), Nonlinear Equations in the Applied Sciences (ed with W F Ames, 1991); *Recreations* Welsh studies, athletics (Canadian National Masters Cross Country and 10,000 metres champion 1981); *Style*— Prof Colin Rogers; ✉ 5E/8 Hampden Street, Paddington, Sydney 2021, NSW (☎ 00 61 2 332 4137); School of Mathematics, University of New South Wales, Sydney 2052, NSW, Australia (☎ 00 61 2 385 2995)

ROGERS, Colin Stuart; s of George Stuart Rogers (d 1982), and Jean Ritchie Christian, of Farningham, Kent; *b* 6 Feb 1947; *Educ* St Olave's GS London, Univ of Essex (BA, MA); *m* 24 Nov 1972, Deborah, *née* Mortimer; 2 s (Benedict Randall b 19 June 1973, Thomas Mortimer b 6 Feb 1977); *Career* with ATV Network then Central Independent Television 1972–80: variously head of scripts, prodr of children's drama, prodr of single plays, ATV rep on ITV Network Children's Prog Ctee and ITV Labour Rels Ctee, latterly prodr of drama series Central Television; freelance prodr 1980–85 (series incl Spyship and Anna of the Five Towns, films incl Three Minute Heroes, Atlantis and The Groundling and the Kite for Play for Today and Space Station Milton Keynes for Screen Two; dir three shorts for The Golden Oldie Picture Show); BBC TV: exec prodr 1986–90, dep head Drama Series and Serials Dept 1986–88, prodr of series incl All Passion Spent 1986 (nominated BAFTA Best Drama Series), A Perfect Spy 1987 (winner TRIC Best BBC TV Series Award 1988, nominated BAFTA Best Drama Series 1988 and Best Mini-series Emmy 1989), Summer's Lease 1989 (nominated BAFTA Best Drama Series 1990); exec prodr Thin Air 1987, Sophia and Constance 1988, Shadow of the Noose 1989, Portrait of a Marriage 1990 (Grand Prize Banff Festival 1991), Spender (created with Jimmy Nail and Ian la Frenais) 1991; estab independent film drama prodn co Deco Films and Television Ltd 1990 (prodns incl continuing series of Resnick drama serials for BBC 1992–), concurrently controller of drama Meridian Broadcasting Ltd 1991–95; at Meridian exec prodr of: Harnessing Peacocks (Gold Nymph Award Best Film and Silver Nymph Award Best Screenplay Monte Carlo Festival 1994) 1993, Under the Hammer 1994, The Ruth Rendell Mysteries 1994 and 1995 (Master of the Moor Silver Medal NY Festival 1995), The Vacillations of Poppy Carew 1994, The English Wife 1995; chm and chief exec Deco Group of Companies 1995– (prodr film Peggy Su 1996); memb Nat Advsy Ctee Kent Literature Festival 1993–; FRTS (memb cncl 1995–); memb: BAFTA, PACT; *Books* A Bunch of Fives (1977); *Clubs* Groucho; *Style*— Colin Rogers, Esq; ✉ Deco Films and Television Ltd, 114 Brackenbury Road, London W6 0BD (☎ and fax 0181 748 0448)

ROGERS, David Bryan; CB (1984); s of Frank and Louisa Rogers; *b* 8 Sept 1929; *Educ* Grove Park Wrexham, UCL (BA); *m* 1955, Marjory Geraldine Gilmour, *née* Horribine; 1 s, 2 da; *Career* inspr of taxes 1953, princ inspr 1968, sr princ inspr 1976, under sec and dir of Operations Bd of Inland Revenue 1978–81, dep sec and DG Bd Inland Revenue 1981–89; memb Cncl UCL 1983–93; *Recreations* piano, organ, singing; *Style*— Bryan Rogers, Esq, CB

ROGERS, David Owen; s of Alan Edgar Rogers (d 1983), of Haslemere, Surrey, and Joan Grace, *née* Thornhill; *b* 5 May 1952; *Educ* Royal GS Guildford Surrey, Kingston-Upon-Hull Coll of Commerce (HND Business Studies); *m* 21 Aug 1982, Deborah June, da of Brian Geoffrey Sharp, of Seaford, E Sussex; 3 da (Jennifer Clare b 1984, Josephine Kate b 1986, Caroline Mary b 1990), 1 s (Timothy Alan b 1993); *Career* Rank Leisure Services Ltd 1973–77, EMI Records Ltd 1978–79, Office of Population Censuses and Surveys 1980–84, house husband 1984–; longstanding memb Lib Pty, fndr memb

SLD (now Lib Democrats); first elected to E Sussex CC 1977, ldr E Sussex CC and chair Policy and Resources Ctee 1993–; memb for: Brighton (St Nicholas) 1977–85, Brighton (Seven Dials) 1985–89, Newhaven 1989–; ldr Lib Democrat Gp (and its precursors: Lib, Alliance, Democrat) E Sussex CC 1977–, elected to Brighton Borough Cncl as memb for St Nicholas Ward 1979–83 and Seven Dials Ward 1983–91, ldr Newhaven Town Cncl 1991–94 (cncllr 1989–); Lewes DC: cncllr Newhaven Meeching Ward 1991–, chm Leisure and Community Servs Ctee 1991–96; chm Lewes Constituency Lib Democrats 1989–91; ALDC (formerly ALC, then ASLDC) 1977–; non-exec dir E Sussex, Brighton & Hove Health Authy 1996; *Style—* David Rogers, Esq; ✉ 74 Fort Rd, Newhaven, East Sussex BN9 9EJ (☎ and fax 01273 512 172)

ROGERS, Sir Frank Jarvis; kt (1988); s of Percy Rogers (d 1960), and Elsie Mary Rogers (d 1956); *b* 24 Feb 1920; *Educ* Wolstanton GS; *m* 1949, Esma Sophia, *née* Holland; 2 da; *Career* military serv 1940–46; journalist; Daily Mirror Newspapers Ltd 1937–49, gen mangr Nigerian Daily Times 1949–52, mangr Argus Melbourne 1952–55, md Overseas Newspapers 1958–60, dir Daily Mirror 1960–63, md IPC 1963–70, chm Nat Newspaper Steering Gp 1970–72, dir Newspaper Publishers' Assoc 1971–73; chm: British Exec Ctee Int Press Inst 1978–88, Exec Ctee Industrial Soc 1976–79, EMAP plc (formerly East Midlands Allied Press Ltd) 1973–90; dir Plessey New Jersey Inc, advsr Corp Affrs Plessey Co Ltd 1973–81, chm Ansafone Ltd 1981–85, dep chm The Telegraph plc 1986–96, dir Telegraph Group Limited 1996–, dir Reuters Founders Share Co 1989–, chm Euro Publishers Cncl 1991–, chm Newspaper Publishers' Assoc 1990–; *Recreations* golf, travel; *Clubs* Moor Park Golf; *Style—* Sir Frank Rogers; ✉ Greensleeves, Loudwater Drive, Loudwater, Rickmansworth, Herts WD3 4HJ; The Daily Telegraph, 1 Canada Square, Canary Wharf, London E14 5DT

ROGERS, Ian Richard; s of Sqdn Ldr R C G T Rogers, of Leith Hill, nr Dorking, Surrey, and Mary Frances, *née* Jory; *b* 5 Dec 1948; *Educ* Truro Public Sch; *m* Paula Louise, *née* Ogden; 1 s (Dominic Ian b 8 April 1969), 1 da (Danielle Louise b 11 Dec 1974); *Career* media mangr Maxwell Clarke 1968–70 (media exec/prodn trainee 1966–67), planner/buyer Lonsdale Crowther 1970–72, group head The Media Department (TMD) 1972–74, advtg and media controller Cadbury Schweppes 1974–76, dep media dir Colman RSCG 1976–80; CIA Group plc: dir of planning and non-bdcast buying 1980–89, dep md 1989–91, md 1991–92; md CIA Media UK Ltd 1992–94, chief exec CIA Medianetwork UK Ltd 1994–95, ret; recipient numerous media awards; FInstD; *Recreations* collecting and restoring classic sports cars, antiques, painting, reading, tennis, squash; *Clubs* Wig & Pen, IOD; *Style—* Ian Rogers, Esq

ROGERS, Jane Rosalind; da of Prof Andrew W Rogers (d 1989), and Margaret Kathleen, *née* Farmer; *b* 21 July 1952; *Educ* New Hall Cambridge (BA), Univ of Leicester (Postgrad Teaching Cert); *m* Michael L Harris; 1 s (Laurence Jay b 1984), 1 da (Kate Lucy b 1981); *Career* novelist and playwright; Arts Cncl writer in residence Northern Coll Barnsley 1985–86, writer in residence Sheffield Poly 1987, Judith E Wilson visiting writer/fell Univ of Cambridge 1991, teacher Creative Writing MA Sheffield Hallam Univ 1994–; memb Soc of Authors; FRSL 1994; *Novels* Separate Tracks (1983), Her Living Image (1984, Somerset Maugham award 1985), The Ice is Singing (1987), Mr Wroe's Virgins (1991), Promised Lands (1995); *TV work* Dawn and the Candidate (C4 1989, Samuel Beckett award 1990), Mr Wroe's Virgins (BBC adaptation 1993); *Recreations* walking, travel, reading; *Style—* Ms Jane Rogers, FRSL; ✉ c/o Pat Kavanagh, Peters Fraser & Dunlop, 503/4 The Chambers, Chelsea Harbour, London SW10 0XF (☎ 0171 344 1000, fax 0171 352 7356)

ROGERS, (Leonard) John; OBE (1979); s of Leonard Samuel Rogers, JP (d 1964) of Croydon, Surrey, and Amy Mary, *née* Martlew (d 1958); *b* 30 Oct 1931; *Educ* Whitgift Sch Croydon, Städtisches und Staatliches Gymnasium Neuss am Rhein, Trinity Coll Cambridge (MA); *m* 16 July 1955, Avery Janet, da of Hugh Griffith Ernest Morgan (d 1968), of Croydon, Surrey; 4 s (Paul b 1956, Nicholas b 1958, Jonathan b 1962, Crispin b 1966); *Career* Nat Serv, E Surrey Regt 1950, Eaton Hall OCS 1951, Lt Intelligence Corps BAOR 1951–52; export contracts administrator (Guided Weapons) Bristol Aircraft Ltd 1958–60, asst sec Bristol Aeroplane Plastics Ltd 1960–62, export contracts mangr (Commercial Aircraft Div) Br Aircraft Corp 1965–73, business dir BAC Commercial Aircraft Div 1973 (sales dir 1977), divnl mktg dir British Aerospace 1978–79, aviation conslt Roconsult AG Zug Schweiz 1980–84; dir: AIM Group plc 1984–93 (non-exec dir 1994–), AIM Aviation Ltd 1984–93; md AIM Aviation (Henshalls) Ltd 1984–93 (aviation business advsr 1994–); memb Assoc Members' Ctee Soc of British Aerospace Cos; Methodist Church: Dorking and Horsham circuit steward 1977–82, memb Euro Affairs Ctee 1980–86 and 1989–91, sec Connexional 1988 Steering Ctee 1986–89, led Wesley 250th Anniversary Pilgrimage to Moravian Church in Herrnhut GDR 1988; memb: Gen Purposes Ctee London Voluntary Serv Cncl 1980–83, Romanian Trade Ctee London C of C 1975–83; Freeman City of London 1979, Liveryman Worshipful Co of Coachmakers and Coach Harness Makers 1979; FInstD 1978, ARAeS 1989; *Recreations* European languages, opera, roses, family history; *Clubs* IOD; *Style—* John Rogers, Esq, OBE; ✉ Willow Pool, Effingham, Surrey KT24 5JG (☎ 01372 458359); AIM Aviation (Henshalls) Ltd, Abbot Close, Oyster Lane, W Byfleet, Surrey KT14 7JT (☎ 01932 351011, fax 01932 352792, telex 928460 WHS G)

ROGERS, Very Rev John; s of William Harold Rogers (d 1982), and Annie Mary, *née* Howells; *b* 27 Nov 1934; *Educ* Jones' West Monmouthshire Sch, St David's Coll Lampeter (BA), Oriel Coll Oxford (MA), St Stephen's House Oxford; *m* 29 July 1972, Pamela Mary, da of Frederick Charles Goddard; 1 s (Paul James Rogers b 17 Aug 1973), 1 da (Sarah Ann (twin)); *Career* ordained: deacon 1959, priest 1960; asst curate Roath St Martin 1959–63, parish priest Dio of Guyana 1963–71; vicar: Caldicot 1971–77, Monmouth 1977–84; rural dean Monmouth 1981–84, rector Ebbw Vale 1984–93, rural dean Blaenau Gwent 1988–93, canon of St Woolos Cathedral 1988–93, dean of Llandaff 1993–; *Recreations* gardening, beer and wine making; *Style—* The Very Rev the Dean of Llandaff; ✉ The Deanery, The Cathedral Green, Llandaff, Cardiff CF5 2YF (☎ 01222 561545)

ROGERS, John Michael Thomas; QC (1979); s of Harold Stuart Rogers, and Sarah Joan Thomas, *née* Bibby; *b* 13 May 1938; *Educ* Rydal Sch, Birkenhead Sch, Fitzwilliam House Cambridge (MA, LLB); *m* 1971, Jennifer Ruth; 1 da (Caitlin Sarah b 1981); *Career* called to Bar Gray's Inn 1963, recorder of the Crown Ct 1976, ldr Wales and Chester Circuit 1990–92, bencher Gray's Inn 1990–; *Clubs* Reform, Pragmatists; *Style—* John Rogers, Esq, QC; ✉ 9 Gough Square, London EC4A 3DE (☎ 0171 353 5371)

ROGERS, Air Chief Marshal Sir John Robson; KCB (1981), CBE (1971); s of B Rogers; *b* 11 Jan 1928; *Educ* Brentwood Sch, RAF Coll Cranwell; *m* 1955, Gytha, *née* Campbell; 2 s, 2 da; *Career* dir-gen Orgn RAF 1977–79, Air Vice-Marshal 1977, AOC Trg Units HQ RAF Support Cmd 1979–81, Air Marshal 1981, Air Memb Supply and Orgn 1981–83, Controller Aircraft 1983–86, Air Chief Marshal 1984; vice chm RAC, chm RAC Motor Sports Assoc; FRAeS; *Recreations* motor sport; *Clubs* RAF, RAC; *Style—* Air Chief Marshal Sir John Rogers, KCB, CBE; ✉ c/o Lloyds Bank, 27 High St, Colchester, Essex

ROGERS, His Hon Judge; John Willis; QC (1975); s of Reginald John Rogers (d 1940); *b* 7 Nov 1929; *Educ* Sevenoaks Sch, Fitzwilliam Coll Cambridge (MA); *m* 1952, Sheila Elizabeth, *née* Cann; 1 da (Mary b 1 Jan 1955), 1 s (James b 9 March 1958); *Career* called to the Bar Lincoln's Inn 1955, bencher 1984; first prosecuting counsel to Inland Revenue S Eastern Circuit 1969–75, recorder 1974–91, hon recorder for City of Canterbury 1985–, circuit judge (SE Circuit) 1991–; chm Advsy Ctee on Conscientious Objectors 1991–; *Recreations* cricket, gardening, music, change ringing; *Clubs* Garrick, MCC, Band of Brothers; *Style—* His Hon Judge Rogers, QC; ✉ 3 Serjeants' Inn, London, EC4Y 1BQ (☎ 0171 353 5537)

ROGERS, Keith (real name Keith Chanter); s of Albert Ernest Chanter, of South Molton, Devon, and Jenny, *née* Jones; *b* 19 June 1947; *Educ* Barnstaple GS Devon; *m* 1977 (m dis 1991), Suzan Mary Jervis; *Career* club DJ 1966–70, music presenter and newsreader Radio Nordsee 1970–72, music presenter and head of news Radio Atlantis 1974, music presenter and head of music Radio Orwell Ipswich 1975–81, music presenter and head of music Essex Radio 1981–89, prog dir Breeze AM from launch 1989–95, freelance 1995–; memb Radio Acad; *Recreations* cinema, theatre, travel, countryside; *Style—* Keith Rogers, Esq

ROGERS, Malcolm Austin; s of James Eric Rogers, and Frances Anne, *née* Elsey; *b* 3 Oct 1948; *Educ* Oakham Sch Rutland, Magdalen Coll Oxford, ChCh Oxford (MA, DPhil); *Career* Nat Portrait Gallery: asst keeper 1974–83, dep dir 1983–94, keeper 1985–94; dir Museum of Fine Arts Boston 1994–; Liveryman Worshipful Co of Girdlers; FSA 1986; *Books* Dictionary of British Portraiture 4 Vols (jt ed, 1979–81), Museums and Galleries of London Blue Guide (1983, 3 edn 1992), William Dobson (1983), John and John Baptist Closterman: A Catalogue of their Works (1983), Elizabeth II: Portraits of Sixty Years (1986), Camera Portraits (1989), Montacute House (1991), Companion Guide to London (ed with Sir David Piper, 1992), The English Face (ed with Sir David Piper, 1992), Boughton House: The English Versailles (contrib, 1992), Master Drawings from the National Portrait Gallery (1993); *Recreations* food, wine, music, travel; *Clubs* Beefsteak, Algonquin Club Boston (hon memb); *Style—* Malcolm Rogers, Esq, FSA; ✉ 20 Charles River Square, Boston, MA 02114, USA (☎ 00 1 617 267 9300)

ROGERS, Martin John; s of Douglas John Rogers, of S Wales, and Mary, *née* Sayce; *b* 21 July 1955; *Educ* Bargod GS, Univ Coll of Wales Aberystwyth (BSc); *m* 1977, Beth, da of Peter Jones; 3 da (Lucy Elizabeth b 31 Jan 1981, Kate Elinore b 2 Feb 1983, Sophie Jane b 11 May 1987); *Career* Pannell Kerr Forster: joined Cardiff Office 1976, ptnr 1985, sr ptnr Derby 1989–96; sr ptnr Coopers & Lybrand Derby 1996–; FCA 1979, MInstD; *Recreations* shooting, sailing, skiing; *Clubs* RAC; *Style—* Martin Rogers, Esq; ✉ Coopers & Lybrand, Wilmot House, St James Court, Friar Gate, Derby DE1 1BT (☎ 01332 372936, fax 01332 254080)

ROGERS, Martin John Wyndham; s of John Frederick Rogers (d 1985), of Oxshott, Surrey, and Grace Mary, *née* Stride (d 1971); *b* 9 April 1931; *Educ* Oundle, Heidelberg Univ, Trinity Hall Cambridge (MA), Univ of Oxford (MA) 1995; *m* 31 August 1957, Jane, da of Harold Alfred Cook (d 1978), of Cobham, Surrey; 2 s (Mark Wyndham Edward b 31 May 1959, Stephen James Wyndham b 17 June 1961), 1 da (Sarah Lucy b 24 June 1966); *Career* Henry Wiggin & Co 1953–55; Westminster Sch 1955–71: asst master 1955–60, sr chem master 1960–64, housemaster 1964–66, under master and master The Queen's Scholars 1967–71; headmaster Malvern Coll 1971–82, chief master King Edward's Sch Birmingham and headmaster of the Schs of King Edward VI in Birmingham 1982–91, dir Farmington Inst for Christian Studies Oxford and fell Manchester Coll Oxford 1991–; seconded as Nuffield res fell (O level chem project) 1962–64, Salters' Co fell Dept of Chem Engrg and Chem Technol Imperial Coll London 1969; chm: Curriculum Ctees of HMC, GSA and IAPS 1979–86, HMC 1987, Arkwright Ctee 1991–, Sanderson Tst 1991–, European Cncl for the Nat Assocs of Independent Schs 1994–; memb Court and Cncl Univ of Birmingham 1985–92; govr: Oundle Sch 1988–, Westonbirt Sch 1991–, Elmhurst Ballet Sch 1991–; memb Cncl GPDST 1991–94, govr English Coll in Prague 1992–; *Books* John Dalton and the Atomic Theory (1965), Chemistry and Energy (1968), Foreground Chemistry Series (ed 1968), Gas Syringe Experiments (1970), Facts, Patterns and Principles (jtly, 1970), Francis Bacon and the Birth of Modern Science (1981); *Recreations* family life, history of science in 16th and 17th centuries; *Clubs* East India; *Style—* Martin Rogers, Esq; ✉ Eastwards, Millwood End, Long Hanborough, Oxfordshire OX8 8BX (☎ 01993 881292, fax 01993 883930); The Farmington Institute, Harris Manchester College, Mansfield Road, Oxford OX1 3TD (☎ 01865 271965/6, fax 01865 271969)

ROGERS, Prof (John) Michael; s of John Patrick Rogers (d 1961), of Dalton-in-Furness, Lancs, and Constance Mary, *née* Fisher (d 1994); *b* 25 Jan 1935; *Educ* Ulverston GS, CCC Oxford (BA, MA), Oriel Coll Oxford (BPhil), Pembroke Coll Oxford (DPhil); *Career* Nat Serv RA 1953–55, later Capt Intelligence Corps TA; res fell Oriel Coll Oxford 1958–61, philosophy tutor Pembroke and Wadham Coll Oxford 1961–65, asst then assoc prof American Univ in Cairo 1965–77, asst then dep keeper Dept of Oriental Antiquities Br Museum 1977–, Khalili prof of Islamic art and archaeology SOAS Univ of London 1991–, Slade prof Univ of Oxford 1991–92; advsr NACF, memb Editorial Ctee Burlington Magazine, corr memb Deutsches Archäologisches Institut (1989); FSA 1974, FBA 1988; Order Egyptian Republic Class II 1969; *Books* The Spread of Islam (1976), Islamic Art and Design 1500–1700 (1983), Süleyman the Magnificent (with R M Ward, 1980), Mughal Painting (1993), The Uses of Anachronism on Methodological Diversity in the History of Islamic Art (1994), Empire of the Sultans. Ottoman art from the collection of Nasser D Khalili (Musée d'art et d'histoire Geneva, 1995); author of numerous articles on arts, architecture and economic history of Islam; *Recreations* music, mountains, botany; *Clubs* Beefsteak; *Style—* Prof Michael Rogers, FBA, FSA; ✉ SOAS, University of London, Thornhaugh Street, Russell Square, London WC1H 0XG (☎ 0171 323 6259, fax 0171 436 3844, telex 291829 SOASP)

ROGERS, Prof Michael Howard; s of Victor George Rogers, BEM (d 1960), of Great Bookham, Surrey, and Amy Rosa, *née* Laskey; *b* 20 May 1930; *Educ* Dorking HS, King's Coll London (BSc, PhD); *m* 21 Dec 1957, (Margaret) Jennifer, da of Joseph Wells Lucas (d 1972), of Dronfield, Derbyshire; 2 s (Keith b 1961, d 1996, Ian b 1965), 1 da (Helen b 1960); *Career* res assoc in astronomy Univ of Illinois 1954–57, sr lectr in mathematics Royal Military Coll of Sci Shrivenham 1957–58, prof of computer sci Univ of Bristol 1966–95 (lectr in mathematics 1958–66); memb cncl Clifton Coll; FBCS 1963, FRSA 1975; *Books* Meta-Programming in Logic Programming (jt ed with H Abrahamson, 1989); *Recreations* music, gardening; *Style—* Prof Michael Rogers; ✉ Woodlands Farm, Abson, Bristol BS15 5TT (☎ 0117 937 2126)

ROGERS, Nicholas Emerson (Nick); s of Reginald Emerson Rogers (d 1983), of 3 Fairfield Rd, Petts Wood, Kent, and Doreen, *née* Burbidge (d 1991); *b* 15 March 1946; *Educ* Charterhouse, Orpington Secdy Modern Sch; *m* 26 Oct 1973 (m dis 1994), Linda Jane; *Career* photographer: The Sunday Independent Plymouth 1968–70, The Reading Evening Post 1970–72; staff photographer The Daily Mail 1973–78; dep picture ed The Observer 1984–86; feature photographer: The Times 1986–90, The European 1990, The Sunday Telegraph 1990–; Kodak Industl and Commercial Photographer of the Year 1987, Feature Photographer of the Year Br Press Awards 1988, commended Nikon Awards 1988; memb: RPS, NUJ, BPPA; *Recreations* photography, sailing, walking, travel; *Style—* Nick Rogers, Esq; ✉ 19 Chatsworth Road, Chiswick, London W4 3HY (☎ 0181 742 8476, car 0860 380347); The Sunday Telegraph, 1 Canada Square, Canary Wharf, London E14 5DT (☎ 0171 538 7372)

ROGERS, Nigel David; s of Thomas Rogers (d 1980), of Wellington, Shropshire, and Winifred May, *née* Roberts; *b* 21 March 1935; *Educ* Wellington GS, King's Coll Cambridge (BA, MA), Hochschule für Musik Munich; *m* 1, 14 Oct 1961, Frederica Bement (d 1992), da of Edmund Parker Lord (d 1985), of Framingham, Mass, USA; 1 da (Lucasta Julia Webster b 26 May 1970); m 2, 1991; *Career* singer and conductor; debut Studio der Frühen Musik, Munich 1961, specialised as leading exponent of baroque style of singing 1964–; performances of baroque operas in England, Germany, Holland, Poland, Switzerland and Austria, world-wide concerts and recitals; numerous recordings incl: Monteverdi 1610 Vespers, Monteverdi Orfeo, songs of John Dowland, Schütz, Christmas Story; Schubert, Die Schöne Müllerin; 17 C Airs de Cour etc; founder: Chiaroscuro Vocal Ensemble 1979, Chiaroscuro Baroque Orch 1987; conducted baroque orchs in Italy, Spain, Switzerland, Lithuania; teacher Schola Cantorum Basiliensis Basle 1972–, prof of singing RCM London 1979–; Hon RCM 1981; *Books* Companion to Baroque Music (Chapter on Voice, 1991); *Recreations* country life, wine, travel; *Style*— Nigel Rogers, Esq; ✉ Royal College of Music, Prince Consort Rd, London SW7 2BS (☎ 0171 589 3643, fax 0171 589 7740)

ROGERS, Nigel Harold John; s of Harold Rogers, of Prittlewell, Essex, and Lorna Mildred Rogers; *b* 18 Sept 1949; *Educ* Southend HS; *m* 1, 1 Oct 1977 (m dis April 1988), Linda Elizabeth Hardy; m 2, 29 Sept 1989, Julia Kim Rogers; 2 da (Sophie Isabella and Lucy Mae (twins) b 30 Jan 1992); *Career* md Octavian Group Ltd 1980–; memb Lloyd's; FCA; *Recreations* skiing, riding, shooting; *Style*— Nigel Rogers, Esq; ✉ Octavian Group Ltd, 84 Fenchurch St, London EC3M 4BY (☎ 0171 265 0371, fax 0171 481 1631)

ROGERS, (Thomas Gordon) Parry; CBE (1991); s of Victor Frank Rogers (d 1947), of Harrow, Middx, and Ella Mary Rogers; *b* 7 Aug 1924; *Educ* West Hartlepool GS, St Edmund Hall Oxford (MA); *m* 1, 9 April 1947 (m dis 1973), Pamela Mary, da of J Leslie Greene (d 1950); 1 s (Michael b 1951), 7 da (Mary b 1948, Natalie b 1949, Patricia b 1955, Barbara b 1957, Bernadette b 1957, Frances b 1962, Philippa b 1964); m 2, 15 Sept 1973, (Patricia) Juliet, da of Richard D Curtis (d 1986); 1 s (Benedict b 1974), 1 da (Ruth b 1979); *Career* Nat Serv WWII 1944–47 RAC and RAEC; personnel mangr Procter & Gamble 1948–54, chief personnel offr Mars 1954–56, personnel dir Hardy Spicer 1956–61, dir of external affrs IBM (UK) 1971–74 (personnel dir 1961–71); Plessey: personnel dir 1974–78, dir personnel and Europe 1978–86, chm Plessey Pension Tst 1978–86; chm Percom Ltd 1985–94; dir: Prima Europe Ltd, Ocean Gp plc 1988–95, BNB Resources plc 1988–94, NB Selection Ltd 1988–94; chm: Salisbury Health Authy 1985–90, Business and Technician Educn Cncl 1986–94, SW London Coll HEC 1988–91, ECCTIS 2000 Ltd 1990–; memb: Clegg Cmmn, Butcher Ctee, DHSS Review, Employment Appeal Tbnl; govr: Ashridge Management Coll 1985–94, Warminster Sch 1989–, St Mary's Sch Shaftesbury 1991–94; Freeman City of London 1987, Liveryman Worshipful Co of Information Technologists; CIMgt 1980, CIPM 1980, FRSA 1978; *Books* Recruitment and Training of Graduates (1967); *Recreations* golf, tennis, birdwatching, music; *Clubs* Savile, Sherborne Golf; *Style*— Parry Rogers, Esq, CBE; ✉ St Edward's Chantry, Bimport, Shaftesbury, Dorset (☎ 01747 852789, fax 01747 851532)

ROGERS, Rev Percival Hallewell (Val); MBE (1945); s of Percy Charles Rogers (d 1956), of Brentwood, Essex, and Olivia Jane, *née* Horne (d 1970); *b* 13 Sept 1912; *Educ* Brentwood Sch, St Edmund Hall Oxford (MA, DipEd), Bishop's Coll Cheshunt, Int Acad for Continuous Educn Sherborne; *m* 1 Jan 1940, (Annie) Mary Stuart, da of Lt-Col James Morwood, IMS (d 1946), of Belfast; 2 s (Julian Hallewell James b 1941, Bruce Henry Arthur b 1946, (k Alpine climbing 1969)), 1 da (Olivia Mary b 1948); *Career* Nat Serv TA 1939, RA 1940, cmmnd 1941 2 Lt RA 1941, War Substantive Lt 1942, Actg Capt 1943, Temp Capt 1944, Actg Maj DAA and QMG Milan 1945, War Substantive Capt and temp Maj 1945 (despatches twice), Maj, released 1946; head of English Dept Haileybury Coll 1936–54, ordained priest St Albans 1948, chaplain Haileybury Coll 1948–54, headmaster Portora Royal Sch Enniskillen 1954–73, chaplain Gresham's Sch Holt 1974–75, dean Int Acad Sherborne 1975–76, asst priest Trinity Church New Orleans 1976–80, dir of ordinands and lay readers Diocese of Clogher 1980–84, priest i/c St Andrew's Sandford on Thames 1985–87; memb: Exec Ctee C of I Bd of Educn 1956–73, Alliance Party for Reconciliation NI 1970–84 (chm Fermanagh Assoc 1983–84); chm Student Christian Movement in Schs Ireland 1956–64, sec UNICEF Co Fermanagh 1982–84, schools lectr for UNICEF Oxford 1987–; memb HMC 1954–73; *Books* A Guide to Divinity Teaching (1962), The Needs of the Whole Man (1971); *Recreations* sailing, boating, chess, music; *Clubs* East India Public Schools and Sports, Union Soc (Oxford); *Style*— The Rev P H Rogers, MBE; ✉ 7 Eyot Place, Oxford OX4 1SA (☎ 01865 244976)

ROGERS, Lady; Ruth; *b* 2 July 1948; *Educ* Colorado Rocky Mountain Sch, Bennington Coll Vermont, London Coll of Printing; *m* 1973, Sir Richard Rogers; 3 step s (Ben b 12 June 1963, Zad b 5 Nov 1965, Ab b 12 July 1968), 2 s (Roo b 18 Jan 1975, Bo b 2 Dec 1983); *Career* Art Dept Penguin Books 1971–73, Richard Rogers Architects 1974–85, chef/owner (with Rose Gray, *qv*) River Cafe 1987–; Italian Restaurant of the Year (The Times) 1988, Best New Restaurant (Courvoisier Best of Best Awards) 1989, Eros Awards (Evening Standard) 1994 and 1995; memb Bd Royal Court Theatre; *Books* The River Cafe Cook Book (with Rose Gray, 1995, Food Book of the Yr Glenfiddich Awards 1996); *Style*— Lady Rogers; ✉ River Cafe, Thames Wharf, Rainville Road, London W6 9HA (☎ 0171 381 8824, fax 0171 381 6217)

ROGERS, Victor Alfred Baden; CBE (1986); s of Henry George Rogers (d 1963), of Norwood Green, Southall, Middx, and Louisa May, *née* Hall (d 1983); *b* 8 March 1926; *Educ* Cranfield Inst of Technol (MSc); *m* 1 April 1950, Jean Valentine, da of Joseph Franklin Stokes (d 1969); 2 s (David Edward b 1954, Peter John b 1962); *Career* Westland Helicopters Ltd: chief designer 1966–72 (Lynx Helicopter 1969–72), tech dir 1972–81 (RAeS Silver medal 1979), dir 1981–84; gp dir and tech dir Westland plc Helicopter and Hovercraft Gp 1984–86; ret 1988; former chm: SBAC (Tech Bd), AECMA (CTI) Europe; former pres RAeS (Yeovil Branch); FRAeS 1963, FIMechE 1972, FEng 1979; *Recreations* music, computers, golf; *Style*— Victor Rogers, Esq, CBE, FEng; ✉ Wrenfield, Bradford Rd, Sherborne, Dorset DT9 6BW (☎ 01935 812007)

ROGERSON, Rt Rev Barry; *see:* Bristol, Bishop of

ROGERSON, Michael Anthony; s of Peter Anthony Rogerson (d 1984), of Virginia Water, Surrey, and Yvonne Marie, *née* Kennedy; *b* 19 Feb 1941; *Educ* Harrow; *m* 27 Sept 1969, Margaret Jane, da of Keith Gordon Blake, CBE (d 1982), of Guildford; 1 s (Richard Pierce Gordon b 1974), 1 da (Belinda Jane b 1971); *Career* Spicer and Pegler: UK 1960–65, Aust 1965–67; Ernst & Whinney 1967–73, ptnr Grant Thorton 1973– (memb Policy Bd 1990–, chm Legal Business Gp 1993–, chm Riche Indust Gps); CBI: memb and past chm London Region, memb Cncl, memb Fin and Gen Purposes Ctee; memb and past chm Marriage Care Cncl; memb Devpt Cncl Univ of Durham; Liveryman Worshipful Co of Skinners 1971; FCA 1965, FIMgt 1982; *Recreations* golf, bridge, gardening, racing; *Clubs* Boodle's, Worplesdon Golf, Trevose Golf; *Style*— Michael Rogerson, Esq; ✉ Plumtree Cottage, Newnham Road, Newnham, Hants RG27 9AE (☎ 01256 767847); Grant Thornton House, Euston Square, London NW1 2EP (☎ 0171 383 5100, fax 0171 387 5356, telex 28984)

ROGERSON, Nicolas; s of Hugh Rogerson (d 1973), and Helen Olivia, *née* Worthington; *b* 21 May 1943; *Educ* Winchester, Magdalene Coll Cambridge (MA); *Career* trainee investmt analyst and staff journalist Investors Chronicle 1964–65, exec Angel Court Consultants 1966–68, currently gp chief exec/dep chm and chm Int Div Dewe Rogerson Ltd (co-fndr 1969); appeals chm King George's Fund for Sailors 1989–; Freeman City of London, memb Worshipful Co of Merchant Tailors 1964; *Recreations* tennis, real tennis, skiing, sailing; *Clubs* Turf, Beefsteak, City of London, Royal Thames Yacht, Racquet (NY),; *Style*— Nicolas Rogerson, Esq; ✉ Dewe Rogerson Group Ltd, 3 1/2 London Wall Buildings, London Wall, London EC2M 5SY (☎ 0171 638 9571, fax 0171 638 7091, mobile 0802 254930)

ROGERSON, Philip Graham; s of Henry Rogerson, and Florence, *née* Dalton; *b* 1 Jan 1945; *Educ* William Hulmes GS Manchester; *m* 21 Dec 1968, Susan Janet, da of Jack Kershaw, of Cleveleys, nr Blackpool, Lancs; 1 s (Simon Andrew b 19 July 1974); 2 da (Penelope Rose b 2 Dec 1971, Hannah Rosemary b 7 April 1988); *Career* various appts with the ICI Group 1978–92 (gen mangr fin ICI plc 1989–92), dep chm British Gas plc 1996– (exec dir 1992–); non-exec dir: Enterprise Oil plc 1987–90, Leeds Permanent Building Society 1994–95, Halifax Building Society 1995–; FCA, MCT; *Recreations* golf, tennis, theatre; *Style*— Philip Rogerson, Esq; ✉ British Gas plc, The Adelphi, John Adam Street, London WC2N 6JT (☎ 0171 821 1444)

ROGISTER, Prof John; s of J J A Rogister (d 1985), of Solihull, and A Rogister, *née* Smal (d 1992); *b* 26 March 1941; *Educ* Solihull Sch, Keble Coll Oxford (pres OU English Club), Univ of Birmingham (BA), Worcester Coll Oxford (DPhil); *m* 1972, Margaret Kathleen, da of late Harold Jury, of New Malden, Surrey; *Career* sr lectr in modern history Univ of Durham 1982– (lectr 1967–82); assoc prof of history Université de Paris X 1982–84; visiting prof Collège de France Paris (Bronze Medal of the Collège) 1987; visiting prof Scuola Normale Superiore Pisa 1988; assoc dir of studies Ecole Pratique des Hautes Etudes (IV Section) Sorbonne Paris 1988–; assoc prof of history Université Paul Valèry Montpellier III 1989–90 (guest prof 1996); pres Int Cmmn for the History of Representative and Parliamentary Insts 1990–; memb Jury for the Prize (lit and history) of the Assoc de la Noblesse de France 1993–; offr Order of the Palmes Acadèmiques (for services to French culture) 1988; memb: Société de l'Histoire de France 1985, Société des Archives Verviétoises (Belgium) 1989; FRHistS 1978; *Publications* Durham University Journal (ed, 1975–81), 1776 American Independence Bicentennial Exhibition Catalogue, National Maritime Museum Greenwich (leading contrib, 1976), Parliaments, Estates and Representation (fndr ed, 1981–90), 16th Biennale Exhibition Catalogue, Casa dell'Uomo (Milan, 1986), Louis XV and the Parlement of Paris 1737–1755 (1994), also author of over 50 articles and reviews; *Recreations* travel, music; *Clubs* United Oxford and Cambridge University, Cercle de l'Union Interalliée (Paris), Fondation Universitaire (Brussels); *Style*— Prof J Rogister; ✉ 4 The Peth, Durham DH1 4PZ (☎ 0191 3864299); Department of History, University of Durham, 43–46 North Bailey, Durham DH1 3EX (☎ 0191 374 2016, fax 0191 374 4754)

ROHATGI, Pradip Krishna (Roy); s of Binay Krishna Rohatgi (d 1961), of Calcutta, India, and Shakuntala Rohatgi; *b* 10 Nov 1939; *Educ* St Xavier's Coll Calcutta, Univ of Calcutta (BCom), Univ of London (BSc); *m* 13 July 1974, Pauline Mary, da of Mervyn Harrold; *Career* sr economist and statistician in industl market res London 1963–66, articled Mann Judd & Co 1966–69; Arthur Andersen: joined 1970, mangr 1973, ptnr 1980, i/c accounting and audit Dubai Office 1980–84, established and ran Indian firm as managing ptnr 1984–89, returned to London as sr ptnr/conslt 1989–91; conslt 1991–; speaker and writer of articles on various business and professional issues; specialist on India related issues; memb: Direct and Indirect Tax Ctee Assoc of C of C in India 1987–89, Exec Ctee Bombay Mgmnt Assoc 1987–89, Main Bd Trade Advsy Ctee for S Asia (DTI) 1992–94, Cncl Rotary Club of London 1992–94; chm Econ Affrs Ctee Indo-American C of C 1986–89, govr Int Students' House London 1991–, hon treas The Children's Med Charity 1992–; ATII 1967, FCA 1969, MBCS 1976, fell Inst of CA's in India 1980; *Recreations* classical guitar, music, fine arts, travel, golf, sailing; *Clubs* Oriental, IOD, Rotary, Royal Over-Seas League, Royal Bombay Yacht; *Style*— Roy Rohatgi, Esq; ✉ 43 Great Brownings, College Road, London SE21 7HP (☎ and fax 0181 670 3512)

RÖHL, Prof John Charles Gerald; s of Dr Hans-Gerhard Röhl (d 1976), of Frankfurt-am-Main, Germany, and Freda Kingsford, *née* Woulfe-Brenan; *b* 31 May 1938; *Educ* Stretford GS, Corpus Christi Coll Cambridge (MA, PhD); *m* 7 Aug 1964, Rosemarie Elfriede, da of Johann Werner von Berg (d 1946), of Hamburg; 1 da (Stephanie Angela b 1965), 2 s (Nicholas John b 1967, Christoph Andreas (twin) b 1967); *Career* RAF 1956–58; prof of history Univ of Sussex 1979– (lectr 1964–73, reader 1973–79, dean Sch of Euro Studies 1982–85); visiting prof of history: Univ of Hamburg 1974, Univ of Freiburg 1977–78; fell: Alexander von Humboldt Fndn 1970–71, Historisches Kolleg Munich 1986–87, Woodrow Wilson Int Center for Scholars Washington DC 1989–90, Inst for Advanced Study Princeton NJ 1994, Moses Mendelssohn Zentrum Potsdam 1996; *Books* Germany Without Bismarck: The Crisis of Government in the Second Reich 1890–1900 (1967), From Bismarck to Hitler: The Problem of Continuity in German History (1970), 1914 - Delusion or Design? The Testimony of Two German Diplomats (1973), Philipp Eulenburgs Politische Korrespondenz (3 vols, 1976–83), Kaiser Wilhelm II - New Interpretations (ed with N Sombart, 1982), Kaiser, Hof und Staat - Wilhelm II und die deutsche Politik (1987), Der Ort Kaiser Wilhelms II in der deutschen Geschichte (ed, 1991), Wilhelm II: Die Jugend des Kaisers 1859–1888 (1993), The Kaiser and his Court: Wilhelm II and the Government of Germany (1994, jt winner Wolfson History Prize 1994); *Recreations* jazz, classical music, walking, bird watching; *Style*— Prof John C G Röhl; ✉ 11 Monckton Way, Kingston, nr Lewes, Sussex BN7 3LD (☎ 01273 472778); School of European Studies, University of Sussex, Brighton BN1 9QN (☎ 01273 678005, fax 01273 623246)

ROITT, Prof Ivan Maurice; *b* 30 Sept 1927; *Educ* King Edward's Sch Birmingham, Balliol Coll Oxford (Domus exhibitioner, BA, DPhil, DSc); *m*; 3 c; *Career* research asst Univ of Leeds 1949–50, postgrad research student Univ of Oxford 1950–52; Middx Hosp Med Sch (now UCL): research fell 1953–65, reader in immunopathology 1965–68, prof and head Dept of Immunology 1968–92, head Dept of Rheumatology Research 1973–92, emeritus prof 1992; head Immunopathology Research Gp Medical Research Cncl 1968; WHO: dir Autoimmune Disorders Reference Library, chm Steering Ctee on Immunological Control of Human Reproduction; dir Multilyte UCL; FRCPath 1974 (MRCPath 1966), FRS 1983, Hon FRSM 1993, Hon FRCP 1995 (Hon MRCP 1985); *Awards* Van Meter Prize American Goitre Assoc 1957, Gairdner Award Toronto 1964, Medal for discovery of thyroid autoimmunity Pisa Univ 1986; *Books* Current Opinion in Immunology, Clinical Immunology (1991), Slide Atlas of Essential Immunology (1992), Encyclopedia of Immunology (1992), Medical Microbiology (1993), Immunology (1993), Essential Immunology (1994); author of over 250 pubns in jls; *Recreations* golf, tennis, music; *Style*— Prof Ivan Roitt; ✉ Department of Immunology, UCL Medical School, Ground Floor, The Windeyer Building, Cleveland Street, London W1P 6DB (☎ 0171 380 9360, fax 0171 380 9400)

ROLAND, Prof Martin; s of Peter Ernest Roland, and Eileen Margaret, *née* Osborne; *b* 7 Aug 1951; *Educ* Rugby, Univ of Oxford (MA, BM BCh, DM, MRCP); *m* Rosalind Jane, *née* Thorburn; 3 s (Christopher, Duncan, Jonathan), 1 da (Alison); *Career* house physician Radcliffe Infirmary Oxford 1975, house surgn Royal United Hosp Bath 1975–76, GP vocational scheme Cambridge 1976–79, lectr in gen practice St Thomas's Hosp Med Sch and princ in gen practice London 1979–83, princ in gen practice Cambridge 1983–93, dir of studies in gen practice Cambridge Univ Sch of Clinical Med 1987–93, prof of gen practice Univ of Manchester and dir of R & D Nat Primary Care R & C Centre 1993–; chm Health Servs and Public Health Research Bd MRC Cncl 1994–; author of numerous pubns on hosp referrals, back pain, use of time and quality of care in gen practice; MFPHM 1987, FRCGP 1994; *Style*— Prof Martin Roland; ✉ National Primary Care Research and Development Centre, Williamson Building, Universiry of Manchester, Oxford Road, Manchester M13 6PL (☎ 0161 275 7636, fax 0161 275 7600)

ROLFE, Christopher John; s of Frank Vere Rolfe, and Nesta Margaret, *née* Smith (d 1996); *b* 16 Aug 1937; *Educ* Truro Cathedral Sch, Humphry Davy Sch, Royal West of England Acad Sch of Architecture (DipArch), Univ of Edinburgh (DipCD, DipTP); *m* 3 Oct 1964, Phyllis Roseline, da of Thomas Henry Harry (d 1972), of Newlyn; 1 s (David

Jon Vere b 27 Nov 1971), 2 da (Kerstin Jane (Mrs W D C Beney) b 17 Feb 1967, Kerry Anne b 15 May 1969); *Career* architect; sr ptnr Christopher Rolfe & Assoc 1964–85, ind chartered architect and planning conslt 1985–; architect and planning conslt to: Bolitho Estates & Trusts 1975–, Barclays Bank Trust Co 1990–, National Trust 1991–; dir Haselden Estates Ltd 1990–93; chm and area rep Penzance Round Table 1968–74, chm St Clare Assoc 1981–82, local advsr to the Royal Nat Mission of Deep Sea Fisherman 1984– (chm Local Advsy Ctee 1994–), clerk to Madron Parish Cncl 1984–, advsr to and tstee Garlidna Almshouses 1986–, clerk to Sir William Matthews and the Thomas Hosking Tst 1991–; RIBA 1964, FRSA 1995; *Books* The Tourist & Leisure Industry (1966); *Recreations* water-colourist, gardening, photography; *Clubs* Penwith Lodge; *Style*— Christopher Rolfe, Esq; ✉ Polteggan Farm, Tremethick Cross, Penzance, Cornwall (☎ 01736 62167)

ROLFE, David John; *b* 2 April 1939; *Educ* King Edward VII Sch Sheffield, Univ of Sheffield; *m*; 3 da; *Career* architect; jt fndr Rolfe Judd Group 1968; Freeman City of London, Liveryman Worshipful Co of Chartered Architects; RIBA 1965; *Recreations* vintage motor sport, travel, music; *Clubs* East India; *Style*— David Rolfe, Esq; ✉ Rolfe Judd Group, Old Church Court, Claylands Road, London SW8 1NZ (☎ 0171 582 7070, fax 0171 735 5141)

ROLFE, Dr William David Ian; s of late William Ambrose Rolfe, and Greta Olwen Jones; *b* 24 Jan 1936; *Educ* Royal Liberty GS Romford, Univ of Birmingham (BSc, MSc, PhD); *m* 1960, Julia Mary Margaret, da of late Capt G H G S Rayer, OBE; 2 c; *Career* demonstrator in geology Univ Coll of N Staffs 1960, Fulbright scholar and asst curator Museum of Comparative Zoology Harvard Coll Cambridge Mass 1961–62; Hunterian Museum Univ of Glasgow: geological curator, lectr then sr lectr in geology 1962–81, dep dir 1981–86; visiting scientist Field Museum of Nat History Chicago 1981, keeper of geology Nat Nuseums of Scotland (Edinburgh) 1986–96; editorial chm of Geological Soc 1973–76, chm Conservation Ctee Geological Soc 1980–85, pres Edinburgh Geological Soc 1989–91; Geological Soc of Glasgow: pres 1973–76, vice pres 1969–72 and 1976, sec 1972–73, cncllr 1964–67, convener Library Improvement Ctee 1966–69; ed: Proceedings of the Geological Soc of Glasgow 1965–68, Scottish Jl of Geology 1967–72; Museums Assoc: diploma tutor 1970–80, fellowship assessor 1975–88; Palaeontological Assoc: pres 1992–94, vice pres 1974–76, sec 1969–74, asst sec 1968–69, cncllr 1965–76; cncllr: Scottish Fedn of Museums 1962–65, 1967–70 and 1975–78, Geological Curators Gp 1967–79; advsr for Treatise on Invertebrate Paleontology Geological Soc of America and Univ of Kansas Press 1972–74; memb: Br Nat Ctee for Geology 1976–81, Touring Exhibitions Panel Cncl for Museums and Art Galleries in Scotland 1980–85, Museum Professionals Gp, Geological Sci Training Awards Ctee NERC 1980–83, Scottish Museum Assts Gp (pres 1971–73), Soc History of Natural History (pres 1996–99, vice pres 1983–85); FGS 1960, FMA 1977, FRSE 1983, FRSA 1985; *Books* Phylogeny and Evolution of Crustacea (ed 1963), Treatise on Invertebrate Paleontology part R (1969), Geological Howlers (1980); various papers on fossil phyllocarid crustaceans and palaeontology and history of 18th century natural sci illustration; *Recreations* visual arts, walking, swimming, music; *Style*— Dr W D Ian Rolfe, FRSE; ✉ 4A Randolph Crescent, Edinburgh EH3 7TH (☎ 0131 226 2094)

ROLINGTON, Alfred; *b* 31 Dec 1950; *Educ* (BA); *Career* dir EMAP Business Publishing 1979–82, md Eastside Publishing 1982–84, chief exec Lloyd's of London Press Business Publishing 1984–92, group md Jane's Information Group 1992–; *Clubs* Ronnie Scott's, Hogarth; *Style*— Alfred Rolington, Esq; ✉ Jane's Information Group, Sentinel House, 163 Brighton Road, Coulsdon, Surrey CR5 2NH (☎ 0181 700 3702, fax 0181 700 3704, e-mail alfred.rolington@janes.co.uk)

ROLL, Rev Sir James William Cecil; 4 Bt (UK 1921), of The Chestnuts, Wanstead, Essex; s of Sir Cecil Ernest Roll, 3 Bt (d 1938), and Mildred Kate (d 1926), da of William Wells, of Snaresbrook, Essex; *b* 1 June 1912; *Educ* Chigwell Sch, Pembroke Coll Oxford, Chichester Theol Coll; *Heir* none; *Career* curate: St James the Great Bethnal Green 1937–39, St Matthew's Custom House 1940–44; hon curate East Ham Parish Church 1944–58, vicar of St John The Divine Becontree from 1958–83 (ret); *Style*— The Rev Sir James Roll, Bt; ✉ 82 Leighcliff Road, Leigh on Sea, Essex SS9 1DN (☎ 01702 713050)

ROLL, Michael; *m* Juliana Markova; 1 s (Maximilian); *Career* musician; debut aged twelve Royal Festival Hall playing Schumann's Concerto under Sir Malcolm Sargent, winner Leeds Int Pianoforte competition aged seventeen, US debut with Boston Symphony Orchestra 1974 (with Sir Colin Davis); worked with numerous major conductors incl: Pierre Boulez, Erich Leinsdorf, Kurt Masur, André Previn, Kurt Sanderling; appeared at festivals incl: Aldeburgh, Bath, Edinburgh, Granada, Hong Kong, Vienna, BBC Proms; given recitals in numerous venues incl: NY, Milan, Berlin, Dresden, Leipzig, London; concerto appearances with: Kurt Masur in Leipzig and London, Valery Gergiev in Leningrad and UK, Sergei Comissiona in Helsinki; performed Beethoven Concerti with Swedish Radio Orch, Rotterdam Philharmonic and Monte-Carlo orchs 1995–96; *Recordings* complete cycle of Beethoven Concerti (first two CDs with RPO and Howard Shelley, first CD voted one of top CD releases for 1996 by BBC Music Magazine); *Style*— Michael Roll, Esq; ✉ c/o Sue Lubbock, 25 Courthope Road, London NW3 2LE (☎ 0171 485 5932, fax 0171 267 0179)

ROLL OF IPSDEN, Baron (Life Peer UK 1977), of Ipsden, Co Oxford; Eric Roll; KCMG (1962, CMG 1949), CB (1956); yr s of Mathias Roll and Fany Roll; *b* 1 Dec 1907; *Educ* Birmingham Univ (PhD); *m* 1934, Winifred, o da of Elliott Taylor; 2 da (Hon Joanna b 1944, Hon Elizabeth (Hon Mrs Foldes) b 1946); *Career* sits as Independent peer in House of Lords; prof econs and commerce Univ Coll Hull 1935–46, under-sec Treasy 1948, dep sec MAFF 1959–61; dep head UK Delgn negotiating EEC entry 1961–63, UK Delgn NATO Paris 1952; exec dir UK IMF and IBRD 1963–64; perm under sec of state Dept of Economic Affrs 1963–65; hon chm Book Devpt Cncl 1967–; dir Bank of Eng 1968–77; chm: S G Warburg & Co 1974–84 (jt chm 1984–86), Mercury Securities 1974–84; pres S G Warburg Gp plc 1986–95; snr advsr SBC Warburg 1995–; dir Times Newspapers Hldgs 1966–83; appeal chm Loan Fund for Musical Instruments; chllr Southampton Univ 1974–84; Grosses Goldene Ehrenzeichen mit Stern Austria, Cdr 1 Class Order of the Dannebrog (Denmark), Offr Legion of Honour, Grand Cordon Order of the Sacred Treasure (Japan); *Style*— The Rt Hon the Lord Roll of Ipsden, KCMG, CB; ✉ 1 Finsbury Ave, London EC2M 2PP

ROLLAND, Lawrence Anderson Lyon; s of Lawrence Anderson Rolland (d 1959), of Leven, and Winifred Anne, *née* Lyon (d 1978); *b* 6 Nov 1937; *Educ* George Watsons Coll Edinburgh, Duncan of Jordanstone Coll of Art Dundee (DipArch); *m* 30 April 1960, Mairi, da of John McIntyre Melville (d 1980), of Kirkcaldy; 2 s (Michael b 1963, Douglas b 1966), 2 da (Gillian b 1961, Katie b 1967); *Career* sole ptnr L A Rolland 1960, jt sr ptnr Robert Hurd 1965, ptnr L A Rolland & Ptnrs 1965, sr ptnr Hurd Rolland Ptnrship; awards and commendations incl: Saltire Soc, Civic Tst, RIBA, Europa Nostra, Times Conservation, Stone Fedn; fndr chm Scottish Construction Indust Gp 1980; memb Ct Univ of Dundee 1993, convenor Advsy Ctee for Artistic Matters for Church of Scotland 1975–80, gen tstee Church of Scotland 1979–; hon fell Bulgarian Inst of Architects 1987; pres: RIAS 1979–81, RIBA 1985–87; FRS 1988, FRSE 1989; *Recreations* music, fishing, shooting and more architecture; *Clubs* Reform; *Style*— Lawrence Rolland, Esq, FRS, FRSE; ✉ School House, Newburn, Upper Largo, Fife (☎ 01333 360383); Rossend Castle, Burntisland, Fife (☎ 01592 873535); 32 Fitzroy Square, London W1P 5HH (☎ 0171 387 9595, fax 0171 387 0725)

ROLLASON, Helen; *b* 11 March 1956; *Educ* Bath HS for Girls, Chelsea Coll of Physical Educn, Dalhousie Univ Canada; *m* 23 March 1980 (m dis 1992); 1 da (Nikki Kate b 17 July 1983); *Career* TV sports journalist; former PE teacher comp schs; joined Essex Radio (from inception), dep sports ed, prodr and dir Cheerleader Productions Channel 4 (asst prodr The Masters from Augusta, The US Open, 1985 Superbowl, Davis Cup final Sweden 1984), reporter Thames Sports, C4 presenter: World Student Games Zagreb 1985, volleyball, swimming, Eng Schs Athletics and World Jr Athletics Championships; jt reporter (ITV) Olympic Games Seoul 1988, former presenter Newsround (BBC), joined BBC Sport 1990, presenter Sport On Friday (Oct-April) 1990–97, first female presenter Grandstand, covered Winter Olympics, Summer Olympics, Paralympics and Cwlth Games; currently: athletics presenter, BBC News Saturday Night Sports presenter, BBC Breakfast Sports presenter; dir Nat Coaching Fndn, memb Lottery Sports Awards Panel; winner BSAD Media Awards for: World Disabled Championships (Grandstand) 1990, Blind Golfers (Sportsnight) 1991, Paralympics (Grandstand) 1992, Special Olympics (Grandstand) 1993; TRIC Sports presenter/reporter 1996; *Recreations* golf, skiing, athletics, tennis, illustration and painting; *Style*— Ms Helen Rollason; ✉ BBC TV Sport, Television Centre, Wood Lane, London W12 7RJ (☎ 0181 576 7514); c/o Knight Ayton Management (☎ 0171 287 4405, fax 0171 434 3075)

ROLLES, Keith; s of Trevor Rolles, of Port Talbot, W Glamorgan, and Betty, *née* Hopkin; *b* 25 Oct 1947; *Educ* Quakers Yard GS Mid Glamorgan, The Royal London Hosp Med Coll (BSc, MB BS, MS); *m* 22 Aug 1970, Sharon, da of Thomas McGrath (d 1979); 2 s (David b 1981, Thomas b 1986); *Career* lectr in surgery and hon conslt surgn Univ of Cambridge and Addenbrooke's Hosp 1984–88, conslt surgn and dir Liver Transplant Unit The Royal Free Hosp 1988–; Hon MA Univ of Cambridge 1983; Hon MS Univ of London 1985; FRCS 1976; *Recreations* squash, tennis, skiing; *Style*— Keith Rolles, Esq; ✉ Academic Dept of Surgery, The Royal Free Hosp and Sch of Medicine, Pond St, Hampstead, London NW3 2QG (☎ 0171 830 2198)

ROLLIN, Peter Hamilton; s of Lawrence Hamilton Rollin, of Diss, Norfolk, and Hedy, *née* Gutgiser (decd); *b* 13 Nov 1942; *Educ* Bedford Mod Sch; *m* 6 April 1976, Elizabeth Mary, da of Maj John Kellock Corbitt, of Diss, Norfolk; 1 s (Matthew b 1977), 1 da (Rachael b 1974); *Career* admitted slr 1969; dep registrar Co Ct 1986, dep dist judge 1991–; memb Law Soc Personal Injury Panel 1994–; former pres Diss Chamber of Trade and Commerce; cncllr: Diss Urban Dist/Town Cncl 1971–77, Norfolk CC 1973–93 (ldr 1987–89); memb Law Soc 1970; *Recreations* choral singing, philately; *Style*— Peter Rollin, Esq; ✉ Jacques, Back St, Garboldisham, Diss, Norfolk (☎ 01953 681362); Park House, Mere St, Diss, Norfolk IP22 3JY (☎ 01379 643555, fax 01379 652221)

ROLLO, 13 Lord (S 1651); Eric John Stapylton Rollo; JP (Perthshire 1962); also Baron Dunning (UK 1869); s of Maj 12 Lord Rollo (d 1947), and his 1 w, Helen, da of Frederick Chetwynd-Stapylton (ggs of 4 Viscount Chetwynd); *b* 3 Dec 1915; *Educ* Eton; *m* 1938, Suzanne, da of W H B Hatton, of Broome House, Broome, Worcs; 2 s, 1 da; *Heir* s, Master of Rollo; *Career* Capt late Gren Guards 1939–45 War; farmer; *Style*— The Rt Hon the Lord Rollo, JP; ✉ Pitcairns, Dunning, Perthshire

ROLLS, Peter John; s of Hector Lionel Rolls (d 1980), and Florence Susie Rolls (d 1989); *b* 7 May 1930; *Educ* Slough GS, Regent St Poly, Harrow Coll of HE, Univ of Surrey (Cert in Scientific Photography, BA, MSc); *m* 7 July 1956, Helen Jane, da of William Kirby; 3 s (Timothy John b 18 June 1957, Christopher Peter b 2 July 1959, Jeremy David b 23 June 1962), 1 da (Alison Jane b 28 Sept 1970); *Career* Nat Serv 1948–50; photographer Miny of Supply 1950–59, sr photographer Miny of Aviation 1959–66, chief photographer Miny of Defence 1966–67, head of printing RAE Farnborough 1967–90, head of profession for MOD(PE) photographers 1989–90, ret 1990; Inst of Incorporated Photographers: chief examiner 1970–74, chm of educn 1976–80; BTEC moderator in photography 1983–95, govr Berkshire Coll of Art 1990–96; conslt: Vocational Standards Cncl 1991–94, Indust Trg Orgn 1995–96; City & Guilds external NVQ verifier 1994–96; President's award Inst of Incorporated Photographers 1975; FBIPP 1972; *Books* Applied Photography (jtly, 1971), Proceedings of 7 International High-Speed Congress (ed, 1975), Microform Systems and Reprography (1980), Minilab Training Primer (jtly, 1993); *Recreations* writing, photography; *Style*— Peter Rolls

ROMANES, (Constance) Margaret; OBE (1981), JP (1965), DL (Dorset 1989); da of Claud Valentine Gee (d 1951), and Hilda, *née* Bentham (d 1968); *b* 9 Aug 1920; *Educ* St Leonard's Sch, Girton Coll Cambridge; *m* 29 June 1943, Giles John Romanes, s of Capt Francis John Romanes (d 1944); 1 s (Julian b 1951, d 1994), 2 da (Jane b 1946, Rosalind b 1947); *Career* dep chm Magistrates' Assoc 1981–87 (vice pres 1990–); chm: Dorset branch Magistrates' Assoc 1981–89 (pres 1990–), Weymouth and Portland Bench 1985–91; contrib to various jls and reader of papers at various int confs; memb: James Ctee (an Interdepartmental Ctee on Distribution of Criminal Business), Portland Borstal Youth Custody Centre Bd of Visitors 1971–86 (chm 1976–81), Salisbury Diocesan Synod 1976–84, Local Parole Review Ctee 1984–86, various govt working parties; Bishop's selector for ACCM 1976–83, chm Dorset Care Tst 1984–94 (vice pres 1994), chm Nat Forum of Care Tsts 1993–95, memb Penal Affairs Consortium 1995–; Lord Chllr's nominee on Legal Aid Duty Slr Ctee 1986–91; *Recreations* music (active memb of orchestras and chamber groups), gardening; *Clubs* RSM; *Style*— Mrs Margaret Romanes, OBE, JP, DL; ✉ Portesham House, nr Weymouth, Dorset DT3 4HE (☎ 01305 871300)

ROME, Alan Mackenzie; s of John Mackenzie Rome (d 1969), and Evelyn Anne, *née* Rae (d 1978); *b* 24 Oct 1930; *Educ* Kings Sch Bruton, Royal W of Eng Acad Sch of Architecture (DipArch); *m* 8 Sept 1956, Mary Lilyan, da of Thomas William Barnard (d 1984); 1 s (Timothy b 1961), 1 da (Judith b 1963); *Career* Nat Serv RE 1949–50; architect; in office of Sir George Oatley 1947–49, asst to S E Dykes Bower (Surveyor of Westminster Abbey) 1955–60, in private practice (initially with Michael Torrens and Alan Crozier-Cole) 1960–; cathedral architect to Deans and Chapters of Bristol and Truro, architect to Bath Abbey and St Mary Redcliffe, consulting architect to Provost and Chapter of Leicester and St Edmundsbury; memb: Organs Advsy Ctee Cncl for the Care of Churches, Churches Conservation Tst, Ctee of Hon Architects Historic Churches Preservation Tst, Bath and Wells Diocesan Advsy Ctee, SPAB; occasional lectr Univ of Bristol; FRIBA, FSA; *Recreations* walking, sketching; *Style*— Alan Rome, Esq; ✉ 11 Mayfair Ave, Nailsea, Bristol BS19 2LR (☎ 01275 853215)

ROMER, Ian Lebeau Ritchie; s of Rt Hon Sir Charles Robert Ritchie Romer (d 1969), of Littlestone, Kent, and Frances Evelyn Lebeau, *née* Kemp (d 1989); previous 3 direct generations (and present) were all educated at Trinity Hall, went to the Chancery Bar and were benchers of Lincoln's Inn; *b* 26 Dec 1929; *Educ* Bryanston, Trinity Hall Cambridge (BA); *m* 1, 1952, Elizabeth, da of James Dales, of Vancouver; 1 s (James b 1955 decd), 1 da (Jane b 1956); m 2, 1960, Mary Rose, da of Col W H Crichton (d 1984), of Polstead, Suffolk; 1 s (Caspar b 1970), 1 da (Emma b 1961); *Career* called to the Bar Gray's Inn 1953, bencher Lincoln's Inn 1981; full-time Commons Cmmr 1993–; *Clubs* Garrick; *Style*— Ian L R Romer, Esq; ✉ 19 Old Buildings, Lincoln's Inn, London WC2 (☎ 0171 831 5061)

ROMER, Mark Lemon Robert; eld s of Sir Charles Robert Ritchie Romer (d 1969, Lord Justice of Appeal), of Littlestone, and Frances Evelyn Lebeau, *née* Kemp (d 1989); f, gf and ggf all members of Court of Appeal, gf going on to House of Lords where he sat with two brothers-in-law (Viscount Maugham, Lord Russell of Killowen); *b* 12 July 1927; *Educ* Bryanston, Trinity Hall Cambridge (MA, LLM); *m* 1, 1953 (m dis 1991), Philippa Maynard, da of Maj Maynard Tomson, MC (d 1984) of Hitchin; 1 s (Stephen b 1957), 2 da (Caroline b 1955, Eugénie b 1961); m 2, 1991, Mary Eileen Hunt, eld da of Dennis and Shandy Hernaman; *Career* served KRRC UK 1945–48; barr 1952; met stipendiary magistrate 1972–96; *Recreations* bird-watching, travel, looking at pictures, painting watercolours; *Style—* Mark Romer, Esq; ✉ Gillings Hill, Arkesden Rd, Clavering, Essex CB11 4QU

ROMER, Stephen Charles Mark; s of Mark Lemon Robert Romer, of Clavering, Essex, and Philippa Maynard, *née* Tomson; *b* 20 Aug 1957; *Educ* King's Coll Sch Cambridge, Radley, Trinity Hall Cambridge (BA, PhD); *m* 17 July 1982 (sep), Bridget Julia, *Née* Strevens; 1 s (Thomas Mark Strevens b 19 June 1985); *Career* Henry fell Harvard Univ 1978–79, teacher British Inst Paris 1983–88 (postgrad scholar 1979–80), asst associé Univ of Paris X 1987–89, asst prof Univ of Łódź Poland (British Cncl post) 1989–90, maître de confs Univ of Tours 1990–; Gregory Award for Young Poets 1985, Prudence Farmer Award New Statesman 1985, Cheltenham/TLS 2nd and 4th Poetry Prizes 1986; *Poetry* Idols (1986, Poetry Book Soc recommendation), Plato's Ladder (1992, Poetry Book Soc choice), Selected Poems of Jacques Dupin (trans, 1992), The New Poetry (contrib to anthology, 1993), Traductions, Passages: Le Domaine Anglais (ed, 1993); *Style—* Stephen Romer, Esq

ROMER-LEE, Alexander Knyvett (Alex); s of Knyvett Romer-Lee, OBE (d 1996), of Green Farm, Hickling, Norfolk, and Jeanne Pamela, *née* Shaw (d 1982); *b* 18 Aug 1953; *Educ* Eton, Institut Universitaire de Technologie Dijon; *m* Janet Christine; 1 da (Katherine Pamela b 6 Jan 1985), 1 s (Jonathan Knyvett b 15 Oct 1987); *Career* Coopers & Lybrand (formerly Deloitte Haskins & Sells): CA 1980, ptnr Southampton 1988, ptnr London 1988–89, managing ptnr Budapest 1990–91, ptnr London 1992–, head of financial servs Central and Eastern Europe 1995–; chm Hungary Sector Gp 1992–; FCA 1991; *Recreations* travel, Burgundy wine, cricket, fishing, Eastern Europe; *Clubs* MCC, East India; *Style—* Alex Romer-Lee, Esq; ✉ Nunns Orchard, Whiteparish, Salisbury, Wilts SP5 2RJ (☎ 01794 884255); Coopers & Lybrand, 1 Embankment Place, London WC2N 6NN (☎ 0171 583 5000)

ROMER-LEE, Robin Knyvett; s of Knyvett Romer-Lee, OBE (d 1996), of Green Farm, Hickling, Norfolk, and Jeanne Pamela, *née* Shaw (d 1982); *b* 27 Oct 1942; *Educ* Eton; *m* 30 March 1968, Annette Millet, da of George Henry Brocklehurst (d 1972); 2 s (Benjamin b 1971, Edward b 1973); *Career* insur broker and memb of Lloyds; dir Sedgwick Europe Risk Services Ltd, chm Sedgwick International Broking Services Ltd 1989; *Recreations* sailing, fishing, gardening; *Style—* Robin Romer-Lee, Esq; ✉ The Old Rectory, Groton, Sudbury, Suffolk CO10 5EE (☎ 01787 210710); Sedgwick House, Sedgwick Centre, London E1 8DX

ROMNEY, 7 Earl of (UK 1801); Sir Michael Henry Marsham; 13 Bt (E 1663); also Baron of Romney (GB 1716) and Viscount Marsham (UK 1801); s of Lt-Col Hon Reginald Marsham, OBE (2 s of 4 Earl of Romney), and Dora, 4 da of Charles North, JP, DL (5 in descent from Hon Roger North, the memoirist and 6 s of 4 Baron North); suc first cous, 6 Earl, 1975; *b* 22 Nov 1910; *Educ* Sherborne; *m* 28 June 1939, (Frances) Aileen (d 1995), o da of Lt-Col James Russell Landale, IA; *Heir* first cous once removed, Julian Marsham; *Career* late Maj RA, served WWII; pres Marine Soc (charity) 1990; *Recreations* foxhunting; *Style—* The Rt Hon the Earl of Romney; ✉ Wensum Farm, W Rudham, King's Lynn, Norfolk (☎ 01485 528249)

ROMSEY, Lord; Norton Louis Philip Knatchbull; s and h of Countess Mountbatten of Burma and of 7 Baron Brabourne; *b* 8 Oct 1947; *Educ* Gordonstoun, Univ of Kent; *m* 1979, Penelope Meredith, only da of Reginald and Marian Eastwood of Palma de Mallorca, Spain; 1 s (Hon Nicholas b 1981), 2 da (Hon Alexandra b 1982, Hon Leonora b 1986, d 1991); *Heir* s, Hon Nicholas Louis Charles Norton Knatchbull b 15 May 1981; *Career* film and TV prodr 1971–80; dir Britt Allcroft Gp Ltd (Thomas the Tank Engine and Friends), chm Friday Productions Ltd; High Steward Romsey 1980; Vice Adm Royal Motor Yacht Club 1985, vice pres Mary Rose Tst; memb Ct Univ of Southampton; Liveryman Worshipful Co of Mercers; *Clubs* Royal Motor Yacht; *Style—* Lord Romsey; ✉ Broadlands, Romsey, Hants SO51 9ZD (☎ 01794 518881)

RONAN, Frank Francis John; s of Patrick Anthony Ronan, of New Ross, Co Wexford, and Theresa, *née* O'Grady (d 1981); *b* 6 May 1963; *Educ* Christian Bros Sch Co Wexford; *Career* author; *Books* The Men Who Loved Evelyn Cotton (1989, Irish Times/Aer Lingus Irish Literature Prize), A Picnic in Eden (1991), The Better Angel (1992), Handsome Men Are Slightly Sunburnt (1996); *Recreations* gardening; *Style—* Frank Ronan, Esq; ✉ c/o Rogers, Colridge & White, 20 Powis Mews, London W11 1SN (☎ 0171 221 3717, fax 229 9084)

RONDEL, Dr Richard Kavanagh; s of William Allen Thomas Rondel (d 1963), of Chelmsford, Essex, and Edna Phyllis, *née* Sayer; *b* 29 Oct 1931; *Educ* King Edward VI Sch Chelmsford, King's Coll London (second MB BS), St George's Hosp Hyde Park Corner London (final MB BS), DipRCOG, DipPharmMed; *m* 1962 (m dis 1992); 1 da (Nicola Louise de Chastelai b 7 Dec 1962), 1 s (Mark Richard de Chastelai b 2 Nov 1963); *Career* house appts St George's Hosp London 1956–58; Nat Serv RAMC, jr specialist in pathology, served Cyprus and Gibraltar 1958–60; registrar and resident med offr St George's Hosp Tooting 1960–62, med advsr John Wyeth Taplow 1963–65, dir of clinical research (UK) CIBA Laboratories Horsham 1965–74, dir of clinical research (Europe, ME and Africa) Bristol Myers International Corp 1975–80, dep chm Iphar Inst for Med Research Munich 1981–83, fndr md Oxford Workshops (int research and consultancy) 1983–; dir: Europharm Ltd 1996–, Pharmakopius International plc 1996–; pres: Br Assoc of Pharmaceutical Physicians 1972–74 (hon life memb 1981), Int Fedn of Assocs of Pharmaceutical Physicians 1978–81; memb Cncl RCP London 1992–; fndn fell Faculty of Pharmaceutical Med 1989 (faculty registrar 1989–95), FRCP 1992; *Books* Adverse Drug Reactions (1973), Clinical Data Management (1994); *Recreations* travel, flying in vintage aircraft; *Clubs* Royal Society of Medicine; *Style—* Dr Richard Rondel; ✉ 2 King George Square, Park Hill, Richmond on Thames, Surrey TW10 6LG (☎ 0181 940 7852); Europharm Ltd, Dorna House, West End, Woking, Surrey GU24 9PW (☎ 01276 858782, fax 01276 858760, mobile 0378 878496)

RONE, Ven James (Jim); s of James Rone (d 1967), of Runcorn, Cheshire, and Bessie Rone (d 1982); *b* 28 Aug 1935; *Educ* Skerry's Coll Liverpool, St Stephen's House Oxford; *m* 1, 1956, Ivy, *née* Mylchreest (d 1970); 1 s (William Geoffrey), 1 da (Ann Carol); m 2, 1976, Mary Elizabeth, da of William Isaac Bancroft Angove; *Career* accountant ICI Ltd 1958–64, co sec/dir Timperley Engineering Ltd and other subsids of Reed International 1965–71, gp chief accountant Leigh and Sillavan Group 1971–73, fin offr Dio of Oxford 1973–79, ordination trg St Stephen's House Oxford 1979–80, curate Stony Stratford Parish Church 1980–82, vicar and rector Fordham with Kennett (Dio of Ely) 1982–89, residentiary canon/canon treas Ely Cathedral 1989–95, archdeacon of Wisbech 1995–; memb Gen Synod C of E 1995–; memb Ecclesiastical Law Soc; FSCA 1971, MInstD 1992; *Recreations* listening to classical music, theatre, rugby and cricket (former player, now spectator), good food and wine; *Clubs* Carlton; *Style—* The Ven the Archdeacon of Wisbech; ✉ Archdeacon's House, 24 Cromwell Road, Ely, Cambs CB6 1AS (☎ 01353 662909, fax 01353 662056)

RONEY, Peter John; *b* 12 Oct 1949; *Educ* Boteler GS Warrington, Univ of Durham (BA); *Career* successively: investment mangr Derbyshire CC, chief investment offr South Yorkshire CC, chief exec Combined Actuarial Performance Services Ltd, md Halifax Financial Services Ltd; currently chief exec Save & Prosper Group Ltd; memb CIPFA, AIIMR; *Style—* Peter Roney, Esq; ✉ Save and Prosper Group Ltd, 20 Finsbury Street, Finsbury Dials, London EC2Y 2AY (☎ 0171 417 2280, fax 0171 417 2393)

RONSON, Gerald Maurice; *b* 26 May 1939; *m* 10 Sept 1967, Gail, *née* Cohen; 4 da; *Career* chief exec: Heron Corporation PLC 1976– (chm 1988–93), Heron International PLC (chm 1983–93); chm and chief exec Snax 24 Corporation Ltd; ambass of Druse Community Mount Carmel; *Clubs* Royal Southern Yacht; *Style—* Gerald M Ronson, Esq; ✉ c/o Heron International plc, Heron House, 19 Marylebone Rd, London NW1 5JL (☎ 0171 486 4477)

ROOCROFT, Amanda Jane; da of Roger Roocroft, of Coppull, Lancs, and Valerie, *née* Metcalfe; *b* 9 Feb 1966; *Educ* Southlands HS, Runshaw Tertiary Coll, Royal Northern Coll of Music; *Career* soprano; winner Decca-Kathleen Ferrier Meml Prize and Silver Medal Worshipful Co of Musicians 1988, Royal Philharmonic Soc/Charles Heidsieck Award for operatic debut 1990; currently studies with Barbara Robotham; *Opera Performances* incl: Fiordiligi in Così fan tutte, Guilietta in I Capuleti e i Montecchi, Mimi in La Boheme, Pamina in The Magic Flute (all Covent Garden), Fiordiligi, Amelia in Simon Boccanegra, Donna Elvira in Don Giovani (all Bavarian State Opera Munich), Fiordilia and Donna Elvira (both Glyndebourne Festival); *Concert Performances* incl: The Proms, London's South Bank, City of Birmingham Symphony Orchestra with Sir Simon Rattle, as well as appearances throughout the rest of the UK and Europe; *Recordings* incl: Vaughan Williams' Serenade to Music (Hyperion), Cosi fan Tutte (with Baroque English Soloists under John Eliot Gardiner, Deutsche Grammophon 1992), solo album Amanda Roocroft (EMI 1994), Mozart and his contemporaries (with the Academy of St Martin in the Fields and Sir Neville Marriner, 1996); *Recreations* reading, cooking, sewing; *Style—* Miss Amanda Roocroft; ✉ c/o Ingpen & Williams Ltd, 14 Kensington Court, London W8 5DN (☎ 0171 937 5158, fax 0171 938 4175)

ROOK, Peter Francis Grosvenor; QC (1991); s of Dr Arthur Rook (d 1991), of Cambridge, and Frances Jane Elizabeth, *née* Knott (d 1990); *b* 19 Sept 1949; *Educ* King's Coll Choir Sch Cambridge, Charterhouse, Trinity Coll Cambridge (open exhibitioner); *m* 2 Sept 1978, Susanna Marian, da of Richard Roland Tewson, of Great Sampford, Essex; 1 s (Joshua b 1983), 2 da (Annabel b 1979, Sophie b 1981); *Career* called to the Bar 1973, 1st standing counsel to Inland Revenue Central Criminal Court and Inner London Courts 1989–91 (2nd standing counsel 1981–89), standing counsel to HM Customs and Excise S Eastern Circuit 1989–91, recorder 1995–; *Books* Sexual Offences (with Robert Ward, 1990); *Recreations* travel, tennis, squash, ornithology, tropical plants; *Clubs* Coolhurst Lawn Tennis and Squash; *Style—* Peter Rook, Esq, QC; ✉ Ground Floor, 5 King's Bench Walk, Temple, London EC4Y 7DN (☎ 0171 797 7600)

ROOKE, Sir Denis Eric; kt (1977), CBE (1970); s of F G Rooke; *b* 2 April 1924; *Educ* Westminster City Sch, Addey and Stanhope Sch, UCL (BSc); *m* 1949, Elizabeth Brenda, *née* Evans; 1 da; *Career* Maj REME 1944–49; devpt engr: S Eastern Gas Bd 1959 (joined 1949), Gas Cncl 1960; chm: British Gas Corporation 1976–86 (dep chm 1972–76), British Gas plc 1986–89; memb: Advsy Cncl for R&D 1972–77, Advsy Cncl for Energy Conservation 1974–77, Offshore Energy Tech Bd 1975–78, British National Oil Corporation (pt/t) 1976–82, NEDC 1976–80, Energy Cmmn 1977–79; pres: IGasE 1975, Welding Inst 1981–83, Pipeline Industs Guild 1981–83, Royal Acad of Engrg (formerly Fellowship of Engrg) 1986–91, Inst of Quality Assurance 1990–92, Br Assoc for the Advancement of Science 1990–91; chm: CNAA 1978–83, Advsy Ctee Nat Museum of Photography, Film and TV 1984–, Royal Cmmn for the Exhibition of 1851 1987– (cmmr 1984–), Tstees Sci Museum 1995– (tstee 1984–); chllr Loughborough Univ 1989–; Hon DSc: Univ of Salford 1978, Univ of Leeds 1980, The City Univ 1985, Univ of Durham 1986, Cranfield Inst of Technol 1987, Univ of London 1991, Loughborough Univ 1994; Hon DEng: Univ of Bradford 1989, Univ of Liverpool 1994; Hon DTech CNAA 1986, Hon LLD Univ of Bath 1987, Hon DUniv Surrey; hon sr fell RCA; hon fell: City and Guilds of London Inst, Humberside Coll of Further Educn, SW Poly (now Univ of Plymouth), Inst of Civil Engrs, Inst of Electrical Engrs, Inst of Chemical Engrs, Inst of Mechanical Engrs, Inst of Gas Engrs, Inst of Energy; Hon Freeman Worshipful Co of Tallow Chandlers; Rumford Medal Royal Soc 1986, Prince Philip Medal Royal Acad of Engrg 1992; FRS 1978, FEng 1977; *Recreations* listening to music, photography; *Clubs* Athenaeum, English-Speaking Union; *Style—* Sir Denis Rooke, CBE, FRS, FEng; ✉ 23 Hardy Rd, Blackheath, London SE3 7NS (☎ 0181 858 6710); 1 Great Cumberland Place, Marble Arch, London W1H 7AL (☎ 0171 723 5173)

ROOKE, His Hon Judge Giles Hugh; TD (1963), QC (1979); s of Charles Eustace Rooke, CMG (d 1947), and Irene Phyllis (d 1969), da of Thomas Main Patterson; *b* 28 Oct 1930; *Educ* Stowe, Exeter Coll Oxford (MA); *m* 1968, Anne Bernadette Seymour, da of His Hon John Perrett (d 1992); 4 s (Alexander b 1969, Nicholas b 1970, George b 1979, Charles b 1989), 1 da (Elizabeth b 1972); *Career* Maj (TA) Kent Yeo 1951–61, KCLY 1961–65; called to the Bar Lincoln's Inn 1957; chm Kent Bar Mess 1975–79, recorder Crown Ct 1975–81, judge SE Circuit (practised as barr from 1957) 1981–, resident judge Canterbury 1995–; hon recorder of Margate 1980–; *Recreations* cultivant son jardin; *Style—* His Hon Judge Rooke, TD, QC; ✉ The Law Courts, Chaucer Road, Canterbury CT1 1ZA

ROOKER, Jeffrey William; MP (Lab) Birmingham Perry Barr (majority 8,590); *b* 5 June 1941; *Educ* Handsworth Tech Sch, Handsworth Tech Coll, Univ of Warwick (MA), Univ of Aston (BScEng); *m* 1972, Angela; *Career* prodn mangr Rola Celestion Ltd 1967–70; lectr Lanchester Poly Coventry 1972–74, memb Birmingham Educn Ctee 1972–74; MP (Lab) Birmingham Perry Barr Feb 1974–, PPS to the Govt Law Officers 1977; oppn front bench spokesman on: social services 1979–80, social security 1981–Nov 1983, Treasy and econ affrs Nov 1983–84, environment 1984–88, community care and social services 1990–92, educn 1992–93, dep shadow leader House of Commons 1994–; memb Public Accounts Ctee 1989–, chair Lab Campaign for Electoral Reform 1989–; memb Cncl of Instn of Prodn Engrs 1975–80; *Style—* Jeffrey Rooker, Esq, MP; ✉ House of Commons, London SW1A 0AA

ROOKLEDGE, Gordon Charles; s of Charles Harcourt Rookledge Collett (d 1954), of Johannesburg, SA, and Elsie Alicia, *née* Goodwin (d 1976); *b* 3 Dec 1933; *Educ* Stanley Park Secdy Sch; *m* 1 April 1960, Jennifer Mary, da of Robert Dampier Lush, of Carshalton, Surrey; 1 s (Gavin Alistair b 1964), 2 da (Sarah Louise b 1962, Emma Constance b 1966); *Career* Nat Serv RA 1952–54; sales rep: Austin Miles Ltd 1954–58, Eros Engraving Ltd 1958–64; sales mangr Westerham Press 1964–68; chm and md: Gavin Martin Ltd 1968–91 (fndr 1968), Sarema Press (Publishers) Ltd (fndr 1973), KGM (Offset) Ltd (fndr 1983); pt/t tutor RCA 1974–84, visiting lectr E Ham Coll of Technol and Middx Poly; proprietor Design Brief magazine 1985–86, fndr jt ed de Worde (quarterly jl of the Wynkyn de Worde Soc) 1993–95; chm Carshalton Soc 1985–96; memb: Beddington, Carshalton and Wallington Archaeological Circle (London), The Regency Soc of Brighton and Hove, Sutton Arts cncl 1995–, Typographic Circle (London), Soc of Genealogists; Freeman: City of London 1993, Worshipful Co of Stationers 1993; *Books* Rookledge's International Typefinder (ed), Rookledge's Handbook of Type Designers (A Biographical Directory from the 15th Century to the present, ed, 1990); *Recreations* film and video, collecting print ephemera, paintings, swimming; *Clubs* Groucho, Chelsea Arts, Wynkyn De Worde Soc (ctee memb); *Style—* Gordon Rookledge, Esq; ✉ Sarema Press (Publishers) Ltd, 15 Beeches Walk, Carshalton Beeches, Surrey SM5 4JS (☎ 0181 770 1953, fax 0181 770 1957)

ROOLEY, Anthony; s of Henry Rooley, and Madge Rooley; *b* 10 June 1944; *Educ* Royal Acad of Music (LRAM); *m* 1967, Carla; 3 da, 1 s (by Emma Kirkby); *Career* lutenist; given concerts in: Europe, USA, Middle E, Japan, S America, NZ, Aust; numerous radio and TV broadcasts in UK and Europe, numerous recordings for Decca, DHM, Virgin

Classics; music admin: Eng Summer Schs 1973–79, The Future of Early Music in Br Conf 1977; fndr Early Music Centre 1976; teacher: RAM 1968, Guildhall Sch of Music and Drama 1971–74, RNCM 1975–76, Univ of Leicester 1976–79, Early Music Centre 1976–80, Schola Cantorum Basel 1985–, Japanese gashkus 1986–, Dartington Int Summer Sch 1986–; music theatre: Cupid and Death 1984, The Marriage of Pantalone 1985, Cupid and Psyche 1987, Venus and Adonis 1988, The Revels of Siena 1988, The Judgement of Paris 1989, Monteverdi's Balli 1990, Monteverdi's Orfeo 1991, Eccle's Semele 1992, Stradella's L'Anime del Purgatorio 1993; co-dir Banquet of the Senses (film) 1993; dir The Consort of Musicke 1969–, artistic dir Musica Oscura (record co); FRAM (1990); *Books* Penguin Book of Early Music (1982), Performance - Revealing the Orpheus within (1990), Routledge Compendium of Contemporary Musical Thought (contrib, 1989), Everyman Companion to Early Music (contrib, 1990); author of various articles for: Guitar Magazine 1976, Lute Soc Jls, Lute Soc Jl of America, Early Music Magazine, Temenos; *Recreations* food, wine, sculpture, gardening, philosophy; *Style—* Anthony Rooley, Esq; ✉ 54A Leamington Road Villas, London W11 1HT (☎ 0171 229 5142, fax 0171 221 1282)

ROOLEY, Richard Herbert; s of George Arthur Rooley, CBE, of Stoke Poges, Bucks, and Valeria, *née* Green (d 1994); *b* 24 April 1940; *Educ* Glasgow Acad, Morrisons Acad, Trinity Coll Dublin (BA, BAI); *m* 25 July 1964, (Ismena) Ruth Rooley, *qv*, da of George Young (d 1956), of Eire; 1 s (George b 1966), 1 da (Ismena b 1968); *Career* Donald Smith & Rooley conslt engrs: joined 1964, assoc 1968, ptnr 1971–91; sr ptnr Rooley Consultants 1991–; ptnr Project Management Partnership 1978–; memb Cncl CIBSE 1972–81 and 1989–92, chm Bldg Servs Res and Info Assoc 1984–86, chm Nat Jt Consultative Ctee 1993; churchwarden Stokes Poges 1980–86, lay chm Burnham Deanery Synod 1985–86; Liveryman Worshipful Co of Engrs (Jr Warden), Master Worshipful Co of Constructors 1992–93; FEng 1989 (hon sec Civil Engrg 1992–95, memb Cncl 1992–95), FICE, FIMechE, FCIBSE, ACIArb, MConsE, fell American Soc of Heating Refrigerating and Air Conditioning Engrs (memb Bd of Dirs 1980–83); *Recreations* golf; *Clubs* RAC; *Style—* Richard Rooley, Esq, FEng; ✉ Greenways, Church Lane, Stoke Poges, Bucks SL2 4PB (☎ 01753 648040, fax 01753 648048)

ROOLEY, (Ismena) Ruth; da of George Young (d 1957), of Bagenalstown, Eire, and Ismena Young, *née* Jeffares; *b* 6 July 1942; *Educ* Alexandra Coll, Trinity Coll Dublin (BA), Cranfield (MBA); *m* 25 July 1964, Richard Rooley, FEng, *qv*, s of George Rooley, of Stoke Poges, Bucks; 1 s (George b 1966), 1 da (Ismena b 1968); *Career* BIIBA (Br Insurance & Investment Brokers Assoc): dir fin servs 1989–91, dir gen 1991–94; exec mangr Int Insurance Indust Gp Coopers & Lybrand 1995–; MIPR; *Recreations* golf; *Clubs* RAC; *Style—* Mrs Ruth Rooley; ✉ Greenways, Church Lane, Stoke Poges, Bucks SL2 4PB (☎ 01753 648040); Coopers & Lybrand, 1 Embankment Place, London WC2N 6NN (☎ 0171 583 5000, direct line 0171 212 3078, fax 0171 212 5510, telex 887470)

ROOM, Adrian Richard West; s of Richard Geoffrey Room, of Littleton Panell, Devizes, Wilts, and Cynthia Ida, *née* West (d 1976); *b* 27 Sept 1933; *Educ* Dauntsey's Sch, Exeter Coll Oxford (MA); *Career* teacher of English and modern languages 1958; lectr in: English and modern languages 1969, Russian 1974 (sr lectr 1980–84); full-time writer 1984–; memb: English Place Name Soc 1980, American Name Soc 1976, Soc of Authors 1980; FRGS 1976; *Books* Place-Names of the World (1974), Great Britain: A Background Studies Dictionary (English-Russian) (1978, revised edn 1997), Room's Dictionary of Confusibles (1979), Place-Name Changes Since 1900 (1980), Naming Names (1981), Room's Dictionary of Distinguishables (1981), Dictionary of Trade Name Origins (1982), Room's Classical Dictionary (1983), Dictionary of Cryptic Crossword Clues (1983), A Concise Dictionary of Modern Place-Names in Great Britain and Ireland (1983), Dictionary of Confusing Words and Meanings (1985), Dictionary of Translated Names and Titles (1985), Dictionary of Irish Place-Names (1986), Dictionary of Britain (1986), Dictionary of True Etymologies (1986), Dictionary of Changes in Meaning (1986), Dictionary of Coin Names (1987), Dictionary of Contrasting Pairs (1988), Dictionary of Astronomical Names (1988), Dictionary of Place-Names in the British Isles (1988), Dictionary of World Place-Names Derived from British Names (1989), Guinness Book of Numbers (1989), A Dictionary of Pseudonyms and their Origins (1989), An A to Z of British Life (1990), Dictionary of Dedications (1990), A Name for Your Baby (1992), The Street Names of England (1992), Brewer's Dictionary of Names (1992), Corporate Eponymy (1992), Place-Name Changes 1990–1991 (1993), The Naming of Animals (1993), A Dictionary of First Names (1994), Hutchinson Pocket Dictionary of First Names (1994), Hutchinson Pocket Dictionary of Confusible Words (1994), African Placenames (1994), Cassell Dictionary of Proper Names (1994), Cassell Dictionary of First Names (1995), Hutchinson Pocket Dictionary of Place Names (1995), Brewer's Dictionary of Phrase and Fable (reviser and ed, 1995), Literally Entitled (1995), An Alphabetical Guide to the Language of Name Studies (1996), Placenames of Russia and the Former Soviet Union (1996), Dictionary of World Placenames (1997); *Style—* Adrian Room, Esq; ✉ 12 High Street, St Martin's, Stamford, Lincs PE9 2LF (☎ and fax 01780 52097)

ROOME, John Walford; s of Maj-Gen Sir Horace Eckford Roome, KCIE, CB, CBE, MC, DL (d 1964), and Helen Isabel, *née* Walford (d 1970); *b* 19 Feb 1928; *Educ* Wellington, Clare Coll Cambridge (MA, LLM); *m* 2 July 1955, (Mary) Katherine, da of James Douglas (d 1958); 1 s (James Henry b 7 Oct 1958), 3 da (Christian b 19 Feb 1957, Frances b 3 July 1960, Annabel b 3 Sept 1964); *Career* RN 1946–48; slr Withers 1953–90 (sr ptnr 1986–90); memb Slrs Disciplinary Tbnl 1987–; Cdre: Royal Yacht Sqdn 1986–91, Royal Ocean Racing Club 1976–78; chm: Offshore Racing Cncl 1978–87 (hon pres 1988–), Review Bd Int Yacht Racing Union 1994–; Younger Brother Trinity House; Portsmouth Naval Base Property tstee 1986–93; *Recreations* sailing (yacht 'Flycatcher'); *Clubs* Royal Yacht Sqdn, Royal Cruising, Royal Ocean Racing, Royal Lymington Yacht, Island Sailing; *Style—* John Roome, Esq; ✉ Riversdale House, Boldre, Lymington, Hants

ROOME, Maj Gen Oliver McCrea; CBE (1973); s of Maj-Gen Sir Horace Roome, KCIE, CB, CBE, MC, DL, late RE (d 1964), and Helen Isabel, *née* Walford (d 1970); *b* 9 March 1921; *Educ* Wellington; *m* 1947, Isobel Anstis, da of Rev A B Jordan (d 1981), of Nottingham; 2 s (Peter b 1951, Harry b 1954), 1 da (Melanie b 1960); *Career* cmmnd RE 1940; WWII served: UK, Western Desert, Sicily, Italy; various appts 1946–68 in UK, Far East, ME and Berlin; IDC 1969, dir of army recruiting 1970–73, chief Jt Servs Liaison Orgn Bonn 1973–76, ret; Col Cmdt RE 1979–84; Co cmmr Scouts IoW 1977–85; High Sheriff IoW 1983–84; DL IoW 1981–96, Vice Lord-Lt IoW 1987–95; *Recreations* sailing (yacht 'Morning Sky'), youth activities; *Clubs* Army and Navy, Royal Yacht Sqdn, Royal Cruising, Royal Ocean Racing, Royal Solent Yacht; *Style—* Maj Gen Oliver Roome, CBE, DL; ✉ The White Cottage, Hill Lane, Freshwater, Isle of Wight PO40 9TQ

ROONEY, Maureen Gowran; OBE (1996); da of James Cunningham, of Blantyre, Lanarks, and Mary, *née* Conroy (d 1994); *b* 27 April 1947; *Educ* Elmwood Convent Bothwell; *m* 30 July 1966, Philip Rooney, s of Hugh Patrick Rooney; 3 da (Marie Elaine b 20 Nov 1967, Phyllis Jane b 1 Dec 1968, Christine b 14 Sept 1972), 1 s (Hugh MacGowan b 10 Nov 1970); *Career* hairdresser 1963–66, machine operator Hoover plc 1974–90, nat women's offr Amalgamated Engineering and Electrical Union 1990–; co-chair Women's Nat Cmmn 1993–96; memb: NEC's Women's Ctee Lab Pty 1989–, General Cncl TUC 1990–, Bd of Mgmnt Adult Literacy & Basic Skills Unit 1992–95, Ctee of Mgmnt Mary MacArthur Holiday Tst 1993–, Nat Constitutional Ctee Lab Pty 1994–, Cncl of Mgmnt Merchant Navy Welfare Bd 1995–; vice pres Nat Childminders' Assoc 1994–96; *Recreations* music, reading, cinema, theatre, knitting and walking; *Clubs* Blantyre Miners' Welfare; *Style—* Mrs Maureen Rooney, OBE; ✉ 84 Goodhart Way, West Wickham, Bromley, Kent BR4 0EY (☎ 0181 289 7837); Amalgamated Engineering and Electrical Union, Hayes Court, West Common Road, Hayes, Bromley, Kent BR2 7AU (☎ 0181 462 7755, fax 0181 315 8234)

ROONEY, Terence; MP (Lab) Bradford North (majority 7,664); *Career* MP (Lab) Bradford N 1990–; *Style—* Terence Rooney, Esq, MP; ✉ House of Commons, London SW1A 0AA (☎ 0171 219 3000)

ROOSE-EVANS, James Humphrey; s of Jack Roose-Evans, and Catharina Primrose, *née* Morgan; *b* 11 Nov 1927; *Educ* Crypt GS Gloucester, St Benet's Hall Oxford (MA); *Career* theatre director and author; fndr: Hampstead Theatre 1959, Bleddfa Trust - Centre for Caring and the Arts in the Welsh Marches 1974; former memb: Drama Panel Welsh Arts Cncl, SE Wales Arts Assoc; has taught regularly at: RADA, Julliard Sch of Music New York, Homerton Coll Cambridge; ordained non-stipendiary Anglican priest 1981 (first Br theatre dir to be also ordained priest); Gian Carlo Menotti artist in residence Charleston Coll Charleston S Carolina 1991–, distinguished visiting fell Ohio State Univ Columbus Ohio 1991; winner 7 awards incl Best Dir and Best Author (84 Charing Cross Rd); *Theatre* prodns in West End incl: An Ideal Husband, The Happy Apple, Private Lives, Cider with Rosie, Under Milk Wood, Mate!, The Seven Year Itch, A Personal Affair, The Best of Friends, Vaclav Havel's Temptation, Pericles, Irving; dir: Chester Mystery Plays (Chester Festival) 1973, French prodn The Best of Friends (Paris) 1989, Christopher Fry's Venus Observed (Chichester Festival Theatre) 1992; *Radio* writer for BBC incl: The Female Messiah (entered for Italia Prize), The Third Adam, Topsy and Ted, Acrobats of God, The Country of the Pointed Firs, The Story of my Life, 84 Charing Cross Road, Re: Joyce!; *Books* Directing a Play (1968), Experimental Theatre (4 edn, 1988), London Theatre (1977), The Adventures of Odd and Elsewhere (new edn, 1988), The Secret of the Seven Bright Shiners (new edn, 1989), Odd and the Great Bear (1973), Elsewhere and the Gathering of the Clowns (1974), The Return of the Great Bear (1975), The Secret of Tippity Witchit (1976), The Lost Treasure of Wales (1977), Inner Journey, Outer Journey (1987, published in America as The Inner Stage), Darling Ma (letters of Joyce Grenfell to her mother, ed 1988), The Time of My Life ENSA (memoirs of Joyce Grenfell, ed 1989), Passages of the Soul - Ritual Today (1994), One Foot on the Stage (authorised biography of Richard Wilson, 1996); *Recreations* writing and creating gardens; *Clubs* Garrick, Dramatists'; *Style—* James Roose-Evans, Esq; ✉ c/o Sheil Land Associates, 43 Doughty Street, London WC1N 2LF (☎ 0171 405 9351, fax 0171 831 2127)

ROOT, Jonathan; *b* 7 April 1949; *Educ* Oakham Sch, Gloucester Coll of Art; *Career* photographer; recent exhbns incl John Hobal Photographic Portrait Awards 1995 and 1996; winner Assoc of Photographers Silver and Merit Awards 1996; memb: Assoc of Photographers 1995, Photographers Gallery 1995; *Recreations* restoring classic cars; *Clubs* Jowett Car, Jupiter Owners Auto; *Style—* Jonathan Root, Esq; ✉ Jonathan Root Photography, 21 Ferdinand Street, Chalk Farm, London NW1 8EU (☎ 0171 485 5522, fax 0171 485 5532, mobile 0468 292666); c/o David Gardiner (☎ 0181 675 3055, fax 0181 675 3440)

ROOTES, 3 Baron (UK 1959); Nicholas Geoffrey Rootes; o s of 2 Baron Rootes (d 1992), and Marian, *née* Hayter; gf 1 Baron Rootes, GBE, founded Rootes Motors; *b* 12 July 1951; *Educ* Harrow; *m* 1976, Dorothy Anne, da of Cyril Walter James Wood (d 1979), of Swansea, and formerly wife of Jonathan Burn-Forti; 1 step s (Dante Burn-Forti b 1965), 1 step da (Lucinda Burn-Forti b 1963); *Heir* cousin, William Brian Rootes b 1944; *Career* journalist, author and copywriter; *Books* The Drinker's Companion (1987), Doing a Dyson (1995); *Recreations* flyfishing, skiing, tennis; *Style—* The Rt Hon the Lord Rootes; ✉ 2 Cedars Road, Barnes, London SW13 OHP

ROOTS, Guy Robert Godfrey; QC (1989); s of William Lloyd Roots, TD, QC, MP (d 1971) of London, and Elizabeth Colquhoun Gow, *née* Gray; *b* 26 Aug 1946; *Educ* Winchester, BNC Oxford (MA); *m* 17 May 1975, Caroline, da of (Alfred Saxon) Godfrey Clarkson (d 1970), of Herts; 3 s (William b 1978, Hamish b 1979, Sam b 1986); *Career* called to the Bar Middle Temple 1969; Harmsworth scholar 1969; Liveryman Worshipful Co of Drapers 1972; *Recreations* sailing, fishing, skiing, photography, woodworking; *Clubs* Itchenor Sailing; *Style—* Guy Roots, Esq, QC; ✉ 2 Mitre Court Buildings, Temple, London EC4Y 7BX (☎ 0171 583 1380, fax 0171 353 7772)

ROPER, Brian; *Educ* Univ of Wales (BSc(Econ)), Univ of Manchester (MA(Econ)); *Career* tutor in economics Univ of Wales Inst of Sci and Technol 1971–72, lectr in economics Teesside Poly 1973–75, sr lectr then princ lectr in economics Leicester Poly 1975–80; Newcastle upon Tyne Poly: head Sch of Economics 1980–85, actg head Faculty of Professional Studies 1985–87, head Dept of Economics and Govt April-Sept 1987, dean Faculty of Social Scis 1987–88 (actg dean July-Sept 1987), actg asst dir (academic) June-Aug 1988, asst dir (resources) 1988–90; dep vice-chllr (academic affrs) and dep chief exec Oxford Poly (later Oxford Brookes Univ) 1991–93, vice-chllr and chief exec Univ of North London 1994–; CVCP: memb 1994–, memb Long Term Strategy Gp 1995–, dir Univs and Colls Staff Devpt Agency 1995–; dir Islington Int Festival 1996–, tstee Cross Millennium Tst 1995–; memb Soc for Research into Higher Educn 1992–; FSS 1975, FIMgmt 1987, FRSA 1995; *Publications* author of numerous conference papers, book chapters, and articles in learned jls; *Style—* Brian Roper, Esq; ✉ University of North London, 166–220 Holloway Road, London N7 8DB (☎ 0171 753 5181, fax 0171 753 5049)

ROPER, Rev Geoffrey Edward Hodgess; s of Rev Frederick Mabor Hodgess Roper (d 1994), and Frances, *née* Brockway; *b* 24 April 1940; *Educ* Christ's Hosp, Magdalen and Mansfield Colls Oxford (MA PPE and Theol); *m* 1967, Janice, da of late Philip Henry Wakeham; 1 s (Jonathan b 1969), 1 da (Lucy b 1973); *Career* steelworks labourer Scunthorpe 1961–62; ordination course 1962–65, ordained Trinity Church Ifield 1965; pt/t industl chaplaincy 1966–71; min: Ifield 1965–71, Streatham 1971–78, Seaford 1978–85; Free Church chaplain Tooting Bec Hosp 1974–78, sr min Chelmsford Gp Utd Reformed Church 1985–95, gen sec Free Church Fed Cncl 1996–; memb Exec Ctee UN Student Assoc 1959–64, chm Seaford Social Responsibility Gp 1979–85, memb Eastbourne Community Health Cncl 1980–85, chm of ctee Friends of Dr Williams's Library 1991–; *Publications* The United Reformed Church - A European Church (with Philip Woods and Sheila Brain, 1994); *Recreations* walking, cycling, visiting art galleries, listening; *Style—* The Rev G H Roper; ✉ The Free Church Federal Council, 27 Tavistock Square, London WC1H 9HH (☎ 0171 387 8413, fax 0171 383 0150)

ROPER, Jeremy James; s of Robert Burnell Roper, CB, of Lindfield, W Sussex, and Mary, *née* Petyt; *b* 13 June 1954; *Educ* King's Coll Sch Wimbledon, Univ of Birmingham (LLB); *m* 20 Sept 1980, Alison Mary, da of Bryan Peter Studwell Cleal, of Wotton-under-Edge, Gloucestershire; 1 s (Richard James b 1987), 2 da (Katharine Mary b 1984, Elizabeth Diana b 1992); *Career* admitted slr 1979; ptnr: Needham and James slrs 1983–93, Dibb Lupton Broomhead 1993–95, Wansbroughs Willey Hargrave 1995–; memb Law Soc 1977; *Recreations* sport, vegetable gardening, theatre; *Style—* Jeremy Roper, Esq; ✉ Wansbroughs Willey Hargrave, Somerset House, Temple Street, Birmingham B2 5DP (☎ 0121 631 4099, fax 0121 631 3781)

ROPER, John Francis Hodgess; s of Rev Frederick Mabor Hodgess Roper, by his w Ellen Frances, *née* Brockway; *b* 10 Sept 1935; *Educ* William Hulme's GS Manchester, Reading Sch, Magdalen Coll Oxford, Univ of Chicago; *m* 1959, Valerie, da of Rt Hon John Edwards, OBE, sometime MP; 1 da; *Career* former econs lectr Manchester Univ; Royal Inst of International Affairs: ed of International Affairs 1983–88, head of Int Security Prog 1985–88 and 1989–90, dir of studies 1988–89; head of Western European

Union Inst for Security Studies Paris 1990–95; Parly candidate: (Lab) Derbyshire High Peak 1964, (SDP) Worsley 1983; MP (Lab and Co-op 1970–81, SDP 1981–83) Farnworth 1970–83; PPS to Min of State for Indust 1978–79, Lab oppn spokesman on Defence (front bench), SDP chief whip 1981–83; vice-chm: Anglo-German Parly Gp 1974–83, Anglo-Benelux Parly Gp 1979–83; Council of Europe: conslt 1965–66, memb Consultative Assembly 1973–80, chm Ctee on Culture and Educn 1979–80, memb WEU 1973–80, chm Ctee on Defence Questions and Armaments WEU 1977–80; chm: Lab Ctee for Europe 1976–80, Cncl on Christian Approaches to Defence and Disarmament 1983–89, GB/East Europe Centre 1987–90; hon treas Fabian Soc 1976–81; memb: Gen Advsy Cncl IBA 1974–79, Cncl Inst of Fiscal Studies 1975–90; vice-pres Manchester Statistical Soc 1971–, tstee History of Parliament Tst 1974–84; *Books* Towards Regional Co-operatives (with Lloyd Harrison, 1967), The Teaching of Economics at University Level (1970), The Future of British Defence Policy (1985), British-German Defence Co-operation (ed with Karl Kaiser, 1988), Franco-British Defence Co-operation (ed with Yves Boyer, 1988), Western Europe and the Gulf (ed with Nicole Gnesotto), Towards a New Partnership: US European Relations in the Post-Cold War Era (ed with Nanette Gantz); *Style—* John Roper, Esq

ROPER, (Mervyn Edward) Patrick; s of Capt Nigel Edward Godfrey Roper, DSO, RN (d 1983), and Marjorie Pamela, *née* Wrench; *b* 5 Oct 1954; *Educ* Marlborough, Coll of Law Surrey; *m* 17 Sept 1977, Sarah-Rose Mary, da of Dr D C Wilkins, CBE, TD; 2 s (Francis b 23 March 1987, Charles b 31 May 1989); *Career* mangr corp servs Turner Kenneth Brown Slrs London (merged with Nabarro Nathanson, May 1995); sec mangr Jupiter Asset Management Ltd 1996–; Liveryman Worshipful Co of Drapers 1980; *Recreations* gardening, cooking; *Clubs* Naval and Military; *Style—* Patrick Roper, Esq; ✉ 19 Criffel Avenue, London SW2 4AY (☎ 0181 674 4541); Jupiter Asset Management Limited, 197 Knightsbridge, London SW7 1RB (☎ 0171 412 0703, fax 0171 581 3857)

ROPER, Stephen John; s of Stanley Dunham Roper, of Lucy's Mill, Mill Lane, Stratford-on-Avon, Warwicks, and Kathleen Nora Theresa, *née* Barry; *b* 14 April 1943; *Educ* Wimbledon Coll, Univ of Durham (BA); *m* 4 May 1969, Sophie Jaqueline, da of Georges Alex, Cmdt (ret) French Army; 2 da (Stephanie b 1970, Joanna b 1971), 1 s (Tristan b 1977); *Career* CA; Pannell Fitzpatrick & Co Kingston Jamaica WI 1971–75, ptnr Eacott Worrall Burnham 1975–; *Recreations* reading, squash, golf; *Clubs* Churchills Camberley Squash, Camberley Heath Golf, Rotary Club of Wokingham; *Style—* Stephen Roper, Esq; ✉ Lavendale House, Broomfield Park, Sunningdale, Berkshire SL5 0JS (☎ 01344 24032); Grenville Court, Britwell Road, Burnham, Bucks SL1 8DF (☎ 01628 665432)

ROPNER, (William Guy) David; s of Sir William Guy Ropner, JP (d 1971), and Margarita (d 1973), da of Sir William Cresswell Gray, 1 Bt; *b* 3 April 1924; *Educ* Harrow; *m* 1, 1955, (Mildred) Malise Hare, da of Lt-Col George Armitage, MC, TD (d 1977); 1 da (Lucy (Mrs C Goelet) b 1957), 3 s (Guy b 1959, Roderick b 1962, Peter b 1964); m 2, 1985, Hon Charlotte Mary Piercy, da of 2 Baron Piercy (d 1981), and formerly w of P E Taddei; 1 s (Nicholas b 1986); *Career* WWII 2 Lt RA, 147 (Essex Yeo) Field Regt RA, Capt 3 Regt RHA Europe and UK 1942–47; joined Sir R Ropner & Co Ltd 1947, dir Ropner PLC (formerly Ropner Holdings Ltd) 1953–94 (chm 1973–84); dir: Mainsforth Investments Ltd 1952–, Cleveland Leasing Ltd 1982–, Guidehouse Expansion Management Ltd 1984–94; memb Gen Ctee Lloyd's Register of Shipping 1961–94; GCBS: vice pres 1978–79, pres 1979–80, chm Lights Advsy Ctee 1978–88, chm of tstees Chamber of Shipping Retirement Benefits Plan 1986–94; chm: MN Welfare Board 1980–93, Cleveland and Durham Industl Cncl 1980–94; memb Cncl Shipwrecked Mariners' Soc 1991–94; memb Lloyd's; *Clubs* St Moritz Tobogganing; *Style—* David Ropner, Esq; ✉ 1 Sunningdale Gardens, Stratford Rd, London W8 6PX

ROPNER, Jeremy Vyvyan; s of John Raymond Ropner (d 1996, s of William Ropner (d 1947), who was 3 s of Sir Robert Ropner, 1 Bt), and Joan, *née* Redhead (d 1993); *b* 3 May 1932; *Educ* Harrow, RNC Dartmouth; *m* 1955, Sally Talbot, da of Maj George Talbot Willcox, MC, and Constance, da of William Ropner *ante*; 1 s (Simon Jock Wilks b 1962) (and 1 s decd), 2 da (Sophia Sally (Mrs Christopher J Mansfield) b 1959, Lisa Cleone Vivian (Mrs Mark Nicole) b 1964); *Career* shipowner; chm: Ropner plc, Ropner Shipping Co Ltd, Hartlepool Water PLC; *Recreations* forestry, golf; *Clubs* Brooks's; *Style—* Jeremy Ropner, Esq; ✉ Firby Hall, Bedale, N Yorks (☎ 01677 422345)

ROPNER, Sir John Bruce Woollacott; 2 Bt (UK 1952), of Thorp Perrow, N Riding of Yorks; s of Sir Leonard Ropner, 1 Bt, MC, TD (d 1977). Sir Leonard's f, William, was 3 s of Sir Robert Ropner, JP, DL, cr a Bt 1904 (*see* Ropner, Bt, Sir Robert); *b* 16 April 1937; *Educ* Eton, St Paul's Sch USA; *m* 1, 1961 (m dis 1970), Anne Melicent, da of late Sir Ralph Delmé-Radcliffe; 2 da (Jenny (Mrs Graham Simpson) b 1963, Katherine (Hon Mrs Henry Holland-Hibbert) b 1964); m 2, 1970 (m dis 1993), Auriol Veronica, da of Capt Graham Lawrie Mackeson-Sandbach, of Caerllo, Llangernyw, Abergele, Denbighshire; 1 s (Henry John William b 1981), 2 da (Carolyn Esme b 1971, Annabel Mariella b 1974); m 3, 6 April 1996, Mrs Niki Tippett; *Heir* s, Henry John William Ropner, b 24 Oct 1981; *Career* dir Ropner plc; high sheriff of N Yorks 1991–92; *Clubs* Brooks's; *Style—* Sir John Ropner, Bt; ✉ Thorp Perrow, Bedale, Yorks (☎ 01677 422710)

ROPNER, Robert Clinton; s and h of Sir Robert Ropner, 4 Bt, *qv*; *b* 6 Feb 1949; *Educ* Harrow; *Style—* Robert Ropner, Esq

ROPNER, Sir Robert Douglas; 4 Bt (UK 1904), of Preston Hall, Stockton-on-Tees, Co Palatine of Durham, and Skutterskelfe Hall, Hutton Rudby, North Riding of Yorks; s of Sir (Emil Hugo Oscar) Robert Ropner, 3 Bt (d 1962); *b* 1 Dec 1921; *Educ* Harrow; *m* 1943, Patricia Kathleen, da of William Edward Scofield, of West Malling, Kent; 1 s, 1 da; *Heir* s, Robert Clinton Ropner, *qv*; *Career* formerly Capt RA; *Style—* Sir Robert Ropner, Bt

ROQUES, (David) John Seymour; s of Frank Davy Seymour Roques (d 1972), and Marjorie Mabel Martina Roques; *b* 14 Oct 1938; *Educ* St Albans Sch; *m* 20 April 1963, (Elizabeth) Anne, da of William John Mallender, of Wootton Courtenay, Somerset; 2 s (David William Seymour b 1966, Edward John Seymour b 1977), 1 da (Sarah Elizabeth b 1968); *Career* Deloitte & Touche (formerly Touche Ross & Co): joined 1957, ptnr 1967, sr ptnr and chief exec 1990–; memb Exec Ctee Deloitte Touche Tohmatsu International 1990–; non-exec dir: British Nuclear Fuels plc 1990–, Portman Building Soc 1995; memb Fin Reporting Cncl 1996–; Liveryman Worshipful Co of Chartered Accountants; MICAS 1962, FRSA 1990; *Recreations* rugby football, racing, opera, gardening; *Clubs* Edgbaston Golf (Birmingham); *Style—* John Roques, Esq; ✉ Deloitte & Touche, Stonecutter Court, 1 Stonecutter Street, London EC4A 4TR (☎ 0171 936 3000, fax 0171 583 1198, telex 884739 TRLNDN G)

ROSBOROUGH, (Robert) John; s of Thomas Uel Rosborough (d 1984), of Belfast, and Maureen Louise, *née* Maultsaid; *b* 19 June 1953; *Educ* Royal Belfast Academical Instn, Queen's Univ of Belfast (BSc); *Career* Downtown Radio: sound engr 1975–77, prodn mangr 1977–79, head of programming 1979–, also head of programming Cool FM 1989–; Freeman Town of Belfast Maine USA 1983; memb: Radio Acad 1983 (cncl memb 1989–), Br Actors' Equity 1984, RTS 1995; AMIEE 1975; *Recreations* travel, swimming, amateur radio, cinema; *Style—* John Rosborough, Esq; ✉ Downtown Radio, Newtownards, Co Down BT23 4ES (☎ 01247 815555, fax 01247 815252)

ROSCOE, (John) Gareth; s of late John Roscoe, and Ann, *née* Jones; *b* 28 Jan 1948; *Educ* Manchester Warehouseman and Clerks Orphan Sch (now Cheadle Hulme Sch), Stretford Tech Coll, LSE (LLB); *m* 1, 29 Aug 1970 (m dis 1979), Helen Jane, da of Geoffrey Duke Taylor, of Skipton, N Yorks; 1 da (Kate b 26 July 1974); m 2, 29 Aug 1980, Alexis Fayrer, da of Raymond Arthur Brett-Holt, of Esher, Surrey; 1 s (Jonathan Hugh b 1 Aug 1983), 1 da (Philippa Claire b 8 Feb 1982); *Career* called to the Bar Gray's Inn 1972, in practice 1972–75; Law Offr's Dept Attorney Gen's Chambers 1979–83, dep slr DOE 1987–89 (legal asst 1975–79, sr legal asst 1979, asst slr 1983–87); legal advsr to: co sec BBC, co sec BBC Worldwide Ltd, dir BBC Worldwide Ltd 1989–96, dir Educational Recording Agency Limited; non-exec memb Optimum NHS Tst 1995–; memb: Bar Cncl 1987–90 (memb Race Relations and Law Reform Ctees), Advsy Ctee Centre for Communications and Law UCL; *Recreations* radio and television, music, horology, motorcycling; *Clubs* Athenaeum; *Style—* Gareth Roscoe, Esq; ✉ Legal Adviser, British Broadcasting Corporation, Broadcasting House, Portland Place, London W1A 1AA (☎ 0171 765 4375/6, fax 0171 765 4381, telex 6371630)

ROSCOE, Robert Simon; *b* 14 April 1949; *Educ* Haberdashers' Aske's; *Career* admitted slr 1976; sr ptnr Victor Lissack & Roscoe 1981– (ptnr 1978–); memb Cncl Law Soc 1992–, chm Criminal Law Ctee Law Soc and chm Jt Ctee with Justices' Clerks Soc 1995–, chm No 14 Regnl Duty Slr Ctee Legal Aid Bd; pres London Criminal Cts Slrs' Assoc 1996; memb Law Soc 1976; *Recreations* Bolton Wanderers FC, Lancashire CCC; *Clubs* MCC; *Style—* Robert Roscoe, Esq; ✉ Victor Lissack & Roscoe, 8 Bow Street, Covent Garden, London WC2E 7AJ (☎ 0171 240 2010, fax 0171 379 4420)

ROSE, Anthea Lorrainne; da of Philip Brown (d 1987), of Edinburgh, and Muriel, *née* Seftor; *b* 2 Dec 1946; *Educ* Lansdowne House Sch Edinburgh (head of school), St Hugh's Coll Oxford (MA), pres Oxford Univ Liberal Club; *m* Aug 1971, Hannan David Rose, s of late Basil Nathan Rose; *Career* admin The Open Univ 1968–69, personnel offr Beecham Pharmaceuticals 1969–71, admin Univ of Kent 1971–76; Chartered Assoc of Certified Accountants: joined 1976, under sec 1982–88, dep chief exec 1988–93, chief exec 1993–; FRSA 1993; *Recreations* travel, wine, food; *Style—* Mrs Anthea Rose; ✉ Chartered Association of Certified Accountants, 29 Lincoln's Inn Fields, London WC2A 3EE (☎ 0171 242 6855, fax 0171 831 8054)

ROSE, Anthony John Wynyard; s of John Donald Rose, FRS (d 1976), and Yvonne Valerie, *née* Evans (d 1996); *b* 22 Jan 1946; *Educ* Oundle; *m* 1972 (m dis 1990), Angela Katherine, da of Wing Cdr Thomas Kenneth Waite (d 1987), of Cheltenham, Glos; 3 s (Dominic John Wynyard b 4 Nov 1984, Alexander Richard Thomas (twin) b 4 Nov 1984, Oliver Louis Christopher b 2 Dec 1986), 1 da (Katherine Lucy b 19 March 1980); *Career* Hon Artillery Co 1970–75; admitted slr 1970; slr Slaughter & May 1970–72 and ICI Ltd 1972–77, ed Aerostat 1975–82, slr then ptnr Charles Russell 1978–92, ptnr and head Commercial Div Barlow Lyde & Gilbert 1992–; currently: dir Chi-Chi's (UK) Limited, dir Paper House Group PLC; author of various articles on Euro competition law and hot air ballooning, awarded Aerostat medal; memb St Barbara Balloon Gp; Freeman Worshipful Co of Salters 1975, Freeman City of London 1975; memb: Law Soc, Int Bar Assoc; *Recreations* ballooning, shooting, fishing, reading, dogs; *Clubs* Hon Artillery; *Style—* Anthony Rose, Esq; ✉ Brook House, Colesbourne, Glos GL53 9NS; Barlow Lyde & Gilbert, Beaufort House, 15 St Botolph Street, London EC3A 7NJ (☎ 0171 782 8457, car 0831 509075)

ROSE, Barry; MBE (1981); s of William George Rose, of Essex, and Beatrice Mary, *née* Castle; *b* 17 July 1923; *m* 20 May 1963, (Dorothy) Jean Colthrup, da of Lt-Col Walter Reginald Bowden; 1 da (Diana b 1964); *Career* editor and publisher; chm own gp of cos 1970–; ed: Justice of the Peace 1944–74, Local Government Review, Family Law and others; memb Pagham Parish Cncl 1951–62; cncllr: Chichester RDC 1951–61, W Sussex CC 1952–73 (ldr Cons Gp 1967–72, alderman 1972), Bognor Regis UDC 1964–68; memb: RDC Assoc 1960–63, CCA 1968–72; various offices held in Cons Pty 1945–74 incl: pres Chichester Divnl Young Cons 1959–69, chm SE Area Cons Local Govt Advsy Ctee 1969–73, chm Chichester Divnl Assoc 1961–69; fndr Assoc of Cncllrs 1960 (pres 1975–86); Parly candidate (Alternative Cons) Old Bexley and Sidcup 1992; memb: Medico Legal Soc, Br Soc of Criminology, Soc of Cons Lawyers, RSL; hon life memb Justices' Clerks Soc 1985, hon memb American Soc of Criminology; Liveryman Worshipful Co of Stationers and Newspapermakers; FRSA; *Books* A Councillor's Work (1971), England Looks at Maud (1972), History of the Poll Tax (1993); *Plays* Change of Fortune (1950), Funny Business (1951); *Recreations* talking politics; *Clubs* Athenaeum, Garrick, United Oxford and Cambridge Univ, MCC; *Style—* Barry Rose, Esq, MBE; ✉ Courtney Lodge, Sylvan Way, Bognor Regis, W Sussex (☎ 01243 861251)

ROSE, Barry Michael; *b* 10 March 1945; *Educ* Univ of Manchester (BSc); *Career* asst investment mangr Co-operative Insurance Society Ltd 1971–76, investmt mangr Scottish Life Assurance Co 1977–88 (investmt sec 1976–77), gen mangr investmt Scottish Provident Institution 1988–93, chief exec Scottish Provident UK 1993–; FIA 1970; *Style—* Barry Rose, Esq; ✉ Scottish Provident UK, 6 St Andrew Square, Edinburgh EH2 2YA (☎ 0131 556 9181, fax 0131 558 2353)

ROSE, Rt Hon Lord Justice; Rt Hon Sir Christopher Dudley Roger; kt (1985), PC (1992); s of Roger Rose (d 1987), of Morecambe, and Hilda, *née* Thickett (d 1986); *b* 10 Feb 1937; *Educ* Morecambe GS, Repton, Univ of Leeds (LLB), Wadham Coll Oxford (BCL); *m* 5 Aug 1964, Judith, *née* Brand; 1 s (Daniel b 1967), 1 da (Hilary b 1969); *Career* lectr in law Wadham Coll Oxford 1959–60 (hon fell 1993), Bigelow teaching fell Law Sch Univ of Chicago 1960–61, barr 1960, QC 1974, recorder of the Crown Court 1978–85, bencher Middle Temple 1983, presiding judge Northern Circuit 1987–90 (practised 1961–85), judge of the High Court of Justice (Queen's Bench Div) 1985–92, a Lord Justice of Appeal 1992–; chm Criminal Justice Consultative Cncl 1994–; govr Pownall Hall Sch 1977–89; memb Senate Inns of Ct and Bar 1983–85; *Style—* The Rt Hon Lord Justice Rose; ✉ Royal Courts of Justice, Strand, London WC2A 2LL

ROSE, Dr (Frank) Clifford; s of James Rose (d 1958), and Clare Rose (d 1960); *b* 29 Aug 1926; *Educ* King's Coll London, Westminster Med Sch (MB BS); *m* 16 Sept 1963, Angela Juliet, da of Eric Halsted (d 1979); 3 s (Sebastian b 1964, Jolyon b 1966, Fabian b 1968); *Career* hon conslt neurologist Charing Cross Hosp 1965–91, physician i/c Dept of Neurology Regnl Neurosciences Centre 1978–91; dir: Academic Neuroscience Unit Charing Cross and Westminster Med Sch 1985–91, London Neurological Centre 1991–; fndr dir Princess Margaret Migraine Clinic 1973–91; prof assoc in human sciences Brunel Univ; sec-treas gen World Fedn of Neurology, scientific advsr Motor Neurone Disease Assoc 1988–91; editor: World Neurology 1990–, Journal of the History of the Neurosciences 1992–; chm: Headache and Migraine Res Gp World Fedn of Neurology 1980–95, Migraine Tst 1987–95; pres Section of Neurology RSM 1990–91, former pres Med Soc of London; Liveryman Worshipful Soc of Apothecaries; hon memb: Neurological Soc of Thailand 1992, Austrian Soc of Neurology 1992, Mexican Assoc for the Study of Headache 1992; FRCP; *Books* author and ed of over 60 books on neurology incl: Advances in Stroke Research (1985), James Parkinson: His Life and Times (1989), Advances in Headache Research (4 edn, 1994); *Recreations* travelling; *Style—* Dr Clifford Rose; ✉ London Neurological Centre, 110 Harley St, London W1N 1AS (☎ 0171 935 3546, fax 0171 935 4172)

ROSE, Sir Clive Martin; GCMG (1981, KCMG 1976, CMG 1967); s of Rt Rev Alfred Rose (d 1971, sometime Suffragan Bishop of Dover), and Lois, *née* Garton (d 1978); *b* 15 Sept 1921; *Educ* Marlborough, ChCh Oxford; *m* 1946, Elisabeth Mackenzie, da of Rev Cyril Lewis, and Effie, *née* Mackenzie; 2 s (Timothy Clive b 1947, Nicholas Martin b 1960), 3 da (Antonia (Mrs David Preston) b 1950, Elisabeth (Mrs Robert Hart) b 1952, Katharine (Mrs John Britten) b 1956); *Career* Rifle Bde 1941–46, Maj (despatches), served UK, Europe, India and Iraq; HM Dip Serv: entered 1948, served India, Germany, France, USA and Uruguay, ambass and head UK Delgn Negotiations on Mutual Reduction of Forces and Armaments (Vienna) 1973–76, dep sec Cabinet Office 1976–79, ambass and

UK perm rep N Atlantic Cncl (Brussels) 1979–82, ret 1982; conslt Control Risks Group 1983–95, memb RCDS Advsy Bd 1985–91, chm Control Risks Information Services Ltd 1991–93 (dir 1986–93); vice patron Royal Utd Servs Inst 1993– (chm Cncl 1983–86, vice pres 1986–93), pres Emergency Planning Assoc 1987–93, vice pres Suffolk Preservation Soc 1988– (chm 1985–88); Hon FICD, FRSA; *Publications* Campaigns against Western Defence: NATO's Adversaries and Critics (1985), The Soviet Propaganda Network: a Directory of Organisations Serving Soviet Foreign Policy (1988); *Style*— Sir Clive Rose, GCMG; ✉ Chimney House, Lavenham, Suffolk CO10 9QT

ROSE, David Jacob Edward; s of Michael Rose, of London, and Susan Phylida, *née* Latham; *b* 21 July 1959; *Educ* Univ Coll Sch, Magdalen Coll Oxford (exhibitioner, BA); *m* 9 Sept 1989, Shyama Deepika Perera, da of Noel Perera; 2 da (Anyusha Kate b 13 July 1991, Tushara Milina b 4 Aug 1994); *Career* news reporter Time Out 1981–84, reporter The Guardian 1984–88 (crime corr 1988–90), home affairs corr The Sunday Times 1990, home affairs corr and chief reporter The Observer 1990–; commended Br Press Awards 1984, special commendation The Howard League for Penal Reform 1993, David Watt Meml Prize 1994; *Books* Beneath the Mountains: Exploring The Deep Caves of Asturias (1987), A Climate of Fear: The Murder of PC Blakelock and the Case of the Tottenham Three (1992), In the Name of the Law: The Collapse of Criminal Justice (Jonathan Cape, 1996); *Recreations* mountaineering and potholing; *Clubs* Alpine; *Style*— David Rose, Esq; ✉ Home Affairs Correspondent, The Observer, 119 Farringdon Road, London EC1R 3ER (☎ 0171 278 2332, fax 0171 713 4286)

ROSE, David Leslie Whitfield; s of Leslie Rose (d 1980), of Leeds, and Joyce, *née* Whitfield (d 1981); *b* 27 Feb 1954; *Educ* Roundhay Sch Leeds, Downing Coll Cambridge, Inns of Ct Sch of Law (MA, LLB); *m* 14 April 1982, Genevieve Mary, da of Thomas Vernon Twigge, of Burley-in-Wharfedale, W Yorks; 1 s (Matthew b 1986), 1 da (Alice b 1989); *Career* called to the Bar 1977, memb NE Circuit and Northern Chancery Bar Assoc; memb NE Circuit Professional Negligence Bar Assoc; treas Leeds N Ward Cons Assoc 1988–89 (chm 1989–91), chm Leeds NE Cons Assoc 1992–95 (dep chm 1990–92); memb Hon Soc of Middle Temple; *Recreations* golf, philately; *Style*— David Rose, Esq; ✉ Atlow, 5 Oaklands Drive, Leeds LS16 8NZ (☎ 0113 281 7543, fax 0113 266 9316); 6 Park Square East, Leeds LS1 2LW (☎ 0113 245 9763 and 0113 226 0226, fax 0113 242 4395)

ROSE, Eliot Joseph Benn (Jim); CBE (1979); s of Col Ernest Albert Rose, CBE (d 1976), of Old Kiln, Churt, Surrey, and Julia, *née* Levy (d 1969); *b* 7 June 1909; *Educ* Rugby, New Coll Oxford; *m* 1, 1940 (m dis 1945), Mollie Lipscombe; m 2, 14 Feb 1946, Susan Pamela, da of Thornely Carbutt Gibson; 1 s (Alan b 1949), 1 da (Harriet b 1950); *Career* sec Lord Baldwin's Fund for German Refugees 1938–39; WWII 1939–45: RAF 1939–41, Govt CCs Bletchley 1941–44, Wing Cdr Dep Dir Intelligence Air Miny 1945; literary ed The Observer 1948–51, first dir Int Press Inst 1951–62, dir Nuffield Survey of Race Relations in Br 1963–69, editorial dir Westminster Press 1970–73, chm and chief exec Penguin Books 1974–80; fndr 33 Club for German Jewish Refugees 1933–39, co-fndr and tstee The Runnymede Tst (chm 1975–90), chm Inter-Action Tst 1968–84, memb Rampton Ctee of Enquiry into Educn of Ethnic Minority Children 1979–81, tstee Writers and Scholars Educnl Tst, conslt UNICEF; US Legion of Merit 1945; *Books* Colour and Citizenship (with Nicholas Deakin, 1969); *Recreations* music, walking; *Clubs* Garrick; *Style*— Jim Rose, Esq, CBE; ✉ 37 Pembroke Square, London W8 6PE (☎ 0171 937 3772); Rocks Farm, Groombridge, Kent (☎ 01892 864 223)

ROSE, Graham David; s of William Rose, of London, and Edna, *née* Fisher; *b* 12 April 1964; *Educ* Northumberland Park Sch Tottenham; *m* 19 Sept 1987, Teresa Julie, da of Albert Michael Humphrey; 1 da (Georgina Charlotte b 6 Dec 1990); *Career* professional cricketer; Middx CCC 1984–86, Somerset 1987– (county cap 1988); fastest century 60 overs (against Devon) 1990; played for Young Eng against Young Aust 1983; *Recreations* wine, gardening and golf; *Style*— Graham Rose, Esq; ✉ c/o Somerset County Cricket Club, The County Ground, St James Street, Taunton, Somerset TA1 1JT (☎ 01823 272946)

ROSE, Gregory; s of Bernard William George Rose, OBE (d 1996), and Molly Daphne Rose, OBE, JP, DL, *née* Marshall; *b* 18 April 1948; *Educ* Magdalen Coll Oxford (BA); *Career* conductor; appts incl: princ conductor London Jupiter Orch, Singcircle, Circle, London Concert Choir; guest appts incl: The London Philharmonic, Ulster Orch, BBC Concert Orch, BBC Singers, Netherland Radio Chamber Orch, Netherland Radio Choir, Nederland Kamerkoor, Groupe Vocal de France, Westdeutscher Rundfunk Chor, Steve Reich and Musicians, Netherlands Wind Ensemble, and also orchs in Eire, Denmark, Norway, Finland, Holland, Poland, Latvia and Estonia; series dir Almeida Festival (Cage at 70 1982, Reich at 50 1986); festivals have included BBC Proms 1978 and 1989, many TV and radio recordings throughout Europe, many compositions published, fndr ctee memb Assoc of Br Choral Dirs, memb SPNM; *Recreations* walking, listening to music; *Style*— Gregory Rose, Esq; ✉ 57 White Horse Rd, London E1 0ND (☎ 0171 790 5883, fax 0171 265 9170)

ROSE, Prof Hilary Ann; da of Arthur Farrow Channell (d 1963), of Orpington, and Sylvia Gladys, *née* Brackenbury; *b* 14 Jan 1935; *Educ* Bromley HS GPDST, LSE (BA), Univ of Bradford (PhD); *m* 1, 31 Dec 1954, John William Chantler (d 1958); 1 s (Simon John b 2 Dec 1955); m 2, 29 June 1961, Steven Peter Russell Rose; 1 s (Benjamin Jacob b 9 March 1963); *Career* res asst Inst of Psychiatry Maudsley Hosp 1963–64, res offr Miny of Housing and Local Govt 1964, asst lectr then lectr LSE 1964–75, prof of social policy Univ of Bradford 1975–; dir W Yorks Centre for Res on Women 1985–94; hon res fell Univ of Essex 1971–72, visiting scholar Bunting Inst Harvard 1979–80, Osher fell The Exploratorium San Francisco 1993; fell: Swedish Collegium for the Advanced Studies of the Social Sciences 1990–91, Centre for the Study of Technol and Culture Univ of Oslo 1992; Hill prof Centre for Advanced Feminist Studies Univ of Minnesota 1992, prof of feminist studies Univ of Gothenberg 1995; memb: Br Sociological Assoc, Women's Study Network (UK); memb Ed Bd: Int Jl of Health Studies, Innovation, Signs - a Jl of Women in Culture and Society, NORA; chm Br Soc for Social Responsibility in Science 1969–71, pres (Sociology) Br Assoc for the Advancement of Science 1987; *Books* Science and Society (with Steven Rose, 1969), The Radicalisation of Science (with S Rose, 1976), The Political Economy of Science (with S Rose, 1976), Countermovements and the Sciences: Yearbook of the Sociology of the Sciences (with Helga Nowotny, 1979), Love Power and Knowledge: towards a feminist transformation of the sciences (1994); *Recreations* music, walking on the Yorkshire moors, gardening, talking with friends; *Style*— Prof Hilary Rose; ✉ 4 Lloyd Square, London WC1X 9BA (☎ 0171 713 1709, fax 0171 833 2563, e-mail h.rose@open.ac.uk); University of Bradford, Bradford BD7 1DP

ROSE, Jeffery Samuel; s of Stanley Rose (d 1983), of London, and Esther, *née* Israel (d 1986); *b* 22 Dec 1924; *Educ* Haberdashers' Aske's Hampstead, Guy's Hosp Univ of London (BDS, FDSRCS, DOrthRCS); *m* 19 Dec 1949, Joyce Rose, da of Julius Bernstein (d 1967), of London; 1 s (Simon b 3 June 1960), 1 da (Ruth b 21 Oct 1956); *Career* Nat Serv Flt Lt RAF 1946–49; sr lectr in orthodontics The London Hosp Dental Sch 1957–67, dental surgn and conslt orthdontist The Royal London Hosp 1967–90; staff examiner in orthodontics Univ of London 1972–76; pres: London Hosp Dental Club 1977–78 (hon treas 1978–87), Br Assoc of Orthodontists 1991–94, Br Orthodontic Soc 1994–95; Br Soc for the Study of Orthodontics: memb 1946, memb Cncl 1961–74, hon treas 1962–70, pres 1972–73, sr vice pres 1976–78, chm Cncl 1980–83, special merit award 1986, life memb 1992; Br Paedodontic Soc: memb 1953, hon sec and treas 1958–61, pres 1964–65; Euro Orthodontic Soc: memb 1954, hon auditor 1956–70, hon treas 1986–92, life memb 1995; memb: Academic Bd London Hosp Med Coll 1975–78, NE Metroplitan Regnl Dental Advsy Ctee, Tower Hamlets Dist Mgmnt Ctee 1976–79, Sub-Ctee in Orthodontics & Paedodontics Univ of London (vice chm 1981–84, chm 1984–87); vice pres: North Western Reform Synagogue 1982–84 (chm 1966–68), Reform Synagogue of GB 1980–83 (chm 1976–79), World Union of Progressive Judaism 1995– (chm Euro Region 1990–95); chm Leo Baeck Coll 1985–88, tstee Reform Fndn Tst 1993–, hon treas Centre for Jewish Educn Tst 1994–; memb: BDA 1946, Royal Soc of Med 1947–83, Br Assoc of Orthodontists 1967, Int Assoc of Dentistry for Children 1969, American Assoc of Orthodontists 1973–89; *Publications* Orthodontic Teaching Models (1954), Atypical Paths of Eruption - Some Causes and Effects (1958), Cases Treated with Extractions of Permanent Canines (jtly, 1960), A Survey of Congenitally Missing Teeth Excluding Third Molars in 6,000 Orthodontic Patients (1966), Early Loss of Teeth in Children (1966), Simple Methods of Retracting Canine Teeth (jtly, 1967), 1,000 Consecutively Treated Orthodontic Cases - a Survey (1977), Choice of Appliances in Relation to Demand for Orthodontic Treatment (1982); *Recreations* Jewish communal work, canal boating; *Style*— Jeffery Rose, Esq; ✉ 9 Meadway Close, London NW11 7BA (☎ 0181 455 5771)

ROSE, John Alexander; s of Alfred Rose (d 1971), and Tamar, *née* Brenner; *b* 15 July 1935; *Educ* The Hall Hampstead, Haberdashers' Aske's Hampstead, Photography Sch Regent St Poly; *m* 29 Dec 1978, Linda Margaret; *Career* fndr own architectural and industl photography business 1956, latterly expanded to incl processing and printing; Masters CPP of Professional Photographers of America; pres BIPP 1974–75; FRPS 1966, FSA 1971, Hon FBIPP 1986 (FBIPP 1966); *Books* How to Run a Photographic Business (1985); *Recreations* walking, holidays, reading; *Style*— John Rose, Esq, FSA; ✉ Harrow Photolabs, 35 Pinner Rd, Harrow HA1 4ES (☎ 0181 427 9022, fax 0181 863 0451)

ROSE, Dr John Luke; s of Dr Howard Farnham Rose (d 1949), of London, and Elizabeth Gwyneth, *née* Willcox (d 1989); *b* 19 July 1933; *Educ* Univ of London, Trinity Coll of Music London (BMus, PhD, LMus TCL); *Career* Nat Serv (as registered conscientious objector, food distribution work) 1952–54; adult educn lectr Univ of Oxford 1958–66, pt/t lectr and teacher Trinity Coll of Music 1958–63 (examiner 1960), pt/t lectr WEA Kent and Surrey 1959–80, pt/t teacher of English, music and art various schs 1959–66, staff tutor Univ of London Senate House 1966–84; dir of studies Proms Summer Sch 1980; lectr and examiner Trinity Coll of Music (Canada, Newfoundland, USA, Fiji, NZ, Aust, India); lectr: V & A, ENO, various univs UK, Canada, USA, NZ, India; full-time composer, writer, pianist, poet and painter 1984–; piano recitals UK and abroad 1959–; presenter BBC progs on music and art; memb: TCM Guild (chm 1961), Union of Grads in Music Cncl, SPNM 1962, Assoc of Univ Teachers 1966–, various Adult Educn Ctees 1966–, Composers' Guild 1967; hon fell Trinity Coll 1961; Royal Philharmonic Soc prizewinner for first and second Symphonies; *Compositions* Symphony No 1 The Mystic (BBC premiere), Symphonic Dances (Hallé), Piano Concerto No 1 (BBC), Overture Macbeth (BBC), Symphony No 2, Violin Concerto (BBC), Hymnos I-X The Pleasures of Youth (Cantata for school choir and orch), 2 String Quartets, Violin Sonata, Blake's Song of Innocence, Te Deum (for organ), Capriccio, Elegy and Scherzetto (for bassoon and piano); piano works incl: Toccata: Ariel, Night Music, 2 Sonatas, Landscapes (for young players), Dance Suite, Apocalyptic visions, The Dance of Spring (rondo for orch) 1993, Piano Concerto No 2 1994; vocal: St Francis (musical), Odysseus (opera), numerous songs, hymns and anthems; *Publications* Wagner's Musical Language (1963), Ludwig, Wagner and the Romantic View (1978), Wagner's Tristan und Isolde, a Landmark in Musical History (1980), Wagner's Music Dramas (a chronological study of his musical works, 1984), Some Basic Facts About Alcohol (1985, 2 edn 1988); *Recreations* reading, gardening, walking, golf, tennis, films, photography, writing poetry, mystical philosophy and meditation, lifelong vegetarian, teetotaller and non-smoker; *Clubs* Foxhills Country; *Style*— Dr John Luke Rose; ✉ Kalon, 113 Farnham Road, Guildford GU2 5PF

ROSE, John Martin; s of Ronald Hilton Rose, of Selsey, W Sussex, and Margaret Joan, *née* Todd; *b* 6 Oct 1934; *Educ* Caterham Sch, DipPR (CAM); *m* 1, 1 Aug 1960 (m dis), Jennifer Jane, da of Charles Hanson; 2 s (Timothy St John Todd b 15 Oct 1961, Christopher Mark b 22 Jan 1963); m 2, 4 Sept 1992, Evelyn Cook, da of Eugenio Oida; *Career* with Hulton Press 1951 (working on Picture Post then Eagle and Girl magazines), sub-ed/corr Caterer & Hotel Keeper 1952; Nat Serv RAF Changi Singapore 1953–54 (Malaya Campaign): prodr/sr announcer Changi Bdcasting Serv (commercial), bdcaster BBC Radio Malaya/Rediffusion Singapore, corr Straits Times, educn offr RAF Labuan, GSM (Clasp) Malaya 1953; successively with West Sussex County Times, Croydon Times then Wallington & Carshalton Times (chief reporter) 1955–58, business and personal managr to Michael Holliday (the singer) 1958, theatre critic/feature writer Leamington Spa Courier (also nat dailies) 1959, feature writer/columnist West Sussex County Times 1960, news corr BBC Home Serv Sussex and Surrey area 1961, PRO Ocean Travel Development 1962–68, assoc dir/head of Tourism Div PPR International Ltd 1968–72, product publicity mangr 3M (UK) Ltd 1972–74, asst dir Food Mfrs' Fedn 1974–79, md Maude-Roxby Sussman Associates PR consltS 1979, chm and md Jonathan Rose Public Relations Ltd 1980–, dir The Evelyn Rose Partnership 1993–; co-ordinator for Chartered Inst of Journalists, ISBA, IPR, NUJ and PRCA Campaign Against Editorial Charges 1994–; script and tech advsr on several films incl A Countess from Hong Kong (with Charlie Chaplin), has scripted and directed other promotional films; fndr: The Seahorse Club (for maritime publicists) 1963, Communicator of the Yr Award 1975; estab various Lib assocs Midlands and Sussex 1959–63, chm Home Counties Young Lib Fedn 1961–63, cncllr and ctee chm Horsham UDC 1962–65 (ldr Lib Gp); co-creator North London Theatre Tst (with Sir Ralph Richardson, later with Sir John Mills) 1982–88, organiser The Sir Ralph Richardson Meml Concert (with Sir John Gielgud, Dame Peggy Ashcroft, etc) 1984; lectr for Industl Soc, IPRA, BAIE, UNA, Conf of Drama Schs, etc; memb: Economic Res Cncl 1966, BAIE 1968 (memb Cncl and dir of Mgmnt Rels 1974–77); FRSA 1968, FIPR 1983 (MIPR 1968, memb Cncl 1978–93); *Recreations* playing piano, composing, wildlife, crosswords, motoring, wine, cooking, country walking, writing, good conversation; *Style*— John M Rose, Esq; ✉ Jonathan Rose Public Relations Ltd, The Old School, Dunwich, Suffolk IP17 3DU (☎ and fax 01728 648570)

ROSE, Joyce Dora Hester; CBE (1981), JP (Herts 1963), DL (Herts 1990); da of Abraham (Arthur) Woolf, of Hampstead, London (d 1972), and Rebecca, *née* Simpson (d 1985); *b* 14 Aug 1929; *Educ* King Alfred Sch London, Queen's Coll London; *m* 6 Oct 1953, Cyril Rose, s of Benjamin Rose, of Bedford (d 1971); 1 da (Gillian b 1955); 2 s (Stephen b 1957, Andrew b 1959); *Career* chm Watford Adult Ct 1990–Dec 1994 (dep chm Family Panel); memb Herts: Magistrates Cts Ctee until 1995, Probation Ctee until 1995; chm Cncl and Nat Exec Magistrates Assoc 1990–93 (chm Herts Branch 1985–90); dir: Apex Tst 1994–, Herts Care Tst 1995–; memb Children Act Advsy Ctee 1991–93; Lib Pty: pres 1979–80, chm 1982–83, chm Women's Lib Fedn 1987–88 (pres 1972 and 1973); former memb: Women's Nat Cmmn, Nat Exec UK Ctee of UNICEF (vice chm 1968–70); Hon LLD Univ of Hertfordshire 1992; *Clubs* Nat Lib; *Style*— Mrs Joyce Rose, CBE, JP, DL; ✉ 38 Main Avenue, Moor Park, Northwood, Middx HA6 2LQ (☎ 01923 821385)

ROSE, Sir Julian Day; 4 Bt (UK 1909), of Hardwick House, Whitchurch, Oxon and 5 Bt (UK 1872), of Montreal, Dominion of Canada; s of Sir Charles Henry Rose, 3 Bt (d 1966), by his w, Hon Phoebe Margaret Dorothy Phillimore, da of 2 Baron Phillimore; also suc kinsman, Sir Francis Rose, 4 Bt 1979; *b* 3 March 1947; *Educ* Stanbridge Earls

Sch Romsey, RADA; *m* 1976, Elizabeth Good, da of Derrol Johnson, of Columbus, Ohio, USA; 1 s (Lawrence Michael b 6 Oct 1986), 1 da (Miriam Margaret b 1984); *Heir* s, Lawrence Michael Rose b 6 Oct 1986; *Career* commenced conversion to organic farming enterprise Hardwick Estate 1975; co-fndr and asst dir Inst for Creative Devpt Antwerp 1975–82, co-fndr The Assoc of Unpasteurised Milk Producers and Consumers 1989; memb: Cncl Soil Assoc 1984–, Bd UK Register of Organic Food Standards, Rural and Agric Affrs Advsy Ctee BBC 1991–94, Cncl Schumacher Soc 1993–, Advsy Cncl for Food Policy Thames Valley Univ 1994–; chm of tstees Sustainable Agriculture, Food and the Environment Alliance 1995–, chm Assoc of Rural Businesses in Oxfordshire 1995–, tstee Dartington Hall Tst; writer and broadcaster on socio-environmental issues; agric correspondent Environment Now 1989; *Style—* Sir Julian Rose, Bt; ✉ Hardwick House, Whitchurch, Oxon RG8 7RB

ROSE, Kenneth Vivian; CBE (1997); s of Dr J Rose; *b* 15 Nov 1924; *Educ* Repton, New Coll Oxford (scholar, MA); *Career* served Welsh Guards 1943–46 (attached Phantom 1945); asst master Eton Coll 1948; memb editorial staff Daily Telegraph 1952–60, fndr and writer Albany column Sunday Telegraph 1961–; FRSL; *Books* Superior Person: a portrait of Curzon and his circle in late Victorian England (1969), The Later Cecils (1975), William Harvey: a monograph (1978), King George V (1983, Wolfson Award for History 1983, Whitbread Award for Biography 1983, Yorkshire Post Biography of the Year Award 1984), Kings, Queens and Courtiers: intimate portraits of the Royal House of Windsor (1985), Founders and Followers: literary lectures on the London Library (contrib, 1992); also author of contribs to Dictionary of National Biography; *Clubs* Beefsteak, Pratt's; *Style—* Kenneth Rose, Esq, CBE, FRSL; ✉ 38 Brunswick Gardens, London W8 4AL (☎ 0171 221 4783)

ROSE, Kevin John; s of Thomas Rose, of Bletchley, Bucks, and Jeanette Iris, *née* Farman; *b* 10 July 1956; *Educ* Bletchley GS; *m* July 1979, Gillian, da of Thomas Lovett; 1 s (Alexander John b 20 Dec 1985); *Career* mktg offr BOC 1976–78 (sales offr 1974–76); VAG (UK) - Volkswagen/Audi: fin controller Sales & Mktg 1978–80, field support mangr 1980–81, fleet ops mangr 1981–84, fleet servs mangr 1984–88, distribution mangr 1988–90, customer servs mangr 1990–91, regnl mangr 1991–93, head of mktg 1993–95; dir Seat UK 1995–; *Recreations* squash, tennis, soccer coaching; *Style—* Kevin Rose, Esq; ✉ 9 Swan Court, Olney, Bucks MK46 4JP (☎ 01234 712357); Seat UK, Seat House, Gatwick Road, Crawley, West Sussex RH10 2AX (☎ 01293 514141)

ROSE, Martin John; s of John Ewert Rose, of Chandlers Ford, Hants, and Margaret Mary, *née* Eames; *b* 21 March 1956; *Educ* St Mary's Coll Southampton, Univ of Warwick (LLB); *m* 7 May 1988, Emma Margaret Havilland, da of Robert Bernard Hutchinson, of Wimborne, Dorset; *Career* called to the Bar Middle Temple 1979, practising barr Western circuit 1980–86, legal conslt The Stock Exchange 1986, sr legal advsr The Securities Assoc 1986–89, sr asst slr Linklaters and Paines 1990–92, gp legal and compliance dir The Smith & Williamson Group 1992–; MSI; *Recreations* gardening; *Style—* Martin Rose, Esq; ✉ Smith & Williamson Securities, 1 Riding House Street, London W1A 3AS (☎ 0171 637 5377)

ROSE, Gen Sir (Hugh) Michael; KCB (1994), CBE (1986), DSO (1995), QGM (1981), ADC Gen (1995); s of late Lt Col Hugh Vincent Rose, IA, and Mrs Barbara Phoebe Masters, *née* Allcard; *b* 5 Jan 1940; *Educ* Cheltenham Coll, St Edmund Hall Oxford (BA, hon fell 1995), Staff Coll, RCDS; *m* 1968, Angela Raye Shaw; 2 s; *Career* cmmnd: Gloucestershire Regt TAVR 1959, RAFVR 1962, Coldstream Guards 1964; served: Germany, Aden, Malaysia, Gulf States, Dhofar, N Ireland (despatches), Falkland Is (despatches); BM 16 Para Bde 1973–75, CO 22 SAS Regt 1979–82, cmd 39 Infantry Bde 1983–85, Cmdt Sch of Infantry 1987–88, dir Special Forces 1988–89, GOC NE Dist and cmd 2nd Infantry Div 1989–91, Cmdt Staff Coll 1991–93, cmd UK Field Army and Inspr Gen of TA 1993–94, Commander UN Protection Force Bosnia-Herzegovina 1994–95, Dep Commander in Chief Land Cmd March-July 1995, Adjutant Gen July 1995–June 1997; chm Army Parachute Assoc, Admiral Army Sailing Assoc, Hon Col Oxford OTC; awarded Legion d'Honneur 1995; *Recreations* skiing, sailing, parachuting; *Style—* Gen Sir Michael Rose, KCB, CBE, DSO, QGM, ADC Gen; ✉ c/o Regimental HQ Coldstream Guards, Wellington Barracks, Birdcage Walk, London SW1E 6HQ

ROSE, Norman Hunter; s of Rev David Douglas Rose, and Catherine Drummond, *née* Pow; *b* 11 March 1949; *Educ* Royal HS Edinburgh, Univ of Edinburgh (LLB); *m* 18 Oct 1980, Kay, da of Gordon Murray Sanderson; *Career* articled clerk A & W M Urquhart WS Edinburgh 1970–72, asst slr Dunfermline Town Cncl 1972–74, dep sec Law Soc of Scotland 1977–85 (asst sec 1974–76), dep dir of company affrs CBI 1985–88, dir of Euro affrs Electronic Data Systems Corp 1989–91 (assoc int gen counsel 1988–89), govt affrs conslt 1992–94, conslt Jackaman Smith & Mulley Slrs Ipswich 1995–, sec Br Paediatric Assoc 1995–96, dir gen Business Servs Assoc 1996–; dir Fedn Against Software Theft 1986–90, memb Bd American Electronics Assoc 1989–91; memb: Law Soc of Scotland 1972, Soc of Writers to HM Signet in Scotland 1972, Soc of Slrs to the Supreme Cts in Scotland 1977; *Recreations* music, hill walking; *Clubs* Law Soc; *Style—* Norman Rose, Esq; ✉ Flat 7, Howard Court, Henry Close, Enfield, Middx EN2 9JT (☎ 0181 245 1170); Red Brick Cottage, 19 The Street, Freston, Ipswich, Suffolk IP9 1AF (☎ 01473 780030); Business Services Association, Mezzanine Floor, Commonwealth House, 1/19 New Oxford Street, London WC1A 1NU

ROSE, Paul Bernard; s of Arthur Rose (d 1974), and Norah, *née* Helman; *b* 26 Dec 1935; *Educ* Bury GS, Univ of Manchester (LLB), Inst of Advanced Legal Studies, Sorbonne; *m* 13 Sept 1957, Eve Marie Thérèse, da of Jean Lapu, of Paris; 2 s (Howard Imre b 25 Jan 1961, Daniel Sean b 18 Oct 1970), 1 da (Michelle Alison b 11 Oct 1964); *Career* called to the Bar Gray's Inn 1958, practising barr 1962–88; legal advsr Cooperative Union Ltd 1958–61, lectr Univ of Salford 1961–63; MP (Lab) Manchester Blackley 1964–79, PPS to Min for Tport 1966–68, frontbencher (Employment), fndr memb SDP; HM coroner Gtr London Southern Dist 1988– (asst recorder 1975–88); pt/t special immigration adjudicator 1987–, pt/t special adjudicator 1993–; pres SE Coroners' Soc; chm NW Sports Cncl 1966–68, memb Cncl of Europe 1968–70; patron St Lucia Soc; assoc Inst of Linguists; memb: Coroners' Soc, Medico-Legal Soc; *Recreations* sport, the arts, computers, writing, travel; *Style—* Paul B Rose, Esq; ✉ 47 Lindsay Drive, Kenton, Harrow, Middlesex HA3 0TA (☎ 0181 204 3076); Coroner's Office, The Law Courts, Barclay Road, Croydon CR9 3NE (☎ 0181 681 5019)

ROSE, Prof Richard; s of Charles Imse, of St Louis, Missouri, USA, and late Mary Conely Rose; *b* 9 April 1933; *Educ* Clayton HS Missouri USA, Johns Hopkins Univ (BA), LSE, Univ of Oxford (DPhil); *m* 1956, Rosemary, da of late James Kenny, of Whitstable, Kent; 2 s, 1 da; *Career* political PR Mississippi River Road 1954–55, reporter St Louis Post - Dispatch 1955–57, lectr in govt Univ of Manchester 1961–66; Univ of Strathclyde: prof of politics 1966–81, dir Centre for the Study of Public Policy 1976–, prof of public policy 1982–; visiting prof European Univ Inst Florence 1976, 1977 and 1993; guest prof: Wissenschaftszentrum Berlin 1988–90, Central Euro Univ Prague 1992–95; Ransone lectr Alabama 1990; fndr memb Exec Ctee Euro Consortium for Political Res 1970, US Ambassador's appointee US-UK Fulbright Educnl Cmmn 1970–75, sec Res Ctee on Political Sociology Int Political Sci Assoc and Int Sociological Assoc 1970–85, fndr memb Exec Ctee Br Politics Gp in the US 1974–; memb: Steering Ctee Choice in Social Welfare Policy Cncl of Euro Studies 1974–77, Home Office Working Pty on the Electoral Register 1975–77; convenor Work Gp on UK Politics Political Studies Assoc 1976–88, conslt to Chm N Ireland Constitutional Convention 1976, memb Cncl Int Political Sci Assoc 1976–82, co-dir 1982 World Congress Programme Rio de Janeiro; conslt: OECD 1980–, World Bank 1992–; UN conslt Pres of Colombia 1990, scientific advsr Paul Lazarsfeld Soc Vienna 1991–; ed Journal of Public Policy 1985– (chm Bd 1981–84); memb Cncl British Irish Studies Assoc 1987–; founding fell Soc for the Advancement of Socio-Economics 1989–; fell: American SSRC Stanford Univ 1967, Woodrow Wilson Int Centre Washington DC 1974; Guggenheim fellowship 1973–74, foreign memb Finnish Acad of Sci and Letters 1985, hon vice pres UK Political Studies Assoc 1986; FBA 1992, FAAAS 1994; *Books* incl: Governing without Consensus - an Irish Perspective (1971), Electoral Behavior (1974), Presidents and Prime Ministers (ed with E Suleiman, 1980), Do Parties Make a Difference? (2 edn, 1984), Understanding Big Government (1984), Ordinary People in Public Policy (1989), Politics in England (5 edition, 1989), Loyalties of Voters (with Ian McAllister, 1990), International Almanac of Electoral History (with T T Mackie, 3 edn, 1991), The Postmodern President - George Bush Meets the World (2 edn, 1991), Lesson - Drawing in Public Policy (1992), Inheritance Before Choice in Public Policy (1994), What is Europe? (1996), How Russia Votes (with Stephen White and I McAllister, 1996); books and articles translated into 14 languages; *Recreations* architecture, historical Britain and modern America, music, writing; *Clubs* Reform, Cosmos (Washington DC); *Style—* Prof Richard Rose, FBA; ✉ Bennochy, 1 East Abercromby Street, Helensburgh, Argyll G84 7SP (☎ 01436 672164, fax 01436 673125); Centre for the Study of Public Policy, Livingstone Tower, 26 Richmond St, Glasgow G1 1XH (☎ 0141 548 3217, fax 0141 552 4711)

ROSE, Dr Stephen John; s of Bernard Rose (d 1967), of London, and Grace Alberta, *née* Hefford; *b* 20 March 1951; *Educ* Highgate Public Sch, Univ of Cambridge, Guy's Hosp London (BA, MA, MB BChir, FRCP, MD); *m* 29 Jan 1983, Beatriz; 2 da (Sybilla Alessandra b 1985, Eilidh Veronica b 1986); *Career* jr doctor Guy's, registrar Westminster Hosp Med Sch London, lectr Univ of Aberdeen, currently conslt and hon sr lectr Dept of Child Health Univ of Birmingham; dir Hopkins and Netherwood Ltd; memb Nat Exec Jr Hosp Drs; *Books* Case Histories in Paediatrics (1984), Early Recognition of Child Abuse (1984), Textbook of Medicine for Medical Students (1986); *Recreations* squash; *Clubs* Univ of Cambridge Union; *Style—* Dr Stephen Rose; ✉ University Dept of Paediatrics, Birmingham Heartlands Hospital, Bordesley Green East, Birmingham B9 5SS (☎ 0121 766 6611, fax 0121 773 6736)

ROSE, Prof Steven P R; s of Lionel Sydney Rose (d 1959), and Ruth, *née* Waxman (d 1988); *b* 4 July 1938; *Educ* Haberdashers' Aske's Sch London, King's Coll Cambridge (state scholar, open scholar, BA), Maudsley Inst of Psychiatry London (Med Res Cncl scholar, PhD); *m* Prof Hilary Rose, prof of social policy, and dir W Yorks Centre for Res on Women Univ of Bradford; 2 s (Simon John Chantler b 2 Dec 1955, Benjamin Jacob b 9 March 1963); *Career* Beit meml fell and Guinness res fell Dept of Biochemistry and New Coll Oxford 1961–63, Nat Inst of Health post-doctoral fell Istituto Superiore di Sanita Rome 1963–64, MRC res staff Nat Inst for Med Res then MRC Metabolic Reactions Res Unit Dept of Biochemistry Imperial Coll London 1964–69, lectr London Univ Extramural Dept 1965–69, prof of biology, chair Dept of Biology and dir Brain and Behaviour Res Gp Open Univ 1969–; visiting appts: res fell Hirnforschungsinstitut Leipzig 1961, sr res fell Australian Nat Univ 1977, prof Univ of Queensland Inst for Med Res 1979, scholar Museum of Comparitive Zoology Harvard Univ 1980, Hill visiting distinguished res prof Univ of Minnesota 1992, Osher fell The Exploratorium San Francisco 1993; scientific sec Science Res Cncl Neurobiology Panel 1968–69, memb Neurochemical Gp (Biochemical Soc) Ctee 1970–75, dir and scientific advsr Edinburgh Science Festival 1991–; pres Biology Section Br Assoc for the Advancement of Sci 1996; memb editorial bds of numerous pubns 1973–; medal of the Univ of Utrecht 1989, PK Anokhin medal Inst of Physiology Moscow 1990, Sechenov medal 1992; fndr memb: Br Res Assoc (memb Ctee 1965–68, 1970–75 and 1988–90), Br Soc for Social Responsibility in Science (memb Ctee 1969–70 and 1974–76); memb: Biochemical Soc, Int Soc for Neurochemistry, Brain Res Assoc, European Brain and Behaviour Soc, European Neurosciences Assoc, European Soc for Neurochemistry; FIBiol 1970, FRSA 1980; *Books* The Chemistry of Life (1966), Science and Society (with Hilary Rose, 1969), The Conscious Brain (1973), No Fire, No Thunder (with Sean Murphy and Alastair Hay, 1984), Not In Our Genes (with Richard Lewontin and Leo Kamin, 1984), Molecules and Minds - Essays on Biology and the Social Order (1988), The Making of Memory (1992, winner Science Book prize 1993), Lifelines (1997); ed of numerous books, author of numerous res papers; *Style—* Prof Steven Rose; ✉ Department of Biology, Open University, Milton Keynes MK7 6AA (☎ 01908 652125, fax 01908 654167)

ROSEBERRY, Michael Anthony; s of Matthew Roseberry, and Jean Roseberry; *b* 28 Nov 1966; *Educ* Durham Sch; *m* 22 Feb 1991, Helen Louise, da of Michael Adamson; 2 da (Jordan Louise b 29 May 1992, Lauren Ella b Feb 1993); *Career* professional cricketer; Middlesex CCC: debut 1986, awarded county cap 1990, over 159 matches; capt Durham CCC 1995–96; England: rep schs under 15 and under 19 (capt for 2 years), memb Young England tour W Indies 1985, capt Young England series v Sri Lanka, memb A tour Aust 1993; awards: Lord's Taverners/MCC Cricketer of the Year 1983, Cricket Soc's Best Young Cricketer of the Year 1984, Middx/Lucozade Player of the Year 1992; *Recreations* golf, rugby, going out; *Style—* Michael Roseberry, Esq; ✉ Durham CCC, County Ground, Riverside, Chester le Street, Co Durham DH3 3QR

ROSEBERY, 7 Earl of (S 1703); Sir Neil Archibald Primrose; 9 Bt (S 1651), DL (Midlothian 1960); also Viscount of Rosebery, Lord Primrose and Dalmeny (both S 1700), Viscount of Inverkeithing, Lord Dalmeny and Primrose (both S 1703), Baron Rosebery (UK 1828), Earl of Midlothian, Viscount Mentmore, and Baron Epsom (all UK 1911); s of 6 Earl of Rosebery, KT, DSO, MC, PC (d 1974, the celebrated race horse owner and s of the Lib PM and Hannah, da of Baron Meyer de Rothschild, through whom Mentmore came into the family), by his 2 w, Hon Dame Eva, *née* Bruce, DBE, JP (da of 2 Baron Aberdare and former w of 3 Baron Belper); *b* 11 Feb 1929; *Educ* Stowe, New Coll Oxford; *m* 1955, (Alison Mary) Deirdre, da of Ronald William Reid, MS, FRCS; 1 s, 4 da; *Heir* s, Lord Dalmeny, *qv*; *Style—* The Rt Hon The Earl of Rosebery, DL; ✉ Dalmeny House, South Queensferry, West Lothian EH30 9TQ (☎ 0131 331 1784, fax 0131 331 1788)

ROSEMONT, David John; s of Leslie Rosemont (d 1964), of Oxted, Surrey, and Elizabeth, *née* Williams (who m 2, 1974, Air Cdre Philip E Warcup); *Educ* Lancing, Architectural Assoc Sch of Architecture; *m* 8 Aug 1975, Elizabeth Abbott (Abbey), da of Frederick Milne Booth Duncan (d 1995), of Ayr, Scot; 2 s (Hugo David b 3 March 1979, Jonathan Duncan b 22 Dec 1980); *Career* architect 1971; assoc: Fairhursts Manchester 1975–77, SKP Architects London 1977–81; commenced private practice David Rosemont Assocs 1981; chm and md: Rosemont Holdings Ltd 1989–, Rosemont Associates Ltd 1989–; chm and dir: Rosemont Building Surveying Ltd 1989–, ARA Structural Engineering Services Ltd 1989–; chm Wandsworth Challenge Partnership 1994–; vice chm Wandsworth C of C 1995–, dir Business Link London South West 1995–; MAE 1988, memb AA, RIBA, MInstD; *Recreations* opera, photography, gastronomy, classic cars, places; *Clubs* Carlton; *Style—* David Rosemont, Esq; ✉ 7 Trinity Crescent, London SW17 7AG (☎ 0181 672 7117); Rosemont Holdings Ltd Group of Companies, 212 St Ann's Hill, London SW18 2RU (☎ 0181 870 8622, 0181 870 9824, fax 0181 870 9885)

ROSEN, Albert; s of Dr Lazar Rosen (d 1951), and Terezie, *née* Ruzickova (d 1971); *b* 14 Feb 1924; *Educ* Vienna Gymnasium, Bratislava Gymnasium, Vienna Music Acad, Prague Conservatory; *m* 1, 1955 (m dis 1961), Anna, *née* Hartlová; 1 s (Alexander b 1956); m 2, 1962 (m dis 1975), Blahoslava, *née* Markvartova; 1 da (Susana b 1964);

Career conductor: State Opera Pilsen 1949, Prague Nat Opera 1959; chief conductor: Prague Smetana Theatre 1965, Radio TV Symphony Orchestra Dublin 1969, Perth Aust 1981, Adelaide Aust 1986; Wexford Festival Opera 1965–88, BBC Philharmonic 1970–88 (touring Greece and Istanbul 1988), San Francisco Opera 1980, Opera du Rhin Strasburg 1982, ENO 1987/88/89, Prague Nat Opera 1989, Vancouver Opera 1991, San Diego Opera 1995; awarded title Conductor Laureate RTE 1994; *Recreations* travel; *Style*— Albert Rosen, Esq; ✉ 70 Haddingon Rd, Dublin 4, Ireland (☎ 00 353 1 6687876); 14700 Praha 4, Pod Lysinami 21, Czech Republic (☎ 00 42 2 4022936)

ROSEN, Emanuel; s of Capt Lionel Rosen, OBE (d 1977), of Hull, and Leah, *née* Levy, of Hull; *b* 23 Sept 1936; *Educ* Hull GS, Univ of Manchester (MD, BSc); *m* 9 Sept 1962, The Hon June Lever, da of Lord Lever of Ardwick (d 1976); 2 s (William David, Edward Leon), 1 da (Caroline Alexandra); *Career* hon conslt surgn Manchester Royal Eye Hosp, lectr in ophthalmology Univ of Manchester, visiting prof Dept of Visual Science UMIST; past pres UK Intraocular Lens Implant Soc, immediate past pres Euro Soc of Cataract and Refractive Surgns; memb Ctee Royal Coll of Surgns of Edinburgh; FRCOphth, FRCSE, FRPS; *Books* Fluorescence Photography of the Eye (1969), Basic Ophthalmoscopy (1972), Intraocular Lens Implantation (1983), Hazards of Light (1986), Visco-elastic Materials (1988), Intercapsular Surgery (1989), Quality of Cataract Surgery (1990); *Recreations* golf, photography; *Clubs* Athenaeum; *Style*— Emanuel Rosen, Esq; ✉ 10 St John Street, Manchester M3 4DY (☎ 0161 832 8778, fax 0161 832 1486)

ROSEN, Prof Michael; CBE (1989); s of Israel Rosen (d 1969), of Dundee, and Lily Rosen, *née* Hyman (d 1996); *b* 17 Oct 1927; *Educ* Dundee HS, Univ of St Andrews (MB ChB); *m* 17 Oct 1955, Sally Barbara, da of Leslie Israel Cohen (d 1960); 2 s (Timothy b 1956, Mark b 1962), 1 da (Amanda (Mrs Kirby) b 1959); *Career* Nat Serv Capt RAMC, served UK, Egypt and Cyprus 1952–54; sr registrar Cardiff 1957, fell Case Western Reserve Univ Cleveland Ohio 1960–61, conslt anaesthetist Cardiff Teaching Hosp 1961–93, hon prof in anaesthetics Univ of Wales 1984–93; dean Faculty of Anaesthetists RCS 1988; pres: Assoc of Anaesthetists of GB and I 1986–88, Coll of Anaesthetists 1988–91; treas World Fedn of Socs of Anesthesiology 1992–; Sir Ivan Magill Gold Medal 1993; Hon LLD Univ of Dundee 1996; hon memb: Aust Soc of Anaesthesiologists 1974, French Soc of Anaesthesiologists 1978, Japanese Soc of Anaesthesiologists 1989, Univ Anaesthetists (USA) 1989; Hon FFARCSI 1990; memb Acad of Med Malaysia 1989; FRCOG 1989, FRCS(Eng) 1994; *Books* Handbook of Percutaneous Central Venous Catheterisation (with I P Latto and W S Ng, 1981, 2nd edn 1992), Obstetric Anaesthesia and Analgesia: Safe Practice (contrib, 1982), Intubation: Practice and Problems (with I P Latto, K Murrin, W S Ng, R S Vaughan and W K Saunders, 1985), Difficulties in Tracheal Intubation (with I P Latto and B Tindall, 1985), Patient-Control Analgesia (with M Harmer and M D Vickers, 1985), Consciousness Awareness and Pain in General Anaesthesia (with J N Lunn, 1987); *Style*— Prof Michael Rosen, CBE; ✉ 45 Hollybush Rd, Cardiff CF2 6SZ (☎ and fax 01222 753893); Department of Anaesthetics, University Hospital of Wales, Heath Park, Cardiff CF4 4XW (☎ 01222 755944, fax 01222 747203)

ROSEN, Michael Wayne; s of Harold Rosen, of London, and Connie Ruby, *née* Isakofsky (d 1976); *b* 7 May 1946; *Educ* Harrow Weald Co GS, Watford Boys' GS, Middlesex Hosp Med Sch London (MB), Wadham Coll Oxford (BA), Nat Film Sch, Univ of Reading (MA); *m* 1, 1976 (m dis 1987), Susanna, da of William Steele; 2 s (Joseph Steele Rosen b 7 July 1976, Eddie Steele Rosen b 9 June 1980); m 2, 1987, Geraldine Clark, da of Jack Dingley; 1 s (Isaac Louis Rosen b 15 June 1987); *Career* writer/bdcaster; presenter: Poems by Post and Meridian Books (BBC World Serv), Treasure Islands (BBC Radio 4), Readabout (Yorkshire TV); writer/presenter: Everybody Here (C4, 1982), Black and White and Read All Over (C4, 1983); performances in schs, colls, libraries and theatres throughout UK 1976–; lectr in Singapore, Aust and Canada; Sunday Times Student Drama award 1968, C Day Lewis fell 1976, Signal Poetry award 1982, The Other Award 1982, Smarties award 1990; memb Br Actors' Equity; *Books* Mind Your Own Business (1974), You Can't Catch Me (1981), Quick Let's Get Out of Here (1983), Don't Put Mustard in the Custard (1985), Hairy Tales and Nursery Crimes (1985), The Wicked Tricks of Till Owlyglass (1989), The Golem of Old Prague (1990), Goodies and Daddies (1991); anthologies: The Kingfisher Book of Children's Poetry (ed, 1985), A Spider Bought a Bicycle (ed, 1986), The Kingfisher Book of Funny Stories (ed, 1988), Rude Rhymes (ed, 1989), A World of Poetry (ed, 1991), The Chatto Book of Dissent (ed with David Widgery, 1991), The Vintage Book of Dissent (ed with David Widgery, 1996); *Plays* Backbone (1969, performed Royal Court), Regis Debray (1971, performed BBC Radio 4); *Recreations* Arsenal FC supporter, reading, second-hand book collecting; *Style*— Michael Rosen, Esq; ✉ Peters Fraser & Dunlop Ltd, 503 The Chambers, Chelsea Harbour, Lots Road, London SW10 0XF (☎ 0171 344 1000)

ROSEN, Murray Hilary; QC (1993); s of Joseph Rosen, and Mercia, *née* Herman, of London; *b* 26 Aug 1953; *Educ* St Paul's, Trinity Coll Cambridge (MA), Brussels Free Univ (dipl); *m* 1975, Lesley, *née* Samuels; 3 da, 1 s; *Career* called to the Bar Inner Temple 1976, memb ad eundem Lincoln's Inn; *Recreations* music, cricket, running; *Style*— Murray Rosen, QC; ✉ 11 Stone Buildings, Lincoln's Inn, London WC2A 3TG (☎ 0171 831 6381, fax 0171 831 2575)

ROSENBERG, Jenifer Bernice; OBE (1989); da of Philip Levene (d 1966), of London, and Jane-Sarah, *née* Kent (d 1982); *b* 1 Oct 1942; *Educ* Our Lady of Zion GS; *m* 1, 1 Aug 1975, Jack Goldstein (d 1975); m 2, 8 Feb 1982, Ian David Rosenberg, s of Alfred Rosenberg (d 1984), of London; *Career* sr buyer Marks & Spencer plc 1960–74, fndr and md J and J Fashions Ltd 1974–92 (sold to Claremont Garments PLC 1992); govr London Inst, vice pres Textile Inst, memb Br Fashion Cncl, tstee Elderly Accommodation Counsel; charities actively involved in: Wellbeing, Action Research, Woman of Distinction Luncheon for Jewish Care (chm), Friends of Bar Ilan Univ Women's Gp (patron), Open the Door Appeal YWCA; fndr dir CILNTEC, md Step Ahead Personnel (recruitment agency); Award from Tyne and Wear Cncl for Industl and Commercial Enterprise (twice), Veuve Clicquot/IOD Business Woman of the Year Award 1986; *Recreations* theatre, photography, music, travelling, bridge; *Style*— Mrs Jenifer Rosenberg, OBE; ✉ 48 Queen's Grove, St John's Wood, London NW8 6HH

ROSENBERG, Michael Samuel; OBE (1995); s of Benjamin Rosenberg (d 1980), and Fanny, *née* Sidenberg (d 1988); *b* 27 June 1939; *Educ* Aldenham; *m* 1965, Jacqueline Ruth; 1 s (Jeremy Philip), 1 da (Juliet Michele); *Career* dir Samuel Montagu & Co 1972–74 (joined 1957), dir United Medical Enterprises Ltd (formerly Allied Investments) 1974–87, chm Raphael Zorn Hemsley Ltd stockbrokers 1994– (dir 1988–); non-exec dep chm David Paradine Ltd; ACIS, AIB; *Recreations* tennis, squash, music; *Style*— Michael Rosenberg, Esq, OBE; ✉ Montrose Securities Ltd, Suite 6, 49 Kensington Court, London W8 5DB (☎ 0171 938 4026, fax 0171 938 4903)

ROSENBERG, Richard Allen (Rich); s of Maurice Stanley Rosenberg (d 1995), of Massachusetts, and Helen, *née* Barkan; *b* 19 Sept 1946; *Educ* Northeastern Univ Mass (BSc), MIT (MSc); *m* 8 Sept 1968, Bernyd, da of Leon Pellows; 2 da (Lisa Michelle b 20 Nov 1972, Amanda Diane b 22 July 1986), 1 s (David Michael b 13 Nov 1975); *Career* Exxon Corporation: various accounting and info systems positions Exxon Company USA 1971–82, admin mangr Baytown Refinery 1982–83, mktg distribution mangr Exxon Co USA 1986–87 (exec asst to pres 1983–84, co-ordination and servs mangr mktg Exxon Co USA 1984–85), asst controller Exxon Co International 1987–90, asst treas Exxon Corp 1990–94, exec dir fin Esso UK plc, Esso Petroleum Co Ltd and Esso Exploration & Production UK Ltd 1994–; dir Britannia Steamship Insurance Association Ltd 1994–; memb US Pres's Private Sector Task Force 1982; *Recreations* golf, tennis, reading, computers; *Style*— Rich Rosenberg, Esq; ✉ Esso UK plc, Esso House, 96 Victoria Street, London SW1E 5JW (☎ 0171 245 3275, fax 0171 245 3154)

ROSENBLOOM, Prof Richard Selig; s of Irving J Rosenbloom (d 1980), and Lillian S Rosenbloom (d 1972); *b* 16 Jan 1933; *Educ* Harvard (AB, MBA, DBA); *m* 14 Oct 1956, Ruth Miriam, *née* Friedlander; 2 s (Joshua b 13 Aug 1958, Daniel b 27 Oct 1963), 1 da (Rachel b 13 Aug 1968); *Career* prof of business admin Harvard Univ 1960–; former non-exec dir Lex Service plc, dir General Instrument Corporation; *Style*— Prof Richard S Rosenbloom; ✉ Harvard Business School, Cambridge, Mass, USA

ROSENBROCK, Prof Howard Harry; *b* 16 Dec 1920; *Educ* Tonman Moseley Sch Slough, Slough GS (Co Major scholar), UCL (Salomons scholar, BSc, PhD, DSc, Clinton prize), Univ of Manchester (MSc); *m* 1950, Cathryn June, *née* Press; 1 s, 2 da; *Career* signals offr RAFVR 1941–46; Radio Transmitter Section GEC Research Lab 1947–48, asst master and mathematics and physics teacher London CC 1948–49, tech asst Electrical Research Assoc 1949–51, asst to engr conslt John Brown & Co Ltd 1951–54, research mangr Constructors John Brown Ltd 1957–62 (joined 1954), on staff Control Gp Univ of Cambridge 1962–66; UMIST: prof of control engrg 1966–87 (now emeritus), vice princ 1977–78; fell UCL 1978; W C Williams lecture Univ of Sheffield 1980, Sir Harold Hartley lecture 1981, Halliburton distinguished lecture series Texas Tech Univ 1985, Cockroft lecture Manchester Technol Assoc 1986; Moulton Medal IChemE 1957, Sir Harold Hartley Medal Inst of Measurement and Control 1970, Control Systems Science and Engrg Award IEEE 1982, Control Achievement Award IEE 1988, Rufus Oldenburger Medal ASME 1994, Nordic Process Control Award 1995; Hon DSc Univ of Salford 1987; memb: Advsy Ctee for Chemical and Process Engrg Mintech 1969–73, Computer Bd DES 1972–76, Br Nat Ctee Int Inst of Applied Systems Analysis 1972–78, IFAC Ctee on Social Effects of Automation 1975–; convenor Working Pty Cncl for Science and Soc on New Technol 1979–81, pres Manchester Medical Engrg Club 1970–71; Inst of Measurement and Control: memb Cncl 1958–66 and 1970–74, chm Control Section 1958–59, memb Educn Ctee 1958–60, vice pres 1971–72, pres 1972–73; IEE: memb Cncl 1966–70, chm Educn and Trg Ctee 1976–77, vice pres 1976–78; SRC: memb Control Panel 1966–72, chm Engrg Computing Requirements Tech Gp 1975–76, memb Engrg Bd 1976–78, memb Special Project in Computing Panel 1978; FIEE, FIChemE, FRS 1976, FEng 1984, ARPS 1990, Hon FInstMC 1992; *Books* Computational Techniques for Chemical Engineers (with C Storey, 1966), Mathematics of Dynamical Systems (with C Storey, 1970), State-Space and Multivariable Theory (1970), Computer-Aided Control System Design (1974), New Technology: Society, Employment and Skill (1981), Designing Human-Centered Technology (1989), Machines with a Purpose (1990), author of numerous scientific pubns; *Style*— Prof Howard Rosenbrock, FEng, FRS; ✉ Linden, Walford Road, Ross-on-Wye, Herefordshire HR9 5PQ (☎ 01989 565372)

ROSENHEAD, Lindsay Margaret; da of Stanislas Eugene Meunier (d 1989), of Epping, Essex, and Louie, *née* Naylor (d 1992); *b* 5 May 1934; *Educ* Southport HS, Southport Sch of Art, St Martin's Sch of Art, Katinka Sch of Dress Design; *m* Martin David Rosenhead, *qv*, s of Prof Louis Rosenhead, CBE (d 1984); 1 da (Annabel Sophie b Jan 1967); *Career* dress designer Julian Rose S Molton St 1954–57; Vogue 1957–67: fashion advsr Vogue Patterns London 1957–61, promotion mangr Vogue Patterns London 1962–63, publicity ed and Paris corr Vogue 1963–67; fashion advsr and head of fashion UK Branch Wool Secretariat 1968–70, ind fashion conslt 1971–, sr lectr in fashion design NE London Poly 1976–82, princ lectr and course dir Fashion BA Harrow 1982–90; Univ of Westminster 1990–96: assoc head Sch of Design and Media, faculty sr tutor; memb: Fashion Gp Paris and London 1963, Textile Inst 1984; *Recreations* music, theatre, walking, skiing, food and wine; *Style*— Mrs Lindsay Rosenhead; ✉ 10 Herons Place, Lion Wharf, Isleworth TW7 7BE (☎ 0181 560 4640, fax 0181 569 8467)

ROSENHEAD, Martin David; s of Prof Louis Rosenhead, CBE (d 1984), of Liverpool, and Esther Rosenhead, JP, *née* Brostoff; *b* 19 May 1935; *Educ* Quarry Bank HS Liverpool, St John's Coll Cambridge (MA, pres Cambridge Union Soc LENT 1956); *m* 20 Jan 1961, Lindsay Margaret Rosenhead, *qv*, da of Stanislas Eugene Meunier, of Epping, Essex; 1 da (Annabel b 26 Jan 1967); *Career* various mgmnt appts ICI 1956–68, business devpt dir Construction Sector Foseco-Minsep plc 1969–70, dir Redland plc 1970–74, non-exec dir Royal Brierley Crystal Ltd 1974–84, business devpt dir Wallpaper Manufacturers Ltd 1974–79, dir Arthur Sanderson and Sons Ltd 1974–79, chm Thomson Shepherd Ltd 1976–78, md Bradfield Brett Holdings Ltd 1978–79; chm: Royal Stafford China Ltd 1980–83, Spartan Holdings Ltd 1980–84, Teakspire Ltd 1980–86; dir: DTELS The Communications Business of the Home Office 1986–94, Profile Consulting Ltd 1988–90, Instrop (Decormetall) Ltd 1989–90; chm and chief exec Response Accessories Ltd 1989–90; chief exec: Seabright Investments Ltd 1994, Seabright Chemicals Ltd 1994; non-exec dir: Cowan De Groot plc 1983–84, Cytotechnics Ltd 1990–94; chm Nicola Martin Tapes Ltd 1990–96, dep chm Hornsea Pottery Ltd 1991–93; business advsr: Suffolk Water plc 1990–92, HM Prison Serv 1992–, Leicestershire CC 1992–94; chm Tst Bd The Allergy Research Fndn 1994–, advsr Harefield Hosp NHS Tst; former Lib Parly candidate; FInstD 1970, FIMgt 1980, FRSM 1996; *Recreations* music, walking, skiing, Europe, hypnosis; *Clubs* Reform; *Style*— Martin Rosenhead, Esq; ✉ 10 Herons Place, Lion Wharf, Isleworth TW7 7BE (☎ 0181 569 9780, fax 0181 569 8467); 12 Latham Rd, Twickenham, Middx TW1 1BN (☎ 0181 891 3705, fax 0181 892 4493, car 0860 396 388)

ROSENTHAL, Jack Morris; CBE (1994); s of Samuel Rosenthal (d 1964), of Manchester and Blackpool, and Leah, *née* Miller (d 1977); *b* 8 Sept 1931; *Educ* Colne GS, Univ of Sheffield (BA); *m* 18 Feb 1973, Maureen Lipman, *qv*, da of late Maurice Julius Lipman, of Hull; 1 s (Adam b 3 Oct 1976), 1 da (Amy b 7 June 1974); *Career* dramatist; 31 original TV films and over 300 TV dramas and comedies incl: Yentl (co-written with Barbra Streisand), The Chain, The Wedding Gift, Eskimo Day (most recently for tv); theatre incl: Smash!, Dear Anyone; winner BAFTA and Int Best Play awards for: The Evacuees, Bar Mitzvah Boy, Spend Spend Spend; winner Int awards for: Ready When You Are Mr McGill, Day To Remember, Bye, Bye, Baby; nat and int nominations for: The Knowledge, P'Tang Yang Kipperbang, London's Burning, Wide-Eyed and Legless; winner of The Br Acad Writer's Award and The RTS Writer's Award, RTS Hall of Fame; Hon MA Univ of Salford 1994, Hon DLitt Univ of Manchester 1995; *Books* author six books of original TV screenplays; *Recreations* listing biographical data for publications such as this; *Clubs* Dramatists'; *Style*— Jack Rosenthal, Esq, CBE; ✉ c/o Casarotto Ramsay Ltd, National House, 4th Floor, 60–66 Wardour Street, London W1V 3HP (☎ 0171 287 4450, fax 0171 287 9128)

ROSENTHAL, Jim; s of Albi Rosenthal, of Oxford; *b* 6 Nov 1947; *Educ* Magdalen Coll Sch Oxford; *m* Chrissy; 1 s (Tom b 14 Jan 1988); *Career* TV sports presenter; Oxford Mail and Times 1968–72, BBC Radio Birmingham 1972–76, BBC Radio Sports Unit 1976–80, with ITV Sport 1980–; TV Sports Presenter of the Year 1990; *Style*— Jim Rosenthal, Esq; ✉ c/o Independent Television Association, 200 Gray's Inn Road, London WC1X 8HF (☎ 0171 843 8137, fax 0171 843 8153)

ROSENTHAL, Norman Leon; s of Paul Rosenthal, and Kate, *née* Zucker; *b* 8 Nov 1944; *Educ* Westminster City GS, Univ of Leicester (BA), Sch of Slavonic and E Euro Studies, Free Univ of Berlin (Kunsthistorisches Seminar); *m* 1989, Manuela Mena Marques; *Career* art exhibitions organiser; first exhibition Artists in Cornwall Leicester Museum and Art Gallery 1965, librarian and res Thomas S Agnew & Sons 1966–68, exhibition offr Brighton Museum and Art Gallery 1970–71 (organised Follies and Fantasies for Brighton Festival), organiser (with Vera Russell) Artists Market (non-profit making gallery Covent Garden) 1972–73, exhibition offr Inst of Contemporary Arts London 1973–76 (organised The German Month 1974, Art into Society - Society into Art, Seven German Artists, The Greek Month 1975), exhibitions sec Royal Acad of Arts 1977–; memb: Bd Palazzo Grassi Venice 1985, Opera Board Royal Opera House Covent Garden; hon fell Royal Coll of Art London 1987, Chevalier des Arts et des Lettres (Cavaliere Ufficiale) 1992, Cross of the Order of Merit of the FRG 1993; *Royal Acad Exhibitions* organiser of all loan exhibitions incl: Robert Motherwell 1978, Post-Impressionism 1979, Stanley Spencer 1980, A New Spirit in Painting 1981, Great Japan Exhibition 1981–82, Painting in Naples, Caravaggio to Giordano 1982, Murillo 1983, The Genius of Venice 1983–84, From Vermeer to De Hooch, Dutch Genre Painting 1984, Chagall 1985, Joshua Reynolds 1986, New Architecture: Foster, Roger, Stirling 1986, The Age of Chivalry 1987, The Early Cézanne 1988, Henry Moore 1988, The Art of Photography 1989, Frans Hals 1990; other exhbn work at the Royal Acad (with Christos M Joachimides): Zeitgeist 1982 (Martin Gropius-Bau Berlin), German Art in the Twentieth Century 1985 (also shown at the Staatsgalerie Stuttgart), British Art in the Twentieth Century 1987 (also shown at the Staatsgalerie Stuttgart), Italian Art in the Twentieth Century 1989 (version shown at Palazzo Grassi Venice), American Art in the Twentieth Century 1993 (at Martin-Gropius-Bau Berlin 1994); *Style*— Norman Rosenthal, Esq; ✉ The Royal Academy of Arts, Burlington House, Piccadilly, London W1V 0DS (☎ 0171 494 5742, fax 0171 287 1796)

ROSENTHAL, Thomas Gabriel (Tom); s of late Dr Erwin Isak Jacob Rosenthal, and Elizabeth Charlotte, *née* Marx (d 1996); *b* 16 July 1935; *Educ* Perse Sch Cambridge, Pembroke Coll Cambridge (MA); *m* Ann Judith Warnford-Davis; 2 s (Adam, Daniel); *Career* 2 Lt RA 1954–56, Lt Cambridgeshire Regt TA 1956–80; md: Thames and Hudson International 1966 (joined Thames and Hudson 1959), Martin Secker and Warburg Ltd 1971 (chm 1980); chm William Heinemann 1980–84, chm and md various subsid cos 1980–84, chm and md Andre Deutsch Ltd (joined 1984); chm Soc of Young Publishers 1961–62; memb: Cambridge Univ Appts Bd 1967–71, Exec Ctee Nat Book League 1971–74, Ctee of Mgmnt and tstee Amateur Dramatic Club Cambridge, Cncl RCA 1982–87, Exec Cncl ICA 1987–; *Books* A Reader's Guide to Modern European Art History (1962), A Reader's Guide to Modern American Fiction (1963), Monograph on Jack B Yeats (1964), Monograph on Ivon Hitchens (with Alan Bowness, 1973), Monograph on Arthur Boyd (with Ursula Hoff, 1986); introductions to: The Financier, The Titan, Jennie Gerhardt (Theodore Dreiser); articles in: The Times, The Guardian, TLS, London Magazine, Encounter, New Statesman, Spectator, Jl of Br Assoc for American Studies, Studio International, Dictionary of National Biography, Nature, The Bookseller; *Recreations* bibliomania, opera, looking at pictures, reading other publishers' books, watching cricket; *Clubs* Garrick, MCC; *Style*— Tom Rosenthal, Esq; ✉ Andre Deutsch Ltd, 106 Great Russell Street London WC1B 3LJ (☎ 0171 580 2746, fax 0171 631 3253)

ROSEWELL, Michael John (Mike); s of Frederick Jack Rosewell (d 1974), of Walton-on-Thames, Surrey, and Anne Emma, *née* Helps (d 1984); *b* 22 Jan 1937; *Educ* Woking GS, LSE (BSc), Westminster Coll (PGCE); *m* 1961, Jill Drusilla, da of Stanley William Orriss; 1 s (Daniel James b 1966), 2 da (Anna-Marie b 1964, Michelle Jane b 1969); *Career* economics master and rowing coach: Ealing GS 1959–64, St George's Coll Weybridge 1964–76, St Edward's Sch Oxford 1976–95; rowing journalist and writer: Surrey Herald 1963–76, Surrey Comet 1967–76, Evening Mail 1968–77, Oxford Times 1976–; features writer Rowing Magazine 1968–, rowing corr The Times 1989–, feature writer Thames User 1992, ed Friends of the Boat Race 1995–, dep ed Regatta Magazine 1996– (features writer 1987–); memb Amateur Rowing Assoc Cncl 1968– (chm Publicity Ctee, chm Jr Rowing Ctee, asst ed Br Rowing Almanack, Eng Rowing Team mangr, memb Exec Ctee, GB Jr Team delegate, GB Jr Crew coach); chief coach: Christ Church 1978–90, Oxford Women's Boat Race Crew 1979–87, Wadham Coll Oxford 1995–, Trinity Coll Oxford 1996–; memb: Sports Writers' Assoc of GB 1990, Br Assoc of Rowing Journalists 1990; vice chm Oxford Branch of Parkinson's Disease Soc 1993–96; *Books* Beginners Guide to Rowing (1970); *Recreations* boating, golf, angling, gardening; *Clubs* Walton Rowing, Leander; *Style*— Mike Rosewell, Esq; ✉ Hillview, Broad Street, Long Compton, Warwicks CV36 5JH (☎ and fax 01608 684709)

ROSIER, (Frederick) David Stewart; s of Air Chief Marshal Sir Frederick Rosier, GCB, CBE, DSO, *qv*, and Hettie Denise, *née* Blackwell; *b* 10 April 1951; *Educ* Winchester Coll, Keble Coll Oxford (BA, MA), RMA Sandhurst; *m* 27 Sept 1975, Julia Elizabeth, da of David Leslie Gomme; 1 s (Charles Frederick James b 8 Dec 1990); *Career* cmmnd 1 The Queen's Dragoon Gds 1973–78, served Germany, NI, UK (Troop Ldr, Intelligence Offr, sqdn 2 i/c; resigned Capt 1978); exec dir S G Warburg & Co Ltd 1984–87 (joined 1978); dir: Warburg Investment Management Ltd 1982–87, Mercury Asset Management Group plc 1987–, Mercury Bank AG 1990– (vice chm 1995–); dep chm Mercury Asset Management plc 1991– (vice chm 1989–91); chm: Mercury Fund Managers Ltd 1991–, Mercury Life Assurance Co Ltd 1992–, Mercury Asset Management Channel Islands Ltd 1992–; cncllr Wandsworth Borough Cncl 1982–86; tstee Burma Star Assoc 1995–; memb Cncl Victory Services Club 1995–; Liveryman Worshipful Co of Coachmakers and Coach Harness Makers; MSI; *Recreations* golf, skiing, shooting; *Clubs* Cavalry & Guards', Hurlingham, Wisley, Valderrama, Fantasians, Swinley Forest; *Style*— David Rosier, Esq; ✉ 99 Thurleigh Road, London SW12 8TY; 33 King William St, London EC4R 9AS (☎ 0171 280 2800, fax 0171 280 2820)

ROSIER, Air Chief Marshal Sir Frederick Ernest; GCB (1972, KCB 1966, CB 1961), CBE (1955, OBE 1943), DSO 1942; s of Ernest George Rosier (d 1942), and Frances Elisabeth, *née* Morris (d 1934); *b* 13 Oct 1915; *Educ* Grove Park Sch Wrexham; *m* 30 Sept 1939, Hettie Denise, da of William Herbert Blackwell (d 1965); 3 s (David, *qv*, b 1951, Nicholas b 1953, John b 1961), 1 da (Elisabeth b 1943); *Career* cmmnd RAF 1935, 43 (F) Sqdn 1936–39, served UK, Western Desert and Europe 1939–45, OC Horsham St Faith 1947, exchange duties with USAF 1948–50, DSD Jt Servs Staff Coll 1950–52, Gp Capt Ops Central Fighter Estab 1952–54, Gp Capt Plans Fighter Cmd 1955–56, IDC 1957, dir Jt Plans Air Miny 1958, chm Jt Planning Staff 1959–61, AOC Air Forces Middle East 1961–63, SASO Tport Cmd 1964–66, AOC in C Fighter Cmd 1966–68, perm mil dep CENTO 1968–70, dep C in C AFCENT 1970–73, ADC to HM The Queen 1956–58, Air ADC to HM The Queen 1972–73; mil advsr and dir BAC 1973–77, dir i/c BAC Saudi Arabia 1977–80; vice pres 8 Army Veterans 1977–, chm of appeals Polish Air Force Benevolent Fund 1975–; Liveryman Worshipful Co of Coachmakers and Harnessmakers 1976, Freeman City of London 1976; Order of Orange Nassau Netherlands 1946, Order of Polonia Restituta Poland 1987; *Clubs* RAF; *Style*— Air Chief Marshal Sir Frederick Rosier, GCB, CBE, DSO; ✉ 286 Latymer Court, London W6 7LD (☎ 0181 741 0765); Ty Haul, Llangollen, Clwyd (☎ 01978 861068)

ROSIN, (Richard) David; s of Isadore Rowland Rosin (d 1993), of Zimbabwe, and Muriel Ena, *née* Wolff; *b* 29 April 1942; *Educ* St George's Coll Salisbury Southern Rhodesia, KCL, Westminster Hosp Sch of Med (MB BS, MS, LRCP, MRCS, Arthur Evans meml prize in surgery, Rogers prize); *m* Michelle Shirley, da of Ivor Moreton (d 1984); 2 da (Natasha Jane b 25 May 1972, Katya Sarah b 4 May 1983), 1 s (Alexei John b 8 Aug 1973); *Career* house physician then house surgn Westminster Hosp 1966–67, ship's surgn P & O Lines 1967, SHO in clinical pathology Westminster Hosp 1968, SHO (latterly Burns Unit) Birmingham Accident Hosp 1969, SHO (rotation) Westminster Hosp 1969–71; registrar: Sutton Hosp Surrey 1971–73, St Helier's Hosp Carshalton 1973–74; clinical asst St Mark's Hosp London 1974–75; sr registrar: Kingston Hosp 1975–77, Westminster Hosp 1977–79 (visiting lectr Univ of Hong Kong Sept-Dec 1978); currently conslt in gen surgery and surgical oncology St Mary's Hosp and conslt surgn King Edward VII's Hosp for Offrs; clinical dir of surgery St Charles' Hosp 1990–92, chm Div of Surgery St Mary's Hosp 1992–95; Runcorn travelling fell 1976, Arris and Gale lectr RCS 1976, Ethicon Fndn scholar 1976 and 1978, Br Jl of Surgery travelling fell 1983, Penrose-May tutor RCS 1985–90, Hunterian prof RCS 1987, Arnott lectr RCS 1991; regnl advsr NW Thames Region RCS(Ed), examiner (MB BS) London and (FRCS) RCS(Ed), intercollegiate specialist examiner in gen surgery; past memb Cncl The Marie Curie Fndn; Freeman: City of London 1972, Worshipful Soc of Apothecaries 1971, Worshipful Co of Barber Surgns 1978; memb: Soc of Minimally Invasive Gen Surgns (fndr and hon sec), Surgical Research Soc, Assoc of Surgns of GB and I (SMIGS rep on Surgical Gastroenterology Ctee), RSM (pres Clinical Section 1982–83, pres Section of Surgery 1992–93, memb Cncl Oncology Section), Br Soc of Gastroenterology, Br Assoc of Surgical Oncology (former hon sec, currently memb Educn Ctee), London Med Soc, Hunterian Soc, Melanoma Study Gp (first hon sec 1986–89, pres 1989–92), World Soc of Hepato-Biliary Surgery, Int Coll of Surgns, Euro Assoc of Endoscopic Surgns, Assoc of Endoscopic Surgns of GB and I (memb Cncl 1995–); FRCS 1971 (memb Cncl 1994–); *Books* Cancer of the Bile Ducts and Pancreas (jt ed, 1989), Head and Neck Oncology for the General Surgeon (jt ed, 1991), Diagnosis and Management of Melanoma in Clinical Practice (jt ed, 1992), Minimal Access Medicine and Surgery - Principles and Practice (ed, 1993), Minimal Access General Surgery (ed, 1994), Minimal Access Surgical Oncology (ed, 1995) and series ed Minimal Access textbooks; also author of various book chapters and published papers; *Recreations* particularly golf, opera, music and theatre, history of medicine and surgery, travelling; *Clubs* Garrick, Coombe Hill Golf, NZ Golf, Roehampton; *Style*— R David Rosin, Esq; ✉ 2 St Simon's Avenue, Putney, London SW15 6DU (☎ 0181 788 6141); 6 Harley Street, London W1N 1AA (☎ 0171 631 3447, fax 0171 631 3459, mobile 0831 655036)

ROSKILL, Hon Julian Wentworth; s of Baron Roskill, PC, DL (d 1996), and Elisabeth Wallace, *née* Jackson; *b* 22 July 1950; *Educ* Horris Hill, Winchester Coll; *m* 1975, Catherine Elizabeth, 2 da of Maj William Francis Garnett, of Quernmore Park, Lancaster; 2 s (Matthew b 1979, Oliver b 1981); *Career* admitted slr 1974; ptnr Rowe & Maw 1988– (head Employment and Industl Rels Gp); memb: Law Soc, City of London Slrs' Co (chm Employment Sub-ctee), Employment Lawyers Assoc; *Recreations* photography, music, theatre, tennis; *Style*— The Hon Julian W Roskill; ✉ Rowe & Maw, 20 Black Friars Lane, London EC4V 6HD (☎ 0171 248 4282, fax 0171 248 2009)

ROSLING, (Richard) Alan; OBE (1994); s of Derek Norman Rosling, of Bucklers Hard, and Joan Elizabeth, *née* Heseltine; *b* 16 Aug 1962; *Educ* Univ of Cambridge (Richmond exhibitioner, BA), Harvard Business Sch (Baker scholar, Harkness fell, MBA); *m* 1990, Sarmila, da of Dr S K Bose; 1 s (Aidan Samya b 2 June 1993); *Career* S G Warburg & Co Ltd 1983–86, Courtaulds Textiles plc 1988–90, Prime Minister's Policy Unit 1991–94, United Distillers 1993–; *Recreations* South Asia, travel, sailing; *Clubs* Royal Southampton, Beaulieu River; *Style*— Alan Rosling, Esq, OBE; ✉ 23 Sutherland Place, London W2 5BZ

ROSLING, Derek Norman; CBE (1988); s of Norman Rosling (d 1984), and Jean, *née* Allen (d 1957); *b* 21 Nov 1930; *Educ* Shrewsbury; *m* (m dis); 2 s (Alan b 1962, John b 1964), 1 da (Jean b 1961); *Career* Hanson plc: fndr dir 1965, dir 1965–94, vice chm 1973–93, ret 1994; FCA, FRSA; *Recreations* sailing, golf, theatre; *Clubs* Royal Yacht Squadron, Royal Southampton Yacht, Brokenhurst Manor Golf; *Style*— Derek N Rosling, Esq, CBE; ✉ Little Salterns, Bucklers Hard, Beaulieu, Hants SO42 7XE

ROSOMAN, Leonard Henry; OBE (1981); s of Henry Edward Rosoman (d 1979), of Cambridge Drive, Lee, London, and Lillian Blanch, *née* Spencer (d 1954); *b* 27 Oct 1913; *Educ* Deacons Sch Peterborough, Univ of Durham, Royal Acad Schs, Central Sch of Arts & Crafts; *m* 1, 21 June 1963 (m dis 1969), Jocelyn, da of late Bertie Rickards, of Melbourne, Aust; m 2, 11 July 1994, Roxanne Wruble Levy, da of late Dr Milton Wruble, of Kalamazoo, Michigan; *Career* Aux Fire Serv 1939–43, Home Office 1943–45, official war artist Admty 1945–46; artist; lectr: Reimann Sch London 1937–39, Camberwell Sch of Art 1946–47, Edinburgh Coll of Art 1948–56, Chelsea Sch of Art 1956–57; tutor RCA 1957–78; exhibitions in London incl: St George's Gallery 1949, Roland Browse & Delbanco Gallery 1954, 1957, 1959, 1965 and 1969, The Fine Art Soc 1974, 1978, 1983 and 1990, Oldham Art Gallery 1977, Imperial War Museum 1989; exhibitions in USA incl: Lincoln Centre NY 1968, State Univ of NY at Albany 1971, Touchstone Gallery NY 1975; major murals incl: Festival of Britain 1951, Diaghilev Exhibition 1954, Brussels World Fair 1958, Shakespeare Exhibition 1964, Royal Acad of Arts 1986, vaulted ceiling Lambeth Palace Chapel 1988; Winston Churchill fell 1966; FRSA 1968, RA 1969, Hon ARCA 1978, Hon RSWS 1979, Hon RWA 1984; *Books* Painters on Painting, Bruegel's Mad Meg (1969); *Recreations* travelling and painting as much as possible; *Clubs* Arts, Chelsea Arts; *Style*— Leonard Rosoman, Esq, OBE, RA; ✉ 7 Pembroke Studios, Pembroke Gardens, London W8 6HX (☎ 0171 603 3638)

ROSS, Alan; CBE (1982); s of John Brackenridge Ross, CBE (d 1958), and Clare Margaret Fitzpatrick (d 1979); *b* 6 May 1922; *Educ* Haileybury, St John's Coll Oxford; *m* 1949 (m dis 1985), Jennifer, da of Sir Geoffrey Fry, KCB, CVO (d 1959), of Wiltshire; 1 s (Jonathan Timothy de Beaurepaire b 1953); *Career* RN 1942–47; asst staff offr Intelligence 16 Destroyer Flotilla 1944, on staff of Flag Offr W Germany 1945, interpreter Br Naval C in C Germany 1946; Br Cncl 1947–50; staff memb The Observer 1952–72, ed London Magazine 1961–, md London Magazine Editions 1961–; Atlantic Award for Literature 1946; FRSL; *Books* Open Sea (1975), Death Valley (1980), Colours of War (1983), Ranji (1983), Blindfold Games (1986), The Emissary (1986), Coastwise Lights (1988), After Pusan (1995); *Recreations* The Turf; *Clubs* Vincent's (Oxford), MCC; *Style*— Alan Ross, Esq, CBE, FRSL; ✉ 30 Thurloe Place, London SW7

ROSS, Alastair Robertson; s of Alexander James Ross (d 1985), of Dunblane, Perthshire, and Margaret Elizabeth McInnes, *née* Robertson (d 1983); *b* 8 Aug 1941; *Educ* McLaren HS Callander Perthshire, Duncan of Jordanstone Coll of Art Dundee (DA); *m* 12 April 1975, Kathryn Margaret Greig, da of late John Ferrier Greig Wilson, of Birmingham; 1 da (Alexandra b 1981); *Career* artist; lectr Duncan of Jordanstone Coll Univ of Dundee 1969– (pt/t 1966–69), tutor Sch of Scottish Artists in Malta 1991–93; recent works incl: bronze for Blackness Devpt Project Dundee, portrait in bronze of Sir Iain Moncreiffe of that Ilk at HM New Register House Edinburgh 1988 (awarded Sir Otto Beit Medal of Royal Soc Br Sculptors 1988); cmmn of a twice life-size torso in bronze for new Rank Xerox HQ Marlow Bucks 1988–89, one-man touring exhbn (26 scupltures) UK and USA 1996–97; awarded: Dickson Prize for Sculpture 1962, Holo-Krome (Dundee) Sculpture Prize and Cmmn 1962, Scottish Educn Dept Travelling Scholarship 1963, Royal Scottish Acad Chalmers Bursary 1964, Royal Scottish Acad Carnegie Travelling Scholarship 1965, Duncan of Drumfork Scholarship 1965, award winner in sculpture Paris Salon Exhibition 1967, awarded Medailles de Bronze 1968 and d'Argent 1970 Société des Artistes Français (membre associé 1970), Sir William Gillies Bequest Fund Award RSA 1989; memb Exec Ctee Fife Branch St John Assoc 1979–, memb Fife Order Ctee Order of St John 1991–; memb Cncl Br Sch at Rome 1990–96; memb Soc Portrait Sculptors 1966; SBStJ 1979, OStJ 1984; Freeman City of London 1989; FRSA 1966, ARBS 1968 (vice pres 1988–90, Scottish rep on cncl 1972–92), professional memb SSA 1969 (cncl memb 1972–75), FSA Scot 1971, FRBS 1975, ARSA 1980, MBIM 1989, Hon FRIAS 1992; *Recreations* heraldry, genealogy, Scottish history;

Clubs St Johns House, Royal Perth, Puffin's (Edinburgh); *Style*— Alastair Ross, Esq; ✉ Ravenscourt, 28 Albany Terrace, Dundee DD3 6HS (☎ 01382 224 235)

ROSS, Alexander (Sandy); s of Alexander Coutts Ross (d 1978), and Charlotte Edwards, *née* Robertson (d 1978); *b* 17 April 1948; *Educ* Grangemouth HS, Univ of Edinburgh (LLB), Moray House Coll; *m* Alison Joyce, *née* Fraser; 3 c (Andrew b 1 Sept 1983, Francis b 29 May 1986, Thomas b 13 July 1992); *Career* articled then slr Edinburgh 1970–74, lectr Paisley Coll of Technol 1974–76, prodr Granada TV Manchester 1977–86, controller of arts and entertainment Scottish TV 1986–, dep chief exec Scottish Television Enterprises; cncllr: Edinburgh Town Cncl 1971–75, Edinburgh Dist Cncl 1974–78; memb BAFTA; *Recreations* reading, golf, music, watching football; *Style*— Sandy Ross, Esq; ✉ 7 Murrayfield Ave, Edinburgh EA12 6AU (☎ 0131 539 1192); Scottish Television, Cowcaddens, Glasgow G2 3PR (☎ 0141 300 3000, fax 0141 300 3717, e-mail 100345.1116@compuserve.com)

ROSS, Alistair Charles; s of Alan Alistair Ross, OBE (d 1984), and Marjorie Evelyn, *née* Catch; *b* 29 Nov 1951; *Educ* Westminster, Charing Cross Hosp Med Sch (MB BS); *m* 19 Nov 1977, Alexandra Jane Elaine, da of Samuel Philippe Alexandre Holland; 1 s (James Alistair George MacKenzie b 1984), 2 da (Katherine Alexandra MacKenzie b 1980, Victoria Isobel MacKenzie b 1982); *Career* surgical registrar The London Hosp 1979–82, sr orthopaedic registrar St Marys Hosp London 1982–88, conslt orthopaedic surgn Royal Utd Hosp and Royal Nat Hosp for Rheumatic Diseases Bath 1988–, dir Bath and Wessex Orthopaedic Res Unit 1988–; Euro travelling scholar Br Orthopaedic Assoc 1987, hon sr lectr Sch of Postgrad Medicine Univ of Bath 1992–; memb: Int Soc of Limb Salvage (ISOLS), European Spine Soc, Br Orthopaedic Oncology Soc, Hip Soc, Rheumatoid Arthritis Surgical Soc; Freeman City of London 1977, Liveryman Worshipful Soc of Apothecaries 1993; LRCP, MRCS 1976, FRCS 1980, FRSM 1982, fell Br Orthopaedic Assoc 1988; *Recreations* music; *Clubs* Leander (Henley-on-Thames); *Style*— Alistair Ross, Esq; ✉ The Bath Clinic, Claverton Down Road, Bath BA2 7BR (☎ 01225 835555)

ROSS, Anthony Lee (Tony); s of Eric Turle Lee Ross (d 1982), and Effie, *née* Griffiths (d 1981); *b* 10 Aug 1938; *Educ* Helsby Co GS, Liverpool Regnl Coll of Art (NND); *m* 1, 16 Sept 1961 (m dis 1971), Carole Dawn, *née* D'Arcy; m 2, 1971 (m dis 1976), Joan Lillian, *née* Allerton; 1 da (Alexandra Ruth b 10 Aug 1971); m 3, 30 June 1979, Zoë, da of Cyril Albert Goodwin, of Cuffley, Hertfordshire; 1 da (Katherine Lee b 12 April 1980); *Career* author and illustrator; drawings in magazines incl Punch, Time and Tide, Town 1962–75, sr lectr Manchester Poly 1965–86, first book published 1973; 26 TV films made with King Rollo Films 1983; exhibitions: London, Holland, Germany, Japan, USA, France; patron: Malcolm Sargent Cancer Fund for Children Readathon, Chelsea Children's Hosp Sch; *Awards* USA, Holland, Japan, Belgium, E Germany, W Germany; *Books* illustrator for over 300 children's books incl: The Reluctant Vampire (by Eric Morecambe, 1982), Limericks (by Michael Palin, 1985), Fantastic Mr Fox (by Roald Dahl, 1988), The Magic Finger (by Roald Dahl, 1989), Alice Through The Looking Glass (by Lewis Carroll, 1992); author of 70 children's books incl: I'm Coming to Get You (1984), I Want my Potty (1986), A Fairy Tale (1991); *Recreations* sailing; *Clubs* Chelsea Arts; *Style*— Tony Ross, Esq; ✉ Andersen Press, 20 Vauxhall Bridge Rd, London SW1V 2SA

ROSS, Lt-Col (Charles) Christopher Gordon; s of Maj Charles Gordon Ross, MC (d 1964), of Moor Park, Herts, and Iris Jefford, *née* Fowler (d 1976); *b* 8 July 1931; *Educ* Marlborough, RMA Sandhurst; *m* 27 April 1963, Fiona Mary Ghislaine Ross, *qv*, da of Gp-Capt Albert Peter Vincent Daly, AFC (d 1985), of Dalysgrove, Co Galway, Ireland; 1 s (Alastair Charles Gordon b 24 Jan 1964), 1 da (Geraldine Catherine Ghislaine b 7 April 1965); *Career* cmmnd 14/20 King's Hussars 1951, Troop Ldr ADC, Capt 1956, Sqdn 2 i/c, Adj, Maj 1963, Sqdn Ldr, Staff Offr, Regt 2 i/c, Lt-Col GSO 1 UKLF 1974, GSO 1 DRAC 1976, resigned 1979; diocesan sec Salisbury Diocese 1979–96, currently orgn, charity and ecclesiastical conslt; lay canon Salisbury Cathedral 1995–; memb Gen Synod Dioceses Cmmn 1991–96; 14/20 King's Hussars Regt Assoc: vice chm 1982–85, chm 1986–91, vice pres 1991–92; chm Sarum St Michael Educnl Charity 1993 (govr 1989–); treas Royal Br Legion Branch; FIMgt 1981; *Recreations* gardening, reading, organising things; *Clubs* Army and Navy, St Moritz Tobogganing; *Style*— Lt-Col Christopher Ross; ✉ The Old Schoolhouse, Quidhampton, Salisbury, Wiltshire SP2 9AT (☎ and fax 01722 743516)

ROSS, David Thomas Mcleod; s of David Ross, and Margert, *née* Mcleod; *b* 3 June 1949; *Educ* Boroughmuir Secdy Sch Edinburgh; *m* 25 Aug 1973, Margaret Gordon Sharpe Ross, da of Robert Charters Russell, of Loanhead; 3 da (Lindsay b 1976, Louise b 1978, Heather b 1984); *Career* CA 1976; md Ivory and Sime plc 1988–90 (joined 1968, dir 1982), ptnr Aberforth Partners 1990–; non-exec dir: Aberforth Smaller Companies Trust plc 1990–94, Aberforth Split Level Trust plc 1990–94, US Smaller Companies Investment Trust plc; memb: Co of Merchants of the City of Edinburgh, High Constables and Guard of Honour Holy Rood House; FCCA; *Recreations* skiing; *Style*— David Ross, Esq; ✉ The Avenue, 40 Greenhill Gardens, Edinburgh, EH10 4BJ (☎ 0131 447 4970); Aberforth Partners, 14 Melville Street, Edinburgh EH3 7NS (☎ 0131 220 0733, fax 0131 220 0735)

ROSS, Rt Hon Lord; Donald MacArthur Ross; PC (1985); s of John Ross, slr; *b* 29 March 1927; *Educ* Dundee HS, Univ of Edinburgh (MA, LLB); *m* 1958, Dorothy, *née* Annand; 2 da; *Career* dean Faculty of Advocates 1973–76, senator Coll of Justice Scotland (Lord of Session) 1977–85, Lord Justice Clerk of Scotland and pres Second Div of the Ct of Session in Scotland 1985– Jan 1997; advocate 1952, QC Scotland 1964, Sheriff Princ Ayr & Bute 1972–73; dep chm Scottish Boundary Cmmn 1977–85, chm of Court Heriot-Watt Univ 1984–90; Lord High Cmmr to Gen Assembly of the Church of Scotland 1990 and 1991; Hon LLD: Edinburgh 1987, Dundee 1991, Abertay Dundee 1994; Hon DUniv Heriot-Watt 1988 FRSE 1988; *Recreations* gardening, walking, travelling; *Clubs* Caledonian, New (Edinburgh); *Style*— The Rt Hon Lord Ross, FRSE; ✉ 33 Lauder Rd, Edinburgh EH9 2JG (☎ 0131 667 5731); Parliament House, Edinburgh EH1 1RQ (☎ 0131 225 2595, fax 0131 220 3730)

ROSS, Donald Nixon; s of Donald Ross (d 1942), of Kimberley, South Africa, and late Jessie Ross; *b* 4 Oct 1922; *Educ* Kimberley HS, Univ of Capetown (BSc, MB ChB), Royal Coll of Surgeons London (FRCS 1949); *m* 5 Feb 1953, Dorothy Maud, da of late James Curtis, of Chepstow; 1 da (Janet Susan b 1958); *Career* res fell Guy's Hosp 1953–58; conslt surgn: Guy's Hosp 1958–68, Nat Heart Hosp 1963–89, Middx Hosp 1968–80; sr surgn Inst of Cardiology 1970–90; Freeman Worshipful Soc of Apothecaries London 1968; Hon: FACS 1976, FACC 1973, FRCS (Thailand) 1987, FRCS Ireland 1984, DSc 1982; FRSM 1996; hon prof Univ of Madras 1995, hon doctorate Univ of Buenos Aires 1996; memb Order of Cedars of Lebanon 1975, Offr's Cross Order Merit Germany 1981, Royal Order of Thailand 1994; *Publications* Hypothermia (1960), Surgeon's Guide To Card Diagnosis (1962), Surgical Cardiology (1969), Biological Tissue in Heart Valve Replacement (1972), Surgery and Your Heart (1982), Principles of Cardiac Diagnosis and Management (1991); contrib to numerous scientific jls and books; *Recreations* horse riding, breeding Arabian horses; *Clubs* Kimberley (SA), Garrick; *Style*— Donald Ross, Esq; ✉ 35 Cumberland Terrace, Regents Park, London NW1 4HP (☎ 0171 935 0756); Rumbolds, Flanders Green, Cottered, Herts (☎ 0176 381 474); 25 Upper Wimpole St, London WIM 7TA (☎ 0171 935 8805, fax 0171 935 9190)

ROSS, Duncan Alexander; CBE (1993); s of William Duncan Ross (d 1982), and Mary, *née* Maciver (d 1985); *b* 25 Sept 1928; *Educ* Dingwall Acad, Univ of Glasgow (BSc); *m* 17 May 1958, Mamie Buchanan Clark, da of Harold Parsons (d 1978); 1 s (Alastair b 1962), 1 da (Deborah b 1959); *Career* various engrg posts S Scotland Electricity Bd 1952–57, various engrg commercial and mgmnt posts Midlands Electricity Bd 1957–77; chm: South Wales Electricity Bd 1981–84 (vice chm 1977–81), Southern Electricity Bd 1984–90, Southern Electric plc 1990–93, ret 1993; FIEE; *Recreations* golf, skiing, boating; *Style*— Duncan A Ross, Esq, CBE; ✉ Winterfold, Hoo Lane, Chipping Campden, Glos GL55 6AZ (☎ 01386 841797, fax 01386 841775)

ROSS, Ernest (Ernie); MP (Lab) Dundee West (majority 10,604); *b* 1942; *Educ* St John's Jr Secdy Sch; *m* 2 s, 1 da; *Career* quality control engr Timex Ltd; joined Lab Pty 1973, MP (Lab) Dundee W 1979–; chair PLP Foreign Affrs Ctee; memb: Select Ctee on Employment, Bd of Govrs Westminster Fndn for Democracy, MSF; *Style*— Ernie Ross, Esq, MP; ✉ House of Commons, London SW1A 0AA

ROSS, Prof Euan Macdonald; s of Dr James Stirling Ross (d 1992), of Redbourn, Herts, and Frances, *née* Blaze; *b* 13 Dec 1937; *Educ* Aldenham, Univ of Bristol (MD, DCH); *m* 11 June 1966, Dr Jean Mary Palmer, da of George Palmer (d 1984); 2 s (Rev Matthew Ross b 1967, James b 1972); *Career* house physician Bristol Royal Infirmary 1962–63, sr house offr Aberdeen and Dundee Teaching Hosps 1963–64, registrar in paediatrics Dundee Teaching Hosps 1964–69, lectr in paediatrics Univ of Bristol 1969–74, sr lectr Middx and St Mary's Med Schs Univ of London 1974–84, conslt paediatrician Central Middx Hosp London 1974–84 and Charing Cross Hosp London 1984–89, prof of community paediatrics King's Coll Univ of London 1989; hon conslt paediatrician King's Healthcare Maudsley Hosp and Lambeth NHS Community Tst; memb: Delegacy King's Coll, Ct Bristol Univ, Br Paediatric Surveillance Unit, Exec Bd Whizz-Kidz charity, Br Dyslexia Assoc; tstee and memb Steering Ctee King's Maudsley Inst of Epileptology; examiner: Univ of Aberdeen, DCCH Royal Coll of Physicians Edinburgh; FRCP 1980, MFPHM 1991; *Books* Paediatric Perspectives on Epilepsy (1985), Epilepsy in Young People (1987), Paediatric Epilepsy (1994); *Recreations* Scottish matters, design, art and photography; *Clubs* Athenaeum, Harvean; *Style*— Prof Euan Ross; ✉ Linklater House, Mount Park Rd, Harrow Hill HA1 3JZ (☎ and fax 0181 864 4746); Department of Community Paediatrics, King's College at Mary Sheridan Centre, 405 Kennington Road, London SE11 4QW (☎ 0171 346 5596, fax 0171 346 5598)

ROSS, Fiona Mary Ghislaine; da of Gp Capt Albert Peter Vincent Daly, AFC (d 1985), of Dalysgrove, Co Galway, and Mary Catherine, *née* Wilson (d 1996); *b* 11 May 1936; *Educ* St Mary's Convent Shaftesbury, Sacré-Coeur Brussels; *m* 27 April 1963, Lt-Col (Charles) Christopher Gordon Ross, *qv*, s of Maj Charles Gordon Ross, MC (d 1964); 1 s (Alastair Charles Gordon b 24 Jan 1964), 1 da (Geraldine Catherine Ghislaine b 7 April 1965); *Career* Nat Fedn of Women's Inst: chm Public Affairs Ctee 1993–94 (vice chm 1992–93, memb 1987–94), chm Int Ctee 1994–, chm Home and Country Ctee 1995–96, memb Exec Ctee 1991–, rep on Consumers in the EC Gp 1990–93, rep Confédération des Organisations Familiales de la Communauté Européenne 1991–, memb Admin Cncl 1992–, rep Assoc Country Women of the World 1991–95, memb Triennial Conf Ctee 1992–95, vice chm UN Ctee 1995–, co-ordinator Agric Ctee 1995–; chm Wilts Fedn of Women's Insts 1984–87 (memb Exec Ctee 1979–87); memb Bd of Mgmnt Jt Equestrian Centre Lackham and Chippenham Colls 1989–96; govr Lackham Coll of Agriculture & Enterprise 1985–89, tstee Friends of Lackham Trust 1985–92; memb Rail (formerly Transport) Users Consultative Ctee for S England 1991–; *Recreations* gardening, reading, badminton, canvas embroidery; *Clubs* Royal Anglo-Belgian; *Style*— Mrs Fiona Ross; ✉ The Old Schoolhouse, Quidhampton, Salisbury, Wiltshire SP2 9AT (☎ 01722 743516)

ROSS, Hugh Robert; s of Flt Lt Robert James Ross, RAF (d 1954), and Marion Bertha, *née* Maidment; *b* 21 April 1953; *Educ* Christ's Hosp Sch Horsham Sussex (RAF Benevolent Fund scholar), Univ of Durham (Kitchener scholar, BA), London Business Sch (NHS scholar, MBA); *m* 7 Aug 1981, Margaret Catherine, da of Joseph Martin Hehir; 1 s (Robert Joseph Hehir Ross b 10 May 1987), 1 da (Kate Mairead Hehir Ross b 6 March 1984); *Career* nat admin trainee Wessex Regnl Health Authy 1976–78, asst sector admin Princess Margaret Hosp Swindon 1978–80, patient servs offr Westminster Hosp London 1981–83 (asst admin 1980–81), dir of operational servs Bart's London 1985–86 (dep unit admin 1983–85); unit gen mangr: City Unit Coventry Health Authy 1986–90, Leicester Gen Hosp 1990–93; chief exec: Leicester Gen Hosp NHS Tst 1993–95, Utd Bristol Healthcare NHS Tst 1995–; memb Alumni Assoc London Business Sch 1987–; FHSM 1989 (dip 1979); *Recreations* golf, travel, real ale; *Style*— Hugh Ross, Esq; ✉ United Bristol Healthcare NHS Trust, Marlborough Street, Bristol BS1 3NU (☎ 0117 928 3605, fax 0117 925 6588)

ROSS, Ian Malcolm MacLean; s of Murdo MacDonald Ross (d 1975), of Flodigarry, Isle of Skye, and Isabel Campbell MacDonald, *née* McCord; *b* 21 Oct 1945; *Educ* Rothesay Acad Isle of Bute, Univ of Glasgow (BSc); *m* 26 Oct 1968, Margaret Eleanor, da of Roelofvinus Johannes van Bogerijen; 1 s (Murdo Roel b 31 March 1975), 1 da (Eleanor Isabel b 14 Nov 1972); *Career* researcher British Steel Corporation 1968–70, mill mangr Culter Guard Bridge Holdings 1970–75, gen mangr then vice pres Avery-Dennison 1975–86, chief exec and dir The Harland Group Ltd 1986–; nat chm CIM 1992–93 (vice chm 1989–92); Freeman City of London, memb Worshipful Co of Marketors; FInstD 1988, FCIM 1989, CChem, FRSC 1992; *Recreations* music, sailing, theatre, rugby; *Clubs* RAC, RNCYC, Rockcliff RFC; *Style*— Ian Ross, Esq; ✉ The Harland Group Ltd, Land of Green Ginger House, Anlaby, Hull HU10 6RN (☎ 01482 56116, fax 01482 53240, car 0831 148671)

ROSS, James H; *Educ* Univ of Oxford (BA), Manchester Business Sch (Dip Business Mgmnt); *m*; 3 c; *Career* served RN 1957–59; British Petroleum: joined 1959, worked variously in UK, France and Africa, involved in demerger Shell-Mex BP and creation of BP Oil Ltd, asst gen mangr BP Tanker Co, dep chm Stolt Tankers and Terminals USA, gen mangr corp planning BP Group, chief exec and md BP Oil International 1986–88, pres and chief exec BP America Inc and an md The British Petroleum Co plc 1988–92; chief exec Cable and Wireless plc 1992–95, chm The Littlewoods Organisation 1996–; non-exec dir McGraw Hill Inc; chm Manchester Business Sch, memb Advsy Bd of Cncl for Strategic and Int Studies, tstee Cleveland Orch; *Style*— James Ross, Esq; ✉ The Littlewoods Organisation, 100 Old Hall Street, Liverpool L70 1AB (☎ 0151 235 2222)

ROSS, James McConville; s of Dr David Sloan Ross, of Elderslie, Renfrewshire, and Maureen, *née* McConville (d 1979); *b* 29 Sept 1960; *Educ* Glasgow HS, Univ of St Andrews (MA); *Career* business ed Reid Business Publishing 1984–85; sr electronics analyst James Capel & Co 1987–90 (analyst 1986–87); head of telecommunications res Hoare Govett (now ABN AMRO Hoare Govett) 1992– (sr electronics analyst 1991–92); *Recreations* skiing, sailing, reading, theatre; *Style*— James Ross, Esq; ✉ ABN AMRO Hoare Govett, 4 Broadgate, London EC2M 7LE (☎ 0171 601 0101)

ROSS, John Eugene; *b* 7 June 1933; *Educ* St Joseph's Coll Beulah Hill London, London Sch of Printing and Graphic Arts; *m* 27 June 1964, Joanna Nicola, da of S A Cloudesley Seddon; 4 s (Christopher John b 16 June 1965, Mark Eugene (twin) b 16 June 1965, Philip Howard b 15 Nov 1966, Henry William b 14 July 1968); *Career* photographer; Zoltan Glass 1952–54, fndr mangr of photographic studio for Colman Prentis and Varley 1954–67, freelance photographer 1967–; chm Ealing Arts Cncl 1988–91 and 1994–; memb: NUJ 1963, AFAEP 1971; *Recreations* the arts - organisation and managment, other voluntary work embracing the arts and cultural relations; *Style*— John Ross, Esq;

✉ John Ross Photography, 62 Tottenham Court Road, London W1P 9RH (☎ and fax 0171 323 4831)

ROSS, Sir (James) Keith; 2 Bt (UK 1960), of Whetstone, Middx; RD (1967); s of Sir James Paterson Ross, 1 Bt, KCVO, FRCS (d 1980; Surgn to HM 1952–64), and Marjorie Burton, *née* Townsend (d 1978); *b* 9 May 1927; *Educ* St Paul's, Middx Hosp Med Sch London (MB BS, MS); *m* 24 Nov 1956, Jacqueline Annella, da of Francis William Clarke (d 1971); 1 s, 3 da (Susan Wendy b 28 Feb 1958, Janet Mary b 20 Nov 1960, Anne Townsend b 10 Sept 1962); *Heir* s, Andrew Charles Paterson Ross b 18 June 1966; *Career* Surgn Lt RNVR 1952–54, Surgn Lt Cdr RNR 1964–72; conslt cardiothoracic surgn Harefield Hosp 1964–67; conslt cardiac surgn: Nat Heart Hosp London 1967–72, Wessex Regn Southampton 1972–90 (conslt emeritus 1990–), King Edward VII Hosp Midhurst 1979–90; pres Soc of Cardiothoracic Surgns 1987–88; memb Cncl RCS 1986–94; FRCS 1956, MS 1965, FRCSEd 1989, FRSM; *Recreations* fly-fishing, painting, golf; *Clubs* MCC, Army and Navy, Royal Lymington Yacht; *Style*— Sir Keith Ross, Bt, RD; ✉ Moonhills Gate, Hilltop, Beaulieu, Hants SO42 7YS (☎ 01590 612104)

ROSS, Lucy; da of Alexander Cameron Ross, of Newhaven, Edinburgh; *b* 17 Nov 1961; *Educ* Tadcaster GS Yorks, Broughton Secdy Sch Edinburgh, Jacob Kramar Coll of Art Leeds, Wimbledon Sch of Art (BA), RCA (MA); *Career* artist; has lectured at various art colls; work in numerous public and private collections; *Exhibitions* incl: solo Arcade Gallery Harrogate 1988, gp exhbn Bankside Gallery 1989, gp exhbn Sue Williams Gallery 1989, solo Berkeley Sq London 1991, solo 369 Gallery Edinburgh 1992, Claudio Cello Madrid 1992, touring Br Cncl exhbn to Eastern former Soviet states and Africa 1993; *Major works* incl: Alterpiece (1991), Ritual (1991), Monument (1992); involved with Glyndebourne Festival Opera prodns 1990–93 incl The Magic Flute, Cosi fan Tutte and Peter Grimes; *Awards* incl: Windsor & Newton Watercolour Award, Latimer Award RSA, Young Artist Delfina Studio Tst Award; *Recreations* film making, photography, mosaic, eating out; *Style*— Ms Lucy Ross; ✉ 42 Grove Park, Camberwell, London SE5 8LG (☎ 0171 737 5681); Stockwell Studios, 35 Jeffreys Road, Stockwell SW4

ROSS, Lt-Col (Walter Hugh) Malcolm; CVO (1994), OBE (1988); s of Col Walter John Macdonald Ross, CB, OBE, MC, TD, JP, DL (d 1982), of Bridge-of-Dee, Castle-Douglas, Kirkcudbrightshire, and Josephine May, *née* Cross (d 1982); *b* 27 Oct 1943; *Educ* Eton, RMA Sandhurst; *m* 31 Jan 1969, Susan (Susie) Jane, da of Gen Sir Michael Gow, GCB, DL, *qv*; 1 s (Hector b 1983), 2 da (Tabitha b 1970, Flora b 1974); *Career* Scots Gds 1964–87; asst comptroller Lord Chamberlain's Office 1987–90, comptroller 1991–, mgmnt auditor The Royal Household 1987–89, Extra Equerry to HM The Queen 1988–, sec Central Chancery of The Orders of Knighthood 1989–90; memb Queen's Body Gd for Scotland (Royal Co of Archers) 1981–; Freeman City of London 1994; *Clubs* Pratt's, New (Edinburgh); *Style*— Lt-Col Malcolm Ross, CVO, OBE

ROSS, Michael David (Mike); s of Patrick James Forrest Ross, and Janet Emily, *née* Forsyth; *b* 9 July 1946; *Educ* Daniel Stewart's Coll Edinburgh; *m* 18 Oct 1973, Pamela Marquis, *née* Speakman; *Career* Scottish Widows: jt asst actuary 1970–75, asst actuary 1975–81, jt actuary 1981–86, asst gen mangr 1986–88, gen mangr 1988–90, actuary to the Society 1988–92, dep md 1990–91, main bd dir 1990–, gp chief exec 1991–; FFA 1969, CIMgt 1991, FRSA; *Publications* various contribs to Transactions of Faculty of Actuaries; *Recreations* golf, curling, skiing, gardening; *Clubs* Caledonian, Lothianburn Golf; *Style*— Mike Ross; ✉ Scottish Widows, PO Box 902, 15 Dalkeith Road, Edinburgh EH16 5BU (☎ 0131 655 6186, fax 0131 662 4394)

ROSS, (Alexander) Michael Murray; s of Donald Ross (d 1982), and Margaret Grant Murray, of Newbury, Berks; *b* 10 Oct 1938; *Educ* Charterhouse; *m* 1962, Jessamine Barbara, da of Jack Desmond Willson; 2 da (Corina Katherine b 1965, Stephanie Tanya b 1966); *Career* Clark Battams CAs London 1957–63, Alexander Grant & Co LA Calif 1963–65, BDO Stoy Hayward (and predecessor firms) 1965– (London 1965–85, Newbury 1985–95, Reading 1995–); appointed by Miny of Agriculture to Exec Ctee of Land Settlement Assoc 1970–78; chm: Educn Ctee of London Soc of CAs 1983–85, Newbury Gp of CAs 1989–91; pres Licensed Victuallers Schs 1993–94; chm: Warnford Investments PLC 1995–, LSA Charitable Trust 1995–; *Recreations* bridge, tennis, golf; *Clubs* Caledonian; *Style*— Michael Ross, Esq; ✉ Garvards Cottage, Woolton Hill, Newbury, Berks RG15 9TY (☎ 01635 253056); BDO Stoy Hayward, 2/10 Bridge Street, Reading, Berks RG1 2LU (☎ 0118 957 6582)

ROSS, Nicholas David (Nick); s of John Caryl Ross, of Surrey, and Joy Dorothy, MBE, *née* Richmond; paternal gf Pinhas Rosen was signatory to Israel's Declaration of Independence and first Min of Justice; *b* 7 Aug 1947; *Educ* Wallington Co GS Surrey, Queen's Univ Belfast (BA); *m* 1 March 1985, Sarah Patricia Ann, da of Dr Max Caplin, OBE, of London; 3 s (Adam Michael b 1985, Samuel Max b 1987, Jack Felix b 1988); *Career* dBC freelance reporter and presenter N Ireland 1971–72; presenter radio: Newsdesk, The World Tonight 1972–74, World at One 1972–75 and 1984, Call Nick Ross 1987–, Radio 4 Gulf News FM 1991; prodr and dir documentaries The Fix and The Biggest Epidemic of Our Times 1981; presenter TV: fndr presenter BBC Breakfast TV, Sixty Minutes 1983–84, Man Alive, Out of Court, Fair Comment 1975–83, Watchdog, Star Memories, Crimewatch UK 1984–, Drugwatch 1985–86, A Week in Politics (Channel 4) 1986–88, various debates (BBC, ITV and BskyB), Crime Limited (BBC) 1993–94, Westminster with Nick Ross 1994–, BBC TV political party conference coverage 1995; chm corp conferences; memb: Govt Ctee on Ethics of Gene Therapy 1990–93, Gene Therapy Advsy Ctee 1993–96, Health of the Nation Working Gp 1991–, Nat Bd for Crime Prevention 1993–, Crime Prevention Agency 1995–, Ctee on the Public Understanding of Science, Med Audit Ctee RCP; chm: Science Book Prize 1991; Advisory bd: Crime Concern, Victim Support; pres Healthwatch, SANEline, Tacade; patron: Prisoners Abroad, Missing Persons Helpline, Patients Assoc; FRSA; *Recreations* scuba diving, skiing; *Style*— Nick Ross, Esq; ✉ c/o BBC Broadcasting House, London W1A 1AA (☎ 0181 752 5993, fax 0171 792 9200)

ROSS, (John) Paul; s of John Ross, and Maureen Martha, *née* Walker; *b* 31 Dec 1956; *Educ* Leyton Sr High, Univ of Kent (BA), Univ of Exeter; *m* 1, 1977 (m dis 1991); 1 s (James John b April 1981); m 2, 1991, Kerensa Jane, *née* Bunce; 4 da (Dorothea Barbara b Feb 1991, Violet Mabel b Aug 1992, Bebe Kerensa b Oct 1994, Hermoine Elizabeth b 26 April 1996); *Career* trainee journalist Western Times; LWT: researcher Current Affairs 1982–84, prodr 1984–85, trainee dir 1985–86, ed 1986–88, reporter Eyewitness 1988–90; ed: Stab in the Dark (Channel 4) 1991, The Word (Planet 24) 1992 and 1993; TV credits as presenter/host/reporter/interviewer incl: Crime Monthly (LWT) 1989–95, The Big Breakfast (Planet 24) 1993 and 1994–95, Good Sex Guide Abroad (ITV) 1995, Jeopardy! (Sky One) 1996, 1 to 3 (Sky One) 1996, Tellystack (UK Gold) 1996–97, All Over the Shop (BBC) 1997, Instant Expert (This Morning, ITV) 1996–97; *Recreations* seeking additional employment; *Style*— Paul Ross, Esq; ✉ Partners in Crime, North House, North Street, Petworth, West Sussex GU28 0DD (☎ 01798 343837, fax 01798 344300)

ROSS, Peter Angus; s of Maj John Milner Ross (d 1979), and Evangeline Joyce, *née* Robertson (d 1982); *b* 25 Feb 1936; *Educ* Glasgow Acad; *m* 16 Aug 1962, Elliot Wallace, da of James Allan Baillie Montgomery (d 1982), of Glasgow; *Career* Nat Serv RA 1954–56; managed farm 1956–58, asst tea taster and rep Wm Wright & Co (Pekoe) Ltd 1958–63; chm: Burnthills Group Ltd and subsids (fndr dir Burnthills (Contractors) Ltd, first memb of the gp 1963), Bowfield Hotel and Country Club Ltd, Goldenbolt International Ltd and assoc cos, Huewind Ltd and assoc cos, Stonefield Castle Hotel Ltd, Covenanters Inn Ltd, Bute Newspapers Ltd, LA Bowl (Ayr) Ltd; dep chm: Mull & West Highland Narrow Gauge Railway Co Ltd, Q96 FM Ltd; farms as Ladyland Estates and Grangehill Estates; underwriting memb Lloyd's 1976–; fndr memb and past pres Johnstone Rotary Club 1975–96 (resigned); received Aims of Industry Award for Scotland 1982; *Style*— P A Ross, Esq; ✉ Grangehill, Beith, Ayrshire, Scotland; 84 High St, Johnstone, Renfrewshire (☎ 01505 324461)

ROSS, (Carl) Philip Hartley; s of John Carl Ross (fndr Ross Foods Ltd); *b* 3 May 1943; *Educ* Shrewsbury; *m* 1, 1968, Pamela Jean, *née* Dixon; 3 da (Rachel b 1969, Kathryn b 1971, Amanda b 1975); m 2, 1985 Joanna Louise, *née* Norton; 2 s (Thomas b 1989, Samuel b 1991); *Career* CA; Peat Marwick Mitchell & Co 1961–65, Forrester Boyd & Co 1965–68; dir Cosalt Ltd 1971–75, md Orbit Holdings Ltd 1972–75, chm: Bristol & West Cold Stores Ltd 1974–83, Philip Ross & Co CAs 1982–, S Cartledge & Son Ltd 1995–; FCA; *Recreations* golf, tennis and fitness; *Style*— Philip Ross, Esq; ✉ Rossa Farm, Rossa Lane, Trusthorpe, Mablethorpe, Lincolnshire LN12 2QH (☎ 01507 441811, fax 01507 443033); Philip Ross & Co, 2a Knowle Street, Mablethorpe, Lincs LN12 2BG (☎ 01507 472727)

ROSS, Ricky; *b* 22 Dec 1957; *Career* singer; fndr memb Deacon Blue 1986–94; 3 UK top ten singles (Real Gone Kid 1988, Four Bacharach and David Songs (EP) 1990, Twist and Shout 1991); albums with Deacon Blue: Raintown (1988, UK no 14), When the World Knows Your Name (1989, UK no 1), Ooh Las Vegas (1990, UK no 3), Fellow Hoodlums (1991, UK no 2), Whatever You Say, Say Nothing (1993, UK no 4), Our Town (1994); organiser: charity album The Tree and the Bird and the Fish and the Bell 1991, The Drumbeat Concert (benefit show) 1992; video The Big Picture 1990; soloist 1995–; albums: Radio On (1996); *Style*— Ricky Ross, Esq; ✉ c/o CEC Management, 6 Warren Mews, London W1P 5DJ (☎ 0171 388 6500, fax 0171 388 6522)

ROSS, Lt Gen Sir Robert Jeremy; KCB (1994, CB 1992), OBE (1978); s of Lt Col Gerald Ross (d 1988), and Margaret Ross-Bell (d 1992); *b* 28 Nov 1939; *Educ* Wellington, CCC Cambridge (MPhil); *m* 15 May 1965, Sara, da of Col W P S Curtis, OBE (d 1965); 1 s (Edward b 1966), 1 da (Annabel b 1968); *Career* entered RM 1957, commando and sea serv 1959–69, Army Staff Coll 1970, staff and commando serv 1971–86, RCDS 1983, Cdr 3 Commando Bde 1986–88, Maj Gen Trg Reserve and Special Forces 1988–90, Maj Gen Commando Forces 1990–93, Cmdt Gen Royal Marines 1993–95; Legion of Merit (US) 1993; *Recreations* skiing, fishing, shooting, walking; *Clubs* Royal Thames Yacht; *Style*— Lt Gen Sir Robert Ross, KCB, OBE; ✉ Barclays Bank plc, 50 Jewry St, Winchester, Hampshire SO23 8RG

ROSS, Stephen Lawrence; s of Julian Ross (d 1988), of London, and Miriam, *née* Gimmack (d 1994); *b* 11 Dec 1950; *Educ* Woodhouse GS; *m* (m dis); 1 s (Daniel Paul b 20 Feb 1979), 1 da (Nicola Jane b 2 Oct 1981); *Career* CA 1974; audit mangr Deloitte Haskin & Sells (London) 1976, ptnr Keane Shaw & Co (London) 1978, sr ptnr Ross Bennet-Smith (London) 1983; FCA; *Recreations* tennis, horse racing, bridge; *Style*— Stephen L Ross, Esq; ✉ Ross Bennet-Smith Chartered Accountants, 112 Jermyn Street, London SW1Y 6LS (☎ 0171 930 6000, fax 0171 930 7070)

ROSS, Stephen William; s of Noel Winston Ross (d 1982), and Evelyn Mary, *née* Emmerson (d 1980); *b* 9 Sept 1948; *Educ* Dover Coll, Univ of Bristol (BScEcon); *m* 1971, Penelope Mary, da of Dr Thomas Simpson; 1 s (Thomas b 1975), 1 da (Jessica b 1977); *Career* hotelier; trainee chef Thornbury Castle (Restaurant of the Year 1969) 1970–72, chef patron Popjoys Restaurant Bath 1973–80 (Michelin star 1975); proprietor: Homewood Park Hotel 1980–90 (Egon Ronay Hotel of the Year 1987), Queensberry Hotel and Olive Tree Restaurant Bath 1988– (Country Hotel of the Year 1994); MHCIMA; *Recreations* cookery and wine, yachting, theatre, elderly motor cars, motorcycling, shooting; *Style*— Stephen Ross, Esq; ✉ Queensbury Hotel, Russel Street, Bath BA1 2QF (☎ 01225 447928, fax 01225 446065)

ROSS, Thomas; s of late Duncan Campbell Ross, and Annie McAskill, *née* Greer (d 1992); *b* 28 June 1941; *Educ* Victoria Drive Sch Glasgow, Royal Coll of Sci and Technol Glasgow, Open Univ (BA 1986); *m* 1964, Olive Constance Patricia, da of Edwin George Leslie Morecroft; 2 da (Linda Jane b 4 May 1967, Lesley Ann b 7 March 1969); *Career* Scottish Television: joined as tech asst 1961, head of installation and vision maintenance 1975, tech co-ordinator Tech Ops Dept 1975–90, tech controller 1990–93; bdcast engrg conslt 1993–; memb: RTS, Tech Performance Working Pty ITC, Tech Ctee ITVA; *Publications* IBA Technical Review - Standards for Television Studio Centre Performance (contrib, 1980); *Recreations* golf, hill walking, sailing; *Style*— Thomas Ross, Esq; ✉ Leadenvalloch, Dollerie, by Crieff, Perthshire

ROSS, Thomas Mackenzie; s of Duncan C Ross, of Muir of Ord, Ross-shire, Scotland, and Elsie, *née* Mackenzie; *b* 4 May 1944; *Educ* Dingwall Acad, Univ of Edinburgh (BSc); *m* Oct 1967, Margaret, da of Robert Dewar; 1 s (Steven Graeme b 1970), 1 da (Elaine Caroline b 1968); *Career* trainee actuary Scottish Life Assurance Co Edinburgh 1966–70, consulting actuary and later vice pres Charles A Kench & Associates Vancouver Canada 1971–76, ptnr Clay & Partners Consulting Actuaries 1976–93, dep chief exec Alexander Clay 1993–; memb Cncl: Faculty of Actuaries 1984–88, Nat Assoc of Pension Funds 1989– (chm 1995–); memb: CBI Pensions Panel 1983–95; fell: Faculty of Actuaries 1970, Canadian Inst of Actuaries 1971, Pensions Management Inst 1987; ASA 1971; *Recreations* horse racing, golf, gardening, hill walking; *Clubs* Naval, Racehorse Owners Assoc, Country Gentlemen's Assoc; *Style*— Thomas Ross, Esq; ✉ Alexander Clay, 67 Grosvenor Street, London W1X 9DB (☎ 0171 318 4100, fax 0171 318 4181)

ROSS, William; MP (UU) Londonderry East (majority 18,527); s of Leslie Alexander Ross (d 1973); *b* 4 Feb 1936; *m* 1974; 3 s, 1 da; *Career* MP (UUP) Londonderry 1974–83 and Londonderry E 1983–, spokesman on agriculture and fisheries; *Recreations* shooting, fishing; *Clubs* Northern Counties, Londonderry; *Style*— William Ross, Esq, MP; ✉ Hillquarter, Turmeel, Dungiven, Londonderry, BT47 (☎ 01504 741428); House of Commons, London SW1 0AA (☎ 0171 219 3571)

ROSS, William Mackie; CBE (1987), TD (1970), DL (1971); s of Harry Caithness Ross (d 1965), and Catherine, *née* Mackie; *b* 14 Dec 1922; *Educ* Johnston Sch, Univ of Durham (MB BS, MD); *m* 17 April 1948, Mary, da of Hedworth Burt, OBE (d 1972); 1 s (Duncan b 1959), 2 da (Heather b 1950, Hilary b 1955); *Career* TA 1951–70, Col RAMC (TA); conslt radiotherapist N Region 1953–87, lectr in radiotherapy Univ of Newcastle 1963–87; pres: Br Inst of Radiology 1978–79, RCR 1983–86; hon fell American Coll of Radiology 1986; FRCS 1956, FRCR 1961, FRCS(Edin) 1994; *Style*— William Ross, Esq, CBE, TD, DL

ROSS COLLINS, Michael Stewart; s of Leslie Ross Collins (d 1984), and Stella Mabel, *née* Stewart; *b* 21 June 1938; *Educ* Harrow; *m* 1972 (m dis 1976), Janette Mary, *née* Bryan; *Career* Lt 1 Bn Royal Fusiliers; chm Ross Collins Ltd Lloyd's insur brokers 1969–81, dir Colne Valley Water Co plc 1975–90; dep chm Sedgwick UK Ltd 1987 (dir 1981–88), chm Sedgwick Risk Management Services 1988–95, dir Sedgwick Europe 1988–92, devpt dir Sedwick Group plc 1995–; dep chm Rickmansworth Water Co plc 1988–90 (dir 1976–90), dir Three Valleys Water plc 1990–, dir NGM Restaurants Ltd 1989–; chm Totteridge branch NSPCC 1982–92; tstee: Sir Halley Stewart Tst, Sir Malcolm Stewart Tst, Fan Museum Tst; Freeman City of London 1961, Master Worshipful Co of Fanmakers 1985–86 (memb Ct of Assts), Liveryman Worshipful Co of Insurers; FInstD; *Recreations* golf, food, wine, travel, gardening, antique furniture, fans; *Clubs* Royal & Ancient, Royal Cinque Ports, Royal St George's, Hadley Wood Golf, Hatfield House Tennis, Moreton Morrell, Saracens, City Livery; *Style*— Michael S Ross Collins, Esq; ✉ Wynches, Much Hadham, Hertfordshire SG10 6BA; Sedgwick Group plc, The Sedgwick Centre, London E1 8DX (☎ 0171 481 5526, fax 0171 481 5149, telex 882131)

ROSS GOOBEY, Alastair; s of George Henry Ross Goobey, and Gladys, *née* Menzies; *b* 6 Dec 1945; *Educ* Marlborough, Trinity Coll Cambridge (BA); *m* 1969, Sarah Georgina Mary, da of Cedric Ernest Stille; 1 da (Charlotte Elizabeth Jane b 4 March 1978), 1 s (George Alastair b 26 Nov 1980); *Career* graduate trainee Investmt Dept Kleinwort Benson Ltd 1968–72, investmt mangr Hume Holdings Ltd 1972–77, pensions fund investmt mangr Courtaulds 1977–81, dir Geoffrey Morley and Partners Ltd 1981–85, chief investmt strategist James Capel and Co 1986–93 (special advsr to the Chllr of the Exchequer HM Treasy 1986–87 and 1991–92), chief exec Hermes Pensions Management Ltd (formerly PosTel Investment Management Ltd) 1993–; chm Private Finance Panel Ltd 1996–; non-exec dir: Scottish Life Assurance Co 1978–86, Cheltenham & Gloucester Building Society 1989–91 and 1992–, TR Property Investment Trust plc 1994–; pres Investment Property Forum 1995–; memb Bd Royal Opera 1995–; Parly candidate (Cons) W Leicester 1979; memb: Goode Ctee on Pensions Law Reform 1992–93, Advsy Ctee on Film Finance 1995–96; Freeman City of London, Liveryman Worshipful Co of Gold and Silver Wyre Drawers; FRSA; *Books* The Money Moguls (1986), Bricks and Mortals (1992), Kluwer Handbook on Pensions (jt ed); *Recreations* music, clarinet, piano, cricket; *Clubs* MCC, Reform, Bottesford CC; *Style*— Alastair Ross Goobey, Esq; ✉ Hermes Pensions Management Ltd, Standon House, 21 Mansell Street, London E1 8AA (☎ 0171 702 0888, fax 0171 702 9452)

ROSS MARTYN, John Greaves; s of Dr William Ross Martyn (d 1996), of Wilmslow, Cheshire, and Ida Mary Martyn, *née* Greaves (d 1993); *b* 23 Jan 1944; *Educ* Repton, Univ of Cambridge (MA, LLM); *m* 4 Aug 1973 (m dis 1996), Pauline, da of Ronald Jennings (d 1979), of Morley, Yorks; 1 s (Philip b 1978), 1 da (Elizabeth b 1975); *Career* asst lectr Birmingham Coll of Commerce 1966–68, called to the Bar Middle Temple 1969, in practice at Chancery Bar 1970–, recorder SE Circuit 1993; memb: Chancery Bar Assoc, Soc of Trust and Estate Practitioners; FCIArb; *Books* Williams, Mortimer and Sunnucks on Executors, Administrators and Probate (jt ed, 1993), Family Provision: Law and Practice (1985), Theobald on Wills (jt ed, 1993); *Recreations* gardening, skiing; *Style*— John Ross Martyn, Esq; ✉ 5 New Square, Lincoln's Inn, London WC2A 3RJ (☎ 0171 404 0404, fax 0171 831 6016, e-mail Chambers@FiveNewSquare.Cityscape.co.uk)

ROSS-MUNRO, (William) Colin Gordon; QC (1972); s of late William Ross-Munro and Adela Chirgwin; *b* 12 Feb 1928; *Educ* Lycée Francais de Londres, Harrow, King's Coll Cambridge (BA); *m* 22 Jan 1958, Janice Jill Pedrana, *née* Brown; 1 da (Victoria d 1974); *Career* served Army Educn Corp and Scots Gds 1946–48; called to the Bar Middle Temple 1951, bencher Middle Temple 1983, head of chambers; *Recreations* tennis, travel; *Clubs* Hurlingham, Queens; *Style*— Colin Ross-Munro, Esq, QC; ✉ 2 Hare Court, Middle Temple, London EC4Y 7BH (☎ 0171 583 1770, fax 0171 583 9269)

ROSS OF ROSS, David Campbell; s of Sheriff Charles Campbell Ross of Shandwick, QC; suc kinswoman Miss Rosa Ross Williamson Ross of that Ilk and Pitcalnie in 1968 as Chief of Clan Ross; *b* 1934; *m* 1958, Eileen, da of Lawrence Cassidy; *Heir* s, Hugh Andrew Campbell (b 1961); *Career* mgmnt conslt; vice pres St Andrew Soc Edinburgh; *Clubs* Royal Northern and Univ; *Style*— David Ross of Ross; ✉ Old School House, Fettercairn, Laurencekirk, Kincardineshire AB30 5JF

ROSS RUSSELL, Graham; *b* 3 Jan 1933; *Educ* Loretto, Trinity Hall Cambridge, Harvard Business Sch; *m* 1963, Jean Margaret, da of the late Col K M Symington; 4 children; *Career* chm EMAP plc until 1994; chm: Securities Inst 1992–, Tunnel Services Ltd 1992–, F&C PEP Investment Tst plc 1993–, Advent Venture Capital Trust plc; Stock Exchange: memb 1965–91, memb Cncl 1973–91, dep chm 1984–88; cmmr Public Works Loan Bd 1981–95, dir Securities and Investmts Bd 1989–93; *Style*— Graham Ross Russell, Esq; ✉ c/o Securities Institute, Centurion House, 24 Monument Street, London EC3R 8AJ

ROSS STEWART, David Andrew; OBE (1985); s of Maj-Gen W Ross Stewart CB, CIE (d 1966), of Caddonfoot, Galashiels, Scotland, and Margaret Jean Denholm, *née* Fraser; *b* 30 Nov 1930; *Educ* Rugby, Clare Coll Cambridge (BA); *m* 23 May 1959, Susan Olive, da of Lt Col W H F Routh (d 1964), of Hillside, Kingston St Mary, Taunton, Somerset; 2 s (James b 20 Sept 1961, Charles b 15 May 1964); *Career* mgmnt trainee Alex Cowan & Sons Ltd 1952–55, asst to gen mangr Alex Cowan & Son (NZ) Ltd 1959–62; gen mangr: Alex Cowan & Sons (Stationery) Ltd London 1962–66, Spicers (Stationery) Ltd Sawston 1966–68; md John Bartholomew & Son Ltd Edinburgh 1968–89; chm: St Andrew Trust plc, EFM Income Trust plc, Quayle Munro Holdings plc; dir Lothian Investment Fund for Enterprise Ltd; convenor: Univ of Edinburgh Advsy Ctee on Business Studies, Fin Ctee Nat Tst for Scotland; fell Scot Cncl Devpt and Indust; *Recreations* fishing, gardening, golf; *Clubs* New (Edinburgh), Hon Co of Edinburgh Golfers, Muirfield Golf; *Style*— David Ross Stewart, Esq, OBE; ✉ 13 Blacket Place, Edinburgh EH9 1RN (☎ 0131 667 3221)

ROSSBERG, Sara Jutta Maria; da of Manfred Rossberg, of Darmstadt, Germany, and Josefine, *née* Kamps (d 1978); *b* 14 Oct 1952; *Educ* Viktoria Sch Darmstadt Germany, Acad of Fine Art Frankfurt/Main, Camberwell Sch of Art and Crafts; *Career* painter (based London 1978–); travelling scholar: German Nat Fndn 1976–77, DAAD 1977–78; *Solo Exhbns* Acad of Fine Art Frankfurt/ Main 1973, Int Art Fair Basle 1986, Kunstkeller Bern 1987, Treadwell Gall 1987, Thumb Gall London 1988, Don't I Know You? retrospective touring show 1989, Rosenberg & Stiebel Inc NY 1990, Louis Newman Galleries LA 1990, Thumb Gall 1991, Stiebel Modern NY 1991, 1993 and 1994, Warrington Mus and Art Gall 1992, Turnpike Gall Leigh 1996; *Gp Exhbns* incl: Summer Show RA 1978, Chelsea Art Soc 1978, Treadwell Gall 1982, various int art fairs UK & abroad 1982–, Art by Woman Wolverhampton Art Gall 1988, self-portrait touring show 1988, Nat Portrait Gall 1989, 1990 and 1993, John Moores 16 Liverpool 1989, Drawing Show Thumb Gall 1988, 1990 and 1995, European Artists Works on Paper Kunstkeller Bern 1990, Discerning Eye Mall Galleries, Portrait Now Nat Portrait Gall, Singer & Friedlander Watercolour touring exhibition 1995; *Awards* Crown Award 1978, prizewinner 16th John Moore's Liverpool Exhbn 1989, commendation BP Awards Nat Portrait Gall 1990; *Recreations* music, running; *Style*— Ms Sara Rossberg; ✉ Rosenberg and Stiebel, 32 East 57th Street, NY 10022, New York, USA (☎ 00 1 212 759 5536)

ROSSDALE, Fleur Viola; da of John Spencer Rossdale, and Lucie Marcelle Louise, *née* Bourcier; *b* 20 March 1957; *Educ* Francis Holland Sch, Florence Univ (Dip); *m* Dec 1982, Fletcher Robinson (m dis 1996); 2 s (George b 1984, William b 1986); *Career* originator of the British Interior Design Exhibition staging first show-house in UK 1982, subsequent series of purpose built interior design led exhbns at The Chelsea Town Hall during 1980's and 90's, estab The British Interior Design Exhibition at Cambridge Gate Regents Park showing work of 30 leading interior designers 1997; *Recreations* include walking, painting, partying and reading; *Clubs* Hurlingham; *Style*— Miss Fleur Rossdale; ✉ 123 Hurlingham Road, London SW6 3NJ (☎ 0171 731 6327, fax 0171 736 3573)

ROSSE, 7 Earl of (I 1806); Sir William Brendan Parsons; 10 Bt (I 1677); also Baron Ballybritt and Oxmantown (I 1795), Lord of the Manors of Towton, Womersley and Woodhall in England and of Parsonstown, Newtown and Roscomroe in Ireland; s of 6 Earl of Rosse, KBE (d 1979), and Anne, *née* Messel (d 1992); half-bro of 1 Earl of Snowdon, *qv*; *b* 21 Oct 1936; *Educ* Grenoble Univ, Ch Ch Oxford (MA); *m* 1966, Alison, da of Maj John Cooke-Hurle, of Startforth Hall, Barnard Castle; 2 s (Lord Oxmantown b 1969, Hon Michael b 1981), 1 da (Lady Alicia b 1971); *Heir* s, Lord Oxmantown, *qv*; *Career* late 2 Lt Irish Gds; UN official: Ghana, Dahomey, Mid-W Africa, Iran, Bangladesh, Algeria 1963–80; dir: Historic Irish Houses and Gardens Assoc 1980–91, Agency for Personal Services Overseas 1981–89, Birr Scientific and Heritage Fndn 1985–, Lorne House Tst 1993–; memb of Irish Govt's Advsy Cncl on Devpt Co-operation 1983–88; Hon FIEI; *Style*— The Rt Hon the Earl of Rosse; ✉ Birr Castle, Co Offaly, Republic of Ireland (☎ and fax 353 509 20056)

ROSSEN, Stig; s of Carlo Rossen, of Kolding, Denmark, and Lone, *née* Kruse; *b* 14 June 1962; *Educ* Kolding Gymnasium Denmark, Guildhall Sch of Music and Drama; *m* 27 Oct 1990 (m dis 1995), Ulrike Yvonne, da of Dr Karl-Albert Schetter, of Munich; 1 da (Josephine Annie b 27 Dec 1990); *Career* musical actor; West End roles: Jean Valjean in Les Misérables (Palace 1990–92, Copenhagen 1993, Asian tour 1996), Anton Fugger in Which Witch (Piccadilly) 1992; other theatre incl: Count Danilo in the Merry Widow, Russian tenor in Fiddler on the Roof, title role in Tordenskiold (Copenhagen) 1993–94, Eisenstein im Fledermaus (Copenhagan) 1995; TV: Roughnecks (BBC) 1994; solo albums: Kerlighed Og Alt Det Der (Denmark only) 1988, Starry Starry Nights 1991, The Impossible Dream 1993; *Recreations* golf, tennis, backgammon, reading; *Style*— Stig Rossen, Esq; ✉ 72 Park Avenue, Bush Hill Park, Enfield, Middx EN1 2HW

ROSSER, Sir Melvyn Wynne; kt (1974), DL (West Glam 1986); s of David John Rosser, of Swansea, and Anita, *née* Rosser; *b* 11 Nov 1926; *Educ* Glanmor Sch Swansea, Bishop Gore GS Swansea; *m* 16 April 1959, (Mary) Margaret; 1 s (Neil), 2 da (Betsan, Mari); *Career* ptnr Deloitte Haskins & Sells: Swansea 1961–66, Cardiff 1966–79, London 1979–86; dir: Nat Bus Co 1969–72, Wales Telecommunications Bd 1970–80, Br Steel Corp 1972–80, Nat Coal Bd 1980–89, W Mids and Wales Regnl Bd Nat West Bank 1986–89; chm: Manpower Services Ctee for Wales 1980–88, chm HTV Group 1986–91; memb: Welsh Econ Cncl 1965–68, Welsh Cncl 1968–80 (chm 1971–80), Royal Cmmn on Standards of Conduct in Public Life 1974, PM's Advsy Ctee on Outside Business Appts 1976–83, Nat Training Agency 1989–91 (chm Training Enterprise and Educn Advsy Gp for Wales 1989–92); pres Univ Coll of Wales Aberystwyth 1985– (vice pres 1977–85); memb: Cncl and Ct of Univ of Wales, memb Gorsedd of Bards; Hon LLD Univ of Wales, hon fell Univ of Glamorgan; FCA; *Recreations* music, gardening, golf; *Clubs* RAC, Cardiff and County; *Style*— Sir Melvyn Rosser, DL; ✉ Corlan, 53 Birchgrove Road, Swansea, W Glamorgan SA7 9JR (☎ 01792 812286)

ROSSER, Michael John (Mike); s of John Desmond Rosser (d 1992), of Enfield, Middx, and Joan, *née* Oakley; *b* 15 Nov 1943; *Educ* Edmonton Co GS; *m* Jo Haigh; 1 s (David John b 18 March 1987), 1 da (Katherine Joan b 31 Aug 1980), 2 step da (Jessica Daisy b 14 May 1986, Pollyanna Rose b 29 Nov 1988); *Career* trainee media planner/buyer Garland Compton advtg agency 1961–64, media planner/buyer Ogilvy & Mather 1964–67; media gp head: Grey London 1967–70, Dorland Advertising 1970–75; media dir Allen Brady & Marsh 1975–77, md J Walter Thompson, JWT Direct and Conquest Media Manchester 1987–91 (media dir J Walter Thompson 1977–86), media dir Poulter Communications Leeds 1991–93, md FDS Director Services 1994– (corp devpt and recovery conslt 1993); FIPA 1988; *Recreations* soccer, cricket, squash, golf (playing and watching); *Style*— Mike Rosser, Esq; ✉ The Royds, 326 Wakefield Road, Denby Dale, Huddersfield (home ☎ 01484 866731, office 01484 604569)

ROSSER, Prof Rachel Mary; da of John Rosser (d 1983), and Madge; *Educ* King's HS Warwick, Newnham Coll Cambridge (BA), St Thomas' Hosp Med Sch (MB BChir), Charing Cross and Westminster Med Sch (PhD); *m* 17 June 1967, Vincent Challacombe Watts, s of Geoffrey Watts (d 1987), of Low Hall, Kirkbymoorside, N Yorks; 1 s (Benjamin b 1977), 1 da (Hannah b 1981); *Career* house offr St Thomas' Hosp 1966–67, house offr and sr house offr 1967–69 (Hackney Hosp, Brook Gen Hosp, Regnl Neurosurgical Unit Central Middx Hosp), research asst and hon registrar Guy's Hosp Med Sch 1969–71, registrar Bethlem Royal and Maudsley Hosps 1971–74, sr registrar 1974–76 (Hammersmith Hosp, King's Coll Dulwich, Maudsley Hosp), reader Charing Cross Med Sch 1983–84 (sr lectr and hon conslt 1976–82), prof of psychiatry UCL 1984– (head of psychiatry 1984–93), sabbatical yr as visiting scholar Univ of Oxford 1993–94; currently dir Churches' Cncl for Health and Healing, hon conslt Camden & Islington Community NHS Tst; author of scientific papers on: quality of life, psychotherapy research, psychosomatic med, post traumatic stress disorder; cncllr Int Coll of Psychosomatic Research 1991– (treas 1983–91); pres: Soc for Psychosomatic Med 1984–86, Psychiatry Section RSM 1991–92; memb UK and Euro Gps for research on quality of life and disasters; FRCPsych 1983 (MRCPsych 1973), FRCP 1984 (MRCP 1971); *Books* Health Care: Priorities and Management (jtly, 1980), Mind Made Disease: A Clinician's Guide to Psychosomatic Research (jtly, 1988), Quality of Life: Assessment and Application (with S R Walker, 1988), Key Issues in Assessing Quality of Life (with S R Walker, 1992); *Style*— Prof Rachel Rosser; ✉ Department of Psychiatry, University College London Medical School, Middlesex Hospital, Mortimer Street, London W1N 8AA (☎ 0171 380 9334, fax 0171 323 1459)

ROSSER, Richard Andrew; JP (1978); s of Gordon William Rosser (d 1985), and Kathleen Mary, *née* Moon (d 1985); *b* 5 Oct 1944; *Educ* St Nicholas GS Northwood, Univ of London (BSc); *m* 17 Nov 1973, Sheena Margaret, da of Iain Denoon; 2 s (Keith Malcolm b 1976, Colin Michael b 1977), 1 da (Rachel Anne b 1980); *Career* Transport Salaried Staff Assoc: res offr 1968–76, fin offr 1976–77, sec London Midland Regn 1977–82, asst gen sec 1982–89, gen sec 1989–; cncllr London Borough of Hillingdon 1971–78 (chm Fin Ctee 1974–78), Parly candidate (Lab) Croydon Central Feb 1974, memb Lab Pty Nat Exec Ctee 1988–; MCIT 1968; *Style*— Richard Rosser, Esq, JP; ✉ Transport Salaried Staffs' Association, Walkden House, 10 Melton Street, London NW1 2EJ (☎ 0171 387 2101, fax 0171 383 0656)

ROSSI, Francis Dominic Nicholas Michael; s of Dominic Rossi, of Kent, and Anne, *née* Traynor; *b* 29 May 1949; *Educ* Sedgehill Sch London; *m* 1, 12 June 1967, Jean, *née* Smith; 3 s (Simon b 1967, Nicholas b 1972, Kieran b 1979); *ptnr* Elizabeth Gurnan; 1 c; m 2, Eileen, da of Michael Quinn; 2 s (Patrick b 1989, Fynn b 1990), 1 da (Kiera Tallulah b 1993); *Career* Status Quo (orignally known as Spectres formed 1962): co-fndr 1967, continual world touring 1967–, Gold and Silver discs every year since 1971; played at: launch of Prince's Trust 1983, Live Aid 1985, Knebworth 1990, Prince's Trust and Help a London Child charity performance Royal Albert Hall 1994; solo career launched 1996, Give Myself to Love (debut single), King of the Doghouse (debut album); ltd edn character jugs issued by Royal Doulton 1993; *Awards* Silver Clef award 1981, Ivor Novello award (for outstanding servs to music indust) 1984, World Music award Monaco 1991, BRIT award (for outstanding servs to music) 1991; *Books* Just for the Record (autobiography, 1993); *Recreations* collecting Koi carp, clay pigeon shooting; *Style*— Francis Rossi, Esq; ✉ c/o The Handle Group of Companies, 1 Albion Place, Galena Road, Hammersmith, London W6 0QT (☎ 0181 846 9111)

ROSSI, Sir Hugh Alexis Louis; kt (1983); *b* 21 June 1927; *Educ* Finchley Catholic GS, King's Coll London (LLB); *m* 1955, (Philomena) Elizabeth, da of Patrick Jennings (d 1951); 1 s, 4 da; *Career* admitted slr 1950; MP (C): Hornsey 1966–83, Hornsey and Wood Green 1983–92; asst Govt whip 1970–72, Euro whip 1971–73, a Lord Cmmr of the Treasy (Govt whip) 1972–74, Parly under sec for the environment Jan-March 1974, oppn spokesman on housing and land 1974–79, min of state NI Office 1979–81, min of state for social security and the disabled DHSS 1981–83, chm Enviroment Select Ctee 1983–92; memb UK Delgn to Cncl of Europe and WEU 1970–73 (dep ldr 1972–73); conslt in environmental law Simmons and Simmons slrs, conslt Wimpey Environmental Ltd 1993–95; former memb Hornsey & Haringey Cncl and Middx CC; chm: Italian Hosp Fund 1992–, UN Assoc (UK) 1992–96, Historic Chapels Tst 1993–; Knight of the Holy Sepulchre 1966, KCSG 1985; FKC 1986, Hon FCIWEM 1990, Hon Fell Inst Waste

Management 1993; *Style—* Sir Hugh Rossi; ✉ c/o Simmons & Simmons, Solicitors, 21 Wilson Street, London EC2M 2TQ (☎ 0171 628 2020)

ROSSI, Mario; s of Carlo Rossi, of Glasgow, and Vitoria, *née* Bertoncini; *b* 11 Feb 1958; *Educ* Glasgow Sch of Art (BA) Royal Coll of Art (MA); *ptnr* Lindsay Alker; 1 da (Vita Rossi); *Career* artist; lectr Goldsmiths' Coll London 1985–90, currently sr lectr in painting Central St Martin's Sch of Art; work in the collections of: Contemporary Arts Soc, V & A, Gallery of Modern Art Edinburgh, Cleveland Art Gallery Middlesbrough, Unilever, Nordstern Cologne, British Council, Glaxo-Welcom, EMI Worldwide, Tetrapak, DTI; Gulbenkian Rome scholar Br Sch at Rome 1982–83, fellowship in creative arts Trinity Coll Cambridge 1987–89, Coopers & Lybrand under 35 award Whitechapel Open 1988, Fulbright fell in visual art 1993–94; *Solo Exhibitions* incl: The Archaeologist (Demarco Gallery, City Arts Centre) 1984, Interim Art 1985, Cleveland Gallery Middlesbrough 1987, Atelier 1 Hamburg 1987, Anderson O'Day Gallery London 1988 and 1990, Ozones (Wren Library, Trinity Coll Cambridge) 1989, Spacex Gallery Exeter 1990, Peter Scott Gallery Lancaster Univ 1991, Oldham Gallery 1991, Angel Row Gallery Nottingham 1991, Anderson O'Day Gallery Economist Bldg St James's 1992, Anderson O'Day Gallery 1993, Northern Arts Sunderland 1995; *Gp Exhibitions* incl: Cross Currents (Third Eye Centre Glasgow) 1979, Scottish Young Contemporaries (Travelling Exhibition) 1981, Expressive Images (New 57 Gallery Edinburgh) 1982, 12 Artisti Britannici A Roma (Palazzo Barberini Rome) 1983, Five Painter (Riverside Studios) 1985, New Image Glasgow (Third Eye Centre Glasgow) 1985, New Art-New World (Sothebys London and NY) 1986, Contemporary British Woodcuts (Worcester Museum) 1986, The Vigorous Imagination-New Scottish Art (Scottish Nat Gallery of Modern Art Edinburgh and touring) 1987, Glasgow Garden Festival 1988, Fire and Metal (Goldsmiths' Gallery) 1988, Whitechapel Open (Whitechapel Gallery) 1988, John Moores 16 (Walker Art Gallery Liverpool) 1989, Scottish Art Since 1900 (Scottish Nat Gallery of Modern Art Edinburgh and The Barbican) 1989–90, Real Life Stories - The Cleveland Collection (Spacex Gallery Exeter) 1990, Post Morality (Kettle's Yard Cambridge) 1990, Post-Modern Prints (V&A) 1991, John Moores 17 (Walker Art Gallery Liverpool) 1991, Cleveland Drawing Bienale Middlesborough 1991, Cross Over (Anderson O'Day Gallery) 1992, The Return of the Cadaure Equis (Drawing Centre NY) 1993; *Clubs* Chelsea Arts; *Style—* Mario Rossi, Esq; ✉ Well Cottage, Cliff End, Pett Level, East Sussex TN35 4EE (☎ and fax 01424 813291)

ROSSITER, Prof Charles Edward; s of Percy Rowland Rossiter (d 1948), of Peru, and Gertrude, *née* Smith (d 1976), of Melbourne, Aust; *b* 5 Dec 1935; *Educ* Framlingham Coll Suffolk, St John's Coll Oxford (BA, MA), Univ of London (DSc); *m* 1, 20 May 1961 (m dis), Averil Elizabeth Margaret Tucker; 1 s (Martin b 1970), 2 da (Jane b 1965, Ann b 1966); m 2, 14 Oct 1988, Jane Elizabeth, da of Joseph Wallace Hughes (d 1963); *Career* assoc prof McGill Univ Montreal 1966–68, head div of computing and statistics Clinical Res Centre MRC 1979–84 (statistician pneumoconiosis unit 1959–79), prof of occupational health and dir TUC Centenary Inst of Occupational Health LSHTM 1984–88 (emeritus prof of occupational health Univ of London 1988), chm Jt Euro Med Res Bd 1988–; Freeman: Worshipful Soc of Apothecaries 1984, City of London 1988; hon fell Faculty of Occupational Med 1984; *Recreations* golf, computing; *Style—* Prof Charles Rossiter; ✉ 10 Mynchen Rd, Knotty Green, Beaconsfield, Bucks HP9 2AS (☎ 01494 670677, fax 01494 670678)

ROSSITER, Rt Rev (Anthony) Francis; s of Leslie Anthony Rossiter (d 1952), and Winifred Mary, *née* Poppitt; *b* 26 April 1931; *Educ* St Benedict's Ealing, Sant Anselmo (LCL) Rome, Lateran Univ; *Career* ordained priest 1955, dep head St Benedict's Sch 1960–67; abbot of Ealing 1967–91; pres Conf of Major Religious Superiors of Eng and Wales 1970–74, vicar for Religious Archdiocese of Westminster 1969–89, vicar of the Abbot Primate 1989–95, Pro-Primate 1995–96; memb Ctee GBA 1983–85, abbot pres Eng Benedictine Congregation 1985– (second asst 1976–85); Hon DD St Vincent Coll Pensylvania 1988; *Style—* The Rt Rev Abbot F Rossiter; ✉ Ealing Abbey, London W5 2DY (☎ 0181 862 2100, fax 0181 810 4725)

ROSSITER, Nicholas Jeremy; s of Anthony Rossiter, of Litton, Somerset, and Anneka, *née* Hooving; *b* 17 July 1961; *Educ* Downside, Oxford Univ (MA); *Career* journalist; gen trainee BBC TV 1986, prodr/dir BBC TV music and arts 1988, contrib to The Listener and other periodicals 1987, dir HRH The Prince of Wales film A Vision of Britain 1988 (BAFTA nomination); other films incl: The Great Picture Chase (with David Puttnam), Monsieur Eiffel's Tower, Rembrandt, The Private Gaze, The Much Loved Friend (portrait of the Nat Gallery), Prague: The City Where Time Stood Still, Relative Values (RTS nomination 1992); exec prodr Sister Wendy's Odyssey, Grand Tour and Story of Painting, exec prodr American Visions (1996); *Books* Ram Ram India (1989); *Recreations* travel; *Style—* Nicholas Rossiter, Esq; ✉ c/o BBC TV Music and Arts, East Tower, Television Centre, Wood Lane, London W12 7RJ (☎ 0181 743 8000)

ROSSLYN, 7 Earl of (UK 1801); Sir Peter St Clair-Erskine; 10 Bt (S 1666); also Baron Loughborough (GB 1780); s of 6 Earl of Rosslyn (d 1977), and Comtesse Athenaïs de Rochechouart-Mortemart; *b* 31 March 1958; *Educ* Eton, Univ of Bristol; *m* 1982, Helen M, el da C R Watters of Sussex; 2 s (Lord Loughborough, Hon Harry b 9 May 1995), 2 da (Lady Alice b 14 June 1988, Lady Lucia b 1993); *Heir* s, Jamie William St Clair-Erskine, Lord Loughborough, b 28 May 1986; *Career* Metropolitan Police 1980–94, Thames Valley Police 1994–; tstee Dunimarle Museum; *Recreations* opera, church music, piano; *Clubs* White's; *Style—* The Rt Hon the Earl of Rosslyn

ROSSMORE, 7 Baron (I 1796 & UK 1838); William Warner Westenra; s of 6 Baron Rossmore (d 1958); *b* 14 Feb 1931; *Educ* Eton, Trinity Coll Cambridge; *m* 1982, Valerie Marion, da of Brian Tobin, of Riverstown, Birr, Ireland; 1 s, 1 step da; *Heir* s, Hon Benedict William Westenra, b 6 March 1983; *Career* 2 Lt Somerset LI; co-fndr Coolemine Therapeutic Community Dublin; *Recreations* drawing and painting; *Clubs* Kildare St & Univ (Dublin); *Style—* The Rt Hon Lord Rossmore; ✉ c/o Lloyds Bank plc, 6 Pall Mall, London SW1

ROSSOR, Dr Martin Neil; s of Harry Bruce Rossor, of Thorpeness, Suffolk, and Eileen, *née* Curry; *b* 24 April 1950; *Educ* Watford GS, Jesus Coll Cambridge (MA, MD, Ralph Horton-Smith Prize), King's Coll Hosp Med Sch (MB BChir, MRCP); *m* 5 July 1973, Eve Beatrix, da of Prof Kurt Lipstein, of Cambridge; 2 s (Alexander b 28 Aug 1979, Thomas b 20 July 1981), 1 da (Charlotte b 31 July 1984); *Career* house offr in gen med KCH and house offr in gen surgery The Brook Hosp London 1974–75, SHO in gen med Bart's 1975–76, SHO in thoracic med The Brompton Hosp 1976–77, SHO in neurology Nat Hosp for Nervous Diseases London 1977–78, registrar in clinical pharmacology and gen med Royal Postgrad Med Sch and Hammersmith Hosp London 1978, clinical scientist MRC Neurochemical Pharmacology Unit and hon registrar in neurology Addenbrooke's Hosp Cambridge 1979–82, sr registrar in neurology Nat Hosp for Neurology and Neurosurgery London 1983–86 (registrar in neurology 1982–83), conslt neurologist to The Nat Hosps for Neurology and Neurosurgery, St Mary's Hosp and the Western Ophthalmic Hosp London 1986–, hon conslt neurologist to St Andrew's Hosp Northampton 1988–, sr lectr Inst of Neurology London 1992–, hon sr fell in molecular genetics St Mary's Hosp Med Sch 1993–, clinical dir for neurology Nat Hosp for Neurology and Neurosurgery 1993–; memb Med Advsy Panel Alzheimer Disease Soc 1986–; ed Alzheimer's Review 1991–, Euro ed Alzheimer's Disease and Associated Orders 1992–, memb Editorial Bd Euro Jl of Neurology 1994–; Freeman City of London, Liveryman Worshipful Soc of Apothecaries; memb Alzheimer's Fndn Assocs, Assoc of Br Neurologists (memb Cncl 1993–), Brain Research Assoc, Br Neuropsychiatry Assoc, Euro Neuroscience Assoc, Harveian Soc, RCPsych (affiliate), RSM, World Fedn of Neurology Dementia (memb Exec Ctee); FRCP 1990; *Books* Unusual Dementias (ed, 1992); also author of numerous book chapters and original papers; *Recreations* English literature, sailing, equestrian sports; *Clubs* Athenaeum; *Style—* Dr Martin Rossor; ✉ St Mary's Hospital, Department of Neurology, Praed Street, London W2 1NY (☎ 0171 725 1236/1756, fax 0171 725 1422)

ROSSWICK, (Robert) Paul; s of John Rosswick (d 1959), and Phoebe, *née* Fagin (d 1982); *b* 1 June 1932; *Educ* Malvern Coll, London Hosp Med Coll (MB BS); *m* 25 March 1962, Elizabeth Rita, da of Horace Cooper; 1 s (Jonathan b 1965), 1 da (Sarah b 1966); *Career* emeritus conslt surgn St George's Hosp London 1970–91, hon sr lectr in surgery St George's Hosp Med Sch, prev first asst in surgery St Georges Hosp 1964–69, Robertson Exchange fellow in surgery Presbyterian-St Lukes Hosp Chicago 1962–63, surgn Royal Masonic Hosp London 1977–91; treas Med Soc London 1994– (pres 1990–91); Freeman City of London 1979, Liveryman Worshipful Soc of Apothecaries 1983; *Recreations* music, photography, freemasonry; *Clubs* RSM; *Style—* Paul Rosswick, Esq; ✉ 79 Harley St, London W1N 1DE (☎ 0171 935 3046, fax 0171 486 3927)

ROSTRON, Chad Kenneth; s of Kenneth William Briggs Rostron, and Rosemary, *née* Arkwright; *b* 6 May 1951; *Educ* Sherborne, Univ of Newcastle (MB BS); *m* Josephine Rose; *Career* conslt ophthalmologist St George's Hosp 1988, hon sr lectr Univ of London 1988; author of pubns on corneal and kerato-refractive surgery; section ed Eye; DO 1979, FRCS 1983, FRCOpth 1989, memb RSM; *Clubs* Royal Soc of Med; *Style—* Chad Rostron, Esq; ✉ 10 Harley St, London W1N 1AA (☎ 0171 483 4921, fax 0171 467 8312)

ROSTRON, Philip; s of Raymond Hugh Riley Rostron (d 1976), and Lilian, *née* Hewson (d 1991); *b* 9 Sept 1951; *Educ* Chadderton GS for Boys; *m* 3 Sept 1977, Caroline Lorraine, da of Rowland Edmunds; 1 s (Gary Paul b 16 Dec 1980), 2 da (Joanna Marie b 25 Oct 1979, Hollie Victoria b 22 Jan 1992); *Career* journalist; Oldham Evening Chronicle 1967–68, Oldham Press Agency 1968–69, Rochdale Observer 1969–71, Daily Telegraph Sydney Aust 1971–73, West Lancashire Evening Gazette Blackpool 1973–78, sports ed Daily Star 1988– (joined 1978); *Books* On The Level (ghosted autobiography of champion racehorse trainer Henry Cecil, 1986); *Recreations* lifelong fan of Oldham Athletic FC, music (favourite singer Scott Walker); *Style—* Philip Rostron, Esq; ✉ Daily Star, 245 Blackfriars Road, London SE1 9UX (☎ 0171 922 7427)

ROSTRON, Timothy Peter (Tim); s of Frank Rostron, of Newbury, Berks, and Mildred Joan, *née* Scull; *b* 1 Oct 1955; *Educ* St Bartholomew's GS Newbury, Winchester Sch of Art (BA); *m* 1987 (m dis), Elizabeth, da of Philip Arnold Draper; *Career* freelance textile designer 1978–79, counterhand ice cream parlour Harrods 1979–80, trainee Doctor newspaper 1980–83, chief sub ed She Magazine 1983–86, features ed Elle Magazine 1987–88; Daily Telegraph: contrib 1986–, asst arts ed 1988–90, ed Weekend section 1990–93, dep arts ed 1993–; *Recreations* learning to drive; *Style—* Tim Rostron, Esq; ✉ The Daily Telegraph, 1 Canada Square, Canary Wharf, London E14 5DT (☎ 0171 538 5000, fax 0171 538 7650)

ROTBLAT, Prof Joseph; CBE (1965); s of late Zygmunt Rotblat, and late Sonia Rotblat; *b* 4 Nov 1908; *Educ* Free Univ of Poland (MA), Univ of Warsaw (DPhys), Univ of Liverpool (PhD), Univ of London (DSc); *Career* res fell Radiological Laboratory Warsaw 1933–39, asst dir Atomic Physics Inst Warsaw 1937–39, Oliver Lodge fell Univ of Liverpool 1939–40, lectr (later sr lectr) Univ of Liverpool 1940–49; worked on atom bomb Liverpool and Los Alamos New Mexico 1939–44; dir of nuclear physics res Univ of Liverpool 1945–49, prof Univ of London and chief physicist Bart's 1950–76, vice dean Faculty of Sci Univ of London 1974–76, treas Bart's Med Coll 1973–76; ed in chief Physics in Medicine and Biology 1960–72; govr: Bart's Med Coll 1977–96, Bart's 1978–; pres: Hosp Physicists' Assoc 1969–70, Br Inst of Radiology 1971–72, Youth Sci Forum 1972–74, Pugwash Confs on Sci and World Affrs 1988–; Hon DSc: Bradford 1973, Liverpool 1989, City Univ 1996; hon fell: UMIST 1985, Queen Mary & Westfield Coll 1996; Dr Sc Honoris Causa: Lomonosov Univ Moscow 1988, Polish Acad of Sciences 1966, American Acad Arts and Sciences 1972, Czechoslovak Acad of Sciences 1988, Ukrainian Acad of Sciences 1994; Order of Merit Polish People's Republic 1987, Order of Cyril and Methodius (first class) Bulgaria 1988, Knight Cdr Order of Merit Federal Republic of Germany 1989; Albert Einstein Peace Prize 1992, Nobel Peace Prize 1995; FRS 1995; *Books* Atoms and The Universe (1956), Science and World Affairs (1962), Aspects of Medical Physics (1966), Scientists in the Quest for Peace (1972), Nuclear Reactors - To Breed or not to Breed (1977), Nuclear Radiation in Warfare (1981), Scientists, The Arms Race and Disarmament (1982), The Arms Race at a Time of Decision (1984), Nuclear Strategy and World Security (1985), Strategic Defence and the Future of the Arms Race (1987), Co-existence, Cooperation and Common Security (1988), Verification of Arms Reductions (1989), Global Problems and Common Security (1989), Nuclear Proliferaton: Technical and Economic Aspects (1990), Building Global Security through Cooperation (1990), Towards a Secure World in the 21st Century (1991), Striving for Peace, Security and Development in the World (1992), A Nuclear-Weapon-Free World: Desirable? Feasible? (1993), A World at the Crossroads (1994), World Citizenship: Allegiance to Humanity (1996); *Recreations* walking, travel; *Clubs* Atheneaum; *Style—* Prof Joseph Rotblat, CBE, FRS; ✉ 8 Asmara Rd, West Hampstead, London NW2 3ST (☎ 0171 435 1471); Flat A, Museum Mansions, 63A Great Russell St, London WC1B 3BJ (☎ 0171 405 6661, fax 0171 831 5651)

ROTH, Andrew; s of Emil Roth (d 1963), of New York, and Bertha, *née* Rosenberg (d 1984); *b* 23 April 1919; *Educ* De Witt Clinton HS NY, Coll of City of New York (BSS), Columbia Univ (MA), Michigan Univ, Harvard Univ; *m* 1, 2 Nov 1941 (m dis 1949), Renee Louise, da of Otto Knitel (d 1962), of NY; m 2, 30 June 1949 (m dis 1984), Mathilda Anna, *née* Friederich; 1 s (Bradley Neil Adrian b 1950), 1 da (Susan Teresa (Terry) b 1953); *Career* USNR Intelligence 1941–45; sr Lt 1945; reader History Dept City Coll NY 1939–40, high school history teacher 1940–41; journalist, foreign corr, author 1945–; memb NUJ; Hon Dr Open Univ 1992; *Books* Japan Strikes South (1941), French Interests and Policies in the Far East (1942), Dilemma in Japan (1945), The Business Background of MPs (1959–70), MP's Chart (1967–87), Enoch Powell Tory Tribune (1970), Can Parliament Decide? (1971), Heath and the Heathmen (1972), Lord on the Board (1972), The Prime Ministers Vol II (1975), Sir Harold Wilson, Yorkshire Walter Mitty (1977), Parliamentary Profiles (1984–85, 1988, 4 edn 1994); *Recreations* sketching, jazz dancing, toin chasing; *Style—* Andrew Roth, Esq; ✉ 34 Somali Rd, London NW2 3RL (☎ 0171 435 6673); Trepwll, Cilreddin Bridge, Llanychaer, Pembrokeshire, Dyfed

ROTH, Prof Klaus Friedrich; s of Franz Roth (d 1937), and Mathilde, *née* Liebrecht; *b* 29 Oct 1925; *Educ* St Paul's, Peterhouse Cambridge (BA), UCL (MSc, PhD); *m* 29 July 1955, Melek, da of Mahmoud Khairy Pasha (d 1954), of Sultana Melek Palace, Heliopolis, Cairo, Egypt; *Career* past master Gordonstoun 1945–46, memb Dept of Mathematics UCL 1948–66; Imperial Coll London: prof of pure mathematics 1966–88, visiting prof 1988–96, hon research fell Dept of Mathematics 1989–; prof Univ of London 1961–89 (emeritus prof 1989–); visiting prof MIT 1965–66 (visiting lectr 1956–57); Fields medal Int Congress of Mathematicians 1958, De Morgan medal London Math Soc 1983, Sylvester medal Royal Soc 1991; hon memb American Acad of Arts and Scis 1966, fell UCL 1979, hon fell Peterhouse Cambridge 1989; memb: London Math Soc 1951, American Math Soc 1956; FRS 1960, Hon FRSE 1993; *Books* Sequences (with H Halberstam, 2 edn 1983); *Recreations* chess, cinema, ballroom dancing; *Style—* Prof Klaus Roth, FRS; ✉ 24 Burnsall St, London SW3 3ST (☎ 0171 352 1363); Colbost, 16a Drummond Rd, Inverness IV2 4NB (☎ 01463 712595)

ROTH, Prof Sir Martin; kt (1972); s of late Samuel Simon Roth, and Regina Roth; *b* 6 Nov 1917; *Educ* Univ of London, St Mary's Hosp (FRCP), MA Cantab; *m* 1945, Constance Heller; 3 da; *Career* formerly sr registrar Maida Vale and Maudsley Hosps, physician Crichton Royal Hosp Dumfries, dir of clinical res Graylingwell Hosp, conslt WHO Expert Ctee on Mental Health Problems of Ageing and the Aged 1958; prof of psychological med Univ of Newcastle upon Tyne 1956–77; Univ of Cambridge: fell Trinity Coll 1977–, prof of psychiatry 1977–85, emeritus prof 1985); visiting asst prof Dept of Psychiatry McGill Univ Montreal 1954, Mayne visiting prof Univ of Qld 1968, Albert Sterne visiting prof Univ of Indiana 1976, Andrew Woods visiting prof 1976; Adolf Meyer lectr APA 1971, Upjohn lectr Univ of Salford 1974, Wade Fndn lectr Univ of Southampton 1975, Jacobson lectr Univ of Newcastle upon Tyne 1983, Linacre lectr St John's Coll Cambridge 1984, Eastman Meml lectr Univ of Rochester NY 1988, F E Williams Lecture Royal Coll of Physicians 1989, Distinguished Guest Lecture Royal Coll of Psychiatrists 1991; memb: Med Conslt Ctee Nuffield Prov Hosp Tst 1962, Standing Med Advsy Ctee Central Health Servs Cncl, Standing Mental Health Advsy Ctee DHSS 1966–75, Scientific Advsy Ctee CIBA Fndn 1970–87, memb Syndicate of Cambridge Univ Press 1979–87, WHO Special Project for Res into the Problems of the Aged 1988–; MRC: memb 1964–68, hon dir Gp for Study of Relationship Between Functional and Organic Mental Disorders 1962–71, Clinical Res Bd 1964–70; distinguished fell American Psychiatric Assoc 1972; Awards: Anna Monika Int Fndn first prize 1977, Gold medal Soc of Biological Psychiatry 1980, Sandoz prize 1985, Kraepelin Gold medal 1986; hon fell: American Coll Neuropsychopharmacology, Aust and NZ Coll of Psychiatry, Canadian Psychiatric Assoc 1972; FRCPSGlas; Hon ScD Trinity Coll Dublin 1977; first pres Royal Coll of Psychiatrists 1971–75 (Fndn fell 1971, hon fell 1975); awarded many nat and int prizes; corresponding memb Deutsche Gesellschaft für Psychiatrie and Nervenheilkunde, hon memb Societe Royale de Medicine Mentale de Belgique; MD, FRCPsych, DPM, FRS 1996; *Publications* incl: Handbook of Anxiety (ed with Graham Burrows and Russell Noyes 1988–), Clinical Psychiatry (with Mayer-Gross and Slater 1954, translated with Slater into Spanish, Italian, Portuguese and Chinese, 3 edn 1977), Psychiatry, Human Rights and the Law (with R Bluglass, 1985), The Reality of Mental Illness (with Jerome Kroll, 1986), Cambridge Examination for Mental Disorders of the Elderly (1988); *Recreations* music, literature, conversation, travel; *Clubs* Athenaeum; *Style*— Prof Sir Martin Roth, FRS; ✉ Trinity College, Trinity Street, Cambridge CB2 1TQ (☎ 01223 338400)

ROTH, Martin Joseph; s of David Roth (d 1958), and Lily Margaret, *née* Watts-Platt (d 1972); *b* 11 May 1924; *Educ* St Paul's, Peter Symonds Sch Winchester, New Coll Oxford (MA); *m* 1951, Jean Patricia, da of Harold Ravenhill Hart; 1 da (Elisabeth Jane b 1952), 2 s (Jeremy David b 1955, Peter John b 1956); *Career* served WWII Queen's Royal Regt (UK) and The Buffs (FE) 1943–46 (scriptwriter Radio SEAC Ceylon 1945–46); called to the Bar Lincoln's Inn 1949, in practice Chancery Bar 1950–87, conveyancing counsel to the Court 1980–87, head chambers 7 New Square 1980–87, bencher Lincoln's Inn 1981, Master of Moots Lincoln's Inn 1984–92, counsel to Crown Estates Cmmrs in common land cases 1985–87; Commons cmmr 1987–92, chief Commons cmmr 1993–96; chm of tstees The Cranston Library, tstee The Holmesdale Museum, tstee Reigate Priory Museum; memb Inst of Conveyancers 1971 (supernumerary 1987); *Recreations* travel, antiquities, numismatics, literature, gardening; *Style*— Martin Roth, Esq; ✉ Fairhall, Colley Lane, Reigate RH2 9JA (☎ 01737 244734)

ROTHENBERG, Helmut; OBE (1990); s of Isak Rothenberg, and Dora, *née* Moses; *b* 22 Jan 1915; *Educ* Musterschule Frankfurt; *m* 23 Aug 1945, Anna Amalia (d 1991), da of Prof Walter Hannes; 3 s (David, John, Robert), 2 da (Eve, Judy); *Career* articled clerk F W Porritt (Chartered Accountant) London; fndr and sr ptnr Blick Rothenberg & Noble 1945–89; dir: James North & Sons Ltd 1961–70 (chm 1968–70), Peter Black Holdings plc 1972–87; conslt Blick Rothenberg (Chartered Accountants) 1989–; govr Mencap City Fndn 1982–, memb Exec Ctee Assoc of Jewish Refugees 1984–88, vice pres Royal Soc of Mentally Handicapped Children and Adults 1991–; *Recreations* opera, theatre, family; *Clubs* Garrick; *Style*— Helmut Rothenberg, Esq, OBE; ✉ 49 Holne Chase, London N2 0QG (☎ 0181 455 1515); Blick Rothenberg, 12 York Gate, London NW1 4QS (☎ 0171 486 0111, fax 0171 935 6852)

ROTHENBERG, Robert Michael; s of Helmut Rothenberg, OBE, and Anna Amalia, *née* Hannes (d 1991); *b* 10 Aug 1950; *Educ* Highgate Sch, Univ of Exeter (BA); *m* 10 July 1981, Philippa Jane, da of Stephen Fraser White, of Gt Doddington; 1 s (Simon b 1983), 2 da (Katie b 1982, Joanna b 1987); *Career* CA 1975–; ptnr Blick Rothenberg Chartered Accountants 1979–, dir Gatton Consulting Group Ltd 1987–92, lectr to professional audiences on taxation and co law 1981–; hon treas Camden CAB 1982–87; FCA, ATII, MAE; *Books* Mastering Business Information Technology (1989), Understanding Company Accounts (4 edn, 1995); *Recreations* travel, skiing, opera, theatre; *Clubs* Garrick, MCC; *Style*— Robert Rothenberg, Esq; ✉ 74 Hillway, Highgate, London N6 6DP (☎ 0181 348 7771); Blick Rothenberg, 12 York Gate, London NW1 4QS (☎ 0171 486 0111, fax 0171 935 6852)

ROTHERHAM, Prof Leonard; CBE (1970); *b* 31 Aug 1913; *Educ* Strutt Sch Belper, UCL; *m* 1937, Nora Mary, *née* Thompson (decd); 1 s, 2 da; *Career* physicist Brown Firth Research Laboratories 1935–46, head of Metallurgy Dept RAE Farnborough 1946–50, dir R&D UKAEA Industl Gp Risley 1950–58, memb for res CEGB 1958–59, head of res Electricity Supply Indust and Electricity Cncl 1965–69, chm Advsy Ctee for Scientific and Tech Info 1970–74; hon prof Univ of Bath 1975– (vice chllr 1969–76); former non-exec dir Chemring Group plc; memb: Def Scientific Advsy Cncl 1967–77 (chm 1974–77), Central Advsy Cncl for Sci and Technol 1968–70, Advsy Cncl for Energy Conservation 1974–79, Advsy for Applied R&D 1976–81; govr Imperial Coll 1977–89; hon fell Inst of Welding 1965, hon life memb American Soc of Mechanical Engrs 1963; Hon LLD Bristol 1972, Hon DSc Bath 1976; fell UCL 1959; Liveryman Worshipful Co of Goldsmiths; FIC 1987, FRS 1963, FEng, FIEE, FIM, FInstP, SFInstE; *Books* Creep of Metals (1951), Research and Innovation (1984), various scientific and technical papers; *Clubs* Athenaeum; *Style*— Prof Leonard Rotherham, CBE, FEng, FRS; ✉ Silver Birches, Sparrows Green, Wadhurst, East Sussex TN5 6DX (☎ 01892 783911)

ROTHERHAM, Miles Edward; s of Leonard Rotherham, CBE, of Horningsham, Wilts, and Nora Mary, *née* Thompson (d 1991); *b* 23 Nov 1941; *Educ* Dulwich, Christ's Coll Cambridge (BA, MA); *m* 8 April 1972, Anne Jennifer, da of Maj Alan Holier James, TD, DL (d 1983), of Northlands, Winterton, South Humberside; 1 s (James b 1976), 1 da (Joanna b 1978); *Career* tech offr INCO 1964–68, sales mangr Int Nickel 1968–78; dir: Amari World Metals 1978–, Br Petroleum Metals Marketing 1979–89, Olympic Dam Marketing 1989–93; chm Miles Metals Ltd 1993–; friend of Battersea Park; Freeman City London 1978, Liveryman Worshipful Co of Goldsmiths 1981; CEng 1979, FIM 1979; *Recreations* antique collecting, boules; *Clubs* Athenaeum; *Style*— Miles Rotherham, Esq; ✉ 13 Soudan Road, London SW11 4HH

ROTHERMERE, 3 Viscount (UK 1919) Vere Harold Esmond Harmsworth; 3 Bt (UK 1910); also Baron Rothermere (UK 1914); patron of three livings; s of 2 Viscount Rothermere (d 1978), and his 1 w Margaret Hunam, *née* Redhead; gn of 1 and last Viscount Northcliffe (d 1922) who founded the Daily Mail 1896, and also gs of 1 Viscount Rothermere who was first Air Sec 1917 and gave the RAF its first twin engine monoplane 1935; *b* 27 Aug 1925; *Educ* Eton, Kent Sch Conn USA; *m* 1, 1957, Patricia Evelyn Beverley (d 1992), da of late John Matthews, FRCS, and former w of Capt Christopher Brooks (gs of 2 Baron Crawshaw); 1 s, 2 da, 1 step da; m 2, 15 Dec 1993, Maiko Jeong-Shun Lee; *Heir* s, Hon Jonathan Harmsworth, *qv*; *Career* chm: Associated Newspapers Ltd 1970–92, Daily Mail and General Trust plc 1978–; tstee Reuters Ltd; pres Cwlth Press Union 1983–89; patron London Sch of Journalism; FRSA, FIMgt; Cdr: Order of Merit (Italy) 1977, Order of Lion (Finland) 1978, Order of Southern Cross (Brazil) 1993, Order of the White Rose of Finland 1995, Order of Merit of the Hungarian Republic (Middle Cross with Star) 1996; *Recreations* reading, painting, sailing, walking; *Clubs* Royal Yacht Sqdn, Beefsteak, The Brook (NY), Boodle's, Travellers' (Paris), Cercle de L'Union Interalliée (Paris); *Style*— The Rt Hon the Viscount Rothermere; ✉ Daily Mail and General Trust plc, Northcliffe House, 2 Derry St, London W8 5TT (☎ 0171 938 6000)

ROTHERWICK, 3 Baron (UK 1939); Sir (Herbert) Robin Cayzer; 3 Bt (UK 1924); eld s of 2 Baron Rotherwick (d 1996), and Sarah Jane, *née* Slade (d 1978); *b* 12 March 1954; *Educ* Harrow, RAC Cirencester; *m* 1982 (m dis 1994), Sara Jane M, o da of Robert James McAlpine, of Tilstone Lodge, Tilstone Fearnall, Tarporley, Cheshire, and late Mrs J McAlpine; 2 s (Hon Herbert Robin b 1989, Hon Henry Alexander b 1991), 1 da (Hon Harriette Jane b 1986); *Heir* s, Hon Herbert Robin Cayzer b 10 July 1989; *Career* late The Life Guards; *Clubs* White's; *Style*— The Lord Rotherwick; ✉ Cornbury Park, Charlbury, Oxford OX7 3EH

ROTHES, 21 Earl of (S before 1457); Ian Lionel Malcolm Leslie; also Lord Leslie and Ballinbreich; s of 20 Earl of Rothes (d 1975), and Beryl Violet, *née* Dugdale (d 1994); 3 Earl k at Flodden 1513, 6 Earl one of first signatories of Nat Covenant 1638, 7 Earl was imprisoned during Cwlth for supporting the King but was rewarded with a Dukedom on the Restoration (regranted Earldom in default of male issue upon his eld da and her descendants male and female 1663) d 1681 when suc by his da, w of 5 Earl of Haddington, on her d in 1700 Rothes passed to her eld s and Haddington to 2 s; *b* 10 May 1932; *Educ* Eton; *m* 8 July 1955, Marigold, o da of Sir David Martyn Evans Bevan, 1 Bt; 2 s; *Heir* s, Lord Leslie, *qv*; *Career* late Sub Lt RNVR; *Style*— The Rt Hon the Earl of Rothes; ✉ Tanglewood, W Tytherley, Salisbury, Wilts

ROTHMAN, Dr Martin Terry; s of Harry Rothman (d 1971), of London, and June, *née* Simmons; *b* 25 May 1948; *Educ* Streatham GS, Strand GS, Univ of Manchester (MB ChB); *m* 13 Sept 1976, Florence, da of Albert Knox, of Warrington, Lancs; 1 s (Alexander Matthew b 31 Oct 1979), 1 da (Emma Rachel b 26 March 1981); *Career* travelling scholar of the MRC 1980–82, Fogarty int fell 1980–82; travelling fellowship: US Nat Inst of Health 1980–82, Faculty in Dept of Cardiology Stanford Univ Calif 1980–82; former conslt cardiologist Royal Brompton Nat Heart and Lung Hosp, conslt cardiologist Royal Hosps NHS Tst (London Chest Hosp) 1982–, interventional cardiologist 1982–; currently dir: Intravascular Res Ltd, Circulation Res Ltd; author of numerous articles and chapters; co-inventor of an intravascular ultrasound device; memb Br Cardiac Soc, former pres Br Cardiovascular Intervention Soc; FRCP 1991; *Recreations* sailing, walking; *Style*— Dr Martin T Rothman; ✉ 16 Pennant Mews, London W8 5JN (☎ 0171 460 5799, fax 0171 460 5797, telex 893589 CROHOS G, car 0860 377441, pager 01893 78 5133)

ROTHNIE, Sir Alan Keir; KCVO (1980), CMG (1967); s of late John and Dora Rothnie, of Aberdeen; *b* 2 May 1920; *Educ* Montrose Acad, Univ of St Andrews; *m* 1953, Anne Cadogan, da of late Euan Cadogan Harris; 2 s, 1 da; *Career* served WWII RN Atlantic and N Russia; joined FO 1945, 1 sec 1952; cnsllr: Baghdad 1963–64, Moscow 1965–68; consul-gen Chicago 1969–72; ambass to: Saudi Arabia 1972–76, Switzerland 1976–80; Hon LLD Univ of St Andrews 1981; *Style*— Sir Alan Rothnie, KCVO, CMG; ✉ Little Job's Cross, Rolvenden Layne, Kent TN17 4PP (☎ 01580 241350)

ROTHSCHILD, Hon Emma Georgina; da of 3 Baron Rothschild, GBE, GM, FRS (d 1990), and his 2 w, Teresa Georgina, MBE, JP, *née* Mayor; *b* 16 May 1948; *Educ* Somerville Coll Oxford (MA), Massachusetts Inst of Technology; *Career* MIT: assoc prof of humanities 1978–80, assoc prof of science technol and society 1979–88; directeur de recherche invité Ecole des Hautes Etudes en Sciences Sociales Paris 1981–82, sr res fell King's Coll Cambridge 1988–, res advsr World Inst for Devpt Econs Res 1989–; memb OECD Gp of Experts on Science and Technology in the New Socio-Economic Context 1976–80, OECD sci examiner Australia 1984–85; memb: Governing Bd Stockholm Int Peace Res Inst 1983–, Governing Bd Stockholm Environment Inst 1989–, Bd Olaf Palme Meml Fund Stockholm 1986–, Royal Cmmn on Environmental Pollution 1986–, Bd British Council 1993–; tstee Inst for Public Policy Res 1988–93; *Books* Paradise Lost: the Decline of the Auto-Industrial Age (1973); author of articles in jls; *Style*— The Hon Emma Rothschild; ✉ King's College, Cambridge CB2 1ST

ROTHSCHILD, 4 Baron (UK 1885); Sir (Nathaniel Charles) Jacob Rothschild; 5 Bt (UK 1847); also a Baron of the Austrian Empire (1822); s of 3 Baron Rothschild, GBE, GM, FRS (d 1990), and his 1 w, Barbara, o da of late St John Hutchinson, KC; *b* 29 April 1936; *Educ* Eton, ChCh Oxford (BA); *m* 1961, Serena Mary, da of Sir Philip Dunn, 2 Bt, and Lady Mary St Clair-Erskine, da of 5 Earl of Rosslyn; 1 s (Hon Nathaniel Philip Victor James b 1971), 3 da (Hon Hannah Mary (Hon Mrs Brookfield) b 1962, Hon Beth Matilda (Hon Mrs Tomassini) b 1964, Hon Emily Magda b 1967); *Heir* s, Hon Nathaniel Philip Victor James Rothschild b 1971, m 13 Nov 1995, Annabella Neilson; *Career* chm St James's Place Capital plc (formerly J Rothschild Holdings plc); chm Bd of Tstees: Nat Gallery 1985–91, National Heritage Meml Fund 1992–; *Clubs* White's; *Style*— The Rt Hon the Lord Rothschild; ✉ The Waddesdon Estate, Buckinghamshire HP18 0JW; 14 St James's Place, London SW1A 1NP (☎ 0171 493 8111, fax 0171 493 5765)

ROTHWELL, Alan George; s of George Rothwell (d 1965), of Warrington, and Emily, *née* Howard; *b* 14 Aug 1953; *Educ* Boteler GS Warrington; *m* 10 March 1979, Brenda; 1 s (Thomas George b 9 Aug 1984), 1 da (Lucy Charlotte b 31 July 1986); *Career* ptnr Chalmers Impey & Co (now Kidsons Impey) 1979; fin dir: Greenalls Retail Management Ltd 1987–89, Greenalls Brewery Ltd 1989–91; gp fin dir Greenalls Group plc 1991–; FCA (ACA 1977); *Recreations* sport, music, theatre, art; *Style*— Alan Rothwell, Esq; ✉ Greenalls Group plc, Wilderspool House, Greenalls Avenue, Warrington WA4 6RH (☎ 01925 651234, fax 01925 413137)

ROTHWELL, Margaret Irene; CMG (1992); da of Prof Harry Rothwell (d 1980), and Martha Annabella, *née* Goedecke (d 1988); *b* 25 Aug 1938; *Educ* Southampton GS for Girls, Lady Margaret Hall Oxford (BA); *Career* FO: joined 1961, second sec UK Delgn to Cncl of Europe Strasbourg 1964–66, second (private) sec to UK Special Representative in Africa Nairobi 1966–68, first sec Washington 1968–72; FCO 1972–76, first sec and head of Chancery Helsinki 1976–79, FCO 1980–82, cncllr and head of Training Dept FCO 1982–84, cncllr and head of Chancery Jakarta 1984–87, cncllr Overseas Inspectorate FCO 1987–90; HM ambass Abidjan 1990– (also accredited in Niger and Burkina Faso); LLD (hc) Univ of Southampton 1994; *Style*— Miss Margaret I Rothwell, CMG; ✉ c/o Foreign & Commonwealth Office, King Charles Street, London SW1A 2AH

ROTHWELL, Peter Francis; s of Prof William Rothwell, and Margaret, *née* Meehan; *b* 13 Sept 1959; *Educ* Manchester GS, St Edmund Hall Oxford (MA); *m* Sara Anne, da of Prof G Randell; 1 da (Emily Laura b 1 Jan 1985); *Career* Thomson Holidays 1982–88 (joined as graduate trainee, successively mktg asst, mktg exec, product mangr, mktg mangr), dir for Europe Jetset International 1988, gen mangr Thomson Worldwide and Citibreaks April-Aug 1989, mktg dir Lunn Poly Ltd Aug 1989–93, purchasing dir Thomson Tour Operations Ltd 1993–94, md tour ops Airtours plc 1995–; MCIM 1989; *Recreations* skiing, squash, sailing; *Style*— Peter Rothwell, Esq; ✉ Managing Director Tour Operations, Airtours plc, Wavell House, Holcombe Road, Helmshore, Rossendale, Lancs BB4 4NB (☎ 01706 240033)

ROUCH, Peter Christopher; QC (1996); s of Rupert Trevelyan Rouch (d 1975), and Doris Linda, *née* Hayes (d 1982); *b* 15 June 1947; *Educ* Canton HS Cardiff, Univ Coll of Wales Aberystwyth (LLB); *m* 1980, Carol Sandra, *née* Francis; 1 s (Robin Benjamin), 1 da (Hannah Jessica); *Career* called to the Bar Gray's Inn 1972, recorder 1992– (asst recorder 1988); *Recreations* skiing, golf, fishing, cinema, reading; *Clubs* Cardiff and County (Cardiff); *Style*— Peter Rouch, Esq, QC; ✉ 9 Mayals Road, Mayals, Swansea, West Glamorgan; Iscoed Chambers, 86 St Helen's Road, Swansea, West Glamorgan SA1 4BQ (☎ 01792 652988); 9–12 Bell Yard, London WC2A 2LF

ROUECHÉ, Mossman (Jr); s of Col Mossman Roueché, of Winter Park, Florida, USA, and Elizabeth Molin, *née* Meier; *b* 14 Dec 1947; *Educ* Montgomery Blair HS Maryland USA, Kenyon Coll Ohio USA (BA), State Univ of NY at Buffalo (MA); *m* 29 July 1972, Charlotte Mary, da of Charles Percy Tunnard Wrinch, of Guernsey, CI; 1 s (Thomas b 1986), 1 da (Alice b 1979); *Career* trainee Standard Chartered Bank plc 1973–75, dir Samuel Montagu & Co Ltd (now subsid of HSBC) 1986–96 (joined 1975), dir of transaction devpt HSBC Markets Ltd 1994–, chm Montagu Pension Trustees Ltd 1995–; memb PCC St Magnus the Martyr Church; *Recreations* archaeology; *Style*— Mossman Roueché, Esq; ✉ 19 Bartholomew Villas, London NW5 2LJ; Box Cottage, Fisher's Lane, Charlbury, Oxon OX7 3RX; HSBC Markets Ltd, Thames Exchange, 10 Queen Street Place, London EC4R 1BQ (☎ 0171 336 3543)

ROUGIER, Maj-Gen (Charles) Jeremy; CB (1986); s of Lt-Col C L Rougier, MC (d 1940), and Marjorie Alice, *née* Tanner (d 1981); *b* 23 Feb 1933; *Educ* Marlborough, Pembroke Coll Cambridge (MA); *m* 5 Dec 1964, Judith Cawood, da of Alan Wheen Ellis (d 1945); 3 s (Johnathan b 1966, Toby b 1967, Fergus b 1970); 1 da (Beth b 1971); *Career* Aden 1960, instr RMA Sandhurst 1961–62; psc 1963, MA to MGO 1964–66, Cdr 11 Engr Sqdn Cwlth Bde 1966–68, jssc 1968, Co Cdr RMA Sandhurst 1969–70, DSD Staff Coll Camberley 1970–72, CO 21 Engr Regt BAOR 1972–74, staff of CDS 1974–77, Cmd Royal Sch of Mil Engrs 1977–79, RCDS 1980, COS HQ N I 1981, ACGS (Trg) 1982–83, dir of Army Trg 1983–84, chm Review of Offr Trg and Educn Study 1985, Engr in Chief (Army) 1985–88, ret; dir RHS Garden Rosemoor 1988–95, ret; FICE (1986); *Recreations* hill walking, DIY, gardening; *Clubs* Army and Navy; *Style*— Maj-Gen Jeremy Rougier, CB; ✉ c/o Lloyds Bank plc, 5 High Street, Bideford, Devon EX39 2AD

ROUGIER, Hon Mr Justice; Hon Sir Richard George; kt (1986); s of George Ronald Rougier, CBE, QC (d 1977), and Georgette, *née* Heyer (the novelist, d 1974); *b* 12 Feb 1932; *Educ* Marlborough, Pembroke Coll Cambridge (BA); *m* 1, 2 June 1962 (m dis 1996), Susanna Allen, da of Harvey Allen Whitworth, MC (d 1959); 1 s (Nicholas Julian b 23 Feb 1966); m 2, 23 Aug 1996, Mrs Judy Williams, da of Thomas Lawrence Seccombe (d 1993); *Career* called to the Bar Inner Temple 1956, bencher 1979, QC 1972, recorder of the Crown Court 1969–86, judge of the High Court of Justice (Queen's Bench Div) 1986–, presiding judge Midland & Oxford Circuit 1990–94; *Recreations* fishing, bridge, golf; *Clubs* Garrick, Rye Golf; *Style*— The Hon Mr Justice Rougier; ✉ Royal Courts of Justice, Strand, London WC2A 2LL

ROUND, Prof Nicholas Grenville; s of Isaac Eric Round, and Laura Christabel, *née* Poole; *b* 6 June 1938; *Educ* Launceston Coll Cornwall, Pembroke Coll Oxford (BA, MA, DPhil); *m* 2 April 1966, Ann, da of Louis Le Vin; 1 da (Grainne Ann b 1968); *Career* Queen's Univ Belfast: lectr in Spanish 1962–71, warden Alanbrooke Hall 1970–72, reader in Spanish 1971–72; Stevenson prof of hispanic studies Univ of Glasgow 1972–94, Hughes prof of Spanish Univ of Sheffield 1994–; former exec memb and vice-chm Clydebank/Milngavie Constituency Lab Pty, former exec memb: Strathclyde West Euro-Constituency Lab Pty, Strathclyde Regnl Lab Pty; MITI 1990; memb: ALL, MHRA, SSMLL, AHGBI, AIH; Oficial de la Orden de Isabel la Católica 1990; FBA 1996; *Books* Unamuno: Abel Sánchez (1974), The Greatest Man Uncrowned: A Study of the Fall of Don Alvaro de Luna (1986), Tirso de Molina: Damned for Despair (1986), On Reasoning and Realism (1991), Libro llamado Fedrón (1993); *Recreations* music, reading, drawing, hill walking, politics, all aspects of Cornwall; *Clubs* Queen's Univ Belfast Student's Union (hon life memb); *Style*— Prof Nicholas Round, FBA; ✉ Flat 12, The Woodlands, 39 Shore Lane, Sheffield S10 3BU (☎ 0114 268 3570); Department of Hispanic Studies, University of Sheffield, Arts Tower, Western Bank, Sheffield S10 2UJ (☎ 0114 276 8555, ext 4401)

ROUNDELL, James; s of Charles Wilbraham Roundell, and Ann, *née* Moore; *b* 23 Oct 1951; *Educ* Winchester, Magdalene Coll Cambridge (BA, Cricket blue); *m* 3 May 1975, Alexandra Jane, da of Sir Cyril Stanley Pickard; 1 s (Thomas b 1979), 1 da (Rebecca b 1982); *Career* Christie's Fine Art Auctioneers: joined 1973, i/c 18th and 19th century English Drawings and Watercolours 1974–76, dir of Old Master & Modern Prints 1976–86, dir of Impressionist and Modern Pictures 1986–95 (during which time handled the sale of two of the three most expensive pictures ever sold); proprietor James Roundell Ltd 1995–; Liveryman Worshipful Co of Grocers 1981 (Freeman 1972); *Books* Thomas Shotter Boys (1975); *Recreations* cricket, sailing, opera; *Clubs* Hurlingham, MCC, I Zingari, various cricket clubs; *Style*— James Roundell, Esq; ✉ James Roundell Ltd, 58 Jermyn Street, London SW1Y 6LX (☎ 0171 499 0722)

ROUNTHWAITE, Francis Anthony; s of George William Rounthwaite (d 1963), and Eileen May, *née* Jones; *b* 3 Jan 1941; *Educ* Newcastle upon Tyne Royal GS, Univ of Durham (BA); *m* 19 March 1966, Shirley Mabel, da of Harold William Perkins, of Lanchester, Tyne & Wear; 1 s (Graham b 1969), 1 da (Julia); *Career* accountant Deloitte Haskins and Sells 1963–66, gen mangr for fin planning Euro operations Massey Ferguson (UK) 1967–70, memb Nat Mgmnt Bd Robson Rhodes (apptd managing ptnr West Midlands 1987) 1970–; capt Berkswell Tennis Club; FCA 1966; *Recreations* golf, tennis, skiing, gardening, music; *Style*— Francis Rounthwaite, Esq; ✉ Robson Rhodes, Centre City Tower, 7 Hill St, Birmingham B5 4UU (☎ 0121 643 5494, fax 0121 643 7738)

ROUNTREE, His Hon Judge Peter Charles Robert; s of Francis Robert George Rountree, MBE (d 1986), of Sark, CI, and Mary Felicity Patricia Rountree, MBE (d 1983); *b* 28 April 1936; *Educ* Uppingham, St John's Coll Cambridge (MA); *m* 20 Dec 1968 (m dis 1996), Nicola Mary, da of Nicholas Norman Norman-Butler, TD, DL (d 1971), of Leez Priory, Hartford End, Essex; 1 s (James Alexander Francis b 7 Dec 1975); *Career* called to the Bar Inner Temple 1961, recorder 1986; circuit judge (SE Circuit) 1986–; *Recreations* sailing, golf, tennis; *Clubs* Royal Yacht Squadron, Bar Yacht (past Cdre), New Zealand Golf, Rye Golf, RAC, Boodle's, Pratt's; *Style*— His Hon Judge Peter Rountree; ✉ Inner London Crown Court, Sessions House, Newington Causeway, London SE1

ROUS, Lt-Gen Hon Sir William Edward; KCB (1992), OBE (mil 1980, MBE mil 1974); s of 5 Earl of Stradbroke (d 1983), by 1 w, Pamela Catherine Mabell (d 1972), da of Capt the Hon E J Kay-Shuttleworth; bro of 6 Earl of Stradbroke, *qv*; *b* 22 Feb 1939; *Educ* Harrow, RMA Sandhurst; *m* 1970, Judith Rosemary, da of Maj Jocelyn Arthur Persse, Rifle Bde (ka 1943); 2 s (James b 1972, Richard b 1975); *Career* cmmnd Coldstream Gds 1959, cmd 2 Bn 1979–81, Brig cmdg 1 Inf Bde 1983–84, dir PR (Army) 1985–87, GOC 4 Armd Div 1987–89, cmdt Staff Coll 1989–91, Military Sec 1991–94, Quartermaster Gen 1994–, Col Coldstream Gds 1994–; *Style*— Lt-Gen the Hon Sir William Rous, KCB, OBE; ✉ RHQ Coldstream Guards, Wellington Barracks, London SW1

ROUSE, Andrew Ernest (Andy); s of Ernest Lionel Rouse, of Upton-on-Severn, and Olive Matilda, *née* Tandy; *b* 2 Dec 1947; *Educ* Newent Secdy Sch, Gloucester Tech Coll; *m* 25 June 1977, Sheila Ann, da of Leslie William Holt; 1 s (Julian Paul b 30 May 1981), 1 da (Victoria Lesley b 8 Dec 1977); *Career* motor racing driver; grass track racing 1965–69, circuit racing in Formula Ford 1969–72 (won SW Championship), began touring car racing winning Castrol Mexico Championship 1972, competed in Br Touring Car Championship 1973–; achievements: 2 litre class champion 1973, 2.5 litre class champion 1974, Br champion 1975, 1983, 1984 and 1985, 3 litre champion 1986, 1988 and 1989; records held in Br Touring Car Championship: most race wins (60), most class wins (82), most wins in a season (9), most consecutive wins (8), most Br titles (4), most class titles (9); also engaged as works driver by Triumph, Jaguar, Ford, Rover and Toyota, 3 times winner Willhire 24 hr race, class champion French Touring Car Championship 1988, competed in numerous int races; md Andy Rouse Engineering Ltd (specialist auto engrs), fndr dir TOCA Ltd (Br Touring Car Championship organisers); *Style*— Andy Rouse, Esq; ✉ Andy Rouse Engineering Ltd, 38 Herald Way, Binley, Coventry CV3 2RQ (☎ 01203 635182, fax 01203 443054)

ROUSE, Anne Barrett; da of William Dashiell Rouse, of Atlantic, Virginia, and Florence Irene, *née* Munson; *b* 26 Sept 1954; *Educ* W Springfield HS, Shimer Coll Ill, Bedford Coll London (BA); *m* 23 Dec 1978, William James Sillett III, s of William James Sillett, Jr; *Career* student nurse Prince of Wales Hosp London 1979–82, staff nurse St Luke's Woodside Hosp London 1982–86; Islington MIND: organiser Mental Health Drop in Centre 1986–88, employment worker 1988–91, dir 1991–; state registered nurse 1982, registered mental nurse 1984; author of articles in The Independent and The Washington Post; poems published in: The Observer, TLS, New Statesman, London Review of Books, London Magazine, Atlantic Monthly; *Poetry* Sunset Grill (1993); anthologies: New Women Poets (ed Carol Rumens, 1990), Poetry Book Society Anthology 3 (ed William Scammell, 1992); *Style*— Ms Anne Rouse; ✉ Bloodaxe Books, PO Box 1SN, Newcastle upon Tyne NE99 1SN

ROUSE, Christopher John; s of Cyril Rouse (d 1995), and Barbara, *née* Walkden; *b* 20 Aug 1941; *Educ* Alleyne's Sch Uttoxeter, The Hotel Sch of Coll of the Fylde; *Career* hotelier; postgraduate mgmnt trg British Transport Hotels (Midland Hotel Manchester, Restaurant la Tour d'Argent Paris, Hotel Nassauer Hof Wiesbaden, Ritz and Palace Hotels Madrid) 1961–65, dep gen mangr Gleneagles Hotel Perthshire 1969–73 (asst mangr and house mangr 1966–69); mangr: Old Course Hotel St Andrews 1973–76, Welcombe Hotel Stratford-upon-Avon 1976–78; gen mangr Turnberry Hotel Ayrshire 1978– (dir of holding co 1993–); memb: Scottish Divnl Ctee BHA 1978–, UK Ctee Leading Hotels of the World 1986–, W of Scotland Ctee IOD 1993–, Walpole Ctee 1993–; hon memb Académie Culinaire de France; fndr memb Connoisseurs Scotland 1991–; Freeman City of London, Liveryman Worshipful Co of Distillers; MIMgt 1976, FHCIMA 1978 (MHCIMA 1961); Master Innholder; *Recreations* travel, golf, wine; *Style*— Christopher Rouse, Esq; ✉ Turnberry Hotel, Turnberry, Ayrshire KA26 9LT (☎ 01655 331000, fax 01655 331706)

ROUSSOUNIS, Dr Socrates Hercules; s of Hercules Rossounis, and Mary, *née* Evagoras; *b* 30 Aug 1937; *Educ* Hawarslian GS Cardiff, St George's Hosp Univ of London (MB BS, DCH, FRCP, DObstRCOG); *m* 22 Nov 1968, Loucia, da of Stephan Stephanou (d 1987); 3 s (Alexander b 24 Feb 1972, Eracles b 2 Sept 1975, Stephan b 1 Oct 1979); *Career* res fell in clinical neurophysicology Hosp for Sick Children Gt Ormond Street 1972–73, sr registrar in paediatrics and developmental medicine Charing Cross Hosp 1973–77, conslt paediatrician St James's Univ Hosp 1977, hon sr lectr in clinical paediatrics Univ of Leeds 1987, medico-legal claims assessor, dir i/c Regnl Child Devpt Centre St James's Univ Hosp Leeds; FRCP 1989; *Publications include* Five Year Follow Up of Very Low Birth Weight Infants: Neurological and Psychological Outcome (Child Care Health and Development, 1993), author of various papers on aspects of paediatric neurology; *Recreations* photography; *Style*— Dr Socrates Roussounis; ✉ 1 Nichols Way, Wetherby, W Yorkshire LS22 6AD (☎ 01937 64178); St James's University Hospital, Leeds LS9 7TF (☎ 0113 243 3144)

ROUT, Owen Howard; s of Frederick Owen Rout (d 1983), and Marion, *née* Salter (d 1972); *b* 16 April 1930; *Educ* Grey HS Port Elizabeth SA; *m* 27 Feb 1954, Jean, da of Alfred Greetham (d 1961); 2 da (Gillian (Mrs Catchpole) b 16 June 1959, Jacqueline (Mrs Brabazon) b 26 Nov 1962); *Career* Barclays Bank: local dir York 1969–71, Chelmsford 1972–75, regnl gen mangr E Mids & E Anglia 1975–77, sr local dir Leeds Dist 1977–81, chm W Yorks Local Bd 1977–81, dir Barclays Bank UK Ltd 1977–87, gen mangr Barclays Bank plc and Barclays plc 1982–87 (exec dir UK ops 1987–90); chm: Barclays Insurance Services Co Ltd and Barclays Insurance Brokers International Ltd 1982–85, Barclays Financial Services Ltd 1988–90, Mercantile Gp plc 1989–92; non-exec chm Starmin plc 1990–93 (non-exec dir 1990–94); dir: Baric Ltd 1982–84, Spreadeagle Insurance Co Ltd 1983–85; non-exec dir Albaraka International Bank Ltd 1990–93; memb Cncl Chartered Inst of Bankers 1985–90 (treas 1986–90), memb Supervisory Bd Banking World Magazine 1986–90, dir Bankers Books Ltd 1986–90; memb Bd of Govrs Anglia Poly Univ 1993–; ACIS, FCIB; *Recreations* watching sport, playing golf, listening to music, gardening; *Clubs* Saffron Walden Golf; *Style*— Owen Rout, Esq; ✉ Pootings, Seven Devils Lane, Saffron Walden, Essex CB11 4BB

ROUTLEDGE, (Katherine) Patricia; OBE (1993); da of Isaac Edgar Routledge (d 1985), of Birkenhead, Cheshire, and Catherine, *née* Perry (d 1957); *b* 17 Feb 1929; *Educ* Birkenhead HS, Univ of Liverpool (BA); *Career* actress and singer; trained Bristol Old Vic and with Walther Gruner Guildhall Sch of Music; *Theatre* first professional appearance as Hippolyta in A Midsummer Night's Dream (Liverpool Playhouse) 1952, first West End appearance in Sheridan's The Duenna (Westminster Theatre) 1954, first Broadway appearance in How's the World Treating You? (Music Box NY, Whitbread Award) 1966, Darling of the Day (Broadway, Antoinette Perry Award) 1968, Love Match (Ahmanson Theatre Los Angeles) 1968–69, Cowardy Custard (Mermaid Theatre) 1972–73, Noises Off (Savoy Theatre) 1981, Queen Margaret in Richard III (RSC (Olivier Award Nomination)) 1984–85, The Old Lady in Candide (Old Vic (Olivier Award)) 1988–89, Come for the Ride (solo show) 1988, Carousel (RNT) 1993; *Television* incl: Sophia and Constance, A Woman of No Importance 1982 (Broadcasting Press Guild Critics Award), A Lady of Letters 1988 (BAFTA Nomination), First and Last, Missing Persons, Victoria Wood - As Seen on TV, Keeping up Appearances (BBC series), lead role in Hetty Wainthropp Investigates; *Style*— Miss Patricia Routledge, OBE; ✉ c/o Marmont Management Ltd, Langham House, 308 Regent Street, London W1R 5AL (☎ 0171 637 3183, fax 0171 323 4798)

ROUTLY, (Ernest) John; s of Dr Ernest Sidney Routly (d 1932); *b* 4 Sept 1914; *Educ* Radley, Gonville and Caius Coll Cambridge; *m* 1939, Alice Janet Routly, JP, *née* Bailey; 2 da; *Career* RAFVR; slr; former dir various cos incl: Rootes Group, William Baird, Andrews Group Holdings; fin advsr Help the Aged and Action Aid; memb Bucks CC 1965–80 (vice chm 1977–79), High Sheriff of Bucks 1972–73; Festiniog Railway Co: dep chm 1953–72, chm 1972–93; chm Festiniog Railway Tst 1954–; dir Romney Hythe and Dymchurch Railway 1986–95; tstee AIDS Caring Education and Training (ACET) 1988–93; *Recreations* railways, genealogy; *Clubs* E India; *Style*— John Routly, Esq; ✉ Ormonde House, 18 St John's Hill, Shrewsbury SY1 1JJ (☎ 01743 231489)

ROUX, Albert Henri; s of Henri Roux (d 1983), and Germaine Roux; bro of Michel André Roux, *qv*; *b* 8 Oct 1935; *Educ* Ecole Primaire St Mandé France; *m* 1959, Monique; 1 s (Michel Albert b 1960), 1 da (Danielle b 1965); *Career* French Mil Serv Algeria; fndr (with bro) Le Gavroche Restaurant 1967 (moved to Mayfair 1981), fndr memb Academie Culinaire de Grande Bretagne, columnist Evening Standard; Maitre Cuisinier de France 1968, Officier du Merite Agricole 1987 (Chevalier 1975); Hon DSc Cncl for Nat Academic Awards 1987; *Books* with Michel Roux: New Classic Cuisine (1983), The Roux Brothers on Patisserie (1986), The Roux Brothers on French Country Cooking (1989), Cooking

For Two (1991); *Recreations* fishing, racing; *Style—* Albert Roux; ✉ Le Gavroche, 43 Upper Brook St, London W1Y 1PF (☎ 0171 408 0881)

ROUX, Michel André; s of Henri Roux (d 1983), and Germaine, *née* Triger; bro of Albert Henri Roux, *qv*; *b* 19 April 1941; *Educ* Ecole Primaire Saint Mandé France, Brevet de Maîtrise (Pâtisserie); *m* 1 (m dis 1979), Françoise Marcelle, *née* Becquet; 1 s (Alain b 1968), 2 da (Christine b 1963, Françine b 1965); m 2, 21 May 1984, Robyn Margaret, *née* Joyce; *Career* French Mil Serv 1960–62; Versailles 1960, Colomb Bechar Algeria 1961–62, awarded the Médaille Commémorative des Opérations de Securité et de Maintien de l'Ordre en AFC avec Agiape Sahara BOPP no 42; commis pâtissier and cuisinièr at Br Embassy Paris 1955–57, commis cook to Miss Cécile de Rothschild Paris 1957–59 (chef 1962–67); restaurants opened in England: Le Gavroche 1967, The Waterside Inn 1972, Le Gavroche (moved to Mayfair) 1981, Roux Britannia 1986; awards: Silver Medal des Cuisiniérs Français (Paris) 1963, Silver Medal Ville de Paris 1966, Silver Medal Sucre Tiré et Soufflé (London) 1970, Prix International Taittinger (2nd, Paris) 1971, Gold Medal Cuisiniérs Français (Paris) 1972, Meilleur Ouvrier de France en Pâtisserie (Paris) 1976, Vermeil Medal du Prestige des Cuisiniérs Français (Paris) 1983, Lauréat Best Menu of the Year Prepared for a Private Function (Caterer and Hotel Keeper) 1984, Lauréat Restaurateur of the Year (Caterer and Hotel Keeper) 1985, Lauréat du Premier Hommage Veuve Cliquot aux Ambassadeurs de la Cuisine Française dans le Monde (Paris) 1985, Lauréat Personality of the Year Gastronomie dans le Monde (Paris) 1985, Lauréat Culinary Trophy Personality of the Year in Pâtisserie (Assoc of French Pâtissiers de la Saint-Michel) 1986, Chevalier de l'Ordre National du Mérite 1987, Officier du Mérite Agricole 1987, The Man of the Year award (RADAR) 1989, Chevalier de l'Ordre des Arts et des Lettres 1990; memb: l'Académie Culinaire de France (UK branch), Assoc Relais et Desserts, Assoc Relais et Chateaux; *Books* New Classic Cuisine (1983), Roux Brothers on Pâtisserie (1986), At Home with the Roux Brothers (1987), French Traditional Country Cooking (1989), Cooking for Two (1991), Desserts, a Lifelong Passion (1994), Sauces (1996); *Recreations* shooting, walking, skiing; *Clubs* The Benedicts; *Style—* Michel Roux, Esq; ✉ The Waterside Inn, Ferry Rd, Bray, Berkshire SL6 2AT (☎ 01628 771966/20691, fax 01628 789182)

ROWALLAN, 4 Baron (UK 1911); John Polson Cameron Corbett; s of 3 Baron Rowallan (d 1993), and his 1 w, Eleanor Mary, *née* Boyle; *b* 8 March 1947; *Educ* Eton, RAC Cirencester; *m* 1, 1971 (m dis 1983), (Susan) Jane Dianne, da of James Green, of S Linden, Longhorsley, Northumberland; 1 s (Hon Jason William Polson Cameron b 1972), 1 da (Hon Joanna Gwyn Alice Cameron b 1974); m 2, 17 April 1984 (m dis 1994), Sandrew Filomena, da of William Bryson, of Holland Green, Kilmaurs, Ayrshire; 1 s (Hon (Jonathan Arthur) Cameron b 1985), 1 da (Hon Soay Mairi Cameron b 1988); m 3, 1995, Claire Dinning, da of Robert Laidler, of Low Fell Gateshead, Yne & Wear; *Heir* s, Hon Jason William Polson Cameron Corbett b 21 April 1972; *Career* estate agent; chm Heritage Circle (UK) Ltd 1980–; dir: Rowallan Activity Centre Ltd, Rowallan Holdings Ltd, Corbett Enterprises Ltd, Rowallan Stabling Co Ltd; chm Turner Dundas Ltd; ARICS; landowner (1000 acres); *Recreations* skiing, riding, commentator; *Style—* The Rt Hon the Lord Rowallan; ✉ Meiklemosside, Fenwick, Ayrshire KA3 6AY (☎ 01560 600769, fax 01560 600335)

ROWAN, Prof Alistair John; s of Francis Peter Rowan (d 1957), and Margaret Gemmell, *née* Scoular (d 1957); *b* 3 June 1938; *Educ* Campbell Coll Belfast, The Edinburgh Coll of Art/Univ of Edinburgh (DipArch, Swimming blue), Magdalene Coll Cambridge (PhD), Univ of Padua; *m* 1968, Ann Martha, da of Charles Percy Tunnard Wrinch; 1 da (Harriet Grace b 1975); *Career* corr Country Life 1967–77 (architectural ed 1966–67), lectr in fine art Univ of Edinburgh 1967–77, prof of history of art Univ Coll Dublin 1977–90, Slade prof of fine art Univ of Oxford 1988, princ Edinburgh Coll of Art 1990–, prof Heriot-Watt Univ 1990–; major works incl: Mr David Bryce (Edinburgh Univ Exhibition) 1976, The Buildings of Ireland - North West Ulster 1979, Designs for Castles and Country Villas by Robert and James Adam 1985, catalogue of Robert Adam Drawings (V & A) 1988, The Buildings of Ireland - North Leinster (with C Casey, 1993), Scottish Country Houses 1600–1914 (with Ian Gow) 1995; memb Historic Buildings Cncl for Scotland 1986–95; pres: The Irish Architectural Archive 1982–87, Heritage Advsy Ctee Dept of the Taoiseach Dublin 1987, Soc of Architectural Historians of GB 1992–96, The Architectural Heritage Soc of Scotland 1992–; chm The Paxton Tst 1993–; memb: Patrick Allan Fraser Tst 1990–, Stanley Mills Preservation Tst 1996–; Silver Medal RSA 1972, Cavaliere del Ordine al Merito 1983; FRSE 1993; *Recreations* gardening and broadcasting; *Style—* Prof Alistair Rowan; ✉ The Edinburgh College of Art, Lauriston Place, Edinburgh EH3 9DF (☎ 0131 221 6060, fax 0131 221 6058)

ROWAN, Patricia Adrienne; da of Henry Matthew Talintyre (d 1962), and Gladys, *née* Gould (d 1992); *Educ* Harrow County GS for Girls; *m* 1 April 1960, Ivan Settle Harris Rowan; 1 s (Matthew Settle Nicholas b 1960); *Career* journalist; Time and Tide 1952–56, Sunday Express 1956–57, Daily Sketch 1957–58, News Chronicle 1958–60, Granada TV 1961–62, Sunday Times 1962–66, ed Times Educational Supplement 1989– (editorial staff 1972–89); Hon FRSA 1989; *Books* What Sort of Life? (1980), Education - The Wasted Years? (contrib, 1988); *Recreations* gardening, cooking, reading; *Clubs* Reform; *Style—* Mrs Patricia Rowan; ✉ Times Supplements Ltd, Admiral House, 66–68 East Smithfield, London E1 9XY (☎ 0171 782 3000, fax 0171 782 3200)

ROWAN, Robert; s of Joseph Rowan (d 1978), of Southend-on-Sea, and Anne, *née* Henderson; *b* 29 Nov 1934; *Educ* Westcliff-on-Sea HS, The Coll of Law; *m* 14 June 1958, Sandra Joyce, da of John Bertram Jackson (d 1974), of Ilford, Essex; 1 s (James Anthony Robert b 1965), 1 da (Claire b 1963); *Career* admitted slr 1970, sr ptnr Carter Faber 1983–91, ptnr Manches & Co 1991–96; hon slr The Cruising Assoc 1985–96; Freeman City of London, Liveryman Worshipful Co of Carmen; memb Law Soc, FCII; *Recreations* sailing, shooting; *Clubs* RAC, Cruising Assoc; *Style—* Robert Rowan, Esq; ✉ Ratcliffes, The Green, Writtle, Essex (☎ 01245 420918)

ROWAN, Thomas Stanley; s of Thomas Rowan (d 1965); *b* 11 April 1935; *Educ* Wellington, Univ of Natal, Gonville and Caius Coll Cambridge (LLB); *m* 1964, Anne Strafford, *née* Sanderson; 1 s (Michael), 1 da (Vanessa); *Career* dir: Singer & Friedlander Investment Management Ltd 1975–, Singer & Friedlander (Jersey) 1976–, Scottish Oriental Smaller Companies Trust PLC; FCA; *Recreations* golf, reading, walking, travel; *Clubs* Leeds; *Style—* Thomas Rowan Esq; ✉ Strafford House, Fulwith Rd, Harrogate, N Yorkshire HG2 8HL (☎ 01423 873137 and 0171 623 3000)

ROWBOTHAM, Brian William; s of Laurence William Edward Rowbotham (d 1967), of Surbiton, and Florence Madge Rowbotham (d 1975); *b* 27 May 1931; *Educ* Oakham Sch; *m* 19 Sept 1959, Carol Ann, da of Henry Nordheim Webster (d 1966), of Wallasey; 3 s (Anthony Charles William, Nigel Henry, Jonathan Brian Nicholas); *Career* Nat Serv Lt RA 1955–57; chm and chief exec Morgan-Grampian plc 1969–86, fndr chm Br Business Press 1984–86; chm: Periodical Publishers Assoc 1985–87, London Newspaper Group 1988–94, Charterhouse Communications Group PLC 1988–, Allied Radio Plc 1994–96; dep chm Adscene Group plc 1987–94; dir Advent Capital (Holdings) PLC 1995–; FCA; *Clubs* RAC; *Style—* Brian Rowbotham, Esq; ✉ Robins Mount, Alma Rd, Reigate, Surrey RH2 ODN (☎ 01737 244860); Brighthold House, Brighton Road, Crawley, W Sussex RH11 9TT (☎ 01293 519161, fax 01293 565663)

ROWBOTHAM, Graham William Henry; s of Frederick Rowbotham, of Canterbury, Kent, and Gladys Emma Ellen, *née* Andrews; *b* 25 June 1948; *Educ* The King's Sch Canterbury, St John's Coll Oxford (MA); *m* 7 Oct 1977, Susan (Sue), da of Anthony Thomas Gordon Turner (d 1980); 3 da (Sophie b 1978, Natasha b 1979, Gemma b 1983); *Career* admitted slr 1973; Arthur Andersen & Co 1969, Slaughter & May 1970–79; Simmons & Simmons: joined 1980, ptnr 1981–, sr ptnr Banking and Capital Markets Gp 1985–; memb Editorial Advsy Bd Int Financial Law Review; memb Worshipful Co of Solicitors 1985; memb: Law Soc, Int Bar Assoc; *Recreations* lawn tennis, golf, real tennis, skiing, walking, reading; *Clubs* Roehampton, Royal Tennis Ct; *Style—* Graham W H Rowbotham, Esq; ✉ Simmons & Simmons, 14 Dominion St, London EC2M 2RJ (☎ 0171 628 2020, fax 0171 588 4129 and 0171 588 9418, telex 888562 SIMMON G)

ROWBOTHAM, Dr Hugo Dalyson; s of George Frederick Rowbotham (d 1975), and Monica Dalyson, *née* Boyle, of Upton, nr Blewbury, Oxfordshire; *b* 30 March 1942; *Educ* Dragon Sch Oxford, Shrewsbury, King's Coll Durham (MB BS, Hockey colours); *m* 8 Sept 1973, Gloria Geraldine; 1 s (Richard b 23 Jan 1976), 2 da (Louisa b 12 Aug 1980, Emily b 23 Feb 1982); *Career* house surgn and physician Newcastle Gen Hosp 1965–66, ENT sr house offr Royal Victoria Infirmary 1966–67, surgical res asst Royal Marsden Hosp 1968–71, private GP 1971–; visiting med offr: King Edward VII Hosp 1975–, The London Clinic 1975–; memb: BMA, Soc of Occupational Med, Sloane Soc, Chelsea Clinical Soc; *Recreations* hockey; *Clubs* Surbiton Hockey, Llamas Hockey, English Nat Ballet Co (Gold Card memb); *Style—* Dr Hugo Rowbotham; ✉ 11 Cromwell Crescent, London SW5 9QW (☎ 0171 603 6967); 147 Harley St, London W1N 1DL (☎ 0171 935 4444, fax 0171 486 3782)

ROWBOTHAM, Dr Thomas Robert (Tom); *b* 9 June 1941; *Educ* Queen's Univ Belfast (BSc, Cross Country capt and blue), Univ of Surrey (MSc), Univ of Nottingham (PhD); *Career* British Telecommunications plc (formerly GPO): exec engr London 1964–68, sr exec engr Microwave Radio Castleton S Wales 1968–74, head Digital Transmission Res Section Martlesham 1974–78, chief of communications R&D Intelsat Washington 1978–80, head Site Servs Div Martlesham 1980–83, head Optical Transmission System Res Div Martlesham 1983–87, gen mangr Network Systems Res Dept Martlesham 1987–89, dir of networks technol Martlesham 1989–93, sr vice pres Concert (a BT/MCI jt venture) 1993–95, dir of Tech Strategy BT 1995–; prof (special chair) Univ of Nottingham 1986–89, visiting prof King's Coll London 1993–; vice pres int affrs IEEE Communications Soc 1992–93, memb Electronics Divnl Bd 1995–; Sporting All Ireland Youths Cross Country Championships Winners medal 1958 and 1959, vice pres British Telecom Research Football Club; FEng 1992, FIEE; *Books* Communications Systems Analysis (with P B Johns, 1972); *Recreations* marathon running; *Style—* Dr Tom R Rowbotham, FEng; ✉ BT Laboratories, Martlesham Heath, Suffolk (☎ 01473 644610, fax 01473 621052, internet rowbott@btlip10.bt.co.uk)

ROWCLIFFE, Simon; *Career* formerly with: Procter & Gamble, various maj London advtg agencies (chm Geers Gross until 1992); currently worldwide co-ordinator Bacardi-Martini business and exec vice pres Europe McCann Erickson Advertising (joined as exec dir 1992); *Style—* Simon Rowcliffe, Esq; ✉ McCann-Erickson Advertising Ltd, 36 Howland Street, London W1A 1AT (☎ 0171 580 6690, fax 0171 915 2031)

ROWDEN, Ray; s of William Charles Rowden (d 1987), of Kent, and Joyce Vera, *née* Wood (d 1983); *b* 11 July 1952; *Educ* Sir William Nottidge Sch Kent; *m* 15 Dec 1973 (m dis 1990), Linda Margaret; 2 da (Helen Louise Victoria b 12 Sept 1974, Elizabeth Christabel b 25 Sept 1980); *partner* Rolf Hind; *Career* trained as: registered mental nurse St Augustine's Hosp Kent 1970–73, SRN Kent and Canterbury Hosp 1976–78, oncology nurse Royal Marsden Hosp London and Surrey 1981; RCN: regnl N Wales 1978–79, sr offr Wales 1978–81, advsr in mgmnt London 1984–86; dir of nursing Royal Marsden Hosp Sutton 1981–84, unit gen mangr Mental Health Servs W Lambeth 1986–89, unit gen mangr Priority Servs W Lambeth DHA 1989–91, chief exec W Lambeth Community Care NHS Trust 1991–93, dir The Inst of Health Services Management 1993–96, dir Commissioning Bd for High Security Psychiatric Services NHS Exec 1996–; memb Open Govt Task Force Dept of Health 1994–, non-exec dir/vice chm Lewisham & Guy's NHS Mental Health Tst 1994–; assoc ed Nursing Times 1986–, memb Ed Advsy Bd Health Services Jl 1993–; memb: Lab Pty 1974–, RCN Nat Cncl 1979–81, staff side Nurses and Midwives Whitley Cncl 1979–81, Cncl for Music in Hosps 1985–, Corp Governance Task Force Dept of Health 1993–; chair NAHAT Primary Care Gp 1992–94; advsr Invitation to the Ballet project (Royal Ballet) 1982–, conslt in nursing and mgmnt to Govt of St Lucia 1990, travel fellowship from King Edward's Hosp fund to examine healthcare in Canada 1984, visiting fell The Kings Fund Coll 1994; MRCN 1970, MHSM 1987; *Books* Managing Nursing (1984); *Recreations* writing, ballet and other dance, music, politics, collecting bronze sculpture and paintings; *Style—* Ray Rowden, Esq; ✉ c/o NHS Executive, 40 Eastbourne Terrace, London W2 3QR

ROWE, Prof Adrian Harold Redfern (Jack); s of Harold Ridges Rowe (d 1945) of Lymington, Hants and Emma Eliza, *née* Matthews (d 1979); *b* 30 Dec 1925; *Educ* King Edward VI GS Southampton, Guys Hosp Dental Sch (BDS, MDS, FDS MCCD RCS); *m* 30 March 1951, Patricia Mary, da of Henry Roland Peter Flett (d 1969), of Forest Hill, London; 3 s (Paul Harold b 1952, Timothy David b 1954, Simon John b 1961); *Career* RADC Lt 1949, Capt 1950–51; head of Dept of Conservative Dental Surgery Guy's Hosp Dental Sch 1967–91; (sr lectr 1963–67), UMDS of Guy's and St Thomas's Hosps: reader in conservative dental surgery 1967–71, prof 1971–91, dean Dental Sch 1985–91, prof emeritus 1991–; chief ed Companion to Dental Studies; memb: UGC Dental Sub Ctee 1974–83, Cncl Med Def Union 1977–96, Bd of Faculty of Dental Surgery RCS 1980–93; dir Med Sickness Soc 1987–95; Colyer Gold Medallist RCS 1993; Liveryman Worshipful Soc of Apothecaries; memb: BDA, FDI, IADR, BES, BSRD; FICD 1969; *Recreations* golf, DIY, gardening, wood turning; *Style—* Prof A H R Rowe; ✉ Manor Lodge, Manor Mews, Ringwould, Deal, Kent CT14 8HT (☎ and fax 01304 375487)

ROWE, Andrew John Bernard; MP (C) Kent Mid (majority 19,649); s of John Douglas Rowe (d 1960), and Mary Katherine Storr; *b* 11 Sept 1935; *Educ* Eton, Merton Coll Oxford (MA); *m* 1, 1960 (m dis), Alison Boyd; 1 s (Nicholas); m 2, 1983, Sheila L Finkle; 2 step da; *Career* asst master Eton Coll 1959–62, princ Scot Office 1962–67, lectr Univ of Edinburgh 1967–74, dir community affrs CCO 1975–79, self employed 1979–83; MP (C) Kent Mid 1983–; Parly private sec to Min for Trade 1992–95, memb Public Accounts Ctee 1995–; tstee Community Serv Vols, pres Kent Co Engrg Soc, vice pres: ACRE, Assoc of County Councils, Kent Assoc of Parish Councils; *Style—* Andrew Rowe, Esq, MP; ✉ House of Commons, London SW1A 0AA (☎ 0171 219 6358, fax 0171 219 3826)

ROWE, Bridget; da of Peter Rowe (d 1996), of Westerham Hill, Kent, and Myrtle, *née* Dodds (d 1996); *b* 16 March 1950; *Educ* St Michael's Sch Limpsfield Surrey, Bromley Technical Coll (HND); *m* James Nolan; 1 s (Peter James b 8 July 1987); *Career* ed: Look Now 1971–76, Woman's World 1976–81; asst ed The Sun 1981–82; ed: Sunday Magazine 1982–86, Woman's Own 1986–90, TV Times 1990–91, Sunday Mirror 1991–92; ed and md The People 1992–96, md Sunday Mirror and The People 1996–; *Recreations* talking, shopping, sleeping; *Style—* Bridget Rowe; ✉ Mirror Group Newspapers, One Canada Square, Canary Wharf, London E14 5AP (☎ 0171 510 3000, fax 0171 293 3405)

ROWE, Heather; da of Leonard Richard Rowe, of Welwyn, Herts, and Enid, *née* Livermore; *b* 16 Oct 1957; *Educ* Welwyn Garden City GS, Univ of Manchester (LLB); *Career* admitted slr 1981, articled clerk and slr Wilde Sapte 1979–83, S J Berwin & Co 1983–85, Durrant Piesse 1985–88, ptnr Lovell White Durrant 1988–; Freeman Worshipful Co of Slrs; memb: Law Soc, Int Bar Assoc, Int C of C; *Recreations* fishing, birdwatching, theatre, opera, cars; *Clubs* Naval, Historic Rally Car Register; *Style—* Miss Heather Rowe; ✉ Lovell White Durrant, 65 Holborn Viaduct, London EC1A 2DY (☎ 0171 236 0066, fax 0171 248 4212, telex 887122 LWD G)

ROWE, Ian Alastair; s of Albert Rowe (d 1947), and Rose Marian, *née* Sheffield (d 1993); *b* 23 June 1931; *Educ* Brentwood Sch; *m* 5 July 1971, Suzy Gay Denise, da of Howard Philip Baker (d 1984), of Knowle, Warwicks; 1 s (Alastair b 1975), 1 da (Samantha b 1972); *Career* Nat Serv 2 Lt Army 1949–51, Capt AVR; chartered accountant; articled clerk 1952–57, Euro fin controller Mead Carney International 1959–64, Euro treasy mangr Occidental Petroleum Corporation 1965–69, chm Meridian Deposit Brokers 1973–89, fin dir Donington Partners Ltd 1990–; FCA 1963 (ACA 1958); *Recreations* amateur competitor motor racing; *Clubs* VSCC, VCC, RREC; *Style*— Ian A Rowe, Esq; ✉ Donington Partners Ltd, Park House, Robin Wood, Kingston Vale, London SW15 3RN (☎ 0181 549 9546)

ROWE, John Richard; s of William Rowe (d 1990), of Hunter Court, Wanstead, London, and Anne, *née* Radley; *b* 1 Aug 1942; *Educ* St Barnabas Secdy Modern Sch; *m* 22 Oct 1966, Rosa Mary, da of Geoffrey Laurence Ball (d 1958), of Woodford Bridge, Essex; *Career* asst film librarian Twentieth Century Fox 1958–61, film researcher Rediffusion TV 1961–72 (progs incl The Life and Times of Lord Mountbatten 1966–68, This Week), head of prodn res Thames TV 1972–82 (progs incl Emmy award winning World at War series 1972–74); Sky TV: head of programming 1982–84, head of prodn 1984–93; prodr Special Projects QVC The Shopping Channel 1994–95 (exec prodr 1993–94); fndr and exec prodr John Rowe Productions (incl prodr of film and TV prodns) 1995–; co-ordinating dir 1987 World Music Video Awards; prodr: The Pet Show series, Live from the Escape, Live from Rotterdam; prodr and dir: A Magical Disney Christmas, Ferry Aid Gala, Deadly Ernest Horror Show series 1989–91; dir Gulf Aid Gala; memb RTS; *Recreations* cinema, walking, reading; *Style*— John Rowe, Esq; ✉ 16 Du Maurier Close, Church Crookham, Fleet, Hants GU13 0YA (☎ and fax 01252 615049)

ROWE, Michael; *Educ* High Wycombe Coll of Art (DipAD), RCA (MA); *Career* in own silversmithing workshop 1972, sunglasses designer Polaroid (UK) Ltd 1971–72; spectacle designer: Optica Info Cncl fashion promotion 1973, Merx International Optical Co 1974–76; visiting lectr: Bucks Coll of Higher Educn 1973–82, Camberwell Sch of Art and Crafts 1976–82; visiting lectr and tutor RCA 1978–84; researcher (with Richard Hughes) into: colouring, bronzing and patination of metals Camberwell Sch of Art and Crafts 1979–82 (work published as manual by Crafts Cncl 1982), ancient patinated surfaces British Museum 1984–87; course leader Dept of Metalwork and Jewellery RCA 1984–; guest lectr: colleges in Dusseldorf, Cologne, Schwabisch Gmund, Pforzheim and Munich 1983, Gerrit Rietreld Academie Amsterdam 1984, Oslo Statens Handverks-Og Kunstindustriskole Norway 1985, Bezaled Coll of Art Jerusalem Israel 1987; guest speaker: Soc of N American Goldsmiths Conf Toronto Canada 1985, Jewellers and Metalsmiths Gp of Aust Fourth Biennial Conf Perth Aust; work in public collections incl: Birmingham City Museum and Art Galleries, Crafts Cncl London, Leeds City Art Gallery, V & A Museum London, Karlsruhe Museum W Germany, Art Gallery of Western Aust Perth, Shipley Art Gallery Gateshead; memb jury: Mecca Dante Stakes Trophy Competition 1981 and 1982, Perrier Trophy Competition 1982, Das Tablett (int silversmithing competition) 1983; Freeman City of London 1983, Freeman Worshipful Co of Goldsmiths 1983; FRSA 1989; *Group Exhibitions* incl: Europalia '73 Brussels 1973, Callab '74 (Br Design and Craft and Philadelphia and World Crafts Exhibition Toronto) 1974, Modern Silver (Lincolnshire and Humberside Arts Assoc) 1977, Southeby Contemporary British Crafts at Auction Munich and London 1980, Galerie Ra Amsterdam 1983, Our Domestic Landscape (one of five selector/writer/exhibitors) London, Manchester and Aberystwyth 1986, Contemporary British Crafts (Br Cncl) 1988, Function Nonfunction (Rezac Gallery Chicago) 1989, New British Design Image and Object (Pompidou Centre Paris and Nat Museum of Modern Art Kyoto Japan) 1990; *Solo Exhibitions* Crafts Cncl Gallery London 1978, V & A Craft Show London 1985, Retrospective Exhibition (Princess of Museum Leeuwarden Holland) 1988, Contemporary Applied Arts London 1988; *Awards* Frogmoor Fndn travelling scholarship 1967, dip World Crafts Cncl 1974, res award Camberwell Sch of Art and Crafts 1978, Sotheby Decorative Arts award 1988; *Style*— Michael Rowe, Esq; ✉ Department of Metalwork and Jewellery, Royal College of Art, Kensington Gore, London SW7 2EU (☎ 0171 590 4444)

ROWE, District Judge Richard Brian (Dick); s of Charles Albert Rowe (d 1967), of Perivale, Middx, and Mabel Florence, *née* Waller (d 1971); *b* 28 April 1933; *Educ* Greenford Co GS, King's Coll London (LLB); *m* 19 March 1959, Shirley Ann, da of William G Symons, of Bournemouth, Hants; 2 da (Melissa Jane b 1965, Hollie Ann b 1968); *Career* Nat Serv RAF 1952–54; Probate Divorce and Admty Div 1954–66, Land Cmmn 1966–69, Lord Chllr's offr House of Lords 1969–75, sec Family Div 1975–79, district judge (formerly registrar) Family Div High Ct 1979–; *Books* Rayden on Divorce (ed, 1967), Tristram and Coote's Probate Practice (ed, 1978, 1983, 1989 and 1995); *Recreations* most sports; *Clubs* MCC; *Style*— District Judge R B Rowe; ✉ Principal Registry Family Division (High Court), Somerset House, Strand, London WC2 1LP

ROWE, Rita; da of Cecil Mason, of St Helens, Merseyside, and Marguarita Helen, *née* Dixon (d 1974); *Educ* St Helens Sch, St Helens Coll Merseyside; *m* 1, 1971, Gerald James Rowe; m 2, 1993, John Fagan Williams, s of Frank Thomas Williams; 1 step da (Kate Brannan); *Career* sales promotions exec Lancashire Evening Telegraph 1974–80, freelance journalist and broadcaster 1980–96, publicity offr Manchester Theatres 1988–94, conslt Staniforth Williams PR 1994–96, fndr and jt md Mason Williams PR 1996–; recipient 10 indust awards for PR work for Boots Opticians, News International, Waddingtons Games and for business achievements; MIPA, MInstD; *Clubs* RAC (by association); *Style*— Ms Rita Rowe; ✉ Ashleigh, 158 Halifax Road, Ripponden, nr Halifax, W Yorkshire HX6 4AH (☎ 01422 823451, fax 01422 824717); Mason Williams, First Floor, Tanzaro House, Ardwick Green, Manchester M12 6FZ (☎ 0161 273 5923, fax 0161 273 7127, mobile 0836 703468)

ROWE, Robert Stewart; CBE (1969); s of James Stewart Rowe, MBE (d 1960), and Anna Gray Gillespie (d 1973); *b* 31 Dec 1920; *Educ* private tutors, Downing Coll Cambridge (MA); *m* 1953, Barbara Elizabeth Hamilton, da of Thomas Austin Hamilton Baynes, OBE (d 1973); 1 s, 2 da; *Career* RAF 1941–46; asst keeper of art Birmingham Art Gallery 1950–56, dep dir Manchester City Art Galleries 1956–58, dir Leeds City Art Gallery, Temple Newsam House and Lotherton Hall 1958–83; memb: Art Panel Arts Cncl of GB 1959–62 and 1969–74, Advsy Cncl V&A Museum 1969–74, Fine Art Advsy Ctee British Cncl 1972–84, Exec Cncl Yorks Arts Assoc 1973–84, Arts Cncl of GB 1981–86; pres Museum Assoc 1973–74, tstee Henry Moore Sculpture Tst 1983–95, chm Bar Convent Museum York 1986–91; Liveryman Worshipful Co of Goldsmiths 1976; Hon LittD Univ of Leeds 1983; *Books* Adam Silver (1965); *Recreations* reading, writing, gardening; *Style*— Robert Rowe, Esq, CBE; ✉ Grove Lodge, Shadwell, Leeds LS17 8LB (☎ 0113 265 6365)

ROWE-BEDDOE, David Sydney; s of Sydney Rowe-Beddoe (d 1937), of Kilgetty, and Gwen Dolan, *née* Evans (d 1967); *b* 19 Dec 1937; *Educ* Llandaff Cathedral Sch, Stowe Sch, St John's Coll Univ of Cambridge (MA), Harvard Univ Graduate Sch of Business Admin (PMD); *m* 1 (m dis 1982), Malinda, o da of Thomas Collison, of California; 3 da (Lisa Dolan b 1964, Samantha Olwen b 1967, Amanda Sian b 1969); m 2, 1984, Madeleine Harrison, o da of late Walter Geminder; *Career* Lt RNVR 1955–58, RNR 1959–66; chief exec Thomas De La Rue & Co 1971–76 (joined 1961); pres: Latin America and Caribbean Revlon Inc 1976–77, Europe ME and Africa Revlon Inc 1977–81, GFTA Trandanalysen BGA Herrdum & Co 1981–87, Morgan Stanley GFTA Ltd 1982–92; chm Cavendish Services Group 1987–94; dir: De La Rue Co plc 1974–76, Morgan Stanley GFTA 1982–92, American Banknote Corporation 1990–, Development Securities plc 1994–; chm: Welsh Development Agency 1993–, Devpt Bd for Rural Wales 1994–; memb: Prince of Wales Ctee 1994–, Welsh Economic Cncl 1994–; govr Welsh Coll of Music and Drama 1993–; Freeman: City of London 1993, Worshipful Co of Broderers 1993; FInstD, FRSA; *Recreations* music, theatre, country pursuits; *Clubs* Cardiff County, Garrick, Turf, The Brook (NY), Automobile (Monaco); *Style*— David Rowe-Beddoe, Esq; ✉ Welsh Development Agency, Principality House, The Friary, Cardiff CF1 4AA (☎ 01222 828667, fax 01222 237166)

ROWE-HAM, Sir David Kenneth; GBE (1986); s of Kenneth Henry Rowe-Ham (d 1990), and Muriel Phyllis Mundy; *b* 19 Dec 1935; *Educ* Dragon Sch, Charterhouse; *m* 1 (m dis 1980), Elizabeth, *née* Aston; 1 s (Adrian); m 2, 1980, Sandra Celia, widow of Ian Glover; 1 s (Mark b 1981), and 1 adopted step s (Gerald); *Career* CA 1962; cmmnd 3 King's Own Hussars; sr ptnr Smith Keen Cutler 1972–82, conslt to Touche Ross & Co 1984–93; chm: Asset Trust plc 1982–89, Jersey General Investment Trust Ltd 1988–89, Olayan Europe Ltd 1989–, Brewin Dolphin Holdings PLC 1992–, APTA Healthcare PLC 1994–, Coral Products PLC 1995–, Gradus Group PLC (jt chm) 1995–; dir: W Canning plc 1981–86, Savoy Theatre Ltd 1986–, Williams Holdings PLC 1992–, CLS Holdings plc 1994–; regnl dir (London) Lloyds Bank 1985–91, memb Advsy Panel Guinness Flight Unit Trust Mangrs Ltd 1985– (chm 1987); Alderman City of London Ward of Bridge and Bridge Without 1976–, Sheriff City of London 1984–85, Lord Mayor of London 1986–87; JP City of London 1976–94, chief magistrate 1986–87; chm: Birmingham Municipal Bank 1970–72, Political Cncl Jr Carlton Club 1977; dep chm Political Ctee Carlton Club 1977–79; memb: Stock Exchange 1964–84, Birmingham City Cncl 1965–72, Ct City Univ 1981–86 (chllr 1986–87), Ct HAC; govr Royal Shakespeare Co, tstee Friends of D'Oyly Carte, pres Black Country Museum Devpt Tst; Liveryman: Worshipful Co of CAs in England and Wales (Master 1985–86), Worshipful Co of Wheelwrights; hon memb Worshipful Co of Launderers; Hon DLitt City Univ 1986; FCA; Commandeur de l'Ordre Mérite (France) 1984, Cdr Order of the Lion (Malawi) 1985, Order of the Aztec Eagle (Class II) Mexico 1985, Order of King Abdul Aziz (Class I) 1987, Grand Officier Order of Wissam Alouite (Morocco) 1987, Order of Diego Losada of Caracas (Venezuela) 1987; Pedro Ernesto medal (Rio de Janeiro) 1987; HM's Cmmn of Lieutenancy for City of London 1987; KJStJ 1986; *Recreations* theatre, shooting; *Clubs* Carlton, Guildhall, Lord's Taverners; *Style*— Sir David Rowe-Ham, GBE; ✉ 140 Piccadilly, London W1V 9FH (☎ 0171 235 4802)

ROWELL, Rt Rev (Douglas) Geoffrey; *see:* Basingstoke, Bishop of

ROWELL, Jack; s of Edwin Cecil Rowell (d 1956), of The Crescent, Hartlepool, and Monica Mary, *née* Day (d 1991); *Educ* West Hartlepool GS, Univ of Oxford (MA); *m* 26 May 1969, Susan Rowell, JP, da of Alan Cooper; 2 s (Dominic John b 27 Aug 1972, Christian Michael b 24 Dec 1974); *Career* with Procter & Gamble until 1976, Lucas Ingredients Bristol 1976–88 (fin dir, chief exec), chief exec Golden Wonder 1988–92, exec dir Dalgety plc 1993–94; chm since 1994: Dolphin Computer Services Ltd, OSI Holdings Ltd, Lyons Seafoods Ltd, Marlar Bennett International Ltd; dir Celsis International plc 1994–; Hon LLD Univ of Bath 1994; FCA; *Rugby career* joined Gosforth (later Newcastle Gosforth), appointed capt and later mangr (winners John Player Cup Final); coach Bath RFC 1977–94; honours with Bath: winners John Player Specials Cup (later Pilkington Cup) 1983/84, 1984/85, 1985/86, 1986/87, 1988/89, 1989/90, 1991/92 and 1993/94, winners Courage League Div 1 1988/89, 1990/91, 1991/92, 1992/93 and 1993/94, winners Middx Sevens 1994; appointed manager England RFU team 1994– (4th place World Cup S Africa 1995); *Recreations* rugby, golf; *Style*— Jack Rowell, Esq; ✉ Dolphin Computer Services Ltd, Mercian Close, Watermoor, Cirencester, Glos GL7 1LT (☎ 01285 647500); c/o The England Rugby Football Union, Rugby Road, Twickenham TW1 1DZ (☎ 0181 892 8161, fax 0181 892 9816)

ROWELL, Prof Neville Robinson; s of Thomas Rowell (d 1971), and Bertha, *née* Robinson (d 1981); *b* 3 Nov 1926; *Educ* Royal GS Newcastle upon Tyne, Univ of Durham (MB BS), Univ of Newcastle (MD), FRCP (London), DCH (England); *m* 5 Aug 1950, Elizabeth Rachel Martin, da of Dr Martin Edwards (d 1967); 3 s (Christopher b 1952, Martin b 1953, Marcus b 1962); *Career* MO RAF 1950–52; house physician, demonstrator in pathology and med registrar Royal Victoria Infirmary Newcastle upon Tyne 1949–58, conslt physician Dept of Dermatology Gen Infirmary Leeds and St James's Univ Hosp Leeds 1962–90, conslt advsr in dermatology DHSS 1978–88, emeritus prof of dermatology Univ of Leeds 1990– (reader 1969–88, prof 1988–90); examiner in med RCP 1980–94; author over 250 articles on autoimmunity, connective tissue diseases and dermatology published in scientific jls; memb: Med Appeals Tbnl DHSS, Court Univ of Leeds 1987–89, Cncl of the Leeds Art Collection Fund 1984–87; vice pres Leeds Civic Tst 1992– (vice chm 1969–92); pres: Br Med Students' Assoc 1971–72, Br Assoc of Dermatologists 1986–87; hon memb: Polish Med Soc 1974, Swedish Dermatological Soc 1975, French Dermatological Soc 1977, German Democratic Republic Dermatological Soc 1987, Br Assoc of Dermatologists; memb BMA, FRSM, FRCP; *Recreations* golf, opera, art and antiques; *Clubs* Alwoodley Golf; *Style*— Prof Neville Rowell; ✉ 16 Park Parade, Harrogate, North Yorkshire HG1 5AF (☎ 01423 566478); Consulting Rooms, Nuffield Hospital, Outwood Lane, Horsforth, Leeds LS18 4HP (☎ 0113 258 8756, fax 0113 258 3108)

ROWLAND, Sir (John) David; kt (1997); s of Cyril Arthur Rowland, and Eileen Mary Rowland; *b* 10 Aug 1933; *Educ* St Paul's, Trinity Coll Cambridge (MA); *m* 18 May 1957, Eileen Giulia, da of Trevor Powell; 1 s (Mark Trevor b 25 Dec 1959), 1 da (Belinda Jane b 25 Aug 1961); m 2, 26 Oct 1991, Diana Louise Matthews, da of Arthur John Dickie; *Career* Matthews Wrightson & Co Ltd 1956–72 (dir 1965), dir Matthews Wrightson Hldgs 1972, chm Stewart Wrightson Hldgs plc 1981–87 (dep chm 1978–81), dir Royal London Mutual Insurance Society 1985–86, chm Westminster Insurance Agencies 1981–88, dep chm Willis Faber plc 1987–88, dir Sedgwick Lloyd's Underwriting Agencies Ltd 1988–92, gp chm and chief exec Sedgwick Gp plc 1989–92 (chief exec 1988–92), chm Lloyd's of London 1993– (memb Cncl 1987–90); non-exec dir SG Warburg Group plc 1992–95; dir: Project Fullemploy 1973–88, Fullemploy Group 1989–91; vice pres Br Insurance and Investmt Brokers' Assoc 1980; memb Cncl Templeton Coll 1980 (chm 1985–92); govr: Coll of Insur 1983–85, St Paul's Schs 1991–; memb: Cncl Industrial Soc 1983–88, Pres's Ctee Business in the Community 1986–92, Cncl for Indust & Higher Educn 1990–92, Contemporary Applied Arts (formerly Br Crafts Centre) 1985–92; Liveryman Worshipful Co of Insurers; Hon MA Univ of Oxford 1993, Hon DPhil London Guildhall Univ 1996; *Recreations* golf, running slowly; *Clubs* MCC, Royal & Ancient Golf, Royal St George's (Sandwich), Royal Worlington & Newmarket, Sunningdale; *Style*— Sir David Rowland; ✉ 105 Barnsbury Street, London N1 1EP (☎ 0171 609 2041); Gifford's Hall, Wickhambrook, Nr Newmarket, Suffolk CB8 8PQ (☎ 01440 820221); Lloyd's, 1 Lime Street, London EC3M 7HL (☎ 0171 327 6611, fax 0171 327 5926)

ROWLAND, Gilbert Raymond David; s of Capt Norman Denis Rowland, and Effy May, *née* McEwen; *b* 8 Oct 1946; *Educ* Catford Secdy Sch, RCM; *Career* harpsichordist; major performances include: Wigmore Hall 1973–75, Greenwich Festival 1975–84, Purcell Room 1979, 1983 and 1985, Berlin 1985, Carlisle 1988, Lancaster 1989 and 1991, broadcasts for BBC Radio 3 1977, 1978, 1983, 1984, and 1985, Peterborough Festival 1992; various solo recordings for Nimbus Records, Scarlatti sonatas for Kingdom Records, keyboard works of Fischer for Keyboard Records, complete harpsichord works of Rameau for Naxos Records, currently recording complete sonatas of Soler for Naxos

Records; piano and harpsichord teacher Epsom Coll 1969–; ARCO 1967, ARCM 1967; *Style—* Gilbert Rowland, Esq; ✉ 418 Brockley Road, London SE4 2DH (☎ 0181 699 2549)

ROWLAND, John; QC (1996); s of Peter Rowland (d 1976), and Marion Agnes *née* Guppy; *b* 17 Jan 1952; *Educ* Aquinas Coll Perth W Aust, Univ of W Australia (BSc Econ), Univ of London (LLB); *m* 8 Dec 1979, Juliet Claire, da of Ernest John Hathaway; 3 s (Benjamin b 1985, Matthew b 1988, Luke b 1990), 2 da (Freya b 1992, Cassia b 1996); *Career* Pilot Offr RAAF 1971–72; tutor Kingswood Coll Univ of W Australia 1973–74; called to the Bar Middle Temple 1979, in practice 1979–; memb: Bar of England and Wales 1979, London Common Law Bar Assoc 1984, COMBAR; *Recreations* cricket, walking, skiing; *Style—* Mr John Rowland, QC; ✉ 4 Pump Court, Temple, London EC4Y 7AN (☎ 0171 353 2656, fax 0171 583 2036)

ROWLAND, Jonathan (Jon); s of David Rowland, and Sara, *née* Porush; *b* 7 Nov 1946; *Educ* Univ Coll Sch London, Architectural Assoc (AA Dipl), Univ of Sussex (MA); *m* 1 Feb 1972, Charlotte Ann, da of Gordon Scott Bessey; 1 da (Abigail Amber b 29 June 1976), 1 s (Adam Benjamin b 30 March 1979); *Career* sr architect Shankland Cox Partnership 1972–77; work incl: architect/social planner Camplands (Jamaica) 1972–73, architect planner Braeton New Town (Jamaica) 1973, project architect Springfield Estate (UK) 1974, sr architect/social planner Rahad Irrigation scheme and Kenana Sugar Development project (Sudan) 1974–76; sr architect Llewelyn-Davies Weeks 1977–78: sr architect/planner Dagat Dagatan (Philippines) 1977–78, sr architect/planner Metro Manila ZIP programme (Philippines) 1978; dir Shankland Cox Partnership 1976–87; work incl: tech expert Kabbutti Upgrading project (Egypt) 1980–82, sr architect/social planner North Peckham Estate (UK) 1982, dep project dir LDDC Southwark Sites 1983, tech expert Mabote Site and Service project Maseru (Lesotho) 1986, assoc Llewelyn-Davies Planning, assoc dir Shenzhen Urban Design Study (China) 1987, urban designer Cardiff Bay Development Corporation 1987–88; tech dir Llewelyn-Davies Planning 1988–; work incl: project dir Barking Reach (UK) 1988, urban regeneration and urban design projects (Leeds and Bristol) 1989–91, project dir Ashford Great Park (UK) 1990–93, urban designer Newburn Haugh (Newcastle) 1994, environmental improvement strategy South Bank (London) 1994; chm the Urban Design Group 1992–; former visiting lectr Architectural Assoc, external examiner Oxford Brookes Univ; memb Editorial Bd Open House; exhibitor at: Royal Acad London, Green Coll Oxford, Wolfson Coll Oxford; memb: RIBA, ARCUK, Royal Anthropological Inst, Urban Design Gp, Land Use Soc; FRSA; *Publications* Community Decay (1973); author of numerous articles in various professional jls; *Recreations* music, art, walking; *Style—* Jon Rowland, Esq; ✉ Urban Design Group, 140a The Broadway, Didcot, Oxon OX11 8RJ (☎ 01235 815907, fax 01235 819606)

ROWLAND, Prof Malcolm; s of Stanley Rowland (d 1973); *b* 5 Aug 1939; *Educ* Univ of London (BPharm, PhD, DSc); *m* 5 Sept 1965, Dawn; 2 da (Lisa Claire b 21 Dec 1968, Michelle b 1 July 1970); *Career* assoc prof of pharmacy and pharmaceutical chemistry Univ of Calif San Francisco 1970–75 (asst prof 1967–71), prof of pharmacy Univ of Manchester 1975– (head Dept of Pharmacy 1988–91), chief exec Medeval Ltd 1983–93 (pres 1993–); pres Euro Fedn of Pharmaceutical Scientists 1996– (vice pres 1994–96); Hon DSc Univ of Poitiers France 1981, Hon DPh Univ of Uppsala Sweden 1989; fell: Inst of Mathematics and its Application 1978, Royal Pharmaceutical Soc of GB 1987 (memb 1965), American Assoc of Pharmaceutical Scientists 1988; *Books* Clinical Pharmacokinetics: Concepts and Applications (with Dr T N Tozer, 3 edn 1995); *Style—* Prof Malcolm Rowland; ✉ Department of Pharmacy, University of Manchester, Manchester M13 9PL (☎ 0161 275 2348, fax 0161 273 8196)

ROWLAND, Richard Arthur Philip; s of William Barry Rowland, of Old Marston, Oxford, and Joyce Mary, *née* Cowdery; *b* 18 July 1944; *Educ* St Paul's, Selwyn Coll Cambridge (MA, LLB); *m* 1, 25 Sept 1971, Cherry Ann (d 1992), da of Kenneth Alexander Adcock; 2 s (Ben Alexander b 20 Sept 1972, Philip Barry b (twin) 20 Sept 1972), 1 da (Tessa Martha b 11 June 1978); m 2, 23 July 1994, Dorota Urszula Zofia, da of Wieslaw Rychlik; *Career* Allen & Overy: articled clerk 1967–69, asst slr 1969–74, ptnr 1974–; memb Ctee City of London Law Soc and Co Law Sub Ctee; *Recreations* print making, music, vintage cars, travel; *Style—* Richard Rowland, Esq; ✉ Allen & Overy, One New Change, London EC4M 9QQ (☎ 0171 330 3000, fax 0171 330 9999)

ROWLAND-HILL, Ian Peter; s of Rowley Dorian Rowland-Hill, of Glos, and Doris Ethel, *née* Talbot; *b* 6 Oct 1948; *Educ* Univ of Reading (BA), Univ of Lancaster (MA); *m* 21 Dec 1991, Barbara, *née* Stapleton; *Career* co dir Brookside Productions Ltd 1982–85, chief exec DBA 1985–; ind memb Parole Bd for England and Wales 1982–85; *Style—* Ian Rowland-Hill, Esq; ✉ Design Business Association, 32–38 Saffron Hill, London EC1N 8FH (☎ 0171 813 3123, fax 0171 813 3132)

ROWLAND PAYNE, Dr Christopher Melville Edwin; s of Maj Edwin Rowland Payne, and Rosemary Ann, *née* Bird; *b* 19 May 1955; *Educ* Clifton Coll, Univ of London, St Bartholomew's Hosp (MB BS, MRCP); *m* 28 May 1994, Wendy Margaret, da of Maxwell Mair, of Bermuda; *Career* conslt dermatologist and landowner; house surgn St Bart's Hosp London 1978; house physician: Med Prof Unit Royal Infirmary Edinburgh 1978, Royal Marsden Hosp 1979; dermatological registrar St Thomas's Hosp London 1980–83, dermatological sr registrar Westminster Hosp 1983–89; professeur universitaire Faculté de Medecine de Paris 1985–86; conslt dermatologist: Kent and Canterbury Hosp 1990–94, William Harvey Hosp Kent 1990–, Chaucer Hosp Kent 1990–, St Saviour's Hosp Kent 1990–, Cromwell Hosp London 1990–, Fitzroy Hosp London 1994–, London Clinic 1995–; clinical prof of dermatology Ross Univ NY 1990–; visiting prof of dermatology Univ of Sci and Technol Kumasi Ghana 1995–; HAC 1974–76; hon memb Société Francaise de Dermatologie; memb: Br Assoc of Dermatologists, Int Soc for Dermatological Surgery; Liveryman Worshipful Soc of Apothecaries, Freeman City of London; Roxburgh prize 1977; Br Assoc of Dermatologists awards: 1984, 1985, 1986, 1988, 1989 and 1993; Dowling Club prizes: 1985, 1986, 1987 and 1988, MRC project grant 1988–89; RCP award 1989; *Publications* contrib: British Medical Journal, Lancet, British Journal of Dermatology and others; *Recreations* shooting, cycling, military history; *Clubs* Cardiff and County; *Style—* Dr Christopher Rowland Payne; ✉ Brogdale, Elham, Kent (☎ 01303 840569, fax 01303 840251); 19 Cambridge Street, London SW1 (☎ 0171 821 5929, fax 0171 233 7393)

ROWLANDS, Prof Brian James; *b* 18 March 1945; *Educ* Wirral GS Cheshire, Guy's Hosp Med Sch (MB BS); *m* 16 Oct 1971, Judith; 1 da (Rachel b 14 March 1975); *Career* lectr Dept of Surgery Univ of Sheffield 1974–77, fell surgical gastroenterology and nutrition Dept of Surgery Univ of Texas Med Sch Houston 1977–78; Univ of Texas Health Sci Centre Houston: instr surgery 1977–78, asst prof of surgery 1978–81, assoc prof of surgery 1981–86; prof and head Dept of Surgery Queen's Univ Belfast 1986–; memb Surgical Res Soc, sec Assoc of Profs Surgery; FRCS 1973, fell American Coll Surgns 1983; FRCSI 1988; *Books* The Physiological Basis of Modern Surgical Care (jt ed, 1988); *Style—* Prof Brian J Rowlands; ✉ Queen's Univ of Belfast, Dept of Surgery, Institute of Clinical Science, Grosvenor Rd, Belfast BT12 6BJ (☎ 01232 240503 ext 2558)

ROWLANDS, Christopher John (Chris); s of Wilfred John Rowlands (d 1978), of Leeds, and Margaretta, *née* Roberts; *b* 29 Aug 1951; *Educ* Roundhay Sch Leeds, Gonville and Caius Coll Cambridge (MA Econ); *m* 1978, Alison Mary, da of Capt Edward Peter Craig Kelly RN; 2 da (Victoria Grace, Amy Louise (twins) b Aug 1981); *Career* Peat Marwick Mitchell: articled clerk 1973–75, CA 1975, mangr 1981, seconded as ptnr Lusaka Zambia 1981–83, sr mangr London Office 1983–85; Asda Group plc: controller business planning Asda Stores 1985–86, divnl dir gp finance 1986–88, dep md/fin dir all gp property devpt and investmt cos 1988–92; HTV Group plc: gp fin dir 1992–93, chief exec 1993–; memb ITVA Cncl 1993– (chm Engrg Policy Gp 1994–); FCA 1975, CIMgt, FRSA; *Recreations* family, theatre, church, skiing, tennis, travel; *Style—* Chris Rowlands, Esq; ✉ HTV Group plc, The Television Centre, Bath Road, Bristol BS4 3HG (☎ 0117 972 2575, fax 0117 971 9215)

ROWLANDS, David; CB (1991); s of George Joseph Rowlands, of Great Crosby, and Margaret, *née* Whittington; *b* 31 May 1947; *Educ* St Mary's Coll Great Crosby, St Edmund Hall Oxford (BA); *m* 8 Nov 1975, Louise Marjorie, da of late George Brown; 2 s (Iain George b 22 March 1980, Simon David b 2 Oct 1982); *Career* DTI: joined 1974, private sec to Min of State for Indust 1978–80, princ 1980–83; Dept of Tport: asst sec 1984–90, under sec 1990–93, dep sec 1993, currently dir of resources; *Style—* David Rowlands, Esq, CB; ✉ Great Minster House, 76 Marsham Street, London SW1P 4DR (☎ 0171 271 5579, fax 0171 271 5936)

ROWLANDS, Edward (Ted); MP (Lab) Merthyr Tydfil and Rhymney (majority 26,713); s of William Samuel Rowlands (d 1966), of Rhondda; *b* 23 Jan 1940; *Educ* Rhondda GS, Wirral GS, King's Coll London; *m* 1968, Janice Williams; 2 s, 1 da; *Career* res asst History of Parly Tst 1963–65, lectr in modern history and govr Welsh Coll of Advanced Technol 1965–66; MP (Lab): Cardiff N 1966–70, Merthyr Tydfil 1972–83, Merthyr Tydfil and Rhymney 1983–; Parly under-sec of state: for Wales 1969–70 and 1974–75, FCO 1975–76; min of state FCO 1976–79; oppn front bench spokesman on: Foreign and Cwlth Affairs 1976–79, Energy 1981–87; chm All Party Gp on Publishing 1983–84, memb Select Ctee on Foreign Affairs 1987–; memb: Governing Body and Exec of Cwlth Inst 1980–91, Academic Cncl Wilton Park 1983–90; judge: Booker McConnell Novel of the Year Competition 1984, Manchester Oddfellows Social Award Book; *Style—* Ted Rowlands, Esq, MP; ✉ 5 Park Crescent, Thomastown, Merthyr Tydfil, Mid Glamorgan (☎ 01685 384912)

ROWLANDS, Rev Canon John Henry Lewis; s of William Lewis Rowlands (d 1986), and Elizabeth Mary, *née* Lewis (d 1973); *b* 16 Nov 1947; *Educ* Queen Elizabeth GS Carmarthen, Saint David's Univ Coll Lampeter (BA), Magdalene Coll Cambridge (MA), Univ of Durham (MLitt), Westcott House Cambridge; *m* 31 July 1976, Catryn Meryl Parry, da of the Reverend Canon Emrys Llewellyn Edwards, of Llys-y-Coed, New Quay, Dyfed; 1 s (William Parri Llywelyn b 1 Sept 1977), 2 da (Sara Kate Llea b 31 March 1979, Elena Angharad Lisa b 17 April 1981); *Career* diocesan youth chaplain Diocese of St David's 1976–79 (curate Rectorial Benefice of Aberystwyth 1972–76), chaplain Saint David's Univ Coll Lampeter 1976–79, dean Faculty of Theology Univ Coll Cardiff (now Univ of Wales Coll of Cardiff) 1993– (lectr 1979–); Saint Michael and All Angels' Theological Coll Llandaff: dir of academic studies 1979–84, sub-warden 1984–88, warden 1988–; dean of divinity Univ of Wales 1991–94; examining chaplain to Archbishop of Wales 1987–91; fell Woodard Corp 1993–; pres Diwinyddiaeth (Guild of Theology Graduates of Univ of Wales) 1989–91; hon canon Llandaff Cathedral 1990–; ex-officio memb Governing Body of Church in Wales 1993–; memb: Academic Bd Univ of Wales 1991–94, Ct Univ of Wales and Wales Coll of Cardiff 1989–, Cncl Cathedral Sch Llandaff 1991–; *Books* Essays on the Kingdom of God (ed, 1986), Church, State and Society - The Attitudes of John Keble, Richard Hurrell Froude and John Henry Newman 1827–1845 (1989); *Recreations* beachcombing, racket games, auctioneering, antique markets, breeding Siamese Sealpoint cats; *Clubs* Captain Scott Soc; *Style—* The Rev Canon John Rowlands; ✉ The Old Registry, Cardiff Rd, Llandaff, Cardiff CF5 2DQ (☎ 01222 563116); St Michael and All Angels' Theological College, Llandaff, Cardiff CF5 2YJ (☎ 01222 563379)

ROWLANDS, John Kendall; s of Arthur and Margaret Rowlands; *b* 18 Sept 1931; *Educ* Chester Cathedral Choir Sch, King's Sch Chester, Gonville and Caius Coll Cambridge (BA, MA); *m* 1, 1957 (m dis 1981), Else A H Bachmann; 1 s, 2 da; m 2, 1982, Lorna Jane Lowe; 1 da; *Career* keeper Dept of Prints and Drawings Br Museum 1981–91 (dep keeper 1974–81), freelance writer and conslt on art 1991–; FSA 1976; *Books* The Paintings of Hans Holbein the Younger (1985), The Age of Dürer and Holbein (1988), Drawings by German Artists in the British Museum: the 15th, and 16th century by artists born before 1530 (1993); *Recreations* making music, rustic pursuits; *Clubs* Beefsteak; *Style—* John Rowlands, Esq, FSA; ✉ c/o The Old Rectory, Silk Willoughby, nr Sleaford, Lincs NG34 8NY

ROWLANDS, Air Marshal Sir John Samuel; GC (1943), KBE (1971, OBE 1954); s of Samuel Rowlands (d 1919), and Sarah Rowlands (d 1943), of Ewloe Green, Ewloe, Chester; *b* 23 Sept 1915; *Educ* Hawarden GS, UCNW Bangor; *m* 1942, Constance, da of Wing Cdr Harry R Wight, MC (d 1947), of Codsall, Staffs; 2 da; *Career* joined RAFVR 1939, Gp Capt 1958, Air Cdre 1963, dir-gen of trg (RAF) MOD 1968–70, Air Vice-Marshal 1968, AOC-in-C Maintenance Cmd 1970–73, Air Marshal 1970, ret 1973; asst princ Sheffield Poly 1974–80; FRAeS, CEng; *Recreations* photography; *Clubs* RAF; *Style—* Air Marshal Sir John Rowlands, GC, KBE

ROWLANDS, (John) Martin; CBE (1980); s of John Walter Rowlands (d 1936), and Mary Ace (Mrs Maitland), *née* Roberts; *b* 20 July 1925; *Educ* Charterhouse, Selwyn Coll Cambridge (MA); *m* 29 Oct 1956, Christiane Germaine Madeleine, da of Justin Lacheny (d 1984); 2 da (Diane Mary b 1957, Noelle Lucy b 1966); *Career* Capt RA serv India and SE Asia 1943–47; Overseas Civil Serv: admin offr Hong Kong 1952–85, sec for Hong Kong Civil Serv 1978–85, memb Hong Kong Legislative Cncl 1978–84, ret 1985; *Recreations* railways, birdwatching; *Clubs* Hong Kong, Hong Kong Jockey; *Style—* Martin Rowlands, Esq, CBE; ✉ Flat 3, 15 Collingham Rd, London SW5 ONU

ROWLEY, Sir Charles Robert; 7 Bt (UK 1836), of Hill House, Berkshire; s of Lt-Col Sir William Joshua Rowley, 6 Bt (d 1971); *b* 15 March 1926; *Educ* Wellington; *m* 1952, Astrid, da of late Sir Arthur Massey, CBE; 1 s (Richard Charles b 1959), 1 da (Caroline Astrid (Mrs Edwin March Phillipps de Lisle) b 1955); *Heir* s, Richard Charles Rowley b 14 Aug 1959; *Style—* Sir Charles Rowley, Bt; ✉ Naseby Hall, Northants NN6 6DP; 21 Tedworth Sq, London SW3 4DR

ROWLEY, Christopher Owen Bergin; s of Owen Rowley (d 1987), and Sylvia Rowley; *b* 12 Aug 1938; *Educ* Rugby, Clare Coll Cambridge (MA); *m* 6 Aug 1964, Anna Mary, da of Roy Clarkson (d 1975), of Oxted, Surrey; 2 da (Katya b 1967, Juliet b 1969); *Career* studio scheduling offr Rediffusion 1962–64; drama coordinating offr ITV 1964–65, KYW-TV Philadelphia and Westinghouse Broadcasting USA 1965–66, prog planning exec Rediffusion TV 1966–67; Thames TV: exec prodr In Sickness and In Health 1971 and Third World War 1972, prodr BAFTA award winning The Sun is God, dep controller factual progs until 1973; IBA TV scheduling offr 1974–84, head of planning TV 1984–90, md Five TV Network Ltd 1990–95; chm West Kent Radio 1992–96; fndr E Sussex Radio Gp 1994, fndr tstee One World Bdcasting Tst; pres Media Soc 1991–93; memb: RTS, Br Acad of Film and TV Arts; Hon DLitt London Guildhall Univ 1994; *Style—* Christopher Rowley, Esq; ✉ Oak House, The Green, Leigh, Tonbridge, Kent TN11 8QL (☎ 01732 833176)

ROWLEY, Prof David Ian; s of Sydney Garnett Rowley (d 1987), and Jessie, *née* Boot (d 1984); *b* 4 July 1951; *Educ* Wheelwright GS Dewsbury, Univ of Aberdeen (BMed Biol, MB ChB), Univ of Sheffield (MD); *m* 5 Aug 1975, Ingrid Ginette, da of K Mueller (d 1985); 1 s (Andrew Graham David b 1979), 1 da (Kristina Ann Ginette b 1976); *Career* lectr in orthopaedic surgery Univ of Sheffield 1981–85, sr lectr in orthopaedic surgery Univ of Manchester 1985–88, sr lectr in orthopaedic mechanics Univ of Salford 1986–88, prof of orthopaedic and trauma surgery Univ of Dundee 1988–; regnl advsr in surgery and examiner RCSEd, ed orthopaedic section Jl of RCSEd; Symes prof and gold medallist RCSEd 1995; FRCSEd, FRCSGlas, FRCS 1980; *Books* Skeletal Injuries in Old Age (1994), Surgery of Disorders of the Foot and Ankle (ed, 1996), Clinical Surgery (co-author and ed, 1996), War Wounds with Fractures: A Guide to Surgical Management (1996); *Style—* Prof David Rowley; ✉ Marclann Cottage, Kellie Castle, Arbirlot, Arbroath, Angus DD11 2PB (☎ 01241 876466, fax 01241 431894), University Department of Orthopaedic Surgery, Royal Infirmary, Dundee DD1 9ND (☎ 01382 322803, fax 01382 202460)

ROWLEY, John Howard; s of Capt Charles Donovan Rowley (d 1935), and Hon Irene Evelyn Beatrice, *née* Molesworth (d 1949); *b* 5 Nov 1931; *Educ* Gresham's Sch Holt, Univ of Reading (BSc); *m* 9 Feb 1963, (Aileen) Margery, da of Capt Robert Clifford Freeman, MC (d 1973); 1 s (Charles b 24 Jan 1969), 1 da (Irene b 18 Aug 1965); *Career* Lt RA 1950–52 (Capt CCF); began teaching in Jamaica 1957; headmaster: de Carteret Prep Sch 1963, Gresham's Sch Holt 1975– (mathematics dept, also i/c target rifle shooting); memb: Ctee BSSRA, Fullbore Ctee CCRS; Cmdt Cadet Competitors Bisley NRA, pres OGRE; *Recreations* fishing, gardening, walking; *Clubs* N London Rifle (Bisley); *Style—* John Rowley, Esq; ✉ Monk's Orchard, Blakeney, Holt, Norfolk (☎ 01263 740 488); Dalnabreac, Acharacle, Argyll (☎ 01967 413668); Gresham's School, Holt, Norfolk (☎ 01263 713271, fax 01263 712 028)

ROWLEY, Sir Joshua Francis; 7 Bt (GB 1786), of Tendring Hall, Suffolk; JP (Suffolk 1978); s of Col Sir Charles Samuel Rowley, OBE, TD, 6 Bt (d 1962); *b* 31 Dec 1920; *Educ* Eton, Trinity Coll Cambridge; *m* 1959, Hon Celia Ella Vere, *née* Monckton, da of 8 Viscount Galway; 1 da; *Career* formerly Capt Gren Gds; dep sec Nat Trust 1952–55, chm W Suffolk CC 1971–74, Suffolk CC 1976–78, DL 1968, High Sheriff 1971, Vice Lord-Lt 1973–78, Lord-Lt 1978–94, JP Suffolk 1978–94; Hon DCL UEA 1991; *Clubs* Boodle's, Pratt's, MCC; *Style—* Sir Joshua Rowley, Bt; ✉ Holbecks, Hadleigh, Ipswich, Suffolk (☎ 01473 823211, 01206 262213)

ROWLEY, Richard Charles; s and h of Sir Charles Robert Rowley, 7 Bt, *qv*; *b* 14 Aug 1959; *Educ* Eton, Exeter Coll Oxford (BA); *m* 3 June 1989, (Elizabeth) Alison, da of late (Arthur) Henry Bellingham (d 1959); 2 s (Joshua Andrew b 1989, William Henry Stuart b 1992); *Style—* Richard Rowley, Esq

ROWLEY-CONWY, Hon Owain Grenville; s and h of 9 Baron Langford, OBE, DL; *b* 27 Dec 1958; *Educ* Marlborough, RAC Cirencester; *m* 3 May 1986 (m dis 1993), Joanna, da of Jack Featherstone, of Clwyd; 1 s (Thomas Alexander b 1987), 1 da (Magdalen Guinevere b 1988); *Style—* The Hon Owain Rowley-Conwy

ROWLEY-HILL, Sir John Alfred; 11 Bt (I 1779), of Brook Hall, Londonderry; s of Sir George Alfred Rowley Hill, 9 Bt (d 1985), and his 2 w, Jessie Anne, *née* Roberts (d 1995); suc half-bro, Sir Richard George Rowley Hill, 10 Bt (d 1992); *b* 29 Feb 1940; *m* 1966 (m dis 1981), Diana Anne, da of Donald Wilfred Walker, of Blaby, Leicester; 1 adopted s (James Richard Rowley-Hill b 27 June 1974), 1 adopted da (Samantha Rowley-Hill b 9 July 1976); *Style—* Sir John Rowley-Hill, Bt; ✉ 12 Ledbury Close, Oadby Grange, Leicester LE2 3PN

ROWLINSON, Prof John Shipley; s of Frank Rowlinson (d 1986), of Wilmslow, Cheshire, and Winifred, *née* Jones; *b* 12 May 1926; *Educ* Rossall Sch Fleetwood Lancs, Trinity Coll Oxford (BSc, MA, DPhil); *m* 2 Aug 1952, Nancy, da of Horace Gaskell (d 1970), of Walkden, Lancs; 1 s (Paul b 1954), 1 da (Stella (Mrs Barczak) b 1956); *Career* res assoc Univ of Wisconsin USA 1950–51, sr lectr in chem Univ of Manchester 1957–60 (res fell 1951–54, lectr 1954–57), prof of chem technol Univ of London 1961–73, Dr Lee's prof of chem Univ of Oxford 1974–93, fell Exeter Coll Oxford 1974–, A D White prof-at-large Cornell Univ USA 1990–96; borough cncllr Sale 1956–59; physical sec and vice pres Royal Soc 1994–, hon foreign memb American Acad of Arts and Sci 1994; hon fell City and Guilds Inst 1986; FRSC, FIChemE, FEng 1976, FRS 1970; *Books* Liquids and Liquid Mixtures (1959), The Perfect Gas (1963), Thermodynamics for Chemical Engineers (1975), Molecular Theory of Capillarity (1982), JD van der Waals, On the Continuity of the Gaseous and Liquid States (ed, 1988), Van der Waals and Molecular Science (1996); *Recreations* mountaineering; *Clubs* Alpine; *Style—* Prof John Rowlinson, FRS, FEng; ✉ 12 Pullen's Field, Oxford OX3 OBU (☎ 01865 67507); Physical and Theoretical Chemistry Laboratory, South Parks Road, Oxford OX1 3QZ (☎ 01865 275973)

ROWLINSON, Stephen Richard; s of Henry Robert Rowlinson (d 1988), of Godalming; *b* 25 Dec 1939; *Educ* Wanstead HS, Univ of Nottingham (BA); *m* 17 Aug 1967, Kathleen Ann (Kathy); 2 s (Benjamin Toby, Thomas Henry); 1 da (Emily Kate Louise); *Career* Sullivan Stauffer Colwell Bayles Inc 1961–62, Harris Lebus Ltd 1962–67, McKinsey and Co Inc 1967–74, TCK Gp Ltd 1974–77, Rowlinson Tomala and Assocs Ltd 1977–80, Bickerton Rowlinson Ltd 1980–84; chm and chief exec offr: Korn/Ferry Int Ltd 1985–89, Penna plc 1989–91, Merton Associates Ltd 1991–96; gp chief exec MSL 1996–; memb Worshipful Co of Upholders; *Recreations* sailing, skiing; *Style—* Stephen Rowlinson, Esq; ✉ 16 Wallside, Barbican, London EC2Y 8BH; MSL plc, 32 Aybrook Street, London W1M 3JL (☎ 0171 487 5000, fax 0171 224 2350)

ROWNTREE, Graham Christopher; s of Christopher Rowntree, of Leicester, and Patricia Jane, *née* Lough; *b* 18 April 1971; *Educ* Hastings HS Hinckley Leics, John Cleveland Coll Hinckley Leics; *Career* rugby union prop; clubs: Nuneaton RFC 1979–86, Leicester RFC 1986– (youth team, first team debut aged 19, winners Pilkington Cup 1993, Courage League Champions 1995); represented: Leicestershire U14, Leicestershire and Midlands U16, U18 and U21, Midlands Div v All Blacks 1993, Barbarians v Newport 1993 and v E Midlands 1994; England: U16, U18, Colts, U21, A tour Canada 1993, memb sr squad tour S Africa 1994, first full cap when came on as sub v Scotland 1995 (sub since 1993), started v Italy and v W Samoa World Cup S Africa 1995, 8 full caps (15 youth and Colts caps); non sporting career currently with P & G Blands Insurance Brokers Leicester; *Recreations* training, training and more training, golf; *Style—* Graham Rowntree, Esq; ✉ c/o Leicester RFC, The Clubhouse, Aylestone Road, Leicester LE2 7LF

ROWSE, Dr Alfred Leslie; CH (1997); s of Richard Rowse (d 1933), of St Austell, and Anne, *née* Vanson (d 1953); *b* 4 Dec 1903; *Educ* St Austell GS, ChCh Oxford (MA, DLitt); *Career* writer; pres Eng Assoc 1951–52, sr res assoc Huntington Library Calif 1962–69, Trevelyan lectr Univ of Cambridge, Bailey lectr McGill Univ Canada, pres Shakespeare Club Stratford-upon-Avon 1970–71; Benson Medal for Servs to Lit RSL, Jenner Gold Medal Royal Instn of Cornwall; Hon DLitt Univ of Exeter, Hon DCL Univ of New Brunswick Canada, Hon DL Lynchburg Coll Virginia; emeritus fell All Souls Coll Oxford (fell 1925–74), FBA, FRSL; *Books* Tudor Cornwall (1941), A Cornish Childhood (1942, with sequels), A Cornishman at Oxford (1942), The Elizabethan Age (4 vols 1950–72), The Churchills (1956 and 1958), The Cornish in America (1969), Shakespeare the Man (1973), Memories of Men and Women (1980), A Life: Collected Poems (1981), Discovering Shakespeare (1989), Friends and Contemporaries (1989), Transatlantic: Later Poems (1989), Four Caroline Portraits (1992), All Souls in My Time (1993), The Regicides (1994), Historians I Have Known (1995); *Clubs* Athenaeum; *Style—* Dr A L Rowse, CH, FBA; ✉ Trenarren House, St Austell, Cornwall PL26 6BH; c/o Curtis Brown, 10 Astor Place, New York 10003, NY, USA

ROWSON, Peter Aston; s of Dr Lionel Edward Aston Rowson, OBE, FRS (d 1989); *b* 8 Oct 1942; *Educ* St Edmunds Coll Ware; *m* 1967, Jennifer Mary, *née* Smyth; 1 s, 2 da; *Career* accountant; fin dir and co sec: Panther Securities PLC, Panther Devpts Ltd, Panther Shop Investmts Ltd, Panther Shop Investments (Midlands) Ltd, Westmead Buildling Company Ltd, Saxonbest Ltd, MRG Systems Ltd, Etonbrook Properties plc, Multitrust Property Investments Ltd; co sec and dir: Yardworth Ltd, Excelchoice Ltd, Snowbest Ltd; co sec: Christchurch Park Properties Ltd, Benfay Investments Ltd; *Style—* Peter Rowson, Esq; ✉ Panther House, 38 Mount Pleasant, London WC1X 0AP (☎ 0171 278 8011)

ROXBURGH, Prof Ian Walter; s of Walter McRonald Roxburgh, and Kathleen Joyce, *née* Prescott; *b* 31 Aug 1939; *Educ* King Edward VII GS Sheffield, Univ of Nottingham (BSc), Univ of Cambridge (PhD); *m* 1960, Diana Patricia, *née* Dunn; 2 s, 1 da; *Career* res fell Churchill Coll Cambridge 1963, lectr in maths King's Coll London 1964–66 (asst lectr 1963–64), reader in astronomy Univ of Sussex 1966–67; Queen Mary & Westfield College (formerly Queen Mary Coll) London: prof of applied maths 1967–87, prof of maths and astronomy 1987–, pro princ 1987, currently dir Astronomy Unit; chm Ctee of Heads of Univ Depts of Mathematics & Statistics 1988–93; conslt Euro Space Agency; Parly candidate: (Liberal) Walthamstow West 1970, (SDP) Ilford North 1983; memb: Euro Physical Soc, Euro Astronomical Soc, Euro Economic Assoc, Br Soc Philosophy of Science, Int Astronomical Union, London Mathematic Soc; FInstP, FRAS; *Style—* Prof Ian W Roxburgh; ✉ 37 Leicester Road, Wanstead, London E11 2DW (☎ 0181 989 7117)

ROXBURGH, Vice Adm Sir John Charles Young; KCB (1972, CB 1969), CBE (1967), DSO (1943), DSC (1942, and Bar 1945); s of Sir (Thomas) James Young Roxburgh (d 1974), and Mona Gladys Mabel, *née* Heymerdinguer (d 1982); *b* 29 June 1919; *Educ* RNC Dartmouth; *m* 1942, Philippa, 3 da of Major Charles Montague Hewlett, MC (d 1944); 1 da (Anthea b 1943), 1 s (Richard Young b 1945); *Career* joined RN 1933 (psc 1955, idc 1962), joined Submarine Branch 1940; served Norway, Bay of Biscay and Med 1940–42; cmd HMS Submarines H43, United and Tapir 1942–45 (Med and Norway), Br Jt Servs Mission Washington 1958–60, dep dir Def Plans (Navy) MOD 1963–65, cmd HMS Eagle 1965–67, Flag Offr Sea Trg 1967–69, Flag Offr Plymouth 1969, Flag Offr Submarines and NATO Cdr Submarines E Atlantic 1969–72, Vice Adm 1970, ret 1972; chm Grovebell Gp Ltd 1972–75, cncllr Surrey CC 1977–81, memb Cncl and Mgmnt Ctee Freedom Assoc 1977–85, pres RN Benevolent Tst 1978–84; *Recreations* golf, sailing, walking, music; *Clubs* Army and Navy, Liphook Golf, Woking Golf; *Style—* Vice Admiral Sir John Roxburgh, KCB, CBE, DSO, DSC*; ✉ Oakdene, Wood Rd, Hindhead, Surrey GU26 6PT (☎ 01428 605600)

ROXBURGH, Dr Stuart Thomas Dalrymple; s of Robert Roxburgh, and Helen Roxburgh; *b* 10 May 1950; *Educ* Camphill Sch, Univ of Glasgow (MB ChB); *m* 25 June 1975, Christine MacLeod Campbell, da of John Ramsay (d 1979); 1 s (Campbell b 27 March 1980), 1 da (Alison b 5 Oct 1982); *Career* conslt ophthalmologist Tayside Health Bd, head Dept of Ophthalmology Univ of Dundee; FRCOphth 1988 (examiner), FRCSEd 1979; *Recreations* golf, hill-walking, painting; *Style—* Dr Stuart Roxburgh; ✉ 4 Craigie Knowes Avenue, Perth, Scotland PH2 0DL (☎ 01738 634347); Ninewells Hospital and Medical School, Dundee (☎ 01382 60111)

ROXBURGHE, 10 Duke of (S 1707); Sir Guy David Innes-Ker; 11 Bt (Premier Bt of Scotland or Nova Scotia, S 1625); also Lord Roxburghe (S before 31 March 1600), Earl of Roxburghe, Lord Ker of Cessford and Cavertoun (both S 1616), Marquis of Bowmont and Cessford, Earl of Kelso, Viscount of Broxmouth (S, with the Dukedom the last Peerages cr in the Peerage of Scotland, 1707), and Earl Innes (UK 1837); s of 9 Duke of Roxburghe (d 1974) and his 2 w (late Mrs Jocelyn Hambro); 1 Earl obtained a charter in 1648 of succession to the honour, to his gs 4 s of his da Countess of Perth, and after him the 3 s successively of his gda Countess of Wigton; Dukedom in remainder to whoever succeeds to Earldom; *b* 18 Nov 1954; *Educ* Eton, Magdalene Coll Cambridge; *m* 1, 1977 (m dis 1990), Lady Jane, *née* Grosvenor, da of 5 Duke of Westminster and Hon Viola Lyttelton, da of 9 Viscount Cobham; 2 s (Marquis of Bowmont and Cessford b 1981, Lord Edward b 1984), 1 da (Lady Rosanagh b 16 Jan 1979); m 2, 3 Sept 1992, Virginia Mary, da of David Wynn-Williams; 1 s (Lord George Alastair b 20 November 1996), 1 da (Lady Isabella May b 7 Sept 1994); *Heir* s, Marquis of Bowmont and Cessford; *Career* formerly Lt RHG/1 Dragoons; landowner, co dir; Liveryman Worshipful Co of Fishmongers; *Recreations* fishing, shooting, golf, cricket, skiing; *Clubs* White's, Turf; *Style—* His Grace the Duke of Roxburghe; ✉ Floors Castle, Kelso, Roxburghshire (☎ 01573 224288); Roxburghe Estate Office, Kelso, Roxburghshire, Scotland (☎ 01573 223333)

ROXBURGHE, Mary, Duchess of; Lady Mary Evelyn Hungerford; *née* Crewe-Milnes; da (by 2 m) of 1 and last Marquess of Crewe; 1 Baron Houghton m sis 3 and last Baron Crewe (extinct 1894), their s 2 Baron cr Earl of Crewe 1895 and a Marquess 1911; *b* 1915; *m* 1935 (m dis 1953), 9 Duke of Roxburghe (d 1974); *Career* bore HM the Queen's Canopy at Coronation of King George VI; *Style—* Mary, Duchess of Roxburghe; ✉ 15 Hyde Park Gardens, London W2 2LU (☎ 0171 262 3349); West Horsley Place, Leatherhead, Surrey

ROY, Prof Donald Hubert; s of William Hadland Roy (d 1987), and Winifred Elizabeth Margaret, *née* Davies (d 1993); *b* 5 April 1930; *Educ* Canton HS Cardiff, Univ of Wales (BA, MA, DipEd), Univ of Paris Sorbonne; *m* 1, 5 Aug 1955 (m dis 1959), Jane Elizabeth Ailwen (Sian); m 2, 25 Jan 1975, Arlette, da of James William Hopper, of Sutton, Surrey; 1 s (Gareth b 1978), 1 da (Francesca b 1980); *Career* Nat Serv cmmnd RAF 1954–56; asst lectr in French Univ of St Andrews 1958–59, lectr in French (former asst lectr) Univ of Glasgow 1959–63, dir and prof of drama (former lectr i/c and sr lectr) Univ of Hull 1963–, visiting prof Univ of Delaware USA 1974, visiting dir Central Univ of Iowa USA 1987; memb Mgmnt Ctee Consortium for Drama and Media in Higher Educn; FRSA 1984; *Books* Molière - Five Plays (1982), Plays by James Robinson Planché (1986), Jacques Copeau and the Cartel des Quatre (1993); *Recreations* reading, gardening, hill-walking; *Style—* Prof Donald Roy; ✉ Department of Drama, University of Hull, Hull, N Humberside HU6 7RX (☎ 01482 465615, fax 01482 466210, telex 592592 KHMAIL G)

ROYALL, District Judge Martyn; s of late Frederick Bertram Royall, of Torquay, and Edna Doreen, *née* Ball; *b* 8 Jan 1948; *Educ* Bishop Wordsworth Sch Salisbury, Coll of Law Guildford; *m* 24 June 1972, Jacqueline Barbara, da of late Jack Thompson; 1 da (Anna Rebecca b 16 Jan 1974), 1 s (Jack Hain b 13 Oct 1975, Thomas Martyn b 2 July 1979); *Career* articled Thomas Eggar & Sons Chichester, qualified slr 1972, ptnr Hawkins 1973–92 (joined 1972), district judge 1992–; pres Kings Lynn W Norfolk Law Soc 1988– (sec 1974–83), chm Nat Young Slrs Gp 1982; memb The Law Soc; *Recreations* outdoor sports (incl shooting); *Clubs* Norfolk; *Style—* District Judge Martyn Royall; ✉ Norwich Combined Court, The Law Courts, Bishopsgate, Norfolk NR3 1UR (☎ 01603 761776)

ROYCE, (Roger) John; QC (1987); s of John Roger Royce (d 1990), of Trig Rock, Cornwall, and Margaret, *née* Sibbald; *b* 27 Aug 1944; *Educ* The Leys Sch Cambridge, Trinity Hall Cambridge (BA); *m* 12 May 1979, Gillian Wendy, da of Geoffrey Guy Adderley, of High Trees, Whitedown Lane, Alton, Hants; 2 s (Andrew David Lyndon b 1986, David John Henry b 1989), 1 da (Joanna Katy Rachel b 1984); *Career* admitted slr 1969, called to the Bar Gray's Inn 1970, bencher 1997, recorder 1986–, head of chambers; sport: Univ of Cambridge Hockey Blue 1965–66, East Hockey 1965–66, West Hockey 1972–73, capt Somerset Hockey 1976, qualified ski instr Austria 1969; *Recreations* skiing, cricket, golf, collecting corkscrews; *Clubs* Hawks, St Enodoc GC; *Style—* John Royce, Esq, QC; ✉ Guildhall Chambers, 23 Broad Street, Bristol BS1 2HG (☎ 0117 927 3366, fax 0117 929 8941)

ROYCE, Norman Alexander; OBE (1993); s of Joseph Samuel Royce (d 1960), of London, and Margaret, *née* Fraser (d 1954); *b* 4 Feb 1915; *Educ* Abbey Sch Beckenham,

Bromley Coll of Art, Architectural Assoc (DipArch); *m* 10 Sept 1948, Molly Walden, da of late Alfred William Clarke, OBE; 3 s (Christopher b 1950, Darryl b 1952, Dominic b 1964), 1 da (Lesley b 1954); *Career* RAF 1940–46: Pilot Staff Offr 1945, Sqdn Ldr, served Europe and ME; pres CIArb 1942, vice pres RIBA 1968 (assoc 1940, fell 1960), pres Concrete Soc 1977; chm: Joint Contracts Tbnl 1978–83, London Ct Int Arbitration 1980, Biggin Hill Airport Consultative Ctee; memb Ctee Royal London Soc for the Blind, vice pres Br Acad of Experts, vice chm Biggin Hill RAF Assoc, chm British Assoc of Aviation Conslts; Freeman City of London 1952; Master: Worshipful Co of Gardeners 1973, Worshipful Co of Fanmakers 1977 (memb Ct of Assts), Guild of Air Pilots and Air Navigators 1981, Worshipful Co of Arbitrators 1983, Worshipful Co of Chartered Architects 1990; CIArb 1957 (former pres); *Recreations* flying, gardening, cricket; *Clubs* Carlton, RAF, City Livery, MCC; *Style*— Norman Royce, Esq, OBE; ✉ 4 Waldron Gardens, Shortlands, Bromley, Kent BR2 0JR (☎ 0181 290 6455, fax 0181 464 3256)

ROYDEN, Sir Christopher John; 5 Bt (UK 1905), of Frankby Hall, Co Palatine of Chester; s of Sir John Royden, 4 Bt (d 1976), of Battle, Sussex, and (Dolores) Catherine (d 1994), da of Cecil Coward, of Lima, Peru; *b* 26 Feb 1937; *Educ* Winchester, ChCh Oxford (MA); *m* 1961, Diana Bridget, da of Lt-Col Joseph Henry Goodhart, MC (d 1975), of Kirkbymoorside, York, by Evelyn, yst da of Henry Beaumont, JP, DL; 2 s (John Michael Joseph b 1965, Richard Thomas Bland b 1967), 1 da (Emma Mary Bridget b 1971); *Heir* s, John Michael Joseph Royden b 17 March 1965; *Career* Nat Serv 2 Lt 16/5 The Queen's Royal Lancers 1955–57; Duncan Fox & Co Ltd 1960–71, stockbroker Spencer Thornton & Co 1971–86, Gerrard Vivian Gray Ltd 1988–; *Recreations* shooting, fishing, gardening; *Clubs* Boodle's; *Style*— Sir Christopher Royden, Bt; ✉ Bridge House, Ablington, Bibury, Glos

ROYDEN, John Michael Joseph; s and h of Sir Christopher John Royden, 5 Bt, *qv*; *b* 17 March 1965; *Educ* Stowe, Univ of Reading (LLB); *m* 1989, Lucilla Mary, da of John Ralph Stourton; 2 da (Charlotte Alice Maude b 1992, Lucinda Catherine Quenelda b 1 Jan 1995); *Career* dir: ECU Capital Markets plc, ECU Group plc, ECU Holdings Ltd, ECU Internet Services plc, The Capital Assured India Fund Ltd, Global Fund Services Ltd, Colour Counsellors Ltd, Colour Counsellors International Ltd; *Recreations* shooting, fishing, stalking, long distance swimming; *Clubs* Boodle's; *Style*— John Royden, Esq; ✉ Flat 2, 8 Nevern Sq, London SW5 9NW (☎ 0171 370 2665)

ROYDON, Terry Rene; s of Leon Roydon, and Lyanne, *née* Hamoniere; *b* 26 Dec 1946; *Educ* Clifton, Univ of London (BSc), Univ of Pittsburgh (MBA); *m* 29 Sept 1972, Carol Joycelyn, da of Stanley Norris; 1 da (Karen b 1977); *Career* md Comben Group plc 1970–84, chief exec Prowting plc 1985–; dir: Nat House Bldg Cncl 1981–, PPS Ltd 1996–; pres: Housebuilder Fedn 1984, European Union of Housebuilders and Developers 1995–; govr St Helen's Sch Northwood 1988–; *Style*— Terry Roydon, Esq; ✉ Prowting plc, Frays Court, 71 Cowley Road, Uxbridge, Middx UB8 2AE

ROYDS, Richard George; s of Nicholas Clyne Royds, and Sally Royds; *b* 15 Nov 1957; *Educ* Charterhouse; *m* Lucinda, da of Richard McClean; 1 s (George), 1 da (Isabella); *Career* sales exec: LWT 1976–79, Capital Radio 1979–82; dir The Media Shop 1982–86; md: Wardley Unit Trust Managers 1986–89, John Govett Unit Trust Managers 1989–92, Mercury Fund Managers Ltd 1992–; dir: Mercury Asset Management plc 1992–, Mercury Life Assurance Co Ltd 1992–; *Recreations* golf, fishing, art, wine, eating, shopping; *Clubs* Sunningdale Golf, Royal St George's Golf, The Golf Match; *Style*— Richard Royds, Esq; ✉ Mercury Asset Management plc, 33 King William Street, London EC4R 9AS (☎ 0171 280 2800, fax 0171 280 2827)

ROYLANCE, Jayne Elizabeth; da of George Russell Spencer Ward (d 1990), of North Walsham, Norfolk, and Kathleen Mary, *née* Lock-Wood; *b* 8 Oct 1947; *Educ* Cromer HS; *m* 7 Oct 1967, John Michael Roylance, s of Robert James Roylance; 1 s (Paul Spencer b 3 Aug 1968), 3 da (Sara Jayne b 24 July 1970, Karen Elizabeth b 6 Aug 1973, Lisa Ann b 1 Jan 1976); *Career* bowls player; Cromer Marrams 1979–86, North Walsham 1986–, represented Norfolk 1980–; achievements incl: won all county honours, England debut 1986, Silver medal triples and fours World Bowls NZ 1988, Bronze medal pairs Cwlth Games NZ 1990, nat indoor singles winner 1992; records: nat fours (skip) 1985, nat triples (skip) 1989, nat two wood singles 1989; also indoor bowls player: int badge holder, won nat honours mixed pairs and mixed fours; *Recreations* squash, working in family business; *Style*— Mrs Jayne Roylance; ✉ c/o North Walsham Bowls & Squash, Tungate Farm, North Walsham, Norfolk (☎ 01692 404966)

ROYLE, Carol Buchanan (Mrs Julian Spear); da of Derek Stanley Royle (d 1990), and Jane Irene, *née* Shortt; *b* 10 Feb 1954; *Educ* Streatham HS for Girls, Pitmans Wimbledon, Central Sch of Speech and Drama; *m* Julian David Barnaby Spear, s of Bernard Spear; 1 s (Taran Oliver Buchanan b 5 Nov 1983), 1 da (Talitha Mary-Jane Buchanan Royle Spear b 31 Aug 1995); *Career* actress; *Theatre* Harrogate Repertory Co 1976–77; RSC 1980–82 and 1990–92 incl: Ophelia in Hamlet and Cressida in Troilus and Cressida 1980–82, Princess of France in Love's Labours Lost and Mrs Arbuthnot in A Woman of No Importance; other roles incl: Titania in A Midsummer Night's Dream (Regent's Park) 1988, Hate in Harold Pinter's Old Times (Birmingham Rep) 1993; *Television* for BBC incl: Blakes 7 1979, Possibilities 1982, Bergerac 1983, Oxbridge Blues 1984, A Still Small Shout 1985, Life Without George (three series) 1987–89, Hedgehog Wedding 1987, Blackeyes 1989, Casualty 1990; for ITV incl: The Professionals 1980, Waxwork 1980, Heartland 1980; for Thames incl: Judgement Day 1983, Ladies in Charge 1985–86, The London Embassy 1987; other credits incl: incl: The Cedar Tree (three series, ATV) 1977–79, Girl Talk (ATV) 1980, The Racing Game (YTV) 1980, Feet Foremost (Granada) 1982, The Outsider (YTV) 1983; *Films* incl: Tuxedo Warrior 1982–83, When the Wall Comes Tumbling Down (EMI) 1984, Deadline (RSPCA) 1988; *Awards* London Drama Critics' Award for Most Promising Actress (for Ophelia) 1980; *Style*— Ms Carol Royle; ✉ c/o Christina Shepherd Ltd, 84 Claverton Street, London SW1 3AX (☎ 0171 630 9191, fax 0171 630 0104)

ROYLE, Dr Edward; s of Fred Royle (d 1973), and Gladys Adelaide, *née* Lane; *b* 29 March 1944; *Educ* King James's GS Almondbury, Christ's Coll Cambridge (BA, MA, PhD); *m* 2 Aug 1968, Jennifer, da of Nicholaas du Plessis (d 1983); 1 da (Catherine Jane); *Career* fell Selwyn Coll Cambridge 1968–72, reader in history Univ of York 1989– (lectr 1972–82, sr lectr 1982–89, head Dept of History 1988–91); local preacher Methodist Church 1965; FRHistS 1975; *Books* Victorian Infidels (1974), Radicals, Secularists and Republicans (1980), Chartism (1980), Social History of Modern Britain 1750–1985 (1987); *Style*— Dr Edward Royle; ✉ Dept of History, University of York, Heslington, York YO1 5DD (☎ 01904 432974)

ROYLE, Joseph (Joe); s of Joseph Royle, of Maghull, Liverpool, and Irene May Royle; *b* 8 April 1949; *Educ* Quarry Bank HS; *m* 6 June 1970, Janet Lilian, da of late Henry Hughes; 3 s (Lee Joseph b 24 March 1971, Darren Henry b 7 March 1974, Mark b 21 March 1981); *Career* professional football manager; former player: Everton, Manchester City, Bristol City, Norwich City; England caps: youth, under 23, 6 full 1971–77, full debut v Malta 1970, 2 goals; manager: Oldham Athletic 1982–94 (League Div 2 champions 1990/91), Everton Nov 1994– (FA Cup winners 1995); Div 2 Manager of the Year 1990/91; honours as player: League Championship Everton 1970, League Cup Manchester City 1976; youngest player to to play in Div 1 for Everton on debut v Blackpool aged 16; *Style*— Joe Royle, Esq; ✉ c/o Everton FC, Goodison Park, Liverpool L4 4EL

ROYLE, Timothy Lancelot Fanshawe; s of Sir Lancelot Carrington Royle, KBE (d 1978); *b* 24 April 1931; *Educ* Harrow, Mons Mil Acad; *m* 1959, Margaret Jill, da of Sir Ivan Rice Stedeford, GBE (d 1975); 2 s, 1 da; *Career* chm: Control Risks Group 1974–91, Westminster Property Group 1983–84, Financial Strategy 1983–84, Berry Palmer & Lyle 1984–91, Hill & Fenley Ltd 1994–, Fanshawe Somerset Ltd 1996–; md: Hogg Robinson UK 1972–81, Hogg Robinson Ltd 1976–81, Hogg Robinson Group 1980–81; dir: Wellmarine Reinsurance Brokers 1975–, Imperio Holdings, Imperio Financial Services, Imperio Ltd, Imperio Reins Co (UK) Ltd; Church Cmmr 1967–83, memb General Synod of C of E 1985–; chm: Lindley Educn Tst 1970–, Christian Weekly Newspapers 1976–; tstee: Wycliffe Coll Oxford, Ridley Coll Cambridge, Charinco, Charifund; Liveryman: Worshipful Co of Marketors, Worshipful Co of Insurers; FCIM; *Recreations* country pursuits, real tennis, skiing; *Clubs* Cavalry and Guards', MCC, St Moritz Tobogganing; *Style*— Timothy Royle, Esq; ✉ Icomb Place, nr Stow-on-the-Wold, Cheltenham, Glos GL54 1JD

ROZENBERG, Joshua Rufus; s of Zigmund Rozenberg (d 1982), and Beatrice Doris, *née* Davies (d 1995); *b* 30 May 1950; *Educ* Latymer Upper Sch Hammersmith, Wadham Coll Oxford (MA); *m* 31 March 1974, Melanie, da of Alfred Phillips; 1 s, 1 da; *Career* trainee journalist BBC 1975, admitted slr 1976, legal affrs corr BBC Radio News 1985, legal corr BBC TV News 1988–; *Books* Your Rights and The Law (with N Watkins, 1986), The Case For The Crown (1987), The Search For Justice (1994), Trial of Strength (1997); *Clubs* Garrick; *Style*— Joshua Rozenberg, Esq; ✉ BBC News, Television Centre, London W12 7RJ (☎ 0181 576 1789, fax 0181 749 9016, e-mail rozenberg@msn.com)

ROZENTAL, HE Andrés; s of Leonid Rozental, of Caracas, Venezuela, and Neoma, *née* Gutman (d 1984); *b* 27 April 1945; *Educ* Univ of Bordeaux (Dip in French Language and Lit), Univ of the Americas (BA), Univ of Pennsylvania (MA Int Rels); *m* 1971, Vivian, da of José Holzer; 2 da (Tamara b 8 Nov 1974, Sandra b 10 March 1979); *Career* Mexican diplomat; joined Foreign Serv 1967, alternate perm rep to OAS Washington 1971–74, cnsllr London 1974–76, princ advsr to Min 1977–79; DG: of Diplomatic Serv 1979, for N American Affrs 1979–82; ambass: to UN Geneva 1982–83, to Sweden 1983–88; sr vice pres Banco Nacional de Mexico (BANAMEX) 1988, dep foreign min 1988–94, ambass to the Ct of St James's 1995–; Polar Star (Sweden) 1983, Civil Merit (Spain) 1991, Order of Merit (France) 1993; *Books* Paradoxes of a World in Transition (jtly, 1993), The United Nations Today: a Mexican Vision (jtly, 1994), Mexican Foreign Policy in the Modern Age (1994), Foreign Ministries: Change and Adaptation (jtly, 1997); *Recreations* swimming, sailing, hiking; *Clubs* Travellers, Canning, Army and Navy; *Style*— HE Mr Andrés Rozental; ✉ Mexican Embassy, 42 Hertford Street, London W1Y 7TF (☎ 0171 495 4024, fax 0171 495 4035)

RUAUX, Her Hon Judge Gillian Doreen; da of Charles Edward Ruaux (d 1977), of Bolton, and Denise Maud, *née* Le Page; *b* 25 March 1945; *Educ* Bolton Sch - Girls' Div Bolton, Univ of Manchester (LLB, LLM); *m* 4 Sept 1968, William Derek Partington, s of Joseph Partington; 1 da (Victoria Louise b 24 Aug 1973); *Career* called to the Bar Gray's Inn 1968 (Gerald Moody scholar), pupillage with H K Goddard, QC, at 9 Albert Sq Manchester then tenancy at same (which transferred to Deans Ct Chambers Manchester), circuit judge (Northern Circuit) 1993–; memb Gray's Inn 1964; *Recreations* opera, theatre, horse-racing and cookery; *Clubs* Bolton Old Links Golf; *Style*— Her Hon Judge Ruaux; ✉ Bolton Combined Court Centre, Blackhorse Street, Bolton, Greater Manchester BL1 1SU

RUBASINGHAM, Arumugam Sinnathamby; s of Arumugam Sinnathamby, and Annaluxmi Kandiah; *b* 14 Nov 1937; *Educ* Sri Lanka (MB BS); *m* 24 March 1969, Parimala, da of Manickam V; 1 s (Lavan 18 Nov 1971), 1 da (Indhu 18 Feb 1970); *Career* sr house offr and sr registrar United Sheffield Hosp 1969–72; sr registrar: Singleton Hosp Swansea 1972–74, Sheffield Hosp 1974–76; conslt ophthalmic surgn Central Nottinghamshire Health Authy 1976–; first chm Fedn of Tamil Assoc; FRCS, FRCOphth, FRCSEd 1973; *Recreations* entertaining and being entertained; *Style*— Arumugam Rubasingham, Esq; ✉ 24 North Park, Mansfield, Nottinghamshire NG18 4PB (☎ 01623 641228); King's Mill Hospital, Mansfield Road, Sutton-in-Ashfield, Notts NG17 4JL (☎ 01623 22515)

RUBENS, Bernice Ruth; da of Eli Reubens (d 1958), of Cardiff, and Dorothy, *née* Cohen (d 1987); *b* 26 July 1928; *Educ* Cardiff HS for Girls, Univ Coll Cardiff (BA); *m* 29 Dec 1947 (m dis), Rudi Nassauer, s of Franz Nassauer; 2 da (Sharon b 1949, Rebecca b 1951); *Career* novelist; documentary film maker; hon vice pres International PEN; Hon Fell Univ of Wales 1984, Hon DLitt Univ of Wales 1991; *Books* Set on Edge (1960), Madame Sousatzka (1962), Mate in Three (1965), The Elected Member (Booker prize 1970), Sunday Best (1972), Go Tell The Lemming (1974), I Sent a Letter to My Love (1976), The Ponsonby Post (1978), A Five Year Sentence (1979), Spring Sonata (1981), Birds of Passage (1982), Brothers (1983), Mr Wakefield's Crusade (1985), Our Father (1987), Kingdom Come (1990), A Solitary Grief (1991), Mother Russia (1992), Autobiopsy (1993), Yesterday in the Back Lane (1995); *Recreations* playing the cello; *Style*— Ms Bernice Rubens; ✉ 111 Canfield Gardens, London NW6 3DY (☎ 0171 625 4845)

RUBENS, Prof Robert David; s of Joel Rubens, of London, and Dinah, *née* Hasseck; *b* 11 June 1943; *Educ* Quintin GS, King's Coll London (BSc), St George's Hosp Med Sch (MB BS), Univ of London (MD); *m* 30 Oct 1970, Margaret, da of Alan Chamberlin, of Burncross, Yorks; 2 da (Abigail b 15 Nov 1971, Carolyn b 10 June 1974); *Career* house and registrar appts 1968–72 (St George's, Brompton, Hammersmith & Royal Marsden Hosps), conslt physician Guy's Hosp 1975–; conslt med offr: Mercantile & General Reinsurance Co plc 1977– (chief med offr 1987–), Legal & General Assurance Society Ltd 1978– (chief med offr 1992–); dir of oncology servs Guy's Hosp 1985–90, prof of clinical oncology UMDS of Guy's and St Thomas's Hosps 1985–; Imperial Cancer Res Fund: memb scientific staff 1972–85, dir Clinical Oncology Unit 1985–; ed-in-chief Cancer Treatment Reviews 1992–; examiner RCP 1987–93; chm: Div of Oncology UMDS of Guy's and St Thomas's Hosp 1989–, EORTC Breast Cancer Co-operative Gp 1991–93; memb: Cncl Assur Med Soc 1982–90, SE Thames Regnl Cancer Ctee 1983–, Assoc of Cancer Physicians 1985; hon dir Inc Homes for Ladies with Limited Income 1983; memb: British Breast Gp 1976, American Assoc for Cancer Res 1977, American Soc of Clinical Oncology 1977; Freeman: City of London 1979, Worshipful Soc of Apothecaries 1978 (Liveryman 1983); memb BMA 1969, FRCP 1984 (MRCP 1969); author of: A Short Textbook of Clinical Oncology (1980), pubns on experimental and clinical cancer therapy; *Recreations* golf, music, reading; *Clubs* Athenaeum, Royal Wimbledon Golf; *Style*— Prof Robert Rubens; ✉ 5 Currie Hill Close, Arthur Rd, Wimbledon, London SW19 7DX (☎ 0181 946 0422); Guy's Hospital, London SE1 9RT (☎ 0181 955 5000)

RUBERY, Dr Eileen Doris; QHP (1993); *b* 16 May 1943; *Educ* Univ of Sheffield (MB, ChB), Univ of London (dip in medical radiotherapy), Univ of Cambridge (PGC in chemical microbiology, PhD); m; 1 da; *Career* Sheffield Royal Infirmary: house physician to Prof G M Wilson (Endocrinology and Therapeutics) 1966–67, house surgn to Prof H L Duthie 1967; MRC research fell 1968–71, Meres' sr research student St John's Coll Cambridge 1971–73; Addenbrooke's Hosp: sr registrar Dept of Radiotherapy and Oncology 1976–78 (registrar 1973–76), Wellcome sr clinical res fell Dept of Clinical Biochemistry and hon conslt Dept of Radiotherapy and Oncology 1978–82; sr res fell and dir Medical Studies Girton Coll Cambridge 1980–82; DHSS (now Dept of Health): sr med offr Toxicology and Environmental Protection (TEP) Div 1983–88, princ med offr TEH and head of Food and Radiation Branch 1988, princ med offr and head Communicable Disease Branch 1988–89, sr princ med offr and head Communicable Disease and Immunisation Div 1989–91, seconded to E Anglian Regnl Health Authy 1991, sr princ med offr and head of Health Promotion (Medical) Div 1991–95, under sec and head of Health Aspects of Environment and Food Div 1995–; pt/t secondment as lectr in public health med Inst of Public Health Univ of Cambridge 1993–; Helen P Tompkinson award BMA; WHO Travelling Fellowship; memb RSM, MRCPath, MFPHM, FRCR, FRSH; *Recreations* reading, theatre, music (classical and opera), travel; *Style*— Dr Eileen Rubery, QHP; ✉ Health Aspects of Environment and Food Division, Room 605A Slapton House, 100 London Road, London SE1 6LW (☎ 0171 972 5001, fax 0171 972 1683)

RUBERY, His Hon Judge; (Reginald) John; s of Reginald Arthur Rubery (d 1964), and Phyllis Margaret, *née* Sidley (d 1992); *b* 13 July 1937; *Educ* Wadham House Hale, King's Sch Worcester; *m* 1, 10 June 1961 (m dis), Diana, da of Maurice Wilcock Holgate; 1 s (Mark John b 7 Feb 1968); m 2, 15 March 1974, Frances Camille, da of Thomas Murphy; 1 step da (Leonie); *Career* admitted slr 1963, ptnr Whitworths Manchester then Taylor Kirkman & Mainprice Manchester 1963–68, cncllr Manchester City Cncl 1968–74, hon sec Law Soc Manchester 1974–78, county court registrar then district judge 1978–95, recorder of the Crown Court 1991–95 (asst recorder 1987–91), circuit judge Midland and Oxford Circuit 1995–; memb: Law Soc, District Judges Assoc, Cncl of Circuit Judges; *Recreations* golf, swimming, gardening; *Clubs* Hale Golf, Nefyn Golf; *Style*— His Hon Judge Rubery; ✉ Birkby, Charnes Road, Ashley, Market Drayton, Shropshire TF9 4LQ

RUBIN, Prof Peter Charles; s of Woolf Rubin (d 1980), of Redruth, Cornwall, and Enis Muriel, *née* Cowling; *b* 21 Nov 1948; *Educ* Univ of Cambridge (MA), Univ of Oxford (DM); *m* 2 Oct 1976, Dr Fiona Anne, da of William Burns Logan (d 1967); 1 s (Jeffrey b 1984), 1 da (Victoria b 1979); *Career* American Heart Assoc fell Stanford Med Center 1977–79, sr registrar in med and clinical pharmacology Glasgow 1979–82, Wellcome Tst sr fell Glasgow 1982–87, prof of therapeutics Univ of Nottingham Med Sch 1987– (chm Dept of Med 1991–); chm SAC in Clinical Pharmacology and Therapeutics RCP 1993–95, memb MRC Grants Ctee 1992–96; examiner: RCP 1996–, Royal Coll of Obstetricians and Gynaecologists 1995–; FRCP 1989, memb Assoc of Physicians 1990; *Books* Lecture Notes on Clinical Pharmacology (edn 5, 1996), Prescribing in Pregnancy (1987, edn 2 1995), Hypertension in Pregnancy (1988); *Clubs* United Oxford & Cambridge Univ; *Style*— Prof Peter Rubin; ✉ Department of Medicine, University Hospital, Nottingham NG7 2UH (☎ 0115 970 9351, fax 0115 942 2232, e-mail peter.rubin@nottingham.ac.uk)

RUBINSTEIN, Felicity Kate; da of Hilary Rubinstein, *qv*, and Helge, *née* Kitzinger; *b* 27 July 1958; *Educ* Godolphin and Latymer, Camden Sch for Girls, Univ of Warwick; *m* 1991, Roland Alexander Philipps, *qv*, s of 3 Baron Milford; *Career* literary; Rosenstone/Wender lit agency NY USA 1980–84, Viking Penguin Inc publishers NY USA 1985–86, dir William Heinemann Ltd publishers UK 1987–88, md Macmillan London publishers UK 1989–93, ptnr Lutyens and Rubinstein Literary Agency 1993–; *Recreations* more reading, food; *Style*— Ms Felicity Rubinstein; ✉ 231 Westbourne Park Rd, London W11

RUBINSTEIN, Hilary Harold; s of Harold Frederick Rubinstein (d 1974), of London, and Lena, *née* Lowy (d 1939); *b* 24 April 1926; *Educ* Cheltenham, Merton Coll Oxford (MA); *m* 6 Aug 1955, Helge, da of Gabriel Kitzinger (d 1963), of Herts; 3 s (Jonathan Paul b 1956, Mark Gabriel b 1961, Ben Hilary b 1963), 1 da (Felicity Kate Rubinstein, *qv*, b 1958); *Career* trainee pilot RAF 1944–47, later Educn Corps and Vocational Advice Serv; editorial dir Victor Gollancz Ltd 1952–63, special features ed The Observer Magazine 1964–65, md AP Watt Ltd Literary Agents 1965–92, md Hilary Rubinstein Books Literary Agents 1992–; memb Cncl Inst of Contemporary Arts 1976–92, tstee Open Coll of the Arts 1987–96; *Books* The Complete Insomniac (1974), The Good Hotel Guide (fndr ed, 1978–), Hotels and Inns - An Oxford Anthology (ed, 1984); *Recreations* hotel-watching, reading in bed; *Style*— Hilary Rubinstein, Esq; ✉ Hilary Rubinstein Books, 61 Clarendon Road, London W11 4JE (home ☎ 0171 727 9550, office ☎ 0171 792 4282, fax 0171 221 5291)

RUBINSTEIN, Michael Bernard; s of Harold Frederick Rubinstein (d 1974), and Lina, *née* Lowy (d 1939); *b* 6 Nov 1920; *Educ* St Paul's; *m* 1955, Joy, *née* Douthwaite; 2 s, 2 da; *Career* served WWII RE TA 1939, Capt RA 1945; admitted slr 1948; Rubinstein Callingham Polden & Gale (formerly Rubinstein Nash & Co): sr ptnr 1976–86, conslt 1986–94; memb Lord Chllr's Ctee on Defamation 1971–74; chm SPNM Tstees 1986–94 (tstee 1967–), vice pres SPNM 1994–; Liveryman Worshipful Co of Musicians; *Books* Wicked, Wicked Libels (ed and contrib, 1972), Rembrandt and Angels (monograph, 1982), Malta's Ancient Temples and Ruts (monograph with Rowland Parker 1988, incorporating The Cart-Ruts on Malta and Gozo, 1984), Music to my Ear (1985); *Clubs* Garrick; *Style*— Michael Rubinstein, Esq; ✉ 1 Walkern Road, Benington, Herts SG2 7LN (☎ 01438 869539)

RUCK, Adam; s of Andrew D'Arcy Ruck (d 1994), of Wrotham, and Patricia, *née* Creasey; *b* 9 Oct 1952; *Educ* Haileybury, New Coll Oxford, Courtauld Inst of Art (MA); *partner* Jane Parritt; 1 s (George Arthur D'Arcy Ruck b 31 Dec 1995); *Career* travel writer/columnist, author; *Books* The Holiday Which? Guide to France (4 edn, 1989), The Holiday Which? Guide to Italy (jtly, 2 edn 1989), The Good Skiing Guide 1985–88 (co-ed), The Holiday Which? Guide to Greece and the Greek Islands (jtly, 1989), AA Explorer France (1992); *Recreations* tennis, skiing, golf; *Clubs* Kandahar, Aberdovey Golf; *Style*— Adam Ruck, Esq; ✉ Pantlludw, Machynlleth, Powys (☎ 01654 702218)

RUCK KEENE, Benjamin Charles (Ben); JP (Oxfordshire 1992); o s of Capt John Henry Ruck Keene, OBE, DSC, RN (d 1967), and Patricia, *née* Gibbons; *b* 2 Sept 1949; *Educ* Ampleforth, Univ of York (BA), Inns of Court Sch of Law; *m* 9 Sept 1972, Frances Anne Marylee, 2 da of Jocelyn Wiseman Fagan Morton; 2 s (Alexander Charles Edward b 21 Aug 1976, Dominic Nicholas John b 14 Feb 1982), 1 da (Hermione Katharine Mary b 28 June 1978); *Career* called to the Bar Gray's Inn 1971, in practice NE Circuit 1972–79, Univ of York 1979–83, assoc dir Credit Suisse Asset Management and memb Stock Exchange 1983–88, fell and bursar Corpus Christi Coll Oxford 1989– (MA by decree 1989); *Clubs* Brooks's, Little Ship; *Style*— Ben Ruck Keene, Esq, JP; ✉ Corpus Christi College, Oxford OX1 4JF (☎ 01865 276736, fax 01865 248910)

RUCK KEENE, David Kenneth Lancelot; s of Thomas Ruck Keene, of Goulds Grove, Ewelme, Oxford, and Anne Coventry, *née* Greig (d 1991); *b* 22 Sept 1948; *Educ* Eton; *m* 30 Oct 1976, Tania Caroline, da of William Anstey Preston Wild; 3 da (Katherine b 1981, Rosanna b 1983, Lucia b 1985); *Career* CA; Rowe & Pitman stockbrokers 1977–86 (ptnr 1982–86), dir SG Warburg Securities 1986–95, dir SBC Warburg 1995–; FCA 1974, MSI; *Recreations* country pursuits, rackets, tennis, golf; *Clubs* White's, Queen's, MCC; *Style*— David Ruck Keene, Esq; ✉ SBC Warburg, 1 Finsbury Ave, London EC2M 2PA (☎ 0171 606 1066, fax 0171 382 4800)

RUCKER, Brig James William Frederick; s of Charles Edward Sigismund Rucker (d 1965), of Ashmore, Salisbury, Wilts, and Nancy Winifred, *née* Hodgson (d 1993); *b* 3 May 1936; *Educ* Charterhouse; *m* 14 Sept 1963, Caroline Lloyd, da of Raymond Wilson Sturge (d 1984), of Ashmore, Salisbury, Wilts; 2 s (Rupert b 1967, Jeremy b 1970), 1 da (Sara b 1964); *Career* Col The QOH, Cdr RAC, BAOR, Brig; DOR MOD; md NAAFI 1987–94; co sec Incorporated Froebel Educational Inst 1995–; *Recreations* shooting, cricket, tennis, gardening; *Clubs* Cavalry and Guards', MCC; *Style*— Brig James Rucker; ✉ Manor Farmhouse, Ashmore, Salisbury, Wilts SP5 5AE; 6 Beechmore Rd, London SW11

RUCKER, Jane; *see:* Campbell Garratt, Jane Louise

RUCKER, His Hon Judge Jeffrey Hamilton; s of Charles Edward Sigismund Rucker, MC (d 1965), of Ashmore, nr Salisbury, Wilts, and Nancy Winifred, *née* Hodgson (d 1993); *b* 19 Dec 1942; *Educ* Charterhouse, Univ of Heidelberg; *m* 15 May 1965, Caroline Mary, da of Col Philip Edward Salkeld (d 1975), of Stour House, Blandford, Dorset; 3 s (Simon b 3 Nov 1970, Nicholas b 26 Sept 1972, James b 3 Feb 1978); *Career* called to the Bar Middle Temple 1967, recorder 1984–88, circuit judge (SE Circuit) 1988–; memb Cncl of Govrs of United Med and Dental Schs of St Thomas' and Guy's Hosps 1991–; *Recreations* sailing, skiing, music; *Style*— His Hon Judge Jeffrey Rucker; ✉ 36 Essex St, London WC2 3AS (☎ 0171 413 0353); Southwark Crown Court, 1 English Grounds, off Battlebridge Lane, London SE1 2HU

RUCKMAN, Eur Ing Robert Julian Stanley; s of William James Ruckman (d 1962), late of Sycamore Rd, Chalfont, and Ida Marjorie, *née* Woodward (d 1989); *b* 11 May 1939; *Educ* Harrow Tech Coll, Cranfield Inst of Tech (MSc); *m* 16 Oct 1965, Josephine Margaret, da of Lieut RNVR George Colin Trentham, DSC (despatches) (d 1979); 1 s (Gordon b 1966), 1 da (Helen b 1973); *Career* chartered engr, systems analyst; memb tech staff Systems Sci Corp Virginia USA 1966, sr engr Kent Instruments 1968, computer mangr Highways Agency DOT (design of Geographical Information Systems (GIS)) 1970–95, ret; author of various publications on digital systems; assessor Br Computer Soc Professional Review Panel, membership advsr IEE 1993–95; CEng, MIEE, MBCS, MinstMC, MCIT, Comp IAP; *Recreations* hill walking, classical music, woodworking; *Clubs* CGA; *Style*— Eur Ing Robert Ruckman; ✉ Flamingo, 13 Alexander Ave, Droitwich, Worcs WR9 8NH (☎ 01905 775286)

RUDD, Lewis Michael Cooper; MBE (1989); s of Dr Alfred Samuel Rudd (d 1996), and Hannah, *née* Marcus (d 1983); *b* 16 Sept 1936; *Educ* Highgate, Magdalen Coll Oxford (MA); *m* 2 Dec 1964, Joan Muriel, da of R N Bower, of Osmanthorpe Manor, Kirklington, Notts; 2 s (Charles b 28 June 1967, Thomas b 2 May 1969), 1 da (Penelope b 4 April 1972); *Career* Nat Serv RASC 1954–56; head of children's programmes Rediffusion TV 1966–68, controller of children's programmes Thames TV 1968–72, asst controller of programmes Southern TV 1972–81, controller of young people's programmes Central TV 1981–94, md FilmFair Ltd 1989–92; Carlton UK Productions: controller of children's and young people's progs 1995–96, a sr exec prodr 1996–; RTS Judges' Award 1993; FRTS 1996; *Style*— Lewis Rudd, Esq, MBE; ✉ Carlton UK Productions Ltd, 35–38 Portman Square, London W1H 0NU

RUDD, Sir (Anthony) Nigel Russell; kt (1996), DL (Derbyshire); s of Samuel Rudd (d 1983), and Eileen, *née* Pinder; *b* 31 Dec 1946; *Educ* Bemrose GS Derby; *m* 20 Sept 1969, Lesley Elizabeth, da of Bernard Thomas Hodgkinson (d 1990); 2 s (Timothy Nigel b 27 May 1971, Edward Thomas b 23 Sept 1973), 1 da (Jennifer Clare b 24 March 1978); *Career* chm: Williams Holdings plc 1982–, Pilkington plc 1995– (dir 1994–), Derby Pride Ltd; non-exec chm: Pendragon plc 1989, East Midlands Electricity plc; non-exec dir Barclays plc 1996–; memb: CBI Pres Ctee, Fndn for Manufacturing and Indust; dir Queen Margaret's Sch York; Liveryman Worshipful Co of Chartered Accountants, Freeman City of London; *Recreations* golf, shooting, tennis; *Clubs* San Lorenzo Golf, Chevin Golf, IOD, London Capital, RAC; *Style*— Sir Nigel Rudd, DL; ✉ Williams Holdings plc, Pentagon House, Sir Frank Whittle Road, Derby DE21 4XA (☎ 01332 202020, fax 01332 202388)

RUDD, His Hon Judge (Julian) Norman Peter Joseph; s of Norman Arthur Rudd, and Winifred Agnes, *née* Sheldrake; *b* 12 May 1943; *Educ* Paston Sch N Walsham, UCL (LLB, LLM); *m* 1968, Judith Margaret, da of Alec Innes Pottinger; 3 s (Aidan b 13 Oct 1970, Edward b 22 Feb 1972, Alex b 7 Sept 1973); *Career* called to the Bar Inner Temple 1969, in practice at Bar Southampton 1970–88, head of chambers 1983–87, recorder 1987–88 (asst recorder 1983–87), circuit judge (Western Circuit) 1988–; chm New Forest Commoner's Tst 1993–; *Recreations* farming; *Style*— His Hon Judge Rudd; ✉ Southampton Combined Court Centre, London Road, Southampton (☎ 01703 228586)

RUDD-JONES, Dr Derek; CBE (1981); s of Walter Henry Jones (d 1966), of Betchworth, Surrey, and Doris Mary, *née* Dawes; *b* 13 April 1924; *Educ* Whitgift Sch Croydon, Repton, Emmanuel Coll Cambridge (BA, MA, PhD); *m* 4 Dec 1948, Joan Hancock, da of Edward Newhouse (d 1962), of Malvern, Worcs; 2 s (Julian b 1955, Nicholas b 1959), 1 da (Clare (Dr Symes) b 1951); *Career* HM Colonial Res Serv 1949–53; Agric Res Cncl postgrad studentship Botany Sch Univ of Cambridge 1945–48, sr scientific offr E African Agric and Forestry Res Orgn 1949–53, NRC postdoctoral fell Univ of Saskatchewan Saskatoon Canada 1952–53, Akers Res Laboratories ICI plc The Frythe Welwyn Herts 1954–56, Jealotts Hill Res Station Bracknell Berks 1956–59, scientific advsr Agric Res Cncl 1959–71 (memb Advsy Ctee on Pesticides 1960–70), fndn chm Br Crop Protection Cncl 1968–72, dir Glasshouse Crop Res Inst Littlehampton 1971–86, visiting fell Univ of Southampton 1975–86, conslt ed 1986–93; author scientific papers in: Nature, Annals Applied Biology; govr W Sussex Inst of Higher Educn 1980–95, memb Scientific Ctee RHS 1982–95, tstee Thomas Phillips Price Tst 1988–93; FIBiol 1965, FIHort 1986; *Books* Healthy Planting Material: Strategies and Technologies (1986); *Recreations* gardening, riding, fly fishing, arboriculture; *Clubs* Farmers'; *Style*— Dr Derek Rudd-Jones, CBE

RUDDELL, Michael Frith (Mike); s of Ven Joseph Frith William Ruddell (d 1992), of Enniscorthy, Ireland, and Anne Rosamond, *née* Yates; *b* 26 Oct 1943; *Educ* Portora Royal Sch Enniskillen, Trinity Coll Dublin (MA, capt of shooting); *m* 7 Sept 1967, Hermione Elizabeth, da of William Braddell-Smith; 2 s (Geoffrey Frith b 12 Sept 1971, Edward William b 30 Jan 1973); *Career* The Boots Company PLC: joined 1966, Personnel Dept 1966–68, Finance Depts 1968–73, Buying and Merchandise Depts 1973–82, dir Timothy Whites 1981, dir Chemist and Beauty Merchandise 1982, dir Boots the Chemists 1982, dir of mktg Boots the Chemists 1983, main bd dir 1984–, large stores dir Boots the Chemists 1986–88, chm and md Boots Properties PLC 1988–96, personnel dir 1996–, tstee Boots Pensions Ltd; chm: A G Stanley Ltd 1994, Childrens World 1994; non-exec dir Community Hospitals Group PLC 1992–; dep chm Nottingham Trent Univ 1996–; *Recreations* travel, tennis, reading, walking; *Style*— Mike Ruddell, Esq; ✉ The Boots Company PLC, Nottingham NG2 3AA (☎ 0115 968 7007)

RUDDOCK, Joan; MP (Lab) Lewisham Deptford (majority 12,238); da of Kenneth Charles Anthony (d 1981), and Eileen Messenger; *b* 28 Dec 1943; *Educ* Pontypool GS for Girls, Imperial Coll London (BSc); *m* 1963 (sep), Keith Ruddock (d 1996), s of Charles Ruddock (d 1966), of Yorks; *Career* mangr Citizens' Advice Bureau Reading, chairperson CND 1981–85; MP (Lab) Lewisham Deptford 1987–, shadow min for transport 1989–92, shadow min Home Office 1992–94, shadow min for environmental protection 1994–; hon fell Goldsmith's Coll; *Style*— Ms Joan Ruddock, MP; ✉ House of Commons, Westminster, London SW1A 0AA

RUDDOCK, Neil; s of Edward Keith Ruddock, of 77 Sandyhurst Lane, Ashford, Kent, and Joyce Freida, *née* Valence; *b* 9 May 1968; *Educ* North Sch for Boys Ashford Kent; *m* 27 May 1989, Sarah-Jane Victoria, da of John Paul Michael Bennett; 1 s (Joshua Paul b 17 Feb 1990), 1 da (Millie-Georgia b 11 July 1992); *Career* professional footballer; apprentice Millwall 1986, Tottenham Hotspur 1986–88, rejoined Millwall 1988, Southampton 1989–92 (over 150 appearances), rejoined Tottenham Hotspur 1992–93; Liverpool: joined 1993–, winners Coca-Cola Cup 1995; rep: Eng Youth, Eng under 19, Eng under 20, Eng under 21; Zenith Data Systems Cup runners-up medal Southampton 1992; Barclays League Young Eagle award London and South 1989; *Recreations* golf, tennis, boxing; *Style*— Neil Ruddock, Esq; ✉ Liverpool FC, Anfield Road, Anfield, Liverpool L4 0TH

RUDGE, Dr Alan Walter; CBE (1995, OBE 1987); *b* 17 Oct 1937; *Educ* London Poly, Univ of Birmingham (PhD Electrical Engrg); *m*; 2 c; *Career* researcher Illinois Inst of Technol Research Inst (IITRI) 1968, on staff Univ of Birmingham until 1974, established Anglo-American Research Centre for Radio Frequency Technol Electrical Research Assoc (ERA) 1974, ERA acquired Research Centre 1979 (md 1979–87); BT plc: joined as dir Research and Technol 1987, memb Mgmnt Bd 1988–, main bd dir 1989–, md devpt and procurement until 1994, dep gp md 1995, dep chief exec 1996–, dir MCI Communication Corp (US assoc co), dir Concert (BT/MCI jt venture); non-exec dir LucasVarity plc 1997–; first chm New Engrg Cncl, chm Engrg and Physical Sciences Research Cncl (EPSRC) 1994–; formerly memb MoD Defence Evaluation and Research Agency Cncl; currently memb: Govt's Advsy Ctee for Science and Technol, DTI Multimedia Indust Advsy Gp; pres IEE 1993 (Faraday medallist 1991), memb Cncl Royal Acad of Engrg 1987–90; visiting prof and external examiner Univ of London; Hon DEng: Univ of Birmingham, Univ of Bradford, Univ of Portsmouth, Nottingham Trent Univ; Hon DSc: Univ of Strathclyde, Univ of Bath, Loughborough Univ; Hon DUniv Surrey; FEng 1984, FRS 1992; *Recreations* sailing, cycling; *Style*— Dr Alan Rudge, CBE, FEng, FRS; ✉ British Telecommunications plc, 81 Newgate Street, London EC1A 7AJ (☎ 0171 356 5135, fax 0171 600 9290)

RUDGE, Anthony John de Nouaille; s of John Edward Rudge (d 1970), and Beryl Florence Doveton, *née* Hamlyn (d 1985); *b* 17 Feb 1931; *Educ* Eton, Ch Ch Oxford (MA); *m* 1961, Kathleen Jill, da of George Craig Watson; 2 s (Anthony Alexander de Nouaille b 12 Feb 1963, Nicholas John de Nouaille b 15 July 1966); *Career* dir: Barclays Bank plc 1972–91 (chm Birmingham Region), Yorkshire Bank Ltd 1980–90, Mercia Sound Ltd 1978–92, W Midlands Devpt Agency 1988–92, Task Undertakings Ltd 1989–92; tstee The Elgar Birthplace 1992, dir The Elgar Fndn 1992; pres Evesham Rowing Club; Hon LLD Univ of Warwick 1991; *Recreations* travel, music, history; *Style*— Anthony Rudge, Esq; ✉ Church Farm, Churchover, nr Rugby, Warwickshire

RUDGE, John Aulton; s of Kenneth James Rudge (d 1993), of Stivichall, Coventry, and Leigh, *née* Soames; *b* 29 Aug 1951; *Educ* Woodlands Sch Coventry, Sch of Architecture Univ of Nottingham (BA, BArch); *m* 19 Aug 1972, Christine, da of William Hollowood (d 1956); 1 s (Robert Aulton b 7 May 1983), 2 da (Alexandra Jane b 25 Sept 1981, Sussanah Kate b 21 April 1987); *Career* architect: Erewash DC Derbyshire 1975–79, de Brant Joyce and Partners London 1979–83; ptnr Percy Thomas Partnership 1986–94 (assoc 1983–86), chief exec Percy Thomas Partnership (Architects) Ltd 1996– (dir 1994–); most notable works incl: Kenstead Hall, London residence for HRH King Fahd of Saudi Arabia, conversion of Grade 2 listed building (7 Albemarle St) into business and fine arts sch for Univ of Notre Dame, Royal Hosp Muscat, Armed Forces Hosp Muscat, Int Covention Centre and Symphony Hall Birmingham, Procurement Exec HQ for the Miny of Defence in N Bristol, West Dorset Hosp (Ph2); dir: The Bristol Initiative 1991–92, Bristol 97 1991–94, DTP Seward 1995; RIBA 1976, ARCUK 1975, FFB 1991; *Style*— John Rudge, Esq; ✉ Percy Thomas Partnership (Architects) Ltd, Capital House, 29 Chapel Street, London NW1 5DH (☎ 0171 262 3484, fax 0171 724 0305, car 0836 630553); Percy Thomas Partnership (Architects) Ltd, 10 Cathedral Road, Cardiff CF1 9YF (☎ 01222 224334, fax 01222 342839)

RUDGE, Peter John Harrington; s of William Charles Rudge (d 1990), of London, and Edna May, *née* Brown (d 1989); *b* 31 Jan 1934; *Educ* Lower Sch of John Lyon Harrow; *m* 1, 8 Aug 1961 (m dis 1980), Lisa Pauline Jean, da of John William Mackareth (d 1983), of Yorks; 1 s (Jeremy Charles Harrington b 9 Nov 1965); m 2, 14 July 1981, Tanis Shelmerdine, da of James Wells-Hunt; *Career* Nat Serv Sub Lt RN 1957–59, served UK and Germany, Lt RNR 1959–62; CA; articled to Thornton and Thornton 1951–57, chief accountant The Chequered Flag (SCS) Ltd 1959–65, fin dir London Lotus Centre Ltd 1965–95; chm: Professional Acceptances Ltd 1965–, EGO Computer Systems Ltd 1978–88; dir Forster and Hales Ltd 1980–, fin dir BA Peters PLC 1988–; chm Gen Cmmrs of Income Tax; FCA; *Recreations* rugby, football, cricket, golf; *Clubs* MCC, Esher RFC, Richmond Golf; *Style*— Peter Rudge, Esq; ✉ Red Rose Motor Company Limited, 4/6 High Street, Edgware, Middlesex (☎ 0181 952 6171)

RUDGE, Stanley Bickerton; s of Alfred Bickerton Rudge, OBE, and Dorothy, *née* Gardiner; *b* 28 Sept 1935; *m* 1962, Beryl Joyce; 2 s (James Edward Bickerton b 11 March 1971, William Bickerton b 16 Feb 1977); 1 da (Vanessa Louise b 12 April 1968); *Career* former ptnr i/c Exec Office and memb Bd of Ptnrs Deloitte & Touche London; FCA, FRGS; *Style*— Stanley Rudge, Esq; ✉ Woodhewers, 19 Murdoch Rd, Wokingham, Berkshire RG40 2DQ (☎ and fax 0118 978 0117)

RUDIN, Richard Duncan (professional name Richard Duncan); s of Arthur Derek Rudin (d 1981), and Margaret, *née* Swale; *b* 24 May 1957; *Educ* John Willmott GS Sutton Coldfield, Sutton Coldfield Coll of FE, Highbury Tech Coll, Open Univ (BA); *m* 30 July 1983, Alison Marjorie, da of David Hay; 1 s (David Duncan Rudin b 2 June 1990); *Career* trainee newspaper reporter (NCTJ) Midland News Assoc 1976–79, newscaster/reporter Beacon Radio 1979–80, presenter/prodr BFBS Germany 1980–84, presenter Metro Radio Newcastle 1984–86, sr presenter Red Rose Radio Preston 1986–89, prog organiser BBC Radio Leeds (and on attachment as prodr BBC Radio Sheffield) 1989–92, prog controller Radio City Gold 1992–95, with media trg and PR Co 1995–, lectr in journalism, public affairs, radio prodn etc City of Liverpool Community Coll 1995–; also freelance comedy writer (work bdcast on Radio 4); nominated Best Outside Bdcast Sony Radio Award 1988; memb Radio Acad 1989; *Recreations* writing, reading, political biographies, histories and theory, walking, playing with son; *Style*— Richard Rudin, Esq; ✉ City of Liverpool Community College, 70 Hope Street, Liverpool L1 9EB (☎/fax 0151 707 8528)

RUDIN, Toni Richard Perrott; s of late Richard William Rudin, and late Sarah Rowena Mary; *b* 13 Oct 1934; *Educ* Bootham Sch, Millfield, RMA Sandhurst, Army Staff Coll, Coll of Law Guildford; *m* Heather Jean, da of late Phillip Tom Farley; 1 s (Simeon b 24 April 1961), 3 da (Elizabeth b 28 Feb 1960, Jaqueline b 27 Dec 1963, Fenella b 13 March 1967); *Career* cmmnd RA 1954, regtl duty 1955–60, long gunnery staff course 1960–61, instructor in gunnery 1961–64, Adjutant City of London Field Regt RA (TA) 1964–65, MOD 1967–69, regtl duty 1969–72, Battery Commander then 2 i/c BAOR Field Regiment; articled clerk 1976–78, slr in private practice 1978–80, sr asst sec The Law Soc 1980–86, sec The Magistrates' Assoc 1986–93, pt/t legal chm Pensions Appeal Tbnls 1994–, gen cmmr of income tax 1995–; memb Law Soc 1978; *Recreations* riding, golf, reading; *Style*— T R P Rudin, Esq; ✉ Otterbank House, 60 Wedgwood Avenue, Blakelands, Milton Keynes MK14 5HX (☎ 01908 610965)

RUDING, Dr (Herman) Onno; s of Dr Roelof Ruding (d 1981), and Annie-Maria, *née* Fehmers; *b* 15 Aug 1939; *Educ* Gymnasium HS, Netherlands Sch of Economics Erasmus Univ Rotterdam (BA, MA, PhD); *m* 17 April 1971, Renée, *née* Hekking; 1 da (Barbara b 1 Sept 1973), 1 s (Martÿn b 8 Feb 1974); *Career* Miny of Finance The Hague 1965–70, Amsterdam-Rotterdam Bank (AMRO Bank) Amsterdam 1971–76, exec dir IMF Washington DC 1977–80, memb Bd of Managing Directors Amsterdam-Rotterdam Bank and chm AMRO International Ltd London 1981–82, Min of Finance of The Netherlands 1982–89 (also chm Interim Ctee IMF 1985–89); chm Bd of Govrs: Asian Development Bank 1984, Inter American Development Bank 1989; chm Christian Federation of Employers (NCW) The Hague and memb Cncl of Presidents UNICE Brussels 1990–92, dir Citicorp 1990–, vice chm Citicorp/Citibank 1992–; non-exec dir: Corning Inc, Corning, Pechiney Paris, Unilever NV, Unilever plc; advsr Robeco Rotterdam; memb Bd of Tstees Mount Sinai Hosp New York; memb: Ctee for Monetary Union, Trilateral Cmmn, Bd of Tax Fndn; *Recreations* golf, history, chess; *Clubs* University, Blind Brook Golf, Noordwÿksche Golf and Country; *Style*— Dr Onno Ruding; ✉ Citicorp/Citibank, 399 Park Avenue, New York, NY 10043, USA (☎ 00 1 212 559 2785, fax 00 1 212 559 4023)

RUDKIN, (James) David; s of David Jonathan Rudkin (d 1995), of Emsworth, Sussex, and Anne Alice *née* Martin (d 1969); *b* 29 June 1936; *Educ* King Edward's Sch Birmingham, Univ of Oxford (MA); *m* 3 May 1967, (Alexandra) Sandra Margaret, da of Donald Thompson (d 1969); 2 s (Jamie b 1972, Tom (twin) b 1972), 2 da (Sophie b 1977, Jess b 1978); *Career* Nat Serv RCS 1955–57, schoolmaster (classics and music) Co HS Bromsgrove Worcs 1961–64; playwright; work incl: Afore Night Come 1960 (staged 1962), The Sons of Light 1964 (staged 1974), Ashes 1972 (staged 1974), Cries from Casement as his Bones are Brought to Dublin 1972 (radio 1973), Penda's Fen 1972 (TV film, shown 1974), The Triumph of Death 1976 (staged 1981), Hansel and Gretel 1979 (staged 1980), Artemis 81 (TV film, shown 1981), The Saxon Shore 1983 (staged 1986), Testimony 1985 (film screenplay, released 1988), author/dir White Lady 1986 (TV film, shown 1987), December Bride 1988 (film screenplay, released 1990), John Piper in the House of Death 1985 (staged 1991), The Lovesong of Alfred J Hitchcock 1989 (radio 1993), The Haunting of Mahler (radio 1994); translations: Hippolytus (Euripides, staged 1978) 1978, Peer Gynt (Ibsen, staged 1982) 1982, Rosmersholm (Ibsen) 1989 (broadcast 1990), When We Dead Waken (Ibsen, staged 1990) 1989, Sir Gawain (TV adaptation, 1991); *Recreations* bridge, languages, geology, music, the sea; *Style*— David Rudkin, Esq; ✉ c/o Casarotto Ramsay Ltd, 60–66 Wardour Street, London W1V 3HP (☎ 0171 287 4450, fax 0171 287 9128)

RUDKIN, Walter Charles; CBE (1981); s of Walter Rudkin (d 1970), of Sleaford, Lincs, and Bertha, *née* Charles (d 1985); *b* 22 Sept 1922; *Educ* Carres GS Lincs, Univ Coll Hull, Univ of London (BSc(Econ)); *m* 8 April 1950, Hilda Mary, da of George Hope (d 1975) of Sunderland; 2 s (Alistair b 1951, Ian b 1957); *Career* WWII Navigator RAF 1942–46; lectr Univ of the Witwatersrand Johannesburg SA 1948–52; MOD: joined 1954, Hong Kong 1956–59, jr directing staff IDC 1962–64, Cabinet Office 1968–71, dir of economics Intelligence 1973–81, dir of economics and logistics Intelligence 1981–82; chm: Bromley Police Community Consultative Gp 1986–88, James Butcher Housing Assoc 1996–; *Recreations* fishing; *Clubs* Royal Cwlth Soc; *Style*— Walter Rudkin, Esq, CBE; ✉ 9 Speen Place, Speen, Newbury, Berks RG14 1RX (☎ 01635 49244)

RUDLAND, Malcolm; s of Harold William Rudland (d 1966), of Leeds, and Marika, *née* Szèll (d 1943); *b* 17 Aug 1941; *Educ* Ashville Coll Harrogate, St Paul's Cheltenham, RAM (BMus); *Career* music teacher Cirencester Sch; conductor; works incl: Fiddler on the Roof, West Side Story, Peter Pan; pianist and organist; music critic for: Times, Opera, Musical Times; hon sec Peter Warlock Soc; FRCO; *Recreations* gliding, walking, reading; *Style*— Malcolm Rudland, Esq; ✉ 32A Chipperfield House, Cale St, London SW3 3SA (☎ and fax 0171 589 9595)

RUDLAND, Margaret Florence; da of Ernest George Rudland (d 1979), and Florence Hilda, *née* Davies; *b* 15 June 1945; *Educ* Sweyne Sch Rayleigh Essex, Bedford Coll Univ of London; *Career* asst mathematics mistress Godolphin and Latymer Sch 1967–70, VSO Ilorin Nigeria 1970–71, asst mathematics mistress Clapham Co Sch 1971–72, asst mathematics mistress and head of mathematics St Paul's Girls' Sch 1972–83, dep headmistress Norwich HS 1983–85, headmistress Godolphin and Latymer Sch 1986–; pres Girls' Sch Assoc 1996; *Recreations* opera, travel, cinema; *Style*— Miss Margaret Rudland; ✉ The Godolphin and Latymer School, Iffley Rd, Hammersmith, London W6 0PG (☎ 0181 741 1936)

RUDMAN, Michael Edward; s of M B Rudman, and Josephine, *née* Davis; *b* 14 Feb 1939; *Educ* St Mark's Sch Texas, Oberlin Coll (BA), St Edmund Hall Oxford (MA); *m* 1, 1963 (m dis 1981), Veronica Anne Bennett; 2 da (Amanda Joan, Katherine Rose); m 2, 1983 (m dis 1994), Felicity Kendal, *qv*; 1 s (Jacob Henry b 1 Oct 1987); *Career* director; pres OUDS 1963–64, asst dir and assoc prodr Nottingham Playhouse and Newcastle Playhouse 1964–68, asst dir RSC 1968; artistic dir Traverse Theatre Club 1970–73, dir Hampstead Theatre 1973–78, dir Lyttelton Theatre 1979–81, assoc dir NT 1979–88, dir Chichester Festival Theatre 1989–90, artistic dir Sheffield Theatres 1992–94; *Theatre* Nottingham Playhouse: Changing Gear, Measure for Measure, A Man for All Seasons, Julius Caesar, Death of a Salesman, Lily in Little India; The Fox and the Fly (RSC Theatregoround) 1968; Traverse Theatre: Curtains 1971, Straight Up 1971, Carravaggio Buddy 1972, The Relapse 1972; Hampstead Theatre: Ride Across Lake Constance 1973, The Show-off 1974, Alphabetical Order 1975, Clouds 1977, Gloo Joo 1978; NT: For Services Rendered 1978, Death of a Salesman 1979, Measure for Measure 1980, The Second Mrs Tanqueray 1981, Brighton Beach Memoirs 1986, Fathers and Sons 1987; West End: Donkeys Years 1976, Clouds 1978, Taking Steps 1980, Brighton Beach Memoirs 1987; NY: The Changing Room 1973, Hamlet 1976, Death of a Salesman 1984, Measure for Measure 1993, Have you Spoken with any Jews Lately? 1994; Chichester Festival Theatre: The Wizard of Oz 1989, The Merry Wives of Windsor 1990, Eurydice 1990, Rumours 1990; Sheffield Theatres: A Midsummer Night's Dream, Jane Eyre, Donkeys Years, Hamlet, Mansfield Park, Grapes of Wrath, Romeo and Juliet; *Clubs* RAC, Royal Mid-Surrey Golf; *Style*— Michael Rudman, Esq; ✉ c/o Peter Murphy, Curtis Brown Group Ltd, 28–29 Haymarket, London SW1Y 4SP (☎ 0171 396 6600, fax 0171 396 0110)

RUDOFSKY, John Alec; s of Alexander Edward Rudofsky (d 1986), and Ethel, *née* Frost; *b* 13 Dec 1951; *Educ* St Clement Danes Sch, Selwyn Coll Cambridge (BA, MA); *m* 1978, Susan Judith, da of late James Ernest Riley; 3 s (James Alexander b 1980, Nicholas John b 1984, Joshua Lewis b 1987); *Career* fin journalist: City Press 1973–76, BBC radio 1973–76, Investors Chronicle 1976–79, Daily Telegraph 1979–86; asst dir and fin communications consult Streets Communications 1987–88, fndr dir and communications conslt Citigate Communications 1988–; *Style*— John Rudofsky, Esq; ✉ Citigate Communications, 26 Finsbury Square, London EC1A 1DS (☎ 0171 282 8000, 0171 282 8010)

RUDOLF, Anthony; s of Henry Cyril Rudolf, (d 1986), of London, and Esther, *née* Rosenberg; *b* 6 Sept 1942; *Educ* City of London Sch, Institut Britannique Paris, Trinity Coll Cambridge; *m* (m dis); 1 s (Nathaniel b 1974), 1 da (Naomi b 1976); *Career* fndr and publisher The Menard Press 1969–; Adam lectr King's Coll London 1990, juror Neustadt Int Prize for Literature Oklahoma 1986, winner H H Wingate/Jewish Quarterly Prize for Non-Fiction 1991 (chm of judges 1996), Hawthornden fell 1993, judge of translation pieces of Br Comparative Literature Assoc 1994–; patron Safer World Fndn; *Books* The Same River Twice: Poems (1976), After the Dream: Poems (1980), Selected Poems of Yves Bonnefoy (1985 and 1995), The Unknown Masterpiece: translation with essay of Balzac's story (1988), Wine from Two Glasses: Poetry and Politics (The Adam Lecture for 1990), At an Uncertain Hour: Primo Levi's War Against Oblivion (1990), I'm Not Even a Grown-Up: The Diary of Jerzy Feliks Urman (1991), The Poet's Voice (poems and translations, 1994), Mandorla (poems, 1995), Engraved in Flesh (on Piotr Rawicz) (1996); *Recreations* talking, walking; *Style*— Anthony Rudolf, Esq; ✉ The Menard Press, 8 The Oaks, Woodside Ave, London N12 8AR (☎ 0181 446 5571)

RUDOLF, Dr Noel de Montjoie; s of Dr Gerald R A de M Rudolf (d 1971, s of Rev Preb E de M Rudolf, CBE, fndr C of E Children's Soc and co-fndr NSPCC), of Clevedon, Somerset, and K Rosemary, *née* Fowles (d 1972); *Educ* Cheltenham, ChCh Oxford (MA, BM BCh), King's Coll Hosp Med Sch; *m* Claudie Lucienne Marcelle, da of M Roger Held, of Alpes-Maritimes; 1 s (Christopher), 2 step-s; *Career* res asst info systems gp Wheatstone Physics Lab and demonstrator King's Coll Univ of London 1959, house physician and surgn Plymouth Hosp 1960, MRC res scholar and fell Univ of Keele

1961–64, registrar Dept of Applied Electrophysiology Nat Hosp London 1965–67; conslt clincial neurophysiologist: Goodmayes, Oldchurch and St Margaret's Hosps Essex 1967–71, Cheyne Centre Chelsea 1971–92, Charing Cross Hosp London 1971–; hon conslt Chelsea and Westminster Hosp 1994–; recognized teacher Univ of London 1986–, hon sr lectr in clinical neurophysiology Charing Cross and Westminster Med Sch 1992–; pt/t private practice 1975–; memb: Cncl C of E Children's Soc (hon vice pres 1994–), Assoc of Br Clinical Neurophysiologists (fndr memb), Br Soc for Clinical Neurophysiology, Int League Against Epilepsy, BMA, RYA; proprietor Mount Pleasant Nursing Home Clevedon 1972–; author of over 60 publications on studies in man of visual perception, thalamus, EEG, epilepsy and evoked potentials; *Recreations* boating, skiing, genealogy, science in religion; *Style*— Dr Noel de M Rudolf; ✉ 22 Devonshire Place, London W1N 1PD (☎ 0171 935 1825, fax 0171 224 7220)

RUE, Dame (Elsie) Rosemary; DBE (1989, CBE 1977); da of Harry Laurence (d 1978), of Chorleywood, and Daisy Annie, *née* Sully (d 1976); *b* 14 June 1928; *Educ* Sydenham HS (GPDST), Univ of Oxford, Univ of London (MB BS); *m* 7 Jan 1950 (m dis 1960), Roger Harry Edward Rue, s of Harry Rue (d 1958), of London; 2 s (Randal b 1952, Rolf b 1955); *Career* gen practice; asst co MO Public Health Serv 1952–65; Oxford RHA: sr admin MO 1971, regnl MO 1973, regnl gen mangr and regnl MO 1984, ret 1988; on secondment as prof of community health LSHTM 1980–82; former pres: Med Women's Fedn, Faculty of Public Health Med RCP (fell 1972); pres BMA 1990–91; currently: vice pres Alzheimers Disease Soc, chm Wyndham Housing Assoc, chm Margaret Pyke Tst; Freedom City of London, Liveryman Worshipful Soc of Apothecaries 1976; Hon MA Univ of Oxford 1988; FRCP 1977, FRCPsych 1980 (hon fell 1990), FRCGP, FRSM, FRCS; *Books* The Oxford Companion to Medicine (contrib); *Style*— Dame Rosemary Rue, DBE; ✉ 2 Stanton St John, Oxford OX33 1ET

RUFFELLE, Frances; da of Norman Albert Ruffell, and Sylvia, *née* Bakel; *b* 29 Aug 1966; *Educ* Gate House Learning Centre, Sylvia Young Theatre Sch; *m* 31 Aug 1990, John Newport Caird, s of George Bradford Caird; 1 s (Nathaniel George b 17 June 1990), 1 da (Eliza Sophie b 15 April 1988); *Career* actress and singer; *Theatre* roles incl: Princess Louisa in The Sleeping Prince (Haymarket) 1983, Dinah in Starlight Express (Apollo) 1984, Eponine in Les Misérables (RSC and Palace 1985, Broadway 1987), Delilah in Apples (Royal Court) 1989, Yonah in Children of Eden (Prince Edward) 1991; *Television* incl: Tuckers Luck (BBC) 1985, Eunice in P'Tang Yang Kipperbang (Channel 4) 1982, Sylvie in The Equalizer (CBS) 1987; *Films* appeared as Angela Hall and Roxanne in the film Wildcats of St Trinians 1980; *Recordings* contrib incl: cast of Les Misérables London 1985 and Broadway 1987, cast of Starlight Express 1984, duet with Christopher Cross on Back of My Mind 1988, featured on Ian Dury's Apples 1989, cast of Children of Eden 1991, duet with Michael Crawford on Michael Crawford Sings Andrew Lloyd Webber 1991; *Awards* for Les Misérables (Broadway): Tony Award for Best Featured Actress, Helen Hayes Award for Best Newcomer, Outer Circle Critics' Award for Best Newcomer, Theatre World Award; *Style*— Ms Frances Ruffelle; ✉ William Morris Agency (UK) Ltd, 31/32 Soho Square, London W1V 6DG (☎ 0171 434 2191, fax 0171 437 0238)

RUFFER, Jonathan Garnier; s of Maj J E M Ruffer; *b* 17 Aug 1951; *Educ* Marlborough, Sidney Sussex Coll Cambridge; *m* 1982, Jane Mary, da of Dr P Sequeira; 1 da (Harriet b 16 Oct 1990); *Career* Myers and Co Stock Exchange; called to the Bar Middle Temple (jr Harmsworth exhibitioner); J Henry Schroder Wagg 1977–79, Dunbar Group Ltd 1980–85 (dir Dunbar Fund Management Ltd 1981-85), dir CFS (Investment Management) Ltd 1985–88, md Rathbone Investment Management 1988–94; dir: Rathbone Bros PLC 1989–94, Odey Asset Management 1992–, Fuel Tech NV 1994–; chief exec Ruffer Investment Managment Ltd 1994–; *Books* The Big Shots (1977); *Recreations* opera, name-dropping; *Clubs* Athenaeum; *Style*— Jonathan Ruffer, Esq; ✉ Harewood Cottage, Ugley Green, Bishops Stortford, Herts CM22 6HW (☎ 01279 813105); Ruffer Investment Management Ltd, 12 Upper Grosvenor Street, London W1X 9PA (☎ 0171 208 0095)

RUFFLES, Philip Charles; s of Charles Richard Ruffles (d 1980), of Westerham Hill, Kent, and Emily Edith, *née* Kemsley; *b* 14 Oct 1939; *Educ* Sevenoaks Sch Kent, Univ of Bristol (BSc); *m* 27 May 1967, Jane, *née* Connor; 2 da (Amy Jane b 12 June 1971, Laura Megan b 31 May 1974); *Career* Rolls-Royce: graduate apprentice 1961–63, engr preliminary design 1963–68, project devpt engr RB211 1968–74, project engr RB211 1974–75, mangr JT1OD Team E Hartford 1976, chief engr RB211 1977–80, head of engrg Helicopters 1981–83, dir of technol 1984–87, dir of design engrg 1987–89, tech dir 1989–90, dir of engrg 1991–; Ackroyd Stuart prize Royal Aeronautical Soc 1987; hon prof Univ of Warwick, Hon DEng Univ of Bristol 1995; FEng 1988, FRAeS, FIMechE; *Recreations* rugby; *Style*— Philip Ruffles, Esq, FEng; ✉ Rolls-Royce plc, PO Box 31, Derby DE2 8BJ (☎ 01332 249701, fax 01332 245253)

RUFUS, Ian Douglas; s of James Douglas Rufus, of Rotherham, S Yorks, and Joyce, *née* Smith; *b* 17 Feb 1949; *Educ* Rotherham GS, Richmond Coll Sheffield (NCTJ Cert); *m* 24 Dec 1973 (m dis 1992), Alison Alexis, *née* Cawley; 2 s (Simon Alexander David b 15 Oct 1976, Timothy Armstrong Douglas b 20 Feb 1982), 1 da (Alexis Amber Davina b 28 April 1979); m 2, 2 Sept 1994, Kate, *née* O'Connor; *Career* mgmnt trainee Jessop-Saville Sheffield 1965–66, reporter S Yorks and Rotherham Advertiser 1966–70, reporter Birmingham Post 1970–71, feature writer Newcastle Journal Newcastle upon Tyne 1971, news prodr BBC Birmingham 1971–73, duty ed LBC London 1973–74, head of news Radio Hallam Sheffield 1974–79, prog controller Mercia Sound Coventry 1979–83, md Humber Bridge Radio (later Viking Radio) Hull 1983, md Mercia Sound 1983–86, md BRMB-FM and XTRA-AM Birmingham and dep gp md Midlands Radio plc 1986–94 area dir GWR plc (Midlands) 1994–; also dir: Independent Radio News, Radio Trent plc, Radio Trent Ltd, Leicester Sound Ltd, Mercia Sound Ltd, RAM FM Ltd; govr Coventry Tech Coll; BRMB-FM won Sony Radio Awards local station of the year 1989 and best breakfast show awards 1989 and 1990, XTRA-AM won Premios Ondas award for Round the World prog; *Recreations* golf, travel; *Style*— Ian Rufus, Esq

RUGBY, 3 Baron (UK 1947), of Rugby, Co Warwick; Robert Charles Maffey; 2 (but eldest surviving) s of 2 Baron Rugby (d 1990), and Margaret, *née* Bindley; *b* 4 May 1951; *m* 1974, Anne Penelope, yr da of David Hale, of Somerden, Chiddingstone, Kent; 2 s (Hon Timothy James Howard b 1975, Hon Philip Edward b 1976); *Heir* s, Hon Timothy James Howard Maffey b 23 July 1975; *Style*— The Rt Hon the Lord Rugby; ✉ House of Lords, London SW1A 0PW

RUGG-GUNN, Prof Andrew John; RD (1979); s of Mark Andrew Rugg-Gunn (d 1988), of Tewkesbury, and Hilda, *née* Rowell (d 1952); *b* 12 June 1939; *Educ* Sherborne, Univ of London (BDS, DSc, Constance Klein prize), Univ of Manchester (PhD); *m* 17 Dec 1966, Diane Vivienne, da of late Henry Marriott; 3 s (Neil Andrew b 25 Aug 1969, Fergus James b 10 March 1971, Peter John b 10 Feb 1980); *Career* dental offr RN 1963–68, Colgate res fell Univ of Manchester 1968–72; Univ of Newcastle upon Tyne: lectr in preventive dentistry 1972–79, reader 1979–88, prof 1988–, head Dept of Child Dental Health 1993–; hon conslt in dental surgery Newcastle Health Authy 1979–; asst scientific ed Br Dental Jl 1992–; Van Den Burghs and Jurgens Nutrition Award 1987, E W Borrow Award Int Assoc for Dental Research 1993, H Trendley Dean Award Int Assoc of Dental Research 1996, Annual Prize Euro Orgn for Caries Research 1996; hon assoc Br Dietetic Assoc 1990; memb: BDA 1963, Br Soc of Paediatric Dentistry 1969, Br Assoc for the Study of Community Dentistry 1970 (pres 1988–89), Int Assoc for Dental Research 1970, Euro Orgn for Caries Research 1972, RSM 1980, Nutrition Soc 1995; LDS RCS 1963, FDS RCS (Edinburgh) 1975; *Books* Fluorides in Caries Prevention (co-author, 1982, 3 edn 1991), Sugarless - the way forward (1991), Nutrition and Dental Health (1993), Sugarless - towards the year 2000 (1994); *Recreations* squash (memb RN team 1966–67 (champion 1967), Cornwall Co team 1967–74, Northumbria Co Veterans team 1984–90 (champion 1986), Vintage team 1994–96 (champion 1995–96)), cricket, walking, travel; *Style*— Prof Andrew Rugg-Gunn; ✉ Department of Child Dental Health, The Dental School, University of Newcastle upon Tyne, Framlington Place, Newcastle upon Tyne NE2 4BW (☎ 0191 222 6000)

RUGGE-PRICE, Sir (Charles) Keith Napier; 9 Bt (UK 1804); s of Lt-Col Sir Charles James Napier Rugge-Price, 8 Bt (d 1966), and Maeve Marguerite (Peggy), *née* de la Peña (d 1995); *b* 7 Aug 1936; *Educ* Middleton Coll Ireland; *m* 1965, Jacqueline Mary, da of Maj Pierre Paul Loranger, MC, CD; 2 s (James b 1967, Andrew b 1970); *Heir* s, James Keith Peter Rugge-Price, b 8 April 1967; *Career* mangr Tomenson-Alexander Ltd Toronto 1971–76; supervisor Employee Benefits City of Edmonton 1976–81; sr mgmnt conslt City of Edmonton 1982–89, supervisor Mgmnt Compensation and Orgn Design 1989–; treas Big Lake Environmental Support Soc; chm St Albert United Church Cncl; vive chm St Albert Museum Management Bd; *Style*— Sir Keith Rugge-Price, Bt; ✉ 2 Lorne Crescent, St Albert, Alberta T8N 3R2, Canada (☎ 403 458 5391); City of Edmonton, 9th Floor Century Place, 9803–102A Avenue, Edmonton, Alberta T5J 3A3 (☎ 403 496 7843)

RUGGLES-BRISE, Guy Edward; TD, DL (Essex 1967); s of Col Sir Edward Ruggles-Brise, 1 Bt, MC, TD, sometime MP Maldon, JP, DL (d 1942), by his 1 w, Agatha, *née* Gurney, of the Norfolk family; hp to bro, Sir John Ruggles-Brise, 2 Bt, CB, OBE, TD; *b* 15 June 1914; *Educ* Eton; *m* 1, 7 Dec 1940, Elizabeth (d 1988), o da of late James Knox, of Smithstone House, Kilwinning, Ayrshire; 3 s (Timothy Edward b 1945, James Rupert b 1947, Samuel Guy b 1956); m 2, 1994, Christine Margaret Fothergill-Spencer, o da of late John A Fothergill; *Career* 104 Essex Yeo 1934–38, 147 Essex Yeo 1938–40, Capt, No 7 Commando 1940, POW Bardia 1941, escaped from Italy 1944; sr ptnr Brewin Dolphin & Co (stockbrokers) 1973–79, ret; memb Stock Exchange 1946–88; pres Pony Riding for the Disabled Tst 1983–84 (chm Exec Ctee 1968–78); High Sheriff of Essex 1967–68; *Recreations* hunting, shooting, fishing; *Clubs* City of London; *Style*— Guy Ruggles-Brise, Esq, TD, DL; ✉ Ledgowan Lodge, Achnasheen, Ross (☎ 01445 720 245); Pitkeathly, Cole End Lane, Wimbish, Saffron Walden, Essex CB10 2UT (☎ 01799 521 215)

RUGGLES-BRISE, Col Sir John Archibald; 2 Bt (UK 1935), of Spains Hall, Finchingfield, Essex, CB (1958), OBE (Mil 1945), TD, JP (Essex 1946); s of Col Sir Edward Archibald Ruggles-Brise, 1 Bt, MC, TD, MP (d 1942); *b* 13 June 1908; *Educ* Eton; *Heir* bro, Guy Edward Ruggles-Brise, TD, DL, *qv*; *Career* formed and commanded Mixed Ack Ack Regt 1942, mangr City Office Employers Liability Assurance 1945–53; Lloyd's underwriter; pres CLA 1957–59 (sponsored first CLA Game Fair 1958); Ld-Lt of Essex 1958–78; chm: Essex Territorial Assoc 1950–58, Standing Cncl Baronetage 1958–63; Church cmmr 1959–64; pro-chllr Essex Univ 1964–74; former govr Felsted and Chigwell Schs; Liveryman Worshipful Co of Spectacle Makers; Hon DUniv Essex; Hon Freeman of Chelmsford; *Clubs* Carlton; *Style*— Col Sir John Ruggles-Brise, Bt, CB OBE, TD, JP; ✉ Spains Hall, Finchingfield, Essex CM7 4PF (☎ 01371 810266)

RUIZ BARRERO, Lorenzo; s of Lorenzo Ruiz Jimenez, of Jorge Juan 55, 28001 Madrid, Spain, and Guadalupe Barrero Alonso (d 1979); *b* 20 March 1946; *Educ* Colegio Sagrados Corazones Madrid (Baccalaureate), Law Faculty Univ of Madrid (LLB); *m* 25 Oct 1978 (m dis 1985), Lady Katherine Lucy Lambart, da of Earl of Cavan (d 1988); 1 s (Lorenzo Cavan b 28 Aug 1980), 1 da (Natasha Pepa b 4 Dec 1982); *Career* slr; in private practice Madrid Spain 1969–75, currently in private practice Messrs Amhurst Brown Colombotti; memb: Madrid Bar Spain, Law Soc; *Books* The Administration of Foreign Estates (contrib, 1988); *Recreations* painting, swimming; *Clubs* RAC; *Style*— Lorenzo Ruiz Barrero, Esq; ✉ 2 Duke St, St James's, London SW1 (☎ 0171 930 2366, fax 0171 930 2250)

RULE, Brian Francis; s of late Sydney John Rule, of Pen-Y-FFordd, Chester, and Josephine, *née* Hegarty; *Educ* Ysgol Daniel Owen Mold, Loughborough Univ of Technol (BSc, MSc); *m* 1 (m dis), Kay; m 2, 31 Dec 1993, Irené Mary; *Career* res asst Loughborough Univ 1963–65, project mangr Glasgow Univ 1965–67, dir of computing Univ of Aberdeen 1974–77 (lectr 1967–71, sr lectr 1971–74); dir: Honeywell Information Systems Ltd London 1977–79, Sci Servs Natural Enviroment Res Cncl 1979–85; dir gen info technol systems MOD 1985–94, md Emeritus Plus Ltd 1994–; memb Antiquarian Horological Soc, dep chm City of Aberdeen Children's Panel 1971–74; *Recreations* antiquarian horology; *Style*— Brian Rule, Esq; ✉ c/o Lloyds Bank plc, 14 Castle Street, Cirencester, Glos

RULE, David Charles; s of Cyril George Leonard Rule (d 1984), and Ivy Macey, *née* Osborne; *b* 17 April 1937; *Educ* Sir Joseph Williamson's Mathematical Sch Rochester, Univ of Birmingham (BDS), LDS RCS, DOrth RCS, FDS RCS 1965, MCCD RCS 1990; *m* 1972, Linda Marion, *née* Meyer; 2 da (Charlotte Bryony b 17 Feb 1977, Rebecca Elizabeth b 1978); *Career* jr house offr Birmingham Dental Hosp 1960; Short Serv Cmmn RADC 1960–63; Eastman Dental Hosp: registrar Dept of Children's Dentistry 1964–65, clinical asst Dept of Oral Surgery 1965, lectr Dept of Children's Dentistry 1965–66, orthodontic course 1966–67, pt/t conslt Dept of Children's Dentistry 1970– (lectr 1967–68, sr registrar 1968–70); hon sr lectr Univ of London, pt/t dean of postgrad dentistry Thames Postgrad Med and Dental Educn, conslt to Navy RADC; hon conslt: Queen Elizabeth Hosp for Children, St Mary's Hosp London, Hammersmith Hosp London; chm Conf of Postgrad Dental Deans and Dirs (UK); memb: Ctee of Mgmnt Eastman Dental Inst, Bd Faculty of Dental Surgery RCS, Bd of Examiners RCS, GDC, SDAC, SCOPME; chm Dental Conslts Ctee Eastman Dental Hosp SHA 1985–90; memb: Bd of Govrs Eastman Dental Hosp 1987–90, Standing Ctee Bd of Studies in Dentistry Univ of London 1984–87; numerous lectureships undertaken worldwide; memb: BDA, Br Soc of Paediatric Dentistry (pres 1988–89), Int Soc of Paediatric Dentistry, Br Soc of Dentistry for the Handicapped (pres 1980–81), Int Assoc of Dentistry for the Handicapped (pres 1988–90), Br Endodontic Soc, Br Soc for the Study of Orthodontics, Br Paediatric Assoc; *Recreations* sailing; *Clubs* MCC; *Style*— David C Rule, Esq; ✉ 7 Malmains Way, Beckenham, Kent BR3 2SA (☎ 0181 650 1895); c/o Dental Department, Thames Postgraduate Medical and Dental Education, 33 Millman Street, London WC1N 8EJ (☎ 0171 831 6222 ext 148, fax 0171 831 5784)

RULE, John Eric; s of Eric Houldsworth Rule, of Guildford, Surrey, and Alpha Rule (d 1988); *b* 15 Nov 1934; *Educ* John Bright GS Llandudno N Wales, Royal GS Guildford; *m* 5 Sept 1959, Georgina Frances, da of Frederick William Luck, of Guildford, Surrey; 1 s (Stephen b 1965), 1 da (Jane b 1961); *Career* Trooper 16/5 Queen's Royal Lancers 1957, cmmnd 2 Lt RAPC 1958, Capt 1958–59; articled clerk Wrigley Cregan Todd & Co 1951–56; Arthur Andersen & Co 1960–89: ptnr 1969–89, Euro banking co-ordination ptnr 1975–83, Euro fin servs co-ordinator 1984–86; chief exec Fin Servs Div Berisford International plc 1989–90; ICAEW: former memb Banking Ctee, former chm Auditing Courses Ctee, former chm Auditing and Accounting Ed Ctee; chm govrs Royal GS Guildford 1988–; FCA 1966 (ACA 1956); *Recreations* gardening, golf; *Clubs* Naval and Military, County (Guildford), NZ Golf; *Style*— John E Rule, Esq; ✉ Fairwinds, 29 Warren Rd, Guildford, Surrey GU1 2HG (☎ 01483 563828)

RULE, Margaret Helen; CBE (1983); da of Ernest Victor Martin (decd), and Mabel, *née* Collins (decd); *b* 27 Sept 1928; *m* 11 June 1949, Arther Walter Thomas Rule, s of Arthur

Walter Rule (decd); 1 s (Nicolas Mark Ulric b 1958); *Career* dir Roman Palace and Museum Fishbourne Chichester 1968–79; The Mary Rose Tst: dir of excavations and salvage 1979–83, dir of res and interpretation 1983–94; formerly chm: Cncl for Nautical Archaeology, Nautical Archaeology Tst; conslt: The Mary Rose Tst, Hamilton/Scourge Ctee Ontario Canada, Maltese Tourist Bd; memb: Govt Advsy Ctee on Historic Wrecks 1976–, Advsy Ctee on Nautical Archaeology USA, Int Advsy Bd Bermuda Underwater Exploration Inst 1995–; govr Portsmouth Univ (formerly Portsmouth Poly); Freeman City of London 1987; Hon DLitt Univ of Liverpool 1983, hon fell Portsmouth Univ 1982; FRSA 1981; *Books* Chichester Excavations (Vol 1, 1976), The Mary Rose (1982), A Gallo-Roman Trading Vessel from Guernsey, Life At Sea: Tudors and Stuarts; author of numerous pamphlets and papers in international jls; *Recreations* anything in, on or under water; *Style—* Mrs Margaret Rule, CBE; ✉ Crofton, East Bracklesham Drive, Bracklesham Bay, West Sussex PO20 8JW (☎ 01243 673502)

RUMBELOW, (Arthur) Anthony; QC (1990); *Educ* Salford GS, Queens' Coll Cambridge (Squire scholar, BA); *Career* called to the Bar Middle Temple 1967 (Harmsworth exhibitioner and Astbury scholar), recorder 1988–; chm Medical Appeal Tbnl; *Style—* Anthony Rumbelow, Esq, QC; ✉ 1 Serjeants' Inn, Fourth Floor, London EC4Y 1NH (☎ 0171 583 1355); 28 St John Street, Manchester M3 4DJ (☎ 0161 834 8418)

RUMBELOW, (Roger) Martin; s of Leonard Douglas Rumbelow (d 1980), and Phyllis Mary, *née* Perkins (d 1984); *b* 3 June 1937; *Educ* Cardiff HS, Univ of Bristol (BSc), Cranfield Inst of Technol (MSc); *m* 24 July 1965, (Marjorie) Elizabeth, da of Charles Richard Glover, of Macclesfield, Cheshire; *Career* Nat Serv RAF pilot and Flying Offr 1955–57; Concorde project mangr Br Aircraft Corp 1973–74 (tech sales 1960–67, dep prodn controller 1967–73); Dept of Trade and Industry: princ 1974–78, asst sec 1978–86, under sec Mgmnt Servs and Manpower Div 1987–92, under sec Electronics and Engrg Div 1992–96; freelance conslt and advsr 1996–; memb Royal Choral Soc; CEng, MRAeS, MInstD; *Recreations* singing, theatre, electronics, computing; *Clubs* RAF; *Style—* Martin Rumbelow, Esq; ✉ The Spinney, The Chase, Knott Park, Oxshott, Surrey KT22 0HR (☎ 01372 842144, internet rumbelow@globalnet.co.uk)

RUMBLE, Peter William; CB (1984); s of Arthur Victor Rumble, and Dorothy Emily, *née* Sadler; *b* 28 April 1929; *Educ* Harwich Co HS, Oriel Coll Oxford (MA); *m* 1953, Joyce Audrey Stephenson; 1 s, 1 da; *Career* entered HM Civil Serv 1952, HM inspr of taxes 1952, princ Miny of Housing and Local Govt 1963, under sec DOE 1977 (asst sec 1972), chief exec Historic Bldgs and Monuments Cmmn 1983–89, tstee American Friends of Eng Heritage 1988–94; memb: Cncl Architectural Heritage Fund 1988– (vice chm 1994–), Ctee S Region Nat Tst 1990–, Churches Conservation Tst (formerly Redundant Churches Fund) 1991–; dir gen Euro Union of Historic Houses Assocs 1990–93; *Recreations* music; *Style—* Peter Rumble, Esq, CB; ✉ 11 Hillside Road, Cheam, Surrey SM2 6ET (☎ 0181 643 1752)

RUMBOLD, Rt Hon Dame Angela Claire Rosemary; DBE (1992, CBE 1981), PC (1991), MP (C) Mitcham and Morden (majority 1,734); da of Prof Harry Jones (d 1986), and Frances Molly Jones (d 1990); *b* 11 Aug 1932; *Educ* Perse Sch Cambridge, Notting Hill and Ealing High Sch, King's Coll London; *m* 15 March 1958, John Marix Rumbold, s of Marix Henry Branscombe Rumbold (d 1980); 2 s (Philip b 15 Sept 1961, Matthew b 3 Dec 1966), 1 da (Polly-Ann (Mrs Postans) b 26 May 1964); *Career* PA to Sir Edward Hulton Hulton Press 1956–58, worked as an exec in husbands business 1958–61; set up BES in 1983; chm Nat Assoc for Welfare of Children in Hosp 1974–77, dep ldr Kingston upon Thames Cncl 1975–83, chm of Local Educn Authorities 1979–80; MP (C) Mitcham and Morden 1982–, PPS to Rt Hon Nicholas Ridley 1983–85, Parly under sec of state for environment 1985–86; min of state: DES 1986–90, Home Office 1990–92; a dep chm Cons Pty 1992–; co chm Women's Nat Ctee 1986–90; Freeman City of London 1988; *Recreations* reading, swimming, music, gardening, ballet; *Style—* The Rt Hon Dame Angela Rumbold, DBE, MP; ✉ House of Commons, London SW1A 0AA

RUMBOLD, Sir Henry John Sebastian; 11 Bt (GB 1779), of Wood Hall, Watton, Herts; s of Sir (Horace) Anthony Claude Rumbold, 10 Bt, KCMG, KCVO, CB (d 1983, formerly an ambass to Thailand and Austria), by his 1 w, Felicity (d 1984), da of late Lt-Col Frederick Bailey and Lady Janet, *née* Mackay (da of 1 Earl of Inchcape); *b* 24 Dec 1947; *Educ* Eton, William & Mary Coll Virginia USA; *m* 1978, Frances Ann, da of late Dr Albert Whitfield Hawkes, and formerly w of Julian Berry; *Heir* kinsman, Charles Anton Rumbold b 1959; *Career* solicitor; currently ptnr Dawson Cornwell & Co, formerly ptnr Stephenson Harwood; *Recreations* riding, shooting, reading; *Clubs* Boodles; *Style—* Sir Henry Rumbold, Bt; ✉ 19 Hollywood Rd, London SW10 9HT; Hatch House, Tisbury, Salisbury, Wilts SP3 6PA; Dawson Cornwell & Co, 16 Red Lion Square, London WC1R 4QT (☎ 0171 242 2556)

RUMBOLD, Sir Jack Seddon; kt (1984), QC (1963); s of William Alexander Rumbold, of Christchurch, NZ, and Jean Lindsay, *née* Mackay; *b* 5 March 1920; *Educ* St Andrew's Coll NZ, Univ of Canterbury NZ (LLB 1940), BNC Oxford (Rhodes scholar, BCL, Cricket blue); *m* 1, 1949, Helen Suzanne, da of Col J B Davis, of Wanganui, NZ; 2 da; m 2, 1970, Veronica Ellie, da of Gilbert Campbell Whigham, of Brookside House, Ascot, and formerly w of (Seymour Henry) Michael Le Fone Hurt; *Career* RN Lt RNVR (despatches) 1941–45; called to Bar Inner Temple 1948, private legal practice; Colonial Legal Serv Kenya 1957–62, AG Zanzibar 1963–64, legal advsr Kenya Govt 1964–66; academic dir British Campus of Stanford Univ USA 1966–1972; chm of Industl Tbnls 1967–1979, pres of Industl Tbnls England and Wales 1979–84; *Recreations* books, music, formerly cricket; *Clubs* Garrick, MCC; *Style—* Sir Jack Rumbold, QC

RUMINS, John Sandford; *b* 16 Dec 1934; *Educ* Univ of Bristol (BA); *m* 13 Sept 1960, (Margaret) Ruth; 1 s (Christopher John b 9 Sept 1965), 2 da (Philippa Ann b 31 Dec 1961, Tanya Helen b 5 July 1969); *Career* RAF 1959–62, PO 1959–61, flying offr 1961–62; CA; qualified with Tansley Witt 1959, Cooper Brothers & Co (later Coopers & Lybrand) 1962–72, head of fin and resource planning div Bank of England 1980–94 (joined 1972), ret; FCA 1959; *Recreations* tennis; *Style—* John Rumins, Esq; ✉ 3 Lyle Park, Sevenoaks, Kent TN13 3JX (☎ 01732 458389)

RUMSEY, (Raymond) Clive; s of Kenneth Walter Rumsey (d 1961), and Florence Alice, *née* Beveridge; *b* 21 March 1930; *Educ* Wimbledon Sch of Art (Nat Dip Design), RCA London (Graphic Design); *m* 4 Sept 1965, Lisa Anne, da of Patrick Vincent McGrath, of Chislehurst, Kent; 1 s (Julian St John b 17 Jan 1968); *Career* Nat Serv RCS 1949–51, NCO draughtsman Sch of Signals Catterick, HQ Southern Cmd Salisbury; Lintas Ltd London 1954–74: art dir, creative dir and head of Dept (seven yrs spent in Europe as agency creative dir); ind advertising conslt 1974–75; McCann-Erickson Advertising: joined 1975, set up Pan-Euro creative unit Euroteam, regnl creative dir (Europe, responsible for creative standards of 22 offices across Europe) 1981–87, dep mangr McCann-Erickson Paris 1987–88; conslt 1988–; *Recreations* travelling, collecting objets d'art; *Style—* Clive Rumsey, Esq; ✉ The Old Cottage, Mount Lane, Barford St Martin, Salisbury, Wilts SP3 4AF (☎ 01722 743 236)

RUMSEY, Stephen John Raymond; s of John William Raymond Rumsey, of Hampstead, and May, *née* Blemings; *b* 6 Nov 1950; *Educ* Windsor GS, LSE (BSc); *m* 3 June 1978, Anne Christine Elaine, da of Arnold Williamson (d 1988); 2 s (James b 1979, Edward b 1981); *Career* investmt mangr Postel Investmt 1977–85, ptnr de Zoete and Bevan 1985–86, chief exec (Bonds) Barclays de Zoete Wedd 1986–93, md Merrill Lynch 1993–; fndr Wetland Tst, Churchill fell 1970; cncllr Royal Borough of Kingston upon Thames 1978–82, dep chm Social Servs Ctee; memb Stock Exchange 1985; memb Cncl: RSPB, BTO; *Recreations* ornithology, agriculture, social servs; *Style—* Stephen Rumsey, Esq; ✉ Merrill Lynch, Ropemaker Place, 25 Ropemaker Street, London EC2Y 9LY (☎ 0171 867 4915, fax 0171 867 4315)

RUNCIE, Baron (Life Peer UK 1991), of Cuddesdon in the County of Oxfordshire; Rt Rev the Rt Hon Robert Alexander Kennedy Runcie; MC (1945), PC (1980); s of Robert Dalziel Runcie (d 1945), of Crosby, Merseyside, and Ann Edna, *née* Benson (d 1949); *b* 2 Oct 1921; *Educ* Merchant Taylors' Crosby, BNC Oxford (MA), Westcott House Cambridge (Dip Theol); *m* 5 Sept 1957, (Angela) Rosalind, da of J W Cecil Turner, MC (d 1968), of Cambridge; 1 s (Hon James b 1959), 1 da (Hon Rebecca (Hon Mrs Tabor) b 1961); *Career* served WWII Scots Gds, tank offr Normandy, Baltic, PA to Br Rep Italy/Yugoslavia Boundary Cmmn 1945–46; ordained 1949, curate All Saints Gosforth 1950–52, chaplain and vice princ Westcott House Cambridge 1953–56, dean Trinity Hall Cambridge 1956–60, princ Cuddesdon Theol Coll 1960–70, Bishop St Albans 1970–80; Archbishop of Canterbury 1980–91; High Steward of Cambridge Univ 1991–; Anglican chm Anglican-Orthodox Joint Doctrinal Cmmn 1973–80, Teape lectr Univ of Delhi 1962, Nobell lectr Harvard Univ 1987; Freeman City of: London, Canterbury, St Albans; Freeman: Worshipful Co of Merchant Taylors, Worshipful Co of Grocers, Worshipful Co of Butchers; Hon Bencher of Gray's Inn 1981; Hon DD: Univ of Oxford 1980, Univ of Cambridge 1981, Univ of the South Sewanee 1981, Univ of St Andrews 1989, Univ of London 1990, King's Coll Toronto 1986, New Raday Coll Budapest 1987, Univ of South Carolina 1987, Yale Univ 1989; Hon DLitt: Univ of Keele 1981, Rikkyo Univ Tokyo 1987; Hon DCL Univ of Kent 1982, Hon LittD Univ of Liverpool 1983; Royal Victorian Chain 1991, Cross of the Order of the Holy Sepulchre 1986, Order of St Vladimir Class II 1975; *Books* Cathedral and City: St Albans Ancient and Modern (ed, 1978), Windows onto God (1983), Seasons of the Spirit (1983), One Light for One World (1988), Theology, University and the Modern World (1988), Authority in Crisis? (1988), The Unity We Seek (1989); *Recreations* opera, reading history and novels, owning Berkshire pigs; *Clubs* Athenaeum, Cavalry and Guards', MCC; *Style—* The Rt Rev the Rt Hon Lord Runcie, PC, MC; ✉ 26a Jennings Road, St Albans, Herts AL1 4PD (☎ 01727 848021, fax 01727 842319)

RUNCIMAN, Hon Sir Steven (James Cochran Stevenson); CH (1984), kt (1958); 2 s of 1 Viscount Runciman of Doxford; *b* 7 July 1903; *Educ* Eton, Trinity Coll Cambridge (hon fell); *Career* historian; prof of Byzantine history Istanbul Univ 1942–45, Br Cncl rep Greece 1945–47; Wolfson Literary Award 1982; Kt Cdr Order of the Phoenix (Greece) 1961, Gold Medal of Honour City of Athens 1991, Order of the Madara Horseman 1st Class (Bulgaria); FBA, CLit 1987; *Books include* A History of the Crusades (in 3 vols), The Sicilian Vespers; *Clubs* Athenaeum; *Style—* The Hon Sir Steven Runciman, CH, FBA; ✉ Elshieshields, Lockerbie, Dumfriesshire (☎ 01387 810280)

RUNCIMAN OF DOXFORD, 3 Viscount (UK 1937); Sir Walter Garrison (Garry) Runciman; 4 Bt (UK 1906), CBE (1987); also Baron Runciman (UK 1933); s of 2 Viscount Runciman of Doxford, OBE, AFC, AE, DL (d 1989), and his 2 wife, Katharine Schuyler, *née* Garrison (d 1993); *b* 10 Nov 1934; *Educ* Eton, Trinity Coll Cambridge; *m* 17 April 1963, Ruth, OBE (1991), memb Advsy Cncl on Misuse of Drugs and chm Mental Health Act Cmmn, da of Joseph Hellman, of Johannesburg, and former w of Denis Mack Smith; 1 s (Hon David Walter), 2 da (Hon Lisa b 18 Aug 1965, Hon Catherine b 18 July 1969); *Heir* s, Hon David Walter Runciman b 1 March 1967; *Career* fell Trinity Coll Cambridge 1959–63 and 1971–; chm: Andrew Weir and Co Ltd, Runciman Investments Ltd; jt dep chm Securities and Investments Bd (memb 1986–); sociologist, former pt/t reader in sociology Univ of Sussex; treas Child Poverty Action Gp 1972–; pres Gen Cncl Br Shipping 1986–87 (vice-pres 1985–86); chm Royal Cmmn on Criminal Justice 1991–93; Liveryman Worshipful Co of Goldsmiths; FBA 1975; *Books* Plato's Later Epistemology (1962), Social Science and Political Theory (1963), Relative Deprivation and Social Justice (1966), A Critique of Max Weber's Philosophy of Social Science (1972), A Treatise on Social Theory Vol I (1983), Vol II (1989); *Clubs* Brooks's; *Style—* The Rt Hon the Viscount Runciman of Doxford, CBE; ✉ House of Lords, London SW1A 0PW

RUNGE, Charles David; s of Sir Peter Runge (d 1970), of High Wycombe, Bucks, and Hon Fiona Margaret Stewart, *née* Macpherson, da of 1 Baron Strathcarron; *b* 24 May 1944; *Educ* Eton, Christ Church Oxford (MA), Manchester Business Sch; *m* 1, 28 July 1969 (m dis 1979), Harriet, da of late John Bradshaw, of Inkpen, Berks; 1 s (Tom b 1971), 1 da (Louise b 1973); m 2, 9 April 1981, Jil, da of John Liddell (d 1987), of Greenock, Scotland; 1 da (Emma b 1986); *Career* Tate & Lyle: md tport 1977–79, chief exec refineries 1979–81, md agribusiness 1983–86, dir corporate affrs 1986–87; chief exec Milk Mktg Bd 1988–91, chief exec Royal Agric Soc of England 1992–; *Recreations* music, walking, fishing; *Clubs* Boodle's, Farmers'; *Style—* Charles Runge, Esq; ✉ The National Agricultural Centre, Stoneleigh Park, Warwickshire CV8 2LZ (☎ 01203 696969)

RUSBRIDGE, Brian John; CBE (1983); s of Arthur John Rusbridge (d 1974), of Appleton, Berks, and Leonora Rusbridge, *née* Hearn (d 1968); *b* 10 Sept 1922; *Educ* Willowfield Sch Eastbourne, Univ of Oxford (Dip Social Admin); *m* 21 July 1951, Joyce, da of Joseph Young Elliott (d 1953), of Darlington; 2 s (Michael John b 1955, Peter Graham b 1958); *Career* personnel mangr ICI Teeside 1949–63, dir industl rels BR Bd 1963–70, div mangr BR London 1970–73, sec, head of orgn and chief employers' negotiator for all local govt employers in UK LACSAB 1973–87, ed The Municipal Year Book 1987–94; chm of E Mosley Cons Assoc; dir: Assoc of Exhbn Organisers 1992–, Newman Books Ltd 1992–94; Freeman City of London 1976, memb Guild of Freeman 1977; MCIT 1964, CIPM 1975 (memb 1947), FRSA 1995; *Recreations* travel, walking, ancient civilisations, resisting developers; *Style—* Brian Rusbridge, Esq, CBE; ✉ 19 Beauchamp Road, E Mosley, Surrey KT8 0PA (☎ and fax 0181 979 4952); The Association of Exhibition Organisers, 26 Chapter Street, London SW1P 4ND (☎ 0171 932 0252, fax 0171 932 0299)

RUSBRIDGE, Prof Michael Geoffrey; s of Col Charles Edward Rusbridge, OBE (d 1996), of Taunton, Somerset, and Ethel May (Elma), *née* Ryder; *b* 3 March 1933; *Educ* Ardingly Coll, Trinity Hall Cambridge (MA, PhD); *m* Eunice Rosemary, da of Charles Gerald John Gerhardt (d 1948), of Okehampton; 1 s (Gerald b 1961), 1 da (Sheila b 1959); *Career* sr scientific offr UK Atomic Energy Authy 1957–67, prof of physics UMIST 1967–94, visiting prof of physics UMIST 1994; CPhys 1968, FInstP; *Recreations* gardening, hill walking, reading, music, nature conservation; *Style—* Prof Michael Rusbridge; ✉ UMIST, PO Box 88, Manchester M60 1QD (☎ 0161 200 3926, fax 0161 200 3941, telex 666094, e-mail m.g.rusbridge@umist.ac.uk)

RUSBRIDGER, Alan Charles; s of G H Rusbridger, of Guildford, Surrey, and Barbara, *née* Wickham (d 1995); *b* 29 Dec 1953; *Educ* Cranleigh Sch, Magdalene Coll Cambridge (MA); *m* 1982, Lindsay, da of Lord Mackie of Benshie, *qv*; *Career* reporter Cambridge Evening News 1976–79, reporter, columnist and feature writer The Guardian 1979–86, TV critic The Observer 1986–87, Washington corr London Daily News 1987, features ed The Guardian 1989–93 (feature writer and ed Weekend Guardian 1987–93), ed The Guardian 1995– (dep ed 1993–95), exec ed The Observer 1996–; commended Br Press Awards 1977 and 1978, What the Papers Say Award for Newspaper Ed of the Year 1996, winner Sysdeco Award for Nat Newspaper Ed of the Year Newspaper Focus Awards 1996; memb NUJ; *Publications* The Guardian Year (ed, 1994); *Recreations* golf, cricket, music; *Style—* Alan Rusbridger, Esq; ✉ The Guardian, 119 Farringdon Rd, London EC1R 3ER (☎ 0171 278 2332, fax 0171 239 9997)

RUSBY, Vice Adm Sir Cameron; KCB (1979), LVO (1965); s of late Capt Victor Evelyn Rusby, CBE, RN, and late Irene Margaret, *née* Gunn; *b* 20 Feb 1926; *Educ* RNC

Dartmouth; *m* 1948, Marion Bell; 2 da; *Career* Dep Supreme Allied Cdr Atlantic 1980–82, ret 1982; cmd offr HMS Ulster 1958–59, exec offr HM Yacht Britannia 1962–65, Dep Dir Naval Signals 1965–68, Cmd Offr HMS Tartar 1968–69, dep asst COS Plans and Policy on Staff of Allied C in C Southern Europe 1969–72, Sr Naval Offr West Indies 1972–74, Rear Adm 1974, Asst Chief Def Staff Ops 1974–77, Vice Adm 1977, Flag Offr Scotland and NI 1977–79; chief exec Scot Soc for the Prevention of Cruelty to Animals 1983–91 pres World Soc for the Protection of Animals 1992–94 (vice pres 1994–96), pres Scottish Cncl King George's Fund for Sailors 1988–96 (life vice pres 1996); *Style*— Sir Cameron Rusby, KCB, LVO; ✉ c/o Bank of Scotland, 70 High St, Peebles EH45 8AQ

RUSH, Michael Allen Frank; s of Colin Charles Rush (d 1968), of Richmond, Surrey, and Muriel Mary, *née* Hinds (d 1968); *b* 2 Jan 1933; *Educ* King's Coll Sch Wimbledon, King's Coll London (BSc); *m* 1, 26 July 1958 (m dis 1979), Janet Larema, da of Lt-Col David George Ogilvy Ayerst, of Burford, Oxon; 1 s (David b 1959), 2 da (Susan b 1961, Lindy b 1970); m 2, 1 Sept 1980, Linda Evelyn, da of Maurice Stratton Townsend, of High Wycombe; *Career* Flying Offr RAF 1954–56; mgmnt conslt A/C Inbucon 1961–65; W S Try Ltd: dir 1968, md 1972, chm of int subsid 1977–85, dep chm main UK subsid 1983–85; formed Michael Rush Associates mgmnt conslts 1985, project mangr Daily Mail and Evening Standard new devpt printing works 1985–93, chm Management Selection Consultants Ltd 1991–; vice chm Chiltern Soc 1995– (hon sec Rivers and Wetlands Conservation Gp 1994–95); MICE 1958, MInstD 1975, FFB 1983; *Recreations* horse riding, hunting, conservation; *Clubs* RAF; *Style*— Michael A F Rush, Esq; ✉ Kingstreet End, Little Missenden, Amersham, Bucks HP7 0RA (☎ 01494 866214, fax 01494 866864)

RUSH, Prof Michael David; s of Wilfred George Rush (d 1983), of Richmond, Surrey, and Elizabeth May Winifred, *née* Gurney (d 1985); *b* 29 Oct 1937; *Educ* Shene GS Richmond Surrey, Univ of Sheffield (BA, PhD); *m* 25 July 1964, Jean Margaret, da of George Telford (d 1987), of Golcar, Huddersfield, Yorks; 2 s (Jonathan b 1968, Anthony b 1971); *Career* Nat Serv RASC 1957–59; Univ of Exeter: asst lectr 1964–67, lectr 1967–81, sr lectr 1981–90, head Dept of Politics 1985–92, reader in Parliamentary Govt 1990–94, prof of politics 1994–; visiting lectr Univ of Western Ontario 1967–68, visiting prof Univ of Acadia Nova Scotia 1981, res fell Carleton Univ Ottawa 1975 and 1992; chm Study of Parliament Gp 1990–93; FRSA 1992; *Books* The Selection of Parliamentary Candidates (1969), The MP and his Information (jtly, 1970), An Introduction to Political Sociology (jtly, 1971), The House of Commons: Services and Facilities (co-ed, 1974), Parliamentary Government in Britain (1981), The House of Commons: Services and Facilities 1972–82 (ed, 1983), The Cabinet and Policy Formation (1984), Parliament and the Public (1976 and 1986), Parliament and Pressure Politics (ed, 1990), Politics and Society: An Introduction to Political Sociology (1992), British Government and Politics Since 1945: Changes in Perspective (co-ed, 1995); *Recreations* listening to classical music, theatre, travel; *Style*— Prof Michael Rush; ✉ 2 St Loyes Rd, Heavitree, Exeter, Devon EX2 5HA (☎ 01392 54089); Department of Politics, University of Exeter, Exeter, Devon EX4 4RJ (☎ 01392 263164)

RUSHDIE, (Ahmed) Salman; s of Anis Ahmed Rushdie (d 1987), and Negin, *née* Butt; *b* 19 June 1947, (Bombay); *Educ* Rugby, King's Coll Cambridge; *m* 1, 1976 (m dis 1987), Clarissa Luard; 1 s; m 2, 1988 (m dis 1993), Marianne Wiggins; *Career* writer; former advertising copywriter; memb: Gen Cncl Camden Ctee for Community Relations 1975–82, Int PEN 1981–, Cncl ICA 1985–, Production Bd BFI 1986–; FRSL 1983; *Books* Grimus (1975), Midnight's Children (1981, Booker Prize, James Tait Black Meml Prize, E-SU Literary Award), Shame (1983, Prix du Meilleur Livre Etranger 1984), The Jaguar Smile: a Nicaraguan Journey (1987), The Satanic Verses (1988, Whitbread Award), Hauroun and the Sea of Stories (1990), Imaginary Homelands (essays, 1991), East, West (1994), The Moor's Last Sigh 1995 (Whitbread Fiction Award 1996, Book of the Year Br Book Awards 1996); *Television films* The Painter and the Pest 1985, The Riddle of Midnight 1988; *Style*— Salman Rushdie, Esq; ✉ Wylie Agency, 36 Parkside, 52 Knightsbridge, London SW1X 7JP (☎ 0171 235 6394)

RUSHFORD, Antony Redfern; CMG (1963); s of Stanley Rushford (d 1952), of New Milton, Hants, and Sarah Beatrice, *née* Gould (d 1979); *b* 9 Feb 1922; *Educ* Taunton Sch, Trinity Coll Cambridge (MA, LLM); *m* 1975, June Jeffery Wells, wid of Roy Eustace Wells (d 1970); 1 step s (Simon), 1 step da (Samantha); *Career* RAFVR (Sqdn Ldr 1946): Active Serv 1943–47, Reserve 1947–59; admitted slr 1944, called to the Bar Inner Temple 1983; asst slr EW Marshall Harvey & Dalton 1948, Home Civil Service Colonial Office 1949–68, joined HM Dip Serv Cwlth Office (later FCO) 1968, ret as dep legal advsr (asst under sec of state) 1982; crown counsel Uganda 1954–63, princ legal advsr Br Indian Ocean Territory 1983, attorney-gen Anguilla and St Helena 1983, legal advsr for Cwlth Sec-Gen to Govr-Gen of Granada, memb Interim Govt, attorney-gen and JP Grenada 1983, legal advsr for Cwlth Sec-Gen St Kitts' and Nevis' independence 1982–83, conslt E Caribbean Cts 1983, conslt maritime legislation for Jamaica Int Maritime Orgn 1983 and 1984, special legal advsr Govt of St Lucia 1982–; sec then pres IDB Inc 1985–86; has drafted many constitutions for UK dependencies and Cwlth countries attaining independence, presented paper on constitutional devpt to meeting of law offrs from smaller Cwlth jurisdictions IOM 1983; UK del and advsr at many constitutional conferences and discussions; CO rep Inst of Advanced Legal Studies, lectr Overseas Legal Offrs Course, memb Editorial Bd Inst of Int Law and Econ Devpt Washington 1977–82, dir of studies Royal Inst of Public Admin 1982–86; fndn memb Exec Cncl Royal Cwlth Soc for the Blind 1969–81 and 1983– (hon legal cnsllr 1984–); memb: Glyndebourne Festival 1950–96, Saudi-Br Soc, Anglo-Arab Assoc, Cwlth Lawyers' Assoc, Cwlth Assoc of Legislative Counsel; govr Taunton Sch 1948, hon legal cnsllr Order of St John 1978–93 (memb Chapter-Gen 1983–94); CStJ; FRSA; *Clubs* Cwlth Tst; *Style*— Antony Rushford, Esq, CMG; ✉ 46 Lower Sloane Street, London SW1W 8BP (☎ 0171 730 4714)

RUSHMAN, Dr Geoffrey Boswall; s of William John Rushman (d 1967), of Northampton, and Violet Helen Elizabeth, *née* Richards; *b* 20 Aug 1939; *Educ* Northampton GS, Univ of London, St Bartholomew's Hosp (MB BS); *m* 12 Oct 1963, Gillian Mary, da of George Leslie Rogers, of Alcester, Warks; 3 da (Alison b 1965, Ruth b 1967, Jacqueline b 1969); *Career* jr anaesthetist St Bartholomew's Hosp 1968–73, conslt anaesthetist Southend Hosp 1974–; Assoc of Anaesthetists prize for contribs to anaesthesia; examiner final FRCA Royal Coll of Anaesthetists 1994– (part I 1991–94) and Coll assessor 1993–; memb Cncl Anaesthetics Section RSM 1985–88 and 1991– (sr sec 1992–93), lay reader Chelmsford Diocese; FFARCS 1970; *Books* Synopsis of Anaesthesia (ed 8–10, 1977, 1982, 1987), Lee's Synopsis of Anaesthesia (11th edn, 1993), MCQ Self Test Companion (1994), A Short History of Anaesthesia (1996), Short Answer Questions in Anaesthesia (1997); *Recreations* skiing, preaching The Gospel, mountain marathons; *Clubs* RSM; *Style*— Dr Geoffrey Rushman; ✉ Department of Anaesthesia, Southend Hospital, Prittlewell Chase, Southend-on-Sea, Essex SSO ORY (☎ 01702 435555 ext 2319)

RUSHMAN, Nigel John; s of Maj Frederick William Edward Henry Rushman, of Lancs, and Irene Vera, *née* Beer; *b* 25 May 1956; *Educ* Gillingham Tech HS, Gravesend GS, Thanet Tech Coll; *m* 1, 21 Sept 1980 (m dis), Deborah Sally, da of Kenneth William White, of London; 1 da (Louise Amanda b 1986); m 2, 28 July 1989, Nicola Susan, da of David Polding, of Cobham, Surrey; 1 da (Sophie b 1995); *Career* md Rushman Lloyd International Ltd; *Recreations* game fishing, skiing, sailing; *Clubs* East India; *Style*— Nigel Rushman, Esq; ✉ Rushman Lloyd International Ltd, 26 Hays Mews, London W1X 7RL (☎ 0171 629 0424, fax 0171 629 1942)

RUSHMAN, Dr Richard William; s of William John Rushman, of Northampton, and Violet Helen Elizabeth, *née* Richards; *b* 29 April 1937; *Educ* Northampton GS, Univ Coll Oxford (open scholar, BA, MA), Univ Coll Hosp Med Sch (Filleter exhibitioner, John Marshall fell, BM BCh, Gold medal in surgery); *m* Ingrid, da of Jan Lubach, of Leiden, Holland; 2 s (Nicholas Richard, Christopher John), 1 da (Helen Ingrid); *Career* conslt orthopaedic surgn Royal Free Hosp London 1974–; hon sec Br Cncl Int Coll of Surgrns 1980–89; FRCS, FRCSEd; *Recreations* skiing, hill walking; *Style*— Dr Richard Rushman; ✉ 47 Hillway, Highgate, London N6 6AH (☎ 0181 348 2480); 72 Harley St, London W1N 1AE (☎ 0171 636 6521, fax 0171 436 2642); Royal Free Hospital, Pond St, Hampstead, London NW3 2QG (☎ 0171 794 0500)

RUSHMORE, Brigadier Frederick Herbert Margetson; CBE (1962, OBE 1956, MBE 1951); s of Frederick Margetson Rushmore, master of St Catharine's Coll Cambridge (d 1933), and Millicent Sarah, *née* Beck (d 1965); *b* 19 May 1915; *Educ* King's Sch Bruton, Christ's Coll Cambridge (BA); *Career* served RA 1935–70 (Burma 1943–44, Korea 1952–53), Brig; dir Nat Assoc of Leagues of Hospital Friends 1970–80, chm General Cmmrs for Income Tax (Holborn Div) 1979–90; *Recreations* music, drama; *Clubs* London Rowing, Leander; *Style*— Brig Frederick Rushmore, CBE; ✉ 71 Lakeside House, Eaton Drive, Kingston upon Thames, Surrey KT2 7RA (☎ 0181 549 1877)

RUSHTON, Prof David Nigel; s of Dr Roland Rushton, of Bromley, and Pamela Anne, *née* Galzini; *b* 21 Dec 1944; *Educ* King's Sch Canterbury, Trinity Coll Cambridge (BA), King's Coll Hosp Med Sch (MB BChir), Univ of Cambridge (MD); *m* 30 March 1968, Anne, da of Leo Gallagher (d 1967), of Liverpool; 2 da (Nicola b 1970, Susannah b 1976), 1 s (Samuel b 1982); *Career* clinical scientific staff MRC Neurological Prostheses Unit 1971–, reader Dept of Neurology Inst of Psychiatry 1990–92, prof of rehabilitation Univ of London (London Hosp Med Coll) 1993–; hon conslt Maudsley Hosp 1979–92, hon conslt neurologist King's Coll Hosp 1984–92; contrib scientific articles on neurology and neurological prostheses; memb: Assoc of Br Neurologists, Physiological Soc, Br Soc for Rehabilitation Med; Freeman Worshipful Co of Spectacle Makers 1979; FRCP 1989; *Books* Treatment in Clinical Medicine - neurological disorders, Handbook of Neuro-Urology, Neurological Prostheses; *Recreations* medieval house reconstruction, steam road vehicles; *Style*— Prof David Rushton

RUSHTON, Ian Lawton; *b* 8 Sept 1931; *Educ* Rock Ferry HS Birkenhead, King's Coll London (BSc); *m* 1, Julia, *née* Frankland (decd); 1 da (Jane b 1960); m 2, 1986, Anita, *née* Stevens; *Career* Mil Serv Flt Lt RAF 1953–56; Royal Insurance: joined 1956, dep gen mangr UK 1972, exec vice pres Royal USA NY 1980, md Royal Insurance (UK) Ltd 1983, dir and gen mangr Royal Insurance plc 1986, vice chm Royal Insurance Holdings plc 1991–93 (dep gp chief exec 1988, gp chief exec 1989–91), dir Aachener und Münchener Beteiligungs AG (Germany) and Mutual & Federal Insurance Co Ltd (S Africa) 1989–93; chm: Fire Protection Assoc 1983–87, Assoc of Br Insurers 1991–93; vice pres Inst of Actuaries 1986–89; chm Hackney Empire Theatre 1995–; memb: Cncl Assoc for Business Sponsorship of the Arts, Ct of Govrs RSC; Freeman: City of London, Worshipful Co of Actuaries, Worshipful Co of Insurers; FIA, FCII, FSS; *Style*— Ian L Rushton, Esq; ✉ 136 Whitehall Court, London SW1A 2EL

RUSHTON, James Edward; s of Edward Sydney Rushton (d 1983), of Wilmslow, Cheshire, and Stella Kathleen Joan Rushton; *b* 8 Aug 1936; *Educ* Repton; *m* 1, 6 June 1963, Fiona Patricia, da of George Stirling Tuite; 2 da (Emma b 1963, Sophie b 1965); m 2, 26 May 1972, Angela Christine, da of Harry Coupe Wrather; 1 s (Daniel b 1973); m 3, 24 June 1983, Marjorie Evelyn, da of James Eric Pickering (d 1958); *Career* chartered surveyor; ptnr Edward Rushton Son & Kenyon 1963 (sr ptnr 1978–); chm Gen Practice Div Educn Ctee 1980–83 (chm Gtr Manchester Branch 1987–88); MRICS Gen Practice Divnl Cncl 1976–84; memb Ctee Greater Manchester Branch IOD; *Recreations* golf, travel, photography; *Style*— James E Rushton, Esq; ✉ Legh House, Wilmslow Road, Mottram St Andrew, Macclesfield, Cheshire (☎ 01625 828901); Edward Rushton Son & Kenyon, 1 St Ann Street, Manchester M2 7LG

RUSHTON, Kenneth John; s of Dr Martin Rushton, of Whitburn, and Halina, *née* Schoenfeld; *b* 6 Oct 1944; *Educ* Uppingham, Trinity Coll Dublin (MA); *m* 2 Sept 1970, Lesley Christine, da of Michael Jackson; 2 s (Patrick b 20 July 1973, Christopher b 13 March 1982), 1 da (Jane b 13 Feb 1976); *Career* ICI: joined 1968, various secretarial appts, Henley Gen Mgmnt Course 1980, asst co sec 1988–96, co sec 1996–; chm Westminster Enterprise Agency, dep chm Business Link London Central, exec memb Business in the Arts; FRSA; *Recreations* theatre, music, opera, skiing, tennis; *Clubs* Royal Society of Arts, Institute of Directors; *Style*— Kenneth Rushton, Esq; ✉ Company Secretary, Imperial Chemical Industries plc, Group Headquarters, No 9 Millbank, London SW1P 3JF (☎ 0171 798 5344, fax 0171 798 5887)

RUSHTON, Dr Neil; s of John Allen Rushton, of Bridlington, Yorks, and Iris, *née* Street (d 1987); *b* 16 Dec 1945; *Educ* Oglethorpe Sch Tadcaster, The Middx Hosp London (MB BS), Univ of Cambridge (MD); *m* 12 June 1971, Sheila Margaret, da of Capt Geoffrey Greville Johnson, of Southwold, Suffolk; 2 s (Mark b 25 Sept 1973, Timothy b 24 Jan 1980), 1 da (Nicola b 15 Aug 1975); *Career* Univ of Cambridge: dir Orthopaedic Res Unit 1983–, fell Magdalene Coll 1984–; hon orthopaedic conslt Addenbrooke's Hosp; Hunterian prof RCS; examiner Univs of Cambridge, Oxford and London; memb Cncl: Br Orthopaedic Assoc (dep ed for Research Jl of Bone & Joint Surgery (B) 1966), Orthopaedic Section RSM; exec memb Euro Orthopaedic Research Soc, fndr memb Br Hip Soc, fell Br Orthopaedic Research Soc, FRSM, FRCS; Hon MA Univ of Cambridge 1979; *Books* Colour Atlas of Surgical Exposures of the Limbs (1985), Orthopaedics - The Principles and Practice of Musculoskeletal Surgery (1987), Body Clock (contrib); *Recreations* dinghy sailing, snow skiing, wines, local radio; *Clubs* RSM, SCGB; *Style*— Dr Neil Rushton; ✉ 37 Bentley Road, Cambridge CB2 2AW (☎ 01223 353624, fax 01223 356889); Orthopaedic Research Unit, University of Cambridge, Box 180, Addenbrooke's Hospital, Cambridge CB2 2QQ (☎ 01223 217551, fax 01223 214094)

RUSSELL, *see:* Hamilton-Russell

RUSSELL, Alec Charles Cumine; s of James Cecil Cumine Russell of Aden, CBE, *qv*, and Diana Margaret, *née* White; *b* 21 Oct 1966; *Educ* Winchester, New Coll Oxford (BA); *Career* Daily Telegraph: Bucharest corr Jan-Dec 1990 (Turkey during Gulf War and Kurdish crisis), Yugoslav War corr 1991–92, SE Europe staff corr (based Bucharest) 1992–93, South Africa corr (based Johannesburg) 1993–; highly commended: Young Journalist of the Year Award 1990, David Blundie Freelance Corr Award 1991; *Style*— Alec Russell, Esq; ✉ The Daily Telegraph, 1 Canada Square, Canary Wharf, London E14 5DT (☎ 0171 538 5000)

RUSSELL, Alexander William; CB; s of William Russell (d 1992), and Elizabeth Wallace Bennett, *née* Russell (d 1992); *b* 16 Oct 1938; *Educ* Royal HS Edinburgh, Univ of Edinburgh (MA), Manitoba Univ (MA); *m* Nov 1962, Elspeth Rae, *née* Robertson; *Career* Scottish Office: asst princ Scottish Devpt Dept 1961–64, private sec to Parly Under Sec of State 1964–65, princ Regnl Devpt Div and Scottish Devpt Dept 1965–72, princ private sec to Sec of State for Scotland 1972–73, Scottish Devpt Dept 1973–76, asst sec Civil Serv Dept 1976–79, under sec Mgmnt and Personnel Office 1979–82, head Treasury MPO Financial Mgmnt Unit 1982–85; HM Customs and Excise: dir of orgn 1985–90, dir customs 1990–93, dep chm 1993–; *Style*— Alexander Russell, Esq, CB; ✉ HM Customs and Excise, New King's Beam House, 22 Upper Ground, London SE1 9PJ (☎ 0171 865 5011, fax 0171 865 5048)

RUSSELL, Andrew Neville; s of Herbert Mark Russell, of Cuckfield, West Sussex, and Phyllis Mary, *née* Slade (d 1989); *b* 30 Oct 1940; *Educ* Highgate Sch; *m* 1964, Audrey Helen Roe; 1 da (Philippa Clare b 1968); *Career* articled clerk Neville Russell 1957–62, accountant Coopers & Lybrand 1963–66, ptnr Caldwell & Braham 1967–73, sr ptnr Neville Russell Brighton 1974–, exec ptnr Neville Russell (UK Partnership) 1982–; treas: Keep Sunday Special Campaign 1982–96, Brighton Int Festival 1988–92 and 1994–; dir: Primavera Chamber Orch 1991–, Brighton and Hove Philharmonic Soc 1993–, Gardner Arts Centre 1994–; Liveryman Worshipful Co of Coachmakers and Coach Harness Makers 1972; FCA 1963; *Recreations* skiing, golf, walking, music, visual arts; *Clubs* The National; *Style*— Andrew N Russell, Esq; ✉ Flat 2, 18 Lewes Crescent, Brighton, E Sussex BN2 1GB (☎ 01273 685459); Neville Russell, 37 Frederick Place, Brighton, East Sussex BN1 4EA (☎ 01273 206788, fax 01273 820901)

RUSSELL, Rt Rev Anthony John; *see:* Dorchester, Bishop of

RUSSELL, Anthony Patrick; s of Dr Michael Hibberd Russell (d 1987), of Little Sutton, S Wirral, and Pamela, *née* Eyre; *b* 11 April 1951; *Educ* The King's Sch Chester, Pembroke Coll Oxford (BA, MA); *Career* called to the Bar Middle Temple 1974, junior Northern Circuit 1977, recorder 1993–96 (asst recorder 1989–93), standing counsel (Criminal) to the Inland Revenue 1994–96; sec Manchester Middle Temple Soc 1986–, memb Bar Cncl 1988–94; memb Cncl Guild of Church Musicians 1985–93 and 1995–; *Recreations* singing, listening to music, video photography, walking in the Peak District; *Clubs* United Oxford and Cambridge Univ; *Style*— Anthony Russell, Esq; ✉ Peel Court Chambers, 45 Hardman Street, Manchester M3 3HA (☎ 0161 832 3791, fax 0161 835 3054)

RUSSELL, Sir Arthur Mervyn; 8 Bt (UK 1812), of Swallowfield, Berkshire; s of Sir Arthur Edward Ian Montagu Russell, 6 Bt (d 1964); suc his, half-bro, Sir George Michael Russell, 7 Bt 1993; *b* 7 Feb 1923; *m* 1, 18 April 1945 (m dis), Ruth, da of Charles George Holloway; 1 s (Stephen Charles b 12 Jan 1949); m 2, 18 Feb 1956, Kathleen Joyce Searle; 1 s (Ian Mervyn b 8 Dec 1957); *Heir* s, Stephen Charles Russell b 12 Jan 1949; *Style*— Sir Arthur Russell, Bt

RUSSELL, Charles Dominic; s and h of Sir Charles Russell, 3 Bt, *qv*; *b* 28 May 1956; *Educ* Worth Abbey Sch; *m* 24 May 1986, Sarah Jane Murray, da of Anthony Chandor, of Blackdown Border, Haslemere, Surrey; 1 s (Charles William b 8 Sept 1988); *Career* antiquarian book dealer; *Style*— Charles Russell, Esq; ✉ Stratton End, Cirencester, Glos

RUSSELL, Sir Charles Ian; 3 Bt (UK 1916), of Littleworth Corner, Burnham, Co Buckingham; s of Capt Sir Alec Charles Russell, MC, 2 Bt (d 1938); *b* 13 March 1918; *Educ* Beaumont Coll, Univ Coll Oxford; *m* 18 Jan 1947, Rosemary (d 1996), da of late Maj Sir John Theodore Prestige, of Bourne Park, Bishopsbourne, Canterbury; 1 s, 1 da; *Heir* s, Charles Dominic Russell b 28 May 1956; *Career* served WWII Capt RHA (despatches); admitted slr 1947, former sr partner Charles Russell & Co of Hale Court Lincoln's Inn London; *Clubs* Garrick, Army and Navy, Royal St George; *Style*— Sir Charles Russell, Bt; ✉ 22 Mullings Court, Cirencester, Glos GL7 2AW

RUSSELL, Christopher Garnet; s of George Percival Jewett (d 1948), of Boscombe, Hants, and Marjorie Alice Boddam-Whetham, *née* Keeling-Bloxam; *b* 6 April 1943; *Educ* Westminster, New Coll Oxford (MA); *m* 23 June 1973, Agatha Mary, da of Stephen Joseph Culkin (d 1984); 1 s (Charles b 1976), 2 da (Claire b 1974, Lucy b 1975); *Career* called to the Bar Middle Temple 1971, ad eundum Lincoln's Inn 1985; *Style*— Christopher Russell, Esq; ✉ 11 Church St, Marcham, Oxon (☎ 01865 391553); 86 Paramount Ct, University St, London WC1 (☎ 0171 383 5943); Penhayle, New Polzeath, Cornwall (☎ 01208 862041); Framfield Place, Framfield, East Sussex (☎ 01825 890021); 12 New Square, Lincoln's Inn, London WC2 (☎ 0171 405 3808, fax 0171 831 7376)

RUSSELL, 5 Earl (UK 1861); Conrad Sebastian Robert Russell; also Viscount Amberley (UK 1861); s of 3 Earl Russell, OM, FRS (d 1970, otherwise Bertrand Russell, the philosopher, writer and savant; ggs of Lord John Russell, of Great Reform Bill fame and twice PM, 3 s of 6 Duke of Bedford and later 1 Earl Russell), by his 3 w, Patricia Helen, *née* Spence; suc half-bro, 4 Earl (d 1987); *b* 15 April 1937; *Educ* Eton, Merton Coll Oxford (BA, MA); *m* 11 Aug 1962, Elizabeth Franklyn, da of Horace Sanders, of Chippenham, Wilts; 2 s (Nicholas Lyulph, Viscount Amberley b 1968, Hon John Francis b 1971); *Heir* s, Nicholas, Viscount Amberley b 1968; *Career* lectr in history Bedford Coll London 1960–74 (reader 1974–79); prof of history Yale Univ USA 1979–84, Astor prof of British history UCL 1984–90, prof of history King's Coll London 1990–, Sir Henry Savile research prof Merton Coll Oxford 1994–95; memb Cncl Royal Historical Soc 1985 (vice pres 1989); Lib Dem spokesman on social security in the House of Lords, vice pres Lib Dem Youth and Students; Hon MA Yale 1979; FBA; *Books* The Crisis of Parliaments: English History 1509–1660 (1971), The Origins of the English Civil War (ed, 1973), Parliaments and English Politics 1621–1629 (1979), The Causes of the English Civil War (Ford Lectures in the University of Oxford 1987–88) (1990), Unrevolutionary England 1603–1642 (1990), The Fall of the British Monarchies 1637–1642 (1991), Academic Freedom (1993); *Style*— The Rt Hon the Earl Russell; ✉ Department of History, King's College, Strand, London WC2 (☎ 0171 836 5454)

RUSSELL, Hon David Whitney Erskine; s and h of 4 Baron Ampthill and his 1 w, Susan Mary, da of Hon Charles Winn (s of 2 Baron St Oswald, JP, DL); *b* 27 May 1947; *Educ* Stowe; *m* 15 Nov 1980, April McKenzie, yst da of Paul Arbon, of New York; 2 da (Christabel b 1981, Daisy b 1983); *Clubs* Turf, White's; *Style*— The Hon David Russell; ✉ Sackville College, East Grinstead, West Sussex

RUSSELL, Prof Donald Andrew Frank Moore; s of Samuel Charles Russell (d 1979), and Laura, *née* Moore (d 1966); *b* 13 Oct 1920; *Educ* King's Coll Sch Wimbledon, Balliol Coll Oxford (BA, MA, DLitt); *m* 22 July 1967, Joycelyne Gledhill Dickinson (Joy) (d 1993), da of Percy Parkin Dickinson (d 1972); *Career* served WWII: Royal Signals 1941–43, Intelligence Corps 1943–45; St John's Coll Oxford: fell 1948–88, univ lectr in classical languages and lit 1952–78, reader in classical lit 1978–85, prof of classical lit 1985–88; J H Gray Lectures Univ of Cambridge 1981; Paddison visiting prof: Univ of N Carolina 1985, Stanford Univ 1989–91; emeritus fell St John's Coll Oxford 1988–; FBA 1971; *Books* Longinus On the Sublime (1964), Plutarch (1972), Ancient Literary Criticism (with M Winterbottom, 1972), Criticism in Antiquity (1981), Menander Rhetor (with N G Wilson, 1981), Greek Declamation (1983), Anthology of Latin Prose (1990), Anthology of Greek Prose (1991), Dio Chrysostom, Orations 7, 12, 36 (1992), Plutarch: Selected Essays and Dialogues (1993), Libanius: Imaginary Speeches (1996); *Style*— Prof Donald Russell, FBA; ✉ 35 Belsyre Court, Oxford OX2 6HU (☎ 01865 556135); St John's Coll, Oxford OX1 3JP

RUSSELL, Edwin John Cumming; s of Edwin Russell (d 1962), and Mary Elizabeth, *née* Cumming (d 1969); *b* 4 May 1939; *Educ* Brighton GS, Brighton Sch of Art, Royal Acad Schs (Cert RAS); *m* 7 Nov 1964, Lorne, da of Lt Cdr J A H McKean, RN (d 1981); 2 da (Rebecca b 21 Jan 1966, Tanya b 25 April 1968); *Career* sculptor; Gold Medal for Sculpture RA, Sir Otto Beit Medal 1991; FRBS 1970; *Works* sculptures incl: Crucifix St Paul's Cathedral 1964, St Catherine Westminster Abbey 1966, Bishop Bubwith W Front Wells Cathedral, forecourt sculpture Rank Xerox Int HQ 1989; shopping centre sculptures: Mad Hatters Tea Party Warrington 1984, Lion and Lamb Farnham 1987 (Best Shopping Centre Award); public works: Suffragette Meml London 1968, First Govr of Bahamas Sheraton Hotel Nassau 1968, Alice and the White Rabbit Guildford (Lewis Carroll commemorative sculpture) 1984, Panda World Wide Fund Int HQ 1988; sundials incl: Jubilee Dolphin dial Nat Maritime Museum Greenwich 1978, sundial Sultan Qaboos Univ Oman 1986, Botanical Armillary sundial Kew Gardens 1987, History of London sundial Tower Hill Underground 1992; *Private Collections* incl: Goodwood House, Arup Assocs, Trafalgar House plc, Cementation Int, John Mowlem & Co, City of London GS; *Recreations* sculpture, mowing the lawn with a tractor; *Style*— Edwin Russell, Esq; ✉ Lethendry, Polecat Valley, Hindhead, Surrey GU26 6BE (☎ 01428 605655)

RUSSELL, Erica Rae; da of Innes Russell, of London, and Joan Rita, *née* Clare; *b* 14 June 1951; *Educ* Secdy Sch Johannesburg S Africa; *Partner* Adam Parker-Rhodes; 2 da (Ruby Russell b 2 Jan 1980, Bronwen Rhodes b 18 May 1982); *Career* freelance animator and film dir; worked in Art Dept Berman's Costumiers 1970, freelance model and prop maker 1972–74, painter and tracer at Richard Williams Studios, then asst to Art Babbit 1975; asst: animator Pink Floyd concert piece 1977, to Paul Vester Speedy Cartoons (film Sunbeam) 1978–80; animator and designer pop promotions and commercials Cucumber Studios 1983–85, fndr Eyeworks animation and design studio (dir Virgin Megastore commercial shown in BFI's Animation Syncopation and on BBC 2's Arts Review), made Feet of Song (winner BFI's Mari Kuttner award for Best Br Animated Film '89, shown at film festivals worldwide incl Modern Art Museum NY and Tate Gallery), guest artist Women Artists of the 20th Century exhibition Wiesbaden 1990, lectr The Museum of the Moving Image and Nat Film Sch; memb ACTT, ASIFA; *Style*— Ms Erica Russell; ✉ 5 Muswell Hill Rd, London N10 3JB (☎ 0181 883 9689)

RUSSELL, Lord Francis Hastings; s (by 2 m) of 13 Duke of Bedford, of Les Ligures, Monte Carlo, and Lydia, Duchess of Bedford, *née* Yarde-Buller; *b* 27 Feb 1950; *Educ* Eton; *m* 1, 1971 (m dis); 1 da (Czarina b 1976); m 2, 1996, Sarah Clemence; *Career* chartered surveyor 1979, md and chm LFR & Co Ltd; ARICS, ASVA (Assoc of Incorporated Soc of Valuers and Auctioneers); *Recreations* skiing, golf; *Style*— The Lord Francis Russell; ✉ 26A Cadogan Square, London SW1X 0JP (☎ 0171 225 3344)

RUSSELL, Sir George; kt (1992), CBE (1985); s of William Henry Russell (d 1972), of Gateshead, Co Durham, and Frances Annie, *née* Atkinson (d 1973); *b* 25 Oct 1935; *Educ* Gateshead GS, Univ of Durham (BA); *m* 19 Dec 1959, Dorothy, da of Ernest Victor Brown (d 1969), of Gateshead, Co Durham; 3 da (Erica Frances b 1963, Livia Jane b 1966, Alison Victoria b 1969); *Career* successively graduate trainee, commercial res offr, sales rep then product manager ICI 1958–67; vice pres and gen mangr: Welland Chemical Co of Canada 1968, St Clair Chemical Co Ltd 1968; dir Luxfer Holdings Ltd 1976; md: Alcan Aluminium (UK) 1977–81, Alcan UK Ltd 1981–82 (asst md 1977–81); md and chief exec British Alcan Aluminium 1982–86; dir: Alcan Aluminiumwerke GmbH Frankfurt 1982–86, Alcan Aluminium Ltd 1987–; chm: Marley plc 1989– (chief exec 1986–89), ITN Ltd 1988–89, 3i Group plc 1993–, Northern Development Company 1994–, Camelot Group plc 1995–; dep chm Channel 4 Television Co Ltd 1987–88; dir: Northern Rock Building Society 1985–, Basys International Ltd 1987–88, Taylor Woodrow plc 1992–; visiting prof Univ of Newcastle upon Tyne 1978–; chm: IBA 1989–90 (memb 1979–86), ITC 1991–96; memb: Bd Northern Sinfonia Orchestra 1977–80, Northern Industl Bd 1977–80, Washington Corp 1978–80, Bd Civil Serv Pay Res Unit 1980–81, Megaw Inquiry into Civil Serv Pay 1981–82, CBI 1984–85, Widdicombe Ctee of Inquiry into Conduct of Local Authy Business 1985–86; tstee: Beamish Museum Tst 1985–89, Thomas Bewick Birthplace Tst 1986–89; Hon DEng Newcastle upon Tyne 1985, Hon DBA Univ of Northumbria 1992, Hon LLD Univ of Sunderland 1995; Hon FRIBA, Hon FRTS; fell Inst of Industl Mangrs; CIMgt, FRSA, FInstD; *Recreations* tennis, badminton, bird watching; *Style*— Sir George Russell, CBE; ✉ 46 Downshire Hill, Hampstead, London NW3 1NX; 3i Group plc, 91 Waterloo Road, London SE1 8XP (☎ 0171 928 3131, fax 0171 401 9057)

RUSSELL, Prof Gerald Francis Morris; s of Maj Daniel George Russell, MC (d 1958), of Ventnor, IOW, and Berthe Marie Mathilde Ghislaine, *née* De Boe (d 1981); *b* 12 Jan 1928; *Educ* George Watson's Coll Edinburgh, Univ of Edinburgh (MB ChB, MD); *m* 8 Sept 1950, Margaret Euphemia, da of John Taylor (d 1956), of Edinburgh; 3 s (Malcolm b 1951, Nigel b 1956, Graham b 1957); *Career* Capt RAMC 1951–53, regtl med offr Queen's Bays; dean Inst of Psychiatry Univ of London 1966–70, prof of psychiatry Royal Free Hosp Sch of Med Univ of London 1971–79, hon conslt psychiatrist Royal Free Hosp and Friern Hosp 1971–79, prof of psychiatry Inst of Psychiatry Univ of London 1979–93, hon conslt psychiatrist Bethlem Royal and Maudsley Hosp 1979–93; dir Eating Disorders Unit Hayes Grove Priory Hosp 1993–; chm Section on Eating Disorders World Psychiatric Assoc 1989–, chm Assoc of Univ Teachers of Psychiatry 1990–94; FRCP, FRCPEd, Hon FRCPsych; *Books* The Neuroses and Personality Disorders, vol 4 of The Handbook of Psychiatry (jtly, 1983), Scientific and Clinical Articles on Eating Disorders; *Recreations* art galleries, photography, music; *Style*— Prof Gerald Russell; ✉ Hayes Grove Priory Hospital, Prestons Road, Hayes, Kent BR2 7AS (☎ 0181 462 7722, fax 0181 462 5028)

RUSSELL, Prof Ian John; s of Phillip William George Russell (d 1975), of Chestfield, Kent, and Joan Lilian, *née* Snook (d 1984); *b* 19 June 1943; *Educ* Chatham Tech Sch for Boys, Queen Mary Coll Univ of London (BSc), Univ of British Columbia (NATO studentship, MSc), Univ of Cambridge (Trinity Hall research studentship, PhD); *m* 20 July 1968, Janice Marion, da of Gladstone Herbert Hall; 1 s (Simon Alexander b 14 Sept 1975), 1 da (Charlotte Louise b 3 Jan 1979); *Career* res fell Magdalene Coll Cambridge 1969–73, SRC res fell Univ of Cambridge 1969–71, Royal Soc res fell King Gustaf V Res Inst Stockholm 1970–71; Univ of Sussex: lectr in neurobiology 1971–79, MRC sr res fell 1979–81, reader 1979–87, prof of neurobiology 1987–; memb: Physiological Soc 1972, Soc of Experimental Biology 1966–1990, Assoc for Res in Otolaryngology 1993–; FRS 1989; *Recreations* hockey, windsurfing, gardening, walking, music, reading and especially my family; *Style*— Prof Ian Russell, FRS; ✉ Martins, Cuilfail, Lewes, East Sussex BN7 2BE (☎ 01273 472351); School of Biological Sciences, University of Sussex, Falmer, Brighton BN1 9QG (☎ 01273 678632, fax 01273 678433, e-mail i.j.Russell@sussex.ac.uk)

RUSSELL, Ven (Harold) Ian Lyle; s of Percy Harold Russell (d 1963), and Emma Rebecca, *née* Jamieson (d 1975); *b* 17 Oct 1934; *Educ* Epsom Coll, London Coll of Divinity (ALCD, BD); *m* 18 Nov 1961, Barbara Lillian, da of Harold Hardman Dixon (d 1968); 2 s (Christopher Ian b 22 Oct 1968, Jonathan Paul b 23 Jan 1973), 1 da (Elizabeth Barbara b 9 Feb 1966); *Career* cmmnd RAF Regt 1953, served Malaya 1954–56; ordained: deacon 1960, priest 1961; curate Iver Bucks 1960–63, priest in charge St Luke's Lodge Moor Sheffield 1963–67, vicar St John Chapeltown Sheffield 1967–75, rural dean Tankersley 1973–75, vicar St Jude's Mapperley Nottingham 1975–89, area dean Nottingham Central Deanery 1986–89, hon canon Southwell Minster 1988–89, archdeacon of Coventry 1989–; memb Gen Synod C of E 1970–75 and 1985–; *Recreations* walking, gardening, photography, sport; *Clubs* RAF; *Style*— The Ven the Archdeacon of Coventry; ✉ 9 Armorial Road, Stivichall, Coventry CV3 6GH (☎ 01203 417750)

RUSSELL, Ian Simon MacGregor; s of James MacGregor Russell, of Dorking, Surrey, and Christine, *née* Clark; *b* 16 Jan 1953; *Educ* George Heriot's Sch Edinburgh, Univ of Edinburgh (BCom); *m* 25 Oct 1975, Fiona; 1 s (Ewan b 7 April 1982), 1 da (Lindsay b 9 July 1989); *Career* audit sr Thomson McLintock 1974–78, accountant Mars Ltd 1978–81, controller Pentos plc 1981–83, sub fin dir Hongkong and Shanghai Banking Corporation 1983–90, controller Tomkins plc 1990–94, fin dir Scottish Power plc 1994–; MICAS 1977; *Recreations* golf, rugby; *Clubs* RAC; *Style*— Ian Russell, Esq; ✉ Scottish Power plc, 1 Atlantic Quay, Glasgow G2 8SP (☎ 0141 248 8200, fax 0141 636 4581)

RUSSELL, Prof James Knox; s of James Knox Russell, and Jane Edgar, *née* Younger; *b* 5 Sept 1919; *Educ* Aberdeen GS, Univ of Aberdeen (BM ChB, MD); *m* 16 May 1964, Cecilia Valentine, MD, DCH, da of Patrick Urquhart (d 1956); 3 da (Janice Valentine b

1950, Hilary Margaret b 1951, Sarah Younger b 1956); *Career* serv WWII, MORAF 1943–46 serv Bomber Cmd in England and W Europe (particular interest in early diagnosis of stress in operational aircrew); trained as obstetrician and gynaecologist under Prof Sir Dugald Baird in Aberdeen 1946–50, chief asst to Prof Harvey Evers Newcastle upon Tyne 1950–58, prof of obstetrics and gynaecology Univ of Newcastle upon Tyne 1958–82 (emeritus 1982–), Cwlth Fund fell USA 1962, dean post graduate medicine 1968–77, conslt in human reproduction WHO 1960–82; examiner obstetrics and gynaecology Univs of: London, Birmingham, Manchester, Aberdeen, Belfast, Liverpool, Tripoli, Kuala Lumpur 1980–82; visiting prof: NY 1967 and 1974, SA 1971 and 1978, Univ of Oviedo 1987; Graham Waite Meml lectr AM Coll of Obstetrics and Gynaecology Dallas 1982; vice chm Mitford PC 1985–92; FRCOG 1958 (memb 1949); *Books* Early Teenage Pregnancy (1982); *Recreations* curing & smoking bacon, salmon, eels, rainbow trout and chicken; *Style*— Prof J K Russell; ✉ Newlands, Tranwell Woods, Morpeth, Northumberland NE61 6AG (☎ 01670 515666)

RUSSELL, Jeremy Jonathan; QC (1994); s of Sidney Thomas Russell, of St Albans, Herts, and Maud Eugenie, *née* Davies; *b* 18 Dec 1950; *Educ* Watford Boys' GS, City of London Poly (BA Business Law), LSE (LLM); *m* 1987, Gillian Elizabeth, da of Hugh Giles; 1 s (Thomas Jonathan Giles b 8 Oct 1988), 1 da (Monica Eugenie Helen b 10 May 1990); *Career* called to the Bar Middle Temple 1975, in practice SE Circuit; *Recreations* reading (particularly military history), gliding, classic cars; *Style*— Jeremy Russell, Esq, QC; ✉ 4 Essex Court, Ground Floor, Temple, London EC4Y 9AJ (☎ 0171 797 7970, fax 0171 353 0998)

RUSSELL, John; s of Harold George Russell, and Joyce Caroline, *née* Morris; *b* 1 June 1953; *Educ* Westcliff HS for Boys, Univ of Southampton (LLB); *m* 23 July 1977, (Ingegerd) Maria, da of Rolf Erik Norén, KVO; 2 da (Samantha b 2 June 1982, Emma b 5 April 1985); *Career* admitted slr 1977, Linklaters & Paines London and Hong Kong 1975–85, investmt banker Merrill Lynch International 1985–88, ptnr Simmons & Simmons 1988–; memb: Law Soc, Capital Markets Forum; MSI; *Recreations* skiing, walking, swimming, sailing; *Style*— John Russell, Esq; ✉ c/o Simmons & Simmons, 21 Wilson Street, London EC2M 2TQ (☎ 0171 628 2020, fax 0171 628 2070)

RUSSELL, John Bayley; s of Frederick Charles Russell (d 1987), of Brisbane, Aust, and Clarice Emily Mander, *née* Jones (d 1959); *b* 22 Jan 1942; *Educ* C of E GS Brisbane Aust, Univ of Queensland (BComm); *m* 27 Sept 1968, Virginia, *née* Winsome; 1 s (Simon b 1972); *Career* Bain & Co Securities: ptnr 1972–, ptnr i/c London Office 1980–84 and 1986–, ptnr i/c NY office 1984–86; memb: Aust-Br C of C, Aust Stock Exchange, Victorian Advsy Ctee; FInstD; *Recreations* golf, reading; *Clubs* Univ and Schs (Sydney); *Style*— John Russell, Esq; ✉ Bain & Co, 115 Houndsditch, London EC3A 7BU (☎ 0171 283 9133, fax 0171 626 7090)

RUSSELL, John Francis; s of Francis Frederick Russell (d 1987), and Barbara Mary, *née* Thornhill (d 1993); *b* 12 Dec 1948; *Educ* Victoria Secdy Modern Sch, Bushey GS, Harrow Tech Coll and Sch of Art; *m* 1, (m dis); 1 s (Drew Francis Robert b 1985), 1 da (Kelly Xenia b 1983); m 2, Jennifer Doherty; 3 da (Gemma Elise Doherty b 1984, Tessa Allanah Doherty b 1992, Alice Imogen Doherty b 21 June 1994); *Career* freelance creative landscape and travel photographer and black and white printer; head: Visual Imaging and Design Bldg Res Estab; many exhibitions of fine art photography; BIPP Jubilee Fellowship Award (Gold medal), RIBA/BIPP Architectural Photographer of the Year, Ilford Photographer of the Year; FBIPP, FRPS; *Recreations* photography, sailing, golf, swimming, travelling; *Style*— John Russell, Esq; ✉ 66 Rowlantt Drive, St Albans, Herts, AL3 4BN (☎ 01727 852799); Audio Visual & Design Service, Department of the Environment, Building Research Establishment, Garston, Watford WD2 7JR (☎ 01923 664354, fax 01923 664094)

RUSSELL, Lynda Jane; da of Ivor Gordon Russell, of Stirchley, Birmingham, and Alison Jeanne, *née* Honeybourne; *b* 15 March 1952; *Educ* Swanshurst Bilateral Sch Kings Heath Birmingham, Royal Coll of Music London (Kathleen Ferrier Meml scholar); *m* 4 Jan 1991, Christopher William Royall, counter-tenor, s of late Gerald William Royall; 2 s (Timothy Gordon Russell Royall b 26 April 1988, Jonathan Charles William b 22 June 1994); *Career* soprano; studied with Meriel St Clair at RCM and with Eugenie Ludwig in Paris and Vienna, prizewinner Hertogenbosch and Paris Competitions; has appeared at numerous international opera houses incl London Colesium, Covent Garden, Madrid, Nice, Venice, Vicenza, Bologna, Rome, Strasbourg and Met Opera NY, given concert and recital performances at numerous European festivals incl Athens, Barcelona, Granada, San Sebastian, Santander, Cuenca, Venice, Berne, Munich, Strasbourg, Dijon, Siena, Glyndebourne and BBC Proms; performed with orchs incl The Sixteen Choir and Orch, London Mozart Players, Bournemouth Symphony Orch, The Philharmonia, RPO and Royal Scottish Orch, worked with conductors incl Libor Pesek, Sir Yehudi Menuhin, Leonard Slatkin, David Hill, Richard Hickox, Simon Rattle, M Rostropovich, Walter Weller and Jesus Lopez-Cobos; *Performances* concert and recital performances incl: Rossini's Stabat Mater Strasbourg and Dijon festivals 1992, Handel's Messiah (with The Sixteen Choir and Orch under Harry Christophers for BBC TV on 250th anniversary of its composition Easter 1992, and with Sir Yehudi Menuhin in Spain and Moscow Autumn 1992), Brahms' Requiem (with Jesus Lopez-Cobos in San Sebastian and with Richard Hickox for BBC TV Wales in Tewkesbury Abbey 1992), Beethoven's Missa Solemnis (with Dresdner Staatskapelle), Mozart's Coronation Mass (with Peter Weller) Madrid, Beethoven's Ninth Symphony (with The Philharmonia under Leonard Slatkin) Royal Festival Hall, Mozart's Mass in C Minor (for RTE) Dublin, Haydn's Creation (with Sixteen Choir and Orch) Madrid, Dvorak's Stabat Mater (with RPO under Libor Pesek) Royal Festival Hall, Teixeira's Te Deum (with Sixteen Choir and Orch) BBC Proms 1992, Britten's Les Illuminations (with LSO under M Rostropovich) Barbican 1993, Britten's Quatre Chansons Françaises (with CBSO under Simon Rattle) Symphony Hall Birmingham 1993; operatic roles: title role in Handel's Partenope (nominated for Soc of West End Theatre Outstanding First Achievement award), various with companies incl Glyndebourne (festival and on tour), Opera North, Opera Northern Ireland and ENO (US tour), made debut at Covent Garden as First Lady in Mozart's Magic Flute Nov 1993; *Recordings* incl: Vaughan Williams' Benedicite (with Bournemouth Symphony Orch under David Hill, Decca Argo) 1992, Teixeira's Te Deum (with The Sixteen Choir and Orch, Collins Classics) 1992, Bach's Christmas Oratorio 1993, Mahler's 4th Symphony with Antoni Wit and Polish Nat Radio Symphony Orch 1993; *Recreations* walking, entertaining, cooking; *Style*— Ms Lynda Russell; ✉ c/o Magenta Music International, 4 Highgate High St, London N6 5JL (☎ 0181 340 8321, fax 0181 340 7823)

RUSSELL, Sir (Robert) Mark; KCMG (1985, CMG 1977); s of Sir Robert Russell, CSI, CIE (d 1972), and Esther Rhona, *née* Murray (d 1983); *b* 3 Sept 1929; *Educ* Trinity Coll Glenalmond, Exeter Coll Oxford (MA); *m* 1954, Virginia Mary, da of George Swire de Moleyns Rogers (d 1957); 2 s (Neil, Alexander), 2 da (Claire, Lesley); *Career* 2 Lt RA 1952–54; joined Dip Serv 1954, third sec FO 1954; second sec: Budapest 1956, Berne 1958; first sec: FO 1961, Kabul 1965 (and head of Chancery), FCO 1967; cnsllr: FCO 1969, (commercial) Bucharest 1970, Washington 1974 (head of Chancery 1977); chief inspr and dep chief clerk FCO 1978, ambassador Ankara 1983, dep under sec of state (chief clerk) FCO 1986, ret 1989; chm Martin Currie European Investment Trust plc, chm C-Mist Ltd, special advsr Scottish Financial Enterprise; chm: Centre for Cwlth, UN and Int Affrs Dundee, Margaret Blackwood Housing Assoc, Scottish Tst for Physically Disabled; memb Bd of Govrs The British Cncl; *Clubs* Royal Cwlth Soc, Royal Over-Seas League, New (Edinburgh); *Style*— Sir Mark Russell, KCMG; ✉ 20 Meadow Place, Edinburgh, Scotland EH9 1JR

RUSSELL, Prof Michael Anthony Hamilton; s of James Hamilton Russell (d 1985), and Hon Kathleen Mary, *née* Gibson; *b* 9 March 1932; *Educ* Diocesan Coll Cape Town SA, Univ Coll Oxford (MA, BM BCh, DPM); *m* 27 Jan 1962, Audrey Anne, da of Archibald Timms (d 1940); 2 s (James Hamilton b 16 March 1974, Nicholas Hamilton b 3 Sept 1977); *Career* house physician and surgn Guy's Hosp London 1957–58, registrar in pathology and sr registrar med Groote Schuur Hosp Univ of Cape Town SA 1959–64, med registrar Ruttonjee Sanatorium Hong Kong 1964–65, registrar and sr registrar in psychiatry Maudsley Hosp London 1965–69, lectr in psychiatry Inst of Psychiatry London 1969–73, sr lectr and hon conslt Maudsley Hosp London 1973–, on MRC External Scientific Staff 1978–, prof of addiction Univ of London Inst of Psychiatry 1992– (reader in addiction 1985–92), hon dir ICRF Health Behaviour Unit Maudsley Hosp London 1988–; numerous papers and articles on tobacco smoking in scientific jls; memb: Cncl Action on Smoking and Health (ASH), Br Assoc of Psychopharmacology; FRCP 1982, FRCPsych 1980, FRSH 1988; *Books* Nicotine Psychopharmacology (with S Wonnacott and I P Stolerman, 1990); *Recreations* reading, swimming, windsurfing, travel; *Style*— Prof Michael Russell; ✉ 14 Court Lane Gardens, Dulwich, London SE21 7DZ (☎ 0181 693 3606); Institute of Psychiatry, The Maudsley Hospital, Denmark Hill, London SE5 8AF (☎ 0171 703 6333, fax 0171 703 6197)

RUSSELL, (Alastair) Muir; s of Thomas Russell (d 1988), and Anne, *née* Muir (d 1977); *b* 9 Jan 1949; *m* 19 Aug 1983, Eileen Alison Mackay, CB, *qv*, da of Alexander William Mackay OBE (d 1967), of Dingwall, Ross-shire; *Career* under sec Housing Environment Dept SO 1992–95, sec and head Agric Environment and Fisheries Dept SO 1995–; non-exec dir Stagecoach Holdings plc 1992–95; *Style*— Muir Russell, Esq; ✉ The Scottish Office, Agriculture, Environment and, Fisheries Department, Pentland House, 47 Robb's Loan, Edinburgh EH14 1TY (☎ 0131 244 6021)

RUSSELL, Sheriff (Albert) Muir Galloway; CBE (1989), QC (Scotland 1965); s of Hon Lord Russell (d 1975, Senator of the Coll of Justice), and Florence Muir, *née* Galloway (d 1983); *b* 26 Oct 1925; *Educ* Edinburgh Acad, Wellington, BNC Oxford (BA), Univ of Edinburgh (LLB); *m* 9 April 1954, Margaret Winifred, da of Thomas McWalter Millar (d 1970), of Edinburgh; 2 s (Douglas b 27 April 1958, Graham b 14 June 1962), 2 da (Anne b 1 Nov 1960, Jennifer b 22 Jan 1964); *Career* Lt Scots Gds 1944–47, served BLA and BAOR; memb Faculty of Advocates (Edinburgh) 1951; standing jr counsel: BOT, Dept of Agric and Forestry Cmmn; Sheriff of Grampian Highlands and Islands at Aberdeen 1971–91, ret; memb Sheriff Ct Rules Cncl 1977–86, vice chm Bd of Mgmnt Southern Gp of Hosps Edinburgh 1964, govr Moray House Coll of Educn 1966–70; *Recreations* golf, music; *Clubs* Royal Northern and Univ (Aberdeen); *Style*— Sheriff Muir Russell, CBE, QC; ✉ Tulloch House, 1 Aultbea, Ross-shire IV22 2JB (☎ 01445 731325); 9 St Fillans Terrace, Edinburgh EH10 5NH

RUSSELL, Dr Nicholas John; s of Dr Michael Hibberd Russell (d 1987), of Little Sutton, Cheshire, and Pamela, *née* Eyre; *b* 23 Feb 1953; *Educ* The King's Sch Chester, Trinity Coll Cambridge (MA, MB BChir), Westminster Hosp Med Sch; *m* 17 Feb 1979, Christine Frances, da of Basil Ivor Lever, of Deanscales, Cockermouth; 2 s (Benjamin b 1979, Julian b 1981), 1 da (Eleanor b 1986); *Career* conslt physician in geriatric med W Cumberland Hosp 1988–; FRCP 1996 (MRCP 1980); *Recreations* tennis, fly fishing; *Style*— Dr Nicholas Russell; ✉ West Cumberland Hospital, Whitehaven, Cumbria CA28 8JG (☎ 01946 693181, fax 01946 513520)

RUSSELL, Rt Hon Sir (Thomas) Patrick; kt (1980), PC (1987); s of Sidney Russell (d 1953), and Elsie Russell (d 1948); *b* 30 July 1926; *Educ* Urmston GS, Univ of Manchester (LLB); *m* 1951, Doreen (Janie) Ireland; 2 da; *Career* called to the Bar Middle Temple 1949, prosecuting counsel to the Post Office Northern Circuit 1961–70, asst recorder Bolton 1964–70, recorder Barrow-in-Furness 1970–71, QC 1971, recorder of the Crown Court 1972–80, bencher Middle Temple 1978, ldr N Circuit 1978–80, judge of the High Court of Justice (Queen's Bench Div) 1980–86, presiding judge N Circuit 1983–86, a Lord Justice of Appeal 1987–96, ret; Hon LLD Univ of Manchester 1988; *Style*— The Rt Hon Sir Patrick Russell; ✉ c/o Royal Courts of Justice, The Strand, London WC2A 2LL

RUSSELL, Peter John; s of Capt Raymond Colston Frederick Russell, of Bristol, and Marjorie Catherine, *née* Lock; *b* 14 Dec 1951; *Educ* Bedminster Down Sch Bristol, Univ of London (BA, LLM); *m* 7 April 1979, Dr Evelyn Mary, da of Sqdn Ldr Lorence Alan Scott, of Bridport, Dorset; 1 s (Timothy Paul b 1985), 1 da (Sarah Anne b 1982); *Career* barr Inner Temple 1975, Northern Circuit 1975–93, lectr in law Univ of Manchester 1975–82; chm Industl Tbnls 1993– (pt/t 1992); memb: Manchester Wine Soc, Manchester Medico-Legal Soc, Hon Soc of the Inner Temple; *Recreations* wine tasting and gardening; *Style*— Peter Russell, Esq; ✉ 18 Elm Rd, Didsbury, Manchester M20 6XD (☎ 0161 434 4306); Alexandra House, 14/22 The Parsonage, Manchester M3 2JA (☎ 0161 833 0581, fax 0161 832 0249)

RUSSELL, Robert Charles (Jack); MBE (1996); s of John Russell, and Jennifer Russell; *b* 15 Aug 1963; *Educ* Archway Comp Sch; *m* 6 March 1985, Aileen Ann; 1 s (Charles David b 1991), 2 da (Elizabeth Ann b 1988, Victoria b 1989), 1 step s (Marcus Anthony); *Career* professional cricketer Gloucestershire CCC 1981– (awarded county cap 1985, caretaker capt 1995–96); England: 49 test matches 1988–, 35 one day ints; tours: Pakistan 1987–88, India and W Indies 1989–90, Aust 1990–91, NZ 1991–92, W Indies 1993/94, S Africa 1995/96; records incl: most dismissals in a match on first-class debut (8 for Glos v Sri Lanka 1981), youngest Glos wicket-keeper (17 years 307 days), hat-trick of catches v Surrey Oval 1986, most dismissals in a test match (11 for England v S Africa, Johannesburg 1995); professional artist; paintings exhibited at Imperial War Museum, Tower of London and others, cmmnd to paint limited edn commemorative pictures of fourth test in Barbados 1994 and fourth test in Adelaide 1995; *Books* A Cricketer's Art (1988), Sketches of a Season (with Christopher Martin-Jenkins, 1989); *Recreations* drawing, painting, sketching, collecting militaria; *Style*— Jack Russell, Esq, MBE; ✉ Jack Russell Gallery, 41 High Street, Chipping Sodbury, Bristol BS17 6BA (☎ 01454 329583, fax 01454 329683)

RUSSELL, Prof Robin Irvine; s of John Russell (d 1952), and Mary Russell (d 1950); *b* 21 Dec 1936; *Educ* Univ of Glasgow (MD, PhD); *m* 18 Aug 1964, Ann, da of Andrew Wallace (d 1977), of Glasgow; 1 s (Bruce b 1965), 1 da (Kara b 1968); *Career* memb med and scientific staff MRC Gastroenterology Unit London 1966–68, lectr in med Univ of Glasgow 1968–70, conslt gastroenterologist in charge Royal Infirmary Glasgow 1970–; visiting prof: Univ of Mississippi, Univ of Singapore, Univ of Toronto; memb: Assoc of Physicians 1976, Br Soc of Gastroenterology 1969; fell American Coll of Nutrition 1984, memb American Gastroenterological Assoc 1985, fell American Coll of Gastroenterology 1985; FRCPE, FRCP Glasgow; *Books* Investigative Tests and Techniques in Gastroenterology (1977), Elemental Diets (1981); *Recreations* golf, travel, literature, music; *Clubs* RSM, New (St Andrews); *Style*— Prof Robin Russell; ✉ Department of Gastroenterology, Royal Infirmary, University of Glasgow, Glasgow G31 2ER (☎ 0141 211 4400, fax 0141 211 4882, e-mail RIRla@clinmed.gla.ac.uk)

RUSSELL, Prof Roy Robert Baird; *b* 7 May 1944, Dublin, Ireland; *Educ* Rossall Sch Fleetwood Lancs, Trinity Coll Dublin (BA), Melbourne Univ (PhD); *m*; 2 c; *Career* research scientist Meat Research Lab CSIRO Brisbane Aust 1970–73, postdoctoral fell Div of Biological Scis Nat Research Cncl of Canada Ottawa 1973–75, sr research fell then dir Dental Research Unit Dept of Dental Scis RCS 1975–91, prof and head Dept of

Oral Biology Univ of Newcastle upon Tyne 1991–; memb MRC/Health Depts Jt Dental Ctee; memb Editorial Bds: Infection and Immunity, Oral Microbiology and Immunology, Microbiology; memb: American Soc for Microbiology, Soc for Gen Microbiology, Int Assoc for Dental Research (past pres Microbiology/Immunology Gp), Br Soc for Dental Research; FDSRCS 1986; *Style*— Prof Roy Russell; ✉ Department of Oral Biology, Dental School, Framlington Place, Newcastle upon Tyne NE2 4BW (☎ 0191 222 7859, fax 0191 222 6137, e-mail r.r.russell@newcastle.ac.uk)

RUSSELL, Rupert Edward Odo; s of David Hastings Gerald Russell (see Debrett's Peerage, Ampthill, B), of London, and Hester Clere, *née* Parsons; *b* 5 Nov 1944; *Educ* Selwyn House Sch Montreal, Rannoch Sch Perthshire; *m* 9 Dec 1981, Catherine Jill, former Lady Brougham and Vaux, da of William Daniel Gulliver (d 1981); *Career* admitted slr 1973; ptnr: Blount Petre and Co 1979–86, Amhurst Brown Martin and Nicholson 1986–87, Payne Hicks Beach 1988–92, REO Russell & Co (own practice) 1992–; vice pres Cities of London and Westminster Cons Assoc (former chm); memb Law Soc 1973; *Recreations* skiing, sailing, fishing, gardening; *Clubs* Buck's (chm); *Style*— Rupert Russell, Esq; ✉ Highleaze, Oare, Marlborough, Wiltshire (☎ 01672 62487/64352, fax 01672 64163)

RUSSELL, Thomas; CMG (1980), CBE (1970, OBE 1963); s of late Thomas Russell OBE, MC; *b* 27 May 1920; *Educ* Hawick HS, St Andrews Univ, Peterhouse Cambridge; *m* 1951, Andrée Irma, *née* Désfossés (decd); 1 s; *Career* Capt Para Regt serv N Africa, Italy; Colonial Admin Serv Solomon Islands 1948, dist cmmr 1948–49 and 1954–56, seconded Colonial Office 1956–57, fin sec 1965, chief sec 1970, govr Cayman Islands 1974–81, rep of Cayman Islands in UK 1982–; *Recreations* anthropology, archaeology; *Clubs* Caledonian, Royal Cwlth Soc; *Style*— Thomas Russell, Esq, CMG, CBE; ✉ 6 Eldon Drive, Farnham, Surrey GU10 3JE; office: Cayman Islands Government Office, 6 Arlington Street, London SW1A 1RE (☎ 0171 491 7772)

RUSSELL, Tony; s of William Russell, of Alton, Hants, and Kathleen Louise, *née* Ludgate; *b* 15 Aug 1946; *Educ* Beaumont Coll, Magdalen Coll Oxford; *m* 1981, Sally Joy, da of Ruben Feldman; 1 s (Ricky Lee b 1981), 1 da (Scarlett Rose b 1984); *Career* radio presenter; scripted/presented features/progs on jazz, blues, country music, folk music, popular music for BBC Radio One, Two, Three, Four, World Service; conslt: BBC 2 TV, Channel 4; co-presented/presented Sounds of Jazz (BBC Radio 2) 1985–90, presented Swing Shift (BFBS) 1988–89, presented weekend breakfast progs (Jazz FM) 1990–91; editor: Old Time Music 1971–, Jazz Express 1982–85, Jazz magazine 1990–; conslt ed The Blues Collection 1993–; *Books* Blacks, Whites and Blues (Studio Vista, 1970); *Style*— Tony Russell, Esq; ✉ Jazz, Guardian Magazines, 75 Farringdon Road, London EC1M 3JY (☎ 0171 713 4205, fax 0171 713 4217)

RUSSELL, Prof William Clelland; s of Hugh McPherson Russell (d 1937), and Nora Catherine, *née* Peoples (d 1983); *b* 9 Aug 1930; *Educ* Allan Glen's Sch Glasgow, Univ of Glasgow (BSc, PhD); *m* 1, 15 Oct 1962, Dorothy Ada, *née* Brown (d 1982); 1 s (Iain Andrew b 1967), 1 da (Lucy Anne b 1965); m 2, 31 March 1985, Reta, *née* Brown; *Career* chemist with Miny of Supply Royal Ordnance Factories Bishopton Renfrewshire and Bridgwater Somerset 1955–56, res chemist J & P Coats Ltd Paisley Renfrewshire 1956–59, Lock res fell Royal Faculty of Physicians and Surgns of Glasgow at Dept of Virology Univ of Glasgow 1959–63, Eleanor Roosevelt Int Cancer fellowship Dept of Med Biophysics Univ of Toronto Canada 1963–64, head Div of Virology Nat Inst for Medical Research Mill Hill London 1973–84 (memb MRC research staff 1964–84), prof of biochemistry Univ of St Andrews 1984–95, emeritus research prof Univ of St Andrews 1995–; ed Journal of General Virology 1972–76, memb Cncl Soc for Gen Microbiology 1987–91 (convener Virus Gp 1984–89); chair Nat Organising Ctee IXth Int Congress of Virology Glasgow 1993; FRSE 1988; *Style*— Prof William Russell, FRSE; ✉ 3 Osborne Terrace, Crail, Fife KY10 3RR (☎ 01333 450614); School of Biological and Medical Sciences, University of St Andrews, Irvine Building, North St, St Andrews, Fife KY16 9AL (☎ 01334 463405, fax 01334 463400, e-mail wcr@st-andrews.ac.uk)

RUSSELL, Hon William Southwell; yr s (by his 1 w, Dorothy) of 26th Baron de Clifford, OBE, TD (d 1982); hp to bro, 27th Baron; *b* 26 Feb 1930; *Educ* Eton, King's Coll Cambridge (BA), Princeton Univ (MScEng); *m* 1961, Jean Brodie, o da of Neil Brodie Henderson, and Conn, da of Adm of the Fleet Sir Charles Madden, 1st Bt, GCB, OM, GCVO, KCMG; 1 s (Miles Edward Southwell b 7 Aug 1966), 2 da (Mary-Jane Sophia b 13 March 1963, Joanna Clare b 23 Jan 1965); *Career* chm and chief exec The Howden Glucose Co Ltd 1973–77, md Ridgways Ltd 1977–80, chm MSS International Ltd 1982–92, md Avebe UK 1986–92; *Recreations* retirement, horse trials, regimental archives of Royal Gloucestershire Hussars; *Style*— The Hon William Russell; ✉ Gilboa Farmhouse, Brokenborough, Malmesbury, Wilts SN16 0HX (☎ 01666 823025)

RUSSELL BEALE, Simon; s of Lt-Gen Sir Peter Beale, RAMC, and Dr Julia Beale, *née* Winter; *b* 12 Jan 1961; *Educ* St Paul's Cathedral Choir Sch, Clifton, Gonville & Caius Coll Cambridge, GSM; *Career* actor; assoc artist RSC; *Theatre* Traverse Theatre credits incl: Die Hose, The Death of Elias Sawney, Sandra Manon; others incl: Look to the Rainbow (Apollo), Women Beware Women (Royal Court), A Winter's Tale, Everyman in His Humour, The Art of Success, The Fair Maid of the West, Speculators, The Storm, The Constant Couple, The Man of Mode, Restoration, Some Americans Abroad, Mary and Lizzie, Playing with Trains, Troilus and Cressida, Edward II, Love's Labour's Lost, The Seagull, Richard III, King Lear, The Tempest, Ghosts, The Duchess of Malfi (Greenwich and West End) 1995, Mosca in Volpone (RNT, Olivier Award for Best Supporting Performance 1996) 1995, Rosencrantz and Guildenstern are Dead (RNT) 1996; *Television* A Very Peculiar Practice, The Mushroom Picker, Down Town Lagos, Persuasion, A Dance to the Music of Time; *Style*— Simon Russell Beale, Esq; ✉ c/o The Richard Stone Partnership, 25 Whitehall, London SW1A 2BS (☎ 0171 839 6421, fax 0171 839 5002)

RUSSELL-JONES, Dr Robin David; s of John Lewis Russell-Jones, JP (d 1970), of Saundersfoot, Pembrokeshire, and Mary Elizabeth, *née* Ebsworth; *b* 5 March 1948; *Educ* Rugby, Peterhouse Cambridge (MA, MB BChir); *m* 1, 1 Nov 1975, Ann Hilary Fair (d 1991), da of Roger Brian Nixon (d 1988), of Leckhampton Hill, Cheltenham; 1 s (Christopher b 1979), 1 da (Joy b 1976); m 2, 18 Sept 1993, Nina, da of Kailash Salooja, of Goring-on-Thames, Oxon; 1 da (Eleanor b 1994); *Career* conslt dermatologist St Thomas Hosp, Ealing Hosp and Hammersmith Hosp 1983–; sr lectr Dept of Med Royal Postgraduate Med Sch London; dir Skin Tumour Unit St John's Inst of Dermatology St Thomas Hosp 1996–; chm: Friends of the Earth Pollution Advsy Ctee, Campaign for Lead Free Air 1984–89; FRCP 1990 (MRCP 1973); *Books* Lead Versus Health (1983), Radiation and Health (1987), Ozone Depletion (1989); *Recreations* skiing, sailing, golf; *Style*— Dr Robin Russell-Jones; ✉ Atholl House, Church Lane, Stoke Poges, Bucks SL2 4NZ

RUSSELL OF ADEN, James Cecil Cumine; CBE (1987, MBE 1980); s of Sidney Cumine Russell (d 1965), of Templecombe, Somerset, and Meriel Eleanor, *née* Fetherstonhaugh (d 1978); *b* 25 June 1933; *Educ* Feltonfleet Sch, Wellington Coll, RMA Sandhurst; *m* 1960, Diana Margaret, da of Richard Leonard White (d 1948); 2 da (Caroline Marguerite Cumine b 10 Aug 1962, Lucy Eleanor Cumine b 14 April 1965), 1 s (Alexander Charles Cumine Russell, *qv*, b 21 Oct 1966); *Career* cmmnd Queen's Own Cameron Highlanders 1953–61, Queen's Own Highlanders (Seaforth and Camerons) 1961–65; admitted slr 1969, ptnr Blount Petre Kramer 1996– (ptnr Blount Petre & Co 1970–95); chm Naval and Military Club 1993–; cncllr (C) Hants CC 1993–, former chm Wessex Area Cons & Unionist Assoc; church warden; memb: Law Soc 1970, City of Westminster Law Soc 1970; *Recreations* shooting, gardening; *Clubs* Naval and Military, Highland Bde, Highland Soc of London; *Style*— James Russell, Esq, CBE; ✉ Blount Petre Kramer Solicitors, 29 Weymouth St, London W1N 4LE (☎ 0171 637 8354, fax 0171 580 6417)

RUSSELL OF LIVERPOOL, 3 Baron (UK 1919); Simon Gordon Jared Russell; s of Capt Hon Langley Russell, MC, s of 2 Baron Russell of Liverpool, CBE, MC; suc gf 1981; *b* 30 Aug 1952; *Educ* Charterhouse, Trinity Coll Cambridge, INSEAD; *m* 1984, Gilda F, yst da of F Albano, of Salerno, Italy; 2 s (Hon Edward Charles Stanley b 1985, Hon William Francis Langley b 1988), 1 da (Hon Leonora Maria Kiloran b 1987); *Heir* s, Hon Edward Charles Stanley Russell b 2 Sept 1985; *Career* mgmnt conslt; Liveryman Worshipful Co of Fishmongers; *Style*— The Rt Hon Lord Russell of Liverpool; ✉ c/o House of Lords, London SW1A 0PW

RUSSELL-ROBERTS, Anthony de Villeneuve; s of Francis Douglas Russell-Roberts (d 1973), and Edith Margaret Gertrudis, *née* Ashton (d 1990); *b* 25 March 1944; *Educ* Eton, New Coll Oxford; *m* 1 (m dis); m 2, 12 Dec 1975, Anne, *née* Dunhill; 1 step s (Ingo Ferruzzi b 19 Feb 1972), 1 step da (Anita Ferruzzi b 19 Dec 1973), 2 da (Tabitha b 10 March 1977, Juliet b 19 Dec 1979); *Career* VSO Br Honduras (now Belize) 1961–62; gen mgmnt trainee Watney Mann 1965–68, ptnr Lane Fox and Ptnrs 1971–76 (joined 1968); stage mgmnt: Glyndebourne Festival Opera 1976, Kent Opera 1977; asst to Gen Dir Royal Opera House 1977–80, artistic admin Theatre Nationale de L'Opera de Paris 1981–83, admin dir Royal Ballet 1983–; *Recreations* gardening, golf; *Clubs* Garrick; *Style*— Anthony Russell-Roberts; ✉ Royal Ballet, Royal Opera House, Covent Garden, London WC2E 7QA (☎ 0171 212 9158, fax 0171 212 9121)

RUSSELL VICK, His Hon Judge; Arnold Oughtred; QC (1980); s of His Hon Judge Sir Godfrey Russell Vick, QC (d 1958), and Marjorie Hester Russell Vick, JP (d 1985), yst da of John A Compston, KC; *b* 14 Sept 1933; *Educ* The Leys Sch, Jesus Coll Cambridge (MA); *m* 5 Sept 1959, Zinnia Mary, da of Thomas Brown Yates (d 1968), of Godalming, Surrey; 2 s (Philip b 1960, Mark b 1964), 1 da (Tessa (Mrs Hendrikz) b 1963); *Career* serv RAF 1952–54, qualified pilot (Flying Offr); called to the Bar Inner Temple 1958, dep recorder Rochester City QS 1971, recorder of the Crown Court 1972–82, circuit judge 1982–, princ co court judge Kent 1990–, designated family judge Medway Care Centre 1991–; memb: Bar Cncl 1964–68, Lord Chllr's Co Court Rules Ctee 1972–80; govr New Beacon Sch Sevenoaks 1982–; memb Ct of Assts Worshipful Co of Curriers (Master 1976–77); *Books* A Hundred Years of Golf at Wildernesse (1990); *Recreations* golf, cricket, gardening, bridge; *Clubs* MCC, Hawks (Cambridge), Wildernesse Golf (Sevenoaks, capt 1978); *Style*— His Hon Judge Russell Vick, QC; ✉ Law Courts, Barker Rd, Maidstone, Kent (☎ 01622 754966)

RUSSILL, Patrick Joseph; *b* 9 Sept 1953; *Educ* Shaftesbury GS, New Coll Oxford (Margaret Bridges organ scholar, MA); *m* 28 April 1979, Jane Mary, *née* Rogers; 3 da (Francesca b 1981, Helen b 1985, Katherine b 1991), 2 s (Benjamin b 1983, Dominic b 1988); *Career* organist, choral dir and church music educator; organist The London Oratory 1977– (asst organist 1976–77), organist for Papal Mass Wembley Stadium 1982; dir: Oxford Chamber Choir 1977–79, London Oratory Jr Choir 1984–, Europa Singers of London 1985–89; Royal Acad of Music: prof in music techniques 1982–87, dir of church music studies and prof in choral conducting 1987–; external examiner for MMus in English Church Music UEA 1991–, visiting prof St George's Coll Jerusalem 1994–; memb Organ Advsy Gp Soc of St Gregory 1978–, memb Exec Ctee Church Music Soc 1990–, tstee Friends of St Marylebone Music 1993–, hon patron Herbert Howells Soc 1993–, memb Ctee Organists' Benevolent League 1994–, memb Cncl Royal College of Organists 1996–; ARCO 1971, Hon RAM 1993 (Hon ARAM 1989); *Performances* organ recitals in UK, Germany, Near East and Asia incl Royal Festival Hall (debut 1986) among many others, UK premièes of work by Hakin and Grier; London Oratory Jr Choir performed at all major London concert venues incl the BBC Proms, over 120 appearances at Royal Opera House Covent Garden, numerous bdcasts on BBC TV and Radio and German radio, recordings on EMI, Hyperion and Deutsche Grammophon Archiv; *Publications* editions of Howells and Sweelinck; music ed The Catholic Hymnbook 1997; author of numerous articles mainly on church music for jls and periodicals incl: Catholic Herald, The Organist, Organists' Review, Church Times, Choir and Organ, Gramophone, The Cambridge Handbook of the Organ 1997; also given lectures to various bodies incl: Incorporated Soc of Organists, Soc of St Gregory, Guild of Church Musicians, Royal Sch of Church Music, Panel of Monastic Musicians, Winchester Diocesan Synod; *Style*— Patrick Russill, Esq; ✉ The Oratory, Brompton Road, London SW7 2RP (☎ 0171 589 4811); Royal Academy of Music, Marylebone Road, London NW1 (☎ 0171 873 7373, fax 0171 873 7374)

RUSSON, David; s of Thomas Charles Russon (d 1962), and Violet, *née* Jarvis; *b* 12 June 1944; *Educ* Wellington GS, UCL (BSc), Univ of York; *m* 29 July 1967, Kathleen Mary, da of Frederick Gregory, of Morecambe, Lancs; 1 s ((Charles) Benedict b 1975), 2 da (Katherine b 1971, Nicola b 1973); *Career* various appts DES 1969–74; British Library: various appts 1974–85, dir Document Supply Centre 1985–88, dir gen for Sci Technol and Indust 1988–91, Bd memb 1988–, dir gen Boston Spa 1991–96, dep chief exec 1996–; dir AVT Communications Ltd 1989–; pres Int Cncl for Scientific and Tech Information 1995– (vice pres 1992–95); contrib to various learned journals; FIInfSc, FRSA; *Recreations* tennis, badminton, golf; *Clubs* National Liberal; *Style*— David Russon, Esq; ✉ March House, Tollerton, York YO6 2ET (☎ 01347 838253); British Library, Boston Spa, Wetherby, W Yorks LS23 7BQ (☎ 01937 546131, fax 01937 546246, telex 557381)

RUSTAGE, Christopher Charles; s of George Roland Rustage (d 1983), of Manchester, and Mary, *née* Killian (d 1993); *b* 7 June 1948; *Educ* De La Salle Coll Manchester, St Joseph's Coll Manchester; *m* 1, 1967 (m dis 1986), Ann, da of Herman Taylor; 2 da (Andre-Jayne b 1967, Joanne Marie b 1971), 1 s (Christopher George b 1974); m 2, Angela Parkin; *Career* franchiser; apprentice motor body fitter 1965–66, specialist importer of blending and roasting teas and coffees, labourer/driver 1968–69, grave digger, brewery asst, asst to lion tamer at Billy Smart's circus, watch assembler and shoe polish manufacturer 1969–73, fndr construction co 1973–79, livestock farmer 1979–83, inventor/manufacturer new health products 1983–87, property speculator and furniture manufacturer 1987–90, fndr Riverside International Ltd (largest privately owned franchising chain in Europe) 1990–; chm The Pet Club Great Britain Ltd; memb Manorial Soc of GB 1972, memb Confedn of Trades & Indust 1983, memb Prince's Tst 1983–84; Lord of the Manor of Edern; *Books* The Fax Book (1983); *Recreations* shooting, boating, travel, country pursuits; *Style*— Christopher Rustage, Esq; ✉ Riverside Group, 75 Mosley Street, Manchester M2 3HR (☎ 0161 839 5737, fax 0161 839 5803)

RUSTIN, Dr Gordon John Sampson; s of Maj Maurice Edward Rustin, MC (d 1972), of Hale, Cheshire, and (Barbara) Joan, *née* Goldstone; *Educ* Uppingham, Middx Hosp Med Sch (MB BS), Univ of London (MSc, MD); *m* 17 Feb 1977, Frances Phyllis, da of Lionel Rainsbury, of London; 1 s (Edward Samuel b 4 May 1981), 1 da (Jessica Leah b 3 Jan 1986); *Career* registrar Whittington Hosp and UCH 1974–76, res fell Hammersmith Hosp 1977–78, sr registrar Charing Cross Hosp 1978–84, sr lectr and hon conslt in med oncology Charing Cross Hosp and Mount Vernon Hosp 1984–95, dir of med oncology Mount Vernon Hosp 1995–; over 150 pubns on: tumour markers, germ cell, trophoblastic ovarian and cervical tumours; memb Testicular and Gynaecological Working Pty MRC, memb Cncl Oncology Section RSM; memb: BMA 1971, RSM 1977, ACP 1985; MRCP 1974, FRCP 1992, BACR 1979; *Recreations* tennis, golf, opera, skiing; *Style*— Dr Gordon Rustin; ✉ 15 Wellgarth Rd, London NW11 7HP (☎ 0181 455 5943); Director of Medical

Oncology, Mount Vernon Hospital, Northwood, Middlesex HA6 2RN (☎ 01923 844389, fax 01923 844138)

RUSTIN, Dr Malcolm Howard Albert; s of Maurice Edward Rustin (d 1973), and Barbara Joan, *née* Goldstone; *b* 6 Nov 1951; *Educ* Uppingham, Middx Hosp Med Sch London (BSc, MB BS, MD, FRCP); *m* Dr Joanna Rustin; *Career* conslt dermatologist; special clinical interest in connective tissue diseases and both a clinical and research commitment to atopic eczema; chm Dermatitis and Allied Diseases Research Tst; Gold medal American Acad of Dermatology; memb Br Assoc of Dermatologists, FRSM; *Publications* author of pubns on the pathogenesis and treatment of atopic eczema; *Style—* Dr Malcolm Rustin; ✉ 53 Wimpole Street, London W1M 7DF (☎ and fax 0171 935 9266); Department of Dermatology, The Royal Free Hospital, Pond Street, London NW3 2QG (☎ 0171 794 0500)

RUTHERFORD, Prof Andrew; CBE (1993); s of Thomas Armstrong Rutherford (d 1935), of Helmsdale, Sutherland, and Christian Proudfoot Russell, MBE, JP (d 1973); *b* 23 July 1929; *Educ* Helmsdale Sch Sutherland, George Watson's Boys' Coll Edinburgh, Univ of Edinburgh (MA), Merton Coll Oxford (BLitt); *m* 4 Sept 1953, Nancy Milroy, da of Dr Arthur Browning (d 1962), of Bathgate, W Lothian; 2 s (Richard Browning, John Arthur Thomas), 1 da (Alison Jean); *Career* Nat Serv cmmnd 2 Lt Seaforth Highlanders 1951–53, serv Somaliland Scouts, Lt 11 Bn Seaforth Highlanders TA 1953–58; lectr Univ of Edinburgh 1956–64 (asst lectr 1955), visiting assoc prof Univ of Rochester NY 1963; Univ of Aberdeen: sr lectr 1964, second prof of English 1965–68, regius prof of English 1968–84, dean Faculty of Arts and Social Sci 1979–82, sr vice-princ 1982–84; Goldsmiths' Coll: London warden 1984–92, prof 1988–92, emeritus prof and hon fell 1992; vice-chllr Univ of London 1994–97; chm of English Bd CNAA 1966–73, Br Cncl Lecture tours 1973–89, pres Int Assoc of Univ Profs of English 1977–80, memb BBC Gen Advsy Cncl 1979–84, chm Literature Advsy Ctee British Cncl 1987–, memb various Scottish Educn Dept Ctees on curriculum and examinations; Hon DLitt State Univ of NY 1990, Hon DUniv Athens 1993, Hon LLD Univ of Aberdeen 1995; Liveryman Worshipful Co of Goldsmiths 1991, Freeman City of London 1990; *Books* Byron - A Critical Study (1961), Kipling's Mind and Art (ed, 1964), Byron - The Critical Heritage (ed, 1970), The Literature of War (1979), Early Verse by Rudyard Kipling 1879–1889 (ed, 1986); *Recreations* shooting; *Style—* Prof Andrew Rutherford, CBE; ✉ Saltoun Hall, Pencaitland, East Lothian EH34 5DS

RUTHERFORD, His Hon Judge; Andrew; s of Robert Mark Rutherford, and Alison Wellington, *née* Clark; *b* 25 March 1948; *Educ* Clifton, Univ of Exeter (LLB); *m* 7 April 1994, Lucy Elizabeth, da of Prof Edmund Bosworth; *Career* called to the Bar Middle Temple 1970, recorder of the Crown Court 1993–95, circuit judge (Western Circuit) 1995–; *Clubs* Bath and County; *Style—* His Hon Judge Rutherford; ✉ Western Circuit Office, Bridge House, Sion Place, Clifton, Bristol BS8 4BN (☎ 0117 974 3763)

RUTHERFORD, Brian William John; *b* 13 Feb 1956; *Educ* LLB; *m* Louise; 3 c; *Career* ptnr Bonar Mackenzie WS 1977–83, vice pres Continental Bank Chicago and London 1983–88, dir Charterhouse Bank Ltd 1988–93, ptnr Dundas & Wilson CS solicitors 1993–; *Style—* Brian Rutherford, Esq; ✉ Dundas & Wilson CS, Boston House, 63/64 New Broad Street, London EC2M 1JR (☎ 0171 256 9191, fax 0171 256 6464)

RUTHERFORD, David John Buckley; OBE (1987); s of Col Alexander John Buckley Rutherford, CVO, CBE (d 1979), of Assendon Lodge, Henley-on-Thames, Oxon, and Joan, *née* Begg (d 1979); *b* 27 July 1930; *Educ* Winchester, Trinity Coll Cambridge (MA); *m* 11 July 1959, Elisabeth Dagmar, da of Henri Thierry-Mieg (d 1938); 3 da (Virginia b 15 Aug 1960, Sophie b 19 Nov 1961, Alice b 21 Sept 1965); *Career* 2 Lt 9 Lancers 1949, City of London Yeo RR TA; dir Martini and Rossi Ltd 1976–96; chm Wine and Spirit Assoc GB 1974–76 and 1988–89; pres FIVS 1989–91; memb Ct of Assts Worshipful Co of Vintners (Master 1994–95); Ordre National du Mérite France 1976, Ordem do Infante Dom Henrique Portugal 1977, Ordine Al Merito della Repubblica Italiana 1982; *Recreations* golf; *Style—* David Rutherford, Esq, OBE; ✉ Martini & Rossi Ltd, 32 Faroe Road, London W14 0EP (☎ 0171 602 3155)

RUTHERFORD, (Gordon) Malcolm; s of Gordon Brown Rutherford (d 1988), of Newcastle upon Tyne, and Bertha, *née* Browne (d 1989); *b* 21 Aug 1939; *Educ* Newcastle Royal GS, Balliol Coll Oxford; *m* 1, 1965 (m dis 1969), Susan Margaret, *née* Tyler; m 2, 24 Feb 1970, Elizabeth Claude Rosemary Maitland, da of Pierre Pelen, of Paris; 3 da (Emma b 15 April 1973, Camilla b 10 Sept 1974, Laetitia b 6 July 1976); *Career* arts ed then foreign ed The Spectator 1962–65, fndr newsletter Latin America 1965; Financial Times: dip corr 1966–69, Bonn corr 1969–74, dep foreign ed 1974–77, asst ed 1977–93, chief political columnist 1977–88, Observer column 1988–90, chief theatre critic 1990–94, obituaries ed 1995–; founding memb: Media Law Group 1983, West-West Agenda 1988; memb Cncl Chatham House; OStJ 1990; *Books* Can We Save the Common Market (1981, 2nd edn 1983); *Recreations* tennis, theatre, reading; *Clubs* Travellers; *Style—* Malcolm Rutherford, Esq; ✉ 89 Bedford Gardens, London W8 7EQ (☎ 0171 229 2063); Financial Times, 1 Southwark Bridge, London SE1

RUTHERFORD, Vice Adm Malcolm Graham; CBE (1991); *b* 21 March 1941; *Educ* Univ of London (BSc), Sch of Languages London (French course); *m* 1969; 2 c; *Career* Italian interpreter 1969; RN 1967–96: served HM Submarines Conqueror and Sceptre until 1978, Nat Defence Coll Latimer 1979, MOD overseer Vickers Shipbuilders 1979–80, MOD London 1980–84, weapons engr surface warship Gulf patrol 1985, two sr posts Procurement Exec 1985–88, Capt 1988, chief exec largest tech trg establishment in Europe 1988–90, Rear Adm 1991, dir personnel MOD 1991–92, Vice Adm 1992, Naval Sec 1992–94, DCDS(S) and Chief Naval Engrg Offr 1994–95, dir i/c reviewing and preparing RN Engrg Branch structure 1995–96; dir Defence Systems GEC Marconi S3I 1996–; Freeman City of London 1996; CEng 1970, FIEE 1985 (RN rep 1988–90), Eur Ing 1989, FRGS; *Recreations* mountaineering, skiing, marathon running, photography, cycling (Channel to Mediterranean 1990), public speaking, current and financial affairs; *Clubs* Garrick, Alpine; *Style—* Vice Adm Malcolm Rutherford, CBE; ✉ c/o Garrick Club, Garrick Street, London WC2E 9AY

RUTHERFORD, Michael John Cloette Crawford (Mike); s of Capt W H F Crawford Rutherford (d 1986), of Farnham, Surrey, and Annette, *née* Downing (d 1993); *b* 2 Oct 1950; *Educ* Charterhouse; *m* 13 Nov 1976, Angela Mary, da of Harry Downing; 2 s (Tom William b 4 Dec 1980, Harry John Crawford b 19 Nov 1987), 1 da (Kate Elizabeth b 19 Oct 1977); *Career* musician; fndr memb Genesis 1966 (with Peter Gabriel, *qv*, and Tony Banks, *qv*), first single released 1969, seventeenth album released 1992; fndr Mike and the Mechanics gp 1985–; top ten single Over My Shoulder 1995 (from album Beggar on a Beach of Gold 1995); *Recreations* polo (Cowdray Park); *Style—* Mike Rutherford, Esq; ✉ c/o Hit & Run Music Ltd, 30 Ives St, London SW3 2ND (☎ 0171 581 0261, fax 0171 584 5774)

RUTHVEN OF CANBERRA, Viscount; Patrick Leo Brer Ruthven; o s and h of 2 Earl of Gowrie, PC, *qv*, and his 1 w, Xandra, *née* Bingley; *b* 4 Feb 1964; *m* Feb 1990, Julie Goldsmith; 1 s (Hon Heathcote Patrick Cornelius Hore b 28 May 1990); *Style—* Viscount Ruthven of Canberra

RUTLAND, 10 Duke of (E 1703); Charles John Robert Manners; CBE (1962); also Earl of Rutland (E 1525), Baron Manners of Haddon (E 1679), Marquess of Granby (E 1703), and Baron Roos of Belvoir (E 1616); s of 9 Duke of Rutland (d 1940), and Kathleen, *née* Tennant (d 1989); and fifteenth in descent from 1 Earl of Rutland's maternal grandmother Anne Plantagenet (sis of Edward IV); *b* 28 May 1919; *Educ* Eton, Trinity Coll Cambridge; *m* 1, 27 April 1946 (m dis 1956), Anne Bairstow, da of Maj William Cumming Bell, of Huddersfield; 1 da; m 2, 15 May 1958, Frances Helen, da of Charles Francis Sweeny (d 1993), of Chesterfield House, South Audley Street, London, and his 1 w, Margaret, Duchess of Argyll (d 1993); 2 s, 1 da (and 1 s decd); *Heir* s, Marquess of Granby; *Career* chm: E Midlands Econ Planning Cncl 1971–74, Leics CC 1974–77; DL and JP Leics; proprietor: Rutland Hotels Ltd, Belvoir Castle (rebuilt by Wyatt in 1800), Haddon Hall Derbyshire; late Capt Grenadier Gds; patron of 11 livings, owner of 18,000 acres; *Style—* His Grace the Duke of Rutland, CBE; ✉ Belvoir Castle, Grantham, Lincs; Haddon Hall, Bakewell, Derbys

RUTMAN, Laurence David; s of Sidney Rutman, and Anne, *née* Smith; *b* 8 Oct 1937; *Educ* Hendon Co Sch, UCL (LLB), Yale Univ (LLM); *m* 26 July 1964, Sandra Christine, da of Philip Colvin; 2 s (Simon b 1966, Paul b 1970), 1 da (Laura b 1968); *Career* slr; ptnr: Paisner & Co 1960–74, Ashurst Morris Crisp 1974– (currently dep sr ptnr and head of Property Dept); *Recreations* music, literature, book collecting; *Style—* Laurence Rutman, Esq; ✉ Broxham House, Four Elms, Edenbridge, Kent; 38 Margaretta Terrace, London SW3; Ashurst Morris Crisp, Broadwalk House, 5 Appold St, London EC2A 2HA (☎ 0171 638 1111, fax 0171 972 7990, telex 887067)

RUTT, Rev (Cecil) Richard; CBE (1973); s of Cecil Rutt, and Mary Hare, *née* Turner; *b* 27 Aug 1925; *Educ* Kelham Theological Coll, Pembroke Coll Cambridge (MA); *m* 1969, Joan Mary Ford; *Career* served RNVR 1943–46; ordained priest 1952, rector St Michael's Seminary (Oryu Dong, Seoul, Korea) 1965–66, bishop of Taejon 1968–74 (asst bishop 1966–68), bishop suffragan of St German's and hon canon St Mary's Cathedral Truro 1974–79, bishop of Leicester 1979–90; ordained Roman Catholic priest 1995; bard of Gorsedd of Cornwall Cornwhylen 1976, hon fell Northumbrian Univs East Asia Centre 1990; Hon DLitt Confucian Univ Seoul 1974; ChStJ 1978; Order of Civil Merit (Peony Class) Korea 1974; *Books* Korean Works and Days (1964), James Scarth Gale and his History of the Korean People (1972), An Anthology of Korean Sijo (1970), The Bamboo Grove (1971), Virtuous Women (translation, 1974), A History of Hand Knitting (1987), The Book of Changes: Zhouyi (1996); *Style—* The Rev Richard Rutt, CBE; ✉ 3 Marlborough Court, Falmouth, Cornwall TR11 2QU (☎ 01326 312276)

RUTTEMAN, Paul Johannes; CBE (1983); s of Cornelis Hendrikus Bernardus Rutteman (d 1962), of Watford, Herts, and Anna Smak (d 1991); *b* 9 Nov 1938; *Educ* Merchant Taylors', LSE (BSc); *m* 1, 1967, Annette Franklin (d 1978); 1 s (John b 2 June 1972), 1 da (Susan b 23 Nov 1970); m 2, 1981, Dorothy Louise, da of John Storie; 2 s (Thomas b 25 Dec 1981, Philip b 1 April 1983); *Career* articled clerk Broads Paterson 1960–64, chartered accountant 1964–, chm Fin Servs Arthur Young 1985–89 (sr tech ptnr 1970–85), ptnr Banking and Fin Servs Indust Gp Ernst & Young 1989–; memb Cncl ICAEW 1978–87, 1989–91 and 1996–, chm Inst Ctee of Fin Servs, pres Groupe d'Etudes des Experts Comptables Brussels 1985–87; FCA (ACA 1964); *Books* author various articles, contrib various books; *Recreations* walking, sailing, photography, family; *Style—* Paul Rutteman, Esq, CBE; ✉ Ernst & Young, Rolls House, Rolls Buildings, Fetter Lane, London EC4A 1NH (☎ 0171 928 2000, 0171 931 1156, fax 0171 405 2147)

RUTTER, Claire; *Educ* Guildhall Sch of Music & Drama (AGSM), Nat Opera Studio (sponsored by Friends of Eng Nat Opera); *m* Stephen Gadd (baritone); *Career* soprano; currently contract princ Scottish Opera; Wigmore Hall recital début 1994; *Roles* with Scottish Opera incl: Violetta in La Traviata, Terinka in The Jacobin, Countess Almaviva in The Marriage of Figaro, Elettra in Idomeneo, Mimi in La Bohème; other prodns incl: Violetta (Welsh Nat Opera), Donna Anna in Don Giovanni (British Youth Opera), Tatyana in Eugene Onegin (Nonsuch Opera), Songs of the Auvergne (with BBC Scottish Symphony Orch); *Recordings* highlights of Madame Butterfly and La Bohème (with RPO) 1997; *Style—* Ms Claire Rutter; ✉ Scottish Opera, 39 Elmbank Crescent, Glasgow G2 4PT (☎ 0141 248 4567, fax 0141 221 8812)

RUTTER, Rev Canon (Allen Edward Henry) Claude; s of Rev Norman Rutter (d 1967), and Hilda, *née* Mason (d 1979); *b* 24 Dec 1928; *Educ* Monkton Combe, Dauntsey's, Queens' Coll Cambridge (MA, DipAgric), Univ of Durham (DipTheol); *m* 26 April 1960, Elizabeth Jane, da of Rt Rev Martin Patrick Grainge Leonard, DSO, MA (Bishop of Thetford, d 1963); 2 s (Christopher b 1962, Timothy b 1965), 2 da (Patricia b 1961, Miranda b 1976); *Career* scientific liaison offr E Malling Res Station Kent 1953–56; curate: Bath Abbey 1959–60, E Dereham Norfolk 1960–64; rector: Cawston Gp (and chaplain Cawston Coll) Norfolk 1964–69, Gingindhlovu Zululand (and agric sec Helwel Diocese of Zululand) 1969–73, Queen Thorne Dorset 1973–; rural dean Sherborne Dorset 1976–87, chm Salisbury Diocesan Lay Educnl and Trg Ctee 1984–92, canon and prebendary Salisbury Cathedral 1986–, diocesan co-ordinator Rural Miny Devpt 1987–92, diocesan rural link offr 1989–92, conslt Archbishops' Cmmn on Rural Areas 1989–91; played cricket for: Univ of Cambridge 1953, Wilts CCC 1948–55, Norfolk CCC 1961–65 (the only clergyman to have played in the Gillette Cup); played hockey for: Cambridge Univ Wanderers, Maidstone; Clergy Golf champion 1977 and 1991; *Recreations* cricket, hockey, golf, farming, gardening, picture framing; *Clubs* Hawks (Cambridge), MCC, Farmers', United Oxford and Cambridge Univ; *Style—* The Rev Canon Claude Rutter; ✉ Trent Rectory, Sherborne, Dorset DT9 4SL (☎ 01935 851049)

RUTTER, Hadyn Michael; s of Herbert Rutter (d 1985), of Winsford, Cheshire, and Mabel Rutter; *b* 29 Dec 1946; *Educ* Verdin GS Winsford, Lincoln Coll Oxford (BA); *m* 1 April 1970, Susan, da of Charles Robert Johnson, of Winsford; 3 da (Tanya b 1974, Amanda b 1977, Lisa b 1981); *Career* admitted slr 1971; Richards Butler & Co London 1969–72, sr ptnr Bruce Campbell & Co Cayman Islands 1977–80 (joined 1972), own practice 1980–; pres Cayman Islands Law Soc 1979 (sec 1975–79); dir: Golf Links Int Ltd, Golf Links Int Inc; organiser World Pro-Am: Arizona, Acapulco, Hong Kong, Dubai, Sun City, Thailand; author Cayman Islands Handbook Tax Guide 1977; Duke of Edinburgh Award (Gold) 1965; *Recreations* cricket, golf, badminton, tennis; *Clubs* Utd Oxford and Cambridge; *Style—* Hadyn Rutter, Esq; ✉ The Mount, Cuddington Lane, Cuddington, Cheshire CW8 2SZ (☎ 01606 883070, fax 01606 889031)

RUTTER, James Edgar; s of Frederick Edgar Rutter (d 1951), of Shelton, Stoke on Trent, and Maggie, *née* Arthan (d 1956); *b* 23 July 1930; *Educ* Longton HS, LSE (BScEcon); *m* 23 May 1953, Margaret Mary, eld da of Benjamin Brian, of Penkhull; 2 s (Mark b 14 Aug 1960, Richard b 13 Jan 1963), 1 da (Sally b 15 Oct 1967); *Career* Nat Serv 1953–55; articled clerk E Downward & Co Hanley 1947–53, accountant Rootes Ltd 1956–58, co sec Agricultural Finance 1958–61, md Peterborough Investment Co 1961–68, lectr Staffordshire Univ (formerly Poly) 1968–; pres: N Staffs Soc of Chartered Accountants 1981–82, Staffs Salop and Wolverhampton Soc of Chartered Accountants 1990–91; contrib articles in: Accountancy (1984), Public Finance and Accountancy (1984), International Accountant (1986); FCA 1964 (ACA 1954); *Recreations* walking, gardening; *Clubs* Trentham RUFC; *Style—* James Rutter, Esq; ✉ 35 Naples Drive, Westlands, Newcastle under Lyme, Staffs ST5 2QD (☎ 01782 632662); Business School, Staffordshire University, Leek Road, Stoke on Trent, Staffs (☎ 01782 412515, fax 01782 744035)

RUTTER, His Hon John Cleverdon; s of Edgar John Rutter (d 1971), of Cardiff, and Nellie, *née* Parker (d 1928); *b* 18 Sept 1919; *Educ* Cardiff HS for Boys, Univ Coll of the SW of Eng Exeter (LLB), Keble Coll Oxford (MA); *m* 4 Sept 1951, Jill (d 1993), da of Maxwell Duncan McIntosh; 1 s (Jeremy b 1953), 1 da (Philippa (Mrs James) b 1955); *Career* serv WWII RA 1939–46, cmmnd 1941, serv overseas; called to the Bar Lincoln's Inn 1948; practising Wales and Chester circuit 1948–66; recorder: Cardiff 1962–66, Merthyr Tydfil 1962–66, Swansea 1965–66; legal memb Mental Health Review Tbnl

Wales 1962–66, Stipendiary Magistrate Cardiff 1966–71, dep chm Glamorgan Quarter Sessions 1969–71, circuit judge Cardiff Crown Ct 1972–90, sr circuit judge 1990–92 (ret); *Recreations* golf, reading; *Style—* His Hon John Rutter; ✉ c/o The Law Courts, Cardiff

RUTTER, Dr (James) Michael; s of James William Rutter (d 1996), of Kendal, and Lily, *née* Harriman (d 1986); *b* 20 Aug 1941; *Educ* Kendal GS, Royal (Dick) Sch of Veterinary Studies Univ of Edinburgh (BVM and S, BSc, PhD); *m* 1 July 1967, Jacqueline Patricia, da of late Thomas Anderson Watson; 1 da (Charlotte Sophie b 6 May 1977); *Career* Univ of Edinburgh: res scholar 1964–67, res asst 1967–69; Inst for Research on Animal Diseases Compton (later Inst for Animal Health): vet res offr 1969–73, princ vet res offr 1973–84, seconded to Dept of Educn and Science 1975–78, head Dept of Microbiology 1984–89, acting head Compton Laboratory 1986–89; dir of Vet Meds MAFF 1989–, chief exec Vet Meds Directorate 1990–; MRCVS 1964; *Books* Perinatal Ill Health in Calves (ed, 1973), Pasteurella and Pasteurellosis (co-ed, 1989); author of numerous scientific articles; *Recreations* gardening, outdoor sports; *Style—* Dr Michael Rutter; ✉ Veterinary Medicines Directorate, Woodham Lane, New Haw, Addlestone, Surrey KT15 3NB (☎ 01932 336911)

RUTTER, Prof Sir Michael Llewellyn; kt (1992), CBE (1985); s of Llewellyn Charles Rutter, and Winifred Olive, *née* Barber; *b* 15 Aug 1933; *Educ* Wolverhampton GS, Bootham Sch York, Univ of Birmingham Med Sch (MB ChB, MD); *m* 28 December 1958, Marjorie, da of Richard Heys (d 1983); 1 s (Stephen b 5 April 1963), 2 da (Sheila b 22 April 1960, Christine b 18 Sept 1964); *Career* memb scientific staff MRC Social Psychiatry Res Unit 1962–65; Inst of Psychiatry Univ of London: sr lectr (later reader) 1966–73, prof of child psychiatry 1973–; hon conslt physician Bethlam Royal and Maudsley Hosps 1966–; hon dir MRC Child Psychiatry Unit Inst of Psychiatry 1984–, hon dir Social Genetic & Developmental Psychiatry Research Centre 1994–; Hon Dr: Univ of Leiden 1985, Catholic Univ Louvain 1990, Univ of Jyvaskyla Finland 1996; Hon DSc: Univ of Birmingham 1990, Univ of Chicago 1991, Univ of Minnesota 1993, Univ of Ghent 1994; Hon MD Univ of Edinburgh 1990; Distinguished Scientific Contribution Award American Psychological Association 1995, Castilla del Pino Prize for Achievement in Psychiatry Cordoba Spain 1995; foreign assoc memb: Inst of Med US Nat Acad of Sciences 1988, US Nat Acad of Educn 1990; foreign hon memb American Acad of Arts and Sciences 1989; founding memb Academia Europaea 1988, hon memb Br Paediatric Assoc 1994; FRS 1987, Hon FRS 1996, hon fell Inst of Child Health 1996; *Books* incl: A Neuropsychiatric Study in Childhood (with P Graham and W Yule, 1970), Maternal Deprivation Reassessed (1972, 2 edn 1981), The Child With Delayed Speech (ed with J A M Martin, 1972), Cycles of Disadvantage: A Review of Research (with N Madge, 1976), Changing Youth in a Changing Society: Patterns of Adolescent Development and Disorder (1979), Developmental Neuropsychiatry (ed 1983), Juvenile Delinquency: Trends and Perspectives (with H Giller, 1983), Language Development and Disorders (ed with W Yule, 1987), Straight and Devious Pathways from Childhood to Adulthood (ed with L Robins, 1990), Developing Minds: Challenge and Continuity Across the Lifespan (with Majorie Rutter, 1993), Child and Adolescent Psychiatry: Modern Approaches (ed with E Taylor and L Hersov, 3 edn 1994), Development Through Life (ed with D Hay, 1994), Stress, Risk and Resilience in Children and Adolescents: Processes, Mechanisms and Interventions (ed with R J Haggerty, L R Sherrod and N Garmezy, 1994), Psychosocial Disorders in Young People: Time trends and their causes (co-edited with David Smith, 1995); *Recreations* grandchildren, fell walking, tennis, wine tasting, theatre; *Style—* Prof Sir Michael Rutter, CBE, FRS; ✉ 190 Court Lane, Dulwich, London SE21 7ED; Institute of Psychiatry, De Crespigny Park, Denmark Hill, London SE5 8AF (☎ 0171 703 5411, fax 0171 708 5800)

RUTTER, Trevor John; CBE (1990, OBE 1976); s of Alfred Rutter (d 1974), of Gwent, and Agnes, *née* Purslow (d 1966); *b* 26 Jan 1934; *Educ* Monmouth Sch, BNC Oxford (BA); *m* 1959, Jo, da of David Barrs Henson (d 1980); 1 s (Orlando); *Career* Br Cncl Indonesia and Munich W Germany 1959–65, first sec FO 1967; Br Cncl: dir in Singapore 1968–71 and Bangkok 1971–75, HQ posts 1975–85 (incl asst dir gen 1982–85), dir in Germany 1986–90, asst dir gen 1990–91, ret; *Style—* Trevor Rutter, Esq, CBE; ✉ 8 De Vere Close, Wivenhoe, Colchester, Essex CO7 9AX (☎ 01206 822562); Niederhutstrasse 49, 53474 Ahrweiler, Germany

RYALL, David John; s of John Bertram Ryall (d 1978), of Shoreham-by-Sea, Sussex, and Gladys Lilian, *née* Bowles (d 1980); *b* 5 Jan 1936; *Educ* Shoreham GS, Wallington GS, RADA (scholar); *m* 1, 1964 (m dis 1984), Gillian, da of Rear Adm Eddison; 1 s (Jonathan Charles b 8 Feb 1966), 1 da (Imogen Victoria b 21 Sept 1967); m 2, 1985, Cathy, da of Benek Buchwald, of Poland; 1 da (Charlotte Maria Grace b 15 Oct 1986); *Career* actor; *Theatre* repertory work at Salisbury, Leicester, Bristol and Birmingham (incl King Lear and The Masterbuilder); with NT at the Old Vic 1965–73: Armstrongs Last Goodnight, The Royal Hunt of the Sun, Rosencrantz and Guildenstern are Dead, A Flea In Her Ear, The Idiot, The Beaux Strategem, The National Health, Jumpers, The Front Page; RNT incl: A Month In The Country, Guys and Dolls, The Beggars' Opera, Coriolanus (Clarence Derwent Award 1985), Animal Farm, A Chorus of Disapproval, Rosmersholm, School for Wives, Wild Oats 1995; devised, directed and performed for NT: A Leap in the Light (works by Edward Bond) 1984, Ego in the Cosmos (Diaries of James Agate) 1989; other appearances incl Twelfth Night (Peter Hall Co) 1991, Venice Preserved (Royal Exchange Co Manchester) 1994; *Television* incl: The Knowledge, The Singing Detective, Inspector Morse, The Men's Room, Shelley, The Borrowers, Casualty, Prime Suspect, To Play the King, Lovejoy, A Touch of Frost, The Final Cut, Jake's Progress, Plotlands; *Film* incl: The Elephant Man, Empire of the Sun, Wilt, Truly Madly Deeply, Revolver, Giorgino, Restoration, Carrington; *Style—* David Ryall, Esq; ✉ c/o Scott Marshall Personal Management, 44 Perryn Road, London W3 7NA (☎ 0181 749 7692, fax 0181 743 1669)

RYALL, Dr Roger Duncan Hall; s of Capt Sydney Kenneth Ryall (d 1947), of Shoreham-by-Sea, and Evelyn Elizabeth, *née* Wright (d 1989); *b* 9 March 1938; *Educ* Wellington, Middx Hosp Med Sch (MB BS, DMRT); *m* 15 June 1963, Rosemary Elizabeth, da of Kenneth David Brough, of London; 1 s (Edward b 1970), 1 da (Vanessa (Mrs Christopher Remington) b 1967); *Career* clinical dir radiotherapy and oncology Wessex Radiotherapy Centre 1978–; pres Hosp Conslts and Specialists Assoc 1982–84 (hon vice pres 1988), registrar Faculty of Clinical Oncology Royal Coll of Radiologists 1990–94; memb Cruising Assoc; memb: RSM, Br Inst Radiology; FRCR; *Books* author of papers on various aspects of cancer res; *Recreations* sailing; *Style—* Dr Roger Ryall; ✉ Hampton House, Headbourne Worthy, Winchester, Hants SO23 7JH (☎ 01962 883270); Wessex Radiotherapy Centre, Royal Southants Hospital, Graham Rd, Southampton (☎ 01703 634288)

RYAN, Chris John; s of Henry Patrick Ryan, of Melton, Suffolk, and Evelyn May, *née* Hill; *b* 16 June 1954; *Educ* Farlingaye Sch Woodbridge, Colchester Sch of Art; *m* 22 June 1982, Vanessa Faith, da of Colin Day; *Career* photographer; trained with Phil Jude, Tony Copeland and Van Pariser; own studio 1981–; major assignments incl: covers for Radio Times and Telegraph, Aston Martin cars, Vogue Espana magazine, annual reports for Duke of Westminster and Societe Generale de Belgique; awards from D & AD and Assoc of Photographers; memb Assoc of Photographers 1976; *Recreations* anything hedonistic; *Style—* Chris Ryan, Esq; ✉ Chris Ryan Studio, 11 Wyfold Rd, Studio 3, London SW6 6SE (☎ 0171 386 8080, fax 0171 386 8041, mobile 0831 806963)

RYAN, David Edward; s of Thomas Ryan (d 1986), and Janet Stafford Ryan; *b* 17 May 1946; *Educ* Hyde GS; *m* 21 Dec 1968, Susan, da of John Cooper (d 1987); 2 s (Mark b 29 Sept 1969, Andrew b 30 July 1971), 1 da (Anna b 21 Nov 1981); *Career* articled Shuttleworth & Haworth, CA 1968, joined Webb Hanson Bullivant & Co 1969 (ptnr 1972); Neville Russell: ptnr 1986, sr ptnr Stockport office 1987–, memb Nat Exec 1996–; dir Stockport Business Venture Ltd, treas Franco-British Business Club; *Recreations* walking, cycling, being out of doors, listening to music, theatre; *Style—* David Ryan, Esq; ✉ Neville Russell, Regent House, Heaton Lane, Stockport SK4 1BS (☎ 0161 477 4750, fax 0161 476 0533)

RYAN, David Stuart; s of David Ryan, of Kingston-upon-Thames, and Eileen Inez, *née* Sullivan (d 1966); *b* 22 Oct 1943; *Educ* Wimbledon Coll, KCL (BA); *m* 16 June 1971, Jacqueline, da of Sydney Wills (d 1989), of Southfields, London; 1 da (Chloe Selena b 1972); *Career* author and advtg copywriter KDM Advertising; *Publications* John Lennon's Secret (1982), India A Guide to the Experience (1983), America A Guide to the Experience (1986), The Lost Journal of Robyn Hood - Outlaw (1989), The Cream of the Troubadour Coffee House (1990), The Blue Angel - Marlene Dietrich's Life and Loves (1993); memb: DMA, IDM, IPG; winner of 24 nat and int advtg awards; *Recreations* photography, travel, poetry; *Clubs* Poetry Soc; *Style—* David Ryan, Esq; ✉ KDM Advertising, Kozmik Press Centre, 83 Gloucester Place, London W1H 3PG (☎ 0171 935 5913, fax 0171 487 4963)

RYAN, Dr David William; s of Leslie Ryan (d 1989), and Fiona, *née* Gregson; *b* 2 May 1946; *Educ* Sheffield City GS, Univ of Sheffield (MB ChB); *m* 24 July 1969, Susan Margaret, da of James Edward Varley (d 1945); 2 s (James b 1973, Charles b 1976); *Career* conslt and hon lectr in anaesthesia Univ of Newcastle upon Tyne 1978–, conslt clinical physiologist 1981–, conslt in charge Intensive Therapy Unit Freeman Hosp 1981–; author of over 120 articles and res papers on intensive therapy, ed Care of The Critically Ill Journal; memb Cncl: Intensive Care Soc 1983–89 (sec 1984–87), World Fedn of Intensive and Critical Care Med 1989– (treas 1993–); memb: BMA 1970, Assoc of Anaesthetists 1972, Intensive Care Soc 1978; FFARCS; *Books* Colour Atlas of Critical and Intensive Care (with G R Park, 1995), Current Practice in Critical Illness Vol 1 (ed); *Recreations* cricket, art; *Style—* Dr David Ryan; ✉ General Intensive Therapy Unit, Freeman Hospital, Newcastle upon Tyne NE7 7DN (☎ 0191 284 3111 ext 26423, fax 0191 223 1180)

RYAN, Maj-Gen Denis Edgar; CB (1987); s of Reginald Arthur Ryan, of Westbury, Wilts, and Amelia, *née* Smith; *b* 18 June 1928; *Educ* Sir William Borlase Marlow Bucks, King's Coll London (LLB); *m* 6 Aug 1955, Jean Mary, da of Charles Waldemar Bentley (d 1963); 1 s (Mark b 1966), 1 da (Amanda (Mrs Jonathan Jardine Paterson) b 1964); *Career* cmmnd RAEC 1950; instr: 3 HEC BAOR 1950–52, SO3 HQ BAOR 1952–54, RMA Sandhurst 1954–56; adj Army Sch of Educn 1956–59, Staff Coll 1960, DAQMG HQ Near E Land Forces (Cyprus) 1961–62, and SO2 Special Ops HQ E Africa (Kenya) 1962–64, SO2 AED 1 MOD 1964–66, GSO2 Intelligence Centre 1966–68, CAES HQ 4 Div BAOR 1968–70, GSO1 Cabinet Office 1970–72, trg devpt advsr Staff Coll 1972–75, Col GS DI4 MOD 1976–78, chief educn offr HQ SE Dist 1978–79, Cdr educn HQ BAOR 1979–82 and UK 1982–84, Dir of Army Educn MOD 1984–87, Col Cmdt RAEC 1990–92, Dep Col Cmdt A G Corps 1992–93; *Recreations* cricket, tennis, rugby, music, theatre; *Clubs* Army and Navy; *Style—* Maj-Gen D E Ryan, CB

RYAN, Sir Derek Gerald; 4 Bt (UK 1919), of Hintlesham, Suffolk; o s of Sir Derek Gerald Ryan, 3 Bt (d 1990), and his 1 w, Penelope Anne, *née* Hawkings; *b* 25 March 1954; *Educ* Univ of California at Berkeley (BAEd); *m* 1986 (m dis 1990), Maria Teresa, da of Juan G Rodriguez, of Lexington, Kentucky; *Heir* kinsman, Desmond Maurice Ryan b 1918; *Career* with Fowler Ferguson Kingston Ruben architects Salt Lake City Utah 1977–79, Atelier d'Urbanisme en Montagne architects/urban planners Chambery France June-Oct 1979; NBBJ architects/planners Seattle Washington 1980–; memb Nat Cncl of Architects Registration Bd (NCARB) 1984; *Recreations* skiing, guitar; *Style—* Sir Derek Ryan, Bt; ✉ 4618 South Austin Street, Seattle, WA 98118–3924, USA (☎ 00 1 206 723 6182); NBBJ, 111 South Jackson Street, Seattle, WA 98104, USA (☎ 00 1 206 223 5204, fax 00 1 206 621 2300)

RYAN, Dr Frank Patrick; s of Francis Ryan (d 1972), of Bolton, Lancs, and Mary Alice, *née* Fitzpatrick; *b* 23 July 1944; *Educ* Thornleigh Coll, Univ of Sheffield Med Sch (MB ChB); *m* 14 Sept 1968, Barbara, da of Frank Horrocks, of Bolton; 1 s (John b 1973), 1 da (Catherine b 1972); *Career* conslt physician Northern Gen Hosp Sheffield; dir Bolton Fine Arts private gallery 1971–79; author, books incl: Sweet Summer (1987), Tiger Tiger (1988), The Eskimo Diet (1990), Goodbye Baby Blue (1990), Tuberculosis: The Greatest Story Never Told (1992), Virus-X (1996); author numerous med pubns; memb Soc of Authors; FRCP 1985, fell Royal Soc of Health; *Recreations* football, walking, painting, appreciation of art; *Clubs* Lansdowne; *Style—* Dr Frank Ryan; ✉ Sheffield District Health Authority (☎ 0114 267 0333)

RYAN, John Gerald Christopher; s of Sir Andrew Ryan, KBE, CMG (d 1949), of E Bergholt, Suffolk, and Ruth Marguerite, *née* Van Millingen (d 1975); *b* 4 March 1921; *Educ* Ampleforth; *m* 3 Jan 1950, Priscilla Ann, da of Austin Blomfield (d 1968), of Chelsea; 1 s (Christopher b 1954), 2 da (Marianne b 1951, Isabel b 1957); *Career* served WWII Lincs Regt UK, India, Burma 1940–46, cmmnd 2 Lt 1941, demobilised Capt 1946; children's author, illustrator and cartoon film maker; cr Captain Pugwash, 35 pubns incl 16 Captian Pugwash titles 1955–, maker of BBC Captain Pugwash films and over 100 others incl Sir Prancelot and Mary Mungo & Midge 1956–80, cartoonist for the Catholic Herald 1964–; memb Soc of Authors; *Recreations* walking; *Style—* John Ryan, Esq; ✉ Gungarden Lodge, The Gungardens, Rye, East Sussex TN31 7HH (☎ 01797 222034)

RYAN, John Patrick; s of James Patrick Ryan (d 1960), of Rhos-on-Sea, N Wales, and Marie Elsie, *née* Gaines (d 1988); *b* 19 Aug 1943; *Educ* St Mary's Coll Rhos-on-Sea N Wales, Queen's Coll Cambridge (MA); *m* 8 Feb 1969, Verna Marguerite, da of Capt Charles Edward Henry Mytton, of Hampstead Garden Suburb; 2 s (Nicholas b 26 Feb 1972, Alastair b 13 Sept 1976), 1 da (Annabel b 22 March 1974); *Career* actuarial supt Guardian Royal Exchange 1968, ptnr James Capel & Co 1972–76, vice pres & princ Tillinghast 1976– (part of Towers Perrin Co); vice pres Inst of Actuaries; assoc Casualty Actuarial Soc USA 1979, memb American Acad of Actuaries USA 1979, fell Inst of Risk Mgmnt 1987; Freeman: City of London, Liveryman Worshipful Co of Needlemakers; FIA 1968, AMIIA 1973; *Recreations* travel, walking, theatre, old buildings, golf, racing; *Style—* John Ryan, Esq; ✉ 15 Priory Gardens, Highgate, London N6 5QY (☎ 0181 348 0195); Old Mill House, West Row Fen, Mildenhall, Suffolk; Tillinghast, Towers Perrin, Castlewood House, 77–91 New Oxford Street, London WC1A 1PX (☎ 0171 379 4000, fax 0171 379 7478, telex 261 411)

RYAN, (Christopher) Nigel John; CBE (1977); s of Brig C E Ryan, MC (d 1981), and Joy, *née* Dodgson; *b* 12 Dec 1929; *Educ* Ampleforth, Queen's Coll Oxford (MA); *Career* chief exec and ed Independent Television News 1969–77, vice pres NBC News (New York) 1977–80, dir of progs Thames Television 1980–82, chm TV-am (News) 1987–92; *Books* A Hitch or Two in Afghanistan (1983), The Scholar and The Gypsy (1992); translations of George Simenon and others; *Clubs* Beefsteak; *Style—* Nigel Ryan, Esq, CBE; ✉ 4 Cleveland Square, London W2 6DH (☎ 0171 723 8552)

RYAN, Sean Matthew; s of Brendan Manus Ryan, of London, and Marion Celia, *née* Hinkley; *b* 14 Sept 1959; *Educ* King's Sch Worcester, Pembroke Coll Oxford (scholar, MA); *m* 12 May 1984, Carmel Mary, da of Kevin Campbell; 1 s (Alastair Matthew b 24 Aug 1988), 1 da (Charlotte Anne b 21 April 1990); *Career* reporter Reading Evening Post 1982–85; Daily Mail 1985–90: investigative reporter 1987–88, asst news ed 1988–89, consumer affairs and environment corr 1989–90; Sunday Times: environment corr

1991–95, science corr 1994–95, dep news ed and sci ed 1995–96, Focus ed 1996–; memb Bd Watch Tst for Environmental Educn 1992–93; Pfizer Award Young Journalist of the Year 1983; *Recreations* walking, running; *Style*— Sean Ryan, Esq; ✉ Sunday Times, 1 Pennington Street, London E1 9XW (☎ 0171 782 5198, fax 0171 782 5612)

RYAN, William Patrick; *Career* Rothmans International BV: chief exec offr Australian associate co Rothmans Holdings Ltd 1989–90 (joined 1966), gp main bd dir 1990–, chief exec tobacco 1991–93, gp chief exec 1993–; *Style*— William Ryan, Esq; ✉ Rothmans International Services Limited, Denham Place, Village Road, Denham, Uxbridge, Middlesex UB9 5BL (☎ 01895 834949)

RYCROFT, Dr Charles; yr s of Sir Richard Rycroft, 5 Bt (d 1925), of Dummer House, Basingstoke, Hants, and Emily Mary, *née* Lowry-Corry (d 1982); *b* 9 Sept 1914; *Educ* Wellington, Trinity Coll Cambridge (exhibitioner, BA), Univ Coll and Univ Coll Hosp London (MB BS, MRCS, LRCP); *m* 1, 1947 (m dis 1963), Chloë, da of late Edouard Majolier; 1 s (Francis Edward b 1950), 2 da (Alice Julia b 1947, Catherine Anne b 1949); m 2, 1978, Jenny, da of late William Pearson; *Career* house physician Maudsley Hosp 1946, private practice in psychotherapy and psychoanalysis 1947–, asst ed Int Jl of Psychoanalysis 1955–58, conslt in psychotherapy Tavistock Clinic 1956–68; book reviewer: Observer, New Society, New Statesman, Times Literary Supplement, NY Review of Books, Modern Painters 1959–; author; *Books* Imagination and Reality (1968), Anxiety and Neurosis (1968), Critical Dictionary of Psychoanalysis (1968), Reich (1971), the Innocence of Dreams (1979), Psychoanalysis and Beyond (1985), Viewpoints (1991); contrib: Psychoanalysis Observed (1965), God I Want (1966), Symbols and Sentiments (1977), The Sources of Hope (1979); *Style*— Dr Charles Rycroft; ✉ 2 Modbury Gardens, London NW5 3QE (☎ 0171 482 1817 (private), 0171 482 6538 (professional))

RYCROFT, Sir Richard Newton; 7 Bt (GB 1784), of Calton, Yorks; s of Sir Nelson Edward Oliver Rycroft, 6 Bt (d 1958); *b* 23 Jan 1918; *Educ* Winchester, Christ Church Oxford (BA); *m* 1947, Ann, da of late Hugh Bellingham Smith; 2 da (Susan Marilda (Mrs Ian Martell) b 1948, Sally Ann (Viscountess FitzHarris) b 1950); *Heir* cous, Richard John Rycroft b 15 June 1946; *Career* master New Forest Foxhounds; memb The Badger Protection Gp; serv WWII Maj (Beds and Herts Regt) on special work in Balkans (despatches); Knight of Order of the Phoenix of Greece (with swords); patron of one living; *Style*— Sir Richard Rycroft, Bt; ✉ Winalls Wood House, Stuckton, Fordingbridge, Hants SP6 2HG (☎ (01425) 2263)

RYDER, Chris; s of Dermod Ryder, and Brigid, *née* Burns; *b* 9 May 1947; *Educ* St MacNissis Coll Garron Tower, St Mary's CBS Belfast; *m* 1967, Anne, da of late John Henry; 3 s (Paul b 6 July 1969, Declan b 5 June 1971, Edward b 14 Aug 1973), 1 da (Michelle); *Career* clerical offr Postmaster-Gen's Dept 1965–66, freelance journalist and publicist 1966–70, advtg and publicity mangr Bass Ireland Ltd 1970–71, freelance journalist 1971–72, news reporter The Sunday Times 1972–88, Irish corr The Daily Telegraph 1988–93; fndr memb NI Community Rels Cncl 1990–94, memb Police Authy for N Ireland 1994–96; *Books* The RUC: A Force Under Fire (1989), The UDR: An Instrument of Peace? (1991); *Recreations* music, reading; *Style*— Chris Ryder, Esq; ✉ 79 Springfield Road, Portavogie, Co Down BT22 1EP (☎ 01247 771875, fax 01247 771148)

RYDER, Edward Alexander; CB (1992); s of Alexander Harry Ryder (d 1992), of Cheltenham, and Gwendoline Gladys, *née* Morris (d 1979); *b* 9 Nov 1931; *Educ* Cheltenham GS, Univ of Bristol (BSc); *m* 24 March 1956, Janet, da of Alfred John Barribal (d 1973); 1 s (Clive b 1961), 1 da (Joanne (Mrs Rockley) b 1959); *Career* Nat Serv Flying Offr RAF 1953–55; civil servant; superintending inspr HM Nuclear Installations Inspectorate 1975–80, head Hazardous Installations Policy Branch Health and Safety Exec 1980–85, HM chief inspr of nuclear installations 1985–91, dir of nuclear safety 1991, ret; jt chm Channel Tunnel Safety Authy 1992–; CPhys; FInstP; *Recreations* golf, concerts; *Style*— Edward Ryder, Esq, CB; ✉ Pinewood, Baskerville Lane, Lower Shiplake, Henley on Thames, Oxon RG9 3JY (☎ 01189 402706)

RYDER, Peter; CB (1994); s of Percival Henry Sussex Ryder (d 1976), and Bridget, *née* McCormack; *b* 10 March 1942; *Educ* Yorebridge GS, Univ of Leeds (BSc, PhD); *m* 24 April 1965, Jacqueline Doris Sylvia, da of Douglas Rigby; 2 s (Andrew Stephen b 9 April 1966, Mark James b 19 Aug 1970), 1 da (Louise Pauline b 4 Feb 1972); *Career* res asst Physics Dept Univ of Leeds 1966–67; Meteorological Office: asst dir Systems Development 1982–84 (Cloud Physics Res 1976–82), dep dir Forecasting Servs 1988–89 (Observational Servs 1984–88), dir of Servs 1989–90; dep chief exec and dir ops Meteorological Office Executive Agency 1990–96; conslt on environmental info servs 1996–; William Gaskell Meml medal 1981, L G Groves Meml prize for Meteorology 1982; FRMS 1968 (memb Cncl 1980–83, memb Editorial Bd Quarterley Jl 1981–84); *Recreations* gardening, walking, fishing, photography, philately; *Style*— Dr Peter Ryder, CB; ✉ 8 Sherring Close, Bracknell, Berks RG42 2LD (☎ and fax 01344 423380, e-mail 106153.2467@compuserve.com)

RYDER, Rt Hon Richard Andrew; PC (1990), OBE (1981), MP (C) Norfolk Mid (majority 18,948); s of (Richard) Stephen Ryder, JP, DL, *qv*, and Margaret, *née* MacKenzie; *b* 4 Feb 1949; *Educ* Radley, Magdalene Coll Cambridge (BA 1971); *m* 1981, Caroline Ryder, MBE, o da of late Sir David Stephens, KCB, CVO; 1 s (decd), 1 da; *Career* journalist, political sec to PM 1975–81; PPS to: Fin Sec to the Treasy 1984, Sec of State for Foreign Affrs 1984–86; chm Cons Foreign and Cwlth Cncl 1984–89; Govt whip 1986–88, Parly sec MAFF 1988–89, econ sec to the Treasy 1989–90, paymaster-gen July-Nov 1990, Parly sec to the Treasy (Govt chief whip) 1990–95; ptnr family farming business; *Style*— The Rt Hon Richard Ryder, OBE, MP; ✉ The House of Commons, London SW1A 0AA

RYDER, Richard Hood Jack Dudley; s of Maj Dudley Claud Douglas Ryder, JP (d 1986), of Rempstone Hall, and Vera Mary, *née* Cook; *b* 3 July 1940; *Educ* Sherborne, Pembroke Coll Cambridge (MA, PhD), Columbia New York (res fell), Univ of Edinburgh (DCP); *m* 24 April 1974, Audrey Jane, da of Frank Rae Arthur Smith; 1 s (Henry Arthur Woden Calcraft Dudley b 1981), 1 da (Emily Nancy Charlotte b 1978); *Career* sr clinical psychologist Oxford 1968–83, princ clinical psychologist Portsmouth 1983–84; memb DHSS Health Advsy Serv 1976–78, chm Cncl RSPCA 1977–79 (vice chm 1990–91, chm Scientific Tech & Acad Ctee 1992–94), memb Cncl Lib Pty 1984–87 (Parly candidate 1983 and 1987), pres SLD Animal Protection Gp 1989–91; chm: Teignbridge NSPCC, Teignbridge Home Start; dir Radon Control Ltd 1990–95, political conslt Political Animal Lobby Ltd; Mellon prof Tulane Univ 1996, FZS, FRSA, AFBPsS; *Books* Victims of Science (1975, 2 edn 1983), Animal Rights - A Symposium (ed, 1979), Animal Revolution (1989), Animal Welfare and the Environment (ed, 1992); *Publications* Speciesism (1970), Painism (1991); *Recreations* philosophy, trees and rhododendrons; *Clubs* Nat Lib, Royal Over-Seas League, Royal Society of Arts; *Style*— Dr Richard D Ryder

RYDER, Sophie Marie-Louise; da of Wilfred Ryder (d 1981), of Twickenham, and Jacqueline, *née* Bazin; *b* 28 Jan 1963; *Educ* Chiswick Comp, Kingston Poly, Royal Acad Schs (dipl); *m* 5 Nov 1989, Harry Scott, s of James Scott; 2 da (Maud Augusta Ryder b 24 Aug 1989, Nell Ryder Lucy b 8 Aug 1991); *Career* sculptor; residencies: Yorkshire Sculpture Park 1986, Grizedale Forest Cumbria 1986, Salisbury Cathedral 1987, Forest of Dean 1988, Kilkenny Eire 1992; *Solo Exhibitions* incl: Edward Totah Gallery London 1987, Salisbury Cathedral 1987, St Paul's Gallery Leeds 1988, Courcoux & Courcoux Salisbury 1989, 1990 and 1992, Berkeley Sq Gallery London 1989, 1995 and 1996, Newport Museum & Art Gallery 1990, Yorkshire Sculpture Park 1991, Collage (Oxford Gallery) 1993, Winchester Cathedral 1994, Charlie Belloc Lowndes Gallery Chicago 1996; *Group Exhibitons* incl: Pick of the Graduates (Christies London) 1984, Dogwork (Interim Art London) 1984, Sophie Ryder & Harry Scott (Gallery 24 London) 1985, Bretton Managerie (Yorkshire Sculpture Park) 1986, Freedom to Touch (Laing Art Gallery Newcastle) 1986, Animal in Photography (Photographers Gallery London) 1987, The Fabricated Landscape (Plymouth City Museum) 1989, Women Artists - Critics Choice (Bruton St Gallery London) 1992, Young British Art (Kunstforening AF 1847 Århus Festival Denmark) 1992, Art in the City (Finsbury Park) 1993, Exhibition for the Blind (Bury St Edmunds Art Gallery) 1993–94, Summer Exhibition (Bruton Gallery Bath) 1994, Young Contemporary's (Berkeley Square Gallery London) 1994, Sculpture in Paradise (Chichester Cathedral) 1994, Sculpture at Goodwood 1994, Minotaurs Myths and Legends (Berkeley Sq Gallery London 1994, Chicago USA 1995); *Public Collections* Newport City Museum, Yorkshire Sculpture Park, Barings Bank Collection, De Beers Collection, Conoco Ltd, Gerard and National Bank, National Trust (Buckland Abbey), The Private Bank and Trust Co Ltd; *Style*— Ms Sophie Ryder; ✉ Lampits Farm, Winson, nr Cirencester, Glos GL7 5ER (☎ 01285 720575)

RYDER, (Richard) Stephen; DL (1973); s of Charles Foster Ryder (d 1942), of Thurlow, Suffolk, and Mabel Elizabeth, *née* Sims (d 1974); *b* 6 Feb 1917; *Educ* Radley, Queens' Coll Cambridge (MA); *m* 12 April 1947, Margaret, da of Neil MacKenzie; 2 s (Rt Hon Richard Andrew Ryder, OBE, MP, *qv*, b 1949, Charles b 1954); *Career* cmmnd KRRC 1940–46, serv UK and ME; farmer and landowner; former chm and pres Suffolk CLA, pres Suffolk Agric Soc 1971, chm Exec Ctee Suffolk Historic Churches Tst 1982–91, pres S Suffolk Cons Assoc 1983–87, lay canon St Edmundsbury Cathedral 1984–91; JP 1956–87, vice pres Suffolk Branch Magistrates' Assoc (former cncl memb); vice chm: W Suffolk CC 1970–74, Suffolk CC 1978–81; High Sheriff Suffolk 1975–76; Freeman City of London 1959, memb Worshipful Co of Salters 1959; *Recreations* visiting old churches, travelling; *Clubs* Farmers', Lansdowne; *Style*— Stephen Ryder, Esq, JP, DL; ✉ Great Bradley Hall, Newmarket, Suffolk CB8 9LT

RYDER, Susan Myfanwy Prudence; da of Capt Robert Edward Dudley Ryder, VC (d 1986), and Hilaré Myfanwy, *née* Green-Wilkinson (d 1982); *b* 14 March 1944; *Educ* Beaufront Sch Camberley, Byam Shaw Sch of Art (David Murray travel scholar, NDD); *m* Martin Graves Bates; 1 s (Oliver Robert Hunter b 29 March 1969), 1 da (Susannah Hilaré Myfanwy b 15 May 1970); *Career* artist; regular exhibitor: Royal Academy Summer Exhbn, Royal Soc of Portrait Painters, New English Art Club; memb New English Art Club 1980, RP 1992; *Solo Exhibitions* Haste Gall 1979 and 1981, W H Patterson 1989 and 1995, Brian Sinfield Gall 1993; *Portraits* HRH The Princess of Wales 1981, Miss Pears 1984, Christina Leder 1988, Miss Nicola Paget 1991, Sir Eric Ash 1993, Lord Porter 1994, HM The Queen 1996; *Awards* Barney Wilkins prize 1990, winner Alexon Portrait Competition 1991, first prize New English Art Club Critic's prize 1993 (second 1992); *Recreations* family and friends; *Style*— Miss Susan Ryder, RP; ✉ 17 Queen's Gate Place, London SW7 5NY (☎ 0171 589 2765 and 01890 840527)

RYDER, Dr Timothy Thomas Bennett; s of Thomas Alfred Ryder, MC (d 1956), and Enid Mary, *née* Sanger (d 1988); *b* 11 Jan 1930; *Educ* Eton, King's Coll Cambridge (BA, MA, PhD); *m* 12 April 1955, Jean (Jill), da of Capt Thomas Herbert Temple; 2 da (Penny (Mrs Burnham) b 1956, Pippa b 1962); *Career* Nat Serv RA 1948–49; Univ of Hull: asst lectr in classics 1955–57, lectr 1957–66, sub-dean Faculty of Arts 1963–66, sr lectr 1966–71, reader 1971–90, dean Sch of Humanities 1987–90; visiting prof of history Michigan State Univ 1966–67 and 1981; reader in classics Univ of Reading 1990–95; memb Cncl: Soc for Promotion of Hellenic Studies 1960–63, 1967–70 and 1975–78, Classical Assoc of GB 1967–70 and 1979–80; *Books* Koine Eirene: General Peace and Local Independence in Ancient Greece (1965), exec ed Ancient History and contrib of 200 articles to Dictionary of World History (1973); *Recreations* travel, cricket (non-playing); *Style*— Dr Timothy Ryder; ✉ c/o University of Reading, Whiteknights, PO Box 218, Reading RG6 2AA (☎ 0118 931 8420)

RYDER, William; s of Leonard Ryder (d 1948), and Bertha, *née* Barlow (d 1980); *b* 17 Oct 1933; *Educ* Batley GS Yorks, Univ of Edinburgh (MB ChB, FRCA); *m* 29 Aug 1958, Christine, da of Lawrence Wileman, of Kidderminster, Worcs; 1 da (Karen b 16 Dec 1965); *Career* cmmnd RAF 1959–62; registrar Cardiff Royal Infirmary 1962–66, sr registrar Royal Victoria Infirmary Newcastle 1966–68, conslt Newcastle Health Authy 1968–, hon lectr Univ of Newcastle 1968–; sr fell Coll of Anaesthetists; memb: Assoc of Anaesthetists, Intensive Care Soc, Anaesthetic Res Soc; *Recreations* marathon running, swimming, dog training; *Clubs* Montagu Court Dining; *Style*— William Ryder, Esq; ✉ 16 Graham Park Rd, Gosforth, Newcastle upon Tyne; Royal Victoria Infirmary, Newcastle upon Tyne NE1 4LP (☎ 0191 232 5131)

RYDER OF EATON HASTINGS, Baron (Life Peer UK 1975), of Eaton Hastings, Oxon; Sir Sydney Thomas (Don) Ryder; kt (1972); s of John Ryder; *b* 16 Sept 1916; *Educ* Ealing Co GS; *m* 1950, Eileen, da of William Dodds; 1 s (Hon Michael John b 1953), 1 da (Hon Jill Patricia b 1950); *Career* ed Stock Exchange Gazette 1950–60, md 1960–63 (jtly 1960–61) Kelly Iliffe Holdings and assoc Iliffe Press Ltd, dir Int Publishing Corp 1963–70, md Reed Paper Group 1963–68, chm and chief exec Reed International Ltd 1968–75, pres Nat Materials Handling Centre 1970–74, dir MEPC Ltd 1972–75; industl advsr to Govt 1974; memb Ct and Cncl Cranfield Inst of Technol 1970–74, vice pres ROSPA 1973–, chm NEB 1975–77; memb: Cncl and Bd of Fells BIM (now Inst of Mgmnt) 1970, Br Gas Corp 1973–79, Cncl UK-SA Trade Assoc 197, Reserve Pension Bd 1973–, Cncl Industl Soc 1971; *Style*— The Rt Hon Lord Ryder of Eaton Hastings; ✉ House of Lords, London SW1A 0PW

RYDER OF WARSAW, Baroness (Life Peer UK 1978), of Warsaw in Poland and of Cavendish, Co Suffolk; (Margaret) Susan Cheshire; CMG (1976), OBE (1957); da of late Charles Ryder; *b* 3 July 1923; *Educ* Benenden; *m* 1959, Gp Capt Lord Cheshire, VC, OM, DSO, DFC (d 1992); 1 s (Hon Jeromy Charles b 1960), 1 da (Hon Elizabeth Diana b 1962); *Career* serv WWII SOE & FANY; social worker, fndr Sue Ryder Fndn for Sick and Disabled All Age Gps; tstee Cheshire Fndn, tstee and co-fndr Ryder-Cheshire Fndn; Hon LLD: Liverpool 1973, Exeter 1980, London 1981, Leeds 1984, Cambridge 1989; Hon DLitt Reading 1982; Hon DCL Univ of Kent 1986, Hon Dr Univ of Essex 1993; Pro Ecclesia et Pontifice Award 1982; Offr's Cross Order of Polonia Restituta 1965, Medal of Yugoslav Flag with Gold Wreath and Diploma 1971, Golden Order of Merit (Poland) 1976, Order of Smile (Poland) 1981, Cdr's Cross Order of Polonia Restituta 1992; *Books* And the Morrow is Theirs (autobiog 1975), Child of My Love (autobiog 1986), Remembrance (annual magazine of the Sue Ryder Foundation); *Clubs* SOE; *Style*— The Rt Hon Baroness Ryder of Warsaw, CMG, OBE; ✉ Sue Ryder Foundation, Cavendish, Sudbury, Suffolk CO10 8AY (☎ 01787 280252)

RYDER RICHARDSON, Julian Charles; s of Edward Ryder Richardson, QC (d 1961), and Marjorie Jesse Gordon, *née* Hollings (d 1961); *b* 4 Sept 1935; *Educ* Charterhouse, Sch of Architecture Regent St Poly (Dip Arch); *m* 1, 1959, Shirley Anne, da of J H Rothera; 2 da (Gail b 30 Nov 1961, Prue Armorel b 1 Sept 1969), 2 s (Edward Simon b 18 Aug 1963, Jonathan Charles b 25 Sept 1965); m 2, Margaret Annear, da of Very Rev Harold E Frankham; *Career* architect; joined Peatfield & Bodgener 1958; Gollins Melvin Ward & Partners (GMW Partnership): joined 1960, associate 1964, ptnr 1971, sr ptnr 1981, jt sr ptnr 1989–; work incl: project architect Commercial Union HQ 1961–69, project architect and mangr BOAC Unit Terminal J F K Int Airport New York 1969–71, Thamesmead Industrialised Building for GLC 1971–75, King Saud Univ Saudi Arabia 1975–80, Minster Court for Prudential Assurance 1986–; overseas work experience in Portugal, Saudi Arabia, Libya, Hong Kong, Belgium and Peru; Freeman City of London 1985, Liveryman Worshipful Co of Chartered Architects; RIBA 1961, MBAE 1991;

Recreations sailing, shooting, cooking; *Clubs* Caledonian, Wig & Pen, Royal Lymington Yacht; *Style*— Julian Ryder Richardson, Esq; ✉ GMW Partnership, PO Box 1613, 239 Kensington High Street, London W8 6SL (☎ 0171 937 8020, fax 0171 937 5815)

RYDILL, Prof Louis Joseph; OBE (1962); s of Louis William Rydill (d 1975), and Queenie Elizabeth, *née* Gallagher (d 1974); *b* 16 Aug 1922; *Educ* Public Central Sch Plymouth, Dockyard Tech Coll Devonport, RNEC Keyham, RNC Greenwich; *m* 11 April 1949, Eva, da of Emanuel Newman (d 1961); 2 da (Sarah (Mrs Ash) b 1950, Jessica b 1959); *Career* asst constructor and constructor RCNC 1945–53, asst prof of naval architecture RNC Greenwich 1953–56, constructor then chief constructor on design of HMS Dreadnought 1956–62, chief constructor on design of aircraft carrier CVAOI 1962–67, prof of naval architecture RNC Greenwich and Univ Coll London 1967–72, asst and dep to dir of submarine project team, dir of warship design and engrg 1976–81, prof of naval architecture Univ Coll London 1981–85, visiting prof of naval architecture at US Naval Acad Annapolis 1985, conslt in ship and submarine design 1985–; hon res fell Univ Coll London 1985; RCNC; FRINA 1967, FEng 1982; co-author of book on submarine design (1994); *Recreations* music, books, plays; *Style*— Prof Louis Rydill, OBE, FEng; ✉ The Lodge, Entry Hill Drive, Bath BA1 5NJ (☎ 01225 427 888)

RYE, Renny Michael Douglas; s of Douglas Rye, of Maidstone, Kent, and Pamela, *née* Whitmore; *b* 2 Dec 1947; *Educ* Maidstone GS, St Catherine's Coll Oxford (BA); *m* 8 Aug 1970, Ann, da of (Andrew Frank) Peter Lynn, of Maidstone, Kent; 1 s (Thomas b 1977), 1 da (Helen b 1974); *Career* BBC: prodn ops asst BBC radio 1971–73, asst floor mangr TV plays dept 1973–79, prodr and asst ed Blue Peter 1979–81; freelance drama dir: The Box of Delights (BBC) 1983–84, The December Rose (BBC) 1985, Casualty (BBC) 1986, The Gemini Factor (Thames) 1987, All our Children (BBC) 1987–89, Agatha Christie's Poirot (LWT) 1988–91, The Other Side of Paradise (Central Films/Grundy) 1991, Lipstick on Your Collar (Whistling Gypsy/Channel 4) 1992, Midnight Movie (feature film) 1993, Chandler & Co (SKREBA/BBC), Kavanagh QC (Central Films) 1994, Karaoke, Cold Lazarus (Whistling Gypsy/BBC/Channel 4) 1995; memb DGGB; *Recreations* cricket, films, music; *Style*— Renny Rye, Esq; ✉ c/o Scott Marshall Personal Management, 44 Perryn Road, London W3 7NA (☎ 0181 749 7692, 743 1669)

RYLANCE, John Randolph Trevor; s of Dr Ralph Curzon Rylance (d 1983), and Margaret Joan Clare, *née* Chambers; *b* 26 Feb 1944; *Educ* Shrewsbury; *m* 14 Dec 1974, Philippa Anne, da of Philip Sidney Bailey (d 1975); 2 da (Georgina b 1976, Charlotte b 1978); *Career* called to the Bar Lincoln's Inn 1968, res asst to Sir Edward Gardner, QC, MP 1971–73, recorder 1993– (asst recorder 1989–93), memb Professional Conduct Ctee Bar Cncl 1992–94; govr Fulham Cross Sch 1977–88, branch chm Fulham Cons Assoc 1983–89 (memb Mgmnt Ctee 1980–90), memb Exec Ctee Fulham Soc 1988–, chm Fulham Palace Tst 1996– (tstee 1991–); *Clubs* Hurlingham; *Style*— John Rylance, Esq; ✉ Francis Taylor Building, Temple, London EC4Y 7BY (☎ 0171 353 7768, fax 0171 353 0659)

RYLAND, David Stuart; s of Sir William Ryland, CB (d 1988), of Croydon, Surrey, and Lady Sybil Ryland; *b* 27 Oct 1953; *Educ* Dulwich, Exeter Coll Oxford; *m* 18 July 1986, Anne Helen, da of Kenneth Wright, of Benfleet, Essex; *Career* admitted slr 1981; Clifford Chance 1981–88, ptnr S J Berwin & Co 1988–; Freeman City of London; memb Law Soc; *Recreations* films, music, sport; *Style*— David Ryland, Esq; ✉ S J Berwin & Co, 222 Grays Inn Rd, London WC1X 8HB (☎ 0171 533 2222, fax 0171 533 2000)

RYLAND, His Hon Judge Timothy Richard Godfrey Fetherstonhaugh; s of Richard Desmond Fetherstonhaugh Ryland (d 1983), and Frances Katharine Vernon, *née* Plummer (d 1990); *b* 13 June 1938; *Educ* St Andrew's Coll, Trinity Coll Dublin (BA, LLB); *m* 22 June 1991, Jean Margaret Muirhead; *Career* called to the Bar Gray's Inn 1961, dep circuit judge 1978, recorder Crown Court 1983, circuit judge (SE Circuit) 1988; *Recreations* opera, wine; *Clubs* Lansdowne, Kildare St and Univ (Dublin); *Style*— His Hon Judge Ryland; ✉ Lamb Building, Temple, London EC4Y 7AS (☎ 0171 797 7788)

RYLE, Evelyn Margaret; da of Paul McConnell Cassidy (d 1966), and Emily Margaret, *née* Wright (d 1982); *b* 26 March 1947; *Educ* King's Park Sch Glasgow (Dux and Gold medal), Univ of Glasgow (Stevenson exchange scholar, MA), Ealing Tech Coll (Dip in Mgmnt Studies); *m* 31 May 1975, Anthony Edward Ryle, OBE; 1 s (David b 1978), 1 da (Frances b 1980); *Career* successively graduate trainee, MBO advsr and systems analyst Dexion-Comino International Ltd 1969–73, Flt Lt and accountant offr Women's RAF 1973–75; systems analyst: Dexion Group 1975–76, Southern Electricity 1976–77; Civil Service: Iron and Steel Div Dept of Indust 1977–78, Commercial Relations and Exports Div Dept of Trade 1978–80, Consumer Affairs Div 1981–84, on leave 1984–86, Vehicles Div DTI 1986–87, asst sec and dep dir Information Technol Services Directorate 1987–90, OCMS Sr Mgmnt Devpt Prog 1990, head Educn and Trg Policy Branch 1990–93, seconded as DG and chief exec The Design Cncl 1993–95, dir Business Competitiveness Government Office for London 1995–96, ret; memb Civil Service Selection Bd Panel of Chairs 1996–; MIMgt 1972, FRSA 1993; *Recreations* family, music, gardening, needlework, walking; *Clubs* RAF; *Style*— Mrs Evelyn Ryle; ✉ Southwood, 34 Fitzroy Road, Fleet, Hants GU13 8JW (☎ 01252 624347, fax 01252 810051, e-mail 106023.1744@compuserve.com)

RYLE, Sallie Elizabeth; da of Barry Davidson Eaton Smith, MBE (d 1995), of Ilkley, Yorkshire, and Mary Elizabeth, *née* Priest; *b* 14 Nov 1950; *Educ* Ilkley GS; *m* 19 Sept 1981, Nicholas Peter Bodley Ryle, s of Michael Thomas Ryle, of Winsford, Exmoor; 1 s (George David Bodley b 6 April 1987), 1 da (Vanessa Isabelle b 25 April 1990); *Career* Yorkshire TV: asst publicity offr 1982–84, head of publicity 1984–87, head of publicity and PR 1987–; memb: Bd of Tstees Eureka! Museum for Children, Leeds C of C Local Affairs Ctee, NUJ, RTS 1989; *Recreations* equestrian sports, tennis, travel; *Style*— Mrs Sallie Ryle; ✉ Yorkshire Television Ltd, The TV Centre, Leeds LS3 1JS (☎ 0113 243 8283, fax 0113 244 0213, telex 557232)

RYLE-HODGES, Carolyn; da of Harry Morton Neal, and Cecilia Elizabeth, *née* Crawford; *b* 10 June 1961; *Educ* Heathfield Sch Ascot, Courtauld Inst of Art Univ of London (BA); *m* 2 June 1988, Rupert Ryle-Hodges, s of Edward Ryle-Hodges; 1 da (Eve b 1 May 1991), 1 s (William b 20 March 1993); *Career* sec and asst to Dirs Redfern Gallery London 1984–86; ptnr Long & Ryle Art Gallery 1988–; corp clients incl: Lloyd Thompson, McKinsey's & Co, Cazenove & Co, Kreditbank, Morgan Grenfell, Société Générale, Mitsui Trust, HM Customs & Excise, Mitsubushi Corp PLC, London Underground Ltd Canary Wharf; memb: Worshipful Co of Carpenters, Friends of the Tate, Friends of the Royal Acad; *Recreations* tennis, fishing, reading, visiting museums, opera, painting, drawing; *Style*— Mrs Carolyn Ryle-Hodges; ✉ 4 Redesdale St, London SW3; Long and Ryle Art Gallery, 4 John Islip St, London SW1P 4PX (☎ 0171 834 1434, fax 0171 821 9409)

RYRIE, Sir William Sinclair; KCB (1982, CB 1979); s of Rev Dr Frank Ryrie; *b* 10 Nov 1928; *Educ* Mount Hermon Sch Darjeeling, Heriot's Sch Edinburgh, Univ of Edinburgh; *m* 1, 1953 (m dis 1969), Dorrit Klein; 2 s, 1 da; m 2, 1969, Christine Gray Thomson; 1 s; *Career* Nat Serv Intelligence Corps Malaya; Colonial Office 1953–63; asst sec Int Monetary Affrs Treasy 1966–69, princ private sec to Chllr 1969–71, under sec Public Sector Gp 1971–75, econ min and head UK Treasy and Supply Delgn Washington and UK exec dir IMF and IBRD 1975–79, second perm sec (Domestic Economy) Treasy 1980–82, perm sec Overseas Devpt Admin 1982–84; exec vice pres and chief exec International Finance Corporation World Bank Washington 1984–93; dir Barings plc 1994–95, chm Barings Emerging Europe Tst 1994–, vice chm ING Barings Holding Company Ltd 1995–; dir: CARE UK 1993–, W S Atkins plc 1994–, First NIS Regnl Fund 1994–, Ashanti Goldfields Co 1995–; dep chm Cwlth Devpt Corp 1994–, pres Edinburgh Univ Devpt Tst 1994–; memb Int Centre for Economic Growth; FRSA 1993; *Books* First World Third World London (1995); *Clubs* Reform; *Style*— Sir William Ryrie, KCB; ✉ Hawkwood, Hawkwood Lane, Chislehurst, Kent BR7 5PN

RYTON, Royce Thomas Carlisle; s of Reginald Thomas Ryton (d 1966), of Ferring, Sussex, and Olive Edwina (d 1963); *b* 16 Sept 1924; *Educ* Lancing, Webber Douglas Acad; *m* 6 Sept 1954, Morar Margaret, da of Capt Edward Coverley Kennedy, RN (ka 1939); 1 da (Charlotte Susan Teresa b 15 Oct 1955); *Career* actor and playwright; serv WWII RN; many years experience in rep tours all over the country incl Sheffield, Birmingham and Cambridge Theatre Cos; appearances incl: Bill in The Unvarnished Truth (also writer, Phoenix Theatre and long US tour) 1978, Terry in The Other Side of the Swamp (also author, Phoenix) 1979, The Tempest and St Joan (Sir Anthony Quayle's Co, Hong Kong and UK tours), Dr Finlay's Case Book, Bloode Water (Ghost Hour series) 1995; author: Crown Matrimonial (over 500 performances at the Haymarket London 1972–74, also on Broadway 1973 and TV), Mother Dear (Ambassadors), The Anastasia File (New York and London and two UK tours), The Royal Baccarat Scandal (Chichester Festival 1988 and Haymarket London 1989), The Little Father (Radio Four) 1990, The Battle of San Remo (Radio Four) 1993, The Scapegoat (Brussels) 1995, Tzar Nicholas II (Radio Four) 1996; memb Br Actors' Equity Assoc; *Recreations* genealogy, Victorian and Russian royalty; *Clubs* Dramatists'; *Style*— Royce Ryton, Esq; ✉ 10 Talbot Lodge, West End Lane, Esher, Surrey KT10 8NE (☎ 01372 470868)

S

SAATCHI, Charles; s of Nathan David Saatchi, and Daisy Saatchi, of London; *b* 9 June 1943; *Educ* Christ's Coll Finchley; *m* 1973, Doris Jean, da of Jack Lockhart of USA; *Career* assoc dir Collett Dickenson Pearce 1966–68, dir Cramer Saatchi 1968–70, dir Saatchi & Saatchi Co plc 1970–93 (hon pres 1993–95), fndr ptnr M&C Saatchi Ltd 1995–; Chm's Award for Outstanding Contribution to Commercials Indust (British TV Advtg Awards) 1994; *Recreations* karting; *Style—* Charles Saatchi, Esq; ✉ c/o Saatchi Gallery, 98a Boundary Road, London NW8 0RH (☎ 0171 624 8299)

SAATCHI, Baron (Life Peer UK 1996), of Staplefield in the County of West Sussex; Maurice Saatchi; s of Nathan David Saatchi and Daisy Saatchi; *b* 21 June 1946; *Educ* LSE (BSc); *m* 1987, Josephine Hart, novelist; 1 s (Hon Edward), 1 step s; *Career* chm Saatchi & Saatchi Co plc 1984–94; fndr ptnr M&C Saatchi Ltd 1995–; fndr Megalomedia (new-media co); memb Bd The London Forum 1992–; *Style—* The Rt Hon Lord Saatchi; ✉ M&C Saatchi Ltd, 34–36 Golden Square, London W1R 4EE (☎ 0171 543 4500, fax 0171 543 4501)

SABBEN-CLARE, James Paley; s of Ernest Elwin Sabben-Clare (d 1993), of Winchester, and Rosamond Dorothy Mary, *née* Scott (d 1993); *b* 9 Sept 1941; *Educ* Winchester, New Coll Oxford (BA, MA); *m* 30 Aug 1969, (Geraldine) Mary, da of (Henry) Stuart Borton (d 1985), of Blandford; 1 s (Matthew b 1973), 1 da (Rebecca b 1971); *Career* Flt Lt RAFVR 1965–81; asst master Marlborough Coll 1964–68, visiting fell All Souls Coll Oxford 1967–68, headmaster Winchester Coll 1985– (second master 1979–85, head of Classics Dept 1969–79); patron Winchester Samaritans, vice pres Winchester Gp for the Disabled; govr: The Pilgrims' Sch, St Swithun's Sch, King Edward VI Sch Southampton, Hordle House Sch; *Books* Caesar and Roman Politics (2 edn, 1981), Fables from Aesop (1976), The Culture of Athens (2 edn, 1980), Winchester Coll (2 edn, 1988), contrib to educnl and classical jls; *Recreations* games, theatre, furniture-making, hill-walking; *Clubs* Jesters, Winchester Amateur Operatic Society (pres); *Style—* James Sabben-Clare, Esq; ✉ Headmaster's House, Winchester College, Winchester, Hampshire SO23 9NA (☎ 01962 854328, fax 01962 842972)

SABBERWAL, Dr Amar Jit Parkash; s of Ram Chand Sabberwal (d 1985), and Vidyawati Thaper (d 1987); *b* 25 Nov 1933; *Educ* Agra Univ (BSc(Eng), Gold Medal, Chllr's Medal), Univ of Manchester (MSc(Tech), PhD); *m* 2 Feb 1963, Jayasree, da of Dr Joti Ranjan Sen; *Career* research engr GKN plc 1958–59, sr research engr NRDC 1959–62, works mangr Indian Cable Co 1963–66, gp ldr Staveley plc 1966–67, engrg dir Ferodo Ltd 1970–73 (engrg mangr 1968–70), md Asbestos Cement Ltd 1974–77, jt md TAC Construction Materials Ltd 1977–81, md T & N Materials Research Ltd 1981–85, md BIP Chemicals Ltd 1986–89, exec dir T & N plc 1989–; non-exec dir: Univ of Salford Holdings plc, Manchester Children's Hosp NHS Tst; chm Ctee for the Employment of People with Disabilities Gtr Manchester; F W Taylor Medal Int Instn for Prodn 1961, Instn Medal Instn of Prodn Engrs 1973; author of numerous papers in jls; FIProdE 1961, FIMechE 1963, FIMgt 1973; *Recreations* weekend gardening, music, reading; *Style—* Dr Amar Sabberwal; ✉ 10 Pinewood, off Park Road, Bowdon, Altrincham, Cheshire WA14 3JQ; T & N plc, Bowdon House, Ashburton Road West, Trafford Park, Manchester M17 1RA (☎ 0161 872 0155, fax 0161 848 8303, car 0836 795021)

SABIN, Paul Robert; s of Robert Reginald Sabin (d 1988), and Dorothy Maude, *née* Aston (d 1992); *b* 29 March 1943; *Educ* Oldbury GS, Univ of Aston (DMS); *m* 19 June 1965, Vivien, da of Harry Furnival; 1 s (Martin Lawrence b 1969), 2 da (Ann Hazel b 1973, Caroline Jane b 1978); *Career* West Bromwich CBC 1959–69, chief fin offr Redditch Devpt Corp 1975–81 (joined 1969); City of Birmingham: joined 1981, city treas 1982–86, dep chief exec 1984–86; chief exec Kent CC 1986–; dir Kent Trg and Enterprise Cncl; Hon Citizen of the City of Baltimore USA 1985; DMS, CPFA 1966, MIMgt, MICMA, FRSA; *Recreations* fine books, music; *Style—* Paul Sabin, Esq; ✉ Kent County Council, Chief Executive's Office, County Hall, Maidstone, Kent ME14 1XQ (☎ 01622 694000, fax 01622 694060)

SABINE, Dr Peter Aubrey; s of Bernard Robert Sabine (d 1970), and Edith Lucy, *née* Dew (d 1989); *b* 29 Dec 1924; *Educ* Brockley Co Sch, Chelsea Poly, Imperial Coll London (BSc, ARCS, PhD, DSc); *m* 13 April 1946, Peggy Willis, da of Harry Augustus Lambert (d 1958); 1 s (Cedric Martin Peter b 1952); *Career* with Geological Survey 1945–84: Geological Museum 1945–50, i/c Petrographical Dept 1950, chief petrographer 1959–70, asst dir field staff 1970, chief geochemist 1977, dep dir (chief sci offr and chief geologist) 1977–84; geological advsr 1984–; contrib to many professional jls and geological maps; Int Union for Geological Sci Cmmn on Systematics in Petrology: memb Sub-Cmmn on Igneous Rocks 1969–, chief UK del 1980–84, chm and cncl memb 1984–92, vice chm 1992–; chm Royal Soc Sub-Ctee on geochemistry 1977–86, visitor Royal Inst 1979–82 (chm Audit Ctee 1989–90); memb: DTI Chemical and Minerals Requirements Bd 1973–82, Minerals Metals and Reclamation Ctee 1983–84, Minerals and Geochemistry Ctees EEC 1975–84 (advsr 1985–86), Ctee of Dirs of W Euro Surveys 1978–84, Steering Ctee Irish Geological Survey 1981–84, Mineral Indust Res Orgn 1983–86, Mineral Soc of America 1953 (fell 1959), Mineral Soc 1945 (cncl memb 1950–53); FGS 1944 (Lyell Fund 1955, cncl memb 1956–67, sec 1959–66, vice pres 1966–67 and 1982–84, sr fell 1994), FRSE 1964, FIMM 1965 (cncl 1976–80), CEng 1971, FRSA 1975, CGeol 1991; *Books* Gemstones (jtly 1983), Chemical Analyses of Igneous Rocks (jtly 1956), Petrography of British Igneous rocks (jtly 1982), Classification of Igneous Rocks (jtly 1989); *Recreations* gardening, genealogy, antique furniture restoration; *Clubs* Athenaeum, Geological Soc (hon memb); *Style—* Dr Peter Sabine, FRSE; ✉ Lark Rise, Camp Road, Gerrards Cross, Buckinghamshire SL9 7PF (☎ 01753 891529)

SACH, Keith Howard; JP (Warwicks 1989); s of Cyril James Sach (d 1989), of Warwicks, and Jessie Annie, *née* Andlaw (d 1990); *b* 13 May 1948; *Educ* Strode's Sch, King George V Sch, St Peter's Coll Birmingham, Open Univ; *m* 14 July 1990, Elizabeth Anne (Mrs Brierley), da of Geoffrey Ball (d 1990); 1 step s (Jonathan b 1976), 2 step da (Alexis b 1973, Kathryn b 1979); *Career* asst master Solihull Sch 1970–79, dir RLSS UK 1979–88 (chief Cwlth sec 1979–86, Cwlth vice pres 1987), md S & P Safety 1988–90, dir Safety Management Partnership Ltd 1992–95, dir Scalefast Systems Ltd 1996–; safety conslt to: HSE, Sports Cncl, Amateur Swimming Assoc, RLSS UK, RLSS Aust, ISRM, ILAM, FIA, Rank Organisation, Biwater Leisure, Circa Leisure plc, D C Leisure, Civic Leisure, Metropolitan Group, Sports and Leisure Management, Fitness Express, local authorities; broadcaster and writer; memb: Indust Lead Body for Sport and Recreation, Safety in Leisure Research Unit (SAIL), Br Assoc for Sport and Law, Br Juvenile and Family Cts Soc; Civil, Criminal and Coroners' Cts expert witness on swimming pool, leisure centre, sport and recreation accidents; chm: Nat Water Safety Ctee 1980–83, Nat Rescue Trg Cncl 1981–88 (tstee 1995–); Hon Constable St Helier Jersey 1984, Hon Citizen Burlington Ontario 1985; *Books* Safety in Swimming Pools (contrib, 1988 and 1997), Recreation Management Factfile (contrib, 1991/92), Handbook of Sports and Recreational Building Design (contrib, 1993), Quality in the Leisure Industry (contrib, 1992), Guide to Risk Assessment (jtly, 1993); *Recreations* theatre, music, travel, swimming; *Clubs* Royal Over-Seas League, Broadgate; *Style—* Keith H Sach, Esq, JP; ✉ High Ash Farm, Great Packington, Warwickshire CV7 7JZ (☎ 0831 608900, fax 0836 003588)

SACHAR, Jasbir Singh; s of late Balwant Singh, and late Inder Kaur, *née* Phul; *b* 12 Dec 1936; *Educ* Punjab Univ Amritsar (BA, BT, MA), Univ of Agra (LLB); *m* 8 Oct 1967, Kanwaljit, da of late Avtar Singh Keer, of India; 1 s (Navi b 22 April 1970), 1 da (Ruby b 26 Aug 1968); *Career* headmaster Govt Middle Sch Chamyari Dist Amritsar 1957–59, princ SGN Int Coll Bareilly India 1964–67; winner numerous prizes for literary and academic achievement; sec Headmasters' Assoc India 1957–59, memb Allahabad Educn Bd 1964–67, pres Asian Welfare and Cultural Assoc E London 1975 (gen sec 1974), PR offr and hon sec Standing Conference of Asian Orgns in UK 1975–, dir of publicity and PR First Int Convention of Overseas Indians (Euro Section) London 1989, fndr and UK delegate First Int Convention NY 1989, hon gen sec Int Punjabi Soc (UK) 1993–; exec memb numerous other nat and int orgns; *Books* Asian Directory and Who's Who editions 1–9 (ed, 1974–94), Asian Observer (ed monthly); *Recreations* gardening, socialising; *Clubs* Rotary Int (Redbridge); *Style—* Jasbir Sachar, Esq; ✉ 47 Beattyville Gardens, Barkingside, Ilford, Essex IG6 1JW (☎ 0181 550 3745, fax 0181 551 0990)

SACHRAJDA, Prof Christopher Tadeusz Czeslaw; s of Czeslaw Sachrajda (d 1959), and Hanna Teresa, *née* Grabowska; *b* 15 Nov 1949; *Educ* Finchley Catholic GS London, Univ of Sussex (BSc), Imperial Coll London (PhD); *m* 31 Aug 1974, Irena, da of Antoni and Antonina Czyzewski; 2 s (Andrew Marian b 22 Sept 1978, Gregory Antoni Czeslaw b 23 Nov 1979), 1 da (Sophie Maria b 31 July 1992); *Career* Harkness fell (for study and travel in USA) Stanford Linear Accelerator Center Stanford Univ Calif 1974–76, fell and staff memb CERN Geneva 1976–79; Physics Dept Univ of Southampton: lectr 1979–86, sr lectr 1986–88, reader 1988–90, prof 1990–, head of dept 1997–; sr fell PPARC (formerly SERC) 1991–96; FRS 1996; *Recreations* family activities, tennis, bridge, walking; *Clubs* Portswood Lawn Tennis; *Style—* Prof Christopher Sachrajda, FRS; ✉ 20 Radway Road, Southampton SO15 7PW (☎ 01703 784208); Department of Physics, University of Southampton, University Road, Highfield, Southampton SO17 1BJ (☎ 01703 592105, fax 01703 593910)

SACHS, John Raymond; s of Andrew Sachs, of Cricklewood, London, and Adelaide Melody, *née* Good; *b* 3 May 1957; *Educ* Belmont Prep, St Paul's; *m* 27 July 1985, Lisa Jayne, da of Brian James; 2 da (Kimberley b 29 Oct 1987, Charlotte Adelaide b 1 Jan 1990); *Career* radio presenter: morning show Capital Radio 1979–91, breakfast show Jazz FM London, Much More Music BBC Radio 2; TV work incl: presenter Four Square (BBC), voice of Take your Pick, event commentator The Gladiators (ITV), star appearances in Brian Conley Show (LWT); TV programme creator (devised format for That's Rich (BBC)), voice-over artist, record, TV and commercials prodr; md: Talking Heads Production Ltd, Talking Heads Voice Over Company; ptnr: Blackburn Sachs Associates, Kilmartin Sachs PR, Laross Hair Products Ltd; Personality of the Year: Variety Club of GB 1988, NY Radio Festival World Awards 1988; Barker Variety Club of GB (vice pres 1991), other charitable involvements incl Children in Need; *Books* Private Files (HarperCollins), Secret Lives (Blake); *Recreations* clay shooting, golf, watersports; *Clubs* RAC, Mossiman's, Tramp; *Style—* John Sachs, Esq; (fax 0181 451 0764, car 0836 758418)

SACHS, MaryLee; da of Richard Charles Sachs (d 1995), of Vista, Calif, and Mary, *née* Wineman; *b* 6 Dec 1958; *Educ* San Diego State Univ Calif (BA Journalism/PR), Ashridge Mgmnt Coll Herts (Leadership Devpt Prog); *m* 14 Oct 1989, Malcolm William Beadling, s of William Beadling; *Career* PR co-ordinator San Diego Civic Light Opera Calif 1980, freelance writer 1981–84, sr account exec The Gable Agency San Diego Calif 1981–82, account supr Cochrane Chase Livingston & Co Inc Newport Beach Calif 1983–84, account mangr rising to bd dir Hill & Knowlton (UK) Ltd London 1984–89, md mktg communications Fleishman Hillard UK Ltd London 1989–91, in own practice The Gable Agency 1991; Hill & Knowlton: rejoined bd 1991, md UK mktg communications 1993–96, chm Euro mktg PR practice 1996–; PR Soc of America Orange County Chapter Award of Excellence (Mktg Communications Prog), IPR Cert of Excellence (Special Progs) 1995; memb: PR Soc of America 1981, Mktg Soc 1989, IPR 1989, IOD 1989, Mktg Gp of GB 1995; *Recreations* skiing, golf, piano, reading, riding, travel; *Style—* Mrs MaryLee Sachs; ✉ Hill & Knowlton (UK) Ltd, 5–11 Theobalds Road, London WC1X 8SH (☎ 0171 413 3000, fax 0171 413 3222, mobile 0385 372517, e-mail msachs@hillandknowlton.com)

SACHS, Hon Mr Justice; Hon Sir Michael Alexander Geddes; kt (1993); s of Dr Joseph Sachs (d 1954), of Penrith, Cumbria, and Ruby Mary, *née* Ross (d 1957); *b* 8 April 1932; *Educ* Sedbergh, Univ of Manchester (LLB); *m* 13 July 1957, Patricia Mary, da of James Conroy (d 1968), of Thrybergh, Yorks; 2 s (Hugh b 1964, Jeromy b 1966), 2 da (Madeleine (Mrs Morgan) b 1959, Elizabeth (Mrs Kirk) b 1962); *Career* admitted slr 1957; ptnr Slater Heelis Manchester 1962–84, recorder of the Crown Ct 1980–84, circuit judge 1984–93; judge of the High Court of Justice (Queen's Bench Div) 1993–; memb No 7 (NW) Legal Aid Ctee 1966–80 (chm 1975–76), chm Greater Manchester Legal Servs Ctee 1977–81, pres Manchester Law Soc 1978–79; memb Ct Univ of Manchester 1977–84, memb Cncl Law Soc 1979–84 (chm Standing Ctee on Criminal Law), hon memb Law Soc 1993; Hon Master of the Bench Middle Temple 1993; Hon LLD Univ of Manchester 1994; Knight of St Sylvester; *Style—* The Hon Mr Justice Sachs; ✉ Royal Courts of Justice, Strand, London WC2A 2LL

SACK, Brian George; MBE (1994); s of Thomas Jacob Sack (d 1972), of London, and Stella May, *née* Blake (d 1962); *b* 29 Jan 1923; *Educ* Hilldrop London, Northern Poly, Coll of Estate Mgmnt, Westminster Coll; *Career* served WWII, fighter pilot RAF; articled pupil to surveyor Potters Bar UDC 1939–45, subsequently qualified as chartered surveyor, on staff Miny of Works until 1951; hotelier; trained under Mrs Ashley Courtenay; business ptnr (with Francis Ernest Coulson) of Sharrow Bay Country House Hotel (joined 1952); ARICS 1951, FHCIMA 1955, memb Br Hotels and Restaurants Assoc

1960, hon memb Académie Culinaire de France; *Awards* listed in Good Food Guide 1960–, memb Relais et Chateaux (oldest membership in UK), Egon Ronay's Restaurant of the Year 1975, Egon Ronay's Hotel of the Year 1980, Egon Ronay's Hosts of the Year 1993 (only hotel in UK to have received these three Gold awards), Egon Ronay/Sunday Times Taste of England Award 1983, RAC Blue Ribbon Award for Excellence 1987–95, Catey Special Award 1988, Cumbria Tourist Bd Award 1988, 3 AA Red Stars, 3 AA Rosettes for Food, AA Care and Courtesy Award 1990, Lancashire Life Lake District Hotel of the Year 1995, Michelin star 1996; *Recreations* music (especially opera), tennis (watching only), motoring, travelling; *Style*— Brian Sack, Esq, MBE; ✉ Sharrow Bay Country House Hotel, Ullswater, Penrith, Cumbria CA10 2LZ (☎ 017684 86301, fax 017684 86349, car 0831 403466)

SACKMAN, Simon Laurence; s of Bernard Sackman (d 1986), and Mamie, *née* Epstein; *b* 16 Jan 1951; *Educ* St Paul's, Pembroke Coll Oxford (BA, MA); *m* 7 Feb 1982, Donna, da of Solomon Seruya, OBE, of Gibraltar; 3 da (Sarah b 1984, Paloma b 1987, Claire b 1992); *Career* Norton Rose: articled clerk 1974–77, asst slr 1977–83, ptnr 1983–, currently head Corp Fin Dept; memb: City of London Slrs Co 1982, Law Soc 1977; *Recreations* theatre, music; *Clubs* City Univ, MCC; *Style*— Simon Sackman, Esq; ✉ Norton Rose, Kempson House, Camomile Street, London EC3A 7AN (☎ 0171 283 6000, fax 0171 283 6500)

SACKS, John Harvey; s of late Joseph Gerald Sacks, of Gloucester Place, London, and Yvonne, *née* Clayton; *b* 29 April 1946; *Educ* Perse Sch Cambridge, Univ of London (LLB); *m* 2 Dec 1969, Roberta Judith, da of late Archy Arenson, of Regent's Park, London; 1 s (David b 19 Jan 1981), 2 da (Deborah b 7 Oct 1972, Rachel b 1 March 1976); *Career* chief exec Arenson Group plc 1982–, chm and md President Office Furniture Ltd; pres Fedn Europenne de Meubles de Bureau 1996–; former chm: Office Furniture and Filing Mfrs' Assoc (OFFMA) 1990–96, London & SE Furniture Manufacturing Assoc; FCA, FRSA; *Recreations* cycling, chess, music; *Clubs* Savile; *Style*— John Sacks, Esq; ✉ Barlogan, Priory Drive, Stanmore, Middx HA7 3HL; Arenson Group PLC, Lincoln House, Colney Street, St Albans, Herts AL2 2DX; (☎ 01923 857211, fax 01923 858387, e-mail JHSacks@aol.com)

SACKS, Chief Rabbi Dr Jonathan Henry; s of Louis David Sacks, of London, and Louisa, *née* Frumkin; *b* 8 March 1948; *Educ* Christ's Coll Finchley, Gonville and Caius Coll Cambridge (MA), New Coll Oxford, London (PhD), Jews' Coll London, Yeshivat Etz Hayyim London; *m* 14 July 1970, Elaine, da of Philip Taylor (d 1986); 1 s (Joshua b 1975), 2 da (Dina b 1977, Gila b 1982); *Career* lectr in moral philosophy Middx Poly 1971–73; Jews' Coll London: lectr Jewish philosophy 1973–76, lectr Talmud and Jewish philosophy 1976–82, Chief Rabbi Lord Jakobovits prof (first incumbent) in modern Jewish thought 1982–, dir rabbinic faculty 1983–90, princ 1984–90, Chief Rabbi of the Utd Hebrew Congregations of the Cwlth 1991–; Sherman lectr Univ of Manchester 1989, Reith Lecturer 1990, visiting prof of philosophy Univ of Essex 1989–90; rabbi: Golders Green Synagogue London 1978–82, Marble Arch Synagogue London 1983–90; editor Le'Ela, A Journal of Judaism Today 1985–90; memb CRAC; Hon DUniv Middlesex 1993; presentation fell King's Coll 1993; *Books* Torah Studies (1986), Tradition and Transition: Essays Presented to Chief Rabbi Sir Immanuel Jakobovits to Celebrate Twenty Years in Office (1986), Traditional Alternatives (1989), Tradition in an Untraditional Age (1990), The Reith Lectures 1990–, The Persistence of Faith (1991), Orthodoxy Confronts Modernity (ed, 1991), Crisis and Covenant (1992), One People? (1993), Will We Have Jewish Grandchildren? (1994), Community of Faith (1995); *Recreations* walking; *Style*— Chief Rabbi Dr Jonathan Sacks; ✉ Office of the Chief Rabbi, 735 High Road, London N12 0US (☎ 0181 343 6301, fax 0181 343 6310)

SACKUR, Stephen John; s of Robert Neil Humphrys Sackur, of Spilsby, W Yorks, and Sallie, *née* Caley; *b* 9 Jan 1964; *Educ* King Edward VI GS Spilsby, Emmanuel Coll Cambridge (BA), Harvard Univ (Henry fellowship); *m* May 1992, Zina, da of Saadallah Sabbagh; *Career* BBC: trainee 1986–87, prodr Current Affairs 1987–89, reporter World At One 1989–90, foreign affairs corr 1990–92, Middle East corr 1992–; *Books* On the Basra Road (1991); *Recreations* football, cinema, books, walking, day dreaming; *Style*— Stephen Sackur, Esq; ✉ BBC News and Current Affairs, BBC Television Centre, London W12 7RJ; BBC, 19 Gabalaya Street, Zamalek, Cairo, Egypt (☎ 00 202 34016982)

SACKVILLE, 6 Baron (UK 1876); Lionel Bertrand Sackville-West; proprietor of Knole, founded around 1456 by Thomas Bourchier (then Archbishop of Canterbury) and expanded in the early seventeenth century by Thomas Sackville, to whom it was made over by Elizabeth I; patron of eleven livings; s of late Hon Bertrand George Sackville-West (bro of 4 Baron and unc of Vita (Victoria) Sackville-West, w of Hon Sir Harold Nicolson, KCVO, CMG) and Eva, da of late Maj-Gen Inigo Richmond Jones, CB, CVO; suc cous 1965; *b* 30 May 1913; *Educ* Winchester, Magdalen Coll Oxford; *m* 1, 1953, Jacobine Napier (d 1971), da of J R Menzies-Wilson and widow of Capt John Hichens, RA; 5 da; m 2, 1974 (m dis 1983), Arlie Roebuck (d 1991), da of Charles Woodhead, of Romany Rye, Brisbane, Aust, widow of Maj Hugh Dalzell Stewart and formerly w of Maj-Gen Sir Francis Wilfred de Guingand, KBE, CB, DSO; m 3, 1983, Jean, JP, da of Arthur Stanley Garton (d 1983), and widow of Sir Edward Imbert-Terry, 3 Bt, MC (d 1978); *Heir* bro, Hugh Inigo Sackville-West; *Career* late Coldstream Gds, served WWII (POW); Lloyd's underwriter, ret; *Style*— The Rt Hon the Lord Sackville; ✉ Knole, Sevenoaks, Kent (☎ 01732 455694)

SACKVILLE, Hon Thomas Geoffrey (Tom); MP (C) Bolton West (majority 1,079); yr s of 10 Earl De La Warr, DL (d 1988); *b* 26 Oct 1950; *Educ* Eton, Lincoln Coll Oxford (BA); *m* 1979, Catherine, da of late Brig James Windsor Lewis; 1 s, 1 da; *Career* formerly merchant banker; MP (C) Bolton W 1983–; PPS to Min of State Treasy 1985–86, PPS to Min of State NI Office 1986–87, PPS to Min of State for Social Security 1987–88, an asst Govt whip 1988–89, a Lord Cmmr of the Treasy (Govt whip) 1989–92, jt Parly under-sec of state Dept of Health 1992–95, Parly under sec of state Home Office 1995–; *Style*— The Hon Tom Sackville, MP; ✉ House of Commons, London SW1A 0AA (☎ 0171 219 4050/3537)

SACKVILLE-WEST, Hugh Rosslyn Inigo; MC; s of late Hon Bertrand Sackville-West (bro of 4 Baron Sackville) and Eva, da of Maj-Gen Inigo Richmond Jones, CB, CVO; hp of bro, 6 Baron; *b* 1 Feb 1919; *Educ* Winchester, Magdalen Coll Oxford; *m* 1957, Bridget Eleanor, da of Capt Robert Lionel Brooke Cunliffe, CBE, RN (ggs of 3 Bt); 2 s, 3 da; *Career* Capt RTR, serv WWII (Croix de Guerre); admin offr N Nigeria 1946–59; ARICS; *Style*— Hugh Sackville-West, Esq; ✉ Knole, Sevenoaks, Kent

SADEQUE, Shahwar; da of Ali Iman (d 1943), of Bangladesh, and Akhtar Banu; *b* 31 Aug 1942; *Educ* Dhaka Univ Bangladesh (BSc), Bedford Coll London (MPhil), Kingston Poly (MSc); *m* 7 Oct 1962, Pharhad Sadeque, s of Abdus Sadeque (d 1961); 1 s (Fahim b 26 Jan 1971), 1 da (Schehrezade b 13 Nov 1963); *Career* computer programmer BARIC Services Ltd 1969–73, physics teacher Nonsuch HS for Girls Sutton 1973–84, pt/t res into application of artificial intelligence and vision systems to mfrg processes Univ of Kingston (formerly Kingston Poly) 1985–92; memb: Cmmn for Racial Equality 1989–93, Bd of Govrs BBC 1990–95, Shadow Bd Southwark Housing Action Tst 1990, Bd Waltham Forest Housing Action Tst 1991–, VAT Tbnls of England and Wales 1991–, Income and Corporation Taxes Tbnl 1992–, Sch Curriculum and Assessment Authy 1993–, Nat Cncl for Educnl Technol 1994–, Metropolitan Police Ctee 1995–, Cncl C&G 1995–, Bd of Govrs Univ of Kingston 1995–; formerly memb various Cons Pty bodies incl Cons Women's Nat Ctee and Bow Gp Educn Standing Ctee, liaises with Home Office and London Borough of Tower Hamlets on Muslim affrs, past govr Riverview Co First Sch, voluntary worker St George's Hosp Tooting, involved with community work for the elderly and charity fundraising (Oxfam and UNICEF); MBCS 1991, FRSA 1994; *Publications* papers: Education and Ethnic Minorities (1988), Manufacturing - Towards the 21st Century (1988), A Knowledge-Based System for Sensor Interaction and Real-Time Component Control (1988); *Recreations* collecting thimbles and perfume bottles, cooking Indian-style, keeping up-to-date with current affairs; *Style*— Mrs Shahwar Sadeque; ✉ 59 Cheam Rd, East Ewell, Epsom, Surrey KT17 3EG (☎ 0181 393 8485, fax 0181 393 4306)

SADGROVE, Very Rev Michael; s of Ralph Sadgrove, of London, and Doreen, *née* Leyser; *b* 13 April 1950; *Educ* Univ Coll Sch London, Balliol Coll Oxford (Liddon student, MA, Denyer and Johnson award), Trinity Theol Coll Bristol; *m* 1974, Elizabeth Jennifer, *née* Suddes; 3 da (Joanna Elizabeth Marie b 1977, Philippa Thomasin Jane b 1979, Eleanor Jemima Clare b 1983), 1 s (Aidan Mark Daniel b 1982); *Career* ordained deacon 1975, priest 1976; licensed to officiate Rural Deanery of Cowley 1975–77; Salisbury and Wells Theol Coll: lectr in Old Testament studies 1977–82, vice princ 1980–82; hon vicar-choral Salisbury Cathedral 1978–82, vicar Alnwick Northumberland 1982–87, chaplain Alnwick Infirmary and to Duke of Northumberland 1982–87, canon residentiary, precentor and vice provost Coventry Cathedral 1987–95, provost of Sheffield 1995–, chaplain Sheffield branch Dunkirk Veterans' Assoc 1995–; memb: English Anglican/RC Ctee 1980–90, Deans and Provosts' Church Music Working Pty 1994–95, Cathedrals Liturgical Gp 1994–, Cathedrals Fabric Cmmn for England 1996–; Bishops' inspr of theol colls and courses 1982–; chm: Precentors' Conf of England and Wales 1991–94, Church Men in the Midlands 1991–95, Sheffield Common Purpose Advsy Gp; tstee: Sheffield GS Tst, Deakin Instn; pres: Sheffield Oratorio Chorus, Sterndale Singers; memb Soc for Old Testament Studies 1978; *Books* A Picture of Faith (1995); contrib: Studia Biblica (1978), Lion Handbook of the World's Religions (1982, 2 edn 1994), Reflecting the Word (1989), Rethinking Marriage (1993), Coventry's First Cathedral (1994), The Care Guide (1995); articles and reviews in theol jls; *Recreations* music (piano, organ, singing), the arts, poetry and literature, bread-making, wine-making, walking the north-east of England, riding Sheffield's trams, a convinced European; *Clubs* Sheffield; *Style*— The Very Rev Michael Sadgrove, Provost of Sheffield; ✉ Provost's Lodge, 22 Hallamgate Road, Sheffield S10 5BS (☎ 0114 266 2373, fax 0114 268 2084); The Cathedral, Sheffield S1 1HA (☎ 0114 275 3434, fax 0114 278 0244)

SADIE, Dr Stanley John; CBE (1982); s of David Sadie, of London (d 1966), and Deborah, *née* Simons (d 1988); *b* 30 Oct 1930; *Educ* St Paul's, Gonville and Caius Coll Cambridge (BA, MA, MusB, PhD); *m* 1, 10 Dec 1953, Adèle (d 1978), da of Henry Bloom (d 1974), of London; 2 s (Graham b 1956, Stephen b 1963), 1 da (Ursula b 1960); m 2, 18 July 1978, Julie Anne, da of Walter McCornack, of Eugene, Oregon; 1 s (Matthew b 1983), 1 da (Celia b 1979); *Career* prof Trinity Coll of Music 1957–65, music critic The Times 1964–81, ed The Musical Times 1967–87; ed: The New Grove Dictionary of Music and Musicians and assoc pubns 1970– (incl The New Grove Dictionary of Opera 1992), Master Musicians series 1976–; gen ed Man and Music series 1989–93; author of studies of: Handel (1962 and 1972), Mozart (1966, 1983 and 1986), Opera (1964 and 1989) and others; chm Handel House Tst 1994; Hon LittD Leicester 1982, Hon RAM 1982; FRCM 1994; *Recreations* watching cricket, reading, opera; *Style*— Dr Stanley Sadie, CBE; ✉ 12 Lyndhurst Rd, Hampstead, London NW3 5NL (☎ 0171 435 2482, fax 0171 435 6481); c/o New Grove Dictionary, 25 Eccleston Place, London SW1W 9NP (☎ 0171 881 8000, fax 0171 881 8496)

SADLEIR, (Franc) Richard; s of Maj Franc Granby Sadleir (ka 1944), of Paignton, Devon, and Josephine Ruth, *née* Hepburn; *b* 27 Dec 1944; *Educ* Marlborough, New Coll Oxford (MA); *m* 25 July 1970, Frances Judith, da of Edward John Wilson (d 1986), of St Agnes, Cornwall; 1 s (Timothy b 1975), 1 da (Rebecca b 1972); *Career* Bank of London and S America Ltd 1967–70, J Henry Schroder and Co Ltd 1970– (dir 1984–); dir The Securities Association Ltd 1986–88; memb Chm's Ctee and chm Compliance Ctee Br Merchant Bankers' Assoc 1991–94; *Recreations* walking, reading, golf; *Style*— Richard Sadleir, Esq; ✉ Fairwinds, Golden Ball Lane, Pinkneys Green, nr Maidenhead, Berks SL6 6NW (☎ 01628 31205); J Henry Schroder and Co Ltd, 120 Cheapside, London EC2V 6DS (☎ 0171 382 6000, fax 0171 382 3950, telex LONDON 885029)

SADLER, Brent Roderick; s of Philip Sadler (d 1959), and Ruth, *née* Dunkerley (d 1996); *b* 29 Nov 1950; *Educ* Royal Masonic Sch Bushey; *m* 17 July 1993, Tess Stimson, *qv*; 1 s (Henry Louis Brent Stimson Sadler b 7 Sept 1994); 2 da from prev marriages (Nicola Louise, Brooke Emma); *Career* news reporter; formerly with: Harrow Observer, Reading Evening Post, Southern TV, Westward TV and HTV Bristol; ITN 1981–91 (ME corr 1986–91); assignments covered incl: hunger strikes Maze Prison Belfast 1981, Falklands war 1982, Israeli invasion of Lebanon 1982, Lebanese civil war 1981–89, Sabra and Chatila massacres 1983, US invasion of Grenada 1986, siege of Bourj al Barajneh Beirut 1987, Iran-Iraq war 1983–88, Gulf war 1991; sr int corr CNN (Rome) 1991–; assignments covered incl: release of Western hostages Beirut 1991, post-war Iraq (incl US missile strikes 1993), Somalia famine 1992–93, Bosnia Herzegovina 1993–96, PLO-Israeli peace agreement 1993, South African elections 1994, US intervention in Haiti 1994, Chechnya rebellion 1995–96, Israeli 'Grapes of Wrath' offensive against Lebanon 1996; winner: Middx Co Press Journalist of the Year 1971, RTS Regional News award 1980, RTS Int News award 1987, BAFTA awards (with ITN team) for quality of coverage from Lebanon (1983) and best actuality coverage of Gulf War (1992), Emmy (US) for Somalia 1993; *Recreations* fly-fishing, skiing, tennis, sailing; *Style*— Brent Sadler, Esq; ✉ CNN, CNN House, 19–22 Rathbone Place, London W1P 1DF (☎ 0171 637 6700)

SADLER, (Arthur) Edward; s of Arthur William Sadler (d 1969), and Hilda, *née* Suckling (d 1984); *b* 27 Oct 1947; *Educ* Adams' GS Newport Shropshire, Univ Coll Oxford (MA), Coll of Law; *m* 1980, Patricia, da of Charles Gill; 1 s (Matthew b 19 July 1981); *Career* articled clerk Farrer & Co 1971–73; ptnr: (specialising in corp tax) Clifford-Turner 1977 (joined Dept of Corp Tax 1973), Clifford Chance (following merger of Clifford-Turner and Coward Chance) 1987–; memb: Corp Tax Sub Ctee of Revenue Ctee Law Soc, Revenue Ctee City of London Solicitors' Co 1978–, Tax Ctee Int Bar Assoc 1980–; Freeman Worshipful Co of Haberdashers 1974; memb: City of London Solicitors' Co, Law Soc, Int Bar Assoc; *Books* Equipment Leasing (with S C Reisbach and Marian Thomas, loose-leaf edn 1993); *Recreations* gardening, opera, hill walking, occasional sailing, Christian activities, 20th Century history; *Style*— Edward Sadler, Esq; ✉ Clifford Chance, 200 Aldersgate Street, London EC1A 4JJ (☎ 0171 600 1000, fax 0171 600 5555)

SADLER, John Stephen; CBE (1982); s of Bernard Eustace Sadler (d 1982), of Bromley, Kent, and Phyllis Dorothy Sadler, *née* Carey (d 1989); *b* 6 May 1930; *Educ* Reading Sch, Corpus Christi Coll Oxford (BA, MA); *m* 1952, Ella, da of John McCleery, of Belfast; 3 s (Stephen, Hugh, Robert); *Career* Civil Serv 1952–66, princ BOT 1958, Br trade cmmr Lagos 1960–64; John Lewis Partnership plc: joined 1966, fin dir 1971–87, dep chm 1984–89; dir: Investment Management Regulatory Organisation Ltd 1987–94, Debenham Tewson & Chinnocks Holdings plc 1987–, AMP Asset Management plc 1991–96, AMP (UK) plc 1991–96; chm: WRC plc 1989–93, UK Bd Australian Mutual Provident Soc 1991–96, Authorised Conveyancing Practitioners Bd 1991–93, West End Central London Bd Sun Alliance Insurance Group 1992–, Alexon Group plc 1993–94, Pearl Group plc 1994–96; memb Monopolies and Mergers Cmmn 1973–85, tstee BT Staff Superannuation Scheme 1983–; *Recreations* golf, rowing, walking; *Clubs* Oriental; *Style*— John Stephen

Sadler, Esq, CBE; ✉ Riverlea, The Warren, Mapledurham, Reading RG4 7TQ; Flat 3, 16 Welbeck Street, London W1M 7PF (☎ 0171 487 4452)

SADLER, Philip John; CBE (1986); s of Edward John Sadler (d 1977), and Adelaide Violet, *née* Parrish (d 1985); *b* 27 Jan 1930; *Educ* Enfield GS, LSE; *m* 11 July 1964, Teresa Jacqueline, da of Victor Coan (d 1949), of London; 2 s (Matthew John b 1965, Jonathan b 1968); *Career* princ scientific offr Civil Serv 1954–64, dir of res Ashridge Management Coll 1964–68 (princ 1969–87), regnl dir Lloyds Bank plc 1985–91, chief exec Ashridge Tst 1988–90 (vice pres 1990–); dir: Williams Lea Group Ltd 1983–, Broadway Lodge Ltd 1983–91; vice pres: Euro Fndn for Mgmnt Devpt 1981–88, Strategic Planning Soc 1984–95; chm Assoc for Mgmnt Educn and Devpt 1991–94, pres Milton Keynes Coll 1994–, chm Dacorum District Citizens' Advice Bureau 1994–; Hon DSc City Univ 1990, Hon DBA De Montfort Univ 1995; BIM Burnham Medal 1982; fell Int Acad of Mgmnt, memb British Acad of Mgmnt; CIMgt, FIPD, FRSA, FInstD; *Recreations* tennis, swimming, classical music; *Style*— Philip Sadler, Esq, CBE; ✉ Shootersway Farmhouse, Shootersway, Berkhamsted, Herts HP4 3TY

SAFINIA, Dr Khosrow; s of Gholam-Reza Safinia (d 1951), and Mehrvash, *née* Mostofi; *b* 18 April 1941; *Educ* Gosforth GS, Sutherland Dental Sch, King's Coll Durham (BDS, LDS RCS, DOrth RCS); *m* 9 April 1973, Dr Shirin Safinia, da of Mohammed-Ali Javad-Shahidi; 2 s (Farhad b 25 July 1975, Bahram b 3 March 1977); *Career* dental surgn; house offr Middx Hosp 1967–68, sr house offr Royal Dental Hosp and St George's Hosp 1968–69, orthodontic course Eastman Dental Hosp Inst of Postgraduate Dental Surgery 1969–70, registrar in orthodontics Eastman Dental Hosp 1970–72, Tweed fndn course Tucson Arizona 1972; private practice: Tehran 1973–84, Harley St London 1984–; assoc prof of orthodontics Univ of Tehran 1973–79, sr dental offr Croydon Health Authy 1984–90, clinical lectr Eastman Dental Hosp Inst of Postgraduate Dental Surgery 1990–; memb: Br Soc for the Study of Orthodontics 1970, American Assoc of Orthodontics 1971, Br Assoc of Orthodontists 1984; fndr memb Iranian Assoc of Orthodontics 1974; fell Pierre Fauchard Acad 1996; *Recreations* skiing, mountain hikes, classical music, photography; *Style*— Dr Khosrow Safinia; ✉ 94 Harley Street, London W1N 1AF (☎ 0171 935 8811, fax 0171 935 8191)

SAGAR, Prof Geoffrey Roger; CBE (1990); s of Eric Sagar (d 1979), of Silverdale, Lancs, and Phyllis Margaret, *née* Rogers (d 1985); *b* 6 March 1933; *Educ* Kirkham GS, Univ of Oxford (MA DPhil); *m* 1 Oct 1955, Margaret Ann, da of William Herbert Beyer (d 1978), of Kennington, Oxford; 1 s (Stephen b 1959), 2 da (Jill b 1957, Helen b 1964); *Career* Nat Serv, RAF Flying Offr 1954–56; Univ Coll of N Wales: lectr 1960–65, sr lectr 1965–77, prof of agricultural botany 1977–95, vice-princ 1981–94, pro-vice-chllr 1994–95, emeritus prof 1995–; dept chm Advsy Ctee on Pesticides, govr Coleg Normal Bangor 1996, memb Cncl Univ of Wales Bangor 1996–; *Recreations* gardening, music, books; *Clubs* Farmers'; *Style*— Prof Geoffrey Sagar, CBE; ✉ Tan Y Graig, Llandegfan, Menai Bridge, Gwynedd (☎ 01248 713144); University of Wales Bangor, Gwynedd (☎ 01248 382525, telex 61100, fax 01248 383876)

SAGE, Morley William; OBE (1984); s of William George Sage (d 1968), of Worle, Weston Super Mare, and Grace Graves, *née* Smith (d 1977); *b* 15 Jan 1930; *Educ* Blundells, Emmanuel Coll Cambridge (MA); *m* 30 April 1955, Enid Muriel, da of Herbert Sim Hirst (d 1987); 1 s (Morley b 1962), 2 da (Caroline b 1957, Fiona b 1960); *Career* chartered electrical engr and conslt; lab and energy mangr Corporate Lab ICI plc 1962–75, dir computing serv Univ of Southampton 1975–88, princ conslt Systems Technol Conslt 1980–; visiting fell Clare Hall Cambridge 1967–69 (life fell 1986); memb: Br Computer Soc 1967, Univ Grants Technol Sub-Ctee 1974–79 (Computer Systems and Electronics Bd 1973–77), Inst of Measurement and Control 1977 (memb cncl 1967–71); chm: Data Communications Protocol Steering Ctee CSERB 1977–81, Inter Univ Ctee on Computing 1983–85, Integrated Prodn Systems SERC 1975–76, Control Engrg Ctee SERC 1974–79 (memb Computing Sci Ctee 1976–79); vice pres IEE 1984–88, dep chm Resources and Methods Ctee ESRC 1982–85; FEng 1987, FIEE 1972, FBCS, FInstMC; *Recreations* reading, gardening, caravanning, DIY, model railways; *Clubs* Royal Cwlth Soc; *Style*— Morley Sage, Esq, OBE, FEng; ✉ Wiltown Place, Wiltown, Curry Rivel, Langport, Somerset TA10 0HZ, (☎ 01458 251407, fax 01458 253376)

SAIDI, Samira Miriam (Sam); da of Hussein Ahmed Saidi, of Manchester, and Elizabeth Anne, *née* Bradshaw; *b* 8 July 1961; *Educ* Bush Davies Schs (ARAD), Royal Ballet Sch; *m* 28 Feb 1987, Alain Jacques Luis Dubreuil, s of Jacques E Dubreuil (d 1989), of Monaco; 1 s (Téo Jacques b April 1993); *Career* dancer Birmingham Royal Ballet (formerly Sadler's Wells Royal Ballet) 1979– (currently first soloist); roles created incl: title role in David Bintley's The Snow Queen, Sybil Vane in The Picture of Dorian Gray, Giselle, Les Sylphides, Alice in Hobson's Choice, Kenneth Macmillan's Quartet, Odette/Odile in Swan Lake, and many other princ roles in co's repertoire; currently re-creating second movement in Massine's Choreatium; active in educn work within co; *Recreations* theatre, interior design, antiques; *Style*— Miss Samira Saidi; ✉ The Birmingham Royal Ballet, Birmingham Hippodrom, Thorp Street, Birmingham B5 4AU (☎ 0121 622 2555, fax 0121 622 5038)

SAINSBURY, Baron (Life Peer UK 1962), of Drury Lane, Borough of Holborn; Alan John Sainsbury; s of John Benjamin Sainsbury, and Mabel Miriam, *née* Van Den Bergh; *see also* Sainsbury, Sir Robert; *b* 13 Aug 1902; *Educ* Haileybury; *m* 1, 1925 (m dis 1939), Doreen Davan (d 1985), da of Leonard Adams; 3 s (Baron Sainsbury of Preston Candover, KG, *qv*, Hon Simon David Davan b 1930, Hon Timothy Alan Davan b 1932); m 2, 1944, Anne Elizabeth (d 1988), da of Paul Lewy; 1 da (Hon Paulette Ann (Hon Mrs Anderson) b 1946); *Career* jt pres J Sainsbury Ltd 1967 (joined 1921, chm 1956–67), Parly candidate (Lib) Div of Suffolk 1929, 1931 and 1935 gen elections, subsequently joined Lab Pty and SDP 1981; *Style*— The Rt Hon the Lord Sainsbury; ✉ J Sainsbury plc, Stamford House, Stamford St, SE1 (☎ 0171 921 6000)

SAINSBURY, David John; s of Sir Robert Sainsbury, *qv*; *b* 24 Oct 1940; *Educ* King's Coll Cambridge, Columbia Graduate Sch of Business NY (MBA); *Career* J Sainsbury plc: joined 1963, dir 1966–, fin controller 1971–73, fin dir 1973–90, dep chm 1988–92, chm 1992–; chm Savacentre Ltd 1984–93, dir Shaw's Supermarkets Inc; visiting fell Nuffield Coll Oxford, chm Governing Body London Business Sch 1991–; tstee SDP 1982–90 (memb Steering Ctee 1981–82); Columbia Business Sch Award for Distinguished Leadership in Business 1990; Hon FEng 1994; *Publications* Government and Industry - A New Partnership (Fabian Soc), Wealth Creation and Jobs (with Christopher Smallwood, Public Policy Centre); *Style*— David Sainsbury, Esq; ✉ J Sainsbury plc, Stamford House, Stamford Street, London SE1 9LL (☎ 0171 921 6000)

SAINSBURY, Jeffrey Paul; s of Walter Ronald Sainsbury, of Cardiff, and Joan Margaret, *née* Slamin (d 1974); *b* 27 June 1943; *Educ* Cardiff HS; *m* 1967, Janet Elizabeth; 1 s (Mark Christopher Paul b 1968), 1 da (Emma Louise b 1971); *Career* qualified CA 1966, md Exchange Registrars Ltd (part of Pannell Kerr Forster); memb: Cardiff City Cncl 1969–96 (Dep Lord Mayor 1977–78, Lord Mayor 1991–92), S Glam CC 1973–76, S Glam Health Authy 1988–90; chm: Cardiff New Theatre 1984–89, Nat Dance Centre of Wales, S Glam TEC; memb Bd Cardiff Bay Devpt Corp 1991–; *Recreations* theatre, music, sport; *Clubs* Cardiff and County; *Style*— Jeffrey Sainsbury, Esq; ✉ 6 Druidstone House, Druidstone Road, St Mellons, Cardiff CF3 9XF (☎ 01633 680397); Exchange Registrars Ltd, 18 Park Place, Cardiff CF1 3PD (☎ 01222 371210, fax 01222 222873, mobile 0378 703946)

SAINSBURY, Sir Robert; kt (1967); s of late John Benjamin Sainsbury, and late Mabel Miriam, *née* Van Den Bergh; *see also* Baron Sainsbury; *b* 24 Oct 1906; *Educ* Haileybury, Pembroke Coll Cambridge; *m* 1937, Lisa Ingeborg, *née* Van Den Bergh (second cousin); 1 s (David John, *qv*), 3 da (1 da decd); *Career* J Sainsbury: joined 1930, dir 1934, jt gen mangr 1938, dep chm 1956, chm 1967, jt pres 1969–; jt fndr Sainsbury Centre for Visual Arts Univ of E Anglia 1973, former tstee and chm Tate Gallery, memb Arts Panel Arts Cncl until 1974, memb Mgmnt Ctee Courtauld Inst of Art 1979–82, hon fell Pembroke Coll Cambridge 1983; Hon Dr RCA 1976, Hon LittD UEA 1977, Hon LLD Univ of Liverpool 1988; FCA 1967 (ACA 1930), Hon FRIBA 1986; *Style*— Sir Robert Sainsbury

SAINSBURY, Roger Norman; s of Cecil Charles Sainsbury (d 1989), of Hitchin, Herts, and Ivy Evelyn, *née* Pettengell; *b* 11 June 1940; *Educ* Eton, Keble Coll Oxford (MA); *m* 16 May 1969, Susan Margaret, da of Henry William Higgs (d 1981); *Career* chartered engr; dir: John Mowlem & Co plc 1982–95, Greater Manchester Metro Ltd 1990–95, UK Detention Services Ltd 1991–95; non-exec chm Thomas Telford Ltd 1993–, vice pres Inst of Civil Engrs; awarded Inst of Civil Engrs: George Stephenson Medal, Reed and Mallik Medal, Parkman Medal; FEng 1986, FICE; *Recreations* gardening, theatre; *Style*— Roger Sainsbury, Esq, FEng; ✉ 88 Dukes Ave, Muswell Hill, London N10 2QA; John Mowlem & Company plc, White Lion Court, Swan Street, Isleworth TW7 6RN (☎ 0181 568 9111, fax 0181 847 4802)

SAINSBURY, Rt Hon Sir Timothy Alan Davan; kt (1995), PC (1992), MP (C) Hove (majority 12,268); yst s (by 1 m) of Baron Sainsbury; *b* 11 June 1932; *Educ* Eton, Worcester Coll Oxford (MA); *m* 26 April 1961, Susan Mary, da of Brig James Alastair Harry Mitchell, CBE, DSO; 2 s (James b 1962, Alexander b 1968), 2 da (Camilla b 1962, Jessica b 1970); *Career* dir J Sainsbury plc 1962–83 and 1995– (non-exec), MP (C) Hove 1973–; PPS to: Sec of State for the Environment 1979–83, Sec of State for Defence 1983; asst Govt whip 1983–85, a Lord Cmmr of the Treasy (Govt whip) 1985–87, Parly under sec of state for defence procurement at MOD 1987–89, Parly under sec of state FCO 1989–90, min of state for trade DTI 1990–92, min of state for industry DTI 1992–94; memb: Cncl RSA 1981–83, Bd of Govrs Westminster Fndn for Democracy; nat chm Conservative Friends of Israel 1995–; Liveryman Worshipful Co of Vintners; hon fell Worcester Coll Oxford 1982, Hon FRICS, Hon FRIBA; *Style*— The Rt Hon Sir Timothy Sainsbury, MP; ✉ House of Commons, London SW1A 0AA

SAINSBURY OF PRESTON CANDOVER, Baron (Life Peer UK 1989), of Preston Candover, Co Hants; Sir John Davan Sainsbury; KG (1992), kt (1980); eldest s (by 1 m) of Baron Sainsbury (Life Peer), *qv*, of Drury Lane; *b* 2 Nov 1927; *Educ* Stowe, Worcester Coll Oxford; *m* 8 March 1963, Anya (Anya Linden, the Royal Ballet ballerina), da of George Charles Eltenton; 2 s (Hon John Julian b 1966, Hon Mark Leonard b 1969), 1 da (Hon Sarah Jane b 1964); *Career* J Sainsbury plc: dir 1958–92, vice chm 1967–69, chm 1969–92, pres 1992–; chm Royal Opera House Covent Garden 1987–91 (dir 1969–85), dir Royal Opera House Tst 1974–84 and 1987–; memb Cncl of Friends of Covent Garden 1969–91 (chm 1969–81); tstee: National Gallery 1976–83, Westminster Abbey Tst 1977–83, Tate Gallery 1982–83, Rhodes Tst 1984–; jt hon treas Euro Movement 1972–75; pres: Br Retail Consortium 1993– (memb Cncl 1975–79), Sparsholt Coll Hants 1993–; memb: Nat Ctee for Electoral Reform 1976–85, President's Ctee CBI 1982–84; vice pres Contemporary Arts Soc 1984– (hon sec 1965–71, vice chm 1971–74); chm: Friends of Covent Garden 1969–81, Benesh Inst of Choreology 1986–87, tstees Dulwich Picture Gallery 1994–, govrs Royal Ballet (govr 1987–); govr Royal Ballet Sch 1965–76 and 1987–91; hon fell Worcester Coll Oxford 1982, hon bencher Inner Temple 1985, Hon DScEcon London 1985, Hon DLitt South Bank Univ 1992, Hon LLD Univ of Bristol 1993; FIGD 1973, Hon FRIBA 1993; Albert Medal RSA 1989; *Clubs* Garrick, Beefsteak; *Style*— The Rt Hon Lord Sainsbury of Preston Candover, KG; ✉ c/o Stamford House, Stamford St, London SE1 (☎ 0171 921 6000)

SAINT, Prof Andrew John; s of Rev Arthur James Maxwell Saint, and Elisabeth Yvetta, *née* Butterfield; *b* 30 Nov 1946; *Educ* Christ's Hosp, Balliol Coll Oxford (BA), Warburg Inst London (MPhil); *Career* teacher Univ of Essex 1971–74, architectural ed The Survey of London 1974–86, historian English Heritage 1986–95, prof of architecture Univ of Cambridge 1995–; Alice Davis Hitchcock Medallion Soc of Architectural Historians (GB) 1978 and 1989; Hon FRIBA; *Books* Richard Norman Shaw (1976), The Image of the Architect (1983), Towards A Social Architecture (1986); *Style*— Prof Andrew Saint; ✉ 14 Denny Crescent, London SE11 4UY (☎ 0171 735 3863); Department of Architecture, University of Cambridge, 1–5 Scroope Terrace, Trumpington Street, Cambridge CB2 1PX (☎ 01223 332964, fax 01223 332950)

SAINT, Dora Jessie; JP; da of Arthur Gunnis Shafe (d 1970), and Grace Lilian, *née* Read (d 1936); *b* 17 April 1913; *Educ* Bromley County Girls' Sch, Homerton Coll Cambridge; *m* 26 July 1940, Douglas Edward John Saint, s of Edward Saint (d 1935); 1 da (Jill b 1941); *Career* author (aka Miss Read); teacher in Middx 1933–40; contrib to: Punch, Times Educnl Supplement, BBC; memb Soc of Authors; *Novels* Village School (1955), Village Diary (1957), Storm in the Village (1958), Thrush Green (1959), Fresh from the Country (1960), Winter in Thrush Green (1961), Miss Clare Remembers (1962), Chronicles of Fairacre (1963), Over the Gate (1964), Market Square (1965), Village Christmas (1966), Fairacre Festival (1968), News from Thrush Green (1970), Tiggy (1971), Emily Davis (1971), Tyler's Row (1972), The Christmas Mouse (1973), Farther Afield (1974), Battles at Thrush Green (1975), No Holly for Miss Quinn (1976), Village Affairs (1977), Return to Thrush Green (1978), The White Robin (1979), Village Centenary (1980), Gossip from Thrush Green (1981), Affairs at Thrush Green (1983), Summer at Fairacre (1984), At Home in Thrush Green (1985), The School at Thrush Green (1987), Mrs Pringle (1989), Friends at Thrush Green (1990); *Children's Books* Hobby Horse Cottage (1958), Hob and the Horse Bat (1965), The Red Bus Series (1965), Changes at Fairacre (1991), Celebrations at Thrush Green (1992); *Non-Fiction* Country Bunch (1963), Miss Read's Country Cooking (1969), Miss Read's Christmas Book (1992); *Autobiography* A Fortunate Grandchild (1982), Time Remembered (1986), Farewell to Fairacre (1993), Tales from a Village School (1994), The Year at Thrush Green (1995), A Peaceful Retirement (1996); *Recreations* reading, theatre-going; *Style*— Mrs Dora Saint, JP; ✉ c/o Michael Joseph Ltd, 27 Wrights Lane, London W8 5TZ

ST ALBANS, Archdeacon of; *see:* Davies, Ven Philip Bertram

ST ALBANS, Bishop of 1995–; Rt Rev Christopher William Herbert; s of Walter Meredith Herbert, of Coleford, Glos, and Hilda Lucy, *née* Dibbin (d 1948); *b* 7 Jan 1944; *Educ* Monmouth, St David's UC Lampeter (BA, Badminton colours), Univ of Bristol (PGCE), Wells Theological Coll; *m* 27 July 1968, Janet Elizabeth, da of Eric Turner, of Headingley, Leeds; 2 s (Robin William b 1970, James Kimbell b 1973); *Career* curate St Paul's Tupsley and asst master Bishop's Sch Hereford 1967–71, dir of educn Diocese of Hereford 1976–81 (advsr in religious educn 1971–76), prebendary Hereford Cathedral 1977–81, vicar St Thomas on the Bourne Farham Surrey 1981–90, dir of post-ordination trg Diocese of Guildford 1983–90, hon canon Guildford Cathedral 1985–95, archdeacon of Dorking 1990–95; chm Pubns Ctee Nat Soc (memb Exec and Standing Ctee), memb numerous diocesan ctees; *Books* The New Creation (1971), A Place to Dream (1976), St Paul's: a Place to Dream (1981), The Edge of Wonder (1981), Listening to Children (1983), On the Road (1984), Be Thou My Vision (1985), This Most Amazing Day (1986), Ways Into Prayer (1987), The Question of Jesus (1987), Alive to God (1987), Help in Your Bereavement (1988), Prayers for Children (1993), Pocket Prayers (1993), The Prayer Garden (1994), Words of Comfort (1994); *Recreations* walking, music, cycling, gardening; *Style*— The Rt Rev Christopher Herbert; ✉ Abbey Gate House, St Albans, Herts AL3 4HD

ST ALBANS, Dean of; *see:* Lewis, Very Rev Christopher

ST ALBANS, 14 Duke of (E 1684); Murray de Vere Beauclerk; also Baron Hedington and Earl of Burford (E 1676), Baron Vere of Hanworth (GB 1750); Hereditary Grand Falconer and Hereditary Registrar of Court of Chancery; s of 13 Duke of St Albans, OBE (d 1988), and his 1 w, Nathalie Chatham (d 1985), da of Percival Walker; gggggs of 1 Duke of St Albans, who was natural s of King Charles II and Eleanor (Nell) Gwynn; *b* 19 Jan 1939; *Educ* Tonbridge; *m* 1, 31 Jan 1963 (m dis 1974), Rosemary Frances, o da of Francis Harold Scoones, MRCS, LRCP, JP; 1 s (Earl of Burford), 1 da (Lady Emma Caroline de Vere (Lady Emma Smellie) b 22 July 1963); m 2, 1974, Cynthia Theresa Mary, da of late Lt-Col William James Holdsworth Howard, DSO, and former w of late Sir Anthony Robin Maurice Hooper, 2 Bt; *Heir* s, Earl of Burford, *qv*; *Career* Govr-Gen Royal Stuart Soc, pres Beaufort Opera; Freeman City of London, Liveryman Drapers' Co; FCA; *Clubs* Hurlingham; *Style*— His Grace the Duke of St Albans; ✉ c/o House of Lords, London SW1A 0PW

ST ALDWYN, 3 Earl (UK 1915); Sir Michael Henry Hicks Beach; 11 Bt (E 1619); also Viscount St Aldwyn (UK 1906), Viscount Quenington (UK 1915); s of 2 Earl St Aldwyn, GBE, TD, PC (d Jan 1992), and Diana Mary Christian, *née* Mills (d July 1992); *b* 7 Feb 1950; *Educ* Eton, Univ of Oxford (MA); *m* 1982, Gilda Maria, o da of Barão Saavedra (d 1984), and Baronesa Saavedra, of Ipanema, Rio de Janeiro, Brazil; 2 da (Lady Atalanta Maria b 1983, Lady Aurora Ursula b 1988); *Heir* bro, Hon David Seymour Hicks Beach b 1955; *Career* commodity broker; Liveryman Worshipful Co of Mercers; *Clubs* Leander, White's; *Style*— The Rt Hon the Earl St Aldwyn; ✉ Williamstrip Park, Coln St Aldwyns, Cirencester GL7 5AT (☎ 01285 750226); 17 Hale House, 34 de Vere Gardens, London W8 5AQ (☎ 0171 937 6223, fax 0171 937 3756); International Fund Marketing (UK) Ltd, 103 Mount Street, London W1Y 5HE (☎ 07000 557558, fax 07000 558559)

ST ANDREWS, Earl of; George Philip Nicholas Windsor; er s and h of HRH The Duke of Kent, KG, GCMG, GCVO (*see Royal Family*); *b* 26 June 1962; *Educ* Eton, Downing Coll Cambridge; *m* 9 Jan 1988, Sylvana Palma (b 28 May 1957), formerly w of John Paul Jones, and da of Max(imilian) Karl Tomaselli and Josiane Preschez; 1 s (Edward Edmund Maximilian George, Lord Downpatrick b 2 Dec 1988), 2 da (Lady Marina-Charlotte Alexandra Katharine Helen b 30 Sept 1992, Lady Amelia Sophia Theodora Mary Margaret b 24 Aug 1995); *Heir* s, Edward Edmund Maximilian George Windsor, Lord Downpatrick b 2 Dec 1988; *Career* attached FCO 1987–88; tstee GB-Sasakawa Fndn 1995–; Christie's 1996–; *Style*— Earl of St Andrews

ST ANDREWS AND EDINBURGH, Archbishop of (RC) 1985–; Most Rev Keith Michael Patrick O'Brien; s of Mark Joseph O'Brien, DSM (d 1988), of Edinburgh, and Alice Mary, *née* Moriarty (d 1955); *b* 17 March 1938; *Educ* St Patrick's HS Dumbarton, Holy Cross Acad Edinburgh, Univ of Edinburgh (BSc), St Andrew's Coll Drygrange, Moray House Coll of Educn (Dip Ed); *Career* Holy Cross Parish Edinburgh 1965–66, sch chaplain and teacher St Columba's Secdy Sch Dunfermline 1966–71; asst priest: St Patrick's Parish Kilsyth 1972–75, St Mary's Bathgate 1975–78; spiritual dir St Andrew's Coll Drygrange 1978–80, rector St Mary's Coll Blairs 1980–85; *Recreations* cycling, hill walking; *Style*— The Most Rev the Archbishop of St Andrews and Edinburgh; ✉ St Bennet's, 42 Greenhill Gardens, Edinburgh EH10 4BJ (☎ 0131 447 3337, fax 0131 447 0816); Diocesan Offices, Gillis Centre, 113 Whitehouse Loan, Edinburgh EH9 1BB (☎ 0131 452 8244, fax 0131 452 9153)

ST ASAPH, Dean of; *see:* Goulstone, Very Rev (Thomas Richard) Kerry

ST AUBIN de TERAN, Lisa Gioconda; da of Cuthbert Jan Alwin Rynveld Carew, of USA, and Joan Mary St Aubin (d 1981); *b* 2 Oct 1953; *Educ* James Allen's Girls' Sch Dulwich; *m* 1, 1970, Jaime Cesar Teran Mejia Ci Fuentes Teran; 1 da (Iseult Joanna Teran St Aubin (Mrs Oswald Michael Radford) b 5 May 1973); m 2, 1982, George Mann Macbeth; 1 s (Alexander Morton George Macbeth b 30 Sept 1982); m 3, 1989, Robbie Charles Duff-Scott, s of Frederick Duff-Scott (d 1989); 1 da (Florence Cameron Alexandra Rose Duff-Scott b 10 July 1990); *Career* plantation mangr and sugar farmer Venezuelan Andes 1972–78; writer; *Awards* Somerset Maugham Award 1983, John Llewelyn Rhys Prize 1983, Eric Gregory Award for Poetry 1983; trans into many languages, public readings worldwide; *Books* Keepers of the House (1983), The Slow Train to Milan (1984), The Tiger (1984), The Bay of Silence (1985), The High Place (poetry, 1986), The Marble Mountain (short stories, 1989), Joanna (1990), Venice the Four Seasons (essays, 1992), A Valley In Italy: Confessions of a House Addict (1994), The Hacienda (memoirs, 1997), The Palace (novel, 1997); *Recreations* reading, falconry, herbal medicines; *Clubs* Groucho; *Style*— Ms Lisa St Aubin de Teran; ✉ c/o A M Heath & Co Ltd, 79 St Martin's Lane, London WC2N 4AA (☎ 0171 836 4271, fax 0171 497 2561)

ST AUBYN, Hon Giles Rowan; LVO (1977); yst s of 3 Baron St Levan (d 1978), and Hon Clementina Gwendolen Catharine, *née* Nicolson (d 1995), da of 1 Baron Carnock; *b* 11 March 1925; *Educ* Wellington, Univ of Glasgow, Trinity Coll Oxford; *Career* master and house master Eton 1947–85; author; FRSL; *Books* Macaulay (1952), A Victorian Eminence (1957), The Art of Argument (1957), The Royal George (1963), A World to Win (1968), Infamous Victorians (1971), William of Gloucester: Pioneer Prince (1977), Edward VII, Prince and King (1979), The Year of Three Kings (1983), Queen Victoria, A Portrait (1991); *Clubs* Beefsteak, The Royal Over-Seas League; *Style*— The Hon Giles St Aubyn, LVO; ✉ Apartment 2, Saumarez Park Manor, Route de Saumarez, Câtel, Guernsey, Channel Islands, GY5 7TH (☎ 01481 51789)

ST AUBYN, Hon (Oliver) Piers; MC (1944); s of late 3 Baron St Levan and Hon Clementina, *née* Nicolson, da of 1 Baron Carnock and sis of Sir Harold Nicolson (the writer, d 1968; *see* Nigel Nicolson); hp of bro, 4 Baron St Levan, DSC; *b* 12 July 1920; *Educ* Wellington, St James's Sch Maryland USA; *m* 1948, Mary Bailey (d 1987), da of Bailey Southwell, of Olievenhoortpoort S Africa; 2 s (James b 1950, Nicholas b 1955), 1 da (Fiona); *Career* served WWII, Capt 60 Rifles and Parachute Regt (despatches); memb Stock Exchange 1949–; ptnr W Greenwell & Co 1957–78; High Sheriff E Sussex 1982–83; *Clubs* House of Lords Yacht, Brooks's; *Style*— The Hon Piers St Aubyn, MC; ✉ Hogus House, Ludgvan, Penzance, Cornwall TR20 8EZ (☎ 01736 740822)

ST AUBYN, Maj Thomas Edward; CVO (1993), DL (1984); s of Capt The Hon Lionel St Aubyn, MVO (d 1964), and Lady Mary, *née* Parker (d 1932); *b* 13 June 1923; *Educ* Eton; *m* 21 Nov 1953, Henrietta Mary, da of Sir Henry Gray Studholme, 1 Bt, CVO (d 1987); 3 da (Sarah b 1955, Caroline b 1957, Clare b 1962); *Career* served in KRRC 1941–62, Italian Campaign 1944–45, seconded to Sudan Defence Force in rank of Bimbashi 1948–52, instr RMA Sandhurst 1955–56; ldr of Tibesti Mountain Expedition 1957 and other Sahara Expdns 1963–71; High Sheriff of Hants 1979–80; HM Body Guard of the Hon Corps of Gentlemen at Arms: memb 1973–, Clerk of the Cheque and Adj 1986–90, The Lieutenant 1990–93; FRGS 1961; *Recreations* shooting, fishing; *Clubs* Army and Navy; *Style*— Maj Thomas E St Aubyn, CVO, DL; ✉ Dairy House Farm, Ashford Hill, Thatcham, Berks RG19 8BL (☎ 01635 298493)

ST CLAIR, William Linn; *b* 7 Dec 1937; *Educ* Edinburgh Acad, St John's Coll Oxford; *children* 2 da (Anna b 1967, Elisabeth b 1970); *Career* writer, formerly under sec HM Treasy, served Admiralty and FCO; conslt OECD 1992–; int pres Byron Soc; fell All Souls Coll Oxford 1992–96 (visiting fell 1981–82), visiting fell Huntington Library Calif 1985; memb Ctee London Library 1996–; FRSL, FBA; *Awards* Heinemann Prize for Lit 1973, Time Life Award for Br Non-Fiction 1990; *Books* Lord Elgin and the Marbles (1967, 2 edn 1983), That Greece Might Still Be Free (1972), Trelawny (1978), Policy Evaluation - A Guide For Managers (1988), The Godwins and the Shelleys - The Biography of a Family (1989), Executive Agencies - A Guide to Setting Targets and Judging Performance (1992); *Recreations* old books, Scottish mountains; *Style*— William St Clair; ✉ 52 Eaton Place, London SW1X 8AL (☎ 0171 235 8329); literary agent: Deborah Rogers, 20 Powis Mews, London W11

ST CLAIR-FORD, Sir James Anson; 7 Bt (GB 1793), of Ember Court, Surrey; o s of Capt Sir Aubrey St Clair-Ford, 6 Bt, DSO, RN (d 1991), and Anne, *née* Christopherson; *b* 16 March 1952; *Educ* Wellington, Univ of Bristol; *m* 1, 1977 (m dis 1985), Jennifer Margaret, da of Cdre J Robin Grindle, RN; m 2, 1987, Mary Anne, da of late Judge Nathaniel Robert Blaker, QC, DL, of Winchester, Hants; *Heir* cousin, Colin Anson St Clair-Ford b 19 April 1939; *Style*— Sir James St Clair-Ford, Bt; ✉ 161 Sheen Lane, London SW14

ST CLAIRE, Marian (Mrs Michael Beare); da of Matthew William Allsopp, of 237 Leyland Lane, Leyland, Lancashire and Margaret Taylor; *b* 11 May 1946; *Educ* Wellfield Secdy Sch Leyland Lancs, Loretto Sch of Dance Southport Lancs, Ballet Rambert Sch London; *m* 2 Aug 1985, Michael Walter Beare, s of Douglas Charles Beare; *Career* ballet dancer; soloist: Ballet Rambert 1966–67 (former memb Corps de Ballet), Cape Town Ballet Co S Africa 1967–69; princ dancer: Scottish Ballet 1969–75, New London Ballet 1975–76; ballerina Dame Margot Fonteyn's Farewell Tour of UK 1976–77, ballerina Harold King's Luch Hour Ballet Arts Theatre London 1978, fndr, ballerina and asst artistic dir London City Ballet Co 1979–91; currently freelance guest ballerina, teacher and répétiteur; guest ballerina: Nat Ballet of Rhodesia 1977, London Festival Ballet 1977–78, Northern Ballet 1978, Wayne Sleep's Hot Shoe Show (London Palladium), Sleep with Friends, Bits and Pieces and World of Dance 1989; performed as guest artist in Canada, Tokyo, Zimbabwe, Stockholm and at Chicago, Cuba, Poland, Spain and Romania dance festivals; guest artist Weiner Ballet Theatre; *Performances* incl: Bluebird Pas de Deux in Sleeping Beauty (Cape Town Ballet and London Festival Ballet), Peasant Pas de Trois and Neopolitan Dance in Swan Lake (Cape Town Ballet), The Misfit (leading role created by Gary Burn, Cape Town Ballet), Beauty in Beauty and the Beast (Scottish Ballet), Sugar Plum Fairy in The Nutcracker (Scottish Ballet), Antonia in Tales of Hoffman (Scottish Ballet), Columbia in Le Carnival (Scottish Ballet), Desdemona in Othello (New London Ballet), Elgie Pas de Deux (New London Ballet), Faust Variations (New London Ballet), Soft Blue Shadows (New London Ballet), leading roles in Giselle (Scottish Ballet, London Festival Ballet, Northern Ballet, London City Ballet), La Sylphide (Scottish Ballet, Northern Ballet, London City Ballet), Cinderella (Northern Ballet, London City Ballet), Carmen (London City Ballet), Swan Lake (London City Ballet), Coppèlia (London City Ballet), La Traviata (London City Ballet); *Recreations* singing, cooking and entertaining, fashion, walking; *Style*— Ms Marian St Claire; ✉ The Garden Flat, 11A Inderwick Rd, Hornsey, London N8 9LB (☎ 0181 341 1272)

ST CLEMENT, Pamela (Pam); *b* 11 May 1942; *Educ* The Warren Worthing, Rolle Coll Devon, Rose Bruford Coll of Drama Kent; *m* 1970 (m dis 1979), Andrew Louis Gordon; *Career* actress; other activities: animal lover and campaigner, gay rights supporter, works with and for AIDS charities; patron: PACE, Open House Project, Animal Welfare Trust (Retirement Home Poject); tstee Iris Tst, memb Ctee Stage for Age, vice pres Scottish Terrier Emergency Care Scheme, vice-pres Pro-Dogs, pres West Herts RSPCA; memb: RSPCA Artists for Animals, Arts for Labour, Inst of Advanced Motorists; *Theatre* incl: Joan Littlewood's Theatre Royal Stratford, Royal Shakespeare Theatre Co (Aldwych and world tour); other credits incl: Stringberg and Chekov (Prospect Theatre Co tour), Macbeth (Thorndike Theatre), I Am A Camera (Yvonne Arnaud Guildford and tour), Once a Catholic (Leeds Playhouse); *Television* incl: Within These Walls (2 series, LWT), Shall I See You Now? (BBC play), A Horseman Riding By (BBC series), Emmerdale Farm (YTV), Shoestring (BBC), Partners in Crime (LWT), Cat's Eyes (TVS), The Tripods (BBC), Not For The Likes Of Us (BBC Play for Today), Pat Butcher in EastEnders (BBC) 1986–; *Films* incl: Hedda, Dangerous Davies, The Bunker, Scrubbers; *Style*— Ms Pam St Clement; ✉ c/o Saraband Associates, 265 Liverpool Rd, London N1 1LX (☎ 0171 609 5313/4, fax 0171 609 2370); BBC TV Studios, Clarendon Rd, Borehamwood, Herts (fax 0181 207 8670)

ST CYRES, Viscount; John Stafford Northcote; s and h of 4 Earl of Iddesleigh; *b* 15 Feb 1957; *Educ* Downside, RAC Cirencester; *m* 14 May 1983, Fiona Caroline Elizabeth, da of Paul Alan Campbell Wakefield, of Barcelona, Spain; 1 s (Thomas Stafford b 1985), 1 da (Elizabeth Rose Adèle b 10 April 1989); *Heir* s, Hon Thomas Stafford Northcote, b 5 Aug 1985; *Career* farmer; *Recreations* shooting, sailing; *Style*— Viscount St Cyres; ✉ Hayne Barton, Newton St Cyres, Devon EX5 5AH

ST DAVIDS, 3 Viscount (UK 1918); Sir Colwyn Jestyn John Philipps; 15 Bt (E 1621); also Baron Strange of Knokin (E 1299), Baron Hungerford (E 1426), Baron de Moleyns (E 1445), and Baron St Davids (UK 1908); s of 2 Viscount St Davids (d 1991), and his 1 w, Doreen Guinness, *née* Jowett (d 1956); *b* 30 Jan 1939; *Educ* Haverfordwest GS, Sevenoaks Sch; *m* 1965, Augusta Victoria Correa Larrain, da of late Don Estanislao Correa Ugarte, of Santiago, Chile; 2 s (Hon Rhodri Colwyn b 1966, Hon Roland Augusto Jestyn Estanislao b 1970); *Heir* s, Hon Rhodri Colwyn Philipps b 16 Sept 1966; *Career* Nat Serv 2 Lt Welsh Guards 1959–61, Securities Agency Ltd 1957–65, Maguire Kingsmill and Co 1965, Kemp-Gee and Co (later Scrimgeour Kemp-Gee and Co) 1968–85 (ptnr 1971), dir Citicorp Scrimgeour Vickers (Securities) Ltd 1985–88, non-exec dir Greig Middleton & Co Ltd 1994– (dir 1989–91, conslt 1991–92); memb Bd Roland House Scout Settlement 1975–77, district cmmr Islington District Scout Cncl 1976–78, memb Baden-Powell Fellowship 1983–, tstee Docklands Scout Tst 1986–90; a Lord in Waiting 1992–94; Dep Speaker in House of Lords 1995–; memb Stock Exchange 1965–93, Liveryman Worshipful Co of Musicians 1971; *Recreations* music, English literature and natural history; *Clubs* City of London, Garrick; *Style*— The Rt Hon the Viscount St Davids; ✉ House of Lords, London SW1A 0PW

ST DAVIDS, Dean of; *see:* Evans, Very Rev (John) Wyn

ST EDMUNDSBURY, Provost of; *see:* Atwell, Very Rev James Edgar

ST EDMUNDSBURY AND IPSWICH, Bishop of 1997–; Rt Rev (John Hubert) Richard Lewis; s of the Ven John Wilfred Lewis (d 1984), and Winifred Mary, *née* Griffin; *b* 10 Dec 1943; *Educ* Radley, King's Coll London (AKC); *m* 17 April 1968, Sara Patricia, da of Canon Gerald Murray Percival (Peter) Hamilton; 3 s (Peter John b 1970, Michael James b 1972, Nicholas Richard b 1975); *Career* curate of Hexham 1967–70, industl chaplain Diocese of Newcastle 1970–77, communications offr Diocese of Durham 1977–82, agric chaplain Diocese of Hereford 1982–87, archdeacon of Ludlow 1987–92, bishop suffragan of Taunton 1992–97; nat chm Small Farmers Assoc 1984–88; *Books* The People, The Land and The Church (jt ed, 1987); *Recreations* kit cars, bricklaying; *Style*— The Rt Rev the Bishop of St Edmundsbury and Ipswich; ✉ Bishop's House, 4 Park Road, Ipswich, Suffolk IP1 3ST (☎ 01473 252829, fax 01473 232552)

ST GEORGE, Charles Reginald; s of William Acheson St George (d 1993), of Morecombe, Lancs, and Heather Atwood, *née* Brown (d 1978); *b* 20 April 1955; *Educ* Henley GS, Univ of Exeter (BA), Queen's Univ Kingston Ontario Canada (MA); *m* 1, 19 July 1980 (m dis 1989); 1 da (Imogen Margaret b 15 Jan 1984), 1 s (Michael John b 31 Dec 1985); m 2, 17 Oct 1991; 1 s (Henry Peter b 19 May 1995); *Career* CBI: sec Smaller Firms Cncl 1979–82, head of secretariat 1982–83; account mangr Ian Greer Associates Ltd 1983–87, md Profile Political Relations Ltd 1989–90 (dir 1987–88), jt md Political Planning Services Ltd 1990–; prospective Lib Parly candidate Guildford 1980–82, Lib Alliance borough cnclr Guildford 1983–87; *Recreations* golf, tennis and skiing; *Style*— Charles St George, Esq; ✉ Political Planning Services, 69 Grosvenor Street, London W1X 9DV (☎ 0171 629 7377)

ST GERMANS, Bishop of 1993–; Rt Rev Graham Richard James; s of Lionel Dennis James, and (Florence Edith) May, *née* James; *b* 19 Jan 1951; *Educ* Northampton GS, Univ of Lancaster (BA), Univ of Oxford (dip in theol), Cuddesdon Theol Coll (cert in theol); *m* 21 Jan 1978, Julie Anne, da of Stanley William Freemantle; 2 da (Rebecca Alice b 5 Oct 1980, Victoria Rachel b 1983, d 1984), 1 s (Dominic Richard b 12 April 1985); *Career* ordained: deacon 1975, priest 1976; asst curate Christ the Carpenter Peterborough 1975–78, priest-in-charge later team vicar Christ the King Digswell Welwyn Garden City Herts 1979–83, selection sec/sec for continuing ministerial educn 1983–85, sr selection sec ACCM 1985–87, chaplain to the Archbishop of Canterbury 1987–93; *Books* Say One for Me (contrib, 1991); *Recreations* theatre, walking, secondhand bookshops; *Style*— The Rt Rev the Bishop of St Germans; ✉ 32 Falmouth Road, Truro, Cornwall TR1 2HX (☎ 01872 73190, fax 01872 77883)

ST GERMANS, 10 Earl of (UK 1815); Peregrine Nicholas Eliot; also Baron Eliot (GB 1784); s of 9 Earl of St Germans (d 1988), by his 1 w Helen Mary (who d 1951, having m 2, 1947, Capt Ralph Benson, Coldstream Gds), da of Lt Charles Walters Villiers, CBE, DSO; *b* 2 Jan 1941; *Educ* Eton; *m* 1, 9 Oct 1964 (m dis 1990), Hon Jacquetta Jean Fredricka Lampson, da of 1 Baron Killearn; 3 s (Lord Eliot, Hon Louis b 11 April 1968, Hon Francis b 16 Nov 1971); m 2, 20 April 1991, Elizabeth Mary, eldest da of Basil James Williams, of France; *Heir* s, Lord Eliot, *qv*; *Career* landowner; 30 yrs in a job without prospects; patron of three livings; *Recreations* sitting still; *Clubs* Pratt's, The Cornish; *Style*— The Rt Hon the Earl of St Germans; ✉ Port Eliot, St Germans, Cornwall (☎ 01503 230211)

ST GILES, Mark Valentine; s of late Austin Loudon Valentine St Giles, and Sybil Gladwin Sykes Thompson; *b* 4 June 1941; *Educ* Winchester, Clare Coll Cambridge (MA); *m* 1966, Susan Janet, da of late Edward Turner; 2 da (Emma b 1968, Lucy b 1970), 1 s (Edward b 1974); *Career* analyst Laurence Keen & Gardner stockbrokers 1964–69, dir Jessel Securities 1969–75, md Allied Hambro Ltd 1975–83, dir Hambros Bank 1975–83, dir (later md) GT Management plc 1983–88, chm Cadogan Management Ltd 1988–93; dir: Framlington Group plc 1989–, International Financial Strategy Ltd 1993–; *Recreations* travel, sailing, gardening; *Style*— Mark St Giles, Esq; ✉ International Financial Strategy Ltd, 19 Buckingham Street, London WC2N 6EF (☎ 0171 976 2500, fax 0171 930 7402)

ST HELENS, 2 Baron (UK 1964); Richard Francis Hughes-Young; s of 1 Baron (sometime Dep Govt Chief Whip, d 1980), and Elizabeth (d 1956), da of late Capt Richard Blakiston-Houston (ggs of Sir Matthew Blakiston, 2 Bt); *b* 4 Nov 1945; *Educ* Nautical Coll Pangbourne; *m* 1983, Mrs Emma R Talbot-Smith; 1 s, 1 da (b 1987); *Heir* s, Hon Henry Thomas Hughes-Young b 7 March 1986; *Style*— The Rt Hon the Lord St Helens; ✉ Marchfield House, Binfield, Berks

ST JOHN, (Oliver) Peter; s of Lt-Col Frederick Oliver St John, DSO, MC (d 1977), and gs of late Sir Frederick Robert St John, KCMG (yst s of late Hon Ferdinand St John, 2 s of 3 Viscount Bolingbroke and St John); through Sir Frederick's w, Isabella Fitz-Maurice (gda of 5 Earl of Orkney), Peter is hp to his 2 cous once removed, 8 Earl of Orkney; *b* 27 Feb 1938; *m* 1, 1963 (m dis 1985), Mary Juliet, da of W G Scott-Brown; 1 s (Oliver Robert b 1969), 3 da (Juliet Elizabeth b 1964, Nicola Jane b 1966, Lucy Margaret b 1972); m 2, 1985, Mary Barbara Huck, da of Dr D B Albertson; 1 step s (Anthony Cameron St John), 3 step da (Dawn Marie Huck, Caroline Jane Huck, Erin Katherine Huck); *Career* lectr UCL 1963–64, assoc prof Univ of Manitoba 1972– (lectr 1964–66, asst prof 1966–72); visiting prof: Carleton Univ 1981–82, Canadian Forces Base Lahr W Germany 1985, 1990 and 1991; memb Advsy Ctee on Acad Relations Dept of External Affairs Canada 1980–90, dir Counter Terror Study Centre 1985–94, pres Agassiz Inst for the Study of Conflict 1994; conslt: Canadian Armed Forces, Air Canada, CBC Radio, US Air Force Special Ops Sch Florida; memb: Royal Inst of Int Affairs 1962, Canadian Inst of Int Affairs 1964 (pres Winnipeg Branch 1971–73), UN Assoc of Canada 1980, Canadian Assoc for the Study of Intelligence & Security 1986; *Books* Fireproof House to Third Option (1977), Mackenzie King to Philosopher King (1984), Air Piracy, Airport Security and International Terrorism: Winning the War Against Hijackers (1991); *Recreations* tennis, squash, swimming, boating, cycling, heritage and photography; *Style*— Peter St John, Esq; ✉ 207 Harvard Avenue, Winnipeg, Manitoba, Canada, R3M 0J9 (☎ 00 1 204 284 1089, fax 00 1 204 453 3615); St John's Coll, Univ of Manitoba, Dysart Road, Fort Garry, Manitoba, Canada R3T 2N2

ST JOHN OF BLETSO, 21 Baron (E 1559); Sir Anthony Tudor St John; 18 Bt (E 1660); s of 20 Baron, TD (d 1978), and Katharine Emily, *née* von Berg; *b* 16 May 1957; *Educ* Diocesan Coll Cape Town, Cape Town Univ SA (BA, BSc, BProc), London Univ (LLM); *m* 16 Sept 1994, Dr Helen Jane Westlake, eldest da of Michael Westlake, of Bath, Avon; 2 s (Hon Oliver Beauchamp b 1995, Hon Alexander Andrew b 29 Aug 1996); *Heir* s, Hon Oliver Beauchamp St John b 11 July 1995; *Career* sits as Independent Peer in Lords (parly interests foreign affairs, environment, financial and legal services), dep chm All Party Parly SA Gp, treas All Party Human Rights Gp, memb EC Select Ctee A (Trade, Finance and Foreign Affairs); solicitor and stockbroker; conslt to Merrill Lynch plc London; chm Eurotrust Ltd; *Recreations* tennis, golf, skiing, running; *Clubs* Western Province Sports, Royal Cape, Hurlingham; *Style*— The Rt Hon The Lord St John of Bletso; ✉ House of Lords, London SW1A OPW; Woodlands, Llanishan, nr Chepstow, Gwent NP6

ST JOHN OF FAWSLEY, Baron (Life Peer UK 1987), of Preston Capes, Co Northants; Norman Antony Francis St John-Stevas; PC (1979); s of late Stephen S Stevas, and Kitty St John O'Connor; *b* 18 May 1929; *Educ* Ratcliffe, Fitzwilliam Coll Cambridge, Christ Church Oxford; *Career* called to the Bar 1952; former jurisprudence tutor; political corr The Economist 1959; author; contested (C) Dagenham 1951, MP (C) Chelmsford 1964–87; under sec of state for Educn 1972–73, min of state for Educn and Science with special responsibility for the Arts 1973–74, oppn spokesman the Arts 1974 and memb Shadow Cabinet 1974–79; Arts min 1979, leader House of Commons and chllr of Duchy of Lancaster 1979–81; vice pres Theatres Advsy Cncl 1983–, chm Royal Fine Art Cmmn 1985–, master Emmanuel Coll Cambridge 1991–; non-exec dir British Sky Broadcasting plc 1991–; former pres Cambridge Union; OStJ 1980, Order of Merit Italy 1965, KSLJ 1963, FRSL 1966; *Clubs* White's, Garrick, Pratt's; *Style*— The Rt Hon the Lord St John of Fawsley, PC; ✉ 47 Ennismore Gardens, London SW7; The Old Rectory, Preston Capes, Daventry, Northamptonshire

ST JOHN PARKER, Michael; s of Rev Canon John William Parker (d 1996), of Lincoln, and Doris Edna, *née* Nurse; *b* 21 July 1941; *Educ* Stamford Sch, King's Coll Cambridge; *m* 5 Aug 1965, Annette Monica, da of Leonard Drake Ugle (d 1976), of West Wickham, Kent; 2 s (Sebastian b 1969, Dominic b 1972), 2 da (Arabella b 1966, Sophia Georgina (Mrs Rupert Bentley) b 1967); *Career* asst master: Sevenoaks Sch 1962–63, King's Sch Canterbury 1963–69, Winchester 1969–70; head of history Winchester 1970–75, headmaster Abingdon Sch 1975– (schoolmaster student ChCh Oxford Trinity Term 1984); memb Cncl Hansard Soc, chm Midland Div HMC 1984, chm Jt Standing Ctee Oxford and Cambridge Schs Examination Bd; govr: St Helen's Sch Abingdon 1975–83, Christ Church Cathedral Sch, Cokethorpe Sch (chm of govrs 1991), Joscas Prep Sch; *Books* The British Revolution - Social and Economic History 1750–1970 (co author 1972), Politics and Industry - the Great Mis-match (contrib 1979), author of numerous articles, pamphlets and reviews; *Recreations* mostly to do with buildings, books, music and gardens; *Clubs* Athenaeum, East India, Leander; *Style*— Michael St John Parker, Esq; ✉ Lacies Court, Abingdon, Oxfordshire (☎ 01235 520163); Abingdon School, Oxfordshire OX14 1DE (☎ 01235 521563)

ST JOHN-SMITH, (Ann Margaret) Emma; da of Rev Roger Douglas St John Smith, of Prestatyn, Clwyd, and Frances Mary, *née* Calderbank; *b* 21 June 1948; *Educ* St Elphin's C of E Public Sch for Girls, Derby and Dist Coll of Technol, Univ of London (BSc (External)); *Career* post grad research and staff appt Royal Instn of GB 1969–72, exhibition work Nat Museum of Wales Cardiff 1972, PR offr Science Museum London (incl regnl outstations) 1973–83, museum mangr Helmshore Textile Museums Lancs 1983–85, press sec Westminster Abbey 1986–; conslt to TV progs: Westminster Abbey: a video history and guide (BBC Enterprises, 1988), Songs of Praise with Bells and Bellringers (BBC, 1992), co-prodr The Abbey - with Alan Bennett (BBC, 1995); memb Cncl Friends of Nat Railway Museum 1977–80; memb LTB Guides Cncl 1995–; hon memb Central Cncl of Church Bellringers 1991–: Freedom City of London 1991, memb Guild of Freemen 1992; MIPR 1977; *Recreations* interior design and decoration, campanology, cooking and entertaining; *Style*— Ms Emma St John-Smith; ✉ Westminster Abbey, The Chapter Office, 20 Dean's Yard, London SW1P 3PA (☎ 0171 976 0983, fax 0171 233 2072)

ST JOHNSTON, Colin David; s of James Hallewell St Johnston, MC, TD, MA (d 1963), and Sheilagh Cassandra, *née* Davidson (d 1973); *b* 6 Sept 1934; *Educ* Shrewsbury, Lincoln Coll Oxford; *m* 1958, Valerie, da of John Thomas Gerald Paget (d 1969); 3 s, 1 da; *Career* Nat Serv N Staffs Regt 1953–55; md Ocean Cory Ltd 1976–85, dir Ocean Transport and Trading plc 1974–88 (dep chief exec 1985–88), non-exec dir FMC plc 1981–83, md Pro Ned Ltd 1989–95; cncl memb: Royal Cwlth Soc for the Blind 1966–95, Industl Soc 1981–96; govr: Camden Sch for Girls 1974–96, Arnold House Sch 1993–; *Recreations* real tennis, opera; *Clubs* MCC, Royal Society of Arts; *Style*— Colin St Johnston, Esq; ✉ 30 Fitzroy Rd, London NW1 8TY (☎ 0171 722 5932, fax 0171 209 4836)

ST JOHNSTON, Sir Kerry; kt (1988); s of (George) Eric St Johnston (d 1978), and (Viola) Rhona, *née* Moriarty (d 1995); *b* 30 July 1931; *Educ* Eton, Worcester Coll Oxford (MA Jurisprudence); *m* 1, 25 Feb 1960, Judith Ann, da of Peter Nicholls (d 1972); 2 s (James b 1963, Rory Tilson b 1966), 1 da (Claire Marie b 1961); m 2, 1980, Charlotte Ann, da of John Scott Limnell Lyon (d 1942); *Career* mil serv XI Hussars (Lt) 1950–51; with Ocean Steamship Co 1955–76 (md 1963–68), fndr dir Overseas Containers 1965 (dep chm 1973–76), pres Private Investment Co for Asia Singapore 1977–81, chm P & O Containers Ltd (formerly Overseas Containers Ltd) 1982–89, md Diehl and St Johnston Ltd 1989–; dir: Royal Insurance 1972–76, Lloyds Bank International 1983–86, P & O Steam Navigation Co 1986–89, Touche Remnant Investment Trust 1982–, Wilrig AS of Oslo 1989–95; *Recreations* fishing, racing, gardening; *Clubs* Boodle's, Beefsteak; *Style*— Sir Kerry St Johnston; ✉ The Garden House, 26 Clapham Common Northside, London SW4 0RL

ST LEVAN, 4 Baron (UK 1887); Sir John Francis Arthur St Aubyn; 5 Bt (UK 1866), DSC (1942), DL (Cornwall 1977); s of 3 Baron (d 1978), and Hon Clementina Gwendolen Catharine, *née* Nicolson (d 1995), da of 1 Baron Carnock and sis of Sir Harold Nicolson (the author, d 1968); *b* 23 Feb 1919; *Educ* Eton, Trinity Coll Cambridge; *m* 1970, Susan, da of late Maj-Gen Sir John Noble Kennedy, GCMG, KCVO, KBE, CB, MC; *Heir* bro, Hon Piers St Aubyn, MC; *Career* slr 1948; Lt RNVR; landowner and farmer, co dir; High Sheriff of Cornwall 1974, Vice Lord Lt of Cornwall 1992–95; fell of Royal Soc for Encouragement of Art; pres: London Cornish Assoc, Friends of Plymouth Museum, W Penwith Nat Tst Assoc, W Cornwall Branch Sail Training Assoc, Penwith and Isles of Scilly Dist Scout Cncl, Cornwall Maritime Trust, Cornwall Church Action with the Unemployed; vice pres: Royal Cornwall Agric Assoc, Royal Bath and West and Southern Counties Soc; bard of Cornwall 1995–; *Books* Illustrated History of St Michael's Mount; *Clubs* Brooks's, Royal Yacht Squadron; *Style*— The Rt Hon the Lord St Levan, DSC, DL; ✉ St Michael's Mount, Marazion, Cornwall

ST MARK, Carole; *b* 1943; *Educ* Douglas Coll Tutgers Univ USA (BA Russian), Pace Univ New York (MBA), Wharton Sch Univ of Pennsylvania (AMP 1988); *Career* early positions with General Electric, St Regis Paper Co and General Foods; Pitney Bowes: joined as dir Human Resources 1980–84, vice pres Strategic Planning 1984–85, vice pres Corp Planning and Devpt (also memb Corp Mgmnt Ctee) 1985–88, pres Pitney Bowes Business Supplies and Services Gp and pres Pitney Bowes Management Services 1988–90, pres Pitney Bowes Logistics Systems and Business Services 1990–94, pres Pitney Bowes Business Services and chm and chief exec Pitney Bowes Management Services Inc 1994– (also memb Mgmnt Ctee); non-exec dir: SuperValu Inc Minneapolis, Grand Metropolitan plc; *Style*— Ms Carole St Mark; ✉ Pitney Bowes Management Services, World HQ, MSC 03–13, 1 Elmcroft Road, Stamford, CT 06926–0700, USA

ST MAUR SHEIL, Michael Patrick; s of John St Maur Sheil, and Doreen Victoria, *née* Bradley; *b* 31 Oct 1946; *Educ* Bloxham Sch, St Edmund Hall Oxford; *m* Janet Susan, o da of Cdr F Allford, RN (ret); 1 s (Ross Patrick), 1 da (Fiona Jean); *Career* photographer (specialising in corp, industl, aerial and travel photography); early career experience working from Black Star photographers' agency NY early '70s (assignments for Time, New York Times, Stern and magazines in Ireland, Beirut and Libya), photographer with Daily Telegraph Magazine 1974–75, photojournalist for numerous pubns 1975–79, corporate work 1980– (clients incl Corbis, National Power, CEC, Merck Sharp & Dohme, Costain, Amec, Samsung, RTZ, US Borax); extensive work for National Geographic (first assignment 1984); *Awards* NY Art Dirs' Assoc: Magazine Cover award 1971, Best Travel Photography for Advertising (colour) 1983, Industl Magazine Cover award 1984; Br Assoc of Ind Eds Best Photography award 1981 and 1993; memb Assoc of Photographers 1976, FRGS; *Publications* Guide to Britain & Ireland (contrib photographer, National Geographic, 1983), Over Europe (contrib photographer, Weldon Owen, 1992); *Recreations* fishing, cricket, photography, mountaineering; *Style*— Michael St Maur Sheil, Esq

ST OSWALD, 5 Baron (UK 1885); Derek Edward Anthony Winn; DL; s of 3 Baron St Oswald (d 1956) and Eve Carew Green (d 1976); suc bro, 4 Baron, MC (d 1984); *b* 9 July 1919; *Educ* Stowe; *m* 1954, Charlotte Denise Eileen, da of Wilfrid Haig Loyd (d 1971), of Oakhill, Seaview, Isle of Wight; 1 s, 1 da; *Heir* s, Hon Charles Rowland Andrew Winn, *qv*; *Career* formerly Lt King's Royal Rifle Corps (Supp Reserve), Capt Parachute Regt (Regular Army Reserve) 1939–46; ADC to govr-gen of NZ 1943–45; substantive Capt Western Desert and N Africa (wounded); asst supt Malayan Police Force 1948–51; pres Wakefield Hospice Appeal Fund; *Books* I Served Caesar (1972); *Recreations* shooting, walking, horse racing; *Clubs* Lansdowne, Special Forces; *Style*— The Rt Hon Lord St Oswald, DL; ✉ Nostell Priory, Wakefield, West Yorkshire

ST PAUL'S, Dean of; *see:* Moses, Very Rev Dr John Henry

ST PIERRE, Roger; s of Alexander Richard St Pierre, MBE, and Caroline Amelia Borrett (d 1985); *b* 8 Nov 1941; *Educ* Ilford County HS; *m* 10 Nov 1975, Lesley, da of Bernard Constantine, of Sheffield; 1 s (Richard b 1976), 2 da (Danielle b 1978, Nicole b 1979); *Career* author and journalist; editor: Disco International 1977–79, Voyager Magazine (British Midland in-flight Magazine) 1986–90, European Hotelier 1992–95, Pocket Guide Series 1993–, Holiday and Leisure World 1995–, Entertain Magazine 1995–, Cycling Today 1996–; contrib to: Debrett's International Collection, Toyota Today, Delegates, London Evening Standard, The Dorchester Magazine, Travel GBI, Renaissance, The Times, Financial Weekly, Wish You Were Here; formerly PR mangr for: Diana Ross, Glen Campbell, Jerry Lee Lewis, Don Williams, Frankie Lane; author of nearly 1,000 record/album sleeve notes; broadcaster BBC and other broadcasting stations; cycle racer in many countries, mangr of int cycle teams; specialist writer on: travel, hotel industry, food and drink, music, motoring, cycling and leisure; memb Br Guild of Travel Writers; *Books* incl: Book of The Bicycle (1973), The Rock Handbook (1986), Illustrated History of Black Music (1986), Marilyn Monroe (1987) Story of The Blues (1993), AA/Thomas Cook Guide to Orlando (1994), McDonalds - A History (1994), Tom Jones - In His Own Words (1996), Know the Game - Cycling (1996); *Recreations* cycling, music, travel; *Style*— Roger St Pierre, Esq; ✉ 24 Beauval Rd, Dulwich, London SE22 8UQ (☎ 0181 693 6463, fax 0181 299 0719)

ST VINCENT, 7 Viscount (UK 1801); Ronald George James Jervis; s of 6 Viscount (d 1940, himself ggs of 2 Viscount, who was in his turn n of 1 Viscount and Earl of St Vincent, whose title commemorated his victory over the Spaniards in 1797 despite being outnumbered 27 to 15 - the name title was chosen by George III himself; St Vincent, more modestly, had suggested Yarmouth and Orford, which did not call to mind his successful action) and Marion, *née* Broun; *b* 3 May 1905; *Educ* Sherborne; *m* 2 Oct 1945, Constance Phillida Anne, da of Lt-Col Robert Hector Logan, OBE, late Loyal Regt; 2 s, 1 da; *Heir* s, Hon Edward Jervis, *qv*; *Career* served WW II, acting Lt Cdr RNVR; JP Somerset 1950–55; *Style*— The Rt Hon the Viscount St Vincent; ✉ Les Charrieres, St Ouen, Jersey, Channel Islands JE3 2LG (☎ 0534 482118)

SAINTE CROIX, Geoffrey de; *see:* de Sainte Croix, Geoffrey Ernest Maurice

SAINTY, Sir John Christopher; KCB (1986); s of Christopher Lawrence Sainty (d 1977), of Hassocks, Sussex, and Nancy Lee, *née* Miller (d 1945); *b* 31 Dec 1934; *Educ* Winchester, New Coll Oxford (MA); *m* 1965, (Elizabeth) Frances, da of Gp Capt Derek James Sherlock, OBE (d 1977); 3 s; *Career* clerk House of Lords 1959, private sec to ldr of House and chief whip 1963, clerk of journals 1965, research asst Inst of Historical Res 1970, reading clerk House of Lords 1974, clerk of the Parliaments 1983–90; memb Royal Cmmn on Historical Manuscripts 1991–; *Style*— Sir John Sainty, KCB; ✉ 22 Kelso Place, London W8 5QG

SALAKO, John Akin; s of Albert Akande Salako (d 1974), of Ilorin, Nigeria, and Jennifer Mary, *née* Fuller; *b* 11 Feb 1969; *Educ* Wildernesse Sch for Boys Sevenoaks; *Career* professional footballer; over 100 appearances Crystal Palace 1987–95 (debut v Barnsley 1987), 14 appearances on-loan Swansea City 1988, transferred to Coventry City FC 1995–; England debut on tour Aust and NZ 1991; jr sport: Surrey football under 16, Kent cross country under 15, Kent CCC under 15; FA Cup runners up medal Crystal Palace 1990; *Recreations* golf, reading, cricket; *Style*— John Salako, Esq; ✉ Coventry City FC, Highfield Road Stadium, King Richard Street, Coventry CV2 4FW

SALAMA, Nabil Youssef; s of Dr Youssef Salama (d 1985), and Malak Zaklama; *b* 5 Dec 1949; *Educ* Med Sch Univ of Cairo Egypt (MB BCh); *m* 30 Aug 1980, Susan Frances, da of James Willson Beale; 1 s (Adam b 5 Sept 1983), 2 da (Georgina b 8 March 1985, Helen Louise b 5 Sept 1990); *Career* conslt oto-laryngologist Lewisham and N Southwark and Greenwich Health Dists 1983–, private conslt Blackheath Hosp 1984–, surgical tutor Lewisham Hosp; author articles in various med jls; memb: BMA, RSM; BAOL, FRCS; *Style*— Nabil Salama, Esq; ✉ Beaumanor, 23 Manor Way, Beckenham, Kent BR3 3LH (☎ 0181 658 3751); The Blackheath Hospital, 40–42 Lee Terrace, Blackheath, London SE3 9UD (☎ 0181 318 7722, fax 0181 318 2542)

SALE, Robert John; DL (Cleveland); s of Lt Col John Walker Sale, OBE (d 1974), of Ilderton Glebe, Wooperton, nr Alnwick, Northumberland, and Nancy Jaqueline Sale; *b* 24 Feb 1930; *Educ* RNC Dartmouth; *m* 14 Jan 1956, Susan, da of Richard Clement Parker (d 1955), of Redlands, nr Cambridge; 1 s (John Richard (Dick) b 1963), 1 da (Lynda Katherine b 1957); *Career* HMS Britannia 1943–47, Midshipman HMS Forth Med Fleet 1947–49, Sub Lt HMS Crispin Home Fleet 1949–50, Lt HMS Consort (served Far E Fleet and Korean War) 1950–53, HMS Diligence 1953–54, Flag Lt to Adm of the Fleet Sir George Creasy C-in-C Portsmouth 1954–55; Barclays Bank UK Ltd: joined 1955, local dir 1962, gen mangr 1977, sr gen mangr 1985–86; dir: Ropner plc, Whitehead Ltd; govr Barnard Castle Sch; investmt advsr Dean and Chapter Durham Cathedral; tstee: Cleveland Community Fndn, Trincomalee Tst; High Sheriff for Co of Durham 1995; FCIB; *Recreations* fishing, shooting, hill walking, tennis, gardening; *Clubs* Royal Ocean Racing; *Style*— Robert Sale, Esq, DL; ✉ Eryholme Grange, nr Darlington, Co Durham DL2 2PQ (☎ 01609 881 230)

SALEM, Daniel Laurent Manuel; s of Raphael Salem (d 1963), and Adriana Gentili di Giuseppe (d 1976); *b* 29 Jan 1925; *Educ* Harvard (BA, MA); *m* 1950, Marie-Pierre, da of René Arachtingi (d 1975); *Career* chm: Condé Nast Publications Ltd 1967–, Condé Nast International Inc 1970–91, Mercury Selected Trust 1974–96, Philharmonia Trust Ltd 1985–92, Mercury Offshore Sterling Trust 1986–96; dep chm Condé Nast Publications Inc 1987–; dir of various other cos; Chevalier de la Legion d'Honneur 1987, Commendatore dell' Ordine al Merito della Repubblica Italiana 1988; *Recreations* music, chess, bridge, backgammon, golf; *Clubs* White's, Portland, Harvard (NYC), Travellers' (Paris); *Style*— Daniel Salem, Esq; ✉ 3 Ennismore Gardens, London SW7 (☎ 0171 584 0466); The Condé Nast Publications Ltd, Vogue House, Hanover Square, London W1 (☎ 0171 499 9080)

SALES, Barry Edward; s of Lawrence Edward Sales (d 1991), of Upwey, Dorset, and Doris May, *née* Heaton (d 1978); *b* 23 Oct 1933; *Educ* Sherborne and Corpus Christi Coll (MA); *m* 14 June 1958, Lois Marshall, da of Dr Roderick Marshall (d 1975), of New York; 2 da (Catherine b 1962, Elizabeth b 1967); *Career* Lt King's African Rifles (Africa Serv Medal 1954); dir Murco Petroleum Ltd 1964–; *Recreations* piano, squash, antiquarian books; *Style*— Barry E Sales, Esq; ✉ 51 Blacketts Wood Drive, Chorleywood, Herts WD3 5PY; Winston House, Dollis Park, London N3 1HZ (☎ 0181 371 3333)

SALES, Christopher Hedley; s of Douglas William Sales (d 1988), and Marjorie Ethel, *née* Keast (d 1992); *b* 24 Oct 1943; *Educ* City of London Sch; *m* 6 June 1970, Lynne Anne; 1 s (Philip b 21 March 1975), 1 da (Josephine b 29 Oct 1980); *Career* chartered accountant Ogden Hibberd Bull & Langton 1966–69 (articled clerk 1961–66), tax accountant British Steel Corporation 1969–73, Clark Battams 1973–82 (asst tax mangr, tax mangr, ptnr 1980), ptnr Clark Whitehill 1982–; UK Taxmaster 1984; Freeman City of London 1984; FCA (ACA 1967), ATII 1970; *Recreations* playing golf, watching Middx CCC; *Clubs* MCC, South Herts Golf, John Carpenter; *Style*— Christopher Sales, Esq; ✉ Clark Whitehill, 25 New Street Square, London EC4A 3LN (☎ 0171 353 1577)

SALIK, Jeffrey David; s of Joe Salik, and Marie, *née* Clare; *b* 27 July 1955; *Educ* City of London Sch (ILEA full scholarship), King's Coll London (BSc); *Career* Renault UK Ltd: after sales mktg analyst 1977–80, parts conslt 1980–81, zone sales mangr 1981–84, regnl publicity mangr 1984–87, network advtg and promotions mangr 1987–91; Honda UK: advtg and mktg mangr 1991–94, aftersales mktg mangr 1994–96; *Style*— Jeffrey Salik, Esq

SALIS, *see:* de Salis

SALISBURY, Bishop of 1993–; Rt Rev David Staffurth Stancliffe; s of Very Rev Michael S Stancliffe (d 1987 formerly Dean of Winchester), and Barbara Elizabeth, da of Rev Canon Tissington Tatlow; *b* 1 Oct 1942; *Educ* Westminster, Trinity Coll Oxford (MA), Cuddesdon Theological Coll; *m* 17 July 1965, Sarah Loveday, da of Philip Sascha Smith, of Mead House, Great Ayton; 1 s (Benjamin b 1972), 2 da (Rachel b 1968, Hannah b 1969); *Career* asst curate of St Bartholomew's Armley 1967–70, chaplain to Clifton Coll Bristol 1970–77, residentiary canon of Portsmouth Cathedral 1977–82, diocesan dir of ordinands and lay ministry advsr Portsmouth 1977–82, provost of Portsmouth 1982–93; chm: Southern Regional Inst 1979–81 and 1984–89, Diocesan Advsy Ctee 1982–93; memb: Gen Synod 1985–, Cathedrals Fabric Cmmn for England 1991–; vice pres Assoc of European Cathedrals 1986–, chm C of E Liturgical Cmmn 1993– (memb 1985–), pres Affirming Catholicism 1994–; Hon DLitt Univ of Portsmouth 1993; *Recreations* old music, Italy; *Style*— The Rt Rev the Bishop of Salisbury; ✉ South Canonry, 71 The Close, Salisbury SP1 2ER (☎ 01722 334031)

SALISBURY, Ian David Kenneth; *b* 21 Jan 1970; *m* 25 Sept 1993, Emma Louise, da of David Grant; *Career* professional cricketer; Sussex CCC 1989–96: debut 1989, awarded county cap 1991; with Surrey CCC 1997–; England: A Team to Pakistan 1990–91, Bermuda and W Indies 1991–92, first full tour to India and Sri Lanka 1992–93, memb team touring W Indies 1993/94, A tour to India 1994–95, A tour to Pakistan winter 1995; 9 tests, 4 one day ints; Wombwell Cricket Lovers' Young Player of the Year, Cricket Writers' Young Cricketer of the Year 1992, one of Wisden's five Cricketers of the Year 1993; *Recreations* watching other sports especially where GB/England is represented, playing as much golf as possible in the off-season, spending time with my wife especially at restaurants over a good bottle of wine, relaxing with friends, attempting DIY, gardening and cooking; *Style*— Ian Salisbury, Esq; ✉ Surrey CCC, The Oval, Kennington, London SE11 5SS (☎ 0171 582 6660, fax 0171 735 7769)

SALISBURY, Dr Jonathan Richard; s of George Richard Salisbury (d 1971), of Hereford, and Patricia Doreen, *née* Jones; *b* 25 June 1956; *Educ* Hereford HS, UCL (BSc), UCH Med Sch (MB BS), King's Coll Sch of Med (MD); *m* 19 May 1984, Alyson Frances, da of Lister Wilfred Bumby (d 1996), of Herne Bay, Kent; 1 da (Elizabeth b 1989), 1 s (Joseph b 1992); *Career* sr lectr in histopathology King's Coll Sch of Med London 1987–, hon conslt histopathologist King's Coll Hosp London 1987–; MRCPath 1986–; *Style*— Dr Jonathan Salisbury; ✉ 155 Abbeville Rd, London SW4 9JJ (☎ 0171 622 2390); Department of Histopathology, King's College School of Medicine, Bessemer Rd, London SE5 9PJ (☎ 0171 346 3093, fax 0171 346 3670)

SALISBURY, 6 Marquess of (GB 1789); Robert Edward Peter Gascoyne-Cecil; DL (Dorset 1974); also Baron Cecil (E 1603), Viscount Cranborne (E 1604), Earl of Salisbury (E 1605); patron of seven livings; s of 5 Marquess of Salisbury, KG, PC, FRS (d 1972), sometime acting Foreign Sec, and Elizabeth Vere (d 1982), da of Rt Hon Lord Richard Cavendish, CB, CMG, bro of 9 Duke of Devonshire; *b* 24 Oct 1916; *Educ* Eton; *m* 18 Dec 1945, Marjorie Olein, da of Capt the Hon Valentine Maurice Wyndham-Quin, RN (d 1983, s of 5 Earl of Dunraven and Mount-Earl); 4 s (and 1 s decd), 1 da; *Heir* s, Viscount Cranborne, *qv*; *Career* Capt Gren Gds; takes Cons whip in the House of Lords; memb editorial bd The Salisbury Review 1982–; pres Royal Assoc British Dairy Farmers; MP (C) W Bournemouth 1950–54; pres Monday Club 1974–81; high steward of Hertford 1972–; *Style*— The Most Hon the Marquess of Salisbury, DL; ✉ Hatfield House, Hatfield, Herts

SALISBURY-JONES, Raymond Arthur; s of Maj-Gen Sir Guy Salisbury-Jones GCVO, CMG, CBE, MC, DL (d 1985), Marshal of Dip Corps 1951–61, and Hilda Violet Helena (d 1995), da of Sir Maurice de Bunsen, 1 and last Bt, HBM Ambass to Madrid (1908–13) and Vienna (1913–14); *b* 31 July 1933; *Educ* Eton, Christ Church Oxford (MA); *Career* 2 Lt Coldstream Guards, serv Canal Zone 1951–53; export mktg mangr Rolls-Royce Motors Ltd 1956–75; dir: Rolls-Royce Motors International Ltd 1973–74, Daniel Thwaites plc 1978–; sr conslt ME Consultants Ltd 1992–; Liveryman Worshipful Co of Grocers; *Recreations* flying, music, skiing; *Clubs* English Speaking Union, Pratt's; *Style*— Raymond Salisbury-Jones, Esq; ✉ 4 Clifton Gardens, London W9 1DT (☎ 0171 289 5169); The Glassmill, 1 Battersea Bridge Road, London SW11 3BG (☎ 0171 924 2980, fax 0171 924 2991)

SALISSE, John; CBE (1986); s of Joseph Salisse (d 1966), of Bournemouth, and Ann, *née* Hull (d 1976); *b* 24 March 1926; *Educ* Portsmouth GS; *m* 7 July 1949, Margaret, da of James Horsfield (d 1950); 1 da (Caroline b 1960); *Career* Marks & Spencer plc 1944–85 (dir 1968–85); chm: CBI Distributive Trades Survey 1983–86 (memb Cncl 1984–89), St Enoch Management Centre Ltd 1986–, Jt London Tourism Forum 1986–96, London Enterprise Agency 1983–88, Retail Consortium 1986–92; dir: London Tourist Board 1984–96 (vice chm 1989–96), Project Fullemploy 1984–86; vice pres Commerce and Distribution Ctee CECD 1986–93; memb: Cncl for Charitable Support 1984–89, CCD Ctee on Commerce and Distribution 1988–93; jt treas Euro Movement 1982–86, tstee Lenta Educn Trust 1987–91; hon sec The Magic Circle 1965–86 (hon vice pres 1975–); memb Fin Ctee RCP 1986–91; Freeman City of London 1992; *Recreations* golf, theatre, history of magic; *Clubs* The Magic Circle, Highgate Golf, The Magic Castle (Los Angeles), IOD, The Savage; *Style*— John Salisse, Esq, CBE; ✉ c/o Midland Bank, 90 Baker St, London W1M 2AX

SALJE, Prof Ekhard Karl Hermann; s of Gerhard Salje, of Hanover, and Hildegard, *née* Drechsler; *b* 26 Oct 1946; *Educ* Herschel Sch Hanover, Univ of Hanover (Dip in Physics, PhD); *m* 19 July 1952, Elisabeth, *née* Démaret; 1 s (Henrik b 26 June 1980), 4 da (Joelle b 16 Oct 1981, Jeanne b 2 April 1983, Léa-Cécile b 4 June 1985, Barbara b 25 April 1990); *Career* prof of crystallography Univ of Hanover 1978–87 (lectr in physics 1975–78); Univ of Cambridge: lectr in mineral physics 1987–88, reader 1988–92, prof 1992–94, prof of mineralogy and petrology 1994–; co-dir IRC in superconductivity 1987–; visiting prof: Univ of Paris 1981–82, Univ of Grenoble 1990–92, Monbusho prof Japan 1996; senator Univ of Hanover 1980–82; Abraham Gottlieb Werner medal 1994; fell: Mineralogical Soc 1990, Acad of Science (Leopoldina) 1994; FInstP 1996, FRS 1996; *Books* Phase Transitions in Ferroelastic and Co-elastic Crystals (1990, 2 edn 1993); author of over 200 scientific pubns; *Recreations* music, painting; *Style*— Prof Ekhard Salje, FRS; ✉ 59 Glisson Road, Cambridge CB1 2HG (☎ 01223 350181); Department of Earth Sciences, University of Cambridge, Downing Street, Cambridge CB2 3EQ (☎ 01223 333481, fax 01223 333478, e-mail es1000@desc.cam.ac.uk)

SALLITT, Timothy William Baines; CBE (1991); s of Brig William Baines Sallitt, OBE (d 1979), and Mary Elaine, *née* Whincup; *b* 21 March 1934; *Educ* Rugby, Bradford Poly, Borough Poly, Georgia Tech Atlanta USA; *m* 14 June 1958, Angela Mary, da of Dr Brian Laidlaw Goodlet, OBE (d 1961); 1 s (Henry b 1962), 2 da (Amelia b 1960, Lucinda b 1965); *Career* Nat Serv 2 Lt RE Cyprus 1955–57; BP 1957–59; divnl mangr: Brush Electrical Engineering 1959–66, Plessey Co 1966–70; sub-co md Hawker Siddeley Group 1970–77, gp dir Hawker Siddeley Group 1977–89, chm ML Holdings plc 1991–; former memb Cncl Electrical Res Assoc, former pres BEAMA, dep chm Export Guarantees Advsy Cncl 1986–89; FIIM; *Recreations* shooting, gardening, crosswords; *Clubs* Boodle's; *Style*— Timothy Sallitt, Esq, CBE; ✉ 61 Sinclair Rd, London W14 0NR (☎ 0171 602 3204); Le Grès, 82110 Lauzerte, France (☎ 00 33 5 63 95 70 23)

SALMON, Jamie Lionel Broome; s of Gerald Mordaunt Broome Salmon, of Kent, and Margaret Ann, *née* Pike; *b* 16 Oct 1959; *Educ* Wellington Coll; *m* Fiona Jane; 2 s (Michael Alan Broome b 16 May 1990, Timothy James Broome b 6 July 1992, Toby Lionel Broome b 23 July 1996); *Career* rugby player and manager; 65 appearances Wellington Rugby Province 1978–83, 200 appearances Harlequins RFC 1982–90; 3 NZ All Black caps 1981, 12 England caps 1985–87; gen mangr Harlequins FC 1993–94 (1 XV mangr 1992–93); dir Pact Print & Design 1989–92; contrib weekly rugby column Daily Telegraph 1989–92, presenter Sky Sports 1994–; *Recreations* golf, cricket; *Style*— Jamie Salmon, Esq; ✉ 43 Gibbon Rd, Kingston, Surrey KT2 6AD

SALMON, Keith John; s of J W Salmon (d 1941), of Kent, and D B E Salmon (d 1990), *née* Evans; *b* 9 Sept 1937; *Educ* Chislehurst GS, Univ of London (BSc); *m* 12 Aug 1971, Denise; 2 da (Jessica Clare b 15 Dec 1972, Emma Louise b 23 July 1974); *Career* studio mangr BBC Radio Drama 1961–65, sound sequence composer BBC Radiophonic

Workshop 1965–67, reporter BBC TV SW Plymouth 1967–68, prodr BBC Radio Nottingham 1968–70, prog organiser BBC Radio Oxford 1970–82, managing ed BBC Radio Norfolk 1982–95; govr Heartsease Sch Norwich; *Recreations* sailing, travel; *Style*— Keith Salmon, Esq; ✉ 7 Eaton Rd, Norwich NR4 6PY (☎ 01603 506620)

SALMON, Prof Michael John; s of Arthur Salmon (d 1972), of Leeds, and May, *née* Dadswell; *b* 22 June 1936; *Educ* Roundhay Sch Leeds, Univ of Leeds (BA, PGCE), Univ of Leicester (MEd); *m* 1, 5 April 1958 (m dis 1973), Angela, da of Leslie Winstone Cookson; 1 s (Andrew John b 17 April 1964); m 2, 17 Aug 1973, Daphne Beatrice, da of Albert Ernest Bird, and Mary, *née* Savage; 1 s (Christopher Michael b 14 Dec 1984); *Career* Flt Lt RAF 1957–62; lectr Letchworth Coll of Technol 1962–65, sr then princ lectr Leeds Coll of Technol 1965–68, princ lectr NE London Poly 1968–71, head Dept of Applied Economics and head Int Office NE London Poly 1971–77, dep dir Chelmer Inst of Higher Educn 1977–83, dir Essex Inst of Higher Educn 1983–89, dir Anglia Higher Educn Coll 1989–91, dir Anglia Poly 1991–92, vice chllr Anglia Poly Univ 1992–95; dir: Proshare Ltd 1991–93, Essex TEC 1989–93; non-exec dir Mid Essex Hosp Servs NHS Tst 1993–95, chm Essex Rivers NHS Trust 1995–; memb various ctees and bds Cncl for Nat Academic Awards 1971–92; memb: Electricity Industry Trg Bd 1973–75, Educn Advsy Cncl IBA 1973–83, Poly and Coll Funding Cncl 1989–93, E Regn Cncl CBI 1989–93, Forum 2000 1993–, CVCP (chm Student Affairs Ctee 1992–95), Academic Ctee Royal Coll of Music 1995–; govr Norwich Sch of Art and Design 1996–; Hon DUniv Anglia Poly Univ 1995; hon fell: Fachochschule für Wirtshaft Berlin 1994, Limburg Hoqeschool Netherlands 1996; FRSA 1982, FIMgt 1982; *Recreations* hill walking, France, gardening; *Style*— Prof Michael Salmon; ✉ Barberries, Runsell Lane, Danbury, Essex CM3 4NY (☎ 01245 223734)

SALMON, Roger Bruce; *b* 1945; *Educ* Malvern Coll, Jesus Coll Cambridge; *m*; 2 c; *Career* various appts rising to dir UK and International Corp Fin Div N M Rothschild and Sons Ltd 1973–90; business conslt and expert witness 1990–93; special advsr to Sec of State for Transport 1993; railway franchising dir and head Office of Passenger Rail Franchising 1993–Oct 1996; *Style*— Roger Salmon, Esq

SALMON, Timothy John (Tim); s of John Frederick Salmon, of Woldingham, and Esmé, *née* Lane; *b* 31 Dec 1960; *Educ* Caterham Sch, Univ of Exeter (BA); *m* 21 July 1990, Helen Sophia, da of Anthony Jessup; *Career* Arthur Andersen: qualified as CA 1985, mangr 1987–, ptnr 1993–; FCA 1995 (ACA 1985); *Recreations* motoring, DIY, gardening, theatre, reading, watching sport; *Clubs* RAC; *Style*— Tim Salmon, Esq; ✉ Arthur Andersen, 1 Surrey Street, London WC2R 2PS (☎ 0171 438 3356, fax 0171 438 2237, mobile 0378 956508)

SALMOND, Alexander Elliot Anderson; MP (SNP) Banff and Buchan (majority 4,108); s of Robert Fyfe Findlay Salmond, of Linlithgow, Scotland, and Mary Stewart Milne; *b* 31 Dec 1954; *Educ* Linlithgow Acad, Univ of St Andrews (MA); *m* 6 May 1981, Moira French McGlashan; *Career* asst economist Govt Econ Serv 1978–80, economist Royal Bank of Scotland 1980–87; MP (SNP) Banff and Buchan 1987–, ldr Scottish Nat Pty 1990– (dep ldr 1987–90); *Publications* numerous articles and conference papers on oil and gas economics; *Recreations* reading, golf; *Style*— Alexander Salmond, Esq, MP; ✉ Constituency Office, 17 Maiden Street, Peterhead, Aberdeenshire AB42 6EE (☎ 01779 470444, fax 01779 474460)

SALOLAINEN, HE Pertti Edvard; *b* 19 Oct 1940, Helsinki; *Educ* MSc (Econ); *m* 1964, Anja, *née* Sonninen; 2 c (Maarit, Markus); *Career* Finnish diplomat; prodr of economic progs The Finnish Broadcasting Co 1965–66 (TV newsreader and ed 1962–65), London corr BBC 1966–69 (London ed 1966); MP Finnish Parl 1970–96, min for foreign trade 1987–95, chm Nat Coalition Pty of Finland 1991–94, dep PM 1991–95; ambassador of Finland to the Ct of St James's 1996–; Finnish Parl: vice chm Social Ctee 1970–75, chm Fin Ctee 1979–87 (memb 1975–87); chm Fin Ctee Interparliamentary Union 1982–87, memb Legal Ctee Nordic Cncl; chm: Bd for GATT Negotiations 1987–95, Bd for Integration Affrs 1989–92, Negotiation Delgn for EEA Agreement 1990–93; responsible min for negotiations Negotiation Delgn for Finland's EU Membership 1993–95; memb: Admin Bd's Work Ctee Outokumpu Mining Co 1979–91, Admin Bd Suomi-Salama Insurance Co 1980–91; dept chief Finnish Employers' Confedn 1969–89; memb Helsinki City Cncl 1972–84; vice pres WWF 1972–89 (fndr Finnish Fund 1972); Int Conservation Award WWF, Golden Medal for Merit Finnish Assoc for Nature Conservation; Grand Cross of the Lion (Finland) 1994; *Style*— HE Mr Pertti Salolainen; ✉ Embassy of Finland, 38 Chesham Place, London SW1X 8HW (☎ 0171 838 6200)

SALOMON, William Henry; s of Sir Walter Hans Salomon (d 1987), of Hamburg, and Kaete Gerda, *née* Jacoby; *b* 20 Sept 1957; *Educ* Lycée Français de Londres, Westminster, Magdalene Coll Cambridge (MA, LLB), Inns of Ct Sch of Law; *m* 4 July 1992, Emma Georgina (Gigi), da of Maj H R Callander, MC; 1 s (Alexander b 26 March 1996), 1 da (Bettina b 9 April 1994); *Career* trainee Welt am Sonntag Hamburg 1974, Brown Shipley & Co Ltd 1978–80, trainee Brown Brother Harriman NY 1980–81, Rea Brothers Ltd 1981–85, Finsbury Asset Management Ltd 1987–; dir: Immuno International AG 1981–, Manganese Bronze (Holdings) plc 1987–, Rea Brothers Group plc 1988– (dep chm), Adam & Harvey Group plc 1991–, Aquila International Fund Ltd 1994–, Ocean Wilson Holdings Ltd 1995–; memb Ct of the Worshipful Co of Pattenmakers; memb Hon Soc of the Inner Temple 1986–; *Recreations* tennis, fishing; *Clubs* Norddeutscher Regatta Verein Hamburg, Rio de Janeiro Country, Carlton, Hurlingham, RAC; *Style*— William Salomon, Esq; ✉ Deputy Chairman Rea Brothers Group PLC, Alderman's Walk, London EC2M 3XR (☎ 0171 623 1155, fax 0171 626 3446)

SALONGA, (Ma) Lea Carmen; da of Feliciano G Salonga, of the Philippines, and Ma Ligaya A Imutan; *b* 22 Feb 1971; *Educ* OB Montessori Center Inc, Ateneo de Manila Univ; *Career* actress and singer; *Theatre* roles incl: title role in Annie (Repertory Philippines) 1980 and 1984, Lucy in The Goodbye Girl (Maverick Prodn) 1982, Rhoda in The Bad Seed (Repertory Philippines) 1981, Addie in Paper Moon (SRO Philippines) 1983, Luisa in The Fantasticks (touring) 1988, Kim in Miss Saigon (London) 1989–90 (NY 1991–92), Eponine in Les Misérables (NY) 1993, Eliza Dolittle in My Fair Lady (Repertory Philippines) 1994; *Recordings* incl: Small Voice 1981, Lea 1983, Lea Salonga 1988, Miss Saigon 1990, Aladdin 1992, The King And I 1992; singing voice of Jasmine in Walt Disney film Aladdin 1992, Lea Salonga (debut album) 1993; *Awards* Aliw Award for Best Child Performer 1981, 1982 and 1983, Cecil Award for Best Recording by a Child 1984, Tinig Award for Outstanding Entertainer 1983, 1984 and 1990, Olivier Award for Best Actress in a Musical 1990, Outer Critics' Circle Award for Best Actress in a Musical 1991, Drama Desk Award for Best Actress in a Musical 1991, Theatre World Award for Outstanding Debut 1991, Tony Award for Best Actress in a Musical 1991; *Recreations* reading, needlepoint, puzzles, Scrabble, theatre, music; *Style*— Ms Lea Salonga; ✉ c/o C Winston Simone Management, 1790 Broadway, New York, NY 10019, USA (☎ 00 1 212 974 5322, fax 00 1 212 974 3988)

SALSBURY, Peter Leslie; *Career* jt md i/c personnel, store ops, store devpt and gp estates Marks and Spencer plc 1994– (previously dir i/c personnel and store operations); non-exec dir NORWEB plc 1992–95; pres Inst of Employment Studies; *Style*— Peter Salsbury; ✉ Marks and Spencer plc, Michael House, Baker Street, London W1A 1DN (☎ 0171 935 4422)

SALT, Anthony William David; s of late Lt-Col Sir Thomas Henry Salt, 3 Bt, JP, DL, and hp of bro, Sir Michael Salt, 4 Bt *qv*; *b* 5 Feb 1950; *Educ* Milton Abbey; *m* 1978, Olivia Anne, yr da of Martin Morgan Hudson; 2 s (Edward James Stevenson b 11 June 1981, Henry Martin Morgan b 17 Dec 1983); *Career* bank official; *Recreations* veteran/vintage cars; *Style*— Anthony Salt, Esq; ✉ Garden Cottage, Everlands, nr Sevenoaks, Kent

SALT, Dr (Robert) Barry; s of Francis Robert Salt (d 1975), and Margaret Jaffray, *née* Incoll (d 1965); *b* 15 Dec 1933; *Educ* Williamstown HS, Melbourne HS, Melbourne Univ, NW Poly London, Birkbeck Coll London (BSc, PhD), London Sch of Film Technique (dip course); *Career* teacher Sunshine HS Melbourne 1955, dancer Ballet Guild Co Melbourne 1955–56, computist Cwlth Aeronautical Res Labs Melbourne 1956, dancer Western Theatre Ballet London 1957, computer programmer Int Computers & Tabulators London 1958–60, lectr in physics Sir John Cass Coll Univ of London 1965–66, dancer Ballet Minerva London 1966, freelance lighting cameraman 1968–71, supply teacher ILEA 1969–70, film teacher and res asst Slade Sch Univ of London 1970, lectr for post grad dip in film studies UCL 1973–78, pt/t lectr Slade Sch London 1978–82, tutor in film-making Sch of Film & TV RCA 1982–87, pt/t tutor in film-making for post grad dip Communications Dept Goldsmiths' Coll Univ of London 1987–88, course dir London Int Film Sch 1988–; visiting lectr film schs and univs England and Europe 1977–; films directed incl: My Name is Errol Addison (documentary) 1965, Pop Up Into a New World (documentary) 1967, The Future Perfect (fictional short) 1968, Six Reels of Film to be Shown in any Order (fiction feature) 1971; organiser and presenter series of progs on film history Nat Film Theatre 1976–; invited speaker at many academic confs on film history in England and Europe 1976–; conslt and writer for Microsoft Encarta 1994–, author of numerous articles on dance, film and science subjects; *Books* Film Style and Technology - History and Analysis (1983, 2 edn 1992); *Recreations* reading; *Style*— Dr Barry Salt; (☎ 0171 240 0168)

SALT, Christopher James; s of Lawrence Athelstan Salt (d 1994), of Woodbury, Devon, and Marion Agnes, *née* Manners; *b* 11 Jan 1946; *Educ* Beaumont Coll Berks, Britannia Royal Naval Coll; *m* 1, 29 Nov 1969, Jennifer, da of Douglas Thomas; 4 da (Rebecca Jane b 8 Aug 1971, Jessica Agnes b 3 Jan 1974, Harriet Clare b 23 Oct 1975, Elizabeth Ann b 1 June 1978); m 2, 16 Sept 1987, Glenys Hilary Smith, da of Cyril Nourse; *Career* Gen List Offr RN 1964–86, customer servs mangr and sales & marketing servs mangr Calor Gas Ltd 1986–91, md Corps of Commissionaires Ltd 1992–; *Recreations* fishing, walking, medieval history; *Style*— Christopher Salt, Esq; ✉ Corps of Commissionaires Management Ltd, Market House, 85 Cowcross Street, London EC1M 6BP (☎ 0171 490 1125, fax 0171 250 1290)

SALT, Julia Ann; da of Kenneth Gordon Richardson, and Nora, *née* McLachlan; *b* 4 May 1955; *Educ* St Mary's Senior HS Hull, St Hilda's Oxford (BA); *m* 29 March 1980, David Sidney Salt, s of John Frederick Salt (d 1987); 1 s (Frederick b 17 July 1985), 1 da (Freya b 12 Aug 1983); *Career* ptnr Allen & Overy 1985–; memb: City of London Solicitors Co 1985, The Law Soc 1977; *Recreations* sailing, riding, birdwatching, opera, languages; *Clubs* Royal Yorks Yacht, Utd Oxford and Cambridge; *Style*— Mrs Julia A Salt; ✉ Oakwell Park, Thorn, Beds LU5 6JH; c/o Allen & Overy, One New Change, London EC4M 9QQ (☎ 0171 330 3000, fax 0171 330 9999)

SALT, Sir (Thomas) Michael John; 4 Bt (UK 1899), of Standon, and of Weeping Cross, Co Stafford; s of Lt-Col Sir Thomas Henry Salt, 3 Bt (d 1965); *b* 7 Nov 1946; *Educ* Eton; *m* 1971, Caroline, eldest da of Henry Robert John Hildyard (d 1986); 2 da (Henrietta Sophia Meriel b 1978, Alexandra Georgia May b 1982); *Heir* bro, Anthony William David Salt *qv*; *Style*— Sir Michael Salt, Bt; ✉ Shillingstone House, Shillingstone, Dorset

SALT, Sir Patrick MacDonnell; 7 Bt (UK 1869), of Saltaire, Yorkshire; s of Cdr Sir John William Titus Salt, 4 Bt, RN (d 1952), and Stella Houlton, *née* Jackson (d 1974); suc bro, Sir Anthony Houlton Salt, 6 Bt, 1991; *b* 25 Sept 1932; *Educ* Stowe; *m* 1976, Ann Elizabeth Mary, da of late Dr Thomas Kay Maclachlan, and widow of Denys Kilham Roberts, OBE; *Heir* kinsman, Daniel Alexander Salt b 1943; *Style*— Sir Patrick Salt, Bt; ✉ Hillwatering Farmhouse, Langham, Bury St Edmunds, Suffolk IP31 3ED

SALTER, David Arthur; s of James Wardel Salter, and Kathleen Wright Salter; *b* 27 Aug 1948; *Educ* Ecclesfield GS, Pembroke Coll Cambridge (MA, LLM); *m* Anne Ruth; 2 s (Robin James Edward b 1 March 1977, William David Wardel b 17 April 1982), 1 da (Alice Rosemary b 9 May 1989); *Career* admitted slr 1972; asst slr: Mills & Reeve Norwich 1972–74 (formerly articled clerk), Barber Robinson Harrogate 1974–75; Booth & Co: asst slr 1975–78, ptnr 1978–, currently head Family Law Dept; recorder of the Crown Court 1995–; memb: Family Proceedings Rules Ctee, Family Div Sub-Ctee Supreme Ct Procedure Ctee; vice chm Slrs' Family Law Assoc; fell Int Acad of Matrimonial Lawyers; govr Harrogate Int Festival, organist and choirmaster Knaresborough Parish Church; ARCO; *Books* Litigation Practice (gen ed), Matrimonial Consent Orders and Agreements (jtly), Humphreys' Family Proceedings (jtly), Family Courts: Emergency Remedies and Procedures (jtly), Pensions and Insurance on Family Breakdown (gen ed), Debt and Insolvency on Family Breakdown (jtly), Butterworths Family Law Service (ed), Family Finance and Tax (jtly); *Clubs* The Leeds; *Style*— David Salter, Esq; ✉ Booth & Co, Sovereign House, South Parade, Leeds LS1 1HQ (☎ 0113 283 2000, fax 0113 283 2060)

SALTER, Joan May; JP (1977); *Career* Vale Royal Borough Cncl: memb 1979–95, chm Environmental Health Ctee 1981–83, chm Planning Ctee 1986–88, Mayor 1989–90; memb Cheshire Family Practitioner Ctee 1981–96, lay memb (for England) GDC 1985–, vice chm Cheshire Family Health Servs Authy 1994–96 (non-exec dir 1990–96); *Style*— Mrs Joan Salter, JP; ✉ Oakmere Hall Farm, Oakmere, Northwich, Cheshire CW8 2EJ

SALTER, Rev (Arthur Thomas) John; TD (1988); er s of Arthur Salter (d 1982), of The Tong-Norton Farm, Tong, nr Shifnal, Shropshire, and Dora May, *née* Wright (d 1985); the Salter family has been seated in Shropshire since the reign of King John, when John de le Sel is mentioned in the records of Shrewsbury Abbey 1211 (*see* Burke's Landed Gentry, 18 edn, vol III, 1972); *b* 22 Nov 1934; *Educ* Wellington GS, King's Coll London (AKC 1960), St Boniface's Theological Coll Warminster; *Career* served Intelligence Corps 1954–55, RAMC 1955–56; ordained: deacon 1961, priest 1962; asst priest: St Peter's Mount Park Ealing 1961–65, St Stephen with St Thomas the Apostle Shepherd's Bush 1965–66, St Alban the Martyr Holborn with St Peter Saffron Hill 1966–70; vicar St Silas with All Saints Pentonville 1970–; priest-in-charge: St Clement Barnsbury and St Michael the Archangel Islington 1970–79, St Dunstan-in-the-West with St Thomas of Canterbury within the Liberty of the Rolls 1979–; chm Ctee The Anglican and Eastern Churches Assoc 1990– (gen sec 1975–90), chaplain Law Courts Branch Edward Bear Fndn for Muscular Dystrophy, chm Wynford Estate's Old People's Club 1971–90; Royal Army Chaplains' Dept 1975–, CF IV (Capt) 1975–81, CF III (Maj); chaplain: 36 Signal Regt 1975–80, 257 (S) Gen Hosp RAMC (V) Duke of York's HQ 1980–94, Reg Army Reserve of Offrs 1994–96; hon chaplain HMTS Lancastria Assoc 1996–; memb Societas Sanctae Crucis (SSC); fell Sion Coll 1979; Freeman City of London 1990; Hon Kt Order of St Michael of the Wing (Royal House of Braganza Portugal) 1984, Companion of Honour Order of Orthodox Hospitallers (Ethnarchy of Cyprus) 1985, Hon Archimandrite's Cross of Byelo-Russian Autocephalic Orthodox Church-in-Exile 1979, Archpriest's Cross of Ethiopian Catholic Uniate Church (Eparchy of Asmara Eritrea) 1980, Archpriest's Cross Exarchate of Pope Shenouda III (Coptic Orthodox Patriarchate of Alexandria) 1981, Locum Tenens Apocrisarios to HAH The Ecumenical Patriarch and Chaplain to HBM Consulate Gen Istanbul 1975; *Recreations* travelling in Eastern Europe, genealogy, reading; *Clubs* Athenaeum, Army and Navy, City Livery, Polish Hearth; *Style*— The Rev John Salter, TD; ✉ St Silas and James Vicarage, 87 Richmond Ave, Islington, London N1 OLX (☎ 0171 607 2865); St Dunstan-in-the-West Vestry, 186A Fleet Street, London EC4 (☎ 0171 405 1929)

SALTER, John Rotherham; s of Herbert Salter (d 1978), of Cooden, Bexhill, and Nora, *née* Waters (d 1978); *b* 2 May 1932; *Educ* Queen Elizabeth's Sch, Ashridge Coll, Lincoln Coll Oxford (MA), King's Coll London; *m* 3 June 1961, Cynthia Rotherham, da of Frederick Brewer (d 1982), of Sevenoaks; 1 s (Jeremy b 1964), 2 da (Rachel b 1962, Christy b 1970); *Career* Nat Serv 2 Lt RA 65 Regt 1952, Lt RA 1953; slr; Denton Hall: ptnr 1961–94, chm Environmental Law Gp 1990–, conslt 1994–; conslt UNIDO 1983–84; vice chm: Int Bar Assoc Ctee of Energy and Nat Resources Law 1976–79, Int Bar Assoc Ctee on Int Environmental Law 1979–82, ABA Ctee on Comparative Govt Law 1988–91; chm: ABA Ctee on Int Law 1993–95, North Sea Gas Gathering Consortium 1979–80, Section on Business Law Int Bar Assoc 1986–88, SBL Ctee on Construction in the Oil Indust 1989–93, IBA Ctee on UN 1995–, Legal Working Gp Int Solid Waste Assoc 1994–, The Care Fndn 1994–, Hospice in the Weald 1995–; tstee: Petroleum Law Educn Tst 1980–, Int Bar Assoc Educn Tst 1983–95; treas Anglo-American Real Property Inst 1985–86; special advsr on int issues to ABA Section of State and Local Govt Law Cncl 1995–; memb Cncl: IBA 1982–90 and 1992–, SBL 1982–, Town and Country Planning Assoc 1984–88, E European Forum 1992–; memb Ctee Br Estonian Latvian and Lithuanian Law Assoc; govr: Lady Boswell's Sch 1980–, Copthorne Sch 1982–; memb: Soc of Chemical Indust 1993–, London Chapter Lambda Alpha International 1993–, London and Middlesex Archaeological Soc 1975–, Soc for Promotion of Roman Studies 1975–, W Kent Branch Oxford Soc 1985–, Gen Ctee Oxford and Cambridge Club 1995–; memb Sr Common Room Lincoln Coll Oxford 1991, hon fell Univ of Dundee 1992, visiting fell and memb of the Court Cranfield Univ 1993, memb Advsy Ctee on Integrated Environmental Mgmnt by Distance Learning Univ of Bath 1994–; occasional lectr at Kings Coll and Imperial Coll London Univ 1993–; legal assoc RTPI 1992, assoc environmental auditor 1993; Freeman: City of London 1984, City of Glasgow 1986; memb Guild of Freemen 1996; Liveryman: Incorporation of Hammermen 1988–, Worshipful Co of Slrs 1989–, Worshipful Co of Fanmakers 1990–; memb Law Soc 1959 (memb Planning Panel 1992–), memb Inst of Waste Mgmnt 1995; FIMgt 1984, FRSA 1984, FRGS 1987, ACIArb 1987, hon memb Bar of Madrid 1987; *Books* Planning Law for Industry (jt ed, 1981), UK Onshore Oil and Gas Law (1986), Oil and Gas Law (contrib, 1984), Halsbury's Laws of England (contrib, 1986), Law of the European Communities (contrib, 1986), Vaughan's Law of the European Communities Service (contrib, 1990), EC Environment and Planning Law (contrib, 1991), Frontiers of Environmental Law (contrib, 1991), Corporate Environmental Responsibility: Law and Practice (1992), Director's Guide to Environmental Issues (1992), European Community Energy Law (contrib, 1994), European Environmental Law (1994), How to Understand an Act of Parliament (jtly, 1996); author of numerous published articles; *Recreations* the arts, archaeology, tennis, sailing; *Clubs* Oxford and Cambridge; *Style—* John Salter, Esq; ✉ Five Chancery Lane, Clifford's Inn, London EC4 1BU (☎ 0171 242 1212)

SALTER, Richard Stanley; QC (1995); s of Stanley James Salter (d 1980), and Betty Maud, *née* Topsom (d 1974); *b* 2 Oct 1951; *Educ* Harrow Co Sch, Balliol Coll Oxford (MA); *m* 11 May 1991, Shona Virginia Playfair, o da of Prof J P Cannon; *Career* called to the Bar Inner Temple 1975, bencher 1991; arbitration sec and membership sec London Common Law and Commercial Bar Assoc 1986–; memb: Cncl of Legal Educn 1990–96 (chm Bd of Examiners 1992–93), Advocacy Studies Bd 1996–; govr Inns of Court Sch of Law 1996–; ACIArb 1983; *Recreations* books, music, theatre, cricket; *Clubs* Savile, Shoscombe Village Cricket; *Style—* Richard Salter, Esq, QC; ✉ 3 Verulam Buildings, Gray's Inn, London WC1R 5NT (☎ 0171 831 8441, fax 0171 831 8479)

SALTER, Prof Stephen Hugh; s of Willoughby de Carle Salter (d 1993), of Mansfield, Notts, and Rachel, *née* Floyd (d 1984); *b* 7 Dec 1938; *Educ* Framlingham Coll, Sidney Sussex Coll Cambridge; *m* 24 April 1973, Prof Margaret Caldwell, da of James Donaldson (d 1947), of Aberfoyle, Perthshire; *Career* apprentice fitter tool maker Saunders Roe Ltd 1956–61, res asst Univ of Cambridge 1962–67, personal chair in engrg design Univ of Edinburgh 1986– (res fell 1967–71, lectr 1971–78, reader 1978–86); author of scientific papers on robotics, renewable energy, mine clearance, the suppression of explosions and hydraulic machines; FRSE 1991; *Recreations* photography, the invention of instruments and tools; *Style—* Prof Stephen Salter, FRSE; ✉ Kings Buildings, Mayfield Rd, University of Edinburgh EH9 3JL (☎ 0131 650 5703, fax 0131 650 5702, e-mail shs@mech.ed.ac.uk)

SALTHOUSE, Dr Edward Charles; s of Edward Salthouse, MBE (d 1965), of Belfast, and Winifred Charles, *née* Boyd (d 1977); *b* 27 Dec 1935; *Educ* Campbell Coll Belfast, Queen's Univ Belfast (BSc, PhD); *m* 1961, Denise Kathleen Margot, da of Dr Joseph Reid (d 1963), of Ballymena, N Ireland; 2 s (Michael, Kevin); *Career* lectr Univ of Bristol 1962–67; Univ of Durham: reader in electrical engrg sci 1962–79, master Univ Coll 1979–, dean Faculty of Sci 1982–85, pro-vice chllr 1985–88; FIEE 1980, FRSA (1986); *Recreations* photography, industl history; *Clubs* Royal Overseas League; *Style—* Dr Edward Salthouse; ✉ The Masters House, The Castle, Durham DH1 3RL; Shieldaig, Hume, Kelso TD5 7TR

SALTIRE, Jonathan Andrew; s of Anthony Saltire (d 1990), of Reading, Berks, and Katharine Saltire; *Educ* King Edward's Sch; *m* 1981, Victoria, *née* Anderson; 1 s (Richard b 1983), 1 da (Alison b 1985); *Career* articled clerk Phillips Davey CAs 1979–81, mgmnt accountant Satterthwaite Instruments Ltd 1981–83, fin dir Clark & Holbrook Ltd 1983–85, md Polymark Technology Inc USA 1988–91 (sr vice pres i/c fin 1985–88), sr ptnr Saltire Associates mgmnt conslts UK 1991–; former district cncllr (Cons); tstee and treas various charities; *Recreations* golf, skiing, tennis, sailing, travel, food and wine; *Style—* Jonathan Saltire, Esq; ✉ Ground Floor Flat, 76 Cromford Road, London SW18 1NY

SALTISSI, Dr Stephen; s of Victor Saltissi, of Leeds, and Betty, *née* Weinman; *b* 21 Sept 1950; *Educ* Roundhay Sch Leeds, King's Coll London (MB BS), Univ of London (MSc, MD); *m* 30 July 1972, Sandra Bernice, da of Maurice Aaron Bellman, of Leeds; 2 da (Nicola b 1978, Caroline b 1980); *Career* sr res fell St Thomas' Hosp 1979–80 (registrar 1977–78); sr registrar: N Tees 1981–82, Newcastle upon Tyne 1982–84; Royal Liverpool Univ Hosp: conslt physician and cardiologist 1984–, clinical sub dean and clinical dir of med; hon lectr Univ of Liverpool 1984–; chm Library Ctee Royal Liverpool Hosp; memb: Br Cardiac Soc 1985, Merseyside and N Wales Assoc Physicians 1984; MRCP 1975, FRCP 1991; *Recreations* tennis, supporter Liverpool FC, travel; *Style—* Dr Stephen Saltissi; ✉ Wansfell, 25 Hillside Drive, Woolton, Liverpool L25 5NR (☎ 0151 428 2034, fax 0151 428 2034); Royal Liverpool University Hospital, Prescot St, Liverpool L7 8XP (☎ 0151 706 3573 (sec), 0151 706 3574 (direct line), fax 0151 706 5833)

SALTONSTALL, James Edwin Rous; s of Peter Rous Saltonstall, (d 1984), of Bridlington, E Yorks, and Antonia, *née* Ernste; *b* 22 July 1947; *Educ* St George's Secdy Sch; *m* 26 June 1971, Christine Ann, da of Norman Woodhouse; 1 s (Jeremy Richard Rous b 11 Dec 1981); *Career* served RN 1962–77; yacht racer and coach; yacht and dinghy racing commencing Royal Yorks Yacht Club 1952, RN dinghy team 1965–77 (capt 1974–76), sr nat racing coach RYA 1977–; attended over 100 int yacht and dinghy events (World, Euro, Olympic); achievements incl: runner-up J24 class World Championships Japan 1985, Euro champion J24 class Germany 1990, nat champion J24 class 1984–85; Yachtsman of the Year 1984 and Special Award 1995; Olympic Team coach Atlanta 1996; *Books* RYA Race Training Manual (3 edn, 1996); *Recreations* sailing; *Style—* James Saltonstall, Esq; ✉ Royal Yachting Assoc, Romsey Rd, Eastleigh, Hants (☎ 01703 627439, fax 01703 629924)

SALTOUN, The Rt Hon Lady (twentieth holder of title; S 1445); Flora Marjory; *née* Fraser; Chief of the Name of Fraser; family granted right to own Univ of Fraserburgh by King James VI; da of 19 Lord Saltoun, MC (d 1979), and Dorothy, da of Sir Charles Welby, 5 Bt, CB, by Maria, sis of 4 Marquess of Bristol; *b* 18 Oct 1930; *Educ* St Mary's Wantage; *m* 1956, Capt Alexander Ramsay of Mar, DL, *qv*, *see* Peerage, Royal Family section and Dalhousie, E; 3 da; *Heir* da, Hon Mrs Nicolson; *Career* sits as Independent in House of Lords; *Clubs* New; *Style—* The Rt Hon the Lady Saltoun; ✉ The House of Lords, London SW1A 0PW

SALUSBURY-TRELAWNY, Sir John Barry; 13 Bt (E 1628), of Trelawny, Cornwall; s of Sir John William Robin Maurice Salusbury-Trelawny, 12 Bt (d 1956), by his 1 w, Glenys Mary, da of John Cameron Kynoch; *b* 4 Sept 1934; *Educ* HMS Worcester; *m* 1958, Carol Knox, yr da of C F K Watson, of The Field, Saltwood, Kent; 1 s, 3 da; *Heir* s, John William Richard Salusbury-Trelawny b 30 March 1960; *Career* Nat Serv RNVR; dir: Martin Walter Group Ltd 1971–74, Korn/Ferry International 1977–83, Morris & Blakey plc 1978–79; chm Goddard Kay Rogers & Associates mgmnt conslts (dir 1984) until 1995; JP Kent 1973–78; FInstM; *Clubs* Army & Navy, Buck's, Royal Cinque Ports Yacht, Royal Naval Sailing Assoc; *Style—* Sir John Salusbury-Trelawny, Bt; ✉ Beavers Hill, Saltwood, Hythe, Kent CT21 4QA (☎ 01303 266476)

SALUSBURY-TRELAWNY, John William Richard; s and h of Sir John Salusbury-Trelawny, 13 Bt *qv*; *b* 30 March 1960; *m* 1, 16 Aug 1980 (m dis 1986), Anita, yr da of Kenneth Snelgrove and Mrs L E Thorpe, of Iver Heath, Bucks; 1 s (Harry John b 10 Dec 1982), 1 da (Victoria Hayley b 31 Aug 1981); m 2, 21 Nov 1987 (m dis 1993), Sandra Patricia, da of Joe and Patricia Thompson, of Seabrook, Kent; 1 s (Thomas Jonathon b 23 March 1989); *Style—* John Salusbury-Trelawny, Esq; ✉ 278 Seabrook Road, Hythe, Kent

SALUSBURY-TRELAWNY, Lt-Col Philip Michael; MC (1945), DL (Cornwall 1982); 2 s of Maj John Salusbury-Trelawny, MC (d 1954, himself ggs of Sir William Salusbury-Trelawny, 8 Bt), of Honiton, Devon, and Louisa Frederika, *née* Mainwaring (d 1985); *b* 11 Nov 1921; *Educ* Winchester; *m* 23 March 1946, Jean Mary (sometime Flt Offr WAAF, d 1988), only da of Col Herbert Cecil Fraser, DSO, OBE, TD (d 1940), of Redlands, Ilkley, Yorks; 1 s (Simon Jonathan b 1948, m 1978 Marian MacAuley), 1 da (Diana Jane b 1947, m 1970 Robert Blake); *Career* served Royal Hampshire Regt 1940; cmmnd Indian Army 1941, 4 Bn Frontier Force Rifles 1941–47, Maj, served Iraq, Western Desert, Cyprus and Italy (MC) 1942–45; transfd British Army (Duke of Cornwall's LI) 1947, various regtl and staff appts in UK and Europe, 5 Bn King's African Rifles Kenya 1958–61, cmd LI Bde Depot Shrewsbury 1964–67 (Lt-Col), ret 1975; regtl sec Light Inf in Cornwall 1979–84; *Recreations* shooting, gardening; *Clubs* Army and Navy; *Style—* Lt-Col Philip Salusbury-Trelawny, MC, DL; ✉ The Bothy, Harrington, nr Spilsby, Lincs PE23 4NH (☎ 01790 752476)

SALVATORI, Roberto Antonio; s of Cornelio Salvatori, of Venezuela, and Elma Valdez; *b* 14 Sept 1961; *Educ* St Mary's Coll Port-of-Spain Trinidad, Guildhall Sch of Music and Drama (Countess of Munster Musical Tst scholar, AGSM), Britten/Pears Sch for Advanced Musical Studies Aldeburgh; *Career* baritone; princ baritone Pavilion Opera 1989–94, princ ENO 1995–; roles with Pavilion Opera incl: Don Giovanni, Count Almaviva in Le Nozze di Figaro, Figaro in Il Barbiere di Siviglia, Enrico in Lucia di Lammermoor, Guglielmo in Cosi Fan Tutte, Belcore in L'Elisir d'Amore, Dr Malatesta in Don Pasquale; roles with ENO incl: Escamillo in Carmen, Ping in Turandot, Marullo in Rigoletto, Marcello in La Boheme; other prodns incl: Giorgio Germont in La Traviata (European Chamber Opera), Scarpia in Tosca (European Chamber Opera), Berkley in Marshner's Der Vampyr (for BBC Television); *Style—* Roberto Salvatori, Esq; ✉ c/o Harold Hold Ltd, 31 Sinclair Road, London W14 0NS (☎ 0171 603 4600, fax 0171 603 0019)

SALVESEN, Robin Somervell; DL (E Lothian 1972); s of Iver Ronald Stuart Salvesen (d 1957), and Marion Hamilton, *née* McClure; bro of Alastair Salvesen; *b* 4 May 1935; *Educ* Cargilfield Sch Edinburgh, Fettes Coll Edinburgh, Univ Coll Oxford, Hendon Tech Coll; *m* 6 Aug 1960, Sari Frances Judith *née* Clarke; 3 s (Francis b 26 Oct 1965, Thomas b 14 May 1967, Iver b 31 Jan 1969); 4 da (Ferelith b 3 May 1961, Alice b 25 Dec 1962, Tabitha b 13 Feb 1964, Emily b 22 June 1970); *Career* 5 Bn QO Nigeria Regt 1955–56, Maj Royal Scots TA 52 Lowland Volunteers 1957–69; chm: Lights Advsy Ctee, Br Shipowners' Assoc, Scot Cncl King George's Fund for Sailors; dir: Christian Salvesen plc, The Murrayfield plc until 1992; dep chm Scot Veterans' Residences, chm Assoc for Protection of Rural Scotland 1994–, Gen Ctee Lloyd's Register of Shipping 1974–91, Merchant Co of the City of Edinburgh, pres Edinburgh Area Scouts 1991–; chm: Bells National Tst, Theodore Salvesen Tst; tstee: Thistle Tst, Novum Tst; elder of St Mary's Church Haddington (chm Congregational Bd 1988–); Liveryman Worshipful Co of Shipwrights; Hon Danish Consul for E Scotland 1972–89; moderator The High Constabulary of The Port of Leith 1994; Silver Jubilee Medal 1977; Royal Order of the Chev of Dannebrog (Denmark) 1981 (first class 1989); memb Queen's Bodyguard for Scotland (Royal Co of Archers) 1965–; FIMgt; *Recreations* shooting with long bow and shotgun; *Clubs* New (Edinburgh); *Style—* Robin S Salvesen, Esq, DL; ✉ Eaglescairnie House, Haddington, E Lothian EH41 4HN (☎ 0162 081261, fax 0162 081775)

SALZ, Anthony Michael Vaughan; s of Michael Salz, of Yelverton, Devon, and Veronica, *née* Hall; *b* 30 June 1950; *Educ* Summerfields Sch, Radley, Univ of Exeter (LLB); *m* 17 May 1975, Sally Ruth, da of Harold J Hagger, of Broughton, Hants; 1 s (Christopher b 1978), 2 da (Emily b 1980, Rachel b 1982); *Career* admitted slr 1974; Freshfields: seconded to Davis Polk and Wardwell NY 1977–78, ptnr 1980–, head of Corp Fin until 1996, sr ptnr 1996–; memb Law Soc; contrib to various learned jls; *Recreations* fly fishing, tennis, golf and the family generally; *Clubs* MCC, Berkshire Golf; *Style—* Anthony Salz, Esq; ✉ Freshfields, 65 Fleet St, London EC4Y 1HS (☎ 0171 936 4000, fax 0171 832 7392)

SALZEDO, Leonard Lopes; s of Samuel Lopes Salzedo (d 1957), of London, and Edna Gladys Gertrude, *née* Kilrow (d 1983); *b* 24 Sept 1921; *Educ* RCM; *m* Patricia Mary, da of Arthur James Clover (d 1972); 2 da (Susan b 21 March 1946, Caroline b 6 Dec 1952); *Career* composer of 17 ballet scores, 18 film scores and numerous orchestral and chamber works; has performed all over UK and in Holland, Germany and Austria; past conductor at Bath and Vienna Festivals, dir of recordings of own work by London Philharmonic and RPO; dir: Ballet Rambert 1966–72, London City Ballet 1982–86; ARCM; Commandeur dans le Conferie des Chevaliers du Sacavin d'Anjou, fell Int Inst of Arts and Letters (Genève et Zurich); *Recreations* photography, travelling, reading; *Clubs* Savage; *Style—* Leonard Salzedo, Esq; ✉ 363 Bideford Green, Leighton Buzzard, Beds LU7 7TX (☎ 01525 371126)

SAMBAR, Dr David H; s of Habib David Sambar (d 1952), of Haifa, and Georgette, *née* El Khoury; *b* 19 Aug 1930; *Educ* Univ of London (BA), American Univ Beirut (MA), Doctorate magna cum laude Faculty Economics and Business Administration Lyons France; *m* 15 Oct 1966, Salma Renee Sambar, da of Labib Y Zacca, of Beirut (d 1982); 1 s (Habib David b 1968), 1 da (Syma Karine b 1970); *Career* Chase Bank Beirut 1955–73 (auditor, asst mangr, mangr, vice pres), vice pres Chase NYC 1973–77, chm Sharjah Investment London 1977–81, Strategic Investmt Planning London 1982–85, chm Sambar International Investments Ltd 1984–, chm British American Properties NY 1990–, chm British American Capital NY 1990–; memb Lloyd's of London 1984–; advsr to various companies, ed of articles and speeches for various US and Euro pubns and professional orgns; tstee Princeton in Asia 1965–, memb Stanford Res Inst 1979–, cnsllr in int affrs

Peoples for UN NYC 1979–, tstee Woman's World Banking 1986–, memb Cons Pty; hon doctorate Mexican Acad of Int Law; fell Atlantic Cncl, FInstD; *Recreations* tennis, skiing; *Clubs* Hurlingham, Institute of Directors, Royal Over-Seas League, RAC; *Style—* Dr David Sambar; ✉ 11 Chelsea Square, London SW3 6LF (☎ 0171 352 1713)

SAMBROOK, Richard Jeremy; s of (Philip) Michael Sambrook (d 1980), of Ashford, Kent, and Joan Hartridge (d 1983); *b* 24 April 1956; *Educ* Maidstone Sch for Boys, Univ of Reading (BA), Birkbeck Coll London (MSc); *m* 3 Oct 1987, Susan Jane, da of John Fisher; 1 s (Huw b 17 July 1992), 1 da (Freya b 20 Jan 1994); *Career* journalist with Thomson Regional Newspapers (on Rhondda Leader and South Wales Echo) 1977–80; BBC: chief sub-ed BBC Radio News 1980–84, prodr BBC TV News 1984–88, dep ed Nine O'Clock News 1988–92, news ed BBC TV and Radio News 1992–96, head of newsgathering BBC News 1996–; memb RTS, FRSA; *Recreations* music, novels, travel; *Style—* Richard Sambrook, Esq; ✉ BBC TV News & Current Affairs, Television Centre, Wood Lane, London W12 7RJ (☎ 0181 576 7994, fax 0181 576 4848)

SAMENGO-TURNER, Fabian Pius; s of late Joseph Frederick Samengo-Turner and Eva Turner; *b* 11 Feb 1931; *Educ* St Benedicts Sch, King's Coll London; *m* 1953, Maureen Ursula, *née* O'Connor; 3 s, 1 da; *Career* Lt Intelligence Corps; md: Laurentide Financial Trust 1962–67, Citibank Financial Trust 1968–72; chm Citibank Financial Trust 1973–74, exec dir Citibank International PLC 1975–95, ret; *Recreations* tennis, motor racing, sailing; *Clubs* RAC, British Racing Drivers'; *Style—* Fabian Samengo-Turner, Esq; ✉ Chapel Row Farm, Bucklebury, Reading, Berks RG7 6PB (☎ 0118 971 2109)

SAMMONS, Geoffrey Tait; CBE (1992); s of Herbert Sammons, CBE (d 1967), and Elsie, *née* Kay (d 1951); *b* 3 July 1924; *Educ* Glenalmond, Univ Coll Oxford (MA); *m* 9 July 1949, Stephanie Anne, da of Stephen Hawley Clark (d 1961); 1 s (Timothy b 1956), 1 da (Anthea b 1952); *Career* RA 1943–45, Lt 8 Medium Regt RA Burma Campaign 1944–45; Allen & Overy Slrs London: joined 1946, ptnr 1953–86, sr ptnr 1981–86; cmmr Bldg Socs Cmmn 1986–92, non-exec dir Spirax Sarco Engineering plc until 1991; govr The Lister Inst of Preventative Med 1987–; memb Law Soc 1949; *Recreations* golf, gardening; *Clubs* Army & Navy; *Style—* Geoffrey Sammons, Esq, CBE

SAMPSON, Anthony Terell Seward; s of Michael Treviskey Sampson (d 1956), and Phyllis, *née* Seward; *b* 3 Aug 1926; *Educ* Westminster (King's scholar), Christ Church Oxford (MA); *m* 1965, Sally Virginia, da of Dr Graeme Bentlif, of Jersey; 1 da (Katherine Alys b 1966), 1 s (Paul Michael b 1968); *Career* served as Sub-Lieut RN 1944–47; ed Drum Magazine Johannesburg 1951–55, editorial staff The Observer London 1955–66, assoc prof Univ of Vincennes Paris 1968–70, chief American correspondent The Observer 1973–74, editorial conslt The Brandt Cmmn 1978–79; chm Soc of Authors 1992–94; tstee Scott Trust 1993–; memb Int Bd Independent Newspapers SA 1995–; FRSL; *Books* Drum, a venture into the New Africa (1956), Anatomy of Britain (1962), The New Europeans (1968), The Sovereign State: The Secret History of ITT (1973), The Seven Sisters (1975), The Arms Bazaar (1977), The Money Lenders (1981), The Changing Anatomy of Britain (1982), Empires of the Sky (1984), The Oxford Book of Ages (with Sally Sampson, 1985), Black and Gold (1987), The Midas Touch (1989), The Essential Anatomy of Britain (1992), Company Man (1995); *Recreations* gardening, opera; *Clubs* Beefsteak, Groucho, Academy; *Style—* Anthony Sampson, Esq; ✉ 27 Ladbroke Grove, London W11 3AY (☎ 0171 727 4188); Quarry Garden, Wardour, Tisbury, Wilts (☎ 01747 870407); c/o Peters Fraser & Dunlop, 503 The Chambers, Chelsea Harbour, London SW10 0XF (☎ 0171 344 1000, fax 0171 352 7356)

SAMPSON, Sir Colin; kt (1993), CBE (1988), QPM (1979), DL (W Yorks 1994); s of James Sampson, of Stanley, nr Wakefield, and Nellie; *b* 26 May 1929; *Educ* Stanley Sch, Univ of Leeds; *m* 1953, Kathleen Stones; 2 s; *Career* Nat Serv Duke of Wellington's Regt; West Riding Constabulary 1949–72 (CID, Fraud Squad, Special Branch), Cmdt Detective Trg Sch Wakefield 1971–72, operational asst Chief Constable W Yorks 1972–76; Dep Chief Constable: Notts 1976–80, W Yorks 1980–83; Chief Constable W Yorks 1983–89; HM Inspector of Constabulary: SE England 1989–90, NE England 1990–91, Scotland 1991–93, ret; currently: chm Cncl Order of St John for W and S Yorks, memb Ct Univ of Leeds, pres W Yorks Scout Assoc, vice pres Yorkshire Soc, chm Kirklees Macmillan Nurse Appeal, pres Wakefield Branch NSPCC; former Barker Variety Club of GB; Hon DUniv Bradford 1988, Hon LLD Univ of Leeds 1990; *Recreations* music, reading, swimming, dog walking; *Style—* Sir Colin Sampson, CBE, QPM, DL; ✉ Kid Royd House, Shepley, W Yorkshire

SAMPSON, Ian Godfrey; JP (1975); s of Geoffrey Morgan Sampson (d 1978), of Peterborough, Cambs, and Dorothy Louise, *née* Dufty (d 1992); *b* 29 May 1941; *Educ* Taunton Sch; *m* 11 July 1964, Gwendolen Celia Anne, da of Neil Cecil Alister Simon (d 1984), of Poole, Dorset; 2 da (Jacqueline b 1970, Philippa b 1972); *Career* HAC TA 1963 (ret 2 Lt); gen mangr Target Unit Trust Group 1975–80, md NM Schroder Unit Trust Group 1980–89, dir NM Schroder Life Assurance Co Ltd 1987–89, md Sun Life Trust Management 1989–92, vice chm Painshill Park Trust Ltd; dir and dep chm LAUTRO 1988–, arbitrator SFA 1994–; borough cncllr 1974–76; *Recreations* restoration of Painshill Park, travel; *Clubs* HAC, United (Guernsey), City of London; *Style—* Ian Sampson, Esq, JP; ✉ 10 Crossway, Walton on Thames, Surrey KT12 3JA (☎ 01932 221363, fax 01932 248779)

SAMPSON, Michael; s of late William Thomas Sampson, of Horsham, Sussex, and Lilian Emma, *née* Edmonds; *b* 27 Sept 1942; *Educ* Collyers Sch Horsham, Univ of Southampton (BScEcon); *m* 7 June 1969, Elizabeth Victoria, da of late Cdr Alfred Bryant Hilliar, of Bishops Caundle, Dorset, and Dorothy Maud, *née* Brendon; 2 da (Anna b 1978, Caroline 1980); *Career* res analyst Simon & Coates stockbrokers 1964–77, Lloyd's investmt mangr 1977–85; dir: John Govett & Co 1986–92, Broadgate Investment Trust 1992–; *Recreations* tennis, golf; *Style—* Michael Sampson, Esq; ✉ Oakhurst, Courtlands, London Road, Tonbridge, Kent TN10 3DA (☎ 01732 354885)

SAMS, Jeremy Charles; s of Eric Sams, of London, and Enid, *née* Tidmarsh; *b* 12 Jan 1957; *Educ* Whitgift Sch Croydon, Magdalene Coll Cambridge, Guildhall Sch of Art; *children* 1 s (Toby Oliver Sams-Friedman b 26 Nov 1994); *Career* composer, director, translator of opera and plays; freelance pianist 1977–82; *Theatre* dir: Schippel, the Plumber, Entertaining Mr Sloane (Greenwich), The Card (Newbury), Wind in the Willows (Tokyo), Neville's Island (Nottingham and West End), Enjoy (Nottingham), Wild Oats (RNT) 1995, The Wind in the Willows (Old Vic) 1995, Passion (Queen's) 1996; translations incl: The Rehearsal (Almeida and Garrick, Time Out Award 1991), Leonce and Lena (Sheffield Crucible), Becket (Theatre Royal Haymarket), The Miser (NT), Les Parents Terribles (RNT), Mary Stuart (RNT) 1996; *Opera* dir: The Reluctant King (Opera North); translations incl: The Magic Flute, Macbeth, Figaro's Wedding, Force of Destiny, La Bohème (ENO), Cosi fan Tutte (Opera 80), Johnny Strikes Up, L'Etoile, Orpheus in the Underworld, The Reluctant King (Opera North); *Scores* over 30 scores for theatre and TV: Kean (Old Vic), The Sneeze, A Walk in the Woods (West End), Persuasion (BAFTA Award for Original TV Music 1996), Have your Cake (BBC) 1997; at the RSC: Temptation, The Tempest, Measure for Measure, Merry Wives of Windsor, Midsummer Night's Dream; at RNT: Sunday in the Park With George (music dir), Ghetto (also lyrics), The Wind in the Willows (also lyrics), Arcadia; *Books* The Miser (trans, Methuen, 1991), The Rehearsal (trans, Methuen, 1991), Les Parents Terribles (trans, Nick Hern 1995), Wild Oats (Nick Hern 1995); *Style—* Jeremy Sams, Esq; ✉ c/o Michael Imison Playwrights Ltd, 28 Almeida Street, London N1 1TD (☎ 0171 354 3174, fax 0171 359 6273)

SAMSON, Prof Thomas James (Jim); s of Edward Samson, of NI, and Matilda Jane, *née* Smyth; *b* 6 July 1946; *Educ* Queen's Univ Belfast (BMus), Univ Coll Cardiff (MMus, PhD, LRAM); *Career* res fell in humanities Univ of Leicester 1972–73; Univ of Exeter: lectr in music 1973–87, head of dept 1986–92, reader in musicology 1987–92, prof of musicology 1992–94; prof of music Univ of Bristol 1994–: memb Cncl RMA; Order of Merit of the Polish Miny of Culture 1989; *Books* Music in Transition: A Study in Tonal Expansion and Atonality (1977), The Music of Szymanowski (1980), The Music of Chopin (1985), Chopin Studies (1988), The Late Romantic Era, Man & Music 7 (1991), The Cambridge Companion to Chopin (1992), Chopin - the Four Ballades (1992), Chopin Studies 2 (with John Rink, 1994), Chopin (Master Musicians, 1996); *Recreations* walking, reading; *Style—* Prof Jim Samson; ✉ Music Department, University of Bristol, Victoria Rooms, Queen's Road, Bristol BS8 1SA (☎ 0117 954 5028)

SAMSOVA, Galina; da of Martin Arkipovich (d 1951), of Lvov, USSR, and Yevdokia, *née* Yerankevich (d 1966); *b* 17 March 1937; *Educ* Comp Sch Lvov, State Ballet Sch Kiev; *Career* dancer Kiev Opera House 1956–60; princ dancer: Nat Ballet of Canada 1961–64, London Festival Ballet 1964–73, New London Ballet (and dir) 1973–78, Sadler's Wells Royal Ballet (and teacher) 1980–90; artistic dir Scottish Ballet 1991–; memb Dance Panel Arts Cncl of GB 1988–90, tstee Dance Teachers Benevolent Fund 1990–; *Recreations* music, reading, gardening; *Style—* Ms Galina Samsova; ✉ The Scottish Ballet, 261 West Princes Street, Glasgow G4 9EE (☎ 0141 331 2931, fax 0141 331 2629)

SAMUEL, Andrew William Dougall; s of Capt Andrew Samuel, RN (d 1952), and Letitia Shearer Samuel; *b* 12 July 1937; *Educ* Hutchesons' Boys' GS Glasgow, Glasgow Sch of Architecture; *m* 1, 20 Feb 1962 (m dis 1981), Sybille Marie Luise; 1 s (Craig Andrew Alexander Porter b 1966), 1 da (Katja Lilian Hamilton b 1969); m 2, 2 Oct 1981, Mary Carswell, da of John Bisset (d 1978), of Homeglen, Carmunock, Glasgow; *Career* chartered architect; princ and dir Andrew Samuel & Co Ltd 1968, chm Townhead Properties Ltd 1980, md Gavin Watson Ltd 1983; holder (with entry in Guinness Book of Records): World Canoeing Record Loch Ness 1975–85, World Canoeing Record English Channel 1976, World Canoeing K2 Doubles Record English Channel 1980–86; World Masters Games (with A Wilson) 1989: first K2 500m, first K2 5000m, third K2 Marathon; Scottish Nat Canoeing Racing Coach 1976–83, registered ICF official (Int Canoe Fedn); chm former E Central Tourist Assoc (Scotland), former chm Central Scotland Tourist Assoc, festival dir Trossachs Water Festival 1973–76, sec Trossachs Tourist Assoc 1969–76 (past pres); memb Ctee: CBI, SPEF; FRIAS, RIBA, FIPD, FFB; *Recreations* boating, travel, canoeing, photography; *Clubs* Trossachs Canoe and Boat, Bowfield Country, West Kilbride Golf; *Style—* Andrew Samuel, Esq; ✉ Woodside Farm, By Beith, Ayrshire, Scotland KA15 1JF

SAMUEL, Anthony John Fulton (Rowley); s and h of Sir John Samuel, 5 Bt; *b* 13 Oct 1972; *Style—* Rowley Samuel, Esq

SAMUEL, Hon Dan Judah; s of 2 Viscount Samuel, CMG (d 1978); hp of bro, 3 Viscount Samuel, *qv*; *b* 25 March 1925; *Educ* Rugby, Balliol Coll Oxford (MA), Sch of Advanced Int Studies Johns Hopkins Univ Washington DC; *m* 1, 1957 (m dis 1977), Esther (Nonni), da of late Max Gordon, of Johannesburg; 1 s (Jonathan Herbert b 1965), 2 da (Lia Miriam (Mrs Glenn H Album) b 1961, Maia Tessa b 1963); m 2, 1981 (m dis 1992), Heather, da of late Angus Cumming, of Haywards Heath; 1 s (Benjamin Angus b 1983), 1 da (Sasha Tamar b 1982); *Career* late Maj Yorks Hussars; dir Shell International Petroleum Co 1973–81, pres Scallop Corporation (NY) 1981–86, business conslt and co dir; dir Asian Inst of Technol (Bangkok) Fndn, dir Br American Educnl Fndn; Cdr Order of Royal Crown of Thailand, Offr Order of the Crown (Belgium); *Recreations* sailing; *Clubs* United Oxford and Cambridge Univ, Special Forces, Hurlingham, Chichester Yacht; *Style—* The Hon Dan Samuel; ✉ 154 Hillspoint Rd, Westport, Connecticut, USA

SAMUEL, 3 Viscount (UK 1937), of Mount Carmel, and Toxteth in the City of Liverpool; David Herbert Samuel; OBE (1996); s of 2 Viscount Samuel, CMG (d 1978, gs of Edwin Samuel, whose yr bro Montagu cr Lord Swaythling), and Hadassah, *née* Goor (d 1986); *b* 8 July 1922; *Educ* High Sch Jerusalem, Balliol Coll Oxford (MA), Hebrew Univ (PhD); *m* 1, 1950 (m dis 1957), Esther, *née* Berelowitz; 1 da (Hon Judith b 1951); m 2, 1960 (m dis 1978), Mrs Rinna Dafni, *née* Grossman; 1 da (Hon Naomi Rachel b 1962); m 3, 1980 (m dis 1993), Mrs Veronika Grimm, *née* Engelhardt; *Heir* bro, Hon Dan Samuel; *Career* Capt RA, served India, Burma and Sumatra 1942–45 (despatches); Weizmann Inst of Sci Israel: academic staff 1949–91, head Chemistry Gp Sci Teaching Dept 1967–84, head Centre for Neurosciences and Behavioural Research 1970–87, dean Faculty of Chemistry 1971–73, currently prof emeritus; post-doctoral fell Chemistry Dept Univ Coll London 1956; research fell: Chemistry Dept Harvard Univ 1957–58, Lab of Chemical Biodynamics (Lawrence Radiation Lab) Univ of Calif Berkeley 1965–66; visiting prof Sch of Molecular Sciences Univ of Warwick 1967, chm Bd of Studies on Chemistry Feinberg Graduate Sch 1968–74, visiting Royal Soc prof MRC Neuroimmunology Unit Zoology Dept UCL 1974–75, visiting prof Pharmacology Dept Yale Sch of Med 1983–84, McLaughlin prof Sch of Med McMaster Univ (Canada) 1984; visiting prof Chemistry Dept Univ of York 1995–96; memb: Bd US-Israel Educnl (Fulbright) Fndn 1969–74 (chm 1974–75), Bd Bat-Sheva de Rothschild Fndn for Advancement of Sci in Israel 1970–84, Bd Israel Center for Scientific and Technol Info 1970–74, Bd of Tstees Nat Inst of Psychobiology in Israel 1973–, Israel Exec Ctee American-Israel Cultural Fndn 1975–87 (chm 1985–87), Academic Advsy Bd Everyman's (Open) Univ 1977–83, Bd of Govrs Tel Aviv Museum of Art 1980–, Ctee for Chemical Educn Int Union of Pure and Applied Chemistry (IUPAC) 1982–90 (nat rep 1973–82), Israel Chem Soc (memb Cncl 1976–84), Royal Chemical Soc 1957– (Fell 1996), Internat Soc Neurochemistry (ISN) 1970–, Int Brain Res Orgn (IBRO) 1984–, Israel Britain and Cwlth Assoc (IBCA) 1984–94, Anglo-Israel Assoc 1985–, Br Israel Arts Fndn 1986–, Bd of Govrs Bezalel Acad of Arts and Design 1977–, Bd Tstees Menninger Fndn (USA) 1989–; Shenkar Coll of Textile Technol and Fashion: memb Bd 1970–87, hon fell 1976, pres 1987–94; memb Editorial Bd: Brain Behaviour and Immunity, Alzheimer Disease and Associated Disorders, Journal of Labelled Compounds and Radiopharmaceuticals; author of over 300 pubns on chemistry, psychopharmacology, animal behaviour, neurochemistry and educn; *Recreations* etching, archery; *Style—* The Rt Hon the Viscount Samuel, OBE; ✉ 1 Pinhas Rosen Street, Flat 4, Herzlia 46590, Israel (☎ 00 972 99553 242, fax 00 972 99552511)

SAMUEL, Edgar Roy; s of Lt Cdr Wilfred Sampson Samuel, RNVR (d 1958), of London, and Viva Doreen, *née* Blashki (d 1977); *b* 13 Dec 1928; *Educ* Univ Coll Sch, Ashbury Sch & Glebe Collegiate Ottawa, City of London Sch, Northampton Poly London (now City Univ), LSE (BA, MPhil); *m* 1956, Ruth Helena (d 1987), da of Joseph Cowen, CBE, of London; 1 s (Jonathan b 1959), 1 da (Deborah (Mrs Nevo) b 1957); *Career* asst steward Eastern Arctic Patrol 1945; optometrist 1950–71 and 1978–83, dir and curator Jewish Museum London 1984–95; vice pres Jewish Historical Soc of Eng (pres 1988–90); FRHistS 1964, FCOptom, DCLP; *Publications* The Portuguese Jewish Community in London (1656–1830) (Jewish Museum, 1992), contrib to Transactions of Jewish Historical Soc of Eng; *Clubs* Reform; *Style—* Edgar Samuel, Esq; ✉ 4 Garden Court, 63 Holden Road, London N12 7DG (☎ 0181 445 1327)

SAMUEL, Geoffrey James; JP; s of late David Leo Samuel, of Heston, and Rose, *née* Simons; *b* 1 Jan 1931; *Educ* St Paul's (Fndn scholar), Pembroke Coll Oxford (MA, state scholar); *m* Aug 1962, Rosemary, da of late Leonard Stanley Hughes; *Career* asst Ashford Co Sch 1954–58, head of dept Sir Walter St John's Sch 1958–69, exchange teacher Howe HS Indianapolis 1960–61, dep head Stanmore Sixth Form Coll 1969–72, headmaster The Heathland Sch 1973–96; sabbatical schoolmaster commoner Pembroke Coll Oxford 1986; lectr: British Cncl, Brunel Univ, Univ of London, Kingston Univ, COSMOS and others; memb Twickenham MBC and London Borough of Richmond upon Thames 1957–78; dep chm Richmond PSD (dep chm licensing 1983–90); former govr: Hounslow Borough Coll, Richmond Adult Coll, Richmond upon Thames Coll, Kneller Sch, Orleans Park Sch (chm 1974–86), Trafalgar Jr Sch; former memb Univ Ct Brunel, memb Sr Common Room Pembroke Coll Oxford; FIMgt, FRSA; *Books* Staff Appraisal in Action (contrib, 1987), Understanding School Management (contrib, 1988); numerous articles in The Times, Guardian, TES, Education and other educnl jls; *Clubs* MCC, Chiswick Bridge, Lensbury, Colourpoint Cat; *Style*— Geoffrey Samuel, Esq, JP; ✉ 25 Thurnby Court, Wellesley Road, Twickenham, Middlesex TW2 5RY (☎ 0181 894 2958)

SAMUEL, Sir John Michael Glen; 5 Bt (UK 1898), of Nevern Square, St Mary Abbots, Kensington, Co London; s of Sir John Oliver Cecil Samuel, 4 Bt (d 1962), and Charlotte Mary Desmond; *b* 25 Jan 1944; *Educ* Radley, Univ Coll London; *m* 1, 24 Sept 1966, Antoinette Sandra, da of late Capt Anthony Hewitt, RE; 2 s (Anthony John Fulton b 1972, Rupert Casper James b 1974); m 2, March 1982, Mrs Elizabeth Ann Molinari, yst da of late Maj R G Curry, of Bournemouth; *Heir* s, Anthony John Fulton Samuel b 13 Oct 1972; *Career* chm: Electric Auto Corporation (Detroit USA) 1978–82, Silver Volt Corporation (Freeport Bahamas) 1980–82, Whisper Electric Car A/S (Denmark) 1985–87, Synergy Research Ltd (UK) 1983–, Clean Air Transport (Hldgs) Ltd 1989–94, Syntech Power Ltd 1994–; MIMechE, CEng; *Recreations* motor racing; *Style*— Sir John Samuel, Bt

SAMUELS, Anita; OBE (1990), DL (Merseyside, 1989); da of Baron Asher Cowan (d 1978), of Liverpool, and Rachel, *née* Dover (d 1978); *b* 12 Feb 1924; *Educ* Belvedere Sch GPDST Liverpool; *m* 1946, Ian Samuels, s of Samuel Samuels; 1 s (Andrew David b 1949), 1 da (Vivienne Lesley b 1950); *Career* formerly: memb and vice chm Liverpool Health Authy, memb Liverpool Family Practitioner Ctee, memb Mental Health Act Cmmn, memb Supplementary Benefits Appeals, vice chm Liverpool Sch of Tropical Med, pres Liverpool Standing Conf of Women's Orgns, pres Merseyside Jewish Welfare Cncl, lay conciliator Liverpool Family Health Services Authy, memb Cncl Univ of Liverpool, memb Mental Health Review Tbnl; High Sheriff for Co of Merseyside 1994–95; JP 1975–94; Hon LLD Univ of Liverpool 1995; *Recreations* opera, concerts, theatre, grandchildren; *Style*— Mrs Anita Samuels, OBE, DL; ✉ 7 The Glen, Liverpool, Merseyside L18 6LB (☎ 0151 724 6113)

SAMUELS, John Edward Anthony; QC (1981); s of Albert Edward Samuels (d 1982), of The Chantry, Reigate, Surrey, and Sadie Beatrice Samuels (d 1991); *b* 15 Aug 1940; *Educ* Charterhouse, Queens' Coll Cambridge (MA); *m* 1967, Maxine, da of Lt-Col F D Robertson, MC, of Oakville, Ontario, Canada; 2 s (David b 1970, Adam b 1973); *Career* called to the Bar Lincoln's Inn 1964, bencher 1990; dep High Ct judge 1983–, recorder Crown Ct 1985–, head of chambers; chm Jt Regulations Ctee of the Inns' Cncl and the Bar Cncl 1987–90; memb: Senate of the Inns of Ct and the Bar 1983–86, Bar Cncl 1992–; asst Parly Boundary Cmmr 1992–; lay chair NHS Complaints Panels 1996–; *Style*— John Samuels, Esq, QC; ✉ 22 Old Buildings, Lincoln's Inn, London WC2A 3UJ (☎ 0171 831 0222, fax 0171 831 2239)

SAMUELS, Dr John Richard; s of Richard Arthur Samuels, of Istead-Rise, Kent, and Iris Molene Phylis, *née* Jenkins; *b* 13 Sept 1952; *Educ* Gravesend Tech HS, Univ Coll Cardiff (BA), Univ of Nottingham (PhD); *m* 1, 7 Sept 1979 (m dis 1985), (Frances) Naomi Field, da of Dr Gerard Field, of Dundas, Ontario, Canada; m 2, 10 Sept 1986, Harriet Annabel, da of Stephen Leslie Rickard, of Newark, Notts; 1 s (William b 1986), 1 da (Jenny b 1984); *Career* archaeologist, writer, lectr and publisher; archaeological field offr Humberside Archaeological Ctee 1975–76, res asst Dept of Archaeology Univ of Nottingham 1976–80, asst dir Rescue Archaeology Unit Univ of Liverpool 1980–81, tutor organiser for Notts in local history and archaeology Workers' Educnl Assoc 1981–89, archaeological conslt 1989–, fndr The Cromwell Press 1986–92, ed East Midlands Archaeology (CBA Gp 14 Jl), ed Nottinghamshire Heritage Magazine 1990–92; memb: Prehistoric Soc 1969–, Soc for Medieval Archaeology 1976–, N Lincs Archaeological Unit Ctee 1976–81, Tst for Lincs Archaeology 1982–89 (memb Exec Ctee 1984–87), Cncl for Br Archaeology (14 Exec Ctee) 1984–, Thoroton Soc 1987–; MIFA 1983, FSA 1993; *Books* Figure Brasses in North Lincolnshire (1976), Aspects of Local History in Aslockton, Whatton and Scarrington Notts (1987), Excavation and Survey of Lydiate Hall, Merseyside (1982), Roman Pottery Production in the E Midlands (1983), Green Fields Beyond (1984), Life & Landscape in E Bridgford 1600–1900 (1985), Discovering Newark-on-Trent (1989), History Around Us (1989), Archaeology in Law (1996); *Recreations* squash, horse riding, walking dogs; *Clubs* Savages; *Style*— Dr John Samuels, FSA; ✉ The Manor, South Street, Normanton on Trent, Newark, Notts NG23 6RQ (☎ 01636 821727)

SAMUELS, Prof Michael Louis; s of Harry Samuels, OBE (d 1976), of London, and Céline, *née* Aronowitz (d 1983); *b* 14 Sept 1920; *Educ* St Paul's, Balliol Coll Oxford (MA); *m* 21 Dec 1950, Hilary Miriam, da of Julius Marcus Samuel, of Glasgow (d 1942); 1 da (Vivien b 1953); *Career* lectr in English language Univ of Edinburgh 1949–59 (asst 1948–49), sr res fell in English language Univ of Glasgow 1989– (prof 1959–89); chm Scottish Studentships Selection Ctee Scottish Educn Dept 1975–88; FRSE 1989; *Books* Linguistic Evolution (1972), A Linguistic Atlas of Late Medieval English (jt ed 1986), The English of Chaucer (with J J Smith, 1988); *Style*— Prof Michael Samuels, FRSE; ✉ 4 Queen's Gate, Dowanhill, Glasgow G12 9DN (☎ 0141 334 4999)

SAMUELSON, David Wylie; s of George Berthold Samuelson (d 1947), and Marjorie Emma Elizabeth, *née* Vint (d 1991); bro of Michael Edward Wylie Samuelson, CBE, *qv* and Sir Sydney Wylie Samuelson, CBE; *m* 1, 1949 (m dis 1973), Joan, da of Philip Woolf; 2 s (Paul, Adam), 2 da (Gail, Zoe); m 2, 1978, Elaine Witz; *Career* served RAF 1944–47; with Br Movietone News 1941–60, fndr dir Samuelson Group plc 1958–84, dir dSam Ltd 1984–; as cameraman filmed in over 40 countries and at 4 Olympic games; original inventions incl: through-the-lens video viewfinders for film cameras, remote control system for Louma camera crane, Samcine inclining prism; winner of many awards incl: SMPTE Special Commendation Award 1978, AMPAS Scientific and Engrg Award 1980, SMPTE Presidential Proclamation Award 1984, Acad Tech Achievement Award 1987, BSC 'Bert Easy' Tech Award 1994; govr London Int Film Sch 1981–94 (chm 1984–86), vice pres Int Union of Film Tech Assocs 1974–80, chm Br Bd of Film Classification 1972–89 (memb 1969–94), memb Br Screen Advsy Cncl 1985–93; FRPS, FBKSTS (pres 1970–72, memb Cncl 1966–78 and 1984–90), FSMPTE, memb ACTT; *Books* Motion Picture Camera and Lighting Equipment, Motion Picture Camera Techniques, The Panaflex Users' Manual, The Cinematographers' Computer Calculator, Motion Picture Camera Data, The Samuelson Manual of Cinematography, American Cinematographer magazine (contrib ed, 1973–83), David Samuelson's Manual for Cinematographers (1993), Hands-on: Manual for Cinematographers; *Recreations* skiing, jogging, work; *Style*— D W Samuelson, Esq; ✉ dSam Ltd, 7 Montagu Mews West, London W1H 1TF (fax 0171 724 4025)

SAMUELSON, James Francis; s and h of Sir Michael Samuelson, 5 Bt; *b* 20 Dec 1956; *Educ* Hailsham; *m* 1987, Caroline Anne Woodley; 2 da (Miranda Alice b 27 May 1990, Naomi Harriet b 1 June 1992); *Style*— James Samuelson Esq; ✉ 3 Manor Cottages, Buckhorn Weston, Gillingham, Dorset SP8 5HH

SAMUELSON, Michael Edward Wylie; CBE; s of George Berthold Samuelson (d 1947), pioneer film prodr making first film 1908, and Marjorie Emma Elizabeth, *née* Vint; bro of David Wylie Samuelson, *qv*, and Sir Sydney Samuelson, CBE; *b* 25 Jan 1931; *Educ* Shoreham GS; *m* Madeleine; 3 s (James b 1962, d 1970, Richard b 1964, Benjamin b 1972), 2 da (Louise b 1959, Emma b 1960, actress as Emma Samms); *Career* photographer RAF 1949–51, stage dir 1952–56, Br Movietone News cameraman 1957–61; Samuelson Group plc 1957–88 (dep chm 1984–88), md Michael Samuelson Lighting Ltd 1989–; credits as dir or prodr or cinematographer on official films to Olympic Games 1968, 1972, 1974, 1976 and 1984 and World Cup Soccer 1966, 1970, 1974, 1982 and 1986; exec crew Variety Club of GB 1967– (chief Barker 1974, memb Exec Bd 1974–), chm Sunshine Coach Scheme GB 1979–85 and 1991 and 1992, tstee Young Variety Club of GB 1980–, chm Worldwide Sunshine Coach 1983–87, memb Cncl Sick Children's Tst 1983–, vice chm and tstee Hospital for Sick Children Great Ormond St Redevelopment Appeal 1984–, chm Great Ormond Street Ltd, chm Appeal Tstees Hosp for Sick Children Great Ormond Street, vice pres Nat Assoc for Maternal and Child Welfare 1978–, pres Variety Clubs International 1987–89, chm bd Variety Clubs International 1989–91; *Recreations* canal boating enthusiast, opera, shooting; *Clubs* MCC; *Style*— Michael Samuelson, Esq, CBE; ✉ 13 Phillimore Place, London W8 7BY (☎ 0171 937 9711); Michael Samuelson Lighting Ltd, Pinewood Studios, Iver Heath, Bucks SL0 0NH (☎ 01753 631133, fax 01753 630485)

SAMUELSON, Sir (Bernard) Michael Francis; 5 Bt (UK 1884), of Bodicote, Banbury, Oxfordshire; s of Sir Francis Samuelson, 4 Bt (d 1981), and Margaret (d 1980), da of Henry Kendal Barnes; *b* 17 Jan 1917; *Educ* Eton; *m* 1952, Janet Amy, da of Lt Cdr Lawrence Garrett Elkington; 2 s, 2 da; *Heir* s, James Francis Samuelson, *qv*; *Career* Lt RA, Burma 1939–45 (despatches); *Style*— Sir Michael Samuelson, Bt

SAMWORTH, David Chetwode; CBE (1985), DL (1984); s of Frank Samworth; *b* 25 June 1935; *Educ* Uppingham; *m* 1969, Rosemary Grace, *née* Hobbs; 1 s (Mark b 1970), 3 da (Mary b 1972, Susannah b 1975, Victoria b 1977); *Career* Lt Sudan and Cyprus; chm Pork Farms Ltd 1968–81, dir Northern Foods Ltd 1978–81; chm: Meat and Livestock Cmmn 1980–84, Samworth Brothers (Holdings) Ltd 1984–; non-exec dir: Imperial Group 1983–85, Thorntons plc 1988–93; pres Br Meat Mfrs Assoc 1988–94; vice chm Leics 33 Hosp Mgmnt Ctee 1970–74, memb Cncl of Univ of Nottingham 1975–76, chm Governing Body Uppingham Sch 1996– (vice chm 1980–89); Liveryman Worshipful Co of Butchers; *Recreations* tennis, hunting; *Style*— David Samworth, Esq, CBE, DL; ✉ PO Box 9, Melton Mowbray, Leicester LE13 0XH

SANBERK, HE Özdem; Turgut and Nimet Sanberk; *b* 1 Aug 1938; *Educ* Galatasaray Lycée, Faculty of Law Univ of Istanbul; *m* Sumru; 1 da; *Career* Turkish diplomat; joined Miny of Foreign Affrs 1963, dep perm del to OECD then to UNESCO Paris 1980–85, subsequently dep dir gen for bilateral economic affrs Miny of Foreign Affrs, advsr for external rels to the PM 1985–87, ambass and perm del to the EC 1987–91, under sec Miny of Foreign Affrs 1991–95, ambass to the Ct of St James's 1995–; *Clubs* Cavalry and Guards', Travellers'; *Style*— HE Mr Özdem Sanberk; ✉ Turkish Embassy, 43 Belgrave Square, London SW1X 8PA (☎ 0171 637 7675, fax 0171 637 3774)

SANCHA, Carlos Luis; s of Luis Antonio José Sancha Lengo (d 1975), and Dorothy Kate Sancha (d 1955); *b* 27 April 1920; *Educ* Lindisfarne Coll, Central Sch of Arts and Crafts, Byam Shaw Sch of Art; *m* 14 Aug 1948, Sheila Neal-Green (d 1994); 3 c (Anita b Dec 1950, Jeremy b Sept 1951, Nicolas b Nov 1957); *Career* portrait painter; apprenticed Carlton Studios 1938–40; joined RAF 1940, cmmnd pilot 1942 (demobbed 1945); painted portraits in: UK, USA, Italy, France and Germany; portraits incl: members of the Royal Family, peers, statesmen and numerous conversation pieces; RP 1973; *Style*— Carlos Sancha, Esq; ✉ 8 Melbury Road, London W14 8LR (☎ 0171 602 3112)

SANCROFT-BAKER, Raymond Samuel; s of Anthony Sancroft-Baker (d 1985), and Jean Norah, *née* Heron-Maxwell (d 1981); *b* 30 July 1950; *Educ* Bromsgrove Sch; *m* 29 Jan 1983, (Daphne) Caroline, da of Gp Capt Maurice Adams, OBE, AFC (d 1976); 2 s (Robert b 1985, Hugh b 1987); *Career* Christie's: head Coin and Metal Dept 1973, dir 1981–, dir Jewellery Dept 1988–; Freeman City of London 1972; Liveryman: Worshipful Co of Wax Chandlers 1973, Worshipful Co of Pattenmakers 1972 (memb Ct of Assts 1987, Master 1994); FRNS 1971, FGA 1992; *Recreations* tennis, squash, wood turning; *Clubs* RAC; *Style*— Raymond Sancroft-Baker, Esq; ✉ 4 Westbourne Park Rd, London W2 5PH (☎ 0171 727 9600); Christie's, 8 King St, St James's, London SW1Y 6QT (☎ 0171 839 9060)

SANCTUARY, Gerald Philip; s of John Cyril Tabor Sanctuary (d 1975), of Laleham-on-Thames, and Maisie Toppin, *née* Brooks (d 1993); *b* 22 Nov 1930; *Educ* Bryanston, Law Soc Sch of Law; *m* 28 July 1956 (m dis 1996), Rosemary Patricia, da of Lt-Col Francis L'Estrange, of Dublin; 3 s (Nigel b 1960, Thomas b 1965, Charles b 1965), 2 da (Celia b 1958, Sophie b 1975); *Career* asst slr Sharrards Kingston on Thames 1955–57, ptnr Hasties Solicitors Lincoln's Inn Fields 1957–63, nat sec Nat Marriage Guidance Cncl 1965–68 (field sec 1963–65), exec dir Sex Info and Educn of USA 1969–71, sec professional and PR Law Soc 1971–78, exec dir Int Bar Assoc 1978–79, legal advsr and sr HQ Co-ordinator Regnl and Local Affrs MENCAP 1979–84, sec Provident Fund NUJ 1984–95; papers presented to confs in Europe, USA and Australasia; jt fndr Family Service Cncl Kenya, treas and Liveryman Guild of Air Pilots and Air Navigators; memb Law Soc 1956–; *Books* Marriage Under Stress (1968), Divorce - And After (1970), Before You See a Solicitor (1973), After I'm Gone - What Will Happen to my Handicapped Child (1984), Shakespeare's Globe Theatre (1992), Running A Marriage Guidance Council, Local Society Handbook, It's Your Law - Law Soc Series (ed, 1973–78); *Recreations* amateur drama, travel, writing, organising murder mystery weekends, recording books for blind people; *Style*— Gerald Sanctuary, Esq; ✉ 99 Beechwood Avenue, St Albans, Herts AL1 4XU (☎ 01727 842666)

SANDALL, Robert Paul; s of Arthur Sandall, of Rippingale, Lincs, and Irene Norah, *née* Chard; *b* 9 June 1952; *Educ* Haberdashers' Aske's Elstree, Lincoln Coll Oxford (exhibitioner, BA), Cornell Univ NY USA; partner, Marina Salandy-Brown; *Career* freelance musican and composer 1976–84, writer, critic and broadcaster 1985–; currently: pop/rock critic Sunday Times, presenter Mixing It BBC Radio 3, presenter VH-1 MTV; regular contrib to: Q, Rolling Stone, Kaleidoscope (Radio 4), Sky News; occasional feature writer and fiction reviewer Sunday Times; memb Performing Rights Soc 1984; *Publications* Rolling Stones: Images of the World Tour 1989–90 (1991); *Recreations* skiing, tennis, scuba diving, fell walking; *Clubs* Green Street; *Style*— Robert Sandall, Esq; ✉ 51 Biscay Road, London W6 8JW (☎ 0181 741 7576); Sunday Times, 1 Pennington St, London E1 5XN (☎ 0171 782 5771, fax 0181 746 3253)

SANDARS, Peta June; *see:* Gurney, Jane

SANDBACH, Richard Stainton Edward; s of Frank Stainton Sandbach (ka 1917), and Beatrice Emmeline, *née* Clifton (d 1963); *b* 13 June 1915; *Educ* Manchester GS, St John's Coll Cambridge (MA, LLM); *m* 10 Sept 1949, (Brenda Mary) Wendy, da of Charles Lionel Osborn Cleminson (d 1958), of the White House, Ickleford, Herts; 2 s (John Christopher Stainton b 1950, Richard Paul Stainton (Dickon) b 1956); *Career* Private VR Suffolk Regt 1939, OCTU 1940, 22 Cheshire Regt 1940–46, Maj Jr Staff Coll 1941, 1 Canadian Army 1943–44, Airborne Corps 1944–46, Lucknow Dist 1946; admitted slr 1946; sr ptnr Greenwoods Peterborough 1970–79 (ptnr 1951–79), clerk Huntingdon Freemen 1968–76; chm: DHSS Local Appeals Tbnl Peterborough 1980–88, Paten & Co Ltd 1988–96, QCCC Ltd 1989–, QCCC Sales Ltd 1991–; fndr chm Minster Gen Housing Assoc Ltd; dir: FB Gibbons & Sons Ltd, Whesby Ltd, Arcade Properties (Peterborough)

Ltd; past pres Peterborough & Dist Law Soc; past chm: City & Cos Club Peterborough, Burgh Soc Peterborough; tstee Peterborough Cathedral Preservation Tst (memb Fin Advsy Ctee); chm Peterborough Diocesan Bd of Fin 1974–84, provincial grand master for Northamptonshire & Huntingdonshire Ancient Free & Accepted Masons of England 1984–90; memb Law Soc 1947; *Books* Introduction to The Book of the Lodge (G Oliver, 1986), Priest and Freemason (1988), Peterborough Booklets 1–5 (1990–92), Notes for a Candidate for Freemasonry (1991), Understanding the Royal Arch (1992), Letter to a Master-Elect (1994), Talks for Lodge and Chapter (1996); *Recreations* hill walking, computers, photography, historic research; *Clubs* United Oxford and Cambridge, City & Counties Peterborough; *Style*— Richard Sandbach, Esq; ✉ 91 Lincoln Road, Peterborough PE1 2SH; (☎ and fax 01733 343012); The Moorings, Fairbourne, Gwynedd; Drumnagarrachan, Kiltarlity, by Beauly, Inverness

SANDBERG, Alexander Christer Edward; s of Oscar Fridolf Alexander Sandberg, OBE (d 1942), and Audrey Maude, *née* Furber (d 1980); *b* 31 July 1923; *Educ* Charterhouse, City and Guilds Coll (BSc); *m* 19 Oct 1957, Aline Isobel, da of Brig W E Duncan, CVO, DSO, MC (d 1969); 3 s (Michael b 1959, Christopher b 1961, Neil b 1965); *Career* Lt RE 1942–45; chm Messrs Sandberg consulting engrs 1955–; former pres Br Section Conseil National des Ingenieurs et des Scientifiques de France, sch govr, past pres City and Guilds Coll Assoc; FCGI, FEng 1987, FICE, FIStructE, FIMechE, FIHT; *Recreations* tennis, golf, sailing; *Clubs* Hurlingham, Anglo Belgian; *Style*— Alexander Sandberg, Esq, FEng; ✉ 16 Thames Quay, Chelsea Harbour, London SW10 0UY (☎ 0171 352 7210); Messr Sandberg, 40 Grosvenor Gardens, London SW1W OLB (☎ 0171 730 3461, fax 0171 730 4972)

SANDBERG, Alexander Logie John; s of John Forbes (d 1963), and Diana Margaret Ina, *née* Hurst; *b* 15 July 1949; *Educ* Hawtreys, Milton Abbey; *m* 15 Sept 1979, Clare Angela Eli, da of Antony Colman; 2 s (James, Edward (twin)), 2 da (Serena, Louisa (twin)); *Career* chm and chief exec College Hill Associates (formerly College Group Limited, PR); *Recreations* tennis, gardening, skiing, shooting; *Clubs* Queen's; *Style*— Alexander Sandberg, Esq; ✉ College Hill Associates, 29 Gresham Street London EC2V 7AH (☎ 0171 457 2020, fax 0171 248 3295)

SANDBERG, Sir Michael Graham Ruddock; kt (1986), CBE (1982, OBE 1977); s of Gerald Arthur Clifford and Ethel Marion Sandberg; *b* 31 May 1927; *Educ* St Edward's Sch Oxford; *m* 1954, Carmel Mary Roseleen, *née* Donnelly; 2 s, 2 da; *Career* served 6 Lancers (Indian Army) and King's Dragoon Gds 1945; Hong Kong and Shanghai Banking Corp: joined 1949, chm 1977–86; treas Univ of Hong Kong 1977–86, chm British Bank of the Middle East 1980–86; dir: International Totalizator Systems Inc, Global Yield Inc, New World Development Ltd, Winsor Ind Corp; memb Exec Cncl of Hong Kong 1978–86, chm Bd of Stewards Royal Hong Kong Jockey Club 1981–86 (Hon Steward 1986), pres Surrey CCC 1987–88; JP Hong Kong 1972–86; Freeman City of London, Liveryman Worshipful Co of Clockmakers; FCIB 1977 (vice-pres 1984–87), FRSA 1983; *Recreations* racing, horology, cricket, bridge; *Clubs* Cavalry and Guards', White's, MCC, Surrey CCC, Portland, Hong Kong; *Style*— Sir Michael Sandberg, CBE; ✉ Waterside, Passfield, Liphook, Hants GU30 7RT (☎ 01428 751225); Domaine de la Haute Germaine, 06510 Le Broc, Alpes Maritimes, France (☎ 00 33 93 29 07 62)

SANDELL, Michael Charles Caines; s of Christopher Sandell (d 1974), of Amesbury, Wilts, and Doris, *née* Waters; *b* 30 Sept 1933; *Educ* Cheltenham, Royal Agric Coll Cirencester; *m* 19 Sept 1959, (Janet) Heather, da of William Duncan Montgomery; 2 da (Camilla b 3 March 1962, Georgina b 1 April 1964); *Career* Nat Serv cmmnd RA, served Gibraltar 1952–53; sr ptnr: Fisher & Co 1981–83, Fisher Hoggarth 1983–; valuer Agricultural Mortgage Corporation plc 1976–; FRICS 1970; *Recreations* shooting, gardening, tennis; *Style*— Michael Sandell, Esq; ✉ Village Farm, Sutton Bassett, Market Harborough, Leicestershire LE16 8HP (☎ 01858 410435); Fisher Hoggarth, Chartered Surveyors, 40 High St, Market Harborough, Leicestershire LE16 7NX (☎ 01858 410200, fax 01858 410207)

SANDELSON, Bernice Helen; da of Maurice Wingate (d 1972), and Bella Davis (d 1991); *b* 29 March 1937; *Educ* Queens Coll London; *m* 10 June 1958, Victor Sandelson; 2 s, 2 da; *Career* owner and md Cartoon Originals 1974–77, proprietor and md Montpelier Sandelson (gallery specialising in 20 C British Art) 1979–; *Recreations* gallery-crawling; *Clubs* Vanderbilt, Chelsea Arts; *Style*— Mrs Bernice Sandelson; ✉ Montpelier Sandelson Ltd, 4 Montpelier St, London SW7 1EZ (☎ 0171 584 0667)

SANDELSON, Neville Devonshire; s of David Sandelson, OBE; *b* 27 Nov 1923; *Educ* Westminster, Trinity Coll Cambridge; *m* 1959, Nana Karlinski, of Neuilly sur Seine; 1 s, 2 da; *Career* called to the Bar Inner Temple 1946; dir of local newspaper and book publishing cos; resumed practice at Bar 1964, dep circuit judge and asst recorder 1977–85; dep chm Westminster and Overseas Trade Services Ltd 1985–90, exec dir Profundis Ltd 1989–; MP (Lab) Hayes and Harlington 1971–74, Hillingdon, Hayes and Harlington (SDP 1981–84) 1974–83, having fought previous elections in other constituencies; fndr memb and treas Manifesto Gp 1975–80, fndr memb SDP 1981; former memb: European Cmmn Lab Ctee for Europe, Wider Share Ownership Cncl 1979–, National Ctee Electoral Reform Cncl 1977–88; jt sec British-Greek Parly Gp, vice-chm SDP Friends of Israel (resigned over Israeli bombardment of Beirut 1982); SDP spokesman on NI and Arts to 1983; vice-chm Afghanistan Support Ctee; co-fndr The Radical Soc 1988 (co-chm 1988–90, hon pres 1990–); *Clubs* Reform; *Style*— Neville Sandelson, Esq; ✉ 71 Valiant House, Vicarage Crescent, London SW11 3LX (☎ and fax 0171 223 5211); Villecelle, 34240 Lamalou-les-Bains, France (☎ 00 33 6795 2502)

SANDEMAN, David Robert; s of Robert John Sandeman, of Bridge of Allan, Stirlingshire, and Enid, *née* Webb; *b* 3 Aug 1954; *Educ* Trinity Coll Glenalmond, UCL (BSc), Wesminster Med Sch London (MB BS, pres Westminster Students' Union); *m* Dr Alison Peters Sandeman, da of William Henry Cowin; 1 da (Isabel Laelia Sandeman b 11 Oct 1988); *Career* pre-registration houseman Westminster Hosp London 1979–80, A&E Luton and Dunstable Hosp 1980, gen surgery registrar (rotation) Birmingham 1980–83, SHO in neurosurgery Bristol 1984, registrar in neurosurgery Liverpool 1984–85 and 1986–87, research registrar UCH London and Inst of Neurology Queen's Square London 1985–86, sr registrar in neurosurgery Manchester Royal Infirmary and Hope Hosp Salford 1987–90, conslt neurosurgn Frenchay Hosp Bristol 1991–; research interests in neuro-oncology and laser application to neurosurgery, pioneer of interactive image directed surgical techniques, minimally invasive neurosurgery, neuro-endoscopy and surgical robotics; memb: Euro Laser Assoc 1987, Soc of Br Neurosurgns 1991, French Neurosurgical Soc 1992, Euro Stereotactic Assoc 1992; *Books* Lasers in Neurosurgery (1990); *Recreations* skiing, cycling, swimming, triathlon, hill walking; *Style*— David R Sandeman, Esq; ✉ Department of Neurosurgery, Frenchay Hospital, Bristol BS16 1LE (☎ 0117 970 1212 ext 2380, fax 0117 970 1161, mobile 0831 451641)

SANDERCOCK, Dr Peter Andrew Gale; s of Capt Michael John Gale Sandercock (d 1996), of Northwood, Middx, and Helen Betty, *née* Howland (d 1995); *b* 16 April 1951; *Educ* Shrewsbury, New Coll Oxford (MA, BMB Ch, DM); *m* 10 Sept 1977, Janet Mary, da of Peter Searell Andrews, of Little Addington, Northants; 3 s (David, Robert, Andrew), 1 da (Eleanor); *Career* actg clinical lectr Univ of Oxford 1981–85, lectr Univ of Liverpool 1985–87, sr lectr Univ of Edinburgh 1988–93, reader in Neurology Univ of Edinburgh 1993–; sec Br Stroke Res Gp; MRCP 1979, FRCP 1992; *Books* Stroke (1987); *Style*— Dr Peter Sandercock; ✉ Dept of Clinical Neuroscience, Western Gen Hosp, Crewe Rd, Edinburgh EH4 2XU (☎ 0131 343 6639, fax 0131 332 5150)

SANDERS, Prof Carol; da of Ronald Humphrey Sanders (d 1957), and Evelyn Maud, *née* Bradbury (now Mrs Payn); *b* 31 Dec 1944; *Educ* Univ of Cambridge (MA), Univ of London (PGCE), Univ of Paris (Doctorat de l'Université); *m* 29 July 1978, Peter Mary Eugene Figueroa, s of Rupert Aston (d 1969); 1 s (James Michael b 1986), 1 da (Emma Michelle b 1982); *Career* lectr in French: Univ of Reading 1969–72, Univ of W Indies 1972–76, Univ of Sussex 1977–84; reader then prof of French Australian Nat Univ Canberra 1984–88, prof of French Univ of Surrey 1988–; fndn pres Assoc for French Language Studies, memb Ctee Soc for French Studies, ed Journal of French Language Studies; FIL, memb Assoc for French Language Studies; Chevalier Des Palmes Académiques France 1983; *Books* F de Saussure - Cours De Linguistique Générale (1979), Cours De Français Contemporain (with M M Gervais, 1986), Lire Le Pacifique (with K Muller, 1989), Franc Exchange (with J Gladkow, 1991), French Today, Language in its Social Context (ed, 1993), Raymond Queneau (1994); *Recreations* travel, reading, writing; *Style*— Prof Carol Sanders; ✉ Department of Linguistic & International Studies, University of Surrey, Guildford GU2 5XH (☎ 01483 300800, fax 01483 302605, telex 859331)

SANDERS, (June) Deidre; da of Philip Ronald Heaton, and Audrey Minton, *née* Harvey (d 1972); *b* 9 June 1945; *Educ* Harrow County GS for Girls, Univ of Sheffield (BA); *m* 12 Dec 1969, Richard James, 2 da (Susan b 1976, Phoebe b 1988); *Career* journalist, author, broadcaster; problem-page ed The Sun, agony aunt BBC TV; memb: Nat Cmmn of Inquiry into the Prevention of Child Abuse, Br Assoc for Counselling; patron Youth Access; Jubilee Medal 1977; *Books* Kitchen Sink or Swim? (1982), Women and Depression (1984), Woman Book of Love and Sex (1985), Woman Report on Men (1987); *Style*— Mrs Deidre Sanders; ✉ PO Box 488, The Sun, Virginia Street, London E1 9BZ (☎ 0171 782 4012)

SANDERS, Dr Eric; s of Albert Sanders, and Caroline, *née* Johnson; *b* 22 Oct 1946; *Educ* Stanley GS Co Durham, Univ of Wales (BSc, MB); *m* 10 July 1971, Dianne Marilyn, da of David Denzil Harris Thomas, of St David's St, Carmarthen; 2 s (Gareth Wyn b 20 June 1974, Gethyn Huw b 21 Sept 1976), 1 da (Angharad Jane b 4 June 1980); *Career* pre-registration house offr Royal Infirmary Cardiff 1971, sr house offr Univ Hosp Wales 1972–74, res registrar and lectr Kruf Inst Renal Disease Royal Infirmary Cardiff 1974–80, conslt physician and dir of dialysis servs W Wales Hosp Carmarthen 1980–93, cons diabetologist N Durham Acute NHS Tst 1993–; dir of med servs W Wales Hosp 1992–; tstee and hon treas Kidney Res Unit Wales Fndn, memb Cncl Wales Diabetes Res Tst, former pres and regnl offr Lions Int Dist 105W; memb: Renal Assoc GB, EDTA; FRCP 1990 (MRCP 1974); *Books* Nephrology Illustrated (1981), Clinical Atlas of the Kidney (1993); *Recreations* local community service, music; *Style*— Dr Eric Sanders; ✉ Dunelm, Ael-y-Bryn, Carmarthen, Dyfed SA31 2HB (☎ 01267 221528); Shotley Bridge Hospital, Consett Road, Co Durham DH8 0NB (☎ 01207 583583)

SANDERS, Geoffrey (Geoff); MBE (1988); s of John Claridge Sanders (d 1979), and Elsie, *née* Boothby (d 1965); *b* 28 Feb 1928; *Educ* Hutton GS nr Preston Lancs, Hull Univ Coll, Univ of London (BA); *m* 16 Aug 1952, Nora Irene, da of Bertie Southgate (d 1965); 2 s (Paul b 24 Oct 1954, Mark b 25 Sept 1957); *Career* dep headmaster King Edward VI Camp Hill Sch for Boys Birmingham 1968–74 (joined 1952, sr history master 1953–68, sr house master 1956–58), headmaster King Edward VI Five Ways Sch Birmingham 1974–90; govr King Edward VI Schs Birmingham 1990– (Bailiff of Fndn 1996–97), tstee Ackers Tst Birmingham 1989–; C of E reader 1954–, fndr chm Br Schs Canoeing Assoc 1970–; chm: Cncl and Exec Br Canoe Union 1973–93, Jubilee Canoeing Fndn 1988–, Nat Cncl for Schs Sports 1989–91 (1979); pres: Solihull Canoe Club 1989–, Br Canoe Union W Midlands Regn 1991–; vice pres Br Canoe Union 1993–; memb SHA; *Books* BCU Coaching Handbook (1964–69), Canoeing for Schools and Youth Groups (1966–); *Recreations* canoeing, caravanning, swimming, industrial archaeology; *Style*— Geoff Sanders, Esq, MBE; ✉ 8 Cransley Grove, Solihull, W Midlands B91 3ZA (☎ 0121 705 2391)

SANDERS, Dr Jeremy Lew (Jerry); s of Dr Kenneth Sanders, of London, and Muriel Nettie, *née* Prepsler; *b* 23 Jan 1952; *Educ* Haberdashers' Aske's Elstree Herts, Univ of Leeds (BA, PhD); *m* July 1977, Crispina Gallego Perez, da of Sr Don Miguel Gallego Varona; 3 da (Emma b 17 May 1978, Melanie b 22 April 1982, Gloria b 15 June 1985), 1 s (Gregory b 28 Feb 1989); *Career* linguist specialist GCHQ Cheltenham 1978–83, features ed Personal Computer World 1983–84, ed Microscope 1984–85, ed PC User 1985–87, fndr ed Parallelogram 1987–91, exec ed PC Magazine 1991–93, ed Computing 1993–96, editorial dir VNU Image Publishing 1996–; UK Press Gazette: Newspaper of the Year for Microscope 1984, Editorial Team of the Year for Computing 1994; *Recreations* formula one motor racing (on TV), Flamenco guitar playing; *Style*— Dr Jerry Sanders; ✉ VNU Business Publications, 32–34 Broadwick Street, London W1A 2HG (☎ 0171 316 9139, fax 0171 316 9161, e-mail jerry_sanders@vnu.co.uk)

SANDERS, Dr John Derek; OBE (1994); s of Alderman John T Sanders, JP (d 1944), and Ethel Mary, *née* Trivett (d 1985); *b* 26 Nov 1933; *Educ* Felsted, Royal Coll of Music (major scholar, ARCM), Gonville & Caius Coll Cambridge (organ scholar, MA, MusB); *m* 22 July 1967, Janet Ann, da of Leonard Dawson (d 1976); 1 s (Jonathan Mark), 1 da (Anna Catharine); *Career* cmmnd offr RA 1956–58; dir of music King's Sch and asst organist Gloucester Cathedral 1958–63; organist and master of choristers: Chester Cathedral 1964–67, Gloucester Cathedral 1967–94; dir of music Cheltenham Ladies' Coll 1968–; pres: Gloucestershire Organists Assoc, Cathedral Organists Assoc 1990–92; former conductor: Gloucestershire Symphony Orch, Gloucester Choral Soc, Gloucester Three Choirs Festival; Freeman City of London 1986, Liveryman Worshipful Co of Musicians 1987; Lambeth Degree Doctor of Music 1990; FRCO 1956, Hon FRSCM 1991; *Publications* Festival Te Deum (1962), Soliloquy for Organ (1977), Toccata For Organ (1979), Te Deum Laudamus (1985), Jubilate Deo (1986), Two Prayers (1989), A Canticle of Joy (1991); *Recreations* gastronomy, travel, walking; *Style*— Dr John Sanders, OBE; ✉ Ridge Cottage, Upton Bishop, Ross-on-Wye, Herefordshire HR9 7UD (☎ 01989 780482)

SANDERS, Michael David; s of Norris Manley Sanders, of Farringdon, Alton, Hants, and Gertrude Florence, *née* Hayley; *b* 19 Sept 1935; *Educ* Tonbridge, Guy's Hosp Med Sch (MB BS, DO); *m* 1 Nov 1969, Thalia Margaret, da of Thomas Garlick (d 1961), of Ashover, Derbyshire; 1 s (Rupert Miles b 16 March 1971), 1 da (Melissa Tryce b 25 May 1973); *Career* house surgn Guys Hosp 1959, res offr Moorfields Eye Hosp 1963–67, Alexander Piggot Werner Meml Fell Univ of California San Francisco 1967–68; conslt ophthalmologist: Nat Hosp Nervous Diseases 1969, St Thomas' Hosp 1972; civil conslt ophthalmology RAF 1972; distinguished lectures: Middlemore Lectre 1985, Percival Hay 1986, Sir Stewart Duke-Elder 1987, Ida Mann 1987, Lettsomian 1988; hon memb Pacific Coast Oto-Ophthalmological Soc, hon conslt Sydney Hosp Univ of Sydney; asst ed British Journal of Ophthalmology, tstee Frost Fndn, med advsr Iris Fund for Prevention of Blindness, pres Int Neuro-Ophthalmology Soc; FRCP, FRCS, FCOpth; *Books* Topics in Neuro-Ophthalmology (1979), Computerised Tomography in Neuro-Ophthalmology (1982); *Recreations* golf; *Clubs* Hurlingham, Hankley Cmmn; *Style*— Michael Sanders, Esq; ✉ 9 Alma Terrace, Allen St, London W8 6QY (☎ 0171 937 7955); Chawton Lodge, Chawton, Alton, Hants (☎ 01420 86681); 8 Upper Wimpole St, London W1M 7TD (☎ 0171 935 5038)

SANDERS, Raymond Adrian; s of Leslie Harry Sanders, and Beatrice Sanders; *b* 13 May 1932; *Educ* Univ of Auckland NZ (LLB), LSE (LLB); *m* 1, 1961 (m dis), Anna Margaret Burton; 1 s; m 2, 1985, Virginia Varnell Dunn; 3 da; *Career* in practice as barr and slr NZ 1956–66, ptnr Jackson Russell and Co Auckland NZ 1962–66, pt/t lectr Univ of Auckland 1960–66 (examiner 1961–66), slr Allen and Overy London 1967–71, in practice as barr 1971–73, DHSS 1973–74 and 1975–84, Law Offrs' Dept 1974–75, legal advsr to Warnock Inquiry (Human Fertilization and Embryology) 1982–84, regnl chm Social Security and Med Appeal Tbnls 1984–86, Social Security cmmr 1986–, Child Support cmmr 1992; *Books* Credit Management (jtly, 1966), Building Contracts and Practice (1967); *Recreations* theatre, music, cycling, tennis; *Style—* Raymond Sanders, Esq; ✉ The Office of the Social Security Commissioners, Harp House, 83 Farringdon St, London EC4

SANDERS, Sir Robert Tait; KBE (1980), CMG (1974); s of Alexander Scott Wilson Sanders (d 1934), of Dunfermline, Fife, and Charlotte McCulloch; *b* 2 Feb 1925; *Educ* Canmore Public Sch Dunfermline, Dunfermline HS, Fettes, Pembroke Coll Cambridge (MA), LSE, SOAS; *m* 1951, Barbara, da of George Sutcliffe (d 1983); 3 s (1 decd); *Career* served Lt 1 Bn Royal Scots 1943–46; dist offr Fiji 1950, sec to Govt Tonga 1956–58, sec to Coconut Indust Inquiry 1963, MLC Fiji 1963–64, sec for Natural Resources 1965–67, actg sec Fijian Affrs 1967, actg chm Native Lands and Fisheries Cmmn 1967, MEC Fiji 1967, sec Chief Min and Cncl of Mins 1967–70; sec to Cabinet 1970–79 (sec foreign affrs 1970–74, sec home affrs 1972–74, sec info 1975–76); treaties advsr to Govt of Fiji 1985–87; author of newspaper and magazine articles; Fiji Independence Medal 1970 (25th Anniversary Independence Medal 1995); *Books* Interlude in Fiji (1963), Fiji Treaties (1987); *Recreations* golf, music; *Clubs* Royal Scots (Edinburgh); *Style—* Sir Robert Sanders, KBE, CMG; ✉ 6 Park Manor, Crieff, Perthshire PH7 4LJ

SANDERS, HE Ronald Michael; *b* 26 Jan 1948; *Educ* Sacred Heart RC Sch Guyana, Westminster Sch (London), Boston Univ, Univ of Sussex; *m* 1975, Susan Ramphal; *Career* high cmmr of Antigua and Barbuda; md Guyana Broadcasting Serv 1973–76, public affrs advsr to PM Guyana 1973–76, lectr in communications Univ of Guyana 1975–76, pres Caribbean Broadcasting Union 1975–76, memb Bd of Dirs Caribbean News Agency 1976–77, conslt to Pres Caribbean Devpt Bank in Barbados 1977–78, special advsr to Min of Foreign Affrs of Antigua and Barbuda 1978–82, dep perm rep to UN in New York 1982–83, ambass extraordinary and plenipotentiary accredited to UNESCO 1983–87 (memb Bd UNESCO 1985–87), high cmmr to the Ct of St James's 1984–87; memb Bd of Dirs: Swiss American Bank and Swiss American Nat Bank of Antigua 1990–, Guyana Telephone and Telegraph Co 1991–95; int rels conslt to Atlantic Tele Network (Inc) 1989–95, advsr on int affrs to Govt of Antigua and Barbuda 1990–91, int rels advsr to Prime Minister of Antigua and Barbuda with rank of ambass 1994–, high cmmr to the Ct of St James's 1995–, non-resident ambass to Germany and France 1996–; memb delgn: Non-Aligned Heads of Govt Conf 1976, Cwlth Heads of Govt 1975, 1983 and 1985; fell Queen Elizabeth House Univ of Oxford 1988 and 1989; memb: Inst of Int Communications, RIIA; *Publications* Broadcasting in Guyana (1978), Antigua and Barbuda: Transition, Trial, Triumph (1984), Inseparable Humanity: An Anthology of Reflections of Shridath Ramphal (ed 1988); several articles in int jls; *Clubs* RAC; *Style—* HE Mr Ronald M Sanders; ✉ 24 Chelmsford Square, London NW10 3AR; High Commission for Antigua and Barbuda, 15 Thayer Street, London W1M 5LD (☎ 0171 486 7073, fax 0171 486 9970)

SANDERS, Prof Roy; s of Leslie John Sanders, and Marguerite Alice, *née* Knight; *b* 20 Aug 1937; *Educ* Hertford GS, Univ of London (BSc, MB BS, FRCS); *m* 1, 25 July 1961 (m dis 1977), Ann Ruth, da of William Costar; 2 s (Andrew St John William b 1965, Charles St John David b 1966), 1 da (Lyvia Ann b 1963); m 2, 6 Jan 1984, Fleur Annette, da of Brian Chandler, of St Gallen, Austria; *Career* HAC Gunner 1957–62, Regt MO 1963–75, HAC Co of Pikemen and Musketeers 1982–, OC HAC Light Cavalry; conslt plastic surgn The Mount Vernon Centre for Plastic Maxillofacial and Oral Surgery; visiting prof UCL; sec: Br Assoc of Plastic Surgns 1986–88, Br Assoc of Aesthetic Plastic Surgns 1985–87; chm Medical Equestrian Assoc 1985–86; pres: Plastic Surgery Section RSM of London 1989–90, Br Assoc of Plastic Surgns 1993; memb Medical Artists' Assoc; Freeman: City of London, Worshipful Company of Barbers of London; Liveryman Soc of Apothecaries of London; *Recreations* equestrian activities, painting in watercolour; *Clubs* Athenaeum; *Style—* Prof Roy Sanders; ✉ 77 Harley St, London WIN 1DE (☎ 0171 935 7417); Upper Rye Farmhouse, Moreton in Marsh, Glos (☎ 01608 650542); Suite 1, 82 Portland Place, London W1 (☎ 0171 580 3541, fax 0171 436 2954)

SANDERS, Dr Samuel Chandrarajan; s of David Selvamanickam Sanders (d 1980), of Jaffna, Sri Lanka, and Harriet Chellammah, *née* Handy; *b* 1 July 1932; *Educ* Jaffna Coll Sri Lanka (MB BS), Univ of Colombo; *m* 30 Jan 1960, Irene Mangayatkarasi, da of Sittampalam Saravanamuttu (d 1971), of Jaffna, Sri Lanka; 1 s (David b 27 Oct 1968), 2 da (Roshini b 15 Nov 1961, Sureshini b 12 Aug 1965); *Career* res house offr Ceylon 1957–58, varied experience in med surgery, neurosurgery, public health and forensic med Sri Lanka 1958–70, postgrad trg in forensic med and clinical therapeutics Univ of Glasgow, Guy's and Edinburgh Royal Infirmary 1971–72, registrar then sr registrar Glasgow Western Dist 1973–76, conslt physician Glasgow Western Dist 1976–96; author various papers on subjects incl cerebral abcesses and epilepsy in the elderly; hon clinical sr lectr Univ of Glasgow, hon lectr Scot Retirement Cncl; med advsr Social Serv Dept Glasgow NW dist; memb: Br Geriatrics Soc, BMA; FRCP; *Books* Advanced Geriatric Medicine (vol 4, contrib, 1984); *Recreations* sport, travel, reading, fishing; *Style—* Dr Samuel Sanders; ✉ 28 Hillfoot Drive, Bearsden, Glasgow G61 3QF (☎ 0141 942 9388)

SANDERS, Dr Stuart; s of David Sadofsky (d 1955), and Florence, *née* Rakusen; *b* 20 Nov 1934; *Educ* Hymers Coll Hull, Univ of Leeds Medical Sch (MB, ChB, FRCGP, MRCS, LRCP, DCH, DObstRCOG, James and Mabel Gaunt Prize in Paediatrics); *m* 15 March 1979, Kathryn, da of Rudolf Bleichroeder; 2 s (Jonathan b 25 Dec 1979, Jeremy b 16 June 1983); *Career* paediatric house physician Leeds Gen Infirmary 1958–59, obstetric house surgn Manygates Maternity Hosp Wakefield 1959, medical sr house offr Pinderfields Gen Hosp Wakefield 1960–61, res pathologist Royal Free Hosp 1961–62, GP NHS 1962–66, paediatric clinical asst Royal Free Hosp 1963–67, sr res fell Hosp for Sick Children Great Ormond St London 1966–74, private physician and princ medical advsr to Sears, Wickes and other public cos and doctor accredited to Swissair and Swiss Embassy 1962–, princ med advsr to The Broadgate Medical Centre; JP 1976–80; chm: St Marylebone Div BMA 1984–87, Ind Doctors Forum 1990–94; Gold Medal Hunterian Soc 1963, Silver Medal Ind Doctors' Forum 1984; Freeman City of London 1978, Liveryman Worshipful Soc of Apothecaries; memb: RSM, Chelsea Clinical Soc, BMA, Cons Medical Soc; *Recreations* family, skiing, bridge, theatre, music; *Clubs* Annabel's, Mark's; *Style—* Dr Stuart Sanders; ✉ 22 Harmont House, 20 Harley Street, London W1 (☎ 0171 935 5687, fax 0171 436 4387, car 0836 625905)

SANDERS, Timothy Simon (Tim); s of Robert Ernest Sanders, and Patricia Anne, *née* Tracy; *b* 13 March 1959; *Educ* Llandovery Coll (Thomas Phillips scholar), Thames Valley GS, Univ of London (LLB); *m* Kathrine, da of Brian Thomas Firth; 1 s (James Thomas b 22 Sept 1986), 1 da (Alice Caroline b 22 March 1992); *Career* articled clerk Corbould Rigby & Co 1981–83, slr Trowers & Hamlins 1984–87, assoc Allen & Overy 1987–91; Theodore Goddard: assoc 1991–92, ptnr 1992–, head Corp Tax Dept 1993–; memb Law Soc 1984; FTII; *Books* Tolleys Indemnities & Warranties (1993); *Recreations* rowing, sailing, golf, national heritage, cinema, theatre, literature; *Style—* Tim Sanders, Esq; ✉ Theodore Goddard, 150 Aldersgate Street, London EC1A 4EJ (☎ 0171 606 8855, fax 0171 606 4390, e-mail timsanders@theodoregoddard.co.uk)

SANDERS, Prof Tom Andrew Bruce; s of John Bruce Sanders (d 1992), of Eastbourne, and Annie, *née* Dewsberry (d 1990); *b* 29 Dec 1949; *Educ* Eastbourne Coll, Queen Elizabeth Coll London (BSc), Univ of London (PhD); *m* 20 Oct 1973, Linda Marie, *née* Fassbender; 1 da (Mila b 30 April 1978), 1 s (Toby b 11 July 1981); *Career* prog assoc UNICEF (Indonesia) 1971–73; res nutritionist SW Thames RHA 1974–77; Queen Elizabeth Coll London: Rank Prize Funds fell 1977–79, res fell 1979–82, lectr in nutrition 1982–84; King's Coll London: lectr in nutrition 1984–91, reader 1991–94, prof of nutrition and dietetics 1994–, head of Dept 1995–; memb: Advsy Ctee on Novel Foods and Processes MAFF/Dept of Health, Nutrition Soc, British Atherosclerosis Discussion Gp (sec), RSM; *Books* The Vegetarian's Healthy Diet Book (1986), The Food Revolution (1991), You Don't Have to Diet (1994) also numerous papers and contribs to scientific jls; *Recreations* surfing, windsurfing, fishing, cinema, theatre, opera; *Style—* Prof T Sanders; ✉ Department of Nutrition and Dietetics, King's College, University of London, Campden Hill Road, London W8 7AH (☎ 0171 333 4273, fax 0171 333 4171, mobile 0468 414337)

SANDERS-CROOK, William Stanley; MBE (1972); s of William Charles Herbert Crook (d 1966), of Twickenham, Middx, and Mary Amelia, *née* Green (d 1986); *b* 2 Nov 1933; *Educ* Latymer Upper Sch, RMA Sandhurst; *m* 1, 5 May 1962; 1 s (William b 1963), 1 da (Deborah b 1972); m 2, 20 Dec 1982, Jean Rosemary, da of Eric Walker (d 1966), of Beaconside, Barnstaple, N Devon; *Career* Regular Army 1953–77; Maj; served infantry and para: BAOR, Suez, Malaya, Borneo, Singapore, MOD, NI, Brunei; writer; dir: John Roberts Conslts 1977–79, Jean Kittermaster PR 1981; MIMgt; *Novels* Four Days (1979), Death Run (1980), Triple Seven (1981), Fighting Back (1992); *Recreations* riding, scuba diving, cabinet making, watercolouring; *Clubs* Special Forces; *Style—* William Sanders-Crook, Esq, MBE; ✉ Jean Kittermaster Public Relations, 239 King's Road, London SW3 5EJ (☎ 0171 352 6811, fax 0171 351 9215)

SANDERSON, Dr Alan Lindsay; s (twin) of 1 Baron Sanderson of Ayot, MC (UK 1960); suc father 15 Aug 1971 and disclaimed his peerage for life 28 Sept 1971; *b* 12 Jan 1931; *Educ* Uppingham, Univ of London (MB BS, MRCP); *m* 1959, Gertrud, da of Herman Boschler; 1 s (Michael b 1959), 4 da (Evelyn b 1961, Frances b 1963, Andrea b 1964, Stephanie b 1970); *Career* conslt psychiatrist Fairfield Hosp; MRCPsych; *Style—* Dr Alan Sanderson; ✉ 2 Caroline Close, London W2 4RW (☎ 0171 229 8533)

SANDERSON, Alison Kimberley; da of Brian Glanville Field, and Barbara Evelyn, *née* Waters; *b* 6 July 1958; *Educ* Twickenham Co Sch for Girls, Thames Valley Sixth Form Coll, Univ of Leeds (BA); *m* Antony Richard Sanderson; 1 da (Katherine Natalie b 2 Feb 1994); *Career* advtg exec; Price Waterhouse CAs 1980–84, Black & Decker Co 1984–90; PepsiCola North America: fin planning mangr Baltimore 1990–92, gp strategic planning mangr Somers NY 1992–93; N Europe planning mangr PepsiCola International Richmond Surrey 1993–94, commercial dir J Walter Thompson Co Ltd 1994–; ACA 1983; *Style—* Mrs Alison Sanderson; ✉ J Walter Thompson & Co Ltd, 40 Berkeley Square, London W1X 6AD (☎ 0171 631 7007, fax 0171 493 8432)

SANDERSON, Arthur Norman; MBE (1985); s of Very Rev Dr William Roy Sanderson, of E Lothian, and Annie Muriel, *née* Easton; *b* 3 Sept 1943; *Educ* Glasgow Acad, Fettes, Corpus Christi Coll Oxford (MA), Univ of Edinburgh (DipEd), Henley Mgmnt Coll (Dip in Management); *m* 30 July 1966, Issy, da of Edward Halliday; 1 s (Angus William b 29 Sept 1968), 1 da (Emma b 27 Jan 1970); *Career* VSO tutor in mathematics and English Foso Trg Coll Ghana 1966–68, economics and careers master Daniel Stewart's Coll Edinburgh 1969–73; British Council: asst dir Kano Nigeria 1974–76, regnl dir Recife Brazil 1976–80, Far East and Pacific Dept London 1980–83, asst then acting rep Ghana 1983–86, regnl dir Glasgow 1986–89, dir Enugu Nigeria 1989–91, dir S India 1991–95, dir Baltic States 1995–; memb General Teaching Cncl of Scotland 1972; *Recreations* hill walking, jogging, golf, languages, Scottish country dancing, classical music; *Style—* Arthur N Sanderson, Esq, MBE; ✉ Lazaretes iela 3, Riga LV1010, Latvia (☎ and fax 00 371 7830031)

SANDERSON, Bryan Kaye; s of Eric Sanderson (d 1973), and Anne, *née* Kaye; *b* 14 Oct 1940; *Educ* Dame Allan's Sch Newcastle upon Tyne, LSE (BSc(Econ)), IMEDE Business Sch Lausanne; *m* Oct 1966, Sirkka Aulikki, *née* Kärki; 1 da (Christina Elvira b Jan 1976), 1 s (Peter James Eric b Sept 1978); *Career* vol serv with UNA Peru 1962–64; British Petroleum: various posts in Oil Supply Dept 1964–73, mangr Supply Co-ordination Branch 1973–76, area co-ordinator France Spain Greece and Turkey 1976–79, gen mangr Oil Supply Dept 1981–84 (asst gen mangr 1979–81), sr corp rep SE Asia 1984–87, md and chief exec BP Nutrition 1987–90, chief exec BP Chemicals 1990–, an md (main bd dir) BP Company plc 1992–; non-exec dir British Steel 1994–; vice pres Chemical Industry Assoc 1994– (memb Sci Cncl 1990–); memb Bd CEFIC 1995–; *Recreations* reading, golf, walking, gardening; *Clubs* Hampstead Golf; *Style—* Bryan Sanderson, Esq; ✉ BP Chemicals, British Petroleum plc, 1 Finsbury Circus, London EC2M 7BA (☎ 0171 496 4748, fax 0171 496 4894)

SANDERSON, Eric Fenton; s of Francis Kirton Sanderson, of Dundee, and Margarita Shand, *née* Fenton; *b* 14 Oct 1951; *Educ* Morgan Acad Dundee, Univ of Dundee (LLB, pres Students' Assoc) Harvard Business Sch (AMP); *m* 26 July 1975, Patricia Ann, da of late Lt-Cdr Donald Brian Shaw, and Mrs Pamela Shaw; 3 da (Anna b 1 June 1979, Caroline b 30 June 1982, Emma b 12 April 1985); *Career* articled clerk Touche Ross & Co Edinburgh, qualified CA 1976; The British Linen Bank Ltd: joined 1976, dir and head corp fin 1984, gp chief exec 1989–; FCIBS 1994 (MCIBS 1990); *Recreations* tennis, gardening, photography; *Clubs* New (Edinburgh); *Style—* Eric Sanderson, Esq; ✉ British Linen Bank Group Ltd, 4 Melville St, Edinburgh EH3 7NZ (☎ 0131 243 8301, fax 0131 243 8310)

SANDERSON, Sir Frank Linton; 3 Bt (UK 1920), of Malling Deanery, South Malling, Co Sussex; er s of Sir (Frank Philip) Bryan Sanderson, 2 Bt (d 1992), and Annette Irene Caroline (d 1967), da of late Col Korab Laskowski, of Warsaw, and gda of Gen Count Edouard de Castellaz; *b* 21 Nov 1933; *Educ* Stowe, Salamanca Univ; *m* 4 April 1961, Margaret Ann (Margot), da of John Cleveland Maxwell (d 1976), of New York, USA; 2 s (David Frank b 1962, Michael John b 1965), 3 da (Caroline Ann b 1966, Nina Margaret b 1968, Katherine Claire b (twin) 1968); *Heir* s, David Frank Sanderson b 26 Feb 1962; *Career* RNVR 1950–65; J H Minet & Co Ltd 1956–93 (dir 1985–93), dir Knott Hotels Co of London 1965–75, dir and chm Humber Fertilisers plc 1972–88; underwriting memb Lloyd's 1957–88; memb Chichester Dio Synod 1980–93; Master Worshipful Co of Curriers 1993–94; *Style—* Sir Frank Sanderson, Bt; ✉ Grandturzel Farm, Burwash, E Sussex TN19 7DE

SANDERSON, Prof John Elsby; s of Arthur John Sanderson, of Rhoose Glamorgan, and Ruth Megan, *née* Griffiths; *b* 1 May 1949; *Educ* Blundell's, Univ of Cambridge (BA, MA, MD), St Bartholomew's Hosp London (MB BChir); *m* 1, 1972 (m dis 1977), Susanna Marion, da of Richard Tewson, of Hempstead, Essex; m 2, 1980, Dr Julia Dorothy Billingham, da of David Billingham, of Crowhurst, Sussex; 1 s (Henry John Elsby b 1981), 1 da (Vanessa Maureen b 1980); *Career* house physician and surgn St Bartholomew's Hosp London 1973–74, sr house physician Brompton and Hammersmith Hosps 1974–75, res fell (cardiology) RPMS Hammersmith Hosp 1975–78, lectr in cardiovascular med Univ of Oxford and John Radcliffe Hosp 1978–81, Wellcome Tst lectr St Mary's Hosp and hon conslt physician Kenyatta Hosp Nairobi 1981–83, conslt physician and cardiologist Taunton and Somerset Hosp and clinical tutor Univ of Bristol 1983–92, sr lectr in med (cardiology) and conslt cardiologist The Chinese Univ of Hong Kong Prince of Wales Hosp 1992–96, prof Dept of Med and head Div of Cardiology The Chinese Univ of Hong Kong 1996–; memb: BMA, Br Cardiac Soc, Br Hypertension Soc, Euro Soc of Cardiology, N American Soc of Electrophysiology; FRCP, FRSTM&H;

fell: American Soc of Angiology, American Soc of Cardiology; *Publications* pubns and papers on cardiomyopathy, tropical heart disease, pacemakers and Ischaemic heart disease; *Recreations* family, music, sailing, tennis and walking; *Clubs* Royal Hong Kong Yacht; *Style—* Prof John Sanderson; ✉ Department of Medicine, The Chinese University of Hong Kong, Prince of Wales Hospital, Shatin, NT, Hong Kong (☎ 00 852 2632 2064, fax 00 852 2637 3852)

SANDERSON, Roy; OBE (1983); s of George Sanderson (d 1938), and Lillian, *née* Charlesworth (d 1939); *b* 15 Feb 1931; *Educ* Leicester, King Richards Royal GS; *m* 25 Aug 1951, Jean Lillian, da of James Booth; 3 s (Roy James, Alan (d 1973), Kevin); *Career* Nat Serv Lance Corpl REME 1949–51; convenor of shop stewards Lucas Aerospace Hemel Hempstead 1952–67; nat sec: EEPTU 1987–92 (asst educn offr 1967–69, nat offr 1969–87), Fedn of Professional Assocs Section AEEU (formerly EEPTU) 1992–93; non-exec dir UKAEA 1987–96; memb: Exec Ctee The Industrial Soc, Armed Forces Pay Review Body, Exec Cncl Confedn of Shipbuilding and Engrg Unions, Econ and Social Ctee of Euro Communities, Employment Appeal Tbnl 1995–, Industl Tbnls 1995–; *Recreations* golf, snooker, supporter of Watford FC; *Clubs* Shendish (Hemel Hempstead); *Style—* Roy Sanderson, Esq, OBE; ✉ 162 Belswains Lane, Hemel Hempstead, Hertfordshire (☎ 01442 242033); Hayes Court, West Common Rd, Hayes, Bromley, Kent (☎ 0181 462 7755)

SANDERSON, Theresa Ione (Tessa); MBE (1985); *b* 14 March 1956; *Educ* Wards Bridge Comp Wednesfield, Wolverhampton and Bilston Coll of Further Educn; *Career* former athlete; represented GB 1974–96 (jr 1973–74); honours at javelin incl: English Schs champion twice, Gold medal Cwlth Games 1978, 1986 and 1990, Silver medal Euro Championships 1978, Gold medal Olympic Games 1984 (Olympic record), Gold medal World Cup 1992, 4th place Olympic Games Barcelona 1992; competed Olympic Games Atlanta 1996; records: UK javelin 1976 and 1983, UK heptathlon 1981; sports presenter Sky News 1989–92; involved with numerous orgns and charities incl: Disabled Olympics (patron), Sickle Cell Anemia, Dance for Everyone, Br Inst for Brain Injured Children, Gt Ormond St, Variety Club, Save the Children; hon fell Wolverhampton Poly, Hon BSc Univ of Birmingham; memb Equity 1990; Female Athlete of the Year Br Athletics Writers' Assoc 1977, 1978 and 1984, Sports Personality of the Year Midland Region Variety Club twice; *Books* Tessa - My Life in Athletics (autobiography, 1985); *Recreations* cardiofunk (low impact aerobic exercise workout); *Clubs* Hounslow Athletics; *Style—* Miss Tessa Sanderson, MBE

SANDERSON, Timothy William; s of Dr Michael William Bristowe Sanderson, and Mrs Kay Glendinning, *née* Holman; *b* 3 March 1958; *Educ* Uppingham, Univ Coll Oxford (MA); *m* 9 Oct 1987, Damaris Stella Lavinia Margot Muir, da of Armitage Clifford Taylor (d 1967), of Hilden Hall, Penn, Bucks; 3 s (Hugh William Muir b 27 Nov 1990, Maximilian Alfred Henry b 14 July 1993, Alexander Edward Rohan b 6 Jan 1996); *Career* Hill Samuel Investment Management Group 1979–90, dir Delaware International Advisers Ltd 1990–; tstee Dunhill Medical Tst; AIIMR; *Recreations* squash, gardening, book collecting, literature, reading, wine, fly fishing; *Clubs* Hurlingham; *Style—* Timothy Sanderson, Esq; ✉ Delaware International Advisers Ltd, 125 Finsbury Pavement, London EC2A 1NQ (☎ 0171 638 2493, fax 0171 638 2099)

SANDERSON OF AYOT, Barony of (UK 1960) *see:* Sanderson, Dr Alan

SANDERSON OF BOWDEN, Baron (Life Peer UK 1985), of Melrose in the District of Ettrick and Lauderdale; Sir (Charles) Russell Sanderson; kt (1981), DL (Roxburgh, Ettrick and Lauderdale 1990); s of Charles Plummer Sanderson (d 1976), of Melrose, Roxburghshire, and (Martha) Evelyn (d 1954), da of Joseph Gardiner, of Glasgow; *b* 30 April 1933; *Educ* St Mary's Sch Melrose, Trinity Coll Glenalmond, Bradford Tech Coll, Scottish Coll of Textiles Galashiels; *m* 5 July 1958, (Frances) Elizabeth, da of Donald Alfred Ramsden Macaulay (d 1982), of Rylstone, Skipton, Yorks; 2 s (Hon (Charles) David Russell b 1960, Hon Andrew Bruce Plummer b 1968 d 1991), 2 da (Hon (Evelyn) Claire (Hon Mrs Walker) b 1961, Hon (Frances) Georgina (Hon Mrs Riley) b 1963); *Career* cmmnd Royal Signals 1952, served 51 (Highland) Inf Div Signal Regt (TA) 1953–56, KOSB (TA) 1956–58; Scottish Cons & Unionist Assoc: vice pres 1975–77, pres 1977–79, hon pres 1996–; Nat Union of Cons Assocs: memb Exec Ctee 1977–86, vice chm 1979–81, chm 1981–86; Min of State Scottish Office 1987–90, chm Scottish Cons Pty 1990–93, vice chm Scottish Peers' Assoc 1996–; ptnr Chas P Sanderson Wool and Yarn Merchants Melrose 1958–87; chm: Edinburgh Financial Trust 1983–87, Shires Investment Trust 1984–87, Hawick Cashmere Co 1991–, The Scottish Mortgage Trust plc 1993– (dir 1991–); dir: Illingworth Morris plc 1981–87 and 1990–92, Clydesdale Bank 1985–87 and 1993– (dep chm 1996–), Woolcombers Plc 1992–95, United Auctions Ltd 1992–, Edinburgh Woollen Mills Ltd 1993–, Caros 1992–95, Watson & Philip Plc 1993–, Morrison Construction Plc 1995–; govr: St Mary's Sch Melrose 1978–87, Scottish Coll of Textiles 1980–87; memb: Cncl Trinity Coll Glenalmond 1982– (chm 1994–), British Cncl Independent Schs 1984–87, Ctee Governing Bodies 1984–87, Ct Napier Univ 1994–; cmmr Gen Assembly Church of Scotland 1972; Liveryman Worshipful Co of Framework Knitters; *Recreations* golf, fishing; *Clubs* Caledonian, Hon Co of Edinburgh Golfers; *Style—* The Rt Hon the Lord Sanderson of Bowden, DL; ✉ Becketts Field, Bowden, Melrose, Roxburgh TD6 0ST (☎ 01835 822736)

SANDFORD, Arthur; DL; s of Arthur Sandford (d 1990), and Lilian Sandford (d 1995); *b* 12 May 1941; *Educ* Queen Elizabeth's GS Blackburn, UCL (LLB); *m* 1963, Kathleen, da of James Entwistle (d 1976); 2 da (Allison b 1967, Janet b 1969); *Career* asst slr Preston CBC 1965–66 (sr asst slr 1966–68), asst slr Hampshire CC 1969–70; Nottinghamshire CC: second asst clerk 1970–72, first asst clerk 1972–74, dep dir of admin 1974–75, dir of admin 1975–77, dep clerk of CC and co sec 1977–78, clerk of the CC and chief exec 1978–90; chief exec The Football League Ltd 1990–92; chief exec Manchester City Cncl 1992–; *Recreations* football, gardening; *Clubs* Royal Over-Seas League; *Style—* Arthur Sandford, Esq, DL; ✉ Fairford House, 66 Loughborough Road, Bunny, Nottingham NG11 6QD (☎ 0115 921 2440)

SANDFORD, Prof Cedric Thomas; s of Thomas Sandford (d 1951), of Bristol, and Louisa Kate, *née* Hodge (d 1971); *b* 21 Nov 1924; *Educ* Univ of Manchester (BA, MA), Univ of London (BA); *m* 1, 1 Dec 1945, Evelyn (d 1982), da of Horace Belch, of Leigh; 1 s (John b 1955), 1 da (Gillian b 1956); m 2, 21 July 1984, Christina Katarin Privett; 1 da (Anna b 1990); *Career* Pilot RAF 1943–46; prof of political economy Univ of Bath 1965–87 (emeritus prof 1987–); consultancies incl: UN, World Bank, IMF, EEC, OECD, Irish Tax Cmmn, UK Inland Revenue; author of many pubns in field of public fin, ptnr Fiscal Publications (publishing firm) 1989–; pres Economics Assoc 1983–86 (memb 1948); memb: Meade Ctee, SW Electricity Consultative Ctee 1981–90, Bath DHA 1984–90, Ofwat Customer Serv Ctee Wessex Region 1996–; active in local and nat affrs of Methodist Church; *Recreations* fishing, gardening, walking; *Style—* Prof Cedric Sandford; ✉ Old Coach House, Fersfield, Perrymead, Bath BA2 5AR (☎ and fax 01225 832683)

SANDFORD, (Christopher) Jeremy; s of Christopher Sandford (d 1985), of Eye Manor, Leominster, and Lettice Macintosh, *née* Rate (d 1993); *Educ* Eton, Oxford (BA); *m* 1, 14 Feb 1957 (m dis 1979), Nell Dunn (author of Poor Cow and Up the Junction), da of Sir Phillip Dunn, 2 Bt (d 1976); 3 s (Roc b 1957, Ruben b 1963, Jem 1967); m 2, 1988, Philippa Sophia Finnis; *Career* writer; formerly: talks and features writer BBC, writer and presenter ITV and BBC Radio, writer and presenter BBC TV women's progs, Thames TV religious broadcasting; poet and musician specialising in Spanish, E European and British gypsy/New Age music performing at festivals, concerts, etc; memb Herefordshire Traveller Support Gp, formerly dir Cyrenians and Simon Community, formerly memb Nat Gypsy Cncl; patron of Shelter, currently running Green and New Age conference facility from Hatfield Court and facilitating music at Oak Dragon and Rainbow Circle camps; *BBC TV Documentaries* incl: Hotel de Luxe, Cathy Where Are You Now?; *Radio, Stage and TV Plays* incl: Cathy Come Home (BBC TV screenplay) 1966, Edna the Inebriate Woman (BBC TV screenplay) 1971, Dreaming Bandsmen, Not Wishing to Return, It Is For Ever, Whelks and Chromium, The Fatted Calf, Death of a Teenager; *Newspaper Series and Enquiries* incl: Families without a Home, The Dossers, Dark Side of Affluence, Reincarnation, The Other Health Service, The Age of Consent; *Books* incl: Synthetic Fun, In Search of the Magic Mushroom, Smiling David, Tomorrow's People, Gypsies, Down and Out in Britain, Figures and Landscapes, Hey Days in Hay, Songs from the Roadside; *Recreations* riding, music, painting, mountain climbing; *Style—* Jeremy Sandford, Esq; ✉ Hatfield Court, Leominster HR6 0SD (☎ 01568 760333)

SANDFORD, 2 Baron (UK 1945); Rev John Cyril Edmondson; DSC (1942); s of 1 Baron Sandford, DL, sometime MP Banbury, Lord Cmmr of the Treasy and Vice-Chamberlain HM's Household 1939–42 (d 1959), by his w Edith, *née* Freeman; *b* 22 Dec 1920; *Educ* Eton, RNC Dartmouth; *m* 4 Jan 1947, Catharine Mary, da of late Rev Oswald Andrew Hunt; 2 s, 2 da; *Heir* s, Hon James Edmondson; *Career* takes Cons whip in House of Lords; RN: midshipman 1940, Med Fleet 1940–41, N African and Sicily Invasions 1942, Normandy Invasions 1944, Signal Offr 1945, House Offr RNC Dartmouth 1947, Flag Lt to Flag Offr cmdg 3 Aircraft Sqdn 1949, Flag Lt to flag offr air (Home) 1951, on Staff C-in-C Far East Station 1953, Cdr 1953, ret 1956; ordained 1958, curate Parish of St Nicholas Harpenden 1958–63, chm Herts CC Social Service 1966–69, exec chaplain to Bishop of St Albans 1965–68, chm bd of Church Army 1969–70; oppn whip House of Lords 1966–70, Parly under-sec of state Dept of Environment 1970–73 and of Dept of Educn and Sci 1973–74; memb Select Ctee on European Community Directive 1978–88; bd memb Ecclesiastical Insurance Office 1978–89; pres: Anglo-Swiss Soc 1976–84, pres Assoc of Dist Cncls 1980–86; Church Cmmr, chm Redundant Churches 1982–89; chm SE Regnl Planning Cncl (SERPLAN) 1981–89; Hon FILA 1971; *Style—* The Rev the Rt Hon the Lord Sandford, DSC; ✉ 27 Ashley Gardens, Ambrosden Avenue, London SW1P 1QD (☎ 0171 834 5722)

SANDFORD, Rear Adm Sefton Ronald; CB (1976); *b* 23 July 1925; *Educ* RNC Dartmouth; *m* 1, 1950, Mary Ann Prins (d 1972); 1 s; m 2, 1972, Jennifer Rachel Newell; 2 da; *Career* served WWII; cmd HMS Protector 1965–67, naval attaché Moscow 1968–70, cmd HMS Devonshire 1971–73, ADC to HM The Queen 1974, Flag Offr Gibraltar 1974–76; a yr bro Trinity House 1968; *Recreations* sailing, photography; *Clubs* Royal Yacht Sqdn, MCC; *Style—* Rear Adm Sefton Sandford, CB; ✉ St Christophe, 47400 Villeton, France (☎ and fax 00 33 53 79 08 52)

SANDHURST, 5 Baron (UK 1871); (John Edward) Terence Mansfield; DFC (1944); s of 4 Baron, OBE (d 1964); *b* 4 Sept 1920; *Educ* Harrow; *m* 1, 1942 (m dis 1946), Priscilla Ann (d 1970), da of late J Fielder Johnson; m 2, 1947, Janet Mary, er da of late John Edward Lloyd, of Long Island, New York; 1 s, 1 da; *Heir* s, Hon Guy Mansfield, QC b 1949; *Career* WWII RAF Bomber Cmd Nos 12, 149 and 419 RCAF Sqdns; md Leslie Rankin Ltd Jersey 1960–92; Hon ADC to Lt-Govr of Jersey 1969–74, pres RAFA Jersey 1968–71; chm No 7 Overseas (Jersey) Sqdn ATC 1982–92, pres 1992–; *Recreations* golf; *Clubs* RAF, MCC, United (Jersey); *Style—* The Rt Hon the Lord Sandhurst, DFC; ✉ La Volière, Les Ruisseaux, St Brelade, Jersey, CI JE3 8DD (☎ 01534 46040)

SANDIFORD, Peter; OBE (1992); s of Jack Sandiford (d 1993), of Exmouth, Devon, and Joan Mary, *née* Mansell; *b* 23 May 1947; *Educ* Watford GS for Boys, UCL (BSc); *m* 1971, Yvonne, da of Harold Haffenden; 1 da (Alexandra Kate b 1974), 1 s (Eliot Paul b 1978); *Career* VSO lectr Malawi Poly 1965–66, archaeologist Miny of Public Building 1968–70; British Council: trainee Madrid 1970–71, asst rep Singapore 1971–75, regnl dir Munich 1981–82 (asst regnl dir 1975–81), staff inspr Mgmnt Gp 1982–84, dir Mgmnt Servs Dept 1984–86, dir Israel 1986–94, regnl dir E and Southern Europe 1995–96, dir Americas 1996–; *Recreations* amateur radio (licensed radio ham); *Style—* Peter Sandiford, Esq, OBE; ✉ The British Council, 10 Spring Gardens, London SW1A 2BN

SANDILANDS, *see also:* Torphichen

SANDILANDS, James Sebastian; s of Sir Francis Edwin Prescott Sandilands, CBE (d 1995), and (Susan) Gillian, *née* Jackson; *b* 15 Oct 1944; *m* 1 July 1972, Gabriele, *née* Mellich, da of Dr Theo Mellich, of Vienna; 1 s (Christopher b 1980); *Career* ptnr: Sheppards and Chase 1966–76, Buckmaster & Moore 1976–85; md Fund Mgmnt Div Credit Suisse Buckmaster & Moore 1985–90, md Quilter Goodison Co Ltd 1992–95 (asst md 1990–92); AIIMR; *Recreations* reading, walking, skiing, opera, theatre; *Style—* James Sandilands, Esq; ✉ 58 Doneraile Street, London SW6 6EP (☎ 0171 736 6923)

SANDISON, Francis Gunn; s of Capt Dr Andrew Tawse Sandison (d 1982), of Glasgow, and Dr Ann Brougham, *née* Austin; *b* 25 May 1949; *Educ* Glasgow Acad, Charterhouse, Magdalen Coll Oxford (BCL, MA); *m* 5 Sept 1981, Milva Lou, da of Prof John Emory McCaw, of Des Moines, Iowa; 1 s (Gavin b 1985); *Career* admitted slr 1974; ptnr Freshfields 1980– (asst slr 1974–80); memb: Law Soc 1974 (memb Revenue Law Ctee 1992–, chm Corporation Tax Sub-Ctee 1993–), City of London Law Soc 1980 (chm Revenue Law Sub-Ctee 1991–), Advsy Bd Fulbright Cmmn 1995–; *Books* Profit Sharing and Other Share Acquisition Schemes (1979), Whiteman on Income Tax (co-author 3 edn, 1988); *Recreations* fishing, wine, photography; *Style—* Francis Sandison, Esq; ✉ Old Barn, Old Barn Lane, Churt, Farnham, Surrey GU10 2NA (☎ 01428 607639); 3 Earl's Court Square, London SW5 9BY (☎ 0171 373 8811); Freshfields, 65 Fleet Street, London EC4Y 1HS (☎ 0171 832 7357, fax 0171 832 7001)

SANDLAND, Eric Michael (Mike); s of Eric Darnley Sandland (d 1989), and Mary Cairns, *née* Blyth (d 1956); *b* 29 April 1938; *Educ* Edinburgh Acad, Trinity Hall Cambridge (MA); *m* 1, 1961 (m dis 1965), Susan, *née* Wright; m 2, 15 Aug 1969, Jacqueline Marie-Therese, *née* Gauthier (d 1990); 3 s (James Alexander b 9 Jan 1980, Peter Michael (twin) b 9 Jan 1980, Thomas William 2 Feb 1982); m 3, 20 July 1991 (m dis 1996), Mrs Ann McMahon; *Career* Norwich Union Life Insur Soc: actuarial student 1961–64, actuarial asst 1964–66, asst sec for France (subsequently sec) 1966–69, gp statistician 1969–72, investmt mangr 1972–86, chief investmt mangr 1986–94; chm: Investmt Ctee Assoc of British Insurers 1988–90, Institutional Shareholders' Ctee 1990–92, Cadbury Ctee; FIA 1964, ASIA/AIIMR 1972; *Recreations* golf, DIY, snooker, bridge, music; *Style—* Mr E M Sandland; ✉ 35 Mount Pleasant, Norwich, Norfolk NR2 2DH (☎ 01603 454212)

SANDLE, Prof Michael Leonard; s of Charles Edward Sandle, and Dorothy Gwendoline Gladys, *née* Vernon; *b* 18 May 1936; *Educ* Douglas HS, Douglas Sch of Art and Technol Doughs, Slade Sch of Fine Art (AFA); *m* 1971 (m dis 1974), Cynthia Dora Koppel; m 2, 1988, Demelza Jane Spargo; 1 s (George Benjamin Charles b 24 May 1992); *Career* various teaching posts in Britain 1961–64, lectr Coventry Coll of Art 1964–68, visiting prof Univ of Calgary Alberta 1970–71, assoc prof Univ of Victoria BC 1972–73, prof in sculpture Fachhochschule für Gestaltung Pforzheim W Germany 1977–80 (lectr 1973–77); has participated in exhibitions internationally 1957–: V Biennale Paris 1966, Documenta IV Kassel W Germany 1968, Documenta VI 1977; works exhibited in public collections including: Arts Cncl of GB, Tate Gallery, Australian Nat Gall Canberra, Metropolitan Museum NY, Stzüki Museum Lodz, Nat Gallery of Warsaw, Wilhelm Lehmbruck Museum Duisburg W Germany, Hakone Open Air Museum Japan; prof Akademie Fur Bildenden Kunste Germany 1980–; RA 1990 (elected ARA 1980), FRBS

1994; *Style*— Prof Michael Sandle, RA; ✉ Schloss Scheibenhardt, D71635 Karlsruhe, Germany (☎ 00 49 721 8686 33)

SANDLER, Prof Joseph John; s of Solomon Sandler (d 1964), of Cape Town, South Africa, and Leah, *née* Kussel (d 1977); *b* 10 Jan 1927; *Educ* Sea Point Boys' Sch Cape Town, Univ of Cape Town (BA, MA, DSc), Univ of London (PhD), Univ of Leiden (MD); *m* 1, 21 Nov 1949, Hannah Miriam (d 1955), da of Dr Ernst Mayer (d 1975), of London; 1 da (Trudy Anne (Mrs McGuinness) b 31 Aug 1950); m 2, 21 Feb 1957, Anne-Marie, da of Col Otto Weil (d 1964), of Geneva, Switzerland; 1 s (Paul Gerard b 2 Dec 1962), 1 da (Catherine Judith (Dr Dedman) b 18 June 1958); *Career* psychoanalyst British Psychoanalytical Soc 1952–, ed British Journal of Medical Psychology 1956–62 and 1968–74, ed International Journal of Psychoanalysis 1968–78 (Internet ed 1996–), fndr ed Int Review of Psychoanalysis 1974–78, prof of psychoanalysis applied to med Univ of Leiden 1968–74, first Sigmund Freud prof of psychoanalysis Hebrew Univ of Jerusalem 1979–84, first holder Freud meml chair of psychoanalysis Univ of London 1984–92, dir Psychoanalysis Unit UCL 1984–92, emeritus prof of psychoanalysis 1992–; pres Euro Psychoanalytical Fedn 1975–79, pres Int Psychoanalytical Assoc 1989–93; sci chm Br Psychonalytical Soc 1986–90; winner Sigourney Award for Outstanding Contribs to Psychoanalysis 1995; Hon FilDr Univ of Lund 1976, Hon LLD Clark Univ 1985; FBPsS 1957 (memb 1947); *Books* Psychosomatic Aspects of Paediatrics (with R MacKeith, 1961), The Patient and the Analyst (with C Dare and A Holder, 1973, 2 ed 1992), The Technique of Child Psychoanalysis (with H Kennedy and R L Tyson, 1980), The Analysis of Defence (with Anna Freud, 1985), From Safety to Superego (1987), Projection Identification Projective Identification (1987), Dimensions of Psychoanalysis (1989), What do Psychoanalysts Want? The Problem of Aims in Psychoanalytic Therapy (with A U Dreher, 1996); *Recreations* reading, teaching, travelling; *Clubs* Reform; *Style*— Prof Joseph Sandler; ✉ 35 Circus Road, London NW8 9JG (☎ 0171 286 3937, fax 0171 289 4800, e-mail Sandler@compuserve100450,1357)

SANDLER, Prof Merton; s of late Frank Sandler, of Salford, Lancs, and the late Edith, *née* Stein; *b* 28 March 1926; *Educ* Manchester GS, Univ of Manchester (MB ChB, MD); *m* 1961, Lorna Rosemary, da of late Ian Michael Grenby, of Colindale, London; 2 s, 2 da; *Career* Capt RAMC; jr specialist in pathology 1951–53, res fell in clinical pathology Brompton Hosp 1953–54, lectr in chem pathology Royal Free Hosp Sch of Med 1955–58; prof of chem pathology Royal Postgrad Med Sch Inst of Obstetrics and Gynaecology Univ of London 1973–91 (now emeritus), conslt chem pathologist Queen Charlotte's Maternity Hosp 1958–91; visiting prof: Univ of New Mexico 1983, Chicago Med Sch 1984, Univ of S Florida 1988; recognised teacher in chem pathology 1960 (examiner various Br and foreign univs and Royal Colls); memb Standing Advsy Ctee Bd of Studies in Pathology Univ of London 1972–76 (Chem Pathology Sub Ctee 1973–); Inst of Obstetrics and Gynaecology: chm Academic Bd 1972–73, chm Bd of Mgmnt 1975–; govr: Br Postgrad Med Fedn 1976–78, Queen Charlotte's Hosp for Women; cncl memb and meetings Sec Assoc of Clinical Pathologists 1959–70, cncl memb Collegium Int Neuro-Psychopharmacologicum 1982–, hon librarian RSM 1987–93; pres: section Med Experimental Med and Therapeutics 1979–80, Br Assoc for Psychopharmacology 1980 (hon memb 1993), Br Assoc for Postnatal Illness 1980–, W London Med Chirurgical Soc 1996–97; chm tstees Nat Soc for Res into Mental Health 1983–, memb Med Advsy Cncls of Migraine Tst 1975–80 (tstee 1987–92, chm Scientific Advsy Ctee 1985–92); memb: Schizophrenia Assoc of GB 1975–78, Parkinson's Disease Soc 1981; chm and sec Biol Cncl Symposium on Drug Action 1979, memb Bd of Mgmnt and chm Awards Sub Ctee Biol Cncl 1983–91 (sec 1985–91); memb Exec Ctee: Marcé Soc 1983–86, Med Cncl on Alcoholism 1987–91, sec and memb of Cncl Harveian Soc of London 1979– (pres 1992), memb Cncl of Mgmnt and patron Helping Hand Organisation 1981–87, foreign corresponding memb American Coll of Neuropsychopharmacology 1975; hon memb: Indian Acad of Neurosciences 1982, Hungarian Pharmacological Soc 1985; jt ed: British Journal of Pharmacology 1974–80, Clinical Science 1975–77, Journal of Neural Transmission 1979–82; jt ed in chief Journal of Psychiatric Research 1982, present or past ed bd memb of 17 other sci jls; lectr to various learned socs incl: 1 Cummings Meml 1976, James E Beall II Meml 1980, Biol Cncl Lecture medal 1984; Anna Monika Int Prize for res on biological aspects of depression 1973, Gold medal Br Migraine Assoc 1974, Senator Dr Franz Burda Int Prize for res on Parkinson's disease 1988, Arnold Friedman Distinguished Clinician/Researcher award 1991; Hon DUniv Semmelweis Univ of Med Budapest 1992; FRCP, FRCPath, FRCPsych, CBiol, FIBiol; *Books* Mental Illness in Pregnancy and the Puerperium (1978), The Psychopharmacology of Aggression (1979), Enzyme Inhibitors as Drugs (1980), Amniotic Fluid and its Clinical Significance (1980), The Psychopharmacology of Alcohol (1980), The Psychopathology of Anticonvulsants (1981), Nervous Laughter (1991); jtly: The Adrenal Cortex (1961), The Thyroid Gland (1967), Advances in Pharmacology (1968), Monoamine Oxidases (1972), Serotonin - New Vistas (1974), Sexual Behaviour: Pharmacology and Biochemistry (1975), Trace Amines and the Brain (1976), Phenolsulphotransferase in Mental Health Research (1981), Tetrahydroisoquinolines and B-Carbolines (1982), Progress towards a Male Contraceptive (1982), Neurobiology of the Trace Amines (1984), Psychopharmacology and Food (1985), Neurotransmitter Interactions (1986), Design of Enzyme Inhibitors as Drugs (Vol I 1987, Vol II 1993), Progress in Catecholamine Research (1988), Migraine: A Spectrum of Ideas (1990), 5–Hydroxytryptamine in Psychiatry (1991), Genetic Research in Psychiatry (1992), Monoamine Oxidase: Basic and Clinical Aspects (1993), Migraine: Pharmacology and Genetics (1996); *Recreations* reading, listening to music, lying in the sun; *Clubs* Athenaeum; *Style*— Prof Merton Sandler

SANDLER, Michael Stephen; s of Carl Bernard Sandler, of Leeds and London, and Taube Irene Barash (d 1980); *b* 17 Oct 1947; *Educ* Leeds GS, Boston Univ (BA); *m* 1973, Gail Michele, da of Dr David Granet, JP, of Scotland; 2 s (Andrew b 1975, Jonathan b 1978); *Career* qualified chartered surveyor; Conrad Ritblat & Co 1971–78, dir Streets Financial Ltd 1979–86, md Kingsway Financial Public Relations (Saatchi & Saatchi Co) 1986–88, md Hudson Sandler Ltd 1988–; ARICS; *Recreations* tennis, theatre, cinema, golf; *Style*— Michael Sandler, Esq; ✉ 2 Marston Close, London NW6 4EU (☎ 0171 328 7510); Hudson Sandler Ltd, 29 Cloth Fair, London EC1A 7JQ (☎ 0171 796 4133)

SANDON, Viscount; (Dudley Adrian) Conroy Ryder; o s of 7 Earl of Harrowby, TD, *qv*; *b* 18 March 1951; *Educ* Eton, Univ of Newcastle upon Tyne, Magdalene Coll Cambridge (MA); *m* 1977, Sarah Nichola Hobhouse (d 1994), o da of Capt Anthony Denys Phillpotts Payne, of Carraway Barn, Carraway Lane, Marnhull, Dorset; 3 s (Hon Dudley Anthony Hugo Coventry b 5 Sept 1981, Hon Frederick Whitmore Dudley b 6 Feb 1984, Hon Henry Mansell Dudley b 13 July 1985), 1 da (Hon Emily Georgina Hobhouse b 13 Jan 1992); *Career* commercial property devpt; exec dir Compton St Securities Ltd 1988–; vice pres Staffs branch Cncl for the Protection of Rural England 1988–95, govr John Archer Sch Wandsworth 1986–88, patron The Guild of Handicraft Tst 1991–, pres The Staffordshire Soc 1995–; FRICS 1992; *Style*— Viscount Sandon; ✉ c/o Sandon Estate Office, Sandon, Stafford ST18 ODA

SANDS, Charles Francis; s of Arthur Langdale Sands (d 1954), and Margaret Soames (d 1978); *b* 9 March 1938; *Educ* Marlborough, Lincoln Coll Oxford (MA); *m* Nov 1965; 2 s (Robert b 1970, David b 1974); *Career* Nat Serv 1956–58, 2 Lt 2 RTR; slr; ptnr Herbert Smith 1972–90, ptnr Allison and Humphreys 1991–; memb: Law Soc, City of London Slrs Co; *Recreations* hunting, golf, tennis, forestry; *Clubs* RAC; *Style*— Charles Sands, Esq; ✉ Forge House, 1–c Ravensdon St, London SE11 4AQ (☎ 0171 735 7010, fax 0171 735 3773)

SANDS, (John) Derek; s of Reginald Sands (d 1971), of Manchester, and Elizabeth, *née* Whitlow (d 1988); *b* 26 Jan 1940; *Educ* Manchester GS, Univ of Manchester (LLB); *m* 1, 7 May 1966, Sylvia Rose Sands (d 1981); 1 s (Christopher Andrew b 12 April 1967), 2 da (Amanda Melanie b 19 Dec 1968, Rachel Elizabeth b 15 Oct 1972); m 2, 10 Sept 1982, Kathleen Sands; *Career* asst slr: Addleshaw Sons & Latham 1965–66 (articled clerk 1961–65), Cartwright & Backhouse 1966–67; ptnr Kirk Jackson 1968– (asst slr 1967–68); Law Soc: memb Cncl 1986–, chm Family Law Ctee 1990–91, current chm Cts and Legal Servs Ctee; chm Manchester Young Slrs' Assoc 1973–74, memn Cncl Manchester Law Soc 1974– (pres 1985–86); memb Law Soc 1965, memb Manchester Law Soc 1965; *Recreations* tennis, swimming, gymnasium pursuits, reading, music, gardening, travel, food, wine; *Clubs* Swinton & Pendlebury Rotary; *Style*— Derek Sands, Esq; ✉ Kirk Jackson, 97–101 Chorley Road, Swinton, Manchester M27 4AB (☎ 0161 794 0431, fax 0161 794 4957, mobile 0973 767174)

SANDS, Jonathan Peter; s of Peter Stuart Sands, of Buxton, Derbys, and Vivianne Anne, *née* Kidd; *b* 27 March 1961; *Educ* Normanton Sch, Stockport Coll of Technol; *m* 17 Sept 1983, Carolyn Jane, da of Norman Fletcher; 2 s (Thomas Charles b 9 March 1986, Henry George b 5 Oct 1993), 1 da (Polly Kate b 17 Sept 1992); *Career* IAS Advertising Macclesfield 1979–82, md Elmwood Design (pt of The Charles Wall Group before MBO 1989) 1985– (joined 1982); recipient numerous design awards incl Design Effectiveness, Clio, Mobius, Int Brand Packaging and NY Festivals; chm DBA 1995–97 (formerly dir); regular lectr at business confs, seminars and at univs on BA and MBA courses; memb DBA, FCSD; *Recreations* fast cars; *Clubs* Groucho's, Harrogate Golf; *Style*— Jonathan Sands, Esq; ✉ Elmwood Design, Elmwood House, Ghyll Royd, Guiseley, Leeds LS20 9LT (☎ 01943 870229, fax 01943 870191)

SANDS, Lawrence Alfred; s of Alfred Lawrence Sands (d 1971), of Weaverham, Cheshire, and Edith Carlihoe, *née* Wright (d 1972); *b* 21 March 1928; *Educ* Northwich Tech Coll, Mid Cheshire Coll of Art & Design; *m* 27 Feb 1953, Jean, da of Arnold Bebbington; 1 s (Stephen Duncan b 28 July 1967), 1 da (Jill Amanda b 28 Jan 1960); *Career* photographer; lectr in portraiture and wedding photography UK, Europe, USA and N Africa; BIPP: licentiate in wedding photography 1959, assoc in commercial photography 1969, N W regnl chm 1972–73, fell in portraiture 1979, chm of A & Q Bd Gen Practice 1989; subject of video 'Award Winning Portraits by Lawrence A Sands'; FRSA 1961, ARPS 1978; *Awards* Ilford Award for Portraiture 1972, Ilford Award for Wedding Photography 1974, BIPP Portrait Award N W Region 1979, BIPP Wedding Photographer of the Year 1982, Craftsman Degree for Services to Photography Professional Photographers of America 1986, BIPP President's Award for Services to Photography 1988, Fuji Professional Award for Services to Photographic Educn 1990; *Recreations* aircraft and flying, old movies (Keaton, Chaplin, Laurel & Hardy, Harold Lloyd), gardening; *Style*— Lawrence Sands, Esq; ✉ Fairways, Malt Kiln Road, Plumley, Knutsford, Cheshire WA16 OTS (☎ 01565 722596); Lawrence Sands, Photographic Services, 8 Malt Rd, Plumley, Knutsford, Cheshire WA16 OTS

SANDS, Peter; s of John Sands, of Whitley Bay, Tyne & Wear, and Jane Caroline, *née* Reay (d 1984); *b* 16 May 1955; *Educ* Whitley Bay GS, Huddersfield Poly (BA); *m* 29 March 1986, Pamela Jean, da of William Maurice Hutchinson; 2 s (Jack William b 1 March 1987, Daniel Peter b 12 July 1988), 1 da (Anna Jane b 24 Feb 1993); *Career* reporter Shields Weekly News (N Shields) 1977–79, sub ed The Northern Echo 1979–81, chief sub ed The Evening Despatch (Darlington) 1981–84; The Northern Echo: night ed 1984–86, asst ed 1986–89, dep ed 1989–90, ed 1990–93; devpt ed Westminster Press 1993–95, dir The Editorial Centre Ltd 1995–; awards (for The Northern Echo): Newspaper Design Award for Provincial Morning Newspapers, Freedom of Information Newspaper Award, Newspaper Indust Awards for Design and Use of Photography 1991, NE Newspaper of the Year 1991; memb Guild of Br Newspaper Eds 1990; *Recreations* spending time with the family, Newcastle Utd FC, Durham CCC, country pubs, newspapers, literature; *Clubs* Durham CCC (vice pres and co-fndr); *Style*— Peter Sands, Esq; ✉ The Editorial Centre, Hanover House, Marine Court, St Leonards, East Sussex (☎ 01424 435991, fax 01424 445547)

SANDS, Philippa Lesley (Pippa); da of Leslie Sands, of Upton, Didcot, Oxfordshire, and Gladys (Bunnie), *née* Robson; *b* 3 Feb 1959; *Educ* Didcot Girls' GS, Univ of Leeds (BSc); *m* Ronald Bruce Owen Burnett, s of Lt-Col Ronald Burnett, OBE; *Career* mktg trainee to product mangr Colgate Palmolive Ltd 1980–82, PR mangr Sterling Health 1985–87 (mktg sr brand mangr 1982–85), dep md Biss Lancaster plc 1989– (account mangr 1987–89, assoc dir 1988–89, dir 1989–94), md Sandpiper Communications 1996–; *Recreations* competitive horse riding (dressage); *Style*— Ms Pippa Sands; ✉ Brockwood, Soldridge, Hants GU34 5QG

SANDS, Roger Blakemore; s of Thomas Blakemore Sands (d 1980), and Edith Malyon, *née* Waldram (d 1986); *b* 6 May 1942; *Educ* Univ Coll Sch Hampstead, Oriel Coll Oxford (scholar, MA); *m* 24 Sept 1966, Jennifer Ann, da of Hugh T Cattell (d 1992); 2 da (b 1972 and 1974); *Career* Clerks Dept House of Commons 1965–, sec to House of Commons Cmmn 1985–87; princ clerk of: Overseas Office 1987–91, Select Ctees and (registrar of Members' Interests) 1991–94, Public Bills 1994–; sec History of Parliament Tst 1974–80, chm Study of Parliament Gp 1993–96 (memb 1970–); *Style*— Roger Sands, Esq; ✉ Public Bill Office, House of Commons, London SW1A 0AA (☎ 0171 219 3000)

SANDWICH, 11 Earl of (E 1660); John Edward Hollister Montagu; also Viscount Hinchingbrooke and Baron Montagu (both E 1660); s of (Alexander) Victor Edward Paulet Montagu (10 Earl of Sandwich, who disclaimed peerages for life 1964; d 1995), and his 1 w, (Maud) Rosemary, *née* Peto; *b* 11 April 1943; *Educ* Eton, Trinity Coll Cambridge (MA); *m* 1 July 1968, (Susan) Caroline, o da of Rev Canon Perceval Ecroyd Cobham Hayman, of Cocking, nr Midhurst, Sussex; 2 s (Viscount Hinchingbrooke, Hon Orlando William b 1971), 1 da ((Lady) Jemima Mary b 1973); *Heir* s, Luke Timothy Charles Montagu, Viscount Hinchingbrooke b 5 Dec 1969; *Career* freelance journalist and editorial conslt; info offr Christian Aid 1974–86, ed Save the Children Fund 1987–92; *Books* Book of the World (1971), Prospects for Africa (jt ed, 1988), Prospects for Africa's Children (1990), Children at Crisis Point (1992); *Style*— The Rt Hon the Earl of Sandwich; ✉ House of Lords, London SW1A OPW

SANDYS, Julian George Winston; QC (1983); s (by 1 m) of Baron Duncan-Sandys, CH, PC; does not use courtesy title of Hon; *b* 1936; *m* 1970, Elisabeth Jane, only da of John Besley Martin, CBE, of Kenton; 3 s, 1 da; *Career* called to the Bar Inner Temple 1959 and Gray's Inn 1970; *Recreations* flying small aeroplanes; *Style*— Julian Sandys, Esq, QC

SANDYS, 7 Baron (UK 1802); Richard Michael Oliver Hill; DL (Worcs 1968); s of 6 Baron Sandys, DL (d 1961), and Cynthia Mary (d 1990), o da of Col Frederic Richard Thomas Trench-Gascoigne, DSO; *b* 21 July 1931; *Educ* RNC Dartmouth; *m* 1961, Patricia Simpson, da of late Capt Lionel Hall, MC; *Heir* The Marquess of Downshire; *Career* sits as a Cons peer in the House of Lords; late Lt Royal Scots Greys; patron of one living; a lord-in-waiting to HM the Queen Jan to March 1974, oppn whip House of Lords 1974–79, Capt HM Body Guard of the Yeomen of the Guard (govt dep chief whip in House of Lords) 1979–82; Liveryman Worshipful Co of Goldsmiths; FRGS; *Clubs* Cavalry & Guards'; *Style*— The Lord Sandys, DL; ✉ Ombersley Court, Droitwich, Worcs WR9 0HH (☎ 01905 620220)

SANFORD, Prof Anthony John; s of Edwin Sanford (d 1970), and Winnifred Olive, *née* Hurdman (d 1981); *b* 5 July 1944; *Educ* Waverley GS, Univ of Leeds (BSc), Pembroke Coll Cambridge (PhD); *m* 1, 3 Sept 1966 (m dis 1986), Valerie Ann, da of Frank Hines (d 1972); 1 da (Bridget Isobel b 27 March 1970); m 2, 24 Jan 1987, Linda Mae, da of John Moxey; 1 s (Anthony Iain Moxey b 2 May 1992), 1 da (Heather Margaret Moxey b 4 May 1995); *Career* lectr in psychology Univ of Dundee 1971–74; Dept of Psychology Univ of Glasgow: sr lectr 1974–80, reader 1980–82, prof 1983–, head of dept 1983–86; Gifford lectr in natural theology 1983; FBPsS, CPsychol; *Books* Understanding Written Language (with S Garrod, 1981), Models, Mind and Man (1983), Cognition and Cognitive Psychology (1985), The Mind of Man (1987), Communicating Quantities (with L Moxey, 1993); *Recreations* hill-walking (Munroist 1991), industrial archeology, music, cooking; *Style*— Prof Anthony Sanford; ✉ Department of Psychology, University of Glasgow G12 (☎ 0141 330 4058, fax 0141 339 8889)

SANGER, Dr Frederick; OM (1986), CH (1981), CBE (1963); s of Frederick Sanger, and Cicely, *née* Crewdson; *b* 13 Aug 1918; *Educ* Bryanston, St John's Coll Cambridge; *m* 1940, M Joan, da of Alfred Howe; 2 s, 1 da; *Career* res scientist Univ Biochemistry Laboratory and MRC Laboratory of Molecular Biol Cambridge 1951–83, ret; winner Nobel Prize for Chemistry 1958 (jt winner 1980); Hon DSc Cambridge 1983; FRS; *Style*— Dr Frederick Sanger, OM, CH, CBE, FRS; ✉ Far Leys, Fen Lane, Swaffham Bulbeck, Cambridge CB5 0NJ (☎ 01223 811610)

SANGER, James Gerald; s of Gerald Fountain Sanger, CBE, JP (d 1981), and (Margaret) Hope Sanger, MBE, *née* Munroe (d 1994); *b* 29 April 1939; *Educ* Shrewsbury, Worcester Coll Oxford (MA), Harvard Business Sch (MBA); *m* 21 Sept 1968, Madeline Mary, da of George William Jack Collis (d 1986); 1 s (Christopher James b 1970), 1 da (Katherine Hope b 1972); *Career* Farrow Bersey Gain Vincent & Co 1962–63 (articled 1957–59), asst to chm Associated Newspapers 1966–68 (joined 1963), md First Investors Ltd 1969–75, dir Henderson Administration 1974–75; fin dir: Blyth Greene Jourdain 1975–77, James Burrough plc 1977–84; exec dir: Tomkins plc 1985–88, Peek plc 1988–; govr: Benenden Sch, Shrewsbury Sch; FCA 1973; *Recreations* squash, tennis, travel, listening; *Clubs* Hurlingham, RAC; *Style*— James Sanger, Esq; ✉ Moreton House, Brightwell-cum-Sotwell, Oxon OX10 0PT (☎ 01491 833655); Peek plc, 309 Reading Road, Henley-on-Thames, Oxon RG9 1EL (☎ 01491 415200, fax 01491 414404)

SANGER, Peter John; s of Percy James Sanger, of Eastcote, Pinner, Middx, and Maude Elizabeth, *née* Smith; *b* 18 Oct 1936; *Educ* Merchant Taylors', Open Univ (BA); *Career* Nat Serv 2 Lt RAOC 1957–59; asst then photographer Thomas Fall Studios 1954–57, lectr Sch of Photography Kodak Ltd 1959–62, lectr then sr lectr in photography Harrow Tech Coll 1962–72, princ lectr in photography Ealing Tech Coll 1972–74, head Dept of Audio-Visual Studies West Surrey Coll of Art and Design 1977–87 (head Dept of Photography 1974–77), asst dir and head Maidstone Coll Kent Inst of Art and Design 1988– (princ Maidstone Coll 1987–88), dir KIAD Enterprises Ltd 1991; photographs published in many books and author numerous articles; exhibitions incl: Points of Contact (Royal Festival Hall) 1969, Images of Malta (Cwlth Inst) 1983, Visited Places (solo, touring); FBIPP 1969, FRPS 1975; *Recreations* travel, photography, classical music, opera; *Style*— Peter Sanger, Esq; ✉ Heddon's Gate, 67 Charlesford Avenue, Kingswood, Maidstone, Kent ME17 3PH (☎ 01622 842193); Kent Institute of Art and Design, Oakwood Park, Maidstone, Kent ME16 8AG (☎ 01622 757286, fax 01622 692003)

SANGSTER, Bruce; s of George Robertson Sangster, and Marie, *née* Davidson; *b* 12 March 1954; *Educ* Broxburn Acad Broxburn; *m* 22 Sept 1979, Jacqueline E R, da of John MacMillan Willison; 1 s (Jamie Sangster b 15 Aug 1982); *Career* commis chef then sr sous chef Old Course Hotel (British Transport Hotels) 1971–80, lectr Kingsway Tech Coll Dundee 1980–81; chef de cuisine: Kirroughtree Hotel Newton Stewart 1981–82, Rothley Court Hotel Rothley Leicestershire 1982–86, Balcraig House Hotel Scone Perthshire 1986–87; exec chef: Murrayshall Country House Hotel Scone Perthshire 1987–93, Lehman Brothers London 1993–; *Awards* Silver Catch Fish Cookery award 1977, Gold medal Cold Fish Dish 1979, Bronze medal Fat Sculpture 1979, Gold medal Gourmet Entrée Dish 1981, semi finalist Br Chef of The Year 1982, finalist Br Chef of The Year 1984 and 1988, third prize Br Chef of The Year 1986 and 1990, AA rosette 1986–87, 1989 and 1990, Michelin Red M award 1987 and 1988, Taste of Scotland Restaurant of the Year 1988, Scottish Hotel Guide Restaurant of the Year 1989, Silver and Bronze award as memb Br Culinary Team at Food Asia '90 1990, winner Egon Ronay British Lamb Chef 1990, Hotel awarded Newcomer of The Year 1990, memb Culinary Olympic Team for Frankfurt 1990, Gold medal St Andrews Food Festival 1991, Gold medal Fat Sculpture Scothot Glasgow 1991, 3 AA Rosettes at Murrayshall 1991, Gold and Bronze medals at Culinary Olympics in Frankfurt (capt Scottish team) 1992, capt British team for Food Asia in Singapore 1994 (Gold medal Nat Hot Kitchen, Silver medal Nat Team Buffet, Nayati Trophy for Most Outstanding Nat Hot Team), third Kikkomans Master Chef of Great Britain 1994, Best Competiton Chef Award Craft Guild of Chefs 1995, Gold medals Team Buffet and Hot Kitchen Hotel Olympia Open Grand Prix 1996, capt Br Nat Team Berlin Culinary Olympics 1996, capt Scottish Nat Team World Culinary Championships Scot Hot Glasgow 1997; entries in Good Food Guide and Egon Ronay 1981–; memb Steering Ctee Scottish Chefs' Assoc 1993; CFA 1975; memb: Master Chefs of GB 1985– (chm Scot Div 1989–), Craft Guild of Chefs 1990; *Style*— Bruce Sangster, Esq; ✉ Lehman Brothers International, One Broadgate, London EC2M 7HA

SANGSTER, Nigel; *Educ* Repton, Univ of Leeds (LLB); *Career* called to the Bar Middle Temple 1976, in practice specialising in criminal law 1977–, head of chambers 1995–; memb Bar Cncl 1994–; *Style*— Nigel Sangster, Esq; ✉ St Paul's Chambers, 5th Floor, St Paul's House, 23 Park Square South, Leeds LS1 2ND (☎ 0113 245 5866, fax 0113 245 5807, mobile 0374 471655)

SANGSTER, Robert Edmund; s of Vernon Edmund Sangster (d 1988), and Margaret Martha Sangster; *b* 23 May 1936; *Educ* Repton; *m* 1 (m dis), Christine; 3 s (Guy, Ben, Adam), 1 da (Kate); m 2 (m dis); m 3, 13 Aug 1985, Susan Mary, da of M Dean, of Isle of Man, and formerly wife of Peter Lilley; 2 s (Sam b 1987, Max Edmund b 1990); *Career* chm: Vernons Organisation 1976–88, Sangster Group Ltd 1988–91; dir Newmarket Thoroughbred Breeders plc 1985–; owner of: The Minstrel (won Derby 1977), Alleged (won Prix de l'Arc de Triomphe 1977 and 1978), Detroit (won Prix de l'Arc de Triomphe 1980) Beldare Ball (won Melbourne Cup 1980), Our Paddy Boy (won Australian Jockey Club Cup 1981), Golden Fleece (won Derby 1982), Assert (won Irish Sweeps Derby 1982), Lomond (won 2000 Guineas 1983), Caerleon (won French Derby 1983), El Gran Señor (won 2000 Guineas and Irish Sweeps Derby 1984), Sadler's Wells (won Irish 2000 Guineas 1984), Gildoran (won Ascot Gold Cup 1984 and 1985 and Goodwood Cup 1984), Committed (won Prix de l'Abbaye de Longchamp and was champion Euro sprinter and Royal Heroine champion of Grass Mare USA 1984), Marooned (won Sydney Cup 1986), Rodrigo de Triano (won 5 gp 1 races, English 2000 Guineas, Irish 2000 Guineas, Middle Park Stakes, Champion Stakes and Juddmonte at York); owner of largest number of winning racehorses 1977, 1978, 1982, 1983 and 1984; *Recreations* golf; *Clubs* Jockey; *Style*— Robert Sangster, Esq; ✉ The Nunnery, Douglas, Isle of Man (☎ 01624 623351); Porte des Isles, Mougins, Cannes, France (☎ 00 33 93 900097); Janes Harbour, Sandy Lane, St James, Barbados (☎ 00 1 809 436 1241); Sangster Group Ltd, Wood Park, Neston, South Wirral L64 7TB (☎ 0151 336 8898, fax 0151 336 8517)

SANKEY, Guy Richard; QC (1991); s of Graham Richard Sankey (d 1996), and Joan, *née* Harrowven (d 1975); *b* 2 April 1944; *Educ* Marlborough, New Coll Oxford (MA Jurisprudence); *m* 1969, Pauline, da of Gerald William Lewis Lamotte; 3 da; *Career* called the Bar Inner Temple 1966, jr counsel to the Crown (Common Law) 1987–91, recorder of the Crown Court 1992–; Liveryman Worshipful Co of Drapers; *Recreations* golf, tennis, skiing; *Clubs* Denham Golf; *Style*— Guy Sankey, QC; ✉ 1 Temple Gardens, Temple, London EC4Y 9BB (☎ 0171 583 1315)

SANKEY, John Anthony; CMG (1983); o s of Henry and Ivy Sankey, of Plumstead Common; *b* 8 June 1930; *Educ* Cardinal Vaughan Sch, Peterhouse Cambridge (MA), NATO Def Coll Rome; *m* 1958, Gwendoline, da of Stanley and Winifred Putman, of Croxley Green; 2 s, 2 da; *Career* Lt RA, served Singapore and Malaya 1951–53; Colonial Office 1953–61, FCO: New York 1961, Guyana 1968, Singapore 1971, Malta 1973, The Hague 1975, special cnsllr African Affrs FCO 1979, high cmmr to Tanzania 1982; perm rep (with personal rank of ambass) to UN, GATT and other int orgns in Geneva 1985–90; sec gen Society of London Art Dealers 1991–96, Britain-Tanzania Soc 1991–; KHS 1996; *Style*— John Sankey, Esq, CMG; ✉ 108 Lancaster Gate, London W2 3NW (☎ and fax 0171 723 2256)

SANKEY, Sara Louise; da of Brian Halsall, of Southport, Merseyside, and Patricia Alice Joy, *née* Austin; *b* 29 Sept 1967; *Educ* Stanley HS; *m* 26 March 1988, Nigel John Sankey, s of Jack Sankey; 1 s (Scott b 17 Nov 1990), 1 da (Sophie b 3 Oct 1994); *Career* badminton player (ladies doubles and mixed doubles); over 240 appearances Churchtown Badminton Club 1979–; England rep at all levels under 12 to sr, currently 68 caps; GB rep Olympic Games Barcelona 1992; honours incl: Silver medal Euro Jr Championships, nat singles and doubles titles all age gps, Gold medals ladies doubles and team event and Silver medal mixed doubles Cwlth Games 1990, winner ladies doubles Dutch Open and Canadian Open 1991, runner-up World Cup ladies Doubles 1992; *Recreations* golf, cooking, looking after my son and daughter; *Style*— Mrs Sara Sankey; ✉ c/o Southport Badminton Club, Drill Hall, Manchester Road, Southport, Merseyside

SANKEY, Vernon Louis; s of Edward Sankey (d 1982), and Marguerite Elizabeth Louise, *née* Van Maurik (d 1962); *b* 9 May 1949; *Educ* Harrow, Oriel Coll Oxford (MA); *m* 5 June 1976, Elizabeth, da of Tom Knights; 3 s (James Edward b 12 May 1979, Mark Henry b 14 July 1981 (twin), William Thomas b 1 Feb 1985), 1 da (Angela Louise b 14 July 1981 (twin)); *Career* Reckitt & Colman plc: mgmnt trainee Food & Drink UK 1971–74, asst mangr Fin & Planning HQ London 1974–76, dir of planning Europe France 1976–78, gen mangr Denmark 1978–80, PA to Chm and Chief Exec HQ 1980–81, md France 1981–85, md Food & Drink Norwich 1985–89, chm and chief exec Reckitt & Colman Inc USA 1989–91, gp dir N America 1989–91, bd memb 1991–, chief exec 1992–; non-exec dir Pearson plc 1993–; memb Int Advsy Bd Korn/Ferry Carré/Orban International 1994–; memb Bd Grocery Mfrs of America (GMA) 1995–; FIMgt 1992, MInstD 1995, memb Mktg Soc 1995; *Recreations* jogging, tennis; *Clubs* Leander (Henley); *Style*— Vernon Sankey, Esq; ✉ Reckitt & Colman plc, One Burlington Lane, London W4 2RW (☎ 0181 747 5615, fax 0181 747 5649)

SANT-CASSIA, Louis Joseph; s of Maj Henri Emmanuel Sant-Cassia, ED (d 1990), of St Paul's Bay, Malta, and Anna, *née* De Piro Gourgion (d 1995); *b* 19 Sept 1946; *Educ* Lyceum Malta, Royal Univ of Malta (MD), Univ of Nottingham (DM); *m* 11 July 1974, Antoinette, da of Gerald H Ferro, MVO, MBE, of Sliema, Malta; 1 s (Henri b 1977), 1 da (Emma b 1980); *Career* cmmnd 1 Bn King's Own Malta Regt 1968–72; res fell Dept of Obstetrics and Gynaecology Nottingham 1981–83, conslt obstetrician and gynaecologist Coventry 1987–; Coventry Dist tutor RCOG 1988–94; visiting sr clinical lectr Univ of Warwick 1993; chm: Coventry Med Res and Ethics Ctee, Med Advsy Ctee Warwickshire Nuffield Hosp; author various pubns on gynaecological oncology, subfertility and recurrent spontaneous abortions; goalkeeper Malta water polo team Med Games 1967; FRCOG 1992 (MRCOG 1979); *Recreations* sailing, gardening, melitensia; *Style*— Louis Joseph Sant-Cassia, Esq; ✉ 11 Dalton Rd, Earlsdon, Coventry CV5 6PB; Four Winds, Stoneleigh Rd, Blackdown, Leamington Spa, Warwicks CV32 6QR (☎ 01926 422147)

SANTER, Rt Rev Mark; *see:* Birmingham, Bishop of

SANTS, Hector William Hepburn; s of (Hector) John Sants, of Finlarig, Killin, Perthshire, and Elsie Ann Watt Hepburn; *b* 15 Dec 1955; *Educ* Clifton, Corpus Christi Coll Oxford (MA); *m* 21 Dec 1987, Caroline Jane, da of Kenneth Ord Mackenzie; 3 s (Hector Alexander b 9 Jan 1989, Edward Kenneth Richard b 16 Oct 1990, Arthur Frederick Joseph b 15 May 1994); *Career* Phillips & Drew stockbrokers: joined 1977, ptnr 1984; dir Phillips & Drew International 1984–86 (md and head NY office 1986–87), first vice pres and head of int securities Union Bank of Switzerland Securities Inc NY 1987–88, head of worldwide broker res Union Bank of Switzerland 1988, head of equities and vice chm UBS (formerly UBS Phillips & Drew) 1988–; memb: Stock Exchange Settlement Servs Bd 1990, Securities and Futures Authy Bd 1993–94, UK Markets Ctee LSE 1994–; ASIA 1979, memb Int Stock Exchange 1984; *Recreations* gardening, stalking, shooting; *Style*— Hector Sants, Esq; ✉ UBS Ltd, 100 Liverpool St, London EC2 2RH (☎ 0171 901 3333)

SAPHIR, Nicholas Peter George; s of Emanuel Saphir, MBE, and Anne Saphir; *b* 30 Nov 1944; *Educ* City of London, Univ of Manchester (LLB); *m* 1971, Ena, da of Raphael Bodin; 1 s; *Career* barr; main bd dir The Albert Fisher Group plc (chief exec Fresh Produce Div), formerly non-exec dir Dairy Crest Ltd, formerly chm Hunter Saphir PLC; former chm: Br Israel C of C, Food From Britain; former memb Food & Drinks EDC; *Recreations* modern art; *Clubs* Farmers'; *Style*— Nicholas Saphir, Esq; ✉ The Albert Fisher Group PLC, C Sefton Park, Bells Hill, Stoke Poges, Bucks SL2 4HS (☎ 01753 677877, fax 01753 664338)

SAPOCHNIK, Carlos Luis; s of Leon Sapochnik (d 1985), of Argentina, and Clara Aronovich; *b* 18 July 1944; *Educ* Buenos Aires Nat Univ, Royal Coll of Art (MA), City Univ; *m* 1966, Victoria, da of Vicente Rosenberg; 1 s (Miquel Vicente b 21 July 1974), 1 da (Manuela Maria b 8 Sept 1972); *Career* freelance graphic designer and illustrator 1970–92; art dir Free Association Books 1984–88, creative dir Burnett Associates 1988–90, dir The Running Head Ltd; publishing clients incl: Methuen & Co, Tavistock Publications, Routledge, Hutchinson Educnl; local govt clients incl: London Borough of Hackney, GLC; theatre clients incl: Royal Court Theatre, Haymarket Leicester, Lyric Hammersmith; other clients incl: Midland Bank, CBS Records; pt/t lectr in graphic design: Chelsea Sch of Art 1981–84, Bath Acad of Art 1982–86; princ lectr in visual communication design Middx Univ 1990–; solo drawing exhibitions: Vortex Gallery 1989, Argile Gallery 1990, Diorama Gallery 1994, Espace Amigorena Paris 1994; two-man drawing exhibitions: Boundary Gallery 1988, Ben Uri Gallery 1996; group exhibitions incl: Dublin Arts Festival 1975, Warsaw Poster Biennale 1976, 1978 and 1980, Lahti Poster Biennale Finland 1978, 1979 and 1983, Brno Graphic Design Biennale Czechoslovakia 1984, 1986, 1988 and 1992, London Group Open 1992, Riviera Gallery 1994, Rexel Derwent Open 1994, Pastel Soc 1994, Ben Uri Gallery 1994, Cheltenham Open 1996; FCSD 1991, memb Soc of Typographic Designers 1987; *Style*— Carlos Sapochnik, Esq; ✉ 6 Ridge Rd, London N8 9LG (☎ 0181 340 4873)

SAPPER, Alan Louis Geoffrey; s of late Max Sapper, and Kate Sapper; *b* 18 March 1931; *Educ* Upper Latymer Sch, Univ of London, Royal Botanic Gardens Kew; *m* Dr Helen Sapper, *née* Rubens; 1 s (Simon), 1 da (Sarah); *Career* gen sec: Writers' Guild of GB 1964–67, Assoc of Cinematograph TV and Allied Technicians 1969–91 (hon memb

1991–); jt gen-sec Broadcasting Cine and TV Entertainment Union 1991–92; memb Gen Cncl TUC 1970–84 (chm 1982); pres: Fedn of Entertainments Unions 1970–91, Int Fedn of Audio-Visual Workers 1974–91; fndr md Interconnect AV global film and TV prodn 1991–; govr: Hammersmith Hosp 1965–72, BFI 1974, Ealing Coll of Higher Educn 1976–78, Nat Film and TV Sch 1980–; chm League for Democracy in Greece 1970; *Publications* On Licence (stage play), Kith and Kin (stage play), The Return (TV play); articles, short stories; *Recreations* taxonomic botany, hill-walking, politics, human nature; *Style—* Alan Sapper, Esq; ✉ 3 Boston Gardens, Chiswick, London W4 2QJ (☎ 0181 742 8512/8313, fax 0181 742 8543)

SAPSFORD, Ralph Neville; s of Roland Geoffrey Sapsford (d 1973), of SA, and Doreen Inez Sapsford; *b* 30 Oct 1938; *Educ* St Andres's Sch Bloemfontein Orange Free State SA, Univ of Cape Town (MB ChB, ChM, class medal for jurisprudence), RCS (cert of completion of higher trg); *m* (m dis 1981) Simone André; 2 s (Wayne b 19 Sept 1965, Lance b 2 Jan 1967), 1 da (Andrea b 18 July 1970); *Career* MPILO Central Hosp Bulawayo Rhodesia: pre-registration house offr in gen surgery then gen med 1963, sr house offr in accident and orthopaedics then gen surgery 1964, registrar in gen surgery 1965; sr house offr in: radiotherapy Western Gen Hosp Edinburgh 1966, orthopaedics Princess Margaret Rose Hosp Edinburgh 1966–67; registrar in cardiothoracic surgery Papworth Hosp Cambridge 1967–68, asst lectr in cardiac surgery Manchester Royal Infirmary 1968; sr registrar in: cardiothoracic surgery Killingbeck Hosp Leeds 1968–69, cardiac surgery Nat Heart Hosp London 1970, cardiothoracic surgery The Middx Hosp London 1970–71; res fell in cardiovascular surgery Dept of Surgery Univ of Alabama Birmingham USA 1972–73, sr registrar in thoracic surgery Harefield Hosp Uxbridge Middx 1974–75; Hammersmith Hosp London: sr registrar in cardiothoracic surgery 1971–72, 1973–74 and 1976–77, conslt/sr lectr in thoracic surgery 1977, ret 1989; hon conslt cardiothoracic surgn to St Mary's Hosp London 1981–90, in private practice Humana Hosp Wellington St John's Wood and Harley St 1990–; B merit award NHS 1987 (C merit award 1983); author of numerous learned articles and pubns; Freeman City of London, memb Worshipful Soc of Apothecaries; FRCS 1967; memb: Soc of Cardiothoracic Surgns GB and I 1969, Br Cardiac Soc 1977, Euro Soc of Cardio-Vascular Surgns 1977; *Recreations* collecting antique pistols and old Jaguars, cabinet making; *Clubs* United Wards; *Style—* Ralph Sapsford, Esq; ✉ 66 Harley St, London W1N 1AE

SAR, HE Gabriel Alexandre; s of Charles Lamine Sar (d 1966), and Anna-Marie, *née* Ka (d 1984); *b* 8 Feb 1945; *Educ* Lycée Faidherbe and Van Vollenhoven Senegal, Univ of Rennes France (BA), Brevet Ecole Nationale d'Administration Senegal, Cert in Diplomatic Studies (Oxford); *m* 16 Dec 1978, Christiane Renée, *née* Vilasco; 1 da (Karine b 22 April 1977), 2 s (Mayécor Charles Lamine b 23 April 1981, Loïc-Alexandre Sar b 9 Dec 1986); *Career* Senegalese diplomat; head Translation Dept Miny of Foreign Affrs 1977–80, first cnsllr London 1980–85, min-cnsllr and head Protocol Dept Foreign Miny 1985–88, min-cnsllr i/c conf and protocol matters at Miny which organised Francophone (May 1989) and Islamic (Dec 1991) Summits held at Dakar 1989–91, diplomatic advsr to Pres Abdou Diouf 1992–93, ambass of the Republic of Senegal to Ct of St James's 1993–; *Recreations* tennis, music, reading; *Style—* HE Monsieur Gabriel Sar; ✉ Senegalese Embassy, 21–24 Cockspur Street, London SW1Y 5BN (☎ 0171 930 7606)

SARCH, Yvonne (The Lady Finsberg); da of Albert Wright (d 1971), and Edith Abigail, *née* Bingham, of Strabane, NI; *b* 13 Nov 1940; *Educ* Clarendon Sch N Wales, Trinity Coll Univ of Dublin (MA), Univ of Manchester (DMS), Univ of London (MA, DipFE); *m* 1, 1967 (m dis 1988), Michael Sarch; 2 s (Patrick b 1968, Adam b 1970); m 2, 1990, Baron Finsberg MBE, JP (Life Peer) (d 1996); *Career* Home Office 1963–65, headmistress Fir Close Sch Lincs 1965–67, lectr Brunel Univ 1967–70, tutor Open Univ 1970–72, conslt James Morrell & Assocs 1972–75, independent economist and managing conslt UK and USA 1975–88, Korn/Ferry International 1988–91, fndr dir Sarch Search International (SSI) 1990–, exec search ptnr Howgate Sable & Partners London 1995–; memb Cncl: RSA, Int Centre for Briefing Farnham Castle; memb Forum International UK; *Books* How to be Headhunted (1990), How to be Headhunted Across Europe (1992); *Recreations* thinking, travelling, tapestry, thrillers; *Style—* Yvonne Sarch; ✉ Howgate Sable & Partners, 35 Curzon Street, London W1V 7AE (☎ 0171 495 1234, fax 0171 495 1700)

SARELL, Sir Roderick Francis Gisbert; KCMG (1968, CMG 1958), KCVO (1971); 2 s of Philip Sarell (d 1942), of Braeside, Ashurstwood, E Grinstead; *b* 23 Jan 1913; *Educ* Radley, Magdalen Coll Oxford; *m* 1946, Pamela Muriel (d 1994), da of Vivian Crowther-Smith; 3 s (Philip, William, Charles); *Career* entered Consular Service 1936, cnsllr and consul gen Rangoon 1953–56, consul gen Algiers 1956–59, cnsllr FO 1960–63; ambass: Libya 1964–69, Turkey 1969–73; Coronation Medal 1953; FRSA 1973; *Clubs* Oriental, Leander, Royal Over-Seas League; *Style—* Sir Roderick Sarell, KCMG, KCVO; ✉ The Litten, Hampstead Norreys, Newbury, Berks (☎ 01635 201274)

SARGANT, Sir (Henry) Edmund; kt (1969); s of Rt Hon Sir Charles Sargant, Lord Justice of Appeal; *b* 24 May 1906; *Educ* Rugby, Trinity Coll Cambridge; *m* 1930, Mary Kathleen (d 1979), da of Tom Lemmey; 1 s; m 2, 1981, Evelyn Noel, *née* Arnold-Wallinger; *Career* served WWII RAF; slr 1930, ptnr Radcliffes & Co 1930–71; pres Law Soc 1968–69; memb Ct of Assts Worshipful Co of Merchant Taylors; *Style—* Sir Edmund Sargant; ✉ 902 Keyes House, Dolphin Square, London SW1V 3NB

SARGANT, Prof Naomi Ellen (Lady McIntosh of Haringey); da of Tom Sargant, OBE, JP (d 1988), of London; *b* 10 Dec 1933; *Educ* Friends Sch Walden, Bedford Coll London; *m* 1, 1954, Peter Joseph Kelly; 1 s (David); m 2, 1962, Andrew Robert McIntosh (Baron McIntosh of Haringey, *qv*); 2 s (Francis, Philip); *Career* pro vice-chllr Student Affairs The Open Univ 1974–78, prof of applied social res 1978–81; chm Nat Gas Consumers' Cncl 1977–80; memb: Nat Consumer Cncl 1978–81, Cmmn on Energy and Environment 1978–81; pres Nat Soc for Clean Air 1981–83; sr commissioning ed (educn) C4 TV 1981–89; actg chief exec The Open Poly 1990, dep chm Poly of E London 1989–92, pres Highgate Hort Soc 1990–; exec memb Nat Inst of Adult Continuing Educn (NIACE) 1992–, pro-chllr Univ of East London 1992–94, vice chm NCVO 1992–, visiting prof Open University 1994–; FRSA, hon fell Royal Coll of Art, MRTS, memb BAFTA; *Recreations* gardening, photography; *Style—* Prof Naomi Sargant; ✉ 27 Hurst Avenue, London N6 5TX (☎ 0181 340 1496, fax 0181 348 4641)

SARGENT, Prof John Reid; s of Alexander George Sargent, of Aberdeen, and Annie, *née* Reid (d 1977); *b* 12 Oct 1936; *Educ* Buckie HS, Robert Gordon's Coll Aberdeen, Univ of Aberdeen (BSc, PhD); *m* 1961, Elizabeth Jean, da of James Buchan; 2 da (Dr Carol Anne Sargent b 1963, Fiona Jean b 1966); *Career* res fell Courtauld Inst of Biochemistry Middlesex Hosp Med Sch 1961–64, lectr Dept of Biochemistry Univ of Aberdeen 1964–70, succesively princ scientific offr, sr princ scientific offr then dir NERC Inst of Marine Biochemistry Aberdeen 1970–85, prof of biological scis Univ of Stirling 1985–, dir NERC Unit of Aquatic Biochemistry 1985–; Bond Gold medal American Oil Chemists' Soc; memb: Biochemical Soc, Marine Biological Assoc of UK, Scottish Assoc of Marine Scis; FIBiol, FRSE 1986; *Recreations* walking, skiing, golf, discussing and thinking; *Style—* Prof John Sargent, FRSE; ✉ 5 Rosebery View, Dalgety Bay, Fife KY11 5YH (☎ 01383 822743); Department of Biological and Molecular Sciences, University of Stirling, Stirling FK9 4LA (☎ 01786 473171)

SARGENT, John Richard (Dick); s of Sir John Philip Sargent, CIE (d 1972), and Ruth Taunton (d 1932); *b* 22 March 1925; *Educ* Dragon Sch, Rugby, ChCh Oxford (BA, MA); *m* 1, 16 July 1949 (m dis 1980), Anne Elizabeth, da of Lt-Col John F Haigh, MBE (d 1976); 1 s (Simon b 1953), 2 da (Sally b 1950, Vicky b 1957); m 2, Oct 1980, Hester Mary, wid of Dr J D E Campbell, 3 step s (Francis, Laurence, Nicholas); *Career* RN 1943–46, Sub Lt RNVR 1945; lectr in economics and fell Worcester Coll Oxford 1951–62, econ conslt HM Treasy 1963–65, prof and fndr memb Dept of Economics Univ of Warwick 1964–73 (pro vice-chllr 1970–72); gp econ advsr Midland Bank 1974–84 (ex-officio ed Midland Bank Review), economic advsr Miny of Technol 1969–71; memb: Doctors and Dentists Pay Review Body 1972–75, Armed Forces Pay Review Body 1972–86, Pharmacists Review Panel 1986–, Cncl Royal Econ Soc 1969–74; govr Nat Inst for Econ Res 1969–, pres Société de Recherches Financières 1985–88 (memb Cncl 1976–92); treas Comforts and Amenities Fund Burford Hosp 1986–, former memb Educn Ctee City of Oxford; author of numerous articles in econ jls; *Books* British Transport Policy (1958); *Recreations* gardening; *Clubs* Reform; *Style—* Dick Sargent; ✉ Trentham House, Fulbrook, Burford, Oxon OX18 4BL (☎ 01993 823525)

SARGENT, Peter Bertram James; s of Maj Bertram Sargent (d 1979), of 61 Maresfield Drive, Pevensey Bay, Sussex, and Hilda, *née* Rooms (d 1985); *b* 8 Nov 1932; *Educ* Sherwood Coll, Naini Tal UP India, The Stationers' Company's Sch London, LSE (BSc Econ); *m* Patricia Ann, da of Harry John William Mason (d 1984), of 33 Mapleton Crescent, Enfield, Middx; *Career* Nat Serv Flying Offr RAF 1957–59; gen mangr admin The Ever Ready Co GB Ltd 1967–69 (mgmnt accountant 1960–67), princ conslt Arthur Young Mgmnt Serv 1969–72, dep controller Barclays Bank Ltd 1972–78, gp planning mangr Grand Metropolitan plc 1978–83, asst corporate controller Europe Engelhard Corp 1983–85, md Sheffield Smelting Co Ltd, dep fin dir Europe Engelhard Corp 1985–90, fin conslt 1991–; Freeman: Worshipful Co of Stationers 1987, City of London 1987; FCA 1957; *Recreations* hockey, cricket, theatre, antiques; *Clubs* Marylebone Cricket, Tulse Hill Hockey, Apostles; *Style—* Peter Sargent, Esq; ✉ 13 East Ridgeway, Cuffley, Potters Bar, Herts EN6 4AW (☎ 01707 873754, fax 01707 872700); Engelhard Limited, Engelhard House, 8 Throgmorton Ave, London EC2N 2DL (☎ 0171 588 4080, fax 0171 374 4632, car 0860 829468, telex 496555)

SARGENT, Prof Roger William Herbert; s of Herbert Alfred Sargent (d 1959), and May Elizabeth, *née* Gill (d 1933); *b* 14 Oct 1926; *Educ* Bedford Sch, Imperial Coll London (BSc, PhD, DIC, DSc(Eng)); *m* 11 Aug 1951, Shirley Jane Levesque, da of Archer Wilfrid Spooner (d 1973); 2 s (Philip Michael b 1 Aug 1954, Anthony John b 26 Dec 1955); *Career* design engr SA l'Air Liquide Paris 1951–58; Imperial Coll London: asst lectr 1950–51, sr lectr 1958–62, prof of chem engrg 1962–66, Courtauld prof of chem engrg 1966–92, dean City and Guilds Coll 1973–76, head Dept of Chem Engrg and Chem Technol 1975–88, dir Interdisciplinary Res Centre for Process Systems Engrg 1989–92, sr res fell 1992–, memb Governing Body 1967–77 and 1979–87; pres Inst of Chem Engrs 1973–74 (vice pres 1969–71 and 1972–73); chm: Chem Engrg and Technol Ctee SRC 1971–73 (memb 1969–73), Process Plant Ctee DTI 1981–87 (memb 1980–81), Engrg and Technol Advsy Ctee Br Cncl 1984–89 (memb 1976–89); memb: Technol Sub Ctee UGC 1984–89, Br-French Mixed Cultural Cmmn 1985–90, Br Nat Ctee for Int Engrg Affairs 1987–89; ed various learned jls and has made a prolific contrib to scientific literature; assoc ed Jl of Optimisation Theory and its Applications 1979–, ed Advsy Bd Computers and Chem Engrg 1987–; foreign assoc US Acad of Engrg 1993; Docteur Honoris Causa: Institut National Polytechnique De Lorraine 1987, Univ de Liège 1995; Hon DSc Univ of Edinburgh 1993; fell Imperial Coll 1994; Hon FCGI 1976, FIChemE 1964, FIMA 1972, FEng 1976; *Style—* Prof Roger Sargent, FEng; ✉ Centre for Process Systems Engineering, Imperial College of Science, Technology and Medicine, London SW7 2BY (☎ 0171 594 6613, fax 0171 594 6606)

SARGENT, Wallace Leslie William; s of Leslie William Sargent (d 1979), and Eleanor, *née* Dennis (d 1964); *b* 15 Feb 1935; *m* 5 Aug 1964, Dr Anneila Sargent, da of Richard Cassells (d 1968), of Burntisland, Fife, Scotland; 2 da (Lindsay Eleanor b 8 July 1970, Alison Clare b 25 Jan 1972); *Career* res fell Caltech 1959–62, sr res fell Royal Greenwich Observatory 1962–64, asst prof of physics Univ of California San Diego 1964–66; Caltech: asst prof 1966–68, assoc prof 1968–71, prof 1971–81, exec offr for astronomy 1975–81 and 1996–, Ira S Bowen prof of astronomy 1981–; visiting fell: Mount Stromlo Observatory Aust Nat Univ 1965 and 1967, Inst of Theoretical Astronomy Univ of Cambridge 1968–72, 1974–75, 1979, 1982 and 1987, Dept of Astrophysics Univ of Oxford 1973, Univ of Groningen 1978, Euro Southern Observatory 1980, 1982 and 1985, Univ of Florence 1981, Institut d'Astrophysique Paris 1984, Royal Observatory Edinburgh 1990, MPIFA Heidelberg 1992, 1993 and 1994; memb: N Hemisphere Review Ctee SRC 1968–69, Visiting Ctee Univ of Arizona 1970–73, Ctee on Space Astronomy and Astrophysics Nat Acad of Sciences 1975–78, Study Gp for Space Telescope Sci Inst Nat Acad of Sciences 1976, Harvard Coll Observatory Visiting Ctee 1979–86 (chm 1987–93), Editorial Bd Annual Reviews of Astronomy and Astrophysics 1977–81, Bd Harvard-Smithsonian Centre for Astrophysics 1983–, Sci Steering Ctee Keck Observatory 1985– (co-chm 1985–89 and 1990–); memb Visiting Ctee: in Astrophysics Stanford Univ 1986, Mount Wilson and Las Campanas Observatories 1987, Astronomy Prog State Univ of NY at Stony Brook 1987, Astronomy Dept U C Berkeley 1988, Space Telescope Sci Inst 1989–91; memb: Astronomy and Astrophysics Survey Ctee Nat Acad of Sciences 1989–91 (co-chm Optical/IR Panel), Space Telescope Advsy Ctee 1990–91; Alfred P Sloane Fndn fell 1968–70, Helen B Warner prize American Astronomical Soc 1969, George Darwin lect RAS 1987, Dirs Distinguished lectr Lawrence Livermore Lab 1988, Dannie Heineman prize 1991, Bruce Gold medal 1994; memb: American Astronomical Union, RAS, Int Astronomical Union; FAAAS 1977, FRS 1981; *Recreations* watching sports, oriental rugs, music, reading; *Clubs* Athenaeum (Pasadena, Ca); *Style—* Wallace Sargent, Esq, FRS; ✉ Astronomy Department, 105–24 California Institute of Technology, 1201 East California Boulevard, Pasadena, CA 91125, USA (☎ 818 356 4055, fax 818 568 1517)

SARGINSON, David Richard; s of Richard Herbert Sarginson (d 1984), and Ursula Rose, *née* Brown (d 1950); *b* 9 May 1936; *Educ* Wrekin Coll Shropshire; *children* 1 s (Mark Richard b 1964), 1 da (Jane Elizabeth b 1962); *Career* slr; HM coroner City of Coventry 1985–, treas Coroners' Soc of England and Wales; fndr of Sarginsons slrs Coventry, pres Warwicks Law Soc 1995; chm and md Sarginson Bros Ltd (manufacturers of foundry equipment and aluminium founders for the automotive industry); *Recreations* France, its life and good food, music; *Clubs* Drapers (Coventry); *Style—* David Sarginson, Esq; ✉ Sarginsons, 10 The Quadrant, Coventry, Warwickshire CV1 2EL (☎ 01203 553181, fax 01203 258573)

SARKANY, Imrich; s of Dr Edmund Sarkany (d 1938), and Maria *née* Pollitzer; *b* 7 Jan 1923; *Educ* St Thomas' Hosp Med Sch; *m* 12 Dec 1956, Helen Ruth Veronica, da of Israel Pomerance, of St Albans; 2 s (Robert b 1962, Andrew b 1965), 1 da (Elizabeth b 1960); *Career* physician (diseases of the skin); conslt dermatologist Royal Free Hosp 1960–89; pres: Br Assoc of Dermatologists 1987–88, Dermatology Section RSM 1981–82, Monosection for Dermato-Venereology of Euro Union of Med Specialists 1987–91, St John's Dermatological Soc 1976–77, Dermatological Dowling Club; memb: Bd of Govrs Royal Free Hosp, Cncl RSM, Bd Euro Acad of Dermatology; fndr chm Br Soc for Investigative Dermatology; *Style—* Imrich Sarkany, Esq; ✉ 2 Romney Close, London NW11 7JD; 132 Harley St, London W1 (☎ 0171 935 3678)

SARKISSIAN, HE Dr Armen; *b* 23 June 1953; *Educ* Dept of Physics Yerevan State Univ Armenia (PhD); *m*; 2 s; *Career* Armenian diplomat and academician; visiting research fell Univ of Cambridge 1984–85; Yerevan State Univ Armenia: assoc prof Dept of Theoretical Physics 1985–90, head Dept of Computer Modelling of Complex Systems 1990–92; visiting prof and hon sr research fell Queen Mary and Westfield Coll London

1992–; Armenian ambass to the Ct of St James's Feb 1993– (chargé d'affaires 1992–93); concurrently: ambass to the Euro Union Nov 1993–, ambass to Belgium, the Netherlands and the Vatican 1995–, head Armenian Mission to the EC 1995–; memb Int Inst of Strategic Studies, hon memb Pan-Armenian Academic and Scientific Soc; FRAS; *Publications* author of three books and numerous academic articles on topics incl political sci, theoretical physics, astrophysics and computer modelling; *Style*— HE Dr Armen Sarkissian; ✉ Embassy of the Republic of Armenia, 25 Cheniston Gardens, London W8 6TG (☎ 0171 938 5435, fax 0171 938 2595)

SARNE, Michael; s of Alfred Scheuer (d 1976), and Agathe, *née* Reiche; *b* 6 Aug 1940; *Educ* BEC Sch, Sch of Slavonic and East European Studies (BA); *m* 15 Jan 1969 (m dis 1982), Tanya, *qv*, da of John Gordon; 1 s (William Mordechai b 30 May 1972), 3 da (Claudia Aviva b 17 Jan 1970, Emma Miriam b 17 Dec 1986, Abigail Leah b 8 Nov 1989); *Career* actor, writer, producer, director and singer; chm Celebrities Guild of GB; memb Bd of Mgmnt: New West End Synagogue, Notting Hill Synagogue; memb: ACTT, AIP, Directors' Guild (GB & USA), Writers' Guild (GB & USA), Equity, Performing Right Soc, BAFTA; *Television* as actor incl: War and Remembrance, Minder, The Knock; screenplays incl: Moonlighting, The Lightship, Ferdydurke; *Films* as actor incl: Every Day's a Holiday, A Place to Go; dir: Road to St Tropez (writer and prodr) 1965, Joanna 1968, Myra Breckinridge 1970, Intimidade 1973, The Punk and the Princess (writer/prodr) 1995; *Recordings* incl: Come Outside, Will I What?, Just for Kicks; *Books* Three Lives of Nigel Kelland (1965), Joanna (1968); *Recreations* tennis, bridge, poetry, painting; *Style*— Michael Sarne, Esq; ✉ c/o British Actors' Equity Association, Guild House, Upper St Martin's Lane, London WC2H 9EG

SARNE, Tanya; *see:* Gordon, Tanya Joan

SAROOP, Narindar; CBE (1982); s of Chief Ram Saroop (d 1988), of Lahore and Chandigarh, and Shyam, *née* Devi (d 1981); *b* 14 Aug 1929; *Educ* Aitchison Coll for Punjab Chiefs Lahore, Indian Mil Acad Dehra Dun India; *m* 1, Oct 1952 (m dis 1967), Ravi Gill, da of the Sardar of Premgarh (d 1968), of Goodwood, Simla, Punjab, India; 1 s (Vijayendra b 1953, d 1983), 2 da (Vaneeta b 1954, Kavita b 1961); m 2, Feb 1968, Stephanie Denise, da of Alexander Panyotis Cronopulo (d 1977), of Zakynthos, Greece; *Career* 2 Royal Lancers (Gardner's Horse), Queen Victoria's Own The Poona Horse; served as: Sqdn Offr, Regtl Signals Offr, Regtl Gunnery Offr, Actg Sqdn Ldr; mgmnt trainee Yule Catto & Co Ltd 1954–55, sr exec Andrew Yule & Co Ltd 1955–61; subsidiary Bd dir: Davy Ashmore Group 1961–64, Turner & Newall Group 1965–71, mgmnt consultancy 1972–76; devpt advsr H Clarkson Group 1976–87, conslt Banque Belge 1987–91; advsr: Cancer Relief Macmillan Fund 1992–95, Coutts & Co 1995–; pres India Welfare Soc 1984–91; memb Cncl: The Freedom Assoc 1980–88, IOD 1983–93; memb: BBC Advsy Panel 1977–80, Charity Review Royal Borough of Kensington and Chelsea 1974–; Parly Candidate (Cons) Greenwich General Election 1979 (first Asian Tory Party candidate this century), cncllr Royal Borough of Kensington and Chelsea 1974–82, vice chm Cons Pty Int Office 1990–92; fndr and chm: Anglo-Asian Cons Soc 1976–79 and 1985–86, The Durbar Club 1981–; *Books* In Defence of Freedom (jtly, 1978), A Squire of Hindoostan (1985); *Style*— Narindar Saroop, Esq, CBE; ✉ 25 de Vere Gardens, London W8

SARUM, Archdeacon of; *see:* Hopkinson, Ven Barnabas John (Barney)

SASDY, Peter George; s of Ernst Sömjén (d 1973), and Magdolna, *née* Révész (d 1985); *b* 27 May 1935; *Educ* Univ of Budapest (BA), Univ of Bristol; *m* Mia Myrtill, da of Ferenc Nadasi; 2 da (Anita Judith b 1970, Carola Marian b 1979); *Career* trainee dir BBC TV, drama dir ATV Network, freelance drama prodr and dir of single plays, drama serials and series; feature films and US mini-series for: BBC TV, LWT, Thames TV, Universal MCA, Warner Brothers, Rank Films, NBC TV, Anglia TV, ABC TV, EMI Films, 20th Century Fox; recent film credits incl: Wuthering Heights (BBC), If Winter Comes (with Paul Scofield, BBC), Minder (pilot for Euston Films), Imaginary Friends (Thames), The Secret Diary of Adrian Mole aged 13 3/4 (Thames), Ending Up (Thames), Sherlock Holmes and the Leading Lady (USA), Witchcraft (BBC), Alexander Korda: I Don't Grow on Trees (Omnibus BBC); Int Emmy Awards nominations 1986 and 1990; memb: Br Film Acad and TV Arts, Directors Guild of America, Directors Guild of GB; *Books* Four Black Cars (co-author, 1958); *Recreations* travel, swimming; *Style*— Peter Sasdy, Esq; ✉ Peter Sasdy Productions Ltd, c/o Robert John Specterman, 315 Oxford Street, London W1R 1LA (☎ 0171 409 3444, fax 0171 355 1005)

SASSOON, Adrian David; s of Hugh Meyer Sassoon, of London, and Marion Julia, *née* Schiff; *b* 1 Feb 1961; *Educ* Eton, Inchbald Sch of Design, Christie's Fine Arts Course; *Career* asst curator Dept of Decorative Arts J Paul Getty Museum Calif 1982–84 (curatorial asst 1980–82), dir Alexander & Berendt Ltd London 1990–92 (asst to md 1987–89); lectr on/dealer in French decorative arts, 18th century Sèvres porcelain and contemporary British ceramics and glass; treas and memb Ctee French Porcelain Soc 1989–95 (joined as memb 1985), memb Cncl The Attingham Tst for the Study of the Country House 1990–95; articles on French 18th century decorative arts in the J Paul Getty Museum Jls 1981–85; *Books* Decorative Arts: A Handbook of the J Paul Getty Museum (1986), Catalogue of Vincennes and Sèvres Porcelain in the J Paul Getty Museum (1991); *Clubs* Lyford Cay (Nassau, Bahamas); *Style*— Adrian Sassoon, Esq

SASSOON, David; s of George Sassoon, and Victoria, *née* Gurgi; *b* 5 Oct 1932; *Educ* Chelsea Coll of Art, RCA; *Career* fashion designer, joined Belinda Bellville 1958, first Ready to Wear Collection 1963, dir 1964, co became Bellville Sassoon 1970, sole shareholder 1983; licencee: Vogue Butterick USA 1966, Japan 1988; *Recreations* theatre, ballet; *Style*— David Sassoon, Esq; ✉ Bellville Sassoon, 18 Culford Gardens, London SW3 2ST (☎ 0171 581 3500)

SASSOON, James Meyer; s of Hugh Meyer Sassoon, of London, and Marion Julia, *née* Schiff; *b* 11 Sept 1955; *Educ* Eton, ChCh Oxford (exhibitioner, MA, Gibbs book prize); *m* 23 Oct 1981, Sarah Caroline Ray, da of Sir (Ernest) John Ward Barnes; 1 s (Frederick b 1 April 1987), 2 da (Alexandra b 6 Nov 1990, Victoria b 4 June 1994); *Career* Thomson McLintock & Co 1977–86, S G Warburg & Co Ltd 1987–95 (dir 1991–95), md SBC Warburg 1995–; contrib articles to art and fin jls; memb: Tate Gallery Patrons of New Art (memb Acquisition Ctee 1986), French Porcelain Soc; FCA 1991 (ACA 1980); *Recreations* travel, the arts, gardening; *Clubs* MCC; *Style*— James Sassoon, Esq; ✉ SBC Warburg, 2 Finsbury Ave, London EC2M 2PP (☎ 0171 860 1090, fax 0171 860 0901)

SATCHELL, Keith; s of Dennis Joseph Satchell, of Hemel Hempstead, and Joan Betty, *née* Elms; *b* 3 June 1951; *Educ* Hemel Hempstead GS, Aston Univ (BSc); *m* 1 July 1972, Hazel Dorothy, da of Douglas Burston, of Birmingham; 2 s (Paul b 1978, Richard b 1980), 1 da (Olivia b 1984); *Career* dir Friends Provident Life Office 1992–; govr Middle Sch Verwood; FIA 1976; *Recreations* sport, reading; *Style*— Keith Satchell, Esq; ✉ Oakfield, 63 Moorlands Road, Verwood, Dorset BH31 7PD (☎ 01202 824118); Friends Provident, 72–122 Castle St, Salisbury, Wilts (☎ 01722 413366)

SATCHELL, (John) Timothy Moffatt (Tim); s of John Frederick Bridge, and Evelyn Adelaide, *née* Calvert; *b* 27 Nov 1946; *Educ* Haileybury and ISC; *m* 5 March 1975, Amanda Rowena, da of Edward Barrington-Smyth; 2 da (Cordelia Victoria b 1 April 1985, Rowena Beatrice b 11 Jan 1988); *Career* newspaper/magazine columnist; asst to Clive Graham Daily Express 1965, subsequently on staff Sunday Express and Daily Mail, int mangr Dart Records and dir Beautiful Music 1970–74; former columns: Bookmarks (Books and Bookmen), Back Page (London Evening News), Mr Pepys (Evening Standard), 7 Days (Hello!), The Insider (Today); ed: London Gossip, Insider; chm Insider Magazines Plc 1995–; Liveryman Worshipful Co of Saddlers; *Books* McQueen (1981), Royal Romance (1986), Astaire (1987), The Newest London Spy (ed Tim Heald, 1988); *Recreations* bees, opera, fashion, farming, the pursuit of excellence; *Clubs* Groucho; *Style*— Tim Satchell, Esq; ✉ 15 Moreton Place, London SW1V 2NL

SATTERTHWAITE, Christopher James; s of Col Richard George Satterthwaite, LVO, OBE (d 1993), of Petersfield, W Sussex, and Rosemary, *née* Messervy; *b* 21 May 1956; *Educ* Ampleforth, Lincoln Coll Oxford (MA); *m* 30 Jan 1988, Teresa Mary, da of Cdr L Bailey; 2 s (James Richard b 29 Oct 1988, Henry Frank b 8 Nov 1989), 1 da (Eleanor Sara b 6 Feb 1992); *Career* graduate trainee H J Heinz Ltd 1979–81, IMP Ltd 1981–93 (md 1987–93), Howell Henry Chaldecott Lury advtg 1993–; *Recreations* fly fishing, bombology, motorbikes; *Clubs* Old Imponians, Vincent's (Oxford); *Style*— Christopher Satterthwaite, Esq; ✉ HHCL Ltd, Kent House, 14–17 Market Place, Great Titchfield Street, London W1N 7AJ (☎ 0171 436 3333, fax 0171 436 2677)

SATTERTHWAITE, Rt Rev John Richard; CMG (1991); s of William Satterthwaite, and Clara Elisabeth Satterthwaite; *b* 17 Nov 1925; *Educ* Univ of Leeds (BA), Community of the Resurrection Mirfield; *Career* history master St Luke's Sch Haifa 1946–48; curate: St Barnabas Carlisle 1950–53, St Aidan Carlisle 1953–54, St Michael Paternoster Royal London 1955–59 (curate-in-charge 1959–65); gen sec C of E Cncl on Foreign Relations 1959–70 (asst gen sec 1955–9), gen sec Archbishop's Cmmn on Roman Catholic Relations 1965–70, vicar St Dunstan in the West 1959–70, bishop suffragan of Fulham 1970, bishop of Gibraltar 1970 (known as bishop of Fulham and Gibraltar until creation of new diocese 1980), bishop of Gibraltar in Europe 1980–93; canon of Canterbury 1963–70, canon of the Old Catholic Cathedral Utrecht 1968–, hon asst bishop Carlisle 1994–; ChStJ 1972; *Clubs* Athenaeum; *Style*— The Rt Rev John Satterthwaite, CMG; ✉ 25 Spencer House, St Paul's Square, Carlisle, Cumbria CA1 1DG (☎ 01228 594055)

SAUGMAN, Per Gotfred; OBE (1990); s of Emanuel A G Saugman (d 1962), and Esther, *née* Lehmann (d 1986); *b* 26 June 1925; *Educ* Gentofte GS, Commercial Coll Copenhagen; *m* 28 Dec 1950, Patricia, da of William Henry Fulford (d 1982); 3 s (Peter b 1951, Philip b 1955, and 1 decd), 1 da (Penelope b 1959); *Career* bookselling and publishing in Denmark, Switzerland, England 1941–49; Blackwell Scientific Publications Ltd (now Blackwell Science Ltd): sales mangr 1952, md 1954–87, chm 1972–90; dir University Bookshops (Oxford) Ltd 1963–88; chm: Wm George's Sons Ltd 1965–87, Blackwell N America Inc 1973–90, Ejnar Munksgaard Publishers Copenhagen 1967–92, Kooyker Boekhandel Leiden 1973–90; fndr and chm of tstees Sunningwell Sch of Art 1972–; memb: Int Publishers Assoc 1976–79, Publishers Assoc of GB and Ireland 1977–82; hon memb Br Ecological Soc 1960–; govr: Oxford Poly 1972–82, Dragon Sch 1975, Headington Sch Oxford 1980; Hon MA Univ of Oxford 1978, hon fell Green Coll Oxford 1981, fell St Cross Coll Oxford 1980; Kt Order of Dannebrog 1972, Chevalier Order of Icelandic Falcon 1984; *Books* From the First Fifty Years (1989, 2nd edn 1993), In the World of the Books (1992), The Way I Think it Was (1992), The Way it Was (1994, Danish edn 1995); *Recreations* reading, art, English watercolours, golf; *Clubs* Athenaeum, RAC, Frilford Golf (Oxford); *Style*— Per Saugman, Esq, OBE; ✉ Sunningwood House, Lincombe Lane, Boars Hill, Oxford OX1 5DZ (☎ 01865 735503, fax 01865 739101)

SAUL, Philip Bycroft; s of Maj John Bycroft Saul, MC (d 1946), and Juliana Margaret, *née* Watson (d 1987); *b* 19 Feb 1933; *Educ* Dover Coll, St Edmund Hall Oxford (MA); *m* 31 July 1956, Jane, da of Maj Gerald William Gostwyck May (d 1962); 2 s (George, Thomas), 3 da (Dorothy, Frances, Lucy); *Career* slr 1959, sr ptnr Stringer Saul 1978–; treas NRA 1991; *Recreations* match rifle shooting (represented England on 11 occasions 1956–92), skiing; *Style*— Philip Saul, Esq; ✉ 6 Wyndham Mews, London W1H 1RS (☎ 0171 262 4013); Marcol House, 293 Regent St, London W1R 7PD (☎ 0171 631 4048, fax 0171 636 2306)

SAUL, Roger John; s of (Frederick) Michael Saul, of Chilcompton, Somerset, and Joan, *née* Legg; *b* 25 July 1950; *Educ* Kingswood Sch Bath, Westminster Coll London; *m* 23 July 1977, Marion Joan, da of Clifford Cameron; 3 s (William Michael, Cameron Robert, Frederick Jakes); *Career* fndr, creator, designer and chief exec of Mulberry 1971–, awarded Queen's Award for Export 1979, 1989 and 1996; BKCEC Exporter of the Year 1987–88, 1990 and 1996, brand label in Br contemporary classic fashion worldwide; memb Bd BKCEC; *Recreations* tennis, historic car racing, skiing, shooting, garden design; *Style*— Roger Saul, Esq; ✉ Mulberry, Kilver Court, Shepton Mallet, Somerset BA4 5NF (☎ 01749 340500, fax 01749 345532)

SAUMAREZ, *see:* de Saumarez

SAUMAREZ SMITH, Dr Charles Robert; s of William Hanbury Saumarez Smith, OBE (d 1994), and Alice Elizabeth Harness, *née* Raven; *b* 28 May 1954; *Educ* Marlborough, King's Coll Cambridge (scholar, MA), Harvard Univ (Henry fellow), Warburg Inst Univ of London (PhD); *m* Romilly Le Quesne, *née* Savage; 2 s (Otto Livingstone b 1987, Ferdinand Le Quesne b 1990); *Career* Christie's research fell and dir of studies (history of art) Christ's Coll Cambridge 1979–82; V & A: asst keeper (responsible for V&A/RCA MA course in history of design) 1982–90, head of research 1990–94; dir National Portrait Gallery 1994–; visiting fell Yale Centre for British Art 1983, Benno M Forman fellowship H F du Pont Winterthur Museum 1988; South Square Fellow RCA 1990; ctee memb: Design History Soc 1985–89, Soc of Architectural Historians 1987–90, Editorial Bd Art History 1988–93, Exec Ctee Assoc of Art Historians 1990–94, Exec Ctee London Library 1992–, Cncl Charleston Tst 1993–; tstee Soane Monuments Tst 1988–; Alice Davis Hitchcock medallion 1990, hon fell RCA 1991, FRSA 1995; *Publications* The Building of Castle Howard (1990), Eighteenth-Century Decoration: Design and the Domestic Interior in England (1993); *Style*— Dr Charles Saumarez Smith; ✉ The National Portrait Gallery, St Martin's Place, London WC2H 0HE (☎ 0171 306 0055, fax 0171 306 0064)

SAUNDERS, Dr Ann Loreille; da of George Cox-Johnson (d 1941), and Joan Loreille, *née* Clowser (d 1980); *b* 23 May 1930; *Educ* Henrietta Barnet Sch, Queen's Coll Harley St, UCL (BA), Univ of Leicester (PhD); *m* 4 June 1960, Bruce Kemp Saunders, s of Kemp Alexander Saunders (d 1973); 1 s (Matthew Kemp b 1964), 1 da (Katherine Sophia Loreille b 1967 d 1984); *Career* dep librarian Lambeth Palace Library 1952–55, asst keeper Br Museum 1955–56, borough archivist St Marylebone Public Library 1956–63, asst to the Hon Editor Journal of the British Archaeological Assoc 1963–75, hon ed Costume Soc 1967–, hon ed London Topographical Soc 1975–; pt/t lectr: Richmond Coll Kensington 1979–92, City Univ 1981–; contrib to various jls incl Geographical Magazine, Burlington Magazine and The London Journal; fell UCL 1991 (hon research fell Dept of History 1995–); Liveryman Worshipful Co of Horners; FSA; *Books* Regent's Park: A Study of the Development of the Area from 1066 to the Present Day (1969), Arthur Mee's King's England Series: London North of the Thames (revised 1972), London: The City and Westminster (revised 1975), Regent's Park (1981), The Regent's Park Villas (1981), The Art and Architecture of London: An Illustrated Guide (won London Tourist Bd award for specialist guidebook of the year 1984, 2 edn 1988, reprinted 1992 and 1996), St Martin in the Fields: A Short History and Guide (1989), The Royal Exchange (1991); *Recreations* reading, embroidery, cooking, walking, studying London, going to exhibitions and the theatre and to churches; *Style*— Dr Ann Saunders, FSA; ✉ 3 Meadway Gate, London NW11 7LA

SAUNDERS, Dr (William) Anthony; s of Robert Valentine Saunders, of Sneyd Park, Bristol, and Mary Isabel, *née* Kerr; *b* 24 June 1940; *Educ* Clifton, Trinity Coll Cambridge (MA, MB BChir, FRCPsych, DPM, DCH); *m* 11 Feb 1967, Angela Pauline, da of Charles Alan Rapson (d 1971), of Topsham, Exeter; 1 s (Jonathan b 7 May 1970), 2 da (Emma b 13 March 1968, Annabel b 29 July 1972); *Career* conslt in child and adolescent pyschiatry 1973–, hon clinical lectr Univ of Southampton 1973–; chm Southampton Child Sexual Abuse Steering Gp, former chm Wessex Child Psychiatrists, past nat chm Ctee of Mgmnt Assoc for Professionals in Servs for Adolescents; *Style*— Dr Anthony Saunders; ✉ Meadow Cottage, Otterbourne, Nr Winchester, Hampshire SO21 2EQ (☎ 01962 713129)

SAUNDERS, Basil; s of Cdr John Edward Saunders, RN (missing presumed dead 1941), and Marjorie, *née* Purdon (d 1983); *b* 12 Aug 1925; *Educ* Merchant Taylors', Wadham Coll Oxford (MA); *m* 1957, Betty, da of Victor Smith (d 1957); 2 s (William, Edward), 4 da (Kate, Louisa, Etta, Charlotte); *Career* Sub Lt RNVR 1943–46; asst d'Anglais College De Tarascon 1951–52, writer General Electric (USA) 1953–54, PR offr BIM 1954–57, conslt Pritchard Wood (later Infoplan) 1958–63, head of PR The Wellcome Fndn 1963–78, dir gen ASLIB 1978–80, conslt Traverse-Healy Ltd 1981–84; dir: Traverse-Healy & Regester Ltd 1984–87, Charles Barker Traverse-Healy 1987–90; freelance PR conslt 1990–; FIPR; *Books* Crackle of Thorns (1968), Bluff Your Way in PR (1991); *Clubs* Savile; *Style*— Basil Saunders, Esq; ✉ 18 Dartmouth Park Ave, London NW5 1JN (☎ 0171 485 4672, fax 0171 482 4994)

SAUNDERS, Christopher John; s of Rupert Henry Saunders (d 1977), of Guildford, Surrey, and Gladys Susan, *née* Harris (d 1975); *b* 7 May 1940; *Educ* Lancing, Fitwilliam Coll Cambridge (MA), Wadham Coll Oxford (CertEd); *m* 27 Oct 1973, Cynthia Elizabeth Saunders, JP, da of Harold Deverel Stiles, TD, JP, of Hove, Sussex; 1 s (Jonathan Mark Christopher b 31 March 1975), 1 da (Lucy Kathryn b 29 Aug 1976); *Career* housemaster Bradfield 1972–80 (asst master 1964–80), headmaster Eastbourne Coll 1981–93, headmaster Lancing Coll 1993–; memb MCC cricket tour 1967, chm Independent Sch FA 1981–; govr: St Andrew's Sch Eastbourne E Sussex, Ashdown House Forest Row E Sussex, Stoke Brunswick Sch Ashurst Wood E Sussex, Holmewood House Langton Green Kent, Horris Hill Newbury Berks, Dorset House Pulborough W Sussex, Chinthurst Sch Tadworth Surrey; memb FA Cncl 1982–; *Recreations* music, theatre, gardening, soccer, cricket; *Clubs* Hawks (Cambridge), MCC; *Style*— Christopher Saunders, Esq; ✉ The Old Farmhouse, Lancing College, West Sussex BN15 0RN (☎ 01273 452213, fax 01273 464720)

SAUNDERS, Christopher Thomas; CMG (1953); s of Thomas Beckenn Avening Saunders (d 1950), and Mary Theodora Slater (d 1928); *b* 5 Nov 1907; *Educ* St Edward's Oxford, ChCh Oxford (MA); *m* 1947, Cornelia Jacomijntje, da of Tjisse Gielstra (d 1957), of The Netherlands; 1 s (John Peter); *Career* economist Univs of Liverpool and Manchester 1930–35; memb Jt Ctee Cotton Trade 1935–40, govt Cotton Control 1940–45; civil servant Miny of Labour and Central Statistical Office 1945–57, dir Nat Inst for Econ and Social Res London 1957–65, res dir UN Econ Cmmn for Europe Geneva 1965–73, prof Sussex Euro Res Centre Univ of Sussex 1973–84, hon fell (pt/t) Science Policy Research Unit Univ of Sussex 1984–; *Books* Seasonal Variations in Employment (1936), Pay Inequalities in EEC (1981); many anonymous contribs to official nat and int reports, numerous journal articles and editing of conference transactions; *Recreations* walking, painting; *Clubs* Reform; *Style*— Christopher Thomas Saunders, Esq, CMG; ✉ 4/17 Gillsland Road, Edinburgh EH10 5BW (☎ 0131 228 6965)

SAUNDERS, Dame Cicely Mary Strode; OM (1989), DBE (1980, OBE 1967); da of Philip Gordon Saunders (d 1961), of The Chase, Hadley Common, Barnet, and Mary Christian Knight (d 1968); *b* 22 June 1918; *Educ* Roedean, St Anne's Coll Oxford, St Thomas's Hosp Med Sch; *m* 1980, Prof Marian Bohusz-Szyszko (d 1995), s of Antoni Bohusz-Szyszko (d 1995), of Wilno, Poland; *Career* fndr and chm St Christopher's Hospice London; former dep chm Attendance Allowance Bd; hon fell UMDS Guy's and St Thomas's Hosps 1993; hon degrees: DSc Yale 1969, DUniv Open Univ 1978, DHL Jewish Theol Seminary of America 1982, LLD Leicester 1983, DUniv Essex 1983, DSc London 1983, LLD Oxford 1986, LLD Cambridge 1986; Gold Medal Soc of Apothecaries of London 1979, Templeton Fndn Award 1981, British Medical Assoc Gold Medal 1987; Liveryman: Worshipful Co of Goldsmiths, Worshipful Soc of Apothecaries; *Recreations* home; *Style*— Dame Cicely Saunders, OM, DBE; ✉ St Christopher's Hospice, 51–59 Lawrie Park Rd, Sydenham SE26 6DZ (☎ 0181 778 9252, fax 0181 659 8680); 50 Lawrie Park Gardens, Sydenham SE26

SAUNDERS, David William; CB (1989); s of William Ernest Saunders, of Hornchurch, Essex, and Lilian Grace, *née* Ward (d 1987); *b* 4 Nov 1936; *Educ* Hornchurch GS, Worcester Coll Oxford (MA); *m* 15 April 1963, Margaret Susan Rose, da of William Colin Bartholomew (d 1980), of London; *Career* Nat Serv RAF 1955–57 (Russian linguist), articled clerk later slr private practice 1960–69; Parly Counsel: asst counsel 1970–75, on loan to Law Cmmn 1972–74, sr asst counsel 1975–78, dep counsel 1978–80, counsel 1980–94, on loan to Law Cmmn as sr draftsman 1986–87, second counsel 1994–96, counsel 1996–; memb Law Soc 1964; *Recreations* bridge, golf, flying; *Style*— David Saunders, Esq, CB; ✉ 104A Belgrave Rd, London SW1V 2BJ (☎ 0171 834 4403); Office of the Parliamentary Counsel, 36 Whitehall, London SW1 (☎ 0171 210 6600)

SAUNDERS, Dean Nicholas; *b* 21 June 1964; *Career* professional footballer; Swansea City 1982–85: apprentice then professional, 49 league appearances and 12 goals, 6 cup appearances; 4 appearances on loan Cardiff City 1985; Brighton & Hove Albion 1985–87: joined on a free transfer, 72 league appearances and 31 goals, 14 cup appearances and 5 goals; Oxford Utd 1987–88: joined for a fee of £60,000, 59 league appearances and 22 goals, 14 cup games and 11 goals; transferred for a fee of £1m to Derby County 1988–91, with Liverpool 1991–92, transferred to Aston Villa 1992–95 (signing fee of £2.9m), transferred to Galatasaray 1995–96, joined Nottingham Forest FC (for fee of £1.5m) 1996–; honours with Aston Villa: runners-up League Championships 1993, winners Coca Cola Cup 1994; over 20 full Welsh caps 1986–; *Style*— Dean Saunders, Esq; ✉ c/o Nottingham Forest FC, City Ground, City Road, Nottingham NG2 5FJ

SAUNDERS, Air Vice-Marshal Derek Arthur (Dusty); CBE; s of Arthur William Edwin Chaplin Saunders (d 1970) and Dorothy May Helen, *née* Ives (d 1985); *b* 14 Nov 1933; *Educ* Dorking County GS, Kings Coll London, Coll of Aeronautics Cranfield; *m* 27 April 1957, (Ada) Margaret, da of John Robert Foster (d 1977); 2 s (Andrew b 1959, Mark b 1962), 1 da (Ailsa b 1964); *Career* RAF 1956–90; CEng, FIEE 1982 (MIEE 1967); *Recreations* caravanning, church music, rural history; *Clubs* Royal Air Force; *Style*— Air Vice-Marshall D A Saunders, CBE

SAUNDERS, Prof George Albert; s of Barnett Stanley Saunders (d 1977), and Lilian Gladys Saunders (d 1976); *b* 4 Jan 1936; *Educ* Caterham Sch, Univ of London (BSc, PhD); *m* 16 April 1960, Linda Mary, da of Edward and Ruth Butt; 2 s (Barnett Edward, Edward Alan); *Career* res fell Univ of California 1962–64, sr lectr (former lectr) Univ of Durham 1964–75, prof of physics Univ of Bath 1975–; FInstP 1970, CPhys 1980; *Recreations* mountaineering, ornithology; *Style*— Prof George Saunders; ✉ School of Physics, University of Bath, Claverton Down, Bath (☎ 01225 826441, fax 01225 826110, e-mail G.A.Saunders@bath.ac.uk)

SAUNDERS, Graham Eric; JP; s of Arthur Frank Saunders (d 1960), of York, and Ivy Ethel Saunders; *b* 3 April 1945; *Educ* Archbishop Holgate's GS York, Univ of Durham (BSc, DipHSM); *m* 20 Dec 1969, Valerie, *née* Barton; 1 da (Elizabeth Helen b 23 Dec 1977), 1 s (Christopher Andrew b 25 Jan 1982); *Career* VSO 1966–67, national admin trainee Sheffield Regnl Hosp Bd 1967–69, dep hosp sec Sunderland Gen Hosp 1969–70, sr admin asst Gp HQ Sunderland Hosp Mgmnt Ctee 1970–72, hosp sec Sunderland Royal Infirmary 1972–74, gen administrator (operational servs) Durham Health Dist 1974–77, dep chief administrator Leeds Eastern Health Dist 1977–81, dist gen mangr Harrogate Health Authy 1985–92 (chief administrator 1982–85), chief exec Harrogate Health Care NHS Trust 1992–; govr Harrogate Coll; MHSM 1970; *Recreations* theatre, opera, good food, jogging (slowly); *Style*— Graham Saunders, Esq, JP; ✉ Harrogate Health Care NHS Trust, Ebor Rise, Cornwall Road, Harrogate HG1 2PU (☎ 01423 885959, fax 01423 501391)

SAUNDERS, (William) Howard; *b* 29 June 1939; *Educ* Alleyns Sch Dulwich; *m* 1, 29 Oct 1960, Rita Doris Hardaway (d 1992), da of Thomas William Hardaway (d 1979); 2 s (Jeremy Howard b 31 March 1965, Jonathan James Howard b 29 July 1972); m 2, 22 May 1996, Moira Ann (sis of Rita Doris Hardaway); *Career* Nat Serv RAPC 1960–62; jt sr ptnr Keith, Bayley, Rogers & Co (formerly Keith Bayley & Rigg) 1982– (joined 1955, ptnr 1970); MSI 1992 (memb Stock Exchange 1970); *Recreations* skiing, tennis, reading news and encyclopedias; *Style*— Howard Saunders, Esq; ✉ Pilgrim House, Pilgrims Way, Westerham, Kent TN16 2DP (☎ 01959 563495); Keith, Bayley, Rogers & Co, Ebbark House, 93–95 Borough High St, London SE1 1NL (☎ 0171 378 0657, fax 0171 378 1795)

SAUNDERS, Iain Ogilvy Swain; s of Leslie Swain Saunders (d 1988), and Elizabeth, *née* Culme Seymour (d 1963); *b* 7 Nov 1947; *Educ* Radley, Univ of Bristol (BSc); *m* 1976, Roberta Ann, da of David Allen Phoenix; 1 da (Christina Ann Swain b 1983); *Career* Arbuthnot Latham 1968–71; Robert Fleming: joined 1971, Jardine Fleming Hong Kong 1976–78, gen mangr Jardine Fleming Tokyo 1978–84, dir Robert Fleming Holdings 1984–, pres and chief exec offr NY office 1985–89, chm Fleming Investment Management London 1990–94, dep chm Robert Fleming Asset Management 1994–; *Recreations* sailing, gardening; *Style*— Iain Saunders, Esq; ✉ Robert Fleming & Co Ltd, 25 Copthall Avenue, London EC2R 7DR (☎ 0171 638 5858, fax 0171 282 4330)

SAUNDERS, Prof John; s of John Saunders, and Queeni, *née* Thomas; *b* 27 Aug 1946; *Educ* Hatfield Secdy Mod Sch, Doncaster Tech Coll Univ of Loughborough (BSc), Cranfield Inst of Technol (MBA), Univ of Bradford (DPhil); *m* 7 Aug 1981, Veronica Wai Yoke, da of Wong Peng Chow; 1 s (Paul), 1 da (Carolyne); *Career* sales and marketing Hawker Siddeley Aviation; lectr: Univ of Bradford Mgmnt Centre, Univ of Warwick Business Sch; prof of marketing Univ of Loughborough and dir Loughborough Univ Business Sch; coordinator of the ESRC Marketing Initiative, ed Int Jl of Research in Marketing, asst ed Br Jl of Management; memb: Senate Chartered Inst of Mktg, Fellowship Ctee of British Acad of Management, Exec Ctee Euro Marketing Acad; FBAM, FCIM, FRSA; *Books* Enterprise (1977), Practical Business Forecasting (1987), The Specification of Aggregate Marketing Phenomina (1987), The Best of Companies (1989), Competitive Positioning (1993), The Marketing Initiative (1994), Principles of Marketing: The European Edition (1996); *Recreations* my family, travel, rock, literature, history, science and technology, exercise, DIY and gardening; *Style*— Prof John Saunders; ✉ 36 Sunnyhill, Burbage, Leicestershire LE10 2SB (☎ 01509 223111)

SAUNDERS, John Henry Boulton; QC (1991); s of Henry George Boulton Saunders (d 1984), and Kathleen Mary, *née* Brandle; *b* 15 March 1949; *Educ* St John's Coll Sch Cambridge, Uppingham (music scholar), Magdalen Coll Oxford; *m* 20 Dec 1975, Susan Mary, da of Charles William Paull Chick (d 1989); 1 s (Daniel Paull b 26 Nov 1985), 2 da (Sarah Kate b 30 Nov 1977, Hannah May b 21 May 1979); *Career* called to the Bar 1972; prosecuting counsel to the DHSS (now DSS) Midland and Oxford Circuit 1983–91, asst recorder 1987–90, recorder 1990–; *Recreations* music, sailing; *Style*— John Saunders, Esq, QC; ✉ 4 Fountain Court, Steelhouse Lane, Birmingham B4 6DR (☎ 0121 236 3476)

SAUNDERS, Prof Kenneth Barrett; s of Harold Nicholas Saunders (d 1993), of Stratton, Cornwall, and Winifred Florence, *née* Gadge (d 1984); *b* 16 March 1936; *Educ* Kingswood Sch Bath, Trinity Hall Cambridge (maj open scholar in classics, MB BChir, MA, MD), St Thomas's Hosp London (univ scholar, Wainbridge prize in med, Seymour Graves Toller prize in med, Bristowe medal in pathology, MRCP 1963, FRCP 1978); *m* 1961, Philippa Mary, da of Col Philip Teviot Harrison; 1 da (Katherine Louise b 1963), 1 s (Stephen Mark b 1966); *Career* jr and research posts St Thomas' Hosp, Hammersmith Hosp and Cardiovascular Research Unit UC San Francisco 1961–72; Middx Hosp Med Sch London: sr lectr in med 1972–79, postgraduate sub-dean 1975–79, reader in med 1979–80; prof of med St George's Hosp Med Sch London 1980–96 (chm of med 1980–90), dean Faculty of Med Univ of London 1990–94, emeritus prof of med Univ of London 1996–; hon conslt physician to the Army 1994–96; memb: Governing Body Br Postgraduate Med Fedn 1990–96, Cncl Sch of Pharmacy Univ of London 1990–96, Jt Planning and Advsy Ctee Dept of Health 1990–94, Med Advsy Ctee Ctee of Vice-Chllrs and Princs 1990–94, Jt Ctee on Higher Med Trg 1990–95; pres Special Advsy Ctee on Gen Internal Med 1990–95; RCP: Tudor Edwards lectr 1987, procensor 1986–87, censor 1987–88, sr examiner 1986–96; memb Cncl RSM 1983–88 (sr hon librarian 1987–88); pres: Euro Soc for Clinical Respiratory Physiology 1986–88, Assoc of Clinical Profs of Med 1993–96; memb GMC 1992–96; memb Editorial Bd Br Jl of Hosp Med 1985–91; memb: Med Research Soc (sec 1978–80), RSM, Assoc of Physicians, Br Thoracic Soc, Euro Respiratory Soc, Classical Assoc, Hellenic Soc, Horatian Soc; *Books* Clinical Physiology of the Lung (1977); author of papers on respiratory med and science in Clinical Science, Thorax, Jl of Physiology; *Recreations* classical literature, especially Homer and Horace, English literature, golf, squash racquets; *Clubs* RAC, Royal Blackheath Golf; *Style*— Prof Kenneth Saunders; ✉ 77 Lee Road, London SE3 9EN (☎ 0181 852 8138, fax 0181 297 8501)

SAUNDERS, Sir Peter; kt (1982); s of Ernest Saunders, and Aletta Saunders; *b* 23 Nov 1911; *Educ* Oundle, Lausanne; *m* 1, 1959, Ann Stewart (d 1976); m 2, 1979, Catherine Imperiali di Francavilla (see Katie Boyle, *qv*); *Career* impresario; served WWII (Capt); early career as film cameraman, film dir, journalist and press agent; theatrical producer 1947–94 (ret); operated rep Royal Artillery Theatre Woolwich 1951 and Prince of Wales Theatre Cardiff 1956; currently chm and md Peter Saunders Group Ltd; currently dir West End Theatre Managers Ltd; fndr Theatre Investment Fund Ltd 1976 (life pres 1995), Theatre Investment Finance Ltd; prodr of over 100 plays incl The Mousetrap (prodr of original show 1952–94, world's longest ever run Dec 1971, rights sold 1994 to consortium headed by Sir Stephen Waley-Cohen, Bt); other West End Prodns incl: Fly Away Peter, The Perfect Woman, Breach of Marriage, My Mother Said, The Hollow, Witness for the Prosecution, The Manor of Northstead, The Water Gipsies, The Bride and the Bachelor, Subway in the Sky, Verdict, The Trial of Mary Dugan, The Unexpected Guest, A Day in the Life of, And Suddenly it's Spring, Go Back for Murder, You Prove It, Fit to Print, Rule of Three, Alfie, The Reluctant Peer, Hostile Witness, Every Other Evening, Return Ticket, Arsenic and Old Lace, Justice is a Woman, As You Like It, Oh Clarence!, On a Foggy Day, The Jockey Club Stakes, Move Over Mrs Markham, Lover, Cockie, Double Edge, A Murder is Announced, The Family Reunion, Cards on the Table; bought Volcano Productions Ltd 1971 (prodns incl No Sex Please We're British, The Mating Game, Lloyd George Knew My Father, At the End of the Day, Touch of Spring, Betzi); lessee Ambassadors Theatre 1958–74, owner Duchess Theatre 1961–68, lessee St Martin's Theatre 1968, owner Vaudeville Theatre 1969–83, owner Duke of York's Theatre 1976–79 (sold to Capital Radio, contractual condition for use as live theatre in perpetuity); prodr over 1,500 programmes for Radio Luxembourg; original dir Yorkshire Television, memb Consortium awarded London Gen Radio Station (became Capital Radio 1973); vice pres: Actors' Benevolent Fund 1972–, Royal Gen Theatre Fund Assoc 1985–; memb Exec Cncl SWET (now SOLT) 1954– (pres 1961–62 and 1967–69, vice pres 1988–94), memb Cncl Theatrical Mgmnt Assoc 1958–64; pres: Stage Golfing Soc 1963, Stage Cricket Club 1956–65; life memb Dogs Home Battersea

1988, govr Christ's Hosp; awarded Silver Heart Award Variety Club of GB 1955; *Publications* The Mousetrap Man (autobiog, 1972), Scales of Justice (play, 1978); *Recreations* cricket, chess, bridge, photography, music of George Gershwin, telephoning, collecting wills; *Clubs* MCC, Highgate Golf; *Style—* Sir Peter Saunders; ✉ Monkswell, Canons Close, The Bishops Avenue, London N2 0BH (☎ 0181 458 4266, fax 0181 905 5925)

SAUNDERS, Prof Peter Robert; s of Albert Edward Saunders, of Orpington, Kent, and Joan Kathleen, *née* Swan; *b* 30 Aug 1950; *Educ* Selhurst GS Croydon, Univ of Kent (BA), Univ of London (PhD); *m* 15 April 1971 (m dis 1990), Susan Elisabeth, da of Dr Frank Ellis, of Redhill, Surrey; 1 s (Michael b 1971), 1 da (Claire Louise b 1973); *Career* res offr Univ of Essex 1973–76, prof of sociology Univ of Sussex 1988– (lectr 1976–84, reader 1984–88); FRSA 1987; *Books* Urban Politics: A Sociological Interpretation (1979), Social Theory and the Urban Question (1981 and 1986), An Introduction to British Politics (1984), Social Class and Stratification (1989), A Nation of Home Owners (1990), Privatisation and Popular Capitalism (1994), Capitalism: A Social Audit (1995), Unequal but Fair? A Study of Class Barriers in Britain (1996); *Style—* Prof Peter Saunders; ✉ School of Social Sciences, University of Sussex, Falmer, Brighton BN1 9QN (☎ 01273 678883, fax 01273 673563)

SAUNDERS, Richard; s of Edward Ernest Saunders (d 1971), of Henley-on-Thames, and Betty, *née* Belsey (d 1993); *b* 4 July 1937; *Educ* St Edmund's Sch Hindhead, Uppingham; *m* 1, 21 Sept 1961, Suzannah, da of Thomas Rhodes-Cooke (d 1985), of Chiswick; 1 s (Andrew b 1964); m 2, 12 June 1970, Alison, da of Maj J A Fiddes (d 1964), of Wimbledon; *Career* 2 Lt LG 1958–60, served in Germany; govr Royal Star and Garter Home 1984–; chartered surveyor; chm Baker Harris Saunders Gp plc 1986–92, conslt Herring Baker Harris Group plc 1992–93; dir: Br Property Fedn 1974–90, St Edmund's Sch Tst Ltd 1978–93, Star and Garter Trading and Promotions Ltd; chm: City Branch RICS 1979–80, Metropolitan Public Gdns Assoc 1984–91; dep for Ward of Candlewick 1983–; Sheriff City of London 1987–88; bd memb Gen Practice Finance Corp 1985–89; govr Bridewell Royal Hosp and King Edward's Sch Witley 1976–93, partnership conslt Christ's Hospital 1993– (govr and almoner 1980–93); memb: Cncl Br Property Fedn 1974–90 (hon treas 1974–85), Ct of Common Cncl Corp of London 1975–; pres Associated Owners of City Properties 1984–86, chm Ex-Servs Resettlement Gp 1991–93; Liveryman and memb Ct of Assts Worshipful Co of Clothworkers 1960 (Warden 1989–90), Liveryman Worshipful Co of Chartered Surveyors 1979–93; FRICS; *Recreations* golf, tennis (lawn and real), music; *Clubs* Cavalry and Guards', MCC, City Livery; *Style—* Richard Saunders, Esq; ✉ 13 Caroline Place, London W2 4AW (☎ 0171 727 1637, fax 0171 243 0643); The Old Rectory, Bagendon, Cirencester, Glos GL7 7DU (01285 831352)

SAUNDERS, Prof Trevor John; s of William John Saunders (d 1976), of Melksham, Wilts, and Phyllis Margaret, *née* Escott (d 1990); *b* 12 July 1934; *Educ* Chippenham GS, UCL (BA), Emmanuel Coll Cambridge (PhD); *m* 5 Sept 1959, Teresa Mary Louisa, da of Albert John Schmitz, of Felixstowe, Suffolk; 2 da (Clare b 14 April 1963, Angela b 7 June 1965); *Career* lectr 1959–72: Bedford Coll London, Univ of Hull, Univ of Newcastle upon Tyne; Univ of Newcastle upon Tyne: sr lectr in classics 1972–78, reader in Greek philosophy 1978, prof of Greek 1978–, head Dept of Classics 1976–82 and 1987–92, memb Senate 1977–80, 1982–85 and 1988–91, dean of Faculty Arts 1982–85, memb Cncl 1984–87 and 1989–92; memb Cncl Univ of Durham 1987–93; visiting memb Inst of Advanced Study Princeton NJ USA 1971–72, 1986 and summer visitor 1993, res fell Humanities Res Centre ANU Canberra 1986, Leverhulme Tst res fell 1992–93, visiting fell Brasenose Coll Oxford 1993; memb Cncl: Soc Promotion of Hellenic Studies 1968–71 and 1974–77, Classical Assoc 1974–79 (pres Northumberland and Durham branch 1984–86); chm Cncl Univ Classics Dept 1981–84; *Books* 3 Penguin Classics: Plato, The Laws (1970), Aristotle, The Politics (revised, 1981), Plato, Early Socratic Dialogues (contrib ed, 1987); Notes on the Laws of Plato (1972), Bibliography on the Laws of Plato (1976), Plato's Penal Code (1991), Aristotle, Politics I and II, Translation and Commentary (1995); *Recreations* railway history, cinema; *Style—* Prof Trevor Saunders; ✉ 27 Moorside South, Newcastle upon Tyne, NE4 9BD (☎ 0191 273 7586); Department of Classics, The University, Newcastle upon Tyne NE1 7RU (☎ 0191 222 7977, fax 0191 222 5432)

SAUNDERS, Prof Wilfred Leonard; CBE (1982); s of Leonard Saunders (d 1962), of Birmingham, and Annie, *née* Vine (d 1973); *b* 18 April 1920; *Educ* King Edward's GS Camp Hill Birmingham, Fitzwilliam House Cambridge (BA, MA); *m* 15 June 1946, Joan Mary, da of Maj W E Rider, TD (d 1949), of Birmingham; 2 s (John b 11 Jan 1948, Peter b 24 Nov 1952); *Career* enlisted Signalman 48 Div Signals TA; served BEF France and Belgium 1940 (evacuated Dunkirk), cmmnd RCS 1942, 1 Army N Africa 1942–43, CMF Italy 1943–46, Capt and Adj 1945, Staff Capt Q at GHQ Caserta 1945–46; dep librarian Inst of Bankers 1948–49, founding librarian Univ of Birmingham Inst of Educn 1949–56, dep librarian Univ of Sheffield 1956–63, seconded UNESCO Uganda 1962, founding dir Postgrad Sch of Librarianship (now Dept of Info Studies) Univ of Sheffield 1963, prof of librarianship and info sci Univ of Sheffield 1968–82 (dean Faculty of Educn Studies 1974–77, emeritus prof 1982); pres Library Assoc 1980, library and info advsy work and consultancy UNESCO, Br Cncl and others 1981–, chm Library and Info Servs Cncl 1981–84, visiting prof Univ of Pittsburgh 1968 and Univ of California Los Angeles 1985; chm Br Cncl's Libraries Advsy Panel 1975–81 (memb 1970–), memb Lord Chllr's Advsy Cncl on Public Records 1986–91; author of numerous pubns on librarianship and info work; Hon LittD Univ of Sheffield 1989; FLA 1952, Hon FIInfSci 1977, Hon FCP 1983; *Recreations* gardening, listening to music, book collecting, walking, dancing; *Style—* Prof Wilfred Saunders, CBE; ✉ 15 Princess Drive, Sawston, Cambridge CB2 4DL

SAUNDERS WATSON, Cdr (Leslie) Michael Macdonald; CBE (1993), DL (Northants 1979); s of Capt Leslie Swain Saunders, DSO, JP, RN, and Elizabeth, da of Vice Adm Sir Michael Culme-Seymour, 4 Bt, KCB, MVO; *b* 9 Oct 1934; *Educ* Eton, RNC Dartmouth; *m* 1958, Georgina Elizabeth Laetitia, da of Adm Sir William Davis, GCB, DSO; 2 s, 1 da; *Career* served RN 1951–71 (Cdr 1969); High Sheriff Northants 1978–79; vice chm Northants Small Industs Ctee 1974–79; chm: Northants Assoc Youth Clubs 1977–91, Heritage Educn Year 1977, Corby Community Advsy Gp 1979–86, Ironstone Royalty Owners Assoc 1979–91, Northants Tourism Advsy Panel 1986–91, Nat Curriculum History Working Gp 1989–91, Heritage Educn Tst 1987–96, Br Library Bd 1990–93, Kettering Gen Hosp Tst 1993–, Friends of Br Library 1994–; memb British Heritage Ctee BTA 1978–88, pres Historic Houses Assoc 1982–88; dir: Lamport Hall Preservation Tst 1978–91, English Sinfonia 1980–, Northants Enterprise Agency 1986–91; tstee: Royal Botanic Gardens Kew 1983–91, Nat Heritage Meml Fund 1987–; CLA: memb Taxation and Legal Ctees 1975–89, Exec Ctee 1975–80 and 1987–92, Fin and Gen Purposes Ctee 1993–, chm Northants Branch 1981–84 (memb 1974–); chm Govrs Lodge Park Comprehensive 1977–83, tstee Oakham Sch 1975–77 (dep pres 1978–82, chm Tax and Parly Ctee 1975–82), Hon DLitt Univ of Warwick 1991; *Recreations* sailing, music, gardening; *Clubs* Brooks's; *Style—* Cdr L M M Saunders Watson, CBE, DL, RN; ✉ Rockingham Castle, Market Harborough, Leics LE16 8TH (☎ 01536 770326); office (☎ 01536 770240)

SAUZIER, Sir (André) Guy; kt (1973), CBE (1959), ED; s of J Adrien Sauzier, of Mauritius; *b* 20 Oct 1910; *Educ* Royal Coll Mauritius; *m* 1936, Thérèse, da of Henri Mallac; 6 s, 2 da; *Career* served WWII Maj Mauritius TF; MLC Mauritius 1949–57, Mauritius rep at Coronation 1953, memb Mauritius Political Delgn to UK 1955, min of Works and Communications 1957–59, gen overseas rep Mauritius Chamber of Agric 1959–79, min plen to EEC 1972–79; *Style—* Sir Guy Sauzier, CBE, ED; ✉ 15 Marloes Rd, London W8 6LQ

SAVAGE, David Jack; s of Arthur Jack Savage (d 1953), of Farnborough, and Sylvia Maude, *née* Bacon (d 1993; descendant of Sir Nicholas Bacon, Lord Keeper of the Great Seal to Queen Elizabeth I); *b* 7 Aug 1939; *Educ* Hurstpierpoint Coll, Univ of London (LLB), Coll of Law; *m* 16 May 1981, Elizabeth Mary, da of late Dr Edmond Louis Ives, and Sheila Ives; 2 s (Nicholas David St John b 1982, Louis Arthur Ives b 1983); *Career* admitted slr 1963; sr ptnr Foster, Savage & Gordon of Farnborough 1984–; NP 1988; cmmr of income tax 1969–90, vice chm N Hants Local Valuation Tribunal 1984–90 (memb 1976–90); pres Hampshire Inc Law Soc 1983–84, dir Slrs' Benevolent Assoc 1984–96; memb: No 3 Southern Area Legal Aid Ctee 1989–, Ctee Berks Bucks and Oxon Law Soc 1990–, Cncl Law Soc 1990– (memb Criminal Law Ctee 1988–); cncllr: Farnborough UDC 1964–73 (vice chm 1972–73), Rushmoor Borough Cncl 1973–80; Parly candidate (Cons): Birmingham Sparkbrook 1974, Birmingham Smallheath 1979; chm of Govrs Farnborough GS 1970–72, dir Aldershot FC 1971, govr Swinton Cons Coll 1971–74, vice pres Aldershot Divnl Cons Assoc 1973– (chm 1969–73); Liveryman: Worshipful Co of Arbitrators 1989, Worshipful Co of Scriveners 1990, Worshipful Co of Woolmen 1991; Freeman City of London 1989; ACIArb 1988; *Recreations* travel (preferably by train), browsing, bricklaying, ornithology; *Clubs* Royal Aldershot Offrs, Law Soc; *Style—* David Savage, Esq; ✉ Ridgeway, 16 Clockhouse Rd, Farnborough, Hants GU14 7QY; Foster Savage and Gordon, 269 Farnborough Rd, Farnborough, Hants GU14 7LX (☎ 01252 541401, fax 01252 373428)

SAVAGE, Sir Ernest Walter; kt (1979); s of late Walter Edwin Savage; *b* 24 Aug 1912; *Educ* Brisbane GS, Scots Coll Warwick Queensland; *m* 1938, Dorothy Winifred, da of A W Nicholls; 1 s, 1 da; *Career* ptnr Coopers & Lybrand Brisbane 1940–76, hon consul for Norway in Brisbane 1950–76; Inst of CA's: memb Nat Cncl 1961–72, nat pres 1968–70, life memb 1978; memb: Bd of Govrs Cromwell Univ 1950–77 (chm 1958–67), Queensland State Cncl of CA's 1951–76 (chm 1958–60 and 1966), Advsy Bd Salvation Army 1981–92; chm: Bank of Queensland 1960–84, Qld Govt Ctee Review of Business Regulations 1985, Public Sector Review Ctee 1987, Geriatric Med Fndn 1986–94, Leukaemia Fdn 1985–94; Knight (1 class) of Order of St Olaf; FCA; *Clubs* Queensland, Brisbane; *Style—* Sir Ernest Savage; ✉ Forest Place, R 42/356 Blunder Road, Durack, Brisbane, Qld 4077, Australia (☎ 017 3722669)

SAVAGE, Francis Joseph (Frank); CMG (1996), LVO (1986), OBE (1989); s of Francis Fitzgerald Savage, and Mona May, *née* Parsons (d 1973); *b* 8 Feb 1943; *Educ* St Stephens RC Sch Welling Kent, North West Kent Coll (county finalist boxing); *m* 6 Aug 1966, Veronica Mary, da of Peter McAleenan, and Nora McAleenan; 2 s (Mark Francis b 14 April 1969, James Christopher b 8 Dec 1971); *Career* FCO 1961–: joined 1961, served in Cairo 1967–70, Washington 1971–73, Aden 1973–74, second sec FCO 1974–78, vice consul then consul (commercial) Düsseldorf 1978–82, first sec and HM consul Peking 1982–86, first sec Lagos and HM consul Benin 1987–90, first sec 1990–93, cnsllr 1993, governor of Montserrat 1993–; memb: Commonwealth Tst, Catenian Assoc; *Recreations* cricket, travel, meeting people, volcano watching, hurricane dodging; *Clubs* Royal Overseas, Kent CC, Peking Cricket; *Style—* Frank Savage, Esq, CMG, LVO, OBE; ✉ Government House, Montserrat, West Indies; Foreign and Commonwealth Office, King Charles Street, London SW1A 2AH (☎ 0171 270 3000)

SAVAGE, Graeme Peter; s of Peter Samuel Savage, of Hove, Sussex, and Patricia, *née* Kerr; *b* 12 Aug 1952; *Educ* Univ of Reading (BA); *m* 1, 12 Dec 1972 (m dis 1992); 1 da (Tamara Jane b 26 Nov 1972), 2 s (Jonathan Peter b 10 Nov 1975, Joseph Graeme b 16 Nov 1979); m 2, Sharon Elizabeth; 2 s (Alexander Gannon b 20 Dec 1990, Connor George b 2 May 1996); *Career* magazine sales rep Thomson Magazines Ltd (grad trainee 1974–75); RIBA Services Ltd: sales rep 1976–77, field sales mangr 1977–78, sales mangr 1978–81, publisher 1981–82, publishing dir 1982–87, dep md 1987–91, md 1991–94; md Wedgwood Markham Associates Ltd 1994–; FInstD 1991–; *Recreations* music, rugby, travel; *Style—* Graeme Savage, Esq; ✉ Wedgwood Markham Associates Ltd, The Coach House, Ealing Green, London W5 5ER (☎ 0181 579 8184, fax 0181 579 3991)

SAVAGE, Peter Edmund Annesley; s of Gordon Annesley (d 1988), and Margaret Emma, *née* Hyson; *b* 25 Nov 1935; *Educ* Welwyn Garden City GS, St Mary's Hosp Med Sch (Warren Low award); *m* 1, 2 Sept 1961 (m dis 1973), Margaret Ann, da of late John Sweetman; 1 s (Michael b 1964), 1 da (Elizabeth b 1965); m 2, 12 Jan 1974, Anne Lowden (d 1989), da of late James Robertson; 2 s (James b 1975, Robert 1976); m 3, 25 Nov 1995, Marjorie Joyce Treanor; *Career* house surgn St Mary's Hosp London 1960, house physician Paddington Gen Hosp London 1961, casualty offr St Mary's Hosp 1962, orthopaedic and gen surgical registrar Worthing Hosp 1963, actg sr registrar W Middx Hosp 1966 (surgical registrar 1965), res registrar St Mary's Hosp London 1967, res registrar NW Met Regnl Hosp Bd 1967; sr registrar: Wexham Park Hosp Slough 1968, St Mary's Hosp London 1969–73 (cardiothoracic 1 asst 1972); conslt surgn Queen Mary's Hosp Sidcup Kent 1974–94, assoc dean of postgrad med (SE Thames) Br Postgrad Med Fedn Univ of London 1991–96, medical dir Queen Mary's Sidcup NHS Trust 1995–; St Mary's Hosp: memb Intensive Therapy Ctee 1974–87, chm Library Ctee 1975–78, chm Med Records Ctee 1975–78, chm Disaster Planning Ctee 1975–95, memb Hosp Mgmnt Team 1980–82, chm Med Staff Ctee 1980–82, chm Med Exec Ctee 1980–82, surgical tutor 1985–90, clinical tutor and dir of med educn 1986–90; chm: Bexley Dist Disaster Planning Ctee 1975–90, Greenwich and Bexley Div BMA 1978; memb: Greenwich and Bexley Area Med Advsy Ctee 1974–79, Bexley Dist Med Ctee 1980–82, Cncl Section of Sugery RSM 1979–81; sec Frognal Med Soc 1988–89; memb: BMA, Hosp Conslts and Specialists Assoc, Assoc of Surgn of GB and I, World Assoc for Emergency and Disaster Med, W Kent Medico-chirurgical Soc, Frognal Med Soc, Int Soc on Disaster Med, Assoc for The Study of Med Educn, Med Writers Gp Soc of Authors; FRSH, FRSM; *Books* Disasters - Hospital Planning (1979), Problems in Peripheral Vascular Disease (1983); author of numerous papers on disaster planning; *Recreations* hill walking; *Style—* Peter Savage, Esq; ✉ 213 Lauderdale Tower, Barbican, London EC2Y 8BY (☎ 0171 562 9955)

SAVAGE, Rick; *b* 2 Dec 1960; *Career* formerly: apprentice footballer Sheffield Utd FC, trainee technician BR; currently bassist; fndr memb Def Leppard 1977; Def Leppard tours: Pyromania 1983, Hysteria 1987, Adrenalize 1992; 1 UK top ten single (Animal 1987), 3 US top ten singles (Hysteria 1988, Pour Some Sugar On Me 1988, Armageddon 1989); albums with Def Leppard: On Through The Night (1980, UK no 15), High 'N' Dry (1981, UK no 26), Pyromania (1983, UK no 2), Hysteria (1987, UK and US no 1), Adrenalize (1992), Retro-Active (1993), Slang (1996); awards incl: Favourite Heavy Metal Artist, Favourite Heavy Metal Album (for Hysteria) American Music Awards 1989; *Style—* Rick Savage, Esq; ✉ c/o Mercury, Chancellors House, 72 Chancellors Road, London W6 9QB (☎ 0181 910 5678, fax 0181 910 5896)

SAVAGE, Valerie (Mrs Paul Ridout); *b* 1944; *Educ* N London Collegiate Sch, Central Sch of Speech & Drama; *m* Paul Ridout; 1 da (Lucy); *Career* speech and language conslt, specialist in communication disorders; formerly chief speech and language therapist Nuffield Hearing and Speech Centre (helped launch Nuffield Dyspraxia Prog), currently in private practice; *Publications* incl professional articles on speech disorders in the pre-school child and teaching progs to treat them; *Recreations* theatre, Indian cookery, horses; *Style—* Miss Valerie Savage; ✉ 97 Harley Street, London W1 (☎ 0171 486 0503; fax 01306 880890)

SAVAGE, Wendy Diane; da of William George Edwards (d 1984), and Anne, *née* Smith (d 1943); *b* 12 April 1935; *Educ* Croydon HS, Girton Coll Cambridge (BA), London Hosp Med Coll (MB BChir); *m* 27 July 1960 (m dis 1973), Miguel Babatunde Richard (Mike) Savage, s of Richard Gabriel Akiwande Savage, of Edinburgh (d 1993); 2 s (Nicholas Richard b 10 June 1964, Jonathan Chukuma b 18 April 1969), 2 da (Yewande Patricia b 9 April 1961, Wendy Claire b 28 May 1962); *Career* res fell Harvard Univ 1962–64, MO Awo-omama and Enugu Nigeria 1964–67; registrar: Kenyatta Hosp Nairobi 1967–69, Royal Free Hosp London 1969–71; various posts Tower Hamlets, Islington Borough and Pregnancy Advsy Serv 1971–73, specialist in obstetrics Cook Hosp NZ 1973–76, lectr London Hosp 1976–77, sr lectr in obstetrics and gynaecology London Hosp Med Coll and hon conslt Royal London Hosp 1977–; hon visiting prof Faculty of Social Scis Middx Univ 1991–; PR Offr Doctors For Women's Choice on Abortion; tstee: Simon Population Tst, Birth Control Campaign; patron Pregnancy Advsy Serv (former tstee); advsr Maternity Alliance; fndr memb: Women in Medicine, Women in Gynaecology and Obstetrics; chair Forum on Maternity and the Newborn RSM 1987–89; memb GMC 1989–; pres: Med Women's Fedn 1992–93, Exec Ctee Safe Motherhood (UK) 1993–94 (resigned); FRCOG 1985 (MRCOG 1971); FRSA 1992; *Books* Hysterectomy (1982), Coping with Caesarian Section and Other Difficult Births (with Fran Reader, 1983), A Savage Enquiry (1986), Caesarean Birth in Britain (with Colin Francome, Helen Churchill and Helen Lewison, 1993); *Recreations* reading novels, playing piano duets, travel; *Style*— Mrs Wendy Savage; ✉ 19 Vincent Terrace, London N1 8HN (☎ 0171 837 7635); Royal London Hospital, Whitechapel, London E1 1BB (☎ 0171 377 7240, fax 0171 377 7160)

SAVERNAKE, Viscount; Thomas James Brudenell-Bruce; only s, and h of Earl of Cardigan; gs of 8 Marquess of Ailesbury; *b* 11 Feb 1982; *Educ* Cothill, Radley; *Style*— Viscount Savernake

SAVIDGE, Dr Geoffrey Francis; *b* 16 Dec 1940; *Educ* Univ of Cambridge (MB BChir, MA), Karolinska Inst Stockholm Sweden (MD); *m* Paula Margaretha; 2 s (Tor b 1964, Kevin b 1975), 1 da (Kim b 1966); *Career* lectr: Dept of Neurology Karolinska Hosp Stockholm 1969–71, Dept of Pathology and Clinical Chemistry St Gorans Hosp Stockholm 1974–77 (Dept of Med 1971–74); res assoc Inst of Coagulation Res Karolinska Inst Stockholm 1976–79, physician Dept of Coagulation Disorders Karolinska Hosp Stockholm 1977–79; St Thomas' Hosp London: dir Haemophilia Reference Centre 1979–, sr lectr and hon conslt 1979, dir of coagulation res Rayne Inst 1988–; memb: Br Soc of Thrombosis and Haemostasis 1983, NY Acad of Sci 1986, American Soc of Haematology 1988, American Heart Assoc 1989, American Assoc for Advancement of Sci; *Books* Factor VIII - von Willebrand Factor (2 vols, 1989); *Recreations* music, reading, sport; *Clubs* United Oxford & Cambridge Univ; *Style*— Dr Geoffrey Savidge; ✉ Haemophilia Centre, St Thomas' Hospital, Lambeth Palace Rd, London SE1 7EH (☎ 0171 620 0378, fax 0171 401 3125)

SAVILE, 3 Baron (UK 1888); George Halifax Lumley-Savile; JP (Borough of Dewsbury 1955), DL (W Yorks 1954); patron of two livings; s of 2 Baron (d 1931), of Rufford Abbey, Ollerton, Notts, and Esmé Grace Virginia (d 1958), da of John Wolton; *b* 24 Jan 1919; *Educ* Eton; *Heir* bro, Hon Henry Lumley-Savile; *Career* formerly Capt Duke of Wellington's Regt, attached 1 Bn Lincs Regt, Burma 1943–44; chm St John Cncl S and W Yorks 1980, pres W Yorks SSAFA 1986; landowner (18,000 acres); CStJ 1983; *Recreations* shooting, listening to classical music; *Clubs* Brooks's, Huddersfield, Sloane; *Style*— The Rt Hon the Lord Savile, JP, DL; ✉ Gryce Hall, Shelley, Huddersfield, W Yorks (☎ 01484 602774); Savile Estate Office, Thornhill, Dewsbury, W Yorks (☎ 01924 462341)

SAVILE, Sir James Wilson Vincent (Jimmy); kt (1990), OBE (1971); s of Vincent Savile, and Agnes, *née* Kelly; *b* 31 Oct 1926; *Educ* St Annes Elementary Sch Leeds; *Career* TV and radio personality; 'Bevin Boy' Coal Mines 1942–48; sometime presenter: Jimmy Savile Show (BBC Radio 1), Jim'll Fix It (BBC1), Mind How You Go (BBC), Top of The Pops (BBC1); voluntary helper: Stoke Mandeville Hosp, Leeds Infirmary, Broadmoor Hosp; major fundraiser for various national charities (runner in London Marathon on numerous occasions); Hon LLD Univ of Leeds 1986; Sony Radio Gold Award 1992; memb Mensa; KCSG (Holy See) 1982; *Books* As It Happens/Love is an Uphill Thing (autobiog 1975), God'll Fix It (1979); *Recreations* running, cycling, wrestling; *Clubs* Athenaeum; *Style*— Sir Jimmy Savile, OBE; ✉ National Spinal Injuries Centre, Stoke Mandeville Hospital, Mandeville Rd, Aylesbury, Bucks HP21 8AL (☎ 01296 315843)

SAVILL, Rosalind Joy; da of Dr Guy Savill, and Lorna, *née* Williams; *b* 12 May 1951; *Educ* Wycombe Abbey, Châtelard Sch Montreux, Univ of Leeds (BA), The Study Centre for the Fine and Decorative Arts (dip); *children* 1 da (Isabella Dove Savill b 23 dec 1989); *Career* museum asst V & A Museum 1973–74; The Wallace Collection: museum asst 1974–78, asst to the dir 1978–92, dir 1992–; fndr ctee memb French Porcelain Soc (chm 1988–94); memb: Advsy Ctee Treasure Houses of Britain exhbn Nat Gall of Art Washington DC 1985, Comité Scientifique Versailles, Tables Royales exhbn Château de Versailles 1993–94, Vetting Ctee Annual Int Ceramics Seminar and Fair London 1981–, Object of the Year Ctee The Grosvenor House Antique Dealers' Fair London 1990–91, Cncl Attingham Summer Sch 1980–92 (fndr chm Scholarship Ctee); author of numerous articles in art jls; FRSA 1990, FSA 1990; *Books* The Wallace Collection - Sèvres Porcelain (1980), Treasure Houses of Britain - Five Hundred Years of Private Patronage and Art Collecting (contrib, 1985), The Wallace Collection Catalogue of Sèvres Porcelain (3 vols, 1988), The Wallace Collection - French Gold Boxes (1991), Boughton House - The English Versailles (contrib, 1992); *Recreations* music, birds, wildlife, gardens; *Style*— Miss Rosalind Savill, FSA; ✉ The Wallace Collection, Hertford House, Manchester Square, London W1M 6BN (☎ 0171 935 0687, fax 0171 224 2155)

SAVILL, Timothy Lydall; s of Edwin Lydall Savill (d 1940), (gs of Alfred Savill, fndr Alfred Savill & Sons, Chartered Surveyors, in 1859) and Margaret H K Thorne (d 1976); uncle Sir Eric Savill, KCVO, MBE, MC, FRICS, fndr the Savill Gardens in Windsor Great Park when dep ranger, also chm Royal Forests, and Keeper of Gardens at Windsor; *b* 25 March 1940; *Educ* Haileybury and Imperial Service Coll Windsor, Radley, Coll of Estate Mgmnt Univ of London; *m* 1, 14 June 1963 (m dis 1973), Sonia Mary Barradale; 1 s (Nicholas b 1966), 1 da (Caroline b 1968); m 2, 1 June 1982 (m dis 1986), Ann Rosemary Stone; *Career* chartered surveyor; fndr dir Timothy Savill & Co; Freeman: City of London, Worshipful Co of Skinners; FRICS; *Recreations* fly-fishing, shooting, gardening, swimming; *Clubs* RAC; *Style*— Timothy L Savill, Esq; ✉ Pikes Farm House, Forest Road, Bill Hill, Wokingham, Berkshire RG40 5QR (☎ 0118 978 3280); PO Box 7, Forest Rd, Bill Hill, Wokingham, Berkshire RG40 5NZ (☎ 0118 978 3280, fax 0118 979 4357)

SAVILLE, Clive Howard; *b* 7 July 1943; *Educ* Bishop Gore GS Swansea, Univ Coll Swansea (BA); *m* 1967, (Camille) Kathleen, da of Edmund St C Burke (d 1979); *Career* Dept for Educn and Employment 1965–; currently dir The Better English Campaign; *Style*— Clive Saville, Esq; ✉ The Better English Campaign, Commonwealth House, 1–19 New Oxford Street, London WC1A 1NU (☎ 0171 404 9911)

SAVILLE, John David; JP; s of Bertie Edward Barrie-Saville, and Catherine, *née* Taysum (d 1965); *b* 5 Jan 1932; *Educ* Aston Commercial Coll; *m* 1; 1 s (David John b 4 April 1964), 2 da (Sharon Ann (Mrs Wilson-Gunn) b 15 Jan 1958, Amanda Theresa (Mrs Cazalet) b 17 Feb 1960); m 2, 20 Dec 1989, Josephine Margaret, da of John Whelan; *Career* Nat Serv Royal Warwicks 1950–52; chm and md J Saville Gordon Group plc 1955–; dir: Industrial Metal Services Ltd, Leigh Interests plc 1989–; memb Ctee Solihull Inst for Med Trg and Res; scout co pres Birmingham; chm The Stonehouse Gang; dir Birmingham Gang Show Ltd; High Sheriff of West Midlands 1996–97; Liveryman Worshipful Co of Pattenmakers; *Recreations* horse riding, skiing, tennis, swimming, walking, light aircraft; *Clubs* Midlands Sporting; *Style*— John D Saville, Esq, JP; ✉ Barrells Park, Ullenhall, Nr Henley in Arden, Warwicks B95 5NQ; J Saville Gordon Group plc, Cranford House, Kenilworth Road, Blackdown, Royal Leamington Spa, Warwicks CV32 6RG (☎ 01926 426526, fax 01926 426026)

SAVILLE, Rt Hon Lord Justice; Rt Hon Sir Mark Oliver; kt (1985), PC (1994); s of Kenneth Vivian Saville, and Olivia Sarah Frances, *née* Gray; *b* 20 March 1936; *Educ* Rye GS, Brasenose Coll Oxford (Vinerian scholar, BA, BCL); *m* 30 June 1961, Jill Whitworth; 2 s (William Christian b 8 March 1962, Henry Oliver b 8 Aug 1964); *Career* Nat Serv 2 Lt Royal Sussex Regt 1954–56; called to the Bar Middle Temple 1962 (bencher 1983); QC 1975, judge of the High Court of Justice (Queen's Bench Div) 1985–94, a Lord Justice of Appeal 1994–; *Recreations* sailing, flying; *Style*— The Rt Hon Lord Justice Saville; ✉ Royal Courts of Justice, Strand, London WC2A 2LL (☎ 0171 936 7067)

SAVIN, Dr John Andrew; s of Lewis Herbert Savin (d 1983), and Mary Helen, *née* Griffith (d 1983); *b* 10 Jan 1935; *Educ* Epsom Coll, Trinity Hall Cambridge (MD), St Thomas' Hosp London (DIH); *m* 31 Oct 1959, Patricia Margaret, da of Cdr Hugh Patrick De Crecy Steel, RN, of St Ann's, York Rd, North Berwick, Lothian; 2 s (William b 1963, Charles b 1968), 2 da (Penelope b 1960, Rosemary b 1964); *Career* RN Surgn Lt 1960–64; registrar Skin Dept St George's Hosp London 1966–68, sr registrar St John's Hosp for Diseases of the Skin 1968–70, conslt dermatologist Royal Infirmary Edinburgh 1971–, sr lectr Dept of Dermatology Univ of Edinburgh 1971–; former: sec Scottish Dermatological Soc, pres Dermatology Section RSM; pres Br Assoc of Dermatologists; memb Med Appeal Tbnl 1975; FRSM, FRCP; *Books* Recent Advances in Dermatology (1980), Common Diseases of the Skin (1983), Common Skin Problems (1988), Clinical Dermatology (1989), Dermatology and The New Genetics (1994); *Recreations* golf, reading, painting; *Clubs* Hon Co of Edinburgh Golfers, Dowling (pres 1992–93); *Style*— Dr John Savin; ✉ 86 Murrayfield Gardens, Edinburgh EH12 6DQ (☎ 0131 337 7768); Dermatology Department, The Royal Infirmary, Edinburgh (☎ 0131 229 2477)

SAVLA, Dr Navin Chandra; s of Bhimsee Dungersee, and Valbai Savla (d 1947); *b* 25 Dec 1943; *Educ* Osmania Univ Hyderabad India (MB BS), Univ of London (DPM); *m* 8 May 1966, Dr Devyani Savla, da of Dr B K Naik; 2 s (Sandeep b 20 July 1970, Siddharth b 26 Nov 1976); *Career* sr registrar in psychiatry Oxford RHA 1972; conslt psychiatrist: St John's Hosp Lincoln 1972–74, India 1974–76; conslt psychiatrist and clinical tutor: Cherry Knowle Hosp Sunderland 1976–82, Claybury Hosp Essex 1982– (chm Div of Psychiatry 1994–); clinical tutor Br Postgrad Med Fndn 1986, hon sr lectr UCL Med Sch; chm Waltham Forest & Redbridge Div Overseas Doctors Assoc, memb World Psychiatrist Assoc; FRCPsych (MRCPsych 1972); *Books* pubns and papers incl: Homicide Behaviour in the Elderly, Depression & Physical Disability in Waltham Forest, Depression & Schizophrenia, Response to ECT - 2 Year Survey in Elderly Depressive, Fluvoxamine versus Dothiepin (article in Br Journal of Clinical Practice, 1991), Failed Discharges (bulletin in Br Journal of Psychiatry, 1995); papers presented at the World Congress of Psychiatry in Rio 1993: Abuse of Psychotropic Drugs, Psychogeriatric Day Hospital Analysis of 50 Consecutive Referrals Undergoing Full Comprehensive Assessment with 50 Retrospective Referrals, Comparison of Clinical Profile (Provision of Services and Carer's Stress Between Pre-senile Dementia and Dementia Over 65 Years); *Style*— Dr Navin Savla; ✉ 80 Overton Drive, Wanstead, London E11 2NW (☎ 0181 989 0859); Claybury Hospital, Woodford Bridge, Woodford Green, Essex IG8 8BY (☎ 0181 505 7171/3360, fax 0181 505 4545)

SAVORY, James Howard; s of Peter Savory, and Rosemary, *née* Blake; *b* 5 May 1953; *Educ* Winchester, Queens' Coll Cambridge (MA); *m* 15 July 1978, Diana Mary, da of Richard Wackerbarth; 1 da (Rebecca b 1982), 2 s (Tom b 1984, Oliver b 1988); *Career* admitted slr 1978; ptnr Slaughter and May 1985–; ATII 1979; *Style*— James Savory, Esq; ✉ Slaughter and May, 35 Basinghall St, London EC2V 5DB (☎ 0171 600 1200, fax 0171 726 0038, 0171 600 0289)

SAVOURS, *see:* Campbell-Savours

SAVVAS, Michael; s of M Savvas, and Rebecca, *née* Hermogenou; *b* 16 March 1957; *Educ* Holloway Sch, London Hosp Med Coll (MB BS, MRCOG); *Career* house surgn N Middx Hosp 1980–81, house physician Whipps Cross Hosp 1981, SHO A/E London Hosp 1982 (Dept of Obstetrics and Gynaecology 1981–82), SHO Dept of Obstetrics and Gynaecology Whipps Cross Hosp 1982–83, SHO/acting registrar Dept of Endocrinology Jessop Hosp for Women Sheffield 1983–84, registrar in obstetrics and gynaecology Westminster Hosp, St Stephen's Hosp and Hillingdon Hosp 1984–86, res registrar KCH and Dulwich Hosp 1986–88, sr registrar KCH, Lewisham Hosp and Greenwich District Hosp 1988–92, conslt Dept of Obstetrics and Gynaecology Lewisham Hosp and hon sr lectr United Med and Dental Schs Guy's and St Thomas's Hosps 1992–; conslt Bridge Fertility Centre; Galen Prize for advances in infertility Hellenic Med Soc; memb: Int Menopause Soc, Br Menopause Soc, Blair Bell Research Soc, Hellenic Med Soc, Int Soc of Gynaecological Endocrinology; FRSM (memb Cncl); author of numerous scientific pubns; *Recreations* classical and medical history, theatre, classical music; *Style*— Michael Savvas, Esq; ✉ Department of Gynaecology, Lewisham Hospital, High Street, Lewisham, London SW13 6LH (☎ 0181 333 3000, fax 0181 690 1963); Bridge Fertility Centre, Emblem House, 27 Tooley St, London SE1 2PR (☎ 0171 403 3363, fax 0171 403 8552); The Blackheath Hospital, 40–42 Lee Terrace, London SE3 9UD (☎ 0181 318 7722)

SAWARD, Rev Canon Michael John; s of Donald Saward (d 1992), and Lily, *née* Kendall (d 1991); *b* 14 May 1932; *Educ* Eltham Coll London, Univ of Bristol (BA), Tyndale Hall Bristol; *m* 3 April 1956, Jackie, da of Col John Atkinson, DSO, OBE, TD; 1 s (Jonathan b 1961), 3 da (Rachel b 1960, Jill b 1965, Susan (twin) b 1965); *Career* 2 Lt RA (Royal W African Frontier Force 1951–52); asst curate: Christ Church Croydon 1956–59, Edgware Parish Church 1959–64; warden Holy Trinity Inter-Church Centre Liverpool 1964–67, sec Liverpool Cncl of Churches 1964–67, C of E radio and TV offr 1967–72, hon curate St John Beckenham 1969–72; vicar: St Matthew Fulham 1972–78, Ealing 1978–91; priest i/c St Paul Northfields Ealing 1986–89, preb Caddington Major in St Paul's Cathedral 1985–91, canon treas St Paul's Cathedral 1991–; ed, journalist, reviewer, broadcaster; London Diocesan Synod 1973–95: memb Bishop's Cncl 1989–91, memb Vacancy-in-See Ctee 1975–95, memb Pastoral Ctee 1989–92, memb Fin Ctee 1989–94; memb: Gen Synod 1975–95, C of E Evangelical Cncl 1976–93, Ealing East Deanery Synod 1978–91, Bowman Charitable Tst 1978–91, Willesden Area Synod 1980–91, Anglican Evangelical Assembly 1983–95; tstee Church Urban Fund (memb Grants Ctee) 1989–90, Church Cmmr for England 1978–93 (memb Bd of Govrs 1986–93, memb Pastoral Ctee 1988–93), dir Jubilate Hymns Ltd 1980–, chm Bowman Ecclesiastical Tstees 1978–91, hon chaplain Royal British Legion Ealing 1979–90, memb St Paul's Cathedral Choir Sch Cncl 1991–, tstee Christian Evidence Soc 1992–; memb Church Pastoral-Aid Soc Cncl 1992–; Freeman City of London 1993; awarded Winston Churchill Travelling Fellowship 1984; *Books* Leisure (1963), Christian Youth Groups (1965), Task Unfinished (1973), Don't Miss the Party (1974), Cracking the God-code (1975), And So to Bed? (1975), God's Friends (1978), All Change (1983), Evangelicals on the Move (1987); *Recreations* hymn-writing, reading (esp military history), music, cricket, travel, food and drink; *Clubs* Athenaeum, Nikaean; *Style*— The Rev Canon Michael

Saward; ✉ 6 Amen Court, London EC4M 7BU (☎ and fax 0171 248 8572, fax 0171 248 3104)

SAWBRIDGE, Edward Henry Ewen; s of Henry Raywood Sawbridge, CBE (d 1990), of The Moorings, Kingsgate, Kent, and Lilian, *née* Wood (d 1991); *b* 14 Aug 1953; *Educ* Radley, Balliol Coll Oxford (MA); *m* 23 July 1983, Angela Rose Louisa, da of Maj Anthony James MacDonald Watt (d 1991), of Longwood, Sunninghill, Berks; 3 s (Jack William Hugo b 1986, Hugh Anthony Edward b 1988, Arthur Henry James b 1991); *Career* Peat Marwick Mitchell & Co 1976–83, ACLI Metals (London) Ltd 1983–85, fin dir Lehman Brothers Commodities Ltd 1985–, exec dir Lehman Brothers International Ltd 1991–; FCA; *Recreations* bridge, fishing, cooking; *Clubs* United Oxford & Cambridge; *Style*— Edward Sawbridge, Esq; ✉ Lehman Brothers International Ltd, 1 Broadgate, London EC2M 7HA (☎ 0171 260 2177, fax 0171 260 2262)

SAWCZUK, Basil; s of Petro Sawczuk, of Brockworth, Glos, and Maria, *née* Perik; *b* 22 May 1954; *Educ* Chosen Hill GS Churchdown, Leicester Poly (DipArch), Open Univ (DipMan), CEM Univ of Reading; *m* 19 May 1979, Sonia Elizabeth, da Stefan Szewczuk (d 1987), of Leicester; 1 s (Luke Sebastian b 24 Oct 1988); *Career* project architect Harper Fairley ptnrs Birmingham 1979–80, assoc Malcolm Payne and Assocs Birmingham 1980–83; DGI: joined 1983, exec dir DGI International plc 1986–91 and Overseas Business Devpt 1992–95, exec DGI Group plc 1991–92; divnl dir (following takeoverby W S Atkins) W S Atkins (Midlands)/Atkins DGI 1996–; responsible for: computer centre GDS Swindon and SWEB HQ Bristol, various projects in Western Siberia, food distribution study in Tyumen region Russia for EC, Paediatric Polyclinic Nefteugansk Russia; memb: Main Ctee Birmingham AA 1980–83 (ed BAA Gazette 1982–83), Ctee Housing Centre Tst 1980, Birmingham and Sutton Coldfield Crime Prevention Panel 1981–82, Ctee of Midland Study Centre 1984, RIBA Parly Action Lobby 1982–83; chm Midland Jr Liaison Organisation 1984; visiting prof Tyumen Univ Russia 1992–93; external examiner: Leicester Sch of Architecture 1990–94, Univ of Nottingham Sch of Architecture 1996–; visiting external lectr: De Montfort Univ Leicester, Univ of Nottingham; Freeman: City of London 1983, Worshipful Co of Arbitrators 1983–94; memb W Midlands Arbitration Discussion Gp 1990, registered mediator 1991; RIBA 1979, FCIArb 1989 (ACIArb 1980, memb Panel of Arbitrators 1991, memb ADR Ctee 1993, chm Ctee Midlands branch 1995), memb Acad of Experts 1990; *Books* Risk Avoidance for the Building Team (1996); various articles in professional jls; *Recreations* photography, reading; *Clubs* The Arbitration; *Style*— Basil Sawczuk, Esq; ✉ Woodlands Cottage, North Littleton, Worcester WR11 5QP (☎ 01386 830782); Atkins DGI, Stoneleigh Deer Park, Stareton, Kenilworth, Warwicks CV8 2LY (☎ 01203 639300, fax 01203 639855)

SAWDY, Peter Bryan; s of Alfred Eustace Leon Sawdy (d 1972), and Beatrice Sawdy (d 1984); *b* 17 Sept 1931; *Educ* Ampleforth, Regent St Poly, LSE; *m* 1, 1955 (m dis 1985), Anne, *née* Stonor (d 1995); 2 da (Caroline Ann b 1957, Susan Angela b 1962); m 2, 1989, Judith Mary, da of Thomas Bowen (d 1989); *Career* joined Brooke Bond Group as trainee then commodity trader 1952, chm Brook Bond Ceylon Ltd 1963–65; Brooke Bond plc: bd dir 1965, jt md 1975, gp chief exec 1977, gp dep chm and chief exec 1981–85; chm: Costain Group plc 1990–93 (dir 1978–), Taylor Chess Ltd 1989–91, Peter Sawdy Associates; dep chm Hogg Group plc 1989– (dir 1985–); dir: Griffin International 1984, Laing Properties 1989–90, Yule Catto PLC 1991–, Lazard Birla Indian Investment Fund 1995–; memb: Cncl Inst of Business Ethics 1992, Corp Panel British Red Cross 1991–; capt Ceylon Nat Rugby Team 1960–64; *Recreations* golf, music, collecting modern first editions; *Clubs* Naval and Military, Royal Ashdown Golf, Royal Mid Surrey Golf; *Style*— Peter Sawdy, Esq; ✉ Peter Sawdy Associates, 13 Clarendon St, London SW1 2EN (☎ 0171 834 2303, fax 0171 976 5410)

SAWKO, Prof Felicjan; s of Czeslaw Sawko (d 1985), and Franciszka, *née* Nawrot (d 1988); *b* 17 May 1937; *Educ* Lilford Hall, Univ of Leeds (BSc, MSc); *m* 18 April 1960, Genowefa Stefania, da of Wladyslaw Bak (d 1973); 4 s (Andrew Martin b 1961, Peter Ian b 1963, Richard Felicjan b 1965, Paul b 1968), 1 da (Barbara Maria b 1962); *Career* asst engr Rendel Palmer & Tritton 1959–62, reader in civil engrg Univ of Leeds 1967 (lectr 1962–67), prof Univ of Liverpool 1967–88, prof of civil engrg Sultan Qaboos Univ 1986–95, ret; DSc Univ of Leeds 1973; *Books* Developments in Prestressed Concrete (1982), Computer Methods for Civil Engineers (1984); *Recreations* bridge, numismatics, travel; *Style*— Prof Felicjan Sawko; ✉ 23 Floral Wood, Liverpool L17 7HR (☎ and fax 0151 727 0913)

SAWTELL, Jeffrey James (Jeff); s of Ivor Charles Sawtell (d 1979), of Ellesmere Port, and Anne, *née* Morris (d 1984); *b* 29 Jan 1946; *Educ* John St Secdy Modern Ellesmere Port, Chester Sch of Art, London Coll of Printing, St Martin's Sch of Art (DipAD), RCA (MA); *m* 1969 (m dis), Trudi Gurling; 1 da (Hannah Rebecca b 1971); partner, Viv Hendry 1993–; *Career* ed Artery 1971–84, artist, writer and pt/t lectr 1972–87; lectr: Wimbledon Sch of Art, Chelsea Coll of Art, Slade Sch, Coventry Poly, London Coll of Furniture, Goldsmith's Coll, Univ of Bremen, Univ of Humboldt; made documentaries in: Portugal, NI, USA, Panama, Guatemala, Jamaica and the UK 1972–87; exhibitions incl: Bookplumbing 1967, Miniatures and Inferences (St Martin's) 1969, Three Schools Exhibition (Royal Acad) 1970, History up to Date (RCA) 1972, The Shrewsbury Affair (TUC Conf, PCL Gallery, Parliament) 1975, Art for Society (Whitechapel Gallery London) 1978, Pentonville Gallery (solo) 1981 and 1984, Wildcat Theatre Gallery Edinburgh 1982, New Beginnings (Pentonville Gallery) 1983, Camden Open 1989, Oriel Gallery 1995 and 1997, Artscape Orkney 1996, Welsh Contemporaries 1996; full-time art feature writer and writer of film, visual art, TV and cultural features The Morning Star 1987–, film critic West End Extra 1993–94, film and art critic London News Talk 1994–95, film biographer Sunday Times 1995; memb: Film Section Critics' Circle 1988 (chm Art & Architecture Section 1995), Broadcasting Press Guild 1991, RCA Soc 1996; *Style*— Jeff Sawtell, Esq; ✉ 19 Lyme St, London NW1 0EH (☎ and fax 0171 267 5803); Morning Star, 1–3 Ardleigh Rd, London N1 4HS (☎ 0171 254 0033 ext 251, fax 0171 254 5950)

SAWYER, Anthony Charles; s of Charles Bertram Sawyer, of Horley, Surrey, and Elisabeth, *née* Spinks (d 1992); *b* 3 Aug 1939; *Educ* Redhill Tech Coll, Croydon Tech Coll; *m* 1962, Kathleen Josephine, *née* McGill; 2 s (Stephen b 1965, Andrew b 1967), 1 da (Sarah Ann b 1969); *Career* Customs and Excise: joined 1963, princ 1978–82, dep collector S Wales 1983–84, collector Edinburgh 1984–88, cmmr of Customs and Excise 1991–, dir Outfield 1991–94 (dep dir 1988–91), dir Ops Prevention 1994–; non-exec dir Royal Bank of Scotland plc 1994–; FIMgt, MInstD, FRSA; *Recreations* sports, music, theatre; *Clubs* National Liberal, Royal Scots (Edinburgh); *Style*— Anthony C Sawyer, Esq; ✉ Commissioner, HM Customs and Excise, New King's Beam House, 22 Upper Ground, London SE1 9PJ (☎ 0171 865 5017, fax 0171 865 5354)

SAWYER, Gp Capt James Nankivell (Jim); CBE (1985); s of Harry Nankivell Sawyer (d 1996), of Wroxham, Norfolk, and Barbara Laidlaw, *née* Hope (d 1990); *b* 29 Oct 1934; *Educ* Langley Sch Loddon Norfolk, RAF Coll Cranwell, RAF Staff Coll Bracknell, Nat Def Coll Latimer; *m* 8 April 1961, Maureen Winifred (Mo), da of Patrick Joseph Tansey (d 1965); 2 s (Richard, Guy), 1 da (Lucy); *Career* cmmnd 1955; pilot on fighter sqdns based in Middle East, exchange posting as pilot US Marines in US and Japan 1963–65, instr and devpt pilot with Central Fighter Estab RAF, Wing Cdr RAF Coningsby 1977–79, then HQ 11 Gp short tour Germany, promotion to Gp Capt 1983, cmd Northern UK Air Def Sector; served in Falklands 1986 and CTTO 1986–89; memb RAFVR(T) 1989–; worked for rehabilitation of alcoholics Scotland 1983–85, youth training instructor, treas/sec St Michael's Church Geldeston, hon sec Waveney Div of SSAFA; *Recreations* reading and writing poetry, walking, cycling, occasional amateur acting, dancing; *Clubs* RAF Assoc; *Style*— Gp Capt Jim Sawyer, CBE; ✉ The Barn, The Street, Geldeston, Beccles, Suffolk NR34 0LN (☎ 01502 717005)

SAX, Richard Noel; s of Lt-Col George Hans Sax, of Leeford Oaks, Whatlington, nr Battle, E Sussex, and Yvonne Anna Marcelle Sax; *b* 26 Dec 1938; *Educ* Tonbridge, St John's Coll Oxford (MA); *m* 8 April 1967, Margaret, da of Ronald Frank Penny (d 1988); 3 da (Catherine b 1968, Josephine b 1971, Charlotte b 1974); *Career* Nat Serv cmmnd 2 Lt RASC 1957, attached 1 Gds Bde Irish Gds Cyprus (GSM Cyprus Clasp), Lt 1959; admitted slr 1967; managing ptnr Rubinstein Callingham 1984–93 (equity ptnr 1968–94), ptnr Manches & Co 1994–; memb Law Cmmn's Working Pty on Family Property 1974, former chm Slrs Family Law Assoc 1987–, memb Law Soc's Family Law Ctee 1990–; dep district judge Princ Registry Family Div; Liveryman Worshipful Co of Skinners; memb Law Soc 1967, fell IAML; *Recreations* current affairs, gardening, history and archaeology, travel, art; *Clubs* MCC; *Style*— Richard Sax, Esq; ✉ 29 Kelsey Way, Beckenham, Kent BR3 3LP (☎ 0181 650 8272); Manches & Co, Aldwych House, 81 Aldwych, London WC2B 4RP (☎ 0171 404 4483, fax 0171 430 1133)

SAXBEE, Rt Rev Dr John Charles; *see:* Ludlow, Bishop and Archdeacon of

SAXBY, Graham; s of Flinton Saxby (d 1972), of Seaton, Devon, and Eleanor Cora, *née* Pratt (d 1985); *b* 4 Nov 1925; *Educ* West Buckland Sch, Univ Coll of S W (now Univ of Exeter), Univ of London (BSc), Univ of Manchester (PGCE), Open Univ (BA (twice)); *m* Christine Mary, da of Ernest Smalley (d 1980); 1 step da; *Career* RAF: joined as photographer 1947, served Singapore, Hong Kong, Bahrain and Germany, latterly chief technician, cmmnd educn offr (technical) 1966, OC Photographic Science Flight Joint Sch of Photography until ret as Sqdn Ldr 1974; Wolverhampton Tech Teachers' Coll (later part of Univ of Wolverhampton): lectr in educnl technol 1974–90, estab Holography Unit 1986, hon res fell in holography 1990–93; tech advsr Holography Dept RCA, holography corr Br Jl of Photography, Distinctions Panel and memb Cncl RPS; *Awards* Technical Writers' award (Specialist Division) 1981, second prize Diplome de la Musée de la Photographie (Prix Louis-Phillipe Clerc) 1983, nominee King Feisal Award for Science Writing 1988, Kraszna-Krausz award for photographic writing 1993, City and Guilds Insignia award (photographic technol) 1970; RPS: memb 1946, fell 1981, hon fell 1988; BIPP: memb 1956, fell 1981; *Books* The Focal Guide to Slides (1979), Holograms: How to Make and Display Them (1980), Newnes Book of Photography (contrib, 1983), Practical Holography (1988), Manual of Practical Holography (1991), author of numerous technical articles in professional jls; *Recreations* photography, music, vegetable gardening; *Style*— Graham Saxby, Esq; ✉ 3 Honor Ave, Goldthorn Park, Wolverhampton, West Midlands WV4 5HF (☎ and fax 01902 341291)

SAXBY, John; s of George Saxby, and Veronica, *née* Flynn; *b* 29 Sept 1949; *Educ* St Mary's Coll Crosby Liverpool, King's Coll London (BA), Univ of Cologne, MA (1992), MBA (1993); *m* 15 Nov 1986, Janet Adelyne, da of Harold Livesey; 1 da (Emily-Jane Christine b 7 Nov 1989); *Career* hosp admin 1974–; chief exec: Royal Cornwall Hospitals NHS Tst 1991–93, Darlington Meml Hosp NHS Tst 1993–; *Recreations* marathon running, board sailing; *Style*— John Saxby, Esq; ✉ Darlington Memorial Hospital, Darlington, Durham DL3 6HX (☎ 01325 380100, fax 01325 743622)

SAXBY, John Christopher Leslie; s of Leslie Eric Saxby (d 1958), and Florence Mildred, *née* Gallimore (d 1983); *b* 2 April 1933; *Educ* Caterham Sch; *m* 19 Oct 1968, Heather Peel, da of Eric Peel Yates (d 1987); 1 s (Robin b 1975), 1 da (Fiona b 1972); *Career* chartered accountant, articled West Wake Price and Co 1951–58, qualified clerk Coopers and Lybrand 1959–65, chief accountant London Merchant Securities plc 1965–70, gp accountant and co sec Carlton Industs plc 1970–81, sr ptnr Saxby and Sinden (previously Saxby and Marner) 1981–; FCA 1957; *Recreations* golf; *Clubs* Worlebury Golf (treasurer), Winscombe Cricket (life memb); *Style*— John Saxby, Esq; ✉ The Orchards, Kenn Road, Kenn, Clevedon, BS21 6TS (☎ 01275 873709); Saxby and Sinden, 36 Cotham Hill, Bristol BS6 6LA (☎ 0117 923 8100); 18 High St, Budleigh, Salterton, Devon EX9 6LQ (☎ 019354 43766)

SAXON, Prof David Harold; s of Rev Canon Eric Saxon, of Bramhall, Manchester, and Ruth, *née* Higginbottom; *b* 27 Oct 1945; *Educ* Manchester GS, Balliol Coll Oxford (Brackenbury scholar, BA, Scott prize, DSc), Jesus Coll Oxford (MA, DPhil); *m* 13 July 1968, Margaret, da of Rev John Flitcroft; 1 s (Philip Jeffrey b 28 Feb 1972), 1 da (Patricia Alice b 6 Dec 1974); *Career* Univ of Oxford: jr res fell Jesus Coll 1968–70, res offr Dept of Nuclear Physics 1969–70; res assoc Columbia Univ 1970–73; Rutherford Appleton Laboratory: res assoc 1974–75, sr scientific offr 1975–76, princ scientific offr 1976–89, grade 6 1989–90; Univ of Glasgow: Kelvin prof of physics 1990–, head Dept of Physics and Astronomy 1996–; dir Scottish Univs Summer Sch in Physics 1993; memb: Selection Panel SERC Particle Physics Experiment 1989–92, High Energy Particle Physics Ctee Inst of Physics 1989–93, Nuclear Physics Div Ctee Inst of Physics 1990–93, Detector Res and Devpt Ctee CERN 1990–93, Particle Physics Ctee SERC 1991–94 (chm 1992), Nuclear Physics Bd SERC 1992–93, UK Ctee on CERN 1992–95, Scientific Policy Ctee CERN 1993–, Physics Res Ctee DESY 1993–, Research Assessment Physics Panel 1996; chm: UK Inst of Physics Conf 1993, Particle Physics Ctee PPARC 1994–95, 27th Int Conf on High Energy Physics 1994; CPhys, FInstP 1985, FRSE 1993; *Style*— Prof David H Saxon, FRSE; ✉ Department of Physics and Astronomy, University of Glasgow, Glasgow G12 8QQ (☎ 0141 330 4673, fax 0141 330 5299)

SAXON, Richard Gilbert; s of Rev Canon Eric Saxon, QHC, of Stockport, and Ruth, *née* Higginbottom; *b* 14 April 1942; *Educ* Manchester GS, Univ of Liverpool (BArch, MCD); *m* 14 Sept 1968, (Elizabeth) Anne, da of Samuel Shaw Tatton, of Barwick in Elmet, Leeds; *Career* Building Design Ptnrship (BDP): assoc 1970–77, ptnr 1977–, head of architectural profession London Office 1991–96, chm London Office 1993–, gp chm 1996–; design ptnr: J P Morgan HQ London 1986–91, Paddington Basin Redevelopment 1989–92, All England Lawn Tennis Club Redevelopment 1992–95, Adam Opel AG Headquarters Rüsselsheim Germany 1993–97; Marks and Spencer Fin Services HQ Chester 1995–; awards incl: RIBA Halifax Bldg Soc HQ 1975, Europa Nostra medal and Civic Tst Durham Milburngate Centre 1978, Civic Tst commendation Merseyside Maritime Museum Masterplan 1981, New City Architecture award JP Morgan HQ 1993; bldg advsr EDC 1984–86; memb: Bldg Sub-Ctee Sci and Engrg Res Cncl 1987–90, Electronic Applications Sub-Ctee NEDO 1991–92, DTI Task Force on Construction Deregulation 1993; pres Br Cncl for Offices 1995–96, chm Good Practice Panel Construction Indust Bd 1996–; Freeman City of London 1988, Liveryman Worshipful Co of Chartered Architects 1989 (memb Ct of Assts 1992–, memb The Bond); RIBA 1968, MIMgt 1986, FRSA 1987, MInstD; *Books* Atrium Buildings, Development and Design: Architectural Press (1983 and 1986, Van Nostrand Reinhold New York 1983 and 1986), Moscow (1987), Kajima Press Japan (1988 and 1993), Bardon Chinese Agency ROC (1994), chapter Atrium Buildings Wiley/AIA Encyclopaedia of Architecture (1988), The Atrium Comes of Age (Longmans 1993), Kenchiku Gijutsu Japan (1995); *Recreations* travel, photography, music, theatre, film, writing; *Style*— Richard Saxon, Esq; ✉ Building Design Partnership, 16 Gresse Street, PO Box 4WD, London W1A 4WD (☎ 0171 631 4733, fax 0171 631 0393, telex 25322)

SAXTON, Patrick Vincent; s of Patrick Cyril Saxton (d 1979), and Zara Pearl, *née* Moore; *b* 6 Sept 1929; *Educ* High Oakham Sch Mansfield; *m* 19 July 1980, Vera Margaret (Vee) (d 1996), da of Alexander John Temple (d 1958), of Sanderstead, Surrey; *Career* Nat Serv RA; Willis Faber and Dumas 1950–53, clerk to Agency Supt Caledonian

Insurance Co 1953–63; Chartered Insurance Institute: Careers Advsy Office 1964–, asst sec 1965–, admin sec 1979–, sec gen 1983–89, Euro conslt 1990–94; sec Insur Indust Trg Cncl 1972–80; chm: Br Insur Law Assoc 1981–83 (vice pres 1994), Insur Trg Ctee of Comité Européen des Assurances, All Saints Educational Tst, Inst of Trg and Devpt 1984–86; pres Insurance Charities 1991–92, pres Insurance Inst of Croydon 1995–96; Freeman City of London 1973; Liveryman: Worshipful Co of Gold and Silver Wyre Drawers 1973, Worshipful Co of Insurers 1984; assoc memb Inst of Insur Sci for Services to Anglo-German Insur Educn; Hon FICG 1977; FCII 1956, FIPD 1978, FIMgt 1982; *Books* Allured to Adventure (1974), Smiling Through (1991); *Recreations* chess, music, photography, watching sport; *Clubs* MCC, Cripplegate Ward; *Style*— Patrick Saxton, Esq; ✉ 24 Lakeside, Wickham Road, Beckenham, Kent (☎ 0181 658 6298); Chartered Insurance Institute, 20 Aldermanbury, London EC2V 7HY (☎ 0171 606 3835, fax 0171 726 0131, telex 957017)

SAXTON, Dr Robert Louis Alfred; s of Capt Ian Sanders Saxton, barr-at-law, of London, and Dr Jean Augusta Saxton, *née* Infield; *b* 8 Oct 1953; *Educ* Bryanston, St Catharine's Coll Cambridge (MA), Worcester Coll Oxford (BMus, DMus); *Career* visiting tutor Univ of Oxford 1980–82, lectr Univ of Bristol 1984–85 (visiting fell 1986), visiting fell Princeton Univ 1986, composer in residence City Univ 1987–89, head of Composition Dept GSMD 1990– (composition tutor 1979–84 and 1986–90); artistic dir Opera Lab 1995–96; composer of over 60 published works; contrib to various music jls; several radio and TV appearances; memb: Cncl SPNM 1978–90 (memb Exec Ctee 1979–82), Artistic Bd Blackheath Concert Halls 1987–89, BBC Score Reading Panel 1988–, Arts Cncl of GB Music Advsy Panel 1989–93, South Bank Artistic Advsy Bd 1991–, Site Devpt Bd South Bank Centre 1996–; PRS 1976, FGSM 1986, MCPS 1990; *Recreations* theatre, cinema, watching cricket, reading biography and history, studying mathematics; *Style*— Dr Robert Saxton; ✉ c/o Chester Music, 8/9 Frith St, London W1V 5TZ (☎ 0171 434 0066, fax 0171 278 6329)

SAXTON, Robert Michael; s of Arthur Colin, and Joyce, *née* Dulson; *b* 12 Aug 1952; *Educ* Magdalen Coll Oxford (MA); *Career* publisher; Studio Vista 1975–80, exec ed Mitchell Beazley 1980–91 (responsible for lists on gardening, design, architecture and photography), editorial dir Duncan Baird Publishers UK 1991– (int co-edn titles and illustrated reference); *Publications* The Promise Clinic (poetry, Enitharmon Press, 1994); *Recreations* hillwalking, ornithology, modern jazz, poetry, cultural astronomy, cookery; *Style*— Robert Saxton, Esq; ✉ Duncan Baird Publishers, Castle House, 75–76 Wells Street, London W1P 3RE

SAY, Rt Rev Dr (Richard) David; KCVO (1988); s of Cdr Richard Say, OBE, RNVR (d 1958), of London, and Kathleen Mary, *née* Wildy (d 1967); *b* 4 Oct 1914; *Educ* Univ Coll Sch, Christ's Coll Cambridge (BA, MA), Ridley Hall Cambridge; *m* 16 Oct 1943, Irene Frances Say, OBE, JP, da of Seaburne Rayner (d 1952), of Exeter; 2 s (Richard William Gurney b and d 1950, William David b 1952), 2 da (Mary Penelope (Mrs Thompson) b 1945, Anne Caroline (Mrs Langley) b 1948); *Career* ordained Canterbury Cathedral: deacon 1939, priest 1940, bishop 1961; curate: Croydon Parish Church 1939–43, St Martin-in-the-Fields 1943–50; gen sec: C of E Youth Cncl 1944–47, Br Cncl of Churches 1947–55; rector of Hatfield Herts and chaplain to 5th Marquess of Salisbury 1955–61, hon canon St Albans 1957–61, 104th Bishop of Rochester 1961–88, chaplain to Pilgrims of GB 1968–, Lord High Almoner to HM The Queen 1970–88, asst Bishop of Canterbury 1988–; C of E del to World Cncl of Churches 1948 1954 and 1961; select preacher: Univ of Cambridge 1954, Univ of Oxford 1963; chaplain and sub-prelate Order of St John 1961, memb House of Lords 1969–88, chm Ctee on State Aid for Churches in Use 1971–90, pro-chllr Univ of Kent 1983–93 (dep pro-chllr 1977–83), memb Court of Ecclesiastical Causes Reserved 1984–92; vice-pres UN Assoc of GB 1986; patron Age Concern England 1994– (chm 1986–89); pres Friends of Kent Churches 1988–; hon memb Inst of RE 1987; Freeman City of London 1953; Hon Freeman: Borough of Tonbridge and Malling 1987, City of Rochester upon Medway 1988; DD Lambeth 1961; Hon DCL Univ of Kent at Canterbury 1987; *Recreations* walking, travel; *Clubs* United Oxford and Cambridge Univ; *Style*— The Rt Rev Dr David Say, KCVO; ✉ 23 Chequers Park, Wye, Ashford, Kent TN25 5BB (☎ 01233 812720)

SAYE AND SELE, 21 Baron (E 1447 and 1603); Nathaniel Thomas Allen Fiennes; DL (Oxon 1979); s of 20 Baron, OBE, MC (Ivo Murray Twisleton-Wykeham-Fiennes, d 1968), and Hersey, da of late Capt Sir Thomas Dacres Butler, KCVO; relinquished by deed poll 1965 the additional surnames of Twisleton and Wykeham; *b* 22 Sept 1920; *Educ* Eton, New Coll Oxford; *m* 1958, Mariette Helena, da of Maj-Gen Sir (Arthur) Guy Salisbury-Jones, GCVO, CMG, CBE, MC (d 1985), and Hilda (d 1995), da of Rt Hon Sir Maurice de Bunsen, 1 and last Bt, GCMG, GCVO, CB; 3 s, 1 da; *Heir* s, Hon Richard Fiennes, *qv*; *Career* Rifle Bde (despatches twice) 1939–45; chartered surveyor; ptnr Laws & Fiennes; regnl dir Lloyds Bank 1983–90; tstee Ernest Cook Tst 1959–95 (chm 1964–90), fell Winchester Coll 1967–83; *Style*— The Lord Saye and Sele, DL; ✉ Broughton Castle, Banbury, Oxon OX15 5EB (☎ 01295 262624)

SAYED, Dr (Zulfiquar) Aly; s of Dr Niwazish Aly Sayed (d 1978), of Civil Lines, Khanewal, and Zubeda, *née* Mumtaz; *b* 23 May 1932; *Educ* Punjab Univ (MB BS), Univ of Edinburgh (MSc, Dip Psych); *m* 12 Oct 1966, (Elva) Arline, da of Joseph Gwilym Jones (d 1979), of St Helens, Lancs; 1 s (Shaun b 1969), 2 da (Zara b 1975, Michelle b 1977); *Career* registrar: United Birmingham Hosps, Nat Hosp Queen Square London; res fell Univ of Edinburgh, sr registrar United Liverpool Hosps, conslt psychiatrist Tameside and Glossop Community and Priority Servs NHS Tst; memb BMA, MIMgt, FRCPsych; *Recreations* good food, travel, reading; *Clubs* Consultants; *Style*— Dr Aly Sayed; ✉ 3 Healey Close, Salford, Greater Manchester M7 3PQ (☎ 0161 792 3930); Tameside General Hospital, Ashton under Lyne, Gtr Manchester (☎ 0161 331 5064)

SAYEED, Dr (Abulfatah) Akram; OBE (1976); s of Mokhles Ahmed (d 1967), of Pirwalistan, Jessore, Bangladesh, and Noor Jehan Begum, *née* Munshi (d 1987); *b* 23 Nov 1935; *Educ* St Joseph's Sch Khulna, Univ of Dhaka (MB BS); *m* 11 Oct 1959, Hosen-ara, da of Al-Haj M Sabet Ali; 2 s (Rana Ahmed b 10 March 1967, Reza Abu b 15 April 1972), 1 da (Dina Jesmin b 17 June 1963); *Career* sr house offr in ophthalmology Dhaka Univ Hosp 1959–60 (house offr 1958–59), rotating internship Monmouth Med Centre Long Branch New Jersey 1960–61, GP 1964– (asst in practice 1963), pt/t MO Leicester Royal Infirmary 1964–89 (sr house offr in ophthalmology 1961–63); author of numerous articles on medico-politics; writer, lectr and broadcaster on med educn and trg in Bangladesh; fndr memb Leicester Cncl for Community Rels 1965–; memb: CRC 1968–77, BBC Asian Programme Advsy Ctee 1972–77, Leics Med Ctee 1977, Leics Family Practitioners' Ctee 1977, Univ Mgmnt Team 1977, Home Sec's Advsy Cncl on Community Rels 1983–88, DHSS Working Gps (Asian health, treatment of overseas visitors); advsr NCCI 1965–68; chm: Stop Rickets Campaign Leics, Standing Conf of Asian Orgns in UK 1973–77 (vice chm 1970–73); UK del First World Conf on Muslim Educn King Abdul Aziz Univ Mecca 1977, vice pres Fedn of Bangladeshi Orgns in UK and Europe 1984, sec Inst of Transcultural Health Care 1985–93, co-ordinator and facilitator in UK for Bangladesh Coll of Physicians and Surgeons 1990–, hon advsr Miny of Health Govt of Bangladesh 1991; memb Editorial Bd: ODA News Review, Asian Who's Who (10 edn, 1994–95); Overseas Doctors' Assoc: fndr chm 1975, gen sec 1975–77, vice pres 1979–84, chm S Trent Div 1981–90, vice chm 1984, chm Annual Representative Meeting 1990–93, chm 1993–; BMA: memb 1961, memb Agenda Ctee 1992 and 1994, pres Leics Div 1993–94 (memb 1975–), memb Gen Med Servs Ctee 1993; memb: Bangladesh Med Assoc UK 1972– (CEC memb 1982–), Ophthalmic Soc of Bangladesh (life memb); Med Journalists' Assoc; FRSM 1981, FODA 1985, Hon FCPS Bangladesh 1992, FCGP (Bangladesh), MRCGP 1992, FRCPE 1994, fell BMA 1995; *Books* Bangladesh Medical Directory (ed 3 edns), Caring for Asians in General Practice (contrib, 1989); *Recreations* reading, oriental music, photography, gardening; *Clubs* Royal Over-Seas League (London and Edinburgh); *Style*— Dr A Akram Sayeed, OBE; ✉ RAMNA, 2 Mickelton Drive, Leicester LE5 6GD (☎ 0116 241 6703); 352 East Park Rd, Leicester LE5 5AY (☎ 0116 273 7569, fax 0116 273 7443)

SAYER, Michael John; s of Maj Douglas James William Sayer, MBE, TD, of Sparham Hall, Norfolk, and Mary Elizabeth, *née* Weddall; *b* 11 Oct 1947; *Educ* Repton, Pembroke Coll Oxford (BA, MA, BLitt); *Career* landowner, author; CLA: memb Norfolk Branch Ctee 1972, memb Water Sub Ctee 1980–84, memb Tax Sub Ctee 1989–93, chm Norfolk Branch 1995–; tax cmmr 1979– (chm St Faith's and Aylsham Div 1988–); memb: Norwich Diocesan Synod 1973–82 (Pastoral Ctee 1974–82), Tax Ctee Historic Houses Assoc 1990–; chm Norfolk Churches Tst 1984–86; jt rep Duke of Norfolk on Commission d'Information et de Liaison des Associations de Noblesse d'Europe (CILANE) 1994–; FSA 1982; *Books* English Nobility: The Gentry, The Heralds and The Continental Context (1979), Norfolk section of Burke's and Savill's Guide to Country Houses, vol III, East Anglia (1981), The Disintegration of a Heritage: Country Houses and their Collections 1979–1992 (1993); *Recreations* history, architecture, shooting; *Clubs* Norfolk; *Style*— Michael J Sayer, Esq, FSA; ✉ Sparham House, Norwich NR9 5PJ (☎ 01603 872268)

SAYER, Paul Anthony; s of John Sayer (d 1992), of South Milford, nr Leeds, and Adelaide, *née* Lambert (d 1985); *b* 4 Oct 1955; *Educ* Tadcaster GS; *m* 31 Jan 1981, Anne, da of James Bell; 1 s (Simon b 19 Dec 1984); *Career* author; shop asst 1973–76, RMN 1979, psychiatric nurse 1976–81 and 1986–89, shop keeper 1981–84, storeman 1984–85, author 1989–; memb: Soc of Authors 1988, Yorkshire Arts 1988; *Books* The Comforts of Madness (1988, Constable Trophy for Fiction, Whitbread First Novel award, Whitbread Book of the Year award), Howling at the Moon (1990), The Absolution Game (1992), The Storm-Bringer (1994), The God Child (1996); *Recreations* lifelong supporter of York City FC, and other hopeless causes; *Style*— Paul Sayer, Esq; ✉ c/o Carol Smith, 25 Hornton Court, Kensington High St, London W8 7RT (☎ 0171 937 4874, fax 0171 938 5323)

SAYER, Philip William; s of Edward George Poulton Sayer, of Basingstoke, Hants, and Jean, *née* Kennedy; *b* 7 Jan 1947; *Educ* Queen Mary's GS Basingstoke Hants; *m* Dec 1984, Joan Katherine, da of Ronald Frederick Taylor; 1 s (Joseph b 21 July 1991), 1 da (Rosie b Sept 1985); *Career* photographer; asst to Maurice Broomfield, photographer Butlins Holiday Camp Bognor 1965–67, photographic printer Derek Robinson Partnership 1967–70, freelance editorial photographer 1970–; currently contrib to various magazines incl: Management Today, Crafts, Blueprint, World of Interiors, GQ (USA), Travel & Leisure (USA), ES, The Times - Saturday Review; currently photographer numerous design gps Europe and USA; solo exhibitions: Portraits for Print (Norwich Sch of Art) 1983, The Face of Craft (Br Crafts Centre) 1984, Portraits (Impressions Gallery York) 1985, permanent exhibition of portraits (The Blueprint Café Design Museum London) 1989, The 100 Mile City (exhibition Architectural Fndn London) 1992, The Making of the Modern World, science museum 1993, The Hermitage, St Petersburg (Pentagram Gallery) 1995; FCSD 1983; *Books* Building of Faith - Westminster Cathedral (1995); *Recreations* painting, cycling, music (jazz, country and western), reading; *Style*— Philip Sayer, Esq; ✉ Philip Sayer Partnership, Lynwood House, Church Road, Cookham Dean, Berkshire SL6 9PD (☎ and fax 01628 890960)

SAYER, Stephen Thomas; s of Charles Martin Sayer, of Epping, Essex, and Justina, *née* Marsden Jones; *b* 8 July 1945; *Educ* Framlingham Coll Suffolk, Coll of Law; *m* 1, 20 July 1968 (m dis 1987), Gillian Susan, da of John Talbot Warwick, of Rustington, Sussex; 2 s (Edward b 1971, Timothy b and d 1973), 1 da (Harriet b 1976); m 2, 30 Jan 1988, Aileen, da of Roy Victor Wegener, of Toowoomba, Queensland, Australia; *Career* admitted slr 1968; ptnr Richards Butler 1974– (asst slr 1968); Freeman City of London 1978, Liveryman Worshipful Co of Slrs 1975; memb: Law Soc 1968, Lawyers Club 1980, The Soc of Eng and American Lawyers, UK Assoc of Euro Law; *Books* contrib to: Longmans Practical Commercial Precedents (1987), International Joint Ventures (1989); *Recreations* real tennis, rackets, theatre, reading; *Clubs* Reform, City of London, Queen's; *Style*— Stephen Sayer, Esq; ✉ Richards Butler, Beaufort House, 15 St Botolph Street, London EC3A 7EE (☎ 0171 772 5730, fax 0171 772 5755, telex 949494 RBLAW G)

SAYERS, Allan Langley; s of Wilfrid William Sayers (d 1977), and Ivy Florence Amelia, *née* Braun (d 1987); *b* 30 June 1939; *Educ* St Paul's; *m* 30 May 1962, Susan Mary, *née* Fisher; 2 s (Andrew John b 18 April 1965, Christopher Allan b 19 Dec 1978); *Career* dir: A Sayers Ltd 1962–86 (chm 1977–86), Menswear Association of Britain 1986–91 (pres 1979–80, dir Menswear Fair Ltd 1978–93); chief exec British Shops and Stores Association 1991–; memb: EDC for the Distributive Trades 1980–85 (Technology Working Pty for the Distributive Trades 1980–83), Mgmnt Bd British Retail Consortium 1993– (Cncl 1980–85), Retail Ctee Br Chambers of Commerce 1993–; UK representative: Euro Assoc of Nat Organisations of Textile Retailers 1992–, Euro Federation of Furniture Retailers 1993–; employers rep Non-Food Wages Cncl 1986–93; chm Wembley Round Table 1970–71, pres Northwick Park Rotary Club 1980–81; Freeman City of London 1994, Liveryman Worshipful Co of Glovers 1994; FIMgt 1979, FRSA 1993; *Recreations* travel, playing at golf, photography, bridge; *Clubs* Northwood Golf; *Style*— Allan Sayers, Esq; ✉ 2 Soval Court, Maxwell Road, Northwood, Middx HA6 2FS (☎ 01923 828685); British Shops and Stores Association, Middleton House, 2 Main Road, Middleton Cheney, Banbury, Oxon OX17 2TN (☎ 01295 712277, fax 01295 711665, car 0831 610884)

SAYERS, Arnold Lewis; CBE (1986), DL (Devon); s of Maj Lorne Douglas Watson Sayers (d 1940), of Alston Hall, Holbeton, Plymouth, and Dame Lucile Newell, JP, *née* Schiff (d 1959); *b* 28 April 1923; *Educ* Wellington Coll, CCC Cambridge (BA); *m* 10 July 1954, Sylvia Penelope, da of late Brig Gen Spencer Vaughan Percy Weston, DSO, MC, of Sevenoaks, Kent; 1 s (Geoffrey b 1965), 3 da (Charlotte b 1956, Priscilla b 1958, Catherine b 1961); *Career* farmer; ldr Devon CC 1981–85 (chm 1988–89); chm: Assoc CC Planning and Transportation Ctee 1981–84, Dartington Cattle Breeding Centre 1966–; dir Devon Waste Management; pres Devon Historic Bldgs Tst; High Sheriff of Devon 1991–92; *Recreations* walking, gardening, music; *Style*— Arnold L Sayers, Esq, CBE, DL; ✉ Carswell, Holbeton, nr Plymouth, Devon PL8 1HH (☎ 01752 830282, fax 01752 830565)

SAYERS, Prof Bruce McArthur; s of John William McArthur Sayers (d 1980), of Melbourne, Aust, and Mabel Florence, *née* Howe (d 1980); *b* 6 Feb 1928; *Educ* Melbourne HS Aust, Univ of Melbourne (BSc, MSc), Univ of London (PhD, DIC, DSc); *Career* professional biophysicist Baker Med Res Inst and Alfred Hosp Melbourne 1949–54; Imperial Coll London: res asst 1954–56, Philips electrical res fell 1956–58, lectr in electrical engrg 1958–62, sr lectr in med electronics 1963–65, reader 1965–68, prof of electrical engrg applied to med 1968–84, head Dept of Electrical Engrg 1979–84, prof of computing applied to med 1984–90, head Dept of Computing 1984–89, Kobler prof of the mgmnt of info technol 1990–93, emeritus prof of computing applied to med Univ of London 1993–, sr res fell and dir Centre for Cognitive Systems 1993–; visiting prof McGill, Melbourne, Rio de Janiero and Toronto Univs; travelling lectr Nuffield Fndn and Nat Res Cncl Canada 19'/1; Univ of Buckingham: memb (Privy Cncl nominee) Academic Advsy Cncl 1988–96, memb Cncl 1994–96; dean City & Guilds Coll 1984–88 and 1991–93; memb: Int Advsy Ctee on Energy Studies Ecole Fédérale Polytechnique de Lausanne 1989–95, Scientific Cncl Int Centre of BioCybernetics Warsaw 1993–; hon conslt Royal Nat Throat Nose and Ear Hosp 1974–93; advsr: Advent Eurofund Ltd 1981–90, Shinan Investment Service SA 1984–87, Advent Capital Ltd 1985–90, Neuroscience Ltd 1985–93, Transatlantic Capital (BioSci) Fund Ltd 1985–; dir: Imperial Software Technology Ltd 1984–90, Imperial Information Technology Ltd 1986–90; pres Section of Measurement in Med Royal Soc of Med 1971–72, vice chm Global Advsy Ctee on Health Res WHO Geneva 1990–94 (temp advsr 1970–87 and 1995–96, memb 1988–94 and 1997–); Freeman City of London 1986, Liveryman Worshipful Co of Scientific Instrument Makers 1985; hon foreign memb Societa Medica Chirurgica di Bologna 1965; hon memb: Med Soc WHO 1974, Eta Kappa Nu 1980; FIEE 1980, FCGI 1983, FEng 1990, FIC 1996; *Recreations* restoring an old house in France; *Clubs* Athenaeum; *Style*— Prof Bruce Sayers, FEng; ✉ 40 Queen's Gate, London SW7 5HR (☎ 0171 581 3690); La Payrastrié, 81360 Montredon-Labessonnié, France (☎ and fax 00 5 33 63 75 10 18); William Penney Building, Imperial College, London SW7 2AZ (☎ 0171 594 8186, fax 0171 589 7953)

SAYERS, Michael Bernard; s of Joseph David Sayers (d 1981), of London, and Miriam May, *née* Konskier (d 1989); *b* 23 April 1934; *Educ* Winchester, Magdalen Coll Oxford (MA); *m* 17 Dec 1958, Peta Ann, da of David Levi, of London; 1 s (Nicholas b 1959), 2 da (Catherine b 1961, Ruth b 1963); *Career* Nat Serv 1952–54: Midshipman 1953, Sub Lt 1954; admitted slr 1960, asst slr Macfarlanes 1960–62 (articled clerk 1957–60), ptnr Norton Rose 1965–94 (asst slr 1962–64); non-exec dir: Emess plc, VCI plc, Persona Group plc, The Monks Investment Trust plc, Fiscal Properties plc, PPP Healthcare Group plc, Leyland Trucks Manufacturing Ltd, Stirling Ltd, The Design Trust; *Style*— Michael Sayers, Esq; ✉ 9 Burgess Hill, London NW2 2BY (☎ 0171 435 4348/5601, fax 0171 435 5487); The Old School House, Holwell, nr Burford, Oxfordshire OX18 4JS (☎ 01993 823084)

SAYERS, Michael Patrick; QC (1988); s of Maj (Herbert James) Michael Sayers, RA (ka 1943), and Sheilah De Courcy Holroyd, *née* Stephenson (d 1969); *b* 28 March 1940; *Educ* Harrow, Fitzwilliam Coll Cambridge (Evelyn Rothschild scholar, MA); *m* 12 March 1976, Moussie Brougham, *née* Hallstrom; 1 s (Frederick b 3 Dec 1981), 1 da (Nicola b 27 Dec 1980), 1 step s (Henry Brougham b 12 Nov 1971); *Career* called to the Bar Inner Temple 1970, bencher 1994; jr Central Criminal Ct Bar Mess 1975–78, supplementary prosecuting counsel to the Crown Central Criminal Ct 1977–88, recorder of the Crown Ct 1986–; memb Ctee Barrs' Benevolent Assoc 1991–; chm Harrow Assoc 1991–; *Recreations* shooting, stalking, theatre, Sweden; *Clubs* Garrick, Pratt's, Queen's, Swinley Forest Golf; *Style*— Michael Sayers, Esq, QC; ✉ 2 King's Bench Walk, Temple, London EC4Y 7DE (☎ 0171 353 1746, fax 0171 583 2051/4571)

SAYLE, Alexei David; s of Joseph Henry Sayle (d 1983), of Liverpool and Malka, *née* Mendelson; *b* 7 Aug 1952; *Educ* Alsop HS Liverpool, Southport Art Sch Lancs, Chelsea Sch of Art (DipAD), Garnet Coll Roehampton London (CertEd); *m* Linda Eleanor, da of Noel Rawsthorn; *Career* comedian, actor and writer; master of ceremonies: Comedy Store Club 1979–80, Comic Strip Club 1980–81; various solo tours as stand-up comedian; *Televison* incl: The Young Ones 1982–85, The Strike 1987, Alexei Sayle's Stuff 1988–91, Night Voice 1990, Itch 1991, Selling Hitler 1991, The All-New Alexei Sayle Show 1994 and 1995, Paris 1995, Sorry About Last Night (writer and actor, BBC) 1995, Great Railway Journeys of the World 1996; *Films* Gorky Park 1983, Supergrass 1985, Siesta 1986, Indiana Jones and the Last Crusade 1989; *Recordings* single released Ullo John! Gotta New Motor? 1984; *Radio* presenter Fourth Column (Radio 4) 1994; *Columnist* Time Out, Sunday Mirror, The Observer Magazine, The Independent, Esquire; *Awards* Best Comedy Awards incl: Pye Radio 1981, RTS 1988, Broadcast Press Guild 1988, International Emmy 1988, Bronze Rose of Montreux; *Books* Train to Hell (1982), Geoffrey the Tube Train and the Fat Comedian (1987), Great Bus Journeys of the World (1988); *Recreations* cycling, shooting, re-using envelopes; *Clubs* The Fridge, Chelsea Arts; *Style*— Alexei Sayle; ✉ c/o Mayer & Eden Ltd, 34 Kingly Court, London W1R 5LE (☎ 0171 434 1242, fax 0171 287 5834)

SAYNOR, John; CMG (1992), JP (Berks 1983); s of Charles Herbert Saynor (d 1985), and Emily, *née* Mundie (d 1994); *b* 28 Sept 1930; *Educ* Doncaster GS; *m* 26 June 1954, Jennifer Ann, da of John Arthur Nelson (d 1968); 2 s (Richard John b 1956, Geoffrey Mark b 1957); *Career* Nat Serv cmmn RASC 1949–51; PO 1951–69, Dept for Nat Savings 1969–74; Cwlth War Graves Cmmn: joined 1974, dir-gen 1989–92; dep chm Maidenhead Magistrates Bench 1993–95, chm High Wycombe YMCA; *Recreations* gardening, golf, bridge, bowls, painting; *Clubs* Maidenhead Golf, Flackwell Heath Bowls; *Style*— John Saynor, Esq, CMG, JP; ✉ 12 The Meadows, Flackwell Heath, High Wycombe, Bucks HP10 9LX (☎ 01628 523459)

SAYWELL, (John Anthony) Telfer; JP (Richmond 1985); s of John Rupert Saywell (d 1948), of Kensington, London, and Winifred, *née* Green (d 1980); *b* 19 Aug 1939; *Educ* Abingdon Sch, Open Univ (BA); *m* 8 June 1968, June Mary, da of Maurice Thomas Hunnable (d 1972), of Rivenhall, Essex; 1 da (Polly b 1969), 2 s (Thomas b 1971, Henry b 1977); *Career* CA; Fincham Vallance & Co 1958–63, Tansley Witt & Co 1963–69; Layton Fern & Co Ltd (coffee and tea specialists): joined 1969, md 1970, chm 1975–; underwriting memb of Lloyd's 1983–; pres UK Coffee Trade Benevolent Soc 1985–86, govr RSC 1982–; treas: Harlequin FC 1971–78, Union Soc City of Westminster 1985–, St Luke's Educnl Centre 1989–; hon auditor Richmond upon Thames Disabled Assoc 1973–, master Billingsgate Ward Club 1987–88; Freeman City of London 1981, memb Ct of Assts Worshipful Co of Carmen 1986; FCA 1964; *Recreations* sailing, studying, skiing; *Clubs* Harlequin FC, Leander, Br Sportsman's, Surrey RFU, Frinton Working Mens'; *Style*— Telfer Saywell, Esq, JP; ✉ 2 Cumberland Rd, Kew Gardens, Richmond, Surrey TW9 3HQ (☎ 0181 940 0298, fax 0181 287 3486); Layton Fern & Co Ltd, 27 Rathbone Place, London WIP 2EP (☎ 0171 636 2237, fax 0171 580 2869)

SCADDING, Dr Glenis Kathleen; *b* 3 Oct 1947; *Educ* Newnham Coll Cambridge (sr scholar, MA), Middx Hosp Med Sch (Florence Johnstone and Stoney clinical studentship, Freeman scholar in obstetrics, MB BChir, MRCP), Univ of Cambridge (MD, Ralph Noble prize, FRCP 1995); *m*; 4 c; *Career* house physician Middx Hosp 1972–73, house surgn Kettering Gen Hosp 1972–73, SHO in neurology Walton Hosp Liverpool 1973–74, MO Shining Hosp Pokhara Nepal 1974–75, SHO Med Unit Brompton Hosp 1974–75, Abbott res fell and hon registrar in endocrinology Royal Free Hosp 1976–80, hon lectr in med Royal Free Med Unit 1978, Wellcome res fell Dept of Neurological Scis 1980–83, sr registrar Dept of Immunology Middx Hosp 1983–87, conslt physician in rhinology and allergy Royal Nat Throat, Nose and Ear Hosp and hon sr lectr Dept of Immunology UCL Sch of Med 1987–, Joseph Sr White fell RCP 1988–92; invited speaker: 7th Int Congress of Paediatric Otorhinolaryngologists Rotterdam 1994, 15th Euro Rhinology Meeting Copenhagen 1994; memb: RSM (memb Cncl Section of Immunology), BMA, Br Soc for Immunology, Antibody Club, Br Soc for Allergy and Clinical Immunology (chm ENT/Allergy Immunology Sub-Ctee), Euro Rhinological Soc, Br Assoc of Paediatric Otolaryngologists; assoc memb: RCPath, Zoological Soc; *Books* Clinical Immunology (co-ed), Immunology of ENT Disorders (ed, 1995); *Style*— Dr Glenis K Scadding; ✉ Royal National Throat, Nose & Ear Hospital, Gray's Inn Road, London WC1X 8DA

SCADDING, Prof John Guyett (Guy); s of John William Scadding (d 1960), of London, and Jessima Alice, *née* Guyett (d 1959); *b* 30 Aug 1907; *Educ* Mercers' Sch, Middx Hosp Med Sch Univ of London (MB BS, MD); *m* 30 Aug 1940, Mabel, da of John Pennington (d 1962), of Cheshire; 1 s (John b 1948), 2 da (Jane (Mrs Jarvis) b 1946, Sarah (Mrs Fielder) b 1950); *Career* WWII served in RAMC 1940–45: M East 1941–45, Maj 1940, Lt-Col 1942; hon conslt in diseases of the chest Army 1952–72 (awarded Guthrie medal 1973); jr hosp appts 1930–33, resident med offr Brompton Hosp 1931–35; Royal (formerly Br) Postgrad Med Sch and Hammersmith Hosp: first asst Dept of Med 1935–45, sr lectr 1945–62; hon conslt physician Hammersmith Hosp 1935–, conslt physician Brompton Hosp 1939–; Inst for Diseases of the Chest Univ of London: dean 1946–60, dir of studies 1950–62, prof of med 1962–72 (emeritus 1972–); Royal College of Physicians: censor 1968–69, second vice pres 1971, Moxon medal 1974; visiting prof: Stanford Univ and Univ of Colorado 1965, McMaster Univ 1973, Univ of Manitoba 1974, Chicago 1976, Dalhousie Univ 1977; pres: Br TB Assoc 1959–61, Med Section RSM 1969–71, Thoracic Soc 1970–71; ed Thorax 1946–60; memb Standing Med Advsy Ctee and Central Health Servs Cncl Miny of Health 1954–66 (chm Standing TB Advsy Ctee), conslt advsr in diseases of the chest DHSS 1960–72, memb Clinical Res Bd MRC 1965–69, chm Industl Med Panel NCB 1962–72; hon memb: Société Francaise de la Tuberculose et des Maladies Respiratoires, Sociedad Espanola de Anatomia Patologica, Canadian Thoracic Soc; Freeman City of London 1950, Liveryman Worshipful Soc of Apothecaries 1950; Doctor Honoris Causa Univ of Reims 1978; FRCP, fell Royal Postgrad Med Sch; *Books* Sarcoidosis (first edn 1967, second edn 1985); *Recreations* music; *Clubs* Athenaeum; *Style*— Prof Guy Scadding; ✉ 18 Seagrave Rd, Beaconsfield, Bucks HP9 1SU (☎ 01494 676033)

SCALES, Prof John Tracey; OBE (1986); s of Walter Laurence Scales (d 1972), of Heathfield, Wierfields, Totnes, and Ethel Margaret, *née* Tracey (d 1949); *b* 2 July 1920; *Educ* Haberdashers' Aske's, King's Coll London, Charing Cross Hosp Med Sch; *m* 22 May 1945, Cecilia May (d 1992), da of Albert Wesley Sparrow (d 1960), of Barnstaple, Devon; 2 da (Sally (Mrs Miller) b 1949, Helen (Mrs Hargreaves) b 1955); *Career* casualty and res anaesthetist Charing Cross Hosp 1944, house surgn Royal Nat Orthopaedic Hosp 1944–45, Capt RAMC 1945–47, Royal Nat Orthopaedic Hosp 1947–87 (hon conslt 1958–), Inst of Orthopaedics Univ of London 1951–87 (prof of biomedical engrg 1974–87); hon conslt: Mount Vernon Hosp 1969–, Royal Orthopaedic Hosp Birmingham 1978–87; emeritus prof Univ of London 1987–, hon conslt and hon dir RAFT Inst of Plastic Surgery Mount Vernon Hosp 1988–93, RAFT dir Pressure Sore Prevention 1994–; memb: Cncl Friends of the RNO Hosp, Action Ctee RNO Hosp; former memb Advsy Panel on Med Engrg Action Res; fndr memb: Euro Soc of Biomechanics, Biological Engrg Soc, Soc for Tissue Viability; MRCS, LRCP 1944, companion fell Br Orthopaedic Assoc 1959, FRCS 1969, CIMechE 1966, FRSM; memb: BSI, ISO (ret 1992), Br Orthopaedic Res Soc; hon memb Br Assoc of Plastic Surgeons 1993, fell Biological Engrg Soc 1994; *Recreations* collecting Goss china; *Style*— Prof John T Scales, OBE; ✉ Fairbanks, Riverview Road, Pangbourne, Berks RG8 7AU; RAFT Institute of Plastic Surgery, Mount Vernon Hospital NHS Trust, Northwood, Middx HA6 2RN (☎ 01923 844371, fax 01923 844031)

SCALES, Prunella Margaret Rumney; *née* Illingworth; CBE (1992); da of John Richardson Illingworth (d 1977), and Catherine, *née* Scales (d 1982); *b* 22 June 1932; *Educ* Moira House Eastbourne, Old Vic Theatre Sch London; *m* 1963, Timothy West, *qv*, s of H Lockwood West, of Brighton, Sussex; 2 s (Samuel b 1966, Joseph b 1969); *Career* actress, dir and teacher; frequent broadcasts, readings, poetry recitals and fringe productions, has directed plays at Bristol Old Vic, Arts Theatre Cambridge, Billingham Forum, Almost Free Theatre London, Nottingham Playhouse, West Yorkshire Playhouse and Nat Theatre of WA Perth, has taught at several drama schools; Hon DLitt: Univ of Bradford 1995, UEA 1996; *Theatre* seasons at Stratford-on-Avon and Chichester Festival Theatre 1967–68; credits incl: The Promise 1967, Hay Fever 1968, It's a Two-Foot-Six-Inches-Above-The-Ground-World 1970, The Wolf 1975, Breezeblock Park 1978, Make and Break (Haymarket) 1980, An Evening with Queen Victoria 1980, The Merchant of Venice 1981, Quartermaine's Terms (Queen's) 1981, When We Are Married (Whitehall) 1986, Single Spies (RNT) 1989, School for Scandal (RNT) 1990, Long Day's Journey into Night (RNT) 1991, Some Singing Blood (Royal Court) 1992, The Editing Process (Royal Court) 1995; *Television* incl: Sybil Fawlty in Fawlty Towers (BBC) 1975–79, Doris and Doreen, A Wife like the Moon, Grand Duo, The Merry Wives of Windsor 1982, Outside Edge, Mapp and Lucia 1985, After Henry 1990, The Rector's Wife (Channel 4) 1994, Signs and Wonders (BBC) 1994, The World of Lee Evans (Channel 4) 1995, Searching (ITV) 1995, Look at the State We're In! (BBC2) 1995, Emma (Meridian/ITV) 1996, Lord of Misrule (BBC) 1996, Breaking the Code (BBC) 1996; *Films* incl: The Lonely Passion of Judith Hearne 1989, A Chorus of Disapproval 1989, Howards End 1990, Wolf 1994, An Awfully Big Adventure 1994, Stiff Upper Lips 1996; *Recreations* gardening, canal boat; *Clubs* BBC; *Style*— Prunella Scales, CBE; ✉ c/o Conway van Gelder Robinson Ltd, 18–21 Jermyn Street, London SW1Y 6HP (☎ 0171 287 0077, fax 0171 287 1940)

SCAMELL, Ernest Harold; s of Capt Ernest Harold Scamell (d 1981), and Lilian Kate, *née* Hall; *b* 9 March 1928; *Educ* Frays Coll Uxbridge, King's Coll London (LLB, LLM, AKC); *m* 1, 22 Aug 1952 (m dis), Patricia Annie, da of Percy Bullock (d 1979); 2 s (Grant b 11 Nov 1956, Adrian b 9 July 1958), 2 da (Joanna b 9 May 1960, Amanda b 19 Oct 1963); m 2, 11 Sept 1977, Ragnhild Bennedsen, da of Viggo Holdt, of Nyborg, Denmark; 1 step c (Cleere b 16 Nov 1967); *Career* called the the Bar Lincoln's Inn 1949; currently memb Chambers Lincoln's Inn (head of Chambers 1971–91); vice provost UCL 1978–84, prof emeritus of English law Univ of London 1990– (reader 1960–66, prof 1966–90); memb Bar Cncl; *Books* Butterworths Property Law Handbook (3 edn, 1994), Land Covenants (1996); *Recreations* flying, model building; *Clubs* Holy Trinity Meccano, The George Formby Soc, Air Touring Flying; *Style*— Ernest Scamell, Esq; ✉ Woodsdale Farmhouse, Pope Street, Godmersham, Kent CT4 7DN; 5 New Square, Lincoln's Inn, London WC2A 3RJ (☎ 0171 404 0404)

SCAMPTON, Ann Barbara; da of John Ewart March, MC (d 1984), and Laura Vera, *née* Vale (d 1981); *b* 2 Feb 1933; *Educ* Cathedral Sch for Girls Shanghai, Lunghwa Acad, Clifton HS for Girls, Royal West of England Acad Sch of Architecture; *m* 7 Aug 1954, Peter Gregory Scampton, s of Gregory Oliver Scampton (d 1970), of Bristol; 3 da (Gillian b 12 June 1959, Sarah b 15 Feb 1961, Katie (twin) b 15 Feb 1961); *Career* architect; founded own practice 1965, amalgamated with Moxley Jenner and Partners 1972, co-fndr dir and co sec Moxley Jenner and Partners (London) Ltd 1986–; govr Clifton HS for Girls Bristol; former pres Bristol Soc of Architects; FRIBA, RWA; *Recreations* painting, sailing; *Clubs* Cruising Assoc; *Style*— Ms Ann Scampton; ✉ Moxley Jenner & Partners (London) Ltd, 47 Clapham High Street, London SW4 7TL (☎ 0171 627 2798, fax 0171 627 2533)

SCANLAN, Charles Denis; s of late Francis Joseph Winsloe Scanlan, and late Eileen, *née* Terry; *b* 23 Dec 1944; *Educ* St Benedict's Sch Ealing, Balliol College Oxford (BA); *m* 11 Sept 1971, Dorothy, da of Frederick Albert Quick, of Laleston, Mid Glam; 2 s (Christopher b 1977, Stephen b 1980); *Career* admitted slr 1970; Simmons & Simmons: articled clerk 1967–70, asst slr 1970–73, ptnr 1973–; Freeman City Slrs Co; memb Law Soc; *Books* Know Your Rights (jtly, 1975); *Style*— Charles Scanlan, Esq; ✉ Simmons & Simmons, 21 Wilson Street, London EC2M 2TX (☎ 0171 628 2020, fax 0171 628 2070)

SCANLON, Baron (Life Peer UK 1979), of Davyhulme, Co Greater Manchester; Hugh Parr Scanlon; s of Hugh Scanlon; *b* 26 Oct 1913, in Australia; *Educ* Stretford Elementary Sch, Nat Council of Labour Colls; *m* 1943, Nora, da of James Markey; 2 da; *Career* apprentice instrument maker; chm Engrg Industry Training Bd until 1982; memb British Gas Corp 1976–, pres AEUW 1968–78 (formerly div organiser and memb London Exec Cncl); Hon DCL Kent 1988; *Style*— The Rt Hon the Lord Scanlon; ✉ 23 Seven Stones Drive, Broadstairs, Kent

SCANNELL, Vernon; *b* 23 Jan 1922; *Educ* Univ of Leeds; *m* 1 Oct 1954, Josephine, da of Lt-Col Claude Higson, of Edenbridge, Kent; 3 s (Toby b 1959, John b 1961, Jacob b 1967), 2 da (Jane b 1955, Nancy b 1957); *Career* 70 Bn Argyll & Sutherland Highlanders 1940–42, 5/7 Bn Gordon Highlanders 1942–45; poet in residence: Berinsfield Oxfordshire 1975–76, King's Sch Canterbury 1979, Wakefield Dist Coll 1987, Mount Sch York 1987; awards: Heinemann Award for Lit 1961, Cholmondeley Poetry Prize 1974, Travelling Scholarship Soc of Authors 1987; FRSL 1961; *Books* A Sense of Danger (1962), Walking Wounded (1965), Epithets of War (1968), The Tiger and the Rose, An Autobiography (1971), New and Collected Poems (1980), Argument of Kings (1987), A Time For Fires (1991), Drums of Morning - Growing Up in the Thirties (1992), Collected Poems 1950–1993 (1993), The Black and White Days, Poems (1996); *Style*— Vernon Scannell, Esq, FRSL; ✉ 51 North Street, Otley, W Yorks LS21 1AH (☎ 01943 467176)

SCARBROUGH, 12 Earl of (E 1690); Richard Aldred Lumley; also Viscount Lumley of Waterford (I 1628), Baron Lumley of Lumley Castle (E 1681), and Viscount Lumley of Lumley Castle (E 1690); s of 11 Earl, KG, GCSI, GCIE, GCVO (d 1969); *b* 5 Dec 1932; *Educ* Eton, Magdalen Coll Oxford; *m* 1970, Lady Elizabeth, *née* Ramsay, da of 16 Earl of Dalhousie, KT, GCVO, GBE, MC; 2 s (Richard Osbert b 18 May 1973, Thomas Henry b 6 Feb 1980), 1 da (Rose Frederica Lily b 31 Aug 1981); *Heir* s, Viscount Lumley, *qv*; *Career* 2 Lt 11 Hussars, Lt Queen's Own Yorks Dragoons, ADC to Govr and C in C Cyprus 1956, Hon Col 1 Bn Yorks Volunteers 1975–88; pres: N Area Royal Br Legion 1984–93, York Georgian Soc 1985–92; memb Royal Cmmn on Historical Manuscripts 1994–; Lord-Lieut of S Yorkshire March 1996– (DL 1974); *Style*— The Earl of Scarbrough; ✉ Sandbeck Park, Maltby, Rotherham, S Yorks S66 8PF (☎ 01302 742210, fax 01302 750090)

SCARD, Dennis Leslie; s of Charles Leslie Scard, of Harrow, and Doris Annie Scard (d 1976); *b* 8 May 1943; *Educ* Lascelles County Secdy Sch, Trinity Coll of Music; *m* Linda Christine, *née* Perry; 2 s from prev m (Timothy Martin b 27 Feb 1969, Christopher Robin b 18 July 1974); *Career* professional musician (horn player) 1962–85 (worked with various symphony and chamber orchs and other musical combinations, opera, ballet, recording and theatre work); Musicians' Union: memb Exec Ctee 1979–85, dist official E and NE area 1985–90, gen sec 1990–; memb Royal Soc of Musicians 1983, FRSA; *Recreations* music, theatre, cooking, walking, home wine-making; *Style*— Dennis Scard, Esq; ✉ Musicians' Union, 60–62 Clapham Road, London SW9 0JJ (☎ 0171 582 5566, fax 0171 582 9805)

SCARDINO, Marjorie Morris; da of Robert Weldon Morris (d 1990), of Texas, and Beth, *née* Lamb; *b* 25 Jan 1947; *Educ* Baylor Univ USA (BA), George Washington Univ Law Sch, Univ of San Francisco Law Sch (JD); *m* 1974, Albert J Scardino; 1 da (Adelaide b 1978), 2 s (William b 1979, Albert b 1984); *Career* ptnr Brannen Wessels Searcy law firm Savannah Ga 1975–85, publisher The Georgia Gazette (winner Pulitzer Prize 1983) 1978–85, pres The Economist Newspaper Group Inc New York 1985–92, chief exec The Economist Group plc London 1992–96, gp chief exec Pearson plc 1996–; dir: W H Smith plc, Con Agra Inc (USA), Public Radio International (USA), The Atlantic Cncl (USA); *Style*— Ms Marjorie Scardino; ✉ Pearson plc, 3 Burlington Gardens, London W1X 1LE (☎ 0171 411 2000, fax 0171 411 2390)

SCARFE, Gerald Anthony; s of Reginald Thomas Scarfe, and Dorothy Edna, *née* Gardner; *b* 1 June 1936; *m* Jane Asher, *qv*, da of Dr Richard Asher (d 1968), of London; 2 s (Alexander David b 16 Dec 1981, Rory Christopher b 10 Dec 1983), 1 da (Katie Geraldine b 11 April 1974); *Career* designer and director; political cartoonist of the Sunday Times 1967–88; designer and dir of animation Pink Floyd's The Wall (MGM); *Theatre* numerous scenery and costume credits incl: Orpheus in the Underworld (London Coliseum), What a Lucky Boy (Manchester Royal Exchange), Ubu Roi (Traverse Theatre), Magic Flute (LA Opera), An Absolute Turkey (Globe), Mind Millie for Me (Haymarket); *Television* dir of films for the BBC: Hogarth 1970, Scarfe by Scarfe 1986, Scarfe's Follies 1987, I Like The Girls Who Do 1988, Scarfe on... 1989, Scarfe on Sex 1991, Scarfe on Art 1991, Scarfe in Paradise 1992, Scarfe on Class 1993; *Films* conslt designer and character design for Walt Disney's Hercules 1997; *Books* Scarfe by Scarfe (1986), Scarfe's Seven Deadly Sins (1987), Scarfe's Line of Attack (1988), Scarfeland (1989), Scarfe on Stage (1992), Scarfe Face (1993); *Recreations* skiing; *Clubs* Brooks's; *Style*— Gerald Scarfe, Esq

SCARFFE, Prof (John) Howard; s of late Andrew Ernest Scarffe, of Douglas, IOM, and Nancy May, *née* Fargher; *b* 11 March 1947; *Educ* King William's Coll IOM, St Bartholomew's Hosp Med Coll Univ of London (MB BS, MD); *m* 8 Jan 1972, Sheila Elizabeth, da of Alfred Coyte, of Broadstairs, Kent; 1 s (Christopher), 1 da (Elizabeth); *Career* house surgn Addenbrooke's Hosp Cambridge 1971–72, sr house offr gen med Bart's 1972–74 (house physician 1971); Univ of Manchester: lectr and hon registrar 1974–76, lectr and hon sr registrar 1976–80, sr lectr and hon conslt 1980–91, reader and hon conslt 1991–96, prof of med oncology and hon conslt 1996–; dir Regnl Acute Leukaemia and Bone Marrow Transplant Unit Christie Hosp; contrib chapters to a number of oncological textbooks; memb: Teaching Faculty Int Union Against Cancer 1980, S Manchester Health Authy 1983–89, NW Regnl Advsy Ctee for Oncology Services 1985–91, Assoc of Cancer Physicians Ctee 1991–94; MRCS 1970, FRCP 1986 (MRCP 1973, LRCP 1970); *Recreations* rugby, walking, reading; *Clubs* Lymm Rugby Football; *Style*— Prof J Howard Scarffe; ✉ Four Winds, Cinder Lane, Thelwall, Cheshire WA4 3JL (☎ 01925 263549); Cancer Research Campaign, Department of Medical Oncology, University of Manchester, Christie Hospital, Wilmslow Rd, Manchester M20 9BX (☎ 0161 446 3748)

SCARISBRICK, Diana; da of Charles Wood (d 1994), and Genevieve, *née* Sutherland (d 1995); *b* 8 Oct 1928; *Educ* Christ's Hosp, St Hugh's College Oxford (exhibitioner, MA); *m* 5 July 1955, Peter Ewald Scarisbrick, s of Charles Ewald Scarisbrick (d 1966); 1 da (Sophie Hastings-Bass b 15 May 1956); *Career* freelance lectr and writer on jewellery and engraved gems; jewellery ed Harpers and Queen Magazine 1990–93; contrib to: Burlington Magazine, Apollo Magazine, Country Life Magazine, Il Giornale Dell'Arte, exhibition and museum catalogues in Britain, Germany, USA and Japan; memb: Soc of Antiquaries, Soc of Jewellery Historians; *Books* The Ralph Harari Collection of Finger Rings (with Prof John Boardman, 1977), Jewellery (1984), Il Valore Dei Gioielli e Degli Orologi da Collezione (1984 and 1987), 2500 Years of Rings (1988), Ancestral Jewels (1989), Rings (1993), Jewels in Britain 1066–1837 (1994), Tudor and Jacobean Jewellery (1995), Chaumet, Master Jewellers from 1780 (1995); *Recreations* walking, sight-seeing; *Style*— Mrs Diana Scarisbrick; ✉ 11 Chester Terrace, London NW1 4ND (☎ 0171 935 9928, fax 0171 487 5634)

SCARLETT, Hon James Harry; s and h of 8 Baron Abinger, DL, *qv*; *b* 28 May 1959; *Educ* BSc, MPhil (Cantab); *Career* FRGS, FLS; *Style*— The Hon James Scarlett

SCARLETT, His Hon James Harvey Anglin; s of Lt-Col James Alexander Scarlett, DSO (d 1925), and Muriel Blease (d 1945); *b* 27 Jan 1924; *Educ* Shrewsbury, ChCh Oxford (MA); *Career* Lt RA 1944–47; called to the Bar Inner Temple 1950, Malayan Civil Serv 1955–58, recorder of the Crown Court 1972–74, circuit judge 1974–89; *Recreations* walking; *Clubs* Athenaeum; *Style*— His Hon James Scarlett; ✉ Chilmington Green, Great Chart, nr Ashford, Kent

SCARMAN, Baron (Life Peer UK 1977), of Quatt, Co Shropshire; Sir Leslie George Scarman; kt (1961), OBE (1944), PC (1973); s of late George Charles Scarman; *b* 29 July 1911; *Educ* Radley, BNC Oxford (MA); *m* 1947, Ruth Clement, da of late Clement Wright; 1 adopted s (John Clement b 1946); *Career* sits as ind peer in House of Lords; called to the Bar Middle Temple 1936; QC 1957, judge of the High Court 1961–72, Lord Justice of Appeal 1972–77, Lord of Appeal in Ordinary 1977–86; chm: Law Cmmn 1965–72, Tbnl Inquiry NI 1969–72; chm and author of report of inquiry into: the Red Lion Square disorders 1975, the Brixton riots 1981; chllr Univ of Warwick 1977–89, visitor St Hilda's Coll Oxford, pres RIPA 1981–87; former memb: Arts Cncl, ENO; pres Thanet Archaeological Soc; hon memb American Philosophical Soc; hon fell: BNC Oxford, LSE; Hon DCL Univ of Oxford 1982; Hon LLD: Univ of Glasgow, Univ of Kent, Univ of Dundee, Univ of London, Univ of Warwick, Univ of Wales, Queen's Univ Belfast, Univ of Freiburg, Univ of Keele, Univ of Exeter; Liveryman Worshipful Co of Dyers; *Style*— The Rt Hon the Lord Scarman, OBE, PC; ✉ House of Lords, London SW1A OPW

SCARPELLO, Dr John Hugh; s of late William John Scarpello, of Sheffield, and Pauline Frances, *née* Berney; *b* 23 July 1947; *Educ* Haberdashers' Askes, Univ of Wales Coll of Med (MB BCh, MD); *m* 20 April 1974, Barbara Jean, da of William John Erasmus; 1 s (Robert John b 27 April 1981), 2 da (Kay Elizabeth b 11 July 1975, Tracey Jane b 30 July 1977); *Career* house offr Univ Hosp of Wales 1971–72, sr house offr Nottingham Gen Hosp 1972–74, med registrar Royal Hosp Sheffield 1974–76, sr registrar Royal Hallamshire Hosp 1976–81, hon clinical tutor Univ of Sheffield 1976–81, conslt physician N Staffs Royal Infirmary 1981–, sr lectr Univ of Keele 1992– (formerly sr res fell); divnl surgn St John Ambulance Stoke Div; memb: Scientific Section Br Diabetic Assoc, Med Res Soc; FRCP 1989 (MRCP 1974); *Recreations* squash, swimming, walking; *Style*— Dr John Scarpello; ✉ Newlyn, Seabridge Lane, Newcastle, Staffs ST5 3LS (☎ 01782 613682); Department of Diabetes and Endocrinology, City General Hospital, Stoke-on-Trent, Staffs ST4 6QG (☎ 01782 741425, fax 01782 741427)

SCARSDALE, 3 Viscount (UK 1911); Sir Francis John Nathaniel Curzon; 11 Bt (S 1636) and 11 Bt (E 1641); also 7 Baron Scarsdale (GB 1761); 30 Lord (territorial lordship) of Kedleston; s of late Hon Francis Nathaniel Curzon (yr bro of 1 & and last Marquess Curzon of Kedleston and s of 4 Baron Scarsdale), and Phyllis, da of Capt Christian Combe, of Strathconan, Ross-shire, by his w, Lady Jane Seymour, da of 3 Marquess Conyngham; *b* 28 July 1924; *Educ* Eton; *m* 1, 1948 (m dis 1967), Solange Yvonne Palmyre Ghislaine (d 1974), da of late Oscar Hanse, of Mont-sur-Marchienne, Belgium; 2 s, 1 da; m 2, 1968, Helene Gladys Frances, da of late Maj William Ferguson Thomson, of Kinellar, Aberdeenshire; 2 s; *Heir* s, Hon Peter Curzon; *Career* late Capt Scots Gds; Shell International Petroleum Co 1948–64, estate mangr Kedleston Estate 1970–77, gave Kedleston Hall & Park to Nat Tst 1987; *Recreations* racing, shooting, piping, photography; *Clubs* County, Derby; *Style*— The Rt Hon the Viscount Scarsdale; ✉ Kedleston Hall, Derby (☎ 01332 840386); Tullich, Strathcarron, Ross-shire

SCHAEFER, Prof Stephen Martin; s of Gerhardt Martin Schaefer, OBE (d 1986), of Bramhall, Cheshire, and Helga Maria Schaefer (d 1992); *b* 18 Nov 1946; *Educ* Manchester GS, Univ of Cambridge (BA, MA), Univ of London (PhD); *m* 26 July 1969, Teresa Evelyn; 2 s (Maximilian b 1974, Joshua b 1977); *Career* London Business Sch: res offr, sr res offr and lectr 1970–79; Stanford Univ asst prof 1979–80; London Business Sch: sr res fell and prof of finance 1981–, dir Inst of Finance and Accounting 1985–92, research dean 1992–95; visiting asst prof: Univ of Chicago, Univ of California at Berkeley 1977; visiting prof: Univ of Venice 1991, Univ of Cape Town; dir: Lawtex plc 1974–91, Securities Assoc 1990–91, Securities and Futures Authy 1991–96; tstee Smith Breeden Mutual Funds; memb American Fin Assoc; *Style*— Prof Stephen Schaefer; ✉ London Business School, Sussex Place, Regents Park, London NW1 4SA (☎ 0171 262 5050, fax 0171 724 3317)

SCHAFFER, Louis Isaac; s of Harry Schaffer (d 1963), and Harriet, *née* Burman (d 1965); *b* 22 April 1930; *Educ* Luton GS, Trinity Coll Cambridge (MA, LLM); *m* 1 Jan 1961, Nina Valerie, da of Raymond Richard Thomas; 2 s (Daniel b 13 Oct 1963, Benjamin b 5 May 1965), 1 da (Rachel b 8 April 1967); *Career* RAOC: 1949–62, Capt 1954; called to the Bar Middle Temple 1955; memb: Brent Police Liaison Gp 1985–89, Bd of Deps of Br Jews 1985–89; *Recreations* walking the dog; *Style*— Louis Schaffer, Esq; ✉ 10 King's Bench Walk, Temple, London EC4Y 7EB (☎ 0171 353 2501, fax 0171 353 0658)

SCHANSCHIEFF, Simon George; OBE (1996), JP (1971); s of Brian Alexander Schanschieff, and Nina, *née* Robinson (d 1990); *b* 22 Oct 1938; *Educ* Oakham Sch Rutland; *m* 27 June 1964, Arman Philippa (Pip), da of Charles Henry Arman (d 1970); 3 s (Guy b 1966, Christopher b 1968, Nicholas b 1978); *Career* qualified CA 1961; ptnr Grant Thornton Northampton 1966–; chm Northants Health Authy 1978–, chm Tstees Oakham Sch 1980–, memb Ctee Northants CCC 1969–; FCA 1971; *Style*— Simon Schanschieff, Esq, OBE, JP; ✉ Old Rectory, Great Billing, Northampton (☎ 01604 407842); Elgin House, Billing Rd, Northampton (☎ 01604 27811)

SCHAPIRA, Prof Anthony Henry Vernon; s of Marcus Schapira (d 1994), of Yorkshire, and Hanna Constance, *née* Glaister (d 1982); *b* 3 Sept 1954; *Educ* Bradford GS, Westminster Med Sch (entrance scholar, Berridge research scholar, BSc, MB BS, MD, DSc, AKC); *m* 1995, Nicola, da of Gavin John Keegan; 1 da (Sarah Victoria Constance b 1983); *Career* house physician to Sir Richard Bayliss, Chief Physician to HM The Queen 1979, med trg Hammersmith and Whittington Hosps, Nat Hosp for Neurology and Neurosurgery and St Thomas's Hosp 1980–84, trg in neurology Royal Free Hosp and Nat Hosp for Neurology and Neurosurgery 1983–88, Wellcome research fell 1985–87; Royal Free Hosp Sch of Med and Inst of Neurology London: sr lectr and conslt in neurology 1988–90, univ chair of clinical neurosciences 1991–; conslt neurologist Royal Free Hosp, Nat Hosp for Neurology and Neurosurgery and Queen Elizabeth II Hosp Welwyn Garden City; hon prof of neurology Mount Sinai Med Sch NY 1995; Queen Square Prize 1986, Graham Bull Prize for Clinical Sci RCP 1995, Buckston Browne Medal Harveian Soc 1995; memb: Movement Disorders Soc, Harveian Soc 1994; FRCP 1992; *Books* Mitochondrial Disorders in Neurology (1994), Mitochondria: DNA, Protein and Disease (1994); *Recreations* chess (Yorkshire champion 1966), motor racing, European history, international affairs; *Clubs* RAC; *Style*— Prof Anthony Schapira; ✉ Department of Clinical Neurosciences, Royal Free Hospital School of Medicine, Rowland Hill Street, London NW3 2PF (☎ 0171 830 2012, fax 0171 431 1577)

SCHAUFUSS, Peter; *b* 26 April 1950; *Educ* Royal Danish Ballet Sch; *Career* ballet dancer, prodr, choreographer; apprenticeship Royal Danish Ballet Co 1965; soloist: Nat Ballet of Canada 1967–68, Royal Danish Ballet 1969–70; princ: London Festival Ballet 1970–74, New York City Ballet 1974–77, National Ballet of Canada 1977–83; artistic dir London Festival Ballet (later English Nat Ballet) 1984–90, dir of ballet Deutsche Oper Berlin 1990–93, artistic dir Royal Danish Ballet 1994–95; presenter Dancer (BBC TV series) 1984; numerous guest appearances with cos incl: Royal Ballet, Nat Ballet of Canada, Ballet National de Marseille, La Scala Milan, Vienna State Opera, Tokyo Ballet Co, American Ballet Theatre, Royal Danish Ballet, Deutsche Oper Berlin, Scottish Ballet, Bavarian State Opera, Paris Opera, Teatro dell'Opera (Rome), Teatro Comunale (Florence); roles created for him in: The Steadfast Tin Soldier 1975, Rhapsodie Espagnole 1975, Phantom of the Opera 1980, Verdi Variations 1982, Orpheus 1982; ballets produced incl: La Sylphide (London Festival Ballet 1979, Ballet National de Marseille 1980, Deutsche Oper Berlin 1982, Stuttgart Ballet 1982, Teatro Comunale Firenze 1983, Vienna State Opera 1990, Opernhaus Zurich 1990, Teatro dell'Opera di Roma 1991, Hessisches Staatstheater Wiesbaden, Ballet du Rhin 1994, Royal Danish Ballet 1994), Napoli (Nat

Ballet of Canada 1981, Teatro San Carlo 1988, English National Ballet 1989), Folktale (Deutsche Oper Berlin 1983), Dances from Napoli (London Festival Ballet 1983, Royal Danish Ballet 1994), Bournonville (Aterballetto 1984), The Nutcracker (London Festival Ballet 1986, Graz Opera Ballet Austria 1992, Deutsche Oper Berlin 1992), Giselle (Deutsche Oper Berlin 1991, Royal Danish Ballet 1995), Tchaikovsky Trilogy (Deutsche Oper Berlin 1993), Swan Lake (Deutsche Oper Berlin 1993), Sleeping Beauty (Deutsche Oper Berlin 1993); choreographer and prodr Hamlet (Royal Danish Ballet 1996); awards: Solo Award (2nd Int Ballet Competition Moscow) 1973, Star of the Year (Federal Republic of Germany) 1978, Soc of W End Theatres Award for Ballet 1979, Evening Standard Award for most outstanding achievement in dance 1979, Manchester Evening News Theatre Award for Dance 1986, Lakerozprisen (Copenhagen) 1988, Berlin Co Award for best ballet prodn of the year (Berlinerzeitung) 1991, Critics' Prize (Edinburgh Festival) 1991; Knight of the Dannebrog 1988, Offr de l'Ordre de la Couronne (Belgium) 1995; *Recreations* boxing; *Style*— Peter Schaufuss, Esq; ✉ c/o Papoutsis Representation Ltd, 18 Sundial Ave, London SE25 4BX

SCHEER, Cherrill Sheila; *née* Hille; da of Maurice Hille (d 1968), and Ray Hille (d 1986); *b* 29 March 1939; *Educ* Copthall Co GS, Architectural Assoc London, Architectural Dept Kingston Sch of Art; *m* 3 Dec 1961, Ian Scheer, s of Oscar Scheer (d 1988); 1 s (Ivan), 1 da (Danielle Ann (Mrs Benson)); *Career* mktg dir Hille International Ltd 1970–83 (mktg mangr 1961–70); dir: Print Forum Ltd 1965–, S Hille & Co (Holdings) Ltd 1970; dir gp mktg: Hille Ergonom plc 1983–89, Scott Howard Furniture Ltd 1989–91, Cherrill Scheer & Associates 1991–; congress dir Design Renaissance 1993 Int Design Congress; vice pres Design & Indust Assoc (chm 1976–78); govr London Guildhall Univ (memb Advsy Bd Sir John Cass Faculty of Arts Design and Manufacture); memb: Fedn of Electronic Industs and Office Furniture, Furniture and Filing Mfrs' Assoc (past chm); FCSD, FInstSMM, FRSA; *Style*— Mrs Cherrill Scheer; ✉ 16 Kerry Ave, Stanmore, Middx HA7 4NN (☎ 0181 954 3839); Cherrill Scheer & Associates, Hille House, 132 St Albans Rd, Watford, Herts WD2 4AE (☎ 01923 242769, fax 01923 228110)

SCHER, Anna Valerie; da of Dr Eric Asher Scher (d 1982), and Constance, *née* Hurwitz (d 1984); *b* 26 Dec 1944; *Educ* St Angela's Coll Cork Eire, Hove Co GS Sussex, Trent Park Coll Cockfosters (Gen Teacher's Cert), Brighton Sch of Music and Drama (Dip in Drama); *m* 1976, Charles Verrall; 1 s (John Benedict b 1980); *Career* fndr and princ Anna Scher Theatre 1968–; drama workshops at: Round House, Sadler's Wells, Unicorn, Young Vic, numerous schs, hosps, libraries; improformances on social issues incl children's rights, AIDS awareness for the Nat Children's Bureau and to Nat AIDS Tst, annual workshops in Ireland and (for the Br Cncl) Scandinavia; TV: First Act (LWT) 1975, The Kids Are United (Man Alive Special, BBC2) 1982, Ain't Many Angels (BBC2) 1980, Acting with Anna (Channel 4) 1983, Anna Scher on Acting (Danish TV) 1985, Desperate to Act (BBC, Radio 5 1991) 1988, Drama with Anna 1988, When Will I be Famous? (ITV) 1988; contribs to: Aquarius, Good Afternoon, Kaleidoscope, Tonight, Woman's Hour, TV-am, Profile, Loose Ends, Prayer for the Day (Radio 4); The Shalom Workshops (Eire, N Ireland, Denmark, Zimbabwe, SA, Israel) 1976–96; assoc RADA 1983; memb: Jury BAFTA 1984, Jury Sony Awards 1987; Community Award Irish Post 1983, Woman of Distinction Award 1988, nominated Woman of Europe 1990; *Books* 100+ Ideas for Drama (with Charles Verrall, 1975), First Act Drama Kit (1976), Another 100+ Ideas for Drama (1987), Desperate to Act (1988); *Recreations* theatre-going, books, radio, restaurants; *Style*— Ms Anna Scher; ✉ The Anna Scher Theatre, 70–72 Barnsbury Rd, London N1 OES (☎ 0171 278 2101, fax 0171 833 9467)

SCHERER, Paul Joseph; s of François Joseph Scherer (d 1961), of Folkestone, Kent, and Florence, *née* Haywood (d 1977); *b* 28 Dec 1933; *Educ* Stonyhurst; *m* 4 April 1959, Mary, da of Claude Fieldus; 1 s (Jonathan b 9 Nov 1961), 3 da (Clare b 14 March 1963, Joanna b 26 June 1965, Lucy b 3 Jan 1968); *Career* Nat Serv 1952–54, cmmnd Buffs (Royal E Kent Regt); publisher; Bailey Bros & Swinfen Ltd 1954–56, jr ed G Bell & Sons Ltd 1956–58, sales mangr Penguin Books 1958–63, gp sales dir Paul Hamlyn Ltd 1963–68, md Int Div William Collins Sons & Co Ltd 1968–77, pres Collins & World USA 1974–75, md Mills & Boon Ltd 1977–82; Transworld Publishers Ltd: md and chief exec 1982–95, chm 1995–96; sr vice pres Bantam Doubleday Dell Publishing Group Inc 1990–96; dir: Bloomsbury Publishing Plc 1993–, Book Tokens Ltd 1995–, Whizzkidz 1996–; chm Curtis Brown Ltd 1996–, memb Bd: Book Devpt Cncl 1971–74, Book Mktg Cncl 1977–84 (chm 1982–84), British Library 1996–; pres The Book Trade Benevolent Soc 1995–; Publishers Assoc Cncl: memb 1982–84 and 1989–94, vice pres 1990 and 1993, pres 1991–93; fndr chm Unicorn Sch Kew 1970–73, govr Worth Sch 1993–96; *Clubs* Hurlingham, Savile; *Style*— Paul Scherer, Esq; ✉ 43a Cheyne Court, London SW3 5TS; Transworld Publishers Ltd, 61–63 Uxbridge Rd, London W5 5SA (☎ 0181 579 2652)

SCHIEMANN, Rt Hon Lord Justice; Rt Hon Sir Konrad Hermann Theodor; kt (1986), PC (1995); s of Helmuth Schiemann (d 1945), and Beate, *née* von Simson (d 1946); *b* 15 Sept 1937; *Educ* King Edward's Sch Birmingham, Freiberg Univ, Pembroke Coll Cambridge (MA, LLB); *m* 1965, Elisabeth Hanna Eleonore, da of late John Holroyd-Reece; 1 da (Juliet b 1966); *Career* jr counsel to the Crown (Common Law) 1978–80; QC 1980, recorder of the Crown Court 1985, bencher Inner Temple 1985, judge of the High Court of Justice (Queen's Bench Div) 1986–95, a Lord Justice of Appeal 1995–; chm Cncl St John's Smith Square 1995– (memb 1984–95, tstee 1990–95), vice chm Parole Bd 1991–92 (memb 1990), govr English Nat Ballet 1995–; *Recreations* music, reading, walking, water sources in Uganda; *Style*— Rt Hon Lord Justice Schiemann; ✉ Royal Courts of Justice, Strand, London WC2A 2LL

SCHIFF, Andras; s of Odon Schiff, and Klara, *née* Csengeri; *b* 21 Dec 1953; *Educ* Franz Liszt Acad of Music Budapest (with Paul Kadosa, Ferenc Rados and Gyorgy Kurtag), private study with George Malcolm; *m* Oct 1987, Yuuko, *née* Shiokawa; *Career* concert pianist; regular orchestral engagements: NY Philharmonic, Chicago Symphony, Vienna Philharmonic, Concertgebouw Orchestra, Orchestre de Paris, London Philharmonic, London Symphony, Royal Philharmonic, Israel Philharmonic, Washington Nat Symphony; festivals incl: Vienna, Feldkirch, Salzburg, Lucerne, Edinburgh and his own annual Chamber Music Festival in Mondsee Austria; *Awards* Premio della Academia Chigiana Siena 1987, Wiener Flotenuhr (Mozart Prize of the City of Vienna) 1989, Bartok Prize 1991; Instrumentalist of the Year: Int Classical Music Awards 1992, Royal Philharmonic Soc 1994; Claudio Arrau Meml Medal Robert Schumann Soc 1994, Kossuth Prize 1996; *Recordings incl* all the Mozart Piano Concertos (with The Camerata Academica Salzburg and Sandor Vegh), Bach Concertos (with The Chamber Orchestra of Europe), all the Schubert Piano Sonatas, Mozart Sonatas and Chamber Music (on Mozart's own instruments); *Recreations* literature, languages, soccer; *Style*— Andras Schiff, Esq; ✉ c/o Terry Harrison Artists Management, The Orchard, Market Street, Charlbury, Oxon OX7 3PJ (☎ 01608 810330, fax 01608 811331)

SCHIFF, Heinrich; *b* 18 Nov 1951; *Career* conductor and cellist; studied cello with Tobias Kuhne and Andre Navarra; debut Vienna and London 1973; conductors worked with (as cellist) incl: Claudio Abbado, Sergiu Celibidache, Sir Colin Davis, Christoph von Dohnanyi, Bernhard Haitink, Nikolaus Harnoncourt, Kurt Masur, André Previn, Giuseppe Sinopoli, Klaus Tennstedt; contemporary performances incl works by Witold Lutoslawski, Hans Werner Henze, Ernat Krenek and John Casken Cello Concerto (world premiere, written for Heinrich Schiff and Northern Sinfonia); professional conductor 1986–; princ guest conductor Deutsche Kammerphilharmonie 1990–92, artistic dir Northern Sinfonia 1990–96, princ conductor Musikkollegium Winterthur and Copenhagen Philharmonic Orch 1995–; guest conductor: Symphony Orch of Hamburg, Frankfurt Museumsgesellschaft Orch, Residentie Orkest Den Haag, Los Angeles Philharmonic, Helsinki Radio Symphony Orch, BBC Nat Orch of Wales, Vienna ORF Symphony Orch, Zurich Tonhalle Orch and Oslo Philharmonic; dir: The Magic Flute (Theatre de la Monnaie Brussels) 1992, Fidelio 1993, The Flying Dutchman (Stadttheater Bern) 1994; numerous recordings on Philips, EMI, Collins, Chandos, Berlin Classics, Deutsche Grammophon, Hyperion and Koch/Schwann; winner Grand Prix du Disque for Shostakovich Cello Concerto (Phillips); *Style*— Heinrich Schiff, Esq; ✉ Künstlersekretariat, Astrid Schoerke, Mönckebergallee 41, D-30453 Hannover, Germany

SCHILD, Geoffrey Christopher; CBE (1993); s of Christopher Schild (d 1963), of Sheffield, and Georgina Schild (d 1970); *b* 28 Nov 1935; *Educ* High Storrs GS Sheffield, Univ of Reading (BSc), Univ of Sheffield (PhD), Univ of Reading (DSc); *m* 1 Aug 1961, Tora, da of Rev Canon Peter Madland (d 1977), of Bergen, Norway; 2 s (Øystein Christopher b 1962, Peter Geoffrey b 1969), 1 da (Ingrid b 1965); *Career* lectr in virology Univ of Sheffield 1963–67; dir: World Influenza Centre at MRC Nat Inst for Med Res 1969–75 (memb scientific staff MRC 1967–75), Nat Inst for Biological Standards and Control 1985– (head Div of Virology 1975–85), MRC Directed Prog of AIDS Res 1987–94; memb: Dept of Health Jt Ctee on Vaccination and Immunisation 1975–, MRC Ctee on Vaccines and Immunological Procedures 1975–, Ctee on Safety of Medicines 1977–, Nat Biological Standards Bd 1985–; chm: MRC Working Gp on Hepatitis Vaccines, Euro Community Working Pty on Biotechnology 1986–93; WHO: memb Special Advsy Gp on Vaccine Devpt 1989–, memb Steering Ctee on AIDS Res 1989–, vice chm Bd of Tstees Int Vaccines Inst Soeul; Freeman City of London 1988; FIBiol 1977, FRCPath 1993, Hon MRCP 1995; *Recreations* ornithology, music; *Style*— Dr Geoffrey C Schild, CBE; ✉ Director National Institute for Biological Standards & Control, Blanche Lane, Potters Bar, Hertfordshire EN6 3QG (☎ 01707 46846/54753, fax 01707 46854)

SCHLAGMAN, Richard Edward; s of Jack Schlagman, of London, and Shirley, *née* Goldston (d 1992); *b* 11 Nov 1953; *Educ* Univ Coll Sch Hampstead, Brunel Univ; *Career* publisher; co-fndr, jt chm and md Interstate Electronics Ltd 1973–86, purchased Bush name from Rank Organisation and renamed IEL Bush Radio Ltd 1981, floated Bush Radio on London Stock Exchange 1984, Bush Radio plc sold 1986; acquired Phaidon Press Ltd 1990, chm and md Phaidon Press Ltd 1990–; memb Exec Ctee Patrons of New Art Tate Gallery; patron: Bayreuth, Salzburger Festspiele; memb: Royal Opera House Trust, Glyndebourne Festival Soc, Designers and Art Dirs Assoc of the UK; FRSA; *Recreations* music, art; *Clubs* Queen's, Chelsea Arts; *Style*— Richard Schlagman, Esq; ✉ Phaidon Press Ltd, Regent's Wharf, All Saints Street, London N1 9PA (☎ 0171 843 1000, fax 0171 843 1010)

SCHLESINGER, Theodore; s of Angel Schlesinger (d 1956), and Areti, *née* Cokino (d 1975); *b* 21 April 1931; *Educ* St Joseph Public Sch Cairo, Univ of London (BSc); *m* 1 (m dis 1973), Patricia, *née* Turley; m 2, 3 Nov 1973, Ann, da of T M Jackson, of The Old Hall Cottage, Cheveley, Newmarket, Suffolk; *Career* mktg mangr American Cyanamid 1954–55, dir of subsid co Gallup Poll 1955–60, chm ERC Statistics International plc 1979– (formed co in 1961); involved in charitable work in Egypt; FRSA; *Recreations* opera, new fiction, gardening, philosophy; *Style*— Theodore Schlesinger, Esq; ✉ The Old Hall, Cheveley, Newmarket, Suffolk (☎ 01638 730334); ERC Statistics International plc, 5–11 Shorts Gardens, Covent Garden, London WC2H 9AT (☎ 0171 497 2312, fax 0171 497 2313, telex 926510)

SCHMIDT, Michael Norton; s of Carl Bernhardt Schmidt (d 1971), and Elizabeth Norton, *née* Hill (d 1990); *b* 2 March 1947; *Educ* The Hill Sch Pottstown PA USA, Christ's Hosp (ESU scholar), Harvard Univ, Wadham Coll Oxford (exhibitioner, MA, pres OU Poetry Soc); *m* (m dis) Claire Patricia Harman; 2 s (Charles Bernhardt b 1980, Benedict William b 1985), 1 da (Isabel Claire b 1982); *Career* Univ of Manchester: Gulbenkian fell of poetry 1971–74, special lectr now sr lectr in poetry Dept of English 1974–, dir The Writing Sch (formerly The Poetry Centre) 1993–; fndr md and editorial dir Carcanet Press Ltd 1969–; fndr and gen ed PN Review (formerly Poetry Nation) 1972–; NW theatre critic The Independent 1986–88, Northern theatre critic The Daily Telegraph 1988–93; Br delegate at literary congresses in Liege Murcia Valencia and Paris; memb Arts Cncl Touring Panel 1991–94; adjudicator Translation Awards Br Comparative Literature Assoc 1992; advsr Finnish Literature Bd 1990–; selector Globe Theatre Awards 1993–; dir Modern Poetry Archive Project Rylands; memb Finnish Literature Soc; FRSL 1994; *Books* British Poetry since 1960 (with G Lindop, 1972), Ten English Poets (1976), Flower and Song: Aztec Poetry (trans with E Kissam, 1977), Fifty Modern British Poets (1979), Fifty English Poets 1300–1900 (1979), Five American Poets (with J Mathias, 1979), Eleven British Poets (1980), British Poetry since 1970 (1980), The Colonist (published as Green Island in USA, 1983, LA Times Book Award, 1984), On Poets & Others (trans, 1986), The Dresden Gate (1988), Reading Modern Poetry (1989), New Poetries (1994); *poetry* Black Buildings (1969), It Was My Tree (1970), Bedlam and the Oakwood (1970), Desert of the Lions (1972), My Brother Gloucester (1976), A Change of Affairs (1978), Choosing a Guest (1983), The Love of Strangers (1988), Selected Poems (1996); *Clubs* PEN; *Style*— Michael Schmidt, Esq, FRSL; ✉ c/o Carcanet Press Ltd, 4th Floor, Conavon Court, 12–16 Blackfriars Street, Manchester M3 5BQ (☎ 0161 834 8730, fax 0161 832 0084)

SCHMIEGELOW, Ian Lunn; *b* 16 March 1943; *Educ* Oundle, Magdalene Coll Cambridge (MA); *m* Penelope (d 1992); 3 da (Alexandra, Catrina, Antonia); *Career* called to the Bar Inner Temple 1967, in practice 1967–69; Hambros Bank Ltd: joined 1969, dir 1978–85, exec dir 1982–85; sr vice pres and chm Mgmnt Cncl for Europe, Middle E and Africa First National Bank of Chicago 1985–87; chm: Hamilton Lunn Ltd 1988–, Brinkley Estates Ltd 1988–; non-exec dir Norsk Hydro (UK) Ltd 1996–; *Clubs* Turf; *Style*— Ian Schmiegelow, Esq; ✉ Hamilton Lunn Ltd, 46 Catherine Place, London SW1E 6HL (☎ 0171 233 7440, fax 0171 233 7442)

SCHOFIELD, Prof Andrew Noel; s of Rev John Nöel Schofield (d 1986), of Fleet, Hants, and Winifred Jane Mary, *née* Eyles; *b* 1 Nov 1930; *Educ* Mill Hill Sch, Christ's Coll Cambridge (MA, PhD); *m* 17 June 1961, Margaret Eileen, da of Oswald Green (d 1963), of Cambridge; 2 s (Ben b 1963, Matthew b 1965), 2 da (Polly b 1962, Tiffany b 1967); *Career* asst engr Scott Wilson Kirkpatrick & Ptnrs (Malawi) 1951–54, lectr Cambridge Univ 1959–68 (res student and demonstrator 1954–59), res fell California Inst of Technol 1963–64, prof of civil engrg Univ of Manchester Inst of Sci and Technol 1968–74, prof of engrg Cambridge Univ 1974–; chm: Andrew N Schofield & Assocs Ltd (ANS&A) 1984–, Centrifuge Instrumentation and Equipment Ltd (ciel) 1987–; FICE 1972, FEng 1986, FRS 1992; *Books* Critical State Soil Mechanics (with C P Wroth, 1968), Land Disposal of Hazardous Waste (with J R Gronow and R K Jain, 1988), Centrifuges in Soil Mechanics (with W H Craig and R G James, 1988); *Style*— Prof Andrew N Schofield, FRS, FEng; ✉ Cambridge University Engineering Department, Trumpington Street, Cambridge CB2 1PZ (☎ 01223 332717/460555, fax 01223 460777)

SCHOFIELD, Angela Rosemary; da of Donald George Tym (d 1958), of Sheffield, and Clara Annie, *née* Bird; *b* 5 July 1951; *Educ* Grange GS Sheffield, Univ of York (BA); *m* 1989, Michael Schofield; *Career* higher clerical offr Royal Hosp Sheffield 1975–76, unit administrator Lightwood House Hosp Sheffield 1976–78, dep sector administrator Royal Infirmary Sheffield 1978–79, sr admin asst Sheffield Area Health Authy 1979–80; hosp administrator: Weston Park Hosp, Charles Clifford Dental Hosp Sheffield 1980–85; unit gen mangr: N Derbyshire Health Authy 1985–88, St Mary's Hosp Manchester 1988–89; sr fell Health Servs Mgmnt Unit Univ of Manchester 1989–92, chief exec

Calderdale Healthcare NHS Trust 1992–95, sr fell Health Servs Mgmnt Unit Univ of Manchester 1995–; chm: Regnl Cncl Trent Region IHSM 1986–87, Quality Assurance Ctee for Managing Health Servs IHSM; *Recreations* horse riding, golf; *Style*— Mrs Angela Schofield; ✉ Health Services Management Unit, Devonshire House, Precinct Centre, Oxford Road, Manchester M13 9PL (☎ 0161 275 2908, fax 0161 273 5245)

SCHOFIELD, Garry Edward; OBE (1994); s of Geoffrey Schofield, of Leeds, and Jean Lines; *b* 1 July 1965; *Educ* Parkside HS; *m* 1984, Adele, da of Robert Stanley Ward; 1 s (Jonathan James b 17 April 1990), 1 da (Danielle Louise b 11 June 1987); *Career* rugby league player; 117 appearances Hull 1983–87 (107 tries); Leeds: joined 1987 (record transfer fee), capt 1989–95, 115 appearances, 82 tries; joined Huddersfield 1996 (record transfer fee); GB: 2 colts caps, 2 under 21 caps, 1 under 24 cap, full debut v France 1984, vice capt tour to NZ and Papua New Guinea 1990, 46 full caps (world record), 31 tries (second highest for GB); Man of Steel and Leeds Player of the Year 1991, Wallace Arnold Player of the Year 1991, Int Player of the Year 1991, Rugby League Writers Sports Award 1996; *Recreations* golf, squash; *Style*— Garry Schofield, Esq, OBE; ✉ c/o Huddersfield Rugby League Club, The Alfred McAlpine Stadium, Stadium Way, Leeds Road, Huddersfield HD1 6PZ

SCHOFIELD, Hugh Robert Armstrong; s of Jack Schofield, of Co Kilkenny, and Ann Margaret, *née* Hurlbut; *b* 19 Aug 1961; *Educ* Clifton Coll Bristol (scholar), St John's Coll Oxford (scholar, BA); *m* June 1993, Rebecca, da of Noel Wain; *Career* BBC Radio: reporter Arabic Service 1984–86, reporter Jerusalem 1986–88, corr Madrid 1988–91, Paris 1991–92, foreign affrs corr 1992–; *Recreations* walking, cooking; *Style*— Hugh Schofield, Esq; ✉ BBC Radio Foreign Affairs Unit, Broadcasting House, London W1A 1AA (☎ 0171 927 4623)

SCHOFIELD, Dr Jennifer Anne; da of Stanley Stephen Goy (d 1979), and Mary Catherine, *née* Jones; *b* 12 July 1946; *Educ* Rosebery GS Epsom Surrey, Middlesex Hospital Med Sch (MB BS); *m* 1 Oct 1977, Neil McCallum, s of Fred Schofield; 3 s (Guy b 11 May 1980, Stuart b 25 Oct 1981, Max b 17 April 1992), 1 da (Olivia b 13 March 1983); *Career* ships surgn MN P&O Shipping Co 1973–74; anaesthetist Duchess of Kent Children's Hosp Hong Kong 1975–76, sr registrar in anaesthetics Hosp for Sick Children Gt Ormond St London 1977, med offr Grendon Underwood Prison Aylesbury 1979–81, conslt anaesthetist Stoke Mandeville Hosp Aylesbury 1981–; chm Oxford Regnl Anaesthetic Advsy Ctee 1991–94; FRCA 1975; *Recreations* needlework, skiing, family life; *Style*— Dr Jennifer Schofield; ✉ Perrotts Farm, Bicester Road, Long Crendon, Aylesbury, Bucks HP18 9BP; (☎ 01844 201585); Anaesthetic Dept (Dr Goy), Stoke Mandeville Hospital, Aylesbury, Bucks HP21 8AL (☎ 01296 315262)

SCHOFIELD, Kenneth Douglas; CBE (1996); s of Douglas Joseph Schofield (d 1978), and Jessie, *née* Gray (d 1994); *b* 3 Feb 1946; *Educ* Auchterarder HS; *m* 12 June 1968, Evelyn May, da of Arthur Gordon Sharp (d 1973); 2 da (Susan b 28 Jan 1971, Evonne b 13 Nov 1973); *Career* mangr Dunblane branch Perth Trustee Savings Bank 1969–71 (joined 1962), George Simms Organisation 1971–74, exec dir and co sec The PGA European Tour 1984– (dep to Press and PR Offr 1971–74, first sec 1975); memb Cncl Jr Golf Fndn; assoc Savings Bank Inst 1966–71; *Books* Pro Golf (1972–75), John Player Golf Yearbook (1973–75); *Recreations* golf, all main sports, walking; *Clubs* Wentworth Club, Crieff Golf, Foxhills County; *Style*— Kenneth D Schofield, Esq, CBE; ✉ PGA European Tour, Wentworth Drive, Virginia Water, Surrey GU25 4LX (☎ 01344 842881, fax 01344 842929)

SCHOFIELD, Leslie James; s of Frank Schofield, of Royton, Oldham, Lancs, and Alice, *née* Wardrop (d 1986); *Educ* Thames Rd Secdy Modern Blackpool, Tech Sch Rochester Kent; *m* 31 March 1967, Daphne Elizabeth Helen; 2 da (Anna b 27 May 1971, Louise b 15 Nov 1974); *Career* actor; served in Fleet Air Arm for 10 years; *Theatre* incl: Arturo Ui (Queen's), The Last Meeting of the Knights of the White Magnolia (Hampstead), Rumblings (Bush); *Television* incl: Oliver Twist, Fifteen Streets, Gentlemen & Players, The Spoils of War, The Fall and Rise of Reginald Perrin, Johnny Briggs, Night on the Tyne, Sherlock Holmes Tricky Business; *Films* incl: Villain, Star Wars, The Eagle has Landed, Force 10 in Navarone, The Wild Geese; *Recreations* golf, enjoying warm weather (Florida); *Clubs* Leatherhead Golf; *Style*— Leslie Schofield, Esq; ✉ c/o Evans and Reiss, 100 Fawe Park Road, Putney, London SW15 2EA (☎ 0181 877 3755, fax 0181 877 0307)

SCHOFIELD, Neill; *b* 2 Aug 1946; *Educ* Univ of Leeds (BA), QMC (MSc); *m* 1969, Carol; 2 da (Catherine, Jane); *Career* DoE 1970–78, Dept of Energy 1978–82, Dept of Employment (now Dept for Educn and Employment) 1982–96; writer and conslt on vocational educn, trg and economic devpt; *Recreations* walking, theatre, family; *Style*— Neill Schofield, Esq; ✉ 3 Dobcroft Close, Sheffield S11 9LL (☎ and fax 0114 236 3978)

SCHOFIELD, Phillip Bryan; s of Brian Homer Schofield, and Patricia, *née* Parry; *b* 1 April 1962; *Educ* Newquay GS; *m* March 1993, Stephanie, da of John Lowe; 2 da (Molly b July 1993, Ruby b 28 Jan 1996); *Career* BBC TV: anchorman Children's TV 1985–87, co-presenter (with Sarah Greene) Going Live until 1993, presenter Schofield's Europe 1990–93, presenter Television's Greatest Hits 1992–93, also The Movie Game (3 series), Schofield's Europe, Take Two (4 series); signed for ITV 1993; presenter: Six Little Angels 1993, Schofield's TV Gold 1993–96, Talking Telephone Numbers 1994–, Schofield's Quest 1994–96, One in a Million 1996; performed title role in Joseph and the Amazing Technicolor Dreamcoat 1992–96 (London Palladium 1992–93, nationwide tour 1993–96); *Awards* Top Man on TV 1987–88, Number 1 TV personality in all maj teenage magazines 1987–88, Best Dressed Man of the Year 1992, Variety Club Show Business Personality of the Year 1992; involved in: Children's Royal Variety Performance 1987–88, Royal Variety Performance 1992, Stars Orgn for Spastics, NSPCC, Br Heart Fndn; *Style*— Phillip Schofield, Esq; ✉ c/o James Grant Management, Syon Lodge, London Road, Syon Park, Middlesex TW7 5BH (☎ 0181 232 4100, fax 0181 232 4101)

SCHOFIELD, Dr Roger Snowden; s of Ronald Snowden Schofield (d 1970), of Leeds, and Muriel Grace, *née* Braime (d 1972); *b* 26 Aug 1937; *Educ* Leighton Park Sch Reading, Clare Coll Cambridge (BA, PhD); *m* 3 Sept 1961, Elizabeth Mary, da of Prof Anthony Clegg Cunliffe, of London; 1 da (Melanie b 1972); *Career* fell Clare Coll Cambridge 1969– (res fell 1962–65), sr res offr Cambridge Group 1966–73, dir SSRC Cambridge Group for the History of Population and Social Structure 1974–94, sr res assoc Cambridge Group for the History of Population and Social Structure 1994–; hon readership in historical demography Univ of Cambridge 1991–; memb: Ctee SSRC Computing Panel 1970–75, Statistics Ctee SSRC 1974–78 (vice chm 1976–78), Software Provision Ctee UK Computer Bd 1977–79; ed: Local Population Studies 1968–, Population Studies 1979–; Br Soc for Population Studies: memb Cncl 1979–87, treas 1981–85, pres 1985–87; memb: Population Investigation Ctee 1976– (treas 1987–), Historical Demography Ctee Int Union for the Scientific Study of Population 1983–91 (chm 1987–91); fell: Royal Historical Soc 1970, RSS 1987; FBA 1988; *Publications* Crisis Mortality (Local Population Studies, 1972), The Population History of England 1541–1871: a reconstruction (with E A Wrigley, 1981, 2 edn 1989), English Marriage Patterns Revisited (Journal of Family History, 1985), The State of Population Theory: forward from Malthus (contrib, 1986), Famine, Disease and Crisis Mortality in Early Modern Society (contrib with J Walter, 1989), The Decline of Mortality in Europe (with David Reher and Alain Bideau, 1991), Old and New Methods in Historical Demography (with David Reher, 1993), British Population Change, 1700–1871 (in R Floud and D McCloskey, The Economic History of Britain: 1700–1871, 1994), English Population History from Family Reconstitution (with E A Wrigley, et al, 1997); various articles on historical demography and research methods; *Style*— Dr Roger Schofield, FBA; ✉ 27 Trumpington St, Cambridge CB2 1QA; Clare College, Cambridge CB2 1TL

SCHOLAR, Dr Michael Charles; CB (1991); s of Richard Herbert Scholar (d 1993), of Truro, Cornwall, and Mary Blodwen, *née* Jones (d 1985); *b* 3 Jan 1942; *Educ* St Olave's and St Saviour's GS, St John's Coll Cambridge (MA, PhD), Univ of California at Berkeley, Harvard Univ; *m* 26 Aug 1964, Angela Mary, da of William Whinfield Sweet (d 1984), of Wylam, Northumberland; 3 s (Thomas b 1968, Richard b 1973, John b 1980), 1 da (Jane b 1976, d 1977); *Career* asst lectr in philosophy Univ of Leicester 1968, fell St John's Coll Cambridge 1969, asst princ HM Treasy 1970, private sec to Chief Sec HM Treasy 1974–76, sr int mangr Barclays Bank plc 1979–81, private sec to PM 1981–83, dep sec HM Treasy 1987–93 (under sec 1983); perm sec: Welsh Office 1993–96, DTI 1996–; ARCO 1965; *Recreations* playing the piano, opera, walking, gardening; *Style*— Dr Michael Scholar, CB; ✉ Department of Trade and Industry, 1 Victoria Street, London SW1H 0ET (☎ 0171 215 5539)

SCHOLES, Richard Thomas; TD; *b* 12 May 1945; *Educ* Stowe; *Career* articled clerk Porter Mattews & Marsden Blackburn 1965–69, Arthur Andersen & Co 1969–70, ptnr Joseph Sebag & Co 1976–78 (joined 1970), Carr Sebag & Co 1978–82, Grieveson Grant 1982–86, dir Kleinwort Benson Securities Limited 1986–; non-exec dir: British Vita PLC, UKF Limited; dep chm RCO Holdings PLC; FCA (ACA 1969); *Recreations* family, country; *Style*— R T Scholes, Esq, TD; ✉ 37 Doneraile Street, London SW6 6EW; Kleinwort Benson Securities Limited, 20 Fenchurch Street, London EC3P 3DB (☎ 0171 623 8000, fax 0171 929 2657)

SCHOLES, Rodney James; QC (1987); s of Henry Scholes (d 1971), of Widnes, and Margaret Bower, *née* Aldred; *b* 26 Sept 1945; *Educ* Wade Deacon GS Widnes, St Catherine's Coll Oxford (BA, BCL); *m* 13 Aug 1977, Katherin Elizabeth (Kate), da of Dermot Keogh (d 1988), of Heaton Mersey; 3 s (Michael b 7 June 1978, Jonathan b 7 Oct 1980, Nicholas b 15 Dec 1982); *Career* called to the Bar Lincoln's Inn 1968, memb Northern Circuit 1968–, recorder of the Crown Court 1986–; *Recreations* watching rugby football; *Style*— Rodney Scholes, Esq, QC; ✉ Byrom Chambers, 61 Fleet Street, London EC4Y 1JK (☎ 0171 353 4363, fax 0171 583 1491); 25 Byrom St, Manchester M3 4PF (☎ 0161 829 2100, fax 0161 829 2101)

SCHOLEY, Sir David Gerald; kt (1987), CBE; *b* 28 June 1935; *Educ* Wellington Coll, ChCh Oxford; *m* 1960, Alexandra Beatrix, da of the Hon George Drew and Fiorenza Drew, of Canada; 1 s, 1 da; *Career* Nat Serv 9 Queen's Royal Lancers 1954–55; with Thompson Graham & Co (Lloyd's Brokers) 1956–58, Dale & Co (Insurance Brokers) Canada 1958–59, Guinness Mahon & Co Ltd 1959–64; SBC Warburg (formerly S G Warburg Group plc): joined S G Warburg & Co Ltd 1965 (dir 1967, dep chm 1977, jt chm 1980–84), chm S G Warburg Group plc 1980–95, chm SBC Warburg (following takeover by Swiss Bank Corporation) July-Nov 1995; chm Int Advsy Cncl Swiss Bank Corporation July 1995–; dir: Mercury Securities plc 1969 (chm 1984–86), Orion Insurance Co Ltd 1963–87, Stewart Wrightson Holdings Ltd 1972–81, Union Discount Co of London Ltd 1976–81, Bank of England 1981–, British Telecommunications plc 1986–94, The Chubb Corporation 1991–, The General Electric Company plc 1992–95; memb Euro Advsy Cncl General Motors 1988–, sr advsr International Finance Corporation Washington 1996–; dir: INSEAD 1992– (chm UK Cncl 1992–, chm Int Cncl 1995–), London First 1993–96; govr/dir BBC 1995– (joined Bd of Dirs 1994); dep chm Export Guarantees Advsy Cncl 1974–75, chm Construction Exports Advsy Bd 1975–78, memb Cncl IISS 1984–93 (hon treas 1984–90); govr: NIESR 1984–, LSE 1993–96; memb: Pres's Ctee Business in the Community 1988–91, Indust and Commerce Gp Save the Children Fund 1989–95 (chm Save the Children Fund 75th Birthday Private Appeal); tstee: Glyndebourne Arts Tst 1989–, Nat Portrait Gallery 1992–; Hon DLitt London Guildhall Univ 1993; FRSA 1987; *Style*— Sir David Scholey, CBE; ✉ SBC Warburg, 1 Finsbury Avenue, London EC2M 2PP (☎ 0171 606 1066, fax 0171 382 4800)

SCHOLEY, Sir Robert; kt (1987), CBE (1982); *b* 8 Oct 1921; *Educ* King Edward VII Sch Sheffield, Univ of Sheffield; *m* 2 da; *Career* served REME 1943–47; engr Steel Peech & Tozer Rotherham 1947, formerley of United Steel Companies Ltd (head office 1972, md Strip Mills Div 1972); Br Steel Corp: memb Bd of Dirs 1973, dep chm and chief exec 1976, chm 1986–92, ret; pres Pipeline Industs Guild 1987–89, dir Eurotunnel Bd 1987–, pres Inst of Metals 1989–90, non-exec dir Nat Health Serv Policy Bd 1989–, vice pres Eurofer 1990– (pres 1985–90), vice chm Int Iron and Steel Inst 1990– (chm 1989–90), ex-chm Ironbridge Gorge Museum Devpt Tst, ex-memb ECSC Consultative Ctee; winner: Bessemer Gold medal Inst of Metals 1988, Gold medal BIM 1988; Hon PhD Engrg Univ of Sheffield 1987; FEng 1990, FIM 1990; *Style*— Sir Robert Scholey, CBE, FEng

SCHOLTENS, Sir James Henry; KCVO (1977, CVO 1963); s of late Theo F J Scholtens; *b* 12 June 1920; *Educ* St Patrick's Marist Brothers' Coll Sale Victoria Aust; *m* 1945, Mary, da of late C D Maguire; 1 s, 5 da; *Career* served RAAF 1942–45; dir Office of Govt Ceremonial and Hospitality Dept of PM and Cabinet 1973–80; dir of Visits to Australia by HM The Queen, HRH The Duke of Edinburgh and members of The Royal Family, Heads of State, Monarchs and Presidents; extra gentleman usher to HM The Queen 1981–; *Clubs* Royal Automobile of Australia (Sydney), Canberra Southern Cross ACT; *Style*— Sir James Scholtens, KCVO; ✉ 74 Boldrewood St, Turner, Canberra, ACT 2612, Australia (☎ 00 61 06 248 6459)

SCHOUVALOFF, Alexander; s of Count Paul Schouvaloff (d 1961), and Anna, *née* Raevsky, MBE (d 1991); *b* 4 May 1934; *Educ* Harrow, Jesus Coll Oxford (MA); *m* 1, 18 Feb 1959 (m dis), Gillian Baker; 1 s (Alexander b 1959); m 2, 18 Nov 1971, Daria Antonia Marie, da of late Marquis de Mérindol, and formerly wife of Hon (Geoffrey) Patrick Hopkinson Chorley; *Career* Nat Serv 2 Lt RMP SHAPE Paris 1957–59, Award of Merit Eaton Hall OCS; asst dir Edinburgh Festival 1965–67; dir: NW Arts Assoc 1967–74, Rochdale Festival 1971, Chester Festival 1973; curator Theatre Museum 1974–89; radio plays Radio Four: Summer of the Bullshine Boys 1981, No Saleable Value 1982; tstee London Archives of the Dance, chm Theatre Design Tst, memb Dance Collection Ctee NY Public Library for the Performing Arts; Polonia Restituta Poland 1971; *Books* Summer of the Bullshine Boys (1979), Stravinsky on Stage (with Victor Borovsky, 1982), Catalogue of Set and Costume Designs in Thyssen-Bornemisza Collection (1987), The Theatre Museum (1987), Theatre on Paper (1990), Léon Bakst - the Theatre Art (1991); *Clubs* Garrick; *Style*— Alexander Schouvaloff, Esq; ✉ 10 Avondale Park Gardens, London W11 4PR (☎ 0171 727 7543)

SCHRODER, (Baron) Bruno Lionel; s of Baron Helmut William Bruno Schroder (d 1969), s of Baron Bruno Schroder or von Schröder, sr ptnr the London branch of the Banking House of J Henry Schroder & Co, cr Freiherr by Kaiser Wilhelm II aboard the yacht 'Hohenzollern' on 27 July 1904; the Baron's er bro Rudolph was cr Freiherr eight months later, and Margaret Eleanor Phyllis (d 1994), eld da of Sir Lionel Darell, 6 Bt, DSO, JP, DL; *b* 17 Jan 1933; *Educ* Eton, Univ Coll Oxford (MA), Harvard Business School (MBA); *m* 30 May 1969, Patricia Leonie Mary (Piffa), da of Maj Adrian Holt (d 1984); 1 da (Leonie b 1974); *Career* 2 Lt The Life Gds 1951–53; dir: Schroders plc 1963– (joined 1960), J Henry Schroder & Co Ltd 1966–, Schroders Inc 1984–; memb Exec Ctee The Air Sqdn, steward of the Argyllshire Gathering; memb Ct of Assts Worshipful Co of Goldsmiths, Liveryman Guild of Air Pilots and Air Navigators; Queen Beatrix of the Netherlands Wedding Medal; *Recreations* flying, stalking, shooting; *Clubs* Brooks's; *Style*— Bruno Schroder; ✉ Schroders plc, 120 Cheapside, London EC2V 6DS (☎ 0171 382 6000, fax 0171 288 2006, telex 885029)

SCHRÖDER, Prof Martin; s of Hermann Schröder (d 1971), and Edith, *née* Kruusna; *b* 14 April 1954; *Educ* Slough GS, Univ of Sheffield (BSc), Imperial Coll London (PhD, DIC); *m* Leena-Kreet, da of Härm Kore; *Career* Royal Society/Swiss Nat Fndn postdoctoral fell Laboratorium für Organische Chemie Eidgenössische Technische Hochschule Zurich Switzerland 1978–80, postdoctoral research asst Univ Chemical Laboratories Cambridge 1980–82; Univ of Edinburgh: sr demonstrator in inorganic chemistry Dept of Chemistry 1982–83, lectr 1983–91, reader 1991–94, personal chair in inorganic chemistry Dept of Chemistry 1994–95; prof of inorganic chemistry Dept of Chemistry Univ of Nottingham 1995–; visiting prof Lash Miller Laboratories Univ of Toronto Canada Jan-May 1990, Mellor visiting prof Univ of Dunedin NZ spring 1995; memb SERC: Inorganic Chemistry Sub-Ctee 1990–93, Ctee to review int collaborations 1992, Ctee to review 21st century materials initiative 1993 and NATO Interview Panel for postdoctoral research fells 1993; memb EPSRC: Instrumentation Ctee 1994, Management Gp for X-ray Crystallographic Nat Serv 1996, chm and memb Inorganic Synthesis Panel; author of over 180 publications in learned jls; CChem, FRSC 1994 (Corday-Morgan Medal and Prize 1989), FRSE 1994 (support research fell 1991–92); *Style*— Prof Martin Schröder, FRSE; ✉ Department of Chemistry, University of Nottingham, University Park, Nottingham NG7 2RD (☎ 0115 951 3490, fax 0115 951 3563)

SCHULTEN, Christopher Francis (Chris); *b* 5 Jan 1953; *Educ* Univ of Manchester (BA History); *m* Oct 1978, Elizabeth; 2 s (Stephen Richard b 25 Sept 1984, Andrew Mark b 22 April 1987); *Career* audit supervisor Arthur Young & Co (London, Manchester, Brussels, Bermuda) 1974–80, comptroller Walton Insurance Ltd (Bermuda) 1980–81, chief accountant Petroleum Products Gp Phillips Petroleum London 1981–84, corp fin mangr DRI Holdings Ltd Staines 1984–86, dep gp fin dir and co sec WPP Group plc London 1986–93, chief exec Richards Butler (slrs) London 1995– (fin dir 1993–95); FCA 1977, MCT 1986; *Recreations* golf, skiing; *Style*— Chris Schulten, Esq; ✉ Richards Butler, Beaufort House, 15 St Botolph Street, London EC3A 7EE (☎ 0171 247 6555, fax 0171 247 5091)

SCHUTZ, Prof Bernard Frederick; s of Bernard Frederick Schutz, of Plainview, NY, and Virginia M, *née* Lefebure (d 1986); *b* 11 Aug 1946; *Educ* Bethpage HS NY, Clarkson Coll of Technol NY (BSc), California Inst of Technol (PhD); *m* 1, 13 Aug 1968 (m dis 1973), Joan Catherine, *née* Rankie; m 2, 16 Sept 1977 (m dis 1981), Susan, *née* Whitelegg; m 3, 22 Dec 1985, Sian Lynette, da of John Alexander Easton Pouncy, of Neath, W Glamorgan; 3 da (Rachel b 1984, Catherine b 1986, Annalie b 1989); *Career* postdoctoral res fell Univ of Cambridge 1971–72, instructor in physics Univ of Yale 1973–74 (postdoctoral res fell 1972–73), prof Univ of Wales Cardiff 1984– (lectr 1974–76, reader 1976–84), dir Max Planck Inst for Gravitational Physics (The Albert Einstein Inst) Potsdam Germany 1995–; memb: American Physical Soc, Soc of Sigma XI; FRAS, FInstP; *Books* Geometrical Methods of Mathematical Physics (1980), A First Course in General Relativity (1985), Gravitational Wave Data Analysis (1989); *Recreations* singing, skiing; *Clubs* Icosahedron; *Style*— Prof Bernard Schutz; ✉ Department of Physics and Astronomy, University of Wales College of Cardiff, PO Box 913, Cardiff CF2 3YB (☎ 01222 874203, fax 01222 874056, telex 498635, e-mail bschutz@astro.cf.ac.uk); MPI Gravitational Physics, Haus der Wirtschaft, Schlaatzweg 1, D-14473 Potsdam, Germany (☎ 00 49 331 2753719, fax 00 49 331 2753798, e-mail schutz@aei-potsdam.mpg.de)

SCHWAB, Ann Dorothy (Annie); da of William Henry Clovis, and Dorothy, *née* Taylor; *b* 28 Nov 1946; *Educ* Burnholme Sch York, Univ of York; *m* 1; 3 s (Barry Devlin b 4 July 1965, Niel Devlin b 12 July 1966, Ian Devlin b 23 July 1968); m 2, 31 Oct 1977, Germain Eric Schwab, *qv*; *Career* hotelier; The Olde Worlde Club York 1972–74, Hans and Gerda's Restuarant Findlenhof Zermatt Switzerland 1976–83, Hotel Poste Zermatt Switzerland 1983–84, Beck Farm Restaurant York 1984–88, Winteringham Fields Winteringham 1988–; memb: Restaurant Assoc 1993, Hospitality Assoc 1993, Cordon Bleu Assoc 1993, Food Writers' Guild, Acad of Food and Wine Serv, Writers' Guild of Great Britain 1994, Euro Toque '96; Which? Good Hotel Guide Humberside Hotel of the Year 1996; *Recreations* journalism; *Clubs* Sloane; *Style*— Mrs Annie Schwab; ✉ Winteringham Fields, Winteringham, South Humberside DN15 9PF (☎ 01724 733096, fax 01724 733898)

SCHWAB, Germain Eric; s of Eric Herbert Schwab (d 1967), of Switzerland, and Therese Marie Anne, *née* Unternahrer; *b* 5 Dec 1950; *Educ* Ecole Chantemerle Moutier Suisse, Ecole D'Aptitude Professionnelle Delémont Suisse, Ecole De Formation Professionnelle de Cuisiner Bienne Suisse, Diplome De Fin D'Apprentis Palais Des Congres Bienne; *m* 31 Oct 1977, Ann Dorothy Schwab, *qv*, da of William Henry Clovis; *Career* chef; Hotel Central Tavanne Switzerland 1970, La Grenette Fribourg Switzerland 1970, Gstaad Palace Gstaad Switzerland 1970, Portledge Hotel Bideford England 1971, Frederick Restaurant Camden London 1971, Chesterfield Hotel Mayfair London 1971, Dorchester Hotel London 1972, St Moritz Club Wardour St London 1973, Seiler Haus Mount Cervin Zermatt Switzerland 1974, Le Mirabeau Hotel Zermatt 1975, Le Bristol Hotel Zermatt 1977, Beck Farm Restaurant Wilberfoss England 1980, Winteringham Fields Winteringham 1988– (Michelin star 1994, Which? Good Hotel Guide Humberside Hotel of the Year 1996); County Restaurant of the Year: Good Food Guide 1990, La Ina 1990; Restaurant of the Year The Independent 1990, English Estates Humberside Rural Employment award 1990, English Estates Humberside county winner (Tourism) 1990, Booker Prize Best Chef and Best Restaurant 1995; memb: Société Master Chefs (UK) Feb 1983, Euro Toque 1990, Académie Culinaire de France; *Recreations* sketching; *Clubs* Sloane; *Style*— Germain Schwab, Esq; ✉ Winteringham Fields, Winteringham, North Lincolnshire DN15 9PF (☎ 01724 733096, fax 01724 733898)

SCHWARZ, Hans; s of Victor Schwarz (d in concentration camp 1941), of Vienna, and Emilie, *née* Gibbs (d 1935); *b* 29 Dec 1922; *Educ* Vienna Secdy Modern, Vienna Art Sch, Birmingham Art Sch; *m* 1944, Lena, da of Frank Jones; 2 s (Stephen b 1945, Julian b 1949); *Career* artist; pt/t teacher: Birmingham Art Sch 1943–53, Camden Arts Centre 1960–66; *Solo Exhibitions* AIA, Thackeray Gall, Camden Arts Centre, Woodland Gall; *Commissions* Nat Portrait Gall, Science Museum, National Maritime Museum; regular exhibitor RA Summer Show and Mall Galls; Hunting Prize for Best Watercolour of the Year 1980; memb: Artists Int Assoc 1955–62, RSBA 1986; NEAC, RWS 1982, RP 1989; *Recreations* walking, swimming; *Style*— Hans Schwarz, Esq, RP; ✉ 1 King George Street, Greenwich, London SE10 8QJ (☎ 0181 691 3446)

SCHWARZ, Jonathan Simon; s of Harry Heinz Schwarz, of SA, and Annette Louise, *née* Rudolph; *b* 20 June 1953; *Educ* Univ of Witwatersrand SA (BA, LLB), Univ of California Berkeley (LLM); *m* 19 Jan 1986, Dr Denise Sheer Schwarz; 3 s (Benjamin b 1987, Daniel b 1989, Adam b 1991); *Career* advocate supreme of SA 1977, High Ct Repub of Botswana 1978; barr and slr Province of Alberta 1981–; int tax ptnr Paisner & Co 1992–; ed Financial Times World Tax Report; memb: Law Soc, Int Bar Assoc, Int Fiscal Assoc, Canadian Bar Assoc, Canadian Tax Fndn; *Style*— Jonathan Schwarz, Esq; ✉ Paisner & Co, 154 Fleet Street, London EC4A 2DQ (☎ 0171 353 0299, fax 0171 583 8621)

SCIAMA, Prof Dennis William; s of Abraham Sciama (d 1969), and Nellie, *née* Ades (1974); *b* 18 Nov 1926; *Educ* Malvern, Trinity Coll Cambridge (BA, PhD); *m* 26 Nov 1959, Lidia, da of Guido Dina (d 1975), of Venice; 2 da (Susan b 26 Oct 1962, Sonia b 30 Oct 1964); *Career* Private REME 1947–49; jr res fell Trinity Coll Cambridge 1952–56, lectr mathematics Univ of Cambridge 1961–70, sr res fell All Souls Coll Oxford 1970–85, extraordinary fell Churchill Coll Cambridge 1986–94, prof of astrophysics Int Sch for Advanced Studies Trieste 1983–; foreign memb: American Philosophical Soc 1982, American Acad Arts and Scis 1983, Accademia Dei Lincei 1984; FRS 1983; *Books* The Unity of the Universe (1959), The Physical Foundations of General Relativity (1969), Modern Cosmology (1971), Modern Cosmology and the Dark Matter Problem (1993); *Style*— Prof Dennis Sciama, FRS; ✉ 7 Park Town, Oxford (☎ 01865 559441); Sissa, Strada Costiera 11, 34014, Trieste, Italy (☎ 00 39 40 3787 475, fax 00 39 40 3787 528)

SCICLUNA, Martin Anthony; s of William and Miriam Scicluna; *b* 20 Nov 1950; *Educ* Berkhamsted Sch Herts, Univ of Leeds (BCom); *m* 28 July 1979, (Katharine) Fenella, da of late Rev Canon Norman Haddock, of Cheltenham, Glos; 2 s (Mark William b 26 April 1984, Edward James b 2 February 1989), 1 da (Claire Alexandra b 11 Aug 1987); *Career* chartered accountant; Touche Ross (now Deloitte & Touche): joined 1973, ptnr 1982–, head London Audit Div 1990–95, chm 1995–; chm London Soc of CAs ICEAW 1988–89, memb Cncl ICEAW 1990–95, memb City Advsy Gp CBI; Freeman City of London, memb Worshipful Co of Chartered Accountants in England and Wales; FCA 1980 (ACA 1976), CIMgt 1996 (MIMgt 1976); *Recreations* tennis, gardening, wine; *Style*— Martin A Scicluna, Esq; ✉ Deloitte & Touche, Stonecutter Court, 1 Stonecutter Street, London EC4A 4TR (☎ 0171 936 3000)

SCLATER, Prof John George; s of John George Sclater, and Margaret Bennet Glen; *b* 17 June 1940; *Educ* Stonyhurst, Univ of Edinburgh (BSc), Univ of Cambridge (PhD); *m* 1, 1968, Fredrica Rose Feleyn; 2 s, (Iain, Stuart); m 2, 1985, Paula Anne Edwards; m 3, Naila Gloria Burchett; *Career* asst res geophysicist Scripps Insitution of Oceanography 1967–72 (postgrad res asst 1965–67), prof MIT 1977–83 (asst prof 1972–77), dir Joint Program in Oceanography and Ocean Engineering (with Woods Hole Oceanographic Institution) MIT 1981–83, The Institution for Geophysics Univ of Texas of Austin 1983–91 (assoc dir, sr res scientist, Shell Distinguished prof in geophysics), prof UCSD/Scripps Instn of Oceanography 1991–; assoc ed Jl of Geophysical Res 1971–74; memb: Ocean Scis Ctee US Nat Acad of Sciences 1972–76, Nat Sci Review Ctee on Oceanography 1974–77, Review Ctee IDOE Nat Sci Fndn 1974, Heat Flow Panel JOIDES 1968–74, Sci Fndn 1974, Ocean Crisis Panel IPOD 1974–76, Indian Ocean Panel JOIDES 1968–74, Indian Ocean Panel Ocean Drilling Prog 1985–88 (Lithesphere panel 1984–86), Ocean Studies Bd/Naval Panel 1985–; chm Ocean Studies Bd US Nat Acad of Scis 1988– (memb 1985–88); FRS; fell: Geological Soc of America, American Geophysical Union; memb: AAPG, Nat Acad of Scis; Rosenstiel Award 1979, Bucher Medal AGU 1985; *Publications* numerous contribs to Jl of Geophysical Res, Bulletin Earthquake Res, Earth and Planetary Sci Letters, Geophysical Jl RAS, Tectonophysics, and other learned jls; *Style*— Prof John Sclater, FRS; ✉ Geological Research Division - 0215, Scripps Instn of Oceanography, University of California, San Diego, La Jolla, CA 92093–0215, USA

SCLATER, John Richard; s of Arthur William Sclater, and Alice, *née* Collett; *b* 14 July 1940; *Educ* Charterhouse, Gonville and Caius Coll Cambridge, Yale, Harvard; *m* 1, 23 Aug 1967 (m dis), Nicola Mary Gloria, o da of late Anthony Charles Cropper, TD, JP, DL, of Tolson Hall, Kendal; 1 s (James Arthur b 17 April 1970), 1 da (Emma Mary b 18 Jan 1972, d 12 July 1993); m 2, 25 April 1985, Grizel Elizabeth Catherine, o da of Lt-Col Herbrand Vavasour Dawson, DL, of Weston Hall, Otley, Yorks; *Career* chm: Hill Samuel Bank Ltd until 1996, Union plc April-Sept 1996 (dir 1981–96), Foreign & Colonial Investment Trust plc, Foreign & Colonial Enterprise Trust PLC, Foreign & Colonial Private Equity Trust PLC, Foreign & Colonial Ventures Ltd, County Catering & Leisure Ltd, Berisford International PLC; dep chm: Yamaichi International (Europe) Ltd, Millennium & Copthorne Hotels PLC; pres The Equitable Life Assurance Society 1994– (dir 1985); dir: Berner Nicol & Co Ltd, James Cropper PLC, Grosvenor Estate Holdings, Holker Estates Co Ltd; tstee The Grosvenor Estate; memb: Cncl of The Duchy of Lancaster, CBI City Advsy Gp; Liveryman Worshipful Co of Goldsmiths; *Recreations* country pursuits; *Clubs* Brooks's, Pratt's, Univ Pitt (Cambridge); *Style*— J R Sclater, Esq; ✉ Sutton Hall, Barcombe, nr Lewes, E Sussex BN8 5EB (☎ 01273 400450, fax 01273 401086); 117 Eaton Square, London SW1W 9AA (☎ 0171 235 0446, fax 0171 235 1228); Yamaichi International (Europe) Ltd, 111 Finsbury Square, London EC2A 1EQ (☎ 0171 330 8000)

SCOBIE, Kenneth Charles; s of Charles Smith Scobie (d 1965), and Shena Bertram, *née* Melrose (d 1990); *b* 29 July 1938; *Educ* Daniel Stewart's Coll, Univ of Edinburgh (CA); *m* 29 Sept 1973, (Adela) Jane, da of Keith Somers Hollebone (d 1991), of Bampton Castle, Oxfordshire; 1 s (Charles b 11 Oct 1976), 1 da (Deborah b 19 May 1975); *Career* CA; profit planning BMC (Scotland) Ltd 1961–63, dep fin dir Motor Car Div Rolls Royce 1963–66, sr mgmnt conslt and ptnr Robson Morrow & Co 1966–70, memb Main Bd and Exec Ctee Black and Decker Euro Gp 1971–72, md Vavasseur SA Ltd 1972–76, chief exec and dir Vernon Orgn 1977, md H C Sleigh UK Ltd 1979–82, gp md Blackwood Hodge plc 1984–90, non-exec dir Albrighton plc 1990–93, dir Postern Executive Group Ltd 1991–, actg chm, dep chm and chief exec Brent Walker Group plc 1991–93; chm: Lovells Confectionery Ltd 1991–, William Hill Group 1992–93, Cardinal Data Ltd 1993–94, Allied Leisure plc 1994–; dep chm/chief exec Addis Ltd 1993–94; non-exec dir: Gartmore Indosuez UK Recovery (Gp) Ltd, Gartmore 1990 Ltd; CA 1961, CIMgt 1987; *Recreations* rugby, golf, tennis, cricket; *Clubs* Stewart's Melville London Scottish RFC, Huntercombe Golf; *Style*— Kenneth Scobie, Esq

SCOBLE, Christopher Lawrence (Chris); s of Victor Arthur Oliphant Scoble (d 1993), of Looe, Cornwall, and Mabel, *née* Crouch; *b* 21 Nov 1943; *Educ* Kent Coll Canterbury, Corpus Christi Coll Oxford (BA); *m* 18 Nov 1972, Rosemary, da of Thomas Henry Hunter (d 1985), of Hamble, Hampshire; 1 s (Sampson b 6 Aug 1973); *Career* asst princ Home Office 1965–69, private sec to Min of State Welsh Office 1969–70; Home Office: princ 1970–78, sec to Advsy Cncl on Penal System 1976–78, asst sec 1978–88, vice chm Media Policy Ctee Cncl of Europe 1985–87; CS (Nuffield and Leverhulme) Travelling fellowship 1987–88; asst under-sec of state Home Office: Broadcasting and Miscellaneous Dept 1988–91, Establishment Dept 1991–94, Police Dept 1994–95; *Style*— Chris Scoble, Esq; ✉ The School House, Church Lane, Sturminster Newton, Dorset DT10 1DH (☎ 01258 473491)

SCOBLE, Peter Ernest Walter; er s of Walter George Scoble (d 1984), and Muriel Phyllis Mary, *née* Buckley; *b* 8 March 1938; *Educ* Malvern; *m* 1, 29 June 1963, (Marjorie) Lesley (d 1988), yr da of James Durban Wilkinson; 1 s (Mark Walter James b 7 Sept 1972), 2 da (Karen Lesley b 20 Oct 1967, Anna Jill b 2 July 1969); m 2, 3 Nov 1990, Carolyn Antonia Pilmore-Bedford, *née* Newnham; *Career* slr; articled clerk Joynson-Hicks & Co, admitted slr 1962; Boodle Hatfield: joined 1962, ptnr 1964–, sr ptnr 1994–; past pres City of Westminster Law Soc, memb Cncl Law Soc 1986–92; chm Papplewick Educnl Tst Ltd; *Recreations* golf, music, philately; *Clubs* MCC, Lowtonian Soc (treas 1995–); *Style*— Peter Scoble, Esq; ✉ Boodle Hatfield, 61 Brook Street, London W1Y 2BL (☎ 0171 629 7411, fax 0171 629 2621)

SCOFIELD, (David) Paul; CBE (1956); s of Edward Henry Scofield (d 1976), of Hurstpierpoint, Sussex, and Mary, *née* Wild; *b* 21 Jan 1922; *Educ* Hurstpierpoint, Varndean Sch for Boys Brighton; *m* 15 May 1943, Joy Mary, da of Edward Henry Parker (d 1947); 1 s (Martin Paul b 6 March 1945), 1 da (Sarah b 22 Aug 1951); *Career* actor; Birmingham Repertory Theatre 1942–45; Stratford-upon-Avon 1946, 1947 and 1948; Hon LLD Univ of Glasgow 1968; Hon DLitt: Univ of Kent 1973, Univ of Sussex 1985; *Theatre incl* Adventure Story and The Seagull (St James's) 1949, Ring Round the Moon (Globe) 1950–52, Much Ado About Nothing (Phoenix) 1952, The River Line (Edinburgh Festival, Lyric Hammersmith, Strand) 1952, Richard II, The Way of the World and Venice

Preserved (Lyric Hammersmith) 1952–53, A Question of Fact (Piccadilly) 1953–54, Time Remembered (New Theatre) 1954–55, Hamlet (Moscow) 1955, Paul Scofield-Peter Brook Season 1956, The Power and the Glory, Hamlet and Family Reunion (Phoenix), A Dead Secret (Piccadilly) 1957, Expresso Bongo (Savile) 1958, The Complaisant Lover (Globe) 1959, A Man for All Seasons (Globe 1960, Anta Theatre NY 1961–62), Coriolanus and Love's Labours Lost (Shakespeare Festival Theatre Stratford, Ontario), King Lear (Stratford and Aldwych 1962–63, Moscow, W Berlin, Prague, Warsaw, Budapest, Bucharest, Belgrade and New York 1964), Timon of Athens (Stratford) 1965, The Government Inspector and Staircase (Aldwych) 1966, Macbeth (Stratford, Russia, Finland) 1967, A Hotel in Amsterdam (Royal Court and New) 1968, Uncle Vanya (Royal Court) 1970, Savages (Royal Court and Comedy) 1973, The Tempest (Wyndham's) 1975, I'm Not Rappaport (Apollo) 1986–87; NT (1971–83): Captain of Köpenick, The Rules of the Game, Volpone, Amadeus, Othello, Don Quixote; Heartbreak House (Theatre Royal Haymarket) 1992, John Gabriel Borkman (RNT) 1996; *Television* numerous TV plays, Martin Chuzzlewit (BBC serial, 1994); *Films* That Lady, Carve Her Name with Pride, The Train, A Man for All Seasons, Bartleby, King Lear, Scorpio, A Delicate Balance, Anna Karenina, Nineteen Nineteen, The Attic, When the Whales Came, Henry V, Hamlet, Utz, Quiz Show (Hollywood, 1993); *Awards* Evening Standard 1956 and 1963, New York Tony 1962, Oscar and Br Film Academy 1966, Danish Film Academy 1971, Hamburg Shakespeare Prize 1972, Variety Club 1956, 1963 and 1987, Evening Standard Award For Best Actor (for John Gabriel Borkman) 1996; *Recreations* walking, reading; *Clubs* Athenaeum; *Style*— Paul Scofield, Esq, CBE

SCOON, HE Sir Paul; GCMG (1979), GCVO (1985), OBE (1970); *b* 1935; *Career* taught in Grenada 1953–67, former Cabinet sec, govr-gen Grenada 1978–92; *Style*— Sir Paul Scoon, GCMG, GCVO, OBE; ✉ PO Box 180, St George's, Grenada (☎ 809 440 2180)

SCOPES, Sir Leonard Arthur; KCVO (1961), CMG (1957), OBE (1946); s of late Arthur Edward Scopes (d 1968), of Monifieth, Angus, by his w Jessie Russell Hendry; *b* 19 March 1912; *Educ* St Dunstan's Coll, Gonville and Caius Coll Cambridge; *m* 21 Dec 1938, Brunhilde Slater, da of late Victor Emmanuel Rolfe, of Worthing; 2 s, 2 da; *Career* memb Br Consular Foreign and Dip Servs 1933–67; vice consul: Antwerp 1933, Saigon 1935, Canton 1937; acting consul Surabaya 1941, vice consul Lourenço Marques 1942, consul Skoplje and Ljubljana 1945, commercial sec Bogota 1947, asst in UN (Econ and Social) Dept of Foreign Office 1950, cnsllr Djakarta 1952, FO inspr 1954; ambass: Nepal 1957–62, Paraguay 1962–67; memb Jt Inspection Unit of UN and Specialised Agencies 1968–71; *Style*— Sir Leonard Scopes, KCVO, CMG, OBE; ✉ Saddlers, Whaddon Hall Mews, Whaddon, Bucks

SCOPES, Richard Henry; s of Eric Henry Scopes, of Funtington, W Sussex, and Ida Lucy Mary (Sally), *née* Hare (d 1991); *b* 6 June 1944; *Educ* Univ Coll Sch, Magdalene Coll Cambridge (LLB); *m* 29 March 1969, Jacqueline Elizabeth Mary, da of Maj Ronald Walter Monk (d 1973), of Blackheath; 1 da (Katie b 1972); *Career* admitted slr 1969; Ashurst Morris Crisp & Co 1963–69, dir Scopes & Sons 1970–75, ptnr Wilde Sapte 1980– (joined 1976); memb City of London Slrs Co 1981; memb: Law Soc, Soc of Practitioners of Insolvency; MIPA; *Recreations* gardening, painting; *Clubs* United Oxford and Cambridge Univ, Royal Over-Seas League; *Style*— Richard Scopes, Esq; ✉ Westfield House, River Hill, Flamstead, Herts AL3 8DA; Wilde Sapte, 1 Fleet Place, London EC4M 7WS (☎ 0171 246 7000, fax 0171 246 7777)

SCORER, Timothy Rowland (Tim); s of Derek Rowland Scorer, TD, of Naples, Florida, USA, and Margaret Shirley, *née* Staveacre; *b* 25 June 1941; *Educ* Repton; *m* 1, 10 Oct 1965 (m dis 1981), Wendy Ann, da of Edward Thomas Glazier (d 1978), of San Antonio, Ibiza; 2 s (Craig b 29 Jan 1967, Jamie b 3 July 1969); m 2, 25 Sept 1982 (m dis 1989), Julia Jane, da of Jeremy John Booth; 1 da (Lucinda b 29 Oct 1987); m 3, 7 May 1993, Julie Emma, da of Alan Baker; 2 s (Alexander b 3 Sept 1992, Cameron b 2 July 1996); *Career* admitted slr 1965; ptnr Josselyn & Sons Ipswich 1967, asst sec Law Soc 1976; ptnr: Barlow Lyde & Gilbert London 1980, Jarvis & Bannister 1992–; chm and fndr Lawyers' Flying Assoc, chm Gen Aviation Safety Cncl, int vice pres Lawyer Pilots' Bar Assoc USA; hon slr: Helicopter Club of GB, Euro Gen Aviation Safety Fndn, Guild of Air Pilots and Air Navigators, Jt Servs' Parachuting Assoc; Freeman City of London 1987, Liveryman Guild of Air Pilots and Air Navigators 1988 (Freeman 1985); memb Law Soc 1966, MRAeS; *Recreations* flying, photography, wine growing, travel; *Style*— Tim Scorer, Esq; ✉ Toad Hall, White Colne, Colchester, Essex CO6 2PW (☎ 01787 224294); Jarvis & Bannister, 3 Gracechurch Street, London EC3V 0AT (☎ 0171 626 1222, fax 0171 626 1218, car 0860 557766)

SCOTLAND, Tony; s of Peter Whitmore Scotland, of Glastonbury, and Elizabeth Anne, *née* Dunn (d 1954); *b* 29 May 1945; *Career* apprentice reporter East Essex Gazette 1961–65, reporter Sydney Morning Herald 1965–66, TV reporter ABC News Hobart Tasmania 1966–68, TV presenter BBC Look East Norwich 1968–69, sub-ed BBC Radio News London 1969–72, prodr The Arts Worldwide BBC Radio 3 1972–80, announcer Radio 3 1972–92; presentation advsr, opera presenter and misc bdcaster Classic FM 1992–; *Books* The Empty Throne - The Quest for an Imperial Heir in the People's Republic of China (1993), Tchaikovsky Ballets in Words and Music (writer and narrator, 1995); *Recreations* travel, printing, curiosities; *Style*— Tony Scotland; ✉ The Pottery, Ham Lane, Ramsdell, Hants RG26 5SD (☎ and fax 0118 981 4844)

SCOTT, *see also:* Maxwell-Scott, Montagu Douglas Scott

SCOTT, Rev Adam; TD (1978); s of Brig Fraser Scott, of Wonersh, and Bridget Penelope, *née* Williams; *b* 6 May 1947; *Educ* Marlborough, ChCh Oxford (BA, MA), City Univ Business Sch (MSc); *m* 30 Sept 1978, Oona MacDonald, PhD, MCSP, da of Prof R J D Graham (d 1950), of St Andrews; *Career* OUOTC 1965–68, CVHQ RA, 94 Locating Regt 1968–81, cmd Reserve Meteorologists, Capt 1975, ret 1981; reader St Aldate's Oxford 1970–75; ordained (Southwark): deacon 1975, priest 1976; asst curate St Michael and All Angels Blackheath Park London 1975–; dean: Ministers in Secular Employment, Woolwich Episcopal Area; trained as intellectual property lawyer 1970–74; called to the Bar Inner Temple 1972; with: ITT 1974–77, PO 1977–81; BT: corporate planner 1981–86, dir Office of Iain Vallance (chm of BT) 1986–88, dir of int affairs 1988–92, dir of customer equipment 1992–94, divnl dir of networks and systems 1995–; fell St Andrews Mgmnt Inst 1994–96, professorial fell Univ of St Andrews 1996–; Freeman City of London 1993; CEng, FIEE 1994 (MIEE 1981); *Recreations* gardening, walking; *Clubs* Cannons; *Style*— The Rev Adam Scott, TD; ✉ 19 Blackheath Park, Blackheath, London SE3 9RW (☎ 0181 852 3286, fax 0181 852 6247)

SCOTT, Dr (Christine) Angela; da of William Hurst Roy Grundy (d 1994), of Salisbury, Wilts, and Margaret, *née* Drury; *b* 19 June 1946; *Educ* Harrogate Coll, King's Coll Med Sch London (MB, BS); *m* 7 June 1969, (John) Nigel (David) Scott, s of Lt-Col George William Inglis Scott, RA, DSO (d 1976); 3 s (Andrew b 1974, Robin b 1976, Alan b 1980); *Career* conslt histopathologist and cytologist to Salisbury Health Care NHS Tst 1981–, med dir of pathology 1989–92; FRCPath 1988; *Recreations* squash, gardening; *Style*— Dr Angela Scott; ✉ Pathology Dept, Salisbury District Hospital, Odstock, Salisbury, Wilts SP2 8BJ (☎ 01722 336262 ext 4110)

SCOTT, Sir Anthony Percy; 3 Bt (UK 1913), of Witley, Surrey; s of Col Sir Douglas Scott, 2 Bt (d 1984), and Elizabeth Joyce, née Glanley (d 1983); *b* 1 May 1937; *Educ* Harrow, ChCh Oxford; *m* 1962, Caroline Teresa Anne, er da of (William Charles) Edward Bacon, of Mobberley, Cheshire; 2 s, (Henry Douglas Edward b 1964, Simon James b 1965), 1 da (Miranda Claire b 1968); *Heir* s, Henry Douglas Edward, *qv*; *Career* called to the Bar Inner Temple 1960; ptnr in stockbroking firm Laurie Milbank & Co 1974–; chm and md L M (Moneybrokers) Ltd 1986–1995; Liveryman Worshipful Co of Haberdashers; *Style*— Sir Anthony Scott, Bt; ✉ Longbarrow, Goodworth Clatford, Andover, Hampshire SP11 7SE

SCOTT, Prof Bill; s of George Barclay Scott (d 1975), of Moniave, Dumfriesshire, and Jeanie Stuart, *née* Waugh (d 1962); *b* 16 Aug 1935; *Educ* Morton Acad, Dumfries Acad, Edinburgh Coll of Art (Dip, postgrad Dip), Ecole des Beaux Arts Paris (travel scholar, Clason Harvie Bequest prize); *m* 25 March 1961, Phyllis Owen, da of William Lauderdale Fisher; 1 s (Ian Alexander b 1 Jan 1962), 2 da (Phyllis Elizabeth b 7 July 1962, Jeanie May b 27 July 1971); *Career* sculptor; temp teacher Fife 1960–61, pt/t teacher Edinburgh Coll of Art 1961–63; Sculpture Sch Edinburgh Coll of Art: lectr 1963–76, sr lectr 1976–90, head Sch of Sculpture 1991, prof 1994; *Solo Exhibitions* Compass Gallery Glasgow 1972, Stirling Gallery 1974, New 57 Gallery Edinburgh 1979, Artspace Art Gallery Aberdeen 1980, Kirkcaldy Museum and Gallery 1985, Talbot Rice Art Centre 1994; *Group Exhibitions* 11 Scottish Sculptors (Fruit Market Gallery, Edinburgh) 1975, Small Sculptures (Scottish Arts Cncl, Edinburgh) 1978, British Art Show (Mappin Gallery Edinburgh, Hatton Gallery and Arnolfini) 1979–80, V Int Exhibition of Small Sculpture Budapest 1981, Built in Scotland (Third Eye Centre Glasgow, City Arts Centre Edinburgh, Camden Arts Centre London) 1982–83, One Cubic Foot Exhibition (Aberdeen & Glasgow) 1986, Scandex Exhibition Norway 1994; *Commissions* New Byre Theatre St Andrews 1969, Cumbernauld Shopping Centre 1980, Kentigern House Glasgow 1985; memb: Cncl Soc of Scottish Artists 1970–73, Bd Fruit Market Gallery 1983–91; chm Awards Panel Arts Ctee Scottish Arts Cncl 1990–93 (memb Art Ctee 1989–93); memb Royal Scottish Acad 1984; *Style*— Prof Bill Scott, Esq

SCOTT, (John) Brough; s of Mason Hogarth Scott (d 1971), of Broadway, Worcs, and Irene Florence, *née* Seely (d 1976); *b* 12 Dec 1942; *Educ* Radley, CCC Oxford; *m* 3 Nov 1973, Susan Eleanor, da of Ronald Grant Macinnes, of Abinger Common, Surrey; 2 s (Charles Ronald Brough b 21 Jan 1976, James Seely b 14 Feb 1979), 2 da (Sophie Diana b 20 July 1974, Tessa Irene b 3 Nov 1984); *Career* amateur and professional jump jockey (100 winners incl Imperial Cup and Mandarin Chase) 1962–70; TV journalist: ITV 1971–84 (chief racing presenter 1979–), Channel 4 1985–; sports journalist: Evening Standard 1972–74, Sunday Times 1974–90, Independent on Sunday 1990–92, Sunday Times 1993–95, Sunday Telegraph 1995–; dir Racing Post 1985– (editorial dir 1988–); Lord Derby Award (racing journalist of the year) 1980, Clive Graham Trophy (services to racing) 1982, Sports Journalist of the Year 1983, Sports Feature Writer of the Year 1985, 1990 and 1993; vice pres Jockeys' Assoc 1969–71; trustee: Injured Jockeys' Fund, Racing Welfare, Professional Riders' Insurance Scheme; *Books* World of Flat Racing (1983), On And Off The Rails (1984), Front Runners (1991), Willie Carson - Up Front (1993), Racing Certainties (1995); *Recreations* riding, making bonfires; *Style*— Brough Scott, Esq; ✉ Racing Post, 120 Coombe Lane, Raynes Park, London SW20 0BA (☎ 0181 879 3377, fax 0181 944 5459, car 0860 334357)

SCOTT, Charles Clive; s of Lt-Col Sir James Walter Scott, 2 Bt (d 1993), of Rotherfield Park, Alton, Hants, and Anne Constantia, *née* Austin; *b* 31 July 1954; *Educ* Eton, Trinity Coll Cambridge (MA), INSEAD (MBA); *m* 6 Oct 1979, Caroline Frances, da of Hugh Grahame Jago; 3 da (Eleanor, Rose, Alice); *Career* dir de Zoete & Bevan Ltd 1988–1995, dir UK Barclays Private Bank Limited 1996–; Freeman City of London 1977, Liveryman Worshipful Co of Mercers 1980; memb Law Soc, MSI; *Clubs* Leander, City University; *Style*— Charles Scott, Esq; ✉ 2 Bunhouse Place, London SW1W 8HU

SCOTT, Charles Thomas; *b* 22 Feb 1949; *Career* accountant Binder Hamlyn 1967–72, Itel Corporation 1972–77, IMS International Inc 1978–90; Cordiant plc (formerly Saatchi & Saatchi Co plc): chief financial and operating offr 1990–93, chief exec 1993–95, chm 1995– (actg chm 1995); FCA 1979 (ACA 1972); *Style*— Charles Scott, Esq; ✉ Cordiant plc, 83/89 Whitfield Street, London W1A 4XA (☎ 0171 436 4000, fax 0171 436 1998, telex 8950391)

SCOTT, Christopher James Anderson; s and h of Sir Oliver Scott, 3 Bt, *qv*; *b* 16 Jan 1955; *Educ* Bryanston, Trinity Coll Cambridge, INSEAD; *m* 23 July 1988, Emma Jane, o da of Michael John Boxhall, of Islington, London; 2 s (Edward James Saim b 25 Oct 1990, Charles James Michael b 26 May 1994), 1 da (Oenone Jennifer Katharine b 19 Feb 1992); *Clubs* Brooks's; *Style*— Christopher Scott, Esq

SCOTT, Rev Dr Claude John; s of Douglas John Ranger Scott (d 1967), and Clarice Amy, *née* Weston (d 1992); *b* 8 Nov 1937; *Educ* Emmanuel GS Swansea, Queen Mary Coll London (BSc, PhD), London Inst of Educn (PGCE); *m* 2 April 1966, Ethne Frances, da of Rev Thomas Henry Stevenson; 2 da (Sarah Claudia b 25 June 1968, Rebecca Gabrielle b 15 Feb 1973), 1 s (Philip Douglas b 5 May 1970); *Career* John Mason HS Abingdon: head Chemistry Dept 1964–68, head Science Dept 1968–71; headteacher Oakmeeds Sch Burgess Hill Sussex 1974–76 (dep headteacher 1971–74), headteacher Thorpe St Andrew Sch Norwich 1977–93, headteacher in industry Colman's of Norwich 1990–92, advsr Norfolk Inspection Advice and Trg Servs 1993–95, currently freelance educnl conslt; in charge science Cothill Sch Abingdon IAPS 1968–71; hon curate Holy Trinity Church Norwich 1991, ordained C of E non-stipendiary miny 1991; memb Nat Cncl SHA 1983–87, memb Bd of Mgmnt Norwich YMCA 1984–88; lay memb Local Advsy Ctee Norwich Magistrates Ct 1990; chm Schools Outreach (Norwich); played Rugby Football seven times for Essex; *Recreations* philately, sailing, travel, music (Norwich Philharmonic Chorus); *Style*— Rev Dr Claude Scott; ✉ 17 Lime Tree Road, Norwich, Norfolk NR2 2NQ (☎ and fax 01603 455686)

SCOTT, Prof Clive; s of Jesse Scott, of Outwell, Cambs, and Nesta Vera, *née* Morton; *b* 13 Nov 1943; *Educ* Bishop's Stortford Coll, St John's Coll Oxford (state scholar, Casberd exhibitioner, MA, MPhil, DPhil); *m* 1, 13 Aug 1965 (m dis 1983), Elizabeth Anne, da of Rowland Drabble; 1 da (Katherine Sophie b 27 Nov 1969), 1 s (Benjamin Nicholas b 24 Aug 1972); m 2, 21 July 1984, Marie-Noëlle, da of Jean Guillot; 2 s (Samuel William b 28 July 1985, Thomas Alexander b 3 Feb 1991); *Career* Univ of East Anglia: asst lectr 1967–70, lectr 1970–88, reader 1988–91, prof of European literature 1991–; dir of studies Br Cncl summer sch for Soviet teachers of English 1983–88; FBA 1994; *Books* French Verse-Art: A Study (1980), Anthologie Éluard (1983), A Question of Syllables: Essays in Nineteenth-Century French Verse (1986), The Riches of Rhyme: Studies in French Verse (1988), Vers Libre: The Emergence of Free Verse in France 1886–1914 (1990), Reading the Rhythm: The Poetics of French Free Verse 1910–1930 (1993); *Style*— Prof Clive Scott, FBA; ✉ School of Modern Languages and European Studies, University of East Anglia, University Plain, Norwich NR4 7TJ (☎ 01603 592135, fax 01603 250599)

SCOTT, Sir David Aubrey; GCMG (1979, KCMG 1974, CMG 1966); s of Hugh Sumner Scott (d 1959), and Barbara Easton Scott, JP (d 1991); *b* 3 Aug 1919; *Educ* Charterhouse, Univ of Birmingham; *m* 1941, Vera Kathleen, da of Maj G H Ibbitson, MBE, RA (d 1958); 1 da (Diana (Lady Unwin)), 2 s (Sir Robert Scott, Andrew); *Career* served WWII RA (Maj); Foreign Serv: high cmmr Uganda and ambass Rwanda 1967–70, asst under sec of state FCO 1970–72, high cmmr NZ and govr Pitcairn Is 1973–75, ambass SA 1976–79; chm: Ellerman Lines 1982–83 (vice chm 1981), Royal Over-Seas League 1981–86, Nuclear Resources Ltd 1984–88; dir: Barclays Bank International 1979–85, Mitchell Cotts Group 1980–86, Bradbury-Wilkinson plc 1984–86; vice pres UK-South Africa Trade Assoc 1981–85, tstee John Ellerman Fndn 1979–, govr Sadler's Wells Tst 1984–89, pres Uganda Soc for Disabled Children 1985–, memb Manchester Olympic Bid Ctee 1988–93; *Books* Ambassador in Black and White (1981); *Recreations* music, birdwatching; *Clubs* Royal Over-Seas League; *Style*— Sir David Scott, GCMG; ✉ Wayside, Moushill Lane, Milford, Surrey GU8 5BQ (☎ 01483 421935)

SCOTT, David Gidley; s of Bernard Wardlaw Habershon Scott, FRIBA (d 1978), of Hitchin, Herts, and Florence May, *née* Wheeler (d 1993); *b* 3 Jan 1924; *Educ* Sutton Valence, St John's Coll Cambridge (MA, LLM); *m* 10 April 1948, (Elinor) Anne, da of Maj Alan Garthwaite, DSO, MC (d 1964), of Penny Bridge, Ulverston; 2 s (Antony b 1956, Robin b 1959), 2 da (Judith b 1952, Dinah b 1961); *Career* WWII RE 1942–47, cmmnd 1944, Troop Cdr Assault Sqdn (wounded Rhine Crossing 1945), Temp Capt (later Actg Maj) cmdg 4 BESD Haifa 1947; called to the Bar Middle Temple 1951, practised Chancery Bar 1952–84, registrar in bankruptcy High Ct 1984–96; vice chm Parish Cncl, former churchwarden and memb PCC; *Recreations* sailing, choral singing; *Clubs* Bar Yacht, Parkstone Yacht; *Style*— David Scott, Esq; ✉ Elm Garth, 45 Benslow Lane, Hitchin, Herts SG4 9RE (☎ 01462 434391)

SCOTT, David Griffiths; s of Wilfred Emberton Scott (d 1967), and Gwenith, *née* Griffiths; *b* 15 Feb 1942; *Educ* Adams GS Newport Shropshire, Christ's Coll Cambridge (MA), London Business School (MSc); *m* 1969 (m dis 1992), Alison Jane Fraser; 1 s (James b 1974), 2 da (Helen b 1971, Katherine b 1976); *Career* md: ISC Alloy Ltd 1975–84, Impalloy Ltd 1978–84, Kleen-e-ze Holdings plc 1984–88, Yale Security Products Ltd 1989–91; dir Ops Bd Newman Tonks plc 1991–94; chief exec Aerospace Division, Intelek plc 1994–; CEng, FIMechE; *Recreations* golf, sailing, cricket; *Style*— David Scott, Esq; ✉ The Barn, Main St, Wick, nr Pershore, Worcs WR10 3NZ (☎ 01386 554185)

SCOTT, Dr David Henry Thomson; *b* 19 Feb 1949; *Educ* George Watson's Coll Edinburgh, Univ of Edinburgh (BSc, MB ChB); *m* 22 July 1972, Dr Mary Scott; 1 s (Angus b 1976), 2 da (Glenda b 1978, Diana b 1980); *Career* intern: Western Memorial Hosp Corner Brook Newfoundland Canada 1972, Charles A Janeway Hosp St John's Newfoundland Canada 1972, house offr Western Gen Hosp Edinburgh 1972–74; registrar Edinburgh Anaesthetic Trg Scheme 1974–76, Astra clinical res fell 1977, lectr Univ of Edinburgh 1978, conslt anaesthetist Royal Infirmary Edinburgh 1979–; Lasarettet i Ljungby Sweden 1978–83; memb: EESSA 1973, AAGBI 1974, SSA 1976, SREEC 1979; FFARCS 1976; *Recreations* electro-mechanical wizardry, skiing, hill walking, malt whisky, fishing; *Clubs* Watsonian; *Style*— Dr David Scott; ✉ Department of Cardiothoracic Surgery, Royal Infirmary of Edinburgh, Lauriston Place, Edinburgh EH3 9YW (☎ 0131 536 3705, fax 0131 229 0659, car 0860 810997)

SCOTT, David Morris Fitzgerald; s of Rev Canon William Morris Fitzgerald Scott (d 1959), of St Aidan's Coll, Birkenhead, Cheshire, and Nora Compigne, *née* Shaw (d 1995); *b* 7 June 1946; *Educ* St Lawrence Coll Ramsgate, The Hotchkiss Sch Lakeville Connecticut USA, CCC Oxford (MA); *m* 10 June 1972, Jacqueline Mary, da of Kenneth Percy Pool; 1 s (Michael b 1981), 2 da (Elizabeth b 1976, Sarah b 1978); *Career* ptnr Kitcat & Aitken 1974–80 (investmt analyst 1967–74), vice pres Bank of NY 1980–83; dir: Warburg Investment Management International 1983–85, Mercury Warburg Investment Management 1985–87, Mercury Rowan Mullens 1987–89, Mercury Asset Management Private Investors Group 1990–; govr: Royal Nat Coll for the Blind, St Lawrence Coll Ramsgate; Freeman City of London, Ct Asst Worshipful Co of Scriveners; lay fell Sion Coll; FInstPet 1974, AIIMR, MSI (Dip); *Recreations* reading; *Clubs* Brooks's, Turf, City of London; *Style*— David Scott, Esq; ✉ Windmill House, Windmill Lane, Wadhurst, East Sussex TN5 6HX (☎ and fax 01892 782683); Mercury Asset Management, 33 King William Street, London EC4 (☎ 0171 280 2800, fax 0171 280 2820, telex 888478)

SCOTT, David Richard Alexander; s of Lt Cdr Robert Irwin Maddin Scott, OBE (d 1968), of Lyddington, Rutland, and (Margaret Sylvia) Daphne, *née* Alexander; *b* 25 Aug 1954; *Educ* Wellington; *m* 1 Aug 1981, Moy, da of Air Chief Marshal Sir John Barraclough, KCB, CBE, DFC, AFC, *qv*; 1 s (Alexander b 8 Aug 1982), 1 da (Arabella b 11 Jan 1985); *Career* CA Peat Marwick Mitchell & Co Blackfriars 1972–81, Channel Four Television Corporation (Channel Four Television Co Ltd until 1993): controller of fin and co sec 1981–88, dir of fin 1988–; FCA 1976; *Recreations* opera, theatre, ballet, bridge, sailing, country pursuits; *Clubs* Guards' Polo; *Style*— David Scott, Esq; ✉ Channel Four TV Corporation, 124 Horseferry Road, London SW1P 2TX (☎ 0171 396 4444, fax 0171 306 8356)

SCOTT, Dr Donald Fletcher; s of Alexander Scott (d 1976), of Cromer, Norfolk, and Jean Scott (d 1976); *b* 29 Nov 1930; *Educ* Thetford GS, Univ of Edinburgh (MB ChB), Univ of London (DPM); *m* 1, 2 Sept 1967, Adrienne Mary (d 1992), da of Dr A A Moffett (d 1984), of Pietermaritzberg, Natal, SA; 1 s (James b 1974), 1 da (Caroline b 1971); m 2, 6 Jan 1994, Mary Caffyn Wright, da of G W Paterson (d 1946), of Gatehouse-of-Fleet, Kirkcudbrightshire; *Career* Nat Serv RAMC 1949–51; conslt clinical neurophysiologist London Hosp 1967–1992, ret; sec EEG Soc Meetings, memb Br Epilepsy Assoc; FRCP 1977; *Books* Neurological and Neurosurgical Nursing (1966), About Epilepsy (1969), Psychology of Work (1970), Fire and Fire Raisers (1974), Understanding EEG (1975), An EEG Data and Retrieval System (1981), Coping with Suicide (1989), Beating Job Burnout (1989), The History of Antiepileptic Treatment (1992); *Recreations* gardening, writing, swimming; *Style*— Dr Donald Scott; ✉ 25 Park Gate, Blackheath, London SE3 9XF (☎ 0181 852 5267)

SCOTT, Douglas Andrew Montagu Douglas; OBE (1994); s of Brig (Claud) Andrew Montagu Douglas Scott (d 1971), and Lady Victoria Doris Rachel Haig (d 1993); *b* 21 June 1930; *Educ* Eton, RMA Sandhurst; *m* 1, 1954 (m dis 1976), Bridget Elizabeth, da of late Air Vice Marshal Sir Robert George, KCMG, KCVO, KBE, CB, MC; 1 s (Adam b 1961, d 1969), 2 da (Emily b 1970, Lucy Rosemary b 1972); m 2, 1977, Daphne Maureen, da of Dr Cyril Shortt, of Glos; *Career* cmmnd Irish Gds 1950, ADC to Govr of South Aust 1953–55, Tubemakers of Australia 1955–63; TI Group 1963–83: dir Accles & Pollock Ltd 1966–76, md TI Chesterfield Ltd 1976–81, dir overseas ops TI Gp 1981–83; recruitment conslt PE International plc 1984–87, chief exec and dir Cancer Relief Macmillan Fund 1987–95 (vice pres 1995–); non-exec dir S Warwicks Gen Hosps NHS Tst 1995–; tstee Global Cancer Concern 1995–, memb Cncl NAHAT 1996–; *Recreations* painting, shooting, gardening, opera; *Clubs* White's, MCC; *Style*— Douglas Scott, Esq, OBE; ✉ Halford House, Shipston-on-Stour, Warks CV36 5BS (☎ 01789 740068, fax 01789 740836)

SCOTT, Douglas Keith (Doug); CBE (1994); s of George Douglas Scott, of Nottingham, and Edith Joyce Scott; *b* 29 May 1941; *Educ* Cottesmore Secdy Modern Sch, Mundella GS Nottingham, Loughborough Teachers' Trg Coll (Cert); *m* 1, 1962 (m dis 1988), Janice Elaine, da of Thomas Arthur Brook, of Notts; 1 s (Michael b 1963), 2 da (Martha b 1973, Rosie b 1978); m 2, 17 Sept 1993, Sharavati (Sharu), da of Ramchandra Sandu Prabhu and Kalyani Ramchandra Prabhu; 1 s (Arran b 1994); *Career* mountaineer; began climbing aged 12, visited Alps aged 17 and every year thereafter; pres Alpine Climbing Gp 1976–82, vice pres Alpine Club, vice pres Br Mountaineering Cncl 1994–; Hon MA: Univ of Nottingham 1991, Loughborough Univ 1994; *Expeditions* first ascents incl: Tarso Teiroko Tibesti Mountains Sahara 1965, Cilo Dag Mountains SE Turkey 1966, S face Koh-i-Bandaka (22500 feet) Hindu Kush Afghanistan 1967, first Br ascent Salathé Wall El Capitain Yosemite 1971, E pillar of Mt Asgard Baffin Island Expedition 1972, SE spur Pic Lenin (7189m) 1974, Mt McKinley (6226m, first alpine ascent of S face via new route, with Dougal Haston) 1976, E face direct Mt Kenya 1976, Orge (7330m) Karakoram Mountains 1977, N Ridge route Kangchenjunga 1977 (and without oxygen 1979), N summit Kussum Kangguru 1979, N face Nuptse 1979, Kangchungtse (7640m, alpine style) 1980, Shivling E pillar 1981, Pungpa Ri (7445m) 1982, Shishapangma S face (8046m) 1982, Lobsang Spire (Karakoram) 1983, Broad Peak (8047m) 1983, E summit and central Mt Chamlang (7287m) 1984, Diran (7260m) 1985, S face Mt Jitchu Drake (6793m) Bhutan 1988, Indian Arête Lotok III 1990, Hanging Glacier Peak S (6220m) 1991; memb other expdns incl: Euro Mt Everest Expedition to SW face 1972; Br Mt Everest Expedition to SW face 1972 (autumn), Br Mt Everest Expedition (reached summit with Dougal Haston, via SW face, first Britons on summit) 1975; *Publications* Big Wall Climbing (1974), Shishapangma Expedition Tibet (1984), Himalayan Climber (1992); contributor to Alpine Journal, American Alpine Journal and Mountain Magazine; *Recreations* rock climbing, photography, organic gardening; *Clubs* Alpine, Nottingham Climbers, Alpine Climbing Gp; *Style*— Doug Scott, Esq, CBE; ✉ Chapel House, Low Cotehill, Carlisle, Cumbria CA4 0EL (☎ 01228 562358)

SCOTT, Lady; Esme; *née* Burnett; CBE (1985); da of David Burnett (d 1968), and Jane, *née* Thornton (d 1967); *b* 1 Jan 1932; *Educ* St George's Sch for Girls Edinburgh, Univ of Edinburgh (MA, LLB); *m* 1, 17 March 1956, Ian Macfarlane Walker (d 1988), s of James Walker (d 1950); 1 s (Angus David Macfarlane b 9 Aug 1960); m 2, 5 Jan 1990, Sir Kenneth Scott, KCVO, CMG, s of Adam Scott; *Career* lectr Queen Margaret Coll Edinburgh 1977–83; chm: Scottish Consumer Cncl 1981–85, Scottish Assoc of CAB 1986–88, Volunteer Devpt Scotland 1989–; vice chm Nat Consumer Cncl 1984–87, cmmr Equal Opportunities Cmmn 1986–90; tstee John Watson's Tst; memb: Scottish Consumer Cncl 1980–81, Scottish Ctee of the Cncl on Tbnls 1986–, Cncl St George's Sch for Girls, Social Security Advsy Ctee 1990–, Direct Mail Services Standards Bd 1990–, Ct Univ of Edinburgh 1989–, Securities & Investments Bd 1991–; FRSA 1987, memb Law Soc of Scotland 1974; *Recreations* crosswords; *Clubs* New (Edinburgh); *Style*— Lady Scott, CBE; ✉ 25a Friary Court, St James's Palace, London SW1A 1BJ

SCOTT, (John) Fenwick Easton; JP; s of Dr (John) Alwyn Easton Scott (d 1955), of Midhurst, and Eveleen Dorothy, *née* Purcell (d 1984); *b* 30 May 1942; *Educ* Cranleigh; *m* 10 Sept 1966, Jayne Anne, da of Douglas Craven Hodgson, of Lincs; 1 s (Simon b 11 Oct 1969), 2 da (Clarissa b 24 Nov 1971, Kirstie b 7 July 1974); *Career* chartered surveyor; head Property Servs Scope; conslt Monkhouse & Partners; gen cmmr for income tax; Freeman City of London, Liveryman Worshipful Co of Armourers and Brasiers; FRICS; *Recreations* golf; *Clubs* W Sussex Golf; *Style*— Fenwick Scott, Esq, JP; ✉ Amblehurst Manor Farm, Wisborough Green, Billinghurst, W Sussex RH14 0EP (☎ 01403 700012)

SCOTT, Finlay McMillan; TD (1984); s of Finlay McMillan Scott (d 1985), and Anne Cameron Robertson, *née* Coutts (d 1972); *b* 25 May 1947; *Educ* Greenock HS, Open Univ (BA), Univ of Durham (MSc); *m* 17 May 1969, Eileen Frances, da of Ronald Francis Marshall; 1 da (Karen Anne Coutts b 21 Dec 1972), 1 s (Finlay Alan McMillan b 18 July 1975); *Career* Dept for Educn 1975–94: under sec (grade 3) 1990, on loan as sec Univs Funding Cncl 1990–92, on loan as sec and dep chief exec Higher Educn Funding Cncl for England 1992–94; chief exec and registrar GMC 1994–; memb: NI Higher Educn Cncl 1994–, Governing Body London Guildhall Univ 1996– TA: Intelligence Corps 1973–76, RAOC 1976–94, Lt Col 1989, Royal Logistic Corps 1994–95; *Recreations* Dartmoor letter boxing, squash, tennis, hill walking; *Style*— Finlay Scott, Esq, TD; ✉ General Medical Council, 178–202 Great Portland Street, London W1N 6JE (☎ 0171 915 3563, fax 0171 915 3640)

SCOTT, (Celia) Gay; da of Ivor Norman Bailey (d 1986), and Enid Alice, *née* Sherwood; *b* 25 March 1944; *Educ* St Angela's Providence Convent London, NW London Poly, Brighton Coll of Librarianship; *m* 18 May 1967, Michael James Frederick Scott, s of Capt John Bristol Irwin Scott (d 1991), of Bedford; 1 s (Charles b 1982); *Career* Membs' Info Serv House of Commons 1973–74, head of Euro Unit Greater London Cncl 1976–80, fndr and dir European Information Ltd (acquired by Eurofi 1982) 1980–, dir Eurofi 1982–; assoc Library Assoc 1967, MIInfSc 1977; *Publications* The European Economic Community (1979), A Guide to European Community Grants and Loans (annually 1980–), Money for Research and Development (jtly, 1986), Eurobrief (monthly 1981–83); *Recreations* riding, walking, cookery, skiing, theatre going, gardening; *Style*— Mrs Michael Scott; ✉ Gorgate Hall, Hoe, Nr Dereham, Norfolk NR20 4HD (☎ and 01362 861011); Eurofi House, 37 London Road, Newbury, Berks RG13 1JL (☎ 01635 31900, fax 01635 37370)

SCOTT, Graham Robert; s of Robert Alexander Scott, of Alness, Ross-shire, and Helen, *née* Tawse (d 1987); *b* 8 Dec 1944; *Educ* Bryanston Sch, Nottingham Univ (BSc); *m* 19 Aug 1967, Wendy Jean, da of Harry Mumford (d 1983); 1 s (Andrew), 1 da (Harriet); *Career* gen mangr Unitrition Int Ltd 1984–86, md BP Nutrition (UK) Ltd 1987–89, area chief exec BP Nutrition Specialities 1989–90, chief exec BP Nutrition Petfoods (now Paragon Petcare International BV) 1991–93, gp chief exec JLI Group plc 1994–95, chief exec NWF Group plc 1995–; CEng 1971, MIChemE 1971; *Style*— Graham Scott, Esq; ✉ Chief Executive, NWF Group plc, Wardle, Nantwich, Cheshire CW5 6BP (☎ 01829 260260)

SCOTT, Dr Hazel R; da of Very Rev Dr Hugh R Wyllie, of Hamilton, Strathclyde, and Eileen, *née* Cameron; *b* 31 Jan 1965; *Educ* Hutchesons' GS, Univ of Glasgow (MB ChB, MRCP); *m* 16 Sept 1994, Alastair E Scott; *Career* sr registrar W Glagow Hosps Univ NHS Tst until 1996, conslt physician (with an interest in respiratory med) Law Hosp NHS Tst 1996–; memb Cncl Royal Coll of Physicians and Surgns of Glasgow 1995–; treas Royal Medicochirurgical Soc of Glasgow 1996–; *Recreations* music, gardening; *Style*— Dr Hazel R Scott; ✉ Department of Medicine, Law Hospital NHS Trust, Carluke, Lanarkshire ML8 5ER (☎ 01698 361100)

SCOTT, Henry Douglas Edward; s and h of Sir Anthony Percy Scott, 3 Bt, *qv*, and Caroline Teresa Anne, er da of (William Charles) Edward Bacon; *b* 26 March 1964; *Educ* Harrow; *m* 1993, Carole Ruth, da of Derek Maddick; *Career* Sugar and Cocoa Depts Philipp Brothers Ltd 1987–, Int Products Div Phibro Energy Ltd 1991–, Hedging Dept Euromin SA London Branch 1992–; *Style*— Henry Scott, Esq; ✉ 59 Church Path, Chiswick, London W4 5BH

SCOTT, Hugh Johnstone; s of Hugh Johnstone Scott (d 1961), and Agnes Alison Leckie, *née* Storie (d 1994); *Educ* Paisley GS, Glasgow Sch of Art (DA), Jordanhill Coll (CertEd); *m* 23 Dec 1960, Mary Smith Craig, da of James Hamilton; 1 s (David b 7 Oct 1961), 1 da (Caroline b 18 Sept 1963); *Career* Nat Serv 1958–60; art teacher various schs 1971–84 (latterly head of art Lomond Sch Helensburgh); full time author 1984–; writer in residence City of Aberdeen 1991 (Scottish Arts Cncl bursary), pt/t lectr in creative writing Adult and Continuing Educn Dept Univ of Glasgow 1988–, tutor with the Arvon Fndn 1994; winner Woman's Realm Children's Story Competition 1982, Scottish Arts Cncl bursary 1988–89, Whitbread Children's Category Book of the Year 1989, Scottish Arts Cncl bursary 1993–94; memb Soc of Authors 1988–; *Books include* The Shaman's Stone (1988), The Plant That Ate The World (1989), Why Weeps The Brogan? (1989, short-listed for the McVitie prize 1990), Freddie and the Enormouse, The Haunted Sand, The Camera Obscura, The Summertime Santa, Something Watching, The Gargoyle (1991), Change the King! (1991), A Box of Tricks (1991), A Ghost Waiting (1993), The Place Between (1994), The Ghosts of Ravens Crag (1996); *Recreations* weight training, reading, exploring England; *Style*— Hugh Scott, Esq; ✉ c/o Walker Books Ltd, 87 Vauxhall Walk, London SE11 5HJ (☎ 0171 793 0909, fax 0171 587 1123)

SCOTT, Iain William St Clair; s of Lt-Col Joseph William St Clair Scott, and Margaret Brown, *née* Rodger (d 1977); *b* 14 May 1946; *Educ* George Watson's Coll Edinburgh; *m* 1 Oct 1971, Noelle Margaret Gilmour (Jill), da of Archibald Gilmour Young (d 1989), of Musselburgh, Edinburgh; 1 s (Ruaridh b 1976), 1 da (Susan b 1973); *Career* CA 1970; Bank of Scotland: cost accountant 1973, asst chief accountant 1981, mangr corp planning 1983, asst gen mangr corporate planning 1985, div gen mangr accounting and fin 1986, gen mangr mgmnt servs 1990, gen mangr Personal Financial and Card Services 1994, gen mangr UK Banking East 1996; chm Cncl Stevenson Coll; FCIBS 1988; *Recreations* golf, curling, squash; *Clubs* Hon Co of Edinburgh Golfers, Bruntsfield Links GS; *Style*— Iain Scott, Esq; ✉ 22 Bramdean Rise, Edinburgh EH10 6JR (☎ 0131 447 2453); 13 Woodlands Road, Lundin Links, Fife; Bank of Scotland, 101 George Street, PO Box 41, Edinburgh EH2 3JH (☎ 0131 243 5855, fax 0131 243 5738)

SCOTT, Sir Ian Dixon; KCMG (1962, CMG 1959), KCVO (1965), CIE (1947); s of Thomas Henderson Scott, OBE, of Selkirk, and Mary Agnes, *née* Dixon; *b* 6 March 1909; *Educ* Queen's Royal Coll Trinidad, Balliol Coll Oxford, LSE; *m* 1937, Hon Anna Drusilla, o da of 1 Baron Lindsay of Birker, CBE (d 1952); 1 s, 4 da; *Career* entered ICS 1932, transferred Political Service 1935, dep private sec to Viceroy 1945–47, first sec UK High Cmmr's Office Pakistan 1947–48, dep dir personnel John Lewis & Co Ltd London 1948–50, entered FO 1950; first sec: British Legation Helsinki 1952–53, British Embassy Beirut 1954; cnsllr 1956–58, IDC 1959, consul gen Leopoldville 1960; ambass: Republic of Congo 1960–61, Sudan 1961–65, Norway 1965–68; dir Clarkson's Holidays Ltd 1969–72 (chm 1972–73); chm Suffolk Area Health Authy 1973–77; memb Cncl Dr Barnardo's 1970–84 (chm 1972–78); memb Bd of Govrs Felixstowe Coll 1971–84 (chm 1972–80); pres Indian Civil Service (Retired) Association 1977–; *Books* Tumbled House, The Congo At Independence; *Recreations* yachting; *Style*— Sir Ian Scott, KCMG, KCVO, CIE; ✉ Ash House, Alde Lane, Aldeburgh, Suffolk

SCOTT, Prof Ian Richard; s of Ernest Richard Scott (d 1971), of Geelong, Aust, and Edith Miriam Scott (d 1976); *b* 8 Jan 1940; *Educ* Geelong Coll, Queen's Coll, Univ of Melbourne (LLB), King's Coll London (PhD); *m* 1 Oct 1971, Ecce Scott, da of Prof Boris Norman Cole, of Leeds; 2 da (Anneke b 1 Jan 1978, Kaatye b 3 Jan 1981); *Career* barr and slr Supreme Ct of Victoria 1964–, called to the Bar Gray's Inn 1995; reader judicial admin Univ of Birmingham 1976–78, dir Inst of Judicial Admin Univ of Birmingham 1976–82, visiting res prof Whittier Coll California 1978–79, Barber prof of law Univ of Birmingham 1978–, exec dir Victoria Law Fndn 1982–84, dean Faculty of Law Univ of Birmingham 1985–94, memb Lord Chllr's Review Body on Civil Justice 1985–88, chm Home Sec's N Yorkshire Magistrates' Courts Inquiry 1989; hon master of the Bench Gray's Inn 1988; *Style*— Prof I R Scott; ✉ Faculty of Law, University of Birmingham, Birmingham B15 2TT (☎ 0121 414 6291)

SCOTT, Ian Russell; s of William Russell Scott (d 1974), of Weymouth, and Winifred Mabel, *née* Morgan; *b* 12 Sept 1942; *Educ* Sherborne, Univ of London (LLB); *m* 3 May 1969, Mary Peverell, da of Robert Riggs Wright, TD, of Piddletrenthide, Dorchester, Dorset; 1 s (William b 1975), 2 da (Katharine b 1971, Louise b 1973); *Career* asst slr Sharpe Pritchard & Co 1967–68, ptnr Ashurst Morris Crisp 1972– (asst slr 1968–72); memb Law Soc 1965; *Recreations* theatre, tennis, hockey, golf, sailing; *Clubs* City of London, Roehampton; *Style*— Ian Scott, Esq; ✉ 15 Briar Walk, London SW15; Moonfleet, Ringstead Bay, Dorchester; Ashurst Morris Crisp, Broadwalk House, 5 Appold Street, London EC2A 2HA (☎ 0171 638 1111, fax 0171 972 7990, telex 887067)

SCOTT, Prof James; s of Robert Bentham Scott (d 1976), and Iris Olive, *née* Hill, of Melton Mowbray, Leics; *b* 13 Sept 1946; *Educ* Univ of London (scholar, BSc), London Hosp Med Coll (MB BS, MSc, MRCP); *m* 1976, Diane Marylin, da of Herbert Lowe; 2 s (William b 30 July 1981, Edward b 10 Sept 1984), 1 da (Lucy b 20 Jan 1990); *Career* house offr: London Hosp 1971–72, Hereford Co Hosp 1972; SHO Midland Centre for Neurosurgery and Neurology and Queen Elizabeth Hosp Birmingham 1972–73; registrar in med: Gen Hosp Birmingham 1973–74, Academic Dept of Med Royal Free Hosp London 1975–76; MRC research fell and hon sr registrar Royal Postgraduate Med Sch and Hammersmith Hosp London 1977–80, Euro Molecular Biology Orgn fell Dept of Biochemistry Univ of Calif San Francisco 1980–83, MRC clinical scientist and hon conslt physician MRC Clinical Research Inst and Northwick Park Hosp 1983–91, hon dir MRC Molecular Med Gp 1992–, prof of med and chm Dept of Med Royal Postgraduate Med Sch Hammersmith Hosp 1992–, dir of med and chief of serv med cardiology Hammersmith Hosps NHS Tst 1994–; Humphrey Davy Rolleston lectr RCP 1989, guest lectr MRS 1990, Pfizer lectr Clinical Research Inst Montreal 1990, guest lectr Japan Atherosclerosis Soc 1992, medallist and visiting prof RSM/American Heart Assoc 1992, Montreal Merck Frosst-McGill lectr in lipid metabolism 1992, Simms lectr 1995; Graham Bull Prize RCP 1989, Squibb Bristol-Myers Award 1993 (for cardiovascular research); memb: Grants Ctee B MRC Systems Bd until 1990, Research Fund Ctee Br Heart Fndn until 1992, Research Ctee RCP 1988–; external examiner (BSc Clinical Scis) 1991 and internal examiner (MB BS) 1993 Univ of London; author of numerous book chapters, reviews and refereed papers; Euro ed Arteriosclerosis, Thrombosis and Vascular Biology (American Heart Assoc jl); memb: Assoc of Physicians of GB and I, Biochemical Soc, RSM, Euro Molecular Biology Orgn 1993; FRCP 1986; *Recreations* family and friends, the twentieth century novel, British impressionist and modern painting, long distance running and swimming; *Style*— Prof James Scott; ✉ Department of Medicine, Royal Postgraduate Medical School, Hammersmith Hospital, Du Cane Road, London W12 0NN (☎ 0181 740 3299, fax 0181 740 4507)

SCOTT, Prof James Alexander; CBE (1985); s of Dr Thomas Scott (d 1976), of Doncaster, and Margaret Lilian, *née* Woodhouse (d 1965); *b* 3 July 1931; *Educ* Doncaster GS, Trinity Coll Dublin (BA, MB, BCh, BAO, MA, MD); *m* 13 July 1957, Margaret Olive, da of Charles Edward Slinger, of Harrogate (d 1976); 1 s (Julian b 1958), 2 da (Kathleen b 1959, Alexandra b 1961); *Career* sr admin med offr Sheffield Regnl Hosp Bd 1971–73, regnl med offr Trent Regnl Health Authy 1973–88, special prof of health care planning Univ of Nottingham 1974–, prof assoc health serv planning Univ of Sheffield 1988–; chm English Regnl MOs Gp 1978–80, pres Hosp Ctee EEC 1980–86, treas Faculty of Community Med RCP 1984–86, chm Med Advsy Ctee Family Health Servs Appeal Unit 1992–94; memb: Health Services Res Ctee MRC 1986–88, Nat Ctee for Review of Blood Transfusion Service 1986–87; chm Bd of Govrs Mid Trent Coll of Nursing and Midwifery 1989–95; Masur fell Nuffield Provincial Hosps Tst 1983; QHP 1980–83; Hon LLD Univ of Sheffield 1983; FFCM 1974, FRCP 1985; *Style*— Prof James Scott, CBE; ✉ 5 Slayleigh Lane, Sheffield S10 3RE (☎ 0114 230 2238)

SCOTT, James Alexander; OBE (1987); s of Douglas McPherson Scott (d 1971), and Mabel Mary, *née* Skepper (d 1962); *b* 30 April 1940; *Educ* Uppingham, Magdalene Coll Cambridge (scholar, MA), London Business Sch (MSc); *m* 24 April 1965, Annette, *née* Goslett; 3 s (David b 8 Jan 1967, Charles b 10 Dec 1971, Alastair b 2 May 1973), 2 da (Joanna b 1 May 1968, Catriona b 20 Oct 1979); *Career* Binder Hamlyn: articled clerk 1961–64, ptnr 1969–, managing ptnr London 1980–88, nat managing ptnr 1988–89; sec Review Bd for Govt Contracts 1969–; memb: Agric Wages Bd for Eng and Wales 1971–86, Pharmacists Remuneration Review Panel 1983, Restrictive Practices Ct 1993–; DTI inspr Atlantic Computers plc 1990; dir: Vestey Group Ltd 1992–, Schroder Exempt Property Unit Tst 1994–; tstee Lonrho Superannuation Scheme 1993–; FCA (ACA 1964); *Recreations* walking, golf, tennis, skiing; *Clubs* Berks Golf, St Enodoc Golf; *Style*— James Scott, Esq, OBE; ✉ Binder Hamlyn, 20 Old Bailey, London EC4M 7BH (☎ 0171 489 9000, fax 0171 489 6291)

SCOTT, James Archibald; CB (1988), LVO (1961); s of James Scott, MBE (d 1983), of Beechhurst, Hawick, Roxburghshire, and Agnes Bone, *née* Howie (d 1985); *b* 5 March 1932; *Educ* Dollar Acad, Univ of St Andrews, Queen's Univ of Ontario (MA); *m* 27 Aug 1957, Elizabeth Agnes Joyce, da of John Trant Buchan-Hepburn (d 1953), of Chagford, St Andrews, Fife; 3 s (Buchan b 1962, Robert b 1964, Hector b 1969), 1 da (Frances (Mrs Rive) b 1960); *Career* RAF Aircrew 1954–56, Flying Offr XI Sqdn 1956; joined CRO 1956; first sec: UK High Cmmn New Delhi 1958–62, UK Mission to UN NY 1962–65; transferred SO 1965, PPS to Sec of State for Scot 1969–71, asst sec Scot Devpt Dept 1971; sec: Scot Educn Dept 1984–87, Indust Dept for Scot 1987–90 (under sec 1976–84); chief exec Scot Devpt Agency 1990–91; exec dir Scottish Financial Enterprise 1991–94; non-exec dir: Scottish Power plc 1992–96, Dumyat Investment Trust plc 1995–; memb Ct Heriot-Watt Univ 1995–; Chevalier dans l'Ordre National du Mérite 1995; FScotvec 1990, FRSE 1993; *Recreations* music, golf; *Style*— James Scott, Esq, CB, LVO, FRSE; ✉ 38 Queen's Crescent, Edinburgh EH9 2BA (☎ 0131 667 8417)

SCOTT, James Empson; s of James Christopher Scott (d 1979), and Phyllis Margaret, *née* Empson (d 1985); *b* 8 Nov 1942; *Educ* King's Sch Canterbury, Oriel Coll Oxford, Middx Hosp Med Sch (MA); *m* 1, 1967 (m dis), Mary, da of Sir Brian Fairfax-Lucy (d 1974); 2 da (Sophie b 1970, Charlotte b 1974); m 2, 1980, Katherine Henrietta, da of Sir Michael Cary (d 1978); 2 s (Matthew b 1984, Ned b 1985), 1 da (Molly b 1990); *Career* successively sr registrar (orthopaedic surgery) Middx Hosp and Royal Nat Orthopaedic Hosp, Fullbright scholar and fell in orthopaedic surgery Massachusetts Gen Hosp, conslt orthopaedic surgn St Stephen's Hosp, St Mary Abbott's Hosp and Westminster Hosps, currently conslt orthopaedic surgn The Chelsea and Westminster Hosp London; asst ed International Orthopaedics, sr exminer (MB BS) Univ of London, memb Cncl Orthopaedic Section RSM; FRCS, FBOA; *Recreations* paintings; *Clubs* Athenaeum, Chelsea Arts; *Style*— James Scott, Esq; ✉ 8 Rectory Grove, London SW4 0EA (☎ 0171 622 0571); The Lister Hospital, Chelsea Bridge Road, London SW1W 8RH (☎ 0171 730 9560, fax 0171 730 7726)

SCOTT, Sir James Jervoise; 3 Bt (UK 1962), of Rotherfield Park, Alton, Hants; s of Sir James Walter Scott, 2 Bt, DL (d 1993), and Anne Constantia, *née* Austin; *b* 12 Oct 1952; *Educ* Eton, Trinity Coll Camb; *m* 13 Oct 1982, Judy Evelyn, da of Brian Trafford, of Tismans, Rudgwick, Sussex; 1 s (Arthur Jervoise Trafford b 2 Feb 1984), 1 da (Alexandra Lilian b 1986); *Heir* s, Arthur Jervoise Trafford Scott b 2 Feb 1984; *Career* ed Big Farm Weekly 1984–88; chm Hampshire branch CLA 1996–; Liveryman Worshipful Co of Mercers; *Style*— Sir James Scott, Bt; ✉ Rotherfield Park, East Tisted, Alton, Hampshire GU34 3QL

SCOTT, James Michael; s of late William George Scott, CBE, RA, of Bennetts Hill Farm, Coleford, Bath, and Hilda Mary, *née* Lucas; *b* 9 July 1941; *Educ* Bryanston, Sorbonne Paris, Slade Sch of Art, UCL; *m* 1, 19 Feb 1966 (m dis 1977), Anna Katherine; 1 s (Alexander Ivan b 10 Sept 1967), 1 da (Rosie Beth Caroline b 5 Sept 1971); m 2, 8 July 1995, Yolanda Orozco; 1 da (Paloma Claire b 3 Aug 1995); *Career* film director and painter; short films: The Rocking Horse 1962, In Separation 1965, A Shocking Accident 1982 (Oscar winner 1983), Crime in The City 1987, People are The Same The Universe Over; pop video Saxon 1983; documentaries: Love's Presentation 1966, R B Kitaj 1967, Richard Hamilton 1969, The Great Ice Cream Robbery 1971, Night Cleaners 1974, '36 to'77 1978, Chance History Art 1979 (Silver Prize Melbourne); features: Adult Fun 1972, Coilin and Platonida 1976, Loser Takes All 1989; TV: Every Picture Tells a Story 1984, Getting Even - A Wimp's Revenge 1985, Inspector Morse 1989; memb: Dirs' Guilds of GB and USA, Br Film Acad, American Acad of Motion Picture Arts; *Recreations* reading, painting, photography; *Style*— James Scott, Esq; ✉ PO Box 4217, Tracy Street, Los Angeles, CA 90027, USA (☎ and fax 00 1 213 953 2761)

SCOTT, Sir (Walter) John; 5 Bt (UK 1907), of Beauclerc, Bywell St Andrews, Co Northumberland; s of Maj Sir Walter Scott, 4 Bt, JP, DL (d 1992), and Diana Mary, *née* Owen (d 1985); *b* 24 Feb 1948; *Educ* privately; *m* 1, 1969 (m dis 1971), Lowell Patria, da of late Gp Capt Pat Vaughan Goddard, of Auckland, NZ; 1 da (Rebecca b 1970); m 2, 1977, Mary Gavin, o da of Alexander Fairly Anderson, of Gartocharn, Dunbartonshire; 1 s (Walter Samuel b 1984), 1 da (Diana Helen Rose b 1977); *Heir* s, Walter Samuel Scott b 6 Dec 1984; *Career* farmer; *Recreations* field sports; *Style*— Sir John Scott, Bt; ✉ Barned House, Gifford, East Lothian EH41 4PJ

SCOTT, John Gavin; s of Douglas Gavin Scott, and Hetty, *née* Murphy; *b* 18 June 1956; *Educ* Queen Elizabeth GS Wakefield, St John's Coll Cambridge (organ scholar, MA, MusB); *m* 28 July 1979, Carolyn Jane, da of David James Lumsden; 1 s (Alexander Gavin b 29 Oct 1987), 1 da (Emma Jane b 27 Dec 1984); *Career* asst organist: Wakefield Cathedral 1970–74, St Paul's and Southwark Cathedrals 1978–84; organist and dir of music St Paul's Cathedral 1990– (sub-organist 1984–90); debut Henry Wood Proms 1977, Royal Festival Hall debut March 1979; frequent solo tours, dir of St Paul's Cathedral Choir in numerous concerts, tours and recordings; awarded first prize: Manchester International Organ Competition 1978, Leipzig J S Bach Competition 1984; Hon RAM 1990; Liveryman Worshipful Co of Musicians; *Recordings* as soloist: Liszt's Ad Nos, Ad Salutarem Undam 1984, Organ Music by Marcel Dupré 1986, Organ Music by Maurice Duruflé 1989, Organ Music by Mendelssohn, Janacek's Glagolitic Mass 1990, Organ Music by Elgar, Harris and Bairstow 1992, Organ Music by William Mathias 1993, Great European Organs No 40 1996; as conductor with St Paul's Choir: Christmas Music 1986, My Soul Doth Magnify the Lord 1987, Herbert Howell's Church Music 1987, My Spirit Hath Rejoiced 1988, Praise to the Lord 1989, The English Anthem 1989, Stainer's Crucifixion 1990, Hear my Prayer 1991, The English Anthem Vol 2 1992, Cathedral Music by Kenneth Leighton 1992, Music by William Croft 1993, The English Anthem Vol 3 1993, RPO Christmas Concert 1993, Christmas Carols from St Paul's 1994, The English Anthem Vol 4 1994, Psalms from St Paul's Vols 1 and 2 1994, The English Anthem Vol 5 1995, Psalms from St Paul's Vols 3 & 4 1995, The English Anthem Vol 6 1996; *Recreations* reading, travel; *Style*— John Scott, Esq; ✉ 5 Amen Court, London EC4M 7BU (☎ 0171 248 6868, fax 0171 248 6868); Magenta Music International Ltd, 4 Highgate High St, London N6 5HX (☎ 0181 340 8321)

SCOTT, John Philip Henry Schomberg; s of Christopher Bartle Hugh Scott, of Galashiels, Scotland, and Anne Margaret D'Arcy, *née* Kerr; *b* 20 July 1952; *Educ* Eton, Magdalene Coll Cambridge (MA), INSEAD Fontainebleau (MBA); *m* 6 Dec 1977, Jacqueline Dawn, da of Maj Colin George Champion Rae, MC, of Little Weston, Somerset; 2 s (Alexander Hugh Frere b 8 Dec 1982, James Julian Frere b 1 April 1985); *Career* Jardine Matheson & Co Ltd Hong Kong 1974–80, dir Lazard Brothers & Co Ltd London 1988– (joined 1981); memb Queen's Body Guard for Scotland (Royal Co of Archers); Freeman City of London 1981, Liveryman Worshipful Co of Grocers 1992; FCII 1980, MSI 1993; *Recreations* outdoor sports; *Clubs* New (Edinburgh); *Style*— John Scott, Esq; ✉ Lazard Brothers & Co Ltd, 21 Moorfields, London EC2P 2HT (☎ 0171 588 2721, fax 0171 628 2485, telex 886438)

SCOTT, (Ian) Jonathan; CBE (1995); s of Col Alexander Brassey Jonathan Scott, DSO, MC (d 1978), of Lasborough, Tetbury, and Rhona Margaret, *née* Stewart; *b* 7 Feb 1940; *Educ* Harrow, Balliol Coll Oxford (BA); *m* 12 June 1965, Annabella Constance Scott, JP, da of Francis William Hope Loudon (d 1985), of Olantigh, Kent, and his w Lady Prudence, *née* Jellicoe, da of 1 Earl Jellicoe; 2 s (Alexander b 1966, Justin b 1970), 1 da (Julia b 1969); *Career* dir: Charterhouse Japhet Ltd 1973–80, Barclays Merchant Bank Ltd 1980–85, Barclays de Zoete Wedd Ltd 1985–92; chm Reviewing Ctee on the Export of Works of Art 1985–95; tstee: Imp War Museum 1984–, V&A Museum 1995–; FSA 1980; *Books* Piranesi (1975), Salvator Rosa (1995); *Clubs* Brooks's; *Style*— Jonathan Scott, Esq, CBE, FSA; ✉ Lasborough Manor, Tetbury, Glos GL8 8UF; Flat 8, 25 Queen's Gate, London SW7 5JE

SCOTT, (Norman) Keith; CBE (1989); s of Norman Scott (d 1986), and Dora Scott (d 1979); *b* 10 Feb 1927; *Educ* Preston GS, Univ of Liverpool Sch of Architecture (BArch, MA), Univ of Liverpool Sch of Planning (DipCD), MIT Cambridge USA (MArch); *m* 19 Jan 1952, Dorothy Anne, da of Frederick Walker (d 1958); 2 s (Quentin Nicholas b 3

Sept 1959, (Timothy) Tarquin b 7 March 1964), 2 da (Louise Amanda b 22 Nov 1953, Hilary Jane b 7 June 1956); *Career* architect to Dean and Chapter Liverpool Cathedral 1979–; chm: Awards Panel RIBA 1982–84, BDP 1984–89 (ptnr 1963, conslt 1989–93); private architect and planning conslt 1993–; memb Bd: Lake Dist Summer Music Festival 1984–95 (chm 1990–95), Rural Buildings Preservation Tst 1994–; govr Lancashire Poly (now Univ of Central Lancashire) 1988–92; life memb Victorian Soc; chm: N Lancs Soc of Architects 1966–67, BDP Music Soc 1968–, Friends of London Int Piano Competition 1991–; memb Lambda Alpha International 1994–; FRIBA, MRTPI; *Books* Shopping Centre Design (1989); *Recreations* music, fell walking, sketching; *Clubs* Oriental; *Style—* N Keith Scott, CBE; ✉ Overleigh House, East Cliff, Preston PR1 3JE (☎ 01772 253545, fax 01772 555354)

SCOTT, Dame (Catherine) Margaret Mary (Mrs Denton); DBE (1981, OBE 1977); da of John Douglas Scott (d 1985), of Swaziland, and Marjorie Heath, *née* Bagley; *b* 26 April 1922; *Educ* Parktown Convent Johannesburg S Africa; *m* 1953, Prof Derek Ashworth Denton; 2 s (Matthew, Angus); *Career* founding dir Australian Ballet Sch 1963–90; memb: Founding Cncl Vic Coll of Arts 1973–87, Bd of Dirs Australian Dance Theatre 1980–83, Dance Panel Australian Cncl 1972–73, Ctee Australian Ballet Soc 1983–84, Jury Int Ballet Competitions Moscow 1981–85; Hon LLD Melbourne Univ 1988, hon life membership The Aust Ballet Fndn 1989; *Recreations* theatre, music, swimming, walking, garden; *Clubs* Alexander, Melbourne; *Style—* Dame Margaret Scott, DBE; ✉ 816 Orrong Rd, Toorak, Melbourne, Vic 3142, Australia (☎ 00 61 3 9827 2640, fax 00 61 3 9826 5457)

SCOTT, Maurice FitzGerald; s of Col Gerald Chaplin Scott, OBE (d 1953), of Ramsey, Isle of Man, and Harriet Mary Geraldine, *née* FitzGerald (d 1983); *b* 6 Dec 1924; *Educ* Campbell Coll Belfast, Wadham Coll Oxford (BA, MA), Nuffield Coll Oxford (BLitt); *m* 30 March 1953, Eleanor Warren (d 1989), da of Norman Dawson (d 1971), of Cults, Aberdeen; 3 da (Alison b 1955, Sheila b 1957, Jean b 1960); *Career* RE 1943–46 (Temp Capt); OEEC Paris 1949–51, PM's Statistical Section under Lord Cherwell 1951–53, Econ Section Cabinet Office 1953–54, NIESR 1954–57, tutor in econs ChCh Oxford (fell) 1957–68, NEDO 1962–63, Devpt Centre of OECD Paris 1967–68, official fell in econs Nuffield Coll Oxford 1968–92 (fell emeritus 1992) FEconS 1950, FBA 1990; *Books* A Study of UK Imports (1963), Industry and Trade in some Developing Countries (with I M D Little and T Scitovsky, 1970), Induction, Growth and Trade - Essays in Honour of Sir Roy Harrod (ed with W A Eltis and J N Wolfe, 1970), Using Shadow Prices (ed with I M D Little, 1976), Project Appraisal in Practice - The Little-Mirlees Method Applied in Kenya (with J D MacArthur and D M G Newbery, 1976), Can We Get Back to Full Employment? (with R A Laslett, 1978), Economic Theory and Hicksian Themes (ed with D Collard, D Helm and A K Sen, 1984), A New View of Economic Growth (1989), Public Policy and Economic Development - Essays in Honour of Ian Little (ed with D K Lal, 1990); *Recreations* walking; *Clubs* Political Economy (Oxford); *Style—* Maurice Scott, Esq; ✉ 11 Blandford Ave, Oxford, OX2 8EA (☎ 01865 559115); Nuffield College, Oxford OX1 1NF (☎ 01865 278500, fax 01865 278621)

SCOTT, Sir Michael; KCVO (1979, MVO 1961), CMG (1977); s of John Scott (d 1957), and Kathleen Scott (d 1983), of Newcastle upon Tyne; *b* 19 May 1923; *Educ* Dame Allan's Sch, Univ of Durham; *m* 1, 1944 (m dis 1967), Vivienne Sylvia Vincent-Barwood (d 1985); 3 s; m 2, 1971, Jennifer Cameron Smith; *Career* served 1942–47 with 1 Gurkha Rifles; Colonial Office 1949–57; HM Dip Serv: dep high cmmr Peshawar Pakistan 1959–62, cnsllr British High Cmmn New Delhi 1963–65, dep high cmmr Nicosia 1968–72, RCDS 1973, ambass to Nepal 1974–77, high cmmr Malawi 1977–79, high cmmr Bangladesh 1980–81, ret; sec-gen Royal Cwlth Soc 1983–88, cncl memb Overseas Devpt Inst 1983–93; dir Tiger Mountain Group 1984–93; tstee: Drive for Youth Charity 1987–93, Int Agric Trg Prog 1988–, King Mahendra Tst for Nature Conservation (UK) 1989–; memb Ctee Britain-Nepal Soc 1991–96; Freeman City of London; *Clubs* Oriental; *Style—* Sir Michael Scott, KCVO, CMG; ✉ 87A Cornwall Gdns, London SW7 4AY (☎ 0171 589 6794)

SCOTT, Maj Gen Michael Ian Eldon (Mike); CB (1997), CBE (1987), DSO (1982); s of Col Eric Scott, and Rose-Anne Scott (d 1994); *b* 3 March 1941; *Educ* Bradfield Coll, RMA Sandhurst; *m* Veronica Daniell; 1 s, 1 da; *Career* cmmnd Scots Gds 1960, served UK, E Africa, N Ireland and BAOR, psc 1974, MA 2 to Chief of Gen Staff, returned N Ireland, Chief of Staff Task Force Delta (now 12 Armd Bde) BAOR, Armed Forces Staff Coll USA, cmd 2 Bn Scots Gds London, Falklands Conflict 1982 and Cyprus, on Directing Staff Staff Coll Camberley 1984, cmd 8 Infantry Bde N Ireland 1984–86, RCDS 1987, Dep Mil Sec (B) MOD 1987–93, GOC Scotland and Govr of Edinburgh Castle 1993–95, Military Secretary 1995–; *Recreations* art, travel, outdoor pursuits; *Style—* Maj Gen M I E Scott, CB, CBE, DSO; ✉ Ministry of Defence (Rm 8270), Main Building, Whitehall, London SW1A 2HB (☎ 0171 218 7581, fax 0171 218 6952)

SCOTT, Michael James; s of Arthur James Scott, and Phyllis, *née* Ravenhill (d 1970); *b* 7 Dec 1942; *Educ* Sutton Valence, Univ of Edinburgh (MA); *m* 10 May 1969, Suzette; 1 s (Edward James b 6 Sept 1980), 1 da (Polly Elizabeth b 2 Sept 1971); *Career* CA 1968; Arthur Andersen 1970–72, ptnr Grant Thornton 1975– (joined 1972, formerly Thornton Baker); *Recreations* skiing, tennis, France; *Clubs* SCGB, DHO, Grasshoppers; *Style—* Michael Scott, Esq; ✉ Grant Thornton, 49 Mill St, Bedford MK40 3LB (☎ 01234 211521, fax 01234 325717)

SCOTT, Rt Hon Sir Nicholas Paul; KBE (1995, MBE 1964), PC (1989), MP (C) Chelsea (majority 12,789); s of Percival John Scott; *b* 5 Aug 1933; *Educ* Clapham Coll, City of London Coll; *m* 1, 1964 (m dis 1976), Elizabeth, da of Robert Robinson, of Thornborough, Bucks; 1 s, 2 da; m 2, 1979, Hon Mrs Tapsell (Hon Cecilia, da of 9 Baron Hawke); 1 s, 1 da; *Career* Parly candidate Islington (C) SW 1959 and 1964; MP (C): Paddington S 1966–Feb 1974, Chelsea Oct 1974–97; PPS to Rt Hon Iain Macleod as Chllr of the Exchequer 1970 and to Rt Hon Robert Carr as Home Sec 1972–74, Parly under sec Dept of Employment 1974, oppn spokesman on housing 1974–75; exec memb 1922 Ctee 1978–81; Parly under sec NI Office Sept 1981–86 (min of state 1986–87), min of state for social security and disabled people 1987–94; dir: A S Kerswill 1970–81, Eastbourne Printers 1970–81, Juniper Studios 1970–81, Bonusbond Holdings 1980–81, Bonusplan Ltd 1977–81, Cleveland Offshore Fund Inc 1970–81, Learplan 1978–81; conslt Hill & Knowlton UK Ltd 1981; former chm Creative Conslts, former md E Allom & Co; govr Br Inst of Human Rights, memb Cncl Community Serv Volunteers, dep chm Br Caribbean Assoc, nat pres Tory Reform Gp, former chm Conservative Parly Employment Ctee, nat chm Young Cons 1963, dir London Office Euro Cons Gp in Euro Parl 1974; JP (Greater London) 1961–86; Liveryman Guild of Air Pilots and Air Navigators; *Clubs* Garrick, Pratt's, Chelsea Arts, MCC; *Style—* The Rt Hon Sir Nicholas Scott, KBE, MP; ✉ House of Commons, London SW1A 0AA

SCOTT, Sir Oliver Christopher Anderson; 3 Bt (UK 1909), of Yews, Undermilbeck, Westmorland; s of Sir Samuel Haslam Scott, 2 Bt (d 1960), and his 2 wife, Nancy Lilian, *née* Anderson (d 1935); *b* 6 Nov 1922; *Educ* Charterhouse, King's Coll Cambridge (MA); *m* 1951, Phoebe Anne, er da of Desmond O'Neill Tolhurst, of Chelsea; 1 s (Christopher James b 1955), 2 da (Hermione Mary (Mrs Miles R Stanford) b 1952, Camilla Nancy (Mrs David B Withington) b 1956); *Heir* s, Christopher James Scott b 16 Jan 1955; *Career* High Sheriff of Westmorland 1966; dir Res Unit of Radiobiology British Empire Cancer Campaign 1966–69, conslt Inst of Cancer Res 1974–82, radiobiologist St Thomas's Hosp London 1982–88; Liveryman Worshipful Co of Skinners; *Clubs* Brooks's; *Style—* Sir Oliver Scott, Bt; ✉ 31 Kensington Square, London W8

SCOTT, Patricia Mary; da of Gordon James Rouse (d 1978), and Hilda May, *née* Marchant; *b* 28 Nov 1954; *Educ* Hreod Burna Sr HS, Portsmouth Poly; *m* 1 Aug 1975, Anthony Vincent Scott, s of Thomas Arthur David Scott; 1 s (Adam James b 27 May 1991); *Career* various appts Thorn Television Rentals Ltd and Thorn EMI plc 1974–85, accountant Burmah Oil Exploration Ltd 1985; Thorn EMI plc: gp tax mangr 1986–89, dir Taxation and Treasury 1989–94; chief exec The Chieveley Consulting Group Ltd 1995–; non-exec dir Warden Housing Assoc 1995–; hon treas St Augustine's Church 1985–, tstee One Small Step charity for the disabled 1993–; govr Downe House Sch 1995–; fell Chartered Assoc of Certified Accountants 1989 (memb 1984); memb: Assoc of Corporate Treasurers 1990, Tax Law Review Ctee 1994–; *Recreations* gardening, poultry keeping, reading; *Style—* Patricia Scott; ✉ Yew Tree House, High Street, Compton, Berkshire RG20 6QT (☎ 01635 579178)

SCOTT, Sir (Charles) Peter; KBE (1978, OBE 1948), CMG (1964); s of Rev John Joseph Scott (d 1947), and Hannah Dorothea, *née* Senior (d 1953); *b* 30 Dec 1917; *Educ* Weymouth Coll, Pembroke Coll Cambridge; *m* 1954, Rachael, yr da of late Cyril Walter Lloyd-Jones, CIE, of Guildford; 1 s (Harry), 2 da (Katherine, Maria); *Career* ICS 1940–47, entered FO 1947, 1 sec Toyko 1949 (2 sec 1948), FO 1950–52, private sec to Gen Lord Ismay at NATO Paris 1952–54; 1 sec: Vienna 1954, British Info Services (NY) 1956; cnsllr and consul-gen Washington 1959–61, idc 1962, head of UK perm mission to Euro Office of UN Geneva 1963–66, min Rome 1966–69, seconded to Centre for Contemporary Euro Studies Univ of Sussex 1969, asst under-sec of state FCO 1970–75, ambass Norway 1975–77; private sec to HRH Prince Michael of Kent 1978–79, treas 1979–81; memb Cncl The Anglo-Norse Soc 1978– (chm Cncl 1979–88); *Recreations* walking; *Clubs* United Oxford and Cambridge Univ, Norfolk (Norwich); *Style—* Sir Peter Scott, KBE, CMG; ✉ Bisley Farmhouse, Irstead, nr Norwich, Norfolk NR12 8XT (☎ 01692 630413)

SCOTT, Peter Denys John; QC (1978); s of John Ernest Dudley Scott, and Joan Steinberg, *née* Clayton-Cooper; *b* 19 April 1935; *Educ* Monroe HS Rochester New York USA, Balliol Coll Oxford (MA); *Career* Nat Serv Lt RHA; called to the Bar Middle Temple 1960, head of chambers; chm Gen Cncl of the Bar 1987 (vice chm 1985–86); *Style—* Peter Scott, Esq, QC; ✉ 4 Eldon Rd, London W8 5PU (☎ 0171 937 3301, fax 0171 376 1169); Fountain Court, Temple, London EC4 9DH (☎ 0171 583 3335, fax 0171 353 0329)

SCOTT, Philip Edward Hannay; s of Edward Beattie Scott, MBE, and Mary, *née* Potter; *b* 6 April 1957; *Educ* Millfield, Cricklade Coll Andover; *m* 23 Sept 1989, Victoria, *née* Byles; *Career* formerly worked in film indust Tor Films Ltd (Tarka the Otter); paralysed in motor racing accident 1977; illustrator 1978–, freelance journalist and broadcaster BBC 1979– (Radio 4, World series, Local Radio); work with the disabled 1979–; achievements incl: fndr memb Project 81, fndr memb Hampshire Centre for Ind Living 1982, became one of first people to be completely supported in the community by a health authy; promotor of interests of the disabled through aviation achievements incl: fndr Operation Ability Ltd 1984, first tetraplegic to pass a Civil Aviation Authy med to gain private pilots' licence, involved first G tests for tetraplegic person 1985; Man of the Year award for serv to disabled community 1988, awarded The Gerald Frewer Meml Trophy 1992; Freeman: City of London, Worshipful Co of Haberdashers 1978; AMRAeS 1985, MIED 1992; *Recreations* art, engineering, travel, chess, calligraphy, aviation; *Style—* Philip Scott, Esq

SCOTT, Philip Gordon; s of John Theophilus Scott (d 1973), of Great Yarmouth, and Grace Virginia, *née* Cole; *b* 6 Jan 1954; *Educ* Great Yarmouth GS, King's Coll London; *m* 9 Feb 1974, Helen Rebecca Evelyn, da of James Richard Blair Fearnley (d 1985); 1 da (Rebecca Jane b 11 Dec 1978), 1 s (John Theophilus b 17 Dec 1980); *Career* Norwich Union: joined 1973, qualified as actuary 1979, asst actuary for NZ 1981–84, asst actuary Investmt Dept Head Office 1984–86, asst investmt mangr 1986–87, investmt mangr 1987–88, sr investmt mangr 1988–92, gen mangr (Fin) 1992–93, gen mangr (Life & Pensions) and dir Norwich Union 1993–; memb Cncl Inst of Actuaries 1994–; FIA 1979, FRSA; *Recreations* sailing, gardening, apples; *Clubs* Annabel's; *Style—* Philip G Scott, Esq; ✉ Whitegate Farm, Fleggburgh, Gt Yarmouth, Norfolk NR29 3DB (☎ 01493 369599); Norwich Union Insurance Group, Surrey Street, Norwich NR1 3PG (☎ 01603 683936, fax 01603 685631, mobile 0860 657337)

SCOTT, Sheriff Richard John Dinwoodie; s of Prof Richard Scott (d 1983), and Mary Ellen Maclachlan (d 1987); *b* 28 May 1939; *Educ* Edinburgh Acad, Univ of Edinburgh (MA, LLB); *m* 1969, Josephine Moretta, da of Allan Holland Blake (d 1954), of Edinburgh; 2 da (Victoria b 1970, Joanna b 1972); *Career* called to the Bar Scotland 1965, advocate in practice 1965–77; Sheriff: Grampian Highland and Is at Aberdeen and Stonehaven 1977–86, Lothian and Borders of Edinburgh 1986–; *Style—* Sheriff Richard Scott; ✉ Sheriff's Chambers, Edinburgh EH1 1LB

SCOTT, Rt Hon Sir Richard Rashleigh Folliott; kt (1983), PC (1991); s of Lt-Col Curtis Wilson Folliott Scott, OBE, 2/9 Gurkha Rifles, and Katharine, *née* Rashleigh; *m* 8 Aug 1959, Rima Elisa, da of Salvador Ripoll and Blanca Korsi de Ripoll, of Panama City; 2 s (Richard Salvador Folliott b 9 June 1960, Jonathan Ripoll Folliott b 21 Dec 1963), 2 da (Katharine Blanca b 27 April 1962, Mariella Louisa (Mrs Karim Lahham) b 4 July 1967); *Career* called to the Bar Inner Temple 1959, QC 1975, bencher 1981, attorney-gen Duchy of Lancaster 1980–83, chm of the Bar 1982–83, judge of the High Court of Justice (Chancery Div) 1983–91, vice-chllr Co Palatine and Duchy of Lancaster 1987–91, Lord Justice of Appeal 1991–94, head Inquiry into defence related exports to Iraq 1992–96, Vice-Chllr of the Supreme Court 1994–, head of Civil Justice 1995–; Hon LLD Univ of Birmingham 1996; *Style—* The Rt Hon Sir Richard Scott; ✉ Royal Courts of Justice, The Strand, London WC2A 2LL

SCOTT, Robin Hugh; *see:* Scutt, Robin Hugh

SCOTT, His Hon Judge Roger Martin; s of Hermann Albert Scott (d 1965), of Morley, Leeds, and Sarah Margaret, *née* Craven (d 1989); *b* 8 Sept 1944; *Educ* Mill Hill Sch, Univ of St Andrews (LLB, univ hockey team); *m* 10 Sept 1966, Diana Elizabeth, da of John Hayes Clark; 2 s (Martin John b 23 Nov 1967, Andrew Charles b 21 March 1970), 1 da (Katherine Anne b 29 July 1972); *Career* called to the Bar 1968, memb NE Circuit 1968–93, pupillage at 38 Park Square Leeds with H A Richardson, a fndr of new chambers at St Paul's House Park Sq 1981 (head of chambers 1985–91), recorder 1989–93 (asst recorder 1985–89), circuit judge (NE Circuit) 1993–; *Recreations* reading, theatre, walking, golf and watching all sports; *Clubs* Yorkshire CCC; *Style—* His Hon Judge Scott; ✉ Teeside Combined Court Centre, Law Courts, Russell Street, Middlesborough, Cleveland TS1 2AE (☎ 01642 34000, fax 01642 34002)

SCOTT, Simon Angus; s of John Moffat Hewitt Scott, of Edinburgh, and Lora, *née* Rutherford (d 1976); *b* 31 May 1956; *Educ* Fettes, RMA Sandhurst (scholarship), Univ of Sussex (BA), Univ of Washington St Louis Missouri USA; *m* 9 June 1984, da of Norman Starrett (d 1987); 1 s (Thomas Starrett b 18 June 1989); *Career* Boys Athletic League NY 1975; Bell Lawrie MacGregor Stockbrokers 1980–81, ptnr Maclean Dubois (Literary Agents) 1981–84; sr copywriter: Marr Associates (Advertising) 1984–86, Hall Advertising 1986–88; creative dir Faulds Advertising 1988–96, fndr ptnr The Union 1996–; awarded: D&AD Silver 1986, other D&AD awards 1983, 1984, 1985 and 1986, Independent Local Radio Gold award 1987, 5 Gold Clio awards, 10 Gold Rose awards, 12 Silver Rose awards, 26 Scotmedia awards; *Books* Hercules the Bear (1981), The Forth Bridge (1983), Forests of Northern England (1983), Coast of Echoes (1984), Prodigal Gun (1984), Startex Assignment (1984); *Recreations* gardening; *Style—* Simon Scott, Esq; ✉ The Union, 1 St Colme Street, Edinburgh EH3 6AA (☎ 0131 220 8250)

SCOTT, Dr (James) Thomas; s of James Basil Spence Scott (d 1937), of London, and Alice Fawsitt, *née* Taylor (d 1987); *b* 10 Nov 1926; *Educ* Univ Coll Sch, St Mary's Hosp Univ of London (MB BS, MD); *m* 29 Oct 1956, Faith Margaret, da of William Ernest Smith (d 1944), of Fishguard, Pembs; 3 s (Humphrey, Matthew, Richard); *Career* RAMC 1952–54; conslt physician: Postgrad Med Sch 1962–65, Hammersmith Hosp 1962–65, Charing Cross Hosp 1966–; hon physician Kennedy Inst of Rheumatology 1966–91, conslt physician in rheumatology Royal Navy 1970–91; past pres Med Soc of London, memb Fin and Exec Ctee Arthritis and Rheumatism Cncl; FRSM 1960, memb Assoc of Physicians 1964, FRCP 1968 (MRCP 1952); hon memb: Australasian Assoc of Rheumatology 1983, American Coll of Rheumatology 1984; *Books* Copeman's Textbook of the Rheumatic Diseases (ed, 5 edn 1978, 6 edn 1986), Arthritis and Rheumatism - The Facts (1980); *Recreations* fly-fishing, numismatics; *Style—* Dr Thomas Scott; ✉ Winter's Lodge, Huish Champflower, Taunton, Somerset TA4 2BZ (☎ 01984 624632); Charing Cross Hospital, Fulham Palace Rd, London W6 8RF (☎ 0181 846 1234)

SCOTT, Dr Walter Grant; s of Thomas Scott (d 1979), and Marion Urie Roberts; *b* 13 May 1947; *Educ* Eastwood HS, Univ of Edinburgh (BSc), Trinity Hall Cambridge (PhD); *m* 1973, Rosemary Ann Clark, da of Alfred W C Lobban (d 1987), of Bedfordshire; 1 s (Matthew), 2 da (Rachel, Diana); *Career* dir Ivory & Sime Ltd 1972–82, sr ptnr Walter Scott & Partners (portfolio mgmnt) 1982–, chm Walter Scott International 1983–; tstee The Walter Scott Research Fndn 1984–; *Recreations* rowing, running, gardening; *Clubs* Leander, New (Edinburgh), New York Athletic; *Style—* Dr Walter Scott; ✉ Millburn Tower, Gogar, Edinburgh (☎ 0131 339 3777)

SCOTT-BARRETT, Lt-Gen Sir David William; KBE (1976, MBE 1956), MC (1945); s of late Brig Rev H Scott-Barrett, CB, CBE; *b* 16 Dec 1922; *Educ* Westminster Sch; *m* 1, 1948, (Marie) Elise, *née* Morris (d 1985); 3 s; m 2, 31 Oct 1992, Judith, widow of Maj John Waring; *Career* cmmnd Scots Guard 1942, served NW Europe WWII, GOC Eastern Dist 1971–73, GOC Berlin 1973–75, Col Cmdt Scottish Div and GOC Scotland 1976–79, govr Edinburgh Castle 1976–79; former dir Arbuthnot Securities; chm Army Cadet Force Assoc 1981–96, dir Haven Project for Mental Health Provision 1983–84; *Style—* Lt-Gen Sir David Scott-Barrett, KBE, MC; ✉ c/o Cavalry and Guards' Club, 127 Piccadilly, London W1V 0PX

SCOTT-BARRETT, Jonathan; s of John Scott-Barrett (d 1968), and Doreen, *née* Robottom (d 1976); *b* 13 April 1944; *Educ* Prince of Wales Sch Nairobi, Ellesmer Coll Shropshire; *m* 1, 1968 (m dis 1980), Jane, *née* Colchester; 2 s (Marcus b 25 Sept 1970, Dominic b 13 July 1972), 1 da (Miranda b 31 July 1977); m 2, 22 Sept 1983, Malise, *née* Menzies; *Career* Capt 15/19 King's Royal Hussars 1963–68; chartered surveyor Savills 1969–72, ptnr Knight Frank & Rutley (Paris) 1972–76, partner Kapnist International Cap d'Antibes 1976–81, dir Hong Kong Hi Speed Ferries Ltd 1982–86, dir Centaur Publishing Ltd (magazine titles incl Marketing Week, Money Marketing, Design Week, Creative Review, also parent co of Linguaphone) 1986–; non-exec dir Hanson plc 1991–; FRICS 1971; *Recreations* tennis, shooting, gym; *Clubs* Cavalry & Guards', Annabel's; *Style—* Jonathan Scott-Barrett, Esq; ✉ Centaur Communications Ltd, St Giles House, 50 Poland Street, London W1V 4AX (☎ 0171 439 4222, fax 0171 734 2947)

SCOTT-GALL, His Hon Judge; Anthony Robert Gall; s of Sidney Robert Gall (d 1994), and Daphne Margaret, *née* Williamson (d 1990); *b* 30 March 1946; *Educ* Stowe, New Coll Oxford (BA Jurisprudence); *m* 8 Sept 1973, Caroline Anne, da of David Charles Roger Scott; 1 s (Alexander David Robert b 6 Aug 1975), 1 da (Henrietta Charlotte Anne b 16 Dec 1976); *Career* called to the Bar Middle Temple 1971, recorder 1993–96, circuit judge (SE Circuit) 1996–; *Recreations* gardening, travel, music, rugby union, cricket, country pursuits; *Clubs* Richmond RFC, Armadillos Cricket; *Style—* His Hon Judge Scott-Gall; ✉ Lewes Combined Court, High Street, Lewes, East Sussex BN7 1YB

SCOTT-GODDARD, Alasdair Craag; s of Victor Albert Scott-Goddard, of Herts, and Stella Olive Ruby, *née* George; *b* 22 Dec 1967; *Educ* Haileybury (scholar); *Career* Maxwell Pergamon Publishing (interactive design) 1988–90, The Mac Consultancy Company (interactive design) 1990–91; ptnr: Zapfactor 1991–93, AMXdigital 1994–; awards incl: BBC Young Film-Maker of the Year, Microsoft Best Multi-Media Title 1990, Creative Review Creative Futures Award 1990; contrib ed Multi-Media Magazine 1992–, judge Creative Review Awards 1995; memb Interactive Designers Assoc 1993; *Recreations* film, travel, dogs; *Clubs* Groucho; *Style—* Alasdair Scott-Goddard, Esq; ✉ AMXdigital Ltd, 124 Cotton Road, London EC2A 3PS (☎ 0171 613 5300, fax 0171 613 5333, mobile 0956 295862)

SCOTT-HARDEN, Anthony Walter; s of Dr Walter Geoffrey Scott-Harden (d 1984), of Scotby, Carlisle, and Charmian Mary, *née* Connell (d 1993); *b* 4 July 1940; *Educ* St Edwards Oxford, Cumberland Westmorland Farm Sch (DipAgric), Coll of Estate Mgmnt; *m* July 1965, Daphne Elizabeth, da of Maj Laurence Wilfred Arnett (d 1966); 1 s (James b 1969), 1 da (Lucy b 1966); *Career* in property; chm Clark Scott-Harden Ltd (chartered surveyors); FRICS 1963; *Recreations* field sports; *Clubs* Turf, White's, Farmers', Northern Counties; *Style—* Anthony Scott-Harden, Esq; ✉ Newbiggin House, Blanchland, Consett, Co Durham DH8 9UD (☎ 01434 675005, fax 01434 675015)

SCOTT-JOYNT, Rt Rev Michael Charles; *see:* Winchester, Bishop of

SCOTT-MANDERSON, Marcus Charles William; s of Dr William Scott-Manderson, and Pamela, *née* Welch; *b* 10 Feb 1956; *Educ* Harrow, ChCh Oxford (BA, BCL), Dept of Forensic Med Univ of Glasgow, The Hague Acad of Int Law The Netherlands 1980; *Career* called to the Bar Lincoln's Inn 1980; sec Family Law Bar Assoc Conciliation Bd; memb: Br Acad of Forensic Sci, Forensisch Medisch Genootschap The Netherlands; *Recreations* ancient history, archaeology, fencing, travel; *Clubs* Lansdowne; *Style—* Marcus Scott-Manderson, Esq; ✉ 17 Burlington Rd, London SW6 4NP (☎ 0171 731 1476); Park House, The Strand, Ashton-in-Makerfield, nr Wigan, Lancs; 4 Paper Buildings, Temple, London EC4Y 7EX (☎ 0171 583 0816, fax 0171 353 4979)

SCOTT PLUMMER, (Patrick) Joseph; s of Charles Humphrey Scott Plummer (d 1991), of Mainhouse, Kelso, Roxburghshire, and Hon Pamela Lilias, *née* Balfour; *b* 24 Aug 1943; *Educ* Radley, Magdalene Coll Cambridge (MA); *m* 1, 12 March 1970 (m dis 1977), Elizabeth-Anne, da of Col Anthony Way, MC, of Kincairney, Murthly, Perthshire; 1 s (Charles b 18 Aug 1972), 1 da (Annabel b 26 June 1974); m 2, 15 Sept 1977, Mrs Christine Margaret Hermione Roberts, da of the Hon Anthony Gerard Bampfylde (d 1968), of Boyton House, Woodbridge, Suffolk; 1 s (Guy b 13 Aug 1978); *Career* ptnr Cazenove and Co 1974–80, md Martin Currie Ltd 1991– (dir 1981–); dir: Candover Investments plc 1987–, The Scottish Eastern Investment Trust plc 1989–; FCA 1967; *Recreations* foxhunting, tennis; *Clubs* New (Edinburgh), Pratt's, Royal Caledonian Hunt; *Style—* Joseph Scott Plummer, Esq; ✉ Mainhouse, Kelso, Roxburghshire (☎ 01573 223327); 29 Castle Terrace, Edinburgh (☎ 0131 229 0228); Martin Currie Ltd, Saltire Court, 20 Castle Terrace, Edinburgh (☎ 0131 229 5252)

SCOTT-WHITE, Raymond; s of Lawson Scott-White, OBE (d 1967), and Muriel Annie, *née* Ward (d 1990); *b* 22 Aug 1934; *Educ* Whitgift Sch Croydon, Imperial Coll London (BSc, ACGI); *m* 6 July 1957, Patricia Anne, da of Ronald John Elmes (d 1981), of Hayes, Kent; 1 s (David Andrew b 9 Nov 1958, d 11 June 1976), 1 da (Sally Anne b 2 Nov 1959); *Career* fndr Scott-White & Hookins conslt engrs 1963; chm Croydon Round Table 1973; Freeman City of London, former Master Worshipful Co of Fan Makers (memb Ct of Assts); CEng, FIStructE, MICE, MIHT, MConsE; *Recreations* golf; *Clubs* Livery, W Sussex Golf; *Style—* Raymond Scott-White, Esq; ✉ London House, 42 West Street, Carshalton, Surrey SM5 2PU (☎ 0181 773 3131, fax 0181 773 2605)

SCOTT-WILSON, John Beaumont; OBE (1987); s of Dr Hew William Scott-Wilson (d 1972), and Beatrice Mary, *née* Jackson (d 1977); *b* 18 Dec 1927; *Educ* Sutton Valence Sch, Downing Coll Cambridge (MA); *m* 1, 2 June 1951, Elizabeth Madeline (d 1992), da of Capt John Charles Grant-Ives (d 1959); 4 s (Timothy b 1952, Christopher b 1954, Peter b 1956, Rhoderick b 1958); m 2, Oct 1993, Andrea Meryl Holtom; *Career* sci offr MOS 1950–56, engr AV Roe and Co, dir Hawker Siddeley Aviation Manchester 1972–77; div dir British Aerospace: Manchester 1977–84, Weybridge 1984–86, Civil Aircraft 1986–88; tech dir British Aerospace Commercial Aircraft Ltd 1989–91; chm NATO Advsy Gp for Aerospace Res and Devpt 1991–94; visiting prof: Univ of Manchester 1992–96, Cranfield Univ 1996–; chm CAA Airworthiness Requirements Bd 1994–; FRAeS 1977, FEng 1985; *Recreations* gardening; *Style—* John Scott-Wilson, Esq, OBE, FEng; ✉ 9 Cadogan Park, Woodstock, Oxford OX20 1UW (☎ 01993 811455)

SCOUGALL, Capt Alexander Cuthbert (Alex); s of James Scougall (d 1968), of Dunning, Perthshire, and Margaret Baldwin Drury Spence, *née* Cuthbert (d 1969); *b* 8 Aug 1939; *Educ* Auchterarder, RNC Dartmouth, RNEC, Univ of Glasgow (MEng, MLitt); *m* 19 Dec 1964, Gillian (Jill), da of Richard Park (d 1966), of Totnes, Devon; 2 da (Sasha b 1967, Kyla b 1972); *Career* HMDY Rosyth 1978–81, staff of 10 Submarine Sqdn 1981–84, HMS Intrepid 1984–86, flag offr submarines 1986–87; MOD: Bath 1987–89, London 1989–94; ret RN 1995; currently dir Nees Ltd; FIMechE 1979 (MIMechE 1973); *Recreations* riding; *Clubs* Liberal; *Style—* Capt Alex Scougall; ✉ Dennis Down House, Hittisleigh, Nr Exeter, Devon

SCOULLER, (John) Alan; s of Charles James Scouller (d 1974), of Banstead, Surrey, and Mary Helena, *née* Pyne (d 1972); bro of Anthony Scouller, *qv*; *b* 23 Sept 1929; *Educ* John Fisher Sch Purley Surrey; *m* 29 May 1954, Angela Geneste, da of Harry Ambrose (d 1937), of Maidstone, Kent; 2 s (James Paul b 1955, Edward John b 1964), 5 da (Catherine Mary b 1956, Frances Elizabeth b 1958, Sarah Margaret b 1961, Helen Louise b 1966, Joanna Clare b 1968); *Career* Nat Serv 1948, cmmnd 2 Lt Queen's Own Royal West Kent Regt 1949, reg cmmn Lt 1951, 1 Bn Malaya 1953–54, Germany 1954, Capt Instructor Sch of Inf (Signals) 1955–56, 1 Bn Cyprus 1957–58, resigned cmmn 1958; Unilever Ltd: personnel mangr Walls Ice Cream Gloucester 1958–62, asst to trg mangr Rotterdam 1962, personnel mangr Domestos Ltd Newcastle upon Tyne 1962–66, personnel mangr Commercial Plastics & Holpak 1966–69; cmmr Cmmn on Industl Relations 1973–74 (dir of industl rels 1969–73), head industl rels Midland Bank Group 1975–88, visiting prof in industl rels Kingston Univ 1988–95, hon sr fell City Univ Business Sch 1989–95; pt/t memb Employment Appeal Tbnl 1976–; memb Educn Bd RC Diocese of Westminster 1989–, govr Letchworth Garden City Heritage Fndn 1995–; FIPD; *Recreations* music, reading, walking, travel, studying employment law; *Style—* Alan Scouller, Esq; ✉ 40 Aubreys, Letchworth, Herts SG6 3TU (☎ 01462 682781)

SCOULLER, Anthony James; s of Charles James Scouller (d 1974), of Banstead, Surrey, and Mary Helena, *née* Pyne (d 1972); bro of Alan Scouller, *qv*; *b* 13 Sept 1936; *Educ* John Fisher Sch Purley; *m* 16 May 1964, Barbara Joy, da of Edward John Lawrence; 1 s (Matthew Edward John), 1 da (Susanna Barbara); *Career* 2 Lt Queen's Own Royal West Kent Regt, active service Cyprus; Beecham Group Marketing 1960–66; J Walter Thompson Inc: London office 1966–69, NY 1969–72, dept mangr Caracas 1972–74, dir London 1975–83; mktg dir: International Distillers and Vinters UK 1983–89, Wyvern International IDV 1989–; dir of wine brands IDV Europe Ltd 1991–, mktg dir IDV UK Ltd 1992–; *Recreations* bridge, horse racing; *Clubs* RAC, Marketing Soc; *Style—* Anthony Scouller, Esq; ✉ IDV UK Ltd, Templefields House, River Way, Harlow, Essex CM20 2EA (☎ 01279 633624)

SCOVELL, Brian Souter; s of Percy Henry John Scovell (d 1991), of IOW, and Maude Janet Scovell (d 1978); *b* 21 Nov 1935; *Educ* Ventnor Coll IOW, Elgin Acad Morayshire, Nat Cncl for the Trg of Journalists (cert, dip); *m* 1 Oct 1965, Audrey Esther, da of Eric William O'Sullivan; 1 s (Gavin Richard Souter b 25 Oct 1969), 1 da (Louise Jayne b 8 Oct 1967); *Career* journalist; trainee reporter Isle of Wight Guardian 1952–57, gen reporter Wolverhampton Express and Star 1957–58; sports reporter: Norwich Evening News and Eastern Daily Press 1958, Press Assoc 1959–60; cricket corr and dep football corr Daily Sketch 1960–71, cricket and football corr Daily Mail 1971–; maj events covered incl: football World Cups 1966, 1982, 1986 and 1990, cricket World Cups 1975, 1979 and 1983, over 200 test matches and 300 int football matches; chm: Football Writers Assoc 1982, Cricket Writers Club 1985–89; Cricket Writer of the Year Wombwell Cricket Lovers Soc 1963, highly recommended in sports news section Sports Cncl Writing Awards 1991; FA soccer coach 1966, MCC cricket coach 1977; *Books* Everything That's Cricket (1963), Whose Side Are You On Ref? (1973), The Big Match (1976), The Diary of a Season (1979), Not Out (1979), Trevor Brooking (1981), Ken Barrington - A Tribute (1982), Glory, Glory (1984), Revelations of a Soccer Manager (1985), The Big Match Soccer Anthology (1987), And the Next Voice You Will Hear (1987), Gary Sobers - Twenty Years at the Top (1988), Handbook of Soccer (1988), Beating the Field - Brian Lara's Story (1995), Dickie: A Tribute to Umpire Dickie Bird (1996); *Recreations* watching and playing cricket, watching and writing on football, going on cricket tours abroad, reading, theatre, walking, cinema; *Clubs* Woodpeckers CC; *Style—* Brian Scovell, Esq; ✉ Daily Mail, Northcliffe House, 2 Derry St, London W8 5TT (☎ 0171 938 6232)

SCOVELL, Edith Joy; da of Frederick George Scovell (d 1951), and Edith Ann, *née* Holl (d 1964); *b* 9 April 1907; *Educ* Casterton Sch, Somerville Coll Oxford (BA); *m* 1937, Charles Sutherland Elton (d 1991); 1 da (Catherine Ingrid b 1940), 1 s (Robert Andrew b 1943); *Career* writer (as E J Scovell); winner Cholmondeley Award 1989, Cheltenham Prize 1991; FRSL 1995; *Books* Shadows of Chrysanthemums (1944), The Midsummer Meadow (1946), The River Steamer (1957), The Space Between (1982), Listening to Collared Doves (1986), Collected Poems (1988), Selected Poems (1991); *Style—* Ms E J Scovell, FRSL; ✉ 51 Diamond Court, 153 Banbury Road, Oxford OX2 7AA (☎ 01865 557644)

SCOWEN, Prof Sir Eric Frank; kt (1973); s of Frank Edward Scowen; *b* 1910; *Educ* City of London Sch, St Bartholomew's Hosp Med Coll Univ of London and KCL (MA, MD, DSc); *Career* physician St Bartholomew's Hosp 1946–75, dir Med Professorial Unit 1955–75, prof of med Univ of London 1961–75 (emeritus prof of med 1975), chm British Pharmacopoeia Cmmn 1963–69; chm: Cncl of Imperial Cancer Research Fund 1967–82 (vice-pres 1982), Ctee on Safety of Medicines 1970–81, Ctee on Review of Medicines 1975–78, Poisons Bd 1976–83, Cncl Sch of Pharmacy Univ of London 1979–88, Clinical Trials Ethical Ctee Royal Coll of Gen Practitioners 1981–88; FRCP, FRCS, FRCPE, FRCPath, FRCGP 1988; Hon LLD Univ of Nottingham, Hon Fell Royal Pharmaceutical Soc, Hon Fell Sch of Pharmacy 1986; *Clubs* Athenaeum; *Style—* Prof Sir Eric Scowen; ✉ Flat 77, 6/9 Charterhouse Sq, London EC1M 6EX (☎ 0171 251 3212)

SCRAFTON, HE Douglas (Doug); *b* 14 July 1949; *m* 1975, Carolyn Patricia, *née* Collison; 1 s (b 1976), 1 da (b 1977); *Career* HM Dip Serv: Office Servs/Supply Dept FCO 1967–69, Rhodesia Dept FCO 1969–70, UK Delgn (later UK Perm Rep) to the EC Brussels (Registry Overseas) 1970–73, archivist Kampala 1973–75, third sec (Aid/Commercial/Info) Mbabane 1975–77, Migration and Visa Dept FCO 1977–79, full time language trg FCO 1979–80, third sec later second sec (Chancery) Jedda 1980–82, second sec (Commercial) Riyadh 1982–84, second sec Cairo 1984–85, Arms Control/Disarmament Dept FCO 1985–87, on secondment to Cabinet Office 1987–89, first sec and head of Chancery Ottawa 1989–92, asst Environment Sci and Energy Dept FCO 1993–95, ambass Republic of Yemen 1995–; *Style—* HE Mr Doug Scrafton; ✉ c/o Foreign and Commonwealth Office (Sana'a), King Charles Street, London SW1A 2AH

SCREECH, Rev Prof Michael Andrew; s of Richard John Screech, MM (d 1986), of Pomphlet, Plymstock, Plymouth, and Nellie Ernestine, *née* Maunder (d 1977); *b* 2 May 1926; *Educ* Sutton HS Plymouth, UCL (BA); *m* 4 April 1956, (Ursula) Anne Grace, da of John William Reeve (d 1960), of Byfleet; 3 s (Matthew Erasmus John b 30 Jan 1960, Timothy Benjamin Mark b 28 Sept 1961, Toby Daniel Luke b 3 Oct 1963); *Career* other rank Intelligence Corps (mainly Far East) 1944–48; successively asst lectr, lectr then sr lectr Univ of Birmingham 1951–61, reader then prof of French UCL 1961–71, Fielden prof of French language and lit UCL 1971–84, Johnson prof Inst for Res in the Humanities Madison Wisconsin 1978, Campion lectr Regina Saskatchewan 1983, Dorothy Ford Wiley prof of Renaissance Culture N Carolina 1986, Zaharoff lectr Oxford 1988; visiting prof: Collège de France 1989, La Sorbonne 1990; sr res fell All Souls Coll Oxford 1984–93, emeritus fell All Souls and extraordinary fell Wolfson Coll Oxford 1993–, occasional lectr Oxford Ministry Course 1994–; ordained deacon 1993, priest 1994; memb comité: d' Humanisme et Renaissance 1958–, des Textes Littéraires Français 1958–, du patronage des Textes Classiques de la Renaissance 1986–; tstee Lambeth Palace Library 1994–; formerly memb Whitchurch Parish Cncl, formerly chm of Mangrs Whitchurch Primary Sch Whitchurch St Mary's PCC; Médaille de la Ville de Tours 1984; fell UCL 1982; DLitt: Birmingham 1960, London 1982, Oxford 1990; Hon DLitt Exeter 1993; FBA 1981, FRSL 1989; Chevalier dans l'Ordre National du Mérite France 1983, Chevalier dans la Légion d'Honneur 1992; *Books* The Rabelaisian Marriage (1958), L'Evangélisme de Rabelais (1959), Marot Evangélique (1967); Rabelais edns: Tiers Livre (1964), Gargantua (1970), Prognostication (1975); Regrets and Antiquitez de Rome (by Du Bellay, ed 1964), Rabelais (1979), Erasmus - Ecstasy and the Praise of Folly (1980), Montaigne and Melancholy (1983), Apology for Raymond Sebond (by Montaigne, trans 1987), A New Rabelais Bibliography (1988), Montaigne - The Complete Essays (1991), Some Renaissance Studies (1992), Clément Marot, a Renaissance poet discovers the Gospel (1993), Erasmus' Annotations on the New Testament (3 vols with Anne Reeve, 1986, 1990 and 1993), Warden Mocket of All Souls College: Doctrina et politia Ecclesiae anglicanae (ed, 1995); *Recreations* walking; *Clubs* Athenaeum; *Style*— The Rev Prof M A Screech, FBA, FRSL; ✉ 5 Swanston Field, Whitchurch-on-Thames, Reading RG8 7HP; All Souls College, Oxford OX1 4AL; Wolfson Coll, Oxford OX2 6UD

SCRIMGEOUR, Alastair James; s of Robin Neville Carron Scrimgeour, of Wiltshire, and Deidre Elizabeth Blundell, *née* Brown; *b* 17 April 1956; *Educ* Eton, Univ of Bristol (BSc Econ); *Career* chartered accountant; ptnr Binder Hamlyn London 1986– (joined 1978); FCA; *Recreations* hunting, point to pointing, tennis; *Clubs* RAC; *Style*— Alastair Scrimgeour, Esq; ✉ The Old School House, Bury, Dulverton, Somerset TA22 9NE (☎ 01398 323715); Binder Hamlyn, 20 Old Bailey, London EC4M 7BH (☎ 0171 489 6170, fax 0171 489 6291, car 0860 283411)

SCRIMGEOUR, Angus Muir Edington; s of Dr David Muir Scrimgeour (d 1977), and May Burton Clair, *née* Edington (d 1988); *b* 19 Feb 1945; *Educ* Westminster, New Coll Oxford (MA), UCL (MSc); *m* 21 Dec 1968, Clare Christian Gauvain, da of Dr Ronald Ormiston Murray, MBE; 1 s (Alexander b 1971); *Career* vice pres Citibank NA 1974–84, chief exec Edington plc merchant bank 1984–90, dep chm Henry Cooke Group 1990–91 (jt chief exec 1988–90), chief exec Bankside Underwriting Agencies Ltd 1992–95; Corporation of Lloyds: dir CSU 1993–96, head of mkt mgmnt 1995–96; conslt to World Bank Washington DC 1996–; *Recreations* farming, design, chess, music; *Clubs* IOD, Berkshire Golf, Manchester Racquet; *Style*— Angus Scrimgeour, Esq; ✉ 46 Chepstow Place, London W2 4TA (☎ 0171 229 1979); Paddock House Farm, Alstonefield, Nr Ashbourne, Derbyshire DE6 2FT

SCRIMGEOUR, Dr John Beocher; s of William Stevenson Scrimgeour (d 1980), of Kelso, Scotland, and Ellen Fernie, *née* Beocher (d 1990); *b* 22 Jan 1939; *Educ* Hawick HS, Univ of Edinburgh Med Sch (MB ChB); *m* 22 Sept 1962, (Margaret) Joyce McDougall, da of Thomas Morrin, of Edinburgh; 1 s (Michael b 1966), 1 da (Jill b 1965); *Career* GP Edinburgh 1963–65, hon sr lectr Dept of Obstetrics and Gynaecology Univ of Edinburgh and conslt in obstetrics and gynaecology Western Gen Hosp Edinburgh 1973–, med dir Western Gen Hosps Tst Edinburgh 1993–; memb The Gynaecological Visiting Soc of GB and Ireland; FRCOG 1982, FRCS 1987, FRCPEd 1993; *Books* Towards the Prevention of Foetal Malformation (1978); *Recreations* golf, tennis and gardening; *Style*— Dr John Scrimgeour; ✉ 4 Kinellan Rd, Edinburgh EH12 6ES (☎ 0131 337 6027); Department of Obstetrics and Gynaecology, Western General Hospital, Crewe Rd, Edinburgh EH4 2XU (☎ 0131 537 1000, fax 0131 537 1002)

SCRIVEN, Rt Rev Henry William; *see:* Europe, Suffragan Bishop in

SCRIVEN, Pamela; QC (1992); da of Maurice Scriven (d 1979), and Evelyn Lavinia, *née* Stickney; *b* 5 April 1948; *Educ* UCL (LLB); *m*; 2 c; *Career* called to the Inner Temple Bar 1970, bencher 1995; recorder of the Crown Ct 1996– (asst recorder 1992–96); memb: Ctee Family Law Bar Assoc 1991–, Bar Cncl Race Relations Ctee 1991–; *Recreations* theatre and travel; *Style*— Pamela Scriven, QC; ✉ 1 King's Bench Walk, 2nd Floor, Temple, London EC4Y 7DB

SCRIVEN, Peter John Keith; s of Sydney Verdun Scriven, of Dudley, W Midlands, and Mona Patricia, *née* Gaston (d 1974); *b* 25 July 1956; *Educ* Alexandra GS Midlands, UCW Aberystwyth (BScEcon), Leicester Poly (DMS); *m*; 2 s (Thomas Edward b Feb 1990, Matthew Alexander b Nov 1994); *Career* UK mktg mangr Barclays Bank 1977–83, investmt mktg mangr Charterhouse Merchant Bank 1983–84, strategic planning mangr Citicorp UK 1984–86, Euro business planning mangr Chase Manhattan Bank 1986–87, gp head of business devpt National and Provincial Building Society 1987–90, sr vice pres and gen mangr Middle East Visa International Service Association 1990–; memb Nat Soc for Cancer Relief, MInstM; *Recreations* flying, skiing, foreign travel, charity work; *Clubs* MCIM, BMAA; *Style*— Peter Scriven, Esq; ✉ PO Box 25,500, Dubai, United Arab Emirates

SCRIVENER, Ronald Stratford; CMG (1965); s of Sir Patrick Stratford Scrivener, KCMG (d 1966), of Gt Bedwyn, Wiltshire, and Margaret Morris, *née* Dorling (d 1972); *b* 29 Dec 1919; *Educ* Westminster, St Catharine's Coll Cambridge; *m* 1, 1947 (m dis 1952), Elizabeth Drake-Brockman; m 2, 1962, Mary Alice Olga Sofia Jane, da of Robert Charlton Lane, and formerly w of Christopher Hohler; 2 step s, 2 step da; *Career* ambass to: Panama 1969–70, Czechoslovakia 1971–74; asst under-sec of State FCO 1974–76; Liveryman Worshipful Co of Scriveners; *Recreations* travel, fishing; *Clubs* White's, Beefsteak, Pratts; *Style*— Ronald Scrivener, Esq, CMG; ✉ 38 Lysia St, London SW6 6NG

SCRIVENOR, Sir Thomas Vaisey; kt (1960), CMG (1956); eld s of John Brooke Scrivenor, ISO (d 1950), of Horncastle, Lincs, and Violet, *née* Vaisey; *b* 28 Aug 1908; *Educ* King's Sch Canterbury, Oriel Coll Oxford (MA); *m* 4 June 1934, Mary Elizabeth, da of late Albert Augustine Neatby, of Court House, Chiselborough, Somerset; 1 s, 3 da; *Career* entered Colonial Office 1930, served in Tanganyika, Palestine and Malta; civil service cmmr Nigeria 1948–53, dep high cmmr Basutoland, Bechuanaland and Swaziland 1953–60; sec Cwlth Agric Bureaux 1961–73; *Style*— Sir Thomas Scrivenor, CMG; ✉ The Old Prebendal House, Shipton-under-Wychwood, Oxfordshire OX7 6BQ

SCROGGS, Cedric Annesley; s of Richard Brian Harry Scroggs, of Crawley, nr Winchester, Hants, and Vera Wesley, *née* Coombs (d 1960); *b* 2 Jan 1941; *Educ* Reading Sch, St John's Coll Oxford (Sir Thomas White scholar, BA); *m* 1964, Patricia Mary Sutherland Ogg, da of late George Sutherland Ogg; 2 s (Duncan John b 1965, James Richard Sutherland b 1971), 1 da (Joanna Mary b 1967); *Career* mktg exec: AEI-Hotpoint Ltd 1962–67, General Foods Ltd 1967–73; mktg dir: Cadbury Ltd 1974–76 (joined 1973), Leyland Cars 1976–78; Fisons plc: md Scientific Equipment Div 1979–81, chm Scientific Equipment Div and main bd dir 1981–92, gp chief exec 1992–93; non-exec dir: Caradon plc 1988–89, Y J Lovell (Holdings) plc 1990; non-exec memb: Milk Mktg Bd 1991, Hillingdon Hosp NHS Tst 1991–92, CBI Nat Mfrg Cncl 1992; visiting fell Nuffield Coll Oxford 1993; pres BEAMA 1991–92; dep chm GENUS Ltd 1995–; non-exec memb Oxfordshire Mental Healthcare NHS Tst 1995–; *Recreations* boating, golf, diving; *Clubs* RAC, Leander, Goring and Streatley Golf; *Style*— Cedric Scroggs, Esq; ✉ The Priory, Brightwell Cum Sotwell, Wallingford, Oxon OX10 0RH (☎ 01491 836188, fax 01491 824437)

SCROPE, Philip Adrian; s of Ralph Henry Scrope (d 1981), and Lady Beatrice Scrope, *née* Savile (d 1973); *b* 4 Jan 1943; *Educ* Ampleforth, RAC Cirencester; *m* 2 April 1975, Penelope Anne, da of Maj Eric Williams, House of Lynturk, Alford, Aberdeenshire; 1 s (Richard b 20 Aug 1977), 1 da (Rosalind b 9 June 1979); *Career* ptnr Smiths Gore Chartered Surveyors and Land Agents; *Style*— Philip Scrope, Esq; ✉ Aydon House, nr Corbridge, Northumberland (☎ 01434 63 2096)

SCROPE, Simon Egerton; s of Richard Ladislas Scrope (d 1990), of Danby House, Middleham, N Yorks, and Lady Jane Egerton (d 1978), da of 4 Earl of Ellesmere; *b* 23 Dec 1934; *Educ* Ampleforth, Trinity Coll Cambridge; *m* 23 July 1970, (Jennifer) Jane, da of Sir Kenneth Wade Parkinson, DL (d 1981), of Aketon Close, Follifoot, Harrogate, N Yorks; 1 s (Simon Henry Richard b 3 Sept 1974), 1 da (Emily Katherine b 24 May 1972); *Career* Nat Serv 2 Lt Coldstream Guards 1953; insurance broker, memb Lloyd's 1956; chm Richards Longstaff Group (now RL Insurance Ltd) 1974–; dir: Gibbs Hartley Cooper Ltd (now HSBC Gibbs) 1993–, R F Kershaw Ltd 1993–; farmer and landowner; memb York Race Ctee; dir: Pontefract Park Racecourse Co Ltd, Hosp of St John and St Elizabeth; *Recreations* shooting, fishing, gardening, racing; *Clubs* Brooks's; *Style*— Simon Scrope, Esq; ✉ Danby on Yore, Leyburn, N Yorks DL8 4PX (☎ 01969 623297); 6 Blomfield Rd, London W9 1AH (☎ 0171 289 2457); HSBC Gibbs, Bishops Court, 27–33 Artillery Lane, London E1 7LP (☎ 0171 247 5433, fax 0171 256 8296)

SCRUTON, Prof Roger Vernon; s of John Scruton, of High Wycombe, Bucks, and Beryl Clarys, *née* Haines (d 1967); *b* 27 Feb 1944; *Educ* Royal GS High Wycombe, Jesus Coll Cambridge (BA, MA, PhD); *m* 1, 1975 (m dis 1979), (Marie Genevieve) Danielle, da of Robert Laffitte, of Orthez, France; m 2, 1996, Sophie Jeffreys, da of late 2 Baron Jeffreys; *Career* called to the Bar Inner Temple 1974, fell Peterhouse Cambridge 1969–71, prof of aesthetics Dept of Philosophy Birkbeck Coll London (formerly lectr and reader), Univ Profs Prog Boston Univ 1992–94; ed Salisbury Review; *Books* Art and Imagination (1974), The Aesthetics of Architecture (1979), The Meaning of Conservatism (1980), Fortnight's Anger (1981), A Dictionary of Political Thought (1983), Sexual Desire (1986), Thinkers of the New Left (1986), A Land Held Hostage (1987), The Philosopher on Dover Beach (1990), Francesca (1991), Xanthippic Dialogues (1993), Modern Philosophy: An Introduction and Survey (1994), Animal Rights and Wrongs (1996), An Intelligent Person's Guide to Philosophy (1996); *Recreations* music, hunting; *Style*— Prof Roger Scruton; ✉ Sunday Hill Farm, Brinkworth, Wilts SN15 5AS

SCRYMGEOUR, Lord; Henry David; s and h of 12 Earl of Dundee, *qv*; *b* 20 June 1982; *Style*— Lord Scrymgeour

SCULLARD, (Rodney) Gordon Boyton; s of George Temple Boyton Scullard (d 1970), and Nellie, *née* Richards (d 1971); *b* 31 Jan 1934; *Educ* St Julians Sch, Ackhursts Sch, Cunninghams Sch; *m* 16 June 1956, Mildred Boyton, da of William Chadwick, of Ruskin Rd, Swalwell, Newcastle upon Tyne; 1 s (Howard Mark Boyton b 25 April 1962), 1 da (Helen Boyton b 25 Nov 1958); *Career* md Rodney Boyton Advertising Ltd 1971, chief exec Ross Woodroff Robertson & Scott Ltd 1981; chm and md: Rex Stewart (Newcastle) Ltd 1984, Alliance International (Newcastle) Ltd 1990–; sr conslt Milgor Partnership Ltd, dir Northern Conservative Club Buildings Ltd; MIPA, MCIM; *Recreations* walking, gardening; *Clubs* Northern Constitutional (chm); *Style*— R G B Scullard, Esq; ✉ 25 Cornmoor Rd, Whickam, Newcastle upon Tyne NE16 4PU (☎ 0191 488 1595); Milgor Partnership Ltd, 28 Front Street, Whickham, Newcastle upon Tyne NE16 4DT (☎ 0191 488 3180, fax 0191 488 3178)

SCULLY, (Marie Elizabeth) Ann; OBE (1995); da of Charles Francis Lyons, and Mary Elizabeth, *née* Godfrey; *b* 21 Nov 1943; *Educ* Notre Dame HS Sheffield, Lanchester Coll Coventry, Univ of London; *m* 1965 (sep 1990), Michael Scully; 2 s (Nicholas b 15 Sept 1972, Peter b 9 Jan 1983), 1 da (Clare b 16 April 1967); *Career* ptnr Chester based business 1980–89; parish cncllr 1975–87, sch govr 1977–94; memb: Nat Assoc of Citizens' Advice Bureaux Merseyside Area Ctee, Mgmnt Ctee Citizens' Advice Bureau Chester, European Coal and Steel Community Consultative Ctee Luxembourg 1990–, BSI Consumer Policy Ctee 1992–94, Bd Investment Mgmnt Regulatory Orgn (IMRO) 1993–; non-exec dir Mid Cheshire Hosp (NHS) Tst 1994–; chm Domestic Coal Consumers Cncl London 1987–95, vice chm Nat Consumer Cncl London 1990–; memb: Energy Advsy Panel 1993–, Cncl of the Banking Ombudsman 1995–, Code of Banking Practice Review Ctee 1996–; cmmr Health & Safety Cmmn 1995–; memb Chester Business Club; *Style*— Mrs Ann Scully, OBE; ✉ Hockenhull House, Hockenhull Lane, Tarvin, Chester CH3 8LB

SCULLY, Prof Crispian; s of Patrick Scully and Rosaleen, *née* Richardson; *b* 24 May 1945; *Educ* Univ of London (BDS, BSc, MB BS, PhD), Univ of Bristol (MD, MDS); *m* 5 Oct 1977, Zoë Boucoumani; 1 da (Frances b 31 Jan 1982); *Career* lectr: Univ of London (oral immunology) 1977–79, Univ of Glasgow (oral medicine and pathology) 1979–81; sr lectr Univ of Glasgow (oral medicine and pathology) 1981–82, prof of oral medicine, surgery and pathology Univ of Bristol 1982–94, head of Sch Univ of Bristol Dental Sch 1986–90, dean and clinical dir Eastman Dental Inst London 1994–; past chm Central Examining Bd for Dental Hygienists; past pres British Soc for Oral Med; past memb Central Research and Devpt Ctee Dept of Health; *Books* incl: Medical Problems in Dentistry (with R A Cawson, 3 edn 1993), Multiple Choice Questions in Clinical Dentistry (with R A Cawson, 1985), Hospital Dental Surgeon's Guide (1985), Slide Interpretation in Oral Diseases and the Oral Manifestations of Systemic Disease (with J P Shepherd, 1986), Dental Surgery Assistant's Handbook (jtly, 2 edn 1993), Colour Aids in Oral Medicine (with R A Cawson, 2 edn 1993), Dental Patient Care (1989), Atlas of Stomatology (with S Flint, 1989), Occupational Hazards to Dental Staff (jtly, 1990), Radiographic Interpretation in Oral Disease (with S Porter, 1991), Clinical Virology in Oral Medicine and Dentistry (with L Samaranayake, 1992), Colour Aids in Medicine and Surgery (with S R Porter, M Gleeson and P Welsby, 1993), Colour Atlas of Oral Diseases in Childhood and Adolescence (with R Welbury, 1993), Colour Atlas of Oral Pathology (with J W Eveson, 1995), Oral Health Care for those with HIV Infection and Other Special Needs (with S Porter, 1995), Innovations and Development in Non-invasive Orofacial Health Care (with S Porter, 1996), Oral Diseases (with S Flint and S Porter, 1996); *Recreations* swimming, hill walking, skiing, travelling, music, windsurfing; *Style*— Prof Crispian Scully; ✉ Eastman Dental Institute, 256 Gray's Inn Road, London WC1X 8LD (☎ 0171 915 1038, fax 0171 915 1039)

SCULLY, Sean; *b* 1945, Dublin; *Educ* Croydon Coll of Art, Univ of Newcastle, Harvard Univ; *Career* artist; lectr: Chelsea Sch of Art and Goldsmiths' Sch of Art 1973–75, Princeton Univ 1977–83; recipient: Guggenheim fellowship 1983, Artist's fellowship (Nat Endowment for the Arts) 1984; subject of numerous articles and reviews; *Solo Exhibitions* incl: Rowan Gallery London 1973, 1975, 1977, 1979 and 1981, Tortue Gallery Santa Monica Calif 1975 and 1976, Duffy-Gibbs Gallery NY 1977, Nadin Gallery NY 1979, Susan Caldwell Gallery NY 1980, Museum fur (Sub-) Kultur Berlin 1981, Sean

Scully: Paintings 1971–81 (Ikon Gallery Birmingham and touring) 1981, David McKee Gallery NY 1983, 1985 and 1986, Gallery S65 Aaslt Belgium 1984, Drawings (Barbara Krakow Gallery Boston Mass) 1985, Monotypes (Pamela Auchincloss Gallery Santa Barbara Calif, David McKee Gallery NY, Douglas Flanders Contemporary Art Minneapolis) 1987, Galerie Schmele Düsseldorf 1987, Art Inst of Chicago 1987, Fuji TV Gallery Tokyo 1988 and 1994, David McKee Gallery NY 1989 and 1990, Whitechapel Art Gallery London and tour 1989, Pastel Drawings (Grob Gallery London) 1989–90, Karsten Greve Gallery Cologne 1990, Galerie de France Paris 1990, Monotypes (Pamela Auchincloss Gallery NY) 1990, Sean Scully - Paintings and Works on Paper 1982–88 (Whitechapel Gallery London, Neubachhaus Munich and Palacio de Velázquez Madrid 1989, Jamileh Weber Galerie Zurich and McKee Gallery NY 1991), Waddington Galleries London 1992 and 1995, The Catherine Paintings (Modern Museum of Fort Worth 1993, Palais des Beaux-Arts Charleroi Belgium and Kunsthalle Bielefeld 1995, Galerie Nationale de Jeu de Paume Paris 1996), Paintings, Works on Paper (Galerie Bernd Kluser Munich) 1993, Galleria Gian Ferrari Arte Contemporanea Milano Italy 1994, Galeria El Diario Vasco San Sebastian Spain 1995, Galerie de l'Ancien Coll Chatellerault France 1995, Bernd Kluser Galerie Munchen Germany 1995, Sean Scully: Twenty Years (Hirshhorn Museum and Sculpture Garden Washington DC, High Museum of Art Atlanta Georgia, La Caixa des Pensiones Barcelona, Museum of Modern Art Dublin and Schirn Kunsthalle Frankfurt) 1995–96, Drawing Exhibition (Graphische Sammlung Munchen and Museum Folkwang Essen) 1996; *Group Exhibitions* incl: John Moores Liverpool Exhibition 8 (prizewinner) 1972, La Peinture Anglaise Aujourd'hui (Museum of Modern Art Paris) 1973, British Painting (Hayward Gallery London) 1974, Certain Traditions (travelling exhibition Canada) 1978, Aspects of All-Over (Harm Boukaert Gallery NY) 1982, Part 1: Twelve Abstract Painters (Siegel Contemporary Art NY) 1984, Art on Paper (Weatherspoon Art Gallery Greensboro N Carolina) 1985, Structure/Abstraction (Hill Gallery Birmingham Mississippi) 1986, Harvey Quaytman & Sean Scully (Helsinki Festival Island) 1987, Logical Foundations (Pfizer Inc NY) 1987–88, Drawings and Related Prints (Castelli Graphics NY) 1989, Drawing: Paul Beus, Paul Rotterdam, Sean Scully (Arnold Herstand & Co NY) 1990, Sean Scully/Donald Sultan: Abstraction/Representation (Stanford Art Gallery Stanford Univ) 1990, Artist in the Abstract (Univ of N Carolina at Greensboro) 1990, La Metafisica della luce (NYC) 1991, Four Series of Paintings (John Berggruen Gallery San Francisco) 1992, workshop (Harvard Univ) 1992, Geteilte Bilder (Museum Folkwang Essen) 1992, Behind Bars, Thread Waxing Space (NYC) 1992, Color Block Prints of the 20th Century (Associated American Artists NYC) 1992, Turner Prize Exhibition (Tate) 1993, Partners (Annely Juda Fine Art London) 1993, British Abstract Art (Flowers East Gallery London) 1994, Seven from the Seventies (Knoedler Gallery NYC) 1995; *Collections* work in numerous public collections worlwide incl: Carnegie Museum of Art Pittsburgh, Museum of Modern Art NY, Arts Cncl of GB, British Cncl, Tate Gallery, V&A, Aust Nat Gallery Canberra; *Style*— Sean Scully; ✉ c/o The Waddington Galleries, 11 Cork Street, London W1X 1PD

SCUPHAM, John Peter; s of John Scupham, OBE (d 1990), of Thorpe St Andrew, Norwich, Norfolk, and Dorothy Lacey, *née* Clark (d 1987); *b* 24 Feb 1933; *Educ* Perse Sch Cambridge, St George's Harpenden, Emmanuel Coll Cambridge (BA); *m* 10 Aug 1957, Carola Nance, da of Hermann Justus Braunholtz, CBE (d 1963); 3 s (Christopher, Giles, Roger), 1 da (Kate); *Career* Nat Serv 1952–54; head of English St Christopher Sch Letchworth 1961–80, fndr The Mandeville Press 1974–; Cholmondeley Award Society of Authors Awards 1996; FRSL; *Books* Prehistories (1975), The Hinterland (1977), Summer Palaces (1980), Winter Quarters (1983), Out Late (1986), The Air Show (1988), Watching the Perseids (1990), Selected Poems (1990), The Ark (1994); *Recreations* book-collecting; *Style*— Peter Scupham, Esq, FRSL; ✉ Old Hall, Norwich Road, South Burlingham, Norwich NR13 4EY

SCURFIELD, Hugh Hedley; s of William Russell Scurfield (d 1981), of Worcestershire, and Elizabeth, *née* Hedley; *b* 9 Dec 1935; *Educ* King's Sch Worcester, Hertford Coll Oxford (MA); *m* 1, 11 July 1959, Ann Beverley; 1 s (Bryan b 1960), 3 da (Jane b 1962, Mary b 1964, Clare b 1967); m 2, 8 Dec 1978, Gillian Myfanwy (Jill), da of Rt Rev Mervyn Charles-Edwards, Bishop of Worcester (d 1983); 1 step s (Timothy b 1966), 3 step da (Anne b 1955, Emma b 1968, Suki b 1973); *Career* gen mangr actuary and dir Norwich Union Insurance Group, ret 1992; dir: Royal Shrewsbury Hosps NHS Tst 1994–, Halifax Life 1994–, Ecclesiastical Insurance Group 1994–, Foundation Health 1994–; chm Shropshire and Mid-Wales Hospice 1993–; FIA (pres 1990–92); rowing: winner at Henley Royal Regatta, rowed for GB and a national selector; *Recreations* large family, home, walking; *Style*— Hugh Scurfield, Esq; ✉ Earnstrey Hill House, Abdon, Craven Arms, Shropshire SY7 9HU (☎ 01746 712579, fax 01746 712631)

SCURLOCK, Prof Ralph Geoffrey; s of Walter Howard Scurlock (d 1992), of Romsey, and Linda May, *née* James (d 1993); *b* 21 Aug 1931; *Educ* Bishop Wordsworth Sch Salisbury, St John's Coll Oxford (MA, DPhil); *m* 7 Aug 1956, Maureen Mary, da of Edwin Leonard Oliver, MM (d 1933); 4 s (Jonathan b 1959, Robin b 1961, Timothy b 1964, Alexander b 1966); *Career* Univ of Southampton: lectr in physics 1959–66, sr lectr 1966–68, reader 1968–85, dir Inst of Cryogenics 1979–, BOC prof of cryogenic engrg 1985–96; series ed OUP 1980–96, series ed Elsevier 1996–; chm Br Cryogenics Cncl 1979–82 and 1991–94, vice chm Int Cryogenic Engrg Ctee 1987–90; FIOP 1971, FIMechE 1982, CEng 1982, FRSA 1989; *Books* Low Temperature Behaviour of Solids (1966), History and Origins of Cryogenics (1992); many other pubns on cryogenics and cryogenic engrg; *Style*— Prof Ralph Scurlock; ✉ 22 Brookvale Rd, Highfield, Southampton SO17 1QP; Institute of Cryogenics, University of Southampton (☎ 01703 554665/592046, fax 01703 593053, telex 47661)

SCURR, Dr Cyril Frederick; CBE (1979), LVO (1952); s of Cyril Albert Scurr (d 1961), of Barnet, and Mabel Rose, *née* Magrath; *b* 14 July 1920; *Educ* Kings Coll London, Westminster Hosp (MRCS, LRCP, MB BS); *m* 23 Aug 1947, Isabel Jean, da of Leonard Spiller (d 1973); 3 s (Martin John b 1950, David Antony b 1955, Andrew James b 1962), 1 da (Judith Ann b 1948); *Career* Maj (specialist anaesthetist) RAMC, served N Africa, Italy, Greece 1942–47; conslt anaesthetist: Westminster Hosp 1949–85, Hosp of St John & St Elizabeth 1950–95 (emeritus 1995); dean Faculty of Anaesthetists 1970–73, pres Assoc of Anaesthetists 1973–76, memb Health Servs Bd 1976–79, Frederick Hewitt lectr RCS 1971; Dudley Buxton Prize 1977, Faculty Gold Medal RCS 1983, John Snow Medal 1984, Magill Centenary Oration 1988; Hon FFARCSI 1977, FFARCS 1953, FRCS 1974, FRCA 1992; *Books* Scientific Foundations of Anaesthesia, Drugs in Anaesthesia; *Recreations* photography, gardening; *Style*— Dr Cyril Scurr, CBE, LVO; ✉ 16 Grange Ave, Totteridge Common, London N20 8AD (☎ 0181 445 7188)

SCURR, John Henry; s of Henry Scurr (d 1981), of Slough, and Joyce, *née* Standerwick; *b* 25 March 1947; *Educ* Langley GS, Middx Hosp Med Sch Univ of London (BSc, MB BS); *m* 1, 16 July 1969 (m dis 1986), Gillian Margaret Mason; m 2, 5 April 1986, Nicola Mary Alexandra, da of Ivor S Vincent (d 1994), of London; *children* 3 s (James b 1976, Edward b 1984, Thomas b 1990), 3 da (Ruth b 1971, Ingrid b 1972, Victoria b 1986); *Career* conslt surgn Middx Hosp and UCH, sr lectr in surgery Univ of London, hon conslt surgn St Luke's Hosp for the Clergy; memb Aeromedical Practitioners Assoc; Freeman Worshipful Soc of Apothecaries 1989, Freeman Guild of Air Pilots and Air Navigators 1994; FRSM 1972, FRCS 1976; *Books* Microcomputer Applications in Medicine (1987); *Recreations* flying, walking; *Clubs* Royal Soc of Medicine; *Style*— John Scurr, Esq; ✉ 5 Balniel Gate, London SW1V 3SD (☎ 0171 834 5578); Lister Hospital, London SW1 (☎ 0171 730 9563, fax 0171 834 6315)

SCUTT, Robin Hugh (known professionally as Scott); CBE (1976); s of late Rev Arthur Octavius Scutt, MA, and Freda May, *née* Palmer; *b* 24 Oct 1920; *Educ* Bryanston, British Institute Paris, Jesus Coll Cambridge (MA); *m* 1, 16 Jan 1943 (m dis 1960), Judy, *née* Watson; 2 s (Mark Oliver b 9 June 1945, (John) Paul b 30 May 1947); m 2, 29 July 1961, Patricia Anne Marie, da of J Pilkington Smith; *Career* Intelligence Corps 1941–42; BBC radio prodr and exec (Euro Serv) 1942–54, BBC TV outside bdcasts prodr 1955–58, BBC Paris rep 1958–62, gen mangr Trans Europe Television 1962, rejoined BBC Outside Bdcasts 1963, BBC prodr 1963–66, asst head BBC TV Presentation 1966, controller BBC Radios 1 and 2 1967–68, BBC2 TV 1969–74, controller Devpt BBC TV 1974–77, dep md BBC TV 1977–80, dir of prodn Nat Video Corp 1981–94; chm United Media Ltd 1983–92, dir LWT Ltd 1981–91; chm: New Technologies Working Party Bdcast Res Unit BFI 1981–83, Int Ctee Monte Carlo Television Festival 1989–; memb Programme Advsy Bd LWT Ltd 1991–93; fell and Gold medallist RTS; Officier de la Légion d'Honneur 1983; Officier de l'Ordre du Mérite Culturel Monaco 1991; FRSA 1985; *Recreations* gardening, theatre, travel; *Clubs* Garrick; *Style*— Robin Scott, Esq, CBE; ✉ The Abbey Cottage, Cockfield, nr Bury St Edmunds, Suffolk IP30 0LY

SEABRIGHT, John Walter (Jack); s of Walter Alexander Seabright (d 1991), of Henley-on-Thames, Oxon, and Emily Gladys, *née* Onion; *b* 2 May 1929; *Educ* Brentwood Sch Essex, Downing Coll Cambridge (MA); *m* 23 Oct 1954, Diana Bartlett, da of George Forrester Fairbairn (d 1966), of Torquay; 2 s (Paul b 1958, Alistair b 1961), 2 da (Theresa b 1960, Lucy b 1963); *Career* dir Coats Patons (UK) 1969–73, md MFI Furniture Group 1974–81, chief exec Henley Distance Learning Ltd 1981–85; chm: Teamband Ltd 1981–, Midlands Convenience Stores plc 1986–91, Compular Ltd 1987–91; dir: Church & Co plc 1982–91, Sperrings Franchising Ltd 1984–86, Clydesdale Group Ltd 1982–85, Thorntons plc 1988–95; *Recreations* walking, travel; *Style*— John W Seabright, Esq; ✉ Wanwood, Park Corner, Nettlebed, Oxon RG9 6DR (☎ 01491 641184); Teamband Ltd, Park Corner, Nettlebed, Oxon

SEABROOK, Air Vice-Marshal Geoffrey Leonard; CB (1965); s of Robert Leonard Seabrook (d 1946); *b* 25 Aug 1909; *Educ* King's Sch Canterbury; *m* 1949, Beryl Mary, *née* Hughes; 1 s, 1 da; *Career* cmmnd RAF 1933; served: Middle East 1935–43, Bomber Cmd 1943–45, Tport Cmd 1945–47, Iraq 1947–49, Signals Cmd 1949–51, Air Miny Orgn and Methods 1951–53, Home Cmd Gp Capt Orgn 1953–56, Far East Air Force 1957–59, idc 1960; Dir of Personnel Air Miny 1961–63, Air Offr Admin Trg Command 1963–66, ret 1966; Air Cdre 1961, Air Vice-Marshal 1964, head of Secretarial Branch RAF 1963–66; FCA 1957 (ACA 1932); *Recreations* golf, sailing; *Clubs* RAF, Piltdown Golf; *Style*— Air Vice-Marshal Geoffrey Seabrook, CB; ✉ Long Pightle, Piltdown, Uckfield, Sussex (☎ 01825 722322)

SEABROOK, Michael Richard; s of Robert Henry Seabrook (d 1983), of Solihull, and Clara, *née* Berry; *b* 24 March 1952; *Educ* King Edward's Sch Birmingham, Univ of Exeter (LLB); *m* 1 Sept 1979, Hilary Margaret Seabrook, JP, da of Anthony John Pettitt, of Bromley; 2 s (Nicholas b 1983, William b 1986); *Career* admitted slr 1976; articled clerk Lovell White & King 1974–76, asst slr Clifford-Turner 1976–79; ptnr: Needham & James 1981–86 (asst slr 1980), Eversheds 1986– (dep sr ptnr 1994–); memb Cncl Birmingham C of C and Indust 1995–, non-exec dir W Mids Enterprise Bd; memb Law Soc 1976; MSI 1992; *Recreations* sporting; *Clubs* Copt Heath Golf, East India and Public Schools, Warwickshire Imps Cricket, Knowle & Dorridge Cricket, Warwickshire Pilgrims Cricket, Bacchanalians Golf Soc; *Style*— Michael R Seabrook, Esq; ✉ 2 Granville Rd, Dorridge, Solihull, West Midlands B93 8BY (☎ 01564 773732); Eversheds, 10 Newhall Street, Birmingham B3 3LX (☎ 0121 233 2001, fax 0121 236 1583)

SEABROOK, Peter John; s of Robert Henry Seabrook (d 1987), of Galleywood, Essex, and Emma Mary, *née* Cottey (d 1989); *b* 2 Nov 1935; *Educ* King Edward VI GS Chelmsford, Essex Inst of Agric Writtle (MHort, Dip Hort); *m* 14 May 1960, Margaret Ruth, da of Arthur Wilfred Risbey, of Churchdown, Glos (d 1990); 1 s (Roger b 9 Feb 1962), 1 da (Alison b 13 May 1964); *Career* Nat Serv RASC 1956–58; author of books and presenter of TV progs on gardening; horticultural advsr and dir Cramphorn plc 1958–66, tech rep Bord na Mona 1966–70, horticultural conslt 1971–; dir: William Strike Ltd 1972–95, Roger Harvey Ltd 1981–; gardening corr: The Sun 1977–, The Yorkshire Post 1981–92; FIHort; *Radio* presenter: In Your Garden 1965–70, Gardeners' Question Time 1981–82; *Television* presenter gardening features on Pebble Mill at One BBC 1 1975–86; presenter: Gardeners' Direct Line BBC TV 1982–90, WGBH TV Boston USA 1975–, Chelsea Flower Show 1976–89, Gardener's World BBC 2 1976–81, Peter Seabrook's Gardening Week BBC 1 1996–; *Books* Shrubs For Your Garden (1973), Complete Vegetable Gardener (1976), Book of the Garden (1979), Good Plant Guide (1981), Good Food Gardening (1983); *Recreations* gardening; *Clubs* Farmers'; *Style*— Peter Seabrook, Esq; ✉ 212A Baddow Rd, Chelmsford, Essex CM2 9QR

SEABROOK, Robert John; QC (1983); s of Alan Thomas Pertwee Seabrook, MBE, of Hindhead, Surrey, and Mary, *née* Parker (d 1977); *b* 6 Oct 1941; *Educ* St George's Coll Harare Zimbabwe, UCL (LLB); *m* 19 Oct 1965, Liv Karin, da of Rev Bjarne Djupvik (d 1983), of Bergen, Norway; 2 s (Justin b 20 Dec 1969, Magnus b 23 April 1975), 1 da (Marianne b 23 Oct 1971); *Career* called to the Bar Middle Temple 1964, bencher 1991, recorder 1984–, leader SE Circuit 1989–92; chm of the Bar Cncl 1994; memb Ct Univ of Sussex 1988–93, govr Brighton Coll 1993–; Master Worshipful Co of Curriers 1995 (Liveryman 1972); memb Les Six; *Recreations* wine, listening to music, travel; *Style*— Robert Seabrook, QC; ✉ 1 Crown Office Row, Temple, London EC4Y 7HH (☎ 0171 797 7500, fax 0171 797 7550, DX 1020)

SEAFIELD, 13 Earl of (S 1701); Ian Derek Francis Ogilvie-Grant; Lord Ogilvy of Cullen and Viscount Seafield (S 1698), Lord Ogilvy of Deskford and Cullen and Viscount Reidhaven (S 1701); s of Countess of Seafield (12 in line, d 1969) and Derek Studley-Herbert (who assumed by deed poll 1939 the additional surnames of Ogilvie-Grant, the present Peer being recognised in those surnames by warrant of Lord Lyon 1971); *b* 20 March 1939; *Educ* Eton; *m* 1, 1960 (m dis 1971), Mary Dawn Mackenzie, da of Henry Illingworth; 2 s (Viscount Reidhaven b 1963, Hon Alexander b 1966); m 2, 1971, Leila, da of Mahmoud Refaat, of Cairo; *Heir* s, Viscount Reidhaven, *qv*; *Clubs* Whites; *Style*— The Rt Hon The Earl of Seafield; ✉ Old Cullen, Cullen, Banffshire

SEAFORD, Very Rev John Nicholas; s of Nicholas Shtetinin Seaford (d 1995), and Kathleen Dorothy, *née* Longbotham (d 1964); *b* 12 Sept 1939; *Educ* Radley, St Chad's Coll Durham (BA, Dip in Theol); *m* 2 Aug 1967, Helen Marian, da of Alexander James Webster (d 1992); 2 s (Nicholas Alexander b 8 Aug 1969, Charles Rupert b 5 Jan 1972), 1 da (Katherine Elizabeth Helen b 11 Aug 1974); *Career* ordained: deacon 1968, priest 1969; curate: St Mark Bush Hill Park 1969–72, St Luke Stanmore Winchester 1972–73; vicar: of Chilworth and North Baddesley 1973–78, of Highcliffe and Hinton Admiral 1978–93; rural dean of Christchurch 1990–93, hon canon of Winchester 1993–, dean of Jersey 1993–, rector of St Helier 1993–; *Recreations* photography, collecting old postcards; *Style*— The Very Rev John Seaford; ✉ The Deanery, David Place, St Helier, Jersey JE2 4TE, CI (☎ 01534 20001, fax 01534 617488)

SEAGROVE, Jennifer Ann (Jenny); da of Derek Claud Seagrove, of Jakarta, Indonesia, and Pauline Marjorie, *née* Pilditch (d 1993); *Educ* St Hilary's Godalming, Queen Anne's Caversham, Kirby Lodge Cambridge, Bristol Old Vic Theatre Sch; *m* 19 May 1984 (m dis 1988), Madhav Sharma; *Career* actress; *Theatre* incl: title role in Jane Eyre (Chichester Festival Theatre), Ilona in The Guardsman (Theatr Clwyd), Bett in

King Lear in New York (Chichester), Present Laughter (Globe), The Miracle Worker (Comedy and Wyndhams), Dead Guilty (with Hayley Mills, Apollo) 1995–96; *Television* incl: Emma Harte in A Women of Substance, Paula in Hold the Dream, title role in Diana, Lucy in Lucy Walker, Laura Fairlie in The Woman in White; for American Television: The Hitchhiker, In Like Flynn, Deadly Games, Incident at Victoria Falls, The Betrothed (with Burt Lancaster); *Films* incl: To Hell and Back in Time for Breakfast, A Shocking Accident, Local Hero, Savage Islands, Tattoo, Moonlighting, The Sign of Four, Appointment with Death, A Chorus of Disapproval, The Guardian, Miss Beatty's Children; *Recreations* country walks with dog, running, writing poetry, gardening, theatre, cinema; *Style*— Miss Jenny Seagrove; ✉ c/o Penny Wesson, Marmont Management, Langham House, 308 Regent Street, London W1R 5AL (☎ 0171 637 3183, fax 0171 323 4798)

SEAL, Dr Barry Herbert; MEP (Lab) Yorkshire West (majority 48,197); s of Herbert and Rose Ann Seal; *b* 28 Oct 1937; *Educ* Univ of Bradford, Harvard Business Sch; *m* 1963, Frances Catherine Wilkinson; 1 s (Robert), 1 da (Catherine); *Career* chem engr, control engr, univ lectr; former ldr Bradford Cncl Labour Gp; MEP (Lab) Yorkshire West 1979–; former ldr Br Lab Gp in Euro Parl; memb Euro Parly: Foreign Affairs Security and Defence Policy Ctee, Tport Ctee, Delgn to USA; *Books* Dissertations on Computer Control; *Recreations* walking, reading, riding; *Style*— Dr Barry Seal, MEP; ✉ City Hall, Bradford BD1 1HY (☎ 01274 726288, fax 01274 752092)

SEAL, David Herbert; s of Maj Jefferson Seal, TD (d 1977), and Florence Eileen, *née* Herbert (d 1980); bro of Michael Seal, *qv*; *b* 7 April 1935; *Educ* Marlborough, Pembroke Coll Cambridge (MA); *m* 19 Nov 1958, Juliet Rose, da of John Perrot (ka Dunkirk 1940); 1 s (John Rupert Jefferson b 1964), 2 da (Kate b 1959, Sarah Juliet b 1962); *Career* ptnr: Jefferson Seal & Co 1956, Seal Arnold 1968, D Q Henriques Seal 1973, Charlton Seal 1976, Jefferson Seal Ltd 1986; memb: Conservative Assoc 1956–71, Stock Exchange 1956, Securities Inst 1992; FInstD; *Recreations* horses, boats, vintage farming; *Clubs* St Helier Yacht, Jersey Riding (vice pres); *Style*— David Seal, Esq; ✉ Holmbury, Augres, Trinity, Jersey JE3 5DA (☎ 01534 861614); PO Box 525 11 Castle Street, St Helier, Jersey JE4 0WZ (☎ 01534 32122, fax 01534 888293)

SEAL, Julius Damien; s of Pulin Behari Seal (d 1982), and Julia Stuart, *née* Hogg; *b* 3 March 1945; *Educ* St Benedict's Sch; *m* 18 Feb 1970, Annie, da of Joseph Joseph, of Kuala Lumpur; 1 s (Giles b 1980), 3 da (Augusta b 1976, Harriet b 1978, Philippa b 1983); *Career* called to the Bar Lincoln's Inn 1967, memb of Inner Temple 1989; *Recreations* show jumping; *Style*— Julius Seal, Esq; ✉ 3 Temple Gardens, Temple EC4 (☎ 0171 583 0832, fax 0171 353 4929)

SEAL, Michael Jefferson; s of Maj Jefferson Seal, TD (d 1977), and Florence Eileen, *née* Herbert (d 1980); bro of David Seal, *qv*; *b* 17 Oct 1936; *Educ* Marlborough; *m* 22 Sept 1962, Julia Mary Seton, da of late Malcolm Sinclair Gaskill, of Hale, Cheshire; 1 s (Jonathan Michael Jefferson), 2 da (Mrs Heather Caroline Seton Manners, Mrs Rosanne Julia Nieboer); *Career* Nat Serv 1955–57, TA 1957–68; The Carborundum Co Ltd 1957–59; ptnr: Jefferson Seal & Co 1961–68 (joined 1959), Seal Arnold & Co 1968–72, D Q Henriques Seal & Co 1972–75, Charlton Seal Dimmock & Co 1975–87; chm: Charlton Seal Ltd 1987–88, Charlton Seal Schaverien Ltd 1988–90; non-exec chm CST Emerging Asia Trust plc 1989–92; dir: Wise Speke Ltd 1990–96, Wise Speke Holdings Ltd 1990–96, Jefferson Seal Ltd (Jersey) 1986–93; memb: Manchester Fin and Professional Forum, Family Welfare Assoc Manchester, Humane Soc of Hundred Salford, Court of Manchester Univ, Gtr Manchester Educnl Tst, Clonter Farm Music Tst, Wood St Mission, The Wythenshawe Hosp Transplant Fund; MSI; *Recreations* opera, country sports; *Clubs* St James's (Manchester); *Style*— Michael Seal, Esq; ✉ The Dene House, Great Budworth, Northwich, Cheshire CW9 6HB (☎ 01606 891555); Wise Speke Ltd, PO Box 512, National House, 36 St Ann Street, Manchester M60 2EP (☎ 0161 839 4222, fax 0161 832 9092)

SEAL, *né* Sealhenry Samuel; *Career* singer and songwriter; debut single Killer (with Adamski) reached UK number 1 for 4 weeks 1990, first solo single Crazy reached number 1 in 3 countries 1990, follow-up single Future Love Paradise 1991; debut album Seal (prodr Trevor Horn) entered UK charts at number 1 in 1991 (also entered US Top 20), released second album Seal in 1994 (UK no 1); Best Male Artist, Best Album, Best Video (for Killer) BRIT Awards 1992, Best Song, Best Record, Best Male Pop Vocal (for Kiss From a Rose) Grammy Awards 1996, International Hit of the Year Ivor Novello Awards 1996; *Style*— Seal

SEALE, Sir John Henry; 5 Bt (UK 1838), of Mount Boone, Devonshire; patron of one living; s of Sir John Carteret Hyde Seale, 4 Bt (d 1964); *b* 3 March 1921; *Educ* Eton, ChCh Oxford; *m* 1953, Ray Josephine, da of late R G Charters, MC, of Christchurch, New Zealand; 1 s, 1 da; *Heir* s, John Robert Charters Seale b 17 Aug 1954; *Career* Capt RA; architect; RIBA; *Style*— Sir John Seale, Bt; ✉ Slade, Kingsbridge, Devon TQ7 4BL

SEALE, John Robert Charters; s and h of Sir John Seale, 5 Bt; *b* 17 Aug 1954; *Educ* Eton, UCNW Bangor; *m* 8 Sept 1996, Michelle Judith, da of K W Taylor, of Mattishall, Norfolk; *Style*— John Seale, Esq

SEALES, Peter Clinton; s of late James M Seales, of Dublin, and late Angela, *née* O'Doherty; *m* Bernadette Rogers; 1 da (Elizabeth Devereaux); *Career* called to the Bar; successively: gp mktg dir Raleigh Industries Ltd, dir E Midlands Electricity Bd, md Potterton International, int mktg dir Ever Ready Holdings; chm PSL Associates 1978–; chief exec: Sea Fish Indust Authy 1982–83, Operation Raleigh 1984–85; former conslt Saatchi & Saatchi Compton, gp mktg dir Wassen International Ltd 1986–92; dir: International Developments Gazzoni 1907 SPA 1992–, Jephson Housing Association Group 1994–; conslt dir Qualitec GB Ltd (custom pharmaceuticals) 1995–, Seal Pharma International Ltd 1996–; hon memb Cncl Operation Innovator 1987–; FInstD 1972; *Recreations* sailing, music; *Style*— Peter Seales, Esq

SEALEY, Barry Edward; CBE (1990); s of Edward Sealey (d 1995), and Queenie Katherine, *née* Hill (d 1981); *b* 3 Feb 1936; *Educ* Dursley GS, St John's Coll Cambridge (MA); *m* 21 May 1960, Helen, da of Dr Frank Martyn (d 1979), of Grimsby; 1 s (Andrew b 1964), 1 da (Margaret (Mrs Cave) b 1962); *Career* Nat Serv RAF 1953–55; Christian Salvesen plc: trainee 1958, dir 1969, md 1981, md and dep chm 1987, dep chm 1989, ret 1990; directorships incl: Scottish Equitable plc 1984–, Scottish American Investment Co 1983–, The Caledonian Brewing Co Ltd 1990–, Wilson Byard plc (chm) 1992–, Stagecoach Holdings plc 1992–, Interface Graphics Ltd (chm) 1992–, Edinburgh Healthcare NHS Tst (chm) 1993–; memb Cncl Industl Soc, dep chm Napier Univ; CIMgt; *Recreations* walking, music; *Clubs* New (Edinburgh); *Style*— Barry E Sealey, Esq, CBE; ✉ 4 Castlelaw Rd, Edinburgh EH13 0DN (☎ 0131 441 2802, fax 0131 441 5576)

SEALY, Prof Leonard Sedgwick; s of Alfred Desmond Sealy (d 1964), of Hamilton, NZ, and Mary Louise, *née* Mark (d 1967); *b* 22 July 1930; *Educ* Stratford HS NZ, Auckland Univ (MA, LLM), Univ of Cambridge (PhD, Yorke prize); *m* 11 Aug 1960, Beryl Mary, da of Richard Edwards; 2 da (Elizabeth Helena b 23 Jan 1963, Louise Caroline b 3 Dec 1969), 1 s (Mark Edward Byers b 4 Sept 1964); *Career* called to the Bar NZ and admitted slr 1953; Univ of Cambridge: univ asst lectr 1959–61, univ lectr 1961–, S J Berwin prof of corp law 1991–; Gonville and Caius Coll Cambridge: fell 1959–, tutor 1960–70, sr tutor 1970–75; ed Cambridge Law Jl 1982–88; gen ed: British Company Law and Practice 1989–, International Corporate Procedures 1991–; *Books* Cases and Materials in Company Law (1971, 6 edn 1996), Benjamin's Sale of Goods (with A G Guest and others, 1974, 4 edn 1992), Company Law and Commercial Reality (1984), Disqualification and Personal Liability of Directors (1986, 4 edn 1993), Guide to the Insolvency Legislation (with D Milman, 1987, 4 edn 1994), Commercial Law, Text and Materials (with R J A Hooley, 1994); *Style*— Prof Leonard Sealy; ✉ Gonville and Caius College, Cambridge CB2 1TA (☎ 01223 332471, fax 01223 332456)

SEAMAN, Christopher Bertram; s of Albert Edward Seaman (d 1960), of Canterbury, Kent, and Ethel Margery, *née* Chambers (d 1985); *b* 7 March 1942; *Educ* Canterbury Cathedral Choir Sch, King's Sch Canterbury, King's Coll Cambridge Scholar MA); *Career* princ timpanist and memb Bd London Philharmonic Orch 1964–68; princ conductor: BBC Scot Symphony Orch 1971–77 (asst conductor 1968–70), Northern Sinfonia Orch 1974–79; chief guest conductor Utrecht Symphony Orch 1979–82, conductor in res Baltimore Symphony Orch 1987–; music dir Naples (Florida) Philharmonic Orch 1993–; appears as guest conductor worldwide; FGSM 1972; *Recreations* people, reading, shopping, theology; *Style*— Christopher Seaman, Esq; ✉ c/o Harrison/Parrott Ltd, 12 Penzance Place, London W11 4PA (☎ 0171 229 9166, fax 0171 221 5042)

SEAMAN, Sir Keith Douglas; KCVO (1981), OBE (1976); s of Eli Semmens Seaman (d 1955), and Ethel Maud Seaman (d 1930); *b* 11 June 1920; *Educ* Unley HS, Adelaide Univ (BA, LLB), Flinders Univ Aust (MA, Dip Hum); *m* 1946, Joan Isabel, da of late Fred Birbeck; 1 s, 1 da; *Career* memb Exec World Assoc of Christian Broadcasting Cos 1960, chm 5KA, 5AU and 5RM Broadcasting Cos 1971–77 (dir 1960), memb Aust Govt Social Welfare Cmmn 1973–76, govr South Australia 1977–82; KStJ 1978; *Style*— Sir Keith Seaman, KCVO, OBE; ✉ 93 Rosetta Village, Victor Harbor, South Australia 5211

SEAMAN, (Marvin) Roy; s of late Charles Seaman, of Harleston, Norfolk, and late Mary Elizabeth, *née* Goldsmith; *b* 11 Sept 1945; *Educ* Stradbroke Sch, RAF Tech Trg Coll; *m* 19 Oct 1976, Judy, da of late Joseph Ragobar, of Marabella, Trinidad; 2 s (Christian b 1978, Jonathan b 1982), 1 da (Michelle Anne b 1981); *Career* RAF 1961–67; int mgmnt conslt to Br firms 1968–81, chm and md Franchise Devpt Services Ltd 1981–; publisher: The Franchise Magazine 1985–, Franchise International 1993–; visiting lectr seminars and colls on franchise and licensing laws; Int Licensing (servs to estab franchisors, prospective franchisors, franchise publications, public relations, seminars, exhibitions and marketing); memb: Int Christian C of C, Full Gospel Businessmen's Fellowship Int, CBI; FInstD, MCIM, MInstEx; *Recreations* deep sea fishing in Caribbean, walking around Norfolk, supporting Norwich City FC, relaxing with family; *Clubs* IOD; *Style*— Roy Seaman, Esq; ✉ Cedar Lodge, Ipswich Rd, Tasburgh, Norfolk (☎ 01508 470686); Franchise Development Services Ltd, Castle House, Castle Meadow, Norwich NR2 1PJ (☎ 01603 620301, fax 01603 630174)

SEARBY, Maj Gen Robin Vincent; s of Air Cdre John Henry Searby, DSO, DFC (d 1986), and Eva, *née* Rowland (d 1976); *b* 20 July 1947; *Educ* Leasam House Sch; *m* 8 May 1976, Caroline Angela, da of late Maj John Beamish, MC; 1 s (Henry b 6 June 1977), 2 da (Louisa b 19 Jan 1979, Alice b 31 March 1981); *Career* RMA Sandhurst 1966–68, 2 Lt 9/12 Royal Lancers (POW) 1968, regtl duty Berlin, BAOR, NI 1968–73, loan serv Dhofar (Sultanate of Oman) 1973–75, regtl duty NI and UK 1976–79, Maj 1979, Army Staff Coll Camberley 1980, GSO II Ops 2 Armd Div BAOR 1981–83, regtl duty 1983–85, Lt-Col dir staff Army Staff Coll 1985–87, CO 9/12 Royal Lancers 1987–89, COS to DRAC 1989–91, Cdr Royal Armoured Corps 1 (BR) Corps 1991–93, Cdr British Forces Former Republic of Yugoslavia 1993, pres Regular Commissions Bd 1994–96, GOC 5 Div 1996–; Distinguished Service Medal (Gallantry) Sultanate of Oman 1975; *Recreations* reading, equitation; *Clubs* Cavalry; *Style*— Maj Gen Robin Searby

SEARLE, Geoffrey John; TD (1976); s of late William Ernest Searle, of Cornwall, and Eileen Edith, *née* Girling; *b* 21 June 1945; *Educ* Bancroft's Sch Woodford Green Essex; *m* 25 Sept 1971, Nicole Nicette Suzanne, da of Gilbert Andre Paul Cochonneau, of Tours, France; 2 s (Dominic b 1973, Yann b 1976), 1 da (Olivia b 1984); *Career* TA RCS 1963–77, ret actg Maj; admitted slr 1968; asst clerk of Cncl Brentwood UDC 1969–73, managing ptnr Denton Hall slrs 1988–92 (asst slr 1973–76, ptnr 1977–94), in own practice 1994–; memb Ctee of Mgmnt Br Chapter of FIABCI (Int Real Estate Fedn) (pres 1996–97), pres Environment and Legislation Ctee FIABCI Worldwide 1994–; memb Int Bar Assoc; fndr memb UK Environmental Law Assoc, assoc memb American Bar Assoc; Freeman City of London, Liveryman Worshipful Co of Slrs; memb Law Soc, FRSA, FIMgt; *Books* Development Land Tax (1985); *Recreations* cinema, reading, walking, cycling, family history, conversation, music; *Clubs* Athenaeum, City Livery; *Style*— Geoffrey Searle; ✉ Planning Solicitor, 32 Centre Point House, St Giles High Street, London WC2H 8LW (☎ 0171 497 3753, fax 0171 240 5818)

SEARLE, Geoffrey William; CBE (1972), DSC (1943); s of William Arthur Searle (d 1957); *b* 11 April 1914; *m* 1940, Constance (d 1996), da of Charles Tyrrell; 1 s (John), 1 da (Heather); *Career* CA 1936; Lt Cdr RNVR; joined BP 1946, dir of fin and planning and chm of Exec Ctee BP Trading Ltd, ret 1974; chm: Star Offshore Services Ltd 1974–80, LASMO plc (formerly London & Scottish Marine Oil plc) 1978–85 (md 1974–78, non-exec dir 1985–86), Assoc of British Independent Oil Exploration Cos (Brindex) 1982, Belden & Blake International Ltd 1986–92; pres Reigate and Surrey County LTC 1980–88; FInstPet 1982; *Books* At Sea Level (1994); *Recreations* golf, music, gardening; *Clubs* Naval, RAC, City of London, Walton Heath Golf; *Style*— Geoffrey Searle, Esq, CBE, DSC; ✉ 20 Beech Rd, Reigate, Surrey RH2 9LR (☎ 01737 245803)

SEARLE, Graham William; *b* 10 May 1935; *Career* gp md Dunhill Holdings plc 1991–93 (gp fin dir 1982–91); non-exec dir Gartmore Emerging Pacific Investment Trust PLC 1992–, dep chm and md Laura Ashley Holdings plc 1994–95, dep chm Monsoon Ltd 1996–; FCA 1961; *Style*— Graham Searle, Esq; ✉ 15 Thurloe Place, Knightsbridge, London SW7 2RZ

SEARLE, Graham William; s of Frederick William Searle (d 1969), and Margaret, *née* Hewitt (d 1961); *b* 26 Sept 1946; *Educ* Sir George Monoux GS Walthamstow, SW Essex Tech Coll, King's Coll London (BSc), Sir John Cass Coll London; *m* 4 Aug 1984 (m dis 1996), Francesca Vivica, *née* Parsons; 1 s (Frederick b 1 June 1991), 1 da (Rebecca b 7 March 1989); *Career* fndr and dir: Friends of the Earth Ltd London 1971, Earth Resources Research Ltd London 1973 (exec dir 1975); advsr Dept of Urban Affrs Fed Govt of Canada 1976, liaison offr Environment Liaison Centre Nairobi Kenya 1977, prog offr UN Environment Prog Nairobi 1978, ind environmental mgmnt conslt 1979–92, exec dir Euro Organic Reclamation and Composting Assoc Brussels and ed Recycling and Resource Management 1991–92, non-exec dir Shanks and McEwan Environmental Services Ltd 1992–94; currently: pres Composting Assoc, hon vice pres Suffolk Wildlife Tst (chm 1994–95); memb: Ind Cmmn on Tport Planning 1973, UK Standing Ctee on Nat Parks 1975, Standing Ctee of UK Waste Mgmnt Advsy Cncl 1975, Environmental Advsy Bd SME, Rivers Advsy Ctee Nat Rivers Authy (Anglia Region) 1988–94, Conservation Working Gp and Broads Plan Steering Ctee Broads Authy 1992–93; FGS; *Books* Project Earth (1973), Changing Directions (contrib, 1974), Rush to Destruction (1975), The Politics of Physical Resources (contrib, 1975), Energy (1977), Automatic Unemployment (co-author, 1979), The Habitat Handbook (1980), Major World Bank Projects (1987); *Recreations* fly-fishing, sea fishing, watching cricket and rugby; *Clubs* Suffolk Agricultural Assoc; *Style*— Graham Searle, Esq; ✉ Blacksmiths Cottage, Huntingfield, Halesworth, Suffolk IP19 0PZ (☎ 01986 798123)

SEARLE, Gregory Mark Pascoe (Greg); MBE (1993); s of Paul Frederick Searle, of Chertsey, Surrey, and Judith Ann (Judy), *née* Brant; bro of Jonny Searle, *qv*; *b* 20 March 1972; *Educ* Hampton Sch Middx, South Bank Univ (BSc); *Career* amateur rower; jr debut for Hampton Sch Club 1988, sr debut Molesey Boat Club 1990; achievements incl: winner schs triple of Schs Head, Nat Schs and Princess Elizabeth Cup Henley 1988, Gold medal Jr World Championships 1989 and 1990 (debut 1988), Bronze medal eights

Sr World Championships 1991 (debut 1990), Gold medal coxed pairs (with bro Jonny) Olympic Games 1992, Bronze medal World Indoor Rowing Championships 1992, Gold medal coxed pairs (with bro Jonny) World Championships 1993, Bronze medal coxless fours Olympic Games Atlanta 1996; first person ever to compete in both Jr and Sr World Championships in same year 1990; chartered surveyor; *Recreations* off road Land Rover driving, rugby, sky diving; *Style—* Greg Searle, Esq, MBE; ✉ 143 Brompton Park Crescent, London SW6

SEARLE, Jonathan William Courtis (Jonny); MBE (1993); s of Paul Frederick Searle, of Chertsey, Surrey, and Judith Ann (Judy), *née* Brant; bro of Greg Searle, *qv*; *b* 8 May 1969; *Educ* Hampton Sch, ChCh Oxford (BA), Coll of Law Lancaster Gate; *Career* slr (employed at Ashurst Morris Crisp) and amateur rower; began rowing at Hampton Sch 1982, memb Molesey Boat Club; achievements incl: UK schs eights champion 1985–87, Gold medal coxless four Jr World Championships 1987 (Silver medal 1986), winner Univ Boat Race with Oxford 1988, 1989 and 1990 (pres univ boat club 1990), Bronze medals eights Sr World Championships 1989 and 1991, winner Tideway Head with Molesey eight 1992, Gold medal coxed pairs (with bro Greg) Olympic Games Barcelona 1992, Gold medal coxed pairs World Championships 1993, Bronze medal coxless fours Sr World Championships 1994, Silver medal coxless fours Sr World Championships 1995, Bronze medal coxless fours Olympic Games Atlanta 1996; *Recreations* playing bridge, art history, opera, Anglo Saxon England; *Style—* Jonny Searle, Esq; ✉ c/o Molesey Boat Club, Barge Walk, Molesey, Surrey (☎ 0181 979 6583)

SEARLE, Ronald William Fordham; s of William James Searle (d 1967), and Nellie, *née* Hunt (d 1991); *b* 3 March 1920; *Educ* Cambridge Sch of Art; *m* 1 (m dis 1967), Kaye Webb, MBE (d 1996), da of Arthur Webb; 1 s (John b 17 July 1947), 1 da (Kate (twin) b 17 July 1947); m 2, 1967, Monica Ilse Koenig; *Career* Sapper 287 Field Co RE 1939–46 (Japanese POW, Siam and Malaya 1942–45, dept psychological warfare Allied Force HQ Port Said Ops 1956; contrib Punch 1947–61, special features artist Life Magazine 1955–62, contrib New Yorker Magazine 1966–, designer commemorative medals to the French Mint 1975– and BAMS 1984–; film designer: John Gilpin, On the Twelfth Day, Energetically Yours, Germany 1960, Toulouse-Lautrec, Dick Deadeye; designer of animation sequences: Those Magnificent Men in their Flying Machines 1965, Monte Carlo or Bust! 1969, Scrooge 1970; one-man exhibitions 1950–88 incl: Leicester Galleries London, Imperial War Museum, Kraushaar Gallery NY, Bianchini Gallery NY, Kunsthalle Bremen, Bibliotéque Nationale Paris, Munich, Neue Galerie Vienna; Awards: LA Art Dirs Club Medal 1959, Philadelphia Art Dirs Club Medal 1959, Nat Cartoonists Soc Award 1959 and 1960, Gold Medal III Biennale Tolentino Italy 1965, Prix de la Critique Belge 1968, Grand Prix de l'Humour Noir (France) 1971, Prix d'Humour Festival d'Avignon 1971, Medal of French Circus 1971, Prix Internationale 'Charles Huard' 1972, La Monnaie de Paris Medal 1974; RDI, AGI; *Books incl* Forty Drawings (1946), John Gilpin (1952), Souls in Torment (1953), Rake's Progress (1955), Merry England (1956), Paris Sketchbook (1957), The St Trinian's Story (with Kaye Webb 1959); with Alex Atkinson: The Big City (1958), USA for Beginners (1959), Russia for Beginners (1960); Refugees (1960), Which Way did He Go? (1961), Escape from the Amazon (1963), From Frozen North to Filthy Lucre (1964), Those Magnificent Men in their Flying Machines (1965), Haven't We Met Before Somewhere? (with Heinz Huber 1966), Searle's Cats (1967), The Square Egg (1968), Hello - Where did all the People Go? (1969), Secret Sketchbook (1970), The Second Coming of Toulouse-Lautrec (1970), The Addict (1971), More Cats (1975), Designs for Gilbert and Sullivan (1975), Paris! Paris! (with Irwin Shaw 1977), Searle's Zoodiac (1977), Ronald Searle (monograph 1978), The King of Beasts (1980), The Big Fat Cat Book (1982), Illustrated Winespeak (1983), Ronald Searle in Perspective (monograph 1984), Ronald Searle's Golden Oldies 1941–1961 (1985), Something in the Cellar (1986), To the Kwai - and Back (1986), Ah Yes, I Remember It Well...: Paris 1961–75 (1987), Non-Sexist Dictionary (1988), Slightly Foxed - but still desirable (1989), Carnet de Croquis (1992), The Curse of St Trinian's (1993), Marquis de Sade meets Goody Two-Shoes (1994); subject of biography Ronald Searle (by Russell Davies, 1990); *Clubs* Garrick; *Style—* Ronald Searle, Esq; ✉ 11 Jubilee Place, London SW3 3TE (☎ 0171 823 3883, fax 0171 823 3363); John Locke Studios, 15 East 76th Street, New York NY 10021 (☎ 00 1 212 288 8010, fax 00 1 212 288 8011)

SEARS, Dr Charles Alistair Newton; s of Dr (Harold) Trevor Newton Sears (d 1996), and Dr Janet Sorley, *née* Conn (d 1994); *b* 30 Dec 1952; *Educ* Sandbach Sch, Middx Hosp Univ of London (MB BS); *m* 6 May 1978, Judith Lesley, da of Dr Leslie Victor Martin, of Oxbridge, Dorset; 3 s (James b 1979, Robert b 1982, Nicholas b 1986); *Career* house offr Middx Hosp 1978; sr house offr: neurosurgery Royal Free Hosp 1978–79, medicine Queen Elizabeth Hosp Birmingham 1979–82; ptnr in gen practice Salisbury 1983–, clinical asst Community Learning Disability Unit Salisbury DHA 1986– (clinical asst Rheumatology 1985–92); trainer in gen practice Salisbury Dist Vocational Trg Scheme; memb: Cncl (Wessex rep) RCGP (memb Wessex Faculty Bd), Bd of Mgmnt Nat Back Pain Assoc 1991–, Undergrad Educn Project Steering Gp Prince of Wales Advsy Gp on Disability 1992–, Rehabilitation Med Ctee RCP 1994–, NHS Exec Commissioning Gp for R & D in Complex and Physical Disability 1994–; RCGP nominee to Back Pain Sub-Gp Clinical Standards Advsy Gp 1992–, memb Med and Social Servs Ctee Muscular Dystrophy Gp of GB and NI 1993–; memb Br Inst of Musculoskeletal Med, MRCGP 1988; *Clubs* Br Inst of Musculoskeletal Med, RYA; *Style—* Dr Charles Sears; ✉ Close House, The Green, Pitton, Salisbury, Wilts SP5 1DZ (☎ 01722 712745); Grove House, 18 Wilton Rd, Salisbury, Wilts SP2 7EE (☎ 01722 333034)

SEATON, Prof Anthony; CBE (1997); s of Dr Douglas Ronald Seaton (d 1986), of Ipswich, Suffolk, and Julia, *née* Harrison; bro of Dr Douglas Seaton, *qv* and James Ronald Seaton, *qv*; *b* 20 Aug 1938; *Educ* Rossall Sch, King's Coll Cambridge (BA, MB, MD); *m* 4 April 1964, Jillian Margaret Duke; 2 s (Andrew b 1966, Jonathan b 1969); *Career* qualified in med 1962, asst prof of med Univ of W Virginia 1969–71, conslt chest physician Univ of Wales 1971–77, dir Inst of Occupational Med Edinburgh 1978–90, prof Univ of Aberdeen 1988– (head Department of Environmental & Occupational Med); author of numerous pubns in jls; memb: Br Occupational Medicine and Thoracic Socs, Ctee on Med Aspects of Air Pollution Dept of Health; chm expert panel on air pollution standards DOE; FRCP 1977 (MRCP 1964), FRCPE 1986, FFOM 1985; *Books* Occupational Lung Diseases (with W K C Morgan 1984), Respiratory Diseases (with D Seaton and A G Leitch, 1989), Thorax (ed, 1977–81), Practical Occupational Medicine (1994); *Recreations* rowing, painting; *Clubs* Edinburgh Univ Staff, St Andrew Boat; *Style—* Prof Anthony Seaton, CBE; ✉ 8 Avon Grove, Barnton, Edinburgh EH4 6RF (☎ 0131 336 5113, fax 0131 336 2710); 71 Urquhart Terrace, Aberdeen AB2 1NJ; Department of Environmental & Occupational Medicine, Medical School, University of Aberdeen, Foresterhill, Aberdeen AB9 2ZD (☎ 01224 681818)

SEATON, Dr Douglas; s of Dr Douglas Ronald Seaton (d 1986), of Ipswich, Suffolk, and Julia, *née* Harrison; bro of Prof Anthony Seaton, CBE, *qv* and James Ronald Seaton, *qv*; *b* 5 Feb 1946; *Educ* Rossall Sch Lancashire, Univ of Liverpool (MB ChB, MD); *m* 1 Aug 1970, Anja Elisabeth, da of Frits Coenraad Neervoort, of Bussum, Netherlands; 3 s (Edward b 31 Aug 1972, Bart b 8 Feb 1974, Michael b 20 May 1978); *Career* sr med registrar United Liverpool Hosps 1976, instr in med W Virginia Univ USA 1977, conslt physician in gen and respiratory med The Ipswich Hosp 1979–, asst ed Thorax 1980–82; author of med papers on respiratory diseases, contrib chapters in med textbooks; MRCP (UK), FRCP (London), MRCS (England); *Books* Crofton and Douglas's Respiratory Diseases (with A Seaton and A G Leitch, 1989); *Recreations* country walking, church architecture; *Style—* Dr Douglas Seaton; ✉ King's Field, 23 Park Rd, Ipswich, Suffolk IP1 3SX (☎ 01473 216671, fax 01473 212011)

SEATON, James Ronald; s of Douglas Ronald Seaton (d 1986), of Ipswich, Suffolk, and Julia, *née* Harrison; bro of Dr Douglas Seaton, *qv*, and Prof Anthony Seaton, CBE, *qv*; *b* 3 March 1955; *Educ* Rossall Sch Fleetwood, Wirral GS Bebington, Univ of Birmingham (BA); *m* 7 Oct 1978, Jessica Ruth, da of Arthur Barwell Hampton; 1 da (Rachel Amelia b 2 Aug 1980), 1 s (Nicholas James b 12 March 1985); *Career* knitwear designer/mfr: J & J Seaton 1978– (2 collections annually), Seaton 1995– (2 collections annually); *Books* The Seaton Collection (1989); *Recreations* yacht sailing, literature, art, classical music, walking, climbing, food and wine; *Style—* James Seaton, Esq; ✉ J & J Seaton, Goetre, Llanfynydd, Carmarthen, Dyfed SA32 7TT (☎ 01558 668825, fax 01558 668875)

SEAWARD, Colin Hugh; CBE (1987); s of Sydney Widmer Seaward (d 1967), and Molly Wendela, *née* Darwen (d 1985); *b* 16 Sept 1926; *Educ* RNC Dartmouth, Univ of Cambridge; *m* 1, Jean, *née* Bugler (d 1971); 3 s (Jonathan Louis b 1952, Nicholas William b 1956, Thomas Edward b 1967), 1 da (Petronella Jane (Mrs Seccombe) b 1950); m 2, Judith Margaret, da of late Canon W T Hinkley, of Alnwick, Northumberland; 2 da (Candida Harriet b 1974, Jessica Lucy b 1976); *Career* War Serv HMS Ajax 1944–45, served Far East 1946–48, Med 1951–52, Admty 1953–55, cmd HMS Aberford 1956–58, Asst Naval Attaché Moscow and Naval Attaché Warsaw 1958–60, HMS Centaur 1960–62, MOD 1962–64, ret; joined HM Dip Serv 1965, dep high cmmr The Gambia 1966–68, FCO 1968–71, Rio de Janeiro 1971, Prague 1972–73, FCO 1973–76, Sr Offrs' War Course RNC Greenwich 1976, cnsllr (econ and commercial) Islamabad 1977–80, HM consul-gen Rio de Janeiro 1980–86, ret 1986, re-employed Protocol Dept FCO 1987–91; sec Anglo-Brazilian Soc 1992–95; Freeman City of London 1987; Hon Citizen State of Rio de Janeiro 1985; *Style—* Colin Seaward, Esq, CBE; ✉ Brasted House, Brasted, Westerham, Kent TN16 1JA

SEAWARD, Prof Mark Richard David; *b* 10 Aug 1938; *Educ* City GS Lincoln, Univ of Birmingham (BSc, Dip Ed), Univ of Nottingham (MSc), Univ of Bradford (PhD, DSc); *Career* head of biology Brigg GS 1960–65, lectr Loughborough Trg Coll 1965–67, sr lectr Trinity and All Saints Colls 1967–73; Univ of Bradford: chm Post Grad Sch of Environmental Sci 1980–88, chm Bd of Studies and Higher Degrees Ctee 1981–84, memb Cncl 1984–90, memb Senate 1984–, prof of environmental biology 1990–, head Dept of Environmental Sci 1991–; ed: The Naturalist, International Lichenological Newsletter; author of over 250 scientific papers and assoc ed of 5 jls; memb Cncl: Br Lichen Soc, Linnean Soc; ed Brontë Soc Transactions, exec memb Yorkshire Naturalists Union; FIBiol, FLS; Nummo Aureo Univ of Wroclaw Poland; *Books* Lichen Ecology (1977), Lichenology in the British Isles 1568–1975 (1977), A Handbook for Naturalists (1980), Urban Ecology (1982), Atlas of the Lichens of the British Isles (1982), Lichen Atlas of the British Isles (1995), Richard Spruce, Botanist and Explorer (1996); *Recreations* book-collecting, music, philately, postal history; *Clubs* Linnean; *Style—* Prof Mark Seaward; ✉ University of Bradford, Bradford BD7 1DP (☎ 01274 384212, fax 01274 384231, telex 51309 UNIBFD G, e-mail m.r.d.seaward@bradford.ac.uk)

SEAWARD, Peter; s of Arthur Jack Seaward and Beatrice May Seaward; *b* 12 Feb 1954; *Educ* Maidstone Coll of Art; *Career* trained in graphic design; photographer; recipient various Assoc of Photographers awards; *Style—* Peter Seaward, Esq; ✉ Holborn Studios, 49 Eagle Wharf Road, London N1 7ED (☎ 0171 608 3249, fax 0171 608 3263)

SEBAG-MONTEFIORE, Charles Adam Laurie; s of Denzil Charles Sebag-Montefiore (d 1996), of London SW6, and Ruth Emily, *née* Magnus; *b* 25 Oct 1949; *Educ* Eton, Univ of St Andrews (MA); *m* 5 Oct 1979, Pamela Mary Diana, da of Archibald Tennant (d 1955), of London SW1; 1 s (Archibald Edward Charles b 1987), 2 da (Elizabeth Anne b 1982, Laura Rose b 1984); *Career* initial career with Touche Ross & Co CAs, ptnr Grieveson Grant & Co 1981–86, dir Kleinwort Benson Securities Ltd 1986–94, dep chm Harvill Press Ltd 1994–, dir Euclidian plc 1994–, tstee Foreign & Colonial Management Common Funds for Growth and Income 1994–; chm: Projects Ctee Nat Art-Collections Fund 1977–86, London Historic House Museums Tst 1992– (tstee 1987–); hon treas: Friends of the Nat Libraries 1990–, Friends of the British Library 1990–95, Friends of Lambeth Palace Library 1990–, The London Library 1991–; govr of Patrons of the Nat Gallery of Scotland 1992–; tstee Samuel Courtauld Tst 1992–; Liveryman Worshipful Co of Spectacle Makers 1973; FCA 1974, FRSA, FSA 1995; *Recreations* visiting picture galleries, collecting books, opera; *Clubs* Brooks's, Beefsteak; *Style—* Charles Sebag-Montefiore, Esq, FSA; ✉ 21 Hazlewell Rd, London SW15 6LT (☎ 0181 789 5999, fax 0181 785 4071)

SEBASTIAN, Timothy (Tim); s of Peter Sebastian, CBE, of Hove, E Sussex, and Pegitha, *née* Saunders; *b* 13 March 1952; *Educ* Westminster, New Coll Oxford (BA), Univ Coll Cardiff (Dip Journalism); *m* 4 June 1977 (m dis 1995), Diane, da of John Buscombe, of Frensham, Surrey; 1 s (Peter b 1981), 2 da (Clare b 1983, Caroline b 1986); *Career* BBC TV: eastern Euro corr 1979–82, Moscow corr 1984–85, Washington corr 1986–89; *Books* Nice Promises (1984), I Spy in Russia (1985), The Spy in Question (1987), Spy Shadow (1989), Saviour's Gate (Bantam Books, 1990), Exit Berlin (1992), Last Rights (1993), Special Relations (1994), War Dance (1995); *Style—* Tim Sebastian, Esq

SEBRIGHT, Sir Peter Giles Vivian; 15 Bt (E 1626), of Besford, Worcs; s of Sir Hugo Giles Edmund Sebright, 14 Bt (d 1985), and his 1 w, Deirdre Ann, née Slingsby Bethell, gggda of 1 Baron Westbury; *b* 2 Aug 1953; *m* 1, 1977 (m dis), Regina Maria, da of Francis Steven Clarebrough, of Melbourne, Australia; 1 s; m 2, Madeleine; 1 s (Dashiell b 1987); *Heir* s, Rufus Hugo Giles Sebright b 31 July 1978; *Style—* Sir Peter Sebright, Bt

SECCOMBE, Baroness (Life Peer UK 1991), of Kineton in the County of Warwickshire; Dame Joan Anna Dalziel Seccombe; DBE (1984), JP (Solihull 1968); da of Robert John Owen (d 1941), of Solihull, W Midlands, and Olive Barlow; *b* 3 May 1930; *Educ* St Martin's Sch Solihull; *m* 1950, Henry Lawrence Seccombe, s of Herbert Stanley Seccombe (d 1951), of Lapworth, Warwickshire; 2 s (Hon Philip Stanley b 1951, Hon Robert Murray b 1954); *Career* memb: West Mids CC 1977–81 (chm Trading Standards 1979–81), Mids Elec Consultative Cncl 1981–90; chm: Cons Womens Nat Ctee 1981–84, Nat Union of Cons & Unionists Assoc 1987–88 (vice-chm 1984–87), Lord Chllr's Advsy Ctee on Magistrates 1975–93, Solihull Bench 1981–84; vice pres Inst of Trading Standards Admin 1992–; memb: West Mids Police Ctee 1977–81 and 1985–91, Offices Ctee 1991–94, Admin and Works sub-Ctee 1991–94, Broadvcasting Ctee 1994–, Finance and Staff sub-Ctee 1994–, Personal Bills Ctee 1994–; vice-chm Cons Party 1987–, govr Nuffield Hosps 1988–, dep chm Nuffield Hosps 1993–, chm tstees of Nuffield Hosps Pension Fund; pres St Enedoc Golf Club 1991–; *Recreations* skiing, golf; *Style—* The Rt Hon Lady Seccombe, DBE, JP; ✉ Trethias, Norton Grange, Little Kineton, Warwicks CV35 0DP (☎ 01926 640562)

SECCOMBE, Sir (William) Vernon (Stephen); kt (1988), JP (Cornwall 1970); s of Stephen Seccombe (d 1964), and Edith Violet, *née* Smith (d 1980); *b* 14 Jan 1928; *Educ* Saltash GS, Plymouth and Devonport Tech Coll; *m* 2 Sept 1950, Margaret Vera, da of Joseph Edgar Profit (d 1988); 4 s (Michael b 1952, Paul b 1953, Tony b 1957, Patrick b 1960); *Career* Nat Serv XII Royal Lancers 1947–49; ret electrical contractor; memb: Saltash Borough Cncl 1953–74, E Cornwall Water Bd 1960–74, Caradon DC 1973–79; traffic cmmr Western Area 1977–81 (dep traffic cmmr 1970–77); chm: Cornwall and Isles of Scilly Health Authy 1981–83, South Western RHA 1983–90, Plymouth Health

Authy 1990–93, Plymouth Hosps NHS Tst; govr Saltash Comp Sch 1970–81; Defence Medal 1945, Queen's Silver Jubilee Medal 1977, Nat Assoc of Boys' Clubs Keystone Gold Award 1984; *Recreations* genealogy, industrial archaeology, gardening; *Style—* Sir Vernon Seccombe, JP; ✉ Chairman, Plymouth Hospitals NHS Trust, Derriford Hospital, Plymouth PL6 8DH (direct ☎ 01752 792762, fax 01752 781041)

SECKER, Prof Philip Edward; s of Cyril Edward Secker (d 1980); *b* 28 April 1936; *Educ* Haberdashers' Aske's, Univ of London; *m* 1968, Judith Andrea, da of Douglas Eric Lee (d 1981); 2 s; *Career* chartered engr; lectr Univ of London 1961–64, visiting asst prof Massachusetts Inst of Tech 1964–65; Univ Coll of N Wales: lectr 1965–69, sr lectr 1969–73, reader 1973–75, prof 1975–80; md IDB (UCNW) Ltd 1971–80, engrg dir Royal Doulton Ltd 1980–87, visiting prof Dept of Physics and Electronics Univ of Keele 1985–; dep chief exec IEE 1990–; *Recreations* flying light aircraft, gardening; *Style—* Prof Philip Secker; ✉ Gwel-Y-Don, Cae Mair, Beaumaris, Gwynedd (☎ 01248 810771)

SECKER-WALKER, Dr Jonathan; s of Geoffrey Secker-Walker (d 1968), of Farnborough, Hants, and Joan Alice, *née* Diplock (d 1995); *b* 19 Oct 1942; *Educ* Sherborne, UCL (BSc), UCH Med Sch (MB BS); *m* 20 July 1968, Jan Lilian, da of Charles James Goodwin, of Ryde, Isle of Wight; 1 s (Thomas Adam b 30 April 1973), 1 da (Katherine Louise b 16 Aug 1971); *Career* registrar (anaesthetics): UCH 1970–72, Gt Ormond St 1972; sr registrar (anaesthetics) St Thomas's Hosp 1973, clinical asst Toronto Sick Children's Hospital 1974, conslt anaesthetist and sr lectr UCH 1975, sr lectr in clinical audit UCL 1988–94, gen mangr UCL Hosps 1992–94, med dir Merrett Health Risk Management Ltd 1994–; hon sr lectr UCL Medical Sch 1994–; FRCA 1972, FRSM; *Recreations* skiing, sailing, walking, theatre; *Style—* Dr Jonathan Secker-Walker; ✉ 40 Woodland Gardens, Highgate Wood, London N10 3UA ☎ 0181 444 9426; The Rayne Institute, 5 University Street, London WC1E 6JJ (☎ 0171 209 6135)

SECOMBE, Sir Harry Donald; kt (1981), CBE (1963); *b* 8 Sept 1921; *Educ* Dynevor Sch Swansea; *m* 1948, Myra Joan Atherton, of Swansea; 2 s, 2 da; *Career* actor, comedian, singer and author; served WWII N Africa and Italy; *Theatre* incl: title role in Pickwick (West End musical, transferred Broadway 1963–65, revived Chichester Festival 1993–94 and tour at Sadler's Wells), The Four Musketeers (Theatre Royal Drury Lane), The Plumber's Progress (Prince of Wales), numerous seasons at London Palladium and ten Royal Command Performances; *Films* incl: Oliver 1968, Song of Norway 1969, and others; *Radio* Educating Archie, The Goon Show 1949–60; *TV* numerous variety shows, presenter Highway (Tyne Tees TV) 1983–93, presenter Sunday with Secombe (STV) 1994; pres Lord's Taverners 1980–81, Barker Variety Club of GB; former chm Stars Organisation for Spastics; pres Br Diabetic Assoc; Hon DMus Wales 1986; FRSA 1971; *Books* Twice Brightly, Goon For Lunch, Katy and The Nurgla, Welsh Fargo, Goon Abroad, The Harry Secombe Diet Book, Harry Secombe's Highway, The Highway Companion, Arias & Raspberries (autobiog, vol 1), The Nurgla's Magic Tear; *Recreations* photography, cricket, golf; *Clubs* Savage; *Style—* Sir Harry Secombe, CBE; ✉ 46 St James's Place, London SW1A 1NS

SECONDÉ, Sir Reginald Louis; KCMG (1981, CMG 1972), CVO (1968, MVO 1957); s of Lt-Col Emile Charles Secondé (d 1952); *b* 28 July 1922; *Educ* Beaumont, King's Coll Cambridge; *m* 1951, Catherine Penelope, da of Thomas Ralph Sneyd-Kynnersley, OBE, MC; 1 s, 2 da; *Career* Maj WWII Coldstream Gds in N Africa and Italy (despatches); Dip Serv 1949–82: UK Delgn to United Nations and British Embassies in Portugal, Cambodia, Poland and Brazil 1949–69, head S European Dept FCO 1969–72, Royal Coll of Defence Studies 1972–73; ambassador: Chile 1973–76, Romania 1977–79, Venezuela 1979–82, ret 1982; *Clubs* Cavalry and Guards'; *Style—* Sir Reginald Secondé, KCMG, CVO; ✉ Gosfield Hall, Gosfield, Halstead, Essex CO9 1SF (☎ 01787 477191)

SECUNDE, Nadine Rekeszus; da of John Philip Secunde, of the USA, and Patricia Margaret, *née* Bousi; *b* 21 Dec 1951; *Educ* Oberlin Conservatory of Music Oberlin Ohio, Univ of Indiana; *m* Heiner Rekeusus; 1 da (Anja Maria b 1989), 1 s (Jan-Philipp b 1992); *Career* soprano; studied with Margaret Harshaw at Univ of Indiana, Fulbright scholarship to Germany 1979, memb Hessisches Staatstheater Ensemble Wiesbaden 1980–84, with Cologne Opera 1984–89, Bayreuth Festspiele 1987–92; numerous guest appearances at major opera houses incl Munich, Vienna, Berlin, San Francisco, Chicago, Paris, Barcelona; *Recordings* incl: Prokofiev's The Fiery Angel (DDG), Strauss' Elektra (Phillips), Bayreuther Ring (Sieglinde), laser disc of Britten's Turn of the Screw; *Recreations* rare books; *Style—* Ms Nadine Secunde; ✉ c/o Ingpen & Williams Ltd, 14 Kensington Court, London W8 5DN (☎ 0171 937 5158, fax 0171 938 4175)

SEDCOLE, (Cecil) Frazer; *b* 15 March 1927; *Educ* Uppingham; *m* 1962, Jennifer B Riggall; 1 s, 1 da; *Career* RAF 1945–48; joined Unilever 1952; dir: Birds Eye Food Ltd 1960–66, Unilever plc and NV 1974–85 (vice chm Unilever plc 1982–85), Tate and Lyle 1982–90; dep chm Reed International 1985–87, vice chm Langnese-Iglo Germany 1966–67, chm UAC International 1976–79; memb: Overseas Ctee CBI 1979–86, BOTB 1982–86, Bd Cwlth Devpt Corp 1984–88; tstee Leverhulme Tst 1982–, govr Queen Elizabeth Fndn for Disabled People 1993–; FCA; *Recreations* golf; *Clubs* RAF; *Style—* Frazer Sedcole, Esq; ✉ Beeches, Tyrrells Wood, Leatherhead, Surrey KT22 PQH

SEDDON, (Edward) Jeremy; s of Col Roland Nelson Seddon, OBE, of Stourton Caundle, Dorset, and Dorothy Ida Kathleen, *née* Canning (d 1982); *b* 14 April 1941; *Educ* Kings Sch Bruton, Univ of Southampton (BSc); *m* 20 Sept 1975, Prudence Mary, da of Arthur William George Clarke (d 1955); 1 s (Thomas b 1985), 2 da (Serena b 1979, Alexandra b 1980); *Career* Associated Electrical Industries Ltd 1958–68, Dalgety Ltd 1968–73, exec chm BZW Ltd India 1995–; Freeman City of London 1976; *Recreations* sailing, music, gardening; *Clubs* Royal Thames Yacht, Special Forces; *Style—* Jeremy Seddon, Esq; ✉ Jesters, Oak Lane, Sevenoaks, Kent TN13 1UF (☎ 01732 461180); BZW Ltd, Ebbgate House, 2 Swan Lane, London EC4R 3TS (☎ 0171 623 2323)

SEDDON, Mark Richard Gwyn; s of John Seddon, of Liverpool, and Dorothy Margaret, *née* Handford; *b* 7 March 1959; *Educ* St Edward's Coll Liverpool, Univ of Liverpool (BA Hons); *Career* stockbroker; Charlton Seal Ltd Manchester 1981–83; assoc dir Neilson Cobbold Ltd (formerly Neilson Milnes Ltd) Liverpool 1993– (joined 1983); local cnclr Roby Ward Knowlsey 1984–92, Parly candidate (Cons) Liverpool Broadgreen 1987; chm N West Young Cons 1981, fndr pres Huyton Rotaract Club 1983, memb Catholic Inst Edwardian Assoc 1989 (sec 1996–97), press offr St Edward's Old Boys RUFC; MSI (pres Liverpool Branch 1993–95 and 1996–97); *Recreations* photography, rugby union, amateur dramatics; *Style—* Mark Seddon, Esq; ✉ Da Pacem, 50 Acacia Ave, Huyton, Merseyside L36 5TP (☎ 0151 489 7932); Neilson Cobbold Ltd, 6th Floor Martins Building, 4 Water St, Liverpool L2 3LF (☎ 0151 236 6666, fax 0151 236 4996)

SEDDON, Nicholas Paul; s of Clive Seddon, of Congleton, Cheshire, and Alison Helen, *née* Dale; *b* 11 July 1960; *Educ* Sandbach GS, Univ of Birmingham (LLB); *m* 22 Oct 1988, Suzanne Elizabeth, da of John Clive Wilson; *Career* admitted slr 1984; ptnr: Needham & James Birmingham 1988–93 (joined 1982), Dibb Lupton Broomhead 1993–; memb: Birmingham Law Soc, Law Soc; *Recreations* motor sport, cycling, photography, wine; *Style—* Nicholas Seddon, Esq; ✉ Arlescote Manor Barn, Arlescote, nr Banbury, Oxon OX17 1DQ; Dibb Lupton Broomhead, Windsor House, Temple Row, Birmingham B2 5LF (☎ 0121 200 5023, fax 0121 212 2730, car 0385 306801)

SEDDON, Dr Richard Harding; s of Cyril Harding Seddon (d 1974), of Bury St Edmunds, and Mary Seddon, *née* Booth (d 1983); *b* 1 May 1915; *Educ* King Edward VII Sch Sheffield, Sheffield Coll of Arts & Crafts, Univ of Reading (PhD); *m* 1946, Audrey Madeline, da of Albert Edward Wareham (d 1973), of Sussex; *Career* artist; vol Lance-Corpl RAOC 1939–40 (invalided after Dunkirk, King's Badge 1940), Co Intelligence Offr Home Guard 1941–43, Instr (Lieut) Reading Univ Sr Training Corps 1943–45; exhibitor at RA, RI and other major galleries 1947–; staff tutor in fine art Univ of Birmingham 1947–47, dir Sheffield City Art Galleries 1948–64, head of art history & liberal studies Buckinghamshire Coll of Technol & Art 1964–80; Royal Soc of Painters in Water Colours: memb Ctee 1974–85, treas 1974–84, pres 1995–96; co-fndr and pres Ludlow Art Soc 1948–64, pres Yorkshire Fedn of Museums of Art Galleries 1954–55, Yorkshire rep Nat Art Collections Fund 1954–64, sec Yorkshire Fact-Finding Ctee of Regionalisation of Art Galleries 1959, dep chm Sheffield Cncl for Gold, Silver and Jewellery Trades 1960–64 (also memb), memb BBC '51 Soc 1960–63; London art critic: Birmingham Post 1965–71, Yorkshire Post 1972–92; hon memb Mark Twain Soc (USA) 1976; Hon RI (1996); civic medal Neuchatel France 1978; ARCA 1939, RWS 1972; *Books* A Hand Uplifted (1963), The Academic Technique of Painting (1960), Art Collecting for Amateurs (1965), Illustrated Dictionary of Art Terms (1984), The Artist's Studio Book (1983); *Recreations* gardening, photography; *Clubs* Arts; *Style—* Dr Richard Seddon; ✉ 6 Arlesey Close, London SW15 (☎ 0181 788 5899)

SEDGEMORE, Brian Charles John; MP (Lab) Hackney South and Shoreditch (majority 9,016); *b* 17 March 1937; *Educ* Heles Sch Exeter, Oxford Univ; *m* (m dis); *Career* civil servant 1962–66, called to the Bar Middle Temple 1966; cnclr London Borough of Wandsworth 1971–74; MP (Lab): Luton West Feb 1974–79, Hackney S and Shoreditch 1983–; PPS to Tony Benn 1977–78, memb Select Ctee on Treasy and Civil Serv 1987–; researcher for Granada TV 1980–84; memb: NUJ, Writers Guild of GB; *Style—* Brian Sedgemore, Esq, MP; ✉ c/o House of Commons, London SW1A 0AA

SEDGWICK, Ivan Harry; *b* 13 Jan 1959; *Educ* Farnborough Sixth Form Coll, Clare Coll Cambridge (MA), City Univ Business Sch (MBA); *m* 1988, Elizabeth, da of late Capt R Heathcote, DSO, RN; 2 s; *Career* Deloitte Haskins & Sells CAs London 1980–81, New Japan Securities London 1981–85, Morgan Stanley International London 1985–89, dir Schroder Securities Ltd 1989–; *Recreations* opera, shooting, fishing; *Style—* Ivan Sedgwick, Esq; ✉ Schroder Securities Ltd, 120 Cheapside, London EC2

SEDGWICK, Dr John Philip; s of Philip Giles Sedgwick (d 1940), and Vera Constance, *née* Everard; *b* 6 Dec 1938; *Educ* Dean Close, Guy's Hosp Med Sch London (MB BS, DA); *m* 1, 23 March 1963 (m dis 1978), Judith Ann, da of Edgar Nelson, of Southampton; 1 s (Philip Giles), 2 da (Nicola Jane, Helen Louise); m 2, 7 April 1982, Anne Louise Warren (d 1991), da of Arthur Henry Dickinson, of Dinnington, nr Doncaster, Yorks; *Career* house surgn Guy's Hosp 1964, house physician Lewisham Hosp 1964–65, sr house offr Royal Sussex Co Hosp 1965–66; med advsr: John Wyeth 1966, Servier Laboratories 1967; GP 1968–75, private practitioner 1975–77, dir health servs Brunel Univ 1978–96, sr clincial occupational health physician Hillingdon Borough; currently MO: Pioneer, Schweppes Beverages, Coca-Cola, Mallinckrodt Veterinary (formerly Pitman-Moore); memb Worshipful Co of Feltmakers 1970; Hon FRSM; *Recreations* golf; *Style—* Dr John Sedgwick; ✉ Ashley Cottage, 3 Ferry Lane, Bray-on-Thames, Berks SL6 2AS

SEDGWICK, (Ian) Peter; *b* 14 Oct 1935; *m* 6 Aug 1956, (Verna) Mary; 1 s (Paul b 17 March 1961), 1 da (Carey Anne b 30 Nov 1962); *Career* National Provincial Bank 1952–59, Ottoman Bank Africa and the ME 1959–69, J Henry Schroder Wagg & Co Ltd 1969–90; gp md investmt mgmnt Schroders plc 1987–95 (vice chm 1995–), pres and chief exec offr Schroders Inc NY 1996–; dir Schroder Nominees Limited 1981–95, chief exec Schroder Investment Management Limited 1985–94, dir Schroder Unit Trusts Limited 1987–95; chm: Schroder UK Growth Fund 1994–, Schroder Wertheim & Co Inc 1996– (non-exec dir 1991–); non-exec dir: Equitable Life Assurance Society 1991–, Drayton Blue Chip Trust plc 1991–, New City & Commercial Investment Trust plc 1992–; chm: Schroder Asian Growth Fund 1991–; *Recreations* golf; *Style—* Peter Sedgwick, Esq; ✉ Schroders plc, 120 Cheapside, London EC2V 6DS (☎ 0171 382 6476, fax 0171 288 2211)

SEDGWICK, Peter Norman; s of Norman Victor Sedgwick, of 25 Allenview Rd, Wimborne, Dorset, and Lorna Clara, *née* Burton; *b* 4 Dec 1943; *Educ* Westminster Cathedral Choir Sch, Downside, Lincoln Coll Oxford (MA, BPhil); *m* 17 Feb 1984, Catherine Jane, da of Barry Donald Thomas and Janet Saunders; 2 s (Richard b 30 Dec 1986, Christopher b 14 April 1988), 2 da (Victoria b 6 July 1989, Rebecca Elizabeth b 3 Dec 1990); *Career* HM Treasy: econ asst 1969, econ advsr 1971, sr econ advsr 1977, under sec 1984, dep dir 1995–; memb London Symphony Chorus 1972– (chm 1979–84); *Recreations* singing, gardening, walking; *Style—* Peter Sedgwick, Esq; ✉ HM Treasury, Parliament St, London SW1 (☎ 0171 270 4430)

SEDLEY, Hon Mr Justice; Hon Sir Stephen John; kt (1992); s of William Sedley (d 1984), and Rachel Sedley (d 1987); *b* 9 Oct 1939; *Educ* Mill Hill Sch, Queens' Coll Cambridge (Open scholar and exhibitioner, BA); *m* 1, 1968 (m dis), Ann Tate; 3 c (Jane May b 5 May 1970, Benjamin Anthony b 9 May 1972, Sarah Ann b 27 Sept 1975); m 2, 1996, Teresa (Tia) Cockrell; *Career* called to the Eng Bar 1964 (called Trinidad and Tobago 1986); QC 1983, asst recorder 1985–92, master of the bench Inner Temple 1989–, judge of the High Court of Justice (Queen's Bench Div) 1992–; memb Int Cmmn on Mercenaries (Angola) 1976, visiting professorial fell Univ of Warwick 1981, memb Mgmnt Ctee Legal Res Inst Univ of Warwick 1981–93, pres Nat Reference Tbnls for coalmining industry 1983–87, visiting fell Osgoode Hall (Toronto) 1987, chair Inquiry into the death of Tyra Henry (Lambeth) 1986–87, fndr memb and dir Public Law Project 1988–93, distinguished visitor Hong Kong Univ 1992, chm Sex Discrimination Ctee Bar Cncl 1992–; Paul Sieghart Meml Lecture on Human Rights 1995; hon prof of law: Univ of Wales at Cardiff 1992–, Univ of Warwick 1993–; hon vice pres Administrative Law Bar Assoc 1993– (memb Ctee 1987–92); *Publications* From Burgos Gaol (translation, 1964), The Seeds of Love (anthology, 1967), Inside the Myth (contrib, 1984), Civil Liberties (contrib, 1984), Police, the Constitution and the Community (contrib, 1985), Challenging Decisions (1986), Public Interest Law (contrib, 1987), Whose Child? (report of the Tyra Henry Inquiry, 1987), Civil Liberties in Conflict (contrib, 1988), Law in East and West (contrib, 1988), Citizenship (contrib, 1991), A Spark in the Ashes: the pamphlets of John Warr (ed with introduction, 1992), Administrative Law and Government Action (contrib, 1995); also various articles in: Public Law, Modern Law Review, Journal of Law and Society, Civil Justice Quarterly, London Review of Books, Industrial Law Journal, Law Quarterly Review; *Style—* The Hon Mr Justice Sedley; ✉ c/o Royal Courts of Justice, Strand, London WC2A 2LL

SEEAR, Baroness (Life Peer UK 1971), of Paddington in the City of Westminster; Beatrice Nancy Seear; PC (1985); da of late Herbert Charles Seear, of Croydon; *b* 7 Aug 1913; *Educ* Croydon HS, Newnham Coll Cambridge, LSE; *Career* ldr of Liberal peers in House of Lords 1984–88, dep leader of Liberal Democrats 1988–; personnel mangr C J Clark Ltd 1936–46, reader in Personnel Mgmnt LSE 1946–78; pres Liberal Pty Orgn 1965–66; author of books on Women's Employment; Hon LLD: Leeds 1979, Bristol 1994; Hon DLitt: Bath 1982, Exeter; Hon Doctorate Middx; *Recreations* gardening, reading, travelling; *Clubs* Royal Commonwealth Soc, Nat Lib; *Style—* The Rt Hon the Lady Seear, PC; ✉ 189b Kennington Rd, London SE11 6ST (☎ 0171 587 0205)

SEED, Paul; *b* 18 Sept 1947; *Educ* Manchester GS, Univ of Manchester (BA, Drama); *Career* director; actor 1970–1981; credits incl: Too Late to Talk to Billy (trilogy, BBC) 1982–83, Wynne & Penovsky (BBC, US title The Man from Moscow) 1984, Inappropriate Behaviour (BBC) 1986, Capital City (Euston Films) 1988–89, House of Cards (BBC) 1990, To Play the King (BBC) 1993, Disaster at Valdez (HBO/BBC) 1992, The Affair

(HBO/BBC) 1994–95, Have your Cake and It (BBC/Initial) 1996; memb Dir Guild of GB; *Style—* Paul Seed, Esq; ✉ c/o Tim Corrie, Peters Fraser & Dunlop Ltd, 503 The Chambers, Chelsea Harbour, Lots Road, London SW10 0XF (☎ 0171 344 1000, fax 0171 352 7356)

SEEKINGS, John Charles; s of Leonard Charles Seekings, of Shrewsbury, and Joan Margaret, *née* Lemming; *b* 25 Oct 1955; *Educ* Worthing Technical HS, Univ of Southampton (BSc); *m* 1 June 1985, Andrea Katrina, da of James Peter Hamilton MBE; 2 da (Charlotte Elise b 30 April 1986, Emily Alexandra b 1 March 1989), 1 s (Matthew Charles b 10 Sept 1991); *Career* freelance stage and prodn mangr (in rep, W End and touring theatres) 1977–78; Royal Opera House: tech mangr 1979–87, asst tech dir 1988–92, dep tech dir 1993–, devpt dir 1995–; TTTS Ltd: conslt to Bd 1992–, dir and chm 1995–; FRGS 1974; *Recreations* family, travel, reading; *Style—* John Seekings, Esq; ✉ Elm Lodge, 84 Bourne Road, Bexley, Kent DA5 1LU; Royal Opera House, 45 Floral Street, Covent Garden, London WC2E 9DD (☎ 0171 212 9386, fax 0171 836 3666)

SEEL, Derek; s of William Alfred Seel (d 1988), and Olive, *née* Greenwell (d 1989); *b* 2 April 1932; *Educ* Stockport Sch, Univ of Manchester (BDS); *m* 27 Feb 1960, Gillian Mary, da of Roy Henderson (d 1966), of Bolton; 2 s (Richard Adrian, Ceri Dan); *Career* conslt orthodontist Univ Hosp Wales 1969–94, dental postgrad dean Univ of Bristol 1987–; memb Cncl RCS 1987–92, dean Faculty of Dental Surgeons RCS 1989–92 (memb Bd 1979–93); Hon DGDP (UK); FDSRCS, MOrth, FRCS, FRCA; *Recreations* music, photography, golf; *Style—* Derek Seel, Esq; ✉ 20 Blenheim Rd, Bristol BS6 7JP (☎ 0117 973 6635)

SEELY, Sir Nigel Edward; 5 Bt (UK 1896), of Sherwood Lodge, Arnold, Notts and Brooke House, Brooke, Isle of Wight; s of Sir Victor Seely, 4 Bt (d 1980), by 1 w, Sybil Helen (later Baroness Paget of Northampton, *née* Gibbons (d 1994), widow of Sir John Bridger Shiffner, 6 Bt; *b* 28 July 1923; *Educ* Stowe; *m* 1, 1949, Loraine, da of late Wilfred W Lindley-Travis; 3 da; m 2, 1984, Trudi, da of Sydney Pacter; *Heir* half-bro, Victor Ronald Seely b 1 Aug 1941; *Career* with Dorland International; *Clubs* Buck's, Royal Solent Yacht; *Style—* Sir Nigel Seely, Bt; ✉ 3 Craven Hill Mews, London W2

SEELY, Hon Peter John Philip; s and h of 4 Baron Mottistone; *b* 29 Oct 1949; *Educ* Uppingham; *m* 1, 1972 (m dis 1975), Joyce, da of Mrs Ellen Cairns, of St Ninians, Stirling; 1 s (Christopher David Peter b 1 Oct 1974); m 2, 1982, Linda, da of W A Swain, of Judds House, Bulphan Fen, Upminster, Essex; 1 s (Richard William Anthony b 1988), 3 da (Penelope Jane b 1984, Jennifer Elizabeth b 1986, Caroline Anne b 1990)); *Style—* The Hon Peter Seely; ✉ Alendale, Uckfield Lane, Hever, Kent TN8 7LJ

SEELY, Maj Victor Ronald; s of late Sir Victor Seely, 4 Bt (d 1980), by his 3 w, Mary, da of late Ronald Collins; hp of half-bro, Sir Nigel Seely, 5 Bt; *b* 1 Aug 1941; *Educ* Eton, RMA Sandhurst, Staff Coll Camberley; *m* 1972, Annette Bruce, da of late Lt-Col J A D McEwen; 1 s (William b 1983), 1 da (Natasha b 1979); *Career* Maj The Royal Hussars (PWO), served on attachment to US Army 1968, served on secondment to Sultan of Oman's Armed Forces 1970–71, ret 1988; dir The Spring Centre charity for special needs children Gloucester 1989–91, advtg conslt 1991–; Liveryman Worshipful Co of Gunmakers; *Recreations* breeding and showing ponies (The Hulverstone Stud), eventing; *Style—* Maj Victor Seely; ✉ Newlands Farm, Farfield Cam, Dursley, Glos GL11 5HE

SEFTON, Catherine; *see:* Waddell, Martin

SEFTON OF GARSTON, Baron (Life Peer UK 1978), of Garston, Co Merseyside; William Henry Sefton; s of George Sefton; *b* 5 Aug 1915; *Educ* Duncombe Rd Sch Liverpool; *m* 1940, Phyllis, *née* Kerr; *Career* sits as Labour peer in House of Lords; leader Liverpool CC 1964–78, oppn leader Merseyside CC 1977–79 (first chm 1973–77); chm: Runcorn Devpt Corpn 1974–81, North West Planning Corpn 1975–80; *Style—* The Rt Hon the Lord Sefton of Garston; ✉ c/o House of Lords, London SW1A 0PW

SEGAL, Prof Anthony Walter; s of Cyril Segal, and Doreen, *née* Hayden; *b* 24 Feb 1944; *Educ* Univ of Cape Town SA (MB ChB, MD), Univ of London (MSc, DSc, PhD); *m* 18 Dec 1966 (m dis), Barbara Ann, da of Justice Solomon Miller (d 1987), of Durban SA; 3 da (Terry b 1969, Jessica b 1972, Penelope b 1976); *Career* Charles Dent Prof of Med Univ Coll and Middx Sch of Med 1986–; FRCP; *Recreations* squash, tennis, sailing, art, theatre; *Style—* Prof Anthony Segal; ✉ Dept of Medicine, University College London, University Street, London WC1E 6JJ (☎ 0171 209 6175, fax 0171 209 6211)

SEGAL, Michael John; s of Abraham Charles Segal (d 1981), of London, and Iris Muriel, *née* Parsons (d 1971); *b* 20 Sept 1937; *Educ* Strode's Sch Surrey; *m* 1 March 1963, Barbara Gina, da of Dr Joseph Leon Fluxman, of Johannesburg, S Africa (d 1954); 1 da (Leila b 10 Sept 1966); *Career* called to the Bar Middle Temple 1962, practised on Midland and Oxford circuit 1963–84; dist judge Princ Registry Family Div 1985–; memb: Queen's Bench Procedure Ctee 1975–80, Civil and Family Ctee Judicial Studies Bd 1990–94; dep stipendiary magistrate 1980–84; memb Medico-Legal Soc, fndr memb Trollope Soc; *Publications* Butterworths Costs Service (jt ed), Supreme Court Practice (jt ed 1993–95); *Recreations* reading, music, logic; *Clubs* Athenaeum; *Style—* Michael Segal, Esq; ✉ 28 Grange Rd, London N6 4AP (☎ 0181 348 0680); Principal Registry, Family Division, Somerset House, London, WC2

SEGAL, Victor Maurice; s of John Segal, of London, and Theresa, *née* Nordman (d 1990); *b* 20 Oct 1940; *Educ* Clifton, The Queen's Coll Oxford (BA, MA); *m* 1, 21 Feb 1967 (m dis 1978), Rosemary, *née* Braunsberg; 1 s (Julian Daniel Joseph b 13 March 1971), 1 da (Alexandra Jane Natasha b 12 June 1969); m 2, 2 Dec 1979, Carol, *née* Norton; *Career* articled clerk Nicholson Graham & Jones 1962–65, admitted slr 1965, Bartlett & Gluckstein 1965–68, dir Singer & Friedlander Ltd 1976– (joined 1968, currently head of int banking); memb: Law Soc 1965, International bankers Club 1981; *Recreations* skiing, golf, tennis, bridge, music, watching Spurs; *Style—* Victor Segal, Esq; ✉ Head of International Banking, Singer & Friedlander Ltd, 21 New Street, Bishopsgate, London EC2M 4HR (☎ 0171 623 3000, fax 0171 623 2122)

SEGALL, Anne (Mrs David Evans); *b* 20 April 1948; *Educ* St Paul's Girls' Sch London, St Hilda's Coll Oxford (BA); *m* David Howard Evans, QC; 2 s (Oliver, Edward); *Career* economics and banking corr Investors' Chronicle 1971–76, banking corr The Economist 1976–80, banking then economics corr Daily Telegraph 1980–; Harold Wincott award 1975; *Recreations* swimming, theatre, reading; *Style—* Ms Anne Segall; ✉ Daily Telegraph (City Office), Salters Hall, 4 Fore Street, London EC2Y 5DT (☎ 0171 538 6911, fax 0171 628 0343)

SEIFERT, John Michael; s of Lt-Col Richard Seifert, and Josephine Jeanette, *née* Harding; *b* 17 Feb 1949; *Educ* Mill Hill Sch, Bartlett Sch of Architecture, UCL (BSc, Dip Arch); *m* 1 Feb 1985, Johanna Marion, da of Elias Hofmann; 2 s (James, Edward), 1 da (Elizabeth), 1 step s (Marlon); *Career* architect; chm John Seifert Ltd; major projects incl: Cutlers Gardens 1983, Mermaid Theatre 1983, Bank of Chicago House 1984, Sheraton Hotel Lagos 1985, Bishopsbridge 1985, MISR Bank Tower 1986, South Quay Plaza 1987, Swiss Banking Corporation 1988, Hambros Bank 1988, Sceptre Court 1988, Greenwich View 1989, Glengall Bridge 1989, Hilton Hotel Paris; major competitions won: Surrey Docks Shopping Centre 1983, Limehouse Basin 1985, Heathrow Hotel 1988, Sandwell Mall 1988; Liveryman Worshipful Co of Glaziers and Painters of Glass 1967; RIBA 1976, CROAIF (France) 1981, NCARB (USA) 1983; registered in Germany; *Recreations* painting, sculpture, numismatics; *Clubs* Carlton, Arts; *Style—* John Seifert, Esq; ✉ John Seifert Architects, 2–20 Capper Street, London WC1E 6JA (☎ 0171 242 1644, fax 0171 379 0099)

SEIFERT, Dr Martin Howard; s of Dr Victor Max Seifert (d 1974), of Winchmore Hill, London, and Sophie Seifert (d 1980); *b* 16 Nov 1939; *Educ* Highgate Sch, London Hosp Med Coll Univ of London (MB BS); *m* Nov 1974, Dr Jackie Morris, *qv*, da of Prof Norman Morris, *qv*, of Hampstead, London; 1 s (Benjamin William D'Avigdor b 1978), 1 da (Victoria Charlotte b 1975); *Career* house surgn The London Hosp 1965, registrar in rheumatology The Middx Hosp 1969 (sr house offr 1967–69), sr registrar and chief asst in rheumatology St Thomas's Hosp 1971–74, res fell in rheumatology Univ of Colorado Med Center Denver USA 1973, conslt rheumatologist St Mary's Hosp London 1974–, conslt physician The Charterhouse Rheumatism Clinic Lndon 1975–84; RCP: hon sec Ctee on Rheumatology, regnl advsr in med for NW Thames Region 1991–95, regnl advsr for continuing med educn 1995–96; RCP rep Central Conslts and Specialists Ctee BMA 1996–; chm Educn Ctee Arthritis and Rheumatism Cncl 1987–90, treas Br Soc for Rheumatology 1984–87 (Heberden Rounds-man 1996); pres Rheumatology and Rehabilitation Section RSM 1989 (vice pres 1990); Med Soc of London: memb Cncl 1990–, hon sec 1993–95, vice pres 1995–96; memb Cncl: RSM 1990–95, Br Soc for Rheumatology 1995– (tstee); numerous papers and contribs to textbooks on rheumatic diseases; FRCP 1980; *Recreations* family, book collecting, the arts, plodding; *Clubs* RSM; *Style—* Dr Martin Seifert; ✉ 45 Whitehall Park, London N19 3TW; The Well House, Sandford St Martin, Chipping Norton, Oxon OX7 7AG; St Mary's Hospital, Praed St, London W2 (☎ 0171 725 1066)

SEIFERT, Dr Ruth; da of Sigmund Seifert (d 1979), and Connie, *née* Shine; *b* 20 Dec 1943; *Educ* Camden Sch for Girls, Guy's Hosp Med Sch London; *m* 1971, Dr Charles Richard Astley Clarke, *qv*, s of Prof Sir Cyril Astley Clarke, KBE, FRS, *qv*; 2 da (Rebecca b 3 Feb 1973, Naomi b 7 Sept 1976); *Career* jr hosp appts 1968–73, post grad trg in psychiatry Maudsley Hosp 1973–80, conslt in pscyhological med Bart's 1980– (dep chm Med Cncl 1988–90), regnl advsr in psychiatry NE Thames RHA 1993–; MO Himal Kisthwar Expdn (to climb Bramah in the Himalayas) 1971; FRCPsych 1988 (MRCPsych 1975); *Recreations* opera, cinema, cooking; *Style—* Dr Ruth Seifert; ✉ Department of Pscyhological Medicine, St Bartholomew's Hospital, West Smithfield, London EC1 (☎ 0171 601 8109)

SEILER, Dr (Edmund) Ronald (Ronnie); TD (1995); s of Dr Henry Edmund Seiler (d 1978), of Edinburgh, and Winifred Marjory, *née* Lindsay (d 1968); *b* 8 March 1934; *Educ* George Watson's Coll Edinburgh, Univ of Edinburgh (MB ChB, DRCOG, DCH, FRCGP, FRCP 1996); *m* 26 March 1966, Anne Christina, da of William Martin McNeill (d 1982), and Dorothy Noel, *née* Maw; 2 da (Catriona Marjory b 22 Feb 1967, Mary Claire McNeill b 16 Jan 1969), 2 s (John Alexander Lindsay b 1 April 1970, Robert William Edmund b 27 April 1973); *Career* house offr Deaconess Hosp then Royal Infirmary Edinburgh 1959–60; Nat Serv Malta, Borneo and Singapore 1960–63; SHO: in obstetrics Forth Park Maternity Hosp Kirkcaldy 1963–64, in paediatrics Royal Hosp for Sick Children Yorkhill Glasgow 1964, in neonatal paediatrics Bellshill Hosp Lanarkshire 1964; trainee GP Dept of Gen Practice Edinburgh 1964–65, SHO/registrar in med Perth Royal Infirmary 1965–66; princ in gen practice: Edinburgh 1966–74, University Health Serv Edinburgh 1974–; lectr Dept of Gen Practice Univ of Edinburgh 1968–74; assoc regional advsr in gen practice 1976–, trainer in gen practice 1979–, chm Assoc of Course Organisers 1984–87; RCGP: chm Educn Ctee SE Scotland Faculty 1970–72, faculty del to UK Cncl 1991–94; pipe major Royal Scottish Pipers Soc 1979–81, RAMC Maj 205 Gen Hosp (TA) Scotland 1983–95, chm local Scout Gp Exec 1985–86; memb: Edinburgh Med Chirurgical Soc, Harveian Soc; *Recreations* golf, piping; *Clubs* Clouston; *Style—* Dr Ronnie Seiler, TD; ✉ 30 Spylaw Bank Road, Edinburgh EH13 0JG (☎ 0131 441 1386); University Health Service, 6 Bristo Square, Edinburgh EH8 9AL (☎ 0131 650 2777, fax 0131 662 1813)

SEITZ, Hon Raymond George Hardenbergh; s of John Francis Regis Seitz, and Helen Stewart Johnson Hardenbergh; *b* 8 Dec 1940; *Educ* Yale Univ (BA); *m* 10 May 1985, Caroline, *née* Richardson; 2 s (Royce Manning Barr b 24 Sept 1966, Thomas McKeen Cutler b 10 April 1974), 1 da (Hillary Helen Brewster b 1 Jan 1969); *Career* American Dip Serv until 1994: consular offr Montreal 1966–69, political offr Nairobi and concurrently vice consul Seychelles 1969–70, princ offr Bukavu Zaire 1970–72, staff offr later dir Secretariat Staff Washington 1972, special asst to DG Foreign Serv 1972–75, political offr London 1975–79 (DG's Award for Reporting), dep exec sec Dept of State Washington 1979–81, dep asst sec for public affrs 1981–82, exec asst to Sec of State 1982–84, min London 1984–89, asst sec of state for Euro and Canadian affrs Washington 1989–91, ambass to Ct of St James's 1991–94; vice chm Lehman Brothers International (Europe) 1996– (sr md 1995–96); non-exec dir: Telegraph Group plc 1994–, Chubb Corporation 1994–, Shandwick plc 1994–, Cable & Wireless plc 1995–, British Airways Plc 1995–, GEC plc 1995–, RTZ-CRA plc 1996–; Presidential Award for Meritorious Service 1986 and 1988; Knight Cdr's Cross (Germany) 1991; hon doctorates: Univ of Reading 1992, Richmond Coll 1992, Univ of Bath 1993, Univ of Leeds 1994, Univ of Durham 1994, Heriot-Watt Univ 1994; Benjamin Franklin Medal RSA 1996; *Recreations* literature, architecture; *Clubs* Garrick, Beefsteak; *Style—* The Hon Raymond Seitz; ✉ Lehman Brothers International (Europe), One Broadgate, London EC2M 7HA (☎ 0171 260 2939, fax 0171 260 2892)

SEKACZ, Ilona Anna; da of Aleksander Sekacz, and Olive, *née* Swithenbank; *b* 6 April 1948; *Educ* Arnold HS Blackpool, Univ of Birmingham; *Career* composer of works for film, television, radio and theatre 1982–; *Recreations* cinema, conservation; *Style—* Miss Ilona Sekacz; ✉ c/o ICM Ltd, Oxford House, 76 Oxford Street, London W1N 0AX (☎ 0171 636 6565, fax 0171 323 0101)

SELBORNE, 4 Earl of (UK 1882); John Roundell Palmer; KBE (1987), DL (Hants 1982); also Baron Selborne (UK 1872), Viscount Wolmer (UK 1882); s of Viscount Wolmer (k on active service 1942; s of 3 Earl) and Priscilla (*see* Baron Newton); suc gf 1971. Lord Selborne's gggf, the 1 Earl, was Lord Chllr 1872–74 and 1880–85 and his ggf was First Lord of the Admiralty 1900–05 and helped establish the RNVR, the RFR, Osborne & Dartmouth Naval Colleges and the Designs Committee which resulted in the Royal Navy being equipped with Dreadnoughts; *b* 24 March 1940; *Educ* Eton, ChCh Oxford; *m* 1969, Joanna Van Antwerp, da of Evan James, of Upwood Park, Abingdon (and sis of Countess Baldwin of Bewdley); 3 s (Viscount Wolmer, Hon George b 1974, Hon Luke (twin) b 1974), 1 da (Lady Emily b 1978); *Heir* s, Viscount Wolmer; *Career* sits as Cons in House of Lords, chm Sub-Ctee D (Agric and Food) House of Lords' Select Ctee on Euro Communities 1991–93, chm Select Ctee on Science and Technology 1993–; chm: Hops Marketing Bd 1978–82, Agric and Food Res Cncl 1983–89 (memb 1975–89, dep chm 1982), Joint Nature Conservation Ctee 1991–, Agricultural Mortgage Corporation 1994–; pres Royal Inst of Public Health and Hygiene 1991–, memb Royal Cmmn on Environmental Pollution 1993–, vice-pres Foundation for Science and Technology 1993–; chllr Univ of Southampton 1996–; former vice-chm Apple and Pear Devpt Cncl, treas Bridewell Royal Hosp (King Edward's Sch Witley) 1972–83; memb Ct of Assts Worshipful Co of Mercers; FRS 1991; *Clubs* Brooks's, Farmers'; *Style—* The Rt Hon the Earl of Selborne, KBE, FRS, DL; ✉ Temple Manor, Selborne, Alton, Hants (☎ 01420 473646)

SELBY, 5 Viscount (UK 1905); Edward Thomas William Gully; o s of 4 Viscount Selby (d 1997), and Mary Theresa, *née* Powell; *b* 21 Sept 1967; *Educ* Harrow; *m* 10 Oct 1992, Charlotte Catherine, yr da of Rolph Brege, of Lomma, Sweden; 1 s (Hon Christopher Rolf Thomas b 18 Oct 1993); *Heir* s, Hon Christopher Rolf Thomas Gully b 18 Oct 1993; *Style*— The Rt Hon the Viscount Selby; ✉ Shuna Castle, Island of Shuna, Argyll; Ardfern House, by Lochgilphead, Argyll PA31 8QN

SELBY, Bishop of 1991–; Rt Rev Humphrey Vincent Taylor; s of Maurice Humphrey Taylor, MBE (d 1987), and Mary Patricia Stuart, *née* Wood; *b* 5 March 1938; *Educ* Harrow, Pembroke Coll Cambridge (BA, MA), Univ of London (MA); *m* 24 April 1965, Anne Katharine, da of Thomas Henry Dart, of Woking, Surrey; 2 da (Katharine b 1966, Elizabeth b 1968); *Career* Nat Serv PO Tech Branch 1956–58; curate: Hammersmith 1963–64, N Kensington 1964–66; rector Lilongwe Malawi 1966–71, chaplain and lectr Bishop Grosseteste Coll Lincoln 1972–74, sec for chaplaincies in higher educn Gen Synod Bd of Educn 1974–80, sec USPG 1984–91 (mission progs sec 1980–84), chm Int and Devpt Affairs Ctee Gen Synod Bd for Social Responsibility 1996–; hon canon: Bristol Cathedral 1986–91, Province of Southern Africa 1989–; *Style*— The Rt Rev the Bishop of Selby; ✉ 10 Precentor's Court, York YO1 2EJ (☎ 01904 656492, fax 01904 655671)

SELBY, Prof Peter John; s of Joseph Selby, and Dorothy, *née* Cross; *b* 10 July 1950; *Educ* Lydney GS, Cambridge Univ (MA, MB, MB BChir, MD); *m* 8 July 1972, Catherine Elisabeth, da of Peter Thomas; 1 s (David b 1985), 1 da (Alexandra b 1980); *Career* conslt physician Royal Marsden Hosp London 1985–88, prof of cancer medicine and conslt physician Univ of Leeds and St James's Univ Hosp Leeds 1988– (dir Imperial Cancer Research Fund Cancer Med Research Unit); ed Br Jl Cancer 1987–92; memb Ctee: Cancer Research Campaign, Assoc of Cancer Physicians, Br Assoc for Cancer Research, Br Oncological Assoc (pres 1992–94), Med Research Cncl, UK Co-ordinator Ctee Cancer Research and Euro Orgn for Research and Treatment of Cancer; FRCP, FRCR; *Books* Hodgkin's Disease (1987), Confronting Cancer: Cause and Prevention (1993), Cancer in Adolescents (1995), Malignant Lymphomas (1995); *Recreations* reading, music, sailing, running; *Style*— Prof Peter Selby; ✉ 17 Park Lane, Roundhay, Leeds LS8; ICRF Cancer Medicine Research Unit, St James's University Hospital, Beckett St, Leeds LS9 7TF (☎ 0113 244 2007, fax 0113 242 9886)

SELBY, Ralph Walford; CMG (1961); s of Sir Walford Selby, KCMG, CB, CVO (d 1965), and Dorothy Orme, *née* Carter (d 1981); *b* 20 March 1915; *Educ* Eton, ChCh Oxford; *m* 8 Dec 1945, Julianna (d 1994), da of Capt Ivan Edward Snell, MC (d 1958), and Marjorie Villiers (d 1981), gda of 4 Earl of Clarendon; 3 da (Virginia, Pamela, Cynthia); *Career* entered HM Dip Serv 1938, Capt Grenadier Gds 1939–45, served in Delhi, The Hague, FO, Tokyo, Copenhagen, Djakarta, Warsaw 1965–66; consul-gen Boston 1966, min Rome 1969, ambass Oslo 1972–75; *Style*— Ralph Selby, Esq, CMG; ✉ Mengeham House, Mengham Lane, Hayling Island, Hants PO11 9JX (☎ 01705 463833)

SELBY, Rona; da of Philip Ronald James, of Dorset, and Agnes Mary, *née* Maycock; *b* 18 March 1953; *Educ* Beckenham GS for Girls, Univ of Exeter (BA); *m* 2 Sept 1978, David Selby; 1 s (Ben b 11 May 1983), 1 da (Tamsin Alexandra b 4 May 1985); *Career* The Bodley Head Publishers 1975–88 (memb Bd 1987–88), publisher Methuen Children's Books 1988–92, conslt S4C Wales 1992, children's book devpt conslt to BBC 1992–96, head of BBC Children's Publishing (Video, Books and Audio) 1996–; *Recreations* swimming, cycling, sailing; *Style*— Mrs Rona Selby; ✉ BBC Worldwide Publishing, Woodlands, 80 Wood Lane, London W12 0TT (☎ 0181 576 2631, fax 0181 576 3027, telex 934678)

SELF, (Hugh) Michael; QC (1973); s of Sir (Albert) Henry Self, KCB, KCMG, KBE (d 1975), and Rosalind Audrey, *née* Otter (d 1987); *b* 19 March 1921; *Educ* Lancing, Worcester Coll Oxford (BA); *m* 1950, Penelope Ann, da of John Drinkwater (d 1936, poet and playwright), and Daisy Kennedy (violinist); 2 da (Susannah, Melanie); *Career* served RN 1941–46, Lt RNVR 1946; called to the Bar Lincoln's Inn 1951, recorder 1975–93, bencher 1980; *Recreations* golf, walking, wine; *Clubs* Savile, West Hove Golf; *Style*— Michael Self, Esq, QC; ✉ 59 Maresfield Gardens, Hampstead, London NW3 (☎ 0171 435 8311); Christmas Cottage, Ingram's Green, Midhurst, W Sussex

SELF, William Woodard (Will); s of Peter John Otter Self, of Canberra, Aust, and Elaine, *née* Rosenbloom; *b* 26 Sept 1961; *Educ* Christ's Coll, Exeter Coll Oxford (MA); *m* June 1989 (m dis 1996), Katharine Sylvia Anthony, da of John Chancellor; 1 s (Alexis b June 1990), 1 da (Madeleine b Sept 1992); *Career* writer; Geoffrey Faber Meml Award 1992; *Books* The Quantity Theory of Insanity (1991), Cock and Bull (1992), My Idea of Fun (1993), Grey Area (1994), Junk Mail (1995), The Sweet Smell of Psychosis (1996); *Style*— Will Self, Esq; ✉ c/o Ed Victor, 6 Bayley Street, Bedford Square, London WC1B 3HB (☎ 0171 304 4100, fax 0171 304 4111)

SELIGMAN, (Richard) Madron; CBE (1994); 4 s of Dr Richard Joseph Simon Seligman, FCGI, FIM (d 1972), and Hilda Mary, *née* MacDowell (d 1966); bro of Sir Peter Seligman, *qv*; *b* 10 Nov 1918; *Educ* Harrow, Balliol Coll Oxford (MA), Sch of Slavonic Studies London Univ; *m* 1947, Nancy-Joan, da of Julian Marks (d 1950); 3 s, 1 da; *Career* Maj 1945, 6 Armd Divnl Signals, North Africa, Italy 1940–46; dir: APV Holdings plc, Fluor GB 1966–83, St Regis Int 1983–85, chm Incinerator Co 1950–89; pres: Oxford Union Soc 1940, Oxford Univ Ski-Team 1938–39, Harrow cricket and rugby teams; MEP (EPP) West Sussex 1979–94; EPP spokesman Ctee for Energy Res and Technol; Hon MEP; *Recreations* skiing, tennis, travel, piano, gardening; *Clubs* Royal Thames Yacht, Royal Inst of International Affairs, MCC, Carlton; *Style*— Madron Seligman, Esq, CBE; ✉ Mile Ash, Towerhill, Horsham, W Sussex RH13 7AG (☎ 01403 240075, fax 01403 261420)

SELIGMAN, Mark Donald; s of Spencer Walter Oscar Seligman, of London, W8, and Joanne Winifred Rhoda, *née* Bye; *b* 24 Jan 1956; *Educ* Eton, Lincoln Coll Oxford (MA), Université de Grenoble, Universität Wien Austria; *m* 17 April 1982, Louise Angela Mary, da of Sir Philip De Zulueta (d 1989); 1 s (Jocelyn David b 9 April 1983), 2 da (Lucinda Marie Joanne b 26 April 1985, Iona Louise b 22 Sept 1990); *Career* Price Waterhouse 1977–80, fin analyst Chloride Group PLC 1981–83, dir SG Warburg & Co Ltd 1989–95 (joined 1983), jt chief exec Corp Fin BZW Ltd 1995–; ACA 1980; *Recreations* stalking, music; *Clubs* Roehampton, Northern Meeting; *Style*— Mark Seligman, Esq; ✉ Barclays de Zoete Wedd Ltd, Ebbgate House, 2 Swan Lane, London EC4R 3TS (☎ 0171 623 2323, fax 0171 956 4612)

SELIGMAN, Sir Peter Wendel; kt (1978), CBE (1969); s of Dr Richard Joseph Simon Seligman, PhD (d 1972), and Hilda Mary, *née* MacDowell (d 1966); bro of Madron Seligman, *qv*; *b* 16 Jan 1913; *Educ* King's Coll Sch, Harrow, Kantonschule Zürich, Gonville and Caius Coll Cambridge (BA); *m* 1937, Elizabeth Lavinia Mary, da of Prof John Laviers Wheatley, ARA (d 1955); 2 s (John, Bruce), 4 da (Hildagrace, Lavinia, Johanna, Gabrielle); *Career* engineer; md APV Holdings Ltd 1942–65 (chm 1965–77), chm British Chemical Plant Manufacturers Assoc 1965–67; dir: St Regis International Ltd 1973–83, Eibis International Ltd 1980–90; chm: Kandahar Ski Club 1972–76, Nat Ski Fedn of GB 1977–81; Liveryman Worshipful Co of Merchant Taylors; FIMechE; *Recreations* carpentry, travel, boating; *Clubs* Hawks', Kandahar Ski (hon memb), Ski Club of Great Britain (hon life memb), Royal Lymington Yacht; *Style*— Sir Peter Seligman, CBE; ✉ 3 Fisherman's Quay, Lymington, Hants SO41 9FW (☎/fax 01590 676569)

SELL, Anthony L; s of Richard Geoffrey Sell (d 1991), and Zena, *née* Goddard; *b* 19 April 1943; *Educ* Christ's Coll Cambridge (open scholar, MA), Univ of Wisconsin (Fulbright scholar), London Business Sch (MSc); m; 3 c; *Career* Organics Div ICI 1965–67, London Business Sch 1967–69, Booz Allen Hamilton 1969–73, International Investment Corporation for Yugoslavia 1973–74, Foseco International 1974–82, commercial dir Metalchem International Ltd 1982–86, DG Buffet Crampon SA 1986–88, commercial dir Boosey & Hawkes plc 1986–89, md Continental Europe Thomas Cook Group Ltd 1989–93, chief exec British Tourist Authority 1993–; *Recreations* playing the clarinet, music, rowing; *Style*— Anthony Sell, Esq; ✉ British Tourist Authority, Thames Tower, Black's Road, London W6 9EL (☎ 0181 563 3031, fax 0181 563 0302)

SELLARS, John Ernest; CBE (1994); s of late Ernest Buttle Sellars, and Edna Grace Mordaunt; *b* 5 Feb 1936; *Educ* Wintringham GS Grimsby, Univ of Manchester (BSc, MSc); *m* 20 Dec 1958, Dorothy Beatrice, da of late Maj Douglas Norman Morrison; 3 da (Karen b 1961, Fiona b 1962, Ann b 1964); *Career* res engr English Electric (GW) Ltd 1958–61, lectr Royal Coll of Advanced Technol (now Univ of Salford) 1961–67, head of mathematics Lanchester Coll of Technol 1967–71, head of computer science Lanchester Poly (now Univ of Coventry) 1971–74, chief offr Business Educn Cncl 1974–83, dir and chief exec Business and Technology Educn Cncl 1983–94, dir City Technol Colls Tst 1989–94; govr London Guildhall Univ 1994–; memb: Engrg Cncl 1994–95, Exec Ctee RoSPA 1994–; hon fell Nene Coll of HE; Hon DUniv Sheffield Hallam Univ; *Recreations* walking, travel; *Clubs* Reform, IOD, Middlesex CCC; *Style*— John Sellars, Esq, CBE; ✉ 306 Cassiobury Drive, Watford, Herts WD1 3AW (☎ 01923 233055)

SELLARS, Dr Leslie; s of Robert Norman Sellars (d 1980), of Flimby, Cumbria, and Hannah Elizabeth, *née* Pickering; *b* 14 Jan 1951; *Educ* Workington GS, Univ of Newcastle upon Tyne (MB BS, MD); *m* 29 June 1974, Joan, da of William Steele (d 1993), of Maryport; 2 da (Kathryn Jane b 1978, Julia Anne b 1979); *Career* registrar in med Royal Victoria Infirmary Newcastle 1977–78, first asst in med (nephrology) Univ of Newcastle upon Tyne 1981–85, conslt physician and nephrologist Royal Hull Hosps Tst 1985–; memb: Renal Assoc 1979, Br Hypertension Soc 1981, Euro Dialysis and Transplant Assoc; FRCPEd 1988, FRCP (London) 1993; *Recreations* fishing, fell-walking; *Clubs* Driffield Anglers, Flimby WMC; *Style*— Dr Leslie Sellars; ✉ 20 The Triangle, North Ferriby, North Humberside HU14 3AT (☎ 01482 631760); The Renal Unit, Hull Royal Infirmary, Analby Road, Hull (☎ 01482 701151)

SELLARS, Prof (Christopher) Michael (Mike); s of Frank Sellars (d 1979), and Olive Margaret, *née* Storey (d 1981); *b* 4 Aug 1935; *Educ* Ackworth Sch, Univ of Sheffield (Ledingham bursary, BMet, PhD, DMet, Metallurgical and Engrg Assoc prize, Brunton medal); *m* 19 March 1960, Mavis Dorothy, *née* Lemmon; 2 s (Neil Robert b 17 March 1963, Ian Anthony b 27 Dec 1964), 1 da (Helen Barbara b 13 Sept 1967); *Career* Tube Investments research fell Univ of Sheffield 1959–60, research metallurgical engr Carnegie Inst of Technol Pittsburgh Pennsylvania 1960–63, sr lectr Univ of Sheffield 1967–74 (lectr 1963–67), section ldr (on study leave) Broken Hill Proprietary Co Ltd Melbourne Aust 1969–70; Univ of Sheffield: reader 1974–83, personal chair 1983–88, POSCO prof of iron and steel technol 1988–, head Dept of Engrg Materials 1991–95, dep dean Faculty of Engrg 1993–96, dean Faculty of Engrg 1996–; Hon CMechD Univ of Navarra Spain 1989, Charles Hatchett Award 1992 and Thomas Medal 1996 Inst of Materials, Honorable Medal Faculty of Metallurgy and Material Engrg Univ of Mining and Engrg Krakow Poland 1994, hon memb Materials Research Soc of India 1994; memb Sheffield Metallurgical and Engrg Assoc (past pres); FIM 1971, FEng 1996; *Publications* author of over 200 pubns in learned soc jls and conf proceedings mainly in fields of physical metallurgy and computer modelling of thermomechanical processing of metals; *Recreations* golf, gardening, reading; *Clubs* Wine Society, Abbeydale Golf; *Style*— Prof Mike Sellars, FEng; ✉ Department of Engineering Materials, The University of Sheffield, Mappin Street, Sheffield S1 3JD (☎ 0114 222 5511, fax 0114 222 5943, e-mail c.m.sellars@sheffield.ac.uk)

SELLERS, Geoffrey Bernard; CB (1991); s of Bernard Whittaker Sellers (d 1991), of Stockport, and Elsie, *née* Coop (d 1963); *b* 5 June 1947; *Educ* Manchester GS, Magdalen Coll Oxford (Mackinnon scholar, BCL, MA); *m* Susan Margaret (d 1995), da of Arthur Donald Faulconbridge (d 1989); 2 s (Daniel b 1981, John b 1987), 2 da (Anna b 1984, Katherine b 1989); *Career* called to the Bar Gray's Inn 1971; legal asst Law Cmmn 1971, Cmmn on Industl Relations 1971–74, Office of Parly Counsel 1974, Law Cmmn 1982–85 and 1991–93, Inland Revenue 1996–; Parly counsel 1987–; *Clubs* RAC; *Style*— Geoffrey Sellers, Esq, CB; ✉ 53 Canonbury Road, London N1 2DG (☎ 0171 359 7606)

SELLERS, Rodney Horrocks (Rod); *b* 25 July 1946; *Educ* Bacup and Rawtenstall GS, LSE (BScEcon), Manchester Business Sch (DipBA); *m* 20 Sept 1975, Judith; 1 s (Richard b 8 March 1980), 1 da (Katie b 9 Feb 1978); *Career* CA; articled with Arthur Andersen and Co London 1967–70, pt/t tutor in accountancy Univ of Manchester 1971–74; British Vita PLC: PA to chief exec 1971–72, fin controller 1973–74, fin dir 1974–91, chief exec 1990–96, dep chm 1996–; dir: Taki Vita SAE, Spartech Corporation; memb: Educn Ctee Manchester Soc of CAs 1976–80, Taxation Ctee Manchester C of C and Indust (MCCI) 1979–81, Euro Study Gp Gtr Manchester Econ Devpt Ltd 1989, City Pride Ctee MCCI 1993, Euro Ctee CBI 1995–, Nat Ctee CBI 1996–; FCA 1970, FRSA 1991, CIMgt 1992; *Recreations* family, gardening, golf; *Clubs* Bolton Golf; *Style*— Rod Sellers, Esq; ✉ British Vita PLC, Soudan Street, Middleton, Manchester M24 2DB (☎ 0161 643 1133, fax 0161 655 3957)

SELLERS, Dr Susan Mary; da of Geoffrey Noel Sellers, of Esher, Surrey, and Mary McNeil, *née* Boswell; *b* 13 Jan 1949; *Educ* Birkenhead HS, Univ of Manchester (MB ChB, MD); *m* 16 July 1983, Andres Lopez, s of Andres Lopez Gil, of Murcia, Spain; 2 s (James b 3 Dec 1984, Teo b 11 Oct 1986), 1 da (Susannah b 24 May 1989); *Career* obstetrician and gynaecologist; registrar Southmead and Frenchay Hosps Bristol 1976–78; John Radcliffe Hosp Oxford: clinical lectr 1982–87, conslt 1988–; memb Cases Ctee Med Protection Soc; FRCOG 1993 (MRCOG 1977); *Recreations* music, family, cookery, travelling; *Style*— Dr Susan Sellers; ✉ Level 4, Women's Centre, John Radcliffe Hospital, Headington, Oxford OX3 9DU

SELLEY, Prof Richard Curtis; JP (1981); s of Harry Westcott Selley (d 1967), and Dorothy Joan, *née* Curtis; *b* 21 Sept 1939; *Educ* Eastbourne Coll, Univ of London (BSc, PhD), Imperial Coll London (DIC); *m* 15 May 1965, Pauline, da of John Fletcher; 2 da (Helen b 24 Aug 1967, Andrea b 2 April 1969); *Career* Imperial Coll London: post doctoral res fell 1963–66, lectr in sedimentology 1966–69, reader in petroleum geology 1974–89, head Dept of Geology 1988–93, prof of applied sedimentology 1989–; visiting res fell Natural History Museum 1990–92; sr sedimentologist Oasis Oil Co of Libya 1969–71, sr geologist Conoco Europe Ltd 1971–74; dir R C Selley & Co Ltd 1982–; dir Tooting Constitutional Club Ltd 1972–; memb Cncl Geological Soc of London 1992– (vice-pres 1992–94, hon sec Foreign and External Affairs 1994–), Cncl Euro Fedn of Geologists 1994–, Cncl Science and Technol Institutes 1994–; memb Geologists Assoc; CGeol, FGS 1962, AAPG 1971, PESGB 1971, SPE 1981; *Books* Ancient Sedimentary Environments (1970), Introduction to Sedimentology (1975), Elements of Petroleum Geology (1985), Applied Sedimentology (1988); *Clubs* Surrey Magistrates', Chaps; *Style*— Prof Richard Selley, JP; ✉ Department of Geology, Royal School of Mines, Imperial College, Prince Consort Rd, London SW7 2BP (☎ 0171 594 6425, fax 0171 594 6464)

SELLIER, Robert Hugh; s of Maj Philip Joseph Sellier (d 1963), and Lorna Geraldine Luxton (d 1983); *b* 15 Nov 1933; *Educ* St Joseph's Coll Oxford, King's Coll Durham (BSc); *m* 1, 16 Aug 1963, late Cynthia Ann, da of Lt-Col F W Dwelly (d 1984); 1 da (Nicola Jane b 1968); m 2, 15 April 1987, Gillian, da of late J Clark; *Career* md: New Ideal Houses 1972–74, Cementation Construction 1979–83; dep md Cementation International 1974–79, chm Cementation Group of Companies 1983–86, group md George Wimpey plc 1986–91, chief exec Y Y Lovell (Holdings) plc 1991–95; non-exec dir Hyder PLC (formerly Welsh Water PLC) 1993–; *Recreations* flying, shooting, scuba diving and skiing; *Style*— Robert H Sellier, Esq; ✉ Archers, Summersales Hill, Crowborough, E Sussex TN6 1UT (☎ 01892 663413)

SELLORS, Patrick John Holmes; LVO (1990); *b* 11 Feb 1934; *Educ* Rugby, Oriel Coll Oxford (BA, BM BCh, MA), Middx Hosp Med Sch (entrance scholar, state scholar, Douglas Cree prize in med); *m*; 3 c; *Career* conslt ophthalmic surgn: Croydon Eye Unit, Royal Marsden Hosp, St Luke's Hosp for The Clergy; hon conslt ophthalmic surgn St George's Hosp, surgn-oculist to HM The Queen; author of various papers for presentation and jls and of chapters in med books; memb Gen Optical Cncl, vice pres Cncl and Exec Ctee Coll of Ophthalmologists, pres Section of Ophthalmology RSM, memb Cncl Med Def Union; tstee Anne Allerton Tst for Ophthalmic Res; Liveryman Worshipful Soc of Apothecaries; FRCS 1965, FCOphth 1990; *Books* An Outline of Ophthalmology (jtly, 1985); *Style—* Patrick J Holmes Sellors, Esq, LVO; ✉ High Burrows, The Drive, Belmont, Surrey SM2 7DP; 149 Harley St, London W1N 2DE

SELLS, Andrew; s of Sir David Perronet Sells (d 1993), and Lady Sells, of Guilden Morden, Royston, Herts; *b* 30 Nov 1948; *Educ* Wellington Coll, Univ of London (MSc); *Career* qualified CA 1972; Schroders plc 1972–82, Thompson Clive & Partners 1982–87, md Nash, Sells & Partners Ltd 1987–; chm: Linden plc, Westerleigh Group plc, R H S Enterprises Ltd; chm Exec Ctee Team 1000, memb Exec Cncl N Wilts Cons Assoc; *Recreations* travel, reading, cricket, hunting; *Clubs* Boodle's, MCC; *Style—* Andrew Sells, Esq; ✉ 10 Kensington Place, London W8 7PT (☎ 0171 727 5080); Sandy Farm, Sopworth, Chippenham, Wiltshire SN14 6PP (☎ 01666 840100); Nash, Sells & Partners Ltd, 25 Buckingham Gate, London SW1E 6LD (☎ 0171 828 6944, fax 0171 828 9958)

SELLS, David James Guthrie; s of Henry James Sells, of Birmingham (d 1967), and Anne Guthrie, *née* Milne (d 1990); *b* 21 Dec 1928; *Educ* King Edward's Sch Birmingham; Merchant Taylors', Lincoln Coll Oxford; *m* 17 Sept 1952 (m dis 1984), Pauline Alice, *née* Hill; 2 s (Adrian David Guthrie b 1957, Christopher James Guthrie b 1961); *Career* news correspondent; Reuters: London 1952–54, Rome 1954–57, Warsaw 1957–60, chief corr Bonn 1960–64, Brussels mangr 1964–65; BBC TV: Beirut 1971–76, Newsday 1976–78, Assignment 1978–79, Newsnight 1980–; BBC Radio presenter: World Tonight 1986–91, World in Focus 1976; *Recreations* reading, swimming, travel; *Style—* David Sells Esq; ✉ Newsnight, BBC TV Centre, London W12 7RJ (☎ 0181 743 8000)

SELLS, Oliver Matthew; QC (1995); s of Sir David Perronet Sells (d 1993), of Royston, Herts, and Beryl Cecilia, *née* Charrington; *b* 29 Sept 1950; *Educ* Wellington Coll, The Coll of Law London; *m* 30 Aug 1986, Lucinda Jane, da of Gerard William Mackworth-Young (d 1984), of Fisherton de la Mere; 1 s (Hugo William b 17 June 1988), 1 da (Rosanna Mary b 30 June 1991); *Career* called to the Bar Inner Temple 1972, bencher 1996; in practice SE Circuit, supplementary counsel to The Crown 1981–86, recorder of the Crown Ct 1991– (asst recorder 1987–91); dir Music for Charity; memb: Gen Cncl of the Bar 1977–80 and 1985–89, Cwlth Law Assoc; hon memb American Bar Assoc; *Recreations* shooting, cricket, fishing; *Clubs* Boodle's, MCC, Norfolk (Norwich); *Style—* Oliver Sells, Esq, QC; ✉ 5 Paper Buildings, Temple, London EC4Y 7HB (☎ 0171 583 6117, fax 0171 353 0075)

SELLS, Robert Anthony; s of Rev William Blyth Sells (d 1977), of Portsmouth, and Eleanor Mary Sells; *b* 13 April 1938; *Educ* Christ's Hosp Sch, Univ of London Guy's Hosp (MB BS); *m* 1, 1964 (m dis 1976), Elizabeth Lucy, *née* Schryver; 2 s (Rupert William Blyth b 1967, Henry Perronet b 1968), 1 da (Katherine b 1970); m 2, 10 May 1977, Dr Paula Gilchrist, da of Stephen Muir (d 1988), of Denbigh, Clwyd; 2 s (Edward Anthony b 1981, Patrick David b 1982); *Career* lectr: Dept of Surgery Univ of London Guy's Hosp 1967–68, Dept of Surgery Cambridge Univ 1968–70; MRC travelling scholar Peter Bent-Brigham Hosp Harvard Univ 1970–71, dir Regnl Transplant Unit; conslt surgn: Royal Liverpool Hosp 1971–78, Liverpool Health Authy 1978–; vice pres The Transplantation Soc 1990– (cncllr 1982–88), pres The British Transplantation Soc 1983–86; MA Cambridge Univ; memb BMA 1962, FRCS, FRCSEd; *Books* Transplantation Today (1982), Organ Transplantation: Current Clinical and Immunological Concepts (1989); *Recreations* conductor, Crosby symphony orchestra; *Clubs* Moynihan Chirurgial, The XX; *Style—* Robert Sells, Esq; ✉ 4 Marine Crescent, Waterloo, Liverpool 22 (☎ 0151 928 3375); Link Unit 9C, Royal Liverpool Hospital, Prescot St, Liverpool L7 8XP (☎ 0151 708 0163, fax 0151 706 5817)

SELSDON, 3 Baron (UK 1932); Sir Malcolm McEacharn Mitchell-Thomson; 4th Bt (UK 1900); s of 2 Baron Selsdon, DSC (d 1963), and his 1 w, Phoebette (d 1991), da of Crossley Swithinbank; *b* 27 Oct 1937; *Educ* Winchester; *m* 1965, Patricia Anne, da of Donald Smith; 1 s; *Heir* s, Hon Callum Malcolm McEacharn Mitchell-Thomson b 7 Nov 1969; *Career* Sub Lt RNVR; banker with Midland Bank Gp, British del to Cncl of Europe and Western European Union 1972–78, chm Ctee of Middle East Trade (Comet) 1979–86, memb British Overseas Trade Bd 1983–86; chm: Greater London and S E Cncl for Sport and Recreation 1978–83; *Recreations* tennis, lawn tennis, skiing, sailing; *Clubs* MCC; *Style—* The Rt Hon the Lord Selsdon

SELWAY, Prof Peter Richard; s of George Ernest Selway (d 1972), of Salisbury, and Elsie Grace, *née* Gough (d 1996); *b* 24 Feb 1942; *Educ* Bishop Wordsworth Sch Salisbury, Univ of Southampton (BSc); *m* 14 Aug 1965, Simone Ann Marie, da of William Francois Tollet; 1 s (Jeremy Richard b 2 Aug 1971), 1 da (Melanie Ann b 23 May 1974); *Career* Standard Telecommunication Laboratories (later STC Technology Ltd, then BNR Europe Ltd, now NORTEL): res engr 1963–71, dept mangr Semiconductor Lasers 1971–80, mangr Components Div 1980–84, dir Materials & Components 1984–87, dir Optoelectronics 1987–94, dir Technology 1994–; visiting prof Dept of Electrical Engrg Imperial College London 1992–; memb: IT & E Panel Technology Foresight 1994–95, User Panel EPSRC 1994–; FInstP 1975, FIEE 1985, FEng 1995; *Recreations* dinghy and windsurfer racing, golf, bridge; *Style—* Prof Peter R Selway, FEng; ✉ 61 West Road, Sawbridgeworth, Herts CM21 0BN (☎ 01279 724127); BNR Europe Ltd, London Road, Harlow, Essex CM17 9NA (☎ 01279 403569, fax 01279 437830, e-mail Peter.Selway.0693515@nortel.co.uk)

SELWOOD, Maj-Gen His Hon Judge David Henry Deering; s of Cdr George Deering Selwood, RN (d 1972), and Enid Marguerite, *née* Rowlinson; *b* 27 June 1934; *Educ* Kelly Coll, Univ Coll of South-West, Law Soc's Sch of Law; *m* 3 Nov 1973, Barbara Dorothea, da of late Dr Kurt Franz Richard Hütter; from previous m 1 s (Stephen b 1963), 1 da (Suzanne b 1966); 2 step-s (Andreas b 1967, Dominic b 1970); *Career* cmmnd (Nat Serv list) RASC 1958; TA (4 Devons) 1959–61, regular cmmn Army Legal Serv Staff List 1961; served on staff: of WO, MOD, HQ BAOR, HQ MELF, HQ FARELF; dir Army Legal Servs 1990–92, dep Col Cmdt Adj Gen's Corps 1996–; admitted slr 1957; recorder: SE Circuit 1985–90, W Circuit 1990–92; circuit judge (SE Circuit) 1992–94, circuit judge (W Circuit) 1994–; res judge Portsmouth Combined Gp of Courts; hon attorney and counsellor US Court of Mil Appeals; *Books* Criminal Law and Psychiatry (co-author, 1987), Crown Court Index (co-author, 1995–); *Recreations* reading, writing, gardening; *Clubs* Army and Navy; *Style—* Maj-Gen His Hon Judge Selwood; ✉ c/o Portsmouth Crown Court, Winston Churchill Avenue, Portsmouth PO1 2EB

SELWYN GUMMER, *see:* Gummer

SEMMENS, Victor Williams; s of Ronald William Semmens, of Somerset, and Cecile Maude, *née* Larter; *b* 10 Oct 1941; *Educ* Blundell's Tiverton; *m* 1964, Valerie Elizabeth Norton, da of John Drummond (d 1981); 2 s (Guy William b 1967, Martin George b 1972); *Career* slr; articled Stolland & Limbrey Pump Ct Temple 1959–64, asst slr then ptnr Wells & Hind Nottingham 1964–89, chm Eversheds 1989–95 (ptnr 1989–); govr The Coll of Law, ret 1995; chm Breedon plc, dir Sheriff Holdings Plc; *Recreations* golf, skiing, sailing; *Style—* Victor Semmens, Esq; ✉ Eversheds, 14 Fletcher Gate, Nottingham NG1 2FX (☎ 0115 936 6000, fax 0115 936 6001)

SEMPER, The Very Rev Canon Colin Douglas; s of William Frederick Semper (d 1982), of Lincoln, and Dorothy Anne, *née* Baxter (d 1978), of Lincoln; *b* 5 Feb 1938; *Educ* Lincoln Sch, Keble Coll Oxford (BA), Westcott House Cambridge; *m* 7 July 1962, Janet Louise, da of Newlyn Harvard Greaves (d 1986), 2 s ((Andrew) Giles b 1963, Hugh Sebastian b 1965); *Career* asst curate Holy Trinity at St Mary Guildford 1963–67, sec Advsy Cncl The Church's Miny 1967–69, prodr BBC and head religious progs radio 1969–82, provost of Coventry 1982–87, canon of Westminster 1987–; Liveryman and Chaplain Worshipful Co of Feltmakers; *Recreations* canals, reading modern novels; *Style—* The Very Rev Colin Semper; ✉ Canon of Westminster, 8 Little Cloister, Westminster Abbey, London SW1P 3PL (☎ 0171 222 5791)

SEMPILL, 21 Lord (S 1489); James William Stuart Whitemore Sempill; s of Ann Moira, Lady Sempill (20 in line; d 1995), and her 2 husband Lt-Col Stuart Whitemore Chant-Sempill, OBE, MC, late Gordon Highlanders (d 1991); *b* 25 Feb 1949; *Educ* Oratory Sch, St Clare's Hall and Hertford Coll Oxford; *m* 1977, Josephine Ann Edith, da of Joseph Norman Rees, of Johannesburg; 1 s (Francis, Master of Sempill b 4 Jan 1979), 1 da (Hon Cosima b 20 April 1983); *Heir* s, Master of Sempill b 4 Jan 1979; *Career* tobacco exec Gallaher Ltd 1972–80, brand mangr South African Breweries Johannesburg 1982–86; account dir: Bates Wells Pty Ltd (Advertising Agency) 1986–87, Partnership in Advertising Johannesburg 1988–90; client serv dir Ogilvy and Mather Cape Town 1990–92, trade mktg dir Scottish & Newcastle Breweries Edinburgh 1993–95; marketing conslt 1995–; *Style—* The Rt Hon the Lord Sempill

SEMPLE, Dr Colin Gordon; s of Dr Thomas Semple, and Elspeth Roubaix, *née* Dewar; *Educ* Loretto, Brasenose Coll Oxford (BA, MA), Univ of Glasgow (MB ChB, MD); *m* 31 March 1979, Elaine Elizabeth, *née* Rankin; 1 s (Alan b 1981), 1 da (Gillian b 1983); *Career* conslt physician Southern Gen Hosp 1988–; author of various papers on diabetes and endocrinology; FRCP (Glasgow and Edinburgh); *Recreations* golf, fishing, gardening; *Style—* Dr Colin Semple; ✉ Medical Unit B, Southern General Hosptial, Glasgow G51 4TF (☎ 0141 201 1100, fax 0141 201 2399)

SEMPLE, Margaret Olivia (Maggie); da of Robert Henry Semple, and Olivia Victorine, *née* Shuffler (d 1992); *b* 30 July 1954; *Educ* Shelburne Girls' HS London, Worcester Coll Worcester (BEd), Univ of London (advanced dip), Univ of Sussex (MA); *m* 21 Sept 1991, Leo Fitzroy Clouden; *Career* teacher Parliament Hill Girls' Sch London 1975–79, ILEA advsy dance teacher White Lion Centre London 1979–80, head of performing arts N Westminster Sch London 1980–88; Arts Cncl London: dir AEMS project 1988–91, dir of educn and trg 1991–; res dir Extemporary Dance Theatre 1985–88; reader Open Univ; pres Laban Guild UK; external examiner: Laban Centre, Univ of Brighton, Central Sch of Speech and Drama; memb Jury Bonnie Bird Choreographic Award 1991–; patron Essex Regnl Dance Cncl; memb: Nat Curriculum Working Gp for Physical Educn 1989–90, Cwlth Inst Educn Ctee 1992–94, Further Educn Funding Cncl's Widening Participation Ctee 1995–, All Souls Gp Oxford 1994–, Cncl of Europe's Expert Gp on Creativity and Youth Initiative; fell Br American Project (BAP) 1992–; UK expert on EC Kaleidoscope Ctee 1994–; contrib to books and jls; FRSA (memb Cncl); *Recreations* leading and participating in dance classes, reading; *Style—* Ms Maggie Semple; ✉ The Arts Council of England, 14 Great Peter Street, London SW1P 3NQ (☎ 0171 973 6507, fax 0171 973 6590)

SEMPLE, Dr Peter d'Almaine; s of Thomas Semple, of Elie, Fife, and Elspeth Roubaix, *née* Dewar; *b* 30 Oct 1945; *Educ* Loretto, Univ of Glasgow (MB ChB, MD); *m* 1979, Judith (Judy) Mairi, da of late Frank Abercromby, of Oban; 2 da (Catriona Mairi b 3 May 1981, Emma Dewar b 15 Dec 1982); *Career* conslt physician and chest specialist Inverclyde Dist 1979–, hon sr clinical lectr Univ of Glagow 1981–; dir of med audit and memb Cncl Royal Coll of Physicians and Surgns of Glasgow 1989–93 and 1995–, past chm Med Audit Ctee Home and Health Dept Scottish Office; various contribs to med periodicals 1975–; past chm W of Scot Branch Br Deer Soc, chm St Petersburg Charity Forum; FRCPGlas 1984, FRCPEd 1988, FRCP (London) 1996; *Recreations* field sports, gardening, golf; *Clubs* Elie Golf House, Royal Gourock Yacht, Town and Country Medical; *Style—* Dr Peter Semple; ✉ High Lunderston, Inverkip PA16 0DU (☎ 01475 522342); Ferrylea, The Shore, Earlsferry, Fife; Inverclyde Royal NHS Tst, Greenock PA16 0XN (☎ 01475 633777, fax 01475 637340)

SEMPLE, Prof Stephen John Greenhill; s of John Edward Stewart Semple (d 1975), and Janet Elizabeth, *née* Casson (d 1978); *b* 4 Aug 1926; *Educ* Westminster, St Thomas's Hosp Med Sch London (MB BS, MD); *m* 5 Aug 1961, Penelope Anne, da of Sir Geoffrey William Aldington, KBE, CMG, of Great Bookham, Surrey; 3 s (Edward Stewart Greenhill b 1965, Robert Mark Greenhill b 1968, David Thomas Greenhill b 1977); *Career* med specialist RAMC 1953–55; St Thomas's Hosp Med Sch London: lectr 1959–61, sr lectr 1961–65, reader 1965–69, prof of med 1969–70; prof of med The Middlesex Hosp Med Sch 1970–91, prof of med and head Dept of Med UCL 1985–91 (emeritus prof of med 1991–), currently visiting prof of med Charing Cross and Westminster Med Sch; memb: Physiological Soc, Med Res Soc, Assoc of Physicians; FRCP; *Publications* Disorders of Respiration (1972); articles in various learned jls incl The Lancet and Jl of Applied Physiology; *Recreations* tennis, music; *Clubs* Queen's; *Style—* Prof Stephen Semple; ✉ White Lodge, 3 Claremont Park Rd, Esher, Surrey KT10 9LT (☎ 01372 465057); Department of Medicine, Charing Cross Hospital, Fulham Palace Road, London W6 8RF (☎ 0181 846 7181, fax 0181 846 7170)

SEN, Srikumar; s of Sukumar Sen (d 1949), of Calcutta, India, and Elalata Mitra (d 1982); *b* 2 Oct 1931; *Educ* Highgate Sch, Jesus Coll Oxford (boxing blue, BA); *m* 15 April 1950, Eileen Fawcett, da of John Haines Oldacre Hartwell; 3 c (Subir Stephen b 21 March 1957, Sarojini Ela Hardy b 29 Nov 1961, Mrinal Fawcett b 19 July 1966); *Career* trainee journalist London Express News and Feature Service 1953–54, trainee The Times 1954–55, managerial asst The Statesman Calcutta 1955–59, head of publicity and PR ICI (India) Ltd 1960–64; sub ed Sports Desk: The Guardian 1965–67, The Times 1967–91; boxing corr The Times 1979–; *Recreations* tennis, squash; *Style—* Srikumar Sen, Esq; ✉ The Times Sports Desk, The Times, 1 Pennington St, London E1 (☎ 0171 782 5960)

SENANAYAKE, Dr Felix; *Educ* St Thomas's Coll Mount Lavinia Sri Lanka (memb Sri Lanka Davis Cup Squad, Sri Lanka Jr Doubles champion, asst sec Ceylon Lawn Tennis Assoc, memb Sri Lanka YMCA Judo Team, karate blackbelt), Univ of Sri Lanka (MB BS), Middx Hosp Med Sch; *m* Pauline, *née* Chalkidou; 2 s; *Career* registrar in radiotherapy Royal Free Hosp, subsquently sr registrar Middx Hosp; Royal Free Hosp: conslt radiotherapist and oncologist 1975–96, dir Dept of Radiotherapy and Oncology 1988–96, chm Oncology Speciality Gp, dep med dir Gray's Inn Div until 1992; conslt radiotherapist and oncologist: The Whittington Hosp, Lister Hosp Stevenage (hon); hon sr lectr in radiotherapy and oncology and recognised teacher at Univ of London; memb Regnl Advsy Ctee on Radiotherapy, chm Int Adjuvant Therapy Orgn; memb: Brain Tumour Working Pty MRC Cancer Therapy Ctee, Head and Neck Collaborative Gp Working Pty UK Co-ordinating Ctee on Cancer Res, Centre Oncologique et Biologique de Recherche Appliquee France (COBRA); *Style—* Dr Felix Senanayake

SENINGTON, David James; s of Victor Samuel Colston Senington, of Bristol, and Ella Matilda, *née* Ridout; *b* 28 March 1947; *Educ* Queen Elizabeth's Hosp Bristol, Coll of Commerce Bristol; *m* 31 Aug 1974, Julie Elizabeth, da of Thomas Park Hill; 1 s (Richard James b 31 December 1980), 1 da (Helen Louisa b 21 June 1984); *Career* reporter New Observer Bristol 1966–67, news sub-ed then features sub-ed Western Daily Press Bristol 1969–70 (reporter 1967–69); travelling 1970–71: Europe, Middle East, India, Australia; Parly reporter The West Australian Perth W Australia 1971; travelling 1971–72:

Australia, New Zealand, Pacific, N America; news sub-ed: Western Daily Press 1972–73, Daily Telegraph London 1973, Daily Mail London 1973–74; travelling 1974–75: N & S America, W & N Africa; freelance sub-ed London 1975–76, contrib Sunday Express 1979–91 (Sunday Times 1977–78); Evening Standard: news sub-ed 1976–79, overnight dep chief sub-ed 1979–84, dep chief sub-ed 1984–85, chief sub-ed 1985–93, copy ed 1993–; memb: NUJ 1966, Soc of Genealogists 1982, Nat Trust 1988; *Recreations* writing, genealogy, numismatics, travel, bricklaying, gardening, reading; *Style—* David Senington, Esq; ✉ Evening Standard, Northcliffe House, 2 Derry St, Kensington, London W8 5EE (☎ 0171 938 6569)

SENIOR, (Alan) Gordon; CBE (1981); s of Oscar Senior (d 1973), of Ash Vale, Surrey, and Helen, *née* Cooper (d 1964); *b* 1 Jan 1928; *Educ* Normanton GS, Univ of Leeds (BSc, MSc); *m* 1, Dec 1954 (m dis 1960), Sheila Mary, da of Ernest Lockyer (d 1959), of Normanton, Yorks; m 2, 29 Nov 1968 (m dis 1978), Lawmary Mitchell, da of Lawrence Champion (d 1981), of Cape Town, SA; 1 s (John b 12 Feb 1970); *Career* served UTC and TA 1945–49; engr; J B Edwards (Whyteleafe) Ltd 1949–51, Oscar Faber & Partners Consulting Engineers 1951–54, W S Atkins Group 1954–80 (tech dir 1967), md Atkins Research and Development 1971; dir: W S Atkins and Partners 1975, Atkins Franlab Ltd 1977; fndr Gordon Senior Associates Consulting Engineers 1980–; dir: ANSEN Ltd 1981–83, McMillan Sloan and Partners 1981–83, Armstrong Technology Services Ltd 1986–87; chm: Surface Engineering and Inspection Ltd (subsid of Yarrow plc) 1983–86, Masta Corporation Ltd 1987–92, Aptech Ltd 1988–89; chm: Indust Advsy Ctee Univ of Surrey 1989–, Greenwich Forum 1991–, QUEST Central Europe Prague 1993–; memb Offshore Safety and Technol Bd of HSE 1985–92; FICE, FIStructE, FSUT; *Books* Brittle Fracture of Steel Structures (co-author, 1970); author of various papers on welding, fatigue, brittle fracture, future devpts offshore and in the oceans and aspects of IT; *Recreations* food, wine, travel, conversation, skiing; *Clubs* Athenaeum; *Style—* Gordon Senior, Esq, CBE; ✉ 3 Briar Patch, Charterhouse, Godalming, Surrey GU7 2JB (☎ and fax 01483 417781)

SENIOR, Grahame; s of Raymond Senior, of Huddersfield, Yorks, and Evelyn, *née* Wood; *b* 21 Oct 1944; *Educ* King James Sch; *m* 10 July 1965, Prudence Elizabeth, da of William Holland; 1 s (Adam Michael b 3 June 1970), 2 da (Claire Elizabeth b 30 Oct 1967, Charlotte Elizabeth b 26 Sept 1980); *Career* mgmnt trainee then asst publicity exec Royal Insurance Group 1963–65, writer Radio Caroline 1965, copywriter Vernons 1965–66, devpt writer Royds 1966–67; Brunnings: copy chief 1967–69, creative dir 1969–73, md 1978–79; fndr Senior King Ltd 1980 (currently chm and chief exec), fndr MKA Films 1981, fndr Media Options Ltd (media independent) 1984; fndr and pres IN Int Network of Agencies; chm Northern Publicity Assoc, organiser Northern NABS fundraising initiatives, fndr Liverpool Gold Medal Awards for Man of the Year; author of various articles and booklets on mktg, market targeting and tourism mktg 1973–87; ACII 1965, MIPA 1967, MInstM 1969; *Recreations* dry fly-fishing, gardening, ballet, tennis, painting, reading, wine, cooking; *Clubs* RAC, IOD; *Style—* Grahame Senior, Esq; ✉ Greenways, Grove Rd, Tring, Herts HP23 5PD (☎ 0144 282 2770); Senior King Ltd, 14–15 Carlisle St, London W1V 5RE (☎ 0171 734 5855, fax 0171 437 1908, mobile 0374 234008)

SENIOR, Dr Michael; DL (Gwynedd 1989); s of Geoffrey Senior (d 1957), of Glan Conwy, N Wales, and Julia Elaine, *née* Cotterell (d 1984); *b* 14 April 1940; *Educ* Uppingham, Open Univ (BA, PhD); *Career* writer and farmer; *Radio Play* The Coffee Table (1964); *Books* Portrait of North Wales (1973), Portrait of South Wales (1974), Greece and its Myths (1978), Myths of Britain (1979), The Age of Myth and Legend in Heroes and Heroines (1980), Sir Thomas Malory's Tales of King Arthur (ed, 1980), The Life and Times of Richard II (1981), Who's Who in Mythology (1985), Conwy: The Town's Story (1977), The Crossing of the Conwy (1991), Son et Lumière Script: A Place in History (1991), Gods and Heroes in North Wales, a Mythological Guide (1992), North Wales in the Making (1995); author of additional local history booklets 1982–90; *Recreations* hill walking, painting, croquet; *Style—* Dr Michael Senior, DL; ✉ Bryn Eisteddfod, Glan Conwy, Colwyn Bay, N Wales LL28 5LF; c/o David Higham Associates Ltd, 5–8 Lower John Street, London W1R 4HA

SENIOR, Robert William; s of Derek Senior, of Cheshire, and Helen Elizabeth, *née* Barr; *b* 5 Dec 1964; *Educ* Frankfurt Int Sch, Br Sch of The Netherlands, Sevenoaks Sch, Univ of Durham (BA); *Career* advtg exec; Burkitt Weinreich Bryant 1987–89, DMB&B 1989–94 (agency bd dir 1993–94), client servs dir Simons Palmer Clemmow Johnson 1994–; *Recreations* sport (former ski instructor), travel, etc; *Style—* Robert Senior, Esq; ✉ Simons Palmer Clemmow Johnson Ltd, 19–20 Noel Street, London W1V 3PD (☎ 0171 287 4455, fax 0171 734 2658, mobile 0831 838455)

SENNITT, His Hon Judge; John Stuart; s of Stuart Osland Sennitt (d 1985), and Nora Kathleen, *née* Stockings (d 1982); *b* 5 March 1935; *Educ* Culford Sch Bury St Edmunds, St Catharine's Coll Cambridge (MA, LLB); *m* 30 April 1966, Janet Ann; 2 da (Tania b 4 April 1967, Caroline b 25 Dec 1979), 1 s (Richard b 8 April 1969); *Career* Admitted slr 1961, ptnr Wild Hewitson & Shaw Slrs Cambridge 1963–83, registrar Cambridge County Court then district judge 1983–94, recorder of the Crown Court 1992–94 (asst recorder 1988–92), circuit judge (SE Circuit) 1994–; *Style—* His Hon Judge Sennitt; ✉ Cambridge County Court, 72–80 Hills Road, Cambridge CB2 1LA

SENTANCE, Andrew William; s of William Thomas Wulfram Sentance, and Lillian, *née* Bointon; *b* 17 Sept 1958; *Educ* Eltham Coll London, Clare Coll Cambridge (MA), LSE (MSc, PhD); *m* 3 Aug 1985, Anne Margaret, da of Raymond Austin Penfold; 1 s (Timothy Michael b 4 March 1989), 1 da (Rebecca Louise b 21 March 1991); *Career* petrol station mangr Petrocell Ltd 1980–81, mgmnt trainee NCB 1982–83; CBI: economist with Economic Affrs Directorate 1986–89, dir economic affrs CBI 1989–93; sr res fell London Business Sch 1994–95, dir Centre for Economic Forecasting London Business Sch 1995–, chief economic advsr Br Retail Consortium 1995–; memb: RPI Advsy Ctee 1989 and 1992–94, CSO Advsy Ctee 1992–93, HM Treasy Ind Panel of Economic Forecasting Advsrs 1992–93, Cmmn on Wealth Creation and Social Cohesion 1994–95, NAPF Retirement Income Inquiry 1994–95, ONS Advsy Ctee 1996–; Soc of Business Economists: memb 1988–, memb Cncl 1991–, chm 1995–; *Recreations* playing piano, guitar, writing and performing music; *Style—* Dr Andrew Sentance; ✉ Centre for Economic Forecasting, London Business School, Sussex Place, Regent's Park, London NW1 4SA (☎ 0171 262 5050, fax 0171 724 6069)

SERGEANT, Annette Lesley; da of John Richard Sergeant, of Scunthorpe, South Humberside, and Dorothy Ruth, *née* Sanderson; *b* 26 Nov 1953; *Educ* John Leggoth GS, Univ of Hull (BSc); *m* 1983 (sep); *Career* trainee postgrad hosps 1976–77, asst admin Whipps Cross Hosp 1977–79, sector admin Barking Hosp 1979–82, unit admin small acute hosps Waltham Forest 1982–85, unit admin then dep gen mangr Whipps Cross Hosp 1985–87, High Fliers training scheme 1987–88, unit gen mangr acute servs Enfield Health Authy 1988–92, chief exec Chase Farm Hosps NHS Tst London 1992–; conslt ed Br Jl of Health Care Mgmnt 1995–; winner Health Service Jl award 1989 (for work on quality); assoc memb Inst of Health Serv Mgmnt 1979; *Recreations* horse riding, travel, golf; *Style—* Miss Annette Sergeant; ✉ Chase Farm Hospital NHS Trust, The Ridgeway, Enfield, Middlesex (☎ 0181 366 9101)

SERGEANT, John; s of Ernest Sergeant (d 1985), and Olive Stevens, *née* Cook, of Devon; *b* 14 April 1944; *Educ* Millfield, Magdalen Coll Oxford (BA); *m* 1969, Mary, *née* Smithies; 2 s (William b 1973, Michael b 1975); *Career* political reporter; appeared with Alan Bennett in his comedy series On The Margin (BBC) 1966, trainee Liverpool Daily Post & Echo 1967–70; BBC TV and Radio: news reporter 1970–80, political corr 1980–88, chief political corr 1988–; assignments as reporter in 25 countries incl: Vietnam, Rhodesia, N Ireland, Turkish invasion of Cyprus, Israeli invasion of Lebanon; also acting corr in Dublin, Paris and Washington, sometime presenter of Radio 4 current affrs programmes incl World at One, Today and PM; winner Broadcasting Press Guild award for most memorable outside bdcast of 1990 (Mrs Thatcher interrupting live bdcast outside Paris Embassy to announce participation in second round of Cons Pty leadership ballot); memb NUJ; *Recreations* sailing; *Style—* John Sergeant, Esq; ✉ BBC Office, Press Gallery, House of Commons, London SW1A 0AA (☎ 0171 219 4765)

SERGEANT, Sir Patrick John Rushton; kt (1984); s of George Sergeant, and Rene Sergeant; *b* 17 March 1924; *Educ* Beaumont Coll; *m* 1952, Gillian, *née* Wilks; 2 da (Harriet, Emma); *Career* Lt RNVR 1945; asst city ed News Chronicle 1948, city ed Daily Mail 1960–84 (dep city ed 1953), fndr and md Euromoney Publications 1969–85 (chm 1985–92, pres 1992–); dir: Associated Newspapers Group 1971–83, Daily Mail and Gen Tst 1983–; Winner Wincott award Financial Journalist of the Year 1979; Freeman City of London; Domus fell St Catherine's Coll Oxford 1988; FRSA; *Books* Another Road to Samarkand (1955), Money Matters (1967), Inflation Fighters Handbook (1976); *Recreations* tennis, skiing, swimming, talking; *Clubs* RAC, Annabel's, Mark's, All England Lawn Tennis and Croquet; *Style—* Sir Patrick Sergeant; ✉ No 1 The Grove, Highgate Village, London N6; Euromoney Publications plc, Nestor House, Playhouse Yard, London EC4V 5EX (☎ 0171 779 8879)

SERLE, Christopher Richard; s of Frank Raymond Serle (d 1988), of Bristol, and Winifred Mary, *née* Pugsley (d 1989); *b* 13 July 1943; *Educ* Clifton, Trinity Coll Dublin; *m* 22 Jan 1983, Anna Catharine, da of Stephen Readhead Southall, of Clifford, Hereford and Worcester; 2 s (Harry b 1983, Jack b 1987); *Career* actor 1964–68, prodr BBC radio and TV 1968–78, TV and radio journalist and presenter; programmes incl: That's Life, In At The Deep End, People, Pick of the Week; *Recreations* gliding, jazz drumming; *Style—* Christopher Serle, Esq; ✉ c/o Curtis Brown, Haymarket House, 28/29 Haymarket, London SW1Y 4SP (☎ 0171 396 6600)

SERMON, (Thomas) Richard; s of Eric Thomas Sermon (d 1978), of Nottingham, and Marjorie Hilda, *née* Parsons (d 1969); *b* 25 Feb 1947; *Educ* Nottingham HS; *m* 10 Oct 1970, Rosemary Diane, da of Thomas Smith (d 1971), of Sheffield; 1 s (Thomas Christopher b 1971), 1 da (Catherine Marjorie b 1975); *Career* co sec Crest Hotels Ltd 1969–74, dep chm Good Relations Gp Ltd 1974–79; md: Shandwick Consultants Ltd 1979–87, Shandwick Consultant Group plc 1987–88; chief exec: Shandwick Europe plc 1988–90, Shandwick International plc 1990–96; chm Shandwick Consultants Ltd 1996–; public relations advsr Goldman Sachs International 1992–96; dir: Lloyd Thompson Group Ltd plc, Wrightson Wood Associates Ltd 1994–, The City of London Sinfonia Ltd 1995–; vice pres RADAR; memb Nat Advsry Cncl on Employment of People with Disabilities (NACEPD) 1994–; chm The London Federation of Clubs for Young People 1996– (hon treas 1995–96); memb cncl: The Foundation for Manufacturing and Industry 1994–, The City and Guilds of London Inst 1994–; Freeman City of London 1968; Ct Asst Worshipful Cos of: Wheelwrights 1990, Chartered Secs and Adminstrators 1991; FCIS 1972; *Clubs* City of London, City Livery, Mark's; *Style—* Richard Sermon, Esq; ✉ Friars Well, Aynho, Banbury, Oxon OX17 3BG (☎ 01869 810284, fax 01869 810634)

SEROTA, Baroness (Life Peer UK 1967), of Hampstead in Greater London; Dame Beatrice Serota; DBE (1992), JP (Inner London); da of Alexander Katz; *b* 15 Oct 1919; *Educ* LSE (BSc, Econ); *m* 1942, Stanley Serota, FICE; 1 s ((Hon) Nicholas Andrew Serota, *qv*, b 1946), 1 da (Hon Judith Alexandra Anne (Hon Mrs Pugh) b 1948); *Career* fndr chm Cmmn for Local Administration 1974–82; memb: LCC 1954–65 (chm Children's Ctee 1958–65), GLC (Lambeth) 1964–67, Advsy Cncl in Child Care and Central Trg Cncl in Child Care 1958–68, Baroness-in-Waiting 1968–69, min of state for health DHSS 1969–70, govr BBC 1977–82, dep speaker House of Lords 1985–, princ dep chm Ctees and chm Select Ctee on the Euro Communities 1986–92; Hon Fell LSE, Hon DLitt Univ of Loughborough; *Style—* The Rt Hon the Baroness Serota, DBE, JP; ✉ The Coach House, 15 Lyndhurst Terrace, London NW3 5QA

SEROTA, Daniel; QC (1989); *b* 27 Sept 1945; *Educ* Univ of Oxford (MA); *m*; 2 da; *Career* called to the Bar Lincoln's Inn 1969; recorder of the Crown Court 1989–; *Style—* Daniel Serota, Esq, QC; ✉ Littleton Chambers, 3 Kings Bench Walk North, Temple, London EC4Y 7HR (☎ 0171 797 8600)

SEROTA, (Hon) Nicholas Andrew; o s of Baroness Serota, *qv*; does not use courtesy prefix of Hon; *b* 27 April 1946; *Educ* Haberdashers' Aske's, Christ's Coll Cambridge (BA), Courtauld Inst (MA); *Career* regnl art offr and exhibition organizer Arts Council of GB 1970–73; dir: Museum of Modern Art Oxford 1973–76, Whitechapel Art Gallery 1976–88, The Tate Gallery 1988–; chm VAAC British Cncl 1992– (memb 1976–); tstee: Public Art Devpt Tst (PADT) 1983–87, Architecture Fndn 1991–, Little Sparta Tst 1995–; Hon DArts City of London Polytechnic 1990, Hon DLitt City Univ 1990, Hon DArts Univ of Plymouth 1993, Hon DLitt Univ of Keele 1994; sr fell RCA 1996; hon fell: Queen Mary and Westfield College Univ of London 1988, Goldsmiths' Coll Univ of London 1994; Hon FRIBA 1992; *Style—* Nicholas Serota, Esq; ✉ The Tate Gallery, Millbank, London SW1P 4RG (☎ 0171 887 8000, fax 0171 887 8007)

SERPELL, Sir David Radford; KCB (1968, CB 1962), CMG (1952), OBE (1944); s of Charles Robert Serpell (d 1949), of Plymouth, and Elsie Leila Serpell (d 1958); *b* 10 Nov 1911; *Educ* Plymouth Coll, Exeter Coll Oxford, Toulouse Univ, Syracuse Univ NY, Fletcher Sch of Law and Diplomacy USA; *m* 1, 1938 (m dis 1971), Ann, da of Prof M S Dooley, of Syracuse, NY; 3 s; m 2, 1972, Doris, da of James Farr, of Burley Gate, Herefordshire; *Career* HM Civil Serv: entered 1939, Ministries of Food, Fuel and Power, Treasy (under sec 1954–60), dep sec Miny of Tport 1960–63, second sec BOT 1963–66, second perm sec 1966–68, second sec Treasy 1968, perm sec Miny of Tport 1968–70, perm sec Dept of Environment 1970–72; chm: Nature Conservancy Cncl 1973–77, Ordnance Survey Review Ctee 1978–79, Ctee to Review BR's Finances 1982; memb British Railways Bd 1974–82; memb: Cncl Nat Tst 1973–77, NERC 1973–76; hon fell Exeter Coll Oxford 1992; FCIT; *Recreations* walking; *Clubs* Utd Oxford and Cambridge Univ; *Style—* Sir David Serpell, KCB, CMG, OBE; ✉ 25 Crossparks, Dartmouth, Devon TQ6 9HP (☎ 01803 832073)

SERRELL-WATTS, D'Arcy John; s of John Serrell-Watts, CBE, JP (d 1975), of Marlow Place, Bucks, and Cynthia Mary, *née* Mason (d 1969); *b* 12 May 1939; *Educ* Harrow, Lincoln Coll Oxford; *m* 1, 1962 (m dis 1972), Lyn, *née* Tippetts; 1 s (Sebastian John b 1965), 1 da (Arabella Alice b 1968); m 2, 1977 (m dis), Linda, *née* Berry; m 3, 30 June 1987, Sylvaine, da of Comte Bernard Robinet de Plas; *Career* md HTS Management Consultants Ltd 1964, vice pres Golightly International NY 1974, treas and dep pres Telecommunications Cncl 1980, md London Car Telephones Ltd 1982; underwriting memb of Lloyd's 1977–96; chm Br Horse Database 1992–96; tstee Nat Hosp Tst; Freeman City of London 1960, Master Worshipful Co of Saddlers 1991 (Warden 1988); *Recreations* shooting, skiing, vegetable gardening; *Clubs* Turf; *Style—* D'Arcy Serrell-Watts, Esq; ✉ Bradwell Lodge, Bradwell-on-Sea, Essex CM0 7PL; 9 Bedford Gardens House, London W8 7EE (☎ 0171 727 2918, fax 0171 221 5949)

SERVICE, Alastair Stanley Douglas; CBE (1995); s of Lt Cdr Douglas Service (d 1976), and Evelyn Caroline, *née* Sharp (d 1986); *b* 8 May 1933; *Educ* Westminster, Queen's Coll Oxford; *m* 1, 1959 (m dis 1984), Louisa Anne Service, JP, *qv*, da of Lt-Col Harold Hemming, OBE, MC (d 1976); 1 s (Nicholas), 1 da (Sophia); m 2, 1992, Zandria Madeleine, da of John E Pauncefort; *Career* writer, former merchant banker and publisher; hon parly campaigns organiser for reforms of family planning, abortion, adoption and divorce laws 1964–75; chm Birth Control Campaign 1970–74, nat chm Family Planning Assoc 1975–79, vice chm Health Educn Cncl 1979–87, gen sec Family Planning Assoc 1980–89, dep chm Health Educn Authy 1987–89; chm: Health Cmmn for Wilts and Bath 1992–96, Wessex Regnl Health Authy 1993–94 (memb 1989–94), Wilts Health Authy 1996–; co-fndr and hon sec ARK (Action for the River Kennet) 1991–; *Books* incl: A Birth Control Plan for Britain (jtly, 1972), Edwardian Architecture (1977), The Architects of London, 1066–Today (1979), Lost Worlds (1981), A Guide to the Megaliths of Europe (1981), Anglo-Saxon and Norman Buildings of Britain (1982), Edwardian Interiors (1982), Victorian and Edwardian Hampstead (1989), The Standing Stones of Europe (1993); *Libretto* The Sky Speaker (opera, composer James Harpham, 1997); *Recreations* cycling, opera (especially Verdi and Bellini), dalmatians, the pursuit of stone circles, mounds and historic buildings; *Clubs* Garrick; *Style—* Alastair Service, Esq, CBE; ✉ Swan House, Avebury, Wilts SN8 1RA (☎ 01672 539312, fax 01672 539634)

SERVICE, Louisa Anne; OBE (1997), JP (1969); da of Lt-Col Henry Harold Hemming, OBE, MC (d 1976), of London, and Alice Louisa Hemming, OBE, *née* Weaver (d 1994); *b* 13 Dec 1931; *Educ* schs in Canada, France, USA and UK, St Hilda's Coll Oxford (BA, MA); *m* 28 Feb 1959 (m dis 1984), Alastair Stanley Douglas Service, CBE, *qv*, s of Lt Cdr Douglas Service (d 1976), of London; 1 s (Nicholas Alastair McFee Douglas b 9 May 1961), 1 da (Sophia Alice Louisa Douglas b 20 April 1963); *Career* export dir Ladybird Electric 1955–59; dir Glass's Information Services Ltd 1971– (dep chm 1976–81, chm 1981–95); jt chm: Municipal Group of Cos 1976– (fin dir 1966–76), Hemming Publishing 1985–; chm: Mayer-Lismann Opera Workshop 1976–91, Youth and Music 1990– (memb Cncl 1987–); memb Cncl: Friends of Covent Garden 1982– (memb Mgmnt Ctee 1982–95), Haydn/Mozart Soc 1990–92; hon sec Womans India Assoc 1967–74, dep chm Paddington Probation Hostel 1976–86; chm: Hackney Juvenile Ct 1975–82, Westminster Juvenile Ct 1982–88, Hammersmith and Fulham Juvenile Ct 1988–92, Hammersmith and Fulham Family Proceedings Ct and Youth Ct 1992–94, Camden Family Proceedings Ct and Youth Ct 1994–; memb: First London Magistrates Cts Ctee 1995–, Dept of Trade's Consumer Credit Appeals Panel 1981–, FIMBRA Appeals Tribunal 1989–92, Adjudication and Appeals Ctee Slrs' Complaints Bureau 1992–93; tstee: Women's India Tst 1989–, Performing Arts Lab 1996– FRGS; *Recreations* music, travel, reading; *Style—* Ms Louisa A Service, OBE, JP; ✉ c/o Hemming Publishing Ltd, 32 Vauxhall Bridge Road, London SW1V 2SS (☎ 0171 973 6404, fax 0171 233 5049)

SESSIONS, John Gibb; *né* Marshall; s of John Craig Marshall, of St Albans, and Esmé Richardson; *b* 11 Jan 1953; *Educ* Verulum Sch St Albans, Univ of Bangor (MA), RADA; *Career* actor; *Theatre* Liverpool Everyman: Chameleon Blue, A Midsummer Night's Dream; Phoenix: The American Napoleon, The Common Pursuit; Riverside Studios: Christmas Show, Salute to Doctor Johnson, Lives of the Great Composers, The Life of Napoleon; Limbo Tales (Gate), Waiting for Godot (Young Vic), One Flew Over the Cuckoo's Nest (Manchester Royal Exchange), Hamlet (Sheffield Crucible), Man is Man (Almeida), The Alchemist (Lyric Hammersmith), The Orton Diaries (NT), Die Fledermaus (Royal Opera House), Tartuffe (Playhouse), Chestnuts Old and New (King's Head), The Life of Napoleon (Albery), Travelling Tales (Haymarket, and nat tour), The Soldier's Tale (Barbican), Daniel in My Night with Reg (Theatre Upstairs Royal Court and Criterion), Paint Said Fred (Royal Academy); *Solo Shows* at: Liverpool Everyman, Young Vic, Cottesloe, Royal Exchange, Gate; *Television* Channel 4 incl: Girls on Top, The Madness Museum, Porterhouse Blue, Gramsci, Whose Line Is It Anyway?, A History of Psychiatry, The Christmas Show; BBC: The Cellar Show, Saturday Review, Laugh I Nearly Paid My Licence Fee, Tender is the Night, The Lenny Henry Show, Jute City, Have I Got News for You, Life with Eliza, The Full Wax, Some Enchanted Evening, On the Spot, Tall Tales, My Night with Reg, Likely Stories; LWT: After Midnight, The Ackroyd Dickens; Yorkshire: The New Statesman, A Day in Summer; Boon (Central), Menace Unseen (Thames), The Tresure Seekers (Carlton); *Radio* incl: New Premises, Whose Line Is It Anyway?, Beachcomber By the Way, Figaro gets Divorced, Poonsh, Aunt Julia and the Scriptwriter, Mightier than the Sword; *Films* incl: Cousin Bette, Faith, The Sender, The Bounty, Gunbus, Whoops Apocalypse, Castaway, Henry V, Sweet Revenge, The Pope Must Die, Princess Caraboo, In the Bleak Midwinter, Pinocchio; *Recreations* socialising, reading, travelling; *Clubs* Groucho; *Style—* John Sessions, Esq; ✉ c/o Markham & Froggatt Ltd, 4 Windmill Street, London W1P 1HF (☎ 0171 636 4412, fax 0171 637 5233)

SETCHELL, David Lloyd; s of Raymond Setchell (d 1967), and Phyllis Jane, *née* Lloyd (d 1952); *b* 16 April 1937; *Educ* Woodhouse GS, Jesus Coll Cambridge (MA); *m* 11 Aug 1962, Muriel Mary, *née* Davies; 1 s (Andrew b 1970), 1 da (Justine (Mrs Nicholas Panay) b 1967); *Career* Peat Marwick London 1960–64, Shawinigan Ltd 1964–71; mktg mangr Gulf Oil Chemicals (Europe) 1971–77 (vice-pres 1978–82), md Gulf Oil 1982–; dir UK Petroleum Industry Assoc; FInstPet (pres 1996–98), FCA; *Recreations* golf, tennis, theatre; *Clubs* Oriental, MCC, St George's Hill Golf, Cotswold Hills Golf; *Style—* David Setchell, Esq; ✉ Gulf Oil (Great Britain) Ltd, Rosehill, New Barn Lane, Cheltenham GL52 3LA (☎ 01242 225300, fax 01242 225213)

SETCHELL, Marcus Edward; s of Eric Headley Setchell (d 1980), of Cambridge, and Barbara Mary, *née* Whitworth (d 1992); *b* 4 Oct 1943; *Educ* Felsted Sch, Univ of Cambridge, St Bartholomew's Hosp Med Coll (MA, MB BChir); *m* 1973, Sarah Loveday, da of Vernon Alfred Robert French (d 1967), of Northwood, Middx; 2 s (Thomas b 1976, David b 1984), 2 da (Anna b 1974, Catherine b 1980); *Career* conslt gynaecologist and obstetrician: St Bartholomew's Hosp 1975–, Homerton Hosp, King Edward VII Hosp for Offrs, St Luke's Hosp for the Clergy; dir Fertility Unit Portland Hosp 1987–94; surgn/gynaecologist to HM The Queen 1990–; regional assessor Maternal Mortality Enquiry 1992–; RSM: memb Cncl, pres Section of Obstetrics and Gynaecology 1994–95; memb Cncl RCOG 1994–; Liveryman Worshipful Soc of Apothecaries; FRCS, FRCSEd, FRCOG; *Publications* Progress in Obstetrics and Gynaecology (1987), General Surgical Operations (1987), Scientific Foundations of Obstetrics & Gynaecology (ed, 1991), Reconstructive Urology (1993), Ten Teachers Gynaecology (1995), Ten Teachers Obstetrics (1995); *Recreations* tennis, skiing, travel, gardening; *Clubs* RSM, Fountain, St Albans Medical; *Style—* Marcus Setchell, Esq; ✉ 64 Wood Vale, London N10 3DN (☎ 0181 444 5266); 149 Harley Street, London W1 (☎ 0171 935 4444)

SETCHELL, Michael Robert; s of George Robert Setchell (d 1989), of Bedford, and Violet, *née* Cooper (d 1996); *b* 22 March 1944; *Educ* Bedford Modern Sch, Guy's Hosp Dental Sch, Univ of London (BDS, LDS, DGDP RCS); *m* 5 Aug 1967, Mary, da of late Cecil Richardson; 1 s (Alexander Michael b 19 April 1976), 1 da (Joanne Mary b 26 May 1973); *Career* dental practitioner; Guy's Hosp London: res house surgn 1966–67, registrar in dental conservation 1967–69, pt/t lectr (Dental Sch) in conservative dentistry 1969–72; pt/t gen practice with Mr C I Hagger Dulwich 1968–70, full time practitioner in Devonshire Place London 1972– (pt/t 1970–72); memb: BDA, The Dental Soc of London (pres 1996–97); *Recreations* gardening, photography, hill walking; *Clubs* Rotary Int, Langley Park Rotary (past pres); *Style—* Michael Setchell, Esq; ✉ Glynn, Setchell & Allan, 35 Devonshire Place, London W1N 1PE (☎ 0171 935 3342)

SETH, Vikram; s of Premnath Seth, and Leila, also *née* Seth; *b* 20 June 1952; *Educ* Doon Sch Dehradun India, Tonbridge Sch, Corpus Christi College Oxford (open scholarship, MA), Stanford University California (MA, full fellowship), Nanjing University China; *Career* writer; sr ed Stanford University Press 1985–86; Guggenheim Fellowship 1986, Commonwealth Poetry Prize 1986, Sahitya Akademi Award 1988, W H Smith Literary Award and Cwlth Writers Prize (for A Suitable Boy) 1994; hon fell Corpus Christi Coll Oxford 1994; *Books* Mappings (poems, Calcutta, 1982), From Heaven Lake - Travels Through Sinkiang and Tibet (1983, Thomas Cook Travel Book Award), The Humble Administrator's Garden (poems, 1985), The Golden Gate - A Novel in Verse (1986), All You Who Sleep Tonight (poems, 1990), Beastly Tales From Here and There - Fables in Verse (Penguin India, 1992), Three Chinese Poets (translations, 1992), A Suitable Boy (novel, 1993), Arion and the Dolphin (libretto, 1994); *Recreations* walking, swimming, music; *Style—* Vikram Seth; ✉ c/o Sheil Land Associates, 43 Doughty St, London WC1N 2LF (☎ 0171 405 9351)

SETHIA, Babulal; s of Babulal Sethia (d 1974), and Joan, *née* Gridley; *b* 9 Feb 1951; *Educ* Rugby, St Thomas's Hosp (BSc, MB BS); *m* 16 Dec 1978, Nicola Jane, da of Alan Thomas Austin, of Edgbaston, Birmingham; 1 s (Ashok James b 1990), 3 da (India Jane b 1984, Nalini Joanne b 1988, Alesha Victoria Margaux b 1991); *Career* conslt cardiac surgn Birmingham Children's Hosp and Queen Elizabeth Hosp 1987–, hon sr lectr Dept of Surgery Univ of Birmingham 1989–; pubns on aspects of acquired and congenital heart disease; FRCS 1981; memb: Soc of Thoracic and Cardiovascular Surgns 1983, Euro Assoc For Cardiothoracic Surgery 1988, Br Cardiac Soc 1989; *Recreations* music, reading, oenology; *Style—* Babulal Sethia, Esq; ✉ The Children's Hosptital, Birmingham B16 8ET (☎ 0121 450 6399, fax 0121 445 1709); Department of Cardiac Surgery, Queen Elizabeth Hospital, Birmingham B15 2TH (☎ 0121 472 1311)

SETON, Sir Iain Bruce; 13 Bt (NS 1663), of Abercorn, Linlithgowshire; s of Sir (Christopher) Bruce Seton, 12 Bt (d 1988); *b* 27 Aug 1942; *Educ* Colchester, Chadacre Agric Inst; *m* 1963, Margaret Ann, o da of Walter Charles Faulkner, of Barlee Road, W Australia: 1 s (Laurence Bruce, m 1990 Rachel, 2 da of Jeffery Woods, of Bridgetown), 1 da (Amanda Jane b 1971); *Heir* s, Laurence Bruce Seton b 1 July 1968; *Style—* Sir Iain Seton, Bt; ✉ PO Box 253, Bridgetown 6255, W Australia

SETON, Sir James Christall; 12 Bt (NS 1683), of Pitmedden, Aberdeenshire; s of Christall Dougal Seton (d 1969), gs of 7 Bt; suc kinsman, Sir Robert James Seton, 11 Bt (d 1993); *b* 21 Jan 1913; *m* 1939, Evelyn, da of Ray Hafer; *Heir* nephew, Charles Wallace Seton b 1948; *Career* corporal US Army; *Style—* Sir James Seton, Bt; ✉ Otterbein-Lebanon, 585 North State Route 741, Lebanon, Ohio 45036–9551, USA

SETON, Lady; Julia; OBE; da of late Frank Clements; *m* 1962, as his 3 w, Sir Alexander Hay Seton, 10 Bt (d 1963); *Career* VMH; writer as Julia Clements; *Books* author of 21 books incl: My Life With Flowers (1993); *Style—* Lady Seton, OBE; ✉ 122 Swan Court, Chelsea Manor St, London SW3 5RU

SEVER, Prof Peter Sedgwick; s of Harry Sedgwick Sever, of London, and Lillian Maria, *née* Moran (d 1990); *b* 23 July 1944; *Educ* Manchester GS, Trinity Hall Cambridge (MA), St Mary's Hosp Med Sch (Lord Moran scholar, MB BChir, Cert of Merit in Therapeutics, FRCP), Univ of London (PhD); *Career* SHO: in gen med and cardiology St Mary's Hosp London 1969–70, in chest diseases The Brompton Hosp 1970; MRC jr research fell Dept of Biochemistry St Mary's Hosp Med Sch and hon med registrar to the Professorial Med Unit 1971–74, lectr in med and pharmacology St Mary's Hosp Med Sch and hon sr registrar St Mary's Hosp 1974–76, sr lectr in med St Mary's Hosp Med Sch and hon conslt physician 1976–89, prof of clinical pharmacology and therapeutics St Mary's Hosp Med Sch 1980–; prog conslt Wellcome Tst/Kenya/St Mary's Research Unit 1980–85, chm Specialist Advsy Ctee on Clinical Pharmacology Jt Ctee on Higher Med Trg 1984–90, memb Br Heart Fndn Grant Awards Ctee 1988–92, govr Imperial Coll of Sci Technol and Med 1989–93, memb Exec Scientific Ctee Euro Soc of Cardiology 1991–93; ed: Clinical Science 1980–87, Jl of Hypertension 1983–89, Jl of Human Hypertension 1987, Jl of Drug Development 1988; memb: Br Pharmacological Soc 1976, Int Soc of Hypertension 1978; sec: London Hypertension Soc 1977–85, Euro Blood Pressure Gp 1979–82; pres Br Hypertension Soc 1989–91; fell Euro Soc of Cardiology; *Books* Clinical Atlas of Hypertension (with Peart and Swales, 1992), Cardiovascular Disease - Practical Issues for Prevention (with Poulter and Thom, 1993), also editor of several books on cardiovascular disease and hypertention and author of over 300 papers on cardiovascular disease and clinical pharmacology; *Recreations* sport (tennis and rugby), theatre, travel; *Clubs* Wig and Pen; *Style—* Prof Peter Sever; ✉ Hedgerley House, Hedgerley, Bucks SL2 3UL; Department of Clinical Pharmacology, Imperial College School of Medicine at St Mary's, Queen Elizabeth the Queen Mother Wing, London W2 1NY (☎ 0171 725 1117, fax 0171 725 6145)

SEVERIN, Prof Dorothy Sherman; da of Wilbur B Sherman, of Dallas, USA, and Virginia, *née* Tucker; *b* 24 March 1942; *Educ* Harvard (AB, AM, PhD); *m* 24 March 1966 (m dis 1979), Giles Timothy Severin; 1 da (Ida); *Career* tutor Harvard Univ 1964–66, visiting lectr Univ of West Indies 1967–68, asst prof Vassar Coll NY 1968–69, lectr Westfield Coll London 1969–82, Gilmour prof of Spanish Univ of Liverpool 1982– (ed Bulletin of Hispanic Studies 1982–); visiting assoc prof: Harvard Univ 1982, Columbia Univ NY 1985, Yale Univ 1985, Univ of California Berkeley 1996; pro vice chllr Liverpool 1989–92; memb: NI HE Cncl 1993–, Int Courtly Lit Soc (former pres Br Branch), Ctee Modern Humanities Res Assoc, Res Panel Humanities Res Bd British Acad 1994–96, Assoc of Hispanists of GB and I; FSA; *Books* Memory in La Celestina (1970), Diego de San Pedro, La pasión trobada (1973), La Lengua de Erasmo romançada por muy elegante estilo (ed, 1975), Diego de San Pedro, Poesía (ed with Keith Whinnom, 1979), Cosas sacadas de la crónica del rey Juan II (ed with Angus Mackay, 1982), Celestina (edns 1969, 1987), Celestina with the Translation of James Mabbe 1631 (ed, 1987), Tragicomedy and Novelistic Discourse in Celestina (1989), Cancionero de Oñate-Castañeda (1990), The Paris Cancioneros (with F Maguire and M Garcia, 1993), Witchcraft in Celestina (1995); *Style—* Prof Dorothy Severin, FSA; ✉ Department of Hispanic Studies, University of Liverpool, PO Box 147, Liverpool L69 3BX (☎ 0151 794 2773/4, fax 0151 794 2774, telex 627095 UNILPL G)

SEVERIN, Giles Timothy (Tim); s of Maurice Watkins, and Inge Severin; *b* 25 Sept 1940; *Educ* Tonbridge Sch, Keble Coll Oxford (MA, BLitt); *m* 1966 (m dis 1979), Dorothy Virginia Sherman; 1 da; *Career* author, film maker, historian, traveller; expeditions: led motorcycle team along Marco Polo route 1961, river Mississippi by canoe and launch 1965, Brendan Voyage from W Ireland to N America 1977, Sindbad Voyage from Oman to China 1980–81, Jason Voyage from Iolkos to Colchis 1984, Ulysses Voyage from Troy to Ithaca 1985, First Crusade route by horse to Jerusalem 1987–88, travels on horseback in Mongolia 1990, trans-Pacific bamboo raft from Hong Kong 1993, Prahu voyage Eastern Indonesia 1996; films: The Brendan Voyage, The Sindbad Voyage, The Jason Voyage, Crusader, In Search of Genghis Khan, The China Voyage; Founder's medal RGS, Livingstone medal RGS (Scotland), Sir Percy Sykes medal RSAA; *Publications:* Tracking Marco Polo (1964), Explorers of the Mississippi (1967), The Golden Antilles (1970), Vanishing Primitive Man (1973), The African Adventure (1973), The Oriental Adventure (1978), The Brendan Voyage (1978), The Sindbad Voyage (1982), The Jason Voyage (1985), The Ulysses Voyage (1987), Crusader (1989), In Search of Genghis Khan (1991), The China Voyage (1994); *Style—* Tim Severin, Esq

SEVERN, Prof Roy Thomas; CBE (1992); s of Ernest Severn (d 1985), of Gt Yarmouth, Norfolk, and Muriel Breeta, *née* Woollatt (d 1978); *b* 6 Sept 1929; *Educ* Deacon's Sch Peterborough, Gt Yarmouth GS, Imperial Coll London (BSc, PhD, DSc); *m* 12 Sept 1957, Hilary Irene, da of Harold Batty Saxton, of Douglas, IOM; 2 da (Fiona Rae b 1960, Elizabeth Louise b 1962); *Career* 2 Lt RE (Survey) 1954–56; lectr Imperial Coll London

1952–54; Univ of Bristol: lectr 1956–65, reader 1965–68, prof 1968–95, pro-vice-chllr 1981–84, currently sr research fell and prof emeritus; memb: UGC Tech Sub Ctee 1982–89, Engrg Bd SERC 1986–90; pres Inst of Civil Engrs 1990–91; FICE, FEng 1982; *Books* Advances in Structural Engineering (1982); *Recreations* sailing, gardening, bee-keeping; *Style*— Prof Roy Severn, CBE, FEng; ✉ Department of Civil Engineering, University of Bristol, Bristol BS8 1TR (☎ 0117 928 7706, fax 0117 928 7783, telex 445938)

SEVERNE, Air Vice-Marshal Sir John de Milt; KCVO (1988, LVO 1961), OBE (1968), AFC (1955), DL (Somerset 1991); s of Dr Alfred de Milt Severne (d 1967), and Joane Mary Margaret, *née* Haydon (d 1994); *b* 15 Aug 1925; *Educ* Marlborough; *m* 1951, Katharine Veronica, da of Capt Vero Elliot Kemball, RN (d 1963); 3 da (Veronica, Amanda, Christina); *Career* joined RAF 1944, Equerry to HRH The Duke of Edinburgh 1958, Station Cdr RAF Kinloss 1971, Cmdt CFS 1974, ret 1980; Capt of The Queen's Flight 1982–89; ADC to HM The Queen 1972–73; pres SW Area RAFA 1981–95; Hon Air Cdre No 3 (County of Devon) Maritime Headquarters Unit RAuxAF 1990–95; winner King's Cup Air Race and Br Air Racing Champion 1960; pres: RAF Equitation Assoc 1976–79 (chm 1973), The Queen's Flight Assoc 1992–, CFS Assoc 1993–, Taunton branch ESU 1996; *Style*— Air Vice-Marshal Sir John Severne, KCVO, OBE, AFC, DL; ✉ c/o RAF Club, 128 Piccadilly, London SW1

SEVITT, Dr Michael Andrew; s of Simon Sevitt (d 1988), of Birmingham, and Betty, *née* Woolf; *b* 13 Oct 1944; *Educ* King Edward's Sch Birmingham, King's Coll Cambridge, UCH Med Sch London; *m* 12 Sept 1970, Dr Jennifer Margaret Duckham, da of William John Duckham, of London, and Peggy Duckham; 1 s (Timothy b 1974), 1 da (Deborah b 1976); *Career* lectr in psychiatry Univ of Southampton 1974–76, conslt in adolescent psychiatry SW Thames RHA 1978–; memb UK Cncl for Psychotherapy; psychiatric advsr: Relate, Samaritans; MRCP 1971, MRCPsych 1974, MInstGPAnal 1979; *Recreations* theatre, music, gardening, wining and dining, follower of Crazy Gang (supporter Wimbledon FC); *Style*— Dr Michael Sevitt; ✉ 7 Upper Park Rd, Kingston upon Thames, Surrey KT2 5LB (☎ 0181 546 4173); Woodside Adolescent Unit, West Park Hospital, Epsom, Surrey KT19 8PB (☎ 01372 729136, fax 01372 727614)

SEWARD, David George; s of Arthur Ernest Seward, of Friern Barnet, London N11, and Vera Evelyn, *née* Todd (d 1989); *b* 23 Jan 1944; *Educ* Woodhouse GS Finchley, St Luke's Coll Exeter; *m* 13 Aug 1966, Barbara Louise, da of William Leslie Nichols (d 1959); 1 s (Jonathan David b 25 Jan 1970), 1 da (Joanna Louise b 4 April 1968); *Career* golf and cricket administrator; playing career: Middlesex Grammar Schs 1959–61, Middlesex Young Amateurs 1960–61, Finchley 1959–66, St Luke's Coll Exeter 1962–65, Taunton 1967–72, Somerset CCC 2nd XI 1967; sec Somerset CCC 1980–82, mktg mangr Nottinghamshire CCC 1983–87, sec Surrey CCC 1987–92, gen mangr Coombe Hill Golf Club Kingston 1992–93, sec Strawberry Hill Golf Club Twickenham 1994–95, sec Wyke Green Golf Club Osterley 1995–; teacher: King's Coll Jr Sch Taunton 1966–69, Priory Jr Sch Taunton 1969–71; dep headteacher Holway Primary Sch Taunton 1971–73; headmaster: Warner C of E Primary Sch Loughborough 1973–76, Wilford C of E Primary Sch Nottingham 1976–80; LTCL; *Recreations* playing golf, piano and organ playing (organist St John the Evangelist Church Taunton and Loughborough Parish Church); *Style*— David Seward, Esq

SEWARD, Desmond; s of Maj W E L Seward, MC (d 1975); *b* 22 May 1935, Paris; *Educ* Ampleforth, St Catharine's Coll Cambridge (BA); *Career* author; Knight SMOM 1978, Gd Cross Constantinian Order of St George 1982; *Books* The First Bourbon (1971), The Monks of War (1972, new edn 1995), Prince of the Renaissance (1973), The Bourbon Kings of France (1976), Eleanor of Aquitaine (1978), The Hundred Years War (1978, new edn 1996), Monks and Wine (1979), Marie Antoinette (1981), Richard III (1983), Naples (1984), Italy's Knights of St George (1986), Napoleon's Family (1986), Henry V (1987), Napoleon and Hitler (1988, new edn 1996), Byzantium (with Susan Mountgarret, 1988), Metternich (1991), Brooks's: a social history (jt ed with Philip Ziegler, 1991), The Dancing Sun (1993); Sussex (1995), The Wars of the Roses (1995); *Recreations* walking, France, Italy; *Clubs* Brooks's, Pratt's; *Style*— Desmond Seward, Esq; ✉ c/o Sheil Land Associates Ltd, 43 Doughty Street, London WC1N 2LF

SEWARD, Prof Gordon Robert; CBE (1990); s of Percy Robert Seward (d 1968), and Ruth Marie, *née* Mackenzie; *b* 18 Dec 1925; *Educ* Grocers Co Sch, Univ of London (MDS, MB BS); *m* 5 May 1962, Dr Margaret Helen Elizabeth Seward, CBE, *qv*; 1 s (Colin Robert b 9 Sept 1966), 1 da (Pamela Elizabeth b 31 May 1964); *Career* Nat Serv Lt and Capt RADC 1949–50, Capt RADC (TA) 167 City of London Field Ambulance 1950–54; Dept of Oral and Maxillofacial Surgery The London Hosp Med Coll: sr lectr 1960–62, reader 1962–68, dean of dental studies 1975–79, prof 1968–90, emeritus prof 1990–; conslt advisor CMO and CDO 1980–86, dean Faculty of Dental Surgery RCS 1986–89; RCS: memb Bd of Faculty Dental Surgery 1977–91, vice dean 1983, dean 1986–89, memb Cncl RCS 1985–84 and 1986–90; memb: City and E London AHA 1976–80, Jt Conslts Ctee 1986–89, Conf Med Royal Colls 1986–89, Dental Educn Advsy Cncl 1975–79; pres London Hosp Dental Club 1983–84; awarded: Tomes medal of BDA 1990, Colyer medal of RCS 1991; Hon FRCSEd 1986, Hon FRCS 1987, Hon FFARCS 1988; memb: BDA, RSM (vice pres Section of Odontology 1975–78, pres 1987–88), EACMFS, BAOMFS (pres 1981–82); FDSRCS; *Books* Outline of Oral Surgery (jtly, 1971), Short Practice of Surgery (contrib, 1976), Surgery of the Mouth and Jaws (contrib, 1986); *Recreations* painting, walking, photography, woodwork; *Style*— Prof Gordon Seward, CBE; ✉ Department of Oral and Maxillo Facial Surgery, St Bartholomew's and the Royal London Hospital Medical College, Turner St, Whitechapel E1 2AD (☎ 0171 377 7050)

SEWARD, Dr Margaret Helen Elizabeth; CBE (1993); da of Frederick Oldershaw, and Gwen, *née* Smith; *b* 5 Aug 1935; *Educ* Latymer Sch London, London Hosp Dental Sch Univ of London (BDS, FDS RCS, MCCD, MDS); *m* 5 May 1962, Prof Gordon Robert Seward, CBE, *qv*; 1 s (Colin Robert b 9 Sept 1966), 1 da (Pamela Elizabeth b 31 May 1964); *Career* registrar Oral Surgery Dept and dental offr to the Nursing Staff London Hosp Whitechapel 1960–62 (resident dental house surgn 1959–60), sr hosp dental offr Highlands Gen Hosp London 1962–64, hon clinical asst Dental Health Study Unit London Hosp Med Coll 1967–75; locum conslt: Highlands Gen Hosp London 1969–70, N Middx Hosp London 1970; pt/t sch/community dental offr Cheshunt Herts 1970–75, pt/t sr research fell Br Postgraduate Med Fndn 1975–77, Cncl of Europe travelling fell The Netherlands 1978, ed Br Dental Jl 1979–92 (ed designate 1978–79); pres: BDA 1993–94 (pres designate 1992), GDC 1994– (memb 1976–); vice chm Standing Dental Advsy Ctee 1990– (memb 1984–), vice dean Bd of Faculty RCS 1990–91 (memb 1980–88), pres Section of Odontology RSM 1991–92; hon pres Women in Dentistry 1988–92; ed Int Dental Jl (Fédération Dentaire Internationale) 1990–; hon memb American Dental Assoc 1992, fell American Coll of Dentists New Orleans 1994, hon fell Acad of Dentistry Int Vancouver 1994; Hon DDSc Univ of Newcastle 1995, Hon DDS Univ of Birmingham 1995, Hon FDS RCSEd 1995; memb Br Paedodontic Soc 1969 (nat sec 1975–78), Br Assoc of Oral and Maxillofacial Surgns 1965, Br Assoc for the Study of Community Dentistry 1974 (fndr memb), Br Dental Eds Forum 1980 (chm 1983–85); chm of govrs The Latymer Sch London 1983–94; author of various book chapters and of numerous papers in learned jls; *Video* Nothing but the Tooth (teething disturbances and treatment); *Recreations* walking, entertaining at home; *Clubs* RSM; *Style*— Dr Margaret Seward, CBE; ✉ General Dental Council, 37 Wimpole Street, London W1M 8DQ (☎ 0171 486 2171, fax 0171 224 3294)

SEWELL, Brian; *Career* art critic The Evening Standard; British Press Awards: Critic of the Year 1988, Arts Journalist of the Year 1994; Hawthornden Prize for Art Criticism 1995; *Books* South from Ephesus (1988), The Reviews that caused the Rumpus (1994), An Alphabet of Villains (1995); *Style*— Brian Sewell, Esq; ✉ The Evening Standard, Northcliffe House, 2 Derry Street, Kensington, London W8 5EE (☎ 0171 938 6000, fax 0171 937 2648)

SEWELL, James Reid; s of James Campbell Sewell, of Glasgow (d 1968), and Iris Eveleen, *née* Reid; *b* 12 April 1944; *Educ* Glasgow HS, Univ of Glasgow (MA), UCL (dip in archive admin); *Career* asst archivist Durham Cty Record Office 1967–70; Corp of London Records Office: asst dep keeper 1970–84, city archivist (formerly dep keeper) 1984–; chm Section of Municipal Archives ICA 1992– (ctee memb 1986–92); fell Guildhall Wine Acad 1993; FSA 1979; *Books* The Russian Journal of Lady Londonderry 1836–37 (with W A L Seaman, 1973), The Artillery Ground and Fields in Finsbury (1977); author of various articles in prof jnls; *Recreations* tennis, orchid growing, antique porcelain, wine; *Clubs* Shirley Park Lawn Tennis (hon sec), Riverside (Croydon); *Style*— James Sewell, Esq, FSA; ✉ Corporation of London Records Office, PO Box 270, Guildhall, London EC2P 2EJ (☎ 0171 332 1250, fax 0171 332 1119)

SEWELL, Prof John Isaac; s of Harry Sewell (d 1975), of Kirkby Stephen, Cumbria, and Dorothy, *née* Brunskill (d 1977); *b* 13 May 1942; *Educ* Kirkby Stephen GS, Univ of Durham (BSc, DSc), Univ of Newcastle upon Tyne (PhD); *m* 6 May 1989, Ruth Alexandra, da of Walter Baxter (d 1986), of Edinburgh; *Career* reader in integrated electronic systems Univ of Hull 1984–85 (lectr 1968–76, sr lectr 1976–84), prof of electronic systems Univ of Glasgow 1985– (dean of engrg 1990–93); visiting research prof Univ of Toronto 1995; winner IEE J J Thomson Premium 1992 (jtly); FIEE 1986, FIEEE 1992; *Recreations* climbing, swimming; *Style*— Prof John Sewell; ✉ 16 Paterson Place Bearsden, Glasgow G61 4RU (☎ 0141 943 0729); Department of Electronics and Electrical Engineering, University of Glasgow, Glasgow G12 8LT (☎ 0141 330 4253, fax 0141 330 4907, telex 777070 UNIGLA G, www http://www.elec.gla.ac.uk, e-mail sewell@elec.gla.ac.uk)

SEWELL, Prof Major Morley Hodkin; s of Major John Sewell (d 1971), and Edith Mary, *née* Hodkin (d 1995); *b* 1 Sept 1932; *Educ* King Edward VII Sch Sheffield, Trinity Hall Cambridge (MA), Sch of Veterinary Med Cambridge (VetMB, MRCVS), PhD (Cantab); *m* 10 Aug 1957, Cynthia Margaret Rose, da of George Hanson; 3 da (Mary Elizabeth (Mrs Packer) b 19 May 1958, Ruth Miriam (Mrs Hutt) b 10 March 1960, Rebecca Ann (Mrs Docea) b 23 May 1961), 1 s (Paul Leonard b 23 Feb 1964); *Career* colonial veterinary research scholar Dept of Animal Pathology Univ of Cambridge 1957–59, veterinary research offr Fed Dept of Veterinary Research Vom Nigeria 1959–63; Univ of Edinburgh: lectr in applied veterinary parasitology 1963–70, sr lectr in veterinary parasitology 1970–79, reader in veterinary parasitology 1980–93, prof of tropical veterinary med 1993–, dean Faculty of Veterinary Med 1994–; memb Cncl RCVS 1993–97; circuit treas Methodist Church; *Recreations* Methodist local preacher, travel, family; *Style*— Prof M M H Sewell; ✉ 14, Craigiebield Crescent, Penicuik, Midlothian EH26 9EQ (☎ 01968 674595); Royal (Dick) School of Veterinary Studies, The University of Edinburgh, Summerhall, Edinburgh EH9 1QH (☎ 0131 650 6102, fax 0131 650 6585, e-mail MMH.Sewell@ed.ac.uk)

SEWELL, Dr Nigel John; s of Charles John Sewell (d 1985), and Vera Kathleen, *née* Swann; *b* 27 April 1948; *Educ* Thames Poly, Int Mgmnt Centres (MBA); *m* 1972, Mary Ann, da of Alfred James Freeman; 2 da (Joy Rosemary b 13 May 1976, Eleanor Mary b 23 March 1979); *Career* legal and co secretarial asst J Lyons and Company Ltd 1967–71, mgmnt trainee SE Thames RHA 1971–73, dep hosp mangr Bromley AHA 1973–75, sector admin King's Health Dist 1975–80, gen mangr Acute Servs Unit Merton and Sutton Health Authy 1986–90 (sector admin 1980–86), chief exec St Helier NHS Tst 1990–; DPhil Int Management Centre 1995, FIMgt 1990, FHSM 1990; *Recreations* opera, swimming; *Style*— Dr Nigel Sewell; ✉ 21 Wilmot Way, Banstead, Surrey SM7 2PZ (☎ 01737 211488); St Helier Hospital, Wrythe Lane, Carshalton, Surrey SM5 1AA (☎ 0181 296 2239)

SEWELL, Rufus Frederick; *b* 29 Oct 1967; *Career* actor; *Theatre* credits incl: Royal Hunt of the Sun, Comedians (both Compass Theatre Co), The Lost Domain (Watermill Theatre Newbury), Peter and the Captain (BAC), Pride and Prejudice (Royal Exchange Manchester), The Government Inspector, The Seagull, As you Like It (all Crucible Sheffield), Making it Better (Hampstead and Criterion), Arcadia (RNT), Translations (Plymouth Theatre NY), Rat in the Skull (Duke of Yorks); *Television* credits incl: The Last Romantics (BBC), Gone to Seed (Central), Middlemarch (BBC), Dirty Something (Skreba), Citizen Locke, Cold Comfort Farm (Thames), Henry IV (BBC); *Films* credits incl: Twenty-One (Anglo Int Films), Dirty Weekend (Michale Winner Ltd), A Man of No Importance (Littlebird Ventures), Carrington (Dora Prodns), Victory (Victory Cinema), Hamlet (Fishmonger Films), The Woodlanders (River Films), The Honest Courtesan (Honest Courtesan NV); *Style*— Rufus Sewell, Esq; ✉ c/o Julian Belfrage Associates, 46 Albemarle Street, London W1X 4PP (☎ 0171 491 4400, fax 0171 493 5460)

SEYMOUR, David; s of Graham Seymour, of Sanderstead, Surrey, and Beatrice (Betty), *née* Watson (d 1992); *b* 24 Jan 1951; *Educ* Trinity Sch Croydon, Queen's Coll Oxford (Open exhibitioner, BA Jurisprudence), Fitzwilliam Coll Cambridge (LLB); *m* 1972, Elisabeth, da of Ronald and Muriel Huitson; 1 s (Nicholas b 16 Feb 1977), 2 da (Rachel b 10 June 1979, Charlotte b 21 Dec 1981); *Career* civil servant; law clerk Rosenfeld Meyer & Susman (attorneys) Beverly Hills Calif 1972–73, called to the Bar Gray's Inn (Holt scholar) 1975; Home Office: joined as legal asst 1976, princ asst legal advsr 1994–96, dep legal advsr 1996–; visiting lectr Sch of Law Univ of Connecticut 1986; *Recreations* hockey, squash, walking; *Clubs* Utd Oxford & Cambridge Univ, MCC; *Style*— David Seymour, Esq; ✉ Deputy Legal Adviser, The Home Office, 50 Queen Anne's Gate, London SW1H 9AT (☎ 0171 273 3000)

SEYMOUR, Jane; da of late John Frankenberg, of Hillingdon, Middx, and Mieke, *née* van Tricht; *b* 15 Feb 1951; *Educ* Wimbledon HS, Arts Educnl Tst; *m* 1, 10 July 1971 (m dis 1976), Michael John Attenborough, *qv*; m 2, 20 Aug 1977 (m dis), Geoffrey Planer; m 3, 18 July 1981, David Flynn, s of Lloyd Flynn, of Santa Barbara, California; 1 s (Sean Michael b 31 July 1985), 1 da (Katherine Jane b 7 Jan 1982); m 4, 1993, James Keach; 2 s (John Stacy b Dec 1995, Kristopher Steven b (twin) Dec 1995); *Career* actress; int ambassador Childhelp USA, nat chm Cityhearts, active involvement in CLIC UK, hon chm RP Fndn USA (fighting blindness), hon citizen Illinois USA 1977; *Theatre* incl: Amadeus (Broadway) 1981, Not Now Darling (Canterbury Repertory), Ophelia in Hamlet (Harrogate Repertory), Lady Macbeth in Macbeth, Nora in A Dolls House; *Television* incl: The Onedin Line 1973, Seventh Avenue 1977, Awakening Land 1978, Battle Star Gallactica 1978, Dallas Cowboy Cheerleaders 1979, East of Eden 1981, The Scarlet Pimpernel 1982, The Haunting Passion 1983, The Phantom of the Opera 1983, The Sun Also Rises 1984, Dark Mirror 1984, The Leather Funnel 1984, Jamaica Inn 1985, The Hanged Man 1985, Obsessed with a Married Man 1985, The Woman He Loved (Golden Globe nomination) 1988, Onassis (Emmy Award) 1988, War and Remembrance (Emmy nomination) 1989, Jack the Ripper 1989, Angel of Death, Matters of the Heart, Are You Lonesome Tonight?; *Films* incl: Oh, What a Lovely War 1969, Sinbad and the Eye of the Tiger 1972, Young Winston 1973, Live and Let Die 1973, Four Feathers, Somewhere in Time 1980, Oh Heavenly Dog 1980, Lassiter 1984, Head Office 1986, The Tunnel 1987, Keys to Freedom 1989, Le Revolution Français; *Books* Jane Seymour's Guide to

Romantic Living (1987); *Style*— Miss Jane Seymour; ✉ c/o London Management, 2–4 Noel Street, London W1V 3RB (☎ 0171 287 9000, fax 0171 287 3036)

SEYMOUR, Lt-Col Michael; MBE (1975); s of Geoffrey Vincent Seymour (d 1991), and Margaret Joan, *née* Underwood (d 1979); *b* 28 Aug 1943; *Educ* Berkhamsted Sch Herts, Aiglon Coll Switzerland, RMA Sandhurst, Staff Coll Camberley; *m* April 1969, (Judith) Linda, da of Gethen Hardwick Eaton Smith; 1 s (Christopher Gethen Hardwick b 1976), 2 da ((Charlotte) Anna Eaton b 1970, Rebecca Margaret Bradford b 1972); *Career* cmmnd Royal Tank Regt 1964, regtl duty Germany, ME and UK 1964–67, instr Jr Leader Regt RAC 1967–69, Regt Adj 1969–71, ADC to Chief of Gen Staff (Gen Sir Michael Carver) 1971–73, Ops Offr N Ireland 1974–75, student Staff Coll Camberley 1975–76, Staff Offr MOD (MI(A)) 1976–78, Sqdn Ldr 1 RTR 1978–81, Directing Staff of Staff Coll Camberley 1981–82, CO 1 RTR 1982–84, Staff Offr UK and Germany 1984–88, ret; exec dir Burson-Marsteller London 1988– (sr cnsllr crisis mgmnt 1988–91, dir issues and crisis mgmnt 1991–96), md issues and crisis mgmnt Burson-Marsteller Europe 1996–; *Recreations* riding, tennis, golf, music, reading; *Style*— Lt-Col Michael Seymour, MBE; ✉ Seymour Farm House, Chicklade, nr Hindon, Salisbury, Wilts SP3 5SU (☎ 01747 820364); 20 Westmoreland Place, London SW1 4AE (☎ 0171 834 0386); Burson-Marsteller, 24–28 Bloomsbury Way, London WC1A 2PX (☎ 0171 831 6262, fax 0171 430 1052, car 0836 217903)

SEYMOUR, Miranda; da of George Fitzroy Seymour, JP, DL (d 1994), of Thrumpton Hall, Nottinghamshire, and Hon Rosemary Nest Scott Ellis, da of 8 Baron Howard de Walden; *b* 8 Aug 1948; *Educ* private sch, Bedford Coll London (BA); *m* 1, 1972 (m dis 1981), Andrew Sinclair; 1 s (Merlin b 1973); m 2, 1989, Anthony Gottlieb; *Career* writer; visiting prof Nottingham Trent Univ 1996; FRSL 1996; *Books* children's books: Mumtaz the Magical Cat (1984), The Vampire of Verdonia (1986), Caspar and the Secret Kingdom (1986), Pierre and the Pamplemousse (1990); The Madonna of the Island - Tales of Corfu (short stories, 1980); historical novels: The Stones of Maggiare (1974), Count Manfred (1976), Daughter of Darkness - Lucrezia Borgia (1977), The Goddess (1978), Medea (1981); modern novels: Carrying On (1984), The Reluctant Devil (1990); A Ring of Conspirators - Henry James and his Literary Circle (biography, 1989) Ottoline Morrell: A Life on the Grand Scale (1992); Robert Graves: Life on the Edge (1995); *Style*— Ms Miranda Seymour, FRSL; ✉ c/o David Higham Literary Agency, 5–8 Lower John St, London W1 (☎ 0171 437 7888, fax 0171 437 1072)

SEYMOUR, Prof Philip Herschel Kean; s of William Kean Seymour (d 1975), of Alresford, Hants, and Rosalind Herschel, *née* Wade, OBE (d 1989); *b* 9 March 1938; *Educ* Kelly Coll Tavistock Devon, Univ of Oxford (BA), Univ of St Andrews (MEd), Univ of Dundee (PhD); *m* 26 Jan 1962, Margaret Jean Dyson (Jane), da of Prof William Ian Clinch Morris, of Springfield, Fife; 2 s (Patrick b 1962, Dominic b 1975), 2 da (Emma b 1964, Mary Marcella b 1978); *Career* Nat Serv RAEC 1957–59; prof Univ of Dundee 1988– (lectr and sr lectr 1966–82, reader 1982–88); chm Scot Dyslexia Assoc 1987; memb Br Psychological Soc; *Books* Human Visual Cognition (1979), Cognitive Analysis of Dyslexia (1986); *Recreations* gardening, fishing; *Style*— Prof Philip Seymour; ✉ Edenfield House, Springfield, by Cupar, Fife (☎ 01334 653177); Department of Psychology, The University, Dundee (☎ 01382 344614, fax 01382 229993, telex 9312110826 DU G)

SEYMOUR, Maj (George) Raymond; CVO (1990), DL (Berks, 1992); s of Sir Reginald Seymour, KCVO (gs of Rt Hon Sir George Seymour, GCB, GCH, PC, and Hon Gertrude, da of 21 Baron Dacre; Sir George was gs of 1 Marquess of Hertford, KG); *b* 5 May 1923; *Educ* Eton; *m* 1957, Hon Mary Quenelda Stanley, da of Gen 1 Baron Ismay (extinct 1965); 1 da, 2 step da; *Career* Maj KRRC, served Palestine, Germany; asst private sec and equerry to HM Queen Elizabeth, The Queen Mother 1993 (equerry 1955); *Recreations* sailing, fishing, shooting; *Clubs* Boodle's; *Style*— Maj Raymond Seymour, CVO, DL; ✉ The Old Vicarage, Bucklebury, Reading, Berks (☎ 0118 971 2504); Appletrees, Swains Rd, Bembridge, Isle of Wight (☎ 01983 872760)

SEYMOUR, Prof Richard; s of Bertram Seymour, of Scarborough, Yorks, and Annie Irenie, *née* Sherwood; *b* 1 May 1953; *Educ* Scarborough HS for Boys, Royal Coll of Art (MA(RCA)); *m* April 1980, Anne Margaret, da of Steven Hart; 1 da (Peggy Teresa b 12 June 1982), 1 s (Arthur William b 25 Sept 1985); *Career* product designer; freelance art dir within various London advtg agencies incl JWT, Holmes Knight Ritchie and Michael Bungey DFS 1977–79, creative dir Blazelynn Advertising London 1979–82 (various D&AD awards), freelance designer working specifically on advtg and new product devpt projects 1982–83, fndr designer Seymour-Furst specialising in film prodn design 1983–84, fndr (with Dick Powell, *qv*) Seymour-Powell 1984– (clients incl British Rail, Yamaha, Tefal, Casio and MZ); external assessor BA Product Design course Central St Martin's Coll of Art and Design 1990– (memb Jt Course Advy Ctee Product Design Dept 1989–90), external examiner RCA Transportation Design course 1993–, visiting prof of product and transportation design RCA 1995–; regular contrib British design press, contrib BBC Design Classics, Designs on Britain and several children's progs featuring design and future thinking 1986; inaugral product design judge BBC Design Awards 1987, memb Panel of Judges D&AD Product Design Section 1987, main speaker Blueprint Moving Up seminars 1988; memb: Exec Ctee Design Business Gp 1988–, Int Advsy Ctee Design Museum 1989–, Steering Ctee Lead Body for Design 1991–, Bd of Tstees Design Museum London 1994–; FRSA 1993, FCSD 1993; *Awards* Best Overall Design and Product Design (for Norton F1 motorcycle) Design Week Awards 1990, D&AD Silver Award (for Technophone Cellular Telephone) 1991, ID Award and D&AD Silver Award (for MuZ Skorpion motorcycle) 1993, winner Product Design category BBC Design Awards 1994, CSD Minerva Award (for MuZ Skorpian) 1994, ID Award (for Sun Voyager) 1994, D&AD President's Award (for outstanding contribution to design) 1995; *Books* The Mirrorstone (conceived and designed 1985, words by Michael Palin, Smarties Award for Innovation in Book Design 1985, Hatchard's Top Ten Authors Award 1985); *Recreations* playing the cello, piano and organ, Early English music, motorcycles; *Style*— Prof Richard Seymour; ✉ Seymour Powell, The Chapel, Archel Road, London W14 9QH (☎ 0171 381 6433, fax 0171 381 9081)

SEYMOUR, Richard William; QC (1991); s of late Albert Percy Seymour, of Bude, Cornwall, and Vera Maud, *née* Greenfield; *b* 4 May 1950; *Educ* Brentwood Sch, Royal Belfast Acad Inst, Christ's Coll Cambridge (MA, scholar, De Hart prize, coll prize); *m* 14 Aug 1971, Clare Veronica, da of Stanley Victor Peskett; 1 da (Victoria Jane Rebecca b 29 Aug 1979), 1 s (Edward Patrick James b 4 Nov 1981); *Career* called to the Bar Gray's Inn 1972 (Holker jr exhbn and sr scholarship), pupil barrister 5 Essex Ct Temple 1972–73, chambers of R I Threlfall QC 1973, in practice 1973–, recorder of the Crown Court 1995– (asst recorder 1991–95); *Books* The Quantum of Damages (jt ed, 1975, 4th edn), Practice and Procedure for the Quantity Surveyor (contrib, 1980, 8th edn), The Architect in Practice (contrib, 1981, 6th edn); *Recreations* archaeology, walking, foreign travel; *Style*— Richard Seymour, Esq, QC; ✉ 4 Raymond Buildings, Gray's Inn, London WC1R 5BP (☎ 0171 405 7211, fax 0171 405 2084)

SEYMOUR, Lord; Sebastian Edward Seymour; s and h of 19 Duke of Somerset; *b* 3 Feb 1982; *Style*— Lord Seymour

SEYMOUR, Timothy Massingham (Tim); s of William George Massingham Seymour, and Georgina Esmée, *née* Rouillard; *b* 29 June 1948; *Educ* Michaelhouse, Univ of Natal (BSc), Oriel Coll Oxford (Rhodes scholar, MA, rugby blue); *Career* articled clerk Price Waterhouse 1974–77, corp fin exec S G Warburg & Co Ltd 1977–80, dir County Bank Ltd 1983–86 (corp fin exec 1980–87), fndr dir Gilbert Eliott Corporate Finance Ltd 1987–90, corp fin dir Rea Brothers Limited 1991–; FCA (ACA 1977); *Style*— Tim Seymour, Esq; ✉ Rea Brothers Limited, Alderman's House, Alderman's Walk, London EC2M 3XR (☎ 0171 623 1155, fax 0171 623 2694)

SEYMOUR-JONES, Carole Veronica; da of John Anthony Seymour-Jones, of Emsworth, Hants, and Elizabeth, *née* Pinches; *b* 3 March 1943; *Educ* St Mary's Calne, Lady Margaret Hall Oxford, Open Univ (BA), Univ of Sussex (MA); *m* 19 Oct 1963 (m dis 1993), Robert Bigland; 3 da (Emma Catherine b 1967, Sophie Victoria b 1969 d 1973, Lucy Camilla b 1974), 1 s (Edward Robert b 1973); *Career* writer; history teacher in secdy schs and Extra-Mural Dept Univ Surrey; memb Soc of Authors 1991, memb PEN 1992; *Books* Beatrice Webb - Woman of Conflict (1992), Refugees (1992), Homelessness (1992), Journey of Faith: The History of the World YWCA 1945–1994 (1994); *Recreations* sailing, skiing; *Style*— Ms Carole Seymour-Jones; ✉ Drovers, Rad Lane, Peaslake, Guildford, Surrey GU5 9PB (☎ and fax 01306 731294)

SEYMOUR-NEWTON, Cyril Terence; s of Maj Cyril Frank Newton (d 1978), of Guernsey, and Mary Jane Frances Fermoix de Chantal Newton, *née* Gallagher (d 1976); *b* 8 Sept 1927; *Educ* Ampleforth, Trinity Coll Cambridge; *m* 31 Jan 1964, Carol, da of Lt-Col Ivor Watkins Birts (ka 1944); 1 s (Rupert Edward Cyril b 3 Nov 1968); *Career* elected underwriting memb Lloyd's 1954 (joined Lloyd's 1949), resigned 1996; dir (at Lloyd's): Seymour-Newton Ltd 1964–89 (fndr and chm), Shead Gray Ltd 1966–72, Halford Shead Underwriting Agencies Ltd 1968–72, Hargreaves Reiss & Quinn Ltd 1979–87, Crump & Johnson Underwriting Agencies Ltd 1980–94, Crump & Cackett Agencies Ltd 1983–94, RK Harrison Underwriting Agencies Ltd 1986–89, Wendover Underwriting Agency Ltd 1987–94; dir: London & Provincial Insurances Ltd 1962–72, Merritt Huthwaite Ltd 1962–64, Seton Wines Ltd 1964–72 (fndr and chm), Halford Shead Life & Pensions Ltd 1968–72; hon treas 1900 Club 1978– (memb Ctee 1970–, hon sec 1973–78), memb Cncl PDSA 1968–82 (dep chm 1971–82); Freeman City of London 1955, Liveryman Worshipful Co of Coachmakers and Coach Harness Makers 1955; *Recreations* reading, music, big game fishing; *Clubs* Brooks's, MCC, 1900, Hawks' (Cambridge); *Style*— C T Seymour-Newton, Esq; ✉ 34 Ennismore Gardens, London SW7 1AE (☎ 0171 584 3143, fax 0171 823 9103)

SEYMOUR-SMITH, Martin; s of Frank Seymour-Smith (d 1972), and Marjorie, *née* Harris (d 1988); *b* 24 April 1928; *Educ* Highgate Sch, St Edmund Hall Oxford (MA); *m* 1952, Janet, da of Dr Lionel de Glanville; 2 da (Miranda b 1953, Charlotte b 1955); *Career* Sgt Br Army served ME 1946–48; schoolmaster 1954–60; freelance writer 1960–, gen ed Gollancz Classics 1967–69; visiting prof and poet in residence Univ of Wisconsin-Parkside 1971–72; Southern Arts prize for non-fiction 1982, Authors' Soc travelling scholarship award 1985; memb Ctee Authors' Soc 1976–79; FRSL 1994; author or ed of over 40 books incl: Tea with Miss Stockport (1963), Shakespeare's Sonnets (ed, 1963), Bluff Your Way in Literature (1 edn 1966, revised 1972), Reminiscences of Norma (1971), Guide to Modern World Literature (1973, revised and rewritten as Macmillan Guide to World Literature, 1985), Robert Graves: His Life and Work (1982, revised 1995), Rudyard Kipling (1989), Dent Dictionary of Fictional Characters (ed, 1991), Hardy (1994), Wilderness (1994), H W Wilson's world Authors (ed, 1996); *Recreations* work, music, reading, travel, animals; *Style*— Martin Seymour-Smith, Esq, FRSL; ✉ 36 Holliers Hill, Bexhill-on-Sea, East Sussex TN40 2DD (☎ and fax 01424 215042, e-mail z,end@globalnet.w.u.k); Shell Land Associates, 43 Doughty St, London WC1N 2LF (☎ 0171 405 9351, fax 0171 831 2127)

SHACKLE, Prof Christopher; s of Francis Mark Shackle (d 1943), and Diana Margaret, *née* Harrington (d 1990); *b* 4 March 1942; *Educ* Haileybury, Merton Coll Oxford (BA), St Antony's Coll Oxford (Dip in Social Anthroplogy, BLitt), Univ of London (PhD); *m* 1, 1964 (m dis), Emma Margaret, *née* Richmond; 2 da (Mary b 15 Feb 1967, Zoe b 13 Sept 1974), 1 s (Guy b 16 April 1969); m 2, Shahrukh, *née* Husain; 1 s (Adam b 24 May 1982), 1 da (Samira b 16 July 1987); *Career* SOAS Univ of London: fell in Indian Studies 1966, lectr in Urdu and Panjabi 1969–79 reader 1979–85, prof of modern languages of S Asia 1985–; FBA 1990 (memb Cncl 1995–90); *Books* Teach Yourself Punjabi (1972), An Anthology of Classical Urdu Love Lyrics (1972), The Siraiki Language of Central Pakistan (1976), A Guru Nanak Glossary (1981), An Introduction to the Sacred Language of the Sikhs (1983), The Sikhs (1984), Urdu Literature (1985), Ismaili Hymns from South Asia (1992), The Indian Narrative (1992), Qasida Poetry in Islamic Asia and Africa (1996); *Style*— Prof Christopher Shackle, FBA; ✉ Department of South Asia, School of Oriental and African Studies, Thornhaugh Street, Russell Square, London WC1H 0XG (☎ 0171 637 2388)

SHACKLETON, Fiona Sara; da of Jonathan Philip Charkham, *qv*, of London, and Moira Elizabeth Frances, *née* Salmon; *b* 26 May 1956; *Educ* Benenden, Univ of Exeter (LLB); *m* 26 Sept 1985, Ian Ridgeway, s of Lt-Col Richard John Shackleton, MBE (d 1977); 2 da (Cordelia Molly Louise b 25 May 1988, Lydia Elizabeth Moira b 6 July 1989); *Career* slr; articled Clerk Herbert Smith & Co 1978–80, admitted 1980; ptnr: Brecher & Co 1981–84 (joined 1980), Farrer & Co 1986– (joined 1984); govr Benenden Sch; memb: Law Soc, International Acad Matrimonial Lawyers, Slrs' Family Law Assoc; *Books* The Divorce Handbook (with Olivia Timbs, 1992); *Recreations* bridge, food and entertaining; *Style*— Mrs Fiona Shackleton; ✉ Farrer & Co, 66 Lincolns Inn Fields, London WC2A 3LH (☎ 0171 242 2022, fax 0171 405 2296, telex 24318)

SHACKLETON, Keith Hope; s of W S Shackleton; *b* 16 Jan 1923; *Educ* Oundle; *m* 1951, Jacqueline Tate; 2 s, 1 da; *Career* artist and naturalist; served RAF Europe and FE 1941–46, civil pilot and dir Shackleton Aviation Ltd 1948–63, full-time painter (mainly marine) 1964–; contrib Animal Magic (BBC TV) 1964–68, formerly presenter Animals in Action (Anglia TV), various trips as naturalist aboard MS Lindblad Explorer incl Antarctic, Arctic, Amazon and Pacific Islands 1969–, various field work and film-commentary assignments incl Himalayas, Andes and Africa; pres: Royal Soc of Marine Artists 1973–78, Soc of Wildlife Artists 1978–83 (fndr memb); vice pres Wildfowl & Wetlands Tst; chm Artists' League of GB; memb: RGS, Zoological Soc of London, NZ Antarctic Soc; Hon LLD Univ of Birmingham 1983; nominated Master Wildlife Artist Leigh Yawkey Woodson Art Museum Wisconsin 1986; represented GB various int dinghy events, crewed winning boat Prince of Wales' Cup for Int Fourteens 4 times; *Books* Tidelines (1951), Wake (1953), Wildlife and Wilderness - An Artist's World (1986), Ship in the Wilderness (1986); illustrated: Wild Animals in Britain (1959), Birds of the Atlantic Ocean, A Sailor's Guide to Ocean Birds; written and illustrated numerous articles for wildlife and yachting magazines; *Recreations* small boat sailing, exploration field work; *Clubs* Itchenor Sailing; *Style*— Keith Shackleton, Esq; ✉ Woodley Wood Farm, Woodleigh, Kingsbridge, South Devon TQ7 4DR

SHACKLETON, Prof Nicholas John; s of Prof Robert Millner Shackleton, FRS, and Gwen Isabel, *née* Harland; *b* 23 June 1937; *Educ* Cranbrook Sch Kent, Clare Coll Cambridge (BA), Univ of Cambridge (MA, PhD, ScD); *m* 1, 1967 (m dis), Judith Carola, *née* Murray; m 2, Vivien Anne, da of John Law; *Career* sr res asst Univ of Cambridge 1965–72; Subdepartment of Quaternary Res Univ of Cambridge: asst dir of res 1972–75, dir 1988–, ad hominem prof 1991– (reader 1987–91); official fell Clare Hall Cambridge 1981– (res fell 1974–81); sr res assoc Lamont-Doherty Geological Res Observatory USA 1975– (sr visiting res fell 1974–75); visiting prof: ETH Zurich 1979, Université Catholique Louvain-La-Neuve Belgium 1994–95; fndr memb Academia Europaea 1988; Hon LLD Dalhousie Univ Halifax Nova Scotia Canada 1996; fell American Geophysical Union 1990, FRS 1985; *Awards* Shephard Medal Soc of Economic Paleontologists and Mineralogists 1985, Carus Medal Deutsche Akademic für Naherforscher 'Leopoldina'

1985, Lyell Medal Geological Soc London 1987, Huntsman Medal Bedford Inst of Oceanography Canada 1990, Crafoord Prize 1995, Wollaston Medal Geological Soc London 1996; *Publications* author/editor of over 200 scientific papers; *Recreations* clarinet playing and researching clarinet history; *Style*— Prof Nicholas Shackleton, FRS; ✉ The Godwin Laboratory, University of Cambridge, Subdepartment of Quaternary Research, Free School Lane, Cambridge CB2 3RS (☎ 01223 334876, fax 01223 334871)

SHAFER, Prof Byron Edwin; *b* 8 Jan 1947; *Educ* Yale Univ (BA), Univ of Calif at Berkeley (PhD, Peter B Odegard prize); *m*; 1 s; *Career* resident scholar Russell Sage Fndn 1977–84, assoc prof of political sci Florida State Univ 1984–85, Andrew W Mellon prof of American Govt Univ of Oxford 1985–; memb Editorial Bd: Jl of American Studies 1986–, Jl of Policy History 1993–; memb: American Political Sci Assoc, American Historical Assoc, Political Studies Assoc UK, Br Assoc for American Studies, Nat Conf of Univ Profs; American Political Sci Assoc: E E Schattschneider award 1980, Franklin L Burdette Pi Sigma Alpha award 1990; author of numerous pubns in learned professional jls; Hon MA Univ of Oxford 1985; *Style*— Prof Byron Shafer; ✉ Nuffield College, Oxford OX1 1NF (☎ 01865 278509, fax 01865 278621)

SHAFFER, Peter Levin; CBE (1987); s of Jack Shaffer (d 1987), of London, and Reka, *née* Fredman; *b* 15 May 1926; *Educ* St Paul's, Trinity Coll Cambridge; *Career* playwright; Five Finger Exercise (1958), The Private Ear, The Public Eye (1961), The Royal Hunt of the Sun (1964), Black Comedy (1965), White Liars (1966), The Battle of Shrivings (1967), Equus (1973), Amadeus (1979), Yonadab (1985), Lettice and Lovage (1987), The Gift of the Gorgon (1992); screenplays: Equus (1977), Amadeus (1984); radio play: Whom Do I Have The Honour of Addressing? (1989); FRSL; *Recreations* walking, music, architecture; *Clubs* Garrick, Arts; *Style*— Peter Shaffer, Esq, CBE, FRSL; ✉ c/o Macnaughton Lord Representation, 200 Fulham Road, London SW10 9PN (☎ 0171 351 5442, fax 0171 351 4560)

SHAH, Navnit Shankerlal; *b* 9 Dec 1933; *Educ* Bombay Univ (MB BS), RCP (DLO), RCS (FRCS); *m* Frances, *née* Murphy; *Career* currently: hon conslt surgn Royal Nat Throat Nose and Ear Hosp London, conslt otologist Nuffield Hearing and Speech Centre London, hon sr lectr Inst of Laryngology and Otology, hon prof Portmann Fndn/Univ of Bordeaux France; memb: Sections of Laryngology and Otology RSM (pres Section of Otology 1990–91), Bd of Dirs Cwlth Soc for the Deaf; formerly: vice dean Inst of Laryngology and Otology, sr lectr/dep dir Professorial Unit and chm Med Cncl Royal Nat ENT Hosp, pres Indian Med Assoc of GB; memb: Br Assoc of Otolaryngologists, Br Assoc of Audiological Physicians, BMA, Med Soc of London; FRSM; *Recreations* reading, current affairs; *Style*— Navnit Shah, Esq; ✉ 80 Harley Street, London W1N 1AE (☎ 0171 580 3664)

SHAH, Samir; s of Amrit Shah, of Bombay, India, and Uma, *née* Chaudhary (d 1973); *b* 29 Jan 1952; *Educ* Latymer Upper Sch London, Univ of Hull (BSc), St Catherine's Coll Oxford (DPhil); *m* 18 Dec 1983, Belkis Bhegani, da of Jan-Mohammed Hassam, of Kampala, Uganda; 1 s (Cimran Temur b 19 Oct 1986); *Career* memb Home Office 1978–79; LWT 1979–87: reporter Skin, researcher Weekend World then series prodr Eastern Eye and Credo, The London Programme; BBC: dep ed news and current affrs progs BBC TV 1987–89, ed weekly and special progs BBC News and Current Affrs 1990–93, head of political progs BBC 1994–; *Recreations* reading, music, sport; *Style*— Samir Shah, Esq; ✉ BBC News and Current Affairs, BBC Television Centre, Wood Lane, London W12 7RJ (☎ 0181 743 8000)

SHAIL, Prof Ronald; s of Thomas Sidney Shail (d 1962), of Middlesbrough, Cleveland, and Leah, *née* Jones (d 1986); *b* 6 July 1935; *Educ* Middlesbrough Boys' HS, Univ of London (BSc, PhD, DSc); *m* 3 Jan 1959, Jean Veronica, da of Leonard Page, of Saltburn-by-Sea; 1 s (John b 1959), 1 da (Helen b 1962); *Career* lectr Dept of Applied Mathematics Univ of Liverpool 1961–66 (asst lectr 1959–61); Univ of Surrey: reader in mathematics 1966–87, prof 1987–, head of Dept of Mathematical and Computing Scis 1989–94; author of some 60 pubns on applied mathematics in scientific jls; exec ed Quarterly Jl of Mechanics and Applied Mathematics 1969–89; FIMA, CMath; *Recreations* model construction, modern history; *Style*— Prof Ronald Shail; ✉ Department of Mathematical and Computing Sciences, University of Surrey, Guildford, Surrey GU2 5XH (☎ 01483 300800)

SHAKER, HE Mohamed I; *b* 1933, Cairo; *Educ* Cairo Univ (LLB), Graduate Inst of Int Studies Univ of Geneva (Docteur es Sciences Politiques); *Career* Egyptian diplomat; chef-de-cabinet Min of State for Foreign Affrs 1974–76, dep chief of mission Washington DC 1976–80, advsr on int nuclear co-operation, arms control and disarmament to Min of Foreign Affrs 1980–82, DG's rep (IAEA) to UN NY 1982–83, dep perm rep to UN NY 1984–86 (dep rep to UN Security Cncl 1984–85), ambass to Austria, perm rep to UN Vienna, resident rep and govr IAEA Bd of Govrs 1986–88, head Dept of Western Europe Miny of Foreign Affrs 1988–, ambass to Ct of St James's 1988–; pres: Third Non-Proliferation Treaty Review Conf Geneva 1985, UN Conf for Promoting Int Co-operation in the Peaceful Uses of Nuclear Energy Geneva 1987; memb: Core Gp Prog for Promoting Nuclear Non-Proliferation (PPNN) 1987–, UN Sec Gen's Advsy Bd on Disarmament Matters 1993– (chm for 1995); *Books* The Nuclear Non-Proliferation Treaty: Origin and Implementation 1959–1979 (Oceana Publications NY, 1980); *Style*— HE Mr Mohamed I Shaker; ✉ Embassy of the Arab Republic of Egypt, 26 South Street, London W1Y 8EL (☎ 0171 499 2401, fax 0171 355 3568)

SHAKERLEY, Charles Frederick Eardley; s of late Maj Sir Cyril Shakerley, 5 Bt and bro of Sir Geoffrey Shakerley, 6 Bt, *qv*; *b* 14 June 1934; *Educ* Harrow, Ch Ch Oxford, Univ of Pennsylvania; *m* 1962, Lucy Carolyn, da of Francis St G Fisher of Cragg, Cockermouth, Cumbria; 3 da; *Career* former memb Stock Exchange, sr ptnr Roger Mortimer & Co 1970–75; chm: Provincial Insurance Co Ltd 1977–94, River & Mercantile Geared Capital & Income Trust; dir: Williams and Glyn's 1980–85, Royal Bank of Scotland Gp 1985, Monks Investment Trust; Liveryman Worshipful Co of Skinners; *Recreations* forestry, shooting, fishing; *Clubs* Brooks's; *Style*— Charles Shakerley, Esq; ✉ Leighton House, Leighton, Welshpool, Powys SY21 8HT (☎ 01938 555562)

SHAKERLEY, Lady Elizabeth Georgiana; *née* Anson; granted style, rank and precedence of an Earl's da 1961; da of Lt-Col Thomas William Arnold, Viscount Anson (d 1958), and H H Princess Anne of Denmark, *née* Anne Bowes-Lyon (d 1980); sis of 5 Earl of Lichfield; *b* 7 June 1941, (HM King George VI stood sponsor); *m* 1972, as his 2 wife, Sir Geoffrey Adam Shakerley, 6 Bt, *qv*; 1 da; *Career* proprietor Party Planners; dir: Kanga, Mosimann's (a members only dining club), Danielle Ryman; chm Cadogan Co; pres Action for ME; *Books* Lady Elizabeth Anson's Party Planners Book (1986); *Style*— The Lady Elizabeth Shakerley; ✉ 56 Ladbroke Grove, London W11 2PB (☎ 0171 727 7686, fax 0171 727 6001)

SHAKERLEY, Sir Geoffrey Adam; 6 Bt (UK 1838), of Somerford Park, Cheshire; s of Maj Sir Cyril Holland Shakerley, 5 Bt (d 1970), and Elizabeth Averil, MBE (d 1990), da of late Edward Gwynne Eardley-Wilmot, gggda of Sir John Eardley Eardley-Wilmot, 1 Bt; bro of Charles Shakerley, *qv*; *b* 9 Dec 1932; *Educ* Harrow, Trinity Coll Oxford; *m* 1, 1962, Virginia Elizabeth (d 1968), da of W E Maskell; 2 s; m 2, 1972, Lady Elizabeth Georgiana Shakerley, *qv*; 1 da; *Heir* s, Nicholas Simon Adam Shakerley, *qv*; *Career* 2 Lt KRRC; md Photographic Records Ltd 1970–; Liveryman Worshipful Co of Skinners; *Books* Henry Moore - Sculptures in Landscape (1978), The English Dog at Home (1986); *Style*— Sir Geoffrey Shakerley, Bt; ✉ 57 Artesian Rd, London W2 5DB

SHAKERLEY, Nicholas Simon Adam; s (by 1 m) and h of Sir Geoffrey Shakerley, 6 Bt, *qv*; *b* 20 Dec 1963; *Style*— Nicholas Shakerley, Esq; ✉ 57 Artesian Rd, London W2 5DB

SHAKESPEARE, John William Richmond; CMG (1985), LVO (1968); s of Dr William Goodman Shakespeare (d 1975), and Ruth, *née* Potter; *b* 11 June 1930; *Educ* Winchester, Trinity Coll Oxford (MA); *m* 1955, Lalage Ann, da of S P B Mais (d 1975); 3 s, 1 da; *Career* served Irish Gds 1949–50, 2 Lt; lectr Ecole Normale Supérieure Paris 1953–54, on editorial staff The Times 1955–59; HM Dip Serv: FCO 1959, served Paris, Phnom Penh, Singapore, Rio de Janeiro, FCO 1969–73, cnsllr Buenos Aires 1973–75, chargé d'affaires Buenos Aires 1976–77, head Mexico and Caribbean Dept FCO 1977–79, cnsllr Lisbon 1979–83, ambass to Peru 1983–87, ambass to Morocco 1987–90, ret; conslt to Clyde & Co 1991–; chm Morgan Grenfell Latin American Companies Trust 1994–; chm Anglo-Portuguese Soc 1994–; *Recreations* swimming, tennis, walking, gardening; *Clubs* Garrick; *Style*— John Shakespeare, Esq, CMG, LVO; ✉ 10 South End Row, London W8

SHAKESPEARE, Nicholas William Richmond; s of John William Richmond Shakespeare, and Lalage Ann, *née* Mais; *b* 3 March 1957; *Educ* The Dragon Sch Oxford, Winchester, Magdalene Coll Cambridge (MA); *Career* asst prodr BBC TV 1980–84, dep arts/literacy ed The Times 1985–87; literary ed: London Daily News 1987, Daily Telegraph 1988–91, Sunday Telegraph 1989–91; *Books* The Men Who Would Be King (1984), Londoners (1986), The Vision of Elena Silves (1989, Somerset Maugham prize), The High Flyer (1993), The Dancer Upstairs (1995); *Recreations* travelling; *Clubs* Beefsteak, Literary Soc; *Style*— Nicholas Shakespeare, Esq; ✉ 71 Oxford Gardens, London W10 5UJ

SHAKESPEARE, Dr (Sir) Thomas William; 3 Bt (UK 1942), of Lakenham, City of Norwich, but does not use the title; er s of Sir William Geoffrey Shakespeare, 2 Bt (d 1996), and Susan Mary, *née* Raffel; *b* 11 May 1966; *Educ* Radley, Pembroke Coll Cambridge (BA 1987, MA, MPhil 1991), King's Coll Cambridge (PhD 1995); issue: (by Lucy Anne Broadhead) Ivy Connor Broadhead b 7 June 1988; (by Judy Brown) Robert Samuel Brown b 19 Nov 1988; *Heir* bro, James Douglas Geoffrey Shakespeare b 12 Feb 1971; *Career* lectr in Sociology Univ of Sunderland; research fell in Sociology Univ of Leeds; *Style*— Dr Thomas Shakespeare; ✉ 13 Wood Terrace, Bill Quay, Gateshead, Tyne and Wear NE10 0UD; University of Leeds, Leeds LS2 9JT (☎ 0113 243 1751, fax 0113 283 4122)

SHALE, Prof Dennis John; s of Samuel Edward Shale, of Leicester, and Winifred Beatrice, *née* Newstead (d 1986); *b* 19 Feb 1948; *Educ* Charles Keene Coll, Univ of Newcastle upon Tyne (BSc, MB BS, MD); *m* 1, 23 March 1970 (m dis 1993), Kathleen Patricia, da of Harry Clark, of Great Glen, Leicestershire; 1 s (Matthew b 1978), 1 da (Victoria b 1975); m 2, 1 May 1993, Pamela Joan, da of Charles Lawrence, of Penarth, S Glam; 1 s (George b 1994), 1 adopted da (Kate b 1987); *Career* lectr in physiology Univ of Newcastle upon Tyne 1976–78, jr trg posts in med Newcastle upon Tyne and Oxford 1978–81, sr registrar in respiratory med Oxford 1981–84, sr lectr in respiratory med Univ of Nottingham 1985–90, David Davies prof of respiratory and communicable diseases Univ of Wales Coll of Med 1991–; author of chapters in books on respiratory med and original articles in aspects of respiratory med incl shock lung and cystic fibrosis in int jls, contrib of editorials and reviews to med jls; assoc ed Thorax 1986; hon regnl advsr to Cystic Fibrosis Tst; memb WHO Advsy Ctee on future mgmnt of cystic fibrosis; memb: Br Thoracic Soc 1983, Med Res Soc 1984, Societas Euro Pneumonology 1985, American Throacic Soc 1989; FRCP 1991 (MRCP 1980); *Recreations* gardening, archaeology, English and American literature, baroque music; *Style*— Prof Dennis Shale; ✉ University of Wales College of Medicine, Section of Respiratory Medicine, Llandough Hospital, Penarth, S Glamorgan CF64 2XX

SHALIT, Jonathan Sigmund; s of David Manuel Shalit, and Sophie Shalit, JP, *née* Gestetner; *b* 17 April 1962; *Educ* City of London; *Career* former exec and graduate trg scheme with Saatchi Group, md Sigmund Shalit & Associates 1987–, md Shalit Entertainment 1987–; memb: The Prince's Tst, Cancer Res Campaign; Freeman City of London, Liveryman Worshipful Co of Coachmakers and Harness Makers; MInstD; *Recreations* sailing, squash and triathlon; *Clubs* Annabel's, RAC, Inst of Directors, Tramp, Queens; *Style*— Jonathan Shalit, Esq; ✉ 2 Charleville Mansions, Charleville Road, London W14 9JB (☎ 0171 385 3695); Sigmund Shalit & Associates, Cambridge Theatre, Seven Dials, Covent Garden, London WC2H 9HU (☎ 0171 379 3282)

SHAMTALLY, Bhye Mahmood (Danny); s of Abdool Raffick Shamtally, of Mauritius, and Bibi Afroze, *née* Hisaindee; *b* 7 June 1951; *Educ* Mauritius Coll, Bhujoharry Coll, Durham Univ Business Sch (MBA); *m* 19 Sept 1973, Carmelita Panaligan, da of late Francisco Panaligan; 1 s (Reza b 2 Dec 1976), 1 da (Natasha b 17 Jan 1979); *Career* staff nurse Belmont Hosp 1974–76, offr-in-charge London Borough of Sutton Social Serv 1977–85 (asst offr-in-charge 1976–77), princ ptnr Private Nursing Homes 1983–; memb: NSPCC, Nat Tst; gold friend Benjamin Waugh Fndn NSPCC; fell Durham Univ Soc 1994; RMN 1974, FIWO 1985, FRSH 1985, MIMgt 1994, FRIPHH 1995; *Recreations* country walks, antiques, collectors cars, poetry; *Clubs* Copthorne and Effingham Country; *Style*— Danny Shamtally, Esq; ✉ Care Unlimied, Standish, Rockshaw Road, Merstham, Surrey RH1 3BZ (☎ 01737 646266, fax 01737 642634)

SHAND, Charles Stuart; s of Maj C W Shand, OBE, BEM (Lord Belhelvie of Whitecains), and Sybil, *née* James; *b* 10 July 1945; *Educ* Portsmouth, London, Seattle, LA and Boston (courses in Engrg, Business Studies and Mktg); *m* 1977, Penelope Sue, da of Sydney John Valentine (d 1969), of Wimbledon; 1 s (Charles William Valentine b 1986); *Career* dir Childs Greene Public Relations Ltd 1971–73, md United Kingdom Sales Promotion Ltd 1971–73, jt md CGA Marketing Group Ltd 1971–73, dir/Euro mangr Young & Rubicam Group Ltd 1973–80, dir J Walter Thompson Ltd 1980–81, int mktg mangr Cadbury Schweppes plc 1981–84, dir of client servs Minale Tattersfield & Partners 1984–88, dir The Page Factory Ltd 1988–91, dep chm Field Wiley & Company Ltd 1988–91, vice chm Shand International Management Ltd 1986–; chm: The Shand Group SC 1992–, Studio 36 International 1992–; dir: Christian Shand BV 1995–, Mission Dynamics Group 1995–; involved with major design projects (corp and brand identities, new product devpt, architectural projects, etc); awards incl: 3 Silver Awards D&AD (for Irish Distillers Packaging 1986, Gold Mastercard (NatWest Bank) 1987 and BP Int Packaging 1991), 2 Certs of Distinction NY Art Dirs' Club (for Hundhaar Schnapps Packaging 1988 and Forte Hotels 1990), Best Literature Award DBA/Mktg Design Effectiveness Awards (for MOMI 1989), Best Brochure Award (for MOMI) and Best Poster Award (for Charlie Chaplin Exhbn, MOMI) NY Festivals (1989); MIAA 1982, MIPR 1984, memb D&AD 1987, FInstD 1989, FRSA 1994, memb Assoc of Masters in Business Admin; *Recreations* cycling, gymnastics, motoring; *Clubs* Headliners' (Dallas, Texas); *Style*— Charles Shand, Esq; ✉ The Shand Group SC, Scottsdale House, 16 Eversley Road, Surbiton, Surrey KT5 8BG (☎ 0181 399 8535, fax 0181 399 3097)

SHAND, His Honour Judge; John Alexander Ogilvie Shand; s of Alexander Shand, MBE, QPM (d 1968), of West Bridgford, Notts, and Marguerite Marie, *née* Farcy (d 1994); *b* 6 Nov 1942; *Educ* Nottingham HS, Queens' Coll Cambridge (MA, LLB, Chancellor's Medal for Law 1965); *m* 1, 18 Dec 1965 (m dis 1988), Patricia Margaret, da of Frederick Toynbee, of Nottingham (d 1958); 2 s (James b 1967, Simon b 1972), 1 da (Juliet b 1969); m 2, 10 Aug 1990, Valerie Jean, da of William Bond, of Lichfield; *Career* called to the Bar Middle Temple 1965; Midland and Oxford circuit 1965–70 and 1973–81, asst lectr fell and tutor Queens' Coll Cambridge 1970–73, chm Industl Tribunals 1981–88, recorder 1981–88; chllr Diocese of Southwell 1981–; chllr Diocese of Lichfield

1989–; circuit judge (Midland and Oxford Circuit) 1988–; *Books* Legal Values in Western Society (co-author, 1974); *Style*— His Honour Judge Shand; ✉ c/o Courts Administrator's Office, Kemley House, Victoria Road, Stafford ST16 2SE (☎ 01785 55219)

SHAND, Kenneth David; s of James Stevenson Shand (d 1993), and Aileen Alicia, *née* Miller; *b* 29 April 1960; *Educ* Glasgow Acad, Univ of Glasgow (LLB Hons, Dip in Professional Legal Practice); *m* 22 June 1985, Valerie Anne, da of Thomas Porter Callaghan; 1 s (Euan Michael b 22 Jan 1990), 1 da (Heather Elizabeth b 23 Nov 1992); *Career* trainee Maclay Murray & Spens, former slr McKenna & Co, re-joined Maclay Murray & Spens as ptnr 1989, co-fndr Brussels office 1993, corp lawyer also actively involved Euro Unit; memb: Law Soc of Scotland (memb Mktg Ctee), Scottish Lawyers' Euro Gp; *Recreations* most sports (particularly football, rugby, golf and tennis), music, theatre; *Clubs* Bruntsfield Links Golfing Society; *Style*— Kenneth Shand, Esq; ✉ Maclay Murray & Spens, 151 St Vincent Street, Glasgow G2 5NJ (☎ 0141 248 5011, fax 0141 248 5819, car 0385 577416)

SHAND, Terence Richard; s of Terence James Shand, and Dorothy Joyce, *née* Shackell; *b* 27 Oct 1954; *Educ* Borehamwood GS; *m* 1 (m dis 1985) Maureen; 1 s (Elliot James b 1977); m 2 (m dis 1995), Arja, da of Paavo Saren; 1 s (Terence Elias b 1984), 1 da (Natalia Sirka b 1988); *Career* dir Stage One Records Ltd 1978–83, chm Castle Communications plc 1983–, dir Alliance Entertainment Corporation; *Recreations* tennis, shooting, music, reading; *Clubs* Carlton; *Style*— Terence Shand, Esq; ✉ 29 Barwell Business Park, Leatherhead Rd, Chessington, Surrey KT9 2NY (☎ 0181 974 1021, fax 0181 974 2674)

SHAND, William Stewart; s of William Paterson Shand (d 1990), of Derby, and Annabella Kirkland Stewart, *née* Waddell (d 1952); *b* 12 Oct 1936; *Educ* Repton, St John's Coll Cambridge (MA, MB BChir, MD); *m* 26 Aug 1972, (Anne) Caroline Dashwood, da of late Patrice Edouard Charvet, of Cheltenham; 2 s (Robert b 1974, James b 1976), 1 step s (Tom b 1967), 2 step da (Claire b 1964, Sophie b 1966); *Career* conslt surgn Bart's 1973–, hon conslt surgn St Mark's Hosp for Diseases of the Colon and Rectum 1985–; Penrose-May teacher RCS (memb Ct of Examiners RCS 1985–91); memb Ct of Assts: Worshipful Soc of Apothecaries 1974, Worshipful Co of Barbers 1981; fell: Assoc of Surgns of GB and I, Hunterian Soc, Harveian Soc of London, Travelling Surgical Soc (pres 1994–), Royal Soc of Med; FRCS 1969, FRCSEd 1970; *Books* The Art of Dying (jtly, 1989); *Recreations* stained-glass window making, painting, fishing, walking; *Style*— William Shand, Esq; ✉ 149 Harley St, London W1N 2DE (☎ 0171 935 4444)

SHANES, Eric; s of Mark Shanes (d 1993), of London, and Dinah, *née* Cohen (d 1977); *b* 21 Oct 1944; *Educ* Whittinghame Coll Brighton, Regent Street Poly Sch of Art, Chelsea Sch of Art (DipAD); *m* Jacky, da of Kenneth Darville (d 1969), of Windsor; 1 s (Mark b 1979), 1 da (Anna b 1976); *Career* author, journalist and artist; classical music critic Daily Mail 1988–89, numerous contribs to Apollo and Modern Painters jls; fndr ed: Turner Studies, Art Book Review; lectr: Chelsea Sch of Art (pt/t) 1966–88, Dept of Art History Univ of Cambridge, Royal Coll of Music; lecture tours: N America 1982, 1983, 1984 and 1986, Switzerland 1987, Malaysia 1988; Br Cncl Cultural Exchange award as official visitor: Romania 1982, Czechoslovakia 1984; Yorkshire Post Art Book award 1979; pres Turner Soc 1994– (chm 1988–94); awarded Nuclear Electric scholarship 1995 (to research and exhibit Turner's Colour-Beginnings at Tate Gallery 1997); fndr chm Save Acton Swimming Baths campaign; *Exhibitions* numerous studio shows of paintings and prints; Splinter Gallery London 1992; guest exhibition curator: J M W Turner - the Foundations of Genius (Taft Museum Cincinnati) 1986, Masterpieces of English Watercolour from the Hickman Bacon Collection and the Fitzwilliam Museum Cambridge (touring Japan) 1990–91; *Books* Turner's Picturesque Views in England and Wales (1979), Turner's Rivers, Harbours and Coasts (1981), The Genius of the Royal Academy (1981), Hockney Posters (1987), Constantin Brancusi (1989), Turner's England (1990), Turner - The Masterworks (1990), Turner's Human Landscape (1990), Dali - The Masterworks (1990), Warhol - The Masterworks (1991), Jack Beal, American Realist (1992), Warhol - The Master Painter (1993), Impressionist London (1994); photographic essay in Gustav Mahler - Songs and Symphonies of Death (Donald Mitchell, 1985); *Recreations* music appreciation, swimming; *Style*— Eric Shanes, Esq; ✉ 7 Cumberland Rd, Acton, London W3 6EX (☎ 0181 992 7985, fax 0181 994 3157)

SHANIN, Prof Teodor; s of Meir Zajdsznur (d 1964), and Rebeka, *née* Jaszunski (d 1988); *b* 29 Oct 1930; *Educ* Univ of Jerusalem (BA), Univ of Birmingham (PhD), Univ of Manchester (MSc); *m* 1 (m dis 1962), Neomi; m 2, 1970, Dr Shulamith Ramon; 2 da (Anna b 1970, Aelita b 1976); *Career* 6 Regt of Commando (Palmakh) Israeli Army 1948–49; probation offr Miny of Welfare (former social worker Youth Care Servs) Tel Aviv 1952–56, dir Rehabilitation Centre (former rehabilitation offr for handicapped) Miny of Labour 1956–63, lectr in sociology Univ of Sheffield 1965–70 (seconded to Centre for Russian and E Euro Studies Univ of Birmingham 1968–70), assoc prof Haifa Univ Israel 1971–73 (sr lectr 1970–71), visiting sr fell St Anthony's Coll Oxford 1973–74, prof of sociology Univ of Manchester 1974– (head of dept 1976–81); fell Wilson Center Washington DC 1987, commoner Trinity Coll Cambridge 1990–91, bd memb Fndn 'Cultural Initiation' Moscow 1991–, co-pres InterCentre Moscow 1993–; memb Br Sociological Assoc; *Books* Peasants and Peasant Societies (1971), The Awkward Class (1972), Russia as a 'Developing Society' (1985), Revolution as a Moment of Truth (1986), Defining Peasants (1990); *Recreations* fell walking, theatre; *Style*— Prof Teodor Shanin; ✉ Department of Sociology, University of Manchester, Manchester M13 9PL (☎ 0161 275 2503)

SHANKS, Duncan Faichney; s of Duncan Faichney Shanks (d 1956), of Uddingston, Strathclyde, and Elizabeth Provan, *née* Clark (d 1943); *b* 30 Aug 1937; *Educ* Uddingston GS, Glasgow Sch of Art (post dip, travelling scholarship to Italy); *m* 1 Aug 1966, Una Brown, da of Laurence George Gordon (d 1965), of Hartwood, Strathclyde; *Career* pt/t lectr Glasgow Sch of Art 1962–79, full time artist 1979–; memb RGI 1982, RSW 1987, RSA 1990 (ARSA 1972); *Recreations* music; *Style*— Duncan Shanks, Esq, RSA

SHANKS, Prof Ian Alexander; s of Alexander Shanks, of Dumbarton, and Isabella Affleck, *née* Beaton; *b* 22 June 1948; *Educ* Dumbarton Acad, Glasgow Univ (BSc), CNAA (PhD); *m* 14 May 1971, Janice Smillie, da of J Coulter, of 3 Aitkenbar Circle, Bellsmyre, Dumbarton, Dunbartonshire; 1 da (Emma b 1977); *Career* projects mangr Scottish Colorfoto Labs Alexandria 1970–72, princ sci offr RSRE Malvern 1973–82, princ scientist Unilever Research 1982–86, visiting prof of Electrical and Electronic Engrg Univ of Glasgow 1985–, chief scientist Thorn EMI plc 1986–94, divnl science advsr Research and Engrg Div Unilever Research 1994–; memb: Optoelectronics Ctee The Rank Prize Funds 1985–, Steering Gp for Science and Engrg Policy Studies Unit 1988–90, Sci Consultative Gp BBC 1989–91, Advsy Bd for the Res Cncls (ABRC) 1990–93; memb Cncl and vice pres The Royal Soc 1989–91; chm Inter-Agency Ctee on Marine Science and Technol 1991–93; Clifford Paterson medal Inst of Physics 1984; FIEE, FRS 1984, FEng 1992, FRSA 1993; *Recreations* music, antique clocks and pocket watches; *Style*— Prof Ian Shanks, FRS, FEng; ✉ King's Close, 11 Main Road, Biddenham, Bedford MK40 4BB (☎ 01234 328773); Unilever Research Colworth Laboratory, Colworth House, Sharnbrook, Bedford MK44 1LQ (☎ 01234 222993)

SHANKS, Dr Jean Mary; da of Peter Martin Shanks (d 1960), and Gwendolen Margaret, *née* Thompson (d 1983); *b* 18 Nov 1925; *Educ* Badminton Sch Bristol, St Hugh's Coll Oxford (BA, BM BCh), Middlesex Hosp Med Sch; *m* 19 Nov 1976, Prince Yuri Nikolaievitch Galitzine, *qv*, s of late Prince Nicolas Alexandrovitch Galitzine; *Career* house physician Princess Alice Hosp Eastbourne 1950–51, lectr Albany Med Sch 1951–52, house surgn Neurosurgical Dept Middlesex Hosp 1952–53, registrar in pathology West Middlesex Hosp, registrar and locum sr registrar in pathology Great Ormond St Hosp; former chm and chief exec offr JS Pathology plc, ret 1994; fndr: Pathology Laboratory Harley St 1958 (became JS Pathology Servs Ltd 1977, then JS Pathology plc, now Unilabs UK), Jean Shanks Fndn 1986–; pres Chelsea Clinical Soc 1994–95; memb Worshipful Soc of Apothecaries; memb: RSM, Hunterian Soc, Med Soc of London, Br Med Assoc, ACP, Soc of Occupational Med; Hon FRCPath 1993; *Publications* Immune Aplastic Haemolytic Anaemia with Thrombocytopaenia (Br Med Jl, 1960), Haemoglobin Values in Business Executives (Br Jl Preventative and Social Med, 1967), Consequences of the provision of laboratory services for the National Health Service by commercial firms: a view from the private sector (Journal of Clinical Pathology Ref 43, 1990); *Recreations* playing the piano, gardening, collecting antiques and paintings, farming; *Style*— Dr Jean Shanks; ✉ 8 South Eaton Place, London SW1W 9JA (☎ 0171 730 3175, fax 0171 824 8174); Holywell Hall, Stamford, Lincs PE9 4DT (☎ 01780 410665, fax 0171 267 1796)

SHANKS, Rev Norman James; s of James Shanks, CBE, of Edinburgh (d 1990), and Marjory Kirkwood, *née* Hind (d 1967); *b* 15 July 1942; *Educ* Stirling HS, Univ of St Andrews (MA), Univ of Edinburgh (BD); *m* 29 July 1968, Ruth, da of Very Rev Dr Hugh Osborne Douglas, KCVO, CBE (former Dean of Chapel Royal in Scotland, d 1987); 2 s (Andrew b 1971, David b 1973), 1 da (Jane b 1969); *Career* civil servant Scottish Office 1964–79, private sec to Sec of State for Scotland 1975–77, chaplain Univ of Edinburgh 1985–88, lectr in theol and church history Univ of Glasgow 1988–95, ldr Iona Community 1995– (memb 1980–); chm: Sec of State's Advsy Ctee on Scotland's Travelling People 1986–88, Edinburgh Cncl of Social Serv 1986–88; convener: Church of Scotland's Church and Nation Ctee 1988–92, Justice, Peace, Social & Moral Issues Cmmn Action of Churches Together in Scotland 1991–95; memb Broadcasting Cncl for Scotland 1988–93; *Style*— The Rev Norman Shanks; ✉ 1 Marchmont Terrace, Glasgow, Scotland G12 9LT (☎ 0141 339 4421); Iona Community, Pearce Institute, Govan Road, Glasgow G51 3UU (☎ 0141 445 4561, fax 0141 445 4295)

SHANKS, Prof Robert Gray (Robin); CBE (1997); s of Robert Shanks, and Mary, *née* Gray; *b* 4 April 1934; *Educ* Methodist Coll Belfast, The Queen's Univ of Belfast (MB, MD, BSc, DSc, MRCP); *m* 10 Dec 1960, Denise Isabel Sheila, da of (Victor) Cecil Woods (d 1971), of Bangor, NI; 4 da (Amanda b 1961, Melanie b 1962, Deborah b 1962, Rachel b 1968); *Career* head of cardiovascular pharmacology Pharmaceutical Div ICI Ltd 1962–66; Queen's Univ of Belfast: lectr and conslt in clinical pharmacology 1967–72, prof of clinical pharmacology 1972–77, Whitla prof and head Dept of Therapeutics and Pharmacology 1977–, dean Faculty of Med 1986–91, pro vice chllr 1991–; pres Ulster Med Soc 1993–94; memb GMC 1987–91; MRIA 1987, FRCP; *Recreations* golf, gardening; *Style*— Prof Robin Shanks, CBE; ✉ Department of Therapeutics and Pharmacology, The Queen's University of Belfast, Whitla Medical Building, 97 Lisburn Rd, Belfast, Northern Ireland BT9 7BL (☎ 01232 335770, fax 01232 438346, telex 274895 QUBADM)

SHANNON, Dr David William Francis; s of William Francis Shannon (d 1979), of Dromore, Co Down, NI, and Elizabeth, *née* Gibson (d 1970); *b* 16 Aug 1941; *Educ* Wallace HS NI, Queen's Univ Belfast (BAgric, PhD), Napier Coll Edinburgh (DMS); *m* 1967, Rosamond Elizabeth Mary, da of Joseph Earls Bond, of Drumlough, Hillsborough, NI; 1 s (Peter David Bruce b 23 July 1975), 1 da (Nicola Elizabeth Jane b 20 Nov 1972); *Career* Poultry Res Centre AFRC: res scientist 1967–86, princ scientific offr 1972–77, head Nutrition Section 1977–78, dir 1978–86; Dept of Animal Sci Univ of Alberta Edmonton 1973–74, chief scientist of agric and horticulture MAFF 1986–95, chief scientist MAFF 1995–; author of numerous articles in scientific press; chm Exec Cncl Cwlth Agric Bureau Int 1989–91; memb: Cncl AFRC 1986–94, BBSRC 1995–, NERC 1995–, Cranfield Univ 1995–, UK Branch World's Poultry Sci Assoc (pres 1986–90), Nutrition Soc; *Recreations* golf, growing fruit; *Style*— Dr David Shannon; ✉ Ministry of Agriculture, Fisheries and Food, Nobel House, 17 Smith Square, London SW1P 3JR (☎ 0171 238 5526, fax 0171 238 5398)

SHANNON, Michael Stuart (Mike); s of Dennis Shannon, of Newport Gwent, and Dorothy Shannon; *b* 28 June 1938; *Educ* Newport HS, UCW Aberystwyth (BSc, DipEd), Univ Coll of N Wales (MEd), Univ of Nottingham, Open Univ Business Sch (FBIM, LHSM); *m* 1, 9 Sept 1961 (m dis 1985), Jacky Townsend; 1 s (Alasdair), 1 da (Kirstie); m 2, 14 Feb 1991, Monica Crimes; *Career* tutor and cnsllr: Cyprus Forces Scheme 1972–74, Open Univ 1975–79; secdy teacher: St Saviour's Sch Poplar London 1961–62, Hartridge Comp 1962–63; RAF: educn offr RAF Hereford 1964–67 and RAF Valley Anglesey 1967–71, offr i/c Near East Air Force Mountain Rescue Team 1971–72, schs offr Limassol Cyprus 1972–74, sr educn and trg offr RAF Coningsby Lincolnshire 1974–77, head Instructional Techniques Dept RAF Sch of Educn RAF Newton 1978–80, staff offr Schs and Community Educn 1980–82; mangr Sir Isaac Pitman Ltd E Africa (Nairobi) 1982–83, md Pitman Central Coll 1983–85, unit gen mangr Acute and Gen Unit Warrington Health Authy 1988–92 (unit gen mangr Mental Illness Unit 1985–88); currently self-employed mngmnt conslt and co dir; govr and chm Fin Sub Gp Whitford VP Sch, sec Pen-y-Gelli Action Gp, sec Whitford Woodland Campaigners; one time Welsh Int at basketball and athletics, Br Univs Br Jr Athletics champion, Combined Servs and RAF basketball rep; *Recreations* mountaineering, rock climbing, birdwatching; *Clubs* Mountain Club of Kenya; *Style*— Mike Shannon, Esq; ✉ Primrose Cottage, Whitford, nr Holywell, Clwyd, North Wales CH8 9AL (☎ 01745 560872)

SHANNON, 9 Earl of (I 1756); Richard Bentinck Boyle; sits as Baron Carleton (GB 1786); also Viscount Boyle and Baron Castle-Martyr (both I 1756); s of 8 Earl of Shannon (d 1963), and Marjorie, *née* Walker (d 1981); *b* 23 Oct 1924; *Educ* Eton; *m* 1, 1947 (m dis 1955), Donna Catherine Irene Helen, da of Marchese Demetrio Imperiali di Francavilla (cr by King Victor Amadeus III of Sardinia 1779), see Katie Boyle, *qv*; m 2, 1957 (m dis 1979), Susan Margaret, da of late John Russell Hogg; 1 s, 2 da; m 3, 1994, Mrs Almine Barton, da of late Rocco Catorsia de Villiers, of Cape Town, South Africa; *Heir* s, Viscount Boyle; *Career* Capt Irish Gds and RWAFF 1942–54; sec Fedn of Euro Indust Co-op Res Orgns 1975–86, chm Fndn Sci and Technol 1977–83; dir Ctee Dirs Res Assoc 1969–85, vice pres Inland Waterways Assoc; dep speaker and dep chm of ctees House of Lords 1968–78, currently chm British-Armenian All-Pty Parly Gp; FRSA, FIMgt, FBHI; *Recreations* horology, inland waterways; *Clubs* White's; *Style*— The Rt Hon the Earl of Shannon; ✉ Pimm's Cottage, Man's Hill, Burghfield Common, Berkshire RG7 3BD

SHANNON, Prof Richard Thomas; s of Edward Arthur Shannon (d 1958), of Auckland, New Zealand, and Grace, *née* McLeod (d 1985); *b* 10 June 1931; *Educ* Mt Albert GS Auckland, Univ of Auckland, Gonville and Caius Coll Cambridge; *Career* lectr in history Univ of Auckland 1961–62, reader in history UEA 1971–79 (lectr 1963–71), prof of modern history Univ of Wales Swansea 1979– (head of dept 1982–88, dean Faculty of Arts 1985–88), visiting fell Peterhouse Cambridge 1988–89, Leverhulme res fell 1988–90; FRHistS 1970; *Books* Gladstone and The Bulgarian Agitation 1876 (1963), The Crisis of Imperialism 1865–1915 (1974), Gladstone, Vol I: 1809–1865 (1982), The Age of Disraeli (1992), The Age of Salisbury (1996); *Recreations* Welsh Border country; *Clubs* Athenaeum; *Style*— Prof Richard Shannon; ✉ Department of History, University of Wales Swansea, Singleton Park, Swansea SA2 8PP (☎ 01792 295225)

SHANNON, Prof Robert William Ernest; *b* 10 Oct 1937; *Educ* Belfast Tech HS, Belfast Coll of Technol (HNC, Inst of Marine Engrs Prize for Heat Engines, Belfast

Assoc of Engrs Prize for Best Student, Capt J S Davidson Meml Prize for Best Student of the Year, Royal Aeronautical Soc (Belfast Branch) Prize for Best Student in Aeronautics), Queen's Univ Belfast (fndn scholar, BSc, PhD); *m* Annabelle; 2 c; *Career* laboratory technician James Mackie & Sons Ltd (Belfast) 1954–55; Short Brothers & Harland Ltd (Belfast): aircraft engrg apprentice 1955–58, aerodynamicist Light Aircraft Div Design Office 1958–62 (pt/t 1959–62), pt/t stressman 1962–63; Queen's Univ of Belfast: asst lectr Dept of Aeronautical Engrg 1963–66, res fell Dept of Mechanical Engrg 1966–70, lectr Dept of Mechanical Engrg 1970; pt/t engrg conslt 1966–70; R&D Div British Gas plc (formerly British Gas Corporation): specialist in fracture 1970–74 (seconded to Civil Engrg Dept Queen's Univ of Belfast 1970–72), successively asst div mangr, mangr, chief project engr, asst dir then dir of on-line inspection 1974–89, HQ dir of engrg res 1989–91, dir of devpt 1991–93; gp dir of special projects British Gas Global 1993–96, ret; professorial fell Queen's Univ of Belfast 1996–; memb Technol and Innovation Ctee CBI 1994–96; memb Advsy Ctee Dept of Mechanical Engrg: Univ of Sheffield 1989–, Univ of Newcastle upon Tyne 1995–; memb: Industl Res and Technol Unit Bd NI Office, Res Ctee Poly and Colls Funding Cncl 1989–92, Mgmnt Bd SEPSU 1991–94; chm Membership Ctee Panel 1 and memb Int Ctee Royal Aeronautical Soc, memb Senate Engrg Cncl; pres: Inst of Gas Engrs 1994–95 (memb Cncl 1990–, chm Fin and Gen Purposes Ctee 1995–96), Inst of Mechanical Engrs 1996–97 (memb Cncl and its Exec Ctee 1989–, memb Res Ctee 1990–, memb Engrg Quality Bd 1993–96, memb Engrg Quality Advsy Bd 1993–96, chm Fin Bd 1994–96); author of numerous pubns concerned with gas pipelines; Gold Medal Inst of Gas Engrs 1982, MacRobert Award 1989, President's Honour Lecture Br Inst of Non-Destructive Testing 1990, Mullard Award Royal Soc 1992; Hon DSc Queen's Univ Belfast; MRAeS, fell Br Inst of Non-Destructive Testing, FIMechE, FIGE, FEng 1987; *Style*— Prof Robert Shannon, FEng; ✉ Lindisfarne, 16 Friths Drive, Reigate, Surrey RH2 0DS (☎ 01737 223559, fax 01737 223559)

SHANNON, William Dermot (Bill); s of Francis Desmond Shannon (d 1972), of Liverpool, and Zita Mary, *née* Sharp; *b* 10 Aug 1944; *Educ* St Edward's Coll Liverpool, Univ of Liverpool (state scholar, BA); *m* 13 Aug 1966, Mavis, da of Harry Bannister; 1 da (Deborah Jane b 9 July 1967); *Career* Cooperative Wholesale Society: market res asst rising to dep mangr market res 1965–70, planning mangr Meat Gp 1970–71, mktg mangr Soft Drinks 1971–75, mktg mangr Wines & Spirits 1975–77, a regnl mktg mangr Central Marketing Div 1977–80; mktg mangr (food) Greater Lancastria Coop 1980–84, mktg mangr United Coop Stoke (following merger of Greater Lancastria with North Midland Coop) 1984; CWS: rejoined as head of Buying Gp Manchester 1984, coop brand mktg mangr 1985–92, gen mangr coop brand gp 1992–96, head of corp affrs 1996–; memb: Chartered Inst of Mktg, Inst of Grocery Distribution, Manchester Statistical Soc, FRSA; *Recreations* local history/archaeology (former chm Lancashire Archaeological Soc), local politics (constituency treas), woodwork; *Style*— Bill Shannon, Esq; ✉ Cooperative Wholesale Society Ltd, PO Box 53, New Century House, Manchester M60 4ES (☎ 0161 827 6270, fax 0161 839 2616, mobile 0831 818644)

SHAO, En; *b* 1954; *Educ* Beijing Centre Music Conservatory, RNCM (Lord Rhodes fellow); *Career* conductor; made to stop music studies due to Cultural Revolution 1966–70; awarded first Eduard Van Beinum Fndn Scholarship 1988, winner Hungarian Television Int Conductor's Competition 1989; second princ conductor Chinese Broadcasting Symphony Orch for 5 years, princ guest conductor Central Philharmonic Orch of China, princ guest conductor Nat Youth Orch China, conductor Hungarian Radio Orch and State Symphony Orch 1989, assoc conductor BBC Philharmonic Orch 1990–92, princ conductor and artistic advsr Ulster Orch 1992–95, currently princ guest conductor Euskadi Symphony Orch Spain and music dir Guildford Philharmonic Orch; guest conductor: Bournemouth Symphony Orch, all BBC Orchs, Northern Sinfonia, Royal Liverpool Philharmonic Orch, Hallé Orch, Royal Scottish Nat Orch, Oslo Philharmonic Orch, Helsinki Philharmonic Orch, Berlin Symphonic Orch, Czech Philharmonic Orch, ABC Orchs Australia 1991, 1993 and 1994, Toronto Symphony Orch, Vancouver Symphony, Colorado Symphony Orch, Nat Symphony Orch Johannesburg (debut 1996); debut BBC Proms 1995; *Recreations* Chinese cooking, contemporary interior design and architecture, ballet, jazz, environmental issues; *Style*— En Shao, Esq; ✉ c/o Deborah Meyer, IMG Artists, Media House, 3 Burlington Lane, London W4 2TH (☎ 0181 233 5814, fax 0181 233 5801)

SHAPER, Prof (Andrew) Gerald; s of Jack Shaper (d 1960), of Cape Town, SA, and Molly, *née* Harris (d 1980); *b* 9 Aug 1927; *Educ* Univ of Cape Town (MB ChB), Univ of Liverpool (DTMandH); *m* 5 July 1952, Lorna June, da of Lt-Col Cyril Ewart Clarke (d 1964), of Zimbabwe; 1 s (Nicholas b 1961); *Career* registrar Hammersmith Hosp and Postgrad Med Sch 1955–56, prof of cardiovascular res Makerere Univ Med Sch Kampala 1957–69 (former lectr, sr lectr, reader), memb scientific staff MRC Social Med Unit LSHTM 1970–75, hon conslt cardiologist UCH 1970–87, prof of clinical epidemiology and head Dept of Public Health and Primary Care Royal Free Hosp Med Sch 1975–92, prof emeritus 1992–; chm: MRC Health Serv Res Panel 1981–86, Heads of Academic Depts of Community Med 1987–90; vice chm Nat Heart Forum; memb: Cncl Cwlth Caribbean Med Research Cncl, Harveian Soc London, Br Cardiac Soc, Atherosclerosis Discussion Gp, Soc for Social Med, Int Epidemiological Assoc; *Books* Medicine in a Tropical Environment (ed 1972), Cardiovascular Disease in the Tropics (ed 1974), Coronary Heart Disease: Risks and Reasons (1988); *Recreations* walking, second-hand and antiquarian books, theatre; *Style*— Prof Gerald Shaper; ✉ 8 Wentworth Hall, The Ridgeway, Mill Hill, London NW7 1RJ (☎ 0181 959 8742); 2 Church Hill, Fremington, Barnstaple, North Devon (☎ 01271 73913)

SHAPIRO, Dr Leonard Melvyn; s of Joseph Shapiro, of London, and Stella, *née* Solomon; *b* 9 March 1951; *Educ* Leyton County HS London, Univ of Manchester (BSc, MB ChB, MD); *m* 1978, Alison Patricia, da of Maj Frederick Howat; 1 s (Paul Richard Howat b 3 May 1984), 1 da (Laura Diana b 10 Sept 1980); *Career* sr registrar Nat Heart Hosp 1983–88, conslt cardiologist Papworth and Addenbrooke's Hosps Cambridge 1988–; special interests: echocardiography, athlete's heart, coronary artery disease, coronary angioplasty, interventional cardiology; co-fndr and founding pres Br Soc of Echocardiography; memb Cardiac Soc, fell American Coll of Cardiology; FRCP 1993 (MRCP 1978); *Books* A Colour Atlas of Hypertension (with K M Fox, 1985, 2 edn with M Bucalter, 1991), A Colour Atlas of Angina Pectoris (with K M Fox and C Warnes, 1986), A Colour Atlas of Heart Failure (with K M Fox, 1987, 2 edn 1995), A Colour Atlas of Physical Signs in Cardiovascular Disease (with K M Fox, 1988), A Colour Atlas of Palpitations and Syncope (with K M Fox, 1989), A Colour Atlas of Congenital Heart Disease in the Adult (with K M Fox, 1989), A Colour Atlas of Coronary Artery Atherosclerosis (1990, 2 edn 1992), Mitral Valve Disease (with F C Wells, 1996), An atlas of echocardiography (with A Kenny, 1997); *Style*— Dr Leonard Shapiro; ✉ Regional Cardiac Unit, Papworth Hospital, Papworth Everard, Cambridge CB3 8RE (☎ 01480 831284, fax 01480 831083)

SHAPLAND, John Russell; s of William Russell Shapland, of Oakcroft, Kerscott, Swimbridge, Barnstaple, N Devon, and Emmeline Gertrude, *née* Andrews; *b* 6 July 1946; *Educ* Queen's Coll Taunton; *m* 1; 1 s (Andrew Russell b 4 March 1969), 1 da (Marilyn Anne b 5 Oct 1972); m 2, 27 March 1982, Patricia Mary, da of Meynell Straw; *Career* dairy farmer 1967–84, hotelier Whitechapel Manor 1987– (conversion from private house 1984–87); Michelin and Egon Ronay stars 1989, Country Restaurant of the Year (Good Food Guide) 1990, 3 rosettes (for food) and 2 red stars (AA) 1991, blue ribbon (RAC) 1991; memb Pride of Britain 1992; *Recreations* running the hotel; *Style*— John Shapland, Esq; ✉ Whitechapel Manor, South Molton, North Devon EX36 3EG (☎ 01769 573377, fax 01769 573797)

SHAPLAND, Maj-Gen Peter Charles; CB (1977), MBE (1960); s of Frederick Charles Shapland (d 1960), of Merton Park, Surrey, and Annie Frances, *née* Carr (d 1970); *b* 14 July 1923; *Educ* Rutlish Sch Merton Park, St Catharine's Coll Cambridge (MA); *m* 1 April 1954, Joyce Barbara, da of Fraser Leopold Peradon (d 1973), of India, Jersey and Chichester; 2 s (Michael b 1958, Timothy b 1962); *Career* served WWII with RE in UK and India, Lt-Col 1965, Brig 1968, Cdr Engr Bde TA & VR 1968, RCDS 1971, dep cdr and COS HQ SE Dist 1972–74; dir volunteers territorials and cadets MOD 1974–78, Hon Col 73 Engr Regt TA 1979–89, sr planning inspr DOE 1980–93, Col Cmdt RE 1981–86, pres Inst RE 1982–87, chm Combined Cadet Force Assoc 1982–; Freeman City of London 1983, Liveryman Worshipful Co of Painter-Stainers 1983; *Clubs* Royal Ocean Racing, Royal Engr Yacht; *Style*— Maj-Gen Peter Shapland, CB, MBE

SHAPLAND, Sir William Arthur; kt (1982); s of Arthur Frederick Shapland, and Alice Maud, *née* Jackson; *b* 20 Oct 1912; *Educ* Tollington Sch Muswell Hill; *m* 1943, Madeline Annie, da of James Amiss; 2 da (Janet, Anne); *Career* Allan Charlesworth & Co CAs: joined 1929, ptnr 1946–55; Blackwood Hodge plc: joined 1946, dir 1946–55, exec dir 1955–64, exec chm 1964–83; tstee dir Bernard Sunley Charitable Fndn 1960–; govr Utd World Coll of the Atlantic, former tstee Charing Cross Sunley Research Centre Tst (resigned 1992), former memb Ct of Univ of Leicester (resigned 1996); vice pres: London Fedn of Clubs for Young People, S London Scouts Cncl; Wayneflete fell Magdalen Coll Oxford 1981, hon fell St Catherine's Coll Oxford 1982; Hon DSc Buckingham 1986, Hon DLitt Univ of Leicester 1983; memb Worshipful Co of Paviors (Master 1980–81, memb Ct of Assts); FCA 1936, Hon FRCS 1978; OStJ 1981, KStJ 1987; *Recreations* golf, fishing, travel; *Clubs* Garrick, City Livery; *Style*— Sir William Shapland; ✉ 44 Beech Drive, London N2 9NY (☎ 0181 883 5073); office: 53 Grosvenor Street, London W1X 9FH (☎ 0171 409 1199)

SHAREEF, HE Dr Abdulkader Abdulwahid Muhammed; *b* 20 June 1944, Zanzibar, Tanzania; *Educ* Islamic Univ of Medina Saudi Arabia (BA Islamic Law), SOAS Univ of London (Dip in Gen Linguistics and Phonetics, BA Arabic/English, MA Linguistics, PhD in Classical Arabic Lit and Islamic Studies); *m* Fatma; 2 c; *Career* Tanzanian diplomat; former appointments incl freelance broadcaster Swahili Section BBC External Serv 1971–82, visiting lectr/asst prof in Arabic and Islamic studies Univ of Manchester 1982–83, lectr/assoc prof in Islamic studies Dept of Near and Middle East Studies SOAS Univ of London 1986 (asst lectr/prof in Arabic 1983–86), head Br appraisal team of Univ of London to Faculty of Law and Shari'a Univ of the UAE al-Ain Abu Dhabi 1987, visiting prof in Islamic studies Univ of Manchester 1989–90 (external examiner in Arabic and Islamic studies 1989–93); Tanzanian ambass to Kingdom of Saudi Arabia (concurrently accredited to Kuwait, Qatar, Bahrain, Oman, UAE, Islamic Republic of Pakistan, Iran, Iraq, Jordan and Israel) 1990–95, Tanzanian ambass to the Ct of St James's (concurrently accredited to Republic of Ireland) 1995–; head Tanzanian delgn to Cwlth Conf on Educn Islamabad Pakistan 1994, memb Tanzanian delgn to Cwlth Heads of Govt Meeting NZ and head Tanzania Sr Officials Meeting Auckland 1995; *Recreations* swimming, squash, cycling, deep-sea fishing, golf; *Style*— HE Dr Abdulkader A Shareef; ✉ Tanzania High Commission, 43 Hertford Street, London W1Y 8DB (☎ 0171 499 8951, fax 0171 491 9321)

SHAREEF, Athar Ali; s of Safdar Ali Shareef (d 1985), of Karachi, Pakistan, and Khurshid, *née* Taki; *b* 27 Nov 1941; *Educ* Royal Coll Colombo Ceylon, Univ of Manchester (BSc); *m* 26 April 1962, Zujajeth (Zuju), da of Dr Hyder Ali Khan (d 1967), of Hyderabad, India; 2 da (Hinna b 1964 d 1978, Juhi b 1975); *Career* chm CMS Conslts 1977–79, vice pres CACI Inc Int 1981–84; dir: Inforem Ltd 1984–87, CSC Europe UK Operations 1991–92; dep chm: Inforem plc 1988–89 (dir 1987–91), CSC Europe 1992–; chm Shamley Green Village Soc 1990–92 and 1995–; memb: Guildford Cons Assoc, Shamley Green Village CC; CEng 1970, FIEE 1991 (MIEE 1970), FInstD; *Recreations* reading, walking, cricket; *Style*— Athar Shareef, Esq; ✉ Pond Cottage, Shamley Green, Guildford, Surrey GU5 0UA (☎ 01483 893125); CSC Europe, 279 Farnborough Road, Farnborough, Hampshire GU14 7LS (☎ 01252 363321, fax 01252 363045)

SHARIF, Omar; *né* Michel Shalhoub; s of Joseph M Shalhoub (d 1978), and Claire Saada; *b* 10 April 1932; *Educ* Victoria Coll Cairo; *m* 1, 5 Feb 1955 (m dis 1967), Faten, da of Ahmed Hamama; 1 s (Tarek b 1957); m 2, 7 Jan 1973; *Career* actor; *Theatre* The Grand Duke in The Sleeping Prince (Chichester & The Haymarket Theatre) 1983–84; *Television* incl: The Far Pavilions (mini series) 1982, Edge of the Wind (BBC Play of the Month) 1984, Huis Clos (Sartre, BBC Play of the Month) 1985, Peter the Great (NBC mini series) 1984–85, Gulliver's Travels (Channel 4) 1996; *Films* incl: Lawrence of Arabia (Oscar nomination, Golden Globe Award) 1962, The Fall of the Roman Empire 1964, Behold a Pale Horse 1964, The Yellow Rolls Royce 1964, Genghis Khan 1965, Dr Zhivago (Golden Globe Award) 1965, The Night of the Generals 1966, Marco the Magnificent 1966, More Than a Miracle 1967, McKenna's Gold 1968, Funny Girl 1968, Mayerling 1968, The Appointment 1969, Che! 1969, The Last Valley 1970, The Horsemen 1971, The Burglars 1971, The Tamarind Seed 1974, Juggernaut 1974, The Mysterious Island of Captain Nemo 1974, Funny Lady 1975, Crime and Passion 1975, Ace up the Sleeve 1976, The Pink Panther Strikes Again 1976, The Right to Love, Ashanti 1979, Bloodline 1979, Oh Heavenly Dog 1980, The Baltimore Bullet 1980, Green Ice 1981, Chanel Solitaire 1981, Top Secret 1984, The Rainbow 1989, Mountains of the Moon 1990, Journey of Love 1990; *Awards* Best Actor in film festivals of: Alexandria, Valencia, Bastia; *Books* The Eternal Male (autobiog, 1977), My Life in Bridge; *Recreations* bridge, owning breeding and racing horses; *Style*— Omar Sharif, Esq; ✉ William Morris Agency (UK) Ltd, 31/32 Soho Square, London W1V 5DG (☎ 0171 434 2191, fax 0171 437 0238)

SHARKEY, Anna; da of William Sharkey, of Glasgow, and Catherine, *née* MacDonald; *Educ* St Catherine's Convent Edinburgh, Royal Acad of Dancing; *m* 1 (m dis 1974), Clive Benabou Cazes (d 1989); m 2, 3 Nov 1976, Jonathan Hugh Cecil, *qv*, s of Professor Lord David Cecil, CH, of Cranborne, Dorset; *Career* actress and singer; memb Catholic Stage Guild; *Theatre* incl: Expresso Bongo 1958, The World of Paul Slickey 1959, Divorce Me Darling 1964, Young Visitors 1969, Gigi 1976, Cowardy Custard 1972, Maggie 1977, The Canterbury Tales 1979, A Little Night Music 1979, A Mummy's Tomb 1980, The Orchestra 1981, HMS Pinafore 1982, Ring Round the Moon 1985, Piaf 1985, Nunsense 1987, The Circle 1988, Twelfth Night 1992, The Importance of Being Earnest 1995; *Opera* incl: L'Elisir D'Amore 1970, Hansel and Gretel 1970, Zaza 1971, Poisoned Kiss 1972, La Vie Parisienne 1974; *Television* incl: Dr Finlay's Casebook, Mammon, Cilla Comedy Six 1974, Girls of Slender Means 1975, Freud Strauss, CQ, Rumpole of the Bailey 1990, Scarfe on Class 1992, The Bill 1993, Trial and Retribution 1996; *Radio* radio incl: Morning Stories, Friday Night is Music Night, Amoung Your Souvenirs, The Oldest Member 1996; *Films* incl: Oliver 1967, The Music Lovers 1968; *Awards* incl: SWET Best Actress in a Musical 1977; *Recreations* cooking, gardening, French operetta; *Style*— Ms Anna Sharkey; ✉ British Actors' Equity Association, 8 Harley Street, London W1N 2AB (☎ 0171 637 9311)

SHARKEY, John; *b* 24 Sept 1947; *Educ* Univ of Manchester (BSc Maths); *m* 3 da; *Career* formerly with: Benton & Bowles, KMP; Saatchi & Saatchi: joined 1984, dep chm 1986, md 1987; chm: BDDP 1990–, Broad Street Group; fndr jt chm and chief exec offr BST-BDDP (formerly Bainsfair Sharkey Trott) 1990–; *Style*— John Sharkey, Esq;

✉ BDDP Holdings (UK) Ltd, 4–6 Soho Square, London W1V 5DE (☎ 0171 287 7778, fax 0171 287 1635)

SHARLAND, Dr Desmond Edward; s of Edward Harry Sharland (d 1964), of London, and Beatrice, *née* Gleeson (d 1952); *b* 13 April 1929; *Educ* Gunnersbury Catholic GS, London Hosp Med Sch (BSc, MB BS, MD); *m* 1, 9 June 1956, Edna (d 1974), da of William Guscott (d 1953); 1 s (Stephen William b 3 April 1957), 1 da (Sarah Jane b 5 May 1961); m 2, 12 April 1986, Dulcie, *née* Newboult; *Career* conslt physician Whittington Hosp 1965–94, hon sr lectr Univ Coll Hosp 1965–94, sr lectr in anatomy Royal Free Hosp Sch of Med 1970–; memb Guild of Catholic Drs; FRSM 1960, FRCP 1975; *Books* Whittington Post-Graduate Medicine (jtly, 1974); *Recreations* cruising and dancing; *Style*— Dr Desmond Sharland; ✉ Cecille Cottage, Church Path, Woodside Lane, London N12 8RH (☎ 0181 445 1214)

SHARLAND, (Edward) John; s of William Rex Sharland (d 1987), and Phyllis Eileen, *née* Pitts (d 1990); *b* 25 Dec 1937; *Educ* Monmouth, Jesus Coll Oxford (BA, MA); *m* 14 Feb 1970, Susan Mary Rodway, da of Douglas Rodway Millard, of Sudbury, Suffolk; 4 da (Nicola b 1971, Sandy b 1972, Philippa b 1974, Rebecca b 1975); *Career* FCO: London 1961–62, second sec (commercial) Bangkok 1962–67, Far E Dept London 1967–69, first sec Vienna 1969–72, first sec and head of Chancery Bangkok 1972–75, first sec (commercial) and consul Montevideo 1976–79, asst Cultural Rels Dept London 1979–82; consul gen: Perth 1982–87, Cleveland 1987–89; high cmmr: Port Moresby Papua New Guinea 1989–91, Victoria Seychelles 1992–95, ret; *Recreations* tennis, bridge, gardening; *Style*— John Sharland, Esq; ✉ Prospect House, 21 Maidstone Road, Lenham, Kent ME17 2QH

SHARMAN, Colin Morven; OBE (1980); *b* 19 Feb 1943; *m* Angela; 1 s (Richard b 1972), 1 da (Sarah b 1969); *Career* qualified chartered accountant Woolgar Hennel & Co 1965; KPMG (and predecessor firms): joined 1966, expanded practice Benelux Scandinavia and the Netherlands 1977–81, large scale investmt London 1981–87, sr ptnr Nat Mktg and Indust Gps and chm KPMG Mktg Ctee 1987–90, sr mgmnt consultancy ptnr 1989–90, sr regnl ptnr for London and South East 1990, chm KPMG Management Consultancy International 1991–94, UK sr ptnr 1994–, currently memb KPMG International Exec Ctee and Euro Bd; non-exec dir UKAEA and AEA Technology; memb Cncl: CBI, Industrial Soc, Assoc of Business Sponsorship of the Arts; chm Audit Ctee London First; past chm Bd of Govrs British Sch in the Netherlands, vice chm Cncl Br Ind Schs in the EC; memb: Advsy Panel Cranfield Business Sch, Bd London Inward, Appeal Ctee Golden Jubilee Appeal Nat Assoc of Almshouses, HRH The Princess Royal's Industry Ctee Animal Health Tst; vice patron Peter May Meml Appeal London Playing Fields Soc; chm Ocean Youth Club; Liveryman Worshipful Co of Gunmakers; Hon MSI, FCA (ACA 1965), CIMgt; *Recreations* outdoor and field sports, shooting, sailing; *Clubs* Carlton, Bembridge Sailing; *Style*— Colin Sharman, Esq, OBE; ✉ Tytherton Lucas, nr Chippenham, Wiltshire; KPMG, 8 Salisbury Square, London EC4Y 8BB (☎ 0171 236 8000, fax 0171 311 3311)

SHARMAN, Helen Patricia; OBE (1992); da of John David Sharman, of Sheffield, and Lyndis Mary, *née* Barrand; *b* 30 May 1963; *Educ* Jordanthorpe Comp Sch Sheffield, Univ of Sheffield (BSc); *Career* dep head Coatings Section MOV Hammersmith (formerly Marconi-Osram Valve, GEC subsid) 1985–87 (joined 1984), res technologist Mars Confectionery Slough 1987–89; selected as UK astronaut for Project Juno (jt venture between USSR and Antequera Ltd) 1989, trained at Yuri Gagarin Cosmonaut Trg Centre USSR 1989–91, became first Br person in space during mission 1991; currently scientific lectr and presenter; Geoffrey Pardoe award RAeS, Bronze medal Br Interplanetary Soc, Friendship of the People of the Soviet Union medal, The Worshipful Guild of Air Pilots and Air Navigators award, Gold Medal of the Royal Aero Club, Pres's Medal of the Soc Chemical Industry, Univ of Sheffield Chancellor's medal for achievement; Freeman City of Sheffield; CChem, Hon FRSC 1993, Hon MSc Univ of Birmingham, Hon DSc Univ of Kent, Hon Master of Univ Univ of Surrey; Hon DTech: Univ of Plymouth 1995, The Robert Gordon Univ 1996; memb Br Interplanetary Soc; sr fell Univ of Sheffield, fell Sheffield Hallam Univ; FRGS 1995, FRAeS 1995 (MRAeS 1991); *Recreations* cycling, swimming, badminton, squash, running, playing piano and saxophone, listening to music, theatre, art, travelling; *Style*— Dr Helen Sharman, OBE; ✉ Fox Artist Management Ltd, Concorde House, 101 Shepherd's Bush Road, London W6 7LP (☎ 0171 602 8822, fax 0171 603 2352)

SHARMAN, Mark; s of Stanley Brian Sharman, of Leamington Spa, Warwicks, and Beryl Mary, *née* Brown; *b* 2 Jan 1950; *Educ* John Port GS Etwall Derbyshire; *m* 1981, Patricia, da of Ivor Goodier (d 1987); 2 s (Matthew b 7 Oct 1981, Luke b 4 Nov 1984); *Career* reporter Derby Evening Telegraph 1967–71, reporter Raymond's News Agency 1971, sports reporter Derby Evening Telegraph 1972, sports sub-ed then chief sub-ed Birmingham Evening Mail 1972–76, sports journalist ATV Ltd Birmingham 1976, sports prodr London Weekend Television 1977–81 (incl prog ed ITV coverage of 1978 World Cup and 1980 Olympics), head of sport, head of news and sport then contoller of news and sport TVS 1981–88 (responsible for ITV network progs incl Emergency 999 and Police International), ed ITV Olympics 1988, md Chrysalis Television plc 1988–91, head of progs London News Network 1992–94, dir of programming Sky Sports 1994–; *Style*— Mark Sharman, Esq; ✉ British Sky Broadcasting Ltd, 6 Centaurs Business Park, Grant Way, Syon Lane, Isleworth, Middx TW7 5QD (☎ 0171 705 3000, fax 0171 705 3421)

SHARMAN, Patrick George; s of Charles A Sharman (d 1988), of Peterborough, and Betty, *née* Roll; *b* 8 July 1939; *Educ* Marlborough, Pembroke Coll Cambridge (MA); *m* 1; 1 s (Robert b 2 April 1969), 1 da (Caroline b 21 Oct 1964); m 2, 26 July 1978, Wendy, *née* Read; 2 s (Timothy b 12 Oct 1978, Algernon b 19 Aug 1980); *Career* admitted slr 1965; articled clerk Theodore Goddard & Co, ptnr Bircham & Co 1968–73, dir and slr Sharman Newspapers Ltd 1973–89, chm Sharman & Co Ltd 1989–; fndr chm Hereward Radio plc, dir Anglia TV Ltd; Freeman City of London, Liveryman City of London Slrs' Co; memb Law Soc 1965; *Recreations* tennis; *Style*— Patrick Sharman, Esq; ✉ 5 Chaucer Road, Cambridge CB2 2EB (☎ 01223 356927); Sharman & Company Ltd, Newark Rd, Peterborough PE1 5TD (☎ 01733 555300, fax 01733 555400, car 0585 679999)

SHARMAN, Peter William; CBE (1984); s of William Charles Sharman (d 1971), and Olive Mabel, *née* Burl (d 1961); *b* 1 June 1924; *Educ* Northgate GS Ipswich, Univ of Edinburgh (MA); *m* 1946, Eileen Barbara, *née* Crix; 1 s, 2 da; *Career* chief gen mangr Norwich Union Insurance Gp 1975–84 (dir 1974–95); dir: Riggs A P Bank Ltd 1976–90, Norwich and Peterborough Building Society 1985–95, Jarrold & Sons Ltd 1987–95; chm: Life Offices Assoc 1977–79, British Insur Assoc 1982–83 (dep chm 1981–82); FIA; *Recreations* golf, tennis, badminton; *Style*— Peter Sharman, Esq, CBE; ✉ 28B Eaton Rd, Norwich NR4 6PZ

SHARP, Sir Adrian; 4 Bt (UK 1922), of Warden Court, Maidstone, Kent; s of Sir Edward Herbert Sharp, 3 Bt (d 1985), and Beryl Kathleen, *née* Simmons-Green (d 1994); *b* 17 Sept 1951; *Educ* Boxhill Sch, Nat Business Coll Cape Town; *m* 1, 1976 (m dis 1986), Hazel Patricia, only da of James Trevor Wallace, of Pietersburg, S Africa, and former w of William Ian Barrett Bothwell; m 2, 1994, Denise, o da of Percy Edward Roberts, of Ironbridge, Shropshire; 1 s (Hayden Sean b 27 Aug 1994); *Heir* s, Hayden Sean Sharp b 27 Aug 1994; *Career* exec mangr Toyota Motor Co; *Style*— Sir Adrian Sharp, Bt; ✉ 27 Donkin Avenue, Tableview 7441, Cape, S Africa; 31 Hamble Court, Broom Park, Teddington, Middx TW11 9RW

SHARP, Anthony Arthur Vivian; s of Vivian Arthur Sharp (d 1978), and Violet Elizabeth, *née* Johnson (d 1981); *b* 5 Nov 1938; *Educ* Repton; *m* 17 Sept 1966, Jill Treharne, da of Hugh Treharne Morgan, OBE (d 1996), of Crowborough, Sussex; 2 da (Antoinette b 1969, Fiona b 1970); *Career* Nat Serv 1957–59, cmmnd Midshipman 1958, RNR 1958–66, Sub Lt 1959, Lt 1962; dir: H Clarkson Ltd 1978–86 (asst dir 1975–78), Clarkson Puckle Ltd 1978–86, Horace Holman Ltd 1986–88, Nelson Hurst and Marsh Agencies Ltd 1988–90, Jardine (Lloyd's Underwriting Agents) Ltd 1990–, Jardine Lloyd's Advisers Ltd 1994–, Anton Members Agency Ltd 1995–; underwriting memb Lloyd's 1972; treas Wivelsfield Cons Assoc 1979–82 (memb Ctee 1978–82); memb: London Ctee Sail Trg Assoc 1968–81, Insur Brokers' Registration Cncl 1983–; *Recreations* tennis, shooting, sailing, skiing; *Clubs* City Univ (memb Ctee 1993–), Lloyd's Yacht, Lloyd's Lawn Tennis; *Style*— Anthony Sharp, Esq; ✉ Jardine Lloyd's Advisers Ltd, Latham House, 16 Minories, London EC3N 1EX (☎ 0171 702 1234. fax 0171 702 4062)

SHARP, Brenda; da of Douglas Sheppard Henderson, of Dereham, Norfolk, and Lily Alice West, *née* Payne (d 1993); *b* 12 Aug 1946; *Educ* Purley Co GS, Brighton Coll of Educn, Coloma Coll Univ of London, Jordanhill Coll of Educn, Univ of Birmingham (Cert Ed, BEd, Dip Ed); *m* 21 Dec 1973, Trevor Leslie Sharp, s of Reginald Stanley Sharp; 1 s (David Alexander b 20 Dec 1977), 1 da (Diana Elizabeth b 3 Dec 1979); *Career* teacher in England, Scotland and France 1967–74, English teacher Hamilton Acad and Claremont HS Scotland 1974–77, area tutor trainer Adult Literacy Scheme Scotland 1978, lectr and head Adult Educn Centre Birmingham 1979–86, lectr FE and co-ordinator Women in Technology Programme Matthew Boulton Coll Birmingham 1984–88, owner and md Fluid Mixers Ltd and Trenda Ltd 1988–92, md Keemix Agitators Ltd 1993–95; non-exec dir: Birmingham Family Health Serv Authy, Women's Engrg Soc (memb Cncl 1988–96, organiser 75th Anniversary Conf 1994), UK ICWES Tst 1992–, Birmingham C of C (BCT Ltd) 1996–; vice chm Branches Forum Nat Childbirth Tst 1982–83; memb: Birmingham Women in Business Assoc 1990–, Exec Ctee Solihull C of C 1990–92, Engrg Advsy Bd Matthew Boulton Coll 1993–, Central Customer Servs Ctee OFWAT 1994–; RSA: memb Manufacturing Initiative Steering Gp for Manufacturing Wealth Creation and the Econ 1992, Midlands Group Ctee 1995–; nat conf mangr Br C of C Nat Conf Birmingham 1996 and Cardiss 1997; asst dist cmmr Solihull N Dist Scouts 1990–93; runner up Midlands Business Woman of the Year 1990 and 1991, Daily Mail/Women into Business Taylor Woodrow Award 1992; FRSA 1990; *Style*— Ms Brenda Sharp; ✉ c/o Cumbria, Larner's Drift, Toftwood, Dereham, Norfolk NR19 1LE

SHARP, (James) Christopher; CBE (1993); s of Stanley Sharp (d 1962), of Stockport, Cheshire, and Annie, *née* Owrid (d 1991); *b* 24 Dec 1939; *Educ* Stockport GS, Pembroke Coll Oxford (MA); *m* 20 July 1963, Mary, da of Roland Bromfield (d 1983), of Shrewsbury; 1 s (Jeremy b 1964), 2 da (Catherine b 1968, Rosemary b 1978); *Career* admitted slr 1966; Salop CC 1963–68, slr G H Morgan and Co Shrewsbury 1968–70, md Northern Rock Building Society 1985– (joined 1970, chief exec 1983–85); dir: Home Housing Association Ltd, Tyne & Wear Development Corporation; chm Tyneside TEC Ltd; vice pres Euro Mortgage Fedn, pres Int Union for Housing Fin; govr: Durham Univ Business Sch, Univ of Northumbria at Newcastle (formerly Newcastle upon Tyne Poly); dir Newcastle Theatre Royal Tst; *Clubs* Northern Counties; *Style*— Christopher Sharp, Esq, CBE; ✉ Northern Rock Building Society, Northern Rock House, Gosforth, Newcastle upon Tyne NE3 4PL (☎ 0191 285 7191, fax 0191 213 0114)

SHARP, David John; s of Norman Sharp, of Viggory Lodge, Horsell Common, Woking, Surrey, and Freda Madeleine, *née* Wakeford; *b* 15 April 1949; *Educ* Lancing, St Mary's Hosp Med Sch London (MB BS, FRCS, MD); *m* 7 Sept 1982, Marisa Nicole, *née* Parnes; 2 s (Oliver b 1985, William b 1986), 1 da (Augusta b 1990); *Career* registrar on orthopaedic higher surgical trg scheme Royal Orthopaedic Hosp Birmingham 1981–83, sr registrar on orthopaedic higher surgical trg scheme Northampton and Royal Postgrad Med Sch London 1983–88, res fell Materials Dept QMC London 1986, conslt orthopaedic surgn The Ipswich Hosp 1988–; memb Br Orthopaedic Res Soc; fell Br Orthopaedic Assoc; *Recreations* vintage car, drawing, squash, opera; *Style*— David Sharp, Esq; ✉ Peartree, Farm, Charsfield, Woodbridge, Suffolk IP13 7QE (☎ 01473 737266)

SHARP, David Stanley; s of Stanley Harold Sharp (d 1981), of Harrogate, Yorkshire, and Emeline Sharp, *née* Smith; *b* 9 July 1942; *Educ* Harrogate GS, St Mary's Hosp Med Sch Univ of London (MB BS, LRCP, MRCS, MRCOG); *m* 3 Dec 1965, Margaret Irene, da of Dr John Sidney Johnston, of Bowdon, Cheshire; 1 s (Paul b 1969), 1 da (Jane b 1966); *Career* obstetrician and gynaecologist 1980–, assoc lectr Univ of Manchester Med Sch 1980–, chm Med Exec Ctee N Manchester Gen Hosp 1988– (clinical dir for obstetrics and gynaecology 1986–); memb Medico Legal Ctee RCOG 1987–90 (memb Cncl 1986–88); memb BMA 1966, FRCOG 1989; *Recreations* golf; *Clubs* Hale Golf, Manchester Golf; *Style*— David Sharp, Esq; ✉ Lyndhurst, 44 Ridgeway Rd, Higher Timperley, Altrincham, Cheshire WA15 7EZ (☎ 0161 980 4984); North Manchester General Hospital, Delaunays Rd, Manchester M8 6RB (☎ 0161 795 4567)

SHARP, Prof Deborah; *b* 11 Nov 1951; *Educ* Lady Margaret Hall Oxford (BA, BM BCh), MRCGP, DRCOG, Univ of London (PhD); *Career* currently prof of primary health care (chair funded by SW RHA) Univ of Bristol; *Books* Prevention of Anxiety and Depression in Primary Care (contrib, 1992); *Style*— Prof Deborah Sharp; ✉ Department of Social Medicine, Canynge Hall, Whiteladies Road, Bristol BS8 2PR (☎ 0117 928 7305, fax 0117 928 7340, mobile 0421 564042, e-mail debbie.sharp@bristol.ac.uk)

SHARP, Dennis Charles; s of Walter Charles Henry Sharp (d 1976), of Bedford, and Elsie, *née* Evans; *Educ* Bedford Mod Sch, AA London (AADipl), Univ of Liverpool (MA); *m* 1, 1963 (m dis 1973), Joanna Leighton, da of William Scales (d 1986); 1 da (Melanie Clare); m 2, 8 Dec 1983, Yasmin, da of C Amirali Shariff; 1 s (Deen b 1984); *Career* architect, writer; Dennis Sharp Architects London 1964–; lectr in architecture Univ of Manchester 1964–68, Leverhulme fell in architecture Univ of Liverpool 1960–63, sr lectr i/c history course AA Sch 1968–72 (sr tutor and lectr 1973–81, gen ed AA (AA Quarterly, AA Papers) 1968–82), visiting prof Columbia Univ of NY 1981, distinguished visiting critic Finnish Assoc of Architects 1980–81, distinguished visiting scholar Univ of Adelaide SA 1984; visiting lectr: Imperial Coll Univ of London 1969–70, Royal Univ of Malta 1971, 1972 and 1974, PNL 1977–78, Univ of Sheffield 1988–89, UCL 1990–92; Graham Fndn lectures Chicago 1974 and 1986; John Player lectr NFT 1977; external examiner: Bartlett Sch UCL 1971–78, Univs of Oxford, Sheffield, Bristol, Liverpool and Kingston, Lanchester Poly, Trent Poly (CNAA); dir CICA 1979–; prof Int Acad of Architecture, special prof Sch of Architecture Univ of Nottingham 1996–; exec ed World Architecture 1989–92, ed International Architecture 1993–94; Silver medal Academie d'Architecture Paris 1991, special mention UIA 1993; ARIBA 1959 (vice pres RIBA 1992–93); *Books* Modern Architecture & Expressionism (1966), Sources of Modern Architecture (1967, 1981), A Visual History of 20th Century Architecture (1972), The Picture Palace (1969), Glass Architecture (ed 1972), The Rationalists (1978), Muthesius H: The English House (ed 1979 and 1987), Illustrated Dictionary of Architects and Architecture (ed 1991), Twentieth Century Architecture: A Visual History (1991), The Bauhaus (1993), Santiago Calatrava (ed, 1992 and 1994), Connell, Ward and Lucas (1994), Bilbao 2000 (1995); *Recreations* photography, investigating towns and buildings; *Clubs* Architecture; *Style*— Dennis Sharp; ✉ Dennis Sharp Architects, 35 Alfred Place, London WC1E 7DP (☎ 0171 436 1607, fax 0171 580 6080)

SHARP, Duncan McCallum; CBE (1994); s of Duncan McCallum Sharp (Sr), of Wakefield, and Marjorie, *née* Lindley; *b* 29 April 1936; *Educ* Queen Elizabeth GS, Univ of Leeds (LLB); *m* 12 Sept 1959, Maureen, da of Percy William Kaye (d 1976); 2 s

(Andrew b 1962, Iain b 1972), 3 da (Janet b 1960, Kathryn b 1965, Alison b 1968); *Career* admitted slr 1959; dep town clerk Bridlington Borough Cncl 1966–69, country prosecuting slr Cumbria CC 1979–86, chief crown prosecutor Cleveland and N Yorkshire 1986–93, chief crown prosecutor CPS Yorkshire 1993–95; *Recreations* gardening, walking, reading, Victorian genealogy; *Style—* Duncan Sharp, Esq, CBE; ✉ 39 Valley View, Wheldrake, York YO4 6AJ (☎ 01904 448595)

SHARP, Sir George; kt (1976), OBE (1969), JP (Fife 1975), DL (Fife 1978); s of Angus Sharp, and Mary, *née* McNee; *b* 8 April 1919; *m* 1948, Elsie May, da of David Porter Rodger, and Williamina, *née* Young; 1 s; *Career* vice chm: Tay Road Bridge Joint Board 1972–78, Forth Bridge Ctee 1972–78; dir Grampian TV 1975–89; memb: Scottish Water Advsy Ctee 1962–69, Scottish Devpt Agency 1975–80, Royal Cmmn on Legal Services in Scotland 1978–80; chm: Forth River Purification Bd 1955–67 and 1975–78, Kirkcaldy Dist Cncl 1958–75, Scottish River Purification Advsy Ctee (and memb) 1967–75, Fife and Kinross Water Bd 1967–75, Fife CC (convenor) 1973–75 (memb 1945–75), Fife Regional Cncl (convenor) 1974–78, Glenrothes Development Corporation 1978–86 (vice chm 1973–78), Scottish Tourist Bd Consultative Cncl 1979–83; memb Potato Mktg Bd 1965–71; pres: Assoc of CCs 1971–73, Convention of Scottish Local Authys 1975–78; mangr tstee Municipal Mutual Insurance 1979–91; memb: Nat Girobank (Scottish Bd) 1984–89, Ctee of Enquiry into Local Government Finance 1974–76, Ctee of Enquiry into Salmon and Trout Fishing; memb Econ and Social Ctee EEC 1982–86; *Style—* Sir George Sharp, OBE, JP, DL; ✉ Strathlea, 56 Station Rd, Thornton, Fife KY1 4AY (☎ 01592 774347)

SHARP, Sir Kenneth Johnston; kt (1984), TD (1960); s of Johnston Sharp (d 1994, aged 103), and late Ann Sharp; *b* 29 Dec 1926; *Educ* Shrewsbury, St John's Coll Cambridge (MA); *m* 1955, Barbara Maud, *née* Keating; 1 s; *Career* Indian Army 1945–48, TA 251 (Westmorland and Cumberland Yeo) Field Regt RA; qualified CA; ptnr: Armstrong Watson & Co 1955–75, Baker Tilly Chartered Accountants 1985–89; head Govt Accounting Serv DTI 1975–83; pres Inst of CAs 1974–75 (memb Cncl 1966–83); Hon Memb of Ct Worshipful Co of CAs (Master 1979–80); FCA 1960 (ACA 1955); *Style—* Sir Kenneth Sharp, TD; ✉ Holly Tree House, Kelliwith, Feock, nr Truro, Cornwall TR3 6QZ

SHARP, Sir Leslie; kt (1996), QPM (1986); s of George James Sharp (d 1970), and Lily Mabel, *née* Moys (d 1983); *b* 14 May 1936; *Educ* Finchley Co GS, Univ of London (LLB); *m* 1, 1956, Maureen Tyson (d 1985); 2 da (Angela b 1957, Amanda b 1975); *m* 2, 1986, Audrey, da of George Sidwell; 2 step da (Susan b 1958, Tina b 1962); *Career* Nat Serv Middx Regt 1954–56; chief supt Met Police 1978–80 (joined 1956), dep chief constable W Midlands Police 1983–88 (asst chief constable (Admin and Supplies) 1980–83), chief constable Cumbria Constabulary 1988–91, chief constable Strathclyde Police 1991–96, ret; awarded Police Long Serv and Good Conduct Medal 1978; Hon LLD Univ of Strathclyde 1995; CIMgt 1986, FRSA 1992; *Recreations* angling, cricket umpire, water colour painting, gardening; *Style—* Sir Leslie Sharp, QPM; ✉ c/o Strathclyde Police HQ, 173 Pitt Street, Glasgow G2 4JS (☎ 0141 204 2626, fax (24 hours) 0141 227 1475, telex 778855)

SHARP, Peter John; s of John Frederick Sharp, of Plumstead, N Norfolk, and Joan Brimelow, *née* Hotchkiss; *b* 16 April 1956; *Educ* Berkhamsted, Univ of Oxford (BA); *m* 22 Dec 1984, Philippa Joanna, da of Sqdn Ldr William Ronald Stanley Body, of Drinkstone Green, Suffolk; 3 s (Samuel Frederick b 1985, William Rodric Peter b 1991, Christopher b 1996), 2 da (Holly Rose b and d 1987, Florence Emily b 1989); *Career* admitted slr 1982; ptnr Wilde Sapte 1984–95 (memb Managing Bd 1990–92), ptnr Le Boeuf Lamb Greene & MacRae (founding English ptnr London office) 1995–; dep chm Prince's Youth Business Tst S London 1993–94 (chm 1991–93); memb Law Soc; *Recreations* motor racing, cycling; *Style—* Peter Sharp, Esq; ✉ Le Boeuf Lamb Greene & MacRae, 2 Suffolk Lane, London EC4R 0AT (☎ 0171 626 3000, fax 0171 626 2623)

SHARP, Richard Adrian William; OBE (1986); s of Frederick George Sharp (d 1964), and Kathleen Muriel, *née* Chandler; *b* 9 Sept 1938; *Educ* Blundell's, Balliol Coll Oxford (MA); *m* 1963, Esther Marian, da of Sir Frederick Johnson Pedler (d 1991), of Moor Park; 2 s (Quentin b 1965, Jeremy b 1967), 1 da (Rachel b 1970); *Career* Nat Serv 1957–59, 2 Lt RM Commandos; asst master Sherborne Sch 1963–68; joined English China Clays 1968, distribution mangr Mainland Europe ECC International 1994–; dir Treneglos Co Ltd; tstee and treas Maitland Tst; pres Nanpean AFC 1969–90, chm SW Cncl for Sport and Recreation 1984–90 (vice chm 1982–84), rugby corr Sunday Telegraph 1976–85; played rugby for: Redruth, Wasps, Bristol, Barbarians, Oxford Univ 1959–62, Cornwall 1957–67 (Capt 1963–65), England 1960–67 (Capt 1963), Br Isles Touring Team 1962; played cricket for Cornwall 1956–69; FILog 1981; *Recreations* golf, gardening, walking; *Clubs* British Sportsman's, Vincent's; *Style—* Richard Sharp, Esq; ✉ Rosenannon, Carlyon Road, St Austell, Cornwall PL25 4LE; ECC International, John Keay House, St Austell, Cornwall PL25 4DJ

SHARP, Sir Richard Lyall; KCVO (1982), CB (1977); s of late Alexander Sharp, Advocate of Aberdeen, by his late w Isabella, OBE; *b* 27 March 1915; *Educ* Fettes, Univ of Aberdeen, Clare Coll Cambridge; *m* 1950, Jean Helen, eld da of Sir James Crombie, KCB, KBE, CMG; 2 s, 2 da (1 da decd); *Career* served WWII Royal Northumberland Fusiliers (POW Singapore and Siam); joined Treasy 1946, IDC 1961, under-sec Prices and Incomes Bd 1966–68, with Treasy 1968–77, ceremonial offr CSD 1977–82; *Style—* Sir Richard Sharp, KCVO, CB; ✉ Home Farm House, Briston, Norfolk NR24 2HN (☎ 01263 860445)

SHARP, Hon Richard Simon; s of Baron Sharp of Grimsdyke (d 1994), and Marion, *née* Freeman; *b* 8 Feb 1956; *Educ* Merchant Taylors', Ch Ch Oxford (MA); *m* 29 Aug 1987, Victoria Susan, da of Lloyd Nelson Hull; 2 s (James Eric Halle b 6 June 1992, Alexander Simon Lloyd b 30 April 1994), 1 da (Caroline Nicola b 17 Oct 1989); *Career* Morgan Guaranty Trust Co 1978–84, md Goldman Sachs International Ltd 1984–; *Recreations* eating, tennis, reading; *Style—* The Hon Richard Sharp; ✉ Goldman Sachs International Ltd, Peterborough Court, 133 Fleet Street, London EC4A 2BB (☎ 0171 774 1000)

SHARP, Steven Michael; s of Clarence Sharp, of Willerby, E Yorks, and Anne, *née* Price; *b* 5 July 1950; *Educ* Ainthorpe HS Kingston-upon-Hull, Hull Poly (Hotel and Catering Institute, City and Guilds of London Institute (distinction), winner Salon Culinaire, ASA Gold medal); *children* 1 da (Emma Louise b 3 Feb 1978), 1 s (Daniel James b 21 Aug 1979); *Career* hotel mgmnt positions 1969–73, sales and mktg mgmnt positions in food distribution 1973–78, dir Bejam Agencies Jersey CI, mktg mangr Bejam Group PLC 1978–83, head of retail mktg Argyll Group PLC 1983–87, mktg dir Asda Group PLC 1987–89, mktg dir Debenhams PLC 1989–92, mktg dir The Burton Group plc 1992–94, chm Steven Sharp plc 1994–; visiting prof Glasgow Caledonian Univ; MCIM; *Recreations* horse riding, shooting, skiing, music, art, advertising; *Style—* Prof Steven Sharp; ✉ 49 Etheldene Avenue, London N10 3QE; Steven Sharp plc, 7 and 8 Bourlet Close, London W1P 7PJ (☎ 0171 636 6800, fax 0171 636 2420)

SHARP, Thomas (Tom); CBE (1987); s of Margaret Sharp, *née* Tout (d 1986); *b* 19 June 1931; *Educ* Univ of Oxford; *m* 24 March 1962, Margaret Lucy, da of Sqdn Ldr Osmund Hailstone, AFC (d 1988), and Sydney Hailstone (d 1989), of Hadlow and Southborough, Kent; 2 da (Helen b 1965, Elizabeth b 1967); *Career* RAF 1949–51; civil servant (mainly with Bd of Trade and related depts) 1954–87, a gen mangr Lloyd's of London 1987–91; memb Lib Dem Pty; cncllr: Surrey CC 1989–, Guildford BC 1991–; chm Surrey Social Servs Ctee 1993–95; *Recreations* walking, reading, music; *Style—* Tom Sharp, CBE; ✉ 96 London Rd, Guildford, Surrey GU1 1TH (☎ 01483 572669)

SHARPE, Andrew; s of late Frank Sharpe, of Glenfield, Leics, and Joyce Marjorie, *née* Slater; *b* 29 April 1949; *Educ* Ashby-De-La-Zouche Boys' GS; *m* 8 July 1972, Sybil Dorothea Sharpe, da of late Harold Myers, of Harborne, Birmingham; *Career* called to the Bar Gray's Inn 1972; practising barrister 1972–; lectr in law Univ of Reading 1971–73; *Recreations* sport, jazz, blues music; *Style—* Andrew Sharpe, Esq; ✉ Spon Chambers, 13 Spon St, Coventry, Warwickshire CV1 3BA (☎ 01203 632977)

SHARPE, David Thomas; OBE (1986); s of Albert Edward Sharpe, of 1 Alma Road, Swanscombe, Kent, and late Grace Emily, *née* Large; *b* 14 Jan 1946; *Educ* GS for Boys Gravesend, Downing Coll Cambridge, Univ of Oxford Med Sch (MB BChir); *m* 23 Jan 1971, Patricia Lilian, da of Brinley Meredith (d 1965); 1 s (Timothy Richard Brinley b 4 Aug 1972), 2 da (Katherine Anna b 24 June 1974, Caroline Louise b 2 Nov 1978); *Career* plastic surgeon; house surgeon Radcliffe Infirmary Oxford 1970–71, sr house offr in plastic surgery Churchill Hosp Oxford 1971–72, Pathology Dept Radcliffe Infirmary 1972–73 (Accident Service 1972), gen surgery Royal United Hosp Bath 1973–75; registrar: Plastic Surgery Unit Chepstow 1976–78 (plastic surgeon 1976), Canniesburn Hosp Glasgow 1978–80; sr registrar in plastic surgery Leeds and Bradford 1980–84, chm and md Plastech Research and Design Ltd 1984–, dir Plastic Surgery and Burns Research Unit Univ of Bradford 1986–, prof of plastic and reconstructive surgery Univ of Bradford; visiting conslt plastic surgeon 1985– (Yorkshire Clinic Bradford, BUPA Hosp Elland W Yorkshire, Cromwell Hosp London), conslt plastic surgeon 1985– (St Luke's Hosp Bradford, Bradford Royal Infirmary, Huddersfield Royal Infirmary); author of various chapters, leading articles and papers on plastic surgery topics, major burn disaster management, tissue expansion and breast reconstruction; memb Cncl British Assoc of Aesthetic Plastic Surgeons 1989– (pres 1996–98); FRCS 1975; *Recreations* painting, shooting, riding, flying (PPL H); *Style—* David T Sharpe, Esq, OBE; ✉ Hazelbrae, Calverley, Leeds LS28 5QQ; The Yorkshire Clinic, Bradford Rd, Bingley, W Yorks BD16 1TW (☎ 01274 560311, fax 01274 510760)

SHARPE, John Harald; s of John William Sharpe (d 1961), of Dore, Sheffield, and Eva Mary, *née* Harrison (d 1994); *b* 31 Dec 1941; *Educ* King Edward VI GS Retford, King Edward VI GS Sheffield, Univ of Liverpool (BSc); *m* 1969, Maureen, da of Roland W Norris, of Umkomaas, Natal, S Africa; 2 s (James Alexander b 29 June 1970, Oliver John b 30 June 1973), 1 da (Sarah Jane b 24 April 1976); *Career* Unilever PLC and subsids: mgmnt trainee 1963–65, various mktg positions in UK, S Africa, USA and Philippines 1965–78, chm Sunlight AG Switzerland 1981–83 (mktg dir 1978–80), sr international mktg and advtg exec detergents 1983–86, chm Elida Gibbs UK 1986–92, chm Birds Eye Wall's 1993–95, chief exec Lever Europe 1995–, pres Unilever Home & Personal Care Europe 1996–; pres Union Savonneries Suisse (Swiss Detergents Assoc) 1981–83, chm Cosmetics Toiletries and Perfumery Assoc UK 1988–90, pres Euro Cosmetics, Toiletries and Perfumery Assoc (COLIPA) 1991–92, chm UK Assoc of Frozen Food Prodrs 1994–95, dir Br Quality Fndn 1994–; FRSA 1993; *Recreations* travel, squash, golf; *Clubs* RAC; *Style—* John Sharpe, Esq; ✉ Lever Europe, Waterloo Office Park Building, Dreve Richelle 161, B-1410 Waterloo, Belgium

SHARPE, Hon Sir John Henry; kt (1977), CBE (1972), JP; s of late Harry Sharpe, and late Jessie, *née* White; *b* 8 Nov 1921; *Educ* Warwick Acad, Mount Allison Commercial Coll Canada; *m* 1948, Eileen Margaret Morrow, of Vancouver, Canada; 1 s (John), 1 da (Kathleen); *Career* served WWII Bermuda Rifles 1939–42, Royal Canadian AF 1942–45 (qualified as navigator in Canada, posted UK and served with RAF Bomber Cmd in ops over Europe); chm Purvis Ltd (joined 1938); MP (UBP) Warwick West Bermuda 1963–93, premier of Bermuda 1975–77 (dep premier 1972–75); min of: fin 1968–75, tport 1980, marine and air servs 1980–81, lab and home affrs 1981–88, delegated and legislative affrs 1989, lab and home affrs 1990–92, delgn and legislative affairs 1992–93, ret Parl 1993; formerly dir Bank of Bermuda Ltd; hon vice patron RAF Assoc, hon life vice pres Bermuda Football Assoc; former chm Bermuda Nat Olympic Cncl, memb Synod C of E, church warden St Mary's Church Warwick; chm: Bd of Inquiry into various Taxi matters 1980 and 1996, Bd of Inquiry into drugs in football 1995; advsr to Cabinet Ctee responsible for Green Paper on Independence for Bermuda 1994; *Recreations* reading, bridge, gardening, tennis, formerly soccer and rugby; *Clubs* Royal Hamilton Amateur Dinghy, Coral Beach and Tennis; *Style—* The Hon Sir John Sharpe, CBE, JP; ✉ Uplands, 26 Harbour Rd, Warwick West, Bermuda; Purvis Ltd, PO Box 461, Hamilton 5

SHARPE, Lee Stuart; s of Leo Sharpe, and Gail Lillian, *née* Noakes; *b* 27 May 1971; *Educ* Hagley RC HS; *Career* professional footballer; Torquay Utd: debut v Exeter City 1987, 14 appearances, 3 goals; transferred to Manchester Utd 1988–96, transferred to Leeds Utd (for fee of £4.5m) 1996–; England: under 21 debut 1989 (winner's medal Under 21 Competition Toulon France 1989), full debut v Republic of Ireland 1991; club honours: Euro Cup Winners' Cup winners 1991, Rumbelows Cup winners 1992 (runners-up 1991), winners inaugural FA Premier League Championship 1992/93, winners League and FA Cup double 1994 and 1996 (setting record), winners Charity Shield 1993 and 1994; Young Player of the Year and Barclays Young Eagle of the Year 1991; *Recreations* snooker in winter, golf in summer, listening to music, sleeping; *Style—* Lee Sharpe, Esq; ✉ c/o Leeds United FC, Elland Road, Leeds, West Yorkshire LS11 0ES

SHARPE, Chief Constable Peter Samuel; QPM (1994); s of Arthur Samuel Sharpe, and May Elizabeth, *née* Ede; *b* 21 Nov 1944; *Educ* Varndean GS Brighton; *m* 1985, Julia Anne, *née* Richens; 1 s; *Career* Sussex Police: joined Brighton Borough Police as constable 1963, various positions rising to rank of chief supt 1988–89; memb staff Police Staff Coll Bramshill 1983–84, dep chief constable Surrey Police 1991–94 (asst chief constable 1989–91), chief constable Herts Police 1994–; *Recreations* cricket, golf; *Clubs* XL; *Style—* Chief Constable Peter Sharpe, QPM; ✉ Hertfordshire Constabulary HQ, Stanborough Road, Welwyn Garden City, Herts AL8 6XF (☎ 01707 354511, fax 01707 354519)

SHARPE, Thomas Anthony Edward; QC (1994); s of James Sharpe (d 1981), of Kent, and Lydia, *née* de Gegg; *b* 21 Dec 1949; *m* 1, 14 June 1974 (m dis), Sheila Carmichael, da of Lord Carmichael of Kelvingrove, *qv*; 2 c; *m* 2, 16 Feb 1988, Phillis, da of late W P Rogers; 2 c; *Career* called to the Bar Lincoln's Inn 1976; fell Wolfson Coll and Nuffield Coll Oxford 1987; *Clubs* Reform; *Style—* Thomas Sharpe, Esq, QC; ✉ 1 Essex Court, Ground Floor, Temple, London EC4Y 9AR (☎ 0171 583 2000, fax 0171 583 0118)

SHARPE, Thomas Ridley (Tom); s of Rev George Coverdale Sharpe (d 1944), and Grace Egerton, *née* Brown (d 1975); *b* 30 March 1928; *Educ* Lancing, Pembroke Coll Cambridge (MA); *m* 1969, Nancy Anne Looper; 3 da (Melanie, Grace, Jemima); *Career* RM 1946–48; social worker Johannesburg SA 1951–52, teacher Natal SA 1952–56, photographer SA 1956–61, deported from SA on political grounds 1961, teacher trg Cambridge 1962–63, lectr in history Cambridge Coll of Arts and Technology 1963–71, novelist 1971–; *Books* Riotous Assembly (1971), Indecent Exposure (1973), Porterhouse Blue (1974), Blott on the Landscape (1975), Wilt (1976), The Great Pursuit (1977), The Throwback (1978), The Wilt Alternative (1979), Ancestral Vices (1980), Vintage Stuff (1982), Wilt on High (1984), Granchester Grind (1995), The Midden (1996); *Recreations* photography, old typewriters, gardening, reading, cats, talking; *Style—* Tom Sharpe, Esq; ✉ 38 Tunwells Lane, Great Shelford, Cambridge CB2 5LJ

SHARPE-NEWTON, Geraldine; da of late Jesse J Sharpe, of New York City, and Adrienne Rosaire; *Educ* Univ of Illinois (BA), Univ of Pittsburgh (MLS Hons); *m* 1, June 1962 (m dis 1974), Thomas Alan Newton; 1 s (Matthew Ross b 1968), 1 da (Jennifer Jesse b 1965); m 2, 1992, John Peter Bluff; *Career* assoc dir special projects Burson Marsteller PR 1974–77, vice pres Niki Singer Inc 1977–79, vice pres dir of PR Simon and Schuster 1979–80; dir Info Servs CBS News 1980–83, head of Press and Public Affrs ITN 1983–91, dir of communications WWF UK 1991–94, sr vice pres International Public Relations Turner Broadcasting System Inc 1994–; memb: IPR, BAFTA, RTS, Media Soc, Foreign Press Assoc, Forum UK, Women in Film and TV, Women in Cable UK; *Recreations* reading, gardening, sailing, hiking, rock collecting; *Clubs* Soho House, Reform, Groucho, Hurlingham; *Style*— Mrs Geraldine Sharpe-Newton; ✉ 29 Albert Mansions, Albert Bridge Road, London SW11 4QB (fax 0171 585 3910); International Public Relations, Turner Broadcasting System Ltd, CNN House, 19–22 Rathbone Place, London W1P 1DF (☎ 0171 637 6733, fax 0171 637 6738)

SHARPEY-SCHAFER, Prof John Francis; s of Prof (Edward) Peter Sharpey-Schafer (d 1964), and Joyce Frances, *née* Adlard; *b* 29 Nov 1938; *Educ* Cheltenham GS, King's Coll Cambridge (BA), Univ of Liverpool (PhD); *m* 1, 14 June 1961 (m dis 1972), Susan Langdale, da of Dr Louis Fitch (d 1950); 2 s (Ben b 27 Feb 1962, Oliver b 16 Dec 1965), 1 da (Hannah b 23 Aug 1963); m 2, 11 Nov 1972, Sylvia Anne, da of Joseph Bosonnet, of Liverpool; 1 s (Kieren b 7 Oct 1982), 2 da (Siobhan b 6 Jan 1974, Barbra b 24 July 1976); *Career* Univ of Liverpool: ICI fell 1963–64, lectr in physics 1964–73, sr lectr 1973–78, reader 1978–88, prof of physics 1988–95; dir National Accelerator Centre South Africa 1995–; sec and chm Edge Hill constituency Lab Pty 1974–80, memb Nuclear Physics Bd SERC 1986–89; FInstP 1974; *Recreations* pursuing beautiful ladies, preferably the wife; *Style*— Prof John Sharpey-Schafer; ✉ National Accelerator Centre, PO Box 72, Faure, ZA-7131 South Africa (☎ 00 27 24 843 3820, fax 00 27 24 843 3525)

SHARPLES, Brian; s of Richard Sharples (d 1960), Bamber Bridge, Preston, and Mary Phyllis, *née* Carr (d 1987); *b* 18 Sept 1936; *Educ* Hutton GS, Harris Tech Coll Preston, Coll of Estate Mgmnt; *m* Annie, da of Joseph Marginson; 3 s (Ian Richard b 14 July 1963, Deryck Alan b 24 Dec 1964, Graeme Brian b 7 May 1966); *Career* quantity surveyor and project mangr with BDP 1961–95 (latterly mgmnt ptnr Manchester office); work incl: Owens Park devpt for Univ of Manchester and Edge Hill Coll Ormskirk, Northwich Town Centre redevpt, Queens Med Centre and Teaching Hosp, Northgate Arena Leisure Centre, study for proposed Design Test and Research Facility Leyland Cars Solihull, St James Hosp Leeds Clinical Sciences Building, Ashworth Special Hosp Liverpool, Leeds Gen Infirmary Phase 1, Fermentation Pilot Plant Wilts, Birkenhead Town Centre shopping devpt, Canary Wharf London shopping devpt, project ptnr for J P Morgan Bank's new HQ at 60 Victoria Embankment London, project mgmnt ptnr CAA NERC devpt Southampton and Harris student residences Manchester; project dir Worcester Royal Infirmary NHS Tst 1995–96; FRICS, ACIArb, memb IQA; *Recreations* golf, general aviation pilot, property development; *Style*— Brian Sharples, Esq

SHARPLES, Hon Christopher John; s of Baroness Sharples, *qv*, and Sir Richard Sharples, KCMG, OBE, MC (assass 1973); *b* 24 May 1947; *Educ* Eton, Business Sch of Neuchatel; *m* 1975, Sharon, da of late Robert Sweeny, DFC; 3 children; *Career* VSO India 1965–66; C Czarnikow Ltd (sugar brokers) 1968–72, co fndr and dir Inter Commodities Ltd (brokers in futures and options, renamed GNI Ltd in 1984 following partial acquisition by Gerrard & National plc) 1972–, chm ICV Ltd (vendors of real-time financial data incl London Stock Exchange trading system) 1981–, dir Intercom Data Systems Ltd (systems integration house) 1982–90, vice chm International Petroleum Exchange 1986–87 (dir 1981–87), dir Hiscox Dedicated Insurance Fund PLC 1995–96; chm: Assoc of Futures Brokers and Dealers (self-regulatory body designated under Fin Servs Act 1986) 1987–91, Securities and Futures Authy 1991–95; memb Takeover Panel 1991–95; served Ctees: London Commodity Exchange (PR), London International Financial Futures Exchange (Clearing), Br Fedn of Commodity Assocs (Taxation), London Commodity Exchange Regulatory Advsy Gp, Advsy Panel Securities and Investmts Bd 1986; MSI; *Recreations* sailing, flying; *Clubs* Royal Yacht Squadron, Air Squadron, White's; *Style*— The Hon Christopher Sharples; ✉ 72 Elm Park Rd, London SW3 6AU (☎ 0171 352 3791, office ☎ 0171 337 3500)

SHARPLES, Baroness (Life Peer UK 1973), of Chawton in Hampshire; Pamela Swan; da of Lt Cdr Keith William Newall, RN (d 1937), and Violet Ruby, *née* Ashton (who m 2, Lord Claud Nigel Hamilton, GCVO, CMG, DSO, s of 2 Duke of Abercorn, and d 1986); *b* 11 Feb 1923; *Educ* Southover Manor Lewes, Florence Italy; *m* 1, 1946, Sir Richard Christopher Sharples, KCMG, OBE, MC, govr of Bermuda (assass in Bermuda 1973), s of Richard William Sharples, OBE; 2 s (Hon Christopher John Sharples, *qv* b 1947, Hon David Richard b 1955), 2 da (Hon Fiona (Hon Mrs Paterson) b 1949, Hon Miranda (Hon Mrs Larkins) b 1951); m 2, 1977, Patrick David de Laszlo (d 1980); m 3, 1983, (Robert) Douglas Swan (d 1995); *Career* served WAAF 1941–46, Armed Forces Pay Review Bd 1979–81; sits as Cons peer in House of Lords; chm TVS Tst 1981–92; *Recreations* golf, tennis, gardening; *Clubs* Royal Cape Golf SA, Mid Ocean Bermuda, Ladies Parliamentary Golf Association; *Style*— The Rt Hon the Lady Sharples; ✉ 60 Westminster Gdns, Marsham St, London SW1P 4JG (☎ 0171 821 1875); Well Cottage, Higher Coombe, Shaftesbury, Dorset SP7 9LR (☎ 01747 852971)

SHARPLES, Prof Robert William; s of William Arthur Sharples (d 1988), of Meopham, Kent, and Joan Catherine, *née* Affleck; *b* 28 May 1949; *Educ* Dulwich Trinity Coll Cambridge (MA, PhD); *m* 24 July 1976, Grace Elizabeth, da of William Nevard (d 1979), of Mill Hill, London; 1 da (Elizabeth b 1984); *Career* res fell Fitzwilliam Coll Cambridge 1972–73; UCL: lectr in Greek and Latin 1973–91, reader in Greek and Latin 1991–94, prof of classics 1994–; sec Cncl of Univ Classical Depts 1983–87; ed Phronesis 1993–; *Books* Alexander of Aphrodisias on Fate (1983), Plato - Meno (1985), Alexander of Aphrodisias - Ethical Problems (1990), Cicero On Fate and Boethius Consolation of Philosophy (1991), Alexander of Aphrodisias - Quaestiones (1992 and 1994), Theophrastus of Eresus (co-author, 1992 and 1995), Stoics, Epicureans and Sceptics (1996); *Recreations* computing, model railways; *Style*— Prof Robert Sharples; ✉ Department of Greek and Latin, University College London, Gower Street, London WC1E 6BT (☎ 0171 380 7492, fax 0171 209 2324, e-mail r.sharples@ucl.ac.uk)

SHARROCK, Ivan; s of William Arthur Sharrock, and Gladys Muriel, *née* Roberts; *b* 17 July 1941; *Educ* Newquay GS, Cornwall Tech Coll; *m* 5 Oct 1974, Suzanne Jacqueline Clare, da of Jack Cecil Edward Haig, of Sutton Coldfield; 1 s (Sky Kelly Ivan b 1975); *Career* sound recordist; memb: Acad of Motion Picture Arts and Sciences, Cinema Audio Soc (USA), BAFTA, BECTU, BKSTS, IATSE Local 659; joined BBC 1961, trained in film sound techniques at Ealing Film Studios 1961–64, outside broadcasts BBC TV 1964–65, freelance sound mixer with Alan King Assocs 1965–81; *Films* has recorded over 60 feature films incl: The Shining, The French Lieutenant's Woman 1981 (Br Acad Award), Greystoke 1984 (Br Acad nomination), The Last Emperor 1987 (Oscar), The Sheltering Sky, Patriot Games, Little Buddha 1993, Mary Shelly's Frankenstein 1994, The Saint 1996; *Recreations* sailing, skiing, windsurfing, music, reading; *Style*— Ivan Sharrock, Esq; ✉ 9 Burghley Road, London NW5 1UG (☎ 0171 267 3170 and 0171 284 4306, fax 0171 284 4250)

SHATTOCK, David John; CBE (1995), QPM (1985); s of Herbert John Shattock (d 1966), and Lucy Margaret, *née* Williams (d 1957); *b* 25 Jan 1936; *Educ* Huish's GS, RCDS; *m* 1, 1956 (m dis 1973); 3 s (Gerard David b 1959, Matthew John b 1962, Julian David William b 1972); m 2, 1 Nov 1973, Freda, da of late William Henry Thums; *Career* Nat Serv RN 1954–56; joined Somerset Constabulary 1956, rising to asst chief constable Avon and Somerset Constabulary 1977; dep chief constable Wilts Constabulary 1983–85; chief constable: Dyfed-Powys Police 1986–89, Avon and Somerset Constabulary 1989–; memb: ACPO, St John Cncl Avon; dir The Bristol Initiative, vice pres Bristol Soc, vice chm Police Athletic Assoc; OStJ 1989; *Recreations* badminton, horse riding, tennis, antique restoration; *Clubs* Shakespeare (Bristol), Bristol Savages; *Style*— David Shattock, Esq, CBE, QPM; ✉ Police Headquarters, PO Box 37, Valley Road, Portishead, Bristol BS20 8QJ (☎ 01275 818181)

SHATTOCK, Sir Gordon; kt (1985); s of Frederick Thomas Shattock (d 1974), of Exeter, Devon, and Rose May Irene, *née* James (d 1988); *b* 12 May 1928; *Educ* Hele's Sch Exeter, RVC London (MRCVS 1951); *m* 17 July 1952, Jeanne Mary (d 1984), da of Austin Edwin Watkins (d 1970), of Exeter; 1 s (Simon John b 1954), 1 da (Clare Lucinda b 1956); m 2, 17 Sept 1988, Mrs David Sale (wid); *Career* sr ptnr St David Veterinary Hosp Exeter 1951–84, dir and vice chm Veterinary Drug Co plc 1982–, divnl bursar Western Area Woodard Sch's 1988–; fndr chm (pres 1989–93) Devon Euro Constituency Cons Cncl; chm: Western Area Cons Pty (Avon, Somerset, Devon and Cornwall) 1982–85 (pres 1989–92), local Cancer Res Campaign 1972–88, Grenville Coll and memb Sch Cncl 1973–88, Exeter Cathedral Music Fndn 1985–; fell Woodward Corp of Schs 1973–88, pres Br Veterinary Hosps Assoc 1974; memb: Exec Cncl Animal Health Tst 1974–, Exeter Health Authy 1985–93, Political Advsy Bd TSW 1985–90, Exec Cncl Guide Dogs for the Blind 1985–; hon memb Br Veterinary Assoc 1989; Freeman City of London 1978, Liveryman Worshipful Co of Farriers (Master 1992–93, memb Ct of Assts); FRSA 1990, Hon FRVC 1994; *Recreations* gardening, restoration of old houses; *Clubs* RSM; *Style*— Sir Gordon Shattock; ✉ Lea House, Bishopsteignton, nr Teignmouth TQ14 9TP (☎ 01626 778888)

SHAUGHNESSY, Alfred James; s of Capt the Hon Alfred T Shaughnessy (ka France 1916), of Montreal, and late Sarah Polk, *née* Bradford (later Lady Legh), of Nashville, Tennessee; *b* 19 May 1916; *Educ* Eton, RMC Sandhurst; *m* 18 Sept 1948, Jean Margaret, da of George Lodge (d 1951), of Kirkella, Hull, Yorks; 2 s (Charles George Patrick b 9 Feb 1955, David James Bradford b 3 March 1957); *Career* playwright, director and screenwriter; WWII cmmnd Capt Grenadier Gds; served 1940–46: Normandy, Belgium, Holland, Germany, demobbed Maj 1946; author of 14 stage plays incl: Release, Holiday for Simon, The Tea-Cosy, Breaking Point, The Heat of the Moment, Old Herbaceous, Love Affair, Double Cut; author of numerous screenplays for films, TV plays, songs and sketches for West End revues and radio plays; nominated US Emmy 1974 and 1975 (scripts for TV series Upstairs, Downstairs), nominated US TV Critics' Circle for Achievement in Writing Award 1976 and 1977; memb Exec Cncl Writers' Guild of GB 1982–88; *Books* Both Ends of the Candle (autobiography, 1978), Sarah, Letters and Diaries of a Courtier's Wife 1906–1936 (1989); novels: Dearest Enemy (1990), Hugo (1994); *Recreations* piano, gardening, walking; *Clubs* Garrick; *Style*— Alfred Shaughnessy, Esq; ✉ The Grange, Yattendon, Thatcham, Berks RG18 0UE; (☎ 01635 201741)

SHAUGHNESSY, 3 Baron (UK 1916); William Graham Shaughnessy; CD; s of 2 Baron (d 1938); 1 Baron Shaughnessy was pres of Canadian Pacific Railway 1899–1918 and chm 1918–23; *b* 28 March 1922; *Educ* Bishop's Coll Sch, Bishop's Univ Lennoxville Canada (BA), Columbia Univ (MSc); *m* 1944, Mary, da of John Whitley (d 1953), of Letchworth, Herts; 1 s (and 1 s decd), 2 da; *Heir* s, Hon Michael Shaughnessy; *Career* WWII Canadian Grenadier Gds, Canadian Army 1941–46, served UK and NW Europe (despatches), ret Maj; co dir; dir: Canada NW Energy Ltd 1955–83 (vice-pres 1969–82), Arbor Memorial Services (Toronto) 1973–, Eurogas Corp (Calgary); tstee Last Post Fund of Canada, pres Royal Cwlth Soc Montreal 1959–61; *Recreations* history, fishing; *Clubs* Cavalry & Guards', University (Montreal), Montreal Racket; *Style*— The Rt Hon the Lord Shaughnessy; ✉ House of Lords, London SW1

SHAVE, Alan William; CVO (1994), OBE (1991); s of William Alfred Shave (d 1990), and Emily, *née* Pullinger (d 1996); *b* 3 Nov 1936; *Educ* George Green's GS Poplar London, Nat Cncl of Journalists (cert); *m* 16 Dec 1961, Lidia Donoso Bertolotto, da of Señor Gumercindo Donoso (d 1993); 1 da (Alison Patricia Anne b 1966), 1 s (David Alan b 1967); *Career* Nat Serv RAF 1957–59; journalist: East London Advertiser 1953–57, Greenock Telegraph 1960, Bristol Evening World 1961; asst information offr Central Office of Information 1961; Cwlth Relations Office (later FCO/Diplomatic Serv): High Cmmn Salisbury Rhodesia 1961–62, High Cmmn Dar es Salaam Tanganyika 1962–64, consulate gen Sydney 1964–66, Embassy La Paz Bolivia 1966–70, FCO 1970–72, Embassy Santiago Chile 1972–76, consulate gen Barcelona 1977–81, consulate gen Milan 1981–84, FCO 1984–88, Embassy La Paz Bolivia 1988–92, govr Anguilla 1992–95, rep for Bolivia Br Exec Service Overseas 1996–; *Recreations* cycle racing, ornithology, travel; *Style*— Alan Shave, Esq, CVO, OBE; ✉ Casilla 3–35183, San Miguel (Calacoto), La Paz, Bolivia

SHAVE, Prof Michael John Ramage; s of Leslie Herbert Shave (d 1982), of Stockport, and Edith Maud, *née* Ramage (d 1957); *b* 10 Aug 1934; *Educ* George Watson's Sch Edinburgh, Hymers Coll Hull, Manchester GS, Wadham Coll Oxford (MA), Univ of Bristol (PhD); *m* 30 July 1959, Ann Morag, da of Donald Kirkpatrick (d 1975), of Manchester; 1 s (Peter Kirkpatrick b 1961), 1 da (Susan Elizabeth b 1964); *Career* asst master: St Edward's Sch Oxford 1957–59, Rugby Sch 1959–64; sr lectr Univ of Bristol 1978–82 (lectr 1964–78), prof of computer sci Univ of Liverpool 1983–; chm Merseyside Branch BCS 1955–88; vice chm Northern Examination and Assessment Bd; Royal Soc Euro fell Université de Grenoble 1978, MBCS 1967, FRSA 1985, CEng 1992; *Books* Data Structures (1975), Computer Service Applied to Business Systems (1982); *Recreations* theatre, concerts, caravanning; *Style*— Prof Michael Shave; ✉ Department of Computer Science, University of Liverpool, PO Box 147, Liverpool L69 3BX (☎ 0151 794 3667, fax 0151 794 3715, telex 627095 UNILPL G)

SHAVE, Terry; *b* 8 June 1952, Suffolk; *Educ* Ipswich Sch of Art, Loughborough Coll of Art (BA), Slade Sch London (higher dip in fine art); *Career* artist; currently head Fine Art Dept Staffordshire Univ; *Solo Exhibitions* Staffordshire Poly Gallery 1983, Some Kind of Eden (Morley Gallery London) 1983, The Minories Colchester (and tour) 1985, Notes from an Ordinary Hell (Ikon Gallery Birmingham) 1986, The Fall to Pandemonium series (Gallery N Kirby Lonsdale Cumbria) 1989, Anderson O'Day Gallery London 1990, Wolf-at-the-Door Gallery Penzance Cornwall 1990, Accumulations (City Museum and Art Gallery Stoke-on-Trent) 1993, Tour to Mead Gallery (Warwick Univ) 1993, Works on Paper (Midlands Contemporary Art Birmingham) 1993, Behind the View (Ainscough Gallery Liverpool) 1995, Loaded (Ikon Gallery Birmingham) 1996; *Group Exhibitions* incl: British Printmaking Now (Thumb Gallery London) 1978, Six Attitudes to Print (Aspex Gallery Portsmouth) 1982, 4th Tolly Cobbold/Eastern Arts Nat Exhibition (prizewinner) 1983, Place (Gimpel Fils London) 1983, John Moores Liverpool Exhibition 15 (prizewinner) 1987, The Presence of Painting (S Bank Centre/Arts Cncl touring) 1989, The Language of Landscape (Anderson O'Day London) 1990, 4 UK Artists (Norlino Gallery NY) 1990, Landscape Visions (selected by Peter Fuller, Pears Gallery Aldeburgh Suffolk) 1990, A Tribute to Peter Fuller (Beaux-Arts Bath) 1990, 11th Bradford Int Print Biennale (RCA London) 1991, Beyond the Wow Factor (New York State Univ USA) 1993, first Harlech Int Contemporary Art Exhibition (invited artist) 1994, Foreign Bodies (Shinjuki Cultural Centre Tokyo Japan) 1996, Warming Up (Arcus Nurnberg Germany) 1996; *Work in Public and Corporate Collections* Arts Cncl of GB, Ipswich Corp, Birmingham Museum and Art Gallery, Stoke-on-Trent Museum and Art Gallery,

Bedfordshire CC, St Thomas's Hosp London, Colgate/Palmolive Ltd, Unilever Ltd, Coopers & Lybrand Ltd, Warwick Univ; work subject of numerous exhibition catalogues, magazine and newspaper articles; *Style*— Terry Shave, Esq; ✉ 19 Park Ave, Wolstanton, Newcastle-under-Lyme, Staffordshire ST5 8AX

SHAW, Maj-Gen Anthony John (Tony); CB (1988), CBE (1985); s of Lt-Col William Arthur Shaw, MC (d 1962), and Ethel, *née* Malley (d 1980); *b* 13 July 1930; *Educ* Epsom Coll, Clare Coll Cambridge (MA, MB BChir), Westminster Hosp (MRCS, LRCP 1954); *m* 12 Aug 1961, Gillian, da of Dr Thomas Arthur Best (d 1974), of Ripley, Yorks; 1 s (David b 1965), 1 da (Fiona b 1963); *Career* cmmnd Lt RAMC 1956, Staff Coll Camberley 1963, served 1956–69 in BAOR, MOD, UK, Malta, Berlin, Malaya, Nepal, Penang, Cameron Highlands, CO Field Ambulance 1969–70, chief instr RAMC Trg Centre 1970–72, NDC 1973, ADGAMS MOD 1973–76, CO Cambridge MH 1977–79, Cdr Med 2 Armd Div BAOR 1979–81 (SE Dist UK 1981), Brig dir of med supply MOD 1981–83, DDGAMS 1983–84, Cdr med UKLF (Maj-Gen) 1985–87, Dir Army Community and Occupational Med 1983–87, DG Army Med Servs 1988–90, civilian med practitioner (MOD) 1991–; pres Standing Med Bd Aldershot; CStJ 1989 (OStJ 1975); DRCOG 1959, DTM & H 1961, FFCM (1983, MFCM 1973), FRCP 1989, fell Med Soc of London; *Recreations* sailing, golf, bridge, gardening; *Clubs* Landsdowne; *Style*— Maj-Gen Tony Shaw, CB, CBE

SHAW, Antony Michael Ninian; QC (1994); s of Harold Anthony Shaw, of Newhaven, Sussex, and Edith Beatrice Sanbach, *née* Holmes, of Iden Green, Kent; *b* 4 Oct 1948; *Educ* King's Sch Canterbury, Trinity Coll Oxford (major history scholar, BA juris); *m* Louise Göta, da of Louis Carl Faugust (d 1971); 1 s (James William Hugo b 19 Jan 1984), 2 da (Antonia Elizabeth Göta b 21 June 1985, Olivia Louise Beatrice b 22 Aug 1990); *Career* res in constitutional law and human rights in Anglophonic Africa financed by Ford Fndn 1970–71, res offr Legal Res Unit Bedford Coll London 1972–75, called to the Bar Middle Temple 1975 (Astbury scholar), visiting lectr London Coll of Printing 1975–76, pupillage 1976, tenancy at 4 Brick Ct chambers of Barbara Calvert, QC, 1977, head of chambers 4 Brick Ct 1988–; criminal defence work including drugs and serious fraud; vice chm Legal Aid and Fees Ctee Bar Cncl 1995–, memb Criminal Bar Assoc; contrib to numerous publications and jls; *Books* Archbold's Criminal Pleadings and Practice (co-ed, 1990–); *Recreations* history, reading; *Style*— Antony Shaw, QC; ✉ 4 Brick Court, Temple, London EC4Y 9AD (☎ 0171 797 7766, fax 0171 797 7700)

SHAW, Sir (Charles) Barry; kt (1980), CB (1974), QC (1964), DL (Co Down 1990); *b* 12 April 1923; *Career* called to the Bar: NI 1948 (bencher 1968), Middle Temple 1970 (hon bencher 1986); dir of Public Prosecutions for NI 1972–89; memb Panel of Chairmen of VAT Tbnls for NI 1991–; *Style*— Sir Barry Shaw, CB, QC, DL; ✉ c/o Royal Courts of Justice, Belfast, Northern Ireland BT1 3NX

SHAW, Prof Bernard Leslie; s of Tom Shaw (d 1971), and Vera (d 1989), *née* Dale; *b* 28 March 1930; *Educ* Hulme GS Oldham, Univ of Manchester (BSc, PhD); *m* 2 June 1951, Mary Elizabeth, da of William Birdsall Neild; 3 s (John Ewart Hardern b 1953, Andrew b and d 1956, Jonathan Bernard b 1960); *Career* sci offr Civil Serv 1953–56, res sci ICI 1956–61, prof Univ of Leeds 1971– (lectr 1962–66, reader 1966–71); FRS 1978; *Recreations* tennis, pottery; *Style*— Prof Bernard Shaw, FRS; ✉ 14 Monkbridge Rd, Leeds LS6 4DX (☎ 0113 275 5895); School of Chemistry, University of Leeds, Leeds LS2 9JT (☎ 0113 233 6401, fax 0113 233 6562, e-mail B.L.Shaw@chem.Leeds.ac.uk)

SHAW, Sir Brian Piers; kt (1986); s of late Percy Augustus Shaw; *b* 21 March 1933; *Educ* Wrekin Coll, CCC Cambridge; *m* 1962, Penelope Gay, *née* Reece; 3 s; *Career* chm Furness Withy & Co 1979–90 (md 1977–87), chm ANZ Grindlays Bank 1987–95; chm Cncl of Euro and Japanese Nat Shipowners' Assocs 1979–84, pres Gen Cncl of Br Shipping 1985–86; chm: Int Chamber of Shipping 1987–92, Port of London Authy 1993–, The Automobile Association Dec 1995– (vice chm 1993–95); non-exec dir Enterprise Oil plc 1986–; past Prime Warden Worshipful Co of Shipwrights; *Recreations* golf, theatre, music; *Clubs* Brooks's, MCC, Denham Golf; *Style*— Sir Brian Shaw; ✉ The Coach House, Biddestone, Wiltshire SN14 7DQ (☎ 01249 713112)

SHAW, (Norman) Carey; s of Norman Henry Shaw, of Wrexham and Swansea, and Mair, *née* Jenkins; *b* 6 May 1940; *Educ* Grove Park GS, Wrexham, Charing Cross Hosp (MB BS); *m* 18 July 1964, Mary Fitzgerald, da of Harold Clarke, of Melton Constable; 3 s (Jeremy b 1968, Timothy b 1970, Jonathan b 1974); *Career* conslt orthopaedic surgn King's Lynn 1974–; memb Central Ctee for Hosp Med Servs 1977–80, chm E Anglian Orthopaedic Advsy Ctee 1984–87, surgical tutor RCS King's Lynn 1984–89, pres W Norfolk and King's Lynn Div BMA 1988–89; FRCS 1970; *Recreations* flying (light aircraft), sailing, photography, computers; *Style*— Carey Shaw, Esq; ✉ Chestnut Byre, Manor Farm, Harpley, King's Lynn (☎ 01485 520646); Orthopaedic Dept, The Queen Elizabeth Hospital, Gayton Rd, King's Lynn PE30 4ET (☎ 01553 613685)

SHAW, Charles de Vere; s of late Capt John Frederick de Vere Shaw, yr s of 6 Bt; hp of unc, Sir Robert Shaw, 7 Bt; *b* 1 March 1957; *Educ* Michaelhouse S Africa; *m* 1985, Sonia, elder da of Thomas Geoffrey Eden, of Wrecclesham, nr Farnham, Surrey; 1 s (Robert Jonathan de Vere b 1988), 1 da (Alexandra Frances b 1986); *Career* businessman; *Recreations* expeditions, sport and wine; *Style*— Charles Shaw, Esq; ✉ Pigeon Farmhouse, Greenham, Newbury, Berks RG19 8SP

SHAW, Prof Charles Timothy (Tim); s of Charles John Shaw (d 1985), and Constance Olive, *née* Scotton (d 1961); *b* 10 Oct 1934; *Educ* Diocesan Coll Rondebosch Cape SA, Witwatersrand Univ (BSc), McGill Univ Montreal Canada (MSc); *m* 1 Sept 1962, Tuulike Raili, da of Dr Artur Aleksander Linari-Linholm (d 1984); 1 s (Jeffrey Charles b 15 Sept 1973), 2 da (Karen b 1 Sept 1963, Nicolette b 29 Jan 1966); *Career* Johannesburg Consolidated Investment Co Group: employed variously 1960–65, head of computing 1966–69, mangr 1969–71, consulting engr (Randfontein Estates, GM Co Ltd, Consolidated Murchison Ltd) 1971–73; consulting engr and dir Rustenburg Platinum Mines Ltd 1973–75, chief consulting engr and alternative dir JCI 1975–77, md Western Areas Gold Mining Co Ltd 1975–77; assoc prof Virginia Poly Inst and State Univ Blacksburg Virginia USA 1977–80, prof of mining Royal Sch of Mines Imperial Coll London 1980– (dean 1991–95); chm Special Sub Ctee on Engrg Qualifications Mining Qualifications Bd 1986–87, ed Mineral Resources Engineering 1988–; memb: Professional Engrs 1977, Scientific Ctee Inst for Archaeo-Metallurgical Studies 1982–92, Safety in Mines Res Advsy Bd UK 1985–88, Ctee of Mgmnt Inst of Archaeology 1985–87, Cncl Royal Sch of Mines Assoc 1982 (pres 1988–89); sec gen Societät der Bergbaukunde (Soc of Mining Professors) 1990–; govr Camborne Sch of Mines 1982–90; fell: South African Inst of Mining and Metallurgy 1961, Inst of Mining and Metallurgy 1980 (memb Cncl 1981–88 and 1989–), Inst of Mining Engrs 1981 (memb Cncl 1988–, pres Southern Counties Branch 1988–89 and 1990–91), Inst of Quarrying 1981; Hon PhD Miskolc University Hungary 1995; CEng 1980; *Style*— Prof Tim Shaw; ✉ Imperial Coll of Science, Technology and Medicine, South Kensington, London SW7 (☎ 0171 589 5111 ext 6401, fax 0171 589 6806)

SHAW, Chris Thomas; s of John Dennis Bolton Shaw (d 1989), of Sussex, and Isabel, *née* Loewe (d 1985); *b* 19 June 1957; *Educ* Westminster, Balliol Coll Oxford; *Career* trainee LBC 1980–81, bulletin ed Independent Radio News 1981–85, chief sub-ed ITN 1987–89 (writer 1985–87), sr prodr Sky News 1990–91; ITN: rejoined 1992, foreign and home news ed Channel 4 News 1992–93, prog ed News at Ten 1993–96, ed ITN news service for Channel 5 1996–; *Style*— Chris Shaw, Esq; ✉ ITN Ltd, 200 Gray's Inn Road, London WC1X 8XZ (☎ 0171 430 4100)

SHAW, Colin Don; CBE (1993); s of Rupert Morris Shaw (d 1980), and Enid Fryer, *née* Smith (d 1955); *b* 2 Nov 1928; *Educ* Liverpool Coll, St Peter's Coll Oxford (BA, MA); *m* 1955, Elizabeth Ann, da of Paul Alan Bowker; 1 s (Giles), 2 da (Tessa, Susan); *Career* called to the Bar Inner Temple 1960; chief sec BBC 1972–76, dir of TV IBA 1977–83, dir Programme Planning Secretariat ITCA 1983–87, dir Broadcasting Standards Cncl 1988–April 1996, ret; memb Arts Cncl 1977–80, govr ESU 1977–83; author of various radio plays and a stage play for children; *Clubs* Reform; *Style*— Colin Shaw, Esq, CBE; ✉ Lesters, Little Ickford, Aylesbury, Bucks HP18 9HS (☎ 01844 339225, fax 01844 338351)

SHAW, (Brian) David; s of Stanley and Sheila Shaw, of Durham; *Educ* Univ of Bradford (BSc, Dip in Mktg); *m* 2 July 1983, Janet; 1 da (Holly b 20 March 1986), 1 s (Alexander b 14 Oct 1987); *Career* Reckitt & Colman: brand mangr 1980–84, market devpt mangr 1984–87, mktg mangr Germany 1987–90, int devpt mangr 1990–92, UK mktg mangr 1992–94, dir of mktg Reckitt & Colman Household Products 1994–; MInstM 1982; *Recreations* running (County Senior Schools 100m champion 1976 and 1977), yoga, tai chi, windsurfing and family; *Style*— David Shaw, Esq; ✉ Reckitt & Colman Household Products Ltd, Dansom Lane, Hull HU8 7DS (☎ 01482 326151, fax 01482 583817)

SHAW, Prof David Aitken; CBE (1989); s of Col John James McIntosh Shaw, MC (d 1940), and Mina, *née* Draper (d 1979); *b* 11 April 1924; *Educ* Edinburgh Acad, Univ of Edinburgh (MB ChB); *m* 22 Oct 1960, Jill, da of Eric Parry, CBE, of Lydiate; 1 s (Andrew b 1965), 2 da (Alison b 1963, Katriona b 1969); *Career* WWII RNVR; Ordinary Seaman 1943, Sub Lt 1944, Lt 1946; lectr in clinical neurology Inst of Neurology Univ of London 1957; Univ of Newcastle upon Tyne: sr lectr in neurology 1964–76, prof of clinical neurology 1976–89, dean of med 1981–89; FRCP 1976, FRCPE 1968, Hon FCST 1988; *Clubs* Athenaeum; *Style*— Prof David Shaw, CBE; ✉ The Coach House, Moor Rd North, Gosforth, Newcastle Upon Tyne NE3 1AB (☎ 0191 285 2029)

SHAW, David Baxter; s of John Knowles Shaw (d 1967), of Sheffield, and Dorothy, *née* Baxter (d 1994); *b* 6 Aug 1936; *Educ* Trent Coll; *m* 14 March 1964, Margaret Mary, da of Walter Edward Moore (d 1976), of Sheffield; 3 da (Katharine b 1964, Elizabeth b 1966, Victoria b 1968); *Career* Nat Serv Lt RA 1959–61; articled Jarvis Barber & Sons 1953–58; ptnr: Forsdike Paterson & Co 1962–67, Moore Fletcher Forsdike & Shaw 1968–75, sr ptnr Shaw Dunk Styring 1975–91, sr ptnr then conslt Hart Shaw 1991–; chm The Manchester Hosiery Gp 1985–; memb Cncl and chm Investigation Ctee ICAEW 1993–, pres Sheffield and Dist Soc of CAs 1976–77; memb Nat Cncl and chm Sheffield Branch IOD 1985–89; memb S Yorks Ctee Prince's Youth Business Tst 1989–; pres Rotary Club of Sheffield 1982; lay treas Sheffield Cathedral 1993–; Freeman: Co of Cutlers in Hallamshire 1974, City of London 1978; Master Worshipful Co of CAs in England and Wales 1989–90 (Liveryman 1978, memb Ct 1979–, Almoner 1991–); FCA 1959; *Recreations* the family, travel, motoring, swimming, photography; *Clubs* Army and Navy; *Style*— David Shaw, Esq; ✉ Kireka House, 527 Fulwood Rd, Sheffield S10 3QB (☎ 0114 230 6431); Hart Shaw, 346 Glossop Rd, Sheffield S10 2HW (☎ 0114 273 8551, fax 0114 276 0934)

SHAW, David Lawrence; MP (C) Dover (majority 833); *b* 14 Nov 1950; *Educ* King's Sch Wimbledon, City of London Poly; *m* 1986, Dr Lesley Christine Shaw, *née* Brown; 1 s (James b 1989), 1 da (Annabel b 1994); *Career* with Coopers & Lybrand 1971–79, County Bank 1979–83, fndr and md Sabrelance Ltd 1983–; The Adscene Group plc; joined Cons Pty 1970, cncllr Royal Borough of Kingston upon Thames 1974–78, Parly Candidate (C) Leigh 1979, vice chm Kingston and Malden Cons Assoc 1979–86, chm Bow Gp 1983–84, MP (C) Dover 1987–; memb Social Security Select Ctee, vice chm Cons Pty Fin Ctee and chm Smaller Businesses Ctee, co-chm All-Pty Dolphin Protection Gp, fndr Bow Gp/Ripon Soc Transatlantic Confs; FCA (ACA 1974); *Style*— David Shaw, Esq, MP; ✉ House of Commons, London SW1A OAA

SHAW, Dr Dennis Frederick; CBE (1974); s of Albert Shaw (d 1957), of Kenton, Middx, and Lily Florence, *née* Hill (d 1968); *b* 20 April 1924; *Educ* Harrow Co Sch, ChCh Oxford, (BA, MA, DPhil); *m* 25 June 1949, Joan Irene, da of Sydney Chandler; 1 s (Peter James b 1951), 3 da (Margaret b 1953, Katherine b 1956, Deborah b 1959); *Career* memb Civil Def Corps 1942–45, jr sci offr MAP 1944–46; Univ of Oxford: demonstrator in physics 1946–49, res offr 1950–57, lectr in physics 1957–75, keeper of sci books 1975–91, professorial fell Keble Coll 1977–91 (fell and tutor in physics 1957–75), emeritus fell 1991; visiting prof of physics Univ of S Tennessee USA 1974, pres Int Assoc of Technol Univ Libraries 1986–90, chm Sci and Technol Libraries Section IFLA 1987–91 (hon treas Special Libraries Ctee IFLA 1991–93, conslt 1993–); memb Press Ctee Int Cncl of Scientific Unions 1991–; memb Oxford City Cncl 1963–67; Home Office: memb Sci Advsy Cncl 1966–78, chm Police Sci Devpt Ctee 1970–74, memb Def Sci Advsy Ctee 1968–95; memb Hebdomadal Cncl Oxford Univ 1980–89; Almoner Christ's Hosp 1980– (chm Educn Ctee 1993–); memb: APS 1957, NYAS 1981; FZS 1970, FInstP 1971, CPhys 1984; *Books* Introduction to Electronics (2nd edn, 1970), Oxford University Science Libraries (2nd edn, 1981), Information Sources in Physics (1985, 3rd edn 1994); *Recreations* enjoying music; *Clubs* Utd Oxford and Cambridge Univ; *Style*— Dr Dennis Shaw, CBE; ✉ Keble College, Oxford OX1 3PG (☎ 01865 272727, fax 01865 272705)

SHAW, Dr Donald George; s of George Shaw (d 1974), of Coventry, and Jane, *née* Humble (d 1955); *b* 21 June 1937; *Educ* Bablake Sch, Univ of Oxford, UCH (MA, MSc, BM BCh); *m* 8 Feb 1964, Anne Patricia, da of Gp Capt L Crocker, CBE, of London, and Lisbon; 2 da (Caroline b 1968, Katherine b 1971); *Career* conslt radiologist: UCH 1970–82, Hosps for Sick Children 1970–; ed British Journal of Radiology 1989–92 (dep ed 1985–89); examiner: RCR 1978–84, Univ of Malaysia 1989; memb: Faculty Bd RCR 1988–91, Cncl RCR 1991–94, Br Inst of Radiology 1989–92, Cncl Br Inst of Radiology 1995–; DMRD, FRCR, FRCP; *Recreations* gardening, music; *Style*— Dr Donald Shaw; ✉ 37 Sandy Lodge Rd, Moor Park, Rickmansworth WD3 1LP

SHAW, Donald Gordon Brian; *b* 14 Jan 1956; *Educ* Edinburgh Acad, Univ of Aberdeen (LLB); *m* 1981, Catherine Ann Shaw; *Career* articled Shepherd & Wedderburn, qualified 1979, currently dep managing ptnr and head Commercial Property Dept Dundas & Wilson (ptnr 1985–); memb Law Soc of Scotland; *Recreations* music, history, art, wine, travel; *Style*— Donald Shaw, Esq; ✉ Deputy Managing Partner, Dundas & Wilson, Saltire Court, 20 Castle Terrace, Edinburgh EH1 2EN (☎ 0131 228 8000, fax 0131 228 8888)

SHAW, Fiona Mary; da of Dr Denis Joseph Wilson, of Cork, Ireland, and Mary Teresa, *née* Flynn; *b* 10 July 1958; *Educ* Scoil Mhuire Cork, Univ Coll Cork, RADA; *Career* actress; Hon LLD Nat Univ of Ireland 1996; *Theatre* Julia in The Rivals (NT) 1983, Mary Shelley in Bloody Poetry (Leicester and Hampstead) 1984; RSC 1985–88: Tatyana Vasilyevna in Philistines, Celia in As You Like It, Madame de Volange in Les Liaisons Dangereuses, Erika Brückner in Mephisto, Beatrice in Much Ado About Nothing, Portia in The Merchant of Venice, Mistress Carol in Hyde Park, Katherine in The Taming of the Shrew, Lady Frampul in New Inn, title role in Electra (Best Actress Olivier Awards 1989, Theatre Critics's Award 1989); title role in Mary Stuart (Greenwich) 1988, Rosalind in As You Like It (Old Vic, Best Actress Olivier Awards 1989), Shen Te/Shui Ta in The Good Person of Sichuan (NT, London Theatre Critics' Award 1989, Best Actress Olivier Awards 1989), title role in Hedda Gabler 1991 (Abbey Theatre Dublin and Playhouse London, nominated Best Actress Olivier Awards 1992, winner London Theatre Critics' Award 1992), Machinal (RNT, Best Actress Evening Standard Award 1993, Best Actress Olivier Awards 1994), Footfalls (Garrick, 1 week) 1994, title role in

Richard II (RNT) 1995, Millamont in The Way of the World (RNT) 1995, The Wasteland (Paris and Canada) 1996; *Television* incl: Elspeth in Fireworks for Elspeth (Granada) 1983, Hedda Gabler 1993, Persuasion 1994, Jane Eyre 1994, The Waste Land (BBC) 1995; *Films* My Left Foot 1988, The Mountains of the Moon 1988, Three Men and a Little Lady 1990, London Kills Me 1991, Super Mario Brothers 1993, Undercover Blues 1993, Anna Karenina 1996, The Butcher Boy 1996; *Books* Players of Shakespeare (1987), Clamorous Voices (contrib, 1988), Conversation with Actresses (1990); *Recreations* travel, reading, walking; *Style*— Miss Fiona Shaw; ✉ Eglantine, Montenotte, Cork, Ireland

SHAW, George Gavin; s of George Bernard James Shaw, and Audry June Rose, *née* Markwick; *b* 18 June 1957; *Educ* Sir Walter St John's GS, Univ of Bristol (BA); *Career* md: Joslin Shaw Ltd 1984–, Shaw PR Co Ltd 1988–; mktg dir Media Contacts 1993–; chm Ctee Sinjuns Club, chm Old Sinjuns AFC; *Recreations* horse racing, shooting, fishing, association football, skiing; *Clubs* White's, Sinjuns; *Style*— George Shaw, Esq; ✉ Media Contacts, Windsor Centre, Windsor Street, Islington, London N1 8QG (☎ 0171 226 9177, fax 0171 359 6351, car 0860 695555, e-mail geo@joshaw.co.uk)

SHAW, Sir (John) Giles Dunkerley; kt (1987), MP (C) Pudsey (majority 8,972); s of Hugh Dunkerley Shaw; *b* 16 Nov 1931; *Educ* Sedbergh, St John's Coll Cambridge; *m* 1962, Dione Patricia Crosthwaite, da of Prof Mervyn Ellison, of Dublin; 1 s, 2 da; *Career* former pres Cambridge Union; Parly candidate (C) Kingston-on-Hull W 1966, mktg dir Confectionery Div Rowntree Mackintosh Ltd 1969–74; MP (C) Pudsey Feb 1974–; Parly under sec of state: NI Office 1979–81, DOE 1981–83, Dept of Energy 1983–84; min of state: Home Office 1984–86, Dept of Indust 1986–87; treas 1922 Ctee 1988–, memb Speaker's Panel of Chairmen 1989–, chm Select Ctee on Sci and Technol 1992–, memb Ctee of Privileges 1994–96, memb Intelligence and Security Ctee 1994–; non-exec dir British Steel plc 1990–; *Recreations* ornithology, fishing; *Style*— Sir Giles Shaw, MP; ✉ House of Commons, London SW1A 0AA

SHAW, (John) Howard; s of Arthur Shaw, and Edith, *née* Richardson, of Oldham, Lancashire; *b* 6 Sept 1946; *Educ* The Hulme GS Oldham, Bristol Poly (LLB); *m* 30 Dec 1972, Mary Charlotte, da of Rev Charles Strong, MBE (d 1959); 2 s (Alister Cameron, Duncan Howard); *Career* grad entry scheme Tstee and Income Tax Dept National Westminster Bank 1970–72; called to the Bar Inner Temple 1973; 3 Dr Johnson's Bldg: pupillage with Adrianne Uziell-Hamilton then K Machin, QC, 1973–74, in practice 1973–87, admin of chambers 1987–90, head of chambers 1990–; *Style*— Howard Shaw, Esq; ✉ The Chambers of Howard Shaw, 3 Dr Johnson's Buildings, Temple, London EC4Y 7BA (☎ 0171 353 8778, fax 0171 353 1926)

SHAW, Dr James Patrick; s of late Henry Shaw, of Edinburgh, and Thomasina Robertina, *née* Hamilton; *b* 3 Dec 1944; *Educ* George Heriot's Sch Edinburgh, Univ of Edinburgh (BDS, PhD); *m* 6 Aug 1971, Katherine May, da of Walter Hunter Gardiner; 2 da (Barbara Lucy b 2 May 1975, Judith Victoria b 16 Sept 1978); *Career* gen dental practitioner 1968–73; Dept of Anatomy Univ of Edinburgh Med Sch: lectr then sr lectr 1973–, head of dept 1995–; CBiol, MIBiol 1983, FDSRCSEd 1993; *Publications* author of book chapters and numerous articles in learned jls; *Style*— Dr James Shaw; ✉ Department of Anatomy, University of Edinburgh Medical School, Teviot Place, Edinburgh EH8 9AG (☎ 0131 650 2998, fax 0131 650 6545, e-mail James.Shaw@ed.ac.uk)

SHAW, Prof Sir John Calman; kt (1995), CBE (1989); s of Arthur John Shaw (d 1978), of Edinburgh, and Dorothy, *née* Turpie (d 1959); *b* 10 July 1932; *Educ* Strathallan Sch, Univ of Edinburgh (BL); *m* 2 Jan 1960, Shirley, da of James Botterill (d 1936), of Yedingham, Yorkshire; 3 da (Jane b 14 Jan 1961, Gillian b 31 Jan 1963, Catherine b 9 Oct 1966); *Career* local sr ptnr Deloitte Haskins & Sells Edinburgh 1980–86 (ptnr 1960–86), chm Scottish Financial Enterprise 1995– (exec dir 1986–90), dep govr Bank of Scotland 1991– (non-exec dir 1990–); non-exec dir: Scottish Mortgage & Trust plc 1982–, Scottish American Investment Company plc 1986– (chm 1991–), TR European Growth Trust plc 1990–, US Smaller Companies Trust plc 1991– (chm), Templeton Emerging Markets Investment Trust plc 1994–, Templeton Latin America Investment Trust plc 1994–, Scottish Metropolitan Property PLC 1994–, Advanced Management Programme in Scotland Ltd 1995– (chm 1995–), Templeton Central and Eastern European Investment Co 1996; visiting prof Univ of Glasgow 1986– (Johnstone Smith prof of accountancy (pt/t) 1972–82); dir: Scottish Industl Devpt Advsy Bd 1987–95, Financial Reporting Cncl 1990–, Scottish Enterprise 1990–96, Univs Funding Cncl (chm Scot Ctee) 1991–93, Scottish HE Funding Cncl 1992– (chm), HE Funding Cncl for Eng 1992–94, Scottish Economic Council 1996–; chm: Br Section and Monetary Panel Euro League for Economic Co-operation 1992–95, David Hume Inst 1995–; dep chm Edinburgh Int Festival Soc 1990–; KStJ 1994; CA 1954 (pres 1983–84), FCMA 1958, MBCS 1975, FRSE 1992; *Books* The Audit Report (1980), Bogie Group Accounts (3 edn, 1973); *Recreations* walking, opera, foreign travel; *Clubs* New (Edinburgh), Western (Glasgow), Caledonian; *Style*— Prof Sir John Shaw, CBE, FRSE; ✉ Bank of Scotland, Head Office, The Mound, Edinburgh EH1 1YZ (☎ 0131 243 5511, fax 0131 243 5546, telex 72275)

SHAW, John Dennis; s of Frederick Shaw, of Chapeltown, Sheffield, and Dorothy, *née* Wilson (d 1958); *b* 11 July 1938; *Educ* Ecclesfield GS, Univ of Sheffield Med Sch (MB ChB); *m* 5 Sept 1964, Margaret, da of William John Jones, of Dymock, Glos; 1 s (Simon b 1966), 1 da (Susan b 1965); *Career* rotating registrar United Sheffield Hosp 1965–67, sr registrar in otolaryngology Cardiff Royal Infirmary and Singleton Hosp Swansea 1967–70, res fell Wayne State Univ Detroit USA 1970, conslt ENT surgn Royal Hallamshire Hosp Sheffield 1971–94, currently hon conslt ENT surgn; memb Cncl Sections of Otology and Laryngology RSM, regnl advsr in otolaryngology RCS Trent, memb Ct of Examiners RCS; FRCSEd 1967, FRCS 1969; *Books* Fibreoptic Endoscopy of the Upper Respiratory Tract; *Style*— John Shaw, Esq; ✉ The Gables, Sandygate Rd, Sheffield S10 5UE (☎ 0114 230 7784)

SHAW, John Frederick; CB (1996); *b* 7 Dec 1936; *Educ* Loretto, Worcester Coll Oxford (MA); *m*, 3 children; *Career* Nat Serv: 2–Lt King's Own Yorkshire Light Infantry Cyprus 1955–57; exec offr Church Commissioners for England 1960–62, accountant Industrial Christian Fellowship 1962–63, various positions HQ Admin staff then head Recruitment Div VSO 1963–73; Dept of Health (formerly DHSS): princ Children's Div 1973–75, asst sec Regnl Liaison Div 1978–82 (princ 1975–78), asst sec Establishments and Personnel Div 1982–86, asst sec Primary Care Review Team 1986–87, under sec Family Practitioner Servs Div 1987–91, dep dir of Performance Mgmnt 1991–93, dep sec and dir of Corp Affairs 1993–95, dep sec and dir NHS Exec 1995–; *Recreations* gardening, singing, amateur dramatics, keeping pigs, active in Church of England affairs; *Style*— John Shaw, Esq, CB

SHAW, Dr Mark Robert; s of William Shaw (d 1993), of Drayton St Leonard, Oxon, and Mabel Courtenay, *née* Bower; *b* 11 May 1945; *Educ* Dartington Hall Sch, Oriel Coll Oxford (BA, MA, DPhil); *m* 11 July 1970, Francesca Dennis, da of Rev Dennis Wilkinson (d 1971); 2 da (Zerynthia b 23 Dec 1972, Melitaea b 19 April 1978); *Career* res asst Dept of Zoology Univ of Manchester 1973–76, univ res fell Univ of Reading 1977–80; Nat Museums of Scotland (formerly Royal Scottish Museum): asst keeper Dept of Natural History 1980–83, keeper of natural history 1983–96, keeper of geology and zoology 1996–; frequent contrib to various pubns on entomology; FRES 1974; *Recreations* field entomology, family life; *Clubs* Univ of Edinburgh Staff; *Style*— Dr Mark R Shaw; ✉ Royal Museum of Scotland, Chambers Street, Edinburgh EH1 1JF (☎ 0131 247 4246, fax 0131 220 4819, e-mail mrs@nms.ac.uk)

SHAW, Martin; s of Albert Cyril Shaw (d 1967), of Leeds, and Letitia Whitehead (d 1978); *b* 31 Oct 1944; *Educ* Leeds GS, UCL (LLB); *m* 1, 19 Aug 1967 (m dis 1995), Christine Helen, da of Maurice Grenville Whitwam (d 1986), of Leeds; 2 s (Simon b 17 March 1973, Jonathan b 4 Aug 1978), 1 da (Sarah b 25 Nov 1970); *m* 2, 2 Aug 1996, Christine Elizabeth St Lawrence, da of Ivor St Lawrence Morris (d 1991), of Collingham, near Leeds; *Career* Simpson Curtis (merged with Pinsent & Co to form Pinsent Curtis, May 1995): articled clerk 1966–69, slr 1969–71, ptnr 1971–, head Corporate Dept 1980–88, managing ptnr 1992–94; chm: Minstergate plc 1985–89, ABI Caravans Ltd 1986–88, Legal Resources Group 1988–91, Minster Corporation plc 1988–90; dir Leeds Business Venture 1982–95; govr: Richmond House Sch 1977–92, Gateways Sch 1985– (currently chm); memb: Headingley Rotary Club, Variety Club of GB (chm Yorkshire region 1995); memb: Slrs Euro Gp 1975, Law Soc 1969, Leeds Law Soc 1969, ABA 1985, IBA 1985; *Recreations* running, golf, squash, tennis; *Clubs* The Leeds, Alwoodley Golf, Chapel Allerton Lawn Tennis & Squash; *Style*— Martin Shaw, Esq; ✉ Moor Lodge, Moor Road, Bramhope, Leeds LS16 9HH (☎ 0113 284 3634); Pinsent Curtis, 41 Park Square, Leeds LS1 2NS (☎ 0113 244 5000, fax 0113 244 8000)

SHAW, Rev (Ralph) Michael; s of late Stanley Shaw, and late Mary Ann Shaw; *b* 20 Sept 1945; *Educ* King Sch Pontefract, Lichfield Theological Coll, Univ of London (DipAE); *m* 26 July 1970, Eileen, *née* Scott; 2 s (Jeremy Paul b 21 March 1974, Matthew David b 13 Dec 1978); *Career* asst curate All Saints Dewsbury 1970, team vicar Redcar in Kirkleatham 1974, youth advsr St Albans Dio 1976, exec dir John Grooms Assoc for Disabled People (charity) 1992–; dir: Dio of St Albans Community Project 1978–91, Mitrecrest Travel 1984–91; chm Prince's Tst-Action Herts 1986–, memb Prince of Wales Gp on Disability, vice chm Townsend C of E Sch 1986–91, govr St John's C of E Sch Digswell 1992–; *Books* Training Games & Exercises (1978); *Recreations* sailing, reading, arts, walking; *Clubs* New Cavendish; *Style*— Rev Michael Shaw; ✉ John Grooms Association for Disabled People, 50 Scrutton Street, London EC2A 4PH (☎ 0171 452 2000, fax 0171 452 2001)

SHAW, Hon Michael Frank; s of Baron Kilbrandon, PC (Life Peer; d 1989); *b* 1944; *m* 1978, Catherine Ballantine; 1 s (Torquil b 1981), 1 da (Tamara b 1980); *Career* md Portmor (Seil Island) Ltd; chm Argyll & The Islands Enterprise, chm West Highlands and Islands of Argyll Tourist Bd until 1994 (ret); vice chm Seil Community Cncl; *Recreations* sailing, shooting, skiing, fishing; *Clubs* New (Edinburgh), Royal Highland Yacht; *Style*— The Hon Michael Shaw; ✉ Kilbrandon House, Balvicar, By Oban, Argyll

SHAW, Michael Hewitt; CMG (1990); s of Donald Smethurst Shaw (d 1982), and Marian Clarissa, *née* Hewitt; *b* 5 Jan 1935; *Educ* Sedbergh, Clare Coll Cambridge (BA, MA), UCL (MA); *m* 10 Aug 1963, Elizabeth Monica, da of Maj-Gen Sir Hubert Elvin Rance, GCMG, GBE, CB (d 1974); 4 da (Melanie b 1964, Sarah b 1968, Lucy b 1970 d 1973, Suzanna b 1973); *Career* Nat Serv 2 Lt RA 1953–55; dist offr and ADC to govr of Tanganyika HMOCS 1959–62; FCO: London 1963 and 1965, second sec The Hague 1964, second sec Vientiane 1966, first sec Valletta 1972, first sec and cnsllr Brussels 1982, cnsllr London 1987–95; postgraduate research student UCL 1993–; chm Assoc for Rural Marley; *Recreations* cricket, theatre, walking; *Clubs* MCC, Army and Navy; *Style*— Michael Shaw, Esq, CMG; ✉ The Close, Marley Common, Haslemere, Surrey GU27 3PT

SHAW, Peter Alan; *b* 31 May 1949; *Career* northern regnl dir Dept of the Environment and Tport 1991–93; Dept for Educn and Employment (previously Dept for Educn): dir of servs 1993–95, ldr Sr Mgmnt Review 1995, dir of sch places, bldgs and governance 1995–; *Style*— Peter Shaw, Esq; ✉ Department for Education and Employment, Sanctuary Buildings, Great Smith Street, Westminster, London SW1P 3BT (☎ 0171 925 5800, fax 0171 925 5379)

SHAW, Capt Peter Jack; CBE (1990); s of Jack Shaw (d 1968), of London, and Gladys Elizabeth, *née* Knight (d 1981); *b* 27 Oct 1924, Geelong, Australia; *Educ* Watford GS, RNC Dartmouth, RN Staff Coll Greenwich, NATO Def Coll Paris; *m* 18 Aug 1951, Pauline, da of Sir Frank William Madge, 2 Bt (d 1962); 1 s (Christopher John b 1957 d 1992), 1 da (Carol Anne (Mrs Livett) b 1952); *Career* WWII 1942–45; served: Russian, Atlantic, Malta convoys, Normandy invasion (on HM Ships: Kenya, Quadrant, Resolution, London, Kelvin); cmd HM LCI (L) 377 1945, staff of Flag Offr Germany 1946–48 and 1951–53, HMS Corunna 1949–51, exec offr HMS Chevron and HMS Whirlwind 1953–55, naval instr RAF Coll Cranwell 1956–58, cmd HMS Venus and HMS Carron 1958, HMS Vigilant 1960, staff of C-in-C Portsmouth 1961–63, MOD 1963–65, SHAPE 1966–68, exec offr RN Coll Greenwich 1968–70, def and naval attache The Hague 1971–73, Capt of the Port and Queen's Harbourmaster Plymouth 1973–76, Capt of the Port and Queen's Harbourmaster Chatham 1976–79, gen sec Interparly Union (Br Gp) 1979–90 (conslt 1990–91), conslt to pres Interparly Cncl 1991–94; exec sec Br Delgn to 30 Interparly Confs incl: Caracas 1979, E Berlin 1980, Manila 1981, Lagos 1982, Rome 1982, Seoul 1983, Geneva 1984, Ottowa 1985, Mexico City 1986, Bangkok 1987, Guatemala 1988; organiser IPU Centenary Conf London 1989; regional organiser Proshare 1994–; FIL 1956, MIMgt 1975; *Recreations* international affairs, foreign languages, domestic pursuits; *Style*— Capt Peter Shaw, CBE, RN; ✉ Woodside Rogate, Petersfield, Hants, GU31 5DJ (☎ 01730 821 344)

SHAW, Prof Richard Wright; s of George Beeley Shaw (d 1965), and Bella, *née* Wright (d 1982); *b* 22 Sept 1941; *Educ* Lancaster Royal GS, Sidney Sussex Coll Cambridge (MA); *m* 2 April 1965, Susan Angela, da of Lewis Birchley; 2 s (David Lewis b 24 Sept 1970, James Lachlan b 29 July 1977); *Career* Univ of Leeds: asst lectr in mgmnt 1964–66, lectr in economics 1966–69; Univ of Stirling: lectr in economics 1969–75, sr lectr in economics 1975–84, head Dept of Economics 1982–84; Paisley Coll: prof and head Dept of Economics and Mgmnt 1984–86, vice princ 1986, princ 1987–92; princ and vice chllr Univ of Paisley 1992–; visiting lectr in economics Univ of Newcastle NSW Australia 1982; dir Renfrewshire Enterprise 1992–, memb Scottish Economic Cncl 1995–; fell Scottish Vocational Educn Cncl 1995, FRSA; *Books* Industry and Competition (with C J Sutton, 1976); *Recreations* walking, listening to music; *Style*— Prof Richard Shaw; ✉ Principal's Suite, University of Paisley, High Street, Paisley PA1 2BE (☎ 0141 848 3000, fax 0141 848 3694)

SHAW, Sir Robert; 7 Bt (UK 1821), of Bushy Park, Dublin; s of Lt-Col Sir Robert de Vere Shaw, 6 Bt, MC (d 1969); *b* 31 Jan 1925; *Educ* Harrow, Oklahoma Univ, Univ of Missouri; *m* 1954, Jocelyn Mary, da of late Andrew McGuffie, of Mbabane, Swaziland; 2 da (Grania b 1955, Reinet b 1960); *Heir* n, Charles de Vere Shaw b 1 March 1957; *Career* Lt RN (ret); professional engr (Alberta); *Style*— Sir Robert Shaw, Bt; ✉ 234–40 Ave SW, Calgary, AB, T2S 0X3, Canada

SHAW, Prof Robert Alfred; s of Walter Schlesinger (d 1964), and Lily Karoline, *née* Plahner (d 1954); *b* 2 Nov 1924; *Educ* Univ of London (BSc, PhD, DSc); *m* 23 Aug 1980, Dr Leylâ Süheylâ Shaw, da of Yusuf Gözen, of Tarsus, Turkey; 1 s (Robert b 28 March 1984), 1 da (Lily b 30 May 1989); *Career* WWII Royal Fusiliers and Queen's Royal Regt UK, India, SE Asia command 1944–47; Birkbeck Coll Univ of London: asst lectr 1953–56, lectr 1956–65, prof of chemistry 1965–90, prof emeritus 1990–; co-dir of an EC sponsored int research project in chemistry with Poland 1994–; author of numerous articles dealing with chemistry, educn, and third world countries; memb Academic Policy Ctee of the Inter-Univ Cncl for Higher Educn Overseas 1976–81, UNESCO conslt to Turkish Govt 1977, main speaker and memb Organising Ctee of Conf sponsored by Institut Mondial du Phosphate Rabat Morocco 1977, main speaker on Life-long Educn in Koblenz W Germany 1978, fndr memb and on steering ctee of Univ of the Third Age London; Dr (hc) Univ Paul Sabatier Toulouse 1978; memb Soc of Chemical Indust; CChem, FRSC;

Recreations reading, music, gardening, travelling, skiing, fencing; *Style*— Prof Robert A Shaw; ✉ Brettargh Holt, Camden Way, Chislehurst, Kent BR7 5HT (☎ 0181 467 5656); Department of Chemistry, Birkbeck College, University of London, Gordon House, 29 Gordon Square, London WC1H 0PP

SHAW, Robert Ian (Bob); s of Robert Shaw (d 1975), of Glasgow, and Lily Shaw (d 1990); *b* 2 Jan 1939; *Educ* Whitehill Sch Glasgow; *m* 19 Aug 1963, Doreen, da of Alexander Archibald; 2 s (Trevor John b 20 Feb 1967, Leonard b 21 Feb 1970); *Career* Peat Marwick McLintock Glasgow 1961–64, Brownlee plc Glasgow 1964–67, Swedish Match Corp (STAB) Glasgow and Surrey 1967–78, EFG plc Edinburgh and Oxford 1978–91, md Tilhill Economic Forestry Ltd (formed by merger of forestry interests of EFG plc and Booker plc) 1991–96, ret; MICAS; *Recreations* golf, gardening; *Style*— Bob Shaw, Esq

SHAW, Prof Robert Wayne; s of Arthur Stanley Shaw, of Colwyn Bay, Clwyd, and Margery Maud, *née* Griffiths; *b* 25 June 1946; *Educ* Priory GS Shrewsbury, Univ of Birmingham (MB ChB, MD), FRCSEd, FRCOG; *m* 6 March 1980, Mary Philomena; 1 s (Robert Andrew b 31 Dec 1982), 1 da (Hilary Mary b 21 June 1985); *Career* prof Dept of Obstetrics and Gynaecology: Royal Free Hosp Sch of Med 1983–92, Univ of Wales Coll of Med 1992–; vice pres RCOG 1995–; dir Wellbeing charity; memb: American Soc of Reproductive Med 1982, Br Fertility Soc 1985; *Books* An Atlas of Endometriosis (1993), Gynaecology (ed jtly, 1993), Endometriosis - Current Understanding and Management (1995); *Recreations* sailing, hill walking; *Clubs* County (Cardiff); *Style*— Prof Robert Shaw; ✉ Department of Obstetrics and Gynaecology, University of Wales College of Medicine, Heath Park, Cardiff CF4 4XW (☎ 01222 743235, fax 01222 743722)

SHAW, Sir Roy; kt (1979); s of late Frederick Shaw, and Elsie, *née* Odgen; *b* 8 July 1918; *Educ* Firth Park GS Sheffield, Univ of Manchester; *m* 1946, Gwenyth Baron; 5 s, 2 da; *Career* writer and lectr; lectr in adult educn Univ of Leeds, prof and dir of adult educn Univ of Keele 1962–75, sec gen Arts Cncl 1975–83; ret; Hon DLitt: City Univ, Univ of Southampton; Hon DUniv Open Univ; *Books* The Arts and the People (1987), The Spread of Sponsorship (1993); *Recreations* arts, walking, swimming; *Clubs* Arts; *Style*— Sir Roy Shaw; ✉ 48 Farrer Rd, London N8 8LB (☎ 0181 348 1857)

SHAW, Sarah Margaret Foulkes; *b* 2 June 1958; *Educ* Penarth GS, Univ of Birmingham (LLB, Sir Henry Barber Law Scholar, Gregory Memorial Prize), Coll of Law; *m* Dr Rory J Shaw; 1 da; *Career* slr Freshfields 1982–86 (articled clerk 1980–82), slr Cadbury Schweppes plc 1986–89, legal advsr Reed International plc 1989–91, gp co sec Signet Group plc 1992–95, partnership sec Frere Cholmeley Bischoff 1996–; memb Law Soc; FRGS; *Style*— Mrs Sarah Shaw; ✉ 26 Hamilton Road, London W5 2EH; (☎ 0181 567 9390); Frere Cholmeley Bischoff, 4 John Carpenter Street, London EC4Y 0NH (☎ 0171 615 8000)

SHAW, Simon (né Simon Griffith); *b* 19 Aug 1956; *Educ* St Paul's, Corpus Christi Coll Cambridge (BA), Bristol Old Vic Theatre Sch; *Career* writer; actor in repertoire, TV, West End etc 1979–; *Books* Murder Out of Tune (1988), Killer Cinderella (1990, Last Laugh Award Crime Writers' Assoc), Bloody Instructions (1991), Dead for a Ducat (1992), The Villain of the Earth (1994, Last Laugh Award Crime Writers' Assoc); *Style*— Simon Shaw, Esq; ✉ 429 Fulham Road, London SW10 9TX

SHAW, Stephen; s of Ivan Shaw, and Phyllis, *née* Niechciki; *b* 20 Dec 1952; *Educ* Harrow Co GS, Univ of Birmingham (LLB); *m* 26 Sept 1978, Fabia Melanie, da of John Alexander; 2 s (Gideon David b 20 Sept 1982, Aaron Alexander b 7 Jan 1987), 2 da (Gabrielle Leah b 25 March 1984, Rachel Rose Sybil b 24 July 1991); *Career* called to the Bar Gray's Inn 1975; ACIArb; *Books* contrib New Law Journal and Estates Gazette on landlord and tenant matters; *Recreations* amateur magic, occasional sleep; *Style*— Stephen Shaw, Esq; ✉ Lamb Chambers, Lamb Building, Temple, London EC4Y 7AS (☎ 0171 797 8300, fax 0171 797 8308)

SHAW, Dr Stephen; s of Walter Arthur Shaw (d 1976), and Gwendolyn Primrose, *née* Cottrell; *b* 26 March 1953; *Educ* Rutlish Sch Merton, Univ of Warwick (BA), Univ of Leeds (MA), Univ of Kent (PhD); *m* 23 April 1977, Christine Elizabeth, da of Michael Robinson; *Career* lectr: Coventry Tech Coll 1975–76, Mid-Kent Coll of Technol 1977–79; res offr: Nat Assoc for the Care and Resettlement of Offenders 1979–80, Home Office 1980–81; dir Prison Reform Trust 1981–; *Recreations* travel, cinema, watching Fulham FC; *Style*— Dr Stephen Shaw; ✉ 8 Caroline Road, Wimbledon, London SW19 3QL (☎ 0181 542 8843); The Prison Reform Trust, 15 Northburgh Street, London EC1V 0AH (☎ 0171 251 5070, fax 0171 251 5076)

SHAW, Hon Thomas Columba; s and h of 3 Baron Craigmyle; *b* 19 Oct 1960; *m* 25 April 1987, (Katherine) Alice, 2 da of David Floyd, OBE, of Combe Down, Bath; 4 s (Alexander Francis b 1 July 1988, Finnian Donald b 28 May 1990, Calum Edward b 4 Jan 1993, another b 9 March 1996); *Style*— The Hon Thomas Shaw; ✉ c/o Rt Hon Lord Craigmyle, 18 The Boltons, London, SW10 9SY

SHAW, Prof (Charles) Thurstan; CBE (1972); s of Rev John Herbert Shaw, CF 1914–18 (d 1945), of Nethercott, Silverton, nr Exeter, Devon, and Grace Irene Woollatt (d 1964); *b* 27 June 1914; *Educ* Blundell's, Sidney Sussex Coll Cambridge (BA, MA, PhD), London Univ Inst of Educn (Post Grad Teachers Dip); *m* 21 Jan 1939, Gilian Ione Maud (d 1992), da of Edward John Penberthy Magor (d 1941), of Lamellen, St Tudy, Bodmin, Cornwall; 2 s (Timothy, Jonathan), 3 da (Rosanne, Gilian, Joanna); *Career* Achimota College Gold Coast 1937–45, Cambridgeshire Educn Ctee 1945–51, Cambridge Inst of Educn 1951–63, prof of archaeology Univ of Ibadan Nigeria 1963–74, dir of studies in archaeology and anthropology Magdalene Coll Cambridge 1975–80; visiting prof: Dept of Anthropology Yale Univ 1979, Dept of Archaeology Univ of Calgary 1980; visiting fell: Clare Hall Cambridge 1973, Inst for Advanced Study Indiana Univ 1984; hon fell Sidney Sussex Coll Cambridge 1994–; memb Cambridge Cncl for Racial Equality 1980–88, fndr and chm Ichnield Way Assoc 1984–90 (pres 1990–), pres Prehistoric Soc 1986–90, vice pres Panafrican Congress on Prehistory 1967–77; Hon DSc: Univ of Nigeria 1983, Univ of Ibadan 1989; Onuna-Ekwulu Ora of Igbo-Ukwu Nigeria 1972, Enyofuonka of Igboland 1989, Onuna Ekwulu Nri 1989, Olokun-Ayala of Ife 1991; Gold Medal Soc of Antiquaries 1990; FRAI 1940, FSA 1947, FBA 1991; *Books* Excavation at Dawu (1961), Archaeology and Nigeria (1963), Igbo-Ukwu: An Account of Archaeological Discoveries in Eastern Nigeria (2 Vols, 1970), Africa and The Origins of Man (1973), Why 'Darkest' Africa? (1975), Unearthing Igbo-Ukwu (1977), Nigeria: Its Archaeology and Early History (1978), The Archaeology of Africa (ed, 1993); *Recreations* walking; *Clubs* Athenaeum; *Style*— Prof Thurstan Shaw, CBE, FSA, FBA; ✉ 26 Peacocks, Great Shelford, Cambridge CB2 5AT (☎ 01223 842283)

SHAW, Rev Prof (Douglas) William David; WS (1951); s of Maj William David Shaw, MC (d 1955), and Nansie, *née* Smart (d 1982); *b* 25 June 1928; *Educ* Loretto, Ashbury Coll Ottawa, Edinburgh Acad, Univ of Cambridge (MA), Univ of Edinburgh (LLB, BD), Univ of Glasgow (Hon DD); *Career* ptnr Davidson & Syme WS Edinburgh 1953–57; ordained minister of Church of Scotland 1960; observer for World Alliance of Reformed Churches at II Vatican Cncl 1962; lectr in divinity New Coll Edinburgh 1963–79; dean Faculty of Divinity and princ New Coll Edinburgh 1974–78; prof of divinity Univ of St Andrews 1979–91, princ St Mary's Coll St Andrews 1986–92; *Books* Who is God? (1968), The Dissuaders (1978), In Divers Manners (ed, 1990), Dimensions - Literary and Theological (ed, 1992), Theology in Scotland (ed); *Recreations* squash, golf, hill walking; *Clubs* Royal and Ancient, New (Edinburgh), Edinburgh Sports; *Style*— The Rev Prof William Shaw; ✉ 40 North Street, St Andrews, Fife KY16 9AQ (☎ and fax 01334 477254)

SHAW OF NORTHSTEAD, Baron (Life Peer UK 1994), of Liversedge in the County of West Yorkshire; Sir Michael Norman Shaw; kt (1982), JP (Dewsbury 1953), DL (W Yorks 1977); eld s of late Norman Shaw; *b* 9 Oct 1920; *Educ* Sedbergh; *m* 1951, Joan Mary Louise, da of Sir Alfred Law Mowat, 2 and last Bt, DSO, OBE, MC (d 1968); 3 s (Hon Charles Michael Mowat b 1952, Hon James William b 1955, Hon Jonathan David b 1957); *Career* MP: (Lib and C) Brighouse and Spenborough 1960–64, (C) Scarborough and Whitby 1966–74, Scarborough 1974–92; PPS: to Min of Lab and Nat Serv 1962–63, to Sec of State for Trad and Indust 1970–72, to Chllr of the Duchy of Lancaster 1973–74; memb UK Delgn Euro Parl 1974–79; Liveryman Worshipful Co of Chartered Accountants; FCA; *Style*— The Rt Hon Lord Shaw of Northstead, JP, DL; ✉ Duxbury Hall, Liversedge, W Yorks WF15 7NR (☎ 01924 402270)

SHAW OF TORDARROCH, John; 22 Chief of the Highland Clan of Shaw; s of late Maj Charles John Shaw of Tordarroch, MBE, TD, DL, JP; *b* 1937; *Educ* Eton, Magdalene Coll Cambridge (MA); *m* 1960, Silvia Margaret, da of late Rev David John Silian Jones; 1 s; *Heir* s, Iain b 1968; *Career* late 2 Lt Seaforth Highlanders 1955–57; memb Royal Co of Archers (Queen's Body Guard for Scotland); hon vice-pres Clan Chattan Assoc (UK); memb standing Cncl of Scottish Chiefs; *Books* A History of Clan Shaw (ed); *Clubs* New, Turf, Puffins; *Style*— John Shaw of Tordarroch; ✉ Newhall, Balblair, by Dingwall, Ross-shire IV7 8LQ

SHAW-STEWART, Sir Houston Mark; 11 Bt (NS 1667), of Greenock and Blackhall, Renfrewshire, MC (1950), TD (1968); s of Lt-Col Sir (Walter) Guy Shaw-Stewart, 9 Bt, MC (d 1976); suc bro, Sir Euan Guy Shaw-Stewart, 10 Bt, 1980; *b* 24 April 1931; *Educ* Eton; *m* 1982, Lucinda Victoria, yr da of Alexander K H Fletcher, of The Old Vicarage, Wighill, nr Tadcaster; 1 s (Ludovic Houston b 1986); *Heir* s, Ludovic Houston Shaw-Stewart b 12 Nov 1986; *Career* 2 Lt RUR Korea 1950, Ayrshire Yeo 1952, ret Maj 1969; jt MFH Lanarkshire and Renfrewshire 1974–78, Vice Lord-Lieut Strathclyde Region 1980–93; memb Queen's Body Guard for Scotland (Royal Co of Archers); *Recreations* shooting and racing; *Clubs* White's, Turf, Pratt's; *Style*— Sir Houston Shaw-Stewart, Bt, MC, TD; ✉ Ardgowan, Inverkip, Greenock, Renfrewshire PA16 (☎ 01475 521226)

SHAWCROSS, Brian Ellis; s of Ellis William Hope Shawcross (d 1981), and Gladys Lily, *née* Cartwright (d 1988); *b* 16 Aug 1938; *Educ* Radley, Sidney Sussex Coll Cambridge (MA); *m* 1, 9 Sept 1961 (m dis 1991), Judy Gwynn, da of Cdr Hugh Vaughan Lavington (d 1957); 1 s (James William Ellis b 5 June 1971), 1 da (Annabel Mary b 9 March 1966); m 2, 26 Feb 1994, Anne Barbara Wilkinson; *Career* chm Hunkydory Designs Ltd 1970–94; dir: Sir Joseph Causton plc 1980–84, Norton Opax plc 1985–86; *Recreations* reading, gardening, travel, music, theatre; *Style*— Brian Shawcross, Esq

SHAWCROSS, Baron (Life Peer UK 1959), of Friston, Co Sussex; Sir Hartley William Shawcross; GBE (1974), kt (1945), PC (1946), QC (KC 1939); s of John Shawcross (d 1968), and Hilda (d 1942); *b* 4 Feb 1902; *Educ* Dulwich, Univ of London, Univ of Geneva; *m* 1, 1924, Rosita Alberta (d 1943), da of William Shyvers (d 1944); m 2, 1944, Joan Winifred (d riding accident 1974), da of Hume Mather (d 1968), of Carlton Lodge, Tunbridge Wells; 2 s, 1 da; *Career* called to the Bar Gray's Inn 1925; chief UK prosecutor Nuremburg Trials, asst chm Sussex QS 1941; rec: Salford 1941–45, Kingston upon Thames 1946–61; JP Sussex 1948–61; former dir: EMI Ltd, Rank Hovis McDougall Ltd, Hawker Siddeley Group, Caffyns Motors Ltd, (and chm) Upjohn & Co Ltd, Times Newspapers, Morgan et Cie SA, Observer Newspapers 1982–94, TVB (Hong Kong) Ltd, Shaw Bros (Hong Kong) Ltd; former chm Int Advsy Cncl Morgan Guaranty Trust Co; MP (Lab) St Helens 1945–58, attorney-gen 1945–51, pres BOT 1951, princ del for UK to Assemblies of UN 1945–50, UK memb Perm Ct of Arbitration The Hague 1950–67; chllr Univ of Sussex 1965–86, chm Int C of C Cmmn on Unethical Practices 1976; Hon FRCS, Hon FRCOG; Kt Grand Cross of Imperial Iranian Order of Homayoon 1965; *Recreations* yachting; *Clubs* Pratt's, RAC, Royal Cornwall Yacht, Royal Yacht Squadron, New York Yacht, Travellers' (Paris); *Style*— The Rt Hon the Lord Shawcross, GBE, PC, QC; ✉ Friston Place, East Dean, nr Eastbourne, East Sussex BN20 0AH (☎ 01323 422206); Anchorage, St Mawes, Cornwall; J P Morgan, 60 Victoria Embankment, London EC4Y 0JP (☎ 0171 325 5133)

SHAWCROSS, His Hon Judge Roger Michael; s of Michael Campbell Shawcross (d 1945), of London, and Friedel Marie Partington, *née* Freund (d 1983); *b* 27 March 1941; *Educ* Radley, Christ Church Oxford (MA); *m* 15 Feb 1969, Sarah, da of Maurice Henry Peter Broom (d 1987), of Farnham, Surrey; 1 s (Philip b 1974), 1 da (Miranda b 1972); *Career* called to the Bar Gray's Inn 1967, recorder Western circuit 1985–93, circuit judge (Western circuit) 1993–; *Recreations* tennis, music, literature, history, travel; *Style*— His Hon Judge Shawcross

SHAWCROSS, (Hon) William Hartley Hume; s (by 2 m) Baron Shawcross (Life Peer); *b* 28 May 1946; *Educ* Eton, Univ Coll Oxford; *m* 1, 1972 (m dis 1980), Marina Warner, *qv*, da of Col Esmond Pelham Warner, TD (d 1982), of Cambridge; 1 s (Conrad Hartley Pelham b 1977); m 2, 1981 (m dis), Michal, da of late A J Levin by his w Leah; 1 da (Eleanor Joan Georgina b 1983); m 3, Oct 1993, Olga Polizzi, *qv*, eldest da of Baron Forte (Life Peer), *qv*, and widow of Marchese Alessandro Polizzi di Sorentino; *Career* writer; columnist The Spectator; *Books* Dubcek, Crime and Compromise, Sideshow, The Quality of Mercy, The Shah's Last Ride, Rupert Murdoch (1992); *Style*— William Shawcross; ✉ c/o Green and Heaton Ltd, 37 Goldhawk Road, London W12

SHAWYER, Peter Michael; s of Edward William Francis Shawyer (d 1986), of Brookmans Park Herts, and Marjorie Josephine Shawyer; *b* 11 Sept 1950; *Educ* Enfield GS, Univ of Sheffield (BA); *m* 23 June 1979, Margot Anne, da of Wing Cdr Norman Edwin Bishop (d 1975), of Sidmouth, Devon; 1 s (Richard b 14 March 1984), 1 da (Emily b 3 Dec 1980); *Career* CA; ptnr (i/c London office) Deloite & Touche (formerly Touche Ross) 1982– (joined 1972), specialist in taxation and author of numerous tax articles in specialist journals; ACA 1975; *Recreations* golf, squash; *Clubs* Enfield Golf; *Style*— Peter Shawyer, Esq; ✉ Deloitte & Touche, Stonecutter Court, 1 Stonecutter Street, London EC4A 4TR (☎ 0171 303 5764, fax 0171 353 9648, telex 884739 TRLNDN G)

SHCHASNY, HE Uladzimir; *b* 25 Nov 1948, Smargon, Belarus; *Educ* Minsk State Inst of Foreign Languages, UN course Moscow; *Career* Belarusian diplomat; USSR Miny of Geology interpreter Pakistan 1969–70 and 1972–74, lectr Minsk State Inst of Foreign Languages 1975–77, student UN course Moscow 1977–78, staff UN Secretariat NY 1978–82; Miny of Foreign Affrs Belarus: staff Press Dept and Dept of Int Orgns 1983–89, asst to Min of Foreign Affrs 1989–91, chief of secretariat 1991–92, dir Dept of Bilateral Cooperation 1992–93; cnsllr-min Lithuania 1994–95 (chargé d'affaires 1993–94), ambass to the Ct of St James's 1995–; *Style*— HE Mr Uladzimir Shchasny; ✉ Embassy of Belarus, 6 Kensington Court, London W8 5DL (☎ 0171 937 3288)

SHEA, Michael Sinclair MacAuslan; CVO (1987, LVO 1985), DL; s of James Michael Shea, of Lenzie; *b* 10 May 1938; *Educ* Gordonstoun, Univ of Edinburgh (MA, PhD); *m* 1968, Mona Grec Stensen, da of Egil Stensen, of Oslo; 2 da; *Career* FO 1963, former 1 sec Bonn, head of chancery Bucharest 1973, DG Br Info Servs NY 1976, press sec to HM The Queen 1978–87; dir of public affairs Hanson plc 1987–93 (now conslt); nat memb for Scot ITC 1996–; visiting prof Strathclyde Graduate Business Sch 1991; chm: Connoisseurs Scotland Ltd 1992–, China Gateway Ltd 1994–; dir: Murray International Trust PLC 1992–, Caledonian Newspapers Ltd 1993–; tstee Nat Galleries of Scotland, govr Gordonstoun Sch, vice chm Fndn of Skin Research, patron The Prince and Princess of Wales Hospice; author; *Books* Britain's Offshore Islands (1981), Tomorrow's Men (1982), Influence (1988), Leadership Rules (1990), Personal Impact (1992), Spin Doctor

(1995), The British Ambassador (1996), To Lie Abroad (1996), and six novels under the name Michael Sinclair; *Recreations* writing, sailing; *Clubs* Garrick; *Style—* Michael Shea, Esq, CVO, DL; ✉ 1 St Colme Street, Edinburgh EH3 6AA

SHEAR, Warren Ivor; s of Alec Shear, of New Wanstead, and Edith Bessie, *née* Onnie (d 1989); *b* 8 Aug 1937; *Educ* East Ham GS, Univ of Sheffield, Royal Coll of Surgeons (LDS); *m* 1961, Marion, da of Aron Hollander; 1 s (Daniel Marc b 3 Dec 1968), 1 da (Sarah Jane b 20 Jan 1970); *Career* dentist; joined Prof H Singer's practice Holland Park 1964, own practice Wimpole St 1967–, pt/t clinical lectr in restorative dentistry Royal Dental Hosp London 1975, pt/t sr clinical lectr in restorative dentistry UCL 1982–91, pt/t UMDS 1992–; memb: RSM 1985, BDA 1962, London Dental Fellowship 1984 (pres 1992–93), Soc for Advancement of Anaesthesia in Dentistry; *publications:* author of various articles published in dental jls; *Recreations* reading, walking, swimming, working for human rights; *Style—* Warren Shear, Esq; ✉ 19 Wimpole St, London W1M 7AD (☎ 0171 580 3863)

SHEARD, (John) Neville; s of Edgar Sheard (d 1982), of Huddersfield, and Kathleen, *née* Frobisher; *b* 7 July 1935; *Educ* Rossall, Exeter Coll Oxford (MA); *m* 1, 26 Feb 1962, Glenys Mary (d 1970); 2 s (Charles b 1962, James b 1965); m 2, 20 July 1973, Elizabeth Mary; 1 s (Jonathan b 1975); *Career* Nat Serv 2 Lt RCS TA; admitted slr 1962, sr ptnr Armitage Sykes Hall Norton Huddersfield 1980– (ptnr 1963–80); non-exec dir Wymas NHS Tst; chm Kirkwood Hospice Huddersfield; memb Law Soc 1962; *Recreations* golf, fell walking; *Style—* Neville Sheard, Esq; ✉ 4 Butternab Rd, Beaumont Park, Huddersfield, W Yorks HD4 7AH (☎ 01484 652996); Armitage Sykes Hall Norton, 72 New North Rd, Huddersfield, W Yorks HD1 5NW (☎ 01484 538121, fax 01484 518968)

SHEARER, Alan; s of Alan Shearer, and Anne, *née* Collins; *b* 13 Aug 1970; *Educ* Gosforth HS Newcastle; *Career* professional footballer; over 100 appearances Southampton FC 1988–92; Blackburn Rovers: transferred for then Br record of £3.2 million 1992–96, winners FA Premier League 1994/95; transferred to Newcastle United for world record fee of £15m 1996–; England: 7 under 17 caps (scored on debut v Eire), 11 under 21 caps (scored twice on debut v Eire, total 13 goals), 1 B cap, 28 full caps (scored on debut v France 1992), memb squad Euro Championship 1992 (Sweden) and Euro 96 (England), capt England 1996–; former rep Newcastle and Northumberland schoolboys; Zenith Data Systems Cup runners-up medal Southampton 1992; youngest player to score a hat-trick in Div 1 (on debut v Arsenal 9 April 1988 aged 17), scorer of over 100 league goals; Sport Writers Player of the Year 1994, PFA Player of the Year 1995; *Recreations* walking my dog; *Style—* Alan Shearer, Esq; ✉ c/o Newcastle United FC, St James's Park, Newcastle upon Tyne NE1 4ST

SHEARER, Anthony Patrick (Tony); s of James Francis Shearer, of London, and Judith Margaret, *née* Bowman; *b* 24 Oct 1948; *Educ* Rugby; *m* 1 Dec 1972, Jennifer, da of Alfred Dixon (d 1981); 2 da (Juliet b 19 Aug 1980, Lauretta b 30 March 1982); *Career* ptnr Deloitte Haskins & Sells 1980–88 (joined 1967), chief operating offr M & G Group plc 1988–96; md: M & G Securities 1991–96, M & G Life and Pensions 1993–96; chief exec Electronic Shase Information Ltd 1996–; govr Rugby Sch 1994–; FCA; *Recreations* skiing, tennis, garden, family, rock 'n' roll; *Clubs* Brooks's, City; *Style—* Tony Shearer, Esq; ✉ 15 Addison Crescent, London W14 8JR (☎ 0171 603 2942)

SHEARER, John Charles Johnston; s of Brig Eric James Shearer, CB, CBE, MC (d 1980), and Phyllis Muriel, *née* Mules (d 1981); *b* 10 Nov 1924; *Educ* Eton, RMA Sandhurst; *m* 1, 1952 (m dis), Sylvia Elizabeth, da of Wilfrid F Coombs (d 1977), of Surrey; 2 s (Charles b 1952, d 1984, Michael b 1961); m 2, 10 April 1975, Ellen Ingeborg, da of Cdr Edward Nennecke, of Hamburg (d 1952); 2 s (Philip b 1974, Edward b 1976); *Career* served Scots Gds 1943–49: 2 Lt 1944, Lt 1944, Capt 1946 (despatches), 24 and 4 Gds Bde 1946–48, ret 1949; ptnr: Thos R Miller & Son 1962–85 (joined 1952), Thos R Miller & Son (Bermuda) 1968–87; dir: Turks Caicos Islands, Hanseatic Consultants Ltd 1974–, Blue Hills Aviation Ltd 1977–95, TCI Sky King 1995–; *Recreations* skiing, fishing, tennis, music, boating; *Clubs* MCC; *Style—* John C Shearer, Esq; ✉ Anstead Brook House, Haslemere Surrey GU27 3BG (☎ 01428 642605, fax 01428 644511)

SHEARER, Magnus Macdonald; JP (Shetland 1969); s of Col Magnus Shearer, OBE, TD, JP (d 1960), and Flora, *née* Stephen (d 1987); *b* 27 Feb 1924; *Educ* Anderson Educnl Inst Shetland, George Watson's Coll Edinburgh; *m* 1949, Martha Nicholson, da of John Henderson, DSM, Master Mariner (d 1957); 1 s; *Career* served RN 1942–46, 2 Lt RA (TA) 1949, Capt TARO 1959; md J & M Shearer Ltd 1960–85; hon consul in Shetland: Sweden 1958–94, West Germany 1972–88; hon sec Lerwick Life Boat Station (RNLI) 1968–92; DL (Shetland 1973), Lord-Lieut for Shetland 1982–94, Hon Sheriff Grampian, Highland and Islands at Lerwick 1993; Knight first class Royal Order of Vasa (Sweden) 1970, Offr first class Order of Merit (FRG) 1983; Cdr Order of Polar Star (Sweden) 1991; *Recreations* reading, bird watching, ships; *Style—* Magnus M Shearer, JP; ✉ 8 Queen's Place, Lerwick, Shetland ZE1 0BZ (☎ 01595 696612)

SHEARER, Dr Raymund Michael; s of Patrick Shearer (d 1959), of Belfast, and Elizabeth, *née* Toolan (d 1957); *b* 6 Nov 1930; *Educ* Irish Christian Brothers Belfast, Queen's Univ Belfast (MB BCh, BAO, MD); *m* 1, 3 Sept 1956, Frances Mary, da of Peter Lenfestey; 3 s (Raymond Patrick b 27 Feb 1958, Cormac Peter b 10 Feb 1960, Lawrence John Paul b 14 Oct 1964), 2 da (Paula Elizabeth b 25 March 1961, Elizabeth Anne b 4 Sept 1962); m 2, 3 March 1987, Deborra Jane, da of Henry Desmond Milling; 2 s (Desmond John b 9 March 1988, Kevin Raymund b 30 April 1989), 1 da (Emer Jane Diana b 27 June 1990); *Career* rotating house offr Mater Infirmorum Hosp Belfast 1954–55, locum tenens 1955, pt/t GP's asst 1955–56, locum tenens 1956, GP's asst 1956–57, GP 1957–, pt/t med dir N & W Community Unit of Mgmnt (unit clinician 1983–94); memb: Eastern (formerly Belfast) Local Med Ctee 1958– (currently chm), NI Gen Med Servs Ctee 1960–, Eastern Health and Social Servs Bd 1978–81, Pemberton Ctee NI (concerning prescribing and social security costs); vice chm NI GP Obstetric Ctee; BMA: memb 1974, NI rep 1990–, currently chm Cncl NI; memb: GMC 1994–, Irish Coll of GPs; *Recreations* ice skating, weight lifting (Bronze medal British Amateur Weight-Lifters' Association 1950); *Style—* Dr Raymund Shearer; ✉ 13 Deramore Drive, Malone Road, Belfast BT9 5JQ (☎ and fax 01232 664421); practice: 26 Springfield Road, Belfast (☎ 01232 323734/248331/325532)

SHEARER, Robert John; s of Lewis George Shearer (d 1985), and Kathleen Mary Justina, *née* Humphreys; *b* 12 March 1939; *Educ* Wellington, Bart's Med Sch Univ of London (MB BS), FRCS 1967; *m* 6 April 1963, Shaune Vanessa, *née* Vance; 1 s (Paul b 23 Sept 1964), 1 da (Rebecca b 13 May 1970); *Career* formerly conslt urologist St George's Hosp, currently conslt urologist and med dir Royal Marsden Hosp; sr lectr Inst of Cancer Res; chm MRC Urology Cancer Working Pty; Liveryman Worshipful Soc of Apothecaries, Freeman City of London; FRSM 1975; *Style—* Robert Shearer, Esq; ✉ Royal Marsden Hospital, Fulham Road, London SW3 6JJ (☎ 0171 352 2166)

SHEARLOCK, Very Rev David John; s of Arthur John Shearlock (d 1947), and Honora Frances Baker, *née* Hawkins; *b* 1 July 1932; *Educ* Surbiton Co GS, Univ of Birmingham (BA), Westcott House Cambridge; *m* 30 May 1959, Jean Margaret, da of John Marr, of Sandlands, Sidbury, Devon; 1 s (Timothy b 1963), 1 da (Ann b 1961); *Career* RA 1950–52, HAC 1952–56; curate: Guisborough Yorkshire 1957–60, Christchurch Priory Hants 1960–64; vicar: Kingsclere Hants 1964–71, Romsey Abbey Hants 1971–82; diocesan dir of ordinands Winchester 1977–82, hon canon of Winchester Cathedral 1978–82, dean of Truro 1982–; Cornwall area chm Royal Sch of Church Music 1983–; chm Truro Victim Support Scheme 1985–95; pres Three Spires Festival 1982–; vice pres: Truro Cancer Relief, Truro RA Assoc; chaplain Cornwall Fire Brigade 1991–; FRSA, FRGS; *Books* The Practice of Preaching (1990), When Words Fail (1996); *Recreations* railways, music, walking, wine making; *Style—* The Very Rev the Dean of Truro; ✉ The Deanery, Lemon St, Truro TR1 2PE (☎ 01872 72661); Maxfield Cottage, Netherbury, Bridport, Dorset; Truro Cathedral Office, 21 Old Bridge St, Truro TR1 2AH (☎ 01872 76782, fax 01872 77788)

SHEARMAN, Prof John Kinder Gowran; s of Brig C E G Shearman, CBE, DSO, MC (d 1968), and Evelyn, *née* White; *b* 24 June 1931; *Educ* Felsted, Courtauld Inst Univ of London (BA, PhD); *m* 1, Jane Dalrymple (d 1982), da of Charles C Smith; 1 s (Michael b 1968), 3 da (Juliet b 1961, Niccola b 1963, Sarah b 1967); m 2, 1983, Deirdre Roskill; *Career* Nat Serv 1949–50; Courtauld Inst Univ of London: asst lectr, lectr and sr lectr 1957–67, reader 1967–74, prof 1974–79, dep dir 1974–78; res fell Inst for Advanced Study 1964; Princeton Univ: prof 1979–87, chm Dept of Art and Archaeology; Harvard Univ: prof 1987–, chm Dept of Fine Arts Harvard Univ 1989–93, Charles Adams univ prof 1994–; Accademia del Disegno (Florence) 1979, Accademia di San Luca (Rome) 1995; Bronze Medal Collège de France 1983; FBA 1976 (Serena Medal 1979), FAAAS 1993; *Books* Andrea Del Sarto (1965), Mannerism (1967), Raphael's Cartoons (1972), Early Italian paintings in the collection of HM The Queen (1983), Funzione & Illusione (1983), Only Connect... (1992); *Recreations* music, sailing; *Clubs* Bembridge Sailing; *Style—* Prof John Shearman, FBA; ✉ 3 Clement Circle, Cambridge, Mass 02138, USA (☎ 00 1 617 876 9548); Department of Fine Arts, Harvard University, Cambridge, MA 02138 (☎ 00 1 617 495 9154, fax 00 1 617 495 1769)

SHEARS, Philip Peter; QC (1996); s of A G Shears (d 1969), and Olave, *née* Grain (d 1967); *b* 10 May 1947; *Educ* Leys Sch Cambridge, Univ of Nottingham (LLB), Univ of Cambridge (LLB); *m* 2, 1990, Sarah; 3 c by prev m (James, Eleanor, Michael); *Career* called to the Bar Middle Temple 1972, memb Midland & Oxford Circuit, recorder of the Crown Court 1990–, specialist in commercial fraud and serious crime; memb Criminal Bar Assoc; *Recreations* sailing, travel, riding; *Style—* Philip Shears, Esq, QC; ✉ 9 Bedford Row, London WC1R 4AZ (☎ 0171 242 3555, fax 0171 242 2511)

SHEASBY, (John) Michael; s of (Herbert) Basil Sheasby, OBE, JP (d 1993), of Maidenhead, Berks, and (Edith) Barbara, OBE, *née* Parker (d 1989); *b* 31 May 1936; *Educ* Haileybury; *m* 3 June 1961, Juliet Sylvia Gillett; 1 s (Christopher Mark Andrew b 30 Nov 1966); *Career* qualified CA 1958; Arthur Young & Co UK and Italy 1953–63, fin dir then md Gp Admin RCA Ltd 1964–81, vice pres fin and planning Squibb Europe Inc 1982–88, fin ptnr Ernst & Young 1989–90, gp controller then dir of gp internal audit Glaxo Wellcome plc (formerly Glaxo Holdings plc) 1990–; advsy dir American C of C 1990–; hon treas British Assoc for the Advancement of Sci 1994–; FCA 1958; *Recreations* watching rugby, sailing, skiing; *Clubs* Harlequins; *Style—* J Michael Sheasby, Esq; ✉ Glaxo Wellcome plc, Glaxo Wellcome House, Berkeley Ave, Greenford, Middx UB6 0NN (☎ 0171 493 4060, fax 0181 966 8330)

SHEBBEARE, Thomas Andrew (Tom); CVO (1996); s of late Robert Austin Shebbeare, and Frances Dare Graham; *b* 25 Jan 1952; *Educ* Malvern, Univ of Exeter (BA Politics); *m* 1976, Cynthia Jane Cottrell; 1 s, 1 da; *Career* World University Service (UK) 1973–75, gen sec British Youth Cncl 1975–80, admin Cncl of Europe 1980–85, exec dir Euro Youth Fndn 1985–88, exec dir The Prince's Tst and sec The Royal Jubilee Tsts 1988–; tstee: Inst for Citizenship Studies 1991–, The Nations Tst 1995–, Gifts in Kind 1996–; *Recreations* family, cooking, food and drink; *Style—* Tom Shebbeare, Esq, CVO; ✉ The Prince's Trust, 18 Park Square East, London NW1 4LH (☎ 0171 543 1234)

SHEDDEN, Prof (William) Ian Hamilton; s of George Shedden (d 1966), of Bathgate, Scotland, and Agnes Hamilton, *née* Heigh (d 1979); *b* 21 March 1934; *Educ* The Acad Bathgate, Univ of Edinburgh (BSc, MB ChB), Univ of Birmingham (MD), City Univ London (Dip Law); *m* 21 March 1960, Elma Joyce, da of Lewis M Jobson (d 1985), of Edinburgh; 3 s (Malcolm b 1960, Andrew b 1962, Colin b 1971), 1 da (Clare b 1968); *Career* cmmnd Capt RAMC 1961–67, regtl MO Hallamshire Bn York and Lancaster Regt 1961–67; lectr Univ of Sheffield 1960–64, sr res fell MRC 1964–67, dir R & D Lilly Industries Ltd 1968–77, vice pres Eli Lilly & Co USA 1977–83, prof of med Univ of Indiana USA 1979–, md Glaxo Group Research Ltd 1983–86; dir: Speywood Holdings, Speywood Group, The Speywood Laboratory 1991–, Speywood Pharmaceuticals 1994–; asst dep coroner City of London 1987–; Freeman City of London 1976, Liveryman Worshipful Soc of Apothecaries 1974; CBiol, FIBiol 1969, FRCPEd 1983, FACP 1981, FFPM 1990, FRCP 1991; *Books* Vinca Alkaloids in the Chemotherapy of Malignant Disease (ed vol 1–3, 1968–70); *Recreations* golf; *Clubs* Naval and Military; *Style—* Prof Ian Shedden; ✉ Brook House, Park Rd, Stoke Poges, Bucks SL2 4PG (☎ 01753 645773, fax 01753 646279, mobiles 0860 664775 and 0836 514149)

SHEDDEN, Rev Gp Capt John; QHC (1994); s of Robert Blair Arnott Shedden (d 1944), of Johnstone, Renfrewshire, and Grace Roberts, *née* Henderson (d 1983); *b* 23 June 1943; *Educ* Johnstone HS, Univ of St Andrews (BD, DipPSS); *m* 5 Jan 1965, Jeannie Lillian, da of Frederick John Gilling; 1 da (Miranda Jane Henderson (Mrs Edwards)), 1 s (John Adair Gilling); *Career* student asst min St Leonard's Church St Andrews 1967–70, asst min Paisley Abbey 1970–72, min Parish of Thornhill 1972–74, social welfare offr Rhodesia 1975–77, chaplain RN 1977–84, min St Mark's Moose Jaw Saskatchewan 1984–86, chaplain RAF 1986– (princ chaplain Church of Scotland and Free Churches 1994–); *Recreations* hill walking, all forms of DIY, music, reading; *Clubs* RAF; *Style—* The Rev Gp Capt John Shedden, QHC; ✉ 8 Millwell Park, Innerleithen, Peebles EH44 6JF (☎ 01896 831532); Chaplaincy Services, HQPTC, RAF Innsworth, Glos GL3 1EZ (☎ 01452 712612 ext 5035, fax 91452 510828)

SHEEHAN, Sheriff Albert Vincent; s of Richard Greig Sheehan, of Bo'ness, and Mary, *née* Moffat; *b* 23 Aug 1936; *Educ* Bo'ness Acad, Univ of Edinburgh (MA, LLB); *m* 1965, Edna Georgina Scott, da of Andrew Hastings, of Coatbridge; 2 da (Wendy b 1968, Susan b 1971); *Career* Capt Royal Scots (The Royal Regt) 1959–61; slr; depute procurator fiscal 1961–71, Leverhulme fell 1971–72, dep crown agent for Scot 1974–79, Scot Law Cmmn 1979–81; sheriff: Edinburgh 1981, Falkirk 1983–; *Recreations* curling, naval history, gardening; *Style—* Sheriff Albert Sheehan; ✉ 63 Murrayfield Gardens, Edinburgh EH12 6DL; Falkirk Sheriff Court, Main Street, Camelon, Falkirk FK1 4AR (☎ 01324 620822)

SHEEHY, Rev Dr Jeremy Patrick; s of Eric Sheehy, of Solihull, W Midlands, and Noreen, *née* Cuffe; *b* 31 Oct 1956; *Educ* Bristol GS, King Edward's Sch Birmingham, Magdalen Coll Oxford (BA Law), St Stephen's House Oxford (Liddon student, BA Theol, Denyer and Johnson prize, Ellerton prize, MA), DPhil (Oxon) 1990; *Career* ordained deacon 1981, priest 1982; fell, dean of divinity, chaplain and tutor New Coll Oxford 1984–90, vicar St Margaret with St Columba Leytonstone 1990–96, priest i/c St Andrew Leytonstone 1993–96, princ St Stephen's House Oxford 1996–; *Style—* The Rev Dr Jeremy Sheehy; ✉ St Stephen's House, 16 Marston Street, Oxford OX4 1JX (☎ 01865 247874, fax 01865 794338)

SHEEHY, Sir Patrick; kt (1991); s of Sir John Francis Sheehy, CSI (d 1949), and Jean Newton Simpson (d 1993); *b* 2 Sept 1930; *Educ* Australia, Ampleforth; *m* 1964, Jill Patricia Tindall; 1 s, 1 da; *Career* Nat Serv 2 Lt Irish Gds 1948–50; British-American Tobacco Co: joined 1950, various appts Nigeria, Ghana, Ethiopia and West Indies, mktg advsr London 1962–67, gen mangr Holland 1967, memb Gp Bd 1970, memb Chm's Policy Ctee and chm Tobacco Div 1975; BAT Industries plc: dep chm 1976–81 (chm BATCo Bd), vice chm 1981–82, chm 1982–95; non-exec dir: British Petroleum Company plc 1984–, Cluff Resources 1992–, Asda Property Holdings 1994–; memb Cncl of Int Advsrs Swiss Bank Corporation 1985–, memb Bd The Spectator 1988–; memb:

President's Ctee CBI, European Roundtable of Industrialists, Action Ctee for Europe, Cncl RIIA; estab Franco British Colloque 1990–, chm Home Office Inquiry into Police Responsibility and Rewards; Chevalier de la Légion d'Honneur (France) 1995; *Recreations* golf, reading, skiing; *Style*— Sir Patrick Sheehy; ✉ c/o British Petroleum Company plc, 1 Finsbury Circus, London EC2M 7BA (☎ 0171 496 4000, fax 0171 496 5656)

SHEEN, Sir Barry Cross Sheen; kt (1978); s of Ronald Cross Sheen (d 1973), and Ethel May, *née* Powell (d 1980); *b* 31 Aug 1918; *Educ* Haileybury, Trinity Hall Cambridge (MA); *m* 1, 27 July 1946, Diane (d 1986), da of Cecil Lucas Donne (d 1957); 3 s (Christopher b 1948, Adrian b 1952, Roderick b 1959); m 2, 5 Nov 1988, Helen Ursula, *née* Woodmansey, wid of Philip Spink; *Career* RNVR 1939–46 (escorting Atlantic and Murmansk convoys, took part in capture of U110), CO HMS Kilkenzie 1943–45; called to the Bar Middle Temple 1947, wreck cmmr, Lloyd's arbitrator in salvage claims, memb Gen Cncl of the Bar 1960–64, jr counsel to Admty 1961–66, QC 1966, bencher 1971, recorder of the Crown Ct 1972–78, judge of the High Ct of Justice Queen's Bench Div (Admiralty Ct) 1978–93; pres Haileybury Soc 1982, chm Assoc of Average Adjusters 1986–87; Liveryman Worshipful Co of Shipwrights 1983; Younger Bro of Trinity House 1993; *Recreations* golf, bowls; *Clubs* Royal Wimbledon Golf, Hurlingham; *Style*— Sir Barry Sheen; ✉ 107 Rivermead Court, London SW6 3SB (☎ 0171 731 7275)

SHEENE, Barry Stephen Frank; MBE (1978); s of Frank Sheene and Iris Sheene; *b* 11 Sept 1950; *Educ* St Martins in the Field; *m* 1984, Stephanie, da of Frederick Harrison; 1 da (Sidonie b 1984), 1 s (Freddie b Nov 1988); *Career* motor cycle racer 1969–84, World Champion 1976–77, more int race wins than any other rider 1974–84, winner Foreign Sportsman awards Italy, Spain and France, survived 2 accidents at high speed 1975 (175 mph) and 1982 (165 mph); dir: Spectra Automotive Products plc Ltd 1983, Barry Sheene Racing Ltd 1972–86; chm Widegate P/L (Commercial Property Co) 1987; presenter ITV Just Amazing 1983–85; helicopter licence 1980, currently presenter Channel 9 TV Aust; 5 year contract with Shell to appear in TV and poster campaigns 1992–, chief exec offr Australian Motor Cycle Grand Prix 1995–96; *Recreations* AS350D Squirrel Helicopter; *Style*— Barry Sheene, MBE; ✉ The Manor House, 2 Riverbend Avenue, Carrara, Gold Coast, Queensland 4211, Australia

SHEEPSHANKS, Robin John; CBE (1990), DL (Suffolk 1979); s of Maj Richard Sheepshanks, DSO, MVO (d 1951), by his w Hon Bridget, *née* Thesiger (d 1983), da of 1 Viscount Chelmsford; *b* 4 Aug 1925; *Educ* Eton; *m* 1951, Lilias Mulgrave, da of Maj Sir Humphrey Noble, 4 Bt, MBE, MC (d 1968), of Walwick Hall; 4 s (David b 1952, Richard b 1955, Andrew b 1960, Christopher b 1964); *Career* Capt 1 King's Dragoon Gds 1943–52; farmer 1952–; chm ADFAM (Suffolk) 1987–, memb E Suffolk CC 1963–74, chm Suffolk CC 1982–84 (memb 1974–93); High Sheriff Suffolk 1981; chm: Suffolk Police Authority, Standing Conference of E Anglian Local Authorities 1987–93, Felix Cobbold Trust 1985–93, Crimestoppers Anglia Region 1994–; dir: Radgrade Ltd 1981–, East Coast Cable Ltd 1989–93; *Recreations* shooting, golf, fishing, gardening; *Clubs* Cavalry and Guards', Pratt's; *Style*— Robin Sheepshanks, Esq, CBE, DL; ✉ The Rookery, Eyke, Woodbridge, Suffolk IP12 2RR (☎ 01394 460226)

SHEERIN, His Hon Judge; John Declan; s of John Patrick Sheerin (d 1969), and Agnes Mary Josephine Sheerin, *née* Keane (d 1975); *b* 29 Nov 1932; *Educ* Wimbledon Coll, LSE (LLB); *m* 1958, Helen Suzanne, da of Philippus Lodewicus le Roux (d 1964); 2 s (Paul, James), 2 da (Sarah, Nicola); *Career* RAF 1958–60, MEAF Nicosia Flying Offr; slr 1957, ptnr Greene & Greene 1962–82; recorder 1979–82, circuit judge (SE Circuit) 1982–, resident judge Cambridge 1992–; *Recreations* Golf; *Clubs* Flempton Golf, Hunstanton Golf; *Style*— His Hon Judge Sheerin; ✉ Cambridge County Court, 72–80 Hills Road, Cambridge CB2 1LA

SHEERMAN, Barry John; MP (Lab) Huddersfield (majority 7,258); s of Albert Sheerman; *b* 17 Aug 1940; *Educ* Hampton GS, LSE, Univ of London (MSc); *m* 1965, Pamela Elizabeth, *née* Brenchley; 1 s, 3 da; *Career* former univ lectr; MP (Lab): Huddersfield E 1979–83, Huddersfield 1983–; memb Public Accounts Ctee 1980–83, chm Parly Advsy Cncl for Tport Safety, co-chm Parly Mfrg Indust Gp, vice chm Parly Univ Gp; oppn front bench spokesman on employment and educn with special responsibility for devpt of educn policy and trg for over-16s 1983–87, spokesman on employment 1987–, home affairs front bench spokesman on police, prisons, crime prevention, drugs, civil defence and fire serv, dep to Rt Hon Roy Hattersley MP 1988–92, shadow min for disability rights 1992–94; chair Networking for Industry (formerly Made In The UK); *Books* Harold Laski (with Isaac Kramnick, 1993); *Style*— Barry Sheerman, Esq, MP; ✉ House of Commons, London SW1A 0AA (☎ 0171 219 5037, office 01924 495277)

SHEFF, Sylvia Claire; MBE (1995), JP (1976); da of Isaac Glickman (d 1981), of Prestwich, Manchester, and Rita, *née* Bor (d 1976); *b* 9 Nov 1935; *Educ* Stand GS for Girls, Univ of Manchester (BA); *m* 28 Dec 1958, Alan Frederick Sheff (d 1986); 1 s (Marcus Jeremy b 1963), 1 da (Janine Rachel b 1960); *Career* teacher 1958–77; fndr and dir Friendship with Israel All Party Gp (in Euro Parl) 1979–90, asst nat dir Cons Friends of Israel 1985–89 (nat projects dir 1974–85), assoc dir Manchester Jewish Cultural Centre 1990–94, int co-ordinator Yeled Yafeh Fellowship Children of Chernobyl Project 1990–94, lectr Jewish Rep Cncl of Gtr Manchester; memb: Bury Family Conciliation Serv Mgmnt Ctee 1985–87, Magistrates Assoc; chm and pres Manchester 35 Gp Women's Campaign for Soviet Jewry 1980– (fndr chm 1972–80), hon sec Nat Cncl for Soviet Jewry UK 1987–89 (memb Cncl 1975–), del Bd of Deps of Br Jews 1987–; *Recreations* bridge, theatre, opera, travel, antiques; *Style*— Mrs Sylvia Sheff, MBE, JP; ✉ 6 The Meadows, Old Hall Lane, Whitefield, Manchester M45 7RZ (☎ 0161 766 4391, fax 0161 766 4391)

SHEFFIELD, Archdeacon of; *see:* Lowe, Ven Stephen Richard

SHEFFIELD, Bishop of 1980–; Rt Rev David Ramsay Lunn; the see was founded in 1914; *b* 1930; *Educ* King's Coll Cambridge (MA), Cuddesdon Theological Coll Oxford; *Career* deacon 1955, priest 1956; curate: Sugley 1955–59, N Gosforth 1959–63; chaplain Lincoln Theological Coll 1963–66, sub-warden 1966–70, vicar St George Cullercoats 1970–75, rector 1975–80 and rural dean of Tynemouth 1975–80; *Style*— The Rt Rev the Bishop of Sheffield; ✉ Bishopscroft, Snaithing Lane, Sheffield, S Yorks S10 3LG (☎ 0114 230 2170, fax 0114 263 0110)

SHEFFIELD, (John) Julian Lionel George; s of John Vincent Sheffield, CBE (himself 4 s of Sir Berkeley Sheffield, 6 Bt, JP, DL); *b* 28 Aug 1938; *Educ* Eton, Christ's Coll Cambridge; *m* 1961, Carolyn Alexandra, er da of the late Brig Sir Alexander Abel Smith, TD, by his 1 w, Elizabeth (da of David B Morgan, of N Carolina); 3 s (John b 1963, Simon b 1964, Lionel b 1969), 1 da (Nicola b 1973); *Career* industrialist; chm: Portals Group plc (papermaking co) 1979–95 (Queen's Award for Export 1966, 1977 and 1982), Norcros plc 1989–96 (joined 1974); dep chm Guardian Royal Exchange 1981–; dir: Inspec Group plc, De La Rue plc, Newbury Racecourse plc; chm North Foreland Lodge Ltd 1987–; Liveryman Worshipful Co of Gunmakers; *Recreations* outdoor sports, collecting; *Clubs* White's, MCC; *Style*— Julian Sheffield, Esq; ✉ Spring Pond, Laverstoke, Whitchurch, Hants RG28 7PD (☎ 01256 895130)

SHEFFIELD, Michael Joseph Forster; OBE, TD, DL (1975); s of Brig Thomas Tredwell Jackson Sheffield, CBE, TD, DL; *b* 11 April 1930; *Educ* Denstone College Staffs, Univ of London (LLB); *m* 1958, Joan Margaret, *née* Ridley; 2 children; *Career* slr; HM coroner: Teesside 1969–73 and 1996–, Cleveland 1973–96; chm: Social Security Appeal Tbnl 1985–, Med Appeal Tbnl 1986–, Disablement Appeal Tbnl 1992–; dir Slrs' Benevolent Assoc 1973– (chm 1986), pres Coroners' Soc of England and Wales 1991–92 (vice pres 1990–91); chm Teesside Cheshire Home 1988–90 (sec 1973–81), tstee Leonard Cheshire Fndn 1994–; vice pres Middlesbrough Rugby Club 1961– (chm 1977–80); govr Middlesbrough HS 1965–67; Royal Signals (NS & TA) 1954–67, Cmdt Durham and S Tyne Army Cadet Force 1977–87, Hon Col Durham Cadet Force 1988–93, memb Cncl Army Cadet Force Assoc 1990–; memb Cncl Order of St John Cleveland, OStJ; *Recreations* tennis, rugby, theatre, military affairs, gardening, bridge; *Clubs* Lansdowne, Cleveland (Middlesbrough); *Style*— Michael Sheffield Esq, OBE, TD, DL; ✉ Ayton House, Easby Lane, Great Ayton, N Yorks (☎ 01642 724310); 9–13 Bedford St, Middlesbrough, Cleveland (☎ 01642 241311, fax 01642 241205)

SHEFFIELD, Provost of; *see:* Sadgrove, Very Rev Michael

SHEFFIELD, Sir Reginald Adrian Berkeley; 8 Bt (GB 1755), of Normanby, Lincolns; DL (Humberside 1985); s of Maj Edmund Sheffield, JP, DL (d 1977), of Sutton Park, Sutton-on-the-Forest, York; (s of 6 Bt), and Nancie Miriel Denise, wid of Lt Cdr Glen Kidston, RN, and yst da of Edward Roland Soames, of Framland House, Melton Mowbray; suc unc, Sir Robert Sheffield, 7 Bt 1977; *b* 9 May 1946; *Educ* Eton; *m* 1, 1969 (m dis 1975), Annabel Lucy Veronica, da of late Timothy Angus Jones, and late Hon Mrs Pandora Astor; 2 da (Samantha Gwendoline (Mrs David Cameron) b 1971, Emily Julia b 1973); m 2, 1977, Victoria Penelope, da of late Ronald Clive Walker, DFC; 1 s (Robert Charles Berkeley b 1984), 2 da (Alice Daisy Victoria b 1980, Lucy Mary b 1981); *Heir* s, Robert Charles Berkeley Sheffield b 1 Sept 1984; *Career* chm Normanby Estate Holdings and subsidiaries; cncllr (C) Ermine Ward Humberside CC 1981–89, vice chm S Humberside Business Advice Centre Ltd; landowner (6,000 acres), memb CLA Lincs Ctee; *Recreations* shooting, stalking; *Clubs* White's, Lincolnshire; *Style*— Sir Reginald Sheffield, Bt, DL; ✉ Thealby Hall, Thealby, Scunthorpe, South Humberside DN15 9AB; Estate Office, Normanby, Scunthorpe, South Humberside DN15 9HS (☎ 01724 720618); 4 Needham Road, London W11 2LR (☎ 0171 727 4160)

SHEGOG, Rev Eric Marshall; s of George Marshall Shegog, of Salford, and Helen, *née* Whitefoot; *b* 23 July 1937; *Educ* Leigh GS, Coll of St Mark and St John, Lichfield Theol Coll, City Univ London (CertEd, DipTheol, MA); *m* 5 Aug 1961, Anne, da of late Elfed Llewellyn Thomas; 2 s (Andrew b 20 May 1963, Simon b 30 May 1966), 1 da (Sarah b 28 July 1969); *Career* Nat Serv RAMC 1955–57, Sgt; asst master Holy Trinity Sch Wimbledon 1960–63, asst curate All Saints Benhilton 1965–68, youth advsr Diocese of Southwark 1968–70, vicar St Michael Abbey Wood 1970–76, chaplain Sunderland City Centre 1976–83, head of religious bdcasting IBA 1984–90, dir of communications C of E 1990–; chm Age Concern Sunderland 1976–83, vice pres Euro Regn World Assoc of Christian Communications; FRSA; *Books* Religious Television: Controversies and Conclusions (contrib, 1990), Religious Broadcasting in the Nineties (contrib, 1991), The Communication of Values (contrib, 1993); *Recreations* gardening, music, jogging; *Style*— The Rev Eric Shegog; ✉ Director of Communications, The Church of England, Church House, Great Smith St, London SW1 3N7 (☎ 0171 222 9011, fax 0171 222 6672)

SHEIKHOLESLAMI, Prof (Ali) Reza; s of Sultan Ali Sultani Sheikholeslami (d 1972), and Shah Zadeh, *née* Mansuri; *b* 21 July 1941; *Educ* Hadaf HS Tehran, Columbia Univ (BA), Northwestern Univ (MA), Univ of California Los Angeles (scholar, DPhil, PhD); *m* 1989, Shirin, da of Ali Khoshnevis; *Career* asst prof of political science Univ of Washington 1975–85, sr res fell Harvard Univ 1985–88; Univ of Oxford: visiting sr fell St Antony's Coll 1988–90, Soudavar prof of persian studies and professorial fell Wadham Coll 1990–; *Books* The Political Economy of Saudi-Arabia, The Structure of Central Authority in Qagar Iran 1871–1896; *Recreations* reading, bicycling, travelling; *Style*— Prof Reza Sheikholeslami; ✉ Oriental Institute, Univ of Oxford, Pusey Lane, Oxford OX1 2LE (☎ 01865 278200, fax 01865 278223)

SHEIL, Hon Mr Justice; Hon Sir John Joseph; kt (1989); Hon Mr Justice Sheil; s of Hon Mr Justice (Charles Leo) Sheil (d 1968), and Elizabeth Josephine, *née* Cassidy (d 1984); *b* 19 June 1938; *Educ* Clongowes Wood Coll, Queen's Univ Belfast (LLB), Trinity Coll Dublin (MA); *m* 18 April 1979, Brenda Margaret Hale, da of Rev Forde Patterson (d 1982), and Elizabeth, *née* Irwin (d 1977); 1 s (Michael Forde b 23 Oct 1980); *Career* called to the Bar: NI 1964, Gray's Inn 1974, Ireland 1976; QC 1975, judge of the High Ct of Justice NI 1989–; *Recreations* golf, travel; *Style*— The Hon Mr Justice Sheil; ✉ Royal Courts of Justice, Chichester St, Belfast BT1 3JF (☎ 01232 235111)

SHEINMAN, Dr Bryan David; s of Neville Sheinman, of London NW11, and Anita Sheinman (d 1988); *b* 23 June 1950; *Educ* Woodhouse GS Finchley, Univ of London (BPharm), Bart's (MB BS), RCP (MRCP), Univ of London (MD); *m* 27 May 1991, Marilyn Phillips, da of Alec Kesselman; *Career* house offr in med and oncology Bart's 1977, house surgn in gen surgery Royal Berks Hosp 1977–78; sr house offr in: med, diabetes, chests and geriatrics Whittington Hosp 1978–79, neurology Bart's 1979–80; registrar in med and cardiology Royal Free Hosp 1980–83, res fell in thoracic med Bart's 1983–86, lectr Cardiothoracic Inst 1986–87; currently: in private practice Harley St, assoc specialist in Chest and Allergy St Mary's Hosp London; memb Worshipful Soc of Apothecaries; memb: Br Thoracic Soc, Br Soc of Allergy and Clinical Immunology, RSM; *Recreations* sailing, jazz; *Style*— Dr Bryan Sheinman; ✉ 120 Harley St, London W1N 1AG (☎ and fax 0171 224 6750); 7 Kidderpore Gardens, London NW3 (☎ 0171 794 0664)

SHELBURNE, Earl of; Charles Maurice Petty-Fitzmaurice; DL (Wiltshire 1990); s (by 1 m) and h of 8 Marquess of Lansdowne, *qv*, and Barbara Stuart Chase (d 1965); *b* 21 Feb 1941; *Educ* Eton; *m* 1, 1965 (m dis 1987), Lady Frances Eliot, da of 9 Earl of St Germans; 2 s (Simon Henry George, Viscount Calne and Calstone b 1970, Hon William Nicholas Charles b 1973), 2 da (Lady Arabella Helen Mary (Lady Arabella Unwin) b 1966, Lady Rachel Barbara Violet (Lady Rachel Spickernell) b 1968); m 2, 1987, Fiona Mary, da of Donald Merritt; *Heir* s, Viscount Calne and Calstone, *qv*; *Career* page of honour to HM The Queen 1956–57; served: Kenya Regt 1960–61, Wiltshire Yeomanry (TA), amalgamated with Royal Yeomanry Regt 1963–73; cncllr: Calne and Chippenham RDC 1964–73, Wilts CC 1970–85, N Wilts DC (chm 1973–76); memb: SW Econ Planning Cncl and chm of its Working Ctee on Population and Settlement Pattern 1972–77, Historic Bldgs and Monuments Cmmn 1983–89, Cncl Duchy of Cornwall 1990–; pres: Wilts Playing Fields Assoc 1965–75, Wilts Assoc of Boys' Clubs and Youth Clubs 1976–, NW Wilts Dist Scout Cncl 1977–88, HHA 1988–93 (dep pres 1986–88), West Country Tourist Bd; Parly candidate (Cons) Coventry NE 1979; Liveryman Worshipful Co of Fishmongers; *Clubs* Turf, Brooks's; *Style*— Earl of Shelburne, DL; ✉ Bowood House, Calne, Wiltshire SN11 0LZ (☎ 01249 812102)

SHELBURNE, Frances, Countess of; Lady Frances Helen Mary; *née* Eliot; da (by 1 m) of 9 Earl of St Germans (d 1988); *b* 1943; *m* 1965 (m dis 1987), Earl of Shelburne, *qv*; *Style*— Frances, Countess of Shelburne; ✉ 29 Narborough Street, Fulham, London SW6 3AP

SHELDON, Hon Sir (John) Gervase Kensington Sheldon; kt (1978); s of Dr John Henry Sheldon (d 1960), of Hopton, Churt, Surrey, and Dr Eleanor Gladys, *née* Kensington (d 1966); *b* 4 Oct 1913; *Educ* Winchester, Trinity Coll Cambridge (MA); *m* 1, 10 Jan 1940, Patricia Mary, da of Lt-Col Arthur Claude Mardon, DSO (d 1950), of Willingdon, Sussex; 1 s (Robin b 1942); m 2, 10 Aug 1960, Janet Marguerite, da of George Wilfrid Seager (d 1979), of Sevenoaks, Kent; 2 s (Jeremy b 1961, Timothy b 1962), 1 da (Sophie b 1964); *Career* served RA (TA) 1939–45 (despatches twice) Egypt, N Africa, Italy, Maj 1943; called to the Bar Lincoln's Inn 1939, judge County Ct 1968–72, circuit judge 1972–78, bencher 1978, judge High Ct of Justice (Family Div) 1978–88 (additional judge High Ct 1988–93), presiding judge Western Circuit 1980–84; *Recreations* shooting, stalking, cricket; *Style*— The Hon Sir Gervase Sheldon; ✉ Hopton, Churt, Surrey GU10 2LD (☎ 01252 792035)

SHELDON, Mark Hebberton; CBE (1997); s of George Hebberton Sheldon (d 1971), and Marie, *née* Hazlitt (d 1974); *b* 6 Feb 1931; *Educ* Stand GS, Wycliffe Coll, CCC Oxford (BA, MA); *m* 16 June 1971, Catherine Eve, da of Edwin Charles James Ashworth (d 1968); 1 s (Edward b 1976), 1 da (Alice b 1972); *Career* Nat Serv Lt Royal Signals 1949–50, TA 1950–53; admitted slr 1957; Linklaters & Paines: articled 1953–56, asst slr 1957–59, ptnr 1959–94, resident ptnr New York 1972–74, sr ptnr 1988–91, jt sr ptnr 1991–93, conslt 1994–96; non-exec dir Coutts & Co 1996–; Law Soc: memb Cncl 1978–96, treas 1981–86, pres 1992–93; pres City of London Law Soc 1987–88; memb: Cncl of JUSTICE 1993–, Advsy Cncl of Centre for Socio-Legal Studies Univ of Oxford 1995–, Panel of Conciliators of Int Centre for Investment Disputes 1995–, Cncl Corp of Lloyd's 1989–90 (chm Working Pty on Voting Rights 1993), Cadbury Ctee on Fin Aspects of Corp Governance 1991–95, Financial Reporting Cncl 1990–, Financial Law Panel 1993–, Sr Salaries Review Body 1994–; tstee Oxford Inst of Legal Practice 1993–; govr Yehudi Menuhin Sch 1996–; memb Ct City of London Slrs' Co 1975– (Master 1987–88); hon bencher Inner Temple 1993; hon memb: Canadian Bar Assoc 1993–, Soc of Public Teachers of Law 1993–; hon fell CCC Oxford 1995; *Recreations* music, English watercolours, wine and food, swimming; *Clubs* Travellers', City of London, Hurlingham; *Style*— Mark Sheldon, Esq, CBE; ✉ 5 St Albans Grove, London W8 5PN (☎ 0171 460 7172, fax 0171 938 4771, messages 0171 937 3120)

SHELDON, Richard Michael; QC (1996); s of Ralph Maurice Sheldon, of Maidenhead, Berks, and Ady, *née* Jaudel; *b* 29 Sept 1955; *Educ* Bolton Sch, Maidenhead GS, Jesus Coll Cambridge (MA, pres CUMC); *m* 1983, Helen Mary, da of John Lake; 1 da (Laura Jane b 1986), 2 s (Nicholas James b 1988, William Mark b 1991); *Career* called to the Bar Gray's Inn 1979; *Recreations* music, bassoon; *Clubs* Halsbury's Laws of England (Vol 7 (2), Companies 4th edn, 1988); *Style*— Richard Sheldon, Esq, QC; ✉ 3/4 South Square, Gray's Inn, London WC1R 5HP (☎ 0171 696 9900, fax 0171 696 9911)

SHELDON, Rt Hon Robert Edward; PC (1977), MP (Lab) Ashton-under-Lyne (majority 10,935); *b* 13 Sept 1923; *m* 1, 1945, Eileen Shamash (d 1969); 1 s, 1 da; m 2, 1971, Mary Shield; *Career* trained as engr; Parly candidate (Lab) Manchester Withington 1959, MP (Lab) Ashton-under-Lyne 1964–; dir Manchester C of C 1964–74 (DAD 1979); chm: Lab Parly econ affrs and fin gp 1967–68, NW Gp Lab MPs 1970–74; oppn spokesman Treasy matters, civil service and machinery of govt 1970–74, memb Public Expenditure Ctee 1972–74 (chm gen sub-ctee); min state: CSD 1974, Treasy 1974–75; fin sec to Treasy 1975–79, oppn front bench spokesman Treasy and econ affrs 1981–83, memb Select Ctee on Treasury and Civil Service until 1981 (and chm sub ctee), chm Public Accounts Ctee 1983– (memb 1965–70 and 1975–79); *Style*— The Rt Hon Robert Sheldon, MP; ✉ 2 Ryder St, London SW1 (☎ 0171 839 4533, fax 0171 930 1528); 27 Darley Ave, Manchester M20 8ZD (☎ 0161 445 3489); House of Commons, London SW1A 0AA (☎ 0171 219 3000)

SHELDON, Timothy James Ralph (Jamie); s of Anthony John Sheldon, and Elizabeth Mary, *née* Ferguson; *b* 9 July 1956; *Educ* Eton, Univ of Exeter (BA); *m* 25 Feb 1984, Susan Jean (Susie), da of John Ridell Best; 1 s (Charles b 14 Oct 1985, Richard b 30 June 1990), 1 da (Sophie b 23 Nov 1987); *Career* CA; Armitage & Norton 1978–82, Robert Fleming & Co Ltd 1982–87; dir: GNI Ltd 1987–, GNI Holdings Ltd 1992–, Gerrard & National Holdings PLC 1994–; non-exec dir Harry Ferguson Ltd 1983–; chm of govrs Hordle House Sch; ACA; *Recreations* sailing, skiing, farming, tennis, squash, piano; *Clubs* Royal Thames Yacht, Royal Yacht Squadron; *Style*— Jamie Sheldon, Esq; ✉ Gerrard & National Holdings plc, Cannon Bridge, 25 Dowgate Hill, London EC4R 2GN (☎ 0171 337 3660, fax 0171 337 3501)

SHELDRICK, Dr (Evelyn) Carol; da of Clement Gordon Sheldrick (d 1979), and Doris Evelyn, *née* Sackett (d 1982); *b* 29 March 1942; *Educ* Woodford HS, Univ of Oxford (MA, BM BChir), Univ of London (MPhil); *m* 17 Dec 1983; *Career* conslt Maudsley Hosp 1978– (formerly house offr, research asst, registrar then sr registrar); author of articles and chapters on changing diagnosis in psychiatry, delinquency and sexual abuse; FRCPsych 1989; *Recreations* music, theatre, gardening, walking; *Style*— Dr Carol Sheldrick; ✉ Maudsley Hospital, Denmark Hill, London SE5 (☎ 0171 919 2546)

SHELFORD, Peter Bengt McNeill; s of Leonard Vere McNeill Shelford (d 1993), and Kerstin Olivia, *née* Lindberg (d 1979); *b* 20 Feb 1951; *Educ* St John's Sch Leatherhead, Guildford Tech Coll, Univ of Southampton, Guildford Coll of Law; *m* 2 July 1977, Patricia Evelyn, da of Comet Norman Pullen; 1 s (Andrew b 21 Sept 1979), 2 da (Sarah b 30 May 1983, Emma b 25 Oct 1985); *Career* Clyde & Co: articled clerk 1973–75, asst slr 1975–79, ptnr 1979– (currently based Hong Kong office); memb Law Soc; *Recreations* tennis, golf, bridge, swimming; *Clubs* Hurst Green Tennis (hon sec 1989–95); *Style*— Peter Shelford, Esq; ✉ c/o Clyde & Co, 51 Eastcheap, London EC3M 1JP (☎ 0171 623 1244); Clyde & Co, 15th Floor, Asia Pacific Finance Tower, Citibank Plaza, 3 Garden Road, Hong Kong (☎ 00 852 2878 8600)

SHELFORD, William Thomas Cornelius (Bill); s of C W Shelford, DL, and Helen Beatrice Hilda, *née* Schuster; *b* 27 Jan 1943; *Educ* Eton, Ch Ch Oxford (MA); *m* 20 March 1971, Annette Betty, *née* Heap Holt; 2 s (Henry b 1973, Thomas b 1980), 1 da (Laura b 1975); *Career* admitted slr 1969; sr ptnr Cameron Markby Hewitt 1990– (ptnr 1970); Liveryman Worshipful Co of Upholders; *Recreations* skiing, gardening; *Clubs* Brooks's, City of London; *Style*— Bill Shelford, Esq; ✉ Chailey Place, Chailey Green, nr Lewes, Sussex BN8 4DA; Cameron Markby Hewitt, Sceptre Court, 40 Tower Hill, London EC3N 4BB (☎ 0171 702 2345)

SHELLEY, Alan John; s of Stanley Arnold Shelley (d 1983), and Ivy May Shelley (d 1995); *b* 7 Aug 1931; *Educ* People's Coll Nottingham; *m* 20 Sept 1958, Josephine Flintoft, da of James Flood (d 1981); 1 s (Matthew b 1965), 1 da (Joanna b 1962); *Career* sr ptnr: Knight Frank & Rutley 1983–92, Knight Frank & Rutley (Nigeria) 1965–79; dir John Holt Investment Co 1981–; chm W Africa Ctee 1985–, gen cmmr of Income Tax 1983–, chm Mansfield Trust, govr RSC; *Recreations* squash, theatre; *Clubs* Oriental, MCC; *Style*— Alan Shelley, Esq; ✉ 54 Bathurst Mews, London W2 2SB (☎ and fax 0171 262 1991)

SHELLEY, Andrew Colin; s of Charles Andrew Shelley (Chief Inspr Essex Constabulary, d 1944), of Chelmsford, and Elizabeth Annie Constance, *née* Harper (d 1985); *b* 17 Jan 1937; *Educ* Royal Masonic Sch, Harvard Business Sch; *m* (m dis); 2 s (Gerald Robin b 1964, Robert Andrew b 1967); *Career* CA; Crittall Manufacturing 1961–65; co sec Munton and Fison Ltd 1968–72 (chief accountant 1965–68), fin dir Muntons plc (formerly Munton and Fison plc) 1972–79; Munton and Fison (Holdings) plc: dir 1979–82, gp chief exec 1982–94, gp md and vice chm 1994–; chm: Muntons Export Ltd, Muntons Microplants Ltd, R M English Grain Ltd, D Quinton & Sons Ltd, C K Squirrell & Sons Ltd, Eling Ltd, Bridlington Farms Ltd, Edward Fison Ltd, Newnham Holdings (Bedford) Ltd, Luzcampo Sociedade Agricola Intensiva do Algarve LDA (Portugal); memb Cncl CBI 1988–91, chm Suffolk TEC 1996– (dir 1989–); pres: E Anglian Dist Soc of CAs 1989–90, Ipswich and Colchester Soc of CAs 1978–79; ICAEW: memb E Anglia Tech Advsy Ctee, memb Nat Tech Advsy Ctee 1978–90, memb Cncl 1981–84 and 1995–, vice chm Industl and Commercial Membs Ctee 1982–84, memb Research Bd 1982–84, vice chm Business Law Ctee 1996–, vice chm Business Bd 1996–, former chm Working Pty on Prevention of Fraud in Industry; Maltsters' Assoc of GB: treas 1986–92 and 1995–, chm 1993–95; Univ Coll Suffolk (assoc coll of UEA): examiner (DMS) 1983–88, govr 1989–92, corp memb 1993–; memb: Univ for Suffolk Task Gp 1994–, Eastern Regnl Ctee FE Funding Cncl 1994–; FCA 1959, AMP Harvard 1981, FIMgt 1982, FInstD 1982, memb Inst of Brewing 1983; *Recreations* gardening, swimming, estate maintenance; *Clubs* Harvard Club of London, Chartered Accountants Dining; *Style*— Andrew Shelley, Esq; ✉ Muntons plc, Cedars Maltings, Stowmarket, Suffolk IP14 2AG (☎ 01449 612400, fax 01449 677800, telex 98205)

SHELLEY, Howard Gordon; s of Frederick Gordon Shelley (d 1979), and Katharine Anne, *née* Taylor; *b* 9 March 1950; *Educ* scholar: Highgate Sch, RCM; *m* 7 June 1975, Hilary Mary Pauline, *née* Macnamara; 1 s (Alexander Gordon b 1979), 1 step s (Peter Cullivan b 1962); *Career* concert pianist and conductor; London debut Wigmore Hall 1971, Henry Wood Prom debut (TV) 1972, conducting debut London Symphony Orch Barbican 1985, concert performances worldwide; has had piano concertos written for him by Cowie, Chapple and Dickinson; performed first cycle of the complete solo piano works of Rachmaninov at Wigmore Hall 1983; Two-Piano duo with Hilary Macnamara (debut 1976); princ guest conductor London Mozart Players 1992– (assoc conductor 1990–92), princ guest conductor Queensland Philharmonic Brisbane 1992–93; memb Worshipful Co of Musicians; FRCM, ARCO; *Recordings* incl: complete solo piano works and concertos of Rachmaninov, Mozart Piano Concertos, Mendelssohn Piano Concertos, Chopin recitals, Schumann recital, Gershwin Piano Concerto and Rhapsodies, Piano Concertos by Vaughan Williams, Tippett, Howard Ferguson and Peter Dickinson; *Awards* Chappell Gold medal 1971, Silver medal of Worshipful Co of Musicians, Dannreuther Concerto prize; *Style*— Howard Shelley, Esq; ✉ 38 Cholmeley Park, Highgate, London N6 5ER; c/o Intermusica Artists Management, 16 Duncan Terrace, London N1 8BZ (☎ 0171 278 5455, fax 0171 278 8434, telex 931 210 2058 sl g)

SHELLEY, Dr (Sir) John Richard; 11 Bt (E 1611) of Michelgrove, Sussex (but does not use the title); s of John Shelley (d 1974); suc gf, Maj Sir John Frederick Shelley, 10 Bt (d 1976); *b* 18 Jan 1943; *Educ* King's Sch Bruton, Trinity Coll Cambridge (MA), St Mary's Hosp Univ of London (MB BChir); *m* 1965, Clare, da of Claud Bicknell, OBE, *qv*; 2 da (Diana Elizabeth b 1970, Helen Ruth b 1972); *Heir* bro, Thomas Henry Shelley b 3 Feb 1945; *Career* general practitioner; ptnr Drs Shelley, Doddington & Gibb (med practitioners); farmer; DObstRCOG, MRCGP; *Style*— Dr John Shelley; ✉ Shobrooke Park, Crediton, Devon EX17 1DG

SHELTON, Graham John; s of Alfred Thomas Shelton (d 1987), of Derby, and Louisa Emily, *née* Clarke (d 1984); *b* 26 Oct 1950; *Educ* Bemrose GS for Boys Derby, Wolverhampton Univ (BA Econ), Univ of Birmingham (scholar, MSocSci), DipHSM 1976; *m* 15 Dec 1979, Noelle Margaret, da of James Minihan, of Limerick, Ireland; 3 s (Matthew William Henry b 31 Dec 1982, James Eoin b 11 Oct 1984, Piers Thomas b 25 Jan 1992), 2 da (Lydia Louise b 9 April 1987, Naomi Marie b 18 July 1989); *Career* trainee in health servs mgmnt Trent RHA, subsequently various appts in W Midlands and E Anglian regions, dep unit admin The Royal Hallamshire Hosp Sheffield 1983–85, unit admin Raigmore Hosp Inverness 1985–86, dir and unit gen mangr Mental Health Servs Norwich Health Authy 1986–93 (acting dist gen mangr 1988–89), chief exec Norfolk Mental Health Care NHS Trust 1993–; former pt/t lectr in health servs mgmnt Sheffield Hallam Univ; author of various jl pubns on mgmnt and mental health servs; MHSM 1976; *Recreations* family, church, music, theatre, memb Norwich Medico Legal Society and Taverham Band; *Style*— Graham Shelton, Esq; ✉ Norfolk Mental Health Care NHS Trust (☎ 01603 421421, fax 01603 421118)

SHELTON, Sir William Jeremy Masefield; kt (1989); s of late Lt-Col Richard Charles Masefield Shelton, MBE, of St Saviour's, Guernsey, and (Ruth Evelyn) Penelope, *née* Coode (d 1992); *b* 30 Oct 1929; *Educ* Radley, Tabor Acad (Mass), Worcester Coll Oxford (MA), Univ of Texas (Austin); *m* 24 Sept 1960, Anne Patricia, da of John Arthur Warder, CBE, of Guernsey; 1 s (Charles b 17 Dec 1972), 1 da (Victoria b 14 Dec 1968); *Career* with Colman Prentis & Varley advertising 1952–55, Corpa (Caracas) 1955–60; md: CPV (International) Bogotá 1960–64, CPV (International) 1967–74, Grosvenor Advertising 1969–74; chm: Fletcher Shelton Delaney & Reynolds 1974–81, GGK London 1984–; cncllr Wandsworth GLC 1967–70, chief whip ILEA 1968–70; MP (C): Clapham 1970–74, Streatham 1974–92; PPS to: Min of Posts and Telecommunications 1972–74, Rt Hon Margaret Thatcher 1975; parly under sec DES 1981–83; memb Cncl of Europe and Western Euro Union 1987–92, chm Access to Justice Ltd 1995–; FIPA; *Clubs* Carlton, Huntercombe Golf; *Style*— Sir William Shelton; ✉ The Manor House, Long Crendon, Bucks HP18 9AN (☎ 01844 208748)

SHEMILT, Elaine Katherine Mary; da of Harold J Shemilt, of Lime Tree Farm, Bagnal, Stoke on Trent, Staffs, and Margarita Isabel Diaz Medina; *b* 7 May 1954; *Educ* Bloomfield Collegiate Sch Belfast NI, Brighton Poly, Winchester Sch of Art (BA), Royal Coll of Art (MA); *m* 1, 1977 (m dis 1984) David A Duly; 2 s (Benjamin b 1979, Emile Joseph b 1980); m 2, 1985, Dr T J C Murphy; 1 da (Genevieve Clare b 1988); *Career* artist; art teacher Winchester 1979–80, artist and printmaker in residence South Hill Park Arts Centre Berkshire 1980–82, fell in fine art and printmaking Winchester Sch of Art 1982–84, sr lectr Duncan of Jordanstone Coll of Art Dundee 1988– (lectr 1985–88), vice chm and dir Dundee Printmakers Workshop/Seagate Gallery Dundee 1989–96, external assessor for printmaking Univ of the W of England 1991–95, external assessor for printmaking Univ of Hull 1996–; memb Scottish Soc of Artists 1992; *Exhibitions* incl: Bexley Heath Kent 1975, Serpentine Gallery London 1976, Guildhall Winchester 1976, Nat Gallery Singapore 1977, RCA London 1977, ICA London 1978, London Poly 1978, Hayward Annual London 1979, RCA London 1980, Ikon Gallery Birmingham 1980, Fylde Arts Assoc 1981, Arteder '82 Muestra International De Arte Grafico Bilbao Spain 1982, RCA 1983, The Nude Cheltenham 1983, The Winchester Gallery 1984, Plymouth Arts Centre 1984, Ferens Art Gallery Hull 1985, Compass Gallery 1985, Landesbank Stuttgart W Germany 1986, Royal Festival Hall London 1987, RSA Diploma Galleries 1987, Kingfisher Gallery Edinburgh 1987, Stamford Theatre and Arts Centre 1988, Gallerie Twerenbold Lucerne Switzerland 1988 and 1990, Andrew Jones Gallery 1988, Bellfrie Gallery Copenhagen Denmark 1988, Soc of Scottish Artists Edinburgh 1989, Paperworks (Seagate Gallery Dundee) 1989, Women's Photography Exhibition (The Small Mansion Arts Centre London) 1990, Kindred Spirits (Ancrum Gallery and Matthew Gallery Duncan of Jordanstone) 1990, Frameworks (BDP Exhibition Preston touring) 1990, 11th Int Bradford Print Biennale (touring) 1990, McManus Gallery group staff exhibition 1990, Lumley-Cazalet Gallery Kensington 1990, 11th Int Print Biennale RCA London 1991, Janus Avivson Gallery Camden London 1992, SSA Edinburgh 1992, The London Group (Barbican), Scotland in New Europe (Demarco Gallery E European Fndn) 1992, installation Bonnington Gallery Nottingham 1993, RSA Annual 1993, installation Seagate Gallery 1993, First Int Print Biennial (Maastricht) 1993, Paperworks (Seagate Gallery) 1993, Stones In Her Pockets (ACAW) 1993 and 1994, Special Photographers Gallery 1993, Stoke Hanley Museum and Art Gallery 1994, Mary Ward Centre Bloomsbury 1994, Courtauld Gallery 1994, Roger Billcliffe Gallery 1994, Seagate Gallery 1994, Phillips Gallery Glasgow 1994, Gallerie Centre d'Art en L'Ile Geneva 1994, Paperworks V (Seagate Gallery) 1994, SSA Annual Exhibition 1994 and 1996, St Magnus Festival Orkney (solo exhbn in collaboration with the festival poet) 1995, Select One (Special Photographers Library exhibition), Lamont Gallery London 1996, Help the Aged Charity 1996, Slade Sch of Art gp show 1996, A Millenium Bestiary Hand Printed Artist's Book 1996, Art Lotto Collective Gallery charity auction 1996, RSA Annual Exhibition 1996, Brave Art Glasgow Mayfest 1996, Networking Gp Edinburgh Festival 1996, Louise Smith Gallery Toronto 1996, RGI Annual Exhibition 1996, Art and Science Richard Demarco E Euro Art Fndn 1996; *Work in Collections* BBC, Bank of America, Landesbank Stuttgart, Kurt Breinlinger Konstanz, Arts Cncl, RCA, Dundee City Museums and Art Galleries, private collections in Europe and Canada; *Important Works* incl: Ritual series 1980–90, installation South Hill Park Arts Centre 1981, Bell Jar series 1988, The Gods and Goddess series (Queen Gunhild, Windeby Girl, Ritual) etchings, lithography and screen prints 1992, installation Tension 1993, installation Strange Fruit Richard Demarco Gallery Edinburgh Festival 1994, Repossessed (solo exhibition accompanying Kevin Crossley-Holland's poems) St Magnus Festival 1995; *Awards* Southern Arts, Arts Cncl, Scottish Arts Cncl, Lincoln and Humberside Arts, Paperworks Purchase prize 1994; *Style—* Ms Elaine Shemilt; ✉ 12 Douglas Terrace, Broughty Ferry, Dundee, Scotland DD5 1EA (☎ and fax 01382 779851); 51 Warrender Park Rd, Edinburgh, Scotland EH9 1EU (☎ 0131 229 8743); Director of Printmakers Workshop and Senior Lecturer in charge of Printmaking, Duncan of Jordanstone College of Art, University of Dundee, 13 Perth Rd, Dundee

SHENKIN, Prof Alan; s of Louis Shenkin, of Glasgow, and Miriam Leah, *née* Epstein; *b* 3 Sept 1943; *Educ* Hutchesons' GS Glasgow, Univ of Glasgow (BSc, MB ChB, PhD); *m* 27 June 1967, Leonna Estelle, da of Godfrey Jacob Delmonte (d 1978), of Glasgow; 1 s (Stephen b 1975), 2 da (Susie b 1970, Trudi b 1971); *Career* lectr in biochemistry Univ of Glasgow 1970–74, Royal Soc Euro exchange fell Karolinska Inst Stockholm 1976–77; conslt in clinical biochemistry Glasgow Royal Infirmary 1978–90 (sr registrar 1974–78), prof of clinical chemistry Univ of Liverpool 1990–, author of various res papers and book chapters on nutritional support and micronutrients; chm Scientific Ctee Assoc of Clinical Biochemists 1994–96, chm and memb Cncl Specialty Advsy Ctee on Chemical Pathology Royal Coll of Pathologists 1995–, memb Cncl Nutrition Soc 1995–; treas Euro Soc of Parenteral and Enteral Nutrition, 1988–92, ctee memb Clinical Metabolism and Nutritional Support Gp of The Nutrition Soc 1988–94; hon memb Czechoslovakian Med Soc and Czechoslovakian Soc for Parenteral and Enteral Nutrition 1990; FRCPath 1990, FRCP(Glas) 1990, FRCP 1993; *Recreations* golf, word games, travel; *Style—* Prof Alan Shenkin; ✉ 10 Rockbourne Green, Woolton, Liverpool L25 4TH (☎ 0151 428 9756); Department of Clinical Chemistry, University of Liverpool, PO Box 147, Liverpool L69 3BX (☎ 0151 706 4232, fax 0151 706 5813)

SHENNAN, Francis Gerard; s of Thomas Gerard Shennan, of Tadley, Hants, and Cecelia, *née* Strype; *b* 14 Sept 1949; *Educ* Preston Catholic Coll, St Joseph's Coll Dumfries, Univ of Edinburgh (LLB); *Career* writer and journalist; news sub ed: Daily Mirror Manchester 1975–76, Scottish Daily Record 1976–88; recruitment columnist the Scotsman 1988–89, fndr The Shennan Agency 1988–, Scot business ed The Sunday Times 1989–90, editorial dir Corporate Advisers Scotland Ltd, dir Footie Index Ltd; law examiner for Scot Nat Cncl for the Trg of Journalists 1981–84, external examiner of media law Napier Poly Edinburgh 1984–92; guest lectr and speaker: Napier Poly, NW Writers' Assoc, SE Writers' Assoc; contrib to: Scotland on Sunday, The Scotsman, The Herald, Sunday Express, Scottish Business Insider, CA Magazine, Investors' Chronicle, Scotish Entrepreneur, Scottish Field, Woman, Woman's Own, Television Weekly; *Books* The Life, Passions, and Legacies of John Napier (1990), Rebels in Paradise: The Inside Story of the Battle for Celtic Football Club (with D Low); *Recreations* travelling, walking; *Style—* Francis Shennan, Esq; ✉ The Shennan Agency, 134 Wilton Street, Glasgow G20 6DG (☎ 0141 946 9030, fax 0141 946 9444)

SHENNAN, Prof Joseph Hugh; s of Hugh Cringle Shennan, and Mary Catherine, *née* Jones; *b* 13 March 1933; *Educ* Univ of Liverpool (BA), CCC Cambridge (Bridges Research Scholar, PhD); *m* 1958, Margaret King, da of William Gladstone Price; 3 s (Andrew b 1959, Robert b 1962, Christopher b 1966); *Career* Nat Serv Mil Intelligence WO 1955–57; asst lectr then lectr in history Univ of Liverpool 1960–65; Univ of Lancaster: successively lectr, sr lectr then reader in history 1965–74, prof and dir Euro studies 1974–79, prof of Euro history and head Dept of History 1979–84, pro vice-chllr (academic) 1985–93, dep vice-chllr 1993–; visiting fell CCC Cambridge 1984–85; external examiner in history various univs; fndr ed European Studies Review (now European History Quarterly) 1970–79, advsy ed European History Quarterly 1979; memb: History Bd CNAA 1982–85, Publications Ctee Advsy Cncl on Public Records 1984; FRHistS 1969; *Books* The Parlement of Paris (1968), Government and Society in France 1461–1661 (1969), The Origins of the Modern European State 1450–1725 (1974), Philippe, Duke of Orléans: Regent of France 1715–1723 (1979), Liberty and Order in Early Modern Europe: The Subject and the State 1650–1800 (1986); author of numerous other articles and chapters in books and learned journals; *Recreations* golf; *Clubs* United Oxford and Cambridge University, Lancaster Golf and Country; *Style—* Prof J H Shennan; ✉ Bull Beck House, Four Acres, Brookhouse, Lancaster LA2 9JW (☎ 01524 770517); Vice-Chancellor's Office, University of Lancaster, Lancaster LA1 4YW (☎ 01524 592003, fax 01524 36841)

SHENTALL, David John Traill; s of Ernest Alan Shentall (d 1992), of Sheffield, and Clara Mary, *née* Traill; *b* 23 March 1940; *Educ* Repton Derby (1st XI football); *m* 5 Sept 1964, Sarah Ann Harriet, da of Charles Burtt Marfleet (d 1967); 1 da (Tessa Clare b 25 Oct 1965), 1 s (Charles Edward Traill b 30 July 1967); *Career* Andels Svineslagteri bacon factory Denmark 1957–58, Wrensons Stores Birmingham 1958–59, John Shentall Ltd family grocery business Chesterfield 1959–60, Fine Fare plc (bought John Shentall) 1960–61, A B Gibson Ltd food distributors Nottingham 1962–73 (md 1969–73), Oriel Foods plc (bought A B Gibson) 1973–75, dir Watson & Philip plc food distributors 1975–81; proprietor Kinloch House Hotel 1981–; 3 Red Stars (AA), 3 Rosettes (for food, AA), Caesar Award (Good Hotel Guide) 1991, Courtesy & Care Award (AA) 1991, Country Hotel of the Year (Johansen Guide) 1994; *Recreations* hotel keeping; *Style—* David Shentall, Esq; ✉ Kinloch House Hotel, by Blairgowrie, Perthshire PH10 6SG (☎ 01250 884237, fax 01250 884333)

SHENTON, David William; s of Sir William Edward Leonard Shenton (d 1967), and Erica Lucy, *née* Denison (d 1978); *b* 1 Dec 1924; *Educ* Westminster Sch, Magdalen Coll Oxford (BA); *m* 1, 1972 (m dis 1987), Della, da of F G Marshall (d 1977), of Sutton, Surrey; m 2, 12 May 1988, Charmian Nancy Lacey, LVO, da of Christopher William Lacey (d 1966), of Walmer, Kent; *Career* WWII Lt Coldstream Gds 1943–46, served Italy (despatches); admitted slr 1951; ptnr Lovell White and King 1955, conslt Lovell White Durrant 1988–89; int arbitrator; conslt Studio Legale Ardito 1990–91; chm Slrs' Euro Gp of Law Soc 1980–81, memb Ctee D of Section on Business Law and Ctee 20 of Section on General Practice Int Bar Assoc 1983– (life chm emeritus Ctee D 1987–); memb: Editorial Ctee International Business Lawyer 1986–88, Chm's Advsy Ctee Int Bar Assoc 1988–90; Freeman City of London 1950; Liveryman: Worshipful Co of Grocers 1954, Worshipful Co of Slrs 1970; *Recreations* sailing, visiting ancient sites and buildings, stone carving, photography; *Clubs* RYS, Household Division Yacht, Cavalry and Guards, Carlton, Justinians; *Style—* David Shenton, Esq; ✉ 16 Eldon Grove, Hampstead, London NW3 5PT (☎ 0171 794 8002, fax 0171 433 3245); The Old Rectory, St James's Street, Yarmouth, IOW PO41 0NU (☎ 01983 760555, messeges 01983 760567, fax 01983 761101)

SHEPARD, Giles Richard Carless; CBE (1994); s of Richard Stanley Howard Shepard, MC, TD, and Kathleen Carless (d 1977); *b* 1 April 1937; *Educ* Eton, Harvard Business Sch; *m* 1966, Peter Carolyn Fern, da of Geoffrey Keighley (d 1966); 1 da, 1 s; *Career* Coldstream Guards 1955–60; dir: Charrington & Co Ltd 1962–64, H P Bulmer & Co Ltd 1964–70; md: Westminster & Country Properties Ltd 1970–76, Savoy Hotel plc 1976–94, The Ritz Hotel London 1995–; dir: Wilton's (St James's) Ltd 1985–, Wentworth Holdings Ltd 1989–96, Guinness Mahon & Co Ltd 1994–; chm Searcy Tansley & Co Ltd 1995–; dir: Kleinwort Development Fund 1991–, London First 1993–95; chm Heritage of London Tst 1994–; memb Nat Exec Br Hospitality Assoc (chm 1992–95), hon catering advsr (with hon rank of Maj Gen) to the Army 1994–; memb: Exec Ctee Cystic Fibrosis Research Tst 1976–93, Cncl Royal Sch of Needlework 1979–94, Royal Parks Advsy Cncl 1992–, Cncl King Edward VII's Hosp 1995–, Cncl Royal United Servs Inst for Defence Studies 1995–; govr Gresham's Sch Holt 1975–, chm City & Guilds of London Art Sch 1982–; memb Cncl Union Jack Club 1978–; High Sheriff of Gtr London 1986–87; memb Ct of Assts Worshipful Co of Fishmongers (prime warden 1987–88), hon memb Académie Culinaire de France; FHICMA; *Recreations* gardening, shooting, embroidery; *Clubs* White's, Pratt's, Beefsteak; *Style—* Giles Shepard, Esq, CBE; ✉ Wallop House, Nether Wallop, Stockbridge, Hampshire SO20 8HE (☎ 01264 781551); The Ritz, 150 Piccadilly, London W1V 9DG (☎ 0171 493 8181, fax 0171 493 5532)

SHEPHARD, Rt Hon Gillian Patricia; PC (1992), MP (C) Norfolk South West (majority 16,931); *b* 22 Jan 1940; *Educ* North Walsham Girls' HS, St Hilda's Coll Oxford; *Career* MP (C) Norfolk South West 1987–; PPS to Economic Sec to Treasy 1988–89, Parly under-sec of state DSS 1989–90, min of state HM Treasy 1990–92, sec of state for employment 1992–93, min of agriculture, fisheries and food 1993–94, sec of state for educn 1994–95, sec of state for educn and employment 1995–; *Style—* The Rt Hon Gillian Shephard, MP; ✉ House of Commons, London SW1A 0AA (☎ 0171 219 3000)

SHEPHARD, Air Cdre Harold Montague; CBE (1974, OBE 1959); s of Rev Leonard Benjamin Shephard (d 1961), of Wareham, Dorset, and Lilian Shephard (d 1982); *b* 15 Aug 1918; *Educ* St John's Leatherhead; *m* 20 May 1939, Margaret Isobel, da of Frederick Girdlestone, of Ewell; 1 s (David Harold Andrew), 1 da (Angela Margaret (Mrs Colgate)); *Career* RAF 1941–74, Air Cdre, provost marshal and dir RAF Security 1971–74; Met Police (CID) 1937–41; MIMgt 1970–74; *Recreations* sport, reading, writing to the press; *Clubs* RAF, Tenterden Golf, Tenterden Cricket (vice pres); *Style—* Air Cdre Harold Shephard, CBE; ✉ 6 Bennetts Mews, West Cross, Tenterden, Kent TN30 6JN (☎ 01580 764945)

SHEPHEARD, Sir Peter Faulkner; kt (1980), CBE (1972); s of Thomas Faulkner Shepheard; *b* 1913; *Educ* Birkenhead Sch, Liverpool Sch of Architecture; *m* 1943, Mary, da of Charles James Bailey; 1 s, 1 da; *Career* architect, town planner and landscape architect; ptnr Shepheard, Epstein & Hunter 1948–89; dean Graduate Sch of Fine Arts Univ of Pennsylvania (USA) 1971–79; *Clubs* Athenaeum; *Style—* Sir Peter Shepheard, CBE; ✉ 21 Well Rd, London NW3 1LH (☎ 0171 435 3019)

SHEPHEARD-HEALEY, Michael Kingsley; s of Patrick Kingsley Shepheard, of London and Rio de Janeiro, and Vivienne, *née* Nathan; *b* 6 Dec 1951; *Educ* Keil Sch Dumbarton Scotland, Glasgow Sch of Art (BA, postgrad dip, Leverhulme travel scholar); *Career* designer: Pushpin Studios, J Walter Thompson NY, McCann Erickson Snazelle Films San Francisco 1976; sr designer J P Coats Glasgow (Jaeger products, Ladybird, Coats Patons) 1977, jr art dir J Walter Thompson Rio de Janeiro 1978–81, dir Rex Stewart and Assocs Glasgow 1981–84; Glasgow Sch of Art: head Dept of Graphic Design, Illustration and Photography 1984–, head Sch of Design and Craft 1993–; freelance designer, many design and painting cmmns incl work for Euro Parliament 1989; work in several private collections; MInstM; *Recreations* drawing and painting, history, fly fishing, sailing; *Clubs* Glasgow Art; *Style—* Michael Shepheard-Healey, Esq; ✉ Glasgow School of Art, 167 Renfrew Street, Glasgow GL1 9LL (☎ 0141 353 4500)

SHEPHERD, Sir Colin Ryley; kt (1996), MP (C) Hereford (majority 3,413); *b* 13 Jan 1938; *Educ* Oundle, Gonville and Caius Coll Cambridge, McGill Univ Montreal; *Career* mktg dir and Parly advsr Haigh Engineering Co Ltd 1963–; MP (C) Hereford Oct 1974–, jt vice chm Cons Parly Agric Ctee 1979–87, memb Select Ctee on House of Commons Servs 1979–, chm Library Sub Ctee 1982–91, chm Catering Sub Ctee 1990–91, chm Catering Ctee 1991–; PPS to sec of State for Wales 1987–90; fell Indust & Parliament Tst, memb Cncl RCVS 1983–, govr Cwlth Inst 1989–, chm Cwlth Parly Assoc 1993–96 (memb Int Exec Ctee 1989–96); *Style—* Sir Colin Shepherd, MP; ✉ Manor House, Ganarew, Nr Monmouth, Gwent (☎ 01600 890220); House of Commons, London SW1A 0AA (☎ 0171 219 3000)

SHEPHERD, (Richard) David; OBE (1979); s of Raymond Oxley Shepherd (d 1960), and Margaret Joyce, *née* Williamson (d 1978); *b* 25 April 1931; *Educ* Stowe; *m* 2 Feb 1957, Avril Shirley, da of Hugh Dowling-Gaywood (d 1940); 4 da (Melinda b 1958, Mandy b 1960, Melanie b 1962, Wendy b 1964); *Career* artist; trained under Robin Goodwin 1950–53, exhibited RA Summer Exhibition 1956, first one man exhibition 1962, painted religious painting of Christ for Army Garrison Church Bordon Hants 1964; *Solo Exhibitions* London 1966, 1978, 1984 and 1988, Johannesburg 1966, NY 1979; *Portraits* HE Dr K Kaunda First Pres of Zambia 1967, HM The Queen Mother 1969, Sheikh Zaid of Abu Dhabi 1970; life story World About Us BBC TV 1971 (The Man Who Loves Giants), BBC documentary Last Train to Mulobezi 1974, series for Thames TV In Search of Wildlife 1988; memb of hon World Wide Fund for Nature, fndr David Shepherd Conservation Fndn (currently focused on endangered mammals), fndr and chm E Somerset Railway; Hon Doctorate Pratt Inst of NY 1971, Hon DSc Univ of Hertfordshire 1990; FRSA 1987; FRGS 1989; Order of Distinguished Service First Div Rep of Zambia; *Books* An Artist in Africa (1967), The Man Who Loves Giants (autobiog, 1975), Paintings of Africa and India (1978), A Brush With Steam (1983), David Shepherd: The Man and His Paintings (1986), David Shepherd - An Artist in Conservation (1992), David Shepherd - My Painting Life (1995), David Shepherd - Only One World; *Recreations* raising funds for wildlife conservation and driving steam locomotives; *Style—* David Shepherd, Esq, OBE; ✉ Winkworth Farm, Hascombe, Godalming, Surrey GU8 4JW (☎ 01483 208220)

SHEPHERD, David Robert; s of Herbert Howell Shepherd (d 1962), of Instow, Bideford, Devon, and Doris Sarah, *née* Smallridge (d 1990); *b* 27 Dec 1940; *Educ* Barnstaple GS, St Luke's Coll Exeter; *partner* Jennifer Margaret Hoare; *Career* cricket umpire; player: English Schs 1959, Devon 1959–64, Gloucestershire CCC 1965–79 (awarded county cap 1969), total 282 first class matches; scored 108 on debut Glos v Univ of Oxford; appointed first class umpire 1981–: first match at Oxford, first one day int England v W Indies 1984, first test match England v Aust 1985, umpired over 30 test matches; other matches umpired incl: World Cup England 1983, World Cup India and Pakistan 1987, MCC Bicentenary Lord's 1987, Asia Cup Sri Lanka, World Cup Aust and NZ 1992, World Cup India, Pakistan and Sri Lanka 1996 (incl final in Lahore), numerous domestic cup finals Lord's; *Recreations* all sports, stamp collecting; *Style—* David Shepherd, Esq; ✉ Test and County Cricket Board, Lords Cricket Ground, London NW8 8QN (☎ 0171 286 4405)

SHEPHERD, Prof (William) Douglas; s of Capt William Davidson Shepherd (d 1995), of Bournemouth, and Jessie, *née* Douglas (d 1988); *b* 14 Sept 1939; *Educ* Bournemouth Sch, Univ of London (BSc); *m* 30 Dec 1967, Eileen May, da of Harry Trafford Stott (d 1974), of Woking; 1 s (Harry b 1985); *Career* technologist BP Res Centre 1965–67, sr lectr Dept of Computer Sci Portsmouth Poly 1967–71, res fell computer laboratory Univ of Kent 1969–70, lectr Dept of Computer Sci Univ of Strathclyde 1971–83; Univ of Lancaster: prof of computing and head of dept 1983–88, dean of Sch of Engrg Computing and Mathematical Scis 1989–92, dir of Information Systems Policy 1992–; sr visitor computer laboratory Univ of Cambridge 1980–81, visiting scientist IBM Euro Network Centre Heidelberg W Germany 1988–89, visiting prof Univ of California Berkeley 1994–95; memb Advsy Panel on Strategy for Communications and Distributed Systems in Successor Prog to Alvey 1987–88, chm Communications and Distributed Systems Club IED 1989–92, chm IEE PGC3 Information Systems and Networks 1994–; MBCS 1970, MIEEE 1988, FIEE 1992; *Books* Local Area Networks: An Advanced Course (1982), Object Oriented Languages (1991), Network and Operating System Support for

Audio and Video (1994); *Recreations* squash, golf and hill walking; *Clubs* Royal Victoria YC, Lancaster Golf and Country; *Style*— Prof Douglas Shepherd; ✉ University of Lancaster, Information Systems Services, Lancaster LA1 4YW (☎ 01524 593827, fax 01524 844011, telex 65111 LANCUL G)

SHEPHERD, Hon Graeme George; s and h of 2 Baron Shepherd, PC, *qv*; *b* 6 Jan 1949; *m* 1971, Eleanor; 1 s (Patrick Malcolm); *Style*— The Hon Graeme Shepherd; ✉ 1a Chelsea Court, 63 Mt Kellett Road, The Peak, Hong Kong

SHEPHERD, Lt-Col Ian; s of Edward Basil Branch Shepherd (d 1980), and Una, *née* Sadler (d 1987); *b* 6 April 1939; *Educ* Queen's Coll of Br Guiana, Dollar Acad, RMA Sandhurst; *m* 19 June 1965, Belinda, da of late Brig Archibald Ian Buchanan-Dunlop, CBE, DSO, of Broughton Place, Broughton, Peebles-shire; 2 s (Rupert Graham b 1968, Christian James b 1971), 1 da (Josephine Mary b 1975); *Career* cmmnd into Royal Highland Fusiliers 1960, Asst Mil Attaché (Tech) Moscow 1981–82; CO Scot Infantry Depot (Bridge of Don) 1984–86, CO Univ of Aberdeen OTC 1986–88, ret 1992; currently regnl organiser (Scotland) Army Benevolent Fund and sec Scottish Nat War Meml; memb Inst of Charity Fundraising Mangrs; chm Mgmnt Ctee Lady Haig's Poppy Factory, memb North, South, East Ctee The Officers' Assoc (Scottish Branch); *Recreations* being an old soldier; *Clubs* Army and Navy; *Style*— Lt-Col Ian Shepherd; ✉ c/o Bank of Scotland, The Mound, Edinburgh EH1 1YZ

SHEPHERD, Prof James; s of James Bell Shepherd, of Ardberg, Bute, and Margaret McCrum, *née* Camick; *b* 8 April 1944; *Educ* Hamilton Acad, Univ of Glasgow (BSc, MB ChB, PhD, FRCP, FRCPath); *m* 5 July 1969, Jan Bulloch, da of William Bulloch Kelly, of Motherwell; 1 s (Ewen James b 7 Feb 1974), 1 da (Fiona Elizabeth b 7 July 1976); *Career* lectr in biochemistry Univ of Glasgow 1969–72; Dept of Pathological Biochemistry Univ of Glasgow and Glasgow Royal Infirmary: lectr 1973–77, sr lectr and hon conslt 1977–84, prof and head of dept 1988–; clinical dir Laboratories Glasgow Royal Infirmary 1993–; asst prof of med Methodist Hosp Houston Texas 1976–77, visiting prof of med Cantonal Hosp Geneva 1984; dir W of Scotland Coronary Prevention Study 1989–96; chm Euro Atherosclerosis Soc 1993–96; memb: Coronary Prevention Gp, Int Atherosclerosis Soc; FRSE 1996; *Books* incl: Lipoproteins in Coronary Heart Disease (jtly, 1986), Atherosclerosis: Developments, Complications and Treatment (jtly, 1987), Lipoprotein Metabolism (1987), Coronary Risks Revisited (ed jtly, 1989), Human Plasma Lipoproteins (ed jtly, 1989), Preventive Cardiology (ed jtly, 1991), Lipoproteins and the Pathogenesis of Atherosclerosis (ed jtly, 1991), Cardiovascular Disease: Current perspectives on the Asian-Pacific Region (ed jtly, 1994), Clinical Biochemistry: An illustrated colour text (co-author, 1995); *Style*— Prof James Shepherd, FRSE; ✉ 17 Barriedale Avenue, Hamilton ML3 9DB (☎ 01698 428259); Department of Pathological Biochemistry, Royal Infirmary, Glasgow G4 0SF (☎ 0141 211 4628, fax 0141 553 1703, telex 779234 HLAGLA G)

SHEPHERD, John H; s of Dr Henry Robert Shepherd, DSC, of Enfield, Middx, and Mimika, *née* Matarki; *b* 11 July 1948; *Educ* Blundell's, St Bartholomew's Hosp Med Coll (MB BS); *m* 27 May 1972, Alison Sheila, da of Capt Henry Stephen Brandram-Adams, MBE, of Wootton, IOW; 1 s (David b 1976), 2 da (Katy b 1978, Emily b 1985); *Career* conslt gynaecological surgn: St Bartholomew's Hosp 1981–, Chelsea Hosp for Women 1983–84, Royal Marsden Hosp 1983–; hon conslt King Edward VII Hosp for Offrs 1993–; author numerous chapters and scientific articles on med topics relating to cancer, gynaecology and obstetrics; memb: Cncl RCOG 1984–87 and 1989–95, Working Pty in Gynaecological Oncology MRC; chm Gynaecological Cancer Sub Ctee of UK Co-ordinating Ctee for Cancer Res; Yeoman Worshipful Soc of Apothecaries; memb: BMA 1971, RSM 1972; FRCS 1975, MRCOG 1978, FACOG 1981, FRCOG 1996; fell: Belgian Royal Acad of Med 1986, Singaporian Acad of Med 1987; memb: Soc of Pelvic Surgns, Soc of Gynaelogic Oncologists, Chelsea Clinical Soc, Academia Europaea, New York Acad of Science; *Books* Clinical Gynaecological Oncology (1985, 2 edn 1990); *Recreations* skiing, sailing, cricket, squash, classical music; *Style*— John Shepherd, Esq; ✉ Pickwick Cottage, 31 College Rd, Dulwich, London SE21 7BG (☎ 0181 693 6342); 149 Harley St, London W1 1AB (☎ 0171 935 4444, fax 0171 935 6224)

SHEPHERD, 2 Baron (UK 1946); Malcolm Newton Shepherd; PC (1965); 2 Baron (UK 1946); s of 1 Baron Shepherd, PC, sometime Chief Labour Whip Lords, Capt Yeomen of the Gd & Hon Corps Gentlemen at Arms, also Nat Agent Lab Pty (d 1954), and Ada, *née* Newton; *b* 27 Sept 1918; *Educ* Friends' Sch Saffron Walden; *m* 15 Nov 1941, Allison, JP, da of Patrick Redmond (d 1980); 2 s (Graeme George b 1951, Douglas Newton b 1954); *Heir* s, Hon Graeme Shepherd; *Career* chm: Mitchell Cotts & Co (FE) Ltd 1950–56, Fielding Brown & Finch (FE) Ltd 1951–62, National Bus Company 1980–85, Cheque Point International 1988–, Czech Banka Cheque joint Prague; dir: Sterling Group of Cos 1976–82, Sum Hung Kai Ltd 1980–85; chief whip House of Lords 1964–67 (oppn chief whip 1960–64), min of state FO 1967–70, lord privy seal and ldr House of Lords 1974–76; chm: MRC 1976–80, Civil Serv Pay Res Unit Bd 1976–81, Packaging Cncl; pres Inst Road Tport Engrs 1987–; *Recreations* golf; *Clubs* Tenterden Golf; *Style*— The Rt Hon the Lord Shepherd, PC; ✉ 29 Kennington Palace Court, Sancroft St, London SE11 (☎ 0171 582 6772); Cheque Point International, Berkeley St, London W1 (☎ 0171 409 0868)

SHEPHERD, Richard Charles Scrimgeour; MP (C) Aldridge Brownhills (majority 11,024); s of Alfred Shepherd; *b* 6 Dec 1942; *Educ* LSE, Johns Hopkins Univ; *Career* dir: Partridges of Sloane Street Ltd, Shepherd Foods Ltd; memb SE Econ Planning Cncl 1970–74; Parly candidate (C) Nottingham E Feb 1974, MP (C) Aldridge Brownhills 1979–, memb Select Ctee on Treasy and CS 1979–, sec Cons Ctees on Euro Affairs and Indust 1980–81; underwriting memb Lloyd's 1974–94; *Style*— Richard Shepherd, Esq, MP; ✉ House of Commons, London SW1A 0AA

SHEPHERD, Robert James (Rob); s of Arthur James Shepherd (d 1989), and Audrey Eleanor, *née* Fewtrell; *b* 1 Oct 1962; *Educ* Ilford Co HS; *m* Susan, da of Ray Lichfield; 2 s (Sebastian b 9 April 1988, Oliver b 24 Jan 1990); *Career* D C Thompson 1981–83, Hayters Sports Reporting Agency 1983–86, chief football writer Today Newspaper 1990–95 (joined 1986), Daily Mail 1995–; memb: Football Writers' Assoc, Sports Writers' Assoc, Young Taverners; *Recreations* football, golf, chess; *Style*— Rob Shepherd, Esq; ✉ Daily Mail, Northcliffe House, 2 Derry Street, Kensington, London E1 9BS (☎ 0171 938 6000)

SHEPHERD, Dr Robert John; s of Reginald John Stuart Shepherd (d 1973), of Gloucester, and Ellen, *née* Pritchard; *b* 16 Jan 1946; *Educ* King's Sch Gloucester, Univ of Liverpool (MB ChB); *Career* med registrar Nat Heart Hosp London, sr med registrar Radcliffe Infirmary Oxford; conslt physician Dept of Med for the Elderly Leics DHA 1977–93, conslt physician Leicester General Hosp NHS Tst 1993–; regional specialty advsr (Trent region) for geriatric med; Br Geriatric Soc: hon dep treas and memb Exec 1996–, memb Cncl 1996–; Trent Br Geriatric Soc: hon treas 1991–93, hon sec 1993–96, chm 1996; memb: BMA, Leics Medical Soc, Leics Medico-legal Soc; MRCP (UK), FRCPEd 1992, FRCP 1995; *Publications* Syncope in Myxoedema due to transient ventricular fibrillation (PostGrad MJ), Normal Pressure Hydrocephalus presenting as Parkinsonian Syndrome (Thorax), Unusual presentation of Systemic lupus erythematosus (Hospital Update, 1996), also author of various other papers; *Recreations* travel, photography, collecting antiques; *Style*— Dr R J Shepherd; ✉ Leicester General Hospital, Gwendolen Road, Leicester LE5 4PW (☎ 0116 249 0490)

SHEPHERD, Stella; *see:* Martin, Stella

SHEPHERD, Prof William; s of William Edward Shepherd (d 1993), of Nottingham, and Mary Elizabeth, *née* Hurst (d 1993); *b* 20 Oct 1928; *Educ* St John's Coll York, Imperial Coll London (BSc), Univ of Toronto Canada (MASc), Univ of London (PhD, DSc); *m* 28 July 1956, Elisabeth Mary, da of Hugh Leslie Gahan (d 1987), of Otford, Kent; 4 s (David William b 1959, Peter Gerald b 1961, Michael John b 1963, Andrew James b 1970 d 1972); *Career* apprentice electrician Nottingham 1942–47; Nat Serv Sergeant instr RAEC 1947–49; sch teacher in Nottingham 1951–52; asst prof Univ of Manitoba Canada 1959–62, princ lectr RMCS 1966–67 (sr lectr 1963–66); Univ of Bradford: reader 1967–78, prof 1978–96, dean Faculty of Engrg 1985–88, pro vice chllr 1988–91, prof of electrical engrg 1994–96; Fulbright prof Univ of Wisconsin Madison USA 1985, Stocker visiting prof Ohio Univ Athens Ohio USA 1993–94 and 1995–96; memb Cncl Institution of Electrical Engrs 1977–80; chm: Yorkshire Centre 1977–78, Scholarships Ctee 1981–83; FIEE, FIEEE; *Books* Thyristor Control of AC Circuits (1975), Energy Flow and Power Factor in Nonsinusoidal Circuits (1979), Power Electronics and Motor Control (1987, 2 edn 1996); *Recreations* music (especially sacred music), tennis, cricket, soccer, gardening (flowers and shrubs), reading biographies, detective stories and cricket books; *Style*— Prof William Shepherd; ✉ 5 Nab Wood Drive, Shipley, W Yorks BD18 4HP (☎ 01274 587153); Department of Electronic and Electrical Engineering, University of Bradford, Bradford, W Yorks BD7 1DP (☎ 01274 384004, fax 01274 384054); Ohio University, USA (e-mail shepherd@bobcat.ent.ohiou.edu)

SHEPHERDSON, Prof John Cedric; s of Arnold Shepherdson, and Elsie, *née* Aspinall; *b* 7 June 1926; *Educ* Manchester GS, Trinity Coll Cambridge (BA, MA, ScD); *m* 1957, Margaret Smith; 1 s, 2 da; *Career* asst experimental offr Aerodynamics and Mathematics Divs Nat Physical Laboratory 1946; Univ of Bristol: asst lectr in mathematics 1946–49, lectr in mathematics 1949–55, reader in mathematics 1955–63, prof of pure mathematics 1964–77, H O Wills prof of mathematics 1977–91, emeritus prof 1991–; memb Inst of Advanced Study Princeton 1953–54; visiting prof: Univ of Calif Berkeley 1966–67 (visiting assoc prof 1958–59), Monash Univ Clayton Victoria Aust 1971, 1986, 1991, 1992 and 1994; visiting scientist IBM Res Laboratories Yorktown Heights NY 1973, 1975 and 1979; memb Advsy Bd Fndns of Computation Laboratory Dept of Computer Sci Univ of Queensland 1987–; memb Editorial Bds Jl of Logic and Computation, Jl of Computer and System Sciences and Jl of Logic in Computer Science 1990–; FIMA 1964 (chm Bristol Branch 1971–72), FBA 1990; memb: London Mathematical Soc, American Mathematical Soc, Assoc for Symbolic Logic, Mathematical Assoc, BAAS; *Publications* papers in mathematical logic and computer sci jls; *Recreations* walking, cycling, skiing, board-sailing, climbing; *Clubs* Fell & Rock Climbing (Lake District); *Style*— Prof John Shepherdson, FBA; ✉ Oakhurst, North Road, Leigh Woods, Bristol BS8 3PN (☎ 0117 973 5410, e-mail john.shepherdson@bris.ac.uk)

SHEPLEY, Christopher John; s of George Frederick Shepley (d 1982), and Florence Mildred, *née* Jepson, of Stockport; *b* 27 Dec 1944; *Educ* Stockport GS, LSE (BA Geography), Univ of Manchester (Dip Town Planning); *m* 1967 (m dis 1992), Jennifer Webber; 1 s (Andrew Michael b 1971), 1 da (Carolyn b 1975); *Career* civil servant; local govt: graduate planner rising to sr planning offr Manchester City Cncl 1966–73, princ planner rising to dep county planning offr Gtr Manchester CC 1973–85, city planning offr rising to dir of devpt Plymouth City Cncl 1985–94; chief planning inspr and chief exec Planning Inspectorate (Civil Service appt) 1994–; hon visiting prof Dept of Planning and Landscape Univ of Manchester 1990–94; memb RTPI 1972 (pres 1989); *Books* The Grotton Papers (1979); *Recreations* music, opera, football, walking, travelling; *Style*— Christopher Shepley, Esq; ✉ Chief Planning Inspector, Department of the Environment, Tollgate House, Houlton Street, Bristol BS2 9DJ (☎ 0117 987 8963, fax 0117 987 8408)

SHEPPARD, Rt Rev David Stuart; *see:* Liverpool, Bishop of

SHEPPARD, Howard; *b* 2 Nov 1944; *Educ* Kingston Sch of Architecture (DArch), Heriot-Watt Univ (MSc); *m*; 3 c; *Career* asst architect Marani Routhwaith & Dick Architects Toronto 1966–67, architect with various private practices 1969–72; GLC: architect planner Transportation and Planning (Central London) 1972–76, project architect Dept of Architecture (Housing) 1976–79, devpt planner Transportation and Planning (NW London) 1979–81; London Docklands Devpt Corp: sr architect planner 1981–86, area dir (Devpt) Wapping and Limehouse 1986–89 (Isle of Dogs and Wapping 1989–91), dir City Design and Planning LDDC 1991– (responsible for statutory planning, urban design and framework planning, architecture, conservation and landscape design); visiting prof of architecture & urban studies Virginia Poly and State Univ USA 1976–77, memb Awards Panel American Inst of Planning (Virginia) Williamsburg 1977, speaker Int Forum Waterfront 2001 Osaka 1991; assoc environmental auditor Environmental Auditors' Registration Assoc; corp memb: RIBA, RTPI; FRSA; *Style*— Howard Sheppard, Esq; ✉ Director of City Design and Planning, London Docklands Development Corporation, 191 Marsh Wall, London E14 9TJ (☎ 0171 512 3000)

SHEPPARD, Maurice Raymond; s of Wilfred Ernest Sheppard (d 1976), and Florence Hilda Sheppard; *b* 25 Feb 1947; *Educ* Haverfordwest GS, Eisteddfod Maldwyn, Loughborough Coll of Art, Kingston Coll of Art (DipAD), RCA (MA); *Career* artist, draughtsman and watercolourist; cmmnd to paint The Golden Valley (for Lord Attenborough's film Shadowlands) 1993; Br Instn Award 1971, David Murray Landscape Award 1972, Geofrey Crawshay Meml travelling scholar Univ of Wales 1973; memb Nat Art Collection Fund; ARWS 1974, RWS 1977, VPRWS 1979, PRWS 1984–87 (tstee 1983–95); *Major Exhibitions* Fairfax-Lucy, Hayes, Sheppard (New Grafton Gallery) 1976, Maurice Sheppard (New Grafton Gallery) 1979, Maurice Sheppard (Christopher Wood Gallery) 1989; *Group Exhibitions* incl: Royal Acad Summer Exhibition 1971–, Royal Watercolour Soc 1974–, Mall Gallery, Agnews, John Nevil Gallery Canterbury, Leonie Jonliegh Gallery Guilford, Tom Caldwell Belfast and Dublin, Prouds Pty Sydney, Mitsokoshi Japan; *Collections* public collections: Br Museum, V & A, Nat Museum of Wales, City of Birmingham Museum and Art Gallery, Beecroft Museum and Art Gallery Westcliffe-on-Sea, Tullie House Museum Carlisle, UCW Aberystwyth; private collections: HM The Queen, Lord Pym, Lord Inglewood, Lady Jane Wellesley, Lady Serena Rothchild, Lady Alice Fairfax-Lucy, Sir Francis Beaumont, Andrew Wilton; corporate collections: Boots plc, WH Smith, Blue Circle plc, HOR Oil (UK) plc, MBNA International Bank of America Ltd (11 works, 1972–95), Canary Wharf Devpt Corp; *Recreations* cycling, music, a small garden, quiet; *Style*— Maurice Sheppard, Esq; ✉ 33 St Martin's Park, Crow Hill, Haverfordwest, Pembrokeshire SA61 2HP (☎ 01437 762659); 14 Apsley St, Rusthall Common, Tunbridge Wells, Kent TN4 8NU

SHEPPARD, Maj Gen Peter John; CB (1995), CBE (1992, OBE 1982); s of Kenneth Wescombe Sheppard, of Pickering, N Yorks, and Margaret, *née* Coleman (d 1993); *b* 15 Aug 1942; *Educ* Welbeck Coll, RMA Sandhurst (RE Instn Prize, rugby 1st XV), Univ of London (BSc(Eng), rugby 1st XV); *m* 15 Aug 1964, Sheila Elizabeth, *née* Bell; 1 da (Sara Jane b 3 August 1968), 1 s (Timothy Peter b 22 Jan 1971); *Career* cmmnd 2 Lt Royal Engrs 1962, Univ of London 1962–65, Lt 1 Div RE Germany then Libya 1966–67; promoted Capt 1968, Intelligence Offr 1 Div RE Germany 1968, 2 i/c 3 Field Sqdn RE England then N Ireland 1968–70, Staff Capt MOD 1970–72, RMCS 1973, psc 1974; promoted Maj 1975, GSO2(W) weapons and fighting vehicles Br Army Staff Washington DC 1975–77, OC 29 Field Sqdn RE Germany then N Ireland 1977–79 (despatches N Ireland 1978), GSO2 HQ 1st Br Corps Germany 1979–80; promoted Lt Col 1980, GSO1 mil ops MOD 1980–82, CO 35 Engr Regt Germany 1982–84; Col 1984, Col Gen Staff HQ 1st Br Corps Germany 1984–86; Brig 1986, Cdr Corps RE HQ 1st Br Corps Germany 1986–89, Dir of Army Plans and Progs MOD 1989–91; Maj Gen 1991, COS BAOR

1991–93, DG Logistic Policy (Army) MOD 1993–94, COS HQ Quartermaster General 1994–96, ret 1996; chief exec Soldiers, Sailors and Airmen's Families Assoc (SSAFA) 1996–; *Recreations* golf, philately, walking, travel; *Clubs* Army and Navy; *Style*— Maj Gen Peter Sheppard, CB, CBE; ✉ SSAFA, 19 Queen Elizabeth Street, Southwark, London SE1 2LP (☎ 0171 403 8783, fax 0171 403 8815)

SHEPPARD, Robin Michael Philpot; s of Derek Geoffrey Philpot Sheppard, of Bath, and Estelle Hope, *née* Craddock; *b* 23 Oct 1954; *Educ* King Edward's Sch Bath, Oxford Poly (BA); *m* 30 Sept 1978, Georgina Mary, da of Charles Morris Baines; 2 s (Samuel Thomas b 7 April 1986, Charles Fredrick b 23 April 1988); *Career* hotelier; trained Adelphi Hotel Liverpool (British Transport Hotels) 1978, asst then sr mangr St Andrews Old Course Hotel 1979, dep mangr Grosvenor Hotel Victoria 1980; gen mangr: Wivenhoe Park Conf Centre 1980–82, Bodsygallen Hall Llandudno 1982, Lygon Arms Broadway 1983–86 (Queen's Award for Indust 1985), Royal Berks Hotel Ascot 1986–88 (Egon Ronay star, RAC blue ribbon and Hilton Hotel of the Yr, voted one of six leading hoteliers by Egon Ronay Guide); md The Windrush Group 1989–92, gen mangr Bath Spa Hotel 1992– (Caterer and Hotelkeeper Hotel of the Yr 1994); designed bottle for and founded the Ty-Nant Spring Water Co (winner Glass Fedn's Bottle of the Yr Award 1989); MHCIMA 1986; *Books* The Adventures of Icycle Tricycle (5 titles for children, 1992); *Recreations* golf, rugby, running; *Clubs* Old Edwardian; *Style*— Robin Sheppard, Esq; ✉ General Manager, Bath Spa Hotel, Sydney, Bath BA2 6JF (☎ 01225 444424, fax 01225 444006)

SHEPPARD OF DIDGEMERE, Baron (Life Peer UK 1994), of Roydon in the County of Essex; Sir Allen John George; kt (1990); s of John Baggott Sheppard (d 1985), and Lily Marjorie, *née* Palmer; *b* 25 Dec 1932; *Educ* Ilford Co HS, LSE (BSc); *m* 1, 1958 (m dis 1980), Damaris, da of David Jones (d 1964); m 2, 1980, Mary, da of Harry Stewart, of London; *Career* with Ford UK and Ford of Europe 1958–68, dir Rootes Group 1968–71, dir British Leyland 1971–75; Grand Metropolitan plc: joined as chief exec subsid Watney Mann & Truman Brewers, gp md 1982, chief exec 1986–93, chm 1987–96; non-exec chm: Unipart Group of Cos 1996–, McBride PLC 1995–, Group Trust plc 1994–, Mallinson Denny Group Ltd 1985–87, UBM until 1985 (dir 1981–85); non-exec dep chm: Meyer International plc until 1994 (dir 1989–94), Brightreasons Group Ltd 1995–96; pt/t memb British Railways Bd 1985–90, non-exec dir Rexam plc (formerly Bowater plc) 1994–95; chm: Business in the Community until 1997, Prince's Youth Business Tst 1990–94, Advsy Bd Br-American C of C 1991–94, London First 1992–, Admin Cncl Prince of Wales's Tsts 1995–; vice pres Brewers Soc 1987–, dep chm Int Business Ldrs Forum 1990–95; memb: Nat Trg Task Force 1989–92, Conservative Party Bd of Mgmnt 1992–, Cncl Animal Health Tst; memb Bd and chm Centenary Campaign Blue Cross; govr and memb Standing Ctee LSE; hon fell: London Business Sch 1993, City & Guilds 1993; Gold Medal Inst of Mgmnt 1993, Int Hall of Fame award Mktg Soc 1994; hon doctorates: Int Mgmnt Centre 1989, Brunel Univ 1994, South Bank Univ 1994; FCMA, FCIS, CIMgt; *Books* Maximum Leadership (jtly, 1995); *Recreations* gardens, reading, red-setter dogs; *Style*— The Rt Hon Lord Sheppard of Didgemere; ✉ House of Lords, London SW1A 0PW

SHEPPERD, Sir Alfred Joseph; kt (1989); s of Alfred Charles Shepperd (d 1939), of London, and Mary Ann, *née* Williams (d 1975); *b* 19 June 1925; *Educ* Archbishop Tenison's Sch, UCL (BScEcon); *m* 1950, Gabrielle Marie Yvette (Gay), da of late France Bouloux; 2 da (Sasha (Mrs Lancaster) b 1959, Rosemary (Mrs Lee) b 1963); *Career* Sub-Lt (A) RNVR UK and Canada 1943–46; fin dir The Wellcome Fndn Ltd 1972–77 (chm and chief exec 1977–90), chm and chief exec Wellcome plc 1986–90; dir: Anglia Maltings (Holdings) Ltd 1972– (chm 1995–96), Mercury Asset Management Group plc 1987–96, Oxford Instrument Group plc 1990–95, Isosceles plc 1991–93, National Transcommunications Ltd 1992–96; memb Advsy Cncl on Sci and Indust (ACOST) 1989–93; Freeman City of London, Liveryman of the Worshipful Soc of Apothecaries 1987; FIMgt 1977; Commandatore della Republica Italy 1983, Encomienda al Merito de Sanidad Spain 1988, Cdr Order of Leopold II Belgium 1989; *Clubs* Oriental, County (Guildford); *Style*— Sir Alfred Shepperd

SHEPPERD, John William; s of John Walter Shepperd, of Lancing, E Sussex, and Joan Mary, *née* Owen; *b* 26 Feb 1951; *Educ* Tottenham GS, UCW Aberystwyth (BSc(Econ)), Univ of Manchester (MA(Econ)); *m* 7 Aug 1975, Margot, *née* Hickey; 2 da (Clare b 19 Sept 1986, Emer b 7 Dec 1990); *Career* lectr Calgary Univ Alberta Canada 1973–78, mangr macroeconomic forecasting Economic Models Ltd 1978–80, economist Laing & Cruickshank 1980–82, economist Mullens & Co 1982–86, dir sterling bond research Warburg Securities 1986–93, chief economist Yamaichi International (Europe) Ltd 1993–; memb: Royal Economic Soc 1972, Soc of Business Economists 1986; *Recreations* tennis, listening to Bob Dylan; *Clubs* Reform; *Style*— John Shepperd, Esq; ✉ 44 Priory Gardens, Highgate, London N6 5QS (☎ 0181 341 9456); Yamaichi International (Europe) Ltd, Finsbury Court, 111–117 Finsbury Pavement, London EC2A 1EQ (☎ 0171 330 8415, fax 0171 330 8434)

SHEPSTONE, Dr Basil John; s of James John Shepstone (d 1957), of Bloemfontein, SA, and Letitia Isabel, *née* Robinson (d 1984); *b* 4 Aug 1935; *Educ* Brebner HS Bloemfontein SA, Univ of the Orange Free State (BSc, MSc, DSc), Univ of SA (BA), Univ of Oxford (BM BCh, MA, DPhil), Capetown Univ (MD); *m* 23 Sept 1961, (Brenda) Victoria, da of James Dudley Alen, of Cambridge; 1 s (Jonathan James b 21 Nov 1962), 1 da (Charlotte Isabel b 8 Dec 1965); *Career* jr lectr in radiation physics Univ of The Orange Free State and hosp physicist Nat Prov Hosp Bloemfontein SA 1958–60, house offr in paediatrics and thoracic surgery United Oxford Hosps 1969, head of Dept of Nuclear Med Univ of Cape Town and Groote Shuur Hosp Cape Town 1972–78 (sr specialist Dept of Radiotherapy 1970–72), dean of degrees Wolfson Coll Oxford 1980–, univ lectr and hon conslt in radiology Oxford Univ and Oxfordshire Health Authy 1981–, head of Dept of Radiology Oxford Univ 1984– (clinical lectr 1978–81), dir of clinical studies Oxford Univ Med Sch 1988–91 (dep dir 1985–88); contrib to jls and books on solid state physics, radiobiology, radiotherapy, radiodiagnosis, nuclear med and med educn; memb: Br Inst of Radiology, Br Nuclear Med Soc; fell Wolfson Coll Oxford; FInstP, LRCP, MRCS, FRCR; *Recreations* art history, reading, travelling; *Style*— Dr Basil Shepstone; ✉ Department of Radiology, University of Oxford, The Radcliffe Infirmary, Woodstock Rd, Oxford OX2 6HE (☎ 01865 224679)

SHER, Antony; s of Emanuel Sher, and Margery, *née* Abramowitz; *b* 14 June 1949; *Educ* Sea Point Boys HS Cape Town SA, Webber-Douglas Acad of Dramatic Art London, Post Grad drama course Manchester Univ Drama Dept and Manchester Poly Sch of Theatre; *Career* actor; assoc artist RSC 1982–94; scriptwriter for TV film Changing Step (BBC) 1990; *Theatre* roles with RSC incl: Richard III, Shylock in Merchant of Venice, The Fool in King Lear, Vindice in The Revenger's Tragedy, Tartuffe, Johnnie in Hello and Goodbye, title role in Singer, title role in Tamburlaine 1993; other roles incl: Arnold in Torch Song Trilogy (Albery) 1985, title role in Arturo Ui (RNT) 1991, Astrov in Uncle Vanya (RNT) 1992, Henry Carr in Travesties (Savoy) 1994, Titus Andronicus (Market Theatre Johannesburg, transfered to RNT) 1995, Stanley (RNT) 1996; *Television* incl: Howard Kirk in The History Man (BBC) 1980, Genghis Cohn (BBC) 1993; *Films* Indian Summer 1996, The Wind in the Willows 1996; *Awards* Best Actor Awards for Richard III incl: Drama Magazine Award 1984, London Standard Award 1985 and Olivier Award 1985; Best Actor Award for Torch Song Trilogy: Olivier Award 1985; *Books* Year of the King (actor's diary and sketchbook, 1985), Middlepost (1988), Characters (painting and drawings, 1989), The Indoor Boy (1991), Cheap Lives (1995); *Style*— Antony Sher, Esq; ✉ c/o Conway van Gelder Robinson Ltd, 18–21 Jermyn Street, London SW1Y 6HP (☎ 0171 287 0077, fax 0171 287 1940)

SHER, Samuel Julius (Jules); QC (1981); s of Philip Sher (d 1985), and Isa Phyllis, *née* Hesselson; *b* 22 Oct 1941; *Educ* Athlone HS, Witwatersrand Univ SA (BCom, LLB), Univ of Oxford (BCL); *m* 29 Aug 1965, Sandra, da of Michael Maris, of Johannesburg, SA; 1 s (Brian b 10 July 67), 2 da (Joanne b 8 Aug 69, Debby b 6 May 74); *Career* called to the Bar Inner Temple 1968, recorder 1987–, bencher 1988, dep judge of the High Ct; *Recreations* tennis; *Style*— Jules Sher, Esq, QC; ✉ 12 Constable Close, London NW11 (☎ 0181 455 2753); Wilberforce Chambers, 8 New Square, Lincoln's Inn, London WC2A 3QP (☎ 0171 306 0102, fax 0171 306 0095)

SHERBORN, Derek Ronald; s of Ronald Thorne Sherborn (d 1971), of Bedfont, Middx, and Evelyn May, *née* Allman (d 1982); *b* 7 May 1924; *Educ* Streatham GS, Streatham Hill Coll; *Career* investigator historic bldgs Miny of Town and Country Planning 1948, ret as princ inspr historic bldgs DOE and Historic Bldgs Cncls 1983; special interests: country houses and contents, historic parks and gdns, theatres, music halls, cinemas; memb: Ctee Regency Soc of Brighton and Hove, Ctee Friends of Brighton Pavilion, Central Cncl of Civic Trust Socs 1996; former vice chm Conservation Areas Advsy Gp Brighton Cncl, pres Kingscliffe Soc, sr tstee Robert McKenzie Charitable Tst; FSA 1960; *Books* The Sherborns of Bedfont 1338–1983 (with Charles Davies Sherborn), articles in Country Life, Architectural Review, Family Tree and elsewhere, The Valley Gardens Conservation Area (report on central Brighton for Brighton Regency Soc, 1993); *Recreations* visiting country houses, churches, art exhibitions, auctions, theatre, opera, ballet; *Style*— Derek Sherborn, Esq, FSA; ✉ Bedfont House, 161 Marine Parade, Brighton, Sussex BN2 1EJ

SHERBORNE, Archeacon of; *see:* Wheatley, Ven Paul Charles

SHERBORNE, Bishop of 1976–; Rt Rev John Dudley Galtrey Kirkham; s of Canon Charles Dudley Kirkham (d 1968), and late Doreen Betty, *née* Galtrey; *b* 20 Sept 1935; *Educ* Lancing, Trinity Coll Cambridge (BA, MA), Westcott House Theological Coll; *m* 1 Oct 1986, Hester Elizabeth Lockett Gregory, da of Reese Blake Lockett (d 1977), of Brenham, Texas, and wid of Thorne Gregory (d 1982); 1 step s (Thorne Gregory Jr), 3 step da (Hester Gregory Hodde, Wynne Gregory Dorsett, Anne Gregory Pace); *Career* cmmnd Royal Hampshire Regt 1954, Seconded to King's African Rifles 1955; asst curate St Mary le Tower Ipswich 1962–65, resident chaplain to Bishop of Norwich 1965–69, priest i/c Rockland St Mary with Hellington 1967–69, chaplain to Bishop of New Guinea 1969–70, asst priest St Martin in the Fields and St Margaret's Westminster 1970–72, chaplain to Thames TV Euston Studios 1970–72, domestic chaplain to Archbishop of Canterbury 1972–76, Archbishop's advsr Headmasters' Conf 1990–93; bishop to Her Majesty's Forces 1992–, hon chaplain to The Princess of Wales Royal Regt, Chaplain in the Grand Priory of the Most Ven Order of St John of Jerusalem; pres Sch Chaplains' Conf 1990–93; memb: Cncl St Luke's Hosp for the Clergy, Dorset Health Tst; govr: Canford Sch, Sherborne Sch for Girls; patron Dorset Assoc of Boys' Clubs; FRGS; *Recreations* running, cross country skiing, woodwork; *Clubs* Army and Navy, Kandahar Ski; *Style*— The Rt Rev the Bishop of Sherborne; ✉ Little Bailie, Sturminster Marshall, Wimborne, Dorset BH21 4AD (☎ 01258 857659, fax 01258 857961)

SHERFIELD, 2 Baron (UK 1964), of Sherfield-on-Loddon, Co Southampton; Christopher James Makins; s of 1 Baron Sherfield, GCB, GCMG, FRS (d 1996), and Alice, *née* Davis (d 1985); *b* 23 July 1942; *Educ* Winchester, New Coll Oxford; *m* 1975, Wendy Cortesi; issue; *Career* HM Dip Serv 1964–74; fell All Souls' Coll Oxford 1963; *Style*— The Rt Hon the Lord Sherfield

SHERIDAN, Cecil Majella; CMG (1961); s of John Peter Sheridan (d 1959), of Liverpool, and Teresa, *née* Myerscough (d 1970); *b* 9 Dec 1911; *Educ* Ampleforth, Univ of Liverpool (Faculty of Law); *m* 19 Sept 1949, Monica, da of late Herbert Frank Ereaut, MBE, of St Helier, Jersey; 2 s (Richard b 1952, Michael b 1956), 1 da (Pauline Monica Ereaut (Mrs William Stephens) b 1950); *Career* WWII: RAFVR 1940–46, Pilot Offr 1941, instr Rhodesian Air Trg Gp 1941–42, RAF Tport Cmd 1943–45, Br Mil Admin Malaya 1945–46, demobbed Sqdn Ldr 1946; admitted slr 1934, slr in private practice 1934–40, colonial legal services 1943–46, state legal advsr and dep public prosecutor Malayan Union and Fedn of Malaya 1946–55; Fedn of Malaya: legal draughtsman 1955–57, slr-gen 1957–59, attorney-gen 1959–63; attorney-gen Malaysia 1963; called to the Bar Inner Temple 1952, slr in private practice (assoc Stephenson Harwood) 1963–65, dir Michael Sheridan & Co Ltd 1983–94; chm: of Traffic Cmmrs E Midlands 1965–81, Licensing Authy for Goods Vehicles E Midlands 1965–83; memb Nottingham Mechanics Inst 1965–83; PMN Fedn of Malaya 1962; *Style*— C M Sheridan, Esq, CMG, PMN; ✉ Roselea Cottage, 65 Main Street, Queniborough, Leics LE7 3DB

SHERIDAN, Christopher Julian; s of Mark Sheridan, and Olive Maud, *née* Hobbs; *b* 18 Feb 1943; *Educ* Berkhamsted Sch; *m* 1972, Diane Virginia, *née* Wadey; 1 da (Kate b 20 April 1974); *Career* Samuel Montagu & Co Ltd: joined International Div 1962, specialised in foreign exchange and foreign treasy markets, exec dir responsible for Dealing Div activities 1974–81, md Dealing Div 1981–84, chief exec 1984–94, dep chm 1988–94; non-exec dir: Yorkshire Building Society 1995–, Hanover Acceptances Ltd 1995–, Prudential Bache International Bank Ltd; memb Partnership Bd Lovell White Durrant; FCIB, CIMgt; *Recreations* theatre, tennis, skiing; *Clubs* Buck's; *Style*— Christopher Sheridan, Esq; ✉ c/o Buck's Club, 18 Clifford Street, London W1X 1RG (☎ 0171 734 2337)

SHERIDAN, David Martin; s of Vernon Arthur Sheridan (d 1990), and Ruth Eleanor, *née* Caminer; *b* 31 Aug 1950; *Educ* Haberdashers' Aske's, King's Coll London (BSc); *m* 1 July 1978, Christine Lesley, *née* White; 2 da (Hillary Ann b 17 June 1984, Deborah Lynn b 15 April 1987); *Career* CA; i/c Statistics Dept Marians Bloodstock Agency 1972–74, buyer Racal-BPL 1974–75, articles Mercer & Hole 1975–78, qualified ACA 1978, exec dir Brand Packaging Jefferson Smurfit Group 1980–82 (joined as PA to divnl fin dir 1978), chm Veruth Holdings Ltd 1991–, md Europa Components & Equipment plc 1991– (fin & mktg dir 1982–90); pres Beds, Bucks & Herts Soc of CAs 1988–89, memb Cncl ICAEW 1993–96 (past memb of numerous ctees); Bd of CAs in Business (BCAB): chm Working Pty 1992, co-vice chm 1993–96, co-opted memb 1996–; memb St Albans Round Table 1983–91, sports offr Area 28 (Round Table) 1989–91; *Recreations* work, more work, my family, squash, riding, crosswords; *Clubs* 41 (St Albans); *Style*— David Sheridan, Esq; ✉ Europa Components & Epuipment plc, Marians House, Barnet Lane, Elstree, Herts WD6 3RD (☎ 0181 953 2379, fax 0181 207 6646, car 01855 521138)

SHERIDAN, Dinah Nadyejda (Mrs Aubrey Ison); da of Fernard Archer Sheridan (d 1958), and Lisa Charlotte, *née* Everth (d 1966, jtly photographers by appt to HM The Queen and Queen Elizabeth The Queen Mother); *b* 17 Sept 1920; *Educ* Sherrards Wood Sch Welwyn Garden City, Italia Conti Stage Sch; *m* 8 May 1942 (m dis 1952), Jimmy Hanley (d 1970); 1 s (Jeremy b 17 Nov 1945), 2 da (Carol Ann b and d June 1944, Jenny b 15 Aug 1947); m 2, 3 March 1954 (m dis 1965), Sir John Davis (d 1993); m 3, 29 May 1986, John Herman Merivale (d 1990); m 4, 17 Sept 1992, Aubrey Ison; *Career* actress; offr sister St John Ambulance Bde; *Theatre* incl: Let's All Go Down The Strand (Phoenix) 1967, A Boston Story (Duchess), Out of the Question (St Martin's), Move Over Mrs Markham (Vaudeville), The Card (Queens), Gentle Hook (Piccadilly), The Pleasure of His Company (with Douglas Fairbanks Jnr, Phoenix), A Murder is Announced (Vaudeville), Half Life (with Sir John Gielgud, Brighton, Richmond, Oxford and Canada), Present Laughter (Vaudeville), The Applecart (with Peter O'Toole, Haymarket), The Kingfisher (tour, Channel Theatre); *Television* incl: The Swish of the Curtain, Just Liz,

Hammer House of Horror, Sink or Swim, Doctor Who Special (The Five Doctors), Winning Streak; recent credits incl: Don't Wait Up (six series, BBC), Keeping Up Appearances (BBC), Us & Them (Yorkshire), Lovejoy (Witzend Prodn), All Night Long (BBC), Countdown; *Film* incl: Genevieve, The Story of Shirley Yorke, The Gilbert & Sullivan Story, Sound Barrier, Appointment in London, Where No Vultures Fly, The Railway Children, The Mirror Cracked; *Recreations* gardening, tapestry, cooking; *Style*— Miss Dinah Sheridan; ✉ c/o Chatto & Linnit, Prince of Wales Theatre, Coventry Street, London W1V 7FE (☎ 0171 930 6677, fax 0171 930 0091)

SHERIDAN, Gail Ruth; da of Isidore Michael Sheridan (d 1987), of Blackpool, and Zelda, *née* Stein; *b* 16 Sept 1943; *Educ* Arnold HS for Girls Blackpool, LSE (BSc); *m* 2 Sept 1972, Darius Jal Sagar, s of Jal Feroze Sagar; 1 s (Aaron b 15 Oct 1984); *Career* PR exec; account exec Gwynne Hart and Assocs 1966, exec Tom-Bay Advertising 1967–68, copywriter Asiatic Advertising Karachi 1967–68, account exec Scientific PR 1968–70, account exec Kingsway PR 1970–72, press offr then publicity mangr Sperry Univac 1972–76, md Sheridan Communications Birmingham and London 1976–94, dir Sheldon Communications Ltd 1994–; ICP Million Dollar Award, fndr memb Birmingham City 2000; MCAM 1969, FIPR 1993 (MIPR 1966); *Recreations* reading, travel; *Style*— Ms Gail Sheridan; ✉ Sheldon Communications Ltd, 28 Museum Street, London WC1A 1LH (☎ 0171 436 1553, fax 0171 436 7825)

SHERIDAN, John Phillip; s of John David Hatton Sheridan (d 1987), of Beckenham, Kent, and Marjorie Eleanor, *née* Rich (d 1995); *b* 18 Feb 1936; *Educ* Dulwich, Royal Veterinary Coll Univ of London (BVetMed); *m* 6 June 1960, Maureen Dorothy, da of William Alfred Sullivan (d 1984), of Hildenborough, Kent; 1 s (Gavin b 1963), 2 da (Corinne b 1961, Bridie b 1966); *Career* gen vet practice: Fakenham Norfolk 1960–61, Reigate Surrey 1961–64, Southwick Sussex 1964; partnership then practice princ 1971–86, md Anicare Gp Servs (mgmnt servs to veterinary profession) 1976–; pres Br Small Animal Veterinary Assoc 1974–75; W Sussex CC: memb 1976–96, chm policy and resources 1989–93, ldr 1984–89; memb Arundel Castle Tstees 1988–, chm Sussex Police Authy 1991–93 (memb 1985–94); MRCVS 1960; *Recreations* skiing, sub aqua; *Style*— John Sheridan, Esq; ✉ High Banks, Bracken Lane, Storrington, Pulborough, W Sussex RH20 3HR (☎ 01903 745341); Anicare Group Services (Veterinary) Ltd, 23 Buckingham Rd, Shoreham-by-Sea, W Sussex BN43 5UA (☎ 01273 463022, fax 01273 463431)

SHERIDAN, Dr (Lionel Astor) Lee; s of Stanley Frederic Sheridan (d 1949), and Anne Agnes, *née* Quednau (d 1980); *b* 21 July 1927; *Educ* Whitgift Sch, Univ of London (LLB, LLD), Queens Univ Belfast (PhD); *m* 1 June 1948, Margaret Helen, da of Louis Charles Béghin (d 1961); 1 s (Peter b 1958), 1 da (Linda b 1955, d 1975); *Career* called to the Bar Lincoln's Inn 1948; pt/t lectr Univ of Nottingham 1949, lectr Queen's Univ Belfast 1949–56, prof of law Univ of Malaya Singapore 1956–63, prof of comparative law Queens Univ Belfast 1963–71, dep princ Univ Coll Cardiff 1977–80 and 1986–87 (prof of law 1971–88, actg princ 1980 and 1987), interim LLM co-ordinator Univ of London 1992–93; chm NI Office of Law Reform Land Law Working Pty 1967–70; LLD Univ of Singapore 1963; Fell UCL 1979; *Books* Fraud in Equity (1957), The Cy-Près Doctrine (with V T H Delany, 1959), Federation of Malaya Constitution (1961), The British Commonwealth: Malaya, Singapore, The Borneo Territories: The Development of their Laws and Constitutions (1961), Constitutional Protection: Expropriation and Restrictions on Property Rights (1963), The Comparative Law of Trusts in the Commonwealth and the Irish Republic (with G W Keeton, 1976), Digest of the English Trusts (with G W Keeton, 1979), The Constitution of Malaysia (with H E Groves, 1987), Equity (with G W Keeton, 1987), The Modern Law of Charities (1992), The Law of Trusts (1993), Chancery Procedure and Anton Piller Orders (1995), Injunctions in General (1995) Injunctions in Particular Cases (1995); *Recreations* sightseeing, reading, theatre going; *Clubs* Athenaeum; *Style*— Dr Lee Sheridan; ✉ Cherry Trees, Broadway Green, Vale of Glamorgan CF5 6SR (☎ 01446 760 403)

SHERIDAN, Paul Richard; TD (1982, Bar 1991); s of Patrick William Sheridan (d 1991), of Grimsby, and Claire Sheridan, JP, *née* Marklew (d 1990); *b* 19 July 1951; *Educ* Havelock Sch Grimsby, Grimsby Coll of Tech, Univ of Kent (BA); *m* 30 Jun 1985, Beverley, *née* Seagger; *Career* RCT TA, Maj 1985–93 (Cadet 1969, 2 Lt 1970, Lt 1972, Capt 1977), Staff Coll (TA) 1991, RARO II 1993–; admitted slr 1979; ptnr Wilkin Chapman 1982–, NP 1985; Cmmr for Oaths 1990; chm League of Friends of Grimsby Hosps 1985–88 (hon membership offr 1988–95), chm Community Fund Raising Panel MRI £1m Scanner Appeal 1992–94; Lord of the Manor of Aspenden Herts 1985–; Freeman City of London 1985, Liveryman Worshipful Co of Carmen 1986; patron Nat Domesday Ctee 1986; memb: Law Soc 1979, Notaries Soc 1985; *Recreations* heraldry; *Clubs* Victory Services, London; *Style*— Paul R Sheridan, Esq, TD; ✉ The Villa, Scartho Road, Grimsby DN33 2AE (☎ 01472 877039); Wilkin Chapman, 46 St Peter's Avenue, Cleethorpes, NE Lincolnshire DN35 8HR (☎ 01472 691285, fax 01472 695872)

SHERIDAN, Peter Warner Alexander; QC (1977); s of Hugo Sheridan (d 1973), of Park Rd, Regents Park, London, and Marie Sheridan (d 1927); *b* 29 May 1927; *Educ* Lincoln Coll Oxford (BA); *Career* called to the Bar Middle Temple 1955, bencher 1988; *Recreations* sports cars, archery, radio, astronomy; *Style*— Peter Sheridan, Esq, QC; ✉ 11 Stone Buildings, Lincoln's Inn, London WC2A 3TG (☎ 0171 831 6381, fax 0171 831 2575, DX 1022 London); 17 Brompton Square, London SW3 (☎ and fax 0171 584 7250); Pile Oak Lodge, Donhead-St-Andrews, nr Shaftesbury, Dorset (☎ 01747 828484)

SHERIDAN, Richard Jonathan; s of Dr Morris (Roger) Sheridan, of London NW11, and late Yvonne, *née* Brook; *b* 20 Dec 1956; *Educ* City of London Sch, Guy's Hosp Med Sch Univ of London; *Career* conslt obstetrician and gynaecologist Watford Gen Hosp; memb Cncl and treas Obstetrics and Gynaecology Section Royal Soc of Med; Freeman City of London, Liveryman Worshipful Soc of Apothecaries; MRCOG 1985, FRCS 1985; *Papers* Fertility in a Male with Trisomy 21 (1989); *Recreations* squash, skiing, riding; *Style*— Richard Sheridan, Esq; ✉ Christmas Cottage, Scatterdells Lane, Chipperfield, Hertfordshire WD4 9EZ (☎ 01923 264105, fax 01923 260943); Watford General Hospital, Vicarage Rd, Watford (☎ 01923 217935)

SHERINGHAM, Teddy; *b* 2 April 1966; *Career* professional footballer; 213 league appearances (33 goals) Millwall 1983–91 (2nd Div champions 1987–88), on loan Aldershot 1984–85, 42 appearances Nottingham Forest 1991–92 (runners up League Cup 1992), joined Tottenham Hotspur 1992–; England: 21 full caps and 5 goals (as at Jan 1997), memb squad Euro 96; winner Golden Boot 1990–91 and 1992–93; *Style*— Teddy Sheringham, Esq; ✉ Tottenham Hotspur FC, 748 High Road, Tottenham, London N17 0AP (☎ 0181 808 6666)

SHERLAW-JOHNSON, Dr Robert; s of Robert Johnson (d 1980), and Helen Smith (d 1976); *b* 21 May 1932; *Educ* Gosforth GS Newcastle upon Tyne, Univ of Durham (BA, BMus), Univ of Leeds (MA, DMus (external)), Univ of Oxford (MA, DMus (external)); *m* 28 July 1959, Rachael Maria, da of Cyril Clarke (d 1974), and Eularia Clarke; 3 s (Christopher b 1962, Austin b 1964, Edward b 1976), 2 da (Rebecca b 1960, Griselda b 1966); *Career* asst lectr in music Univ of Leeds 1961–63, dir of music Bradford Girls' GS 1963–65, lectr in music Univ of York 1965–70, fell Worcester Coll 1970, univ lectr in music Univ of Oxford; recordings (as pianist) of Catalogue of D'Oiseaux, Messiaen, later works by Liszt, own piano works; composer of: 3 piano sonatas, piano concerto, clarinet concerto, Opera The Lambton Worm, Carmina Vernalia, 2 string quartets, various songs and other chamber works; FRAM; *Books* Messiaen (1975, 2 edn 1989); *Recreations* collecting playing cards, croquet, bell-ringing; *Style*— Dr Robert Sherlaw-Johnson; ✉ Malton Croft, Woodlands Rise, Stonesfield, Oxon (☎ 01993 891318); Worcester College, Oxford (☎ 01865 278300); Faculty of Music, St Aldates, Oxford (☎ 01865 276125, fax 01865 276128)

SHERLING, Clive Richard; s of Philip Sherling, of Northwood, Middx, and Maureen Vivienne, *née* Gulperin; *b* 20 Oct 1949; *Educ* Woodhouse GS, LSE (BSc Econ); *m* 3 March 1993, Sally Ann; 2 s (Adrian Mark, William David (twins) b 31 Oct 1977); *Career* articled clerk then ptnr Arthur Andersen 1970–87, with Apax Partners & Co Ventures Ltd 1987–; former chm Sports Aid Fndn Charitable Tst, chm Football Licencing Authy, memb Cncl Br Venture Capital Assoc; MSI; FCA (ACA 1973); *Recreations* soccer, theatre, walking; *Style*— Clive Sherling, Esq; ✉ Lincoln House, Woodside Hill, Chalfont Heights, Gerrards Cross, Bucks SL9 9TF (☎ 01753 887454); Apax Partners & Co Ventures Ltd, 15 Portland Place, London W1N 3AA (☎ 0171 872 6336, fax 0171 872 8999)

SHERLOCK, Dr Alexander; CBE (1989); s of Thomas Sherlock, MM (d 1971), of Bognor Regis, Sussex, and Evelyn Mary, *née* Alexander (d 1990); *b* 14 Feb 1922; *Educ* Magdalen Coll Sch Oxford, Stowmarket GS, London Hosp (MB BS); *m* 1, 24 March 1945, Clarice Constance (Peggy) (d 1975), da of Edward G Scarff (d 1976), of Stowmarket, Suffolk; 1 s (Jim b 18 Feb 1951), 2 da (Penny b 10 March 1946, Clare b 6 March 1960), 1 step da (Sandra b 18 Aug 1948); m 2, 1976, Eileen, da of Leslie Hall (d 1976), of Bawtry; *Career* Flt Lt RAF 1946–48; med practitioner and conslt 1948–79; called to the Bar Gray's Inn 1961; asst dep coroner St Pancras 1971–72; memb: Felixstone UDC 1960–74, E Suffolk CC 1966–74, Suffolk CC 1974–79; MEP (EDG) S W Essex 1979–89; chm Fire and Public Protection Ctee 1977–79; vice-pres: Inst of Environmental Health Offrs, Trading Standards Inst; OStJ 1974; FRSA 1987; *Recreations* walking, gardening; *Clubs* RAF, Royal Belgian Automobile; *Style*— Dr Alexander Sherlock, CBE; ✉ 58 Orwell Road, Felixstowe, Suffolk IP11 7PS (☎ 01394 284503)

SHERLOCK, David Christopher; s of Frank Ernest Sherlock (d 1987), and (Emily) Edna, *née* Johnson (d 1993); *b* 6 Nov 1943; *Educ* Blakesley Sch, Rutlish Sch Merton, Coll of Art & Industl Design Newcastle upon Tyne, Univ of Nottingham (BA, MPhil); *m* 1, 1969 (m dis 1975) Jean, *née* Earl; m 2, 1976, Cynthia Mary, da of Norman Lovell Hood; 1 s (Nicholas David b 12 Oct 1978), 1 da (Zoë Virginia Mary b 10 Feb 1977); *Career* Nottingham Coll of Art & Design 1967–70, Trent Poly 1970–74, dep dir Nat Coll of Art & Design Dublin 1975–80; princ: Winchester Sch of Art 1980–87, Central St Martin's Coll of Art & Design 1988–91; asst rector London Inst 1988–91, dir of devpt RCA 1991–93, regnl sr inspr and nat sr inspr for art and design Further Educn Funding Cncl 1993–; conslt industl designer and sometime advsr to EC, UN and govts of Bangladesh, Somalia, Ghana, Portugal and Turkey; chm Bd of Tstees Fndn for HE in Art and Design; FRSA 1975, FCSD 1990; *Recreations* sailing, mountain biking; *Clubs* Royal Southern Yacht; *Style*— David Sherlock, Esq; ✉ Woodside, Park Rd, Winchester, Hampshire SO22 6AA (☎ 01962 854661)

SHERLOCK, Nigel; DL (Tyne and Wear 1995); s of Horace Sherlock (d 1967), and Dorothea, *née* Robinson (d 1980); *b* 12 Jan 1940; *Educ* Barnard Castle Sch, Univ of Nottingham (BA); *m* 3 Sept 1966, Helen Diana Frances, da of M Sigmund; 2 s (Andrew b 27 July 1968, Mark b 7 July 1976), 1 da (Emma b 5 Sept 1970); *Career* stockbroker; chm Wise Speke Ltd 1993–; dir London Stock Exchange 1995–; vice chm Bd Assoc of Private Client Investment Managers and Stockbrokers (APCIMS); High Sheriff of Tyne and Wear 1990–91; chm Cncl Univ of Newcastle, dir Northern Sinfonia Orchestra (former chm), vice pres (former chm) Northumberland Co Scout Assoc; vice pres Northumbria Coalition Against Crime; memb Cncl St John's Coll Univ of Durham; Freeman City of Newcastle Upon Tyne; Hon Bro Trinity House Newcastle 1995; MSI; AIIMR, FIMgt, FRSA; *Recreations* the countryside, music, theatre and rugby football; *Clubs* Brooks's, City of London, New (Edinburgh), Northern Counties (Newcastle); *Style*— Nigel Sherlock, Esq; ✉ 14 North Ave, Gosforth, Newcastle Upon Tyne NE3 4DS (☎ 0191 285 4379); Wise Speke, Commercial Union House, 39 Pilgrim St, Newcastle Upon Tyne NE1 6RQ (☎ 0191 201 3800)

SHERLOCK, Prof Dame Sheila Patricia Violet; DBE (1978); da of Samuel Philip Sherlock (d 1979), and Violet Mary Catherine Beckett (d 1969); *b* 31 March 1918; *Educ* Folkestone Co Sch, Univ of Edinburgh (MD), Yale; *m* 1951, Dr D Geraint James, *qv*; 2 da (Amanda, Auriole); *Career* physician and lectr in med Postgrad Medical Sch of London 1948–59, prof of med Univ of London Royal Free Hosp Sch of Med 1959–83; Rockefeller fell Yale; memb Senate Univ of London 1976–81, sr censor and vice pres Royal Coll of Physicians of London 1976–77; Hon MD: Lisbon, Oslo, Leuven 1985, Trinity Coll Dublin 1992, Valladolid 1994; Hon LLD Aberdeen 1982; Hon DSc: City Univ (NY), Yale 1983, Univ of Edinburgh 1985, Univ of London 1989, Univ of Barcelona 1991, Univ of Mainz 1992; other hon degrees: Univ of Padua 1995, Univ of Wisconsin 1995, Univ of Cambridge 1995, Univ of Toronto 1996; Hon FACP, Hon FRCP (C), Hon FRCPI, Hon FRCPGlas, Hon FRCS; FRCP, FRCPEd, FRACP; *Books* Diseases of the Liver and Biliary System (10 edn, 1996); *Recreations* cricket, travel; *Style*— Prof Dame Sheila Sherlock, DBE; ✉ 41 York Terrace East, London NW1 4PT (☎ 0171 486 4560); Royal Free Hospital, London NW3 2QG (☎ 0171 431 4589)

SHERMAN, Sir Alfred; kt (1983); s of Jacob Vladimir Sherman, and Eva, *née* Goldental; *b* 10 Nov 1919; *Educ* Hackney Downs Co Secdy Sch, LSE (BScEcon); *m* 1958, Zahava (d 1993), da of Dr Gideon Levin; 1 s (Gideon); *Career* journalist and public affrs advsr, leader writer Daily Telegraph, conslt; co fndr (with Sir Keith Joseph, MP, and Mrs Margaret Thatcher, MP) Centre For Policy Studies 1974, speech writer and aide to Mrs Thatcher 1974–83; external affairs advsr to Radovan Karadzic (Pres of Republika Srpska) 1993–94; *Clubs* Reform; *Style*— Sir Alfred Sherman

SHERMAN, Sir Lou (Louis); kt (1975), OBE (1967), JP (Inner London); *m* Sally, CBE, JP; *Career* chm Housing Corporation 1977–80, dep chm Harlow Development Corporation, initiator Lea Valley Regnl Park Authy; *Style*— Sir Lou Sherman, OBE, JP

SHERRARD, Michael David; QC (1968); s of Morris Sherrard (d 1965), and Ethel, *née* Werbner (d 1983); *b* 23 June 1928; *Educ* King's Coll London (LLB); *m* 6 April 1952, Shirley, da of Maurice and Lucy Bagrit (both d 1973); 2 s (Nicholas b 9 June 1953, Jonathan b 5 Aug 1957); *Career* called to the Bar Middle Temple 1949, treas Middle Temple 1996; memb Winn Ctee on Personal Injury Litigation 1966–68, recorder of the Crown Ct 1974–93, master of the Bench Middle Temple 1977, bench rep on Senate 1978–80, inspr Dept of Trade under Companies Acts (London Capital Gp) 1975–77; chm Normansfield Hosp Public Inquiry 1977–78, memb Bar Assoc of City of NY 1986–95, memb Cncl of Justice 1985–, dir Middle Temple Advocacy 1994–; FRSA 1991; *Publications* contrib British Accounting Standards - The First 10 years (1981); *Recreations* travel, listening to opera, oriental art; *Style*— Michael Sherrard, Esq, QC; ✉ 26 Eton Avenue, London NW3 3HL (☎ 0171 431 0713, fax 0171 433 1605); Crooked Beams, 4 Church Road, Alderton, Glos (☎ 01242 680268); The Treasury, Middle Temple, London EC4Y 9AT (☎ 0171 477 4815, fax 0171 427 4817)

SHERRARD, Scott Rathman; s of John Alfred Sherrard, of Buckhaven, Fife, and Mary Stephen, *née* Stiven; *b* 19 May 1954; *Educ* Dundee HS, Galashiels Acad, Gonville and Caius Coll Cambridge (BA, vice pres JCR); *m* 1, 7 July 1978, Lorna Jane (d 1985), da of Allan William Clark; 1 s (Nicholas Clark Stiven b 25 Dec 1982); m 2, 28 Aug 1987, Susan Elizabeth, da of William Graham Clark; 1 da (Katherine Jane b 15 Sept 1988); *Career* Scottish & Newcastle Breweries Ltd: joined as mgmnt trainee 1975, brand mangr 1976–78, mktg mangr 1978–81; fndr ptnr: Cockman Thompson Wilding Ltd 1981–83, Grierson Cockman Craig & Druiff Ltd 1983–85; Grey London Ltd advtg agency: planning dir 1985–88, creative devpt dir 1988–90, md 1990–95; chief exec The Cambridge Centre 1995–; chm Collett Dickenson Pearce 1995–; writer/prodr of musical for Edinburgh Festival; chm Borders Young Libs; *Recreations* children, piano, golf, fishing; *Clubs* Audley Fly Fishing; *Style*— Scott Sherrard, Esq; ✉ c/o Collett Dickenson Pearce & Partners Ltd, 33–34 Soho Square, London W1V 6DP (☎ 0171 292 4005)

SHERRARD, Simon Patrick; s of Patrick Sherrard, and Angela Beatrice, *née* Stacey (d 1988); *b* 22 Sept 1947; *Educ* Eton; *m* 23 Aug 1975, Sara Anne, da of Maj Peter Pain Stancliffe, MBE; 1 s (James b 19 Oct 1984), 3 da (Emma b 11 Jan 1977, Kate b 4 Aug 1978, Polly b 6 April 1983); *Career* Samuel Montagu & Co Ltd 1968–74, Jardine Matheson & Co Ltd Hong Kong 1974–84, md Bibby Line Group Ltd Liverpool 1985–; non-exec dir: Cooke Bros (Tattenhall) Ltd 1991–, Lloyd's Register of Shipping 1992–; Liveryman Worshipful Co of Shipwrights; *Recreations* tennis, farming; *Clubs* White's, MCC, I Zingari; *Style*— Simon Sherrard, Esq; ✉ Bibby Line Group Ltd, 105 Duke St, Liverpool L1 5JQ (☎ 0151 708 8000, fax 0151 794 1099, car 0836 263156)

SHERRATT, Brian Walter; OBE (1995); s of late Walter Eric Sherratt, and Violet Florence, *née* Cox-Smith; *b* 28 May 1942; *Educ* Univ of Leeds (BA, PGCE), Univ of London (AcDipEd, MA); *m* 1966, (Pauline) Brenda Hargreaves; 2 s, 2 da; *Career* asst master Normanton GS 1965–67, head Religious Studies Dept Selby GS 1967–70, sr lectr in religious studies and warden Avery Hill Coll of Educn 1970–73, asst master Kidbrooke Sch 1970–71, warden Mile End Teachers' Centre Avery Hill Coll 1971–73, dep head Sandown Court Sch Tunbridge Wells 1976–79 (sr master 1973–76), headmaster and warden Kirk Hallam Sch and Community Centre 1979–84, headmaster Great Barr Grant-Maintained Sch Birmingham 1984–; hon lectr Sch of Educn Univ of Birmingham 1988–; memb: Ct Univ of Birmingham 1986–90, Centre for Policy Studies 1994–, Organising Ctee Going for Green 1994–96, Politeia 1995–; non-exec dir Going for Green Limited 1996– (also memb); FIMgt 1984, FRSA 1984; *Publications* Gods and Men: a survey of world religions (1971), Opting for Freedom: a stronger policy on grant-maintained schools (Centre for Policy Studies, Policy Study No 138, 1994), Grant-Maintained Status: considering the options (1994), Conservative Secretaries of State and Radical Educational Reform Since 1979 (co-author, 1997); contrib TES; *Recreations* the environment, classical music, literature, antiques, buildings; *Style*— Brian Sherratt, Esq, OBE; ✉ Great Barr Grant-Maintained School, Aldridge Road, Birmingham B44 8NU (☎ 0121 366 6611, fax 0121 366 6007)

SHERRIN, Ned (Edward George); CBE (1997); s of Thomas Adam Sherrin (d 1965), of Lower Farm, Kingweston, Somerset, and Dorothy Finch, *née* Drewett (d 1974); *b* 18 Feb 1931; *Educ* Sexey's Bruton, Exeter Coll Oxford (MA); *Career* producer, director, presenter and writer for film, theatre, radio and television; 2 Lt Royal Corps of Signals 1949–51; called to the Bar Gray's Inn; ATV 1956–58, BBC 1958–65 (TW3, Tonight); *Theatre* incl: Side by Side by Sondheim, Jeffrey Bernard is Unwell, The Mitford Girls, Sing a Rude Song, Mr and Mrs Nobody, Ratepayer's Iolanthe, Metropolitan Mikado, Bookends, Victor Spinetti's Private Diary, Our Song (London and Athens), A Passionate Woman 1994, Salad Days (Vaudeville) 1996; *Radio* Loose Ends; *Films* incl: The Virgin Soldiers 1967, The National Health 1972; *Books* Cindy Ella or I Gotta Shoe, Rappell 1910, Benbow Was His Name, A Small Thing Like an Earthquake (autobiography), Cutting Edge, Loose Neds, Ned Sherrin's Theatrical Anecdotes, Ned Sherrin in his Anecdotage (1993), Oxford Dictionary of Humorous Quotations (ed, 1995), Scratch an Actor (novel, 1996), Diary: Sherrin's Year (1996); *Recreations* eating, theatre; *Clubs* Groucho; *Style*— Ned Sherrin, Esq, CBE

SHERRINGTON, Prof David; s of James Arthur Sherrington, KSG (d 1986), of Middlesbrough, Cleveland, and Elfreda, *née* Cameron (d 1996); *b* 29 Oct 1941; *Educ* St Mary's Coll Middlesbrough, Univ of Manchester (BSc, PhD); *m* 20 July 1966, Margaret, da of Richard Gee-Clough (d 1980), of Blackpool, Lancashire; 1 s (Andrew Damian b 20 Feb 1967), 1 da (Lesley Jane b 14 Jan 1971); *Career* lectr in theoretical physics Univ of Manchester 1967–69 (asst lectr 1964–67), prof of physics Imperial Coll London 1983–89 (lectr in theoretical solid state physics 1969–74, reader 1974–83), Wykeham prof of physics Univ of Oxford 1989–, Ulam scholar Los Alamos Nat Laboratory 1995–96; jls ed: Communications on Physics 1975–78, Advances in Physics 1984–, Journal of Physics A: Mathematical and General 1989–93; contrib many articles in scientific jls; fell New Coll Oxford 1989–; hon MA Univ of Oxford 1989; FInstP 1974, fell American Physical Soc 1984; FRS 1994; *Books* Phase Transitions in Soft Condensed Matter (co-ed, 1989), Spontaneous Formation of Space - Time Structures and Criticality (co-ed, 1991), Phase Transitions and Relaxation in Systems with Competing Energy Scales (co-ed, 1993), Physics of Biomaterials: Fluctuations, Selfassembly and Evolution (co-ed, 1995); *Style*— Prof David Sherrington, FRS; ✉ Theoretical Physics, Univ of Oxford, 1 Keble Rd, Oxford OX1 3NP (☎ 01865 273947, fax 01865 273418, e-mail D.Sherrington1@physics.ox.ac.uk)

SHERRY, Patrick; *b* 29 Sept 1947; *Educ* Univ of Birmingham (BCom), London Stock Exchange Exam; *m*; 4 c; *Career* chartered accountant and mgmnt conslt; joined Coopers & Lybrand 1969, subsequently with Hoare Govett, rejoined Coopers & Lybrand (ptnr 1986–, former chm Int Financial Servs Gp, former managing ptnr Int Affrs in UK Firm, memb Int Exec Ctee and int exec ptnr Coopers & Lybrand International 1995–); FCA; *Style*— Patrick Sherry, Esq; ✉ Coopers and Lybrand, 1 Embankment Place, London WC2N 6NN (☎ 0171 212 4910, fax 0171 212 5100)

SHERSBY, Sir (Julian) Michael; kt (1995), MP (C) Uxbridge (majority 13,179); s of William Henry Shersby, and Elinor Shersby; *b* 17 Feb 1933; *Educ* John Lyon Sch Harrow on the Hill; *m* 1958, Barbara Joan, da of John Henry Barrow; 1 s, 1 da; *Career* MP (C) Uxbridge 1972–; PPS to Min of State for Aerospace and Shipping 1973–74; memb: House of Commons Public Accounts Select Ctee 1983–, Speaker's Panel of Dep Chairmen 1983–, Exec Ctee UK Branch CPA 1988–; Parly advsr to Police Fedn of England and Wales 1989–; cncllr: London Borough of Paddington 1959–64, Westminster City Cncl 1964–71 (chm Children's Ctee 1964–67); dir The Sugar Bureau 1966–67 (dir gen 1977–88, Parly advsr 1988–96), sec UK Sugar Indust Assoc 1978–88; memb Court Brunel Univ 1975–, pres London Green Belt Cncl 1989–, pres Uxbridge Victim Support Scheme 1993–; Hon DUniv Brunel 1994; FIPR 1994; *Recreations* theatre, travel, fishing; *Clubs* Carlton, Conservative (Uxbridge); *Style*— Sir Michael Shersby, MP; ✉ House of Commons, London SW1A 0AA (☎ 0171 219 3000, fax 0171 219 5948)

SHERSTON-BAKER, Sir Robert George Humphrey; 7 Bt (GB 1796), of Dunstable House, Richmond, Surrey; o s of Sir Humphrey Dodington Benedict Sherston-Baker, 6 Bt (d 1990), and Margaret Alice, *née* Binns; *b* 3 April 1951; *m* 2 Nov 1991, Vanessa R A, yst da of C E A Baird, of Grouville, Jersey, CI; 1 s (David Arbuthnot George b 1992), 1 da (Amy Margaret b 8 Feb 1994); *Heir* s, David Arbuthnot George Sherston-Baker b 24 Nov 1992; *Style*— Sir Robert Sherston-Baker, Bt; ✉ Wealden House, North Elham, Kent CT4 6UY

SHERWEN, J Timothy R; s of A R Sherwen, of Tonbridge, Kent, and Catherine Joyce Sherwen (d 1982); *b* 21 Nov 1937; *Educ* Tonbridge, Selwyn Coll Cambridge (BA); *m* 1969, Mary Christiane, da of Gerald Charles Stokes (d 1980); 1 s; *Career* md Thomas Nelson & Sons Ltd 1982, dir Centaur Communications Ltd 1989, exec chm Linguaphone Institute Ltd 1990– (chm Linguaphone Group plc 1986–); Parly candidate Faversham 1979; *Recreations* sailing, music, riding; *Style*— Timothy Sherwen, Esq; ✉ Linguaphone Institute Ltd, St Giles House, 50 Poland St, London W1V 4AX (☎ 0171 287 4050, fax 0171 734 0006, telex 261352)

SHERWOOD, Bishop of 1989–; Rt Rev Alan Wyndham Morgan; s of Albert Wyndham Morgan (d 1987), and Daisy Eleanor, *née* Campbell (d 1991); *b* 22 June 1940; *Educ* Boys' GS Gowerton, St David's UC Lampeter (BA, colours in tennis, hockey and badminton), St Michael's Coll Llandaff; *m* 25 Jan 1965, (Margaret) Patricia, da of William Oswald Williams (d 1985); 1 s (Jonathan Charles b 7 Jan 1966), 1 da (Eleanor Jane b 22 Aug 1968); *Career* asst curate: Llangyfelach with Morriston 1964–69, Cockett 1969–71, St Mark's Coventry 1972; team vicar St Barnabas Coventry E 1972–78, bishop's offr for social responsibility Diocese of Coventry 1978–83, archdeacon of Coventry 1983–89; memb Gen Synod 1981–89, chm House of Clergy Coventry Diocesan Synod 1982–88; vice pres Nat Cncl for Voluntary Orgns (chm 1986–89); pres: Nottingham Assoc of Voluntary Orgns, Nottingham Help the Homeless Assoc; memb Governing Cncl Family Policy Studies Centre; chm: Notts Child Care Forum, Mansfield Social Strategy Gp, Mansfield Educn Forum; vice chm Notts Health Authy Local Ethics Ctee; pres Mansfield DIAL (Disabled Info Advice Line); bd dir N Notts TEC, chm N Notts TEC Additional Needs 1990–96; chm Gen Synod Bd of Social Responsibility's Working Pty which produced pubn Something to Celebrate; *Publications* Working Together: Partnerships in Local Social Service (1981), A Time to be Born and a Time to Die (1985), Partnership for Health (1987); *Recreations* walking, reading, gardening; *Style*— The Rt Rev the Bishop of Sherwood; ✉ Sherwood House, High Oakham Rd, Mansfield, Notts NG18 5AJ (☎ 01623 657491, fax 01623 662526)

SHERWOOD, Dr Anthea Joy; da of Antony Hugh William Sherwood (d 1963), and Gladys Lilian, *née* Spackman (d 1968); *b* 21 July 1949; *Educ* Crediton HS for Girls, Univ Coll London (BSc), Univ Coll Hosp Med Sch (MB BS); *m* 10 April 1979, Evan Richard Llewelyn Davies, s of David Ronald Davies (d 1994); 2 s (Huw b 1982, Owen b 1985); *Career* John Marshall fell; lectr and registrar Inst of Child Health and GOS, lectr and sr registrar UCH 1978–79, registrar in histopathology Plymouth Hosp 1979–81, conslt histopathologist Torbay Hosp 1981–87, conslt histopathologist Derriford Hosp 1987–; hon conslt histopathologist to the RN; cncl memb Assoc of Clinical Pathologists 1988–91; memb: BMA, IAP; FRCPath 1992 (MRCPath 1980); *Recreations* gardening, family life; *Clubs* Wrangaton Golf; *Style*— Dr Anthea Sherwood; ✉ The Department of Histopathology, Derriford Hospital, Derriford Rd, Plymouth (☎ 01752 792352)

SHERWOOD, (Robert) Antony Frank; CMG (1981); s of Frank Henry Sherwood (d 1964), and Mollie, *née* Moore (d 1952); *b* 29 May 1923; *Educ* Christ's Hosp, St John's Coll Oxford (MA); *m* 21 Nov 1953, Margaret Elizabeth, da of Frank and Vera Simpson; 2 s (Simon b 1956, Jeremy b 1957), 2 da (Deborah b 1954, Harriet b 1958); *Career* RAF 1942–46; Br Cncl 1949–81: Turkey, Nigeria (twice), Syria, Uganda, Somalia, UK, ret as asst DG 1981; Help The Aged: chm International Ctee 1988–92 (memb 1982–94), tstee 1988–94; ed Directory of Statutory and Voluntary Health Social and Welfare Servs in Surrey 1986 and 1987; vice chm Mgmnt Ctee Guildford Inst Univ of Surrey; *Recreations* reading, travel, genealogy; *Style*— Antony Sherwood, CMG; ✉ 18 Rivermount Gardens, Guildford, Surrey GU2 5DN (☎ 01483 38277)

SHERWOOD, James Blair; s of William Earl (d 1996), and Florence Balph Sherwood; *b* 8 Aug 1933; *Educ* Yale Univ (BA); *m* 31 Dec 1977, Shirley Angela, da of Geoffrey Masser Briggs (d 1993), of Hinton Waldrist, Oxon; 2 step s (Charles Nigel Cross b 1959, Simon Michael Cross b 1960); *Career* Lt (jr grade) US Naval Reserve 1955–58; mangr French Ports and asst gen freight traffic mangr United States Lines Co (Le Havre and NY) 1959–62, gen mangr Container Transport International Inc 1963–64, fndr and pres Sea Containers Group (Bermuda) 1965–, chm Orient-Express Hotels Inc 1987–; estab Harry's Bar (with Mark Birley) London 1979; restored and brought into regular service the Venice Simplon-Orient-Express 1982; dir: Illustrated London News Partnership, Through Transport Mutual Insurance Association Ltd, Harry's Bar Ltd, Hotel Cipriani SpA; tstee Solomon R Guggenheim Fndn NY; *Recreations* tennis, skiing, golf, sailing; *Clubs* Pilgrims, Mory's, Hurlingham, Mark's; *Style*— James Sherwood, Esq; (☎ 0171 805 5000)

SHERWOOD, John Herman Mulso; s of Rev Edward Charles Sherwood (d 1946), and Naomi Claire, *née* Flecker (d 1936); *Educ* Marlborough, Oriel Coll Oxford (open scholar, MA); *m* 1952, Joan Mary, *née* Yorke; 1 da (b 13 Oct 1954); *Career* Intelligence Corps 1940–45; control cmmn for Germany 1945–46, BBC 1946–73 (head of French Service 1963–73); memb: Detection Club 1957, CWA 1960, Soc of Authors 1976; *Books* author of No Golden Journey (a biography of uncle, James Elroy Flecker); crime novels incl: A Botanist at Bay (1987), The Mantrap Garden (1986), Flowers of Evil (1987), Menacing Groves (1988), A Bouquet of Thorns (1989), The Sunflower Plot (1990), The Hanging Garden (1991), Creeping Jenny (1992), Bones Gather no Moss (1994), Shady Borders (1996); *Recreations* gardening, crime writing; *Clubs* Oriental; *Style*— John Sherwood, Esq; ✉ Northend Cottage, 36 The High St, Charing, Ashford, Kent TN27 0HX (☎ 01233 713226)

SHERWOOD, Kenneth Alan; s of Frederick Sherwood (d 1950), of Pinner, and Winifred Edith Maud, *née* White (d 1987); *b* 20 May 1935; *Educ* Merchant Taylors'; *m* 18 Feb 1961, Jennifer Edith, da of Geoffrey Higginson Allard (d 1986), of Watford; 1 s (Graham b 1961), 2 da (Heather b 1964, Frances b 1966); *Career* Kidsons Impey (formerly Chalmus Impey then Hodgson Impey) chartered accountants: ptnr 1968–94, nat tech ptnr 1978–93, dir of professional servs 1990–93, conslt 1994–96; memb Cncl ICAEW 1977–83, pres AAT 1988–89 (memb Cncl 1983–91), chm ICAEW Ctee on Housing Assocs 1976–94, hon treas Notting Hill Housing Tst 1988–91, chm Hightown Praetorian Housing Assoc 1990–95 (memb Ctee 1980–), hon treas Berkhamsted Town Hall Tst 1981–86 and 1990– (vice chm 1986–90), chm Berkhamsted Citizens Assoc 1974–76; Liveryman Worshipful Co of CAs; Freeman City of London; *Recreations* gardening, walking, reading, theatre, local community gps; *Style*— Kenneth Sherwood, Esq; ✉ Rhenigidale, Ivy House Lane, Berkhamsted, Herts HP4 2PP (☎ 01442 865158)

SHERWOOD, (Peter) Louis Michael; s of Peter Louis Sherwood, and Mervyn De Toll; *b* 27 Oct 1941; *Educ* Westminster, New College Oxford (BA, MA), Stanford Univ Sch of Business (MBA); *m* 22 Aug 1970, Nicole, da of Albert Dina, of Voiron, France; 1 s (Christopher b 1974), 2 da (Anne b 1975, Isabelle b 1978); *Career* corp fin exec Grenfell & Co Ltd 1965–68, asst to Chm Fine Fare Ltd 1968–69, md Melias Ltd 1969–72, retailing exec Cavenham Ltd 1972, dir Anglo-Continental Investment & Finance Co Ltd 1972–79, sr vice pres for devpt Grand Union Co (New Jersey) 1979–85, pres Gt Atlantic & Pacific Tea Co 1985–88, dir Gateway Corporation 1988–89, chm and chief exec Gateway Foodmarkets Ltd 1988–89; non-exec dir: EBC Group plc 1990–, Clerical Medical & General Life Assurance Society 1990–, Birmingham Midshires Building Society 1991–96, United Bristol Healthcare NHS Trust 1991–, ASW Holdings plc 1993–; non-exec chm: Magnet Group plc 1990–92, HTV Group plc 1991– (non-exec dir 1990–), New Look plc 1994–96; chm: Bristol C of C and Initiative 1993–95 (non-exec dir 1989–), Centre for the Performing Arts (Bristol) Ltd 1995–, dep chm Bristol Bristol 2000 Ltd 1995–; *Recreations* mountain walking, running, fine wine collecting, English watercolours collecting; *Clubs* Lansdowne; *Style*— Louis Sherwood, Esq; ✉ 10 College Rd, Clifton, Bristol BS8 3HZ

SHERWOOD, Martin William; s of Peter Louis Sherwood (d 1992), and Mervyn, *née* De Toll, of London; *Educ* Westminster, New Coll Oxford (BA); *Career* grad trainee, account exec and supervisor Ogilvy Benson & Mather advtg agency 1967–74, mktg mangr, sales mangr, controller shop-in-shops, then md (subsid) Debenhams plc 1974–85, md Retail Detail Ltd 1985–87, md MMI plc financial mktg gp (memb FIMBRA, PRCA, BES Assoc) 1987–94, chief exec Investment Finance Div Mills & Reeve (lawyers) 1994–, dir BES/EIS companies; non-exec dir Shops Bd Notting Hill Housing Trust 1981–, memb NEDO Ctee 'Better Made in Britain' 1984, fndr and non-exec tstee CRUSAID 1986–; MIPR 1989; *Recreations* charity, bridge, music; *Style*— Martin Sherwood, Esq; ✉ Mills

& Reeve, Francis House, 112 Hills Road, Cambridge CB2 1PH (☎ 01223 364422, fax 01223 355848)

SHERWOOD, Oliver Martin Carwardine; s of Nathaniel Edward Carwardine Sherwood, of Easthorpe, nr Colchester, Essex, and Heather Patricia Motion, *née* Carolin; *b* 23 March 1955; *Educ* Radley; *c* 1 s (Peter Frederick Carwardine b 27 Oct 1986), 1 da (Davina Ruth b 7 July 1984); *Career* racehorse trainer; asst trainer to: G Pritchard-Gordon Newmarket 1975–76, Arthur Moore Ireland 1976–79, Fred Winter Lambourn 1979–84; racehorse trainer Rhonehurst Upper Lambourn 1984–; trainer of 325 winners incl winners of: EBF Novice Hurdle Final Cheltenham 1986, Glenlivet Hurdle Liverpool 1987, Sun Alliance Novices Hurdle Cheltenham 1987 and 1988, Sun Alliance Novices Steeplechase Cheltenham 1988, Bic Razor Gold Cup Handicap Hurdle Lingfield 1989, Rapid Raceline Scottish Champion Hurdle Ayr 1989, Gerry Fielden Hurdle Newbury 1989, Charles Heidsieck Champagne Bula Hurdle Newbury 1989, New Year's Day Hurdle Windsor 1990, ASW Hurdle Ascot 1990, Ekbalco Handicap Hurdle Newcastle 1990, Hennessy Cognac Gold Cup Steeplechase Newbury 1990, Tingle Creek Handicap Chase Sandown 1990, Baring Securities Tolworth Hurdle Sandown 1990, First Nat Steeplechase Ascot 1990, Cheltenham Grand Annual Challenge Cup Handicap Chase Cheltenham 1991, BMW Champion Novices' Hurdle Punchestown 1991, Challow Hurdle 1994, Tote Gold Trophy 1994; champion amateur rider (ridden 95 winners incl 3 Nat Hunt Cheltenham Festival winners); *Recreations* shooting, cricket; *Style*— Oliver Sherwood, Esq; ✉ Rhonehurst, Upper Lambourn, nr Newbury, Berkshire RG16 7RG (☎ 01488 71411, fax 01488 72786)

SHETH, Pranlal; CBE (1994); s of Purashotam Virji Sheth (d 1936), and Sakarben Sheth (d 1985); *b* 20 Dec 1924; *m* 1951, Indumati, da of Dr Chaganlal Druva (d 1958); 1 s (Sunil), 1 da (Vandna); *Career* journalist Kenya 1943–52, chm Nyanza Farmers Co-op Soc 1954–60, called to the Bar Lincoln's Inn 1962; memb: Central Agric Bd Kenya 1963–66, Econ Planning and Devpt Cncl Kenya 1964–66; dep chm Asian Hosp Authy 1964–66; chief ed Gujarat Samacher Weekly 1972–73; gp sec Abbey Life Group of Cos: 1971–77 (legal advsr and dir 1980–88, sometime dir various subsids), legal dir Hartford Europe gp of cos 1977–86, gp sec ITT gp of cos in UK 1983–86, dir Reed Executive plc 1990–93; dep chm CRE 1977–80, memb Independent Television Cmmn 1991–95 (memb IBA 1990–91); chm: Abbey Ethical Unit Tst Advsy Bd 1988–96, Victim Support Ltd 1995–; vice pres UK Immigrants Advsy Serv 1986–92; memb: N Metropolitan Conciliation Ctee Race Rels Bd 1973–77, BBC Consultative Gp on Industry and Business Affrs 1986–89, Shop and Premises Ctee Oxfam 1988–93, Victim Support Advsy Bd 1995–; tstee: Project Fullemploy (charitable tst) 1977–89, Sangam 1979–, Runnymede Tst 1987–, Urban Tst 1987–, Windsor Fellowship 1987–, Womankind Worldwide 1988–96, Shelter 1989–90, Immigrants Aid Tst 1989–, One World Broadcasting Tst 1991–, Gujarati Literary Acad 1992–; dir: Roundhouse Arts Centre 1986–91, One World Online Ltd 1995–; patron Int Centre for Child Studies, vice patron UK Assoc Int Year of the Child 1978–80; hon legal advsr and memb Exec and Gen Cncls Nat Assoc of Victim Support Schemes 1988–96; memb: Gen Cncl of the Bar, Bar Assoc for Commerce Fin and Indust, Br Insurance Law Assoc, Life Assurance Legal Soc; govr Univ of N London 1979–; FInstD, FIMgt; *Recreations* music, theatre, sports, literature; *Clubs* Royal Over-Seas League, Cwlth Tst; *Style*— P Sheth, Esq, CBE; ✉ 70 Howberry Rd, Edgware, Middx (☎ 0181 952 2413, fax 0181 952 5332)

SHEW, Edmund Jeffrey; s of Edmund Robert Shew (d 1952), of Bosbury, Herefordshire, and Dorothy May, *née* Teague (d 1988); *b* 23 Dec 1936; *Educ* Rossall Sch Fleetwood; *m* 1, 24 June 1960 (m dis); 1 s (Michael b 14 June 1962), 1 da (Dorothy b 19 May 1966); m 2, 21 Nov 1987, Vivien Dawn, da of Meirion Jones; *Career* Nat Serv RAF 1960–62; articled clerk 1954–59, ptnr Stanley Marsh & Co CAs St Helens 1962–66, princ Edmund Shew & Co CA St Helens 1966–; pres Liverpool Soc of CAs 1983–84, memb Cncl ICAEW 1989–95; memb Worshipful Co of CAs in Eng and Wales; memb: Guild of Freemen of the City of London, The Guild of Tax Advsrs; FCA (ACA 1960), ATII 1963, FCCA 1983, FIMgt 1986; *Recreations* secretary of St Helens & District Scout Assoc, classical music, gardening, art, theatre, agriculture; *Clubs* City Livery; *Style*— Edmund Shew, Esq; ✉ 46 Crank Rd, Billinge, nr Wigan, Lancs WN5 7EZ (☎ 01744 895361); 8 Le Golf, Gros Bissinges, 74500 Evian-les-Bains, France (☎ 00 33 4 50 75 27 91); Edmund Shew & Co, 35 Westfield St, St Helens, Merseyside WA10 1QD (☎ 01744 730888, fax 01744 451785)

SHIACH, Allan George; s of Maj Gordon Leslie Shiach, WS (d 1948), and Lucie Sybil, *née* de Freitas; *b* 16 Sept 1941; *Educ* Gordonstoun, McGill Univ (BA); *m* 12 Nov 1966, Kathleen Beaumont, da of Richard B Swarbreck (d 1977), of Rhodesia; 2 s (Dominic Leslie b 1967, Luke Allan b 1974), 1 da (Philippa Lucie b 1969); *Career* chm Macallan-Glenlivet plc 1980–96, dir Rafford Films Ltd 1984–; screenwriter/producer 1970–; writer/co-writer: Don't Look Now 1975, Castaway 1985, The Girl from Petrovka 1978, DARYL 1984, Tenebrae 1982, Joseph Andrews 1979, The Witches 1988, Cold Heaven 1990, Two Deaths 1995, The Preacher's Wife 1996, In Love and War 1996, Regeneration 1996, and others; memb Cncl of Scotch Whisky Assoc; dir: Scottish Television plc, Caledonian Publishers Ltd; chm: Scottish Film Cncl, Scottish Screen; govr British Film Inst; Freeman City of London 1988, Liveryman Worshipful Co of Distillers; memb: BAFTA, WGA, American Acad of Motion Picture Arts and Scis; *Clubs* Savile; *Style*— Allan Shiach, Esq; ✉ 16 The Boltons, Chelsea, London SW10 9SU (☎ 0171 370 2694, fax 0171 373 4044)

SHIACH, Sheriff Gordon Iain Wilson; s of John Crawford Shiach (d 1978), and Florence Bygott, *née* Wilson; *b* 15 Oct 1935; *Educ* Lathallan, Gordonstoun, Univ of Edinburgh (MA, LLB); *m* 1962, Margaret Grant, da of Donald Duff Smith, of Grantown-on-Spey; 2 da (Katherine d 1996, Alison); *Career* advocate 1960–72 (Edinburgh); Sheriff: Fife and Kinross at Dunfermline 1972–79, Lothian and Borders at Linlithgow 1979–84, Lothian and Borders at Edinburgh 1984–; Hon Sheriff at Elgin 1986–; memb: Cncl Sheriffs' Assoc 1989–95 (pres 1993–95), Standing Ctee on Criminal Procedure 1989–93, Bd Lothian Family Mediation Serv 1989–93, Parole Bd for Scotland 1990–, Cncl Faculty of Advocates 1993–95, Shrieval Trg Gp 1994–95, Review Gp on Social Work Nat Standards for Throughcare 1994–95; *Recreations* walking, swimming, music, art, film, theatre; *Clubs* New (Edinburgh); *Style*— Sheriff Gordon Shiach; ✉ Sheriffs' Chambers, Sheriff Court House, 27 Chambers Street, Edinburgh EH1 1LB (☎ 0131 225 2525, fax 0131 225 4422)

SHIELD, Dr Michael James; s of Joseph Wishart Shield, DSC, and Phyllis Mabel Rosina Liffin, *née* Bullivant; *b* 17 Oct 1949; *Educ* Cheltenham, Univ of London, Middx Hosp Med Sch (MB BS); *m* 27 March 1976, Amelia Joan, da of Leyshon Edward Thomas (d 1956); 1 s (James b 1981), 1 da (Zabrina b 1983); *Career* WHO fellowship in tropical diseases trg prog; sr lectr and hon conslt microbiologist St Mary's Hosp 1980–81, dir Med Dept UK and Republic of Ireland and bd dir G D Searle & Co Ltd UK 1986–; FRCPath, MFPM; *Recreations* golf, photography, travel, whale watching, house renovation; *Style*— Dr Michael Shield, Esq; ✉ G D Searle & Co Ltd, PO Box 53, Lane End Rd, High Wycombe, Bucks HP12 4HL (☎ 01494 521124)

SHIELDS, Elizabeth Lois; da of Thomas Henry Teare (d 1977), and Dorothy Emma Elizabeth, *née* Roberts-Lawrence (d 1977); *b* 27 Feb 1928; *Educ* Whyteleafe Girls' GS Surrey, UCL (BA), Univ of York (MA); *m* 12 Aug 1961, David Cathro Shields, s of Arthur William Strachan Shields; *Career* teacher: classics at St Philomena's Carshalton, Jersey Coll for Girls, St Swithun's Winchester, Trowbridge HS, Queen Ethelburga's, Harrogate, Malton Sch; lectr Univ of Hull 1989–; lectr WEA Leeds and York 1991–; memb Lib Dem Pty, cncllr Ryedale DC May 1980, MP (Lib Dem) Ryedale May 1986–June 1987, re-selected prospective Parly candidate Ryedale, Lib Dem spokesman on the environment for Yorks and Humberside 1990–; chm: Ryedale Dist Cncl 1989–90, Ryedale DC Community Servs 1991–, Ryedale Housing Assoc 1990–91, Malton Sch PTA, chm govrs Langton CP Sch 1992–; memb govrs Norton Sch 1980–92, patron Malton and Norton Boys' Club, pres Ryedale Motor Neurone Disease Assoc 1990–, pres Ryedale Cats Protection League 1991–; *Clubs* Nat Lib, Ryedale House; *Style*— Mrs Elizabeth Shields; ✉ Firby Hall, Kirkham Abbey, Westow, York YO6 7LH (☎ 01653 81 474)

SHIELDS, Frank Cox; s of Joseph F Shields (d 1973), of Dublin, and Alice, *née* Cox (d 1972); *b* 10 Sept 1944; *Educ* Harvard Coll (AB), Wharton Sch of Fin and Commerce (MBA); *m* 9 Oct 1971, Elizabeth Jean, da of John Blythe Kinross, CBE, of London; 2 s (Oliver b 1975, Alexander b 1980), 1 da (Henrietta b 1973); *Career* res staff LSE 1969–71; stockbroker: Cazenove & Co 1971–73, Grieveson Grant & Co 1973–78; exec dir: European Banking Co Ltd 1978–85, EBC AMRO Bank Ltd 1985–86; sr rep Maruman Securities Co Ltd London 1987, dir and gen mangr Maruman Securities (Europe) Ltd 1987–92, sr private banker and vice-pres Merrill Lynch International Bank Ltd 1992–94, head of real estate and tstee services National Bank of Kuwait (International) PLC 1995–; *Recreations* architecture, reading, travel; *Clubs* Buck's, The Nassau (Princeton NJ); *Style*— Frank Shields, Esq; ✉ 24 Church Row, Hampstead, London NW3 6UP (☎ 0171 435 1175); National Bank of Kuwait (International) PLC, 13 George Street, London W1H 5PB (☎ 0171 224 2277, fax 0171 935 8280, telex 892348)

SHIELDS, (Robert) Michael Coverdale; *b* 23 Jan 1943; *Educ* Durham Johnston GS, Univ of Durham (BSc), Univ of Newcastle (DipTP); *m* Dorothy Jean; 2 s (Paul, Mark), 1 da (Emma); *Career* planning asst City of Newcastle upon Tyne 1964–65, planning asst rising to sr planning asst Durham CC 1965–69, princ planning asst rising to asst city planning offr Nottingham City Cncl 1969–73, dep dir of planning Leeds City Cncl 1973–78, city tech servs offr and dep chief exec Salford City Cncl 1978–83; chief exec: Trafford BC 1983–87, Trafford Park Development Corp 1987–; dir: Northbank Industrial Park Management Company Ltd, Trafford Business-Education Partnership, Manchester Business Link; memb: Bd of Mgmnt Manchester Coll of Nursing and Midwifery, Trafford Gp MCCI, Planning Advsy Gp Univ of Manchester, Steering Ctee NW Engrg Educn Club; non-exec chm Salford Univ Business Services Ltd; pro-chllr and dep chm of cncl Univ of Salford, govr Altrincham GS for Boys (chm 1988–93); MRTPI 1968, FRGS 1968, FRSA 1988; *Recreations* reading, cinema and theatre, DIY, badminton, philately; *Style*— Michael Shields, Esq; ✉ Trafford Park Development Corporation, Trafford Wharf Road, Wharfside, Trafford Park, Manchester M17 1EX (☎ 0161 848 8000, fax 0161 848 8638)

SHIELDS, Sir Neil Stanley; kt (1964), MC (1946); s of Archie Shields (d 1958), and Hannah Shields (d 1976); *b* 7 Sept 1919; *m* 1970, (Gloria) Dawn, *née* Wilson; *Career* Maj NW Europe 1940 and 1944–46; dir Central and Sheerwood plc 1969–84; chm: Anglo Continental Investment & Finance Co Ltd 1965–74, Standard Catalogue Co Ltd 1976–84, Holcombe Holdings plc 1978–84, Trianco Redfyre Ltd 1979–84; md Chesham Amalgamations & Investments Ltd 1968–78 (dir 1964–84); chm Cmmn for the New Towns 1982–95; dep chm London Transport 1989–93 (chm 1988–89, memb 1986–93, chm LT Property Bd 1986–95); chm London Area Nat Union of Conservative and Unionist Assocs 1961–63; memb Cncl Aims of Indust 1975–; govr Bedford Coll 1983–85; hon memb RICS 1993; *Recreations* reading, music, wining and dining; *Clubs* Carlton, HAC; *Style*— Sir Neil Shields, MC; ✉ 12 London House, Avenue Rd, London NW8 7PX

SHIELDS, Prof Sir Robert; kt (1990), DL (Merseyside 1991); s of Robert Alexander Shields (d 1947), of Paisley, Scotland, and Isobel MacDougall, *née* Reid (d 1982); *b* 8 Nov 1930; *Educ* John Neilson Inst Paisley, Univ of Glasgow (MB ChB, MD), FRCS, FRCSEd; *m* 19 Jan 1957, (Grace) Marianne, da of George Swinburn (d 1953), of London; 1 s (Andrew Duncan Robert b 1966), 2 da (Gillian Elizabeth b 1959, Jennifer Anne b 1962); *Career* RAMC: Nat Serv 1954–56, Lt 1954, Capt 1955, Maj (TA) 1956–61; Regtl MO: 1 Bn Argyll and Sutherland Highlanders 1954–56, 7 Bn Argyll and Sutherland Highlanders (TA) 1956–61, Hon Col Liverpool Univ OTC; Western Infirmary Glasgow: house offr 1953–54, sr house offr 1956–57, registrar in surgery 1958–59; Univ of Glasgow: Hall tutorial fell 1957–58, lectr in surgery 1959–62; res asst Dept of Surgical Res Mayo Clinic USA 1959–60, sr lectr then reader in surgery Welsh Nat Sch of Med 1962–69; Univ of Liverpool: prof of surgery 1969–96 (prof emeritus 1996–), dean Faculty of Med 1982–85; hon conslt surgn Royal Liverpool Univ Hosp and Broadgreen Hosp 1969–96 (conslt emeritus Royal Liverpool Hosp 1996–); memb Liverpool Health Authy 1974–78, vice chm Mersey RHA 1983–85 (memb Res Ctee 1976–93); pres: Liverpool Med Inst 1988–89, Merseyside, Cheshire and Lancs Cncl on Alcoholism 1993–94; regnl advsr RCS 1986–93, chm Mil Educn Ctee Univ of Liverpool 1987–93, vice chm Specialist Trg Authy 1996–; pres: Sugical Res Soc 1983–85, Assoc of Surgns of GB and I 1986–87, Br Soc of Gastroenterology 1990–91 (hon memb), James IVth Assoc of Surgns 1993–, Royal Coll of Surgns of Edinburgh 1994–; memb: GMC 1984–94, MRC 1987–92; Hon DSc Univ of Wales 1990; hon fell: American Coll of Surgns 1990, American Surgical Assoc 1992, Coll of Med S Africa 1991, HKCS 1996, Acad of Med Singapore 1996; Hon FRCPSGlas 1993, Hon FRCSI 1996, Hon FRCPEd 1996; *Books* Surgical Emergencies II (1979), Surgical Management (1983), Gastroenterological Emergencies (1992), Portal Hypertension (1992); *Recreations* sailing, reading; *Clubs* Army and Navy; *Style*— Prof Sir Robert Shields, DL; ✉ Strathmore, 81 Meols Drive, West Kirby, Wirral L48 5DF (☎ 0151 632 3588) Royal College of Surgeons of Edinburgh, Nicolson Street, Edinburgh EH8 9DW (☎ 0131 527 1635, fax 0131 557 9771)

SHIER, Jonathan Fraser; s of Frank Eric Shier (decd), and Margery Mary, *née* Dutton (d 1995); *b* 18 Oct 1947, Melbourne, Australia; *Educ* Geelong C of E GS Aust, Monash Univ Melbourne (LLB, BEC); *Career* private sec to Dep Senate Ldr and AG of Aust 1973–76, mktg controller and dir of sales and mktg Scottish TV 1977–85, dir of sales and mktg Thames TV plc 1985–93, dep chief exec Thames TV plc 1990–93; chm ITV Marketing Ctee 1989–91; chief exec offr Central and Eastern Europe Nethold 1994–; *Recreations* travel, theatre, music, diving; *Clubs* Annabel's, Hurlingham, IOD; *Style*— Jonathan Shier, Esq; ✉ Nethold Central Europe, Planetenweg 8, 2132 HP Hoofddorp, The Netherlands (☎ 00 31 2356 86789, fax 00 31 2356 86646)

SHIFFNER, George Frederick; s of late Capt George Edward Shiffner (gs of 4 Bt); hp of kinsman, Sir Henry Shiffner, 8 Bt; *b* 3 Aug 1936; *Educ* Wellington; *m* 1961, Dorothea Helena Cynthia, da of late T H McLean; 1 s, 1 da; *Career* photographer, ABIPP; *Style*— George Shiffner, Esq; ✉ 14 Coggeshall Rd, Braintree, Essex (☎ 01376 322524); Searles, Alderford Street, Sible Hedingham, Essex (☎ 01787 460486)

SHIFFNER, Sir Henry David; 8 Bt (UK 1818), of Coombe, Sussex; s of Maj Sir Henry Burrows Shiffner, 7 Bt, OBE (d 1941); *b* 2 Feb 1930; *Educ* Rugby, Trinity Hall Cambridge; *m* 1, 1951 (m dis 1956), Dorothy, da of W G Jackson, of Coventry; 1 da (Elizabeth Marilyn b 1953); m 2, 1957 (m dis 1970), Beryl, da of George Milburn, of Saltdean, Sussex; 1 da (Linda Mary b 1957); m 3, 1971, Joaquina Ramos Lopez, of Madrid; *Heir* kinsman, George Frederick Shiffner, *qv*; *Career* company dir; *Style*— Sir Henry Shiffner, Bt

SHILLING, David; s of Ronald Shilling, and Gertrude Shilling; *b* 27 June 1953; *Educ* St Paul's; *Career* designer; designs incl: menswear, womenswear, lingerie, furs, jewellery, fine china limited edition pieces, ceramic tiles, wallpapers, upholstery fabrics and designs for film, theatre, ballet and opera; important shows incl: The Hats (Ulster Museum exhibition, exhibited Worthing, Plymouth, Salisbury, Durham, Leeds and

Exeter Museums) 1981–, David Shilling - A Decade of Design (Chester Museum) 1991; other exhibitions incl: Angela Flowers London, Tino Ghelfi Vicenza Italy, Rendezvous Gallery Aberdeen, Phillip Francis Sheffield, Richard Demarco Gallery Edinburgh, Sotheby's Stockholm, Salamo-Caro Gallery Cork St London 1993, British Cncl Koln 1995; work in museum collections: V & A London, Met NY, Los Angeles County, Mappin Gallery Sheffield, Musée de l'Art Décoratif Paris; UN sr conslt for design and product adaptation for developing countries (projects in S America, Asia and Africa) 1990–; pres Valdivia Ecuador; *Books* Thinking Rich (1986); *Recreations* sleeping on aeroplanes, jet-skiing, jam making; *Style*— David Shilling, Esq; ✉ 5 Homer St, London W1H 1HN (☎ 0171 262 2363, fax 0171 262 2363)

SHILLING, David Roger; s of Roger Shilling, and Rita Shilling; *b* 28 July 1954; *Educ* Woodroffe Sch Lyme Regis, Bournemouth & Poole Coll of Art and Design (DipAD, SIAD, MCAM); *m* Frances Louise; 2 da (Vienna, Lydia); *Career* Picador Design 1973–74, Dayton Groom and Saunders 1974–77, Mallard Advertising 1977–82, Monitor Advertising 1982–85, creative dir David Pilton Advertising 1990– (bd dir 1993); IPA Agency TV Prodr Dip 1989; MIPA; *Recreations* playing guitar, running (completed 3 London Marathons 1991–93, NY Marathon in 3 hrs 30 minutes), TV and cinema, writing, board sailing; *Style*— David Shilling, Esq; ✉ David Pilton Advertising Ltd, Royalty House, 72–74 Dean Street, London W1V 6AE (☎ 0171 439 1228, fax 0171 734 7121)

SHILLINGTON, Sir (Robert Edward) Graham; kt (1972), CBE (1970, OBE 1959, MBE 1951), DL (Co Down 1975); s of Maj D Graham Shillington, DL, MP (d 1944); *b* 2 April 1911; *Educ* Sedbergh, Clare Coll Cambridge; *m* 1935, Mary E R Bulloch (d 1977); 2 s, 1 da; *Career* chief constable RUC 1970–73 (dep chief constable 1969–70); *Recreations* golf, gardening; *Clubs* Royal Over-Seas League, Royal Belfast Golf; *Style*— Sir Graham Shillington, CBE, DL; ✉ Ardeevin, 184 Bangor Road, Holywood, Co Down, NI BT18 0BY

SHIMELL, William Douglas John; s of William George Shimell, of Cawsand, Cornwall, and F Elizabeth Bowen; *b* 23 Sept 1952; *Educ* Westminster Abbey Choir Sch, St Edward's Sch Oxford, Guildhall Sch of Music, National Opera Studio; *Career* baritone; *Roles* incl: Count Almaviva in The Marriage of Figaro (Glyndebourne Festival 1984, La Scala Milan 1987 and 1989, Geneva Opera 1989, Vienna Staatsoper 1990, 1993, 1994 and 1995, Zurich Opera 1990, Chicago Lyric Opera 1991), Marcello in La Bohème (Royal Opera House Covent Garden 1990, Vienna Staatsoper 1991, San Francisco 1993, Metropolitan NY 1996), title role in Don Giovanni (WNO 1984, ENO 1985, Amsterdam 1989 and 1992, Zurich 1991, Aix-en-Provence Festival 1993, Munich 1994, Berlin 1994, San Francisco 1995), Dandini in La Cenerentola (Glyndebourne Touring Opera 1983, Le Chatalet Paris 1986), Malatesta in Don Pasquale (Netherlands Opera) 1987, Nick Shadow in The Rake's Progress (San Francisco Opera 1988, Opèra de Lyon 1995), Guglielmo in Cosi fan Tutte (Covent Garden, Geneva Opera, Zurich Opera, Tokyo, Bolshoi Theatre Moscow with La Scala Co 1989), Don Alfonso in Cosi fan Tutte (Rome 1995, Paris 1996), Dourlinski in Lodoiska (La Scala Milan under Riccardo Muti, also recorded live for Sony) 1991; *Recordings* Joseph in Berlioz L'Enfance du Christ (with English Chamber Orch under Leger, Thames Television), Bach B minor Mass (with Chicago Symphony Orch under Sir Georg Solti, Decca), Vaughan Williams Sea Symphony (with Royal Liverpool Philharmonic under Vernon Handley, EMI), Lambert Summer's Last Will and Testament (with English Northern Philharmonic under David Lloyd-Jones), Stravinsky Pulcinella (with Amsterdam Concertgebouw under Chailly, Decca), title role in Don Giovanni (with Vienna Philharmonic under Riccardo Muti, EMI); *Style*— William Shimell, Esq; ✉ c/o IMG Artists, Media House, 3 Burlington Lane, Chiswick, London W4 2TH (☎ 0181 747 9977, fax 0181 742 8758)

SHINDLER, Dr Colin; s of Israel Shindler, of Prestwich, Manchester, and Florence, *née* Weidberg; *b* 28 June 1949; *Educ* Bury GS Lancs, Gonville and Caius Coll Cambridge (BA, MA, PhD); *m* 23 Sept 1972, (Nancy) Lynn, da of Prof Robert Stephen White, of Santa Barbara, Californa, USA; 1 s (David b 1977), 1 da (Amy b 1975); *Career* film, television writer and producer: res fell American Film Inst Beverly Hills 1972; as prodr incl: Love Story series (BBC) 1981, East Lynne (BBC) 1982, The Worst Witch (Central, American Cable Emmy) 1985, A Little Princess (LWT, BAFTA) 1986, Lovejoy (BBC, series V 1993, series VI 1994), Wish Me Luck (LWT) 1987, 1914 All Out (YTV, first prize Reims Int Film Festival) 1989; as writer and prodr: Young Charlie Chaplin (Thames/PBS, US Prime Time Emmy nomination), The Scarlet Thread (NBC) 1992, Madson (BBC) 1995; author of screenplay Buster (feature film) 1988; memb BAFTA; *Books* Hollywood Goes to War (1979), Buster (1988), Hollywood in Crisis (1996); *Recreations* cricket, soccer, golf, tennis, badminton, theatre, music, fell walking in the Lake District; *Style*— Dr Colin Shindler; ✉ c/o ICM Ltd, Oxford House, 76 Oxford Street, London W1N 0AX (☎ 0171 636 6565, fax 0171 323 0101)

SHINDLER, Geoffrey Arnold; s of Israel Shindler, of Manchester, and Florence, *née* Weidberg (d 1962); *b* 21 Oct 1942; *Educ* Bury GS, Gonville and Caius Coll (WM Tapp scholar, MA, LLM); *m* 20 Feb 1966, Gay, da of late Harry Kenton; 3 da (Freya b 29 Dec 1966, Nicola b 8 Oct 1968, Caroline b 29 Jan 1971); *Career* ptnr March Pearson & Skelton 1971–86 (articled clerk 1966–68, asst slr 1968–71), ptnr Halliwell Landau Manchester 1986–; memb: Bd of Visitors HM Prison Manchester 1973–84, Salford FPC 1984–89, Exec Ctee NW Arts 1984–91, chm Local Review Ctee (Parole) HM Prison Manchester 1979–84; hon assoc Centre For Law and Business Univ of Manchester 1990–, chm Soc of Tst and Estate Practitioners 1994–, dir Opera North 1995–, chm Ctee Inst for Fiscal Studies NW region 1996–; recipient Muriel Goodwin trophy 1993; memb: Manchester Literary and Philosophical Soc, Law Soc; MSI; *Books* Law of Trusts (with K Hodkinson, 1984); *Recreations* theatre, opera, books; *Clubs* St James's (Manchester), Lancashire CCC, MCC, Portico Library; *Style*— Geoffrey Shindler, Esq; ✉ 10 Bury Old Road, Prestwich, Manchester M25 0EX (☎ 0161 740 2291); Halliwell Landau, St James's Court, Brown St, Manchester M2 2JF (☎ 0161 835 3003, fax 0161 835 2994)

SHINGLER, Timothy Hugh; s of Hugh Shingler (d 1993), and Enid Mary, *née* Stuffins; *b* 10 Aug 1955; *Educ* Bromley Tech HS for Boys; *m* 1, 1979 (m dis 1985), Laura Muriel, *née* Mill; 1 da (Sarah Laura b 23 Dec 1983); m 2, 11 June 1988, Susan, da of Dennis Arthur Edgar Elmes; 1 da (Helen Elizabeth b 21 April 1992); *Career* geological data supervisor and co scout Shell UK Exploration and Production 1973–81, sr project co-ordinator Petroleum Information Ltd 1981–86, assoc Petroleum Servs Div James Capel & Co 1990–91 (oil exec 1986–89), gp head Petroleum Servs Gp Arthur Andersen 1991–; dir Borough 19 Motor Club Ltd; memb Petroleum Exploration Soc of Great Britain 1986–; MInstPet 1986; *Recreations* motor sport, skiing, gardening, cooking; *Style*— Timothy Shingler, Esq; ✉ Arthur Andersen, 1 Surrey Street, London WC2R 2PS (☎ 0171 438 3880, fax 0171 438 3881)

SHINGLES, Godfrey Stephen (Geoff); CBE (1987); s of Sidney Shingles, and Winifred, *née* Moss; *b* 9 April 1939; *Educ* Paston Sch N Walsham Norfolk, Univ of Leeds (BSc); *m* (m dis); 2 s (Jonathan b 19 Feb 1968, James b 29 April 1970); *Career* Digital Equipment Co 1965–94 (latterly chm and chief exec), chm Videologic PLC 1996– (dep chm 1994–96); dir: Gatton Consulting Group 1994–, European Data Systems Ltd, Interregnum Venture Marketing Ltd; chm: ProMetrics Group Ltd, ABSA Consulting; Liveryman Worshipful Co of Info Technologists; FInstD, FBCS, FIEE; *Recreations* painting, skiing, sailing, rugby, ballet; *Clubs* Royal Ocean Racing; *Style*— Geoff Shingles, Esq, CBE

SHINGLES, Raymond Edward Laws; MBE (Mil 1945); s of Charles Edward Shingles (d 1948), and Lillie Waldock (d 1957); *b* 11 March 1913; *Educ* Cranleigh Sch; *m* 1952, Phyllis Willan, da of Lt-Col Charles Edward Jefferis, of Cookham House Hotel (d 1963); 2 s (Justin, Rupert); *Career* Lt-Col 9 JAT Regt Indian Army, served in forces 1939–46, passed Staff Coll Quetta, served in India; slr Supreme Ct, ptnr Linklaters & Paines 1950–74; dir: Air Products Ltd 1957–80, Brown Shipley Holdings plc 1969–74, Brown Shipley & Co Ltd 1969–74, Bowthorpe Holdings Ltd 1970–76, Hongkong & Shanghai Banking Corporation (Jersey) Ltd 1975–84, Fleming Albany American Fund Ltd 1978–91, Brown Shipley (Jersey) Ltd 1977–87, Brown Shipley (Guernsey) Ltd 1977–87, Brown Shipley Sterling Bond Fund Ltd 1978–88, Brown Shipley International Currency Fund Ltd 1982–88, Brown Shipley International Bond Fund Ltd 1983–88, Brown Shipley Sterling Capital Fund Ltd 1979–88, Robert Fleming (Jersey) Ltd 1977–, Robert Fleming Investment Management (Jersey) Ltd 1985–, Property Security Investsment Trust (CI) Ltd 1984–; *Recreations* horse racing, golf; *Clubs* Channel Islands Race and Hunt, La Moye Golf; *Style*— Raymond Shingles, Esq, MBE; ✉ La Sergenté, La Grande Route de Rozel, St Martin, Jersey, CI JE3 6AX (☎ 01534 854967)

SHINGLETON, Andrew Philip; s of Wilfrid James Shingleton (d 1984), of Suffolk, and Grace Bernadina Shingleton, *née* Pole; *b* 28 June 1943; *Educ* Douai Sch; *m* 1, 1967, Vanessa Jane (d 1977), da of Capt John Liley, of Marbella; 3 s (Toby John-James b 1972, Alexander William (b 1975), Barnaby Andrew (twin) b 1975); m 2, 1982, Wendy Elizabeth, da of Alec Barnes, of S Lancing; *Career* McCann Erickson Advertising: dir 1987–, vice pres McCann Erickson Worldwide 1994–; MIPA 1972, memb CAM 1973; *Recreations* walking the Cornish cliffs, golf, 18th century French history; *Style*— Andrew P Shingleton, Esq; ✉ Bossiney, Orchehill Avenue, Gerrards Cross SL9 8QH (☎ 01753 887985); McCann Erickson Advertising, 36 Howland Street, London W1A 1AT (☎ 0171 580 6690)

SHIPLEY, (Norman) Graham (de Mattos); s of Capt Norman Douglas Holbrook Shipley (d 1979), of Bromborough, Wirral, Merseyside, and Lesley Cynthia, *née* Stott; *b* 10 Jan 1948; *Educ* King's Sch Chester, Trinity Coll Cambridge (BA, Dip Computer Sci, MA), Inns of Ct Sch of Law; *m* 11 Sept 1982, Helen Rhian, da of David Neville de Mattos, of Witchampton, Wimborne, Dorset; 2 da (Jemima, Kate); *Career* called to the Bar Lincoln's Inn 1973; currently specialising in: patent, copyright, trade mark law, confidential information, computer law, entertainment law; *Recreations* electronics, motor cycling, DIY, children, Japanese cookery; *Clubs* Wig & Pen; *Style*— Graham Shipley, Esq; ✉ New House Farm, Purton End, Debden, Saffron Walden, Essex CB11 3JT (☎ 01799 540565, fax 01799 541906); 19 Old Buildings, Lincoln's Inn, London WC2A 3UP (☎ 0171 405 2001, fax 0171 405 0001)

SHIPPEY, Prof Thomas Alan; s of Ernest Shippey (d 1962), and Christine Emily, *née* Kjelgaard; *b* 9 Sept 1943; *Educ* King Edward's Sch Birmingham, Queens' Coll Cambridge (BA, MA, PhD); *m* 1, 27 Dec 1966 (m dis 1983), Susan Margaret, da of John Veale, of Bingley, W Yorks; 1 s (John b 1973), 2 da (Louise b 1970, Gillian b 1972); m 2, 19 June 1993, Catherine Elizabeth, da of John Barton, of Bromley, Kent; *Career* lectr Univ of Birmingham 1965–72, fell St John's Coll Oxford 1972–79, prof of Eng language and medieval Eng lit Univ of Leeds 1979–93, Walter Ong chair Dept of English St Louis Univ 1993–; *Books* Old English Verse (1972), Poems of Wisdom and Learning in Old English (1976), Beowulf (1978), The Road to Middle-Earth (1982), Fictional Space (1991), Fiction 2000 (1992), Oxford Book of Science Fiction Stories (1992), Oxford Book of Fantasy Stories (1994); *Recreations* walking, running, science fiction; *Style*— Prof Thomas Shippey; ✉ English Department, St Louis University, St Louis, MO 63103, USA (☎ 00 1 314 977 7196, fax 00 1 314 977 1514, e-mail shippey@sluvca.slu.edu)

SHIPSTER, Col John Neville; CBE (1973), DSO (1944); s of Col G C Shipster, MC (d 1941); *b* 31 Jan 1922; *Educ* Marlborough; *m* 1948, Cornelia Margarethe, *née* Arends; 2 s, 1 da; *Career* WWII served 2 Punjab Regt Indian Army, CO 1 Bn Middlesex Regt 1965–67, Cdr British Forces Belize 1970–73, Cmdt Def NBC Sch 1974; Dep Col Queen's Regt 1975; *Recreations* golf, sailing; *Clubs* Army and Navy; *Style*— Col John Shipster, CBE, DSO; ✉ Deben House, 41 Cumberland St, Woodbridge, Suffolk (☎ 0139 43 3957)

SHIPWRIGHT, Adrian John; s of Jack Shipwright, and Jennie, *née* Eastman; *b* 2 July 1950; *Educ* King Edward VI Sch Southampton, ChCh Oxford (BA, BCL, MA); *m* 17 Aug 1974, Diana Evelyn, da of Percival Denys Treseder (d 1971); 1 s (Henry b 1983), 1 da (Fiona b 1985); *Career* asst slr Linklaters & Paines 1977, official student and tutor in law Christ Church Oxford 1977–82, ptnr Denton Hall Burgin & Warrens 1984–87 (asst slr 1982–84), hon lectr in laws King's Coll London 1986–90, ptnr S J Berwin & Co 1987–92 (conslt 1992), prof of business law King's Coll London 1992–96; called to the Bar Lincoln's Inn 1993, in practice Pump Ct Tax Chambers; memb Tst Law Ctee; govr King Edward VI Sch Southampton 1982–96; FRSA, AIIT; *Books* CCH British Tax Reporter Vol 5 (1986) Tax Planning and UK Land Development (1988, 2 edn 1990), Capital Gains Tax Strategies in the New Regime (1989), UK Tax and Intellectual Property (1990, 2 edn 1996), VAT, Property and the New Rules (1990), Strategic Tax Planning (ed and contrib), Textbook on Tax Law (1996); *Recreations* music; *Style*— Adrian Shipwright, Esq; ✉ 55 Homlesdale Rd, Teddington, Middx TW11 9LJ; c/o Pump Court Tax Chambers, 16 Bedford Row, London WC1R 4EB (☎ 0171 414 8080, fax 0171 414 8099)

SHIRAISHI, Yuko; da of Masahiro Shinoda, of Tokyo, Japan, and Kazuko Shiraishi; *b* 6 March 1956; *Educ* Shinmei Jr Sch Tokyo, Myojyo HS Tokyo, Chelsea Sch of Art (Br Cncl scholar, BA, MA); *m* 1983, David Juda, *qv*; *Career* artist; solo exhibitions: Curwen Gallery 1984, Edward Totah Gallery 1988, 1990 and 1992, Shigeru Yokota Gallery Tokyo 1989 and 1992, Galerie Konstruktiv Tendens Stockholm 1990 and 1994, Artsite Bath 1990, Margaret Lipworth Fine Art Florida 1991, Cairn Gallery Nailsworth 1991, Galerie Lupke Frankfurt 1992, Gallery Kasahara 1993 and 1996, ACP Viviane Ehri Galerie Zürich 1994 and 1996, Galerie Hans Mayer Düsseldorf 1996, EAF Adelaide 1996; selected group exhibitions: New Contemporaries (ICA) 1980, Whitechapel Open Exhibition 1985, 1989, 1990 and 1992, The Presence of Painting: Aspects of British Abstraction 1957–88 (Arts Cncl Mappin Gallery Sheffield and touring) 1988, From Prism to Paintbox Colour Theory and Practice in Modern British Painting (Oriel Gallery Clwyd) 1989, Kunstlerinnen des 20 Jahrhunderts (Museum Wiesbaden Germany) 1990, Geteilte Bilder (Folkwang Museum, Germany) 1992, A Sense of Purpose (Mappin Art Gallery Sheffield) 1992, Recent British Painting (Arts Cncl touring exhbn) 1993, Zwei Energie Haus fur Konstructive und Konkrete Kunst (Zurich) 1993; Jerwood Painting Prize Royal Scottish Acad Edinburgh/The Royal Acad of Arts London 1994; work in the collections of: Unilever, Br Museum, YKK Japan, IBM, Arthur Andersen collection, Seibu Japan, McCrory Corporations NY, London & Continental Bankers Ltd, Ove Arup, Arts Cncl of GB, Contemporary Art Soc, Graves City Art Gallery Sheffield, Ohara Museum Japan, Weishaupt Forum Germany; *Style*— Ms Yuko Shiraishi; ✉ Acme Studio, Studio F, 11–31 Orsman Rd, London N1 (☎ 0171 739 8949); c/o Annely Juda Fine Art, 23 Dering Street, London W1R 9AA (☎ 0171 629 7578, fax 0171 491 2139)

SHIRLEY, Vera Stephanie (Steve); OBE (1980); da of Arnold Buchthal (d 1970), and Margaret, *née* Schick (d 1987); arrived in UK on Kindertransport as child refugee in 1939; f moved from being friendly enemy alien (one of the Dunera boys) prior to UK Army, to US Army (serving at Nuremberg trials) later German equivalent of High Ct Judge, changed name on naturalisation to Brook to honour Rupert Brooke; *b* 16 Sept 1933; *Educ* Sir John Cass Coll London (BSc); *m* 14 Nov 1959, Derek George Millington Shirley, s of George Millington Shirley (d 1970); 1 s (Giles Millington); *Career* PO Res Station Dollis Hill 1951–59, CDL 1959–62, fndr dir FI GROUP plc 1962–93 (ceded control to workforce 1991, life pres 1993–), non-exec dir: AEA Technology plc (formerly

UKAEA) 1992–, Tandem Computers Inc 1992–; chair Women of Influence 1993; memb: Computer, Systems and Electronics Requirements Bd 1979–81, Electronics and Avionics Requirements Bd 1981–83; memb: Cncl Industl Soc 1984–90, Nat Cncl for Vocational Qualifications 1986–89, Br-N American Ctee 1991–, Cncl 1992 Cwlth Studies Conf; winner: RITA award (recognition of IT achievement) 1985, BIM (now Inst of Mgmnt) Gold medal 1991; US Nat Women's Hall of Fame 1995; tstee Help The Aged 1987–90, pres Br Computer Soc 1989–90 (vice pres 1979–82); Freeman City of London 1987, Master Worshipful Co of Info Technologists 1992–93; fndr chair of Tstess The Kingwood Tst Charity 1994–, patron Disablement Income Gp 1989–; memb Cncl Buckingham Univ 1993–96; hon fell: Manchester Metropolitan Univ 1989, Staffs Univ 1991, Sheffield Hallam Univ 1992; Hon DSc: Buckingham Univ 1991, Aston Univ 1993, Nottingham Trent/Southampton Inst 1994; Hon DTech Loughborough Univ 1991, Hon DLitt De Montford Univ 1993, Hon DBA Univ of the West of England 1995, Hon DTech Univ of Kingston 1995; Hon FGIA 1989, FBCS 1971, CIMgt 1984, CEng 1990; *Publications* articles in professional jls; *Recreations* sleep; *Style—* Mrs Steve Shirley, OBE; ✉ 47 Thames House, Phyllis Court Drive, Henley on Thames, Oxon RG9 2NA (☎ and fax 01491 579004)

SHIRLEY-QUIRK, John Stanton; CBE (1975); s of Joseph Stanley Shirley-Quirk, and Amelia Shirley-Quirk; *b* 28 Aug 1931; *Educ* Holt Sch Liverpool, Univ of Liverpool (BSc, DipEd); *m* 1, 1955, Patricia, *née* Hastie (d 1981); 1 s, 1 da; m 2, 1981, Sara V, *née* Watkins; 1 s, 2 da; *Career* bass-baritone singer; Offr Educn Branch RAF 1953–57; asst lectr in chemistry Acton Tech Coll 1957–61, lay clerk St Paul's Cathedral 1961–62; professional singer 1961–: Elegy For Young Lovers (Glyndebourne Opera) 1961, Curlew River 1964, The Burning Fiery Furnace 1966, The Prodigal Son 1968, Owen Wingrave 1970, Death in Venice 1973, Confessions of a Justified Sinner 1976, The Ice Break 1977; world wide appearances and tours incl: America 1966, Aust 1967, Metropolitan Opera NY 1974; numerous recordings: operas, songs, cantatas etc; memb Voice Faculty: Peabody Conservatory Baltimore Maryland 1991–, Carnegie Mellon Univ Pittsburgh 1994–; memb Ct Brunel Univ 1977; Hon RAM 1972; Univ of Liverpool Chem Soc medal 1965, Sir Charles Santley Meml gift Worshipful Co of Musicians 1969; Hon DMus Univ of Liverpool, Hon DUniv Brunel Univ; *Recreations* trees, canals, clocks; *Style—* John Shirley-Quirk, CBE; ✉ c/o Dr Kate Shirley-Quirk, The Mill House, Church Road, Pangbourne, Berks, RG8 7BB; 6062 Red Clover Lane, Clarksville, Maryland 21029, USA (☎ 00 1 410 531 1315, fax 00 1 410 531 3335, e-mail jssq@peabody.jlu.edu)

SHIVAS, Mark; s of James Dallas Shivas (d 1986), of Banstead, Surrey, and Winifred Alice, *née* Lighton (d 1978); *b* 24 April 1938; *Educ* Whitgift Sch, Merton Coll Oxford (MA); *Career* co-fndr and asst ed Movie Magazine 1961–64, dir, prodr and presenter Granada TV 1964–68, drama prodr BBC TV 1969–79; prodns incl: The Six Wives of Henry VIII, Casanova, To Encourage the Others, The Evacuees, 84 Charing Cross Road, Abide with Me, The Glittering Prizes, Rogue Male, She Fell Among Thieves, Professional Foul, On Giants Shoulders, Telford's Change; dir Southern Pictures 1979–81 (exec prodr Winston Churchill the Wilderness Years and Bad Blood); prodr Channel 4: The Price 1985, What if it's Raining? 1986, The Storyteller 1987; BBC TV: head of drama gp 1988–93, head of films 1993–; exec prodr: Truly, Madly, Deeply 1991, Enchanted April, The Grass Arena, The Snapper, Priest, Small Faces, Jude, The Van; film prodr: Moonlighting 1982, A Private Function 1985, The Witches 1989; FRTS; *Recreations* swimming, gardening, Italy; *Clubs* Groucho; *Style—* Mark Shivas, Esq; ✉ BBC TV, Wood Lane, London W12 7RJ (☎ 0181 743 8000, fax 0181 749 9331)

SHNEERSON, Dr John Michael; s of Gregory Shneerson, of Orpington, Kent, and Alfreda, *née* Ledger (d 1980); *b* 27 Sept 1946; *Educ* St Paul's, St Edmund Hall Oxford (MA, DM), St Mary's Hosp London; *m* 15 March 1975, Dr Anne Shneerson, da of Dr Kenneth Maclean, of Oxted, Surrey; 1 s (Robert b 1983), 2 da (Joanna b 1979, Catherine b 1981); *Career* sr registrar Westminster & Brompton Hosps London 1978–80; conslt physician: Newmarket Gen Hosp 1980–, Papworth Hosp 1980–, Addenbrooke's Hosp 1980–96, W Suffolk Hosp 1980–; dir: Assisted Ventilation Unit Newmarket Gen Hosp 1981–92, Respiratory Support and Sleep Centre Papworth Hosp 1992–; FRCP 1986; *Recreations* squash, golf, tennis, gardening; *Style—* Dr John Shneerson; ✉ Papworth Hospital, Papworth Everard, Cambridge CB3 8RE (☎ 01480 830541, fax 01480 830620)

SHOHET, Philip Samuel David; s of Emile Shohet (d 1968), and Rhoda, *née* Goldstone (d 1986); *b* 24 Aug 1944; *Educ* Manchester GS; *m* (m dis), Mavis Elizabeth Lock; *Career* articled with Binder Hamlyn until 1969, mgmnt consultancy work in 1970's, first commercial dir Inst of Chartered Accountants in England and Wales until 1985, md Buckmans Ltd 1985–; regular contrib to nat and professional media on accountancy matters; ACA 1969; *Recreations* tennis, squash, reading, classical music, horse riding, dining out; *Clubs* Reform; *Style—* Philip Shohet, Esq; ✉ Buckmans Ltd, 410 Strand, London WC2R 0NS (☎ 0171 836 8866)

SHONE, Richard Noel; *b* 8 May 1949; *Educ* Wrekin Coll Shropshire, Clare Coll Cambridge (BA); *Career* writer; assoc ed The Burlington Magazine 1979–; selected and catalogued: Portraits by Duncan Grant (1969), Portraits by Walter Sickert (1990); co-selector Sickert exhibition RA 1992–93, purchaser Arts Cncl Collection 1994–96, selector New Contemporaries exhibition Liverpool and London 1996; contrib numerous articles on modern Br art and Bloomsbury to: The Spectator, The Observer, Art in America, The Burlington Magazine; closely involved in restoration and opening of Charleston Farmhouse Sussex (home of Vanessa Bell and Duncan Grant) 1980–; memb: Jury Turner Prize 1988, Advsy Ctee Govt Picture Collection 1990–94; *Publications* Bloomsbury Portraits: Vanessa Bell, Duncan Grant and their Circle (1976, new edn 1993), The Century of Change: British Art Since 1900 (1977), Sisley (1979), Augustus John (1979), The Post Impressionists (1980), Walter Sickert (1988), Rodrigo Moynihan (1988), Alfred Sisley (1992); *Style—* Richard Shone, Esq; ✉ The Burlington Magazine, 12–14 Duke's Road, London WC1

SHOOTER, Prof Reginald Arthur; CBE (1980); s of Rev Arthur Edwin Shooter, TD, and Mabel Kate, *née* Pinniger; *b* 4 April 1916; *Educ* Univ of Cambridge (MA, MD); *m* 4 Dec 1946, Jean, da of Prof T W Wallace, CBE, MC, FRS, of Long Ashton Res Station; 1 s (Adrian), 3 da (Joanna, Felicity, Anthea); *Career* Surgn Lt RNVR 1943–46; Rockefeller travelling fell 1950–51, prof of med microbiology Univ of London 1961–81, bacteriologist Bart's 1961–81, dean of Med Coll Bart's 1972–81; memb: Public Health Lab Servs Bd 1970–82, City and E London AHA 1974–81, Scientific Advsy Cncl Stress Fndn 1980–88, Gloucester Health Authy 1981–85; tstee: Mitchell City of London Tst 1958–82, Jenner Tst 1989–; chm Dangerous Pathogens Advsy Gp 1975–81; govr: Bart's 1972–74, Queen Mary Coll 1972–81; Pybus medal N of Eng Surgical Soc 1979; FRCP, FRCS, FRCPath; *Recreations* fishing, gardening; *Style—* Prof Reginald Shooter, CBE; ✉ Eastlea, Back Edge Lane, Edge, Stroud, Glos GL6 6PE (☎ 01452 812408)

SHORE, Andrew; s of Frank Shore (d 1969), of Oldham, Lancs, and Edith, *née* Ashton (d 1963); *b* 30 Sept 1952; *Educ* Counthill GS Oldham, Univ of Bristol (BA), Royal Northern Coll of Music, London Opera Centre; *m* 1976, Fiona Mary, da of John Macdonald; 3 da (Sarah Jane b 12 Sept 1983, Emily Ann b 22 Sept 1985, Harriet Mary Edith b 16 March 1990); *Career* stage mangr and singer Opera for All tours (Frosch in Die Fledermaus, Fiorello in The Barber of Seville, Giacomo in Fra Diavolo, Marquis in La Traviata) 1977–79; Kent Opera: joined chorus 1979, subsequent roles incl Antonio in Marriage of Figaro, Pasha Selim in Il Seraglio, Dr Bartolo in The Barber of Seville, Papageno in The Magic Flute, deviser and presenter of educnl material; Opera North roles incl: debut as King Dodon in The Golden Cockerel 1985, Sacristan in Tosca, Leander in The Love for Three Oranges, Varlaam in Boris Godunov, Don Inigo in L'Heure Espagnole, Dr Bartolo, The Mayor in The Thieving Magpie, Don Jerome in Gerhard's Duenna, Geronimo in Cimarosa's Secret Marriage, title roles in Don Pasquale, Gianni Schicchi, King Priam and Wozzeck; Scottish Opera roles incl: debut as Mr Flint in Billy Budd 1987, Baron in La Vie Parisienne, Don Alfonso in Cosi Fan Tutte; English National Opera roles incl: debut as Cappadocian in Salome 1987, Doeg in Philip Glass's Planet 8, Don Alfonso, Falstaff, Papageno, Frank in Die Fledermaus, Dr Bartolo, Don Pasquale; Glyndebourne Festival roles incl: debut as Baron Douphol in La Traviata 1988, Vicar in Albert Herring, Falstaff, and Dr Bartolo and Don Alfonso with Glyndebourne Touring Opera; debut as Dr Bartolo: with Welsh Nat Opera 1990, in Vancouver and Ottawa 1991; debut at Royal Opera House Covent Garden as Baron Trombonok in Rossini's Il Viaggio a Reims 1992, debut at the Paris Opera, Bastille as Sacristan in Tosca 1995, debut as Dulcamara in L'Elisir d'amore San Diego 1996; prodr for various amateur and professional gps: Nabucco, Manon Lescaut, Carmen, Orpheus in the Underworld, Bastien and Bastienne, Der Freischütz, Hugh the Drover, La Traviata, Romeo & Juliet, Handel's Faramondo, Wolf-Ferrari's School for Fathers; winner Tim Brandt award in Opera Prodn 1977; *Recordings* Nightingale by Charles Strouse 1983, Barber of Seville (role of Dr Bartolo) 1995; *Style—* Andrew Shore, Esq; ✉ Athole Still International Management, Foresters Hall, 25–27 Westow Street, London SE19 3RY (☎ 0181 771 5271, fax 0181 771 8172)

SHORE, Darryl Francis; *b* 30 Aug 1946; *Educ* De La Salle Coll Sheffield, Sheffield Univ Med Sch (MB ChB); *Career* house surgn Royal Infirmary Sheffield 1972 (house physician 1971–72), demonstrator in pathology Univ of Sheffield 1972–73, sr house offr orthopaedic surgery Royal Hosp Sheffield 1973, sr house offr in gen surgery Bristol Royal Infirmary 1974 (sr house offr in urology 1973–74), sr house offr in orthopaedic surgery Dept of Orthopaedics Bristol 1974–75, registrar in paediatric surgery Children's Hosp Sheffield 1975–76, registrar in gen and vascular surgery Royal Infirmary Sheffield 1976 (registrar in gen surgery 1975); registrar in cardiothoracic surgery: Royal Infirmary and Children's Hosp and Cardiothoracic Unit Northern Gen Hosp Sheffield 1976–78, Brompton Hosp London 1978; res fell in cardiothoracic surgery Albert Einstein Coll of Med NY USA 1979; sr registrar in cardiothoracic surgery: Brompton Hosp London 1980, Hosp for Sick Children Gt Ormond St London 1981; sr registrar in cardiac surgery Nat Heart Hosp London 1982, conslt in cardiac surgery to the Southampton and SW Hampshire Health Authy and clinical teacher Univ of Southampton 1982–87; Royal Brompton Hosp: conslt cardiac surgn in adult and paediatric cardiac surgery 1987–, clinical dir of surgery 1990–95; *Publications* incl: Urinary Lithiasis in Childhood in the Bristol Clinical Area (jtly in Br Jl of Urology, 1975), Results of Mitral Valvuloplasty with Suture Plication Technique (jtly in Jl of Thoracic and Cardiovascular Surgery, 1980), Atresia in Left Atrio-Ventricular Connection (jtly in Br Heart Jl, 1982), Oral Verapamil Fails to Prevent Supraventricular Tachycardia Following Coronary Artery Surgery (jtly in Int Jl of Cardiology, 1985), Thirteen Years Evaluation of the Bjork-Shiley Isolated Mitral Valve Prosthesis (jtly in Jl of Cardiovascular Surgery, 1989), Surgical Treatment for Infarct-Related Ventricular Septal Defects (jtly in Jl of Thoracic Surgery, 1990); *Style—* Darryl Shore, Esq; ✉ Royal Brompton Hospital, Sydney St, London SW3 6NP (☎ 0171 351 8211)

SHORE, Dr Elizabeth Catherine; *née* Wrong; CB (1978); da of Edward Murray Wrong (d 1928), and Rosalind Grace Smith (d 1983); *b* 19 Aug 1927; *Educ* Newnham Coll Cambridge, Bart's; *m* 1948, Rt Hon Peter David Shore, MP, *qv*, s of Robert Norman Shore (d 1942); 2 s (Piers (d 1977), Crispin), 2 da (Thomasina, Tacy); *Career* dep chief MO DHSS 1977–84, postgrad med dean NW Thames Region 1985–93, assoc dean of postgrad med educn N Thames Region 1993–95, sr research fell in med in old age Charing Cross and Westminster Med Sch 1993–; Child Accident Prevention Tst: cncl chm 1985–88, chm of Professional Ctee 1988–90, tstee 1985–93; pres Med Women's Fedn 1990–92 (ed Medical Woman 1992–); GMC: memb 1989–94, memb Standards Ctee 1989–90, memb Professional Conduct Ctee 1990–92, memb Educn Ctee 1991–92; chm Career Progress of Doctors Ctee BMA 1994–95; memb Cncl PSI 1991–; *Recreations* swimming, reading; *Style—* Dr Elizabeth Shore, CB; ✉ 23 Dryburgh Road, London SW15 1BN

SHORE, Rt Hon Peter David; PC (1967), MP (Lab) Bethnal Green and Stepney (majority 12,230); *b* 20 May 1924; *Educ* Quarry Bank HS Liverpool, King's Coll Cambridge; *m* 1948, Dr Elizabeth Catherine Shore, CB, *qv*, *née* Wrong; 1 s, 2 da (and 1 s decd); *Career* Parly candidate (Lab): St Ives (Cornwall) 1950, Halifax 1959; MP (Lab): Stepney 1964–74, Tower Hamlets, Stepney and Poplar 1974–83, Bethnal Green and Stepney 1983–; head Lab Res Dept 1959–64, PPS to Harold Wilson as PM 1965–66, jt Parly sec Miny of Technol 1966–67 and Dept of Econ Affrs 1967, sec of state for econ affrs 1967–69, min without portfolio and dep ldr House of Commons 1969–70, oppn spokesman on Europe 1971–74, trade sec 1974–76, environment sec 1976–79; memb Shadow Cabinet and chief oppn spokesman on: foreign affrs 1979–80, Treasy and econ affrs 1981–Nov 1983, Trade and Indust and shadow ldr of The House Nov 1983–87; memb Select Ctee on Foreign Affrs 1987–; memb Nolan Ctee 1995; *Recreations* swimming; *Style—* The Rt Hon Peter Shore, MP; ✉ 23 Dryburgh Rd, London SW15

SHORROCK, (John) Michael; QC (1988); s of James Godby Shorrock (d 1987), and Mary Patricia, *née* Lings; *b* 25 May 1943; *Educ* Clifton Coll, Pembroke Coll Cambridge (MA); *m* 25 Nov 1971, Marianne, da of Jack Mills (d 1983); 2 da (Amabel b 13 Dec 1971, Rose b 1 Sept 1974); *Career* called to the Bar Inner Temple 1965, bencher 1995, recorder of the Crown Court 1982–, head of chambers; memb Criminal Injuries Compensation Bd 1995–; *Style—* Michael Shorrock, Esq, QC; ✉ Peel Court Chambers, 45 Hardman Street, Manchester M3 3HA (☎ 0161 832 3791, fax 0161 835 3054)

SHORT, Prof (Charles) Alan; s of Charles Ronald Short, of Hillingdon, Middx, and Dorothea Henrietta Winterfeldt; *b* 23 March 1955; *Educ* Lower Sch of John Lyon Harrow, Trinity Coll Cambridge (MA), Harvard Univ Graduate Sch of Design; *m* 12 April 1985, The Noble Romina Scicluna Patrizia Corinne Desirée, da of Alan Edward Marshall (d 1983), and the Noble Mignon Scicluna-Marshall; *Career* architect; ptnr Edward Cullinan Architects 1981–86; fndr: Peaké, Short & Ptnrs 1986, Short, Ford and Associates 1992; visiting prof De Montfort Univ 1994–; winner Green Building of the Year Award for Queens Building Leicester 1995; DipArch, RIBA; *Recreations* collecting drawings, restoration of family home (Palazzo Parisio Malta); *Clubs* Chelsea Arts; *Style—* Prof Alan Short; ✉ Short, Ford and Associates, Prescott Studios, 15 Prescott Place, London SW4 (☎ 0171 720 9994)

SHORT, Clare; MP (Lab) Birmingham Ladywood (majority 15,283); da of Frank Short, and Joan Short; *b* 15 Feb 1946; *Educ* Univ of Keele, Univ of Leeds (BA); *m* 1981, Alexander Ward Lyon (d 1993), former MP (Lab) York; *Career* civil servant Home Office 1970–75; dir: All Faiths for One Race Birmingham 1976–78, Youth Aid and the Unemployment Unit 1979–83; MP (Lab) Birmingham Ladywood 1983–, chm All Pty Parly Gp on Race Rels 1985–86, memb Home Affrs Select Ctee 1983–85; front bench spokesperson on: employment 1985–88, social security 1988–91, environmental protection 1992–93, women 1993–95; elected to Shadow Cabinet 1995; chief oppn spokesperson on: tport 1995–96, overseas devpt 1996–; memb Lab Pty NEC 1988–; *Publications* Talking Blues - A Study of Young West Indians' Views of Policing (1978), Handbook of Immigration Law (1978), Dear Clare (1991); *Recreations* family and friends, swimming; *Style—* Clare Short, MP; ✉ House of Commons, London SW1A 0AA

SHORT, (Bernard) David; CBE (1995); s of Bernard Charles Short (d 1970), and Ethel Florence, *née* Matthews (d 1990); *b* 9 June 1935; *Educ* St Edmund Hall Oxford (MA); *m* 3 Sept 1960, Susan Yvonne, da of Charles Henry Taylor; 2 s (Nicholas b 1970, Timothy b 1973), 1 da (Katharine b 1972); *Career* Royal Scots 1953–56, cmmnd 2 Lt 1954, Lt 1955; teacher Ingliz Erkek Lisesi Istanbul 1960–65, lectr Univ of Fukuoka Kyushu Japan 1963–65, asst lectr Garretts Green Tech Coll Birmingham 1966–67, sr lectr Henley Coll of Further Educn Coventry 1971–73, head Dept of Gen Studies Bournville Coll of Further Educn Birmingham 1973–76 (lectr 1967–71), HM inspr of schs 1976–93 (staff inspr 1984, chief inspr further educn 1986–93), head Further Educn Support Unit Dept for Educn and Employment 1993–96; tstee The Croft Tst 1996–; FRSA 1991; *Books* A Guide to Stress in English (1967), Humour (1971); *Recreations* music, boats, gardening; *Style*— David Short, Esq, CBE; ✉ 40 The Avenue, Andover, Hampshire SP10 3EP

SHORT, Dr David James; s of Jesse Short (d 1955), of Bolton, Lancs, and Elaine Alice, *née* Lunn; *b* 11 Oct 1936; *Educ* Bolton Sch, Univ of Durham, Univ of Bristol, Univ of London; MSc, MRCS, LRCP, DIH, Dip Aviation Med; *m* 1, July 1961, Jennifer, da of Arthur Law (d 1982); 1 da (Gillian Andrea Claire b 28 Jan 1963); m 2, 31 May 1978, Sondra Nicholson Archer; 1 da (Elizabeth Francis Emily b 18 Nov 1983); *Career* offr and pilot RAF 1960–68: flying trg, sqdn pilot, duty combat survival instr; Sqdn Ldr RAuxAF, Sqdn Ldr RAF Med Branch, recalled serving as forward specialist med offr Gulf War 1990; house and res positions Bristol Maternity Hosp 1973–74, GP trainee Cheddar Somerset 1975, MO Br Aerospace Riyadh 1975–76, flying doctor Australian outback 1976, hon clinical asst in cardiology and respiratory physiology UCH London, princ in gen practice and hosp practitioner Brixham 1977–80, princ in gen practice Bristol 1981–85, specialist advsr Bristol Airport Mgmnt Ctee 1981–85, sr MO BR Western Region 1985– (latterly memb Exec); accredited specialist in occupational med Jt Ctee Higher Med Trg 1987; lectr and examiner Red Cross and St John Ambulance Bde 1977–80, hon memb Torbay Hosps Dist Mgmnt Team 1978–80, locum physician Saudi Arabia Armed Forces 1981–, clinical teacher gen practice Univ of Bristol 1981–85, aviation med examiner CAA 1982–, lectr and examiner first aid at work (Health and Safety Exec) 1985–; numerous articles in learned jls; MFOM, MIMgt; *Recreations* flying fast aerobatic light aircraft, outdoor pursuits, photography; *Clubs* RAF; *Style*— Dr David Short; ✉ 12 Whitesfield Road, Nailsea, Bristol BS19 2DT (☎ 01275 855294); Medical Centre, Temple Gate House, Temple Gate, Bristol BS1 6PX (☎ 0117 934 8981)

SHORT, Nigel David; s of David Malcolm Short, of Cheshire, and Jean, *née* Gaskill; *b* 1 June 1965; *Educ* Bolton Sch; *m* 24 Aug 1987, Rhea Argyro, da of Nikolaos Karageorgiou; 1 da (Kyveli Aliki b 7 July 1991); *Career* professional chess player; int master 1980, grandmaster 1984; achievements incl: Br lightning chess champion 1978 and 1980, equal first Br Championship 1979, runner-up World Jr Championship 1980, Br champion 1984 and 1987, memb England Olympiad team 1984–92 (Silver medals 1984, 1986 and 1988, Bronze medal 1990), World Championship candidate 1985–94 (defeated Anatoly Karpov in semi-finals Spain 1992, finalist 1993, challenger to World Champion Garry Kasparov 1993), English champion 1991; other titles won: BBC Master Game 1981, OHRA Tournament Amsterdam 1982, Baku Azerbaijan 1983, Wijk Aan Zee 1986 and 1987, Reykjavik 1987, first equal Subotica Interzonal 1987, Hastings 1988 and 1989, VSB Amsterdam 1988 (first equal 1991 and 1992); highest ever rating achieved by Br player (2685) 1992; fndr memb and dir Professional Chess Assoc 1993; Hon Fell Bolton Inst of HE; *Recreations* politics, music, swimming; *Style*— Nigel Short, Esq

SHORT, (Orville) Peter; s of Francis Augustus Short (d 1970), and Lucy Minnie Edwards (d 1968); *b* 23 Nov 1927; *Educ* Priory Sch for Boys Shrewsbury, Sch of Architecture, Univ of Liverpool; *m* 2 April 1961, Fiona Mary, da of George Francis McConnell (d 1978); 1 s (Stephen b 1962), 1 da (Rachel b 1963); *Career* Nat Serv KOYLI Berlin, DCLI Jamaica; chartered architect 1957; Salop Co Architects, Sir Percy Thomas & Son, IDC & Turriff Tech Servs, sr ptnr Peter Short & Ptnrs (Architectural and Planning Conslts) 1971–87, princ Peter Short architect 1987–; memb Worcester Festival Choral Soc 1968– (memb Ctee 1985–86); memb church choirs: St Giles Shrewsbury 1939–45, Abbey Shrewsbury 1955–64, St Nicholas Alcester 1964–; memb Alcester: Civic Soc (public footpath sub-ctee for Heart of England Way, produced footpath booklets), Rotary Club 1981–94; RIBA (ARIBA 1957); *Recreations* tennis, badminton, walking, watching cricket, singing, watercolour painting; *Clubs* Alcester Tennis, Alcester Unionist, Worcestershire CCC; *Style*— Peter Short, Esq; ✉ 46 Birmingham Road, Alcester, Warwickshire B49 5EP (☎ 01789 762731); Peter Short, Chartered Architect, 9c High Street, Alcester, Warwickshire B49 5AE (☎ 01789 764250)

SHORT, Philip; s of Wilfred Short (d 1976), and Marion, *née* Edgar; *b* 17 April 1945; *Educ* Sherborne, Queens' Coll Cambridge (MA); *m* 1, 9 Aug 1968 (m dis), Christine Victoria, da of (Francis) Donald Baring-Gould; 1 s (Sengan b 1 March 1971); m 2, 1 Sept 1992, Renquan, da of Zhen Gu; 1 s (Benedict b 10 May 1993); *Career* correspondent BBC Moscow 1974–76, Peking 1977–81, Paris 1981–90, Tokyo 1990–; *Books* Banda (1974), The Dragon and The Bear (1982); *Recreations* Chinese porcelain; *Style*— Philip Short, Esq; ✉ BBC, 4th Floor, NTV Yonbancho-Bekkan, 5–6 Yonbancho, Chiyoda-Ku, Tokyo 102, Japan (☎ 00 813 32880011, fax 00 813 32880010)

SHORT, Renée; *Educ* Nottingham Co GS, Univ of Manchester; *m* 2 da; *Career* freelance journalist; memb: Watford RDC 1952–64, Herts CC 1952–67; contested (Lab): St Albans 1955, Watford 1959; MP (Lab) Wolverhampton NE 1964–87; chm: Parly Select Ctee for Social Servs 1979–87, Parly and Scientific Ctee 1982–85 (vice pres 1986, now life memb); memb: Lab NEC 1970–81 and 1983–87, MRC 1988–93; vice pres: Health Visitors' Assoc 1987–, Campaign for Nursery Educn 1983–, Br Assoc for Early Childhood Educn, Women's Nat Cancer Control Campaign (WNCCC); memb: Inst of Med Ethics' Working Pty on Ethical Implications of AIDS 1991–93, RCP Working Pty on Homelessness, BMA/RCOG Working Pty on Infertility 1991; chm Rescare 1986–90 (now patron), pres Action for the Newborn; chm: Theatres' Advsy Cncl 1974–80, Celebrities Guild 1989–92; hon memb Cncl NSPCC; assoc memb Cwlth Parly Assoc; hon fell Wolverhampton Poly (now Wolverhampton Univ) 1987; Hon FRCPsych 1988, Hon MRCP 1989; *Books* The Care of Long Term Prisoners (1979); *Recreations* theatre, music; *Style*— Mrs Renée Short; ✉ 70 Westminster Gardens, Marsham St, London SW1P 4JG (☎ 0171 828 6110)

SHORT, Rodney Neil Terry; s of late Flt Lt Cyril Herbert Terry Short, AFC, of Burnham-on-Sea, Somerset, and Deborah Allen, *née* Hobbs; *b* 4 Aug 1946; *Educ* Sherborne, Coll of Law, INSEAD (MBA); *m* 16 April 1977, Penelope Anne, da of late Capt Emile William Goodman, OBE; 1 s (Jonathan b 1980), 1 da (Anna b 1983); *Career* admitted slr 1970, asst slr Freshfields 1970–73 and 1974–77, Corp Fin Dept Kleinwort Benson 1974–75; Clifford Chance (formerly Coward Chance) 1977–: Dubai office 1978–81, Bahrain office 1981–83, ptnr 1982–, Paris office 1989–91; Freeman City of London Solicitors' Co 1983; memb: Law Soc 1970, IBA 1982; *Recreations* tennis, golf, shooting, skiing; *Clubs* Roehampton; *Style*— Rodney Short, Esq; ✉ 1 Vineyard Hill Road, London SW19 7JL (☎ 0181 879 1677); Clifford Chance, 200 Aldersgate Street, London EC1A 4JJ (☎ 0171 600 1000, fax 0171 600 5555)

SHORT, HE Roger Guy; MVO (1971); s of Harold Short (d 1973), and Alice Ames Short; *b* 9 Dec 1944; *Educ* Malvern, Univ Coll Oxford (MA); *m* 19 June 1971, (Sally) Victoria, da of Bernard Thomas Taylor; 1 s (Thomas b 1988), 2 da (Katherine b 1978, Elizabeth b 1982); *Career* FCO: entered 1967, third and second sec Ankara 1969, FCO 1974, commercial consul Rio de Janeiro 1978, first sec and head of Chancery Ankara 1981, cnsllr FCO 1984, head of Chancery, cnsllr and consul gen Oslo 1986–91, head Personnel Services Dept FCO 1990–94, ambass Sofia 1994–; *Style*— HE Mr Roger Short, MVO; ✉ c/o FCO (Sofia), King Charles Street, London SW1A 2AH

SHORTALL, Michael Patrick; Lord of Ballylorcan, Anglo-Norman Territorial Barony (Irish) dating from before 1208, although first authenticated use dates from 1408; s of John Shortall (d 1967), and Mary Shortall (d 1967); *b* 16 March 1934; *Educ* Medway Coll, RMA Sandhurst, Staff Coll Camberley; *m* 7 June 1969, Patricia Hastings, da of Cdr John Manwaring Parker, RN (d 1979); 1 da (Clare b 1979); *Career* Maj cmdg Sqdn, Europe, N Ireland, Middle East and Far East; ADC to COS N Army Gp, DAA and QMG; logistic ops MOD, ret 1972; chartered surveyor, chm and md Auction Centre Ltd; fine art auctioneer and valuer, md Auction Centres; writer on antiques for Bristol, Somerset and Dorset magazines and newspapers, broadcaster and lectr on antiques and auctions, antiques expert Coast to Coast TVS, Meridian TV and HTV; FRICS, FSVA; *Recreations* sailing, music; *Clubs* MCC; *Style*— Michael Shortall of Ballylorcan; ✉ Auction Centres, Main Hall, Main Street, Mudford, Yeovil, Somerset BA21 5TE (☎ 01935 851511)

SHORTER, John; s of Frank Charles Shorter (d 1966), and Ada, *née* Leeder (d 1983); *b* 22 Sept 1942; *Educ* Hove Co GS, Univ of Sussex (BA), Univ of Lancaster (MA); *m* 30 July 1966, Margot Gertrud, da of Fritz Kleiner; 1 s (Christian Andreas b 1 Sept 1968), 1 da (Siham Andrea b 30 Oct 1972); *Career* VSO Univ of Huê Vietnam 1961–62; teacher Berlitz Sch: Mainz 1963–66, Casablanca 1966–67; British Council: asst rep Kuwait 1971–73, asst regnl dir Zagreb 1973–76, dir Ahwaz 1977–79, English language offr Warsaw 1979–84, dir Al-Khobar 1985–86, dir Jeddah 1986–88, head English Language Promotion Unit 1988–90, dir Qatar 1990–94, dir Bahrain 1994–; Merit medal Univ of Poznan 1984; *Recreations* good food, walking, reading, travel, alsatians; *Clubs* Royal Over-Seas League; *Style*— John Shorter, Esq; ✉ The British Council, PO Box 452, Manama, Bahrain (☎ 00 973 261 555, fax 00 973 241 272)

SHORTER, John Jeffery; s of Charles Jeffery Shorter (d 1968), of East Wittering, Sussex, and Adelaide, *née* Deacon; *b* 28 Sept 1936; *Educ* Reading Sch, Chichester HS, Brocklands Tech Coll (ONC Mech Engrg) Kingston Tech Coll; *m* 1, 1961 (m dis 1968), Judith, da of James Shattock; m 2, 1968, Vera Threadgold, da of Cecil Triggs; 3 da (Joanne b 16 Sept 1971, Toni b 1 Feb 1973, Louise b 21 Sept 1975); m 3, 16 Sept 1996, Judi Gray; *Career* engr apprentice Vickers Armstrong (Aircraft) Ltd Weybridge 1953–58 (design draughtsman in engine installations Vanguard VC 10), design draughtsman CF Taylor (Unity Designs) 1963–66; Chas A Blatchford & Sons Ltd: design draughtsman 1966–69, prodn mangr 1969–71, chief engr 1971–84, tech dir 1984–87, tech and mktg dir 1987–92, dir and gen mangr Products Div 1992–; memb Br Design Awards Judging Panel 1990, del ISO Tech Ctee on Physical Testing of Prostheses, UK rep for Interbor, conslt to UNIDO on artificial limb mfrg; *awards* Br Design Cncl Awards and Queen's Awards for Technol 1976 (for Modular Assembly Prosthesis) and 1990 (for Endolite System); memb: Instn of Engrg Designers 1969, Inst of Industl Mangrs 1972, Int Soc for Prosthetics and Orthotics; MIMgt 1979, MInstD 1984; *Recreations* golf, off-shore sailing; *Clubs* Basingstoke Golf, Rotary (Basingstoke & Deane); *Style*— John Shorter, Esq; ✉ Chas A Blatchford & Sons Ltd, Research & Development Unit, Unit 6, Sherrington Way, Basingstoke, Hampshire (☎ 01256 465771, fax 01256 810450, car 0589 896757)

SHORTIS, Maj-Gen Colin; CB (1988), CBE (1980, OBE 1977, MBE 1972); *b* 18 Jan 1934; *Educ* Bedford Sch; *m* 1957, Sylvia Mary Jenkinson; 2 s, 2 da; *Career* Cdr 8 Inf Bde 1978–80, RCDS 1981, Cdr Br Mil Advsy and Trg Team Zimbabwe 1982–83, Dir of Inf 1983–86, GOC NW District 1986–89, Col Cmdt Prince of Wales Divn 1983–89, Col Devonshire and Dorset Regt 1984–90; govr: Plymouth Coll, Uffculme Sch; tstee Army Museums Ogilby Tst; *Recreations* sailing; *Clubs* Army and Navy; *Style*— Maj-Gen Colin Shortis, CB, CBE; ✉ South Farm, Blackborough, Cullompton, Devon EX15 2JE

SHOTTER, Very Rev Edward Frank; s of Frank Edward Shotter (d 1970), and Minnetta, *née* Gaskill (d 1976); *b* 29 June 1933; *Educ* Humberstone Fndn Sch Clee, St David's Coll Lampeter, Univ of Wales (BA), St Stephen's House Oxford; *m* 9 Dec 1978, Dr Jane Edgcumbe, da of Dr John Oliver Pearce Edgcumbe; 2 s (James b 1982, Piers b 1984), 1 da (Emma b 1987); *Career* ordained: deacon 1960, priest 1961; asst curate St Peter's Plymouth 1960–62, intercollegiate sec Student Christian Movement London 1962–66; dir: London Medical Gp 1963–89, Inst of Medical Ethics 1974–89; chaplain Univ of London 1969–89, prebendary St Paul's Cathedral London 1977–89, dean of Rochester 1989–; memb Gen Synod 1994–; jt chm Kent Ecumenical Police Chaplaincy Ctee 1993– (Force chaplain 1995–); chm Governing Body King's Sch Rochester 1989–, pres St Bartholomew's Hosp Rochester 1989–, dir Firmstart Medway 1991–; chm: Medway Enterprise Agency 1993–, Medway Business Support Partnership 1994–, Medway Business Point Ltd 1996–; vice pres Inst of Med Ethics 1994– (Amulree fell 1991–); chm: Working Party on Ethics of Prolonging Life and Assisting Death 1993–, Univ of Greenwich Research Ethics Ctee 1995–; memb: Ctee on Welfare of Czech and Slovak Med Students in Britain 1968–69, Editorial Bd Journal of Medical Ethics (fndr 1975), Archbishop of Canterbury's Cnsllrs on Foreign Rels 1971–82, BCC East West Rels Advsy Ctee 1971–81, Educn Ctee St Christopher's Hospice 1982–89; sec Assoc of English Cathedrals 1994–; FRSM; Patriarchal Cross Romanian Orthodox Church 1975; *Books* Matters of Life and Death (ed, 1970), Life Before Birth (jt author, 1986); *Recreations* Romania, domestic architecture, hill walking; *Clubs* Reform; *Style*— The Very Rev the Dean of Rochester; ✉ The Deanery, Rochester, Kent ME1 1TG (☎ 01634 844023, fax 01634 401410); Northseat of Auchedly, Tarves, Aberdeenshire AB41 0NB

SHOVELTON, Walter Patrick; CB (1976), CMG (1972); s of Sydney Taverner Shovelton, CBE (d 1968), and May Catherine Kelly (d 1958); *b* 18 Aug 1919; *Educ* Charterhouse, Keble Coll Oxford (MA); *m* 1968, Helena, da of Denis George Richards, OBE; *Career* Maj WWII 1940–46; civil servant; dep sec 1946–78, dir gen GCBS 1978–85; dir Br Airports Authy 1982–85, vice chm The Maersk Co Ltd 1987–96 (dir 1985–87), dir Maersk Air Ltd 1993–95; chm Birmingham Euro Airways 1988–93; advsr: House of Lords Ctee on Euro Communities 1985–86, House of Commons Select Ctee on Tport 1986; chm Maritime Ctee William & Mary Tercentenary Tst 1985–89; Offr of the Order of Orange Nassau; *Recreations* golf; *Clubs* Brooks's, Royal Ashdown Forest Golf, Rye Golf, Hampstead Golf, Seniors Golf; *Style*— W P Shovelton, Esq, CB, CMG; ✉ 63 London Rd, Tunbridge Wells, Kent TN1 1DT (☎ 01892 527885)

SHRAGER, Robert Neil; s of Benjamin Shrager, of London, and Rose Ruth, *née* Kempner; *b* 21 May 1948; *Educ* Charterhouse, St John's Coll Oxford (MA), City Univ (MSc); *m* 1982, Elizabeth Fiona, da of Mortimer Stuart Bogod (d 1964); 2 s (James b 1985, Edward b 1987); *Career* dir: Morgan Grenfell & Co Limited 1985–88, Dixons Group plc 1988–; non-exec dir RJB Mining PLC 1994–; *Recreations* family, golf, arts, walking; *Clubs* RAC; *Style*— Robert Shrager, Esq; ✉ Woodstock, 5 Hollycroft Avenue, London NW3 7QG (☎ 0171 435 4367); Dixons Group plc, Maylands Avenue, Hemel Hempstead, Herts HP2 7TG (☎ 01442 354506)

SHRANK, Dr Alan Bruce; s of Philip Shrank, of London, and Hetty, *née* Rosenberg; *b* 18 Aug 1932; *Educ* City of London Sch, Magdalen Coll Oxford, Middx Hosp London (MA, BM BCh); *m* 12 March 1960, Lucy Rose Désirée, da of Lt Chesley Gordon Murcell (d 1970); 1 s (Alexander b 9 Sept 1970), 1 da (Catherine b 23 March 1973); *Career* Corpl Air Trg Corps 1947–48; conslt dermatologist: Ibadan Univ 1962–63, Shropshire Health Authy 1967–; chm: Computer Gp Br Assoc of Dermatologists 1986–89 (memb 1970), Regnl Advsy Ctee of Dermatology 1989–; memb Med Appeal Tbnl 1989–; author of numerous articles on epidemiology of skin diseases; borough cncllr Shrewsbury and Atcham Borough Cncl 1970–83, memb TUC Health Servs Ctee 1979–84, pres Hosp

Conslts and Specialists Assoc 1984–86, vice pres Nat Pure Water Assoc 1984–94; memb RSM 1960, FRCP 1977; *Books* International Coding Index for Dermatology (jtly, 1978); *Recreations* furniture making, fell walking, fighting for lost causes; *Style*— Dr Alan Shrank; ✉ Shropshire Nuffield Hospital, Shrewsbury, Shropshire SY3 9DP (☎ 01743 353441)

SHRAPNEL, John Morley; s of Norman Shrapnel, of Far Oakridge, Glos, and Mary Lillian Myfanwy, *née* Edwards; *b* 27 April 1942; *Educ* Stockport Sch Cheshire, City of London Sch, St Catharine's Coll Cambridge (MA); *m* 1975, Francesca Anne, da of Sqdn Ldr Anthony Charles Bartley, and Deborah Kerr, the actress; 3 s (Joe Sebastian b 1976, Alexander Carey b 1979, Thomas Heydon b 1981); *Career* actor; fndr memb Nat Youth Theatre; *Theatre* in rep Nottingham Playhouse and Birmingham; NT: Banquo in Macbeth, Pentheus in the Bacchae, Endicott in Front Page, Orsino in Twelfth Night 1973–75; Timon in Timon of Athens (Bristol Old Vic) 1979; RSC: Agamemnon in The Greeks 1980, Jeremy in May Days 1985, Sigmund in The Archbishop's Ceiling 1986, Foustka in Havel's Temptation 1988, Oedipus in Oedi pus Rex 1989, Angelo in Measure for Measure 1990, Creon in Thebans 1991–92, Azriel in The Dybbuk 1991–92, Claudius in Hamlet 1992–93; other roles incl: Leonard Brazil in City Sugar (premiere, Bush), Brutus in Julius Caesar (Riverside); West End credits incl: Andrey in Three Sisters, Tesman in Hedda Gabler, Gibbs in Pinter's The Hot House; *Television* Earl of Suffolk in Elizabeth R, McKendrick in Professional Foul, Erzberger in Gossip from the Forest, Hardinge in Edward and Mrs Simpson, Sakharov in People from the Forest, Glyde in Woman in White, Myshlaevsky in White Guard, Cyril Burt in The Intelligence Man, Creon in Sophocles' Theban Plays, BBC Shakespeare Series (Hector in Troilus and Cressida, Alcibiades in Timon of Athens, Kent in King Lear), Rev Eland in the Burston Rebellion, Steyne in Vanity Fair, Blake in Potter's Black-Eyes, Schulte-Hiller in Selling Hitler, Dr Jacobs in GBH, Dunning in Between The Lines, Archibald Hall in The Ladies' Man, Kavanagh QC, Black Easter, McIntyre in Bodyguards; *Radio* extensive radio work incl: Morse in Inspector Morse, Death and the Maiden, Gielgud's celebratory King Lear; *Film* Petya in Nicholas and Alexandra, Fr James in Pope Joan, Semper in Wagner, Lionel in Personal Services, Zdhanov in Testimony, Mendalbaum in How to Get Ahead in Advertising, Cinca in Two Deaths, Skinner in 101 Dalmations; *Recreations* mountaineering, walking, skiing, music, reading, family; *Style*— John Shrapnel, Esq; ✉ c/o ICM Ltd, Oxford House, 76 Oxford Street, London W1N 0AX (☎ 0171 636 6565, fax 0171 323 0101)

SHREEVE, Ven David Herbert; s of Hubert Ernest Shreeve (d 1965), of Oxford, and Ivy Eleanor, *née* Whiting; *b* 18 Jan 1934; *Educ* Southfield Sch Oxford, St Peter's Coll Oxford (MA), Ridley Hall Cambridge; *m* 12 Dec 1957, Barbara, da of Arthur Thomas Fogden (d 1964), of Oxford; 1 da (Gillian Barbara b 1960), 1 s (Ian David b 1962); *Career* ordained deacon Exeter 1959, priest 1960; asst curate St Andrew's (Plymouth) 1959–64; vicar: St Anne (Bermondsey) 1964–71, St Luke (Eccleshill) 1971–84; rural dean Calverley 1978–84, hon canon Bradford Cathedral 1983–84, archdeacon Bradford 1984–; memb: Dioceses Cmmn, Gen Synod 1977–90 and 1993–; *Recreations* walking, camping, jogging, photography; *Style*— The Ven the Archdeacon of Bradford; ✉ Rowan House, 11 The Rowans, Baildon, Shipley, W Yorks BD17 5DB (☎ 01274 583735, fax 01274 586184)

SHREEVE, Robert; s of Frank William Shreeve (d 1986), of Derby, and Dorothy, *née* Hill (d 1987); *b* 6 March 1950; *Educ* Bemrose GS Derby, Univ of Sussex (BA); *m* 13 August 1982, Margaret Mary, da of Alfred Sommi; 2 s (Daniel Gresley b 16 Dec 1982, Jack Hamilton b 27 Oct 1986), 1 step s (Lindsay Thomas Sharp b 21 Nov 1975); *Career* coll dir Hutchinson Publishing Group 1972–77, univ publisher (social science) Macmillan 1977–79, publisher Papermac 1979–82, editorial dir Sphere Books 1982–86, md The Network Club 1986–88, ind consIt 1988–90, md Virgin Publishing Ltd 1990–; *Recreations* trout fishing, boating, food and drink, photography, cinema, collecting contemporary art; *Style*— Robert Shreeve, Esq; ✉ Virgin Publishing, 332 Ladbroke Grove, London W10 5AH (☎ 0181 968 7554, fax 0181 968 0929, mobile 0831 606835)

SHRESTHA, HE Surya Prasad; s of late L P Shrestha, and G K Shrestha; *b* 1 March 1937; *Educ* Tribhuvan Univ (MA), LSE (dip in econ & social admin); *m* 1958, Ginni; 2 s, 2 da; *Career* Nepalese diplomat; section offr Parliament Secretariat & Miny of Devpt 1958–63, under sec Miny of Home and Panchayat 1963–65, under sec Election Cmmn 1965–66, zonal cmmr Bagmati Zone 1974–78 (jt zonal cmmr 1970–74), acting sec Home & Panchayat Miny 1978–79, sec of Industry and Commerce 1979–83, jt memb Nat Planning Cmmn 1983–85, chief election cmmr appointed by HM The King conducted gen and local elections under Panchayat system 1985–91, chief election cmmr under present Constitution of Nepal conducted gen election under multi-party democratic system 1991–93, ambass of Nepal to the Ct of St James's 1993–; chm: Nepal Industrial Devpt Corp (NIDC) 1981, Commercial Bank of Nepal 1982, Asian Productivity Orgn (APO) Tokyo 1980–83 (previously vice chm); memb: Central Ctee Nepal Red Cross Soc 1974–78, Nepal Leprosy Relief Assoc 1975–, High Level Decentralization Ctee 1984; Nepalese rep at numerous int confs; dir Nepal Rastra Bank Governing Body 1980; Nepalese decorations: Prabal Gorkha Dakshin Bahu III class 1966, Vikhyat Trishakti Patta III class 1973, Prasiddha Prabal Gorkha Dakshin Bahu II class 1976, Suvikhyat Trishakti Patta II class 1991; *Recreations* reading and gardening; *Style*— HE Mr Surya Shrestha; ✉ Royal Nepalese Embassy, 12a Kensington Palace Gardens, London W8 4QU (☎ 0171 229 1594, fax 0171 792 9861)

SHREWSBURY, Bishop of 1994–; Rt Rev David Marrison Hallatt; s of John Vincent (d 1980), of Birkenhead, Cheshire, and Edith Elliott, *née* Leighton (d 1989); *b* 15 July 1937; *Educ* Birkenhead Sch, Univ of Southampton (BA), St Catherine's Coll Oxford (MA); *m* 19 Aug 1967, Margaret, da of Edmund Smitton (d 1995), of Aughton, Ormskirk, Lancs; 2 s (Jonathan David b 1972, Timothy James b 1974); *Career* curate St Andrew's Maghull Liverpool 1963–67, vicar All Saints Totley Sheffield 1967–75, team rector St James and Emmanuel Didsbury 1975–89, archdeacon of Halifax 1989–94; *Recreations* walking, cycling, birdwatching, crosswords, listening to music, theatre; *Style*— The Rt Rev the Bishop of Shrewsbury; ✉ 68 London Road, Shrewsbury, Shrewsbury, Shropshire SY2 6PG (☎ 01743 235867, fax 01743 243296)

SHREWSBURY AND WATERFORD, 22 Earl of (E 1442, I 1446 respectively); Charles Henry John Benedict Crofton Chetwynd Chetwynd-Talbot; DL (Staffs); Premier Earl (on the Roll) in peerages both of England and Ireland; Baron Talbot (GB 1723), Earl Talbot and Viscount Ingestre (GB 1784); Hereditary Lord High Steward of Ireland and Great Seneschal; patron of 11 lvings; s of 21 Earl (d 1980) by 1 w, Nadine, Countess of Shrewsbury; *b* 18 Dec 1952; *Educ* Harrow; *m* 1974, Deborah Jane, da of Noel Staughton Hutchinson, of Ellerton House, Sambrook, Salop; 2 s (Viscount Ingestre b 11 Jan 1978, Hon Edward William Henry Alexander b 18 Sept 1981), 1 da (Lady Victoria Jane b 7 Sept 1975); *Heir* s, Viscount Ingestre; *Career* dep chm Britannia Building Soc 1988–91 (dir 1983–92); princ The Shrewsbury Partnership; patron St Giles Hospice, hon pres SSAFA (Wolverhampton); vice pres: Shropshire Bldg Preservation Tst, Staffordshire Small-bore Rifle Assoc; pres: Bldg Socs Assoc, British Institute of Innkeepers 1996–; chm Firearms Consultative Ctee 1994–; dir: Banafix Ltd 1996–, PMI Ltd 1996–; patron Albrighton Moat Project; chllr Wolverhampton Univ 1993–; Hon LLD Wolverhampton Univ 1994; *Recreations* all field sports; *Style*— The Rt Hon the Earl of Shrewsbury and Waterford, DL; ✉ Wanfield Hall, Kingstone, Uttoxeter, Staffs ST14 8QT (☎ and fax 01889 500 275)

SHRIMPLIN, John Steven; s of John Reginald Shrimplin (d 1977), of Chelmsford, Essex, and Kathleen Mary, *née* Stevens; *b* 9 May 1934; *Educ* Colchester Royal GS, King's Coll London (BSc); *m* 17 August 1957, Hazel, da of Frederick Baughen (d 1969), of Coventry, Warwickshire; 2 s (Peter b 1960, Russell b 1963); *Career* Guided Weapons Dept Royal Aircraft Estab Farnborough 1956–66, Def Operational Estab W Byfleet 1966–71, attended JSSC 1971, Def Res and Devpt Staff Br Embassy Washington USA 1972–73, asst dir (Future Aircraft Systems) MOD Procurement Exec 1974–79, asst chief scientist RAF MOD 1979–83, head of Weapons Dept Royal Aircraft Estab Farnborough 1983–85, minister/cncllr Def Equipment 1985–88, dep head Br Def Staff Br Embassy Washington 1985–88, dir of Sci Studies MOD 1988–90, dep dir gen Br Nat Space Centre 1991–94, ind consIt 1995–; UK rep Euro Long Term space Policy Ctee 1995–; FRAeS; *Recreations* walking, gardening, travel; *Style*— John Shrimplin, Esq; ✉ 7 Clarewood Drive, Camberley, Surrey GU15 3TE (☎ and fax 01276 64459)

SHRIMPLIN, Roger Clifford; s of Clifford Walter Shrimplin (d 1987), and Grace Florence, *née* Davis; *b* 9 Sept 1948; *Educ* St Albans Sch, Jesus Coll Cambridge (MA, DipArch); *m* 21 Sept 1974, Catalina Maria Eugenia, da of L Alomar-Josa (d 1982); 3 s (Robert b 1977, Richard b 1980, Edward b 1985); *Career* architect; ptnr and princ C W & R C Shrimplin (Chartered Architects and Chartered Town Planners) 1975–; occasional lectr: Univ of Cambridge Sch of Architecture, Architectural Assoc; external examiner Bartlett Sch of Architecture Univ of London; chm Tstees of Temple Island Henley; memb cncl: ARCUK 1985–88 and 1994–, RIBA 1995–; memb various ctees of RIBA, ARCUK and ACE; Lord of the Manor of Shimpling Norfolk 1987; Freeman and Liveryman: City of London, Worshipful Co of Glaziers & Painters of Glass 1974 (memb Ct of Assts); chm The London Stained Glass Repository; RIBA 1974, FRTPI 1985, FCIArb 1986, MIL 1994, Arquitecto Colegiado (Baleares) 1990; *Style*— Roger Shrimplin, Esq; ✉ 11 Cardiff Road, Luton, Bedfordshire LU1 1PP

SHRIMPTON, David Everard; s of Col G H T Shrimpton, CBE, TD, of Dulwich, and Joyce Margaret, *née* Little; *b* 19 May 1943; *Educ* Dulwich; *m* 25 Oct 1969, Rosemary Sarah, da of Frank Victor Fone; 3 s (Matthew John b 3 Nov 1972, Benjamin James b 24 May 1975, Daniel Thomas b 11 April 1978); *Career* student trainee mangr Deloitte Haskins & Sells 1961–75, princ Industl Devpt Unit DTI 1975–77, corp fin exec Midland Bank plc 1977–79; BDO Stoy Hayward: ptnr in charge corporate finance 1979–89, gen practice ptnr 1989–; dir: Fulham FC, Broomleigh Housing Assoc; Freeman City of London, Liveryman Worshipful Co of Chartered Accountants; FCA 1967; *Recreations* tennis, rugby and Fulham FC; *Style*— David Shrimpton, Esq; ✉ BDO Stoy Hayward, 8 Baker St, London W1M 1DA (☎ 0171 486 5888, fax 0171 487 3686)

SHRIMSLEY, Bernard; s of John Shrimsley (d 1975), and Alice Shrimsley (d 1942); *b* 13 Jan 1931; *Educ* Kilburn GS; *m* 1952, Norma Jessie Alexandra, da of Albert Porter (d 1959), of Southport; 1 da; *Career* RAF 1949–51; journalist and author; Press Assoc 1947–48, Southport Guardian 1948–49 and 1951–53, Daily Mirror 1953–58, dep northern ed Sunday Express 1958–61, northern ed Daily Mirror 1961–64; ed: Liverpool Daily Post 1968–69, The Sun 1972–75, News of the World 1975–80, The Mail on Sunday 1982; dir News Group Newspapers Ltd 1975–80, dir (later vice chm) Mail on Sunday Ltd 1981–82; assoc ed Daily Express 1986–96; memb: Press Cncl 1989 (vice chm 1990), judge Br Press Awards 1988–95, Def Press and Broadcasting Ctee 1989–93; *Books* The Candidates (1968), Lion Rampant (1984); *Clubs* Garrick; *Style*— Bernard Shrimsley, Esq

SHRUBSALL, Brian Thomas Edward; s of Thomas Bertie Charles Shrubsall, and Eva Allen; *b* 23 Sept 1940; *Educ* Westlands Sch, Sittingbourne & Medway Coll; *m* 14 March 1964, Dawn, da of Norman Marcus Bassart Camp (d 1986), of Faversham, Kent; 2 s (Ian b 1967, David b 1970); *Career* dir Swan Hill plc (formerly Higgs and Hill plc); also chm BIDS Ltd, dir Ian David Ltd; FCIOB, FFB; *Recreations* golf, racehorse owner, sport, theatre; *Clubs* Wentworth; *Style*— Brian Shrubsall, Esq; ✉ Greenworth House, Lake Rd, Virginia Water, Surrey GU25 4QW (☎ 01344 844708); Swan Hill plc, Crown House, Kingston Rd, New Malden, Surrey KT3 3ST (☎ 0181 942 8921, fax 0181 949 9280, telex 28345)

SHUBIK, Irene; da of Joseph Leib Meyerov Shubik (d 1958), of Vitebsk, Russia, and Sara Soloweiczyk (d 1961); *Educ* Havergal Coll Toronto Canada, Univ Coll Toronto (BA, Epstein award for short story competition), UCL (MA); *Career* staff writer Encyclopaedia Britannica Films Inc Chicago USA 1958, story ed on Armchair Theatre and originator Sci Fiction series Out of This World in Drama Dept ABC TV 1960, story ed Story Parade BBC TV 1963; prodr BBC: Out of the Unknown 1966–67, Thirteen Against Fate 1966, Wednesday Play (later Play For Today) 1967–72, Wessex Tales 1973, two stories by Isaac Bashevis Singer for Playhouse 1974–75, Rumpole 1975 (Play For Today); wrote and directed Scrolls From The Son of A Star for BBC, Chronicle and Israel TV 1974–75; prodr: Rumpole Thames TV 1977–79, Staying On, Granada TV deviser and writer Jewel In The Crown 1979–82; freelance writer and prodr 1982–; *Awards* BAFTA Award for best single prodn (Edna The Inebriate Woman) 1971, Critics' Circle Award (Edna The Inebriate Woman) 1972, first prize Trieste Sci Fiction Festival (The Machine Stops) 1967, Jury Award Jerusalem Film Festival (Scrolls From The Son of A Star) 1976, Gold Drama Award NY Festival and nominated Best Foreign Import of The Year NY Times (Staying On) 1981; *Books* Play For Today: The Evolution of TV Drama (1975), The War Guest (1986), The Mind Beyond (ed and contrib, 1976); *Recreations* learning Russian; *Clubs* BAFTA; *Style*— Ms Irene Shubik; ✉ Garden Flat, 25 St James's Place, London SW1A 1HH (☎ and fax 01726 290776)

SHUBROOK, Brian Ralph; s of Ronald Kenneth Shubrook, and Audrey Gwendoline, *née* Jones; *b* 22 June 1950; *m* 20 May 1972, Pauline, da of George Frederick Edgill, MBE, of Leigh-on-Sea, Essex; 2 da (Nicola Jane b 9 Aug 1974, Jessica Anne b 8 Jan 1979); *Career* sr foreign exchange dealer Lloyds Bank Int London 1968–74, foreign exchange mangr Banco de Santander London 1974–81, treas Bayerische Hypotheken und Wechsel Bank London 1981–86, first vice pres and treas Swiss Volksbank London 1986–93, treas mangr Bayersiche Hypotheken-und Wechsel Bank AG (Hypobank) 1993–94, asst gen mangr Treasury Banco Santander London 1994–95, treas Bank Brussels Lambert London 1995–; chm Foreign Exchange Ctee Foreign Banks Assoc London, tstee Lupus UK Aid Gp charity; *Recreations* golf, squash, tennis; *Style*— Brian Shubrook, Esq; ✉ Starlings, 36A Monkhams Ave, Woodford Green, Essex IG8 0EY (☎ 0181 505 6876); Bank Brussels Lambert, 6 Broadgate, London EC2M 2AJ (☎ 0171 392 5508, fax 0171 398 5518, mobile 0410 005895, car 0374 737381)

SHUCKBURGH, Julian John Evelyn; s of Sir Evelyn Shuckburgh, GCMG, CB (d 1994), and Hon Nancy, *née* Brett, da of 3 Viscount Esher; *b* 30 July 1940; *Educ* Winchester, Peterhouse Cambridge (law tripos); *m* 1, 1963 (m dis 1969), Faith, da of Sir Paul Wright, *qv*; 1 da (Matilda b 1965), 1 s (Benjamin b 1967); m 2, 1976 (m dis 1992), Sarah, eld da of Sir David Willcocks, *qv*; 2 da (Amy b 1977, Hannah b 1979), 1 s (Alexander b 1982); *Career* publisher; Methuen & Co: publicity asst 1961, asst ed Academic Dept 1963, commissioning ed Academic Dept 1964–65; Weidenfeld & Nicolson Ltd: sr ed Reference Books 1965, sr ed Academic Dept 1966–68, dir Academic Dept 1968–72; read for the Bar Middle Temple 1972–73; editorial dir W H Allen Ltd 1973–75, publishing dir and md of Pitkin Pictorials Ltd Garrod & Lofthouse (Printers) 1975–78, md and fndr Shuckburgh Reynolds Ltd 1978–87, md Barrie & Jenkins Ltd 1987–, assoc publisher Ebury Press 1992–, publishing dir Condé Nast Books 1992–; *Books* The Bedside Book (1979), The Second Bedside Book (1981); *Recreations* music (memb Bach Choir), walking, classic car rallying, food and wine; *Style*— Julian Shuckburgh, Esq; ✉ 22 Ellingham Road, London W12 9PR (☎ 0181 749 7197); Random House UK Ltd, 20 Vauxhall Bridge Road, London SW1V 2SA (☎ 0171 973 9044)

SHUCKBURGH, Sir Rupert Charles Gerald; 13 Bt (E 1660), of Shuckburgh, Warwickshire; s of Sir Charles Gerald Stewkley Shuckburgh, 12 Bt, TD, JP, DL (d 1988), and his 2 w Nancy Diana Mary, OBE (d 1984), da of late Capt R Egerton Lubbock, RN, bro of 1 Baron Avebury; *b* 12 Feb 1949; *Educ* Worksop Coll; *m* 1, 1976 (m dis 1987), Judith, da of late William Gordon Mackaness, of Paddock Lodge, Everdon, Daventry; 2 s (James Rupert Charles, Peter Gerald William b 1982); m 2, 5 Sept 1987, Margaret Ida, da of late William Evans, of Middleton, Derbyshire; *Heir* s, James Rupert Charles Shuckburgh b 4 Jan 1978; *Style*— Sir Rupert Shuckburgh

SHUFFREY, Ralph Frederick Dendy; CB (1983), CVO (1981); s of Frederick Arthur Shuffrey, MC (d 1982), of Windmill House, Uppingham, Rutland, and Mary, *née* Dendy (d 1951); *b* 9 Dec 1925; *Educ* Shrewsbury, Balliol Coll Oxford; *m* 1953, Sheila, da of Brig John Lingham, CB, DSO, MC (d 1976); 1 s, 1 da; *Career* served Army 1944–47, Capt (occupation of Greece); joined Home Office 1951, dep under sec of state and princ estab offr 1980–84; hon sec Soc for Individual Freedom 1985–89; chm: The Cranstoun Projects Ltd 1988–, Fire Serv Res and Trg Tst 1989–; *Clubs* Reform; *Style*— Ralph Shuffrey, Esq, CB, CVO; ✉ Flat D, Campden House, 29 Sheffield Terrace, London W8 7ND (☎ 0171 229 4536)

SHUGAR, Douglas Richard; s of Harry William Shugar (d 1973), and Patricia Elsie, *née* Wilson; *b* 27 Aug 1960; *Educ* City of London Sch, Exeter Coll Oxford (MA); *Career* Macfarlanes: articled clerk 1984–86, asst slr 1986–92, ptnr 1992–; memb Assoc of Pension Lawyers; *Style*— Douglas Shugar, Esq; ✉ Macfarlanes, 10 Norwich Street, London EC4A 1BD (☎ 0171 831 9222, fax 0171 831 9607)

SHUKMAN, David Roderick; s of Dr Harold Shukman, of St Antony's Coll Oxford, and Rev Dr Ann Shukman, *née* King-Farlow; *b* 30 May 1958; *Educ* Eton, Univ of Durham (BA); *m* Jessica Therese, da of David Pryce-Jones; 2 s (Jack b 5 Dec 1989, Harry b 20 April 1992), 1 da (Kitty b 3 Nov 1994); *Career* reporter Coventry Evening Telegraph 1980–83; BBC: news trainee 1983–85, reporter BBC TV Northern Ireland 1985–87, defence and foreign affrs corr BBC TV News and Current Affrs 1987–95, Brussels corr 1995–; memb: Int Inst for Strategic Studies 1988, Royal Inst for Int Affrs 1988; *Books* All Necessary Means: Inside the Gulf War (with Ben Brown, 1991), The Sorcerer's Challenge: Fears and Hopes for the Weapons of the Next Millenium (1995); *Recreations* tennis, reading; *Style*— David Shukman, Esq; ✉ BBC Bureau, IPC, Boulevard Charlemagne 1, 1040 Brussels, Belgium (☎ 00 32 2 230 2120, fax 00 32 2 230 2688)

SHULMAN, Alexandra (Mrs Paul Spike); da of Milton Shulman, *qv*, and Drusilla Beyfus, *qv*; *m* 26 May 1994, Paul Spike, s of late Rev Dr Robert W Spike, of New York City, NY, and Alice Spike of El Paso, Texas, USA; 1 s (Samuel Robert b 6 April 1995); *Career* successively: features ed Tatler Magazine, women's ed Sunday Telegraph, features ed Vogue Magazine; ed: GQ Magazine 1990–92, Vogue Magazine 1992–; *Style*— Ms Alexandra Shulman; ✉ Editor, Vogue Magazine, Vogue House, Hanover Square, London W1R 0AD (☎ 0171 499 9080, fax 0171 493 1345)

SHULMAN, Jeremy Ian; s of David Shulman (d 1974), of Leeds, and Lilo Shulman; *b* 3 March 1952; *Educ* Leeds GS, Univ of Birmingham (LLB); *m* 6 Nov 1977, Angela Elaine Lewin; 1 s (David Charles b 1 Oct 1979); *Career* admitted slr 1975; currently chm Shulmans (fndr 1981); nat chm Young Slrs' Gp 1986–87, memb Cncl Law Soc 1991–; govr Park Lane Coll Leeds, former memb Gen Advsy Cncl IBA, chm Local Radio Advsy Ctee; memb JNF Massada Fellowship; memb Law Soc 1975; *Recreations* playing tennis and golf, walking (particularly in Yorshire Dales), watching cricket and rugby, music, reading; *Clubs* Moor Allerton Golf, Chapel Allerton Lawn Tennis and Squash, Leeds Club; *Style*— Jeremy Shulman, Esq; ✉ Shulmans, 21 York Place, Leeds LS1 2EX (☎ 0113 245 2833, fax 0113 246 7326)

SHULMAN, Milton; s of Samuel Shulman and Ethel Rice; *Educ* Univ of Toronto (BA), Osgood Hall Ontario Canada (barr); *m* 1956, Drusilla Beyfus, *qv*, da of Norman Beyfus; 1 s (Jason), 2 da (Alexandra Shulman, *qv*, Nicola); *Career* Maj Canadian Armoured Corps 1940–46 (despatches); writer; Evening Standard: film critic 1948–53, theatre critic 1953–92, TV critic 1966–72; TV exec: Granada 1958–62, Rediffusion 1962–64; film critic Vogue 1975–87, political and social columnist Evening Standard and Daily Express 1973–89, arts and gen columnist Evening Standard 1992–; regular memb Radio 4 Stop The Week 1972; memb Advsy Cncl Br Theatre Museum 1983–86; *Books* Defeat in West (1948), How to be a Celebrity (1950), Preep (1964), Preep in Paris (1967), Kill Three (1967), Preep and The Queen (1970), Ravenous Eye (1973), Least Worst Television in the World (1973); *Clubs* Hurlingham, Garrick; *Style*— Milton Shulman, Esq; ✉ 51 Eaton Square, London SW1W 9BE (☎ 0171 235 7162, 0171 823 1366)

SHULMAN, Neville; OBE (1990); s of J W Shulman (d 1971), and A Shulman; *b* 2 Dec 1939; *m* 8 Jan 1970, Emma, *née* Broide; 2 s (Alon Hamilton b 9 Sept 1970, Lee Hamilton b 23 June 1973), 1 da (Lauren Hamilton b 8 Aug 1984); *Career* CA in private practice 1961–; ed magazine Industry 1967 and 1968; mangr actors and film dirs 1973–, prodr theatrical prodns, documentaries and short films; chm and dir Int Theatre Inst 1985–, chm Land and City Families Tst 1987–, tstee Camden Arts Centre 1988–; sec Fedn of Industrial Devpt Assocs 1965–68, offr and memb Theatres Advsy Cncl 1985–, vice pres Nat Children's Home 1989–; prison visitor Pentonville 1966; pres Rotary Club of London 1992–93 (vice pres 1991–92); Liveryman of the Worshipful Co of Blacksmiths 1992; Freeman of the City of London 1992; Hon Col Tennessee Army 1977–; memb NUJ 1967–; FCA 1961, FRGS 1990, FRSA 1992; *Books* Exit of a Dragonfly (1985), Zen In the Art of Climbing Mountains (1992), On Top of Africa (1995); *Recreations* contemporary art, travel, archaeology, film, theatre; *Clubs* The Explorers; *Style*— Neville Shulman, Esq, OBE; ✉ 4 St George's House, 15 Hanover Square, London W1R 9AJ (☎ 0171 486 6363, fax 0171 408 1388)

SHURMAN, Laurence Paul Lyons; s of Joseph Shurman (d 1964), and Sarah, *née* Lyons; *b* 25 Nov 1930; *Educ* Newcastle upon Tyne Royal GS, Magdalen Coll Oxford (MA); *m* 22 Nov 1963, Mary Seamans, da of the late Orin McMullan; 2 s (Daniel b 1965, Morley b 1966), 1 da (Ruth b 1970); *Career* admitted slr 1957; fndr: Shurman & Bindman 1961, Shurman & Co 1964 (amalgamated with Kingsley Napley 1967); managing ptnr Kingsley Napley 1975–88, Banking Ombudsman 1989–96; chm Br and Irish Ombudsman Assoc 1993–95; govr: (vice chm) Channing Sch 1985–, Newcastle upon Tyne Royal GS 1991–; legal memb Mental Health Review Tbnl 1976–94, memb Cncl Justice 1973–, pres City of Westminster Law Soc 1980–81, chm Crossroads 1997–; Gilbert lectr 1990, Ernest Sykes Meml lectr 1991; memb Law Soc 1957; *Books* The Practical Skills of the Solicitor (1981, 1985), Atkins Encyclopaedia of Court Forms Vol 26 (contrib section on Mental Health Review Tbnls); *Recreations* law reform, literature, fell walking, swimming; *Clubs* Leander; *Style*— Laurence Shurman, Esq; ✉ 14 Southwood Avenue, London N6 5RZ (☎ 0181 348 5409)

SHUTE, Kenneth; s of Stanley Oswald Shute, of 3 South Close, Llanfrechfa, Gwent, and Elizabeth Hannah, *née* Davies; *b* 22 Dec 1945; *Educ* Jones West Monmouth Sch Pontypool, St Thomas' Hosp London (MB BS, MS, FRCS); *m* 28 June 1975, Jennifer Catherine, da of Dr Robert William Burchfield, CBE, of The Barn, 14 The Green, Sutton Courtenay, Oxon; 1 s (Daniel b 2 Aug 1980), 1 da (Susannah b 13 July 1982); *Career* conslt surgn gen and vascular Royal Gwent Hosp 1982–; memb Vascular Surgical Soc of GB, patron Pontypool Rugby Club, hon surgn Monmouthshire Rugby Football Club; *Recreations* skiing, squash, rugby; *Style*— Kenneth Shute, Esq; ✉ Royal Gwent Hospital, Newport, Gwent (☎ 01633 252244)

SHUTTLE, Penelope Diane; da of Jack Frederick Shuttle, of Middlesex, and Joan Shepherdess Lipscombe; *b* 12 May 1947; *m* Peter William Redgrove, *qv*, s of G J Redgrove, of Hampstead; 1 da (Zoe b 1976); *Career* writer and poet; *Radio* plays: The Girl who Lost her Glove 1975 (jt third prize winner Radio Times Drama Bursaries Competition 1974), The Dauntless Girl 1978; poetry recorded for Poetry Room Harvard; Arts Cncl Award 1969, 1972 and 1985, Greenwood Poetry Prize 1972, EC Gregory Award for Poetry 1974, Authors' Fndn Grant 1993; *Novels* An Excusable Vengeance (1967), All the Usual Hours of Sleeping (1969), Wailing Monkey Embracing a Tree (1974), The Terrors of Dr Treviles (with Peter Redgrove, 1974), Rainsplitter in the Zodiac Garden (1976), Mirror of the Giant (1979); *Poetry* Nostalgia Neurosis (1968), Midwinter Mandala (1973), Photographs of Persephone (1973), Autumn Piano (1973), Songbook of the Snow (1973), The Hermaphrodite Album (with Peter Redgrove, 1973), Webs on Fire (1977), The Orchard Upstairs (1981), The Child-Stealer (1983), The Lion from Rio (1986), Adventures with my Horse (PBS Recommendation 1988), Taxing The Rain (1992), Building a City for Jamie (1996); *Psychology* The Wise Wound (with Peter Redgrove, 1978 re-issued 1986 and 1994), Alchemy for Women (with Peter Redgrove, 1995); *Recreations* gardening, walking, iyengar yoga; *Style*— Ms Penelope Shuttle; ✉ c/o David Higham Associates, 5–8 Lower John Street, Golden Square, London W1R 4HA (☎ 0171 437 7888, fax 0171 437 1072)

SHUTTLEWORTH, 5 Baron (UK 1902); Sir Charles Geoffrey Nicholas Kay-Shuttleworth; 6 Bt (UK 1850), DL (Lancs); s of 4 Baron Shuttleworth, MC (d 1975), and Anne Elizabeth (d 1991), da of late Col Geoffrey Francis Phillips, CBE, DSO; *b* 2 Aug 1948; *Educ* Eton; *m* 1975, Ann Mary, da of James Whatman and former w of late Daniel Henry Barclay; 3 s; *Heir* s, Hon Thomas Kay-Shuttleworth; *Career* dir Burnley Building Society 1978–82, chm National and Provincial Building Society 1994–96 (dir and dep chm 1983–93), dep chm Abbey National plc 1996–; chartered surveyor; ptnr Burton Barnes and Vigers 1977–96; dir Rank Foundation 1993–; memb Bd Skelmersdale Development Corporation 1982–85; govr Giggleswick Sch N Yorks 1982– (chm of Govrs 1984–); chm Rural Devpt Cmmn 1990–; memb Cncl Lancaster Univ 1990–93; Hon Col 4 Bn The Queen's Lancashire Regt; Lord-Lieut of Lancashire 1996–; FRICS; *Clubs* Brooks's; *Style*— The Rt Hon the Lord Shuttleworth, DL; ✉ Leck Hall, Carnforth, Lancs; 14 Sloane Ave, London SW3 (☎ 0171 589 8374)

SHUTTLEWORTH, Dr Kenneth Owen; s of Owen William Shuttleworth, of Birmingham, and Ilene Doris, *née* Peakman; *Educ* Handsworth GS Birmingham, City of Leicester Poly (Dip Arch); *m* 30 May 1987, Seana Ann, da of Patrick James Brennan; 1 s (Jo b 28 April 1990), 1 da (Jaime b June 1993); *Career* architect; Harry Bloomer & Sons 1972–73, Essex Goodman & Suggitt Birmingham 1973–74; currently ptnr/dir Foster & Partners (formerly Sir Norman Foster & Partners, joined 1974); projects incl: Willis Faber & Dumas Ipswich, Hong Kong Bank Hong Kong, Televisa Mexico, Century Tower Tokyo, ITN HQ London, BP HQ London, King Faisal Fndn Riyadh, Cranfield Library, Nîmes Mediatech France, Hong Kong Airport, British Gas Thames Valley Park; Hon Dr of Design De Montfort Univ 1994; memb: ARCUK 1977, RIBA 1977; *Awards* RIBA: Willis Faber & Dumas 1977, Stansted Airport (Nat Award) 1992, Sackler Galleries (Best Building of the Year) 1993 (Nat Award 1992); Civic Tst: Renault Centre Swindon 1984, Stansted Airport Terminal 1992 (also Concrete Soc Award 1992), Crescent Wing Sainsbury Centre for Visual Arts 1992; Royal Gold Medal for Architecture 1983; numerous other awards; *Recreations* drawing, design, photography, landscape; *Style*— Dr Kenneth Shuttleworth; ✉ Director, Foster & Partners, Riverside 3, 22 Hester Road, London SW11 4AN (☎ 0171 738 0455, fax 0171 738 1107)

SHUTTLEWORTH, Maj Noel Charles; s of Rev Richard Charles Shuttleworth (d 1955), and Doris Marian, *née* Sims (d 1978); *b* 4 Jan 1933; *Educ* Haileybury and ISC, RMA Sandhurst; *Career* Scots Guards 1953–63, served Germany, Canada, Kenya, UK, ret Maj 1963; fndr and chm The English Courtyard Assoc 1979– (winners of 6 Civic Tst Commendations, 10 Housing Design awards from DOE, RIBA and NHBC for excellence in housing design), dir Les Blancs Bois Ltd Guernsey 1987–; chm The Elderly Accommodation Cncl 1992– (govr 1987–); vice pres Devizes Constituency Cons Assoc 1980– (chm 1977–80); *Recreations* cricket (played for Kenya and E Africa 1962–63), tennis; *Clubs* Cavalry and Guards'; *Style*— Maj Noel Shuttleworth; ✉ 38 St John's Rd, Hampton Wick, Middx; Crabtree, Savernake Forest, Marlborough, Wiltshire; The English Courtyard Association, 8 Holland Street, London W8 4LT (☎ 0171 937 4511, fax 0171 937 3890)

SHUTZ, Roy Martin; s of Joseph Shutz (d 1969), of Birmingham, and Alice, *née* Susz (d 1989); *b* 23 Jan 1943; *Educ* King Edward's Five Ways Sch Birmingham, Univ of Birmingham (LLB), Coll of Law; *Career* teacher Longsands Sch Cambridge 1966–68, admin asst Univ of Warwick 1968–69, asst to Academic and Fin Secs LSE 1969–74, chm Romar Investments Ltd 1969–; barr 1974–90; Barnet Borough Cncl: memb 1982–, chm Educn Ctee 1985–90, mayor 1990–91, leader 1991–94; memb Middx Area Probation Ctee 1986–94, non-exec dir Barnet Community Healthcare Tst 1991–94; FInstD; *Recreations* golf, rugby union (chm Mill Hill RFC 1996–), singing, theatre; *Clubs* Aldenham Golf, Warwickshire Co Cricket; *Style*— Roy Shutz, Esq; ✉ 6 Trinity Avenue, London N2 0LX (☎ and fax 0181 883 1205)

SIBLEY, Dame Antoinette; DBE (1996, CBE 1973); da of Edward George Sibley, of Kent, and Winifred Maude, *née* Smith; *b* 27 Feb 1939; *Educ* Arts Educnl Sch Tring Herts, Royal Ballet Sch; *m* 1, 1964 (m dis 1973), Michael George Somes, CBE (d 1994); m 2, 1974, Richard Panton Corbett, s of William Corbett, of Shropshire; 1 s (Isambard b 1980), 1 da (Eloise b 1975); *Career* graduated into the Royal Ballet 1956, took over the role of Odette/Odile in Swan Lake at short notice Covent Garden 1959, promoted to soloist 1959 and to princ dancer 1960; noted for interpretation of Aurora in Sleeping Beauty, title role in Giselle, title role in Ashton's Cinderella, Juliet in Macmillan's Romeo and Juliet, Titania in The Dream (created for her by Ashton), title role in Manon (created for her by Macmillan), Dorabella (created for her by Ashton), Chloe in Ashton's Daphnis and Chloe, Ashton's A Month in the Country, numerous other roles; has toured N and S America, USSR, Aust and Europe; prima ballerina role in film Turning Point; pres Royal Acad of Dancing 1991– (vice pres 1989–91); *Publications* Sibley and Dowell (1976), Antoinette Sibley (1981), Antoinette Sibley - Reflections of a Ballerina (1986); *Recreations* opera going, reading, music; *Style*— Dame Antoinette Sibley, DBE; ✉ c/o The Royal Opera House, Covent Garden, London WC2

SIBLEY, Edward; s of William Sibley (d 1941), of Rhymney, Gwent, and Myfanwy, *née* Williams (d 1987); *b* 21 July 1935; *Educ* Rhymney GS Gwent, UCW Aberystwyth (LLB, Samuel Evans Prize), Coll of Law; *m* 3 Aug 1957, Sonia, da of Harold Beynon; 2 s (Stephen b 6 Dec 1965, Neil Edward b 24 May 1970), 1 da (Deborah Jane b 1 Dec 1962); *Career* articled clerk Clifford-Turner 1962–65, admitted slr 1965, ptnr Berwin & Co 1967 (joined as asst slr 1965), sr ptnr Berwin Leighton (fndr ptnr 1970), qualified NY Bar USA 1985; memb Worshipful Co of Slrs 1985; memb: Law Soc, ABA, IBA, UIA; *Recreations* skiing, running, opera, theatre, literature; *Clubs* Reform; *Style*— Edward Sibley, Esq; ✉ Berwin Leighton, Adelaide House, London Bridge, London EC4R 9HA (☎ 0171 623 3144, fax 0171 623 4416)

SIBLEY, Richard Edmonde Miles Phillippe; s of William Alfred Sibley, JP (d 1992), of Street Farm, Crowfield, Suffolk, and Florence May, *née* Marsh; *b* 23 May 1949; *Educ* Clark's Coll London, Anglican Regnl Coll; *m* 5 June 1976, Hannelore, da of Hans Njammasch, of W Germany; 1 s (Alexander b 21 March 1979); *Career* chief exec Ogilby Housing Society Ltd 1987–, chm Calderwood Housing Assoc 1992– (co sec 1970–75); dir Sibley Property Co Ltd; chm NE London Valuation Ct (rating) 1981–90 (memb 1976); chm London (NE) Valuation and Community Charge Tbnl 1990–; rotarian 1982– (pres

1993–94); Freeman City of London 1980, Liveryman Worshipful Co of Coopers 1980 (Upper Warden 1994–95, pres Soc of the Livery 1993–94); *Recreations* painting, politics, farming; *Clubs* Bishopsgate Ward; *Style*— R E M P Sibley, Esq; ✉ 60 Parkstone Ave, Emerson Park, Hornchurch, Essex RM11 3LS (☎ 01708 471320); Ogilby Housing Society Ltd, Estate Office, Greenways Court, Butts Green Rd, Hornchurch, Essex RM11 2JL (☎ 01708 475115/6)

SICHEL, Ronald James; s of Walter Adolf Sichel (d 1989), Chalfont St Peter, Bucks, and Thea Anna, *née* Tuchler; *b* 22 May 1940; *Educ* Repton, L'Ecole Superieure Neuchâtel Switzerland; *m* 16 Jan 1965 (m dis 1979), Colette Jeannine, da of Dr Charles Stagnaro (d 1983), of St Raphael, France; 1 s (Edward b 27 June 1973); *Career* wine shipper: H Sichel and Sons Ltd 1960, dir 1969–79, vice chm 1979–88, chm 1988–94; dir John Rigby & Co (Gunmakers) Ltd 1995–; memb Worshipful Co of Founders 1963 (memb Ct 1996–), Freeman City of London 1963; *Recreations* fly-fishing, competition pistol and rifle shooting, game shooting, skiing, painting, golf, photography; *Clubs* Buck's; *Style*— Ronald Sichel, Esq; ✉ 53 Cadogan Square, London SW1X 0HY (☎ 0171 235 3321, fax 0171 235 1728); John Rigby & Co (Gunmakers) Ltd, 66 Great Suffolk Street, London SE1 0BU (☎ 0171 620 0690, fax 0171 928 9205, car 0860 258468)

SIDDALL, Sir Norman; kt (1983), CBE (1975), DL (Notts 1988); *b* 4 May 1918; *Educ* Univ of Sheffield (BEng); *m* 1943; 2 s, 1 da; *Career* National Coal Board: chief mining engr 1966–67, dir-gen of prodn 1967–71, bd memb 1971–83, dep chm 1973–82, chm 1982–83; former non-exec dir CIN Management Ltd; Hon DSc Univ of Nottingham; CEng, FEng 1979, FIMinE, CIMgt; *Style*— Sir Norman Siddall, CBE, DL, FEng; ✉ Brentwood, High Oakham Rd, Mansfield, Notts NG18 5AJ

SIDDALL, Robert Guy; s of Sir Norman Siddall, *qv*, of Mansfield, Notts, and Pauline, *née* Arthur; *b* 28 Jan 1945; *Educ* Nottingham HS, Univ of Nottingham (BSc); *m* 1970, Gillian Elaine, da of Philip Morley, and Violet, *née* Fenton; 4 da (Anna-Louise b 1973, Naomi Sarah b 1975, Charlotte Elaine b 1978, Laura Mary b 1980); *Career* National Coal Board 1968–95; trainee 1966–68, various jr mgmnt positions 1968–71, undermangr Sherwood Colliery 1971–73, dep mangr Rufford Colliery 1973–75, colliery mangr Blidworth Colliery 1975–80, sr mining engr Planning & Surveying North Notts 1980–83, chief mining engr Doncaster area 1983–85; dep dir: Mining North Derbyshire 1985–87, Selby North Yorks 1987–88, Mining North Yorks area 1988–90; gp dir: North Yorks Gp 1990–91, South Yorks Gp 1991–93; dir Opencast 1991–93; conslt 1995; dir Shelton Trenching Systems Ltd 1996–; pres: Midland Inst of Mining Engrs 1992–93, Instn of Mining Engrs 1995–96; winner Futers Medal Instn of Mining Engrs 1992; author of several pubns in tech jls; FIMinE, FIMgt, FEng 1995; *Recreations* industl archaeology; *Style*— Robert Siddall, Esq, FEng; ✉ Fir Tree Farm, Darfield, Barnsley, South Yorkshire S73 9JB (☎ 01226 751762, fax 01226 755481)

SIDDLE, Prof Kenneth; s of Fred Siddle, of Morecambe, Lancs, and Vera, *née* Sunderland; *b* 30 March 1947; *Educ* Morecambe GS, Downing Coll Cambridge (scholar, Bye fell, MA, PhD); *m* 1, 1971 (m dis 1994), Yvonne Marie, *née* Kennedy; 1 s (Paul b 1977); m 2, 1996, Anne Elizabeth Willis; *Career* lectr Dept of Med Biochemistry Welsh Nat Sch of Med 1971–78; Univ of Cambridge: Meres sr student for med res St John's Coll 1978–81, fell Churchill Coll 1982–, Wellcome lectr Dept of Clinical Biochemistry 1981–90, prof of molecular endocrinology 1990–; visiting scientist Joslin Diabetes Center and Harvard Med Sch 1989–90; chm Biochemical Jl 1995–; memb: Biochemical Soc 1970–, Br Diabetic Assoc 1972–, Br Soc for Cell Biology 1980–, Assoc of Clinical Biochemists 1985–; sr treas Cricket Club Univ of Cambridge; author of over 100 articles in scientific jls; *Recreations* mountaineering, cricket, gardening; *Clubs* Lancashire CC, Hawks'; *Style*— Prof Kenneth Siddle; ✉ Department of Clinical Biochemistry, University of Cambridge, Addenbrooke's Hospital, Cambridge CB2 2QR (☎ 01223 336789, fax 01223 330598)

SIDDONS, Peter Robert; s of (Arthur) Harold Makins Siddons, of Farnham, Surrey, and Joan Richardson, *née* McConnell (d 1949); *b* 26 June 1943; *Educ* Harrow, Jesus Coll Cambridge (MA); *m* 12 Oct 1974 Elvina Lucy, da of Maj Roger Alexander Howard; 3 ç (Philippa Sarah b 7 March 1977, Alastair Mark b 29 July 1978, Melanie Sarah b 30 Aug 1980); *Career* Coopers & Lybrand: articled clerk Cooper Brothers & Co 1965–68, ptnr 1974, seconded to HM Treasury 1978–79, ptnr-in-charge Litigation Support Unit 1985–87, ptnr-in-charge London Audit Div 1985–88, fin dir and memb Bd 1988–94, ptnr-in-charge Risk Mgmnt 1994–; special tstee St George's Hosp 1981–94 (chm 1984–94), tstee Harrow Club 1983–96, govr Harrow Sch 1993–; FCA 1979 (ACA 1968); *Recreations* golf, theatrical art research; *Clubs* West Sussex Golf; *Style*— Peter Siddons, Esq; ✉ Coopers & Lybrand, 1 Embankment Place, London WC2N 6NN (☎ 0171 213 4585, fax 0171 213 4433)

SIDEY, Air Marshal Sir Ernest Shaw; KBE (1972), CB (1965); s of Thomas Sidey (d 1943), of Alyth, Perthshire; *b* 2 Jan 1913; *Educ* Morgan Acad Dundee, Univ of St Andrews; *m* 1946, Doreen Florence, da of Cecil Ronald Lurring, of Dublin, Eire; 1 da (and 1 da decd); *Career* RAF (UK and Burma) WWII, Air Cdre 1961, PMO Tport Cmd 1965–66, dep dir gen RAF Med Servs 1966–68, Air Vice-Marshal 1966–71, PMO Strike Cmd 1968–70, dir gen RAF Med Servs 1971–74 (ret), Air Marshal 1971; QHS 1966–74; dir gen Chest, Heart and Stroke Assoc 1974–85, govr Royal Star and Garter Home 1974–86; MD, FFCM, DPH; *Recreations* racing, golf, bridge; *Clubs* RAF; *Style*— Air Marshal Sir Ernest Sidey, KBE, CB; ✉ Callums, Tugwood Common, Cookham Dean, Berks SL6 9TU

SIDMOUTH, 7 Viscount; John Tonge Anthony Pellew Addington; kt of Malta (1962); s of 6 Viscount Sidmouth (d 1976, himself fourth in descent from 1 Viscount, PM 1801–04), and Gladys Mary Dever (d 1983); *b* 3 Oct 1914; *Educ* Downside, BNC Oxford; *m* 1, 1940, Barbara Mary Angela (d 1989), da of Bernard Rochford, OBE; 2 s (1 decd), 5 da; m 2, 2 Oct 1993, Marie Thérèse, da of His Hon late Sir Joseph Alfred Sheridan, and widow of Francis Anthony Baring Pollen; *Heir* s, Hon Jeremy Addington; *Career* Colonial Serv E Africa 1938–54; md Joseph Rochford & Sons Ltd; memb Cncl and chm Glasshouse Ctee NFU 1962–69; memb: ARC 1964–74, Central Cncl for Agric Co-operation 1970–73, Lords Select Ctee on Euro Community 1984–87; pres Nat Cncl on Inland Tport 1978–84, tstee John Innes Fndn 1974–90, chm Governing Body Glasshouse Crop Res Inst 1981–84; pres St Gregory's Soc (old boys of Downside) 1980–83; *Style*— The Rt Hon the Viscount Sidmouth; ✉ 12 Brock Street, Bath BA1 2LW

SIDNEY, Elizabeth Anne; *Educ* Sherborne Sch for Girls, Univ of Oxford (MA), Univ of London (MA); *m* (m dis), Deryck Malcolm Sidney; 1 s, 3 da; *Career* psychologist Civil Service Cmmn 1957–72, trg dir Family Planning Assoc 1970–74, fndr and managing ptnr Mantra Consultancy Group (conslts and trainers in public and private sectors UK, Europe, USA, India, Far East); memb Kensington Chelsea and Westminster Area Health Authy 1972–80, pres Women's Liberal Fedn 1982–84, chm Lib Pty Policy Panel on Employment 1980–83, dep chm Candidates Ctee Lib Pty 1986–87, pres Women Liberal Democrats 1988–91, chm Liberal Democrats Working Pty on Industl Democracy 1990–, exec memb Int Network of Liberal Women 1991–, Liberal Democrat rep on Exec Women's Nat Cmmn 1993–; tstee: New Economics Fndn 1980–, Environmental Law Assoc 1996–; chm The Green Alliance 1984–89; former JP; CPsychol, FBPsS, FPTD, FRSA; *Books* The Skills of Interviewing (1961), Case Studies of Management Initiative (1967), The Industrial Society (1970), Skills with People: A Guide for Managers (1973), Future Woman: How to Survive Life (1982), ed Managing Recruitment (1989), One to One Management (1991); *Recreations* political work, environment, travel; *Clubs* RSA; *Style*— Ms Elizabeth Sidney; ✉ 25 Ellington Street, London N7 8PN (☎ 0171 607 6592); Mantra Consultancy Group (☎ 0171 609 9055, fax 0171 609 9447)

SIDWELL, Prof (John William) Martindale; s of John William Sidwell, and Mary, *née* Martindale; *b* 23 Feb 1916; *Educ* Wells Cathedral Sch; *m* 5 Sept 1944, Barbara Anne, da of Edwin Hill; 2 s (Peter, Timothy); *Career* N Somerset Yeo TA 1937, acting Lance Corpl 1939–42 (boarded out); sub organist Wells Cathedral, dir of music Warwick Sch 1943–46, organist Holy Trinity Church Leamington Spa 1943–46; organist and dir of music: Hampstead Parish Church 1946–92, St Clement Danes Church (central church of RAF) 1957–92; prof: Royal Sch of Church Music 1958–63, Trinity Coll of Music 1955–63, Royal Acad of Music 1963–82; fndr and conductor: Hampstead Choral Soc 1946–81, London Bach Orchestra 1967–81, Martindale Sidwell Choir 1954, St Clement Danes Music Soc, St Clement Danes Chorale; guest conductor: BBC Symphony Orchestra, BBC Singers, LSO; conductor for numerous broadcasts and recordings; winner Harriet Cohen Bach medal; FRAM, FRCO; *Clubs* Savage, Wig & Pen; *Style*— Martindale Sidwell, Esq; ✉ 1 Frognal Gardens, Hampstead NW3 6UY (☎ 0171 435 9210)

SIEFF, Hon David Daniel; s (by 1 m) of Baron Sieff of Brimpton (Life Peer); *b* 1939; *Educ* Repton; *m* 1962, Jennifer, da of H Walton, of Salford Priors, Worcs; 2 s (Simon Marcus b 1965, Jonathan David b 1966); *Career* Marks & Spencer plc: corp and external affrs dir until 1997, non-exec dir 1997–; chm FIBI Bank (UK) 1994–; chm Nat Lottery Charities Bd, memb Bd Business in the Community; *Style*— The Hon David Sieff; ✉ Marks and Spencer plc, Michael House, Baker Street, London W1A 1DN (☎ 0171 935 4422)

SIEFKEN, Prof Hinrich Gerhard; s of Werner Johann Hinrich Siefken (d 1968), and Lisel, *née* Menne (d 1963); *b* 21 April 1939; *Educ* Carl Duisberg Gymnasium Leverkusen, Univ of Tübingen (DPhil), Univ of Nottingham (DLitt); *m* 1 Aug 1968, Marcia Corinne, da of Harry Birch (d 1989), of Sheffield; 1 s (Kristian Hinrich b 8 August 1973), 1 da (Brigitte Christiane 14 March 1970); *Career* tutor Univ of Tübingen 1962–65, lectr Univ Coll of N Wales Bangor 1965–66, wissenschaftlicher asst Univ of Tübingen 1966–67, sr lectr St David's Univ Coll Lampeter 1973–79 (asst lectr 1967–68, lectr 1968–73), prof of German Univ of Nottingham 1979– (head Sch of Modern Languages 1986–88, dean Faculty of Arts 1988–92, dir Inst of German, Austrian and Swiss Affrs 1992–94); ed Trivium 1978–79 (subject ed 1974–79), gen ed Renaissance and Modern Studies 1986–88, memb Editorial Bd New Manchester German Texts 1986–91; memb: English Goethe Soc, Deutsche Thomas Mann Gesellschaft, Deutsche Schiller Gesellschaft; *Books* Kudrunepos (1967), Ungeduld und Lässigkeit - Kafka (1977), Thomas Mann - Goethe Ideal der Deutschheit (1981), Theodor Haecker (1989), Theodor Haecker, Tag - und Nachtbücher (ed, 1989), Die Weisse Rose, Student Resistance to National Socialism (ed, 1991), Resistance to National Socialism: Arbeiter, Christen, Jugendliche, Eliten (ed, 1993), Die Weisse Rose und ihre Flugblätter (1994), Theodor Haecker: Leben und Werk (ed, 1995), Kunst und Widerstand (ed, 1995); *Recreations* music, walking, gardening; *Style*— Prof Hinrich Siefken; ✉ 6 Mountsorrel Drive, Westbridgford, Nottingham NG2 6LJ (☎ 0115 981 1617); Department of German, University of Nottingham, University Park, Nottingham NG7 2RD (☎ 0115 951 5816, fax 0115 951 5812)

SIEGEL, Jeffrey; s of Harold Siegel, and Ruth Berman (d 1972); *b* 18 Nov 1942; *Educ* Chicago Musical Coll, Royal Acad of Music London, Juilliard Sch of Music (Dr of Musical Arts 1971); *m* 20 May 1973, Laura, da of Edmund Mizel; 1 s (Noah b 1988), 1 da (Rachel b 1983); *Career* piano soloist with world's leading orchestras including: LSO, London Philharmonic, Royal Philharmonic, Philharmonia, Hallé Orchestra, Birmingham Symphony, New York, Chicago, Boston, Philadelphia, Cleveland; solo concerts at: Carnegie Hall, Queen Elizabeth Hall, Festival Hall; *Style*— Jeffrey Siegel, Esq; ✉ Robert Gilder & Co, Enterprise House, 59–65 Upper Ground, London SE1 9PQ (☎ 0171 928 9008, fax 0171 928 9755)

SIEGHART, Mary Ann Corinna Howard; da of Paul Sieghart (d 1988), and Felicity Ann, *née* Baer; *b* 6 Aug 1961; *Educ* Cobham Hall, Bedales, Wadham Coll Oxford (major scholarship, 1st in PPE); *m* 17 June 1989, David Stephens Prichard, s of Maj Michael Prichard; 2 da; *Career* journalist Eye to Eye Publishing 1978–79, reporter Sunday Express 1979, arts ed rising to news ed Cherwell 1979–80, ldr and feature writer Daily Telegraph 1980–82, Eurobond corr rising to Lex Columnist Financial Times 1982–86, city ed Today 1986, political corr The Economist 1986–88, presenter The World This Week 1988; The Times: ed op-ed page 1988–91, arts ed 1989–90, currently asst ed and political leader writer; chairwoman The Brains Trust (BBC 2), contrib Start the Week (Radio 4); runner up young journalist of the year Br Press Awards 1983, Harold Wincott prize for Young Financial Journalist of the Year 1983, winner Laurence Stern fellowship 1984 (worked for the Washington Post); *Recreations* tobogganing, trekking in remote places, doodling, classic cars, reading novels on holiday, listening to music; *Style*— Ms Sieghart; ✉ The Times, 1 Pennington St, London E1 (direct ☎ 0171 782 5160, fax 0171 782 5229)

SIEMENS, Herman Werner; s of Prof Dr Hermann Werner Siemens (d 1969), of Leiden, The Netherlands, and Berta Luise, *née* von Müller (d 1985); *b* 21 May 1925; *Educ* Leiden Gymnasium Sch, Delft Technol Univ (MSc), Universidad Del Valle (MBA); *m* 7 June 1955, Cornélie, da of Herman Constantyn, Count Schimmelpenninck (d 1948), of The Hague; 1 s (Herman Werner b 1963 m Rosy Brega), 4 da (Louise b 1956 m Dr Ignazio Savona, Clara b 1957 m Richard Charles Furse, Sabine b 1959 m Maurits, Baron Van Hövell tot Westerflier, Julie b 1961 m Gonzague Marie Petit-Trabal); *Career* res engr Centre à l'Energie Atomique Paris 1953, former exec with aluminium companies in Colombia, Denmark, Nigeria and UK, pres and chief exec Aluminio Alcan de Colombia SA Cali Colombia 1961–69, md and chief exec Aluminord AS Copenhagen Denmark 1969–75, chm and chief exec Alcan Aluminum of Nigeria Ltd and Alcan Aluminum Products Ltd (both in Lagos) 1978–83, sr ptnr Siemens Mgmnt Conslts London, sr conslt for ILO Geneva, memb Westminster Christian Cncl Homelessness Ctee; memb London Diocesan Synod (House of Laity), memb London Diocesan Bd for Schs (memb Educn Ctee), govr St George's Sch Hanover Square; FInstD; *Recreations* music, riding, sailing, squash; *Clubs* Lagos Yacht, Metropolitan (Lagos); *Style*— Herman W Siemens, Esq; ✉ Kendal Lodge, 19 Garrad's Rd, London SW16 1JX (☎ and fax 0181 677 2585); 108 Riouwstraat, 2585 HH, The Hague, The Netherlands (☎ 00 31 70 350 4018); 3940 Côte-des-Neiges, appt C-42, Montreal, Quebec H3H 1W2, Canada (☎ 00 1 514 934 0176)

SIGWART, Dr Ulrich; s of Dr August Robert Sigwart, and Elizabeth Augusta Sigwart; *b* 9 March 1941; *Educ* Univ of Basel, Univ of Munster Medical Sch, Univ of Freiburg; *m* 2 Sept 1967, Christine Rosemary, da of Peter Sartorius; 2 s (Philip Martin Christopher b 10 Aug 1970, Jan Michael Pierre b 27 April 1973), 2 da (Ann Elizabeth b 27 Feb 1969, Catherine Isabel b 15 Oct 1976); *Career* intern Community Hosp Lörrach, res Framington Union Hosp 1968–71, chief of cath lab Gollwitzer Meier Inst Bad Oeynhausen 1973–79, chief of invasive cardiology Univ Hosp Lausanne 1979–89, conslt cardiologist and dir of invasive cardiology Royal Brompton London; academic career: prof of med Univ of Düsseldorf, assoc prof of cardiology Univ of Lausanne; memb Editorial Bd: Clinical Cardiology, Herz & Gefässe, Cardiac Imaging, Interventional Cardiology; memb: Br Cardiac Soc, American Heart Assoc, Swiss Soc of Cardiology, German Soc of Cardiology; chm: Working Gp on Myocardial Function, Working Gp on PTCA & Lysis SSC; FRCP, FACC, FESC, FACA; *Books* Automation in Cardiac Diagnosis (1978), Ventricular Wall Motion (1984), Coronary Stents (1992), Endoluminal Stents (1995); *Recreations* flying, sailing, music, skiing, photography; *Style*— Dr Ulrich Sigwart; ✉ 7 Sydney Place,

London SW7 3NL (☎ 0171 581 5991); Royal Brompton Hospital, Sydney Street, London (☎ 0171 351 8615, fax 0171 351 8614)

SIKORA, Prof Karol; s of Witold Karol Sikora (d 1966), and Thomasina Sikora; *b* 17 June 1948; *Educ* Dulwich, Univ of Cambridge (MA, PhD, MB BChir), Middx Hosp; *m* 6 Dec 1975, Alison Mary; 1 s (Simon b 1977), 2 da (Emma b 1980, Lucy b 1982); *Career* former dir Ludwig Inst for Cancer Res Cambridge; currently: prof and head Dept of Clinical Oncology Royal Postgrad Med Sch Hammersmith, jt dir of cancer servs Hammersmith and Charing Cross Hosps, dep dir (clinical) Imperial Cancer Research Fund; FRCR 1980, FRCP 1987; *Books* Monoclonal Antibodies (1984), Fight Cancer (1989), Treatment of Cancer (1995), Cancer: a positive approach (1995); *Recreations* boating; *Clubs* Athenaeum, Polish Hearth; *Style*— Prof Karol Sikora; ✉ Department of Clinical Oncology, Hammersmith Hospital, London W12 0HD (☎ 0181 740 3060, fax 0181 743 8766)

SILBER, (Rudolf) Martin; s of Paul Silber (d 1931), and Vally, *née* Schlochauer (d 1944); *b* 22 Sept 1918; *Educ* Univ of London, London Sch of Building (HND); *m* 1, 9 Jan 1938 (m dis 1948), Irene, da of Thomas Arnold White (d 1936), of Australia; 1 s (Paul Dorian b 1939); m 2, 10 Sept 1949, Ila MacNeill, da of Dr William Fraser (d 1971); 1 s (Andrew Ernest b 1954), 1 da (Lucy Anne b 1950); *Career* WWII cmmnd RE 1940–46, serv Egypt, Persia and Iraq, SO WO Ctee (Fortification and Works Europe); dist surveyor: Lambeth (responsible for NT) 1965–75, City of London (responsible for Barbican Devpt and Nat West Tower) 1975–79; ptnr Silber & James 1979–; former pres: Dist Surveyors' Assoc 1966, Assoc of Architects & Surveyors 1963, Faculty of Bldg 1970; Freeman City of London, Liveryman Worshipful Co of Fan Makers; CEng, FIStructE, FIAS, ACIArb; *Recreations* music, theatre, gourmet; *Clubs* Nat Lib; *Style*— Martin Silber, Esq; ✉ Crittle's Court, Wadhurst, East Sussex TN5 6BY (☎ 01892 783743)

SILBER, Stephen Robert; QC (1987); s of Julius Joseph Silber (d 1975), of London, and Marguerite Silber; *b* 26 March 1944; *Educ* William Ellis Sch, Trinity Coll Cambridge, UCL; *m* 1982, Frances Nina Lucinda, da of Lt Col D St J Edwards; 1 s, 1 da; *Career* called to the Bar Gray's Inn 1968, bencher Gray's Inn 1994, memb Judicial Studies Bd (Criminal Law Ctee) 1994–, law cmmr for Eng and Wales 1994–, recorder of the Crown Court 1987–; *Recreations* photography, walking, watching sport; *Style*— Stephen Silber, Esq, QC; ✉ Law Commission, Conquest House, 37/38 John Street, London WC1N 2BQ (☎ 0171 453 1246, fax 0171 453 1297)

SILBERSTON, Prof (Zangwill) Aubrey; CBE (1987); s of Louis Silberston (d 1975), of London, and Polly, *née* Kern (d 1976); *b* 26 Jan 1922; *Educ* Hackney Downs Sch London, Jesus Coll Cambridge (BA, MA), Univ of Oxford (MA); *m* 1, 1945 (m dis), Dorothy Marion, da of A S Nicholls (d 1965), of London; 1 s (Jeremy b 1950), 1 da (Katharine b 1948 d 1982); m 2, 1985, Michèle, da of Vitomir Ledić, of Zagreb; *Career* Royal Fusiliers 1942–45, served in Iraq, Egypt, N Africa and Italy; economist Courtaulds Ltd 1946–50; Univ of Cambridge: res fell St Catharine's Coll 1950–53, lectr in economics 1951–71, fell St John's Coll 1958–71; official fell Nuffield Coll Oxford 1971–78 (dean 1972–78); Univ of London: prof of economics Imperial Coll 1978–87, prof emeritus Univ of London 1987–, sr res fell Mgmnt Sch Imperial Coll 1987–; dir Brussels Office London Economics 1992–; memb: Monopolies Cmmn 1965–68, Bd Br Steel Corp 1967–76, Royal Cmmn on the Press 1974–77, Royal Cmmn on Environmental Pollution 1986–96, Restrictive Practices Ct 1986–92; vice pres Royal Econ Soc 1992– (memb 1946, sec gen 1979–92), pres Confedn of Euro Econ Assocs 1988–90, specialist advsr Sub-ctee B European Communities Ctee House of Lords 1993; *Books* The Motor Industry (jtly, 1959), Economic Impact of the Patent System (jtly, 1973), The Steel Industry (jtly, 1974), The Multi-Fibre Arrangement and the UK Economy (1984), The Future of the Multi-Fibre Arrangement (1989), Beyond the Multi-Fibre Arrangement (jtly, 1995), Environmental Economics (ed, 1995), The Changing Industrial Map of Europe (jtly, 1996); *Recreations* opera, ballet; *Clubs* Travellers'; *Style*— Prof Aubrey Silberston, CBE; ✉ Imperial College, 53 Princes Gate, London SW7 2PG (☎ 0171 594 9354, fax 0171 594 9353)

SILK, *see:* Kilroy-Silk

SILK, Dr David Baxter A; *b* 14 April 1944; *Educ* Univ of London (MB BS, LRCP, MRCP); *Career* lectr in med Dept of Med and Gastroenterology St Bartholomew's Hosp London 1971–75, MRC Travelling fell and visiting assoc prof Univ of Calif San Francisco USA 1975–76, sr lectr and conslt Liver Unit King's Coll London 1976–78, conslt physician and co dir Dept of Gastroenterology and Nutrition Central Middx Hosp London 1978–; appointed to Editorial Bd: Gut 1978, Jl of Clinical Nutrition and Gastroenterology 1985, Gastroenterology in Practice 1987; chm Br Soc of Parenteral and Enteral Nutrition 1975; memb: Euro Soc of Parenteral and Enteral Nutrition, American Soc of Parenteral and Enteral Nutrition; Research medal The British Soc of Gastroenterology; memb Assoc of Physicians, MRCS 1968, MD 1974, FRCP 1983; *Books* Nutritional Support in Hospital Practice (1983), Artificial Nutrition Support in Clinical Practice (1994); author of over 300 articles in learned jls; *Style*— Dr David Silk; ✉ Dept of Gastroenterology and Nutrition, Central Middx Hospital, Acton Lane, Park Royal, London NW10 7NS

SILK, Dennis Raoul Whitehall; CBE (1995), JP (Oxon 1973); s of Rev Dr Claude Whitehall Silk (d 1974), and Louise Enicita, *née* Dumoret (d 1936); *b* 8 Oct 1931; *Educ* Christ's Hosp Horsham, Sidney Sussex Coll Cambridge (MA, Cricket blues 1953, 1954 and 1955, Rugby Football blues 1953 and 1954); *m* 6 April 1963, Diana Merilyn, da of William Frank Milton (d 1970), of Taunton, Somerset; 2 s (Thomas b 1967, William b 1970), 2 da (Katharine b 1964, Alexandra b 1966); *Career* housemaster Marlborough Coll 1957–68 (asst master 1955–68), warden Radley Coll 1968–91; non-exec dir Ecclesiastical Insurance Co; dir: Rank Fndn, Imperial War Museum; memb: Ctee MCC 1965–89 (pres 1992–94), TCCB 1984– (chm 1994–); *Books* Cricket for Schools (1964), Attacking Cricket (1965); *Recreations* gardening, fishing, reading; *Clubs* Hawks, E India Sports, Devonshire; *Style*— Dennis Silk, Esq, CBE, JP; ✉ Sturts Barn, Huntham Lane, Stoke St Gregory, nr Taunton, Somerset TA3 6EG (☎ 01823 490348, fax 01823 490641)

SILK, Donald; s of Robert Silk (d 1991), of London, and Polly, *née* Silk (d 1980); *b* 6 Sept 1928; *Educ* Magdalen Coll Sch Oxford, New Coll Oxford (BA, MA), Hague Acad of Int Law (Certificat d'Assiduité), London Graduate Sch of Business Studies; *m* 1, 8 Feb 1959 (m dis 1969), Angela Kate, da of Harry Buxton (d 1973), of London and Manchester; 2 s (Benjamin b 1960, Joseph b 1961); 1 da (Rebecca b 1966); m 2, 6 April 1983, Hilary Wells, da of George William Jackson (d 1985), of Chesterfield, Derbyshire; 1 s (James b 1984), 1 da (Polly Georgina Charlotte b 1986); *Career* Nat Serv Sgt instr RAEC 1947–49, memb HAC; dir Silk's Estates Investments Ltd 1949–69, slr and cmmr for oaths 1956–, chm Property Equity and Life Assurance Co 1969–88; hon vice pres Zionist Fedn 1971– (chm 1967–71), former common councilman City of London, former memb Bd of Deps of Br Jews, tstee Chichester Festival Theatre; Freeman City of London; memb: City of London Slrs Co 1971, Law Soc; SSC 1956; *Recreations* food and wine, theatre, opera, travel, yachting, watching polo; *Style*— Donald Silk, Esq; ✉ 69 Charlbury Rd, North Oxford OX2 6UX (☎ 01865 513881)

SILK, Rt Rev Robert David; s of Robert Reeve Silk (d 1990), and Winifred Patience Silk (d 1985); *b* 23 Aug 1936; *Educ* Gillingham GS, Univ of Exeter (BA), St Stephen's House Oxford; *m* 21 Sept 1957, Joyce Irene, da of Richard Bracey (d 1981, Brig in the Salvation Army); 1 s (Richard b 1967), 1 da (Mary b 1970); *Career* deacon 1959, priest 1960; curate: St Barnabas Gillingham 1959–63, Holy Redeemer Lamorbey 1963–69; priest-in-charge of The Good Shepherd Blackfen 1967–69; rector: Swanscombe 1969–75, Beckenham St George 1975–80; proctor in convocation 1970–, memb of the Liturgical Cmmn 1976–91, archdeacon of Leicester 1980–94, prolocutor of the Convocation of Canterbury 1980–94, team rector of the Holy Spirit Leicester 1982–88; chm Leicester Cncl of Faiths 1986–93, moderator Churches' Cmmn for Inter-Faith Relations (formerly Ctee for Rels with People of Other Faiths) 1990–93, bishop of Ballarat Victoria Aust 1993–; *Publications* Prayers For Use At The Alternative Services (1980), Compline - An Alternative Order (1980), In Penitence and Faith (1988); *Recreations* theatre, watching rugby football, Richard III; *Clubs* Athenaeum; *Style*— The Rt Rev the Bishop of Ballarat; ✉ Diocesan Registry, PO Box 89, Ballarat, Victoria, Australia 3350 (☎ 00 61 53 311183, fax 00 61 53 332982)

SILKIN, Jon; s of late Joseph Silkin, and Doris, *née* Rubenstein (d 1996); *b* 2 Dec 1930; *Educ* Wycliffe Coll, Dulwich; *m* 9 March 1974 (m dis 1995), Lorna, *née* Tracy; 3 s (Adam (decd), David, Richard), 1 da (Rachel); *Career* journalist 1947–48, Nat Serv Sgt Instr Educn Corps 1948–50, manual labourer 1950–56, teacher of English to foreign students in language sch 1956–58; poet: awarded Gregory Fellowship in Poetry Univ of Leeds 1958–60, undertook res on poets of WWI 1962, Beck visiting lectr Denison Univ Ohio 1965, teacher Writers Workshop Univ of Iowa 1968–69, visiting lectr Aust Arts Cncl and Univ of Sydney 1974–, C Day Lewis Fellowship London 1976–77, teacher of creative writing Coll of Idaho 1978, Bingham poet Univ of Louisville 1981, Elliston poet Univ Cincinnati 1983; visiting poet: visiting poet Mishkenot Sha'ananim Jerusalem 1980, at yearly fest of Univ of Notre Dame 1985, Writers Conf of Univ of N Alabama, The American Univ 1989, Univ of Iowa 1991, Tsukuba Univ 1991–94; co-ed Stand Magazine (literary quarterly); FRSL 1987; *Books* The Peacable Kingdom (1954), The Two Freedoms (1958), The Re-ordering of the Stones (1961), Nature with Man (1965), Poems New and Selected (1966), Amana Grass (1971), Out of Battle (Criticism of Poets of WWI 1972, new edn 1987), Poetry of the Committed Individual (Anthology of Poetry from Stand, 1973), The Principle of Water (1974), The Little Time-keeper (1976), The Penguin Book of First World War Poetry (ed, 1979), The Psalms with their Spoils (1980), Selected Poems (1980, 1988), Gurney: A Play in Verse (1985), The War Poems of Wilfred Owen (ed, 1985, new edn 1994), The Penguin Book of First World War Prose (ed with Jon Glover, 1989), The Ship's Pasture (poems 1986), The First Twenty-Four Years (1987), The Lens-Breakers (1992), The Life of Free and Metrical Verse in Twentieth Century Poetry (1996); *Style*— Jon Silkin, Esq; ✉ 13 Queens Terrace, Newcastle upon Tyne, Tyne and Wear NE2 2PJ (☎ 0191 281 2614, fax 0191 273 3280)

SILLARS, James; s of Matthew Sillars (d 1987), and Agnes, *née* Sproat (d 1942); *b* 4 Oct 1937; *Educ* Ayr Acad; *Career* mgmnt conslt; MP (Lab 1970–76, SLP 1976–79) S Ayrshire 1970–79, MP (SNP) Glasgow Govan 1988–92; jt fndr Scot Lab Pty 1976, joined SNP 1980 (former dep ldr); formerly: railway fireman, radio operator RN, firefighter, Labour Pty official and trade union official, chief exec Scottish Consultants International; asst sec Gen Arab-Br C of C; *Style*— James Sillars, Esq; ✉ 97 Grange Loan, Edinburgh EH9 2ED (☎ 0131 667 6658)

SILLARS, Michael Gordon; s of Derek Gordon Sillars, of Greendales, Nether Silton, Thirsk, North Yorkshire, and Patricia Dora, *née* Lovell; *b* 2 Aug 1943; *Educ* Forres Sch Rondebosch Cape Town SA, Diocesan Coll Rondebosch Cape Town SA; *m* 16 June 1973 (sep 1991), Lavinia Charlotte, da of Eric James Fletcher; 2 da (Amanda Louise b 16 July 1976, Emma Charlotte b 23 Nov 1979); *Career* Peat Marwick Mitchell & Co: articled clerk Middlesbrough 1963–69, qualified chartered accountant 1969, London 1970–71, Johannesburg SA 1971–73; Haggie Rand Ltd Johannesburg SA: chief accountant Haggie Rand Industrial Products Ltd 1973–74, fin accountant Haggie Steel Ropes Ltd 1974–75, project accountant Haggie Rand Wire Ltd 1975–77; ptnr: H H Kilvington Chartered Accountants Hartlepool Cleveland 1978–80 (joined 1977), WT Walton & Son Hartlepool (following merger) 1980–87, BDO Binder Hamlyn (following merger) 1987–91, Waltons & Clark Whitehill Waltons (following merger) 1991–; chm: Teeside Soc of Chartered Accountants 1989–90, CAs Panel to Cleveland Police Fraud Squad 1991–; FCA 1979 (ACA 1969); *Recreations* golf, tennis, music, art and drawing, photography; *Clubs* West Hartlepool; *Style*— Michael Sillars, Esq; ✉ Waltons & Clark Whitehill Waltons, 40 Victoria Road, Hartlepool, Cleveland (☎ 01429 234414)

SILLERY, William Moore; s of William Sillery, of Belfast, and Adeline, *née* Moore; *b* 14 March 1941; *Educ* Methodist Coll Belfast, St Catharine's Coll Cambridge (MA); *m* 19 Aug 1963, Elizabeth Margaret, da of James S Dunwoody, of Belfast; 2 da (Clare, Jane); *Career* Belfast Royal Acad: head modern languages 1968, vice princ 1974, dep headmaster 1976, headmaster 1980–; memb: NI Ctee Univs Funding Cncl 1988–92, Belfast Educn and Library Bd 1994–; educn advsr Ulster TV; memb HMC; *Recreations* reading, golf, bridge; *Clubs* East India, Belvoir Park Belfast; *Style*— William Sillery, Esq; ✉ Ardmore, 15 Saintfield Rd, Belfast BT8 4AE (☎ 01232 645260); Belfast Royal Academy, Belfast BT14 6JL (☎ 01232 740423)

SILLEY, Jonathan Henry; s of Henry Arthur John Silley, CBE (d 1972), and Betty Stewart, *née* Cotton (d 1981); *b* 2 May 1937; *Educ* Winchester; *m* 17 June 1961, Alison Mary, da of Richard Kenneth May (d 1965), of Purley, Surrey; 3 da (Jennifer Mary b 1964, Jane Elizabeth b 1965, Nichola Anne b 1969); *Career* Nat Serv 1955–57, 2 Lt Queen's Royal Regt; joined Samuel Hodge Gp 1959; dir: Surface Protection 1959–84 (chm 1971–84), E Wood Ltd 1963–84 (chm 1971–84), S Hodge Ltd 1965– (chm and md 1971–), Hodge Clemco Ltd 1965– (chm 1971–), Victor Pyrate Ltd 1965– (chm 1971–), Hodge Separators Ltd 1976– (chm), Stetfield Ltd 1987– (chm), Western Selection plc 1988–91, Teknequip Ltd 1993– (chm); memb HAC 1988; *Recreations* golf, tennis, racquets; *Clubs* City of London; *Style*— Jonathan Silley, Esq; ✉ Oudle House, Much Hadham, Herts SG10 6BT (☎ 0127 984 2359); Samuel Hodge Ltd, Queen Alexandra House, 2 Bluecoats Avenue, Hertford SG14 1PB (☎ 01992 558675)

SILLITOE, Alan; s of Christopher Archibald (d 1959), and Sabina Burton (d 1986); *b* 4 March 1928; *Educ* Radford Boulevard Sch Nottingham; *m* 19 Nov 1959, Ruth, da of Leslie Alexander Jonas Fainlight, of Sussex; 1 s (David Nimrod Sillitoe, *qv*, b 1962), 1 da (Susan Dawn b 1961); *Career* air traffic control 1945–46, RAF wireless operator 1946–49; writer 1948–; visiting prof of English de Montfort Univ Leicester 1993–96; Hon Degree: Manchester Poly 1976, Nottingham Poly 1990, Nottingham Univ 1994; *Books* Saturday Night and Sunday Morning (1958, Authors' Club award 1958, film 1960, play 1964), The Loneliness of the Long Distance Runner (1959, Hawthornden prize, film 1962), Key to the Door (1961), Raw Material (1972), The Widower's Son (1976), The Storyteller (1979), Her Victory (1982), The Lost Flying Boat (1983), The Open Door (1989), Last Loves (1990), Leonard's War (1991), Snowstop (1993), Life Without Armour (autobiog, 1995), Leading the Blind (1995); poetry collections incl: The Rats and Other Poems (1960), A Falling Out of Love (1964), Show on the North side of Lucifer (1979), Tides and Stone Walls (1986); for children: Marmalade Jim City Adventures (1967), Marmalade Jim at the Farm (1980), Marmalade Jim and the Fox (1985); *Recreations* short wave world morse code listening, travel; *Clubs* Savage; *Style*— Alan Sillitoe, Esq; ✉ c/o The Savage Club, 1 Whitehall Place, London SW1A 2HD

SILLITOE, David Nimrod; s of Alan Sillitoe, *qv*, of London, and Ruth Esther, *née* Fainlight; *b* 30 March 1962; *Educ* City of London Sch, Kingsway Princeton Coll of Further Educn, Hammersmith and W London Coll, NE London Poly; *m* Julia Ruth; 1 s (Jed Ethan b 2 June 1996); *Career* photographer; freelance: Mail on Sunday 1986–87, with The Independent and The BBC Central Stills Library and contrib to Reflex Agency 1987–88, The Guardian 1988; staff photographer The Guardian 1989–; memb NUJ; *Books* Alan Sillitoe's Nottinghamshire (photographs, 1987); *Recreations* motorcycle touring, recorded music and radio, shooting; *Clubs* Nat Pistol Assoc, Sportsmans Assoc of GB, Motorcycle Action Gp; *Style—* David Sillitoe, Esq; ✉ The Guardian, 119 Farringdon Rd, London EC1R 3ER (☎ 0171 278 2332)

SILLITOE, Leslie Richard; OBE (1977), JP (1963); s of Leonard Richard Sillitoe (d 1926), and Ellen, *née* Sutton (d 1933); *b* 30 Aug 1915; *Educ* St George's Sch, St Giles Sch, Stoke-on-Trent Sch of Art, Stoke-on-Trent Tech Coll; *m* 1939, Lucy, da of Arthur Goulding (d 1923); 2 da (Christine Ann, Margaret Leslie); *Career* Nat Serv WWII with N Staffs Regt, RE, and RA, served with Br Liberation Army and BAOR (Normandy to Hartz Mountains), Sr NCO 30 Corps (France, Belgium, Holland, Luxembourg and Germany, Territorial Efficient Serv medal 1945); modeller ceramics indust 1931–63, gen pres Ceramic and Allied Trade Union 1961–63 (organiser 1963–67, asst gen sec 1967–75, gen sec 1975–80), dep chm Ceramic Glass Mineral Prods Trg Bd 1977–83; chm: Nat Jt Cncl for Ceramic Indust 1975–80, N Staffs Manpower Ctee 1975–83; pres N Staffs Trades Cncl 1963–81, memb Stoke-on-Trent City Cncl 1953–83, hon memb N Staffs Med Inst, vice chm Museums Ctee; Lord Mayor Stoke-on-Trent 1981–82 (dep Lord Mayor 1982–83); memb: W Midland TAVRA 1979–83 and 1995–, Ctee Staffs War Pensions 1980–, Cncl Univ of Keele 1989–; chm: Friends of the Staffs Regt 1982–, Stoke-on-Trent Branch Normandy Veterans 1986–, John Baskeyfield VC Meml Ctee; vice pres Pottery and Glass Benevolent Inst 1980–; re-elected to Stoke-on-Trent City Cncl 1986–; memb Ctee N Staffs Special Adventure Playground 1996; Freeman City of Stoke-on-Trent 1993; *Recreations* walking, photography, swimming, history; *Clubs* Gideons Int, Longton Rotary (pres 1987–88); *Style—* Leslie Sillitoe, Esq, OBE, JP; ✉ 19 Sillitoe Place, Penkhull, Stoke-on-Trent ST4 5DQ (☎ 01782 847866)

SILLS, Dr John Anthony; s of Oliver Anthony Sills, of Barton, Cambridge, and Joan, *née* Webster; *b* 7 Sept 1943; *Educ* Perse Sch Cambridge, Queens' Coll Cambridge, Bart's Med Sch (MA, MB BChir, FRCP, DCH); *m* 24 June 1974, Hope Glen Milne, da of James Paterson Forsyth; 2 s (Benjamin b 29 Dec 1975, Daniel b 17 Dec 1979), 2 da (Laura b 9 Feb 1978, Emily b 16 May 1983); *Career* sr registrar Royal Hosp For Sick Children Edinburgh 1974–78, conslt paediatrician Royal Liverpool Children's Hosp Alder Hey and Whiston Hosp Prescot 1978–; memb: Nat Tst Scotland, Br Paediatric Assoc, BAPSCAN; *Books* Surgical Management of Rheumatoid Arthritis (contrib), author of papers on paediatrics and paediatric rheumatology; *Recreations* classical music, jazz, films, skiing, windsurfing, Liverpool FC; *Style—* Dr John Sills; ✉ Royal Liverpool Children's Hospital NHS Trust, Alder Hey, Eaton Rd, Liverpool L12 2AP (☎ 0151 252 5541); Whiston Hospital, Prescot, Merseyside L35 1DR (☎ 0151 430 1452)

SILSOE, 2 Baron (UK 1963); Sir David Malcom Trustram Eve; 2 Bt (UK 1943), QC (1972); s of 1 Baron Silsoe, GBE, MC, TD, QC (d 1976), by his 1 w, Marguerite (d 1945), da of Sir Augustus Meredith Nanton; *b* 2 May 1930; *Educ* Winchester, ChCh Oxford; *m* 1963, Bridget Min, da of Sir Rupert Hart-Davis, *qv*; 1 s (Hon Simon Rupert), 1 da (Hon Amy Comfort b 13 June 1964); *Heir* s, Hon Simon Rupert Trustram Eve b 17 April 1966; *Career* barr 1955, bar auditor Inner Temple 1965–70, bencher 1970; *Style—* The Rt Hon the Lord Silsoe, QC; ✉ Neals Farm, Wyfold, Reading, Berks RG4 9JB; 2 Mitre Court Buildings, 2nd Floor, Temple, London EC4Y 7BX (☎ 0171 583 1380, fax 0171 353 7772)

SILVER, Clinton Vita; CBE (1993); s of Sidney (Mick) Silver (d 1973), of London, and Mina, *née* Gabriel (d 1980); *b* 26 Sept 1929; *Educ* Upton Park Sch, City of London Coll, Univ of Southampton (BSc(Econ)); *m* 1973, Patricia Ann (Jill), da of John Vernon (d 1958); 1 s (Michael John b 1974), 1 da (Suzy Jane b 1978); *Career* Nat Serv 1950–52; Marks and Spencer plc: joined 1952, alternate dir 1974–78, dir 1978–94, md 1990–94, dep chm 1991–94; chm Br Fashion Cncl 1994–97; non-exec dir: Hillsdown Holdings plc 1994–, Tommy Hilfiger Corp 1994–, Pentland Group plc 1994–; memb: Bd Youth and Music, Appeal Bd Univ of Southampton, Varifone Inc 1997–; chm: Israel/Diaspora Tst, Jewish Assoc for Business Ethics; vice pres Br Overseas Trade Gp for Israel, vice chm Bd of Caldicott Sch; CIMgt, Companion Textile Inst; *Recreations* family, garden, music; *Style—* Clinton Silver, Esq, CBE; ✉ 47 Baker Street, London W1A 1DN (☎ 0171 268 6537, fax 0171 268 2648)

SILVER, Prof Ian Adair; s of Capt George James Silver (d 1937), and Nora Adair, *née* Seckham (d 1979); *b* 28 Dec 1927; *Educ* Rugby, Corpus Christi Coll Cambridge (MA), Royal Veterinary Coll London (FRCVS); *m* 30 June 1950, Marian (d 1994), da of Dr Frederick John Scrase (d 1981); 2 s (Alastair b 1960, Angus b 1963), 2 da (Alison b 1956 (who m Andrew Lorimer Hunter, *qv*), Fiona (Mrs Rainer Grün) b 1959); *Career* RN 'Y' Scheme 1945, seconded Cambridge Univ, trans to Tech & Scientific Regt 1948; Univ of Cambridge: demonstrator in zoology 1952–57, lectr in anatomy 1957–70, fell and sr graduate tutor Churchill Coll 1965–70; Univ of Bristol: prof of comparative pathology 1970–81, prof and chm Dept of Pathology and Microbiology 1981–93 (emeritus prof of pathology 1993–), dean Faculty of Medicine 1987–90, sr research fell 1995–; prof of neurology Univ of Pennsylvania USA 1977–; visiting prof: Louisiana Tech Univ USA 1973, Cayetana Heredia Univ Lima Peru 1976; Royal Soc prof Federal Univ Rio de Janeiro Brazil 1977; chm Southmead Health Servs NHS Trust 1992– (non-exec dir 1991–92); memb Research Cncl Ctees: MRC, SERC, AFRC, ARC; pres: RCVS 1985–86 and 1987, Int Soc for Study of O Transport to Tissue 1977 and 1986; *Books* edited 7 scientific books, published over 200 learned papers; *Recreations* exploration, DIY, fishing; *Style—* Prof Ian Silver; ✉ c/o Dept of Anatomy, School of Veterinary Science, Southwell Street, University of Bristol, Bristol BS2 8EJ (☎ 0117 928 8362, fax 0117 925 4794)

SILVER, Leslie Howard; OBE (1982); s of Harry Silver, and Bessie, *née* Hoffman; *b* 22 Jan 1925; *m* 1, Anita (d 1983); 1 s (Mark b 1960), 2 da (Hilary b 1948, Jane b 1950); m 2, 29 April 1984, Sheila Estelle; *Career* WWII Warrant Offr RAF 1943–46; pres: Paintmakers Assoc of GB, Oil Colour Chemists Assoc, Paint Res Assoc, Paint Indust Club; chm: Leeds Utd FC until 1996 (joined board 1981), Bd of Govrs Leeds Metropolitan Univ (formerly Leeds Poly); Hon DTech Leeds Poly 1990; MIMgt; *Style—* Leslie Silver, Esq, OBE; ✉ c/o Leeds Utd FC, Elland Road, Leeds LS11 0ES (☎ 0113 271 6037)

SILVER, Lynne; *see:* Woolfson, Lynne

SILVER, Max Joseph; s of Benjamin Silver (d 1981), of Cardiff, and Rose, *née* Spira (d 1941); *b* 14 April 1925; *Educ* City of Cardiff HS, Univ of Wales (BSc), Croydon Poly (Dip Telecoms); *m* 4 Feb 1964, Muriel, da of Jack Grasin (d 1960), of Palmers Green, London; 1 s (Jonathan b 1970), 1 da (Rochelle b 1965); *Career* electronics res worker GEC Wembley 1947–50, res and prodn mgmnt with assoc co of GEC on airborne def projects 1950–59, with Elliot Automation and md Associated Automation Ltd (later part of GEC) 1960–70, company doctor Philips Group and Pye of Cambridge Sub Gp 1971–80, princ of consultancy on company acquisitions and mergers (with contracts to PA Consulting and M & A International mgmnt conslts) 1980–; advsr to Educn Ctee Brent Cncl, vice chm of Govrs Kilburn Poly 1982–86; CEng, FIEE, FIERE, FIMfgE, FIMgt, FSCA, FMS, FFA; *Recreations* reading, gardening, travel; *Style—* Max Silver, Esq; ✉ The Penthouse, Cedarwood Lodge, Orchard Drive, Edgware, Middx HA8 7SD (☎ 0181 958 7885)

SILVER, Petronilla; da of Prof Peter Hele Spencer-Silver, of London, and Patricia Anne, *née* Cuffe; *b* 16 Sept 1950; *Educ* Godolphin and Latymer GS London, Redland Coll of Educn Bristol (DipEd); *Career* sec and sales asst Redfern Gallery London 1973–77, dir The Contemporary Art Society 1981–93 (organising sec as asst 1977–81), freelance contemporary art advsr 1993–; memb: Museums Assoc, Newlyn Art Gallery, Penzance Arts Club, Chelsea Arts Club, Friends of the Tate; *Clubs* Chelsea Arts (hon memb); *Style—* Miss Petronilla Silver; ✉ 5 Knowsley Road, London SW11 5BN

SILVER, Prof Robert Simpson; CBE (1967); s of Alexander Clark Silver (d 1962), of Montrose, Angus, and Isabella Simpson (d 1950); *b* 13 March 1913; *Educ* Montrose Acad, Univ of Glasgow (MA, DSc); *m* 1937, Jean McIntyre (d 1988), da of Alexander Bruce (d 1937), and Elizabeth, *née* Livingstone (d 1950); 2 s; *Career* engrg scientist, consultant, James Watt prof of mechanical engrg Univ of Glasgow 1967–79, prof emeritus 1979–, prof of mechanical engrg Heriot-Watt Coll Edinburgh 1962–66; G & J Weir Ltd: head of res 1939–46, chief of R & D 1956–62, head of devpt 1956–58, dir 1958–62; res physicist ICI Ltd 1936–39, dir of res Federated Foundaries Ltd 1948–54, chief design engr John Brown Land Boilers Ltd 1954–56; Hon DSc Strathclyde 1984; UNESCO Sci Prize 1968, foreign assoc of US Acad of Engrg 1979; FInstP 1942, FIMechE 1953, FRSE 1963; *Books* Introduction to Thermodynamics (1971), The Bruce (A Play in 3 acts, performed Edinburgh Int Festival, 1986), The Picture (play, performed King's Head Theatre Islington, 1991), Conflicts and Contents (Poems of the Quarter Century 1930/55) (1992); *Recreations* fly-fishing, poetry; *Style—* Prof Robert Silver, CBE, FRSE; ✉ 5 Panmure Street, Montrose, Angus, Scotland DD10 8EZ (☎ 01674 677793)

SILVERLEAF, (Alexander) Michael; QC (1996); s of David James Silverleaf, of Wimbledon, and Rachel, *née* Hardstone; *b* 2 Nov 1953; *Educ* King's Coll Sch Wimbledon, Imperial Coll London (BSc Physics); *partner* since 1985, Joanne Ruth, da of Walter John Welch; 3 da; *Career* called to the Bar Gray's Inn 1980, in practice in intellectual property, jr counsel in patent matters to the Treasy 1991–96; *Books* Passing Off Law and Practice (with John Drysdale, 1986, 2 edn 1995); *Recreations* motor racing, squash; *Style—* Michael Silverleaf, Esq, QC; ✉ 11 South Square, 2nd Floor, Gray's Inn, London WC1R 5EU (☎ 0171 405 1222, fax 0171 242 4282)

SILVERMAN, Prof Bernard Walter; s of Elias Silverman, of London, and Helen, *née* Korn (d 1989); *b* 22 Feb 1952; *Educ* City of London Sch, Univ of Cambridge (MA, PhD, ScD); *m* 9 March 1985, Dr Rowena Fowler; 1 s (Matthew b 1989); *Career* res fell Jesus Coll Cambridge 1975–77, devpt mangr Sinclair Radionics Ltd 1976–77, lectr Univ of Oxford 1977–78; Univ of Bath: lectr 1978–80, reader 1981–84, prof of statistics 1984–93, head Sch of Mathematical Sciences 1988–91; prof of statistics Univ of Bristol 1993–; ed International Statistical Review 1991–, author of over seventy papers in jls; Chartered Statistician; hon sec Royal Statistical Soc 1984–90, fell Inst of Mathematical Statistics USA 1986–; Guy Medal in Bronze Royal Statistical Soc 1984, President's Award Ctee of Presidents of Statistical Socs USA 1991, Guy Medal in Silver Royal Statistical Soc 1995; *Books* Density Estimation for Statistics and Data Analysis (1986), Nonparametric Regression and Generalized Linear Models (with P J Green, 1994); *Style—* Prof Bernard Silverman; ✉ School of Mathematics, University Walk, Bristol BS8 1TW (☎ 0117 928 7968, fax 0117 928 7999)

SILVERMAN, Jon; s of Leonard Silverman, of Leeds, and Lili; *b* 22 July 1949; *Educ* Enfield GS, Selwyn Coll Cambridge (MA); *m* 15 Sept 1974, Jacqui, da of Raymond Mellor; 2 s (Alex b 27 Jan 1981, Daniel b 23 April 1983); *Career* trainee journalist Thomson Orgn, reporter and feature writer Evening Post Luton 1971–74, reporter Radio Hallam Sheffield 1974–75; BBC Radio: BBC Radio Sheffield 1975–77, sub-ed Newsroom London 1977–78, Parly journalist and political correspondent Westminster 1978–83, news reporter 1983–87, European reporter Paris 1987–89, home/legal affairs correspondent 1989–; radio presenting incl: PM, Today, World This Weekend; memb: High Court Journalists Assoc, Crime Reporters' Assoc, NUJ; Bar Cncl Legal Reporting Award for Bdcasting 1992, Radio Journalist award Sony Radio Awards 1996; Cropwood fell Cambidge Inst of Criminology 1991; *Books* Cropwood Conference Papers (contrib, 1992), Crack of Doom (1994); *Recreations* football, theatre; *Style—* Jon Silverman, Esq; ✉ Social Affairs Unit, BBC Radio News and Current Affairs, Broadcasting House, London W1A 1AA (☎ 0171 765 5502, fax 0171 636 4295)

SILVERMAN, Prof (Hugh) Richard; s of S G Silverman (d 1985), and N E Silverman, *née* Braley, of New South Wales; *b* 23 Sept 1940; *Educ* Brighton Coll of Art and Craft (DipArch), Univ of Edinburgh (MSc); *m* 24 Feb 1963, Aase Kay, da of Knud Sonderskov Madsen; 2 da (Jennifer Solvej b 24 April 1971, Sophia Annelise b 23 Nov 1974); *Career* dir Alec French Partnership (Architects) Bristol 1984–86, prof and head The Welsh Sch of Architecture Cardiff 1986–; memb: Bd Cardiff Bay Devpt Corp 1990– (chm Devpt Advsy Panel); ARIBA 1965, FRSA 1989; *Style—* Prof Richard Silverman; ✉ Welsh School of Architecture, University of Wales, King Edward VII Avenue, Cardiff CF1 3AP (☎ 01222 874431, fax 01222 874926)

SILVESTER, Peter; s of Eric William James Silvester, and Dorothy May, *née* Collier; *b* 21 Jan 1936; *Educ* Godalming GS; *m* 8 Feb 1964, Christine Catherine; *Career* Nat Serv RAF SAC; Friends Provident Life Office: asst gen mangr 1981–87, gen mangr (investmt) 1987–88, dir and gen mangr investmt 1988–94, gp investmt dir Friends Provident and md FP Asset Management Group 1994–96, ret; non-exec dir: Presidio Oil Co Inc, Ivory and Sime Discovery Trust, Friends Provident Ethical Investments Trust, Esprit (Luxembourg); chm Land on Capital Holdings Ltd; formerly vice pres The Pensions Mgmnt Inst and past pres Insur Lawn Tennis Assoc, memb RSPB; FIA 1971, FPMI 1979, FInstD, MSI, FRSA; *Recreations* skiing, fishing, golf, tennis; *Style—* Peter Silvester, Esq

SILVESTER, Simon Charles Arthur; s of Oliver Dutton Silvester (d 1987), and Rowena Anne, *née* Davies; *b* 25 Jan 1962; *Educ* The King's Sch Chester, Trinity Hall Cambridge (MA, ed Cantab magazine); *Career* account planner Boase Massimi Pollitt advtg 1983–87, copywriter Delaney Fletcher Delaney 1987–89, sr planner Gold Greenlees Trott 1989–90; planning dir: Burkitt Edwards Martin 1990–95, Alto European Network 1991–95; one year sabbatical 1995–96, md Silvester Research Ltd 1996–; awards: Merit NY One Show 1988, Silver ILR Radio Awards 1988, Pyramid Epica Awards 1988, Merit Euro Awards 1988; main speaker (at invitation of Belgium Economics Min) Euro Union Summit on Youth 1993; memb: MRS 1983, Mktg Soc 1992; *Publications* Spoilt Brats (1990), Invasion of Essex Men (1991), Eurokids - The Single Youth of the Single Market (1992), Is Research Killing Advertising? (1992); *Recreations* travel, parties, art; *Style—* Simon Silvester, Esq; ✉ (web ref www.silvester.com)

SIM, Peter Anderson; s of Stuart Anderson Sim (d 1970), and Bertha Roberts (d 1980); *b* 16 July 1939; *Educ* High Wycombe Royal GS, Coll of Estate Mgmnt; *m* 8 Oct 1966, Gillian Margaret Anne, da of Thomas Cedric Nicholson (d 1960); 2 s (Andrew b 1968, David b 1970), 1 da (Christina b 1976); *Career* dir Taylor Woodrow Property Co 1974, md Property Legal & General 1974–89; dir: Legal & General Investment Management (Holdings) Ltd, Legal & General Assurance (Pensions Management) Ltd, Legal & General Property Ltd, Cavendish Land Co Ltd, Watling Street Properties Ltd, Paramount Reality Holdings Ltd, Bridge End Properties Ltd, Glanfield Securities Ltd, Investment Property Databank Ltd, Gosvenor Herries Educational Trust Ltd; chm and md Wildoak Properties Ltd 1989–93, property dir: Cadogan Estates Ltd 1993–, Chelsea Land Ltd, Cadogan Holdings Co; memb: Asset Valuation Standards Ctee RICS 1982–94, Devpt and Planning Practice Panel 1994–; Liveryman Worshipful Co of Chartered Surveyors; FRICS; *Recreations* gardening, swimming; *Style—* Peter Sim, Esq; ✉ 3 Blaenavon, Caversham Heights, Berks RG4 7XQ (☎ 0118 946 2540); Cadogan Estates Ltd, 18 Cadogan Gardens, London SW3 2RP (☎ 0171 730 4567)

SIMCOX, Richard Alfred; CBE (1975, MBE 1956); s of late Alfred William Simcox, and Alice Simcox; *b* 29 March 1915; *Educ* Wolverhampton, Gonville and Caius Coll Cambridge; *m* 1951, Patricia Elisabeth, *née* Gutteridge; 1 s, 2 da; *Career* Br Cncl 1943–75: rep Jordan 1957–60, rep Libya 1960, cultural attaché Br Embassy Cairo 1968–71, rep Iran 1971–75; govr Gabbitas-Thring Educnl Tst until 1994; *Style—* Richard Simcox,

Esq, CBE; ✉ Little Brockhurst, Lye Green Rd, Chesham, Bucks HP5 3NH (☎ 01494 783797)

SIME, Peter Ernest Miller; s of Ian Falconer Sime, and Marjorie Joan Thompson, *née* Miller; *b* 18 Nov 1954; *Educ* Crewe Co GS, Jesus Coll Oxford (MA), Birkbeck Coll London (MSc); *m* 16 Dec 1989, Vanessa Jane, da of Leslie and Doreen Nokes; *Career* CA; Deloitte Haskins & Sells 1976–83, fin dir and co sec Gardner Lohmann ltd 1983–85, head of enforcement Assoc of Futures Brokers & Dealers Ltd 1988–90 (compliance mangr 1985–88), head of market supervision London Int Fin Futures Exchange 1990–91, dir of accounting SFO 1991–94, head of regulatory control C S First Boston 1994–; ACA 1979; *Recreations* flying, mountaineering; *Style*— Peter Sime, Esq; ✉ The Barn, Haffenden Quarter, Smarden, Kent TN27 8QR; C S First Boston, One Cabot Square, London E14 4QJ (☎ 0171 516 1263)

SIMEON, Sir John Edmund Barrington; 7 Bt (UK 1815), of Grazeley, Berks; s of Sir John Walter Barrington Simeon, 6 Bt (d 1957); 1 Bt m da and heir of Sir FitzWilliam Barrington 10 Bt, extinct 1833; *b* 1 March 1911; *Educ* Eton, ChCh Oxford; *m* 10 July 1937, Anne Robina Mary, er da of Hamilton Dean; 1 s, 2 da; *Heir* s, Richard Edmund Barrington Simeon, *qv*; *Career* served WWII RAF 1939–43, invalided out with rank of Flt Lt, emigrated to Canada 1951, civil servant Dept of Social Welfare Govt Br Columbia 1951–75; *Style*— Sir John Simeon, Bt; ✉ 987 Wavertree Rd, N Vancouver, BC V7R 1S6, Canada

SIMEON, Prof Richard Edmund Barrington; s and h of Sir John Simeon, 7 Bt, *qv*, by his w, Anne Mary Dean; *b* 2 March 1943; *Educ* St George's Sch Vancouver, Br Columbia Univ (BA), Yale Univ (MA, PhD); *m* 1, 6 Aug 1966 (m dis 1989), Agnes Joan, o da of George Frederick Weld; 1 s (Stephen George Barrington b 1970), 1 da (Rachel Elizabeth b 1973); m 2, 17 April 1993, Maryetta Cheney; *Career* prof Dept of Political Studies Queen's Univ Kingston Canada 1968–91, prof of political sci and law Univ of Toronto 1991–; dir: Inst of Intergovernmental Relations Queen's Univ 1976–83, Sch of Public Admin Queen's Univ 1986–91; res co-ordinator Royal Cmmn on the Economic Union and Canada's Devpt Prospects 1983–85, vice chm Ontario Law Reform Cmmn 1989–95; *Books* Federal-Provincial Diplomacy (1972), Federalism and the Economic Union (with K Norrie and M Krasnick, 1985), Politics of Constitutional Change (ed with Keith Banting, 1984), State, Society and the Development of Canadian Federalism (with Ian Robinson, 1990), In Search of a Social Contract (1994), Rethinking the Federal Idea: Citizens, Politics and Markets (ed with K Knop, S Ostry and K Swinton, 1995), Degrees of Difference: Canada and the United States in a Changing World (with K Banting and G Hoberg, 1996); *Style*— Prof Richard Simeon; ✉ Department of Political Science, University of Toronto, Toronto, Ontario, Canada M5S 1A1 (☎ 00 1 416 978 3346, fax 00 1 416 978 5566)

SIMEONE, Reginald Nicola (Reggie); CBE (1985); s of Nicola Francisco Simeone (d 1985), of Horsham, Sussex, and Phyllis Simeone, *née* Iles (d 1985); *b* 12 July 1927; *Educ* Raynes Park GS, St John's Coll Cambridge (MA); *m* 2 April 1954, Josephine Frances, da of Robert Hope (d 1979), of Beverley, Yorks; 2 s (Nigel b 1956, Robert b 1961); *Career* Nat Serv RN instr Lt (meteorologist) 1947–50, Admty 1950–59; UKAEA 1959–90: Fin Branch 1959–61, Econs and Progs Branch 1961–65, chief personnel offr AWRE 1965–69, princ estab offr 1970–76, authy personnel offr 1976–84, comptroller of fin and admin 1984–87, memb Bd for Fin and Admin 1987–88, advsr to chm 1988–90; exec vice pres Euro Atomic Energy Soc 1987–90; chm Police Ctee for AEA Constabulary 1986–90; advsr to chm Nuclear Electric plc 1990–96; FRMetS; *Recreations* travel, music, theatre; *Clubs* United Oxford and Cambridge Univ; *Style*— Reginald N Simeone, Esq, CBE; ✉ 31 Portsmouth Avenue, Thames Ditton, Surrey KT7 0RU (☎ 0181 398 0428)

SIMEONS, Charles Fitzmaurice Creighton; DL (Beds 1987); s of Charles Albert Simeons (d 1957), and Vera Hildegarde, *née* Creighton (d 1982); *b* 22 Sept 1921; *Educ* Oundle, Queens' Coll Cambridge (MA); *m* 1, 10 March 1945, Rosemary Margaret (d 1991), da of Ashley Tabrum, OBE; 1 s (Peter), 1 da (Jennifer (Mrs Bishop)); m 2, 5 Dec 1991, Constance Anne Dowson, da of Frederick George Restell (d 1974); *Career* cmmnd RA 1942, 52 Field Regt, serv 8 Indian Div ME and Italy, Maj; md British Gelatine Works 1957, Croda Gelatins 1968–70, MP (C) Luton 1970–74, environmental control conslt 1974–, health and safety advsr Control of Toxic Substances 1980–, int market res studies communication with govt covering Europe, Japan and the US; business advsr Prince of Wales Business Tst 1993–; memb Luton Rotary Club 1951–91 (pres 1960–61, hon memb 1996), dist govr Rotary Int Dist 109 1967–68, memb Holt Rotary Club 1992–; pres: Luton and Dunstable C of C 1967–68, Luton and Dist Dunkirk Veterans 1963–94 (patron 1994–); chm: Luton Cons Assoc 1960–64, Ampthill Cheshire Home 1963–72, Cancer Res Campaign Luton 1963–80, Nat Children's Home Luton 1976–90; hon sec: Union of Ind Companies 1978–80, 8 Indian Officers Assoc 1983–; memb: Customer Consultative Ctee Anglia and Thames Water 1984–89, Small Firms Panel ABCC 1985–89, Eastern Customer Servs Ctee Office of Water Servs 1990–96; conf dir Advsy Ctee on Protection of the Seas 1989 (London) and 1991 (Brussels), fndr patron Pensthorpe Waterfowl Tst 1990–, fndr chm Friends of Pensthorpe Waterfowl Tst 1993–95, organiser Kelling Hosp Gala 1996; JP Luton 1959–74; Freeman City of London 1969, memb Ct of Assts Worshipful Co of Feltmakers (Liveryman 1969, Master 1987–88), memb Worshipful Co (formerly Guild) of Water Conservators 1991; FIIM 1975; *Books* Coal: Its Role in Tomorrow's Technology (1978), Water As An Alternative Source of Energy (1980); *Recreations* charitable activities, watching most sports, walking the dogs; *Clubs* City Livery, Clover (8 Indian Offrs, hon sec); *Style*— Charles Simeons, Esq, DL; ✉ Mill Leet, High Street, Cley-next-the-Sea, Norfolk NR25 7RR (☎ 01263 740772, fax 01263 741198)

SIMKIN, (Richard) Graham; s of Frederick Simkin (d 1986), and Edna, *née* Turner; *b* 14 July 1952; *Educ* Univ of Leeds (LLB); *m* 6 July 1974, Susan Mary, da of Rev Keith Shackleton (d 1974); 1 s (Matthew b 1989), 3 da (Elizabeth b 1980, Sarah b 1981, Rachel b 1986); *Career* slr; ptnr Boodle Hatfield 1978–90, seconded to Terre Armée Internationale SA as directeur juridique 1980–83, head corp serv Boodle Hatfield 1988–90; Terre Armée Group: main bd dir 1989–, dep chief exec 1990–91, chief exec 1991–93; chief exec Terre Armée Internationale SA 1994–; ptnr Graham Simkin & Co 1990–94; memb Law Soc 1976; *Recreations* theatre, photography; *Clubs* RAC; *Style*— Graham Simkin, Esq; ✉ Terre Armée International SA, 36 Avenue Raymond Poincaire, 75116 Paris, France (☎ 00 33 1 53 70 61 14, fax 00 33 1 53 70 63 20); Groupe TAI, Hamilton House, Marlowes, Hemel Hempstead, Herts HP1 1BB

SIMKISS, Prof Kenneth; s of Clifford Simkiss (d 1970), of Poulton-le-Fylde, Lancs, and Edith Howe (d 1978); *b* 4 July 1934; *Educ* Blackpool GS, Univ of London (BSc, DSc), Univ of Reading (PhD); *m* 25 March 1961, Nancy Carolyn, da of Dr Travis Bain McGilvray, of Michigan, USA; 2 s (Douglas Eric b 1964, Gregory Daryl b 1970), 1 da (Gillian Varina b 1966); *Career* prof Dept of Zoology Queen Mary Coll Univ of London 1968–72 (lectr 1958–65); Univ of Reading: reader in physiology and biochemistry 1965–68, prof Dept of Zoology 1972–, currently head of research Sch of Animal & Microbial Scis; memb Cncl: Soc for Experimental Biology 1975–77, Zoological Soc 1978–80, Marine Biological Assoc 1979–82, 1983–86 and 1987–91, Freshwater Biological Assoc 1980–84; FIBiol 1973; *Books* Bird Flight (1963), Calcium in Reproductive Physiology (1967), Bone and Biomineralisation (1975), Biomineralisation (1989); *Recreations* music, art; *Style*— Prof Kenneth Simkiss; ✉ School of Animal & Microbial Sciences, PO Box 228, University of Reading, Reading RG6 6AJ (☎ 0118 931 8460, fax 0118 931 6562, telex 847813 ROLIBG)

SIMM, Robert James (Bob); s of Alfred Simm (d 1992), of Manchester, and Vera, *née* Lowe; *b* 2 March 1948; *Educ* St John's Coll, Univ of Lancaster (BA); *m* 7 May 1977, Sally Elizabeth, da of Edward McNamara; 2 s (Richard James Alfred b 5 Jan 1982, James Edward Alexander b 26 April 1984), 1 da (Katherine Elizabeth Jane b 4 April 1989); *Career* Marks and Spencer plc: grad trainee 1971–74, Head Office 1974–75, head Store Mgmnt Trg 1975–77; sr mangr Price Waterhouse 1977–84; KPMG Peat Marwick: head Human Resources 1984–85, ptnr 1985–94, chm Int Human Resources Steering Ctee 1986–91, sr ptnr Mgmnt Consulting 1990, memb Bd 1991, chm UK Mgmnt Consulting 1993–94; art consIt and gallery owner 1995–; Inst of Mgmnt Consultants: chm UK Professional Devpt Ctee 1988–90 (London Regnl Ctee 1985–88), currently memb Cncl; memb Cncl Management Consultants Assoc, memb Devpt Ctee Nat Portrait Gallery; MITD 1974, memb Inst of Transactional Analysis 1975, FIMC 1985, ACA 1991, FRSA 1992; *Recreations* collecting and sponsoring art; *Style*— Bob Simm, Esq; ✉ 23 Greenhill, Prince Arthur Road, London NW3 5UB (☎ 0171 794 6982); Graham Gallery, 1 Castle Street, Tunbridge Wells, Kent (☎ 01892 526695)

SIMMERS, Graeme Maxwell; OBE (1982); s of William Maxwell Simmers (the Scottish rugby int, d 1972), and Gwenyth Reinagle, *née* Sterry (Wightman Cup tennis champion); gm Mrs C R Sterry, *née* Cooper (5 times Wimbledon tennis champion); *b* 2 May 1935; *Educ* Glasgow Acad, Loretto; *m* 10 Sept 1965, Jennifer Margaret Hunter, da of William Roxburgh, OBE, of Fife; 2 s (Mark William b 1967, Peter Hunter Maxwell b 1973), 2 da (Corinne Charlotte b 1969, Kirstin Margaret b 1970); *Career* Nat Serv Lt RM 1959–61; CA 1959, ptnr Kidson Simmers 1959–88, chm Scottish Highland Hotels Group Ltd 1972–92, non-exec dir Stirling Royal Infirmary NHS Tst 1993–; chm Hotel and Catering Benevolent Assoc Scotland 1984–87; memb: Scottish Tourist Bd 1979–86, Nat Exec Br Hospitality Assoc 1991–; chm Championship Ctee Royal and Ancient Golf Club 1988–91, govr The Queen's Coll Glasgow 1989–93, chm Scottish Sports Cncl 1992–; chm of govrs Loretto Sch, elder and treas of Killearn Kirk; *Recreations* golf, tennis, skiing; *Clubs* R & A, All England Lawn Tennis; *Style*— Graeme M Simmers, Esq, OBE; ✉ Kincaple, Boquhan, Balfron, Glasgow G63 0RW (☎ 01360 440375, fax 01360 440985)

SIMMONDS, Andrew Keith John (Andy); s of Reginald Arthur Simmonds (d 1989), and Hilda Violet, *née* Hunniset; *b* 10 Aug 1952; *Educ* Rye GS, Univ of Manchester (BSc); *m* 1978, Janet, da of A Stanley Hore; 2 da (Beth b 1981, Laura b 1984); *Career* articled clerk Deloitte & Co CAs 1973–77, sr lectr Accountancy Tuition Centre 1977–85 (lectr in financial accounting 1977–80), princ Tech Dept Touche Ross (now Deloitte & Touche) 1985–; advsr Accounting Standards Bd; memb: ICAEW Tech Advsy Ctee, London Soc of Chartered Accountants (former chm); FCA (ACA 1977); *Books* Mastering Financial Accounting (Macmillan, 1986), Mergers, Acquisitions & Goodwill (Touche Ross, 1986), Accounting for Europe (Touche Ross, 1989), Accountants Digest: Accounting for Subsidiary Undertakings (Accountancy Books, 1992); *Recreations* music, golf; *Style*— Andy Simmonds, Esq; ✉ Deloitte & Touche, Hill House, 1 Little New Street, London EC4A 3TR (☎ 0171 303 4605, fax 0171 353 9820, e-mail andy_simmonds@ deloitte.touche.co.uk)

SIMMONDS, David Anthony Kenward; JP (Hertfordshire 1980); s of Maurice Alan Charles Simmonds (d 1983), and Florence Mary, *née* Kenward, of Orchard End, Nan Clarks Lane, Mill Hill, London; *b* 8 Sept 1939; *Educ* Stowe, Univ of London (BSc); *m* 1, 23 Sept 1963 (m dis 1974), Carole Anne, da of Geoffrey Charles Thomas Parkes (d 1987); 2 da (Jane b 1965, Lucy b 1968); m 2, 27 March 1975, Valerie, da of John Barsley (d 1972); 2 s (Matthew b 1975, Mark b 1978); *Career* chartered surveyor Hendon; chm Hendon Round Table 1974–75; Barnet PSA: dep chm Juvenile Panel 1988–, chm Licensing Ctee 1990–95, dep Bench chm 1992–96; Freeman City of London 1963, Liveryman Worshipful Co of Tallow Chandlers 1963 (memb Ct of Assts 1994–96); FRICS 1972 (ARICS 1963); *Recreations* travel, gardening, wine, philately, railways; *Clubs* MCC; *Style*— David Simmonds, Esq, JP; ✉ Little Orchard, Barnet Lane, Elstree, Herts WD6 3QX (☎ 0181 207 1232); Burroughs House, The Burroughs, Hendon NW4 4AP (☎ 0181 202 8181, fax 0181 202 3383)

SIMMONDS, Jeremy Basil Canter; RD (1979); s of Reginald Arthur Canter Simmonds (d 1974), of Woodlands Farm, Cookham Dean, Berks, and Betty, *née* Cahusac; *b* 2 July 1941; *Educ* Trinity Coll Glenalmond, Keble Coll Oxford (BA); *m* 4 March 1967, Sally, da of John Bertrand Aust (Capt RA, d 1979), formerly of Tugwood, Cookham Dean; 2 s (Timothy b 1967, Michael b 1970), 2 da (Anne b 1973, Clare b 1973); *Career* London Div RNR 1963–82, ret with rank of Lt Cdr; Radcliffes & Co: articled 1965–67, admitted slr 1967, asst slr 1967–69, ptnr 1969–73; Glovers (formerly Glover & Co): sr banking ptnr 1973–, sr ptnr 1996–; memb Nat Cncl Nat Asthma Campaign, memb Cncl The Shellfish Assoc of GB; Freeman City of London 1980, Liveryman Worshipful Co of Fishmongers 1980; memb Law Soc 1967; *Recreations* walking, photography; *Clubs* Naval; *Style*— Jeremy Simmonds, Esq, RD; ✉ Woodmancutts, Church Rd, Cookham Dean, Maidenhead, Berks SL6 9PJ (☎ 01628 474991); Glovers, 115 Park St, London W1Y 4DY (☎ 0171 629 5121, fax 0171 491 0930)

SIMMONDS, Prof Kenneth; s of Herbert Marshall Simmonds, and Margaret, *née* Trevurza; *b* 17 Feb 1935; *Educ* Univ of NZ (BCom, MCom), Harvard Univ (DBA), LSE (PhD), Univ of de Deusto Spain (MGCE), JDipMA; *m* 19 June 1960, Nancy Miriam, *née* Bunai; 2 s (John, Peter), 1 da (Jane); *Career* clerk Guardian Trust Company Wellington NZ 1950–53, asst co sec Gordon & Gotch Ltd Wellington 1953–55, chief accountant William Cable Ltd Wellington 1955–59; conslt: Arthur D Little Inc Cambridge Mass 1959–60, Harbridge House Inc Boston 1962–64; sr lectr Cranfield Inst of Tech 1963–64, asst prof of int business Indiana Univ Bloomington 1964–66, prof of mktg Univ of Manchester 1966–69, Ford Fndn prof of int business Univ of Chicago 1974–75, prof of mktg and int business London Grad Sch of Business 1969–, mktg advsr International Publishing Corporation 1967–78; dir: British Steel Corporation 1970–72, Redpath Dorman Long Ltd 1972–74, EMAP plc 1981–, MIL Research Group plc 1986–89, Aerostructures Hamble Ltd 1990–92; chm Planners Collaborative 1985–88; govr London Business Sch 1980–86, chm London Business Group 1988–91, chief ed International Journal of Advertising 1982–; memb: Textile Cncl UK 1968–70, Ctee Social Science Res Cncl UK 1971–72, Ctee CBI 1971–74, Electrical Engrg Econ Devpt Ctee UK 1982–86; fell: NZ Soc of Accountants, NZ Inst of Cost and Mgmnt Accountants, Acad of Int Business; FCIS, FCMA, FCIM; *Books* International Business and Multinational Enterprises (1973, 4 edn 1989), Case Problems in Marketing (1973), Strategy and Marketing (1982, 2 edn 1986), Short Cases in Marketing (1987); *Style*— Prof Kenneth Simmonds; ✉ London Business School, Regents Park, London NW1 4SA (☎ 0171 262 5050)

SIMMONDS, Nigel; s of John Desmond Simmonds, and Hazel May, *née* Bartlett; *b* 1 Aug 1962; *m* 19 July 1986, Louise Margaret, da of Anthony Kempton; *Career* Walker Crips Weddle Beck plc: joined as messenger 1979, dir 1990–; *Style*— Nigel Simmonds, Esq; ✉ Walker Crips Weddle Beck plc, Sophia House, 76–80 City Rd, London EC1Y 2BJ (☎ 0171 253 7502, fax 0171 253 7500)

SIMMONDS, Richard James; CBE (1996); s of Reginald A C Simmonds, and Betty, *née* Cahusac; sis Posy Simmonds the illustrator and cartoonist; *b* 1944; *m* 1967, Mary, *née* Stewart; 1 s, 2 da; *Career* nat vice chm Young Cons 1973–75, fndr vice chm Young Euro Democrats 1974; PA to Rt Hon Edward Heath, MBE, MP 1973–75, PPS to Sir James Scott-Hopkins as Ldr EDG 1979–82; MEP (EPP): Midlands West 1979–84, Wight and Hampshire East 1984–94; spokesman: Youth and Educn 1982–84, Budget Control 1984–87; Br whip 1987–89, chief whip 1992–94; chm The Countryside Cmmn 1995–;

memb Berkshire CC (chm 4 ctees) 1972–79; memb: Agric and Budget Control Ctees, Environment, Public Health & Consumer Protection Ctee; chm Bd of Govrs Berks Coll of Agric 1979–91, fndr pres Mounted Games Assoc 1984–, travelling fell Waitangi Fndn 1995–96, memb Cncl PDSA 1995–, pres-elect Jersey Cattle Soc 1996, fell Parl and Indust Tst (attached to Marks and Spencer and DuPont International); Liveryman Worshipful Co of Gunmakers; *Publications* The Common Agricultural Policy, A Sad Misnomer (1979), A to Z of Myths and Misunderstandings of EEC (1981, 1988 and 1992), World Hunger - The European Community's Response (1981), European Parliament Report on Farm Animal Welfare (1985, 1987 and 1990), The Production, Processing, Politics and Potential of New Zealand Meat (1996); *Recreations* resisting bureaucracy, getting things done; *Clubs* Carlton, Tamworth, Ancient Britons; *Style—* Richard Simmonds, Esq, CBE; ✉ Dyars, Cookham Dean, Berkshire SL6 9PJ

SIMMONDS, Stefan Marshall; s of late Paul Benjamin Simmonds, of Bradford, and Edna Margaret Simmonds; *b* 16 Aug 1945; *Educ* Bradford Tech Coll; *m* 1970, Shahnaz, da of late Col Ambass Sadeghian, of Tehran, Iran; 3 da (Shaeda, Samantha, Sara); *Career* chm: Drummond Group plc, Marshall Fairley Investments Ltd property devpt, mgmnt and investment co; *Style—* Stefan Simmonds, Esq; ✉ Drummond Group plc, Drummond House, PO Box 18, Lumb Lane Mills, Bradford, W Yorks BD8 7RP (☎ 01274 721435)

SIMMONS, His Honour Judge Alan Gerald; s of Maurice Simmons (d 1949), of Bedford, and Sophie, *née* Lasserson (d 1952); *b* 7 Sept 1936; *Educ* Bedford Modern and Quintin Sch; *m* 26 Nov 1961, Mia, da of Emanuel Rosenstein (d 1957), and Lisa, *née* Rinsler (d 1981); 1 s (Richard b 1964), 1 da (Joanne b 1966); *Career* Nat Serv RAF 1956–58; dir: Aslon Laboratories Ltd, Record Productions (Surrey) Ltd, Ashcourt Ltd; called to the Bar Gray's Inn 1968, Holker Sr Exhibition, Lee Essay Prize, recorder 1989 (asst recorder 1985), circuit judge (SE Circuit) 1990–; memb: Bd of Deps of Br Jews 1982–88, Mental Health Review Tbnl; former memb Cncl of United Synagogues; *Recreations* music, reading, fencing; *Style—* His Honour Judge Simmons; ✉ South Eastern Circuit Office, New Cavendish House, 18 Maltravers Street, London WC2R 3EU (☎ 0171 936 7235)

SIMMONS, Allan Frank; s of Michael Philip Simmons (d 1971), and Elda Dineen, *née* Malpas; *b* 7 June 1943; *Educ* Bournemouth Sch for Boys; *m* 9 Sept 1967, Elizabeth Ann, da of Edwin Waring Mathison; 2 s (Jonathan Michael Harman b 9 May 1973, Alexander Waring b 3 June 1975), 1 da (Katie Ann b 14 April 1980); *Career* Malpas Simmons (merged with Smith and Williamson CAs 1987): trainee 1959, ptnr 1969–; memb British Inst of Agricultural Consultants; FCCA (ACCA 1967); *Recreations* sailing, walking, reading; *Clubs* Poole Yacht; *Style—* Allan Simmons, Esq; ✉ Smith and Williamson, 21 Chipper Lane, Salisbury, Wilts SP1 1BG (☎ 01722 411881)

SIMMONS, Prof Ian G; s of Charles Frederick Simmons (d 1984), of Iver, Bucks, and Christina Mary, *née* Merrills; *b* 22 Jan 1937; *Educ* Slough GS, UCL (BSc, PhD); *m* 28 July 1962, Carol Mary, da of John Saunders (ka 1941), of Ealing, W London; 1 s (David b 1968), 1 da (Catherine b 1966); *Career* ACLS fell Univ of California Berkeley 1964–65, Churchill Meml fell 1971; prof: Univ of Bristol 1978–81, Univ of Durham 1981– (sr lectr 1970–76, reader 1976–78); Sir James Knott Fndn fell 1992–93; memb: Cncl for Nat Parks; Bergwanden medal Kirchberg Austria 1988; DLitt Dunelm 1990; FSA 1981, memb Academia Europaea 1994; *Books include* Biogeographical Processes (1982), Changing the Face of the Earth (1989, 2 edn 1996), British Prehistory: the Environment (jt ed, 1981), Earth Air and Water (1991), Interpreting Nature: Cultural Constructions of Environment (1993), Environmental History (1993), The Environmental Impact of Later Mesolithic Cultures (1996), Humanity and Environment: a Cultural Ecology (1996); *Recreations* all high culture except ballet; *Clubs* St Aidan's Coll SCR; *Style—* Prof I G Simmons, FSA; ✉ Science Laboratories, South Road, Durham DH1 3LE (☎ 0191 374 2464, fax 0191 374 2456, e-mail I.G.Simmons@durham.ac.uk)

SIMMONS, Marion Adèle; QC (1994); da of Sidney Simmons (d 1983), of London, and Bella, *née* Byer; *b* 11 April 1949; *Educ* Hendon County GS, Queen Mary Coll London (LLB, LLM); *Career* called to the Bar Gray's Inn 1970, asst recorder 1990–, Master of the Bench Gray's Inn 1993–; *Style—* Ms Marion Simmons, QC; ✉ 3–4 South Square, Gray's Inn, London WC1R 5HP (☎ 0171 696 9900, fax 0171 696 9911)

SIMMONS, Michael; s of Frederick Simmons, and Eveline Irene, *née* Jeffries; *b* 17 Oct 1935; *Educ* Scarborough Boys' HS, Univ of Manchester (BA); *m* 1963, Angela, da of Alec Thomson, and Sybil Thomson; 2 s (Stephen b 19 Oct 1967, Alastair b 12 Jan 1970); *Career* reporter Macclesfield Advertiser 1960–61, reporter and drama critic Newcastle upon Tyne Evening Chronicle 1961–62, reporter political staff Glasgow Herald 1962–67, E Europe corr Financial Times 1967–73; The Guardian: third world review ed 1977–81, E Europe ed 1986–90, community affrs corr 1993–95, society dep ed 1995–; *Books* Berlin: The Dispossessed City (1988), The Unloved Country: A Portrait of East Germany (1989), The Reluctant President: A Political Life of Vaclav Havel (1991); *Recreations* cricket, hill walking; *Clubs* Trinity Cricket; *Style—* Michael Simmons, Esq; ✉ The Guardian, 119 Farringdon Rd, London EC1R 3ER (☎ 0171 278 2332, fax 0171 239 9787)

SIMMONS, Air Marshal Sir Michael George; KCB (1989, CB 1988), AFC (1976); s of George Martin Simmons (d 1990), and Thelma Alice Cecilia, *née* Howie (d 1975); *b* 8 May 1937; *Educ* Shrewsbury, RAF Coll Cranwell; *m* 23 May 1964, Jean, da of Arthur Aliwell (d 1990); 2 da (Susan Jean (Mrs Christopher Vaughan) b 17 Nov 1965, Sally Ann b 22 March 1968); *Career* cmmnd 1958, 6 Sqdn Cyprus 1959–61, ADC to AOC-in-C FTC 1961–64, 39 Sqdn Malta 1964–67, 51 Sqdn Wyton 1967–69, RN Staff Coll 1970, MOD 1971–72, OC XV Sqdn Germany 1973–76, MOD 1976–79, OC RAF Cottesmore 1980–82, MOD 1982–84, SASO Headquarters Strike Cmd 1984–85, AOC 1 Gp RAF 1985–87, ACAS 1987–89, Dep Controller Aircraft MOD 1989–92; ADC to HM The Queen 1980–81; sec Cncl of Justice for Animals and Humane Slaughter Assoc 1992–, chief exec Universities Fedn for Animal Welfare 1993–; *Recreations* golf, horology, walking; *Clubs* RAF; *Style—* Air Marshal Sir Michael Simmons, KCB, AFC; ✉ c/o Council of Justice to Animals and Humane Slaughter Association, 34 Blanche Lane, South Mimms, Potters Bar, Herts EN6 3PA

SIMMONS, Dr Paul Douglas; s of Gordon Edward Frank Simmons (d 1976), and Joan Madeline, *née* Eade; *b* 4 Oct 1947; *Educ* Felixstowe GS, Univ of Leeds (MB ChB); *m* 4 Sept 1982, Ruth Danae, da of Rev Gp Capt Kenneth James Holt; *Career* hon conslt physician St Paul's Hosp London 1980–93; conslt physician: Leicester Royal Infirmary 1980–82, Bart's London 1982– (sr registrar 1976–80, hon lectr 1982–); hon conslt physician St Luke's Hosp for the Clergy 1986–; lately chm: Genito-urinary Regnl Advsy Ctee, NE Thames RHA; hon med consIt Soc of Health Advsrs in STD; Liveryman Worshipful Soc of Apothecaries; FRCP 1992 (MRCP 1976); *Recreations* gardening; *Style—* Dr Paul Simmons; ✉ St Bartholomew's Hospital, West Smithfield, London EC1A 7BE (☎ 0171 601 8090)

SIMMONS, Richard John; CBE (1995); s of John Eric Simmons, and Joy Mary, *née* Foat; *b* 2 June 1947; *Educ* Moseley GS Birmingham, LSE (BSc), Univ of California Berkeley Business Sch; *m* 23 April 1983, Veronica, da of Richard Sinkins; 1 s, 1 da; *Career* CA; asst sec to IASC 1973–75, currently UK sr audit ptnr Arthur Andersen; non-exec dir Cranfield Info Technol Inst 1987–89; memb Advsy Bd Royal Acad of Arts, hon treas Political Ctee Carlton Club; chm Bow Gp 1980–81; FCA 1971; *Recreations* horse racing, tennis, gardening; *Style—* Richard Simmons, Esq, CBE; ✉ Arthur Andersen, 1 Surrey St, London WC2R 2PS (☎ 0171 438 3302)

SIMMS, Alan John Gordon; s of Edward Gordon Clark, formerly Januszkiewiscz (d 1981), of Aigburth, Liverpool, and Hilda Mary, *née* Gordon; *b* 3 April 1954; *Educ* Liverpool Collegiate GS, Univ of London (LLB); *m* 2 Aug 1980, Julia Jane, da of Paul Ferguson, of Leintwardine, Shropshire; 1 s (Jack Edward Paul Januszkiewiscz b 28 Feb 1996), 1 da (Charlotte Jane Januszkiewiscz (twin)); *Career* called to the Bar Lincoln's Inn 1976; ad eundum Northern Circuit 1980–; memb Criminal Bar Assoc; sec Inst of Advanced Motorists 1986–88, chm ROSPA Chester (ROSPA Advanced Drivers Assoc Class One and Diploma holder), memb's rep Nat Exec Ctee Royal Soc of Prevention of Accidents, legal memb Mental Health Review Tbnl 1994–; memb: Br Motor Racing Marshals Club, Br Automobile Racing Club (Oulton Park), Hon Soc of Lincoln's Inn 1976, Br Acad of Forensic Sci 1978, Bar Assoc of Commerce Fin and Indust 1980, Br Psychological Soc 1994, Forensic Sci Soc 1995; *Recreations* reading, motor racing, motor racing marshalling, road safety, blues and jazz music, guitar playing, crime (theory only); *Style—* Alan Simms, Esq; ✉ Chavasse Court Chambers, 2nd Floor, Chavasse Court, 24 Lord St, Liverpool (☎ 0151 707 1191)

SIMMS, (Dr) Brendan Peter; s of David John Simms, of Dublin, and Anngret, *née* Erichson; *b* 3 Sept 1967; *Educ* St Kilian's German Sch Dublin, Heinrich-Hertz Gymnasium Bonn, Trinity Coll Dublin (scholar, Gold medal), Univ of Tübingen, Peterhouse Cambridge; *m* 3 Sept 1993, Anita Mary, da of Richard John Bunyan; *Career* res fell Christ Church Coll Oxford 1992–93, fell and dir of studies in history Peterhouse Cambridge 1993–; *Books* The Impact of Napoleon (1997), The Struggle for Mastery in Germany, 1780–1850 (1997); *Recreations* hill walking, football; *Style—* Brendan Simms; ✉ Peterhouse, Cambridge CB2 1RD (☎ 01223 338200)

SIMON, Sir David Alec Gwyn; kt (1995), CBE (1991); s of Roger A Simon (d 1993), of Shoreham, and Barbara, *née* Hudd; *Educ* Christ's Hosp, Gonville and Caius Coll Cambridge (MA), INSEAD (MBA); *m* 1, 1964 (m dis 1987), Hanne, *née* Mohn; 2 s; m 2, 1992, Sarah, *née* Smith; *Career* British Petroleum plc: mktg dir BP Oil UK 1980–82, md BP Oil International 1982–85, a gp md 1986–95, chief operating offr 1990–92, gp dep chm 1990–95, gp chief exec 1992–95, chm 1995–; memb Court of Bank of England 1995–; non-exec dir: Grand Metropolitan plc 1989–, The RTZ Corporation plc 1995– (non-exec dir CRA Ltd Dec 1995–); memb: Supervisory Bd Allianz AG 1996–, Int Cncl and UK Advsy Bd INSEAD, Advsy Cncl Deutsche Bank; Liveryman: Worshipful Co of Tallow Chandlers, Worshipful Co of Carmen; *Recreations* music, golf, reading; *Style—* Sir David Simon, CBE; ✉ The British Petroleum Company plc, Britannic House, 1 Finsbury Circus, London EC2M 7BA (☎ 0171 496 4000, fax 0171 496 4572)

SIMON, 3 Viscount (UK 1940); Jan David Simon; s of 2 Viscount Simon, CMG (d 1993), and (James) Christie, *née* Hunt; *b* 20 July 1940; *Educ* Westminster, Dept of Navigation Univ of Southampton, Sydney Tech Coll; *m* 26 April 1969, Mary Elizabeth, da of late John Joseph Burns (d 1966), of Sydney, NSW; 1 da (Fiona Elizabeth Christie b 1971); *Heir* none; *Career* MN 1958–68; nautical research 1968–70; Shipbroker 1970–82; former examiner Advanced Motorists Aust; Master Mariner; *Recreations* classical music, motor vehicles; *Clubs* Oriental; *Style—* The Viscount Simon; ✉ House of Lords, London SW1A 0PW

SIMON, Josette; da of Charles Simon, of Leicester, and Eileen, *née* Petty; *Educ* Alderman Newton's GS for Girls, Central Sch of Speech Training and Dramatic Art; *Career* actress; Hon MA Univ of Leicester (for services to the Arts) 1995; *Theatre* RSC: Macbeth, Antony and Cleopatra, Much Ado About Nothing, The Tempest, Peer Gynt, The Custom of the Country, The Merchant of Venice, Love's Labours Lost, Golden Girls, The Party, The War Plays, The Mystery of the Charity of Joan of Arc, Measure for Measure; RNT: The White Devil, After the Fall (Best Actress Evening Standard Drama Awards 1990, Plays and Players Awards 1990, Critics' Circle Awards 1991, London Theatre Awards 1991, Laurence Olivier Awards 1991); others incl Ibsen's The Lady from the Sea (Lyric Hammersmith) 1994, The Taming of the Shrew (Leicester Haymarket) 1995; concert performances: The Fairy Queen (with The Sixteen, conducted by Harry Christophers, Tel Aviv) 1994, King Arthur (with Les Arts Florrissante, conducted by William Christie, France) 1995; *Television* incl: Blake's Seven, The Squad, The Cuckoo Waltz, Pob's Programme, 123 Go, Umbrella, The Sharpeville Six, Somewhere to Run, Trumpet of a Prophesy, Here is the News, King, Tecx, The Dogs and Freedom, Thompson, The Pyrates, When Love Dies, Capital City, Runaways, Nice Town, Seekers, Henry IV, Bodyguards, Kavanagh QC; *Radio* incl: Goldoni's Mirandolina, Cromwell Mansions, Dictator Gal (nominated Prix Futura Award Berlin 1993), Gertrude Stein's Listen to Me, The Roads of Freedom, Sealed with a Kiss, Medea, Selections from the Old Testament, Something Understood, Poetry Please; *Films* incl: Dardanelle, Cry Freedom, Milk and Honey (Best Actress: Atlantic Film Festival Canada 1988, Paris Film Festival 1990; nominated Best Actress Canadian Acad Award 1989), A Child from the South, Bitter Harvest, Bridge of Time; *Recreations* learning French and Italian, playing the saxaphone, reading, cinema, music, travel, gardening, cooking; *Style—* Josette Simon; ✉ c/o Markham & Froggatt Ltd, Julian House, 4 Windmill Street, London W1P 1HF (☎ 0171 636 4412, fax 0171 637 5233)

SIMON, Hon Peregrine Charles Hugo; QC (1991); s (by 2 m) of Baron Simon of Glaisdale (Life Peer); *b* 1950; *Educ* Westminster Sch, Trinity Hall Cambridge (MA); *m* 1980, Francesca, da of Maj T W E Fortescue Hitchins, of Border Lodge, Brewham, Somerset; 2 s ((Alexander Edward) Orlando b 1986, Ferdinand William Hugo b 1989), 2 da (Polly Harriet Artemis b 1982, Lucy Persephone Frances b 1984); *Career* called to the Bar Middle Temple 1973, memb Midland & Oxford Circuit; *Style—* The Hon Peregrine Simon, QC; ✉ Midge Hall, Glaisdale, Whitby, N Yorks

SIMON, Peter Walter; s of Prof Walter Simon (d 1981), and Kate, *née* Jungmann (d 1984); *b* 25 Nov 1929; *Educ* Thames Valley Sch, LSE (BSc, PhD); *m* 1960, Sheila Rose, da of James Brimacombe (d 1985); 1 s (Nicholas b 1961), 1 da (Susannah b 1964); *Career* dir: Legal and General Group plc and subsids, Lion Holdings 1974–87, Victory Insurance Holdings 1984–87, The British Land Co plc 1987–, Concord Financial Advsrs UK Ltd 1987–88; vice chm Export Fin Co Ltd 1984–89; chm: Cogent Ltd 1984–88, Conrad Ritblat Residential Properties Ltd 1989–96; ACII; *Recreations* cricket, hockey, golf, bridge; *Clubs* MCC, East India Sports, Teddington Cricket, Teddington Hockey, Lord's Taverners; *Style—* Peter W Simon, Esq; ✉ 54 Ormond Ave, Hampton, Middlesex TW12 2RX (☎ 0181 979 2538)

SIMON, Robin John Hughes; s of Most Rev William Glyn Hughes Simon, Archbishop of Wales (d 1972), and Sarah Ellen (Sheila), *née* Roberts (d 1963); *b* 23 July 1947; *Educ* Cardiff HS, Univ of Exeter (BA), Courtauld Inst of Art (MA); *m* 1, 1971, Margaret, *née* Brooke; m 2, 1979, Joanna, *née* Ross; 1 s (Benet Glyn Hughes b 1974), 2 da (Alice Emily Hughes b 1976, Poppy Candida Hughes b 1991); *Career* univ lectr in history of art and English 1972–78, hist bldgs rep The Nat Tst 1979–80, dir Inst of Euro Studies London 1980–90, art critic The Daily Mail 1990– (arts corr 1987–90), ed Apollo magazine 1990–; selector: The Discerning Eye 1992, The Critics' Choice: New British Art 1993; visiting prof of history of art and architecture Westminster Coll 1989; memb: Ctee Courtauld Inst Assoc of Former Students 1991–, Cncl The Walpole Soc 1992–96, Advsy Cncl Paul Mellon Centre for Studies in British Art 1993–96, Exec Ctee Assoc of Art Historians 1993–96, Ctee of Honour Lord Leighton Centenary Tst 1994–96, The Johnson Club 1995–; Delmas fndn fell Venice 1978; *Books* The Art of Cricket (with Alastair Smart, 1983), The Portrait in Britain and America (1987); articles in various jls, papers and magazines; *Recreations* cricket (capt Poor Fred's XI), music; *Clubs* Garrick; *Style—* Robin

Simon, Esq; ✉ Apollo, 29 Chesham Place SW1X 8HB (☎ 0171 235 1676, fax 0171 235 1673)

SIMON, Roger; 2 Baron Simon of Wythenshawe (UK 1947), but does not use title; s of 1 Baron (d 1960); *b* 16 Oct 1913; *Educ* Gresham's, Gonville and Caius Cambridge; *m* 1951, (Anthea) Daphne, da of Sidney May; 1 s, 1 da (Margaret); *Heir* s, (Hon) Matthew Simon b 10 April 1955; *Style*— Roger Simon, Esq; ✉ Oakhill, Chester Av, Richmond, Surrey

SIMON OF GLAISDALE, Baron (Life Peer UK 1971), of Glaisdale, in N Riding, Yorks; Jocelyn Edward Salis Simon; kt (1959), PC (1961), DL (N Yorks 1973); s of Frank Cecil Simon, of 51 Belsize Park, London NW3; *b* 15 Jan 1911; *Educ* Gresham's Sch Holt, Trinity Hall Cambridge; *m* 1, 1934, Gwendolen Helen (d 1937), da of E J Evans; m 2, 1948, Fay Elizabeth Leicester, JP, da of Brig H Guy A Pearson, of Jersey; 3 s (Hon Peregrine Charles Hugo b 1950, Hon (Benedict) Mark Leicester b 1953, Hon (Dominic) Crispin Adam b 1958); *Career* called to the Bar 1934, KC 1951, MP (C) Middlesbrough W 1951–62, jt Parly under sec of state Home Office 1957–58, fin sec to the Treasy 1958–59, slr-gen 1959–62, pres Probate Divorce and Admty Div High Ct of Justice 1962–71, Lord of Appeal in Ordinary 1971–77, er bro Trinity House; hon LLD Univ of Cambridge, hon Docteur-en-Droit Laval Univ Quebec; *Style*— The Rt Hon the Lord Simon; ✉ House of Lords, London SW1A 0PW

SIMONDS-GOODING, Anthony James Joseph; s of Maj Hamilton Simonds-Gooding, of Buncar House, Dooks, Glenbeigh, Co Kerry, Eire, and Dorothy, *née* Reilly; *b* 10 Sept 1937; *Educ* Ampleforth, Britannia RNC Dartmouth; *m* 1, 1961, Fiona; 4 s (Rupert, Benedict, George, Harry d 1996), 2 da (Lucinda, Dominique); m 2, 8 July 1982, Marjorie Anne, da of William John Pennock (d 1987); 1 step s (Daniel Porter); *Career* RN 1953–59; Unilever 1960–73, Whitbread & Co plc 1973–85 (mktg dir, md, gp md), chm and chief exec all communication and advertising companies worldwide for Saatchi & Saatchi plc 1985–87, chief exec British Satellite Broadcasting 1987–90, chm Ammirati Puris Lintas Ltd (formerly S P Lintas) 1994–96; currently chm Design and Art Directors Assoc; non-exec dir: Robinson & Sons Ltd 1993–, Newell & Sorrell 1996–, Clark & Taylor 1996–, Community Hospitals plc; dir: Inst of Contemporary Art, Cancer Relief Macmillan Fund, Brixton Prison Board; *Recreations* family, opera, tennis, fishing, reading, painting, travelling, skiing; *Clubs* Hurlingham; *Style*— Anthony Simonds-Gooding, Esq; ✉ c/o Design and Art Directors Association, 85 Vauxhall Walk, London SE11 (☎ 0171 582 6487)

SIMONIS, Peter George; *b* 3 June 1926; *Educ* Cranleigh Sch; *m* 1956, Erica, da of Eric Marsden; 1 s, 1 da; *Career* Lt RNVR; dir Burmah Oil Co Ltd 1970–79, chm Haden plc 1979–87; dir: Ellerman Lines Ltd 1979–83, The Morgan Crucible Co plc 1983–96, Rowan Cos Inc (USA) 1985–, Gibraltar Shiprepair Ltd 1985–90, Haden MacLellan Holdings plc 1987–, Whessoe plc 1988–, Holt Lloyd Group Ltd 1995–, Jordec Group plc 1996–; chm: Br American Offshore Ltd, Teredo Petroleum plc 1990–93, Inspectorate plc 1992–; Liveryman Worshipful Co of Tallow Chandlers; *Clubs* Oriental; *Style*— Peter Simonis, Esq; ✉ British American Offshore Ltd, 79 Park Street, London W1 (☎ 0171 499 2957, fax 0171 409 2738)

SIMONS, Prof John Philip; s of Mark Isaac Simons (d 1973), of London, and Rose, *née* Pepper (d 1962); *b* 20 April 1934; *Educ* Haberdashers' Aske's, Sidney Sussex Coll Cambridge (BA, PhD, ScD); *m* 1, 1 Dec 1956, Althea Mary (d 1989), da of Robert Douglas Screaton (d 1988), of Nottingham; 3 s (Thomas John b 1960, Joseph Robert b 1962, Benjamin David b 1965); m 2, 25 Jan 1992, Mrs Elizabeth Ann Corps; *Career* Univ of Birmingham: ICI fell 1960, reader 1975, prof of photochemistry 1979–81; prof of physical chemistry Univ of Nottingham 1981–93, Dr Lee's prof of chemistry Univ of Oxford and fell Exeter Coll 1993–; memb: SERC Chemistry Laser Facility Ctees, NATO Sci Ctees; pres Faraday Div Royal Soc of Chemistry 1993–95; CChem, FRSC 1979, FRS 1989; *Books* Photochemistry and Spectroscopy (1970); *Recreations* verse; *Style*— Prof John Simons, FRS; ✉ Physical and Theoretical Chemistry Laboratory, University of Oxford, South Parks Road, Oxford OX1 3QZ (☎ 01865 275402, fax 01865 275410)

SIMONS, Jonquil Edwina; da of Jack Albert Simons (d 1996), of Brighton, and Rose Simons; *b* 3 March 1953; *Educ* Brighton & Hove HS for Girls GPDST; *m* 1990, Robert David Tracy, s of Arthur Herbert Tracy (d 1962); *Career* asst to Publicity Mangr Robert Hale & Co publishers 1971–72, publicity asst Evans Bros educnl publishers 1972–73, PR asst Sussex Police 1973–76, PRO Gardner Centre Theatre Sussex 1976–77, assoc dir Public Relations Counsel Ltd PR consultancy 1980–82 (account exec 1977–80), head of PR Alan Pascoe Associates Ltd 1982–84, freelance PR conslt 1984–88, ptnr The Matthews Simons Partnership 1988–93, princ The Simons Partnership 1993–; Inst of PR: chm London & SE Gp Ctee 1986 and 1987 (memb 1983–93, hon sec 1983–85), memb Cncl 1989, 1990 and 1991, memb Educn and Trg Ctee 1989–95, chm Student Devpt Working Pty 1993, judge Sword of Excellence 1992 and 1993, memb Fells Forum Working Pty 1996–; memb British MENSA; FIPR 1991 (MIPR 1981); *Recreations* theatre, canal and river cruising; *Style*— Ms Jonquil Simons; ✉ The Simons Partnership, 16 Marina Approach, West Quay Marina, Yeading, Middx UB4 9TB (☎ 0181 842 2078, fax 0181 842 3464, mobile 0860 466959)

SIMONS, (Alfred) Murray; CMG (1983); s of Louis Simons (d 1950), and Fay Simons (d 1996); *b* 9 Aug 1927; *Educ* City of London Sch, Magdalen Coll Oxford (MA), Columbia Univ NY; *m* 1975, Patricia Jill, da of David Murray Barclay (d 1959); 2 s (Julian b 1977, Jonathan b 1978); *Career* HM Dip Serv 1951–85; first sec: Office of Cmmr-Gen for SE Asia and Singapore 1958–61, Br High Cmmn New Delhi 1964–68; Br Embassy Washington 1971–75, head of SE Asia Dept FCO 1975–79, consul-gen Montreal 1980–82, ambass and head of UK Delgn (negotiations on mutual reduction of forces and armaments and assoc measures in Central Europe, at Vienna) 1982–85; pres John Carpenter Club 1993; Freeman City of London 1990; *Recreations* theatre, tennis; *Style*— Murray Simons, Esq, CMG; ✉ 128 Longland Drive, Totteridge, London N20 8HL (☎ 0181 446 3163)

SIMONS, Paul; s of Francis Simons (d 1964), and Kathleen, *née* Ruddy (d 1983); *b* 11 March 1948; *Educ* Bridley Moor HS, Kingston Poly, Univ of Lancaster (MA); *m* 1 (m dis), Lesley Bailey; 2 s (Neil b 27 Dec 1968, Nicholas b 6 Sept 1971); m 2, Ann, da of William Perry, of Long Ashton, Bristol; 1 s (Harry Jonathan b 27 Oct 1991 d 7 Jan 1993), 1 da (Kate b 7 Dec 1984); *Career* Cadbury Schweppes 1972–75 (asst product mangr, product mangr), gp product mangr Imperial Tobacco Foods 1975–76, mktg mangr United Biscuits 1976–78, Cogent Elliott 1978–84 (account dir, client serv dir); Gold Greenlees Trott 1984–88 (client serv dir, dep md, vice chm), chm and chief exec Simons Palmer Clemmow Johnson Ltd 1988–; chm: Manning Gottlieb Media Ltd, Maher Bird Associates Ltd; estab Harry Simons Tst to provide funds for res into Reyes Syndrome 1993; rock musician (guitar) 1963–67, played with several bands (started first band with late John Bonham of Led Zeppelin), released various unsuccessful records; MIPA, FInstD, fell Marketing Soc; author numerous articles; *Recreations* gym, sailing, concerts, travel; *Style*— Paul Simons, Esq; ✉ 3 The Gables, Vale of Health, Hampstead, London NW3 1AY (☎ 0171 794 8822); Simons Palmer Clemmow Johnson Ltd, 19–20 Noel St, London W1V 3PD (☎ 0171 287 4455, fax 0171 734 2658)

SIMONS, Susannah Catherine; da of Peter Simons, of Windsor, and Betty, *née* Edwards; *b* 19 April 1948; *Educ* Langley GS Berks, GSM; *m* 17 July 1976, Richard Percival Taylor, s of Percival Taylor; 1 s (Sebastian Richard b 29 Oct 1982), 1 da (Sarah Kate b 7 May 1980); *Career* TV and radio presenter; radio drama studio mangr BBC 1970–73 (BBC trainee 1969), prodr and presenter Capital Radio 1973; presenter: IRN 1975, Tonight (BBC) 1977, PM (BBC Radio) 1977, various BBC Radio 4 news and current affairs progs 1977–87 (The World at One, The World This Weekend, Radio 4 Budget Special, 1981 Royal Wedding, 1987 General Election, also The Jimmy Young Show on Radio 2 and The News Quiz), The Business Programme (Channel 4) 1986, Business Daily (Channel 4) 1987, Today (Radio 4), Answering Back (Channel 4) 1992, Classic FM 1992–, Around Westminster (BBC 2) 1993, TUC Conf coverage (BBC 2) 1995; dir Business Television 1990–92; tstee: Nat Youth Dance Tst, More House Sch; Variety Club Female Radio Personality of the Year 1984, Broadcasting Press Best Radio Prog 1992; AGSM, FRSA; *Recreations* reading, theatre, opera, walking, skiing, cooking; *Style*— Ms Susannah Simons; ✉ Classic FM, Academic House, 24–28 Oval Road, London NW1 (☎ 0171 284 3000)

SIMPKIN, Andrew Gordon; s of Ronald William Simpkin, of Menorca, and Garry, *née* Braidwood; *b* 31 March 1947; *Educ* Chethams Hosp Sch Manchester; *m* 9 Sept 1972, Gail Yvonne, da of John Hartley Turner, of Knutsford, Cheshire; 2 s (Robert Gordon b 1974, James William b 1976); *Career* slr; ptnr: Ogden & Simpkin 1973–78, Pannone & Partners 1978–; non-exec dir Trafford Park Estates plc 1986–; memb: Young Slrs' Gp Law Soc 1972–82, Equal Opportunities Cmmn 1986–91; *Recreations* mountaineering; *Clubs* Law Soc, St James's; *Style*— Andrew G Simpkin, Esq; ✉ Pannone & Partners, 41 Spring Gardens, Manchester M2 2BB (☎ 0161 832 3000, fax 0161 834 2067, telex 66817 2)

SIMPKIN, Dr Paul; s of Leslie Simpkin (d 1968), and Cynthia, *née* Wardle; *b* 17 Aug 1945; *Educ* Queen Elizabeth GS Wakefield, St Thomas's Hosp Med Sch London (scholar, MB BS); *m* 1980, Marie-Louise, da of Dr Albert Edward Meechan Sieger; 2 da (Arabella Louise b 1981, Victoria Lucy b 1983); *Career* hon clinical asst Chest Dept St Thomas's Hosp 1975–80 (jr med appts 1970–75); conslt staff physician: GLC 1975–86, ILEA 1975–90; consulting occupational health physician 1980–, med advsr London Residuary Body 1986–93, md Medicine At Work Ltd 1989–; med advsr to numerous cos, professional instns and local govt authorities; MRCP (UK) 1974, AFOM 1982; *Style*— Dr Paul Simpkin; ✉ 2 Upper Wimpole Street, London W1M 7TD (☎ 0171 935 5614)

SIMPSON, His Hon Judge; Alan; s of William Henry Simpson (d 1994), of Blackpool, and Gladys, *née* Locke (d 1973); *b* 17 April 1937; *Educ* Leeds GS, CCC Oxford (MA); *m* 20 Nov 1965, Maureen, da of John Patrick O'Shea; 1 da (Sheenagh b 2 Feb 1967), 1 s (Matthew b 1 Oct 1968); *Career* called to the Bar Inner Temple 1962 (scholar), recorder of the Crown Court 1975–85, circuit judge (NE Circuit) 1985–; *Recreations* sport, especially cricket, football, boxing (admin steward BBBC), reading, music; *Style*— His Hon Judge Simpson; ✉ Leeds Combined Court Centre, Oxford Row, Leeds LS1 3BG

SIMPSON, Alan; MP (Lab) Nottingham South (majority 3,181); s of Reg Simpson, and Marjorie Simpson; *b* 20 Sept 1948; *Educ* Bootle GS, Nottingham Poly (BScEcon); *children* 1 da, 2 s; *Career* pres Nottingham Poly Students' Union 1969–70, asst gen sec Nottingham Cncl of Voluntary Serv 1970–74 (estab Home Office pilot project for non-custodial treatment of young offenders 1971), community worker on anti-vandalism project 1974–78, res and info offr Nottingham Racial Equality Cncl 1979–92, MP (Lab) Nottingham South 1992–; cncllr Notts CC 1985–93; sec Socialist Campaign Gp of Labour MPs 1994–; memb UNISON; author of various books and articles on community development, housing, employment, policing policies, Europe and racism; *Recreations* sport, vegetarian cooking, music, reading; *Style*— Alan Simpson, Esq, MP; ✉ House of Commons, London SW1A 0AA

SIMPSON, Alan Francis; s of Francis Simpson (d 1947), and Lilian, *née* Ellwood (d 1988); *b* 27 Nov 1929; *Educ* Mitcham GS; *m* 1958, Kathleen (d 1978), da of George Phillips (d 1975); *Career* author and scriptwriter 1951– (in collaboration with Ray Galton, *qv*); *Theatre* incl: Way out in Piccadilly 1966, The Wind in the Sassafras Trees 1968, Albert och Herbert (Sweden) 1981; *Television* incl: Hancock's Half Hour 1954–61, Comedy Playhouse 1962–63, Steptoe and Son 1962–74, Galton and Simpson Comedy 1969, Clochmerle 1971, Casanova 1974, Dawson's Weekly 1975, The Galton and Simpson Playhouse 1976, Camilo e Filho (Portugal Steptoe) 1995, Paul Merton In Galton & Simpson's... (series) 1996; *Radio* with Ray Galton: Hancock's Half Hour 1954–59, Steptoe and Son 1966–73, The Frankie Howerd Show, Back with Braden; *Films* incl: The Rebel 1960, The Bargee 1963, The Wrong Arm of the Law 1963, The Spy with a Cold Nose 1966, Loot 1969, Steptoe and Son 1971, Den Siste Fleksnes (Norway) 1974; *Awards* incl: Scriptwriters of the Year (Guild of TV Prodrs and Dirs) 1959, Best TV Comedy Series (Steptoe and Son, Screenwriters Guild) 1962/3/4/5, John Logie Baird Award 1964, Best Comedy Series (Steptoe and Son, Dutch TV) 1966, Best Comedy Screenplay (Screenwriters Guild) 1972; *Books* with Ray Galton: Hancock (1961), Steptoe and Son (1963), The Reunion and Other Plays (1966), Hancock Scripts (1974), The Best of Hancock (1986), Hancock - The Classic Years (1987), The Best of Steptoe and Son (1988); *Recreations* gastronomy, football, travelling, after dinner speaking; *Clubs* Hampton Football (pres); *Style*— Alan Simpson, Esq; ✉ c/o Tessa Le Bars Management, 54 Birchwood Road, Petts Wood, Kent BR5 1NZ (☎ and fax 01689 837084)

SIMPSON, Alasdair John; s of James White Simpson (d 1987), and Joan Margaret, *née* Ebsworth (d 1997); *b* 10 March 1943; *Educ* Queen Elizabeth GS Carmarthen, Univ of London (LLB); *m* 11 March 1966, (Judith) Jane, da of Sidney Zebulin Manches, of St John's Wood, London; 1 s (Thomas), 2 da (Emily, Sarah); *Career* admitted slr 1967; sr ptnr Manches & Co 1981– (asst slr 1967, ptnr 1968); memb The Law Soc 1967; *Recreations* tennis, thoroughbreds, claret and Provence; *Clubs* RAC, Turf; *Style*— Alasdair Simpson, Esq; ✉ Flat 9, 33 Knightsbridge, London SW1X 7NL (☎ 0171 838 9706); Messrs Manches & Co, Aldwych House, 81 Aldwych, London WC2B 4RP (☎ 0171 404 4433, fax 0171 430 1133, car 0836 271586)

SIMPSON, Anthony Maurice Herbert; TD (1973); s of Lt-Col M R Simpson, OBE, TD, DL (d 1981), and Renée Claire Lafitte (d 1973), of Leicester; *b* 28 Oct 1935; *Educ* Rugby, Magdalene Coll Cambridge (MA, LLM); *m* 1961, Penelope Gillian, da of Howard Dixon Spackman (d 1965), of Swindon; 1 s, 2 da; *Career* serv TA 1960–73, Maj 1968; called to the Bar Inner Temple 1961; MEP (C) Northamptonshire 1979–94; memb Euro Cmmn Legal Serv 1975–79, quaestor of Euro Parl 1979–87 and 1989–94, inspr Euro Cmmn 1994–; *Recreations* walking, travelling; *Style*— Anthony Simpson, Esq, TD; ✉ Bassets, Great Glen, Leics LE8 9GQ (☎ 0116 259 2386)

SIMPSON, Brian; MEP (Lab) Cheshire E (majority 39,279); s of John Hartley Simpson (d 1991), of Golborne, Lancashire, and Freda, *née* Mort; *b* 6 Feb 1953; *Educ* Golborne Comp Sch Wigan, West Midlands Coll of Educn Walsall (Cert Ed); *m* 2 Aug 1975, Linda Jane, da of late Harold Gwynn; 1 s (Mark Bevan b 22 Dec 1981), 2 da (Rachel Anne b 21 July 1979, Bethan Victoria b 30 May 1989); *Career* memb Merseyside Police Authy 1981–86, dep chm Liverpool Airport 1981–86; rep: Liverpool Speke Ward Merseyside CC 1981–86, Penketh and Cuerdley Ward Warrington Borough Cncl 1987–91 (dep chm of fin 1987–89); MEP (Lab) Cheshire East 1989–; memb: Br Southern Slav Assoc, Gt Central Steam Railway Loughborough, E Lancs Railway Bury, League Against Cruel Sports; life govr RNLI; life memb Assoc of Independent and Railway Preservation Socs; *Recreations* rugby league, cricket, steam railways; *Clubs* Golborne Sports and Social (Golborne Wigan, life memb), Lancs CCC; *Style*— Brian Simpson, Esq, MEP; ✉ Gilbert Wakefield House, 67 Bewsey Street, Warrington WA2 7JQ (☎ 01925 654074)

SIMPSON, Air Cdre Charles Hunting; CBE (1961); s of John Andrew Simpson (d 1936, Maj Calcutta Light Horse), of Elmdon, IOW, and Winifred Elizabeth Louise, *née* Hunting (d 1952); *b* 11 Feb 1915; *Educ* Oundle, Pembroke Coll Cambridge (MA); *m* 1945, Beatrice Gillian Patricia, da of Capt Arthur Noel Vernon Hill-Lowe (d 1964), of Court of Hill, Shrops; 2 da; *Career* joined RAF 1937, Bomber and Flying Trg Cmds 1939–45, Air Attaché Stockholm 1946–48, Cdr Univ of Cambridge Air Sqdn 1948–50, Staff Coll 1951,

Air Staff Policy 1951–53, dep dir Air Intelligence 1953–54, Asst Cmdt RAF Staff Coll Andover 1954–58, Gp Capt 1954, Cdr RAF E Africa 1958–61, ret 1961 with rank of Air Cdre; Freeman City of London, Liveryman Worshipful Co of Gunmakers; FRMets, FBIS, FRAeS; *Recreations* yachting, racing, pottery; *Clubs* Royal Yacht Squadron, Boodle's, RAF; *Style*— Air Cdre Charles Simpson, CBE; ✉ Fugelmere Grange, Fulmer, Slough, Bucks SL3 6HN (☎ 01753 662051)

SIMPSON, Christopher Liddon; s of ffreebairn Liddon Simpson, of South Kensington, London, and Dorina, *née* Ilieva (d 1991); *b* 5 Aug 1952; *Educ* St Edmund's Sch, Ealing Sch of Art and Photography; *m* 3 Dec 1988, Sophie Louise, da of David Alexander Caruth; 2 s (Jack Liddon b 22 Jan 1992, Fergus Alexander b 14 April 1995); *Career* photographer; early career experience working as student observer Vogue Studios London, stills photographer for French series Paul et Virginie and travel photographer for English Vogue and Mauritius Govt Tourist Office 1973; worldwide fashion and beauty photographer 1974–91: based London 1974–79, based Paris (working for French mags incl Elle, L'Officiel, Marie France, etc) 1979–84, based Sydney (working for mags incl Australian Vogue and Studio International) 1984, based London (with various exhbns incl Chelsea Arts Club, Special Photographers Gallery, Hamiltons, Woods Gallery, Assoc of Photographers) 1985–91; advtg, landscape, portrait, motor and location photographer 1991–; Freeman: City of London 1985, Worshipful Co of Skinners 1985; memb: Assoc of Photographers 1974, RPS 1991; *Awards* winner various awards in Fashion & Beauty, Landscape and Portrait categories Assoc of Photographers (formerly AFAEP) 1986–; *Recreations* scuba diving, swimming, fishing, gardening; *Clubs* Chelsea Arts, Grand Bay Yacht (Mauritius); *Style*— Christopher Simpson, Esq; ✉ Chris Simpson & Associates, 2 Felden Street, London SW6 5AF (☎ 0171 371 9244, fax 0171 731 7917)

SIMPSON, David; s of David Donald Simpson, of Dundee, and Elizabeth, *née* McGaw; *b* 9 Aug 1949; *Educ* Morgan Acad Dundee, Univ of Aderdeen; *Career* business mangr publication Univ of Aberdeen 1973–74, dep ed Accountancy Age 1974–76, journalist Sunday Express 1976–79, city correspondent The Guardian 1979–86 (also business correspondent), industl ed and dep ed business news The Observer 1986–88, dir Dewe Rogerson Ltd 1988–95 (latterly head of PR), chief exec Ludgate Communications Ltd 1995–, chm Ludgate Design Ltd 1995–, dir Ludgate Asia; *Style*— David Simpson, Esq; ✉ Ludgate Communications Ltd, 111 Charterhouse Street, London EC1M 6AA (☎ 0171 253 2252)

SIMPSON, Prof David Ian Hewitt; s of Harold George Simpson, of Belfast, and Helena, *née* Hewitt; *b* 4 Jan 1935; *Educ* Campbell Coll Belfast, The Queen's Univ of Belfast (MB BCh, BAO, MD); *m* 28 July 1960, Cintra Marguerite, da of Donald Sidney Caldwell (d 1970); 3 s (Andrew b 1962, Gawain b 1965, Jonathan b 1966), 1 da (Alexandra b 1964); *Career* med res offr: East African Virus Res Inst Entebbe Uganda 1962–65, Microbiological Res Estab 1966–71, MRC Laboratory Kisumu Kenya 1971–73; sr lectr and conslt London Sch of Hygiene and Tropical Medicine 1973–78, conslt and dir PHLS Special Pathogens Laboratory CAMR Porton 1978–83, prof of microbiology The Queen's Univ of Belfast 1983–; memb various govt and MRC ctees; FRCPath 1983; contrib to various textbooks; *Style*— Prof David Simpson; ✉ Fallow Hill, 129 Ballylesson Road, Belfast BT8 8JU (☎ 01232 826300); Department of Microbiology & Immunobiology, The Queen's University of Belfast, Grosvenor Road, Belfast BT12 6BA (☎ 01232 240503)

SIMPSON, David Macdonald; s of James Simpson (d 1990), of Perth, and Helen Macdonald, *née* Butters; *b* 25 May 1941; *Educ* Fettes, ChCh Oxford (MA); *m* Elizabeth Cochran, da of James Cochran Hamilton (d 1987), of Paisley; 1 s (Andrew b 1971), 1 da (Shona b 1974); *Career* gen mangr and sec Standard Life Assurance Co 1994–96 (investmt mangr 1973–88, gen mangr (investment) 1988–94); hon sec Faculty of Actuaries; FFA 1966; *Recreations* golf, curling, hill walking, skiing; *Clubs* Elie Golf House, Bruntsfield Links GS, Honourable Company of Edinburgh Golfers; *Style*— David Simpson, Esq; ✉ 6 Cumlodden Avenue, Edinburgh EH12 6DR (☎ 0131 337 3641)

SIMPSON, David Martin Wynn; s of William Wynn Simpson, OBE (d 1987), of Northwood, and Winifred Marjorie, *née* Povey, of Bristol; *b* 31 Jan 1938; *Educ* Queen's Coll Taunton, Christ's Coll Cambridge (MA); *m* 6 Dec 1968, Susan Katharine, da of Robert Windsor, of Steyning; 4 da (Amanda b 1964, Phillippa b 1966, Vanessa b 1970, Fiona b 1971); *Career* slr, sr ptnr Trump & Ptnrs 1968, chm Legal Aid Ctee 1987, pres Bristol Law Soc 1989; chm Wrington Div Gen Cmmrs of Taxes 1986; pt/t chm Industrial Tribunals, pt/t immigration adjudicator; MIMgt, FCIArb, FInstD, MIPA; *Recreations* flying, gardening, swimming; *Style*— David Simpson, Esq; ✉ The Post House, Burrington, Bristol BS18 7AA (☎ 01761 462664); Trump & Partners, 34 St Nicholas Street, Bristol BS1 1TS (☎ 0117 929 9901, fax 0117 929 8232)

SIMPSON, Prof David Rae Fisher; s of David E Simpson (d 1986), and Roberta Muriel, *née* Wilson (d 1995); *b* 29 Nov 1936; *Educ* Gordonstoun, Univ of Edinburgh (MA), Harvard (PhD); *m* 1 March 1980, Barbara Dianne Goalen, da of Norward James Inglis, and Gladys Elliot Inglis; 1 s (Fergus Rae Goalen b 1981), 1 step s (Donald Mclean b 1967), 1 step da (Jacqueline Barbara b 1966); *Career* instr in economics Harvard Univ 1963–64, assoc statistician UN Headquarters New York 1964–65, lectr in political economy UCL 1967–69, prof of economics Univ of Strathclyde 1975–89, dir The Fraser of Allander Inst Univ of Strathclyde 1975–80, economic advsr Standard Life Assurance Co 1989–; *Books* Problems of Input-Output Tables and Analysis (1966), General Equilibrium Analysis (1975), The Political Economy of Growth (1983), The Challenge of New Technology (1988), The End of Macroeconomics (1994); *Recreations* reading, walking, swimming; *Style*— Prof David Simpson; ✉ Standard Life, 30 Lothian Road, Edinburgh EH1 1YD (☎ 0131 245 0813, fax 0131 245 2198)

SIMPSON, David Richard Salisbury; OBE (1989); s of late Richard Salisbury Simpson, and Joan Margaret, *née* Braund; *b* 1 Oct 1945; *Educ* Merchiston Castle Sch Edinburgh; *Career* VSO teacher W Pakistan 1963–64; CA; joined Peat Marwick Mitchell & Co 1964–72, Scottish dir Shelter (Campaign for the Homeless) 1972–74; dir: Amnesty Int (Br Section) 1974–79, Action on Smoking and Health (ASH) 1979–90; fndr and dir International Agency on Tobacco and Health 1991–; Hon MFPHM 1991; *Recreations* reading, music, hill-walking, Orkney; *Style*— David Simpson, Esq, OBE; ✉ 24 Highbury Crescent, London N5 1RX (☎ 0171 359 7568)

SIMPSON, Dorothy; *née* Preece; *b* 20 June 1933; *Educ* Bridgend GS for Girls Glamorgan, Univ of Bristol (BA, Teaching Dip); *m* 1961, Keith Taylor Simpson; 2 s, 1 da; *Career* French and Eng teacher: Dartford GS for Girls 1955–59, Erith GS 1959–61; Eng teacher Senacre Sch Maidstone 1961–62, marriage guidance cnsllr 1969–82; author; memb: Soc of Authors, CWA of GB, Mystery Writers of America; *Novels* Harbingers of Fear (1977); with series character Detective Inspector Luke Thanet: The Night She Died (1981), Six Feet Under (1982), Puppet for a Corpse (1983), Close Her Eyes (1984), Last Seen Alive (1985, Silver Dagger award CWA), Dead on Arrival (1986), Element of Doubt (1987), Suspicious Death (1988), Dead by Morning (1989), Doomed to Die (1991), Wake the Dead (1992), No Laughing Matter (1993), A Day for Dying (1995); *Uncollected Short Stories* The Wisp of Sound (Ellery Queen's Mystery Magazine, Nov 1977), The Sanctuary (Alfred Hitchcock's Mystery Magazine, April 1978), Boxes within Boxes (Ellery Queen's Mystery Magazine, March 1980), Two's Company (John Creasey's Crime Collection, 1984), The Person Inside (Ellery Queen's Mystery Magazine, April 1987), A Man in a Million (Ellery Queen's Mystery Magazine, Dec 1995); *Collected Short Stories* Just Deserts (in A Dead Giveaway, collected crime stories, 1995); *Recreations* reading, gardening, painting; *Style*— Ms Dorothy Simpson; ✉ c/o Peter Robinson, Curtis Brown, 4th Floor, Haymarket House, 28–29 Haymarket, London SW1Y 4SP (☎ 0171 396 6600)

SIMPSON, Air Vice-Marshal (Charles) Ednam; s of Charles Walker Clark Simpson (d 1970), of Stirling, and Margaret Gourlay, *née* Doig (d 1970); *b* 24 Sept 1929; *Educ* Stirling HS, Falkirk HS, Univ of Glasgow (MB ChB), Univ of London (MSc); *m* 2 May 1955, Margaret Riddell, da of (Robert) Wallace Hunter (d 1981), of Glasgow; 2 s (David b 1956, Ian b 1957), 1 da (Fiona b 1960); *Career* joined RAF 1955, Staff Offr (aviation med) Br Def Staff Washington DC 1975, dep dir health and res RAF 1979; offr cmdg RAF hosps: Wegberg 1981, Princess Alexandra Hosp Wroughton 1982; dir health and res RAF 1984, asst surgn-gen (environmental health and res) 1985, princ MO RAF Strike Cmd 1986–88; dir RAF Benevolent Fund (Scotland) 1989–94; HM Cmmr Queen Victoria Sch Dunblane 1990–; QHS 1984–89; MFCM, FFOM; *Recreations* golf, bird-watching; *Clubs* RAF; *Style*— Air Vice-Marshal Ednam Simpson; ✉ Am Bruach, Kippen, Stirling FK8 3DT (☎ 01786 870281)

SIMPSON, George; s of William Simpson (d 1979), of Dundee, Scotland, and Eliza Jane, *née* Wilkie (d 1982); *b* 2 July 1942; *Educ* Morgan Acad Dundee, Dundee Inst of Technol (Dip in Business Admin); *m* 5 Sept 1963, Eva, da of William Chalmers, of Dundee; 1 s (George Anthony b 22 Feb 1965), 1 da (Gillian b 23 Oct 1966); *Career* sr accountant Scottish Gas 1964–68, sr fin position British Leyland 1969–77, fin dir Leyland Truck & Bus Ltd 1978–79; md: Coventry Climax 1980–82, Freight Rover 1983–85, Rover Group Commercial Vehicles 1986–87; chief exec Leyland DAF 1987–88, chm and chief exec Rover Group PLC 1989–92, memb Supervisory Bd DAF NV 1989–94, chm Rover Group and dep chief exec British Aerospace plc (parent co) 1992–94, chief exec Lucas Industries plc 1994–96, md GEC plc 1996–; non-exec dir: ICI plc 1995–, Pilkington plc 1992–, NW Venture Capital Fund Ltd; pres SMMT 1995– (formerly vice pres), pres West Midlands Development Agency 1993–, vice pres Inst of the Motor Indust; industl prof Univ of Warwick 1991–, memb Govt's Advsy Ctee on Business and Environment 1991–93; memb Senate Engrg Cncl; FCCA, ACIS, FIMI, FCIT, FRSA; *Recreations* golf; *Clubs* Royal Birkdale Golf, Wisley Golf, Leamington and County Golf; *Style*— George Simpson, Esq; ✉ General Electric Company plc, 1 Stanhope Gate, London W1A 1EH (☎ 0171 493 8484, fax 0171 493 1974)

SIMPSON, Dr Graeme Kenneth; s of late Kenneth Caird Simpson, of Grangemouth, Stirlingshire, and Edna Muriel, *née* Graham; *b* 25 Sept 1956; *Educ* Grangemouth HS, Univ of Edinburgh Med Sch (BSc, MB ChB); *m* 6 May 1978, Jacqueline Sara, da of late Andrew Auchterlonie, of Edinburgh; 1 s (David Malcolm b 1978), 2 da (Elspeth Margaret b 1981, Patricia Hannah b 1984); *Career* sr house offr Med Renal Unit Royal Infirmary Edinburgh 1981–82 and Med Unit Roodlands Hosp Haddington 1982–83 (house surgn 1981), registrar in med Eastern Gen Hosp Edinburgh 1983–86 (house physician 1980–81), sr registrar in gen and geriatric med Newcastle upon Tyne 1986–89, consl t physician and clinical dir geriatric med Royal Alexandra Hosp Paisley 1989–; memb: Collegiate Membs Ctee RCP 1985–89 (chm and memb College Cncl 1988–89), Br Geriatric Soc; life memb Royal Med Soc; MRCP 1983, FRCPE 1995; *Books* contrib Body Weight Control (1988); *Recreations* golf, swimming, carpet making; *Style*— Dr Graeme Simpson; ✉ Weybridge, 18 Stanely Drive, Paisley, Strathclyde; Royal Alexandra Hosp, Paisley, Strathclyde

SIMPSON, Graham; s of Geoffrey Albert Simpson, of Grays, Essex, and Sarah Elizabeth, *née* Thompson; *b* 5 Sept 1951; *Educ* Torells Boys' Sch, Univ of S California, Architectual Assoc Sch of Architecture (AADipl), Univ of Westminster (RIBA); *m* 16 Aug 1980 (m dis 1990); 1 s (Bertram Rupert Oscar), 1 da (Chloë March Louise); *Career* architect; CZWG 1987–90 (projects: The Circle London SE1 apartments, houses, business units, shops and courtyards), Prince Turki Abdullah Abdulrahman 1991–95 (projects: private residences in Riyadh and Sydney), Sir Norman Foster and Partners 1995– (projects: Al Faisaliah Centre, Riyadh hotel, apartments, office, banquet hall and retail centre); RIBA; *Recreations* cricket, skiing; *Clubs* Middx CCC; *Style*— Graham Simpson, Esq; ✉ 45 Anstice Close, Chiswick, London W4 2RL (☎ 0181 747 1720); PO Box 352, Riyadh 11411, Saudi Arabia (office ☎ 00 966 1 462 3508, home ☎ 00 966 1 465 7778 ext 25, home fax 00 966 465 7541)

SIMPSON, Harry Arthur (aka Camp-Simpson); AE; s of Cyril Simpson (d 1950), of Ferndown, Dorset, and Nellie, *née* Buckley (d 1967); *b* 16 Dec 1914; *Educ* Moseley GS Warwicks; *m* 1, 10 July 1943 (m dis 1983), Lilian Jackson, *née* Macdonald; 1 s (Roger Graham b 13 Feb 1948, d 1974), 2 da (Dianne Gail b 13 March 1945, Julie Jackson b 11 Dec 1956); m 2, 9 May 1984, Deborah Jane, da of Philip J Camp, of Bookham, Surrey; *Career* Nat Serv WWII RAF, specialist 'N' Symbol Award 1942, Pilot Gen Duties, Sqdn Ldr; contract Bakelite Ltd 1930–39; fndr chm and chief exec Flexible Abrasives Ltd 1947–65, dir John Oakey & Sons Ltd 1963–65, fndr chm and chief exec Arrow Abrasives Ltd 1966–93, sr ptnr Scart Associates International 1994–; FRMetS, FInstD; *Recreations* yachting, golf, fishing; *Clubs* Royal Thames Yacht, RAC, RAF; *Style*— Harry Simpson, Esq, AE; ✉ Little Langley Farm, Langley, Liss, W Sussex GU33 7JW (☎ 01730 892142); Scart Associates International (fax 01730 895797, mobile 0468 903804)

SIMPSON, Prof Hugh Walter; s of Rev Ian Simpson (d 1976), and Dr Elenora Simpson, *née* Howie (d 1989); *b* 4 April 1931; *Educ* Bryanston, Univ of Edinburgh (MB ChB, MD), Univ of Glasgow (PhD); *m* 21 March 1959, Myrtle Lilias, da of Maj H Emslie; 3 s (Lt-Col Robin Gordon b 5 Jan 1960, Bruce Brian b 7 Feb 1961, Rory Drummond b 13 Jan 1968), 1 da (Rona O'Clanise b 17 June 1962); *Career* med offr Br Antarctic Survey Hope Bay 1955–58, leader of many scientific expeditions to polar regns, pathologist then prof and head of div Glasgow Royal Infirmary and Univ of Glasgow 1959–93, sr res fell Univ of Glasgow and Dept of Surgery Royal Infirmary 1993–; inventor of Chronobra for detection of breast pre-cancer risk; author of over 150 scientific pubns; chm Ethical Ctee; Polar medal 1964, Mungo Park medal 1970, J Y Simpson medal lecture RCS Edinburgh 1995; FRCPath, FRCP; *Recreations* skiing; *Style*— Prof Hugh Simpson; ✉ 7 Cleveden Crescent, Glasgow G12 0PD (☎ 0141 357 1091); Farleitter, Kincraig, Inverness-shire PH21 1NU (☎ 01540 651 288); University Department of Surgery, Glasgow Royal Infirmary, Glasgow G4 OSF (☎ and fax 0141 357 1091)

SIMPSON, Ian; s of Herbert William Simpson (d 1972), of Sunderland, Co Durham, and Elsie, *née* Jagger (d 1991); *b* 12 Nov 1933; *Educ* Bede GS Sunderland, Sunderland Coll of Art, RCA; *m* 26 July 1958 (m dis 1982), Joan, da of Donald Charlton (d 1958), of Sunderland; 2 s (Robert b 2 Sept 1962, Howard b 13 Feb 1964), 1 da (Katharine b 8 March 1967); m 2, 26 March 1982, Birgitta, da of Yngve Brädde (d 1976), of Björketorp, Sweden; *Career* Nat Serv RAF 1953–55; head Dept of Co-ordinated Studies Hornsey Coll of Art 1969–72 (head Dept of Visual Res 1967–69), visiting prof Syracuse Univ NY 1977, head St Martin's Sch of Art 1986–88 (princ 1972–86), asst rector London Inst 1986–88, conslt Open Coll of the Arts, freelance artist and writer 1988–; one man exhibitions: Cambridge 1975, Durham 1977, Hambledon Gallery Blandford 1985, Chappel Galleries Essex 1994; broadcast wrote and presented: Eyeline 1968, Picture Making 1973, Reading the Signs 1976; chm Fine Art Bd CNAA 1976–81 (memb Cncl 1974–80), conslt Leisure Study Gp 1986–87; ARCA 1958, FSAE 1976, FRSA 1983; *Books* Eyeline (1968), Drawing Seeing and Observation (1973), Picture Making (1973), Guide to Painting and Composition (1979), Painters Progress (1983), An Encyclopaedia of Drawing Techniques (1987), A Course in Painting (1988), The Challenge of Landscape Painting (1990), The New Guide to Illustration (ed, 1990), Anatomy of Humans (1991), Collins Complete Painting Course (1993), Collins Complete Drawing Course (1994); *Recreations* reading, music; *Style*— Ian Simpson, Esq; ✉ Motts Farm House, Chilton St, Clare, Sudbury, Suffolk CO10 8QS (☎ 01787 277835)

SIMPSON, Sheriff Ian Christopher; s of Maj David Francis Simpson, WS (d 1994), of St Andrews, and Joss, *née* Dickie (d 1975); *b* 5 July 1949; *Educ* Trinity Coll Glenalmond, Univ of Edinburgh (LLB); *m* 7 Aug 1973, (Christine Margaret) Anne, da of Duncan D Strang, of Crieff; 2 s (Richard David b 1977, Graham Mark b 1979); *Career* appointed Sheriff of S Strathclyde Dumfries and Galloway (floating) 1988, Sheriff at Airdrie 1991–; memb Faculty of Advocates 1974; *Recreations* golf; *Clubs* Royal and Ancient, Dunbar Golf; *Style*— Sheriff Ian Simpson; ✉ 30 Cluny Drive, Edinburgh, Scotland EH10 6DP (☎ 0131 447 3363); Airdrie Sheriff Court, Sheriff Court House, Graham Street, Airdrie

SIMPSON, James; s of William Watson Simpson, of N Baddesley, Southampton, Hants, and Beatrice Hilda, *née* Dixon; *b* 16 April 1944; *Educ* Barton Peveril GS Eastleigh Hants, Univ of London (LLB); *m* 28 Dec 1968 (m dis 1982), Patricia Vivian (Tricia), da of Michael Joseph Sheridan, of Southampton; 1 s (Toby b 1973), 1 da (Charlotte b 1975); *Career* RNR 1965, cmmnd Sub Lt 1966, Lt 1969, resigned cmmn 1974; admitted slr 1969, asst litigation slr Coffin Mew & Clover Southampton 1969–70, prosecuting slr Hants CC Portsmouth 1970–72; Brutton & Co Fareham: asst slr 1972–73, ptnr 1973–87, sr ptnr 1987–89; dep High and Co Ct registrar 1978–89; called to the Bar Middle Temple 1990; hon sec Hants Inc Law Soc 1987–89, pt/t chm Industl Tbnls 1996–; fndr chm Hamble Valley Round Table 1975–76 (chm Area I 1981–82); ward cncllr Fareham Borough Cncl 1978–82; *Recreations* flying, foreign travel, photography, golf; *Clubs* Naval, Hamble Valley Stick, Grenelefe FL Golf; *Style*— James Simpson, Esq; ✉ Bell Yard Chambers, 116–118 Chancery Lane, London WC2A 1PP (☎ 0171 306 9292); 12 East Street, Titchfield, Hants PO14 4AD (☎ 01329 846639)

SIMPSON, Jeremy Miles; s of Gordon Simpson (d 1984), of Glastonbury, and Barbara, *née* Wilkes (d 1976); *b* 25 Nov 1933; *Educ* Malvern, Clare Coll Cambridge (MA); *m* 21 July 1956, Penelope Ann Mary, da of Harvey James (d 1979), of Hayle, Cornwall; 1 s (Mark b 1962), 4 da (Clare b 1957, Rebecca b 1961, Miranda b 1962, Catherine b 1964); *Career* Lt RN 1955–58; md Tan Sad Chair Co 1967–69, chm Giroflex Ltd 1972–86, md Papropack Ltd 1972–86, chm Gordon Russell plc 1986–89, non-exec dir Havelock Europa plc 1989–90, ptnr and mktg mangr Ergo Systema Lisbon Portugal 1990–93, chm Mines & West Holdings plc 1993–; Freeman City of London 1988, memb Worshipful Co of Furniture Makers; Finnish Order of the Lion (First Class) 1986; *Books* Mind the Gap (novel, as Jeremy Miles, 1993); *Recreations* family, reading, walking, travel; *Clubs* United Oxford and Cambridge Univ, Cavalry and Guards'; *Style*— Jeremy Simpson, Esq; ✉ Mines & West Holdings plc, 94 Plomer Green Lane, Downley, High Wycombe, Bucks HP13 5TX (☎ 01494 534411)

SIMPSON, Joe; s of Lt-Col I L Simpson, and Geraldine Elizabeth, *née* McGuire; *b* 13 Aug 1960; *Educ* Ampleforth, Univ of Edinburgh (MA); *Career* author, mountaineer, guide and lectr; memb Alpine Climbing Gp; expeditions incl: 1st ascent W face Siula Grande and 1st ascent E face Seria Central Cordillera Huayhuash Peru 1985, 1st ascent Tupopdam Pakistan 1988, 1st Br expedition to climb Ama Dablam Solo Khumbu Nepal 1990, 1st ascent E face Pachermo Nepal 1991, 1st ascent North Spur Ranrapalca 1994, other expeditions to Nepal, India, Pakistan, Peru, Ecuador, Patagonia and Africa; active memb Greenpeace; *Books* Touching the Void (1988, trans into 14 foreign languages, winner Boardman Tasker Prize 1988, NCR Book Award for Non-Fiction 1990, Literaturpreis des Deutschen Alpenvereins 1990, Cardo d'argento Premio ITAS del libro di Montagna 1993), The Water People (novel, 1992), This Game of Ghosts (autobiography, 1993), Storms of Silence (non-fiction, 1996); *Recreations* photography, paragliding, gardening, rock climbing, surfing, diving, fishing, travel; *Style*— Joe Simpson; ✉ c/o Vivienne Schuster, Curtis Brown, 4th Floor, Haymarket House, 28–29 Haymarket, London SW1Y 4SP (☎ 0171 396 6600)

SIMPSON, John; s of William Thomas Simpson (d 1979), and Mary, *née* Wise (d 1976); *b* 15 May 1943; *Educ* St Bonaventure GS London; *m* 1967 (m dis 1990), Ina Signd, *née* Janke; 1 da (Victoria b 1970), 1 s (Michael b 1972); *Career* trainee mangr rising to asst export mangr Norcross plc 1960–64; Bunzl plc: joined as sales mangr 1964, various positions rising to md of subsid Rolex Paper Co and dir 5 other subsids 1973; dep chm and chief exec The Mayflower Corporation plc (automotive and other engrg component mfrs) 1989– (fndr chm and chief exec 1973 until Stock Exchange listing 1989); FRCA 1994; *Recreations* reading, golf, motor racing, cars, art, music, tennis, philosophy, antiques, business, conversation, collecting first edition books, gardens, people; *Clubs* St James', Wentworth Golf; *Style*— John Simpson, Esq; ✉ The Mayflower Corporation plc, Mayflower House, London Road, Loudwater, High Wycombe, Bucks HP10 9RF (☎ 01494 450145, fax 01494 450607)

SIMPSON, Prof John Alexander; s of Henry Keith Lindsay Simpson (d 1941), of Greenock, and Mrs Simpson (d 1972); *b* 30 March 1922; *Educ* Greenock Acad, Univ of Glasgow (MB ChB, MD, DSc 1993), Univ of Edinburgh (DSc 1992); *m* 15 Dec 1951, Elizabeth Marguerite Hood, da of Dr James Hood Neill (d 1958), of Edinburgh; 2 s (Henry Keith Lindsay b 1952, Neill John b 1954), 1 da (Guendolen Hope b 1960); *Career* surgn Lt RNVR 1945–48; MRC fell Nat Hosp for Nervous Diseases London 1953–55, conslt physician Western Infirmary Glasgow 1956, reader in neurology (formerly sr lectr) Univ of Edinburgh 1956–64; physician i/c: Regnl Neurological Unit Edinburgh 1956–64, Dept of Neurology Inst of Neurological Sciences Glasgow 1964–87; hon conslt neurologist to Br Army 1965–81, ed Jl of Neurology Neurosurgery and Psychiatry 1970–79, conslt neurologist to Civil Serv Cmmn 1974–87, emeritus prof of neurology Univ of Glasgow 1987– (lectr in med 1950–56, prof of neurology 1964–87); vice pres Myasthenia Gravis Assoc, former chm Scot Epilepsy Assoc; FRCPE 1961, FRCP 1963, FRCPG 1964, FRSE 1969; Istiqlal Decoration (first class) Hashemite Kingdom of Jordan 1973; *Books* Applied Neurophysiology (with W Fitch, 1988); *Recreations* sailing, violin playing, painting; *Style*— Prof John A Simpson, FRSE; ✉ 87 Glencairn Drive, Glasgow G41 4LL (☎ 0141 423 2863)

SIMPSON, John Andrew; s of Robert Morris Simpson, and Joan Margaret, *née* Sersale; *b* 13 Oct 1953; *Educ* Dean Close Sch Cheltenham, Univ of York (BA, hockey colours), Univ of Reading (MA); *m* 25 Sept 1976, Dr Hilary Simpson, da of Edmund Wilfred Croxford; 2 da (Katharine Jane b 1982, Eleanor Grace b 1990); *Career* ed Concise Oxford Dictionary of Proverbs 1978– (2nd edn 1992), sr ed Supplement to the Oxford English Dictionary 1980–84 (asst ed 1976–78), chief ed Oxford English Dictionary 1993– (ed new words 1984–85, co-ed 1986–93), ed Oxford Dictionary of Modern Slang (with John Ayto) 1992, ed Oxford English Dictionary Additions series Vols 1 and 2 (with Edmund Weiner) 1993; fell Kellogg Coll Oxford 1991–; memb: English Faculty Oxford 1993–, Philological Soc 1994–; *Recreations* cricket, computing; *Style*— John Simpson, Esq; ✉ Chestnut Lodge, St Mary's Close, Wheatley, Oxford OX33 1YP (☎ 01865 875140); Oxford English Dictionaries, Oxford University Press, Great Clarendon Street, Oxford OX2 6DP (☎ 01865 267728, fax 01865 267810)

SIMPSON, Very Rev Dr John Arthur; s of Arthur Simpson (d 1958), and Mary Esther, *née* Price (d 1982); *b* 7 June 1933; *Educ* Cathays HS Cardiff, Keble Coll Oxford (BA, MA), Clifton Theol Coll; *m* 15 Aug 1968, Ruth Marian, da of Leo Dibbens (d 1966); 1 s (Damian b 1972), 2 da (Rebecca b 1970, Helen b 1974); *Career* curate: Leyton 1958–59, Christ Church Orpington 1959–62; tutor Oak Hill Coll London 1962–72, vicar Ridge Herts 1972–79, dir Ordinands and Post-Ordination Trg Diocese of St Albans 1975–81, hon canon St Albans Cathedral 1977–79, residentiary canon St Albans and priest i/c of Ridge 1979–81, archdeacon of Canterbury and residentiary canon of Canterbury Cathedral 1981–86, dean of Canterbury 1986–; dir Ecclesiastical Insurance Group 1983–; chm: (Canterbury) Cathedral Gifts Ltd 1986–, The Canterbury Cathedral Co Ltd 1989–; chm Govrs King's Sch Canterbury 1986–; Hon DD Univ of Kent 1994; *Recreations* travel, theatre, opera; *Clubs* Athenaeum; *Style*— The Very Rev the Dean of Canterbury; ✉ The Deanery, Canterbury, Kent CT1 2EP; Cathedral House, 11 The Precincts, Canterbury CT1 2EH (☎ 01227 762862, fax 01227 762897)

SIMPSON, John Cody Fidler-; CBE (1991); s of Roy Simpson Fidler-Simpson (d 1980), of Dunwich, Suffolk, and Joyce Leila Vivienne, *née* Cody (d 1983); *b* 9 Aug 1944; *Educ* St Paul's, Magdalene Coll Cambridge (MA); *m* 14 Aug 1965 (sep 1984), Diane Jean, da of Dr Manville Petteys, of La Jolla, Calif, USA; 2 da (Julia Anne b 1969, Eleanor Mary b 1971); *partner*, Tira, da of Harry Shubart, of Evanston, Illinois, USA; *Career* with the BBC; sub ed Radio News 1966, corr Dublin 1972; foreign corr: Brussels 1975, Johannesburg 1977; diplomatic corr TV News 1978, political ed 1980, presenter Nine O'Clock News 1981, diplomatic ed 1982, foreign affairs ed 1988–; BAFTA Richard Dimbleby Award 1992, RTS TV Journalist of the Year 1990; FRGS 1990; *Books* The Best of Granta (jt ed, 1966), Moscow Requiem (novel, 1980), A Fine and Private Place (novel, 1982), The Disappeared (1985), Behind Iranian Lines (1988), Despatches from the Barricades (1990), From the House of War (1991), The Darkness Crumbles (1992), In the Forests of the Night (1993), Lifting the Veil (jtly, 1995); *Recreations* books, travelling, diving; *Clubs* Athenaeum, Chelsea Arts, Queen's; *Style*— John Simpson, Esq, CBE; ✉ BBC Television Centre, Wood Lane, London W12 7RJ (☎ 0181 743 8000)

SIMPSON, Prof John Harold; s of Frederick Harold Simpson (d 1990), of Clifton, York, and Margaret Morrison, *née* Lees-Wallace; *b* 21 May 1940; *Educ* Bootham Sch York, Exeter Coll Oxford (BA), Univ of Liverpool (PhD, DSc); *m* 31 Aug 1964, Frances Mary, da of Thomas Estell Peacock (d 1989); 3 da (Amanda b 1967, Rachel b 1968, Joanna b 1970); *Career* Univ of Wales Bangor: lectr in physical oceanography 1965, res fell Nat Inst of Oceanography 1969–70, personal chair in physical oceanography 1982, established chair in physical oceanography 1986–, head Sch of Ocean Scis 1996–; visiting prof of physical oceanography Virginia Inst of Marine Sciences USA 1989; NERC: memb Ctee AAPS 1975–79, memb Cncl 1982–88, chm North Sea Project Scientific Steering Gp 1987–92, chm LOIS Shelf Edge Study Steering Gp 1992–; memb Cncl Scottish Marine Biological Assoc 1985–91, pres Challenger Soc for Marine Sci 1994–96; *Recreations* hill walking, windsurfing, gardening; *Style*— Prof John Simpson; ✉ School of Ocean Sciences, University of Wales, Bangor, Menai Bridge, Anglesey LL59 5EY (☎ 01248 351151, fax 01248 716367)

SIMPSON, Lt-Col John Rowton; TD (1963), DL (1972); s of Lt-Col Maurice Rowton Simpson, OBE, TD, DL (d 1981), of Leicester, and Renée Claire, *née* Lafitte; *b* 19 Sept 1926; *Educ* Rugby, Magdalene Coll Cambridge (MA, LLM); *m* 8 Oct 1959, Roxane Eveline, da of William Pickford (d 1984), of Leicester; 2 s (Jeremy b 17 Nov 1963, Matthew b 29 Sept 1966), 1 da (Lucy b 28 Dec 1970); *Career* Coldstream Gds 1944, cmmnd 2 Lt Gordon Highlanders 1945, Lt Sierra Leone Regt 1946 (Capt 1947), transfd to reserve 1948, Maj RA TA 1958 (Lt 1951, Capt 1954), RE TA 1961 (Lt-Col 1965), Sherwood Foresters 1966, reserve RE 1968; admitted slr 1953; ptnr Herbert Simpson & Co 1960; sr ptnr: Stone & Simpson 1978, Harvey Ingram Stone & Simpson 1988–91; memb TAVR Assoc E Midlands 1958–95 (chm Cadet Ctee 1985–89); hon sec Westleigh RFC 1954–59; capt Leicestershire GC 1972; vice chm Leicestershire Sports and Recreation Advsy Cncl 1976–; chm City of Leicester Sports and Recreation Advsy Cncl 1976–88; pres: Leicestershire Rugby Union 1979, 1980 and 1985 (ctee memb 1959–), Rugby Football Union 1988 (ctee memb 1968–95); Freeman City of London; memb Worshipful Co of Framework Knitters; memb Law Soc; *Recreations* rugby football, golf; *Clubs* E India; *Style*— Lt-Col John R Simpson, TD, DL; ✉ 16 Knighton Grange Rd, Leicester LE2 2LE (☎ 0116 270 5753)

SIMPSON, His Hon Judge Keith Taylor; *b* 8 May 1934; *Educ* privately, Jesus Coll Oxford (MA); *m* 1961, Dorothy Preece; 2 s, 1 da; *Career* called to the Bar Middle Temple 1958, in gen common law practice, circuit judge (SE Circuit) 1990–; *Recreations* walking, gardening, tennis, fishing, reading, opera; *Style*— His Hon Judge Keith Simpson; ✉ c/o The Law Courts, Barker Rd, Maidstone, Kent ME16 8EQ (☎ 01622 754966)

SIMPSON, Keppel Moore; s of George William Simpson (d 1983), of Liverpool, and Ethel Annie, *née* Moore (d 1975); *b* 10 Aug 1933; *Educ* Abergele GS, Univ of Liverpool (BEng); *m* Barbara Pauline (d 1994); 1 s (Mark b 1958), 3 da (Philippa b 1960, Caroline b 1962, Amanda b 1965); *Career* Sub Lt RN 1953–55; dir: Conf Européene des Postes et des Telecommunications 'Eurodata' Programme 1971–73, Intelsat Permanent Management Arrangements 1974–76, PA International Management Consultants Ltd 1976–84, Sundridge Park Management Centre Ltd 1979–84, PA International Holdings Ltd 1982–84, Yeoward Bros Ltd 1983–, Ercol Furniture Ltd 1992–, Ballet Rambert 1995–; chm PA International Management Consultants Inc 1980–84; prog dir UK Nat Microelectronics Awareness Prog 1978; fndr memb: Workaid, Chesham Prep Sch Tst Ltd; CEng, MIEE, FIMC; *Clubs* Naval, RNVR Yacht; *Style*— Keppel Simpson, Esq; ✉ 8 Shardeloes, Amersham, Bucks HP7 0RL (☎ 01494 724984, fax 01494 721785)

SIMPSON, Rear Adm Michael Frank; CB (1985); s of Robert Michael Simpson, and Florence Mabel Simpson; *b* 27 Sept 1928; *Educ* King Edward VI Sch Bath, RNEC Manadon, RAF Tech Coll Henlow; *m* 1973, Sandra, *née* Cliff; 2 s, 1 da; *Career* joined RN 1944, Air Engr Offr 1952; served: FAA Sqdns, cruisers and carriers; US Navy 1964–66, Ark Royal 1970–72, supt RN Aircraft Yard Fleetlands 1978–80; Cdre RN Barracks Portsmouth 1981–83, dir-gen Aircraft (Navy) 1983–85; dir Field Aircraft Services of Croydon 1985–, md Hunting Airmotive Ltd 1988–94, dir Hunting Aviation Ltd 1988–, chm Aircraft Engrg Div Hunting Aviation 1994–; CEng, FRAeS, FIMechE; *Style*— Rear Adm Michael F Simpson, CB; ✉ Keppel, Blackhills, Esher, Surrey KT10 9JW; Hunting Aviation Ltd, Aircraft Engineering Division, 12 Imperial Way, Croydon, Surrey CR9 4LE (☎ 0181 688 7777, fax 0181 688 6603)

SIMPSON, Norman; s of James Robert Simpson (d 1942), of Warsop, Notts, and Alice May Lody, *née* Eaton (d 1982); *b* 22 Sept 1933; *Educ* Warsop Infants' and Secdy Sch, Mansfield Technical Sch, Mansfield Sch of Art, Nottingham Sch of Architecture, Nottingham Poly (Dip Landscape Design); *m* 2 Sept 1958, Margaret Audrey, da of Frederick Israel Woodhouse (d 1969), of Sutton in Ashfield, Notts; *Career* architect; over 40 leisure projects throughout UK; award-winning projects incl: W Burton 'A' Power Station (Civic Tst Award 1968 and Countryside Award 1970), Nat Watersport Centre Holme Pierrepont; former chm East Midland Landscape Group; memb: The Assoc of Consulting Architects 1980, The Assoc for the Studies in Conservation of Historic Bldgs 1981; assoc Inst of Sport and Recreation Mgmnt, ARCUK 1964, FRIBA 1968 (ARIBA 1964), ALI 1976, FIMgt 1982; *Recreations* photography and sketching; *Clubs* Rotary (Nottingham North, former pres); *Style*— Norman Simpson; ✉ Studio, 22 Pentwood Avenue, Arnold, Nottingham NG5 8RR (☎ 0115 967 0107, fax 0115 967 1182)

SIMPSON, Paul Graham; s of Graham James Simpson, of Nuneaton, Warwicks, and Valerie Ann, *née* Chilton; *b* 27 Aug 1961; *Educ* Manor Park GS Nuneaton, King Edward VI Coll Nuneaton, Univ of Kent at Canterbury (BA); *Career* editorial asst MW Publishers Edgware 1982–84; Litho Week (Haymarket Publishing): reporter 1984–85, features ed 1985, news ed 1985, dep ed 1986–87, ed 1987–90 (youngest ever ed); ed: Newspaper Focus magazine (Haymarket Publishing) 1990–94, Four Four Two magazine (Haymarket Publishing) 1994–96, The Box 1996–; nominated Ed of the Year Periodical Publishers Assoc 1992; Newspaper Focus nominated for Business Magazine of the Year Media Week Awards 1991, awarded Business Magazine of the Year by the Periodical Publishers Assoc Awards 1992; *Books* Construction Yearbook (1983), British Printing

Industry (1987), European Printing Industry (1992); *Recreations* reading American thrillers, writing, listening to Elvis Presley records; *Style*— Paul Simpson, Esq; ✉ Haymarket Publishing, 38 Hampton Road, Teddington, Middlesex TW11 0JE (☎ 0181 943 5053)

SIMPSON, Peter; *Educ* Bournemouth and Poole Coll of Art; *m* Dec 1970, Jennifer Carol, *née* Johnson; 2 da (Rebecca Caroline b 21 Sept 1972, Naomi Rosalind Mary b 18 July 1975); *Career* ceramic designer; currently asst dean Sch of Art and Design Univ of Derby; *Exhibitions* incl: one-man exhibition (Pace Gallery and Design Centre London) 1970, Ceramics '71 (Bradford City Art Gallery and Design Centre London) 1971, More British Potters (Keetles Yard Cambridge) 1972, International Ceramics '72 (V & A) 1972, Craftsman's Art (V & A) 1973, Modern British Crafts (Royal Scottish Museum Edinburgh) 1973, Gordon Baldwin, Peter Simpson (British Crafts Centre London) 1974, Chunichi 3 Int Exhibition of Ceramic Art Tokyo 1975, 6 Studio Potters (V & A Museum) 1976, 2-man show (British Crafts Centre London) 1979, 4-man show (CPA London) 1980, Pottery Now (Sotheby's Gallery Belgravia London) 1985; numerous works in public collections incl Royal Scottish Museum (Edinburgh) and V & A Museum (London); visiting tutor and lectr in ceramics; memb Craftsmen Bursary Panel Southern Arts Assoc 1976–79 (memb Visual Arts Panel 1976–78), exhibition memb The Contemporary Applied Arts London; *Style*— Peter Simpson, Esq; ✉ School of Art and Design, University of Derby, Britannia Mill, Mackworth Road, Derby DE22 3BL (☎ 01332 622222)

SIMPSON, His Hon Judge Peter Robert; s of Surgn Capt Donald Lee Simpson, RN (d 1985), of Barnet, Herts, and Margaret Olive, *née* Lathan; *b* 9 Feb 1936; *Educ* St John's Coll Southsea Hants; *m* 1, 1968 (m dis 1994), Mary Elizabeth, da of late Thomas Kirton; 2 s; m 2, 1995, Megan Elizabeth, only da of late Kenneth John Dodd; *Career* admitted slr 1960; called to the Bar Inner Temple 1970, ad eundem Lincoln's Inn 1972, practised on the South Eastern Circuit then at Chancery Bar (mainly in property and conveyancing matters), rec 1987–89, appointed circuit judge (SE Circuit) 1989, second judge Mayors & City of London Court 1994–; former memb Herts and Essex Sessions bar mess; *Recreations* reading legal and political biographies, dipping into books of history, listening to music, playing chess, dining out; *Clubs* Guildhall; *Style*— His Hon Judge P R Simpson; ✉ 12 New Square, Lincoln's Inn, London WC2A 3SW; Mayors and City of London Court, 32 Threadneedle Street, London EC2R 8AY

SIMPSON, Dr Robert Wilfred Levick; s of Robert Warren Simpson, and Helena Hendrika, *née* Govaars; *b* 2 March 1921; *Educ* Westminster City Sch; *m* 1, 1946, Bessie Fraser (d 1981); m 2, 1982, Angela Mary Musgrave; *Career* BBC music prodr 1951–80; composer of 11 Symphonies, 15 String Quartets, many other chamber and orchestral works, 3 concertos; memb: CND, Peace Pledge Union, Musicians Against Nuclear Arms, Royal Astronomical Soc, Br Astronomical Assoc, Inc Soc of Musicians, Composers' Guild of GB, Assoc of Professional Composers; *Books* Carl Nielsen, Symphonist (1952 and 1979), The Essence of Bruckner (1966 and 1977, revised edn 1992), The Symphony (ed, 1967), Beethoven's Symphonies (1970), The Proms and Natural Justice (1981); *Recreations* astronomy; *Style*— Dr Robert Simpson; ✉ Siocháin, Killelton, nr Camp, Tralee, County Kerry, Republic of Ireland (☎ 00 3536630213)

SIMPSON, Robin Muschamp Garry; QC (1971); s of Ronald Simpson (d 1957), of Aldeburgh, Suffolk, and Lila, *née* Muschamp (d 1951); *b* 19 June 1927; *Educ* Charterhouse, Peterhouse Cambridge (MA); *m* 1, 13 Oct 1956 (m dis 1968), Avril Carolyn, da of Dr J E M Harrisson, of Bovey Tracey, S Devon; 1 s (Charles b 17 Oct 1961), 1 da (Anna b 13 Aug 1963); m 2, 23 March 1968, Faith Mary, da of Dr F G Laughton-Scott, of London W1; 1 s (Hugo b 14 March 1972), 1 da (Kate b 14 Oct 1968); *Career* called to the Bar Middle Temple 1951; memb Central Criminal Ct Bar Mess, practising SE Circuit, recorder Crown Ct 1976–86, Master of Bench Middle Temple 1979, appeal steward Br Boxing Bd of Control; *Recreations* real tennis, sailing; *Clubs* MCC, Garrick, Aldeburgh Yacht; *Style*— Robin Simpson, Esq, QC; ✉ 116 Station Road, Barnes, London SW13 0NB (☎ 0181 878 9898)

SIMPSON, Dr Roderick Howard Wallace; s of Dr Robert Wallace Simpson (d 1991), of Salisbury, and Betty Noreen, *née* Mollett (d 1994); *b* 10 Jan 1951; *Educ* King's Sch Bruton, Univ of St Andrews (BSc), Univ of Dundee (MB ChB), Univ of Stellenbosch (MMed); *m* 10 Nov 1979, (Alethea) Avrille, da of Cecil Alfred Milborrow, of Johannesburg, SA (d 1993); 3 s (Andrew b 1980, Richard b 1983, Nicholas b 1993), 1 da (Eleanor b 1987); *Career* registrar in pathology Guy's Hosp 1976–79, lectr in pathology Univ of Stellenbosch 1980–82, sr lectr in pathology and neuropathology Univ of Witwatersrand SA 1982–85, conslt pathologist and sr lectr Univ of Exeter and Royal Devon and Exeter Hosps 1985–; author of 3 chapters in med textbooks and various pubns in med jls on aspects of histopathology (in particular tumours of the head and neck); MRCPath 1983; *Recreations* cricket, travel, dining well with good company, the past; *Clubs* East India; *Style*— Dr Roderick Simpson; ✉ Iron Pool, Dry Lane, Christow, nr Exeter, Devon EX6 7PF (☎ 01647 252034); Area Department of Pathology, Church Lane, Heavitree, Exeter, Devon EX2 5DY (☎ 01392 402941)

SIMPSON, William George; s of William Anion Simpson (d 1961), of Liverpool, and Sarah Jane Simpson (d 1972); *b* 27 June 1945; *Educ* Liverpool Inst, Univ of Liverpool (BA), Univ of Aberdeen (Gilroy scholar), MA (Dublin); *m* 2 Nov 1968, Margaret Lilian, da of Bertram Pollard, of Liverpool; 2 da (Nicola Margaret b 1969, Fiona Sarah b 1974); *Career* asst librarian Univ of Durham 1969–73, John Rylands Library Univ of Manchester 1973–85 (asst librarian, sub-librarian, sr sub-librarian); univ librarian: Univ of Surrey 1985–90, Univ of London 1990–94; librarian and college archivist Trinity Coll Dublin 1994–; memb: SCONUL 1985–, Br Library London Servs Advsy Ctee 1990–94, Nat Cncl for Orientalist Library Resources 1991–, An Chomhairle Leabharlanna 1995–, COLICO 1995–, Mgmnt Ctee Nat Preservation Office 1996–; chm: American Studies Library Gp 1987–94, Guildford Inst 1987–90; dir: CURL 1992–, IRIS 1994–; ALA, FRSA, FRAS; *Publications* Libraries, Languages and the Interpretation of the Past (1988); author of articles and reviews in learned and professional jls; *Recreations* astronomy, genealogy, languages, travel; *Style*— William Simpson, Esq; ✉ Cranhurst, Station Rd, Farncombe, Godalming, Surrey GU7 3NF (☎ 01483 415815); Trinity College Library, College Street, Dublin 2, Ireland (☎ 003531 608 1665, fax 003531 671 9003)

SIMPSON, Sir William James; kt (1984); s of William Simpson, and Margaret, *née* Nimmo; *b* 1920; *Educ* Victoria Sch, Falkirk Tech Sch; *m* 1942, Catherine McEwan Nichol; 1 s; *Career* Sgt Argyll and Sutherland Highlanders 1939–45; gen sec Foundry Section AUEW 1967–75, memb Race Relations Bd 1967–74, chm Lab Pty 1972–73, memb Flixborough Inquiry 1973–74, chm Advsy Ctee on Asbestos 1976–79, former chm Health and Safety Cmmn; *Books* Labour - The Unions and The Party (1973); *Style*— Sir William Simpson; ✉ 11 Strude Howe, Alva, Clackmannanshire, Scotland (☎ 01259 60859)

SIMPSON-ORLEBAR, Sir Michael Keith Orlebar; KCMG (1991, CMG 1982); s of Aubrey Orlebar Simpson (d 1933), and Laura Violet, *née* Keith-Jones; *b* 5 Feb 1932; *Educ* Eton, ChCh Oxford (MA); *m* 19 April 1964, Rosita, da of Ignacio Duarte (d 1959); 2 s (Aubrey b 1965, Edward b 1966), 1 da (Charlotte b 1972); *Career* Nat Serv Lt KRRC 1950–51; HM Dip Serv: entered 1954, Tehran 1955–57, FO 1957–62, Bogota 1962–65, FCO 1966–68, Paris 1969–72, Tehran 1972–76, FCO 1977–80, min Rome 1980–83, head Br Interest Section Tehran 1983–85; ambassador: Lisbon 1986–89, Mexico City 1989–92 (ret); DG Hispanic and Luso Brazilian Cncl (Canning House) 1992–96; *Recreations* gardening, fishing; *Style*— Sir Michael Simpson-Orlebar, KCMG

SIMS, Prof Andrew Charles Petter; s of Dr Charles Henry Sims (d 1994), of Exeter, and Dr Norah Winnifred Kennan, *née* Petter; *b* 5 Nov 1938; *Educ* Monkton Combe Sch, Emmanuel Coll Cambridge, Westminster Hosp Med Sch London (MA, MB BChir, MD); *m* 25 April 1964, Ruth Marie, da of Dr John Cuthbert Harvey (d 1988), of Birmingham; 2 s (David b 1965, John b 1968), 2 da (Mary b 1966, Ann b 1970); *Career* house surgn Westminster Hosp 1963–64, registrar Manchester Royal Infirmary 1965–68, conslt psychiatrist All Saints' Hosp Birmingham 1971–76, sr lectr and hon conslt psychiatrist Univ of Birmingham 1974–79, prof of psychiatry Univ of Leeds 1979–; memb GMC; pres RCPsych 1990–93 (dean 1987–90); chm: Confidential Inquiry into Homicides and Suicides of Mentally Ill People 1992–95, Schizophrenia Report of Clinical Standards Advsy Gp 1993–95; fell Coll of Physicians and Surgns Pakistan 1994; FRCPsych 1979, FRCPEd 1993, Hon FRCPsych 1994, MD Lambeth 1995; *Books* Neurosis in Society (1983), Psychiatry CMT (5 edn, 1983), Lecture Notes in Behavioural Science (1984), Symptoms in the Mind (1988), Anxiety in Clinical Practice (1988), Angsttherapie in der Klinischen Praxis (1993), Psychiatry (6 edn, 1993), Speech and Language Disorders in Psychiatry (1995), Symptoms in the Mind (2 edn, 1995); *Recreations* music, theatre, hill walking, gardening; *Clubs* Christian Medical Fellowship, RSM, Athenaeum; *Style*— Prof Andrew Sims; ✉ Department of Psychiatry, St James's University Hospital, Leeds, West Yorkshire LS9 7TF

SIMS, Bernard John; s of John Sims (d 1949), of London, and Minnie, *née* Everitt (d 1962); *b* 13 May 1915; *Educ* Wimbledon Coll London, LSE (LLB); *m* 27 April 1963, Elizabeth Margaret Eileen, da of Philip Edward Filbee (d 1960), of St Leonards on Sea, Sussex; *Career* WWII: RA 1940–42, RAOC 1942–45, SO HQ AA Cmd 1943–45, Capt 1944, SO Northumbrian Dist Northern Cmd 1945; slr 1938, lectr Law Soc's Sch of Law 1945–47, sr legal asst Bd of Inland Revenue 1947–53, legal advsr Indust and Commercial Fin Corp 1953–61, chief examiner and moderator Law Soc 1953–81; chm Editorial Bd: Simon's Taxes 1970–, Inheritance Tax 1991–; Freeman: City of London 1951, Worshipful Co of Slrs; memb Law Soc 1938, FIT 1965; Kt Cdr of the Equestrian Order of the Holy Sepulchre 1967; *Books* Controls on Company Finance (1958), Estate Duty Changes (1969), Capital Duty (1975), Halsbury's Laws of England (contrib, 4 edn 1983, reissue 1996 and conslt on stamp duties), Sergeant and Sims on Stamp Duties (11 edn 1995); *Recreations* music; *Clubs* City Livery, Lansdowne; *Style*— Bernard Sims, Esq; ✉ 89 Dovehouse St, Chelsea, London SW3 6JZ (☎ 0171 352 1798)

SIMS, Frank; s of Frank Sims (d 1986), and Doris Elizabeth, *née* Hayes; *b* 21 July 1943; *Educ* Hitchin GS, Univ of Sheffield (BA); *m* 29 Oct 1966, Jean Caroline, da of Edward Francis Whitworth; 1 s (Richard b 1974), 1 da (Claire b 1972); *Career* CA; Price Waterhouse 1967–72, Wallace Sassoon Bank 1972–74, Binder Hamlyn 1974– (ptnr); Freeman City of London 1977, Liveryman Worshipful Co of Glovers; FCA 1970; *Recreations* golf, music, travel; *Clubs* Wig and Pen; *Style*— Frank Sims, Esq; ✉ 52 Russell Rd, Buckhurst Hill, Essex IG9 5QE (☎ 0181 505 0019); Binder Hamlyn, 20 Old Bailey, London EC4M 7BH (☎ 0171 489 6168, fax 0171 489 6293)

SIMS, Frank Alexander; OBE (1986); s of Frank Howell Sims (d 1980), of Bognor Regis, and Mary, *née* Laidlaw (d 1994); *Educ* Chichester HS for Boys, Univ of Nottingham (BSc); *m* 11 June 1956, Kathleen Veronica, da of Rodney Vernon Fox-Kirk (d 1986); 1 s (Anthony James Alexander b 15 Feb 1960), 1 da (Amanda Jane b 27 March 1957); *Career* Nat Serv 1955–57, sapper and OCTU trg 1955–56, Military garrison engr (West Kent Area) 1956–57; resident engr Corby Development Corporation 1954–55 (asst engr 1953–54), tech staff offr on attachment to Military Experimental Estab 1957; W Riding CC: asst bridge engr 1957–59, resident engr 1959–61, princ asst engr (Bridges) 1961–63, chief asst county engr (Bridges) 1963–68, superintending engr Road Construction Sub-Unit 1968–73; exec dir of engrg (chief offr) W Yorkshire Metropolitan CC 1973–86, chief exec Pell Frischmann Consultants Ltd 1986–; memb: Res Ctee on Bridges Road Research Laboratory, Bridge Design Ctee Miny of Transport, Computers in Construction Industry, Working Party Miny of Building and Public Works, Reclamation and Waste Disposal Working Party Inst of Municipal Engrs, Structural Codes Advsy Ctee IStructE, Advsy Ctee Dept of Civil and Structural Engrg Univ of Sheffield, Nat Steering Ctees and BSI Ctees on Eurocodes, Exec Ctee Inst of Highways and Transportation Yorkshire and Humberside; chm: BSI Steel Concrete Bridge Code Ctee, Structural Engrg Gp Bd; jt chm: Eurocode Advsy Panel ICE, Standing Ctee on Structural Safety; specialist advsr Assoc of Met Authorities, former chm Advsy Ctee Dept of Civil Engrg Univ of Leeds; Concrete Soc: fndr memb Yorkshire and Humberside Branch, former chm Prestressed Concrete Ctee, memb Int Panel, former memb Cncl, vice pres; memb Cncl Concrete Bridge Development Group 1992; winner Lewis Angell medal and prize Inst of Municipal Engrs 1982; author of numerous technical papers concerning design construction and maintenance of highways & bridges, waste management and assoc subjects; fell: Inst of Municipal Engrs, Inst of Waste Mgmnt; FEng 1982, FICE, FIHT, FRSA 1996; *Recreations* gardening, DIY, music, walking, fishing, golf; *Style*— Frank Sims, Esq, OBE, FEng; ✉ Pell Frischmann Consultants Ltd, George House, George St, Wakefield, W Yorkshire WF1 1LY (☎ 01924 368145, fax 01924 376643)

SIMS, Prof Geoffrey Donald; OBE (1971); s of Albert Edward Hope Sims, and Jessie Elizabeth Sims; *b* 13 Dec 1926; *Educ* Wembley Co GS, Imperial Coll of Sci and Technol (BSc, ARCS, MSc, PhD, DIC); *m* 9 April 1949, Pamela Audrey, da of Thomas Edwin Richings; 1 s (Graham b 12 Jan 1950), 2 da (Patricia b 7 Feb 1953, Anne b 16 Sept 1960); *Career* res physicist GEC Wembley 1948–54, seconded to work with Prof D Gabor (Nobel Laureate) Imperial Coll 1950–54, sr sci offr UKAEA Harwell, lectr (later sr lectr) Dept of Electrical Engrg UCL 1956–63; Univ of Southampton: prof and head Dept of Electronics 1963–74, dean Faculty of Engrg and Applied Sci 1967–70, sr dep vice chllr 1970–72; vice chllr Univ of Sheffield 1974–90; memb: Br Library Organising Ctee 1971–73, Annan Ctee on the Future of Broadcasting 1974–77; chm Engrg Advsy Ctee BBC 1981–90, vice chm Br Cncl Ctee Int Cooperation Higher Educn 1985–90 (memb 1981–94), hon dep treas Assoc of Cwlth Univs 1983–90, chm Cncl for Educn in the Cwlth 1990–96, memb Conf of Euro Rectors Perm Ctee 1981–94 (memb Bureau 1984–94), pres Liaison Ctee Rectors Confs of Memb States of Euro Communities 1987–89; fell Midland Chapter Woodard Sch 1977–, Custos Worksop Coll 1984–92, Guardian of the Standard of Wrought Plate within the Town of Sheffield 1984–, Capital Burgess Sheffield Church Burgesses Tst 1988–89 (memb 1984–, chm Educnl Fndn 1992–); memb Royal Naval Engrg Coll Advsy Cncl 1988–95 (chm Res Ctee 1990–95); Hon DSc Univ of Southampton 1980, Hon LLD Univ of Dundee 1987, Hon ScD Alleghany Coll 1989, Hon DSc Queen's Univ Belfast 1990, Hon LLD Univ of Sheffield 1991; hon fell Sheffield Hallam Univ (formerly Sheffield City Poly) 1990; Symons Medal ACU 1991; FIEE 1963, FEng 1980, FCGI 1980; *Books* Microwave Tubes and Semiconductor Devices (with I M Stephenson, 1963), Variational Techniques in Electromagnetism (1965); *Recreations* golf, travel, music; *Clubs* Athenaeum; *Style*— Prof Geoffrey Sims, OBE, FEng; ✉ Ingleside, 70 Whirlow Lane, Sheffield S11 9QF (☎ and fax 0114 230 3113)

SIMS, George Frederick Robert; s of George Sims (d 1976), and Ada, *née* Harrison (d 1954); *b* 3 Aug 1923; *Educ* Lower Sch of John Lyon Harrow; *m* 7 Aug 1943, Beryl, *née* Simcock; 2 s (Christopher b 12 July 1944, Timothy b 25 June 1962), 1 da (Linda b 29 April 1947); *Career* Army Service Special Communications Unit No 1 1942–47; author; jr reporter Press Association 1940–42, dealer in rare books 1947–87; memb: Crime Writers' Assoc 1966, Detection Club 1989; *Books* The Terrible Door (1964), Sleep No More (1966), The Last Best Friend (1967), The Sand Dollar (1969), Deadhand (1971),

Hunters Point (1973), The End of the Web (1976), Rex Mundi (1978), Who is Cato? (1981), The Keys of Death (1982), Coat of Arms (1984), The Rare Book Game (1985), More of the Rare Book Game (1988), Last of the Rare Book Game (1990), The Despain Papers (1992), A Life in Catalogues (1994); *Recreations* swimming in warm seas, walking in the Hambleden Valley, watching people; *Style*— George Sims, Esq; ✉ Peacocks, Hurst, Berkshire RG10 0DR (☎ 0118 934 1030)

SIMS, Surgn Cdr Harrington; s of Enoch Sims (d 1940), and Mary Hannah, *née* Murphy (d 1963); *b* 13 April 1930; *Educ* Wath GS, Univ of Sheffield (MB ChB); *m* 4 July 1953, Joyce, da of Haydn Parkin (d 1987); 3 s (Christopher Martin, Andrew Jon, David Murray); *Career* permanent RN med serv 1955–74, advsr in genito-urinary med and dermatology to Dir Gen Naval Med Serv 1965–74; hon clinical lectr in genitourinary med Univ of Sheffield 1975–77, physician i/c Genito-Urinary Med Dept Norwich Health Authy 1977–; memb WM Navy Lodge London 1982–83, chm Norwich Conslt Staff 1988–89; FRCPE 1982; *Recreations* music (especially Elgar), history, gardening; *Clubs* Royal Over-Seas League; *Style*— Surgn Cdr Harrington Sims; ✉ Barleycorn, Old Brewery Lane, Reepham, Norwich NR10 4NE (☎ 01603 870722); Norfolk and Norwich Hospital, Brunswick Rd, Norwich, Norfolk (☎ 01603 667369)

SIMS, John Haesaert Mancel; s of Capt Harold Mancel Sims (d 1958), of London, and Jeanie Emilie Anne, *née* Haesaert (d 1965); *b* 16 Dec 1929; *Educ* Highfield Sch Wandsworth, Brixton Sch of Bldg; *Career* Nat Serv RE 1948–50; various appts with quantity surveyors' firms in private practice 1950–73, in sole practice as bldg contracts conslt; lectr, writer and arbitrator 1973–, author of numerous articles on bldg contracts for Building 1975–89; pres Soc of Construction Arbitrators 1992–95, chm Chartered Inst of Arbitrators 1994–95 (vice pres 1991–95), memb DTI Departmental Advsy Ctee on Arbitration Law 1990–; Freeman City of London 1981, Liveryman Worshipful Co of Arbitrators 1982; FRICS 1967 (ARICS 1954), FCIArb 1970, MAE 1988, FRSA 1995; *Books* with Vincent Powell-Smith: Building Contract Claims (1983, 2 edn 1988), Contract Documentation for Contractors (1985, 2 edn 1990), Determination and Suspension of Construction Contracts (1985), The JCT Management Contract: A Practical Guide (1988), Construction Arbitrations (1989), The Arbitration Act 1996: A Practical Guide (with Margaret Rutherford, QC, 1996); *Recreations* classical music, choral singing, reading; *Clubs* Wig and Pen; *Style*— John H M Sims, Esq; ✉ 15 Cheyne Place, London SW3 4HH (☎ 0171 353 0643); 41 Paradise Walk, London SW3 4JL (☎ 0171 352 1401, fax 0171 352 1402)

SIMS, Monica Louie; OBE (1971); da of Albert Charles Sims (d 1959), of Gloucester, and Eva Elizabeth, *née* Preen; *Educ* Denmark Rd HS for Girls Gloucester, St Hugh's Coll Oxford (MA, LRAM, LGSM); *Career* tutor in English and drama Dept of Adult Educn Univ Coll of Hull 1947, educn tutor Nat Fedn of Women's Insts 1950; BBC: radio talks prodr 1953, TV prodr 1956, ed Women's Hour 1964, head of children's progs (TV) 1967, Controller Radio 4 1979, dir of progs (radio) 1983; dir of prodn Children's Film and Television Foundation 1985–; vice pres Br Bd of Film Classification; memb Cncl Univ of Bristol; FRSA 1984; *Recreations* theatre, cinema, gardening; *Style*— Miss Monica Sims, OBE; ✉ 97 Gloucester Terrace, London W2 3HB (☎ 0171 262 6191); Children's Film and Television Foundation, Elstree Studios, Borehamwood, Herts WD6 1JG (☎ 0181 953 0844, fax 0181 207 0860, telex 922436 EFILMS G)

SIMS, Neville William; MBE (1974); s of William Ellis Sims (d 1954), of Whitchurch, Cardiff, and Ethel Stacey Colley, *née* Inman (d 1980); *b* 15 June 1933; *Educ* Penarth Co Sch; *m* 2 April 1964, Jennifer Ann, da of Horace George Warwick, of Rhiwbina, Cardiff; 2 s (Jeremy b 1971, Matthew b 1981), 2 da (Heather b 1973, Caroline b 1980); *Career* articles with T H Trump, qualified CA 1957; Ernst & Young: ptnr 1960–85, managing ptnr Cardiff Office 1974–84, ret 1985; conslt Watts Gregory & Daniel 1986–; dir: Compact Cases Ltd Caerphilly 1986–89, Peter Evans Flooring Ltd 1992–; chm: Wales Area Young Cons 1960–63, Barry Cons Assoc 1962–72, Govrs Howell's Sch Llandaff Cardiff 1981–; hon treas: YWCA Centre Cardiff 1963–70, Cardiff Central Cons Assoc 1987–93; pres S Wales Soc of CAs 1977–78, chm CAs for Business in Wales (CABW) 1992–; memb: Welsh Regnl Bd Homeowners' Friendly Soc 1984–88, Standing Fin Ctee Welsh Nat Bd for Nursing, Midwifery and Health Visiting 1989–93, Post Office Users' Cncl for Wales 1992–, Exec UK 200 Group; memb Cncl: ICAEW 1981–, AAT 1989–92; FCA; *Recreations* theatre, music, gardening, walking; *Clubs* Cardiff Business, Cardiff and County; *Style*— Neville Sims, Esq, MBE; ✉ The Chimes, 15 Westminster Crescent, Cyncoed, Cardiff CF2 6SE (☎ 01222 753424, fax 01222 383022)

SIMS, Sir Roger Edward; kt (1996), JP, MP (C) Chislehurst (majority 15,276); s of Herbert William Sims (d 1981), of Chislehurst, and Annie Amy, *née* Savidge (d 1987); *b* 27 Jan 1930; *Educ* City Boys' GS Leicester, St Olave's GS Tower Bridge London; *m* 15 June 1957, Angela, da of John Robert Mathews (d 1951), of Chislehurst; 2 s (Matthew Robert b 31 March 1962, Toby Edward b 27 July 1966), 1 da (Virginia Claire b 29 May 1959); *Career* Campbell Booker Carter Ltd 1953–62, advsr Dodwell & Co Ltd 1974–90 (dept mangr 1962–74), dir Inchcape International Ltd 1981–90; memb Chislehurst and Sidcup UDC 1956–62, JP Bromley 1960–72, chm Juvenile Court 1970–72, MP (C) Chislehurst 1974–, PPS to Home Sec 1979–83, vice chm Cons Health Ctee; chm 1912 Club; memb: Central Exec Ctee NSPCC 1980–93 (pres Bromley and Dist Branch), Gen Med Cncl 1989–; MCIM; *Recreations* swimming, singing (Royal Choral Soc); *Clubs* Bromley Cons; *Style*— Sir Roger Sims, JP, MP; ✉ House of Commons, London SW1A 0AA (☎ 0171 219 5000/4404, fax 0171 219 4746)

SIMS-WILLIAMS, Prof Nicholas John; s of Rev Michael Vernon Sims Sims-Williams (d 1992), and Kathleen Marjorie, *née* Wenborn (d 1996); twin bro of Prof Patrick Sims-Williams, FBA, *qv*; *b* 11 April 1949; *Educ* Borden GS Sittingbourne, Trinity Hall Cambridge (BA, MA, PhD); *m* 1 July 1972, Ursula Mary Judith, da of (George) Hugh Nicholas Seton-Watson, CBE, FBA (d 1984); 2 da ((Jennifer) Helen Seton b 1986, Frances Mary Seton b 1989); *Career* res fell Gonville and Caius Coll Cambridge 1975–76; Univ of London: lectr in Iranian languages SOAS 1976–89, reader in Iranian studies 1989–94, prof of Iranian and Central Asian studies 1994–; res reader British Acad 1992–94; sec Corpus Inscriptionum Iranicarum; Prix Ghirshman Institut de France 1988; corresponding fell Aust Acad of Scis 1989; FBA 1988; *Books* The Christian Sogdian Manuscript C2 (1985), Sogdian and Other Iranian Inscriptions of the Upper Indus, I (1989) and II (1992), Documents Turco-Sogdiens du IXe-Xe Siècle de Touen-Houang (with James Hamilton, 1990), Partita (1993); *Recreations* composing music, playing French horn; *Style*— Prof Nicholas Sims-Williams, FBA; ✉ 11 Park Parade, Cambridge CB5 8AL (☎ 01223 368903); School of Oriental and African Studies, University of London, Thornhaugh St, Russell Square, London WC1H 0XG (☎ 0171 637 2388, fax 0171 436 3844, telex 262433 W 6876)

SIMS-WILLIAMS, Prof Patrick; s of Rev Michael Vernon Sims Sims-Williams (d 1992), and Kathleen Marjorie, *née* Wenborn (d 1996); twin bro of Prof Nicholas Sims-Williams, FBA, *qv*; *b* 11 April 1949; *Educ* Borden GS Sittingbourne, Trinity Hall Cambridge (MA), Univ of Birmingham (PhD); *m* 1986, Dr Marged Haycock, da of Emrys J Haycock; 1 da (Gwen Kathleen b 11 Nov 1990), 1 s (Gwilym Emrys b 10 Sept 1993); *Career* Univ of Cambridge: fell St John's Coll 1977–93, lectr Dept of Anglo-Saxon, Norse and Celtic 1977–93, reader in Celtic and Anglo-Saxon 1993; prof of Celtic studies Univ of Wales Aberystwyth 1994–; British Acad research reader 1988–90; ed Cambrian Medieval Celtic Studies; O'Donnell lectr: Univ of Oxford 1981–82, Univ of Edinburgh 1986; Sir Israel Gollancz prize British Acad; FBA 1996; *Books* Religion and Literature in Western England, 600–800 (1990), Britain and Early Christian Europe (1995); *Recreations* music, sailing, carpentry; *Style*— Prof Patrick Sims-Williams, FBA; ✉ Department of Welsh, University of Wales, Aberystwyth, Dyfed SY23 2AX (☎ 01970 622137)

SIMSON, Peregrine Anthony Litton; s of Brig Ernest Clive Litton Simson, of Aston Rowant, Oxon, and Daphne Camilla Marian, *née* Todhunter (d 1982); *b* 10 April 1944; *Educ* Charterhouse, Worcester Coll Oxford (BA); *m* 6 May 1967 (m dis 1979), Caroline Basina, da of Frank Hosier (d 1962), of Wexcombe Manor, Marlborough, Wilts; 1 s (Christian Edward Litton b 9 April 1970), 1 da (Camilla Basina Litton b 12 July 1972); *Career* slr; ptnr: Clifford-Turner 1972–87, Clifford Chance (merged firm of Clifford Turner and Coward Chance) 1987–; Liveryman Worshipful Co of Slrs 1974; memb Law Soc 1970; *Recreations* shooting, tennis, travel; *Clubs* City, Hurlingham, Annabel's; *Style*— Peregrine Simson, Esq; ✉ Corn Hall, Bures St Mary, Suffolk; Clifford Chance, 200 Aldersgate Street, London EC1A 4JJ (☎ 0171 600 1000)

SINCLAIR, Dr Allan; s of Henry Williamson Sinclair (d 1988), of Glasgow, and Mary, *née* Turner (d 1955); *b* 9 Oct 1929; *Educ* Perth Academy, Hillhead HS Glasgow, Univ of Glasgow (MB ChB); *m* 4 Sept 1961, Isobel Alexander, da of John McCowan Stevenson (d 1987), of Hamilton; 3 s (John b 1962, Allan b 1965, Martin b 1968); *Career* Capt RAMC 1954–56; sr registrar and conslt in psychiatry St Andrew's Hosp Northampton 1960–68, conslt in psychiatry Lanarkshire Health Bd 1968–94; med dir: Lanarkshire Community and Priority Services Unit 1994–95, Lanarkshire Health Care NHS Tst 1995–96; former chm: Lanarkshire Div of Psychiatry, Med Staff Assoc Monklands Hosp; elder Hamilton Old Parish Church; FRCPGlas 1976, FRCPsych 1987; *Recreations* fishing, golf, classical literature; *Clubs* Hamilton Golf, New Club St Andrews, Bothwell and Blantyre Angling; *Style*— Dr Allan Sinclair

SINCLAIR, Dr Andrew Annandale; s of Stanley Charles Sinclair CBE (d 1973), and Kathleen, *née* Nash-Webber; *b* 21 Jan 1935; *Educ* Eton, Trinity Coll Cambridge, Harvard Univ, Columbia Univ; *m* 1 (m dis 1971), Marianne Alexandre; 1 s (Timon Alexandre); m 2 (m dis 1984), Miranda Seymour; 1 s (Merlin George); m 3, 25 July 1984, Sonia, Lady Melchett; *Career* Ensign Coldstream Gds 1953–55; ed and publisher Lorrimer Publishing 1968–87, md Timon Films 1968–; FRSL 1970, FSAH 1970; *Novels* The Breaking of Bumbo (1957), My Friend Judas (1958), The Project (1960), The Hallelujah Bum (1963), The Raker (1964), Gog (1967), Magog (1972), A Patriot for Hire (1978), The Facts in the Case of E A Poe (1980), Beau Bumbo (1985), King Ludd (1988), In Love and Anger (1994); *Non-Fiction* Prohibition The Era of Excess (1962), The Available Man The Life Behind the Mask of Warren Gamaliel Harding (1965), The Better Half The Emancipation of the American Woman (1965), A Concise History of the United States (1967), The Last of the Best - The Aristocracy of Europe in the Twentieth Century (1969), Che Guevara (1970), Dylan Thomas - Poet of His People (1975), The Savage - A History of Misunderstanding (1977), Jack - A Biography of Jack London (1977), John Ford (1979), Corsair - The Life of J Pierpont Morgan (1981), The Other Victoria - The Princess Royal and the Great Game of Europe (1981), The Red and the Blue (1986), Speigel (1987), War Like a Wasp (1989), The War Decade (1989), The Need to Give the Patrons and the Arts (1990), The Naked Savage (1991), The Sword and the Grail (1992), Francis Bacon, His Life and Violent Times (1993), In Love and Anger: A View of the 'Sixties (1994), Arts & Cultures: A History of the Fifty Years of the Arts Council of Great Britain (1995), Jerusalem: The Endless Crusade (1996); *Recreations* visiting ruins; *Clubs* Chelsea Arts, The Garrick; *Style*— Dr Andrew Sinclair; ✉ 16 Tite St, London SW3 4HZ (☎ 0171 352 7645)

SINCLAIR, Dr Bruce David; s of William Sinclair, of Comins Coch, Aberystwyth, and Muriel Elma, *née* Bruce; *b* 18 April 1961; *Educ* Ardwyn GS and Penglais Comp Aberystwyth, Univ of St Andrews (Thomson entrance bursary, BSc, PhD, J F Allen prize, Neil Arnot prize, class medal); *m* 17 Aug 1991, Marina Elizabeth, da of John Kenneth Blair, and Carita Maria, *née* Schwela; 2 s (Callum Dennis b 28 June 1993, Paul Bruce b 30 Oct 1995); *Career* Sch of Physics and Astronomy Univ of St Andrews: res asst in nonlinear optics in fibres 1986–87 then in diode pumped lasers 1987–89, Wolfson lectr (temp) in laser physics 1989, lectr 1989–96, sr lectr 1996–; Inst of Physics: local organiser Scot branch 1991–, hon sec Quantum Electronics Group 1994–97 (ctee memb 1992–95); volunteer ENABLE, hon pres Students Voluntary Serv Univ of St Andrews; *Books* contrib chapter to Optoelectronic Devices (ed Des Smith, 1995); also author of over 20 publications in refereed jls and over 32 papers at confs and tech meetings; *Recreations* family, tandem, gardening, walking, swimming, DIY; *Style*— Dr Bruce Sinclair; ✉ School of Physics and Astronomy, University of St Andrews, North Haugh, St Andrews, Fife KY16 9SS (☎ 01334 463118, fax 01334 463104)

SINCLAIR, Charles James Francis; s of Sir George Evelyn Sinclair, CMG, OBE, *qv*, of Carlton Rookery, Saxmundham, Suffolk, and Katharine Jane, *née* Burdekin (d 1971); *b* 4 April 1948; *Educ* Winchester, Magdalen Coll Oxford (BA); *m* 1974, Nicola, da of Maj W R Bayliss, RM; 2 s (Jeremy b 1977, Robert b 1979); *Career* CA 1974; Dearden Farrow CAs London 1970–75, fin accountant Associated Newspaper Group 1975; Associated Newspapers Holdings Ltd: asst md 1986, dep md 1987, md 1988, md and gp chief exec Daily Mail and General Trust plc 1989–; non-exec dir: Schroders plc 1990–, Reuters Holdings PLC 1994–; chm of tstees Minack Theatre Tst (Porthcurno Cornwall); FCA 1980; *Recreations* opera, fishing, skiing; *Clubs* Athenaeum, Vincent's; *Style*— Charles Sinclair, Esq; ✉ Daily Mail and General Trust plc, Northcliffe House, 2 Derry St, London W8 5TT (☎ 0171 938 6614, fax 0171 938 3909)

SINCLAIR, 17 Lord (S *c* 1449, confirmed 1488–9); Charles Murray Kennedy St Clair; CVO (1990, LVO 1953); s of 16 Lord Sinclair, MVO, JP (d 1957); 1 Lord resigned the Earldoms of Orkney and Caithness to the crown 1470, 10 Lord obtained Charter under Gt Seal 1677 confirming his honours with remainders to male heirs whatsoever; *b* 21 June 1914; *Educ* Eton, Magdalene Coll Cambridge; *m* 1968, Anne Lettice, da of Sir Richard Cotterell, 5 Bt, CBE, TD; 1 s, 2 da (Hon Laura b 1972, Hon Annabel b 1973); *Heir* s, Master of Sinclair b 9 Dec 1968; *Career* Maj Coldstream Gds; memb Queen's Body Guard for Scotland (Royal Co of Archers), Portcullis Pursuivant of Arms 1949–57, York Herald 1957–68, hon genealogist to Royal Victorian Order 1960–68, an extra equerry to HM Queen Elizabeth The Queen Mother 1953–; Lord-Lieut Dumfries and Galloway (Dist of Stewartry) 1982–89 (Vice Lord-Lieut 1977–82, DL Kirkcudbrightshire 1969), rep peer for Scotland 1959–63; *Clubs* New (Edinburgh); *Style*— The Rt Hon the Lord Sinclair, CVO; ✉ Knocknalling, St John's Town of Dalry, Castle Douglas, Kirkcudbrightshire DG7 3ST (☎ 0164 43 221)

SINCLAIR, Dr Clive John; s of David Sinclair, of Hendon, London, and Betty, *née* Jacobovitch; *b* 19 Feb 1948; *Educ* UEA (BA), Univ of Calif Santa Cruz, Univ of Exeter, UEA (PhD); *m* 1979, Frances, da of Sydney Redhouse (d 1994); 1 s (Seth Benjamin b 1981); *Career* writer; copywriter Young & Rubicam 1973–76, literary ed The Jewish Chronicle 1983–87, British Cncl writer in residence Univ of Uppsala Sweden 1988; Bicentennial Arts fell 1980–81, Somerset Maugham prize 1981, one of 20 Best Young British Novelists 1983; memb: Soc of Authors, PEN 1979–; FRSL 1983; *Fiction* Bibliosexuality (1973), Hearts of Gold (short stories, 1979), Bedbugs (short stories, 1982), Blood Libels (1985), Cosmetic Effects (1989), For Good or Evil (short stories, 1991), Augustus Rex (1992), The Lady with the Laptop (short stories, 1996); *Misc* The Brothers Singer (biog, 1983), Diaspora Blues (travel, 1987); *Recreations* travel & football & letter writing; *Style*— Dr Clive Sinclair, FRSL; ✉ Rogers Coleridge & White, 20 Powis Mews, London W11 1JN (☎ 0171 221 3717, fax 0171 229 9084)

SINCLAIR, Sir Clive Marles; kt (1983); s of George William Carter Sinclair, and Thora Edith Ella, *née* Marles; *b* 30 July 1940; *Educ* Highgate Sch, Reading Sch, St George's Coll Weybridge; *m* 1962 (m dis 1985), Ann, *née* Trevor Briscoe; 2 s, 1 da; *Career* ed Bernards (publishers) 1958–61; chm: Sinclair Radionics 1962–79 (produced pocket TV), Sinclair Research Ltd 1979–, Cambridge Computer Ltd 1986–90; fndr Sinclair Browne (publishers) 1981–85 (annual Sinclair Prize for Fiction); dir: Shaye Communications Ltd 1986–91, Anamartic Ltd; visiting fell Robinson Coll Cambridge 1982–85; chm Br MENSA 1980–; Hon DSc: Bath 1983, Warwick 1983, Heriot Watt 1983; visiting prof: Imperial Coll of Sci and Technol 1984–92 (hon fell 1984), UMIST 1984 (hon fell); Mullard award Royal Soc 1984; *Publications* Practical Transistor Receivers (1959), British Semiconductor Survey (1963); *Recreations* music, poetry, mathematics, science, poker; *Clubs* Chelsea Arts; *Style*— Sir Clive Sinclair; ✉ 7 York Central, 70 York Way, London N1 9AG (☎ 0171 837 6316); Sinclair Research Limited, 7 York Central, 70 York Way, London N1 9AG (☎ 0171 837 6150, fax 0171 278 3101)

SINCLAIR, David Grant; s of Leslie Sinclair (d 1978), of London, and Beatrice Zena, *née* Samuel (d 1979); *b* 12 Feb 1948; *Educ* Latymer Upper Sch; *m* 7 June 1970, Susan Carol, da of Alexander Merkin (d 1963), of London; 2 s (Alexander James b 1972, Julian Lloyd b 1974); 1 da (Olivia Lesley b 1982); *Career* fndr and sr ptnr Sinclair Silverman CAs 1972–; jt fndr and dir International Corporate Compliance Ltd and assoc cos 1991–; fndr and chm Master Financial Services Ltd and assoc cos 1982–, chm Motivision Worldwide plc and subsids 1993–; recognised expert in forensic accounting; FCA 1978 (ACA 1972); *Recreations* bridge, charity work; *Style*— David G Sinclair, Esq; ✉ Sinclair Silverman, Roman House, 296 Golders Green Road, London NW11 9PT (☎ 0181 455 0011, fax 0181 455 1199, mobile 0385 287237)

SINCLAIR, David William Jonathan; s of James Daniel Sinclair, of Glasgow, and Barbara Kathleen, *née* Barclay-Bishop; *b* 24 Oct 1952; *Educ* Eltham Coll London, Univ of Warwick (BA); *m* 1 May 1986, Prudence Evelyn, da of late Sir Evelyn Hone; 1 s (Jack b 23 Dec 1990), 1 da ((Josephine) Faith b 23 Aug 1989); *Career* music writer and broadcaster; former drummer/vocalist in groups incl: Empire Made 1976–77, Tidal Waveband 1977–78, Blunt Instrument 1978–79, London Zoo 1979–81, TV Smith's Explorers 1981–82, Laughing Sam's Dice 1983–85; contrib to magazines and newspapers incl: One Two Testing 1983–85, Guitar Heroes 1983–84, The History of Rock 1983–84, Kerrang! 1983–85, The Times 1985–, Q Magazine 1986–, Billboard (ed Global Music Pulse column) 1991–, Rolling Stone 1992–; researcher BBC TV (progs incl Eight Days A Week, Wogan, The Rock'n'Roll Years and Rock School) 1984–86; regular appearances on: Sunday Edition (BBC Radio 5) 1991–92, Sunrise Morning News (Sky TV) 1991–92, The Breakfast Show (BBC GLR) 1992–; *Books* Tres Hombres - The Story of ZZ Top (1986), Rock on CD - The Essential Guide (1992, revised and updated 1993); *Recreations* tennis, badminton, bridge; *Clubs* Polytechnic of Central London; *Style*— David Sinclair, Esq; ✉ The Times, 1 Pennington St, Wapping, London E1 9XN (☎ 0171 782 5000, fax 0171 782 5046)

SINCLAIR, Sir George Evelyn; kt (1960), CMG (1956), OBE (1950); s of Francis Sinclair (d 1953), of Chynance, St Buryan, Cornwall; *b* 6 Nov 1912; *Educ* Abingdon Sch, Pembroke Coll Oxford (MA); *m* 1, 1941, Katharine Jane (d 1971), da of Beauford Burdekin (d 1963), of Sydney, NSW, and Mrs K P Burdekin (d 1964); 1 s (Charles James Francis Sinclair, *qv*), 3 da; m 2, 1972, Mary Violet, wid of G L Sawday; *Career* WWII RWAFF (W Africa) 1940–43, temp Maj; entered Colonial Serv 1936, Gold Coast 1936–40, Colonial Office 1943–45, sec Elliot Cmmn on Higher Educn in W Africa 1943–45, Gold Coast 1945–55, regnl offr Trans-Volta Togoland 1952–55, dep govr Cyprus 1955–60, ret 1961; political work in UK and overseas 1960–64; memb Wimbledon Borough Cncl 1962–65; MP (C) Dorking 1964–1979; dir Intermediate Technol Devpt Gp 1979–82 (vice pres 1966–79), fndr tstee Physically Handicapped & Able Bodied; fndr memb Human Rights Tst 1971–74, memb Bd Christian Aid 1973–78; memb Cncl: Oxford Soc 1982–93, Overseas Servs Resettlement Bureau; memb Assoc of Governing Bodies of Public Schs (chm 1979–84); memb Bd of Govrs: Abingdon Sch 1971–88 (chm 1973–80), Felixstowe Coll 1980–87, Campion Sch Athens 1983–; chm Independent Schs Jt Cncl 1980–83, tstee Runnymede Trust 1969–75; conslt: UN Fund for Population Affairs, Int Planned Parenthood Fedn; special advsr Global Ctee of Parliamentarians on Population and Devpt; chm UK Consultative Ctee for Oxford Conf of Global Forum of Spiritual and Parly Leaders on Human Survival 1988; hon fell Pembroke Coll Oxford; *Recreations* golf, fishing, gardening; *Clubs* Athenaeum, Aldeburgh Yacht, Aldeburgh Golf, Royal Cwlth Soc; *Style*— Sir George Sinclair, CMG, OBE; ✉ Carlton Rookery, Saxmundham, Suffolk IP17 2NN (☎ 01728 602217, fax 01728 604917)

SINCLAIR, Wing Cdr Gordon Leonard; OBE (1996), DFC (1940); s of William Francis Sinclair (d 1924), Katharine, *née* Sweibinz (1968); *b* 15 Aug 1916; *Educ* Eastbourne Coll; *m* 1952, Lady Bridget Ellinor Fortescue, da of 6th Earl Fortescue, and Marjorie, *née* Trotter; 2 s (Alan Gordon William b Sept 1956, Robert Alistair b Feb 1965), 2 da (Fiona Caroline b Nov 1958, Joanna Rosalind b Oct 1963); *Career* Union Cold Storage Co 1934–37; RAF 1937–56: Wing Cdr Fighter Cmd, pilot Battles of France and Britain, personal air secretary to Sec of State for Air 1946–48, Staff Coll 1948, advsr to Lebanese Army 1952–54; Morgan Crucible Co 1956–58, dep dir Br Steel Exports Assoc 1958–72, London dir Usinor Steel Co France 1972–82, ind steel conslt 1983–; pres Int Steel Trade Assoc 1990– (chm 1983, 1988 and 1989); pres The Royal Soc for the Prevention of Accidents 1992–95 (dep pres 1985–92), chm Woodford Valley Cons Assoc 1986–; War Cross of Valour (Czechoslavakia) 1940, The Order of George of Podgrad (Czechoslavakia) 1991; *Recreations* shooting, fishing, golf, gardening; *Clubs* RAF, Pratt's; *Style*— Wing Cdr Gordon Sinclair, OBE, DFC; ✉ Fairwood House, Great Durnford, Salisbury, Wiltshire SP4 6BD (☎ 01980 623372)

SINCLAIR, Iain Macgregor; s of Dr Henry Macgregor Sinclair (d 1989), of Bridgend, Glamorgan, and Doris, *née* Jones (d 1991); *b* 11 June 1943; *Educ* Cheltenham Coll, London Sch of Film Technique, Trinity Coll Dublin, The Courtauld Inst; *m* (Mary) Annabel Rose, *née* Hadman; 1 s (William Llewelyn b 21 Oct 1975), 2 da (Farne b 8 July 1972, Madeleine b 14 Jan 1980); *Career* writer; *Books* incl: The Kodak Mantra Diaries (historical documentary, 1971), Lud Heat (poetry/essays, 1975), Suicide Bridge (poetry/essays, 1979), White Chappell, Scarlet Tracings (fiction, 1987), Flesh Eggs and Scalp Metal (poetry, 1989), Downriver (fiction, 1991), Radon Daughters (fiction, 1994); *Style*— Iain Sinclair, Esq; ✉ c/o John Parker, MBA Literary Agents, 45 Fitzroy St, London W1P 5HR (☎ 0171 387 2076, fax 0171 387 2042)

SINCLAIR, Sir Ian McTaggart; KCMG (1977, CMG 1972), QC (1979); s of John Sinclair (d 1950), of Whitecraigs, Renfrewshire, and Margaret Wilson Gardner, *née* Love (d 1965); *b* 14 Jan 1926; *Educ* Merchiston Castle Sch, King's Coll Cambridge (BA, LLB); *m* 24 April 1954, Barbara Elizabeth, da of Stanley Lenton (d 1982), of Grimsby; 2 s (Andrew b 1958, Philip b 1962), 1 da (Jane b 1956); *Career* Intelligence Corps 1944–47; called to the Bar Middle Temple 1952 (bencher 1980); entered Dip Serv 1950; legal cnsllr: NY and Washington 1964–67, FCO 1967–71; dep legal advsr FCO 1971–72, second legal advsr 1973–75, legal advsr 1976–84; barr 1984–; memb Int Law Cmmn 1981–86; memb Institut de Droit Int 1987– (assoc memb 1983–87); hon memb: American Soc of Int Law 1987, Permanent Ct of Arbitration 1992–; FRGS 1987; *Books* Vienna Convention on the Law of Treaties (1973, 2 edn 1984), International Law Commission (1987); *Recreations* golf, bird-watching, reading; *Clubs* Athenaeum; *Style*— Sir Ian Sinclair, KCMG, QC; ✉ 2 Hare Court, Temple, London EC4Y 7BH (☎ 0171 583 1770, fax 0171 583 9269)

SINCLAIR, Jeremy; s of Donald Alan Forrester Sinclair (d 1987), of London; *b* 4 Nov 1946; *m* Jan 1976, Jacqueline Margaret, da of Jack Metcalfe (d 1994); 2 s (Leon b 21 Oct 1981, David b 13 March 1985), 1 da (Naomi b 26 Jan 1979); *Career* worldwide creative dir and Euro chm Saatchi & Saatchi plc until 1995 (resigned); ptnr M&C Saatchi 1995–; *Style*— Jeremy Sinclair, Esq; ✉ M&C Saatchi Ltd, 36 Golden Square, London W1R 4EE (☎ 0171 543 4500)

SINCLAIR, Kenneth Brian; s of Joseph Frederick Sinclair, and May, *née* Haddon; *b* 14 March 1931; *m* 5 Jan 1957, Yvonne Joan, da of Walter Henry Tucker; 1 s (Keith Andrew Brian b 1 May 1960); *Career* Pagle Star Insurance 1949–54, NCB 1954, ptnr David A Bevan Simpson 1960–70 (joined 1954); exec ptnr de Zoete and Bevan 1974; chm Barclays de Zoete Wedd Securities Ltd 1990–94, vice chm BZW Holdings Ltd 1990–94; dir: Barclays Bank plc 1988–94, Medeva plc 1991–; *Recreations* bridge, chess, watching football; *Clubs* City of London; *Style*— Kenneth Sinclair, Esq; ✉ Medeva plc, 10 St James St, London SW1A 1EF (☎ 0171 839 3888, fax 0171 930 1514)

SINCLAIR, Air Vice-Marshal Sir Laurence Frank; GC (1941), KCB (1957, CB 1946), CBE (1943), DSO (1940, bar 1943); s of late Frank Sinclair, Nigerian Political Serv; *b* 1908; *Educ* ISC, RAF Coll Cranwell; *m* 1941, Valerie (d 1990), da of Lt-Col Joseph Dalton White; 1 s (Mark), 1 da (Susan); *Career* Sqdn Ldr 1938, CO No 110 (Blenheim) Sqdn 1940, CO RAF Watton 1941, CO No 324 Wing N Africa 1943, Gp Capt 1943–44, ADC to HM King George VI 1943–49, AOC Tactical Bomber Force, MAAF, SASO, Balkan Air Force, 1944, AOC No 2 Gp BAFO 1949–50, asst cmdt RAF Staff Coll Bracknell 1950; cmdt: RAF Coll Cranwell 1950–52, Sch of Land-Air Warfare Old Sarum 1952–53; Air Vice-Marshal 1952, asst chief of air staff (ops) 1953–55, AOC Br Forces Arabian Peninsula 1955–57, cmdt Jt Servs Staff Coll 1958, ret 1960; controller: Ground Servs Miny Aviation 1960–61, Nat Air Traffic Control Servs 1962–66; Legion of Merit USA 1943, Légion d'Honneur France 1944, Partisan Star with gold leaves (Yugoslavia); *Recreations* fishing; *Clubs* RAF; *Style*— Air Vice-Marshal Sir Laurence Sinclair, GC, KCB, CBE, DSO; ✉ The Old Prebendal House, Shipton-under-Wychwood, Oxford OX7 6BQ (fax 01993 832031)

SINCLAIR, Dr Leonard; s of Sidney Sinclair (d 1973), of London, and Blanche, *née* Appele (d 1988); *b* 23 Sept 1928; *Educ* Rochelle Sch, Raine's Fndn Sch, Middx Hosp Med Sch Univ of London (Neyerstein scholar, James McIntosh scholar, BSc, MB BS, Lyell Gold medal, Football colours); *m* 22 March 1959, Ann, da of Frederick Franks; 1 da (Judith b 19 Dec 1959), 3 s (Jonathan b 31 Oct 1962, David b 5 Feb 1964, Anthony b 27 Aug 1969); *Career* house surgn and house physician: Southend Gen Hosp 1954–56, Queen Elizabeth Hosp for Children 1956–57 (med registrar 1960–62); house physician Whittington Hosp 1957, jr lectr and hon registrar Guy's Hosp Med Sch 1957–60, sr paediatric registrar Westminster and Westminster Children's Hosp 1962–66, hon conslt paediatrician Hosp of St John and St Elizabeth 1965–75; conslt paediatrician: St Stephen's Hosp 1966–88, Westminster Hosp 1973–, Royal Nat Throat Nose and Ear Hosp 1969–, Westminster Children's Hosp 1988–, Charing Cross Hosp 1988; New Heath Tst fell 1959–61; visiting prof: Mount Sinai Hosp 1969, St Sophia's Children's Hosp Univ of Rotterdam 1983, hon sr lectr Faculty of Med Univ Coll London 1984; dep pres Paediatric Section RSM 1974–75 (sec Paediatric Section 1971–73); DCH 1957, FRCP 1974 (MRCP 1960), FRSM 1966, memb BPA 1968, fell Soc for Endocrinology 1968, memb BMA 1969; *Books* Metabolic Disease in Childhood (1979), Enfermedades Metabolicas en la Infancia (1981), BMA Complete Family Health Encyclopedia (paediatric section, 1990); author of other scientific and med papers; *Recreations* tennis, old books, other people's problems; *Clubs* Athenaeum, Royal Society of Medicine; *Style*— Dr Leonard Sinclair; ✉ 152 Harley St, London W1 (☎ 0171 935 0444)

SINCLAIR, Master of; Hon Matthew Murray Kennedy St Clair; s and h of 17 Lord Sinclair, CVO; *b* 9 Dec 1968; *Educ* Glenalmond, RAC Cirencester; *Career* assoc memb Royal Inst of Chartered Surveyors (ARICS); *Clubs* New (Edinburgh); *Style*— The Master of Sinclair; ✉ 1 St Bernards Crescent, Edinburgh EH4 1NR

SINCLAIR, Lady (Euphemia) Meredith; raised to the rank of an Earl's da 1948; da of Rev the Hon Charles Augustus Sinclair (d 1943; s of 16 Earl of Caithness), and Mary Ann, *née* Harman (d 1938); *b* 22 Oct 1915; *Career* SRN; *Style*— The Lady Meredith Sinclair; ✉ 5a Mulberry Drive, Wheatley, Oxon OX33 1UT (☎ 01865 873876)

SINCLAIR, Michael; *see:* Shea, Michael Sinclair MacAuslan

SINCLAIR, Nicholas Hilary; s of Hugh Sinclair (d 1962), actor, of Sussex, and Rosalie, *née* Williams; *b* 28 Jan 1954; *Educ* Christ's Hosp Horsham, Univ of Newcastle upon Tyne; *Career* photographer; SE Arts photography bursary 1983, artist in residence Esher Coll Surrey 1984; visiting lectr: Univ of Sussex 1984, Univ of Cambridge 1986, Northbrook Coll Horsham 1983–94, West Dean Coll Chichester 1984–90, London Coll of Printing 1991–92; visual arts and film critic BBC Radio Sussex 1982–85, chm North Star Studios 1983–93, visual arts organiser Gardner Arts Centre Univ of Sussex 1984–85, memb Photography Panel SE Arts 1985–89; work published in Harpers and Queen, The Guardian, The Times, New Scientist, The Independent Sunday Review, Design Week, World of Interiors, Creative Camera, Br Jl of Photography; *Exhibitions* individual: Gardner Arts Centre Univ of Sussex 1983, Photogallery St Leonards-on-Sea 1985, Photography Centre of Athens 1986, West Dean Coll Chichester 1990, Brighton Museum and Art Gallery 1995, Tom Blau Gallery London 1996; group incl: Behind the Auguste Mask (circus photographs, National Theatre) 1985, Brewery Arts Centre Kendal 1986, Central Sch of Art London 1987, Hove Museum and Art Gallery 1988, Circus Comes To Town (Northern Centre for Contemporary Art) 1989, Volkshochshule Stuttgart 1990 (Br Cncl touring W Germany) 1990–91, Nat Portrait Gallery London 1994, Joseloff Gallery Hartford USA 1995; work in the collection of Nat Portrait Gallery; *Books* Behind the Auguste Mask (1985), Sussex Churches and Chapels (1989), Portraits (1993), The Chameleon Body (1996); *Recreations* swimming, music, theatre, cinema; *Style*— Nicholas Sinclair, Esq; ✉ North Star Studios, 65 Ditchling Road, Brighton BN1 4SD (☎ and fax 01273 730289)

SINCLAIR, Sir Patrick Robert Richard; 10 Bt (NS 1704), of Dunbeath, Caithness; s of Alexander Robert Sinclair (d 1972, bro of 8 Bt), and Mabel Vera, *née* Baxendale (d 1981); suc his cousin, Sir John Rollo Norman Blair Sinclair, 9 Bt (d 1990); *b* 21 May 1936; *Educ* Winchester, Oriel Coll Oxford (MA); *m* 1974, Susan Catherine Beresford, eldest da of Geoffrey Clive Davies, OBE, of Holbrook, Ipswich, Suffolk; 1 s (William Robert Francis b 1979), 1 da (Helen Margaret Gwendolen b 1984); *Heir* s, William Robert Francis Sinclair b 27 March 1979; *Career* RNVR; called to the Bar Lincoln's Inn 1961, bencher 1994, in practice at Chancery Bar; *Clubs* Pin Mill Sailing (Suffolk); *Style*— Sir Patrick Sinclair of Dunbeath, Bt; ✉ 5 New Square, Lincoln's Inn, London WC2A 3SA (☎ 0171 404 0404)

SINCLAIR, Roderick John (Rod); s of Maj-Gen Sir John Sinclair, KCMG, OBE (d 1977), and Esme Beatrice, *née* Sopwith (d 1983); *b* 10 July 1944; *Educ* Gordonstoun; *m* 1 (m dis 1976), Lucinda Mary Martin-Smith; m 2, 15 May 1977, Sarah Margaret, da of Brig Harold Dolphin; 1 s (James Alexander b 1984), 1 da (Natasha Esme b 1982); *Career* short serv cmmn Scots Gds 1963–66; stockbroker L Messel & Co 1969–77, ptnr De Zoete & Bevan 1977–85, dir Barclays De Zoete Wedd Securities Ltd 1985–93, dir Instinet International Ltd 1993–, strategic int mktg dir Reuters 1995–, dir Securities and Futures Authy 1994–; chm: Broker Services Ltd 1987–88, Thamesway Investment Services 1987–94; memb Int Stock Exchange 1978; *Recreations* tennis, skiing; *Clubs* Boodle's; *Style*— Rod Sinclair, Esq; ✉ Downgate Farm, Steep Marsh, Petersfield, Hants GU32

2BP (☎ 01730 263321); Reuters Ltd, 85 Fleet Street, London EC4P 4AJ (☎ 0171 542 5434, fax 0171 542 5320)

SINCLAIR, Thomas Humphrey; s of William Sinclair Boston (d 1972), and Jean, *née* Matthews; *b* 17 Aug 1938; *Educ* Oundle, RAC Cirencester; *m* 2, 30 May 1970, Ann Pauline, da of Flt Lt Harold Rowson (d 1983); 2 s (Michael, John); *Career* Nat Serv 1958–60; chm William Sinclair Holdings plc 1984– (md 1978); dir Elsoms (Spalding) Ltd; *Recreations* golf, tennis; *Style*— Thomas Sinclair, Esq; ✉ William Sinclair Holdings plc, Firth Road, Lincoln LN6 7AH (☎ 01522 537561, fax 01522 560648)

SINCLAIR-LOCKHART, Sir Simon John Edward Francis; 15 Bt (NS 1636), of Murkle, Co Caithness, and Stevenson, Co Haddington; s of Sir Muir Edward Sinclair-Lockhart, 14 Bt (d 1985), and Olga Ann, *née* White-Parsons; *b* 22 July 1941; *m* 1973, Felicity Edith, da of late Ivan Lachlan Campbell Stewart, of Havelock North, NZ; 2 s (Robert Muir b 1973, James Lachlan b (twin) 1973), 1 da (Fiona Mary b 1979); *Heir* s, Robert Muir Sinclair-Lockhart b 12 Sept 1973; *Style*— Sir Simon Sinclair-Lockhart, Bt; ✉ 13 Franklin Terrace, Havelock North, New Zealand

SINCLAIR OF CLEEVE, 3 Baron (UK 1957); John Lawrence Robert Sinclair; o s of 2 Baron (d 1985), and Lady Sinclair of Cleeve, *née* Patricia Hellyer; *b* 6 Jan 1953; *Educ* Winchester Coll, Bath Univ, Manchester Univ; *Heir* none; *Career* design and technol; workshop technician in an Inner London Comprehensive Sch, designer of recycled furniture; *Recreations* mime, motorcycling, music; *Clubs* Scala Cinema; *Style*— J L R Sinclair, Esq

SINDEN, Donald Alfred; CBE (1979); s of Alfred Edward Sinden (d 1972), and Mabel Agnes, *née* Fuller (d 1959); *b* 9 Oct 1923; *m* 3 May 1948, Diana, da of Daniel Mahony (d 1981); 2 s (Jeremy b 14 June 1950, d 29 May 1996, Marcus (Marc), *qv* b 9 May 1954); *Career* actor; first stage performance 1942; assoc artist RSC 1967–; pres: Fedn of Playgoers' Socs 1968–93, Royal Theatrical Fund 1983–, Theatre Museum Assoc 1985–1995; tstee Br Actors' Equity Assoc 1988–; FRSA *Television* incl: Two's Company, Never the Twain, Discovering English Churches; *Films* Rank Orgn 1952–60 appearing in 23 films incl: Doctor in the House, The Cruel Sea; *Awards* incl: Drama Desk Award (for London Assurance) 1974, Variety Club of GB Stage Actor of 1976, Evening Standard Drama Award Best Actor 1977 (both for King Lear); *Books* A Touch of the Memoirs (autobiog, 1982), Laughter in the Second Act (autobiog, 1985), The Everyman Book of Theatrical Anecdotes (ed, 1987), The English Country Church (1988), The Last Word (ed, 1994); *Recreations* serendipity; *Clubs* Garrick (tstee), Beefsteak, MCC; *Style*— Donald Sinden, Esq, CBE; ✉ 60 Temple Fortune Lane, London NW11 7UE

SINDEN, Marcus Andrew (Marc); s of Donald Alfred Sinden, CBE, *qv*, of London, and Diana, *née* Mahony; *b* 9 May 1954; *Educ* Hall Sch Hampstead, Edgeborough Surrey, Stanbridge Earls Hants, Bristol Old Vic Theatre Sch; *m* 20 Aug 1977, Joanne Lesley, da of Geoffrey Gilbert, of Dorset; 1 s (Henry b 1980), 1 da (Bridie b 1990); *Career* actor 1978– and producer 1996–; jeweller and goldsmith H Knowles-Brown Ltd Hampstead 1973–78; artistic dir Mermaid Theatre 1993–94; md Smallhythe Productions Ltd; Freedom City of London, Liveryman Worshipful Co of Innholders; FZS; *Theatre* as prodr That Good Night; as actor West End incl: Enjoy, Her Royal Highness, Underground, School for Scandal, Two into One, Ross, Over My Dead Body, The Beaux Stratagem; other roles incl: John Bulls Other Island (Dublin), Major Barbara (Chichester Festival Theatre), There's a Girl in my Soup, Dangerous Obsession, Private Lives, Mansfield Park, Sting in the Tale; numerous rep; *Television* incl: Crossroads, Home Front, Magnum PI, Country Boy, Bergerac, Never the Twain, Rumpole of the Bailey, Emmerdale, Century Falls, The Politicians Wife, Against All Odds, The Island; *Films* The Wicked Lady, Clash of Loyalties, White Nights, Manges D'Homme, The Mystery of Edwin Drood, Carry On Columbus, Decadence, Princess, The Brylcreem Boys; *Recreations* theatrical history, zoology, ethology, cricket, motor racing, history of stunt-work; *Clubs* Green Room; *Style*— Marc Sinden, Esq; ✉ c/o Hilary Gagan Assoc, Caprice House, 3 New Burlington Street, London W1X 1FE

SINFIELD, Prof (Robert) Adrian; s of Robert Ernest Sinfield (d 1983), of Diss, Norfolk, and Agnes Joy, *née* Fouracre (d 1995); *b* 3 Nov 1938; *Educ* Mercers' Sch, Balliol Coll Oxford (BA), LSE (Dip); *m* 17 Sept 1964, Dorothy Anne, da of George Stanley Palmer (d 1992), of Watford; 2 da (Beth b 1965, Laura b 1969); *Career* jr admin Lutheran World Service Hong Kong 1961–62, res asst LSE 1963–64, res assoc NY State Mental Health Res Unit Syracuse 1964–65, Univ of Essex 1965–79 (asst lectr, lectr, sr lectr, reader sociology); prof of social policy Univ of Edinburgh 1979–95 (emeritus 1995–); visiting posts: Graduate Sch of Social Work and Soc Res Bryn Mawr Coll Pa 1969, NY Sch of Social Work Univ of Columbia 1969, Euro Chair of Social Policy Eötvös Laránd Univ Budapest 1996; conslt: on long term unemployed OECD Paris 1965–68, on industl social welfare UN NY 1970–72, on income maintenance servs N Tyneside CDP 1975–78; exec Child Poverty Action Gp 1974–78, co-fndr and chm Mgmnt Ctee Unemployment Unit 1981–91; pres: Sociology and Social Policy British Assoc for Advancement of Science 1993, Social Policy Assoc 1996– (chm 1986–89); *Books* The Long-Term Unemployed (1968), Industrial Social Welfare (1971), What Unemployment Means (1981), The Workless State (co-ed with Brian Showler, 1981), Excluding Youth (co-author, 1991), The Sociology of Social Security (co-ed, 1991), Poverty, Inequality and Justice (ed, 1993), The Routes to Welfare in Denmark and the United Kingdom (co-author, 1996); *Recreations* reading, walking, travel; *Style*— Prof Adrian Sinfield; ✉ 12 Eden Lane, Edinburgh EH10 4SD (☎ 0131 447 2182); University of Edinburgh, Department of Social Policy, Adam Ferguson Building, George Square, Edinburgh EH8 9LL (☎ 0131 650 3924, fax 0131 650 3919, e-mail Adrian.Sinfield@ed.ac.uk)

SINGER, Prof Albert; s of Jacob Singer (Capt in Polish Army, d 1989), of Sydney, Aust, and Gertie, *née* Sadik (d 1986); *b* 4 Jan 1938; *Educ* Sydney GS, Univ of Sydney (MB BS, PhD), Univ of Oxford (DPhil); *m* 27 June 1976, Talya, da of Maurice Goodman (d 1991); 3 da (Leora b 1978, Rebecca b 1980, Alexandra b 1983); *Career* Nat Serv Royal Aust Air Force 1956–57, Univ Sqdn Flt Lt 1960, active serv with RAAF Reserve in Vietnam 1968–69; Commonwealth fell Oxford 1970, visiting fell to Europe and USA 1968–69, pt/t conslt WHO 1969–70, in res 1970–73, sr lectr then reader Univ of Sheffield 1973–80, conslt gynaecologist Whittington Hosp London 1980–, prof UCL; has published extensively on subject of gynaecological surgery and res into causes of female cancer; served on numerous govt panels and ctees primarily concerned with female cancer, memb Med Ctee of Women's Nat Cancer Control Campaign; memb RSM, FRCOG; *Books* The Cervix (with J Jordan), The Colour Atlas of Gynaecological Surgery (6 vols with David Lees), Lower Genital Tract Pre-Cancer (with J Monaghan); *Recreations* sport, especially tennis, swimming and sailing; *Clubs* Oxford and Cambridge; *Style*— Prof Albert Singer; ✉ 148 Harley Street, London W1N 1AH (☎ 0171 935 1900, fax 0181 458 0168)

SINGER, Aubrey Edward; CBE (1984); s of Louis Henry Singer, and Elizabeth, *née* Walton; *b* 21 Jan 1927; *Educ* Bradford GS; *m* 1949, Cynthia Adams; 1 s, 3 da; *Career* BBC TV: joined 1949, asst head of outside broadcasts 1956–59, head of sci features 1959–61, head of Features Gp 1967–74, controller BBC2 1974–78, md BBC Radio 1978–82, dep dir gen BBC 1982–84, md BBC TV 1982–84; chm White City Films 1984–, dir Goldcrest Films and TV 1988–90; vice pres RTS 1982–88 (fell 1978), memb Ctee Nat Museum of Photography Film and TV Bradford 1985–, fell Royal Asiatic Soc; Hon DLitt Univ of Bradford 1984; *Recreations* walking; *Clubs* Savile; *Style*— Aubrey Singer, Esq, CBE; ✉ White City Films, 79 Sutton Court Rd, Chiswick, London W4 3EQ (☎ 0181 994 6795, 0181 994 4856, fax 0181 995 9379)

SINGER, His Hon Judge; Harold Samuel Singer; s of Ellis Singer (d 1982), and Minnie, *née* Coffman (d 1964); *b* 17 July 1935; *Educ* Salford GS, Fitzwilliam House Cambridge (MA); *m* 1966, Adele Berenice, da of Julius Emanuel; 1 s (Andrew b 1967), 2 da (Rachel b 1970, Victoria b 1974); *Career* called to the Bar Gray's Inn 1957, recorder of the Crown Court 1981–84, circuit judge (Northern Circuit) 1984–; *Recreations* music, reading, painting, photography; *Style*— His Hon Judge Singer; ✉ c/o Northern Circuit Office, 15 Quay Street, Manchester M60 9FD

SINGER, Nicky Margaret; da of Geoffrey William Singer (d 1970), and Sheila Anne, *née* King (d 1987); *b* 22 July 1956; *Educ* Queen Anne's Sch Caversham, Univ of Bristol (BA); *m* 17 Sept 1983, (Timothy) James Stephen King-Smith; 2 s (Roland James Singer-Kingsmith 28 Dec 1987, Edmund John Singer-Kingsmith b 26 Sept 1991), 1 da (Molly Rose Singer-Kingsmith b 23 July 1996); *Career* assoc dir of lectures and seminars ICA 1980–83, researcher Voices (C4) 1983–84, programme conslt for David Puttnam at Enigma Film and TV 1984–85, literature offr SE Arts 1985–86, co-fndr and co-dir Performing Arts Labs charity 1987–; presenter six films Labours of Eve (BBC) 1995; chair Literature Ctee Brighton Festival 1988–93; short drama cmmnd The Sins of the World (C4) 1990; *Novels* To Still the Child (1992), To Have and to Hold (1993), What She Wanted (1996); author of numerous short stories; *Style*— Ms Nicky Singer; ✉ c/o Lutyens & Rubinstein, 231 Westbourne Park Road, London W11 1EB (☎ 0171 792 4855, fax 0171 792 4833)

SINGER, Dr Norbert; CBE (1990); s of Salomon Singer (d 1970), and Mina, *née* Korn (d 1976); *b* 3 May 1931; *Educ* Highbury Co Sch, QMC London (BSc, PhD); *m* 23 May 1980, Dr Brenda Margaret Walter, da of Richard Walter, of Tunbridge Wells; *Career* res chemist and project ldr Morgan Crucible Co Ltd 1954–57; N London Poly 1958–70 (lectr, sr lectr, princ lectr, dep head of Dept of Chemistry), head of Dept of Life Sciences Poly of Central London 1971–74 (prof 1972–74), asst dir then dep dir Poly of N London 1974–78, vice chllr Univ of Greenwich 1992–93 (dir Thames Poly 1978–92), visiting prof Univ of Westminster 1996–; chm: Bexley Health Authy 1993–94, Oxleas NHS Tst (formerly Bexley Community Health NHS Tst) 1994–; memb Cncl CNAA 1982–88, chm Reviews Co-ordination Ctee 1984–87, chm CNAA CATCOM 1990–92; memb Governing Body: The London Inst, Nene Coll, Rose Bruford Coll (chm 1994–), Connaught Sch; govr St Peter's CEP Sch; Hon DSc Univ of Greenwich 1993; fell Queen Mary and Westfield Coll Univ of London 1993; CChem, FRSC 1964 (MRSC 1951); *Recreations* walking, reading; *Style*— Dr Norbert Singer, CBE; ✉ Croft Lodge, Bayhall Road, Tunbridge Wells, Kent TN2 4TP (☎ 01892 523821)

SINGER, Hon Mr Justice; Hon Sir (Jan) Peter; kt (1993); s of late Dr Hanus Kurt Singer, and Anita, *née* Muller; *b* 10 Sept 1944; *Educ* King Edward's Sch Birmingham, Selwyn Coll Cambridge; *m* 2 Jan 1970, Julia Mary, da of Norman Stewart Caney (d 1988); 1 s (Luke b 1985), 1 da (Laura b 1983); *Career* called to the Bar Inner Temple 1967, recorder of the Crown Court 1987–93 (asst recorder 1983–87), QC 1987, bencher 1993; judge of the High Court of Justice (Family Div) 1993–; Family Law Bar Assoc: sec 1980–83, treas 1983–90, chm 1990–92; Bar nominee: Matrimonial Causes Rule Ctee 1981–85, Nat Legal Aid Ctee Law Soc 1984–89; memb: Senate of the Inns of Court and the Bar 1983–86, Legal Aid and Fees Ctee Bar Cncl 1986–92; ex officio memb: Gen Cncl of the Bar 1990–92, Bar Ctee Gen Cncl of the Bar 1990–92; vice pres Int Acad of Matrimonial Lawyers (Euro Chapter) 1992–93; *Recreations* travel, walking, gardening; *Style*— The Hon Mr Justice Singer; ✉ Royal Courts of Justice, Strand, London WC2A 2LL

SINGER, Susan Honor; da of Brig John James McCully, DSO, (d 1985), and Honor Goad, *née* Ward (now Mrs Edward Basil Elliott), of Deal, Kent; *b* 23 Feb 1942; *Educ* St Mary's Calne, Open Univ (BA), Garnett Coll (PGCE); *m* 18 April 1964, Christopher Ronald Morgan Singer; 1 s (Humphrey Stewart Morgan b 14 Dec 1965), 2 da (Charlotte Honor b 20 Sept 1967, Hermione Juliet b 24 Jan 1971); *Career* set up and ran pre-sch playgp 1968–74; St Paul's Girls' Sch: mathematics teacher 1980–91, head of Middle Sch 1988–91, head of mathematics 1990–91; headteacher Guildford High Sch 1991–; memb: Girls' Sch Assoc 1991–, SHA 1991–; RSA 1994; *Recreations* off shore sailing, reading, theatre, concerts, skiing; *Style*— Mrs Susan Singer; ✉ Guildford High School, London Road, Guildford GU1 1SJ (☎ 01483 561440, fax 01483 306516)

SINGH, Dr Ajeet; s of Wir Singh (d 1961), and Jagchanan Kaur; *b* 6 June 1935; *Educ* King George Med Coll Lucknow India (MB BS), Univ of Bombay (DA); *m* 5 Aug 1962, Sharda, da of Mangesh Nadkarny, of Bankikiodla, India; 1 s (Bobby b 15 June 1963), 2 da (Aarti, Vineeta); *Career* asst prof of anaesthetics Bombay 1964–67, sr registrar anaesthesia Liverpool 1969–72, conslt anaesthetist West Midland RHA 1972–; former dir Midland Community Radio Coventry, former chm Radio Harmony Coventry, fndr memb and former pres Rotary Club of Coventry Jubilee, former memb Exec Ctee Relate Rugby; memb: Assoc of Anaesthestists GB and Ireland, Intractable Pain Soc, Midland Soc of Anaesthetists, Rugby Med Soc; former minute sec Obstetric Anaesthetist Soc; FFARCS; *Publications* author of six papers in professional jls; *Recreations* music, photography, painting, broadcasting; *Clubs* Rotary (Coventry), Whitefield Golf (fndr memb), Rugby 16; *Style*— Dr Ajeet Singh; ✉ Hospital of St Cross, Barby Road, Rugby CV22 5PX (☎ 01788 545207)

SINGH, Prof Ajit; *b* 11 Sept 1940; *Educ* Punjab Univ (BA), Howard Univ Washington DC (MA), Univ of Cambridge (MA), Univ of California at Berkeley (PhD); *Career* Univ of Cambridge: research offr 1964–65, asst Univ lectr 1965–68, Univ lectr 1968–91, ad hominem reader 1991–95, prof of economics 1995–; Queens' Coll Cambridge: lectr and fell 1965, dir of studies in economics 1972–95, sr fell 1992; Dr William M Scholl visiting prof of int economics Univ of Notre Dame USA 1987–94; currently ed Cambridge Jl of Economics; conslt: ILO Geneva 1988–, World Bank Washington DC 1989–, UNCTAD 1990–, South Cmmn and subsequently South Centre 1990–; sr economic advsr: Govt of Mexico 1978–82, Govt of Tanzania 1982–85; *Publications* author of numerous essays, book chapters and articles in learned economic jls; *Style*— Prof Ajit Singh; ✉ Queens' College, Cambridge CB3 9ET; Faculty of Economics and Politics, University of Cambridge, Austin Robinson Building, Sidgwick Avenue, Cambridge CB3 9DD (fax 01223 335475, e-mail Ajit.Singh@econ.cam.ac.uk)

SINGH, Amolak; *b* 16 June 1934; *Educ* King Edward VII Sch Taiping Malaysia, Elphinstone Coll Univ of Bombay, Nair Hosp Dental Coll Univ of Bombay (BDS), Royal Dental Sch Queen's Univ Belfast (LDS RCS), King's Coll London (external LLB, Dip in Med Ethics and Law), Law Section Central London Poly, Holborn Law Tutors, RCS (DGDP RCS 1992); *m*; *Career* princ in gen dental practice 1961–; memb GDC, gen sec Gen Dental Practitioners' Assoc 1991–, pres Anglo-Asian Odontological Gp 1993–; memb: Dental Advsy Ctee BUPA, Cncl Br Heart Fndn 1990–92, Industl Tbnl Panel and Special Race Panel of Industl Tbnls (Sec of State appointment); chm Cncl of Managerial and Professional Staffs; author of numerous pubns on legal and medico-legal interests; memb BDA, assoc memb Law Soc; *Recreations* skiing in the Alps, reading, walking, swimming, gardening; *Style*— Amolak Singh, Esq; ✉ 144 Long Lane, Bexleyheath, Kent DA7 5AH (☎ 0181 303 3120)

SINGH, Prof Ghan Shyam; s of Thakur Kaloo Singh, and Gulab, *née* Kunwar; *b* 24 Jan 1929; *Career* Muslim Univ Aligarh India 1954–57, Bocconi Univ Milan Italy 1963–65, Queen's Univ Belfast 1965–92 (prof emeritus 1992–); currently visiting prof Urbino Univ Italy; *Books* Leopardi and the Theory of Poetry (1964), Le poesie di Kabir (ed with Ezra Pound 1966), Leopardi e L'Inghilterra (1968), Poesie di Thomas Hardy (ed 1968), Contemporary Italian Verse (1968), A Critical Study of Eugenio Montale's Poetry Prose and Criticism (1973), Ezra Pound (1979), T S Eliot Poeta Drammaturgo Critico (1985), Neanche un minuto (1986), The Circle and Other Poems: Olga and Pound (1988), Ezra Pound Centenary (1990), Leopardi e i poeti inglesi (1991), Poesie d'amore alle moglie (ed 1993), The Sayings of Ezra Pound (1994), Ezra Pound as Critic (1994), F R Leavis: A Literary Biography (1995); *Recreations* reading, travelling; *Style*— Prof G Singh; ✉ The Queen's University of Belfast, Belfast, Northern Ireland (☎ 01232 245133 ext 3583, fax 01232 247895, telex QUBADM 74487)

SINGH, Harjit; s of Sewa Singh Alg (d 1965), of Tanzania, and Alg Waryam Kaur, *née* Oberoi; *b* 19 Feb 1934; *Educ* Magna Cum Laude (LLB), Univ of London (LLM); *m* 12 Nov 1969, Harsharan Bir Kaur, da of Maj Gurdial Singh (d 1970), of Chandigarh, Punjab, India; 2 s (Jasdeep b 21 June 1972, Dalbir b 25 April 1979), 1 da (Arshdeep b 15 Dec 1970); *Career* called to the Bar Lincoln's Inn 1956; practised at E African Bar 1957–71, memb SE Circuit 1975–, head of chambers 2 Middle Temple Lane; pres: Tanzania Table Tennis Assoc 1964–67, Tanzania Hockey Assoc 1967–70; chm Wandsworth Anglo-Asian Conservatives 1979–82; currently pres Int Human Rights Orgn (UK); *Books* Tanganyika Law Society's Draft Constitution of Tanzania (1961); *Recreations* hockey, cricket, reading, political history and religion, chess; *Style*— Harjit Singh, Esq; ✉ 32 Malbrook Road, Putney, London SW15 6UF (☎ 0181 7886328); 2 Middle Temple Lane, Temple, London EC4Y 9AA (☎ 0171 3531356, 0171 3531357, fax 0171 583 4928)

SINGH, HE Laleshwar Kumar Narayan; s of late Mr and Mrs Narayan; *b* 2 April 1941, Windsor Forest, W Coast, Demerara, Guyana; *Educ* Windsor Forest Govt Sch, Indian Educn Tst Coll, Univ of London (external LLB); *m* 10 Sept 1971, Latchmin, *née* Ramrattan; 2 c (Ashwindra b 22 Nov 1976, Vashti b 17 Oct 1987); *Career* early career working for British Rail, despatch clerk with Olney Amsden Ltd; called to the Bar Lincoln's Inn 1969, Inner London Magistrates' Ct Serv 1971–93, Ct Clerk trg course 1980–82, offr to the Ctee of Magistrates Inner London Cmmn Area; Guyanese high cmmr to Ct of St James's 1993–, concurrently non-res ambass to the Netherlands, France and Russian Fedn; *Style*— HE Mr Laleshwar Singh; ✉ Guyana High Commission, 3 Palace Court, Bayswater Road, London W2 4LP (☎ 0171 229 7684/8, fax 0171 727 9809)

SINGH, Prof Madan Gopal; s of Gurbachan Singh, of Chandigarh, India, and Pushpa, *née* Bawa; *b* 17 March 1946; *Educ* Univ of Exeter (BSc), Univ of Cambridge (PhD), France (Docteur ès Sciences), Univ of Manchester (MSc); *m* 1, 1 July 1969 (m dis 1979), Dr Christine Mary, *née* Carling; m 2, 24 Nov 1979, Dr Anne-Marie Claude, da of Francis Bennavail, of Mont de Marsan, France; 2 s (Alexandre b 11 April 1980, Christophe b 9 June 1985); *Career* fell St John's Coll Cambridge 1974–77, Maître de Conferences Associé Univ of Toulouse 1976–78, chargé de recherche au CNRS 1978–79; UMIST: prof of control engrg 1979–87, head Control Systems Centre 1981–83 and 1985–87, prof of information engrg 1987–, chm Computation Dept 1994–; vice chm SECOM IFAC 1981–84, chm IMACS Tech Ctee TC18 1987–, vice pres IEEE Systems Man and Cybernetics Soc 1990– (pres 1994 and 1995); visiting prof: Beijing Univ of Aeronautics and Astronautics 1987–, Ecole Centrale de Lille 1990–, Theseus Institut 1993–94, Ecole Normale Superieure de Paris 1994, IUSPIM 1994; Outstanding Contribution Award 1991, Nörbert Weiner Award IEEE SMC Soc 1993; Chev dans l'Ordre des Palmes Academiques (France) 1994; Hon DEngg Univ of Waterloo Canada 1996; CEng, FIEE 1984, FIEEE 1989, FBCS 1994; *Books* Systems: Decomposition, Optimisation and Control (with A Titli, 1978), Applied Industrial Control - An Introduction (with J P Elloy, R Mezencev and N Munro, 1980), Large Scale Systems Modelling (with M S Mahmound, 1981), Large Scale Systems: Theory and Applications (ed with A Titli, 1981), Parallel Processing Techniques for Simulation (ed with A Y Allidina and B K Daniels, 1987), Knowledge Based and Other Approaches to Reliability (ed with G Schmidt, S Tzafestas and K Hindi, 1987), Systems and Control Encyclopedia (ed, vols 1–8 1987, vol 9 1990, vol 10 1992); *Recreations* tennis, swimming, walking; *Style*— Prof Madan Singh; ✉ Computation Department, UMIST, Sackville Street, Manchester M60 1QD (☎ 0161 2003347, fax 0161 2003346)

SINGH, Dr Manmeet; s of Dr Bakhtawar Singh (d 1968), of Kisumu, Kenya, and Sukhbir Kaur, *née* Soin (d 1994); *b* 26 June 1935; *Educ* Kisumu HS Kenya, Univ of London (MB BS); *m* 11 Aug 1968, Seema Manmeet, da of Jabar Jang Singh (d 1985), of Toronto, Canada; 1 s (Sadmeet b 1970), 1 da (Aushima b 1973); *Career* sr lectr in urology Univ of London Hosp Medical Coll 1973–75, conslt urological surgn Whipps Cross Hosp 1975–, hon sr clinical lectr UCL Inst of Urology 1986–; fell: Hunterian Soc, Société Internationale d'Urologie; FRCS, FRSM; *Books* Urology (contrib, 1976), Current Operative Urology (contrib, 1984), Tropical Urology and Renal Disease (contrib, 1984); *Recreations* books, photography, African history, vintage cars; *Clubs* RSM; *Style*— Dr Manmeet Singh; ✉ 97 Hainault Rd, Chigwell, Essex 1G7 5DL (☎ 0181 500 6137), Department of Urology, Whipps Cross Hosp, Whipps Cross Rd, Leytonstone, London E11 (☎ 0181 593 5522); 152 Harley St, London W1 1AE (☎ 0181 559 2339)

SINGH, His Hon Judge; Mota; QC (1978); s of Dalip Singh, and Harnam Kaur; *b* 26 July 1930; *Educ* Duke of Gloucester Sch Nairobi; *m* 9 Nov 1950, Swaran, da of Gurcharan Singh Matharu, BEM (d 1987); 2 s (Satinder b 1956, Jaswinder b 1958), 1 da (Paramjeet b 1951); *Career* called to the Bar Lincoln's Inn 1956, recorder 1979–82, circuit judge (SE Circuit) 1982–; late city cncllr and alderman of Nairobi, sec Law Soc of Kenya, vice chm Kenya Justice, memb and chm London Rent Assessment Ctee, memb Race Rels Bd UK; vice pres Family Serv Units; patron: Anne Frank Fndn, St George's Hosp Tooting, Swami Narayan Mandir Neasden; Hon LLD Guru Nanak Dev Univ 1981; *Recreations* reading; *Clubs* MCC; *Style*— His Hon Judge Mota Singh, QC; ✉ 3 Somerset Rd, Wimbledon, London SW19 5JU; office (☎ 0171 522 7203); Southwark Crown Court, 1 English Grounds, off Battlebridge Lane, London SE1 2HU

SINGH, Rameshwar (Ray); s of Brijmohan Singh (d 1960), and Ramkumari; *Educ* Cncl of Legal Educn London; *m* 2 Sept 1968, Gwynneth Dorothy, da of late David Llewellyn Jones, of Ty-Draw, Cilfrew, Neath; 3 s (David-Marc Ramesh b 20 Sept 1969, Rodric Andrew b 6 Nov 1971, Richard Owain b 16 March 1974); *Career* barr at law; local Bar jr Swansea; Wales and Chester circuit: dep jr 1989, jr 1990–; dep dist judge; chm Child Support Appeals Tribunal; past chm Indian Soc of W Wales, W Glamorgan Community Relations Cncl (hon pres); memb: W Glamorgan Drugs Prevention Cncl, Race Rels Ctee Gen Cncl of the Bar, Family Ct Servs Ctee; memb: Bar Cncl, Hon Soc of Middle Temple, Family Law Bar Assoc, Criminal Law Bar Assoc, Crown Courts Users' Ctee, Area Criminal Justice Liaison Ctee, Family Court Services Ctee; CRE Cmmr for Wales 1996–; *Recreations* cooking, watching cricket, rugby, walking; *Clubs* Glamorgan CCC (vice pres), Swansea Rugby (patron), Neath CC (vice pres), Bonymaen RFC (hon legal advsr); *Style*— Ray Singh, Esq; ✉ Maranatha, Cilfrew, Neath, West Glamorgan SA10 8NE (☎ 01639 635387), Angel Chambers, 94 Walter Rd, Swansea SA1 5QA (☎ 01792 464623, fax 01792 648501)

SINGH, Dr Waryam; s of the late L R Brara, and the late Karmawali; *Educ* (MB BS, DLO); *m* 30 Jan 1980, Maya Sudha; 1 s (Arjun), 1 da (Amrita); *Career* conslt otolaryngologist Lothian Health Bd and hon sr lectr in otolaryngology Univ of Edinburgh 1980–; hon prof USA, Germany, Czechoslovakia and Japan; contrib clinical papers to numerous pubns and books, also ed and publisher, organiser and symposium dir of Int Voice Symposium 1987, 1991 and 1993, and Int Oncology Symposium 1993, inventor of Singh Speech Valve, dir Voice Research Laboratory; pres: Lothian BMA, Union of Euro Phoniatricians, Assoc of Head and Neck Oncologists of GB, World Congress in Phoniatrics and Phonosurgery 1995; fndr pres Br Assoc of Phoniatricians; chm Scot Div Overseas Drs Assoc Edinburgh, liaison offr Bd of Union of Euro Phoniatricians for GB; memb: The Euro Acad of Facial Surgery, Int Assoc of Logopedics and Phoniatricians, The Scot Otolaryngologist Soc, Br Assoc of Otolaryngologists, The Overseas Drs Assoc, BMA, RSM; hon memb: Hungarian Otolaryngology Soc, Acad of Czechoslovakian Medical Socs and Czechoslovakian Soc of Otolaryngology and Head and Neck Surgery, Int Acad of Otolaryngology and Head and Neck Surgery, Russian Assoc of Phoniatrics and Phonopeds, Italian Assoc of Phoniatrics and Logopedics, Lithuanian Otolaryngologic Soc; Comite d'honneur Assoc Des Reeducateurs Des Mutiles De La Voix France; nominated for Great Scot of the Year award 1991; FRCS 1977; *Recreations* photography, travel, cricket, music, poetry; *Style*— Dr Waryam Singh; ✉ St John's Hospital, Livingston, W Lothian, Scotland (☎ 01506 419666)

SINGHVI, HE Dr Laxmi Mall; s of Dashrath Mall Singhvi and Akal Kaur Singhvi; *b* 9 Nov 1931; *Educ* Allahabad Univ (BA), Rajasthan Univ (LLB), Univ of Cambridge, Harvard Univ Law Sch (LLM), Cornell Univ Law Sch (SJD); *m* 1957, Kamla Baid; 1 s (Dr Abhishek Manu), 1 da (Mrs Abhilasha Sunil Lalbhai); *Career* jurist, constitutional expert, parliamentarian, sr advocate Supreme Ct, human rights exponent, author, poet, philosopher and litterateur; memb academic and res staff Univ of Calif Berkeley 1955–56; MP (Ind) Lok Sabha 1962–67, dep ldr Indian Delgn to Cwlth Parly Conf 1964, fndr chm Inst of Constitutional and Parly Studies 1964–79; memb: all Parly Select Ctees on constitutional matters 1962–67, Govt of India Ctee on Information and Bdcasting Media 1964–67, Govt of India Ctee on Legal Aid and Processual Justice 1972–73; chm: Rajasthan Law Reforms, Legal Servs and Legal Aid Cmmn 1973–75, Govt of India Ctee on Revitalization of Rural Local Self-Govt 1986–87; life memb Cwlth Parly Assoc, assoc life memb Inter Parly Union; sr standing counsel: Govt of India 1967–71, State of UP 1968–72; advocate gen State of Rajasthan 1972–77; Supreme Ct of India: advocate 1951–67, sr advocate 1967–; pres Bar Assoc 1978, 1979, 1980, 1981 and 1982 (formerly vice pres), fndr pres Bar Assoc Tst 1979; tstee Int Legal Center NY 1967–74, sec gen 4th Cwlth Law Conf 1971, chm World Colloquim on Legal Aid in London 1975; fndr pres Indian Centre for the Independence of Judges and Lawyers 1979–, fndr chm Indian Nat Centre for Human Rights Educn and Res 1980; vice chm UN Human Rights Sub-Cmmn 1981 (memb 1978–81), pres World Congress on Human Rights 1990–; Indian high commissioner to Court of St James's 1991–; ldr India's Human Rights Delgn to UN confs in Bangkok, Geneva and Vienna 1993; a pres Parliament of World's Religions 1993; chm: Indian Fedn of UNESCO Assocs 1971–91, Indian Nat Ctee for Abolition of Death Penalty 1977–, Asian Conf on Approaches to Human Rights 1985, Centre for the Study of Law and Society Inst of Sociology and Communication 1989, Centre for the Study of Law and Soc New Delhi; fndr memb Family Planning Fndn of India; fndr chm Dishantar theatre movement 1962, chm Nat Sch of Drama 1978–82, pres emeritus Authors' Guild of India (pres 1985–90), tstee Jnanpith; Rotary Fndn fell Harvard Univ 1952–53, hon rotarian, Paul Harris fell, chief guest and keynote speaker 75th anniversary Rotary Fndn Rotary Int Conf Orlando Florida USA; Inter Faith Gold Medallion Award Int Cncl of Christians and Jews, Royal Asiatic Soc Annual Lecture 1991, Sir Francis Yonghusband Lecture 1993, Sir Robert Rede Lecture Univ of Cambridge 1993, a pres Cncl to the World Parl of Religions Chicago 1993; Hon Nyayavacaspati Gurukul Hardwar 1968; hon Tagore law prof Univ of Calcutta 1975–; hon prof of law Delhi and Andhra Univs; hon visiting prof of law Univ of Leicester 1992, hon prof Univ of Hull 1993; hon patron: Cwlth Legal Educn Assoc 1983 (fndr chm 1972), Int Centre for Public Law Inst of Advanced Legal Studies London 1992–; hon bencher and Master Middle Temple 1987; Hon LLD: Jabalpur Univ 1983, Banaras Hindu Univ 1984, Univ of Jodhpur 1992, Univ of Buckingham 1992, Univ of N London 1993, De Montfort Univ 1994, Jodhpur Univ 1994, Univ of Leicester 1996, Univ of London 1996, Univ of Westminster 1996; Hon DLitt: Univ of Tamil Nadu 1991, Osmania Univ India 1994; Hon Freeman Worshipful Co of Arbitrators London 1994; fndr memb Indian Law Inst; life memb: Indian Soc of Int Law, Inst of Public Admin; *Books* incl: Horizons of Freedom (1969), Law and Poverty (ed, 1970), Indian Federalism (1974), Law Day (1979), Legal Aid (1985), Independence of Justice (1985), Freedom on Trial (1991), Sandhya Ka Suraj (collection of Hindi poems); author and ed of numerous monographs, res papers and literary essays; Towards A New Global Order (festchrift vol in hon of Dr L M Singhvi, 1993); *Recreations* poetry, performing arts (especially theatre), gardening; *Clubs* Athenaeum; *Style*— HE Dr Laxmi Mall Singhvi; ✉ The High Commission of India, India House, Aldwych, London WC2B 4NA; 9 Kensington Palace Gardens, London W8 (office ☎ 0171 836 2556/8484 ext 110); B-8, South Extension Part-II, New Delhi-110049, India

SINGLETON, (Richard John) Basil; s of Richard Carl Thomas Singleton, of Crumlin, Co Antrim, and Marion Frances, *née* Campbell (d 1981); *b* 25 April 1935; *Educ* Foyle Coll Londonderry, Campbell Coll Belfast, Hong Kong Univ; *m* 14 Sept 1957, Florence Elizabeth, da of Albert McRoberts, of Dunmurry, Co Antrim (d 1981); 1 s (Richard David b 1961, d 1975), 1 da (Wendy Marion Jane b 1964); *Career* RA 1953–55; Ulster TV Ltd: mktg exec 1959–64, mktg mangr 1965–73; md AV Browne Advertising Ltd 1973–82, chm and chief exec Basil Singleton Ltd 1982–; dir: Brookville Ltd 1982–, Contactors Communications Ltd 1986–; memb Belfast Jr Chamber of Commerce 1961–75; chm: Publicity Assoc of NI 1969–70, Ulster Branch Irish Hockey Union 1976–88; MCIM, MIPR; *Recreations* hockey, tennis; *Clubs* Ulster Reform; *Style*— Basil Singleton, Esq; ✉ Basil Singleton Ltd, 72 Circular Road, Belfast, County Antrim BT4 2GD (☎ 01232 768330)

SINGLETON, Dr (William) Brian; CBE (1974); s of William Max Singleton (d 1977), and Blanche May Singleton (d 1975); *b* 23 Feb 1923; *Educ* Queen Elizabeth GS Darlington, Royal (Dick) Sch of Vet Studies Univ of Edinburgh; *m* 1947, Hilda, da of Herbert A Stott (d 1974); 2 s (Neil, Mark), and 1 s decd, 1 da (Maxine); *Career* vet advsr ITA 1968–, pres RCVS 1969–70; served on Govt Ctee of Inquiry into the Future Role of the Vet Profession in GB (chm Sir Michael Swann) 1971–76, visiting prof of surgery Ontario Vet Coll Guelph Canada 1973–74, hon vet advsr Jockey Club 1977–88; pres: Br Small Animal Vet Assoc 1960–61, World Small Animal Vet Assoc 1975–77; dir Animal Health Tst 1977–88, pres Br Equine Vet Assoc 1987–88, memb UGC working Pty on Veterinary Educn into the 21 Century; FRCVS 1976; Diplomate American Coll of Vet Surgns 1972, Dalrymple Champney Br Vet Assoc highest honour for meritorious servs to the vet profession 1987, Hon Dr of Vet Med and Surgery Univ of Edinburgh 1993; *Recreations* gardening, sailing, bird watching; *Clubs* Farmers'; *Style*— Dr Brian Singleton, CBE; ✉ Vine Cottage, Blakeney, Norfolk, NR25 7BE (☎ 01263 740246, fax 01263 741174)

SINGLETON, Roger; CBE (1997); s of Malcolm Singleton (ka 1944), and Ethel, *née* Drew; *b* 6 Nov 1942; *Educ* City GS Sheffield, Univ of Durham (MA), Univ of Bath (MSc), Univ of London (Dip Soc Studies), Univ of Leeds (CertEd); *m* 30 July 1966, Ann, da of late Lawrence Edmond Hasler; 2 da (Jane b 1968, Katharine b 1969); *Career* various appts in care and educn of deprived and delinquent young people 1961–71, professional advsr to Children's Regnl Planning Ctee 1971–74, sr dir Barnardo's 1984– (dep dir 1974–84), contribs to various jls; chm Nat Cncl of Voluntary Child Care Organisations 1990–92, former memb Nat Youth Bureau Mgmnt Ctee, memb Central Cncl for Educn and Trg in Social Work, memb various Govt ctees and inquiries; CIMgt 1994, FRSA 1991; *Recreations* house and garden; *Clubs* Reform; *Style*— Roger Singleton, Esq, CBE; ✉ Barnardo's, Tanners Lane, Barkingside, Ilford, Essex IG6 1QG (☎ 0181 550 8822, fax 0181 551 6870)

SINGLETON, Valerie; OBE (1994); da of Wing Cdr Denis Gordon Singleton, OBE, and Catherine Eileen Singleton, LRAM; *b* 9 April 1937; *Educ* Arts Educnl Sch London,

RADA; *Career* broadcast personality and writer; Bromley Rep 1956–57; subsequently: No 1 tour Cambridge Arts Theatre, theatre work, TV appearances in Compact and Emergency Ward 10, top voice over commentator for TV commercials and advtg magazines; BBC 1: continuity announcer 1962–64, presenter Blue Peter 1962–72, Nationwide 1972–78, Val Meets the VIPs (3 series), Blue Peter Special Assignment (4 series), Blue Peter Royal Safari with HRH The Princess Anne, Tonight and Tonight in Town 1978–79, Blue Peter Special Assignments Rivers Yukon and Niagara (1980); BBC 2: Echoes of Holocaust 1979, The Migrant Workers of Europe 1980, The Money Programme 1980–88; Radio 4: PM 1981–93, several appearances Midweek; freelance broadcaster and travel writer 1993–; Channel 4: presenter Back-Date (daily quiz prog) 1996; numerous appearances in TV advertising; memb Equity; *Recreations* travelling, photography, exploring London, sailing, walking, visiting salesrooms, museums; *Style*— Miss Valerie Singleton, OBE; ✉ c/o Arlington Enterprises, 1–3 Charlotte St, London W1 (☎ 0171 580 0702)

SINGLETON-GREEN, Brian; s of John Singleton-Green (d 1974), and Edna, *née* Hargreaves; *b* 26 April 1951; *Educ* Eltham Coll, Clare Coll Cambridge; *m* 26 April 1986, Barbara Ann, *née* Dyer; *Career* Deloitte & Co 1973–76, H M Treasy 1977–78, Binder Hamlyn 1979–80, Tech Directorate ICAEW 1980–89, ed Accountancy 1990–; FCA 1976; *Style*— Brian Singleton-Green, Esq; ✉ Accountancy, 40 Bernard Street, London WC1N 1LD (☎ 0171 920 8878, fax 0171 833 2085)

SINHA, Indra; s of Capt Bhagvati Prasad Sinha, of Bombay and Goa, India, and Irene Elizabeth, *née* Phare (d 1986); *b* 10 Feb 1950; *Educ* Mayo Coll Ajmer Rajasthan India, Oakham Sch Rutland, Pembroke Coll Cambridge (BA); *m* 9 Sept 1978, Viktoria Jane Yvette, da of Maj Arthur Henry Lionel Pilkington; 1 da (Tara Pauline Elizabeth b 6 Oct 1981), 2 s (Dan Alexander Iqbal b 28 Aug 1984, Samuel Barnaby Prem b 14 May 1988); *Career* writer and advtg exec; advtg copywriter: The Creative Business 1976–79, Ogilvy & Mather 1980–83; Collett Dickenson Pearce & Partners: copywriter 1984–95, head of copy 1988–93, dep creative dir 1993–94, exec creative dir 1994–95; chm and creative ptnr Chaos Communication Ltd 1995; memb D&AD; *Books* Kama Sutra (new trans, 1980), Tantra (1994), The CyberGypsies (1997); *Recreations* travelling, cybertravel, music, entomology; *Clubs* Sussex CCC; *Style*— Indra Sinha, Esq; ✉ Merrywell, Gatehouse Lane, Framfield, E Sussex TN22 5PP (☎ 01825 890399, fax 01825 890259, mobile 0468 738830, e-mail indra.sinha@virgin.net)

ŠINKOVEC, HE Matjaž; s of Ivan Šinkovec (d 1974), of San Francisco, and Vilma, *née* Likar (d 1991), of Ljubljana; *b* 22 May 1951; *Educ* Lone Mountain Coll, Univ of San Francisco (BA, MA); *m* 12 Dec 1981, Magdalena, da of Josip Novak; 2 s (Boštjan b 26 Feb 1983, Aleš b 26 Sept 1985); *Career* Slovenian diplomat and politician; journalist Daily Delo 1974, desk offr Dept for Developed Countries Slovenian Foreign Miny 1978–84, int sec Confedn of Trade Unions of Slovenia 1984–90, MP and chm Int Relations Cmmn Parly of the Republic of Slovenia 1990–92, ambass extraordinary and plenipotentiary of the Republic of Slovenia to the Ct of St James's 1992–; Slovenian rep to numerous int confs; memb Cncl Govt Coalition 1990–91, fndr memb Social Democratic Party of Slovenia (vice pres in charge of int relations 1988–92, Parly ldr 1990–92); author, co-author, trans or ed of over 100 articles, essays and pubns; *Recreations* swimming, sailing, travel; *Style*— HE Mr Matjaž Šinkovec; ✉ Zg.Pirniče 139, 61215 Medvode, Slovenia (☎ 00 386 61 621 039); Embassy of Slovenia, Suite 1, Cavendish Court, 11–15 Wigmore Street, London W1H 9LA (☎ 0171 495 7775, fax 0171 495 7776)

SINNATT, Maj-Gen Martin Henry; CB (1984); s of Dr Oliver Sturdy Sinnatt (d 1965), and Marjorie Helen, *née* Randall (d 1964); *b* 28 Jan 1928; *Educ* Hitchin GS, Hertford Coll Oxford, RMA Sandhurst; *m* 20 July 1957, Susan Rosemary, da of Capt Sydney Landor Clarke (d 1966); 4 da (Jacqueline Margaret b 22 April 1959, Katherine Susan b 30 March 1961, Nicola Jane b 16 Aug 1963, Victoria Helen b 1 Oct 1965); *Career* RTR 1948–84; served: W Germany, Korea, Hong Kong, Aden, Norway; CO 4 RTR BAOR 1969–71, cdr RAC 1 Corps BAOR 1972–74, dir operational requirements MOD 1974–77, dir combat devpt 1979–81, COS and head UK Delgn 'Live Oak' SHAPE 1982–84; ret 1984; sr exec and sec Kennel Club 1984–93; Freeman City of London 1981; *Recreations* golf, gardening, travel, medieval history; *Style*— Maj-Gen Martin Sinnatt, CB; ✉ Meadowside Farmhouse, Tulls Lane, Standford, Bordon, Hants GU35 8RB

SINNOTT, Kevin Fergus; s of Myles Vincent Sinnott (d 1974), of Wales, and Honora, *née* Burke (d 1993); *b* 4 Dec 1947; *Educ* St Roberts Aberkenfig, Cardiff Coll of Art (fndn course), Glos Coll of Art and Design (DipAD), RCA (MA); *m* 30 Aug 1969, Susan Margaret, da of Lawrence Hadyn Forward; 3 s (Matthew b 22 Aug 1971, Gavin b 6 June 1975, Thomas b 4 March 1983), 1 da (Lucy Anne b 24 Aug 1984); *Career* artist; visiting lectr: Ruskin Sch of Drawing Oxford 1975–76, Canterbury Coll of Art 1981–88; pt/t teacher St Martin's Sch of Art London 1981–93; *Solo Exhibitions* House Gallery London 1980 and 1983, Ikon Gallery Birmingham 1980, Riverside Studios London 1981, Gallery Gwyn Hodges Oxford 1981, St Paul's Gallery Leeds 1981, Blond Fine Art London 1982 and 1984, Chapter Arts Centre Cardiff 1984, Bernard Jacobson Gallery (London 1986, London and NY 1987, NY 1988, London 1990), Jan Turner Gallery LA 1987, Roger Ramsay Gallery Chicago 1988, Anne Berthoud Gallery London 1990, Flowers East London 1992 and 1994; *Group Exhibitions* incl: Whitechapel Open London 1978 and 1980, John Moore's Liverpool 1978, 1980 and 1991, Ruskin Sch of Art Oxford 1981, Blond Fine Art London 1982–85, LA Louver Gallery California 1986, Bernard Jacobson Gallery London 1986, Lefevre Gallery London 1988, The Contemporary Arts Centre Cincinnati 1988; *Work in Public Collections* Br Cncl, Arts Cncl of GB, Courtauld Inst (Contemporary Art in the East Wing), RCA, The Whitworth Manchester, Br Museum, Wolverhampton City Art Gallery, Metropolitan Museum of Art NY, Deutsche Bank AG London, Unilever, Contemporary Art Soc of Wales, The Nat Museum of Wales; *Clubs* Chelsea Arts; *Style*— Kevin Sinnott, Esq; ✉ c/o Flowers East, 199/205 Richmond Road, London E8 3NJ (☎ 0171 985 0067)

SINNOTT, Stephen; s of Stephen Sinnott, of Penwortham, Lancs, and Mary Agnes, *née* Makin; *b* 24 June 1951; *Educ* Abbotsford Road Secdy Modern, West Dery Comp, Middlesex Poly (BA), Edge Hill Coll of HE (PGCE); *m* 8 Jan 1972, Mary, da of William Crossman; 1 s (Stephen William b 4 Aug 1977), 1 da (Kate Elizabeth b 28 May 1980); *Career* teacher Shorefields Comp Toxteth Liverpool 1975–79, head of economics Broughton HS Preston 1979–; NUT: memb Nat Exec for Lancs and IOM 1986–92, vice pres 1992–94, pres 1994–95; *Style*— Stephen Sinnott, Esq; ✉ 12 Hollywood Avenue, Penwortham, Preston, Lancs PR1 9AS (☎ 01772 742620); National Union of Teachers, Hamilton House, Mabledon Place, London WC1H 9BD

SINTON, Andy; *b* 19 March 1966; *Career* professional footballer (midfielder); Cambridge Utd 1982 (93 league appearances, 13 goals), transferred to Brentford 1986 (for £30,000, 149 appearances, 28 goals), transferred to Queen's Park Rangers 1989 (for £350,000, 160 appearances, 22 goals), transferred to Sheffield Wednesday 1993 (for £2.75 million), transferred to Tottenham Hotspur FC 1996; 12 full England caps; *Style*— Andy Sinton, Esq; ✉ Tottenham Hotspur FC, White Hart Lane, 748 High Road, Tottenham, London N17 0AP

SINYOR, Gary Ellis; s of Samuel Joseph Sinyor, and Claire, *née* Mizrahi; *b* 1 June 1962; *Educ* Manchester GS, Robinson Coll Cambridge (MA), Nat Film and TV Sch; *Career* film writer/prodr/dir; writer/prodr The Unkindest Cut (nominated Best Short Film BAFTA 1990), prodr The Korda Film, co-writer/co-prodr/co-dir Leon the Pig Farmer (Charles Chaplin award for first feature film Edinburgh Film Festival 1992, Int Critics' prize Venice Film Festival 1992), writer/dir/co-prodr Solitaire for 2 1994, writer One For The Road (Channel 4) 1995, co-writer/co-prodr/dir Stiff Upper Lip 1996; Most Promising Newcomer Award Evening Standard Film Awards 1994; *Style*— Gary Sinyor, Esq; ✉ Cavalier Features, 8–10 Great Titchfield Street, London W1P 7AA (fax 0171 436 0066)

SINYOR, Joe; s of Samuel Joseph Sinyor, and Claire, *née* Mizrahi; *b* 16 Aug 1957; *Educ* Manchester GS, Jesus Coll Cambridge (BA), London Business Sch (MBA); *m* 22 Dec 1987, Pamela Caroline Neild, da of Michael Collis; 2 s (Joshua Samuel Michael b 18 Nov 1988, Benjamin Johnathan b 30 June 1990), 1 da (Jessica Claire Rachael b 1 Jan 1994); *Career* slr Nabarro Nathanson London 1979–81, corp fin exec J Henry Schroder Wagg 1984–85, sr engagement mangr McKinsey & Co Inc 1985–90, gp chief exec Pepe Group PLC 1990–93, md Dillons The Bookstore 1994–; memb Cncl Booksellers' Assoc 1995–; *Recreations* family, opera, walking, skiing; *Style*— Joe Sinyor, Esq; ✉ Dillons UK Ltd, The Royal House, Prince's Gate, Homer Road, Solihull, West Midlands B91 3QQ (☎ 0121 703 8000, fax 0121 711 7476)

SISSON, Brig Arthur Alexander; CBE (1978); s of Prof Geoffrey Roy Sisson, OBE (d 1964), and Lucy Cameron, *née* Ward (d 1982); *b* 30 May 1924; *Educ* Highgate Sch, Univ of Edinburgh; *m* 1 Oct 1951, Pamela, da of Maj John Chadwick (d 1981); 2 s (Richard b 1957, Peter b 1962), 2 da (Jennifer b 1954, Sarah Jane b 1965); *Career* cmmnd RA 1945; served: SE Asia, India, Palestine, Malaya, Cyprus, Aden; intro Army bulk refuelling system 1970–79, initiated DROPS (demountable rack system), dir logistic orgn and devpt MOD (Army) 1976–79; mgmnt and def conslt 1979–; FMS; *Reports* Logistic Concept 1985–2005 (1979), Vulnerability of the British LOC in Europe (1985); *Recreations* butterfly conservation, racing, computers; *Style*— Brig Arthur Sisson, CBE; ✉ 10 Castelnau, Barnes, London SW13 9RU

SISSON, Dr Charles Hubert; CH (1993); s of Richard Percy Sisson (d 1958), and Ellen Minnie, *née* Worlock (d 1955); *b* 22 April 1914; *Educ* Fairfield Secdy Sch Bristol, Univ of Bristol (BA), Univs of Berlin and Freiburg, Sorbonne; *m* 19 Aug 1937, Nora, da of Anthony Huddleston Gilbertson (d 1954), of Bristol; 2 da (Janet, Hilary); *Career* Sgt Intelligence Corps 1942–45, served India; Miny of Lab: asst princ 1936, under sec Dept of Employment 1962–72; Simon sr res fell Univ of Manchester 1956–57; Hon DLitt Bristol 1980; FRSL 1972; *Books* The Spirit of British Administration, with some European comparisons (1959), Christopher Homm (novel, 1965), English Poetry 1900–1950 (1971), In the Trojan Ditch (collected poems and selected translations, 1974), The Avoidance of Literature (1978), Collected Poems (1984), God Bless Karl Marx (poems, 1987), On the Look-out: A Partial Autobiography (1989), In Two Minds: Guesses at other Writers (1990), English Perspectives (1992), Antidotes (poems, 1991), Is There a Church of England? (1993), What and Who (poems, 1994), Poems: Selected (1995); translations incl: Dante, Virgil, Lucretius, Du Bellay, Catullus, Racine; *Recreations* gardening, washing up; *Style*— Dr Charles Sisson, CH, FRSL; ✉ Moorfield Cottage, The Hill, Langport, Somerset TA10 9PU (☎ 01458 250845)

SISSON, Rosemary Anne; da of Prof Charles Jasper Sisson (d 1965), and Vera Kathleen Ginn; *b* 13 Oct 1923; *Educ* Cheltenham Ladies' Coll, UCL (BA), Newnham Coll Cambridge (MLit); *Career* WWII with Royal Observer Corps 1943–45; lectr in English: Univ of Wisconsin 1949–50, UCL 1950–55, Univ of Birmingham 1956–58; The Writers' Guild of GB: co-chm 1979 and 1980, pres 1995; tstee The Theatre of Comedy; charity work: writer of SSAFA's The Great Event (HM The Queen's 40th Anniversary prog) 1991, Joy to the World 1989, 1990, 1992, 1993, 1994 and 1995; contrib to TV series: Upstairs, Downstairs, The Duchess of Duke Street, The Young Indiana Jones Chronicles (1991, 1992, 1993 and 1994), Ruth Rendell Mysteries (1992), and adaptations for TV and radio; *Stage Plays incl* The Queen and the Welshman (1957), Fear Came to Supper (1958), The Splendid Outcasts (1958), Home and the Heart, The Royal Captivity (1960), Bitter Sanctuary (1963), I Married a Clever Girl, A Ghost on Tiptoe (with Robert Morley), The Dark Horse (1979); *Novels incl* The Exciseman (1972), The Killer of Horseman's Flats (1973), The Stratford Story (1975), The Queen and the Welshman (1979), Escape from the Dark (1976), The Manions of America (1981), Bury Love Deep (1985), Beneath the Visiting Moon (1986), The Bretts (1987, televised 1987), Rosemary for Remembrance (collected poems, 1995); also six children's books; *Recreations* riding, travel; *Clubs* BAFTA; *Style*— Miss R A Sisson; ✉ Andrew Mann Ltd, 1 Old Compton St, London W1V 5PH (☎ 0171 734 4751)

SISSONS, Dr Clifford Ernest; s of George Robert Percival Sissons (d 1964), and Elsie Emma, *née* Evans (d 1993); *b* 26 Jan 1934; *Educ* Liverpool Inst HS for Boys, Univ of Liverpool Med Sch (MB ChB); *m* 28 Dec 1956, Mary Beryl, da of James Davies (d 1941); 2 s (Mark Christopher John, Guy Richard James), 1 da (Amanda Jane Elizabeth); *Career* Nat Serv Capt RAMC 1959–61; house physician and house surgn Liverpool Stanley Hosp 1958–59; med registrar: Birkenhead Gen Hosp 1962–67, Professorial Med Unit Liverpool Royal Infirmary 1967–69; sr med registrar David Lewis Northern and Sefton Gen Hosp Liverpool 1969–72, conslt physician Wrexham War Memorial and Maelor Hosps 1972–; memb Cncl RCP 1985–87 (regnl advsr 1982–87), examiner in med RCP (London) 1991–; memb: BMA, Br Soc of Echocardiography, Br Hyperlipidaemia Assoc; FRCP 1977 (MRCP 1966); *Recreations* languages, travel, reading, painting; *Style*— Dr Clifford Sissons; ✉ Wrexham Maelor Hosp, Crosenwydd Rd, Wrexham, Clwyd (☎ 01978 291100)

SISSONS, (Thomas) Michael Beswick; s of Capt T E B Sissons (ka 1940), and Marjorie, *née* Shepherd; *b* 13 Oct 1934; *Educ* Winchester, Exeter Coll Oxford (BA, MA); *m* 1, 1960 (m dis), Nicola Ann, *née* Fowler; 1 s, 1 da; m 2, 1974 (m dis), Ilze, *née* Kadegis; 2 da; *Career* Nat Serv 2 Lt 13/18 Royal Hussars 1953–55; lectr in history Tulane Univ New Orleans 1958–59, freelance writer and journalist 1958–60, AD Peters & Co Ltd Literary Agency 1959–88 (dir 1965, chm and md 1973–88), jt chm The Peters Fraser & Dunlop Group Ltd 1994– (jt chm and md 1988–94), dir London Broadcasting Co 1973–75; pres Assoc of Authors' Agents 1978–81, memb Ctee MCC 1984–87 and 1993– (chm Arts and Library Sub-ctee 1985–93, chm Mktg and Public Affrs Sub-ctee 1995–), memb Bd BFSS 1994–95; *Books* Age of Austerity (ed with Philip French 1963, 2nd edn 1986); *Recreations* riding, gardening, cricket, music; *Clubs* Groucho, MCC; *Style*— Michael Sissons, Esq; ✉ The White House, Broadleaze Farm, Westcot Lane, Sparsholt, Wantage, Oxon OX12 9PZ (☎ 01235 751215, fax 01235 751561); Peters Fraser & Dunlop, 503 The Chambers, Chelsea Harbour, Lots Rd, London SW10 01XF (☎ 0171 344 1000, fax 0171 351 1756)

SISSONS, (John Gerald) Patrick; s of Gerald William Sissons (d 1966), and Georgina Margaret, *née* Cockin (d 1960); *b* 28 June 1945; *Educ* Felsted, St Mary's Hosp Med Sch London (MB BS, MD); *m* April 1971 (m dis 1985), Jennifer Anne Scovell; 2 da (Sarah b 1973, Rebecca b 1974); *Career* registrar and hon lectr Royal Post Grad Med Sch London 1973–76, NIH Fogarty fell and asst memb Scripps Clinic San Diego USA 1977–80, reader in infectious diseases Royal Post Grad Med Sch 1987 (Wellcome sr lectr 1980–86), prof of med Univ of Cambridge 1988–; fell Darwin Coll Cambridge; FRCP, FRCPath; *Recreations* travel; *Style*— Patrick Sissons, Esq; ✉ Department of Medicine, University of Cambridge Clinical School, Hills Road, Cambridge CB2 2QQ (☎ 01223 336849)

SISSONS, Peter George; s of George Robert Percival Sissons (d 1964), and Elsie Emma, *née* Evans (d 1993); *b* 17 July 1942; *Educ* Liverpool Inst HS for Boys, Univ Coll Oxford (MA); *m* Sylvia; 2 s (Michael Peter, Jonathan Richard), 1 da (Kate Victoria); *Career* TV journalist and presenter; ITN 1964–78: gen trainee then script writer, gen reporter, foreign correspondent, news ed, indust correspondent, indust ed; presenter News at One 1978–82, presenter Channel Four News 1982–89, chm Question Time BBC TV 1989–93, presenter 6 O'Clock News BBC 1989–93, presenter 9 O'Clock News BBC 1994–; Broadcasting Press Guild's Best Front of Camera Performer 1984, Royal TV Soc's Judges Award 1989; *Recreations* relaxing; *Style*— Peter Sissons, Esq; ✉ c/o BBC TV Centre, Wood Lane, London W12 7RJ (☎ 0181 743 8000)

SITKOVETSKY, Dmitry; s of Julian Sitkovetsky, violinist, and Bella Davidovich, pianist; *b* 1954, Baku, USSR; *Educ* Moscow Conservatoire, Juilliard Sch NY; *Career* violinist; winner Kreisler competition Vienna 1979; fndr and music dir New European Strings 1990–; artistic dir: Korsholm Festival Finland 1983–93, Umea Festival Sweden 1991–93, Seattle International Music Festival 1993–; principal conductor of Ulster Orchestra 1996–; guest conductor: Stuttgart Chamber Orch, MDR Leipzig Orch, Tasmanian Symphony Orch, chamber ensemble of St Martin in the Fields (tour of Germany) 1994, Vienna Virtuosi; worked with numerous major conductors incl Claudio Abbado, Vladimir Ashkenazy, Andrew Davis, Sir Colin Davis, Christoph Dohnanyi, Alexander Lazarev, Erich Leinsdorf, Sir Neville Marriner, Gennadi Rozhdestvensky, Wolfgang Sawallisch and Michael Tilson Thomas; given recital performances at various international venues and festivals incl Salzburg, Lucerne, Edinburgh, Ravinia and Mostly Mozart, BBC Proms (première of Casken's Violin Concerto) 1995; was the first postwar Russian emigré musician to return to Moscow at the official invitation in 1988; subject of South Bank Show 1993; *Recordings* incl: Bach, Mozart, Elgar, Bartok, Prokofiev and Shostakovich violin concerti, chamber works by Brahms, Grieg, Ravel and Prokofiev, own string trio transcription of Bach's Goldberg Variations, Beethoven Violin Concerto (with Acad of St Martin in the Fields, under Sir Neville Marriner), Elgar Violin Concerto (with RPO under Sir Yehudi Menuhin), Bartok Violin Concertos (with Philharmonia under Libor Pesek); *Publications* author of several transcriptions incl: Bach Goldberg Variations for String Trio and Goldberg Variations for String Orch, Dohnanyi Serenade, Shostakovitch String Symphony Opus 73 for String Orch, Tchaikovsky String Symphony Opus 30; *Style*— Dmitry Sitkovetsky, Esq; ✉ c/o Deborah Meyer, IMG Artists (Europe), Media House, 3 Burlington Lane, Chiswick, London W4 2TH

SITWELL, Francis Trajan Sacheverell; yr s of Sir Sacheverell Sitwell, 6 Bt, CH (d 1988); bro and h of Sir Reresby Sitwell, 7 Bt, *qv*; *b* 17 Sept 1935; *Educ* Eton; *m* 21 June 1966, Susanna Carolyn, 3 da of late Rt Hon Sir Ronald Hibbert Cross, 1 Bt, KCMG, KCVO; 2 s (George Reresby Sacheverell b 22 April 1967, William Ronald Sacheverell b 1969), 1 da (Henrietta Louise Vereker b 1973); *Career* late Sub Lt RN; assoc dir Charles Barker City Ltd 1969; memb Cncl London Philharmonic Orch 1965; MIPR 1969; *Clubs* Brooks's; *Style*— Francis Sitwell, Esq; ✉ 20 Ladbroke Grove, London W11; Weston Hall, Towcester, Northants NN12 8PU

SITWELL, Sir (Sacheverell) Reresby; 7 Bt (UK 1808), of Renishaw, Derbyshire; DL (Derbyshire 1984); s of Sir Sacheverell Sitwell, 6 Bt (d 1988), by his w, Georgia Louise, *née* Doble (d 1980); *b* 15 April 1927; *Educ* Eton, King's Coll Cambridge; *m* 1952, Penelope, yr da of Col Hon Donald Alexander Forbes, DSO, MVO (d 1938), s of 7 Earl of Granard; 1 da (Alexandra Isobel Susanna Edith (Mrs Richard Hayward) b 1958); *Heir* bro, Francis Trajan Sacheverell Sitwell, *qv* b 17 Sept 1935; *Career* former Lt 2 Bn Grenadier Gds, BAOR Germany 1946–48; advtg and PR exec 1948–60, vending machines operator 1960–70, wine merchant 1960–75; landowner 1965–; Lord of the Manors of Eckington and Barlborough in Derbyshire and of Whiston and Brampton-en-le-Morthen in South Yorks; High Sheriff of Derbyshire 1983; Freeman City of London 1984; *Publications* Mount Athos (with J Julius Norwich and A Costa, 1964), Hortus Sitwellianus (epilogue, 1984); *Recreations* travel, music, architecture, racing; *Clubs* White's, Brooks's, Pratt's, Pitt (Cambridge), Soc of Dilettanti; *Style*— Sir Reresby Sitwell, Bt, DL; ✉ Renishaw Hall, Renishaw, nr Sheffield S31 9WB (☎ 01246 432042); 4 Southwick Place, London W2 2TN (☎ 0171 262 3939)

SIXSMITH, (George) Martin; s of George Francis Sixsmith, of Belvoir Road, Walton, Cheshire, and Joyce Lythgoe, *née* Sutton; *b* 24 Sept 1954; *Educ* The Manchester GS, Sorbonne Univ Paris, New Coll Oxford (open scholar, MA), Leningrad Polytechnical Inst USSR, Harvard Univ USA, St Antony's Coll Oxford; *m* 4 Sept 1976, Mary Winifred, da of Francis Cooney; 2 s (Patrick Martin b 7 Jan 1983, Daniel Thomas b 30 Oct 1985), 2 da (Joanna Mary b 19 Dec 1979, Rebecca Helen b 11 Oct 1988); *Career* Harkness fell and tutor in slavics Harvard Univ 1977–79; BBC: trainee journalist London 1980–82, Western Europe reporter Brussels 1982–85 then Geneva 1985–86, Eastern Europe corr Warsaw 1986–88, Moscow corr TV News 1988–91, Washington corr TV News 1991–94, Moscow corr TV News 1994–; memb Young Königswinter Confs 1986; memb NUJ; *Books* Vladislav Xodasevic: k 40–letiju so dnja smerti (critical biog of Vladislav Khodasevich the Russian poet, Vestnik Paris, 1979), The Harvard Guide to France (E P Dutton NY, 1980), Jobit's Journal: A history of the French campaigns in Ireland (trans, 1982), Moscow Coup: the death of the Soviet system (Simon & Schuster, 1991); *Recreations* serious music, Russian literature, Liverpool FC, my four children; *Style*— Martin Sixsmith, Esq; ✉ BBC Television News, Wood Lane, London W12 7RJ (☎ 0181 743 8000)

SIZER, Prof John; CBE (1989); s of John Robert Sizer, and Mary Sizer; *b* 14 Sept 1938; *Educ* Univ of Nottingham (BA), Loughborough Univ (DLitt); *m* 1965, Valerie Davies; 3 s; *Career* accountancy asst Ross Group Ltd Grimsby 1954–57, sr cost clerk Eskimo Foods Ltd Cleethorpes 1957–58, asst accountant Clover Dairies Ltd Grimsby 1958–61, fin advsr Guest Keen & Nettlefolds Ltd 1964–65, Univ of Edinburgh 1965–68 (teaching fell, lectr), London Graduate Sch of Business Studies 1968–70 (sr lectr in accounting, asst academic dean); Loughborough Univ: prof of fin mgmnt 1970–96, dean Sch of Human & Environmental Studies 1973–76, sr pro-vice chllr 1980–82, fndr and head Dept of Mgmnt Studies 1971–80, 1982–84 and 1990, dir Business Sch 1991–92, visiting prof 1996–; visiting prof Univ of Lancaster 1993–94, memb Science and Engrg Base Coordinating Ctee 1993–, memb Steering Gp Technol Foresight Prog 1996–; chief exec and memb Scottish Higher Education Funding Cncl 1992–; Nat Forum for Mgmnt Educn & Devpt 1987–96 (memb Exec Ctee, chm Fin and Resourcing Ctee), advsr Business & Mgmnt Studies UFC 1989–92; memb: Univ Grants Ctee 1984–89, Jt CVCP/UFC Steering Ctee on Performance Indicators 1989–92, UFC NI Ctee 1989–92; chm: OECD/IMHE 1980–84, Soc for Res into Higher Educn 1992–93; memb Editorial Bd: Financial Accountability and Management 1985–, Higher Education 1990–, Education Economics 1993–, Tertiary Education and Management 1994–; advsr Bertelsmann Fndn Germany 1989–90; fell Chartered Inst of Mgmnt Accountants; *Books* An Insight into Management Accounting (1969, 3 edn 1989), Case Studies in Management Accounting (1974), Perspectives in Management Accounting (1981), Resources and Higher Education (jt ed, 1983), A Casebook of British Management Accounting (jtly 1984, 1985), Institutional Responses to Financial Reductions in the University Sector (1987); *Recreations* enjoying Scotland, walking; *Style*— Prof John Sizer, CBE; ✉ Ettrick, Main Street, West Linton, Peebleshire EH46 7EE (☎ 01968 660103); Scottish Higher Education Funding Council, Donaldson House, 97 Haymarket Terrace, Edinburgh EH12 5HD (☎ 0131 313 6502, fax 0131 313 6531)

SKAE, John Robin; JP; s of Reginald John Skae (d 1988), and Gwendoline Catharine Bleackley Skae (d 1981); *b* 11 July 1936; *Educ* Oundle; *m* 1 Sept 1961, Cynthia Fay, da of Norman Louis Forrest (d 1988), of Stoke-on-Trent; 1 s (Christopher b 13 Sept 1962), 2 da (Jennifer b 18 March 1965, Joanna b 16 Dec 1968); *Career* dir and co sec Bamfords Ltd Uttoxeter Staffs 1964–74, gp sec Dowty Group plc Cheltenham 1974–85, co sec Midland Bank plc London 1985–93; dir: Skipton Building Soc 1994–, Homeloan Management Ltd 1995–, Commercial Mortgage Systems Ltd 1995–; FCA 1962; *Recreations* sport, music, countryside, gardening; *Style*— John Skae, Esq, JP; ✉ Thornhill, Gambles Lane, Woodmancote, Cheltenham, Glos GL52 4PU; The Skipton Building Society, The Bailey, Skipton, North Yorkshire BD23 1DN (☎ 01756 7005000)

SKAN, Martin; s of Reginald Norman Skan (d 1985), of Worcester, and Millicent May, *née* Vaughan (d 1977); *b* 28 Dec 1934; *Educ* Haileybury, Harvard Sch California (exchange scholar); *m* 1, 1970 (m dis 1988), Sally Elizabeth Margaret, da of John Eric Wade; 2 da (Lara Julie b 1971, Tilly Matina b 1975); m 2, 1989, Brigitte Berta, da of late Erwin Heinrich Joos, of Winterthur, Switzerland; *Career* cmmnd Dorset Regt 1955–57; British Market Research Bureau Ltd (subsid of JWT Advertising) 1957–58, Kinloch (PM) Ltd 1958–89; dir: Skan Taylor & Co Ltd 1959–65, J A & P Holland Ltd 1962–65, Parkinsons (Doncaster) Ltd 1962–65, Holland Distributors Ltd 1962–65, Harper Paper Group (and subsid cos) 1962–65, LMS (Consultants) Ltd 1986–91; chm Chewton Glen (Hotels) Ltd 1966–; for Chewton Glen Hotel: Egon Ronay Hotel of The Year award 1976, Michelin Star 1981–, Times Hotel Restaurant of the Year 1990, Tourism Catey award 1990, American Express Country Hotel of the Year 1991 and 1992, 5 Red Stars (AA and RAC) 1993; Personality of the Year 1990, Master Innholder 1991, Hotelier of the Year 1991; fndr memb The Walpole Ctee; hon memb Académie Culinaire de France; Freeman City of London 1991; *Recreations* tennis, golf, cycling, skiing; *Clubs* IOD, Brockenhurst Golf, Royal Lymington Yacht; *Style*— Martin Skan, Esq; ✉ Chewton Glen Hotel, Christchurch Rd, New Milton, Hants BH25 6QS (☎ 01425 275341, fax 01425 272310)

SKED, Gordon George; *b* 20 March 1947, Perth, Scotland; *Educ* Dollar Acad; *m*; 2 da (b 1967 and 1971); *Career* automotive designer; student apprentice then jr stylist Rootes Motors (later Chrysler UK) 1965–70; Rover Group (and predecessor cos British Motor Corporation, Leyland Cars and Austin Rover): sr stylist Austin Morris Ltd Birmingham 1970–72, leading project stylist Austin Morris Ltd 1972–77, exec designer Jaguar Rover Triumph Ltd Solihull 1977–80, chief designer Leyland Cars 1980–82, studio dir Austin Rover Group 1982–87, dir product design Austin Rover Group 1987–89, dir of product design Rover Group Ltd (incl Land Rover Ltd) 1989–95; pt/t shadow design dir (involved in restructuring) Design Cncl 1994; fndr Gordon Sked Design Associates (independent design conslt) 1995–; chair: Judging Panel RSA Annual Bursary, Jury BBC Design Awards 1994; winner Minerva Design Mgmnt Prize Chartered Soc of Designers 1993; Hon DTech Univ of Coventry 1995; FCSD 1981 (vice pres 1988–90), FRSA; *Projects* for Rootes incl Avenger Estate, Chrysler Europe products and Dodge trucks; for Rover and predecessors incl: exterior concept design ADO74 (proposed Mini replacement) and ADO88 (later Austin Metro) 1972, Triumph TR7 replacement proposal 1977, final exterior design of Austin Metro 1979, Rover SD1 (2000–3500 range) 1982, devpt of Rover Vitesse 1981–82, responsibility for Project XX (later Rover 800, in collaboration with Honda) 1980–85, MG EX-E concept car 1985 (winner Auto and Design Award), Rover CCV coupé concept car 1986 (winner Auto and Design Award and Premier Br Coachbuilder Award), Rover 200/400 (with Honda) 1985–89, Project Synchro (later Rover 600, with Honda) 1989–93 (Design Cncl Prize), new of Rover 800 1991, MGF, New Rover 200 1995, New Rover 400 1995; *Recreations* art, photography, all aspects of automotive and design interest, golf, music, travel; *Style*— Gordon G Sked; ✉ Gordon Sked Design Associates, 11 The Elms, Leek Wootton, Warwick CV35 7RR (☎ and fax 01926 859721)

SKEET, Muriel Hilda Henrietta; da of Col Frederick William Claude (d 1974), of Colchester, Essex, and Mabel Constance, *née* Pitt-King (d 1976); *b* 12 July 1926; *Educ* Endsleigh House, London Univ (MPH, DipH and TM), Yale Univ; *Career* trg Middx Hosp and London Sch of Hygiene and Tropical Med 1949 (SRN), ward and admin sister Middx Hosp 1949–60, field work organiser operational res unit Nuffield Provincial Hosps Tst 1961–64, res organiser Dan Mason Nursing Ctee of Nat Florence Nightingale Meml Ctee of GB and NI 1965–70, chief nursing offr and nursing advsr BRCS and St John of Jerusalem and BRCS Jt Ctee 1970–78, res conslt WHO SE Asia 1970, Euro del and first chm bd of Cwlth Nurses' Fedn 1971, Leverhulme Fellowship 1974–75, health servs advsr and conslt WHO and other int agencies and orgns 1978–; memb: Hosp and Med Servs Ctee 1970, Ex-Servs War Disabled Help Ctee 1970, Br Cwlth Nurses War Meml Fund 1970 ctee and cncl, Br Cwlth Nurses War Meml Fund 1970, mgmnt cncl Nat Florence Nightingale Meml Ctee 1970, cncl Queen's Inst of Dist Nursing 1970, cncl of nurses Royal Coll of Nursing; MRSH, FRSN, FRCN 1977, memb RSM 1980; *Books* Waiting in Outpatients' Departments (1965), Marriage and Nursing (1968), Home from Hospital (1970), Home Nursing (1975), Health Needs Help (1977), Health Auxiliaries in the Health Team (jtly, 1978), Self Care for the People of Developing Countries (1979), Discharge Procedures (1980), Notes on Nursing 1860 and 1980 (1980), Emergency Procedures and First Aid for Nurses (1981), The Third Age (1982), Providing Continuing Care for Elderly People (1983), First Aid for Developing Countries (1983), Protecting the Health of the Elderly (1983), Know Your Own Body (1987), Add Life to Years (1989), Tropical Health: concise notes (1989), Better Opportunities for Disabled People (1989); various articles for professional jls; *Recreations* music, opera, painting, reading; *Clubs* Arts, Royal Over-Seas League; *Style*— Miss Muriel Skeet; ✉ c/o Royal Over-Seas League, Over-Seas House, St James's Street, London SW1

SKEET, Sir Trevor Herbert Harry; kt (1986), MP (C) Bedfordshire North (majority 11,618); s of Harry May Skeet; *b* 28 Jan 1918; *Educ* King's Coll Auckland NZ, Univ of NZ (LLB); *m* 1, 1957, Elizabeth (decd), da of Montague Gilling, of Bedford; 2 s; m 2, 1985, Valerie A E Benson; *Career* Lt RNZNVR; barr and slr NZ, barr UK; MP (C): Willesden E 1959–64, Bedford 1970–83, Bedfordshire N 1983–; chm Parly and Scientific Ctee 1983–88, memb Select Ctee on Science and Technology 1992; *Recreations* walking, travel, gardening; *Clubs* Royal Cwlth Soc, Army and Navy; *Style*— Sir Trevor Skeet, MP; ✉ The Gables, Milton Ernest, Beds MK44 1RS (☎ 01234 822307)

SKEGGS, Dr David Bartholomew Lyndon; s of Dr Basil Lyndon Skeggs (d 1956), of Herts, and Gladys Jessie, *née* Tucker (d 1978); *b* 26 Aug 1928; *Educ* Winchester, Oriel Coll Oxford, St Bart's Hosp London; *m* 16 Nov 1957, Anne, da of H N Hughes, of Worcs; 2 da (Lucinda b 1960, Imogen b 1963); *Career* RN 1954–56; Surgn Lt Cdr RNR 1956–70; dir of radiotherapy Royal Free Hosp London 1966–86, hon conslt Royal N Hosp London and Lister Hosp Stevenage, chm Dept of Radiotherapy and Oncology Cromwell Hosp London 1992–; past memb Bd of Examiners Part 1 FRCR, sr examiner DMRT 1970–75; use of computerised radiotherapy and devpt of computerised 3–D radiotherapy treatment planning; memb Bd of Visitors for prisons; memb Cncl Wycombe Abbey Sch; Liveryman Worshipful Soc of Apothecaries; *Books* contribs: Maingot's Textbook of Surgery, Shaw's Textbook of Gynaecology, Scott Brown's Textbook of ENT Surgery; *Recreations* gardening, music, travel, competitive games; *Style*— Dr David Skeggs; ✉ The Coach House, Barnes Common, London SW13 OHS (☎ and fax 0181 876 7929); 152 Harley St, London W1N 1HH (☎ 0171 935 0444)

SKELDING, Barry Howard; s of Denis Howard Skelding, of Barton-on-Sea, Hants, and Stella, *née* Scott Elliott; *b* 2 Jan 1945; *Educ* The Stationers' Co's Sch; *m* 27 Aug 1977, Margaret Marion, da of Gordon David Carnegie (d 1969); 2 da (Katie b 1981, Sarah b 1983); *Career* admitted slr 1970; assoc ptnr Gamlens 1970, gp property slr EMI Ltd 1970–80, ptnr Rowe and Maw 1980–92, assoc Jaques & Lewis and Eversheds 1993–95, ptnr Park Nelson 1995–; memb: Law Soc 1970, City of London Slrs' Co 1995; Freeman City of London 1996; *Recreations* lawn tennis, squash rackets, music; *Clubs* Cumberland, Herts Country; *Style*— Barry H Skelding, Esq; ✉ 2 Folly Pathway, Radlett, Herts WD7 8DS

SKELLERN, Peter; s of John Skellern, of Derbyshire, and Margaret, *née* Spencer (d 1987); *b* 14 March 1947; *Educ* The Derby Sch Bury Lancs, Guildhall Sch of Music and Drama (AGSM); *m* 1970, Diana Elizabeth, da of Edward Dampier Seare; 1 s (Timothy Seare b 29 Nov 1971), 1 da (Katherine Daisy b 22 June 1974); *Career* pianist; trombonist Nat Youth Brass Band 1963, memb March Hare pop gp 1968–70; wrote song You're a Lady (reached No 1 in 6 countries) 1972, writer for Stop the Week (BBC Radio 4) 1970s, made autobiographical TV series 1981, scriptwriter, composer and actor Happy Endings TV series of mini-musicals 1982, co-wrote (with Richard Stilgoe) and appeared in Who Plays Wins (Vaudeville) 1985; *Recordings* 15 albums incl: Astaire (1980), Oasis (with Julian Lloyd Webber and Mary Hopkin, 1982); *Books* Trolls (musical for children, 1990, published by J B Cramer); *Recreations* sailing; *Clubs* Lord's Taverners; *Style—* Peter Skellern, Esq

SKELLEY, Dr Eva; da of Dr Francis Kosek, of Brno, Czechoslovakia, and Blazena Koskova (d 1982); *b* 7 Oct 1932; *Educ* Charles Univ Prague Czechoslovakia (MA, PhD, Dip); *m* 26 July 1957, Jeff Skelley, s of Francis Skelley; 1 da (Danielle Barbara); *Career* Radio Prague: translator, reporter, broadcaster; md Collets Holdings 1981–92, publisher European Bookseller magazine 1992–; govr Univ of Brighton 1991–; *Books* Soviet Satire (gen ed, 1968), Soviet Scene (co-ed 1987), Perestroika in Action (1988), One Way Ticket to Democracy (1989), Perestroika - The Crunch is Now (1990); *Recreations* skiing, gardening, music, travel; *Style—* Dr Eva Skelley; ✉ 19 Baskerville Road, London SW18 3RW

SKELMERSDALE, 7 Baron (UK 1828); Roger Bootle-Wilbraham; s of Brig 6 Baron Skelmersdale, DSO, MC (d 1973), and Ann (d 1974), da of Percy Quilter and gda of Sir Cuthbert Quilter, 1 Bt; *b* 2 April 1945; *Educ* Eton, Lord Wandsworth Coll; *m* 1972, Christine, da of Roy Morgan, of Hamel Evercreech, Somerset; 1 s, 1 da (Hon Carolyn Ann b 1974); *Heir* s, Hon Andrew Bootle-Wilbraham b 9 Aug 1977; *Career* horticulturist; dir Broadleigh Nurseries 1991– (md 1973–81); pres Somerset Tst for Nature Conservation 1980–, pres Br Naturalists Assoc 1980–95; Lord-in-Waiting to HM The Queen 1981–86; Parly under sec of state: DOE 1986–87, DHSS 1987–88, DSS 1988–89, NI Office (DHSS and Agric) 1989–90; dep chm of Ctees House of Lords 1991–95, dep speaker House of Lords 1995–; parly conslt 1991–; memb Jt Ctee on Statutory Instruments 1991–, memb Sub Ctee B (Euro energy, indust and tport) 1996–; chm The Stroke Assoc 1993–; govr Castle Sch Taunto 1992–96; memb Royal Horticultural Soc; FLS; *Recreations* gardening, reading, bridge; *Style—* The Rt Hon Lord Skelmersdale; ✉ c/o House of Lords, London SW1A OPW (☎ 0171 219 3224, fax 0171 630 0088)

SKELTON, John Martin; s of Martin Oliver Skelton, and Marie Lillian, *née* Bartlett; *b* 22 May 1952; *Educ* Westminster, BNC Oxford (BA); *m* 3 Sept 1982, Clare Louise; 2 s (Simon Martin Sheridan, James John), 1 da (Georgina Louise); *Career* admitted slr 1977; ptnr: Withers 1980–87 (asst slr 1977–79), Macfarlanes 1987–; *Style—* John Skelton, Esq; ✉ 46 Blackheath Park, London SE3 9SJ; Macfarlanes, 10 Norwich Street, London EC4A 1BD (☎ 0171 831 9222, fax 0171 831 9607)

SKELTON, John Stephen; MBE (1989); s of Godefroy Skelton (d 1979), of Wellingborough, and Margaret Evangeline, *née* Gill (d 1981); *b* 8 July 1923; *Educ* Norwich Cathedral Choir Sch, Bablake Sch Coventry, City of Coventry Sch of Art; *m* 1948, Myrtle, da of John Bromley Martin; 1 s (Jonathan Gill b 1949), 2 da (Helen Mary b 1951, Rebecca Alys b 1968); *Career* cmmnd Capt RA, served India Burma Malaya 1942–47; sculptor; Arts Cncl rep Royal Soc of Br Sculptors Scottish Public Sculpture Scheme 1965–70, artist in residence Bishop Otter Coll Chichester 1989–90; works incl: all sculpture for Christ Church Coventry (12 works) 1956, sculpture of Salomé (Hopetoun House Edinburgh) 1963, meml to Merchant Navy (Winchester Cathedral) 1959, Variation on the Willendorf Venus (exhibited at Henry Moore Study Centre Leeds) 1963, Aftermath of War (now at Herbert Art Gall Coventry) 1965, Our Lady of Pity (Norwich Cathedral) 1967, Lady Macbeth (Shakespeare Centre Stratford upon Avon), Rhythmic Form (now at Univ of Chigaco) 1967, Axis Mundi (Bishop Otter Coll) 1990; portraits: Sir Joseph Simpson (St Paul's Cathedral) 1969, Ivor Novello (St Paul's Cathedral) 1973, Carl Ebert (Glyndebourne Opera House) 1981; memorials to: The Great Commanders (St Paul's Cathedral Crypt), Winston Churchill (St Paul's Cathedral), Earl Mountbatten (Romsey and Royal Thames YC), Mary Rose meml to Unknown Sailor (Portsmouth Cathedral), Korean War Meml (Royal Engrs Chatham), George Eliot and John Clare (Poets' Corner Westminster Abbey); work in collections incl: Toledo Museum of Art USA, Shakespeare Centre Stratford upon Avon, Br Museum, Chichester City Museum, Plymouth Art Gallery, HM The Queen, Coventry Art Gallery; rep GB Int Yugoslavian Sculpture Symposium 1964 and UN Pavilion Yugoslavia 1966; Royal Soc of Br Sculptors Silver medal 1975; fell Royal Soc of Br Sculptors 1963, fell Soc of Designer Craftsmen, FRSA 1964; *Recreations* water colours; *Clubs* Art Workers' Guild; *Style—* John Skelton, Esq, MBE; ✉ Blabers Mead, Streat, Hassocks, East Sussex BN6 8RR (☎ 01273 890491, workshop and fax 01273 890839)

SKELTON, Rt Rev Kenneth John Fraser; CBE (1972); s of Henry Edmund Skelton (d 1957); *b* 16 May 1918; *Educ* Dulwich, Corpus Christi Coll Cambridge; *m* 1945, Phyllis Barbara, da of James Emerton; 2 s, 1 da; *Career* ordained 1941, rector of Walton-on-the-Hill Liverpool 1955–62, bishop of Matabeleland 1962–70, asst bishop of Durham, rural dean of Wearmouth and rector of Bishopwearmouth 1970–75, 96 bishop of Lichfield 1975–84, asst bishop Dio of Sheffield and Derby 1984–; *Books* Bishop in Smith's Rhodesia (1985), The Overseas Bishoprics' Fund 1941–91 (1991); *Style—* The Rt Rev Kenneth Skelton, CBE; ✉ 65 Crescent Rd, Sheffield S7 1HN (☎ 0114 255 1260)

SKELTON, Nick David; s of David Frank Skelton, of Odnull Farm, Wase Lane, Berkswell, and Norma, *née* Brindley; *m* 25 Oct 1982, Sarah Sue Poile, da of Charles Edwin Edwards; 2 s (Daniel b 9 April 1985, Harry b 20 Sept 1989); *Career* show jumper; ridden 100 World Cup classes and 60 Nations Cup teams; jr Euro champion 1975, winner 10 classes Wembley 1981, 3 team Gold medals Euro Championships (individual Bronze), team Silver medal and 2 team Bronze medals World Championships (individual Bronze), winner Hickstead Derby 3 times (runner up twice); Grand Prix wins: Dublin 3 times, NY twice, Aachen Germany 3 times; GB high jump record Olympia 1975; *Recreations* skiing, farming; *Style—* Nick Skelton, Esq; ✉ c/o British Show Jumping Association, British Equestrian Centre, Stoneleigh, Kenilworth, Warwickshire CV8 2LR

SKELTON, Robert William; OBE (1989); s of John William Skelton (d 1989), of South Holmwood, Surrey, and Rosa Ellen Victoria Ena, *née* Wright (d 1969); *b* 11 June 1929; *Educ* Tiffins Sch Kingston; *m* 31 July 1954, Frances, da of Lionel Aird (d 1990), of Clapham; 3 s (Oliver b 1957, Gregory b 1959, Nicholas b 1962); *Career* V & A: dep keeper Indian Section 1972–77 (asst keeper 1960–72), keeper Indian Dept 1978–88; tstee: Asia House Tst 1977–, The Indian Nat Tst for Art and Cultural Heritage (INTACH) 1991–; memb Cncl: Soc for S Asian Studies 1984–94, Royal Asiatic Soc 1970–73, 1975–78 and 1988–92; *Books* Indian Miniatures from the XVth to XIXth Centuries (1961), Rajasthani Temple Hangings of The Krishna Cult (1973), Indian Painting (jtly, 1978), Arts of Bengal (jtly, 1979), The Indian Heritage (jtly, 1982); *Recreations* chamber music, walking; *Style—* Robert Skelton, Esq, OBE; ✉ 10 Spencer Road, S Croydon, Surrey CR2 7EH (☎ and fax 0181 688 7187)

SKENE, Charles Pirie; OBE (1992); *b* 30 April 1935; *Educ* Loretto; *m* 9 May 1964, Alison Jean Katherine Lamont; 1 s (Richard b 1967), 2 da (Jennifer b 1966, Pamela b 1972); *Career* gp chm and chief exec of The Skene Group of Companies; pres: Jr Chamber Aberdeen 1967, Aberdeen C of C 1983–85, Assoc of Scot Chambers of Commerce 1985–86; nat sec Jr Chamber Scot 1970 (dir 1969), fndr Aberdeen Civic Soc 1968; chm: NE Branch of Lorettonian Soc 1976–86, Royal Northern and Univ Club 1981–82, Industry Year Grampian Area 1986, Industry Matters Grampian Area 1987–89; indust consIt Scot Educn Indust Ctee 1986–87, former memb Exec Ctee Scot Cncl Devpt and Indust, dir Aberdeen and NE Soc for the Deaf 1973–, assessor to Dean of Guild 1983–95, govr The Robert Gordon Univ 1985–; memb: Economic Affrs Ctee SCUA 1986–, Exec Ctee CBI (Scot) 1988–94 and 1995–, Open Univ Enterprise in Higher Educn Advsy Ctee for Scot 1990–91; chm: RGIT Enterprise Mgmnt Ctee 1988–93, Scot Industrialists' Cncl Grampian Branch, Scotland Educn Ctee CBI 1993–94, Enterprise Gp CBI (Scot) 1994–; donor of the annual Skene Aberdeen Int Youth Festival Award 1976–; initiator: Skene Young Entrepreneurs Award 1987–, Scotland Tomorrow (televised banquet); author of paper Educating Scotsmen and Women 1987; MSC Fit for Work Award, Euro Year of the Environment (conservation award, design award commendation); FRSA, FBIPP; *Style—* Charles P Skene, Esq, OBE; ✉ The Skene Group, 23 Rubislaw Den North, Aberdeen AB15 4AL

SKENE OF SKENE, Danus George Moncrieff; s of Robert William Dugald Skene (d 1981), of Pitlour, Strathmiglo, Fife, and Elizabeth Diana Wolfe, *née* Sutherland (d 1996); *b* 2 April 1944; *Educ* Eton, Univ of Sussex (BA), Univ of Chicago (MA), Univ of Aberdeen (MEd); *m* 1977, Anne Audrey, da of Donald Campbell (d 1962); 2 da (Hannah Dorothea b 1979, Abigail Mary Elspeth b 1985), 1 s (Dugald Alexander b 1982); *Career* tutor Makerere Univ College Uganda 1966–68, lectr Univ of Durham 1970–71, civil servant HM Treasy 1971–72, teacher 1977–79 and 1984–, dir Scottish Churches Action for World Devpt 1980–83, educnl co-ordinator Perth and Kinross Region 1989–; memb Gen Teaching Cncl 1976; Parly candidate: (Lab) Kinross and W Perthshire 1974 (both elections), (Lib) N Tayside 1983, (Alliance) Moray 1987; cncllr Perth & Kinross 1980–84; Chief of Clan Skene 1994–; *Books* Just Sharing (with Duncan Forrester, 1987); *Recreations* traditional music, walking the hills; *Style—* Danus Skene of Skene; ✉ Pitlour, Strathmiglo, Fife KY14 7RS (☎ 01337 860754)

SKIDELSKY, Baron (Life Peer UK 1991), of Tilton in the County of East Sussex; Robert Jacob Alexander Skidelsky; s of Boris J Skidelsky (d 1982), and Galia V, *née* Sapelkin (d 1987); *b* 25 April 1939; *Educ* Brighton Coll, Jesus Coll Oxford (BA, MA, DPhil); *m* 2 Sept 1970, Augusta Mary Clarissa, da of John Humphrey Hope (d 1974); 2 s (Hon Edward b 1973, Hon William b 1976), 1 da (Hon Juliet b 1981); *Career* res fell Nuffield Coll Oxford 1965–68, assoc prof Johns Hopkins Univ USA 1970–76; Univ of Warwick: prof of int studies 1978–90, prof of political economy 1990–; memb: Lord Chllr's Advsy Cncl on Public Records 1987–92, Schools Examination and Assessment Cncl 1992–93 (resigned); chm: Charleston Tst 1987–92, Social Market Fndn 1991–, Hands Off Reading Campaign 1994–; tstee Humanitas 1991–; FRHistS 1973, FRSL 1978, FBA 1994; *Books* Politicians and the Slump (1967), English Progressive Schools (1970), Oswald Mosley (1975), John Maynard Keynes (I 1983, II 1992), World After Communism (1994); *Recreations* tennis, bridge, opera; *Style—* The Rt Hon Lord Skidelsky, FBA; ✉ Tilton House, Firle, E Sussex BN8 6LL (☎ 01323 811570); University of Warwick, Coventry CV4 7AL

SKIDMORE, (Frederic) David; OBE (1984); s of Frederick Ernest Skidmore, of Bexhill on Sea (d 1990), and Mary Elizabeth Skidmore (d 1980); *b* 10 Dec 1939; *Educ* Gonville and Caius Coll Cambridge (MA, MB BChir, MD), Birmingham Med Sch; *m* 12 July 1966 (m dis 1983), Yvonne, da of John Steel (d 1979); 1 s (David James Benedict b 1970), 1 da (Rebecca Mary b 1969); m 2, 1983, Diana Sarah; *Career* former: demonstrator in anatomy Cambridge, Br Heart Fndn res fell, lectr in surgery Univ of Manchester; currently: conslt surgn Dartford and Gravesham DHA, hon sr lectr Dept of Surgery Med Sch UCL; Freeman: City of London, Worshipful Co of Tylers and Bricklayers, Worshipful Soc of Apothecaries; memb: Royal Inst of Int Affrs, Royal Society of Medicine, Br Assoc for Surgical Oncology; FRCSEd 1968, FRCS 1970; *Books* Studies on Development of the Heart and Great Vessels (1973); *Recreations* swimming, windsurfing, ornithology; *Clubs* Hawk's (Cambridge), Otter, Carlton; *Style—* David Skidmore, Esq, OBE; ✉ London Bridge Hospital, London SE1 2PR (☎ 0181 318 6923, car 0836 714317, fax 0181 852 6919)

SKILBECK, (Norman) Stewart; s of Neilson Skilbeck (d 1978), of Northallerton, and Alice, *née* Jamieson; *b* 8 Dec 1947; *Educ* Durham Cathedral Chorister Sch, Durham Sch; *m* 16 Aug 1975, Margaret Rosamund, da of Albert Alma Wilson (d 1978), of The Grange, Camblesforth, Selby; 2 s (John b 1977, William b 1980), 1 da (Jennifer b 1983); *Career* CA; in practice 1972–78, fin dir Grindlays Humberclyde 1979–84; dir Vintage Car Dept Sotheby's 1990–94 (conslt 1984–89), dir Brooks Auctioneers 1994–; FCA 1971; *Recreations* music, travel, gardening; *Clubs* Veteran Car, Rolls-Royce Enthusiasts; *Style—* Stewart Skilbeck, Esq; ✉ The Villa, Main Street, Hemingbrough, Selby, North Yorkshire (☎ 01757 638312); Brooks Auctioneers, 81 Westside, London SW4 9AY (☎ 0171 228 8000, fax 0171 585 0830)

SKILTON, Prof David John; s of Henry Charles Stanley Skilton, of London, and Iris Flora Marion, *née* Redfern (d 1975); *b* 10 July 1942; *Educ* Tollington GS London, King's Coll Cambridge (MA, MLitt), Univ of Copenhagen; *m* 1, 29 Oct 1976 (m dis 1981), Marvid Elaine Graham, da of David King Wilson (d 1976), of Glasgow; m 2, 12 April 1984, Joanne Vivien, da of Norman Louis Papworth, of Huntingdonshire; 1 s (Adam Jonathan b 1989), 1 da (Hannah Catherine b 1985); *Career* sr lectr Univ of Glasgow 1978–80 (lectr 1970–80), dean Faculty of Arts St David's Univ Coll Lampeter 1983–86 (prof of English 1980–86), prof of English and head of Dept of English UWIST 1986–88; Univ of Wales Cardiff: prof of English and head Sch of English Studies Communication and Philosophy 1988–, dep princ 1992–95, pro-vice chllr 1995–96; memb Nat Curriculum English Working Gp 1988–89, literary advsr to Trollope Soc 1988–, tstee and chair of Advsy Bd Roald Dahl Arts Project Tst; *Books* Anthony Trollope and his Contemporaries (1972), Defoe to the Victorians: Two Centuries of the English Novel (1978), The Complete Novels of Anthony Trollope (gen ed), Critical Approaches: The Early and Mid-Victorian Novel (1992), Anthony Trollope, An Autobiography (ed); *Recreations* music; *Style—* Prof David Skilton; ✉ University of Wales, Cardiff, PO Box 94, Cardiff CF1 3XB (☎ 01222 874040, fax 01222 874502, e-mail skilton@cf.ac.uk)

SKINGSLEY, Air Chief Marshal Sir Anthony Gerald; GBE (1992), KCB (1986, CB 1983); s of Edward Roberts Skingsley; *b* 19 Oct 1933; *Educ* Univ of Cambridge (MA); *m* 1957 Lilwen Dixon; 2 s, 1 da; *Career* joined RAF 1955, OC RAF Laarbruch (Germany) 1974–76, HQ 2 ATAF (ACOS Offensive Ops) 1977–78, Hon ADC to HM The Queen 1976–77, RCDS course 1978, Dir Air Plans MOD 1979–80, ACOS Plans and Policy SHAPE 1980–83, Cmdt RAF Staff Coll Bracknell 1983–84, Asst Chief of Air Staff 1985–86, Air Memb for Personnel 1986–87, C-in-C RAF Germany, Cdr 2 Allied Tactical AF 1987–89, Dep C-in-C AFCENT 1989–92; currently: pres RAF Assoc Luxembourg, vice pres Anglo-German Officers' Assoc, vice pres Forces Help Soc and Lord Roberts Workshops, memb Presidential Advsy Cncl Atlantic Assoc; *Recreations* off-shore sailing, golf, travel; *Clubs* RAF; *Style—* Air Chief Marshal Sir Anthony Skingsley, GBE, KCB; ✉ c/o National Westminster Bank plc, 43 Swan St, West Malling, Kent ME19 6LE

SKINNER, Alan Kenneth; s of Kenneth Alfred Skinner of Hindhead, Surrey, and Millicent Louise, *née* Chapman; *b* 27 Aug 1948; *Educ* Sutton Valence; *m* 24 March 1973, Heather, da of Peter Campbell; 1 da (Hannah b 13 June 1978); *Career* Edward Moore & Sons (now Moores Rowland): articled clerk 1966–70, qualified 1970, ptnr 1975, sr ptnr Kingston upon Thames office 1975–; chm Accreditation of Trg Offices Surrey Bd ICAEW 1984–93, jt chm Kingston CAs Practitioners Gp, chm SW London Dist Soc of

CAs 1981–82, external examiner Accountancy Fndn Course Kingston Univ 1986–94; non-exec dir Kingston Hosp 1990–; memb Kingston Round Table 1976–89; FCA 1979 (ACA 1970); *Recreations* walking, travel, DIY; *Style*— Alan Skinner, Esq; ✉ Green Hayes, Forest Rd, Pyrford, Woking, Surrey GU22 8LU; Moores Rowland, Applemarket House, 17 Union St, Kingston upon Thames, Surrey KT1 1RP (☎ 0181 549 6399, fax 0181 549 6209)

SKINNER, Prof Andrew Stewart; s of Andrew Paterson Skinner (d 1975), of Cardross, Dunbartonshire, and Isabella Bateman, *née* Stewart (d 1986); *b* 11 Jan 1935; *Educ* Kiel Sch Dumbarton, Cornell Univ, Univ of Glasgow (MA, BLitt); *m* 29 Aug 1966, Margaret Mary Dorothy, da of William Robertson (d 1986), of Alloway, Ayrshire; *Career* Queen's Univ Belfast 1960–62, Queen's Coll Dundee 1962–64; Univ of Glasgow: lectr 1964, reader 1976, head Dept of Political Economy 1979–86, dean Faculty of Social Scis 1980–83, clerk of senate 1983–90, Daniel Jack chair of political economy 1985–94, Adam Smith chair 1994–, vice princ (Arts) 1991–96; FRSE 1988, FRSA 1991, FBA 1993; *Books* Principles of Political Economy (ed Sir James Steuart, 1966), Adam Smith - The Wealth of Nations (ed with R H Campbell and W B Todd, 1976), A System of Social Science - papers relating to Adam Smith (1979, 2 edn, 1996), Adam Smith Reviewed (ed with P Jones, 1992); *Recreations* gardening; *Clubs* The University; *Style*— Prof Andrew Skinner, FRSE, FBA; ✉ Glen House, Cardross, Dunbartonshire G82 5ES (☎ 01389 841603); Department of Political Economy, University of Glasgow, Glasgow G12 8RT (☎ 0141 330 4657, fax 0141 330 4940, telex 777070 UNIGLA)

SKINNER, Angus; s of Dr Theodore Skinner (d 1988), and Morag, *née* MacKinnon (d 1989); *b* 4 Jan 1950; *Educ* Univ of Edinburgh (BSc), Univ of London, Univ of Strathclyde (MBA); *m* (sep 1995); 1 s (Aidan b 11 July 1980), 2 da (Jenny b 20 Sept 1982, Caitlin b 9 May 1985); *Career* social worker Cheshire and Kent Cncls 1971–75, social work mangr Lothian and Borders Cncls 1975–91, chief inspr Scottish Office 1992– (chief social work advsr 1991–92); *Books* Another Kind of Home (1992); *Recreations* sometimes; *Style*— Angus Skinner, Esq; ✉ Scottish Office, Room 31, James Craig Walk, Edinburgh EH1 3BA (☎ 0131 244 5414, fax 0131 244 5496)

SKINNER, Dennis Edward; MP (Lab) Bolsover (majority 20,660); s of Edward Skinner; *b* 11 Feb 1932; *Educ* Tupton Hall GS, Ruskin Coll Oxford; *m* 12 March 1960, Mary, da of James Parker; 1 s, 2 da; *Career* former miner; joined Lab Pty 1950, MP (Lab) Bolsover 1970–; NEC: memb Lab Pty Home Policy Ctee 1978–, memb Lab Pty Orgn Policy Ctee 1978, Lab Pty chm 1988–89; memb: Campaign Gp Labour MPs 1982–, Lab Pty Youth Ctee until 1982, Tribune Gp until 1982; memb Clay Cross Cncl 1960–72, pres Derbyshire Miners 1966–70; *Style*— Dennis Skinner, Esq, MP; ✉ House of Commons, London SW1A 0AA

SKINNER, (Thomas) James Hewitt; s and h of Sir (Thomas) Keith Hewitt Skinner, 4 Bt, *qv*; *b* 10 Sept 1962; *Style*— James Skinner, Esq; ✉ Wood Farm, Reydon, nr Southwold IP18 6SL

SKINNER, Jeremy John Banks; s of R Banks Skinner (d 1978), of Moor Park, Herts, and Betty, *née* Short; *b* 15 Nov 1936; *Educ* Rugby, Clare Coll Cambridge (BA); *m* 31 Aug 1963, Judith Anne, da of Jack William Austin (d 1986), of Letchworth, Herts; 1 s (Spencer b 13 July 1966), 2 da (Sophie (Mrs Payne) b 24 Nov 1964, Sasha b 9 July 1968); *Career* Nat Serv 2 Lt 16/5 The Queen's Royal Lancers 1956–57; ptnr Linklaters & Paines 1967–; non-exec dir Tarquin plc; memb: Cncl Inst of Fiscal Studies, Int Bar Assoc, Governing Body Rugby; memb Ct of Assts Worshipful Co of Cordwainers (former Master); *Recreations* hunting; *Style*— Jeremy Skinner, Esq; ✉ Stocking Farm, Stocking Pelham, nr Buntingford, Herts (☎ 01279 777556); Barrington House, 59/67 Gresham St, London EC2 (☎ 0171 606 7080)

SKINNER, Sir (Thomas) Keith Hewitt; 4 Bt (UK 1912), of Pont Street, Borough of Chelsea; s of Sir (Thomas) Gordon Skinner, 3 Bt (d 1972), and his 1 w, Mollie Barbara, *née* Girling (d 1965); *b* 6 Dec 1927; *Educ* Charterhouse; *m* 29 April 1959, Jill, da of late Cedric Ivor Tuckett, of Tonbridge, Kent; 2 s; *Heir* s, (Thomas) James Hewitt Skinner, *qv*; *Career* dir Reed International 1980–90, chm and chief exec Reed Publishing 1982–90; *Style*— Sir Keith Skinner, Bt; ✉ Wood Farm, Reydon, nr Southwold IP18 6SL

SKINNER, Michael Gordon (Mick); s of Geordie Skinner, of Newcastle upon Tyne, and Chrissie, *née* Jackson; *b* 26 Nov 1958; *Educ* Wallbottle GS; *m* Anna, *née* Palmer; 1 da (Emily Elizabeth b 4 July 1995); *Career* former rugby union flanker; clubs: Blaydon RFC 1974–79, Blackheath RFC 1979–84 and 1992–94, Harlequins FC 1984–92 (winner John Player Cup 1988 and Pilkington Cup 1991); capt Barbarians' Easter tour of Wales 1990; rep: Blaydon Colts (winner Durham Co Colts Cup), Northumberland U21, Kent, London Div, England B (debut v France 1987); England: debut v France 1988, memb World Cup runners-up team 1991 (was the only England forward to score a try in the World Cup), memb Grand Slam winning team 1992, 21 caps; freelance computer consult; *Style*— Mick Skinner, Esq; ✉ Blackheath FC, The Rectory Field, Charlton Rd, Blackheath, London SE3 (☎ 0181 858 1578)

SKINNER, Peter; MEP (Lab) Kent W (majority 16,777); s of James and Jean Skinner; *Educ* Univ of Bradford (BSc), Univ of Warwick (postgrad cert in industl rels), Univ of Greenwich (PGCE); *m* 14 July 1990, Julie Doreen; *Career* industl rels offr 1982–84, union organiser 1984–86, lectr NW Kent Coll and Univ of Greenwich 1989–94, MEP (Lab) Kent W 1994–; *Recreations* most sports, especially football; *Style*— Peter Skinner, Esq, MEP; ✉ The Labour Party, JC House, Priory Hill, Dartford, Kent DA1 2ER (☎ 01322 281500)

SKINNER, Prof Quentin Robert Duthie; s of Alexander Skinner, CBE (d 1979), and Winifred Rose Margaret, *née* Duthie; *b* 26 Nov 1940; *Educ* Bedford Sch, Gonville and Caius Coll Cambridge (BA, MA); *m* 31 Aug 1979, Dr Susan Deborah Thorpe James, da of Prof Derrick James, of London; 1 s (Marcus b 13 July 1982), 1 da (Olivia b 7 Dec 1979); *Career* Univ of Cambridge: fell Christ's Coll 1962–, prof of political sci 1978–96, regius prof of modern history 1996–; Hon LittD: Univ of Chicago 1992, Univ of E Anglia 1992; FRHS 1970, FBA 1980; *Books* The Foundations of Modern Political Thought (2 vols, 1978), Machiavelli (1981), Meaning and Context (1988), Reason and Rhetoric in the Philosophy of Hobbes (1996); *Style*— Prof Quentin Skinner, FBA; ✉ Christ's College, Cambridge, Cambs, CB2 3BU

SKINNER, Richard; *Career* radio and TV personality; BBC Radio 1 1973–92: fndr presenter/reporter Newsbeat 1973–79, hosted Rock On, Saturday Live, Rockshow and The Saturday Sequence, specialist interviewer of most major int rock stars; BBC Radio 1 documentary series incl: Beeb's Lost Beatles Tapes (Sony Award), profiles of Mark Knopfler, Elton John and Ronnie Spector; BBC TV: former regular presenter Top of the Pops and Whistle Test, one hour special documentaries (for BBC 2) interviewing Genesis, Joni Mitchell, Bryan Ferry, Paul McCartney and Peter Gabriel; presenter The Morning Show GLR 1990–92, jt programming dir and morning show presenter Virgin Radio (national independent radio station) 1993– Oct 1996; other work: opening voice and anchorman (for BBC TV) Live Aid 1985, The Nelson Mandela Tribute (for BBC) 1987, also regular contrib to BBC World Service, The British Forces Broadcasting Service and Westwood One radio networks (USA); *Style*— Richard Skinner, Esq; ✉ c/o Virgin Radio, 1 Golden Square, London W1R 4DJ (☎ 0171 434 1215)

SKINNER, Robin Charles Owen; s of Michael Owen Skinner (d 1993), and Patricia Alma, *née* Benson-Young, of Chichester, W Sussex; *b* 20 Sept 1949; *Educ* Rugby, Fitzwilliam Coll Cambridge (MA, rugby blue, rugby fives blue), Coll of Law Guildford; *m* 21 July 1973, Jillian Mary, da of Benjamin Ian Gilmour Mantle, of Cambridge; 2 s (Charles b 30 May 1974, Toby b 24 June 1976), 1 da (Emily b 20 Oct 1982); *Career* articled Linklaters & Paines 1974; admitted slr 1975; sr ptnr Rawlison & Butler 1984–; Liveryman Worshipful Co of Cordwainers (Steward Warden 1988); *Recreations* tennis, golf, family; *Clubs* Hawk's (Cambridge), City Livery, Royal Ashdown Golf; *Style*— Robin Skinner, Esq; ✉ 21 Gateways, Guildford, Surrey GU1 2LF; Rawlison & Butler, Griffin House, 135 High St, Crawley, West Sussex RH10 1DQ (☎ 01293 527744, fax 01293 520202)

SKIPPER, David John; s of Herbert George Skipper (d 1962), and Edna Skipper (d 1993); *b* 14 April 1931; *Educ* Watford GS, Univ of Oxford (MA); *m* 1955, Brenda Ann, da of late Alfred George Williams; 3 s (Andrew David b 19 April 1961, Jonathan Philip b 12 May 1963, Timothy Peter b 4 April 1967), 1 da (Elisabeth Lucy b 6 June 1969); *Career* served RAF 1954–57; asst master: Radley Coll 1957–63, Rugby Sch 1963–69; headmaster: Ellesmere Coll Salop 1969–81, Merchant Taylors' Sch 1981–91; dir: Westminster Centre for Educn 1991–96, South Bank Univ Secdy PGCE by Distance Learning 1992–; chm: Govrs Quainton Hall Sch, Soc of Sch Masters; Liveryman Worshipful Co of Merchant Taylors; fell Woodard Corporation; *Recreations* walking, gardening, reading, wood, fungi, herbs; *Style*— David Skipper, Esq; ✉ Doltons Farm, Newport Road, Woburn MK17 9HX (☎ 01525 290093, office ☎ 0171 815 8020)

SKIPWITH, Alexander Sebastian Grey d'Estoteville; s (by 1 m) and h of Sir Patrick Skipwith, 12 Bt; *b* 9 April 1969; *Educ* Harrow, Kent Univ, Chelsea Coll of Art and Design; *Career* dir and sec Britain's In-line Skating Assoc 1995–; freelance graphic designer 1994–; *Clubs* Chelsea Arts; *Style*— Alexander Skipwith, Esq; ✉ 2 Russell Road, London W14 8JA (☎ 0171 371 1568)

SKIPWITH, Sir Patrick Alexander d'Estoteville; 12 Bt (E 1622), of Prestwould, Leicestershire; s of Grey d'Estoteville Townsend Skipwith (ka 1942), and Sofka (d 1994), da of Prince Peter Alexandrovitch Dolgorouky; suc gf, Sir Grey Humberston d'Estoteville Skipwith 1950; *b* 1 Sept 1938; *Educ* Harrow, Trinity Coll Dublin (MA), Imperial Coll London (PhD); *m* 1, 24 June 1964 (m dis 1970), Gillian Patricia, adopted da of late Charles Frederick Harwood; 1 s, 1 da; m 2, 1972 (separated 1986), Ashkhain, da of late Bedros Atikian, of Calgary, Alberta, Canada; *Heir* s, Alexander Sebastian Grey d'Estoteville Skipwith b 9 April 1969; *Career* marine geologist: Ocean Mining Inc 1966–70; Directorate-Gen of Mineral Resources Jeddah Saudi Arabia 1970–73; geological ed Bureau de Recherches Géologiques et Minières Jeddah Saudi Arabia 1973–86; md Immel Publishing Ltd 1988–89; freelance editing (GeoEdit), translating and public relations 1986–96; head of translation BRGN Orléans France 1996–; memb: Euro Assoc of Science Editors, Société Française des Traducteurs; AMSTRAD; IMM; *Recreations* riding, sailing, hill walking; *Clubs* Chelsea Arts; *Style*— Sir Patrick Skipwith, Bt; ✉ 76 rue de Pont-aux-Moines, 45450 Donnery, France (☎ 00 33 02 38 59 24 13, fax 00 33 02 38 59 28 98)

SKIPWITH, Peyton Stephen; s of Sir Grey Humberston d'Estoteville Skipwith, 12 Bt (d 1950), and Cynthia, *née* Egerton Leigh (d 1995); *b* 30 June 1939; *Educ* Canford; *m* 1 Oct 1971, Anne, da of Cecil England Barren, of Seasalter, Kent; 1 s (Grey b 1981), 2 da (Selina b 1972, Amber b 1974); *Career* dep md The Fine Art Soc; hon curator The Art Workers' Guild; contrib to: The Connoisseur, Apollo, Burlington Magazine; *Style*— Peyton Skipwith, Esq; ✉ The Fine Art Society, 148 New Bond St, London W1Y 0JT (☎ 0171 629 5116)

SKIPWORTH, Mark; s of George Skipworth, of Kingston-upon-Hull, and Jean Marjorie Skipworth; *b* 27 Jan 1959; *Educ* Sydney Smith Sch Hull, St John's Coll Oxford (BA); *m* 29 Aug 1981, Julie Alison Patricia, da of Frank Deegan; 2 s (Hunter b 31 Oct 1987, Patrick b 2 May 1992), 1 da (Zoe b 16 April 1994); *Career* reporter Sheffield Star 1980–84, writer Which? Magazine 1984–89, reporter Daily Telegraph 1989; The Sunday Times: consumer affairs correspondent 1990–93, dep insight ed 1994–95, news ed 1995–; *Awards* Yorkshire Young Journalist of the Year 1982, Nat Newspapers' Consumer Journalist of the Year 1991, commended Reporter of the Year (Br Press Awards) 1991, Scoop of the Year 1994, What the Papers Say Investigations of the Year 1994, Br Press Awards Exclusive of the Year 1994, Br Press Awards Team Journalism Award 1994; *Books* Oxford Type: The Best of ISIS (with Andrew Billen, 1984), The Scotch Whisky Book (1987), Class (with Greg Hadfield, 1994); *Recreations* sleep; *Style*— Mark Skipworth, Esq; ✉ The Sunday Times, 1 Pennington Street, London E1 9XW (☎ 0171 782 5667, fax 0171 782 5731)

SKLAR, Dr Jonathan; s of Vivian Sklar, of London, and Joyce, *née* Longworth (d 1991); *b* 9 June 1949; *Educ* Latymer Upper Sch, Royal Free Hosp Univ of London, Inst of Psychoanalysis London; *children* 2 da (Clea b 1 Aug 1978, Livia b 31 Oct 1981); *Career* sr registrar in psychiatry Friern and Royal Free Hosps 1978–79, sr registrar in psychotherapy Tavistock Clinic 1979–83, conslt psychotherapist Cambridge Health Authy 1983–95; head of Dept of Psychotherapy Cambridge 1989–95, visiting prof Arhus Univ and Psychiatric Hosp Denmark 1991–92, in private psychoanalytic practice 1995–; sec psychotherapy exec of Joint Ctee of Higher Psychiatric Trg 1990–92; Freedom City of Cusco Peru 1989; LRCP, MRCS 1973, MB BS 1974, MRCPsych 1977, assoc memb Br Psychoanalytical Soc 1984 (memb 1991), Examination Notes for the MRC Psych Part 1 (with B Puri, 1989); *Recreations* reading, opera; *Clubs* Mossiman's; *Style*— Dr Jonathan Sklar; ✉ 20 Elstow Grange, Brondesbury Park, London NW6 7DW (☎ 0181 830 0237)

SKORUPSKI, Prof John Maria; s of Wactaw Skorupski (d 1991), of Warsaw, and late Wanda, *née* Pankiewicz; *b* 19 Sept 1946; *Educ* St Benedict's Sch Ealing, Christ's Coll Cambridge (MA), Univ of Cambridge (PhD); *m* 18 Sept 1971, Barbara, da of Ernest Robert Taylor; 2 da (Katharine Wanda Taylor b 3 Nov 1978, Julia Zofia Taylor b 9 Feb 1982); *Career* visiting lectr Univ of Ife Nigeria 1971–72, visiting prof Univ of Louvain Belgium 1974; res fell UC Swansea Univ of Wales 1974–76, lectr Depts of Philosophy Univ of Glasgow 1976–84, prof of philosophy Univ of Sheffield 1984–90, prof of moral philosophy Univ of St Andrews 1990–; gen ed: OUP OPUS paperbacks, The International Research Library of Philosophy; memb Editorial Bd: Ratio and The Philosophical Quarterly Utilitas; pres Aristotelian Soc 1990–91; hon fell Centre for the Study of Political Thought Jagiellonian Univ Krakow 1991–; memb Exec Ctee Mind Assoc 1992–; FRSE 1992; *Books* Symbol and Theory, A Philosophical Study of Theories of Religion in Social Anthropology (1975), John Stuart Mill (1989), English Language Philosophy 1750–1945 (1993); *Recreations* walking, skiing, music; *Style*— Prof John Skorupski, FRSE; ✉ Department of Moral Philosophy, University of St Andrews, St Andrews, Fife KY16 9AL (☎ 01334 462483)

SKREIN, (Stephen Peter) Michael; *b* 31 Jan 1947; *Educ* Univ Coll Sch, Univ of Oxford (AM), Univ of Southern Calif (MA), Coll of Law; *Career* Richards, Butler & Co: admitted slr 1973, ptnr Richards Butler 1976–, head Commercial Litigation Gp 1990–96; memb Honor Soc of Phi Kappa Phi; Freeman City of London, Liveryman City of London Slrs' Co; memb: Law Soc, Int Bar Assoc, Copinger Soc, Baltic Exchange; *Style*— Michael Skrein, Esq; ✉ Richards Butler, Beaufort House, 15 St Botolph Street, London EC3A 7EE (☎ 0171 247 6555, fax 0171 247 5901)

SKYNNER, Dr (Augustus Charles) Robin; s of Reginald Charles Augustus Skynner (d 1965), of Two-Waters-Foot, nr Liskeard, Cornwall, and Mary Flemming, *née* Johns (d 1966); *b* 16 Aug 1922; *Educ* St Austell Co Sch Cornwall, Blundell's, Univ of London (MB BS, DPM); *m* 1, 12 July 1948 (m dis 29 April 1959), Geraldine Annella; m 2, 8 May 1959, Prudence Mary (d 1987), da of John Francis St Aubyn Fawcett (d 1954); 1 s (David b 1961), 1 da (Rosemary b 1963); *Career* WWII serv: RAF 1940, pilot trg cmmnd 1941, active serv pilot 21 Sqdn 2 Tactical Airforce, demobbed 1946; appts as conslt psychiatrist 1959–, physician i/c Dept of Psychiatry Queen Elizabeth Hosp for Children

1965–70, sr tutor in psychotherapy and hon conslt Bethlem Royal and Maudsley Hosp 1971–82; fndr memb: Group-Analytic Practice 1960–, Inst of Gp Analysis 1968–; fndr memb and first chm Inst of Family Therapy 1976–78, memb Cncl Tavistock Inst of Med Psychology 1988–92, regular columnist The Guardian 1989–94; advsr London Diocese Pastoral Work Devpt Scheme, conslt Gp and Family Dynamics Exploring Parenthood; FRCPsych, fndr memb Assoc of Family Therapy; memb American Family Therapy Acad; distinguished affiliate memb and approved supervisor American Assoc of Family and Marital Therapists, hon memb Euro Assoc of Family Therapy; *Books* One Flesh, Separate Persons: Principles of Family and Marital Psychotherapy (1976), Families and How to Survive Them (with John Cleese, *qv*, 1983), Explorations with Families: Group Analysis and Family Therapy (1987), Institutes and How to Survive Them: Mental Health Training and Consultation (1989), Life and How to Survive It (with John Cleese, *qv*, 1993), Family Matters (1995); *Recreations* country pursuits, windsurfing; *Style—* Dr Robin Skynner; ✉ 88 Montagu Mansions, London W1H 1LF (☎ 0171 935 3103/3085)

SKYRME, Sir (William) Thomas Charles; KCVO (1974), CB (1966), CBE (1953), TD (1949), JP (Oxon 1948), DL (Glos 1983); s of C G Skyrme of Monmouth; *b* 1913; *Educ* Rugby, New Coll Oxford, Dresden Univ, Paris Univ; *m* 1, 1938 (m dis 1953), Hon (Barbara) Suzanne Lyle (d 1994), yr da of 1 Baron Lyle of Westbourne (d 1954); 1 s, 2 da (*see* Sir Gerard Waterlow, Bt); m 2, 1957, Mary, da of Dr R C Leaning; *Career* WWII RA (wounded twice), Lt-Col; called to the Bar Inner Temple 1935 (Master of the Bench 1988), in practice Western circuit, sec to Lord Chllr 1944–48, sec of Cmmns 1948–77; pres Cwlth Magistrates' and Judges' Assoc 1970–79, (life vice pres 1979), chm Magistrates' Assoc of Eng and Wales 1979–81 (vice pres 1981–), gen cmmr Income Tax 1977–88, cmmr Broadcasting Complaints Cmmn 1981–87 (chm 1985–87), memb Top Salaries Review Bd 1981–90, chm Judicial Salaries Ctee 1984–90; chm Batsford Fndn 1983–96; Freeman City of London 1970, HM Lt City of London 1977–; FRGS; *Books* The Changing Image of the Magistracy (1979), History of the Justices of the Peace (1991); *Clubs* Army and Navy, Hurlingham; *Style—* Sir Thomas Skyrme, KCVO, CB, CBE, TD, JP, DL; ✉ Casa Larissa, Klosters, Switzerland; Elm Barns, Blockley, Moreton-in-Marsh, Glos

SLACK, His Hon Judge; John Kenneth Edward; TD (1964), DL (Bucks 1995); s of Ernest Edward Slack (d 1967), of Broadstairs, Kent, and Beatrice Mary, *née* Shorten (d 1972); *b* 23 Dec 1930; *Educ* Univ Coll Sch, St John's Coll Cambridge (MA, Cricket blue); *m* 4 April 1959, Patricia Helen, da of William Keith Metcalfe (d 1979), of Southport, Lancs; 2 s ((Mark) Christopher b 1960, Martin Andrew b 1962); *Career* Nat Serv: Capt RAEC 1949–51, TA; RA Middx Regiment (DCO) 1951–64; slr 1957, ptnr Freeborough Slack & Co 1958–76, recorder Crown Ct 1972–77, circuit judge (SE Circuit) 1977–; memb Cncl Univ Coll Sch 1974–90 (chm 1980–88); Club Cricket Conference: capt 1959–64, active vice pres 1969–77, pres 1978; capt Bucks CCC 1967–69, played rugby for Middlesex; *Recreations* golf; *Style—* His Hon Judge Slack, TD, DL; ✉ c/o Crown Court, 38 Market Square, Aylesbury, Bucks HP20 1XD (☎ 01296 434401, fax 01296 435665)

SLACK, Dr Richard Charles Bewick; s of Dr Horace George Bewick Slack (d 1966), of Bramhall, Cheshire, and Dorothy Edith, *née* Smith; *b* 4 March 1944; *Educ* Manchester GS, Jesus Coll Cambridge (MA, MB BChir); *m* 10 May 1969, Dr Patricia Mary Slack, da of Dr Arthur Hamilton Cheshire (d 1982), of Brewood, Staffs; 2 s (Benjamin b 1972, William b 1974), 2 da (Clare b 1976, Eleanor b 1981); *Career* house surgeon St Mary's Hosp London 1969–70; lectr: Middx Hosp Med Sch 1971–73, Univ of Nairobi 1973–77; sr lectr Univ of Nottingham 1978–, hon conslt PHLS and Nottingham Health Authy 1978–, conslt in communicable disease control 1990–, temp conslt WHO Special Programme AIDS 1987–88; memb: Exec Soc of Public Health, Exec Assoc of Med Microbiologists, Nottingham Medico-Chirurgical Soc; MRCPath 1977; *Books* Medical Microbiology (1992), Antimicrobial Chemotherapy (1995), Public Health (ed); *Recreations* fell walking, skiing, forestry; *Style—* Dr Richard Slack; ✉ 5 Magdala Road, Mapperley Park, Nottingham, NG3 5DE (☎ 0115 960 5940); Department of Microbiology, University of Nottingham Medical School, Queen's Medical Centre, Nottingham NG7 2UH (☎ 0115 942 1421, fax 0115 942 2190); Department of Public Health, Nottingham Health Authority (☎ 0115 912 3350, fax 0115 912 3351)

SLACK, Timothy Willatt; LVO (1995); s of Cecil Moorhouse Slack, MC (d 1986), and Dora, *née* Willatt (d 1978); *b* 18 April 1928; *Educ* Winchester, New Coll Oxford (MA); *m* 1, 31 Aug 1957, Katharine (d 1993), da of Norman Hughes (d 1982); 1 s (Henry b 1962), 3 da (Caroline b 1960, Louisa b 1966, Rebecca b 1969); m 2, 19 July 1996, Shuna, da of Lt-Col James Black; *Career* Nat Serv RN; asst master: Lycée de Garcons Rennes France 1951–52, Schule Schloss Salem W Germany 1952–53, Repton Derbys 1953–59; headmaster: Kambawsa Coll Burma 1959–62, Bedales Sch Hants 1962–74, Hellenic Coll London 1983–84; dir: FCO Wiston House Conf Centre 1977–83 (asst dir 1975–77), Nat Tenants Resource Centre 1990–; princ St Catharine's Fndn Cumberland Lodge Windsor 1985–95; Parly candidate: (Lib) Petersfield Feb and Oct 1974, (Alliance) Enfield Southgate 1984, (Alliance) Fareham 1987; chm: Soc of Headmasters of Ind Schs 1965–67, of govrs Royal Sch Windsor Gt Park 1988–95, Cwlth Round Table 1994–; *Style—* Timothy Slack, Esq, LVO; ✉ Hamlet House, Hambledon, Hants PO7 4RY (☎ 01705 632358)

SLACK, Sir William Willatt; KCVO (1990); s of Cecil Moorhouse Slack, MC (d 1986), and Dora, *née* Willatt (d 1979); *b* 22 Feb 1925; *Educ* Winchester, New Coll Oxford (MA), Middx Hosp Med Sch (BM, BCh); *m* 28 July 1951, Dr Joan Wheelwright, da of Lt-Col Talbot H Wheelwright, OBE (d 1938); 2 s (Robert b 1953, Graham b 1955), 2 da (Diana b 1962, Clare b 1966); *Career* conslt surgn and sr lectr in surgery Middx Hosp 1962–90; surgn King Edward VII Hosp for Offrs 1975–91; author of various surgical articles in med jls and textbooks; Sergeant-Surgn to HM The Queen 1983–90; dean: Middx Hosp Med Sch 1983–87, Univ Coll and Middx Sch of Med 1987–90; formerly memb: NE Thames RHA, Conf Met Deans, Conf Deans UK Med Schs; hon fell UCL; memb Ct of Assts Worshipful Co of Barbers (Master 1991–92); FRCS, FRSM (pres Coloproctology Section 1980); *Recreations* croquet, gardening; *Style—* Sir William Slack, KCVO; ✉ Hillside Cottage, Tower Hill, Stawell, Somerset TA7 9AJ (☎ and fax 01278 722 719)

SLADE, Adrian Carnegie; CBE (1988); s of George Penkivil Slade, KC (d 1942), and Mary Albinia Alice, *née* Carnegie (d 1988); *b* 25 May 1936; *Educ* Eton, Trinity Coll Cambridge (BA); *m* 22 June 1960, Susan Elizabeth, da of Edward Forsyth (d 1978); 1 s (Rupert b 15 Jan 1965), 1 da (Nicola b 28 March 1962); *Career* dir S H Benson (advertising) 1969–71, co fndr and chm Slade Hamilton Fenech 1986–91 (previously Slade Bluff & Bigg 1975–86, Slade Monico Bluff 1971–75), dir Longslade Media Trg 1991–; mgmnt Wandsworth Cncl for Community Rels 1967–81; chm: Orange Tree Theatre Ltd Richmond, ONE plus ONE Marriage and Partnership Research; Parly Candidate: (Lib) Putney 1966 and 1974, (Alliance) Wimbledon 1987; memb GLC Richmond, ldr Alliance Gp 1981–86; pres Lib Pty 1987–88, jt pres Lib Democrats 1988 (vice pres 1988–89); *Recreations* theatre, music, photography, piano playing; *Style—* Adrian Slade, Esq, CBE

SLADE, Sir (Julian) Benjamin Alfred; 7 Bt (UK 1831), of Maunsel House, Somerset; s of Capt Sir Michael Niall Slade, 6 Bt (d 1962), and Angela (d 1959), da of Capt Orlando Chichester; *b* 22 May 1946; *Educ* Millfield; *m* 1977 (m dis 1991), Pauline Carol, da of Maj Claude Myburgh; *Career* chm and md Shirlstar Holdings Ltd, dir Pyman Bell Ltd; Freeman City of London 1979, memb Worshipful Co of Ironmongers; *Recreations* racing, polo, bridge; *Clubs* Turf, Old Somerset Dining; *Style—* Sir Benjamin Slade, Bt; ✉ 25 Chelsea Square, London SW3 6LF (☎ 0171 352 4573); Maunsel, North Newton, Bridgwater, Somerset (☎ 01278 663413); Shirlstar Holdings Ltd, Fifth Floor, Hayes Gate House, 27–33 Uxbridge Road, Hayes, Middlesex UB4 0JN (☎ 0181 573 0005, fax 0181 573 0069)

SLADE, Rt Hon Sir Christopher John; kt (1975), PC (1982); s of George Penkivil Slade, KC (d 1942), and Mary Albinia Alice Slade; *b* 2 June 1927; *Educ* Eton, New Coll Oxford; *m* 1958, Jane Gwenllian Armstrong, da of Rt Hon Sir Denys Buckley, MBE; 1 s, 3 da; *Career* called to the Bar 1951, QC 1965, attorney-general Duchy of Lancaster 1972–75, bencher Lincoln's Inn 1973, treas Lincoln's Inn 1994, judge High Ct of Justice (Chancery Div) 1975–82, judge Restrictive Practices Ct 1980–82 (and pres 1981–82), Lord Justice of Appeal 1982–91; dep chm Appeals Ctee Panel on Takeovers and Mergers; memb Ct Assts Worshipful Co of Ironmongers (Master 1973); *Clubs* Garrick; *Style—* The Rt Hon Sir Christopher Slade; ✉ 16 Elthiron Road, London SW6 4BN (☎ 0171 731 0938)

SLADE, David; TD (1973); s of Dr David Adrian Slade (d 1984), of York, and Jean Mary, *née* Marshall (d 1991); *b* 3 July 1941; *Educ* St Peter's York, Emmanuel Coll Cambridge (MA, LLM); *m* 1967, Barbara Lilian Ruth, da of William Douglas Draffan; 3 s (Edward b 9 Sept 1970, William b 18 Oct 1972, d 1974, Alexander b 10 July 1975), 1 da (Georgina b 23 Nov 1976); *Career* admitted slr 1966, ptnr Constant & Constant 1972–85 (asst slr 1966–72), sr ptnr Stephenson Harwood 1996– (joined as ptnr 1985); memb Airborne Artillery TA 1960–73; Liveryman Worshipful Co of Shipwrights; memb Law Soc; *Recreations* collecting paintings, theatre, tennis, gardening; *Style—* David Slade, Esq, TD; ✉ Stephenson Harwood, 1 St Paul's Churchyard, London EC4M 8SH (☎ 0171 329 4422)

SLADE, Elizabeth Ann; QC (1992); da of late Dr Charles Paul Slade, and Henriette, *née* Dub; *b* 12 May 1949; *Educ* Wycombe Abbey Sch, Lady Margaret Hall Oxford (MA, exhbner); *m* 1975, 2 da; *Career* called to the Bar Inner Temple 1972, bencher 1990, chm Employment Law Bar Assoc 1995–97; *Books* Tolleys Employment Handbook (ed then co-ed, 1–7 edn, 1978–90); *Recreations* walking, swimming, tennis, opera, music, visiting art galleries, family activities; *Style—* Miss Elizabeth Slade, QC; ✉ 11 King's Bench Walk, Temple, London EC4Y 7EQ

SLADE, Julian Penkivil; s of George Penkivil Slade, KC (d 1942), of London, and Mary Albina Alice, *née* Carnegie (d 1988); *b* 28 May 1930; *Educ* Eton, Trinity Coll Cambridge (BA); *Career* composer and author; BASCA Gold Badge of Merit 1987; *Musical Plays* incl: Bang Goes the Meringue! Lady May (1951), Christmas in King Street (with Dorothy Reynolds, 1952), The Duenna (1953), The Merry Gentleman (1953), Salad Days (1954–60), Free as Air (1957), Hooray for Daisy (1959), Follow that Girl (1960), Wildest Dreams (1961); *Other Musicals* incl: The Comedy of Errors (1954), Vanity Fair (1962), Nutmeg and Ginger (1963), Sixty Thousand Nights (1966), The Pursuit of Love (1967), Winnie the Pooh (1970), Trelawny (1972), Out of Bounds (1975), Love in a Cold Climate (Thames TV, 1981), Now We Are Sixty (1986), Salad Days (adapted for BBC Radio 2 1994, Vaudeville Theatre 1996); *Publications* scripts incl: Salad Days, Free as Air, Follow that Girl, The Duenna, The Merry Gentleman, Trelawny; *Books* Nibble The Squirrel (for children, 1946); *Recreations* going to theatre and cinema, drawing, listening to music; *Style—* Julian Slade, Esq; ✉ 86 Beaufort Street, London SW3 6BU (☎ 0171 376 4480)

SLADE, Laurie George; s of Humphrey Slade (d 1983), of Nairobi, Kenya, and Constance Laing, *née* Gordon; *b* 12 Feb 1944; *Educ* Duke of York Sch Nairobi, Magdalen Coll Oxford (MA); *Career* called to the Bar Lincoln's Inn 1966, advocate High Court Kenya 1976, 14 years in consumer dispute resolution, legal advsr and registrar Chartered Inst of Arbitrators and dep registrar London Court of Int Arbitration 1982–88, ombudsman Insurance Ombudsman Bureau London 1994–96 (dep ombudsman 1988–94), SIB independent investigator 1996–; assoc Br and Irish Ombudsman Assoc; FCIArb 1993; *Style—* Laurie Slade, Esq; ✉ Securities and Investments Board, Gavrelle House, 2–14 Bunhill Row, London EC1Y 8RA (☎ 0171 638 1240, fax 0171 382 5907)

SLADEN, Angus Murray; s of Sqdn Ldr Algernon Ivan Sladen, DSO (d 1976), and Dorviegelda Malvina, *née* MacGregor; *b* 17 Dec 1950; *Educ* Stowe, Univ of Texas; *m* 1989, Sarah, da of John William Hayter, DL, of Cagebrook, Hereford; 1 s (Archie Jack Murray b 28 June 1996), 2 da (Olivia b 24 June 1992, Georgina b 23 March 1994); *Career* insur broker 1974–; dir Wendover Underwriting Agency Ltd (merged with Barder & Marsh 1993), md Barder & Marsh (renamed Marlborough Underwriting Agency Ltd 1995) 1993–; *Recreations* shooting, stalking, fishing; *Clubs* Boodle's, Pratt's, City of London; *Style—* Angus Sladen, Esq; ✉ 14 Shafto Mews, London SW1; Marlborough Underwriting Agency Ltd, River House, 119/121 Minories, London EC3N 1DR (☎ 0171 709 0219)

SLANE, Viscount; Alexander Burton Conyngham; s and h of Earl of Mount Charles, *qv*; *b* 30 Jan 1975; *Style—* Viscount Slane

SLANEY, Prof Sir Geoffrey; KBE (1984); s of Richard Slaney, and Gladys Lois Slaney; *b* 19 Sept 1922; *Educ* Brewood GS, Univs of Birmingham, London and Illinois; *m* 1956, Josephine Mary Davy; 1 s, 2 da; *Career* Barling prof and head Dept of Surgery Queen Elizabeth Hosp Birmingham 1971–87 (now emeritus prof of surgery); hon conslt surgn: Utd Birmingham Hosps and Regnl Hosp Bd 1959–87, Royal Prince Alfred Hosp Sydney 1981–; pres Royal Coll of Surgeons 1982–86; Hon Freeman Worshipful Co of Barbers; *Style—* Prof Sir Geoffrey Slaney, KBE; ✉ 23 Aston Bury, Edgbaston, Birmingham B15 3QB (☎ 0121 454 0261)

SLAPAK, Maurice; s of Abraham Szlapak (d 1965), of Nairobi, and Rachel Szlapak; *b* 15 Feb 1930; *Educ* Prince of Wales Sch Nairobi, Millfield, Downing Coll Cambridge (MA, MB MChir); *m* 16 June 1960, Catherine Elisabeth, da of Arthur Ellis (d 1966), of Ottawa, Canada; 2 da (Gabrielle Isobel b 16 Jan 1964, Alexander Rachel b 10 Feb 1968); *Career* Capt RAMC: RMO i/c Household Cavalry Regt 1959, MO i/c SHAPE Paris; assoc prof of surgery Harvard Med Sch 1972, co chm first Int Symposium Organ Preservation 1973, sr asst surgn Univ of Cambridge 1972–75, conslt and co dir Transplant Unit St Mary's Hosp Portsmouth, Hunterian prof of surgery RCS, memb Editorial Advsy Bd Transplantation Proceedings; pres: World Transplant Games, Transplant Section Royal Soc of Med; fndr and pres Transplant Olympic Games 1978, vice pres Euro Soc for Organ Transplantation; FRCS 1964, FRCS (Canada) 1967, FACS 1971; *Publications* Experimental and Clinical Methods in Fulminant Liver Failure Support (1973), The Acute Abdomen (in Tice Sloane Practice of Medicine, 1972); *Recreations* tennis, squash, windsurfing, reading; *Clubs* All England Lawn Tennis, Queen's, Hurlingham; *Style—* Maurice Slapak, Esq; ✉ Abbey House, Itchen Abbas, Hants SO21 1BN (☎ 01962 779233, fax 01962 779673); 37 Rutland Gate, London SW5; Cromwell Hospital (☎ 0171 370 4233)

SLATER, Dr Alan John; *b* 20 Oct 1948; *Educ* Univ of Birmingham (MB ChB), Open Univ (BA); *m* 30 June 1973, Jane Slater; 2 da (Jenny b 1976, Gill b 1978); *Career* res assoc MRC Leukaemia Trials Welsh Nat Sch of Med Cardiff 1974–76, registrar in radiotherapy and oncology Velindre Hosp Cardiff 1976–79, resident res fell Princess Margaret Hosp Toronto 1979–81, clinical scientist MRC Addenbrooke's Hosp Cambridge 1981–82; conslt in clinical oncology; Clatterbridge Centre for Oncology, BUPA Murrayfield Hosp, Ysbyty Glan Clwyd 1982–; dir of med servs Clatterbridge Centre for Oncology NHS Tst 1992–94; author of numerous papers and chapters on oncology; memb Mersey Conslts and Specialists Ctee; visiting conslt: Nobles' Isle of Man Hosp, Countess of Chester Hosp, Grosvenor Nuffield Hosp; FRCR 1980; *Recreations* horticulture, steam railways, postal history; *Style—* Dr Alan Slater; ✉ 5 Burlingham

Ave, West Kirby, Wirral, L48 8AJ (☎ 0151 625 9868); Clatterbridge Centre for Oncology, Bebington, Wirral L63 4JY (☎ 0151 334 1155, fax 0151 334 0882, e-mail alans@ccotrust.co.uk)

SLATER, Arnold; s of Arnold Slater, of Holmfirth, Yorks, and Pauline Margaret, *née* Shaw-Parker; *b* 26 March 1948; *Educ* Hadham Hall Sch, Regent St Poly; *m* 21 Oct 1972, Judith Helen, da of Philip Ellison, of Bishops Stortford, Herts; 1 s (Ross Adrian b 24 Sept 1973), 1 da (Anthea Helen b 15 Feb 1978); *Career* chief photographer Herts and Essex Observer 1973–78; photographer: Press Assoc 1978–87, London Daily News 1987, Sunday People 1987–88, Daily Mirror 1988–; winner: Simeon Edmunds award for best young press photographer, Ilford Press Photographer of the Year 1987; *Recreations* squash, skiing, fly tying, fly fishing; *Style—* Arnold Slater, Esq; ✉ c/o The Picture Desk, The Daily Mirror, One Canada Square, Canary Wharf, London E14 5AP (☎ 0171 510 3000)

SLATER, Dr David Homfray; CB (1996); s of William Dennis Slater, and Edna Florence, *née* Homfray; *b* 16 Oct 1940; *Educ* Ardwyn GS, Univ Coll of Wales (BSc), Univ of Wales (PhD); *m* 18 April 1964, Edith Mildred, da of Geoffrey Edward Price; 4 da (Ellen Louise b 7 March 1965, Sian Juliet b 1 July 1966, Melanie Lynne b 18 March 1968, Emma Wynne b 22 Feb 1970); *Career* res asst The Ohio State Univ 1966–69, sr res fell Univ of Southampton 1969–70, lectr Dept of Chemical Engrg and Technol Imperial Coll Univ of London 1970–75, ptnr Cremer & Warner 1979–81 (conslt 1975–79), fndr dir Technica Ltd (London) 1981, chm and chief exec Technica Inc (USA) 1987–91, dir and chief inspr HM Inspectorate of Pollution 1991–95, dir Pollution Prevention and Control and chm Policy Gp The Environment Agency 1995–; prof Warren Centre for Advanced Engineering Univ of Sydney 1985–86, hon prof of life sciences Univ Coll of Wales 1991–; CChem, CEng, FRSC; *Recreations* music, horses, walking the dogs; *Clubs* Athenaeum; *Style—* Dr David Slater, CB; ✉ The Environment Agency, 2 Marsham Street, London SW1P 3PY (☎ 0171 276 8080, fax 0171 276 8800)

SLATER, Duncan; CMG (1982); *b* 15 July 1934; *m* 1972, Candida Coralie Anne Wheatley; 1 s, 2 da; *Career* joined FO 1958; served: Abu Dhabi, Islamabad, New Delhi; head of chancery Aden 1968–69, FO 1969, special asst to Sir William Luce 1970–71, first sec UK Representation to EEC Brussels 1973–75, UK rep to Int Atomic Energy Agency and UN Industl Devpt Orgn 1975–78, cnsllr and head of chancery Lagos 1978–81 and on staff of Govt House Salisbury 1979–80, ambass to Muscat 1981–86, asst under sec of state FCO 1986–92, high cmmr Malaysia 1992–94, ret; chm: Research Inst for the Study of Conflict and Terrorism 1994–, GEC Marconi (Projects) Ltd; *Style—* Duncan Slater, Esq, CMG; ✉ 15 Marlborough Street, London SW3 3PS (☎ 0171 225 0799)

SLATER, Prof Gillian Lesley; da of Leonard William Henry Filtness (d 1978), of Sutton, Surrey, and Adeline Mary, *née* Rowland; *b* 13 Jan 1949; *Educ* Sutton HS for Girls, St Hugh's Coll Oxford (IBM scholar, MSc, DPhil, MA); *m* 1, 1970 (m dis 1983), John Bruce Slater; 2 da (Rosemary Jane Slater b 16 May 1977, Eleanor Ann Slater b 21 Jan 1981); m 2, 1988, Ian David Huntley, s of Desmond Ernest Huntley; *Career* lectr in mathematics Poly of S Bank 1973–79, sr lectr then princ Sheffield City Poly 1979–86; Manchester Metropolitan Univ (formerly Manchester Poly): head Dept of Mathematics and Physics 1986–89, asst dir and dean of sci and engrg 1989–92, pro-vice-chllr 1992–94; vice-chllr Bournemouth Univ 1994–; FIMA (1982), CMath 1991, FRSA 1992; *Books* Essential Mathematics for Software Engineers (1987), Mathematics for Software Construction (with A Norcliffe, 1991); also author of numerous articles in learned jls; *Recreations* gardening, music; *Style—* Prof Gillian Slater; ✉ Bournemouth University, Fern Barrow, Poole, Dorset BH12 5BB (☎ 01202 595006, fax 01202 595069)

SLATER, Prof (James) Howard; s of Arthur Robert Frank Slater, of Tiverton, Devon, and Mildred Dorothy, *née* White; *b* 16 Dec 1947, Tamale, Gold Coast (now Ghana); *Educ* Worthing Tech HS, UCL (BSc, PhD, DSc); *m* 13 Sept 1969, Georgette Eloise Edwina, da of Cecil Edwin Baldwin (d 1995); 2 da (Elisabeth b 15 Nov 1977, Catherine b 20 June 1979); *Career* lectr in microbiology Univ of Kent at Canterbury 1972–75, sr lectr in environmental sciences Univ of Warwick 1979–82 (lectr 1975–79), visiting prof in microbiology Univ of Connecticut 1982, prof of applied microbiology UWIST then Univ of Wales Cardiff 1982–; ed 5 books and author of numerous scientific pubns, holder various patents; sr res conslt BioTechnica Int Inc 1982–84, res dir Biotal Ltd 1984–88; dir: Int Inst of Biotechnology 1990–95, Carbury Herne Ltd 1990–; FIBiol 1984, fell Int Inst of Biotechnol 1988, FRSA 1991; *Recreations* photography, sailing, travelling, sports-watching; *Style—* Prof Howard Slater; ✉ School of Pure and Applied Biology, University of Wales Cardiff, PO Box 915, Cardiff CF1 3TL (☎ 01222 874771, fax 01222 874771, e-mail sabjhs@cardiff.ac.uk. and 106270,1206@compuserve.com)

SLATER, James Derrick (Jim); s of Hubert Slater, and Jessica Slater; *b* 13 March 1929; *Educ* Preston Manor County Sch; *m* 1965, Helen Wyndham Goodwyn; 2 s, 2 da; *Career* articled clerk to chartered accountants 1946–53, accountant then gen mangr to a group of metal finishing cos 1953–55, sec Park Royal Vehicles Ltd 1955–58, dir AEC Ltd 1959, dep sales dir Leyland Motor Corporation 1963, chm Slater Walker Securities Ltd (formerly H Lotery & Co Ltd) 1964–75 (md 1964–72), dir British Leyland Motor Co 1969–75, chm Salar Properties Ltd 1983–; columnist Financial Mail on Sunday 1994–; FCA 1963 (ACA 1953); *Books* Return to Go (autobiography, 1977), The Zulu Principle (1992), Investment Made Easy (1994), Pep Up Your Wealth (1994), Beyond the Zulu Principle (1996); children's books incl: Goldenrod, Goldenrod and the Kidnappers, Grasshopper and the Unwise Owl, Grasshopper and the Pickle Factory, The Boy who Saved Earth, A Mazing Monster Series, Roger the Robot Series; *Recreations* salmon fishing, bridge, chess; *Style—* Jim Slater, Esq; ✉ 67 Victoria Road, Kensington, London W8 5RH

SLATER, Adm Sir John Cunningham Kirkwood (Jock); GCB (1992, KCB 1988), LVO (1971), ADC (1995); s of Dr James K Slater, OBE (d 1965), of Edinburgh, and Margaret Claire Byrom, *née* Bramwell; *b* 27 March 1938; *Educ* Edinburgh Acad, Sedbergh; *m* 1972, Ann Frances, da of late William Patrick Scott, OBE, DL, of Orkney Islands; 2 s (Charles b 1974, Rory b 1977); *Career* RN; Equerry to HM The Queen 1968–71; CO: HMS Jupiter (frigate) 1972–73, HMS Kent (guided missile destroyer) 1976–77; Royal Coll of Def Studies 1978; CO: HMS Illustrious (aircraft carrier) 1981–83, HMS Dryad & Capt Sch of Maritime Ops 1983–85; ACDS (Policy and Nuclear) 1985–87; Flag Offr Scotland and N Ireland, Naval Base Cdr Rosyth, NATO Cdr N sub area E Atlantic, Cdr Nore sub area Channel 1987–89, Chief of Fleet Support 1989–91, C-in-C Fleet, Allied C-in-C Channel and C-in-C Eastern Atlantic 1991–92, Vice Chief of the Def Staff 1993–95, First Sea Lord and Chief of Naval Staff 1995–, First and Princ ADC to HM The Queen 1995–; vice chm RUSI 1993–95 (vice pres 1995–); Er Bro Trinity House 1995 (Yr Bro 1978), Freeman City of London 1989, Liveryman Worshipful Co of Shipwrights 1991; *Recreations* outdoor; *Clubs* Army and Navy; *Style—* Adm Sir Jock Slater, GCB, LVO, ADC; ✉ c/o The Naval Secretary, Victory Building, HM Naval Base, Portsmouth, Hants

SLATER, Kenneth Frederick; s of Charles Frederick Slater (d 1929), and Emily Gertrude, *née* Rodmell (d 1959); *b* 31 July 1925; *Educ* Hull GS, Univ of Manchester (BSc); *m* 1965, Marjorie Gladys, da of Horace Beadsworth (d 1942); *Career* leader UK team of nat experts for definition of NATO Air Defence Ground Environment Malvern 1964, head of Ground Radar and Air Traffic Control Gp 1971, head of Applied Physics Dept and dep dir Royal Signals and Radar Estab (RSRE) Malvern 1976, head of Civil and Mil Systems Dept and dep dir RSRE 1977, dir Admty Surface Weapons Estab Portsmouth 1978, engrg dir Marconi Underwater Systems Ltd Waterlooville 1984–88; engrg conslt 1988–; visiting prof UCL; memb Senate Engrg Cncl; Liveryman Worshipful Co of Engrs; FEng 1985, FIEE; *Publications* articles for scientific jls and conferences incl articles in the Dictionary of Applied Physics and the Encyclopaedia Britannica; *Recreations* yacht ('Ripples'), music, photography, walking; *Clubs* RN Sailing Assoc; *Style—* Kenneth Slater, Esq, FEng; ✉ Valinor, Blackheath Way, W Malvern, Worcs WR14 4DR (☎ and fax 01684 567641)

SLATER, Prof Peter James Bramwell; *b* 26 Dec 1942; *Educ* Univ of Edinburgh (BSc, PhD, DSc); *m*; 2 s; *Career* demonstrator Zoology Dept Univ of Edinburgh 1966–68 (Shaw Macfie Lang fell 1964–66), lectr in biology Univ of Sussex 1968–84; Univ of St Andrews: Kennedy prof of natural history 1984–, chm Dept of Zoology and Marine Biology 1984–87, head Sch of Biological and Medical Scis 1992–; pres Assoc for the Study of Animal Behaviour 1986–89 (hon sec 1973–78), chm Heads of Univ Biological Scis UK 1994–96; FRSE 1991; *Books* Sex Hormones and Behaviour. Studies in Biology (1978), Animal Behaviour (ed jtly, vol 1 Causes and Effects 1983, vol 2 Communication 1983, vol 3 Genes, Development and Learning 1983), An Introduction to Ethology (1985), The Collins Encyclopedia of Animal Behaviour (ed, 1986), Behaviour and Evolution (ed jtly, 1994), Bird Song: Biological Themes and Variations (jtly, 1995); *Style—* Prof Peter Slater, FRSE; ✉ School of Biological and Medical Sciences, Bute Medical Building, University of St Andrews, St Andrews, Fife KY16 9TS (☎ 01334 463500, fax 01334 463600, e-mail pjbs@st-andrews.ac.uk)

SLATER, Richard; s of Dennis Slater (d 1979), and Freida, *née* Hodgson; *b* 18 Aug 1948; *Educ* UCS, Pembroke Coll Cambridge (MA); *m* Julie Norma, da of Gordon Jolley Ward; 2 s (Samuel Rupert b 1980, Frederick James b 1985), 1 da (Amy Louise b 1982); *Career* Slaughter and May: articled clerk 1970–72, asst slr 1972–79, ptnr 1979–, Hong Kong Office 1981–86; memb Law Soc 1972; *Recreations* tennis, theatre, cinema, opera, travel, photography, horse racing, watching football, rugby and cricket; *Clubs* Hampstead Cricket (Tennis Section), The Hong Kong, Ladies' Recreation (Hong Kong); *Style—* Richard Slater, Esq; ✉ Slaughter and May, 35 Basinghall Street, London EC2V 5DB (☎ 0171 600 1200, fax 0171 600 0289)

SLATER, William Bell; CBE (1982), VRD (1959); s of William Bell Slater (d 1985), of 15 King's Walk, W Kirby, Wirral, Cheshire, and May Slater; *b* 7 Jan 1925; *Educ* Lancaster Royal GS; *m* 1950, Jean Mary, da of George William Kiernan (d 1964); 2 s; *Career* War Serv RM Commando Capt Far East, RM Res 1949–63, Lt-Col and CO Mersyside Unit 1959–63, Hon Col 1986–91; chm: Thos & Jno Brocklebank 1972–85 (dir 1966–85, joined as trainee 1947), Cunard Brocklebank Ltd 1975–85 (dir 1967–85), Cunard Ship Management Services Ltd 1970–85, Cunard International Services Ltd 1972–85, Albion & Overseas Shipping Agency Ltd 1972–85, Charles Howson & Co Ltd 1972–85, Moss Tankers Ltd 1972–85, Port Line Ltd 1975–85 (dir 1972–85), Cunard Shipping Services Ltd 1972–85, Cunard International Technical Services Ltd 1974–85, Transworld Leasing Ltd 1977–85, Heavy Lift Cargo Airlines Ltd 1978–85; dir: Cunard Steam-Ship Co plc 1972–85 and 1986–88 (md Cargo Shipping and Aviation Div 1974–85), Cunard Group Pension Tstees Ltd 1972–88, Osmarine International Ltd 1972–85, Trafalgar House Trustees Ltd 1978–88; dir Port Line Assoc cos: ACTA/ANL Assets Ltd 1975–85, ACT (A) Leasing Ltd 1975–85, Blueport ACT (NZ) Ltd 1976–85, Blue Star Port Lines Management 1974–85, ACT (A) Investments (Australia) Ltd 1978–85; chm Associated Container Transportation (Australia) Ltd 1982–85 (dir 1974–85); chm Cunard Assoc cos: Associated Container Transportation 1982–85 (dir 1974–85), Atlantic Container Line Ltd 1977–78 and 1983–84 (dir 1968–85); chm Mersey Docks & Harbour Co 1987–93 (dep chm 1985–87, dir 1980–93); dir Trafalgar House plc 1975–88; gen cmmr of Income Tax 1987–; memb Gen Cncl of Br Shipping 1975–85, pres Br Int Freight Assoc (previously Inst of Freight Forwarders Ltd) 1987–88 (external dir 1989–94), FCIT (vice-pres 1984–87), Order of El Istiglal (2nd Class) Jordan 1972; *Recreations* swimming, gardening, walking, (previously rugby, cricket); *Clubs* Naval; *Style—* William Slater, Esq, CBE, VRD; ✉ Gayton Court, 419 Woodham Lane, Woodham, Addlestone, Surrey KT15 3PP (☎ 01932 349389)

SLATFORD, Rodney Gerald Yorke; s of Frederick Charles Slatford (d 1951), and (Irene) Vida Yorke, *née* Robinson (d 1991); *b* 18 July 1944; *Educ* Bishop's Stortford Coll Herts, RCM; *Career* double bassist, broadcaster; memb Nat Youth Orch of GB 1961–62, RCM 1963–65; princ bass: London Soloist's Ensemble 1965, Midland Sinfonia (later English Sinfonia) 1965–74, Nash Ensemble of London 1965–94, Purcell Room recital debut 1969, freelance Acad of St Martin-in-the-Fields 1972–74, co-princ double bass English Chamber Orch 1974–81, soloist Henry Wood Promenade Concert 1974, Wigmore Hall Double Bass Forum 1974, world recital tour (India, Sri Lanka, Singapore, Aust, NZ, Nepal) 1975, soloist Aix Festival English Chamber Orch 1977, artist in residence (one month) Cairo Conservatoire 1981, artist in residence Kusatsu Int Summer Acad Japan 1984; md and fndr Yorke Edn 1969–, prof RCM 1974–84, fndr and dir Isle of Man Int Double Bass Competition and Workshop 1978, examiner for Assoc Bd Royal Schs of Music 1979–96, admin Young Musicians Scheme Greater London Arts Assoc 1980–82, chm ESTA Music Competition Report 1982, head of School of Strings RNCM 1984– (sr tutor in double bass 1980–84), fndr and chm The Yorke Tst 1984–, guest tutor Beijing Conservatoire 1984, organiser Manchester Bass Week 1985, reg presenter BBC Radio 3 1986–, guest tutor Toho Sch of Music Tokyo 1988, chm ESTA Int Conf Manchester 1989; memb: Advsy Ctee Br Cncl Music 1989, Gowrie Ctee review of the London Music Conservatoires 1990, Exec Ctee European String Teachers' Assoc; chm Br Branch ESTA 1992–96; has made numerous bdcasts and recordings, juror and examiner at numerous nat and int venues, has lectured extensively since 1964, author of various reports and contrib to Grove's Dictionary of Music; Hon RCM 1976, FRNCM 1987; *Recreations* music publishing, gardening, cooking, walking; *Style—* Rodney Slatford, Esq; ✉ c/o Royal Northern College of Music, 124 Oxford Rd, Manchester M13 9RD (☎ 0161 273 6283)

SLATTERY, David Antony Douglas; MBE (1958); s of Rear Adm Sir Matthew Sausse Slattery, KBE (d 1990), of Warninglid, Sussex, and Mica Mary, *née* Swain; *b* 28 Jan 1930; *Educ* Ampleforth, St Thomas' Hosp London (MB BS); *m* 1, 5 May 1954 (m dis 1973), Mary Winifred, da of Robert Miller (d 1942); 2 s (Nicholas b 1955, Simon b 1961), 2 da (Penelope b 1957, Jennifer b 1962); m 2, 22 Feb 1974, Claire Louise, da of Maj L B McGuinness (d 1972); 1 s (Benjamin b 1979); *Career* Capt RAMC 1954–58; MO E Midlands Gas Bd 1959–69, SMO Br Steel Corpn 1969–73, CMO Rolls-Royce plc 1973–91; conslt occupational physician (regnl advsr occupational health) Mersey RHA 1992–94, independent conslt occupational physician 1994–; visiting prof of occupational health Univ of Liverpool 1992–; civilian advsr occupational med RAF, memb Advsy Bd Civil Serv Occupational Health Serv until 1991, dean Faculty of Occupational Med RCP until 1991, FRCP, FFOM; *Recreations* fishing, shooting, history; *Style—* David Slattery, Esq, MBE; ✉ 99 South Quay, Wapping Dock, Liverpool L3 4BW (☎ and fax 0151 707 2022)

SLATTERY, Tony Deklan; s of Michael Slattery, and Margaret Slattery; *b* 9 Nov 1959; *Educ* London Catholic GS, Trinity Hall Cambridge (exhibitioner, MA, pres Footlights); *Career* writer, improviser and performer; repertoire incl: drama, revue, film, comedy, presenting, soap opera, current affrs; *Theatre* work incl: Edinburgh Fringe Festival, Me and My Girl (West End), Comedy Store Leicester Square, Radio Times (Queen's Theatre London); *Television* incl: Whose Line Is It Anyway? (Channel 4), This is David Harper (Channel 4), Drowning in the Shallow End (BBC), writer and presenter Saturday Night at the Movies (ITV), S & M (Channel 4), Just A Gigolo (ITV) 1993; *Films* incl: Peter's Friends (dir Kenneth Branagh) 1992, The Crying Game (dir Neil Jordan) 1992;

Recreations bad musicals, good white wine, Victoria Wood; *Style*— Tony Slattery, Esq; ✉ c/o ICM Ltd, Oxford House, 76 Oxford Street, London W1N 0AX (☎ 0171 636 6565, fax 0171 323 0101)

SLAUGHTER, Giles David; s of Gerald Slaughter (d 1945), of Harpenden, Herts, and Enid Lilian, *née* Crane (d 1987); *b* 11 July 1937; *Educ* Royal Masonic Sch Bushey Herts, King's Coll Cambridge (BA, MA); *m* 14 Aug 1965, Gillian Rothwell, da of Philip Rothwell Shepherd (d 1981); 3 da (Miranda b 1966, Victoria b 1967, Imogen b 1976); *Career* Nat Serv 2 Lt 1 Bn Suffolk Regt 1955–57; housemaster Ormiston House Campbell Coll Belfast; headmaster: Solihull Sch West Midlands 1973–82, Univ Coll Sch Hampstead 1983–96; memb HMC 1973–96; govr: Cobham Hall Sch, Godolphin and Latymer Sch, King's Coll Sch, Aldwickbury Sch; JP Solihull 1977–82; FRSA; *Recreations* theatre, gardening, cricket, golf; *Style*— Giles Slaughter, Esq; ✉ 6 Church Lane, Lower Ufford, Woodbridge, Suffolk (☎ 01394 461281)

SLAY, Prof Desmond; s of Wilfred Charles Slay (d 1986), of Oxford, and Doris Elizabeth, *née* Walker (d 1978); *b* 30 Dec 1927; *Educ* Lord Williams's GS Thame, Univ of Oxford (MA), Univ of Wales (PhD); *m* 10 April 1958, Leontia Mary Cecilia, da of Bernard Patrick Alphonsus McCartan (d 1966), of Belfast; 4 s (Gregory b 1959, Benet b 1961, Jonathan b 1965, Matthew b 1965), 1 da (Deborah b 1960); *Career* Dept of English UWA: asst lectr 1948–50, lectr 1950–62, sr lectr 1962–72, reader 1972–78, acting head of dept 1976–78, Rendel prof of English and head of dept 1978–90, res prof 1990–95; former memb Aberystwyth Round Table, memb Viking Soc for Northern Res (pres 1970–72), fndr chm and memb 41 Club for former tablers 1972–, area sec Ceredigion Scout Cncl 1990– (dist sec 1983–90); The Scout Assoc Medal of Merit 1991; Knight of the Order of the Falcon (Iceland) 1992; *Books* Codex Scardensis (1960), The Manuscripts of Hrólfs Saga Kraka (1960), Romances (1972), Proceedings of the First International Saga Conference (jtly 1973), Mirmanns Saga (1996); *Recreations* supporting scouting; *Style*— Prof Desmond Slay; ✉ 52 Maeshendre, Waunfawr, Aberystwyth, Ceredigion SY23 3PS (☎ 01970 623841)

SLAYMAKER, Paul Ellis; s of Ellis Hamilton Slaymaker, of Surrey, and Barbara Joan, *née* Langfield; *b* 10 March 1945; *Educ* Sunbury GS (BA), Ealing Tech Coll; *m* 1968, Ann Elizabeth, da of Edward Michael Frederick Piercey (d 1982), of IOW; 1 s (Nicholas b 1978), 1 da (Emma b 1975); m 2, 1991, Frances Margaret Illingworth; *Career* advertising; mgmnt conslt McKinsey & Co Inc 1975–76, head of mktg CPC (UK) Ltd 1977–80, dep md Leo Burnett Ltd 1980–86; Delaney Fletcher Bozell: md 1986–95, exec vice pres Bozell Worldwide 1995–; *Recreations* photography, flying, shooting; *Style*— Paul Slaymaker, Esq; ✉ Bozell Worldwide, 25 Wellington Street, London WC2E 7DA (☎ 0171 836 3474)

SLEDGE, The Ven Richard Kitson; s of Sidney Kitson Sledge (d 1968), and Mary Sylvia, *née* Harland, of Sandal, Wakefield; *b* 13 April 1930; *Educ* Epsom Coll, Peterhouse Cambridge (MA); *m* 12 April 1958, Patricia Henley, da of Gordon Sear (d 1985), of Dunstable; 2 s (Timothy b 1964, Nicholas (decd)), 2 da (Elizabeth b 1959, Hilary b 1966); *Career* ordained deacon 1954, priest 1955; curate of: Emmanuel Plymouth Devon 1954–57, St Martin, St Stephen and St Laurence Exeter 1957–63; rector of Dronfield Derbyshire 1963–78, rural dean of Chesterfield 1972–78, rector of Hemingford Abbots Cambs 1978–89; hon canon of Ely 1978–, archdeacon of Huntingdon 1978–96, Bishop of Ely's sr chaplain 1996–; *Style*— The Ven Richard Sledge; ✉ 7 Budge Close, Brampton, Huntingdon, Cambs PE18 8PL

SLEE, Very Rev Colin B; *b* 1945; *Educ* Ealing GS, King's Coll London (BD, AKC, Univ of London Rowing colours), St Augustine's Coll Canterbury; *m* 1971, Edith, *née* Tryon; *Career* ordained: deacon 1970, priest 1971 (St Francis Norwich); curate St Mary the Great with St Michael Cambridge and chaplain Girton Coll Cambridge 1973–76, chaplain and tutor King's Coll London 1976–82, sub-dean Cathedral and Abbey Church of St Alban 1982–94, provost The Cathedral and Collegiate Church of St Saviour and St Mary Overie Southwark 1994–; tstee: Crisis, Parents for Children; govr Inform; *Recreations* rowing, bee-keeping, gardening; *Style*— The Very Rev the Provost of Southwark; ✉ Provost's Lodging, 51 Bankside, London SE1 9JE; Southwark Cathedral, Montague Close, London SE1 9DA (☎ 0171 407 3708, fax 0171 357 7389)

SLEE, William Robert; *b* 13 Jan 1941; *Educ* Holy Cross Coll Massachusetts (BSc); *m* 1981, Heidi, *née* Burklin; 2 s (Alexander, Maximilian); *Career* vice pres and Euro petroleum coordinator Citibank 1963–73, md and chief operating offr European Banking Co Ltd 1973–84; gp md Schroders plc 1984–, vice chm J Henry Schroder & Co Ltd 1995–; *Recreations* sailing, tennis; *Clubs* Royal Southampton Yacht, Royal Lymington Yacht; *Style*— William Slee, Esq; ✉ Schroders plc, 120 Cheapside, London EC2V 6DR (☎ 0171 382 6000, fax 0171 382 6669, telex 885029)

SLEEMAN, Prof Brian David; s of Richard Kinsman Sleeman, of Virginia Water, Surrey, and Gertrude Cecilia, *née* Gamble; *b* 4 Aug 1939; *Educ* Canterbury Rd Sch Morden Surrey, Tiffin Boy's Sch Kingston Surrey, Battersea Coll of Technol (BSc), Univ of London (PhD), Univ of Dundee (DSc); *m* 7 Sept 1963, Juliet Mary, da of Frederick James John (d 1972); 2 s (Matthew b 19 Feb 1969, David b 12 June 1972), 1 da (Elizabeth b 15 Sept 1966); *Career* Univ of Dundee: asst lectr 1965–67, lectr 1967–71, reader 1971–78, prof of applied analysis 1978–93, head Dept of Mathematics and Computer Sci 1986–89, Ivory prof of mathematics 1993–95, hon prof of mathematics 1995–; prof of applied mathematics Univ of Leeds 1995–; various hon visiting professorships at univs in: USA, Canada, Sweden, France, Chile, China; chm Scot Branch for Inst of Mathematics and its applications 1982–84, pres of Edinburgh Mathematical Soc 1988–89; FIMA 1972, FRSE 1976, CMath 1991; *Books* Multiparameter Spectral Theory in Hilbert Space (1978), Differential Equations and Mathematical Biology (1983); *Recreations* choral music, hill walking; *Style*— Prof Brian Sleeman, FRSE; ✉ School of Mathematics, University of Leeds, Leeds LS2 9JT (☎ 0113 233 5188, fax 0113 242 9925, e-mail bds@amsta.leeds.ac.uk)

SLEEMAN, His Hon Judge; Stuart Philip; s of His Hon Colin Sleeman, of Dorking, Surrey, and Margaret Emily, *née* Farmer; *b* 9 May 1947; *Educ* Cranleigh Sch, Merton Coll Oxford (MA Jurisprudence); *m* 22 Sept 1973, Elisabeth Nina, *née* Brann; 1 s (Dominic Philip b 22 Sept 1976), 2 da (Anna Louise b 23 July 1979, Miriam Claire Dorothy b 7 Jan 1984); *Career* called to the Bar Gray's Inn 1970 (scholar), recorder of the Crown Court 1989–93 (asst recorder 1986–89), circuit judge (SE Circuit) 1993–; chm Old Cranleighan Soc 1985– (hon sec 1978–85), govr Cranleigh Sch 1989–; *Recreations* hockey, music, gardening, bridge; *Style*— His Hon Judge Sleeman; ✉ Kingston Crown Court, Canbury Park Road, Kingston upon Thames, Surrey KT2 6JU

SLEEP, Wayne Philip Colin; s of Stanley Sleep, of Plymouth, and Joan Gwendoline Maude Sleep (d 1994); *b* 17 July 1948; *Educ* West Hartlepool Tech Sch, Royal Ballet Sch Richmond Park (Leverhulme scholarship); *Career* dancer, choreographer; joined Royal Ballet 1966 and in 1973 became princ dancer in over 50 leading roles incl: Puck in The Dream, Jester in Cinderella, Blue Boy in Les Patineurs, Petrushka, Alain and Widow Simone in La Fille Mal Gardée, Dr Coppélius in Coppèlia (ENB tour) 1994; roles created for him by Sir Frederick Ashton incl: Koila in A Month in the Country, G R Sinclair in Elgar's Enigma Variations, Squirrel Nutkin and one of the Bad Mice in the film The Tales of Beatrix Potter; worked with other choreographers incl: Dame Ninette De Valois, Sir Kenneth Macmillan, Rudolph Nureyev, Joe Layton, Norman Main, Nigel Lythgoe; choreographer of: David and Goliath (London Contemporary Dance), dance sequence in Death on the Nile, The Hot Shoe Show (BBC TV), Harry Nilsson's The Point (and played leading role, Mermaid), Savoy Suite (Savoy Theatre reopening benefit for ENB) 1993, Promenade (for ENB Sch Festival) 1994; acting roles incl: Ariel in The Tempest (New Shakespeare Co), Truffelino in The Servant of Two Masters, title role in Pinocchio (Birmingham rep), Tony Lumpkin in She Stoops to Conquer (BBC Radio), the Soldier in The Soldiers Tale (Festival Hall), The First Great Train Robbery, The Virgin Soldiers, original co of Cats 1981, Song and Dance 1982, Emcee in Gillian Lynn's Cabaret (West End), played in numerous pantomime seasons; formed own dance gp with nat and int tours under the names of Dash, The Hot Shoe Show and Bits and Pieces 1982–85, made several guest appearances Royal Opera House 1990, made ballet dance video Step into Ballet 1991, dir Carnival for the Birds (Royal Opera House), toured UK with cabaret show, revival of Song and Dance (West End and UK tour) 1992, Hollywood and Broadway - The Musicals (with Lorna Luft) 1992, directed royal ballet gala for Benesh Dance Notation charity 1993, Wayne's World of Dance tour 1993, Hollywood and Broadway Part II (UK tour) 1994, starred in and choreographed royal charity gala 90 Years of Dance 1995; Show Business Personality of the Year 1983, two entries in Guiness Book of Records; Hon DUniv Exeter; FRSA; *Books* Variations on Wayne Sleep (1982); *Clubs* Groucho; *Style*— Wayne Sleep, Esq; ✉ c/o Brian Marshall, 20 Guernsey Way, Hardwick, Banbury, Oxon OX16 7UE (☎ 01295 257729)

SLEIGH, Prof (James) Douglas; s of Andrew Scott Sleigh (d 1958), of Glasgow, and Margaret Handbury Lennox, *née* Jefferson (d 1938); *b* 5 July 1930; *Educ* Glasgow Acad, Univ of Glasgow (MB ChB); *m* 4 Sept 1956, Rosemary Margaret, da of David Falconer Smith (d 1972); 2 s (Andrew Falconer b 1957, David Douglas b 1960); *Career* Nat Serv Lt RAMC 1954–55, Capt RAMC 1955–56, pathologist Mil Hosp Tidworth Hants; registrar Dept of Bacteriology Western Infirmary Glasgow 1956–58, lectr Dept of Bacteriology Univ of Edinburgh 1958–65, conslt pathologist Dunbartonshire Area Laboratory 1965–69, prof Dept of Bacteriology Univ of Glasgow 1988–94 (sr lectr then reader 1969–88), latterly at Royal Infirmary Glasgow (formerly Western Infirmary Glasgow), ret 1994; author of numerous pubns in med lit and editorial contrib to the British Medical Journal and The Lancet; FRCPath, FRCPG; *Books* Notes on Medical Bacteriology (with M C Timbury, 1981, 4 edn 1994); *Recreations* bargain hunting, spending time on the Isle of Arran; *Clubs* Univ of Glasgow, Coll; *Style*— Prof Douglas Sleigh; ✉ 63 Newton Grove, Glasgow G77 5QJ (☎ 0141 616 2409)

SLEIGH, Prof Michael Alfred; s of Cyril Button Sleigh (d 1978), of Bath, and Ida Louisa, *née* Horstmann (d 1987); *b* 11 June 1932; *Educ* Taunton Sch, Bristol GS, Univ of Bristol (BSc, PhD, DSc); *m* 28 Dec 1957, Peggy, da of Maurice Arthur Mason (d 1982), of Calne, Wilts; 2 s (Roger b 1960, Peter b 1965), 1 da (Anne b 1962); *Career* Nat Serv Flying Offr RAF Educn Branch 1957–58; lectr in zoology Univ of Exeter 1958–63, lectr and reader in zoology Univ of Bristol 1963–74, prof of biology Univ of Southampton 1975–; sec Soc for Experimental Biology (nat) 1965–69, vice pres Int Soc of Protozoologists 1987–88 (pres Br section 1982–85); memb: Marine Biological Assoc of the UK, Freshwater Biological Assoc; FIBiol 1977; *Books* The Biology of Cilia and Flagella (1962), The Biology of Protozoa (1973), Cilia and Flagella (1974), Microbes in the Sea (1987), Protozoa and other Protists (1989); *Recreations* travel, gardening, microscopy, walking, photography, natural history; *Style*— Prof Michael Sleigh; ✉ Department of Biology, School of Biological Sciences, University of Southampton, Biomedical Sciences Building, Bassett Crescent East, Southampton SO16 7PX (☎ 01703 594397, fax 01703 594269)

SLEIGHT, Sir Richard; 4 Bt (UK 1920), of Weelsby Hall, Clee, Co Lincoln; s of Sir John Frederick Sleight, 3 Bt (d 1990), and Jacqueline Margaret, *née* Carter; *b* 27 May 1946; *m* 1978, Marie-Thérèse, da of O M Stepan, of London; 2 s (James Alexander b 1981, Nicholas Edward b 1985); *Heir* s, James Alexander Sleight b 5 Jan 1981; *Style*— Sir Richard Sleight, Bt; ✉ c/o National Westminster Bank, 6 High Street, Teddington, Middx

SLESSOR, Gp Capt John Arthur Guinness; CVO (1995), DL (Hants 1989); s of Marshal of the RAF Sir John Slessor, GCB, DSO, MC (d 1979), and Hermione Grace, *née* Guinness (d 1970; direct descendant of 2 Duke of Cleveland, natural s of King Charles II and Barbara Villiers, who was cr Duchess with remainder to her s); *b* 14 Aug 1925; *Educ* Eton, ChCh Oxford; *m* 6 Oct 1951, Ann Dorothea Gibson; 1 s (Anthony b 1954), 1 da (Catherine (Mrs Rupert Prichard) b 1955); *Career* joined RAF 1943, served N France 1944, cmmnd 1945, various flying appts 1946–59 (incl Germany and Rhodesia), USAF Acad Colorado 1960–62, OC 83 Sqdn (V-Force) 1962–65, MOD 1966–68, Air Attaché Madrid 1968–70, OC RAF Odiham 1971–73, Chief Intelligence Offr RAF Germany 1973–75, MOD 1976–77, ret 1978; sec Overseas Rels HQ St John Ambulance 1978–89, pres Andover Div St John Ambulance (Alton Div 1988–94); govr Alton Coll 1990–94; Gentleman Usher to HM The Queen 1978–95 (Extra Gentleman Usher 1995–); CStJ 1990 (OStJ 1981); *Recreations* country pursuits; *Clubs* RAF; *Style*— Gp Capt J A G Slessor, CVO, DL; ✉ Grateley Lodge, Grateley, Andover, Hants SP11 8JP (☎ 01264 889314)

SLEVIN, Dr Maurice Louis; s of David Slevin, of Cape Town, South Africa, and Nita, *née* Rosenbaum; *b* 2 July 1949; *Educ* De La Salle Coll East London South Africa, Univ of Cape Town South Africa (MB ChB); *m* 1, 5 Jan 1975 (m dis 1988), Cherry Lynn; 2 da (Lindi b 1978, Amy b 1981); m 2, 1993, Nicola Jane Harris; 1 da (Susannah b 1996); *Career* med registrar Groote Schuur Hosp Cape Town South Africa 1977, registrar and sr registrar Dept of Med Oncology Bart's Hosp London 1978–82, conslt physician and med oncologist Depts of Med Oncology Bart's and Homerton Hosps London 1982–; chm Br Assoc Cancer United Patients MRCP 1978, MD 1984, FRCP 1989; *Books* Randomised Trials in Cancer: A Critical Review by Sites (jt ed, with Maurice Staquet), Challenging Cancer: From Chaos to Control, Cancer: The Facts (with Michael Whitehouse, 1996); *Style*— Dr Maurice Slevin; ✉ Dept of Medical Oncology, St Bartholomew's Hospital, West Smithfield, London EC1A 7BE (☎ 0171 606 6662, fax 0171 796 3979); 149 Harley St, London W1N 1HG (☎ 0171 224 0685)

SLIGO, 11 Marquess of (I 1800); Jeremy Ulick Browne; sits as Baron Monteagle (UK 1806); also Baron Mount Eagle (I 1760), Viscount Westport (I 1768), Earl of Altamont (I 1771), Earl of Clanricarde (I 1543 and 1800, with special remainder); s of 10 Marquess of Sligo (d 1991), and José, *née* Gauche; *b* 4 June 1939; *Educ* St Columba's Coll, RAC Cirencester; *m* 1961, Jennifer June, da of Maj Derek Cooper, MC, of Dunlewey, Co Donegal, and Mrs C Heber Percy; 5 da (Lady Sheelyn Felicity b 1963, Lady Karen Lavinia b 1964, Lady Lucinda Jane b 1969, Lady Clare Romane b 1974, Lady Alannah Grace b 1980); *Heir* cousin, Sebastian Ulick Browne b 27 May 1964; *Clubs* Kildare Street; *Style*— The Most Hon the Marquess of Sligo; ✉ Westport House, Westport, Co Mayo, Republic of Ireland

SLIM, Hon Hugo John Robertson; 2 s of 2 Viscount Slim, OBE; *b* 1961; *Educ* Eton, St John's Coll Oxford (MA); *m* 28 Sept 1991, Rebecca, da of late Prof Philip Abrams, and of Prof Sonia Jackson, of Bristol; 1 da (Jessica Charlotte Abrams b 1 Nov 1994); *Career* Save The Children Fund: Morocco 1983, Sudan 1985, Ethiopia 1986; United Nations Ethiopia 1987–88, conslt Rural Evaluations Ethiopia and Bangladesh 1989–90; Save the Children Fund: Turkey 1991, Occupied Territories 1991–92, London 1992–94; dir Centre for Devpt and Emergency Planning Oxford Brookes Univ 1994–; Liveryman Worshipful Co of Clothworkers; FRGS; *Publications* Registration in Emergencies (Oxfam, 1990), Listening for a Change (1993), A Feast of Festivals (1996); *Style*— The Hon Hugo Slim; ✉ c/o Oxford Brookes University, Gypsy Lane, Headington, Oxford OX3 0BP (☎ 01865 741111)

SLIM, 2 Viscount (UK 1960); John Douglas Slim; OBE (1973), DL (Greater London 1988); s of Field Marshal 1 Viscount (Sir William Joseph) Slim, KG, GCB, GCMG, GCVO,

GBE, DSO, MC, sometime GOC Allied Land Forces SE Asia, govr-gen Aust and govr and constable Windsor Castle (d 1970), and Aileen, *née* Robertson (d 1993); *b* 20 July 1927; *Educ* Prince of Wales Royal Indian Mil Coll Dehra Dun; *m* 1958, Elisabeth, da of Arthur Rawdon Spinney, CBE (decd); 2 s, 1 da; *Heir* s, Hon Mark Slim; *Career* cmmnd Indian Army 6 Gurkha Rifles 1945–48, Lt Argyll and Sutherland Highlanders 1948, Staff Coll 1961, Jt Serv Staff Coll 1964, Cdr 22 SAS Regt 1967–70, GSO1 (Special Forces) HQ UK Land Forces 1970–72, ret 1972; dep chm Peek plc (chm 1976–91; dir Trailfinders Ltd and various other cos; pres Burma Star Assoc; vice-pres Br-Aust Soc; vice-chm Arab-Br C of C and Indust 1977–96; Master Worshipful Co of Clothworkers 1995–96; FRGS 1983; *Clubs* White's, Special Forces; *Style—* The Rt Hon the Viscount Slim, OBE, DL; ✉ c/o House of Lords, Westminster, London SW1A 0PW

SLIM, Hon Mark William Rawdon; s and h of 2 Viscount Slim, OBE; *b* 13 Feb 1960; *m* 15 Feb 1992, Harriet Laura, yr da of Jonathan Harrison, of Beds; 1 s (Rufus William Rawdon b 15 April 1995); *Career* ptnr BH2 (property advsrs) (City of London office); Liveryman Worshipful Co of Clothworkers; *Recreations* shooting, fishing, dogs; *Clubs* White's; *Style—* The Hon Mark Slim; ✉ BH2, 66 Gresham Street, London EC2V 7NP (☎ 0171 600 5000)

SLINGER, His Hon Judge; Edward; s of Thomas Slinger (d 1957), of Lancs, and Rhoda, *née* Bradshaw (d 1987); *b* 2 Feb 1938; *Educ* Accrington GS, Balliol Coll Oxford (BA); *m* 31 July 1965, Rosalind Margaret, da of Stanley Albert Jewitt, of Chiddingfold, Surrey; 2 s (Giles b 1969, Fergus b 1975), 2 da (Nicola b 1967, Emma b 1971); *Career* admitted slr 1961; dep dist registrar High Court 1981–88, recorder of the Crown Court 1992–95 (asst recorder 1988–92, Higher Courts Advocacy Qualification 1994), circuit judge (Northern Circuit) 1995–; vice chm: Lancs CCC 1987–, TCCB Disciplinary Ctee 1989– (memb 1987–); memb TCCB Working Pty on Structure of First Class Cricket; *Clubs* Lancashire CCC (tstee), MCC; *Style—* His Hon Judge Slinger; ✉ c/o Courts Administrator's Office, 10 Winckley Square, Preston, Lancs PR1 3JJ (☎ 01772 821451, fax 01772 884767)

SLIPMAN, Sue; OBE (1994); da of Max Slipman (d 1971), of London, and Doris *née* Barham (d 1972); *b* 3 Aug 1949; *Educ* Stockwell Manor Sch, Univ of Wales (BA), Univ of London (PGCE); 1 s (Gideon Max b 1988); *Career* pres NUS 1977–78, vice chm Br Youth Cncl 1977–78, memb Cncl the Open Univ 1978–81, memb City and Guilds Numeracy Examination Bd 1984, chm Ctee of Mgmnt Workbase 1981–86; memb: Exec Ctee 300 Group 1985, Advsy Cncl for Adult and Continuing Educn 1978–, Nat Union of Public Employees 1970–85, EC Econ and Social Ctee 1990–92; dir: Nat Cncl for One Parent Families 1985–95, London East TEC 1989–, London TEC Cncl 1995–96, Gas Consumers' Cncl 1996–; memb Working Gp on Women's Issues to Sec of State for Employment 1992–, chm Lead Body for National Vocational Qualifications in advice, guidance and counselling; author of chapters in: The Re-Birth of Britain 1983, Public Issues, Private Pain 1988; FRSA 1990; *Books* Helping Ourselves to Power: A Training Manual for Women in Public Life Skills (1986), Helping One Parent Families to Work (1988), Maintainance: A System to Benefit Children (1989), Making Maintainance Pay (1990); *Recreations* swimming; *Style—* Ms Sue Slipman, OBE; ✉ Gas Consumers Council, Abford House, 15 Wilton Road, London SW1

SLIWERSKI, Trevor Zygmunt; s of Zdzislaw Andrzej Sliwerski, of Ben Rhydding, Ilkley, W Yorks, and Irene Sliwerski (d 1990); *b* 30 Dec 1950; *Educ* John Fisher Sch Purley Surrey; *m* Lynn, da of Leonard Arthur Francis (d 1991); 1 s (Jeremy Andrew Zbigniew b 1987), 1 da (Claire Louise b 1983); *Career* dealer: Savory Milln 1968–71, R Layton 1971–74, Nomura 1978–80; dir RBT Fleming 1980–85, dir i/c Japanese equity warrants Baring Securities 1985–95, AJG Investments Ltd 1995–; prop Noah's Ark Nursery 1990–; *Recreations* walking, flying; *Clubs* Surrey Walking, Stock Exchange Athletic; *Style—* Trevor Sliwerski, Esq; ✉ AJG Investments Ltd, Three Quays, Tower Hill, London EC3R 6DS (☎ 0171 867 0023, fax 0171 867 8998); Noah's Ark Nursery, Blackhorse Road, Woking, Surrey GU22 0RE (☎ 01483 233832, fax 01483 234317)

SLOAM, Nigel Spencer; s of Maurice Sloam (d 1991), of London, and Ruth, *née* Davis; *b* 17 Dec 1950; *Educ* Haberdashers' Aske's, Corpus Christi Coll Oxford (BA, MA); *m* 3 Sept 1978, Elizabeth Augusta, da of Arnold Hertzberg; 1 s (Oliver Julian Richard b 1983), 1 da (Natalia Sylvia Caroline b 1979); *Career* trainee actuary Messrs Bacon & Woodrow 1972–76, actuary Sahar Insurance Co of Israel 1976–77, mangr Actuarial Dept Charterhouse Magna Assurance Co 1977–78, dir Messrs Bevington Lowndes Ltd 1978–79, princ and ptnr Nigel Sloam & Co 1979–; Freeman City of London, Liveryman Worshipful Co of Basketmakers; FIA 1977, AFIMA 1979, ASA 1987; *Clubs* Utd Oxford and Cambridge Univ, City Livery, PHIATUS, Goose and Beast (pres); *Style—* Nigel Sloam, Esq; ✉ Nigel Sloam & Co, Annandale, West Heath Ave, London NW11 7QU (☎ 0181 209 1222, fax 0181 455 3973

SLOAN, Sir Andrew Kirkpatrick; kt (1991), QPM; s of Andrew Kirkpatrick Sloan, of Kirkcudbright, and Amelia Sarah, *née* Vernon; *b* 27 Feb 1931; *Educ* Kirkcudbright and Dumfries Acad, Open Univ (BA), Storvik; *m* 1953, Agnes Sofie, da of Nils Jaeger Aleksander, of Norway (d 1975); 3 da (Ann-Soffi, Dorothy, Janet); *Career* RN 1947–53, served in cruisers and submarines in Home Waters, Mediterranean and Caribbean, petty offr; West Yorks Police (reaching rank of Chief Supt) 1955–66, Asst Chief Constable Lincs Police 1976–79, nat co-ordinator Regnl Crime Squads England & Wales 1979–81, dep chief constable Lincs Police 1981–83; chief constable: Beds Police 1983–85, Strathclyde 1985–91, ret; *Recreations* walking, travel, conversation; *Style—* Sir Andrew Sloan, QPM; ✉ Royal Bank of Scotland PLC, 151 High Street, Dumfries DG1 2RA

SLOAN, Eur Ing Gordon McMillan; s of Samuel Sloan, of Muirkirk, Ayrshire, Scotland, and Christine McMillan, *née* Turner; *b* 30 Dec 1934; *Educ* Muirkirk Sch, Kilmarnock Acad, Glasgow Royal Tech Coll; *m* 5 Aug 1961, Patricia Mary, da of William Stewart McKim (d 1979); 1 s (John), 4 da (Christine, Elizabeth, Mary, Rachel); *Career* dir: Parsons Brown & Newton Consulting Engineers 1973–81, McMillan Sloan & Partners Consulting Engineers 1981–; notable works incl: studies, master plans, reports and detailed plans for major new ports at Dammam (Saudi Arabia), and Muara (Brunei), study and re-devpt plan with designs for Cardiff Port, design of floating port Aqaba (Jordan), detailed study of abandonment and removal of major N Sea prodn platform; Freeman City of London 1967, Liveryman Worshipful Co of Turners 1968 (memb Ct of Assts 1987, Upper Warden 1994–95, Master 1995–96, Dep Master 1996–97); CEng 1967, FInstPet 1974, FIMechE 1978, MSocIS (France) 1978, FPWInst 1988, Eur Ing 1989; *Recreations* music appreciation, property renovation and restoration; *Style—* Eur Ing Gordon Sloan; ✉ 32 Murray Rd, Wimbledon, London SW19 4PE (☎ 0181 946 3201, fax 0181 947 0767)

SLOAN, Ronald Kenneth (Ronnie); *b* 21 July 1943; *Educ* Edinburgh Acad; *m* 29 May 1965, Sandra; 2 s (Elliot b 1969, Moray b 1971), 1 da (Hazel b 1978); *Career* Standard Life 1960–67, Friends Provident 1967–70; dir: Antony Gibbs Pensions Ltd 1970–71, Martin Paterson Assocs Ltd 1972–87; divnl dir and actuary Buck Paterson Conslts Ltd 1987–93, ind conslt actuary 1993–94, ptnr Punter Southall & Co 1994–; pres Edinburgh Academical RFC 1992–94 (capt 1973–74), govr Scottish Sports Aid Fndn, chm Raeburn Place Appeal; fundraiser for Children 1st (formerly RSSPCC) running 29 marathons dressed as tartan Superman in Edinburgh, Glasgow, Aberdeen, Dundee, Dublin, London, Snowdonia, NY, Boston, Athens, Venice, Berlin, Amsterdam, Frankfurt and Lausanne raising over £150,000 to date; FFA 1967, FPMI 1977, FInstD 1980; *Recreations* tennis, rugby, marathons, Scottish country dancing; *Clubs* New (Edinburgh); *Style—* Ronnie Sloan, Esq; ✉ 20 Lomond Road, Edinburgh EH5 3JR (☎ and fax 0131 552 3062)

SLOANE, Ian Christopher; s of Albert Henry Sloane (d 1968), and Ivy Rose, *née* Dennis; *b* 28 Jan 1938; *Educ* Lewes Co GS, Poly of Central London (DMS); *m* 1968, (Phyllis) June Barton; 2 s (Nicholas Ian b 20 Aug 1971, Peter Andrew b 6 May 1974); *Career* Nat Serv HM Forces 1957–59; HM Dip Serv: MECAS 1960–61, vice-consul Khartoum 1961–64, vice-consul Algiers 1964–67, vice-consul Saigon 1967, second sec Dacca 1967, second sec Lahore 1967–70, Poly of Central London 1970, FCO 1971–73, second sec UK Delgn to Disarmament Conf Geneva 1973–74, head of chancery and consul Seoul 1974–77, first sec Bonn 1977–83, first sec FCO 1983–85, first sec Moscow 1985, first sec Ankara 1985–88, FCO 1989–90, consllr NY 1990–94, HM ambass and consul-gen Ulaanbaatar Mongolia 1994–Jan 1997, ret; *Recreations* tennis, bridge, collecting antique maps; *Style—* Ian Sloane, Esq; ✉ c/o Foreign & Commonwealth Office, King Charles Street, London SW1A 2AH

SLOANE, Prof Peter James; s of John Joseph Sloane (d 1992), of Cheadle, Cheshire, and Elizabeth, *née* Clarke; *b* 6 Aug 1942; *Educ* Cheadle Hulme Sch, Univ of Sheffield (BA), Univ of Strathclyde (PhD); *m* 30 July 1969, Avril Mary, da of Kenneth Urquhart (d 1984), of Morayshire; 1 s (Christopher Peter b 1971); *Career* asst lectr and lectr in political economy Univ of Aberdeen 1966–69, lectr in industl econmics Univ of Nottingham 1969–75, econ advsr Unit for Manpower Studies Dept of Employment 1973–74, prof of economics and mgmnt Paisley Coll 1975–84; Univ of Aberdeen: prof of political economy 1984–, Jaffrey prof of political economy 1985–, vice-princ and dean of social scis and laws 1996–; visiting prof: McMaster Univ Hamilton Ontario Canada 1978 (Cwlth fell), Indiana Univ 1996; memb: Sec of State for Scotland's Panel of Econ Conslts 1981–91, Cncl Scottish Econ Soc 1983–, Ct Univ of Aberdeen 1987–91 and 1993–97, ESRC 1979–85; memb: Royal Economic Soc, Br Univs Industl Rels Assoc, Euro Assoc of Labour Economists; *Books* Changing Patterns of Working Hours (1975), Sex Discrimination in the Labour Market (with B Chiplin, 1975), Sport in the Market? (1980), Women and Low Pay (ed 1980), The Earnings Gap Between Men and Women in Great Britain (1981), Equal Employment Issues (with H C Jain, 1981), Tackling Discrimination in the Workplace (with B Chiplin, 1982), Labour Economics (with D Carline, et al 1985), Sex at Work: Equal Pay and the Comparable Worth Controversy (1985); plus contributions to various academic jls; *Recreations* sport; *Clubs* Royal Cwlth Soc; *Style—* Prof Peter Sloane; ✉ Hillcrest, 45 Friarsfield Rd, Cults, Aberdeen AB1 9LB (☎ 01224 869412); Department of Economics, University of Aberdeen, Edward Wright Building, Dunbar St, Aberdeen AB24 3QY (☎ 01224 272166, fax 01224 272181, telex 73458 UNIABN G)

SLOCOCK, (David) Michael; s of Maj Arthur Anthony Slocock (d 1995), and Elizabeth Anthea, *née* Sturdy (d 1990); *b* 1 Feb 1945; *Educ* Radley, Lincoln Coll Oxford (BA); *m* 12 April 1969, Theresa Mary, da of Maj Anthony Clyde-Smith (d 1989), of Jersey, CI; 2 s (Julian Mark Anthony b 1973, Mark David Philip b 1976), 1 da (Lucinda Sheila Mary b 1971); *Career* The Sunday Telegraph 1967–69, Hill Samuel & Co Ltd merchant bankers 1969–71, dir various cos including Normans Group plc, Empire Plantations & Investments, L K Industrial Investments 1971–79; chief exec: Normans Group plc 1973–90, Catalogue Shopping Corporation 1991–; *Recreations* sailing, gardening; *Clubs* Royal Southern Yacht; *Style—* Michael Slocock, Esq; ✉ Southover House, Tolpuddle, Dorchester, Dorset DT2 7HF (☎ 01305 848220, fax 01305 848516)

SLOCOMBE, Sue; OBE (1994); da of Capt Leonard William Ellis, MBE (d 1977), and Phyllis Muriel, *née* Chick (d 1984); *b* 8 June 1949; *Educ* Nailsea GS, Bedford Coll of Physical Educ, Univ of Bristol; *m* 5 Aug 1972, Martin Charles Slocombe, s of Charles Slocombe (d 1976); *Career* teacher Clifton HS for Girls 1970–74; lectr: Coll of St Matthias 1974–76, Faculty of Educn Bristol Poly 1976–93; currently princ lectr and dir of studies Univ of the West of England (formerly Bristol Poly); sportswoman: int hockey player: Outdoor World Cup 1979, Euro Bronze medallist 1985, indoor capt 1985–88; coach England Ladies Sr Hockey Team 1986–94 (Euro Silver medal 1987, 4th in World Cup 1990, Euro Gold medal 1991), coach GB Ladies Olympic Hockey Squad 1993– (asst coach 1989–90, 4th in Atlanta Olympic Games 1996); memb: Coaches Advsy Panel Br Olympic Assoc, Exec Bd Nat Coaches Assoc 1993–, Exec Bd Nat Coaching Fndn 1993–, Sports Cncl Women in Coaching Advsy Gp 1993–; involved in hockey coaching to club and int standard (also children's hockey coach); winner Coach of the Year award 1991; memb: NASC, PE Assoc of GB and NI, BAALPE; *Books* Indoor Hockey (1985), Make Hockey Fun - Hockey for 8–12 year olds (1985); *Style—* Mrs Sue Slocombe, OBE; ✉ Brackenwood, 2 Folleigh Close, Long Ashton, Bristol BS18 9HX (☎ 01275 394116); Director of Studies (Schools Liaison), Faculty of Education, University of West of England, Redland Hill, Bristol BS6 6U2 (☎ 0117 974 1251, fax 0117 973 2251)

SLOGGETT, Jolyon Edward; OBE (1995); s of Edward Cornelius Sloggett (d 1974), of Harrow, Middx, and Lena May, *née* Norton; *b* 30 May 1933; *Educ* John Lyon Sch, Univ of Glasgow (BSc); *m* 4 July 1970, Patricia Marjorie Iverson, da of Leonard Artemus Ward, of Steyning, W Sussex; 2 da (Alexandra, Clementine); *Career* joined RNVR 1955, Nat Serv 1957–58, cmmnd temporary Actg Sub Lt(E) 1957, RNEC 1957, HMS Camperdown 1958, sr engrg offr 51 minesweeping sqdn 1958, resigned as Lt(E) from RNR 1964; ship designer WM Denny & Bros Ltd 1956–57 and 1959–60; Houlder Bros & Co Ltd: naval architect 1965–68, mangr new projects 1968–72, exec dir fin and devpt 1972–78, exec dep chm Houlder Offshore; md Br Shipbuilders: mktg and product devpt 1978–79, offshore 1979–81; chm Vickers Offshore (P & D) Ltd 1979–80, conslt Jolyon Sloggett Assocs 1981–86; sec Inst of Marine Engrs 1986–; vice pres Old Lyonian Assoc; Liveryman Worshipful Co of Shipwrights; FIMarE, FRINA 1972, FICS 1967; *Books* Shipping Finance (1984); *Recreations* gardening, woodwork, sailing; *Style—* Jolyon Sloggett, Esq, OBE; ✉ Annington House, Steyning, W Sussex BN44 3WA (☎ 01903 812259, fax 01903 879043); Institute of Marine Engineers, 76 Mark Lane, London EC3R 7JN (☎ 0171 481 8493, fax 0171 488 1854)

SLOGGETT, Jonathan Frank; *b* 19 Jan 1950; *Educ* St Joseph's RC Coll Beulah Hill, Univ Coll Oxford (PPE, MA), Univ of Papua New Guinea (MEcon); *Career* tutor in economics Univ of Papua New Guinea 1971–73; Dover Harbour Bd: economist 1973–77, dir admin and fin 1977–80, dep md 1980–83, md 1983–; FCIT; *Publications* Port Economics (Proc ICE, pt 1 88, 1990); *Style—* Jonathan Sloggett, Esq; ✉ Dover Harbour Board, Harbour House, Dover, Kent CT17 9BU (☎ 01304 240400, fax 01304 240465)

SLOGROVE, Richard Paul; s of Wing Cdr A P H Slogrove (d 1974), and Margaret Anne (Margot), *née* Hannam-Clark; *b* 1 Nov 1945; *Educ* The King's Sch Ely, RAF Coll Cranwell (Sword of Honour, Queen's Medal), Univ of London (BA); *m* 6 June 1970, Judyth Anne, da of James Peacock; 1 da (Emma b 1 June 1972); *Career* RAF 1963–76 (Sqdn Ldr); md Telex UK Ltd 1985–88; Memorex Telex: vice pres Personal Computer Div 1988–90, pres Canada 1990–92, vice pres N America Sales and Serv 1992–94; dir of global mktg British Telecommunications plc 1994–; non-exec dir Mediaset SpA 1996–; memb Cncl Inst of Educn Univ of London; memb Mktg Soc 1995; *Recreations* gardening, music; *Clubs* RAF; *Style—* Richard Slogrove, Esq; ✉ British Telecommunications plc, BT Centre (A801), 81 Newgate Street, London EC1A 7AJ (☎ 0171 356 6721, fax 0171 356 4905)

SLOMAN, Prof Aaron; s of Reuben Sloman, and Hannah, *née* Rest; *b* 30 Oct 1936; *Educ* Cape Town Univ (BSc), Univ of Oxford (DPhil); *m* 29 May 1965, Alison Mary, da of Wilfred Dresser; 2 s (Benjamin b 1967, Jonathan b 1973); *Career* Univ of Oxford: Rhodes scholar 1957–60, St Antony's scholar 1960–62; lectr in philosophy Univ of Hull 1962–64, sr visiting fell Univ of Edinburgh 1972–73; Univ of Sussex: lectr in philosophy 1964–76, reader in philosophy and artificial intelligence 1976–84, prof of artificial intelligence and cognitive sci 1984–91; prof of artificial intelligence and cognitive science Univ of Birmingham 1991–; fell American Assoc for Artificial Intelligence 1991 (research prof 1994–); *Books* The Computer Revolution in Philosophy (1978); *Style—* Prof Aaron Sloman; ✉ School of Computer Science, The University of Birmingham, Edgbaston, Birmingham B15 2TT (☎ 0121 414 4775, fax 0121 414 4281, e-mail A.SLOMAN@cs.bham.ac.uk)

SLOMAN, Sir Albert Edward; kt (1987), CBE (1980); s of Albert Sloman (d 1969), of Launceston, Cornwall, and Lillie Brewer (d 1973); *b* 14 Feb 1921; *Educ* Launceston Coll Cornwall, Wadham Coll Oxford (MA, DPhil); *m* 4 Aug 1948, Marie Bernadette, da of Leo Bergeron (d 1976); 3 da (Anne Veronique b 1949, Isabel Patricia b 1952, Bernadette Jeanne b 1955); *Career* Flt Lt RAF 1939–41, night-fighter pilot 219 and 68 Sqdns, served UK, N Africa, Malta and Sicily (despatches); lectr in Spanish Univ of California Berkeley USA 1946–47, reader in Spanish Univ of Dublin 1947–53, fell Trinity Coll Dublin 1950–53, Gilmour prof of Spanish Univ of Liverpool 1955–62 (dean Faculty of Arts 1960–62), vice chllr Univ of Essex 1962–87; chm: Ctee of Vice Chllrs Princs 1981–83, Br Acad Studentship Ctee 1965–87, Bd of Govrs Centre for Info on Language Teaching in Res 1979–87, Overseas Res Students Fees Support Scheme 1980–87, Univs Cncl for Adult Continuing Educn 1984–87, Ctee for Int Co-operation in Higher Educn 1985–88, Selection Ctee of Cwlth Scholarship Cmmn 1986–93, Inspection of Ruskin Coll Oxford 1986–87, Int Bd Utd World Coll 1988–92; memb: Economic and Social Ctee EC 1973–82, Bd Br Cncl 1985–88; vice chm Assoc of Cwlth Univs 1985–87, vice pres Int Assoc of Univs 1970–75; dir: Isys plc 1985–, Close Bros Ltd, Bessa Companies 1992–; pres The Penzance Library 1990–96; Reith lectr 1963, Guildhall Granada lectr 1969; Hon Doctorate: Univ of Nice 1974, Univ of Essex 1988, Univ of Liverpool 1989; *Recreations* travel, walking; *Clubs* Savile; *Style—* Sir Albert E Sloman; ✉ 19 Inglis Rd, Colchester, Essex CO3 3HU (☎ 01206 47270)

SLOT, His Hon Judge; Peter Maurice Joseph; s of Joseph Slot (d 1969), and Marie Slot (d 1971); *b* 3 Dec 1932; *Educ* Bradfield, St John's Coll Oxford; *m* Sept 1962, Mary, da of John Lewis; 3 da, 2 s; *Career* called to the Bar 1957, recorder 1974–80, circuit judge (SE Circuit) 1980–; memb Ctee Surrey Family Mediation Serv; *Recreations* music, golf, argument; *Clubs* Walton Heath Golf; *Style—* His Hon Judge Slot; ✉ Guildford Crown Court, Mary Road, Guildford, Surrey

SLOWE, Victoria Jane (Vikki); da of David Ross, of London, and Sybil, *née* Harris; *b* 24 May 1947; *Educ* Camden Sch for Girls, London Coll of Fashion (City & Guilds Dip); *m* 1966, Martin A M Slowe; 2 da (Emily b 1970, Hannah b 1973); *Career* abstract artist of constructions and prints; fell Royal Soc of Painter-Printmakers; *Group Exhibitions* incl: Realities Nouvelles Paris, VOK Moscow, NY, Ottawa, Singapore, Royal Academy, Royal W of England Academy and Royal Soc of Painter-Printmakers London; *Collections* incl: Smithsonian Instn Washington DC, Tel Aviv Museum, Ashmolean Museum Oxford; *Recreations* exhibitions, travel, theatre; *Style—* Mrs Vikki Slowe

SLYNN OF HADLEY, Baron (Life Peer UK 1992), of Eggington in the County of Bedfordshire; Sir Gordon Slynn; kt (1976), PC (1992); er s of John and Edith Slynn; *b* 17 Feb 1930; *Educ* Sandbach Sch, Goldsmiths' Coll, Trinity Coll Cambridge; *m* 1962, Odile Marie Henriette, da of Pierre Boutin; *Career* called to the Bar Gray's Inn 1956, bencher 1970, treas 1988; lectr in air law LSE 1958–61, jr counsel Miny of Labour 1967–68, jr counsel Treasy 1968–74, recorder 1971 (hon recorder Hereford 1972–76), QC 1974, leading counsel Treasy 1974–76, judge of the High Court of Justice (Queen's Bench Div) 1976–81, pres Employment Appeal Tbnl 1978–81, judge Ct of Justice of Euro Communities 1988–91 (advocate gen 1981–88), a Lord of Appeal in Ordinary 1992–; visiting prof of law: Univ of Durham 1981–88, KCL 1986–90 and 1995–, Univ of Technol Sydney 1990–; chief steward Hereford 1978– (dep chief steward 1977–78); hon vice pres Union Internationale des Avocats 1976–; pres Bentham Club 1992, Holdsworth Club 1993; fell Int Students' Tst 1985– (govr 1979–85 and 1992–), govr Sadlers Wells Theatre 1988–95, chm Exec Cncl Int Law Assoc 1988–; pres Acad of Experts 1992–96; hon memb: Canadian Bar Assoc, Colegio de Abagados de Buenos Aires; hon fell American Coll of Trial Lawyers; memb American Law Inst; Master Worshipful Co of Broderers 1994–95; Hon Decanus Legis Mercer USA; hon fell: Univ Coll Buckingham 1982, St Andrews Coll Sydney 1991, Liverpool John Moores Univ 1992, Goldsmiths' Coll London 1993, King's Coll London 1995; Hon LLD Univs of: Birmingham 1983, Buckingham 1983, Exeter 1985, Technol Sydney 1991, Bristol Poly (CNAA) 1992, Sussex 1992, Stetson USA 1993, Saarlaudes 1994, Staffordshire 1994; Hon DCL: Univ of Durham 1989, City Univ 1994; Hon DUniv Univ Museo Social Buenos Aires 1994; Cordell Hull Medal Stamford Univ Al 1993; visitor: Mansfield Coll Oxford 1996–, Univ of Essex 1996–; memb Cncl Pilgrims 1992–; Commandeur d'Honneur de Bontemps de Medoc et des Graves, Commandeur Confrerie de St Cunibert (Luxembourg), Chevalier de Tastevin; FCIArb; *Clubs* Beefsteak, Garrick, Athenaeum; *Style—* The Rt Hon Lord Slynn of Hadley, PC; ✉ House of Lords, London SW1A 0PW

SMALE-ADAMS, (Kenneth) Barry; OBE (1991); s of Douglas William Smale-Adams; *b* 30 June 1932; *Educ* St John's Coll Johannesburg, Camborne Sch of Mines; *m* 1953, Marion June, *née* Hosken; 2 s (Mark, Jeremy), 1 da (Deborah); *Career* mining engr; Anglo American Corporation of SA 1953–59, gen mangr Associated Mines Malaysia Ltd 1960–65, res mining advsr Hellenic Industrial Development Bank Athens 1965–67, The Rio Tinto Zinc Corporation 1967–87 (exec dir Con Zinc Rio Tinto Malaysia Ltd and Rio Tinto Bethlehem Indonesia 1967–72), gen mangr and dir Rio Tinto Fin and Exploration Ltd 1973–80, md RTZ Deep Sea Mining Enterprises Ltd 1974–87, chm Riofinex Ltd 1976–83 (dep chm 1983–87), consulting engr to mining dir 1983–87; non-exec dir Robertson Group plc, chm Robertson Mining Fin 1987–89, dir Anglesey Mining plc 1988–, chm Plateau Mining plc 1990–93 (ret), conslt 1993–; pres Inst of Mining and Metallurgy 1983–84, chm Court of Govrs Camborne Sch of Mines 1984–93, memb Cncl Univ of Exeter; FIMM, Assoc Camborne Sch of Mines, FEng 1983; *Recreations* fishing, reading, music, theatre, sports; *Style—* Barry Smale-Adams, Esq, OBE, FEng; ✉ 4 The Hermitage, Richmond, Surrey TW10 6SM (☎ 0181 948 3439, fax 0181 948 0487)

SMALL, David Purvis; CMG (1988), MBE (1966); s of Joseph Small (d 1958), of Wishaw, Scotland, and Ann Purvis (d 1983); *b* 17 Oct 1930; *Educ* Our Lady's HS Motherwell; *m* 12 Oct 1957, Patricia, da of John Kennedy (d 1980); 3 s (Joseph b 25 March 1959, John b 10 Aug 1960, David b 30 June 1965); *Career* Nat Serv RAF, serv Egypt Sudan Eritrea and Kenya 1949–51; clerical offr Admty (Civil Serv) 1953 (asst sec 1955–60), CRO 1961, Madras 1962–64, FCO 1965, second sec Ibadan 1964–68, first sec and head of Chancery Quito 1968–73 (former second sec and consul), first sec FCO 1973–76, first sec and head of Chancery Dacca 1976–80, first sec commercial Stockholm 1980–82, cnsllr commercial and econ Copenhagen 1982–87, high cmmr Georgetown Guyana and ambass Paramaribo Suriname 1987–90; *Recreations* golf, soccer, gardening; *Clubs* Cowal Golf; *Style—* David P Small, Esq, CMG, MBE; ✉ Ashbank, Strachur, Argyll PA27 8BX (☎ 01369 860282)

SMALL, Harry; s of Eric James Small, of London, and Brenda, *née* Bedford; *b* 20 April 1957; *Educ* St Alban's Boys' GS, Oriel Coll Oxford (BA, MA); *Career* asst slr Linklaters & Paines 1981–86 (articled clerk 1979–81); Baker & McKenzie: assoc Hong Kong 1986–87, assoc London 1987–89, ptnr Intellectual Property/IT Dept 1989–; visiting lectr in trade mark law Queen Mary Coll London 1984–85, lectr in designs law IP Dip Univ of Bristol 1993–, expert EU Economic and Social Ctee on various EU copyright proposals 1990–; author of numerous articles on IT matters; memb: Law Soc England 1981–, Law Soc Hong Kong 1986–87, Computer Law Gp 1990–, Soc for Computers and Law 1993–; *Recreations* travel, food, drink, sleeping; *Clubs* Lansdowne; *Style—* Harry Small, Esq; ✉ Baker & McKenzie, 100 New Bridge Street, London EC4V 7JA (☎ 0171 919 1000, e-mail harry_small@bakermck.com)

SMALL, Prof John Rankin; CBE (1991); s of David Carmichael Small (d 1960), and Annie, *née* Stirling (d 1985); *b* 28 Feb 1933; *Educ* Univ of London (BSc Econ); *m* 17 Aug 1957, Rena, da of John Wood (d 1980); 1 s (John Rankin b 1962), 2 da (Karen Elaine b 1960, Mandy Jayne b 1965); *Career* accountant Dunlop Rubber Co 1956–60, lectr Univ of Edinburgh 1960–64, sr lectr Univ of Glasgow 1964–67, prof of accountancy and fin Heriot-Watt Univ 1967– (dep princ 1990–95); chm: Accounts Cmmn Scot 1983–92, Nat Appeal Panel for Entry to Pharmaceutical Lists Scot 1987–96; bd memb Scottish Homes 1993–; dir: Environmental Resource Technology Ltd, Edinburgh Instruments Ltd; Hon DLitt Heriot-Watt Univ; FCCA 1958, FCMA 1960; *Books* Introduction to Managerial Economics (1967), Accounting (1991); *Style—* Prof John Small, CBE; ✉ 39 Caiystane Terrace, Edinburgh, Scotland EH10 6ST (☎ 0131 445 2638); Heriot-Watt University, Lord Balerno Building, Riccarton, Edinburgh EH14 4AS (☎ 0131 449 5111, fax 0131 449 5153)

SMALL, HE Joseph; *b* 1937, Borrisoleigh, Co Tipperary; *Educ* UC Dublin; *m*; 4 c; *Career* Irish Dip Serv; third sec Dept of Foreign Affrs 1963–65, third sec Paris 1965–67, second sec Perm Representation of Ireland to UN 1967, first sec Lagos 1968–70, first sec Headquarters 1970–72, cnsllr (dep head of mission) Washington 1973–76, asst sec Headquarters 1976–81, ambass to Aust (and concurrently to NZ and Indonesia) 1981–87, ambass to Austria (and concurrently to Czechoslovakia, Hungary and Yugoslavia) 1987–91, head of delgn to the Conf on Security and Cooperation in Europe 1987–89, ambass to Ct of St James 1991–95; *Style—* Mr Joseph Small

SMALLBONE, Graham; s of Dr Eric George Smallbone (d 1964), and Jane Jack, *née* Mann (d 1987); *b* 5 April 1934; *Educ* Uppingham (music scholar), Worcester Coll Oxford (Hadow music scholar, BA, MA); *m* 2 April 1959, Dorothea Ruth, da of late Dr Marcus Löw; 2 s (Ian Eric Christopher b 1965, Patrick Marcus b 1971), 2 da (Claire Dorothea b 1960, Hilary Jane b 1962); *Career* Nat Serv Lt RA 1952–54; asst master Oundle Sch 1958–61; dir of music: Dean Close Sch 1961–66, Marlborough Coll 1967–71; precentor and dir of music Eton Coll 1971–85, headmaster Oakham Sch 1985–96; chm Fabrics Advsy Ctee Peterborough Cathedral; govr: Yehudi Menuhin Sch, Nat Youth Orchestra; pres: Music Masters' Assoc 1975, Int Cello Centre 1985; warden Sch Music Section ISM 1977; conductor: Cheltenham Chamber Orch 1963–66, N Wilts Orch 1966–71, Windsor and Eton Choral Soc 1971–85; ARCO, ARCM, FRSA 1990; *Recreations* golf, photography; *Clubs* East India; *Style—* Graham Smallbone, Esq; ✉ The Old Manse, 56 High Street, Chinnor, Oxon OX9 4DH (☎ and fax 01844 354572)

SMALLEY, Very Rev Dr Stephen Stewart; s of Arthur Thomas Smalley, OBE, of Banstead, Surrey (d 1975), and May Elizabeth Selina, *née* Kimm (d 1986); *b* 11 May 1931; *Educ* Battersea GS, Jesus Coll Cambridge (MA, PhD), Eden Theol Seminary USA (BD); *m* 13 July 1974, Susan Jane (d 1995), da of Wing Cdr Arthur James Paterson, of Banstead, Surrey (d 1987); 1 s (Jovian b 1977), 1 da (Evelyn b 1983); *Career* asst curate St Paul's Church Portman Square 1958–60; chaplain Peterhouse Cambridge 1960–63 (acting dean 1962–63); lectr and sr lectr: Univ of Ibadan Nigeria 1963–69, Univ of Manchester 1970–77; vice provost Coventry Cathedral 1986 (canon residentiary and precentor 1977–86), dean of Chester Cathedral 1987–; *Books* Christ and Spirit in the New Testament (ed with B Lindars, 1973), John: Evangelist and Interpreter (1978), 1, 2, 3 John (1984), Thunder and Love (1994); *Recreations* music, drama, literature, travel; *Clubs* City (Chester); *Style—* The Very Rev Dr Stephen S Smalley; ✉ The Deanery, 7 Abbey St, Chester CH1 2JF (☎ 01244 351380); The Old Hall, Longborough, Moreton-in-Marsh, Glos GL56 0QS (☎ 01451 832350); Cathedral Office, 1 Abbey Square, Chester CH1 2HU (☎ 01244 324756)

SMALLMAN, Barry Granger; CMG (1976), CVO (1972); s of Charles Stanley Smallman, CBE, ARCM (d 1981), of Worthing, Sussex, and Ruby Marian, *née* Granger (d 1949); *b* 22 Feb 1924; *Educ* St Paul's, Trinity Coll Cambridge (MA); *m* 6 Sept 1952, Sheila Maxine, da of William Henry Knight, of Sissinghurst, Kent; 2 s (Mark b 1955, Robin b 1957), 1 da (Joy b 1953); *Career* served 1939–45, Lt Intelligence Corps; Br dep high cmmr Sierra Leone 1963–64 and NZ 1964–67, IDC 1968, consul-gen Br Embassy Thailand 1971–74, Br high cmmr Bangladesh 1975–78, Dip Serv resident chm Civil Service Selection Bd 1978–81, Br high cmmr Jamaica and ambass Haiti 1982–84; chm Cncl Benenden Sch 1986–92; memb Cncl: St Lawrence Coll Ramsgate 1984–, The Leprosy Mission 1984–96, The Soc for Promoting Christian Knowledge 1984– (vice chm 1993–); fndr and dir Granger Consultancies 1984–94; *Recreations* reading, writing, short stories and verse, singing, piano, bird watching, tennis, golf; *Style—* Barry Smallman, Esq, CMG, CVO; ✉ Beacon Shaw, Benenden, Kent TN17 4BU (☎ and fax 01580 240 625)

SMALLMAN, Prof (Edward) Raymond; CBE (1992); s of David Smallman, and Edith, *née* French; *b* 4 Aug 1929; *Educ* Rugeley GS, Univ of Birmingham (BSc, PhD, DSc); *m* 6 Sept 1952, Joan Doreen, da of George Faulkner, of Wolverhampton; 1 s (Robert Ian b 1959), 1 da (Lesley Ann (Mrs Grimer) b 1955); *Career* sr scientific offr AERE Harwell 1953–58; Univ of Birmingham: lectr Dept of Physical Metallurgy 1958–63, sr lectr 1963–64, prof of physical metallurgy 1964–69, Feeney prof of metallurgy and materials sci 1969–93, head Physical Metallurgy and Sci of Materials 1969–81, head Dept Metallurgy and Materials 1981–88, dean Faculty of Sci and Engrg 1984–85, dean Faculty of Engrg 1985–87, vice princ 1987–92, prof of metallurgy and materials sci 1993–; Sir George Beilby Gold medal 1969, Rosenhain medal 1972, Elegant Work prize 1979, Platinum medal 1989; pres Birmingham Metallurgical Assoc 1972, vice pres Metals Soc 1980–85, vice pres Inst of Materials 1995– (memb Cncl 1992–), pres Federated Euro Materials Socs 1994– (vice pres 1992–94); SERC: memb Materials Cmmn 1988–92, memb Cncl 1992–94; Warden Assay Office Birmingham 1994–; non-exec dir Univ Hosp Birmingham NHS Tst 1995–; Hon DSc: Univ of Wales, Univ of Novi Sad Yugoslavia 1990; hon foreign memb: China Ordnance Soc 1993, Czech Soc for Metal Sci 1995; FIM 1965, FRS 1986, FEng 1991; *Books* Modern Physical Metallurgy (1962, 4 edn 1985), Modern Metallography (1966), Structure of Metals and Alloys (1969), Defect Analysis in Electron Microscopy (1975), Vacancies '76 (1976), Metals and Materials (1994); *Recreations* golf, bridge, travel; *Clubs* Athenaeum, South Staffs Golf; *Style—* Prof Raymond Smallman, CBE, FRS, FEng; ✉ 59 Woodthorne Rd Sth, Tettenhall, Wolverhampton WV6 8SN (home ☎ and fax 01902 752545, work ☎ 0121 414 5223, fax 0121 414 5247, telex SPAPHYG 338938)

SMALLMAN, Timothy Gilpin; s of Stanley Cottrell Smallman (d 1965), of Kenilworth, Warwicks, and Grace Mary Louise, *née* Wilson (d 1990); *b* 6 Nov 1938; *Educ* Stowe; *m* 18 April 1964, Jane, da of Edward Holloway (d 1988), of Acocks Green, Birmingham; 2 s (Guy b 1965, Simon b 1967); *Career* chm: Smallman Lubricants (Hereford) Ltd 1972, WF Smallman and Son Ltd 1978 (md 1965); chm and md Smallman Lubricants Ltd 1978, chm Coronet Oil Refineries Ltd 1979, nat pres Br Lubricants Fedn Ltd 1983–85 (dir 1977–89), chm Needwood Oils and Solvents Ltd 1984; FInstD 1965, FInstPet 1968; *Recreations* golf, bridge, ornithology, nature and wildlife conservation; *Clubs* Copt Heath Golf; *Style—* Timothy Smallman, Esq; ✉ Luddington Manor, nr Stratford-upon-Avon CV37 9SJ; W F Smallman & Son Ltd, 216 Great Bridge St, W Bromwich, W Midlands (☎ 0121 557 3372)

SMALLWOOD, Air Chief Marshal Sir Denis Graham; GBE (1975, CBE 1961, MBE 1951), KCB (1969, CB 1966), DSO (1944), DFC (1942); s of Frederick William Smallwood, of Moseley, Birmingham; *b* 13 Aug 1918; *Educ* King Edward's Sch Birmingham; *m* 1940, Frances Jeanne (d 1992), da of Walter Needham, of Birmingham; 1 s (Christopher), 1 da (Johanna); *Career* RAF 1938; served WWII as fighter pilot Fighter Cmd nos 605, 87 and 247 Hurricane Sqdns 1939–42, ldr Spitfire Wing 1943–44; dir staff RAF Staff Coll Haifa 1945–46, asst sec Chiefs of Staff Ctee 1947–49, dir staff Jt Servs Staff Coll 1950–53, Cdr RAF Biggin Hill 1953–55, dir staff IDC 1955–56, Gp Capt Plans Air Task Force Suez Campaign 1956, Cdr RAF Guided Missiles Station Lincs 1959–61, AOC and Cmdt RAF Coll of Air Warfare, Manby 1961, Air Cdre 1961, Asst Chief of Air Staff (Ops) 1963–65, Air Vice Marshal 1963, AOC 3 Gp Bomber Cmd 1965–67, SASO Bomber Cmd 1967–68, COS Strike Cmd 1969, Air Marshal 1969, Cdr Br Forces Near East and AOC-in-C NEAF and Admin of Sovereign Base Areas of Akrotiri and Dhekelia Cyprus 1969–70, Vice-Chief of Air Staff 1970–73, AOC-in-C Strike Cmd 1974, Air Chief Marshal 1973, C-in-C UK Air Forces 1975–76; ADC to HM The Queen 1954–59, mil advsr Br Aerospace 1977–83; chm/pres Air League 1977–84 (now life vice pres); Freeman City of London, Liveryman Guild of Air Pilots and Air Navigators; FRSA, FRAeS; *Books* RAF Biggin Hill; *Recreations* equitation, gardening, swimming, wild life, hiking, antiques; *Clubs* RAF, Les Ambassadeurs; *Style*— Air Chief Marshal Sir Denis Smallwood, GBE, KCB, DSO, DFC; ✉ 27 Swinnerton House, Phyllis Court Drive, Henley-on-Thames, Oxfordshire RG9 2HU

SMALLWOOD, John Frank Monton; CBE (1991); s of Frank T Smallwood (d 1982), and Edith, *née* Stanford (d 1957); *b* 12 April 1926; *Educ* City of London Sch, Peterhouse Cambridge (scholar, MA); *m* 14 June 1952, Jean Margaret, da of Horace Thomas Lovell (d 1981); 1 s (Christopher John b 1956), 2 da (Elizabeth Mary (Mrs King-Fisher) b 1953, Patricia Anne (Mrs Wyer) b 1958); *Career* served RAF (Japanese translation and interrogation) 1944–48, PO 1945, FO 1946; Bank of England: joined 1951, private sec to Govrs 1959–62, advsr 1967–69, auditor 1969–74, dep chief accountant 1974–79, ret 1979; memb: Church Assembly Gen Synod 1965– (memb Standing Ctee 1971–95), Central Bd of Fin 1965– (dep vice chm 1972–82); Church Cmmr 1966– (memb Bd of Govrs 1966–, memb Gen Purposes Ctee 1968–), memb C of E Pensions Bd 1985–96, chm Southwark Dio Bd of Fin 1975– (memb 1962–), vice chm Southwark Ordination Course Cncl 1981–94 (memb 1960–94, treas 1960–70); tstee: City Parochial Fndn 1969– (vice chm 1977–81, chm 1981–92), Tst for London 1986– (chm 1986–92), Lambeth Palace Library 1977–, Overseas Bishoprics Fund 1977– (chm 1991–); lay reader 1983–; *Recreations* family, music, church finances, genealogy, church history; *Style*— John Smallwood, Esq, CBE; ✉ Downsview, 32 Brockham Lane, Brockham, Betchworth, Surrey RH3 7EL (☎ 01737 842032)

SMART, Adrian Michael Harwood; s of Harold Leslie Harwood Smart (d 1976), of Cuckfield, Sussex, and Moira, *née* Scanlon (d 1986); *b* 20 Nov 1935; *Educ* Eastbourne Coll; *m* 14 Sept 1963, Anne Sara, da of Richard Buxton Morrish; 1 s (Richard Anthony Harwood b 29 March 1967), 1 da (Amanda Hilary Harwood b 6 Oct 1964); *Career* Slaughter and May: articled clerk 1957–61, asst slr 1961–68, ptnr 1969–93; dir: Baring Stratton Investment Trust plc 1994–, Pillar Property Investments plc 1994–; memb Bd of Mgmnt Royal Alexandra and Albert Sch Fndn 1996–; *Recreations* gardening, fishing, stalking; *Clubs* Boodle's, City of London, Hong Kong; *Style*— Adrian M H Smart, Esq; ✉ Little Santon Farm, Trumpet Hill, Reigate Heath, Surrey RH2 8QY (☎ 01737 242285, fax 01737 226577)

SMART, (Elizabeth) Ann; da of William Jeffrey Hughes (d 1962), and Nancy Elizabeth, *née* Williams; *b* 30 April 1934; *Educ* The Queen's Sch Chester, St Anne's Coll Oxford (MA, BCL, Winter Williams prize in law); *m* 1958, John (Ian) Morrison Smart, s of Peter Fernie Smart (d 1972); 2 da (Jane Elizabeth Morrison b 20 Nov 1962, Helen Victoria Morrison b 11 Oct 1964), 1 s (Timothy William Morrison b 2 July 1966); *Career* called to the Bar Middle Temple 1959; asst lectr Univ of Manchester 1957–58, lectr Magdalen Coll Oxford 1958–61; St Hugh's Coll Oxford: lectr 1972–77, fell and sr tutor in law 1977–95, CUF lectr 1977–90, admissions tutor 1980–85, fell emeritus 1995–; special post Bodleian Law Library Oxford 1990– Sept 1996; served on Dover Ctee on Admissions Procedures 1982–83; hon bencher Middle Temple 1989; currently govr Canford Sch and Sherborne Sch for Girls; *Books* Chitty on Contracts (jt ed 22nd and 23rd edns); *Recreations* opera, gardening; *Style*— Mrs E A Smart; ✉ Horseshoe House, Wootton, Woodstock, Oxon OX20 1DR (☎ and fax 01993 811307)

SMART, Clive Frederick; s of Charles Frederick Smart (d 1983), of Altrincham, Cheshire, and Gladys, *née* Morton; *b* 14 April 1932; *Educ* Manchester GS; *m* 22 June 1957, Audrey (d 1982), da of Stanley Walker Brown (d 1965), of Altrincham; 2 s (David b and d 1959, Philip b 1971), 4 da (Karen b 1958, Angela b 1960, Valerie b 1962, Nicola b 1966); *Career* CA; articled clerk Edwin Guthrie & Co CAs 1949, Peat Marwick 1954–58, gen mangr Halle Concerts Soc 1960–91 (co sec 1958–90); arts mgmnt conslt 1991–; chm Assoc of Br Orchestras Tst; hon memb: Royal Northern Coll of Music, Inc Soc of Musicians; Hon MA Univ of Manchester 1992; Queen's Silver Jubilee medal; FCA 1954, FRSA 1987; *Recreations* sailing, photography, gardening, music; *Clubs* Royal Over-Seas League; *Style*— Clive Smart, Esq; ✉ 297 Washway Rd, Sale, Cheshire (☎ 0161 962 1707)

SMART, Geoffrey John Neville; s of John Frederick Smart (d 1979), of Lincoln, and Elsie, *née* Blunt; *b* 19 Sept 1946; *Educ* Lincoln Sch, Emmanuel Coll Cambridge (MA); *m* 5 Nov 1970, Karen Martha Margareta, da of Maj August Wilhelm Cordes; 3 da (Katherine b 1974, Harriet b 1976, Clare b 1978); *Career* analyst Mgmnt Dynamics Ltd 1967–70, ptnr Deloitte Haskins & Sells 1980–89 (mgmnt conslt 1970–74, mangr 1974–80), ptnr Coopers & Lybrand 1980–; *Recreations* golf, theatre, music; *Clubs* RAC; *Style*— Geoffrey Smart, Esq; ✉ Coopers & Lybrand, 1 Embankment Place, London WC2N 6NN (☎ 0171 213 5186, fax 0171 213 2406)

SMART, Prof Sir George Algernon; kt (1978); s of Algernon Smart (d 1952), and Mary Ann Smart (d 1984); *b* 16 Dec 1913; *Educ* Uppingham, Univ of Durham (BSc, MD); *m* 1939, Monica Helen, da of Joseph Ernest Carrick; 2 s, 1 da; *Career* prof of med Univ of Durham and Newcastle upon Tyne 1956–71; dir British Postgraduate Medical Fedn and prof of med Univ of London 1971–78; vice pres and sr censor RCP 1972, life vice pres RNLI; hon fell Coll of Physicians and Surgns Pakistan; *Books* Fundamentals of Clinical Endocrinology (co-author); *Style*— Prof Sir George Smart; ✉ Taffrail, Crede Lane, Old Bosham, Chichester, Sussex PO18 8NX

SMART, Prof (Arthur David) Gerald; CBE (1991); s of Arthur Herbert John Smart (d 1979), of Seaton, Devon, and Amelia Olwen Mona, *née* Evans (d 1967); *b* 19 March 1925; *Educ* Rugby, King's Coll Cambridge (MA), Regent St Poly (DipTP); *m* 18 June 1955, Anne Patience, da of Charles William Baxter, CMG, MC (d 1969), of Storrington, Sussex; 2 da (Amelia b 1 May 1959, Susan (Mrs Ridout) b 9 July 1960); *Career* planner in local govt 1950–75, co planning offr Hants CC 1963–75, head of Bartlett Sch of Architecture and Planning UCL 1975–80, prof of urban planning (later emeritus prof) Univ of London 1975–85; conslt Countryside Cmmn 1989–90; memb: Cncl Solent Protection Soc, Governing Body British Assoc for Central and E Europe 1986–96, various govt ctees on planning 1963–77, Cncl RSPB 1985–90; chm: Milford-on-Sea Parish Cncl 1989–93 (currently memb), Structure Plan Examinations in Public DOE; ARICS 1953, FRTPI 1964, FRSA 1982; *Recreations* ornithology, sailing, walking, music; *Clubs* Royal Lymington Yacht; *Style*— Prof Gerald Smart, CBE; ✉ 10 Harewood Green, Keyhaven, Lymington, Hants SO41 0TZ (☎ 01590 645475)

SMART, Sir Jack; kt (1982), CBE (1976), JP (Castleford, 1960), DL (West Yorkshire, 1987); s of James William Smart (d 1968), and Emily, *née* Greenanay (d 1955); *b* 25 April 1920; *Educ* Altofts Colliery Sch; *m* 1941, Ethel, da of Henry King (d 1963), of Cutsyke, Castleford; 1 da (Joan); *Career* miner 1934–59; mayor Castleford 1962–63; memb: Wakefield Metropolitan Dist Cncl 1973– (leader 1973–), Layfield Ctee of Inquiry on Local Govt Fin; chm Wakefield DHA 1977–88, former chm Assoc of Met Authys, pres The Yorkshire Soc 1980; hon fell Bretton Coll; Hon Freeman City of Wakefield Met Dist Cncl 1985; FRSA; *Recreations* golf, swimming; *Style*— Sir Jack Smart, CBE, JP, DL; ✉ Churchside, Weetworth, Pontefract Rd, Castleford, W Yorks (☎ 01977 554880)

SMART, Nicholas Ormond Edward; *b* 25 Dec 1952; *Educ* Hardye's Sch Dorchester, Plymouth Poly (BSc); *Career* Barclays Bank plc 1971–73, Agricultural Central Trading Ltd 1973–76, Plymouth Poly 1976–79, postgraduate res Ecology and Conservation Unit UCL 1979–82, Woodlands project offr RSPB 1983–86, Conservation Offices WWF 1986; British Council: acting head Overseas Services Secretariat 1986–87, asst dir Kano 1987–88, asst rep Lagos 1988–89, asst dir Johannesburg 1989–91, dir Cape Town 1991–95; devpt conslt 1995–; author of various pubns; *Recreations* ornithology, photography, environmental conservation, travel; *Style*— Nicholas Smart, Esq; ✉ PO Box 210, Steenberg, Cape Town 7947, South Africa (☎ 021 788 8828, fax 021 788 8399, e-mail smart.nd@iafrica.com)

SMART, Prof (Roderick) Ninian; s of late Prof W M Smart, FRSE, and Isabel, *née* Carswell; *b* 6 May 1927; *Educ* Glasgow Acad, Queen's Coll Oxford (Major open scholar, BA, BPhil); *m* 1954, Libushka Baruffaldi; 4 c; *Career* 2 Lt, Capt Army Intelligence Corps 1945–48 (overseas service in Ceylon); lectr in philosophy UCW Aberystwyth 1952–56, lectr in history and philosophy of religion Univ of London 1956–61 (acting head of Dept 1959), H G Wood prof of theology Univ of Birmingham 1961–67; prof of religious studies: Univ of Lancaster 1967–82 (hon prof 1982–89, prof emeritus 1989, pro vice chllr 1969–72), Univ of Calif Santa Barbara 1976– (J F Rowny Prof of Comparative Religions); author of numerous articles and reviews; visiting lectr in philosophy: Yale Univ 1955–56, Banaras Hindu Univ 1960; visiting prof: Univ of Wisconsin 1965, Princeton 1971, Univ of Otago NZ 1981, Univ of Queensland Aust 1980 and 1985, St Martin's Coll of Educn Lancaster 1980–89, Univ of Cape Town SA 1982, Harvard Univ 1983, United Theol Coll India 1984, Univ of Hong Kong 1989; dir Schools Cncl Projects on Secdy and Primary Religious Educn Univ of Lancaster 1969–79; memb: Archbishops' Cmmn of Christian Doctrine (C of E) 1966–70, Cncl American Soc for the Study of Religion 1979– (pres 1984–87); pres: Shap Working Party on World Religions in Educn 1977– (co chm 1968–77), Br Assoc for the History of Religions 1981–85, Oxford Soc of Historical Theology 1981–82; vice pres: World Congress of Faiths 1978–79, Inst of Religion and Theology of GB and Ireland 1978–82 (gen sec 1974–78); editorial conslt The Long Search BBC TV 1974–77, external examiner for numerous undergraduate and graduate degrees, numerous special lectures worldwide; Hon DHumane Letters Loyola Univ 1968; Hon DLitt: Univ of Glasgow 1984, Kelaniya Univ Sri Lanka 1991, Univ of Lancaster 1995; Hon DUniv Stirling 1986, Univ of Middx 1996; hon prof of religious studies: Univ of Wales 1987–, Univ of Stirling 1988–; *Books* incl: Reasons and Faiths (1958), The Teacher and Christian Belief (1966), The Yogi and the Devotee (1968), The Message of the Buddha (1975), The Religious Experience (1979, 5 edn 1996), Religion and Politics in the Contemporary World (with Peter Merkl, 1983), Worldviews (1983), Religion and the Western Mind (1989), The World's Religions (1989), Buddhism and Christianity: Rivals and Allies (1993), Religions of Asia (1993), Religions of the West (1993), Doctrine and Argument in Indian Philosophy (2 edn, 1993), Choosing a Faith (1995), Religion and Nationalism (1995), Dimensions of the Sacred (1996), Smart Verse (1996), Reflections in the Mirror of Religion; *Recreations* cricket, poetry, tennis; *Clubs* Athenaeum; *Style*— Prof Ninian Smart; ✉ Department of Religious Studies, University of California Santa Barbara, CA 93106, USA (☎ 00 1 805 893 3564, fax 00 1 805 893 2059)

SMART, (Alexander Basil) Peter; CMG (1990); s of (Henry) Prescott Smart (d 1981), of Houghton le Spring, Co Durham, and (Mary) Gertrude, *née* Todd; *b* 19 Feb 1932; *Educ* Ryhope GS Co Durham; *m* 24 Sept 1955, Joan Mary, da of Alex Cumming (d 1973); 3 s (Peter b 1960, Michael (twin) b 1960, Jeremy b 1966); *Career* 2 Lt RAEC 1951–53, supervising offr for educn Gibraltar Cmd 1951–52; Foreign (later HM Dip) Serv: joined 1953, Duala French Cameroons 1956, Cyprus 1956–59, Seoul Korea 1959–63, Rangoon Burma 1968–71, head communications tech servs dept FCO 1975–77, cnsllr later dep high cmmr Canberra 1977–82, dep head mission Prague 1983–86, Br high cmmr Seychelles 1986–89, Br ambass Fiji and Br high cmmr Tuvalu and Nauru 1989–92, ret 1992; FRSA; *Recreations* music and the arts, exploring little-used roads; *Style*— Peter Smart, Esq, CMG; ✉ Jay House, Deanwood Rd, Jordans, Beaconsfield, Bucks HP9 2UU (☎ 01494 676630)

SMART, Richard Anthony; s of James Clifford Smart (d 1972), of Neath, West Glamorgan, and Rose Beryl, *née* Penn (d 1991); *b* 8 March 1942; *Educ* Neath GS; *m* 3 Oct 1968, Gaynor, da of Oswald Isaac (d 1965); 2 s (Matthew James b 4 Oct 1974, Jonathan Anthony (twin) b 4 Oct 1974); *Career* CA 1966; joined Deloitte Plender Griffiths & Co 1959; ptnr: Deloitte Haskins & Sells 1976–90, Cork Gully 1990, Coopers & Lybrand (formerly Coopers & Lybrand Deloitte) 1990–; memb: Insolvency Practitioners Assoc 1976, Inst of Credit Mgmnt 1988, Soc of Practitioners of Insolvency 1990; FCA 1977; *Recreations* sport and music; *Clubs* Cardiff and County; *Style*— Richard A Smart, Esq; ✉ Coopers & Lybrand, Churchill House, Churchill Way, Cardiff CF1 4XQ (☎ 01222 237000, fax 01222 345626)

SMEDLEY, Hon Mr Justice; Hon Sir (Frank) Brian; kt (1995); s of Leslie Smedley (d 1970); *b* 28 Nov 1934; *Educ* West Bridgford GS, Univ of London (LLB); *Career* called to the Bar Gray's Inn 1960, recorder of the Crown Court 1971–84, memb Senate of Inns of Court and the Bar 1973–77, QC 1977, circuit judge 1987–95, Central Criminal Court 1987, sr judge Sovereign Base Areas Cyprus 1991–95, judge of the High Court of Justice 1995–; *Recreations* travel, gardening; *Clubs* Garrick; *Style*— Hon Mr Justice Smedley; ✉ c/o Royal Courts of Justice, Strand, London WC2A 2LL

SMEDLEY, Sir Harold; KCMG (1978, CMG 1965), MBE (1946); s of Ralph Davies Smedley (d 1954), of Worthing; *b* 19 June 1920; *Educ* Aldenham, Pembroke Coll Cambridge; *m* 1950, Beryl, da of Harold Brown, of Wellington, NZ; 2 s, 2 da; *Career* Nat Serv RM WWII, served UK, Med and W Europe; entered Dominions Office 1946, private sec to Sec of State Cwlth Rels Office 1954–57, Br high cmmr Ghana 1964–67, ambass Laos 1968–70, asst under sec FCO 1970, sec gen Cmmn on Rhodesian Opinion 1971–72, high cmmr Repub of Sri Lanka and ambass to Maldives Repub 1973–75, high cmmr in NZ and govr of Pitcairn 1976–80; chm Bank of NZ (London) 1983–90 (dep chm 1981–83); pres: Hakluyt Soc 1987–92, W Sussex Assoc for the Blind 1990–; vice chm Victoria League 1981–90, memb W Sussex CC 1989–93; *Clubs* United Oxford and Cambridge Univ, Cwlth Tst; *Style*— Sir Harold Smedley, KCMG, MBE; ✉ 11A Beehive Lane, Ferring, West Sussex BN12 5NN

SMEDLEY, Peter Lawrence; s of Graham Powell Smedley (d 1983), of Carmichael's House, Carmichaels, Longforgan, Dundee, Tayside, and Jean Grace, *née* Ludlow (d 1996); *b* 20 Jan 1939; *Educ* King's Sch Canterbury, RAC Cirencester; *m* 1977, Christine June, da of Donald William Howard; *Career* fndr light aircraft business in SA 1971–72; National Canning Company (family business) 1963–65, fndr own co Smedley Powell & Co (surveying and land agency) 1965, purchased Ston Easton Park 1977, undertook restoration 1977–82, opened as hotel 1982 (winner Egon Rony Gold Plate Hotel of the Year), dir (with estate mgmnt responsibilities) family farming co Scotland 1985; awarded RAF Flying Scholarship; *Recreations* shooting, garden planning, numismatology;

Style— Peter Smedley, Esq; ✉ Ston Easton Park, Ston Easton, Bath, Somerset BA3 4DF (☎ 01761 241 631, fax 01761 241 377)

SMEE, Clive Harrod; CB (1997); s of Victor Woolley Smee (d 1991), of Kingsbridge, Devon, and Leila Olive, *née* Harrod (d 1956); *b* 29 April 1942; *Educ* Royal GS Guildford, LSE (BEcon), Business Sch Indiana Univ (MBA), Inst of Cwlth Studies Oxford; *m* 5 April 1975, Denise Eileen, da of Edward Ernest Sell (d 1968), of Shafton, Yorks; 1 s (David b 1981), 2 da (Anna b 1978, Elizabeth b 1985); *Career* Br Cncl Nigeria 1966–68, econ advsr ODM 1969–75, sr econ advsr DHSS 1975–82, Nuffield and Leverhulme travelling fell USA and Canada 1978–79, advsr Central Policy Review Staff 1982–83, sr econ advsr HM Treasy 1983–84; chief econ advsr: DHSS 1984–89, Dept of Health 1989–; conslt NZ Govt 1988 and 1991; visiting prof of econ Univ of Surrey 1995–; chm Social Policy Working Pty OECD 1987–89; *Recreations* running, gardening, family; *Style*— Clive Smee, Esq, CB; ✉ c/o Department of Health, Skipton House, 80 London Road, London SE1 6LW (☎ 0171 972 5220, fax 0171 972 5187)

SMEETON, David; s of Lt Cdr Donald Edward Smeeton (ka 1940, served HMS Glorious), and Enid Mona, *née* Brockman; *b* 16 Sept 1936; *Educ* Malvern Coll; *m* 22 Aug 1959, Diana Mary, da of William John (Jack) Pitts; 1 s (Jonathan Donald b 18 Feb 1963, d 1987), 1 da (Rachel Mary b 1 March 1965); *Career* reporter Western Morning News Plymouth 1955–60; BBC: regnl reporter Plymouth 1960–63, reporter BBC national news London 1963–65, educn corr 1968–70 (educn reporter 1965–68), home affrs corr 1970–73, Tokyo corr 1973–78, educn and local govt corr London 1978–81, Bonn corr 1981–86, W of England corr 1986–94; freelance journalist and bdcaster 1994–; Winston Churchill fell USA 1968; memb: Cncl St John Ambulance Devon, Educn Ctee SW RSA, Soc of Industl and Emergency Serv Offrs, Inst of Journalists, Radio Acad; *Recreations* walking, canoeing, Dartmoor and West Country history, amateur dramatics; *Style*— David Smeeton, Esq; ✉ 41 Mead Drive, Thurlestone, Kingsbridge, Devon TQ7 3TA

SMELLIE, Keith Graham; s of Prof James Maclure Smellie (d 1961), and Hilda Kathleen, *née* Lamsdale (d 1996); *b* 8 April 1934; *Educ* Repton; *m* 13 August 1960, Meriel Hill, da of George Benjamin Hill Parkes (d 1991); 4 c (Tiona Jayne b 16 Feb 1962, Alastair James b 14 Nov 1963, Stuart Guy b 2 Feb 1967, Justin Charles b 1 May 1968); *Career* Nat Serv cmmnd RA 1953; articled clerk Impey Cudworth & Co Birmingham, qualified chartered accountant 1961, memb Birmingham Stock Exchange 1965, dir Albert E Sharp & Co 1988– (ptnr Albert E Sharp & Co 1967–88), fndr dir NMW Computers plc 1972–91; memb Stock Exchange Midlands & Western Unit Ctee Birmingham 1972–88; ACA 1961, memb Int Stock Exchange 1965, AIIMR 1967; *Style*— Keith Smellie, Esq; ✉ South Lawn, Rowington, Warwick CV35 7AA (☎ 01926 843247); Albert E Sharp, Temple Court, 35 Bull Street, Birmingham B4 6ES (☎ 0121 200 2244, fax 0121 683 7300)

SMERDON, Richard William; s of late John Conran Smerdon, of Cheltenham, and late Monica Rosewarne, *née* Woollen; *b* 20 May 1942; *Educ* King Edward GS Aston Birmingham, Christ Church Oxford (open Smith choral scholar, exhibitioner, MA); *m* 1, 13 Aug 1966 (m dis 1991), Alison Lorna, *née* Webb; 1 s (Edward b 14 May 1968), 2 da (Helen b 2 Jan 1970, Jane b 26 August 1972); m 2, 19 Oct 1991, Caroline Mary Kynaston Bowden, da of John Kynaston Williams; *Career* asst slr Slaughter and May 1965–69 (articled 1963–65), currently ptnr Osborne Clarke (ptnr Bristol 1970–87, founding ptnr London 1987–90, sr ptnr 1990–96); memb Stock Exchange (Midland and Western) Working Pty on Smaller Co Markets 1994; founding chm Coach House Small Business Centre 1982–85, chm Bath Festival Fndn 1988–91; memb Law Soc; *Books* Butterworth's Company Law Service (co-ed, 1987); *Recreations* singing early music, eating and entertaining, accompanying wife, reading books on cricket; *Style*— Richard Smerdon, Esq; ✉ Osborne Clarke, 6 Middle Street, London EC1A 7JA (☎ 0171 600 0155, fax 0171 726 2772); Osborne Clarke, 30 Queen Charlotte Street, Bristol BS99 7QQ (☎ 0117 923 0220)

SMETHURST, Dr (John) Michael; CBE (1996); s of Albert Smethurst (d 1973), of Barrow-in-Furness, and Nelly, *née* Kitchin (d 1985); *b* 25 April 1934; *Educ* William Hulme's GS Manchester, Univ of Manchester (BA); *m* 2 Jan 1960, Mary, da of Ernest Edwin Clayworth (d 1986), of Manchester; 1 s (Matthew b 1966), 1 da (Laura b 1964); *Career* sch master 1956–60, lectr and coll librarian Lancaster Coll of Art 1960–63, tutor librarian Bede Coll Durham 1963–66, librarian Inst of Educn Univ of Newcastle 1966–69, dep librarian Univ of Glasgow 1969–72, univ librarian Univ of Aberdeen 1972–86, DG Humanities and Social Scis 1986–91, DG London Br Library 1991–95 (dep chief exec 1995–96); former chm: Friends of Aberdeen Art Gallery, Aberdeen Maritime Museum Appeal; pres: Friends of Aberdeen Univ Library 1986–, Scottish Library Assoc 1983, Liber Ligue Int Des Bibliotheques Européens de Researches 1989–94; chm: Standing Conf of Nat and Univ Libraries 1983–85 and 1989–90 (memb Cncl 1981–92), Library and Info Servs Ctee Scotland 1980–86, Int Ctee ESTC 1986–96, Tstees of the Brotherton Collection Univ of Leeds 1987–, Consortium of European Research Libraries 1992–; tstee Nat Library of Scotland 1975–86; memb Bd: Br Library 1986–96, Research Libraries Group (USA) 1992–96; hon memb SLA, hon res fell UCL 1986–; Hon DLitt Sheffield 1996; ALA; *Books* various articles in professional jls and other pubns; *Recreations* music, gardening, art, travel; *Clubs* Athenaeum; *Style*— Dr Michael Smethurst, CBE; ✉ Romney, 72 Grove Rd, Tring, Herts HP23 (☎ 01442 825465)

SMETHURST, Richard Good; s of Thomas Good Smethurst (d 1981), of Abingdon, Oxfordshire, and Madeleine Nora, *née* Foulkes (d 1987); *b* 17 Jan 1941; *Educ* Liverpool Coll, Worcester Coll Oxford (Henriques scholar), Nuffield Coll Oxford (G Webb Medley jr scholar, BA, MA); *m* 1964, (Dorothy) Joan, da of William James Mitchenall (d 1951), of Shrewsbury; 2 s (James b 1971, Jonathan b 1979), 2 da (Katharine b 1969, Frances b 1976); *Career* fell and tutor in econs St Edmund Hall Oxford 1965–66 (res fell 1964–65), conslt UN/FAO World Food Prog Inst for Cwlth Studies Oxford 1965–66; Univ of Oxford: fell and tutor in econs Worcester Coll and univ lectr in econs 1967–76, dir Dept for External Studies and professorial fell Worcester Coll 1976–86; dep chm Monopolies and Mergers Cmmn 1986–89 (pt/t memb 1978–86); Univ of Oxford: chm Gen Bd of The Faculties 1989–91, Provost Worcester Coll 1991–; pt/t econ advsr HM Treasy 1969–71, pt/t policy advsr PM's Policy Unit 1975–76, non-exec dir Investmt Mgmnt Regulatory Orgn 1987–; memb: Advsy Cncl for Adult and Continuing Educn DES 1977–83, Continuing Educn Standing Ctee UGC/NAB 1984–88, Cncl Templeton Coll Oxford Centre for Mgmnt Studies 1982–; chm: Unit for Devpt of Adult Continuing Educn 1991–92, Academic Consultative Ctee Open Univ 1986–92, Advsy Bd Music at Oxford 1988–; tstee Euro Community Baroque Orchestra 1986–93, pres WEA Thames and Solent, life govr Liverpool Coll; fndn hon fell Rewley House Oxford 1990, hon fell St Edmund Hall Oxford 1991; *Publications* Impact of Food Aid on Donor Countries (with G R Allen, 1967); contrib: New Thinking About Welfare (1969), The Economic System in the UK (1977, 2 edn 1979), New Directions in Adult and Continuing Education (1979), Continuing Education in Universities and Polytechnics (1982); various articles in Jl of Development Studies and Oxford Review of Education; *Recreations* good food; *Style*— Richard Smethurst, Esq; ✉ The Provost's Lodgings, Worcester College, Oxford OX1 2HB (☎ 01865 278362, fax 01865 793106)

SMETS, Pascale Charlotte Marie; da of Luc Lois Clement Smets, and Jennifer Evelyn, *née* Popper; *b* 26 Oct 1964; *Educ* Farnborough Hill Convent Hants, Alleyn's Sch Dulwich, Chelsea Sch of Art & Design, St Martin's Sch of Art & Design (BA); *m* 12 Dec 1992, (Matt Pritchett, *qv*, s of Oliver Pritchett; 2 da (Edith b 13 April 1994, Mary b 29 Jan 1996); *Career* fashion designer; knitwear designer rising to designer on main sportswear collection Daniel Hechter SIPC 1986–88, designer for 'Studio' collection (day and evening wear) Jean Muir Ltd 1988–89, fndr own label Pascale Smets Ltd 1989–; freelance collections for: Int Wool Secretariat, Carrington Viyella, Pied à Terre's clothing line; nominee New Generation Award Br Fashion Awards 1992, included in Best of Br Women 1993; *Recreations* cooking, entertaining, gardening; *Style*— Ms Pascale Smets

SMIDDY, (Francis) Paul; s of Francis Geoffrey Smiddy, of Leeds, and Thelma Vivenne Smiddy; *b* 13 Nov 1953; *Educ* Winchester, Univ of Manchester; *m* 2 Sept 1978, Katy, da of Stewart MacDougall Watson, OBE, of Newport, Gwent; 2 s (Oliver b 1980, Alexander b 1982); *Career* mangr Price Waterhouse 1978–82, fin analyst J Sainsbury 1982–84, res analyst Capel-Cure Myers 1984–85, assoc dir Wood Mackenzie 1985–88; dir: Retail Res Kleinwort Benson Securities 1988–93, Retail Res Nomura Research Institute - Europe Ltd 1993–95, Credit Lyonnais Laing 1995–; Freeman Guild of Air Pilots and Air Navigators; FCA 1988; *Recreations* flying, motor sport, squash, France, skiing; *Style*— Paul Smiddy, Esq; ✉ Credit Lyonnais Laing, Broadwalk House, 5 Appold Street, London EC2A 2DA (☎ 0171 588 4000)

SMIETANA, Krzysztof; Wlodzimierz Smietana, of Krakow, Poland, and Irena, *née* Ludwig (d 1985); *b* 11 Oct 1956; *Educ* Secdy Music Sch Krakow, Krakow Acad of Music, Guildhall Sch of Music and Drama; *Career* violinist; formerly soloist with the Polish Chamber Orch, came to London 1980 to study under Yfrah Neaman at (and now teacher at) the Guildhall Sch of Music; performed throughout Europe, made several tours of Germany, appeared at most major London venues, regularly bdcast on BBC Radio 3, guest leader LSO; prizewinner numerous int competitions, winner numerous Polish honours; FGSM 1996; *Recordings incl* Panufnik's Violin Concerto (CD Review magazine CD of the Month) 1989, Fauré Sonantas (CD for Meridian, Retailers Assoc Award for Best Chamber Music Recording 1995) 1993; *Style*— Krzysztof Smietana, Esq; (☎ 0171 354 8506, fax 0171 359 4249)

SMIETON, Dame Mary Guillan; DBE (1949); da of John Guillan Smieton, and Maria Judith, *née* Toop; *b* 5 Dec 1902; *Educ* Perse Sch Cambridge, Wimbledon HS, Bedford Coll London, Lady Margaret Hall Oxford (MA); *Career* asst keeper PRO 1925–28, Miny of Labour and Nat Serv 1928–59, gen sec Women's Vol Servs 1938–40, on loan to UN as dir of personnel 1946–48, perm sec Miny of Educn 1959–63, UK rep UNESCO Exec Bd 1962–68; hon fell: Lady Margaret Hall Oxford 1959, Bedford Coll 1971, Royal Holloway Bedford New Coll 1985; tstee Br Museum 1963–73, cncl chm Bedford Coll 1963–70; memb: Advsy Cncl on Public Records 1965–73, Standing Cmmn on Museums and Galleries 1970–73; vice pres Museums Assoc 1974–77; *Clubs* United Oxford and Cambridge University; *Style*— Dame Mary Smieton, DBE; ✉ 14 St George's Rd, St Margaret's on Thames, Middlesex TW1 1QR (☎ 0181 892 9279)

SMILEY, Col David de Crespigny; LVO (1952), OBE (Mil, 1945), MC (1943, and bar 1944); s of Maj Sir John Smiley, 2 Bt (d 1930), and Valerie, da of Sir Claude Champion de Crespigny, 4 Bt (d 1978); *b* 11 April 1916; *Educ* Nautical Coll Pangbourne, RMC Sandhurst; *m* 28 April 1947, Moyra Eileen, da of Lt-Col Lord Francis George Montagu Douglas Scott, KCMG, DSO (d 1952; yst s of 6 Duke of Buccleuch), and widow of Maj Hugo Douglas Tweedie, Scots Gds (ka 1945); 2 s (Xan Smiley, *qv*, Philip David Smiley, *qv*); *Career* cmmnd Royal Horse Gds (The Blues) 1936; served WWII with 1 Household Cav Regt in M East (despatches) 1940–42, SOE 1943–45, in Balkans 1943–44, Far East 1945; Staff Coll 1946, asst mil attaché Warsaw 1947, cmd RHG 1952–54, mil attaché Stockholm 1955–58 (Kt Cdr of Order of Sword of Sweden 1957), Cdr Armed Forces of Sultan of Oman 1958–61, mil advsr to Imam of Yemen 1963–68; memb HM Body Guard of Hon Corps of Gentlemen-at-Arms 1966–68; Order of Skanderbeg (Albania), Order of Freedom 1st Class (Albania); *Books* Arabian Assignment (1975), Albanian Assignment (1984), Irregular Regular (1993); *Recreations* watching TV, cooking, reading; *Clubs* White's, Special Forces, MCC; *Style*— Col David Smiley, LVO, OBE, MC; ✉ 30 Kensington Mansions, Trebovir Road, London SW5 9TQ (☎ 0171 373 6765, fax 0171 373 6669)

SMILEY, Lt-Col Sir John Philip; 4 Bt (UK 1903), of Drumalis, Larne, Co Antrim, and Gallowhill, Paisley, Co Renfrew; o s of Sir Hugh Houston Smiley, 3 Bt, JP, DL (d 1990), and Nancy Elizabeth Louise Hardy, *née* Beaton (sis of late Sir Cecil Beaton); *b* 24 Feb 1934; *Educ* Eton, RMA Sandhurst; *m* 2 Nov 1963, Davina Elizabeth, eldest da of Denis Charles Griffiths (d 1949), of Orlingbury Hall, nr Kettering, Northants; 2 s (Christopher Hugh Charles b 1968, William Timothy John b 1972), 1 da (Melinda Elizabeth Eirène (Mrs Jonathon Baker) b 1965); *Heir* s, Christopher Hugh Charles Smiley b 7 Feb 1968; *Career* cmmnd Grenadier Guards 1954, served in BAOR Cyprus and Hong Kong, ADC to Govr of Bermuda 1961–62, ret 1986; dir of admin Russell Reynolds Assocs 1986–89; govr Oundle Schs 1987–; memb Ct of Assts Worshipful Co of Grocers 1987– (Master 1992–93); *Clubs* Army and Navy; *Style*— Lt-Col Sir John Smiley, Bt; ✉ Cornerway House, Chobham, nr Woking, Surrey GU24 8SW (☎ 01276 858992)

SMILEY, Philip David; s of Col David de Crespigny Smiley, LVO, OBE, MC, *qv*, of London, and Moyra Eileen, *née* Montagu-Douglas-Scott; *b* 26 Aug 1951,,W Germany; *Educ* Eton, Univ of St Andrews (MA); *m* 3 March 1995, Sohyung, da of Genand Mrs Young-Woo Kim; 1 s (Francis Hugh Kim b 13 Jan 1996); *Career* HM Overseas Colonial Serv 1974–85: Miny of Home Affrs Solomon Islands 1974–76, Judicial Dept Solomon Islands 1976–80, Civil Serv Branch Hong Kong 1981–83, Economic Servs Branch Hong Kong 1983–85; WI Carr Group 1985–90: research co-ordinator and dir Hong Kong 1985–87, md WI Carr (Far East) Ltd Hong Kong 1988–89, gp dir of fin and admin London 1989–90; Jardine Fleming Group 1990–: dir Jardine Fleming Securities Ltd, dir Jardine Fleming Broking Ltd, dir JF Asia Select Ltd, md JF Singapore, branch mangr Seoul Office 1990–96; dir Hyundai International Merchant Bank 1990–95; chm: Br C of C Korea, Bd Euro C of C Korea 1995–96; Solomon Islands Independence Medal 1976; *Recreations* winter sports, collecting books, travel, dogs; *Clubs* White's, Special Forces, Foreign Correspondents (Hong Kong), Hong Kong; *Style*— Philip Smiley, Esq; ✉ 157 Mount Pleasant Road, Singapore (☎ 00 65 250 7424); Jardine Fleming International Securities Ltd, 42–01 Republic Plaza, 9 Raffles Place, Singapore (☎ 00 65 439 6308, fax 00 65 536 7509)

SMILEY, Xan de Crespigny; s of Col David de Crespigny Smiley, LVO, OBE, MC, *qv*, and Moyra, widow of Maj Hugo Tweedie, and da of Lt-Col Lord Francis Montagu Douglas Scott, KCMG, DSO (6 s of 6 Duke of Buccleuch and Queensberry); *b* 1 May 1949; *Educ* Eton, New Coll Oxford (MA); *m* 1983, Hon Jane Acton, 6 and yst da of 3 Baron Acton, CMG, MBE, TD (d 1989); 2 s (Ben Richard Philip de Crespigny b 1985, Adam David Emerich b 1988), 2 step da (Charlotte Pugh b 1978, Rebecca Pugh b 1979); *Career* journalist and broadcaster; commentator BBC Radio External Serv current affrs 1974–75, corr Spectator and Observer in Africa 1975–77, dir Africa Confidential newsletter 1981- (ed 1977–81); publisher The Soviet Analyst 1990–91; Noel Buxton lectr in African politics 1980; ldr writer The Times 1982–83; The Economist 1983–86: foreign affrs, staff writer, Middle East ed; Moscow corr Daily Telegraph 1986–89, Washington corr The Sunday Telegraph 1990–92; The Economist: political ed 1992–94, Euro corr 1994–95, Euro ed 1996–; *Recreations* food, sport (memb Br ski team 1969, winner of Downhill Oxford v Cambridge 1969), shooting, travel, genealogy; *Clubs* White's, Beefsteak, Polish Hearth; *Style*— Xan Smiley, Esq; ✉ 36 Rectory Grove, Clapham, London SW4 0EB; The Economist, 25 St James's Street, London SW1A 1HG (☎ 0171 830 7000, fax 0171 930 5549)

SMILLIE, James; s of Maj Robert Smillie (d 1977), of Stanmore, Middx, and Jean Young, *née* Burnside (d 1970); *b* 7 June 1929; *Educ* Merchant Taylors'; *m* 1, 19 June 1949 (m dis

1978), Brenda, da of Herbert Lionel Kelsey, of Harrow, Middx; 4 da (Anne Patricia (Mrs Palmer) b 22 Jan 1958, Sheena Jane (Mrs Owen) b 26 July 1959, Elizabeth Dawn (Mrs Ferrigno) b 10 Dec 1963, Susan Carole b 14 Dec 1965); m 2, 7 March 1981, Chloë Ann, *née* Rich; *Career* Nat Serv 2 Lt/Actg Capt RASC 1953–55; CA; Ramsay Brown & Co 1947–53, Rootes Group Coventry 1955–56; Stratstone Ltd (subsid Thomas Tilling Ltd) 1956–: co sec, dir, md (mgmnt buy-out 1982), chm and md 1982–92 (sold 1992), non-exec chm 1992–94; chm Stratstone Leasing Ltd 1982–92, sr ptnr Rover Transport Co 1968–84, non exec dir Great Southern Group plc 1987– (chm 1989–94), dep chm SCI (UK) PLC 1994–, chm Amersham (Holdings) Ltd 1992–, chm Jaguar Dealer Cncl 1982–89; pres Motor Agents' Assoc 1988–89 (dep pres 1987–88), vice-pres Motor Trade Benevolent Soc 1988–89; memb: Stanmore (later Beaconsfield) Cons Assoc 1961–84, Chesham and Amersham Cons Assoc 1984–; life govr Imp Cancer Res Fund 1987–; Liveryman Worshipful Co of Coachmakers and Coach Harness Makers 1975 (memb Ct 1983, sr warden 1995, master 1996–97); CA (Scot) 1953, FIMI 1978, FInstD; *Recreations* golf, theatre, Glyndebourne; *Clubs* Carlton, RAC, Denham Golf; *Style*— James Smillie, Esq; ✉ Whyteposts, 66 High St, Old Amersham, Bucks (☎ and fax 01494 434547)

SMILLIE, (William) John Jones; s of John Smillie (d 1978), and Emily Mary Caroline, *née* Jones (d 1981); *b* 18 Feb 1940; *Educ* Lauriston Sch Falkirk, Territorial Sch Stirling, Stirling HS; *Career* Scottish hotel family background, trained in all hotel depts in Scotland and Paris with extensive kitchen work, progressed to mgmnt with Edward R Barnett Ltd industl caterers (now taken over by Grand Metropolitan Group), responsible for 50 outlets throughout Scotland, England and Wales (asst gen mangr 1964–67); House of Commons Catering Dept: personnel mangr 1967, asst to catering mangr 1970, gen mangr 1971, head of dept 1980–91; fndr memb Wine Guild of UK 1984; chief exec Gatehouse Records 1992–, dir Miller Morelle Designs 1993–, dir Kick FM Ltd 1996–; chm Newbury Community Radio Assoc 1996–; memb: Br Inst of Cleaning Science 1976, Hine Soc 1979, Restaurateurs' Assoc of GB 1983, Br Epilepsy Assoc 1981 (vice pres), League Against Cruel Sports 1983, Paddle Steamer Preservation Soc 1993; contrib various articles to catering trade papers; hon memb Le Conceil Culinaire Français de Grande Bretagne 1990; FHCIMA 1979, ACF 1972, FCFA 1967; *Recreations* theatre, ballet, music, piano, motoring, boating, radio presenter and producer, travel, gourmandising, jazz music, rock music, intervals at the opera; *Style*— John Smillie, Esq; ✉ The Gatehouse, 90 Wimbledon Parkside, London SW19 5LT (☎ 0181 780 9350, fax 0171 823 8905)

SMITH, Adrian Ewart; s of Frank Ewart Smith (d 1977), of Semley, Wilts, and Winnie Wilson (d 1967); *b* 10 Aug 1935; *Educ* Bournemouth Sch, LSE, Univ of Cambridge; *m* 29 July 1972, Hilary Kathryn, da of Kenneth Pearson (d 1985), of Doncaster, Yorks; 1 s (Kieron Alexander b 1977), 1 da (Claire Querida b 1975); *Career* RAF 1953–55; Shell Petroleum Co 1963–67, Miny of Tport 1967–68, Bd of Trade 1968–70, Dept of Employment 1970–73, Euro Cmmn Brussels 1978–81, FCO 1973–92 (PM's office 1982–83 and 1989); memb: Industrial Tbnl Southampton 1992–, Immigration Appeal Tbnl London 1993–, Child Support Appeal Tbnl 1993–; vice chm Southampton Community Health Servs Tst 1992–; *Style*— Adrian Smith, Esq; ✉ The Old Post Office, Walditch, nr Bridport, Dorset DT6 4LD (☎ 01590 623322)

SMITH, Sir Alan; kt (1982), CBE (1976), DFC (1941, and Bar 1942), DL (Kinross 1967); s of Capt Alfred Smith, MN (d 1931), of Sunderland, and Lilian, *née* Robinson (d 1956); *b* 14 March 1917; *Educ* Bede Coll Sunderland; *m* 1, 10 July 1943, Margaret Stewart (d 1971), da of Herbert Charles Todd (d 1954), of St Ronans, Kinross; 3 s (Michael Charles b 1948, Bruce Alan b 1948, Stuart Duncan b 1956), 2 da (Susan Janet Anstead b 1945, Ailsa Hilda b 1959); m 2, 1977, Alice Elizabeth, da of Robert Stewart Moncur (d 1961); *Career* served WWII pilot RAF 1939–45; chief exec Todd & Duncan Ltd 1946–60, chm and chief exec Dawson International 1960–82 (life pres 1982–); chm: Scottish Cashmere Association 1964–92, Gleneagles Hotels 1982–84, Quayle Munro Ltd 1983–90; dir Global Recovery Investment Trust 1981–86; memb Bd: Scottish Devpt Agency 1981–86, Scottish Tourist Bd 1982–85; cncllr Kinross Borough Cncl 1952–65, provost of Kinross 1959–65, cncllr Tayside Region 1979–90; CTI; *Recreations* sailing, swimming; *Clubs* Lansdowne; *Style*— Sir Alan Smith, CBE, DFC, DL; ✉ Ardgairney House, Cleish, by Kinross KY13 7LG (☎ 01577 850265); c/o Dawson International plc, Lochleven Mills, Kinross, Scotland KY13 7DH (☎ 01577 863521, telex 76168)

SMITH, Alan Christopher; CBE (1996); s of Herbert Sidney Smith (d 1986), of Birmingham, and Elsie Blanche, *née* Ward (d 1989); *b* 25 Oct 1936; *Educ* King Edward's Sch Birmingham, Brasenose Coll Oxford (BA); *m* 12 Oct 1963, Anne Elizabeth, da of John Gill Boddy, of Braunston, nr Rugby; 1 s (Mark b 1965), 1 da (Lara b 1969); *Career* Nat Serv 2 Lt RCS 1956; former cricket player: capt Oxford Univ CC 1959–60, Warwicks CCC 1958–78 (capt 1968–74), 6 tests for England; cricket admin: England selector 1969–73 and 1982–86, England mangr W Indies 1981 and NZ/Pakistan 1984, gen sec Warwicks CCC 1976–86, chief exec TCCB 1987–96; dir: Aston Villa FC 1972–78, Royds Advtg and Mktg 1970–86; *Recreations* cricket, both football codes, golf, motoring, bridge; *Clubs* MCC, I Zingari, Vincent's (Oxford); *Style*— Alan Smith, Esq, CBE; ✉ The Old Farmhouse, Wyck Rissington, Cheltenham, Glos GL54 2PN (☎ 01451 820509)

SMITH, Alan Frederick; *b* 21 July 1944; *children* 1 da (Julia Ann 1961), 1 s (Michael b 1963); *Career* Colchester Borough Cncl 1961–66, Ipswich Borough Cncl 1966–73, asst county treas Suffolk CC 1973–74, fin mangr Anglian Water 1974–75, asst fin dir Southern Water Authy 1975–80, fin dir Anglian Water Authy 1980–90, gp md Anglian Water plc 1990– (gp fin dir 1989–90); non-exec dir Peptide Theraputics Group plc; dir and govr St Felix Sch; memb CIPFA; *Style*— Alan Smith, Esq; ✉ Anglian Water plc, Ambury Rd, Huntingdon, Cambridgeshire PE18 6NZ (☎ 01480 443177)

SMITH, Prof Alan Gordon Rae; s of Alan Fife Smith (d 1976), and Jean Reid, *née* Lightbody (d 1971); *b* 22 Dec 1936; *Educ* Glasgow HS, Univ of Glasgow (Macfarlane scholar, MA), Univ of London (PhD); *m* 1972, Isabel, da of Neil McKechnie Robertson and Helen Brown; 1 s (Donald Alan Neil b 1979), 1 da (Stella Jean b 1975); *Career* research fell Inst of Historical Research Univ of London 1961–62; Univ of Glasgow: asst lectr in modern history 1962–64, lectr 1964–75, sr lectr 1975–85, reader 1985–92, head Dept of Modern History 1991–94, prof of modern history 1992–95, head Sch of History and Archaeology 1993–95, chm of history examiners 1993–94, prof in early modern history 1995–; memb Governing Bd Inst of Historical Research Univ of London 1994–; FRHistS (memb Cncl 1990–94), FRSE 1996; *Publications* author of ten books incl: Servant of the Cecils (1977), The Emergence of a Nation State (1984); *Recreations* watching sport; *Style*— Prof Alan Smith, FRSE; ✉ 5 Cargil Avenue, Kilmacolm, Inverclyde, Scotland PA13 4LS; Department of Modern History, University of Glasgow, Glasgow G12 8QQ (☎ 0141 330 5480)

SMITH, Alan K P; *Educ* Univ of Edinburgh; *Career* exec dir Marks & Spencer plc 1978–93 (joined 1964), chief exec Kingfisher plc 1993–95, chm Storehouse plc 1996–; non-exec dir: Colefax & Fowler Group plc, Booker plc 1995–; memb Bd South Bank Centre; *Style*— Alan Smith, Esq; ✉ Storehouse plc, Marylebone House, 129–137 Marylebone Road, London NW1 5QD (☎ 0171 262 3456, fax 0171 706 4072)

SMITH, Alec Quinton; JP (Herts); s of Thomas Quinton Smith (d 1953), of London Colney, Herts, and Irene Ethel, *née* Eames (d 1958); *b* 15 Dec 1927; *Educ* St Albans GS for Boys, Sch of Architecture and Surveying Northern London Poly, Brunel Univ (MA); *m* 1, 19 July 1952, Monica Joan (d 1991), da of Thomas William Hill (d 1965), of London Colney, Herts; 1 s (Graham b 1956), 1 da (Andrea b 1954); m 2, 20 Nov 1992, Barbara Joyce, da of late Alfred Leopold Gerhard; *Career* 5002 Sqdn RAF 1946–48; sr ptnr V B Johnson and Partners Chartered Surveyors 1952–90; chm: Beds and Herts Chartered Surveyors 1973, Masterbill Micro Systems Ltd 1981–91; dir Fencing Contractors Assoc 1983–; chief exec Nat Fencing Trg Authy 1991–95; tstee Lucy Kemp-Welch Meml Tst; court chm Watford Bench of Magistrates; Freeman City of London 1981, Liveryman Worshipful Co of Arbitrators 1981; FRICS 1960, FCIArb 1972 (panel memb 1972–), MScL 1987; *Recreations* photography, very light gardening; *Style*— Alec Smith, Esq, JP; ✉ The Corners, 23 Finch Lane, Bushey, Herts (☎ 0181 950 3811)

SMITH, Alex; MEP (Lab) Scotland South (majority 45,155); *Career* MEP (Lab) Scotland S 1989–; *Style*— Alex Smith, Esq, MEP; ✉ c/o European Parliament, 93–113 Rue Belliard, 1040 Brussels, Belgium

SMITH, Sir Alexander Mair (Alex); kt (1975); s of John Smith; *b* 15 Oct 1922; *Educ* Univ of Aberdeen (PhD); *m* 1, 1956, Doris, *née* Patrick (d 1980); 3 da; m 2, 1984, Jennifer, *née* Pearce; *Career* physicist with UKAEA 1952–56, dir and chief scientist Rolls Royce & Associates Ltd 1967–69 (head of advanced res Rolls Royce 1956–67), dir Manchester Poly 1969–81; chm: Ctee of Dirs of Polys 1974–76, Schs Cncls 1975–78; memb: Univ Grants Ctee 1974–76, BBC Gen Advsy Cncl 1978–81, RSA Cncl 1979–84; vice pres City & Guilds of London Inst 1981–91; FInstP; *Recreations* golf; *Style*— Sir Alex Smith; ✉ Flat Two, 6 Hall Road, Wilmslow, Cheshire SK9 5BW (☎ 01625 522011)

SMITH, Dr (Edward) Alistair; CBE (1982); s of Archibald Smith (d 1977), of Fintray, Aberdeenshire, and Jean Milne, *née* Johnston; *b* 16 Jan 1939; *Educ* Aberdeen GS, Univ of Aberdeen (MA, PhD); *Career* Univ of Aberdeen: lectr in geography 1963–88, dir Devpt Tst 1982–90, dir Overseas Office 1988–; memb Grampian Health Bd 1983–91; pres Scottish Cons and Unionist Assoc 1979–81, dep chm Scottish Cons Pty 1981–85; memb: Scot Vocational Educn Cncl Bd 1989–93, Ctee for Scotland Nature Conservancy Cncl 1989–91, NE Regnl Bd Nature Conservancy Cncl for Scotland 1991–92; *Books* Europe: A Geographical Survey of the Continent (with R E M Mellor, 1979); *Recreations* photography, travel, music; *Style*— Dr Alistair Smith, CBE; ✉ 68A Beaconsfield Place, Aberdeen AB2 4AJ (☎ 01224 642932, fax 01224 642932); University of Aberdeen, Regent Walk, Aberdeen AB9 1FX (☎ 01224 272090, fax 01224 272576, e-mail intoff@admin.aberdeen.ac.uk)

SMITH, Dr Alistair Fairley; s of Dr Arthur Fairley Smith (d 1972), and Jane Meikle Marshall Bird (d 1980); *b* 5 Oct 1935; *Educ* Bootham Sch York, Univ of Cambridge (MA, MD); *m* 13 Sept 1961, Carol Ann, da of Edmond Stephen Smith; 1 s (Charles b 1967), 1 da (Helena b 1964); *Career* house offr London Hosp 1960–61, jr asst pathologist Addenbrooke's Hosp Cambridge 1962–65, lectr (later sr lectr) in clinical chemistry Univ of Edinburgh 1965–, hon conslt Royal Infirmary of Edinburgh NHS Tst, head Diagnostic Med Serv Royal Infirmary Edinburgh; FRCPE 1964, FRCPath 1967; *Books* Multiple Choice Questions on Lecture Notes on Clinical Chemistry (1981), Lecture Notes on Clinical Biochemistry (jtly 5 edn, 1993); *Recreations* golf, bridge; *Clubs* Royal Burgess Golf, Bruntsfield Links Golf; *Style*— Dr Alistair Smith; ✉ 38 Cammo Rd, Edinburgh EH4 8AP (☎ 0131 339 4931); Department of Clinical Biochemistry, The Royal Infirmary NHS Trust, Edinburgh EH3 9YW (☎ 0131 536 2697, fax 0131 536 2758, e-mail A.F.Smith@ed.ac.uk)

SMITH, Allan Keppie; CBE; s of Allan Smith (d 1977), of Kincardineshire, and Margaret Isobel, *née* Keppie (d 1992); *b* 18 May 1932; *Educ* Univ of Aberdeen (BSc); *m* 2 Sept 1965, Mary Bridget, *née* Love, of Paisley; 1 s (Stephen Allan b 4 March 1971), 3 da (Valerie May b 18 May 1976, Fiona Margaret Keppie b 5 Dec 1981, Leanne Isabel b 20 May 1983); *Career* Nat Serv 1953–55, cmmnd REME 1954; Babcock and Wilcox: graduate trainee 1955–57, welding engr Metallurgical and Welding Dept 1957–62, facilities engr Indust Engrg Dept 1962–65, indust engrg mangr 1965–74, production dir Renfrew Works 1974–76; md: Renfrew and Dumbarton Works 1976–86, Babcock Thorn Ltd 1986–93, Rosyth Royal Dockyard plc 1986–93; dir Babcock International Group PLC 1989–93; md Facilities Mgmnt Div Babcock International Group 1991–; chm: Babcock Rosyth Defence Ltd 1993–, Rosyth Royal Dockyard PLC 1993–, Babcock New Zealand Ltd 1994–, Railcare Ltd 1995–; former pres Scot Engrg Employers Assoc, past chm Cncl Welding Inst, past memb Scot Indust Devpt Advsy Bd, fell Paisley Univ, chm Integrated Graduate Devpt Scheme Mgmnt Ctee; FEng 1990, FIMechE, FWeldI; *Recreations* DIY, shooting, gardening, restoration of farm carts; *Style*— Allan Smith, Esq, CBE, FEng; ✉ Rosyth Royal Dockyard, Rosyth, Fife KY11 2YD (☎ 01383 422001, fax 01383 417774, car 0835 343231)

SMITH, Allen Donald Warren; OBE (1984); s of Donald Charles Wesley Smith (d 1983), and Olive Kathleen Smith (d 1979); *b* 20 Oct 1922; *Educ* Ipswich Sch, Norwich City Coll (BSc(Eng) London); *m* 12 Aug 1949, June Mary, da of Kenneth Pearce (d 1946); 3 s (Andrew b 1951, Christopher b 1953, Nicholas b 1958); *Career* RAF Airfield Construction Serv 1944–47, Flt Lt, serv France, Belgium, Holland, Germany and Singapore; various engrg appts 1948–62: E Suffolk CC, Surrey CC, W Riding of Yorks CC, Somerset CC, Sir Alexander Gibbs Partners (Conslt Engrs); dep county surveyor: E Sussex CC 1962–68, Kent CC 1968–71; county surveyor Kent 1972–84, conslt transportation planning and highways; pres County Surveyor's Soc 1978–79, chm Frittenden Parish Cncl (Kent), memb RAC Public Policy Ctee 1984–94, former chm Engrg Cncl Regnl Orgn Kent and Sussex; Freeman City of London 1984, Liveryman Worshipful Co of Engrs 1984; FEng 1983, FICE, FIHT, MIWM; *Books* A History of the County Surveyors' Society 1885–1985 (1985); *Recreations* music, gardening, reading; *Clubs* RAC; *Style*— Allen Smith, Esq, OBE, FEng; ✉ Kippens, Frittenden, Cranbrook, Kent TN17 2DD (☎ 01580 852358)

SMITH, Prof (Ernest) Alwyn; CBE (1986); s of late Ernest Smith, and late Constance Barbara, *née* Webster; *b* 9 Nov 1925; *Educ* Queen Mary's Sch Walsall, Univ of Birmingham (MB, ChB, PhD); *m* 6 May 1950, Doreen Florence, da of John Preston (d 1974); 1 s (Jeremy b 1954), 1 da (Wendy b 1960); *Career* RM Lt 1943–46; prof Univ of Manchester 1967–90, pres Faculty of Community Med RCP UK 1981–86; Medaille D'Argent Academie Nationale De Medecine France; *Books* The Science of Social Medicine (1968), Genetics In Medicine (1966), Recent Advances In Community Medicine (1982 and 1985); *Recreations* sailing, birdwatching, walking; *Style*— Prof Alwyn Smith, CBE; ✉ Plum Tree Cottage, Arnside, via Carnforth LA5 0AH (☎ 01524 761976)

SMITH, Dr Andrew Benjamin; s of Benjamin Butler Smith, of Stonehaven, Grampian, and Elsie Marjory, *née* Flemming; *b* 6 Feb 1954; *Educ* Mackie Acad Stonehaven, Univ of Edinburgh (BSc), Univ of Exeter (PhD); *m* 18 Aug 1976, Mary Patricia Cumming, da of David Cumming Simpson; 2 da (Katherine Heather b 22 Jan 1985, Fiona Margaret b 18 April 1987); *Career* post-doctoral research asst Univ of Liverpool 1979–81 and 1982–83 (temp lectr in geology 1981–82), research scientist Dept of Palaeontology The Natural History Museum 1983–; Bicentenary Medal Linnean Soc 1993, Bigsby Medal Geological Soc 1995; Hon DSc Univ of Edinburgh 1989; FRSE 1996; *Books* Echinoid Palaeolbiology (1984), Systematics and the fossil record: discovering evolutionary patterns (1994); *Style*— Dr Andrew Smith, FRSE; ✉ Department of Palaeontology, The Natural History Museum, Cromwell Road, London SW7 5BD (☎ 0171 938 8925, fax 0171 938 9277)

SMITH, Andrew Charles; QC (1990); *Educ* Univ of Oxford (BA); *Career* called to the Bar Middle Temple 1974; *Style*— Andrew Smith, Esq, QC; ✉ Fountain Court, Temple, London EC4Y 9DH

SMITH, Andrew David; MP (Lab) Oxford East (majority 7,538); s of late David E C Smith, and Georgina H J Smith; *b* 1 Feb 1951; *Educ* Reading Sch, St John's Coll Oxford (BA, BPhil); *m* 26 March 1976, Valerie, da of William Labert; 1 s; *Career* Oxford City

Cncl: cncllr 1976–87, chm Recreation and Amenities Ctee 1980–83, chm Planning Ctee 1985–87, chm Race and Community Relations Ctee 1985–87; relations offr Oxford and Swindon Co-op Soc 1979–87; MP (Lab) Oxford E 1987–; memb Social Servs Select Ctee 1988–89; oppn front bench spokesman: on higher educn 1988–92, on Treasy & econ affrs 1992–94; shadow chief sec to Treasy 1994–96, shadow sec of state for tport 1996–; memb Parly Panel Union of Shop Distributive and Allied Workers 1986, jt sec All Pty Gp for Overseas Devpt 1987–94; chm Govrs of Oxford Brookes Univ (formerly Oxford Poly) 1987–93; *Clubs* Blackbird Leys Community Assoc; *Style*— Andrew Smith, MP; ✉ 4 Flaxfield Rd, Blackbird Leys, Oxford OX4 5QD; Constituency (☎ 01865 772893); House of Commons, London SW1 (☎ 0171 219 5102)

SMITH, Prof Andrew Paul; *b* 3 Aug 1952, Liss, Hampshire; *Educ* Cambridgeshire HS, UCL (BSc, PhD); *m*; 1 s, 2 da; *Career* post-doctoral res fell Dept of Experimental Psychology Univ of Oxford 1976–82, scientist MRC Perceptual and Cognitive Performance Unit Univ of Sussex 1982–88, Charles Hunnisett res fell Laboratory of Experimental Psychology Univ of Sussex 1989–90, dir Health Psychology Res Unit and reader Sch of Psychology UWCC 1990–93, prof Dept of Psychology Univ of Bristol 1993–; memb Mgmnt Ctee Agro-Food Quality Link Prog; CPsychol, FBPsS; *Publications* author of numerous articles in learned periodicals; *Style*— Prof Andrew Smith; (☎ 0117 928 8453, fax 0117 928 8671)

SMITH, Anne; QC (Scot 1993); da of John Mather (d 1963), of London, and Jessica, *née* Douglas; *b* 16 March 1955; *Educ* Jordanhill Coll Glasgow, Cheadle County GS for Girls, Univ of Edinburgh (LLB Hons, medallist in Criminal Law); *m* 22 Sept 1979, David Alexander Smith, WS, s of William Duncan Smith; 1 s (William Iain b 6 Aug 1983), 1 da (Charlotte Alexandra b 14 Aug 1985); *Career* apprenticed Shepherd & Wedderburn, WS 1977–79, pupil of Lord McGhie 1979–80, admitted Faculty of Advocates 1980, in full time practice 1980–; *Recreations* being with my children, music (piano and flute), aerobics, hill-walking, gardening, skiing; *Style*— Mrs Anne Smith, QC; ✉ Bank House, Albert Terrace, Edinburgh EH10 5EA (☎ 0131 447 1449, fax 0131 447 0435); Advocates' Library, Parliament House, Edinburgh EH1 1RF (☎ 0131 226 5071, fax 0131 225 3642)

SMITH, Anthony David; CBE (1987); s of Henry Smith (d 1951), and Esther, *née* Berdiowsky (d 1967); *b* 14 March 1938; *Educ* Harrow Co Sch, Brasenose Coll Oxford (BA); *Career* current affrs prodr BBC TV 1960–71, fell St Antony's Coll Oxford 1971–76, dir BFI 1979–88, memb Bd Channel Four TV Co 1980–84, pres Magdalen Coll Oxford 1988–; memb: Acton Soc Trust 1978–, Writers and Scholars Educn Tst 1982–, Arts Cncl of GB 1990–; *Books* The Shadow in the Cave: The Broadcaster, the Audience and the State (1973), British Broadcasting (1974), The British Press since the War (1976), Subsidies and the Press in Europe (1977), The Politics of Information (1978), Television and Political Life (1979), The Newspaper: An International History (1979), Newspapers and Democracy (1980), Goodbye Gutenberg - The Newspaper Revolution of the 1980's (1980), The Geopolitics of Information (1980), The Age of Behemoths - the Globalisation of Mass Media Firms (1991), From Books to Bytes (1993); *Style*— Anthony Smith, Esq, CBE; ✉ Albany, Piccadilly, London W1V 9RP (☎ 0171 734 5494); Magdalen College, Oxford (☎ 01865 276101)

SMITH, Anthony John Francis; s of Hubert J F Smith (d 1984), of Dorset, and Diana, *née* Watkin (d 1990); *b* 30 March 1926; *Educ* The Dragon Sch Oxford, Blundell's Sch Devon, Balliol Coll Oxford (MA); *m* 1, 1 Sept 1956 (m dis 1983), Barbara Dorothy, da of Maj-Gen Charles Richard Newman CB, CMG, DSO (d 1954), of Ottery St Mary, Devon; 1 s (Adam b 1963), 2 da (Polly b 1968, Laura b 1969); m 2, 1984, Margaret Ann (formerly Mrs Holloway), da of George Hounsom (d 1987); 1 s (Quintin b 1986); *Career* RAF 1944–48; reporter Manchester Guardian 1953–57, sci corr Daily Telegraph 1957–63, freelance broadcaster, author and journalist 1964–; FRGS 1966, FZS 1969; *Books* Blind White Fish in Persia (1953), High Street Africa (1961), Throw Out Two Hands (1963), The Body (1968), The Dangerous Sort (1970), Mato Grosso (1971), The Human Pedigree (1975), Wilderness (1978), A Persian Quarter Century (1979), The Mind (1984), Smith & Son (1984), The Great Rift (1988), Explorers of the Amazon (1990), The Free Life (1994); for children: Which Animal Are You? (1988), Best Friends (1990), Swaps (1992), The Free Life (1995), Sex, Genes and All That (1997); *Recreations* ballooning; *Clubs* Explorers (NY); *Style*— Anthony Smith, Esq; ✉ 10 Aldbourne Rd, London W12 (☎ 0181 248 9589); St Aidan's, Bamburgh, Northumberland

SMITH, Anthony Patrick; s of Edward Smith, and Gladys, *née* Green; *b* 7 Aug 1939; *Educ* Latymer Sch, Open Univ (BA), Poly of Central London (MA); *m* 1965, Barbara Marie, *née* Johnson; 1 da (Vanessa); *Career* registered general and psychiatric nurse; former dir of nurse educn School of Nursing Univ of Southampton; currently chief exec offr English National Board for Nursing, Midwifery and Health Visiting; former memb UK Nursing Delgn to America, Forence Nightingale scholar and fell Florence Nightingale Fndn; RGN, RMN; *Recreations* keen collector of Staffordshire pottery, countryside, Labrador dogs; *Clubs* Sloane; *Style*— Anthony Smith, Esq; ✉ English National Board for Nursing, Midwifery and Health Visiting, Victory House, 170 Tottenham Court Road, London W1P 0HA (☎ 0171 388 3131, fax 0171 383 4031)

SMITH, Antony Gervase; s of Gervase Gorst Smith, JP (d 1963), and Gladys Alford (d 1968); *b* 31 July 1927; *Educ* Haileybury; *m* 4 Nov 1955, Penelope, da of Pearson Faux, of Durban, Natal (d 1964); 1 s (Julian Gervase b 21 Feb 1958), 2 da (Miranda b 9 March 1962, Philippa b 30 April 1963); *Career* Belt of Honour 60th Rifles OCTU, served KRRC 1945–48, Capt Queen Victoria's Rifles 1948–52; dir Long Till & Colvin 1960–68, md Astley & Pearce (Sterling) 1980, chm MH Cockell Ltd 1987; Liveryman Worshipful Co of Turners 1969; *Recreations* shooting, walking a labrador; *Clubs* Army & Navy, Royal Green Jackets; *Style*— Antony Gervase Smith, Esq; ✉ Cozen's House, Orcheston, Salisbury, Wilts SP3 4RW (☎ 01980 620257)

SMITH, (Brian) Arthur John; s of Sydney Frederick Smith, of Bath, and Hazel Nora, *née* Kirk; *b* 27 Nov 1954; *Educ* Roan Sch, Univ of East Anglia (BA); *Career* writer and comedian; former teacher and road sweeper, fndr memb National Revue Co (produced 5 series of The Good Human Guide on BBC Radio 2 and 4), as solo comedian hosted First Exposure (BBC) and Paramount City (BBC), reg contrib Loose Ends (Radio 4), fndr comedy double act Fiasco Job Job with Phil Nice (C4 series Arthur and Phil Go Off 1985); author of plays: Live Bed Show (nominated for Perrier and Independent Theatre Awards 1989, Garrick Theatre 1995), Trench Kiss, An Evening With Gary Lineker (with Chris England, Edinburgh Festival then Duchess Theatre (nominated Best Comedy Olivier Awards 1992)) 1991–92, Arthur Smith Sings Andy Williams (Edinburgh, London, NY) 1992–93, Sod (with Nigel Cole) 1993; presenter: Arthur Smith on the Floor (BBC Radio 5) 1994, Sentimental Journeys (BBC Radio 4) 1994; wrote and performed Hamlet 1995; *Books* Trench Kiss (1990), An Evening With Gary Lineker (with Chris England, 1992); *Recreations* smoking, sleeping; *Clubs* Players, Macreadies, Arthur Cravan Soc (chm 1990–); *Style*— Arthur Smith, Esq

SMITH, Barrie Edwin; OBE (1994), JP (Sheffield, 1979); *m* June; 2 da (Dawn, Helen); *Career* chartered accountant; Nat Serv 1959–61; articled clerk JE Forsdike & Co 1953–58; Franklin Greening: audit mangr 1961, ptnr 1964, co merged with Pannell Kerr Forster 1971, taxation ptnr 1971, managing ptnr 1988–92, chm S Yorks practice 1993–96, conslt 1996–; dir: Congregational & General Insurance plc, Congregational & General Charitable Trust, Northern General Hosp Tst, Health & Care plc, Knowle House (Services) Limited; past pres: Sheffield Chamber of Commerce (memb of Cncl and Econ and Industl Affairs Ctee), Sheffield and District Soc of CA, Rotary Club of Abbeydale; elder Central United Reformed Church, tstee S Yorks Historic Churches Tst, life patron S Yorks Opera; Freeman City of London, memb Worshipful Co of CAs; MInstD, FRSA, FIMgt; *Recreations* gardening, maintaining a Victorian house, keeping fit by running, badminton, walking, keen interest in soccer; *Style*— Barrie E Smith, Esq, OBE, JP; ✉ Pannell Kerr Forster, Knowle House, 4 Norfolk Park Road, Sheffield S2 3QE (☎ 0114 276 7991, fax 0114 275 3538)

SMITH, (Donald) Barry; *b* 22 May 1948; *m* 1 Nov 1975, Sophie Janina, *née* Pasko (Rachel b 1978, Claire b 1980, Alice b 1986); *Career* divnl fin accountant Showerings Vine Products & Whiteways Ltd 1971–78, accountant CH Beazer Holdings plc 1973–78, sr ptnr Rossiter Smith & Co Chartered Accountants 1978–; Dolphin Packaging plc: fin dir 1987–89, chm 1989–90, dep chm 1990–; FCA 1971, ATII 1972; *Style*— Barry Smith, Esq; ✉ Rossiter Smith & Co, Bank House, 1 Burlington Road, Bristol BS6 6TJ (☎ 0117 973 0863, fax 0117 923 7929)

SMITH, Prof Barry Edward; s of Ernest Edward Smith (d 1977), and Agnes Mary, *née* DeFraine (d 1957); *b* 15 Nov 1939; *Educ* Dr Challoner's GS Amersham, Royal Melbourne Tech Coll, Hatfield Tech Coll, Univ of Exeter (BSc), Univ of E Anglia (PhD); *m* 7 Sept 1963, Pamela Heather, *née* Pullen; 1 da (Tamzin Sarah b 23 Nov 1964), 1 s (Joel Dominic Barnaby b 4 Feb 1968); *Career* trainee chemist ICIANZ Central Res Laboratories 1956–59, lab asst Polymers Div ICI 1959–60, Univ of Exeter 1960–64, Univ of E Anglia 1964–66, res fell Univ of Washington Seattle 1966–68, SRC res fell Physical Chemistry Laboratory Univ of Oxford 1968–69, sr princ scientific offr ARC Unit of Nitrogen Fixation 1985 (sr scientific offr 1969–74, princ scientific offr 1974–85), asst dir Unit of Nitrogen Fixation 1986, head and dep chief scientific offr Nitrogen Fixation Laboratory AFRC Inst of Plant Science Res 1987–; Univ of Sussex: hon reader Sch of Chemistry and Molecular Sciences Univ of Sussex 1985, hon reader in biochemistry Sch of Biological Sciences 1986, hon professorial fell 1989–95; hon prof Sch of Chemical Scis Univ of E Anglia 1995–; visiting prof Univ of Essex 1988–; memb Int Steering Ctee for Int Symposia on Nitrogen Fixation 1988–, convenor Enzyme Cmmn Panel on Nomenclature of Molybdenum Enzymes; memb: Biochemical Soc, Br Biophysical Soc; ed Biochemical Jl, author of numerous pubns in scientific jls; MRSC; *Recreations* gardening and bridge; *Style*— Prof Barry Smith; ✉ Nitrogen Fixation Laboratory, John Innes Centre, Colney, Norwich NR4 7UH (☎ 01603 456900 ext 2720, fax 01603 455030/454970)

SMITH, Barry Howard; *b* 8 Sept 1949; *Educ* QMC London (LLB); *Career* admitted slr 1974; media and entertainment ptnr Richards Butler 1980–; *Recreations* art, cinema, theatre; *Style*— Barry Smith, Esq; ✉ Richards Butler, Beaufort House, 15 St Botolph St, London EC3A 7EE (☎ 0171 247 6555, telex 949494 RBLAW G, fax 0171 247 5091)

SMITH, (John) Brian; s of Sydney John Smith (d 1979), of Beaconsfield, and Florence May Dean Smith; *b* 5 June 1928; *Educ* Bradford GS, Sidney Sussex Coll Cambridge (MA); *m* 23 July 1953, Joan Margaret, da of Horace Newton Jennings (d 1951), of Bradford; 2 s (Timothy b 1954, Nicholas b 1962), 2 da (Penelope b 1956, Joanna b 1963); *Career* dir: The Rank Organisation 1976–83, Manganese Bronze Holdings plc 1984–93, Gerald Gobert Holdings Ltd 1985–95; chm: J B Smith Consultants Ltd 1983–, Eagle Trust plc 1989–96, Samuelson Group plc 1990–, D Pavis Group Ltd 1991–93, Visual Action plc 1996–; dep chm: British Bd of Film Classification 1992–, LEP Group plc 1992–96; memb Bucks CC 1985–89; Freeman: City of London, Worshipful Co of Scientific Instrument Makers; FInstD, CIMgt 1981; *Recreations* golf, tennis, bridge; *Style*— Brian Smith, Esq; ✉ Hebden House, Eghams Close, Beaconsfield, Bucks HP9 1XN (☎ 01494 673063, fax 01494 676212, car 0836 229819)

SMITH, Brian; CMG (1993), OBE (1975); s of Charles Francis Smith (d 1966), and Grace Amelia, *née* Pope (d 1972); *b* 15 Sept 1935; *Educ* Hull GS, Open Univ (BSc); *m* 1955, Joan Patricia, da of Ernest John Rivers (d 1991); 1 s, 2 da; *Career* RAPC 1954–57; HM Dip Serv 1952–54 and 1957–94: FO 1952, Bahrain 1957, Qatar 1959, vice consul Luxembourg 1960, Morocco 1962, Iran 1964, Switzerland 1967–69, FCO 1969, Uganda 1973, Iran 1975–77, FCO 1977, dep consul gen NY USA 1979, commercial cnsllr Bonn FDR 1982–86, overseas inspector FCO 1986; Br high cmmr: Botswana 1989–91, Trinidad 1991–94, ret; *Recreations* horse riding, reading, embroidery; *Style*— Brian Smith, Esq, CMG, OBE; ✉ c/o Foreign & Commonwealth Office, King Charles Street, London SW1

SMITH, Dr (Eric) Brian; s of Eric Smith, and Dilys Olwen, *née* Hughes; *b* 10 Oct 1933; *Educ* Mold Alun Sch, Wirral GS, Univ of Liverpool (BSc, PhD); *m* 1, 31 Aug 1957 (m dis 1977), Margaret; 2 s (Mark b 10 Sept 1961, Nicholas b 27 Jan 1965), 1 da (Caroline b 14 Jan 1960); m 2, 9 July 1983, Regina Arvidson Ball; *Career* Univ of Oxford: ICI fell 1959–60, fell St Catherine's Coll and lectr in physical chemistry 1960–88, master St Catherine's Coll 1988–93 (vice master 1984–85); vice chllr Univ of Wales Cardiff 1993–; FRCS; *Books* Basic Chemical Thermodynamics (1973–1980), Intermolecular Forces (jtly, 1981), Forces Between Molecules (jtly, 1986); *Recreations* mountaineering; *Clubs* Alpine, Gorphwysfa; *Style*— Dr Brian Smith; ✉ University of Wales, Cardiff, PO Box 920, Cardiff CF1 3XP (☎ 01222 874 835, fax 01222 874 879)

SMITH, Dr (Norman) Brian; CBE (1980); s of Vincent Smith (d 1963), and Louise, *née* Horsfield; *b* 10 Sept 1928; *Educ* Sir John Deane's GS Northwich, Univ of Manchester (BSc, MSc, PhD); *m* 2 April 1955, Phyllis, da of Edmund and Sarah Ellen Crossley; 2 s (Clive b 1959 d 1964, David b 1961), 1 da (Jane b 1962); *Career* tech offr ICI Terylene Cncl 1954; ICI Fibres Div: textiles devpt dir 1969, dep chm 1972, chm 1975–78; dir ICI Ltd 1978–85; chm: ICI America Inc 1981–85, ICI of Canada Ltd 1981–85; dir: Fiber Industries Inc 1972–83, Canadian Industries Ltd 1981–85; Lister & Co plc: non-exec dir 1985–90, dep chm 1990–91, chm 1991–94; chm: MB Group plc (formerly Metal Box plc) 1986–89 (dep chm 1985), BAA plc 1991–, Hydron Ltd 1994–, Cable & Wireless plc 1995– (non-exec dir 1988–June 95); non-exec dir: Carrington Viyella 1979–81, Davy Corporation plc 1986–91, Yorkshire Chemicals plc 1990–91, Berisford International plc 1990–96, Mercury Communications Ltd 1990–93; chm: Man-Made Fibres Producers Ctee 1976–78, Wool Textile EDC 1979–81, BOTB N American Advsy Gp 1983–87, Priorities Bd for Res and Devpt in Agric and Food 1987–92, Heatherwood and Wexham Park Hosps NHS Tst 1991–, Standing Conf on Schools' Science and Technol 1992–96; pres Br Textile Confederation 1977–79, memb BOTB 1980–81 and 1983–87, dir Oxford Diocesan Board of Finance 1990–; Freeman City of London 1986, Liveryman Worshipful Co of Glovers 1986; Hon DBA, IMC Buckingham 1990; FTI 1981, CIMgt 1985, FCIM; *Recreations* sailing, tennis, gardening; *Clubs* Brooks's; *Style*— Dr N Brian Smith, CBE

SMITH, Rt Rev Brian Arthur; *see:* Tonbridge, Bishop of

SMITH, Prof Brian Clive; s of Cyril Ernest Smith, of Barton-on-Sea, Hants, and Hilda Jane, *née* Padengtion; *b* 23 Jan 1938; *Educ* Colfe's GS, Univ of Exeter (BA, PhD), McMaster Univ Ontario Canada (MA); *m* 27 Aug 1960, Jean, da of Frank Baselow, of Norwich; 1 s (David William b 22 Aug 1968), 1 da (Rebecca Jane b 23 Aug 1963); *Career* lectr in politics Univ of Exeter 1963–70, lectr in public admin Civil Service Coll 1970–72, reader in politics Univ of Bath 1980–89 (sr lectr in politics 1972–80), head Dept of Political Sci and Social Policy Univ of Dundee 1989–93, currently dean of arts and social scis Univ of Dundee; memb Political Studies Assoc; *Books* Regionalism in England (1964), Field Administration - An Aspect of Decentralisation (1967), Advising Ministers (1969), Administering Britain (with J Stanyer, 1976), Policy Making in British Government (1976), Government Departments - An Organisation Perspective (with D C Pitt, 1980), The Computer Revolution in Public Administration (ed with D C Pitt, 1984), Decentralisation - The Territorial Dimension of the State (1985), Bureaucracy and Political Power (1987), Progress in Devlopment Administration (ed, 1992), Understanding Third World Politics (1996); *Recreations* walking, travel; *Style*— Prof

Brian Smith; ✉ Dean of Arts and Social Sciences, University of Dundee, Dundee DD1 4HN (☎ 01382 23181, fax 01382 201604)

SMITH, Brian Roy; s of Arthur Roy Smith (d 1971), and Phyllis Edith Smith (d 1990); *b* 18 Aug 1937; *Educ* Sir George Monoux GS; *m* 4 July 1959, Barbara Gladys, da of James Richard Beasley (d 1980); 1 s (Stewart Spencer b 26 Jan 1963), 1 da (Justine Caroline b 10 April 1967); *Career* RAF 1956–58; English & American INSOE Co 1959–68, B R Smith and Others (Lloyd's Syndicate) 1969–; chm Garwyn Ltd 1972–; dir: Reed Stenhouse Syndicates Ltd 1976–85, Bankside Syndicates Ltd 1985–, Bankside Members Agency Ltd 1985–, Bankside Underwriting Agencies Ltd 1985–, Cotesworth and Co Ltd 1985–; memb Lloyd's 1972– (memb Non Marine Assoc Ctee 1985–), non-exec dir QBE Lloyd's Agency 1996–; *Recreations* golf, tennis, theatre, opera, boating; *Clubs* Weald Park Golf; *Style*— Brian Smith, Esq; ✉ Bishops Hall, Lambourne End, Essex (☎ 0181 500 6510); B R Smith and Others, 120 Middlesex St, London EC1 (☎ 0171 247 0304)

SMITH, Brian Stanley; s of Ernest Stanley Smith (ka 1943), of Leeds, and Dorothy Maud Smith; *b* 15 May 1932; *Educ* Bloxham, Keble Coll Oxford (BA, MA); *m* 28 Sept 1963, Alison Margaret, da of Robert George Alexander Hemming, of Cardross, Dumbarton; 2 da (Frances b 1964, Jennifer b 1966); *Career* archivist: Worcs 1956–58, Essex 1958–60, Glos 1961–68 (co archivist 1968–79); pt/t ed Victoria Co Hist Glos 1968–70, sec Royal Cmmn on Historical Manuscripts 1982–92 (asst sec 1980–81); vice pres Bristol and Glos Archaeological Soc 1987– (ed 1971–79, pres 1986–87); FSA 1972, FRHistS 1980, FRSA 1991, memb Soc of Archivists (chm 1979–80); *Books* History of Malvern (1964, second edn 1987), History of Bristol and Gloucestershire (1972, third edn 1996), The Cotswolds (1976), History of Bloxham School (1978), Manuscript sources for the history of St Helena (1996); *Recreations* mountaineering, gardening, historical research; *Style*— Brian Smith, Esq, FSA; ✉ Bryn Farm, Vowchurch Common, Hereford HR2 0RL (☎ 01981 550623)

SMITH, Brian Ward; s of Frederick George Smith (d 1979), and Violet Barbara, *née* Whitbread (d 1983); *b* 15 July 1937; *Educ* Trinity Sch of John Whitgift Croydon, Christ's Coll Cambridge (coll scholar, BA), Univ of Calif at Berkeley (Fulbright scholar, MS); *m* 9 Feb 1963, Ann Buckingham; 2 s (Jonathan Ward b 26 May 1966, Matthew Simon (twin)), 1 da (Sarah Jane b 18 June 1969); *Career* civil and structural engr; design engr Ove Arup and Partners 1961, Univ of California 1962–64; Flint & Neill (consulting engrs): joined 1964, assoc 1974, ptnr 1977, sr ptnr 1993–; memb Exec Cncl Int Assoc for Shell and Spatial Structures, Building Research Estab visitor 1992–97; author of various specialist articles for the technical press; FICE, FIStructE, FASCE, MConsE, FEng 1994; *Recreations* painting/drawing, walking, skiing; *Clubs* Ski Club of GB; *Style*— Brian Smith, Esq, FEng; ✉ Flint & Neill Partnership, 6th Floor, 21 Dartmouth Street, London SW1H 9BT (☎ 0171 227 1950, fax 0171 227 1951)

SMITH, (William Wilson) Campbell; s of Stanley Smith (d 1993), of Glasgow, and Winifred Agnes Erskine, *née* Wilson; *b* 17 May 1946; *Educ* Glasgow Acad, St Catharine's Coll Cambridge (exhibitioner, MA), Univ of Glasgow (LLB); *m* 13 April 1974, Elizabeth Margaret, da of Maj Tom Richards; 2 da (Emma Jane Campbell b 24 May 1977, Catherine Elizabeth Campbell b 30 Oct 1979); *Career* trainee slr Biggart Lumsden & Co Glasgow (qualified 1972), asst slr Herbert Smith & Co London 1972–73, ptnr Biggart Baillie & Gifford Slrs Glasgow 1974–; Freeman City of Glasgow; memb: Incorporation of Barbers Glasgow 1970– (deacon 1989–90), Incorporation of Cordiners Glasgow 1975–; memb: Law Soc of Scot 1972, Int Bar Assoc; *Recreations* barbershop singing, golf, croquet; *Clubs* Royal Scottish Automobile, Glasgow Golf; *Style*— Campbell Smith, Esq; ✉ Parklea, 16 Dargarvel Avenue, Dumbreck, Glasgow G41 5LU (☎ 0141 427 0267); Biggart Baillie & Gifford, Dalmore House, 310 St Vincent Street, Glasgow G2 5QR (☎ 0141 228 8000, fax 0141 228 8310)

SMITH, Carl Bernard; s of Peter Smith, West Bridgford, Nottingham, and Ada Elizabeth, *née* Barclay (d 1990); *b* 1 Dec 1961; *Educ* West Bridgford Comp Sch, Basford Hall Coll (City & Guilds exam, ONC, HND), Trent Poly (BSc); *m* 1985, Rosalind Ann, da of Geoffrey Stanforth (d 1971); 1 s (Benjamin Carl b 29 Oct 1987), 1 da (Lydia Ann b 7 Sept 1989); *Career* rower; memb: Nottingham Boat Club, Nottingham County Rowing Assoc; eleventh place Men's Quad Sculls Jr World Championship Moscow 1979; World Championships (Men's Lightweights): ninth place Single Sculls Munich 1981, Silver medal Coxless Fours Duisberg 1983, Bronze medal Coxless Fours Montreal 1984, eighth place Double Skulls Hazelwinkel 1985, Gold medal Double Sculls Nottingham 1986, Bronze medal Double Skulls Copenhagen 1987, eighth place Single Fours Milan 1988, Bronze medal Eights Tasmania 1990; Henley Royal Regatta: winner Wyfold Challenge Cup (Coxless Fours) 1982 and 1984, winner (record time) Ladies Challenge Plate (Eights) 1989, winner Thames Challenge Cup (Eights) 1990; winner Grand Challenge Cup (Eights) Japanese Henley Royal Henley Regatta Tokyo 1990; Cwlth Games Edinburgh 1986: Bronze medal Men's Heavyweight Double Sculls, Bronze medal Men's Lightweight Single Sculls; Nat Championships of GB: Gold medal Jr Men's Quad Sculls 1979, Bronze medal Men's Lightweight Double Sculls 1980, Men's Lightweight Single Sculls (Gold medal 1981, Silver medal 1982), Gold medal Men's Lightweight Coxless Fours 1983 and 1984, Gold medal Men's Heavyweight and Men's Lightweights Double Sculls 1985, Gold medal Men's Heavyweight and Men's Lightweights Eights (record times) 1990; Head of the River Race for Scullers: Gold medal Men's Lightweight Single Sculls 1982–86 and 1988–90, winner Heavyweight Div 1985; Head of the River Race for Fours: Gold medal Men's Heavyweight Quad Sculls 1985–88 and 1990, Heavyweight Div 1985; Gold medal Men's Heavyweight Quad Sculls Head of the River Race for Fours 1985–88 and 1990; Lucerne Int Regatta: Bronze medal Men's Lightweight Coxless Fours 1983, Gold medal Men's Lightweight Double Sculls 1986–87, fifth Men's Lightweight Single Sculls 1988, Silver medal (world record in heat) Men's Lightweight Eights 1990 (fourth 1989); Gold medal (world record time) World Rowing Championships Vienna 1991; Gold medal World Lightweight Championships Montreal 1992, fifth World Championships 1993, 18th place World Lightweight Double Sculls Finland 1995, 4th place World Lightweight Eights Strathclyde 1996; winner: Henley Royal Regatta Stewards' Challenge Cup 1992, UK Nat Championships, Lightweight Eights Pairs Int Regatta 1994, Gold medal Lucerne Regatta Lightweight Eights 1994, Gold medal Lightweight Eights World Rowing Championships Indianapolis 1994; *Awards* Nottingham Boat Oarsman of the Year 1986, Ted Moult Meml Award for E Midland Sports Aid 1989, Minet Trophy for Int Rower of the Year 1994; *Style*— Carl Smith, Esq; ✉ 33 Jumelles Drive, Calverton, Nottingham NG13 6QD (☎ 0115 965 3160); Nottinghamshire County Rowing Association, National Water Sports Centre, Holme Pierrepont, Nottingham; Mrs M Marshall, 60 Green Lane, Ockbrook, Derby DE7 3SE (☎ 01332 673619)

SMITH, Sheriff Charles; s of Charles Smith (d 1973), of Perth, and Mary Allan, *née* Hunter (d 1988); *b* 15 Aug 1930; *Educ* Kinnoull Sch, Perth Acad, Univ of St Andrews (MA, LLB); *m* 1959, Janet Elizabeth, da of James Hurst (d 1942); 1 s (Charles), 1 da (Jennifer); *Career* admitted slr 1956; princ Perth 1961–82; temp sheriff 1977–82; sheriff: of Glasgow and Strathkelvin 1982–86, of Tayside Central and Fife at Perth 1986–91, of Tayside Central and Fife at Cupar and Dundee 1991–; memb: Perth Town Cncl 1966–68, Cncl Law Soc of Scotland (convenor various ctees) 1977–82, Cncl Sheriffs' Assoc 1988–91; *Recreations* tennis, golf, croquet; *Style*— Sheriff Charles Smith; ✉ c/o Sheriff Court, Cupar, Tayside (☎ 01334 652121)

SMITH, Sir Charles Bracewell; *see:* Bracewell-Smith, Sir Charles

SMITH, Charles John Wolstenholme; s of Dr Maurice Wolstenholme Smith, of Leamington Spa, Warks, and Winifred Daisy, *née* Parr; *b* 7 Dec 1940; *Educ* Uppingham; *m* 2 Nov 1968, Jennifer Ann, da of John Robinson Bennett; 2 s (Edward Charles Wolstenholme b 15 Dec 1970, Henry James Wolstenholme b 23 Dec 1973); *Career* articled Burgis & Bullock Leamington Spa 1959–64, joined Foster & Stephens 1964 (became Touche Ross & Co); ptnr: Touche Ross & Co 1967–92, Gearey Smith & Windle 1992–; FCA 1974 (ACA 1964); *Recreations* horse riding, golf, tennis; *Clubs* Olton Golf; *Style*— Charles Smith, Esq; ✉ Gearey Smith & Windle, One Waterloo Street, Birmingham B2 5PG (☎ 0121 633 0633, fax 0121 632 5433)

SMITH, Christopher Gordon; s of Maj (Joseph) Gordon Smith, of St Aster, Duras 47120, France, and Sheila Mary, *née* Gleeson (d 1982); *b* 3 Sept 1952; *Educ* The Abbey Sch Fort Augustus; *m* 16 Aug 1980, Jean Helen, da of (James Craufuird) Roger Inglis, of Gifford, E Lothian, Scotland; 1 s (Jeremy b 14 June 1983), 1 da (Camilla b 4 June 1985); *Career* dir: C R McRitchie & Co Ltd (co sec 1977–84), Norloch Ltd (co sec 1977–84); dir Noble Grossart Ltd 1989– (treas 1985, asst dir 1987–89); *Recreations* squash, skiing, running; *Clubs* Edinburgh Sports; *Style*— Christopher G Smith, Esq; ✉ 1 Wester Coates Terrace, Edinburgh EH12 5LR; Noble Grossart Ltd, 48 Queen St, Edinburgh (☎ 0131 226 7011, fax 0131 226 6032)

SMITH, Rev Christopher Hughes; s of Rev Bernard Hughes Smith (d 1963), of Petts Wood, Orpington, Kent, and Dorothy Lucy, *née* Parker (d 1985); *b* 30 Nov 1929; *Educ* Bolton Sch, Emmanuel Coll and Wesley House Cambridge (BA, MA); *m* 28 July 1956, (Margaret) Jean, da of Frank Passmore Smith (d 1960), of Middlesbrough; 3 s (Jeremy b 1959, Philip b 1962, Robert b 1964), 1 foster s (Ernest b 1962); *Career* Nat Serv RAOC 1948–50, Sgt 1950; intercollegiate sec Student Christian Movement 1955–58, Leicester (S) Methodist Circuit 1958–65, Birmingham (SW) Methodist Circuit 1965–74, chm Birmingham Methodist Dist 1974–87, Lancaster Methodist Circuit 1987–88, gen sec Div of Educn and Youth 1988–95; pres Methodist Conf 1985–86, jt pres Birmingham Cncl of Christian Churches 1976–87, pres Nat Christian Educn Cncl 1995–; dir Methodist Newspapers Co Ltd; tstee Nat Assoc of Christian Communities and Networks, govr Queen's Coll Birmingham; Hon MA Univ of Birmingham 1985, hon fell Selly Oak Colls Birmingham 1992; *Books* Music of the Heart: Methodist Spirituality; *Recreations* walking, books, gardening; *Style*— The Rev Christopher Hughes Smith; ✉ 12 Spean Court, Wollaton Road, Nottingham NG8 1GL (☎ 0115 928 5662)

SMITH, Christopher Robert (Chris); MP (Lab) Islington South and Finsbury (majority 10,652); s of Colin Smith, and Gladys, *née* Luscombe; *b* 24 July 1951; *Educ* George Watson's Coll Edinburgh, Pembroke Coll Cambridge (PhD), Harvard (Kennedy scholar); *Career* cncllr London Borough of Islington 1978–83 (chief whip 1978–79, chm Housing Ctee 1981–83); Parly candidate (Lab) Epsom and Ewell 1979, MP (Lab) Islington S and Finsbury 1983–; ASTMS branch: sec 1978–80, chm 1980–83; memb Cncl for Nat Parks, housing devpt worker, memb Environment Select Ctee 1983–87; chm: Tribune Group of MPs 1988–89 (sec 1984–88), Lab Campaign for criminal justice 1985–88; oppn front bench spokesman on Treasy and econ affrs 1987–92, memb Shadow Cabinet 1992–, chief oppn spokesman on environmental protection 1992–94, shadow nat heritage sec 1994–95; chief oppn spokesman on: social security 1995–96, health 1996–; pres Lab Environment Capaign (SERA) 1992–; chm Bd Tribune Newspaper 1990–93, chm Bd New Century Magazine 1993–96; memb: Bd of Shelter 1987–92, Exec Ctee NCCL 1986–88, Bd Sadler's Wells Theatre 1986–93, Exec Ctee Fabian Soc 1992– (vice chm 1995–96), Exec Ctee Nat Tst 1995–, tstee John Muir Tst 1991–; *Recreations* literature, music, theatre, mountaineering; *Style*— Chris Smith, Esq, MP; ✉ House of Commons, London SW1A 0AA (☎ 0171 219 5119)

SMITH, Sir Christopher Sydney Winwood; 5 Bt (UK 1809) of Eardiston, Worcestershire; s of Sir William Sydney Winwood Smith, 4 Bt (d 1953); *b* 20 Sept 1906; *m* 1932, Phyllis Berenice, yst da of late Thomas Robert O'Grady; 6 s, 3 da; *Heir* s, Robert Christopher Sydney Winwood Smith, *qv*; *Style*— Sir Christopher Smith, Bt; ✉ Junction Rd, via Grafton, NSW, 2460, Australia

SMITH, Prof (Christopher) Colin; s of Alfred Edward Smith (d 1969), of Brighton, and Dorothy May, *née* Berry (d 1984); *b* 17 Sept 1927; *Educ* Varndean Sch for Boys Brighton, Univ of Cambridge (MA, PhD, LittD); *m* 14 Aug 1954, Ruth Margaret, da of Harry James Barnes (d 1987), of Brighton; 1 s (Roderick b 1958 d 1960), 3 da (Jennifer b 1960, Rebecca b 1961, Jocelyn b 1964); *Career* Dept of Spanish Univ of Leeds: asst lectr 1953–56, lectr 1956–64, sr lectr 1964–68, sub dean of arts 1963–67; Univ of Cambridge: lectr in Spanish 1968–75, fell St Catharine's Coll 1968–, prof of Spanish 1975–90; visiting prof Univ of Virginia USA 1981; memb Assoc of Hispanists of GB (pres 1977–79), corresponding memb Royal Spanish Acad 1993; Comendador de número de la Orden de Isabel la Católica (Spain) 1988; *Books* Spanish Ballads (1964), Collins English/Spanish, Spanish/English Dictionary (1971, 3 edn 1992), The Poema de mio Cid (1972, 3 edn 1994), Estudios Cidianos (1977), Place-names of Roman Britain (with A L F Rivet, 1979), The Making of the Poema de mio Cid (1983), Christians and Moors in Spain (1989, 2 vols); *Recreations* natural history (especially entomology), archaeology; *Style*— Prof Colin Smith; ✉ 56 Girton Rd, Cambridge CB3 0LL (☎ 01223 276 214); St Catharine's Coll, Cambridge CB2 1RL

SMITH, Colin Deverell; *b* 21 May 1947; *Career* Safeway plc (formerly Argyll Group plc): joined 1979, fin controller and co sec Argyll Foods 1980–83, co sec and gp fin controller 1983–89, main bd dir 1984–, fin dir 1989–93, gp chief exec 1993–; *Style*— Colin Smith, Esq; ✉ Safeway plc, Safeway House, Millington Road, Hayes UB3 4AY (☎ 0181 848 8744)

SMITH, Colin Ferguson; s of Henry Ferguson Smith, of Kinlet, Salop, and Barbara Catharine, *née* Tangye; *b* 12 Oct 1932; *Educ* Leighton Park Sch Reading, Gonville and Caius Coll Cambridge (MA, LLB); *Career* Tangyes Ltd: prodn controller 1960–62, chief buyer 1962–64, co sec and accounts mangr 1964–67; asst co sec Central Wagon Co Ltd 1967–69, dir Smith Keen Cutler Ltd 1986–92 (ptnr and res mangr 1971–86); memb Stock Exchange; FCIS 1971; *Clubs* Carlton; *Style*— Colin Smith, Esq; ✉ 55 Warwick Crest, Arthur Road, Birmingham B15 2LH; The Clos Mill, St Clears, Dyfed, Wales (☎ 0121 454 4698)

SMITH, Colin Hilton; s of Reginald Walter Smith (d 1982), and Barbara, *née* Milligan; *b* 21 Feb 1953; *Educ* Falmouth Sch of Arts, RCA, Yale Univ; *m* 1, 1976 (m dis 1980), Barbara Ann, da of William Henry Spicer; m 2, 1983 (m dis 1992), Rosemary Victoria, da of Gerald Henry Dean; 1 s (William Lawrence Hilton b 1986); *Career* artist; *Solo Exhibitions* Nicola Jacobs Gallery London 1982, 1984, 1987 and 1989, Ruth Siegal NY 1986, Anderson O'Day Gallery London 1991, Kunstlandschaft Europa Kunstverein Freiburg 1991, Gallery Three Zero NYC 1993, Big Paintings for the Barbican London 1993, Galleri M Stockholm 1995, The Chelsea Arts Club 1995, Univ of Northumbria Gallery 1995, Wilmer Cutler and Pickering Berlin 1995, Galleria Arte X Arte Buenos Aires 1996; *Gp Exhibitions* Falmouth Sch of Art 1974–75, PCL Gallery London 1977, New 57 Gallery London 1977, The First Exhbn Nicola Jacobs Gallery 1979, Sculpture and works on paper Nicola Jacobs Gallery 1980, Fourteenth Int Festival of Painting Cagnes-sur-Mer-France 1982, Tolly Cobbold Eastern Arts Fourth Nat Exhbn and tour 1983, The Figurative Exhibition II Nicola Jacobs Gallery 1983, New Talent Hal Bromm NYC 1984, The Image as Catalyst Ashmolean Museum 1984, Royal Over-Seas League Annual Exhbn (jt first prize winner) 1987, Academicians Choice (Mall Galleries London and The Eye Gallery Bristol) 1990, The London Gp Exhbn RCA 1990, Forgrounds and Distances touring 1992–93, Retour á la Peinture Montreal 1992, The Figure The City

NYC 1993, Ian Jones and Colin Smith (Barbican) 1993, John Moores Exhbn 18 (Walker Art Gallery Liverpool) 1993, Painting The City (Corr Contemporary Art London) 1995, Mostra 1996, (Br Sch at Rome), The Motor Show - Cars in Art (touring exhbn) 1996; *Collections* Galerie de Beerenburght Holland, RCA, Unilever London, Arts Cncl of GB, Prudential Holborn, Pepsi Cola London, Contemporary Art Soc, Arthur Andersen Ltd, British Airways, EMI Ltd, Kettering Art Gallery, Carlton Communications, Coopers Lybrand, Virgin Airways London, The Duke and Duchess of Westminster, Amerivox Scandanavia Stockholm, Arthur Andersen Newcastle, Wilmer cutler and Dickering Berlin, BML Corp Mgmnt Frankfurt, Scottish Equitable Edinburgh; Great London Arts Assoc Award 1982, London Arts Bd Award 1995, Abbey Award in Painting Br Sch at Rome 1996; Harkness fell and res assoc Faculty of Fine Art Yale Univ 1983–86; *Publications* An Interview with Richard Diebenkorn (Artscribe 1992), Karl Weschice (The Whistler Magazine, 1996); *Recreations* reading, films; *Clubs* Chelsea Arts; *Style—* Colin Smith, Esq; ✉ 59 Whipps Cross Rd, London E11 1NJ (☎ 0181 989 6607)

SMITH, His Hon Judge Colin Milner; QC (1985); s of Alan Milner Smith, OBE, of Otford, Kent, and Vera Ivy, *née* Cannon (d 1973); *b* 2 Nov 1936; *Educ* Tonbridge, BNC Oxford (MA), Univ of Chicago (JD); *m* 14 Dec 1979, Moira Soraya, da of Charles Reginald Braybrooke, (d 1989) of Lower Layham, Suffolk; 1 s (Alexander b 1982), 1 da (Camilla b 1987); *Career* Nat Serv Lt RM (3 Commando Brig) 1955–57; called to the Bar Gray's Inn 1962, recorder 1987–91, circuit judge (SE Circuit) 1991–; *Recreations* cricket, skiing, reading; *Clubs* MCC; *Style—* His Honour Judge (Colin) Smith, QC; ✉ 3 Verulam Buildings, Gray's Inn, London WC1R 5NT (☎ 0171 831 8441)

SMITH, Colin Roderick; CVO (1984), CBE (1995), QPM (1987); s of Humphrey Montague Smith, OBE, of Bexhill, and Marie Louvain, *née* Prior (d 1988); *b* 26 March 1941; *Educ* Dorking County GS, Bexhill GS, Univ of Birmingham (BSoc Sc); *m* 5 Aug 1961, Patricia Joan, da of Charles Coppin (d 1962); *Career* Lt 18 Co (Amph) RASC 1959–62; constable rising to chief supt East Sussex Constabulary (later Sussex Police) 1962–77, asst chief constable Thames Valley Police 1977–82, dep asst cmmr Metropolitan Police 1982–85 (fndr Royalty and Diplomatic Protection Dept), chief constable Thames Valley Police 1985–91, HM Inspector of Constabulary 1991–; ACPO 1990 (chm: SE Region, Gen Purposes Ctee, Negotiating Ctee), co-dir Extended Interview Board 1988–91; *Publications* various professional papers on police related subjects; *Recreations* horse riding; *Clubs* RAC; *Style—* Colin Smith, Esq, CVO, CBE, QPM; ✉ Bridge House, Sion Place, Clifton Down, Bristol BS8 4XA (☎ 0117 973 6400, fax 0117 923 8009)

SMITH, Colin Roland Francis; s of Roland Smith (d 1993), of Sutton Coldfield, and Anne, *née* Colley (d 1954); *b* 6 Sept 1944; *Educ* John Willmott GS; *m* Sylvia, da of Sydney Skillett, of Guernsey; 1 s (Gavin b 1966), 1 da (Helena b 1964); *Career* harbour corr Guernsey Evening Press 1962–63; reporter on several local newspapers and Daily Sketch until 1968; The Observer: joined 1968, chief roving corr 1972–77, ME corr (based in Cyprus, Cairo and Jerusalem) 1977–85, chief roving corr 1985–88, Asia ed based in Bangkok 1988–90, asst ed and roving corr 1990, Washington corr 1993; roving corr The Sunday Times 1993–94; contrib: The Oldie 1994–, The Sunday Telegraph 1995–, The Sunday Times 1995–, Punch magazine 1996–; Int Reporter of the Year 1975 and 1985; *Books* Carlos - Portrait of a Terrorist (1976, revised edn 1995); *Novels* Cut-Out (1980), The Last Crusade (1991); *Recreations* tennis, military history; *Style—* Colin Smith, Esq; ✉ PO Box 827, Nicosia, Cyprus (☎ and fax 00 357 2 497953)

SMITH, Sir Cyril; kt (1988), MBE (1966), DL (Greater Manchester 1991); *b* 28 June 1928; *Educ* Rochdale GS for Boys; *Career* MP (Lib until 1988, Lib Dem 1988–92) Rochdale 1972–92, Lib chief whip 1975–76; cncllr Rochdale BC 1952–66, Alderman 1966–74, Mayor of Rochdale 1966–67, memb Rochdale Metropolitan Dist Cncl 1974–75; county pres Greater Manchester N Scouts 1994–; Freeman Borough of Rochdale 1992; Hon DEd Metropolitan Univ Manchester 1976, Hon LLD Univ of Lancaster 1993; *Recreations* listening to music, reading, TV; *Clubs* National Liberal (chm 1987–88); *Style—* Sir Cyril Smith, MBE, DL; ✉ 14 Emma St, Rochdale, Lancs (☎ 01706 48840)

SMITH, Dr Cyril Stanley; CBE (1985); s of Walter Charles Smith (d 1932), of London, and Beatrice May Smith (d 1978); *b* 21 July 1925; *Educ* Plaistow Municipal Secdy Sch, LSE (MSc), Univ of London (PhD); *m* 1, 1949 (m dis 1968), Helena Ursula; 2 da (Vanessa (Mrs Hallam) b 1952, d 1989, Emma Josephine b 1956, d 1978); m 2, 8 May 1968, Eileen Cameron, da of Samuel Dentith (d 1976), of Salford; *Career* Dorset Regt 1943–47; dir Dept of Youth Work Univ of Manchester 1961–70, dir of social policy studies Civil Serv Coll 1971–75, sec SSRC 1975–85; chm Br Sociological Assoc 1972–74, memb Sec of State's Ctee on Inequalities in Health (DHSS) 1977–80; author of various books and articles on adolescence, leisure, social sciences; chm Br Assoc for Servs to the Elderly 1988–90; *Books* Adolescence (1968), The Wincroft Youth Project (1972), Leisure & Society in Britain (jt ed, 1973); *Recreations* football; *Clubs* West Ham FC; *Style—* Dr Cyril Smith, CBE

SMITH, Dr Cyril William; s of Reginald William Smith (d 1971), of Great Massingham, Norfolk, and Maud Evelyn Smith (d 1978); *b* 7 Jan 1930; *Educ* Douai Sch, Univ of Exeter (BSc), Univ of London (BSc, PhD); *m* 14 June 1958, Eileen Dorothy, da of Cyril Jackson (d 1955), of Norwich; 3 s (Andrew b 1959, Paul b 1960, Martin b 1962); *Career* asst exp offr TRE Malvern 1947–56, res fell Imperial Coll London 1956–59, physics master Downside Sch 1959–64, sr lectr Univ of Salford 1973–89 (lectr 1964–73), conslt 1989–; scientific advsr to Environmental Med Fndn; CEng, FIEE, CPhys, MInstP, life SMIEEE, MIPEMB; *Books* Electromagnetic Man (1989 and 1990, French edn 1995); *Recreations* walking, gardening, travel, international cookery; *Style—* Dr Cyril Smith; ✉ Medical Instrumentation Division, Salford University Business Services Ltd, PO Box 50, Salford M6 6BY (☎ 0161 736 8921, fax 0161 745 5999/7308)

SMITH, David; s of Walter Horace Smith (d 1960), and Annie, *née* Matthews (d 1971); *b* 18 July 1927; *Educ* Burton GS, Univ of Sheffield (BSc, PhD); *m* 1951, Nancy Elizabeth, da of Harold Hawley (d 1968); 2 s, 3 da; *Career* vice pres Exxon Chemical Co 1971–78, chm and md Esso Chemical Ltd 1979–86; petroleum and chemical consIt 1987–; memb Cncl Chemical Indust Assoc 1982–86, pres Southampton C of C 1990–91; dir Assoc of Br C of C 1992–95; chm govrs Southampton Inst of Higher Educn 1990–; *Recreations* golf, cricket; *Clubs* MCC, Royal Winchester Golf; *Style—* David Smith, Esq

SMITH, Prof (Anthony) David; s of Rev William Beddard Smith (d 1985), and Evelyn, *née* Eagle (d 1987); *b* 16 Sept 1938; *Educ* Kingswood Sch Bath, ChCh Oxford (Bostock exhibitioner, BA, MA, DPhil); *m* 1, 1962 (m dis 1974), Wendy Diana, *née* Lee; 1 s (Richard David b 1968), 1 da (Catherine Anne b 1965); m 2, 1975, Dr Ingegerd Östman; 1 s (Niklas Carl William b 1987); *Career* Univ of Oxford: Royal Soc Stothert res fell 1966–70, res lectr Christ Church 1966–71, Wellcome res fell 1970–71, univ lectr in pharmacology and student of Christ Church 1971–84, prof and head Dept of Pharmacology 1984–, hon dir MRC Anatomical Neuropharmacology Unit 1985–, fell Lady Margaret Hall Oxford 1984–; ed and contrib articles in various jls; memb: Gen Bd of the Faculties Oxford 1980–84, Neurosciences Bd MRC 1983–85; Docktor honoris causa Szeged 1993; seventh Gaddum Meml Prize Br Pharmacological Soc 1979, Decade of the Brain lectr 1993, memb Norwegian Acad of Sci and Letters 1996; memb: Physiological Soc, Pharmacological Soc; *Recreations* music, travel; *Style—* Prof David Smith; ✉ Department of Pharmacology, Mansfield Road, Oxford OX1 3QT (☎ 01865 271883, fax 01865 271882)

SMITH, Prof (Norman John) David; s of Norman Samson Smith (d 1962), of Kensington, London, and Eileen Tatton, *née* Oakley (d 1971); *b* 2 Feb 1931; *Educ* King's Coll Sch, King's Coll Hosp Med Sch Univ of London (BDS, MPhil), Univ of London (KCHMS BDS), Royal Free Hosp Sch of Med (MSc); *m* 1, 2 Oct 1954 (m dis), Regina Eileen, da of Reginald Lugg (d 1961), of Highgate, London; 1 s (Malcolm David Oakley b 1964); m 2, 21 Sept 1983, Mary Christine, da of Alfred Thomas Pocock (d 1977); 1 da (Clare Zillah Mary b 1983); *Career* served MN, apprentice Pacific Steam Navigation Co 1948–52, offr serv Royal Mail Lines 1953–58, gen dental practice/jr hosp experience 1964–73, head Dept of Dental Radiology King's Coll Sch of Med 1973–, civil conslt (dental radiology) to RAF 1990–96; memb: Southwark Cncl 1974–78, GLC 1977–86, Thames Water Authy 1977–83, South East Thames RHA 1978–86, Hon Co of Master Mariners; Hon DUniv Open Univ 1993; *Books* Simple Navigation by the Sun (1974), Dental Radiography (1980), Dental Radiography (2 edn, 1988); *Recreations* nature, photography, walking; *Style—* Prof David Smith; ✉ Department of Dental Radiology, King's College School of Medicine & Dentistry, Caldecot Rd, London SE5 9RW (☎ 0171 737 4000 ext 2503)

SMITH, David Andrew; s of John William Smith (d 1968), of London, and Patricia Mary Smith; *b* 5 March 1952; *Educ* Finchley GS, Lincoln Coll Univ of Oxford (MA, ed Cherwell (Univ newspaper)); *m* 18 Oct 1980, Pamela, da of Douglas Keith Reading; 2 s (Mark Patrick Reading b 30 Dec 1982, Matthew Louis Reading b 29 May 1986); *Career* corr Italy Reuters 1977–78 (Spain 1975–76); ITN corr: Africa 1979–81, Israel 1982–86, Soviet Union 1988–90, USA 1991–; visiting prof Univ of Michigan 1986–87; International Reporter of the Year (for despatches from Lebanon) RTS Awards 1983; *Books* Mugabe (1981), Prisoners of God - The Conflict of Arab and Jew (1987); *Style—* David Smith, Esq

SMITH, His Hon Judge David Arthur; QC (1982); s of Arthur Heber Smith (d 1983), of Kent, and Marjorie Edith Pounds, *née* Broome (d 1989); *b* 7 May 1938; *Educ* Lancing, Merton Coll Oxford (MA); *m* 1967, Clementine, da of William Taylor Gordon Urquhart (d 1977); 2 s (Rupert b 1969, Julian b 1970); *Career* official princ Archdeaconry of Hackney 1973–, recorder of the Crown Ct 1978–86, circuit judge (Western Circuit) 1986–; wine treas Western Circuit 1980–86; memb Parole Bd 1989–94; treas Cncl of Her Majesty's Circuit Judges 1991–; sec Int Bee Res Assoc 1963–; *Style—* His Hon Judge David Smith, QC; ✉ The Law Courts, Small Street, Bristol

SMITH, David Arthur George; OBE (1996), JP (Bradford 1975); s of Stanley George Smith (d 1967), of Bath, and Winifred May Francis Smith (d 1985); *b* 17 Dec 1934; *Educ* City of Bath Boys' Sch, Balliol Coll Oxford (BA, DipEd, MA); *m* 31 Aug 1957, Jennifer, da of John Ronald Anning (d 1963), of Launceston; 1 s (John b 1962), 2 da (Sarah b 1961, Charlotte b 1967); *Career* asst master Manchester GS 1957–62, head of history Rossall Sch 1963–70; headmaster: King's Sch Peterborough 1970–74, Bradford GS 1974–96; JP Peterborough 1972–74; chm HMC 1988; FRSA 1985; *Books* Left and Right in Twentieth Century Europe (1970), Russia of the Tsars (1970); *Recreations* walking, writing; *Clubs* Athenaeum (Bradford); *Style—* David Smith, Esq, OBE, JP; ✉ c/o Bradford Grammar School, Bradford, W Yorks BD9 4JP

SMITH, David Bruce Boyter; OBE (1994); s of Bruce Aitken Smith (d 1993), of Dunfermline, and Helen Brown, *née* Boyter; *b* 11 March 1942; *Educ* Dunfermline HS, Univ of Edinburgh (MA, LLB); *m* 7 Aug 1965, Christine Anne, da of Robert McKenzie (d 1972); 1 s (Andrew b 1 Aug 1969), 1 da (Caroline b 1 July 1974); *Career* admitted slr 1968, NP 1969, slr Standard Life Assurance Co 1969–73; Dunfermline Building Society: sec 1974, gen mangr 1981, dep chief exec 1986, chief exec 1987–; memb Cncl NHBC 1987–, dep chm Glenrothes New Town Devpt Corp 1990–96, dir Fife Enterprise Ltd 1991–, Building Socs Investor Protection Bd 1991–, chm BSA Scottish Ctee 1996– (vice chm 1994–96), memb Cncl BSA London 1996–, vice chm Northern Assoc Building Socs 1996–, memb Scottish Conveyancing Bd 1996–, memb Scottish Advsy Bd BT 1996–; memb Ct and finance convener Univ of Edinburgh 1991–, vice chm Lauder Coll 1993–, life tstee Carnegie Dunfermline and Hero Fund Tsts, dir Scottish Fisheries Museum Tst Ltd 1992–; memb Law Soc of Scotland 1968; FRSA 1992, FInstD 1994 (chm Scottish Div 1994–); *Recreations* golf, sailing, the arts; *Clubs* New (Edinburgh), Forth Cruising, Dunfermline Golf; *Style—* David Smith, Esq, OBE; ✉ 4 Garvock Hill, Dunfermline, Fife KY12 7TZ (☎ 01383 723863); Dunfermline Building Society, Caledonia House, Carnegie Avenue, Fife KY11 5PJ (☎ 01383 627727, fax 01383 627802)

SMITH, Sheriff David Buchanan; s of William Adam Smith (d 1955), of Elderslie, Renfrewshire, and Irene Mary Calderwood, *née* Hogarth (d 1976); *b* 31 Oct 1936; *Educ* Paisley GS, Univ of Glasgow (MA), Univ of Edinburgh (LLB); *m* 1 April 1961, Hazel Mary, da of James Alexander Walker Sinclair, MBE (d 1960), of Edinburgh; 2 s (David Ewan b 1962, d 1986, Patrick Sinclair b 1965), 1 da (Alison Mary b 1963); *Career* advocate 1961–75, standing jr counsel to Scottish Educn Dept 1968–75; tutor Faculty of Law Univ of Edinburgh 1964–72; sheriff of N Strathclyde at Kilmarnock 1975–; pres Kilmarnock and Dist History Gp, treas The Sheriffs' Assoc 1979–89 (archivist 1989–), tstee Scot Curling Museum Tst 1980–, pres Ayr Curling Club 1995–96; FSA (Scot); *Books* Curling: an Illustrated History (1981), The Roaring Game: Memories of Scottish Curling (1985), The Sheriff Court (in The Stair Memorial Encyclopedia of the Laws of Scotland vol 6, 1988), George Washington Wilson in Ayrshire (1991); *Recreations* history of the laws and institutions of Scotland, curling, collecting curliana, music, architecture; *Style—* Sheriff David B Smith; ✉ Sheriff Court House, Kilmarnock, Ayrshire KA1 1ED (☎ 01563 520211, fax 01563 543568)

SMITH, Sir David Cecil; kt (1986); s of William John Smith, and Elva Emily, *née* Deeble; *b* 21 May 1930; *Educ* St Paul's, Queen's Coll Oxford (MA, DPhil); *m* 1965, Lesley Margaret, da of Henry John Mollison Mutch (d 1946); 2 s (Adam, Cameron), 1 da (Bryony); *Career* 2 Lt RA 1955–56; Swedish Inst scholar Uppsala Univ 1951–52, Brown res fell Queen's Coll Oxford 1956–59, Harkness fell Berkeley Univ California 1959–60, lectr Dept of Agric Oxford Univ 1960–74, tutorial fell and tutor for admissions Wadham Coll Oxford 1971–74 (Royal Soc res fell 1964–71), Melville Wills prof of botany Univ of Bristol 1974–80 (dir of biological studies 1977–80), Sibthorpian prof of rural economy Oxford Univ 1980–87, princ and vice chllr Univ of Edinburgh 1987–94, pres Wolfson Coll Oxford 1994–; Hon DSc: Liverpool 1986, Exeter 1986, Hull 1987, Aberdeen 1990, Napier 1993, Oxford Brookes 1996; Hon DL: Pennsylvania 1990, Queen's (Ontario) 1991; Hon DUniv Heriot-Watt 1993, Hon Dr (hc) Edinburgh 1994; FRS 1975, FRSE 1988; *Books* The Biology of Symbiosis (with A Douglas, 1987); *Clubs* Farmers'; *Style—* Sir David Smith, FRS, FRSE; ✉ Wolfson College, Oxford OX2 6UD (☎ 01865 274101, fax 01865 274136)

SMITH, David Henry; s of Charles Henry Smith (d 1990), and Elizabeth Mary, *née* Williams (d 1963); *b* 3 April 1954; *Educ* West Bromwich GS, Univ Coll Cardiff (BSc(Econ), Tassie medallion), Birkbeck Coll London (MSc(Econ)); *m* 1980, Jane Howells; 2 s (Richard Howell b 1981, Thomas David b 1983), 2 da (Emily Victoria b 1987, Elizabeth Jane b 1992); *Career* econ report writer Lloyds Bank 1976–77, economist Henley Centre 1977–79, econ writer Now! magazine 1979–81, asst ed Financial Weekly 1981–84, econ corr The Times 1984–89, econ ed The Sunday Times 1989– (currently also policy advsr); commended Journalist of the Year Br Press Awards 1992, Business Columnist of the Year Periodical Publishing Assoc Awards 1995 and 1996; *Books* The Rise and Fall of Monetarism (1987), North and South (1989, 2 edn, 1994), Mrs Thatcher's Economics (1989), Mrs Thatcher's Economics: Her Legacy (1991), From Boom to Bust (1992), UK Current Economic Policy (1995); *Recreations* golf, squash, occasional tennis; *Clubs* St James's Squash; *Style—* David Smith, Esq; ✉ The Sunday Times, 1 Pennington Street, London E1 9XW (☎ 0171 782 5750, fax 0171 782 5237)

SMITH, Rt Rev David James; *see:* Bradford, Bishop of

SMITH, Dr David John Leslie; s of Arthur George Smith (d 1975), and Gertrude Mary Duce, *née* Buck; *b* 8 Oct 1938; *Educ* North Glos Tech Coll (HND), Coll of Aeronautics (MSc), Univ of London (PhD), RCDS; *m* 14 April 1962, Wendy Lavinia, da of Frederick James Smith (d 1955); 2 da (Andrea, Penelope); *Career* Nat Gas Turbine Estab: scientific offr 1961, head turbomachinery dept 1976; student RCDS 1979, dir aircraft mechanical and electrical equipment controllerate of aircraft MOD (PE) 1980, head aerodynamics dept Royal Aircraft Estab 1981; dep dir: Marine Technol Admty Res Estab 1984, planning Admiralty Res Estab 1986; head of def res study team and asst under sec state civilian mgmnt specialists MOD 1988–91, dir Gp Servs Def Res Agency until 1994; CEng 1972, FRAeS 1986; *Recreations* gardening, painting oil and watercolour; *Style*— Dr David Smith

SMITH, David Thomas; s of David Smith, of Lowestoft, Suffolk, and Lilian Florence, *née* Mills; *b* 13 April 1920; *Educ* Roman Hill Sch Lowestoft, Lowestoft Tech Coll, Lowestoft and Norwich Schs of Art, Slade Sch of Art UCL (dip); *m* Elizabeth, da of Dr A J Hawes, MC, MD; 2 da (Caroline b 1950, Sarah b 1953); *Career* art master Framlingham Coll Suffolk 1939–40, served RAF 1940–45, art master Langford Grove Girls Sch Barcombe Mills Sussex 1945–48, lectr in painting Sch of Art Regent St Poly London 1951–65, sr lectr Chelsea Sch of Art 1965–79; official artist British Antarctic Survey 1975–79 and 1980, awarded grant to record Finnish Lapland by Finnish FO 1979, artist for Trinity House 1982–84 (leading to film An Artist in Antarctica); RE 1951; *Exhibitions* over 60 solo exhbns and numerous gp exhbns incl: Antarctica (Commonwealth Inst London) 1977, Antarctica (Bankside Gallery London) 1981, Mitsukoshi Galleries Tokyo, Kobe and Hiroshima 1983, Christensen's Museum and Art Gallery Norway 1983, Lighthouses of England and Wales (Commonwealth Inst) 1985, Journeys over Land and Sea (New Acad Gallery London) 1988, invited retrospective Evesham Arts Festival 1990, various RA, RWS and RE exhbns; *Awards* Knapping Prize RSBA 1948, Abbey Major Rome Scholarship 1949; *Books* illustrator: View from the Sea by Cdr Richard Woodman, The Discovery of Antarctica by Prof Antony Fogg, CBE, FRS; *Recreations* music (RSM Gold Medal for piano); *Clubs* Antarctic, British Antarctic Survey; *Style*— David Smith, Esq

SMITH, Denis; s of Harold Smith (d 1990), of Stoke-on-Trent, and Emily Anne, *née* Bullock (d 1975); *b* 19 Nov 1947; *Educ* Queensberry Road Secdy Sch; *m* 7 Oct 1967, Kathryn Elizabeth, da of Thomas Finney; 2 s (Paul Denis b 16 April 1969, Thomas James b 5 March 1978), 1 da (Rebecca Emily b 6 June 1971); *Career* professional football manager; player Stoke City 1966–82: 407 league appearances, 34 League Cup appearances, 22 FA Cup appearances; player-mangr York City 1982–87: 37 league appearances, 2 League Cup appearances, 4 FA Cup appearances; mangr: Sunderland 1987–91, Bristol City 1992–93, Oxford Utd 1993–; achievements as player: England Schs Trophy Stoke-on-Trent 1962–63, represented Football League v Irish League 1971, League Cup medal Stoke City 1972, FA Cup semi-finalist Stoke City 1971 and 1972; honours as mangr: Div 4 Championship York City 1984, Div 3 Championship Sunderland 1988, promotion to Div 1 Sunderland 1990, promotion to Div 1 Oxford Utd; full coaching licence FA 1979; *Recreations* reading, walking, watching cricket and athletics; *Style*— Denis Smith, Esq; ✉ Manager, Oxford Utd FC, Manor Ground, Headington, Oxford OX3 7RS (☎ 01865 61503)

SMITH, Derek Graham; s of Albert Edward Smith (d 1993), and Rosetta Alexandra, *née* Lyme; *b* 16 May 1947; *Educ* Royal Liberty Sch Essex, Univ of Kent (BA); *m* 25 April 1981, Margaret Elizabeth, *née* Harris; 1 da (Michelle Helen b 7 Sept 1982), 1 s (Fraser James b 8 June 1987); *Career* Coopers and Lybrand 1969–77: joined as articled clerk 1969, subsequently supervisor then mangr; Neville Russell 1977–: mangr then sr mangr, ptnr 1980–, chm Mgmnt Bd London Office 1991–, nat managing ptnr 1993; chm: Nat IT Ctee, Nexia Int Audit and IT Ctee; memb Cncl St Martins Ongar Church; Freeman City of London 1992; FCA 1972, FIMC 1987; *Books* Management and Control of Time in an Accountancy Practice (1982); *Recreations* DIY, local church; *Clubs* National; *Style*— Derek Smith, Esq; ✉ Springfield Orchard, Epping Road, Ongar, Essex CM5 0BD; Neville Russell, 24 Bevis Marks, London EC3A 7NR (☎ 0171 377 1000, fax 0171 377 8931)

SMITH, Derek Ronald; s of Frederick Richard Smith, of Jaywick, Essex, and Louisa Alice, *née* Wylde (d 1993); *b* 20 May 1950; *Educ* William Penn Comp, Univ of Surrey (BSc), Open Univ (Dip in Mgmnt, MBA); *m* 29 Sept 1973, Olwyn Mary, da of late Jack Lloyd; 2 s (Kieran James, Elian Lloyd), 2 da (Liane-Louise, Jaimé Lloyd); *Career* asst to md Roberts' Capsule Stopper Co 1968–70, rock drill sales engr Ingersoll Rand 1970–71, theatre technician 1972–79; Thames Television plc: joined as bdcast engr 1979, tech mangr 1989–92; controller of operations Central Independent Television 1992; memb Soc of Motion Picture Technicians and Engrs 1981, MIMgt 1987; *Recreations* walking, continuing education, literature, music, drawing; *Style*— Derek Smith, Esq

SMITH, Derek Vincent; s of Arthur Edmund Smith, of Cheshire, and Hazel, *née* Proudlove (d 1989); *b* 26 Sept 1948; *Educ* Sale Co Boys' GS, Univ Coll Swansea (BSc(Econ)), Univ of Strathclyde (postgrad dip in Russian); *m* 25 July 1970, Carol Anne Susan, da of Roy Cunio; 1 da (Claire-Louise b 17 Nov 1976), 1 s (Matthew James b 24 Oct 1978); *Career* NHS nat admin trainee Scotland 1972–74, asst sector administrator Falkirk and Dist Royal Infirmary 1974–76, administrator (serv planning) Ayrshire and Arran Health Bd 1976–79, dist planning offr Southmead Dist Avon Area Health Authy 1979–82; Frenchay Hosp Bristol: administrator 1982–85, gen mangr 1985–87; district gen mangr S Bedfordshire Health Authy 1987–90; chief exec: Camberwell Health Authy 1990–93, King's Healthcare NHS Trust 1993–; Dip HSM 1975, MHSM 1979; *Recreations* squash rackets, tennis, classical music, sailing; *Style*— Derek Smith, Esq; ✉ King's Healthcare NHS Trust, King's College Hospital, Denmark Hill, London SE5 9RS (☎ 0171 346 3161, fax 0171 346 3436)

SMITH, Prof (Stanley) Desmond; s of Henry George Stanley Smith (d 1969), and Sarah Emily Ruth Weare; *b* 3 March 1931; *Educ* Cotham Bristol, Univ of Bristol (BSc, DSc), Univ of Reading (PhD); *m* 1 July 1956, Gillian Anne, da of Howard Stanley Parish; 1 s (David), 1 da (Nicola); *Career* SSO RAE Farnborough 1956–59; res asst Meteorology Dept Imperial Coll London 1959–60, reader Univ of Reading 1966–70 (lectr 1960–66), prof of physics and dept head Heriot-Watt Univ 1970–; chm and dir: Edinburgh Instruments Ltd 1971–, Edinburgh Sensors Ltd 1988–; dir Edinburgh C of C 1981–84; memb: cabinet ACOST 1987–88 (formerly ACARD 1985–87), Def Sci Advsy Cncl MOD 1985–91; FRMetS 1962, FRSE 1973, FInstP 1976, FRS 1976; *Recreations* mountaineering, skiing, tennis, golf, raising the temperature; *Clubs* Royal Soc; *Style*— Prof Desmond Smith, FRS, FRSE; ✉ Tree Tops, 29D Gillespie Road, Colinton, Edinburgh EH13 0NW (☎ 0131 441 7225); Physics Department, Heriot-Watt University, Riccarton, Edinburgh EH14 4AS (☎ 0131 451 3021, fax 0131 449 5542, telex 72553 EDINST G)

SMITH, (Brian) Douglas; s of Henry Charles Smith (d 1958), of Crouch End, London, and Ruby Constance, *née* Hall (d 1976); *b* 17 Aug 1935; *Educ* Stationers' Co Sch Hornsey, King's Coll London, LSE (BA, Cricket purple); *m* 1, 1961, Verity Anne, da of late William Wright; 2 da (Tracy McClure b 1965, Francesca McClure b 1967); m 2, 1985, Mary Barbara, *née* Gillman; 1 da (Rebecca Barbara); *Career* London publicity offr Cons Party Central Office 1960–62, head of publicity Fire Protection Assoc 1962–64, sec Int Cooperation Year Ctee 1964–66, dir Intercapita Public Relations 1966–68, assoc dir Planned Public Relations 1968–71, dir MDA Public Relations 1971–85; chm: Parliamentary Monitoring Services Ltd 1985–, PMS Publications Ltd 1985–; md PRCI Ltd (later Countrywide Political Communications) 1985–90, chief exec Westminster Advisers Ltd 1990–; exec dir Centre for Euro Political Communication Studies 1993–; cncllr Hornsey Borough Cncl 1961–65 (chm Housing Ctee 1963–65); Haringey Cncl: cncllr 1964–86, dep ldr Cons Gp 1966–70, dep mayor 1968–69, chm Planning and Devpt Ctee 1968–70, chm Personnel Ctee 1969–71, ldr Cons Oppn 1980–84; chm PR Consits Assoc 1984–85 (treas, vice chm), pres IPR 1990 (chm Govt Affrs Gp 1986–87), pres CERP Consultants 1992–94; PR Week Award for outstanding career achievement in PR 1990, hon PR advsr UK Scout Movement 1965–; MCAM, FIPR; *Publications* Lobbying the UK Parliament (with Arthur Butler, 1984); *Recreations* watching and talking cricket, visiting old pubs; *Clubs* Kent CCC, Foreign Press Assoc; *Style*— Douglas Smith, Esq; ✉ 20 Highgate Heights, 77 Shepherds Hill, London N6 5RF (☎ 0181 348 4964); Parliamentary Monitoring Services, 19 Douglas Street, Westminster SW1P 4PA (☎ 0171 233 8283)

SMITH, (Fraser) Drew; s of Capt Frank Smith, and Beatrice, *née* Blank; *b* 30 March 1950; *Educ* Westminster; *m* 19 June 1987, Susan Mary, da of Liam Maloney; 1 s (Oliver b 1988), 1 da (Grace b 1989); *Career* IPC Magazines 1968–72, Westminster Press 1972–80, Consumers' Assoc 1981–90, freelance writer Drew Smith Associates 1990–; creator Food File (C4) 1992, ed Taste Magazine 1991–94, publisher Intercity Guides 1992 and 1993; chm Guild of Food Writers 1994–95, dir of food policy London Docklands, friend of McCarrison Soc, friend of Nat Organic Centre; *Books* Good Food Guide (1983–90), Good Food Directory (1986), Modern Cooking (1990), Food Watch (1994 and 1995), Baby Watch (1995); *Recreations* life; *Style*— Drew Smith, Esq

SMITH, Sir Dudley Gordon; kt (1983), DL (Warwickshire 1988), MP (C) Warwick and Leamington (majority 8,935); s of Hugh William Smith (d 1977), of Cambridge, and Florence Elizabeth Smith (d 1967); *b* 14 Nov 1926; *Educ* Chichester HS; *m* 1, 1958 (m dis 1974); 1 s, 2 da; m 2, 1976, Catherine, o da of late Thomas Amos, of Liverpool; *Career* mgmnt consit and former journalist; asst news editor Sunday Express 1953–59, divnl dir Beecham Group 1966–70; Parly candidate (C) Peckham Camberwell 1955; MP (C): Brentford and Chiswick 1959–66, Warwick and Leamington 1968–; oppn whip 1964–66; Parly under sec of state Dept of Employment 1970–74, Parly under sec of state for Army MOD 1974; vice chm Parly Select Ctee on Race Rels and Immigration 1974–79, UK del to Cncl of Europe and WEU 1979– (sec gen European Democratic Gp 1983–), chm WEU Def Ctee 1989–93, pres WEU Assembly 1993–96; fndr memb OSCE (formerly CSCE) Assembly 1992–; chm United and Cecil Club 1975–80; Freeman City of London, Liveryman Worshipful Co of Horners; Insignia of Cdr Order of Isabella The Catholic (Spain) 1994, Insignia of The Horseman of Madara First Class (Bulgaria) 1994; *Books* Harold Wilson: A Critical Biography (1963); *Recreations* travel, books, music, preservation of wild life; *Style*— Sir Dudley Smith, DL, MP; ✉ Church Farm, Weston-under-Wetherley, nr Leamington Spa, Warwicks (☎ 01926 852425); House of Commons, Westminster, London SW1A 0AA (☎ 0171 219 3445)

SMITH, Edward Richard; s of Albert Edward Smith (d 1961), of Finchley, London, and Elsie Florence, *née* Turner (d 1995); *b* 19 March 1936; *Educ* Highgate Sch; *m* 10 Sept 1960, Pamela Margaret, da of Alfred Montague Mundy (d 1977), of Gidea Park and Tunbridge Wells; 2 s (Donald Edward Philip b 1966, Philip Richard Jeremy b 1969); *Career* Nat Serv RAOC 1954–56; Martins Bank Ltd 1954–68; dir: Hill Samuel Bank Ltd 1974–90, Gross Hill Properties Ltd 1983–91, Sydney and London Properties Ltd 1986–91, Consolidated Land Properties Ltd 1988–91, Ascot Holdings plc 1988–93, European Equity Corporation Ltd 1988–90, Waterglade International Holdings PLC 1990–92; proprietor Felstead Books, ptnr Phildon Consits; Freeman City of London, Liveryman Worshipful Co of Pattenmakers; FCIB 1980, FRSA 1994; *Recreations* antiquarian books, gardening, travel; *Clubs* East India, RAC, MCC; *Style*— Edward R Smith, Esq; ✉ Phildon Lodge, Seal Hollow Rd, Sevenoaks, Kent TN13 3SL (☎ 01732 456928, fax 01732 740253)

SMITH, Prof Edwin; s of Albert Edwin Smith, and Sarah Ann Smith (d 1990); *b* 28 July 1931; *Educ* Chesterfield GS, Univ of Nottingham (BSc), Univ of Sheffield (PhD); *m* 15 March 1958, Patricia Georgina, da of Frederick Walter Gale; *Career* AEI Research Lab Aldermaston 1955–61, CEGB Research Labs Leatherhead 1961–68; Univ of Manchester: prof of metallurgy 1968–88, dean Faculty of Science 1983–85, pro-vice-chllr 1985–88; prof emeritus and hon fell Univ of Manchester-UMIST Materials Science Centre 1988–; currently conslt to major UK and US orgns; FIM, FRS 1996; *Recreations* general sporting interests (has run 14 marathons); *Style*— Prof Edwin Smith, FRS; ✉ Manchester University-UMIST Materials Science Centre, Grosvenor Street, Manchester M1 7HS (☎ 0161 200 3556, fax 0161 200 3586)

SMITH, Elizabeth Jean; da of Lt-Gen Sir Robert Hay, KCIE (d 1980), of Denholm, Roxburghshire, and Mary Carnegie, *née* McAusland, MBE; *b* 15 Aug 1936; *Educ* St George's Sch Edinburgh, Univ of Edinburgh (MA); *m* 23 Feb 1960, Geoffrey Peter Smith, s of William Stanley Smith (d 1958), of Wallasey, Cheshire; 1 s (Graham b 1968), 1 da (Catherine b 1965); *Career* BBC: studio mangr 1958–61, prodr radio news 1961–70, dep ed consumer affrs Radio 4 1970–78, prodr TV current affrs 1978–79, sr asst Secretariat 1979–81, Cwlth fellowship to study the impact of satellite TV on India 1984, asst head central talks and features World Service 1981–84, head current affrs World Service 1984–88, controller English servs World Service 1988–94; sec gen Commonwealth Broadcasting Assoc 1994–; monthly columnist for The Listener 1975–78; memb: Cncl Radio Acad 1992–95, Cncl Royal Inst of Int Affrs 1992–95; *Books* Healing Herbs (jtly, 1978), Sambo Sahib (1981); *Style*— Mrs Elizabeth Smith; ✉ 12 Highbury Terrace, London N5 1UP (☎ 0171 226 3519); Room 312, BBC, Yalding House, 152–156 Great Portland Street, London W1N 6AJ (☎ 0171 765 5151/5144, fax 0171 765 5152)

SMITH, Brig Eric David; CBE (1975, MBE 1951), DSO (1945); s of Christopher Smith (d 1958), and Jessica Lucy, *née* Bartram (d 1965); *b* 19 Aug 1923; *Educ* Allhallows Sch Devon; *m* 5 Jan 1957, Jill Helene, da of Brig J C Way Cott, OBE (d 1981); 2 da (Joanna (Mrs Davis) b 1959, Beverly (Mrs Stark) b 1962); *Career* cmmnd 7 Gurkha Rifles 1942, active service Italy and Greece 1944–45 (wounded), operational serv Malaya 1950–54, student Staff Coll Camberley 1956, operational serv Borneo 1963–64 (badly injured in helicopter 1964), operational serv Sabah 1965, Co 1/2 Gurkha Rifles 1965–68, Col Bde of Gurkhas 1970–71, Brig cmdg Br Gurkhas Nepal 1971–74, Hon Col 7 Gurkha Rifles 1975–83, ret active list 1978; special advsr to Commons Def Ctee on Bde of Gurkhas Report 1988–89; author; chm Sidmouth Town Cncl 1988–90; *Books* Britain's Brigade of Gurkhas (1973), Battles For Cassino (1975), East of Kathmandu (1976), Even the Brave Falter (1978), Battle for Burma (1979), Malaya and Borneo (counter-insurgency) (1985), Johnny Gurkha, Victory of a Sort (1988), Wars Bring Scars (1994); *Recreations* keen on all sport until loss of right arm (now a spectator), walking; *Style*— Brig Eric Smith, CBE, DSO; ✉ 2 Balfour Mews, Sidmouth, Devon EX10 8XL

SMITH, Dr Francis William; s of Capt William Smith, RAMC (d 1978) of Harare, Zimbabwe, and Frances Marrianne May, *née* Emslie (d 1992); *b* 8 Jan 1943; *Educ* Prince Edward Sch Harare Zimbabwe, Univ of Aberdeen (MB ChB, DMRD, MD); *m* 5 Dec 1970, Pamela Anne, da of James Cox (d 1958), of Gateshead, Co-Durham; 1 s (James b 1976), 1 da (Jane b 1971); *Career* dir of clinical magnetic resonance res Aberdeen Royal Infirmary 1980 (conslt in nuclear med 1979–); chief ed Magnetic Resonance Imaging 1985–91, assoc ed Jl of Magnetic Resonance Imaging 1991–; club doctor: Montrose Football Club 1990–95, Dundee United Football Club 1995–; pres Soc for Magnetic Resonance Imaging 1983; FFR, RCSI 1978, FRCPE 1992, Dip in Sports Med 1992; *Books* magnetic Resonance in Medicine and Biology (1984), Practical Nuclear Medicine (1989); *Recreations* swimming, walking, entomology, fly fishing, golf; *Style*— Dr Francis Smith; ✉ 7 Primrosehill Road, Cults, Aberdeen, Scotland AB15 9ND (☎ 01224 868745);

Department of Nuclear Medicine, Aberdeen Royal Infirmary, Foresterhill, Aberdeen AB25 2ZD (☎ 01224 681818, fax 01224 840700)

SMITH, Frank Arthur; s of George Frederick Stanley Smith (d 1984), of Nottingham, and Doris Hannah, *née* Simcock (d 1984); *b* 18 Dec 1941; *Educ* King Edward VII Sch Sheffield, Trinity Coll Oxford (MA); *m* 1, 14 Oct 1967, Eva June (d 1990), da of George Henry Larner, of Haverfordwest; 1 s (Thomas Louis b 19 March 1972), 1 da (Anna Margaret b 23 March 1969); m 2, 23 Oct 1993, Karin Ulrika, da of Axel Ludwig Bäck, of Eksjö, Sweden; 3 step da (Anna Rachel b 7 June 1963, Miriam Elna b 28 Dec 1966, Rebecca Karin b 4 Dec 1968); *Career* Robson Rhodes 1963– (nat tax ptnr 1983–93), seconded as head Int Dept Salustro Reydel Paris 1993–; memb Tax Ctee ICAEW 1984–93, memb Tax Ctee London C of C and Indust 1978–86; tstee Geffrye Museum 1989–; memb Ctee Otter Housing Soc 1991–93; FCA 1966, fell Chartered Inst of Taxation 1978; *Recreations* walking, reading, gardening, jazz, cinema; *Style*— Frank Smith, Esq; ✉ 14 Rue de Birague, 75004 Paris, France (☎ 00 33 1 48 04 85 74); Salustro Reydel, 8 Avenue Delcassé, 75008 Paris, France (☎ 00 33 1 53 77 38 75, fax 00 33 1 53 77 39 08); Eastnor Garden House, 73 Tranquil Vale, Blackheath, London SE3 0BP (☎ 0181 852 6390); Robson Rhodes, 186 City Rd, London EC1V 2NU (☎ 0171 251 1644, fax 0171 250 0801)

SMITH, Prof Frank Thomas; s of Leslie Maxwell Smith, of Havant, Hants, and Catherine Matilda, *née* Wilken; *b* 24 Feb 1948; *Educ* Kinson CP Sch, Bournemouth GS, Jesus Coll Oxford (BA, DPhil); *m* 16 Sept 1972, Valerie Sheila, da of Albert Alfred Hearn; 3 da (Helen b 1976, Natalie b 1978, Amy b 1987); *Career* res fell Theoretical Aerodynamics Unit Southampton 1972–73, lectr Imperial Coll London 1973–78, visiting prof Univ of W Ontario 1978–79, reader and prof Imp Coll 1979–84, Goldsmid prof in applied maths UCL 1984–; FRS 1984; *Books* Boundary - Layer Separation (with Prof Susan Brown 1987); *Recreations* sports, reading, family; *Style*— Prof F T Smith, FRS; ✉ Mathematics Department, University College, Gower St, London WC1E 6BT (☎ 0171 387 7050 ext 2837)

SMITH, Gary Andrew; s of Walter Henry Smith (d 1984), and Claire Elizabeth, *née* Copps; *b* 13 Oct 1958; *Educ* Colfes GS; *m* 18 April 1990 (m dis); 1 s (Darren Anthony b 13 Sept 1986); *Career* bowls player; England int 1982–; Eng Indoor Pairs winner 1986, 1991 and 1994, Br Isles Pairs winner 1987, 1992 and 1995, World Indoor Pairs runner-up 1987, 1994 and 1996, UK Indoor Singles champion 1988, Eng Indoor Singles champion 1988, Eng Indoor Fours winner 1983, 1984, 1988, 1989, 1990, 1994 and 1996, Br Isles Indoor Fours winner 1989, 1990, 1991 and 1995, Eng Outdoor Mixed Pairs winner 1991, England Outdoor Pairs winner 1992, Br Isles Outdoor Pairs winner 1993, World Indoor Pairs winner 1993, Cwlth Games pairs bronze medalist 1994; sec and treas Eng Bowls Players Assoc, sec Professional Bowls Assoc; with Barclays Bank 1976–92, mktg mangr Botra Bowlswear 1992–; ACIB; *Recreations* bowls, music, gardening; *Clubs* Cyphers, Blackheath and Greenwich; *Style*— Gary Smith, Esq; ✉ 42A Macoma Road, Plumstead, London SE18 2QP (☎ and fax 0181 317 0903)

SMITH, Geoffrey Edwin; OBE (1981); s of Curtis Edwin Smith, (d 1993), and Mabel Alice, *née* Bacon (d 1971); *b* 9 Nov 1930; *Educ* Hertford GS; *m* 5 April 1958, (Jeanette) Jan Mary, da of Rex Saynor (d 1976), of Mirfield; 1 s (Jeremy Redington b 12 March 1969), 1 da (Charlotte Victoria b 2 Oct 1964); *Career* RAF 1949; sr asst co librarian Herts CC, dep co librarian Hants Co Library 1959–63, co librarian Leicestershire CC 1963–73, dir libraries and information serv Leicestershire CC 1973–90; T C Farries and Co: dir 1990–94, vice chm 1992–94, conslt 1994–; sr res fell Loughborough Univ 1987–; memb: Library Assoc Cncl 1962–79, Library Advsy Cncl 1972–78, Library and Information Servs Cncl 1985–88; Soc Co Librarians: memb Exec Ctee 1963–89, vice pres 1982–88, pres 1989; FRSA, FIMgt, FLA 1956; *Recreations* swimming, cinema; *Clubs* Society of Bookmen; *Style*— Geoffrey Smith, Esq, OBE; ✉ 16 Soar Rd, Quorn, Loughborough, Leics LE12 8BW (☎ 01509 412 655)

SMITH, Wing Cdr Geoffrey Wilfred Tracey; s of Claude Smith (d 1974), of Upper Poppleton, York, and Doris Lilian Tracey Smith (d 1977); *b* 18 March 1927; *Educ* West Hartlepool GS, Downing Coll Cambridge (MA, MB BChir), St Bart's Hosp; *m* 22 Dec 1954 (m dis 1977), (Barbara) Megan, da of William Ashley, DSM (d 1946), of Cairo; 1 s (Nigel b 1963); m 2, 16 Feb 1978, Teresa Jeanne, da of late Robert Audley Furtado, CB, of Langton Herring, Dorset; *Career* Lt HLI 1945–48, RAF 1959–75 (ret Wing Cdr); conslt ophthalmology RAF 1971–75, asst ophthalmic surgn Guy's Hosp 1976–78, sr conslt Miny of Public Health Qatar 1978–85; pty candidate (Lab) Fylde constituency 1987, Euro Parly candidate (Lab) Lancs Central 1989, Parly candidate (Lab) S Ribble Lancs 1992; former chm Monks Orchard Branch (Croydon NE) Lab Pty; FRCSEd 1971, FRCOphth 1989; *Recreations* organist; *Clubs* The Golfers; *Style*— Wing Cdr Geoffrey Smith; ✉ Fig Tree Cottage, 18 Church Street, Uckfield, E Sussex TN22 1BJ (☎ 01825 765781)

SMITH, Prof George David William; s of George Alfred William Smith (d 1989), and Grace Violet Hannah Dayton, *née* Bloom; *b* 28 March 1943; *Educ* St Benedict's Sch Aldershot, Salesian Coll Farnborough Hants, CCC Oxford (open scholar, graduate scholar, MA, DPhil); *m* 1968, Josephine Ann, da of Edwin Walter Halford; 2 s (Timothy George Edwin b 1969, Richard Charles Edwin b 1972); *Career* Univ of Oxford: SRC research fell 1968–70, postdoctoral research fell 1970–75, sr research fell 1975–77, lectr in metallurgy 1977–92, George Kelley reader in metallurgy 1992–96, prof of materials science 1996–; research fell Wolfson Coll Oxford 1972–77 (jr research fell 1968–72), emeritus fell St Cross Coll Oxford 1992– (fell 1977–91), professorial fell Trinity Coll Oxford 1996– (tutorial fell 1991–95); md Kindbrisk Ltd 1987– (winner R&D 100 award 1993); memb: Inst of Materials (formerly Inst of Metals) 1963–96, ASM Int (formerly American Soc for Metals) 1981–, Materials Research Soc (USA) 1987–, Minerals, Metals and Materials Soc (USA) 1992–; Sir George Beilby medal and prize 1985; Inst of Metals: Vanadium Award (jtly) 1985, Rosenhain medal and prize 1991; CEng 1978, CPhys 1996; FInstP 1996 (MInstP 1978), FIM 1996, FRS 1996; *Books* Atom Probe Microanalysis: Principles and Application to Materials Problems (with M K Miller, 1989), Atom Probe Field Ion Microscopy (jtly, 1996); *Recreations* walking, fishing, birdwatching, travel; *Style*— Prof George Smith, FRS; ✉ Department of Materials, University of Oxford, Parks Road, Oxford OX1 3PH (☎ 01865 273762, fax 01865 273789, e-mail george.smith@materials.oxford.ac.uk)

SMITH, Prof Gerald Stanton; s of Thomas Arthur Smith (d 1974), of Manchester, and Ruth Annie, *née* Stanton; *b* 17 April 1938; *Educ* Stretford GS, Sch of Slavonic and E Euro Studies Univ of London (BA, PhD), Univ of Oxford (DLitt 1996); *m* 2 Aug 1961 (m dis 1981), Frances, da of Percy Wetherill (d 1993), of Deganwy, N Wales; 1 s (Ian b 1964), 1 da (Gillian b 1963); m 2, 16 Feb 1982, Barbara, da of Maj John Henry Heldt (US Army, d 1986), of Sarasota, Florida; 1 step s (Gus b 1969), 1 step da (Elizabeth b 1971); *Career* RAF 1957–60, Corpl 1959 Jt Servs Sch for Linguists 1958, RAF Gatow Berlin 1959–60; jazz musician London 1960–64; lectr in Russian: Univ of Nottingham 1964–71, Univ of Birmingham 1971–79; res fell Univ of Liverpool 1979–82; visiting prof: Indiana Univ 1984, Univ of California Berkeley 1984; private scholar Social Scis and Humanities Res Cncl of Canada 1985, John Simon Guggenheim meml fell 1986, prof of Russian and fell New Coll Oxford Univ 1986–; memb Br Assoc for Slavonic Soviet and E Euro Studies; *Books* Songs to Seven Strings (1985), Contemporary Russian Poetry: A Bilingual Anthology (1993); *Recreations* jazz music (founder of Jazz Orchestra Nottingham 1968), watching water; *Style*— Prof Gerald Smith; ✉ Taylor Institution, Oxford University, St Giles, Oxford OX1 3NA (☎ 01865 270476)

SMITH, Sir (Thomas) Gilbert; 4 Bt (UK 1897) of Stratford Place, St Marylebone, Co London; s of Sir Thomas Turner, 3 Bt (1961); *b* 2 July 1937; *Educ* Huntley Sch, Nelson Coll; *m* 1962, Patricia Christine, da of David Cooper, of Paraparaumu, New Zealand; 2 s, 1 da; *Heir* s, Andrew Thomas Smith b 17 Oct 1965; *Style*— Sir Gilbert Smith, Bt; ✉ PO Box 654, Masterton, New Zealand

SMITH, Gillian Sara; da of Nathan Abraham Oppenheim, of Edinburgh, and Eve Renee, *née* Halson; *b* 26 Jan 1953; *Educ* St George's Sch for Girls Edinburgh, Newnham Coll Cambridge (MA, Roman Law Prize); *m* 5 Oct 1987, Lindsay Meredith Smith; 1 s (Simon Alexander b 25 May 1989); *Career* asst slr Linklaters & Paines 1977–81 (articled clerk 1975–77), in-house counsel Nordic Bank 1981–83; S J Berwin & Co: joined 1983, ptnr 1985–, seconded Watchell Lipton Rosen & Katz New York 1987–89, banking ptnr S J Berwin & Co 1989–, head of Banking 1992–; chair Banking Specialist Gp Interlaw (int assoc of ind law firms); *Recreations* ancient languages, cooking, gardening; *Style*— Mrs Gillian Smith; ✉ S J Berwin & Co, 222 Grays Inn Road, London WC1X 8HB (☎ 0171 533 2222, fax 0171 533 2000, direct ☎ 0171 533 2647)

SMITH, Godfrey; s of Flying Offr Reginald Montague Smith, RAF (d 1975), of Bexhill, and Ada May, *née* Damen; *b* 12 May 1926; *Educ* Surbiton Co Sch, Eggar's GS, Worcester Coll Oxford (MA, pres union); *m* 23 June 1951, Mary, da of Jakub Schoenfeld (d 1966), of Vienna; 3 da (Deborah b 1956, Amanda b 1959, Candida b 1964); *Career* RAF 1944–47; Sunday Times: PA to Lord Kemsley 1951, news ed 1956, asst ed 1959, magazine ed 1965–72, dir 1968–81, assoc ed 1972–91, ed Weekly Review 1972–79, columnist 1979–; Regent's lectr Univ of Calif 1970; author; FRSL 1995; *Novels* The Flaw in the Crystal (1954), The Friends (1957), The Business of Loving (1961, Book Soc choice), The Network (1965), Caviare (1976); *Non-fiction* The English Companion (1984), The English Season (1987, revised edn 1994), The English Reader (1988); *Anthologies* The Best of Nat Gubbins (1978), A World of Love (1982), Beyond the Tingle Quotient (1982), How it Was in the War (1989), Take the Ball and Run (1991); *Recreations* chums; *Clubs* Garrick, Savile, Leander, MCC; *Style*— Godfrey Smith, Esq, FRSL; ✉ 10 Kensington Park Mews, London W11 2EY (☎ 0171 727 4155); Village Farmhouse, Charlton, Malmesbury, Wilts SN16 9DL (☎ 01666 822479, fax 01666 824094)

SMITH, Gordon Walkerley; JP (1977); s of George Arthur Smith (d 1976), and Elsie, *née* Johnson (d 1993); *b* 20 March 1933; *Educ* St James Sch Grimsby, Hull Coll of Architecture; *m* 15 Sept 1956, Anne, da of George Adam Young (d 1978); 1 s (David b 1957), 1 da (Diane b 1961); *Career* architect; princ Sir Charles Nicholson Gp; diocesan surveyor: Lincoln 1970, Southwell 1974; fell Woodard Corpn 1976, Custos St James Sch Grimsby 1985; chm Gy and Cleethorpes Branch NSPCC 1992; Liveryman Worshipful Co of Paviors; FRIBA; *Recreations* reading, gardening, walking, music; *Style*— Gordon W Smith, Esq, JP; ✉ Walkerley House, Barnoldby le Beck, nr Grimsby DN37 0AS (☎ 01472 827665); Sir Charles Nicholson Group, The Old Rectory, Bargate, Grimsby DN34 4SY (☎ 01472 355288)

SMITH, Graham Alan; s of Sydney Horace Smith (d 1970), and Joan Olive, *née* Tame; *b* 29 Oct 1947; *Educ* Beckenham GS for Boys; *m* Aug 1978, Joan Louise; 1 s (Patrick Henry James Smith b Nov 1984); *Career* sales asst then exec ABC TV/Thames TV 1966–70, media gp head Boase Massimi Pollitt Advertising 1970–73, successively business devpt mangr, business devpt dir then vice chm Saatchi & Saatchi Advertising 1973–92, exec vice pres Ogilvy & Mather Europe 1992–94, dir and ptnr Leopard Advertising Ltd 1994–; memb Mktg Soc 1986; *Recreations* motor racing, photography, cricket; *Style*— Graham Smith, Esq; ✉ Leopard Advertising Ltd, 40 Marsh Wall, London E14 9TP (☎ 0171 512 1000, fax 0171 512 1999)

SMITH, Graham Frederick; s of Archibald Frederick Smith, of High Wycombe, Bucks, and Janet Mearing, *née* Hall; *b* 17 Feb 1943; *Educ* Royal GS High Wycombe; *m* 8 Oct 1966, Wendy Elizabeth, da of John Maltby (d 1982), of Oxford; 1 s (Andrew b 1968), 2 da (Lucy b 1972, Melanie b 1976); *Career* ptnr Ernst & Young (CAs) 1975–; former chm High Wycombe Lawn Tennis Club, Bucks County Tennis Colour 1967; FCA 1964; *Recreations* golf, garden, music; *Style*— Graham F Smith, Esq; ✉ Crabtrees, Nairdwood Lane, Prestwood, Great Missenden, Bucks HP16 0QH (☎ 01494 865128); Ernst & Young, Becket House, 1 Lambeth Palace Rd, London SE1 7EU (☎ 0171 928 2000, fax 0171 928 1345)

SMITH, Graham Paul; s of James Alfred Smith (d 1985), and Elsie Winifred, *née* Cleathero; *b* 25 Dec 1949; *Educ* Royal GS High Wycombe, Univ of Durham (BA), Osgoode Hall Law School Toronto (LLM); *m* 14 Sept 1991, Mary, da of Edward T Ray (d 1986), of Southwold, Suffolk; 1 da (Charlotte b 1994); *Career* slr Supreme Ct 1975; ptnr: Clifford-Turner 1981–87, Clifford Chance 1987–; memb Computer Law Assoc; Liveryman Worshipful Co of Slrs; memb Law Soc 1975; *Books* contrib chapters to: The Encyclopaedia of Information Technology Law (1990), Computer Law (3 edn, 1996); *Recreations* opera, cricket; *Clubs* MCC, RAC; *Style*— Graham Smith, Esq; ✉ Clifford Chance, 200 Aldersgate Street, London EC1A 4JJ (☎ 0171 600 1000, fax 0171 600 5555, telex 887847)

SMITH, Graham Richard Elliott; s of Donald Smith (d 1978), and Betty Lillian, *née* Elliott; *b* 24 Feb 1958; *Educ* Royal GS Guildford, Univ of Nottingham (BA); *m* 19 Sept 1987, Sharon Elizabeth Peterson, da of Aubrey Owen Mulroney, of Nortonbury, Morgans Rd, Hertford, Herts; 2 s (Sebastian Guy Elliott b 5 November 1991, Willem Peter Elliott b 5 April 1994)), 1 da (Leone Jane Peterson b 4 June 1990); *Career* admitted slr 1982; ptnr Wilde Sapte 1987– (articled clerk 1980–82, slr 1982–87); Freeman Worshipful Co of Slrs 1986–; memb: Law Soc, Int Bar Assoc; *Recreations* skiing, fine wine, travel; *Style*— Graham Smith, Esq; ✉ Wilde Sapte, 1 Fleet Place, London EC4M 7WS (☎ 0171 246 7000, fax 0171 246 7777)

SMITH, Graham William; CBE (1990); s of William George Smith, of Salisbury, Wilts, and Edith May, *née* Bown (d 1992); *b* 15 Aug 1939; *Educ* Bishop Wordsworth Sch Salisbury, Univ of Durham (CSS), Univ of Newcastle upon Tyne (post grad dip); *m* 6 Dec 1958, Jeanne Lilian Ann, da of Thomas George Goodyear; 2 s (Adrian Graham b 18 May 1959, Julian William b 22 May 1968), 1 da (Emma Jane b 4 Nov 1963); *Career* probation officer Durham City 1965–69, sr probation officer Durham and HM Prison 1969–71; Inner London Probation Serv: asst chief probation officer 1973–78, dep chief probation officer 1978–81, chief probation officer 1981–92; HM Chief Inspr of Probation 1992–; Home Office Dept of Health review on mentally disordered offenders 1991; memb: Home Sec's Advsy Bd on Restricted Patients 1986–92, Lord Chancellor's Advsy Ctee on Legal Educn and Conduct 1991–, Cncl Inst of Criminology; govr Nat Inst of Social Work 1992, chm Assoc of Chief Officers of Probation 1988–89; visiting prof UN Asia and Far East Inst Tokyo 1981–83; memb Penological Ctee Cncl of Europe 1994–; Margaret Mead Award Int Assoc of Residential and Community Alternatives 1990; Freeman City of London 1974; *Recreations* reading, all sport, gardening, travel, grandchildren; *Style*— Graham Smith, Esq, CBE; ✉ The Cottage, Swanley Village Rd, Swanley Village, Kent BR8 7NG (☎ 01322 665427); Home Office, 50 Queen Anne's Gate, London SW1H 9AT (☎ 0171 273 2690)

SMITH, Prof Hamilton; s of Alexander Forrest Smith, of Kilsyth, and Elsie May Annie, *née* Dinnick (d 1988); *b* 27 April 1934; *Educ* Kilsyth Acad, Univ of Glasgow (BSc, PhD); *m* 14 May 1962, Jacqueline Ann, da of Robert Brechin Spittal (d 1983); *Career* Univ of Glasgow: MRC fell 1960–63, special res fell 1963–64, lectr then sr lectr in forensic med 1964–84, reader in forensic med and sci 1984–87, prof of forensic med and toxicology 1987–; author of several scientific papers; FRSC 1973, FRCPath 1984, FRSE 1991; *Books* Glaister's Medical Jurisprudence and Toxicology (edn 13, 1973); *Recreations* golf, gardening; *Clubs* Royal Scottish Automobile, New (St Andrews); *Style*— Prof Hamilton Smith, FRSE; ✉ Department of Forensic Medicine and Science, University of Glasgow, Glasgow G12 8QQ (☎ 0141 339 8855, fax 0141 330 4602)

SMITH, Hon (William) Henry Bernard; s and h of 4 Viscount Hambleden, *qv*; *b* 18 Nov 1955; *m* 1983, Sara Suzanne, da of Joseph F Anlauf, of Palos Verdes Estates, California, USA; 2 da (Sara Marie Celeste b 1986, Alexandra Patricia b 1989); *Style*— The Hon Henry Smith; ✉ 109 Eccleston Mews, London SW1X 8AQ (☎ 0171 235 4785)

SMITH, Prof Henry Sidney (Harry); s of Prof Sidney Smith (d 1979), of Barcombe, Sussex; *b* 14 June 1928; *Educ* Merchant Taylors', Christ's Coll Cambridge (BA, MA), DLit (London); *m* 18 May 1961, Hazel (d 1991), da of Francis Robert Flory (d 1929); *Career* Nat Serv RCS 1946–49; lectr in Egyptology Univ of Cambridge 1959–63 (asst lectr 1954–59), semi-ret pt/t prof of Egyptology UCL 1986–93 (reader in Egyptian archaeology 1963–70, Edwards prof of Egyptology and head of dept 1970–88); field dir of Egypt Exploration Soc (Nubian Survey 1961, Kor 1965, N Saqqara 1971–81, Memphis 1981–88); fell Christ's Coll Cambridge 1955–63; FBA; *Books* A Visit to Ancient Egypt: Life at Memphis and Saqqara, The Fortress of Buhen (vol 1 1979, vol 2 1976), Saqqara Demotic Papyri (with W J Tait, 1985), The Anubieion at Saqqara (vol 1 with D G Jeffreys, 1988, vol 2 with Lisa L Giddy, 1992); *Recreations* travel, fine art; *Style*— Prof H S Smith, FBA; ✉ Ailwyn House, High Street, Upwood, Huntingdon, Cambridgeshire PE17 1QE (☎ 01487 812196); Department of Egyptology, University College London, Gower St, London WC1E 6BT (☎ 0171 387 7050 ext 2885)

SMITH, Horace Anthony; s of Osbourne Smith (d 1975), and Gertrude Mabel, *née* Reason; *b* 17 Jan 1941; *Educ* De Aston Sch Market Rasen; *m* 1, 4 June 1959 (m dis 1981), Catherine Mary, da of Flt Lt J A Tindall, DFC, of E Yorks; 2 s (David b 1960, Richard b 1962); m 2, 30 Aug 1984, Imelda, da of Jesus Paez, of Manila; 2 da (Annalisa b 1985, Emma Jade b 1987); *Career* sr exec offr Dept of Employment 1965–73, overseas dir Professional and Exec Recruitment 1973–85, dir International Training and Recruitment Link (ITRL) 1985–93, md Coppas International Group Ltd 1989–93, dir Associated Health Care Consultants Ltd 1990–93; regnl dir Europe Middle and Far East National Safety Cncl (USA) and International Safety Cncl 1993–; MRGS 1974, MICD 1994; *Books* Guide to Working Abroad (1983, 1985, 1986, 1987, 1988, 1990, 1992, 1993); *Recreations* cricket, horseracing, bridge, Oriental studies; *Clubs* IOD, Lions Int; *Style*— Horace Smith, Esq; ✉ International Safety Council, 21 Tilton Rd, Borough Green, Kent TN15 8RS (fax 01732 886581, fax 01732 886582)

SMITH, Iain Crichton; OBE (1980); *b* 1928; *m*; *Career* poet, novelist and short story writer in English and Gaelic; English teacher 1955–77; full time writer 1977–; visiting prof Univ of Dundee; essays about work edited by Colin Nicolson (Edinburgh Univ Press); Hon Doctorate: Univ of Dundee 1983, Univ of Glasgow 1984, Univ of Aberdeen 1988; FRSL; *Awards* Poetry Book Soc Recommendations 1972, 1975, 1989 and 1992, Poetry Book Soc Choice 1984, eight Arts Cncl awards, PEN Award 1970, Cwlth Poetry Prize (European Section) 1986, Saltire Prize 1992, Forward Award 1995, Cholmondeley Award 1996; *Novels* incl: Consider the Lilies, The Last Summer, In the Middle of the Wood, An Honourable Death (1992); *Poetry* incl: Collected Poems, Ends and Beginnings (1994); *Short Stories* incl: Short Stories; Bibliography (1990); *Recreations* reading detective stories; *Style*— Iain Crichton Smith, Esq, OBE, FRSL; ✉ Tigh-na-Fuaran, Taynuilt, Argyll PA35 1JW (☎ 018662 463)

SMITH, Dr Ian Edward; s of David N Smith, of Dundee, and Netty T, *née* Millar; *b* 16 May 1946; *Educ* Dundee HS, Univ of Edinburgh (Ettles scholar, Leslie Gold medal), Univ of Illinois (Carnegie scholar), Harvard Univ; *m* 1978, Suzanne D, *née* Mackey; 3 da (Emily b 31 Oct 1979, Rebecca b 24 March 1982, Kate b 12 Dec 1984); *Career* Edinburgh Royal Infirmary: house physician 1971–72, house surgn 1972, SHO Dept of Med 1972–73, med registrar Professorial Unit 1973; locum sr med registrar Med Professorial Unit Royal Marsden Hosp 1974–75 (med registrar 1973–74), Royal Marsden res fell Dept of Med and Biophysics Inst of Cancer Research 1975–76, UICC travelling fell Sidney Farber Cancer Inst Harvard Med Sch 1976–77, lectr in med Inst of Cancer Research and hon sr med registrar Royal Marsden Hosp 1977–78, conslt med oncologist Royal Marsden Hosp 1978–, head Section of Med Inst of Cancer Research 1991– (hon sr lectr 1979–); clinical dir Cancer Research Campaign 1992; chm: Sub-Ctee UK Coordinating Ctee on Cancer Research, Advsy Ctee on Med Oncology RCP; former pres Edinburgh Royal Med Soc; memb: American Soc of Clinical Oncology 1980, Br Assoc for Cancer Research 1981, Br Assoc for Cancer Physicians 1982, Euro Soc of Med Oncology 1986, Br Oncological Assoc 1986; *Books* Autologous Bone Marrow Transplantation in Solid Tumours (jt ed, 1984), Medical Management of Breast Cancer (jt ed, 1991); author of over 200 pubns on breast cancer, lung cancer and cancer biology; *Style*— Dr Ian Smith; ✉ 59 Marryat Road, Wimbledon, London SW19 (☎ 0181 947 3921); Royal Marsden Hospital, Downs Road, Sutton, Surrey SM2 5PT (☎ 0181 642 6011, fax 0181 643 0373)

SMITH, Ian Newell; s of Harry Smith (d 1985), of Kenilworth, and Edith Mary, *née* Newell; *b* 27 July 1933; *Educ* Malvern; *m* 3 Oct 1964 (José) Jillian, da of Flt Lt John Foster Drake, DFC, BEM (d 1959); 1 da (Anna Louise b 9 Sept 1965); *Career* Pilot Offr RAF 1958; admitted slr 1957, sr ptnr Seymours Slrs Coventry 1960–; non-exec dir Coventry Building Society 1973– (chm 1985–87 and 1991–96); pres Warwickshire Law Soc 1994; tstee: Edwards Charity 1962, Coventry Nursing Tst 1972– (chm 1984–), Helen Ley House 1975–, Warwicks Boys Tst 1977–, Samuel Smiths Charity 1987–; sec: Milverton Lawn Tennis 1960–62, Leamington and Dist Round Table (chm 1967–68); Freeman City of Coventry 1960; memb: Drapers' Guild Coventry 1986 (Master 1992), Broadweavers and Clothiers' Co Coventry 1988 (clerk 1988–96); memb Law Soc 1957; *Recreations* golf, sailing, skiing, choral singing, gardening; *Style*— Ian Smith, Esq; ✉ Hexworthy, Birches Lane, Kenilworth (☎ 01926 853238); Seymours, Queens House, Queens Rd, Coventry (☎ 01203 553961, fax 01203 251634)

SMITH, Dr Ian Robertson; s of Robert Smith (d 1988), of Paisley, and Mary Elizabeth Boyd, *née* Loudon (d 1951); *b* 1 Aug 1943; *Educ* Paisley GS, Univ of Glasgow (MB ChB); *m* 1968, Margaret Foster, da of Provost Harry Clunie (d 1993); 1 da (Angela Elizabeth b 9 Nov 1969), 1 s (Michael Stuart b 31 July 1971); *Career* house physician Paisley Infirmary 1968–69, house surgn Inverness Royal Infirmary 1969, SHO in obstetrics Inverness Raigmore 1969–70, GP Inverness 1970–; chm Ness DOC (GP Cooperative) 1996–; gen practice trainer 1986–95, assoc advsr in gen practice 1987–92; memb Highland Health Bd Gp Educn Ctee 1978–; memb: BMA 1970, Highland Med Soc 1970 (pres 1994–95); FRCGP 1991 (hon sec N of Scotland Faculty 1975–87, chm N of Scotland Faculty 1991–93); *Recreations* medical advisor Caledonian Thistle Football Club; *Clubs* Nairn Golf, Inverness 41 Curling; *Style*— Dr Ian Smith; ✉ Dromard, 43 Midmills Road, Inverness IV2 3NZ (☎ 01463 236741); Ardlarich Medical Practices, 15 Culduthel Road, Inverness IV2 4AG (☎ 01463 712233)

SMITH, Ivo; s of Guy Sydney Smith (d 1972), of Market Rasen, Lincs, and Florence Maud, *née* Titmarsh (d 1981); *b* 31 May 1931; *Educ* De Aston GS Market Rasen Lincs, Jesus Coll Cambridge (MA, MChir), Saint Mary's Hosp Med Sch Univ of London; *m* 17 Feb 1962, Janet, da of George James Twyman (d 1936), of Deal, Kent; 1 da (Mary b 1965), 2 s (Robin b 1966, Simon b 1969); *Career* Nat Serv RAF (Educn Branch) 1950–51; conslt surgn, lectr and author on surgery of the breast and the breast in art; memb of Pensions Appeals Tribunals; Freeman City of London 1965, Liveryman Worshipful Soc of Apothecaries 1964; FRCS; *Recreations* my family, fishing, farming; *Style*— Ivo Smith, Esq; ✉ 229 Princes Gardens, London W3 0LU (☎ 0181 992 0939)

SMITH, Prof Ivor Ramsay; s of Howard Smith (d 1966), of Birmingham, and Elsie Emily, *née* Underhill (d 1980); *b* 8 Oct 1929; *Educ* Univ of Bristol (BSc, PhD, DSc); *m* 3 Jan 1962, Pamela Mary, da of Alfred Voake (d 1976), of Birmingham; 3 s (Laurence David b 12 May 1963, Andrew Paul b 25 June 1965, Michael Jonathan b 8 Nov 1968); *Career* design and devpt engr GEC Birmingham 1956–59, reader (also lectr and sr lectr) Univ of Birmingham 1959–74; Loughborough Univ of Technol: prof of electrical power engrg 1974–, head Dept of Electronic and Electrical Engrg 1980–90, dean of engrg 1983–86, pro vice chllr 1987–91; dir: Loughborough Consultants Ltd 1980–, E Midlands Regnl Technol Network (Qazar 7) 1989–; CEng 1974, FIEE 1974, FEng 1988; *Recreations* gardening, walking, reading; *Style*— Prof Ivor Smith, FEng; ✉ 83 Nanpantan Rd, Loughborough, Leics LE11 3ST; Department of Electronic & Electrical Engineering, University of Technology, Loughborough, Leics LE11 3TU (☎ 01509 222821, fax 01509 222854, telex 34319, e-mail i.r.smith@lut.ac.uk)

SMITH, Jack; s of John Edward Smith (d 1984), and Laura Amanda, *née* Booth (d 1949); *b* 18 June 1928; *Educ* Netheredge GS Sheffield, Sheffield Coll of Art, St Martins Sch of Art, RCA (ARCA); *m* 23 June 1956, Susan, da of Brig Gen Hugh Marjoribanks Craigie Halkett (d 1951); *Career* Nat Serv RAF 1946–48; artist; exhibitions: Beaux Arts Gallery London 1952–58, Catherine Viviano Gallery NY 1958, 1962 and 1963, Whitechapel Gallery 1959 and 1971, Matthiesen Gallery 1960 and 1963, Grosvenor Gallery 1965, Marlborough Fine Art 1968, Fischer Fine Art 1981 and 1983, 1983, Angela Flowers Gallery 1990, 1991, 1992 and 1996; work shown: Venice Biennale 1956, Br Painting Madrid 1983 et al; work in permanent collections incl: Tate Gallery, Arts Cncl, Contemporary Art Soc, Br Cncl; *Style*— Jack Smith, Esq; ✉ 29 Seafield Rd, Hove, East Sussex BN23 2TP (☎ 01273 738 312)

SMITH, James Boyd; GM (1943); s of James Hughes Smith (d 1950); *b* 9 Feb 1920; *Educ* George Heriot's Sch Edinburgh, Univ of Edinburgh; *m* 1946, May, *née* Campbell; 1 s (Peter), 1 da (Pamela); *Career* served WWII Capt RE; chartered electrical engr; joined Ferranti plc 1947; dir of various subsidiary cos: Ferranti Offshore Systems 1974–85, Ferranti Cetec Graphics 1977–85, TRW Ferranti Subsea 1977–85, asst gen mangr Ferranti Edinburgh 1980–83, pt/t advsr 1983–85; dir Wolfson Microelectronics Ltd 1984–93; memb Ct Univ of Edinburgh 1975–84; hon fell Univ of Edinburgh 1989; FRSE 1977 (memb Cncl 1992–95); *Recreations* organ playing, genealogy, gardening; *Clubs* New (Edinburgh); *Style*— James Smith, Esq, GM, FRSE; ✉ 28 Murrayfield Road, Edinburgh EH12 6ER (☎ 0131 346 8604)

SMITH, James Cadzow; CBE; s of James Smith (d 1954), of Edinburgh, and Margaret Ann, *née* Cadzow (d 1982); *b* 28 Nov 1927; *Educ* Bellevue Sch Edinburgh, Heriot-Watt Coll, Univ of Strathclyde; *m* 1954, Moira Barrie, da of Joseph Watt Hogg; 1 s (Norman Barrie b 1955), 1 da (Elaine Margaret b 1958); *Career* NI Electricity Serv 1973–77 (dir of Engrg, dep chm and chief exec), chm E Midlands Electricity Bd 1977–82, chm Eastern Electricity Bd 1982–90, chm and chief exec Eastern Electricity plc 1990–93, chm Eastern Group plc (formerly Eastern Electricity) 1993–95; dir N M Rothschild; chm Bd of Mgmnt Royal Greenwich Hosp Sch Holbrook; vice pres Int Union for Electro-heat 1985–88, visiting prof of electrical engrg Univ of Strathclyde; memb Worshipful Co of Engrs, Freeman City of London; Hon LLD Univ of Strathclyde; FIEE 1960 (pres 1989–90), fell Inst of Mechanical and Marine Engrs 1960, FRSE 1981, FEng 1984; *Recreations* mountaineering, skiing, music, theatre; *Clubs* Caledonian, Alpine; *Style*— James C Smith, CBE, FEng, FRSE

SMITH, Dr James Cuthbert (Jim); s of Leslie Cuthbert Smith, of Pinner, Middx, and Freda Sarah, *née* Wragg; *b* 31 Dec 1954; *Educ* Latymer Upper Sch, Christ's Coll Cambridge (MA, Frank Smart prize in zoology), Univ of London (PhD); *m* 22 Sept 1979, Fiona Mary, da of David Mackie Watt; 1 s (Angus James MacDougall b 15 May 1994); *Career* NATO postdoctoral fell Sidney Farber Cancer Inst and Harvard Med Sch 1979–91, ICRF postdoctoral fell 1981–84, head Div of Developmental Biology Nat Inst for Med Research 1991– (memb scientific staff 1984, sr scientist 1990); scientific fell Zoological Soc, Wellcome visiting prof 1991–92, int res scholar Howard Hughes Med Inst 1993–; memb Editorial Bd: The New Biologist 1989–91, Development, Cell, Trends in Genetics, Cell Growth and Differentiation, Current Biology; author of numerous pubns and articles in scientific jls; Scientific medal Zoological Soc 1989, Otto Mangold prize German Soc for Developmental Biology 1991; chm British Soc for Developmental Biology 1994–, memb Euro Molecular Biology Orgn 1992 (medal 1993); FRS 1993; *Recreations* riding, reading, talking, cycling; *Style*— Dr Jim Smith, FRS; ✉ Division of Developmental Biology, National Institute for Medical Research, The Ridgeway, Mill Hill, London NW7 1AA (☎ 0181 913 8524, fax 0181 913 8584)

SMITH, James Edward; s of James Joseph Smith, of Liverpool, and Dorothy, *née* Roberts; *b* 31 March 1950; *Educ* Univ of Liverpool (BA, Duke of Edinburgh Gold award), Liverpool Univ Business Sch (Post Grad Degree in Mktg), Inst of Mktg (Dip MInstM); *m* 1979, Celia Margaret, da of John Nairm; 2 da (Emma Lindsey b 25 Sept 1980, Rebecca Caroline b 20 July 1982); *Career* articled clerk Harwood Banner & Co 1968–71, mktg mangr Mobil Oil 1971–73, student 1973–74, mktg mangr Lonhro 1974–76, mktg dir rising to md Graham Poulter Group 1976–85, client servs dir J Walter Thompson 1988–90 (bd dir 1985–88); chm: JWT Group Manchester until 1996, chm Conquest Creative Services; MInstM; *Recreations* music, wine, skiing, basketball (10 caps England Youth Int), travel; *Clubs* Young Presidents' Organisation; *Style*— James Smith, Esq

SMITH, James Michael (Jim); s of James Smith (d 1965), of Sheffield, and Doris, *née* Rawson; *b* 17 Oct 1940; *Educ* *irth Park GS; *m* 29 July 1961, Yvonne, da of Richard Hammond; 3 da (Alison Jane b 11 Jan 1963, Suzanne Elizabeth b 5 July 1965, Fiona Yvonne b 25 Jan 1968); *Career* professional football manager; former player: Sheffield Utd (no first team appearances), Aldershot (league debut 1961), Halifax Town, Lincoln City, Boston Utd, Colchester Utd; mangr: Boston Utd, Colchester Utd, Blackburn Rovers 1975–78, Birmingham City 1978–82, Oxford Utd 1982–85, Queen's Park Rangers 1985–88, Newcastle Utd 1988–91, Portsmouth 1991–95, Derby County 1995–; coach Middlesbrough 1991 (asst mangr); honours as mangr: Eastern Floodlight League Boston Utd, promotion to Div 3 Colchester Utd 1974, promotion to Div 1 Birmingham City 1980, Div 3 Championship Oxford Utd 1984, Div 2 Championship Oxford Utd 1985, promotion to Premier League Derby County 1995/96, runners up League Cup Queen's Park Rangers 1986, FA Cup semi-finalists 1992; league promotion play-offs reached: Newcastle Utd 1989–90, Middlesbrough 1990–91, Portsmouth 1992–93; Bells Mangr of the Month award 15 times; chief exec League Managers' Assoc 1995; *Books* Bald Eagle (1990); *Recreations* golfing, gardening; *Style*— Jim Smith, Esq; ✉ c/o Derby County FC, Baseball Ground, Derby DE23 8NB (☎ 01332 340105)

SMITH, Jan Eileen; da of Harold Douglas Smith, of Morecambe, and Lena, *née* Barrett; *b* 5 April 1947; *Educ* Convent Sch Lusaka Zambia, Casterton Sch Kirkby Lonsdale Cumbria, Carlisle & County HS Carlisle Cumbria, Univ Coll of Rhodesia Salisbury Rhodesia (BA of Univ of London); *m* 28 April 1973, Ian Dudley Brawn, s of late John Dudley Brawn; *Career* Int Div Midland Bank plc London: graduate trainee 1970–72, area rep trade devpt 1972–76, asst mktg mangr Corp Devpt Area 1978–79; TSB England & Wales plc/TSB Group London: mangr market/product devpt Mktg Div 1983–86 (asst mangr 1980–83); sr mangr market planning and devpt Mktg Dept Lloyds Bank plc London 1986–88, mktg dir First Direct-Midland Group plc London 1989–90, dir of network mktg TSB Bank plc 1990–92; mktg dir Mazda Cars (UK) Ltd 1992–95, gp strategic dir RAC 1995–; winner Product Excellence Award The Mktg Soc 1990; memb: Women's Advtg Club of London, The Marketing Soc; MInstD, FIDM (fndr memb);

Recreations motor racing, Jaguar cars, reading, ballet, swimming; *Clubs* RAC, Jaguar Drivers'; *Style*— Miss Jan E Smith; ✉ RAC Motoring Services, 14 Cockspur Street, London SW1Y 5BL (☎ 0171 389 8925, fax 0171 389 8905)

SMITH, Hon Mrs Justice; Hon Dame Janet Hilary (Dame Janet Mathieson); DBE (1992); da of Alexander Roe Holt (d 1970), and Margaret Holt, *née* Birchall (d 1991); *b* 29 Nov 1940; *Educ* Bolton Sch; *m* 1, 6 June 1959 (m dis 1982), Edward Stuart Smith, s of Edward Austin Carruthers Smith (d 1990); 2 s (Richard b 1959, Alasdair b 1963), 1 da (Rachel b 1962); m 2, 12 Oct 1984, Robin Edward Alexander Mathieson, s of Alexander John Mathieson, MC (d 1974), of Yoxall, Staffs; *Career* called to the Bar Lincoln's Inn 1972, QC 1986, recorder of the Crown Court 1988, memb Criminal Injuries Compensation Bd 1988–92, judge of the High Court of Justice (Queen's Bench Div) 1992–, judge Employment Appeal Tbnl 1994–, presiding judge (NE Circuit) 1995–; *Style*— The Hon Mrs Justice Smith, DBE; ✉ Royal Courts of Justice, Strand, London WC2A 2LL

SMITH, Joan Alison; da of Alan Smith (d 1985), and Ann Anita, *née* Coltman; *b* 27 Aug 1953; *Educ* Girls GS Stevenage, HS for Girls Basingstoke, Univ of Reading (BA); *Career* journalist: Evening Gazette Blackpool 1976–78, Piccadilly Radio Manchester 1978–79, Sunday Times 1979–84; freelance writer 1984–; *Books* Clouds of Deceit (1985), A Masculine Ending (1987), Why Aren't They Screaming? (1988), Misogynies (1989), Don't Leave Me This Way (1990), Femmes de Siècle (ed, 1992), What Men Say (1993), Full Stop (1995), Hungry For You: From Cannibalism to Seduction - A Book of Food (1996); *Style*— Ms Joan Smith; ✉ Rogers, Coleridge and White, 20 Powis Mews, London W11 1JN (☎ 0171 221 3717, fax 0171 229 9084)

SMITH, (Edward Ernest) John; s of Ernest Frederick Smith, DCM, of Chiswick, London, and Elizabeth, *née* Reilly; *b* 13 Aug 1950; *Educ* Latymer Upper Sch London, Emmanuel Coll Cambridge (MA, MD, BChir), St Thomas's Hosp Med Sch; *m* 23 April 1984, Muriel Susan, da of Daniel Shannon, of Ayr; 1 s (David b 1989), 2 da (Susan b 1985, Katherine b 1987); *Career* conslt cardiothoracic surgn St George's Hosp London and Royal Surrey Co Hosp Guildford; memb BMA 1974; FRCS 1978; *Recreations* opera, golf, skiing; *Clubs* London Rowing, Royal Wimbledon Golf; *Style*— John Smith, Esq; ✉ Homewood, 4A Drax Avenue, Wimbledon SW20 0EH (☎ 0181 946 1893); 97 Harley St, London W1N 1DF (☎ 0171 486 2090)

SMITH, Sir John Alfred; kt (1994), QPM (1986); s of Alfred Joseph Smith (d 1988), of Clacton, Essex, and Ruth Alice, *née* Thorpe; *b* 21 Sept 1938; *Educ* St Olave's and St Saviour's GS London SE, Police Staff Coll; *m* 28 May 1960, Joan Maria, da of James Noel Francis (d 1979); 1 s (Martin John b 1965), 1 da (Amanda Jayne (Mrs Hale) b 1962); *Career* joined Met Police 1962, foot beat duty Carter St 1962–66, special course Staff Coll 1966, Inspr Bow St and West End Central Stations 1968–73, Obscene Pubns Branch New Scotland Yard 1973–76, Lewisham Div 1976–77, head Central Drugs Squad 1977–79 (sr cmd course 1978), Cdr 1981, P Dist Bromley and Lewisham Police 1980–81, Dep Chief Constable Surrey Constabulary 1981–84, Met Police 1984–90, head Force Reorganisation Team and Force Inspectorate 1985–87, Asst Cmmr Mgmnt Support Dept 1987–89, Asst Cmmr Specialist Ops Dept 1989–90; HM Inspr of Constabulary 1990–91, Dep Cmmr Met Police 1991–95; pres Assoc of Chief Police Offrs 1993–94 (memb 1981); chm Towards Employability Group 1994–95; formerly: vice pres Surrey Assoc of Youth Clubs, vice pres Surrey PHAB, tstee Crimestoppers Tst; currently: dir Sabrewatch Ltd, conslt IBM (UK) Ltd, advsr on security and crowd control FA of Eng, memb Ctee and dir Automobile Assoc; Freeman City of London 1981; *Recreations* golf, gardening; *Clubs* Crystal Palace FC; *Style*— Sir John Smith, QPM; ✉ 23 Winterbourne, Horsham, West Sussex RH12 5JW (☎ and fax 01403 260935)

SMITH, John Allan Raymond; s of Alexander MacIntyre Smith (d 1979), of Edinburgh, and Evelyn Joyce, *née* Duthie (d 1988); *b* 24 Nov 1942; *Educ* Boroughmuir Sch Edinburgh, Univ of Edinburgh (MB, ChB), Univ of Aberdeen (PhD); *children* 2 s (Richard b 1967, Michael b 1968), 3 da (Jane b 1966, Sheri b 1970, Sara b 1975); m 18 April 1979, Valerie, da of James Fullalove (d 1988), of Eaglescliffe; *Career* house offr Royal Infirmary Edinburgh 1966–67, Dept of Surgery Univ of Aberdeen 1974–76, sr surgical registrar Aberdeen Teaching Hosp 1976–78, sr lectr in surgery Univ of Sheffield and hon conslt surgn Royal Hallamshire Hosp 1978–85, conslt surgn Northern Gen Hosp Sheffield 1985–; contrib of numerous chapters in textbooks; memb Cncl Royal Coll of Surgeons of Edinburgh; FRCS and FRSCEd 1972; *Books* Pyes Surgical Handicraft: Complications in Surgery; *Style*— John A R Smith, Esq; ✉ 4 Endcliffe Grove Ave, Sheffield S10 3EJ (☎ 0114 268 3094); Northern General Hospital, Herries Rd, Sheffield S5 7AU (☎ 0114 243 4343)

SMITH, Dr John Derek; s of Richard Ernest Smith (d 1933), of Mayfield, Wetherby, Yorks, and Winifred Strickland, *née* Davis (d 1932); *b* 8 Dec 1924; *Educ* King James's GS Knaresborough, Clare Coll Cambridge (MA, PhD); *Career* scientific staff ARC Virus Res Unit Cambridge 1945–59, res fell Clare Coll Cambridge 1949–52, visiting scientist Inst Pasteur Paris 1952–53, Rockefeller Fndn fell Univ of California Berkeley 1955–57, sr res fell California Inst of Technol 1959–62, memb scientific staff MRC Laboratory of Molecular Biology Cambridge 1962–88, ret; Sherman Fairchild Distinguished Scholar California Inst of Technol 1974–75; FRS 1976; *Recreations* travel, cuisine; *Style*— Dr John Smith, FRS; ✉ 12 Stansgate Avenue, Cambridge CB2 2QZ (☎ 01223 247 841)

SMITH, John Ernest; s of Ernest Theodore Smith, of Chigwell, and Sybil Margaret, *née* Jones; *b* 30 March 1949; *Educ* Chigwell Sch; *m* 2 Sept 1971, Jill Kathleen, da of Leonard Victor George Dennis, of Wanstead, London; 1 s (Richard b 1979), 1 da (Sarah); *Career* qualified CA 1971; Ernst & Young (formerly Arthur Young): ptnr 1978–90, nat dir of business servs 1982–85, regnl managing ptnr 1989–90; dir: Security Design Associates Ltd 1990–, C P Holdings Ltd 1991–; pres CA Students Soc London 1983–85, chm London Soc CA 1986–87, memb Cncl ICAEW 1987–93 (chm Res Bd 1988–90, chm Ethics Ctee 1989–90), chm Agric Trg Bd 1989–92; ind memb Agric Wages Bd Eng and Wales 1987–89; Liveryman Worshipful Co of Chartered Accountants; FCA; *Recreations* golf, cricket, football, food and drink; *Clubs* MCC, Wig and Pen; *Style*— John E Smith, Esq; ✉ 10 Bearswood End, Beaconsfield, Bucks HP9 2NR (☎ 01494 671275); C P Holdings Ltd, C P House, Otterspool Way, Watford, Herts WD2 8HG (☎ 01923 250500, fax 01923 221628)

SMITH, Prof John Harold; s of Reginald William Smith (d 1967), of Hythe, Kent, and Cicely Doreen, *née* Page (d 1984); *b* 21 April 1927; *Educ* Harvey GS Folkestone, LSE (BA); *m* 13 Jan 1951, Jean, da of Henry John Horton, MBE (d 1973), of Hythe, Kent; 2 s (Christopher b 1953, Nigel b 1954), 1 da (Rachel b 1964); *Career* RNVR 1944–48; res worker Acton Soc Tst 1950–52, lectr LSE 1952–64; Univ of Southampton: prof of sociology 1964–91, dean of Faculty of Social Scis 1967–70, dep vice-chllr 1974–78, curator and chm Hartley Library 1983–87, emeritus prof 1991; visiting prof Aston Business Sch 1996–; contrib to numerous articles in scientific jls; memb: Cncl CNAA 1967–74, Educn Ctee King's Fund 1970–76, Cncl Central Cncl for Educn and Trg in Social Work 1971–78, DHSS Small Grants Ctee 1975–79, Mgmnt Cncl Southern Arts Assoc 1978–91, Advsy Ctee Open Univ 1986–93, sec of state Advsy Ctee on the Arts and Heritage 1990–96, Southern Arts Bd 1991–95; govr King Alfred's Coll Winchester 1976–89; chm John Hansard Memorial Tst 1995–; memb Br Sociological Assoc 1952–; FRSA 1978; *Books* Management under Nationalization (1954), Industrial Sociology (1961), Married Women Working (1963), Manpower Policy and Employment Trends (1967), Select List of British Parliamentary Papers (1979); *Recreations* walking, photography; *Style*— Prof John Smith; ✉ Rutland Lodge, South Parade, Ledbury, Herefordshire HR8 2HB 01531 633449); Aston Business School, Aston University, Aston Triangle, Birmingham B4 7ET (☎ 0121 359 3611, fax 0121 359 6384, e-mail (JANET) BUSINESSS@UK.AC.ASTON)

SMITH, John Herbert (Jack); CBE (1977); s of Thomas Arthur Smith (d 1979), of Shipley, West Yorks, and Pattie, *née* Lord (d 1962); *b* 30 April 1918; *Educ* Salt HS Shipley Yorks; *m* 22 Sept 1945, Phyllis (Mary), da of Jacob Baxter (d 1949), of Bradford, Yorks; 2 s (Robert b 1946, Nigel b 1952), 3 da (Helen b 1949, Rosamond b 1953, Alison b 1956); *Career* WWII, RAMC N Africa and Italy 1940–46; dept clerk and chief fin offr Littleborough Lancs 1946–48, various posts West Midlands Gas Bd 1949–61, chief accountant Southern Gas Bd 1961–65, dep chm E Midlands Gas Bd 1968–72 (dir of fin and admin 1965–68), dep chm and chief exec Br Gas Corp 1976–83 (memb for fin 1973–76), memb Mgmnt Ctee Lazard American Exempt Fund 1976–91; chm: Moracrest Investments 1977–85, Nationalised Industs Fin Panel 1978–83; dep chm Mgmnt Ctee Pension Fund Property Unit Tst 1984–89 (memb 1975), chm United Property Unit Tst 1986–89 (memb 1983); memb: Trilateral Cmmn 1976–85, Br American Property Unit Tst 1982–93, Cncl ICAEW 1977–81; FCA 1939, memb IPFA 1949, CGASE 1968, FRSA 1985; *Recreations* piano playing, walking; *Style*— Jack Smith, Esq, CBE; ✉ 81 Albany, Manor Rd, East Cliff, Bournemouth, Dorset BH1 3EJ (☎ 01202 298 157)

SMITH, Sir John Lindsay Eric; CH (1994), kt (1988), CBE (1975), JP (1964, Berks), DL (1978); s of Capt E C E Smith, MC, of Ashfold, Handcross, Sussex; *b* 3 April 1923; *Educ* Eton, New Coll Oxford; *m* 1952, Christian Margaret, da of Col Ughtred Elliott Carnegy of Lour, DSO, MC (d 1973); 2 s (Adam Carnegy Eric b 1953, Bartholomew Evan Eric b 1955), 3 da (Emma Victoria Eric b 1956, d 1983, Serena Mary (Hon Mrs Nicholas Soames) b 1959, Clare Elizabeth Dido (Mrs Simon Sheffield) b 1962); *Career* served RNVR 1942–46; dir: Coutts & Co 1950–93, Rolls Royce 1955–75, Financial Times 1959–68; dep govr Royal Exchange Assurance 1961–66; MP (C) Cities of London and Westminster 1965–70; High Steward Maidenhead 1966–75; memb: Historic Buildings Cncl 1971–78, Redundant Churches Fund 1972–74, Nat Heritage Memorial Fund 1980–82; Lord-Lt Berks 1975–78, dep chm Nat Tst 1980–85 (memb Exec Ctee 1961–85); fell Eton Coll 1974–89; hon fell New Coll Oxford 1979; Hon FRIBA; Liveryman Worshipful Co of Fishmongers; KStJ; *Style*— Sir John Smith, CH, CBE, JP, DL; ✉ Shottesbrooke Park, Maidenhead, Berks SL6 3SW

SMITH, Sir Joseph William Grenville; kt (1991); s of Douglas Ralph Smith (d 1987), of Cardiff, and Hannah Leticia Margaret, *née* Leonard (d 1968); *b* 14 Nov 1930; *Educ* Cathays HS Boys Cardiff, Welsh Nat Sch of Med (MB BCh), Univ of London, Univ of Wales (MD); *m* 3 Aug 1954, Nira Jean, da of Oliver Davies (d 1964), of Burry Port, Carms; 1 s (Jonathan b 1955); *Career* Nat Serv RAF 1954–56, Flying Offr Med Branch (later Flt Lt), MO RAF SYLT, 2 TAF BAOR; lectr (later sr lectr) bacteriology and immunology London Sch of Hygiene and Tropical Medicine 1960–65, conslt clinical bacteriologist Radcliffe Infirmary Oxford 1965–69, head of bacteriology Wellcome Res Laboratories 1969, princ in gen practice Islington 1970–71, dep dir epidemiological res lab Public Health Laboratory Serv 1971–76; dir: Nat Inst for Biological Standards and Control 1976–85, Public Health Laboratory Serv of England and Wales 1985–92; chm Bd of Mgmnt LSHTM 1995–; memb: Br Pharmacopoea Cmmn 1976–85, Cncl Royal Coll of Pathology 1988–90, MRC 1988–92; FRCPath 1975, FFPHM 1976, FRCP 1987; *Books* Tetanus (jtly, 1969); *Style*— Sir Joseph Smith; ✉ 95 Lofting Road, London N1 1JF

SMITH, Kate; da of Reginald Ernest Bayston, of Co Durham, and Mabel, *née* Jackson; *b* 8 May 1951; *Educ* Orpington Co Secdy Sch Kent, Wilby Carr HS Doncaster Yorkshire, Doncaster Coll of Technol, Univ of Leeds (BA), Wine & Spirit Educn Tst (higher cert in wines & spirits, instructors cert in wines & spirits Dip pt A&B); *m* 14 Oct 1973, Richard Francis Smith, s of late William Henry Bernard Smith; 2 s (Giles Edward b 25 April 1983, Rupert James b 29 Aug 1995); *Career* asst mangr Restaurant and Banqueting Div Trust House Forte London 1974–75, lectr in food and beverages North Devon Coll 1976–77; Royal Garden Hotel London: project mangr Garden Cafe 1978, acting banqueting mangr 1978–80, promotions mangr 1980; sales and mktg dir Hyatt Carlton Tower London 1982, conslt Rank Hotels Ltd 1982–84, dir Smith Giddings Ltd (parent co of The Beetle & Wedge Hotel Moulsford-on-Thames Oxon); winner: Pub of the Year Award The Royal Oak 1985, Badoit Restaurant of the Year Award Beetle & Wedge 1991, Gonzalez Byass Customer Care Award Beetle & Wedge 1992, Good Hotel Guide Cesar Award 1993, Hosts of the Year Egon Ronay Guide Beetle & Wedge 1995; Master Innholder until 1995, memb Academie Culinaire de France; *Recreations* skiing, theatre, interior design, wine and food; *Style*— Mrs Kate Smith; ✉ The Beetle & Wedge Hotel, Moulsford-on-Thames, Oxford OX10 9JF (☎ 01491 651381, fax 01491 651376)

SMITH, Prof Keith; s of Joseph Smith (d 1972), and Catherine Maria, *née* Carr (d 1985); *b* 9 Jan 1938; *Educ* Hyde County GS Cheshire, Univ of Hull (BA, PhD); *m* 29 July 1961, Muriel Doris, da of George Hyde (d 1988); 1 s (Matthew b 1968), 1 da (Fiona b 1966); *Career* tutor in geography Univ of Liverpool 1963–65, lectr in geography Univ of Durham 1965–70, prof of geography Univ of Strathclyde 1982–86 (sr lectr 1971–75, reader 1975–82); Univ of Stirling: prof of environmental science 1986–, head Sch of Natural Sciences 1994–96, dean Faculty of Natural Sciences 1996–; FRSE 1988; *Books* Water in Britain (1972), Principles of Applied Climatology (1975), Human Adjustment to The Flood Hazard (1979), Environmental Hazards (1992, 2 edn 1996); *Recreations* gardening, hill-walking; *Style*— Prof Keith Smith, FRSE; ✉ 11 Grinnan Rd, Braco, By Dunblane, Perthshire, Scotland FK15 9RF (☎ 01786 880359); Faculty of Natural Sciences, University of Stirling, Stirling, Scotland FK9 4LA (☎ 01786 467750, fax 01786 446896)

SMITH, Keith D; s of Charles Henry Denis Smith, of West Sussex, and Renée Hilda, *née* Marriner; *b* 21 Sept 1948; *Educ* Hampton Sch, Univ of Durham (BA), Univ of Sussex (MA); *m* 1, 1 April 1972 (m dis 1986), Jacquelyn Patricia; m 2, 20 Sept 1991, Susan Patricia; 2 s (Samuel Henry Victor b 9 July 1989, Abel Charles Haverford b 13 Sept 1990), 1 da (Abigael Alice Victoria b 12 March 1992); *Career* graduate trainee Wasey Pritchard-Wood 1971–73, sr planner Doyle Dane Bernbach 1973–74, account dir McCann-Erickson 1974–77, bd dir Grey Advertising 1977–81, jt fndr ptnr Wright & Partners 1981–85 (sold to Ayer Barker); TBWA: dep md TBWA Holmes Knight Ritchie (London) 1985–94, dir Europe, ME and India (Brussels) 1994–96, chm Asia Regn 1996–; winner Duke of Edinburgh's Award; memb Marketing Soc 1989; *Recreations* cricket, soccer, squash, bull-fighting; *Clubs* MCC, Lansdowne; *Style*— Keith Smith, Esq; ✉ TBWA Lee Davis, 8/F CC Wu Building, 302–308 Hennessy Road, Wanchai, Hong Kong (☎ 00 852 28 33 20 33, fax 00 852 28 34 58 77)

SMITH, Kenneth David; s of Percival Smith (d 1985), and Doris Lillian, *née* Townsend; *b* 27 Feb 1944; *Educ* Beckenham Tech Sch, Beckenham Art Sch, SE London Tech Coll; *m* 1 (m dis 1993); 1 s, 2 da; m 2, 19 Nov 1993, Marilyn Susan, *née* Brittain; *Career* designer; Elsom Pack Roberts (chartered architects, and town planners) 1978–86, ptnr EPR Design Partnership 1985–89, md EPR Design Ltd 1988–92, md KDS & Associates 1992–; memb City Architecture Forum; Freeman: City of London 1981, Worshipful Co of Paviors (ctee memb 1988–); FCSD; *Recreations* art, theatre, music; *Clubs* RAC; *Style*— Kenneth Smith, Esq; ✉ 10 Edward Henry House, Cornwall Road, Waterloo, London SE1 8YF; KDS & Associates Ltd, 201 The Blackfriars Foundry, 156 Blackfriars Road, London SE1 8EN (☎ 0171 721 7091, fax 0171 721 7093)

SMITH, Lance Clifford Redfern-; s of George Morritt Refern-Smith (d 1990), of Cobham, Surrey, and Joan Grace, *née* Creasey; *b* 20 Jan 1950; *Educ* Wrekin Coll, Cambridge Poly (BA); *m* 5 July 1974, (Anne) Fiona, da of late David Edwin Bull; 1 s (Rory Oliver Redfern-Smith b 8 Feb 1981), 2 da (Gemma Abigail Redfern-Smith b 30

June 1978, Tamsin Annabel Redfern-Smith b 29 July 1984); *Career* retail mktg accountant Petrofina (UK) Ltd 1971, Smith & Nephew 1972–75 (brand mangr rising to product gp mangr Toiletry), commercial mangr Building Products Div Olin Corp 1975–77, Polycell (UK) Ltd 1977–80 (new products devpt mangr, Trade Div mangr, mktg mangr, trade devpt mangr), IMP Ltd 1980–91 (account dir, bd dir, md, chief exec offr), chief operating offr Darcy Masius Benton & Bowles Ltd 1992–; chm: DMB&B Portugal, DMB&B Financial; dir: DMB&B Inc, DMB&B Holdings Ltd; *Recreations* hunting (Southdown & Eridge), riding, shooting, fly-fishing; *Clubs* Champneys; *Style*— Lance Smith, Esq; ✉ D'Arcy Masius Benton & Bowles, 123 Buckingham Palace Road, London SW1W 9DZ (☎ 0171 630 0000, fax 0171 630 0033)

SMITH, Lance, né Tchisic; s of Dragan Tchisic, of Serbia, and Lilian May, *née* Smith (d 1990); *b* 8 Oct 1950; *Educ* Reed's Sch Cobham Surrey, Camberwell Sch of Arts and Crafts London, Royal Academy Schools London; *m* 1987, Putrisha, da of Soloman Fintan Lawlor (d 1975); 1 s (Ludovic b 29 Dec 1992); *Career* artist; *Solo Exhibitions* Painting and Drawings (Fabian Carlsson Gallery London and Arnolfini Gallery Bristol, illustrated catalogue) 1986, Forum Int Kunstmesse Zurich 1987, Paintings and Drawings 1984–88 (Turnpike Gallery Leigh Gtr Manchester, South Hill Park Arts Centre Bracknell, The Minories Colchester, The Arts Cncl Gallery Belfast and Hendriks Gallery Dublin, illustrated catalogue) 1988, Fabian Carlsson Gallery (London) 1989, Blasón Gallery (London, illustrated catalogue) 1990, Sammlung Hauser and Wirth Zürich and Goldach 1992, Galerie Andy Jllien Zürich 1992, Galerie Helmut Pabst Frankfurt 1994, Galerie Arte Nuova Flawil 1994; *Group Exhibitions* incl: Nat Open Art Exhibition TSWA (Newlyn and Penwith Galleries, Cornwall and nat tour, illustrated catalogue) 1984, Second Int Contemporary Art Fair (London) 1985, Tolly Cobbold/Eastern Arts Fifth Nat Exhibition (Fitzwilliam Museum, Cambridge and tour, illustrated catalogue) 1985, Contemporary Art Fair (Galleri Mustad Stockholm) 1986, Fabian Carlsson Gallery (London) 1986, New Year - New York (Fabian Carlsson Gallery London) 1987, The Romantic Tradition in Contemporary British Painting (Sala de Exposiciones Comunidad, Autónoma de la Region de Murcia, Circulo de Bellas Artes Madrid and Ikon Gallery Birmingham, illustrated catalogue) 1988, Landscape and Beyond (Cleveland Gallery Middlesbrough) 1988, Salama-Caro Gallery (London) 1988, Second Int Festival of Art (Baghdad) 1988, The Drawing Show (Thumb Gallery London) 1988 and 1990, Reflexions Abstraites (Galerie Faris Paris) 1989, Galeri B & W (St Galen Switzerland) 1990, Gruzelier Modern and Contemporary Art London 1990, Hope Suffrance Print Studios London 1991, Collection Hauser and Wirth Zürich 1992 and 1993; work in public collections incl Fitzwilliam Museum Cambridge and Fndn Hauser and Wirth Zürich; work in private collections throughout Eng, Denmark, France, Germany, Ireland, Monaco, NZ, Spain, Sweden, Switzerland and USA, *Awards* Arts Cncl of GB award 1980; first prize: Tolly Cobbold/Eastern Arts Fifth Nat Exhibition 1985, Second Int Festival of Art Baghdad 1988; *Clubs* Chelsea Arts (hon memb); *Style*— Lance Smith, Esq; ✉ 17 Reardon House, Reardon St, London E1 9QJ (☎ 0171 481 4508); Carysfort Rd Studios, 53b Carysfort Rd, London N16 9AD (☎ 0171 923 3346); c/o Iwan Wirth and Ursula Hauser, Sammlung Hauser and Wirth AG, Sonneggstrasse 84, CH-8006, Switzerland

SMITH, Lawrence George Albert; s of Lawrence Cyril Smith (d 1966), of Kidderminster, Worcs, and Ida Mildred Smith, *née* Moule (d 1970); *b* 17 Dec 1930; *Educ* King Charles I Sch Kidderminster, Univ of Birmingham (LLB); *m* 12 Nov 1955, Tess, da of Bertram Bishop (d 1957), of Worcs; 3 da (Sally b 1960, Rachel b 1963, Rebecca b 1968); *Career* Nat Serv Lt S Staffs Regt BAOR 1955; admitted slr 1954; ptnr Thursfields 1964–92, NP 1977–, clerk Clare Witnell & Blount Charity 1973–91; dep chm Kidderminster Cons Assoc 1971–73, pres Kidderminster and Dist C of C 1984–86; assoc Inst of Euro Law Univ of Birmingham 1991–, dir West Mercia Chamber of Commerce and Industry Ltd 1992–, memb Nat Cncl Assoc of British C of Cs 1993–95, govr Kidderminster Coll 1994–96; *Recreations* rugby football, sailing, rambling, politics; *Style*— Lawrence Smith, Esq; ✉ Bracton House, 5 Westville Ave, Kidderminster, Worcs DY11 6BZ (☎ 01562 824806); Thursfields, 14 Church St, Kidderminster (☎ 01562 820575, fax 01562 66783, telex 337837)

SMITH, Sir Leslie Edward George; kt (1977); *b* 15 April 1919; *Educ* Christ's Hosp; *m* 1, 1943, Lorna Pickworth; 2 da; m 2, 1964, Cynthia Holmes; 1 s, 1 da; *Career* The BOC Group: joined 1956, gp md 1969–72, chm and chief exec 1972–79, chm 1979–85; dir Cadbury Schweppes 1977–87; memb: Exec Ctee King Edward VII Hosp for Offrs 1978–87, NEB 1979; pt/t memb British Gas Corpn 1982–90; FCA; *Style*— Sir Leslie Smith; ✉ Norton Hall, Mickleton Chipping, Campden, Glos GL55 6PX (☎ 01386 438790)

SMITH, Llewellyn Thomas; MP (Lab) Blaenau Gwent (majority 30,067); *Career* MP (Lab) Blaenau Gwent 1992–; *Style*— Llewellyn Smith, Esq, MP; ✉ House of Commons, London SW1A 0AA (☎ 0171 219 3000)

SMITH, Prof Lorraine Nancy; da of Geoffrey Leonard Millington, of Ottawa, and Ida May, *née* Attfield; *b* 29 June 1949; *Educ* Hillcrest HS Ottawa, Univ of Ottawa (BScN), Univ of Manchester (MEd, PhD); *m* Christopher Murray, s of Herbert Murray Smith (d 1990); 1 s (Nicholas Geoffrey Murray b 13 Nov 1979), 1 da (Jennifer Eugenie b 17 Dec 1983); *Career* staff nurse 1971–75, sister 1975–76; lectr Dept of Nursing Studies Univ of Manchester 1976–90; Univ of Glasgow: prof 1990–, head of dept 1990–; memb: Acute Healthcare Res Ctee 1991–94, UK Clinical Standards Advsy Gp 1994–, Turning Point (Scotland), RCN; *Recreations* bridge, sailing, reading, skiing; *Clubs* S Caernarvonshire Yacht; *Style*— Prof Lorraine N Smith; ✉ Department of Nursing Studies and Midwifery, University of Glasgow, 68 Oakfield Avenue, Glasgow G12 8LS (☎ 0141 330 4051, fax 0141 307 8039)

SMITH, Dame Margaret Natalie Cross (Maggie); DBE (1990, CBE 1970); da of Nathaniel Smith, and Margaret Little, *née* Hutton; *b* 28 Dec 1934; *Educ* Oxford HS for Girls, Oxford Playhouse Sch; *m* 1, 1967 (m dis 1975), Robert Stephens, actor (later Sir Robert Stephens; d 1995); 2 s (Christopher (actor under name of Chris Larkin), Toby); m 2, 1975, Beverley Cross, *qv*; *Career* actress; debut as Viola in Twelfth Night (OUDS) 1952, NY debut as comedienne in New Faces (Ethel Barrymore Theatre) 1956; dir United Br Artists 1982–; Hon DLitt: Univ of St Andrews 1971, Univ of London 1991, Univ of Cambridge 1994; Shakespeare Prize 1991, BAFTA Special Achievement Award 1993, Channel 4 Lifetime Achievement Award 1995; *Theatre* for Old Vic Co 1959–60 credits incl: The Double Dealer, As You Like it, Richard II, The Merry Wives of Windsor, What Every Woman Knows; for Nat Theatre credits incl: The Recruiting Officer 1963, Othello, The Master Builder, Hay Fever 1964, Much Ado About Nothing, Miss Julie 1965, A Bond Honoured 1966, The Beaux' Stratagem (also USA) 1970, Hedda Gabler (Evening Standard Best Actress Award) 1970, War Plays 1985, Coming in to Land 1986; at Festival Theatre Stratford Ontario: Antony and Cleopatra, The Way of the World, Measure for Measure, The Three Sisters 1976, A Midsummer Night's Dream, Richard II, The Guardsman, As You Like it, Hay Fever 1977, As You Like It, Macbeth, Private Lives 1978, Virginia, Much Ado About Nothing 1980; other credits incl: Share My Lettuce (Lyric Hammersmith) 1957, The Stepmother (St Martin's) 1958, Rhinoceros (Strand) 1960, Strip the Willow (Cambridge) 1960, The Rehearsal (Globe) 1961, The Private Ear and the Public Eye (Globe (Evening Standard Drama Award Best Actress)) 1962, Mary Mary (Queen's (Variety Club of GB Best Actress of the Year)) 1963, The Country Wife (Chichester) 1969, Design for Living (LA) 1971, Private Lives (Queen's 1972, Globe 1973, NY 1975 (Variety Club of GB Stage Actress Award 1972)), Peter Pan (Coliseum) 1973, Snap (Vaudeville) 1974, Night and Day (Phoenix) 1979, Virginia (Haymarket (Standard Best Actress Award 1982)) 1981, The Way of the World (Chichester and Haymarket (Evening Standard Best Actress Award 1985)) 1984, Interpreters (Queen's) 1985, Lettice and Lovage (Globe 1987, NY 1990 (Tony Award Best Leading Actress 1990)), The Importance of Being Earnest (Aldwych) 1993, Three Tall Women (Wyndam's (Evening Standard Best Actress Award 1994)) 1994 and 1995, Talking Heads (Chichester) 1996; *Television* incl: Bed Among the Lentils (as part of Alan Bennett's Talking Heads, BBC (RTS Award)) 1989, Memento Mori (BBC) 1992, Suddenly Last Summer (BBC) 1993; *Films* The VIP's 1963, The Pumpkin Eater 1964, Young Cassidy 1965, Othello 1966, The Honey Pot 1967, Hot Millions 1968 (Variety Club of GB Award), The Prime of Miss Jean Brodie 1968 (Oscar, SFTA Award), Oh! What a Lovely War 1968, Love and Pain (and the Whole Damned Thing) 1973, Travels with my Aunt 1973, Murder by Death 1976, California Suite 1977 (Oscar), Death on the Nile 1978, Quartet 1981, Clash of the Titans 1981, Evil Under the Sun 1982, The Missionary 1982, A Private Function 1984 (BAFTA Award Best Actress 1985), The Loves of Lily 1985, A Room with a View 1986 (Variety Club of GB Award, BAFTA Award Best Actress 1986), The Lonely Passion of Judith Hearne 1989 (Evening Standard British Films Award 1988, BAFTA Award Best Film Actress 1988), Hook 1992, Sister Act 1992, The Secret Garden 1993, Richard III 1996, First Wives Club 1996, Washington Square 1997; *Style*— Dame Maggie Smith, DBE; ✉ c/o Write on Cue, 29 Whitcomb Street, London WC2H 7EP (☎ 0171 839 3040, fax 0171 839 3055)

SMITH, Dame Margot; DBE (1974); da of Leonard Graham-Brown, MC, FRCS (d 1950); *b* 5 Sept 1918; *Educ* Hilders Hindhead, Westonbirt Glos; *m* 1, 1938 (m dis 1947), as his 1 w, Bertram Aykroyd (d 1983), yst s of Sir Frederic Alfred Aykroyd, 1 Bt; 1 s (Sir James Alexander Frederic Aykroyd, 3 Bt, *qv*), 1 da; m 2, 1947, Roy Smith, MC, TD (d 1983); 1 s; *Career* chm: Yorks Cons Women's Ctee 1963–66, Nat Cons Women's Ctee 1969–72, Nat Union of Cons & Unionist Assocs 1973–74; memb NSPCC Central Exec Ctee 1969–85; *Recreations* riding, gardening; *Style*— Dame Margot Smith, DBE; ✉ Howden Lodge, Spennithorne, Leyburn, N Yorks (☎ 01969 623621)

SMITH, Mark Aynsley; s of Frank Sidney Smith (d 1987), and Sheila Gertrude, *née* Cowin (d 1987); *b* 24 May 1939; *Educ* KCS Wimbledon; *m* 3 Oct 1964, Carol Ann, da of Harold Jones (d 1983); 1 s (Jeremy b 1973), 1 da (Melissa b 1975); *Career* chartered accountant Peat Marwick Mitchell & Co London 1958–66; SBC Warburg: joined 1966, dir 1971, vice chm 1990–93, non-exec dir 1993–95; dir: The Laird Group plc 1993–, Renold plc 1994–, Bradford & Bingley Building Society 1994–; Br Merchant Banking and Securities Houses Assoc: memb Corp Fin Ctee 1988–92, dep chm 1989–90, chm 1991–92; memb Take-Over Panel 1991–92; govr Milbourne Lodge Jr Sch Esher Surrey; FCA 1973 (ACA 1963); *Recreations* golf, walking, collecting; *Style*— Mark Smith, Esq; ✉ 38 Meadway, Esher, Surrey KT10 9HF (☎ 01372 462689, fax 01372 468595)

SMITH, Martin Gregory; s of Archibald Gregory Smith, OBE (d 1981), of St Albans, and Mary Eleanor Smith (d 1976); *Educ* St Albans Sch, St Edmund Hall Oxford (BA, MA), Stanford (MBA, AM); *m* 2 Oct 1971, Elise Becket, da of late George Campbell Becket, of Lakeville, Conn, USA; 1 s (Jeremy b 28 Jan 1974), 1 da (Katie b 5 Aug 1975); *Career* asst brewer Arthur Guinness Son and Co Dublin Ltd 1964–69, engagement mangr McKinsey and Co Inc 1971–74, vice pres and dir head of corp fin Citicorp Int Bank Ltd 1974–80, sr vice pres and chm Bankers Trust International Ltd 1980–85; chm Phoenix Group Ltd 1995–; dir Phoenix Securities Ltd 1983–; chm: Phoenix Fund Managers Ltd 1991–, Jupiter Extra Income Trust plc, SMA (Holdings) Ltd; dir: Orion Group plc, Silver Platter International NV, Methuen Group Ltd; vice chm and memb Bd of Govrs of the South Bank, chm South Bank Site Devpt Bd, chm Bd of Tstees and dir Orchestra of the Age of Enlightenment; *Recreations* music, hunting, sailing, skiing, tennis; *Clubs* Brooks's, Royal St George Yacht (Dublin), Corinthian Yacht, Cirencester Golf; *Style*— Martin Smith, Esq; ✉ The Phoenix Partnership, One Laurence Pountney Hill, London EC4R 0EU (☎ 0171 638 2191, fax 0171 638 0720)

SMITH, Martin Stephen; s of Cyril George Smith, of Coulsdon, Surrey, and Irene Mildred, *née* Harrison; *b* 1 July 1952; *Educ* Purley GS, Fitzwilliam Coll Cambridge (MA); *m* 24 Feb 1979, Krystyna Maria, da of Josef Parkitny; 2 da (Louisa Aniela b 10 Nov 1982, Natalia Maria b 24 Sept 1985); *Career* freelance writer 1974, account mangr Ogilvy Benson & Mather advtg 1976–78 (copywriter 1975–76), account supervisor Saatchi & Saatchi 1978–80, account dir TBWA 1980–82; Bartle Bogle Hegarty: fndr ptnr 1982–, chm Lexington Street (below-the-line gp) 1989–, dep chm 1991–, md 1996–; *Style*— Martin Smith, Esq; ✉ 19 Grand Avenue, London N10 3AY; Bartle Bogle Hegarty, 60 Kingly Street, London W1R 6DS (☎ 0171 734 1677, fax 0171 437 3666)

SMITH, Maureen; *b* 30 July 1947; *m* 8 Nov 1978, Alan Lewis Sutherland; 1 da (Natasha b 1980); *Career* md: BBDO PR Ltd 1972 (dir 1971), Good Relations Ltd 1973; chief exec: Good Relations Group Ltd 1975, Good Relations Group plc; chm The Communication Group plc (PR consultancy); *Style*— Ms Maureen Smith; ✉ The Communication Group plc, 19 Buckingham Gate, London SW1E 6LB (☎ 0171 630 1411, fax 0171 931 8010)

SMITH, Maxwell; TD (1967); *b* 19 Dec 1929; *Educ* Royal Liberty Sch Romford, Univ of London (BSc, DipEd); *m* 29 Sept 1956, Anne; 1 s (Duncan b 1970), 2 da (Helen (Mrs Notter) b 1962, Isobel (Mrs Smales) b 1965); *Career* RE TA 1951–67 (Maj 1964–67); South Bank Poly: head Dept of Estate Mgmnt 1970–77, dean of Faculty 1972–77, asst and dep dir 1977–86; co dir and mgmnt conslt 1986–, memb and vice chm Corp Southwark Coll 1992–, chief exec Co of Chartered Surveyors Youth Trg Tst 1991–92; chm: CNAA Surveying Bd 1975–81, SERC Bldg Sub-Ctee 1980–86; memb Gen Cncl RICS 1975–86 (divnl pres 1977–78); memb Worshipful Co of Chartered Surveyors 1977; hon fell South Bank Univ 1988; FRICS 1965 (ARICS 1951), MIMgt 1969; *Books* Manual of British Standards in Building Construction & Specification (second edn, 1987), South Bank Century (1992); *Recreations* walking, music, painting; *Style*— Maxwell Smith, Esq, TD; ✉ 50 Pickwick Rd, Dulwich Village, London SE21 7JW (☎ 0171 274 9041)

SMITH, Melvyn Kenneth (Mel); s of Kenneth Smith (d 1984), of Chiswick, London, and Vera Ellen Elizabeth, *née* Flemming; *b* 3 Dec 1952; *Educ* Latymer Upper Sch Hammersmith London, New Coll Oxford; *m* 30 April 1988, Pamela, *née* Gay Rees; *Career* actor, writer and director; dir: TalkBack, Smith Jones Brown & Cassie; *Theatre* Charlie's Aunt 1983 (actor), The Gambler (author, actor and dir), Not In Front Of The Audience (actor and dir), Big in Brazil (dir), Summer With Monica (dir): asst dir Royal Court prodns: When Did You Last See My Mother, Nobody Knew They Were There, Dr Jekyll and Mr Hyde; assoc dir Crucible and Young Vic prodns: Carnation Gang, Old Times, My Fair Lady, Hitting Town, Loot; *Television* comedy series incl: Not the Nine O'Clock News 1979–82, Alas Smith & Jones (with Griff Rhys Jones) 1984–, The World According to Smith & Jones 1986–87, Small Doses 1989, Colin's Sandwich, Smith and Jones 1991–; drama incl: Muck & Brass, Milner 1994; dir numerous TV commercials; *Film* Morons From Outer Space (author of screenplay) 1985, Wolves From Willoughby Chase 1988, Wilt 1989, Lame Ducks 1991, Princess Bride, Restless Natives, Number One, Bullshot, Slayground, National Lampoon's European Vacation II, Bloody Kids, Babylon, The Tall Guy (dir, 1989), Radioland Murders (dir, 1994); *Records* Bitter & Twisted, Scratch 'n' Sniff, Alas Smith & Jones, Not the Nine O'Clock News, Rockin' around the Christmas Tree (with Kim Wilde); *Awards* Emmy Award for Alas Smith & Jones, Br Comedy Top Entertainment Series Award for Smith & Jones 1991, Br Comedy Top Entertainment Performer (with Griff Rhys Jones) for Smith & Jones 1991; *Books* The Lavishly Tooled Smith & Jones (1986), Janet Lives With Mel and Griff (1988), Head to Head (1992); *Clubs* Groucho; *Style*— Mel Smith, Esq; ✉ c/o Anna Wilks, TalkBack, 33 Percy Street, London W1P 9FG (☎ 0171 631 3940, fax 0171 631 4273)

SMITH, Most Rev Michael; *see:* Meath, Bishop of (RC)

SMITH, (James David) Michael (Mike); s of William Smith (d 1988), and Elizabeth Mary, *née* Lewis; *b* 24 Sept 1939; *Educ* Midsomer Norton GS, UCL (BSc); *m* 1974, Susan Sheridanne, da of David William Burges; 2 s (Guy Edward b 1977, Owen James b 1979); *Career* various positions in Chemicals and Carbon Dioxide Divs The Distillers' Co 1960–69; BTR plc: md BTR Silvertown Ltd 1973–76 (chemical plant business mangr 1969–72, dir and commercial mangr 1972–73), chief exec Industl Products Gp 1976–79, dir BTR Industries Ltd (and chief exec various divs) 1979–87, exec dir Europe BTR plc 1988–95 (non-exec dir 1995–96); dir: Octopus Publishing Group plc 1985–88, Bullough plc 1996–, Cobham plc 1996–; chm APV plc 1996– (dir 1995–); *Recreations* rugby, golf, skiing, squash, reading, theatre, wine, music; *Style—* Mike Smith, Esq; ✉ Meadowcroft, Sterlings Field, Cookham Dean, Berks SL6 9PG (☎ 01628 488109, fax 01628 488109, car 0831 621193)

SMITH, Michael John; s of late Reginald Charles George Smith, of Ashford, Kent, and late Kate, *née* Godden; *b* 9 March 1943; *Educ* Ashford GS; *m* 15 Sept 1965 (m dis 1978), Anne; 1 s (Ian Michael Sommerfield b 1969), 1 da (Samantha Jane b 1967); *Career* md CAP Group 1981–88 (joined 1963), jt md Sema Group plc 1988–89, chm and chief exec Thorn EMI Software 1989–91, chm and chief exec Data Sciences Ltd 1991–93; dir DEGW International Ltd 1989–; tstee Leadership Tst; Liveryman Worshipful Co of Information Technologists 1988; FIMgt 1986; Lord of the Manor Hawridge and Cholesbury 1987; *Style—* Michael Smith, Esq; ✉ Hawridge Court, Hawridge, Bucks HP5 2UG (☎ 01494 758240)

SMITH, Michael John; s of Frank Smith (d 1988), of Cowbridge, S Glam, and Marjory Smith (d 1987); *b* 23 Sept 1939; *Educ* City of London Sch; *m* 20 Aug 1966, Diane, *née* White; 2 s (Jeremy b 26 June 1970, Philip b 24 May 1972); *Career* journalist: Wilson Daily Times N Carolina USA 1960–62, Enfield Herald N London 1963–65; PR Bullock & Turner 1965–69; Golley Slater PR Cardiff: fndr and md 1969–95, chm 1995–; chm Inst of PR Wales Gp 1987–; course dir Postgraduate Dip in Public and Media Relations Univ of Wales Coll of Cardiff; FIPR; *Style—* Michael Smith; ✉ Golley Slater Public Relations Ltd, 9–11 The Hayes, Cardiff, South Glamorgan CF1 1NU (☎ 01222 388621, fax 01222 228554)

SMITH, Michael John; s of Jack Smith (d 1962) of London, and Ada, *née* Cotton; *b* 12 Feb 1933; *Educ* Aylesbury C of E Sch Highwood, Mill Hill Sch; *m* 1, 1959 (m dis 1974), Genifer, *née* Joseph; 2 s (Steven Alexander b 25 July 1963, Timothy Daniel b 7 June 1971); m 2, 6 Aug 1976, Lorna, da of Henry White (d 1990), of Dublin; 1 step s (Stefan Prescott b 1967), 1 step da (Nadia Prescott b 1963); *Career* articled to Goodman & Mann Auctioneers Surveyors & Valuers 1950–54; valuer: Cecil Lewis 1954–56, Moss & Partners 1956–61; founding jt sr ptnr (with Harold Melzack) Smith Melzack & Company 1961–; Freeman: City of London 1987, Worshipful Co of Plumbers 1989; fell: Valuers Inst 1963 (memb 1958), Incorporated Soc of Valuers and Auctioneers 1968; assoc The Zoological Soc 1970, memb The Firemark Circle 1980, Lloyd's underwriting memb 1973; *Recreations* golf, foreign travel; *Clubs* Arts, Lloyd's Yachting, Coombe Hill Golf (former membership chm); *Style—* Michael Smith, Esq; ✉ Smith Melzack, 17/18 Old Bond St, London W1 (☎ 0171 493 1613, fax 0171 493 5480)

SMITH, Michael (Paul) Marshall; s of Prof David M Smith, of Loughton, Essex, and Margaret, *née* Harrup; *b* 3 May 1965; *Educ* Chigwell Sch Essex, Kings Coll Cambridge (MA); *Partner* Paula Grainger; *Career* writer; ptnr Smith & Jones Film Production; Cambridge Footlights: memb 1984–87, memb Ctee 1987, performer/writer nat tour 1987 and tour of USA 1988; memb: Equity, Musicians Union; *Awards* Icarus Award 1990, BFS Award for Best Short Story 1990, 1991 and 1996, August Delerth Award for Best Novel 1994; *Books* Only Forward (1994), Spares (1996); short stories incl: Dark Terrors, Dark Voices, Dark Lands, The Mammoth Books, Omni; film and television adaptations: Clive Barker's Weaveworld, Robert Faulcon's Nighthunter, Douglas Adams's Dirk Gently; writer/performer (as Michael Rutger) And Now In Colour (BBC Radio 4, 2 series and 2 Christmas specials); *Recreations* music, art and design, foreign travel, cats (owner Spangle and Lintilla); *Style—* Michael Marshall Smith, Esq; ✉ c/o Caradoc King, AP Watt Limited, 20 John Street, London WC1N 2DR (☎ 0171 405 6774)

SMITH, Mike; s of Reginald George Smith, (d 1976), of Chelmsford, and Barbara, *née* Martin; *b* 23 April 1955; *Educ* King Edward VI Sch Chelmsford; *m* 21 June 1989, Sarah Greene, television presenter, da of Harry Greene, of London NW5; *Career* broadcaster; Capital Radio 1978–82, BBC Radio 1 1982–84 and 1986–88, BBC TV Breakfast Time 1983–86, also ITV and LBC Radio; presenter: Capital Radio and Radio 1 Breakfast Shows 1980–88, That's Showbusiness (BBC 1) 1989–96, Body Heat (ITV) 1994–96; *Recreations* motor racing, flying; *Clubs* Royal Automobile; *Style—* Mike Smith, Esq; ✉ c/o Jonathan Altaras Associates, 27 Floral Street, London WC2E 9DP (☎ 0171 836 8722, fax 0171 836 6066)

SMITH, (George) Neil; CMG (1987); s of George William Smith (d 1982), of Sheffield, and Ena Hill (d 1993); *b* 12 July 1936; *Educ* King Edward VII Sch Sheffield; *m* 5 May 1956, Elvi Vappu, da of Johannes Hämäläinen (d 1962), of Finland; 1 s (Kim b 1959), 1 da (Helen b 1957); *Career* joined Dip Serv 1953, Nat Serv RAF 1954–56; commercial attaché Br Embassy Rangoon 1958–61, second sec (commercial) Br Embassy Berne 1961–65, Dip Serv Admin 1965–66, first sec Cwlth Office 1966–68, Br Mil Govt Berlin 1969–73, FCO (European Integration and N America Depts) 1973–77, cnsllr (Commercial) Br Embassy Helsinki 1977–80, HM Consul Gen Zurich and Principality of Liechtenstein 1980–85, head of Trade Rels and Exports Dept FCO 1985–88, ambass to Republic of Finland 1989–95, ret; sec-gen Soc of London Art Dealers 1996–; *Recreations* music and golf; *Clubs* Travellers'; *Style—* Neil Smith, Esq, CMG; ✉ c/o Travellers' Club, 106 Pall Mall, London W1

SMITH, Prof Neilson Voyne (Neil); s of Voyne Smith (d 1991), and Lilian Freda, *née* Rose (d 1973); *b* 21 June 1939; *Educ* Trinity Coll Cambridge (BA, MA), UCL (PhD); *m* 2 July 1966, Dr Saraswati Keskar, da of Dr Govind Raghunath (d 1963); 2 s (Amahl b 4 June 1967, Ivan b 13 July 1973); *Career* lectr in linguistics and W African languages SOAS 1970–72 (lectr in W African languages 1964–70), prof of linguistics UCL 1981– (reader in linguistics 1972–81, head Dept of Phonetics and Linguistics 1982–90); memb: Linguistics Assoc GB (pres 1980–86), Philological Soc 1964– (sometime memb Cncl), SSRC 1973–89; pres Assoc of Heads and Professors of Linguistics 1993–94; *Books* An Outline Grammar of Nupe (1967), The Acquisition of Phonology (1973), Modern Linguistics (with Deirdre Wilson, 1979), Mutual Knowledge (ed, 1982), The Twitter Machine (1989), The Mind of a Savant (with I Tsimpli, 1995); *Recreations* travel, music, walking; *Style—* Prof Neil Smith; ✉ 32 Long Buftlers, Harpenden, Herts AL5 1JE (☎ 01582 761313); Department of Phonetics and Linguistics, University College London, Gower St, London WC1E 6BT (☎ 0171 380 7173, fax 0171 383 4108, e-mail neil@linguistics.ucl.ac.uk)

SMITH, Norman Jack; s of Maurice Leslie Smith (d 1967), of Newton Abbot, Devon, and Ellen Dorothy, *née* Solly (d 1994); *b* 14 April 1936; *Educ* Henley GS, Oriel Coll Oxford (MA), City Univ (MPhil); *m* 4 March 1967, Valerie Ann, da of Capt Arthur Ernest Frost (d 1978), of Ramsgate, Kent; 1 s (Malcolm b 1970); 1 da (Gail b 1974); *Career* market analyst Dexion Ltd 1957–60, commercial evaluation mangr Vickers Ltd 1960–69, business devpt mangr Baring Bros and Co Ltd 1969–80; dir: Burntisland Engineers and Fabricators Ltd 1974–76, Zenith Reed Ltd 1975–76, International Economic Services Ltd 1975–76, SAI Tubular Services Ltd 1983–88, Atkins Oil and Gas Engineering Ltd 1984–86, Smith Rea Energy Analysts Ltd 1985–, Gas Transmission Ltd 1989–, Smith Rea Energy Aberdeen Ltd 1990–; dir gen Offshire Supplies Office 1978–80; chm: British Underwater Engineering Ltd 1981–83, Mentor Engineering Consultants Ltd 1988–92; md Smith Rea Energy Associates Ltd 1983–; memb Norwegian Petroleum Soc, FInstPet, FInstD, fell Soc of Business Economists; *Recreations* archaeology, walking, swimming, gardening; *Clubs* United Oxford and Cambridge, Oil Industries; *Style—* Norman Jack Smith, Esq; ✉ Smith Rea Energy Associates Ltd, Hunstead House, Nickle, Chartham, Canterbury, Kent CT4 7PL (☎ 01227 738822, fax 01227 738866)

SMITH, Paul Andrew; s of Kenneth Desmond Smith, and Joy, *née* Moore; *b* 15 April 1964; *Educ* Heaton GS Newcastle upon Tyne; *m* (sep); 2 s (Oliver James b 1988, Michael Paul b 1993); *Career* professional cricketer; Warwickshire CCC: debut 1982, awarded county cap 1986; youth player: Northumberland CCC 1971–80, Northumberland under 13, under 15, under 19, N of Eng 1979, England under 19 v Young Aust; world record most consecutive partnership over 50 (11 with Andy Moles), youngest Warwicks player to score 1000 runs in a season 1984 and 1500 runs in a season 1986, 2 first class hat-tricks v Northants 1989 and Sussex 1990; honours with Warwickshire: Nat West Trophy 1989 and 1993, winners Benson & Hedges Cup 1994 (man of the match award, runners up 1984), winners Britannic Assurance Co Championship 1994, winners Axa Equity & Law Trophy 1994; all-rounder of the year Warwickshire 1986 and 1989, benefit year 1995; Advtg and PR Dept Birmingham Post and Mail Newspaper Group off-season 1986–88, classic car restorer Earlsway Classics Halesowen; *Recreations* restoration of classic cars; *Style—* Paul Smith, Esq; ✉ c/o Warwickshire County Cricket Club, County Ground, Edgbaston, Birmingham B5 7QU (☎ 0121 446 4422)

SMITH, Paul B; CBE (1994); s of Harold Smith, of Beeston, Notts, and late Marjorie Smith; *b* 5 July 1946; *Educ* Beeston Fields Sch Beeston Notts; *Career* clothes designer; fndr Paul Smith Ltd Nottingham 1970; currently wholesales in 34 countries around the world with Paul Smith shops in London, Nottingham, NY, Paris, Hong Kong, Singapore, Taiwan, Thailand, Korea and 147 in Japan; finalist Design Cncl's Prince Philip Prize for the Designer of the Year 1992 and 1993; Hon MDes Nottingham Poly (now Nottingham Trent Univ) 1991; RDI 1991; *Style—* Paul Smith, Esq, CBE; ✉ Paul Smith Ltd, 40–44 Floral Street, London WC2E 9DJ (☎ 0171 836 7828)

SMITH, Paul David John; s of Ernest Smith, of Walton on the Naze, Essex, and Margaret Lillian, *née* Taylor; *b* 12 June 1949; *m* Helen Mary, *née* Verlander; 2 s (Joel Julian, Giles James); *Career* jr art dir Davis and Page 1968–70; art dir: Charles Barker Ltd 1970–72, Vernons 1972–73, Royds 1973, Collett Dickinson and Pearce 1973–75 (dir 1975–87); creative dir Allen Brady & Marsh 1987–91, int creative dir Lowe Howard-Spink 1991–94, exec creative dir Grey Advertising 1995– (jt gp creative dir 1994–95); many nat and int awards incl 4 D&AD Silver awards; *Recreations* tennis; *Style—* Paul Smith, Esq; ✉ Grey Advertising Ltd, 215–227 Great Portland Street, London W1N 5HD (☎ 0171 636 3399)

SMITH, Paul John; s of John Joseph Smith, of Sunderland, Tyne and Wear, and Mary Patricia, *née* Maher; *b* 25 July 1945; *Educ* Ampleforth, Univ of Newcastle (MB BS); *m* 14 July 1972, Anne Westmoreland Snowdon; 1 s (Mark b 1977), 3 da (Jaime b 1980, Victoria b 1982, Francesca b 1982); *Career* asst lectr in anatomy 1969–71; surgical registrar: Glasgow Western Infirmary 1971–76, Wexham Park Hosp 1976–78; res asst Microsurgical Laboratory Univ of Louisville 1978; Christine Kleinert fell in hand surgery Louisville 1978, resident and instructor in plastic surgery Duke Univ N Carolina 1979; conslt plastic surgn: Mount Vernon Hosp 1982–, Gt Ormond St Hosp for Sick Children 1988–; memb: Cncl Br Hand Soc 1988–90, Editorial Bd Journal of Hand Surgery 1989–91; sec Plastic Surgery Royal Soc of Med 1990; FRCSGlas 1974; Hayward foundation scholar 1978, 1st prize American Assoc Hand Surgery Toronto 1979, Pulvertaft Prize British Hand Soc 1983; memb: BMA, RSM, BSSH, BAPS, BAAPS; *Books* Principles of Hand Surgery (1990); *Recreations* skiing; *Style—* Paul Smith, Esq; ✉ Kimble Farm, Fawley, Henley, Oxon RG9 6JP (☎ 01491 638870); Wellington Hospital, London W1 (☎ 01491 638030)

SMITH, Peter Alan; s of Dudley Vaughan Smith (d 1983), and Beatrice Ellen, *née* Sketcher; *b* 5 Aug 1946; *Educ* Mill Hill Sch, Univ of Southampton (BSc); *m* 2 Oct 1971, Cherry, da of Thomas A Blandford (d 1986); 2 s (Nicholas David b 1975, Richard James b 1977); *Career* RAFVR 1964–67, cmmnd actg PO 1967; Coopers & Lybrand: joined 1967, ptnr 1975–, managing partner London City Office 1989–, memb Ptnrship Bd 1990–, chm 1994–; chm Int Banking Indust Ctee 1988–90; memb: Fin Ctee The Nat Tst 1991–, Prince of Wales Business Leaders' Forum 1994–, President's Ctee CBI 1995–, Ctee on Corp Governance 1996–; former hon treas UK Housing Tst; Liveryman Worshipful Co of CAs 1993; CIMgt, FCA, FRSA; *Books* Housing Association Accounts and their Audit (1980); *Recreations* golf, gardens; *Clubs* Carlton, Beaconsfield Golf; *Style—* Peter Smith, Esq; ✉ The Old Vicarage, Hughenden, High Wycombe, Bucks HP14 4LA (☎ 01494 530364); Coopers & Lybrand, 1 Embankment Place, London WC2N 6NN (☎ 0171 213 4586, fax 0171 822 4652, telex 884730)

SMITH, Peter Alexander Charles; OBE (1981); s of Alexander Smith, and Gwendoline, *née* Beer; *b* 18 Aug 1920; *Educ* St Paul's; *m* 1, 1945, Marjorie May, *née* Humphrey (d 1983); 1 s; m 2, 1994, Jeanette Gwendoline, *née* Middleditch; *Career* served WWII RA; admitted slr 1948; chm Securicor Group plc 1974–95 (chief exec 1974–85), dir Fitch Lovell 1982–90, non-exec chm Metal Closures Group plc 1983–87 (dir 1972–87, dep chm 1981–83), chm Br Security Indust Assoc 1977–81; pres Royal Warrant Holders Assoc 1982–83 (memb Cncl 1976–, vice pres 1981–82), vice pres Forest Philharmonic Symphony Orch 1991–; FRSA; *Recreations* golf, music, photography; *Clubs* British Racing Drivers'; *Style—* Peter Smith, Esq, OBE; ✉ Securicor Gp plc, Sutton Park House, 15 Carshalton Rd, Sutton, Surrey SM1 4LE (☎ 0181 770 7000)

SMITH, Peter John; *b* 31 Dec 1936; *Educ* Rastrick GS Brighouse W Yorks; *m* Marie Louise; 1 s, 1 da; *Career* local govt treas; trainee Huddersfield CBC 1953–59, acct Bradford CBC 1959–61, asst chief acct Chester CBC 1961–63, computer mangr Keighley Municipal Borough Cncl 1963–66, asst city treas Gloucester CBC 1966–69, dep borough treas Gateshead CBC 1969–73; Tyne and Wear CC: asst co treas 1973–74, dep co treas 1974–80, co treas (incl treas of Northumbria Police Authy, Northumbria Probation and After-Care Ctee, Newcastle Airport, Northumbria Tourist Bd) 1980–86, gen mangr Tyne and Wear Residuary Body 1985–88; freelance conslt 1988–89, exec dir Westgate Trust plc 1990–92; chm Gateshead Healthcare Tst 1992–; memb: Bd of Tyne & Wear Passenger Tport Exec 1981–86, Ctee N American Property Unit Tst 1981–93, Bd Northern Investors Co 1984–87; IPFA; *Style—* Peter Smith, Esq

SMITH, Peter Michael; s of Peter William Smith (d 1944), of Reading, and Margaret, *née* Gilchrist (d 1971), of St George's College, Weybridge; *b* 10 Jan 1938; *m* 6 Dec 1975, Sarah Diana, da of John Seyfried; 2 s (Benjamin b 18 June 1977, Matthew b 17 Oct 1981); *Career* served BSA Police Rhodesia 1956–59; Barclays Bank plc 1955–56, Barclays Bank International 1959–62; PR and marketing management: Total Oil Products Central Africa 1962–66, Gallaher plc 1966–69; PR advsr Booker McConnell plc (responsible for early development of Booker Prize for Fiction) 1970–78, public affrs mangr Powell Duffryn plc 1978–85, head of corporate relations Reed International plc 1985–87, dir UK Radio Developments 1990–92, jt managing ptnr City and Corporate Counsel (co-fndr 1987) 1987–93, tstee One World Broadcasting Trust 1991–96, fndr chief exec The Strategic Partnership (London) Ltd 1994–; dir: Threadneedle Group PLC (co-fndr 1987), Hollis Directories, A T Hudson Ltd, Elixir Marketing Communications; chm Worldaware (Centre for World Development Educn) 1992–95 (currently vice pres), chm RSA Tomorrow's Company Inquiry Network 1993–95; councillor London Borough of Camden 1968–71; Parly Candidate (C): Rowley Regis and Tipton 1970, West Bromwich West Feb 1974; joined SDP 1982, currently memb Social and Liberal Democratic Party; memb Nat Cncl and Exec Ctee Euro Movement in UK 1981–82; chm PR Educn and Res Tst 1984–89; Royal Cwlth Soc: dep chm 1980–83, currently vice pres, founder and chm Focus Gp 1975, pres Focus Gp 1978–83; Inst of PR: chm City and Fin Gp 1981–82, pres 1984, chm Govt Affrs Gp 1991–95; Investor Relations Soc: co-fndr 1980, memb Ctee 1980–92, chm 1986–89; memb Professional Affrs Ctee Investor Relations Soc; awarded Stephen Tallents Medal 1995; FIPR, FRSA, FInstD; *Recreations* golf, reading, music; *Clubs* IOD, Royal Commonwealth Soc; *Style*— Peter Smith, Esq; ✉ 6 Hawksmoor Mews, Cable Street, London E1 0DG (☎ 0171 791 3003); The Strategic Partnership (London) Ltd, 211 Piccadilly, London W1V 9LD (☎ 0171 917 2949, fax 0171 895 1376)

SMITH, Peter Vivian Henworth; CB (1989); s of Vivian Smith (d 1973), of Clacton-on-Sea, Essex, and Dorothea, *née* Ovenden (d 1941); *b* 5 Dec 1928; *Educ* Clacton Co HS, BNC Oxford (BA, BCL, MA); *m* 19 Feb 1955, Mary Marjorie, da of Frank John Willsher (d 1947), of Clacton-on-Sea; 5 da (Kathleen b 1955, Jacqueline b 1958, Susan b 1961, Linda b 1962, Johanna b 1967); *Career* RASC 1947–49, 2 Lt 1948, RARO 1949–70 (Lt); called to the Bar Lincoln's Inn 1953, practised at Bar 1953–55; joined HM Overseas Legal Serv 1955; resident magistrate Nyasaland 1955–64, sr resident magistrate Malawi 1964–69, puisne judge Malawi 1969–70; HM Customs and Excise (England): legal asst 1970–72, sr legal asst 1972–76, asst slr 1976–82, princ asst slr 1982–86, slr 1986–89; legal advsr: Broadcasting Standards Cncl 1989–, Govt Dept 1990–, Registry of Bldg Socs 1990–92; chm Clacton-on-Sea Cncl of Churches 1989–91; *Recreations* bridge, classical music, computers; *Style*— Peter Smith, Esq, CB; ✉ Likabula, 14 St Albans Rd, Clacton-on-Sea, Essex CO15 6BA (☎ 01255 422053); Broadcasting Standards Council, 5–8 The Sanctuary, London SW1P 3JS (☎ 0171 233 0544, fax 0171 233 0397)

SMITH, His Hon Judge Peter William; s of William Smith (d 1995), and Bessie, *née* Hall (d 1986); *b* 31 Dec 1945; *Educ* Arnold Sch Blackpool, Downing Coll Cambridge (MA); *m* Vanessa, da of John Wildash; 1 s (Matthew b 29 May 1974); *Career* called to the Bar Middle Temple 1969, in practice Northern Circuit, circuit judge (Northern Circuit) 1994–; *Style*— His Hon Judge Peter Smith; ✉ c/o Northern Circuit Office, 15 Quay Street, Manchester M60 9FD

SMITH, Peter Winston; QC (1992); s of George Arthur Smith (d 1993), and Iris Muriel, *née* Winstanley (d 1986); *b* 1 May 1952; *Educ* Bridlington Sch E Yorks, Selwyn Coll Cambridge (MA), Coll of Law Chancery Lane London (Hardwicke scholar, Tancred scholar, Megarry pupillage award); *m* 13 Sept 1980, Diane, da of Charles Webster Dalgliesh; 2 da (Laura b 13 July 1980, Katy b 15 Feb 1982), 1 s (James b 3 May 1983); *Career* called to the Bar Lincoln's Inn 1975, pupillage Joseph Turner of Liverpool 1975–76, examiner of title HM Land Registry 1976–82, lectr Univ of Manchester 1977–83; practising N Circuit: 460 Royal Exchange Manchester 1979–87, 40 King St Manchester 1987–; asst recorder 1994–, dep High Ct judge 1996–; *Books* Conveyancing Law-Practice (2 edn 1982); *Recreations* reading military history, football, memb Titanic Historical Soc; *Style*— Peter Smith, Esq, QC; ✉ 40 King Street, Manchester M2 6BA (☎ 0161 832 9082, fax 0161 835 2139)

SMITH, Philip Henry; s of Alfred Henry Smith (d 1977), of Leicester, and Georgina May, *née* Ives (d 1969); *b* 24 Nov 1946; *Educ* Loughborough Coll GS, Leicester Regnl Coll of Technol, Nottingham Poly; *m* 27 Dec 1968, Sonia Idena, da of Ivan Garnet Moody (d 1964), of Leicester; 2 s (Christian Philip b 13 June 1972, Philip Raoul b 28 Feb 1975), 1 da (Melissa b 21 June 1969); *Career* sr audit asst Leics CC 1964–69, gp accountant Lusaka City Cncl Zambia 1969–72, branch accountant Dairy Produce Bd Zambia 1972–74, divnl dir and sec Dorada Hldgs plc 1974–81, divnl fin dir Brook Tool Engrg Hldgs plc 1981–83, gp treas Asda Gp plc 1983–91, dir of treasy National Power plc 1991–; vice pres Leicester City Football Club plc, chm Padbury Utd Football, life memb Clifton Rangers Youth Football, vice pres Padbury Cricket Club; memb IPFA 1971, FCMA 1974, FIMgt 1974, FCT 1988 (elected memb Cncl 1996); *Recreations* sports, wine, gardening, political and economic affairs; *Style*— Philip H Smith, Esq; ✉ The Old White Horse, Main St, Padbury, Buckingham, Bucks MK18 2AY (☎ 01280 814848); National Power plc, Senator House, 85 Queen Victoria Street, London EC4V 4DP (☎ 0171 615 3159, fax 0171 615 3151, telex 883141)

SMITH, Philip Henry; s of Reginald Smith, and Grace, *née* Howgate; *b* 14 July 1934; *Educ* Leeds GS, Univ of Leeds (MB ChB); *m* 13 Aug 1960, Margaret, da of Wilfred Glover (d 1967); 1 s (Richard b 1965 d 1988), 4 da (Alison (Mrs Dawson) b 1962, Catherine b 1964 d 1964, Anne b 1967, Rosemary b 1967); *Career* Nat Serv and OC 50 FST Br Cameroons, OC Surgical Div Tidworth Mil Hosp; head Dept of Urology St James Hosp Leeds 1967–, urologist to Regnl Spinal Injuries Unit Pinderfields Hosp Wakefield 1967–91; sec Urology Gp of European Orgn for Res on Treatment of Cancer 1979–82 (chm 1976–79); chm: Prostatic Cancer Sub Gp MRC 1985, Urology Working Party MRC 1988–91; memb: BAUS, Spinal Injuries Assoc, Int Soc of Urology and of Paraplegia; FRCS 1960; *Books* Bladder Cancer (ed, 1984), Combination Therapy in Urological Malignancy (ed, 1988); *Recreations* grandchildren, gardening; *Style*— Philip Smith, Esq; ✉ Department of Urology, St James Hospital, Leeds LS9 7TF (☎ 0113 243 3144, fax 0113 283 6975)

SMITH, Phylis Janet; da of Donald Watt, of Jamaica, and Rose, *née* MacLean; *b* 29 Sept 1965; *Educ* St John Wall Roman Catholic Sch; *m* 1 June 1988, Robert Smith, s of Robert Smith; 1 s (Robert Daniel Smith b 1988); *Career* athlete (400m runner); Cosford Games 1986, first int GB v Spain Madrid 1986, with Wolverhampton and Bilston until 1990, with Wigan Harriers 1991–93, with Sale 1993–; fourth 4x400m final World Championships Tokyo 1991, Bronze medallist 4x400m Olympic Games Barcelona 1992 (finalist in individual event), 400m champion AAA Olympic Trials 1992 and 1996, Bronze medallist 4x400m World Championships Stuttgart 1993, AAA 400m champion 1993, Euro Bronze medallist 400m 1994 (fourth 4x400m final), Gold medallist 4x400m Cwlth Games 1994 (fourth 400m final), memb GB Olympic Squad Atlanta 1996; UK record holder 4x400m World Championships 1991; UK 200m champion 1990 and 1992; Access Athlete of the Year 1989; nurse Maternity Unit Dudley Road Hosp Birmingham, residential social worker Braybrook House Wednesfield Wolverhampton; *Recreations* gardening, reading; *Style*— Mrs Phylis Smith

SMITH, Rae; da of Christine White (now Mrs Smith), and adopted da of Rex Howard Smith, of Shropshire; sister of Charlotte Emily Smith; father Kevin Duggan, of Dublin; *b* 8 Sept 1962; *Educ* Sir John Talbot's Sch, Central Sch of Art & Design; *Career* theatre designer and director; began career asst designer Glasgow Citizen's Theatre; worked Mladinsko, Ljubljana and Red Pilot Theatres (Slovenija, former Yugoslavia) 1988–90; assoc artist and designer Lyric Hammersmith 1996; *Productions* incl: installation artist and designer for Theatre de Complicité's Almeida season 1990 and The Visit (RNT) 1991, Gormenghast (David Glass Co) 1992, The Street of Crocodiles (Theatre Complicité, RNT) 1992, It's Staring you Right in the Face 1992, Dinner for Ralph Ralph 1992, Madness in Valencia (The Gate) 1992, The Europeans (Wrestling Sch) 1993, Shameless (Opera Circus) 1993, Wise Guy Scapino (Theatr Clwyd) 1993, Julius Caesar (English Shakespeare Co) 1993, A Midsummer Nights' Dream (Lyceum Edinburgh) 1993, Death of a Salesman (West Yorkshire Playhouse) 1994, The Magic Flute (Opera North) 1994, Henry VI (part 3, RSC), Some Voices (Royal Court) 1994, Mosquito Coast (Young Vic) 1994, Charley's Aunt (Manchester Royal Exchange), Lucky (also dir, Young Vic), The Letter (Lyric (dir Neil Bartlett, *qv*)) 1995, The Phoenician Women (RSC) 1995, Crocodile Looking at Birds (co-designer Rosa Maggiora, *qv*) 1995, Silence Silence Silence (Mladinsko, Sloveija) 1996, Don Giovanni (WNO) 1996, Endgame (Donmar) 1996; *Awards* incl: Soc of British Theatre Designer Award (funded working sabbatical Japan), Margaret Woodward Award (funded working sabbatical Indonesia); Manchester Evening News Awards incl: Best Touring Prodn (Henry VI, RSC), Best Main Prodn (Wise Guy Scapino, Theatre Clywd), Best Touring Prodn (The Street of Crocodiles); also for The Street of Crocodiles: 4 Olivier Award nominations, Sainsbury Arts Award, Dublin Theatre Festival Award for Best Visiting Prodn, L'Académie du Thétre Award for Best Foreign Prodn, Prudential Arts Award, Barcelona Critics' Award for Best Foreign Prodn and Alicia Best Touring Prodn 1992; Time Out Awards incl: Madness in Valencia (The Gate), The Visit (RNT); *Recreations* canoeing, javelin, walking in the country, drinking and talking with good friends; *Style*— Rae Smith; ✉ Ivy House, Rowe Lane, Welshampton, Ellesmere, Shropshire SY12 0QD

SMITH, Sir Raymond Horace; KBE (1967, CBE 1960), AFC (1968); s of Horace P Smith (d 1965), of London, and Mabelle E, *née* Couzens (d 1960); *b* 18 March 1917; *Educ* Salesian Coll London, Barcelona Univ Spain; *m* 1943, Dorothy, da of Robert Cheney Hart (d 1946), of London; 3 s; *Career* serv WWII with Br Security Co-ordination W Hemisphere (USA, Canada, Caribbean and S America), civil attaché Br Embassy Caracas 1941, negotiator for sale of British owned railway cos to S American Govts 1946–53; pres British Cwlth Assoc of Venezuela 1955–57; consultant to: Rolls Royce, Fairey Engineering, Hawker Siddeley, Brackett; chm Hawker Siddeley Venezuela; CRAeS; *Recreations* Cresta Run, tennis, skiing, water skiing; *Clubs* White's, Naval and Military, Country, Jockey (Caracas); *Style*— Sir Raymond Smith, KBE, AFC; ✉ Quinta San Antonio, Calla El Samancito, Caracas Country Club, Caracas, Venezuela (☎ 32 92 18/33 36 96); 37 Lowndes St, London SW1 (☎ 0171 235 6249); Calle Real de Sabana Grande, Edificio Las Américas, Chacaíto, Caracas, Venezuela (☎ 71 40 18/ 72 92 29; telex 21644)

SMITH, Dr Richard Michael; s of Louis Gordon Smith (d 1971), of Essex, and Elsie Fanny, *née* Ward; *Educ* Earls Colne GS Essex, UCL (BA, Rosa Morison prize), St Catherine's Coll Cambridge (MA, PhD); *m* 1971, Margaret Anne, da of William D McFadden; *Career* post doctoral res fell Univ of Chicago 1971–73, lectr in population studies Plymouth Poly 1973–74; Univ of Cambridge: asst lectr in population and historical geography 1974–76, fell Fitzwilliam Coll 1977–83; Univ of Oxford: lectr in historical demography 1983–89, professorial fell All Souls Coll 1983–94, reader in history of med and dir Wellcome Unit for the History of Med 1990–94; Univ of Cambridge: fell Downing Coll, reader in historical demography and dir Cambridge Gp for the History of Population and Social Structure 1994– (sr res offr 1976–81, asst dir 1981); Fndn lectr Fitzwilliam Coll Cambridge 1989, Sir John Neal's lectr UCL 1995; FRHistS 1985, FBA 1991; *Books* Sources on English Society 1250–1800: The Sir Nicholas Bacon Collection (1973), Bastardy and its Comparative History (1980), Land, Kinship and Life-Cycle (1984), The World We Have Gained: Histories of Population and Social Structures (1986), Life, Death and the Elderly: Historical Perspectives (1991), Medieval Society and the Manor Court (1996); *Recreations* walking in Norfolk, listening to music; *Style*— Dr Richard Smith, FBA; ✉ Cambridge Group for the History of Population and Social Structure, 27 Trumpington Street, Cambridge CB2 1QA (☎ 01223 333181, fax 01223 333183)

SMITH, Prof Richard Sydney William; s of Sydney Frederick Smith, and Hazel Nora, *née* Kirk; *b* 11 March 1952; *Educ* Roan GS for Boys, Univ of Edinburgh Med Sch (BSc, MB ChB), Graduate Sch of Business Stanford Univ (MSc); *m* Oct 1977, Linda Jean, da of Alexander Rae Arnott; 2 s (Freddie Paris b April 1982, James Arthur b Feb 1984), 1 da (Florence Harriet Rose b March 1991); *Career* house offr: Eastern Gen Hosp Edinburgh 1976–77, Dunfermline and West Fife Hosp 1977; jr doctor Auckland and Green Lane Hosps Auckland NZ 1977–78, chief exec BMJ Publishing Group and ed British Medical Journal 1991– (asst ed 1979–91); special prof of medical journalism Dept of Med Univ of Nottingham 1993–; television doctor: BBC Breakfast Time 1982–86, TV-AM 1988–89; *Awards* Med Journalists' Assoc Young Journalist of the Year 1980, Periodical Publishers' Assoc Specialist Writer of the Year 1981, runner up Med Journalists' Assoc Journalist of the Year 1983 and 1985; memb: BMA 1979, Med Journalists' Assoc 1980; fell Acad of Gen Educn Manipal Karnataka India 1993; MFPHM 1991, FRCPE 1992, MRCP 1993; *Books* Alcohol Problems (1982), Prison Health Care (1984), Unemployment and Health (1987), The Good Health Kit (1987); *TV* That's Family Life (BBC1, 1983), Compulsions (Thames, 1987), Fashion Victims (BBC2, 1991), Breakthrough or Ballyhoo (BBC2, 1992); *Recreations* music (particularly jazz and chamber), theatre, wine, running, hill walking; *Style*— Prof Richard Smith; ✉ British Medical Journal, BMA House, Tavistock Square, London WC1H 9JR (☎ 0171 387 4499, fax 0171 383 6418)

SMITH, Dr Robert Carr; CBE (1989); s of late Edward Albert Smith, of Herts, and Olive Winifred, *née* Carstairs; *b* 19 Nov 1935; *Educ* Queen Elizabeth's Sch Barnet, Univ of Southampton (BSc), Univ of London (PhD); *m* 1960, Rosalie Mary, da of Talbot Victor Spencer, of Sussex; 1 s (James b 1965), 1 da (Georgina b 1968); *Career* vice-chllr Kingston Univ (formerly Kingston Poly) 1982–, previously prof of physical electronics Univ of Southampton; dir: Higher Education Statistics Agency, AZTEC (Kingston, Merton and Wandsworth Trg and Enterprise Cncl), Univs' and Colls' Employers' Assoc; chm Polys and Colls Employers' Forum 1988–90; memb Cncl: for Industry and Higher Educn, Polys and Colls Funding 1988–93; *Recreations* travelling, visual arts, book collecting; *Style*— Dr Robert Smith, CBE; ✉ Maybury House, Swanmore Green, Church Road, Swanmore, Southampton SO32 2PA (☎ 01489 891013); Kingston University, River House, 53–57 High Street, Kingston upon Thames, Surrey KT1 1LQ (☎ 0181 547 7010, fax 0181 547 7009)

SMITH, Robert Christopher Sydney Winwood; s and h of Sir Christopher Smith, 5 Bt, *qv*; *b* 1939; *m* 1971, Roslyn Nellie, eldest da of late James Keith McKenzie, of Sydney, NSW; 1 s (Craig Robert Winwood b 1974), 1 da (Robyn Louise Winwood b 1978); *Style*— Robert Smith, Esq; ✉ 13 Siren Street, Port Maquarie, NSW, Australia

SMITH, Sir Robert Courtney; kt (1987), CBE (1980); s of John Smith, JP, DL (d 1954), of Glasgow and Symington, and Agnes, *née* Brown (d 1969); *b* 10 Sept 1927; *Educ* Kelvinside Acad Glasgow, Sedbergh, Trinity Coll Cambridge (BA, MA); *m* 6 March 1954, Moira Rose, da of Wilfred Hugh Macdougall (d 1948), of Glasgow; 2 s (Nigel b 1956 d 1971, Christopher b 1961), 2 da (Lorna (Mrs Bromley-Martin) b 1958, Rosalind (Mrs Lindsay Buchan) b 1964); *Career* RM 1945–47, RMFVR 1951–57; CA 1953; ptnr Arthur Young McClelland Moores 1957–78; chm: Standard Life 1982–88, Alliance Trust 1984–96; dir: Bank of Scotland, British Alcan Aluminium plc, Edinburgh Investment Tst plc, Sidlaw Group plc, Volvo Truck and Bus Ltd; dir Merchants House of Glasgow, pres Business Archives Cncl Scotland, tstee Carnegie Tst for Univs of Scotland, memb Scottish Industs Devpt Bd 1972–88 (chm 1981–88), chllr's assessor Univ of Glasgow 1984–96; Hon Col Royal Marines Reserve Scot 1992–96; Hon LLD: Univ of Glasgow 1978, Univ of Aberdeen 1991; FRSE 1988; *Recreations* gardening, racing; *Clubs* East India, Western (Glasgow), Hawks' (Cambridge); *Style*— Sir Robert Smith, CBE, FRSE; ✉ North Lodge, Dunkeld, Perthshire PH8 0AZ (☎ 01350 727574)

SMITH, Robert Daglish; s of Robert Ramsay Smith (d 1992), of Sidcup, Kent, and Jessie, *née* Daglish; *b* 2 July 1934; *Educ* Dulwich Coll (State scholar), Queens' Coll Cambridge (MA); *m* 1984, Ursula, da of Peter Josef Stollenwerk; *Career* Nat Serv 2 Lt Royal Signals 1953–55; The King's Sch Canterbury 1960–65 (dir King's Week Arts Festival 1962–65), lectr Newland Park Coll of Educn Bucks 1965–67, Wells Management

Consultants Ltd 1968–70, freelance mgmnt conslt in fundraising (arts admin) 1970–74, dir E Midlands Arts Assoc 1974–80 (sec then chair Standing Ctee of Regnl Arts Assocs 1976–80), exec dir UK Ctee for UNICEF (UN Children's Fund) 1980–; cmmr Howard League Inquiry into Violence in Penal Institutions for Young People 1994–95; memb Cncl (treas) Children's Rights Office 1995–; FRSA 1990; *Recreations* music, opera, theatre, travel; *Style*— Robert D Smith, Esq; ✉ Executive Director, UNICEF (UK), 55 Lincoln's Inn Fields, London WC2A 3NB (☎ 0171 405 5592, fax 0171 405 2332)

SMITH, Sir Robert Hill; 3 Bt (UK 1945), of Crowmallie, Co Aberdeen; s (by 2 m) of Sir Gordon Smith, 2 Bt, VRD (d 1983); *b* 15 April 1958; *Educ* Merchant Taylors', Aberdeen Univ; *m* 13 Sept 1993; *Heir* bro, Charles Gordon Smith, b 21 April 1959; *Recreations* sailing; *Clubs* Royal Thames Yacht; *Style*— Sir Robert Smith, Bt; ✉ Crowmallie, Pitcaple, Aberdeenshire

SMITH, Robert James; s of Mervyn Daniel Smith (d 1982), of Wickwar, Glos, and Marjorie Irene, *née* Griffin; *b* 22 July 1945; *Educ* King's Coll Taunton, Royal Holloway Coll Univ of London (BA); *m* 20 Aug 1970, Anne Rosemary, da of Brendan Fitzpatrick (d 1993), of London; 1 s (Daniel b 1983), 1 da (Kate b 1979); *Career* managing ed Gower Press Ltd Xerox Corp Inc 1971–75, editorial mangr Octopus Books Ltd 1975–78, ed dir Ebury Press Nat Magazine Co Ltd 1979–85, publishing dir Sidgwick and Jackson Ltd 1985–90, chm and md Smith Gryphon Ltd 1990–; *Recreations* conservation, theatre, local history, collecting antiques and antiquarian books; *Clubs* Groucho; *Style*— Robert Smith, Esq; ✉ Smith Gryphon Ltd, 12 Bridge Wharf, 156 Caledonian Road, London N1 9UU (☎ 0171 278 2444, fax 0171 833 5680)

SMITH, Robert James; s of James Alexander Smith, of Crawley, Sussex, and Rita Mary, *née* Emmott; *b* 21 April 1959; *Educ* Notre Dame Middle Sch Crawley, St Wilfrid's Comp Crawley; *m* 13 Aug 1988, Mary Theresa, da of John Richard Poole; *Career* pop singer, musician and song-writer; stage debut with Malice (school group) 1976, name changed to Easy Cure (debut concert 1977), band now called The Cure (debut concert 1978); first tours: Britain 1979, Europe 1979, USA 1980, Antipodes 1980, Japan 1984; has performed in over 1000 concerts worldwide; other work incl: guitarist Siouxsie and the Banshees Sept-Oct 1979 and Oct 1982–May 1984, co-fndr The Glove (studio project, one album Blue Sunshine) 1983; *Albums* Three Imaginary Boys (US version Boys Don't Cry) 1979, Seventeen Seconds 1980, Faith 1981, Pornography 1982, Japanese Whispers (compilation) 1983, The Top 1984, Concert (live) 1984, The Head on the Door 1985, Standing on a Beach (compilation) 1986, Kiss Me Kiss Me Kiss Me 1987, Disintegration 1989, Mixed Up (compilation) 1990, Entreat (live) 1991, Wish 1992, Show (live) 1993, Paris (live) 1993, Wild Mood Swings 1996; *Videos* incl: Staring at the Sea (singles compilation) 1986, The Cure in Orange (concert) 1986, Picture Show (singles compilation) 1991, Playout (live) 1991, Show (concert) 1993; *Awards* Best Video (for Lullaby) BPI 1989, Best US Radio Song (for Lovesong) ASCAP 1989, Best British Group BPI 1990, Best Video (for Friday I'm in Love) MTV 1992, Best US Radio Song (for Friday I'm in Love) ASCAP 1993; *Publications* Ten Imaginary Years (offical Cure biography, jtly 1987), Songwords (co-author and ed, 1989); *Recreations* deep sea diving, hot air ballooning, reading, writing, staring into space...; *Style*— Robert Smith, Esq; ✉ Fiction Records, 97 Charlotte St, London W1P 1LB (☎ 0171 323 5555, fax 0171 323 5323)

SMITH, Robert Lee; s of John Joseph Smith, and Joan Margaret, *née* Parry; *b* 9 Feb 1952; *Educ* St Dunstan's Coll, Magdalene Coll Cambridge (open scholar, MA); *m* 24 May 1986, Susan Elizabeth, da of Raymond and Elizabeth Armfield; 1 da (Anna Elizabeth b 15 Sept 1989), 1 s (Andrew John b 18 July 1991); *Career* admin trainee 1974–76; Dept for Educn and Employment: princ private sec to Sec of State 1985–87, under sec 1994–95, dir for Pupils, Parents and Youth 1995–; co-chm Inst of Mgmnt Civil Serv Network 1995–; *Recreations* folk dancing and music, package holidays; *Style*— Robert Smith, Esq; ✉ Department for Education and Employment, Sanctuary Buildings, Great Smith Street, London SW1P 3BT (☎ 0171 925 5510, fax 0171 925 6986)

SMITH, Robert Walter; s of (Robert) Harvey Smith, and Irene, *née* Shuttleworth; *b* 6 May 1961; *Educ* Cavendish Sch, Cottingley Middle Sch, Beckfoot GS; *m* 2 April 1988, Leanne Carole, da of Leslie Noel Alston; *Career* professional horseman; Euro Bronze medallist 1977, Sunday Times Cup Grand Prix of GB Rider of the Year award 1979, nat champion 1988, King George Cup 1979 and 1988, Cock of the North 1988 and 1989, Nations Cup winner Rome 1988 and Aachen 1989, Dubai Cup 1989, gentleman's champion 1989; memb Br teams in Nation's Cup for twelve years; *Recreations* tennis, boxing, skiing, golf, running; *Style*— Robert Smith, Esq

SMITH, Robin Anthony; TD (1978, Bar 1984), DL (W Yorks 1991); s of Tom Sumerfield Smith (d 1990), of Wetherby, and Mary, *née* Taylor; *b* 15 Feb 1943; *Educ* St Michael's Coll Leeds, Univ of Manchester (LLB); *m* 5 Oct 1967, Jennifer ELizabeth, da of Eric Anthony Roslington (d 1978), of Leeds; 1 s (Jonathan b 1969), 1 da (Sarah b 1972); *Career* cmmnd KOYLI 1966, 5 Bn The Light Inf 1967–86, ret as Lt-Col 1986; admitted slr 1966; Dibb Lupton Broomhead (formerly Dibb Lupton) ptnr 1968–87, managing ptnr 1987–93, sr ptnr 1993–; memb Law Soc 1966– (memb Cncl 1982–91); govr Stonyhurst Coll 1990–; *Recreations* cricket, golf, tennis; *Clubs* Army and Navy, Leeds, Alwoodley Golf, MCC; *Style*— Robin Smith, Esq, TD, DL; ✉ Dibb Lupton Broomhead, 125 London Wall, London EC2Y 5AE (☎ 0171 814 6469, fax 0171 600 1751)

SMITH, Robin Arnold; s of John Arnold Smith, and Joy Lyall; *b* 13 Sept 1963, Durban, SA; *Educ* Northlands Boys' HS Durban SA; *m* 21 Sept 1988, Katherine; 1 s (Harrison b Dec 1990), 1 da (Margaux b July 1994); *Career* professional cricketer; Natal SA 1980–85; Hampshire CCC: debut 1982, awarded county cap 1985, Benson & Hedges Cup winners 1988 and 1992 (Man of the Match), NatWest Trophy winners 1991 (Man of the Match); England: over 58 test caps 1988–, 64 one day ints, highest test score 175 v W Indies 1991; tours: India 1988 (cancelled), Nehro Cup 1988/89, India and W Indies 1989/90, Aust 1990/91, NZ and Aust (incl World Cup) 1991/92, India and Sri Lanka 1992/93, W Indies 1993/94, South Africa 1995/96; dir: Mazuri Sports helmets and sunhats, Judge Tours; *Recreations* reading, fishing, keeping fit, golf; *Style*— Robin Smith, Esq; ✉ c/o Hampshire CCC, County Cricket Ground, Northlands Rd, Southampton SO9 2TY (☎ 01703 333788)

SMITH, Robin Barker; s of Arthur Smith of Clandown, Somerset, and Mary, *née* Thompson; *b* 22 Aug 1946; *Educ* Ulverston GS, Univ of Leeds (MB ChB, ChM), Univ of Oxford (MA), Univ of Chicago; *m* 4 Dec 1971 (m dis 1987), Judith Mary, da of Robert Walton Anderson (d 1986); 1 s (Matthew Robert b 18 Feb 1978), 1 da (Victoria Clare b 5 Feb 1975); m 2, 21 Sept 1990, Carol Jane, da of Joseph Peden; *Career* surgical tutor Radcliffe Infirmary Oxford 1975–81 (registrar 1973–75), res fell Univ of Chicago 1979–80; conslt surgeon Royal United Hosp Bath 1981–; FRCS (1975); *Books* chapters in various surgical texts 1980–88; *Recreations* skiing, tennis, music, reading; *Style*— Robin Barker Smith, Esq; ✉ Homefield, Widcombe Hill, Bath BA2 6EA (☎ 01225 64718); Longwood House, The Bath Clinic, Claverton Down Rd, Bath (☎ 01225 835555)

SMITH, Rt Rev Robin Jonathan Norman; *see:* Hertford, Bishop of

SMITH, Baron (Life Peer UK 1978), of Marlow, Co Bucks; Sir (Edwin) Rodney Smith; KBE (1975); o s of Dr Edwin Smith; *b* 10 May 1914; *Educ* Westminster, London Univ (MS, BS, MRCS, LRCP, FRCS); *m* 1, 1938 (m dis 1971), Mary Rodwell; 3 s (Hon Martin Rodney b 1942, Hon Andrew Edward Rodney b 1948, Hon Robert Aidan Rodney b 1956), 1 da (Hon Elinor b 1950); m 2, 1971, Susan, da of Dr Rowdon Marrian Fry; *Career* pres RCS 1973–77, chm Conference of Royal Colls (UK) 1976–78, pres Royal Soc of Med 1978; examiner in surgery London Univ; consulting surgn: St George's Hosp (surgn 1946), Wimbledon Hosp, Royal Prince Alfred Hosp Sydney NSW; memb House of Lords Bridge Team in matches against Commons since 1979; *Style*— The Rt Hon the Lord Smith, KBE; ✉ Dower Cottage, Marlow Common, Bucks

SMITH, Dr Roger; s of Sylvanus Joseph Smith (d 1973), of Newcastle under Lyme, Staffs, and Winifred Beatrice, *née* Adams (d 1979); *b* 3 Feb 1930; *Educ* Newcastle under Lyme HS, Trinity Coll Cambridge (MA, MD), UCH London (PhD); *m* 25 June 1955, Barbara Ann, da of Harold Willatt (d 1987), of Newcastle under Lyme, Staffs; 1 s (Julian b 22 May 1960); 3 da (Philippa b 7 Dec 1956, Clare b 6 April 1962, Katharine b 3 April 1966); *Career* served: Rifle Bde 1948, Intelligence Corps 1949; sr Wellcome res fell UCH London 1965–68, clinical reader Nuffield Depts of Med and Orthopaedic Surgery Oxford 1969–77, fell Nuffield Coll Oxford 1971–77, conslt physician in metabolic med John Radcliffe Hosp and Nuffield Orthopaedic Centre Oxford 1977–95, hon conslt physician Nuffield Orthopaedic Centre Oxford 1995–; fell Green Coll Oxford 1984–95 (emeritus fell 1995); memb Cncl RCP 1985–89 (regnl advsr 1981–85), chm Med Staff Cncl and Med Exec Ctee Oxford Hosps 1987–89; memb: Scientific Advsy Ctee Brittle Bone Soc, Soc for Relief of Paget's Disease (chm), Cncl Nat Osteoporosis Soc, Assoc of Physicians, FRCP; *Books* Electrolyte Metabolism in Severe Infantile Malnutrition (1968), Biochemical Disorders of the Skeleton (1979), Osteoporosis 1990 (1990); *Recreations* badminton, tennis; *Style*— Dr Roger Smith; ✉ 6 Southcroft, Elsfield Rd, Old Marston, Oxford OX3 0PF; Nuffield Orthopaedic Centre Headington, Oxford OX3 7LD (☎ 01865 741155)

SMITH, Roland Hedley; CMG (1994); s of Alan Hedley Smith, of Sheffield, and Elizabeth Louise, *née* Froggatt; *b* 11 April 1943; *Educ* King Edward VII Sch Sheffield, Keble Coll Oxford (BA, MA); *m* 27 Feb 1971, Katherine Jane, da of Philip Graham Lawrence (d 1975), of Brighton; 2 da (Rebecca b 1972, Ursula b 1975); *Career* HM Dip Serv: third sec FO 1967, second sec Moscow 1969, second later first sec UK Delgn to NATO Brussels 1971, first sec FCO 1974, first sec and cultural attaché Moscow 1978, FCO 1980, attached to Int Inst for Strategic Studies 1983, political advsr and head of Chancery Berlin 1984, Sci Energy and Nuclear Dept FCO 1988, head of Non Proliferation and Def Dept FCO 1990–92, min and dep permanent rep UK Delgn to NATO Brussels 1992–95, dir (Int Security) FCO 1995–; *Books* Soviet Policy Towards West Germany (1985); *Recreations* music, choral singing; *Clubs* Royal Cwlth Soc; *Style*— Roland Smith, Esq, CMG; ✉ c/o Foreign & Commonwealth Office, London SW1A 2AH (☎ 0171 270 3000)

SMITH, Sheriff Ronald Good; s of Adam Smith (d 1961), and Selina Spence, *née* Wotherspoon (d 1969); *b* 24 July 1933; *Educ* King's Park Sr Secondary Sch, Univ of Glasgow (BL); *m* 16 Feb 1962, Joan Robertson Beharrie, of Perth; 2 s (Douglas Adam b 1964, Andrew John b 1967); *Career* Nat Serv 1952–54, served in Korea and Keyna (Corpl); slr 1962–84; appointed Sheriff 1984; *Style*— Sheriff Ronald G Smith; ✉ 29 Broomcliff, 30 Castleton Drive, Newton Mearns, Glasgow G77 5LG

SMITH, (Charles) Russell; CBE; *Career* co-fndr Allied Textile Companies plc 1963 (chm until 1991); non-exec dir: Lloyds Bank plc 1986–, Lloyds Abbey Life plc 1988–, Lloyds Merchant Bank (Holdings) Ltd 1989–, Heywood Williams Group plc 1990; former pres Br Textile Confedn; *Style*— Russell Smith, Esq, CBE; ✉ Lloyds Bank plc, 71 Lombard Street, London EC3P 3BS (☎ 0171 626 1500)

SMITH, Sally Lou; da of Arthur L Jones (d 1977), of Bradford, Penn, and Agnes, *née* Atwood (d 1987); *b* 6 Aug 1925; *Educ* Wellesley Coll Mass USA (BA), Camberwell Sch of Arts and Crafts; *m* 5 July 1952 (m dis 1962), Charles Ross Smith, s of Charles Ross Smith (d 1957), of Pa, USA; *Career* bookbinder; work on flood-damaged books Biblioteca Nazionale Florence 1966–68, pres Designer Bookbinders 1979–81, solo bookbinding exhibition Wellesley Coll Mass USA 1982 (also at Centro Del Bell Libro Ascona Switzerland 1974); work in public collections: Br Library, V & A, Birmingham Reference Library, NY Public Library, Rosenbach Collection USA, Lilley Library USA, Wellesley Coll Library USA, Univ of Texas Humanities Res Centre, Br Crafts Cncl, Royal Library The Hague, Eton Coll Library; Maj J R Abbey award for Bookbinding 1965, Sunday Telegraph Br Crafts award for Bookbinding 1977; fell Designer Bookbinders 1965, memb Art Workers' Guild 1975; *Recreations* reading, walking, friends; *Style*— Mrs Sally Lou Smith; ✉ 6 Leighton Grove, London NW5 2RA (☎ 0171 267 7516)

SMITH, Simon Timothy; s of Peter Smith (d 1991), and June Ann Smith, of Melbourne; *b* 29 April 1960; *Educ* Gowerton GS West Glamorgan, King Edward VI Sch Lichfield, Univ of Lancaster (BA), Magdalene Coll Cambridge (MA, rugby blues, athletics half blue); *m* 11 July 1986, Dr Paula Jane Smith, da of Eric David Nock; 2 s (Samuel David b 6 June 1990, George Peter b 8 Jan 1992), 1 da (Elizabeth Anne b 3 Jan 1995); *Career* rugby union player (right wing); clubs: Lichfield 1978–79, Vale of Lune 1979, Fylde 1979–82, over 150 appearances Wasps 1983–91, Old Blues (Christ's Hosp Old Boys) 1991–92; England: 6 sch under 19 caps 1979, students rep 1982, full debut v Romania 1985, Five Nations debut v France 1985, 9 caps scoring 3 tries; chartered surveyor: Richard Ellis 1984–88, Fletcher King plc 1988–90, Conrad Ritblat (assoc dir and head of Industl Dept) 1990–92; pt/t rugby coach Eton Coll and Richmond under 21's 1992–93, master Eton Coll 1993–95, master/asst housemaster Cranleigh Sch 1995–; contrib article to Estates Gazette 1991; ARICS 1986; *Recreations* committed Christian, golf, tennis; *Style*— Simon Smith, Esq; ✉ Wasps FC, Repton Ave, Sudbury, nr Wembley, Middlesex HA0 3DW (☎ 0181 903 6066)

SMITH, Stan; *b* 3 April 1929, Hull; *Career* artist; Ruskin Sch of Drawing and Fine Art Univ of Oxford: head of fine art 1979–87, also variously dep/actg Ruskin master, admissions tutor and chm of examiners (MA Oxon); pres The London Gp 1977–93 (hon life pres 1993), fndr memb and vice chm Soc of Landscape Painters 1989–; organiser of exhbns for: GLC, London Gp (S London Art Gallery, Barbican Centre, Morley Gallery, Gulbenkian and Moore Galleries), Arts Cncl of GB, Lancs and Cornwall CCs, Ashmolean Museum Oxford; tutor in drawing RCA 1974–79 (MA RCA); sometime course dir: Florida State Univ, Univ of Oxford, UCLA, RCA; visiting lectr: Chelsea Sch of Art, London Coll of Printing, Brighton Coll of Art, Falmouth Sch of Art, N Staffs Poly; conslt ed Artist's and Illustrator's Magazine, conslt BBC2 prog A Feeling for Paint, delegate on symposium Images and Understanding (with Prof Sir Ernst Gombrich, Dr Jonathan Miller and Prof Colin Blakemore), occasional broadcaster; fell Linacre Coll Oxford 1981; memb Soc of Authors 1987, RWS 1992; *Solo Exhibitions* Falmouth Sch of Art 1978, Morley Gallery 1980, Ruskin Sch of Drawing 1985, Preston Poly 1986, Artspace Gallery 1987, Gallery 10 1990, Galleria Internationale Portugal 1991, Chelsea Arts Club 1994; *Group Exhibitions* numerous incl: 20th Century Br Art Fair, Arts Club Dover St, Bankside Gallery London, Battersea Arts Centre, Business Art Gallery, Camden Arts Centre, The Cartoon Gallery London, Chelsea Arts Club, Connaught Brown, RA Summer Exhbns, RCA, Mall Galleries, Morley Gallery, Richard Delmarco Gallery, Smith's Gallery, Whitechapel Art Gallery, Bede Gallery Jarrow, Gardner Centre for the Arts Univ of Sussex, Ruskin Sch Oxford, John Moores Biennales Liverpool, Newcastle Poly, Newlyn Gallery St Ives, Pavilion Gallery Brighton, Walker Art Gallery Liverpool; *Collections* work in numerous private and public collections incl: National Collection (Chantrey Bequest), Br Museum, others in Amsterdam, Bali, Hong Kong, Iceland, Italy, LA, NY, Dubai; *Awards* Hunting Group Prize 1987, Daler Rowney Prize RA Summer Exhbn 1985, runner-up Charles Wollaston Award for most distinguished work in RA Summer Exhbn 1983; *Books* How to Draw and Paint (1980), The Artist's Manual (ed jtly, 1981), The Figure: Drawing and Painting (1983), Drawing and Sketching (1984), The Complete Drawing Course (1994), The Complete Watercolour Course (1996); *Clubs* Chelsa Arts (chm 1995–), Groucho; *Style*— Stan Smith, Esq; ✉ 11 Buckingham Place, Brighton, E Sussex BN1 3TD

SMITH, Col Stanley Jackman; s of George Stanley Smith (d 1960), of Purley, Surrey, and Dorothy Ellen, *née* Jackman (d 1980); *b* 16 Sept 1921; *Educ* St Paul's, The Law Soc's Sch of Law; *m* 15 Feb 1958, Gisela, da of Kurt Flessa, of Minden, Germany; 3 da (Karoline Susanne b 4 Feb 1959, Jennifer Christine b 9 June 1960, Helen Deborah b 20 April 1962); *Career* articled clerk Evill & Coleman Solicitors London 1938–42, admitted slr 1944; served Army 1942–75: RA 1942–43, Intelligence Corps 1943–46 (active serv Burma Campaign 1944–45), Staff Capt (Legal) and Dep Asst Judge Advocate Gen (Indian Army) 1946–47, Prosecuting Offr Japanese and German War Crimes Trials (Singapore, Malaya, Burma, Borneo, Hong Kong, Germany) 1946–50, Mil Dept Office of the Judge Advocate Gen of the Forces 1947–48, joined Directorate of Army Legal Services 1948, promoted Maj 1951, Dep Asst Dir Army Legal Services 1951–60 (served BAOR, Korea (active serv), Japan, Middle East Land Forces, Egypt, Kenya), promoted Lt Col 1960, Asst Dir Army Legal Services 1960–67 (War Office, BAOR), promoted Col 1967, Dep Dir Army Legal Services (Far East Land Forces 1969–71, MOD 1971–73), CO Army Legal Aid Section Germany 1973–75, Col RARO 1975–; decorations: 1939–45 Star, Burma Star, Defence Medal 1939–45, War Medal 1945, Queen's Medal for Korea, UN Medal for Korea 1953; prosecuting slr Hampshire Constabulary 1975–85; lay memb Investigation Ctee ICAEW 1988–, summary writer Criminal Appeal Office of Court of Appeal (Criminal Div) 1989–; memb: Law Soc 1959, Int Soc for Military Law and the Law of War (UK Gp) 1993; *Recreations* reading history, gardening, walking, The USA; *Clubs* Army and Navy; *Style—* Col Stanley Smith; ✉ 5 St Lawrence Close, Stratford-Sub-Castle, Salisbury, Wiltshire SP1 3LW (☎ 01722 500133)

SMITH, Prof Stanley William (Stan); s of Stanley Smith (d 1980), of Warrington, and Edith, *née* Barlowe; *b* 12 Jan 1943; *Educ* Boteler GS, Jesus Coll Cambridge (MA, PhD); *m* (m dis); 1 da (Caroline Elizabeth b 2 July 1965), 2 s (Philip Malcolm b 2 Oct 1967, Stephen Mark b 31 March 1971); *Career* asst lectr in English Univ of Aberdeen 1967–68; Univ of Dundee: lectr in English 1968–85, sr lectr 1985–88, reader 1988–89, chair 1989–, head of dept 1989–92 and 1992–94; visiting prof: Univ of Florence 1987, Univ of Zaragoza 1996; memb: Steering Ctee Standing Conf of Arts and Social Sciences 1990–, Bd Euro Soc for the Study of English 1992–93, SOED Postgraduate Awards Ctee 1993–; chm Cncl for Univ English 1991–93 (memb Steering Ctee 1989–93), vice chm Scottish Ctee of Profs of English 1993–95 (memb 1990–); poetry reviews ed The Literary Review 1979–81; gen ed: Longman Critical Reader series 1988–, Longman Studies in Twentieth Century Literature 1991–; *Books* A Sadly Contracted Hero: The Comic Self in Post-War American Fiction (1981), Inviolable Voice: History and Twentieth-Century Poetry (1982), Twentieth-Century Poetry (ed, 1983), W H Auden (1985), Edward Thomas (1986), W B Yeats: A Critical Introduction (1990), The Origins of Modernism: Eliot, Pound, Yeats and the Rhetorics of Renewal (1994), Auden issue: Critical Survey (ed, 1994), W H Auden (1996); *Recreations* classical music, chess, foreign travel, archaeology; *Style—* Prof Stan Smith; ✉ Department of English, University of Dundee, Dundee DD1 4HN (☎ 01382 344411, fax 01382 345503)

SMITH, Prof Stephen Kevin; s of Albert Smith, DFC, of 4 Wellington Court, Wellington Rd, Birkenhead, and Drusilla, *née* Hills; *b* 8 March 1951; *Educ* Birkenhead Sch, Univ of London (MB BS, MD); *m* 8 July 1978, Catriona MacLean, da of Alan Maclean Hobkirk, of 53 Netherby Rd, Edinburgh; 1 s (Richard Alan), 2 da (Lucinda Jane, Alice Charlotte); *Career* lectr Univ of Sheffield 1982–85, conslt in obstetrics and gynaecology MRC Reproductive Biology Unit and Lothian Health Bd 1985–88, prof of obstetrics and gynaecology Univ of Cambridge 1988–; author of various scientific and med pubns; MA (Cantab), Fell Fitzwilliam Coll, MRCOG, MRCS, LRCP; *Recreations* keep-fit, football, politics, military history, music; *Style—* Prof Stephen Smith; ✉ Department of Obstetrics and Gynaecology, University of Cambridge Clinical School, The Rosie Maternity Hospital, Cambridge CB2 2SW (☎ 01223 336871, fax 01223 248811)

SMITH, (Albert) Stephen William; s of Tom Smith (d 1993), of Bury, Lancs, and Marjorie, *née* Sarbutt (d 1979); *b* 19 Oct 1948; *Educ* Bury Church Sch, Bury Technical Coll, Manchester Poly (gen catering dip); *Career* restaurateur; trainee mangr rising to catering mangr Ferranti Ltd 1968–76, gp catering mangr Ward and Goldstone Ltd Salford 1976–80, catering advsr Stockport Sch Meals Serv 1980–84, chef/proprietor Restaurant Nineteen Bradford 1984–; Egon Ronay Restaurant of the Year finalist and 1 Star 1988, Michelin Red M 1988, Yorkshire Post Restaurant of the Decade 1980s, Yorkshire Life Restaurant of the Year 1990 and 1995, Good Food Guide County Restaurant of the Year 1991 and 1993, Michelin star 1994–, 3 rosettes AA Restaurant Guide 1994–; MHCIMA; memb: Restaurant Assoc of GB, Master Chefs of GB; *Recreations* swimming, keep fit; *Style—* Stephen Smith, Esq; ✉ Restaurant Nineteen, North Park Road, Bradford, W Yorkshire BD9 4NT (☎ 01274 492559, fax 01274 483827)

SMITH, Stewart Ranson; CBE (1987); s of John Smith (d 1980), of Ashington, Northumberland, and Elizabeth Atkinson, *née* Barnes; *b* 16 Feb 1931; *Educ* Bedlington GS, Univ of Nottingham (BA, MA), Yale Univ USA (MA); *m* 2 Jan 1960, (Lee) Tjam Mui Smith; *Career* Nat Serv RAEC 1955–57; Br Cncl: asst rep Singapore 1957–59, HQ London 1959–61, dir Br Inst Curitiba Brazil 1961–65, asst rep Sri Lanka 1965–69, seconded to ODA London 1970–73, rep Kenya 1973–76, controller Overseas B HQ 1976–80, rep Spain 1980–87, controller Higher Educn Div 1988, controller Europe Div 1989–90, jefe de gabinete Madrid Capital Europea de Cultura '92 1990–92, advsr on external relations Complutense Univ of Madrid 1992–95; Cruz Oficial del Orden Isabella la Catolica 1989; *Recreations* cricket, music; *Style—* Stewart R Smith, Esq, CBE; ✉ Flat 1, Cumberland House, Clifton Gardens, London W9 1DX

SMITH, Stuart Crawford; s of David Norman Smith, of Spain, and Sheila Marie, *née* Hallowes; *b* 17 Sept 1953; *Educ* City of Bath Boys' Sch, Wadham Coll Oxford (major scholar, BA), Univ of Sussex (MA); *m* 23 Dec 1987, Hilary Joy Phillips; *Career* ed Marketing Week Magazine 1988– (joined as sub ed 1982); *Recreations* skiing, reading, swimming; *Style—* Stuart Smith, Esq; ✉ Centaur Publishing, St Giles House, 49–50 Poland St, London W1V 4AX (☎ 0171 439 9429, fax 0171 439 9669)

SMITH, Terence Barriston (Terry); s of Herbert William Smith, of Arundel, Sussex, and Elsie Eva, *née* Hasker; *b* 12 July 1941; *Educ* N Hammersmith Sch of Art, Ealing Tech Coll, Open Univ (BA); *m* (m dis), Marion; 1 da (Justine Emma b 2 Aug 1966), 1 s (Richard Adam b 19 Jan 1968); *partner* Jean Douglas-Withers; *Career* mgmnt trainee Metal Box Co 1960–62; systems analyst: Ford Motor Co 1962–65, J Stone Ltd 1965–67; BBC: systems analyst 1967–68, sr systems analyst 1968–70, chief systems analyst 1970–73, asst head of TV computer projects 1973–76, head of TV computer servs 1976–91, head of IT BBC TV 1991–95; dir and ptnr Business Solutions Partnership 1995–; Freeman City of London 1988, Liveryman Worshipful Company of Information Technologists 1988; FBCS 1976, CEng; *Recreations* golf, opera, cricket, wine; *Clubs* Gerrards Cross Golf, Harleford Golf Middlesex CC; *Style—* Terry Smith, Esq; ✉ Badgers Mount, Bottle Square Lane, Radnage, Bucks HP14 4DP (☎ 01494 483647); Business Solutions Partnership, Wyke House, Bulstrode Way, Gerrards Cross, Bucks SL9 7QU

SMITH, Terence Charles (Terry); s of Ernest George Smith (d 1985), of London, and Eva Ada, *née* Bruce; *b* 15 May 1953; *Educ* Stratford GS, Univ Coll Cardiff (BA), Mgmnt Coll Henley (MBA); *m* 31 Aug 1974, Barbara Mary, da of Ivor Thomas George, of Ebbw Vale; 2 da (Katy b 1981, Emily b 1984); *Career* Barclays Bank 1974–83: mgmnt trainee, branch mangr, fin mangr; bank analyst W Greenwell and Co 1984–86; Barclays de Zoete Wedd 1986–88: dir, bank analyst, head of fin desk; bank analyst James Capel and Co 1989–90, dep md and head of UK company research UBS Phillips & Drew 1990–92 (dismissed following publication of book on suspect UK financial accounting techniques), ptnr Collins Stewart stockbrokers 1992–; rated leading banking sector analyst 1984–90; ACIB, memb Stock Exchange; *Books* Accounting for Growth (1992, 2 edn 1996); *Recreations* riding, motorcycling, sailing; *Style—* Terry Smith, Esq; ✉ 9 Springfield Place, Springfield Green, Chelmsford, Essex CM1 5ZA (☎ 01245 268209); 64 Trafalgar Court, Glamis Rd, Wapping, London E1 9TF (☎ 0171 488 3496); Collins Stewart & Co, 21 New Street, London EC2M 4HR (☎ 0171 283 1133)

SMITH, Terence Denby (Terry); s of Sydney Smith (d 1986), of Wakefield, Yorkshire, and Florence Evelyn, *née* Lister; *b* 28 Jan 1934; *Educ* Wheelwright GS Dewsbury Yorks; *m* 1, 1957 (m dis 1980), Audrey Booth; 2 s (Howard Michael b 1965, David Mathew b 1968); m 2, 1983, Pamela Elaine Leather; *Career* professional journalist 1951–60, fndr Mercury Press Agency Ltd 1960; Radio City plc: fndr 1973, md 1973–92, chm 1992–; chm: Broadcast Marketing Services Ltd 1982–86, EMAP Radio Ltd (now owners of Radio City) 1992–, City FM Ltd, Radio City Gold Ltd, Independent Radio News Ltd 1988–; dir: Liverpool Empire Theatre Trust Ltd 1980–, Liverpool FC and Athletic Grounds PLC 1992–; dir: Satellite Media Services Ltd 1988–95, UK Advertising Ltd 1993–96, Media Projects Ltd 1993–; chm Assoc of Ind Radio Cos 1983–85; *Recreations* football, golf, winter sports; *Clubs* Royal Liverpool Golf, Liverpool Artists, Liverpool Racquet; *Style—* Terry Smith, Esq; ✉ Radio City, 8–10 Stanley Street, Liverpool L1 6AF (☎ 0151 227 5100, fax 0151 471 0330)

SMITH, Thomas William David; s of George Ernest Smith, of Sheffield, and Dora Staniforth; *b* 4 Aug 1939; *Educ* Selwyn Coll Cambridge (MA, MB BChir), St Mary's Hosp Med Sch (FRCS, FRCSE); *m* 24 Nov 1967, Christina Mary, da of William O'Connor, of Dublin; 3 s (Nicholas William Patrick b 1968, Thomas Fitzgerald George b 1972, Hugh Francis Niall b 1974), 2 da (Gillian Mary b 1970, Alexandra Gwen b 1972); *Career* orthopaedic registrar Oxford 1968–70, sr orthopaedic registrar Sheffield 1970–73, lectr Univ of Sheffield 1973–76, conslt orthopaedic surgn Sheffield 1976–; *Recreations* fly fishing, skiing; *Style—* Thomas Smith, Esq; ✉ Cleveland House, 3 Whitworth Rd, Sheffield, South Yorkshire S10 3HD (☎ 0114 230 8398); Orthopaedic Department, Northern General Hospital, Herries Rd, Sheffield S5 7AU (☎ 0114 243 4343)

SMITH, Timothy John; MP (C) Beaconsfield (majority 23,597); s of late Capt Norman Wesley Smith, CBE (sometime Cdre Orient Steam Navigation Co), and late Nancy Phyllis, da of Engr Capt F J Pedrick, RN; *b* 5 Oct 1947; *Educ* Harrow, St Peter's Coll Oxford (MA); *m* 1980, Jennifer Jane, da of late Maj Sir James Sidney Rawdon Scott-Hopkins, MP, MEP; 2 s (Henry b 1982, Charles b 1984); *Career* articled Gibson Harris & Turnbull 1969–71, sr auditor Peat Marwick Mitchell 1971–73, co sec Coubro & Scrutton Holdings 1973–79, MP Ashfield 1977–79, sec Parly and Law Ctee ICAEW 1979–82; MP (C) Beaconsfield 1982–, PPS to Rt Hon Leon Brittan 1983–85, Parly under sec NI Office Jan-Oct 1994, memb NI Select Ctee 1994–, vice chm Cons Backbench Fin Ctee 1987–92, sec Cons Backbench Trade and Indust Ctee 1987–92, memb Public Accounts Ctee 1987–92 and 1995–, vice chm and jt treas Cons Pty 1992–94; FCA; *Style—* Timothy Smith, Esq, MP; ✉ House of Commons, London SW1 (☎ 0171 219 3000)

SMITH, Prof Sir Trevor Arthur; kt (1996); s of late Arthur James Smith, of Newnham-on-Severn, Gloucs, and Vera Gladys, *née* Cross; *b* 14 June 1937; *Educ* LSE (BSc); *m* 1, 14 Feb 1960 (m dis 1973), Brenda Susan, *née* Eustace; 2 s (Adam James William b 6 June 1964, Gideon Matthew Kingsley b 14 May 1966); m 2, 9 Aug 1979, Julia Donnithorne, *née* Bullock; 1 da (Naomi Thérèse b 8 June 1981); *Career* school teacher LCC 1958–59, temp asst lectr Univ of Exeter 1959–60, res offr Acton Soc Tst 1960–62, lectr in politics Univ of Hull 1962–67 visiting assoc prof California State Univ Los Angeles 1969; QMC (later QMWC) London: lectr (later sr lectr) in political studies 1967–83, head of dept 1972–85, dean of social studies 1979–82, prof 1983–91, pro-princ 1985–87, sr pro-princ 1987–89, sr vice princ 1989–91; vice chllr Univ of Ulster 1991–; dir: Job Ownership Ltd 1978–85, New Society Ltd 1986–88, Statesman and Nation Publishing Co Ltd 1988–90, Gerald Duckworth & Co Ltd 1990–95; chm Political Studies Assoc of UK 1988–89 (vice pres 1989–91, pres 1991–93); govr: Sir John Cass and Redcoats Sch 1979–84, Univ of Haifa 1985–92, Bell Educn Tst 1988–93; memb Tower Hamlets DHA 1987–91 (vice chm 1989–91), vice pres Patients Assoc of UK 1988–, dep pres Inst of Citizenship Studies 1991–; pres Belfast Civic Tst 1995–; memb: Administrative Bd Int Assoc of Univs 1995–96, Editorial Bd *Government and Opposition* 1995–, Bd A Taste of Ulster 1996–; Parliamentary candidate (Lib) Lewisham West 1959; tstee Joseph Rowntree Reform Trust Ltd 1975–87 (chm 1987–); Hon LLD: Dublin 1992, Hull 1993, Belfast 1995, Nat Univ of Ireland 1996; FRHistS 1986, CIMgt 1992, FRSA 1994, hon memb of the Senate of the Fachhochsule Augsberg 1994; *Clubs* Reform; *Style—* Prof Sir Trevor Smith; ✉ University of Ulster, Coleraine, Co Londonderry, Northern Ireland BT52 1SA (☎ 01265 324329, fax 01265 324901)

SMITH, William James; s of William Smith, and Alice, *née* Divers; *b* 2 Dec 1954; *Educ* St Aloysius Coll Glasgow, Heriot-Watt Univ (BSc); *m* 3 July 1978, Marion Anne, da of Hugh Charles Slevin (d 1989); 1 s (Alastair b 1983), 3 da (Sarah b 1981, Hannah b 1985, Moya b 1994); *Career* asst investmt mangr Standard Life Assur Co 1977–84, jt md Prudential-Bache 1986–90, dir BZW Securities 1990–96, dep chm BZW Asset Management 1996–; FFA 1982, FIMA 1993; *Recreations* running; *Style—* William Smith, Esq; ✉ BZW Asset Management, Seal House, 1 Swan Lane, London EC4R 3UD (☎ 0171 775 6264, fax 0171 775 6243)

SMITH, Dr (Ronald) William James (Bill); s of Ronald Sidney James Smith, and Amy Elizabeth Dinah Smith; *b* 12 Feb 1943; *Educ* Neath GS, Welsh Nat Sch of Med (MB BCh, MRCGP), London Sch of Hygiene and Tropical Med (MSc, Chadwick medal), Royal Coll of Obstetricians and Gynaecologists (dip); *m* 2 April 1966, Susan Louise, da of Percival Joseph Sadler; 3 da (Victoria Jane (Mrs Fenerty) b 12 July 1967, Josephine Clare b 14 Dec 1968, Samantha Fay (Mrs Ray) b 9 April 1970); *Career* house surgn Cardiff Royal Infirmary 1967–68, house physician Neath General Hosp 1968; RAMC: Capt 1968–73, Maj 1973–81, Lt Col 1981–85; conslt in public health med East Suffolk 1985–90; dir of public health med: Pembrokeshire 1990–91, Mid Glamorgan 1991–; fell Faculty of Public Health Med; *Recreations* gardening, walking, sailing, reading; *Style—* Dr Bill Smith; ✉ Mid Glamorgan Health Authority, District Headquarters, Albert Road, Pontypridd CF37 1LA

SMITH-BINGHAM, Col Jeremy David; s of Col Oswald Cyril Smith-Bingham (d 1979), of Glos, and Vera Mabel Johnson (d 1989); *b* 29 July 1939; *Educ* Eton, Sandhurst; *m* 22 July 1969, Priscilla Mary, da of Lt-Col Godfrey Sturdy Incledon-Webber, TD (d 1986); 3 s (Richard David b 1970, Alexander John b 1973, Guy Jeremy b 1978); *Career* cmmnd Royal Horse Gds (The Blues) 1959, served England, Cyprus, N Ireland, Germany, CO The Blues and Royals 1982–85, Lt-Col cmdg Household Cavalry 1990–, Silver Stick-in-Waiting 1990–93, Chief of Staff London Dist 1993–94, DG Br Equestrian Fedn 1994–; Liveryman Worshipful Co of Haberdashers; *Recreations* skiing, tennis, rackets, water sports, riding; *Clubs* White's, Cavalry and Guards'; *Style—* Col Jeremy Smith-Bingham; ✉ St Brannocks House, Braunton, Devon EX33 1HN (☎ 01271 812270)

SMITH-DODSWORTH, David John; s and h of Sir John Christopher Smith-Dodsworth, 8 Bt, *qv*; *b* 23 Oct 1963; *Educ* Ampleforth; *Career* farmer; *Style—* David Smith-Dodsworth, Esq; ✉ Thornton Watlass Hall, Ripon, Yorkshire

SMITH-DODSWORTH, Sir John Christopher; 8 Bt (GB 1784), of Newland Park and Thornton Watlass, Yorks; s of Sir Claude Matthew Smith-Dodsworth, 7 Bt (d 1940); *b* 4 March 1935; *Educ* Ampleforth; *m* 1, 1961 (m dis 1971), Margaret Anne, da of Alfred Jones, of Pludds, Glos; 1 s (David John b 1963), 1 da (Cyrilla Denise b 1962); m 2, 1972,

Margaret Theresa (d 1990), da of Henry Grey, of Auckland, NZ; 1 s (Daniel Leui'i b 1974); m 3, 10 March 1991, Lolita, da of Romeo Pulante, of Laur, Philippines; 1 s (John Joseph b 12 April 1995), 1 da (Joanna Marie b 23 April 1992); *Heir* s, David John Smith-Dodsworth b 23 Oct 1963; *Publications include* New Zealand Ferns and Allied Plants (with P J Brownsey, 1989), New Zealand Native Shrubs and Climbers (1991); *Style*— Sir John Smith-Dodsworth, Bt

SMITH-GORDON, Sir (Lionel) Eldred Peter; 5 Bt (UK 1838); s of Sir Lionel Eldred Pottinger Smith-Gordon, 4 Bt (d 1976); *b* 7 May 1935; *Educ* Eton, Trinity Coll Oxford; *m* 1962, Sandra Rosamund Ann, da of late Wing Cdr Walter Farley, DFC; 1 s (Lionel George Eldred b 1964), 1 da (Isobel Charlotte Laura b 1966); *Heir* s, Lionel George Eldred Smith-Gordon b 1 July 1964; *Career* chm: Consolidated Holdings (Gresham) Ltd 1976–, Smith-Gordon and Co Ltd scientific, technical and med publishers 1988–; *Style*— Sir Eldred Smith-Gordon, Bt; ✉ 13 Shalcomb Street, London SW10 (☎ 0171 352 8506)

SMITH-GORDON, Lionel George Eldred; s and h of Sir (Lionel) Eldred Peter Smith-Gordon, 5 Bt, *qv*; *b* 1 July 1964; *Educ* Eton, Westfield Coll and King's Coll Univ of London; *m* 10 April 1993, Kumi, o da of Masashi Suzuki, of Japan; *Career* with J P Morgan 1986–; *Style*— Lionel Smith-Gordon, Esq; ✉ 424 West End Avenue 19K, New York, New York 10024, USA

SMITH-MARRIOTT, Sir Hugh Cavendish; 11 Bt (GB 1774), of Sydling St Nicholas, Dorset; s (by 1 m) of Sir Ralph George Smith-Marriott, 10 Bt (d 1987); *b* 22 March 1925; *Educ* Bristol Cathedral Sch; *m* 1953, Pauline Anne (d 1985), da of Frank Fawcett Holt, of Bristol; 1 da (Julie Anne (Mrs David A Graveney) b 1958); *Heir* bro, Peter Francis Smith-Marriott b 14 Feb 1927; *Recreations* chm Old Cathedralians Soc; *Clubs* Gloucestershire CCC, MCC, Durham CCC, Bristol Savages, Bristol RFC, Old Cathedralians Soc; *Style*— Sir Hugh Smith-Marriott, Bt; ✉ 26 Shipley Rd, Westbury-on-Trym, Bristol BS9 3HS

SMITH-MAXWELL, Archie Lonsdale Shipley; s of Lt Col John Douglas Hamilton Smith-Maxwell (d 1959), and Winifred Joan, *née* Formby; *b* 6 March 1927; *Educ* Eton; *m* 28 Nov 1950, Patricia Mary Wentworth, da of Maj Philip Wentworth Bell (d 1961); 2 s (Charles James Lonsdale b 1952, Philip John b 1953); *Career* served 1 The Royal Dragoons 1944–49; MFH The Ledbury 1966–76; livestock and bloodstock breeder (int judge); pres Irish Draught Horse Soc of GB; memb: S Worcs Cons Assoc, Br Legion; *Recreations* field sports; *Clubs* Cavalry and Guards'; *Style*— Archie Smith-Maxwell, Esq; ✉ Welland Lodge Farm, Upton-on-Severn, Worcestershire WR8 0SS (☎ 0168459 2161)

SMITH OF GILMOREHILL, Baroness (Life Peer UK 1995), of Gilmorehill in the District of the City of Glasgow; Elizabeth Margaret Smith; DL (City of Edinburgh); da of late Frederick William Moncrieff Bennett; *b* 4 June 1940; *Educ* Univ of Glasgow; *m* 5 July 1967, Rt Hon John Smith, QC, MP (d 1994), son of late Archibald Leitch Smith, of Dunoon, Argyll; 3 da (Hon Sarah b 22 Nov 1968, Hon Jane b 28 July 1971, Hon Catherine b 4 May 1973); *Career* memb Press Complaints Cmmn 1995–; non-exec dir Scottish TV; chm Edinburgh Festival Fringe Soc; cncl memb: British Heart Fndn, Russo-British Chamber of Commerce; memb governing body of British Assoc for Central and Eastern Europe; *Style*— The Rt Hon Lady Smith of Gilmorehill, DL; ✉ c/o House of Lords, London SW1A OPW

SMITHAM, Peter; s of Brinley James Smitham, and Violet May, *née* Linden; *b* 11 May 1942; *Educ* Univ Coll Swansea (BSc), Univ of Salford (DMS), Stanford Univ California (Sr Exec Prog); *m* Lynne Helen, *née* Wolfendale; 2 da (Andrea, Samantha); *Career* mgmnt Co-operative Wholesale Society 1964–67, ops dir then gen mangr ITT 1967–71, gen mangr Barclay Securities 1971–73, md Jermyn Holdings 1973–83, md European electronics Lex Service plc 1983–85, managing ptnr Schroder Ventures 1994– (ptnr 1985–); dir various other companies; *Style*— Peter Smitham, Esq; ✉ Schroder Ventures, 20 Southampton Street, London WC2E 7QG (☎ 0171 632 1031, fax 0171 497 2174)

SMITHERS, Prof Alan George; s of Alfred Edward (d 1976), of London, and Queenie Lilian, *née* Carmichael (d 1994); *b* 20 May 1938; *Educ* Barking Abbey, King's Coll London (BSc, PhD), Univ of Bradford (MSc, PhD); *m* 27 Aug 1962, Angela Grace, da of David Wykes, of Exeter; 2 da (Vaila Helen b 1967, Rachel Hilary b 1969); *Career* lectr in botany Birkbeck Coll London 1964–67, sr lectr in educn Univ of Bradford 1969–75 (research fell 1967–69), prof of educn Univ of Manchester 1976–96, prof of educn (policy research) Brunel Univ 1996–; fell Soc for Res in Higher Educn, former memb Nat Curriculum Cncl, memb Beaumont Ctee on Nat Vocational Qualifications, CPsychol; *Books* Sandwich Courses: An Integrated Education? (1976), The Progress of Mature Students (with A Griffin, 1986), The Growth of Mixed A Levels (with P Robinson, 1988), The Shortage of Mathematics and Physics Teachers (with P Robinson, 1988), Increasing Participation in Higher Education (with P Robinson, 1989), Graduates in the Police Service (with S Hill and G Silvester, 1990), Teacher Provision in the Sciences (with P Robinson, 1990), Gender, Primary Schools and the National Curriculum (with P Zientek, 1991), The Vocational Route into Higher Education (1991), Teacher Provision: Trends and Perceptions (with P Robinson, 1991), Staffing Secondary Schools in the Nineties (with P Robinson, 1991), Every Child in Britain (Report of Channel 4 Education Commission, 1991), Beyond Compulsory Schooling (with P Robinson, 1991), Technology in the National Curriculum (with P Robinson, 1992), Technology at A Level (with P Robinson, 1992), Assessing the Value (with C Marsden, 1992), General Studies: Breadth at Level? (with P Robinson, 1993), Changing Colleges: Further Education in the Market Place (with P Robinson, 1993), All Our Futures: Britain's Education Revolution (1993), Technology Teachers (with P Robinson, 1994), The Impact of Double Science (with P Robinson, 1994), Post-18 Education: Growth, Change, Prospect (with P Robinson, 1995), Affording Teachers (with P Robinson, 1995), Co-Educational and Single Sex Schooling (with P Robinson, 1995); *Recreations* theatre, walking, swimming; *Style*— Prof Alan Smithers; ✉ Centre for Education and Employment Research, Brunel University, St Margaret's Road, Twickenham TW1 1PT (☎ 0181 891 8288, fax 0181 891 8286)

SMITHERS, Andrew Reeve Waldron; s of Prof Sir David Waldron Smithers, MD, FRCP, FRCS, FRCR (d 1995), of Ringfield, Knockholt, Kent, and Gwladys Margaret, *née* Angel; gs of Sir Waldron Smithers, MP for 30 yrs Chislehurst and Orpington; *b* 21 Sept 1937; *Educ* Winchester, Clare Coll Cambridge (MA); *m* 8 June 1963, (Amanda) Jill, da of Edward Gilbert Kennedy; 2 s ((Matthew) Pelham b 10 Oct 1964, (Jonathan) Kit b 6 Dec 1967); *Career* chm: Whatman plc (fomerly Whatman Reeve Angel plc) 1969– (dir 1960–), Smithers & Co Ltd (Economic Consits) 1989–; dir: S G Warburg Securities 1967–89 (joined co 1962), Mercury Selected Trust 1977–; *Recreations* conversation, reading, performing arts, cricket, tennis; *Clubs* Brooks's; *Style*— Andrew Smithers, Esq; ✉ Smithers & Co Ltd, 20 St Dunstan's Hill, London EC3R 8HL (☎ 0171 283 3344, fax 0171 283 3345)

SMITHERS, Sir Peter Henry Berry Otway; kt (1970), VRD (and clasp); s of Lt-Col H O Smithers, JP, of Itchen Stoke House; *b* 9 Dec 1913; *Educ* Harrow, Magdalen Coll Oxford (MA, DPhil); *m* 1943, Dojean, da of T M Sayman of St Louis, USA; 2 da; *Career* WWII Lt Cdr RNVR, Naval Staff France 1940, Br Embassy Washington 1940–46, Mexico, Central American Republics, Panama 1942–46; called to the Bar: Inner Temple 1936, Lincoln's Inn 1937; memb Winchester RDC 1946–49; MP (C) Winchester 1950–64; PPS Colonial Office 1952–59; Vice Chm Cons Parly Foreign Affrs Ctee 1959–61, Parly Under Sec of State FO 1962–64; del Consultative Assembly Cncl of Europe 1952–56, UK del to UN Gen Assembly 1960–62, sec gen Cncl of Europe 1964–69; Master Worshipful Co of Turners 1955, Liveryman Goldsmiths Co 1949; sr fell UN Inst for Trg and Res 1969–72; Hon DJur Zurich Univ 1969, Marzotto Prize (Italy) 1969, Alexander von Humboldt Gold Medal 1970, Chevalier de la Légion d'Honneur, Aguila Azteca Mexicana, Medal of Honour Parly Assembly of the Cncl of Europe 1984, RHS Gold Medal (8 times) for Photography, RHS Veitch Meml Medal (Gold) for Servs to Horticulture 1994; 23 one man shows of photography in museums and insts in the US and Europe; hon citizen Commune of Vico Morcote 1994, hon citizen of Switzerland 1995; *Books* Life of Joseph Addison, Adventures of a Gardener (1995); *Recreations* gardening; *Clubs* Carlton, Everglades (Palm Beach), Bath & Tennis (Palm Beach); *Style*— Sir Peter Smithers, VRD; ✉ CH-6921, Vico Morcote, Switzerland (☎ 00 41 91 691973, fax 00 41 91 691692, Internet 100436.163@compuserve.com)

SMITHIES, Karen; OBE (1994); da of Terry Hicken, of Coalville, and Josephine Anne, *née* Spouge; *b* 20 March 1969; *Educ* Ibstock HS, King Edward VII Coll; *m* 28 April 1990, (Robert) Dean Smithies, s of Don Smithies (d 1994); *Career* amateur cricketer; Newark and Sherwood CC (formerly Nottingham Women's CC) 1983–; capt under 18 boy's local team 1985/86; England: 2 one day ints v India 1986, 2 tests and 2 one day ints v Aust 1987, memb team to Aust 1988, memb team touring NZ and Aust 1991/92, winners Women's World Cup 1993, Sports Writers of Great Britain Team of the Year 1993, Daily Express Team of the Year 1993, Sunday Telegraph Team of the Year 1993; worked in print finishing firm 1987–89, currently a dep mangr Coral Racing Ltd (joined 1990); *Recreations* running, going out for meals, looking after hubby; *Style*— Mrs Karen Smithies, OBE; ✉ c/o Women's Cricket Association, Warwickshire County Cricket Ground, Edgbaston Road, Birmingham B5 7QX (☎ 0121 440 0520, fax 0121 446 6344)

SMITHSON, Rt Rev Alan; *see:* Jarrow, Bishop of

SMITHSON, Dr (William) Henry; s of Ronald Geoffrey Smithson (d 1965), of Wetherby, W Yorks, and Harriet, *née* Gregson; *b* 12 March 1951; *Educ* Leeds GS, Univ of Dundee (MB ChB, DRCOG, MRCGP); *m* 24 June 1982, Jeanne Rachael, da of John Edmund Smales, of Roos, E Yorks; 1 s (William John b 6 May 1984), 1 da (Elizabeth Anne b 13 June 1988); *Career* GP trainee York Vocational Trg Scheme 1977–80, assoc family physician The PAS Manitoba Canada 1980–82, princ in gen practice Escrick York 1982–; GP trainer 1986–91, business mangr Yorkshire Medicine 1988–94, vol trg course organiser York 1991–; RCGP: memb Yorks Faculty 1989–, faculty rep on Cncl 1991–94, vice chm Yorks Faculty 1993–, Prince of Wales Educational Fell in Epilepsy 1996; memb Epilepsy Task Force 1993–; memb: BMA 1982, York Med Soc 1983; professional memb Br Epilepsy Assoc 1994; *Recreations* cricket, writing, foreign travel, golf; *Clubs* York Wanderers Cricket, Fulford Golf (York); *Style*— Dr Henry Smithson; ✉ Drs Belbin, Smithson & Butlin, The Surgery, Escrick, York YO4 6LE (☎ 01904 728243, fax 01904 728826)

SMITHSON, Peter Denham; s of William Blenkiron Smithson (d 1974), and Elizabeth, *née* Denham (d 1978); *b* 18 Sept 1923; *Educ* The GS Stockton-on-Tees, The Sch of Architecture Univ of Durham, Newcastle upon Tyne, Royal Acad Schs London; *m* 18 Aug 1949, Alison Margaret (d 1993), da of Ernest Gill (d 1980); 1 s (Simon), 2 da (Samantha Target, Soraya Wilson); *Career* RE 1942–45; architect in private practice; maj projects (with Alison Smithson) incl: Hunstanton Secdy Modern Sch 1950–54, The Economist Bldg St James St 1959–64, Robin Hood Gdns Tower Hamlets 1963–72, Garden Bldg St Hilda's Coll Oxford 1967–70, Second Arts Bldg 1978–81 and Amenity Bldg 1978–85 Univ of Bath, Sch of Architecture and Bldg Engrg Univ of Bath 1982–88, Arts Barn Univ of Bath 1980–90, The Yellow Lookout Lauenforde 1991, Hexenbesenraum Bad Kaulstafen 1991–96; visiting prof: Delft, Munich, Harvard, Bath; memb The Boltons Assoc; *Books* with Alison Smithson: Ordinariness and Light (1970), Without Rhetoric (1973), The Shift (1982), The 30's (1985), Upper Lawn (1986), Italian Thoughts (1993), Changing the Art of Inhabitation (1994); *Style*— Peter Smithson, Esq; ✉ Cato Lodge, 24 Gilston Rd, London SW10 9SR (☎ 0171 373 7423)

SMITHWICK, Michael Stewart; s of Everard Edward Smithwick (d 1976), of Talywain, Monmouthshire, and Eva, *née* Riddington (d 1980); *b* 6 July 1941; *Educ* Stationers' Co Sch, Univ of Leicester (BA), Univ of Lancaster (MSc); *m* 1 Aug 1964, Karen Dorothy, da of John Alfred Stevenson; 2 s (Marcus Jonathan Justin b 13 Feb 1968, Jason Michael Lance b 22 May 1969), 1 da (Sarah Annabel b 24 Jan 1971); *Career* Dexion Ltd 1959–64 (graduate trainee, distribution promotion offr, product mangr), agric mktg mangr Saville Tractors Ltd 1965–66, Massey Ferguson Ltd 1966–71 (regnl mangr south, Euro mktg mangr), BOC Group 1971–80 (mktg dir then dir and gen mangr Electric Welding, md Sparklets International Group), md Nicklin Advertising Ltd 1980–92, md Esprit Sponsorship Ltd 1992–; non-exec dir: Edwards High Vacuum International Ltd 1975–77, TSL Group PLC 1988; MIPA 1982; *Recreations* reading, painting (appreciation rather than practice); *Style*— Michael Smithwick, Esq; ✉ Esprit Group, 176 Blackfriars Road, London SE1 8ER (☎ 0171 928 5055)

SMITS, Coenraad Henri (Coen); s of Gerardus Wilhelmus Smits (d 1982), and Johanna Christina Louise, *née* Taconis; *b* 9 July 1958; *Educ* Erasmus Univ Rotterdam (MEconSci, winner H J Kuhlmeyer prize); *Career* brand positions Sarah Lee 1985–87, sr brand positions Heineken Breweries 1987–89; The Coca-Cola Co: mktg mangr Coca-Cola Netherlands 1989–91, mktg dir Coca-Cola GB 1991–92, category devpt mangr and global brand mangr The Coca-Cola Co Atlanta 1992–95, mktg dir Turkey Region 1995–; *Books* Marketing Information Systems (1985); *Recreations* sailing, field hockey, squash, golf; *Style*— Coen Smits, Esq; ✉ Coca-Cola Turkey Region Office, Fahrettin Kerim Gokay Caddesi, 35, Altunizade, Istanbul, Turkey (☎ 00 90 216 327 0000, fax 00 90 216 326 3232)

SMOUHA, Brian Andrew; s of Wing Cdr Edward Ralph Smouha, OBE (d 1992), and Yvonne Annie, *née* Ades; *b* 3 Sept 1938; *Educ* Harrow, Magdalene Coll Cambridge; *m* 28 Dec 1961, Hana Smouha, da of Simon Btesh (d 1974); 2 s (Joe b 21 Jan 1963, Stephen b 12 April 1965); *Career* CA; ptnr Touche Ross (now Deloitte & Touche) 1970–, seconded under-sec industl devpt unit Dept of Indust 1979–80; liquidator of: Banco Ambrosiano 1983, BCCI 1991; dir British Maritime Technology; pres Cambridge Athletics Union 1961, rep UK at athletics; FCA 1973; *Recreations* skiing, tennis; *Style*— Brian Smouha, Esq; ✉ Deloitte & Touche, Stonecutter Court, 1 Stonecutter Street, London EC4A 4TR (☎ 0171 936 3000, car 0860 336600, fax 0171 583 1198, telex 884739 TRLUNDN G)

SMOUT, Prof (Thomas) Christopher; CBE (1994); s of Arthur Smout (d 1961), of Sheriffs Lench, Evesham, Worcs, and Hilda, *née* Follows (d 1979); *b* 19 Dec 1933; *Educ* Leys Sch Cambridge, Clare Coll Cambridge (MA, PhD); *m* 15 Aug 1959, Anne-Marie, da of Alfred Schoøning, of Charlottenlund, Denmark; 1 s (Andrew b 1963), 1 da (Pernille Anne b 1961); *Career* prof of econ history Univ of Edinburgh 1971 (asst lectr 1959); Univ of St Andrews: prof of Scottish history 1980–91, dir St John's House Centre for Advanced Historical Studies 1992–; historiographer royal Scotland 1993–; memb Royal Cmmn on Ancient and Historical Monuments (Scotland), dep chm Bd Scottish Nat Heritage until 1996, tstee Nat Museum of Scotland until 1995; hon fell Trinity Coll Dublin 1995, Hon DSocSc Queen's Univ Belfast 1995, Hon DSSS Univ of Edinburgh 1996; FRSE 1978, FBA 1988, FRSA 1991, FSA (Scot) 1991; *Books* A History of the Scottish People (1969), A Century of the Scottish People (1986), Scottish Voices (with Sydney Wood, 1990), Prices, Food and Wages in Scotland 1550–1780 (with A J S Gibson, 1995); *Recreations* birds, butterflies, dragonflies and bees; *Style*— Prof Christopher Smout, CBE, FRSE; ✉ Chesterhill, Shore Rd, Anstruther, Fife KY10 3DZ (☎ 01333 310330); St John's House Centre for Advanced Historical Studies, University of St Andrews, St Andrews, Fife (☎ 01334 476161)

SMYTH, Christopher Jackson; s of Col Edward Hugh Jackson Smyth, of Churt, Surrey, and Ursula Helen Lucy, *née* Ross (d 1984); *b* 9 Aug 1946; *Educ* St Lawrence

Coll, Trinity Hall Cambridge (MA); *m* 9 Dec 1972, Jane Elizabeth, da of Dr Robert Alexander Porter (d 1981); 3 da (Debbie-Jayne b 1976, Sophie b 1979, Amanda b 1982); *Career* Lt RN 1966–76, Lt Cdr Sussex Div RNR 1978–82; called to the Bar Inner Temple 1972, in practice SE Circuit, recorder of the Crown Court (asst recorder 1991); *Recreations* sailing, fly-fishing; *Clubs* Army and Navy, RNSA; *Style—* Christopher Smyth, Esq; ✉ 1 Crown Office Row, Temple, London EC4Y 7HH (☎ 0171 797 7500, fax 0171 797 7550, telex 24988 ICOR G); Crown Office Row Chambers, Blenheim House, 120 Church St, Brighton BN1 1WH (☎ 01273 625625, fax 01273 698888)

SMYTH, His Hon Judge; David William; QC (1989); s of William McKeag Smyth (d 1954), and Eva Maud, *née* Moran (d 1992); *b* 12 Nov 1948; *Educ* Methodist Coll Belfast, Queen's Univ Belfast (Porter scholar, LLB Hons); *m* 23 July 1977, Anthea Linda Hall-Thompson, DL, da of Lloyd Hall-Thompson (former MP, d 1992); 3 da (Rachel Anthea b 13 Feb 1979, Hannah Sophia b 31 Dec 1983 d 1984, Rebecca Charlotte b 21 May 1987), 1 s (Alasdair Lloyd William b 26 Aug 1980); *Career* called to the NI Bar 1972, political res London 1972–74, called to the Bar Gray's Inn 1978, called to the Bar of Ireland 1989, County Ct judge Fermanagh and Tyrone 1990–; chm Legal Aid Advsy Bd NI 1994–, chm NI Cncl on Alcohol 1996–; *Recreations* cycling, hill walking, history, opera, theatre; *Style—* His Hon Judge Smyth, QC; ✉ Royal Courts of Justice, Chichester Street, Belfast BT1 3JE (☎ 01238 511621)

SMYTH, (Joseph) Desmond; s of Andrew Smyth (d 1991), and Annie Elizabeth, *née* Scott; *b* 20 April 1950; *Educ* Limavady GS, Queen's Univ Belfast; *m* 23 April 1975, (Irene) Janette, da of John Dale (d 1991); 1 s (Stuart b 1976), 1 da (Kerry b 1978); *Career* Ulster Television: accountant 1975–76, co sec and fin controller 1976–83, md 1983–; dir NIE plc 1996–; pres NI Chamber of Commerce and Indust 1991–92; chm: Prince's Youth Business Tst in NI, Youth Enterprise Scheme (NI); FCA, FRTS, MInstD; *Recreations* cycling, cinema, fishing; *Style—* Desmond Smyth, Esq; ✉ Ulster Televison plc, Havelock House, Ormeau Road, Belfast BT7 1EB (☎ 01232 328122)

SMYTH, Rev (William) Martin; MP (Ulster Unionist) Belfast South (majority 10,070); s of James Smyth, JP (d 1982), of Belfast, and Minnie Kane; *b* 15 June 1931; *Educ* Methodist Coll Belfast, Magee Univ Coll Londonderry, Trinity Coll Dublin (BA, BD), Presbyterian Coll Belfast; *m* 1957, Kathleen Jean, da of David Johnston (d 1978), of Ballymatoskerty, Toomebridge; 2 da (and 1 da decd); *Career* ordained Raffrey Presbyterian Church 1957, installed Alexandra (Belfast) 1963–82, minister without charge April 1982; grand master: Grand Orange Lodge of Ireland 1972–96, World Orange Cncl 1973–82; hon dep grand master Orange Order: USA, NZ, NSW; hon past grand master Canada; elected NI Assembly Oct 1982–86, chm of Assembly Health and Social Services Ctee; MP (UU) Belfast S 1982–, Ulster Unionist Pty spokesman on health, social servs, chief whip 1995–; vice chm Parly Social Servs Panel; memb: Br Exec IPU 1985–92 and 1994, Social Servs Select Ctee 1983–90, UK Exec CPA 1989–, Health Select Ctee 1991–; vice chm Br-Brazilian Gp, sec Br-Israel Gp; treas: Br-Namibia Gp, Br-Morocco Gp; *Recreations* reading, photography, travel; *Style—* The Rev Martin Smyth, MP; ✉ 6 Mornington, Annadale Ave, Belfast BT7 3JS, N Ireland; office: 117 Cregagh Rd, Belfast BT6 0LA, N Ireland (☎ 01232 457009, fax 01232 450837); House of Commons, London SW1 (☎ 0171 219 4198, fax 0171 219 2347)

SMYTH, Peterjohn Jeremy Vignaux; s of late Eric Thomas William Smyth, and Olive Cecily Smyth; *b* 14 April 1940; *Educ* Ampleforth (Cambridge exhibitioner), Clare Coll Cambridge (BA, Dip Arch); *m* Jan 1966, Julia, da of Hubert Alwyn Child; 1 s (Timothy Christian b 15 Sept 1966), 2 da (Rhoda b 9 Jan 1970, Dorothy Vignaux b 21 April 1973); *Career* architect; Morton Lupton & Smith Wallingford Berks 1963–66; Percy Thomas Partnership (Architects) Ltd (formerly Sir Percy Thomas & Son then Percy Thomas Partnership): joined 1966, assoc 1972–80, ptnr 1980–94, dir 1994–; ldr and co-ordinating architect Prince of Wales' new urban village Poundbury (Dorchester) 1993; memb Urban Villages Forum 1994–; work experience incl healthcare, housing and gen architecture projects; contrib articles to various pubns and sometime speaker and lectr; RIBA 1966; *Awards* winner int competition for 600 bed hosp Cairo 1975, int competition for 1000 bed hosp Avellino (Italy) 1992; *Recreations* golf; *Style—* Peterjohn Smyth, Esq; ✉ Percy Thomas Partnership (Architects) Ltd, 10 Cathedral Road, Cardiff, S Glamorgan CF1 9YF (☎ 01222 224334)

SMYTH, Reginald; s of Richard Oliver Smyth and Florence, *née* Pearce; *b* 10 July 1917; *Educ* Galleys Field Sch Hartlepool Cleveland; *m* 1949, Vera, *née* Toyne; *Career* served Royal Fus 1936–45; Civil Serv 1945–55; cartoonist (as Reginald Smythe) Mirror Publications 1955–; creator Andy Capp: daily comic strip 1956–, musical 1982–, TV series 1986–; Best Br Cartoon Strip Awards 1961–65, Premio Cartoon award Lucca 1969, Best Cartoon award Genoa 1973, Best Strip Cartoon USA Cartoonist Assoc 1974, Italian Strip award Derthona 1978; memb: Nat Cartoonists Soc, C of E; *Books* World of Andy Capp (annual, 1957–), Andy Capp (annual, 1968–); *Style—* Reginald Smyth, Esq; ✉ Whitegates, Caledonian Rd, Hartlepool, Cleveland TS25 5LB

SMYTH, His Hon Judge (James) Robert Staples; s of Maj Robert Smyth, of Gaybrook, Mullingar, Co Westmeath (d 1952), and Mabel Anne Georgiana, *née* MacGeough-Bond (d 1985); *b* 11 July 1926; *Educ* St Columba's Coll Dublin, Merton Coll Oxford (BA, MA); *m* 3 April 1971, Fenella Joan, da of Ian Blair Mowat, of Bridge of Weir, Renfrewshire; 1 s (Ralph b 1976); *Career* served WWII RAF; called to the Bar Inner Temple 1949; resident magistrate Northern Rhodesia 1951–55, dep chm Agric Land Tbnl 1974, stipendiary magistrate West Midlands 1978, recorder of the Crown Court 1983–86, circuit judge (Midland and Oxford Circuit) 1986–; *Recreations* shooting, fishing; *Style—* His Hon Judge Robert Smyth; ✉ Leys, Shelsley Beauchamp, Worcester WR6 6RB

SMYTH, (John) Rodney; s of John Clifford Smyth, of Heswall, Merseyside, and Norah Myfannwy, *née* Powell; *b* 23 Aug 1953; *Educ* Shrewsbury, Magdalene Coll Cambridge (MA); *m* 20 July 1990, Sarah, *née* Johnson; 1 s (Edward John Richard b 13 Oct 1995); *Career* barr 1975–79; admitted slr 1980; asst slr Holman Fenwick & Willan 1980–82, ptnr Lovell White Durrant (formerly Durrant Piesse) 1985–95 (asst slr 1982–85), asst compliance offr L G T Asset Management plc 1995–; memb Law Soc; *Recreations* birdwatching, paintings; *Style—* Rodney Smyth, Esq; ✉ Brickhouse Farm, Main Rd, St Mary Hoo, Rochester, Kent ME3 8RP (☎ 01634 270 326); L G T Asset Management plc, Alban Gate, 14th Floor, 125 London Wall, London EC2Y 5AS (☎ 0171 710 4567, fax 0171 696 0966, telex 886100)

SMYTH, Stephen Mark James Athelstan; s of Marcus Smyth (d 1965), of Walnut Tree Cottage, Ditchling, and Ann, *née* Symons; *b* 28 Dec 1946; *Educ* Hurstpierpoint Coll, Alliance Francaise; *m* 22 May 1981, Bridget Rosemary Diana, da of Maj (Arthur) Creagh Gibson (d 1970), of Glenburn Hall, Jedburgh; 2 da (Lalage Vivien b 5 Jan 1986, India b 24 May 1989); *Career* called to the Bar Inner Temple 1974, asst recorder 1994–; chm Churchill Clinic IVF Ethical Ctee 1995; *Recreations* books, sailing; *Clubs* Bosham Sailing; *Style—* Stephen Smyth, Esq; ✉ 2 Harcourt Buildings, Temple, London EC4 (☎ 0171 353 2112, fax 0171 353 8339)

SMYTH, Dr Sir Timothy John; 2 Bt (UK 1956), of Teignmouth, Co Devon; s of Julian Smyth (d 1974, himself 2 s of Brig Rt Hon Sir John Smyth, 1 Bt, VC, MC (d 1983)), and his w Philomena Mary, *née* Cannon; *b* 16 April 1953; *Educ* Univ of NSW (MB BS, LLB, MBA); *m* 1981, Bernadette Mary, da of Leo Askew; 2 s, 2 da; *Heir* s, Brendan Julian Smyth b 4 Oct 1981; *Career* hosp mangr; *Style—* Dr Sir Timothy Smyth, Bt; ✉ Hunter Area Health Service, New Lambton, NSW 2305, Australia

SNAGGE, Col Carron Edward Mordaunt; s of Maj Ralph Mordaunt Snagge, MBE, TD, of Cowes, IOW, and Pamela Mordaunt, *née* Scrimgeour; *b* 23 June 1951; *Educ* Eton; *m* 15 Dec 1973, Jennifer Anne, da of (John) Dugald Thomson, of Darling Point, Sydney, Australia; 1 s ((Thomas) Henry Dugald b 15 April 1984), 3 da (Emily Jane b 20 Aug 1977, Jemima Alice b 8 May 1979, Cecily Rose b 17 May 1989); *Career* Cadet Mons OCS 1970; 1 Bn Royal Green Jackets: 2 Lt (Germany and NI) 1971, Capt (Dover, NI, Cyprus and Hong Kong) 1975, Co Cdr (Falkland Islands and Tidworth) 1984, 2 i/c (Germany) 1988, CO (NI, Germany and Dover) 1991–93; other appts: Platoon Cdr Jr Inf Bn Shorncliffe 1972, Lt Regtl Careers Course Sandhurst 1974, Adj Rifle Depot Winchester 1979, Maj Co Cdr Rifle Depot 1980, student Australian Cmd and Staff Coll 1983, COS Br Forces Belize 1986, Lt-Col Staff Offr MOD London 1989, instr Army Staff Coll 1994, Col Staff Offr Headquarters NI 1994–97, Col Staff Offr York 1997–; Freeman City of London 1972, Liveryman Worshipful Co of Skinners 1978; *Recreations* sailing, sub aqua diving, hill walking; *Clubs* Royal Yacht Sqdn, Army and Navy; *Style—* Col Carron Snagge

SNAGGE, Air Cmdt Dame Nancy Marion; DBE (1955, OBE 1945); da of late Henry Thomas Salmon; *b* 2 May 1906; *Educ* Notting Hill High Sch; *m* 1962, Thomas Geoffrey Mordaunt Snagge, DSC (d 1984); *Career* joined WAAF 1939, offr in the WAAF and WRAF 1939–, ADC to HM King George VI 1950–52, ADC to HM The Queen 1952–56, dir WRAF 1950–56; *Style—* Air Cmdt Dame Nancy Snagge, DBE, AE; ✉ The Dower House, 5 Headbourne Worthy House, Winchester, Hampshire SO23 7JG

SNAILHAM, (George) Richard; s of Capt William Rushton Snailham (d 1942), and Mabel, *née* Wilson (d 1989); *b* 18 May 1930; *Educ* Oakham, Keble Coll Oxford; *m* 19 Jan 1990, Dr Christina March; *Career* Nat Serv 1948–50, Duke of Wellington's Regt, Intelligence Corps MI8; schoolmaster: Alleyn Ct Sch Westcliff 1954–55, Clayesmore Sch Iwerne Minster Dorset 1955–57, Exeter Sch Devon 1957–65; sr lectr RMA Sandhurst 1965–90, author and feature writer Operation Raleigh 1990–92, tour gp ldr Voyages Jules Verne and ACE Study Travel 1993–; semi finalist Mastermind 1973, semi finalist Brain of Britain 1976, twice winner Busman's Holiday 1987; fndr memb Scientific Exploration Soc 1969 (hon vice pres), pres Globetrotters Club 1977–90, sec Young Explorers Trust 1986–90, chm Winston Churchill Fellowship Surrey and West Sussex 1984–91; expeditions to: Ethiopia 1966 and 1972, Blue Nile 1968, Dahlak Islands 1970–71; other expeditions to: Zaire River 1974–75, Ecuador 1976 and 1996, Kenya (Op Drake) 1980, Kenya (Op Raleigh) 1986, 1989, and 1994, Botswana 1991, Chile and Mongolia (Op Raleigh) 1992; RGS: fell 1973, Mrs Patrick Ness award 1980, memb Cncl 1986–88, hon foreign sec 1990–95; *Books* The Blue Nile Revealed (1970), A Giant Among Rivers (1976), Sangay Survived (1978), Normandy and Brittany (1986); *Recreations* writing articles, giving travel and expedition talks; *Clubs* Globetrotters, Mastermind, Constitutional (Windsor); *Style—* Richard Snailham, Esq; ✉ 13 Gloucester Place, Windsor, Berks SL4 2AJ (☎ and fax 01753 863357)

SNAITH, Prof Martin Somerville; s of Gp Capt Leonard Somerville Snaith, CB, AFC, DL (d 1985), and Joyce Edith, *née* Taylor; *b* 20 May 1945; *Educ* Bedford Sch, Trinity Coll Dublin (MA, BAI, MSc, ScD), Univ of Nottingham (PhD); *m* 15 June 1974, Jane Dorothy Elizabeth, da of Aubrey Alexander Maxwell Clark, of Bushmills, Co Antrim, NI; 1 s (Timothy James b 15 Nov 1982), 1 da (Lucinda Jane b 18 May 1979); *Career* materials engr Kenya Govt, post-doctoral res fell Trinity Coll Dublin, lectr Queen's Univ Belfast, prof of highway engrg Univ of Birmingham (ODA sr lectr), pro-vice-chllr Univ of Birmingham; memb: Gaffney Ctee (and author Snaith Report for NI), EPSRC Inland Surface Tport Prog Advsy Gp; rep athletics Ireland 1969; Freeman City of London 1989, Liveryman Worshipful Co of Paviors; FICE 1986, FIHT 1987, FIEI 1987; *Recreations* shooting, skiing, fishing, coin collecting; *Clubs* Kildare Street and Univ (Dublin), Athenaeum, Nairobi; *Style—* Prof Martin Snaith; ✉ 281 High St, Henley-in-Arden, Warwickshire B95 5BG (☎ 01564 793223); School of Civil Engineering, University of Birmingham, Edgbaston, Birmingham B15 2TT (☎ 0121 414 5161, fax 0121 414 5160, telex 333762 UOBHAM G)

SNAITH, Dr (Richard) Philip; s of Herbert Longridge Snaith (d 1960), of Darlington, and Katherine Elizabeth, *née* Smith (d 1958); *b* 1 May 1933; *Educ* Sedbergh, Guy's Hosp Med Sch Univ of London (MD); *m* 21 April 1972, Joanna; 2 s (Douglas b 1959, Julian b 1961), 1 da (Polly b 1965); *Career* conslt psychiatrist Stanley Royal Hosp Wakefield 1967–77, sr lectr in psychiatry Univ of Leeds 1977–, hon conslt psychiatrist St James Univ Hosp Leeds 1977–; FRCPsych 1977; *Books* Clinical Neurosis (1991); *Recreations* fell walking; *Style—* Dr Philip Snaith; ✉ 30 Gledhow Wood Rd, Leeds LS8 4BZ; Dept of Psychiatry, Clinical Sciences Building, St James's Univ Hospital, Leeds LS9 7TF (☎ 0113 243 3144)

SNAPE, Peter Charles; MP (Lab) West Bromwich East (majority 2,813); s of Thomas & Kathleen Snape; *b* 12 Feb 1942; *Educ* St Joseph's Stockport, St Winifred's Stockport; *m* 1963 (m dis 1980); 2 da; *Career* former railway signalman then guard, soldier (RE & RCT), British Rail clerk; MP (Lab) W Bromwich E Feb 1974–, memb Cncl of Europe and WEU 1975, asst Govt whip 1975–77, Lord Cmmr of the Treasury (Govt whip) 1977–79; oppn front bench spokesman: on defence and disarmament 1981–82, home affrs 1982–83, transport 1983–92; *Style—* Peter Snape, Esq, MP; ✉ House of Commons, London SW1A 0AA

SNASHALL, Dr David Charles; s of Cyril Francis Snashall, of London, and Phyllis Mary, *née* Hibbitt (d 1970); *b* 3 Feb 1943; *Educ* Haberdashers' Aske's Hatcham GS, Univ of Edinburgh (MB ChB), London Sch of Hygiene and Tropical Med (MSc, DIH, DTM&H), Univ of Wales Cardiff (LLM 1996); *children* (Lesley b 1963, Rebecca b 1978, Corinna b 1996); *Career* resident posts in hosp med and gen practice UK, Canada and France 1968–75, chief MO Majes Consortium Peru 1975–76, chief med advsr Tarmac 1977–81, project MO Mufindi Project 1981–82, chief MO Costain Group of Companies 1982–89, med advsr to House of Commons 1982–91, hon conslt and clinical dir of staff occupational health servs W Lambeth Health Authy 1982–93, sr lectr in occupational health United Med and Dental Schs of Guy's and St Thomas' Hosps 1982–, chief med advsr FCO 1989–, clinical dir occupational health servs Guy's and St Thomas' Hosp Tst 1993–; memb: Health Servs Advsy Ctee HSE (BMA nominated) 1987–, GMC 1989–96, Editorial Ctee Occupational and Environmental Med 1994–; SE Thames regnl speciality advsr 1989–; FFOM 1987 (AFOM 1981, MFOM 1983), FRCP 1993 (MRCP 1972); *Publications* incl Searching for Causes of Work-related Diseases: An Introduction to Epidemiology at the Work Site (jtly, 1991); *Recreations* travel, European languages, jazz music, mountaineering, cooking, gardening; *Clubs* Ronnie Scott's; *Style—* Dr David Snashall; ✉ 2 Charity Cottages, Petsoe End, Olney, Buckinghamshire MK46 5JN (☎ 01234 711072); United Medical and Dental Schools of Guy's and St Thomas' Hospitals, Occupational Health Department, St Thomas' Hospital, London SE1 7EH (☎ 0171 928 9292 ext 2302)

SNEATH, Christopher George; s of Arthur George Sneath (d 1972), and Dorothy, *née* Knight (d 1989); *b* 27 June 1933; *Educ* Canford Sch Dorset; *m* 12 May 1962, Patricia Lesley, da of Anthony Spinks (d 1982); 1 s (James Rupert b 19 Jan 1966), 1 da (Deborah Jane b 16 July 1963); *Career* CA 1957; sr ptnr specialising in int business matters KPMG Peat Marwick 1978–94 (ptnr 1971–94), dep sec gen Peat Marwick International 1978–80; dir: Spirax-Sarco Engineering plc, Saracens plc, Enfield Community Care NHS Tst; vice pres and hon treas Saracens RFC, vice chm of Govrs Queenswood Sch Herts, tstee The Sir Thomas Lipton Meml Hostel; receiver gen Order of St John, KStJ 1991; FCA; *Books* Guide to Acquisitions in the US (1989); *Recreations* watching cricket and rugby football, maintaining Lotus motor cars; *Clubs* Carlton, Hadley Wood Golf, Marylebone Cricket, Pilgrims; *Style*— Christopher Sneath, Esq; ✉ 109 High Street, London N14 6BP (☎ 0181 447 8325, fax 0181 447 8328); 4 Chatsworth Gardens, Eastbourne, Sussex BN20 7JP (☎ 01323 725709)

SNEATH, Christopher Gilbert; s of Colin Frank Sneath, of Brookmans Park; *b* 25 June 1938; *Educ* Framlingham Coll Suffolk; *m* 25 May 1963, Elizabeth Mary, da of Bernard Stephen Copson, Little Heath, Potters Bar, Herts; 2 da (Lucy Jane b 1965, Julia Elizabeth b 1967); *Career* Nat Serv RCS 1957–59; md Flakt Barrett & Wright Group Ltd 1971–92, dir Phab UK Ltd 1991, sales and mktg dir A G Manly Group Ltd 1992–, dir C J Bartley & Co Ltd 1995–; pres Heating & Ventilating Contractors Assoc 1990–91 and 1996; capt Brookmans Park Golf Club 1980–81 (pres 1994–), chm London Area Clubs Physically Handicapped Able Bodied 1987, assessor Latham Review of Construction Industry 1994; memb Worshipful Co of Painter-Stainers 1991; companion memb Chartered Inst of Bldg Servs Engrs 1983; *Recreations* golf, marathon running; *Clubs* Brookmans Park Golf, RAC; *Style*— Christopher Sneath, Esq; ✉ 31 Brookmans Ave, Brookmans Pk, Hatfield, Herts AL9 7QH (☎ 01707 658709, fax 01707 661570); A G Manly Group Ltd, 36–60 Burr Road, Wandsworth, London SW18 4SQ (☎ 0181 874 8122, fax 0181 874 9391)

SNEDDEN, David King; s of David Snedden; *b* 23 Feb 1933; *Educ* Daniel Stewart's Coll Edinburgh; *m* 1958; 2 s (Keith b 1961, Stuart b 1963), 1 da (Ann); *Career* formerly: investmt advsr Guinness Mahon Ltd, dir Radio Forth Ltd, memb Press Cncl; md: Belfast Telegraph Newspapers 1966–70 (dir 1979–82), Scotsman Publications 1970–79; Thomson Regional Newspapers Ltd: dir 1974–, gp asst md 1979–80, jt md 1980–82; Trinity International Holdings plc: md and chief exec 1982–93, non-exec dir 1993–, chm 1994–; exec chm Headway Home and Law Publishing Group Ltd 1993, chm Norcor Holdings plc 1994–; non-exec dir BSkyB Ltd 1994–; dir: Reuters Holdings plc 1987–94, The Press Assoc 1984–92 (chm 1989–91); *Recreations* golf, fishing; *Clubs* Caledonian, Bruntsfield Links Golfing Soc, Isle of Harris Golf; *Style*— David Snedden, Esq; ✉ Flat 29, Ravelston Heights, Edinburgh EH4 3LX (☎ 0131 343 3290)

SNEDDON, Alan Drysdale; *b* 29 Feb 1932; *Educ* Allan Glen's Sch Glasgow; *m* Janette; 1 da (Ailsa); *Career* with Scottish Mutual Assurance Society until 1961: Co-operative Insurance Society (CIS): joined as jr actuary 1961, gen mangr and actuary (life) 1979–87, chief gen mangr (chief exec) 1987–97; FFA; *Recreations* tennis, badminton, gardening, rugby football, good food and wine; *Style*— Alan Sneddon, Esq; ✉ Co-operative Insurance Society Ltd, Miller Street, Manchester M60 0AL (☎ 0161 832 8686, fax 0161 837 4048)

SNEDDON, Hutchison Burt; CBE (1983, OBE 1968), JP (1964); s of Robert Cleland Sneddon, of Wishaw, Lanarks, and Catherine McDade, *née* McComisky (d 1978); *b* 17 April 1929; *Educ* Wishaw HS, Burnbank Tech Coll; *m* 3 Oct 1960, Elizabeth Ross, da of Allan Jardine (d 1963); 1 s (Cleland b 1967), 2 da (Joanne (Mrs Graeme McNaught) b 1961, Irene (Mrs Michael Rayner) b 1964); *Career* Nat Serv NCO RE 1950–52; served: Sch of Survey Newbury, II Armd Div HQ Herford W Germany 1951–52; air photographic interpreter; construction engr 1953–64; Br Gas: tech sales mangr 1964–71, area mangr 1971–79, sales mangr (special projects) 1983–89; memb: W Regnl Hosp Bd 1968–70, Motherwell and Wishaw Burgh Cncl 1958–75 (provost 1971–75), Scottish Tourist Bd 1969–83, JP Advsy Ctee 1975–92; chm Motherwell Dist Cncl 1974–77; Scottish chm: Nat Bldg Agency 1977–82 (dir 1974–82), Housing Corp 1980–83 (memb 1977–83); chm Cumbernauld Devpt Corp 1979–83, vice pres Confedn of Scottish Local Authys 1974–76; sec Wishaw Branch Nat Bible Soc of Scotland 1986–, pres World Fedn of Burns Clubs 1989–90; chm: Gas Higher Mangrs Assoc 1986–88 (asst gen sec 1988–92), North and South Lanarkshire JP Advsy Ctees; HM Lord-Lieut Strathclyde Region Co of Lanarkshire (Dist of Monklands, Motherwell, Hamilton, E Kilbride and Clydesdale) 1992– (DL 1989); hon pres RM Assoc Lanarkshire 1993–; City of Schweinfurt Gold Medal of Freedom 1975; *Recreations* watching football, philately; *Style*— Hutchison Sneddon, Esq, CBE, JP; ✉ 36 Shand St, Wishaw, Lanarks ML2 8HN (☎ 01698 73685)

SNELGROVE, Rt Rev Donald George; TD (1973); s of William Henry Snelgrove (d 1956), of London and Plymouth, and Beatrice, *née* Upshall; *b* 21 April 1925; *Educ* Christ's Coll Finchley, Devonport HS, Queens' Coll Cambridge (MA); *m* 1949, Sylvia May, da of Charles Lowe (d 1962), of Derbyshire; 1 s (John b 1956), 1 da (Elizabeth b 1957); *Career* Sub Lt RNVR UK and Far East 1943–46; Royal Army Chaplains Dept 1960–74; ordained St Paul's Cathedral 1950; curate: St Thomas Oakwood 1950–53, St Anselm Hatch End 1953–56; vicar: Dronfield Derbyshire 1956–62, Hessle 1963–70; rural dean of Kingston upon Hull 1966–70, canon and prebendary of York 1969–81, rector of Cherry Burton 1970–78, archdeacon of the E Riding 1970–81, bishop of Hull 1981–94, hon asst bishop of Lincoln 1995–; chm Central Church Fund; dir: Central Bd of Fin of C of E 1975–, Ecclesiastical Insurance Group 1978–94, Church Schools Co Ltd 1981–, Allchurches 1992–; *Style*— The Rt Rev D G Snelgrove, TD; ✉ Kingston House, Park View, Barton-upon-Humber, N Lincs DN18 6AX (☎ and fax 01652 634484)

SNELL, Phillip John; s of Henry Lye Taylor Snell, of Pinner, and Mabel Violet, *née* Malyon; *b* 31 Jan 1941; *Educ* Pinner Co GS, King's Coll London (BA), Birkbeck Coll London (MA); *m* 24 June 1967, Rosemary Anne, da of Frederick George Shave; 3 s (James Phillip b 26 Jan 1972, Douglas Paul b 19 Sept 1974, Alistair John b 3 Oct 1977); *Career* res offr Cwlth Relations Office 1963–64, inspector of taxes Bd of Inland Revenue 1964–67, teacher Pinner GS 1967–70, teacher and dir of studies Kingsbury HS 1970–78; Preston Manor HS: first dep head 1978–82, headmaster 1982–88; headmaster Kingsbury HS 1988–; SHA: sec Area 5 1990–92, memb Nat Cncl 1992–95, memb Exec Ctee 1994–95; govr Univ of Westminster 1995–; chm British Assoc for Local History 1983–87; vice pres Pinner Local History Soc; FRSA 1995; *Recreations* classical music, art, local history; *Style*— Phillip Snell, Esq; ✉ Kingsbury High School, Princes Avenue, London NW9 9JR (☎ 0181 204 9814, fax 0181 206 0715)

SNOAD, Harold Edward; s of Sidney Edward Snoad, of Eastbourne, Sussex, and Irene Dora, *née* Janes; *b* 28 Aug 1935; *Educ* Eastbourne Coll; *m* 1, 21 Sept 1957 (m dis 18 June 1963) Anne Christine, *née* Cadwallader; m 2, 6 July 1963, Jean, da of James Green (d 1968), of London; 2 da (Helen Julie b 1969, Jeanette Clare b 1975); *Career* Nat Serv RAF 1954–56; with BBC 1957–96: prodr and dir 1970–83, exec prodr and dir 1983–96; currently working freelance 1996–; produced and directed many successful comedy series for the BBC incl: The Dick Emery Show, Rings on their Fingers, The Further Adventures of Lucky Jim, Tears Before Bedtime, Hilary, Don't Wait Up, Ever Decreasing Circles, Brush Strokes, Keeping up Appearances; dir feature film Not Now Comrade, re-wrote Dad's Army for radio; scripted original comedy series: Share and Share Alike and It Sticks Out Half a Mile (radio), High and Dry (TV); *Books* Directing Situation Comedy (1988); *Recreations* swimming, gardening, theatre going, DIY, motoring; *Style*— Harold Snoad, Esq; ✉ Fir Tree Cottage, 43 Hawkewood Rd, Sunbury-on-Thames, Middx TW16 6HL (☎ 01932 785887)

SNODGRASS, Prof Anthony McElrea; s of William McElrea Snodgrass (d 1934), and Kathleen Mabel, *née* Owen (d 1988); *b* 7 July 1934; *Educ* Marlborough, Worcester Coll Oxford (MA, DPhil); *m* 1, 1959 (m dis 1978), Ann Elizabeth, da of Halford John Vaughan; 3 da (Nell Catherine b 1961, Rachel Ann b 1963, Elspeth Mary b 1964); m 2, 1983, Annemarie, da of late Ernst Künzl; 1 s (Thomas Anthony b 1986); *Career* Nat Serv Pilot Offr RAF 1953–55, student Br Sch at Athens 1959–60; Univ of Edinburgh: lectr in classical archaeology 1961–69, reader 1969–75, ad hominem prof 1975–76; Laurence prof of classical archaeology Univ of Cambridge 1976–, fell Clare Coll Cambridge 1977–; Sather prof of classics Univ of California at Berkeley 1984–85, Geddes-Harrower prof of classical archaeology Univ of Aberdeen 1995–96; chm Antiquity Publications Ltd 1987–; fndr memb Humanities Research Bd British Acad 1994–95; memb: Soc for the Promotion of Hellenic Studies 1961, Soc for the Promotion of Roman Studies 1963; FSA 1978, FBA 1979; *Books* Early Greek Armour and Weapons (1964), The Dark Age of Greece (1971), Archaeology and the Rise of the Greek State (1977), Archaic Greece (1980), Narration and Allusion in Early Greek Art (1982), An Archaeology of Greece (1987); *Recreations* mountaineering, skiing; *Clubs* Alpine, Alpine Ski; *Style*— Prof Anthony Snodgrass, FSA, FBA; ✉ Faculty of Classics, Sidgwick Avenue, Cambridge CB3 9DA (☎ 01223 335155/335152, fax 01223 335409)

SNODGRASS, John Michael Owen; CMG (1981); s of Maj William McElrea Snodgrass (d 1934), and Kathleen Mabel, *née* Owen (d 1988); *b* 12 Aug 1928; *Educ* Marlborough, Univ of Cambridge (MA); *m* 1957, Jennifer, da of Robert James (d 1970), of S Rhodesia; 3 s (Andrew, Peter, James); *Career* HM Dip Serv: consul gen Jerusalem 1970–74, cnsllr British Embassy S Africa 1974–77, head of S Pacific Dept FCO 1977–80; ambass to: Zaire, Congo, Rwanda and Burundi 1980–83, Bulgaria 1983–86; ret; *Recreations* skiing, travel; *Style*— John Snodgrass, Esq, CMG; ✉ The Barn House, North Warnborough, Hants RG29 1ET (☎ 01256 702816)

SNOW, Adrian John; s of Edward Percy John Snow, of Middleton-on-Sea, W Sussex, and Marjory Ellen, *née* Nicholls; *b* 20 March 1939; *Educ* Hurstpierpoint Coll, Trinity Coll Dublin (BA, MA, HDip in Ed), Univ of Reading (MEd); *m* 1963 (m dis 1994), (Alessina) Teresa, da of Charles Arthur Kilkelly, of Far Field, Killiney Hill Rd, Killiney, Co Dublin; 1 s (Robin Edward Charles b 1965), 1 da (Susan Alessina b 1963); *Career* PO RAF 1962; asst master: New Beacon Prep Sch 1958–59, King's Sch Sherborne 1963–64, Dublin HS (pt/t) 1964–65, Brighton Coll 1965–66; The Oratory: head of econ and political studies 1966–73, head of history 1967–73, housemaster 1967–73, actg headmaster 1972–73, headmaster 1973–88, warden to the govrs The Oratory Sch Assoc 1989–93; dir: Oratory Construction Ltd 1988–93, Oratory Trading Ltd 1989–93; govr: Prior Park Coll 1980–87, Moreton Hall 1984–93, The Highlands Reading 1985– (chm), St Edward's Reading 1985– (chm), St Mary's Ascot 1986–94; pres Old Oratorian Cricket Club 1994–; Tennis and Rackets Assoc: memb Tennis Ctee 1990–95 (chm Devpt Sub-Ctee 1993–), devpt offr 1994–; vice chm Berkshire Ctee The Princes Tst 1990; chm Friends of Hardwick Tennis Court 1996– (hon treasurer 1990–96); *Recreations* gardening, real tennis; *Style*— Adrian Snow, Esq; ✉ 103 Poole Keynes, Cirencester, Gloucestershire GL7 6EG

SNOW, Antony Edmund; s of Thomas Maitland Snow, CMG, of Montreux, Switzerland, and Phyllis Annette Hopkins, *née* Malcolmson; *b* 5 Dec 1932; *Educ* Sherborne, New Coll Oxford; *m* 31 March 1961, Caroline, da of Comar Wilson (d 1961), of Oakley Manor, nr Basingstoke, Hants; 1 s (Lucian b 21 Aug 1965), 2 da (Arabella b 1 Feb 1964, Henrietta b 2 April 1970); *Career* 10 Royal Hussars, cmmnd 1952–53; dep chm Charles Barker & Sons 1971–76, vice pres Market Planning Steuben Glass NY 1976–78, dep dir Corning Museum of Glass USA 1978–79, dir Rockwell Museum USA 1979–83; dir: Charles Barker plc 1983–90 (chm and chief exec 1983–87), Hogg Group plc 1988–94; chm Hill and Knowlton (UK) Ltd 1992– (chm Mgmnt Ctee Europe 1994–); tstee: Arnott Museum USA 1980–84, Corning Museum of Glass USA 1983–, V & A Museum 1995–; chm Fraser Tst 1996–; memb: Ctee of Mgmnt Courtauld Inst of Art 1985–89, Exec Ctee Nat Art Collections Fund 1985–, Cncl RCA 1994–; cncllr Design Cncl 1989–94, tstee Monteverdi Choir 1988–, memb AMAC Ctee English Heritage 1989–92; FRSA, FIPA, FIPR; *Recreations* English watercolours; *Clubs* Cavalry and Guards', City of London; *Style*— Antony Snow, Esq; ✉ 16 Rumbold Rd, London SW6 2JA (☎ 0171 731 2881); Fyfield Hill Barn, Marlborough, Wilts (☎ 01672 86498)

SNOW, Jonathan George (Jon); s of Rt Rev George D'Oyly Snow, Bishop of Whitby (d 1977), and Joan Monica, *née* Way; *b* 28 Sept 1947; *Educ* St Edward's Sch Oxford, Univ of Liverpool; 2 da (Leila Snow Colvin b 1982, Freya Snow Colvin b 1986); *Career* dir New Horrizon Youth Centre Covent Garden 1970–73; journalist: LBC and IRN 1973–76, ITN 1976– (Washington corr 1983–86, diplomatic ed 1986–89); presenter Channel Four News 1989–; visiting prof Nottingham Trent Univ; memb NUJ; *Books* Atlas of Today (1987), Sons and Mothers (1996); *Style*— Jon Snow; ✉ ITN Ltd, 200 Gray's Inn Road, London WC1X 8XZ (☎ 0171 430 4237, fax 0171 430 4609)

SNOW, Rear Adm Kenneth Arthur; CB (1987); s of Arthur Chandos Pole-Soppitt (d 1986, assumed the surname of Snow by deed pole), and Evelyn Dorothea, *née* Joyce (d 1957); *b* 14 April 1934; *Educ* St Andrews Coll Grahamstown, S African Nautical Coll; *m* 1956, Pamela Elizabeth Terry, da of Ald Frank Harold Ernest Sorrell, of Southsea, Hants; 1 s (Christopher b 1958), 2 da (Vanessa b 1960, Penelope b 1965); *Career* cadet RN 1952, cmd HMS Kirkliston 1962, 1st Lt HMY Britannia 1968–69, cmd HMS Llandaff 1970, HMS Arethusa 1979, HMS Hermes 1983, Rear Adm 1984; Receiver-Gen and Chapter Clerk Westminster Abbey 1987–; Liveryman Worshipful Co of Horners; FNI 1992; *Recreations* painting, gardening; *Clubs* Army and Navy; *Style*— Rear Adm Kenneth Snow; ✉ 2 The Cloister, Westminster Abbey, London SW1 3PA; The Chapter Office, 20 Deans Yard, Westminster Abbey, London SW1P 3PA

SNOW, Peter John; s of Brig John Fitzgerald Snow, CBE (Somerset LI, d 1973), and Peggy Mary, *née* Pringle (d 1970); *b* 20 April 1938; *Educ* Wellington Coll, Balliol Coll Oxford (BA); *m* 1, 30 Sept 1964 (m dis 1975), Alison Mary, da of late George Fairlie Carter, of Piltdown, Sussex; 1 s (Shane Fitzgerald b 1966), 1 da (Shuna Justine b 1968); m 2, 15 May 1976, Ann Elizabeth, da of Dr Robert Laidlaw MacMillan, of Toronto, Canada; 1 s (Daniel Robert b 1978), 2 da (Rebecca Olwen b 1980, Katherine Peggy b 1983); *Career* Nat Serv 2 Lt Somerset LI 1956–58; dip and def corr ITN 1966–79 (reporter and newscaster 1962–), presenter BBC TV Newsnight and election progs 1979–; *Books* Leila's Hijack War (1970), Hussein: A Biography (1972); *Recreations* tennis, sailing, skiing, model railways; *Style*— Peter Snow, Esq; ✉ c/o BBC TV, BBC TV Centre, Wood Lane, London W12 7RJ (☎ 0181 749 7512)

SNOW, Philip Albert; OBE (1985, MBE 1979), JP (Warwicks 1967–76, W Sussex 1976); s of William Edward Snow, FRCO (d 1954), and Ada Sophia, *née* Robinson; bro of late Baron Snow of Leicester, CBE (Life Peer, aka C P Snow, the author); *b* 7 Aug 1915; *Educ* Alderman Newton's Sch Leicester, Christ's Coll Cambridge (MA); *m* 1940, (Mary) Anne, da of Henry Harris (d 1970), of Leicester; 1 da (Stefanie Dale Vivien Vuikamba b 1947, m Peter Waine, *qv*); *Career* author, bibliographer, administrator; HM Colonial Admin Serv: admin offr, estab and protocol offr, magistrate, provincial cmmr and asst colonial sec Fiji and Western Pacific 1937–52 (ADC to Govr and C-in-C Fiji 1939, Fiji Govt liaison offr with US and NZ forces WWII, dep sheriff Colony of Fiji 1940–52, official memb Legislative Cncl Fiji 1951); passed Govt examinations in law, Fijian language & customs and Hindi (in Devanagri script) with distinction; vice pres Fiji Soc 1944–52; fndr: Suva Cricket Assoc 1939, Nadi Cricket Assoc 1942, Lautoka Cricket Assoc 1943, Fiji Cricket Assoc 1946 (vice patron 1952–); memb founding ctee: Union Club Suva 1944, Fuji Arts Club 1945; bursar Governing Body Rugby Sch 1952–76, organiser Rugby Sch Appeal 1954–59, tstee Rugby Sch 1914–18 and 1939–45 War Meml Funds 1954–76; memb Jt Ctee Governing Bodies of Schs Assoc 1959–65, chm Ind Schs Bursars' Assoc 1962–65 (memb Ctee 1956–59, vice chm 1959–62), perm Fiji rep on Int Cricket Conf and Cncl 1965–94 (30 year record for ICC), organiser visit by HM The Queen and HRH The Duke of Edinburgh to Rugby Sch for 400th anniversary and other Quatercentenary celebrations 1967, memb first Cricket World Cup Ctee 1970–75, designer Fiji cricket centenary stamps Fiji Govt 1974, liaison offr and actg mangr first Fiji cricket team England 1979, first chm Assoc Memb Countries of Int Cricket Conf 1982–87, first pres

Worthing Soc 1983– (vice chm 1977–83), literary executor and executor of Lord Snow; former first class cricketer; memb teams: Christ's Coll Cambridge 1935–38 (capt 1936–37), Cambridge Crusaders 1935–38, Leicestershire CCC 1946 (capt 2nd XI 1936–38), Sir Pelham Warner's XI 1946, Fiji nat first class team touring NZ (capt) 1948, MCC (elected playing memb) 1951 (capt and mangr MCC teams 1951–65), Authors 1951–58, Googlies 1952–65, Rugby CC 1952–65 (jt holder record opening batting partnership); elected special hon life memb MCC for servs to int cricket 1970; Foreign Specialist Award USA Govt 1964, Fiji Independence Silver Jubilee Medal 1995; FRAI 1952, FRSA 1984; *Publications* Civil Defence Services, Fiji (1942), Sources Describing Fijian Customs for Fijian Examination Candidates (ed with G K Roth, 1944), Civil Service Journal Fiji (ed, 1945), Cricket in the Fiji Islands (introduction by Sir Pelham Warner, 1949), Rock Carvings in Fiji (1950), Report on the Visit of Three Bursars to the United States of America and Canada in 1964 (1965), Best Stories of the South Seas (1967), Bibliography of Fiji, Tonga and Rotuma (Vol I, 1969), The People from the Horizon: an illustrated history of the Europeans among the South Sea Islanders (jtly with Stefanie Snow Waine, 1979, runner-up Best History/Biography Award Arts Cncl of GB), Stranger and Brother: a Portrait of C P Snow (1982), Years of Hope (1996), A Time of Renewal (1997); contrib to Daily Telegraph, The Times and various periodicals, numerous bdcasts, articles and reviews on cricket and the Pacific in jls, various forewords, prefaces and introductions to books; *Recreations* formerly cricket, table tennis for Univ of Cambridge and Cambridgeshire (won RMS Queen Mary championship 1964), chess for Univ of Cambridge, deck tennis (won Liners' championships 1938–51), tennis (for Suva); *Clubs* MCC, Hawks (Cambridge), Mastermind, Stragglers of Asia CC (hon memb), De Flamingo's (Amsterdam, hon memb); *Style*— Philip Snow, Esq, OBE, JP; ✉ Gables, Station Rd, Angmering, W Sussex BN16 4HY (☎ 01903 773594)

SNOW, Hon Philip Charles Hansford; s of Baron Snow, CBE (C P Snow, the author and public servant, d 1980), and Pamela Hansford Johnson, CBE (the novelist, d 1981); *b* 26 Aug 1952; *Educ* Eton, Balliol Coll Oxford; *m* 19 Sept 1987, Amanda, er da of Sir Clive Anthony Whitmore, GCB, CVO, *qv*; 1 s (Alexander Daniel Hansford b 6 Dec 1994), 1 da (Renata Maria Hansford b 20 Nov 1992); *Career* writer on China and int affairs; res assoc Oriental Inst Univ of Oxford; memb: Royal Inst of Int Affairs, GB-China Centre; cncl memb China Soc; *Books* The Star Raft: China's Encounter with Africa (1988); *Style*— The Hon Philip Snow

SNOW, Surgn Rear Adm Ronald Edward; CB (1991), LVO (1972), OBE (1977); s of Arthur Chandos Pole Snow (formerly Soppitt, name changed by deed poll, d 1984), of Cape Town, SA, and Evelyn Dorothea, *née* Joyce (d 1956); *b* 17 May 1933; *Educ* St Andrew's Coll Grahamstown S Africa, Trinity Coll Dublin (MA, MB BCh, BAO), RCS Ireland (DA), RCP Ireland (MFOM), LMCC; *m* 16 Dec 1959, Valerie Melian, da of Raymond Arthur French (d 1981), of Dublin, Ireland; 2 da (Suzanne Lynn, Nicola Jane); *Career* MO HMS Victorious 1966; MO Submarine Escape Trg Tank, HMS Dolphin 1967; princ MO HM Yacht Britannia 1970; asst to SMO (Admin) RN Hosp Haslar 1972; duties with MDG(N) as Naval Health 2 MOD (Navy) 1973; dir of Studies Inst Naval Med 1975; duties with MDG(N) as dep dir of med personnel (Naval) 1977; Staff MO to Surgn Rear Adm (Naval Hosps) 1980; Fleet MO to CINCFLEET and med advsr to CINCHAN and CINCEASTLANT 1982; MO i/c Inst of Naval Med 1984; Queen's Hon Physician (QHP) 1974–91; Asst Surgn Gen (Serv Hosps) and Dep Med Dir-Gen (Naval) 1985; Surgn Rear Adm (Support Med Servs) 1987; Surgn Rear Adm (operational med servs) 1989–91; OStJ 1986; *Recreations* Nat Hunt racing, cruising; *Style*— Surgn Rear Adm Ronald Snow, CB, LVO, OBE; ✉ c/o Naval Secretary, Ministry of Defence, Victory Building, HM Naval Base, Portsmouth PO13 L5

SNOW, Terence Clive; s of Ernest William George Snow (d 1968), and Elsie May, *née* Baynes (d 1992); *b* 18 Sept 1931; *Educ* Poly of N London Sch of Architecture; *m* 28 March 1953, Phyllis, da of Frank Mann (d 1971); 4 s (Graeme b 1956, David b 1958, Phillip b 1960, John b 1969), 1 da (Patricia b 1971); *Career* Nat Serv RAF 1956–58; conslt Architects Co-Partnership 1995– (dir 1973–, md 1991–95); vice pres RIBA 1979–81 (memb Cncl 1979–86); chm: RIBA Services Ltd 1982–94, Library Planning Consultants Ltd 1982–94, National Building Specification Ltd 1982–94; dir RIBA Cos Ltd 1986–, chm NBS Servces Ltd 1990–94; FRIBA 1970 (ARIBA 1960); *Recreations* magic; *Clubs* The Magic Circle; *Style*— Terence Snow, Esq; ✉ Architects Co-Partnership, Northaw House, Potters Bar, Herts EN6 4PS (☎ 01707 651141, fax 01707 652600)

SNOWBALL, Joseph; s of Joseph Snowball (d 1960), and Gwendoline Alice, *née* Miles (d 1990); *b* 30 April 1946; *Educ* Cardiff HS; *m* 24 Oct 1970, Priscilla, da of Joseph Bennett; 1 s (Joseph Philip b 7 Sept 1973), 1 da (Carys Anne b 17 March 1976); *Career* Coopers & Lybrand CAs: articled clerk with predecessor firm 1962–68, ptnr in associate firm Lagos Nigeria 1978–81, ptnr in UK firm S Wales 1981–88, ptnr Gloucester office 1988–94; ptnr Gloucester office Guilfoyle Sage & Co 1994–; FCA 1978 (ACA 1968); *Recreations* golf, rugby; *Clubs* Ross on Wye Golf; *Style*— Joseph Snowball, Esq; ✉ Guilfoyle Sage & Co, 58 Eastgate Street, Gloucester GL1 1QN (☎ 01452 309363, fax 01452 311088)

SNOWDON, 1 Earl of (UK 1961); Antony Charles Robert Armstrong-Jones; GCVO (1969); also Viscount Linley (UK 1961); s of Ronald Owen Lloyd Armstrong-Jones, MBE, QC, DL (d 1966), of Plas Dinas, Caernarfon, and Anne, *née* Messel, later Countess of Rosse (d 1992); *b* 7 March 1930; *Educ* Eton, Jesus Coll Cambridge; *m* 1, 6 May 1960 (m dis 1978), HRH The Princess Margaret Rose (*see* Royal Family), yr da of HM the late King George VI; 1 s, 1 da; m 2, 15 Dec 1978, Lucy Mary, da of Donald Brook Davies, of Hemingstone Hall, Ipswich, and formerly w of Michael Lindsay-Hogg (film dir, s of Edward Lindsay-Hogg, gs of Sir Lindsay Lindsay-Hogg, 1 Bt, JP); 1 da (Lady Frances b 17 July 1979); *Heir* s, Viscount Linley (*see Royal Family section*); *Career* photographer; artistic advsr Sunday Times and Sunday Times Publications 1962–90, The Telegraph Magazine 1990–, consultative advsr to Design Cncl London 1962–87, editorial advsr Design Magazine 1962–87; designer: Snowdon Aviary for London Zoo (in collaboration with Cedric Price and Frank Newby) 1965, for investiture of HRH the Prince of Wales at Caernarfon Castle (in collaboration with Carl Toms, CBE and John Pound, CBE) 1969, electrically-powered wheelchair for disabled people (Chairmobile) 1972; pres: Contemporary Art Soc for Wales, Civic Tst for Wales, Welsh Theatre Co, Gtr London Arts Assoc, Int Year of Disabled People England (1981), ADAPT (Access for Disabled People to Arts Premises Today) 1995–; vice pres Bristol Univ Photographic Soc; memb: Cncl of Nat Fund for Research into Crippling Diseases, Faculty of Designers for Industry, The Prince of Wales Advsy Gp on Disability; patron: Metropolitan Union of YMCAs, British Water Ski Fedn, Welsh Nat Rowing Club, Physically Handicapped and Able-Bodied, Circle of Guide Dog Owners, Demand, Disabled Water Skiing Assoc; fndr Snowdon award Scheme for Disabled Students 1980; provost Royal Coll of Art 1995– (sr fell 1986); fell Manchester Coll of Art and Design; Hon DUniv Bradford 1989; Hon LLD: Univ of Bath 1989, Univ of Southampton 1993; Constable of Caernarfon Castle 1963–; Liveryman Worshipful Co of Clothworkers; RDI, FRSA, FSIAD, FRPS; *Exhibitions* Photocall (London 1958), Assignments (Photokina 1972), London (1973), Brussels (1974), Los Angeles, St Louis, Kansas, New York, Tokyo (1975), Sydney and Melbourne (1976), Copenhagen (1976), Paris (1977), Amsterdam (1977); Serendipity (Brighton 1989, Bradford 1989, Bath 1990); *Television* TV films: Don't Count the Candles (CBS 1968, winner two Hollywood Emmys, St George Prix, Venice Dip, Prague and Barcelona Film Festival award), Love of a Kind (BBC 1969), Born to be Small (ATV 1971, Chicago Hugo award), Happy being Happy (ATV 1973), Mary Kingsley (BBC 1975), Burke and Wills (1975), Peter, Tina and Steve (ATV 1977), Snowdon on Camera (BBC 1981, BAFTA nomination); *Awards* Art Dirs Club of NY Certificate of Merit 1969; Soc of Publication Designers: Cert of Merit 1970, Designers Award of Excellence 1973; Wilson Hicks Cert of Merit for Photocommunication 1971, Design and Art Directors award 1978, Royal Photographic Soc Hood award 1979; *Books* Malta (in collaboration with Sacheverell Sitwell, 1958), London (1958), Private View (in collaboration with John Russell and Bryan Robertson, 1965), Assignments (1972), A View of Venice (1972), The Sack of Bath (1972), Inchcape Review (1977), Pride of the Shire (in collaboration with John Oaksey, 1979), Personal View (1979), Tasmania Essay (1981), Sittings (1983), My Wales (in collaboration with Viscount Tonypandy, 1986), Israel - a First View (1986), Stills 1984–1987 (1987), Public Appearances 1987–1991 (1991), Wild Flowers (1995), Snowdon on Stage (1996); *Style*— The Rt Hon the Earl of Snowdon, GCVO; ✉ 22 Launceston Place, London W8 5LR (☎ 0171 937 1524, fax 0171 938 1727)

SNOWDON, Graham Richard; s of Thomas Richard Snowdon (d 1970), of Doncaster, and Edna Mary, *née* Storm; *b* 8 Feb 1944; *Educ* Doncaster GS; *m* 5 Aug 1967, Peta Dawn, da of Frederick Alfred Rawlings (d 1992), of Lowestoft; 1 s (Frazer Richard b 6 March 1974), 1 da (Jessica Louise b 21 March 1972); *Career* jr reporter: Barnsley Chronicle 1960–61, Yorkshire Evening News 1961–63; family sports agency Doncaster 1963–64, competitions press offr RAC Motor Sport Div London 1964–66, northern press offr RAC Manchester 1966–70, freelance sports journalist 1969– (contrib to Daily Telegraph (as Graham Richards), Guardian and Press Assoc), ptnr (with Peta Snowdon) Snowdon Sports Editorial 1970– (sports press agency and official collators of nat sporting leagues and competitions), conslt Guinness Book of Records 1971–95; *Recreations* food and drink, walking, travel, motoring, autonumerology; *Clubs* Assoc Internationale des Journalistes du Cyclisme, Assoc Internationale de la Presse Sportive; *Style*— Graham Snowdon, Esq; ✉ 6 Hallam Grange Croft, Fulwood, Sheffield, S Yorks S10 4BP (☎ 0114 230 2233); 43 Eastgate, Pickering, N Yorks YO18 7DU (☎ 01751 477581); Snowdon Sports Editorial, PO Box 154, Sheffield S10 4BW (☎ 0114 230 3093, fax 0114 230 3094, car 0378 134830)

SNOWMAN, Daniel; s of Arthur Mortimer Snowman (d 1982), and Bertha, *née* Lazarus; *b* 4 Nov 1938; *Educ* Jesus Coll Cambridge, Cornell Univ NY (MA in Political Sci); *m* 17 Dec 1975, Janet Linda, *née* Levison; 1 s (Benjamin b 1977), 1 da (Anna b 1978); *Career* bdcaster, writer and lectr; lectr Univ of Sussex 1963–67; prodr features arts and education BBC Radio 1968–95; prodns incl: A World in Common, The Vatican, Reith Lectures, Northern Lights (BBC Arctic Festival), variety of historical and cultural programmes; visiting prof of History California State Univ 1972–73; contrib to British and US newspapers and jls; *Books* America Since 1920 (1968), Eleanor Roosevelt (1970), Kissing Cousins: An Interpretation of British and American Culture, 1945–75 (1977), If I Had Been ... Ten Historical Fantasies (1979), The Amadeus Quartet: The Men and the Music (1981), The World of Plácido Domingo (1985), Beyond the Tunnel of History (1990), Pole Positions: The Polar Regions and the Future of the Planet (1993), Plácido Domingo's Tales from the Opera (1994), Fins de Siècle (with Lord Briggs, *qv*, 1996); *Recreations* singing with London Philharmonic Choir (former chm); *Style*— Daniel Snowman, Esq; ✉ 46 Molyneux Street, London W1H 5HW (mobile/voicemail 0956 628265)

SNOWMAN, (Michael) Nicholas; s of Kenneth Snowman and Sallie, *née* Moghi-Levkine (d 1995); *b* 18 March 1944; *Educ* Highgate Sch, Magdalene Coll Cambridge (BA); *m* 1983, Margo Michelle Rouard; 1 s; *Career* asst to Head of Music Staff Glyndebourne Festival Opera 1967–69, co-fndr and gen mangr London Sinfonietta 1968–72, admin Music Theatre Ensemble 1968–71, artistic dir Institut de Recherche et de Co-ordination Acoustique/Musique (IRCAM) Centre d'Art et de Culture Georges Pompidou 1972–76, co-fndr Ensemble InterContemporain 1975– (artistic advsr 1975–92, memb Bd 1992–), chief exec The South Bank Centre 1992– (gen dir (Arts) 1986–92); memb Music Ctee Venice Biennale 1979–86; Festival d'Automne de Paris: artistic dir Stravinsky 1980, Webern 1981, Boulez 1983; prog conslt Cité de la Musique La Villette Paris 1991; memb Br Section Franco-Br Cncl 1995; Officier Ordre des Arts et des Lettres 1990 (Chevalier 1985), Order of Cultural Merit (Poland) 1990, Chevalier dans l'Ordre National du Mérite (France) 1995; *Books* The Best of Granta (co-ed, 1967), The Contemporary Composers (series ed, 1982–); author of papers and articles on music and cultural policy; *Recreations* films, eating, spy novels; *Clubs* Garrick; *Style*— Nicholas Snowman; ✉ Royal Festival Hall, South Bank Centre, London SE1 8XX (☎ 0171 921 0608)

SNYDER, Michael John; s of Percy Elsworth Snyder (d 1953), and Pauline Edith, *née* Davenport; *b* 30 July 1950; *Educ* Brentwood Sch, City of London Coll; *m* 14 Dec 1974, Mary Barbara, da of Rev Wilfrid Edgar Dickinson; 2 da (Julia Caroline b 10 Nov 1976, Susanna Jane b 9 Sept 1978); *Career* CA; Kingston Smith: joined 1968, ptnr 1974, managing ptnr 1979–, sr ptnr 1990–; chm Cheviot Capital Ltd; dir: Group Consultancy (Computer Services) Ltd, Kingston Smith Financial Services Ltd; chm: London Practioner Bd LSCA, Assoc of Practising Accountants; memb: Ct of Common Cncl City of London, dep chm Finance Ctee, Establishment Ctee, Policy and Resources Ctee, City Lands and Bridge House Estates Ctee, Music and Drama Ctee Guildhall Sch of Music and Drama, Bd of Govrs City of London Sch for Girls; chm Barbican Residential Ctee; Freeman City of London 1980, Liveryman and memb Ct of Assts Worshipful Co of Needlemakers, Liveryman Worshipful Co of Tallow Chandlers; hon treas Bow Bells Assoc, hon treas and govr Brentwood Sch; FCA 1978 (ACA 1973), FInstD, MSI, SFA registered rep; *Recreations* inland waterways, forestry, music, bridge; *Clubs* City Livery (hon treas), Cordwainer Ward, Bishopgate Ward, City Pickwick (hon treas); *Style*— Michael Snyder, Esq; ✉ Kingston Smith, Devonshire House, 60 Goswell Road, London EC1M 7AD (☎ 0171 566 4000, fax 0171 566 4010, car tel 0836 733 761)

SOAMES, Hon Emma Mary; *née* Soames; da of Baron Soames, GCMG, GCVO, CH, CBE, PC (Life Peer; d 1987), and Hon Mary Soames, DBE, *qv*, *née* Spencer-Churchill; sis of Hon Rupert Soames, *qv* and Hon Nicholas Soames, MP, *qv*; *b* 6 Sept 1949; *m* 4 July 1981 (m dis 1989), James MacManus, assist ed The Times, s of Dr Niall MacManus, of Warwick Sq, London SW1; 1 da (Emily Fiona b 1983); *Career* journalist Evening Standard, former ed Literary Review, features ed Vogue, ed Tatler, freelance journalist, dep ed The Oldie 1991–92, ed ES Magazine (Evening Standard) 1992–94, ed Telegraph Magazine 1994–; tstee Addictive Diseases Tst; *Clubs* Groucho, Academy; *Style*— The Hon Emma Soames; ✉ 26 Eland Road, London SW11 5JY

SOAMES, Eveline Virginia (Evie) (Lady Duff Gordon); da of Samuel Soames, of London, and Margaret Temple Dolan (d 1983); *b* 30 April 1947; *Educ* Downe House Sch, Trinity Coll Dublin (BA); *m* 1975, Sir Andrew Duff Gordon, 8 Bt, *qv*; 3 s (William b 1977, Thomas b 1979, Frederick b 1981); *Career* dir Charles Barker 1975–, md Charles Barker Watney Powell 1976–91, chief exec Charles Barker Public Affairs 1991–; dir: Liberty plc, Franco-Br Parly Rels Ctee 1975–; *Clubs* Kington Golf; *Style*— Ms Evie Soames; ✉ Charles Barker plc, 56 Dean Street, London W1V 6HX (☎ 0171 494 1331)

SOAMES, Baroness; Hon Mary; *née* Spencer Churchill; DBE (1980, MBE Mil 1945); da of late Rt Hon Sir Winston Leonard Spencer Churchill, KG, OM, CH, TD, PC, FRS (d 1965, gs of 7 Duke of Marlborough), and Baroness Spencer Churchill (Dame Clementine Ogilvy, GBE, cr Life Peeress 1965, da of late Col Sir Henry Montague Hozier, KCB, bro of 1 Baron Newlands, and Lady (Henrietta) Blanche Ogilvy, da of 5 (10 but for attainder) Earl of Airlie, KT); *b* 1922; *m* 1947, Capt Christopher Soames (later Baron Soames, GCMG, GCVO, CH, CBE, PC, d 1987); 3 s, 2 da; *Career* formerly Jr Cdr ATS;

memb Cncl Winston Churchill Memorial Tst 1978–97 (chm of tstees 1991–), chm Royal Nat Theatre Bd 1989–95; patron Nat Benevolent Fund for the Aged 1978–; govr Harrow Sch 1981–95; hon fell Churchill College Cambridge; Hon DLitt Sussex 1989; Chevalier de la Légion d'Honneur (France) 1995; *Books* Clementine Churchill by Her Daughter Mary Soames (1979), A Churchill Family Album (1982), The Profligate Duke: George Spencer Churchill, 5th Duke of Marlborough and his Duchess (1987), Winston Churchill: His Life as a Painter - A Memoir by his daughter Mary Soames (1990); *Style—* The Lady Soames, DBE

SOAMES, Hon (Arthur) Nicholas Winston; MP (C) Crawley (majority 7,765); s of Baron Soames, GCMG, GCVO, CH, CBE, PC (Life Peer; d 1987), and Hon Mary, DBE, *qv, née* Spencer-Churchill, da of late Sir Winston Churchill and Baroness Spencer-Churchill; bro of Hon Rupert Soames, *qv* and Hon Emma Soames, *qv*; *b* 12 Feb 1948; *Educ* Eton; *m* 1, 1981 (m dis 1988), Catherine, da of Capt Tony Weatherall, of Dumfries; 1 s (Arthur Harry David b 1985); m 2, 21 Dec 1993, Serena Mary, da of Sir John Lindsay Eric Smith, CBE, JP, DL, *qv*, of Shottesbrooke Park, Maidenhead, Berks; 1 da (Isabella b 1996); *Career* served 11 Hussars 1967–70, extra equerry to HRH The Prince of Wales 1970–72, Lloyd's insurance broker 1972–74, PA to Sir James Goldsmith 1974–76, PA to US Senator Mark Hatfield 1976–78, asst dir Sedgwick Group 1979–81; Parly candidate (C) Central Dumbartonshire 1979, MP (C) Crawley 1983–, PPS to Rt Hon John Selwyn Gummer as Min of State for Employment and Chm of the Cons Party 1984–86, sec Cons Foreign Affrs Ctee 1986–87, PPS to the Rt Hon Nicholas Ridley 1987–89, PPS to Sec of State DTI 1989–92, Parly sec Min of Agric Fisheries and Food 1992–94, min of state (Armed Forces) Min of Defence 1994–; *Clubs* White's, Turf, Pratt's; *Style—* The Hon Nicholas Soames, MP; ✉ The House of Commons, London SW1 0AA

SOAMES, Hon Rupert Christopher; s of Baron Soames, GCMG, GCVO, CH, CBE, PC (Life Peer; d 1987), and Hon Mary Soames, DBE, *qv, née* Spencer-Churchill; bro of Hon Emma Soames, *qv* and Hon Nicholas Soames, MP, *qv*; *b* 18 May 1959; *Educ* Eton, Worcester Coll Oxford (BA, pres Oxford Union 1980); *m* 1988, Camilla Rose, eldest da of Sir Thomas Raymond Dunne, of Gatley Park, Leominster, Herefordshire; 2 s (Arthur Christopher b 3 Feb 1990, Jack Winston b 20 Sept 1994), 1 da (Daisy b 2 April 1992); *Career* GEC plc: joined 1981, currently md subsid Avery Berkel UK; *Clubs* Turf, White's; *Style—* The Hon Rupert Soames; ✉ Avery Berkel UK, Sertec House, West Bromwich Road, Tame Bridge, Walsall, West Midlands WS5 4BD (☎ 01922 434343)

SOAR, Adrian Richard; s of Reginald Herbert Soar (d 1984), and Kathleen Mary, *née* Watson (d 1995); *b* 5 March 1941; *Educ* Tonbridge (scholar), Jesus Coll Oxford (exhibitioner, MA); *m* 1973, Michaela Joana Coltofeanu; 1 s (Daniel Nicholai b 4 Feb 1976), 1 da (Laura Eleanor b 8 July 1978); *Career* Macmillan Ltd 1969–: export mangr 1969–71, md Macmillan India Ltd 1972–73, marketing dir Macmillan Press Ltd 1973–78, md Macmillan Press Ltd 1979–85, chm Macmillan Press Ltd and Macmillan Education Ltd 1985–94, md Book Publishing Gp Macmillan Ltd 1994–; *Recreations* cooking, work, reading, gardening, sailing; *Style—* Adrian Soar, Esq; ✉ Macmillan Publishers Ltd, 25 Eccleston Place, London SW1W 9NF

SOBERS, Sir Garfield St Auburn (Garry); kt (1975); *b* 28 July 1936, Bridgetown, Barbados; *Educ* Bay St Sch Barbados; *m* 1969, Prudence Kirby; 2 s, 1 da; *Career* cricketer; played in 93 test matches for WI (39 as capt) 1953–74, capt WI and Barbados teams 1964–74, capt Notts CCC 1968–74, ret; held world records in test cricket: 365 not out, 26 centuries, 235 wickets, 110 catches; memb Appeal Panel Immigrations Dept 1982; *Books* Cricket Advance (1965), Cricket Crusader (1966), Cricket in the Sun (1967); *Style—* Sir Garry Sobers

SOBOLEWSKI, Dr Stanislaw; s of Kazimierz Sobolewski (d 1979), of Scunthorpe, and Bronislawa Sobolewska (d 1989); *b* 9 Feb 1943; *Educ* Bialystok GS Poland, Med Acad of Bialystok Poland (MB BS), Univ of Bradford (PhD); *m* 1, 1968 (m dis 1976), Elizabeth, *née* Olszewska; 1 s (Edward b 1974), 2 da (Marta b 1970, Anastasia b 1972); m 2, Patricia, da of George Pearson (decd), of Rawmarsh, Rotherham, S Yorks; *Career* Grajewo Hosp Poland 1967, Olecko Hosp Poland 1968–70, sr house offr in rheumatology Harrogate 1971–72, registrar in pathology Sheffield 1974–77 (registrar in clinical haematology 1972–74), sr registrar in haematology Leeds and Bradford, conslt haematologist Trent RHA S Lincs Dist Boston; regnl rep RCPath, fndr chm Trent Region Haematology Sub Ctee, chm Boston Leukaemia and Cancer Fund, memb Med Exec Ctee Pilgrim Hosp; ACP 1974, memb Br Soc of Haematology 1976, MRCS 1976, LCRP 1976, MRCPath 1979; *Books* A New Function of Megakaryocytes in Malignancy (1986); *Recreations* classic cars restoration, swimming, football; *Clubs* Polish Social (Scunthorpe); *Style—* Dr Stanislaw Sobolewski; ✉ Pinewood, 32 Linden Way, Boston, Lincs PE21 9DS (☎ 01205 351655); Consultant Haematologist, Pilgrim Hospital, Sibsey Rd, Boston Lincs PE21 9QS (☎ 012053 64801)

SODOR AND MAN, Bishop of 1989–; Rt Rev Noel Debroy Jones; CB (1986); s of Brinley Jones, of Gwent, and Gwendoline Alice, *née* White (d 1988); *b* 25 Dec 1932; *Educ* West Monmouth Sch for Boys, St David's Coll (BA), Wells Theol Coll; *m* 1969, Joyce Barbara Leelavathy, da of Arumugam Arulanandam (d 1979), of Singapore; 1 s (Benjamin b 1972), 1 da (Vanessa b 1970); *Career* clerk in Holy Orders 1955, parishes Dio of Monmouth; vicar of Kano N Nigeria 1960, chaplain Royal Navy 1962, chaplain of the Fleet 1984–; Hon Chaplain to HM The Queen 1983; GSM; *Recreations* formerly rugby, squash, music, family; *Clubs* Sion Coll, Army and Navy; *Style—* The Rt Rev the Lord Bishop of Sodor; ✉ Bishop's House, Quarterbridge Road, Douglas, IOM IM2 3RF

SOFER, (Hon Mrs) Anne Hallowell; da of Baron Crowther (Life Peer, d 1972); does not use courtesy style of Hon; *b* 1937; *Educ* St Paul's Sch, Swarthmore Coll USA, Somerville Coll Oxford (MA); *m* 1958, Jonathan Sofer, barrister-at-law; 2 s, 1 da; *Career* sec Nat Assoc of Govrs and Mangrs 1972–75, additional memb ILEA Educn Ctee 1974–77, cncllr (Lab until 1981 whereafter SDP) GLC for St Pancras N 1977–86, chm ILEA Schs Sub Ctee 1978–81, chief educn offr London Borough of Tower Hamlets 1989–; columnist The Times 1983–87; dir Channel Four Television Co Ltd 1981–83, tstee Nuffield Fndn 1991–, vice chm National Children's Bureau 1996–; *Books* The School Governors' Handbook (with Tyrrell Burgess, 1978 and 1986), The London Left Takeover (1987); *Style—* Mrs Anne Sofer; ✉ 46 Regent's Park Rd, London NW1 7SX (☎ 0171 722 8970)

SOKOLNICKI, Count Juliusz (Nowina-); s of Count Antoni (Nowina-) Sokolnicki (d 1946) of the manors of Siedlemin and Izabelin Poland and Irena, *née* Skirmunt (d 1981); *b* 16 Dec 1920; *Educ* Joseph Pilsudski Coll Pinsk, Warsaw Univ; *m* 1, Elizabeth Mary Krokowski, *née* Mayal (d 1982); m 2, 29 July 1983, Margaret Thornburn (d 1992), da of Francis Docherty (d 1947); m 3, 23 Sept 1993, Avril Dalgleish; *Career* Cadet Offr 84 Bn Polish Armed Forces during campaign in Poland Sept 1939, captured by Russians, escaped, active in Polish underground, arrested by Gestapo Aug 1940, released 1942 and rejoined underground in Lublin, Capt 1943, escaped to Italy after Warsaw Rising, Lt-Col 1945; active in Polish political organisations in Britain since 1947; chm Polish Nat Revival Movement 1954; memb Cncl of Republic of Poland in exile 1954–72 (vice-chm 1963–67); ed fortnightly jl Rzeczpospolita Polska 1967–71; min of information Govt in Exile 1967–71, and home affairs 1970–71; pres of the Republic of Poland in Exile 1972–90 (relinquished office after free elections in Poland); a fndr Central Euro Cncl New York 1986 (membership comprising seven govts or monarchs in exile from Albania, Bulgaria, Croatia, Czechoslovakia, Estonia, Poland and Roumania); vice-pres London Appreciation Soc 1981; memb: Royal Soc of St George, Club des Intellectuels Français 1979, Polish Nobility Assoc in USA 1982, Bd of Humanity International Washington DC; delegate for England to Institut Héraldique, Historique et Généalogique de France 1971; Hon Citizen: State of Texas 1982, State of Nebraska 1982, City of Minneapolis 1982, City of Baltimore 1985; Freeman City of London 1993; Grand Master Order of St Stanislas 1979–, Hon Lt-Col State of Alabama Militia 1981, recteur honoraire de l'Institut de Documentation et d'Etudes Européannes Bruxelles 1981, hon prof of political science Institut St Irène France, Dr of Art and Philosophy Academia Int Americana Mexico 1981, hon life memb Augustan Soc (USA) 1982, senator Int Parliament for Safety and Peace 1982, patron Fndn of the Families of Poland 1991; orders and decorations include: Order of Besa (Albania) 1988, Order of the White Eagle (Poland), Order of Polonia Restituta (Poland), Cdr Merito Commercial (Mexico) 1979, Order of Masaryk (Czechoslovakia) 1987, Grand Collar Equitem Crucis Hierosolimae (Patriarchate of Antioch) 1982, Grand Croix Etoile de la Paix (France) 1948, Etoile Civique Medaille d'Or (France) 1980, Grand Croix Encouragement Public (France) 1982, Medaille de Vermeil Grand Prix Humanitaire (France) 1980, Order of Palmetto (S Carolina) 1992, Distinguished Service Medal of the S Carolina State Guard 1992, Niadh Nask 1st Class (from The MacCarthy Mor) 1992; *Recreations* travelling, painting; *Clubs* Special Forces; *Style—* Count Juliusz Sokolnicki; ✉ 9 York Place, Castle Gardens, Colchester, Essex CO1 2RF (☎ 01206 865591)

SOKOLOV, Dr Avril; da of Frederick Cresswell Pyman (d 1966), and Frances Gwenneth, *née* Holman (d 1964); *b* 4 May 1930; *Educ* École de Jeune Filles Lausanne, Newnham Coll Cambridge (exhibitioner, Arthur Hugh Clough Scholar, BA), PhD (Cantab); *m* 1963, Kirill Konstantinovich Sokolov, s of Konstantin Mikhailovich Sokolov (d 1972); 1 da (Irina b 1965); *Career* Br Cncl scholar Leningrad 1959–61, freelance translator, researcher and writer Moscow 1963–74; Univ of Durham: pt/t lectr 1976–78, lectr 1978–86, sr lectr 1986–89, reader 1989–96, reader emeritus 1996–; memb Assoc of Writers (Translating Sector); FIL 1949, FBA 1996; *Books* Life of Aleksander Blok vol 1: The Distant Thunder (1979), Life of Aleksander Blok vol 2: The Release of Harmony (1980), History of Russian Symbolism (1994); also translated numerous books, articles and poetry; *Recreations* art, theatre, travelling; *Style—* Dr Avril Sokolov, FBA; ✉ Department of Russian, School of Modern European Languages, University of Durham, Elvet Riverside, New Elvet, Durham DH1 3JT (☎ 0191 374 287, fax 0191 374 7795)

SOLANDT, Jean Bernard; s of Alfred Ernest Solandt (d 1977), and Mathilde, *née* Braun (d 1991); *b* 23 Dec 1936; *Educ* Lycée Pasteur and Collège Technique Commercial Strasbourg France; *m* 6 Aug 1966, Sheila, da of Capt James William Hammill, OBE (d 1974); 1 s (Jean-Luc), 1 da (Nathalie Claire); *Career* banker; Société Générale (Strasbourg, Paris and London) 1954–68; Schroder Group: joined 1968, gp md Fin Markets Div Schroders plc 1984–, 1984–, dir Schroder Wertheim & Co Inc 1986–, dir Schroder Wertheim Holdings Inc 1986–, dir Schroders Asia Ltd 1991–, chm Schroder France SA 1992–, dir J Henry Schroder Bank AG 1993–, dir Schroder Structured Investments Inc 1995–, Schroder & Co Ltd 1995– (vice chm 1984–94); non-exec dir: Woolwich Building Society 1993–, Banca Woolwich SpA Banque Woolwich 1994–; *Recreations* golf, skiing, reading, music, motoring, walking; *Style—* Jean Solandt, Esq; ✉ 27 Heathgate, London NW11 7AP; J Henry Schroder & Co Ltd, 120 Cheapside, London EC2V 6DS (☎ 0171 382 6818)

SOLANKI, Ramniklal Chhaganlal; s of Chhaganlal Kalidas Solanki (d 1963), and Ichchhaben Chhaganlal Solanki (d 1993); *b* 12 July 1931; *Educ* Irish Presbyterian Mission Sch Surat, MTB Coll Gujarat Univ (BA), Sarvajanik Law Coll Surat (LLB); *m* 16 June 1955, Parvatiben Ramniklal, da of Makanji Dullabhji Chavda (d 1979); 2 s (Kalpesh b 9 Nov 1960, Shailesh b 3 June 1964), 2 da (Sadhana (Mrs Ravindra Karia) b 18 May 1956, Smita (Mrs Mukesh Thakkar) b 5 July 1958 d 1994); *Career* sub ed Nutan Bharat and Lok Vani Dailies Surat 1954–56, freelance columnist for several newspapers while serving State Govt in India 1956–63, London corr Gujarat Mitra Surat 1964–68, Euro corr Janmabhoomi Gp of Newspapers Bombay 1968–; ed and md: Garavi Gujarat Newspapers 1968–, Asian Trader 1985–, Asian Hotel & Caterer 1995–; md Garavi Gujarat Property Ltd 1982; Reporter of the Year Award 1970; memb: Asian Advsy Ctee BBC 1976–80, Nat Centre for Indian Language Trg Steering Gp 1978, Exec Ctee Gujarati Arya Kshtriya Maha Sabha UK 1979–84, Exec Ctee Gujarati Arya Assoc 1974–84 (vice-pres 1980–83), CPU 1964–, Foreign Press Assoc 1984–, Parly Press Gallery House of Commons, Cwlth Press Union (full memb); organiser Asian Trader of the Year Awards 1989–, sec Indian Journalists Assoc of Europe 1978–79; memb Guild of Br Newspaper Eds 1976; tstee Mahatma Gandhi Meml Tst; *Recreations* reading, writing, meeting people, politics, travelling; *Style—* Ramniklal Solanki, Esq; ✉ Garavi Gujarat Publications, Garavi Gujarat House, 1 Silex St, London SE1 0DW (☎ 0171 928 1234, fax 0171 261 0055, e-mail garavi@gujarat.demon.co.uk)

SOLE, David Michael Barclay; OBE (1993); *b* 8 May 1962; *Educ* Univ of Exeter; *Career* former rugby union player (prop); former clubs: Exeter Univ, Toronto Scottish, Bath (John Player Cup winners 1987); current club Edinburgh Academicals; Scotland: B debut 1983, full debut v France 1986, capt 1989–92, capt Grand Slam winning team 1990, 44 caps; memb Br Lions tour to Aust 1989 (3 test appearances), capt Barbarians v All Blacks 1989, capt Home Unions v Europe 1990 (in aid of Romanian Appeal); grain buyer; *Style—* David Sole, Esq, OBE; ✉ c/o Edinburgh Academicals, Raeburn Place, Edinburgh

SOLE, Brig Denis Story; CVO (1971), OBE (1964); s of Brig Denis Mavesyn Anslow Sole, DSO (d 1962), and Lilian May, *née* Story (d 1974); *b* 26 July 1917; *Educ* Cheltenham, Sandhurst Staff Coll Quetta; *m* 5 March 1957, Susan Margaret, da of Maj Cecil Arnold Williams (d 1951); 1 s (Simon John b 1960), 1 da (Sarah Elizabeth b 1958); *Career* served in The Border Regt 1937, Palestine 1937–39, India, Burma 1939–48, AAG Royal Nigerian Mil Forces 1959–62; def advsr to Br High Cmmn Zambia 1964–66, def and mil attache Turkey 1968–72; *Recreations* sailing, shooting, fishing, tennis; *Clubs* Army and Navy; *Style—* Brig Denis S Sole, CVO, OBE

SOLESBURY, William Booth; s of William Solesbury, and Hannah Solesbury; *b* 10 April 1940; *Educ* Hertford GS, Univ of Cambridge (BA), Univ of Liverpool (MCD); *m* 1966, Felicity; 1 s, 2 da; *Career* London CC 1961–65; planning asst: London Borough of Camden 1965–66, City of Munich 1966–67, Miny of Housing 1967–72; NATO res fell Univ of Calif Berkeley 1973, Dept of the Environment 1974–89, Gwilym Gibbon res fell Nuffield Coll Oxford 1989–90, sec Econ and Social Res Cncl UK 1990; currently conslt; *Publications* Policy in Urban Planning (1974); various articles in Public Administration, Policy and Politics; *Recreations* home life, films, reading, travel; *Style—* William Solesbury, Esq

SOLEY, Clive Stafford; MP (Lab) Hammersmith (majority 4,754); *b* 7 May 1939; *Educ* Downshall Secondary Modern, Newbattle Abbey Adult Educn Coll, Strathclyde Univ (BA), Southampton Univ (Dip Applied Soc Servs); *Career* probation offr 1970–75, sr probation offr 1975–79; MP (Lab): Hammersmith N 1979–83, Hammersmith 1983–; oppn front bench spokesman: on NI 1981–82 and 1983–84, on home affrs 1984–87, on housing and local govt 1987–89, on housing and planning 1989–92; chm NI Affairs Select Ctee 1995– (memb 1994–); memb Standing Ctee: Prevention of Terrorism Bill 1983–84, Criminal Justice Bill 1987–88, Housing Bill 1987–88, Local Govt & Housing Bill 1988–89, Planning & Compensation Bill 1990–91, Freedom & Responsibility of the Press Bill 1992–93; fell Industry and Parliament Tst; memb GMB; *Recreations* walking, photography, scuba diving; *Style—* Clive Soley, Esq, MP; ✉ House of Commons, London SW1A 0AA (☎ 0171 219 5118/5490, home 0171 740 7585, fax 0171 219 5974)

SOLIMAN, Dr John Iskandar; s of Iskandar Soliman, and Ines, *née* Abdallah; *b* 24 Sept 1926; *Educ* Alexandria Univ (BSc, MSc), Univ of London (PhD); *m* 17 July 1953 (m dis 1981), Gabrielle, da of John Zammit; 1 s (Andre b 1955), 1 da (Monette b 1956); *Career* lectr Alexandria Univ Egypt 1948–61, sr sci offr Br Iron and Steel Res Assoc London 1961–62, lectr QMC 1962–87, chm Int Cmmns Europe, organizer Int Confs Europe, prof Univ of Rome 1981–; visiting prof to Univs in USA and Europe, conslt to multinational cos; author of numerous articles in jls; MIMechE; memb: Soc of Automotive Engrs USA, VDI Germany, SIA France, ATA Italy, ASME, IEEE (USA), SME (USA); *Clubs* Anglo Belgian, Annabel's; *Style*— Dr John Soliman; ✉ 42 Lloyd Park Ave, Croydon, CR0 5SB (☎ 0181 681 3069, fax 0181 686 1490)

SOLMAN, Robert Frederick; s of Edward Vickery Solman (d 1977), of Spire House, Comberton, Kidderminster, and Marjorie Anne Watts, *née* Styles; *b* 27 Jan 1934; *Educ* Sebright Sch, Univ of Birmingham (LLB); *Career* called to the Bar Middle Temple 1958, in practice Midlands and Oxford Circuit, recorder 1985–; *Style*— Robert Solman, Esq; ✉ Roydfield, Blakedown, nr Kidderminster, Worcs DY10 3JJ (☎ 01562 700 275); 5 Fountain Court, Steelhouse Lane, Birmingham (☎ 0121 606 0500, fax 0121 606 1501)

SOLOMON, David; s of Leslie Ezekiel Solomon, of London, and Peggy, *née* Shatzman; *b* 6 Aug 1948; *Educ* Clarks Coll, City of London Coll; *m* 15 July 1973 (m dis 1986), Sarah-Lou Reekie; 1 s (Tony Daniel b 1980); *Career* began in advertising with Garland-Compton, fndr Pink-Soda Fashion Co 1983– (opened Euro Office in Paris 1988); winner Queen's Award for Export Achievement 1987, BKCEC Award for Export Achievement (awarded by The Princess Royal); MInstMSM; *Recreations* marathon, running, tennis; *Style*— David Solomon, Esq; ✉ 22 Eastcastle St, London W1N 7PA (☎ 0171 636 9001, fax 0171 637 1641, telex 22827 PK SODA G)

SOLOMON, David Joseph; s of Sydney Solomon (d 1963), of Bournemouth, Hants, and Rosie, *née* Joseph (d 1978); *b* 31 Dec 1930; *Educ* Torquay GS, Univ of Manchester (LLB); *m* 5 April 1959, Hazel, da of Joseph Boam, of London; 1 s (Jonathan b 1961), 2 da (Ruth b 1963, Joanne b 1966); *Career* slr; ptnr Nabarro Nathanson 1961–68; D J Freeman: head Property Dept 1976–90, chief exec 1990–93, sr ptnr 1992–96; chm Carter Asian Arts plc; pres Highgate Literary and Scientific Instn 1993–; memb: Cncl Oriental Ceramics Soc 1989–92 and 1994–, The Architecture Club; tstee Public Art Devpt Tst; Freeman Worshipful Co of Slrs; memb Law Soc; *Recreations* Chinese ceramics, music, architecture, modern art, wine; *Clubs* Athenaeum; *Style*— David Solomon, Esq; ✉ Russell House, 9 South Grove, London N6 6BS (☎ 0181 341 6454); Longecourt Les Culetre, 21230 Arnay le Duc, France (☎ 00 33 80 90 05 55)

SOLOMON, Gerald Oliver; s of Thomas Oliver Solomon (d 1987), of Barnard Castle, Co Durham, and Florence, *née* Towers (d 1978); *b* 18 June 1935; *Educ* King James I GS Bishop Auckland, UCL (LLB); *m* 4 May 1957, Norma, da of Harold Crofton Barron, BEM (d 1965), of Barnard Castle, Co Durham; 1 s (Jeremy b 1959 d 1981), 1 da (Amanda b 1963); *Career* Lloyds Bank 1958–95 (ret): asst treas 1976–79, dep chief accountant 1979–80, regnl dir S Wales 1980–82, gen mangr UK Retail Banking 1982–93, md Agricultural Mortgage Corp 1993–95; dir: Jt Credit Card Co Ltd (Access) 1984–90, Visa International (EMEA) 1989–95; memb Cncl of Banking Ombudsman 1987–90; Freeman City of London 1970; FCIB 1983; *Recreations* golf, fell walking; *Clubs* Royal Over-Seas League, United (Jersey); *Style*— Gerald Solomon, Esq; ✉ Littlegarth, Churchfields Ave, Weybridge, Surrey KT13 9YA (☎ 01932 847337)

SOLOMON, Sir Harry; kt (1991); s of Jacob Eli Solomon (d 1987), and Belle Brechner (d 1951); *b* 20 March 1937; *Educ* St Albans Sch, Law Society Sch of Law; *m* Judith Diana, da of Benjamin Manuel (d 1974); 1 s (Daniel Mark b 2 Sept 1965), 2 da (Louise Sara b 3 July 1964, Juliet Kate b 6 Aug 1969); *Career* admitted slr 1960, in private practice 1960–75; Hillsdown Holdings plc: co-fndr 1974, md 1975–84, chm and chief exec 1984–93 (jt chm 1984–87), non-exec dir 1993–; chm RCP Help Medicine Appeal, dir Nat Heart Charity CORDA; Hon FRCP; *Recreations* jogging, cricket, tennis, collecting of historical autographed letters; *Style*— Sir Harry Solomon; ✉ Hillsdown Holdings plc, Hillsdown House, 32 Hampstead High St, London NW3 1QD (☎ 0171 794 0677, fax 0171 435 1355, telex 297220)

SOLOMON, John William; s of George William Solomon (d 1957), of Roehampton, London, and Ivy Louie (Pat), *née* Castle (d 1991); *b* 22 Nov 1931; *Educ* Charterhouse; *m* 1, 25 July 1953 (m dis 1972), Anne, da of (David) Robert Thomas Lewis (d 1979), of Carshalton, Surrey; 3 s (Andrew b 1954, John b 1956, Gregory b 1964); m 2, 5 Dec 1972, Barbara Arthur; *Career* md: William P Solomon Ltd 1957–83 (joined 1951), John Solomon Inc Ltd 1983–93; Tobacco Trade Benevolent Assoc: hon treas 1970–76, vice chm 1976–82, chm 1982–86, vice pres 1980–; chm Imported Tobacco Prods Advsy Ctee 1976–80, 1984–86 and 1990–; The Croquet Assoc: chm 1962–64, vice pres 1975–83, pres 1983–; nat titles in assoc croquet: ten GB Open Championship, ten GB Mens Championship, ten GB Open Doubles Championship, one GB Mixed Doubles Championship, nine times holder Presidents Cup, twice winner NZ Open Championship, twice winner NZ Open Doubles Championship, four times winner Championship of Champions; govr Sevenoaks Sch 1992–; Worshipful Co of Tobacco Pipe Makers and Tobacco Blenders: Freeman 1960, Liveryman 1962, memb Court 1974, Master 1989–90; *Books* Croquet (1966); *Recreations* music, golf, acting, croquet; *Clubs* Hurlingham; *Style*— John Solomon, Esq; ✉ Kingswood Place, Horsham Road, Findon, Worthing, West Sussex (☎ 01903 873921)

SOLOMON, Jonathan; s of Samuel Solomon, ICS (d 1988), of London, and Moselle Solomon; *b* 3 March 1939; *Educ* Clifton, King's Coll Cambridge (MA); *m* 6 Oct 1966, Hester Madeline, da of Orrin McFarland, of Florida; 1 s (Gabriel b 27 April 1967); *Career* supervisor Sidney Sussex Coll Cambridge 1960–72, lectr Extra-Mural Dept Univ of London 1963–70; princ 1967–72: Bd of Trade (asst princ 1963–67), DTI, Treasy; asst sec 1973–80: Dept of Prices and Consumer Protection, Dept of Indust; under sec Dept of Indust 1980–85; Cable and Wireless plc: dir Special Projects 1985–87, dir Corp Strategy 1987–88, Corp Business Devpt 1988–92, exec dir Strategy and Corp Business Development 1993–; dir: Int Digital Communications 1987–, Tele 2 1990–, Nahodkha and Sakhalin Telecommunications 1991, Hongkong Telecom 1996; *Recreations* sport, research, futurology, writing; *Clubs* English Speaking Union, RAC; *Style*— Jonathan Solomon, Esq; ✉ 12 Kidderpore Gardens, London NW3 (☎ 0171 794 6230); Cable and Wireless plc, 124 Theobalds Road, London WC1 (☎ 0171 315 4611)

SOLOMON, Prof Louis; s of Samuel Solomon (d 1976), of Johnannesburg, and Ann, *née* Miller (d 1976); *b* 31 May 1928; *Educ* SA Coll Sch Cape Town, Univ of Cape Town (MB ChB, MD); *m* 1 July 1951, Joan Sarah, da of Philip Mendelsohn, of Johannesburg; 1 s (Ryan b 1956), 1 da (Caryn b 1953); *Career* prof of orthopaedic surgery: Univ of the Witwatersrand Johannesburg 1967–85, Univ of Bristol 1985–; memb: Int Hip Soc, Br Orthopaedic Assoc; *Books* with A G Apley: Apley's System of Orthopaedics and Fractures (1993), A Concise System of Orthopaedics and Fractures (1994); *Recreations* cycling; *Style*— Prof Louis Solomon; ✉ Dept of Orthopaedic Surgery, Bristol Royal Infirmary, Bristol BS2 8HW (☎ and fax 0117 973 3953)

SOLOMON, Nathaniel; s of Leopold Solomon (d 1984), and Fanny, *née* Hartz (d 1991); *b* 20 Nov 1925; *Educ* Owen's Sch London, Emmanuel Coll Cambridge (MA); *m* 24 Feb 1951, Patricia, da of Arthur Creak (d 1954); 2 s (Max b 1957, Justin b 1962), 1 da (Claire b 1959); *Career* Midshipman Fleet Air Arm 1944–47; joined Unilever 1949; dir: United Africa Co Ltd 1964–72, William Baird PLC 1972–74; md Associated Leisure PLC 1974–84, chm Pleasurama plc 1984–88; dir: Bally Manufacturing Corp 1989–91, Jefferies International, Harrap Publishing Group 1989–92, Cardinal Business Group 1992–; chm: JPI Group 1991–95, Crown Leisure 1993–; Tottenham Hotspur plc: chm 1991, dep chm 1991–92, life vice pres 1992–; CIMgt 1986; *Recreations* bridge, tennis, wine, opera, theatre, watching soccer (especially Tottenham Hotspur); *Clubs* Reform, Harvard Business Sch, The Wimbledon; *Style*— Nathaniel Solomon, Esq; ✉ 96 Kensington High Street, London W8 4SG (☎ 0171 937 7733, fax 0171 937 8185)

SOLOMON, Stephen Edward; s of Maj William Edward Solomon (d 1977), and Winifred Constance, *née* Day; *b* 29 Nov 1947; *Educ* Royal GS Guildford Surrey, Univ of Manchester; *m* (m dis 1995) Maureen Diane, da of William Robert Wilkins, of Tenby, Dyfed; 2 s (Robert William Petrie b 1980, John Christopher Petrie b 1981); *Career* admitted slr 1973; ptnr: Crossman Block and Keith slrs 1978–87 (joined 1976), Withers Crossman Block 1988–89, Crossman Block 1989–93; tstee The Law Debenture Corp plc 1994–95, W Davies & Son 1996–; memb: Guildford Round Table 1979–89, Guildford XRT 1988–90; memb: Law Soc; *Recreations* golf, skiing, gliding, astronomy, plumbing; *Clubs* Bramley Golf; *Style*— Stephen Solomon, Esq; ✉ 79 Strathcona Avenue, Bookham, Surrey KT23 4HR (☎ 01372 456009)

SOLOMONS, Anthony Nathan; s of Lesly Emmanuel Solomons (d 1938), and Susy, *née* Schneiders; *b* 26 Jan 1930; *Educ* Oundle; *m* 16 Dec 1958, Jean, da of Dr Jack Joseph Golding; 2 da (Nicola Jane b 2 June 1960, Jennifer Anne b 30 June 1963); *Career* Nat Serv cmmnd Dorset Regt 1953–54; Singer & Friedlander Ltd: joined 1958, chief exec 1973, chm 1976–; chm: Singer & Friedlander Group plc 1987–, Peoples Phone Plc 1995–; dir: Bullough plc, Burford Group Plc; memb Educnl Assets Bd; FCA, FIMgt; *Clubs* Carlton; *Style*— Anthony Solomons Esq; ✉ Singer & Friedlander, 21 New Street, London EC2M 4HR (☎ 0171 623 3000, fax 0171 623 2122, telex 886977); 10 Constable Close, London NW11 6TY (☎ 0181 458 6716)

SOLTI, Sir Georg; KBE (1971, Hon CBE 1968); *b* 21 Oct 1912, Budapest; *Educ* Liszt Acad of Music Budapest; *m* 1, 1946, Hedwig Oeschli; m 2, 1967, Anne Valerie Pitts; 2 da (Gabrielle b 1970, Claudia b 1973); *Career* studied under Kodály, Bartók, Dohnányi; won First Prize as pianist Concours Int Geneva 1942; former conductor and pianist Budapest State Opera; musical dir: Bavarian State Opera 1946–52, Frankfurt Opera 1952–61, Covent Garden Opera 1961–71 (music dir laureate 1992–), Chicago Symphony Orchestra 1969–91 (music dir laureate 1991–), Orchestre de Paris 1971–75; princ conductor and artistic dir LPO 1979–83 (conductor emeritus 1983–92); Hon FRCM 1980; Hon DMus: Univ of Leeds 1971, Oxford 1972, Yale 1974, De Paul 1975, Harvard 1979, Furman 1983, Surrey 1983, London 1986, Rochester 1987, Durham 1995; prof honoris causa Baden-Württemberg 1985; Knight Commander's Cross with Badge and Star (Fed Republic of Germany) 1986, Middle Cross of the Order of the Merit with Star (Republic of Hungary) 1993, Grosses Verdienstskreuz mit Stern und Schulterband (FDR) 1993, Cdr of the Order of Leopold (Belgium) 1993, Mil Order of Santiago do Espada (Portugal) 1994; adopted UK citizenship 1972; *Awards* Medal of Merit Chicago 1987, Gold Medal Royal Philharmonic Soc 1989, Hans Richter Medal Vienna Philharmonic Orch 1993, 31 Grammy Awards 1993, Von Bülow Medal Berlin Philharmonic Orch 1993, Kennedy Center Honor 1993; *Style*— Sir Georg Solti, KBE; ✉ Ingpen & Williams Ltd, 14 Kensington Court, London W8 5DN (☎ 0171 937 5158, fax 0171 938 4175)

SOLTMANN, Diana-Margaret; da of HE Dr Otto Soltmann, of Koblenz, W Germany, and Ethel Margaret, *née* Oakleigh-Walker; *b* 29 Oct 1952; *Educ* Rosemead Sch Littlehampton, Univ of Keele (BA), LSE (Dip Personnel Mgmnt); *m* 16 June 1980, Timothy Congreve Stephenson, *qv*; 3 s (Christopher (Kit) b 2 Feb 1983, William b 8 July 1985, James b 1 Dec 1989); *Career* dir: Good Relations Technol 1978–85, The Communication Group 1985–89; head corp communications Blue Arrow plc 1988–89, md Millbank Public Relations (MBO of Royle Communications) 1990–; chm S London Ctee for the Employment of People with Disabilities 1994–; AIPM, MIPR; *Recreations* reading, theatre; *Style*— Miss Diana Soltmann; ✉ Millbank Public Relations Ltd, 33 Great Portland Street, London W1N 6EY (☎ 0171 436 2100, fax 0171 436 2600)

SOLWAY, Gordon R; *Career* The Boots Company plc: joined 1961, dir 1979–, i/c N American pharmaceuticals ops 1986–91, md Boots Pharmaceuticals 1992–95; md Knoll Pharmaceuticals 1995–96, ret; *Style*— Gordon Solway, Esq

SOLYMAR, Prof Laszlo; *b* 24 Jan 1930; *Educ* Tech Univ of Budapest (Dip of Electrical Engrg, PhD); *m* 2 da (Gillian Kathy Lacey-Solymar b 1963, Lucy Suzanne Solymar b 1970); *Career* lectr Tech Univ Budapest 1952–53; res engr: Res Inst for Telecommunications Budapest 1953–56, Standard Telecommunications Laboratories Ltd Harlow Essex 1956–66; Univ of Oxford: fell and tutor BNC 1966–86, lectr Dept of Engrg Sci 1971–86, Donald Pollock reader in engrg sci Dept of Engrg Sci 1986–, professorial fell Hertford Coll 1986–, prof of applied electromagnetism 1992–; visiting positions and consultancies: visiting prof Laboratoire de Physique Ecole Normale Superieure Univ of Paris 1965–66, visiting prof Tech Univ of Denmark 1972–73, conslt Tech Univ of Denmark 1973–76, visiting scientist Thomson-CSF Res Laboratories Orsay France 1984, conslt BT Res Laboratories 1986–88, conslt Hirst Res Laboratories GEC 1986–88, visiting prof Dept of Physics Univ of Osnabruck Germany 1987, visiting prof Optical Inst Tech Univ Berlin 1990, conslt Pilkington plc 1990, visiting prof Dept of Physics of Materials Univ Autonoma Madrid 1993/95; author of 3 radio plays for BBC Radio 4 (with late John Wain) 1991: Anaxagoras, Archimedes, Hypatia; Winner Faraday Medal IEE 1992; FIEE 1978, FRS 1995; *Books* Lectures on the Electrical Properties of Materials (with D Walsh, 1 edn 1970), Superconductive Tunnelling and Applications (1972), A Review of the Principles of Electrical and Electronic Engineering (4 volumes, ed, 1974), Lectures on Electromagnetic Theory (1 edn, 1976), Volume Holography and Volume Gratings (with D J Cooke, 1981), Solutions Manual to Accompany Lectures on the Electrical Properties of Materials (1988) Lectures on Fourier Series (1989); *Recreations* languages, twentieth century history particularly that of the Soviet Union, theatre, chess, skiing, swimming; *Style*— Prof Laszlo Solymar; ✉ Department of Engineering Science, University of Oxford, Oxford OX1 3PJ (☎ 01865 273110, fax 01865 273905)

SOMERLEYTON, 3 Baron (UK 1916); Sir Savile William Francis Crossley; 4 Bt (UK 1863), KCVO (1994), JP (Lowestoft), DL (Suffolk 1964); s of 2 Baron, MC, DL (d 1959), and Bridget, Baroness Somerleyton (d 1983); *b* 17 Sept 1928; *Educ* Eton; *m* 1963, Belinda Maris, da of late Vivian Loyd, of Kingsmoor, Ascot; 1 s (Hon Hugh b 1971), 4 da (Hon Isabel (Hon Mrs (Mark) Cator) b 1964, Hon Camilla (Hon Mrs Sandy Soames) b 1967, Hon Alicia b 1969, Hon Louisa b 1974); *Heir* s, Hon Hugh Francis Savile Crossley b 27 Sept 1971 (page of honour to HM The Queen 1983–84); *Career* cmmnd Coldstream Gds 1948, Capt 1956; former co cnllr E Suffolk, non-political lord-in-waiting to HM The Queen (permanent) 1978–91; Master of the Horse 1991–; farmer; patron of one living; dir Essex and Suffolk Water plc; landowner (5000 acres); *Recreations* hunting, shooting; *Clubs* Pratt's, White's; *Style*— The Rt Hon the Lord Somerleyton, KCVO, JP, DL; ✉ Somerleyton Hall, nr Lowestoft, Suffolk NR32 5QQ (☎ 01502 730308/730224, fax 01502 732143)

SOMERS COCKS, Hon Anna Gwenllian (Hon Mrs Allemandi); da of John Sebastian Somers Cocks, CVO, CBE (d 1964), and Marjorie Olive, *née* Weller, and sister of 9 Baron Somers; raised to the rank of a baron's da 1996; *b* 18 April 1950; *Educ* Convent of the Sacred Heart Woldingham, St Anne's Coll Oxford (MA), Courtauld Inst Univ of London (MA); *m* 1, 1971 (m dis 1977), Martin Alan Walker; m 2, 1978 (m dis 1990), John Julian Savile Lee Hardy; 1 s (Maximilian John Lee b 10 Feb 1980), 1 da (Katherine Isabella Eugenia b 15 Feb 1982); m 3, 30 Nov 1991, Umberto Allemandi; *Career* asst keeper: Dept of Metalwork V & A 1973–85, Dept of Ceramics V & A 1985–87; ed Apollo 1987–90, ed-in-chief The Art Newspaper 1994–95 and 1996– (ed

1990–95), chm Umberto Allemandi & Co Publishing (publishers of The Art Newspaper) 1995–; memb Cons Advsy Ctee on the Arts and Heritage; expert advsr to Heritage Lottery Fund; memb Worshipful Co of Goldsmiths 1989; FSA; *Publications* The Victoria and Albert Museum - The Making of the Collection (1980), Princely Magnificence - Court Jewels of the Renaissance (ed and jt author, 1980), Renaissance Jewels, Gold Boxes and Objets de Vertu in the Thyssen Bornemisza Collection (1985); *Recreations* skiing, entertaining, travelling, walking; *Clubs* Reform; *Style*— Hon Anna Somers Cocks, FSA; ✉ San Defendente 52, Canale d'Alba, Piedmont, Italy

SOMERSET, David Henry FitzRoy; s of Brig Hon Nigel FitzRoy Somerset, CBE, DSO, MC (d 1990; s of 3 Baron Raglan), and Phyllis Marion Offley, *née* Irwin (d 1979); *b* 19 June 1930; *Educ* Wellington Coll, Peterhouse Cambridge (MA); *m* 1955, Ruth Ivy, da of Wilfred Robert Wildbur (d 1978), of King's Lynn, Norfolk; 1 s (Henry b 1961), 1 da (Louise b 1956); *Career* joined Bank of England 1952, personal asst to md of Int Monetary Fund Washington DC 1959–62, private sec to govr of Bank of England 1962–63, chief cashier and chief of Banking Dept Bank of England 1980–88 (ret 1988); dir: Prolific Group plc 1988–93, Yamaichi Bank (UK) plc 1988–95; chm London Advsy Bd Bank Julius Baer & Co Ltd 1991–; cmmr English Heritage 1988–91; fell and fin advsr Peterhouse Cambridge 1988–; memb Cncl of Friends of Peterhouse 1981–, chm Old Wellingtonian Soc 1988–, govr Wellington Coll 1989–; FCIB; *Recreations* gardening, shooting, racing; *Clubs* Boodle's; *Style*— D H F Somerset, Esq; ✉ White Wickets, Boars Head, Crowborough, Sussex TN6 3HE (☎ 01892 661111, fax 01892 667281)

SOMERSET, Hon Geoffrey; 2 surv s of 4 Baron Raglan, JP (d 1964); bro and hp of 5 Baron Raglan, JP, DL; *b* 29 Aug 1932; *Educ* Westminster, RAC Cirencester; *m* 6 Oct 1956, Caroline Rachel, o da of Col Edward Roderick Hill, DSO, JP, DL, of Stanford-in-the-Vale, Oxon; 1 s (Arthur b 27 April 1960), 2 da (Belinda (Mrs Nicholas Boyd) b 9 Feb 1958, Lucy b 8 Feb 1963); *Career* Nat Serv with Grenadier Gds 1952–54; instr Standard Motor Co Ltd Coventry 1958–60, gp marketing mangr Lambourn Engrg Gp 1960–71, dir Trenchermans Ltd 1971–79, underwriting memb of Lloyd's 1981; memb: Berks CC 1966–75 (chm Children's Ctee and Mental Welfare Sub Ctee), Newbury Dist Cncl 1979–83 (chm Recreation and Amenities Ctee), Oxfordshire Valuation Court 1988–, Oxfordshire CC 1988–93; Freeman City of London, Liveryman Worshipful Co of Skinners 1968; *Recreations* shooting, gardening, conservation; *Style*— The Hon Geoffrey Somerset; ✉ Manor Farm, Stanford-in-the-Vale, Faringdon, Oxon SN7 8NN (☎ 01367 710558, fax 01367 710116)

SOMERSET, Jane, Duchess of; Gwendoline Collette (Jane); *née* Thomas; 2 da of late Maj John Cyril Collette Thomas, N Staffordshire Regt, of Burn Cottage, Bude, Cornwall; *m* 18 Dec 1951, 18 Duke of Somerset (d 1984); 2 s (19 Duke, Lord Francis Seymour), 1 da (Lady Anne Seymour); *Style*— Her Grace Jane, Duchess of Somerset; ✉ Bradley Cottage, Maiden Bradley, Warminster, Wiltshire BA12 7HW

SOMERSET, 19 Duke of (E 1547); Sir John Michael Edward Seymour; 17 Bt (E 1611), DL (Wilts 1993); also Baron Seymour (E 1547); s of 18 Duke of Somerset, DL (d 1984), and Gwendoline Collette (Jane), née Thomas; *b* 30 Dec 1952; *Educ* Eton; *m* 20 May 1978, Judith-Rose, da of John Hull; 2 s (Lord Seymour, Lord Charles Thomas George b 1992), 2 da (Lady Sophia b 1987, Lady Henrietta Charlotte b 1989); *Heir* s, Sebastian Edward, Lord Seymour, b 3 Feb 1982; *Career* pres RFS 1993–; FRICS; *Style*— His Grace the Duke of Somerset, DL; ✉ c/o House of Lords, London SW1

SOMERSET JONES, Eric; QC (1978); s of late Daniel and late Florence Somerset Jones; *Educ* Birkenhead Inst, Lincoln Coll Oxford (MA); *m* 1966, Brenda Marion, da of late Hedley Shimmin; 2 da (Wendy b 1967, Felicity b 1970); *Career* served RAF Coll Cranwell, link trainer instr SE Asia Cmd; called to the Bar Middle Temple 1952, Bencher 1988; memb Lord Chllr's County Cts Rule Ctee 1975–78, recorder Crown Ct (authorised for Official Referee business) 1975–; memb Gen Cncl of the Bar 1991–93; *Recreations* family pursuits, travel, listening to music, photography; *Clubs* Royal Chester Rowing; *Style*— Eric Somerset Jones, Esq, QC; ✉ Goldsmith Building, Temple, London EC4Y 7BL (☎ 0171 353 7881, fax 0171 353 5319); Southmead, Mill Lane, Willaston Wirral, Cheshire L64 1RL (☎ and fax 0151 327 5138); 12 Marryat Square, London SW6 6UA (☎ 0171 381 5360)

SOMERTON, Viscount; James Shaun Christian Welbore Ellis Agar; s and h of 6 Earl of Normanton; *b* 7 Sept 1982; *Style*— Viscount Somerton

SOMERVILLE, Ian Christopher; *b* 2 Oct 1948; *Educ* St Edwards Coll Liverpool, Imperial Coll London (BSc); *m* 11 July 1970, Felicity Ann; *Career* taxation mangr Arthur Andersen & Co (London and Manchester) 1976–82, VAT ptnr Coopers & Lybrand 1985– (sr taxation mangr 1982–85); sometime chm Stockport Family Practitioner Ctee, memb Ctee Family Welfare Assoc Manchester 1980–85; chm: N Cheshire Branch BIM 1984–85, Nat Tech Ctee of the VAT Practitioners' Gp 1992–96; FCA 1978 (ACA 1973), FIMgt 1984; *Books* Tolley's VAT Planning (contrib, 1986–96), ICAEW Taxation Service (contrib, 1988–91), VAT Planning For Property Transactions (Woodhead Faulkner, 1990), The 1993 EC VAT System: Are You Ready? (1992); *Recreations* music, gardening, cats; *Style*— Ian Somerville, Esq; ✉ Coopers & Lybrand, 9 Greyfriars Road, Reading RG1 1JG (☎ 0118 959 7111, fax 0118 960 7700)

SOMERVILLE, Dr Jane; da of Capt Bertram Platnauer, MC, of London, and Pearl Annie, *née* Backler (d 1969); *b* 24 Jan 1933; *Educ* Queen's Coll London, Guy's Hosp Med Sch London (MB BS, MD); *m* 2 Feb 1957, Walter Somerville, s of Patrick Somerville (d 1954), of Dublin; 3 s (Lorne b 1963, Rowan b 1966, Crispin b 1972), 1 da (Kate b 1961); *Career* sr lectr Inst of Cardiology London 1964–74, hon conslt physician Hosp For Sick Children 1968–88; hon sr lectr: Nat Heart and Lung Inst Univ of London 1974–, Inst of Child Health until 1988; conslt physician and cardiologist Royal Brompton and Nat Heart Hosp (formerly Nat Heart Hosp) 1974–, conslt cardiologist St Bartholomew's 1988–; memb Ctee on Cardiology RCP 1985–90, advsr on congenital heart disease for The Sec of State's Hon Med Advsy Panel On Driving And Disorders Of The Cardiovascular System 1986; chm Working Party Grown Up Congenital Heart Defects for British Cardiac Soc, chm Working Gp Grown Up Congenital Heart Disease European Soc of Cardiologists; memb Bd of Govrs Queen's Coll London; FACC 1972, FRCP 1973; *Recreations* collecting blue opaline and objet d'art, studying Fabergé, growing orchids, roof gardening; *Style*— Dr Jane Somerville; ✉ Director of Grown Up Congenital Heart Unit, Royal Brompton National Heart and Lung Hospital, Sydney St, London SW3 6NP (☎ 0171 351 8602/8600/8200, fax 0171 351 8201)

SOMERVILLE, Julia; *b* 1947; *Career* newscaster; BBC 1973–87, with ITN 1987–; *Style*— Ms Julia Somerville; ✉ ITN, 200 Gray's Inn Road, London WC1X 8XZ (☎ 0171 833 3000)

SOMERVILLE, Julian John Fitzgerald; s of Michael Fitzgerald Somerville, of Alfredston Place, Wantage, Oxon, and Barbara, *née* Gregg (d 1982); *b* 21 June 1944; *Educ* Kings Sch Canterbury, Trinity Coll Dublin (BA, MB BCh, MA, MD, FRCSEd); *m* 29 Aug 1970, (Irene) Dione, da of Willoughby Eric O'Connell Cole Powell (d 1954); 1 s (Nigel John Powell b 12 May 1972), 1 da (Grainne b 26 May 1975); *Career* Maj RAMC TA (joined 1973); internship Sir Patrick Duns Hosp Dublin 1970–71, anatomy demonstrator Trinity Coll Dublin 1971–72, res fell Sir Patrick Duns Hosp Dublin 1972–73, surgical and urological registrar King Edward VIII Hosp Durban SA 1973–81, registrar and sr registrar in Urology Leeds Gen Infirmary Yorks 1981–85; conslt urologist Halifax Gen Hosp Yorks 1985–; memb: BMA, Br Assoc of Urological Surgns 1982; *Recreations* sailing; *Style*— Julian Somerville, Esq; ✉ White Chimneys, Rawson Ave, Halifax, West Yorkshire HX3 0LR (☎ 01422 341997); The BUPA Hospital, Elland, nr Halifax, W Yorkshire HX5 9EB (☎ 01422 375577)

SOMERVILLE, Dr Kevin William; *b* 21 Nov 1950; *Educ* Lynfield Coll Auckland, Univ of Auckland (sr scholar in human biology, BSc, MB ChB, Beecham prize in physiology, sr prize in med, T W J Johnson prize in postgraduate med), Univ of Nottingham (DM); *Career* house offr posts in Auckland and Nelson 1974–76, med registrar Auckland and Greenlane Hosps 1976–79, clinical research fell Gastrointestinal Unit Western General Hosp Edinburgh 1979–80, lectr and hon sr registrar Dept of Therapeutics Univ of Nottingham 1981–85, conslt gen physician Middlemore Hosp Auckland 1986, sr registrar Div of Geriatric Med Radcliffe Infirmary Oxford 1986–89, sr lectr Dept of Med Bart's Med Coll and London Sch of Med and Dentistry 1989–, clinical dir Dept of Med for the Elderly Bart's NHS Gp 1989–95; research and pubns on disease aetiology and pharmaco-epidemiology in older people; Elizabeth Brown Prize Br Geriatrics Soc 1987; memb: Br Geriatrics Soc, American Geriatrics Soc, Christian Med Fellowship, E London and The City Ethics Ctee; FRACP 1981, FRCP 1995; *Style*— Dr Kevin Somerville; ✉ Department of Medicine for the Elderly, St Bartholomew's Hospital Medical College, West Smithfield, London EC1A 7BE (☎ 0171 601 7842, fax 0171 601 8465)

SOMERVILLE, Brig Sir (John) Nicholas; kt (1985), CBE (1978); yr s of Brig Desmond Henry Sykes Somerville, CBE, MC (d 1976), of Skibbereen, Co Cork, and Moira Burke, *née* Roche (d 1976); *b* 16 Jan 1924; *Educ* Winchester; *m* 6 Aug 1951, Jenifer Dorothea, da of Capt W M Nash, OBE, of Skibbereen, Co Cork; 1 s (Robin b 1959), 2 da (Philippa b 1953, Penelope b 1954); *Career* enlisted 1942, cmmnd 2 Lt 24 Regt SWB 1943, active serv D Day to VE Day intelligence offr (later Adj and Co Cdr) 1944–45, signal offr (later Adj) 1 SWB Palestine and Cyprus 1945–48, instr RMA Sandhurst 1949–52, Staff Coll Camberley 1954, DA & QMG (ops and plans) BAOR 1955–57, Co Cdr 1 SWB Malayan Emergency 1958–59, Brevet Lt-Col 1963, jssc 1963, GSO1 (plans) HQ FARELF 1964–66, CO 1 SWB Hong Kong and Aden 1966–68, instr Jt Servs Staff Coll 1969, cmdt Jr Div Staff Coll 1970–73, Brig dir army recruiting 1973–76, Regular Cmmns Bd 1976–79; devpt co-ordinator Royal Cwlth Soc 1980–81, md Saladin Security Ltd 1981–85, self-employed conslt personnel selection 1985–, voluntary conslt on Parly Selection Bd Procedure Cons Pty; *Recreations* sailing; *Clubs* Landsdowne; *Style*— Brig Sir Nicholas Somerville, CBE; ✉ Deptford Cottage, Deptford Lane, Hook, Hants RG29 1BS (☎ 01256 702796)

SONDHEIMER, Prof Ernst Helmut; s of Max Sondheimer (d 1982), and Ida, *née* Oppenheimer (d 1993); *b* 8 Sept 1923; *Educ* Univ Coll Sch, Trinity Coll Cambridge (MA, PhD, ScD); *m* 18 Aug 1950, Janet Harrington, da of Edgar Harrington Matthews (d 1968); 1 s (Julian b 1952), 1 da (Judith (Mrs Robertson) b 1956); *Career* WWII Cavendish Laboratory Cambridge 1944–45; fell Trinity Coll Cambridge 1948–52; Univ of London: lectr in mathematics Imperial Coll of Science and Technol 1951–54, reader in applied maths Queen Mary Coll 1954–60, prof of maths Westfield Coll 1960–82 (prof emeritus 1982–); ed Alpine Journal 1986–91; memb Highgate Literary and Sci Inst; fell: King's Coll London 1985–, Queen Mary and Westfield Coll London 1989–; memb London Mathematical Soc 1963–; *Books* Green's Functions for Solid State Physicists (with S Doniach, 1974), Numbers and Infinity (with A Rogerson, 1981), papers on the electron theory of metals; *Recreations* mountains, growing alpines, reading history; *Clubs* Arts, Alpine; *Style*— Prof Ernst Sondheimer; ✉ 51 Cholmeley Crescent, London N6 5EX (☎ 0181 340 6607)

SONNABEND, Yolanda; da of late Dr H Sonnabend, and late Dr F Sandler; *b* 26 March 1935, Rhodesia; *Educ* Eveline HS Rhodesia, Académie des Beaux-Arts Geneva, McGill Univ, Slade Sch of Fine Art London (Boise post grad travelling scholarship); *Career* artist; visiting tutor: Camberwell Sch of Art 1964–70, Central Sch of Art (stage design) 1969–; lectr Slade Sch of Fine Art 1988–; Travel award to Venice 1977, Br Cncl grant to Prague (Baroque Theatre) 1979, Arts Cncl bursary to Geneva (mask making) 1979; *Solo Exhibitions* Whitechapel Art Gallery 1975, Serpentine Gallery 1985–86, Fischer Fine Art 1989; numerous gp exhibitions 1956–, designed plays, operas and ballet; ballet designs incl: Requiem, My Brother My Sisters, Swan Lake (Royal Ballet) 1987, costumes for Bayadère (Royal Ballet) 1988; *Public Collections* Arts Cncl of GB, British Cncl, Theatre Museum, V & A, Nat Portrait Gallery (portraits incl Stephen Hawkings and Sir Kenneth Macmillan), Science Museum, Unilever, Library of Performing Arts, Lincoln Center NYC, Unilever; *Style*— Ms Yolanda Sonnabend

SOOKE, Thomas Peter; s of Dr Paul Sooke (d 1992), of London, and Gertrude, *née* Klinger (d 1969); *b* 8 Jan 1945; *Educ* Westminster, Pembroke Coll Cambridge (MA), Columbia Univ New York (MBA); *m* 6 June 1975, Ceridwen Leeuwke, da of Derek Matthews; 1 s (Alastair b 1981), 1 da (Leonie b 1985); *Career* Price Waterhouse 1968–70, Wallace Bros Bank 1972–76, dir Granville Holdings plc and Venture Funds 1976–87 (co fndr Br Venture Capital Assoc 1983), corp fin ptnr Deloitte & Touche 1988–91, fndr ptnr CitiCourt & Co 1991–; non exec dir Baronsmead Investment Trust plc, Quester VCT plc and private cos; FCA 1979; *Recreations* tennis, golf, old watercolours; *Clubs* United Oxford and Cambridge, Isle of Purbeck Golf; *Style*— Thomas Sooke, Esq; ✉ CitiCourt & Co, 190 Strand, London WC2R 1JN (☎ 0171 240 2791, fax 0171 240 2792)

SOOLE, Michael Alexander; s of Brian Alfred Seymour Soole (d 1974), and Rosemary Una, *née* Salt; *b* 18 July 1954; *Educ* Berkhamsted Sch, Univ Coll Oxford (MA); *Career* called to the Bar Inner Temple 1977, practising barr 1978–; Parly candidate Aylesbury (SDP/Liberal Alliance) general elections 1983 and 1987; pres Oxford Union 1974, memb Bd Christian Aid 1991–; *Recreations* conversation, beagling; *Style*— Michael Soole, Esq; ✉ 9 Charlton Place, London N1 8AQ (☎ 0171 359 0759); 5 Bell Yard, London WC2A 2JR (☎ 0171 333 8811, fax 0171 333 8831)

SOOTHILL, Prof Peter William; *b* 30 Oct 1957; *Educ* Guy's Hosp Med Sch London (MB BS), Univ of London (BSc, MD, MRCOG); *Career* KCH London: lectr then hon sr registrar in obstetrics and gynaecology and dir Day Assessment Unit 1989–91, subspeciality fell/sr registrar in fetal med 1991–92; sr lectr in obstetrics and gynaecology UCL Med Sch and Inst of Child Health Univ of London 1992–95, hon conslt UCH (dir Fetal Med Unit) and Gt Ormand St Hosp London 1992–95, prof of maternal and fetal med Univ of Bristol 1995–; author of numerous articles in learned jls; *Style*— Prof P W Soothill; ✉ University Department of Obstetrics and Gynaecology, Fetal Medicine Research Unit, St Michael's Hospital, Southwell Street, Bristol BS2 8EG (☎ 0117 928 5513, fax 0117 928 5683)

SOPER, Baron (Life Peer UK 1965), of Kingsway, London Borough of Camden; Rev Donald Oliver Soper; s of Ernest Frankham Soper (d 1962), of Wallington, Surrey, and Caroline Amelia, *née* Pilcher; *b* 31 Jan 1903; *Educ* Haberdashers' Aske's, St Catharine's Coll Cambridge, Wesley House Cambridge, LSE (PhD); *m* 3 Aug 1929, Marie Gertrude (d 1994), da of late Arthur Dean, of Norbury; 4 da (Hon Ann Loveday Dean (Hon Mrs Horn) b 15 April 1931, Hon Bridget Mary Dean (Hon Mrs Kemmis) b 17 Dec 1933, Hon Judith Catharine Dean (Hon Mrs Jenkins) b 25 Oct 1942, Hon Caroline Susan Dean (Hon Mrs Blacker) b 11 Aug 1946); *Career* sits as Lab Peer in House of Lords; min: South London Mission 1926–29, Central London Mission 1929–36; supt min W London Mission 1936–78, chm Shelter 1974–78; pres: League Against Cruel Sports, Christian Socialist Movement, Fellowship of Reconciliation, Methodist Conference (1953); World Methodist Peace Prize 1982; open-air speaker: Tower Hill every Wednesday for last 70 years, Hyde Park every Sunday; Hon DD Cambridge; *Books* Aflame with Faith, It is Hard to Work for God, The Advocacy of the Gospel, All His Grace, Christianity and Politics, Calling for Action (Autobiography),

Practical Christianity Today, Will Christianity Work?; *Style*— The Rev the Rt Hon the Lord Soper; ✉ 19 Thayer Street, London W1M 5LJ

SOPER, Rt Rev (Andrew) Laurence; OSB; s of Alan Soper, of Angmering-on-Sea, W Sussex, and Anne, *née* Morris; *Educ* St Benedict's Sch Ealing, St Benet's Hall Oxford, Collegio Sant Anselmo Rome (STL, STD), St Mary's Twickenham (PGCE); *Career* Barclays Bank 1960–64; entered monastery Ealing 1964; ordained: deacon (Assisi) 1969, priest 1970; St Benedict's Abbey Sch Ealing: teacher 1973–83, bursar 1975–91, master i/c St Benedict's Middle Sch 1978–84, prior 1984–91, abbot 1991–, episcopal vicar for Religious in Archdiocese of Westminster Western Area 1995; del to Gen Chapter (sec) 1985 and 1989; pt/t chaplain Harrow Sch 1981–91, asst visiting chaplain Feltham Young Offenders Instn 1988–; chm Union of Monastic Superiors 1995–; Freeman City of Norcia Italy; FRSA 1975; *Books* The Thoughts of Jesus Christ (1970), T H Green as Theologian (1972); *Recreations* walking; *Style*— The Rt Rev Laurence Soper, OSB; ✉ Ealing Abbey, Charlbury Grove, Ealing, London W5 2DY (☎ 0181 862 2100)

SOPHER, Ivan; s of James Joseph Sopher, of 22 Manor Hall Ave, London, and Sophie Sopher; *b* 27 Aug 1949; *m* 1973, Helen; 1 s, 2 da; *Career* sole proprietor Ivan Sopher & Co CAs; dir: Professional Publications Ltd, Delta Financial Management plc, DJS Securities Ltd; FCA, FCCA, ATII, MIMgt; *Recreations* travel, sport; *Style*— Ivan Sopher, Esq; ✉ 5 Elstree Gate, Elstree Way, Borehamwood, Herts WD6 1JD

SORABJI, Prof Richard Rustom Kharsedji; s of Prof Richard Kaikushru Sorabji (d 1950), of Oxford, and Mary Katharine Monkhouse (d 1990); *b* 8 Nov 1934; *Educ* Charterhouse, Pembroke Coll Oxford (BA, BPhil); *m* 1958, Margaret Anne Catherine, da of Kenneth Taster (d 1958); 1 s (Richard Jon Francis b 29 March 1959), 2 da (Cornelia Katharine b 23 Dec 1961, Tahmina Lucy b 28 Dec 1964); *Career* positions rising to assoc prof with tenure Sage Sch of Philosophy Cornell Univ NY 1962–69; Univ of London: positions rising to current position of prof of ancient philosophy Dept of Philosophy KCL 1970–, chm Bd of Philosophical Studies 1979–82, head Philosophy Dept KCL 1984–85 (acting head 1975, 1983 and 1987), designer and first dir King's Coll Centre for Philosophical Studies 1989–91, fell KCL 1990–, dir Inst of Classical Studies 1991–; pres Aristotelian Soc 1985–86, fndr and organiser Int Project on the Aristotle Commentators 1985–; memb Common Room: Wolfson Coll Oxford 1991–, Pembroke Coll Oxford 1992–; sr fell Cncl of Humanities Princeton Univ 1985, sr res fell Soc of the Humanities Cornell Univ 1979, Townsend lectr Cornell Univ 1991; Choice Award for Outstanding Academic Books 1989–90; FBA 1989; *Books* Aristotle on Memory (1972), Articles on Aristotle (co-ed, 4 vols, 1975–79), Necessity, Cause and Blame (1980), Time, Creation and the Continuum (1983), Philoponus and the Rejection of Aristotelian Science (ed, 1987), Aristotle Transformed: The Ancient Commentators and Their Influence (ed, 1989) Translations of the Ancient Commentators on Aristotle (ed of 21 vols, 40 more in prep, 1987–), Matter, Space and Motion (1988), Animal Minds and Human Morals (1993); *Recreations* archaeology, architecture; *Style*— Prof Richard Sorabji, FBA; ✉ Department of Philosophy, King's College, Strand, London WC2R 2LS (☎ 0171 873 2231, fax 0171 836 1799)

SORENSEN, Eric; *b* 1944; *Educ* Bedford Sch, Univ of Keele (BA); *m*; 2 s, 1 da; *Career* voluntary work in India then various posts DOE, private sec to Rt Hon Peter Shore as Sec of State for the Environment 1977, regnl dir Manchester Office Depts of Environment and Tport 1980–81, head Merseyside Task Force 1981–84, head Inner Cities Directorate (responsible for DOE urban policy) 1984–87, head of Cabinet Office Urban Policy Unit 1987–88, dir of personnel DOE 1988–90, dep sec Housing and Construction Command 1990–91, chief exec London Docklands Devpt Corp 1991–; *Style*— Eric Sorensen, Esq; ✉ London Docklands Development Corporation, Thames Quay, 191 Marsh Wall, London E14 9TJ (☎ 0171 512 3000, fax 0171 512 0777)

SORENSEN, (Nils Jorgen) Philip; *see:* Philip Sorensen, (Nils Jorgen) Philip

SORKIN, (Alexander) Michael; s of Joseph Sorkin, of London (d 1984), and Hilda Ruth, *née* Fiebusch; *b* 2 March 1943; *Educ* St Paul's Manchester Univ (BA); *m* 27 Nov 1977, Angela Lucille, da of Leon Berman (MC), of London; 1 s (Jacob b 1983), 2 da (Zoe b 1979, Kim b 1980); *Career* Hambros Bank Ltd: joined 1968, dir 1973, exec dir 1983, vice chm 1987–95, dep chm 1995–; dir Hambros PLC 1986–; *Recreations* opera, golf, tennis; *Style*— Michael Sorkin, Esq; ✉ Hambros Bank Ltd, 41 Tower Hill, London EC3N 4HA (☎ 0171 480 5000, fax 0171 702 9262)

SORRELL, John W; CBE (1996); *m* Frances Newell, *qv*; 3 c; *Career* fndr and co chm Newell & Sorrell Ltd (identity and design consits) 1976–; vice pres CSD 1989–92; chm: DBA 1990–92, Design Cncl 1994–; memb: BR Architecture and Design Panel 1991–93, RSA Design Advsy Gp 1991–93; govr Design Dimension 1991–93; speaker and lectr on corporate identity: Mgmnt Res Gp Inst of Mgmnt, Elisava Sch of Design Barcelona, Singapore Design Forum; chm DTI Trade Mission to India; hon memb Romanian Design Centre; memb: D&AD, Strategic Planning Soc, IOD; FCSD, FRSA; *Recreations* arboriculture, Arsenal, art; *Clubs* Groucho; *Style*— John Sorrell, Esq, CBE; ✉ Newell & Sorrell Ltd, 4 Utopia Village, Chalcot Rd, London NW1 8LH (☎ 0171 722 1113, fax 0171 722 0259)

SORRELL, Martin Stuart; s of Jack Sorrell, of Mill Hill, London NW7; *b* 14 Feb 1945; *Educ* Haberdashers' Aske's, Christ's Coll Cambridge, Harvard Business Sch; *m* 1971, Sandra Carol Ann, *née* Finestone; 3 s; *Career* gp fin dir Saatchi & Saatchi Co plc (business serv) 1977–86, gp chief exec WPP Group plc (mktg servs) 1986–; non-exec dir Storehouse plc 1994–; memb: Governing Body London Business Sch, Advsy Bd Instituto de Estudios Superiores de la Empresa (IESE), Advsy Bd Judge Inst for Mgmnt Studies; tstee: Univ of Cambridge Fndn, Princess Royal Tst for Carers; *Recreations* skiing; *Clubs* Reform, Harvard, MCC; *Style*— Martin Sorrell, Esq; ✉ WPP Group plc, 27 Farm St, London W1X 6RD (☎ 0171 408 2204)

SORRELL, Richard; s of Alan Sorrell (d 1994), of Thundersley, Essex, and Elizabeth, *née* Tanner (d 1971); *b* 24 Sept 1948; *Educ* Eton House Sch Thorpe Bay Essex, Walthamstow Art Sch, Kingston Coll of Art (DipAD Fine Art), Royal Acad Schs (Post Grad Cert, bronze and silver medals); *m* 1974, Dodie, da of Michael Burke; 2 s (William b 1978, Edmund b 1981); *Career* artist (painter, draughtsman and printmaker) 1972–; memb Art Workers' Guild, ctee memb Nat Artists' Assoc 1995–; RWS 1978 (ARWS 1975), RBA 1989 (ARBA 1988), NEAC 1995; *Works* aerial views incl Blickling Hall, Ickworth and Uppark (all for National Tst), Stonor Park for Lord Camoys, Antony House for Sir Richard Carew-Pole, Settrington House for Sir Richard Storey, Buscot Park for Lord Faringdon, Summer Fields Sch Oxford, Channel Tunnel workings Shakespeare Cliff for V&A; *Exhibitions* incl: Royal Acad 1971–, Royal Watercolour Soc 1975–, Royal Soc of Br Artists 1988–, Nat Portrait Gallery 1980, 1983 and 1984, Lutyens Exhbn Hayward Gallery 1980, Artists in National Parks (V&A) 1988, Agnews 1990, Cadogan Gallery 1982; *Collections* work in public collections incl: V&A, Museum of London, National Tst, Worshipful Co of Fishmongers; *Style*— Richard Sorrell, Esq

SORRIE, Dr George Strath; CB (1993); s of Alexander James Sorrie (d 1945), and Florence Edith, *née* Strath (d 1994); *b* 19 May 1933; *Educ* Robert Gordon's Coll Aberdeen, Univs of Aberdeen, London and Dundee (MB ChB, DPH, DIH, FFOM); *m* 22 Sept 1959, Gabrielle Ann, da of late James Baird; 3 da (Rosalind b 1961, Ann b 1962, Catherine b 1977); *Career* Flt Lt Med Branch RAF 1958–61; lectr in epidemiology Univ of London 1965–67, GP Rhynie Aberdeen 1967–73, dep dir of med servs Health and Safety Exec 1980–87 (med advsr 1973–80), dir and med advsr Civil Serv Occupational Health Serv 1987–93; FFOM RCP; *Style*— Dr George Sorrie, CB; ✉ 30 Irvine Crescent, St Andrews, Fife (☎ 01334 474510)

SOUBRY, Anna Mary; da of David Stuart Soubry (d 1985), and Frances Margaret, *née* Coward; *b* 7 Dec 1956; *Educ* Hartland Comp Worksop Notts, Univ of Birmingham (LLB); *children* 2 da (Amelia Anne Gordon b 8 July 1990, Rosamund Mary Gordon b 22 August 1991); *Career* presenter Grampian TV then Central TV; presenter: Heart of the Country, Central Weekend, This Morning, The Time The Place, Speak Out, Crimestalker II, Right or Wrong; exec NUS 1980, hon pres Univ of Stirling 1981; *Recreations* cooking, eating, football, music; *Style*— Ms Anna Soubry; ✉ c/o Julie Irelaw-Chapman, The Ship, 74 Vicarage Road, Pitstone, Beds LU7 9EY (☎ 01296 662441)

SOUHAMI, Mark J; s of John F Souhami (d 1996), and Freda Souhami; *b* 25 Sept 1935; *Educ* St Marylebone GS; *m* 1964, Margaret, da of Joseph Austin; 2 da (Emma b 1966, Charlotte b 1968); *Career* Dixons Group plc: joined as gp mktg dir 1970, md Retail Div 1973, gp main bd dir 1978–, gp md 1986–92, dep chm 1992– (pt/t 1994–); chm Br Retail Consortium; memb Metropolitan Police Ctee 1995; *Clubs* Savile, RAC, Naval and Military; *Style*— Mark Souhami, Esq; ✉ Dixons Group plc, 29 Farm Street, London W1X 7RD

SOULBURY, 2 Viscount (UK 1954); James Herwald Ramsbotham; also Baron Soulbury (UK 1941); s of 1 Viscount, GCMG, GCVO, OBE, MC, PC (d 1971); *b* 21 March 1915; *Educ* Eton, Magdalen Oxford; *m* 1949, Anthea Margaret (d 1950), da of late David Wilton; *Heir* bro, Hon Sir Peter Edward Ramsbotham, GCMG, GCVO, *qv*; *Style*— The Rt Hon the Viscount Soulbury; ✉ c/o The House of Lords, Westminster, London SW1

SOUNDY, Andrew John; s of Maj Harold Cecil Soundy, MBE, MC, TD (d 1969), and Adele Monica Templeton, *née* Westley; *b* 29 March 1940; *Educ* Boxgrove Sch Guildford, Shrewsbury, Trinity Coll Cambridge (BA, MA); *m* 12 Oct 1963, Jill Marion, da of Frank Nathaniel Steiner, of Gerrards Cross, Bucks; 1 s (Mark b 1964), 2 da (Emma b 1967, Victoria b 1969); *Career* admitted slr 1966; sr ptnr Ashurst Morris Crisp slrs; non-exec dir EW Fact PLC; farmer and breeder of pedigree cattle; *Recreations* opera, tennis, good living; *Clubs* Cavalry and Guards'; *Style*— Andrew J Soundy, Esq; ✉ Ashurst Morris Crisp, Broadwalk House, 5 Appold Street, London EC2A 2HA (☎ 0171 638 1111, fax 0171 972 7990, telex 887067)

SOUNESS, Graeme James; s of James Souness, and Elizabeth, *née* Ferguson (d 1984); *b* 6 May 1953; *Educ* Carrickvale Secdy Sch; *m* 1; 2 s (Fraser b 29 May 1980, Jordan Cameron b 17 March 1985), 1 da (Chantelle Karen b 20 June 1975); *m* 2, 1 June 1994, Karen Patricia; *Career* professional football manager; player: Tottenham Hotspur 1969–73, Middlesbrough 1973–78, Liverpool 1978–84, Sampdoria Italy 1984–86, Scotland 1975–86 (54 full caps); mangr: Glasgow Rangers 1986–91 (also player 1986–90), Liverpool 1991–94, Galatasaray (Turkey) 1995–96, Southampton 1996–; achievements as player for Liverpool incl: 3 Euro Cup Winners medals (v Bruges 1978, Real Madrid 1981, Roma 1984), 5 League Championship medals 1979–84, 4 League Cup winners medals 1981–84; achievements as mangr Rangers: Scottish League Championship 1987, 1989, 1990 and 1991, Skol Cup 1987, 1988, 1989 and 1990; achievements as mangr Liverpool: FA Cup 1992; achievements as mangr Galatasaray: Turkish Cup 1996; *Books* No Half Measures (with Bob Harris, 1984), A Manager's Diary (1990); *Recreations* gardening; *Style*— Graeme Souness, Esq; ✉ c/o Southampton FC, The Dell, Milton Road, Southampton SO9 4XX

SOUSTER, Peter John Robertson; s of Eric George Souster (d 1987), and Lillian, *née* Robertson; *b* 22 March 1944; *Educ* Whitgift Sch, Queens' Coll Cambridge (Golf blue); *m* 1975, Anna Geraldine, da of Andrew Frederick Smith; 1 s (Timothy Michael Peter b 1978), 1 da (Rachel Catherine Anna b 1980); *Career* Peat Marwick Mitchell: articled clerk 1966–69, Hong Kong office 1973–75, London office 1974–78; ptnr Baker Tilly (formerly Howard Tilly & Co) 1981– (joined 1978); *Books* The Responsible Director (1986, reprinted as Directors - Your Responsibilities and Liabilities,1993); *Recreations* golf, squash; *Clubs* Hawks' (Cambridge), Chartered Accountants Golfing Soc; *Style*— Peter Souster, Esq; ✉ Baker Tilly, 2 Bloomsbury Street, London WC1B 3ST (☎ 0171 413 5100, fax 0171 413 5101)

SOUTAR, Air Marshal Sir Charles John Williamson; KBE (1978, MBE 1958); s of Charles A Soutar, and Mary H Watson; *b* 12 June 1920; *Educ* Brentwood Sch, London Hosp; *m* 1944, Joy Dorée Upton; 1 s, 2 da; *Career* RAF 1946, QHS 1974–81, PMO Strike Cmd 1975–78, Dir-Gen RAF Med Servs 1978–81; CStJ 1972; *Clubs* RAF; *Style*— Air Marshal Sir Charles Soutar, KBE; ✉ Oak Cottage, High St, Aldeburgh, Suffolk

SOUTAR, (Samuel) Ian; s of James Soutar, of Ballymena, NI, and Maud, *née* McNinch (d 1992); *b* 2 June 1945; *Educ* Ballymena Acad, Trinity Coll Dublin (BA); *m* 10 August 1968, Mary Isabella, da of William Boyle (d 1951), of Ballymena, NI; 1 s (Michael b 26 Dec 1971), 1 da (Kim b 16 July 1973); *Career* FCO 1968; third sec then second sec UK Delgn to EC 1970–72, second sec Br Embassy Saigon 1972–74, first sec FCO 1974 and 1981–86, private sec to Parly Sec FCO Affrs 1976–77, first sec Br Embassy Washington DC 1977–80, dep high Cmmr Br High Cmmn Wellington NZ 1986–91, Royal Coll of Defence Studies 1991, head Info Systems Div (Ops) 1992–95, head Library and Records Dept 1995–; *Recreations* walking, listening to music; *Style*— Ian Soutar, Esq; ✉ Library and Records Department, Foreign & Commonwealth Office, Downing Street West, London SW1A 2AL (☎ 0171 270 3925)

SOUTER, Hon Amanda Elizabeth; da and co-heiress presumptive of 25 Baron Audley, *qv*; *b* 5 May 1958; *Style*— The Hon Amanda Souter; ✉ c/o Friendly Green, Cowden, nr Edenbridge, Kent TN8 7DU

SOUTER, William Alexander; s of William Souter (d 1951), and Jean Smith, *née* Troup (d 1975); *b* 11 May 1933; *Educ* George Watson's Boy's Coll Edinburgh, Univ of Edinburgh (MB ChB); *m* 12 Sept 1959, Kathleen Bruce, da of William Caird Taylor (d 1935); 1 s (Ewen b 1966), 2 da (Catriona b 1960, Lorna b 1962); *Career* sr registrar Orthopaedic Dept Edinburgh Royal Infirmary and Princess Margaret Rose Orthopaedic Hosp 1965–68, conslt orthopaedic surgn Princess Margaret Rose Orthopaedic Hosp Edinburgh 1968–, hon sr lectr Orthopaedic Dept Univ of Edinburgh, visiting prof Bioengineering Dept Univ of Strathclyde 1985–; fndr memb and first hon sec European Rheumatoid Arthritis Surgical Soc 1979–83 (pres elect 1993–95, pres 1995–), chm EULAR Standing Ctee on Surgery of Rheumatoid Disease 1987–95; memb: Editorial Bd Jl of Bone and Joint Surgery 1981–84, Cncl British Orthopaedic Assoc 1986–88 and 1993–95, Cncl Royal Coll of Surgeons of Edinburgh 1988–93 and 1993–98; first pres and memb Br Elbow and Shoulder Soc 1987–; Br Soc for Surgery of the Hand: memb Cncl 1976–78, vice pres 1992, pres 1993; Br Orthopaedic Assoc and Br Orthopaedic Res Soc 1968, Rheumatoid Arthritis Surgical Soc 1974; FRCSEd 1960; *Recreations* gardening, photography, music, skiing, golf; *Style*— Mr William A Souter; ✉ Old Mauricewood Mains, Penicuik, Midlothian EH26 0NJ (☎ 01968 672609); Consultant Orthopaedic Surgeon, Surgical Arthritis Unit, Princess Margaret Rose Orthopaedic Hosp, Frogston Rd, Edinburgh EH10 7ED (☎ 0131 536 4600, fax 0131 536 4601)

SOUTH, Sir Arthur; kt (1974), JP (Norwich 1949); s of Arthur South; *b* 29 Oct 1914; *Educ* City of Norwich Sch; *m* 1, 1937 (m dis 1976), May Adamson; 2 s; *m* 2, 1976, Mary June (d 1982), widow of Robert Carter, JP, DL; *Career* Lord Mayor of Norwich 1956–57 (cncllr 1935–41 and 1946–61); chm: Norwich, Lowestoft and Gt Yarmouth Hosp Mgmnt Ctee 1966–74 (memb 1948–74), Norfolk AHA 1974–78, E Anglian RHA 1978–87; former chm Labour Party Gp Norwich City Cncl; Hon Freeman City of Norwich 1984; Hon DCL UEA 1989; *Recreations* football, bowls, cricket; *Clubs* MCC, Mitre Bowls, Norfolk Cricket, Norwich City FC (former chm and dir); *Style*— Sir Arthur South, JP; ✉ 23 Hall Lane, Drayton, Norwich, Norfolk NR8 6DR

SOUTHAM, Prof John Chambers; s of Frank Lloyd Southam (d 1975), of Leeds, and late Marjorie, *née* Chambers; *b* 3 Feb 1934; *Educ* Leeds GS, Univ of Cambridge (MA, MD), Univ of Leeds; *m* 27 Aug 1960, Susan, da of Reginald Alfred Saxty Hill (d 1977), of Hereford; 2 s (Philip b 1963, Jeremy b 1966); *Career* lectr in oral pathology Univ of Sheffield 1963–70, dean of dental studies Univ of Edinburgh 1983–88 (sr lectr in dental surgery 1970–77, prof of oral med and pathology 1977–93), vice dean Faculty of Dental Surgns Royal Coll of Surgns Edinburgh 1994– (sec 1991–94); memb Gen Dental Cncl 1984–94; FDSRCSEd 1981, FRCPath 1983; *Books* Oral Pathology (with J V Soames, 1993); *Recreations* gardening, walking, travelling, scouting; *Clubs* Royal Society of Medicine; *Style*— Prof John Southam; ✉ 13 Corstorphine House Ave, Edinburgh EH12 7AD (☎ 0131 334 3013)

SOUTHAM, Neil Leon Fordyce; s of Leonard Walter Southam, of Chestfield, Kent, and Christina Watt, *née* Fordyce; *b* 25 March 1933; *Educ* Chislehurst and Sidcup Co GS for Boys, North London Poly (DipArch); *m* 5 March 1960, Diana Margaret, da of Leslie Horace Leslie-Smith; 4 da (Fiona Forbes, Kirsten Margaret, Morna Ann, Andrea Macpherson); *Career* GMW (formerly Gollins, Melvin and Ward): architectural asst 1956, assoc 1964, ptnr 1971, sr ptnr 1981–; Freeman City of London, Liveryman Worshipful Co of Chartered Architects; ARIBA 1970, FFB 1985; *Recreations* sailing, scuba diving, book collecting; *Clubs* Caledonian; *Style*— Neil Southam, Esq; ✉ The End, Ways End, Camberley, Surrey GU15 2JU (☎ 01276 24520); 29 Heron Place, 9 Thayer Street, London W1M 5LF; GMW Partnership, PO Box 1613, 239 Kensington High Street, London W8 6SL (☎ 0171 937 8020, fax 0171 937 5815)

SOUTHAMPTON, 6 Baron (GB 1780); Charles James FitzRoy; o s of Charles FitzRoy (d 1989), who suc as 5 Baron Southampton 1958, but disclaimed his peerage for life, and his 1 w, Margaret, *née* Drake (d 1931); *b* 12 Aug 1928; *Educ* Stowe; *m* 29 May 1951, Pamela Anne, da of late Edward Percy Henniker; 1 s (Hon Edward Charles b 8 July 1955), 1 da (Hon Geraldine Anne (Hon Mrs Fuller) 1951), and 1 s decd; *Heir* s, Hon Edward Charles FitzRoy, *qv*; *Career* Master: the Easton Harriers 1968–71, the Blankney Foxhounds 1971–72; *Style*— The Rt Hon the Lord Southampton; ✉ Stone Cross, Stone Lane, Chagford, Devon

SOUTHAN, His Hon Judge Robert Joseph; s of Thomas Southan (d 1962), of Warwicks, and Kathleen Annie, *née* Beck (d 1987); *b* 13 July 1928; *Educ* Rugby, St Edmund Hall Oxford (MA), UCL (LLM); *m* 1960, Elizabeth Andreas, da of Clive Raleigh Evatt, QC (d 1984), of Aust; 1 s (Richard b 1962, d 1984), 1 da (Anne b 1969); *Career* called to the Bar: England and Wales 1953, New South Wales 1974; recorder Crown Ct 1982, circuit judge (SE Circuit) 1986–; *Recreations* sailing, skiing, tennis, squash, theatre, opera; *Clubs* Royal Corinthian Yacht, Bar Yacht, Cumberland Lawn Tennis; *Style*— His Hon Judge Robert Southan; ✉ Harrow Crown Court, Hailsham Drive, Harrow, Middx HA1 4TU (☎ 0181 424 2294)

SOUTHBY, Sir John Richard Bilbe; 3 Bt (UK 1937), of Burford, Co Oxford; 3 Bt (UK 1937); s of Sir (Archibald) Richard Charles Southby, 2 Bt, OBE (d 1988) and his 2 w, Olive Marion (d 1991), da of late Sir Thomas Bilbe-Robinson, GBE, KCMG; *b* 2 April 1948; *Educ* Peterhouse Rhodesia, Loughborough Univ (BSc); *m* 1971, Victoria Jane, da of John Wilfred Sturrock, of Tettenhall, Wolverhampton; 2 s (Peter John b 20 Aug 1973, James William b 1984), 1 da (Sarah Jane b 1975); *Heir* s, Peter John Southby b 20 Aug 1973; *Career* currently gen mangr East Midlands Electricity plc Northampton; chm: Milton Keynes Large Employers Assoc, Milton Keynes Police Area Advisory Team; memb bd: Milton Keynes Economic Partnership, Milton Keynes Theatre & Gallery Co; FIMgt, MIEE; *Recreations* gardening, DIY, skiing, travel; *Clubs* Milton Keynes Rotary; *Style*— Sir John Southby, Bt; ✉ Lomagundi, High Street, Nash, Bucks MK17 0EP

SOUTHCOTT, Barry John; *b* 27 March 1950; *Educ* Latymer Upper Sch, Univ of Bradford (BScEcon); *m* 1978, Lesley Anne, *née* Parkinson; 2 s; *Career* investmt analyst Phillips & Drew 1971–75; CIN Management Ltd: joined 1975, md Marketable Securities Div 1983–93, chief exec 1993–; dir: British Investment Trust plc, BZW Convertible Investment Trust plc; memb: Investmt Ctee Nat Assoc of Pension Funds 1986–90, Quotations Ctee Stock Exchange 1992–, Exec Ctee Inst Fund Mgmnt Assoc 1995–; AMIIMR 1973, MSI 1993; *Style*— Barry Southcott, Esq; ✉ CIN Management Ltd, PO Box 10, Hobart House, Grosvenor Place, London SW1X 7AD (☎ 0171 245 6911)

SOUTHEND, Archdeacon of; *see:* Jennings, Ven David Willfred Michael

SOUTHERN, Sir Richard William; kt (1974); s of Matthew Henry Southern; *b* 8 Feb 1912; *Educ* Newcastle upon Tyne Royal GS, Balliol Coll Oxford; *m* 1944, Sheila, *née* Cobley, widow of Sqdn Ldr C Crichton-Miller; 2 s; *Career* served WWII: Oxford and Bucks LI, Durham LI, RAC, Political Intelligence Dept FO; historian; fell and tutor Balliol Coll Oxford 1937–61 (hon fell 1966–), jr proctor Univ of Oxford 1948–49, Birkbeck lectr in ecclesiastical history Trinity Coll Cambridge 1959–60, Chichele prof of modern history Univ of Oxford 1961–69; pres: St John's Coll Oxford 1969–81 (hon fell 1981–), Royal Historical Soc 1968–72, Selden Soc 1973–76; also hon fell: Sidney Sussex Coll Cambridge, Exeter Coll Oxford; Hon DLitt Univs of: Glasgow, Durham, Cambridge, Bristol, Newcastle upon Tyne, Warwick, Columbia, The South; Hon LLD Harvard; FBA; *Style*— Sir Richard Southern, FBA; ✉ 40 St John Street, Oxford OX1 2LH

SOUTHERN, Sir Robert; kt (1970), CBE (1953); s of Job Southern, of Whitefield; *b* 17 March 1907; *Educ* Stand GS, Co-op Coll Univ of Manchester; *m* 1933, Lena, da of George Henry Chapman, of Whitefield; 1 s, 1 da; *Career* gen-sec Co-operative Union Ltd 1948–72; *Style*— Sir Robert Southern, CBE; ✉ Spurr House, Pole Lane, Unsworth, Bury, Lancs BL9 8QL (☎ 0161 766 6652)

SOUTHESK, Earl of; David Charles Carnegie; styled Earl of Macduff 1961–92; s and h of 3 Duke of Fife, *qv* (*see* Peerage, Royal Family Section); *b* 3 March 1961; *Educ* Eton, Pembroke Coll Cambridge (MA), RAC, Univ of Edinburgh (MBA); *m* 1987, Caroline Anne, o da of Martin Bunting; 3 s (Lord Carnegie b 1 July 1989, Hon George William Carnegie b 23 March 1991, Hon Hugh Alexander Carnegie b 10 June 1993); *Heir* s, Charles Duff Carnegie, Lord Carnegie; *Career* stockbroker; formerly with Cazenove & Co and Bell Lawrie Ltd, currently CA Reeves & Neylan; memb Worshipful Co of Clothworkers, Freeman of City of London 1987; MICAS; *Style*— Earl of Southesk; ✉ Kinnaird Castle, Brechin, Angus DD9 6TZ

SOUTHEY, Sir Robert John; kt (1976), AO (1993), CMG (1970); s of late Allen Hope Southey, and late Ethel Thorpe McComas, MBE; *b* 20 March 1922; *Educ* Geelong GS, Magdalen Coll Oxford (MA); *m* 1, 1946, Valerie Janet Cotton (d 1977), da of Hon Sir Francis Grenville Clarke, KBE, MLC (d 1955); 5 s; m 2, 1982, Marigold Merlyn Baillieu, da of Sidney Myer (d 1934), and Dame (Margery) Merlyn Myer, DBE (d 1982); *Career* WWII Coldstream Gds 1941–46, served N Africa and Italy, Capt 1944; dir: Buckley & Nunn 1958–78, BP Company of Australia Ltd 1965–91, ICL (Australia) Pty Ltd 1977–90, NatWest Finance Australia Ltd 1983–85, NatWest Australia Bank Ltd 1985–87, General Accident Fire & Life Assurance Corporation plc 1968–89 (chm Aust Advsy Cncl), Wm Haughton & Co Ltd 1953–80, Kawasaki (Australia) Pty Ltd 1986–; chm NZI Insurance Australia Ltd 1989–92; memb Fed Exec Lib Pty 1966–82, pres Lib Pty Victoria 1966–70, fed pres Lib Pty 1970–75; chm: Aust Ballet Fndn 1980–90, Nat Cncl Aust Ballet 1991–95; *Recreations* music, fishing; *Clubs* Cavalry and Guards', MCC, Leander, Melbourne; *Style*— Sir Robert Southey, AO, CMG; ✉ 16 Horsburgh Grove, Armadale, Vic 3143, Australia

SOUTHGATE, Crispin John; s of Brig John Terence Southgate, OBE, and Stancia Lillian, *née* Collins; *b* 16 Feb 1955; *Educ* Christ's Hosp Horsham, Merton Coll Oxford (MA); *m* 15 Sept 1979, Joanna Mary, da of Gerald Norman Donaldson, TD; 2 s (William b 1987, Richard b 1990), 1 da (Eleanor b 1985); *Career* Price Waterhouse & Co 1977–82; Charterhouse Bank Ltd: joined 1982, dir 1987, md 1992–94; dir: S G Warburg 1994–95, Merrill Lynch 1996–; treas Rainer Fndn 1984–; ACA 1980; *Style*— Crispin Southgate, Esq; ✉ Merrill Lynch International Ltd, Ropemaker Place, 25 Ropemaker Street, London EC2Y 9LY (☎ 0171 867 2000, fax 0171 867 2370)

SOUTHGATE, Very Rev John Eliot; s of Reginald Henry Southgate; *b* 2 Sept 1926; *Educ* City of Norwich, Univ of Durham; *m* 1958, Patricia Mary, *née* Plumb; 2 s, 1 da; *Career* ordained Leicester 1955, vicar of Plumstead Southwark 1962, rector of Charlton Southwark 1966, dean of Greenwich 1968, archdeacon of Cleveland York 1974, dean of York 1984–94, ret; chm Nat Assoc of Victim Support Schemes 1988–93, church cmmr 1989–94, chm Assoc of English Cathedrals 1990–94; Hon DUniv York 1989; *Recreations* music; *Clubs* Yorkshire, Royal Commonwealth, Royal Over-Seas League; *Style*— The Very Rev John Southgate; ✉ 39 Churchfields, Hethersett, Norfolk NR9 3PH (☎ and fax 01603 812116)

SOUTHGATE, Robert; s of Robert Bevis Southgate (d 1958), and Anne, *née* Boyes (d 1985); *b* 20 Jan 1934; *Educ* Morecambe GS; *m* 7 Sept 1957, Elizabeth, da of Robert Benson; 4 s (Paul Robert b 30 Nov 1958, Mark Nicholas b 6 Oct 1960, Jonathan Michael b 8 March 1962, Andrew James b 28 Sept 1965); *Career* reporter Morecambe Guardian 1949–52, sub-ed News Chronicle 1955–56, night chief sub-ed Daily Mirror Manchester 1956–60, night ed Daily Herald 1960–62, freelance newscaster/reporter BBC and ABC 1962–64, dep Northern ed The Sun 1964–68, newscaster/reporter ITN 1968–79, reporter Thames News and TV Eye Thames Television 1979–82, controller of news and current affrs TVS 1982–85; Central Television: controller of news and regnl progs 1985–92, md Central Broadcasting 1993–94 (dep md 1992–93), ret as md 1994; non-exec dir: Meridian Television 1993–, 021 Television 1993–94, Central Television 1994–; ed The Cook Report (Central) 1995; memb Arts Cncl of England 1994– (memb Arts Cncl of GB 1992–94), chm W Midlands Regnl Arts Bd, memb City of Birmingham Touring Opera, dep chm Birmingham Royal Ballet; *Recreations* theatre, opera; *Style*— Robert Southgate, Esq; ✉ Central Television, Central House, Broad Street, Birmingham B1 2JP (☎ 0121 643 9898, fax 0121 643 8369)

SOUTHWARD, Dr Nigel Ralph; CVO (1995, LVO 1985); s of Sir Ralph Southward, KCVO, *qv*, of 9 Devonshire Place, London W1, and Evelyn, *née* Tassell; *b* 8 Feb 1941; *Educ* Rugby, Trinity Hall Cambridge (MA, MB BChir); *m* 24 July 1965, Annette, da of Johan Heinrich Hoffmann, of Strandvejen, Skodsborg, Denmark; 1 s (Nicholas b 1966), 2 da (Karen b 1968, Emma b 1970); *Career* house surgn Middlesex Hosp 1965, house physician Royal Berkshire Hosp Reading 1966, house physician Central Middlesex Hosp 1966, casualty MO Middlesex Hosp 1967, visiting MO King Edward VII Hosp for Offrs 1972–; apothecary to HM The Queen, apothecary to the household and to the households of: HM Queen Elizabeth the Queen Mother, the Princess Margaret Countess of Snowdon, Princess Alice Duchess of Gloucester, the Duke and Duchess of Gloucester, Duke and Duchess of Kent and Prince and Princess Michael of Kent 1975–; Liveryman Worshipful Soc of Apothecaries; *Recreations* sailing, hunting, skiing; *Clubs* RYS, RCC; *Style*— Dr Nigel R Southward, CVO; ✉ 9 Devonshire Place, London W1N 1PB (☎ 0171 935 8425, fax 0171 224 0533, mobile 0836 757557)

SOUTHWARD, Sir Ralph; KCVO (1975); s of Henry Stalker Southward, of Cumberland; *b* 2 Jan 1908; *Educ* Glasgow HS, Univ of Glasgow (MB ChB), MRCP Londond; *m* 1935, Evelyn, da of J G Tassell, of Harrogate; 4 s (one of whom Dr Nigel Ralph Southward, CVO, *qv*); *Career* med practitioner; Mil Serv RAMC (med specialist and Col), served N Africa, India, Ceylon 1940–45; apothecary to: Royal Household 1964–74, HM Queen Elizabeth the Queen Mother 1966–87, TRH the Duke and Duchess of Gloucester 1966–75, HM The Queen 1972–74; Hon Freeman Worshipful Soc of Apothecaries 1975; FRCP 1970; *Recreations* fishing (trout, salmon), golf, travel; *Style*— Sir Ralph Southward, KCVO; ✉ 9 Devonshire Place, London W1N 1PB (☎ 0171 935 7969); Amerden Priory, Taplow, Maidenhead, Berks SL6 0EE (☎ 01628 23525)

SOUTHWARK, Archbishop and Metropolitan of (RC) 1977–; Most Rev Michael George Bowen; s of late Maj C L J Bowen, and Lady Makins; *b* 23 April 1930; *Educ* Downside, Trinity Coll Cambridge, Gregorian Univ Rome; *Career* 2 Lt Irish Gds 1948–49; wine trade 1951–52, English Coll Rome 1952–59, ordained 1958, curate Earlsfield and Walworth South London 1959–63, theology teacher Beda Coll Rome 1963–66, chllr Diocese of Arundel and Brighton 1966–70, bishop of Arundel and Brighton 1971–77 (coadjutor bishop 1970–71); vice pres Bishops' Conf of England and Wales 1996–; Freeman City of London 1984; *Recreations* golf, tennis; *Style*— The Most Rev Michael G Bowen, Archbishop of Southwark; ✉ Archbishop's House, 150 St George's Road, Southwark, London SE1 6HX (☎ 0171 928 2495/5592, fax 0171 928 7833)

SOUTHWARK, Provost of; *see:* Slee, Very Rev Colin B

SOUTHWARK, Bishop of 1991–; Rt Rev Robert (Roy) Kerr Williamson; s of late James Williamson, of Belfast, and late Elizabeth, *née* Kelly; *b* 18 Dec 1932; *Educ* Elmgrove Sch Belfast, Oak Hill Theol Coll London; *m* 1956, Anne Boyd, da of late John Smith, of Belfast; 3 s (Stephen b 1958, Jonathan b 1965, Andrew b 1966), 2 da (Gillian b 1959, Katharine b 1968); *Career* ordained: deacon 1963, priest 1964; curate of Crowborough Sussex 1963–66; vicar: Hyson Green Notts 1966–71, St Ann with Emmanuel Notts 1971–76, Bramcote 1976–79; archdeacon of Notts 1978–84, bishop of Bradford 1984–91; chm Central Religious Bdcasting Advsy Ctee 1993–, co-chair Interfaith Network for the UK 1994–; Hon DLitt Univ of Bradford; *Recreations* home, family, bird watching, music, watching TV sport, reading; *Style*— The Rt Rev the Bishop of Southwark; ✉ Bishop's House, 38 Tooting Bec Gardens, London SW16 1QZ (☎ 0181 769 3256, fax 0181 769 4126)

SOUTHWELL, Bishop of 1988–, Rt Rev Patrick Burnet Harris; s of Edward James Burnet Harris, and Astrid, *née* Kendall; *b* 30 Sept 1934; *Educ* St Albans Sch, Keble Coll Oxford (MA); *m* 1968, Valerie Margaret Pilbrow; 2 s, 1 da; *Career* asst curate St Ebbe's Oxford 1960–63, missionary with S American Missionary Soc 1963–73, archdeacon of Salta Argentina 1969–73, diocesan bishop Northern Argentina 1973–80, rector Kirkheaton and asst bishop Diocese of Wakefield 1981–85, sec Partnership for World Mission 1986–88, asst bishop Diocese of Oxford 1986–88; *Recreations* ornithology, S American Indian culture, music, harvesting; *Style*— The Rt Rev the Bishop of Southwell; ✉ Bishop's Manor, Southwell, Notts NG25 0JR

SOUTHWELL, 7 Viscount (I 1776); Sir Pyers Anthony Joseph Southwell; 10 Bt (I 1662); also Baron Southwell (I 1717); s of late Hon Francis Joseph Southwell, 2 s of 5 Viscount; suc unc 1960; *b* 14 Sept 1930; *Educ* Beaumont Coll, RMA Sandhurst; *m* 1955, Barbara Jacqueline, da of A Raynes; 2 s; *Heir* s, Hon Richard Southwell; *Career* Capt (ret) 8 Hussars 1951–55; company dir; int mgmnt and mktg conslt; *Clubs* MCC; *Style*— The Rt Hon the Viscount Southwell; ✉ PO Box 2211, 8062 Paphos, Cyprus (fax 00 357 6 253066)

SOUTHWELL, Richard Charles; QC (1977); s of late Sir Philip Southwell, CBE, MC, and Mary, *née* Scarratt; *m* 1962, Belinda Mary, da of late Col F H Pownall, MC; 2 s, 1 da; *Career* called to the Bar Inner Temple 1959, jt head of chambers; dep pres Lloyd's Appeal Tbnl; judge of the Cts of Appeal of Jersey and Guernsey, dep judge of the High Ct; *Style*— Richard Southwell, Esq, QC; ✉ 1 Hare Court, Temple, London EC4Y 7BE (☎ 0171 353 3171, fax 0171 583 9127)

SOUTHWOOD, Prof Sir (Thomas) Richard Edmund; kt (1984), DL (1993); s of Edmund William Southwood (d 1984), of Parrock Manor, Gravesend, and Ada Mary (d 1949), da of Ven Archdeacon Thos R Regg, of Newcastle, NSW; *b* 20 June 1931; *Educ*

Gravesend GS, Imperial Coll London (BSc, PhD, DSc), Univ of Oxford (MA, DSc); *m* 1955, Alison Langley, da of Arthur Langley Harden (d 1983), of Fallows Green, Harpenden, Herts; 2 s (Richard, Charles); *Career* prof of zoology and applied entomology Univ of London and head of Dept of Zoology Imperial Coll London 1967–79, Linacre prof of zoology and head of dept Univ of Oxford 1979–93, vice chllr Univ of Oxford 1989–93, prof of zoology Univ of Oxford 1993–; dir Glaxo Wellcome plc (formerly Glaxo Holdings Plc) 1992–; fell Merton Coll Oxford 1979–, fell Eton Coll 1993–; co-chm UK Round Table on Sustainable Devpt 1995–; chm Bd of Tstees Br Museum (Nat Hist) 1980–84 (memb 1973), chm Royal Cmmn on Environmental Pollution 1981–86 (memb 1974–), vice pres Royal Soc of London 1982–84 (fell 1987), pres Royal Entomological Soc of London 1983–85, prof at large Cornell Univ USA 1985–91, prof of environmental scis policy Central Euro Univ Budapest 1991–95; chm Nat Radiological Protection Bd 1985–94 (memb 1981–94); memb: Academia Europaea 1989, Pontifical Acad of Sci 1992; foreign memb: American Acad of Arts and Scis 1980, Norwegian Acad of Sci and Letters 1987, US Nat Acad of Scis 1988, Royal Netherlands Acad of Arts & Scis 1995; Hon DSc: Griffith, East-Anglia, Liverpool, McGill, Warwick, Durham, Sussex, Victoria; Hon LLD: London, Brookes, Bristol; Hon Doctorate Lund; Cavaliere Ufficiale Republica d'Italia 1991, Ordem de Merito (II) Republic of Portugal 1993; fell Imperial Coll, hon fell Westminster Coll 1995; Hon FRCP, Hon FRCR; *Books* Land and Water Bugs of the British Isles (with D Leston, 1959), Life of the Wayside and Woodland (1963), Ecological Methods (1966, 2 edn 1978), Insects on Plants (jtly, 1984), Insects & The Plant Surface (jtly, 1986), Radiation and Health (jtly, 1987); *Recreations* reading, natural history; *Clubs* Athenaeum, Oxford and Cambridge; *Style*— Prof Sir Richard Southwood, DL, FRS; ✉ Merton College, Oxford OX1 4JD (☎ 01865 276310); Zoology Department, South Parks Rd, Oxford OX1 3PS (☎ 01865 271255, fax 01865 310447, e-mail richard.southwood@zoo.ox.ac.uk)

SOUTTER, Lucy Caroline; da of David Fraser Soutter, of Glos, and Joyce Elizabeth Anne, *née* Smith; *b* 17 March 1967; *Educ* Charlton Park Convent for Girls Cheltenham, St James Secretarial Coll London; *Career* squash player; Br number 1, world number 2 1987; represented England: under 16's 4 times (capt), under 19's 19 times, sr's 27 times; Br under 16 Open champion 1981, 1982 and 1983, Br under 19 Open champion 1983 and 1984, world sr masters champion (invitation) 1984, world jr champion 1984, Br sr champion 1985, 1989 and 1990 (runner-up 1987), world sr team champions 1985, 1987 and 1990, Br under 23 Open champion 1987 and 1988, Portugese Open champion 1988, Swiss Open champion 1988, Edmonton women's int champion 1988, third place Calgary Women's Int Open 1991; asst England squash team manager 1994; exec memb Women's Int Squash Players' Assoc 1987–91, memb Representative Panel Ctee SRA 1993 and 1994; resident squash and tennis professional Roehampton Club 1992–; pts I, II and III Squash Rackets Assoc qualified coach, pt 1 elementary, tennis coach 1993, pt 2 intermediate LTA Coaches Award 1994; *Recreations* health and fitness, sport, reading, music, horticulture; *Style*— Miss Lucy Soutter; ✉ 6 Manor Park, Richmond, Surrey TW9 1XZ (☎ 0181 241 1325)

SOUTTER, William Patrick (Pat); s of William Paterson Soutter, of Glasgow, and Eleanore Louise, *née* Siekawitch; *b* 12 Jan 1944; *Educ* Glasgow HS, Univ of Glasgow (MB ChB, MD), Univ of Strathclyde (MSc); *m* 30 June 1973, Winifred Christine, da of William Hanworth, of Paisley; 2 da (Elizabeth b 1980, Eleanor b 1986); *Career* lectr in obstetrics and gynaecology Univ of Glasgow 1978–81, sr lectr in obstetrics and gynaecology Univ of Sheffield 1981–85, reader in gynaecological oncology Inst of Obstetrics and Gynaecology 1985–; ed Br Jl of Obstetrics & Gynaecology; FRCOG 1988; *Recreations* fishing, golf; *Style*— Pat Soutter, Esq; ✉ Institute of Obstetrics & Gynaecology, Royal Postgraduate Medical Sch, Hammersmith Hospital, Du Cane Rd, London W12 0HS (☎ 0181 383 326, fax 0181 383 8065)

SOWARD, Prof Andrew Michael; *b* 20 Oct 1943; *Educ* St Edward's Sch Oxford, Queens Coll Cambridge (open exhibition, BA, PhD, Rayleigh essay prize), Univ of Cambridge (ScD); *m* 1968; 1 da, 1 s; *Career* visiting memb Univ of NY Courant Inst of Mathematical Sciences 1969–70; visiting fell Co-op Inst for Res in Environmental Sciences Boulder Colorado 1970–71; Univ of Newcastle upon Tyne: SRC res fell Oct-Nov 1971, lectr Dec 1971–81, reader in fluid mechanics 1981–86, head Dept of Applied Mathematics 1985–88, prof of fluid dynamics 1986–95, head Div of Applied Mathematics 1989–95; prof of applied mathematics Univ of Exeter 1996–; res and teacher Inst of Geophysics and Planetary Physics Univ of California LA 1977–78; on staff Geophysical Fluid Dynamics Summer Sch Woods Hole Oceanographic Instn Mass USA July-Aug 1978 and 29 June-2 Aug 1987; ed Jl of Geophysical and Astrophysical Fluid Dynamics 1991– (memb Editorial Bd 1986–89, assoc ed 1989–90); FRS 1991; *Publications* Rotating Fluids in Geophysics (co-ed with P H Roberts, 1978), Stellar and planetary magnetism (vol 2 The Fluid Mechanics of Astrophysics and Geophysics, ed, 1983), Dynamo Theory of Planetary Magnetism (special issue of Geophysics & Astrophysics Fluid Dynamics, co-ed with F H Busse, 1988), Geomagnetism and Palaeomagnetism (NATO ASI Series C, co-ed, 1989), also author of over 60 scientific papers; *Style*— Prof Andrew Soward, FRS; ✉ Department of Mathematics, University of Exeter, Exeter EX4 4QE (☎ 01392 263263, fax 01392 263997)

SOWDEN, Dr David Stewart; s of John Stewart Sowden (d 1980), and Elisabeth Ann, *née* Barford (d 1991); *b* 27 April 1956; *Educ* Cranbourne Bilateral Sch, Leeds Med Sch (MB ChB, DRCOG, DCH, MRCGP, DFFP); *m* 1981, Dr Maureen Patricia Burnett; *Career* house offr: (surgery) Leeds Gen Infirmary 1979–80, (med) Chapel Allerton Hosp Leeds 1980; GP vocational trg scheme Lincoln 1980–83, ptnr and full time princ in gen practice Measham 1983–; Univ of Leicester: clinical tutor to Univ Dept of Gen Practice 1983–, regnl advsr Gen Practice Postgraduate Educn Dept 1995– (assoc regnl advsr 1991–95); Leicester Vocational Trg Scheme: vocational trainer 1986–, vocational course organiser 1988–91; FRCGP (memb Cncl); *Recreations* golf, Alpine skiing, photography, travel; *Style*— Dr David Sowden; ✉ 18 Tower Gardens, Ashby de la Zouch, Leics LE65 2GZ (☎ 01530 270667); Measham Medical Unit, Measham, nr Swadlincote, Derbys DE12 7HR (☎ 01530 270667)

SOWDEN, Terence Cubitt; QC (1989); s of late Capt George Henry Sowden, RNR, and Margaret Duncan, *née* Cubitt; *b* 30 July 1929; *Educ* Victoria Coll, Overseas Nautical Training Coll, Hendon Tech Coll London, Univ of London; *m* 1955, Doreen Mary Lucas (d 1983); 1 s (Gary), 2 da (Sally Ann Dallimore, Jayne); *Career* called to the Bar Middle Temple 1951, advocate Royal Ct of Jersey 1951, private practice in Jersey and then with Crill, Cubitt Sowden & Tomes Advocates and Solicitors (sr ptnr 1962–83), States dep St Helier No 1 Dist 1961–64, HM Slr Gen for Jersey 1986–93, Juge d'Instruction for Jersey 1994–; former memb Bd Channel Television, former dep chm Royal Bank of Scotland (Jersey) Ltd; memb Br swimming team for tour to Denmark and Sweden 1949, holder of records for Corbière to St Helier and Sark to Guernsey long distance swims; *Books* The Jersey Law of Trusts (with Paul Matthews, 1988, 3 edn 1994); *Recreations* writing, walking the low tide; *Style*— Mr T C Sowden, QC

SOWERBUTTS, Rev Janet Elise; da of Francis Alfred Owen Sowerbutts (d 1964), and Esmeralda Helen, *née* Woodward (d 1967); *b* 17 Aug 1938; *Educ* Westcliff HS for Girls, Westminster Coll Cambridge; *Career* co dir Messrs James Brodie & Co (Export Ltd) 1962–69, Atlantic sec Girls' Bde 1970–75, ordained minister Utd Reformed Church 1978, Cheshunt chair Westminster Coll Cambridge 1985, provincial moderator Thames North Province 1990– (first woman to be appointed); *Style*— The Rev Janet Sowerbutts; ✉ Thames North Province, The City Temple, Holborn Viaduct, London EC1A 2DE (☎ 0171 583 8701)

SOWERBY, Amanda Louise (*née* Smith); da of Geoffrey Norman Smith, of Dewsbury, West Yorkshire, and Kathleen, *née* Heaton; *b* 29 Jan 1963; *Educ* Westborough HS Dewsbury, Whitcliffe Mount Sixth Form Coll, Wheelwright Coll Dewsbury; *m* 7 May 1987, Mark Richard Sowerby, s of John William Sowerby; 2 s (Joseph Richard b 28 June 1989, Thomas Mark b 5 April 1993); *Career* hockey player; former clubs: Wakefield, Laund Hill Ladies; currently with Doncaster (top team premier div) and also Yorkshire rep (top Co in England 1994, top scorer); England caps: under 21, under 23, full debut 1987, over 40 caps; achievements incl: Silver medal Euro Cup London 1987, fourth place World Cup Sydney 1990, scored 2 goals v USA Wembley 1987 (player of match award), Euro Cup Gold Medal Brussels 1992; former employment: supervisor Dewsbury Sports Centre, residential child care offr Doncaster; currently: pt/t PE instr Barnsley Coll, level 3 nat hockey coach; *Recreations* most sports, walking, music, reading especially Ludlum or King; *Style*— Mrs Amanda Sowerby; ✉ 28 Briestfield Road, Grange Moor, Wakefield, West Yorkshire WF4 4DX (☎ 01302 851406); c/o All England Hockey Association, Milton Keynes

SOWREY, Air Marshal Sir Frederick Beresford; KCB (1978, CB 1968), CBE (1965), AFC (1954); s of Gp Capt F Sowrey, DSO, MC, AFC (d 1968), of Eastbourne, and Warsash; *b* 14 Sept 1922; *Educ* Charterhouse; *m* 1946, Anne Margaret, da of Capt C T A Bunbury, OBE, RN (d 1951), of Crowborough; 1 s, 1 da; *Career* RAF 1940, served WWII in Fighter Reconnaissance Units in Euro Theatre, Gp Capt 1962, Air Cdre 1965, SASO Air Forces, ME Aden, dir Overseas Def Policy MOD 1968–70, SASO RAF Trg Cmd with rank of Air Vice-Marshal 1970–72, Cmdt Nat Def Coll 1972–75, dir gen RAF Trg 1975–77, UK Rep Perm Mil Deputies Gp CENTO as Air Marshal 1977–79; res fell Int Inst for Strategic Studies 1980–81; author of and contrib to articles and reviews in military and def jls incl D Day Encyclopedia; pres: Sussex Industl Archaeology Soc (chm 1981–93), First World War Aviation Historians 1982–, Military Commentators Circle 1984–; vice pres Victory Servs Assoc (chm 1985–89, pres 1989–93), vice pres RAF Historical Society 1986– (chm 1996), memb Bd of Conservators of Ashdown Forest 1983–; *Recreations* early motoring, industrial archaeology, sussex countryside; *Clubs* RAF; *Style*— Air Marshal Sir Frederick Sowrey, KCB, CBE, AFC; ✉ c/o National Westminster Bank, 67 High Street, Staines, Middlesex

SPACIE, Maj-Gen Keith; CB (1987), OBE (1974); s of Frederick Percy Spacie (d 1981), and Kathleen, *née* Wrench (d 1989); *b* 21 June 1935; *m* 16 Sept 1961, Valerie Elise, da of Lt-Col Harry William Wallace Rich (d 1971); 1 s (Dominic b 1964); *Career* RMA Sandhurst 1954–55, cmmnd Royal Lincolnshire Regt 1955, transferred Para Regt 1959, cdr Ind Para Co 1964–65, Army Staff Coll 1965–66, DAA & QMG Para Bde 1968–70 instr RMA Sandhurst 1970–72, Nat Def Coll 1972–73, cdr 3 Bn Para Regt 1973–75, NATO staff SHAPE, 1976–78, instr Nat Def Coll 1978–79, cdr 7 Field Force 1979–81, RCDS 1982, mil cmmr and cdr Br Forces Falkland Islands 1983–84, dir Army Trg 1984–87; md Cranfield Education and Training Ltd 1987–89, dir Sudbury Consultants Ltd 1989–; visiting fell Univ of Surrey; MInstD; *Recreations* cross country running, military history, country pursuits; *Clubs* Army and Navy, Thames Hare and Hounds; *Style*— Maj-Gen Keith Spacie, CB, OBE; ✉ c/o Army and Navy Club, Pall Mall, London SW1Y 5JN; business address: 2 Park Chase, Guildford, Surrey GU1 1ES (☎ 01483 301736, fax 01483 569547)

SPACKMAN, Dr John William Charles; s of Lt-Col Robert Thomas Spackman, MBE (d 1984), and Ann, *née* Rees (d 1984); *b* 12 May 1932; *Educ* Cyfarthfa Castle GS Merthyr Tydfil, Wellington GS, Royal Mil Coll of Sci, Univ of London (external BSc, PhD), UMIST (MSc); *m* 2 April 1955, Jeanette Vera, da of George Samuel (d 1956); 2 s (Michael b 1956, David b 1964), 1 da (Sarah b 1959); *Career* Nat Serv 1950–52; cmmnd RAOC 1952, regtl appts 1952–72, Lt-Col Project Wavell 1969–72, Lt-Col GSO1 RARDE 1972–75, Col sr mil offr Chemical Def and Microbiological Def Estab Porton Down 1975–78, branch chief Info Systems Div SHAPE 1978–80, Brig, dir Supply Computer Servs 1980–83, ret Brig 1983; dir (under sec) operational strategy DHSS 1983–87; dir: Computing and Info Servs Br Telecom UK 1987–90, ACT Logsys 1990–93, Intelligent Networks Ltd 1991–94, John Spackman Associates Ltd 1990–, European Telecommunications Informatics Service 1990–93, Information Systems Div Govt of Malta 1993–95; sr conslt Office of the Chairman MSV Ltd Govt of Malta 1995–; govr Int Cncl for Computer Communication 1989–; Freeman City of London 1987, Liveryman Worshipful Co of Info Technologists 1989; MIMgt 1970, MInstD 1983, FBCS 1987, CEng 1990; *Recreations* gardening, rock climbing, mountaineering, opera; *Clubs* Naval and Military, Casino Maltese (Malta); *Style*— Dr John Spackman

SPACKMAN, Michael John; s of Geoffrey Bertram Spackman (d 1976), and Audrey Ivy Elizabeth, *née* Morecombe; *b* 8 Oct 1936; *Educ* Malvern Coll, Clare Coll Cambridge (MA), Queen Mary Coll London (MScEcon); *m* 27 Feb 1965, Judith Ann, da of Walter Henry Leathem (d 1966); 2 s (Sean Michael b 1968, Keir David b 1972), 2 da (Juliet Sarah Helen Christina b 1977, Helena Claire Nicola b 1982); *Career* Mil Serv 2 Lt RA 1955–57; physicist UKAEA Capenhurst 1960–69, sr physicist/engr The Nuclear Power Group Ltd 1969–71, princ scientific offr then econ advsr Dept of Energy 1971–77, dir of econs and accountancy Civil Serv Coll 1979–80; HM Treasy: econ advsr 1977–79, head Public Servs Econs Div 1980–85, under sec and head Public Expenditure Econs Gp 1985–91 and 1993–95; chief econ advsr Dept of Tport 1991–93; Gwilym Gibbon fell Nuffield Coll Oxford 1995–96, special advsr National Economic REsearch Associates 1996–, visiting research assoc LSE 1996–; *Recreations* climbing; *Style*— Michael Spackman, Esq; ✉ 44 Gibson Square, Islington, London N1 0RA (☎ 0171 359 1053, fax 0171 288 1270)

SPACKMAN, Michael Kenneth Maurice; s of Harry Maurice Spackman (d 1984), of Godalming, and Mary Madeline (Molly) Pinson (d 1959); *b* 2 Feb 1926; *Educ* Marlborough; *m* 9 Jan 1960, Ann Veronica, da of Francis Mervyn Cook (d 1979), of Burford; 2 da (Henrietta b 1960, Catriona b 1962); *Career* Lt attached Indian RA; merchant banker; dir Singer & Friedlander Investment Management Ltd 1986–90, First Spanish Investment Trust 1987–96, Vallehermoso SA 1990; *Recreations* horse trials, tennis; *Style*— Michael Spackman, Esq; ✉ Hydestile Paddock, Hambledon Road, Godalming, Surrey GU8 4DE (☎ 01483 417564)

SPACKMAN, Susan Jane; da of William John Wotton, of Devon, and Dorothy Wotton, *née* Cooper; *b* 14 March 1947; *Educ* St Dunstan's Abbey Plymouth, Tavistock Comprehensive, Plymouth Poly Sch of Architecture (Dip Arch); *m* 28 Aug 1970, Richard Benjamin James; 1 s (Edward b 1979), 1 da (Clair b 1974); *Career* chartered architect; principal Crookes & Spackman; ARIBA (chm Plymouth Branch 1987–89), nat jt vice pres The Assoc of Conslt Architects 1987–89 (representing the Assoc of Conslt Architects with The Campaign for the Bar, investigating Law Reform for all professionals with respect to liability); chm of mktg S Western Regn RIBA 1993–95, sec Western chapter BAWE (British Assoc of Women Entrepreneurs) 1993–96; *Recreations* equestrianism; *Style*— Mrs Susan J Spackman; ✉ Briar House, 243 Whitchurch Road, Tavistock, Devon PL19 9EG (☎ 01822 615221); Crookes & Spackman, The Old Stables, Paddons Row, Tavistock, Devon PL19 0HF (☎ 01822 614222, fax 01822 617764)

SPALDING, Prof (Dudley) Brian; s of Harold Andrew Spalding, and Kathleen Constance Spalding; *b* 9 Jan 1923; *Educ* King's Coll Sch Wimbledon, Univ of Oxford (BA, MA), Univ of Cambridge (PhD, ScD); *m* 1, Eda Isle-Lotte Goericke; 2 s, 2 da; m 2,

Colleen King; 2 s; *Career* prof of heat transfer Imperial Coll 1958–88 (emeritus prof 1988–); md Concentration Heat & Momentum Ltd (CHAM) 1970–; Reilly prof Purdue Univ Indiana 1978–79; awards incl; Medaille d'Or (Inst Francais de l'Energie) 1980, Bernard Lewis medal 1982, Luikov medal 1986; foreign memb: Russian Acad of Sciences 1994, Ukrainian National Acad of Sciences 1994; hon prof USTC Hefei China 1988; FRS 1983, FIMechE, FInstE, FIChemE, ASME, FEng 1989; *Books* incl: Some Fundamentals of Combustion (1955), Convective Mass Transfer (1963), Heat and Mass Transfer in Recirculating Flows (jtly, 1969), Engineering Thermodynamics (with Cole, 1974), Genmix (1978), Combustion and Mass Transfer (1974); *Recreations* computing, jogging; *Style*— Prof Brian Spalding, FRS, FEng; ✉ Concentration Heat and Momentum Ltd, Bakery House, 40 High St, London SW19 5AU (☎ 0181 947 7651, fax 0181 879 3497)

SPALDING, Frances; da of Hedley Stinston Crabtree (d 1985), and Margaret, *née* Holiday (d 1989); *b* 16 July 1950; *Educ* Farringtons Sch Chislehurst, Univ of Nottingham (BA, PhD); *m* 20 April 1974 (m dis 1991), Julian Spalding; 1 s (Daniel b 11 Aug 1983); *Career* art historian and biographer; lectr Sheffield City Polytechnic 1978–88, currently freelance; ed The Charleston Magazine 1992–, research co-ordinator for the Writers-in-Prison Ctee English PEN 1991–93; FRSL 1984; memb: Soc of Authors, PEN; *Publications* Magnificent Dreams: Burne-Jones and the late Victorians (1978), Whistler (1979), Roger Fry: Art and Life (1980), Vanessa Bell (1983), British Art since 1900 (1986), Stevie Smith: A Critical Biography (1988), Twentieth Century Painters & Sculptors (Dictionary of British Art series, 1990), Dance till the Stars Come Down: A Biography of John Minton (1991), Virginia Woolf: Paper Darts (selected and introduced, 1991), Whistler (1994); *Recreations* music; *Style*— Frances Spalding, FRSL; ✉ c/o Coleridge & Rogers, 20 Powis Mews, London W11

SPALDING, John Anthony (Tony); s of John Eber Spalding (d 1964), of Wrexham, Clwyd, and Katherine, *née* Davies; *b* 17 Feb 1938; *Educ* Wellington, Brasenose Coll Oxford; *m* (m dis); 2 da; *Career* journalist 1959–61, Public Affairs Dept Ford Motor Co 1961–64 and 1966–73, PR offr Vauxhall Motors Ltd Ellesmere Port 1964–66; dir of PR: British Leyland 1974–79 (car PR mangr 1973), Wilkinson Match 1979–80, Spillers 1980, Dalgety 1980–81; dir of communications Sea Containers/Seaco 1981–84, dir of public affairs Battersea Leisure/Alton Towers 1984–85, dir of external affairs Whitbread 1985–86; dir of public affairs: Dalgety 1986–89, Vauxhall Motors Ltd 1989–; FIPR 1988, FIMI 1989, FRSA 1988; *Style*— Tony Spalding, Esq; ✉ Vauxhall Motors Limited, Griffin House, Osborne Road, Luton, Beds LU1 3YT (☎ 01582 427620, fax 01582 426926)

SPALDING, John Oliver; CBE (1988); s of John Spalding, OBE (d 1954), of Manchester, and Winifrid Ethel, *née* Trigger (d 1965); *b* 4 Aug 1924; *Educ* William Hulme's GS Manchester, Jesus Coll Cambridge (MA); *m* 20 Sept 1952, Mary Whitworth, da of James Birch Hull (d 1972), of Manchester and Eastbourne; 1 s (Simon John b 1960), 1 da (Sarah Mary b 1958); *Career* RA 1943–47, attached IA (5 Indian Field Regt and Mountain Artillery Trg Centre Ambla), overseas serv in Burma, Singapore, Java and India, Capt RA; admitted slr 1952; articled clerk to Sir Derek Hilton Manchester 1949–52, asst slr Manchester Corp 1952–55, asst slr rising to sr slr Hampshire CC 1955–62; Halifax Building Society: asst slr 1962–64, Head Office slr 1964–74, gen mangr 1970, dir 1975–88, dep chief gen mangr 1981, chief exec 1982–88; dir NMW Computers plc 1989–91; chm: Future Constitution and Powers of Bldg Socs Working Pty (The Spalding Ctee) 1981–83, Calderdale Small Business Advice Centre 1983–88; memb: Cncl Bldg Socs Assoc 1981–88, Farrand Ctee on Conveyancing 1984, Nat House-Bldg Cncl 1985– (chm 1988–92); memb Law Soc; *Recreations* boating and bird watching; *Style*— John Spalding, Esq, CBE; ✉ Water's Edge, Springe Lane, Swanley, Nantwich, Cheshire CW5 8NR (☎ 01270 524520, car 0836 629006)

SPALDING, Julian; s of Eric Spalding, and Margaret Grace, *née* Savager; *b* 15 June 1947; *Educ* Chislehurst and Sidcup GS for Boys, Univ of Nottingham (BA, Dip Museums Assoc); *m* 1, 1974 (m dis 1991), Frances; 1 s; *m* 2, Gillian, *née* Tait; *Career* art asst: Leicester Museum and Art Gallery 1970–71, Durham Light Infantry Museum and Arts Centre 1971–72; keeper Mappin Art Gallery 1972–76; dir: Sheffield City Cncl 1982–85 (dep dir 1976–82), Manchester City Art Galleries 1985–89, Glasgow Museums 1989–; acting dir Nat Museum of Labour History 1987–88; dir: Niki de Saint Phalle Fndn 1995–, Scottish Football Museum Tst 1995–; BBC broadcaster (talks and reviews incl Third Ear (BBC Radio Three) 1988); chm Exhibitions Sub Ctee Arts Cncl 1981–82 and 1986; memb: Art Panel 1978–82, Art Galleries Assoc 1987– (fndr and memb Ctee 1976–), Visual Arts Advsy Ctee Br Cncl 1990–; master Guild of St George John Ruskin's Guild 1996 (companion 1978, dir 1983); Crafts Cncl: memb Projects and Orgn Ctee 1985–87, memb 1986–, memb Purchasing Ctee 1986, memb Exhibitions Ctee 1986–90; FMA 1983; *Books* L S Lowry (1979), Three Little Books on Painting (1984), Is There Life in Museums? (1990); exhibition catalogues incl: Modern British Painting (1975), Glasgow's Great British Art Exhibition (1990), Gallery of Modern Art Glasgow (1996); contrib to Burlington Magazine; *Style*— Julian Spalding, Esq; ✉ Art Gallery and Museum, Kelvingrove, Glasgow G3 8AG (☎ 0141 287 2600, fax 0141 287 2608)

SPALDING, Richard Lionel; s of Frederick Lionel Spalding, MD, FRCS (d 1966), of Worcester, and Ines Sylvia, *née* Salkeld (d 1994); *b* 21 May 1938; *Educ* Malvern; *m* 14 Sept 1963, Cicely Jane, da of late Philip Cecil King-Lewis; 1 s (William Joseph b 11 May 1973), 2 da (Henrietta Jane b 5 Nov 1966, Frederica Victoria b 7 Dec 1968); *Career* Hubert Leicester & Co accountants Worcester 1957–63, KPMG 1963– (managing ptnr Guildford Office 1986–91, head of UK trg 1992–); ACA 1963; *Recreations* operas, gardens, churches, Spain; *Clubs* Brooks's; *Style*— Richard Spalding, Esq; ✉ Sheriff's Lench Manor, Evesham, Worcestershire WR11 5SR; KPMG, PO Box 695, 8 Salisbury Square, London EC4Y 8BB (☎ 0171 311 1000, fax 0171 311 3311)

SPALDING, Ruth Jeanie Lucile (Mrs Ruth O'Brien); da of late Henry Norman Spalding, of Oxford, and late Nellie Maud Emma, *née* Cayford; *Educ* Headington Sch Oxford, Somerville Coll Oxford (MA); *children*; 1 da (Jeanie Moyo); *Career* author and lectr; formerly: stage actor and dir, typist, adult educn lectr and advsr in art and crafts and social studies, gen sec Assoc of Head Mistresses; fndr and dir Oxford Pilgrim Players (later Rock Theatre Company); author as Marion Jay of: With This Sword (documentary/play, Royal Festival Hall), The Word (play, BBC TV), Pleasure or Pain in Education, Mistress Bottom's Dream; author as Ruth Spalding of: The Improbable Puritan (biog, Whitbread Literary award 1975, a BBC TV Book of the Year), The Diary of Bulstrode Whitelocke 1605–1675 (ed 1990, reprinted 1991), Contemporaries of Bulstrode Whitelocke 1605–1675 (1990), Dr Thomas Winston 1575–1655 (article for Dictionary of National Biography, 1996); feature articles in The Times, feature and documentary progs BBC radio; FRHistS, FRSA; memb: Soc of Authors, Br Actors Equity Assoc; *Recreations* walking, theatre, organic gardening, foreign travel; *Clubs* English-Speaking Union; *Style*— Ruth Spalding; ✉ 34 Reynards Rd, Welwyn, Herts AL6 9TP (☎ 01438 714696)

SPALL, Timothy; *Career* actor; hon vice-pres The Archie and Gwen Smith Memorial Tst Fund; *Theatre* NT incl: Bottom in A Midsummer's Night Dream, Ligurio in Mandragola, Dauphin in Saint Joan, Le Bourgeois Gentilhomme; RSC incl: Andre in The Three Sisters, Rafe in Knight of the Burning Pestle, Waxford Squeers/Mr Folair in Nicholas Nickleby, Simple in The Merry Wives of Windsor, Ivan in Suicide, Mech in Baal; Birmingham Rep incl: Boucicault in Heavenly Bodies, Gratiano in The Merchant of Venice, Harry Trevor/Baptista in Kiss Me Kate, Lawrence in Mary Barns (also Royal Court); other credits incl: Martin in Aunt Mary (Warehouse), Khlestakov in The Government Inspector (Greenwich), Vic Maggot in Smelling A Rat (Hampstead), Derek in Screamers (Playhouse Studio Edinburgh); *Television* BBC incl: Phil in A Nice Day at the Office, Jimmy Beales in Roots, Chico in La Nona, Francis Meakes in Broke, Paul in Body Contact, Clevor Trevor in Arena - Night Moves, Hawkins in Guest of the Nation, Gordon in Home Sweet Home, Sgt Baxter in A Cotswold Death, Yepikhodov in The Cherry Orchard, Shorty in The Brylcreem Boys, Wainwright in Vanishing Army, Pathologist in Murder Most Horrid, Dread Poets Society; other credits incl: Barry in Auf Wiedersehen Pet (Witzend Prodns for Central TV), Webster in Boon (Central), Frank Stubbs in Frank Stubbs Promotes (2 series, Noel Gay TV for Carlton), Kevin in Outside Edge (3 series, Central (Best TV Comedy Drama Br Comedy Awards 1994 for series I & II), Donald Caudell in Stolen (LWT), Porfiry in Great Writers - Dostoyevsky (LWT), Lyndon in Dutch Girls (LWT), Pilot in A Class Act (Meridian), Andrei in The Three Sisters, Pig Robinson in The Tale of Little Pig Robinson; *Films* incl: Cunningham in Young Indie, Aubrey in Life is Sweet, Eric Lyle in The Sheltering Sky, Ramborde in 1871, Hodkins in White Hunter Black Heart, Igor in To Kill A Priest, Peck in Dream Demon, Reverant Miln in Robinson Crusoe, Nick Watt in The Nihilist's Double Vision, Polidari in Gothic, Paulus in The Bride, Douglas in Remembrance, Harry in Quadrophenia, Jim in SOS Titanic, Afican Footsteps, Maurice in Secrets and Lies 1996; *Clubs* Colony, Dean Street Soho; *Style*— Timothy Spall; ✉ c/o Markham & Froggatt Ltd, Julian House, 4 Windmill Street, London W1P 1HF (☎ 0171 636 4412, fax 0171 637 5233)

SPALTON, David John; s of John Roland Spalton, of Duffield, Derbyshire, and Gertrude Edna, *née* Massey; *b* 2 March 1947; *Educ* Buxton Coll Derbyshire, Westminster Med Sch (MB BS); *m* 26 May 1979, Catherine, da of Donald George Bompas, CMG, of Petts Wood, Kent; 3 s (George b 1980, James b 1983, Benjamin b 1992); *Career* sr registrar Moorfields Eye Hosp 1976–77; conslt ophthalmic surgn: Charing Cross Hosp 1981–82, St Thomas' Hosp 1982; hon conslt ophthalmic surgn Royal Hosp Chelsea, hon sr lectr in ophthalmology UMDS; Liveryman Worshipful Soc of Apothecaries; memb RSM, MRCP 1973, FRCS 1975, FRCOphth 1988, FRCP 1990; *Books* Atlas of Clinical Ophthalmology (1985); *Recreations* fly fishing; *Style*— David Spalton, Esq; ✉ 59 Harley St, London W1N 1DD (☎ 0171 935 6174, fax 0171 636 5199)

SPARK, Dame Muriel Sarah; DBE (1993, OBE 1967); da of Bernard Camberg, and Sarah Elizabeth Maud, *née* Uezzell; *b* 1918; *Educ* James Gillespiés Sch for Girls Edinburgh, Heriot Watt Coll Edinburgh; *m* 1937 (m dis), Sydney Oswald Spark; 1 s (Samuel Harry Louis b 1938); *Career* gen sec The Poetry Soc, ed The Poetry Review 1947–49; hon memb American Acad of Arts and Letters 1978; Hon DLitt: Strathclyde 1971, Edinburgh 1989, Aberdeen 1995; Hon DUniv Heriot-Watt; Commandeur de l'Ordre des Arts et des Lettres France 1996 (Officier 1988), CLitt 1991 (FRSL 1963), FRSE 1995; *Books* critical and biographical: Selected Poems of Emily Brontë (ed, 1952), Child of Light - Reassessment of Mary Shelley (1951, revised as Mary Shelley 1987), John Masefield (1953, 1962 and revised 1992), The Brontë Letters (ed, 1954), Curriculum Vitae (autobiography, 1992), The Essence of the Brontës (1993); poetry: The Fanfarlo and other Verse (1952), Collected Poems I (1967), Going Up to Sotheby's and other Poems (1982); fiction: The Comforters (1957), Robinson (1958), The Go-Away Bird (1958), Memento Mori (1959, adapted for stage 1964, and BBC TV 1992), The Ballad of Peckham Rye (1960, Italia Prize for dramatic radio 1962), The Bachelors (1960), Voices at Play (1961), The Prime of Miss Jean Brodie (1961, adapted for stage 1966 and revived 1994, filmed 1969, BBC TV 1978), Doctors of Philosophy (play, staged 1962, published 1963), The Girls of Slender Means (1963, adapted for radio 1964, BBC TV 1975), The Mandelbaum Gate (1965, James Tait Black Memorial Prize), Collected Stories 1 (1967), The Public Image (1968), The Very Fine Clock (for children, 1969), The Driver's Seat (1970, filmed 1974), Not to Disturb (1971), The Hothouse by the East River (1973), The Abbess of Crewe (1974, filmed 1977), The Takeover (1976), Territorial Rights (1979), Loitering with Intent (1981), Bang-Bang You're Dead and other Stories (1982), The Only Problem (1984), The Stories of Muriel Spark (1985), A Far Cry from Kensington (1988), Symposium (1990), Harper and Wilton (story, signed limited edn, 1996), Reality and Dreams (1996); for children: The French Window and The Small Telephone (1993); *Recreations* reading, travel; *Style*— Dame Muriel Spark, DBE; ✉ c/o David Higham Associates Ltd, 5–8 Lower John St, Golden Square, London W1R 4HA

SPARKES, David; s of Wing Cdr Ronald George Sparkes, ret, of Woodham, Co Durham, and Eileen Violet, *née* Temperley; *b* 19 June 1946; *Educ* King Alfred Sch Plon W Germany, Old Swinford Hosp Sch Stourbridge Worcs, Newcastle upon Tyne Coll of Art and Industl Design (Dip, LSIAD); *m* 27 Sept 1969, Susan Louisa, da of Eden Sidney Wilkes; 2 da (Sally b 12 Sept 1973, Alice b 6 Aug 1976); *Career* designer Property Dept C & A 1968–69, contracts mangr (office design) Dexion 1969–72, sr designer (store design) Dixons 1972–73, mangr (office design) Ford of Europe 1973–76, mangr (store design) Debenhams 1976–80, dir Retail Div AID 1980–92, dir (interiors) Conran Design 1982–84, dir (interiors/retail) DIA Interiors 1984–86, jt md Sparkes Orr Design Consultants London 1986–; major design projects incl: Somerfield (new trading concept of Gateway) 1989–90 (winner Retails Environments category Design Week Awards 1991), Dales (new discount trading concept for Asda) 1992–93, Shoe Express (new discount trading concept for BSC) 1993, Forte Spa Leisure Club 1993, Littlewoods Chain Stores 1994; MCSD 1979; *Recreations* photography, motorbikes, cinema, books; *Style*— David Sparkes, Esq; ✉ Sparkes Orr Design Consultants, 5 Dryden Street, Covent Garden, London WC2E 9NB (☎ 0171 829 8306)

SPARKES, Prof John Jackson; s of Malcolm Sparkes (d 1933), of Jordans Bucks, and Elizabeth, *née* Jackson (d 1968); *b* 4 Dec 1924; *Educ* Bootham Sch York, Univ of Manchester (BSc), Univ of Essex (PhD); *m* 30 Aug 1952, Sheila Margaret, da of late John Wells; 2 s (Julian Malcolm b 7 Nov 1956, Kevin John b 20 Jan 1958), 1 da (Camilla Jane Elizabeth b 25 Sept 1959); *Career* Admiralty Signal Estab Haslemere 1944–46; hosp physicist: Middlesex Hosp 1946–47, St Mary's Hosp London 1948–49; sch teaching: Ardingly Coll Sussex 1949–51, Watford GS 1951–52; physicist British Telecommunications Research Taplow Bucks 1952–62, sr lectr Imperial Coll London 1962–67, reader in electronics Univ of Essex 1967–70; The Open Univ: prof of electronics 1970–93 (pt/t following early retirement 1986), pro vice chancellor 1972–74, dean of technology 1974–84, emeritus 1993; MIEE 1957, SMIEEE (NY) 1960, FEng 1984; *Books* Junction Transistors, (1966), Transistor Switching and Sequential Circuits (1969), Semiconductor Devices (1987, 2nd edn 1994), Open Learning and Distance Education with Computer Support (jt author, 1992), Electronics (with D Crecraft and D Gorham, 1993); *Recreations* philosophy of science, golf, higher education; *Style*— Prof John Sparkes, FEng; ✉ Long Gable, 40 Sheethanger Lane, Felden, Hemel Hempstead, Herts HP3 OBQ (☎ 01442 251388)

SPARKS, Ian Leslie; s of Ronald Leslie, of Southport, Merseyside, and Hilda, *née* Bullen; *b* 26 May 1943; *Educ* Holt HS Liverpool, Brunel Univ (MA); *m* 1 July 1967, Eunice Jean, da of Reginald Robinson (d 1983); 1 da (Clare b 1973); *Career* social worker Merseyside 1971, asst divisional dir Barnardos 1974, chief exec The Children's Soc 1986– (social work dir 1981); tstee: Br Agencies for Adoption and Fostering (hon treas), National Children's Bureau, National Cncl of Voluntary Child Care Organisations; chm Christian Child Care Network, vice chm Int Anglican Family Network; memb Br Assoc of Social Workers; *Recreations* piano playing, gardening in miniature; *Style*— Ian Sparks, Esq; ✉ The Children's Society, Edward Rudolf House, Margery St, London WC1X 0JL (☎ 0171 837 4299, fax 0171 837 0211)

SPARKS, Prof (Robert) Stephen John; s of Kenneth Grenfell Sparks, and late Ruth Joan, *née* Rugman; *b* 15 May 1949; *Educ* Wellington, Bingley GS Yorks, Imperial Coll London (BSc, PhD); *m* 19 June 1971, Ann Elizabeth, da of Frederick Currie Talbot (d 1986); 2 s (Andrew Robert James b 24 Aug 1978, Daniel Joseph b 1 May 1982); *Career* Royal Exhibition of 1951 fell Univ of Lancaster 1974–76, NATO fell Univ of Rhode Island 1976–78, lectr in geology Univ of Cambridge 1978–89, prof of geology Univ of Bristol 1989–; pres Geological Soc of London 1994–; memb: Grants Ctee NERC 1985–88, various ctees Royal Soc; Wager Medal Int Assoc of Volcanology and Chemistry of the Earth's Interior, Bigsby Medal Geological Soc London; FRS 1988, FGS; *Books* Tephra Studies (co-ed with S Self, 1980), author of 130 published scientific papers; *Recreations* soccer, squash, tennis, cricket, music, theatre; *Style—* Prof Stephen Sparks, FRS; ✉ Walnut Cottage, Brinsea Road, Congresbury BS19 5JF (☎ 01934 834306); Department of Geology, University of Bristol, Bristol BS8 1RJ (☎ 0117 928 7789)

SPARROW, Bryan; CMG (1992); *b* 8 June 1933; *Educ* Hemel Hempstead GS, Pembroke Coll Oxford; *m* 1958, Fiona Mylechreest; 1 s, 1 da; *Career* Dip Serv; served: Belgrade, Moscow, Tunis, Casablanca, Kinshasa, Prague, Belgrade; ambass Cameroon 1981–84, non-res ambass Central African Republic and Equatorial Guinea 1982–84, Canadian Nat Def Coll 1984–85; consul gen: Toronto 1985–89, Lyons 1989–92; ambass Croatia 1992–94, ret; *Style—* Bryan Sparrow, Esq, CMG; ✉ c/o Foreign and Commonwealth Office, King Charles Street, London SW1A 2AH

SPARROW, (Albert) Charles; QC (1966); *Educ* Univ of London (LLB); *Career* called to the Bar: Gray's Inn 1950 (treas 1994), Lincoln's Inn 1967; head of chambers 13 Old Square; hon legal advsr Cncl for Br Archaeology 1966–, hon cnsllr to Freemen of Eng and Wales 1978–; KStJ; FSA; *Style—* Charles Sparrow, Esq, QC; ✉ 13 Old Square, Lincoln's Inn, London WC2A 3UA (☎ 0171 242 6105, fax 0171 405 4004)

SPARROW, Derek Tuart; s of Sydney Sparrow (d 1976), of Lytham St Annes, Lancs, and Dagmar May, *née* Wisternoff (d 1976); *b* 11 April 1935; *Educ* Denstone Coll Uttoxeter Staffs, Keble Coll Oxford (MA); *m* 16 Aug 1958, Doreen Beryl, da of Frank Keener (d 1975), of Hove, E Sussex; 2 s (Simon Charles Tuart b 1964, Christopher b 1965), 1 da (Sarah May b 1963); *Career* Nat Serv 2 Lt RA 1953–55; admitted slr 1961; asst examiner accounts Law Soc 1966–88; dir: Portman Building Society 1973–90, Old Ship Hotel (Brighton) Ltd 1977–, Downs Crematorium Ltd 1979–95; pres Sussex Law Soc 1984; tstee Brighton Festival Tst 1978–, sec Trg and Enterprise Sussex C of C 1990–, pres Sussex Co Golf Union 1994–, tstee Mid-Sussex NHS Tst 1996–; Freeman: City of London 1968, Worshipful Co of Curriers (Master 1986); memb: Law Soc 1961–, IOD 1979–; *Books* Accounting for Solicitors (1965), Some Aspects of the Family Company (with M J Long, 1979); *Recreations* golf, reading, after dinner speaking; *Style—* Derek Sparrow, Esq; ✉ 52 Brittany Road, Hove, East Sussex BN3 4PB (☎ 01273 420993); Donne Mileham & Haddock, 42 Frederick Place, Brighton, E Sussex BN1 1AT (☎ 01273 329833, fax 01273 739764)

SPARROW, Sir John; kt (1984); s of Richard Albert Sparrow, and Winifred Sparrow; *b* 4 June 1933; *Educ* Stationers' Company's Sch, LSE (BScEcon); *m* 1967, Cynthia Naomi Whitehouse; *Career* with Rawlinson & Hunter CAs 1954–59, Ford Motor Co 1960, AEI Hotpoint Ltd 1960–63, United Leasing Corporation 1963–64, Morgan Grenfell 1964–88; dir: Federated Chemicals (formerly Greeff Chemicals) 1969–78 (chm 1974–78), Morgan Grenfell & Co Ltd 1970–82 and 1983–86, Morgan Grenfell Group plc (formerly Morgan Grenfell Holdings Ltd) 1971–82 and 1983–88, Harris Lebus 1973–79, United Gas Industries 1974–82 (dep chm 1981–82), Gas and Oil Acreage 1975–78, Tioxide Group 1977–78; chm Wormald International Holdings (formerly Mather & Platt) 1979–81; seconded as head of Central Policy Review Staff Cabinet Office 1982–83; chm: Morgan Grenfell Asset Management Ltd 1985–88, Morgan Grenfell Laurie Holdings Ltd 1985–88; dir: Coalite Group plc 1974–82 and 1984–89, Short Bros plc 1984–89 (dep chm 1985–89), ASW Holdings plc 1987–93, Regalian Properties plc 1990–93, Metropolitan & Country Racecourse Management & Holdings Ltd 1991–; dep chm National & Provincial Building Society 1994–96 (memb London Advsy Bd 1986–89, dir 1989–96); Cons cncllr in Enfield 1961–62; memb: Peterborough Development Corporation 1981–88; chm: Process Plant EDC 1984–85, Ctee of Enquiry into the Future of the National Stud 1985, National Stud 1988–91, Universities Superannuation Scheme Ltd 1988–96, Horserace Betting Levy Bd 1991–, Racecourse Technical Services Ltd 1991–94, Horseracing Forensic Laboratory Ltd 1991–; vice chm Govrs LSE 1984–93; hon fell: Wolfson Coll Cambridge 1987, LSE 1994; FCA 1957; *Recreations* reading, walking, racing, cricket, crosswords; *Clubs* MCC; *Style—* Sir John Sparrow; ✉ 52 Grosvenor Gardens, London SW1W 0AU (☎ 0171 333 0043, fax 0171 333 0041)

SPATHIS, Dr Gerassimos Spyros (Memos); s of Spyros Andrew Spathis (d 1975), of Cephalonia, Greece, and Olga, *née* Georgopoulos; *b* 20 April 1935; *Educ* The King's Sch Canterbury, Exeter Coll Oxford (MA, DM), Guy's Hosp London; *m* 3 June 1967, Maria, da of Demetrius Messinezy, of Tinos and Geneva; 2 da (Anna b 1969, Sonia b 1971); *Career* various positions held at: Guy's Hosp, Osler Hosp Oxford, Addenbrooke's Hosp Cambridge, St Thomas's Hosp, Central Middlesex and Middlesex Hosps London; physician St Helier Hosp Carshalton 1972, hon physician Royal Marsden Hosp Sutton, hon sr lectr St George's Hosp Med Sch, first sub dean St Helier Hosp 1986–93; vice chm SW Thames RHA 1989–93 (memb 1984–93), memb Cncl NAHAT 1989–93; Liveryman Worshipful Soc of Apothecaries; FRCP 1977, DPMSA; *Recreations* hill walking, photography; *Style—* Dr G S Spathis; ✉ St Anthony's Hospital, London Rd, N Cheam (☎ 0181 337 6691)

SPAVEN, Dr Patrick John; s of John Basil Spaven (d 1960), and Marie, *née* Burford; *b* 2 Nov 1949; *Educ* Felsted, Univ of Sussex (MA), Univ of Warwick (PhD); *m* 1976, Kirsti, da of Hans-Jacob Hallvang; 1 s (Thomas b 8 June 1983), 1 da (Rebecca b 10 Oct 1990); *Career* tutor in industl studies Univ of Sheffield 1974–76, Nuffield research assoc Univ of Warwick 1976–77, industl relations offr Advisory Conciliation and Arbitration Service 1977–80; British Council: industl relations advsr 1980–84, asst rep Kenya 1984–88, head of employment relations 1988–91, dir Barcelona 1991–; hon memb Anglo-Catalan Soc 1993–; MIPM 1984; *Style—* Dr Patrick Spaven; ✉ Institut Britanic, C/Amigo 83, 08021 Barcelona, Spain

SPAWFORTH, David Meredith; s of Lawrence Spawforth (d 1965), and Gwendoline, *née* Meredith; *b* 2 Jan 1938; *Educ* Silcoates Sch, Hertford Coll Oxford (MA); *m* 17 Aug 1963, Yvonne Mary, da of Roy Gude (d 1987); 1 s (Graham David b 22 Dec 1964), 1 da (Fiona Jane b 20 Sept 1968); *Career* asst master Winchester Coll 1961–64, house master Wellington Coll 1967–80 (asst master 1964–67), headmaster Merchiston Castle Sch Edinburgh 1981–; govr of various schs, memb HMC; FRSA; *Recreations* walking, theatre, France; *Clubs* East India; *Style—* David Spawforth, Esq; ✉ Headmaster's House, Merchiston Castle School, Colinton, Edinburgh EH13 0PU (☎ 0131 441 3468 and 0131 441 1722, fax 0131 441 6060)

SPEAIGHT, Anthony Hugh; QC (1995); s of George Victor Speaight, of Kew Gardens, Surrey, and Mary Olive, *née* Mudd; *b* 31 July 1948; *Educ* St Benedict's Sch Ealing, Lincoln Coll Oxford (MA); *m* 3 Aug 1991, Gabrielle Anne Kooy-Lister; 2 s (Edmund William Laurier b 18 July 1992, Lawrence Frederick Joseph b 28 May 1996), 1 da (Isabella Louise Annunziata b 14 Sept 1994); *Career* called to the Bar Middle Temple 1973; elected memb Gen Cncl of the Bar 1987–91, memb Bar Cncl Working Pty on Televising Cts 1988; chm Editorial Bd Counsel (jl of the Bar of Eng and Wales) 1991–95; nat chm Fedn of Cons Students 1972–73, chm Youth Bd of the Euro Movement (UK) 1974–75, dep chm Cons Gp for Europe 1977; Freeman City of London; Schuman Silver medal (awarded by FVS Fndn of the FDR) 1976; *Books* The Law of Defective Premises (with G Stone, 1982), The Architects Journal Legal Handbook (jtly, 1985–95); *Recreations* fox-hunting, theatre, cricket; *Clubs* Carlton, Hurlingham; *Style—* Anthony Speaight, Esq, QC; ✉ 12 King's Bench Walk, Temple, London EC4 (☎ 0171 583 0811, fax 0171 583 7228)

SPEAR, Prof Walter Eric; s of David Spear (d 1945), of London, and Eva, *née* Reineck (d 1978); *b* 20 Jan 1921; *Educ* Musterschule Frankfurt am Main, Univ of London (BSc, PhD, DSc); *m* 15 Dec 1952, Hilda Doris, da of John Charles King (d 1985), of London; 2 da (Gillian b 1961, Kathryn b 1963); *Career* lectr in physics (later reader) Univ of Leicester 1953, Harris prof of physics Univ of Dundee 1968–91, prof emeritus 1991–; author of numerous res papers on electronic and transport properties in crystalline solids, liquids and amorphous semi-conductors; Europhysics Prize of Euro Physical Soc 1977, Max Born Medal and Prize Inst of Physics and German Physical Soc 1977, Makdougall-Brisbane Medal of RSE 1981, Maxwell Premium of IEE 1981 and 1982, Rank Prize for Optoelectronics 1988; Mott Award 1989, Rumford Medal of RS 1990; FInstP 1962, FRSE 1972, FRS 1980; *Recreations* music, literature; *Style—* Prof Walter Spear, FRS, FRSE; ✉ 20 Kelso Place, Dundee DD2 1SL (☎ 01382 667649)

SPEARING, Prof Anthony Colin; s of Frederick Spearing, and Gertrude, *née* Calnin; *b* 31 Jan 1936; *Educ* Alleyn's Sch Dulwich, Jesus Coll Cambridge (MA); *m* 1961; 1 s, 1 da; *Career* res on Piers Plowman under supervision of CS Lewis and Elizabeth Salter 1957–60; Univ of Cambridge: WM Tapp fell Gonville & Caius Coll 1959–60, asst lectr in English 1960–64, supernumerary fell Gonville and Caius Coll 1960; Queens' Coll: asst dir of studies in English 1960–67, lectr in English 1964–85, dir of studies in English 1967–85, sec Faculty of English 1970–71, chm Degree Ctee Faculty of English 1977–79, reader in Medieval English lit 1985–87, chm Faculty of English 1986–87, official fell 1960–87, life fell 1987–; Univ of Virginia: visiting prof of English 1979–80 and 1984, Center for Advanced Studies 1987–89, prof of English 1987–89, William R Kenan prof of English 1989–; external examiner: Univ of Bristol 1974, MA in Medieval Studies Univ of York 1974–76; Studentship Selection Ctee UK Dept of Education and Science 1976–79, William Matthews lectr Birkbeck Coll Univ of London 1983–84; Lansdowne visiting fell Univ of Victoria BC 1993; visiting lectr at numerous univs in Britain, Europe, Canada and USA; *Books* Criticism and Medieval Poetry (1964, 2 edn 1972), An Introduction to Chaucer (with Maurice Hussey and James Winny, 1965), The Gawain Poet: A Critical Study (1970), Chaucer: Troilus and Criseyde (1976), Medieval Dream-Poetry (1976), Medieval to Renaissance in English Poetry (1985), Readings in Medieval Poetry (1987), The Medieval Poet as Voyeur (1993); contrib to numerous learned jls; *Style—* Prof A C Spearing; ✉ Department of English, Bryan Hall, University of Virginia, Charlottesville, Va 22903, USA

SPEARING, (David) Nicholas; s of George David Spearing, of Caterham, Surrey, and Josephine Mary, *née* Newbould; *b* 4 May 1954; *Educ* Caterham Sch, Hertford Coll Oxford (BA, MA); *m* 20 Sept 1980, Annemarie, da of Ernest Thomas John Gatford (d 1989), of Smallfield, Surrey; 2 da (Laura b 1982, Elizabeth b 1987), 2 s (James b 1989, George b 1992); *Career* slr; articled Gordon Dadds & Co 1976–78; Freshfields: asst slr 1978–84, ptnr 1984–; past chm Law Soc Slrs' Euro Gp; memb: Jt Law Soc, Bar Competition Law Working Pty; memb City of London Slrs Co; *Books* contrib: Encyclopaedia of Forms and Precedents (1985), Butterworths Competition Law (1991); author of articles in professional jls; *Recreations* reading, tennis, golf; *Style—* Nicholas Spearing, Esq; ✉ The Coach House, St Mary's Abbey, Woolmer Hill, Haslemere, Surrey GU27 1QA (☎ 01428 653 210, fax 01428 661 570); Whitefriars, 65 Fleet Street, London EC4Y 1HS (☎ 0171 936 4000, fax 0171 832 7001)

SPEARING, Nigel John; MP (Lab) Newham South (majority 2,502); s of T A E Spearing, of Hammersmith; *b* 8 Oct 1930; *Educ* Latymer Upper Sch, St Catharine's Coll Cambridge; *m* 1956, Wendy, da of Percy Newman, of Newport; 1 s, 2 da; *Career* Nat Serv RCS ranks and cmmn 1950–52; teacher Wandsworth Sch 1956–68, dir Thameside R & D Group 1968–69, housemaster Elliott Sch Putney 1969–70; Parly candidate (Lab) Warwick and Leamington 1964; co-opted GLC Planning and Tport Ctees 1966–73; MP (Lab): Acton 1970–Feb 1974, Newham S May 1974– (by-election); pres Socialist Environment and Resources Assoc 1977–86, chm Anti-Common Market Campaign 1977–83; memb Select Ctees on: Members' Interests 1973–74, Procedure 1975–79, Overseas Devpt 1972–74 and 1977–79, Sound Bdcasting 1978–83, Foreign Affairs 1979–87, Euro Legislation 1979– (chm 1983–92); chm PLP Parly Affairs Ctee 1989–; memb Bd Christian Aid 1987–91, a vice pres River Thames Soc 1975–; *Style—* Nigel Spearing, Esq, MP; ✉ House of Commons, London SW1A 0AA

SPEARING, Roger Edward; s of Edward George Spearing (d 1986), and Joan Audrey, *née* Greaves, of Aldeburgh, Suffolk; *b* 19 Feb 1946; *Educ* Felsted; *m* 24 July 1971, Lindy Frances, da of Walter Freeman (Mickie), of Chigwell, Essex; 3 da (Emma b 1976, Charlotte (twin) b 1976, Victoria b 1982); *Career* CA; Chalmers Impey & Co 1964–72, tech mangr Save & Prosper Group Ltd 1972–79, co fndr and dir Sun Life Unit Services Ltd 1980–89, dir Valens Associates Ltd 1991–94, co-fndr and md The Langton Partnership Ltd 1992–94, conslt George Rutt & Co; FCA 1979 (ACA 1968); *Recreations* equestrian activities; *Style—* Roger Spearing, Esq; ✉ Hastingwood Farm, Hastingwood, Essex CM17 9JX (☎ 01279 422718)

SPEARMAN, Sir Alexander Young Richard Mainwaring Spearman; 5 Bt (UK 1840), of Hanwell, Middlesex; s of Sir Alexander Bowyer Spearman, 4 Bt (d 1977); *b* 3 Feb 1969; *Heir* unc, Dr Richard Ian Campbell Spearman b 14 Aug 1926; *Style—* Sir Alexander Spearman, Bt; ✉ Zorgvliet, 3 Sir George Grey Street, Oranjezicht 8001, Cape RSA

SPEARMAN, John Litting; s of Thomas Spearman, and Elizabeth Alexandra, *née* Leadbeater; *b* 25 Nov 1941; *Educ* Trinity Coll Dublin (MA Mathematics); *m* 1, 1966, Susan Elizabeth, *née* Elwes; 1 da (Laragh Elizabeth Jane), 1 s (Thomas Crawford John); m 2, 1988, Angela Josephine, *née* van Praag; *Career* graduate trainee Unilever 1964, account dir Lintas Advtg 1969, account dir and assoc bd dir Leo Burnett 1969–73, account dir, md then chm and chief exec Collett Dickenson Pearce 1973–90, chm Lazer Sales (sales and mktg subsid of LWT) 1990–92, chief exec Classic FM Radio 1992–; chm Playback (mgmnt trg video co) 1990–; bd dir Royal Philharmonic Orch 1993–96, memb Industry Lead Body for Design, patron dir RIBA, tstee World Monuments Fund, chm Classic FM Charitable Tst 1992–, pres Music Therapy Appeal Ctee; memb Arts Cncl; *Recreations* music, theatre, reading, gardening, walking, skiing, sailing; *Clubs* Royal Irish Yacht, Hurlingham, Mark's; *Style—* John Spearman, Esq; ✉ Classic FM Radio, Academic House, 24–28 Oval Road, London NW1 7DQ (☎ 0171 713 2629, fax 0171 713 2630)

SPEARMAN, Richard; QC (1996); s of Clement Spearman, CBE, of 56 Riverview Gardens, Barnes, London, and Olwen Regina, *née* Morgan; *b* 19 Jan 1953; *Educ* Bedales Sch, King's Coll Cambridge (MA); *m* 30 April 1983, Alexandra Elizabeth, da of Bryan A Harris, of Churchills, Sidmouth, Devon; 3 da (Olivia b 6 July 1985, Annabel b 11 Oct 1987, Lucinda b 16 Jan 1992); *Career* called to the Bar Middle Temple 1977; *Books* Sale of Goods Litigation (with F A Philpott, 1983, 2 edn 1994); *Recreations* tennis, skiing; *Clubs* Brooks's, Hurlingham, MCC; *Style—* Richard Spearman, Esq, QC; ✉ 5 Raymond Buildings, Gray's Inn, London WC1R 5BP (☎ 0171 242 2902, fax 0171 831 2686)

SPEARMAN, Dr Richard Ian Campbell; s of Sir Alexander Young Spearman, 3 Bt (d 1959), and Dorothy Catherine (d 1982); hp of nephew, Sir Alexander Spearman, 5 Bt; *b* 14 Aug 1926; *Educ* Clayesmore Sch, S London Coll, Birkbeck Coll London (BSc), UCL

(PhD, DSc); *Career* biologist; Microbial Dept Hon Sch of Hygiene 1948–49, Infestation Control Div MAFF 1949–52, Nat Inst for Med Research 1952–54, Genetics Dept UCL 1954–57, MRC research staff 1957–70, res conslt 1970–86, hon sr lectr UCL 1970–; memb: Soc of Experimental Biology, Br Ecological Soc, Int Cmmn for Avian Anatomical Nomenclature 1971–86; chm Integument Sub-Ctee 1985–86, fndr memb European Soc for Dermatological Research 1971–90, memb Mgmnt Ctee London Skin Club 1977–81, pres Euro Soc for Comparative Skin Biology 1978–82, chm Int Cmmn on Skin Biology of Int Union for Biological Sciences 1979–82, memb Mgmnt Ctee Biological Cncl 1980–92, memb Royal Soc and Inst of Biology Jt Ctee on Biological Educn 1980–86, ed Biological Cncl Conference Guide 1981–89 (and Handbook 1989–91); CBiol, FIBiol, FLS (vice-pres 1977–79), Scientific FZS; author of over 80 research papers, reviews and books, mainly on cell biology, skin biology (especially keratinization) and ornithology; *Books* The Integument, Comparative Biology of Skin, The Skin of Vertebrates, The Biochemistry of Skin Disease; *Recreations* travel, natural history, local history, music; *Style—* Dr Richard Spearman; ✉ 70 Hatherley Road, Winchester, Hants SO22 6RR (☎ 01962 852010)

SPECULAND, Bernard; s of Cyril Speculand (d 1953), and Hannah, *née* Shelower; *b* 26 Aug 1949; *Educ* City of Norwich GS, Univ of Bristol (BDS, MDS); *m* 19 Dec 1975, Christine, da of Alec Turner; 1 s (Alex b 1982), 2 da (Caroline b 1977, Mary b 1980); *Career* sr registrar: Royal Adelaide Hosp 1977, Bristol Royal Infirmary, Bristol Dental Hosp and Frenchay Hosp 1978–85; conslt oral and maxillo-facial surgn City Hosp Birmingham 1985–; pres Birmingham Medico Legal Soc 1993–95 (vice pres 1991–93); fell BAOMS, FRACDS 1977, FDSRCS 1975, FFDRCSI 1975; *Books* The Mouth and Peri-Oral Tissues in Health and Disease (contrib, 1989); *Recreations* squash, running, windsurfing; *Style—* Bernard Speculand, Esq; ✉ Department of Oral Surgery & Orthodontics, City Hospital, Birmingham B18 7QH (☎ 0121 554 3801)

SPEDDING, Prof Sir Colin Raymond William; kt (1994), CBE (1988); s of late Rev Robert K Spedding, and Ilynn, *née* Bannister; *b* 22 March 1925; *Educ* Univ of London (BSc, MSc, PhD, DSc); *m* 6 Sept 1952, Betty Noreen (d 1988), da of late A H George; 2 s (Peter George b 1954 d 1958, Geoffrey Robert b 1957), 1 da (Lucilla Mary (Mrs Weston) b 1960); *Career* Sub Lt RNVR 1943–46; Grassland Res Inst 1949–75 (dep dir 1972–75); Univ of Reading: visiting prof then pt/t prof Dept of Agric and Horticulture 1970–75, prof of agric systems Dept of Agric 1970–90, head Dept of Agric and Horticulture 1975–83, dir Centre for Agric Strategy 1981–90, dean Faculty of Agric and Food 1983–86, pro vice chllr 1986–90, emeritus prof 1990–; dir and dep chm Lands Improvement Holdings plc; dir Centre for Economic and Environmental Devpt; pres: Euro Assoc of Animal Prodn Study Cmmn on Sheep and Goat Prodn 1970–76, Br Soc of Animal Prodn 1979–80; ed Agricultural Systems 1976–88, vice chm Prog Ctee Int Livestock Centre for Africa Addis Ababa 1980–83 (memb 1976–80); chm: Bd of UK Register of Organic Food Standards 1987–, Farm Animal Welfare Cncl 1988–, Nat Resources Policy Gp Inst of Biology 1988–92, Apple and Pear Res Cncl 1989–, Scientific Advsy Panel of World Soc for Protection of Animals 1989–, Kintail Land Res Fndn 1990–, Nat Equine Forum 1992–, CSTI 1994–; pres Inst of Biology 1992–94 (vice pres 1987–91); sr conslt to Agric & Food Res Cncl 1992–94; memb: Media Resource Services Steering Ctee 1985–, Governing Body Inst of Grassland and Environmental Res 1987–91, Cncl of Mgmnt PDSA 1988–, Food Safety Policy Gp Inst of Biology 1990–92; conslt dir Centre for Agric Strategy; patron: Family Farmers' Assoc, Nat Sci Centre; vice patron Fruit Culture Tst; awards: Canadian Inst of Agric Recognition Award 1971, George Hedley Meml Award 1971, Wooldridge Meml lectr and medallist (BVA) 1982, Massey Ferguson National Agricultural Award 1991, Hawkesbury Centenary Medal of Honour Univ of Western Sydney Aust 1991, Bawden Meml lectr 1992, Hammond Meml lectr 1995, Hume Meml lectr 1996, Paul Lynch address 1996; Hon DSc Reading 1995; hon life memb Br Soc of Animal Sci, hon assoc RCVS 1994, Hon FIBiol 1994; FZS 1962, FIBiol 1967, CBiol 1984, FRASE 1984, FIHort 1986, FRAgS 1986, FRSA 1988, MInstD 1992, FLS 1994; *Books* Sheep Production and Grazing Management (2 edn, 1970), Grassland Ecology (1971), Grasses and Legumes in British Agriculture (ed with E C Diekmahns, 1972), The Biology of Agricultural Systems (1975), Vegetable Productivity (ed, 1981), Biological Efficiency in Agriculture (with J M Walsingham and A M Hoxey, 1981), Fream's Agriculture (ed, 1983), An Introduction to Agricultural Systems (2 edn, 1988), Fream's Principles of Food & Agriculture (ed, 1992), Agriculture and the Citizen (1996); *Clubs* Athenaeum, Farmers'; *Style—* Prof Sir Colin Spedding, CBE; ✉ Vine Cottage, Orchard Rd, Hurst, Berks RG10 0SD (☎ 0118 934 1771, fax 0118 934 2997)

SPEED, Gary Andrew; s of Roger Speed, of 8 Courtland Drive, Aston Park, Deeside, Clwyd, and Carol, *née* Huxely; *b* 8 Sept 1969; *Educ* Deeside HS, Hawarden HS; *Career* professional footballer; Leeds Utd: joined from school 1986, first team debut v Oldham Athletic 1989, over 100 appearances, League Championship winners 1992; transferred Everton FC (fee £3.5m) 1996; Wales caps: 6 youth, 2 under 21, 4 full; *Recreations* golf, snooker, cricket, fishing, films, TV, fashion; *Style—* Gary Speed, Esq; ✉ c/o Everton FC, Goodison Park, Liverpool L4 4EL

SPEED, James Nicholas; s of J R G Speed, of The Cedar House Gallery, Ripley, Surrey, and J Speed, *née* Williamson; *b* 24 Dec 1958; *Educ* Wellington; *Career* hotelier; three year's experience at The Lancaster Hotel Paris, currently md Durrant's Hotel London; Which London Hotel of the Year 1992 and 1993; *Recreations* buying and collecting fine art at auction and The Cedar House Gallery Ripley, collecting fine wines, house restoration; *Style—* James Speed, Esq; ✉ Durrants Hotel, George Street, London W1H 6BJ (☎ 0171 935 8131, fax 0171 487 3510)

SPEED, Sir (Herbert) Keith; kt (1992), RD (1967), DL (Kent 1996), MP (C) Ashford (majority 17,359); s of Herbert Victor Speed (d 1971), of Bletchley, Bucks, and Alice Dorothy Barbara, *née* Mumford; *b* 11 March 1934; *Educ* Bedford Modern, RNC Dartmouth, RNC Greenwich; *m* 14 Oct 1961, Peggy Voss, da of Cedric Cyril Clarke (d 1983); 3 s (Herbert Mark Jefferey b 1963, Crispin Nicholas b 1965 d 1967, Nicholas William b 1968), 1 da (Emma Jane b 1970); *Career* offr RN (incl Korean War) 1947–57, Lt Cdr RNR; sales mangr Amos (Electronics) 1957–60, mktg mangr Plysu Products 1960–65, CRD 1965–68; MP (C): Meriden 1968–74, Ashford 1974–; asst Govt whip 1970–71, Lord Cmmr of the Treasy (Govt whip) 1971–72; Parly under sec: DOE 1972–74, MOD (RN) 1979–81; oppn spokesman: on environment 1975–77, on home affrs 1977–79; Parly conslt to Professional Assoc of Teachers 1982–, memb Parly Assembly Cncl of Europe and Western Euro Union 1987–; dir Folkestone Water Co 1986–, chm Local Council Leasing Plc 1995–; patron: E Ashford Rural Tst, Ashford Branch BDA; *Books* Blueprint for Britain (1964), Sea Change (1982); *Recreations* classical music, opera, reading; *Clubs* Garrick, Hurst Castle Sailing; *Style—* Sir Keith Speed, RD, DL, MP; ✉ House of Commons, London SW1 1AA (☎ 0171 219 4516)

SPEED, Sir Robert William Arney; kt (1954), CB (1946), QC (1963); s of Sir Edwin Arney Speed (d 1941), of Remenham House, Henley-on-Thames, and Ada Frances, *née* Ross (d 1953); *b* 18 July 1905; *Educ* Rugby, Trinity Coll Cambridge (MA); *m* 25 April 1929, Phyllis (d 1991), da of Rev Philip Armitage (d 1960), of Farne, Nettlebed, Oxon; 1 s (John b 30 March 1934, d 1992), 1 da (Sarah b 5 April 1931, d 24 Aug 1976); *Career* called to the Bar Inner Temple 1928, princ asst slr to HM Procurator Gen and Treasy 1945–48, slr BOT 1948–60, bencher 1961, counsel to the Speaker 1960–80; *Recreations* golf; *Clubs* United Oxford and Cambridge, Hon Co of Edinburgh Golfers, Huntercombe Golf; *Style—* Sir Robert Speed, CB, QC; ✉ Upper Culham, Wargrave, Reading, Berks RG10 8NR (☎ 01491 574271)

SPEIGHT, Martin Peter; s of Peter John Speight, of Hassocks, Sussex, and Valerie, *née* Brown; *b* 24 Oct 1967; *Educ* Hurstpierpont Coll, Univ of Durham (BA, cricket palatinate); *partner* Lisa Montague; *Career* professional cricketer Sussex CCC 1986– (awarded county cap 1991); represented: Combined Univs in Benson & Hedges Cup 1986–89 (reached quarter finals 1989), England Schs under 15's 1984, England Young Cricketers' tour Sri Lanka 1987; professional cricket coach Wellington NZ winters 1989–93 and 1995–96, player Wellington State team Shell Trophy 1990, 1993 and 1995–96; memb Professional Cricket Assoc; artist; work incl paintings of cricket grounds at Arundel, Hove, Southampton, Oval, Colchester, Eastbourne, Horsham, Worcester, Lords Abergavenny and The Basin Reserve NZ; Christmas cards published 1994; *Books* A Cricketer's View (book of cricket ground paintings, 1995); *Recreations* most sports including golf, hockey, squash, rowing and rugby; *Style—* Martin Speight, Esq; ✉ 45 Maldon Road, Brighton, East Sussex, BN1 5BD; c/o Sussex CCC, The County Ground, Eaton Rd, Hove, E Sussex BN3 3AN (☎ 01273 732161, fax 01273 771549)

SPEIR, Sir Rupert Malise; kt (1964); 3 s of Lt-Col Guy Speir (whose mother was Hon Emily Gifford, 3 da of 2nd Baron Gifford), by his w Mary (6 da of John Fletcher of Saltoun, JP, DL, whose w Bertha was a member of the Talbot family of Lacock Abbey & hence a connection of William Henry Fox Talbot, the pioneer of photography); *b* 10 Sept 1910; *Educ* Eton, Pembroke Coll Cambridge; *Career* served WWII Intelligence Corps (Lt-Col 1945); chm: Matthew Hall & Co until 1982, Common Bros; employee J Henry Schroder Wagg, dir Lloyds Bank N Regnl Bd; slr 1936; MP (C) Hexham 1951–66, PPS to: Min State FO & Parly Sec CRO 1956–59, Parly & Financial Sec Admiralty & Civil Lord of the Admiralty 1952–56; contested (C): Linlithgow 1945, Leek 1950; vice pres Keep Britain Tidy Gp; Liveryman Worshipful Co of Fishmongers; *Style—* Sir Rupert Speir; ✉ Birtley Hall, Hexham, Northumberland NE48 3HL (☎ 01434 230275)

SPEKE, (Ian) Benjamin; s of Col Neil Hanning Reed Speke, MC, TD (d 1996), of Aydon White House, Corbridge, Northumberland, and Averil Allgood, *née* Straker; *b* 12 March 1950; *Educ* Eton; *m* 30 July 1983, Ailsa Elizabeth, da of Matthew Hall Fenwick, of Capheaton, Newcastle upon Tyne; 1 s (Toby b 1989), 2 da (Zara b 1988, Thea b 1990); *Career* 9/12 Royal Lancers (Prince of Wales) 1968–72, Northumberland Hussars (Queen's Own Yeo) 1974–87; Pinchin Denny 1974–77, Hoare Govett Equity sales 1977–80, ptnr Wise Speke & Co 1980–87, dir Wise Speke Ltd 1987–; memb Int Stock Exchange 1980; *Recreations* field sports; *Clubs* Pratt's, Turf, Northern Cos; *Style—* Benjamin Speke, Esq; ✉ Thornbrough High House, Corbridge, Northumberland NE45 5PR (☎ 01434 633080); Wise Speke Ltd, Commercial Union House, 39 Pilgrim St, Newcastle upon Tyne NE1 6RQ (☎ 0191 201 3800, fax 0191 201 3801)

SPELLAR, John Francis; MP (Lab) Warley West (majority 5,472); s of William David Spellar; *b* 5 Aug 1947; *Educ* Dulwich, St Edmund Hall Oxford; *m* 1981, Anne; 1 da; *Career* nat offr EETPU 1969–82 and 1983–92; Parly candidate (Lab) Bromley 1970; MP (Lab): Birmingham Northfield 1982–83 (also contested 1983 and 1987), Warley W 1992–; memb Commons Select Ctee on Energy 1982–83, sec All Pty Construction Ctee 1992–, oppn whip (Employment and Trade and Indust) 1992–94, oppn spokesman on NI 1994–95, oppn spokesman on Defence 1995–; *Recreations* reading, gardening; *Clubs* Rowley Regis and Blackheath Labour; *Style—* John Spellar, Esq, MP; ✉ House of Commons, London SW1A 0AA (☎ 0171 219 5800)

SPELMAN, Richard; *b* 1946; *Educ* CIM (grad), Harvard Business Sch Advanced Mgmnt Program (grad); *m*; 2 da; *Career* The Halifax Building Society: joined as mgmnt trainee Lincolnshire 1964, assr dist mangr Wimbledon office 1969–73, asst advtg mangr Head Office 1973–79, advtg mangr 1979–82, mktg controller 1982–85, memb Exec 1985–, asst gen mangr mktg servs 1985–89, gen mangr mktg 1989–95, dir of banking and business devpt 1995, dir of distribution 1996–; dir: Halifax Estate Agencies Ltd, Halifax General Insurance Services Ltd; HM Treasy advsr to Govt on advtg 1990–; former memb Exec Ctee and former chm Press Cncl Incorporated Soc of Br Advertisers, memb Cncl Advtg Standards Bd of Fin; *Clubs* Reform, Harvard (Boston); *Style—* Richard Spelman, Esq; ✉ Halifax Building Society, Trinity Rd, Halifax, West Yorkshire HX1 2RG (☎ 01422 333333, fax 01422 333567)

SPENCE, Prof Alastair Andrew; CBE (1993); s of James Glendinning Spence (d 1964), of Doonfoot, Ayr, and Margaret, *née* Macdonald (d 1986); *b* 18 Sept 1936; *Educ* Ayr Acad, Univ of Glasgow (MB ChB, MD); *m* Maureen Isobel, da of David Aitchison (d 1948), of Prestwick, Ayrshire; 2 s (Andrew b 15 May 1965, Stuart b 17 Sept 1966); *Career* prof and head Univ Dept of Anaesthesia Western Infirmary Glasgow 1969–84, prof of anaesthetics Univ of Edinburgh 1984–; Royal Coll of Anaesthetists: vice pres 1988–91, pres 1991–94, pres Scottish Soc of Anaesthetists 1995–96, memb Clinical Standards Advsy Gp 1994–, memb Scottish Sub-Ctee Advsy Ctee on Distinction Awards 1994– (med vice chm 1995–); chm: Bd Br Jl of Anaesthesia 1983–91, UK Anaesthetic Res Soc; Hon FDS RCS Eng; FRCA 1963, FRCP Glas and Ed, FRCSEd and Eng; *Books* Respiratory Monitoring in Intensive Care (1982), Norris and Campbell's Anaesthesia, Resuscitation and Intensive Care (7 edn, 1989); *Recreations* golf, gardening; *Clubs* Caledonian; *Style—* Prof Alastair Spence, CBE; ✉ Harewood, Kilmacolm PA13 4HX; 3–9 Dun-Ard Gdns, Edinburgh EH9 2HZ (☎ 0131 667 0231); Department of Anaesthetics, Royal Infirmary, Edinburgh EH3 9YW (☎ 0131 536 3654, fax 0131 536 3672)

SPENCE, Christopher A; MBE (1992); s of Robert Donald Spence (d 1993), of Ifield, and Margaret, *née* Summerford (d 1994); *b* 24 April 1944; *Educ* Bromsgrove Sch Worcs; *m* 1990, Nancy Corbin, da of late Max Meadors; *Career* freelance cnsllr 1976–86; London Lighthouse: fndr dir 1992–96, pres 1997–; fndr chair Pan London HIV/AIDS Providers Consortium 1992–96; dir of courses Urban Ministry Project, lectr Counselling Dip Course London; dir Task Force, private sec to Speaker of the House of Lords; *Books* A Homecoming and the Harvest - A Counsellor's View of Death, Dying and Bereavement, At Least 100 Principles of Love (with Nancy Kline), AIDS: An Issue for Everyone, AIDS: Time to Reclaim Our Power, On Watch: Views from the Lighthouse; *Style—* Christopher Spence, Esq, MBE; ✉ London Lighthouse, 111 Lancaster Road, London W11 1QT (☎ 0171 792 1200, fax 0171 229 1258)

SPENCE, Christopher John; s of Brig Ian Fleming Morris Spence, OBE, MC, TD, ADC (d 1966), of London, and Ruth, *née* Peacock (d 1961); *b* 4 June 1937; *Educ* Marlborough; *m* 1, 1960 (m dis 1968), Merle Aurelia, er da of Sir Leonard Ropner, 1 Bt, MC, TD (d 1977); 1 s (Jeremy b 1964 (d 1982)), 1 da (Miranda (Mrs Patrick Barran) b 1963); m 2, 1970, Susan, da of Brig Michael Morley, MBE (d 1990), of Wiltshire; 1 s (Jonathan b 1975), 1 da (Lara b 1972); *Career* 2 Lt 10 Royal Hussars (PWO) 1955–57, Royal Wilts Yeo 1957–66; memb London Stock Exchange 1959–78; chm English Trust Co Ltd 1991– (md 1978–91); High Sheriff of Berkshire 1996–97; *Recreations* racing, shooting, golf; *Clubs* Jockey, Pratt's, Cavalry and Guards', City of London, Swinley Forest Golf; *Style—* Christopher Spence, Esq; ✉ Chieveley Manor, Newbury, Berks RG20 8UT (☎ 01635 248208); 18A Maunsel Street, London SW1 (☎ 0171 828 1484); 12A Charterhouse Square, London EC1M 6AX (☎ 0171 608 0888)

SPENCE, Prof David Allan; s of Allan Lemuel Spence (d 1942), of Auckland, NZ, and Dorothy Louisa, *née* Matthews (d 1982); *b* 3 Jan 1926; *Educ* King's Coll Auckland NZ, Clare Coll Cambridge (MA, PhD), Univ of Oxford (DSc); *m* 19 March 1955, Isobel Begg, da of Robert Maxton Ramsay (d 1957), of Glasgow; 2 da (Anne (Mrs Young) b 1956, Barbara b 1960), 2 s (Paul b 1961, James b 1968); *Career* jr lectr Maths Dept Auckland UC (now Univ of Auckland NZ); flying offr RNZAF (Def Sci Branch) 1949–50; Aero Dept Royal Aircraft Estab Farnborough Hants 1952–64 (sr princ sci offr (individual merit) 1963); Univ of Oxford: Dept of Engrg Sci 1964–81, reader in theoretical mechanics 1977–81, fell Lincoln Coll 1964–81 and 1989–, currently with OCIAM (Oxford Centre for Industl & Applied Mathematics); Imperial Coll of Sci and Tech and Med London: prof of mathematics 1981–91, sr res fell 1991–95, prof emeritus 1991–; FRAeS, FIMA, CEng; *Publications* IMA Jl of Applied Mathematics (ed, 1975–91); jl contribs on aero-, fluid- and geomechanics; *Recreations* gardening, golf, hill walking; *Clubs* Climbers; *Style*— Prof David Spence; ✉ 16 Dunstan Road, Old Headington, Oxford OX3 9BY (☎ 01865 65663); Oxford Centre for Industrial and Applied Mathematics (☎ 01865 270510, fax 01865 270515)

SPENCE, David Lane; s of Dr A S Spence, and Edith F, *née* Lane; *b* 5 Oct 1943; *Educ* Fettes; *m* 1966, Beverley Esther, da of Gp Capt Jasper Cardale (d 1981); 1 s (William b 1978), 2 da (Sally b 1976, Sarah b 1980); *Career* CA; C F Middleton & Co 1962–67; Grant Thornton (formerly Thornton Baker): joined 1967, ptnr 1970, ptnr Euro practice 1974–79, chm Investigations Panel 1975–84 and 1990–, exec ptnr 1984–89; DTI inspector 1989 and 1992; Liveryman Worshipful Co of Glaziers; vice pres ICAS, chm CAs Joint Ethics Ctee; *Recreations* golf, skiing, opera; *Clubs* Caledonian, Royal & Ancient Golf, Sunningdale Golf; *Style*— David Spence, Esq; ✉ Grant Thornton House, Melton St, Euston Square, London NW1 2EP (☎ 0171 383 5100, fax 0171 387 5371)

SPENCE, Ian Richard; s of John Jack Spence (d 1976), and Floretta Eva, *née* Bate (d 1968); *b* 15 Oct 1938; *Educ* Dulwich Coll, Jesus Coll Cambridge (BA); *m* 1971, Anne, da of Col Arundel Kiggell; 2 da (Jacqueline b 1973, Fiona b 1975); *Career* civil servant; Inland Revenue: joined 1962, various policy and mgmnt appointments incl 2 secondments rising to dir Int Div 1991–; memb: Permanent Scientific Ctee Int Fiscal Assoc, Ctee of Fiscal Affairs OECD; *Recreations* tennis, opera, golf, bridge, cycling, sailing; *Clubs* Athenaeum, Dulwich Sports; *Style*— Ian Spence, Esq; ✉ Director, International Division, Board of Inland Revenue, Strand Bridge House, Strand, London WC2R 1HH (☎ 0171 438 6762, fax 0171 438 6396)

SPENCE, James William (Bill); DL (Orkney 1988); s of James William Spence, of Stromness, Orkney, and Margaret Duncan, *née* Peace; *b* 19 Jan 1945; *Educ* Firth Jr Secdy Sch Orkney, Leith Nautical Coll Edinburgh, Robert Gordon's Inst of Technol Aberdeen (Master Mariner), Univ of Wales Cardiff (BSc); *m* 31 July 1971, Margaret Paplay, da of Henry Stevenson (d 1983), of Stromness, Orkney; 3 s (James b 1976, Steven b 1978, Thomas b 1980); *Career* Merchant Navy 1961–74; apprentice deck offr Watts Watts & Co Ltd 1961–65, certificated deck offr P & O Steam Navigation Co Ltd 1965–74; Micoperi SpA 1974–75, temp asst site co-ordinator Scapa Flow Project; John Jolly: mangr 1975, jr ptnr 1976–77, sr ptnr 1977–78, md and proprietor 1978–; consul Norway 1978 (vice consul 1976–78), vice consul The Netherlands 1978–94, chm Assoc of Hon Norwegian Consuls in the UK and Ireland 1993–95 (vice chm 1991–93); station hon sec RNLI Kirkwall Lifeboat 1987–96 (dep Launching Authy 1976–87); memb: Kirkwall Community Cncl 1978–82, Orkney Pilotage Ctee 1979–88; chm: Kirkwall Port Employers' Assoc 1979–87 (memb 1975), Bd of Tstees Pier Arts Centre Tst Orkney 1989–91 (tstee 1980–91), Br Horse Soc Orkney Riding Club 1985–92 (memb 1984); MNI 1972, MICS 1979; Cdr Royal Norwegian Order of Merit 1987, Chevalier in the Order of Orange-Nassau (Netherlands) 1994; *Recreations* oenophilist, equestrian matters, Orcadian history; *Clubs* Caledonian; *Style*— J William Spence, Esq, DL; ✉ Alton House, Kirkwall, Orkney KW15 1NA; John Jolly, PO Box 2, 21 Bridge St, Kirkwall, Orkney KW15 1HR (☎ 01856 872268, fax 01856 875002, car 0585 200860, telex 75253)

SPENCE, John Alexander; s of James Alexander Spence (d 1960), of Maidstone, Kent, and Edith Charlotte, *née* Barden; *b* 11 April 1936; *Educ* Maidstone Tech Sch, Royal Dockyard Sch Chatham; *m* 2 July 1973, Patricia, o da of Oliver G A Pocock; *Career* engr (ret 1984); non-exec dir Radio Invicta Ltd, non-exec chm/dir various small private cos; chm: Kent Ambulance Serv 1986–93, Medway HA 1986–93, Medway NHS Tst 1993–; memb Shadow Bd W Kent Health Commissioning Agency 1991–93, formerly memb Cncl NAHA; vice pres Gillingham Cons Assoc 1973– (chm 1963–66, hon treas 1966–73); memb Kent CC 1973–93 (chief whip Cons Gp 1985–92), memb ACC 1982–93 (memb Police Ctee 1982–93, chm Local Govt Fin Ctee 1991–93), chm UK Standing Ctee on Local Govt Superannuation 1992–93; Kent Police Authy: memb 1973–93, vice chm 1973–77, chm 1981–86; memb Police Negotiating Bd and Central Ctee for Common Police Servs 1982–89, memb Police Trg Cncl and Bd of Govrs Bramshill Police Staff Coll 1989–93; memb: Cncl Univ of Kent, Chatham Historic Dockyard Tst, Exec Bd Kent Inst of Med and Health Scis, Ct Rochester Bridge Tst (Sr Warden 1992–94); pres New Coll of Cobham 1991–94, chm Bridge Wardens Coll Univ of Kent 1996; varied charitable work; hon fell S Bank Univ; FRSA; *Recreations* The National Trust; *Style*— John A Spence, Esq; ✉ 175 Fairview Avenue, Gillingham, Kent ME8 0PX (☎ 01634 232538); Medway NHS Trust, Medway Hospital, Windmill Road, Gillingham, Kent ME7 5NY (☎ 01634 830000 ext 3122, fax 01634 829470, mobile 0860 304130)

SPENCE, Prof John Edward (Jack); s of John Herbert Spence (d 1946), of Krugersdorp, SA, and Violet, *née* Brown (d 1976); *b* 11 June 1931; *Educ* Boys HS Pretoria SA, Univ of Witwatersrand Johannesburg SA (BA), LSE (BSc); *m* 27 June 1959, Susanne Hilary Spence; 1 da (Rachel b 1967); *Career* lectr Dept of History and Politics Univ of Natal Pietermaritzburg SA 1958–60, Rockefeller jr res fell LSE 1960–62, reader Dept of Governmental Political Theory Univ Coll Swansea 1972–73 (asst lectr 1962–63, lectr 1963–68, sr lectr 1968–72), prof Dept of Politics Univ of Leicester 1973–91 (head of Dept of Politics 1974–81 and 1986–91, pro vice chllr 1981–85), dir of studies Royal Inst of Int Affrs 1991–; pres African Studies Assoc UK 1977–78, chm Br Int Studies Assoc 1986–88, memb Hong Kong Cncl for Academic Awards 1986–90; memb: Royal Inst of Int Affrs 1961, Int Inst of Strategic Studies 1967; *Books* Republic Under Pressure (1965), Lesotho-Politics of Dependence (1968), Political and Military Framework of Investment in South Africa (1976), British Politics in Perspective (ed with R Borthwick, 1985), Change in South Africa (1994); *Recreations* collecting Faber poetry volumes, walking dogs; *Clubs* Travellers'; *Style*— Prof J E Spence; ✉ Castle View Farm, Bringhurst, nr Market Harborough, Leicestershire; Royal Institute of International Affairs, 10 St James's Square, London SW1Y 4LE (☎ 0171 957 5700, fax 0171 957 5710)

SPENCE, Malcolm Hugh; QC (1979); s of Dr Allan William Spence (d 1990), and Martha Lena, *née* Hutchison (d 1981); *b* 23 March 1934; *Educ* Stowe, Gonville and Caius Coll Cambridge (MA, LLM); *m* 18 March 1967, (Jennifer) Jane, da of Lt-Gen Sir George Sinclair Cole, KCB, CBE (d 1973); 1 s (Robert William b 1971), 1 da (Annabelle Irene b 1969); *Career* Nat Serv 1 Lt Worcestershire Regt 1952–54; called to the Bar Gray's Inn 1958 (James Mould scholar, sr Holker exhibitioner, Lee prizeman), bencher Gray's Inn 1988; entered Chambers of John Widgery, QC, pupil to Nigel Bridge (now Lord Bridge of Harwich) 1958; chm of Panel Examination in Public of Hartlepool and Cleveland Structure Plans 1979; asst recorder 1982–85, recorder 1985–; chm Local Planning and Environment Bar Assoc 1994–; landowner (1100 acres); *Books* Rating Law and Valuation (jtly, 1961); *Recreations* trout fishing, golf; *Clubs* Hawks (Cambridge); *Style*— Malcolm Spence, Esq, QC; ✉ 2 Gray's Inn Square, London WC1 (☎ 0171 242 4986, fax 0171 405 1166); Scamadale, Arisaig, Inverness-shire (☎ 01687 450698, fax 01687 450303)

SPENCE, Prof Robert; s of Robert Whitehair Spence (d 1988), and Minnie Grace, *née* Wood (d 1984); *b* 11 July 1933; *Educ* Hymers Coll Hull, Hull Coll of Technol (BSc), Imperial Coll London (DIC, PhD, DSc); *m* 18 April 1960, Kathleen, da of George Potts, of Whyteleafe, Surrey; 1 s (Robert b 1963), 1 da (Merin b 1966); *Career* Imperial Coll London: lectr 1962, reader 1968, prof of info engrg 1984–; founding dir and chm Interactive Solutions Ltd 1985–90; author of numerous papers; FIEE, FIEEE, FCGI, FRSA; FEng 1990; Officier De L'ordre Du Palme Academique (France) 1996; *Books* Linear Active Networks (1970), Tellegen's Theorem and Electrical Networks (1970), Resistive Circuit Theory (1974), Modern Network Theory - An Introduction (1978), Sensitivity and Optimisation (1980), Circuit Analysis by Computer (1986), Tolerance Design of Electronic Circuits (1988); *Recreations* concrete aspects of gardening, bass player in steel band; *Style*— Prof Robert Spence, FEng; ✉ Department of Electrical and Electronic Engineering, Imperial College of Science Technology and Medicine, Exhibition Rd, London SW7 2BT (☎ 0171 594 6259, fax 0171 581 4419, telex 929484)

SPENCE, Roy Archibald Joseph; s of Robert Spence (d 1988), of Belfast, and Margaret, *née* Gilmore; *b* 15 July 1952; *Educ* Queen's Univ Belfast (MB BCh, MD); *m* 26 Sept 1979, Diana Mary, da of Dr C Burns, OBE (d 1989), of Ballymoney; 2 s (Robert b 20 July 1982, Andrew b 14 Sept 1984), 1 da (Katharine b 11 Feb 1987); *Career* conslt surgn Belfast City Hosp 1986–; exec dir Belfast City Hosp Tst Bd; hon lectr in surgery Queen's Univ of Belfast; author 150 jl papers, 11 chapters in books; memb: BMA, Assoc of Surgns, Br Soc of Gastroenterology, World Assoc of Hepato-Biliary Surgns; chm Community Rels Ctee Police Authy NI 1996– (memb Police Authy 1994–); memb Bd of Govrs and Bd of Tstees Wallace HS Lisburn; FRCSEd 1981, FRCSI 1981; *Books* Pathology for Surgeons (1986, 2nd edn 1993); *Recreations* fishing; *Style*— Roy Spence, Esq; ✉ 7 Downshire Crescent, Hillsborough, Co Down, Northern Ireland BT26 6DD (☎ 01846 682362); Level 2, Belfast City Hosp, Lisburn Rd, Belfast BT9 7AB (☎ 01232 329241)

SPENCE, Saxon May; *née* Fairbairn; da of George Frederick Fairbairn (d 1981), and Ann May, *née* Northcott (d 1992); *b* 25 Feb 1929; *Educ* Ealing Girls' GS, UCL (BA), Sch of Educn; *m* 12 May 1952, John George Spence, s of Jack Spence (d 1953); 1 s (Ian b 1961), 1 da (Catherine b 1956); *Career* cncllr Exeter City Cncl 1972–74, cncllr Devon CC 1973–77 and 1981– (ldr Lab Gp 1985–, dep ldr 1973–77 and 1981–85); memb: Nat Jt Ctee Working Women's Orgns 1973–85, Nat Lab Women's Ctee 1973–85 (chm 1979–80), Bd SWEB 1978–81, Devon Regnl Ctee Co-op Retail Servs 1978–, Women's Nat Cmmn 1982–85, Devon and Cornwall Area Manpower Bd 1983–88, Assembly of Euro Regions 1993–, Assoc of CCs 1985–89 and 1993–, Educn Ctee Assoc of CCs 1985– (vice chm 1993–94, chm 1994–); vice chm NEOST 1994–, chm CLEA 1994–95 and 1996– (vice chm 1995–96), memb Bd Nat Youth Agency 1996–; vice chm: Western Regnl Tport Users' Consultative Ctee 1985–88 (memb 1975–88), Exeter and Devon Arts Centre Bd 1989– (memb 1987–), Exeter Cncl for Voluntary Service 1989–92 (memb 1963–); govr Exeter Coll 1972–93 (chm of Govrs 1985–89), vice chm of Govrs Rolle Coll 1981–88, govr The Staff Coll 1986–, chair Exeter Community Educn Govrs 1994–; *Recreations* reading, travelling, walking, theatre, music; *Clubs* Pinhoe and Whipton Labour; *Style*— Mrs Saxon Spence; ✉ 5 Regent's Park, Exeter, Devon EX1 2NT (☎ 01392 271785, fax 01392 51096); Devon County Council, County Hall, Exeter, Devon (☎ 01392 382502)

SPENCE, His Hon Judge; Stanley Brian; s of George Henry Spence (d 1941), and Sarah, *née* Hoad (d 1961); *b* 3 May 1937; *Educ* Portsmouth GS, Britannia Royal Naval Coll Dartmouth; *m* 3 April 1961, Victoria Rosaleen, da of Lionel Charles Tapper; 1 s (Adrian Charles b 8 Nov 1961), 1 da (Henrietta Louise b 12 Aug 1965); *Career* RN Supply and Secretariat specialisation, RNC Dartmouth 1953–57, HMS Eagle 1957–59, staff of FO2FEF 1959–60, RNC Greenwich 1961, staff SORS Portsmouth 1961–62, sec to Capt (F) 3rd FS 1962–64, HMS St Vincent 1964–66; called to the Bar 1968; DBSO Singapore 1969–70, asst sec to Cdr Far East Fleet and Fleet legal advsr 1970–71, sec to Cdr Far East Fleet and Fleet legal advsr 1971–, SSO 8th FS (HMS Leander) 1972–74, legal advsr staff CINC Naval Home Command 1974–75, voluntary ret from RN 1975; Office of Judge Advocate Gen (Army & RAF): dep judge advocate 1975–79, asst judge advocate gen 1979–91; recorder 1987–91, circuit judge (SE Circuit) 1991–; *Recreations* maintaining cottage in France, drinking wine; *Style*— His Hon Judge Spence; ✉ The Crown Court, Artillery House, Tilehurst Road, Reading, Berkshire RG3 2JF (☎ 0118 959 5934)

SPENCE, Chief Constable William Arthur; QPM (1990); *b* 20 Nov 1943; *Educ* Ellon Acad, Univ of Strathclyde (LLB), Open Univ (BA); *m* Hazel; 2 da (Shona, Maureen); *Career* Strathclyde Police: constable Renfrew & Bute Constabulary 1962 (joined as cadet), various ranks rising to asst chief constable 1986–88; chief constable Tayside Police 1995– (dep chief constable 1988–95); Scottish Cmd Course 1979, Chief Offrs' Course Bramshill Staff Coll 1991; liaised with Swedish Nat Police Euro Football Championships 1992; pres ACPO in Scotland 1996–97; tstee: Police Dependants' Tst, Prince's Tst; advsr Convention of Scottish Local Authorities (Protective Servs Forum); memb Ct Univ of Abertay Dundee; *Recreations* genealogy, reading, gardening, theatre; *Clubs* Chief Constable's; *Style*— Chief Constable William Spence, QPM; ✉ Tayside Police HQ, PO Box 59, West Bell Street, Dundee DD1 9JU (☎ 01382 223200, fax 01382 225772, e-mail forcedev@taysidepolice.gov.uk)

SPENCER, Prof Anthony James Merrill; s of James Lawrence Spencer (d 1961), of Streetly, Staffs, and Gladys, *née* Merrill; *b* 23 Aug 1929; *Educ* Queen Mary's GS Walsall, Queens' Coll Cambridge (BA, MA, ScD), Univ of Birmingham (PhD); *m* 1 Jan 1955, Margaret, da of Ernest Albert Bosker (d 1949), of Walmley, Sutton Coldfield; 3 s (John b 1957, Timothy b 1960, Richard b 1963); *Career* Private 1 Bn West Yorks Regt 1948–49, res assoc Brown Univ USA 1955–57, sr scientific offr UKAEA 1957–60, prof of theoretical mechanics Univ of Nottingham 1965–94 (lectr 1960–63, reader 1963–65), prof emeritus 1994; visiting prof: Brown Univ 1966 and 1971, Lehigh Univ 1978, Univ of Queensland Aust 1982; Erskine fell Univ of Canberbury NZ 1985; memb: Mathematics Ctee SRC 1978–81, Mathematical Scis Sub Ctee UGC 1983–87; FRS 1987; *Books* Deformations of Fibre-Reinforced Materials (1972), Engineering Mathematics (2 vols, 1977), Continuum Mechanics (1980); *Style*— Prof Anthony Spencer, FRS; ✉ 43 Stanton Lane, Stanton-on-the-Wolds, Keyworth, Nottingham NG12 5BE (☎ 0115 937 3134); Department of Theoretical Mechanics, University of Nottingham, University Park, Nottingham NG7 2RD (☎ 0115 951 3838, fax 0115 951 3837)

SPENCER, 9 Earl (GB 1765); Charles Edward Maurice Spencer; also Viscount Spencer, Baron Spencer (both GB 1761), and Viscount Althorp (GB 1765 and UK 1905); s of 8 Earl Spencer, LVO, DL (d 1992), and his 1 w, Hon Frances Ruth Burke Roche, da of 4 Baron Fermoy; bro of Diana, Princess of Wales (*see* Royal Family); *b* 20 May 1964; *Educ* Maidwell Hall, Eton, Magdalen Coll Oxford; *m* 16 Sept 1989, (Catherine) Victoria, o da of John Lockwood, of Barnes, London; 1 s (Louis Frederick John, Viscount Althorp b 14 March 1994), 3 da (Lady Kitty Eleanor b 28 Dec 1990, Lady Eliza Victoria b 10 July 1992, Lady Katya Amelia b (twin) 10 July 1992); *Heir* s, Louis Frederick John, Viscount Althorp b 14 March 1994; *Career* page of hon to HM The Queen 1977–79; TV correspondent NBC News 1987–91 and 1993–96, reporter Granada Television 1991–93; *Clubs* Brooks's; *Style*— The Rt Hon the Earl Spencer; ✉ Althorp, Northampton NN7 4HG

SPENCER, Christopher Paul; er s of Anthony John Spencer, of Cornerstones, Beechwood Ave, Weybridge, Surrey, and Elizabeth (d 1991), da of Engr Rear Adm David John Carruthers, CBE, RN; *b* 7 July 1950; *Educ* St George's Coll Weybridge; *m* 28 June 1975, Margaret Elizabeth, da of Lt-Col Cyril Meredith Battye Howard, OBE, of Rowan Cottage, Rydens Ave, Walton-on-Thames, Surrey; 2 da (Katherine b 13 Aug 1978, Anna Lisa b 24 July 1981); *Career* CA; ptnr: Midgley Snelling Spencer & Co 1978–83, Pannell Kerr Forster (CI) 1984–; chm Guernsey Branch IOD 1994–96, memb Guernsey C of C, pres Guernsey Soc of Chartered and Certified Accountants; FCA; *Recreations* sailing, skiing, tennis; *Clubs* United, Guernsey Yacht, Ski Club of GB; *Style*—

Christopher Spencer, Esq; ✉ La Chimere, George Rd, St Peter Port, Guernsey (☎ 01481 711040); Pannell Kerr Forster, Suites 13/15, Sarnia House, Le Truchot, St Peter Port, Guernsey (☎ 01481 727927, fax 01481 710511, telex 4191177 Panker G)

SPENCER, Sir Derek Harold; kt (1992), QC (1980), MP (C) Brighton Pavilion (majority 3,675); s of Thomas Harold Spencer, of Waddington, Lancs, and Gladys, *née* Heslop (d 1989); *b* 31 March 1936; *Educ* Clitheroe Royal GS, Keble Coll Oxford (MA, BCL); *m* 1, 30 July 1960 (m dis), Joan, da of late James Nutter, of Clitheroe, Lancs; 2 s (David John b 1966, Andrew Duncan b 1970), 1 da (Caroline Jane b 1964); m 2, 26 Nov 1988, Caroline Alexandra, da of Dr Franziskus Pärn, of Hamburg; 1 s (Frederick Thomas Francis b 27 Oct 1990); *Career* 2 Lt KORR 1954–56, served Nigeria; called to the Bar Gray's Inn 1961, recorder of Crown Ct 1979–92, bencher Gray's Inn 1991, slr-gen 1992–; MP (C): Leicester South 1983–87, Brighton Pavilion 1992–; jt sec Cons Back Bench Legal Ctee 1985–86; PPS: to David Mellor as Min of State at the Home Office 1986, to Sir Michael Havers as Attorney Gen 1986–87; vice chm St Pancras N Cons Assoc 1977–78, cncllr London Borough of Camden 1978–83 (dep ldr Cons Gp 1980–81); *Recreations* reading, swimming, travelling; *Style*— Sir Derek Spencer, QC, MP; ✉ House of Commons, London SW1A 0AA (☎ 0171 219 3000, fax 0171 219 2582)

SPENCER, Geoffrey Thomas; s of James William Spencer, and Doris Winifred, *née* Gillingham; *b* 16 May 1946; *Educ* Cheshunt GS, City of London Coll; *m* 1, 24 June 1974 (m dis 1989), Barbara; 1 s (Alexander James b Oct 1983), 1 da (Hilary Jane b Sept 1978); m 2, 9 March 1989, Diane, da of Sidney Collins; *Career* Coutts & Co: asst mangr Business Devpt Div 1972–74, account mangr Cavendish Square Branch 1974–78, mangr Kensington Branch 1978–82, mangr Mktg and Planning Dept Branch Banking Div 1982–83, head Int Banking Div 1986–88 (sr mangr 1983–84, dep head 1984–86), assoc dir 1986, head Commercial Banking Gp 1988, memb Main Bd 1989–90; dir Coutts & Co (Nassau) Ltd 1985–90, md Coutts Fin Co 1988–90; London gen mangr CBI-TDB Union Bancaire Privée 1990–93, dir CentreTrust Ltd Jersey 1991–93, sr vice pres Int Client Banking Republic National Bank of New York (London branch) 1993–95, head Private Banking Brown, Shipley & Co Ltd 1995–, dir KBL-Brown, Shipley (Jersey) Ltd 1995–; ACIB 1970, FCIB 1988; *Recreations* badminton, gardening, travel, music; *Clubs* Overseas Bankers'; *Style*— Geoffrey Spencer, Esq; ✉ Brown, Shipley & Co Ltd, Founders Court, Lothbury, London EC2R 7HE (☎ 0171 606 9833, fax 0171 606 5899)

SPENCER, Prof Harrison C; *b* 22 Sept 1944, Baltimore, Maryland, USA; *Educ* Haverford Coll Pennsylvania (BA), The Johns Hopkins Univ Sch of Med Baltimore Maryland (MD), Univ of Calif Sch of Public Health Berkeley Calif (MPH), London Sch of Hygiene and Tropical Med London (DTM&H); *Career* intern (med) Vanderbilt Univ Hosp Nashville Tennessee 1969–70, US Public Health Serv resident (med and preventive med) Univ of Calif Berkeley 1970–72, epidemic intelligence serv offr Centers for Disease Control Atlanta Georgia 1972–74, resident (internal med) Univ of Calif San Francisco 1974–75, MO Central America Research Station San Salvador El Salvador 1975–77, MO Bureau of Tropical Diseases Centers for Disease Control Atlanta 1977–79, sr physician and malaria co-ordinator Clinical Research Centre Kenya Med Research Inst Nairobi and sr lectr Dept of Community Med Univ of Nairobi Med Sch 1979–84, SMO WHO Geneva 1984–87, chief Parasitic Diseases Branch Div of Parasitic Diseases Centers for Infectious Diseases and Centers for Disease Control & Prevention Atlanta Georgia 1987–91, dean (prof Depts of Tropical Med and Biostatics & Epidemiology) Sch of Public Health & Tropical Med Tulane Univ New Orleans Louisiana 1991–95 (concurrently prof Grad Faculty Tulane Univ, adjunct prof Dept of Med Tulane Univ Med Sch), dean London Sch of Hygiene & Tropical Med 1996–; memb Bd: Nat Cncl Int Health USA 1992–, Bureau of Governmental Research USA 1992–; US Public Health Serv: Commendation Medal 1984 and 1991, Oustanding Serv Medal 1989; memb: American Soc of Tropical Med and Hygiene (memb Cncl 1991–), American Public Health Assoc, E African Soc of Parasitology; fell: American Coll of Physicians, American Coll of Preventive Med, Soc of Tropical Med and Hygiene; *Books* International Health and Development (jtly, in preparation), various book chapters; author of numerous academic pubns in learned jls; *Style*— Prof Harrison C Spencer; ✉ London School of Hygiene & Tropical Medicine, Keppel Street, London WC1E 7HT (☎ 0171 927 2237, fax 0171 323 4562)

SPENCER, (Richard) Harry Ramsay; s of Col Richard Augustus Spencer, DSO, OBE (d 1956), and Maud Evelyn, *née* Ramsay (d 1989); hp (to Barony only), of 3 Viscount Churchill; *b* 11 Oct 1926; *Educ* Wellington, Architectural Assoc (AADipl); *m* 1, 1958, Antoinette Rose-Marie (d 1994), da of Godefroy de Charrière, of Préverenges, Lausanne, Switzerland; 2 s (Michael b 1960, David b 1970); m 2, 18 Aug 1995, Elisabeth Monk; *Career* former Lt Coldstream Gds; ret architect; RIBA; *Recreations* the arts; *Style*— Harry Spencer, Esq; ✉ The Old Vicarage, Vernham Dean, Hants SP11 0EN (☎ 01264 737386)

SPENCER, Herbert; s of Harold Spencer, and Sarah Ellen, *née* Tagg; *b* 22 June 1924; *m* 27 Sept 1954, Marianne Möls, *née* Dordrecht; 1 da (Mafalda Saskia b 1958); *Career* RAF 1942–45; dir Lund Humphries Publishers 1970–88, prof of graphic arts Royal Coll of Art 1978–85; memb Stamp Advsy Ctee PO 1968–94, int pres Alliance Graphique Int 1971–73, Master Royal Designers for Indust and vice pres Royal Soc of Arts 1979–81; conslt: W H Smith Ltd 1973–96, Tate Gallery 1981–89; one man exhibitions of paintings: Bleddfa Tst 1986, Gallery 202 London 1988–89 and 1990, Eva Jekel 1992; one man exhibition of photographs Zelda Cheatle Gallery London 1991; photographs in permanent collection of V&A Museum; ed: Typographica 1949–67, Penrose Annual 1964–73; RDI 1965, FRSA 1965, DrRCA 1970, hon fell RCA 1985; *Books* Traces of Man (photographs, 1967), The Visible Word (1968), London's Canal (2 edn, 1976), Pioneers of Modern Typography (3 edn, 1990), The Liberated Page (2 edn, 1990); *Clubs* Chelsea Arts; *Style*— Herbert Spencer, Esq; ✉ 75 Deodar Rd, Putney, London SW15 2NU (☎ and fax 0181 874 6352); Runnis Chapel, Dutlas, Knighton, Powys LD7 1UF (☎ 01547 510648)

SPENCER, Ivor; DL (London 1985); *b* 20 Nov 1924; *m* 1948; 1 s (Nigel), 1 da (Philippa); *Career* professional toastmaster; fndr and life pres Guild of Professional Toastmasters 1956–, estab Guild of Professional Toastmasters Best After-Dinner Speakers Award of the Year (recipients incl Baroness Thatcher, Lord Redcliffe Maud, Sir Peter Ustinov, Bob Monkhouse, Denis Norden and Lord Tonypandy); officiated at over 1000 Royal events UK and overseas (first toastmaster to achieve this 1992); princ: Ivor Spencer International School for Butler Administrators and Personal Assistants 1981–, Ivor Spencer Sch for Professional Toastmasters; chm and md Ivor Spencer Enterprises Ltd; *Recreations* after-dinner speaking; *Clubs* IOD; *Style*— Ivor Spencer, Esq, DL; ✉ 12 & 14 Little Bornes, Alleyn Park, Dulwich, London SE21 8SE (☎ 0181 670 5585/8424, fax 0181 670 0055, car 0860 313835)

SPENCER, James; QC (1991); s of James Henry Spencer, and Irene Dulcie, *née* Wilson; *b* 27 May 1947; *Educ* The King's Sch Pontefract, Univ of Newcastle upon Tyne (LLB); *m* 8 July 1968, Patricia (Patsy), da of Jack Johnson, MBE, of Pontefract; 2 s ((James) Adam b 1976, (John) Joseph b 1979), 1 da ((Jane) Emma b 1971); *Career* admitted slr 1971, called to the Bar Gray's Inn 1975, recorder of the Crown Ct 1990–; *Style*— James Spencer, Esq, QC; ✉ 11 King's Bench Walk, Temple, London EC4Y 7EQ (☎ 0171 353 3337)

SPENCER, John Hall; *b* 17 April 1928; *Educ* Bedford Sch, RNC Greenwich, Harvard Univ; *m* 1 Dec 1953 (m dis 1967), Edite, da of late Gen Jacques Pommes-Barrere; 2 s (William b 1955, Patrick Henri b 1958), 1 da (Catherine M L b 1961); *Career* offr RM 1945–51; William Mallinson & Sons (Australasia) Pty 1952–54, Management Research Groups London 1954–57, Beaverbrook Newspapers 1957–59, Cons Central Office 1959–61, J Walter Thompson 1961–82, md John Spencer Associates 1982–94; chm Activities Ctee London Fedn of Boys Clubs 1982– (memb Exec 1972–), MIPA 1960, MIPR 1961; *Books* The Business of Management (with Sir Roger Falk, 1959), Battle for Crete (1962), The Wall is Strong (1966), The Surgenor Campaign (1972); *Recreations* hunting, golf, travel, the theatre; *Clubs* Carlton, Army & Navy, RAC, Rye Golf; *Style*— John Spencer, Esq; ✉ 76 Millbank Court, John Islip St, London SW1P 4LG (☎ 0171 828 4886, fax 0171 834 6405)

SPENCER, Prof John Rason; *Educ* Univ of Cambridge (LLB, MA); *Career* Univ of Cambridge: asst lectr Law Faculty 1973–76, lectr 1976–91, reader 1991–95, prof 1995–; fell Selwyn Coll Cambridge 1970–; *Style*— Prof J R Spencer; ✉ Selwyn College, Cambridge CB3 9DQ

SPENCER, John Southern; s of Robert Southern Spencer, and Marjorie Turner, *née* Frankland; *b* 10 Aug 1947; *Educ* Sedbergh, Queens' Coll Cambridge (MA); *children* 1 s (David b 1981), 2 da (Hazel b 1985, Emily b 1988); *Career* slr, ptnr John Spencer 1975; Rugby Union; formerly: Capt Yorkshire, Capt Univ of Cambridge (3 Blues), Capt Barbarians, Capt England (16 Caps), British Lions Tour 1971; pres: Wharfedale RUFC, Grassington Angling Club; tstee Upper Wharfedale Immediate Care Scheme, vice chm Govrs Ermysted's GS Skipton, govr Malsis Sch Cross Hill N Yorks; memb Law Soc; *Recreations* rugby, squash, cricket; *Clubs* The Sportmans, Wig & Pen, The Rugby; *Style*— John Spencer, Esq; ✉ High Pasture, Moor Lane, Threshfield, Skipton, N Yorks BD23 5NS (☎ 01756 752456); 6A Station Rd, Grassington, Skipton, N Yorks BD23 5NQ (☎ 01756 753015, fax 01756 753020)

SPENCER, John William James; s of Capt John Lawrence Spencer, DSO, MC (d 1967), and Jane Lilian, *née* Duff; *b* 26 Dec 1957; *Educ* Sedbergh, Magdalene Coll Cambridge (MA); *m* 2 Oct 1987, Jane Elizabeth, da of Andrew Young (d 1974); 1 s (Charles b 1990), 2 da (Rosanagh b 1991, Caitlin b 1996); *Career* dir: Dewey Warren & Co Ltd 1986–88, PWS North America 1988–89, Ballantyne McKean & Sullivan (Lloyd's brokers) 1989–95, Lloyd's America Ltd 1995–; *Style*— J W J Spencer, Esq; ✉ Ghyllas, Sedbergh, Cumbria LA10 5LT; 8 Bushwood Road, Kew, Surrey TW9 3BQ (☎ 0181 940 9814)

SPENCER, Jonathan Page; s of John Austin Spencer, of Bath, and Doreen, *née* Page (d 1991); *b* 24 April 1949; *Educ* Bournemouth Sch, Downing Coll Cambridge (MA), Univ of Oxford (ICI res fell, jr res fell Christchurch, DPhil); *m* 1976, Caroline Sarah; 2 da, 1 s; *Career* DTI: admin trainee 1974–77, princ 1977–83, private sec to Secs of State 1982–83, asst sec 1983–91, under sec and head Insurance Div (Insurance Directorate since 1996) 1991–; author of various articles in scientific jls; *Recreations* making and listening to music, keeping the house up and the garden down; *Style*— Jonathan Spencer, Esq; ✉ Insurance Directorate, Department of Trade and Industry, 1 Victoria Street, London SW1H 0ET (☎ 0171 215 0120, fax 0171 215 0239)

SPENCER, Michael Warlow; s of Arthur Cyril Dennis Spencer, of Cumbria, and Joyce Spencer; *b* 30 Sept 1958; *Educ* Sedbergh, Univ of Southampton; *m* 11 June 1994, Katy, da of Dr Gareth Jones; 1 s (Huw b 8 March 1995); *Career* graduate trainee United Newspapers 1980–83, Raymonds News Agency 1983–84, BBC Local Radio 1984–85, Granada TV News 1985–88, reporter/prodr BBC Documentaries and BBC Youth and Entertainment 1988–90; Granada Television: prodr 1990–92, ed regnl features 1992–93, head of news and features 1993–94, head of regnl progs 1994–; memb BAFTA 1993; *Recreations* squash, hill walking, sailing; *Style*— Michael Spencer, Esq; ✉ Granada Television Ltd, Granada TV Centre, Quay Street, Manchester M60 9EA (☎ 0161 827 2011)

SPENCER, Paul Arnold; s of John Spencer, of Yorkshire, and Maria Helena, *née* Rosenbroek; *b* 1 Feb 1960; *Educ* Beverley GS, Univ of Nottingham; *m* Karen Lesley; 1 s (Angus); *Career* prodr Radio Comedy BBC 1983–89, freelance TV prodr 1989–91; head of comedy: Central TV 1991–94, Carlton TV 1994–95; controller of network comedy ITV Network Centre 1995; currently head of comedy Carlton UK Productions 1995–; *Recreations* renovating my crumbling home; *Clubs* Lansdowne, Soho House; *Style*— Paul Spencer, Esq; ✉ Carlton UK Productions, 135–38 Portman Square, London W1H 9FH (☎ 0171 486 6688, fax 0171 486 1132)

SPENCER, Prof Paul Samuel John; OBE (1994); s of Albert Owen Spencer (d 1986), of Leicester, and Constance Christina, *née* Brass; *b* 24 Oct 1934; *Educ* Wyggeston Sch Leicester, Leicester Colls of Art and Technol, Univ of London; *m* 17 Aug 1957, Avril Dorothy, da of Thomas Spriggs (d 1972), of Leicester; 1 s (Jonathan b 1963), 2 da (Isobel b 1961, Rosemary b 1965); *Career* pre-registration pharmacist Middx Hosp London 1957–58, asst lectr Sch of Pharmacy Univ of London 1959–62, princ pharmacologist Allen & Hanburys (now Glaxo Research) Ware Herts 1962–65, sr lectr then reader in pharmacology Sch of Pharmacy Univ of Aston 1965–70, head of sch Welsh Sch of Pharmacy UWIST Cardiff 1978– (prof of pharmacology 1971–), first dean Faculty of Health and Life Sciences Univ of Wales Coll Cardiff 1988–91, dep princ and pro-vice chllr Univ Wales Cardiff 1994–97; author of over 120 res and professional articles and reviews specialising in pharmacology of psychotropic drugs and pharmaceutical educn; former memb: Educn Ctee and various working parties on professional educn and pharmacology RPharmS, Medicines Cmmn 1992–95, various CNAA Ctees, CRM Psychotropics Sub Ctee; currently memb: Standing Pharmaceutical Ctee for England and Wales, Welsh Standing Pharmaceutical Ctee in Welsh Office; Hon DSc De Montfort Univ 1994 (former chm); FIBiol 1972, FRPharmS 1978, MCPP 1981, CBiol 1984; *Recreations* music, photography, sport; *Style*— Prof Paul Spencer, OBE; ✉ c/o Welsh School of Pharmacy, UWC, King Edward VII Avenue, Cathays Park, Cardiff CF1 3XF (☎ 01222 874781, fax 01222 874149)

SPENCER, Ritchie Lloyd; s of Capt P Lloyd Spencer; *b* 27 Sept 1942; *Educ* St Bees Sch, Univ of Manchester (BA), LSE; *m* 1965, Catherine Dilys, da of Dr John Naish; 3 s (Hal b 1968, Patrick b 1969, James b 1972); *Career* dir Sunderland Shipbuilders Ltd 1972–76, md Reliant Motors plc Tamworth Staffs 1977–87, dir Nash Industries plc 1980–87, chief exec GKN Powder Metallurgy Div 1987–90; chm: Bound Brook Lichfield Ltd 1987–90, Firth Cleveland Sintered Products Ltd 1987–90, Sheepbridge Sintered Products Ltd 1987–90; pres: Bound Brook Italia SpA Brunico 1987–90, Saini SpA Milan 1987–90; dir: Mahindra Sintered Products Pune Ltd India 1987–90, Sintermex SA de CV Mexico 1987–90; md: European Industrial Services Ltd 1990–94, Nettlefolds Ltd 1990–94, Unifix Ltd 1990–94, Unifix (Belgium) NV/SA 1990–94, Unifix (Netherlands) BV 1990–94, EIS Depots Ltd 1990–94; chief exec Hoesch Woodhead Ltd 1994–; cncl memb Soc Motor Manufacturers & Traders 1978–87, chm Motor Indust Res Assoc 1984–; MIPM; *Recreations* theatre, music, gardening, tennis, skiing; *Style*— Ritchie Spencer, Esq; ✉ Skelbrooke Hall, Skelbrooke, nr Doncaster, S Yorks (☎ and fax 01302 728408); Dorlinn View, Argyll Terrace, Tobermory, Isle of Mull (☎ 01688 302324); Hoesch Woodhead Ltd, 177 Kirkstall Road, Leeds LS4 2AQ (☎ 0113 244 1202)

SPENCER, Robin Godfrey; s of Eric Spencer (d 1992), of Chester, and Audrey Elaine, *née* Brown; *b* 8 July 1955; *Educ* King's Sch Chester, Emmanuel Coll Cambridge (MA); *m* 5 Aug 1978, Julia Margaret Eileen, da of Eric John Bennet Burley, of Chester; 3 da (Jennifer b 1983, Susanna b 1984, Laura b 1987); *Career* called to the Bar Gray's Inn 1978, in practice Wales and Chester Circuit, asst recorder of the Crown Ct 1993–; *Recreations* cricket, music; *Style*— Robin Spencer, Esq; ✉ Sedan House, Stanley Place, Chester CH1 2LU (☎ 01244 348282, fax 01244 342336)

SPENCER, HE Rosemary Jane; CMG (1991); da of Air Vice-Marshal Geoffrey Roger Cole Spencer, CB, CBE (d 1969), and Juliet Mary, *née* Warwick (d 1994); *b* 1 April 1941; *Educ* Upper Chine Sch, Shanklin IOW, St Hilda's Coll Oxford (BA); *Career* HM Dip Serv: FO 1962–65, Br High Cmmn Nairobi 1965–67, FCO 1967–70, second sec and private sec to Hon Sir Con O'Neill EC negotiating team Brussels 1970–71, first sec Office of UK Rep to EC Brussels 1972–73, Br High Cmmn Lagos 1974–77, asst head Rhodesia Dept FCO 1977–79, RCDS 1980, cnsllr Br Embassy Paris 1980–84, cnsllr (external relations) Office of UK Rep to EC Brussels 1984–87, head of Euro Community Dept External FCO 1987, asst under sec of state Public Depts FCO 1989–93, min in charge Br Embassy Office Berlin 1993–96, ambass to The Netherlands 1996–; govr Upper Chine Sch IOW 1984–94 (chm Governing Bd 1989–92); *Recreations* country walking, domestic arts, reading; *Clubs* Oxford & Cambridge, Royal Commonwealth Society; *Style*— HE Miss Rosemary Spencer, CMG; ✉ Foreign and Commonwealth Office (The Hague), King Charles St, London SW1A 2AH

SPENCER, Shaun Michael; QC (1988); s of Edward Michael Spencer, of Leeds, and Barbara Joan Patricia Spencer; *b* 4 Feb 1944; *Educ* Cockburn HS, Univ of Durham (LLB); *m* 9 June 1971, Nicola, da of Frederick George Greenwood, of Tockwith, N Yorks; 3 s (Robert Phillip b 1972, Samuel James Edward b 1982, Edward Frederick Claudio b 1993), 2 da (Eleanor Jane b 1979, Elizabeth Anne b 1980); *Career* lectr in law Univ of Sheffield 1966–68 (asst lectr in law 1965–66), called to the Bar Lincoln's Inn 1968 (Hardwicke & Mansfield scholar), barr N Eastern Circuit 1969–, recorder of the Crown Ct 1985–, head of chambers; Master of Hounds Claro Beagles 1982–88; *Recreations* cookery, books, singing; *Style*— Shaun Spencer, Esq, QC; ✉ 34A Rutland Drive, Harrogate, N Yorks HG1 2NX (☎ 01423 523162); 6 Park Square, Leeds LS1 2LW (☎ 0113 245 9763, fax 0113 242 4395)

SPENCER, Thomas Newnham Bayley (Tom); MEP (EPP) Surrey (majority 27,018); s of Thomas Henry Newnham Spencer (d 1979); *b* 10 April 1948; *Educ* Nautical Coll Pangbourne, Univ of Southampton; *m* 1979, Elizabeth Nan, *née* Bath; 2 da and 1 step da; *Career* Peat Marwick Mitchell CAs 1972–75, asst dir Britain in Europe referedum campaign 1975, J Walter Thompson advtg 1975–79; MEP (EPP): Derbyshire 1979–84, Surrey West 1989–94, Surrey 1994–; Cons spokesman on: Social Affairs and Employment 1979–82, External Trade 1982–84; assoc dean Templeton Coll Oxford 1984–89 (exec dir European Centre for Public Affrs 1987–89), Cons dep chief whip European Parliament 1989–91, permanent rapporteur EPP 1991– (chm British Section EPP 1994); memb: Environment, Public Health and Consumer Affrs Ctee, Foreign Affrs Ctee; *Recreations* gardening, opera; *Clubs* Carlton; *Style*— Tom Spencer, Esq, MEP; ✉ Barford Court, Lampard Lane, Churt, Surrey GU10 2HJ (☎ 01428 712375)

SPENCER-NAIRN, Angus; s of Michael Alastair Spencer-Nairn, of Baltilly House, Ceres, Fife, and Ursula Helen, *née* Devitt; *b* 23 Jan 1947; *Educ* Eton, RAC (MRAC); *m* 6 July 1968, Christina Janet, da of late Col Hugh Gillies, of Kindar House, New Abbey, Dumfriesshire; 1 s (Michael b 1975), 1 da (Fiona b 1974); *Career* CA; sr ptnr Rawlinson & Hunter, in practice St Helier Jersey; *Recreations* motor racing, flying, tennis, deer stalking, golf; *Clubs* Royal and Ancient Golf (St Andrews), New (Edinburgh); *Style*— Angus Spencer-Nairn, Esq; ✉ La Fontaine, Rue Du Pont, St John, Jersey, CI JE3 4FF (☎ 01534 861716); Ordnance House, Box 83, 31 Pier Rd, St Helier, Jersey, CI (☎ 01534 875141, fax 01534 32876, telex 4192075)

SPENCER-NAIRN, Sir Robert Arnold; 3 Bt (UK 1933), of Monimail, Co Fife, DL (District of Fife 1995); s of Lt-Col Sir Douglas Leslie Spencer Spencer-Nairn, TD, 2 Bt (d 1970), and his 1 w, Elizabeth Livingston Henderson; *b* 11 Oct 1933; *Educ* Eton, Trinity Hall Cambridge; *m* 1963, Joanna Elizabeth, da of late Lt Cdr George Stevenson Salt, RN, s of 2 Bt (cr 1899); 2 s (James Robert b 1966, Andrew George b 1969), 1 da (Katharine Elizabeth b 1964); *Heir* s, James Robert Spencer-Nairn b 7 Dec 1966; *Career* late Lt Scots Gds; *Style*— Sir Robert Spencer-Nairn, Bt, DL; ✉ Barham, Cupar, Fife KY15 5RG

SPENCER-SMITH, Sir John Hamilton; 7 Bt (UK 1804), of Tring Park, Herts; s of Capt Sir Thomas Cospatric Spencer-Smith, 6 Bt (d 1959), and Lucy Ashton, da of late Thomas Ashton Ingram; *b* 18 March 1947; *Educ* Milton Abbey, Lackham Coll of Agric; *m* 1980 (m dis 1992), Mrs Christine Sandra Parris, da of late John Theodore Charles Osborne, of Durrington, Worthing, Sussex; 1 da (Jessica Kirsten b 1985); *Heir* kinsman, Michael Philip Spencer-Smith b 1952; *Career* owner Hazel House Quarantine Kennels Midhurst; *Recreations* watching polo; *Clubs* Cowdray Park Polo; *Style*— Sir John H Spencer-Smith, Bt; ✉ Hazel House Quarantine Kennels, Elsted Marsh, Midhurst, W Sussex

SPENCER WATSON, Mary; da of George Spencer Watson, RA (d 1934), of London, and Hilda Mary, *née* Gardiner (d 1953); *b* 7 May 1913; *Educ* Schs of Sculpture: Bournemouth, Slade, Royal Acad (prize winner), Central; Ossip Zadkine Paris; *Career* sculptor; winner European Woman of Achievement Award EUW; solo exhibitions: Heals Mansard Gallery 1937, Foyles Art Gallery London 1945, Shire Hall Dorchester 1945, Dorset County Museum Dorchester 1976, 1982 and 1991, Civic Centre Southampton 1982, Stour Gallery Blandford 1983, New Art Centre London 1985 and 1990, Pelter Sands Art Gallery Bristol 1988; gp exhibitions incl: Royal Acad London, Fine Art Soc, Woman's Int Soc, Nat Soc, Crafts Centre London, Basle Art Fair, Portland Tout Quarry Dorset, Olympia Art Fair, Hannah Peschar Sculpture Garden Surrey, Roche Ct Sculpture Garden Wilts, Rutherford Art Centre, Millfield Sch; recent installation of symbolic beasts of the four evangelists at Wells Cathedral; architectural work for: Guildford Cathedral (two wooden angels in the children's chapel), Harlow New Town, Austin Car Works Longbridge Birmingham, Stevenage New Town, Cambridge (two colls), Queen's Hospital Belfast, St Bartholomew's Hostel London, Wyke Regis Dorset, St Etheldreda Chesfield Park Herts; teacher at various schs incl: Poole Art Coll, Clayesmore Sch 1943–48; memb: Woman's Int Soc, Nat Soc London; *Recreations* riding; *Style*— Mary Spencer Watson; ✉ Dunshay, Langton Matravers, Swanage, Dorset BH19 3EB

SPENS, David Patrick; QC (1995); s of Lt-Col Hugh Stuart Spens, MB, MBE, TD (d 1988), and Mary Jean Drake, *née* Reinhold; *b* 2 May 1950; *Educ* Rugby, Univ of Kent (BA); *m* 7 April 1979, Daniele, da of Robert William Irving, MBE (d 1994); 2 da (Dominique b 1982, Sophie b 1986); *Career* called to the Bar Inner Temple 1973; jr counsel to the Crown at the Central Criminal Ct 1988–95, recorder of the Crown Ct 1994–; *Recreations* opera, tennis, travel, catamaran sailing, throwing parties; *Style*— David Spens, Esq, QC; ✉ 6 King's Bench Walk, Temple, London EC4Y 7DR (☎ 0171 583 0410, fax 0171 353 8791)

SPENS, John Alexander; RD (1970), WS; s of late T P Spens and Nancy Farie Spens (d 1996); *b* 1933; *Educ* BA, LLB; *m* Finella Jane Gilroy; 2 s, 1 da; *Career* Carrick Pursuivant of Arms 1974–85, Albany Herald of Arms 1985–; ptnr Maclay Murray & Spens (Slrs) 1960–90 (conslt 1990–); dir: Scottish Amicable Life Assurance Soc 1963– (chm 1978–81), Standard Property Investment PLC 1977–87; *Style*— John Spens, Esq, RD, WS, Albany Herald of Arms; ✉ The Old Manse, Gartocharn, Dunbartonshire G83 8RX (☎ 01389 83329)

SPENS, 3 Baron (UK 1959); Patrick Michael Rex; s of 2 Baron Spens (d 1984), and Joan Elizabeth (d 1994), da of late Reginald Goodall; *b* 22 July 1942; *Educ* Rugby, CCC Cambridge (MA); *m* 1966, Barbara, da of Rear-Adm Ralph Fisher, CB, DSO, OBE, DSC (d 1988); 1 s, 1 da (Hon Sarah b 1970); *Heir* s, Hon Patrick Nathaniel George Spens b 14 Oct 1968; *Career* dir Morgan Grenfell & Co Ltd 1973–82, md Henry Ansbacher & Co 1982–87, currently princ Patrick Spens & Co; FCA; *Style*— The Rt Hon Lord Spens; ✉ Gould, Frittenden, Kent TN17 2DT

SPERRYN, Simon George; s of George Roland Neville Sperryn, of Hampton Lucy, Warwickshire, and Wendy, *née* King; *b* 7 April 1946; *Educ* Rydal Sch Clwydd, Pembroke Coll Cambridge (MA), Cranfield Sch of Mgmnt (MBA); *m* 11 Sept 1993, Jessica Alice Hayes; *Career* Chamber of Industry and Commerce: Birmingham 1967–77, chief exec Northants 1979–85, chief exec Manchester 1986–92, chief exec London 1992–; chm Manchester Camerata Ltd 1989–92; dir Manchester Trg and Enterprise Cncl 1990–92; Assoc of Br Chambers of Commerce: memb Nat Cncl 1986–, memb Bd of Mgmnt 1990–94; pres Br Chambers of Commerce Executives 1994–95; FIMgt, FRSA; *Recreations* singing, drawing; *Style*— Simon Sperryn, Esq; ✉ Deynes House, Deynes Lane, Debden, Saffron Walden, Essex CB11 3LG (☎ 01799 540232); London Chamber of Commerce and Industry, 33 Queen Street, London EC4R 1AP (☎ 0171 248 4444, fax 0171 489 0391, telex 888941 LCCIG)

SPICELEY, Peter Joseph; MBE; s of Robert Joseph Spiceley (d 1974), and Lucy Violet, *née* Gore; *b* 5 March 1942; *Educ* Trinity Sch of John Whitgift Croydon; *m* 6 Nov 1965, Cecilia, da of Dr Jorge Emilio Orozco (d 1989); 2 da (Anamaria b 1967, Jacqueline Suzanne b 1970); *Career* diplomat; FO London 1961, Br Embassy Bogota Colombia 1964–66, Br Embassy Lima Peru 1969–72, Br Embassy Yaoundé Cameroon 1972–74, Br Consulate Douala Cameroon 1974–76, Br Embassy Quito Ecuador 1976–81, FCO London 1982–86 (1967–69), Br Consulate Miami USA 1986–90, FCO 1991–94, dir of trade promotion Br Consulate General Sydney Aust 1994–; *Style*— Peter Spiceley, Esq, MBE; ✉ c/o Foreign & Commonwealth Office, King Charles St, London SW1A 2AH

SPICER, Sir James Wilton; kt (1988), MP (C) Dorset West (majority 8,010); s of James Spicer and Florence Clara Spicer; *b* 4 Oct 1925; *Educ* Latymer Sch; *m* 1954, Winifred Douglas Shanks; 2 da; *Career* Regular Army 1943–57; Parly candidate (C) Southampton Itchen by-election 1971, MP (C) Dorset W Feb 1974–, UK memb Euro Parl 1975–78, MEP (EDG) Wessex 1979–84; chm: Cons Political Centre 1969–72, Cons Gp for Europe 1975–78; chief whip of Cons Gp in Euro Parl 1976–80, memb Select Ctee Agric 1984–85, appointed vice chm Cons Party and chm Int Office 1984–92, chm Bd of Govrs Westminster Fndn for Democracy 1992–; chm British-Turkish Parly Gp, chm Fitness for Indust, chm Thames and Kennet Marina Ltd; *Style*— Sir James Spicer, MP; ✉ Whatley, Beaminster, Dorset (☎ 01308 862337); House of Commons, London SW1A 0AA

SPICER, John Vincent; s of Herbert Gordon Spicer, of Billericay, Essex, and Doreen Mary, *née* Collings; *b* 2 March 1951; *Educ* Billericay Comp Sch, Univ of Sheffield (BA); *m* 23 June 1973, Patricia Ann, da of Raymond Sidney Bracher (d 1986), of Harlow, Essex; *Career* business planner Kodak 1975–77, strategic planner Whitbread plc 1978–82, brewery analyst Grenfell & Colegrave 1982–84; dir and brewery analyst: Kleinwort Benson Securities Ltd 1986–91, SBC Warburg 1991–; MSI; *Recreations* opera, golf, squash, hill walking; *Style*— John Spicer, Esq; ✉ Flat 9, 56 Holland Park, London W11 3RS (☎ 0171 229 0316); SBC Warburg, 1 Finsbury Ave, London EC2M 2PA (☎ 0171 606 1066, telex 937011)

SPICER, Sir (William) Michael Hardy; kt (1996), MP (C) Worcestershire South (majority 16,151); s of Brig Leslie Hardy Spicer (d 1981), of Whitley Bay, Northumberland, and Muriel Winifred Alice Spicer; *b* 22 Jan 1943; *Educ* Wellington, Emmanuel Coll Cambridge (MA); *m* 1967, Patricia Ann, da of Patrick Sinclair Hunter (d 1981); 1 s, 2 da; *Career* former asst to ed The Statist, dir Cons Systems Res Centre 1968–70, md Economic Models Ltd 1970–80; MP (C) Worcs S 1974–, PPS to Trade Mins 1979–81, vice chm Cons Pty 1981–83, dep chm Cons Pty 1983–84, Parly under sec of state Dept of Transport 1985–86, min for aviation 1986–87, Parly under sec of state Dept of Energy 1987–90, min for housing and planning 1990, chm Parly Office of Sci and Technol 1992, chm Parly and Scientific Ctee 1996–; chm Assoc of Electricity Prodrs 1991–; govr Wellington Coll 1992–; *Books* Final Act (1983), Prime Minister, Spy (1986), Cotswold Manners (1989), Cotswold Murders (1991), Cotswold Mistress (1992), A Treaty Too Far - A New Policy for Europe (1992), Cotswolds Moles (1993), The Challenge of the East (1996); *Recreations* painting, writing, tennis; *Style*— Sir Michael Spicer, MP; ✉ House of Commons, London SW1A 0AA (☎ 0171 219 3000)

SPICER, Sir Nicholas Adrian Albert; 5 Bt (UK), of Lancaster Gate, Borough of Paddington; s of (Sir) Peter James Spicer, 4 Bt, who did not use the title (d 1993), and Margaret, *née* Wilson; *b* 28 Oct 1953; *Educ* Eton, Birmingham Univ (MB ChB); *m* 1992, Patricia Carol, 2 da of Warwick Dye, of Auckland, NZ; 2 s (James Peter Warwick b 12 June 1993, Andrew Nicholas Kingsley b 1 Aug 1995); *Heir* s, James Peter Warwick Spicer b 12 June 1993; *Career* medical practitioner; Liveryman Worshipful Co of Fishmongers; *Style*— Sir Nicholas Spicer, Bt; ✉ 6 Linton Lane, Bromyard, Herefordshire HR7 4DQ

SPICER, Paul Cridland; s of John Harold Vincent Spicer, of 24 Newcastle Rd, Chester-Le-Street, Co Durham, and Joan Sallie, *née* Hickling; *b* 6 June 1952; *Educ* New Coll Sch Oxford, Oakham Sch Rutland, Univ of London (BMus), Univ of Durham (PGCE), RCM (ARCO, ARCM, Walford Davies prize, Top Organ award); *Career* asst dir of music Uppingham Sch 1974–78, dir of music Ellesmere Coll 1978–84, prodr BBC Radio Three 1984–86, sr prodr Radio Three Midlands 1986–90, artistic dir Lichfield Int Arts Festival 1990–; dir: Chester Bach Singers 1982–84, Leicester Bach Choir 1984–92, Birmingham Bach Choir 1992–, Royal Coll of Music Chorus 1996–; fndr dir Finzi Singers 1987–; princ conductor Royal Coll of Music Chamber Choir 1995–, guest conductor Netherlands Radio Choir 1995–; memb Cncl: Assoc of Br Choral Dirs 1989–92, Birmingham Contemporary Music Gp 1991–94; vice chm British Arts Festivals Assoc 1994–; tstee Finzi Tst and chm Finzi Tst Festivals, dir Abbotsholme Soc; memb RCO; freelance record prodr, frequent bdcaster and organ recitalist Radio 3; composer of organ, instrumental and chamber music; *Compositions* princ works incl: On The Power of Sound (chorus and orchestra), The Darling of The World (chorus and orchestra), Piano Sonata, Song for Birds (cycle), Dies Natalis (a Capella), Kiwi Fireworks (organ); church music incl: Come Out Lazar, Magnificat and Nunc Dimittis; *Publications* English Pastoral Partsongs; *Recreations* architecture, prints (old and contemporary), promoting British music; *Style*— Paul Spicer, Esq; ✉ 1 The Close, Lichfield, Staffs WS13 7LD (☎ and fax 01543 250627); 7 The Close, Lichfield, Staffs WS13 7LD (☎ 01543 257298)

SPICER, Paul George Bullen; s of Col Roy Godfrey Bullen Spicer, CMG, MC (d 1946), and Margaret Ina Frances, *née* Money; *b* 6 Feb 1928; *Educ* Eton; *m* 10 Sept 1954, June Elizabeth Cadogan, da of Antony Fenwick (d 1954), of Kiambu, Kenya, and Brinkburn Priory, Northumberland; 1 s (Rupert b 1955), 1 da (Venetia b 1959); *Career* Lt Coldstream Gds 1945–49, served UK, Palestine and Libya; Shell International Petroleum: joined 1949, London, Kenya, Tanzania, USA, Canada, South Africa and Cyprus, rising to md Overseas until 1970; Lonrho plc: joined 1970, main bd dir 1978–94, dep chm 1991–94; *Recreations* books, music, horses; *Clubs* Brooks's, White's; *Style*— Paul Spicer, Esq; ✉ 22 Ovington Gardens, London SW3 1LE

SPICKERNELL, Rear Admiral Derek Garland; CB (1974); s of Cdr Sydney Garland Spickernell, RN (ka 1940), and Florence Elizabeth Curtis, *née* March (d 1980); *b* 1 June 1921; *Educ* RNEC Keyham; *m* 1946, Ursula Rosemary Sheila, da of Frederick Cowslade Money (d 1953), of Newbury; 2 s (Richard, John (decd)), 1 da (Susan); *Career* Rear Adm MOD Whitehall 1971–75, dir gen Br Standards Instn 1981–86, vice pres Int Standards Orgn Geneva 1985–88; *Recreations* Golf; *Style*— Rear Admiral Spickernell, CB; ✉ Ridgefield, Shawford, Hants (☎ 01962 712157)

SPIEGELBERG, Richard George; s of Francis Edward Frederick Spiegelberg (d 1979), and Margaret Neville, *née* Clegg; *b* 21 Jan 1944; *Educ* Marlborough, Hotchkiss Sch USA,

New Coll Oxford (MA); *m* 1, 1970 (m dis 1979), Coralie Eve, *née* Dreyfus; 2 s (Rupert b 1971, Maximilian b 1974); *m* 2, 1980, Suzanne Louise *née* Dodd; 1 s (Assheton b 1981), 1 da (Henrietta b 1984); *Career* Economist Intelligence Unit 1965–67, business journalist and mgmnt ed The Times 1967–74, princ Dept of Indust 1974–75, NEDO 1975–76; assoc dir: J Walter Thompson & Co 1976–80, Coopers & Lybrand 1980–84; dir and jt md Streets Fin 1984–87, exec dir corp communications Merrill Lynch Europe Ltd 1987–; *Books* The City (1973); *Recreations* walking, golf, opera; *Clubs* Brooks's; *Style*— Richard Spiegelberg, Esq

SPIEGELBERG, (Anthony) William Assheton; MBE (1997), TD (1970), DL (Cheshire 1995); s of Francis Edward Frederick Spiegelberg (d 1979), of Tarporley, and Margaret Neville, *née* Clegg; *b* 10 Dec 1936; *Educ* Marlborough, Magdalene Coll Cambridge (MA History); *m* July 1973, Mary Rose, *née* Birch, wid of the Hon Hugh Stanley; 1 da (Diana Mary Frances b 14 Jan 1977), 2 step s (Lord Derby, *qv*, Hon Peter Stanley); *Career* Nat Serv 2 Lt 5 Royal Inniskilling Dragoon Gds 1955–57; chartered accountant 1965; The Greenalls Group plc: joined 1965, co sec 1980–; Maj Cheshire Yeo (TA) 1957–74, Hon Col Cheshire Yeo Sqdn Queen's Own Yeo 1993–; chm of govrs Grange Sch Hartford Cheshire 1987–, chm Warrington Charities Tst 1989, chm of tstees Aintree Racecourse Charitable Appeal Tst 1995; Freeman Worshipful Co of Distillers 1996; ACA 1965, memb ACT 1975; *Recreations* shooting, golf, skiing; *Clubs* Cavalry & Guards; *Style*— William Spiegelberg, Esq, MBE, TD, DL; ✉ The Greenalls Group plc, Wilderspool House, Greenalls Avenue, Warrington WA4 6RH (☎ 01925 651234, fax 01925 413137)

SPIERS, (John) Anthony; *b* 19 Sept 1944; *Educ* Bishop Vesey's GS Sutton Coldfield Warwickshire; *m* 1971, Catherine Anne; 3 s (Jonathan (by first w), Benjamin b 1972, Gerald b 1973), 2 da (Catherine b 1975, Hannah-May b 1981); *Career* slr; ptnr Peter Peter & Wright 1970–96; clerk to Blanchminster Charity 1976–84; memb Cornwall CC 1981–88, dir Solicitors' Benevolent Assoc 1991–93, chm Devon and Exeter Soc of Tst and Estate Practitioners 1992–94, sec Devon and Exeter Law Soc 1994–; FRSA (memb Cncl 1995–, chm SW Regnl Ctee 1996–); *Recreations* fishing, reading, walking; *Style*— Anthony Spiers, Esq; ✉ Woolstone Mill, Bude, Cornwall EX23 0NB (☎ 01288 361800)

SPIERS, Sir Donald Maurice; kt (1993), CB (1987), TD (1966); s of Harold Herbert Spiers (d 1968), and Emma, *née* Foster (d 1978); *b* 27 Jan 1934; *Educ* Trinity Coll Cambridge (MA); *m* 13 Dec 1958, Sylvia Mary, da of Sammuel Lowman (d 1963); 2 s (Simon b 1965, Philip b 1969); *Career* 2 Lt RE 1952–54, devpt engr de Havilland 1957–60, operational res Air Miny 1961–66, scientific advsr Far East AF 1967–70, asst chief scientist RAF 1971–78, MOD PE 1978–84, dep controller Aircraft 1984–86, Controller Estabs Res & Nuclear Programmes 1987–89, Controller Aircraft 1989–94; aerospace conslt 1994–; non-exec dir: Computing Devices Co Ltd 1994–, Meggitt plc 1995–, Smiths Industries Aerospace and Defence Ltd 1995–; pres Royal Aeronautical Soc 1995–96; *Style*— Sir Donald Spiers, CB, TD; ✉ 20 Paddock Close, Camberley, Surrey GU15 2BN (☎ 01276 28164)

SPIERS, Dr John Raymond; s of H H Spiers (d 1956), and Kate, *née* Root (d 1976); *b* 30 Sept 1941; *Educ* Red Hill Sch E Sutton, Hornsey Coll of Art and Design, Catford Coll of Commerce, Univ of Sussex (BA); *m* 24 June 1967 (m dis 1981), Prof Margaret Ann Spiers, da of Leonard Forbes Boden, OBE (d 1987); 1 s (Ruskin b 19 June 1968), 1 da (Jehane b 21 Jan 1972); *Career* publisher and journalist 1960–; fndr, chm and md: The Harvester Press Ltd 1970–88, Harvester Microform Publications Ltd 1973–87, Wheatsheaf Books Ltd 1980–88; fndr and chm John Spiers Publishing Ltd 1988–; memb: Advsy Bd Centre for Study of Social History Univ of Warwick 1979–82, Chllr's Advsy Gp Univ of Sussex 1986–; a special advsr to Rt Hon Sir Peter Morrison, MP (Dep Chm) Cons Central Office 1989–90; chm: Univ of Sussex Alumni Soc 1983–, Brighton Theatre Ltd 1984, Brighton Business Group 1989–95, Brighton Health Authy 1991–92, Brighton Healthcare NHS Tst 1992–94, David Salomon's Mgmnt Devpt Centre (SETRHA) 1993–94, Brighton Healthcare Arts Tst 1993–94, Advsy Bd Centre for Health Care Mgmnt Univ of Nottingham 1994–96, The Patients' Assoc 1995– (actg chief exec 1995–96); tstee: Brighton Int Arts Festival 1989–96, Choice in Educn (grant maintained schs) 1989–92, Grant Maintained Schs Fndn 1992– (vice chm 1992–), The Trident Tst 1992– (vice chm 1993, chm 1994–); founding dir Southern Sound Radio PLC 1980–87; dir: Radical Soc 1988– (co chm 1990–), Center for Intelligence Studies Washington DC 1990–93; distinguished sr fell Center for Cons Studies Washington DC 1992; conslt dir Cons Central Office 1990–95, health policy advsr The Social Market Fndn 1994–; pres Brighton Kemp Town Cons Assoc 1991–95, dep treas Cons Pty SE Area England 1990–92; memb: Advsy Cncl IEA Health Unit 1989–92, Communications Advsy Gp and Patients' Charter Advsy Gp NHS Mgmnt Exec 1991–94, Strategic Ctee on Women's Issues SE Thames RHA 1992–, King's Fund NAHAT Public Participation Advsy Gp 1992, Governance in the NHS (Induction and Trg) Working Pty NHS Mgmnt Exec 1993, Ministerial Advsy Gp on Design in Healthcare 1993–, PM's Advsy Panel on The Citizen's Charter 1994, Policy Advsy Gp Inst of Health Services Mgmnt 1994–, NHSME Working Pty on Open Govt 1994, Bd Int Health Care Mgmnt Inst 1994–, NHS Exec Patient Responsiveness Gp 1996–; Nat Assoc of Health Authorities and Tsts: memb Cncl 1992–94, memb Exec 1993–94, vice chm Provider Ctee 1993–94, chm Conf Ctee 1993–94 (memb 1992); visiting fell: NHS Staff Coll Wales 1995–, King's Fund Mgmnt Coll 1996–; JP (East Sussex) 1989–91; Queen's Award for Export Achievement 1986; Hon DUniv Sussex 1994; Companion of the Guild of St George 1981; FRSA 1994; *Books* The Rediscovery of George Gissing (with Pierre Coustillas, 1971), The Invisible Hospital and The Secret Garden: An Insider's Account of the NHS Reforms (1995), Who Owns Our Bodies: Making Moral Choices in Health Care (1996), Sense and Sensibility in Health Care (co-author, 1996), How to be a Street-Smart Patient (1997); *Recreations* collecting books, reading them, canal boats, walking, travelling in railway carriages, natural history; *Clubs* Carlton; *Style*— Dr John Spiers; ✉ 44 St Thomas's Street, Old Portsmouth, Hampshire PO1 2EX (☎ 01705 297534, fax 01705 811450)

SPIERS, Judith Marilyn (Judi); da of Leonard David Spiers (d 1987), and Fay, *née* Sugarman; *Educ* Notre Dame Convent Plymouth, Rose Bruford Coll of Speech and Drama Sidcup Kent; *Career* actress Belgrade Theatre in Education Co Coventry 1973–75, announcer then prog presenter Westward TV 1975–85 (franchise taken over by TSW 1982); presenter BBC TV incl: Bazaar 1985–87, Daytime Live 1987–, Daytime UK 1990, Pebble Mill 1992–95; others incl: Road Runner (HTV and WTV) 1993–94, Judi Spiers Show (BBC Radio 2), Cable Travel TV; appearances in TV dramas: Heather Anne (TSW), Where There's a Will (TSW), Virtual Murder (BBC), Baywatch (ITV), The Governor, Wally K Daly Alternative DJ Show (radio drama); completed Lombard RAC Rally 1989; *Recreations* swimming, reading, cooking, skiing, scuba diving, snorkelling, gardening, travelling; *Style*— Ms Judi Spiers; ✉ c/o Jon Roseman, JRA Agencies Ltd, 46 Sutton Court Road, London W4 4NN (☎ 0181 742 0552, fax 0181 742 0554)

SPIERS, Shaun Mark; MEP (Lab Co-op) London SE (majority 8,022); s of (Charles) Gordon Spiers (d 1990), and Ann Kathleen, *née* Hutton; *b* 23 April 1962; *Educ* Brentwood Sch Essex, St John's Coll Oxford (BA), King's Coll London (MA); *Career* political offr SE Co-op 1987–94, MEP (Lab Co-op) London SE 1994–; *Clubs* Bromley Labour, Lewisham Labour; *Style*— Shaun Spiers, Esq, MEP; ✉ Sunways House, 298 Broadway, Bexleyheath, Kent DA6 8AH (☎ 0181 298 9339, fax 0181 298 9959)

SPILG, Dr Walter Gerson Spence; s of George Spilg, JP (d 1966), and Fanny, *née* Cohen (d 1978); *b* 27 Oct 1937; *Educ* Hutchesons' GS Glasgow, Univ of Glasgow (MB ChB); *m* 1 Sept 1965, Vivien Anne, da of Edwards Burns (d 1963), of Glasgow; 1 s (Edward George b 1968), 2 da (Sandra Jane b 1966, Jillian Deborah b 1971); *Career* house offr Stobhill Hosp Glasgow 1964–65, registrar in pathology Glasgow Royal Infirmary 1966–68 (Coats Perman scholar Univ Dept of Pathology 1965–66), lectr in pathology Univ of Glasgow 1969–72, conslt pathologist Victoria Infirmary Glasgow 1972– (sr registrar 1968–69, in administrative charge 1986–); hon clinical sr lectr Univ of Glasgow; memb: Area Medical Sub-Ctee in Laboratory Medicine, BMA, ACP (pres Caledonian Branch 1995–), Pathological Soc of Great Britain and Ireland, Int Acad of Pathology, Forensic Med (Scotland) Ctee, Panel of Examiners RCPSGlas; FRCPath 1982, FRCPG 1988; *Recreations* bridge, reading; *Style*— Dr Walter Spilg; ✉ 4B Newton Court, Newton Grove, Newton Mearns, Glasgow G77 5QL (☎ 0141 639 3130); Pathology Department, Victoria Infirmary, Glasgow G42 9TY (☎ 0141 201 5662, fax 0141 201 5672)

SPILLER, Prof Eric; s of Leonard Spiller, of Wombourne, Staffs, and Helen, *née* Holder; *b* 19 Aug 1946; *Educ* Central Sch of Art & Design London, Royal Coll of Art London (MA); *m* Carolyn; 2 s (Charles b 12 Sept 1974, Rufus b 8 Nov 1977), 1 da (Nancy b 11 July 1980); *Career* jewellery designer and lectr: pt/t lectr Fashion Dept Harrow Sch of Art 1971–73, lectr in silversmithing and jewellery 1973–75, Dept of Three-Dimensional Studies NI Poly, lectr i/c of jewellery 1975–81 (Dept of Design Grays Sch of Art, Robert Gordons Inst of Technol Aberdeen), prog ldr BA (Combined Studies) Crafts Crewe and Alsager Coll of Higher Educn 1981–83, princ lectr/dep head of dept 1983–85 (Dept of Silversmithing Jewellery and Allied Crafts, Sir John Cass Faculty of Art City of London Poly); head of sch: Sch of Design Portsmouth Coll of Art Design and Further Educn 1985–87, Grays Sch of Art Robert Gordons Inst of Technol Aberdeen 1987–92, asst princ The Robert Gordon Univ 1992–; visiting lectr: Univ of Ulster, West Surrey Coll of Art, Loughborough Coll of Art, S Glamorgan Inst of Higher Educn, Brighton Poly, San Diego State Univ; public collections incl: Goldsmiths Hall, Crafts Cncl, W Midlands Arts, NW Arts, Aberdeen Art Gallery, Scot Crafts Collection; private collections worldwide; numerous exhibitions incl: Craftmans Art (V & A) 1973, Aberdeen Art Gallery 1977, New Jewellery (Royal Exchange Theatre Manchester) 1984, New York 1983, Kyoto 1984, Tokyo 1984–85, Munich 1989 and 1991; memb Cncl: Crafts Cncl 1993–, Scottish Arts Cncl 1994– (chm Craft Ctee 1994–); FRSA; *Style*— Prof Eric Spiller; ✉ Faculty of Design, The Robert Gordon University, Garthee Road, Aberdeen AB10 7QB (☎ 01224 263750, fax 01224 263737)

SPILLER, John Anthony; MBE (1979); s of C Finn and step-s of C H Spiller (d 1993), and Sarah, *née* Walsh (d 1988); *b* 29 Dec 1942; *Educ* Bideford Sch, N Devon Tech Coll, Bideford Art Coll; *m* 1 Sept 1972, Angela, da of Surtees Gleghorn (d 1971); 1 s (Ben b 23 Feb 1976), 1 da (Sarah b 16 July 1974); *Career* chm Devon Young Liberals 1960–62, asst agent to Mark (Lord) Bonham-Carter Torrington Parly Constituency 1962–64, constituency agent Cornwall N Parly Constituency to John W Pardoe MP 1965–71; N regnl organiser and election agent: to Cyril Smith, MP Rochdale By-Election, to Alan Beith, MP Berwick-upon-Tweed By-Election 1972; nat agent Lib Central Assoc 1973–78, advsr to Joshua Nkomo African Peoples Union Zimbabwe (then Rhodesia) Independence Elections 1979–80, marginal seats advsr (UK) Lib Pty 1981–82, sec gen Lib Pty 1983–86, liaison offr for Devonshire PHAB 1991–92; co sec Estuary Seascapes Ltd 1994–, sr exec Western Approaches Ltd 1992–96; nat pres Assoc of Lib Agents and Organisers 1983–84; memb: Bd Mgmnt Gladstone Benevolent Fund 1980–95 (sec and tstee 1995–), Shelter, RNLI (S West); delegate Democracy conf Vilnius Lithuania 1992 and 1994, Electoral Reform Soc delegate Democracy Conf Tallin Estonia 1995; delegate: Citizens and Democracy Conf Moscow Russia 1995, Democracy Conf Yerevan Repub of Armenia 1995; Office for Democratic Instns and Human Rights (ODIHR) observer for state elections Repub of Georgia Nov 1995, Office of Int Monitoring (OSCE) observer for elections Bosnia and Herzegovina Sept 1996; *Recreations* travel, watching amateur boxing, music (folk); *Style*— John Spiller, Esq, MBE; ✉ 5 Royston Rd, Bideford, Devon EX39 3AN (☎ 01237 477173, fax 01237 477573); Keogh, Moycullen, County Galway, Eire

SPILLER, Richard John; s of Capt Michael Macnaughton Spiller, of Belfast, and Agnes Gall, *née* Algie; *b* 31 Dec 1953; *Educ* Royal Belfast Academical Inst, Univ of Exeter (LLB), City of London Poly (MA); *m* 17 Sept 1982, Hilary, da of William Wright, of Kingston-on-Thames, Surrey; 1 s (James b 1984), 1 da (Emily b 1987); *Career* admitted slr 1980; ptnr D J Freeman 1985–; Freeman: City of London 1986, Worshipful Co of Slrs 1986 (memb Commercial and Insurance Law Sub Ctees); memb Law Soc; *Style*— Richard Spiller, Esq; ✉ D J Freeman, 43 Fetter Lane, London EC4A 1NA (☎ 0171 583 4055, fax 0171 353 7377)

SPILMAN, John Ellerker; JP (1984), DL (Humberside, 1990); s of Maj Harry Spilman, MC, JP, DL (d 1980), and Phyllis Emily, *née* Hind; *b* 9 March 1940; *Educ* Sedbergh, RAC Cirencester; *m* 25 Oct 1975, Patricia Mary, da of Gilbert Sutcliffe (d 1988), of Cleethorpes; 1 s (David b 1984), 1 da (Joanna b 1980); *Career* md farming co, dir Aylesby Manor Farms Ltd; High Sheriff Humberside 1989–90; church warden; tstee: Stanford Charity, McAulay Meml Tst; *Recreations* fishing, shooting, tennis, music, Rotary (club pres 1991–92); *Clubs* Farmers; *Style*— John E Spilman, Esq, JP, DL; ✉ Aylesby Manor, Grimsby, S Humberside (☎ 01472 871800); Manor Farm, Aylesby, Grimsby (☎ 01472 872550, fax 01472 873032)

SPINETTI, Victor George Andrew; s of Guiseppe Spinetti (d 1985), and Lily, *née* Watson; *b* 2 Sept 1933; *Educ* Monmouth, Cardiff Sch of Music and Drama; *Career* actor and director; fell Coll of Music and Drama Cardiff; *Theatre* with Joan Littlewood's Theatre Workshop Stratford East 1959–65; numerous West End and Broadway appearances 1964–; one man show Victor Spinetti's Very Private Diary (Edinburgh Festival 1981, Donmar and Apollo Theatres London 1989, Sydney Opera House 1990, New York 1992); recent theatre incl: Windy City, Pirates of Penzance, Super Ted, Peter Pan, Comic Cuts, Oliver, One for the Pot; RSC at Stratford 1995–96; debut as dir NT 1968; plays dir incl: Hair (Amsterdam and Rome), Jesus Christ Superstar (Paris), Deja Revue (London); devised and wrote revue Off The Peg (Arts Theatre), co-author (with John Lennon) play In His Own Write; *Television* recent credits incl: The Paradise Club, Vincent van Gogh, Singles, Maxwell's House, An Actor's Life for Me, Secrets (by Judith Krantz); *Films* recent credits incl: Voyage of the Damned, Mistral's Daughter, Sins, Under the Cherry Moon, The Attic, The Krays; *Awards* winner of Broadway Tony Award and Paris Int Festival first prize (for Oh! What A Lovely War 1965); *Recreations* reading, writing, walking; *Style*— Victor Spinetti, Esq; ✉ c/o Barry Burnett Organisation Ltd, Suite 42–43, Grafton House, 2–3 Golden Square, London W1R 3AD (☎ 0171 437 7048/9, fax 0171 734 6118)

SPINK, Brian Maurice; s of Henry Lewis Spink (d 1986), of N Devon, and Marjorie Rose, *née* Sandell (d 1976); *b* 3 July 1934; *Educ* Lawrence Coll Birmingham, Birmingham Sch of Speech and Drama, RADA; *m* 1, 1962 (m dis 1986), Jennifer Ann, da of Léon Goossens; 1 s (Alexander b 1964), 2 da (Susannah b 1966, Léonie b 1971); *m* 2, 1995, Madeleine Newbury; *Career* actor; *Theatre* Jesus in York Mystery Plays 1957, seasons at Hornchurch, Leatherhead, Oxford and Nottingham; at Old Vic (early 1960's): Paris in Romeo and Juliet, Orsino and Antonio in Twelfth Night, Hastings in Richard III, Sebastian in The Tempest, Flamineo in The White Devil; Azdak in Caucasian Chalk Circle (Citizens' Theatre Glasgow), Winterhalter (opposite Ingrid Bergman) in Water of the Moon, Brutus and Orsino in Shakespeare season (Comedy Theatre), Morosini in The Heretic (Duke of York's), Vallance in Thunderbolt (Arts), Giles Ralston and Major Metcalf in The Mousetrap (Ambassadors and St Martin's); RNT: Mathematician in The Trojan War Will Not Take Place, Viceroy in The Spanish Tragedy, She Stoops to

Conquer (tour), Ventidius and Proculeius in Antony and Cleopatra, one man show of own narrative poem The Red Train; Caedmon in Christopher Fry's One Thing More: Or Caedmon Construed (Whitby Festival) 1989; dir Christopher Fry's Thor With Angels (performed in London churches), dir John Gabriel Borkman 1995; *Film/Television* incl: Julius Caesar, King and Country, Riviera Police, Twelfth Night, A Very Public Affair, Invasion, Sister Dora, Don Quixote, Rumpole of the Bailey, The Road to 1984, Prime Suspect III; *Publications* The Red Train (Arvon Fndn Award Sotheby's Int Competition 1982), contrib New Poetry 6 (ed Ted Hughes); *Recreations* walking long distances, reading, listening to music; *Style*— Brian Spink, Esq

SPINK, Ian Alexander; s of John Arthur Spink, of Melbourne, Australia, and Lorna Kathleen, *née* Hart; *b* 8 Oct 1947; *Educ* Highett HS, Aust Ballet Sch; *m* 1, 1972 (m dis 1975), Gail Mae Ferguson; m 2, 1986 (m dis 1992), Michele Ashmore Smith; *Career* dancer Australian Ballet Co 1968–74, dancer and choreographer Dance Co of NSW 1975–77, dancer Richard Alston & Dancers Co 1978–79, fndr, dancer, dir and choreographer Ian Spink Dance Group 1978–82, co-fndr Second Stride (dance theatre) 1982 (became sole dir 1988), currently freelance choreographer and dir; choreography incl: theatre choreography for RSC, Ro Theatre (Holland) and The Crucible (Sheffield), opera choreography for Opera North, WNO, Royal Opera House, Scot Opera, Opera de Nice, ENO and Glyndebourne Festival Opera; directed: Fugue by Caryl Churchill (Channel 4) 1988, Judith Weir's The Vanishing Bridegroom (Scot Opera) 1990, The Pelican (Glasgow Citizens Theatre) 1992, Orlando (Battignano Opera Festival) 1992; directed and choreographed 15 devised works for Second Stride incl: Bacleuheim 1939 1995, Hotel 1996, Wierd Actions 1996; *Recreations* music, cooking, gardening; *Style*— Ian Spink, Esq; ✉ Dernol School, Llangurig, Llanidloes, Powys SY18 6RZ

SPINK, Dr Robert; MP (C) Castle Point (majority 16,830); *b* 1 Aug 1948; *Educ* Univ of Manchester (BSc(Eng)), Cranfield (MSc(IndustEng), CDipAF, PhD); *m* 1968, Janet; 4 c; *Career* served RAF 1964–66, invalided; apprentice then engr EMI Electronics Ltd 1966–77, industrial mgmnt conslt 1977–80, dir and co-owner Seafarer Navigation International Ltd 1981–84, conslt industrial engr 1984–, dir Bournemouth International Airport plc 1989–93; MP (C) Castle Point 1992–; memb: Educn Select Ctee 1992–94, Bd Parly Office of Science and Technol 1993–; PPS to Ann Widdecombe Home Office 1994–; Dorset CC: cncllr 1985–93, dep ldr Cons Gp 1989–90, memb Dorset Police Authy 1985–93; CEng, MIMC, MIMgt; *Style*— Dr Robert Spink, MP; ✉ House of Commons, London SW1A 0AA (☎ 0171 219 6237, fax 0171 219 0402 and 01268 792992, mobile 0468 981666)

SPIRA, Peter John Ralph; s of Dr Jean-Jacques Spira (d 1970); *b* 2 March 1930; *Educ* Eton, King's Coll Cambridge; *m* 1, 1957, Meriel, *née* Gold; m 2, 1969, Anne Marie Marguerite Renée, *née* Landon; 6 c; *Career* SG Warburg & Co Ltd 1957–74 (vice chm 1971–74, non-exec dir until 1982), fin dir Sotheby Parke Bernet Group plc 1974–82, vice chm Goldman Sachs Int Corpn London 1982–87, dir Société Générale de Surveillance Holding SA Geneva 1987, dep chm County NatWest Ltd 1988–91, dir NatWest Investment Bank Ltd 1988–92, dir Smithers & Co Ltd 1991–, dep chm SGS Holding UK Ltd 1995–; dir Nat Film Fin Corp 1981–86, FCA; *Recreations* music, reading, photography, carpentry; *Style*— Peter Spira, Esq; ✉ 63 Bedford Gardens, London W8 7EF (☎ 0171 727 5295, fax 0171 221 3865); France (☎ 00 33 04 70 06 46 68, fax 00 33 04 70 06 43 09)

SPITTLE, His Hon Judge; Leslie; s of Samuel Spittle (d 1942), and Irene, *née* Smith; *b* 14 Nov 1940; *Educ* Acklam Hall GTS, Constantine Coll of Technol, Univ of Hull (LLB); *m* 7 Sept 1963, Brenda, da of Charles Alexander Clayton (d 1961); 3 s (Nicholas b 21 June 1968, Jonathan b 23 Sept 1971, Matthew b 14 Dec 1981); *Career* Univ of Hull Air Sqdn RAFVR; mgmnt trainee 1956–62, lectr and sr lectr Teeside Poly 1965–70; called to the Gray's Inn 1970, recorder 1990–96, circuit judge (NE Circuit) 1996–; former: chm Round Table, chm Yarm Sch Assoc, vice chm govrs Kirklevington Sch; ACIS 1960; *Recreations* amateur dramatics, golf, various charitable bodies; *Clubs* Eaglescliffe Golf, Rotary (Teeside West); *Style*— His Hon Judge Spittle

SPITTLE, Dr Margaret Flora; da of Edwin William Spittle (d 1977), of Tunbridge Wells, and Ada Florence, *née* Axam; *b* 11 Nov 1939; *Educ* King's Coll London (MSc, AKC), Westminster Hosp Med Sch (DMRT), FRCP; *m* 2 Jan 1965 (m dis 1977), Clive Lucas Harmer, s of Cecil Norman Harmer (d 1986), of Westcliff-on-Sea; 2 da (Kasha Jane Lucas b 1968, Victoria Margaret Lucas b 1971); m 2, 31 May 1986, David John Hare, s of John Robinson Hare (d 1982), of Southrepps; *Career* conslt clinical oncologist Meyerstein Inst of Clinical Oncology The Middx Hosp, The St John's Dermatology Centre St Thomas' Hosp and the Cromwell Hosp 1971–; vice pres and dean Royal Coll of Radiologists 1994–, vice pres RSM 1994– (pres Radiology Section 1989, Oncology Section 1987); pres Head and Neck Oncologists of GB 1991; memb: Govt Ctee on Breast Screening, Nat Radiological Protection Bd, Govt Ctee on Med and Radiation in the Environment; Freeman City of London, Liveryman Worshipful Soc of Apothecaries (memb Ctee); memb BMA, FRCR; *Recreations* family, golf, music, flying; *Style*— Dr Margaret Spittle; ✉ The Manor House, Beaconsfield, Claygate, Surrey KT10 0PW (☎ 01372 465540, fax 01372 470470); Meyerstein Institute of Clinical Oncology, The Middlesex Hospital, Mortimer St, London W1N 8AA (☎ 0171 380 9090, fax 0171 436 0160)

SPITTLE, Eur Ing Robert; s of William Charles Spittle, of 24 Shires House, Eden Grove Road, Byfleet, Surrey, and Ellen, *née* Angel; *b* 14 March 1955; *Educ* Highlands CS Sch, Guildford Co Tech Coll, Poly of the South Bank (BSc); *m* 21 May 1977, Lydia Shirley, da of Leonard Taylor; 1 da (Cally b 16 Dec 1980); *Career* design engr in building servs mech engrg Kennedy and Donkin International Consulting Engineers 1971–78, project engr The Raven Group (design and build contractors) 1978–82, project mangr then UK internal mech engrg conslt The Central Consulting Services Group IBM (UK) Ltd, property mgmnt 1982–87, engrg ptnr Building Design Partnership (building design conslts) 1989– (mech engrg assoc 1987–89); memb: Chartered Inst of Building Services Engrs 1982, American Soc of Heating Refrigeration and Air Conditioning Engrs 1986; CEng 1986, MIMechE 1990, Eur Ing 1990, MConsE 1993; *Recreations* swimming, running, windsurfing; *Style*— Eur Ing Robert Spittle; ✉ Building Design Partnership, 16 Greese St, London W1A 4WD (☎ 0171 631 4733, fax 0171 631 0393, car 0831 475 879)

SPOFFORTH, (David) Mark; s of Michael Gordon Spofforth (d 1987), and Joan Mary, *née* Marsh; *b* 26 July 1956; *Educ* Bradfield, Univ of Durham (BSc); *m* 31 July 1983, Dorothy Lesley, *née* Payne; 1 da (Gemma Mary b 17 Nov 1987), 1 s (Peter Michael b 25 Jan 1990); *Career* articled clerk Coopers & Lybrand 1980–82, ptnr Spofforths CAs 1984– (joined 1983); ICAEW: memb Tech Ctee 1985–94, memb Cncl 1993–, chm Gen Practitioner Bd 1995– (memb 1993–); memb Main Ctee SE Soc of CAs 1990–; Freeman City of London, memb Ct Worshipful Co of Horners, memb Worshipful Co of CAs; FCA 1982, FRSA 1994; *Recreations* rugby, skiing, scuba diving; *Clubs* City Livery, Carlton; *Style*— Mark Spofforth, Esq; ✉ Spofforths, Tudor Court, 52 Richmond Road, Worthing, East Sussex BN11 1PR (☎ 01903 234943, fax 01903 203474, mobile 0860 927297)

SPOKES, Christopher Daniel; s of John Dacre Spokes (d 1976), and Joyce Margaret, *née* Sheppard; *b* 29 July 1947; *Educ* Wellingborough Sch, Northampton Coll of Technol, Northampton Coll of Agric (NCA), Shuttleworth Coll (NDA), UCW Aberystwyth (BSc Econ); *m* May 1983, Gillian Stewart, da of Alec Neil Donaldson; 1 s (Alexander James b Oct 1987), 1 da (Charlotte Kate b April 1985); *Career* articled clerk Cooper Bros (later Coopers & Lybrand) 1973–76; Bidwells chartered surveyors: joined 1977, ptnr 1986–, currently head Client Accounting gp; pres Cambridge Soc of Chartered Accountants 1990–91, current chm Business Membs Gp E Anglian Soc of Chartered Accountants; FCA 1981 (ACA 1976); *Recreations* tennis, billiards, cinema, walking; *Clubs* Farmers; *Style*— Christopher Spokes, Esq; ✉ Brooklands House, 167 Caxton End, Bourn, Cambridge CB3 7ST (☎ 01954 719288); Bidwells, Trumpington Rd, Cambridge CB2 2LD (☎ 01223 841841)

SPOKES, John Arthur Clayton; QC (1973); s of Peter Spencer Spokes (d 1976), of Oxford, and Lilla Jane, *née* Clayton (d 1979); *b* 6 Feb 1931; *Educ* Westminster, Brasenose Coll Oxford (MA); *m* 30 Dec 1961, Jean, da of Dr Robert McLean (d 1972), of Carluke; 1 s (Andrew), 1 da (Gillian); *Career* called to the Bar Gray's Inn 1955, bencher 1985–, recorder of the Crown Ct 1972–93; chllr Diocese of Winchester 1985–93; chm Data Protection Tbnl 1985–; *Clubs* United Oxford and Cambridge; *Style*— J A C Spokes, Esq, QC; ✉ 3 Pump Court, Temple, London EC4Y 7AJ (☎ 0171 353 0711, fax 0171 353 3319)

SPOKES SYMONDS, Ann; da of Peter Spencer Spokes (d 1976), and Lilla Jane, *née* Clayton (d 1979); *b* 10 Nov 1925; *Educ* The Masters Sch Dobbs Ferry NY, St Anne's Coll Oxford (MA); *m* 1980, (John) Richard Symonds, s of Sir Charles Symonds, KBE, CB (d 1978); 2 step s (Jeremy, Peter (twins)); *Career* memb Oxford City Cncl 1957–95 (hon alderman 1995–), Parly candidate gen elections of 1959, 1966 and 1970, lord mayor of Oxford 1976–77, chm Oxfordshire CC 1981–83; memb W Regnl Bd Central Independent TV (formerly ATV) 1978–92 (dir 1978–81), admin Social Servs to 1980, chm ACC Social Servs Ctee 1978–82; memb: Prince of Wales Advsy Gp on Disability 1983–90, Hearing Aid Cncl 1987–89, Bd of Anchor Housing Assoc 1976–83 and 1985–94; organising sec Age Concern Oxford 1968–80; patron Age Concern England 1994– (chm 1983–86, vice pres 1987–94); FRSA 1991; *Books* Celebrating Age - An Anthology (1987), Havens Across the Sea (1990), Storks, Black Bags and Gooseberry Bushes (1993); *Recreations* photography, travel, lawn tennis, swimming, golf; *Style*— Mrs Ann Spokes Symonds; ✉ 43 Davenant Rd, Oxford OX2 8BU

SPON-SMITH, Robin Witterick; s of Alan Witterick Spon-Smith, and Joyce Margaret, *née* Bache (d 1988); *b* 11 Oct 1942; *Educ* Eltham Coll London, LLM (Greenwich Univ) 1996; *m* 11 June 1966, Jennifer Dorothy, da of William Frederic Delabere Walker; 2 s (Jolyon b 1973, Phillip b 1975); *Career* 1 Bn London Scottish (TA) 1960–65; admitted slr 1965, called to the Bar Inner Temple 1976; recorder 1987–; cncllr London Borough Bromley 1968–71, govr Eltham Coll 1974–96; Freeman City of London 1980; *Books* The Law Society's Guide to Oaths and Affirmations (1993, 2 edn 1996); *Style*— Robin Spon-Smith, Esq; ✉ 1 Mitre Court Buildings, Temple, London EC4Y 7BS (☎ 0171 797 7070, fax 0171 797 7435)

SPOONCER, Rachel Anne; da of Ronald Clifford Spooncer, of Wilmslow, Cheshire, and Anne Patricia, *née* Mair; *b* 25 Oct 1953; *Educ* Manchester HS for Girls, Univ of Birmingham (BSc, Garner Prize); *m* 14 July 1990, Dr James Hugh Steven, s of Hugh Reid Mowat Steven; *Career* technol mangr KLEA Engineering ICI 1987–95, ops mangr ICI Engineering Technology 1995–; winner MacRobert Award 1993; FIChemE 1994, FEng 1996; *Recreations* skiing, gardening, walking, cycling; *Style*— Mrs Rachel Spooncer, FEng; ✉ ICI Engineering Technology, PO Box No 8, The Heath, Runcorn, Cheshire WA7 4QD (☎ 01928 513598)

SPOONER, Dr David; s of Rev Reginald H Spooner (d 1982), and Lucy Ellen, *née* Read; *b* 12 Jan 1949; *Educ* Magdalen Coll Sch Brackley, Univ of Birmingham (MB, BSc); *m* Diana Lilian, da of Frederick John Mason, of Banbury; 2 s (John, Andrew), 1 da (Rebecca); *Career* res fell Cancer Res Inst Sutton Surrey 1979–81, sr registrar in radiotherapy Royal Marsden Hosp London 1981–82 (registrar 1976–79); conslt in radiotherapy and oncology: Queen Elizabeth Hosp, Birmingham Children's Hosp, Royal Orthopaedic Hosp Birmingham; memb Cncl Royal Coll of Radiologists; FRCP, FRCR; *Style*— Dr David Spooner; ✉ Birmingham Oncology Centre, Queen Elizabeth Hospital, Edgbaston B15 2TH (☎ 0121 472 1311 ext 3134, fax 0121 627 2902)

SPOONER, Dr Derek John; s of Harry Spooner (d 1968), and Vera Lois, *née* Manning (d 1993); *b* 14 Oct 1943; *Educ* Taunton's Sch Southampton, St Catharine's Coll Cambridge (MA, PhD); *m* 26 July 1969, Christine Elizabeth, da of Arthur Nuttal Simpson, of Looe, Cornwall; 2 da (Catherine b 1974, Helen b 1978); *Career* sr lectr Dept of Geography Univ of Hull 1985– (lectr 1968–85, head of dept 1986–89 and 1995–96, dean of sch 1996–97); visiting prof: Univ of Maryland 1976, Univ of W Virginia 1985; ed: Regnl Studies Assoc newsletter 1986–89, Geography (jl of the Geographical Assoc) 1989–95, The Regnl Review of the Yorks and Humberside Regnl Res Observatory 1996–; memb: Regional Studies Assoc, RGS, Geographical Assoc; *Books* Mining and Regional Development (1981); *Recreations* cricket, birdwatching, travel; *Clubs* Hull Cricket (capt 1975, 1977, 1990 and 1991); *Style*— Dr Derek Spooner; ✉ School of Geography and Earth Resources, The University, Hull HU6 7RX (☎ 01482 465554, fax 01482 466340)

SPOONER, Edgar; *b* 10 Sept 1916; *Educ* Barmouth GS; *Career* field offr Ordnance Survey 1937–39 and 1946–47, serv 512 Field Survey Co Royal Engrs 1939–46, various local govt appts in Mid Wales 1947–76, dir Powys Rural Cncl 1976–81; chm Radio Maldwyn (incremental ILR station for Mid-Wales and Borders) 1990–93 (pres 1993–95); mayor of Newtown 1979–81 and 1989–90 (cncllr 1974–91), cncllr Montgomeryshire Dist Cncl 1987–95; SBStJ; *Recreations* classical music, flat green bowling (pres Welsh Bowling Assoc 1986); *Style*— Edgar Spooner, Esq; ✉ 14 Glandulas Drive, Newtown, Powys SY16 4JB (☎ 01686 625352)

SPOONER, Prof Frank Clyffurde; s of Harry Gordon Morrison Spooner (d 1967), and Ethel Beatrice, *née* Walden (d 1985); *b* 5 March 1924; *Educ* Christ's Coll Cambridge (BA, MA, PhD, LittD); *Career* WWII RNVR 1942–46, Sub Lt (S); served: HMS Shippigan, HMS Swiftsure, HMS Newfoundland, HMS Rame Head; chargé de recherches Centre Nat de la Recherche Scientifique Paris 1949–50, Allen scholar Univ of Cambridge 1951, fell Christ's Coll 1951–57; Cwlth Fund fell: Univ of Chicago 1955–56, Univs of NY, Columbia and Harvard 1956–57, Ecole Pratique des Hautes Etudes Paris 1957–63; lectr Ctee for Advanced Studies Univ of Oxford 1958–59, lectr in economics Harvard Univ 1961–62; Irving Fisher res prof of economics Yale Univ 1962–63; Univ of Durham: lectr 1963–64, reader 1964–66, prof 1966–85, emeritus prof of econ history 1985; Leverhulme fell 1977–79 and 1985–86; Prix Limantour, Lauréat de l'Académie des Sciences Morales et Politiques (1957); FRHistS 1970, FSA 1983; *Books* L'Économie mondiale et les frappes monétaires en France 1493–1680 (1956), The international economy and monetary movements in France, 1493–1725 (1972), Risks at Sea: Amsterdam insurance and maritime Europe, 1766–1780 (1983); *Recreations* music, walking, photography; *Clubs* United Oxford and Cambridge Univ; *Style*— Prof Frank Spooner; ✉ 31 Chatsworth Ave, Bromley, Kent BR1 5DP; Department of Economics, 23–26 Old Elvet, Durham DH1 3HY (☎ 0191 374 2272)

SPOONER, Graham Michael; s of Ronald Sidney Spooner (d 1968), of Westcliff-on-Sea, Essex, and Kitty Margaret, *née* Cole (d 1985); *b* 23 Aug 1953; *Educ* Westcliff HS, St John's Coll Cambridge (MA); *m* Virginia Mary, *née* Barker; *Career* ICFC (now part of 3i Group plc): joined 1974, area mangr Nottingham 1983, local dir in London 1986, dir 3i plc 1987–93, head of corp fin Olliff & Partners PLC 1993–95, dir Rea Brothers Limited 1995–96, dir of corp fin Kidsons Impey 1996–; *Recreations* sports, classic cars, heritage, travel; *Clubs* United Oxford and Cambridge Univ; *Style*— Graham Spooner, Esq; ✉ 4 Barrow Court, Barrow Gurney, Bristol BS19 3RW (☎ 01275 463314); 22 Remington Street, London N1 8DH (☎ 0171 253 2729); Kidsons Impey, Spectrum House, 20–26 Cursitor Street, London EC4A 1HY (☎ 0171 405 2088, fax 0171 831 2206)

SPOONER, Sir James Douglas; kt (1981); o s of Vice Adm Ernest John Spooner, DSO (d 1942), and Megan, *née* Foster (d 1987); *b* 11 July 1932; *Educ* Eton, ChCh Oxford; *m* 1958, Jane Alison, da of Sir Gerald Glover (d 1986); 2 s, 1 da; *Career* former ptnr Dixon Wilson & Co CAs; chm: Coats Viyella 1969–89, Morgan Crucible 1983–; dir: John Swire & Sons 1970–, J Sainsbury 1981–94, Barclays Bank 1983–94; chm Tstees British Telecom Pension Scheme 1992–; chm Navy Army and Air Force Inst 1973–86, pres KIDS (handicapped children's charity); fell and chm Cncl King's Coll London 1986–, dep chm Royal Opera House Covent Garden 1987–, govr Royal Acad of Music 1996–; fell Eton Coll 1990–; FCA; *Recreations* history, music, shooting; *Clubs* White's, Beefsteak; *Style—* Sir James Spooner; ✉ Swire House, 59 Buckingham Gate, London SW1E 6AJ

SPOONER, Raymond Philip; s of Henry James Spooner (d 1989), and Ethel, *née* Phillips (d 1986); *b* 31 Aug 1934; *Educ* Addey and Stanhope Sch London, City Univ London (MSc); *m* 23 Oct 1954, Beryl Jean, da of Percy Charles Bratton (d 1973); 1 s (Kevin Paul b 2 Oct 1956 d 1985), 1 da (Yvette Kay Dawn b 14 Oct 1958); *Career* Sgt Intelligence Corps 1952–54, TA 1954–62; co sec 1963–67; lectr: Queen Elizabeth Trg Coll for the Disabled Leatherhead 1967–72, SW London Coll 1972–82 (also dep head of Accountancy Dept); sr lectr in accountancy and audit South Bank Poly 1982–90; currently: princ Ray Spooner and Co (accountants and mgmnt consults), dir and chief exec Arranbee Consultancy Servs Ltd (conslts in internal auditing and mgmnt control); author of Spooner Report (brought about the creation of UK professional qualification for internal auditors); govr: Inst of Internal Auditors UK 1976–78, SW London Coll 1970–81; memb Cncl Inst of Co Accountants; pres: Soc of Co and Commercial Accountants 1987–88, Bookham and Horsley Rotary Club 1988–89; Freeman: City of London 1978, Worshipful Co of Secs and Admins 1978; MIMgt 1967, FSCA 1968, ACIS 1971, FIIA 1986; *Recreations* bridge, DIY, singing; *Clubs* Barn Operatic Soc (Bookham); *Style—* Raymond Spooner, Esq; ✉ Conifers, Orestan Lane, Effingham, Surrey KT24 5SN (☎ 01372 457248); Arranbee Consultancy Services Ltd and Ray Spooner and Co, Tredan House, Church Rd, Bookham, Surrey KT23 3JG (☎ 01372 458995)

SPOONER, Richard Hamilton; s of Derek Richard Spooner (d 1978), and Patricia Sackville, *née* Hamilton; *b* 17 Feb 1952; *Educ* King's Sch Ely, Lanchester Sch of Business Studies (BA); *m* 8 April 1978, Susan Elizabeth Ann, da of Anthony John Rowntree; 3 da (Victoria, Catherine, Elizabeth); *Career* audit mangr Howard Tilly 1976–79, chief accountant Yeoman Aggregates Ltd 1979–83; dir: Yeoman Heavy Haulage Ltd 1980–83, Buckingham Computers Ltd 1981–84, HTA 1983–88; md: Howard Tilly Associates Ltd 1984–88, H T A Property Systems Ltd 1987–; chm Baker Tilly Consulting 1988–; ptnr: Howard Tilly 1986–88, Baker Tilly 1988–; ACA, MInstD, MIMgt; *Recreations* tennis, cricket, bridge, good food; *Style—* Richard Spooner, Esq; ✉ Orchard House, off Elkins Rd, Hedgerley, Bucks (☎ and fax 01753 645357); Baker Tilly, 2 Bloomsbury St, London WC1B 3ST (☎ 0171 413 5100, fax 0171 413 5101, car 0831 173907)

SPOOR, Roger Charlton; OBE (1988), RD, DL (1988); s of Kenneth Spoor (d 1983), of Newcastle, and Dorothy, *née* Dickinson; *b* 21 April 1932; *Educ* Sedbergh; *m* 6 Oct 1956, Susan Elizabeth, da of Jack Edmund Daniels; 2 c (Nicola Jane b 9 Jan 1959, Mark b 7 April 1960); *Career* Nat Serv 1955–57; Tyne Div RNR 1950, ret Lieut Cdr 1971; articled clerk Percy F Ward & Co 1950–55; ptnr: J C Graham & Spoor 1958–70, Ernst & Young (formerly Arthur Young) 1970–92; memb Exec Ctee Arthur Young 1975–84; dir: Northern Football Ground Co Ltd, Newcastle St Cuthbert Estates Ltd, Calvert Trust, Northumbria Calvert Trust Ltd, Exmoor Calvert Trust Ltd, Newcastle City Health NHS Trust, Northern RHA 1990–94; memb Ctee N Soc of Chartered Accountants 1973–80 (pres 1979–80), chm N Soc Courses Ctee 1974–79; memb: NE Electricity Bd 1981–89, Tyne & Wear Residuary Body 1985–88, Northumberland Nat Parks Ctee 1985–90, Ctee IOD 1978–94 (hon sec N Counties Branch 1971–78), TAVR Assoc Employers' Liaison Ctee 1987–94, Ctee Nat Advsy Ctee on Employment of Disabled People 1991–; hon treas Univ of Newcastle 1978–93 (chm Fin Ctee 1978–93), chm N Fin Forum 1989–94, dir BEAM Ltd (Pinetree Centre) 1990–; Northern Football Club: hon treas 1958–75, memb Mgmnt Ctee 1958–79, pres 1978–79; chm Murray House Community Centre & Youth Club 1972–76 (hon treas 1959–72); Calvert Trust: tstee 1974–, chm Mgmnt Ctee Kielder Adventure Centre 1981–86 (chm Working Party 1979–81), chm Northumbria Calvert Trust; pres Jubilee Sailing Tst 1989–; Newcastle Upon Tyne Cncl for the Disabled (The Dene Centre): vice chm 1972–86, chm Information & Advsy Ctee 1982–86, chm 1986–92, vice pres 1994–; hon sec Ret Offrs Assoc 1981–91; winner Founding Societies Centenary award Inst of Chartered Accountants 1991; High Sheriff for County of Tyne and Wear 1994–95; Freeman City of Newcastle upon Tyne 1983, Hon Freeman Newcastle Trinity House 1995; Hon DCL Univ of Newcastle 1991; FCA 1955; *Recreations* fishing, shooting, watercolour painting, debating; *Clubs* Army & Navy, Northern Counties, Northumberland Golf; *Style—* Roger Spoor, Esq, OBE, RD, DL; ✉ 5 Graham Park Road, Newcastle upon Tyne NE3 4BH (☎ 0191 285 1238)

SPORBORG, Christopher Henry; s of Henry Nathan Sporborg, CMG (d 1985), of Albury, Ware, Herts, and Mary, *née* Rowlands; *b* 17 April 1939; *Educ* Rugby, Emmanuel Coll Cambridge; *m* 1961, Lucinda Jane, da of Brig Richard Nigel Hanbury (d 1971), of Braughing, Herts; 2 s (William b 1965, Simon b 1972), 2 da (Sarah (Mrs James Hopkins) b 1964, Eliza (Mrs James S de Uphaugh) b 1967); *Career* Nat Serv Lt Coldstream Gds; Hambros Bank Ltd 1962–95; dep chm Hambros PLC (dir 1983); chm: Hambro Countrywide plc 1986–, Hambro Insurance Services Group PLC 1992–, Atlas Copco Group in GB 1984–, BFSS Investments Ltd 1980–; dep chm C E Heath PLC 1994–; jt master Puckeridge Foxhounds, fin steward The Jockey Club 1995–; landowner; *Recreations* racing, hunting (MFH); *Clubs* Boodle's, Jockey; *Style—* Christopher Sporborg, Esq; ✉ Brooms Farm, Upwick Green, Ware, Herts (☎ 01279 771444); Hambros PLC, 41 Towerhill, London EC3N 4HA (☎ 0171 480 5000, fax 0171 865 1529)

SPOTSWOOD, Marshal of the Royal Air Force Sir Denis Frank; GCB (1970, KCB 1966, CB 1961), CBE (1946), DSO (1943), DFC (1942); s of Frank Henry Spotswood (d 1957), of Elstead, Surrey, and Caroline Spotswood (d 1984); *b* 26 Sept 1916; *m* 1942, Ann, da of Solomon Child (d 1968); 1 s; *Career* joined RAF 1936, served WWII in Europe, N Africa and SE Asia (despatches twice), Gp Capt 1954, ADC to HM The Queen 1957–61, Actg Air Cdre 1958, Cdr RAF Coll Cranwell 1958–61, Air Cdre 1960, AVM 1961, Asst COS Air Def Div SHAPE 1961–63, AOC 3 Gp Bomber Cmd 1964–65, C-in-C RAF Germany 1965–68, Cdr 2 Allied TAF 1966–68, Air Marshal 1965, Air Chief Marshal 1968, AOC-in-C RAF Strike Cmd 1968–71, Air ADC to HM The Queen 1970–74, Chief of Air Staff 1971–74, Marshal of the RAF 1974; vice chm Rolls Royce 1974–80, chm Smiths Industries Aerospace Cos 1980–83 (dir 1983–91), dir Dowty Group 1980–87; chm Royal Star and Garter Home 1980–86 (govr 1975–); FRAeS; Offr Legion of Merit (USA); *Recreations* golf, bridge, rugby (spectator), rowing (spectator); *Clubs* RAF, Royal Aeronautical Soc, Phyllis Court, Huntercombe Golf; *Style—* Marshal of the Royal Air Force Sir Denis Spotswood, GCB, CBE, DSO, DFC; ✉ Coombe Cottage, Hambleden, Henley-on-Thames, Oxon RG9 6SD

SPOTTISWOOD, Air Vice-Marshal James Donald (Don); CB (1988), CVO (1977), AFC (1971); s of James Thomas Spottiswood (d 1981), of Hartlepool, and Caroline Margaret, *née* Taylor (d 1989); *b* 27 May 1934; *Educ* West Hartlepool GS, Univ of Boston (MA); *m* 3 April 1957, Margaret Maxwell, da of John James Harrison (d 1939), of Wingate; 2 s (Ian b 1960, David b 1963), 1 da (Lynne b 1958); *Career* joined RAF: 1951, 139 Sqdn 1954, CFS 1956 Flt Cdr RAF Halton 1959, Flt Cdr 617 Sqdn 1963, RNSC 1965, Personal SO C-in-C Middle East 1966, Sqdn-Cdr 53 Sqdn 1968, JSSC 1970, Station Cdr RAF Thorney Is 1971, Station Cdr and Dep Capt Queens Flt 1974, gp dir RAF Staff Coll Bracknell 1977, RCDS 1978, Int Mil Staff NATO HQ 1979, DG of Trg 1983, AOC Trg Units 1985, ret 1989; vice pres Shorts Support Services Div and md and chief exec Airwork Ltd; chm: RAF Gliding and Soaring Assoc 1983–89, Br Gliding Assoc 1989–; *Recreations* gliding, sailing, golf; *Clubs* RAF; *Style—* Air Vice-Marshal Don Spottiswood, CB, CVO, AFC

SPOTTISWOODE, Clare Mary Joan; da of Tony and Charlotte Spottiswoode; *b* 20 March 1953; *Educ* Cheltenham Ladies Coll, Clare Coll Cambridge (MA), Yale Univ (Mellon fellowship, MPhil); *m* 1977, Oliver Richards, s of Robin Richards; 3 da (Imogen b 15 Sept 1980, Camilla b 13 April 1982, Olivia b 8 May 1990), 1 s (Dominic b 9 Dec 1991); *Career* economist HM Treasy 1977–80, sole proprietor Spottiswoode Trading (import business) 1980–84, chm and md Spottiswoode & Spottiswoode (microcomputer software house) 1984–90, tutor London Business Sch and software conslt 1990–93, dir gen Ofgas 1994–; non-exec dir Booker plc 1995–; CIGE 1994; *Books* Quill (1984), Abacus (1984); *Recreations* children, gardening, theatre; *Style—* Ms Clare Spottiswoode; ✉ Director General, Ofgas, Stockley House, 130 Wilton Road, London SW1V 1LQ (☎ 0171 932 1661, fax 0171 932 1662)

SPRAGUE, Christopher William; s of Coulam Alfred Joseph Sprague, of New Malden, Surrey, and Joan Gertrude, *née* Jackson (d 1986); *b* 19 Aug 1943; *Educ* St Edward's Sch Oxford, Christ Church Oxford (MA); *m* 24 April 1971, Clare, da of Dr John Russell Bradshaw (d 1968), of Topsham, Devon; 4 da (Katharine b 1972, Alison b 1974, Hannah b 1979, Alexandra b 1981); *Career* articled Simmons & Simmons, admitted slr 1970; ptnr Ince & Co 1975– (asst slr 1970–75), specialist in insur and maritime law, lectr on maritime law and assoc subjects; subscribing memb Assoc of Average Adjusters, supporting memb London Maritime Arbitrators Assoc, memb Law Soc; memb Thames Regnl Umpires Cmmn (sec 1981–88), holder of FISA int rowing umpire's license; Liveryman: Worshipful Co of Barbers, City of London Solicitors' Co; *Recreations* reading, history, rowing, bellringing; *Clubs* United Oxford and Cambridge, London Rowing, Leander, Carlton; *Style—* C W Sprague, Esq; ✉ Pasturewood, Woodhill Lane, Shamley Green, Guildford, Surrey GU5 0SP

SPRATT, Prof Brian Geoffrey; s of Clarence Albert Spratt (d 1966), of Rye, E Sussex, and Marjory Alice, *née* Jeffreys; *b* 21 March 1947; *Educ* Tonbridge, UCL (BSc, PhD); *m* 1, 18 Nov 1986 (m dis 1995), Jennifer Kathleen, da of Donald Broome-Smith; 1 s (Timothy Peter b 22 April 1988); m 2, Jiaji Zhou; 1 s (Henry Jestyn); *Career* res fell Dept of Biochemical Scis Princeton Univ 1973–75, res fell Dept of Genetics Univ of Leicester 1975–80; Univ of Sussex: lectr in biochemistry 1980–87, reader 1987–89, prof of molecular genetics and Wellcome Tst princ res fell 1989–; Squibb lectures Rutgers Univ 1985; Fleming award Soc for Gen Microbiology 1982, Pfizer academic award 1983, Hoechst-Roussel award American Soc for Microbiology 1993; FRS 1993; *Publications* author of numerous publications on microbiology in learned jls; *Style—* Prof Brian Spratt, FRS; ✉ Flat 4, 10 Fourth Avenue, Hove, East Sussex BN3 2PH (01273 728984); School of Biological Sciences, University of Sussex, Brighton BN1 9QG (☎ 01273 678309, fax 01273 678433)

SPRATT, Sir Greville Douglas; GBE (1987), TD (1962, and bar 1968), JP (City Bench 1978), DL (Gtr London 1986); er s of Hugh Douglas Spratt, of Henley-on-Thames, and Sheelah Ivy, *née* Stace; *b* 1 May 1927; *Educ* Leighton Park Sch, Charterhouse; *m* 1954, Sheila Farrow, yst da of late Joseph Wade, of the Old Mill, Langstone, Hants; 3 da; *Career* Coldstream Gds 1945–46, cmmnd 1946, seconded to Arab Legion, served Palestine, Jordan and Egypt 1946–48, GSO III (Ops and Intelligence) 1948; joined HAC as Private 1950, re-cmmnd 1950, Capt 1952, Maj 1954, CO (Lt-Col) 1962–65, Regtl Col 1966–70, memb Ct of Assts HAC 1960–70 and 1978–95; Lloyd's 1948–61 (underwriting memb 1950–); J & N Wade Gp of Cos: joined 1961, dir 1969–76, md 1972–76 (when gp sold); regnl dir and chm (City and West End) National Westminster Bank 1989–92; dir: Williams Lea Gp 1989–96, Forest Mere Ltd 1991–95 (chm 1993–95), Charterhouse Enterprises Ltd 1989–95, Craigie Taylor Int; chm Claremount Underwriting Agency Ltd 1994–; memb City TAVRA 1960– (vice chm 1973–77, chm 1977–82), vice pres TAVRA for Gtr London 1994– (memb Exec and Fin Ctee 1977–94, chm 1992–94); Hon Col: City and NE sector London ACF 1983–, 8 Bn The Queen's Fusiliers 1988–92, The London Regt 1992–95; cncl memb Reserve Forces Assoc 1981–84, pres London Fedn of Old Comrades Assocs 1983–, dep pres London Br Red Cross 1983–91 (vice-pres 1993–); patron: Emily Appeal, Alzheimer's Disease Soc; memb: Blackdown Ctee Nat Tst 1977–87, Ctee Guildhall Sch of Music and Drama 1978–80 and 1989– (hon memb GSMD 1988), Court City Univ 1981– (chllr 1987–88), Governing Bodies of Girls' Schs Assoc 1982–90, City of London Police Ctee 1989–91, Planning & Communications Ctee 1990–91, Surrey Scout Cncl 1990–; govr: St Ives Sch 1976– (vice chm 1977–86, chm 1986–90), King Edward's Sch Witley 1978– (vice pres 1989–95), Christ's Hosp 1978–95, Bridewell Royal Hosp 1978–95, City of London Sch for Girls 1981–82, Malvern Girls' Coll 1982–90, St Paul's Cathedral Choir Sch 1985–, Charterhouse 1985– (chm Governing Body 1989–95), City of London Freemen's Sch 1992–95; life govr Corp of the Sons of the Clergy 1985–, patron Int Centre for Child Studies 1985–, vice pres Not Forgotten Assoc 1990–; Royal Br Legion: pres Haslemere 1989–, vice pres St James' 1991–; chm: Action Research 1989– (memb Haslemere Ctee 1971–82, memb Cncl 1982–), Anglo Jordanian Soc 1991–; ADC to HM The Queen 1973–78, Alderman City of London (Castle Baynard Ward) 1978–95, Sheriff City of London 1984–85, Lord Mayor of London 1987–88; church cmmr 1993–95; tstee: Chichester Theatre, Endowment of St Paul's Cathedral, Children's Res Int, Carthusian Tst, Castle Baynard Educnl Tst, Trekforce; special tstee St Bartholomew's Hosp 1990–95, patron Surrey Charity Gp 1989–93; Freeman City of London 1977, Liveryman Worshipful Co of Ironmongers 1977 (Master 1995–); Hon DLitt City Univ 1988; FRSA, KStJ 1987 (OStJ 1985); Chevalier de la Légion d'Honneur 1961, Commandeur de l'Ordre Nationale du Mérite (France) 1984, Cdr Order of the Lion (Malawi) 1985, memb Nat Order of Aztec Eagle (Mexico) 1985, Order of Merit (Norway) 1988, Order of Merit (Senegal) 1988; *Recreations* tennis, music, military history, stamp, coin and bank note collecting; *Clubs* Cowdray Park Golf, United Wards, City Livery, Guildhall; *Style—* Sir Greville Spratt, GBE, TD, JP, DL; ✉ West Kingsley Place, Kingsley Green, West Sussex GU27 3LR (☎ 01428 644367)

SPRENT, Prof Janet Irene; OBE (1996); da of James William Findlater, and Dorothy May Findlater; *b* 10 Jan 1934; *Educ* Slough HS for Girls, Imperial Coll of Science and Technol London (BSc, ARCS), Univ of Tasmania (PhD), Univ of London (DSc); *m* 1955, Peter Sprent; *Career* scientific offr Rothamsted Experimental Station 1954–55, ICIANZ res fell Univ of Tasmania 1955–58, botany mistress Rochester Girl's GS 1959–61, lectr then sr lectr Goldsmiths' Coll London 1960–67; Univ of Dundee: successively res fell, lectr, sr lectr and reader 1967–89, dean Faculty of Sci and Engineering 1987–89, prof of plant biology 1989–, head Dept of Biological Scis 1992–95, dep princ 1995–; hon res prof Scottish Crop Res Inst 1991–; chm of govrs MacAuley Land Use Res Inst 1995– (govr 1990–); various overseas visits and int meetings in respect of nitrogen fixing crops and tree research; memb: NERC 1991–95, Scottish HEFC 1992–96, Jt Nature Conservation Ctee, Panel for Individual Merit Promotions UK Res Cncl; memb: Soc for Experimental Biology, Soc for Gen Microbiology, Botanical Soc of Scotland, Aust Soc of Plant Physiologists; fell Linnaean Soc, FRSA, FRSE 1990; *Books* The Ecology of the Nitrogen Cycle (1987), Nitrogen Fixing Organisms: Pure and Applied Aspects (with P Sprent, 1990), Advances in Legume Systematics, 5. The Nitrogen Factor (co-ed with D McKey, 1994), numerous book chapters and papers in scientific jls; *Recreations* hill-walking, flying (St John's Air Wing), gardening, music; *Style—* Prof Janet Sprent,

OBE, FRSE; ✉ 32 Birkhill Avenue, Wormit, Newport on Tay, Fife DD6 8PW (☎ and fax 01382 541706); Department of Biological Sciences, University of Dundee, Dundee DD1 4HN (☎ 01382 344279)

SPRIGGE, Prof Timothy Lauro Squire; s of Cecil Jackson Squire Sprigge (d 1959), of Rome and London, and Katriona, *née* Gordon Brown (d 1965); *b* 14 Jan 1932; *Educ* Gonville and Caius Coll Cambridge (MA, PhD); *m* 4 April 1959, Giglia, da of Gavin Gordon (d 1965); 1 s (Samuel Felix b 1961), 2 da (Georgina Nessie b 1960, Lucy Cecilia b 1960); *Career* lectr in philosophy UCL 1961–63, reader in philosophy Univ of Sussex 1963–69 (lectr 1963–70), prof of logic and metaphysics Univ of Edinburgh 1979–89; prof emeritus and endowment fell Univ of Edinburgh 1989–; vice chm (formerly chm): Advocates for Animals Soc, St Andrew Animal Fund; memb: Aristotelian Soc, Mind Assoc, Scottish Philosophical Club; FRSE 1993; *Books* The Correspondence of Jeremy Bentham Vols 1 and 2 (ed, 1968), Facts, Words and Beliefs (1970), Santayana: An Examination of his Philosophy (1974), The Vindication of Absolute Idealism (1983), Theories of Existence (1984), The Rational Foundations of Ethics (1987), James and Bradley: American Truth and British Reality (1993); *Recreations* backgammon; *Style—* Prof Timothy Sprigge, FRSE; ✉ 31A Raeburn Place, Edinburgh EH4 1HU (☎ 0131 315 2443); David Hume Tower, Univiversity of Edinburgh, George Square, Edinburgh (☎ 0131 667 1011 ext 6212)

SPRING, Richard John Grenville; MP (C) Bury St Edmunds (majority 18,787); s of late H J A Spring, and Marjorie, *née* Watson-Morris (d 1995); *b* 24 Sept 1946; *Educ* Rondebosch Cape Province SA, Univ of Cape Town, Magdalene Coll Cambridge; *m* 13 Dec 1979 (m dis 1993), Hon Jane Henniker-Major, da of 8 Baron Henniker, KCMG, CVO, MC, DL, *qv*; 1 s, 1 da; *Career* vice pres Merrill Lynch Ltd 1976–86 (joined 1971), dep md Hutton International Associates 1986–88, exec dir Shearson Lehman Hutton 1988–90, md Xerox Furman Selz 1990–92; Parly candidate (C) Ashton-under-Lyne 1983, MP (C) Bury St Edmunds 1992–; memb House of Commons Select Ctee for: Employment 1992–94, N Ireland 1994–; PPS to: Sir Patrick Mayhew as Sec of State for N Ireland 1994–95, Rt Hon Tim Eggar as Min of State DTI 1996, Hon Nicholas Soames and James Arbuthnot as Mins of State MOD 1996–; vice chm Cons Backbench Arts and Heritage Ctee 1992–94; jt sec: N Ireland Cons Backbench Ctee 1993–95, All Pty Drugs Misuse Gp; vice chm All Pty Racing and Bloodstock Gp; vice chm Small Business Bureau 1992– (chm of its Parly Advsy Gp 1992–), pres Bow Gp Arts and Heritage Gp 1992–; held various offices Westminster Cons Assoc 1976–87; *Recreations* country pursuits, tennis, swimming; *Clubs* Boodle's, Farmers' (Bury St Edmunds); *Style—* Richard Spring, Esq, MP; ✉ House of Commons, London SW1A 0AA

SPRING RICE, Hon Charles James; s and h of 6 Baron Monteagle of Brandon; *b* 24 Feb 1953; *Educ* Harrow; *m* 1987, Mary Teresa Glover; 4 da (Helena Maire b 1987, Charlotte Etain b 1988, Agnes Imogen b 1991, Thea Teresa b 1995); *Career* head of English Holy Family Coll Walthamstow 1992–; *Style—* Charles Spring Rice, Esq; ✉ 26 Malvern Rd, London E8 3LP

SPRINGBETT, David John; *b* 2 May 1938; *Educ* Dulwich Coll London; *m* 3 s (Bruce b 1965, Duncan b 1967, d 1977, Jack b 1985), 4 da (Sally b 1963, Lucy b 1964, Zoe b 1980, Josie b 1981); *Career* insurance and reinsurance broker; underwriting memb Lloyd's; memb Cncl, hon librarian and memb Expert Ctee Royal Philatelic Soc; Britain's Salesman of the Year 1981; *Style—* David Springbett, Esq; ✉ The Abbey House, Huntercombe Lanes, Taplow, Berks SL6 0PQ (☎ 01628 663306, fax 01628 660835)

SPRINGETT, Rod; *Educ* Colchester Sch of Art, Royal Coll of Art (MDes); *m* 1968, Rosaleen, *née* Tucker; 2 s (Matthew b 5 Sept 1972, Thomas b 13 Sept 1975); *Career* designer Klein Peters Consultancy 1967–68, designer/art dir London Weekend Television Publications 1968–70, ptnr Springett Wuttke Ltd 1970–76, chm Springett Associates Ltd 1994– (founded 1976); work selected, exhibited and published in design competitions and pubns incl D&AD, NY Art Dirs' Club and Design Cncl exhbns; recipient: D&AD Silver Award, Clio Award, Star-Pack Gold Award, DBA Design Effectiveness Award; reg contrib of articles to design and mktg jls incl: Design, Design Week, Graphics International, Marketing, Marketing Week, RSA Jl; pt/t tutor then visiting lectr RCA 1977–78; visiting lectr: London Business Sch 1992, Glasgow Coll of Art 1993–, Falmouth Coll of Art 1995; external advsr in graphic design CNAA 1986–92; variously external examiner of design degree courses for RCA, Kent Inst, De Montfort Univ and Colchester Inst; memb D&AD 1968–90 (reg exhibitor and jury memb, twice elected to Exec Ctee, fndr memb Student Award Scheme), FRSA 1972 (memb 1969, reg jury memb Student Design Awards, memb Design Advsy Gp 1994–), FCSD 1980 (memb Graphics Advsy Gp 1989–); *Style—* Rod Springett, Esq; ✉ Springett Associates Ltd, 13 Salisbury Place, London W1H 1FJ (☎ 0171 722 6903)

SPRINGMAN, Prof Sarah Marcella; *b* 26 Dec 1956; *Educ* Wycombe Abbey Sch, Univ of Cambridge (Roscoe Meml prize, college prize, MA, MPhil, PhD, Squash blue, BUSF Cycling champion); *Career* Univ of Cambridge Officer Training Corps TA: commissioned 1978, trg offr 1978, cmd Royal Engineer Wing 1980 and 1983–85, Lt 1980, Capt 1983–86; Sir Alexander Gibb & Partners: various positions Geotechnical Dept, seconded to Public Works Dept and Monasavu Hydro-Electric Scheme Fiji, Adelaide and Canberra Offices 1975–83; Univ of Cambridge: SERC studentship Dept of Engrg 1983–84, research asst Soil Mechanics Gp Dept of Engrg 1985–89, res fell Magdalene Coll 1988–90, lectr Soil Mechanics Gp 1993–96 (asst lectr 1990–93), fell and college lectr in Soil Mechanics Magdalene Coll 1991–96; govr: Marlborough Coll 1991–95, Wycombe Abbey Sch 1993–96, World Masters Games 1992–; memb: Women's Engineering Soc 1983, British Geotechnical Soc 1988; CEng, MICE 1983, MIRE 1990, FRSA 1993; *Sporting Career* 11 times British Triathlon champion, European Triathlon champion 1985, 1986 and 1988, 5 European Team Gold medals, S Pacific Squash champion 1982, vice pres Int Triathlon Union 1992–96 (co-chair Women's Cmmn 1990–92), memb Great Britain Sports Cncl 1993–96 (UK Sports Cncl 1996–); Cosmopolitan-Clairol Women of Achievement Award 1991; *Style—* Prof Sarah Springman; ✉ Institut fur Geotechnik, Eidgenossische Technische Hochschule, Zurich CH 8093, Switzerland (☎ 00 41 1 633 2525, fax 00 41 1 633 1079)

SPROAT, Iain MacDonald; MP (C) Harwich (majority 17,159); s of William and Lydia Sproat; *b* 8 Nov 1938; *Educ* Melrose, Winchester, Magdalen Coll Oxford; *m* 1979, Judith Kernot, *née* King; 1 step s (Charles); *Career* MP (C) Aberdeen S 1970–83, Parly candidate Roxburgh and Berwickshire 1983, MP (C) Harwich 1992–; PPS to sec of State for Scotland 1973–74; memb: Br Parly Delgn to oversee S Vietnamese Elections 1973, Br Parly Delgn to Soviet Union 1974; chm Soviet & East Euro Gp of Cons Foreign Affairs Ctee 1975–81; leader Cons Gp on Scottish Select Ctee 1979–81, chm Scottish Cons Ctee 1979–81; leader Br Parly Delgn to Austria 1980; Parly under-sec of state Dept of Trade 1981–83; special advsr to PM Gen Election 1987, Parly under-sec of state Dept of National Heritage 1993–95, min of state Dept of National Heritage 1995–; conslt N M Rothschild & Sons Merchant Bankers Ltd 1983–; chm: Milner and Co Ltd, Cricketers' Who's Who Ltd; former dir D'Arcy Masius Benton and Bowles Ltd, dir Coll of Petroleum Studies Oxford; tstee: African Medical and Research Fndn 1987–, Scottish Self-Governing Schs Tst; Cricket Writer of the Year Wombwell Cricket Lovers' Soc 1983; *Books* Cricketers' Who's Who (ed annually, 1980–), Wodehouse at War (1981), Edward Heath - A Pictorial Biography, The British Prime Ministers (contrib); with Adam Sykes: The Wit of Sir Winston, The Wit of Westminster, The Wit of the Wig, The Harold Wilson Bunkside Book, The Cabinet Bedside Book; *Clubs* Oxford and Cambridge; *Style—* Iain Sproat, Esq, MP; ✉ Snore Hall, nr Downham Market, Norfolk PE38 0LN; House of Commons, London SW1A 0AA

SPROT OF HAYSTOUN, Lt-Col Aidan Mark; MC (1944), JP (Peeblesshire 1966); yr s of Maj Mark Sprot of Riddell, JP, DL (d 1946), of Riddell, Roxburghshire, and Meliora (d 1979), er da of Sir John Adam Hay, 9 Bt, of Haystoun and Smithfield; *b* 17 June 1919; *Educ* Stowe; *Career* landowner, farmer; Lt-Col served Royal Scots Greys 1940–62; pres Lowlands of Scotland TA & VRA 1986–89; Lord-Lt of Tweeddale (formerly Peeblesshire) 1980–94 (DL 1966–80); memb: Royal Co of Archers (Queen's Body Guard for Scotland), Peeblesshire CC 1963–75; hon sec Royal Caledonian Hunt 1964–74; dir Peeblesshire Branch Red Cross 1966–74 (now patron); county cmmr Peeblesshire Scout Assoc 1968–73 (now pres) and pres Borders Area Scout Assoc 1993–; Medal of Merit Scout Assoc 1993; pres Lothian Fedn of Boys' Clubs 1988–; Hon Freeman Tweeddale Dist 1994; *Recreations* country pursuits, motor-cycle touring; *Clubs* New (Edinburgh); *Style—* Lt-Col Aidan Sprot of Haystoun, MC, JP; ✉ Crookston, by Peebles EH45 9JQ (☎ 01721 740209)

SPROTT, Duncan; s of Hugh Sprott, and Brenda, *née* Grieves; *b* 2 Dec 1952; *Educ* Newport GS Essex, Univ of St Andrews, Heatherley Sch of Art; *Career* writer; *Books* 1784 (1984), The Clopton Hercules (1991, US title The Rise of Mr Warde), Our Lady of the Potatoes (1995); *Style—* Duncan Sprott, Esq; ✉ c/o Faber & Faber Ltd, 3 Queen Square, London WC1N 3AU (☎ 0171 465 0045)

SPRY, Christopher John; s of Reginald Charles Spry (d 1962), and Kathleen Edith, *née* Hobart; *b* 29 Aug 1946; *Educ* Sir Roger Manwood's Sch Sandwich, Univ of Exeter (BA); *m* 1968 (m dis 1989), Jean Banks; 2 s (Matthew Alan b 16 Aug 1974, Michael John b 24 Nov 1978); m 2, 1989, Judith Christina, *née* Ryder; *Career* nat trainee 197–69, admin asst Doncaster Royal Infirmary 1969–70, dep hosp sec Lewisham Hosp 1970–73, hosp sec Nottingham Gen Hosp 1973–75, dist admin S Nottingham 1978–81 (asst dist admin 1975–78), dist gen mangr Newcastle Health Authy 1984–89 (dist admin 1981–84), regnl gen mangr SW Thames RHA 1989–94, regnl dir S Thames Region of NHS Executive 1994–96, chief exec Gtr Glasgow Health Bd 1996–; memb: ACARD Working Gp on UK Med Equipment Indust 1986–, IHSM Working Party on Alternative Delivery and Funding of Health Servs 1988–; MIHSM 1972; *Recreations* swimming, books, enjoying townscapes; *Style—* Christopher J Spry, Esq; ✉ Greater Glasgow Health Board, 225 Bath Street, Glasgow G2 4JT (☎ 0141 201 4641, fax 0141 201 4901)

SPRY, Sir John Farley; kt (1975); s of Joseph Farley Spry (d 1923); *b* 11 March 1910; *Educ* Perse Sch, Peterhouse Cambridge; *m* 1 (m dis 1940); 1 s, 1 da; m 2, 1953, Stella Marie (d 1995), da of Sydney Carlisle Fichat; *Career* slr; asst registrar of titles and conveyancer Uganda 1936–44, asst dir Land Registration Palestine 1944–48, puisne judge Tanganyika 1961–64, vice pres Court of Appeal East Africa 1970–75 (justice of appeal 1964–70), chm Pensions Appeal Tribunal England 1975–76; Gibraltar: chief justice 1976–80, cmmr for revision of laws 1981–85, pres Court of Appeal 1983–86; chief justice British Indian Ocean Territory 1981–84, chief justice St Helena 1983–92, pres Br Antarctic Territory Court of Appeal 1991–, justice of appeal Falkland Islands 1991–95; *Books* Sea Shells of Dar es Salaam (Parts: 1 1961, 2 1964, revised 1968), Civil Procedure in East Africa (1969), Civil Law of Defamation in East Africa (1976); *Recreations* conchology; *Style—* Sir John Spry; ✉ 15 de Vere Gardens, London W8

SPURGEON, Peter Gregory; s of Philip George Spurgeon (d 1959), and Ruth Elsie Martin, *née* Shewring; *b* 23 March 1939; *Educ* Sudbury GS Suffolk; *m* 8 June 1963, Jacqueline Merle, da of Donald Holtam; 1 da (Michaela (Mrs Fishwick) b 4 Feb 1964), 1 s (Gregory b 24 March 1967); *Career* MOD (incl Nat Serv Singapore) 1958–62; Home Office: immigration offr 1962–67, various positions rising to grade 7 Criminal Policy Dept 1967–83, head Security Branch 1983–86, chief inspr Drugs Branch 1986–89, head Fire Servs Div 1989–92; dir Criminal Injuries Compensation Bd (CICB) 1992–, chief exec Criminal Injuries Compensation Authy (CICA) 1996–; *Recreations* guitar, gardening, swimming, travel, grandchildren minding; *Style—* Peter Spurgeon, Esq; ✉ Criminal Injuries Compensation Authority, Morley House, 26–30 Holborn Viaduct, London EC1A 2JQ (☎ 0171 842 6802, fax 0171 436 0804)

SPURGEON, Maj-Gen Peter Lester; CB (1980); s of Harold Sidney Spurgeon (d 1959), of Suffolk, and Mrs Emily Anne Spurgeon, *née* Bolton; *b* 27 Aug 1927; *Educ* Merchant Taylors Sch Northwood; *m* 1959, da of Cyril Bland Aylward, of Bournemouth (d 1972); 1 s (Simon), 1 da (Nicola); *Career* RM 1946–80; Col Commandant Royal Marines 1987–90; Maj-Gen cmdg Trg and Res Forces RM 1977–80, chief exec Royal Agric Benevolent Inst 1982–91; pres RM Assoc 1986–90; *Recreations* gardening, golf; *Clubs* Army & Navy; *Style—* Maj-Gen P L Spurgeon, CB; ✉ c/o Lloyd's Bank, 1 High St, Oxford OX1 4AA

SPURLING, (Susan) Hilary; da of Judge Gilbert Alexander Forrest (d 1977), and Emily Maureen, *née* Armstrong; *b* 25 Dec 1940; *Educ* Clifton HS Bristol, Somerville Coll Oxford; *m* 4 April 1961, John Spurling; 2 s (Nathaniel Stobart b 1974, Gilbert Alexander Fettiplace b 1977), 1 da (Amy Maria b 1972); *Career* Spectator: arts ed 1964–69, lit ed 1966–69; book reviewer: The Observer 1970–87, Daily Telegraph 1987–; *Books* Ivy When Young - The Early Life of I Compton-Burnett 1884–1919 (1974), Handbook to Anthony Powell's Music of Time (1977), Secrets of a Women's Heart - The Later Life of I Compton-Burnett 1919–69 (1984), Elinor Fettiplace's Receipt Book (1986), Paul Scott: a life (1990), Paper Spirits (1992); *Style—* Ms Hilary Spurling; ✉ David Higham Associates, 5–8 Lower John St, Golden Square, London W1R 4HA

SPURLING, John Antony; s of Antony Cuthbert Spurling (d 1984), and Elizabeth Frances, *née* Stobart (d 1990); *b* 17 July 1936; *Educ* Dragon Sch, Marlborough, St John's Coll Oxford (BA); *m* 4 April 1961, Susan Hilary, da of Gilbert Alexander Forrest; 2 s (Nathaniel Stobart b 31 May 1974, Gilbert Alexander Fettiplace b 2 Dec 1977), 1 da (Amy Maria b 6 May 1972); *Career* Nat Serv 2 Lt RA 1955–57; plebiscite offr Southern Cameroons 1960–61, BBC Radio announcer 1963–66, freelance writer and broadcaster 1966–, Henfield writing fell Univ of E Anglia 1973, art critic The New Statesman 1976–88; playwright and novelist; *Plays* for stage: Macrune's Guevara (Nat Theatre) 1969, In the Heart of the British Museum (Traverse Theatre Edinburgh) 1971, The British Empire Part One (Birmingham Repertory Theatre) 1980, Coming Ashore in Guadeloupe (Cherub Co Harrogate, Edinburgh and London) 1982–83, Racine at the Girls' Sch (Cheltenham Literary Festival) 1992; for BBC Radio 3: Dominion Over Palm and Pine 1982, The Christian Hero 1982, The Day of Reckoning 1985, Discobolus 1989, The Butcher of Baghdad 1993 (also staged by Cherub Co London 1993), MacRune's Guevara 1993; *Novels* The Ragged End (1989), After Zenda (1995); *Style—* John Spurling, Esq; ✉ c/o Patricia MacNaughton, MLR, 200 Fulham Rd, London SW10 9PN (☎ 0171 351 5442, 0171 376 5575, fax 0171 351 4560)

SPURR, Margaret Anne; *née* Spurr; OBE (1994); da of John William Spurr, and Anne Spurr; *b* 7 Oct 1933; *Educ* Abbeydale Girls' GS Sheffield, Univ of Keele (BA, PGCE); *m* 7 Nov 1953, John Spurr; 1 s (David b 2 Nov 1959), 1 da (Jane b 26 Aug 1961); *Career* tutor English literature: Univ of Glasgow 1971, Univ of Keele 1972–73; headmistress Bolton Sch Girls' Div 1979–94; govr BBC 1993, chm BBC English Nat Forum 1994–; sr examiner Univ of London 1971–80; memb: Scholarship Selection Ctee English Speaking Union 1983–93, CBI Schs' Panel 1985–88, Nat Ctee Women in Indust Year 1986–88; Bd of pres Girls' Schools Assoc 1985–86, chm Nat Isis Ctee 1987–90; chm Scholaservices 1988–; ed Annual Directory Soc of Educn Conslts 1991–93; govr Stafford Coll; memb Governing Cncl: Liverpool John Moores 1995–, Keele Univ 1996–; Hon DLitt Univ of Keele 1995; FRSA 1991; *Recreations* gardening, theatre, poetry; *Clubs* Reform; *Style—* Mrs John Spurr, OBE; ✉ The Old Vicarage, Croxden, Uttoxeter ST14 5JQ (☎ 01889

507 214); English National Forum, BBC, Room 617, Broadcasting House, London W1A 1AA (☎ 0171 580 4468)

SPURRELL, Dr Roworth Adrian John; s of Ivor Pritchard Spurrell (d 1968), and Marjorie, *née* Cheney; *b* 27 May 1942; *Educ* Oundle, Univ of London (MD, BSc, MB BS); *m* 28 April 1973, Susan Jane, da of George Kemp (d 1984); 2 da (Emma Louise, Clare Alexandra); *Career* registrar in cardiology: St George's Hosp London 1969–70, Nat Heart Hosp 1970–71; sr registrar in Cardiology Guy's Hosp 1971–74, conslt in charge of cardiology Bart's Hosp 1976– (conslt 1974–); FRCP, FACC; *Recreations* sailing, flying; *Clubs* Royal Yacht Sqdn, RAF; *Style*— Dr Roworth Spurrell; ✉ 10 Upper Wimpole St, London W1M 7TD (☎ 0171 935 3922)

SPURRIER, Peter Brotherton; s of Eric Jack Spurrier, MBE, of Storrington Sussex, and Frances Mary, *née* Brotherton; *b* 9 Aug 1942; *Educ* Gayhurst Prep Sch Gerrards Cross, Chetham's Hosp Sch, Manchester Coll of Art and Design (NDD) 1964; *m* 1973, Hon Elizabeth Jane, da of Baron Maude of Stratford-upon-Avon, TD, PC (d 1993); 2 s (Benedict b 1979, Thomas b 1982), 1 da (Lucinda b 1985); *Career* Esquire in the Venerable Order of St John currently design conslt; dir Maritime Insignia 1994–; memb Cncl The Heraldry Soc, chm Soc of Heraldic Arts 1991; FRSA; Freeman City of London; Freeman and Liveryman Worshipful Co of Painter-Stainers 1985; memb Chartered Soc of Designers; OStJ 1990; *Recreations* beagling, fishing, painting; *Style*— Peter Spurrier, Esq; ✉ 15 Morella Rd, Wandsworth Common, London SW12 8UQ (☎ 0181 675 1431)

SPURRIER, Roger Hawley; s of Rev Henry Cecil Marriott Spurrier (d 1954), of Roughton, Lincs, and Olive Victoria, *née* Hawley (d 1981); *b* 15 Feb 1928; *Educ* Marlborough; *m* 1, 1955, Margaret Judith Briony (d 1987), da of John Otto Richards, of NZ; 2 s (Timothy John b 1957, Roger Dermot b 1958); m 2, 1992, Barbara Ruth Spratt; *Career* land agent; sr ptnr Jas Martin & Co; FRICS; *Style*— Roger Spurrier, Esq; ✉ The Old Rectory, Blankney, Lincoln (☎ 01526 320483); Jas Martin & Co, 8 Bank St, Lincoln (☎ 01522 510234, fax 01522 511274)

SPURRIER-KIMBELL, David Henry; s of Norman Kenneth Bernard Kimbell, FRCOG (d 1982), of Warmington, Northants, and Mary Pamela, da of Sir Henry Spurrier; *b* 24 Sept 1944; *Educ* Oundle, Heidelberg Univ; *m* 25 July 1970, Maureen Patricia, da of Dr Eric Charles Elliot Golden; 1 s (Henry b 1986), 2 da (Antonia b 1977, Deborah b 1979); *Career* Br Leyland Motor Corp Ltd 1966–78, overseas dir Leyland Vehicles Ltd 1978, joined Spencer Stuart & Assocs Ltd London 1979 (int ptnr 1983, md UK 1985, int chm 1987); *Recreations* golf, tennis; *Clubs* Oriental; *Style*— David Spurrier-Kimbell, Esq; ✉ Chalkpit House, Ecchinswell, Hants RG20 4UQ (☎ 01635 298269); Spencer Stuart and Associates Ltd, 16 Connaught Place, London W2 2ED (☎ 0171 493 1238)

SPURWAY, (Marcus) John; s of Marcus Humphrey Spurway (d 1994), of Goudhurst, Kent, and Eva, *née* Mann (d 1980); *b* 28 Oct 1938; *Educ* Archbishop Tenison's Sch Croydon; *m* 23 Oct 1963, Christine Kate, da of Robert Charles Townshend (d 1981), of Canterbury; 2 s (Marcus John Charles b 1967, Edward Lewis David b 1969); *Career* Nat Serv 4 Regt RHA; insur broker; dir Morgan Reid & Sharman Ltd (Lloyd's brokers, formerly B & C Aviation Insurance Brokers); specialist in aviation insur; *Books* Aviation Insurance Abbreviations, Organisations and Institutions (1983), Aviation Insurance, The Market and Underwriting Practice (1991), Aviation Law and Claims (1992); *Style*— John Spurway, Esq; ✉ Lomeer, Common Road, Sissinghurst, Kent TN17 2JR; Morgan Reid & Sharman Ltd, 6 Alie Street, London E1 8DD (☎ 0171 488 9000, fax 0171 480 6914)

SPYER, Prof Kenneth Michael (Mike); s of Harris Spyer (d 1982), of Wanstead, and Rebecca, *née* Jacobs (d 1982); *b* 15 Sept 1943; *Educ* Coopers Company's Sch, Univ of Sheffield (BSc), Univ of Birmingham (PhD, DSc); *m* 25 Aug 1971, Christine, da of John Roland Spalton; 2 s (Simon Jeremy b 20 Nov 1976, Nicholas Henry b 26 Oct 1979); *Career* res fell Dept of Physiology Univ of Birmingham Med Sch 1969–72, Royal Soc Euro prog fell Instituto di Fisiologia Umana Pisa 1972–73, sr res fell Department of Physiology Univ of Birmingham Med Sch 1978–80 (res fell 1973–78); Royal Free Hosp Sch of Med: Sophia Jex-Blake prof of physiology Dept of Physiology 1980–, dir British Heart Fndn Neural Control Gp 1985–, chm Basic Med Sciences 1991–; jt head Depts of Physiology Royal Free Hosp Med Sch and UCL 1994–; Crisp lectr Univ of Leeds 1988, Glaxo lectr Dept of Pharmacology Univ of Edinburgh 1993; visiting prof: Univ of Shanghai 1989, Georg-August Univ Göttingen 1990, Northwestern Univ Chicago 1990, Univ Vittoria Brazil 1991; chm: Physiological/Pharmacological Panel Wellcome Tst 1993–96, Euro Biomedical Research Assoc 1996–; memb Ctee: Animal Procedures Home Office 1990–, Benevolent Fund Physiological Soc 1993–; memb Scientific Panel Brain Research Tst 1993–, hon life memb Centre for Neuroscience UCL 1984, field ed News in Physiological Science 1992–96; Wolfson Univ Award 1989–92; Hon MD Univ of Lisbon 1991; memb: Physiological Soc 1972–, Brain Research Assoc 1973–, Euro Neuroscience Assoc 1976–, Research Defence Soc 1976– (hon sec 1986–89), Int Brain Research Orgn 1980–, Harveian Soc 1983– (hon sec 1987–89), Zoological Soc 1983–, Clinical Autonomic Soc 1983–, German Physiological Soc 1984–93, Soc for Neuroscience 1986–; author of numerous pubns in learned jls; *Recreations* armchair sports, flyfishing, travelling (particularly in Italy), gardening, books, fine arts; *Style*— Prof Mike Spyer; ✉ Department of Physiology, University College London, Gower Street, London WC1E 6BT (☎ 0171 387 7050); Department of Physiology, Royal Free Hospital School of Medicine, Rowland Hill Street, London NW3 2PF (☎ 0171 431 0009)

SQUIRE, David Michael; s of Denis Arthur Squire, of Esher, Surrey, and (Patricia) Mary Joyce, *née* Davis; *b* 26 Feb 1949; *Educ* St Edward's Sch Oxford, Univ Coll Oxford (MA); *m* 1 June 1974, Karen StClair, da of Peter Edward Hook (d 1982); 3 da (Isabelle b 1976, Eleanor b 1980, Madeline b 1982); *Career* CA 1973; ptnr Price Waterhouse 1981– (joined London Office 1970); tstee Ealing Jr Music Sch 1996–; FCA 1979; *Recreations* sailing, tennis, family history, hill walking; *Style*— David Squire, Esq; ✉ 2 St Stephen's Ave, London W13 8ES (☎ 0181 997 5906, e-mail 100277.243@compuserve.com); Price Waterhouse, Southwark Towers, 32 London Bridge Street, London SE1 9SY (☎ 0171 939 3000, 0171 939 2426, fax 0171 378 0647, e-mail David_Squire@Europe.notes.pw.com)

SQUIRE, Giles; professional name of Peter Giles Eyre-Tanner; s of Peter Ralph Eyre-Tanner, of Oak Tree House, Bucks, and Jean Rae, *née* Beaver; *b* 7 Feb 1954; *Educ* Wellington Coll Crowthorne Berks; *m* 2, 21 May 1988, Julie Anne, da of Brian Jay Stokoe; 1 s (Giles Lawrence b 14 Aug 1980), 1 da (Lucy Victoria b 28 July 1989); *Career* head of special programming UBN 1973–74 (disc jockey 1970–73), songwriter 1980–84; Metro Radio: joined 1974, sr presenter 1983–84, presentation prodr 1984–87, sr prodr 1987, asst prog controller 1987–88, prog controller Metro FM 1988–89, assoc dir of progs 1989–91, prog controller Metro FM and GNR 1991–, prog dir Metro FM 1992–, gp controller Tyne Tees 1993, currently md TFM Radio (part of EMAP plc); Sony best pop prog award 1987; memb: Performing Rights Soc, BASCA, Equity; *Style*— Giles Squire, Esq; ✉ Metro FM, EMAP plc, Radio House, Swalwell, Newcastle upon Tyne NE99 1BB (☎ 0191 420 0971, fax 0191 488 8611)

SQUIRE, Air Marshal Peter Ted; DFC (1982), AFC (1979); s of Wing Cdr Frank Squire, DSO, DFC (d 1992), and Margaret Pascoe, *née* Trump (d 1980); *b* 7 Oct 1945; *Educ* King's Sch Bruton, RAF Coll Cranwell; *m* 10 Oct 1970, Carolyn; 3 s (Christopher b 8 May 1972, Richard b 11 Sept 1974, Edward b 11 Sept 1980); *Career* cmmnd RAF 1966, advanced flying and operational trg 1966–68, pilot No 20 Sqdn Singapore (Hunters and Pioneers) 1968–70, flying instr RAF Valley (Hunters) 1970–73, Sqdn Ldr 1973, Flt Cdr No 3(F) Sqdn Germany (Harriers) 1975–78, memb UK Air Forces TACEVAL Team HQ Strike Cmd 1978–80, attended Royal Naval Staff Coll Greenwich 1980, CO No 1(F) Sqdn RAF Wittering (Harriers) 1981–83, ldr Cmd Briefing and Presentation Team then PSO to AOC-in-C HQ Strike Cmd 1984–86, promoted Gp Capt 1985, CO Tri-National Tornado Trg Estab RAF Cottesmore 1986–88, Air Plans Dept MOD London 1988–89, promoted Air Cdre 1989, Dir Air Offensive MOD 1989–91, promoted Air Vice-Marshal 1991, Sr Air Staff Offr HQ Strike Cmd and Dep Chief of Staff Ops UK Air Forces 1991–93, AOC No 1 Gp 1993–94, Asst Chief of Air Staff 1994–95, promoted Air Marshal 1996, dep CDS Programmes and Personnel 1996–; pres RAF Cricket Assoc; *Recreations* cricket, golf; *Style*— Air Marshal P T Squire, DFC, AFC; ✉ Ministry of Defence, Main Building, Whitehall, London SW1A 2HB

SQUIRE, Rachel; MP (Lab) Dunfermline West (majority 7,484); *b* 13 July 1954; *Educ* Godolphin and Latymer Girls' Sch, Univ of Durham (BA), Univ of Birmingham; *m* 6 July 1984, Allan Lee Mason; *Career* social worker Birmingham City Cncl 1975–81; area offr NUPE: Liverpool 1981–82, Ayrshire 1982–83, Renfrewshire 1983–85, all of Scotland 1985–92; MP (Lab) Dunfermline W 1992–; memb: Amnesty International, WEA; *Recreations* historic buildings, archaeology, reading; *Style*— Ms Rachel Squire, MP; ✉ House of Commons, London SW1A 0AA; (☎ 01383 622889, fax 01383 623500)

SQUIRE, Robin Clifford; MP (C) Hornchurch (majority 9,165); *b* 12 July 1944; *Educ* Tiffin Sch Kingston-upon-Thames; *m* Susan Fey, *née* Branch; 1 step s, 1 step da; *Career* cncllr London Borough of Sutton 1968–82 (ldr 1976–79), dep chief accountant Lombard North Central Ltd 1972–79, chm Gtr London Young Cons 1973, vice chm Nat Young Cons 1974–75; Parly candidate (C) Havering Hornchurch 1974, MP (C) Hornchurch 1979–; sec Cons Parly Euro Affrs Ctee 1979–80, vice chm Cons Parly Trade Ctee 1981–83, chm Cons Parly Environment Ctee 1990–91 (vice chm 1985–90); memb: Select Ctee on Environment 1979–83 and 1987–91 (Cons ldr 1982–83), Select Ctee on Euro Legislation 1985–88; PPS to: Min of State Dept of Tport 1983–85, Rt Hon Chris Patten MP as Cons Pty Chm 1991–92; Parly under-sec of state: DOE 1992–93, DFE 1993–95, Dept for Educn and Employment 1995–; chm Cons Action on Electoral Reform 1983–86, memb Bd of Mgmnt Shelter 1982–91; successful sponsor of Local Govt (Access to Information) Act 1985; Freedom of Information Award as individual who had most advanced freedom of information in 1985; FCA (ACA 1966); *Books* Set the Party Free (jtly, 1969); *Recreations* bridge, rugby, films; *Style*— Robin Squire, Esq, MP; ✉ House of Commons, London SW1A 0AA (☎ 0171 219 4526, fax 0171 219 2546)

SQUIRE, Dr (Clifford) William; CMG (1978), LVO (1972); s of Clifford John Squire (d 1938), of Gt Yarmouth; *b* 7 Oct 1928; *Educ* Royal Masonic Sch, St John's Coll Oxford (MA), Univ of London (PhD), Coll of Europe Bruges; *m* 1, 6 July 1959, Marie José (d 1973), da of René Paul Carlier (d 1978), of Paris; 2 s (Stephen b 1961, Christophe b 1963, decd), 2 da (Catherine b 1960, Anne Louise b 1965); m 2, 22 May 1976, Sara Laetitia, da of Michael Duncan Hutchison, of Richmond, Surrey; 1 s (James b 1977), 1 da (Emma b 1979); *Career* Br Army 2 Lt, Palestine and Greece 1947–49; HM overseas civil serv asst dist offr Nigeria 1953–59; HM Diplomatic Serv Foreign Office, Bucharest, United Nations NY, Bangkok, Washington 1959–79; ambass to Senegal 1979–82, FCO 1982–84, ambass to Israel 1984–88; devpt dir Univ of Cambridge 1988–96, fell Wolfson Coll Cambridge 1988–96; *Clubs* Travellers (London); *Style*— Dr William Squire, CMG, LVO; ✉ c/o Royal Bank of Scotland, Drummonds, Whitehall, London SW1A 3DX

SQUIRES, Leslie Mervyn; s of Capt Leslie Squires (d 1971), of Folkestone, Kent, and Antoinette, *née* Georgiou (d 1992); *b* 8 July 1947; *Educ* Gordon Sch; *m* 5 May 1971, Jane Barkby, da of Victor Harold Pochin, of Dartford, Kent; 1 s (Jonathan b 25 May 1975), 1 da (Joanna b 1 Sept 1978); *Career* civil servant 1964–67, administrative offr Lloyds Register of Shipping 1967–69, new business exec Lloyds & Scottish Ltd 1969–72, regnl mangr Western Tst & Savings 1972–74, dir Jonathan Wren & Co Ltd 1975–79, md Jonathan Wren City 1977–79, gen mangr Fin Recruitment 1979–81, dir and fndr Anderson Squires 1981–90, trg mangr Acuma (American Express Group) 1991–93, mgmnt conslt Ark Management Resources Ltd 1993–94, estab fin advsr Friends Provident 1995–; CInstSMM 1980, FInstD 1986, MIMgt 1986; *Recreations* travel, current affairs, sport, music; *Clubs* Sidcup Rugby Football, St John's Operatic Soc Sidcup; *Style*— Leslie Squires, Esq

SQUIRES, Richard John; s of Richard George Squires (d 1982), of Dulwich, and Lilian Florence, *née* Fuller (d 1987); *b* 9 Dec 1937; *Educ* Alleyns Sch Dulwich; *m* 19 Aug 1961, Valerie Jean, da of Richard Wotton Wood, of Southfields, Wimbledon; 1 s (Paul Julian b 1970), 1 da (Fiona Jane b 1967); *Career* asst actuary: Imperial Life Assurance of Canada 1963–65, Canada Life Co 1965–68; dir Save & Prosper Group Ltd 1981–94 (gp actuary 1969–89), ptnr Watson Wyatt Partners 1990–; Freeman City of London, Liveryman Worshipful Co of Actuaries; FIA 1962; *Recreations* golf, gardening, painting; *Clubs* Bletchingley Golf, City Livery; *Style*— Richard Squires, Esq; ✉ 6 The Highway, Sutton, Surrey SM2 5QT (☎ 0181 642 7532); Watson Wyatt Partners, Watson House, London Rd, Reigate, Surrey RH2 9PQ (☎ 01737 241144, fax 01737 241496, telex 946070)

SRISKANDAN, Kanagaretnam; s of Kanagaretnam Kathiravelu (d 1980), of Sri Lanka, and Kanmanyammal, *née* Kumaraswamy (d 1991); *b* 12 Aug 1930; *Educ* Central Coll Jaffna Ceylon, Royal Coll Colombo Ceylon, Univ of Ceylon (BSc, tennis colours); *m* 23 June 1956, Dorothy, da of Louis Harley (d 1964), of Kandy, Sri Lanka; 2 s (Kumar b 1957, Ranjan b 1959), 1 da (Shiranee b 1964); *Career* asst engr: PWD Ceylon 1953–56, Sir William Halcrow & Ptnrs London 1956–58; section engr Tarmac Civil Engineering 1958–59; West Riding of Yorkshire CC: asst engr 1959–61, sr engr 1961–64, princ engr 1964–68; Dept of Transport: superintending engr Midland Rd Construction Unit 1968–71, asst chief engr and Head of BES Div 1971–74 (head of BET Div 1974–76), dep chief highway engr 1976–80, chief highway engr 1980–87; divnl dir Mott MacDonald 1988–93; conslt Mott MacDonald 1993–; CEng 1958, FIHT 1974, FICE 1978, FIStructE 1985; *Publications* numerous papers on Engineering and Management topics; *Recreations* gardening, golf; *Style*— Kanagaretnam Sriskandan, Esq; ✉ 21 Bonar Place, Chislehurst, Kent BR7 5RJ

STABB, His Hon Sir William Walter; kt (1981), QC (1968); 2 s of Sir Newton John Stabb, OBE (d 1931), and Ethel Mary, *née* Townsend, DBE (d 1961); *b* 6 Oct 1913; *Educ* Rugby, Univ Coll Oxford; *m* 1940, Dorothy Margaret, *née* Leckie; 4 da; *Career* RAF 1940–46; called to the Bar 1936; bencher Inner Temple 1964– (treas 1985), official referee of the Supreme Court 1969–, circuit judge, sr official referee 1978–85, ret; *Style*— His Hon Sir William Stabb, QC; ✉ Old Barn Cottage, Chipperfield, Kings Langley, Herts WD4 9BH (☎ 01923 263124)

STABLE, His Hon (Rondle) Owen Charles; QC (1963); s of Rt Hon Sir Wintringham Stable, MC (d 1977), of Plas Llwyn Owen, Llanbrynmair, Powis, and Lucie Haden, *née* Freeman; *b* 28 Jan 1923; *Educ* Winchester; *m* 6 April 1949, Yvonne Brook, da of Lionel Brook Holliday, OBE (d 1965), of Copgrove Hall, Boroughbridge, Yorkshire; 2 da (Emma (Mrs Hay), Victoria); *Career* WWII Capt RB 1940–46; called to the Bar Middle Temple 1948; bencher 1969, dep chm Herts Quarter Sessions 1963–71, recorder of Crown Cts 1972–79, circuit judge 1979; resident judge: Wood Green Crown Ct 1980–81, Snaresbrook Crown Ct 1982–95; sr circuit judge 1982–95; Bd of Trade inspector: Cadco Gp of Cos 1963–64, HS Whiteside and Co Ltd 1965–67, Int Learning Systems Corp Ltd 1969–71, Pergamon Press 1969–73; memb: Gen Cncl of the Bar 1962–64, Senate of 4 Inns of Ct 1971–74, Senate of Inns of Ct and the Bar 1974–75; chllr Dio of Bangor 1959–88, memb Governing Body of Church in Wales 1960–88, layreader Dio of St Albans 1961–; chm Horserace Betting Levy Appeal Tbnl 1969–74; *Books* A Review of Coursing (with R M Stuttard, 1971); *Recreations* playing the flute; *Clubs* Boodle's; *Style*— His Hon Owen Stable, QC; ✉ Bucklers Hall, Much Hadham, Herts SG10 6EB (☎ 01279 842604)

STABLEFORD, Brian Michael; s of William Ernest Stableford, of Denton, Lancashire, and Joyce Wilkinson; *b* 25 July 1948; *Educ* Manchester GS, Univ of York (BA, DPhil); *m* 1, 1973 (m dis 1983), Vivien Wynne, da of Caradog Owen; 1 s (Leo Michael b 5 April 1975), 1 da (Katharine Margaret b 21 Oct 1978); m 2, 1985, Roberta Jane, da of Charles Cragg; *Career* lectr Sociology Dept Univ of Reading 1976–88; freelance writer (latterly full time); pt/t lectr in cultural and media studies Univ of the West of England 1995–; *Awards* incl: European SF Award 1984, Distinguished Scholarship Award Int Assoc for the Fantastic in the Arts 1987, J Lloyd Eaton Award 1987, Pioneer Award Science Fiction Research Assoc 1996; *Fiction and Science Fiction* incl: Hooded Swan (series, 1972–78), Realms of Tartarus (1977), Man In a Cage (1976), The Mind Riders (1976), Daedalus (series, 1976–79), The Last Days of the Edge of the World (1978), The Walking Shadow (1979), Asgard (trilogy, 1982–90), The Empire of Fear (1988), The Werewolves of London (trilogy, 1990–94), Sexual Chemistry - Sardonic Tales of the Genetic Revolution (1991), Young Blood (1992), Genesys (trilogy, 1995–97), The Hunger and Ecstasy of Vampires (1996); *Non-Fiction* incl: The Science in Science Fiction (1982), The Third Millennium (1985), Scientific Romance in Britain (1985), The Way to Write Science Fiction (1989); *Reference* contribs incl: The Encyclopedia of Science Fiction, The Survey of Science Fiction Literature, Anatomy of Wonder, Science Fiction Writers, The Survey of Modern Fantasy Literature, Supernatural Fiction Writers, The Cambridge Guide to Literature In English, Fantasy Literature, Horror Literature; *Style*— Brian Stableford, Esq; ✉ 113 St Peter's Rd, Reading, Berks RG6 1PG (☎ 0118 961 6238)

STABLEFORD, Howard; s of Keith Stableford, and Thelma May, *née* Fleming; *b* 12 April 1959; *Educ* Hutton GS Preston, Univ Coll Durham (BA); *m* 8 June 1991, Lizanne Kay, *née* Scott; 2 da (Shelby Elizabeth b 4 Nov 1993, Peyton Alexandra b 24 Sept 1995); *Career* television presenter; BBC Radio Lancashire 1981–82, BBC Radio Northampton 1982–84, BBC TV 1984–; programmes incl: Newsround, Beat the Teacher, Open Forum, Tomorrow's World, The Eleventh Hour; *Recreations* Harley-Davidson motorcycles, running, scuba diving; *Style*— Howard Stableford, Esq; ✉ BBC Science and Features, White City, 20 Wood Lane, London W12 7DT (☎ 0181 752 6681, fax 0181 752 6019)

STABLEFORTH, Dr David Edward; s of Edward Victor Stableforth (d 1975), of Weymouth, Dorset, and Una Alice Stableforth; *b* 23 Feb 1942; *Educ* Truro Sch Cornwall, St Catharine's Coll Cambridge, St Mary's Hosp Paddington; *m* 11 May 1967, Penelope Jane, da of David Ivor Phillips, MC (d 1976), of Finchley, London; 1 s (William b 1973), 2 da (Abigail b 1972, Emily b 1979); *Career* sr med registrar Brompton Hosp and St James' Hosp Balham 1973–77, conslt physician Birmingham Heartlands Hosp and hon sr lectr Univ of Birmingham 1977–; pres Midland Thoracic Soc; memb: Br Thoracic Soc, BMA; FRCP 1985; *Recreations* walking, cycling, sailing and canoeing, theatre and concert-going; *Style*— Dr David Stableforth; ✉ Birmingham Heartlands Hospital, Bordesley Green East, Birmingham B9 5ST (☎ 0121 766 6611)

STACE, Victoria Penelope (Vikki); da of Leonard H Stace (d 1981), of Cheltenham, and Gina, *née* Pluckrose; *b* 21 Aug 1950; *Educ* Malvern Girls' Coll, Univ of Bristol; *m* (m dis 1990), Gavin J Graham; 1 s (Toby James Christopher b 8 June 1984), 1 da (Chloe Alexandra b 23 July 1982); *Career* PR conslt; formerly: English teacher Nepal, journalist; PR officer with publishing co for 15 years (promotions incl: Shirley Conran's Superwoman, John Hackett's The Third World War, Longman's Chronicle Of The Twentieth Century); mktg dir Sidgwick & Jackson, fndr Vikki Stace Associates subsequently Powerhouse 1985– (consumer and corp PR consultancy); former chm Publishers Publicity Assoc, several times winner of Promotion of the Year Award; MIPR; *Recreations* golf, tennis, skiing, opera, theatre, gardening; *Clubs* Riverside Racquet, Groucho's; *Style*— Ms Vikki Stace; ✉ 38 Sterndale Rd, London W14 0HS (☎ 0171 603 4524); Yew Tree House, Sopworth, nr Malmesbury, Wilts (☎ 01454 283344); Powerhouse, 12 Berghem Mews, Blythe Road, London W14 0HN (☎ 0171 371 2600, fax 0171 371 4099, e-mail 106146.1530@compuserve.com)

STACEY, Gloria Rose; da of Solomon Israel Cooklin (d 1950), and Amelia Simmie, *née* Nieman (d 1989); *Educ* Thornbank Sch Malvern Worcs, Kenton Coll Middx, City & Guilds Sch of Art; *m* 1954 (m dis 1987), Nicholas Anthony Howard Stacey, *qv*, s of Marius Szecsi; *Career* artist specializing in collage pictures; dir Swedish Fashions 1953–60; exhibitions: Lasson Gall London 1971, Marcel Bernheim Paris 1973, Fabian Carlsson Sweden 1978, Galleri Fleming Sweden 1978; pictures in numerous public and private collections; *Recreations* swimming, gardening, Dachshunds, looking at paintings, cooking; *Style*— Mrs Gloria Stacey; ✉ 12a Shelley Court, Tite Street, London SW3 4JB

STACEY, Air Vice-Marshal John Nichol; CBE (1972), DSO (1945), DFC (1943); s of Capt Herbert Chambers Stacey (d 1966), of Rhydyfantwn, Moylegrove, nr Cardigan, S Wales, and Brittannia May, *née* Davies (d 1972); *b* 14 Sept 1920; *Educ* Whitgift Middle Sch; *m* 29 April 1950, Veronica, da of Air Vice-Marshal Harry Vivian Satterly, CB, CBE, DFC (d 1982); 2 da (Amanda (Mrs Reuter) b 1953, Caroline (Mrs Russell) b 1956); *Career* served WWII (despatches 3 times), CO 160 Liberator Sqdn Ceylon as Wing Cdr 1944–45, asst air attaché Washington DC 1947–48, RAF Staff Coll Bracknell 1949, instructional staff Bracknell 1958–60, CO Royal Malayan AF 1960–63 (Johan Mangku Negara Malaya 1963), CO RAF Station Laarbruch Germany 1963–66, Air Offr Cmdg the ATC and Air Cadets 1968–71, AOA Air Support Cmd 1974–75, ret RAF 1975; dir Stonham Housing Assoc 1976–82; memb: Tunbridge Wells Health Authy 1981–85, RAF Housing Assoc 1982–86, High Weald Housing Assoc 1989– (chm 1992–); tstee: Housing Assoc Charitable Tst 1978–86, Bedgebury Sch Governing Cncl 1983–, Tunbridge Wells Cancer Help Centre 1983–94; pres: Royal Air Force Assoc Headcorn 1973–, Royal British Legion Goudhurst 1992–; *Recreations* golf, DIY; *Clubs* RAF, Dale Hill Golf; *Style*— Air Vice-Marshal John Stacey, CBE, DSO, DFC

STACEY, Prof Margaret (Meg); da of Conrad Eugene Petrie (d 1953), and Grace Priscilla, *née* Boyce (d 1949); *b* 27 March 1922; *Educ* City of London Sch for Girls, LSE (BSc); *m* 1945, Frank Arthur Stacey (d 1977); 3 s (Richard John b 1951, Peter Frank b 1955, Michael Read b 1958), 2 da (Patricia Ann b 1948, Catherine Margaret (Kate) b 1954); *Career* lab offr Royal Ordnance Factory 1943–44, tutor Oxford 1944–51; Univ Coll Swansea: res offr and fell Lower Swansea Valley Project 1961–63, sr lectr in sociology 1970–74 (lectr 1963–70), dir Medical Sociology Res Centre 1972–74; Univ of Warwick: prof of sociology 1974–89, chm Dept of Sociology 1974–79, chm Graduate Sch of Interdisciplinary Women's Studies 1985–89, chm Mgmnt Ctee Nursing Policy Studies Centre 1985–89, emeritus prof of sociology 1989–; memb SSRC: Sociology Ctee 1969–71, Panel on Health and Health Policy 1976–77; Br Sociological Assoc: memb Exec Ctee 1965–70 and 1975–79, hon gen sec 1968–70, chm 1977–79, pres 1981–83, memb Woman's Caucus 1974–; pres: Soc for the Social History of Medicine 1987–88, Section N (Sociology) BAAS 1990; memb Cncl: Sci and Sociology Working Party on Expensive Med Techniques 1979–82, Nat Academic Awards Health and Med Servs Bd 1980–83, Sci and Soc 1982–91; scientific advsr: Euro Regn Dir WHO 1985–88, Chief Scientist Children's Res Liaison Gp and Nat Perinatal Epidemiology Unit DHSS 1980–85, Thomas Coram Unit 1984–89, (pregnancy studies) Thomas Coram Unit Univ of London 1985–94, S Warks RHA Survey of Training Needs of the Mentally Handicapped 1986–88, Res Ctee West Midlands RHA 1987–90, Univ Coll of N Wales Longitudinal Study of Ageing 1987–92; memb Editorial Bd: Jl of Med Ethics 1977–82, Sociology 1978–82; editorial advsr: Social Sci and Medicine, Jl of the Sociology of Health and Illness, Sociological Review, Jl of Medical Ethics; memb: Welsh Hosp Bd 1970–74 (chairperson Working Party on Children in Hosp in Wales 1970–72), Michael Davies Ctee Hosp Complaints Procedure 1971–73, GMC 1976–84, Steering Ctee Forum on Quality in Health Care RSM, Exec Ctee Human Values in Health Care Forum; pres Assoc for the Welfare of Children in Hosp, govr Coventry Univ (formerly Coventry Poly) 1988–94, memb S Warwicks Community Health Cncl 1992–94; chm S Warwicks Maternity Services Liaison Ctee 1994–; hon fell Univ Coll Swansea 1987–, Lucile Petry Leone prof Univ of Calif San Francisco 1988; FRSM 1978; *Books* Tradition and Change: a study of Banbury (1960), Methods of Social Research (1969), Power Persistence and Change: a second study of Banbury (with E Batstone, C Bell and A Murcott, 1975), Health Care and Health Knowledge (co-ed M Reid, C Heath, R Dingwall, 1977), Women, Power and Politics (with Marion Price 1981, Fawcet Prize 1982), Concepts of Health, Illness and Disease: a comparative perspective (ed with Caroline Currer, 1986), The Sociology of Health and Healing (1988), Beyond Separation: further studies of children in hospital (with D Hall, 1979), Overviews of Research on the Care of Children in Hospital (with S Roche, 1984–92), Regulating British Medicine: The General Medical Council (1992), Changing Human Reproduction: Social Science Perspectives (ed, 1992); *Recreations* gardening, walking; *Style*— Prof Meg Stacey; ✉ 8 Lansdowne Circus, Leamington Spa, Warwickshire CV32 4SW (☎ and fax 01926 312094); Department of Sociology, University of Warwick, Coventry CV4 7AL (☎ 01203 523072, fax 01203 523497)

STACEY, Rear Adm Michael Lawrence; CB (1979); s of Maurice Stacey (d 1971), and Dorice Evelyn, *née* Bulling (d 1967); *b* 6 July 1924; *Educ* Epsom Coll; *m* 1955, Penelope Leana, da of Alister Riddoch (d 1968); 2 s (Hugo, Mark); *Career* various sea appts and cmds 1942–70; dep dir Naval Warfare 1970–72, i/c HMS Tiger 1973–75; ADC 1975; asst Chief of Naval Staff (Policy) 1975–76, Flag Offr Gibraltar 1976–79; dir Marine Pollution Control Unit Dept of Tport 1979–88, int consltt on marine pollution 1988–; memb Advsy Ctee on Protection of the Sea; Younger Brother of Trinity House; memb Ctee of Mgmnt RNLI; Liveryman Worshipful Co of Shipwrights; FNI, FIMgt; *Recreations* fly-fishing, sailing; *Clubs* Army and Navy; *Style*— Rear Adm Michael Stacey, CB; ✉ Little Hintock, 40 Lynch Rd, Farnham, Surrey GU9 8BY (☎ 01252 713032, fax 01252 724638)

STACEY, Nicholas Anthony Howard; s of Marius Stacey (d 1945), and Lilian, *née* Balkanyi (d 1996); *Educ* Jesuit Gymnasium, Commercial Acad Hungary, Univ of Birmingham, Univ of London, Columbia Univ NY (Fulbright sr research fell); *m* 1 (m dis 1986), Gloria Rose Stacey, *qv*; m 2, 10 March 1987, Marianne Luise Ehrhardt, *qv*; *Career* editorial staff Financial Times 1945–46, asst sec Chartered Assoc of Certified Accountants 1947–51, asst ed The Director (jl of IOD) 1953–54, econ and mktg advsr GEC plc 1955–62; chm: Nicholas Stacey Associates 1960–, Chesham Amalgamations & Investments Ltd 1962–83, Cel-Sci Corp Washington DC 1983–90, Integrated Asset Management 1984–86; dir Octagon Oil & Gas Ltd 1991–; chm of tstees Soc for the Promotion of New Music 1969–86; memb: Consultative Ctee for Indust Bd of Trade 1958–62, Ctee Byam Shaw Sch of Drawing and Painting 1964–65, Heath Ctee 1964, London Ctee Lucy Cavendish Coll Cambridge 1978–83, US-UK Educnl (Fulbright) Cmmn 1983–90, Governing Ctee Br Fulbright Scholars Assoc 1982–89; fell Chartered Inst of Secretaries and Administrators; *Books* English Accountancy, A Study in Social and Economic History (1954), Changing Pattern of Distribution (1960), Industrial Market Research (1963), Mergers In Modern Business (1976), Living in an Alibi Society (1989); *Recreations* skiing, walking, music, swimming; *Clubs* Reform, Chelsea Arts (hon memb); *Style*— Nicholas Stacey, Esq; ✉ c/o Reform Club, Pall Mall, London SW1Y 5EW

STACEY, Rev Nicolas David; s of David Henry Stacey (d 1986), and Isobel Ewen, *née* Part; *b* 27 Nov 1927; *Educ* RNC Dartmouth, St Edmund Hall Oxford (MA), Cuddesdon Theol Coll Oxford; *m* 19 July 1955, Anne Caroline Mary, eld da of 2 Viscount Bridgeman, KBE, CB, DSO, MC, JP (d 1982); 1 s (David Robert b 10 May 1958), 2 da (Caroline Jill b 28 Aug 1956, Mary Elizabeth b 15 May 1961); *Career* Midshipman RN 1945–46, Sub-Lt 1946–48; asst curate St Mark's Portsmouth 1953–58, domestic chaplain to Bishop of Birmingham 1958–60, rector of Woolwich 1960–68, dean London Borough of Greenwich 1965–68, dep dir Oxfam 1968–70; dir of social services London Borough of Ealing 1971–74, Kent CC 1974–85; social services conslt 1985–88, dir Aids Policy Unit 1988–89, chm East Thames Housing Gp 1993–; dep chm Television South Charitable Tst 1988–92, six preacher Canterbury Cathedral 1984–90; int sprinter 1948–52, Br Empire Games 1949, Olympic Games 1952, pres Oxford Univ Athletic Club 1951, capt Combined Oxford and Cambridge Athletics Team 1951; *Books* Who Cares (autobiography, 1971); *Recreations* golf; *Clubs* Beefsteak, Vincent's (Oxford), Royal St George's Golf (Sandwich); *Style*— The Rev Nicolas Stacey; ✉ The Old Vicarage, Selling, Faversham, Kent (☎ 01227 752833, fax 01227 752889)

STACEY, Thomas Charles Gerard (Tom); s of David Henry Stacey (d 1986), and Isobel Gwen, *née* Part; *b* 11 Jan 1930; *Educ* Eton, Worcester Coll Oxford; *m* 5 Jan 1952, Caroline Susan, da of Charles Nightingale Clay (d 1961); 1 s (Sam b 1966), 4 da (Emma b 1952, Mathilda b 1954, Isabella b 1957, Tomasina b 1967); *Career* formerly: staff writer Picture Post, chief roving corr The Sunday Times and others; author and screenwriter; works incl: The Hostile Sun (1953), The Brothers M (1960), Summons to Ruwenzori (1963), To-day's World (1970), Immigration and Enoch Powell (1972), The Living and The Dying (1976), The Pandemonium (1980), The Worm in the Rose (1985), Deadline (novel and screenplay, 1988), Bodies and Souls (short stories, 1989), Decline (1991); chm: Stacey International 1974–, Kensington Film Co 1990–; fndr and dir Offender's Tag Assoc; awarded John Llewellyn Rhys Meml prize 1953, Granada award (as foreign corr) 1961; FRSL 1977 (memb Cncl 1987–92); *Recreations* trees, music; *Clubs* White's, Beefsteak, Pratt's; *Style*— Tom Stacey, Esq, FRSL; ✉ 128 Kensington Church St, London W8 4BH (☎ 0171 221 7166, fax 0171 792 9288)

STACK, Rt Rev Mgr George; s of Gerald Stack, and Elizabeth, *née* McKenzie; *b* 9 May 1946; *Educ* St Aloysius Coll Highgate, St Edmund's Coll Ware, St Mary's Coll Strawberry Hill (BEd); *Career* ordained priest 1972, curate St Joseph's Hanwell 1972–75, Diocesan Catechetical Office 1975–77, curate St Paul's Wood Green 1977–83, parish priest Our Lady Help of Christians Kentish Town 1983–90, vicar gen Archdiocese of Westminster 1990–93, prelate of honour to His Holiness 1993, admin Westminster Cathedral 1993–; *Style*— The Rt Rev Mgr George Stack; ✉ Cathedral Clergy House, 42 Francis Street, London SW1P 1QW (☎ 0171 798 9055)

STACK, (Maurice) Neville; s of Maurice Stack (d 1970); *b* 2 Sept 1928; *Educ* Arnold Sch; *m* 1953, Molly, *née* Rowe; 1 s, 1 da; *Career* journalist; Express and Star 1950, Sheffield Telegraph and Kemsley Nat Newspapers 1955, northern news ed IPC Nat Newspapers 1971, sub ed Daily Express 1973, ed Stockport Advertiser 1974, ed-in-chief Leicester Mercury 1974–87, dir F Hewitt & Co Ltd Leicester 1985–88, editorial conslt Straits Times Singapore 1988–89; Europe columnist: New Zealand Herald, Straits Times, The Hindu Madras; writer, int editorial conslt to newspapers, authority on journalist trg, lectr; Hon MA Univ of Leicester 1988; press fell Wolfson Coll Cambridge 1987–88; cncl memb Guild of British Newspaper Editors 1992–93; *Books* The Empty Palace (1977), Editing for the Nineties (1988); *Recreations* writing, computing, travelling, enjoying music and art; *Style*— Neville Stack, Esq; ✉ 34 Main St, Belton-in-Rutland, Leics LE15 9LB (☎ and fax 01572 718718)

STACK, (Ann) Prunella (Mrs Brian St Quentin Power); OBE (1980); da of Capt Edward Hugh Bagot Stack, 8 Gurkha Rifles (d 1914), and Mary Meta Bagot Stack (d 1935), fndr Women's League of Health and Beauty 1930; *b* 28 July 1914; *Educ* The Abbey Malvern Wells; *m* 1, 15 Oct 1938, Lord David Douglas-Hamilton (ka 1944), yst s of 13 Duke of Hamilton and 10 Duke of Brandon (d 1940); 2 s (Diarmaid Hugh b 17 June 1940, Iain b 16 Aug 1942); m 2, 22 July 1950, Alfred Gustave Albers (d 1951), o s of late N W Albers, of Newlands, Cape, S Africa; m 3, 15 May 1964, Brian St Quentin Power, 2 s of late Stephen Power, of Querrin, Co Clare; *Career* ldr The Women's League of Health and Beauty 1935 (pres 1982), memb Nat Fitness Cncl 1937–39, vice pres Outward Bound Tst 1980–; *Books* The Way to Health and Beauty (1938), Movement is Life (1973), Island Quest (1979), Zest for Life (1988), Style for Life (1990); *Recreations* poetry, music, travel; *Style*— Miss Prunella Stack, OBE; ✉ 14 Gertrude St, London SW10 (☎ 0171 351 3393)

STACKHOUSE, Glynne Charles; s of Frederick Charles Stackhouse (d 1981), of Walsall, Staffs, and Mabel, *née* Boonham (d 1986); *b* 23 Feb 1941; *Educ* Queen Mary's GS Walsall, Merton Coll Oxford (BA, MA); *m* 17 July 1971, Patricia Irene, da of Mr & Mrs Harold Henry Rogers; 1 da (Julia Clare b 26 Sept 1974), 1 s (Damian Charles Andrew b 31 March 1976); *Career* pt/t lectr Trinity Coll of Music London 1965–66, dir of music Wallingford GS Berks 1966–70; British Cncl: asst dir Libya 1971, asst dir Italy 1971–75, dir Botswana 1975–79, asst then dep dir Staff Trg 1979–85, dir Hamburg 1985–89, head Music Dept 1989–96; ind music conslt 1996–; *Recreations* music, theatre, food and drink, travel, pretending to garden, reading; *Style*— Mr Glynne Stackhouse

STACY, Graham Henry; CBE (1993); s of Norman Winny Stacy (d 1980), and Winifred Frances, *née* Wood (d 1985); *b* 23 May 1933; *Educ* Stationers' Company's Sch; *m* 19 July 1958, Mary, da of Cyril Arthur Fereday; 4 c (Richard Graham b 13 June 1963, Julia Caroline b 30 July 1964, Helen Clare (twin) b 30 July 1964, Caroline Jane b 18 Sept 1967); *Career* Nat Serv 1955–57, Sub Lt RN; articled clerk Walter Smee Will & Co 1950–55, qualified CA 1955; Price Waterhouse 1957–93: ptnr 1968–93, nat tech ptnr 1976–88; memb: UK Auditing Practices Ctee 1976–84, UK Accounting Standards Ctee 1986–90, UK Accounting Standards Bd (ASB) 1990–94, Monopolies and Mergers Cmmn 1995–; chm ASB Public Sector Ctee 1991–95; treas Sanctuary Housing 1995–, nat treas United Reformed Church 1995–; FCA (ACA 1955); *Recreations* bridge, tennis, DIY; *Style*— Graham Stacy, Esq, CBE; ✉ 31 Fordington Road, Highgate, London N6 4TD (☎ 0181 444 9314)

STACY, Neil Edwin; s of Edwin Frank Dixon Stacy, of Hinton, Gloucestershire, and Gladys Emily, *née* Wallis (d 1980); *b* 15 May 1941; *Educ* Hampton GS, Magdalen Coll Oxford (MA, DPhil); *Career* actor; *Theatre* incl: The Soldier's Fortune, A Room with a View, The Importance of Being Earnest, Richard II (Prospect Prodns 1964–68), Enemy (Saville) 1969, The Recruiting Offr (Bristol and Edinburgh Fest) 1979, A Patriot for Me (Chichester Festival) 1983, Canaries Sometimes Sing (Albery) 1987, Captain Carvallo (Greenwich) 1988, Blithe Spirit (Lyric Hammersmith) 1989, Single Spies (RNT tour) 1990, The Letter (Lyric Hammersmith) 1995; *Television* incl: War and Peace, Barlow at large, Colditz, The Pallisers, To Serve Them all my Days, Shackleton, The Fourth Arm, Duty Free, Three up Two Down, The House of Windsor; *Recreations* medieval history; *Style*— Neil Stacy, Esq; ✉ c/o Michael Whitehall Ltd, 125 Gloucester Road, London SW7 4TE (☎ 0171 244 8466, fax 0171 244 9060)

STADLEN, Nicholas Felix; QC (1991); s of Peter Stadlen (d 1996), concert pianist and former Daily Telegraph chief music critic, and Hedi, *née* Simon; *b* 3 May 1950; *Educ* St Paul's (scholarship), Hackley Sch NY (English Speaking Union scholar), Trinity Coll Cambridge (open scholar, BA, pres Cambridge Union); *m* 9 Dec 1972, Frances Edith, da of Maj T E B Howarth, MC (d 1988); 3 s (Matthew Benedict b 1979, William Gabriel b 1981, Thomas Barnaby b 1986); *Career* called to the Bar Inner Temple 1976; sec Br Irish Assoc 1973–74, memb Public Affrs Ctee Bar Cncl 1987; *Publications* Convention - an Account of the 1976 Democratic Party Presidential Convention (contrib, 1976), Gulbenkian Foundation Reports on Drama and Music Education (jtly, 1974 and 1975); *Recreations* listening to classical music; *Style*— Nicholas Stadlen, Esq, QC; ✉ Fountain Court, Temple, London EC4Y 9DH (☎ 0171 583 3335, fax 0171 353 0329)

STAFFORD, Bishop of 1996–; Rt Rev Christopher John Hill; s of Leonard Hill (d 1991), and Frances Vera, *née* Bullock; *b* 10 Oct 1945; *Educ* Sebright Sch Worcs, King's Coll London (BD, MTh, Relton Prize for Theol, AKC); *m* 1976, Hilary Ann, da of Geoffrey James Whitehouse; 3 s (Vivian John b 1978, Adrian Hugh b 1982, Edmund James b 1983), 1 da (Felicity Ann b 1980); *Career* ordained deacon 1969, priest 1970; asst curate Dio of Lichfield: St Michael Tividale 1969–73, St Nicholas Codsall 1973–74; asst chaplain to Archbishop of Canterbury for foreign rels 1974–81, Archbishop's sec for ecumenical affrs 1982–89, hon canon Canterbury Cathedral 1982–89, chaplain to HM the Queen 1987–96, canon residentiary St Paul's Cathedral 1989–96 (precentor 1990–96), hon canon Lichfield Cathedral 1996–; co-sec Archbishop of Canterbury's Cmmn on Women in the Episcopate 1989–93; Anglican sec: Anglican-RC Int Cmmn (I) 1974–82 and (II) 1983–89, Anglican-Lutheran Euro Cmmn 1981–82, Anglo-Nordic/Baltic Cmmn 1989–92; Anglican co-chm London Soc for Jews and Christians 1991–96, Anglican chm C of E French Protestant Conversaions 1994–; memb: London Soc for the Study of Religion 1990–, Ecclesiastical Law Soc 1990– (vice-chm 1993–), Legal Advsy Cmmn Gen Synod 1991–, Cncl for Christian Unity 1992–; chm Cathedrals' Precentors Conf 1994–96; *Recreations* Radio 3, mountain walking, detective stories, Italian food, unaffordable wine, industrial archaeology, GWR; *Clubs* Nikaean, Athenaeum, Odd Volumes, Nobodies Friends; *Style*— The Rt Rev the Bishop of Stafford; ✉ Ash Garth, 6 Broughton Crescent, Barlaston, Stoke-on-Trent, Staffs ST12 9DD (☎ 01782 373308, fax 01782 373705)

STAFFORD, 15 Baron (E 1640); Francis Melfort William Fitzherbert; DL (Staffs 1994); s of 14 Baron (d 1986), and Morag Nada, da of late Lt-Col Alastair Campbell, of Altries, Milltimber, Aberdeenshire; *b* 13 March 1954; *Educ* Ampleforth, Reading Univ, RAC Cirencester; *m* 1980, Katharine Mary, 3 da of John Codrington, of Barnes, London; 2 s (Hon Benjamin John Basil b 1983, Hon Toby Francis b 1985), 2 da (Hon Teresa Emily b 1987, Hon Camilla Rose Jane b 1989); *Heir* s, Hon Benjamin Fitzherbert b 8 Nov 1983; *Career* pro-chllr Keele Univ 1993–; non-exec dir: Tarmac Ind Products Div 1987–93, Mental Health Fndn Mid Staffs 1991–, Hanley Economic Building Soc 1993–; patron and pres of various orgns in Staffordshire; govr Harper Adams Agric Coll 1990–; *Recreations* cricket, shooting, golf; *Clubs* Army & Navy, Lord's Taverners; *Style*— The Rt Hon the Lord Stafford, DL; ✉ Swynnerton Park, Stone, Staffordshire ST15 0QE

STAFFORD, Baroness; Morag Nada; *née* Campbell; yr da of late Lt-Col Alastair Campbell, of Aberdeenshire; *m* 1952, 14 Baron Stafford (d 1986); 3 s (15 Baron, Hon Thomas, Hon Philip), 3 da (Hon Aileen, Hon Caroline, Hon Wendy); *Career* first lady pres Staffordshire Agric Soc 1969 (re-elected pres 1989, patron 1990), pres Midland Area NSPCC 1972–87, Northern Area pres St John Ambulance 1972–82, county pres St John Ambulance 1982–95; DStJ; *Recreations* gardening, fishing, shooting, photography, tennis; *Clubs* Army & Navy; *Style*— The Rt Hon Morag, Lady Stafford; ✉ Beech Farm House, Beech, Stoke-on-Trent, Staffordshire ST4 8SJ (☎ 01782 796519)

STAFFORD, Peter Moore; s of Harry Shaw Stafford (d 1981), of Holmes Chapel, Cheshire, and May Alexandra, *née* Moore (d 1994); *b* 24 April 1942; *Educ* Charterhouse; *m* 29 Sept 1973, Elspeth Anne, da of James Steel Harvey; 2 c (Gayle b 3 Sept 1975, Christopher b 9 March 1977); *Career* Garnett Crewdson & Co Manchester: articled clerk 1960–64, CA 1964–66; Arthur Andersen 1966–68; ptnr: Garnett Crewdson & Co 1968–71, Spicer & Oppenheim 1971–90 (national managing ptnr 1990), Touche Ross (now Deloitte & Touche) 1990– (all following mergers); chm Touche Ross Bd of Ptnrs 1992–95 (memb 1990–); memb Cncl for Industry and Higher Educn 1993–; govr Terra Nova Sch Tst Ltd; FCA (ACA 1965); *Recreations* travel, gardening, restoring antique launches; *Style*— Peter Stafford, Esq; ✉ Deloitte & Touche, Abbey House, 74 Mosley St, Manchester M60 2AT (☎ 0161 228 3456, fax 0161 228 2021)

STAFFORD-CLARK, Maxwell Robert Guthrie Stewart (Max); s of David Stafford-Clark, and Dorothy Crossley, *née* Oldfield; *b* 17 March 1941; *Educ* Felsted, Riverdale Country Day Sch NYC, Trinity Coll Dublin; *m* 1, 1971, Carole, *née* Hayman; m 2, 1981, Ann, *née* Pennington; 1 da (Kitty b 28 Aug 1988); *Career* artistic director; Traverse Theatre Edinburgh 1968–70, Traverse Theatre Workshop 1971–72, Joint Stock Theatre Group 1974–79, Royal Court Theatre 1979–93, Out of Joint Theatre Group 1993–; visting prof Royal Holloway and Bedford Coll, Univ of London 1993–94, Maisie Glass prof Univ of Sheffield 1995–96; *Books* Letters to George (1988); *Style*— Max Stafford-Clark, Esq; ✉ 7 Gloucester Crescent, London NW1 (☎ 0171 485 9911); c/o Out of Joint, 20–24 Eden Grove, London N7 8ED (☎ 0171 609 0207, fax 0171 609 0203)

STAHL, Andrew; s of Adam Jack Stahl, of London, and Sheena Penelope, *née* Simms; *b* 4 July 1954; *Educ* Slade Sch of Fine Art; *m* 1988, Jean Oh Mei Yen, da of Henry Oh Sui Hong; *Career* artist; visiting lectr in painting Slade Sch of Fine Art and Chelsea Sch of Art; *Solo Exhibitions* Air Gallery London 1981 and 1983, Paton Gallery London 1984 and 1988, Flowers East 1992, Worthing Museum and Art Gallery 1993, Prints and Drawings (Flowers East) 1993, Maidstone Library Gallery 1994, Flowers East 1995, Wolverhampton Art Gallery and Museum 1995; *Group Exhibitions* incl: British Drawing (Hayward Gallery) 1982, Pagan Echoes (Riverside Studios) 1983, selections from 10 years at Air (Air Gallery) 1985, 17 International Festival of Painting Cagnes France 1985, Walking & Falling (Interim Art & Kettles Yard Cambridge) 1986, British Painting (touring Malaysia, Singapore, Hong Kong, Thailand) 1987, Artists Choice (V & A Museum) 1987, London Group (RCA) 1988, Figuring out the 80's (Laing Art Gallery Newcastle), Whitechapel Open 1989, Rome Scholars 1980–90 (RCA) 1990, Selected Line (William Jackson Gallery) 1992, Biella Print Biennale 1993, 5 Artists (Angela Flowers Gallery) 1994, East Open Exhbn (Norwich Art Gallery) 1994, John Moores Liverpool Exhibition 1995; *Work in Public Collections* Metropolitan Museum of Art New York, Arts Cncl of GB, Br Cncl, Contemporary Arts Soc, Br Museum, City Museum Peterborough, Leicestershire Educn Authy *Awards* Abbey Major Rome Scholarship 1979–81, fellowship in printmaking RCA 1989, Rome Award in painting Br Sch at Rome 1989, Wingate scholarship to travel in Far East 1991; *Style*— Andrew Stahl, Esq; ✉ 1 Domingo St, London EC1Y 0TA

STAINER, John Martin; s of Ivan Walter Thomas Stainer (d 1988), of The Mill, Burcombe, Salisbury, Wilts, and Muriel Alison, *née* West; *b* 1 Sept 1948; *Educ* Kingston GS; *m* 12 Nov 1966, Paula Marguerite, da of Wilf Househam; 2 s (James Andrew b 12 Feb 1968, Jonathan Mark b 3 Oct 1978), 1 da (Karen Juliette b 12 March 1967); *Career* S H Benson: mgmnt trainee 1966, asst prodn mangr Benson Recruitment Advertising 1967, account exec 1969; account exec Benton & Bowles 1969–71; Benton & Bowles Recruitment: fndr 1971, account dir 1974, bd dir 1978, md 1982, chm 1986; chm Bernard Hodes Advertising (formerly B & B Bernard Hodes Advertising after merger 1989) 1991–, sr ptnr The Let's Talk Partnership 1995–; former Middx co hockey player and England trialist; Freeman City of London 1976; MIPA 1976; *Recreations* family, cricket, hockey, golf, music; *Clubs* Surrey CCC, Glamorgan CCC, Gloucestershire CCC, Malden Wanderers CC, Old Kingstonian Hockey, Kingswood Golf and Country; *Style*— John Stainer, Esq; ✉ 71 Longdown Lane South, Epsom, Surrey KT17 4JJ (☎ 01372 722928); Bernard Hodes Advertising, Griffin House, 161 Hammersmith Rd, London W6 8BS (☎ 0181 846 9666/01372 749925, fax 0181 748 0311)

STAINTON, Sir (John) Ross; kt (1981), CBE (1971); s of George Stainton, and Helen, *née* Ross; *b* 27 May 1914; *Educ* Malvern; *m* 1939, Doreen Werner; 3 da; *Career* Imperial Airways 1933–40; served RAF WWII; BOAC: mangr N America 1949–54, commercial dir 1964, dir 1968–74, dep md 1968, md 1971, chm and chief exec 1972–74; BA (following merger of BEA and BOAC 1974): dir 1974–, dep chm and chief exec 1977–79, chm 1979–81; vice pres Private Patients Plan plc; FCIT (pres 1970–71), FRSA; *Style*— Sir Ross Stainton, CBE; ✉ c/o RAF Club, 128 Piccadilly, London W1V 0PY (☎ 0171 499 3456)

STAIR, 14 Earl of (S 1703); Sir John David James Dalrymple; 15 Bt of Stair (S 1664) and 11 of Killock (S 1698); also Viscount Stair and Lord Glenluce and Stranraer (S 1690), Viscount Dalrymple and Lord Newliston (S 1703), Baron Oxenfoord (UK 1841); s of 13 Earl of Stair, KCVO, MBE (d 1996), and Davina Katharine, *née* Bowes Lyon; *b* 4 Sept 1961; *Educ* Harrow; *Heir* bro, Hon David Hew Dalrymple b 20 March 1963; *Career* cmmnd Scots Gds 1982; *Style*— The Rt Hon the Earl of Stair; ✉ Lochinch Castle, Stranraer, Wigtownshire

STALLARD, Baron (Life Peer UK 1983), of St Pancras in the London Borough of Camden; Albert William Stallard; s of Frederick Stallard, of Tottenham; *b* 5 Nov 1921; *Educ* Low Waters Public Sch, Hamilton Acad Scotland; *m* 1944, Julie, da of William Cornelius Murphy, of Co Kerry; 1 s (Hon Richard b 1945), 1 da (Hon Brenda b 1949); *Career* engr 1937–65, tech trg offr 1965–70; memb St Pancras Borough Cncl 1953–59 (alderman 1962–65); chm: Public Health Ctee 1956–59 and 1962–65, Housing and Planning Dept 1956–59; memb Camden Borough Cncl 1965–70 (alderman 1971–78); MP (Lab): St Pancras North 1970–74, Camden Div of St Pancras North 1974–83; PPS: Min of Agric 1973–74, min of Housing and Construction 1974–76; govt whip 1978–79 (asst 1976–78), Lords Cmmr Treasy, chm Lords All Party Gp on Ageing 1989–; memb and chm Camden Town Disablement Advsy Ctee 1951–83, vice pres Camden Assoc of Mental Health; memb AEU Order of Merit 1968, former memb Inst of Trg & Devpt; *Style*— The Rt Hon the Lord Stallard; ✉ c/o House of Lords, London SW1A 0PW

STALLWORTHY, Jon Howie; s of Sir John Arthur Stallworthy (d 1993), and Margaret Wright, *née* Howie (d 1980); *b* 18 Jan 1935; *Educ* Rugby, Univ of Oxford (BA, MA, BLitt); *m* 25 June 1960, Gillian (Jill), da of Sir Claude Humphrey Meredith Waldock, CMG, OBE, QC (d 1981); 2 s (Jonathan b 1965, Nicolas b 1970), 1 da (Pippa b 1967); *Career* Nat Serv 1953–55, 2 Lt Oxon and Bucks LI, seconded Royal W African Frontier Force; visiting fell All Souls Coll Oxford 1971–72, dep academic publisher OUP 1972–77, Anderson prof of Eng lit Cornell Univ 1977–86, professorial fell Wolfson Coll and reader in Eng lit Univ of Oxford 1986–92, ad hominem prof of English lit Univ of Oxford 1992–; FRSL, FBA 1990; Hon DUniv Surrey; *Books* incl: Between the Lines, WB Yeats's Poetry in the Making (1963), Vision and Revision in Yeats's Last Poems (1969), Alexander Blok, The Twelve and Other Poems (trans with Peter France, 1970), Wilfred Owen (winner Duff Cooper Meml Prize, W H Smith & Son Literary Award, E M Forster Award, 1974), The Penguin Book of Love Poetry (ed, 1973), Wilfred Owen - The Complete Poems and Fragments (ed, 1983), Boris Pasternak, Selected Poems (trans with Peter France, 1984), The Oxford Book of War Poetry (ed, 1984), The Anzac Sonata - New and Selected Poems (1986), First Lines - Poems Written in Youth from Herbert to Heaney (ed, 1987), Henry Reed - Collected Poems (ed, 1991), Louis MacNeice (1995, winner Southern Arts Lit Prize), The Guest from the Future (1995); *Style*— Prof Jon Stallworthy; ✉ Long Farm, Elsfield Rd, Old Marston, Oxford OX3 OPR; Wolfson Coll, Oxford OX2 6UD (☎ 01865 274100)

STAMER, Sir (Lovelace Anthony); 5 Bt (UK 1809), of Beauchamp, Dublin; s of Sir Lovelace Stamer, 4 Bt (d 1941), and Mary, *née* Otter (d 1974; her mother Marianne was seventh in descent from 4 Baron North); *b* 28 Feb 1917; *Educ* Harrow, Trinity Coll Cambridge (MA), RAC Cirencester; *m* 1, 1948 (m dis 1953), Stella Huguette, da of late Paul Burnell Binnie; 1 s, 1 da; m 2, 1955 (m dis 1959), Margaret Lucy, da of late Maj T A Belben, IA; m 3, 1960 (m dis 1968), Marjorie June, da of late T C Noakes; m 4, 1983, Elizabeth Graham Smith (d 1992), da of late C J R Magrath; *Heir* s, Peter Tomlinson Stamer (Sqdn Ldr RAF, ret); *Career* PO RAF 1939–41, 1 Offr Air Tport Aux

1941–45; exec dir: Bentley Drivers Club Ltd 1969–73, Bugatti and Ferrari Owners Clubs 1973–74; hon tres Ferrari Owners Club 1976–81; *Style*— Sir Anthony Stamer, Bt; ✉ 5 Windrush Court, 175 The Hill, Burford, Oxfordshire OX18 4RE (☎ 01993 823849)

STAMER, Peter Tomlinson; s and h of Sir (Lovelace) Anthony Stamer, 5 Bt, and his 1 w, Stella Huguette, *née* Binnie; *b* 19 Nov 1951; *Educ* Malvern, Univ of Southampton; *m* 1979, (m dis 1989) Dinah Louise; 1 s (William Peter Alexander b 20 Sept 1983), 1 da (Antonia Louise b 1981); *Career* Br Aircraft Corp 1970–71; RAF 1972–89 (Photographic Interpretation branch 1977–89), Sqdn Ldr 1988; furniture maker/restorer 1990–93, Starlight Yachts (Poole) 1994, Česká Kooperativa (insurance co, Prague) 1994–; *Style*— Peter Stamer, Esq; ✉ c/o Lloyds Bank, 31 Sloane Square, London SW1W 8AG

STAMMERS, Lionel John; s of Frederick Arthur Stammers, and Dorothy Irene, *née* Heales (d 1987); *b* 11 May 1933; *Educ* Harlow Coll London (BSc Econ); *m* 5 Aug 1957, Sybil Ann, da of William James Wescott; 2 da (Jane Emma b 1963, Susan Fiona b 1965); *Career* non-exec dir: BTR plc 1988–93 (exec dir until 1988), BBA Group plc 1989–93, Hays plc, McKechnie plc, Bullough plc, Tomkins plc, Barlo plc; *Style*— Lionel Stammers, Esq; ✉ Hays plc, Hays House, Millmead, Guildford, Surrey GU2 5HJ (☎ 01483 302203)

STAMP, Ewen George Morrell; TD (1979); s of Col (John George) Morrell Stamp, TD, of Cambridge, and Marian Lomax, *née* Robinson (d 1987); *b* 16 Aug 1939; *Educ* Gordonstoun; *m* 19 Sept 1970, Mary Frances, da of Philip Erskine Hodge, of Lewes, Sussex; 3 da (Jane b 23 Jan 1973, Amy b 8 May 1975, Helen b 7 Dec 1979); *Career* articled clerk Winter Robinson Sisson & Benson 1958–63, with Deloitte Plender Griffiths 1964–68, co sec Blagden & Noakes (Hldgs) Ltd (now Blagden Industries plc) 1968–80, gp fin dir Hemming Group Ltd 1980–91, ptnr G M Stamp & Co CAs 1992–; head of mgmnt support Assoc of Payment Clearing Servs 1993–; Freeman City of London 1976; HAC (TA) Capt 1964–79 (memb Ct of Assts 1979–89); FCA 1977; *Recreations* sailing; *Clubs* HAC, Royal Harwich Yacht; *Style*— Ewen Stamp, Esq, TD; ✉ 43 Shenfield Place, Shenfield, Brentwood, Essex CM15 9AH

STAMP, Gavin Mark; s of Barry Hartnell Stamp, of Hereford, and Norah Clare, *née* Rich; *b* 15 March 1948; *Educ* Dulwich, Gonville and Caius Coll Cambridge (MA, PhD); *m* 12 Feb 1982, Alexandra Frances, da of Frank Artley, of Redcar; 2 da (Agnes Mary b 1984, Cecilia Jane b 1986); *Career* architectural historian and author; lectr Mackintosh Sch of Architecture Glasgow; contrib: The Spectator, Daily Telegraph, Independent, Herald, Architects Jl, Private Eye; chm Thirties Soc (now the Twentieth Century Soc), fndr and chm Alexander Thomson Soc 1991; Hon FRIAS 1994; *Books* The Architects Calendar (1974), The Victorian Buildings of London (with C Amery, 1980), Temples of Power (text only, 1979), Robert Weir Schultz and His Work for The Marquesses of Bute (1981), The Great Perspectivists (1982), The Changing Metropolis (1984), The English House 1860–1914 (1986), Telephone Boxes (1989), Greek Thomson (ed with S McKinstry, 1994); *Style*— Gavin Stamp; ✉ 1 Moray Place, Strathbungo, Glasgow G41 2AQ (☎ and fax 0141 423 3747)

STAMP, Gerard Christopher; s of Barry Hartnell Stamp, of Withington, Herefordshire, and Norah Agnes, *née* Rich; *b* 22 March 1955; *Educ* King Edward VI Sch Norwich, Bristol Poly (BA); *m* 21 Sept 1985, Jacqui, da of Alan Newman; 1 s (Rupert Charles b 11 July 1994), 1 da (Eleanor Rose b 1 April 1990); *Career* freelance designer/illustrator 1976–79; art dir: Boase Massimi Pollit advtg 1979–81, KMP 1981–82, Foote Cone and Belding 1982–84, Tony Hodges & Partners 1984–89; creative dir Bates Dorland (formerly BSB Dorland) 1991–94 (joined 1989), exec creative dir Leo Burnett 1994–; awards incl: 6 Campaign Poster Silvers, 2 Campaign Press Silvers, 3 D&AD Silvers, 2 Cannes Silver Lions, 4 Cannes Gold Lions, 2 Creative Circle Silvers, Creative Circle Gold; *Recreations* watercolourist and etcher, jazz pianist; *Style*— Gerard Stamp, Esq; ✉ 3 Bell Yard, Gunton Hall, Norfolk NR11 7HL (☎ 01263 768885); Leo Burnett Ltd, The Leo Burnett Building, 60 Sloane Avenue, London SW3 3XB (☎ 0171 591 9111, fax 0171 591 9126/7)

STAMP, Dr Gillian Penelope; da of late Guy St John Tatham, of Johannesburg; *Educ* Univ of Witwatersrand (BA), Brunel Univ (MA) BIOSS Brunel Univ (PhD); *m* 27 Dec 1958, Hon (Jos) Colin Stamp, s of 1 Baron Stamp, GCB, GBE (d 1941); 2 s (Robbie, Jonathan); *Career* dir Brunel Inst of Orgn and Social Studies (BIOSS) Brunel Univ; res consultancy work for numerous nat and int cos; visiting prof Indian Inst of Technol New Delhi; memb Ed Bd: International Journal of Career Management, Indian Journal of Training and Development; memb Cncl St George's House Windsor 1995; Hon DPhil 1991; FRSA 1992; *Publications* Well-Being at Work (with Colin Stamp, 1993); *Style*— Dr Gillian Stamp; ✉ 12 Ullswater Road, London SW13 (☎ 0181 748 2782, fax 0181 255 7579); Brunel Institute of Organisation and Social Studies, Brunel University, Uxbridge, Middlesex (☎ 01895 270072, fax 01895 254760)

STAMP, Malcolm Frederick; *b* 29 Dec 1952; *Educ* Stand GS; *Career* unit gen mangr (Acute) N Manchester HA 1985–88; dist gen mangr: Crewe HA 1988–90, Liverpool HA 1990–92; chief exec: Royal Liverpool Univ Hosp Tst 1992–94, Norfolk & Norwich Health Care NHS Tst 1994–; regnl rep NAHAT Cncl; former chm of govrs Peel Brow Primary Sch; memb Inst of Mgmnt Servs, MHSM; *Recreations* football, reading, family; *Style*— Malcolm F Stamp, Esq; ✉ Norfolk & Norwich Health Care NHS Trust, Norfolk & Norwich Hospital, Brunswick Road, Norwich, Norfolk NR1 3SR (☎ 01603 287207, fax 01603 287547)

STAMP, Terence Henry; s of Thomas Stamp (d 1983), and Ethel Esther *née* Perrot (d 1985); *b* 22 July 1938; *Educ* Plaistow Co GS; *Career* actor; Doctor of Arts (hc) 1993; *Films* incl: Billy Budd 1960, The Collector 1964, Far from the Madding Crowd 1966, Tales of Mystery 1967, Theorom 1968, Meeting with Remarkable Men 1977, Superman I and II 1977, The Hit 1984, Legal Eagles 1985, Wall Street 1987, Young Guns 1988, The Sicilain 1988, Alien Nation 1989, Prince of Shadows 1991, Priscilla, Queen of the Desert 1994; *Books* Stamp Album (1987), Coming Attractions (1988), Double Feature (1989), The Night (novel, 1992); *Recreations* film; *Clubs* New York Athletic; *Style*— Terence Stamp, Esq; ✉ c/o Markham & Froggatt Ltd, Julian House, 4 Windmill Street, London W1P 1HF (☎ 0171 636 4412, fax 0171 637 5233)

STAMP, 4 Baron (UK 1938) Trevor Charles Bosworth Stamp; s of 3 Baron Stamp (d 1987); *Educ* Leys Sch, Gonville and Caius Cambridge (BA), St Mary's Hosp Med Sch (MB BCh); *m* 1, 1963 (m dis 1971), Anne Carolynn, da of John Kenneth Churchill, of Tunbridge Wells; 2 da; m 2, 1975, Carol Anne, da of Robert Keith Russell, of Farnham, Surrey; 1 s, 1 da; *Heir* s, Hon Nicholas Charles Trevor Stamp b 1978; *Career* med registrar Professorial Med Unit St Mary's Hosp 1964–66; Dept of Human Metabolism UCH and Med Sch: hon sr registrar 1968–73, hon sr lectr 1972–73; conslt physician and dir Dept of Bone and Mineral Metabolism Inst of Orthopaedics Royal Nat Orthopaedic Hosp 1974–; hon conslt physician and sr lectr Middx Hosp and UCL Sch of Med 1974–; Prix André Lichtwitz France 1973; FRCP 1978; *Style*— The Lord Stamp; ✉ 15 Ceylon Road, London W14 0PY; Royal National Orthopaedic Hospital, Stanmore, Middx

STANBRIDGE, Air Vice-Marshal Sir Brian Gerald Tivy; KCVO (1979, MVO 1958), CBE (1974), AFC (1952); s of Gerald Edward Stanbridge (d 1966); *b* 6 July 1924; *Educ* Thurlestone Coll Dartmouth; *m* 1, 1949 (m dis 1984), (Kathleen) Diana, *née* Hayes; 2 da; m 2, 1984, Jennifer Anne; *Career* Air Vice-Marshal Burma Campaign 1944–45, personal pilot and flying instr to HRH the Duke of Edinburgh 1954–58, sec to COS Ctee 1971–73, defence serv sec to HM The Queen 1975–79 (ret); dir gen Air Transport Users' Ctee 1979–85; *Recreations* bridge, computers, DIY; *Clubs* RAF; *Style*— Air Vice-Marshal Sir Brian Stanbridge KCVO, CBE, AFC; ✉ 20 Durrant Way, Sway, Lymington, Hants S041 6DQ (☎ 01590 683030)

STANBRIDGE, Ven Leslie Cyril; *b* 19 May 1920; *Educ* Bromley GS Kent, St John's Coll Durham, Univ of Durham (BA, DipTheol, MA); *Career* local govt offr 1936–46; served RAPC 1940–45; curate of Erith Kent 1949–51, tutor and chaplain St John's Coll Durham 1951–55, vicar of St Martin Hull 1955–64, rector of Cottingham 1964–72, archdeacon of York 1972–88, canon of York 1968–, succentor canonicorum 1988–; *Recreations* fell walking, cycling; *Style*— The Ven Leslie C Stanbridge; ✉ 1 Deangate, York YO1 2JB (☎ 01904 621174)

STANBROOK, Clive St George Clement; OBE (1988), QC (1989); s of Ivor Robert Stanbrook, former MP for Orpington, and Joan, *née* Clement; *b* 10 April 1948; *Educ* Dragon Sch Oxford, Westminster, UCL (LLB); *m* 3 April 1971, Julia Suzanne, da of Victor Hillary; 1 s (Ivor Victor Hillary), 3 da (Fleur Elizabeth, Sophie Noelette, Isabella Grace); *Career* called to: the Bar Inner Temple 1972, the Turks and Caicos Bar 1986, the NY Bar 1988; bd memb World Trade Center Assoc (London) 1977–83, fndr and sr ptnr Stanbrook & Hooper (int lawyers) Brussels 1977–; pres Br C of C for Belgium and Luxembourg 1985–87; *Books* Extradition the Law and Practice (jtly, 1980), Dumping Manual on the EEC Anti Dumping Law (1980), International Trade Law and Practice (co ed, 1984), Dumping and Subsidies (jtly, 1996); *Recreations* tennis, sailing; *Style*— Clive Stanbrook, Esq, OBE, QC; ✉ Stanbrook & Hooper, 42 Rue du Taciturne, Brussels 1000, Belgium (☎ 00 32 2 230 5059, fax 00 32 2 230 5713)

STANCLIFFE, David Staffurth; *see:* Salisbury, Bishop of

STANDAGE, Simon; *Career* fndr memb: English Concert 1973, Salomon String Quartet 1981, Collegium Musicum 90 1990; prof of baroque violin Royal Academy of Music and Dresdner Akademie für Alte Musik; assoc dir Academy of Ancient Music 1991–95; recordings incl: Vivaldi Four Seasons (nominated for Grammy Award), Mozart Concertos, numerous works by Vivaldi, Telemann and Haydn; *Style*— Simon Standage, Esq; ✉ Collegium Musicum 90, 106 Hervey Road, Blackheath, London SE3 8BX (☎ 0181 319 3372, fax 0181 856 1023)

STANDEN, Clive Struan; s of Roy Standen (d 1991), and Peggy, *née* Horne; *b* 31 Aug 1952; *Educ* Royal GS Guildford, Br Sch of Osteopathy (Dip), Univ of Wales (MA Ethics & Healthcare); *m* 1974, Anne Margaret, da of John Shee; 1 da (Rebecca b 11 Dec 1978), 2 s (Thomas b 12 Aug 1980, Joseph b 28 March 1986); *Career* practising osteopath 1972–; princ and chief exec Br Sch of Osteopathy 1990– (memb Faculty 1979–); chm Cncl of Independent Colls and Research Instns 1991–, memb Validation Bd Open Univ 1992–; extensive lecturing and examining overseas; memb Gen Cncl and Register of Osteopaths 1978; *Recreations* tennis, squash, climbing, gardening, cooking, reading; *Style*— Clive Standen, Esq; ✉ 3 The Drive, Kettering, Northants NN15 7EX (☎ 01536 513605); The British School of Osteopathy, 1–4 Suffolk Street, London SW1Y 4HG (☎ 0171 930 9254, fax 0171 839 1098, mobile 0802 846081)

STANDEN, John Francis; s of Dr Edward Peter Standen (d 1976), and Margaret, *née* O'Shea; *b* 14 Oct 1948; *Educ* St James' Sch Burnt Oak, Univ of Durham (BA); *m* 9 Aug 1975, Kathleen Mary, da of Joseph Quilty, of Co Galway, Ireland; 2 s (Luke b 1981, Owen b 1984), 1 da (Aine b 1979); *Career* dir Barclays Merchant Bank Ltd 1986–; Barclays de Zoete Wedd Ltd: md Corp Fin 1990–92, chief exec offr Corp Finance UK 1992–93, chief exec Corp Finance Worldwide 1993–95, chief exec offr Emerging Markets 1995–; ACIB 1974; *Recreations* relaxing, walking, family fun, theatre, opera; *Style*— John Standen, Esq; ✉ The Blue House, Thorley Street, nr Bishops Stortford, Herts CM23 4AL (☎ 01279 508 413); Barclays de Zoete Wedd, Ebbgate House, 2 Swan Lane, London EC4 (☎ 0171 623 2323, fax 0171 775 1764, telex 923141)

STANDING, John Ronald; Sir John Ronald Leon, 4 Bt, but prefers to be known by professional name of John Standing; s of Sir Ronald George Leon, 3 Bt (d 1964), and his 1 w, Dorothy Katharine (the actress Kay Hammond; d 1980), da of Cdr Sir Guy Standing, KBE (d 1937), and who m 2, Sir John Clements, CBE; *b* 16 Aug 1934; *Educ* Eton, Millfield, Byam Shaw Sch of Art; *m* 1, 1961 (m dis 1972), Jill, da of Jack Melford, actor; 1 s (Alexander John b 1965); m 2, 7 April 1984, Sarah Kate, da of Bryan Forbes, *qv*, film dir; 1 s (Archie b 28 July 1986), 2 da (India b 25 June 1985, Octavia b 3 Nov 1989); *Heir* s, Alexander John Leon, *qv*; *Career* actor; 2 Lt KRRC 1953–55; artist (watercolours); *Theatre* incl: The Importance of Being Earnest 1968, Ring Round the Moon 1969, Arms and the Man 1970, Sense of Detachment 1972, Private Lives 1973, St Joan 1973, Jingo 1976, The Philanderer 1978, Plunder 1978, Close of Play 1979, Tonight at 8.30 1981, Biko Inquest 1984, Rough Crossing 1985, Hayfever (Albery) 1992, A Month in the Country (Albery) 1994, Son of Man (RSC) 1996; *Television* UK incl: The First Churchills, Charley's Aunt, Tinker Tailor Soldier Spy; USA incl: Lime Street 1985, Murder She Wrote 1989, LA Law 1990; *Films* incl: King Rat 1965, Walk Don't Run 1965, The Eagle Has Landed 1976, Rogue Male 1976, The Legacy 1977, Mrs Dalloway; *Recreations* painting, fishing; *Clubs* MCC; *Style*— John Standing, Esq; ✉ c/o ICM Ltd, Oxford House, 76 Oxford Street, London W1N 0AX (☎ 0171 636 6565, fax 0171 323 0101)

STANDRING, Robert Cumberland; s of George Lancelot Standring (d 1987), of East Sheen, London, and Ethel Mary, *née* Reid (d 1975); *b* 1 Feb 1929; *Educ* Westminster; *m* 9 Nov 1963, Eileen Margaret, da of Charles Frederick Greenslade (d 1958); 1 s (Rev Rupert Benjamin Charles Standring b 2 Nov 1968), 1 da (Charlotte Katharine Alexandra b 11 April 1970); *Career* Nat Serv RAMC 1947–49; Legal & General Group 1946–87; Nat Viewers and Listeners Assoc: hon treas 1977–92, exec chm 1990–92; chm Int Congress for the Family UK Ltd 1989–93; dir: Aldro School Educational Trust Ltd 1985–, World Horizons Ltd 1989–93; memb Horsley PCC 1995–; Liveryman Worshipful Co of Vintners 1959; APMI 1978, AIA 1970; *Clubs* National (at Carlton); *Style*— R C Standring, Esq

STANES, Ven Ian Thomas; s of Sydney Stanes (d 1966), of Bath, and Iris, *née* Hulme; *b* 29 Jan 1939; *Educ* City of Bath Boys' Sch, Univ of Sheffield (BSc), Linacre Coll Oxford (MA), Wycliffe Hall Oxford; *m* 8 Sept 1962, Sylvia Alice, da of George John Drew; 1 da (Sally Rachael b 12 Aug 1968), 1 s (Alan Thomas (decd) b 18 Jan 1971); *Career* ordained: deacon 1965, priest 1966; curate Holy Apostles Leicester 1965–69, vicar St David's Broom Leys Coalville (Dio of Leicester) 1969–76, priest/warden Marrick Priory (Dio of Ripon) 1976–82, offr for mission miny and evangelsm Willesden (Dio of London) 1982–92, continuing ministerial educn offr Willesden 1984–92, preb St Paul's Cathedral 1989–92, archdeacon of Loughborough (Dio of Leicester) 1992–; *Recreations* hockey, rock climbing, walking, photography, singing, music and art appreciation, drama; *Style*— The Ven the Archdeacon of Loughborough; ✉ The Archdeaconry, 21 Church Road, Glenfield, Leics LE3 8DP (☎ 0116 231 1632, fax 0116 232 1593)

STANESBY, Rev Canon Derek Malcolm; s of Laurence John Charles Stanesby (d 1991), of Congleton, Cheshire, and Elsie Lilian, *née* Stean (d 1959); *b* 28 March 1931; *Educ* Orange Hill Sch Edgware, Northampton Poly London, Leeds Univ (BA), Coll of the Resurrection Mirfield, Manchester Univ (MEd, PhD); *m* 29 July 1958, Christine Adela, da of David Payne (d 1985), of Tamworth, Staffs; 3 s (Michael b 1961, Mark b 1963, Peter b 1966), 1 da (Helen b 1959); *Career* GPO Radio Research Station Dollis Hill 1947–51; RAF 1951–53, PO, Navigator; ordained Norwich Cathedral 1958; curate: Norwich 1958–61, Southwark 1961–63; vicar St Mark Bury 1963–67, rector St Chad Ladybarn 1967–85, canon of Windsor 1985–; memb Archbishop's Cmmn on Christian Doctrine 1986–91; author of various articles; *Books* Science, Reason and Religion (1985);

Recreations hill walking, sailing, woodwork, idling; *Style*— The Rev Canon Derek Stanesby; ✉ 4 The Cloisters, Windsor Castle, Berks SL4 1NJ (☎ 01753 864142)

STANFIELD, Brian John; *b* 12 July 1934; *Educ* London (LLB); *m* 1956, Janet Margery Mary; 1 s, 1 da; *Career* slr 1959; legal dir UK Grand Metropolitan plc 1986–92; asst dir Inst for Citizenship Studies 1992–93, pt/t chm Industl Tribunals 1992–; pres City of Westminster Law Soc 1979; Liveryman Worshipful Co of Makers of Playing Cards; *Recreations* theatre, music; *Clubs* Savile; *Style*— Brian Stanfield, Esq; ✉ Cheriton, 35 Worple Rd, Epsom, Surrey

STANFIELD, Prof Peter Robert; s of Robert Ainslie Stanfield, of Woodstock, Oxford, and Irene Louisa, *née* Walker; *b* 13 July 1944; *Educ* Portsmouth GS, Univ of Cambridge (MA, PhD, ScD); *m* 21 Sept 1987, Philippa, da of Eric Moss, of Willoughby, Lincolnshire; 2 step s (Edward MacMillan Barrie b 1968, William MacMillan Barrie b 1970); *Career* SRC res fell MBA laboratory Plymouth 1968–69, fell Clare Coll Cambridge, univ demonstrator in physiology Univ of Cambridge 1969–74; Univ of Leicester: lectr in physiology 1974–81, reader 1981–87, prof 1987–, head Dept of Physiology 1989–93; visiting prof: Purdue Univ Indiana 1984–85, Univ of Illinois at Chicago 1993–; ed Journal of Physiology 1980–88, field ed Pflügers Archiv (European Jl of Physiology) 1993–; memb Physiological Soc 1973– (memb Ctee 1985–90 and 1995–, hon sec 1996–); *Books* Ion Channels: Molecules in Action (with D J Aidley, 1996); author of scientific papers on physiology of cell membranes; *Recreations* walking, gardening, music; *Style*— Prof Peter Stanfield; ✉ Department of Cell Physiology and Pharmacology, University of Leicester, PO Box 138, Leicester LE1 9HN (☎ 0116 252 3300, fax 0116 223 1401)

STANFORD, Adrian Timothy James; s of Ven Leonard John Stanford (d 1967), formerly Archdeacon of Coventry, and Dora Kathleen, *née* Timms (d 1939); *b* 19 July 1935; *Educ* Rugby, Merton Coll Oxford (MA); *Career* Nat Serv 2 Lt The Sherwood Foresters 1954–55; merchant banker; dir Samuel Montagu & Co Ltd 1972–95 (joined 1958); chm Louis Franck INSEAD Scholarship Fund, advsr Royal Fine Art Cmmn Tst, tstee Old Broad St Charity Tst; *Recreations* gardening, architecture; *Clubs* Boodle's, Brooks's; *Style*— Adrian Stanford, Esq; ✉ The Old Rectory, Preston Capes, nr Daventry, Northamptonshire NN11 3TE; 47 Ennismore Gardens, London SW7 1AH

STANFORD, James Keith Edward; s of late Lt-Col J K Stanford, OBE, MC, and late Eleanor Stanford; *b* 12 April 1937; *Educ* Rugby, RMA Sandhurst; *m* 1964, Carol Susan Harbord; 1 da (Melissa (Viscountess Folkestone)), 1 s (Charles); *Career* served 17/21 Lancers 1955–65 (Capt); IBM Corp 1965–72, in industry and the City 1973–90 (chm Daniel Brown Corp 1987–90), currently dir-gen Leonard Cheshire Fndn; vice chm Holiday Care Service; *Recreations* country activities; *Clubs* Cavalry and Guards'; *Style*— James Stanford, Esq; ✉ Grange Farm, Spratton, Northampton NN6 8LA (☎ 01604 846500); Leonard Cheshire Foundation, 26–29 Maunsel Street, London SW1P 2QN (☎ 0171 828 1822, fax 0171 976 5704)

STANFORD, Peter James; s of Reginald James Hughes Stanford, of Wirral, Merseyside, and Mary Catherine, *née* Fleming; *b* 23 Nov 1961; *Educ* St Anselm's Coll Birkenhead, Merton Coll Oxford (BA); *m* 1995, Siobhan Cross; *Career* reporter The Tablet 1983–84, ed The Catholic Herald 1988–92 (news ed 1984–88), freelance journalist and broadcaster 1984– (incl BBC, The Guardian, The Sunday Times, The Independent, The Independent on Sunday, New Statesman, Daily Telegraph, presenter C4 series Catholics and Sex and on Viva! Radio); chm ASPIRE (Assoc for Spinal Res, Rehabilitation and Reintegration), dir CandoCo Dance Co; *Books* Hidden Hands: Child Workers Around the World (1988), Believing Bishops (with Simon Lee, 1990), The Seven Deadly Sins (ed, 1990), Catholics and Sex (with Kate Saunders, 1992), Basil Hume (1993), Lord Longford (1994), The Catholics and Their Houses (with Leanda de Lisle, 1995), The Devil: A Biography (1996); *Recreations* soap operas, vases, photography, old cars; *Clubs* Academy; *Style*— Peter Stanford, Esq; ✉ 41 Crossley Street, London N7 8PE (☎ 0171 607 1656)

STANFORD-TUCK, Michael David; s of Wing Cdr Roland Robert Stanford-Tuck, DSO, DFC (d 1987), of Sandwich Bay, Kent, and Joyce, *née* Carter (d 1985); *b* 3 Nov 1946; *Educ* Radley, Univ of Southampton (LLB); *m* 30 June 1973, Susan Penelope, da of Raymond John Lilwall, of St Peters, Broadstairs, Kent; 1 s (Alexander b 1976), 2 da (Olivia b 1978, Camilla b 1984); *Career* admitted slr 1972; barr and attorney Supreme Ct of Bermuda 1978; ptnr: Appleby Spurling & Kempe Bermuda 1978–83, Taylor Joynson Garrett London 1985–; memb Ctee The Bermuda Soc; Liveryman City of London Slrs Co 1989 (Freeman 1973), Freeman City of London 1989; memb Law Soc; *Recreations* golf, gardening, shooting, skiing; *Clubs* Royal St George's Golf; *Style*— Michael Stanford-Tuck, Esq; ✉ Taylor Joynson Garrett, Carmelite, 50 Victoria Embankment, London EC4 (☎ 0171 353 1234, fax 0171 936 2666, telex 268014)

STANFORTH, Prof Anthony William; s of William Reginald Stanforth (d 1979), and Kathleen Helen, *née* Oldham (d 1985); *b* 27 July 1938; *Educ* Ipswich Sch, Univ of Durham (BA, MA), Heidelberg Univ, Marburg Univ (DPhil); *m* 2 Jan 1971, Susan Margaret, da of William James Vale (d 1992), of Oulton Broad; 2 s (Robert b 16 Feb 1976, Andrew b 7 Jan 1979); *Career* asst lectr Univ of Manchester 1964–65, lectr then sr lectr Univ of Newcastle 1965–81 (Earl Grey fell 1961–64), visiting asst prof Univ of Wisconsin 1970–71, prof of languages Heriot-Watt Univ 1981–; FRSA 1983, Hon FIL 1994; *Books* Die Bezeichungen für 'gross', 'klein','viel' und 'wenig' im Bereich der Germania (1967), Deutsche Einflüsse auf den englischen Wortschatz in Geschichte und Gegenwart (1996); *Recreations* opera; *Style*— Prof Anthony Stanforth; ✉ School of Languages, Heriot-Watt University, Riccarton, Edinburgh EH14 4AS (☎ 0131 4495111)

STANGER, David Harry; OBE (1987); s of Charles Harry Stanger, CBE (d 1987), of Knole, Long Sutton, Somerset, and Florence Bessie Hepworth, *née* Bowden; *b* 14 Feb 1939; *Educ* Oundle, Millfield; *m* 20 July 1963, Jill Patricia, da of Reginald Arthur Barnes, of Chessbord, Troutstream Way, Loudwater, Chorley Wood, Herts; 1 s (Edward b 1972); 2 da (Vanessa b 1966, Miranda b 1967); *Career* served RE 1960–66, seconded Malaysian Engrs 1963–66, operational serv Kenya, Northern Malaysia and Sarawak, Capt RE; joined R H Harry Stanger 1966, ptnr Al Hoty Stanger Ltd 1975; chm: Harry Stanger Ltd 1972–90, Stanger Consultants Ltd 1990–93; memb: Steering Ctee NATLAS 1981–85, Advsy Cncl for Calibration and Measurement 1982–87; chm: Assoc of Consulting Scientists 1981–83, NAMAS Advsy Ctee 1985–87, Standards Quality Measurement Advsy Ctee 1987–91; sec gen Union Int des Laboratoires 1984–93, vice pres IQA 1986– (chm Cncl 1990–93); Freeman Co of Water Conservators 1989–; chm: Br Measurement and Testing Assoc 1990–93, Advsy Bd Brunel Centre for Mfrg Metrology 1991–93; first sec gen Euro Orgn for Testing and Certification 1993– (UK rep on Cncl 1990–93); *Recreations* collecting vintage wines; *Clubs* Carlton; *Style*— D H Stanger, Esq, OBE; ✉ Avenue Louis Lepoutre 116, B-1050 Brussels, Belgium (☎ 32 2 346 4371); European Organisation for Testing and Certification (EOTC), Egmont House, rue d'Egmontstraat 15, B-1000 Brussels, Belgium (☎ 00 32 2 502 4141, fax 00 32 3 502 42 39)

STANGER, Keith Burroughs; s of Eric Alfred (d 1971), of Gildersome, Yorks, and Mary, *née* Burroughs; *b* 17 Sept 1939; *Educ* Leeds GS, Univ of St Andrews (MA), Harvard Business Sch (PHD); *m* 29 April 1967, Susan Margaret, da of Reginald Arthur Banham d (1969), of Buenos Aires; 2 s (Julian Patrick b 1971, Edward Alexander b 1974); *Career* Bank of London and South America (Argentina, Paraguay, Colombia) 1964–72, chief accountant Bank of London and Montreal 1972–76; with Lloyds Bank International: in USA 1976–80, in Uruguay and Brazil 1980–86; Lloyds Bank plc London: gen mangr strategic planning 1985–88, gen mangr corp banking and treasy 1988–89, gen mangr fin 1990–91; gen mangr Union National Bank 1991–94 (ret); memb Putney Soc, Basset Hound Club, Albany Bassets Club; FRGS; *Recreations* tennis, climbing, walking, antique maps; *Clubs* Montevideo Cricket; *Style*— Keith Stanger, Esq; ✉ 9 Spencer Walk, London SW15 (☎ 0181 789 1866); Moulin du Pont, Nanteuil Auriac de Bourzac, 24320 Verteillac, France

STANGROOM SPRINTHALL, Sonya Mary; da of Samuel Frederick Coates-Sprinthall (d 1973), and Dorothy Mary, *née* Philipson-Atkinson; *b* 19 Aug 1940; *Educ* Lancaster Coll of Art (NDD); *m* 3 Aug 1963 (m dis 1984), James Edward Stangroom, s of Alfred William Stangroom (d 1986); *Career* artist; thirteen one woman exhibitions; gp exhibitions incl: Young Contemporaries London 1961, Mansard Gallery London 1969–75, Graves Open Exhibition Sheffield, Mappin Art Gallery; mural cmmns: Sheffield Corpn Dept of Education, two murals for Richmond Coll of Educn; memb: Br Inst of Persian Studies, Soc for the Promotion of Byzantine Studies; *Recreations* archaeology (draughtsman Siraf Persian Gulf 1968), Islamic architecture and art, the study of Russian ikons; *Style*— Sonya Stangroom Sprinthall

STANHOPE, Hon William Henry Leicester; s and h of Viscount Petersham, *qv*; *b* 14 Oct 1967; *Educ* Aysgarth Sch, Aiglon Coll; *Recreations* skiing, fishing, shooting; *Style*— The Hon William Stanhope; ✉ 61 B/C Stanhope Gardens, London SW7 5RF

STANIER, Capt Sir Beville Douglas; 3 Bt (UK 1917), of Peplow Hall, Hodnet, Shropshire; s of Brig Sir Alexander Beville Gibbons Stanier, 2 Bt, DSO, MC, JP, DL (d 1995), and Dorothy Gladys, *née* Miller (d 1973); *b* 20 April 1934; *Educ* Eton; *m* 23 Feb 1963, (Violet) Shelagh, da of Maj James Stockley Sinnott (ka 1942), of Tetbury, Glos; 1 s (Alexander b 1970), 2 da (Henrietta b 1965, Lucinda (Mrs James Martin) b 1967); *Heir* s, Alexander James Sinnott Stanier b 1970; *Career* serv Welsh Gds 1952–60 (2 Lt 1953, Lt 1955, Capt 1958), UK, Egypt, Aust; ADC to Govr-Gen of Aust (Field Marshal Viscount Slim) 1959–60; stockbroker, ptnr Kitcat & Aitken 1960–76; farmer 1974–; conslt Hales Snails Ltd 1976–88; memb Whaddon Parish Cncl 1976– (chm 1983–); *Recreations* shooting, cricket; *Clubs* MCC; *Style*— Capt Sir Beville Stanier, Bt; ✉ Kings Close House, Whaddon, Bucks MK17 0NG (☎ 01908 501738); Home Farm, Shotover Park, Wheatley, Oxford OX33 1QP (☎ 0378 305419)

STANIER, Field Marshal Sir John Wilfred; GCB (1982, KCB 1978), MBE (1961), DL (Hampshire 1986); s of Harold Allan Stanier (d 1932), and Penelope Rose, *née* Price (d 1974); *b* 6 Oct 1925; *Educ* Marlborough, Merton Coll Oxford; *m* 1955, Cicely Constance, da of Cmdr Denis Malet Lambert, DSC; 4 da (Emma, Harriet, Miranda, Candia); *Career* cmmnd QOH 1946, served in N Italy, Germany, Hong Kong; cmd: Royal Scots Greys 1966–68, 20 Armoured Bde 1969–71; GOC1 Div 1973–75, Cmdt Staff Coll Camberley 1975–78, Vice CGS 1978–80, Col Royal Scots Dragoon Guards 1979–84, ADC Gen to HM The Queen 1981–85, Col Cmdt RAC 1982–85, C-in-C UKLF 1981–82, CGS 1982–85, Constable HM Tower of London 1990–96; *Recreations* sailing, fishing; *Clubs* Cavalry and Guards'; *Style*— Field Marshal Sir John Stanier, GCB, MBE, DL; ✉ c/o Messrs Coutts & Co, 440 Strand, London WC2R 0QS

STANIFORTH, Adrian Martyn Christopher (Kim); s of Adrian Wheatley Staniforth (d 1971), of Todwick, Sheffield, and Doris Annie, *née* Wiles (d 1984); *b* 27 Feb 1936; *Educ* Ackworth Sch, Univ of Manchester (BA); *m* 29 Aug 1964, Margaret, da of James Hardman, of Sheffield (d 1980); 2 s (Dominic b 1965, Rupert b 1969), 2 da (Amanda b 1967, Arabella b 1970); *Career* CA 1960; Spicer and Peggler London 1961–62, sr ptnr Barber Harrison and Platt 1963–; ICAEW: memb Cncl 1973–80, chm Examinations Ctee 1978–80, memb Educn and Trg Directorate 1978–82, memb Ethics Ctee 1985–; chm Cncl St Luke's Hospice 1970–, pres Sheffield Jr C of C 1970–71, chm Yorkshire Regnl Gp of Jr Chambers 1973, tstee Sheffield Town Tst, non-exec dir Central Sheffield Univ Hosp Tst 1991–; chm of govrs Sheffield HS 1995–; Freeman: City of London 1979, Worshipful Co of CAs 1979; *Recreations* walking, swimming, skiing, sailing, wine, appreciating the arts; *Style*— Kim Staniforth, Esq; ✉ 2 Rutland Park, Sheffield S10 2PD (☎ 0114 266 7171, fax 0114 266 9846)

STANLEY, Ailsa; OBE (1976); da of Albert Smith (d 1979), of Hull, and Ellen, *née* Dunn (d 1962); *b* 3 June 1918; *Educ* Eversleigh HS Hull, Woods Coll Hull; *m* 19 June 1948, Harry Ronald Stanley, s of Harry Stanley; *Career* sec London N Eastern Railway Co 1934–38, sec to gen mangr Hull Daily Mail 1938–39, organiser Hull Daily Mail Comfort Fund 1939–45, business mangr and ed monthly jl 1946–48, sometime freelance journalist Nottingham Evening Post, ed The Soroptimist (jl of the Fedn of Soroptimist Clubs of GB & I) 1962–90, ed The International Soroptimist 1976–91; currently life pres Radio Trent (fndr bd memb 1975–) and RAM FM Ltd; life vice pres Mapperley Hosp League of Friends (fndr memb 1955, sometime chm), formerly memb Metrication Bd, memb Consumer Policy Ctee BSI 1965– (chm 1967–70), memb Mgmnt Ctee Nottingham CAB (co fndr, sometime chm), memb Bd Nottingham Playhouse; JP Nottingham 1957–88; *Recreations* walking, theatre, entertaining; *Clubs* Soroptimist International of Nottingham, European Union of Women, Fawcett Soc; *Style*— Mrs Ailsa Stanley, OBE; ✉ Radio Trent Ltd, 29–31 Castle Gate, Nottingham NG1 7AP (☎ 0115 952 7000, fax 0115 952 7003)

STANLEY, His Hon Judge; Derek Peter; s of (Ronald) Peter Stanley (d 1972), of Birmingham, and Vera Kathleen, *née* Sterry-Cooper; *b* 7 Aug 1947; *Educ* Solihull Sch, Inns of Ct Sch of Law; *m* 10 July 1971, Gabrielle Mary, da of (Kenneth) Nigel Tully; 2 da (Louise b 22 May 1972, Alice b 25 March 1976), 1 s (Francis b 19 Feb 1978); *Career* called to the Bar Gray's Inn 1968, in practice Birmingham Bar 1968–94 (head of Chambers 1988–92), recorder of the Crown Court 1988–94, circuit judge (Midland & Oxford Circuit) 1994– (princ cts Birmingham and Wolverhampton); memb Bar Cncl 1988–91; *Recreations* church music, squash, tennis; *Clubs* Edgbaston Priory (Birmingham), The Last Slursh Club; *Style*— His Hon Judge Stanley; ✉ c/o Midland & Oxford Circuit Office, The Priory Courts, 33 Bull Street, Birmingham B4 6DW

STANLEY, Rt Hon Sir John Paul; kt (1988), PC (1984), MP (C) Tonbridge and Malling (majority 21,558); s of Harry Stanley (d 1956), and Maud Stanley (d 1993); *b* 19 Jan 1942; *Educ* Repton, Lincoln Coll Oxford; *m* 1968, Susan Elizabeth Giles; 2 s, 1 da; *Career* Cons Res Dept (Housing) 1967–68, res assoc IISS 1968–69, fin exec RTZ Corporation 1969–74; MP (C) Tonbridge and Malling Feb 1974–, memb Parly Select Ctee on Nationalised Industs 1974–76, PPS to Rt Hon Margaret Thatcher 1976–79, min for housing and construction with rank of min of state (DOE) 1979–83, min of state for armed forces MOD 1983–87, min of state for NI 1987–88; memb Parly Select Ctee on Foreign Affrs 1992–; *Recreations* music, arts, sailing; *Style*— The Rt Hon Sir John Stanley, MP; ✉ House of Commons, London SW1A 0AA

STANLEY, Martin Edward; s of Edward Alan Stanley, of Northumberland, and Dorothy, *née* Lewis; *b* 1 Nov 1948; *Educ* Royal GS Newcastle upon Tyne, Magdalen Coll Oxford (exhibitioner, BA); *m* 1971 (m dis 1991), Marilyn Joan, *née* Lewis; 1 s (Edward b 8 April 1983); partner Janice Munday; *Career* various positions Inland Revenue 1971–80; DTI: various positions 1980–90, princ private sec 1990–92, head Engrg, Automotive and Metals Div 1992–96, chief exec Oil, gas and petrochemicals Supplies Office 1996–; *Recreations* travel, walking, sailing; *Style*— Martin Stanley, Esq; ✉ OSO, DTI, 151 Buckingham Palace Road, London SW1W 9SS (☎ 0171 215 4258)

STANLEY, Oliver Duncan; s of late Bernard Stanley, and late Mabel *née* Best; *b* 5 June 1925; *Educ* Rhyl GS, ChCh Oxford (MA), Harvard Univ; *m* 7 Sept 1954, Ruth Leah Stanley, JP; 1 s (Julian b 1958); 3 da (Nicola b 1955, Katherine b 1960, Sarah b 1963); *Career* served 8 Hussars 1943–47; called to the Bar Middle Temple 1963; HM inspr of taxes 1952–65, dir Gray Dawes Bank 1966–72, chm Rathbone Brothers plc 1987– (dir 1971–87), dir Axa Equity & Law plc 1992–, chm Profile Books 1996–; memb: Cncl of

Legal Educn 1992–96 Nat Museums and Galleries Merseyside Devpt Tst 1994–96; govr IOC Law Sch 1996–; *Books* Guide to Taxation (1967), Taxology (1971), Creation and Protection of Capital (1974), Taxation of Farmers and Landowners (6 edn, 1995); *Recreations* music, tennis, French; *Clubs* Travellers'; *Style*— Oliver Stanley, Esq; ✉ Rathbone Brothers plc, University House, 13 Lower Grosvenor Place, London SW1W 0EX

STANLEY, Prof Peter; 2 s of Albert Edward Stanley (d 1964), of Ilkeston, Derbyshire, and Rhoda, *née* Clifford (d 1994); *b* 20 March 1930; *Educ* Ilkeston GS, Selwyn Coll Cambridge (MA), Univ of Nottingham (PhD); *m* 31 July 1952, Rennie Elizabeth (d 1 June 1954), da of Joseph Wilkinson of Ilkeston, Derbyshire (d 1933), 1 da (Elizabeth b 4 March 1954); m 2, 5 July 1980, Kathleen Mary (Kate), da of Samuel Evans (d 1981), of Stapleford, Notts; 1 s (Jonathan b 1 July 1982); *Career* Nat Serv 2 Lt RCS 1949–51; tech asst Rolls-Royce Ltd Derby 1954–57; Dept of Mechanical Engrg Univ of Nottingham: sr res asst 1957–61, lectr 1961–71, sr lectr 1971–75, reader 1975–78; prof of mechanical engrg Univ of Manchester 1979–96, prof emeritus 1996–; memb Qualifications Bd Award Ctee IMechE; chm: Editorial Bd Jl Strain Analysis, Jt Br Ctee Stress Analysis; MSc Univ of Manchester 1983, DSc 1992; FIMechE 1979 (MIMechE 1966), CEng, FInstP 1970 (AInstP 1959), CPhys; *Books* Computing Developments in Experimental and Numerical Stress Analysis (ed, 1976), Fracture Mechanics in Engineering Practice (ed, 1977), Non-Linear Problems in Stress Analysis (ed, 1978), Stability Problems in Engineering Components and Structures (jt ed, 1979), Structural Integrity Assessment (ed, 1992), Engineering Integrity Assessment (jt ed, 1994); numerous papers in tech jls; *Recreations* walking, swimming, English Heritaging, Jonathan; *Style*— Prof Peter Stanley; ✉ 7 Croft Road, Wilmslow, Cheshire SK9 6JJ (☎ 01625 527702); Manchester School of Engineering, University of Manchester, Simon Building, Oxford Rd, Manchester M13 9PL (☎ 0161 275 4303, fax 0161 275 4346)

STANLEY, Peter Henry Arthur; s of Col F A Stanley, OBE (d 1979), of Bramshott Lodge, Liphook, Hants, and Ann Jane, *née* Collins; *b* 17 March 1933; *Educ* Eton; *m* 1, 7 May 1965 (m dis), Gunilla Margaretha Antonia Sophie, da of Count Wilhelm Douglas (d 1987), of Schloss Langenstein, Baden Wurttemberg; 1 s (Robin b 1968), 1 da (Louisa b 1966); m 2, 21 May 1990 (m dis), Mrs Lucy Campbell, da of James A Barnett, of Bel Air, California, USA; *Career* Grenadier Gds 1951–53; CA; trainee Dixon Wilson 1953–58, Peat Marwick (NY and Toronto) 1959–60, ptnr Hill Chaplin & Co (stockbrokers) 1961–68, chm and chief exec offr Williams De Broe PLC 1984–93 (dir 1968–93), chm BWD Securities plc 1995– (dir 1994–); memb Cncl Stock Exchange 1979–86, dir Securities Assoc 1986–91 (chm Capital Ctee); FCA 1958; *Recreations* tennis, golf, shooting; *Clubs* White's, Swinley Forest Golf, All Woodley Golf; *Style*— Peter Stanley, Esq; ✉ Cundall Hall, Helperby, Yorks YO6 2RP (☎ 01423 360252)

STANLEY, Hon Richard Morgan Oliver; s of Lt-Col the Hon Oliver Stanley, DSO (d 1952), and Lady Kathleen Thynne (d 1977), da of 5 Marquess of Bath; raised to rank of a Baron's s 1973; yr bro of 8 Baron Stanley of Alderley; *b* 30 April 1931; *Educ* Winchester, New Coll Oxford (MA); *m* 27 July 1956, Phyllida Mary Katharine, 3 da of Lt-Col Clive Grantham Austin, JP, DL (d 1974), of Micheldever, and Lady Lilian Lumley, sis of 11 Earl of Scarbrough; 2 s (Martin Thomas Oliver b 1957, Oliver Hugh b 1959), 2 da (Serena Emma Rose (Mrs Matthew Jebb) b 1961, Laura Sylvia Kathleen (Mrs David Barbour) b 1968); *Career* Lt Coldstream Gds 1950–51; dir: Metal Box Co Ltd 1979–85, UKPI (dep chm) 1985–86, Friends' Provident Instn 1986–, Pantheon Investment Participations plc 1987–, GA Properties Ltd 1988–92, Drawlane Transport Gp plc 1989–92; chm British Bus plc 1992–94; Warden Bradfield Coll; govr Thomas Coram Fndn; Freeman City of London, Liveryman Worshipful Co of Tinplate Workers; *Clubs* Boodle's; *Style*— The Hon Richard Stanley

STANLEY, Hon Richard Oliver; s and h of 8 Baron Stanley of Alderley; *b* 24 April 1956; *Educ* St Edward's Sch Oxford, Univ Coll London (BSc); *m* 1983, Carla, er da of Dr K T C McKenzie, of Solihull, 1 s (Oliver Richard Hugh b 1986 d 1989), 3 da (Maria Elizabeth Jane b 1988, Imogen Alexandra Ruth b 1990, Hermione Helena Rose b 1992); *Style*— The Hon Richard Stanley

STANLEY OF ALDERLEY, 8 Baron (UK 1839); Sir Thomas Henry Oliver Stanley; 14 Bt (E 1660), DL (Gwynedd 1985); also Baron Sheffield (I 1783) and Baron Eddisbury of Winnington (UK 1848); s of Lt-Col the Hon Oliver Hugh Stanley, DSO, JP, DL (d 1952, s of 4 Baron; descended from Sir John Stanley of Weever, yr bro of 1 Earl of Derby), and Lady Kathleen, *née* Thynne (d 1977), da of 5 Marquess of Bath; suc cous, 7 Baron (who preferred to be known as Lord Sheffield) 1971; *b* 28 Sept 1927; *Educ* Wellington Coll; *m* 30 April 1955, Jane Barrett, da of late Ernest George Hartley; 3 s (Richard, Charles, Harry), 1 da (Lucinda); *Heir* s, Hon Richard Stanley; *Career* Capt (ret) Coldstream Gds and Gds Ind Parachute Co; farmer in Anglesey and Oxfordshire; chm Thames Valley Cereals Ltd 1979–81; govr St Edwards Sch Oxford 1979–, memb RNLI Ctee of Mgmnt 1981– (chm Fund Raising Ctee 1986–94); sits as Cons in House of Lords; *Recreations* sailing, fishing, skiing; *Clubs* Farmers'; *Style*— The Rt Hon the Lord Stanley of Alderley, DL; ✉ Trysglwyn Fawr, Rhosybol, Amlwch, Anglesey (☎ 01407 830 364); Rectory Farm, Stanton St John, Oxford (☎ 0186 351214)

STANLEY PRICE, His Hon Peter; QC (1956); s of Herbert Stanley Price (d 1957); *b* 27 Nov 1911; *Educ* Cheltenham, Exeter Coll Oxford; *m* 1, 1946, Harriett Ella Theresa, *née* Pownall (d 1948); 2 s (twins); m 2, 1950, Margaret Jane, wid of William Hebditch (d 1941); 1 da; *Career* called to the Bar Inner Temple 1936, bencher 1963; recorder: Pontefract 1954, York 1955, Kingston-upon-Hull 1958; chm N Riding of Yorks QS 1958–70, judge of appeal Jersey and Guernsey 1964–69, recorder Sheffield 1965–69, circuit judge (formerly judge of Central Criminal Ct) 1969–84; pres Nat Reference Tbnl: Conciliation Scheme for Deputies employed in Coal-Mining Industry 1967–79, Conciliation Scheme for Coal-Mining Industry 1979–83; *Recreations* birds and trees, gardening, shooting; *Clubs* Brooks's; *Style*— His Honour Peter Stanley Price, QC; ✉ Church Hill, Great Ouseburn, York (☎ 01423 330252)

STANSALL, Paul James; s of James Douglas Stansall (d 1984), of Newark, Notts, and Vera Jean, *née* Hall; *b* 21 Sept 1946; *Educ* Winifred Portland Secdy Tech Sch Worksop Notts, RCA (MA), Leicester Poly (DipArch); *m* 1 Jan 1970 (m dis 1993), Angela Mary, da of Alexander Burgon (d 1954), of Beeston, Notts; 1 da (Alexandra b 1984); *Career* res asst Univ Coll London (memb Space Syntax Res Team) 1975–80, assoc DEGW Architects Planners and Designers (memb ORBIT 2 Team) 1980–89, visiting prof Cornell Univ 1987–88, founding ptnr Allinson Stansall Partnership conslt architects 1989–90, dir Tectus Architecture Ltd 1991–; visiting tutor in property mgmnt Civil Service Coll 1991–, visiting lectr UCL and Univ of Strathclyde 1993; memb Editorial Bd Jl of Property Mgmnt 1993; conslt to Nat Audit Office and various govt depts on space use and mgmnt; published numerous res papers and articles 1974–; memb Labour Pty; RIBA 1987, memb ARCUK 1981; *Recreations* history of science, walking, cooking; *Style*— Paul Stansall, Esq; ✉ 59 Dukes Avenue, London N10 2PY (☎ 0181 444 4586); Tectus Architecture Ltd, 8–9 Stephen Mews, London W1P 1PP (☎ 0171 436 4050, fax 0171 436 8451)

STANSBIE, (John) Michael; s of John Albert Stansbie, MBE, of Willersey, Nr Broadway, Worcs, and Norah Lydia, *née* Hopkins; *b* 2 Oct 1941; *Educ* Bolton Sch, Christ Church Oxford (MA), Middlesex Hosp Med Sch (BM BCh); *m* 12 April 1969, Patricia, da of Joseph Arthur Dunn of St Arvans, Chepstow, Gwent; 2 s (Nicholas b 1973, Nigel b 1975); *Career* house surgn Middlesex Hosp London 1967, house physican Hillingdon Hosp Middlesex 1967–68, casualty offr Kettering Gen Hosp 1969, ENT registrar and sr ENT house offr Queen Elizabeth Hosp Birmingham 1970–71, sr ENT registrar West Midlands Trg Scheme 1972–76, conslt ENT surgn Walsgrave Hosps NHS Tst Coventry 1977–; West Midlands regnl advsr in otolaryngology RCS 1988–94, chm W Midlands Region Trg Sub-Ctee in Otolaryngology 1991–94, sec Midland Inst of Otology 1981–90; chm Coventry and Dist Branch Br Cactus and Succulent Soc 1987–90; FRCS 1972, FRSM 1977; *Recreations* natural history, cactus collecting and judging; *Style*— Michael Stansbie, Esq; ✉ 76 Bransford Ave, Cannon Park, Coventry CV4 7EB (☎ 01203 416755); ENT Department, Walsgrave Hospital, Clifford Bridge Rd, Coventry (☎ 01203 538966)

STANSBY, John; s of Dumon Stansby (d 1980), and Vera Margaret, *née* Main (d 1972); *b* 2 July 1930; *Educ* Oundle, Jesus Coll Cambridge (scholar, MA); *m* 22 July 1966, Anna-Maria, da of Dr Harald Kruschewsky; 1 da (Daniela b 1967), 1 step s (Oliver b 1957), 1 step da (Veronica b 1960); *Career* Nat Serv cmmnd Queen's Royal Regt with Somaliland Scouts Br Somaliland 1949–50, Essex Regt TA 1950–55; domestic fuels mktg mangr Shell Mex & BP Ltd 1955–62, sr mktg conslt AIC Ltd 1962–65, dir Rank Leisure Services Ltd 1966–70, dir Energy Div P&O Steam Navigation Co 1970–74; chm: Dumon Stansby & Co Ltd 1974–, UIE (UK) Ltd (Bouygues Offshore) 1974–, SAUR (UK) Ltd 1986–89, Bouygues (UK) Ltd 1986–91, Cementation-SAUR Water Services PLC 1986–88, SAUR Water Services plc 1988–89, London Minsk Development Co plc 1993–96; dep chm: London Tport Exec 1978–80, Energy Resources Ltd 1990–92; FInstPet, FCIT, FRSA; *Recreations* music, theatre, swimming; *Clubs* Travellers; *Style*— John Stansby, Esq; ✉ 19 Brook Green, London W6 7BL (☎ 0171 603 0886, fax 0171 602 7488)

STANSFIELD, George Norman; CBE (1985, OBE 1980); s of George Stansfield (d 1975), of Cheadle Hulme, and Martha Alice, *née* Leadbetter; *b* 28 Feb 1926; *Educ* Liscard HS; *m* 1947, Elizabeth Margaret, da of Hugh Williams, of Colwyn Bay, Clwyd; *Career* RAF 1944–47; Miny of Food and Supply 1948–58; personal asst to: Dir-Gen of Armaments Prodn War Office 1958–61, Cwlth Rels Office 1961–62; HM Dip Serv 1965: second sec Calcutta 1962–66 and Port of Spain 1966–68, first sec FCO 1968–71 and (Commercial) Singapore 1971–74; special aide to Earl Mountbatten of Burma on visits to Singapore in 1972 and 1974; HM consul: Durban 1974–78, FCO 1978; cnsllr 1980, head Overseas Estate Dept FCO 1980–82, Br high cmmr Solomon Islands 1982–86, conslt Training Dept FCO 1986–; *Recreations* sailing, cine photography, wild life; *Clubs* Royal Southampton Yacht, Civil Serv; *Style*— George Stansfield, Esq, CBE; ✉ Deryns Wood, Westfield Rd, Woking, Surrey (☎ 01483 728678)

STANSFIELD, Lisa; da of Keith Stansfield, and Marion, *née* Kelly; *b* 11 April 1966; *Educ* Redbrook Middle Sch and Oulder Hill Community Sch Rochdale Lancs; *partner* Ian Owen Devaney; *Career* pop singer; formed band Blue Zone (with Andy Morris and Ian Devaney) 1986; solo albums: Affection (UK no 2) 1989, Real Love 1991 (jt album sales of over 8m), So Natural (1993); recorded version of Cole Porter's Down In The Depths for Red Hot and Blue LP (raising funds for Aids Research) 1990; numerous maj tours 1990–92 incl Rock in Rio concert (audience 100,000) 1990 and world tour (UK, Europe, N America, Japan and SE Asia) 1992; other charity work: Trading Places (breast cancer), Prince's Tst, Simple Truth concert (for the Kurds), Red Hot and Blue and Red Hot and Dance, Freddie Mercury Tribute concert for Aids Awareness (Wembley Stadium, audience 75,000) 1992; *Awards* Best Female Artist BRIT Awards 1990–91 and 1991–92 (Best Newcomer 1989–90), Best Contemporary Song (All Around The World) Ivor Novello Awards 1990, Best Int Song Ivor Novello Awards 1991, Best New Artist Silver Clef Awards 1990, Best Newcomer US Billboard Awards 1990, Best New Female Singer Rolling Stone magazine 1991, Best Br Artist World Music Awards Monte Carlo 1991, two Grammy Award nominations 1991; *Recreations* painting, cooking, crosswords, drinking; *Style*— Ms Lisa Stansfield; ✉ c/o 24 Madrid Road, Barnes, London SW13 9PD (☎ 0181 748 5591)

STANSFIELD SMITH, Sir Colin; kt (1993), CBE (1988); s of Mr Stansfield Smith, and Mary, *née* Simpson; *b* 1 Oct 1932; *Educ* William Hulmes GS, Univ of Cambridge (MA, DipArch); *m* 17 Feb 1961, Angela Jean Earnshaw, da of Eric Maw (d 1970), of Rustington, Sussex; 1 s (Oliver b 1970), 1 da (Sophie b 1967); *Career* Nat Serv Intelligence Corps 1951–53; ptnr Emberton Tardrew & Partners 1965–71, dep co architect Cheshire CC 1971–73, co architect Hants 1973, prof of architectural design Sch of Architecture Portsmouth Univ 1990; vice pres RIBA 1983–86; chm Estates Sub Ctee MCC 1978–84; Royal Gold Medal for Architecture RIBA 1991; ARIBA; *Recreations* painting, golf; *Clubs* MCC, Hockley Golf; *Style*— Prof Sir Colin Stansfield Smith, CBE; ✉ Three Minsters House, 76 High Street, Winchester, Hants SO23 8UL (☎ 01962 847800)

STANSGATE, Viscountcy of; *see:* Benn, Rt Hon Anthony Neil Wedgwood, MP

STANTON, David; *b* 5 Nov 1942; *Educ* Worcester Coll Oxford (BA), LSE (MSc); *Career* Nuffield fell Central Planning Bureau Uganda 1965–67, lectr Brunel Univ 1967–70, on staff Highway Economics Unit Miny of Tport 1970–71, economic advsr DOE 1971–74, economic advsr HM Treasy 1974–75, seconded as sr economic advsr Hong Kong Govt 1975–77; Dept of Employment: sr economic advsr Unit for Manpower Studies 1977–80, economic analyst Economics Branch 1980–83, dir EMRU 1983–87, chief economist 1988–92; dir Analytical Servs Div DSS 1992–; *Style*— David Stanton, Esq; ✉ Analytical Services Division, Department of Social Security, The Adelphi, 1–11 John Adam Street, London WC2N 6HT (☎ 0171 962 8611, fax 0171 962 8795)

STANTON, Stuart Lawrence; s of Michael Arthur Stanton (d 1968), and Sarah, *née* Joseph; *b* 24 Oct 1938; *Educ* City of London Sch, London Hosp Med Sch (MB BS); *m* 1, 25 Feb 1965; 3 da (Claire b 1967, Talia b 1970, Joanna b 1972); m 2, 17 Feb 1991; 1 s (Noah b 1994), 1 da (Tamara b 1991); *Career* conslt urogynaecologist St George's Hosp 1984–, hon sr lectr St George's Hosp Med Sch 1984–; assoc Br Assoc of Urological Surgns; memb: Blair Bell Res Soc, Int Continence Soc; MRCS LRCP 1961, FRCS 1966, FRCOG 1987; *Books* Clinical Gynaecologic Urology (1984), Surgery of Female Incontinence (co ed with Emil Tanagho, 1986), Principles of Gynaecological Surgery (1987), Gynaecology in the Elderly (1988), Gynaecology (co-ed, 1992); *Recreations* photography, travel, opera, theatre; *Style*— Stuart Stanton, Esq; ✉ Flat 10, 43 Wimpole St, London W1M 7AF (☎ 0171 486 0677, fax 0171 486 6792)

STAPLE, Alan Edward; s of William Staple, of Stoke-sub-Hamdon, and Elizabeth Paula, *née* Blakey-Milner (d 1989); *b* 21 April 1960; *Educ* Helston Sch, Brunel Univ (BSc, pt/t MEng, Metal Box prize), Univ of Bath (pt/t MBA); *m* 25 Sept 1982, Amanda Jayne, da of Colin Beck; 1 s (Henry William b 4 April 1991), 1 da (Laura Roseanna b 20 July 1988); *Career* Westland Helicopters: undergraduate apprentice 1978–83, control systems engr 1983–85, project ldr (Active Vibration Control) 1985–91, asst chief systems engr 1991–94, chief electrical systems engr 1994–; Archimedes Award (jtly) for innovative advance in product design made possible by electronic control 1988, Howard Hughes Award American Helicopter Soc 1990; *Style*— Alan Staple, Esq; ✉ Westland Helicopters Ltd, Yeovil, Somerset BA20 2YB (☎ 01935 703876, fax 01935 702042)

STAPLE, Rev David; OBE (1995); s of William Hill Staple (d 1983), and Elsie, *née* King (d 1984); *b* 30 March 1930; *Educ* Watford Boys' GS, Christ's Coll Cambridge (Bishop Gell's Hebrew Prize 1953, MA), Regent's Park and Wadham Coll Oxford (MA), Univ of London (external BD); *m* 23 July 1955, Margaret Lilian, da of Wilfred Ernest Berrington (d 1975); 1 s (Martin Hugh b 1958), 3 da (Rosemary Jane (Mrs Sherwood) b 1961, Eleanor Ruth (Mrs White) b 1962, Hilary Margaret (Mrs Hines) b 1964); *Career* Baptist minister: West Ham Central Mission 1955–58, Llanishen Cardiff 1958–74, College Road Harrow 1974–86; gen sec Free Church Fed Cncl 1986–96 (gen sec emeritus 1996–); Baptist Missionary Soc Gen Ctee: memb 1965–83, chm 1981–82, hon life memb 1983–; memb: Cncl Regent's Park Coll Oxford 1964–, Governing Body Regent's Park Coll Oxford

1967–, Baptist Union Cncl 1970–96; govr Westhill Coll Birmingham 1986–96; FRSA 1995; *Recreations* fellwalking, music; *Style—* The Rev David Staple, OBE; ✉ 1 Althorp Road, St Albans, Hertfordshire AL1 3PH (☎ 01727 810009, fax 01727 867888)

STAPLE, George Warren; CB (1996); s of Kenneth Harry Staple, OBE (d 1978), and Betty Mary, *née* Lemon; bro of William Philip Staple, *qv*; *b* 13 Sept 1940; *Educ* Haileybury; *m* Jan 1968, Olivia Deirdre, da of William James Lowry (d 1952), of Mtoko, Southern Rhodesia; 2 da (Alice b 1969, Polly b 1970), 2 s (Harry b 1976, Edward b 1978); *Career* admitted slr 1964; ptnr Clifford Chance (formerly Clifford-Turner) 1967–92; DTI inspr: Consolidated Gold Fields plc 1986, Aldermanbury Trust plc 1988 (reported Dec 1990); dir the Serious Fraud Office 1992–; chm of tbnls Securities and Futures Authy 1988–92; memb: Commercial Court Ctee 1978–92, Court of Govrs London Guildhall Univ 1982–94, Cncl Law Soc 1986– (treas 1989–92); *Recreations* cricket, hill walking; *Clubs* Brooks's, City of London, MCC; *Style—* George Staple, Esq, CB; ✉ Serious Fraud Office, Elm House, 10–16 Elm Street, London WC1X 0BJ (☎ 0171 239 7300, fax 0171 837 1689)

STAPLE, William Philip; s of Kenneth Harry Staple, OBE (d 1978), and Betty Mary, *née* Lemon; bro of George Warren Staple, CB, *qv*; *b* 28 Sept 1947; *Educ* Haileybury, Law Soc Coll of Law; *m* 14 May 1977 (m dis 1986), Jennifer Frances, da of Brig James Douglas Walker, OBE, of Farnham; 1 s (Oliver b 1980), 1 da (Sophia b 1982); *Career* called to the Bar 1970, exec Cazenove & Co 1972–81, dir N M Rothschild and Sons Ltd 1986–94 (asst dir 1982–86), DG Panel on Takeovers and Mergers 1994–96, returned as dir N M Rothschild and Sons 1996–; non-exec dir Grampian Holdings plc 1984–91; *Recreations* fishing, tennis, theatre; *Clubs* White's, City of London; *Style—* William Staple, Esq; ✉ N M Rothschild & Sons Ltd, New Court, St Swithin's Lane, London EC4P 4DU (☎ 0171 280 5000, fax 0171 280 5389)

STAPLES, (Hubert Anthony) Justin; CMG (1981); s of Francis Hammond (d 1970), of Sussex, and Catherine Margaret Mary, *née* Pownall (d 1981); *b* 14 Nov 1929; *Educ* Downside, Oriel Coll Oxford (MA); *m* 1962, Susan Angela, da of William Langston Collingwood Carter (d 1976), of Oxford; 1 s (Roderick), 1 da (Antonia); *Career* joined Dip Serv (formerly Foreign Serv) 1954, served in Bangkok, Berlin, Vientiane, Brussels (UK Delgn NATO) and Dublin; HM ambass: Bangkok 1981–86, Helsinki 1986–89, ret; pres Anglo-Finnish Soc 1993–; *Recreations* skiing, riding, golf; *Clubs* Travellers'; *Style—* Justin Staples, Esq, CMG; ✉ 48 Crescent Road, Kingston, Surrey KT2 7RF

STAPLETON, Anthony Elliott Hopewell; s of Lt-Col B A Stapleton, CBE, MC, TD, of Birralee, Manor Lane, Gerrards Cross, Bucks, and Ann Elliott, *née* Batt (d 1973); *b* 11 Aug 1940; *Educ* Wrekin Coll Wellington Shropshire; *m* 29 Aug 1964, Deana Mary, da of James McCauley; 1 s (Andrew Elliot b 7 April 1969); *Career* trainee Selfridges London 1958–61, asst mangr Lewis's Leicester 1961–62, asst buyer Lewis's London 1962, asst to Gen Mangr (on acquisition of Ilford Store) 1962–63, sales mangr Lewis's Bristol 1963–67, special accounts controller S Reece & Son Liverpool 1967–68; floor controller: Lewis's Liverpool 1969–70 (asst to Promotions Dir 1968–69), Lewis's Birmingham 1970–73; asst gen mangr: Lewis's Leicester 1973–74, Lewis's Birmingham 1974–76; gen mangr Selfridges Oxford 1976–79, merchandise dir Selfridges London 1979–85, gen mangr John Radcliffe Hosp Oxford 1985–93, Associated Nursing Services plc 1994–96, Speciality Care plc 1996–; chm Oxford Crime Prevention Ctee 1977–79, memb Oxford St Traders' Assoc 1979–85, memb Steering Ctee Better Made in Britain 1983, exec Textile Benevolent Assoc 1980–85, memb Clothing Panel NEDO 1980–85; *Recreations* family, home brewing, gardening, photography, travel; *Clubs* Oxford Management; *Style—* Anthony Stapleton, Esq; ✉ Cedars, Slade End, Brightwell cum Sotwell, nr Wallingford, Oxford OX10 0RQ (☎ 01491 38886); Speciality Care plc, Hamilton House, London EC4Y 0HA (mobile 0850 805986)

STAPLETON, David Eric Cramer; s of Edward Eric Stapleton (d 1957); *b* 7 Nov 1933; *Educ* Ampleforth, RAC Cirencester, Harvard Business Sch; *m* 1960, Annabel Alison, da of Sir Gerald Gordon Ley, 3 Bt, TD, of Lazonby Hall; 4 da; *Career* former ptnr W I Carr and memb Stock Exchange, ret; dir: Hunters of Brora, Scottish Asian Investment Trust, Marlin Fund Management UK Ltd; *Recreations* shooting, fishing; *Clubs* Buck's, Kildare Street; *Style—* David Stapleton, Esq; ✉ Armathwaite Place, Armathwaite, Carlisle, Cumbria (☎ 01697 472225); Marlin Fund Management UK Ltd, One Rosehill Business Park, Carlisle (☎ 01228 514144)

STAPLETON, Air Vice-Marshal Deryck Cameron; CB (1960), CBE (1948), DFC (1941), AFC (1939); s of John Rouse Stapleton, OBE (d 1985), of Sarnia, Natal; *Educ* King Edward VI Sch Totnes; *m* 1942, Ethleen Joan Clifford, da of Sir Cuthbert William Whiteside (d 1969); 3 s; *Career* joined RAF 1936, served Trans-Jordan and Palestine 1937–39, WWII ME, Sudan, N Africa, Iraq, UK and Italy, OC 14 Sqdn RAF 1940–41, OC 254 Wg RAF 1944–45, asst sec (Air) War Cabinet Offs 1945–46, sec COS Ctee MOD 1947–49; OC: RAF Odiham 1949–51, RAF Oldenburg 1955–57; dir Jt Plans Air Miny 1961–62, chm Jt Def Plans MOD 1963–64, Air Vice-Marshal 1963, AOC No 1 Gp Bomber Cmd 1964–66, Cmdt RAF Staff Coll Bracknell 1966–68, ret 1968; BAC area mangr Libya 1969–70, BAC rep Iran 1970–79, md Irano-Br Electronics 1978–79, BAe rep China and chm British Commercial Cos Assoc Peking 1979–83; *Style—* Air Vice-Marshal Deryck Stapleton, CB, CBE, DFC, AFC; ✉ c/o National Westminster Bank, Leicester Square, London WC2

STAPLETON, Very Rev Henry Edward Champneys; s of Edward Parker Stapleton, OBE (d 1971), of Hutton Buscel, Scarborough, N Yorks, and Frances Mary, *née* Champneys (d 1981); *b* 17 June 1932; *Educ* Lancing, Pembroke Coll Cambridge (MA), Ely Theol Coll; *m* 14 Nov 1964, Mary Deborah, da of Canon Baldwin Sparrow Sapwell (d 1981), of Attleborough, Norfolk; 2 da (Helen Mary Champneys Cooper b 1969, Catherine Jane Champneys b 1971); *Career* ordained: deacon 1956, priest 1957; curate St Olave's York 1956–59, Pocklington 1959–61; vicar Seaton Ross with Everingham and Bielby and Harswell 1961–67, rural dean Weighton 1966–67, rector Skelton 1967–75, vicar Wroxham & Hoveton St John 1975–81; priest i/c: Belaugh 1976–81, Hoveton St Peter 1979–81; canon residentiary and precentor Rochester Cathedral 1981–88, dean of Carlisle 1988–; memb: Churches Conservation Tst, Royal Cmmn on Historical MSS 1992–; church cmmr 1993–; tstee: Historic Churches Preservation Tst, Incorporated Church Bldg Soc; FSA 1976; *Books* Skelton Village - The Continuing Community (1971), A Skilful Master Builder (1975), Heirs Without Title (1974), The Model Working Parson (1976), Churchyards Handbook (3 edn, 1988); author of many articles & parish histories; *Recreations* archaeology, genealogy; *Style—* The Very Rev the Dean of Carlisle, FSA; ✉ The Deanery, Carlisle, Cumbria CA3 8TZ (☎ 01228 23335)

STAPLETON, Wing Cdr (Erik) Julian; MBE (1981); s of Air Vice-Marshal Frederick Snowden Stapleton, CB, DSO, DFC (d 1974), and Anne Sofie, *née* Schibsted; *b* 5 Jan 1945; *Educ* Framlingham Coll, RAF Coll Cranwell; *m* 17 Nov 1973, Anne-Sofie, da of Björn Steenstrup, of Oslo, Norway; 1 s (Stephen b 1976), 1 da (Sonia b 1974); *Career* cmmnd RAF 1967; served UK, Peru, Hong Kong, Malta, Maldive Is, Europe, ADC to AOC in C Strike Cmd 1974–76, MOD Harrogate 1976–78, Unit Cdr RAF Church Fenton 1979, HQ RAF Support Cmd 1980–81, RAF Staff Coll 1982, MOD London 1983–84, Dir Staff RAF Staff Coll 1985–86, Station Cdr RAF Chilmark 1987–88, ret RAF 1988; Marshall of Cambridge: exec asst to chm 1988–89, head supply and support servs 1990–94, head of corp servs 1995–96; ind conslt 1996–; MCIPS, MInstPet, MIMgt; *Recreations* shooting, skiing, tennis, wind-surfing, philately; *Clubs* RAF, Den Norske; *Style—* Wing Cdr Julian Stapleton, MBE; ✉ Denham Hall, Denham, Bury St Edmunds, Suffolk IP29 5EL (☎ 01284 811188)

STAPLETON, Nigel John; s of Capt Frederick Ernest John Stapleton, of Winchmore Hill, London, and Katie Margaret, *née* Tyson; *b* 1 Nov 1946; *Educ* City of London Sch, Fitzwilliam Coll Cambridge (BA, MA); *m* 20 Dec 1982, Johanna Augusta, da of Johan Molhoek, of Vienna, Austria; 1 s (Henry James b 1988), 1 da (Elizabeth Jane Cornelia b 1990); *Career* Unilever plc: various commercial appts 1968–83, vice pres fin Unilever (United States) Inc 1983–86; dep chm Reed International plc 1994– (fin dir 1986–96), chm Reed Elsevier plc 1996– (chief fin offr 1993–96); non-exec dir Allied Domecq plc (Allied-Lyons plc until 1994) 1993–, chm Lexis-Nexis 1995–; memb Fin Reporting Review Panel; FCMA 1987 (ACMA 1972); *Recreations* classical music, travel, tennis, opera; *Clubs* United Oxford & Cambridge Univ; *Style—* Nigel Stapleton, Esq; ✉ Reed Elsevier plc, 6 Chesterfield Gardens, London W1A 1EJ (☎ 0171 491 8269, fax 0171 491 8311)

STARK, Sir Andrew Alexander Steel; KCMG (1975, CMG 1964), CVO (1965), DL (Essex 1981); s of Thomas Bow Stark (d 1917), and Barbara Black, *née* Steel (d 1954); *b* 30 Dec 1916; *Educ* Bathgate Acad, Univ of Edinburgh (MA); *m* 24 Aug 1944, (Helen) Rosemary Oxley, da of Lt-Col John Oxley Parker, TD (d 1981), of Faulkbourne, Essex; 3 s (Antony, Michael, Donald b 1953 d 1970); *Career* served WWII Green Howards and staff appts, Maj 1945; entered FO 1948; served Vienna, Belgrade, Rome, Bonn; ambass attached to UK mission UN 1968, under sec gen UN 1968–71, ambass Denmark 1971–76, dep under sec FCO 1976–78; dir: The Maersk Co 1978–90 (chm 1978–87), Scandinavian Bank 1978–88, Carlsberg Brewery 1980–87; advsr on Euro affrs to Soc of Motor Mfrs and Traders 1978–89; chm: Anglo-Danish Soc 1983–95, Anglo-Danish Trade Advsy Bd 1983–93, Rural Community Cncl of Essex 1990–93; pro chllr Univ of Essex 1983–95 (chm Cncl 1983–89), pres Br Assoc of Former UN Civil Servants 1989–94; Hon DUniv Essex 1990; Grosses Verdienstkreuz German Fed Republic 1965, Grand Cross Order of the Dannebrog (Denmark) 1974; *Recreations* shooting, golf; *Clubs* Travellers', MCC; *Style—* Sir Andrew Stark, KCMG, CVO, DL; ✉ Fambridge Hall, White Notley, Witham, Essex CM8 1RN (☎ 01376 583117)

STARK, Ian David; MBE (1989); s of late Alexander Ross Stark, and Margaret Barrie, *née* Grubb; *b* 22 Feb 1954; *Educ* Galashiels Acad; *m* 30 Nov 1979, Janet Dixon, da of Dr George Ballantyne McAulay; 1 s (Timothy b 8 Aug 1981), 1 da (Stephanie b 3 June 1980); *Career* three day eventer; team Silver medallist LA Olympics 1984, team Gold and individual Bronze medallist Euro Championships 1985, team Gold medallist World Championships 1986, champion Badminton Horse Trials 1986, team Gold and individual Silver medallist Euro Championships 1987, first and second place Badminton 1988, team Silver and Individual Silver medallist Seoul Olympics 1988, team Gold medallist Euro Championships 1989, team Silver and individual Silver medallist Stockholm World Championships 1990, individual and team Gold medallist Euro Championships Punchestown Ireland 1991, memb team Olympic Games Barcelona 1992 and Atlanta 1996; *Books* Flying Scott (with Janet Stark 1988), Murphy Himself & Glenburnie (with Janet Stark and Gillian Newsum 1992); *Clubs* British Horse Soc; *Style—* Ian Stark, Esq, MBE; ✉ Haughhead, Ashkirk, Selkirk, Borders TD7 4NS (☎ 01750 32238)

STARKEY, Sir John Philip; 3 Bt (UK 1935) of Norwood Park, Parish of Southwell and Co of Nottingham, DL (Notts 1981); s of Lt-Col Sir William Randle Starkey, 2 Bt (d 1977); *b* 8 May 1938; *Educ* Eton, Ch Ch Oxford (MA), Sloan fell London Business Sch; *m* 1966, Victoria Henrietta Fleetwood, da of late Lt-Col Christopher Herbert Fleetwood Fuller, TD; 1 s, 3 da; *Heir* s, Henry John Starkey b 13 Oct 1973; *Career* cmmnd Rifle Bde 1956–58; merchant banker and agriculturalist; with Antony Gibbs & Sons Ltd 1961–71; chm J L Maltby Ltd; JP Notts 1982–88; church cmmr 1985–91; High Sheriff of Notts 1987–88; memb Exec Ctee and chm E Midlands Region Nat Tst 1986–; chm Notts Branch Country Land Owners Assoc 1977–80; vice pres (UK) Confederation of European Agric 1988–; pres Newark Chamber of Commerce 1980–82; memb Ct Cncl Univ of Nottingham 1980–; memb Archbishop of Canterbury's Cmmn on Rural Areas (ACORA); *Recreations* cricket; *Style—* Sir John Starkey, Bt, DL; ✉ Norwood Park, Southwell, Notts NG25 0PF

STARKIE, Martin Sidney; s of Henry Starkie (d 1947), of Burnley, Lancs, and Pauline Anne, *née* Martin (d 1971); *b* 25 Nov 1922; *Educ* Burnley GS, Exeter Coll Oxford (BA, MA, pres John Ford Soc, fndr and first pres William Morris Soc, capt athletics, fndr and first pres OU Poetry Soc and OU Bdcasting Soc), LAMDA (ALAM); *Career* actor/dramatist and prodr/director; actor Shanklin Theatre Co 1947–48, actor and poetry reader BBC 1948, numerous leading roles BBC TV and Radio 1949–64, actor and dir Watergate Theatre London 1949–53, asst dir to Esmé Percy 1949–53, writer and presenter Schools TV (Rediffusion/ITV) 1962–65; chm and md: Classic Presentations Ltd 1960–, Chanticleer Presentations Ltd 1967–; fndr and dir Chaucer Festival: Canterbury 1985 (London 1987), Chaucer Centre Canterbury 1985–, Chaucer Heritage Tst 1992–; tstee Peter Nathan Cultural and Charitable Tsts 1967, memb Cncl Kensington Soc 1992, conslt Thorney Island Soc Westminster 1995; FRSA 1997; *Productions* trans (with D Rancic) Turgenev's Torrents of Spring (dramatised/prodr Oxford Playhouse 1959, adapted for BBC with Brian Deakin 1963), dramatised/dir A Beach of Strangers (Criterion London) 1967, prodr Holy Bedroc (by Kevin Sheldon & Sir Adrian Beecham, LAMDA) 1967; writer/prodr/dir numerous prodns of The Canterbury Tales incl: Oxford Playhouse (first stage version) 1964, Phoenix Theatre London (the musical) 1968, Eugene O'Neill Theatre NY (5 Tony nominations) 1969, TV series from The Canterbury Tales (BBC) 1969, Her Majesty's Theatre Melbourne 1976, Shaftesbury Theatre (Coghill 80th Birthday) 1979; prodn conslt for 12 international prodns 1969–73; recent dir/prodr credits incl: The Canterbury Tales (Arts Theatre) 1991, When Knights Were Bold (Mermaid Theatre), Man with Sparrow (White Bear Theatre, Brighton Marlborough Theatre) 1993, Killing Time (Jermyn Street Theatre), Aspects of Eve (Pentameters Theatre Hampstead) 1995, Love, Lust and Marriage (Gulbenkian Theatre Canterbury 1995, Arts Theatre Lodnon 1996); *Recordings* incl: Shakespeare's Sonnets and Scenes from the Plays (HMV Victor Records) 1964, The Canterbury Pilgrims (Polydor/DGG (Grammy nomination for Best Spoken Word Recording)) 1968, The Death of Patroclus with Vanessa Redgrave (77 Records) 1968, The Canterbury Tales with Prunella Scales 1982 (EMI, re-issued 1995), The Canterbury Tales with Fenella Fielding (Durkin/Hayes Canada) 1995; conslt Chaucer's Work, Life and Times (CD-ROM for Primary Source Media) 1995; *Publications* Oxford Poetry (ed with Roy MacNab, 1946), Canterbury Tales (the musical with Nevill Coghill, 1968), More Canterbury Tales (the musical with Nevill Coghill, 1976), Officina Bodoni ed of Chaucer's Prologue (Chanticleer Presentations Ltd, 1989); *Recreations* reading, listening to chamber music, playing the piano, people, cats, travel; *Clubs* Arts Theatre, Oxford University; *Style—* Martin Starkie, Esq; ✉ Chaucer Heritage Centre, 22 St Peter's Street, Canterbury, Kent CT1 2BQ (☎ 01227 470379, fax 01227 761416)

STARKIE, (Thomas) Oliver Matthew; s of Dr Ernest Thomas Winstanley Starkie, and Nancey Elizabeth, *née* Colvin; *b* 1 May 1943; *m* 5 Oct 1968, Joan, da of James Ian Ogilvie Brewster, of Short Hill, Livesey Rd, Ludlow, Shropshire; 1 s (Christopher James Winstanley b 10 Sept 1971), 1 da (Claire Anne b 24 March 1977); *Career* CA; sr ptnr Starkie & Ptnrs; FCA 1968, ATII 1968; *Recreations* lawn tennis, lacrosse; *Style—* Oliver Starkie, Esq; ✉ 7A Harlestone Rd, Northants NN5 7AE (☎ 01604 750080, fax 01604 759927)

STARKIN, Ivan; s of Julian Starkin (d 1972), and Anne Mary, *née* Lewis (d 1978); *b* 3 Dec 1935; *Educ* Northern Poly Sch of Architecture (DipArch); *m* 1, 27 March 1960, Lucille Maureen; 2 s (Stewart b 17 July 1961, Jeremy b 11 April 1964), 2 da (Emma b 31 March 1966, Caroline b 22 Oct 1970); m 2, 1 Sept 1976, Jacqueline Susan, *née* Wills; 1 s (Ben b 23 July 1982), 1 da (Samantha b 5 July 1980); *Career* architect, md ICSA Ltd 1982– (specialist in office devpts and private hosps); ARIBA; *Recreations* painting and sketching, theatre; *Style—* Ivan Starkin, Esq; ✉ ISCA Ltd, Crips House, 4–8 Whites Grounds, London SE1 3LA (☎ 0171 407 0011 and 0181 693 1122, fax 0171 407 0033, car 0831 402493)

STARLING, David Henry; s of Brig John Sieveking Starling, CBE (d 1986), of Jersey, and Vivian Barbara, *née* Wagg (d 1983); *b* 11 Aug 1935; *Educ* Eton; *m* 1 Aug 1967, Judith Penelope, er da of Sir Laurence Lindo, GCVO, CMG, OJ; 1 s (Christopher Henry Boris b 9 Aug 1969), 1 da (Belinda Jane 7 April 1972); *Career* cmmnd RN 1953–58; sr ptnr Galloway & Pearson stockbrokers 1983–84 (joined 1959), dir W I Carr Group following takeover of Galloway & Pearson 1984–94, conslt Hambros Equities UK Ltd 1994; memb Cncl Stock Exchange 1975–79; *Recreations* sailing, ceramics; *Clubs* Boodle's, Royal Naval Sailing Assoc; *Style—* David Starling, Esq

STARLING, Melvin James; s of James Albert Starling, and Jean, *née* Craddock; *b* 15 July 1954; *Educ* Vyners GS Andover, UCL (BSc, DipArch); *m* 26 July 1978, Miriam Claire; 1 da (Jemma Alice b 23 May 1984), 1 s (Thomas William b 15 May 1986); *Career* ptnr Pringle Brandon Architects 1986–; RIBA 1985; *Recreations* golf, sport, family; *Clubs* RAC; *Style—* Melvin Starling, Esq; ✉ Pringle Brandon Architects, 10 Bonhill Street, London EC2M 2PS (☎ 0171 377 6782, fax 0171 247 5600)

STARMER-SMITH, Nigel Christopher; s of Harry Starmer-Smith, and Joan Mary, *née* Keep (d 1985); *b* 25 Dec 1944; *Educ* Magdalen Coll Sch Oxford, Univ Coll Oxford (MA, rugby blues); *m* 25 Aug 1973, Rosamund Mary, da of Wallace Bartlett; 1 da (Charlotte Alice Mary b 2 May 1975 d 1991); 2 s (Charles Jeremy Nigel b 5 June 1978, Julian Edward Giles b 9 April 1982); *Career* schoolmaster Epsom Coll Surrey 1967–70, BBC Radio Outside Bdcasts 1970–73, sports commentator and presenter BBC TV (mainly rugby union and hockey) 1973–, ed in chief Rugby World magazine 1984–93; minister's rep on Southern Sports Cncl 1989–93; *Former Sportsman* rugby: Oxford Univ, Oxfordshire, Harlequins, Surrey, Barbarians, England; hockey: Oxford Univ, Oxfordshire; cricket: Territorial Army; *Books* The Official History of the Barbarians (1977), Rugby - A Way of Life (1986); numerous rugby annuals and books; *Recreations* tennis, golf, piano-playing, family; *Clubs* Leander, Harlequin FC, Wig & Pen; *Style—* Nigel Starmer-Smith, Esq; ✉ c/o BBC Sport & Events Group, Kensington House, Richmond Way, London W14 0AX

START, Glenn William; s of William Alfred John Start, of Leytonstone, and Marjorie Masie, *née* Short; *b* 23 Jan 1950; *Educ* Aveley Tech HS; *m* 20 Aug 1972, Pauline Maria Olga, *née* Beckman; 1 da (Felicity Louise b 30 Aug 1980), 1 s (Gregory William b 5 May 1982); *Career* articled clerk Elliotts CAs (became Kidsons Impey 1990) 1967–74, CA 1974, ptnr 1976, memb Kidsons Nat Exec 1989, managing ptnr East region 1990– (London 1989); Freeman City of London 1989, Liveryman Worshipful Co of Gold and Silver Wyre Drawers 1990; FCA; *Clubs* City Livery; *Style—* Glenn Start; ✉ Kidsons Impey, Carlton House, 31–34 Railway Street, Chelmsford, Essex CM1 1NJ (☎ 01245 269595, fax 01245 354285)

STARY, Erica Frances Margaret; da of Eric Halstead Smith (d 1987), and Barbara Maud, *née* Creeke (d 1947); *b* 20 Jan 1943; *Educ* Hunmanby Hall, LSE (LLM); *m* 1, 1966; m 2, 1971, Michael McKirdy Anthony Stary, s of John Henry Stary (presumed dead 1939); 1 da (Philippa b 1977); *Career* admitted slr 1965; lectr then sr lectr Coll of Law 1966–73, Inland Revenue 1974–75, asst ed then ed British Tax Review 1976–, tech offr Inst of Taxation 1981–86, city lawyer 1986– (currently in own tax practice), dep district judge 1994–, asst recorder 1996–; frequent lectr and author on taxation matters; memb Nat Ctee of Young Slrs 1969–77, chm London Young Slrs Gp 1972, dir Slrs Benevolent Assoc 1973–77, dir and tstee London Suzuki Group and Tst 1984–89, asst clerk then clerk Second East Brixton Gen Cmmrs of Income Tax 1987–; memb Cncl: Chartered Inst of Taxation 1989– (chm Technical Ctee 1993–94), Assoc of Taxation Technicians 1991– (pres 1994–95); tstee: Nat Children's Orch 1989–, Tax Advsrs Benevolent Assoc 1996–; Liveryman City of London Solicitors' Co, memb Ct of Assts Guild of Tax Advrs 1995–; FTII 1984; *Recreations* sailing, music, theatre; *Style—* Mrs Michael Stary; ✉ Erica Stary & Co, PO Box 56, London N1 9BH

STARZEWSKI, Tomasz Jacek; s of Wojtek Starzewski, of London, and Maria Piotrowicz Starzewska; *b* 13 Aug 1961; *Educ* Emmanuel Sch, St Martin's Sch of Art; *Career* fashion designer (couture/ready-to-wear); worked from parents' home before moving to Fulham, opened first shop Old Brompton Rd 1990, second shop subsequently opened Pont Street (exclusively for bridal and couture collections); launched The House of Tomasz Starzewski Pont St 1991 (The Asprey Group being majority shareholders since 1993), opened new flagship store Sloane Street 1996; exports to USA, Canada, Europe, Middle and Far East; Br Fashion Awards: nominee Best Couture Designer 1990, subsequently nominee Glamour Category 3 times; *Recreations* cooking, bridge, travelling, antique hunting, the art of conversation; *Clubs* Tramps; *Style—* Tomasz Starzewski, Esq; ✉ The House of Tomasz Starzewski, 177–178 Sloane Street, London SW1X 9QL (☎ 0171 235 4526)

STASSINOPOULOS, Mary; da of John Stassinopoulos (d 1975), of Athens, and Pauline, *née* Kalliodis; *b* 9 Jan 1943; *Educ* Greece, Geneva Univ; *m* 1, 1963 (m dis 1977), Michael E Xilas; 1 s (Elias b 1965), 1 da (Irene b 1967); m 2, 1985, John G Carras; *Career* fell Imperial Soc of Teachers of Dancing; dir Vacani Sch of Dancing (sch under patronage of HM Queen Elizabeth the Queen Mother), examiner and memb Ctee Cecchetti (classical ballet) Soc; *Recreations* theatre, classical music, reading; *Clubs* Harry's Bar; *Style—* Miss Mary Stassinopoulos; ✉ 20 Norfolk Rd, London NW8 6HG (☎ 0171 586 3691); Vacani School of Dancing, St Michael's House, 2 Elizabeth Street, London SW1W 9RB (☎ 0171 823 5461)

STATHAM, Sir Norman; KCMG (1977, CMG 1967), CVO (1968); s of Frederick Statham, and Maud, *née* Lynes; *b* 15 Aug 1922; *Educ* Seymour Park Cncl Sch, Manchester GS, Gonville and Caius Coll Cambridge; *m* 1948, Hedwig Gerlich; 1 s (and 1 s decd), 1 da; *Career* served WWII and Intelligence Corps until 1947; Manchester Oil Refinery Ltd and Petrochemicals Ltd 1948–50; FO (later FCO): joined 1951, head Euro Economic Integration Dept (rank of cnsllr) 1965–68 and 1970–71, consul-gen São Paulo 1968–70, min (econ) Bonn 1971–75, asst and dep under sec 1975–76, ambass Brazil 1977–79; vice pres British C of C in Germany 1981–85, pres COBCOE 1982–84, FCO special rep for Br-German Co-operation 1984–86; *Recreations* calligraphy, reading, birdwatching; *Style—* Sir Norman Statham, KCMG, CVO; ✉ 11 Underhill Park Rd, Reigate, Surrey RH2 9LU

STATON, Roger Anthony; s of Harry James Staton (d 1977), of Coventry, and Janet, *née* Palmer; *b* 25 Nov 1945; *Educ* Bablake Sch Coventry, Univ of Manchester (BSc); *m* 23 May 1970, Angela, da of Joseph Armstrong; 2 s (David b 14 Sept 1971, Adam b 5 Aug 1973); *Career* trg offr GEC Telecommunications Ltd Coventry 1968–69 (apprentice 1963–68), prodn ed The Rugby Review 1969–71, dep ed Radio Communication magazine; account exec: Scott Mactaggart Associates 1973–74, Golley Slater Public Relations 1974–75; fndr md Roger Staton Associates 1976–; dir: The Pegasus Press Ltd 1984–, The RSA Group Ltd 1985–, ArtHaus Visual Communications Ltd 1987–; MIPR; *Recreations* reading, classic cars, cooking, walking; *Clubs* Wig and Pen; *Style—* Roger Staton, Esq; ✉ Roger Staton Associates Ltd, Old Trinity Church, Trinity Road, Marlow, Bucks SL7 3AN (☎ 01628 487222, fax 01628 487223)

STAUGHTON, Rt Hon Lord Justice; Rt Hon Sir Christopher Stephen Thomas Jonathan Thayer Staughton; kt (1981), PC (1988); yr s of Simon Thomas Samuel Staughton, and Edith Madeline, *née* Jones; *b* 24 May 1933; *Educ* Eton, Magdalene Coll Cambridge; *m* 1960, Joanna Susan Elizabeth, see Lady Staughton, er da of George Frederick Arthur Burgess; 2 da; *Career* served 2 Lt 11 Hussars; called to the Bar Inner Temple 1957 (reader 1996, treas-elect 1997), QC 1970, recorder of the Crown Ct 1972–81, judge of the High Court of Justice (Queen's Bench Div) 1981–87, a Lord Justice of Appeal 1987–; *Style—* The Rt Hon Lord Justice Staughton; ✉ Royal Courts of Justice, Strand, London WC2A 2LL (☎ 0171 936 6000)

STAUGHTON, Lady; Joanna Susan Elizabeth; da of George Frederick Arthur Burgess (d 1963), and Lilian Margaret Colvin, *née* Bovill; *b* 29 Dec 1937; *m* 16 Aug 1960, Rt Hon Sir Christopher Stephen Thomas Jonathan Thayer Staughton, *qv*; 2 da (Catharine Elizabeth b 11 June 1961, Sarah Louisa Margaret (Mrs Niall Donaldson) b 17 May 1963); *Career* sch care worker Inner London 1966–71; chm Herts Family Health Services Authy 1987–96; memb: Inner London Juvenile Panel 1970 (chm 1992–94), Police Complaints Bd 1976–85, S Westminster PSD 1980–90, Cncl Child Accident Prevention Tst 1991–, Cncl Nat Children's Bureau 1991–, Cncl NAHAT 1993–96, Cncl Br Heart Fndn 1994–; pres: Relate (Watford) 1992–, Rickmansworth Scouts 1994–; memb St Albans Abbey Music Tst 1995–; govr various schs incl Francis Holland Schs 1971–; High Sheriff for Co of Hertfordshire 1994–95; Freeman City of London 1995; *Recreations* swimming, walking, needlework; *Style—* Lady Staughton; ✉ c/o Royal Courts of Justice, Strand, London WC2A 2LL

STAUGHTON, Dr Richard Charles David; s of Thomas Richard Staughton (d 1989), and Bardi Dorothy, *née* Cole (1989); *b* 15 Aug 1944; *Educ* Wellingborough Sch, Emmanuel Coll Cambridge (MA), Bart's Med Coll (MB BChir); *m* 1, 1979 (m dis 1988), Jenny, da of Sir Anthony Quayle (d 1989); 1 s (Jack Anthony b 29 Dec 1982); m 2, 1991, Clare, o da of Sir Mark Evelyn Heath, KCVO, CMG, *qv*; *Career* successively: house surgn then SHO Bart's, registrar King Edward VII Hosp Windsor, registrar (dermatology) St Thomas' Hosp, sr registrar (dermatology) Westminster Hosp, conslt dermatologist Addenbrooke's Hosp Cambridge; currently conslt dermatologist Chelsea and Westminster Hosp and hon conslt to King Edward VII Hosp for Offrs Beaumont St, Royal Hosp Chelsea and Royal Brompton Hosp; hon corresponding memb Soc Français de Dermatologie; memb: Br Assoc of Dermatologists, St John's Soc (pres 1987); FRCP; *Books* Cutaneous Manifestations of HIV Disease (1988), Vulval Disease (1994); *Recreations* gardening, matters Orcadian; *Clubs* Garrick; *Style—* Dr Richard Staughton; ✉ Chelsea and Westminster Hospital, 369 Fulham Road, London SW10 9NH; Lister Hospital, Chelsea Bridge Road, London SW1W 8RH (☎ 0171 730 8308, fax 0171 823 5541)

STAUGHTON, Simon David Howard Ladd; s of Simon Staughton (d 1967), and Madeline Somers-Cox, *née* Jones (d 1974); *b* 24 Jan 1931; *Educ* Eton; *m* 12 Oct 1957, Olivia Katharine, da of Egbert Cecil Barnes (d 1987); 1 s (James b 1959), 2 da (Julia b 1960, Fiona b 1963); *Career* 2 Lt 10 Royal Hussars (PWO); sr ptnr Lee & Pembertons solicitors 1986–96, chm St Austell Brewery Co Ltd; *Clubs* Cavalry and Guards'; *Style—* David Staughton, Esq; ✉ The Old Rectory, Latimer, Bucks HP5 1UA (☎ 01494 764567); 45 Pont Street, London SW1X 0BX (☎ 0171 589 1114)

STAUNTON, Edmund George; DL (Notts 1991); s of Maj Reginald Evelyn Boothby (d 1976), of Burwell Hall, Louth, Lincs, and Frances Katherine, *née* Staunton; assumed the name of Staunton by deed poll 1956; *b* 25 April 1943; *Educ* Eton, Royal Agric Coll; *m* 7 March 1970, Elizabeth Anne, da of John Peter Foster, OBE, of Harcourt, Hemingford Grey, Huntingdon; 2 s (William b 1972, Robert b 1974); *Career* farming and estate mgmnt; chm (Notts area) Country Landowners' Assoc 1984–86, pres (Notts area) Ramblers' Assoc 1987–90, pres (Notts area) Fedn of Young Farmers' Clubs 1990–91, pres (Notts area) Farming and Wildlife Advsy Gp 1992–, memb (Midland area) Landowners' Panel Agricultural Land Tbnl; ARICS 1970; *Style—* Edmund Staunton, Esq, DL; ✉ Staunton Hall, Near Orston, Nottingham

STAUNTON, Marie; da of Austin Staunton, of Grange-over-Sands, Cumbria, and Ann, *née* McAuley; *b* 28 May 1952; *Educ* Larkhill House Sch Preston Lancs, Univ of Lancaster (BA), Coll of Law; *m* 15 March 1986, James Albert Provan, s of William Provan, of Wallaceton, Bridge of Earn, Perthshire; 2 da (Lucy Maryanne b 1987, Amy Claire b 1994); *Career* slr; legal offr Nat Cncl for Civil Liberties, dir Br Section Amnesty Int (memb Int Exec Ctee); ed Solicitors Journal; publishing dir FT Law and Tax; FRSA; *Recreations* walking, gardening, children, theatre; *Style—* Ms Marie Staunton; ✉ 18 Grove Lane, London SE5 8ST (☎ 0171 701 9191); Longmans Law Tax and Finance, 21–27 Lamb's Conduit, London WC1N 3NJ (☎ 0171 242 2548, fax 0171 831 8119)

STAUNTON, Stephen (Steve); *b* 19 Jan 1969; *Career* professional footballer (defender); League debut on loan with Bradford; clubs: Liverpool 1986–91 (FA Cup winners 1989, League champions 1990), joined Aston Villa for £1.1m 1991– (League runners-up 1993, winners Coca Cola Cup 1994 and 1996); Ireland: 63 full caps; *Style—* Steve Staunton; ✉ Aston Villa FC, Villa Park, Trinity Road, Birmingham B6 6HE (☎ 0121 327 2299)

STAVELEY, Maj-Gen Robert; s of Brig Robin Staveley, DSO (d 1968), of Fleet, Hants, and Ilys Evelyn, *née* Sutherland (d 1977); *b* 3 June 1928; *Educ* Wellington, RMA Sandhurst, Staff Coll Camberley, RCDS; *m* 15 March 1958, Airlie Jane Rachel, da of Maj-Gen William H Lambert, CB, CBE (d 1978), of Dartmouth, Devon; 1 s (Robin b 3 Feb 1961), 1 da (Anabel Jane (Mrs Peter Merriman) b 9 March 1963); *Career* cmmnd RA 1948, BAOR 1948–51, ADC to GOC Malta 1951–53, Air OP pilot Malayan Emergency 1954–57 (despatches), ADC to GOC in C Northern Cmd 1957–58, Indian Staff Coll 1959, SO and missile battery cdr BAOR 1960–65, instr Staff Coll 1966–68, cmd 47 Lt Regt RA UK and Hong Kong 1969–71, CRA 2 Div BAOR 1973–74, RCDS 1975, COS Army Logistic Exec 1979–82, Col Cmdt RA 1982–87; controller and dir of admin Norton Rose slrs 1983–91; tstee and memb Cncl Douglas Haig Meml Homes 1982–97, govr Royal Sch Hampstead 1992– (chm of govrs 1993); memb Guild of Air Pilots and Air Navigators 1983, FIMgt 1983; *Recreations* offshore sailing, skiing, good food, music; *Clubs* Army and Navy, Royal Ocean Racing, Royal Artillery Yacht (Cdre 1980–83, Adm 1991–97); *Style—* Maj-Gen Robert Staveley; ✉ Cox & Kings, 7 Pall Mall, PO Box 1190, London SW1Y 5NA

STAVELEY, Adm of the Fleet Sir William Doveton Minet; GCB (1984, KCB 1981), DL (Kent 1992); s of Adm Cecil Minet Staveley, CB, CMG (d 1934), and Margaret Adela, *née* Sturdee (d 1960); gs of Gen Sir Charles Staveley and of Adm of the Fleet Sir Doveton Sturdee, Bt; *b* 10 Nov 1928; *Educ* West Downs, Winchester, RNC Dartmouth, RNC Greenwich; *m* 1954, Bettina Kirstine, da of L R A Shuter (d 1960); 1 s (Richard), 1 da (Juliet); *Career* joined RN 1942, served HM Yacht Britannia 1957, subsequently in Far East, Middle East and Mediterranean Cmdg HM Ships Houghton, Zulu, Intrepid and Albion, Dir Naval Plans Naval Staff 1974–76, Flag Offr 2 Flotilla 1976–77, Flag Offr Carriers and Amphibious Ships and NATO Cdr Carrier Striking Gp 2 1977–78, COS to C-in-C Fleet 1978–80, Vice Chief of Naval Staff 1980–82, Allied C-in-C Channel, C-in-C Eastern Atlantic Area and C-in-C Fleet 1982–85, Chief Naval Staff and First Sea Lord 1985–89, First and Princ Naval ADC to HM The Queen 1985–89; chm: Royal London Hosp and Assoc Community Servs NHS Tst 1991–92, Chatham Historic Dockyard Tst 1991–, Br Sch of Osteopathy 1991–96, NE Thames RHA 1993–94, N Thames RHA 1994–96; memb: Gen Cncl King Edward VII's Hosp Fund for London 1993–96, Cncl Univ of Kent 1992–, London Advsy Ctee English Heritage 1990–; govr Sutton Valence Sch 1990–92; pres Kent Branch Royal British Legion 1992–, a vice pres Falkland Islands Assoc 1991–; Freeman City of London, Liveryman Worshipful Co of Shipwrights, yr bro Trinity House; CIMgt; *Recreations* country sports, gardening,; *Clubs* Boodle's, RNSA;

Style— Adm of the Fleet Sir William Staveley, GCB, DL; ✉ Chatham Historic Dockyard Trust, The Historic Dockyard, Chatham, Kent ME4 4TE (☎ 01634 812551, fax 01634 826918)

STEADMAN, Anne Mary (Mrs Brian Mitchell); da of Victor William Arthur Sheppard, of Bognor Regis, Sussex, and Joyce Helen, *née* Carter; *b* 20 May 1947; *Educ* Colston's Girls' Sch Bristol; *m* 1, 1 Oct 1966 (m dis 1977), Christopher St Jermain Steadman, s of Brian St Jermain Steadman, TD (d 1961); 1 s (James b 1970), 1 da (Millie b 1972); m 2, Brian Edward Mitchell, s of Eric James Mitchell, of Middleton on Sea, Sussex; *Career* sr ed Financial Mail Johannesburg SA 1975–79, property corr Financial Weekly 1980–82; dir: Brian Mitchell Assocs Ltd 1982–85, City & Commercial Communications plc 1985–90; ARICS 1970 (hon sec 1971–73); *Recreations* most sports as a spectator, particularly football and cricket; *Style*— Ms Anne Steadman; ✉ 95 High St, Thames Ditton, Surrey (☎ 0181 398 0871)

STEADMAN, (Roger) Evan; s of Edward John Steadman (d 1982), and Nellie Maud, *née* Evans (d 1985); *b* 17 Aug 1938; *Educ* Ilford County HS; *m* 22 Dec 1963, Patricia, da of late Peter Reginald Hignett; 1 s (Ben Charles b 1965), 2 da (Rebecca Louise b 1967, Victoria Suki b 1976); *Career* fndr The Evan Steadman Communications Group (sold to Maxwell Communications 1988), currently chm Evan Steadman Productions Ltd; former chm: Maxwell Business Communications Group Ltd, MBC Exhibitions Ltd, Evan Steadman Communications Group, Bush Steadman & Partners Ltd (PR conslts), The Assoc of Exhibition Organisers; *Books* Earthquake (1968); *Recreations* producing musicals, sponsoring artists, doing nothing in the sunshine; *Style*— Evan Steadman, Esq; ✉ 37 Chelsea Crescent, London SW10 0XF (☎ 0171 352 1001); 15 Passage de la Trinité, Port la Galère, 06590 Théoule, France (☎ 00 33 93 75 02 21); Evan Steadman Productions Ltd, 12 Rose & Crown Walk, Saffron Walden, Essex CB10 1JH (☎ 01799 528292, fax 01799 528268, car 0831 484278)

STEADMAN, Howard Ian; s of Maurice Steadman, and Gertrude Steadman; *b* 17 Dec 1939; *Educ* Kilburn GS, Jesus Coll Oxford (MA); *m* 30 March 1969, Joy Elaine, da of Harry Fisher; 1 s (Richard b 1970), 2 da (Elizabeth b 1973, Victoria b 1980); *Career* McAnally Montgomery and Co stockbrokers 1966–74 (ptnr 1971–74), The British Petroleum Pension Trust Ltd 1974– (portfolio mangr 1982–); memb Stock Exchange 1971–74, AIIMR 1966; *Recreations* bridge, badminton, tennis; *Style*— Howard Steadman, Esq; ✉ BP Pension Services Ltd, Britannic House, 1 Finsbury Circus, London EC2M 7BA (☎ 0171 496 5609, fax 0171 496 5581, telex 94021211 BPPS G)

STEAFEL, Sheila; da of Harold Steafel, of S Africa, and Eda, *née* Cohen; *b* 26 May 1935; *Educ* Barnato Park Johannesburg Girls' HS, Univ of the Witwatersrand (BA), Webber Douglas Sch of Drama; *m* 1958 (m dis 1964), Harry H Corbett; *Career* actress; numerous TV series, one woman shows and radio; *Theatre* incl: Billy Liar 1960, How the Other Half Loves 1972, Harpo in A Day in Hollywood, revival of Salad Days 1976, A Night in the Ukraine 1979, with Players Theatre Old Time Music Hall 1979, Twelfth Night 1983, The Duenna 1983, the witch in Humperdinck's Hansel and Gretel 1983; RSC incl: Mistress Quickly in Merry Wives of Windsor 1985, Barbican season 1986, Ivanov 1989, Much Ado About Nothing 1989, Lady Tailbush in The Devil is an Ass 1995, Nurse in The Relapse 1995, Martha in Faust 1995; Façade with Mozart Players 1988–89; *Films* incl: Baby Love 1969, Some Will Some Won't 1969, Tropic of Cancer 1970, Percy 1971, SWALK 1971, The Waiting Room 1976, Bloodbath in the House of Death 1983; *Style*— Ms Sheila Steafel; ✉ 6 James Ave, London NW2 4AJ; c/o Scott Marshall Personal Management, 44 Perryn Road, London W3 7NA (☎ 0181 749 7692, fax 0181 740 7342)

STEANE, Dr Patricia Ann; da of George Glenwright (d 1989), and Louie Margery, *née* Hail (d 1963); *b* 3 April 1938; *Educ* Trowbridge Girls' HS, Hitchin Girls' GS, Royal Free Hosp Univ of London (MB BS); *m* 15 Oct 1960, Henry Alfred Steane, s of Alfred Steane (d 1986); 1 s (Robert b 2 June 1968), 1 da (Katherine b 23 Oct 1965); *Career* house surgn Royal Free Hosp 1962 (sr house offr anaesthetics 1963–64), house physician Bedford Gen Hosp 1963, registrar anaesthetics W Herts Hosp 1964–65, sr registrar anaesthetics Swansea Hosps 1971–77 (clinical asst 1966–70), conslt anaesthetist Singleton and Morriston Hosps Swansea 1977–, med dir Swansea NHS Tst 1993–; memb: Assoc of Anaesthetists, BMA, Welsh Med Ctee 1984–86, W Glamorgan Health Authy 1988–90; FFARCS 1971; *Recreations* tennis, music, swimming, skiing; *Clubs* Royal Over-Seas League; *Style*— Dr Patricia Steane; ✉ Medical Directors Office, Singleton Hospital, Sketty, Swansea SA2 8QA (☎ 01792 285166)

STEARNS, Michael Patrick; s of Cdr Eric Gascoyne Stearns, OBE, and Evelyn, *née* Sherry; *b* 19 Jan 1947; *Educ* Guy's Hosp Univ of London (BDS, MB BS); *m* Elizabeth Jane Elford Smith; *Career* registrar (later sr registrar) Guy's Hosp 1977–84; conslt head and neck surgn and otolaryngologist: Royal Free Hosp 1984–, Barnet Gen Hosp 1984–; sec Euro Acad of Facial Surgery 1989–; fell: Univ of Washington 1982, Univ of Oregon 1983; FRCS 1978, FRSM 1982; *Recreations* flying; *Style*— Michael Stearns, Esq; ✉ Suite 14, 30 Harley Street, London W1N 1AB (☎ 0171 631 4448)

STEARS, Michael John; s of Frank Albert Stears (d 1984), of Hastings, E Sussex, and Elsie Ellis, *née* Munns (d 1985); *b* 25 Aug 1934; *Educ* Harrow Art Coll, Southall Tech Coll; *m* 15 Sept 1960, Brenda Doreen, da of William Albert George Livy, of Stoke Poges, Bucks; 2 da (Jacqueline Anne b 2 March 1961, Janet Madeline b 6 July 1962); *Career* designer and creator of special effects for films; Nat Serv, served RMP (Signals) 1952–54; pres Br Sight Hound Field Assoc (BSFA); ACTT 1954, BKSTS 1979; pres 3 Jays Illusions Inc USA; *Films* incl: Reach for the Sky 1956, Carve Her Name with Pride 1958, Operation Amsterdam 1960, The Guns of Navarone 1961, Dr No 1962, Call Me Bwana 1963, From Russia With Love 1963, Goldfinger 1964, Thunderball (Oscar) 1965, You Only Live Twice 1967, Chitty Chitty Bang Bang 1968, OHMS 1969, Fiddler on the Roof 1971, The Pied Piper 1972, Theatre of Blood 1973, The Black Windmill 1974, That Lucky Touch 1975, One of Our Dinosaurs is Missing 1976, Star Wars (Oscar) 1977, The Martian Chronicles 1979, Outland 1980, Megaforce 1982, Sahara 1984, Haunted Honeymoon 1985, Murder by Illusion 1987, Navy SEALS 1988; *Recreations* breeding, showing & luring Russian wolf hounds, model aircraft; *Clubs* The Borzoi, The Northern Borzoi Assoc, Soc of Model Aeronautical Engrs, The Acad of Model Aeronautics (USA); *Style*— Michael Stears, Esq; ✉ 6 Crossways, Wilton Court, Park Lane, Beaconsfield, Bucks (☎ 01494 681795)

STEBLES, Andrew Gordon; s of Capt George Douglas Stebles (d 1983), and Stella Swan (d 1987); *b* 12 March 1950; *Educ* Queen Elizabeth GS Wakefield, Downing Coll Cambridge (BA, MA); *m* 20 Sept 1975, Diane Vivien, da of Gordon William Samuel Johnson of Bromely, Kent; 3 s (Paul Michael Alexander b 15 Aug 1979, Mark Christopher James b 9 July 1981, Jonathan Simon Philip b 17 March 1986); *Career* Blue Circle Industries plc: joined 1972, chief programmer 1978–80, systems assur and standards mangr 1980–83, data admin mangr 1983–85; database admin mangr Corp of Lloyds 1985–86, sr mangr Lloyds TSB Group plc (formerly Lloyds Bank plc) 1995– (sr devpt mangr 1986–95); *Recreations* cycling, swimming, gardening; *Style*— Andrew Stebles, Esq

STEDALL, Robert Henry; s of Lt-Col M B P Stedall, OBE, TD (d 1982), of Hurstgate, Milford, Godalming, Surrey, and Audrey Wishart, *née* Cottam; *b* 6 Aug 1942; *Educ* Marlborough, McGill Univ Montreal (BCom); *m* 24 June 1972, Elizabeth Jane (Liz), da of C J J Clay (d 1988), of Lambertts, Hascombe, Godalming, Surrey; 2 s (Oliver Marcus b 1976, James Robert b and d 1978), 1 da (Victoria Patricia b 1979); *Career* CA 1967 (articled McClelland Moores & Co 1964–68); Bowater Corporation Ltd 1968–82: cash controller 1968–72, fin dir Far E 1972–75; fin dir Ralli Bros Ltd 1975–82, md Engelhard Metals 1982–84, dir of fin designate Greenwell Montagu 1984–85, fin dir Gartmore Investment Management 1985–88, dir of admin Nat Employers Life Assurance Co Ltd 1989–91, dir and gen mangr Fin and Admin Lombard North Central plc 1992–96; chm Dunsfold Parish Cncl; Liveryman Worshipful Co of Ironmongers (Master 1989); *Recreations* gardening, tennis, golf, bridge; *Clubs* Boodle's; *Style*— Robert Stedall, Esq; ✉ Knightons, Dunsfold, Godalming, Surrey GU8 4NU (☎ 01483 200 245)

STEDMAN, John Edward Rooney; s of John Edward Stedman, MC (d 1983), of Blackheath, London, and Emily Rosina Yeo, *née* Rooney (d 1975); *b* 18 May 1936; *Educ* Rugby, Univ Coll London (BA); *Career* schoolmaster Stubbington House, King's Sch Worcester and Summerfields 1957–66, dir English Language Tutors Sussex 1967, sr ptnr English Language Tutors Madrid 1968–, dir European Holiday Courses SA Madrid 1968–; tstee Tello Fernandez Trust Madrid 1989–; landowner in Cumberland until 1989, 28 lord of the manor of Irthington Cumberland; reader C of E 1962–; memb: Inst of Heraldic and Genealogical Studies, Heraldry Soc, White Lion Soc, Prayer Book Soc; govr Corpn of the Sons of the Clergy 1993; FRSA 1963; *Recreations* art, heraldry, opera, country pursuits; *Clubs* Lansdowne; *Style*— John Stedman, Esq; ✉ Chateau de Malussen, Sarrazac 24800, France (☎ 00 33 5 53 52 24 06); Villaneuva 30, 28001 Madrid, Spain (☎ 00 34 1 577 8277); Santalucia Lovell, Serrano 1, 28001 Madrid, Spain

STEDMAN, Patricia Rosamund Kathleen; da of Capt Leonard Gordon Stedman, MC (d 1961), of SA, and Diana Josephine Steere (Mrs Maurice Ashley Brown, d 1980); *b* 17 Feb 1938; *Educ* St Mary's Gerrards Cross Bucks, Catherine Judson's Secretarial Coll London; *Career* secretarial and stockbroking asst J A Brewin (later Brewin Dolphin) London 1957–66, managing exec Brewin Dolphin country stockbrokers Jersey 1976–86 (fndr 1973), md Jersey Overseas Investment Management Ltd (formerly Strabo Investment Management Ltd) 1989 (fndr and md 1986), fndr Patricia Stedman Investment Management 1989; MSI 1993; *Recreations* riding and racing, sailing, travelling; *Clubs* Royal Channel Is Yacht; *Style*— Miss Patricia Stedman; ✉ The Stable Flat, Northdale, St Ouen, Jersey, Channel Islands JE3 2DU (☎ 01534 483122, fax 01534 485224)

STEED, Mark Wickham; s of Richard David Steed, and Jennifer Mary, *née* Hugh-Jones; gs of Henry Wickham Steed, editor of The Times; *b* 31 Oct 1952; *Educ* Downside; *m* 3 June 1989, Carola Dawn (m dis 1994), da of Dorian Joseph Williams, of Foscote Manor, Buckingham; *Career* CA; dir: Oxford Investments Ltd 1981–86, Beckdest Ltd 1981–88, Colt Securities Ltd 1983–95, Global Portfolio Management Ltd 1996–; MSI, MCIM; *Recreations* shooting; *Clubs* Naval and Military; *Style*— Mark Steed, Esq; ✉ Keepers Cottage, The Shaw, Leckhampstead, Buckingham MK18 5PA; 605 Nelson House, Dolphin Square, London SW1V 3NZ

STEEDMAN, Prof Carolyn Kay; da of Ellis Kay Pilling (d 1977), of Streatham Hill and Gypsy Hill, London, and Edna Dawson (d 1983); *b* 20 March 1947; *Educ* Rosa Bassett GS for Girls London, Sch of Eng and American Studies Univ of Sussex (BA), Newnham Coll Cambridge (MLitt, PhD); *m* 1971 (m dis 1986), Mark Jerome Steedman, s of George Steedman, of Newton-upon-Rawcliffe, Yorks; *Career* class teacher in primary schs in E Sussex and Warwicks 1974–81, project asst Schs Cncl Language in the Multicultural Primary Classroom Project Dept of Eng Univ of London Inst of Educn 1982–83, fell Sociological Res Unit Univ of London Inst of Educn 1983–84, reader Dept of Arts Educn Univ of Warwick 1991–93 (lectr 1984–88, sr lectr 1988–91), prof of social history Centre for the Study of Social History Univ of Warwick 1995– (reader 1993–95); visiting prof of history Univ of Michigan Ann Arbor 1992; ed History Workshop Journal 1983–; memb Panel for Validation and Review Cncl for Nat Academic Awards; external examiner: Univ of Portsmouth (formerly Portsmouth Poly) 1990–93, Univ of Keele 1992–; *Awards* elected Helen Gamble res student Newnham Coll Cambridge 1970–71, Nuffield Fndn small grant in social scis for work on Margaret McMillan (1860–1931) and the idea of childhood 1983, History Twenty Seven Fndn grant Inst of History Res 1983, elected Sr Simon res fell Dept of Sociology Univ of Manchester 1990–91; *Publications* incl: The Tidy House: Little Girls Writing (1982, awarded Fawcett Soc Book prize 1983), Policing the Victorian Community: the Formation of English Provincial Police Forces 1856–1880 (1984), Language Gender and Childhood (jt ed, 1985), Landscape for a Good Woman (1986), The Radical Soldier's Tale (1988), Childhood Culture and Class In Britain: Margaret McMillan 1860–1931 (1990), Past Tenses: Essays on Writing, Autobiography and History 1980–90 (1992), Strange Dislocations: Childhood and the Idea of Human Interiority 1780–1930 (1995); *Style*— Prof Carolyn Steedman; ✉ University of Warwick, Coventry CV4 7AL (☎ 01203 523523 ext 3624, e-mail aerag.cvs@uk.ac.warwick)

STEEDMAN, Robert Russell; OBE (1997); s of Robert Smith Steedman (d 1950), of Sevenoaks, Kent, and Helen Hope, *née* Brazier; *b* 3 Jan 1929; *Educ* Loretto, School of Architecture Edinburgh Coll of Art (DA), Univ of Pennsylvania (MLA); *m* 1, July 1956 (m dis 1974), Susan Elizabeth, da of Sir Robert Scott, GCMG, CBE (d 1982), of Peebles, Scotland; 1 s (Robert Scott b 1958), 2 da (Helena Elizabeth b 1960, Sarah Aeliz b 1962); m 2, 23 July 1977, Martha, da of Rev John Edmund Hamilton; *Career* Nat Serv Lt RWAFF 1947–48; ptnr Morris and Steedman Edinburgh 1959–; memb: Countryside Cmmn for Scotland 1980–88, Royal Fine Art Cmmn for Scotland 1984–95; sec Royal Scottish Acad 1983–90 (memb Cncl 1981–, dep pres 1982–83), dir Friends of the Royal Scottish Acad 1985–; govr Edinburgh Coll of Art 1974–88, memb Edinburgh Festival Soc 1978–; former cncl memb: Royal Incorporation of Architects in Scotland, Soc of Scottish Artists, Scottish Museums 1984–90; chm Central Scotland Woodlands Tst 1984–87; awards: Civic Tst (ten times) 1963–88, Br Steel 1971, Saltire 1971, RIBA award for Scotland 1974 and 1989, Euro Architectural Heritage Medal 1975, Assoc for the Protection of Rural Scotland 1977, 1983 and 1989; FRSA 1979, RIBA, FRIAS, ALI, RSA; *Clubs* New (Edinburgh), Royal and Ancient (St Andrews); *Style*— Robert Steedman, Esq, OBE, RSA; ✉ 38 Young Street, North Lane, Edinburgh EH2 4JD; (☎ 0131 226 6563, fax 0131 220 0224)

STEEDMAN, Prof (Robert) Scott; s of Robert Russell Steedman, of Blebocraigs, Fife, Scot, and Susan Elizabeth Sym, *née* Scott; *b* 10 Sept 1958; *Educ* Edinburgh Acad, UMIST (BSc), Queens' Coll Cambridge (MPhil), St Catharine's Coll Cambridge (PhD); *m* 5 Sept 1981, Zoreh, da of Dr Ebrahim Kazemzadeh (d 1993), of Mashad, Iran; 1 s (Nicholas Robert Cyrus b 1985), 1 da (Hannah Hope Eliza b 1990); *Career* fell St Catharine's Coll Cambridge 1983–93, lectr Dept of Engineering Univ of Cambridge 1983–90, with EQE (safety and risk mgmnt conslts) 1990–92, dir Gibb Ltd (engrg conslts) 1993–; visiting prof MIT 1987, Royal Acad of Engrg visiting prof of engrg design Univ of Wales Cardiff 1996–; memb Senate Engrg Cncl 1996–; FICE 1994 (MICE 1988), FRSA 1996; *Books* Geotechnical Centrifuge Modelling (contrib, 1995); *Recreations* the children, skiing, messing about in boats; *Clubs* New (Edinburgh); *Style*— Prof Scott Steedman; ✉ 3 Surley Row, Caversham, Berkshire RG4 8ND (☎ 0118 946 3254)

STEEDS, Prof John Wickham; s of John Henry William Steeds (d 1987), of London, and Ethel Amelia, *née* Tyler; *b* 9 Feb 1940; *Educ* Haberdashers' Aske's, UCL (BSc), Univ of Cambridge (PhD); *m* 7 Dec 1969, Diana Mary, da of Harry Kettlewell (d 1984), of Harlaxton; 2 da (Charlotte b 7 Dec 1971, Lucy b 12 Dec 1973); *Career* res fell Selwyn Coll Cambridge 1964–67; Dept of Physics Univ of Bristol: lectr 1967–77, reader 1977–85, prof 1985–, dir Interface Analysis Centre 1990–; memb Sci and Engrg Cncl Ctees 1982–88, chm Sci Res Fndn Emerson Green 1988–, chm Cmmn on Electron Diffraction Int Union of Crystallography; Holweck Medal and Prize Inst of Physics and Sociét Française de Physique (1996); FRS 1988, FInstP 1991; *Books* Introduction to Anisotropic

Elasticity Theory of Dislocations (1973), Electron Diffraction of Phases in Alloys (1984); *Recreations* tennis, cycling, travel; *Style*— Prof John Steeds, FRS; ✉ 21 Caynge Square, Clifton, Bristol BS8 3LA (☎ 0117 973 2183); Physics Department, University of Bristol, Bristol BS8 1TL (☎ 0117 928 8730, fax 0117 925 5624, e-mail J.W.Steeds@bristol.ac.uk)

STEEL, Sir David Edward Charles; kt (1977), DSO (1940), MC (1945), TD; s of Gerald Arthur Steel, CB; *b* 29 Nov 1916; *Educ* Rugby, Oxford Univ (BA); *m* 3 Nov 1956, Ann Wynne, da of Maj-Gen Charles Basil Price, CB, DSO, DCM, VD, CD (d 1975); 1 s (Richard), 2 da (Nicola, Caroline); *Career* served WWII 9 Queen's Royal Lancers France, M East, N Africa, Italy (despatches thrice); slr Linklaters & Paines 1948, legal asst BP 1950, pres BP N America 1959–61, md Kuwait Oil 1962–65; BP: md 1965–75, dep chm 1972–75, chm 1975–81; dir: Bank of England 1978–85, Kleinwort Benson Gp (formerly Kleinwort Benson Lonsdale) 1985–92; tstee The Economist 1979–96, chm Wellcome Trust 1982–89 (tstee 1981–89), pres London Chamber of Commerce and Indust 1982–85; chm: Govrs Rugby Sch 1984–88, Lenta Educn Tst 1986–90, London Educn Business Partnership 1986–89; hon fell Univ Coll Oxford 1981, Hon DCL City Univ 1983; Hon Freeman Worshipful Co of Tallow Chandlers 1980; Order of Taj III (Iran) 1974, Cdr Order of Leopold (Belgium) 1980; *Recreations* golf, gardening; *Clubs* Cavalry and Guards', MCC, Hurlingham, Royal and Ancient (St Andrews); *Style*— Sir David Steel, DSO, MC, TD

STEEL, Rt Hon Sir David Martin Scott; KBE (1990), PC (1977), DL (Ettrick and Lauderdale and Roxburghshire 1990), MP (Lib Dem) Tweeddale, Ettrick and Lauderdale (majority 2,520); s of Very Rev Dr David Steel; *b* 31 March 1938; *Educ* Prince of Wales Sch Nairobi, George Watson's Coll Edinburgh, Univ of Edinburgh (MA, LLB); *m* 1962, Judith Mary, da of W D MacGregor, CBE; 2 s, 1 da; *Career* sometime journalist, asst sec Scottish Lib Pty 1962–64, BBC TV interviewer in Scotland 1964–65 and later presenter of religious programmes for STV, Granada and BBC; MP (Lib until 1988, now Lib Dem): Roxburgh, Selkirk and Peebles 1965–83, Tweeddale, Ettrick and Lauderdale 1983–; pres Anti-Apartheid Movement of GB 1966–69, memb Parly Delgn to UN 1967, sponsored Abortion Act 1967, Lib chief whip 1970–75, spokesman on foreign affrs 1975–76, ldr of Lib Pty 1976–88, memb Select Ctee on Privileges 1979–86, pres Lib International 1994–96; tstee Shelter 1970– (former chm Shelter Scotland), memb Br Cncl of Churches 1971–74, rector Edinburgh Univ 1982–85; Freedom of Tweeddale 1988, Freedom of Ettrick and Lauderdale 1990; Chubb fell Yale Univ 1987, Hon Doctorate Univ of Stirling 1991, Hon DLitt Univ of Buckingham 1993, Hon DUniv Heriot Watt Univ 1996; Cdr's Cross of the Order of Merit (Germany) 1992; *Books* Boost for the Borders (1964), Out of Control (1968), No Entry (1969), The Liberal Way Forward (1975), A New Political Agenda (1976), Militant for the Reasonable Man (1977), A House Divided (1980), Partners in One Nation (1985), Border Country (with Judy Steel, 1985), The Time Has Come (1987), Mary Stuart's Scotland (with Judy Steel, 1987), Against Goliath (1989); *Recreations* classic cars, fishing; *Style*— The Rt Hon Sir David Steel, KBE, DL, MP; ✉ House of Commons, London SW1A 0AA

STEEL, David William; QC (1981); s of Sir Lincoln Steel (d 1985), and Barbara Isobel Thorburn, *née* Goldschmidt (d 1994); *b* 7 May 1943; *Educ* Eton, Keble Coll Oxford (MA); *m* 1970, Charlotte Elizabeth, da of Lt Cdr David A R M Ramsay, DSM (d 1981); 2 s (Jonathan b 1971, Timothy b 1974); *Career* called to the Bar Inner Temple 1966, bencher 1991; jr counsel to Treasury (Admiralty and Common Law) 1978–81, recorder 1988–, head of chambers; wreck cmmr for Eng and Wales 1982–; memb: Panel Lloyd's Salvage Arbitrators 1981–, Lord Chllr's Advsy Ctee on Legal Educn and Conduct; ed: Temperley, Merchant Shipping Acts (1975), Kennedy on Salvage (1985); *Recreations* shooting, fishing; *Clubs* Turf; *Style*— David Steel, Esq, QC; ✉ Chinnor Hill Manor, Chinnor, Oxford OX9 4BG

STEEL, Elizabeth Anne; da of William Frederick Steel (d 1961), and Amy Winifred Steel (d 1975); *b* 3 July 1936; *Educ* St Bernard's Convent Sch Slough, Univ of Reading (BSc, MSc); *Career* behavioural endocrinologist; asst in res Sub-Dept of Animal Behaviour Madingley Cambridge 1960, visiting res worker Inst of Animal Behavior Rutgers Univ New Jersey USA 1964, pharmaceutical res Aspro-Nicholas Research Inst Wexham Bucks 1965; Univ of Cambridge: univ res assoc Sub-Dept of Animal Behaviour 1966, chief res officer MRC Unit on Devpt and Integration of Behaviour Madingley 1985–89, sr res assoc Dept of Psychiatry 1990–92; *Recreations* riding, walking, taking the lid off things; *Style*— Miss Elizabeth Steel; ✉ Department of Zoology, Downing St, Cambridge (☎ 01223 336600)

STEEL, Her Hon Judge; Elizabeth Mary; DL (Merseyside 1991); da of His Hon Judge Edward Steel (d 1976), of Warrington, Cheshire, and Mary Evelyn Griffith, *née* Roberts (d 1987); sis of Hon Mrs Justice Steel, *qv*; *b* 28 Nov 1936; *Educ* Howells Sch Denbigh, Univ of Liverpool (LLB); *m* 8 April 1972, Stuart Christie, *qv*, s of Samuel Albert Christie; 1 da (Elspeth Victoria b 19 Nov 1976), 1 s (Iain Duncan b 17 Feb 1978); *Career* asst slr Percy Hughes & Roberts 1960–67 (articled clerk 1955–60); ptnr: John A Behn Twyford & Co 1968–80 (asst slr 1967–68), Cuff Roberts North Kirk 1980–91; recorder 1989–91, circuit judge (Northern Circuit) 1991–; nat vice chm Young Cons 1965–67; memb: Cripps Ctee 1967–69, Race Relations Bd 1970–78, Gen Advsy Cncl BBC 1979–82; chm: NW Advsy Cncl BBC 1979–82, Steering Ctee Hillsborough Slrs Gp 1989–91; dep and vice chm Bd of Dirs Liverpool Playhouse 1980–88 (memb Bd 1968–94, vice pres 1994–); Liverpool Law Soc: vice pres 1988–89, pres 1989–90, memb Ctee, former chm Legal Educn Sub Ctee; non-exec dir Bd Royal Liverpool Univ Hosp Tst 1990–91; memb: Law Soc 1960, Liverpool Law Soc 1960; *Recreations* theatre (watching professional and performing/directing amateur), music, needlework, cooking, reading, entertaining, being entertained; *Clubs* University Women's, Athenaeum (Liverpool); *Style*— Her Hon Judge Steel, DL; ✉ The Queen Elizabeth II Law Courts, Derby Square, Liverpool L2 1XA (☎ 0151 473 7373)

STEEL, Hon Mrs Justice; Hon Dame (Anne) Heather; DBE (1993); da of His Hon Edward Steel (d 1976), of Warrington, Cheshire, and Mary Evelyn Griffith, *née* Roberts (d 1987); sis of Her Hon Judge Elizabeth Steel, *qv*; *b* 3 July 1940; *Educ* Howells Sch Denbigh North Wales, Univ of Liverpool (LLB); *m* 1967, David Kerr-Muir Beattie, s of Harold Beattie (d 1957), of Manchester; 1 da (Elinor b 1970), 1 s (Andrew b 1972); *Career* called to the Bar Gray's Inn 1963, practised Northern Circuit, prosecuting counsel for DHSS 1984–86, recorder of the Crown Court 1984–86, circuit judge 1986–93, judge of the High Court of Justice (Queen's Bench) 1993–; memb Judicial Studies Bd Criminal Ctee 1992–95; pres Faculty of Law Soc Univ of Liverpool 1994–, pres Merseyside Medico-Legal Soc 1992–94 (patron); bencher Gray's Inn 1993; memb Cncl Rossall Sch; Liveryman Worshipful Co of Pattenmakers, Freeman City of London; *Recreations* theatre, art, antiques, gardening; *Style*— The Hon Mrs Justice Steel, DBE; ✉ The Royal Courts of Justice, Strand, London WC2A 2LL

STEEL, John Brychan; QC (1993); s of Lt-Col John Exton Steel, of Swindon Hall, nr Cheltenham, Glos, and Marianne Valentine, *née* Brychan Rees; *b* 4 June 1954; *Educ* Harrow, Univ of Durham (BSc in Chemistry); *m* 6 June 1981, Susan Rebecca, da of Dr Robert Fraser (d 1979), of Yarm, County Durham; 2 s (Charles John Robert b 1984, Henry James Edward b 1989), 1 da (Sophie Rosanagh b 1986); *Career* Lt Inns of Ct and City Yeomanry TA 1977–81; called to the Bar Gray's Inn 1978, appointed to Attorney General's List of Bar Counsel 1989; dep chm Ski Club of GB 1989–91; chm: Kandahar Ski Club 1992–, Great Tew Trust; dir Busoga Tst; *Recreations* skiing, walking, flying; *Clubs* RAC, Kandahar (dir and chm), Ski Club of GB; *Style*— John Steel, Esq, QC; ✉ 4–5 Gray's Inn Square, Gray's Inn, London WC1R 5AY (☎ 0171 404 5252, fax 0171 242 7803); Great Rollright Manor, Chipping Norton, Oxon OX7 5RH (☎ 01608 730131, fax 01608 737480)

STEEL, Prof (Christopher) Michael; s of Very Rev Dr David Steel, of Edinburgh, and Sheila Eunice Nanette, *née* Martin (d 1993); *b* 25 Jan 1940; *Educ* Prince of Wales Sch Nairobi, George Watson's Coll Edinburgh, Univ of Edinburgh (Ettles scholar, BSc, MB ChB, PhD, DSc, Leslie Gold Medal in Med); *m* 1 Aug 1963, Judith Margaret, da of Frederick David Spratt; 2 s (Andrew David b 15 Feb 1968, Robert Michael b 22 Nov 1969), 1 da (Heather Judith b 3 May 1974); *Career* jr hosp appts Edinburgh Teaching Hosps 1965–68, univ research fell Edinburgh Med Sch 1968–71, MRC travelling research fell Univ of Nairobi Med Sch 1972–73, memb Clinical Scientific Staff MRC Human Genetics Unit Edinburgh 1973–94 (asst dir 1979–94), prof of med sci Univ of St Andrews 1994–; T P Gunton Award BMA (for research and educn in the cancer field) 1993–94; memb UK Gene Therapy Advsy Ctee 1994–; FRCPE, FRCSEd, FRCPath, FRSE 1994; *Books* Biochemistry: A Concise Text for Medical Students (1992); *Recreations* golf, skiing, theatre; *Clubs* RSM; *Style*— Prof Michael Steel, FRSE; ✉ University of St Andrews, School of Biological and Medical Sciences, Bute Medical Building, St Andrews, Fife KY16 9TS (☎ 01334 463558, fax 01334 463482, mobile 0860 255684)

STEEL, Patricia Ann; OBE (1990); da of Thomas Norman Steel (d 1970), of Huddersfield, Yorks, and Winifred, *née* Pearson (d 1974); *b* 30 Oct 1941; *Educ* Hunmanby Hall nr Filey, Univ of Exeter (BA); *Career* Parly liaison Chamber of Shipping UK and Br Shipping Fedn 1968–71, sec Inst of Highways and Tportation 1973–90, memb Occupational Pensions Bd 1979–83; non-exec dir London Regnl Tport 1984–91; dir: Docklands Light Railway Ltd 1984–91 (chm 1988–89), Victoria Coach Station Ltd 1988–91; memb Street Works Advsy Ctee 1987–95, public affairs advsr Babtie Group 1992–, memb Mgmnt Bd Transport Res Laboratory 1992–96, non-exec dir Richmond Twickenham and Roehampton NHS Healthcare Tst 1992–; *Recreations* politics, music, travel; *Style*— Miss Patricia Steel, OBE; ✉ 7 The Strathmore, 27 Petersham Rd, Richmond, Surrey

STEEL, Robert John Beveridge; *b* 6 Aug 1954; *Educ* Whitehill Sch Glasgow, Mackintosh Sch of Architecture Univ of Glasgow (BArch, DipArch, Joe Park student prize in architecture); *m*; 1 c; *Career* architectural asst: Dorward Matheson Gleave and Partners 1974–76, Fewster Valentine and Partners 1976–78, Rayack Construction Ltd 1978–80, McLean Gibson and Associates 1980–83; architect Building Design Partnership 1983–87; Reiach and Hall Architects: architect 1987–89, assoc 1989–91, dir 1991–; RIBA 1987, ARIAS 1987, memb ARCUK 1987; *Awards* for Lanark Architectural Heritage Trail: CDC Environmental Award Scheme 1986, Civic Tst Award 1988; for Life Association of Scotland HQ Edinburgh: EAA Silver Medal Commendation 1990, Patent Glazing Contractors Assoc Award 1991, Civic Tst Award 1991; for Strathclyde Graduate Business Sch Glasgow: Scottish Civic Tst Dip of Excellence 1992, Civic Tst Commendation 1993, RIBA Regional Award 1993; for Wemyss Bay Station Restoration: Int Brunel Award 1994, Ian Allan Railway Heritage Award 1994, Civic Tst Commendation 1994; *Recreations* architecture (issues, trends, debate), golf, skiing, swimming, badminton, travel, music, cinema; *Style*— Robert Steel, Esq; ✉ 20 Farm Court, Kirkland Park, Bothwell, Lanarkshire G71 8BU (☎ 01698 854645); Reiach and Hall Architects, 6 Darnaway Street, Edinburgh EH3 6BG

STEEL, Prof Robert Walter; CBE (1983); s of Frederick Grabham Steel (d 1948), and Winifred Barry, *née* Harrison (d 1974); *b* 31 July 1915; *Educ* Great Yarmouth GS, Cambridge and Co HS, Jesus Coll Oxford (BSc, MA); *m* 9 Jan 1940, Eileen Margaret, da of Arthur Ernest Page (d 1941), of Bournemouth; 1 s (David Robert b 1948), 2 da (Alison Margaret b 1942, Elizabeth Mary b 1945); *Career* Nat Serv WWII Naval Intelligence 1940–45; geographer Ashanti Social Survey Gold Coast 1945–46, lectr (later sr lectr) in cwlth geography Univ of Oxford 1947–56 (fell Jesus Coll 1954–56, hon fell 1982); Univ of Liverpool: John Rankin prof of geography 1957–74, dean Faculty of Arts 1965–68, pro vice chllr 1971–73; princ Univ Coll Swansea 1974–82, vice chllr Univ of Wales 1979–81; hon dir Cwlth Geographical Bureau 1972–81; chm: Univs' Cncl for Adult and Continuing Educn 1976–80, Lower Swansea Valley Devpt Gp 1979–88, Govrs Westhill Coll Birmingham 1981–95 (vice chm Cncl of Church and Assoc Colls 1988–90, pres 1990–94), Wales Advsy Body for Local Authy Higher Educn 1982 86, Cwlth Human Ecology Cncl 1988–90; Swansea Festival of Music and the Arts 1982–95, Swansea Civic Soc 1988–; Hon DSc Univ of Salford 1977, Hon LLD Wales 1983, Hon LLD Univ of Liverpool 1985, Hon DUniv Open Univ 1987, Hon LLD Univ of Birmingham 1996; fell: Univ Coll of Swansea 1991, Selly Oak Coll Birmingham 1995, Trinity Coll Carmarthen 1995; FRGS 1939; memb: Inst of Br Geographers 1939– (pres 1969, ed 1950–61), Geographical Assoc 1946– (pres 1973), African Studies Assoc UK 1963– (pres 1973), Royal African Soc 1939– (vice pres 1977–), Cncl Nat Univ of Lesotho 1981–85, Cncl Univ of Swaziland 1987–91; *Recreations* walking, gardening, travel, reading, music; *Clubs* Royal Cwlth Soc; *Style*— Prof Robert Steel, CBE; ✉ 12 Cambridge Rd, Langland, Swansea SA3 4PE (☎ 01792 369 087)

STEEL, Roger Cameron; s of David Ian Steel, of Scarborough, N Yorks, and Sylvia Margaret, *née* Youngman (d 1966); *b* 18 Feb 1952; *Educ* Scarborough HS for Boys, UCL (LLB); *m* 14 June 1975, Harriet Dorothy (Prue), da of George Michael Gee, of Coombe Bissett, Wilts; 2 da (Louise b 1982, Eleanor b 1985); *Career* admitted slr 1976 specialising in employment law; Frere Cholmeley Bischoff (formerly Frere Cholmeley): qualified 1976, ptnr 1982–; memb: Employment Lawyers Assoc, Int Bar Assoc, Law Soc, City of London Law Soc; *Recreations* swimming, photography, travel; *Style*— Roger Steel, Esq; ✉ Squirrels Wood, Park Lane, Ashtead, Surrey KT21 1EY (☎ 01372 272083); Frere Cholmeley Bischoff, 4 John Carpenter Street, London EC4Y 0NH (☎ 0171 615 8000, fax 0171 615 8080)

STEELE, Arthur David McGowan; s of David McGowan Steele (d 1981), of Melbourne, and Agnes Claire, *née* Turner (d 1991); *b* 16 Dec 1935; *Educ* Geelong Coll, Univ of Melbourne (MB BS); *Career* Active Citizen Military Forces Aust 1954–61, cmmnd Lt 1957; conslt ophthalmic surgn Moorfields Eye Hosp 1976–, author papers on corneal and cataract surgery; treas Royal Ophthalmological Soc of UK 1979–88 (sec 1977–79), hon treas Royal Coll of Ophthalmologists 1988–91; Yeoman Worshipful Soc of Apothecaries 1985; FRCS 1971, FRACO 1976, FRCOphth 1988; *Books* Cataract Surgery (ed, 1984), Manual of Corneal Surgery (1992); *Recreations* music, literature, theatre; *Clubs* athenaeum; *Style*— Arthur Steele, Esq; ✉ 62 Wimpole Street, London W1M 7DE (☎ 0171 637 7400); Moorfields Eye Hospital, City Road, London EC1V 2PD

STEELE, John H; *b* 1941, Lenoir, N Carolina; *Educ* N Carolina State Univ (BEng, MEng); *m* Merida; *Career* Exxon Corporation: joined 1965, various technical and mgmnt appts in Oil & Gas Production USA 1965–76, California District Mangr Exxon USA 1976–78, prodn mangr EPMI 1978–82, dir Esso Exploration and Production Norway 1982–85, divnl mangr Exxon USA New Orleans 1985–92, prodn ops mangr then vice pres prodn Exxon USA Houston 1992–94, md Esso Exploration and Production UK Ltd and dir Esso UK plc 1995–; memb Texas Register of Professional Engrs, memb UKOOA, memb Soc of Petroleum Engrs, FInstPet; *Recreations* golf, ballet, opera; *Style*— John Steele, Esq; ✉ Esso UK plc, Esso House, 96 Victoria Street, London SW1E 5JW (☎ 0171 834 6677)

STEELE, John Roderic; CB (1978); s of Harold G Steele (d 1968), of Wakefield, and Doris, *née* Hall (d 1986); *b* 22 Feb 1929; *Educ* Queen Elizabeth GS Wakefield, Queen's Coll Oxford (MA); *m* 22 Sept 1956, (Margaret) Marie, da of Joseph Stevens (d 1963), of Ingleton, Yorks; 2 s (Richard b 1957, David b 1963), 2 da (Alison b 1959, Elisabeth b

1965); *Career* Civil Serv; asst princ Miny of Civil Aviation 1951–54, private sec to Parly sec 1954–57; princ: Road Tport Div 1957–60, Sea Tport Div 1960–62, shipping policy 1962–64; asst sec shipping policy Bd of Trade 1964–67, cnsllr (shipping) Br Embassy Washington 1967–71, asst sec (Civil Aviation Div) DTI 1971–73; under sec: Space Div 1973–74, shipping policy 1974–75, Gen Div Bd of Trade 1975–76; dep sec: Bd of Trade 1976–80, Dept of Indust 1980–81; DG (tport) Cmmn of Euro Communities 1981–86; dir P&O Container Line 1987–, chm P&O European Transport Service 1989–, non-exec dir Peninsular & Oriental Steam Navigation Co 1992–95; memb: Prisma Transport Consultants 1986–, Dover Harbour Bd 1990–92; FCIT; *Recreations* cricket, tennis, opera; *Clubs* United Oxford and Cambridge, Philippics; *Style—* J R Steele, Esq, CB; ✉ Brocas Oast, Hever, nr Edenbridge, Kent; Sq Ambiorix 30, BTE 30, 1040 Bruxelles, Belgium; c/o Prisma Transport Consultants, 16 rue Bellot Case 269, 1211 Geneve 12, Switzerland

STEELE, Mavis Mary; MBE (1983); da of Alexander McLeod Steele (d 1966), of 45 Kenton Park Ave, Kenton, Harrow, Middx, and Evelyn Violet, *née* Crane (d 1960); *b* 9 Sept 1928; *Educ* Claremont Ave Comp Sch; *Career* int bowler; England Outdoor: singles winner 1961, 1962 and 1969, pairs winner 1964 and 1971, triples winner 1968, fours winner 1963–69; Middx: singles winner 1955, 1958–59, 1961–62, 1965–70, 1976 and 1986; two wood winner 1970–72 and 1980, pairs winner 1964, 1967, 1971–72, 1982, 1985 and 1994, triples winner 1953, 1968, 1971 and 1973, fours winner 1958, 1963, 1966, 1969, 1976, 1985 and 1992, Outdoor int 1959–96, Indoor int 1979, 1980, 1981, 1985–96, World Championships NZ singles and pairs Silver medal winner 1973, World Championships Canada fours Gold medal winner and triples Silver medal winner 1981, Cwlth Games Aust triples Bronze medal winner 1982; England indoor: singles winner 1989, two wood triples winner 1989, fours winner 1991; hon asst sec English Women's Bowling Assoc, pres Middx County Women's Bowling Assoc 1971 and 1992, hon treas Middx County Women's Bowling Assoc, pres English Women's Indoor Bowling Assoc 1990–91, chm English Women's Umpires Assoc; tstee English Bowling Assoc Charity Tst; *Recreations* bowls; *Clubs* Sunbury Sports Bowls, Egham Indoor Bowls; *Style—* Miss Mavis Steele, MBE; ✉ 45c Woodthorpe Rd, Ashford, Middx TW15 2RP (☎ 01784 259568)

STEELE, Maj-Gen Michael Chandos Merrett; MBE (1972), DL (Surrey 1996); s of William Chandos Steele (d 1969), of Kingswood, Surrey, and Daisy Rhoda, *née* Merrett (d 1956); *b* 1 Dec 1931; *Educ* Westminster Sch, RMA Sandhurst; *m* 1961, Judith Ann, da of Edward James Huxford, of Grimsby; 2 s (Timothy, Jeremy), 1 da (Elizabeth); *Career* cmmnd RA 1952, BMRA Welsh Div 1965–67, BM 8 Inf Bde Londonderry 1970–72, CO 22 AD Regt RA 1972–74, GI HQDRA 1974–76, Cmd 7th Artillery Bde 1976–78, Nat Defence Coll Canada 1978–79, BGS Def Sales Organization MOD London 1979–82; Chief Jt Services Liaison Orgn Bonn 1983–86, Hon Col 104 Air Defence Regt RA (V) 1987–96, Col Commandant RA 1988–94, Regtl Comptroller RA 1989–; chm The Tree Cncl 1994–96; *Recreations* tennis, gardening, walking; *Style—* Maj-Gen Michael Steele, MBE, DL; ✉ Elders, Masons Bridge Rd, Redhill, Surrey RH1 5LE (☎ 01737 763982)

STEELE, Prof Raymond; s of William Henry Steele (d 1971), of Southend on Sea, and Madeline Mable, *née* Wilkinson (d 1965); *b* 9 July 1934; *Educ* Univ of Durham (BSc), Loughborough Univ of Technol (PhD, DSc); *m* 2 da (Lorna, Susan); *Career* res engr EK Cole 1959–61 (indentured apprentice 1950–55), devpt engr Cossor Radar and Electronics 1961–62, R&D engr Marconi 1962–65; sr lectr: RNC Greenwich 1965–68, Loughborough Univ of Technol 1968–79; scientist Bell Laboratories USA 1979–83, dir Plessey Res Roke Manor 1983–86, prof of communications Univ of Southampton 1983–, md Multiple Access Communications Ltd 1986–; memb: Advsy Bd IEEE Personal Communications, Advsy Bd Int Jl of Wireless Information Networks, IEEE Vehicular Technol Soc AVANT GARDE 1996; adjudicator of research proposals Euro Cmmn 1991 and 1995; sr tech ed USA IEEE Communications Magazine; awarded: Marconi Premium (with co-authors) 1979–89, Bell System Tech Jl's Best Mathematics Communications Techniques, Computing and Software and Social Sciences paper 1981; fell USA Inst of Electrical and Electronic Engrs; FEng 1992, FIEE, CEng; *Books* Delta Modulation (1975), Digital Communication (contrib, 1986), Mobile Radio Communications (ed, 1992), Source-Matched Mobile Communications (1995), ed Pentech Press Digital Cellular Radio Series; *Recreations* oil painting, ballroom dancing, music; *Style—* Prof Raymond Steele, FEng; ✉ Electronic and Computer Science Department, University of Southampton, Southampton SO9 5NH (☎ 01703 592881, fax 01703 593045); Multiple Access Communications Ltd, Epsilon House, Enterprise Rd, Chilworth Research Centre, Southampton SO16 7NS (☎ 01703 767808, fax 01703 760602)

STEELE, Richard Charles; s of Maj Richard Orson Steele, MBE (d 1984), of Gloucester, and Helen Curtis, *née* Robertson (d 1995); *b* 26 May 1928; *Educ* Ashburton Coll Devon, UCNW (BSc), Univ of Oxford; *m* 12 Dec 1956, Anne Freda, da of Hugh White Nelson (d 1978), of New Milton, Hants; 2 s (Richard Hugh b 21 June 1958, John David b 9 Aug 1964), 1 da ((Anne) Mary b 18 Jan 1960); *Career* Gunner 66 Airborne Anti-Tank Regt 1946–48; asst conservator of forests Tanganyika 1951–63, head Woodland Mgmnt Section Nature Conservancy 1963–72, head terrestrial and freshwater life scis NERC 1972–78, head Div of Scientific Servs Inst of Terrestrial Ecology 1978–80, DG Nature Conservancy Cncl 1980–88, conslt in nature conservation and forestry 1988–93; memb Cncl Nat Tst 1987–94, memb Southern Regnl Ctee Nat Tst; FICFor 1968 (former pres), FIBiol 1974, FIMgt 1980; *Books* Monks Wood: A Nature Reserve Record (ed 1972); *Recreations* gardening, walking; *Style—* Richard Steele, Esq; ✉ 1 Birdhaven, Wrecclesham, Farnham, Surrey GU10 4PB (☎ 01252 726219)

STEELE, Stuart James; s of James Richard Steele (d 1973), of Ealing, London, and Margaret Glass, *née* Leonard (d 1984); *b* 13 Jan 1930; *Educ* Westminster, Trinity Coll Cambridge (MA, MB BChir), Middx Hosp Med Sch; *m* 23 Oct 1965, Jill Westgate, da of Jack Westgate Smith (d 1991), of Watford, Herts; 2 s (Andrew James b July 1968, Alasdair Malcolm b Aug 1970); *Career* Nat Serv Gunner and 2 Lt RA; WHO fell USA 1969; sr lectr in obstetrics and gynaecology Middx Hosp Med Sch 1969–73; hon conslt: Middx Hosp and the Hosp for Women 1969–95, The Margaret Pyke Centre for Family Planning 1970–, UCL Hosps 1986–; reader in obstetrics and gynaecology: Middx Hosp Med Sch 1973–87, UCL 1987–95; dir Dept of Obstetrics and Gynaecology Middx Hosp Med Sch 1973–86, assoc dir Dept of Obstetrics and Gynaecology UCL 1987–95; vice pres Royal Scot Corp, elder Church of Scot; FRCS 1962, FRCOG 1974, MFFP 1993; *Books* Gynaecology, Obstetrics and the Neonate (1985); *Recreations* gardening, theatre, opera, ballet; *Clubs* Caledonian, RSM; *Style—* Stuart Steele, Esq; ✉ 35 Tring Avenue, London W5 3QD; London Women's Clinic, 113–115 Harley Street, London W1N 1DG (☎ 0171 487 5050)

STEELE, Thomas Graham (Tom); s of Thomas Steele (d 1979), of Lesmahagow, Lanarkshire, and Helen, *née* Thomson (d 1984); *b* 11 May 1945; *Educ* Larkhall Acad, Skerry's Coll; *m* 15 August 1969, Fiona, da of Max McAuslane; 1 s (Thomas Maxwell b 22 May 1976), 1 da (Eilidh Sheena b 10 Oct 1977); *Career* journalist: Dumfries & Galloway Standard 1962–64, Scottish Daily Mail 1964–67 (parly corr 1965–67), BBC 1967–73, Radio Clyde 1974–75; Radio Forth: head of news 1975–79, prog dir 1979–96, md 1996–; memb Scottish Broadcasting Editors 1984; *Awards* Trics Award 1977, Emergency Programming Award Sony Awards 1979, Arts Coverage Award (for Edinburgh Festival) Sony Awards 1985, Broadcasting Excellence International Festival of New York 1988, Paters Award for Radio Excellence Australia 1989, best UK arts programming Sony 1994; *Recreations* sailing, golf, conversation; *Style—* Tom Steele, Esq; ✉ Radio Forth Ltd, Forth House, Forth Street, Edinburgh EH1 3LF (☎ 0131 556 9255, fax 0131 557 8489)

STEELE, Tommy; né Thomas Hicks; OBE (1979); s of Thomas Walter Hicks (d 1980), and Elizabeth Ellen Bennett (d 1982); *b* 17 Dec 1936; *Educ* Bacon's Sch for Boys Bermondsey; *m* 1960, Ann, *née* Donoghue; 1 da (Emma b 1969); *Career* actor; stage debut (Sunderland) 1956, London stage debut (Dominion Theatre) 1957; *Theatre* incl: Buttons in Rodgers and Hammerstein's Cinderella (Coliseum) 1958, Tony Lumpkin in She Stoops to Conquer (Old Vic) 1960, Arthur Kipps in Half a Sixpence (Cambridge Theatre London 1963–64, Broadhurst Theatre NY 1965), Truffaldino in The Servant of Two Masters (Queen's) 1969, Dick Whittington (London Palladium) 1969, Meet Me in London (Adelphi) 1971, Jack Point in The Yeomen of the Guard (City of London Festival) 1978, The Tommy Steele Show (Palladium) 1973, Hans Andersen (Palladium) 1974 and 1977, one-man show (Prince of Wales) 1979, Don Lockwood in Singin' in the Rain (also dir) 1983 and 1989, Some Like it Hot (London) 1992, one-man show (Price of Wales) 1995; *Films* Kill Me Tomorrow 1956, The Tommy Steele Story, The Duke Wore Jeans, Tommy the Toreador, Light Up the Sky, It's All Happening, The Happiest Millionaire, Half a Sixpence 1967, Finian's Rainbow, Where's Jack?; *Other Work* incl: Quincy's Quest (wrote and acted for TV) 1979, My Life, My Song (composed and recorded) 1974, A Portrait of Pablo (composed) 1985, Rock Suite - an Elderly Person's Guide to Rock (composed) 1987, dir Singin' in the Rain (nat tour) 1994–95; *Books* Quincy (1981), The Final Run (1983); *Recreations* squash, painting; *Style—* Tommy Steele, Esq, OBE; ✉ c/o IMG Artists Europe, Axis Centre, Burlington Lane, London W4 2TH (☎ 0181 233 5805, fax 0181 233 5301)

STEELE-BODGER, Prof Alasdair; CBE (1980); s of Henry William Steele-Bodger (d 1952), of Tamworth, Staffs, and Katherine, *née* Macdonald (1983); *b* 1 Jan 1924; *Educ* Shrewsbury, Gonville and Caius Coll Cambridge (MA, Triple blue), Royal Dick Veterinary Coll, Univ of Edinburgh (BSc); *m* 4 Sept 1948, Anne Chisholm, da of Capt Alfred William John Finlayson, RN (d 1957), of Ringwood, Hants; 3 da (Catherine b 1954, Fiona b 1956, Gillie b 1957); *Career* veterinary surgn; gen practice Lichfield Staffs 1948–77, conslt practice Fordingbridge Hants 1977–79, prof of veterinary clinical studies Univ of Cambridge 1979–90; visiting prof Univ of Toronto 1973; hon veterinary conslt: to Br Agricultural Export Cncl 1967–88, to Nat Cattle Breeders' Assoc (now Nat Cattle Assoc) 1979–; EEC official veterinary expert 1973–; dir Bantin & Kingman Ltd (now B & K Universal Ltd) 1980–; pres: BVA 1966 (memb Cncl 1957–85, hon memb 1985), RCVS 1972 (memb Cncl 1960–90); memb: Cncl Royal Agricultural Soc of Eng 1967–, Horserace Scientific Advsy Ctee 1973–92, Bd of Advsrs Univ of London 1984–, Home Office Panel of Assessors under Animal (Scientific Procedures) Act 1986–; chm Advsy Bd Br Veterinary Formulary 1987–96; vice pres Inst of Animal Technol 1988–; Crookes' Prize 1970, Dalrymple-Champneys Cup and Medal 1972; Ehrenbürger der Tierarztl Hochschule Hannover 1992; Hon FRCVS 1975, hon fell RASE 1993 (hon vice pres 1996–), ARAgS 1996; *Recreations* walking, fishing, travel, golf; *Clubs* Farmers, Hawks (Cambridge); *Style—* Prof Alasdair Steele-Bodger, CBE; ✉ The Old House, Walton-on-Trent, Derbyshire DE12 8LL (☎ 01283 716961, fax 01543 254680)

STEELE-PERKINS, Crispian; s of Dr Guy Steele-Perkins, of Robin Hill, Deepdene Park, Exeter, and Sylvia de Courcey Steele-Perkins; *b* 18 Dec 1944; *Educ* Marlborough, Guildhall Sch of Music; *m* 29 April 1967, Angela (d 1991), da of William Scambler Hall (d 1967); 1 s ((Michael) Guy b 28 Oct 1970), 2 da (Emma Victoria b 20 March 1968, Kathleen (twin) b 28 Oct 1970); *Career* trumpeter, specialising in Baroque period; with Sadler's Wells Opera/ENO 1966–73, dir London Gabrieli Brass Ensemble 1973–84, with English Chamber Orch 1973–76, asst princ trumpeter Royal Philharmonic Orch 1976–80, prof of trumpet Guildhall Sch of Music 1980–90, solo trumpeter with City of London Sinfonia and The King's Consort 1980–, gives about 50 solo recitals and masterclasses a year; made over 800 recordings (incl 80 film soundtracks and 12 solo albums) incl: Six Trumpet Concertos, Shore's Trumpet, The Proud Trumpet, The King's Trumpeter, The Well-Tempered Trumpet, Italian Trumpet Sonatas, Brass Music of the Baroque, Splendour of the Baroque; *Style—* Crispian Steele-Perkins, Esq; ✉ c/o Anglo-Swiss Artists' Management, 59 St Martin's Lane, London WC2N 4JS (☎ 0171 240 4411, fax 0171 240 4424)

STEEN, Anthony David; MP (C) South Hams (majority 13,711); s of late Stephen N Steen, of London; *b* 22 July 1939; *Educ* Westminster, Univ of London; *m* Carolyn Steen, JP, *née* Padfield; 1 s (Jason), 1 da (Xanthe); *Career* youth club ldr in E London Settlement 1959–64, called to the Bar Gray's Inn 1962, practised 1962–76; fndr dir: Task Force 1964–68, YVF 1968–74; Lloyd's underwriter; MP (C): Liverpool Wavertree 1974–83, South Hams 1983–; memb Select Ctee on Immigration and Race Relations 1975–79, jt nat chm Impact 80s Campaign 1980–82, Cons Central Office co-ordinator for Critical Seats 1982–87, memb Select Ctee on Environment 1989–92, PPS to Sec of State for Nat Heritage 1992–94, Prime Minister's appointee to generate new activity amongst MPs in constituency work 1994; chm: Cons Party Backbench Ctee on Cities, Urban and New Town Affrs 1979–83, Urban and Inner City Ctee 1983–87, Cons Backbench Sane Planning Gp 1987–92; vice chm: Health and Social Servs Ctee 1979–81, Environment Ctee 1979–81, Cons Deregulation Ctee 1993–; sec All Party Caribbean Gp 1979– (currently vice chm), chm All Party Papua New Guinea Gp, exec memb Population and Devpt Gp 1989–; memb: Child Abuse All Party Ctee, House of Commons Catering Ctee 1991–95; chm West County Members 1992–94; advsr: English Vineyards Assoc, British Midland Airways; conslt The Communications Group plc; vice pres: Int Centre foir Child Studies, Assoc of District Cncls; memb Cncl for Christians and Jews; tstee: Educn Extra, Dartington Summer Arts Fndn; advsy tutor to Sch of Environment PCL 1982–83; *Publications* Tested Ideas for Political Success (1976, revd dns 1983 and 1991), New Life for Old Cities (1981), Public Land Utilisation Management Schemes (PLUMS) (1988); *Recreations* cycling, swimming, piano playing, tennis; *Clubs* Royal North Cape, RAC, Brixham & Totnes Conservative, Lords & Commons Cycle; *Style—* Anthony Steen Esq, MP; ✉ House of Commons, London SW1A 0AA (☎ 0171 219 5045)

STEEN, Martin Gamper; s of Dr Terence Ross Steen (d 1987), and Ingeborg, *née* Gamper; *b* 4 Sept 1954; *Educ* Clifton, Univ of London (LLB); *m* 18 Jan 1977, Charlotte Elizabeth, da of Dr Michael John Goring, of Stanford; 1 s (Michael Terence b 1988), 2 da (Anna Charlotte b 1983, Laura Ingeborg b 1985); *Career* called to the Bar Inner Temple 1976, practising Albion Chambers Bristol 1977–, acting stipendiary magistrate 1994; *Style—* Martin Steen, Esq; ✉ Albion Chambers, Broad St, Bristol BS1 1DR (☎ 0117 927 2144)

STEEN, (David) Michael Cochrane Elsworth; s of Prof Robert Elsworth Steen, MD (d 1981), and Elizabeth Margaret, *née* Cochrane; *b* 5 March 1945; *Educ* Eton, Oriel Coll Oxford (MA); *m* 18 Dec 1971, Rosemary Florence, da of Maj William Bellingham Denis Dobbs; 1 s (Peter b 1977), 3 da (Jane b 1973, Lucy b 1975, Rosalie b 1977); *Career* KPMG (formerly Peat Marwick Mitchell & Co): joined 1968, ptnr 1982–, head of audit servs 1987–90, head of UK insurance practice 1991–92, bd memb 1992–, head of risk mgmnt 1996–; FCA, ARCM; *Books* Guide to Directors Transactions (1983), Audits & Auditors - What the Public Thinks (1989); *Recreations* music (organ playing), riding, reading; *Clubs* Kildare Street, Carlton, Leander; *Style—* Michael Steen, Esq; ✉ Nevilles, Mattingley, Hants RG27 8JU (☎ 0125 676 2144); 5 Vicarage Gate, London W8 4HH (☎ 0171 937 6558); KPMG, 8 Salisbury Square, London EC4Y 8BB (☎ 0171 311 8345, fax 0171 311 8885, telex 8811541 KPMGLO G)

STEEN, Prof William Maxwell; s of late Stourton William Peile Steen, and Marjorie Gordon, *née* Maxwell; *b* 30 Sept 1933; *Educ* Kingswood Sch Bath, Univ of Cambridge (MA), Imperial Coll London (PhD, DIC); *m* April 1960, Margaret, da of John Thomas

Porkess Frankish, of Scunthorpe; 1 s (Philip b 6 Oct 1963), 1 da (Melanie b 6 May 1965); *Career* Nat Serv Pilot RAF 1952–54; process engr APV Co Ltd 1958–62, Methodist Missionary Soc Bankura Christian Coll India 1962–65, sr lectr Imperial Coll London 1985–87 (lectr 1965–85), James Bibby prof of engrg manufacture Univ of Liverpool 1987–; pres Liverpool Metallurgical Soc 1991–92; Freeman City of London 1983, Liveryman Worshipful Co of Goldsmiths; fell Laser Inst of America, pres Assoc of Industl Laser Users; FIM, FIEE, CEng; *Publications* over 250 incl: Laser Material Processing (1993); *Recreations* gardening, swimming, real tennis; *Clubs* Athenaeum (Liverpool, proprietor); *Style*— Prof William Steen; ✉ PO Box 147, Liverpool L69 3BX (☎ 0151 794 4839/40, fax 0151 794 4892, telex 627095)

STEER, Dr Christopher Richard; s of Eric Arthur Steer (d 1975), of Chistlehurst, Kent, and Joan, *née* Bowden; *b* 30 May 1947; *Educ* St Olaves GS London, Univ of Edinburgh (BSc, MB ChB, DCH Glas), FRCPE; *m* 20 Dec 1970 (m dis 1986), Patricia Ann, da of James Gallacher (d 1985); 1 s (Paul Christopher), 1 da (Jane Elizabeth); m 2, 1986, Patricia Mary Lennox; 1 s (Jamie Alisdair), 1 da (Rosemary Gillian); *Career* conslt paediatrician Fife 1983, clinical dir Acute Unit Fife Health Bd 1990–; memb: BMA 1978, Scott Paediatric Soc 1978, Paediatric Res Soc 1978, BPA 1980; *Recreations* gardening; *Style*— Dr Christopher Steer; ✉ 14 Bellhouse Rd, Aberdour, Fife KY3 0TL (☎ 01383 860738); Paediatric Department, Victoria Hospital, Hayfield Rd, Kirkcaldy, Fife KY2 5AH (☎ 01592 643355)

STEER, Clive Allen; s of Allan Edwin Steer (d 1986), of Guildford, Surrey, and Majorie, *née* Allen (d 1976); *b* 11 May 1938; *Educ* Northmead Sch Guildford, Royal Aircraft Estab Coll Farnborough, Central Sch of Art and Design London; *m* 24 Feb 1962, Janet, da of Arthur F E Evans, OBE; 1 s (Jonathan b 21 Sept 1967), 3 da (Rebecca b 8 Feb 1966, Georgina b 27 Oct 1970, Jacqueline b 23 Sept 1972); *Career* industl designer; Rediffusion Vision Limited London 1964–69, head of industl design Philips Electrical (UK) Ltd 1969–79, Philips Singapore 1979–82, assoc Business Design Group 1985–89, dir On the Line Design (conslts) 1989–90, princ Steer Associates 1990–94, accompanying offr FCO 1994–95, design counsellor Business Link Thames Valley 1995–; speaker on design and mktg at Design Cncl courses; awards: Design Cncl award for Philips Design Team Product (consumer and contract goods) 1975, 1984 Oscar for Invention and Gold medal Int Exposition of Invention Geneva; former: memb Judging Panel Design Cncl Consumer and Contract Goods Awards, memb Jury Bursary Awards RSA, chm Product Gp (A1) CSD, chm Membership Bd CSD, memb Fellowship Bd CSD, govr St Martin's Sch of Art, vice pres and memb Cncl CSD; FRSA 1978, FCSD 1979; *Style*— Clive Steer, Esq; ✉ Westview, Shere Rd, West Horsley, Leatherhead, Surrey KT24 6EW (☎ 01483 284686)

STEER, David; QC (1993); s of Alcombe Steer, of St Helens, Merseyside, and Nancy, *née* Smart; *b* 15 June 1951; *Educ* Rainford HS, Manchester Poly (BA Law); *m* 28 Sept 1974, Elizabeth May, da of James Basil Hide; 1 s (Oliver James Alcombe b 9 Aug 1982); *Career* called to the Bar Middle Temple 1974, recorder 1991–, jt head of chambers 1992–; memb Bar Cncl 1995–96; *Recreations* carriage driving, rugby league, horticulture; *Style*— David Steer, Esq, QC; ✉ Pyke's Farm, Clay Lane, Eccleston, St Helens WA10 5PX (☎ 01744 36952); 5th Floor, Corn Exchange Building, Fenwick Street, Liverpool L2 7QS (☎ 0151 227 1081, fax 0151 236 1120)

STEER, Lt-Col Peter Frank; s of Alfred Albert (Peter) Steer (d 1995), of Bovey Tracey, Devon, and Gertrude Elizabeth, *née* Murrin (d 1989); *b* 1 May 1933; *Educ* Newton Abbot GS; *m* 21 Aug 1956, Rosina, da of late George William Ethelston, of Oswestry, Salop; 1 s (Martin b 1957), 1 da (Susan b 1960); *Career* cmmnd RA (short serv cmmn) Mons OCS 1952, regular cmmn 1956; Troop Offr 31 Trg Regt RA, 61 Light Regt RA Korea 1953–54, Adventure Trg Instr 64 Trg Regt RA 1954–57, 12 LAA Regt (Adj) BAOR, Regtl Serv 33 Para Light Regt RA and 7 Para Regt RHA Cyprus, Libya, Bahrain and Gulf 1959–83, Canadian Army Staff Coll 1963–65, GS02 (Intelligence) HQ 1 Div BAOR 1965–68, cmd 39 (Roberts) Battery of Jr Ldrs Regt RA 1968–69, 7 Para Regt RHA cmd I (Bull's Troop) Battery Malaya and N Ireland 1969–71, Instr Jr Div Staff Coll Warminster 1971–73, Lt-Col and Chief Special Projects HQ Afnorth Oslo 1973, GSOI Review Study Ammunition Rates and Scales MOD 1976, Head African Section DI4 Def Int Staff MOD 1976, ret Nov 1979, recalled to serv Dec 1979 as int co-ordinator mil advsrs staff to Govr of Rhodesia/Zimbabwe during ceasefire and election supervision, ret 1980; recruitment conslt, gen mangr Securiguard; Br Schs Exploring Soc: exec dir 1981–93 (expdns incl Greenland 1982–83, Arctic, Norway 1984, Alaska 1985, Papua New Guinea 1987); pt/t Opportunities Devpt Offr Aldershot and Dist MENCAP 1995–; chm govrs Greenfields Primary Sch Hartley Wintney 1976–90; FRGS, MIM; *Recreations* riding, hill walking, cross country skiing, expeditioning; *Clubs* Special Forces; *Style*— Lt-Col Peter Steer; ✉ Nightingales, West Green Rd, Hartley Wintney, Hants RG27 8RE (☎ 01252 843688)

STEFANOU, Stelio H; s of George Stefanou (d 1979), of Surbiton, Surrey, and Katina, *née* Heracleiou; *b* 6 Nov 1952; *Educ* Hollyfield Sch Surbiton, Tiffin GS Kingston upon Thames Surrey, Imperial Coll Univ of London (BSc); *m* 3 Sept 1977, Rosemarie Ann, da of Sydney Gordon, of London; *Career* product devpt Johnson Matthey 1974–77, mktg exec Esso UK plc 1977–80, dir John Doyle Construction Ltd 1980–87, gp md and chief exec John Doyle Group plc and chm each gp subsid 1987–; CBI: chm Hertfordshire County Gp 1992–94, memb Nat Cncl 1994–, chm Eastern Regnl Cncl 1995– (vice chm 1994–95); memb Lighthouse Club; Freeman City of London 1994, Liveryman Worshipful Co of Founders; ARCS 1974, FInstD; *Recreations* travel, food; *Style*— Stelio H Stefanou, Esq; ✉ Holwellbury House, nr Holwell, nr Hitchin, Herts SG5 3SD; John Doyle Group plc, John Doyle House, Little Burrow, Welwyn Garden City, Herts AL7 2SP (☎ 01707 329481, fax 01707 328213)

STEIN, Christopher Richard (Rick); s of Eric Stein (d 1965), of Cornwall, and Dorothy Gertrude, *née* Jackson; *b* 4 Jan 1947; *Educ* Uppingham, New Coll Oxford (BA); *m* 21 Sept 1975, Jill, da of Jack Newstead; 3 s (Edward b 16 Jan 1979, Jack b 31 Oct 1980, Charles b 14 Sept 1985); *Career* chef and restaurateur; estab (with Jill Stein) The Seafood Restaurant Cornwall 1975–; ratings: 1 Star Egon Ronay Guide, 4/5 Good Food Guide, 3 Rosettes AA Guide, Red M Michelin Guide, Black Four Leaf Clover Ackerman Guide; winner Badoit/Decanter Restaurant of the Year award 1989, Egon Ronay Restaurant of the Year 1995; presenter Rick Stein's Taste of the Sea (BBC 2) 1995 (Television Programme of the Year Glenfiddich Awards 1996), presenter Rick Stein's Fruits of the Sea (BBC 2) 1997; BBC Good Food TV Personality of the Year 1996; other business interests: St Petroc's Hotel and Bistro, The Middle Street Café, Stein's Delicatessen; *Books* English Seafood Cookery (1988, Glenfiddich Food Book of the Year award 1989), Rick Stein's Taste of the Sea (1995, André Simon Cookery Book of the Year 1996, BBC Good Food of the Year 1996), Fish (1996), Fruits of the Sea (1997); *Recreations* surfing; *Style*— Rick Stein, Esq; ✉ Seafood Restaurant, Riverside, Padstow PL28 8BY (01841 532485, fax 01841 533344)

STEIN, Keith Peter Sydney; s of Victor Stein (d 1984), and Pearl Stein; *b* 27 July 1945; *Educ* Preston Manor GS, Univ of Leeds (BA), LSE (MSc); *m* 13 Dec 1970, Linda, da of Michael Collins (d 1976); 1 s (Jonathan), 1 da (Nicole); *Career* sr operational res Int Wool Secretariat 1968–70, Mgmnt Servs Div and Foods Div Unigate plc 1971–76 (sr conslt, ops mangr, div planning mangr, special projects dir, commercial accountant), ptnr and nat dir, mgmnt consultancy 1977–86, strategic mgmnt Arthur Young 1986–89; Ernst & Young Management Consultants: sr ptnr 1989–, dir of int privatisation 1993–, head of PFI/project fin 1996; FCMA 1976, MIMC 1981; *Recreations* cricket (played for county, schools and university), soccer, table tennis, golf, skiing, bridge; *Style*— Keith Stein, Esq; ✉ Valley View, Rasehill Close, Rickmansworth, Herts WD3 4EW (☎ 01923 779134); Ernst & Young Management Consultants, Becket House, 1 Lambeth Palace Road, London SE1 7EU (☎ 0171 931 3972, fax 0171 928 1345, telex 885234 ERNSLOG)

STEIN, Prof Peter Gonville; JP (1970); s of Walter Oscar Stein (d 1967), of London and Montreux, and Effie Drummond, *née* Walker (d 1969); *b* 29 May 1926; *Educ* Liverpool Coll, Gonville and Caius Coll Cambridge (MA, LLB), Collegio Borromeo Pavia, Univ of Aberdeen (PhD); *m* 1, 22 July 1953 (m dis 1978), Janet Mary, da of Clifford Chamberlain (d 1969), of Manor House, Desborough, Northants; 3 da (Barbara b 1956, Penelope b 1959, Dorothy b 1960); m 2, 16 Aug 1978, Anne Mary Howard, da of Harrison Sayer (d 1980), of Seven Dials, Saffron Walden, Essex; *Career* joined RN 1944, Japanese translator 1945, Sub-Lt (sp) RNVR 1945–47; slr of the Supreme Ct 1951; dean Faculty of Law Univ of Aberdeen 1961–64 (prof of jurisprudence 1956–68); Univ of Cambridge: regius prof of civil law 1968–93, fell Queens' Coll 1968– (vice pres 1974–81), chm Faculty Bd of Law 1973–76; fell Winchester Coll 1976–91; memb: Bd of Mgmnt Royal Cornhill and Associated (Mental) Hosps 1963–68 (chm 1967–68), Sec of State for Scotland's Working Pty on Hosp Endowments 1966–69, Univ Grants Ctee 1971–75; pres Soc of Public Teachers of Law 1980–81; memb: US-UK Educnl Cmmn (Fulbright) 1985–91, Academia Europaea 1989; Hon Dr Juris Göttingen 1980; Hon Dott Giur Ferrara 1991; FBA 1974; foreign fell: Accademia di Scienze Morali e Politiche (Naples) 1982, Accademia Nazionale dei Lincei (Rome) 1987, Koninklijke Academie voor Wetenschappen (Brussels) 1991; corresponding fell Accademia degli Intronati (Siena) 1988; QC (Honoris Causa) 1993; *Books* Fault in the Formation of Contract in Roman Law and Scots Law (1958), Regulae Iuris: From Juristic Rules to Legal Maxims (1966), Legal Values in Western Society (with J Shand, 1974), Adam Smith's Lectures on Jurisprudence (jt ed, 1978), Legal Evolution (1980), Legal Institutions, the Development of Dispute Settlement (1984), The Character & Influence of the Roman Civil Law: Historical Essays (1988), The Teaching of Roman Law in England Around 1200 (with late F de Zulueta, 1990), Notaries Public in England since the Reformation (ed and contrib, 1991), Röisches Recht und Europa (1996); *Style*— Prof Peter Stein, JP, QC, FBA; ✉ Wimpole Cottage, 36 Wimpole Rd, Great Eversden, Cambridge CB3 7HR (☎ 01223 262349); Queens' College, Cambridge CB3 9ET (☎ 01223 335511)

STEINBERG, Gerald; MP (Lab) City of Durham (majority 15,058); *Career* MP (Lab) City of Durham 1987–; *Style*— Gerald Steinberg, Esq, MP; ✉ House of Commons, London SW1A 0AA (☎ 0171 219 3000)

STEINBERG, Prof Hannah; da of late Dr Michael Steinberg, and Marie, *née* Wein; *Educ* Putney HS, Queen Anne's Sch Caversham, Univ of Reading (Cert in Commerce), Denton Secretarial Coll, UCL (BA, PhD, Trouton Scholar), Univ of London (post grad studentship, pres Univ Union); *Career* sec to md Omes Ltd until 1944; University Coll London: joined 1950 as hon research asst, asst lectr then lectr in pharmacology, reader in psychopharmacology, prof of psychopharmacology (first in Western Europe) 1970–92, head of Psychopharmacology Gp 1979–92, hon research fell in psychology 1992–; emeritus prof Univ of London 1989–; hon research prof Sch of Psychology Middx Univ 1992–; hon consltg clinical psychologist Dept of Psychological Med Royal Free Hosp 1970, visiting prof in psychiatry McMaster Univ Ontario (week long assignment) 1971; vice pres: Collegium Internationale Neuro-Psychopharmacologicum 1968–74 (emeritus fell 1995–), Br Assoc for Psychopharmacology 1974–76 (hon memb 1989–); convener Academic Women's Achievement Gp 1979–92, special tstee Middx Hosp 1988–92; memb Editorial Bd: British Journal of Pharmacology 1965–72, Psychopharmacologia 1965–80, Pharmacopsychoecologia 1987–; memb: MRC Working Parties, Experimental Psychological Soc, Br Pharmacological Soc, Euro Behavioural Pharmacology Soc (fndr memb 1986), Euro Coll of Neuro-Psychopharmacology (fndr memb 1986), Br Assoc of Sport and Exercise Sciences (accredited sport and exercise scientist 1992–), European Health Psychology Soc; dir Art Research, Creativity and Health 1991–96; chartered psychologist, fell Br Psychological Soc (ed Bulletin 1955–62), distinguished affiliate American Psychological Assoc Div of Psychopharmacology 1978; *Books* Animals and Men (trans and jt ed, 1951), Animal Behaviour and Drug Action (jt ed, 1963), Scientific Basis of Drug Dependence (1968), Psychopharmacology: Sexual Disorders and Drug Abuse (jt ed, 1972), Exercise Addiction (jt ed, 1995), Quality and Quantity in Sport and Exercise Psychology (jt ed, 1996), How Teams Work (jt ed, 1996); author of scientific, semi-popular articles and chapters on psychopharmacology, physical exercise and mental health, academic women's issues and also planning in conservation areas; *Style*— Prof Hannah Steinberg; ✉ School of Psychology, Middlesex University, Queensway, Enfield, Middlesex EN3 4SF (☎ 0181 362 5000, direct line 0181 362 6075, fax 0181 362 5343, e-mail Hannah3@mdx.ac.uk)

STEINBERG, Dr (Victor) Leonard; s of Nathan Steinberg (d 1947), of London, and Sarah, *née* Bardiger; *b* 26 Aug 1926; *Educ* Shoreham GS, Regent Street Poly, St Bartholomew's Hosp (MB BS, DPhysMed, FRCP London and Edinburgh); *m* 25 Jan 1953, Leni, da of Max Ackerman (d 1964), of London; 3 s (Nathan Anthony b 28 Nov 1953, Michael John b 8 Feb 1955, Stephen David b 30 Jan 1960); *Career* conslt rheumatologist: Enfield Gp of Hosps 1959–67, Central Middx Hosp 1960–91 (hon conslt 1991–), Wembley Hosp 1967–95; former pres Section of Rheumatology RSM, past pres London Jewish Med Soc; memb: Br Soc of Rheumatology, Harveian Soc of London, Br Med Acupuncture Soc; Freeman City of London, Liveryman Worshipful Soc of Apothecaries of London; memb BMA; *Recreations* swimming, walking, opera, theatre, clay pigeon shooting; *Clubs* RAC; *Style*— Dr Leonard Steinberg; ✉ 22 Holne Chase, London N2 (☎ 0181 458 27264); 29–31 Devonshire Street, London W1N 1RF

STEINBY, Prof Eva Margareta; da of Kaarlo Erkki Wilén and Doris Margareta Steinby; *b* 21 Nov 1938; *Educ* Univ of Helsinki (Hum Kand, Fil Kand, Fil Lic, Fil Dr), Univ of Oxford (MA); *Career* Institutum Romanum Finlandiae Rome: asst 1973–77, dir 1979–82 and 1992–94; docent in history Univ of Helsinki 1977–, sr research fell Finnish Acad Helsinki 1985–92, prof of archaeology of the Roman Empire and fell All Souls Coll Univ of Oxford 1994–; visiting fell All Souls Coll Oxford 1990–91; fell: Suomen Historiallinen Seura 1978, Societas Scientiarum Fennica 1983, Pontificia Accademia Romana di Archeologia 1993–95 (corresponding fell 1982); corresponding fell Deutsches Archaologisches Institut 1984, Medaglia d'Oro per Benemeriti Culturali (Italy) 1983, offr 1st class Order of White Rose (Finland) 1991; *Books* La cronologia delle figlinae doliari urbane (1976), Lateres signati Ostienses (vols I-II, 1977–78), Indici complementari ai bolli doliari urbani (CIL, XV, 1, 1987), Lacus Iurturnae I (ed, 1989), Lexicon Topographicum Urbis Romae (5 vols, 1993–); also author of numerous articles in Italian, German and Finnish learned jls; *Style*— Prof Eva Margareta Steinby; ✉ University of Oxford Institute of Archaeology, 36 Beaumont Street, Oxford OX1 2PG (☎ 01865 278248, fax 01865 278254); All Souls College, Oxford OX1 4AL (☎ 01865 279379)

STEINER, Prof George; s of F G Steiner (d 1968), and E Steiner (d 1981); *b* 23 April 1929; *Educ* Paris (BèsL), Univ of Chicago (BA), Univ of Harvard (MA), Univ of Oxford (DPhil), Univ of Cambridge (PhD); *m* 7 July 1955, Zara; 1 s (David b 1958), 1 da (Deborah b 1960); *Career* memb staff the Economist London 1952–56, Inst for Advanced Study Princeton 1956–58, Gauss lectr Princeton 1959–60, fell Churchill Coll Cambridge 1961; lectures: Massey 1974, Leslie Stephen Cambridge 1986, W P Ker Univ of Glasgow 1986, Page Barbour Univ of Virginia 1987; Fulbright professorship 1958–69, O Henry short story award 1958, Guggenheim fellowship 1971–72, prof of English and comparative literature Univ of Geneva 1974–94, visiting prof Collège de France 1992, visiting prof of Euro and comparative literature Univ of Oxford 1994, Lord Weidenfeld visiting prof of comparative literature Univ of Oxford 1994–95; Zabel award of Nat Inst of Arts and Letters of the US 1970, Faulkner Stipend for Fiction PEN 1983, Gifford Lectr 1990, corresponding memb Germany Academy, hon memb American Acad of Arts and Sciences, Legion d'Honneur, hon fell Balliol Coll Oxford 1995; doctorate (hc) Univ of Louvain 1980; Hon DLitt Univs of: East Anglia 1976, Bristol 1989, Glasgow 1990, Liège 1990, Ulster 1993, Durham 1995; Hon DLitt: Kenyon Coll USA 1996, Trinity Coll Dublin 1996; FRSL 1964; *Books* Tolstoy or Dostoevsky (1958), The Death of Tragedy (1960), Anno Domini (1964), Language and Silence (1967), Extraterritorial (1971), In Bluebirds Castle (1971), The Sporting Scene: White Knights in Reykavik (1973), After Babel (1975), Heidegger (1978), On Difficulty and other Essays (1978), The Portage to San Cristabal of AH (1981), Antigones (1984), George Steiner, a reader (1984), Real Presences (1989), Proofs and Three Parables (1992, winner Macmillan Silver Pen Award for Fiction PEN), No Passion Spent (1996), The Deeps of the Sea and Other Fiction (1996), Home in English (ed, 1996); *Recreations* chess, music, hill walking, old English sheepdog; *Clubs* Athenaeum, Savile, Harvard Club of NYC; *Style*— Prof George Steiner; ✉ Churchill College, University of Cambridge, Cambridge CB3 0DS

STEINER, Jeffrey Josef; s of Beno Steiner, and Paula Borstein; *b* 3 April 1937; *Educ* Bradford Inst of Technol Yorkshire, City and Guilds Inst London; *m* 1, 1957 (m dis 1970), Claude; 1 s (Eric b 25 Oct 1961), 2 da (Natalia b 14 Sept 1965, Thierry Tama Tama (foster) b 31 Dec 1970); m 2, 6 March 1976 (m dis 1983), Linda, *née* Schaller; 1 s (Benjamin b 3 April 1978), 1 da (Alexandra b 1980); m 3, 19 March 1987, Irja, *née* Eckerbrant Bonnier; *Career* mangr Metals and Controls Div Texas Instruments 1959–60 (mgmnt trainee 1958–59), pres Texas Instruments 1960–66 (Argentina, Brazil, Mexico, Switzerland, France), pres Burlington Tapis 1967–72, chm and pres Cedec SA Engrg Co 1973–84, chm, pres and chief exec offr The Fairchild Corporation (NYSE) 1985–, chm and chief exec offr Banner Aerospace Inc (NYSE); memb: Anti-Defamation League, Boys Town of Italy, Montefiore Med Centre, Bd Israel Museum; hon doctorate Yeshiva Univ 1994; Chevalier de l'Ordre des Arts et des Lettres 1990, Chevalier de l'Ordre National du Mérite 1992; *Recreations* tennis, sailing, art collecting; *Clubs* Annabel's, Polo of Paris, Racing de France, Harry's Bar, St James's, Mark's; *Style*— Jeffrey Steiner, Esq; ✉ 6 Cheyne Walk, London SW3; The Fairchild Corporation, 110 East 59th St, New York, NY 10022, USA (☎ 00 1 212 308 6700 and 703 478 5800, fax 00 1 212 888 5674)

STEINER, Prof Robert Emil; CBE (1979); s of Rudolf Steiner (d 1958), of Vienna, and Clary, *née* Nördlinger (d 1921); *b* 1 Feb 1918; *Educ* Theresiamische Academie and Franz Josephs Realgymnasium Vienna, Univ of Vienna, Univ Coll Dublin (MB, ChB, MD); *m* 17 March 1945, Gertrude Margaret, da of Fritz Konirsch (d 1943), of Castlebar, Co Mayo, Ireland; 2 da (Hilary Clare b 1950, Ann Elizabeth b 1953); *Career* WWII; MO Emergency Med Serv: Guy's Hosp 1941, Macclesfield Infirmary 1941–42, Winwick Emergency Hosp 1942–44; trainee diagnostic radiologist Sheffield Royal Infirmary 1944, dir Dept of Diagnostic Radiology Hammersmith Hosp 1957–60 (dep dir 1950–57); prof of diagnostic radiology: Dept of Diagnostic Radiology Hammersmith Hosp, Univ of London, Royal Postgrad Med Sch 1960–83 (emeritus prof 1984–); pres: Br Inst of Radiology 1972–73, Royal Coll of Radiologists 1977–79; formerly: dep chm Nat Radiological Protection Bd, civilian conslt radiology to Med Dir Gen (Naval), conslt advsr in radiology to Dept of Health; Hon: FACR 1965, FCRA 1971, FFR RCSI 1972; DMR 1945, FRCR 1948, FRCP 1965, FRCS 1982; author of over 250 scientific pubns and 5 books; *Recreations* gardening, swimming, walking, music; *Clubs* Hurlingham; *Style*— Prof Robert Steiner, CBE; ✉ 12 Stonehill Rd, East Sheen, London SW14 8RW (☎ 0181 876 4038); NMR Unit, University of London, Hammersmith Hospital, Du Cane Rd, London W12 OHS (☎ 0181 740 3298, 0181 743 2030)

STEINER, Rear Adm (Ottakar Harold Mojmir) St John; CB (1967); s of Ferdinand Steiner (d 1961), and Alice Mary Dorothea, *née* Whittington (d 1964); *b* 8 July 1916; *Educ* St Paul's; *m* 1, 1940 (m dis 1974), Evelyn Mary, da of Henry Thomas Young; 1 s (Anthony St John, OBE b 1942), 1 da (Angela St John b 1948); m 2, Edith Eleanor Powell, wid of Sqdn Ldr J A F Powell; 1 step s (Jonathan Powell b 1955); *Career* joined RN 1934; served 1935–44: HMS Frobisher, HMS Orion, HMS Southampton, HMS Electra, HMS Courageous, HMS Ilex, HMS Havelock; sqdn torpedo offr HMS Superb 1945–47, staff of C-in-C Far East 1948–50, naval staff Admty 1950–52, exec offr HMS Ceylon 1953–54, exec offr HMS Daedalus 1955–56, naval staff Admty 1956–57, Capt 3 Destroyer Sqdn and CO HMS Saintes 1958–59, naval advsr to UK High Cmmr Canada 1960–62, Capt HMS Centaur 1963–65, asst chief Def Staff 1966–68; ADC to HM The Queen 1965; chm: Whitbread Round the World Races 1972–78, Transglobe Expedition 1979–80, Shipwrecked Fisherman and Mariners Royal Benevolent Soc; cdre RNSA 1974–76 (life vice-cdre 1978); Freeman City of London 1966, memb Worshipful Co of Coachmakers and Coach Harness Makers 1966; *Recreations* sailing, golf, bowls, garden; *Style*— Rear Adm O St John Steiner, CB

STEINFELD, Alan Geoffrey; QC (1987); s of Henry C Steinfeld (d 1967), of London, and Deborah, *née* Brickman; *b* 13 July 1946; *Educ* City of London Sch, Downing Coll Cambridge (BA, LLB); *m* 19 Feb 1976, Josephine Nicole, da of Eugene Gros, of London; 2 s (Martin b 28 Jan 1980, Sebastian b 1 Nov 1981); *Career* called to the Bar Lincoln's Inn 1968 (bencher 1996), dep judge of the High Court 1994–; *Recreations* lawn tennis, skiing, sailing, opera, cinema, lying in Turkish baths; *Clubs* RAC, Cumberland Lawn Tennis; *Style*— Alan Steinfeld, Esq, QC; ✉ 21 Wadham Gardens, London NW3 3DN (☎ 0171 483 3450); Jardin des Hesperides, Antibes, France; 24 Old Buildings, Lincoln's Inn, London WC2A 3UJ (☎ 0171 404 0946, fax 0171 405 1360)

STEINFELD, Michael Robert; *b* 3 Dec 1943; *Educ* William Ellis Sch London, Pembroke Coll Oxford (BA); *m* 28 May 1980, Elizabeth Ann, *née* Watson; 2 da (Rebecca Hannah b 25 Feb 1981, Jemimah Francine b 15 Oct 1983), 1 s (Jonathon Henry b 29 Oct 1992); *Career* Titmuss Sainer & Webb (now Titmuss Sainer Dechert): articled clerk 1968–70, asst slr 1970–72, ptnr 1972–; memb Law Soc; *Recreations* sport, food, cinema, newspapers, music, France; *Style*— Michael Steinfeld, Esq; ✉ Titmuss Sainer Dechert, 2 Serjeants' Inn, London EC4Y 1LT (☎ 0171 583 5353, fax 0171 353 3683)

STELL, Christopher Fyson; OBE (1989); s of Herbert Stell (d 1967), of Liverpool, and Caroline Irene, *née* Fyson (d 1982); *b* 26 Jan 1929; *Educ* Liverpool Coll, Univ of Liverpool (BArch, MA); *m* 17 Aug 1957, Dorothy Jean, da of Wilfred Hugh Mackay (d 1986), of Havant, Hants; 2 s (John b 1958, Edward b 1962); *Career* conslt Royal Commission on Historical Monuments (England) 1989– (architectural investigator 1955–89); numerous contribs to learned jls; hon vice pres Royal Archaeological Inst, hon sec Ancient Monuments Soc; memb Listed Buildings Advsy Cee Methodist Church, tstee Historic Chapels Tst; ARIBA 1956, FSA 1964; *Books* An Inventory of Nonconformist Chapels and Meeting-Houses in Central England (1986), South-West England (1991), North of England (1994); *Recreations* book binding, photography; *Clubs* Athenaeum; *Style*— Christopher Stell, Esq, OBE, FSA; ✉ Frognal, 25 Berks Hill, Chorleywood, Herts WD3 5AG (☎ 01923 282044); Hob Lane House, Brearley, Luddendenfoot, Halifax, Yorks HX2 6JF; Royal Commission on Historical Monuments (England), 55 Blandford Street, London W1H 3AF

STELLA-SAWICKI, Dr Marek Andrzej; s of Jan Stella-Sawicki (d 1984), of Poland, and Stanislawa, *née* Lissowska; *b* 21 Feb 1948; *Educ* Henry Jordan Sch, Tech Univ Cracow (MSc), King's Coll London (PhD); *m* 27 July 1974, Teresa, da of Capt Antoni Witczak (d 1973), of London; 2 da (Dominika Helena b 1976, Joanna Jadwiga b 1978); *Career* sr systems engr United Biscuits (McVities) Ltd 1975–78, sr projects engr Metal Box PLC 1978–82, projects engrg mangr Computer Field Maintenance Ltd 1982–85, gen mangr DPCE Computer Servs PLC 1985–86, dir engrg ops MBS PLC 1986–88, dir Computacenter Ltd 1988–95, mktg and tech dir Computeraid Services Limited 1995–; conslt Cover Pubns 1976–79, ed Video World 1979–81, publishing dir and editorial dir Video Press 1981–85; sponsorship: W Middx Lawn Tennis Club, Video Press Falklands Appeal; memb Cncl: Engrg Inst, AFSM (USA); FIEE; *Books* Investigation into Computer Modelling Simulation and Control of the Stirling Engine (1978), Video A-Z (10 vols, 1981–83), A-Z of Personal Computers (10 vols, 1983–86), Which Appliance (2 edns, 1984–86); *Recreations* skiing, shooting, tennis, target shooting (Bisley); *Clubs* Hurlingham, Leander, West Middx Lawn Tennis, Nat Rifle Assoc; *Style*— Dr Marek Stella-Sawicki; ✉ Computeraid Services Limited, Cygnus House, 1 The Southwood Crescent, Apollo Rise, Farnborough, Hampshire GU14 0NL (☎ 01252 548888, fax 01252 547669, car 0836 681567)

STELLINI, Salv J; s of Joseph Stellini (d 1969), and Victoria Stellini (d 1979); *b* 19 July 1939; *Educ* Royal Univ of Malta (BA), Univ of Alberta Canada (MA), LSE (Foreign Serv Cert); *m* 1969, Lucinda, *née* Flannery; 1 s (Luke b 1975), 1 da (Alexia b 1972); *Career* teacher 1959–64; Maltese Foreign Serv: joined 1966, second sec NY 1968–71, Head Office 1971–74, first sec London 1974–77, asst dir Cwlth Secretariat London 1977–79, Head Office 1979–81, resigned 1981; int mktg mangr Farsons (Malta) 1981–87; rejoined Foreign Serv 1988, ambass of Malta to Washington 1988–91, high cmmr of Malta to Ct of St James's 1991–96; *Recreations* walking, reading, theatre; *Style*— Mr Salv J Stellini

STEMBRIDGE, David Harry; QC (1990); s of Percy Gladstone Stembridge (d 1959), of Droitwich, and Emily Winifred, *née* Wright; *b* 23 Dec 1932; *Educ* Bromsgrove, Univ of Birmingham (LLB); *m* 2 April 1956, Theresa Cecilia, da of Max Furer, of Mulhouse, France; 3 s (Michael b 1957, Peter b 1960, Philip b 1968), 1 da (Helen b 1963); *Career* called to the Bar Gray's Inn 1955, in practice Midland and Oxford Circuit, recorder Crown Ct 1977–; *Recreations* organ, sailing; *Clubs* Bar Yacht; *Style*— David Stembridge, Esq, QC; ✉ 5 Fountain Court, Steelhouse Lane, Birmingham B4 6DR (☎ 0121 606 0500, fax 0121 606 1501); 199 Strand, London WC2R 1DR (☎ 0171 379 9779, fax 0171 379 9481)

STEMMER, Philip; s of Emanuel Stemmer, of London, and Regina Stemmer; *b* 12 Dec 1949; *Educ* Manchester Jewish GS, Turner Dental Sch Manchester (BDS, represented Univ of Manchester soccer team); *m* 22 Dec 1976, Elissa, da of Myer Freedman; 1 s (Raphael Steven b 22 Dec 1993), 4 da (Shiri Debra b 12 Aug 1979, Daniella Civia b 15 Dec 1981, Natalie Ruth b 30 Nov 1985, Anna Sophie Rose b 14 Dec 1994); *Career* dental surgn; gen practice (with Phillip Wander) Manchester 1974–76, opened new practice Manchester 1976–84, opened branch practice Droylsden 1982–84, practised in Israel 1984–86 (affiliated to Periodontal Dept Tel Aviv Dental Sch), in private practice Harley St then Devonshire Place 1986–, owner of practice North Finchley 1987–89, opened UK's first fresh breath centre to combat oral malodour 1995; memb: BDA, Alpha Omega, Dental Post Grad Soc of Manchester, Insight Gp; rep Lancs Chess Team 1964; *Recreations* swimming, music (opera, cantorial, good modern), chess; *Style*— Philip Stemmer, Esq; ✉ 2 Devonshire Place, London W1N 1PA (☎ 0171 935 7511/0407, mobile 0831 115406)

STEMPLOWSKI, HE Ryszard; s of Kazimierz Stemplowski, of Poland, and Eugenia, *née* Białecka; *b* 25 March 1939; *Educ* Tech Lycée Bydgoszcz, Tech Univ of Wrocław, Wrocław Univ (LLM), Inst of History (Polish Acad of Scis) Warsaw (PhD); *m* 1, 1964 (m dis 1968), Anita, *née* Zajaczkowska; m 2, Irena, *née* Zasłona; 2 da (Maria b 1976, Zofia b 1978); *Career* Polish diplomat; research fell Inst of History Polish Acad of Scis Warsaw 1973–90, chief of the Chancellory of the SEJM (Chamber of Deputies) 1990–93, Polish ambass to Ct of St James's 1994–; visiting fell St Antony's Coll Oxford 1974, Alexander von Humboldt fell and visiting scholar Univ of Cologne 1981–82; *Books* Dependence and Defiance: Argentina and Rivalries among USA, UK and Germany (1930–46) (Warsaw, 1975), State Socialism in Real Capitalism (Warsaw, 1996); also author of books and papers in on state and nation building processes and int rels (economics, migrations, diplomacy, political ideas) in the 20th century; *Recreations* music, astrophysics; *Clubs* Athenaeum, Army & Navy, Travellers, Rotary; *Style*— HE Mr Ryszard Stemplowski; ✉ 4 Templewood Avenue, London NW3 7XA; Polish Embassy, 47 Portland Place, London W1N 3AG (☎ 0171 580 2969, fax 0171 323 4018)

STENHAM, Anthony William Paul (Cob); s of Bernard Basil Stenham (d 1972); *b* 28 Jan 1932; *Educ* Eton, Trinity Coll Cambridge (MA); *m* 1, 1966 (m dis), Hon Sheila Marion, da of 1 Baron Poole, PC, CBE, TD (d 1993); m 2, 1983, Anne Martha Mary O'Rawe; 2 da (Polly Elizabeth Josephine b 1986, Daisy Constance b 1990); *Career* called to the Bar Inner Temple 1955, chartered accountant 1958; Price Waterhouse 1955–61, Philip Hill Higginson Erlanger 1962–64, fin dir and jt md William Baird & Co 1964–69; Unilever NV and plc 1969–86: fin dir 1970–86, chm Unilever United States Inc 1978–79, corp devpt dir 1984–86; md NY and chm Europe, ME and Africa Bankers Trust Co 1986–90; dir and dep chm VSEL Consortium plc 1987–95; dir: Equity Capital for Industry 1976–81, Capital Radio plc 1982–94, Virgin Group plc 1986–89, Colonial Mutual (UK Holdings) Ltd 1987–92, The Rank Organisation plc 1987–, Rothmans International plc 1988–95, Rothmans International BV 1995–, Unigate plc 1989–, STC plc 1990–91; chm Arjo Wiggins Appleton plc 1991–, dep chm Telewest Communications plc 1994–; non-exec dir: Standard Chartered plc 1991–, Worms et cie 1991–96, Trafalgar House plc 1993–96; chm Advsy Bd Inst of Contemporary Arts 1987–89 (chm Cncl 1977–87), memb Cncl Architectural Assoc 1982–84; Royal Coll of Art: memb Ct 1978–, memb Cncl 1978–81, chm Cncl and pro-provost 1979–81, hon fell 1980; govr: Museum of London 1986–93, Theatres Tst 1989–96, Design Museum 1992–96; FRSA, FRCA; *Recreations* cinema, opera, painting; *Clubs* Beefsteak, White's; *Style*— Cob Stenham, Esq; ✉ 4 The Grove, London N6 6JU (☎ 0181 340 2266); Arjo Wiggins Appleton plc, 25 St James's Street, London SW1A 1HA (☎ 0171 839 7771, fax 0171 839 8881)

STENHOUSE, Sir Nicol; kt (1962); s of late John Stenhouse; *b* 14 Feb 1911; *Educ* Repton; *m* 1951, Barbara Heath Wilson (d 1991); 2 s, 1 da; *Career* chm and md Andrew Yule & Co Ltd Calcutta 1959–62; pres Bengal C of C and Indust (Calcutta) and Assoc C of C of India 1961–62; *Style*— Sir Nicol Stenhouse; ✉ 3 St Mary's Court, Sixpenny Handley, nr Salisbury, Wilts SP5 5PH

STENLAKE, Prof John Bedford; CBE (1985); s of Frank Stenlake (d 1940), of Ealing, London, and Blanche, *née* Bedford (d 1969); *b* 21 Oct 1919; *Educ* Ealing GS, Birkbeck Coll Univ of London (BSc), Sch of Pharmacy Univ of London (PhD, DSc); *m* 14 July 1945, Anne Beatrice, da of Frank Douglas Holder, DL, OBE, MC, JP (d 1978), of Chelmsford; 5 s (Timothy b 1946, Robert b 1948, Christopher b 1951, William b 1953, Richard b 1957), 1 da (Marion b 1961); *Career* WWII RAF Flt Lt 1942–45; Boots The Chemist 1935–39; demonstrator, asst lectr then lectr in pharmaceutical chemistry Sch of Pharmacy Univ of London 1945–52, sr lectr in pharmaceutical chemistry Royal Coll of Sci and Technol Glasgow 1952–61, prof of pharmacy Univ of Strathclyde 1961–82 (hon prof 1982–95, emeritus prof 1993); inventor of atracurium besylate (Tracrium) muscle relaxant used in surgical anaesthesia and intensive care (Queen's award for Technological Innovation); memb: Ctee on Safety Meds 1970–79, Lanarkshire Health Bd 1977–83; leader UK delgn to the Euro Pharmacopoeia Cmmn 1980–88, chm Br Pharmacopoeia Cmmn 1980–88 (memb 1963–, vice chm 1978–80), memb Meds Cmmn 1984–91; author of many reviews, papers and articles concerned with original research in medicinal and pharmaceutical chemistry; Hon DSc Univ of Strathclyde 1988; CChem, FRSC, FRPharmS, FRSE 1964; *Books* Practical Pharmaceutical Chemistry (with A H

Beckett, 1962), Foundations of Molecular Pharmacology (1979), Chapters in Burger's Medicinal Chemistry (4 edn, 1980), Handbook of Experimental Pharmacology (vol 49, 1986), Medicinal Chemistry, The Role of Organic Chemistry in Drug Research (1986); *Recreations* reading, gardening; *Clubs* Royal Commonwealth Society; *Style*— Prof John Stenlake, CBE, FRSE; ✉ Mark Corner, Twynholm, Kirkcudbright DG6 4PR (☎ 01557 860242)

STENNING, Christopher John William (Kit); s of Col Philip Dives Stenning, of Sunnyside, Elie, Fife, and Cynthia Margaret, *née* Rycroft; *b* 16 Oct 1950; *Educ* Marlborough; *m* 19 Sept 1981, Ruth Marian, da of late George Thomas Chenery Draper; 1 s (Jonathan b 1985), 1 da (Rachel b 1983); *Career* slr 1970–82, slr to Prudential Corp 1982–88, dir of corp fin David Garrick 1988–90, proprietor Kit Stenning Assocs 1990–91, ptnr Messrs Kennedys Slrs 1991–; Freeman: City of London 1971, Worshipful Co of Haberdashers 1971; *Books* The Takeover Guide (1988); *Recreations* sport; *Clubs* Hurlingham; *Style*— Kit Stenning, Esq

STENNING, Prof Keith; s of Luis Charles Stenning (d 1992), of Beaconsfield, and Marjorie, *née* Warren; *b* 15 June 1948; *Educ* High Wycombe Royal Grammar, Trinity Coll Oxford (exhibitioner, MA), Rockefeller Univ (PhD); *m* 1980, Dr Lynn Michell, da of Maj Leonard Dodd; 1 s (Nye b 2 June 1981); *Career* res assoc Rockefeller Univ 1975–76, lectr in psychology Univ of Liverpool 1976–83; Univ of Edinburgh: lectr in cognitive science 1983–88, dir Human Communication and Res Centre 1988–, professorial fell 1988–; author of numerous papers on human information processing; *Recreations* sailing; *Style*— Prof Keith Stenning; ✉ Human Communication Research Centre, University of Edinburgh, 2 Buccleuch Place, Edinburgh EH8 9LW (☎ 0131 650 4444, fax 0131 650 4587)

STEPHEN, (John) David; s of John Stephen (d 1968), and Anne Eileen Stephen (d 1991); *b* 3 April 1942; *Educ* Luton GS, King's Coll Cambridge (MA), Univ of Essex (MA); *m* 28 Dec 1968, Susan Dorothy, *née* Harris; 3 s (John b 1972, Edward b 1977, Alexander b 1982), 1 da (Sophy b 1974); *Career* Runnymede Tst 1970–75 (dir 1973–75), Latin American regnl rep Int Univ Exchange Fund 1975–77, special advsr to Sec of State for Foreign and Cwlth Affrs 1977–79, freelance writer and conslt 1979–84, memb Gen Mgmnt Bd and dir of corporate rels Cwlth Devpt Corpn 1984–92, princ offr Exec Office of the Sec-Gen United Nations NYC 1992–96, dir UN Verification Mission Guatemala 1996–; Parly candidate (Alliance) N Luton 1983 and 1987; *Style*— David Stephen, Esq

STEPHEN, Col George McLaughlin; OBE (1979); s of Dr George Mackie Stephen (d 1951), and Charlotte Baron, *née* McLaughlin (d 1963); *b* 12 May 1938; *Educ* Epsom Coll; *m* 1, 20 July 1963 (m dis 1988), Caroline Barbara, *née* Grotrian; 1 s (Aidan Diarmid Grotrian b 3 Sept 1970); m 2, 25 May 1988, Rozanne Shirley, da of Col M P Robinson, OBE, TD, DL, of Carleton Lodge, Carleton, W Yorks; *Career* Nat Serv Seaforth Highlanders and Cameronians (Scottish Rifles) 1957–68, Scots Greys 1968–71 (psc 1972), Scots Dragoon Guards 1971–78 (NDC 1978), Lt-Col and CO 13/18 Royal Hussars RAC 1978–81, exchange offr Cmd and Staff Coll Aust 1981–84, Col MOD 1984–88; memb and vice pres Int Affrs Int League for Protection of Horses, pres Br Percheron Horse Soc 1992; memb: Nat Equine Welfare Cncl, BHS, BFSS; memb Queen's Body Guard for Scotland (Royal Company of Archers) 1987; Haute Dignitaire D'Honneur Grande Chancellerie Int de l'Ordre Equestre de Saint Georges de France; Freeman Worshipful Co of Farriers; *Recreations* riding, shooting, reading, art, music; *Clubs* Cavalry and Guards'; *Style*— Col George Stephen, OBE; ✉ Anne Colvin House, Snetterton, nr Norwich, Norfolk NR16 2LR (☎ 01953 498682, fax 01953 498373); Kirkburn House, Ettrick, Selkirkshire, Scotland TD7 5JA

STEPHEN, Prof Kenneth William; s of William Stephen (d 1970), and Agnes Eleanor, *née* Rankin; *b* 1 Oct 1937; *Educ* Hillhead HS, Univ of Glasgow (BDS, DDSc); *m* Anne Seymour, da of John Gardiner; 1 da (Linda Jane b 22 Nov 1966), 1 s (Grant MacLean b 8 Sept 1970); *Career* general dental practitioner 1960–64, house offr Dept of Oral Surgery Glasgow Dental Hosp 1964–65; Univ of Glasgow: lectr in conservative dentistry 1965–68, sr lectr in oral med 1971–80 (lectr 1968–71), reader 1980–84, head Dept of Oral Med and Pathology 1980–92, prof of community dental health 1984–95, prof of Dental Public Health 1995–, head Dept of Adult Dental Care 1992–95; conslt in charge Glasgow Sch of Dental Hygiene 1979–96; hon lectr in oral physiology Univ of Newcastle 1969–70; memb: Int Assoc for Dental Res, Fédération Dentaire Internationale, Euro Orgn for Caries Res, BDA, Br Soc for Dental Res; hon memb: Finnish Dental Soc 1979, Hungarian Dental Assoc 1993; pres Glasgow Odontological Soc 1995 (vice pres 1994–95); ORCA Rolex prize 1990, E W Borrow Meml award IADR 1992; HDD 1965, FDS 1967; author of 140 papers in scientific jls and contrib to 11 books; *Recreations* skiing, hillwalking, gardening, swimming, cycling; *Style*— Prof Kenneth Stephen; ✉ University of Glasgow Dental School, 378 Sauchiehall Street, Glasgow G2 3JZ (☎ 0141 211 9854, fax 0141 332 7053)

STEPHEN, Dr (George) Martin; s of Sir Andrew Stephen, KB (d 1980), of Sheffield, and Frances, *née* Barker; *b* 18 July 1949; *Educ* Uppingham, Univ of Leeds (BA), Univ of Sheffield (DipEd, DPhil); *m* 21 Aug 1971, Jennifer Elaine, da of George Fisher, of Polloch Lodge, Polloch, Invernesshire; 3 s (Neill b 22 July 1976, Simon b 31 Aug 1978, Henry b 20 March 1981); *Career* various posts in remand homes 1966–71, teacher of English Uppingham Sch 1971–72, housemaster and teacher of English Haileybury Sch and ISC 1972–83, second master Sedbergh Sch 1983–87, headmaster The Perse Sch 1987–94, high master The Manchester Grammar Sch 1994–; assoc memb of the room Gonville & Caius Coll Cambridge 1988–94; HMC: memb 1987–, chm Community Serv Ctee 1992–, memb HMC/GSA Univ Working Pty 1994–; memb: The Naval Review 1991–, CSU Educn Advsr Ctee, Cncl The Project Tst; govr: Withington Sch Manchester 1994–, Pownall Hall Sch Wilmslow 1994–; FRSA 1996; *Books* An Introductory Guide to English Literature (1982), Studying Shakespeare (1982), British Warship Designs Since 1906 (1984), English Literature (1986, 2 edn 1991), Sea Battles in Close Up (1987, 2 edn 1996), Never Such Innocence (1988, 3 edn 1993), The Fighting Admirals (1990), The Best of Saki (1993, 2 edn 1996), The Price of Pity (1996); *Recreations* sailing, fishing, rough shooting, writing, theatre; *Clubs* East India Devonshire Sports & Public School (hon memb); *Style*— Dr Martin Stephen; ✉ 143 Old Hall Lane, Manchester M14 6HL (☎ 0161 224 3929); The Manchester Grammar School, Manchester M13 0XT (☎ 0161 224 7201, fax 0161 257 2446)

STEPHEN, Michael; MP (C) Shoreham (majority 14,286); s of late Harry L Stephen, and Edna Stephen; *b* 25 Sept 1942; *Educ* King Henry VIII Sch Coventry, Stanford Univ (LLM), Harvard Univ; *m* 27 May 1989, Virginia Mary, da of late Charles de Trensé; *Career* admitted slr 1964, called to the Bar Inner Temple 1966; Lt The Life Gds 1966–70; Harkness Fellowship USA (LLM Stanford) 1970–72, research fell Harvard Univ 1972, asst legal advsr to UK Ambassador to UN 1972, practising barr 1972–87; Parly candidate (C) Doncaster N 1983, MP (C) Shoreham 1992–; PPS to MAFF 1996–; author of Bail (Amendment) Act 1993, vice chm Cons Parly Home Affairs and Legal Ctees, memb Environment Select Ctee and Euro Standing Ctee 1994–; Industry and Parliament Tst Fellowship (British Rail) 1993–94; CCncllr Dunmow Div Essex 1985–91, memb Nat Exec Assoc of CCs 1989–91; memb: Royal United Services Inst, Int Inst for Strategic Studies, Royal Inst of Int Affrs 1984–; author of pamphlets and articles on Home Office and legal affrs, foreign affrs and housing; *Style*— Michael Stephen, Esq, MP; ✉ House of Commons, London SW1A 0AA (☎ 01426 247908)

STEPHEN, Rt Hon Sir Ninian Martin; KG (1994), AK (1982), GCMG (1982), GCVO (1982), KBE (1972), PC (1979); s of late Frederick Stephen; *b* 15 June 1923; *Educ* George Watson's Edinburgh, Edinburgh Acad, St Paul's, Melbourne Univ; *m* 1949, Valery, da of A Q Sinclair; 5 da; *Career* Lt 2 AIF; barr and slr 1949, barr Vic 1952, QC 1966, judge Supreme Ct of Vic 1970–72, justice of High Court of Australia 1972–82, hon bencher Gray's Inn 1981, govr gen of Australia 1982–89, Aust ambass for the environment 1989–92; judge Int Criminal Tbnls for former Yugoslavia and for Rwanda 1993–; chm Nat Library of Aust 1989–94; Hon LLD: Sydney 1984, Melbourne 1985, Griffith 1988; Hon DLitt Western Australia 1992; Hon Liveryman Worshipful Co of Clothworkers 1991; KStJ 1982, Cdr Légion d'Honneur 1994; *Style*— The Rt Hon Sir Ninian Stephen, KG, AK, GCMG, GCVO, KBE; ✉ 193 Domain Road, South Yarra, Vic 3141, Australia

STEPHENS, Air Cmdt Dame Anne; DBE (1961, MBE 1946); da of late Gen Sir Reginald Byng Stephens, KCB, CMG; *b* 4 Nov 1912; *Educ* privately; *Career* joined WAAF 1939, served UK, Belgium, Germany 1939–45; WRAF: inspr 1952–54, dep dir 1954–57, dir 1960–63; staff offr HQ 2 TAF 1957–59, promoted Air Cmdt 1960; Hon ADC to HM The Queen 1960–63; *Style*— Air Cmdt Dame Anne Stephens, DBE; ✉ The Forge, Sibford Ferris, Banbury, Oxfordshire (☎ 01295 780452)

STEPHENS, Arthur Edward; s of Ora V Stephens (d 1975), of Houston, Texas, and Ada, *née* Sadler; *b* 23 May 1948; *Educ* Univ of Texas at Austin (BBA, BSc (Mech Eng)), Columbia Univ (MBA); *m* 31 Oct 1977, Jennifer Frances, da of Hugh and Gwyneth Roberts; *Career* Frank E Basil Inc: asst vice-pres 1972–74, vice-pres Athens Greece 1974–77; dep gen mgr Saudi Maintenance Co Riyadh Saudi Arabia 1977–82; Frank E Basil Inc: mgr Business Devpt Athens Greece 1982–83, vice-pres Finance, Personnel and Admin Washington DC 1983–86; pres Brown & Root Services Corporation and vice-pres Brown & Root Inc Houston Texas 1986–94, pres Houston Executive Air Services Inc 1986–94, chief exec Brown & Root Ltd London 1994–, sr vice-pres and regl mgr Brown & Root Inc 1994–; memb Bd: Dawson Industries Perth Australia 1992–94, Contracts Services Assoc Washington DC 1987–95; memb: Advsy Visiting Ctee Dept of Mech Engrg Univ of Texas 1994–96, OLG Houston Sch Bd 1993–94; registered professional engr Texas; Samuel F Bronfman Fell Columbia Univ 1971; memb American Soc of Mech Engrs 1969; *Clubs* RAC, IOD; *Style*— Arthur E Stephens; ✉ Brown & Root Ltd, 150 The Broadway, Wimbledon, London SW19 1RX (☎ 0181 544 6601, fax 0181 544 6950)

STEPHENS, Aylwin Kersey (Kerry); s of Sidney Stephens (d 1969), of Dorking, Surrey, and Joan, *née* Kelsey; *b* 16 Jan 1947; *Educ* Truro Sch Cornwall; *m* 1, 28 Nov 1978, Lorraine Naomi Tomlinson (d 1986); m 2, 14 June 1990, Emma Frances Catherine Griffiths, da of Colin Brook; 2 s (Rupert Hugh Kersey b 17 April 1993, Anthony Alexander Aylwin b 10 April 1995); *Career* articled clerk J Hulbert Grove & Co 1964–69; Deloitte Plender & Griffiths (later Deloitte & Co, then Deloitte Haskins & Sells) 1969–85: corporate and int tax specialist, ptnr London Tax Dept 1978, resigned partnership 1985; in private practice specialising in corporate and int tax 1985–87; readmitted ptnr Deloitte Haskins & Sells (now Coopers & Lybrand) 1987–; FCA 1969; *Recreations* work, walking, good hotels, 50's rock 'n' roll, 16th century; *Style*— Kerry Stephens, Esq; ✉ Coopers & Lybrand, Harman House, 1 George Street, Uxbridge, Middx UB8 1QQ (☎ 01895 273333, fax 01895 256413)

STEPHENS, Barbara Marion; da of late Sydney Davis Webb, and Edna Marion, *née* Finch; *b* 25 Aug 1951; *Educ* Colchester County HS, Mid-Essex Tech Coll (HNC in Engineering), N E London Poly (Dip in Mgmnt Studies), City Univ (MBA); *m* 28 March 1970, Trevor James Stephens; *Career* mech technician apprentice Marconi Co 1969–73, various tech and managerial posts Marconi Communication Systems Ltd 1973–88, asst indust advsr then indust advsr NEDO 1988–92; W Cumbria Devpt Agency: dir of ops 1993–95, chief exec 1995–; memb Cncl (now Senate) Engrg Cncl 1990–, fell Smallpeice Tst 1994–; memb: Advsy Cncl for the Devpt of RN Personnel 1995–, Higher Educn Funding Cncl for England 1995–; IEng 1976, AMIPE 1976, MIEIE 1992, FIMgt 1994 (MBIM 1978), FRSA 1992; *Recreations* embroidery, reading, letter writing, encouraging women to pursue careers in industry; *Style*— Ms Barbara Stephens; ✉ West Cumbria Development Agency, Thirlmere Building, Derwent Howe, Workington, Cumbria CA14 3YP (☎ 01900 65656, fax 01900 67587)

STEPHENS, Brian John; s of George Henry Stephens, of Southampton, and Marie Stephens; *b* 14 Dec 1946; *Educ* King Edward VI GS Southampton; *m* 5 April 1968, Rosemary Ann; 1 s (Marc b 1969), 1 da (Paula b 1970); *Career* BBC: engr 1965, studio mangr 1967, radio prodr 1977, ed of progs Radio 2 1991– (sr prodr 1986); tstee Mother Christmas Charity; *Recreations* cycling, reading, cooking, music on CD; *Style*— Brian Stephens, Esq; ✉ BBC Radio Two, Broadcasting House, London W1A 1AA (☎ 0171 765 4995)

STEPHENS, Dr John David; s of Sydney Brooke Stephens (d 1982), and Thora Gladys Stephens (d 1993); *b* 9 April 1944; *Educ* Highfields GS Wolverhampton, Guy's Hosp Med Sch (MB BS, MD); *m* 19 July 1967 (m dis 1976), Amanda; 1 s (Damian b 1 Nov 1969); *Career* house physician and surgn Royal Surrey Co Hosp Guildford 1967–68, house surgn Guy's Hosp 1968–69, house physician Churchill Hosp Oxford 1969–70, registrar in med UCH 1970–72, registrar in cardiology Brompton Hosp 1972–73 (house physician 1970), res fell in cardiology Harvard Univ Med Sch Boston USA 1973–74, sr registrar in cardiology St Bartholomew's Hosp 1974–81, conslt cardiologist and head of Cardiovascular Res Unit Oldchurch Hosp Romford and Royal London Hosp (Royal Hosps Tst) 1981–; author of pubns in various int med jls on original res in coronary blood flow, congestive heart failure and cardiovascular pharmacology; memb Br Cardiac Soc; FRCP 1993 (MRCP 1970); *Books* Cardiovascular Responses to Vasodilators in Man (1979); *Recreations* skiing, opera; *Clubs* RAC; *Style*— Dr John Stephens; ✉ 93 Harley Street, London W1N 1DS (☎ 0171 637 5881)

STEPHENS, John Lindsay; s of Rev Grosvenor Stephens (d 1992), and Olive, *née* Voysey-Martin (d 1987); *b* 23 July 1951; *Educ* Christ's Hosp, Lanchester Poly (BA); *m* 30 Aug 1975, Nicola Elizabeth (Nikki), da of Neville Brouard, of Les Eturs, Catel, Guernsey, CI; 1 s (David b 1982), 1 da (Joanna b 1980); *Career* admitted slr 1977; ptnr Simmons and Simmons; memb: Nat Tst, Residents Action Gp WABF, Weald of Kent Preservation Soc; *Recreations* family, music, food and wine, photography, working out; *Clubs* City of London, Frittenden Tennis, King George's Sports and Social, RAF; *Style*— John Stephens, Esq; ✉ Simmons & Simmons, 21 Wilson Street, London EC2M 2TX (☎ 0171 628 2020, fax 0171 628 2070)

STEPHENS, Prof Kenneth Gilbert; s of George Harry Stephens (d 1972), and Christiana, *née* Jackson (d 1986); *b* 3 May 1931; *Educ* Bablake Sch Coventry, Univ of Birmingham (BSc, PhD); *m* 1, 7 Dec 1957 (m dis 1980), Miriam Anne, da of Tom Sim, of Newbury, Berks; 1 s (Ian b 1963), 1 da (Jane b 1961); m 2, Elizabeth Carolynn, da of Howard Jones, of Oxted, Surrey; *Career* res physicist AEI Aldermaston 1955–62, chief physicist Pye Laboratories Cambridge 1963–66; Univ of Surrey: lectr 1966–67, reader 1967–78, prof 1978–96 (prof emeritus 1996), head of Dept of Electronic and Electrical Engrg 1983–91, dean Faculty of Engrg 1992–96; author various articles on ion implantation of materials in scientific jls; govr Royal GS 1977– (chm 1996–); FInstP 1972, FIEE 1979; *Recreations* watching cricket, gardening, music, reading; *Clubs* Blackheath CC (Surrey), MCC; *Style*— Prof Kenneth Stephens; ✉ 10 Brockway Close, Merrow, Guildford, Surrey GU1 2LW (☎ 01483 575087); Department of Electronic and Electrical Engineering, University of Surrey, Guildford GU2 5XH (☎ 01483 259136)

STEPHENS, Malcolm George; CB (1991); s of late Frank Ernest Stephens, and Annie Mary Janet, *née* Macqueen; *b* 14 July 1937; *Educ* St Michael and All Angels and Shooters Hill GS, St John's Coll Oxford (Casberd scholar, MA); *m* 5 Dec 1975, Lynette Marie, da of late John Patrick Caffery; *Career* Dip Serv: joined 1953, Ghana 1959–62, Kenya 1963–65, Exports Credits Guarantee Dept 1965–82, princ 1970, seconded to Civil Service Staff Coll as dir of economics and social admin course 1971–72, asst sec 1974, estab offr 1977, under sec 1978, head project gp 1978–79, princ fin offr 1979–82; int fin dir Barclays Bank International 1982, export fin dir and dir Barclays Export Servs with Barclays Bank 1982–87, chief exec Export Credits Guarantee Dept 1987–92, chief exec London C of C and Indust 1992–93, sec gen Int Union of Credit and Investmt Insurers (Berne Union) 1992– (pres 1989–92); dir: European Capital 1992–, Maj Projects Assoc 1996–; memb: Overseas Projects Bd 1985–87, British Overseas Trade Bd 1987–92, Inst of Credit Mgmnt; fell Inst of Export, FIB; *Recreations* gardening, fitness centre, reading; *Clubs* Travellers'; *Style*— Malcolm Stephens, Esq, CB; ✉ 111 Woolwich Road, Bexleyheath, Kent DA7 4LP (☎ 0181 303 6782); International Union of Credit and Investment Insurers (Berne Union), 35 Old Queen Street, London SW1H 9JA (☎ 0171 799 2990, fax 0171 799 2991)

STEPHENS, His Honour Judge (Stephen) Martin; QC (1982); s of Abraham Stephens (d 1977), of Swansea, and Freda, *née* Ruck (d 1995); *b* 26 June 1939; *Educ* Swansea GS, Wadham Coll Oxford (MA); *m* 1965, Patricia Alison, da of Joseph Morris (d 1981), of Nottingham; 1 s (Richard b 1966) and 1 s decd, 1 da (Marianne b 1971); *Career* called to the Bar Middle Temple 1963, recorder of the Crown Court 1979–86, circuit judge (Wales and Chester Circuit) 1986–; memb: Criminal Ctee Judicial Studies Bd 1995–, Parole Bd 1995–; *Recreations* theatre, cricket; *Style*— His Honour Judge Stephens, QC; ✉ c/o Swansea Crown Court, St Helens Road, Swansea

STEPHENS, Meic; s of Herbert Arthur Lloyd Stephens (d 1984), of Pontypridd, and Alma, *née* Symes (d 1994); *b* 23 July 1938; *Educ* Pontypridd Boys' GS, UCW Aberystwyth (BA), Univ of Rennes (DipFrench), UCNW Bangor (DipEd); *m* 14 Aug 1965, Ruth Wynn, da of Rev John Ellis Meredith (d 1981), of Aberystwyth; 1 s (Huw b 1981), 3 da (Lowri b 1966, Heledd b 1968, Brengain b 1969); *Career* teacher of French Ebbw Vale GS 1962–66, ed Poetry Wales 1965–73, journalist Western Mail Cardiff 1966–67, lit dir Welsh Arts Cncl 1967–90; ed, journalist, literary conslt 1990–, columnist Western Mail 1991–; dir Combrógos Literary Agency; visiting prof of English Brigham Young Univ Utah USA 1991, pt/t lectr Univ of Glamorgan 1994–; hon fell St David's Univ Coll Lampeter 1986–, life memb the Welsh Acad 1990; memb: The Kilvert Soc, The Radnorshire Soc, The Hon Soc of Cymmrodorion London; sec Rhys Davies Tst; hon memb White Robe Gorsedd of Bards 1976; *Books* Triad (1963), The Lilting House (co-ed, 1969), Writers of Wales (co-ed, 86 vols, 1970–), Artists in Wales (ed, 3 vols, 1971/73/77), The Welsh Language Today (ed, 1973), Exiles All (1973), A Reader's Guide to Wales (ed, 1973), Linguistic Minorities in Western Europe (1976), Green Horse (co-ed, 1978), The Arts in Wales 1950–75 (ed, 1979), The Curate of Clyro (ed, 1983), The Oxford Companion to the Literature of Wales (ed, 1986), A Cardiff Anthology (ed, 1987), The White Stone (trans, 1987), A Book of Wales (ed, 1988), A Dictionary of Literary Quotations (1989), The Gregynog Poets (ed, 12 vols 1989–90), The Bright Field (ed, 1991), The Oxford Illustrated Literary Guide to Great Britain and Ireland (ed, 1992), A Most Peculiar People (ed, 1992), Changing Wales (ed, 12 vols 1992–), A Rhondda Anthology (ed, 1993), Take Wales: Cinema in Wales (1993), Literature in 20th Century Wales: a Select Bibliography (1995), The Collected Poems of Harr Webb (ed, 1995), For the Sake of Wales (trans, 1996), The Basques (trans, 1996), The Collected Poems of Glyn Jones (ed, 1996), The Collected Stories of Rhys Davies (ed, 3 vols, 1996); *Recreations* the world of Wales; *Style*— Meic Stephens, Esq; ✉ 10 Heol Don, Whitchurch, Cardiff CF4 2AU (☎ 01222 623359)

STEPHENS, Nicholas Edward Egerton; s of Brian Alexis Fenwick Stephens, of Shrewsbury, and Cynthia Mary Denise, *née* Prideaux-Brune; *b* 12 May 1946; *Educ* Charterhouse; *m* 10 Sept 1970, Avril Rose, da of Morgan Henry Birch Reynardson; 2 da (Samantha Jane b 12 June 1975, Clare Diana b 17 June 1978); *Career* Champagne Laurent Perrier 1964–65, articled clerk R M March Son & Co (chartered accountants) 1965–69, Ionian Bank 1969–72, ptnr James Capel & Co 1978–80 (joined 1972), ptnr then dir (on incorporation) Albert E Sharp & Co 1980–; Parly candidate (Cons) Walsall North Gen Election 1983; High Sheriff of Shropshire 1995–96; co cmmr of scouts 1983–88, fell Woodard Corpn 1987–, custos Ellesmere Coll 1992–; Freeman Worshipful Co of Glaziers and Painters of Glass 1995; FCA; *Recreations* shooting, fishing, golf, tennis, opera, skiing; *Clubs* Boodle's, Pratt's, MCC, St Moritz Toboganning; *Style*— Nicholas Stephens, Esq; ✉ Grafton Lodge, Montford Bridge, Shrewsbury SY4 1HE (☎ 01743 850262); Albert E Sharp, Edmund House, Newhall Street, Birmingham B3 3ER (☎ 0121 200 2244)

STEPHENS, Rev Prof (William) Peter; s of Alfred Cyril William Joseph Stephens (d 1942), of Penzance, Cornwall, and Jennie Eudora, *née* Trewavas (d 1983); *b* 16 May 1934; *Educ* Truro Sch, Univ of Cambridge (MA, BD), Univ of Strasbourg (Docteur es Sciences Religieuses), Univ of Lund, Univ of Münster; *Career* asst tutor in Greek and New Testament Hartley Victoria Coll Manchester 1958–61, methodist minister Nottingham and univ chaplain 1961–65, minister Shirley Church Croydon 1967–71, Ranmoor chair in church history Hartley Victoria Coll Manchester 1971–73 (Fernley Hartley lectr 1972), Randles chair in historical and systematic theol Wesley Coll Bristol 1973–80, James A Gray lectr Duke Univ N Carolina 1976; Queen's Coll Birmingham: res fell 1980–81, lectr in church history 1981–86, Hartley lectr 1982; prof of church history Univ of Aberdeen 1986– (dean Faculty of Divinity 1987–89); memb Bristol City Cncl 1976–83; memb Central Ctee Conf of European Churches 1974–92; *Books* The Holy Spirit in the Theology of Martin Bucer (1970), Faith and Love (1971), Methodism in Europe (1981), The Theology of Huldrych Zwingli (1986), Zwingli - An Introduction to His Thought (1992), The Bible The Reformation and the Church (ed, 1995); *Recreations* tennis, squash, skiing, hill-walking, theatre, opera; *Style*— The Rev Prof Peter Stephens; ✉ Faculty of Divinity, University of Aberdeen, King's College, Old Aberdeen AB24 3UB (☎ 01224 272383, fax 01224 273750)

STEPHENS, Philip Francis Christopher; s of Haydn Stephens, of London, and Teresa, *née* Martin; *b* 2 June 1953; *Educ* Wimbledon Coll, Worcester Coll Oxford (BA); *partner* Patricia Jean Hemingway; 1 da (Jessica Rose b 24 Nov 1989), 1 s (Benedict Haydn b 24 Mar 1993); *Career* asst ed Europa Publications 1974–76, ed Commerce International 1976–79, corr Reuters London and Brussels 1979–83; Financial Times: econs corr 1983–88, political ed 1988–94, assoc ed and political commentator 1995–; Fulbright fell; commended Br Press Awards 1991; *Books* Politics and the Pound: The Conservatives' Struggle with Sterling (1996); *Style*— Philip Stephens, Esq; ✉ Financial Times, 1 Southwark Bridge, London SE1 (☎ 0171 873 3000)

STEPHENS, William R (Bill); s of James Stephens (d 1982), of Uttar Pradesh, India, and Creina Grace, *née* Williams; *b* 7 May 1948; *Educ* Lord Weymouth Sch Warminster Wilts, Oxford Poly (HND); *m* 10 Dec 1976, Margaret Louise, da of Thomas Hill; 2 da (Katherine Marisa b 30 Nov 1979, Cara Jane b 5 June 1982); *Career* in hotel mgmnt with Grand Metropolitan Hotels 1969–71, sales trainee rising to SE England regnl mangr Walt Disney Productions London 1971–75, independent sales mangr Seven Keys (Australian film distribution co) 1975–77, gen mangr rising to md UK distribution and dir of overseas sales (Europe, Middle E and Africa) Sunn Classic Productions 1977–84; Channel Four Television: joined as programme sales mangr 1984, later film sales mangr, head of film and programme sales 1988–93, dir of sales Channel Four International Ltd 1993–; memb BAFTA 1990; *Recreations* golf, cinema, travel; *Clubs* Stanmore Golf; *Style*— Bill Stephens, Esq; ✉ Channel Four Television, 124 Horseferry Road, London SW1P 2TX (☎ 0171 306 8746, fax 0171 306 8361, mobile 0385 234381)

STEPHENSON, (Robert) Ashley Shute; LVO (1989, MVO 1979); s of James Stephenson (d 1960), and Agnes Maud, *née* Shute (d 1983); *b* 1 Sept 1927; *Educ* Heddon-on-the-Wall Sch, Walbottle Secdy Sch; *m* 21 May 1955, Isabel, da of Edward Dunn (d 1960); 1 s (Ian Ashley b 1964), 1 da (Carol b 1959); *Career* apprentice Newcastle upon Tyne Parks Dept 1942; served RASC Palestine and Cyprus 1946; landscape gardener Donald Ireland Ltd 1949, student RHS's gardens Wisley 1952; The Royal Parks: joined 1954, supt Regent's Park 1969, supt Central Royal Parks 1972, bailiff 1980–90; landscape conslt Trusthouse Forte (now Forte) 1990–93; freelance gardening corr (gardening corr The Times 1982–87), contrib to TV and radio progs; chm Britain in Bloom 1991, dir Gardens for Pleasure 1987–94; memb: Ctee London Children's Flower Soc, Ctee Royal Gardeners' Benevolent Fund, Ctee Rotten Row 300, Prince of Wales Royal Parks Tree Ctee 1979, Floral Ctee RHS 1981–; pres Br Pelargonium and Geranium Soc 1983–94, chm SE in Bloom Ctee English Tourist Bd 1990– (judge Britain in Bloom competition), hort advsr Cincinnati Flower and Garden Show Soc USA 1990–; vice pres PHAB 1992; MIHort; *Books* The Garden Planner (1981); *Recreations* golf, walking, reading, gardening; *Clubs* Arts; *Style*— Ashley Stephenson, Esq, LVO; ✉ 17 Sandore Rd, Seaford, East Sussex BN25 3PZ (☎ 01323 891050)

STEPHENSON, (Robert Noel) David; OBE; s of Capt Arthur Charles Robert Stephenson, MC (d 1965), and Margaret, *née* Smyth (d 1975); *b* 10 June 1932; *Educ* Loretto Sch; *m* 19 Nov 1966, Heather June, da of George Weatherston, of Gosforth, Newcastle upon Tyne; 2 s (Mark b 8 June 1968, John b 3 Oct 1972), 1 da (Julia b 27 July 1969); *Career* CA 1955, Peat Marwick Mitchell Canada 1956–60, Scottish & Newcastle Breweries Ltd 1960–91; memb Bd: Tyne & Wear Enterprise Tst 1983–91, Theatre Royal Tst 1988–93, Tyneside Trg and Enterprise Cncl 1989–91, Newcastle Building Soc, High Gosforth Park Ltd, Home Housing Assoc; chm Area Manpower Bd N Tyne 1984–88, Tyneside Stables Project Ltd 1985–91; govr: Loretto Sch 1986–94, Newcastle upon Tyne Poly 1988–91; memb Cncl Univ of Newcastle upon Tyne 1984–88; hon fell Northumbria Univ at Newcastle; FCA 1960, FRSA; *Recreations* golf, fishing, gardening; *Style*— David Stephenson, Esq, OBE; ✉ Newton Low Hall, Felton, Northumberland NE65 9LD (☎ 01665 575617)

STEPHENSON, (Marjorie) Gail; da of James Midgley (d 1978), and Ina, *née* Simpson (d 1992); *b* 28 July 1953; *Educ* Pendleon HS for Girls Salford, Manchester Sch of Orthoptics Manchester Royal Eye Hosp (DBO), Manchester Poly; *m* 27 July 1974, Barry James Stephenson, s of James Henry Stephenson; 1 da (Rebecca Kathy b 11 Dec 1981); *Career* sr orthoptist Royal Albert Edward Infirmary Wigan 1974–76, student teacher Manchester Royal Eye Hosp 1976–78; orthoptic teacher Manchester Royal Eye Hosp: full time 1978–81, pt/t 1982–91; pt/t locum head of Trg Sch Leeds Gen Infirmary 1987–89, pt/t research orthoptist St Paul's Eye Hosp Liverpool 1989–91, full time head Dept of Orthoptics Univ of Liverpool 1991– (responsible for writing and introducing one of UK's two 3 yr honours degree courses in orthoptics); invited memb Woman of the Yr Lunch (Savoy Hotel) 1993 and 1994; Br Orthoptic Soc: chm Nat Scientific Ctee 1989–92, chm Nat Educn Ctee 1990–92, memb Nat Exec Cncl 1989–, memb Working Pty into Post-Basic Orthoptic Qualifications 1989–, Br rep on selection panel for Int Orthoptic Assoc Fellowship 1990–, chm Professional Devpt Ctee 1992–; Orthoptists Bd Cncl for Professions Supplementary to Med: memb 1990–, memb Registration Ctee 1990–, memb Disciplinary Ctee 1990–, chm Educn Ctee 1994–95; examiner (final examination) DBO 1991, external examiner (BSc Orthoptics) Glasgow Caledonian Univ 1994; memb Editorial Bd Br Orthoptic Jl 1991–, reviewer of neuro-ophthalmology papers submitted to Br Jl of Ophthalmology 1993–, author of various pubns, book reviews and presentations; *Recreations* all sport, watching tennis and football, playing tennis and squash, swimming; *Style*— Ms Gail Stephenson; ✉ Department of Orthoptics, PO Box 147, University of Liverpool, Liverpool L69 3BX (☎ 0151 794 5731, fax 0151 794 5781, mobile 0374 752849)

STEPHENSON, Geoffrey Charles; s of Edmund Charles Stephenson, and Hilda Rose, *née* Bates; *b* 19 Aug 1943; *Educ* Bromley GS; *m* 3 Sept 1966, Margaret, da of Frank Wirth (d 1989); 1 s (Alistair James b 2 May 1974), 2 da (Louise Elizabeth b 26 March 1970, Rebecca Dorothy b 8 Feb 1972); *Career* Legal and General Assurance Society Ltd 1964–72; called to the Bar Gray's Inn 1971, ad eundem Lincoln's Inn 1991, admitted to State Bar Texas 1991; chm Sundridge Park Lawn Tennis and Squash Rackets Club; FCII; *Recreations* sport; *Clubs* Sundridge Park Lawn Tennis and Squash Rackets, British Sub-Aqua; *Style*— Geoffrey Stephenson, Esq; ✉ 2/3 Grays Inn Square, London WC1R 5JH (☎ 0171 242 4986, fax 0171 406 1166, car 0850 131467)

STEPHENSON, Prof Geoffrey Michael; s of Maurice Stephenson (d 1958), of Kenton, Harrow, Middx, and Laura, *née* Sharp (d 1975); *b* 16 April 1939; *Educ* Harrow County Sch for Boys, Univ of Nottingham (BA, PhD); *m* 1, 14 April 1962 (m dis 1981), Marguerite Ida, da of James Lindsay (d 1986), of Kettering; 1 s (Lawrence James b 1963), 1 da (Katherine b 1965); m 2, 9 July 1982 (m dis 1987) Gillian Sarah, da of Geoffrey Wade, of Cheadle Hulme; m 3, 10 Jan 1989, Jennifer Ann, da of Frederick Williams, of St Mellon, Cardiff, and Elsie Williams; 1 s (David Field William b 1989); *Career* res psychologist Balderton Hosp 1960–61, lectr in psychology Univ of Keele 1962–66, reader in psychology Univ of Nottingham 1976–78 (lectr 1966–74, sr lectr 1974–76), prof of social psychology Univ of Kent Canterbury 1978– (dir Inst of Social and Applied Psychology 1986–93); ed: Br Jl of Social Psychology 1978–84, Social Behaviour Int Jl 1986–90, Community and Applied Social Psychology 1991–, Issues in Criminological and Legal Psychology 1992–; chartered psychologist; memb: Br Psychological Soc 1960– (chm Social Psychology Section 1977–80), Euro Assoc of Experimental Social Psychology 1972– (pres 1984–87); chm: IBA Advtg Advsy Ctee 1988–90, ITC Advtg Advsy Ctee 1991–92; memb Governing Body Christchurch Coll Canterbury 1989–; FBPsS 1980–; *Books* incl: The Development of Conscience (1966), The Social Psychology of Bargaining (with Ian Morley, 1976), The Psychology of Criminal Justice (1992), Employment Relations (jt ed, 1992), Suspicion and Silence: The Right to Silence in Police Investigations (jt ed, 1994); *Recreations* sailing, classical music (violin playing), cooking; *Clubs* Faversham Lab Party, Kent CCC; *Style*— Prof Geoffrey Stephenson; ✉ Institute of Social and Applied Psychology, The University, Canterbury, Kent (☎ 01227 764000, telex 965449, fax 01227 763674)

STEPHENSON, Sir Henry Upton; 3 Bt (UK 1936), of Hassop Hall, Co Derby, TD; s of Lt-Col Sir (Henry) Francis Blake Stephenson, 2 Bt, OBE, TD, JP, DL (d 1982), and Joan, *née* Upton; *b* 26 Nov 1926; *Educ* Eton; *m* 1962, Susan, da of late Maj John Ernest Clowes, of Clifton, Ashbourne, Derbyshire; 4 da (Fiona Kathleen b 1964, Annabel Mary b 1965, Emma Frances b 1968, Lucy Clare b 1970); *Heir* 1 cous, Timothy Hugh Stephenson b 5 Jan 1930; *Career* High Sheriff of Derbyshire 1975; late Capt Yorkshire Yeo; dir Stephenson Blake (Holdings) Ltd and Thos Turton & Sons Ltd; *Style*— Sir Henry Stephenson, Bt, TD; ✉ Tissington Cottage, Rowland, Bakewell, Derbyshire

STEPHENSON, Prof (James) Ian Love; s of James Stephenson (d 1979), of Hunwick, Bishop Auckland, and May, *née* Emery (d 1966); *b* 11 Jan 1934; *Educ* Blyth GS, Univ of Durham (BA); *m* 3 Jan 1959, Kate, da of James Robert Brown (d 1987), of Ponteland; 1 s (Stephen b 1964), 1 da (Stella b 1970); *Career* artist; Hatton Sch, then tutorial student, then studio demonstrator King's Coll Newcastle upon Tyne (pioneered first modern art fndn course in UK) 1955–58, Boise Sch Italy 1959, visiting lectr Poly Sch of Art London 1959–62, visiting painter Chelsea Sch of Art 1959–66, dir fndn studies Dept of Fine Art Univ of Newcastle (first perceptual and conceptual UK syllabus) 1966–70, dir postgrad painting Chelsea Sch of Art (inspired many successful artists) 1970–89, int course ldr

Voss Summer Sch 1979, vice pres Sunderland Arts Centre 1982–84; fine art advsr Canterbury Art Coll 1974–79, Royal Acad steward Artists Gen Benevolent Inst 1979–80, first UK specialist advsr CNAA 1980–83; memb: Visual Arts Panel Northern Arts Assoc Newcastle 1967–70, Fine Art Panel NCDAD 1972–74, Perm Ctee New Contemporaries Assoc (revived annual nat student exhibitions) 1973–75, Fine Art Bd CNAA 1974–75; former examiner at various polys; sr postgrad examiner: Univ of London 1975–83, Heriot-Watt and Edinburgh Univs 1989–96; memb: Advsy Ctee Nat Exhibition of Children's Art Manchester 1975–92, Working Pty RA Jubilee Exhibition 1976–77, Selection Ctee Arts Cncl Awards 1977–78, Painting Faculty Rome and Abbey Major Scholarships 1978–82, Recommending Ctee Chantrey Bequest 1979–80, Boise Scholarship Ctee UCL 1983; chm Ctee David Murray Studentship Fund 1990; hon life memb: Mark Twain Soc 1978, Accademia Italia 1980; hon memb CAS 1980–81; RA 1986 (ARA 1975); *Exhibitions* incl: Br Painting in the Sixties London 1963, Mostra di Pittura Contemporanea Amsterdam and Europe (Int Marzotto European prizewinner) 1964–65, 9o Biennio Lugano 1966, 5e Biennale and 18e Salon Paris 1967, Recent Br Painting London and world tour 1967–75, Junge Generation Grossbritannien Berlin 1968, Retrospective Newcastle 1970, La Peinture Anglaise Aujourd'hui Paris 1973, Elf Englische Zeichner Baden Baden and Bremen 1973, Recente Britse Tekenkunst Antwerp 1973, 13a Bienal São Paulo and Latin America 1975, Arte Inglese Oggi Milan 1976, Retrospective London and Bristol 1977, Englische Künst der Gegenwart Bregenz 1977, Br Painting 1952–77 London 1977, Color en la Pintura Britanica Rio de Janeiro and Latin America 1977–79, Abstract Paintings from UK Washington 1978, Retrospective Birmingham and Cardiff 1978, Royal Acad of Arts Edinburgh 1979–80, Art Anglais d'Aujourd'hui Geneva 1980, Br Art 1940–80 London 1980, Colour in Br Painting Hong Kong and Far East 1980–81, Contemporary Br Drawing Tel Aviv and Near East 1980–82, The Deck of Cards Athens and Arabia 1980–82, A Taste of Br Art Today Brussels 1982, Arteder Muestra Internacional Bilbao 1982, La Couleur en la Peinture Britannique Luxembourg and Bucharest 1982–83, Int Print Biennales Bradford 1982, 1984 and 1986, 15a Bienale Ljubljana 1983, V&A Mortlake Display London 1996 (only artist to attend visit by HM The Queen to Nat Museum); *Illustrator* Cubism and After (BBC film) 1962, Contemporary Br Art 1965, Private View 1965, Blow Up (MGM film) 1966, Art of Our Time 1967, Recent Br Painting 1968, Adventure in Art 1969, In Vogue 1975, Painting in Britain (1525–1975) 1976, Br Painting 1976, Contemporary Artists 1977, 1983 and 1989, Contemporary Br Artists 1979, Tendenze e Testimonianze 1983; *Collections* work in various incl: Birmingham Bristol and Leeds City Art Galleries, Tate Gallery, Gulbenkian Foundation, Madison Art Center, V & A Br and Welsh Nat Museums; *Style*— Prof Ian Stephenson, RA; ✉ c/o Royal Academy of Arts, Piccadilly, London W1V 0DS

STEPHENSON, His Hon Judge; Jim; s of Alexander Stephenson (d 1958), of Heworth, Co Durham, and Norah Stephenson (d 1988); *b* 17 July 1932; *Educ* Royal GS Newcastle upon Tyne, Exeter Coll Oxford (BA); *m* 1964, Jill Christine, da of late Dr Edward William Lindeck, of Yew Tree Cottage, Fairwarp, Sussex; 3 s; *Career* called to the Bar Gray's Inn 1957, memb Gen Cncl of the Bar 1961–64, jr North-Eastern Circuit 1961, recorder Crown Ct 1974–83, circuit judge (NE Circuit) 1983–; pres NE Br Magistrates' Assoc 1988–92; additional memb of the Bd Faculty of Law Newcastle upon Tyne 1984–90, govr Newcastle Prep Sch 1985–92; *Recreations* history, walking, music; *Clubs* Durham Co; *Style*— His Hon Judge Stephenson; ✉ Newcastle upon Tyne Crown Court, Quayside, Newcastle upon Tyne NE1 3LA (☎ 0191 201 2000)

STEPHENSON, John; s of George Stephenson, of Eastbourne, E Sussex, and Joyce, *née* Sirett (d 1992); *b* 28 May 1952; *Educ* Ewell Castle Sch Ewell Surrey, Kingston Art Sch (BA), RCA (MA); *partner* Lesja Liber; 3 c (Natalka Liber Ivanovna Stephenson b 5 Dec 1985, Samuel Liber Ivanovich and Hana Liber Ivanovna Stephenson (twins) b 13 July 1989); *Career* special effects/puppet designer/film maker and commercials director; creative supr Jim Henson's Creature Shop 1986–; other work incl shop interiors for Ryder branches London 1981; currently dir Jim Henson Organisation and Jim Henson Productions; advsr/interim shadow design dir Design Cncl 1994; *Films* earlier work incl: The Dark Crystal 1980, Return to Oz 1983, Greystoke - The Legend of Tarzan Lord of the Apes 1984, various other films and videos 1984–86; more recent work incl: Teenage Mutant Ninja Turtles 1990, The Flintstones 1993 (Scientific and Engrg Award Acad of Motion Picture Arts & Scis), Pinocchio (2nd unit dir) 1996; *Style*— John Stephenson, Esq; ✉ Jim Henson Organisation, 30 Oval Road, London NW1 7DE (☎ 0171 428 4000)

STEPHENSON, Maj-Gen John Aubrey; CB (1982), OBE (1971); s of Reginald Jack Stephenson (d 1976), of Weymouth, Dorset, and Florence, *née* Pick (d 1947); *b* 15 May 1929; *Educ* Dorchester GS, RMA Sandhurst, RMCS Shrivenham, Staff Coll Camberley, RCDS; *m* 29 July 1953, Sheila, da of Henry Douglas Colbeck (d 1978), of Newcastle upon Tyne; 2 s (Guy b 1957, Peter b 1963), 1 da (Susan b 1955); *Career* joined Royal Artillery (despatches) 1951, pilot 652 Air Op Sqdn RAF 1954–56, Capt 1 Regt RHA 1956–58, Capt 39 Missile Regt 1960–61, Maj Combat Devpt MOD London 1963–64, Batty Cdr (Maj) 25 Field Regt RA 1965–67, CO 16 Light Air Def Regt RA 1969–71, Col project mangr 155 MM Systems 1971–73, Brig Cdr 1 Artillery Bde 1975–77, Brig SMO RARDE 1977–78, Maj Gen DGW/A MOD London 1978–80, VMGO MOD London 1980–81; defence conslt 1990–93; md Weapon Systems Ltd 1982–90, dir ATX Ltd 1984–86; pres Royal Br Legion Houghton 1987–, govr Dorchester Thomas Hardye Sch 1984–96, Churchwarden St Peters Stockbridge 1990–95; FIMgt 1977; *Recreations* fishing, sailing, walking, reading, history, travel; *Clubs* Royal Over-Seas League; *Style*— Maj-Gen John Stephenson, CB, OBE; ✉ Collingwood, 27 Trafalgar Way, Stockbridge, Hants SO20 6ET (☎ 01264 810458)

STEPHENSON, Rt Hon Sir John Frederick Eustace Stephenson; kt (1962), PC (1971); 2 s of Sir Guy Stephenson, CB (er s of Sir Augustus Keppel Stephenson, KCB, KC), by his w Gwendolen, da of Rt Hon John Gilbert Talbot, PC, JP, DL, MP, sometime Parly sec BOT and s in his turn of Hon John Chetwynd Talbot (4 s of 2 Earl Talbot); *b* 28 March 1910; *Educ* Winchester, New Coll Oxford (MA, hon fell); *m* 1951, Hon (Frances) Rose, yr da of Baron Asquith of Bishopstone, PC (*see* Stephenson, Hon Lady); 2 s (David b 1954, Daniel b 1960), 2 da (Mary b 1952, Laura b 1958); *Career* WWII RE and Intelligence Corps served Middle East and NW Europe, Lt-Col 1946; called to the Bar Inner Temple 1934, QC 1960; recorder: Bridgwater 1954–59, Winchester 1959–62; chllr Diocese: Peterborough 1956–62, Winchester 1958–62; High Court judge (Queen's Bench) 1962–71, dep chm Dorset QS 1962–71, Lord Justice of Appeal 1971–85; *Books* A Royal Correspondence (1938); *Recreations* reading, music, golf; *Clubs* MCC, Hurlingham, Royal Wimbledon Golf; *Style*— The Rt Hon Sir John Stephenson; ✉ 26 Doneraile Street, London SW6 6EN (☎ 0171 736 6782)

STEPHENSON, John Patrick; s of Patrick Tinsley Stephenson, of Stebbing, nr Dunmow, Essex, and Evelyn Dorothea Margaret, *née* Orriss; *b* 14 March 1965; *Educ* Felsted, Univ of Durham (BA, Cricket palatinate); *m* 24 Sept 1994, Fiona Maria, da of Michael J Luckhurst, of Redbourn, nr St Albans, Herts; *Career* professional cricketer; capt Durham Univ 1986 and Combined Univs 1987; Essex CCC 1984–: debut 1985, awarded county cap 1989, 188 appearances; Hampshire CCC 1995– (capt 1996); overseas teams: Fitzroy/Doncaster CC Melbourne 1983–84 and 1987–88, Boland CC SA 1988–89, Gold Coast Dolphins and Bond Univ Queensland 1990–91 and 1991–92; England: schs tour Zimbabwe 1982–83, 1 Test match v Aust Oval 1989, A tour Zimbabwe 1990, capt under 25 v India 1990, A tour W Indies 1992; most sixes by an Englishman 1989, shared double hundred opening partnership with Graham Gooch both innings v Northants 1990; honours with Essex CCC: County Championship 1986, 1991 and 1992 (runners up 1989 and 1990), Refuge Cup 1989, runners up Benson & Hedges Cup 1989, runners up John Player League 1986; *Recreations* alternative modern music, modern literature; *Style*— John Stephenson, Esq; ✉ c/o Hampshire CCC, Northlands Road, Southampton, Hampshire

STEPHENSON, Lt-Col John Robin; CBE (1994, OBE (Mil) 1976); s of John Stewart Stephenson (d 1975), and Edith Gerda Greenwell Stephenson (d 1975); *b* 25 Feb 1931; *Educ* Christ's Hosp, RMA Sandhurst; *m* 27 Jan 1962, Karen Margrethe, da of August Hansen Koppang (d 1973); 1 s (Robin b 1967), 2 da (Celia b 1963, Kristina b 1964); *Career* cmmnd Royal Sussex Regt 1951, Platoon Cdr Egypt 1951–53, Lt 1953, instr Regtl Depot 1953–54, ADC and Company 2 i/c Korea 1955–56, Company 2 i/c Gibraltar 1956–57, Capt 1957, instr Mons Offr Cadet Sch 1958–60, Company Cdr NI 1960–61, Company Cdr Regtl Depot 1962–64, Maj 1963, GSO3 Libya 1964–65, Company Cdr Germany 1966–67, Infantry rep Sch of Signals 1968–70, Bn 2 i/c NI 1970–72, Lt-Col 1972, Sr Offrs' War Course 1972–73, CO 5 Bn Queen's Regt 1973–76, dep pres Regular Cmmns Bd 1976, SO UK C in C's Ctee 1977–79, resigned cmmn 1979; sec: MCC 1987–93 (asst sec 1979–86, managed MCC tours to Bangladesh 1979–80, E Africa 1980–81, Canada 1985 and Kenya 1993), Int Cricket Cncl (formerly Conf) 1987–93; govr: Clayesmore Sch 1988–, St Bede's Sch Eastbourne 1988–94; chm of Govrs Leaden Hall Sch Salisbury 1995–; Order of Orange-Nassau 1972; *Recreations* cricket, rugby, football, squash, golf, boating and gardening; *Clubs* MCC, IZ, Free Foresters, XL (pres 1994–96), Stragglers of Asia CC (pres 1994–), East India; *Style*— Lt-Col John Stephenson, CBE; ✉ Plum Tree Cottage, Barford St Martin, nr Salisbury, Wiltshire SP3 4BL (☎ 01722 743443)

STEPHENSON, John William; JP (1980); s of Kenneth George Stephenson (d 1979), and Madeline Alice, *née* Ounsworth (d 1974); *b* 23 June 1938; *Educ* Harrow Co Sch; *m* 7 Sept 1963, Lesley Helen, da of Flt Lt Harold Douglas Hopper (d 1980); 2 da (Joanna Margaret b 1968, Sarah Elizabeth b 1970); *Career* surveyor; Fuller Peiser: joined 1959, ptnr 1970, opened Sheffield office 1972, currently sr ptnr Sheffield Office; memb Wood Ctee to review rating of plant and machinery 1991; tstee Sheffield Town 1986; chm Sheffield Chamber Music Festival Ltd 1993– (dir and vice chm 1988–93); FRICS 1970; *Recreations* music, literature, walking; *Clubs* Sheffield, Royal Over-Seas League; *Style*— John Stephenson, Esq, JP; ✉ Borgen, Grindleford, Sheffield S30 1HT (☎ 01433 630288); Fuller Peiser, Chartered Surveyors, Willis House, Peel Street, Broomhill, Sheffield S10 2PS (☎ 0114 266 6630, fax 0114 268 0077, car 0836 242685)

STEPHENSON, Timothy Congreve; s of Augustus William Stephenson, of Saxbys Mead, Cowden, nr Edenbridge, Kent, and Mary Gloria (d 1992), only and posthumous child of Maj William La T Congreve, VC, DSO, MC; *b* 7 March 1940; *Educ* Harrow, London Business Sch; *m* 1, 14 April 1966 (m dis 1980), Nerena Anne, da of Maj the Hon William Nicholas Somers Laurence Hyde Villiers; 2 s (Guy b 1969, Frederick b 1978), 2 da (Lucinda b 1967, Henrietta b 1975); m 2, 16 June 1980, Diana-Margaret Soltmann, *qv*, da of HE Dr Otto Soltmann, of Koblenz, Germany; 3 s (Christopher b 1983, William b 1985, James b 1989); *Career* Welsh Gds 1959–65; Gallaher Ltd 1965–79, md Grafton Ltd and chm Grafton Office Products Inc 1980–86, md Stephenson Cobbold Ltd 1987–, chm Stephenson and Co 1996–; former memb Industl Tbnls and fndr memb Bd of Lab Rels (ACAS) NI; MInstD, FRSA; *Recreations* bridge, shooting, gardening; *Clubs* Brooks's, Beefsteak, Pratt's, City of London; *Style*— T C Stephenson, Esq; ✉ Stephenson and Co, Dudley House, 169 Piccadilly, London W1V 9DD (☎ 0171 495 6428, fax 0171 495 6432)

STEPHENSON, Timothy Hugh; TD, JP (Sheffield); only s of William Raymond Shirecliffe Stephenson (d 1977), himself 2 s of Sir Henry Kenyon Stephenson, 1 Bt, DSO, VD; hp to 1 cous, Sir Henry Upton Stephenson, 3 Bt, TD, *qv*; *b* 5 Jan 1930; *Educ* Eton, Magdalene Coll Cambridge; *m* 1959, Susan Lesley, yr da of late George Arthur Harris, of Sheffield; 2 s (Matthew Francis Timothy b 1960, Oliver George b 1962); *Clubs* Cavalry and Guards', The Sheffield; *Style*— Timothy Stephenson, Esq, TD, JP; ✉ Lomberdale Hall, Bakewell, Derbyshire

STEPTOE, Prof Andrew Patrick Arthur; s of Patrick Christopher Steptoe, CBE (d 1988), and Sheena McLeod, *née* Kennedy (d 1990); *b* 24 April 1951; *Educ* Uppingham, Gonville and Caius Coll Cambridge (choral exhibitioner, hon sr scholar and Swann prize for biology, MA), Magdalen Coll Oxford (DPhil, MA (incorporated)), Univ of London (DSc); *m* 1, 1980 (m dis 1984), Jane Furneaux, da of Hugh Horncastle; 1 s (William Arthur Hugh b 1981); m 2, 1991, Frances Jane, da of Peter Wardle; 1 s (Matthew Peter Steptoe Wardle b 1984); *Career* Dept of Psychiatry Univ of Oxford: MRC research student 1972–75, MRC trg fell 1975–77; St George's Hosp Med Sch London: lectr in psychology 1977–81, sr lectr 1981–87, reader 1987–88, prof of psychology 1988–; visiting prof Dept of Public Health Univ of Tokyo 1992; memb: Research Progs Bd ESRC 1994–96, Educn and Psychosocial Research Ctee Cancer Research Campaign 1994–; assoc ed: Psychophysiology 1982–86, Jl of Psychophysiology 1987–89, Annals of Behavioral Med 1991–, Br Jl of Clinical Psychology 1992–95, Jl of Psychosomatic Research 1994– (asst ed 1989–93), Int Jl of Rehabilitation and Health 1995–; ed Br Jl of Health Psychology 1995–; memb Editorial Bd: Psychology and Health, Int Jl of Behavioral Med, Homeostasis and Self-Regulation, Patient Educn and Counseling; essay prize in clinical psychology (Mental Health Fndn) 1972, Kenneth Reeves essay prize (Soc for Psychosomatic Research) 1977; hon fell Swedish Soc of Behavioural Med 1988; memb: Int Soc of Behavioural Med (pres 1994–96), Soc for Psychosomatic Research (pres 1983–85), Soc for Psychophysiological Research USA (memb Bd of Dirs 1984–87); FBPsS (memb Scientific Affrs Bd 1991–93); *Books* Psychological Factors in Cardiovascular Disorders (1981), Problems of Pain and Stress (1984), Health Care and Human Behaviour (with A Mathews, 1984), Essential Psychology for Medical Practice (with A Mathews, 1988), Stress, Personal Control and Health (with A Appels, 1989), Psychosocial Processes and Health (with J Wardle, 1994); non-medical: The Mozart-Da Ponte Operas: The Cultural and Musical Background to Le nozze di Figaro, Don Giovanni and Cosi fan tutte (1988); *Recreations* music, theatre, reading, family; *Style*— Prof Andrew Steptoe; ✉ Deparment of Psychology, St George's Hospital Medical School, University of London, Cranmer Terrace, London SW17 0RE (☎ 0181 725 5603, fax 0181 767 2741, e-mail asteptoe@sghms.ac.uk)

STEPTOE, Roger Guy; s of Charles Steptoe, of Winchester, and Norah Constance, *née* Shaw; *b* 25 Jan 1953; *Educ* Univ of Reading (BA), Royal Acad of Music (LRAM); *Career* composer and pianist; composer-in-residence Charterhouse 1976–79; RAM: admin Int Composer Festivals 1987–93, prof of composition 1980–91; festival dir Clerkenwell Music Series 1996– (artistic dir 1994–96); works regularly as a soloist, chamber pianist and accompanist, compositions performed internationally; has performed in: UK, IOM, Russia, Sweden, Portugal, Spain, Scotland, Germany, USA; memb: Inc Soc of Musicians, Composers' Guild of GB, Royal Soc of Musicians; ARAM 1986; *Compositions* incl: King of Macedon (opera), Concertos for cello, oboe, tuba, clarinet and flute, 2 String Quartets, Piano Trio, various song cycles for all voices and piano, instrumental works for different combinations, Oboe Quartet, 2 Piano Sonatas, 2 Violin Sonatas, In Winter's Cold Embraces Dye (for soprano, tenor, chorus and chamber orch), Life's Unquiet Dream (for baritone, chorus and chamber orch), Cheers! (for chamber orch), The Passionate Shepherd to his Love (for childrens' voices); *Recordings* incl: the Songs of Ralph Vaughan Williams with Peter Savidge, the Piano Quartets of Walton and Frank Bridge; *Recreations* music, gardening, food and drink and seeing friends; *Style*— Roger Steptoe, Esq; ✉ Malaval par St Solve, 19130 Objat, France; c/o Alfred Lengnick & Co, Pigeon

House Meadow, 27 Grove Road, Beaconsfield, Bucks HP9 1UR (☎ 01494 681216, fax 01494 670443)

STERLING, John Adrian Lawrence; s of Francis Thomas Sterling (d 1942), of Melbourne, Aust, and Millicent Lloyd, *née* Pitt (d 1989); *b* 17 April 1927; *Educ* Scotch Coll Melbourne, CEPS Mosman NSW, Barker Coll NSW, Univ of Sydney (LLB); *m* 6 Nov 1976, Caroline Snow, da of Octavius Samuel Wallace (d 1984), of Strabane, Co Tyrone; *Career* admitted to the Bar NSW Aust 1949, called to the Bar Middle Temple 1953, dep DG Int Fedn of Phonographic Indust 1961–73, professorial fell Queen Mary and Westfield Coll 1996, visiting sr research fell King's Coll London 1996; memb: Intellectual Property and Data Protection Ctees Br Computer Soc, Exec Ctee Br Literary and Artistic Copyright Assoc; *Books* various publications incl: The Data Protection Act (1984), Copyright Law in the UK and the Rights of Performers, Authors and Composers in Europe (1986), Encyclopedia of Data Protection (co-ed, 1991), Intellectual Property Rights in Sound Recordings, Film and Video (1992, supplement 1994); *Recreations* reading, music, medieval iconography; *Style—* Prof J A L Sterling; ✉ Lamb Chambers, Lamb Building, Temple, London EC4Y 7AS (☎ 0171 797 8300, fax 0171 797 8308)

STERLING, Prof Michael John Howard; s of Richard Howard Sterling, of Hampton, Middx, and Joan Valeria, *née* Skinner; *b* 9 Feb 1946; *Educ* Hampton GS, Univ of Sheffield (BEng, PhD, DEng, Hon DEng 1995); *m* 19 July 1969, Wendy Karla, da of Charles Murray Anstead (d 1978), of Milton Libourne, Wilts; 2 s (Christopher b 1972, Robert b 1975); *Career* AEI student apprentice 1964–68, res engr GEC Elliot Process Automation 1968–71, sr lectr in control engrg Univ of Sheffield 1978–80 (lectr 1971–78), prof of engrg Univ of Durham 1980–90; vice chllr and princ Brunel Univ 1990–; chm: Higher Educn Statistics Agency 1992–, Higher Educn Statistics Agency Mgmnt Ctee 1992–93, Jt Performance Indicators Working Gp HEFCE/SHEFC/HEFCW 1992–95, Universities Statistical Record Review Gp 1992–95, Sub-Ctee on Res Performance Indicators CVCP/UFC 1992–93, Electro Mechanical Engrg Ctee SERC 1989–91 (memb 1987–89), SERC Electrical and Power Industs Sub-Ctee 1987–89, SERC/Central Electricity Generating Bd Co-funded Res Ctee 1987–92; memb: Electricity Supply Res Cncl 1987–89, Engrg Bd SERC 1989–92, Mechanical, Aeronautical and Prodn Engrg Assessment Sub-Panel HEFCE 1992 and 1996, Performance Indicators Ctee CVCP/UFC 1991–93, Cncl IEE 1991–93, CICHE 2 Br Cncl 1991–, CVCP Euro Ctee 1991–96, Quality Assessment Ctee HEFCE 1992–95, Standing Ctee for Educn, Trg and Competence to Practise Royal Acad of Engrg 1993–, Main Ctee CVCP 1990–, Cncl CVCP 1994–95, CVCP Student Numbers Steering Group 1995–, CVCP Info Systems Sector Gp 1995–; corresponding memb CVCP Research and Knowledge Transfer Steering Gp 1996; memb Engrg Cncl 1994– (Standing Ctee for the Engrg Profession 1994–, Standing Ctee for the Regions and Assembly 1994–); chm: OCEPS Ltd 1990–, WASMACS Ltd 1994–; govr: Burnham GS Burnham Bucks 1990–, Hampton Sch Hampton Middx 1991–; CEng 1975, FInstMC 1983 (vice pres 1985–88, pres 1988, memb Cncl 1983–91), FRSA 1984, FIEE 1985, FEng 1991; *Books* Power System Control (1978); author of 120 papers in learned jls; *Recreations* gardening, DIY, computers, model engineering; *Style—* Prof Michael Sterling, FEng; ✉ Brunel University, Uxbridge, Middlesex UB8 3PH (☎ 01895 274000, fax 01895 232806, telex 261173 G)

STERLING, Dr (Isobel Jane) Nuala; CBE (1993); da of Prof Fred Bradbury (d 1948), and Florence Jane, *née* Ratcliff (d 1982); *b* 12 Feb 1937; *Educ* Friends' Sch Saffron Walden, King's Coll London, St George's Hosp London (MB BS); *m* 26 August 1961, Dr Graham Murray, s of George Sterling (d 1987); 5 s (Charles b 1963, Guy b 1967, Andrew b 1974, Mark b 1977, Thomas b 1981), 1 da (b and d 1972); *Career* St George's Hosp London: house physician/surgn 1960–61, sr house offr 1961–62, med registrar 1965–67; in gen practice Oxford 1968–69, lectr Dept of Med Univ of California San Francisco 1969–70, conslt physician in geriatric med Southampton Univ Hosps 1979– (sr registrar then lectr Dept of Med 1972–79); pres Med Women's Fedn 1989–90, chm Standing Med Advsy Ctee 1990–94 (memb 1984–96), memb Clinical Standards Advsy Gp 1992–94; FRCP 1982 (MRCP 1971); *Recreations* music, orchids, gardening, Chinese porcelain; *Style—* Dr Nuala Sterling, CBE; ✉ Royal South Hants Hospital, Brinton's Terrace, Southampton, Hants SO14 0YG

STERLING OF PLAISTOW, Baron (Life Peer UK 1991), of Pall Mall in the City of Westminster; Sir Jeffrey Maurice Sterling; CBE (1977); s of late Harry Sterling, and Alice Sterling; *b* 27 Dec 1934; *Educ* Reigate GS, Preston Manor Co Sch, Guildhall Sch of Music; *m* 1985, Dorothy Ann, *née* Smith; 1 da; *Career* Paul Schweder and Co (Stock Exchange) 1955–57, G Eberstadt & Co 1957–62, fin dir General Guarantee Corp 1962–64, md Gula Investments Ltd 1964–69, chm Sterling Guarantee Trust plc 1969 (merged with P&O 1985), memb Bd of Dirs British Airways 1979–82, chm The Peninsular and Oriental Steam Navigation Company 1983– (dir 1980–); special advsr to Sec of State for Industry (later Trade and Industry) 1982–90; World ORT Union: memb Exec 1966–, chm Orgn Ctee 1969–73, chm ORT Technical Servs 1974–, vice pres British ORT 1978–; pres: Gen Cncl of Br Shipping 1990–91, EC Shipowners' Assocs 1992–94; dep chm and hon treas London Celebrations Ctee for Queen's Silver Jubilee; Motability: chm Exec Ctee 1977–, vice chm 1977–94, chm 1994–; chm: Young Vic Co 1975–83, Bd of Govrs Royal Ballet Sch 1983–; govr Royal Ballet 1986–; Hon Capt RNR 1991, elder brother Trinity House 1991; Freeman City of London; Hon DBA Nottingham Trent Univ 1995, Hon DCL Univ of Durham 1996; Hon FIMarE 1991, Hon FICS 1992, Hon MRICS 1993; FISVA 1995; *Recreations* music, swimming, tennis; *Clubs* Garrick, Carlton, Hurlingham; *Style—* The Rt Hon the Lord Sterling of Plaistow, CBE; ✉ The Peninsular and Oriental Steam Navigation Company, Peninsular House, 79 Pall Mall, London SW1Y 5EJ (☎ 0171 930 4343, fax 0171 930 8572, telex 885551)

STERN, Charles Roger; *b* 16 April 1950; *Educ* Marlborough, Univ of Cambridge (MA), London Business Sch (MSc); *m* 24 July 1973, Nicola Kay (d 1991); 3 s (Oliver James b 29 May 1978, William Mark b 13 April 1980, Thomas Joseph b 11 May 1984); *Career* planning asst Delta Group Overseas Ltd 1973–76; fin dir: Delta RA Ltd 1976–79, Delta Group Industrial Services Division 1979–84; md Delta Group Australia 1984–86, gp fin dir Aegis Group plc 1986–92, fin dir United News & Media plc (formerly United Newspapers plc) 1992–; ACMA; *Style—* Charles Stern, Esq; ✉ United News & Media plc, Ludgate House, 245 Blackfriars Road, London SE1 9UY (☎ 0171 921 5000, car 0802 203720)

STERN, (John) Chester; s of Julius Charles Stern (d 1983), of Littlehampton, Sussex, and Bertha Margaret, *née* Baker; *b* 6 Sept 1944; *Educ* Parktown Boys' HS Johannesburg SA, Broad Green Coll Croydon Surrey; *m* 25 March 1967, Rosemary Ann, da of Wilfred Harold Symons; 2 da (Carolyn Joy b 28 Sept 1969, Paula Jane b 26 Feb 1972); *Career* asst librarian Wills Library Guy's Hospital Medical Sch 1964–65, ed asst Food Processing & Marketing 1965–66, freelance broadcaster BBC Radio London 1970–74, freelance sportswriter The Sunday Telegraph 1973–76; Metropolitan Police New Scotland Yard: publicity asst 1966–68, head of News Gp 1968–71, PRO Traffic Warden Service 1971–74, press and publicity offr London Airport Heathrow 1974–75, press and publicity offr S London 1975–77, head Press Bureau 1977–82; crime corr The Mail on Sunday 1982–; pres Crime Reporters' Assoc 1995 (chm 1993); Winston Churchill fell 1975; FRGS 1964, MIPR 1971; *Books* Dr Iain West's Casebook (1996); *Recreations* badminton, tennis, squash, golf; *Clubs* Mensa, Groucho; *Style—* Chester Stern, Esq; ✉ The Mail on Sunday, Associated Newspapers Ltd, Northcliffe House, 2 Derry St, Kensington, London W8 5TS (☎ 0171 938 7031, fax 0171 937 3829)

STERN, Dr Gerald Malcolm; s of Aaron Nathan Stern (d 1975), of London, and Rebecca, *née* Marks (d 1981); *b* 9 Oct 1930; *Educ* Thomas Parmiters Sch, London Hosp Med Coll (MB BS, MD); *m* 27 Sep 1962, Jennifer Rosemary, da of Maj Alfred Charles Pritchard (d 1974); 2 s (Robert Max James b 24 April 1965, Edward Gerald Matthew b 7 April 1972), 1 da (Melanie Rosemary b 6 July 1963); *Career* temp cmmn Surgn Lt RNVR 1956–58; currently emeritus conslt neurologist UCHs and Nat Hosp for Neurology and Neurosurgery London; memb Bd of Govrs Nat Hosp for Nervous Diseases 1982–; chm Medicine Advsy Panel Parkinson's Disease Soc, vice pres RSM 1996; memb: Assoc of Br Neurologists 1964– (pres 1994–95), Assoc of Physicians of GB and Ireland; FRCP 1970 (memb Cncl 1982); Ehrenmitgleid Osterreichishe Parkinson Gesellschaft (1986); *Books* Parkinson's Disease (1989); *Recreations* music, squash; *Clubs* Athenaeum; *Style—* Dr Gerald Stern; ✉ Woolavington Wing, The Middlesex Hospital, Mortimer Street, London W1 (☎ 0171 388 0640, fax 0171 436 5859)

STERN, Dr Jeremy Samuel; s of Harold Ian Stern, of Sheffield, and Daphne, *née* Moses; *b* 12 Jan 1967; *Educ* Ecclesfield Sch Sheffield, King Edward VII Sch Sheffield, Christ's Coll Cambridge (MA), UCL, Middx Sch of Med London (MB BChir); *Career* house surgn Basildon and Orsett Hosps 1991–92, house physician Southampton Gen Hosp 1992, sr house offr in med Guy's Hosp 1992–94, registrar in geriatics St George's Hosp London 1994–95; registrar in neurology: Atkinson Morley's Hosp 1995–96, Chelsea & Westminster Hosp 1996–; memb Exec Ctee Tourette Syndrome (UK) Assoc; memb (youngest ever) GMC 1994–; memb Br Neuropsychiatry Assoc 1992, MRCP 1994; *Recreations* eating, playing the piano, bassoon and didgeridoo, history of medicine; *Clubs* Archers Addicts, Richard Cloudsley Dining Society; *Style—* Dr Jeremy Stern; ✉ Chelsea & Westminster Hospital, 639 Fulham Road, London SW10 9NH (☎ 0181 746 8000)

STERN, Linda Joy; QC (1991); da of Lily Rachel Saville, *née* Gold (decd); *b* 21 Dec 1941; *Educ* St Paul's Girls' Sch; *m* 1, 1961, Michael Brian Rose (d 1976); 2 s; m 2, 1978, Nigel Maurice Stern; *Career* called to the Bar Gray's Inn 1971, recorder of the Crown Court 1990–; FRSA; *Recreations* reading, opera, concert and theatre going; *Style—* Mrs Linda J Stern, QC; ✉ 5 King's Bench Walk, Temple, London EC4Y 7DN (☎ 0171 797 7600, fax 0171 797 7648)

STERN, Michael Charles; MP (C) Bristol North West (majority 45); s of Maurice Leonard Stern (d 1967), of Finchley, and Rose, *née* Dzialosinski; *b* 3 Aug 1942; *Educ* Christ's Coll GS Finchley; *m* 1976, Jillian Denise, da of Raymond Denis Aldridge, of York; 1 da (Katharine b 1980); *Career* ptnr: Percy Phillips & Co 1964–80, Halpern & Woolf 1980–92; conslt Cohen Arnold & Co 1992–; chm Bow Group 1977–78, Parly candidate (C) Derby S 1979, MP (C) Bristol NW 1983–; PPS to: Hon Peter Brooke as Min of State Treasy 1986–87 and as Paymaster Gen 1987–89, John Redwood as Min for Corp Affrs 1990–91; memb: Select Ctee on Energy 1990–92, Public Accounts Ctee 1992–: a vice chm Cons Pty 1991–92; co-opted memb Educn Ctee London Borough of Ealing 1980–83; FCA; *Recreations* fell-walking, bridge, chess; *Clubs* United & Cecil, London Mountaineering; *Style—* Michael Stern, Esq, MP; ✉ House of Commons, London SW1A 0AA

STERN, Prof Nicholas Herbert; s of Adalbert Stern, and Marion Fatima, *née* Swann; *b* 22 April 1946; *Educ* Latymer Upper Sch, Univ of Cambridge (BA), Univ of Oxford (DPhil); *m* 7 Sept 1968, Susan Ruth, da of Albert Edward Chesterton (d 1978), of Pinner, Middx; 2 s (Daniel b 1979, Michael b 1980), 1 da (Helen b 1976); *Career* fell and tutor in econs St Catherine's Coll Oxford, lectr in industl maths Univ of Oxford 1970–77; prof of econs: Univ of Warwick 1978–85, LSE 1986– (Sir John Hicks prof of econs 1990–); chief economist European Bank for Reconstruction & Devpt 1994–; memb: Ctee Oxfam Africa 1974–79, Asia Ctee 1986–89; ed Jl of Public Economics 1981; fell Econometric Soc 1978; FBA 1993; *Books* Crime, the Police and Criminal Statistics (with R Carr-Hill, 1979), Palanpur: The Economy of an Indian Village (with C Bliss, 1982), The Theory of Taxation for Developing Countries (with D Newbery, 1987), The Theory and Practice of Taxation for Developing Countries (with E Ahmad, 1991); *Recreations* walking, reading, watching football; *Style—* Professor Nicholas Stern, FBA; ✉ Chief Economist, EBRD, One Exchange Square, London EC2A 2EH (☎ 0171 338 6805, fax 0171 338 6110)

STERNBERG, Michael Vivian; s of Sir Sigmund Sternberg, JP, *qv*, and Beartrice Ruth, *née* Schiff (d 1994); *b* 12 Sept 1951; *Educ* Carmel Coll Wallingford, Queens' Coll Cambridge (MA, LLM); *m* 20 July 1975, Janine Lois, da of Harold Levinson; 1 s (Daniel Isaiah b 24 Sept 1982), 2 da (Rachel Serena b 2 Feb 1980, Sarah Jessica b 4 Jan 1988); *Career* called to the Bar Gray's Inn 1975; asst sec Family Law Bar Assoc 1986–88; tstee: London Jewish East End Museum 1984–94, Sternberg Charitable Settlement; memb Cncl of Christians and Jews 1988, Lloyd's underwriter 1978–; Freeman City of London, Liveryman Worshipful Co of Horners 1987; Medaglia D'Argento di Benemerenza of the Sacred Military Constantinian Order of St George 1990; *Recreations* walking, reading, wine, theatre, amusing children; *Clubs* Reform, City Livery; *Style—* Michael Sternberg, Esq; ✉ 4 Paper Buildings, Temple, London EC4Y 7EX (☎ 0171 583 0816, fax 0171 353 4979)

STERNBERG, Sir Sigmund; kt (1976); s of Abraham Sternberg (d 1935), of Hungary, and Elizabeth Sternberg (d 1991); *b* 2 June 1921, Budapest; *m* 1970, Hazel (Lady Sternberg, JP), da of Albert Everett-Jones; 1 step s, 1 step da; 1 s (Michael Vivian Sternberg, *qv*) and 1 da from prev m; *Career* served WWII, Civil Defence Corps; former ring-dealing memb London Metal Exchange, Lloyd's underwriter 1969–; chm: Martin Slowe Estates Ltd 1971–, ISYS plc 1973–; instituted research gp for Lab Shadow Cabinet 1973–74; Fabian Soc: chm Appeals Ctee 1975–77, memb Econ and Indust Ctee 1976, treas Appeal Ctee 1995–; dep chm Lab Fin and Indust Gp 1972–93; chm: St Charles Gp HMC 1972–93, NW Metropolitan RHB 1974; memb: Camden and Islington AHA 1974–77, Gen Purposes Ctee NAMH 1972; hon treas Cruse Bereavement Care 1981–82, pres Friends of Cruse 1993–; vice pres Royal Coll of Speech and Language Therapists, chm Inst for Archaeo-Metallurgical Studies; chm Exec Ctee Int Cncl for Christians and Jews, memb Bd of Deputies of Br Jews, govr Hebrew Univ of Jerusalem, tstee Manor House Tst (Sternberg Centre for Judaism) 1984– (chm 1993–), convenor Religious Press Gp; vice pres: Reform Synagogues of GB 1991, Cncl of Christians and Jews 1992– (hon treas 1977–92); memb: Cncl Inst of Business Ethics, Ct Univ of Essex; judge Templeton Fndn 1988–92; JP Middx 1965, memb Cwlth Magistrates' and Judges' Assoc 1985; Paul Harris fell Rotary Fndn of Rotary Int 1989, speaker chm Rotary Club of London 1980–83 and 1993–; hon memb: Rotary Club Budapest 1989, Highgate Rotary 1990; Order of the Orthodox Hospitallers 1st Class with Star and Badge of Religion 1986, OstJ 1988, Brotherhood Award Nat Conf of Christians and Jews Inc 1980, KCSG 1985, Silver Pontifical Medal 1986, Benemerenti Medal (Vatican) 1988 (in Silver 1990), Good Servant Medal Canadian CCJ 1991, Silver Jerusalem Mayoral Award 1991, Man of Reconciliation Award Warsaw Univ 1995, Order of the Gold Star (Hungary) 1990, Hungarian CCJ Award 1995, Medaglia d'Argento di Benemerenza Sacred Mil Constantinian Order of St George 1991, Cdr's Cross 1st Class (Austria) 1992, Cdr's Cross Order of Merit (Poland) 1992, Cdr of the Order of Civil Merit (Spain) 1993, Cdr's Cross Order of Merit (Germany) 1993; Liveryman Worshipful Co of Horners, Freeman City of London; FRSA 1979, Hon FRSM 1981, Hon FCST 1989; *Recreations* golf, swimming; *Clubs* Reform, City Livery; *Style—* Sir Sigmund Sternberg; ✉ 80 East End Rd, London N3 2SY (fax 0171 485 4512)

STEUART FOTHRINGHAM, Robert; DL (Angus 1985); eld s of Maj Thomas Scrymsoure Steuart Fothringham, MC, DL, JP, TD (d 1979, 2 s of Lt-Col Walter Thomas James Scrymsoure Steuart Fothringham, of Pourie-Fothringham and Tealing, Angus, and of Grantully and Murthly, Perthshire, who took the name Steuart on succeeding

Sir Archibald Douglas Stewart, 8 and last Bt, in the lands of Grantully and Murthly in 1890), and Carola Mary (d 1989), da of Maj the Hon Charles Hubert Francis Noel, OBE (d 1947); bro of Henry Steuart Fothringham of Grantully, OBE, *qv*; *b* 5 Aug 1937; *Educ* Fort Augustus Abbey, Trinity Coll Cambridge, RAC Cirencester; *m* 16 Feb 1962, Elizabeth Mary Charlotte (d 1990), da of Thomas Hope Brendan Lawther (d 1994), of Earl's Court, London SW5; 2 s (Thomas b 1971, Lionel b 1973), 2 da (Mariana (Mrs Pease) b 1966, Ilona b 1969); *Career* CA; memb Royal Co Archers; *Recreations* shooting, fishing, archery, music; *Clubs* Puffin's, Turf, New (Edinburgh); *Style*— Robert Steuart Fothringham, Esq, DL; ✉ Fothringham, Forfar, Angus DD8 2JP (☎ 01307 820231); Murthly Castle, Murthly, Perth PH1 4HP (☎ 01738 710397)

STEUART FOTHRINGHAM OF GRANTULLY, Henry; OBE (1995); yst s of Maj Thomas Scrymsoure Steuart Fothringham, 21 of Pourie-Fothringham, MC, DL, JP (d 1979), of Fothringham, Forfar, Angus, and Carola Mary (d 1989), da of Maj the Hon Charles Hubert Francis Noel, OBE (d 1947); bro of Robert Steuart Fothringham, DL, *qv*; inherited the barony of Grantully from uncle, Maj Patrick Scrymsoure Steuart Fothringham, 22 of Grantully, DSO (d 1953); *b* 15 Feb 1944, Edinburgh; *Educ* Fort Augustus Abbey, RAC Cirencester; *m* 20 May 1972, Cherry Linnhe Stewart, 14 of Achnacone, o surviving da of Brig Ian Macalister Stewart, 13 of Achnacone, DSO, OBE, MC, DL (d 1987), of Achnacone, Appin, Argyll; 3 s (Patrick b 23 April 1973, Charles b 6 April 1974, Ian b 13 Jan 1976); *Career* landowner, specialist in Scottish silver, writer and researcher; proprietor Grantully Castle Antiques 1966–68; ptnr (with late bro, Walter): specialising in Scottish silver 1968–72, promoting Norman Orr (crystal engraver, artist and designer) 1968–89; dir: Fothringham Enterprises 1990–, Logierait Bridge Co 1995–; memb: Tay Salmon Fisheries Bd 1977–80, Reviewing Ctee on the Export of Works of Art 1982–94, Advsy Cncl on the Export of Works of Art 1982–94; govr Heartland Radio Foundation Ltd 1995–; Freeman: Worshipful Co of Goldsmiths 1993, City of London 1994; memb: The Silver Soc 1977 (memb Cncl 1991–, vice chm 1992–93, chm 1993–94), The Stewart Soc 1963 (memb Cncl 1968–82 and 1988–, hon vice pres 1971–, tstee 1975–, memb Benevolent Fund 1975–82 and 1993–, vice pres 1992–95, pres 1995–), Incorporation of Goldsmiths of the City of Edinburgh 1990– (memb Deacon's Cncl 1991–, memb Investment Ctee 1991–95), various historical and Scottish learned socs; MInstD, FRSA, FSA(Scot), FRPSL; *Books and Publications* The Family of Fothringham of Pourie (1990, 3 edn 1995); contrib: Jackson's Silver and Gold Marks of England, Scotland and Ireland (1989), Scottish Gold and Silver Work (ed, 1991 edn); author of numerous articles in learned jls, book and exhbn reviews for various pubns; *Recreations* Scottish silver studies, books, history, writing, the Arts and Sciences, Scotland, the countryside, trees and gardens, genealogy, Indian telegraphy, compulsive research, polymathy, etc; *Clubs* City Livery, Royal Over-Seas League, Antiquaries Dining (Edinburgh), Puffins (Edinburgh); *Style*— Henry Steuart Fothringham, Esq, OBE; ✉ The Lagg, Aberfeldy, Perthshire PH15 2EE (☎ 01887 820020, fax 01887 829582, car 0831 843061); Achnacone, Appin, Argyll PA38 4BE (☎ 01631 730239)

STEVELY, Prof William Stewart; s of Robert Reid Stevely (d 1992), of Saltcoats, Ayrshire, and Catherine Callow, *née* Stewart; *b* 6 April 1943; *Educ* Ardrossan Acad, Univ of Glasgow (BSc, DipEd), Univ of Oxford (DPhil); *m* 1968, Sheila Anne, *née* Stalker; 3 s, 2 da; *Career* successively asst lectr, lectr then sr lectr in biochemistry Univ of Glasgow 1968–88; Univ of Paisley (formerly Paisley Coll of Technol): prof and head Dept of Biology 1988–92, vice princ 1992–; memb: Nat Bd for Scotland of Nursing Midwifery and Health Visiting 1993–, Scottish HE Funding Cncl 1994–; memb: Biochemical Soc 1968, Soc of Gen Microbiology 1973, Inst of Environmental Sci 1990; FIBiol 1988; *Style*— Prof William Stevely; ✉ University of Paisley, Paisley, Renfrewshire PA1 2BE (☎ 0141 848 3672)

STEVEN, Alasdair Robert Malcolm; s of James White Robertson Steven (d 1970), and Helen Mary, *née* Urquhart (d 1989); *b* 1 May 1942; *Educ* Trinity Coll Glenalmond, Univ de Grenoble; *Career* various fin insts 1964–76, ind theatrical prodr 1976–79, freelance journalist 1979–; reviewer opera and ballet Birmingham Post, contrib numerous pubns on the arts, writer various TV scripts incl The Three Tenors (Channel 4) 1990 and various progs incl Nureyev Gala at the London Coliseum; *Recreations* gardening, food, wine and the French; *Style*— Alasdair Steven, Esq; ✉ Poirier, 8a St Dunstan's Rd, London W6 8RB (☎ 0181 748 6897); Place de la Mairie, Incourt, France 62770 (☎ 00 33 2103 2451)

STEVEN, Stewart Gustav; s of Rudolph Steven, and Trude Steven; *b* 30 Sept 1935; *Educ* Mayfield Coll Sussex; *m* 1965, Inka Sobieniewska; 1 s (Jack); *Career* political reporter Central Press Features 1961–63, political corr Western Daily Press 1963–64; Daily Express: political reporter 1964–65, dip corr 1965–67, foreign ed 1967–72; Daily Mail: asst ed 1972–74, associate ed 1974–82; ed: Mail on Sunday 1982–92, Evening Standard 1992–95; columnist Mail on Sunday 1996–, chm Liberty Publishing Ltd 1996–; hon perpetual student Bart's Hosp 1993; chm: Equity Theatre Cmmn 1995–, Nat Campaign for the Arts 1995–; memb Bd: Better English Campaign 1995–, Thames Advsy Gp 1995–, London Film Cmmn 1996–; *Books* Operation Splinter Factor (1974), The Spymasters of Israel (1976), The Poles (1982); *Recreations* swimming, pool maintenance; *Clubs* Groucho, Surrey CCC; *Style*— Stewart Steven, Esq; ✉ c/o Liberty Publishing Ltd, Trevor House, 100 Brompton Road, London SW3 1ER (☎ 0171 225 6763/6717, fax 0171 225 6720)

STEVENS, Alan Michael; s of Raymond Alfred George Stevens, of Bournemouth, and Joan Patricia, *née* Drury; *b* 8 April 1955; *Educ* Malvern, Selwyn Coll Cambridge (MA); *m* 2 May 1987, Lynn Sarah, da of Henry B Hopfinger, of Coventry; 2 s (Thomas b 1990, Benjamin b 1992), 2 da (Eloise b 1988, Natalia b 1993); *Career* admitted slr 1980; ptnr Linklaters & Paines 1987– (joined 1978); memb Law Soc, Freeman Worshipful Co of Slrs; *Recreations* tennis, skiing, sailing; *Clubs* Royal Hong Kong Yacht; *Style*— Alan Stevens, Esq; ✉ Putney, London; Linklaters and Paines, Barrington House, 59–67 Gresham St, London EC2V 7JA (☎ 0171 606 7080, fax 0171 606 5113, telex 884349/888167)

STEVENS, Anthony John (Tony); s of John Walker Stevens (d 1930), and Hilda, *née* Stevens (d 1990); *b* 29 July 1926; *Educ* Long Eaton Co GS, Univ of Liverpool (BVSc, MRCVS), Univ of Manchester (Dip Bacteriology); *m* Patricia Frances, da of Robert Gill (d 1974); 1 s (Timothy Mark), 2 da (Carol Anne, Heather Frances); *Career* MAFF: res offr 1952–53, vet investigation offr 1953–65, superintending investigation offr 1965–68, dir Vet Investigation Serv 1968–71, dir Vet Field Servs 1971–78, dir Vet Laboratories 1978–86; conslt and specialist advsr Food and Agricultural Orgn UNO (various periods 1960–90); memb Cncl RCVS (postgrad vet dean London and SE 1986–95); vice pres Zoological Soc of London, vice chm Surrey Industl History Gp, formerly pres Surrey Small Shepherds Club; Hon MA Univ of Cambridge 1962; *Books* Handbook of Veterinary Laboratory Diagnosis FAO (1963); *Recreations* farming, archaeology, canals, riding; *Style*— Tony Stevens, Esq; ✉ Marigold Cottage, Great Halfpenny Farm, Halfpenny Lane, Guildford, Surrey GU4 8PY (☎ 01483 65375)

STEVENS, Auriol; da of Capt E B K Stevens, DSO, RN (d 1971), and Ruth, *née* Pugh; *b* 4 Nov 1940; *Educ* Somerville Coll Oxford (BA), Univ of London (external dipl); *m* 1, 1962 (m dis 1987), Prof Hugh Stephenson; 2 s (b 1965, b 1970), 1 da (b 1966); m 2, 1988, Dr John Ashworth, *qv*; 4 step c; *Career* fashion model and design asst Mattli 1961–62, freelance feature writer and photographer in UK, US and W Germany 1962–72, resources ed, features ed then dep ed Times Educnl Supplement 1972–78, educn corr The Observer 1978–83, reporter/presenter A Week in Politics C4 TV 1983–86, dir Universities Information Unit CVCP 1986–92, ed Times Higher Educn Supplement 1992–; dir Higher Education: the Offical Fair Company 1990–92, memb Cncl Policy Studies Inst 1985–91, chm of govrs Elliott Sch Putney 1981–85 (govr 1973–85); FRSA 1992; *Books* Clever Children in Comprehensive Schools (1978); *Recreations* domestic arts, hill walking, photography; *Style*— Ms Auriol Stevens; ✉ Times Supplements Ltd, Admiral House, 66–68 East Smithfield, London E1 9XY (☎ 0171 782 3375, fax 0171 782 3000, e-mail astevens@THES.co.uk)

STEVENS, Brian Turnbull Julius; s of Maj John Osmond Julius Stevens, MBE, and Kathleen, *née* Forman; *b* 3 Nov 1938; *Educ* Eton; *m* 5 Dec 1970, The Hon Henrietta Maria, da of Lt-Col 1 Baron St Helens, MC (d 1980); 3 da (Flora Matilda Julius b 25 Feb 1973, Harriet Maria Julius b 11 Jan 1975, Louisa Elizabeth Julius b 15 Oct 1976); *Career* admitted slr 1962; currently ptnr Withers: memb Law Soc; *Recreations* field sports and gardening; *Clubs* Boodle's, Pratt's; *Style*— Brian Stevens, Esq; ✉ Withers, 12 Gough Square, London EC4 (☎ 0171 936 1000, fax 0171 936 2589, telex 24213 WITHER G)

STEVENS, David Franklin; s of John Stanley Stevens (d 1969), of Guildford, Surrey, and Margaret Madelene, *née* Gale (d 1949); *b* 8 Jan 1928; *Educ* Sherborne; *m* 1947, Patricia Mary, da of Charles Campbell; 1 s (Alastair David b 1948), 1 da (Bryony Jane Carolyn b 1951); *Career* Nat Serv Capt Queen's Royal Regt, served Far East 1946–48, TA 1S9/23 SAS 1953–60; Rigby & Evens Ltd wine shippers Bristol 1949–63 (MW 1961), md Rigby & Evens (Liverpool) Ltd 1963–69, dir Matthew Clark & Sons (Holdings) Ltd London 1967–81, chm Rigby & Evens (Wine Shippers) Ltd Liverpool and London 1969–76; estab own wine consultancy 1981–87, first exec dir Inst of Masters of Wine 1987–94 (chm 1973–74, pres 1994–97); wine columnist Literary Review 1987–92; memb Wine Ctee Int Wine and Food Soc; Freeman City of London, Liveryman Worshipful Co of Distillers 1993; memb: Confrerie des Chevaliers du Tastevin, Academie du Vin de Bordeaux, Commanderie du Bon Temps de Medoc et des Graves; *Books* contrib: Wines of the World (ed Serena Sutcliffe, 1979), Oxford University Press Companion to Wine (Jancis Robinson, 1994); *Recreations* writing, travelling, good wine, the cinema, all sports (active tennis player); *Style*— David Stevens, Esq; ✉ The Three Cottages, Meadle, nr Aylesbury, Bucks HP17 9UD (☎ 01844 343825)

STEVENS, Dr David Laurence; s of Laurence Sydney Stevens (d 1987), of Ampney Crucis, Cirencester, Gloucestershire, and Ida May, *née* Roberts (d 1989); *b* 15 Sept 1938; *Educ* High Pavement Sch, Nottingham and Guy's Hosp Med Sch Univ of London (MB BS, MD); *m* 20 Feb 1965, (Karin) Ute, da of Friedrich Heinrich Rudolf Holtzheimer (d 1966), of Berlin; 2 s (Michael b 1967, Andrew b 1970); *Career* registrar in neurology Derbyshire Royal Infirmary 1966–67, sr registrar in neurology Leeds Gen Infirmary 1967–73, res fell dept of genetics Univ of Leeds 1969–70; conslt neurologist 1973–: Gloucestershire Royal Hosp, Cheltenham Gen Hosp, Frenchay Hosp Bristol; memb ed bd Br Jl of Hosp Med 1985–, assoc ed Journal of Neurological Sciences 1990–; author of articles on neurology in med jls, contribs to various books; Sec Gen Res Gp on Huntington's Chorea World Fedn of Neurology 1983–91 (memb res ctee 1973–); past pres SW England Neurosciences Assoc 1984–85; memb Assoc of Br Neurologists; FRCP 1980 (MRCP 1966); *Books* Handbook of Clinical Neurology (contrib); *Recreations* travel, photography, skiing, talking (a lot); *Style*— Dr David Stevens; ✉ Department of Neurology, Gloucestershire Royal Hospital, Gloucester GL1 3NN (☎ 01452 394634, fax 01452 394499)

STEVENS, Prof Denis William; s of William James Stevens (d 1977), of Croydon, and Edith Ruby, *née* Driver (d 1977); *b* 2 March 1922; *Educ* Royal GS High Wycombe, Jesus Coll Oxford (MA); *m* 1, 1949, Sheila Elizabeth, da of John Holloway; 2 s (Anthony Vincent b 20 May 1950, Michael David b 20 Sept 1956), 1 da (Daphne Elizabeth b 28 Jan 1953); m 2, 1975, Lillian Elizabeth, da of John Kwasny; *Career* served RAF Intelligence India and Burma 1942–46; BBC Music Dept 1949–54 (first broadcast performances of major works by Charpentier, Dufay, Dunstable, Monteverdi, Telemann and Vivaldi), visiting prof Cornell Univ 1955 and Columbia Univ 1956, Royal Acad of Music 1960, pres and artistic dir Accademia Monteverdiana 1961–, visiting prof Univ of California Berkeley 1962, distinguished visiting prof Pennsylvania State Univ 1962–64, prof of musicology Columbia Univ 1965–74, visiting prof Univ of California Santa Barbara 1975, distinguished visiting prof Univ of Washington Seattle 1976, visiting prof Univ of Michigan Ann Arbor 1977; visiting prof Goldsmiths Coll London 1995, visiting prof Académie Musicale de Villecroze 1996; contrib to congresses in: London, Oxford, Cologne, Salzburg, Paris, Wégimont, Corrèze, Moscow, New York, New Haven, Washington, Rochester (NY), San Diego, Los Angeles and St Louis; organiser and leader of Rockefeller Congress at Bellagio 1974; co-fndr Ambrosian Singers 1952, sec Plainsong and Medieval Music Soc 1958–62; conducted Accademia Monteverdiana at Prom Concerts 1967–74 and at various int music festivals incl Edinburgh, Bath, London, Salzburg, Lucerne, Gstaad, Lisbon and Bordeaux, numerous recordings and bdcasts (TV and radio); Hon DHL Fairfield Univ Connecticut 1967; Freeman City of London 1961, Liveryman Worshipful Co of Musicians 1961; Hon RAM 1960; *Books* The Mulliner Book: A Commentary (1953), Thomas Tomkins (1957), The Pelican History of Music (1957–65), History of Song (1959), Tudor Church Music (1960), Treasury of English Church Music Vol 1 (1965), Musicology (1980), Musicology in Practice (1987), Monteverdi (1978), The Joy of Ornamentation (1989), Letters of Monteverdi (1995), Early Music (1996); contrib: Encyclopedia Britannica, Grove's Dictionary, Die Musik in Geschichte und Gegenwart, Enciclopedia della Musica; *Recreations* travel, photography; *Clubs* Garrick; *Style*— Prof Denis Stevens, CBE; ✉ 3 The Quadrangle, Morden College, London SE3 0PW

STEVENS, Handley Michael Gambrell; s of Dr Ernest Norman Stevens (d 1991), and Dr Kathleen Emily Gambrell (d 1986); *b* 29 June 1941; *Educ* The Leys Sch, Phillips Acad Andover Mass, King's Coll Cambridge (MA); *m* 5 March 1966, Anne Frances, da of Robert Ross, of Evesbatch, Hereford and Worcester; 3 da (Hilary b 1970, Lucy b 1971, Mary b 1980); *Career* Dip Serv 1964–70 (Kuala Lumpur 1966–69); asst private sec Lord Privy Seal 1970–71, Civil Serv Dept 1970–73, DTI 1973–83, under sec Dept of Tport 1983–94 (Int Aviation 1983–87, Finance 1988–91, Public Tport in London 1991–94); research assoc Euro Inst LSE 1994–; *Recreations* Anglican lay reader, music, walking; *Style*— Handley M G Stevens, Esq; ✉ 55 St George's Drive, London SW1V 4DF (☎ 0171 834 0336)

STEVENS, Sir Jocelyn Edward Greville; kt (1996), CVO (1992); s of Maj (Charles) Greville Bartlett Stewart-Stevens, formerly Stevens, JP (d 1972, having m subsequently (1936) Muriel Athelstan Hood, *née* Stewart, 10 Lady of Balnakeilly, Perthshire, and adopted (1937) the name Stewart-Stevens), and late Mrs Greville Stevens (d 1932), da of Sir Edward Hulton (who owned the Evening Standard until 1923, when he sold it to 1 Baron Beaverbrook); *b* 14 Feb 1932; *Educ* Eton, Trinity Coll Cambridge; *m* 1956 (m dis 1979), Jane Armyne, LVO (1993), da of John Vincent Sheffield; 2 s (1 decd), 2 da; *Career* Nat Serv The Rifle Bde 1950–52; journalist Hulton Press Ltd 1955–56, chm and md Stevens Press Ltd and ed of Queen Magazine 1957–68, dir Beaverbrook Newspapers 1971–77 (md 1974–77), md Evening Standard Co Ltd 1969–72, md Daily Express 1972–74, dep chm and md Express Newspapers 1975–81, dir Centaur Communications Ltd 1982–85, publisher and ed The Magazine 1982–84, rector and vice provost RCA 1984–92, chm English Heritage 1992–; dep chm Independent Television Commission 1991–96; non-exec dir: Lowe Group plc 1988–90, The Television Corporation 1996–; chm The Silver Trust 1989–93, pres The Cheyne Walk Trust 1989–93; govr: ICSTM 1985–92, Winchester Sch of Art 1986–89; Hon DLitt Loughborough Univ; sr fell RCA, hon fell

CSD; FRSA; *Recreations* skiing; *Clubs* White's, Buck's, Beefsteak; *Style*— Sir Jocelyn Stevens, CVO; ✉ 14 Cheyne Walk, London SW3 5RA; English Heritage, 23 Savile Row, London W1X 1AB (☎ 0171 973 3334, fax 0171 973 3379)

STEVENS, John Christopher Courtney; MEP (C) Thames Valley (majority 758); *b* 23 May 1955; *Educ* Winchester, Magdalen Coll Oxford (BA); *Career* foreign exchange dealer Bayerische Hypotheken Wechselbank Munich 1976–77; fin corr Il Messaggiero Rome 1978; foreign exchange dealer: Banque Indosuez Paris 1979–80, Morgan Grenfell & Co Ltd London 1980–84, dir Morgan Grenfell International (and head of Euro Govt Bond Trading) 1985–89, advsr on foreign exchange and interest rates to J Rothschild Investment Management 1989–; MEP (C) Thames Valley 1989–; *Books* A Conservative European Monetary Union (1990); *Style*— John Stevens, Esq, MEP; ✉ 39 St James's Place, London SW1A 1NS (☎ 0171 493 8111, fax 0171 493 0673)

STEVENS, Dr (Katharine) Lindsey Haughton; da of Richard Haughton Stevens (d 1977), of Sheringham, Norfolk, and Rachel Vera Joyce, *née* Huxstep; *b* 17 July 1954; *Educ* Harrogate Ladies' Coll, Runton Hill and Gresham's Schs, Churchill Coll Cambridge (MA), Middx Hosp Med Sch (MB BCh); *m* 1989, David Barrett McCausland, s of John McCausland, of Pett, Hastings; 2 s (Duncan James Stevens McCausland b 1989, Theodore Richard Stevens McCausland b 1994), 1 da (Beth Mary Stevens McCausland b 1991); *Career* conslt/mangr Accident and Emergency St George's Hosp 1985–96, clinical dir Accident and Emergency Services St Helier Hosp 1996–; hon sr lectr Univ of London 1985–, instr in advanced trauma life support RCS 1989, instructor in paediatric advanced life support 1992, fndr St George's Start-a-Heart campaign and fund 1986; res into: psychological effects of trauma and bereavement, domestic violence, water safety, resuscitation, cardiac illness, physiotherapy; dep dist surgn St John Ambulance Bde; memb Br Assoc of Accident and Emergency Med 1985, editorial rep Accident and Emergency Section RSM 1995– (treas 1992–95); regnl sub-speciality advsr RCS 1990; memb RSM 1989; FFAEM 1993, FRCP 1994 (MRCP 1983); *Books* Emergencies in Obstetrics and Gynaecology; *Style*— Dr Lindsey Stevens; ✉ Accident and Emergency Department, St Helier Hospital, Wrythe Lane, Carshalton, SM5 1AA (☎ 0181 296 2276)

STEVENS, Dr Martin John; s of John Frederick Stevens (d 1972), of Aldeburgh, Suffolk, and Lucy Thelma, *née* Clark; *b* 5 June 1942; *Educ* The GS Leiston Suffolk, St Thomas's Hosp Med Sch; *m* 14 Oct 1978, (Gwyneth) Sandra George, da of Alec Thomas, of Rotherham, S Yorks; 2 s (John Joseph Benjamin b 23 Aug 1979, James Frederick Martin Zacharia b 18 June 1981); *Career* conslt and clinical dir the psychiatry of old age E Suffolk Health Authy 1977–; memb Section for Psychiatry of Old Age of RCPsych, examiner for MRCPsych; FRCPsych 1986, FRCP 1995; *Recreations* chorister (bass) St Mary le Tower Church Ipswich; *Style*— Dr Martin Stevens; ✉ 55 Henley Road, Ipswich, Suffolk (☎ 01473 251265); Department of Geriatric Psychiatry, Minsmere House, The Ipswich Hospital, Heath Rd, Ipswich, Suffolk (☎ 01473 712233)

STEVENS, Patrick Tom; s of Tom Stevens, of Norfolk, and Gwendoline, *née* Nurse; *b* 21 Aug 1949; *Educ* Paston GS Norfolk; *Career* tax specialist Coopers & Lybrand 1975–79, tax ptnr BDO Stoy Hayward (and predecessor firms) 1979–96, tax ptnr Ernst & Young 1996–; Liveryman Worshipful Co of Glass Sellers; FCA 1972, ATII 1975; *Recreations* theatre, golf; *Style*— Patrick Stevens, Esq; ✉ 11A London Road, Southborough, Tunbridge Wells, Kent; Ernst & Young, Rolls House, Rolls Buildings, Fetter Lane, London EC4 (☎ 0171 931 2334, fax 0171 353 8134)

STEVENS, Peter Charles; s of Dennis Charles Stevens (d 1988), and Monica, *née* Jenkinson (d 1991); *b* 2 Aug 1943; *Educ* Central Fndn Boys' GS London, St Martin's Sch of Art London, RCA London (MDes, prize for three dimensional design, travelling scholarship to Europe); *m* (m dis); 2 s (Luke b 8 March 1972, Timothy b 10 Jan 1980); *partner* Melanie Jane Wood; *Career* vehicle designer; Ford Motor Co 1970–73, Ogle Design 1973–75, own consultancy Peter Stevens Design 1976–85, chief designer (styling) Lotus Cars 1985–89, Jaguar Sport 1989–90, chief designer (styling) McLaren Cars 1990–93; sometime visiting lectr RCA; Br Design award Design Cncl for Lotus Elan 1990, runner-up Duke of Edinburgh's Designer of the Year award 1991; *Recreations* motorsport, race team management, sailing, boating, painting, old cars; *Style*— Peter Stevens, Esq

STEVENS, Peter Rupert; s of Surgn Capt R W Stevens, RN; *b* 14 May 1938; *Educ* Winchester, Taft Sch (USA); *m* 1963, Sarah Venetia Mary, da of late Air Vice-Marshal H A V Hogan, CB, DSO, DFC; 3 children; *Career* 2 Lt KRRC; stockbroker; sr ptnr Laurie Milbank 1981–86 (ptnr 1969–86), head Sterling Fixed Interest and International Chase Manhattan Gilts Ltd; chief exec GT Management plc 1989–94; dir Corporate Governance LGT Gp 1994–; memb: Stock Exchange Cncl 1974–87 and 1988–91 (dep chm 1988–90), Bd of The Securities & Futures Authy 1986–; *Recreations* opera, gardening, country pursuits; *Style*— Peter Stevens, Esq; ✉ Highmead House, Alton, Hants GU34 4BN (☎ 01420 83945)

STEVENS, Raymond (Ray); s of Brian Charles Stevens, of High Wycombe, and Jane, *née* Vasallo; *b* 26 July 1963; *Educ* St Bernard's Catholic Sch; *partner* Natalie France, da of Raymond Jackson; 1 s from previous partner (Louis Charles Blount Stevens b 13 Feb 1989); *Career* judoist (currently under 95kg div); took up judo with Micklefield Judo Club High Wycombe 1973, joined Budokwai Judo Club London to train with Neil Adams 1982, int debut 1980; honours incl: Gold medal Nat Jr Championships 1982, Gold medal All England Championships 1983, Gold medal Br Championships 1984, 1985 and 1986, Gold medal Br Masters 1985, Silver medal Br Open 1985, Gold medal Cwlth Games Edinburgh 1986, Gold medal Welsh Open 1986, Gold medal Yugoslavia Open 1989, Gold medal Cwlth Games Auckland 1990, Gold medal Br Open 1990, 1994 and 1995, Silver medal Olympic Games Barcelona 1992, Gold medal Scottish Open 1994, Silver medal European Championships 1994, Silver medal Prague Open 1995, team Gold medal Europa Cup 1995; former joiner and roof tiler, currently pt/t personal fitness trainer and model; *Recreations* all sports (particularly golf and tennis), music, films; *Style*— Ray Stevens, Esq; ✉ 10 St Olaves Mansions, Walnut Tree Walk, Kennington, London SE11 6DW; Metropolitan Health Club, Burns Rd, Battersea, London (☎ 0171 228 4400)

STEVENS, Richard William; s of late William Edward Stevens, and late Caroline Alice, *née* Mills; *b* 1 Oct 1924; *Educ* Dorking GS, Regent St Poly (BSc); *m* 5 July 1947, Anne Clara (d 1994), da of Dudley Victor Hammond; 1 s (Paul b 7 May 1952), 1 da (Nicole b 12 Aug 1956); *Career* designer; Siemens Electric Lamps and Supplies Ltd 1945–52, Metropolitan Vickers Ltd 1952–54; chief designer Atlas Lighting Ltd 1958–63 (designer 1954–58), industl design mangr Standard Telephones and Cables Ltd 1963–69, design mangr Post Office Telecommunications (later British Telecom) 1969–83, sr industrialist Design Cncl 1983–87, jt-fndr Richard Stevens Design Associates 1988–94; pres Soc of Industl Artists and Designers (now CSD) 1972–73, memb Bd and treas ICSID 1973–77; Gold medal 11th Milan Triennale 1957, 3 Design Centre awards London 1960, RSA Presidential award for Design Mgmnt (awarded to PO) 1977; RDI 1973, FCIBS, FCSD; *Style*— Richard Stevens, Esq; ✉ Hazel Cottage, Ewood Lane, Newdigate, Dorking, Surrey RH5 5AR (☎ 01306 631239)

STEVENS, Dr Robert Bocking; s of John Skevington Stevens, and Enid Dorothy, *née* Bocking; *b* 8 June 1933; *Educ* Oakham Sch, Keble Coll Oxford (MA, BCL, DCL, hon fell), Yale Univ (LLM); *m* Katherine Booth; *Career* called to the Bar Gray's Inn 1956; successively: foreign assoc Haight Gardner Poor and Havens NYC, pupil to R A MacCrindle 3 Essex Ct Temple; subsequently joined Midland Circuit, Essex Ct Chambers since 1965, counsel Covington and Burling (int commercial law and competition law) Washington and London 1991–; Yale Univ: asst prof of law 1959–61, assoc prof 1961–65, prof 1965–76; prof of law, adjunct prof of history and provost Tulane Univ 1976–78; pres Haverford Coll 1978–87; Univ of Calif Santa Cruz: fell Cowell Coll and prof of history 1987–93, chllr 1987–91; master Pembroke Coll Oxford 1993–; visiting appts Northwestern Univ, Univ of E Africa, Stanford Univ, UCL, Univ of Texas, Brookings Instn; former conslt for various US federal govt depts and UN Devpt Prog, former legal advsr to govts of Tanzania, the Bahamas and the E African community; memb Nat Cncl on the Humanities 1985–92; currently memb: Research Ctee American Bar Fndn, Bd Nat Inst for Social Servs Info, Editorial Bd American Jl of Legal History, Bd of Mgmnt Socio-Legal Centre Oxford (hon fell); chm Marshall Aid Meml Cmmn, govr Abingdon Sch, vice chm Bentham Ctee; former tstee: New Orleans Museum of Art, Santa Cruz Symphony, Vermont Law Sch; former memb: Nat Bd of Med Examiners, Bd US Merchant Marine Acad, various other educnl and arts bodies; Hon LLD: NY Law Sch 1984, Univ of Pennsylvania 1985, Villanova Univ 1987; Hon DLitt Haverford Coll 1991; *Books* author of several books incl studies of competition law, social legislation and the legal profession and judiciary in US and UK; most recent books: Law and Politics (1978), The American Law School (1983), The Independence of the Judiciary: The View from the Lord Chancellor's Office (1993); *Recreations* antiques, walking, politics and tennis; *Clubs* Reform; *Style*— Dr Robert Stevens; ✉ Master's Lodgings, Pembroke College, Oxford OX1 1DW (☎ 01865 243482, fax 01865 276446); Covington and Burling, Leconfield House, Curzon Street, London W1Y 8AS (☎ 0171 495 5655, fax 0171 495 3101)

STEVENS, Prof Stanley James; s of Harold Stevens (d 1987), of 84 Sandalwood Rd, Loughborough, and Gladys Mary, *née* Swain (d 1981); *b* 11 April 1933; *Educ* Bablake Sch Coventry, Univ of Nottingham (MSc), Cranfield Inst of Technol (MSc), Univ of Loughborough (PhD); *m* 1 Sept 1956, Rita Lillian Stevens, da of Charles Lloyd (d 1986), of 5 Meredith Rd, Coventry; 2 da (Carol Anne b 3 June 1961, Kathryn Diane b 3 Nov 1965); *Career* engrg apprenticeship Armstrong-Siddely Motors Ltd 1950–55, project engr Siddeley Engines Ltd Bristol 1955–61; Loughborough Univ of Technol: lectr in aeronautics 1961–70, sr lectr 1970–76, reader 1976–81, prof of aircraft propulsion 1987–; ctee memb Loughborough Royal Aeronautical Soc, pres Leicestershire Lawn Tennis Assoc; Freeman City of Coventry 1956; MIMechE, MRAeS, CEng; *Recreations* tennis, walking, water colour painting; *Style*— Prof Stanley Stevens; ✉ 101 Valley Road, Loughborough, Leicestershire LE11 3PY (☎ 01509 215139); Department of Aeronautical & Automotive Engineering and Transport Studies, Loughborough University of Technology, Loughborough, Leicestershire LE11 3TU (☎ 01509 223404, fax 01509 267613, telex 34319)

STEVENS, Stuart Standish; s of Maj Edward Aloysious Stevens (d 1948), and Virginia Mary, *née* D'Vaz; *b* 30 April 1947; *Educ* St Joseph's Euro HS Bangalore S India (pres Old Boys Assoc UK branch), Acton County GS, Royal Holloway Coll Univ of London; *m* (m dis); 3 s (Uther Edward b 1984, Stuart William b 1989, Alexander George b 1993), 1 da (Isabella Eda b 1986); *Career* called to the Bar Gray's Inn 1970; head of Chambers; specialist in white collar and corp fraud; Freeman City of London 1991; *Style*— Stuart Stevens, Esq; ✉ Holborn Chambers, The Chambers of Stuart Stevens, 6 Gate Street, Lincoln's Inn Fields, London WC2 (☎ 0171 242 6060, fax 0171 242 2777)

STEVENS-PRIOR, Terence Frank; s of Rodney Frank Stevens, of Waiheke Island, Auckland, NZ, and Marie Elsie, *née* Pitt; *b* 11 June 1962; *Educ* Auckland GS, Selwyn Coll Aukland; *m* 27 June 1992, Sophie Charlotte, da of Roy Leonard Prior, of London; *Career* graphic artist Prints Graphic Air Studio Auckland 1980–82, art dir Ogilvy & Mather Advertising Auckland 1983–84; art dir/creative gp head: SSC&B Lintas Auckland 1984–85, Rialto Advertising Auckland 1985–89; art dir/writer BBDO London 1989–90, creative dir Saatchi and Saatchi Copenhagen 1990–93 (concurrently freelance dir with Productionsselskabet Films), sr art dir The Leith Agency Edinburgh 1993, currently freelance; awards incl: 2 Bronze, 2 Silver and 3 Gold (NZ Advtg Inst), Bronze (Creative Circle London), Silver (Award Show Australia), Gold (London Int Advtg), Gold (Aurora Prize), Gold (Swedsh Advtg Awards), Bronze and Gold (Inter Scandinavian Swans), 3 Golds (Danish Advtg Awards), 4 Golds (Creative Circle Denmark), Bronze and Silver Lions (Cannes Int Film Festival), Commendation (D&AD) 1994; *Recreations* surfing, skiing, swimming, cinema, chess, reading, painting, travel; *Clubs* The Fork Chess (Copenhagen), Dragons Chess (Edinburgh); *Style*— Terence Stevens-Prior, Esq; ✉ 60 Dundas Street, Edinburgh EH3

STEVENSON, Dr David John Douglas; s of Dr Douglas Stuart Stevenson, MBE (d 1951), of Glasgow, and Mary Edith, *née* Lang (d 1981); *b* 6 Jan 1933; *Educ* Ardvreck Sch Perthshire, Oundle, Univ of Cambridge (MA), Univ of Glasgow (MB ChB, MD, DPH), Univ of Liverpool (DTM & H); *m* 29 July 1967, Anna Marie (Rie), da of Povl Sigismund Skadegård (d 1977), of Rungsted Kyst, Denmark; 2 s (Bjorn b 1968, Alan b 1974), 1 da (Ellen b 1969); *Career* house surgn Western Infirmary Glasgow 1957, house physician Stobhill Hosp Glasgow 1957–58, diocesan medical offr Dio of Nyasaland (Univs Mission to Central Africa) 1958–63, govt med offr Malawi 1965–66, lectr in tropical diseases Univ of Edinburgh 1966–72, sr lectr in int community health Sch of Tropical Med Univ of Liverpool 1972–90 (on loan to Tribhuwan Univ Nepal 1974–75); hon fell Univ of Edinburgh 1991–; Parly candidate (SNP): Glasgow Woodside 1964, Edinburgh South 1970, Euro Parl elections Lothian 1979 and 1984; memb: Inc of Hammermen (Glasgow) 1933, Inc of Bakers (Glasgow) 1942; Freeman City of Glasgow 1933; FFPHM 1993; *Books* Davey and Lightbody's The Control of Disease in the Tropics (ed 1987); *Recreations* bagpipe and shawm music, parapsychology; *Clubs* Edinburgh University Staff; *Style*— Dr David Stevenson; ✉ 22 Blacket Place, Edinburgh, Scotland EH9 1RL (☎ 0131 667 3748); Department of Public Health Sciences, University of Edinburgh Medical School, Teviot Place, Edinburgh EH8 9AG (☎ 0131 650 3228, fax 0131 650 6909, e-mail D.Stevenson@ed.ac.uk)

STEVENSON, Dr Derek Paul; CBE (1972); s of Frederick Paul Stevenson (d 1949), and Blanch Maud, *née* Coucher (d 1948); *b* 11 July 1911; *Educ* Epsom Coll, Univ of London and Guy's Hosp; *m* 10 May 1941, Pamela Mary, da of Lt-Col Charles Jervelund, OBE (d 1962); 2 s (John b 1944, Timothy b 1948), 1 da (Wendy b 1942); *Career* regular offr RAMC, MO Sandhurst, overseas serv Malaya, Singpore, China, Capt 1937, WWII served BEF 1939–40, Adj RAMC depot 1940–42, WO 1942–46, Maj 1942, Lt-Col 1943, asst dir gen Army Med Servs WO 1943; sec BMA 1958–76, chm Cncl World Med Assoc 1969–71, vice pres Private Patients Plan, conslt Med Insur Agency; cncllr West Sussex CC 1980–85, Chichester Local Health Authy 1983–85, memb Med Servs Bd 1977–79; Hon LLD Univ of Manchester 1964; memb BMA, MRCS, LRCP, Hon FRCGP 1992; *Recreations* golf, gardening; *Clubs* Athenaeum; *Style*— Dr Derek Stevenson, CBE; ✉ 19 Marchwood Gate, Chichester, West Sussex PO19 4HA (☎ 01243 774237)

STEVENSON, George William; MP (Lab) Stoke-on-Trent South (majority 6,909); s of Harold Stevenson, of Maltby, Yorkshire, and Elsie, *née* Bryan; *b* 30 Aug 1938; *Educ* secdy modern sch; *m* 1958, Doreen June (d 1989), da of Joseph Parkes; 2 s (Leslie Alan b 8 Jan 1961, Andrew Mark b 19 Feb 1966), 1 da (Jacqueline b 15 Nov 1959); m 2, 1 June 1991, Pauline Margaret, *née* Brookes; *Career* MEP (Lab) Staffs E 1984–94, MP Stoke-on-Trent S 1992–; memb Euro Select and Standing Ctees; chair: PLP Agriculture Ctee, All Pty Tibet Gp; Stoke-on-Trent City Cncl: dep ldr 1972–83, chm Highways Ctee; Staffordshire CC: dep ldr 1981–85, chm Social Services and Establishment Ctees; chm: Br Labour Gp Euro Parl 1987–88, Euro Parly Delgn for Relations with South Asia 1989; *Recreations* reading, travel; *Style*— George Stevenson, MP; ✉ Stoke South Constituency

Office, 2A Stanton Road, Meir, Stoke-on-Trent ST3 6DD (☎ 01782 593393, fax 01782 593430); House of Commons, London SW1A 0AA (☎ 0171 219 5012, fax 0171 219 2688)

STEVENSON, Henry Dennistoun (Dennis); CBE (1981); s of Alexander James Stevenson, of Scotland, and Sylvia Florence, *née* Ingleby; *b* 19 July 1945; *Educ* Edinburgh Acad, Glenalmond Coll, King's Coll Cambridge; *m* 15 Feb 1972, Charlotte Susan, da of Air Cdre Hon Sir Peter Beckford Rutgers Vanneck, GBE, CB, AFC; 4 s (Alexander, Heneage, Charles, William); *Career* chm: SRU Group 1972–96, Intermediate Technology Development Group 1984–90, GPA Group plc 1993–; dir: British Technology Group 1979–89, London Docklands Development Corporation 1981–88, Tyne Tees TV 1982–87, Pearson plc 1988–, Manpower plc 1988–, Thames Television plc 1991–93, J Rothschild Assurance plc 1991–, English Partnerships 1993–, British Sky Broadcasting Group plc 1994–; independent memb Takeover Panel 1992–; chm: Aycliffe & Peterlee Corporation 1972–81, Nat Assoc of Youth Clubs 1972–80, Sinfonia 21 1989–, Tstees of Tate Gallery 1989–; *Recreations* tennis, violin, reading; *Clubs* MCC, Brooks's; *Style*— Dennis Stevenson, Esq, CBE; ✉ SRU Ltd, 78/80 St John St, London EC1M 4HR (☎ 0171 250 1131, fax 0171 250 1952)

STEVENSON, Hugh Alexander; *b* 7 Sept 1942; *Educ* Harrow, Univ Coll Oxford (BA); *m* 23 Oct 1965, Catherine, *née* Peacock; 2 s, 2 da; *Career* Linklaters & Paines slrs 1964–70, joined S G Warburg & Co 1970, dir S G Warburg Group plc 1987–95, chm Mercury Asset Management Group plc 1992– (dir 1986–); *Style*— Hugh Stevenson, Esq; ✉ Mercury Asset Management Group plc, 33 King William Street, London EC4R 9AS (☎ 0171 280 2800)

STEVENSON, Dr Jim; s of George Stevenson (d 1982), and Frances Mildred Groat (d 1974); *b* 9 May 1937; *Educ* Kirkham GS, Univ of Liverpool (BSc, PhD); *m* 5 Jan 1963, Brenda, da of Thomas Edward Cooley (d 1967); 1 s (Michael b 17 Nov 1963), 1 da (Rachel b 21 Nov 1968); *Career* NATO res fell Univ of Trondheim Norway 1963–65, lectr in biochemistry Univ of Warwick 1965–69; BBC Open Univ: prodr 1969–76, ed sci progs 1976–79, head of progs 1979–82; dep sec BBC 1982–83, head of educnl bdcasting services and educn sec BBC 1983–89; chief exec Educational Broadcasting Services Trust 1988–; memb: Int Inst of Communications, Soc of Satellite Professionals, RTS; *Recreations* television, good company, food and drink; *Style*— Dr Jim Stevenson; ✉ 34 Vallance Rd, London N22 4UB (☎ 0181 889 6261); The Educational Broadcasting Services Trust, 36–38 Mortimer St, London W1N 7RB (☎ 0171 765 5023, fax 0171 580 6246)

STEVENSON, John; CBE (1987); *b* 15 June 1927; *Educ* Henry Smith Sch Hartlepool, Univ of Durham (LLB), Univ of Oxford (MA); *m* 29 March 1956, Kathleen, *née* Petch; 1 s (Mark Petch b 1962), 1 da (Jane Clare b 1960); *Career* admitted slr 1952; clerk of the peace and co slr Gloucestershire CC 1969–74, chief exec Buckinghamshire CC 1974–80, sec Assoc of CCs in Eng and Wales 1980–87; Deputy Licensing Authority: Metropolitan and S Eastern Traffic Areas 1988–96, Eastern Traffic Area 1990–96, Western Traffic Area 1991–96; vice pres Inst of Trading Standards Admin; hon fell Univ of Birmingham 1981–, visiting fell Nuffield Coll Oxford 1982–90; memb Law Soc; *Style*— John Stevenson, Esq, CBE; ✉ 1 Hales Meadow, Harpenden, Hertfordshire AL5 4JB (☎ 01582 761393)

STEVENSON, Juliet Anne Virginia; da of Brig Michael Guy Stevens, MBE, and Virginia Ruth, *née* Marshall; *b* 30 Oct 1956; *Educ* Hurst Lodge Sch Berks, St Catherine's Sch Surrey, RADA (Gold Bancroft Medal); *partner* Hugh Brody; 1 da (Rosalind b 1994); *Career* actress; currently assoc artist RSC; *Theatre* RSC 1978–86 incl: Madame de Tourvel in Les Liaisons Dangereuses, Rosalind in As You Like It, Cressida in Troilus and Cressida (nominated for Olivier Best Actress Award), Isabella in Measure for Measure (nominated for Best Actress Award, winner Drama Magazine Best Actress Award), Titania/Hippolyta in A Midsummer Night's Dream, Susan in The Witch of Edmonton, Clara Douglas in Money, Lady Percy in Henry IV Parts I and II, Miss Chasen in Once in a Lifetime, Yeliena in The White Guard, Aphrodite/Artemis in Hippolytus, Octavia/Iras in Antony and Cleopatra, Caroline Thompson in The Churchill Play; other credits incl: Emma/Betsy in Other Worlds (Royal Court) 1982, Paulina in Death and the Maiden (Royal Court and Duke of York's, Best Actress Time Out Awards and Olivier Awards 1992), Anna in Burn This (Hampstead/Lyric), Fanny in On the Verge (Sadler's Wells), title role in Yerma (NT) 1987 (nominated for Olivier Best Actress Award), Hedda in Hedda Gabler (NT) 1989, Galactia in Scenes from an Execution (Mark Taper Forum Los Angeles), The Duchess of Malfi (Wyndham's) 1995; *Television* for BBC incl: Nora in a Dolls House, Claire in The March, Rape Victim in Omnibus - Rape, Lucy Sadler in Aimée, Ruth in Out of Love, Hilda Spencer in Stanley, Rosalind in Life Story (winner Ace Cable TV Network Award Best Supporting Actress), Antigone in Oedipus at Colonus, title role in Antigone, Elizabeth Von Reitburg in Freud, Fliss in Bazaar and Rummage, Joanna Langton in Maybury; other credits incl: Margaret in In The Border Country (Channel 4), Vicky in Living With Dinosaurs (Jim Henson Organisation, winner Emmy Award for Best Children's Film), Barbara Mallen in The Mallens (Granada), The Politician's Wife (Channel 4, The Broadcasting Press Guild Award for Best Actress 1996) 1995; *Films* incl: Nina in Truly Madly Deeply (BBC/Samuel Goldwyn), Alice in Ladder of Swords (Magnaserve Ltd), Cissie II in Drowning By Numbers (Allarts Enterprises), Fraulein Burstner in The Trial, Isobel in The Secret Rapture 1994, Mrs Elton in Emma (Miramax) 1996; *Books* Clamorous Voices (co-author, 1988), Shall I See You Again (co-ed, 1994); *Recreations* talking, walking, reading, piano, travelling, cinema, theatre, music; *Style*— Juliet Stevenson

STEVENSON, Rt Rev Dr Kenneth William; *see:* Portsmouth, Bishop of

STEVENSON, Michael Charles; s of Michael Anthony Stevenson, and Ena Elizabeth Stevenson, of Doncaster; *b* 14 Aug 1960; *Educ* Doncaster GS, Christ Church Oxford (Open scholarship, MA); *m* 1987, Deborah Frances, da of Lord Taylor of Gosforth, *qv*; 1 s (Thomas b 1991), 1 da (Celia b 1994); *Career* BBC: trainee BBC Radio Sport 1983–84, prodr Talks & Documentaries BBC Radio 1984–88, prodr On the Record BBC1 1988–90, chief asst Policy & Planning BBC 1990–91, dep ed On the Record 1991–92, sec of the BBC 1992–96, dep dir Regnl Bdcasting 1996–; tstee BBC Children in Need; *Recreations* tennis, music; *Clubs* Vanderbilt Racquet; *Style*— Michael Stevenson, Esq; ✉ The British Broadcasting Corporation, Broadcasting House, London W1A 1AA (☎ 0171 765 5172)

STEVENSON, Maj-Gen Paul Timothy; OBE (1985, MBE 1975); s of Ernest Stevenson, of Wortley, Wotton under Edge, Glos, and Dorothy Trehearn (d 1985); *b* 3 March 1940; *Educ* Bloxham Sch; *m* 26 June 1965, Ann Douglas, da of Col Douglas Burns Drysdale DSO, OBE (d 1990); 1 s (Jonathan b 1970), 1 da (Iona b 1968); *Career* joined RM 1958, 41 Commando 1960–62, 45 Commando (Aden) 1962–63, HMS Mohawk 1965–68, 45 Commando 1973–75, HMS Bulwark 1975–76, Falklands campaign SO1 plans 1982, CO 42 Commando 1983–84, dir personnel 1987–88, Cmd Br Forces Falkland Islands 1989–90; clerk to Worshipful Co of Carpenters 1991; modern pentathlon Br team 1962–69, biathlon Br team 1965; *Recreations* field sports, golf, gardening, skiing; *Clubs* Army and Navy; *Style*— Maj-Gen Paul Stevenson, OBE; ✉ c/o Lloyds Bank, Wotton under Edge, Glos GL12 7DA

STEVENSON, Robert Wilfrid (Wilf); s of James Alexander Stevenson (d 1993), and Elizabeth Anne, *née* Macrae; *b* 19 April 1947; *Educ* Edinburgh Acad, Univ Coll Oxford (MA), Napier Poly pt/t (FCCA); *m* 1, 15 April 1972 (m dis 1979), Jennifer Grace, da of David Grace Antonio (d 1986), of Edinburgh; m 2, 19 April 1991, Elizabeth Ann, da of John Cavin Minogue, of Harrogate; 2 da (Iona Jane Minogue b 13 March 1992, Flora Kathleen Minogue b 19 Dec 1994), 1 s (Tobin James Minogue b 28 July 1993); *Career* res offr Univ of Edinburgh Students' Assoc 1970–74, sec Napier Univ Edinburgh 1974–87, dir Br Film Inst 1988– (dep dir 1987–88); hon prof Univ of Stirling 1991–; *Recreations* cinema, hill walking, bridge; *Style*— Wilf Stevenson, Esq; ✉ British Film Institute, 21 Stephen Street, London W1P 1PL; (☎ 0171 957 8903, fax 0171 436 0437, telex 27624 BFILDNG, e-mail wilf.stevenson@bfi.org.uk)

STEVENSON, Dr Ronald; s of George Stevenson, of Blackburn (d 1969), and Elizabeth Blundell (d 1989); *b* 6 March 1928; *Educ* Royal Manchester Coll of Music (special distinction), Conservatorio di Santa Cecilia Rome; *m* 1952, Marjorie Spedding; 1 s (Gordon b 1953), 2 da (Gerda b 1956, Savourna b 1961); *Career* freelance composer, pianist, broadcaster and teacher 1966–; sr lectr in composition and piano Univ of Cape Town 1962–65; visiting prof of piano lit Shanghai Conservatory 1985, visiting prof Julliard Sch of Music NY 1987; regular broadcaster on music of Busoni (26 BBC Radio progs 1970–80), writer and performer TV documentary on Busoni (BBC 2) 1974, writer and broadcaster series of radio progs on Scots pipe, harp and fiddle 1981; Harriet Cohen Int Music Award 1966, Scottish Arts Cncl Living Artists' Award 1966; vice pres Workers' Music Assoc, patron Euro Piano Teachers' Assoc; supporter Rudolf Steiner Trg Centre Garvald (for young handicapped people); Dr hc Univ of Stirling 1996; memb Royal Soc of Musicians of GB, memb Composers' Guild of GB; fell Royal Manchester Coll of Music 1966, Hon FRIAS 1992; *Compositions* Passacaglia on DSCH 1962, Piano Concerto No 1 1966, Border Boyhood Song-cycle (cmmnd by Peter Pears) 1971, Piano Concerto No 2 1972 (BBC Proms), Violin Concerto The Gypsy (cmmnd by Sir Yehudi Menuhin) 1992, Cello Concerto in memoriam Jacqueline du Pre (cmmnd by Royal Scottish Nat Orch) 1995; *Books* An Introduction to Western Music (1971), Bernhard Ziehn: Canonic Studies (1976), The Paderewski Paradox (1992); contrib various articles in learned jls; Ronald Stevenson (biography by Malcolm MacDonald, 1989); *Recreations* walking, poetry, literature; *Clubs* Scottish Arts (hon memb); *Style*— Dr Ronald Stevenson; ✉ Townfoot House, West Linton, Peeblesshire EH46 7EE (☎ 01968 660511)

STEVENSON, Ross Calvin; s of Robert Stevenson, and Doreen, *née* Reid; *b* 15 Jan 1959; *m* Annabel, da of Gordon Johnson; 1 s (Josh b 9 June 1991), 1 da (Gemma b 9 June 1991); *Career* various positions rising to conference and banqueting mangr The Gleneagles Hotel Perthshire 1979–88, res mangr The Moat House Int Glasgow 1988–92, gen mangr Briggens House Hotel Herts 1992–95, gen mangr The Royal Crescent Hotel Bath 1995–; vice chm Bath Conference Cabinet; MInstD 1995; *Recreations* cycling, running, reading; *Style*— Ross Stevenson, Esq; ✉ Royal Crescent Hotel, 15–16 Royal Crescent, Bath, Somerset BA1 2LS (☎ 01225 739955, fax 01225 339401)

STEVENSON, Sir Simpson; kt (1976); s of Thomas Henry Stevenson, of Greenock; *b* 18 Aug 1921; *Educ* Greenock HS; *m* 1945, Jean Holmes, da of George Henry Holmes; *Career* chm Bd Western Regnl Hosp 1967–73, memb Inverclyde DC 1974–; chm: Scottish Health Servs Common Agency 1973–77, Gt Glasgow Health Bd 1973–83, Consortium of Local Authorities Special Programme 1974–83; memb Royal Cmmn on NHS 1976–79; Hon LLD Univ of Glasgow 1982; *Style*— Sir Simpson Stevenson; ✉ The Gables, 64a Reservoir Road, Gourock, Renfrewshire (☎ 01475 631774)

STEVENSON, (Arthur) William; TD (1980), QC (1996); s of Arthur John Stevenson, and Olivia Diana, *née* Serocold (d 1996); *b* 17 Oct 1943; *Educ* Marlborough, Trinity Coll Oxford (Evan Williams exhibitioner, MA); *m* 31 May 1969, Bridget Laura, da of late Laurence Frederick York; 1 da (Rebecca Clare b 25 April 1971), 2 s (Henry Laurence b 10 Jan 1973, Robert Frederick John b 13 April 1978); *Career* called to the Bar Lincoln's Inn 1968 (Hardwicke and Droop scholar), in practice London, recorder of the Crown Ct 1992–; *Recreations* country sports, skiing, sailing; *Clubs* Royal Thames Yacht, Bar Yacht; *Style*— William Stevenson, Esq, TD, QC; ✉ 1 Paper Buildings, Temple, London EC4Y 7EP (☎ 0171 583 7355, fax 0171 353 2144)

STEWARD, Rear Adm Cedric John; CB (1984); s of Ethelbert Harold Steward (d 1977), and Anne Isabelle, *née* West (d 1986); *b* 31 Jan 1931; *Educ* Northcote Coll Auckland, Britannia RNC Dartmouth, Greenwich Naval Coll, NDC Latimer (jssc), RCDS; *m* 1952, Marie Antoinette, da of Arthur Gordon Gurr (d 1951), of Sydney, NSW; 3 s (Mark, Bretton, John); *Career* served Korea 1951 and 1954; Staff Royal Aust Naval Coll Jervis Bay 1959–62, RNZNLO and dep head NZ Defence Liaison Staff Canberra 1969–73, Capt 11 Frigate Sqdn 1974–75, Dep Chief of Naval Staff 1979–81, Cdre Auckland 1981–83, Chief of Naval Staff 1983–86; owner Antric Park Horse Stud 1986–; memb Aust Naval Inst; *Recreations* philately, boating, golf, tennis, equestrian, fishing; *Clubs* Helensville Golf, Auckland RC (Ellerslie); *Style*— Rear Adm Cedric Steward, CB

STEWART, *see:* Shaw-Stewart

STEWART, Sir Alan D'Arcy; 13 Bt (I 1623), of Ramelton, Co Donegal; s (by 1 m) of Sir Jocelyn Harry Stewart, 12 Bt (d 1982); *b* 29 Nov 1932; *Educ* All Saints, Bathurst NSW; *m* 1952, Patricia, da of Lawrence Turner, of Ramelton; 2 s, 2 da; *Heir* s, Nicholas Courtney D'Arcy Stewart b 4 Aug 1953; *Career* yacht builder, marine engr; *Style*— Sir Alan Stewart, Bt; ✉ One Acre House, Church St, Ramelton, Co Donegal

STEWART, Alastair James; s of Gp Capt James Frederick Stewart, of Winslow, Bucks, and Joan Mary, *née* Lord; *b* 22 June 1952; *Educ* St Augustine's Abbey Sch, Univ of Bristol; *m* 8 April 1978, Sally Ann, da of Frederick Harold Rudolph Jung (d 1968); 2 s (Alexander b 1982, Frederick b 1993), 1 da (Clementine b 1985); *Career* dep pres NUS 1974–76; Southern Independent TV: editorial trainee 1976, industl reporter and presenter of progs (incl Energy - What Crisis?) 1976–80; ITN: industl corr 1980–82, newscaster (incl News at Ten and Channel 4 News) 1982–89 and 1990–92, Washington corr 1990; news anchor London News Network 1993–; presenter: Alastair Stewart's Sunday (BBC Radio 5) 1994, The Sunday Programme (GMTV) 1994, Police Stop! (Carlton TV/ITV Network) 1994–, Missing (LWT/ITV Network) 1993–, Police, Camera, Action! (Carlton TV/ITV Network) 1995–; presenter various news progs incl: The Budget 1982–92, General Election 1987 and 1992, State Opening of Parliament 1988–89, weddings of Prince of Wales and Duke of York; patron The Zito Tst, vice patron Mental Health Fndn; *Recreations* reading, music, antique maps; *Style*— Alastair Stewart, Esq; ✉ London News Network, The London Television Centre, Upper Ground, London SE1 9LT (☎ 0171 827 7700, 0171 827 7780)

STEWART, Sheriff Alastair Lindsay; QC (Scot 1995); s of Alexander Lindsay Stewart (d 1977); *b* 28 Nov 1938; *Educ* Edinburgh Acad, St Edmund Hall Oxford, Univ of Edinburgh; *m* 1, 1968 (m dis), Annabel Claire, da of Prof William McCausland Stewart (d 1989); 2 s; m 2, 1991, Sheila Anne, da of David Hynd Flockhart, wid of William Neil Mackinnon; *Career* tutor Faculty of Law Univ of Edinburgh 1963–73, standing jr counsel Registrar of Restrictive Trading Agreements 1968–70, advocate depute 1970–73; Sheriff: South Strathclyde, Dumfries and Galloway at Airdrie 1973–79, Grampian, Highland and Islands at Aberdeen 1979–90, Tayside, Central and Fife at Dundee 1990–; temp judge Supreme Cts of Scotland 1996–; govr Robert Gordon's Inst of Technol 1982–90; chm: Grampian Family Conciliation Serv 1984–87, Scottish Assoc of Family Conciliation Servs 1986–89; ed Scottish Civil Law Reports 1992–95; *Recreations* reading, music, walking; *Style*— Sheriff Alastair Stewart, QC; ✉ Sheriff's Chambers, Sheriff Court House, Dundee DD1 9AD (☎ 01382 229961)

STEWART, Sir Alastair Robin; 3 Bt (UK 1960), of Strathgarry, Co Perth; s of Sir Kenneth Dugald Stewart, 1 Bt, GBE (d 1972), and Noel, *née* Brodribb (d 1946); suc bro, Sir David Brodribb Stewart, 2 Bt (d 1992); *b* 26 Sept 1925; *Educ* Marlborough; *m* 1953, Patricia Helen, MBE, RIBA, da of late John Alfred Merrett, of Pondhead Farm, Forest Green, Surrey; 1 s (John Kenneth Alexander b 1961), 3 da (Judith Patricia b 1954, Lucy Janetta b 1956, Catherine Helen b 1958); *Heir* s, John Kenneth Alexander Stewart b 1961;

Career Lt Royal Glos Hussars; md Stewart & Harvey Ltd (ret); *Style*— Sir Alastair Stewart, Bt; ✉ Walter's Cottage, Little Baddow, Chelmsford, Essex CM3 4TQ

STEWART, Alec James; s of Mickey J Stewart (the England cricket official); *b* 8 April 1963; *Educ* Tiffin Sch; *Career* professional cricketer; Surrey CCC: joined 1981, awarded county cap 1985, capt 1992–; England: debut on tour WI 1989/90, memb tour Aust and NZ 1990/91, vice capt tour NZ and World Cup squad Aust 1992, India and Sri Lanka 1992/93, memb team touring W Indies 1993/94 (vice capt), Aust 1994/95 and S Africa 1995/96, memb team touring Zimbabwe and New Zealand 1996–97; first Englishman to score 2 centuries against W Indies in same test (fourth test) 1994; jt world record 11 catches in a match Surrey v Leics 1989; *Style*— Alec Stewart, Esq; ✉ c/o Surrey County Cricket Club, Kennington Oval, London SE11 5SS (☎ 0171 582 6660)

STEWART, Alexander Christie; s of Lt-Col Robert Christie Stewart, CBE, of Arndean, Dollar, Clackmannanshire, Scotland, and Ann Grizel, *née* Cochrane; *b* 21 June 1955; *Educ* Gordonstoun; *m* 24 April 1986, Katherine Lake, da of Denys Barry Herbert Domvile; 1 s (Archie b 10 June 1989), 1 da (Georgina b 11 Oct 1987); *Career* racehorse trainer 1983–; trained winners incl: Mtoto, Opale, Waajib, Dubian, Ghariba, Life at the Top, Daarkom, Braashee, Al Maheb, Filia Ardross and Wagon Master; *Recreations* shooting; *Style*— Alexander Stewart, Esq; ✉ Clarehaven Stables, Newmarket, Suffolk CB8 7BY (☎ 01638 667323, fax 01638 666389)

STEWART, (John) Allan; MP (C) Eastwood (majority 11,688); s of Edward MacPherson Stewart by his w Eadie Barrie; *b* 1 June 1942; *Educ* Bell Baxter HS (Cupar), Univ of St Andrews, Harvard; *m* 1973, Marjorie Sally (Susie), *née* Gourlay; 1 s, 1 da; *Career* lectr in political economy Univ of St Andrews 1965–70; CBI 1971–78: head Regnl Devpt Dept 1971–73, dep dir econs 1974, Scottish sec 1974, Scottish dir 1978; cncllr Bromley 1975–76, Parly candidate (C) Dundee East 1970; MP (C): Renfrewshire E 1979–83, Eastwood 1983–; parly under sec Scottish Office 1981–86 (responsible for home affrs and environment in Scottish Office April 1982), Scottish min for Indust and Educn 1983–86, Scottish min for Indust and Local Govt 1990–95; *Books* The Long March of the Market Men (with Harry Conroy, 1996); *Recreations* hedgehogs, bridge; *Style*— Allan Stewart, Esq, MP; ✉ House of Commons, Westminster, London SW1A 0AA (☎ 0171 219 5110)

STEWART, Angus; QC (Scot 1988); s of Archibald Ian Balfour Stewart, CBE, and Ailsa Rosamund Mary Massey; *b* 14 Dec 1946; *Educ* Edinburgh Acad, Balliol Coll Oxford (BA), Univ of Edinburgh (LLB); *m* 14 June 1975, Jennifer Margaret, da of John Faulds Stewart (d 1980), of Edinburgh; 1 da (Flora b 13 Sept 1981); *Career* barr 1975–; keeper of the Advocate's Library 1994–; tstee: Int E Boat Class Assoc 1993–, Nat Library of Scotland 1994–, Stewart Heritage Tst 1994–; *Style*— Angus Stewart, Esq, QC; ✉ 8 Ann Street, Edinburgh EH4 1PJ (☎ 0131 332 4083)

STEWART, Dr (George) Barry; s of Robert Temple Stewart, of Sunderland, Tyne and Wear, and Sarah Alice, *née* Robson; *b* 3 Sept 1943; *Educ* Robert Richardson GS, Univ of Nottingham (LLB), Fitzwilliam Coll and Inst of Criminology Univ of Cambridge (Dip in Criminology, JD); *Career* called to the Bar Gray's Inn 1968, attorney and cnsllr at Law Federal Cts USA, memb Bar of NY 1987, barrister Kings Inns Dublin 1994, head of chambers, sr memb Cleveland Bar; Methodist preacher, Danby circuit N Yorks accredited 1964; *Recreations* reading, foreign travel; *Style*— Dr G Barry Stewart; ✉ Ridge Hall, Ridge Lane, Staithes, Saltburn-by-the-Sea, Cleveland TS13 5DX (☎ 01947 840511); Cleveland Chambers, Borough Road, Middlesbrough, Cleveland TS1 3AA (☎ 01642 226036)

STEWART, Brian John; CBE (1996); s of Ian Mann Stewart, and Christina Stewart; *b* 9 April 1945; *Educ* Perth Acad, Univ of Edinburgh (MSc); *m* 16 July 1971, Seonaid; 2 s (Alistair b 1974, Duncan b 1980), 1 da (Emily b 1976); *Career* articled clerk J & R Morison CAs Perth 1962–67, chief mgmnt accountant Ethicon Ltd Edinburgh 1969–76; Scottish and Newcastle plc: joined 1976, various commercial and financial positions in Scottish Brewers and William Younger subsids and Retail and Beer Prodn divisions, corp devpt dir 1985–88, gp fin dir 1988–91, gp chief exec 1991–; non-exec dir: Booker plc 1993–, Standard Life Assurance Company; memb Ct Univ of Edinburgh 1991–, vice chm Brewers' and Licensed Retailers' Assoc (formerly Brewers' Soc) 1994–; MICAS 1967; *Recreations* golf, skiing; *Style*— Brian Stewart, Esq, CBE; ✉ Scottish & Newcastle plc, 111 Holyrood Road, Edinburgh EH8 8YS (☎ 0131 556 2591, fax 0131 556 4665)

STEWART, Callum John Tyndale; s of Air Vice-Marshal William K Stewart CB, CBE, AFC, QHP (d 1967), of Farnborough, Hants, and Audrey Wentworth, *née* Tyndale (who m 2 1970, Sir Bryan Harold Cabot Matthews, CBE (d 1986); *b* 2 Feb 1945; *Educ* Wellington Coll; *m* 1, 18 July 1975 (m dis 1982), Elaine Alison, da of Francis Bairstow (d 1979); m 2, 20 April 1991, Anna Rosemary, da of Peter Balmer (d 1995); 2 s (Rory William Kilpatrick b 13 Feb 1992, Finlay James Heriot b 19 May 1993); *Career* exec dir Bland Welch & Co Ltd 1963–72; dir: CE Heath (International) Ltd 1972–75, Fielding & Ptnrs 1975–86 (dep chm 1984–86), CE Heath plc 1986–; *Recreations* tennis, jogging slowly, antiques; *Style*— Callum Stewart, Esq; ✉ CE Heath plc, 133 Houndsditch, London EC3A 7AH (☎ 0171 234 4000)

STEWART, Danielle Caroline; da of Edward Elieza Harris, of London, and Deanna Sylvia, *née* Levy (now Mrs Morgan-Russell); *b* 6 Nov 1961; *Educ* Sutton HS for Girls (GPDST), Nonsuch HS for Girls, Kingston Poly; *m* 2, 17 July 1993, John P Forristal; *Career* articled clerk: Myers Davis CAs 1980–82, Halpern & Woolf CAs 1982–84; audit sr rising to audit mangr Bright Grahame Murray 1985–87, self-employed 1987–88, ptnr Warrener Stewart & Co 1988–; dir: A Plus Ltd, Warrener Stewart Ltd, A Plus Group of Companies (A Plus Software Ltd, A Plus Collaborative Group Ltd, A Plus Computer Services Ltd); devised and released Auditplus audit system 1991; memb CCAB Working Pty on Accounting Standards Exemptions, vice chm Auditing Practices Bd Working Pty on Small Co Auditing Standards; ICAEW: memb Tech Directorate, memb Audit Faculty Ctee; LSCA: memb Main Ctee, vice chm Tech Ctee; winner Young Accountant of the Year Award 1994; FCA; *Books* Auditplus (1991); *Recreations* show jumping and horse riding generally; *Style*— Ms Danielle C Stewart; ✉ Warrener Stewart & Co, Harwood House, 43 Harwood Road, London SW6 4QP (☎ 0171 731 6163, fax 0171 731 8304)

STEWART, David Charles; s of Andrew Graham Stewart (d 1964), of Corsliehill, Houston, Renfrewshire, and Barabel Ethel, *née* Greig (d 1985); *b* 23 June 1936; *Educ* Winchester, Trinity Coll Cambridge (BA); *m* 16 Nov 1978, Wendy Ann, da of John McMillan (d 1951), of Kingswood, Surrey; 1 s (Jonathan b 1979), 3 da (Tara b 1981, Serena b 1983, Fleur (twin) b 1983); *Career* Nat Serv 2 Lt Royal Scots Greys 1956–57; dir: The Victaulic Co Ltd 1965, Stewarts and Lloyds Plastics Ltd 1965; md Victaulic plc 1983–95; *Style*— David Stewart, Esq; ✉ The Brewery House, Old, Northamptonshire NN6 9RH (☎ 01604 781577)

STEWART, David Howat; s of William Gray Stewart (d 1980), and Helen Dorothy, *née* Howat (d 1986); *b* 27 Oct 1945; *Educ* Grangefield GS Stockton-on-Tees; *m* 1, 1968 (m dis 1985), Gillian; 2 da (Caroline Victoria b 1977, Sarah Louise b 1982); m 2, 1985, Susan Andrea, da of Brig George Laing, CBE (ADC to HM The Queen 1962, d 1986); 2 s (Harry George William b 1985, Freddie George Howat b 1991); *Career* Nat Westminister Bank Group 1963–70, exec dir County NatWest Ltd 1970–87, gen mangr and chief exec Creditanstalt-Bankverein (London Branch) 1987–91, head of Branch Banking and a md Hill Samuel Bank Ltd 1991–93, commercial banking dir TSB Bank plc (now Lloyds TSB) 1993–96, banking conslt 1996–; ACIB 1967; *Recreations* music; *Style*— David Stewart, Esq; ✉ c/o DIBC (UK) Ltd, 9 North Audley Street, London W1Y 1WF (☎ 0171 495 2288, fax 0171 839 9250)

STEWART, Capt Sir David John Christopher; 7 Bt (UK 1803), of Athenree, Tyrone; s of Sir Hugh Charlie Godfray Stewart, 6 Bt (d 1994), and his 1 w, Rosemary Elinor Dorothy, *née* Peacocke (d 1986); *b* 19 June 1935; *Educ* Bradfield, RMA Sandhurst; *m* 7 Nov 1959, Bridget Anne, er da of late Patrick Wood Sim; 3 da (Siobhan Amanda (Mrs Toby Holland) b 1961, Selina Godfray b 1964, Sophie Caroline (Mrs Jonathan A'Court-Wills) b 1966); *Heir* half-bro, Hugh Nicholas Stewart b 1955; *Career* Capt (ret) Royal Inniskilling Fus (seconded Trucial Oman Scouts); sometime dir Maurice James (Hldgs) Ltd; memb Fine Art Trade Guild; *Clubs* MCC; *Style*— Capt Sir David Stewart, Bt; ✉ Tower View, 8 Silver St, Wiveliscombe, nr Taunton, Somerset TA4 2PA

STEWART, David Purcell; s of Maurice Edward Stewart (d 1967), of Epsom, Surrey, and Joyce Ethel Stewart, of Worthing, Sussex; *b* 8 Sept 1941; *Educ* Rutlish Sch Merton Park; *m* 14 Sept 1968, Judith Esther, da of Charles Owen (d 1983), of Bexleyheath; 1 da (Susannah Celia b 23 April 1977); *Career* Coopers & Lybrand (following merger with Deloitte Haskins & Sells): joined 1958, ptnr 1967, nat tax ptnr 1982–90, exec ptnr i/c Central London office 1990–94, chm Euro Human Resource Advsy Gp 1994–; Freeman City of London 1982; FCA 1963, FInstD 1982; *Recreations* numismatics, theatre, opera, cricket; *Clubs* RAC, MCC; *Style*— David Stewart, Esq; ✉ The Oast House, Best Beech, Wadhurst, Sussex TN5 6JH; Coopers & Lybrand, 1 Embankment Place, London WC2N 6NN (☎ 0171 583 5000)

STEWART, Ed; *né* Mainwaring; s of R M Mainwaring (d 1989), of Church Knowle, Dorset, and Peggy Stewart, *née* Fraser; *b* 23 April 1941; *Educ* Glengyle Putney, Eagle House Sandhurst, St Edward's Oxford; *m* Chiara Francesca Marinella, da of James McGrath Henney; 1 s (Marco Ray James b 23 March 1977), 1 da (Francesca b 27 May 1975); *Career* TV and radio presenter; *Radio* Keith Prowse Records 1960–61; Hong Kong 1961–65: Radio Hong Kong, Commercial Radio, Rediffusion; Radio London (offshore) 1965–67; BBC Radio 1 1967–79: Junior Choice, Sunday Sport, Newsbeat, Roadshow; BBC Radio 2 1980–84 (Ed Stewart Show, Family Favourites), ILR Radio Mercury 1984–90, BBC Radio 2 1990–; *Television* Exit The Way Out Show (Rediffusion) 1967, Anything You Can Do (Granada) 1969, Stewpot (LWT) 1970–71, Ed and Zed (BBC) 1970, Crackerjack (BBC) 1975–79, Wish You Were Here? (Thames) 1982–84, QVC 1993–; winner: Variety Club Broadcaster of the Year 1975, The Sun Top Children's Personality 1975; capt Variety Club of GB Golfing Soc 1983 and 1984; Bait Rat Grand Order of Water Rats; nat vice pres PHAB, pres PHAB Surrey; *Recreations* golf, cricket, tennis, football, cycling, travelling; *Clubs* Wig & Pen; *Style*— Ed Stewart, Esq; ✉ BBC Radio 2, Broadcasting House, London W1A 1AA

STEWART, Ewen; s of late Duncan Stewart, of Kinlocheil, and Kate, *née* Blunt; *b* 22 April 1926; *Educ* Univ of Edinburgh (BSc, MA, LLB); *m* 1959, Norma Porteous, da of late William Charteris Hollands, of Earlston (d 1992); 1 da; *Career* agric economist E of Scotland Coll of Agric 1946–49; practised at Scottish Bar 1952–62, lectr in agric law Univ of Edinburgh 1957–62, former standing jr counsel Miny of Fuel and Power; Parly candidate (Lab) Banffshire 1962; Sheriff: Wick Caithness 1962–92, Dornoch and Sutherland 1977–92, Tain Ross and Cromarty 1977–92, Stornoway Western Isles 1990–92, ret; *Style*— Ewen Stewart, Esq; ✉ 16 Bignold Court, George Street, Wick, Caithness KW1 4DL

STEWART, Prof Sir Frederick Henry; kt (1974); s of Frederick Stewart, and Hester, *née* Alexander; *b* 16 Jan 1916; *Educ* Fettes, Univ of Aberdeen (BSc), Emmanuel Coll Cambridge (PhD); *m* 1945, Mary Florence Elinor Stewart, *qv*, da of Frederick Albert Rainbow (d 1967); *Career* mineralogist ICI Ltd (Billingham Div) 1941–43, lectr in geology Univ of Durham 1943–56, regius prof of geology Univ of Edinburgh 1956–82; chm: NERC 1971–73, Advsy Bd for the Res Cncls 1973–79; memb: Cncl for Scientific Policy 1967–71, Advsy Cncl for Applied R & D 1976–79; tstee Br Museum (Natural History) 1983–87; Hon DSc: Univ of Aberdeen, Univ of Leicester, Heriot-Watt Univ, Univ of Durham, Univ of Glasgow; FRS 1964, FRSE 1957, FGS; *Clubs* New (Edinburgh); *Style*— Prof Sir Frederick Stewart, FRS, FRSE; ✉ 79 Morningside Park, Edinburgh (☎ 0131 447 2620); House of Letterawe, Lochawe, Argyll (☎ 01838 200329)

STEWART, George Girdwood; CB (1979), MC (1945), TD (1954); s of Herbert Alexander Stewart (d 1966), and Janetta Dunlop, *née* Girdwood (d 1988); *b* 12 Dec 1919; *Educ* Kelvinside Acad Glasgow, Univ of Glasgow, Univ of Edinburgh (BSc); *m* 1950, Shelagh Jean Morven, da of Dr R R Murray; 1 s (Alan b 1955), 1 da (Sara b 1953); *Career* served RA 1940–46 (dispatches), Cmd Offr 278 (L) Field Regt RA (TA) 1957–60; Forestry Cmmn 1948–79: conservator W (Scotland) 1967–69, cmmr for forest and estate mgmnt 1969–79; pres Scot Ski Club 1971–75, vice-pres Nat Ski Fedn of GB and chm Alpine Racing Ctee 1975–78; memb Cncl Nat Tst for Scotland 1975–79, rep Branklyn Garden 1980–84, regional rep Central and Tayside 1984–88, forestry advsr 1988–93; memb: Environment Panel BR Bd 1980–90, memb Countryside Cmmn for Scot 1981–88; chm Scot Wildlife Tst 1981–87, specialist advsr to House of Lords Select Ctee on EEC Forestry Policy 1986, memb Cairngorm Recreation Tst 1986–; advsr Highlands and Islands Enterprise Cairngorm Estate 1987–; pres Scot Nat Ski Cncl 1988–94; assoc dir Oakwood Environmental 1991–; winner Nat Serv to Sport Award (Scot) 1995; FRSA; FICFor, Hon FLI; *Recreations* skiing, tennis, studying Scottish painting; *Clubs* Ski Club of GB; *Style*— George Stewart, Esq, CB, MC, TD; ✉ Stormont House, Mansfield Rd, Scone, Perth PH2 6SA (☎ 01738 551815)

STEWART, Gillian; da of Gordon Anderson Stewart (d 1988), and Iris, *née* Ross; *b* 21 Oct 1958; *Educ* Inverness Royal Acad, Univ of Edinburgh (BSc); *Career* golfer; amateur record: Scot under-19 stroke play champion 1975, Scottish girl international 1975–77, Br girls champion 1976, Scottish women's champion 1979 (1983 and 1984), runner-up Br Championship 1982, runner-up Spanish Championship 1984, IBM Euro Open champion 1984, Helen Holm Trophy winner 1981–84; int appearances: Scot Ladies Home Int 1979–84, Scot Ladies Euro team Championship 1979, 1981 and 1983, GB Cwlth team 1979–83, GB Vagliano Trophy Team 1979, 1981 and 1983, GB Curtis Cup team 1980–82, GB World Cup team 1982–84, Avia Watches Golfer of the Year 1984; turned professional 1985, won Ford Classic at Woburn 1985 and 1987, won Princess Lall Meriem Cup (Morocco) 1994, fourth in WPGA Order of Merit 1986, seventh in WPGET Order of Merit 1990; holder of Euro record for the most consecutive cuts made on tour (79 between 1986 and 1991); memb: Women Professional Golfers Euro Tour, PGA; *Recreations* all aspects of golf, hill-walking, cycling, spectating at major sporting events; *Style*— Miss Gillian Stewart; ✉ 14 Annfield Road, Inverness, Scotland IV2 3HX (☎ 01463 231477)

STEWART, Gordon; s of Archibald Leitch Stewart, of Luton, Beds, and Christina Macpherson, *née* Taylor (d 1976); *b* 18 April 1953; *Educ* Luton GS, Univ of Durham (BA); *m* 2 Oct 1982, Teresa Violet, da of Sir James Holmes Henry, 2 Bt, CMG, MC, TD, QC, of Hampton, Middx; 2 s (Edmund James b 24 May 1985, Roland Valentine b 16 Jan 1988); *Career* asst slr Slaughter & May 1978–83 (articled clerk 1976–78); ptnr Simmons & Simmons 1985– (asst slr 1983–85); memb Law Soc; *Recreations* food and wine; *Style*— Gordon Stewart, Esq; ✉ Simmons & Simmons, 21 Wilson Street, London EC2M 2TX (☎ 0171 628 2020, fax 0171 628 2070)

STEWART, Gordon Colin; s of Alan Alexander Fergus Stewart, of Glasgow, and Helen Somerville, *née* Curr; *b* 16 May 1956; *Educ* Buckhurst Hill Co HS Essex, Hutchesons' Boys GS Glasgow, Univ Coll Oxford (MA); *m* 1987, Fiona Annabel, da of Jack Gatchfield, of Welwyn Garden City, Herts; 2 da (Jessica b 1989, Amelia b 1995), 1 s (Alexander b 1992); *Career* ptnr: Cameron Markby 1983–88 (articled and asst slr 1978–83), Allen & Overy 1989–; pres Soc of Practitioners in Insolvency 1996–97; memb Consumer & Commercial Law Ctee Law Soc 1991– (also chm Insolvency Law Sub-Ctee), slr memb Lord Chllr's Insolvency Rules Ctee 1993; memb: City of London Slrs' Co, Int Bar Assoc 1995; *Books* Administrative Receivers and Administrators (1987), Leasing Law in the European Union (contrib, 1994); *Recreations* running, golf, literature, humour; *Clubs* Roehampton, Holmes Place Health (Barbican); *Style*— Gordon Stewart, Esq; ✉ Allen & Overy, One New Change, London EC4M 9QQ (☎ 0171 330 3000, fax 0171 330 9999)

STEWART, Ian Graham; s of John Meldrum Stewart (d 1968), and Ann Mitchell, *née* Warne; *b* 14 Feb 1948; *Educ* Cowdenbeath HS, Univ of Edinburgh (MA, MSc), UCNW; *m* 28 July 1973, Patricia Ann, da of Paul Garston Stevens; 2 da (Clare Elizabeth b 15 June 1978, Sonia Caroline b 5 March 1978); *Career* British Council: teacher Rautaruukki Steel Works Finland 1969–70, teacher Oporto 1971–73, lectr Univ of Tabriz 1973–75, lectr Khartoum Poly 1975–77, asst dir Finland 1978–82, English language offr Morocco 1982–84, desk offr English Language Div 1984–88, English language offr Thailand 1988–92, asst dir English Language Div 1992–94, dir Croatia 1994–; *Books* Nucleus Chemistry and Nucleus Geology (with C Barron, 1976); *Recreations* badminton, walking, reading, amateur meteorology; *Style*— Ian Stewart, Esq; ✉ The British Council, Ilica 12/1, PO Box 55, 10001 Zagreb, Croatia

STEWART, James Cecil Campbell; CBE (1960); s of late James Stewart, and Mary Stewart; *b* 25 July 1916; *Educ* Armstrong Coll, King's Coll Durham Univ; *m* 1946, Pamela Rouselle, da of William King-Smith; 1 da; *Career* radar Telecommunication Res Estab 1939–45, nuclear weapons and power UKAEA Harwell 1946–49 and UKAEA Risley 1949–63, memb Bd of UKAEA and CEGB 1963–69, dir National Nuclear Corporation Ltd 1969–82; chm: Br Nuclear Forum 1974–92, NNC Pension Tstee Ltd 1979–92, Int Advsy Ctee CONCORD Denver USA 1986–94; *Recreations* tending a garden; *Clubs* East India, Les Ambassadeurs; *Style*— James Stewart, Esq, CBE; ✉ White Thorns, Higher Whitley, Warrington WA4 4QJ (☎ 01925 730377)

STEWART, James Harvey; s of Harvey Stewart, of Fochabers, Moray, and Annie, *née* Gray; *b* 15 Aug 1939; *Educ* Peterhead Acad, Univ of Aberdeen (MA), Univ of Manchester (Dip Soc Admin); *m* 24 April 1965, Fiona Maria Maclay, da of John Reid (d 1973), of Peterhead; 3 s (Iain b 1969, Alasdair b 1972, Gordon b 1974), 1 da (Marie b 1966); *Career* hosp sec Princess Margaret Rose Orthopaedic Hosp Edinburgh 1965–67, dep gp sec York A Hosp Mgmnt Ctee 1968–73 (princ admin asst 1967–68), area admin Northumberland AHA 1973–82, dist admin Northumberland Health Authy 1982–83, regnl admin E Anglian RHA 1983–85; chief exec: Barking Havering and Brentwood Health Authy 1985–93, Barking and Havering Health Authy 1993–95; conslt in healthcare mgmnt 1995–; AHSM; *Recreations* music, reading, football and rugby, food, wine; *Clubs* Rotary Club of Cambridge, Cambridge Univ RUFC, London Hosp Officers'; *Style*— James H Stewart, Esq; ✉ 85 Main Street, Hardwick, Cambridge CB3 7QU (☎ 01954 210961)

STEWART, James Michael; s of Surgn Lt-Col John M Stewart, and Dr Margaret J W, *née* Robertson; *b* 5 Sept 1960; *Educ* Sedbergh, Univ of Exeter (BA), Univ of Kingston (MBA); *Career* KMG Thompson McLintock 1982–86; Peter Leonard Associates: joined 1986, fin dir 1987–89, md 1989–92; founding ptnr Winter Stewart Associates London 1992–; *Recreations* squash, swimming, running, gym; *Style*— James Stewart, Esq; ✉ Winter Stewart Associates, Mandeville Courtyard, 142 Battersea Park Road, London SW11 4NB (☎ 0171 498 2253, fax 0171 498 2279)

STEWART, James Simeon Hamilton; QC (1982); s of Henry Hamilton Stewart, MA, MD, FRCS (d 1970), and Edna Mary, *née* Pulman; *b* 2 May 1943; *Educ* Cheltenham, Univ of Leeds (LLB); *m* 19 April 1972, Helen Margaret, da of (Thomas) Kenneth Whiteley (d 1993); 2 da (Alexandra b 18 Jan 1974, Georgina b 27 Nov 1975); *Career* called to the Bar Inner Temple 1966, practising N Eastern Circuit and London, recorder of the Crown Ct 1982–, master Inner Temple 1992–, dep High Ct judge 1993–, jt head of chambers 1996–; *Recreations* cricket, gardening, tennis; *Clubs* Bradford, Leeds Taverners; *Style*— James Stewart, Esq, QC; ✉ Park Court Chambers, 40 Park Cross St, Leeds S1 2QH (☎ 0113 243 3277, fax 0113 242 1285, telex 666135)

STEWART, Prof John David; s of David Stewart (d 1970), and Phyllis, *née* Crossley (d 1986); *b* 19 March 1929; *Educ* Stockport GS, Balliol Coll Oxford, Nuffield Coll Oxford; *m* 27 July 1953, Theresa, da of John Raisman (d 1980); 2 s (David b 7 Oct 1955, Henry b 27 June 1959), 2 da (Lindsey b 16 Feb 1957, Selina b 12 March 1962); *Career* Industl Rels Dept NCB; Inst of Local Govt Studies Univ of Birmingham: sr lectr 1966–67, assoc dir 1970–76, prof 1971–96, dir 1976–83, hon prof 1996–; head of Sch of Public Policy Univ of Birmingham 1990–92; memb Layfield Ctee on Local Govt Fin, vice pres RIPA 1988–92; *Books* British Pressure Groups (1958), Management in Local Government (1971), Corporate Planning in Local Government (with R Greenwood, 1974), The Responsive Local Authority (1974), Approaches in Public Policy (jt ed with S Leach, 1982), The Case for Local Government (with G Jones, 1983), Local Government: Conditions of Local Choice (1983), The New Management of Local Government (1986), Understanding the Management of Local Government (1988, 2 edn 1995), Local Government in the 1990s (jt ed with G Stoker, 1995), The General Management of Local Government (with Michael Clarke, 1990), Choices for Local Government (with Michael Clarke, 1991), The Politics of Hung Authorities (with S Leach, 1992), Management in the Public Domain (with Stewart Ranson, 1994), The Changing Organisation and Management of Local Government (with Steve Leach and Keiron Walsh, 1994), Citizenship: Community, Rights and Participation (with David Prior and Keiron Walsh, 1995); *Style*— Prof John Stewart; ✉ 15 Selly Wick Rd, Birmingham B29 7JJ (☎ 0121 472 1512)

STEWART, Sheriff John Hall; s of Cecil Francis Wilson Stewart (d 1964), and Mary Fyffe, *née* Hall; *b* 15 March 1944; *Educ* Airdrie Acad, Univ of St Andrews (LLB); *m* 29 Nov 1968, Marion, da of Donald MacCalman (d 1978); 1 s (Alan Breck b 1973) 2 da (Rohan Mhairi b 1975, Katryn MacCalman b 1978); *Career* enrolled slr 1971–77, advocate 1978–85, sheriff S Strathclyde Dumfries and Galloway at Airdrie 1985–; memb Faculty of Advocates 1978; *Recreations* scuba diving, golf, spectator rugby football and soccer; *Clubs* Uddinton Rugby Football (past pres), Uddington Cricket and Sports (pres); *Style*— Sheriff John H Stewart; ✉ 3 Fife Crescent, Bothwell, Glasgow G71 8DG (☎ 01698 853854); Sheriff's Chambers, Sheriff Court House, Hamilton

STEWART, John Young (Jackie); OBE (1972); s of Robert Paul Stewart (d 1972), and Jean Clark Young; *b* 11 June 1939; *Educ* Dumbarton Acad; *m* 1962, Helen McGregor; 2 s (Paul Stewart, *qv*, b 1965, Mark b 1968); *Career* former racing driver; memb Scottish and Br Team for clay pigeon shooting; former Scottish, English, Irish, Welsh and Br Champion, won Coupe des Nations 1959 and 1960; first raced 1961, competed in 4 meetings driving for Barry Filer Glasgow 1961–62, drove for Ecurie Ecosse and Barry Filer winning 14 out of 23 starts 1963, 28 wins out of 53 starts 1964, drove Formula 1 for Br Racing Motors (BRM) 1965–67 then for Ken Tyrrell 1968–73, has won Australian, NZ, Swedish, Mediterranean, Japanese and many other non-championship maj int motor races, set new world record by winning 26 World Championship Grand Prix (Zandvoort) 1973, 27 (Nürburgring) 1973, third in World Championship 1965, second in 1968 and 1972, World Champion 1969, 1971 and 1973; fndr Stewart Grand Prix (preparation of Formula 1 racing team, in conjunction with Ford, for 1997 season); Br Automobile Racing Club Gold Medal 1971 and 1973, Daily Express Sportsman of the Year 1971 and 1973, BBC Sports Personality of the Year 1973, Segrave Trophy 1973, Scottish Sportsman of the Year 1968 and 1973, USA Sportsman of the Year 1973; film: Weekend of a Champion 1972; Hon PhD Lawrence Inst of Technology USA 1986, Hon PhD Glasgow Caledonian Univ 1993, Hon DEng Heriot-Watt Univ 1996; *Books* World Champion (with Eric Dymock, 1970), Faster! (with Peter Manso, 1972), On the Road (1983), Jackie Stewart's Principles of Performance Driving (with Alan Henry, 1986), The Jackie Stewart Book of Shooting (1991); *Recreations* tennis, shooting, golf; *Clubs* RAC, RSAC, Br Racing Drivers', Royal and Ancient Golf (St Andrews), Scottish Motor Racing; *Style*— Jackie Stewart, Esq, OBE; ✉ Stewart Grand Prix, 16 Tanners Drive, Blakelands, Milton Keynes MK14 5BW (☎ 01908 216122, fax 01908 216892)

STEWART, Marshall; s of Frederick Stewart (d 1988), and Gwendoline Miriam, *née* Bryant; *b* 23 Aug 1936; *m* 1977, Emma Christine, da of late J L Wood, of Harthill, Yorks; *Career* provincial and national newspapers 1952–63; ed the Today prog BBC London 1970–74 (various BBC editorial posts 1963–69), chief ed IRN and LBC 1974–77, head of information BBC London 1978–82; Central Independent Television: dir of public affrs 1982–87, dir of corporate strategy and main bd dir 1987–92, corp advsr 1992–94, dir Central Television Enterprises 1990–94; chm Harthill Communications Ltd 1992–, corp advsr Independent Television News 1992–; dir Informed Sources International Ltd 1993–96; memb Cncl RTS 1979–81, memb BAFTA, memb Assoc of European Journalists; *Recreations* theatre; *Clubs* Garrick; *Style*— Marshall Stewart, Esq; ✉ 3 Motcomb Street, London SW1X 8JU (☎ 0171 235 9894, fax 0171 935 2215)

STEWART, Lady; Mary Florence Elinor; da of Frederick Albert Rainbow (d 1967), and Mary Edith, *née* Matthews (d 1963); *b* 17 Sept 1916; *Educ* Eden Hall Sch Penrith Cumberland, Skellfield Sch Topcliffe Yorks, Univ of Durham (BA, MA); *m* 24 Sept 1945, Prof Sir Frederick Henry Stewart, *qv*, s of Frederick Robert Stewart (d 1974); *Career* pt/t lectr in Eng Univ of Durham 1948–56 (asst lectr 1941–45); novelist 1954–; memb PEN 1955–, hon fell Newnham Coll Cambridge 1986; *Books* Madam Will You Talk? (1954), Wildfire at Midnight (1956), Thunder on the Right (1957), Nine Coaches Waiting (1958), My Brother Michael (1959), The Ivy Tree (1961), The Moonspinners (1962), This Rough Magic (1964), Airs Above the Ground (1965), The Gabriel Hounds (1967), The Wind Off the Small Isles (1968), The Crystal Cave (1970, Frederick Niven Award), The Little Broomstick (1971), The Hollow Hills (1973), Ludo and the Star Horse (1974, Scottish Arts Cncl Award), Touch Not the Cat (1976), The Last Enchantment (1979), A Walk in Wolf Wood (1980), The Wicked Day (1983), Thornyhold (1988), Frost on the Window and Other Poems (1990), Stormy Petrel (1991), The Prince and the Pilgrim (1995); *Recreations* gardening, painting, playing the piano, crosswords; *Clubs* New (Edinburgh); *Style*— Lady Stewart; ✉ c/o Hodder and Stoughton Publishers, 338 Euston Road, London NW1 3BH (☎ 0171 873 6000, fax 0171 636 9851)

STEWART, Col (Robert) Michael; OBE (1973), TD (1964), DL (Cleveland, 1975); s of Col Evan George Stewart, DSO, OBE (d 1958), of St Pauls Coll Hong Kong, and Dorothy Sarah, *née* Lander (d 1990); *b* 17 May 1931; *Educ* Monkton Combe Sch, UCL (BSc), Univ of London (Postgrad Dip); *m* 20 Oct 1962, (Vera) Patricia, da of Andrew Catley Hills (d 1983), of Sevenoaks, Kent; 2 da (Frances b 1963, Isobel b 1965); *Career* Army: cmmnd Royal Signals 1950, served in Austria and Germany 1950–51, in 56, 50 and 34 Signal Regts TA 1951–73, CO 34 Regt 1970–73, Col 1973; Dep Cmd: NE Dist TA 1973–76, 12 Signal Bde 1976–79; Cleveland County Cadet Cmdt 1979–84, Hon Col 34 Signal Regt 1981–88, Col Cmdt Royal Signals 1987–93, Hon Col Cleveland ACF 1992–; ICI: plant mangr 1956–59, design engr 1959–66, sec mangr 1966–74, mangr Supply Dept 1974–77, works engr 1977–78, works mangr 1978–81; gen mangr Phillips-Imperial Petroleum Ltd 1981–92, private sector liaison mangr City Challenge 1993–; dir Tees and Hartlepool Port Authy 1985–94; chm: Royal Jubilee Tst Ctee for Cleveland 1981–85, 'Indust Year 1986' Steering Ctee for Cleveland; TAVRA: chm N Eng 1984–90, chm Cncl Jt Civilian Staff Ctee 1987–90, memb TAVR Advsy Ctee 1987–90, vice chm Cncl 1988–90, tstee Cncl's Pension Fund 1992–; High Sheriff of Cleveland 1990–91; civil rep Cncl of RFEA 1986–; pres: Guisborough Branch Royal Br Legion 1989–, Cleveland SATRO 1990–, Langbaurgh Dist Scouts 1992–; dir N Tees Health NHS Tst 1991–; vice chm of govrs Prior Purseglove Coll 1992–, tstee Cleveland Community Fndn 1993– (dep chm 1995–), govr HMS Trincomalee Tst 1993– (vice chm 1994–), chm E Middlesbrough Community Venture Bd 1994–; ADC to HM the Queen 1975–80; MIEE 1960, MInstMC 1962, FRSA 1986; *Recreations* skiing, sailing, climbing; *Clubs* Army and Navy; *Style*— Col Michael Stewart, OBE, TD, DL; ✉ Hutton House, Hutton Gate, Guisborough, Cleveland TS14 8EQ (☎ 01287 632420); City Challenge, Southlands Centre, Ormesby Road, Middlesbrough, Cleveland TS3 0HB (☎ 01642 300699, fax 01642 300681)

STEWART, Michael James; s of John Innes MacIntosh Stewart (d 1994), and Margaret, *née* Hardwick (d 1979); *b* 6 Feb 1933; *Educ* St Edward's Sch Oxford, Magdalen Coll Oxford (BA, MA); *m* 23 June 1962, Hon Frances Julia, da of Baron Kaldor, FBA (Life Peer, d 1986); 1 s (David b 1974), 3 da (Lucy b 1964, Anna b 1966, d 1978, Kitty b 1970); *Career* econ advsr HM Treasy 1961–62 (econ asst 1957–60), sr econ advsr Cabinet Office 1967 (econ advsr 1964–67), econ advsr Kenya Treasy 1967–69, reader in political economy UCL 1969–94, emeritus 1994, special advsr to Foreign Sec 1977–78; *Books* Keynes and After (1967), The Jekyll and Hyde Years (1977), Controlling the Economic Future (1983), Apocalypse 2000 (with Peter Jay, 1987), Keynes in the 1990's (1993); *Recreations* looking at paintings, eating in restaurants; *Clubs* United Oxford and Cambridge Univ; *Style*— Michael Stewart, Esq; ✉ 79 South Hill Park, London NW3 2SS (☎ 0171 435 3686)

STEWART, Mike (*né* Michael Stewart Mrowiec); s of Francis Joseph Mrowiec (d 1990), and Frances, *née* Lyall; *b* 30 Jan 1946; *Educ* Henry Cavendish Sch Derby, Central Sch Derby, Sch for Business and Language Studies Oostkamp Bruges Belgium; *m* Barbara Kosilla; *Career* reporter and sports ed Staffordshire Advertiser and Chronicle 1965–71, chief reporter and news ed Staffordshire Newsletter 1971–73, sr newsman BRMB Radio Birmingham 1974–76, head of news and sport Beacon Radio Wolverhampton 1976–81, head of news and sport and prog controller Radio West Bristol 1981–84, prog controller Radio Broadland Norwich 1984–90, gp prog dir East Anglian Radio Group 1990– (comprising Broadland FM, SGR-fm Ipswich and Bury St Edmunds, SGR Colchester and Amber Radio), md SGR (Suffolk Gp Radio) Ipswich Bury St Edmunds and Colchester 1996–; MInstD 1993; *Recreations* music, badminton, sport, films, food and wine; *Style*— Mike Stewart, Esq; ✉ East Anglian Radio, St George's Plain, 47–49 Colegate, Norwich NR3 1DB (☎ 01603 630621, fax 01603 666252)

STEWART, Sir (James) Moray; KCB (1995, CB 1990); *b* 21 June 1938; *Educ* Marlborough, Univ of Keele; *Career* breakdown and info serv offr AA 1956–57, asst master Northcliffe Sch Bognor Regis 1957–58, asst princ Air Miny 1962–66, princ MOD 1966–70, first sec UK Delgn to NATO 1970–73, asst under sec of state MOD 1980–84, asst sec gen Defence Planning and Policy NATO 1984–86, dep under sec of state MOD 1986–90, second permanent under sec of state MOD 1990–96; vice chm Civil Serv RFU, chm Civil Serv Healthcare; memb Pegusus Tst; tstee Imperial War Museum, cmmr Queen Victoria Sch Dunblane; Hon DLitt Univ of Keele 1995; memb IISS, memb RUSI; *Recreations* reading, walking, listening to music; *Clubs* Royal Over-Seas League, Farmers', New (Edinburgh); *Style*— Sir Moray Stewart, KCB

STEWART, Dame Muriel Acadia; DBE (1968); da of late James Edmund Stewart; *b* 22 Oct 1905; *Educ* Gateshead GS, Univ of Durham (BA); *Career* teacher: Newcastle upon Tyne 1927–29, Northumberland 1929–70; nat pres Nat Union of Teachers 1964–65, headmistress Shiremoor Middle Sch 1969–70; chm Schools Cncl 1969–72, vice chm

Bullock Ctee 1972–74, memb Northumberland Educn Ctee 1981–89, pres Lib Democrat Educn Assoc; Hon MEd Univ of Newcastle; *Style*— Dame Muriel Stewart, DBE; ✉ 102 Great North Road, Gosforth, Newcastle upon Tyne NE3 5JR

STEWART, Nicholas John Cameron; QC (1987); s of John Cameron Stewart, and Margaret Mary, *née* Botsford; *b* 16 April 1947; *Educ* Worcester Coll Oxford (Open exhibitioner, PPE), Cert Dip Accounting and Finance; *m* 1974, Pamela Jean, *née* Windham; 1 s (Senan 11 Dec 1981), 2 da (Rosalind 8 Feb 1984, Olivia 3 Aug 1986); *Career* called to the Bar Inner Temple 1971; dep High Court judge (Chancery Div) 1991–; chm Bar Human Rights Ctee of England and Wales 1994–, dir of publications Union Internationale des Avocats 1994–; narrator/presenter No Further Questions (BBC Radio 4, two series); *Style*— Nicholas Stewart, Esq, QC; ✉ 4 New Square, Lincoln's Inn, London WC2A 3RJ (☎ 0171 404 3800, fax 0171 404 3900, e-mail 100745.2517@compuserve.com)

STEWART, Norman Macleod; s of George Stewart (d 1965), and Elspeth, *née* Stewart (d 1982); *b* 2 Dec 1934; *Educ* Elgin Acad, Univ of Edinburgh (BL); *m* 17 July 1959, Mary Slater, da of William Campbell (d 1977); 4 da (Gillian b 1961, Alison b 1964, Carol b 1967, Morag b 1969); *Career* asst slr Alex Morison and Co WS Edinburgh 1957–58; Allan Black and McCaskie Elgin: asst slr 1959–61, ptnr 1961–84, sr ptnr 1984–; chm Elgin & Lossiemouth Harbour Bd 1993–; former pres: Edinburgh Univ Club of Moray, Elgin Rotary Club; former chm Moray Crime Prevention Panel, former sec Lossiemouth Hersbruck (Bavaria) Twin Town Assoc, former treas Moray GC, former memb Cncl Soc of Slrs in the Supreme Ct (Scot); The Law Soc of Scot: cncl memb 1976–89, convenor Public Rels Cmmn 1979–81, convenor Professional Practice Cmmn 1981–84, vice pres 1984–85, pres 1985–86; hon memb American Bar Assoc 1985; memb: Law Soc of Scot, Int Bar Assoc, Cwlth Lawyers' Assoc; *Recreations* travel, music, golf, Spain and its culture; *Clubs* New (Edinburgh); *Style*— Norman Stewart, Esq; ✉ Argyll Lodge, Lossiemouth, Moray IV31 6QT (☎ 0134381 3150); Allan Black and McCaskie, 151 High St, Elgin, Moray IV30 1DX (☎ 01343 543355, fax 01343 549667)

STEWART, Patrick Hewes; s of Alfred Stewart (d 1984), of Mirfield, W Yorks, and Gladys, *née* Barrowclough (d 1979); *b* 13 July 1940; *Educ* Mirfield Secdy Modern, Bristol Old Vic Theatre Sch; *m* 1966 (m dis 1992), Sheila Falconer; 1 s (Daniel b 20 Oct 1968), 1 da (Sophie b 29 June 1973); *Career* actor and dir; assoc artist RSC 1967 (now hon artist); *Theatre* roles incl: King John, Shylock, Henry IV, Cassius, Titus Andronicus, Oberon, Leontes, Enobarbus (SWET Award), Touchstone and Launce, title role in Yonadab (NT) 1986; other credits incl: George in Who's Afraid of Virginia Woolf? (Young Vic) 1987 (London Fringe Best Actor Award), A Christmas Carol 1993; *Television* incl: Sejanus in I Claudius, Karla in Tinker Tailor Soldier Spy and Smiley's People, Salieri in The Mozart Inquest, Oedipus in Oedipus Rex, Rev Anderson in The Devil's Disciple, Jean in Miss Julie, Claudius in Hamlet, Capt Jean-Luc Picard in Star Trek: The Next Generation 1987– (two Best Actor Awards and a nomination, American TV Awards), also dir various episodes of The Next Generation (winner Emmy for A Fistful of Datas); *Films* incl: Hedda, Dune, Lady Jane, Excalibur, LA Story, Death Train 1993, Robin Hood: Men in Tights 1993, Gun Men 1993, Jeffrey 1996, Star Trek: First Contact 1996; *Recreations* walking, scuba, travel; *Style*— Patrick Stewart; ✉ Peters Fraser & Dunlop Ltd, 503 The Chambers, Chelsea Harbour, Lots Road, London SW10 0XF (☎ 0171 352 4446, fax 0171 352 7356)

STEWART, Paul Evan; s of John Young (Jackie) Stewart, OBE, *qv*, and Helen, *née* McGregor; *b* 29 Oct 1965; *Educ* Aiglon Coll Villars Switzerland, Duke Univ N Carolina (BA); *m* Victoria; 1 s (Dylan Young); *Career* motor racing driver; began competing in Dunlop Autosport Star of Tomorrow and Jr Formula Ford 1600 Championships 1987, sixth place Br Formula Ford 2000 Championship 1988, winner Daytona 24–hr Race GTO Class 1989, drove in Formula 3 1989–90 and Int Formula 3000 1991–93; co-fndr (with Jackie Stewart) Paul Stewart Racing, team competes in Formula 3 and Formula Vauxhall, also co-fndr Stewart Grand Prix 1995; *Awards* Br Formula 3 Championship: winners 1992, 1993 and 1994 (record), record-breaking 100th win 1995, winners 1996; Formula Vauxhall Championship: winners 1993, 1994, 1995 and 1996; *Recreations* guitar, skiing, tennis; *Style*— Paul Stewart, Esq; ✉ Paul Stewart Racing (UK) Ltd, 16 Tanners Drive, Blakelands, Milton Keynes, Bucks MK14 5BW (☎ 01908 216122, fax 01908 216133)

STEWART, Peter Antony Eabry; s of James Oswald Stewart (d 1981), and Beryl Nesta, *née* Eabry (d 1974); *b* 25 April 1928; *Educ* Queen Elizabeth's Hosp Bristol, Cranfield Univ (MSc, Young Prize, DSc); *m* 1951 (m dis 1989); 3 s (Paul Eabry, Mark Eabry, Charles Edward); *Career* student apprenticeship Engine Div Bristol Aeroplane Co 1945–49 (detail draughtsman 1949–51); design draughtsman: Rocket Missile Div Armstrong Whitworth Aircraft Coventry 1951–52, Rocket Missile Div D Napier & Son Luton 1952–54; devpt engr Rocket Motors Willcocks Clevedon (experimental engrs) 1954–55, design engr Rocket Motors Bristol Aerojet Ltd Banwell 1955–58, rocket propulsion specialist and trials team ldr (UK & Aust) Black Knight Rocket Project Saunders Roe Ltd (IOW) 1958–60, rocket and satellite systems engr Advanced Projects Gp Astronautics Div Hawker Siddeley 1960–62, engr future projects Bristol Siddeley 1962–68, chief Advanced Projects Gp Rolls Royce Bristol 1968–92; chief exec Stewart Associates 1992–; visiting prof: Cranfield Univ 1990–93, Aerospace Dept Univ of Bristol 1991–; holder of 11 patents and author of 37 pubns; Queen's Award for Technological Achievement 1978; FRAeS 1975 (Ackroyd Stuart Prize 1983), FIMechE 1975, FIEE, FInstP, FRPS 1975, FIMgt, fell Royal Astronomical Soc, FGS, fell Br Interplanetary Soc, assoc IOD, FEng 1991 (McRobert Award 1985); *Recreations* hill walking, speleology, skiing, sailing, consciousness studies; *Style*— Prof Peter Stewart, FEng; ✉ Stewart Associates, 9 Beaufort, Harford Drive, Frenchay, Bristol BS16 1NP (☎ and fax 0117 956 5700)

STEWART, Col Robert Christie; CBE (1983), TD (1962); s of Maj Alexander C Stewart, MC (d 1927), of Arndean, by Dollar, Scotland, and Florence Hamilton, *née* Lighton (d 1982); *b* 3 Aug 1926; *Educ* Eton, Univ of Oxford (BA, MA); *m* 21 May 1953, Ann Grizel, da of Air Chief Marshal Hon Sir Ralph Alexander Cochrane, GBE, KCB, AFC (d 1977); 3 s (Alexander, John, David), 2 da (Catriona (Mrs Marsham), Sara (Mrs Anthony Scott)); *Career* Lt Scots Gds 1944–49, 7 Bn Argyll and Sutherland Highlanders TA 1951–65, Lt-Col 1963–66, Hon Col 1/51 Highland Volunteers 1972–75; landowner; Lord-Lt Kinross-shire 1966–74, Lord-Lt Clackmannanshire 1994–; chm Perth and Kinross CC (memb 1953–75), chm and pres Bd of Govrs East of Scotland Coll of Agric 1970–83; *Recreations* shooting, golf, the country; *Clubs* Royal Perth Golfing Soc, County; *Style*— Col Robert C Stewart, CBE, TD; ✉ Arndean, Dollar, Scotland FK14 7NH (☎ 01259 742527, fax 01259 743888)

STEWART, Robin Milton; QC (1978); s of Brig Guy Milton Stewart (d 1943), and Dr Elaine Oenone, *née* Earengey; *b* 5 Aug 1938; *Educ* Winchester, New Coll Oxford (MA); *m* 8 Sept 1962, Lynda Grace, da of Arthur Thomas Albert Medhurst (d 1976); 3 s (Andrew Douglas Lorn b 1964, James Milton b 1966, Sholto Robert Douglas b 1969); *Career* called to the Bar: Middle Temple 1963, King's Inns Dublin 1975; prosecuting counsel to Inland Revenue (NE Circuit) 1976–78, recorder Crown Court 1978–, bencher Middle Temple 1988, head of chambers; dir Bar Mutual Indemnity Fund Ltd 1988–93; memb Professional Conduct Ctee Bar Cncl 1991–93, chm Professional Negligence Bar Assoc 1991–93, former memb Hexham UDC and Tynedale DC; Parly candidate (C) Newcastle upon Tyne W 1974; Freeman City of London, Liveryman Worshipful Co of Glaziers 1966; *Recreations* gardens, silver, pictures, opera, Scottish family history; *Clubs* Oriental; *Style*— R M Stewart, Esq, QC; ✉ Little Chart, 46 Oak Hill Rd, Sevenoaks, Kent TN13 1NS (☎ 01732 453475); Les Mias, 16270 Nieuil, France (☎ 00 33 545 71 15 36); 4 Brick Court, Temple, London EC4Y 9AD (☎ 0171 353 5875); Chambers: 199 Strand, London WC2R 1DR (☎ 0171 379 9779, fax 0171 379 9481)

STEWART, Robin Reith Wittet; s of Dr James Stewart (d 1955), and Veronica Mary, *née* Wittet (d 1991); *b* 11 Aug 1935; *Educ* George Watson's Coll Edinburgh, Univ of Edinburgh (MA), Univ of Cambridge (BA), Univ of Manchester (DSA); *m* Sara Elizabeth Gartly, da of John Sutherland (d 1974); 2 da (Hilary Stewart b 27 Oct 1965, Lindsay Jane Stewart b 17 June 1969); *Career* trainee in hosp admin Western Regnl Hosp Bd Glasgow 1958–61, sr admin asst Glasgow Royal Infirmay 1961–63, dep sec and treas Bd of Mgmnt Glasgow Royal Infirmary and Associated Hosps 1963–70, sec Northern Regnl Hosp Bd Inverness 1970–74, gen mangr Highland Health Bd 1985–94 (sec 1974–85), dir Inverness and Nairn Enterprise 1991–; pres Inverness-shire Red Cross 1994–, memb Scottish Cncl Red Cross 1996–; memb Hosp Ctee EC 1978–88 (ldr UK Delgn 1986–88); formerly: chm Scottish Div IHSM, treas Inverness Dist Sports Cncl, pres Inverness Choral Soc; FHSM 1972 (AHSM and medal 1961); *Recreations* choral singing, Church of Scotland elder; *Style*— Robin Stewart, Esq; ✉ 20 Crown Avenue, Inverness IV2 3NF (☎ 01463 236493)

STEWART, Roderick David (Rod); *b* 10 Jan 1945; *Career* singer and songwriter; apprentice Brentford FC 1961; performed with bands The Five Dimensions, The Hoochie Coochie Men, The Soul Agents, Steampacket, The Shotgun Express; albums: Truth (with Jeff Beck Group, 1967, reached UK no 8), Cosa Nostra - Beck Ola (with Jeff Beck Group, 1969, UK no 39), An Old Raincoat Won't Ever Let You Down (1969), First Step (with The Faces, 1970, UK no 45), Gasoline Alley (1970, UK no 62), Long Player (with The Faces, 1971, UK no 31), Every Picture Tells A Story (1971, UK no 1), A Nod's As Good As A Wink...To A Blind Horse (with The Small Faces, 1971, UK no 2), Never A Dull Moment (1972, UK no 1), Sing It Again Rod (compilation, 1973, UK no 1), Ooh La La (with Small Faces, 1973, UK no 1), Coast to Coast Overture And Beginners (live, with The Faces, 1974, UK no 3), Smiler (1974, UK no 1), Atlantic Crossing (1975, UK no 1), A Night On The Town (1976, UK no 1), The Best of The Faces (compilation, 1977, UK no 24), The Best of Rod Stewart (compilation, 1977, UK no 1), Foot Loose And Fancy Free (1977, UK no 3), Blondes Have More Fun (1978, UK no 3), Rod Stewart's Greatest Hits (1980, UK no 1), Foolish Behaviour (1980, UK no 4), Tonight I'm Yours (1981, UK no 8), Absolutely Live (1982, UK no 35), Body Wishes (1983, UK no 5), Love Touch (1986, UK no 5), Out of Order (1988, UK no 11), The Best of Rod Stewart (1989, UK no 3), Storyteller 1964–90 (box set, 1989), Vagabond Heart (1991, UK no 2), The Best of Rod Stewart (compilation, 1993, UK no 3); recipient of numerous awards; *Style*— Rod Stewart, Esq

STEWART, Sir Ronald Compton; 2 Bt (UK 1937), of Stewartby, Co Bedford; DL (1974); s of Sir (Percy) Malcolm Stewart, 1 Bt, OBE (d 1951); *b* 14 Aug 1903; *Educ* Rugby, Jesus Coll Cambridge; *m* 1936, Cynthia Alexandra, OBE, JP (d 1987), da of late Harold Farmiloe 1987); *Heir* none; *Career* chm London Brick Co Ltd 1966–79; High Sheriff Bedfordshire 1954, DL 1974–88; *Style*— Sir Ronald Stewart, Bt, DL; ✉ Maulden Grange, Maulden, Bedfordshire

STEWART, Roy Irvine; CBE (1985), DL (1992); s of James Irvine Stewart (d 1976), of Tynemouth, and Ida Vera, *née* Pacey (d 1990); *Educ* South Shields Central HS; *Career* co sec to Bellway plc 1966–85; dir Mawson & Wareham (Music) Ltd 1972–; chm IOD (Northern Counties) 1995–, chm Northumbria Ambulance Serv Nat Health Tst 1990–94, chm Diocese of Newcastle Parsonages Bd 1985–, pres Northumbria Cons Euro Constituency 1987–, co cmmr Scout Assoc Co Durham 1972–91, hon treas Tynemouth Dist Scout Cncl 1992–, chm Newcastle Cathedral Tst 1993– (memb 1982–90 and 1992); memb: Exec Ctee Gateshead Dispensary Tst 1986–, Exec Ctee Northumberland Co Scout Cncl 1993–, Fairbridge Regnl Ctee 1993–; Tynemouth and Whitley Bay Cons Assoc: hon treas 1980–83, chm 1985–88 and 1993–96, pres 1983–85 and 1996–; former JP N Tyneside; High Sheriff Tyne & Wear 1988–89; Freeman City of London 1989, memb Worshipful Co of Chartered Accountants; FCA; *Recreations* music, bridge, motor cycling; *Clubs* Northern Counties; *Style*— Roy I Stewart, Esq, CBE, DL; ✉ Brockenhurst, 2 The Broadway, Tynemouth NE30 2LD (☎ 0191 257 9791, fax 0191 296 4917); 31 Percy Gardens, Tynemouth NE30 4HQ (☎ 0191 257 4562)

STEWART, Dr Sir (John) Simon Watson; 6 Bt (UK 1920), of Balgownie; er s of Sir (John) Keith Watson Stewart, 5 Bt (d 1990), and Mary Elizabeth, *née* Moxon; *b* 5 July 1955; *Educ* Uppingham, Charing Cross Hosp Med Sch (MD, FRCP, FRCR); *m* 3 June 1978, Catherine Stewart, da of (Henry) Gordon Bond, of Shiplake, Oxon; 1 s ((John) Hamish Watson b 12 Dec 1983), 1 da (Anna Rebecca Watson b 1 May 1987); *Heir* s, (John) Hamish Watson Stewart b 12 Dec 1983; *Career* conslt in clinical oncology St Mary's Hosp Paddington; sr lectr Royal Postgraduate Med Sch Hammersmith Hosp; Freeman City of London 1980, memb Worshipful Co of Merchant Taylors 1980; *Recreations* skiing, sail boarding; *Clubs* Oriental; *Style*— Dr Sir Simon Stewart, Bt; ✉ 38 Dukes Avenue, Chiswick, London W4 4AE (☎ 0181 995 2213); Dept of Oncology, St Mary's Hospital, Praed Street, London W2 (☎ 0171 725 1132)

STEWART, Stephen Paul; QC (1996); s of Cyril Stewart (d 1994), and Phyllis Mary, *née* Hough; *b* 9 Oct 1953; *Educ* Stand GS Whitefield, St Peter's Coll Oxford (MA); *m* 5 July 1980, Dr M Felicity Stewart, da of (Anthony) Martyn Dyer; 1 da (Eleanor Catherine Anne b 3 Oct 1984), 1 s (Peter Edward John b 21 Dec 1989); *Career* called to the Bar Middle Temple 1975 (Harmsworth Major exhibitioner and scholar), in practice Northern Circuit, asst recorder 1995–; *Recreations* running, music; *Clubs* Alderley Edge Cricket; *Style*— Stephen Stewart, Esq, QC; ✉ 25 Byrom Street, Manchester M3 4PF (☎ 0161 829 2100, fax 0161 829 2101)

STEWART, Sir William Duncan Paterson; kt (1994); *b* 7 June 1935; *Educ* Dunoon GS, Univ of Glasgow (BSc, PhD, DSc); m; 1 s; *Career* asst lectr Univ of Nottingham 1961–63, lectr Univ of London 1963–68; Univ of Dundee: prof of biology 1968–94, vice princ 1985–87; chief exec Agric and Food Res Cncl 1988–90; Cabinet Office: chief scientific advsr 1990–95, head of Office of Science and Technol 1992–95; memb: NERC, AFRC, Advsy Bd for Res Cncls, Advsy Cncl on Science and Technol, Royal Cmmn on Environmental Pollution, NEDO Working Pty on Biotechnology, Cabinet Ctee on Science and Technol, Official Ctee on Science and Technol, MAFF Priorities Bd, Def Scientific Advsy Ctee, DTI Innovation Advsy Bd, Energy Advsy Ctee on R & D, BNSC Res Bd, EC Res Cncl; 20 hon degrees from Univs incl Univ of Edinburgh and Univ of Glasgow; author of over 300 scientific pubns; CBiol; FRS, FRSE 1973; *Recreations* observing homo sapiens; *Clubs* Athenaeum, Dundee United; *Style*— Sir William Stewart, FRS, FRSE

STEWART, William Gladstone; *b* 15 July 1935; *Educ* Shooters Hill GS London, Woolwich Poly London; *m* 1960 (m dis 1976), Audrey Ann, da of Charles Harrison; 1 s (Nicholas b 1961); 2 other c (Barnaby 1976, Hayley b 1980); *partner*, Laura Calland; 2 da (Isobel b 1989, Hannah b 1994); *Career* RAEC King's African Rifles 1952–55; Redcoat Butlins 1958, BBC TV 1958–67 (directors' course 1965), freelance prodr, broadcaster and writer 1967–; prodns incl: The Frost Programme, David Frost, Live from London, Father Dear Father, Bless This House, The Price is Right, The Thoughts of Chairman Alf, Tickets for the Titanic, The Lady is a Tramp, The Nineteenth Hole, Fifteen-to-One (also presenter); co-fndr (with Colin Frewin) Sunset and Vine 1976, fndr md Regent Productions 1982–; Fellow Royal Television Society 1996; *Recreations* the English language, music, tennis, riding; *Clubs* Reform; *Style*— William G Stewart, Esq;

✉ Regent Productions Ltd, 6 Putney Common, London SW15 1HL (☎ 0181 789 5350, fax 0181 789 5332)

STEWART, Prof William James; s of James W Stewart, of Hindhead, Surrey, and Margaret M Stewart; *b* 13 July 1947; *Educ* Blundell's, Imperial Coll London (BSc, MSc); *m* 1976, Dr Jill A Stewart, da of F E Chapman; 2 c (Alexander b 6 June 1983, Antonia b 1 May 1986); *Career* chief scientist GEC-Marconi Materials Technology Caswell (joined 1971); visiting prof: Imperial Coll London, UCL, Univ of Southampton; contrib to numerous books and jls; granted numerous patents for inventions in field of optics; memb: Editorial Bd Journal of Optical Communications, BBSRC Engrg Ctee; chm ECOC/IOOC 1997; Worshipful Co of Scientific Instrument Makers award for achievement; memb Optical Soc of America, MIEEE/LEOS, MIEE, MInstD; FEng 1989; *Recreations* woodwork; *Style*— Prof William Stewart, FEng; ✉ Marconi, Caswell, Towcester, Northants NN12 8EQ (☎ 01327 356715, fax 01327 356775, e-mail w.stewart@ieee.org)

STEWART-CLARK, Alexander Dudley; s and h of Sir John Stewart-Clark, 3 Bt, MEP, *qv*; *b* 21 Nov 1960; *Educ* Worth Abbey; *Career* md Challenge F Timber Ltd (formerly Douglas Timber Ltd) 1988–; *Books* Hydroscopics of Oak (1987), Amazon Reforestation - The Williams Theory, The Consequence of Burning Rubber Elements in the Atmosphere (1992); *Recreations* rugby, tennis; *Style*— Alexander Stewart-Clark, Esq; ✉ Puckstye House, nr Cowden, Kent TN8 7ED; 28 Fairfield St, London SW18 1DW

STEWART-CLARK, Sir John (Jack); 3 Bt (UK 1918), of Dundas, W Lothian; MEP (Cons) Sussex East and Kent South (majority 6,212); s of Sir Stewart Stewart-Clark, 2 Bt (d 1971), and Jane Pamela, *née* Clarke (d 1993); *b* 17 Sept 1929; *Educ* Eton, Balliol Coll Oxford, Harvard Business Sch; *m* 1958, Lydia, da of James William Loudon, of Valkenswaard, The Netherlands; 1 s (Alexander Dudley, *qv*, b 1960), 4 da (Daphne b 1959, Nadia (Mrs Patrick J Waterfield) b 1963, Zarina b 1965, Natalie b 1969); *Heir* s, Alexander Dudley Stewart-Clark b 21 Nov 1960; *Career* late Coldstream Gds; Parly candidate (Cons & Unionist) Aberdeen N 1959; MEP (EDG): E Sussex 1979–94, E Sussex and Kent S 1994–; treas European Democratic Gp 1979–92, vice pres European Parliament 1992–; chm EP Delgn to Canada 1979–82, vice-chm EP Delgn to Japan 1986–89; ctee spokesman on: external affrs 1979–83, institutional affrs 1983–85, youth, culture, educn and media 1989–92, civil liberties 1992–; dir: Oppenheimer International Ltd until 1984, Low & Bonar 1982–95, Cope Allman International Ltd until 1983, AT Kearney Management Consultants 1985–92, Pioneer Concrete Holdings Ltd 1989–; memb Bd Tstee Savings Bank Scotland 1986–89; md: J & P Coats (Pakistan) Ltd 1961–67, J A Carp's Garenfabrieken (Helmond) Holland 1967–70, Philips Electrical Ltd London 1971–75, Pye of Cambridge Ltd 1975–79; former memb Cncl Royal United Servs Inst, chm Supervisory Bd Euro Inst for Security 1984–86, tstee dir Euro Centre for Work and Soc 1983–; chm: EPIC (Euro Parliamentarians & Industrialists Cncl) 1984–, European Action Cncl for Peace in the Balkans 1995–; pres CRONWE (Conf Regnl Orgns of NW Europe) 1987–93; memb Royal Co of Archers (Queen's Bodyguard for Scot); *Publications* European Competition Law (jtly), It's My Problem as Well: Drugs Prevention and Education (jtly); *Recreations* golf, tennis, music, travel, vintage cars; *Clubs* White's, Royal Ashdown Forest Golf; *Style*— Sir Jack Stewart-Clark, Bt, MEP; ✉ Puckstye House, Holtye Common, nr Cowden, Kent TN8 7EL (☎ 01342 850285, fax 01342 850789)

STEWART-LIBERTY, Oliver James; s of Arthur Ivor Stewart-Liberty, MC, TD (d 1990), of Pipers, The Lee, Great Missenden, Bucks, and his 1 w, Rosabel Fremantle, *née* Fynn; *b* 9 Oct 1947; *Educ* Bryanston Sch; *m* 16 Sept 1972, Anne Catherine, da of Frank Arthur Bicknell, of London; 1 s (Charles b 1978), 1 da (Alexandra b 1980); *Career* dir Liberty plc 1977–95 (currently major shareholder); *Recreations* shooting, cricket, tennis, boules; *Clubs* Hurlingham; *Style*— Oliver Stewart-Liberty, Esq; ✉ c/o Liberty plc, 212 Regent Street, London W1R 6AH (☎ 0171 734 1234)

STEWART OF ARDVORLICH, Alexander Donald; DL (Perthshire 1988); s of John Alexander McLaren Stewart of Ardvorlich, TD, JP, DL (d 1985), and Violet Hermione, *née* Cameron (d 1979); *b* 18 June 1933; *Educ* Wellington, Univ of Oxford (BA), Univ of Edinburgh (LLB); *m* 4 Dec 1970, Virginia Mary, da of Capt Peter Washington (d 1983), of Pine Farm, Wokingham, Berks; 1 s (James b 1980), 5 da (Sophie b 1972, Emily b 1974, Theresa b 1976, Catrina b 1978, Petra b 1982); *Career* admitted slr (WS) 1961, ptnr McGrigor Donald Glasgow 1965–93; dir: Scottish Amicable Life Assurance Soc 1986– (chm), Murray Split Capital Trust plc; hon consul for Thailand 1983–; *Recreations* field sports, winter sports, music; *Style*— Alexander Stewart of Ardvorlich, DL; ✉ Ardvorlich, Lochearnhead, Perthshire FK19 8QE

STEWART OF DALBUIE, George Prince McKean; s of George Stewart (d 1942), of Bothwell, Lanarkshire, and Eileen Eva, *née* Atkinson (d 1942); *b* 2 Nov 1925; *Educ* Glenalmond, Univ of Glasgow (MA); *m* 17 July 1952, Jean Thomson, da of John McNaught (d 1971); 2 s (George b 1953, Roderick b 1961), 1 da (Ann b 1956); *Career* served in RNAS 1943–47; dir Alexander Dunn Ltd 1958–70, md Airdun Ltd 1970–87; dir and gen mangr Creda Ltd (Glasgow) 1987–90, dir Midscot Training Services Ltd 1987–; memb Inc of Masons (Glasgow) 1926; Freeman Citizen of Glasgow 1926; FSA Scot 1991; *Recreations* gardening, watercolours, antiquities; *Clubs* Western; *Style*— George Stewart of Dalbuie; ✉ Dalbuie, Southend, Argyll PA28 6PJ

STEWART-RICHARDSON, Alastair Lucas Graham; s of Lt-Col Neil Graham Stewart-Richardson, DSO (d 1934), and Alexandra, *née* Ralli (d 1972); *b* 29 Nov 1927; *Educ* Eton, Magdalene Coll Cambridge (MA); *m* 29 May 1969, (Diana) Claire, da of Brig George Streynsham Rawstorne, CBE, MC (d 1962); 2 s (James George b 1971, Hugh Neil b 1977), 1 da (Sarah Alexandra b 1974); *Career* called to the Bar Inner Temple 1952, bencher 1978; memb Panel of Arbitrators Lloyd's Form of Salvage Agreement 1995; cmmr of Income Tax for Inner Temple 1982; *Style*— Alastair Stewart-Richardson, Esq; ✉ 7 King's Bench Walk, Temple, London EC4Y 7DS (☎ 0171 583 0404, fax 0171 583 0950, telex 887491 KBLAW)

STEWART-RICHARDSON, Ninian Rorie; s of Sir Ian Rorie Hay Stewart-Richardson (d 1969), and Audrey Meryl Odlum (who m 2, 1975, Patrick Allan Pearson Robertson, CMG); hp of bro Sir Simon Alaisdair (Ian Neile) Stewart-Richardson, 17 Bt, *qv*; *b* 20 Jan 1949; *Educ* Rannoch Sch Perthshire, Commercial Pilot Trg; *m* 21 Oct 1983, Joan Kristina, da of Howard Smee, of Rio de Janeiro; 2 s (Edward Rorie b 22 July 1988, William Howard b 15 Aug 1990), 1 da (Olivia Joan b 16 March 1987); *Career* late commercial air pilot; industrialist Brazil Ultra Violet Application to Indust; *Recreations* sailing, skiing; *Style*— Ninian Stewart-Richardson, Esq; ✉ Rua Nice 132, Jardim Mediterraneo, Granja Vianna, Cotoa 06700, São Paulo, Brazil

STEWART-RICHARDSON, Sir Simon Alaisdair (Ian Neile); 17 Bt (NS 1630), of Pencaitland, Haddingtonshire; s of Sir Ian Rorie Hay Stewart-Richardson, 16 Bt (d 1969), by his 2 w, Audrey Meryl Odlum (who m 2, 1975, Patrick Allan Pearson Robertson, CMG); *b* 9 June 1947; *Educ* Trinity Coll Glenalmond; *Heir* bro, Ninian Rorie Stewart-Richardson, *qv*; *Recreations* music, theatre, sailing; *Style*— Sir Simon Stewart-Richardson, Bt; ✉ Lynedale, Longcross, nr Chertsey, Surrey KT16 0DP (☎ 01932 872329)

STEWART-SMITH, Christopher Dudley; CBE (1995); s of Ean Stewart-Smith (d 1964), and Edmee, *née* von Wallerstain und Marnegg; *b* 21 Jan 1941; *Educ* Winchester, King's Coll Cambridge, MIT; *m* 1964 (m dis 1989), Olivia Barstow; 1 s, 2 da; *Career* Courtaulds Ltd 1962–65, McKinsey & Co Inc 1966–71, Sterling Guarantee Tst/P&O Group 1971–86; chm: Butlers Warehousing and Distribution Ltd 1971–85, Earls Court & Olympia Ltd 1974–85, Sterling Guards Ltd 1974–85, Sutcliffe Catering Group Ltd 1975–85, P & O Cruises Ltd 1985–86, Swan Hellenic Cruises 1985–86, Conder Group plc 1987–92, Collett Dickenson Pearce International 1990–91, Healthcall Group plc 1991–, London and Henley plc 1995–; dir: Williamson Tea Holdings plc 1986–93, George Williamson & Co Ltd 1986–93, Life Sciences International plc 1987–, Erith plc 1992–95; vice pres Olympia Int Showjumping 1977–85; memb Royal Tournament Ctee 1976–85; chm: Br Exhibitions Promotion Cncl 1984–85, London C of C and Indust 1988–90, Producer Responsibility Group/Valpak 1994–95; pres Assoc of Br Chambers of Commerce 1992–94; hon memb: Royal Smithfield Club 1985–, Cncl Worldaware 1988–, Southern Advsy Bd of NatWest Bank plc 1988–92, Cncl of Mgmnt Acad of St Martins in the Fields 1988–93; currently Warden Worshipful Co of Grocers (Liveryman 1972, memb Ct of Assts 1992); FRSA 1984; *Clubs* Travellers'; *Style*— Christopher Stewart-Smith, Esq, CBE; ✉ 52 Westbourne Terrace, London W2 3UJ (☎ 0171 262 0514, fax 0171 723 5956)

STEWART-SMITH, John Ronald; s of Maj James Geoffrey Stewart-Smith (d 1938), of Falcon Hill Kinver, nr Stourbridge, Worcs, and Bertha Mabel Milner, *née* Roberts; *b* 23 Feb 1932; *Educ* Marlborough, Waitaki (NZ); *m* 22 Oct 1955, Catherine May, da of Walter Douglas Montgomery Clarke, JP (d 1948), of Bombay, India; 1 s (Geoffrey b 1958), 2 da (Joanna b 1960, Nicola b 1962); *Career* gp mktg dir Glover Gp Ltd 1976–79, projects dir and co sec Dashwood Finance Co Ltd 1983–, dir Kowloon Shipyard Co Ltd 1983–; CEng, MIMechE 1967, MIMarE 1969, MInst Export 1974, FIMarE 1989; *Recreations* bridge, tennis, skiing; *Style*— John Stewart-Smith, Esq; ✉ Dashwood Finance Co Ltd, Georgian House, 63 Coleman St, London EC2R 5BB (☎ 0171 588 3215, fax 0171 588 4818, telex 885624)

STEWART-WILSON, Lt-Col Sir Blair Aubyn; KCVO (1994, CVO 1989, LVO 1983); s of Aubyn Harold Raymond Wilson (d 1934), and Muriel Athelstan Hood Stewart-Stevens, *née* Stewart (d 1982); *b* 17 July 1929; *Educ* Eton, RMA Sandhurst; *m* 1962, (Helen) Mary, da of Maj Wilfred Michael Fox (d 1974), of Taunton; 3 da (Alice (Mrs Jonathan Young) b 1963, Sophia (m (Alastair) Bruce McIntosh, *qv*) b 1966, Belinda b 1970); *Career* cmmnd Scots Gds 1949; served UK, Germany, Far East and NZ, Lt-Col 1969; def mil and air attaché Vienna 1975–76; dep master of HM Household and equerry to HM The Queen 1976–94, extra equerry to HM The Queen 1994–, HM's tstee Royal Armouries Bd 1995–; Major Atholl Highlanders; *Recreations* shooting, fishing; *Clubs* Pratt's, White's; *Style*— Lt-Col Sir Blair Stewart-Wilson, KCVO; ✉ c/o Royal Bank of Scotland plc, 84 Atholl Road, Pitlochry PH16 5BJ

STEWART-WILSON, Col Ralph Stewart; MC (1944); s of Aubyn Harold Raymond Wilson (d 1934), of Aust, and Muriel Athelstane Hood Stewart-Stevens, *née* Stewart (d 1982); 11 Laird of Balnakeilly; ggs of Charles Wilson, pioneer grazier in NSW and Victoria; *b* 26 Jan 1923; *Educ* Eton; *m* 4 Oct 1949, Rosalind, da of Lt-Col H S O P Stedall, OBE, TD (d 1989), of Oxon; 1 s (Capt Aubyn Stewart-Wilson b 1963), 2 da (Maria (Mrs C Bremridge) b 1952, Lorna (Mrs L Heaton) b 1954); *Career* soldier and farmer; served Rifle Bde, 60 Rifles, Staffordshire Regt 1941–68; theatres of ops incl: Tunisia 1942–43, Italy and Austria 1944–45, Kenya 1956, Malaya 1956–57; appts incl: BM7 Armd Bde 1954–56, Jt Planning and Def Policy Staffs, 2 i/c 60 Rifles 1963–64, CO 1 Bn The Staffordshire Regt 1964–66; memb Queen's Body Guard for Scotland (Royal Co of Archers), Capt in Atholl Highlanders; former pres Atholl NFU for Scotland, pres The Stewart Soc 1989–92, memb Br Onithologists Union; *Recreations* ornithology, shooting; *Clubs* Royal and Ancient Golf (St Andrews); *Style*— Col Ralph S Stewart-Wilson of Balnakeilly, MC; ✉ Pitlochry, Perthshire PH16 5JJ (☎ 01796 472059)

STEWARTBY, Baron (Life Peer UK 1992), of Portmoak in the District of Perth and Kinross; Sir (Bernard Harold) Ian Halley Stewart; kt (1991), RD (1972), PC (1989); s of Prof Harold Charles Stewart, CBE, DL, and his 1 w Dorothy Irene, *née* Löwen (d 1969); *b* 10 Aug 1935; *Educ* Haileybury, Jesus Coll Cambridge (MA), LittD Cambridge 1978; *m* 8 Oct 1966, Hon Deborah Charlotte Stewart, JP, eldest da of 3 Baron Tweedsmuir (2 s of 1 Baron Tweedsmuir, otherwise known as John Buchan, the author); 1 s (Hon Henry Ernest Alexander Halley b 1972), 2 da (Hon Lydia Barbara Rose Anne Phoebe b 1969, Hon (Dorothy) Louisa Charlotte Amabel b 1970); *Career* served RNVR 1954–56, Lt-Cdr RNR; with Seccombe Marshall & Campion (bill brokers) 1959–60; chm: The Throgmorton Trust plc 1990–, Delian Lloyd's Investment Trust plc 1993–95; dep chm: Standard Chartered plc 1993–, Angerstein Underwriting Trust plc 1995–; dir: Brown Shipley & Co (merchant bankers) 1971–83, Diploma plc 1990–, Portman Building Society 1995–; dir Securities and Investments Bd 1993–; MP (C): Hitchin Feb 1974–83, N Herts 1983–92; oppn spokesman Banking Bill 1978–79, PPS to Rt Hon Sir Geoffrey Howe (as Chllr of the Exchequer) 1979–83, under sec MOD (Def Procurement) Jan-Oct 1983, econ sec Treasy with special responsibility for monetary policy and fin instns 1983–87, min of state for the Armed Forces 1987–88, min of state NI 1988–89; memb: Public Expenditure Ctee 1977–79, Public Accounts Ctee 1991–92; former jt sec Cons Parly Fin Ctee; chm Br Acad Ctee for Sylloge of Coins of Br Isles 1993– (memb 1967–), vice chm Westminster Ctee Protection of Children 1975–92, vice pres Herts Soc 1974–; memb Cncl Haileybury 1980–95 (life govr 1977); tstee Sir Halley Stewart Tst 1978–; hon fell Jesus Coll Cambridge 1994; FBA 1981, FRSE 1986, FSA, FSA Scot, KStJ 1992 (CStJ 1986, vice pres St John Ambulance Herts 1978–); *Books* The Scottish Coinage (1955, 1967), Coinage in Tenth-century England (with C E Blunt and C S S Lyon, 1989); *Recreations* history, real tennis; *Clubs* MCC, Hawks, RAC; *Style*— The Rt Hon Lord Stewartby, PC, RD, FRSE, FSA, FBA; ✉ c/o House of Lords, London SW1A OPW

STEYN, David Andrew; s of John Hofmeyr Steyn, *qv*, and Daphne Mary, *née* Nelson; *b* 13 Sept 1959; *Educ* Robert Gordon's Coll Aberdeen, Univ of Aberdeen (LLB); *m* 9 June 1990, Tanya Susan, da of Elisabeth and Lyon Roussel; 1 s (James Philip b 17 Oct 1992), 2 da (Elisabeth Daphne b 28 March 1991, Sophie Rebecca b 1 Oct 1996); *Career* md Quaestor Investment Management Ltd 1989–; *Recreations* theatre, politics; *Style*— David Steyn, Esq; ✉ 70 Lansdowne Road, London W11 2LR; Quaestor Investment Management Ltd, River Plate House, Finsbury Circus EC2M 7TT

STEYN, Baron (Life Peer UK 1995), of Swafield in the County of Norfolk; Sir Johan van Zyl Steyn; kt (1985), PC (1992); *b* 15 Aug 1932; *Educ* Jan van Riebeeck Sch Cape Town S Africa, Univ of Stellenbosch S Africa (BA, LLB), Univ Coll Oxford (Cape Province Rhodes scholar, MA); *m* Susan Leonore, *née* Lewis; 2 s and 2 da by prev m; *Career* barr S Africa 1958–73 (sr counsel), barr England 1973–, QC 1979, bencher Lincoln's Inn 1985, High Court judge Commercial Court 1985, Supreme Ct Rule Cmmn 1985–89, chm Race Rels Ctee of Bar 1987–88, presiding judge Northern Circuit 1989–91, Lord Justice of Appeal 1992–94; Lord of Appeal in Ordinary 1995–; chm: Departmental Advsy Ctee on Arbitration Law 1990–94, Lord Chllr's Advsy Ctee on Legal Educn and Conduct 1993–96; *Clubs* Garrick; *Style*— The Rt Hon Lord Steyn, PC; ✉ House of Lords, London SW1A 0PW

STEYN, John Hofmeyr; s of Johannes Stephanus Steyn (d 1937), and Blanka, *née* Hablutzel (d 1990); *b* 3 Oct 1929; *Educ* Univ of Cape Town (MB ChB), Univ of Aberdeen (PhD); *m* 6 April 1952, Daphne Mary, *née* Nelson; 5 s (John Peter b 1955, David Andrew Steyn, *qv* b 1959, Michael Paul b 1960, Richard Stephen b 1961, Gordon Philip b 1963), 2 da (Anne Scott b 1954, Catherine b 1958); *Career* conslt urologist Aberdeen Royal Infirmary 1967–93, sr lectr Univ of Aberdeen 1967–93, ret; hon treas Royal Coll of Surgns of Edinburgh 1993–, chm Albyn Hosp Aberdeen 1995–; FRCS 1957, FRCSEd 1973; CStJ; *Clubs* Royal Northern and Univ; *Style*— John Steyn, Esq; ✉ c/o The Royal

College of Surgeons of Edinburgh, Nicolson Street, Edinburgh EH8 9DW (☎ 0131 527 1600, fax 0131 557 6406)

STIBBON, Gen Sir John James; KCB (1988), OBE (1977); s of Jack Stibbon (d 1939), and Elizabeth Matilda, *née* Dixon (d 1968); *b* 5 Jan 1935; *Educ* Portsmouth Southern GS, RMA Sandhurst, RMCS (BSc Eng); *m* 10 Aug 1957, Jean Fergusson, da of John Robert Skeggs, of Newquay, Cornwall; 2 da (Jane b 1958, Emma b 1962); *Career* cmmnd RE 1954, Staff Capt War Office 1962–64, Adj 32 Armd Engr Regt 1964–66, instr RAC Centre 1967–68, OC 2 Armd Engr Sqdn 1968–70, DAA md QMG 12 Mech Bde 1971–72, GSO1 (DS) Staff Coll 1973–75, CO 28 Amphibious Engr Regt 1975–77, Asst Mil Sec MOD 1977–79, Cmd 20 Armd Bde 1979–81, Royal Coll of Def Studies 1982, Cmdt RMCS 1983–85, Asst Chief of Def Staff (operational requirements) MOD 1985–87, Master Gen of the Ordnance 1987–91, chief Royal Engr 1993–; Col Cmdt: RAPC 1985–92, RPC 1986–91, RE 1988–; chm: Royal Star and Garter Home 1991–, Gordon Sch Fndn 1992–; currently dir: Chelworth Ltd, Chemring Group plc, ITT Defence, DESC; hon vice pres FA 1987–93; Hon DSc CIT 1989; CEng, FICE 1989; *Recreations* watercolour painting, association football, palaeontology; *Style*— Gen Sir John Stibbon, KCB, OBE; ✉ Clifton House, Vicarage Lane, Shrivenham, Swindon, Wilts SN6 8DT

STIBBS, Prof (Douglas) Walter Noble; s of Edward John Stibbs (d 1922), of Sydney, Australia, and Jane, *née* Monro (d 1963); *b* 17 Feb 1919; *Educ* Sydney Boys' HS, Univ of Sydney (BSc, MSc), New Coll Oxford (DPhil); *m* 8 Jan 1949, Margaret Lilian Calvert, da of Rev John Calvert (d 1949), of Sydney, Australia; 2 da (Helen b 1956, Elizabeth b 1959); *Career* lectr Dept of Mathematics and Physics New England Univ Coll Armidale NSW 1942–45, sr sci offr Cwlth Solar Observatory Canberra 1945–51 (res asst 1940–42), Radcliffe travelling fell Radcliffe Observatory Pretoria SA and Univ Observatory Oxford 1951–54, princ sci offr UKAEA Aldermaston 1955–59; Univ of St Andrews: Napier prof of astronomy and dir of Univ Observatory 1959–89, sr prof Senatus Academicus 1987–89, emeritus prof 1990–; visiting prof of astrophysics Yale Univ Observatory 1966–67, Br Cncl visiting prof Univ of Utrecht 1968–69, prof Collège de France Paris 1975–76 (Médaille du Collège 1976); Univ Coll London: external expert (Appointments and Promotions) 1970–74 and 1976–80, external examiner (BSc Astronomy) 1977–81; visiting fell Mount Stromlo Observatory and memb Astrophysical Theory Centre Sch of Mathematics Australian Nat Univ Canberra 1990–; memb: Int Astronomical Union 1951– (pres Fin Ctee 1964–67, 1973–76 and 1976–79), Br Nat Ctee for Astronomy 1964–76, Advsy Ctee for Meteorology in Scotland 1960–69 (also 1972–75 and 1978–80), Science Res Cncl 1972–76, Royal Greenwich Observatory Ctee 1966–70 (memb Bd of Visitors 1963–65), Royal Observatory Edinburgh Ctee 1966–76 (chm 1970–76), Astronomy Space and Radio Bd 1970–76, SA Astronomical Advsy Ctee 1972–76; chm: Astronomy Policy and Grants Ctee 1972–74, N Hemisphere Observatory Planning Ctee 1970–74; FRAS 1942 (memb Cncl 1964–67 and 1970–73, vice pres 1972–73), FRSE 1960 (memb Cncl 1970–72); *Books* The Outer Layers of a Star (with Sir Richard Woolley, 1953); *Recreations* music (clavichord and organ), ornithology, photography, golf, long-distance running (17 marathons during 1983–87 incl: Athens, Berlin, Boston, Edinburgh 3h 59m 23s, Honolulu, London, Paris; 13 half marathons, gold medallist Australian Veterans Games 1991); *Clubs* Royal and Ancient (St Andrews); *Style*— Prof D W N Stibbs, FRSE; ✉ Mount Stromlo Observatory, Australian National University, Weston Creek Post Office, Canberra ACT 2611, Australia

STIBY, Robert Andrew; JP (1980); s of Maj Arthur Robert Charles Stiby, TD, JP (d 1987), of Reigate, and Peggy, *née* Hartley (d 1973); *b* 25 May 1937; *Educ* Marlborough, London Coll of Printing (Dip in Printing Mgmnt); *m* 1, 1962 (m dis 1976); 1 s (Jonathan b 10 May 1963), 1 da (Emma b 17 Sept 1965); m 2, 1980 (m dis 1984); m 3, 30 May 1986, Julia, da of Sidney Fuller, of Canterbury; 1 da (Renata b 5 Nov 1971); *Career* Nat Serv 1955–57; md and chm Croydon Advertiser Group of Newspapers 1969–83, dir Portsmouth & Sunderland Newspapers Ltd 1983–87, chm and chief exec Radio Investments Ltd 1972–, chm The Local Radio Company Ltd 1996–; dir: Capital Radio 1972–, Minster Sound Radio plc 1991–, Island FM 1992–, Wessex FM 1993–, Orchard Media Ltd 1994–, Talk Radio UK 1994–; md Cable Guide Ltd 1987–90; chm of govrs London Coll of Printing 1979, dir Fairfield Halls 1993–; pres Newspaper Soc 1983–84; pres Croydon Boys' Club 1988–93; *Recreations* hill walking, painting; *Clubs* Reform, MCC, North Weald Gp; *Style*— Robert Stiby, Esq, JP; ✉ Tower House, Outwood Lane, Bletchingley, Surrey RH1 4LR (☎ 01883 743979); Radio Investments Ltd, Croudace House, 97 Godstone Road, Caterham, Surrey CR3 6XQ (☎ 01883 341517, fax 01883 341729)

STICKNEY, (Robert) Paul; s of Charles Stickney (d 1966), and Kathleen Mary, *née* Ford (d 1987); *b* 6 Sept 1944; *Educ* Yeovil Sch, Portsmouth Poly Sch of Architecture (Dip Arch); *m* 13 Sept 1969, Dorothy Dawn, da of Alfred Edward Shaw (d 1971); 1 s (Richard b 1972), 1 da (Jenny b 1976); *Career* architect; Portsmouth City Architects Dept 1968–71, sr architect Bailey Piper Stevens Partnership 1971–73; chm Leslie Jones Architects (joined 1973, assoc 1974, ptnr 1977); memb Bd Br Cncl of Shopping Centres; memb RIBA 1970; *Recreations* literature and visual arts; *Style*— Paul Stickney, Esq; ✉ Leslie Jones, 35 Portland Place, London W1N 3AG (☎ 0171 255 1150, fax 0171 580 4891); Little Court, 25 Ashley Drive, Walton on Thames, Surrey KT12 1JL

STIGWOOD, Robert Colin; s of late Gordon Stigwood, of Beaumont, Adelaide, and Gwendolyn Burrows; *b* 1934; *Educ* Sacred Heart Coll; *Career* theatre, film, television and record prodr; came to England 1956, subsequently held a variety of jobs incl mangr halfway house for delinquents in Cambridge, opened talent agency in London 1962, first independent record prodr in England with release of single Johnny Remember Me (liquidated firm 1965), business mangr Graham Bond Orgn, co-md NEMS Enterprises 1967, fndr Robert Stigwood Orgn 1967, fndr RSO Records 1973, dir Polygram 1976; Int Prodr of Year (ABC Interstate Theatres Inc) 1976; *Stage Musicals* in England and US incl: Oh! Calcutta, The Dirtiest Show in Town, Pippin, Jesus Christ Superstar, Evita, Sweeney Todd, Grease; *Television* in England and US incl: The Entertainer, The Prime of Miss Jean Brodie (series); *Films* incl: Jesus Christ Superstar, Bugsy Malone, Tommy, Saturday Night Fever, Grease, Sgt Pepper's Lonely Hearts Club Band, Moment by Moment, The Fan, Times Square, Grease 2, Staying Alive, Gallipoli; *Recreations* sailing, tennis; *Style*— Robert Stigwood, Esq; ✉ Robert Stigwood Organisation Ltd, Barton Manor, East Cowes, Isle of Wight PO32 6LB (☎ 01983 280676, fax 01983 293923)

STILES, George; s of John Leslie Stiles (d 1967), of Haywards Heath, Sussex, and Joy Irene, *née* Baker (d 1985); *b* 9 Aug 1961; *Educ* Greshams Sch Norfolk, Univ of Exeter (BA); *partner* Hugh Vanstone, *qv*; *Career* composer; memb: BASCA, Musicians Union, Equity, PRS, Mercury Workshop; numerous TV and Radio appearances as Stiles and Drewe; *Theatre* credits with lyricist Anthony Drewe incl: Tutankhamun (Northcott Theatre & Imagination Building London) 1984, Just So (also Cameron Mackintosh prodn Watermill Theatre 1989, Tricycle Theatre 1990) 1985, The Ugly Duckling or The Aesthetically-Challenged Farmyard Fowl (Watermill Theatre 1993, Bay Street Theatre Long Island 1995), Stiles and Drewe - Warts and All (revue with Jenna Russell, Aled Jones, Alison Jiear) 1995; song contribs incl: The Challenge (Shaw Theatre) 1992, The Mercury Workshop Musical Revue (Jermyn Street) 1994, The Shakespeare Revue (RSC, Barbican, Vaudeville, nat tour); credits with lyricist Paul Leigh incl: Moll Flanders (Lyric Hammersmith 1993, Theatre Royal York 1995 and 1996), Tom Jones (Theatre Royal York) 1996, The Three Musketeers (scheduled 1998, Plymouth Theatre Royal and Chichester Festival); other credits incl: musical dir and composer for Barry Humphries' Look at me when I'm Talking to You, composer for Habeas Corpus (Donmar Warehouse); currently writing new musical version of Peter Pan; *Recordings* Moll Flanders, The Shakespeare Revue, The Challenge, We Can Be Kind, Musical of the Year, Hey Mr Producer; *Awards* Vivian Ellis Prize (for Just So), TMA Regional Theatre Award for Best Musical (for Moll Flanders) 1995, The Orchestra's Prize and Best Song (for Peter Pan), 2nd Prize Musical of the Year (for The Three Musketeers) 1996; nominated London Drama Critics Award for Best Musical and Most Promising Newcomers (for Just So) 1990; *Publications* Moll Flanders (Samuel French, 1995); *Style*— George Stiles, Esq; ✉ c/o M L R, 200 Fulham Road, London SW10 9PN (☎ 0171 351 5442, fax 0171 351 4560)

STILL, Brig Nigel Maxwell; CBE (1983); s of Brig George Bingham Still, OBE (d 1965), of London, and Violet Winifred, *née* Maxwell (d 1980); *b* 27 March 1936; *Educ* Marlborough, Clare Coll Cambridge (BA); *m* 3 April 1965, Mary Richenda, da of Maj P J D Macfarlane, of Moulsford, Oxon; 1 s (George b 1973), 1 da (Caroline b 1967); *Career* cmmnd 17/21 Lancers 1958 (Adj 1960), instr RMA Sandhurst 1962, Sqdn Ldr 17/21 Lancers 1965, Army Staff Course 1966, GSO 2 (Armd) HQ Army Strategic Cmd 1968, DAMS Mil Sec's Dept MOD 1972, CO 17/21 Lancers 1975, GSO 1 (Directing Staff) Aust Army Staff Coll 1977, Col GS (OR) 17 MOD 1979, Coll Cdr RMA Sandhurst 1982, Cdr 43 Inf Bde 1984, ret 1987; dir of admin Lyddon (Stockbrokers) Cardiff 1987–88; *Recreations* golf, cricket, rugby football, music; *Clubs* I Zingari (cricket); *Style*— Brig Nigel M Still, CBE; ✉ c/o Midland Bank plc, Wellington Square, Minehead, Somerset

STILL, Dr Ronald McKinnon; s of Ronald Still (d 1980), of Helensburgh, and Nan, *née* McKinnon; *b* 20 March 1932; *Educ* Hermitage Sch Helensburgh, Univ of Glasgow (MB ChB) 1956; *m* 23 Nov 1963 (m dis 1987), Patricia Ann, da of Maj K J Jones (d 1989); 1 s (Jamie b 3 May 1972), 2 da (Sarah b 30 Nov 1966, Shona b 12 June 1969); *Career* short serv cmmn RAMC, seconded as Capt Malaya Mil Forces 1957–60; house offr: Glasgow Royal Infirmary 1956–57, Oakbank Hosp Glasgow 1961, Queen Mother's Hosp 1962, Western Infirmary 1963; registrar Stobhill and Queen Mother's Hosps 1963–66, sr registrar Glasgow Teaching Hosp 1966–67, conslt obstetrician and gynaecologist Stobhill Hosp Glasgow 1967–96 (house offr 1961); currently conslt gynaecologist: Glasgow Nuffield Hosp, Ross Hall Hosp, HCI Clydebank; hon clinical sr lectr Univ of Glasgow; memb Osprey Gynaecological Soc; MRCOG 1963, FRCOG 1973; *Recreations* golf, music; *Clubs* Royal and Ancient (St Andrews), Glasgow Golf, Milngavie Golf; *Style*— Dr Ronald Still; ✉ 9/5 Whistlefield Court, 2 Canniesburn Road, Bearsden, Glasgow G61 1PX (☎ 0141 942 3097); Stobhill General Hospital, Glasgow (☎ 0141 201 3000); Royal Maternity Hospital, Glasgow (☎ 0141 221 3400)

STILLWELL, Michael Ian; s of Alan Bertram Stillwell (d 1985), of London, and Dorothy Elizabeth, *née* Peel; *b* 22 Nov 1938; *Educ* Rutlish Sch Merton, INSEAD Fontainebleau; *m* 1962, Susan, da of William Brown; 2 s (Andrew Michael b 1967 d 1989, Nicholas John b 1968); *Career* CA; articled Clerk Myrus Smith & Walker London 1957–62; Cooper Brothers & Co (now Coopers and Lybrand): Singapore 1963–65, res mangr Ipoh Malaysia 1965–67, ptnr Kuala Lumpur Malaysia 1968–69, ptnr London 1972, seconded to Italian firm Milan 1972–74, ptnr UK 1974–94, staff ptnr London 1982–84, dir Human Resources 1985–87, dir Int Affairs 1988–94; hon treas: RIIA 1991–94, The Br Sch at Rome 1996–; memb Mgmnt Ctee Wiltshire Friendly Soc Ltd 1995–, tstee International Sacred Literature Trust 1995–; FCA 1972, MInstD, FRSA 1995; *Books* European Financial Reporting - Italy (1976); *Recreations* mountain walking, music, golf; *Clubs* Orchardleigh Golf; *Style*— Michael Stillwell, Esq; ✉ Snarlton Farm, Wingfield, Wilts BA14 9LH (☎ and fax 01225 762373)

STIMPSON, Paul Michael; s of Michael Frederick Stimpson, of Epsom Downs, Surrey, and Jean Lilian Winifred, *née* Allen; *b* 25 July 1959; *Educ* Glyn GS, W London Inst of Higher Educn (BA); *m* 26 May 1984, Patricia Fraser, da of Harry Garnet St Hill; 3 s (Michael b 29 Sept 1985, Philip (twin) b 29 Sept 1985, Richard b 10 April 1989), 1 da (Tamara b 22 May 1995); *Career* basketball player; clubs: Crystal Palace 1976–87 (Nat League debut 1977), Kingston 1987–88 and 1989–90, Solent 1988–89; 112 caps England 1979–88 (capt 1982–87), memb GB Olympic team 1980 and 1984, memb GB team World Student Games 1981; honours: Nat Schs under 19 winner 1977, Jr Nat Cup winner 1977 and 1978, 5 Nat League titles, 7 Nat Championships, 4 Nat Cups, Gold medal Cwlth Games NZ 1982; most capped player in Britain (first player to reach 100 caps), English Player of the Year 1983, Minet Olympic Award for Sporting Excellence 1988; memb English Basketball Fellowship; competitor Superstars (BBC TV) 1982; teacher 1981–84, mktg mangr Zodiac Toys 1987–90, vice pres basketball ISL Marketing AG Lucerne Switzerland 1992– (basketball mangr 1990–92); *Books* Basketball: the Skills of the Games (1986, 1996); *Recreations* cricket, skiing, family; *Style*— Paul Stimpson, Esq; ✉ Kreuzbuchstrasse 30, CH-6045 Meggen, Switzerland (☎ 00 41 41 3771151); ISL Marketing AG, Zentralstrasse 1, PO Box 3339, CH-6002 Lucerne, Switzerland (☎ 00 41 41 249595, fax 00 41 41 249797)

STIMSON, Theresa Josephine (Tess); da of Michael Stimson, and Jane, *née* Bower; *b* 17 July 1966; *Educ* Notre Dame Convent Sch Lingfield, St Hilda's Coll Oxford; *m* 17 July 1993, Brent Sadler, *qv*; 1 s (Henry Louis Brent Stimson Sadler b 7 Sept 1994); *Career* writer and freelance journalist; prodr ITN 1987–91; assignments incl: King's Cross fire 1987, Purley rail disaster 1988, European elections 1989, Thatcher resignation 1990, Gulf war 1990–91, McCarthy and Mann Beirut hostage releases 1991, N Ireland 1987–91; author and freelance journalist 1991–; assignments incl: Waite release 1991, S Africa 1992–94, Somalia famine 1992–93, Iraq 1992–93; *Books* Yours Till the End (Sunnie and Jackie Mann biog, 1992); *Novels* Hard News (1993), Soft Focus (1995), Pole Position (1996); *Recreations* rock-climbing, tennis, water and snow skiing; *Clubs* Academy; *Style*— Tess Stimson Sadler; ✉ c/o Mandarin Fiction, Michelin House, 81 Fulham Road, London SW3 (☎ 0171 581 9393)

STING, *né* Gordon Matthew Sumner; *b* 2 Oct 1951; *m* 20 Aug 1992, Trudie Styler; 2 s, 3 da; *Career* musician and actor; teacher St Paul's Primary Sch Cramlington 1971–74, memb The Police 1977–86; Police albums: Outlandos D'Amour (1978, reached UK no 6), Regatta De Blanc (1979, UK no 1), Zenyatta Mondatta (1980, UK no 1), Ghost In The Machine (1982, UK no 1), Synchronicity (1983, UK no 1), Every Breath You Take - The Singles (compilation, 1986, UK no 1); solo albums: Dream Of the Blue Turtles (1985, UK no 1), Bring On The Night (live, 1986), Nothing Like The Sun (1987, UK no 1), The Soul Cages (1991, UK no 1), Ten Summoner's Tales (1993), Mercury Falling (1996); films: Quadrophenia 1979, Radio On 1980, Brimstone And Treacle 1982, Dune 1984, The Bride 1985, Plenty 1985, Bring On The Night (concert) 1985, Stormy Monday 1988, Julia 1988, The Grotesque 1995, Mercury Falling 1996; winner of Ivor Novello, BRIT and Grammy Awards (4 in 1994); co-fndr Rainforest Fndn; Hon DMus Univ of Northumbria at Newcastle; *Style*— Sting; ✉ c/o Firstars/Talent Bank Management, Bugle House, 21A Noel Street, London W1V 3PD (☎ 0171 439 2282, fax 0171 439 7649)

STINTON, Dr Darrol; MBE (1964); s of Ernest Thomas Stinton (d 1980), and Vera, *née* Hall (d 1988); *b* 9 Dec 1927; *Educ* Beverley GS; *m* 1, March 1952, Barbara, *née* Chapman; 1 s (Julian b 1957), 1 da (Caroline b 1959); m 2, June 1971, Christine Diane, da of Frederick Miller Roehampton (d 1994); 1 s (Matthew b 1973); m 3, July 1976, Ann Jacqueline Frances, da of Robert Spence Adair (d 1978), 1 step s (Terence Gent Eggett b 1971), 1 da (Penelope b 1977); *Career* Blackburn and De Havilland aircraft cos; cmmnd RAF 1953–69, Empire Test Pilot Sch 1959, qualified test pilot Air Registration Bd 1969–, Air Worthiness Div of CAA until 1989, vice pres Royal Aeronautical Soc 1989–92; md Darrol Stinton Ltd Int Aero-Marine Conslts 1982–; sr visiting fell Loughborough Univ of Technol 1990–95; PhD, CEng, FRAeS, FRINA, MIMechE; *Books* textbooks and papers on aircraft design, flight testing and sailing craft design; *Recreations* subaqua, sailing, writing; *Clubs* RAF; *Style*— Dr Darrol Stinton, MBE; ✉ 40 Castle St, Farnham, Surrey GU9 7JB (☎ 01252 713120)

STIRLING, Sir Angus Duncan Aeneas; kt (1994); s of Duncan Alexander Stirling (d 1990), and Lady Marjorie Stirling; *b* 1933; *Educ* Eton, Trinity Coll Cambridge; *m* 1959, Armyne Morar Helen, er da of Mr and Hon Mrs William Schofield, of Masham, Yorks; 1 s, 2 da; *Career* former dep sec Gen Arts Cncl of GB, DG The Nat Trust 1983–95 (dep dir 1979–83), chm Royal Opera House Covent Garden 1991–96 (dir 1979–96), sr policy advsr Nat Heritage Meml Fund 1996, chm Greenwich Fndn for the Royal Naval Coll 1996–; chm: Friends of Covent Garden 1981–91, Policy Ctee CPRE 1996–; memb: Bd of Govrs Byam Shaw Sch of Art 1965–90, Advsy Cncl LSO 1979–, Crafts Cncl 1980–85, Theatres' Tst 1983–90, Heritage of London Tst 1983–95, Heritage Educn Tst 1985–96, Samuel Courtauld Tst 1990–; Royal Ballet: memb Bd 1979–96 (dep chm 1989–91), govr 1988–96; tstee The World Monuments Fund in Britain 1996–; memb Ct of Assts Worshipful Co of Fishmongers 1991; Hon DLit Univ of Leicester 1995; *Clubs* Garrick, Brooks, Grillions; *Style*— Sir Angus Stirling; ✉ 25 Ladbroke Grove, London W11 3AY

STIRLING, Prof Charles James Matthew; s of Brig Alexander Dickson Stirling, DSO (d 1961), and Isobel Millicent, *née* Matthew (d 1984); *b* 8 Dec 1930; *Educ* Edinburgh Acad, Univ of St Andrews (BSc), King's Coll London (PhD, DSc); *m* 1 Sept 1956, Eileen Gibson, da of William Leslie Powell (d 1974), of Bournemouth; 3 da (Catherine (decd), Julia, Alexandra); *Career* res fell: Civil Serv Porton 1955–57, ICI Edinburgh 1957–59; lectr in chemistry Queen's Univ Belfast 1959–65, reader in organic chemistry King's Coll London 1965–69, head of dept UCNW 1981–90 (prof of organic chemistry 1969–90), prof of organic chemistry Univ of Sheffield 1990– (head Dept of Chemistry 1991–94); RSC: pres Perkin Div Royal Soc of Chemistry 1989–91, chm Confs Ctee; pres Section B (Chemistry) Br Assoc for the Advancement of Sci 1990; chm: Menai Bridge Cncl of Churches 1982–83, Bangor Monteverdi Singers 1974–89; gave Christmas lectures for Royal Instn (BBC (TV) 2) 1992; memb Organic Div Int Union of Pure and Applied Chemistry 1991–95; Hon DSc Univ of St Andrews 1994; public orator Univ of Sheffield 1995–; FRS 1986, FRSC 1967; *Books* Radicals in Organic Chemistry (1965), Organosulphur Chemistry (ed, 1975), Chemistry of the Sulphonium Group (ed, 1982), Chemistry of Sulphones and Sulphoxides (ed with S Patai and Z Rappoport, 1988); *Recreations* choral music, collection of chiral objects, furniture restoration; *Style*— Prof Charles Stirling, FRS; ✉ Department of Chemistry, University of Sheffield, Sheffield S3 7HF

STIRLING, Derek William; s of William James Stirling (d 1966), of Salisbury, Wilts, and Mary Violet, *née* Phillips (d 1974); *b* 15 Dec 1931; *Educ* Beckenham GS, Poly of Central London, Open Univ (BA); *m* 1958, Margaret Ann, da of Frederick Thomas Davis; 2 s (Christopher Derek b 1960, Julien James b 1962), 1 da (Katrina Jane b 1959); *Career* RAF signals Hong Kong 1950–52, applied photographer MoD 1956–58, head Dept of Photography Film and Television Salisbury Coll of Art and Design 1958–92, princ Salisbury Coll of Art and Design 1991–92; BIPP: chm Educn and Trg Ctee 1984–90 (memb 1982–), memb Cncl 1985–94 and 1996–, vice pres 1989, pres 1990–91, memb Editorial Cmmn 1992–, memb Fin and Resources Cmmn 1992–, chm BPA Educn Ctee 1991–; external verifier City & Guilds NVQs 1994–; chm of Judges Ilford Photographic Awards 1991, judge Br Telecom Press Awards 1990; memb: Cncl Br Photographic Assoc 1989, Vocational Standards Cncl 1987, Br Sound and Television Soc until 1994, Royal Photographic Soc until 1994; FBIPP 1989 (ABIPP 1962), memb PPPITO 1992 (chm Educn Ctee 1993–); *Recreations* tennis, badminton, golf, travel, music; *Style*— Derek Stirling, Esq; ✉ Braewood, The Croft, Bishopstone, Salisbury, Wiltshire SP5 4DF (☎ 01722 780470, e-mail 100411.327@Compuserve.com)

STIRLING, Sheriff Hamish; s of James Stirling, FRSE (d 1986), of Aberdeen, and Anne Wood, *née* Black; *b* 9 July 1938; *Educ* Liverpool Coll, Robert Gordons Coll Aberdeen (MA, LLB); *m* 15 Aug 1963, Margaret Davidson, da of late Harry Bottomley; 2 s (Grigor b 28 Aug 1964, Euan b 26 Oct 1966), 1 da (Rhona Elizabeth b 20 Aug 1970); *Career* slr Elgin 1961–63; procurator fiscal depute: Dundee 1963–70, Jedburgh 1970–74, Glasgow 1974–75; admitted Faculty of Advocates 1976; temp sheriff 1982–92, sheriff S Strathclyde Dumfries & Galloway and Hamilton 1992–; *Recreations* golf, foreign travel, music; *Clubs* Deer Park Golf; *Style*— Sheriff Hamish Stirling; ✉ Sheriff's Chambers, Hamilton Sheriff Court, 4 Beckford Street, Hamilton ML3 6AA (☎ 01698 282957)

STIRLING, Prof (Arthur) Paul; s of A O Stirling (d 1957), and Lily Jane Stirling; *b* 13 Oct 1920; *Educ* Whitgift Sch Croydon, Exeter Coll Oxford (MA, DPhil); *m* 3 April 1948, Margaret L; 2 s (Nicholas b 1952, Simon b 1960), 2 da (Elisabeth Webster b 1956, Catharine b 1958); *Career* RN 1941–45, Lt RNVR; lectr in anthropology LSE 1952–65; visiting prof of sociology Middle East Tech Univ of Ankara 1983–86, prof emeritus and res conslt Univ of Kent at Canterbury 1984 (prof of sociology and social anthropology 1965–84), hon res fell SOAS London; visitor HM Borstal Dover, jt fndr Canterbury Assoc for Mental Health Health; founding chm: Chaucer Housing Assoc, Gp for Anthropology in Policy and Practice; memb Assoc of Social Anthropologists, FRAI; *Books* Turkish Village (1965), Culture and Economy: Changes in Turkish Villages (1993); *Style*— Prof Paul Stirling; ✉ Eliot College, University of Kent at Canterbury, Canterbury CT2 7NS (☎ 01227 764000); Honorary Research Fellow, School of Oriental and Afrcan Studies, University of London, Russell Square, London WC1H 0XG

STIRLING-HAMILTON, Sir Malcolm William Bruce; 14 Bt (NS 1673), of Preston, Haddingtonshire; o s of Sir Bruce Stirling-Hamilton, 13 Bt (d 1989), and Stephanie (who m 2, 1990, Anthony Cole Tinsley), eldest da of Dr William Campbell, of Alloway, Ayrshire; *b* 6 Aug 1979; *Educ* Stowe; *Heir* kinsman, Rev Andrew Robert Hamilton b 5 Sept 1937; *Style*— Sir Malcolm Stirling-Hamilton, Bt; ✉ Narborough Hall, Narborough, King's Lynn, Norfolk PE32 1TE

STIRLING OF FAIRBURN, Capt Roderick William Kenneth; TD (1965), JP (Ross and Cromarty 1975); s of Maj Sir John Stirling, of Fairburn, KT, MBE (d 1975), of Fairburn, Muir of Ord, Ross-shire, and Marjorie Kythé, *née* Mackenzie of Gairloch; *b* 17 June 1932; *Educ* Harrow, Univ of Aberdeen Sch of Agric; *m* 26 Oct 1963, Penelope Jane, da of Lt-Col Charles Henry Wright, TD, DL (d 1978), of Shadforth, Co Durham, formerly of Tuthill, Haswell, Co Durham; 4 da (Charlotte (Mrs Hingston) b 1965, Katharine (Mrs Sanders) b 1967, Jane b 1968, Fiona b 1971); *Career* Nat Serv Scots Gds 1950–52, cmmnd 1951, Seaforth Highlanders and Queen's Own Highlanders TA 1953–69, ret Capt; dir: Scottish Salmon and White Fish Co Ltd 1972–91 (chm 1980–91), Moray Firth Salmon Fishing Co Ltd 1973–91, Highland Opportunity 1992–96; vice chm Red Deer Cmmn 1975–89 (memb 1964–89); chm: Highland Ctee Scottish Landowners Fedn 1974–79, Scatwell and Strathconon Community Cncl 1975–88, Scottish Accident Prevention Cncl 1984– (vice pres 1991 and 1992, chm Water and Leisure Safety Cmmn 1993–94); pres Highlands, Islands and Moray Branch Scots Guards Assoc 1995–; gen cmmr for income tax 1975–91; memb Ross and Cromarty Dist Cncl 1984–96; Lord-Lieutenant Ross and Cromarty and Skye and Lochalsh 1988 (DL Ross and Cromarty 1971); *Recreations* field sports, gardening, curling; *Clubs* New (Edinburgh); *Style*— Capt Roderick Stirling of Fairburn, TD, JP; ✉ Arcan, Muir of Ord, Ross and Cromarty IV6 7UL (☎ 01997 433207); Fairburn Estate Office, Urray, Muir of Ord, Ross and Cromarty IV6 7UT (☎ 01997 433273, fax 01997 433274)

STIRLING OF GARDEN, Col James; CBE, TD; s of Col Archibald Stirling of Garden, OBE, DL, JP (d 1947); *b* 8 Sept 1930; *Educ* Rugby, Trinity Coll Cambridge; *m* 1958, Fiona Janetta Sophia, da of Lt-Col D A C Wood Parker, OBE, TD, DL (d 1967), of Keithick, Coupar Angus, Perthshire; 2 s, 2 da; *Career* cmmnd 1 Bn Argyll and Sutherland Highlanders 1950, served Korea (wounded), transferred 7 Bn (TA) 1951, Lt-Col cmdg 1966, CO 3 Bn 1968; hon Col 3/51 Highland Vols TA; Scottish dir Woolwich Building Soc, ptnr Kenneth Ryden and Ptnrs (chartered surveyors), dir Scottish Widows Soc 1976; pres Highland TAVRA 1991– (chm 1982–87); DL Stirlingshire 1969, HM Lord Lt of Central Region (Dists of Stirling and Falkirk) 1983–; FRICS; Prior of the Order of St John of Jerusalem in Scotland 1995, KStJ; *Clubs* New (Edinburgh); *Style*— Col James Stirling of Garden, CBE, TD; ✉ Garden, Buchlyvie, Stirling (☎ 01360 85212)

STIRRAT, Prof Gordon Macmillan; s of Alexander Stirrat (d 1989), and Mary Caroline, *née* Hutchinson (d 1987); *b* 12 March 1940; *Educ* Hutchesons GS Glasgow, Univ of Glasgow (MB ChB), Univ of Oxford (MA), Univ of London (MD); *m* 2 April 1965, Janeen Mary, da of Hugh Brown (d 1983); 3 da (Lorna Margaret b 1966, Carolyn Jane b 1967, Lindsay Ann b 1970); *Career* lectr Univ of London 1970–75, clinical reader Univ of Oxford 1975–82; Univ of Bristol: prof of obstetrics and gynaecology 1982–, dean Faculty of Med 1990–93, pro-vice-chllr 1993–97; memb: South West RHA 1984–90, Bristol & Weston Health Authy 1990–91, Bristol & Dist Health Authy 1991–96, GMC 1993–97, Christian Med Fellowship; FRCOG 1981; *Books* Obstetrics Pocket Consultant - Aids to Obstetrics & Gynaecology; *Recreations* fly fishing, walking, writing, photography; *Clubs* United Oxford and Cambridge Univ; *Style*— Prof Gordon Stirrat; ✉ Department of Hospital Medicine, Division of Obstetrics and Gynaecology, University of Bristol, Bristol BS2 8EG (☎ 0117 928 5291, fax 0117 927 2792, e-mail g.m.stirrat@bristol.ac.uk)

STIRRUPS, David Robert; s of Robert James Stirrups (d 1987), and Eunice Nora, *née* Palmer; *b* 23 June 1948; *Educ* Gillingham GS, Univ of Sheffield (BDS), Open Univ (BA), Sheffield Poly (MSc); *m* 22 July 1971, Anne Elizabeth; 1 s (Robert b 1980), 2 da (Kathleen b 1975, Rosemary b 1978, d 1978); *Career* conslt orthodontist Gtr Glasgow Health Bd 1980–93, currently prof of orthodontics Univ of Dundee; chm Scot Ctee for Hosp Dental Servs 1988–93; memb: Central Ctee for Hosp Dental Servs 1988–93, Dental Cncl RCPS Glas 1988–92; FDSRCS 1974, RCPSGlas; *Recreations* orienteering; *Clubs* Perth; *Style*— Prof David Stirrups; ✉ Dundee Dental Hospital, Park Place, Dundee DD1 4HN (☎ 01382 635961, e-mail d.r.stirrups@dundee.ac.uk)

STIRTON, Prof Charles Howard; s of late Dr Charles Aubrey Stirton, of Natal, S Africa, and Elizabeth Maud, *née* Inglesby; *b* 25 Nov 1946; *Educ* St Charles's Coll Pietermaritzburg, Univ of Natal (MSc), Univ of Cape Town (PhD, S African Assoc of Botanists Jr Medal), Naval Gymnasium S Africa (Dip in Engine Room Mechanics); *m* Jana Žantovská, da of late Žantovsky; 1 da (Elishka Kara Marie b 9 March 1988); *Career* PRO Natal branch Wildlife Soc of S Africa Jan-May 1966, lawyers' clerk Paola & Wright June-Oct 1966, mangr Pobana Trading Store Nov 1966–Feb 1967, chief professional offr Botanical Research Inst S Africa 1979–82 (sr professional offr 1975–78, S African liaison botanist London 1979–82), B A Krukoff botanist for neotropical legume research Royal Botanic Gardens Kew 1982–87, assoc prof Dept of Botany Univ of Natal 1988–90, freelance journalist 1990; Royal Botanic Gardens Kew: research co-ordinator for economic botany progs 1990–92, dep dir and dep dir of science 1992–95, dep dir and dir of sci and horticulture 1995–96; dir National Botanic Garden of Wales 1996–; sr res fell Univ of Birmingham 1992–96, hon prof Univ of Reading 1995–; chair Plants Sub-ctee Species Survival Cmmn IUCN 1994–96; fndr pres and hon life memb Natal Evolutionary Biology Soc; tstee: ILDIS, Bentham-Moxon Tst, Pat Brenan Meml Fund; CIBiol, MIBiol, MIMgt, MInstD, FLS; *Books* Plant Invaders - Beautiful But Dangerous, Advances in Legume Biology, Advances in Legume Systematics No 3, Problem Plants of Southern Africa, Weeds in a Changing World; author of over 90 scientific papers in learned jls; *Recreations* gardening, reading, collecting postal history, pottery and postcards, cinema, conservation; *Style*— Prof Charles Stirton; ✉ National Botanic Garden of Wales, Neuadd Deg, Middleton Hall, Llanarthne, Carmarthenshire SA32 8HW (☎ and fax 01558 668768)

STISTED, Brig (Joseph) Nigel; OBE (1978); o s of Joseph Laurence Heathcote Stisted (d 1975), of Fordlands, Catsfield, Sussex, and Katherine Dorothea, *née* Sayer (d 1977); *b* 23 July 1931; *Educ* Winchester, RMA Sandhurst; *m* 11 Aug 1962, Judith Ann, o da of Col Duncan Arthur Davidson Eykyn, DSO, DL (d 1986), of Penicuik, Midlothian; 2 s (Charles b 21 July 1963, William b 12 April 1965); *Career* joined Army 1950, commissioned The Royal Scots 1952; served 1 Bn: Berlin, Korea, Egypt, Cyprus, Scotland, Suez Ops; Adj Depot The Royal Scots 1957–58; ADC to GOC Br Sector Berlin 1959–60, Instr RMA Sandhurst 1960–61, Staff Coll Camberley 1962, BM 155 (Lowland) Bde 1963–65, cmd 1 Bn The Royal Scots 1965–67, Jt Servs Staff Coll 1967, asst mil advsr Br High Cmmn Ottawa 1968–70, 2 i/c 1 Bn The Royal Scots 1970–71, CO 1 Bn 1971–73 (despatches 1972), AAG Scot Div Edinburgh 1974–76, cmd New Coll (SMC) RMA Sandhurst 1976–79, Brig Inf HQ UKLF 1980, cmd 52 Lowland Bde 1980–83, ret on med grounds 1983; elected memb Queen's Body Gd for Scotland (Royal Co of Archers) 1966 (non-active list 1992); *Clubs* Royal Scots (Edinburgh); *Style*— Brig Nigel Stisted, OBE; ✉ c/o The Bank of Scotland, New Town Branch, 103 George Street, Edinburgh EH2 3HR

STITT, Iain Paul Anderson; s of John Anderson Stitt, and Elise Marie, *née* Dias; *b* 21 Dec 1939; *Educ* Ampleforth, RNC Dartmouth; *m* 1 July 1961, Barbara Mary, da of Richard Bertram George, of Carlisle (d 1986); 2 s (Jonathan b 1964, Paul b 1965), 3 da (Philippa b 1962, Kristina b 1966, Francesca b 1968); *Career* served Royal Navy 1958–66; Arthur Andersen: joined 1966, tax ptnr 1974, office managing ptnr Leeds Office 1975–81, UK dir of tax competence 1981–88, office managing ptnr EC office in Brussels 1988–91, managing ptnr Int Tax Gp 1991–96; memb Cncl Inst of Taxation 1969–89 (pres 1982–84), memb Tax Technical Ctee ICAEW 1984–96; memb Hon Co of CAs in Eng and Wales; MRIN 1961, FTII 1969 (ATII 1964), FCA 1975 (ACA 1970); *Books* Deferred Tax Accounting (1986), Taxation and the Single Market (1991); *Recreations* boats, skiing, classical music; *Clubs* Royal Automobile, Royal Over-Seas League, Cruising Association, Bruxelles Royal Yacht; *Style*— Iain Stitt, Esq; ✉ 2 Hereford Rd, Harrogate, North Yorkshire HG1 2NP (☎ 01423 563846, fax 01423 501237)

STOBART, Paul Lancelot; s of George Lancelot Stobart, of La Massana Parc, Andorra, and Elizabeth Carla, *née* Bruxby; *b* 31 May 1957; *Educ* Peterhouse Sch Zimbabwe, Oriel Coll Oxford (BA Jurisprudence, Golf blue); *m* Nicola (Nikki) Mary, da of late Robert Clyde Norton Scott; 1 da (Alice Lucy b 14 Dec 1995); *Career* Price Waterhouse London 1980–84 (qualified CA 1983), Hill Samuel London & NY 1984–88; Interbrand Group plc: dir 1988–94, chm Europe 1995–96; dir Sage Group plc 1996–; ACA; *Books* Brand Power (ed, 1994); *Recreations* golf, cricket, theatre; *Clubs* Oxford and Cambridge Golfing Soc, Royal St George's Golf; *Style*— Paul Stobart, Esq; ✉ The Sage Group plc, Benton Park Road, Benton Park, Newcastle upon Tyne NE7 7LZ (☎ 0191 255 3000, fax 0191 255 0306)

STOBO, James; CBE (1996, OBE 1983), DL (1987); s of Alexander Hamilton Stobo (d 1968), of Fishwick, and Mary Gilchrist Young (d 1983); *b* 9 Dec 1934; *Educ* Edinburgh Acad; *m* 28 Oct 1963, Pamela Elizabeth Mary, da of James Herriot (d 1941), of Duns; 1 s (Herriot b 1974), 2 da (Laurna b 1966, Carolyn b 1969); *Career* farmer at Fishwick 1952–91; dir: John Hogarth Ltd Kelso, Moredun Scientific Ltd Edinburgh; memb Home Grown Cereals Authy 1971–76; pres: NFU Scot 1973–74, Animal Disease Res Assoc 1980–95; past chm and pres Scot Assoc of Young Farmers Clubs, past pres Royal Smithfield Club; vice pres Scot Nat Fatstock Club; chm: Scot Seed Potato Devpt Cncl 1988–95, Longridge Towers Sch Govrs, Pentlands Science Parl Ltd; FRAgS 1987;

Recreations game shooting, photography; *Clubs* Caledonian, Farmers'; *Style—* James Stobo, Esq, CBE, DL; ✉ Nabdean, Berwick on Tweed TD15 1SZ (☎ 01289 386224, fax 01289 386384, car 0831 885 218)

STOCK, Christopher John Robert; s of Dr John Peter Penderell Stock (d 1973), of Newcastle under Lyme, Staffs, and Sybil, *née* Bashford; *b* 1 May 1938; *Educ* Yarlet Hall, Clifton, Univ of St Andrews (BDS), Univ of London (MSc); *m* 12 Oct 1963, Diana Mary, da of Reginald Adolph Lovatt Wenger; 2 da (Corinne Alison b 16 July 1968, Sally Penderell b 18 Nov 1971); *Career* Royal Army Dental Corps 1962–78 (ret Lt-Col as clinical advsr in advanced conservation), pt/t in endodontic practice and sr res fell Eastman Dental Hosp London 1978–; memb: Br Endodontic Soc (sec and pres 1982), Fedn Dentaire Internationale; fell Int Coll of Dentists; *Books* Endodontics in Practice (1985, 2 edn 1990), A Colour Atlas of Endodontics (1988), Color Atlas and Text of Endodontics (1995); *Recreations* golf, photography, collecting prints; *Clubs* North Hants Golf, St Enodoc Golf, Royal and Ancient Golf; *Style—* Christopher Stock, Esq; ✉ Heather House, Pines Rd, Fleet, Hampshire GU13 8NL (☎ 01252 616220); The Endodontic Practice, Lister House, 11/12 Wimpole St, London W1M 7AB (☎ 0171 636 7900)

STOCK, Michael (Mike); s of William Ralph Stock (d 1978), and Joan, *née* Stringer; *b* 3 Dec 1951; *Educ* Swanley Comp Swanley Kent, Univ of Hull; *m* 1975, Frances Roberta, da of Kevin Wilcox; 2 s (Matthew b 29 Aug 1982, James b 22 April 1988), 1 da (Amy b 30 Sept 1992); *Career* song writer, record producer and musician (signed first publishing deal 1970); memb bands: The Pact (sch band), Mirage 1976–84, Nightwork 1981–84; fndr ptnr Stock Aitken Waterman (with Pete Waterman and Matt Aitken) 1984; has won numerous Silver, Gold and Platinum Discs since 1985 for writing and/or producing artists incl: Princess, Hazell Dean, Dead or Alive, Bananarama, Mel and Kim, Sinitta, Rick Astley, Kylie Minogue, Brother Beyond, Jason Donovan, Donna Summer, Sonia, Big Fun, Cliff Richard, Sybil, World Wrestling Federation; estab new record label and prodn house 1994; currently working with Matt Aitken writing and/or producing artists incl: Jocelyn Brown, Kym Mazelle, Darren Day and Robson and Jerome; involved with charity work incl SAW Goes to the Albert (Royal Marsden Hosp) and records: Let It Be (Ferry Aid), The Harder I Try (Young Variety Club of GB), Help (Comic Relief), Let's All Chant, I Haven't Stopped Dancing Yet and Use It Up and Wear It Out (Help a London Child), Ferry 'Cross the Mersey (Mersey Aid), Do They Know It's Christmas? (Ethiopia Famine Appeal), You've Got a Friend (Childline); *Awards* BPI Best British Producers 1988; Music Week top Producers for: Singles (1st) and Albums (3rd) 1987, Singles (1st) and Albums (1st) 1988 and 1989; Ivor Novello Awards (UK): Songwriters of the Year 1987, 1988 and 1989, Writers of Most Performed Works 1987, 1988 and 1989; BMI Awards (USA) Writers of Most Performed Works 1987, 1988 and 1989; Jasrac Awards (Japan) and Cash Awards (Hong Kong) Writers of the Most Performed Foreign Works 1989; *Recreations* sport; *Style—* Mike Stock, Esq; ✉ c/o Modal Production Group Ltd, Century House, 100 Union Street, London SE1 (☎ 0171 928 4444, fax 0171 928 0920)

STOCKDALE, David Andrew; QC (1995); s of John Ramsden Stockdale (d 1987), and Jean Stewart, *née* Shelley; *b* 9 May 1951; *Educ* Giggleswick Sch, Pembroke Coll Oxford (MA); *m* 1 June 1985, Melanie Jane, da of Anthony Newis Benson, of Adlington, Cheshire; 1 s (William Benson b 13 March 1988), 3 da (Verity Katharine b 8 Sept 1989, Grace Elizabeth b 27 Sept 1991, Bridget Claudia b 17 Feb 1994); *Career* called to the Bar Middle Temple 1975, in practice Northern Circuit 1976–, recorder of the Crown Court 1993– (asst recorder 1990–93); govr Giggleswick Sch 1982–; memb: Professional Negligence Bar Assoc, Personal Injuries Bar Assoc; *Recreations* family, the outdoors, remote Scotland; *Clubs* Sloane; *Style—* David Stockdale, Esq, QC; ✉ Deans Court Chambers, Cumberland House, Crown Square, Manchester M3 3HA (☎ 0161 834 4097, fax 0161 834 4805)

STOCKDALE, Dr Elizabeth Joan Nöel; *Educ* Univ of Aberdeen Faculty of Medicine (MB ChB), Dip in Med Radiodiagnosis (London 1977), FRCR (1979), Univ of Strathclyde Grad Business Sch (MBA 1995), memb Coll of Paediatrics and Child Health (1996); *m* 26 May 1979, Christopher Leo Stockdale; 2 s (David Leo Andrew b 1983, Alexander James b 1984), 1 da (Jane Frances b 1981); *Career* house surgn Aberdeen Royal Infirmary and house physician Woodend Gen Hosp Aberdeen 1972–73, sr house surgn Professorial Surgical Unit Great Ormond St London 1974, registrar and sr registrar Dept of Diagnostic Radiology St George's Hosp London 1975–79 (with appts to The Royal Nat Orthopaedic Hosp, Atkinson Morleys Hosp, The Royal Marsden Hosp and St James's Hosp), conslt radiologist to the Grampian Health Bd 1980–, hon clinical sr lectr Univ of Aberdeen 1980–; former pres Aberdeen and NE Branch Med Women's Fedn, chm Grampian Div BMA 1995–; memb: S Radiological Soc 1980, Euro Soc of Paediatric Radiologists 1980, Br Paediatric Assoc 1986, S Surgical Paediatric Soc 1986, Br Inst Radiology 1990, Br Med Ultrasound Soc 1990, S Soc of Paediatric Radiologists 1996; *Recreations* theatre, travel, classical music; *Style—* Dr Elizabeth Stockdale; ✉ 1 Grant Road, Banchory, Kincardineshire AB31 5UW (☎ 01330 823096); Department of Diagnostic Radiology, Aberdeen Royal Infirmary, Foresterhill, Aberdeen AB9 2ZG; Department of Diagnostic Radiology, Royal Aberdeen Children's Hospital, Cornhill Rd, Aberdeen AB9 2ZG (☎ 01224 681818 ext 52697)

STOCKDALE, Mark Timothy Charles; s of Arthur Ernest Stockdale (d 1993), and Dorothy Eillen Stockdale; *b* 27 March 1961; *Educ* BSc (Economics & Statistics), MA (Marketing); *m* 1990, Cathy, da of Royden Moulder; 1 s (Jordan b 24 April 1994), 1 da (Kristen b 24 May 1996); *Career* advtg exec; account planner: Allen Brady & Marsh 1984–86, J Walter Thompson 1986–88; sr planner Leagas Delaney Partnership 1988–92, exec planning dir Leo Burnett 1995– (bd planning dir 1992–95); reg contrib to indust jls; memb: MRS, Account Planning Gp; *Recreations* listening to and playing music, eating good food as often as possible, drinking to excess whenever allowed; *Style—* Mark Stockdale, Esq; ✉ Leo Burnett Ltd, The Leo Burnett Building, 60 Sloane Avenue, London SW3 3XB (☎ 0171 591 9111)

STOCKDALE, Sir Thomas Minshull; 2 Bt (UK 1960), of Hoddington, Co Southampton; er s of Sir Edmund Villiers Minshull Stockdale, 1 Bt, JP (d 1989), and Hon Louise Fermor-Hesketh (d 1994), da of 1 Baron Hesketh; *b* 7 Jan 1940; *Educ* Eton, Worcester Coll Oxford (MA); *m* 1965, Jacqueline, da of Ha-Van-Vuong, of Saigon; 1 s (John Minshull b 1967), 1 da (Charlotte Fermor b 1970); *Heir* s, John Minshull Stockdale b 13 Dec 1967; *Career* called to the Bar Inner Temple 1966, bencher Lincoln's Inn 1994; memb Ct of Assts Worshipful Co of Fishmongers; *Recreations* shooting, travel; *Clubs* Turf, MCC; *Style—* Sir Thomas Stockdale, Bt; ✉ Manor Farm, Weston Patrick, Basingstoke, Hampshire RG25 2NT (☎ 01256 862841)

STOCKEN, (George Hubert) Anthony; s of George Walter Stocken (d 1974), of Wilts, and Olga Germaine, *née* Helson; *b* 30 June 1929; *Educ* King's Coll Taunton, Royal West of England Acad, Univ of Bristol; *m* 7 Sept 1956, Pauline Denise Cruse, da of Arthur Ford (d 1987), of Hampshire; 1 s (Michael George Anthony b 1956), 1 da (Sarah Ann b 1958); *Career* chartered architect; princ in private architectural practice; Architectural Heritage Year award 1975, Times RICS Conservation award 1976, Civic Tst Commendation award 1986; cncllr Salisbury 1968–74 (dist cncllr 1973–83, chm Dist Cncl 1976–77), mayor of City of Salisbury 1975–76, chm Salisbury Round Table 1966–67, vice chm Nat Assoc of Chartered Tstees; chm: Sarum 76 Salisbury Recreation Centre, Salisbury Branch Nat Fed of Old Age Pensioners Assoc 1975–82 (pres 1982), Salisbury Dist Queen's Silver Jubilee Appeal Fund, Prince's Tst for Wiltshire; former tstee Salisbury Almshouse and Welfare Charities, fndr memb Sarum Housing Assoc, fndr chm Rehabilitation Engrg Movement Advsy Panel in Salisbury Dist, chm Workface Community Serv Scheme; memb: Salisbury DHA 1981–83, Salisbury Dist Health Cncl 1983–87; chm of govrs Salisbury Coll of Technol 1979–81, vice chm of govrs Bishop Wordsworth GS 1980–83; govr: Exeter House Sch for Disabled Children, St Martin's CE Junior Aided Sch; fndr chm Cncl for Sport and Recreation in Salisbury Dist, chm Westwood Sports Centre 1970–89, memb Cncl Salisbury Festival; patron: Salisbury Playhouse, St Edmunds Art Centre; chm Wilts Assoc of Boys Clubs and Youth Clubs 1977–89, fndr chm Salisbury Boys Club 1974–76 (pres 1977), memb Nat Cncl of Boys Club 1974–90, chm Nat Devpt of Boys Club 1983–86; Liveryman and memb Ct of Assts Coach Makers and Coach Harness Makers of London (chm Livery Ctee 1983–85); ARIBA, FFAS, FRSA, FFB; *Recreations* horse riding, hunting, swimming, walking; *Clubs* Naval, Royal Soc of Arts, RIBA; *Style—* Anthony Stocken, Esq; ✉ Bodrigy, Cadgwith, The Lizard, Helston, Cornwall; Beckford House, Quavey Road, Redlynch, Salisbury, Wilts

STOCKEN, Oliver Henry James; s of Henry Edmund West Stocken (d 1980); *b* 22 Dec 1941; *Educ* Felsted, Univ Coll Oxford; *m* 1967, Sally Forbes, da of John Dishon, of Aust; 2 s, 1 da; *Career* md Barclays Aust 1982–84; dir: N M Rothschild & Sons 1972–77, Esperanza Ltd 1977–79, Barclays Merchant Bank Ltd 1979–86, Barclays de Zoete Wedd 1986–93 (fin dir 1991–93); fin dir Barclays Bank 1993–; Liveryman Worshipful Co of Coachmakers & Coach Harness Makers; FCA 1967; *Style—* Oliver Stocken Esq; ✉ Barclays plc, 54 Lombard Street, London EC3P 3AH (☎ 0171 699 5000)

STOCKING, Barbara Mary; da of Percy Frederick Stocking, of Rugby, Warwickshire, and Mary, *née* Catling (d 1993); *b* 28 July 1951; *Educ* Univ of Wisconsin Madison (MS), Univ of Illinois Urbana, New Hall Cambridge (BA, New Hall Coll prize, sec Cambridge Univ Social Servs Orgn); *m* 3 Oct 1981, Dr Robert John MacInnes, s of Dr Iain MacInnes, of Maidenhead; 2 s (Andrew Tom b 3 June 1986, Stephen Courtney b 12 Sept 1989); *Career* staff assoc Nat Acad of Scis Washington DC 1974–76, jt res fell Nuffield Provincial Hosp Tst and Centre for Med Res Univ of Sussex 1977–79, sec to WHO Ind Cmmn (Onchocerciasis Control Prog) 1979–81, sr Nuffield res fell 1981–83, fell in health policy, innovation and evaluation Kings Fund Coll 1983–86, dir Kings Fund Centre for Health Servs Devpt 1987–93; chief exec: Oxford RHA 1993–94, Anglia and Oxford RHA 1994–96; regional dir Anglia and Oxford NHS Exec 1996–; memb: Riverside Health Authy 1985–89, Advsy Ctee Nat Perinatal Epidemiology Unit 1986–89, Advsy Ctee UK Harkness Fellowships 1989–95, Central R&D Ctee NHS 1991–96; MHSM; *Books* The Image and the Reality: A Case Study of the Impacts of Medical Technology (with S L Morrison, 1978), Patterns for Uncertainty (ed with G McLachlan and R F A Shegog, 1979), Initiative and Inertia - Case Studies in the Health Service (1985), In Dreams Begins Responsibility - A Tribute to Tom Evans (ed, 1987), Expensive Medical Technologies (ed, 1988), A Study of the Diffusion of Medical Technology in Europe (series ed, 1991), Criteria for Change (the history and impact of consensus development conferences in UK, with Bryan Jennett and Jackie Spiby, 1991), Medical Advances (the future shape of acute services, 1992); *Recreations* all things foreign (especially visiting France), music (including opera); *Clubs* UK Women's Forum; *Style—* Ms Barbara Stocking; ✉ Anglia and Oxford Regional Health Authority, 6–12 Capital Drive, Linford Wood, Milton Keynes MK14 6QP (☎ 01908 844400)

STOCKPORT, Bishop of 1994–; Rt Rev Geoffrey Martin (Geoff) Turner; s of Ernest Hugh Turner (d 1985), of Bebington, and Winifred Rose, *née* Martin (d 1985); *b* 16 March 1934; *Educ* Bideford GS, RMA Sandhurst, Oak Hill Theol Coll; *m* 6 July 1959, Gillian, da of Arthur Kingsley Chope; 1 da (Sarah b 1960), 2 s (Mark b 1961, John b 1963); *Career* ret Capt RA 1960; curate: St Stephen Tonbridge 1963–66, St John Parkstone 1966–69; vicar: St Peter Derby 1969–73, Christ Church Chadderton 1973–79; rector St Andrew Bebington 1979–93, hon canon Chester Cathedral 1989–93, rural dean N Wirral 1990–93, archdeacon of Chester 1993–94; *Recreations* literature, sport; *Clubs* National Liberal; *Style—* The Rt Rev the Bishop of Stockport; ✉ Bishop's Lodge, Back Lane, Dunham Town, Altrincham WA14 4SG (☎ 0161 928 5611, fax 0161 929 0692)

STOCKTON, 2 Earl of (UK 1984); Alexander Daniel Alan Macmillan; also Viscount Macmillan of Ovenden; s of Rt Hon Maurice Victor Macmillan, PC, MP (Viscount Macmillan of Ovenden, d 1984), and Katharine, Viscountess Macmillan of Ovenden, DBE, *qv*; gs of 1 Earl of Stockton (d 1986); *b* 10 Oct 1943; *Educ* Eton, Ecole Politique Université de Paris, Univ of Strathclyde; *m* 1, 1970 (m dis 1991), Hélène Birgitte (Bitta), da of late Alan Douglas Christie Hamilton, of Stable Green, Mitford, Northumberland; 1 s (Daniel Maurice Alan, Viscount Macmillan of Ovenden b 1974), 2 da (Lady Rebecca Elizabeth b 1980, Lady Louisa Alexandra b 1982); m 2, 23 Dec 1995, Miranda Elizabeth Louise, formerly w of Sir Nicholas Keith Lillington Nuttall, 3 Bt, and previously of late Peter Richard Henry Sellers, CBE, and da of Richard St John Quarry and Diana, Lady Mancroft; *Heir* s, Viscount Macmillan of Ovenden; *Career* book and magazine publisher; journalist Glasgow Herald 1965–66, reporter Daily Telegraph 1967, foreign corr Daily Telegraph 1968–69, chief Euro corr Sunday Telegraph 1969–70; dep chm Macmillan Ltd 1972–80, chm Macmillan Publishers 1980–90, pres Macmillan Ltd 1990–; govr English Speaking Union 1978–84 and 1986–93; chm: Central London TEC 1990–95, London TEC Gp 1991–94; memb Sec of State's TEC Advsy Gp 1991–94; Worshipful Co of Merchant Taylors: Liveryman 1972, memb Ct of Assts 1987, Master 1992–93; Liveryman Worshipful Co of Stationers & Newspaper Makers 1973 (memb Ct of Assts 1996); Hon DUniv Strathclyde 1993; Hon DLitt de Montfort 1993, Westminster 1995; FIMgt, FRSA, Hon FISVA 1996; *Recreations* shooting, fishing, photography, conversation; *Clubs* Beefsteak, Buck's, Carlton, Garrick, Pratts, White's; *Style—* The Rt Hon the Earl of Stockton; ✉ Macmillan Publishers Ltd, 25 Eccleston Place, London SW1W 9NF (☎ 0171 881 8000)

STOCKWELL, Anthony Howard; s of F H C Stockwell, of Enfield, Middx, and G B Stockwell, *née* Colledge; *b* 14 Jan 1949; *Educ* The Grammar Sch Enfield, Clare Coll Cambridge (exhibitioner, BA); *m* K Richardson; *Career* slr; ptnr and head Banking Dept Stephenson Harwood (formerly articled clerk and asst slr); winner Daniel Reardon prize (Law Soc); Freeman City of London, Freeman and Liveryman City of London Slrs' Co; memb: The Law Soc 1974, City of London Law Soc (memb Banking Law and Professional Practice Sub-ctees); *Style—* Anthony Stockwell, Esq; ✉ Stephenson Harwood, One St Paul's Churchyard, London EC4M 8SH (☎ 0171 329 4422, fax 0171 606 0822)

STOCKWIN, Prof James Arthur Ainscow; s of Wilfred Arthur Stockwin (d 1991), of Sutton Coldfield, and Dr Edith Mary, *née* Ainscow (d 1983); *b* 28 Nov 1935; *Educ* King Edward's Sch Birmingham, Exeter Coll Oxford (MA), Aust Nat Univ (PhD); *m* 30 Jan 1960, Audrey Lucretia Hobson, da of Eric Stuart Wood (d 1996); 2 da (Katrina Mary (Mrs Bennett) b 19 Nov 1961, Jane Clare (Mrs Skirrow) b 26 Jan 1964), 2 s (Rupert Arthur b 1 Oct 1966, Timothy James b 20 Dec 1968, d 1987); *Career* Aust Nat Univ Canberra 1964–81: lectr, sr lectr, reader; Nissan prof of modern Japanese studies and dir Nissan Inst of Japanese Studies Univ of Oxford 1982–, professorial fell St Antony's Coll 1982–; pres Br Assoc of Japanese Studies 1994–95; *Books* The Japanese Socialist Party and Neutralism (1968), Japan: Divided Politics in a Growth Economy (1975, 2 edn 1982), Dynamic and Immobilist Politics in Japan (ed and part-author, 1988), The Establishment of the Japanese Constitutional System (by Junji Banno, trans 1992), The Story of Tim (1993); *Recreations* languages; *Style—* J A A Stockwin; ✉ Nissan Institute of Japanese Studies, 27 Winchester Road, Oxford OX2 6NA (☎ 01865 274573, fax 01865 274574)

STODART OF LEASTON, Baron (Life Peer UK 1981), of Humbie, in the District of E Lothian; (James) Anthony Stodart; PC (1974); s of Col Thomas Stodart, CIE, IMS (d 1934), and Mary Alice, *née* Coullie; *b* 6 June 1916; *Educ* Wellington; *m* 1940, Hazel Jean (d 1995), da of Lt Ronald James Usher, DSC, RN (d 1948); *Career* sits as Cons peer in House of Lords; farmer; MP (C) Edinburgh W 1959–74 (stood as Lib Berwick & E Lothian 1950, C Midlothian and Peebles 1951, Midlothian 1955), under sec of state for Scotland 1963–64, min of state for Agric and Fisheries 1972–74 (Parly sec 1970–72); chm: Agric Credit Corp 1975–87, Ctee of Inquiry into Local Govt in Scotland 1980, Manpower Review of Vet Profession in UK 1984–85; dir FMC 1980–82; *Recreations* playing golf and preserving a sense of humour; *Clubs* New (Edinburgh), Hon Co of Edinburgh Golfers, Cavalry and Guards'; *Style—* The Rt Hon the Lord Stodart of Leaston, PC; ✉ Lorimers, N Berwick, E Lothian (☎ 01620 892457); Leaston, Humbie, E Lothian (☎ 01875 833213)

STODDARD, Christopher James; s of Frederick Stoddard, of Congleton, Cheshire, and Millicent, *née* Barnett; *b* 2 June 1947; *Educ* Newcastle HS, Univ of Sheffield (MB ChB, MD); *m* 26 June 1971, Margaret Elizabeth, da of Reginald Bailey (d 1977); 1 s (James Edward b 12 Oct 1977), 1 da (Emma Louise b 3 Oct 1975); *Career* surgical registrar Royal Infirmary Sheffield 1974–76, clinical fell in surgery McMaster Med Centre Hamilton Ontario 1978–79, sr lectr in surgery Liverpool 1981–86, conslt surgn Royal Hallamshire Hosp Sheffield 1986– (lectr in surgery 1977–78); memb: Surgical Res Soc, Br Soc of Gastroenterology; FRCS 1976; *Books* Complications of Minor Surgery (1986), Complications of Upper Gastrointestinal Surgery (1987); *Recreations* golf, gardening; *Style—* Christopher Stoddard, Esq; ✉ Royal Hallamshire Hospital, Glossop Road, Sheffield S10 2JF (☎ 0114 276 6222); Blaenwern, 12 Slayleigh Lane, Fulwood, Sheffield, S Yorks (☎ 0114 230 9284); 27 Wilkinson St, Sheffield, S Yorks (☎ 0114 272 3711)

STODDART, Anne Elizabeth; CMG (1996); *b* 29 March 1937; *Career* FO 1960–63 and 1967–70, third then second sec Br Military Govt Berlin 1963–67, first sec econ Br Embassy Ankara 1970–73, head of Chancery Br High Cmmn Colombo 1974–76; asst head: West Indian and Atlantic Dept FCO 1977–78, Maritime Aviation and Environment Dept FCO 1979–81; dep UK Perm Rep to the Cncl of Europe Strasbourg 1981–87, head Import Policy Branch External Euro Policy Div DTI 1987–91, dep perm rep Econ Affairs UK Mission to the UN Geneva 1991–96; *Style—* Miss Anne Stoddart, CMG; ✉ Flat 1, 63 The Avenue, Richmond, Surrey TW9 2AH (☎ 0181 948 2497)

STODDART, Christopher West; s of Dr Ian West Stoddart, of Winchester, and Bridget, *née* Pilditch; *b* 10 April 1950; *Educ* Winchester, Churchill Coll Cambridge (open exhibitioner, BA); *m* 1, 1972 (m dis 1977), Deborah, da of John Ounsted; m 2, 1985, Dr Hazel Collins, da of the Hon Robert H Grasmere; *Career* graduate trainee Dept of the Environment 1971–75, res sec Centre for Environmental Studies 1976–80, sec ITV Companies Assoc 1981–82 (regnl companies sec 1980–81), dir of resources Tyne Tees Television Ltd 1983–88 (gen mangr 1982–83), md and chief exec Satellite Information Services Ltd 1988–92, md GMTV Ltd 1992–; *Recreations* mountaineering, skiing, windsurfing; *Clubs* Austrian Alpine; *Style—* Christopher Stoddart, Esq; ✉ GMTV Ltd, The London Television Centre, Upper Ground, London SE1 9LT (☎ 0171 827 7000)

STODDART, John Joseph; s of John Stoddart, of Liverpool, and Patricia, *née* Taylor; *b* 6 June 1957; *Educ* St Joan of Arc RC Secdy Modern; *m* 19 July 1980, Deborah Ann, da of Ronald André Lefebvre; *Career* served Grenadier Gds 1972–78 (joined aged 15); photographer 1978– (based Liverpool until 1984, London thereafter); early editorial work for magazines incl The Face and NME, currently working throughout Europe and USA; perm exhbn L'Express (Joseph Sloane Sq); Portrait Photographer of the Yr 1989; *Recreations* photography, art; *Style—* John Stoddart, Esq; ✉ 1 Lawrence Mansions, Lordship Place, Chelsea, London SW3 5HU (☎ 0171 351 7480)

STODDART, Prof John Little; CBE (1994); s of late John Little Stoddart, and late Margaret Pickering, *née* Dye; *b* 1 Oct 1933; *Educ* South Shields HS for Boys, Univ Coll Durham (BSc), Univ of Wales (PhD), Univ of Durham (DSc); *m* 1957, Wendy Dalton, *née* Leardie; 1 s (decd), 1 da (Janet); *Career* Nat Serv Sgt RA 1954–56 (served UK, Hong Kong, Malaya); dir Welsh Plant Breeding Station Aberystwyth 1987–88 (res scientist 1965–87), res dir AFRC Inst Grassland and Environmental Res 1988–93; memb: AFRC Strategy Bd, Animals Res Ctee, Plants & Environmental Res Ctee 1988–93, AFRC/NERC Jt Agriculture & Environment Prog Mgmnt Ctee 1988–93, Forestry Res Co-ordination Ctee 1988–93, Biotechnology Jt Advsy Bd 1988–93, RASE Symposia 1992 Strategy Gp; min's memb Cncl of Nat Inst for Agricultural Botany 1978–93; chm ODA Plant Sci Prog Advsy Cmmn 1995–; hon prof Univ Coll of Wales 1983–, visiting prof Univ of Reading 1984–92; non-exec dir Derwen NHS Tst 1994–; tstee Stapledon Meml Tst 1996–; FIBiol 1984, ARPS 1985, FRAgS 1993; *Publications* contrib author to numerous refereed papers and reviews; *Recreations* photography, golf, model making, swimming; *Style—* Prof John Stoddart, CBE; ✉ Institute of Biological Sciences, University of Wales, Aberystwyth, Dyfed SY23 3DA (☎ 01970 622316, fax 01970 622350); home (☎ and fax 01970 623893)

STODDART, John Maurice; CBE (1995); s of Gordon Stoddart (d 1983), of Wallasey, and May, *née* Ledder (d 1969); *b* 18 Sept 1938; *Educ* Wallasey GS, Univ of Reading (BA); *Career* head Dept of Econ and Business Studies Sheffield Poly 1970–72, asst dir NE London Poly 1972–76, dir Humberside Coll 1976–83, currently vice-chllr and princ Sheffield Hallam Univ (previously Sheffield City Poly); dir: Sheffield Sci Park 1988–, Sheffield TEC 1990–; memb: CNAA 1980–86, Nat Forum Mgmnt Educn and Devpt 1987–, Cncl for Educn and Trg in Social Work 1989–93, Cncl for Indust and Higher Educn 1990–94; chm: Ctee of Dirs of Polys 1990–93 (vice chm 1988–90), Higher Educn Quality Cncl 1992–; Hon DEd CNAA 1992, Hon DLitt Coventry 1993, Hon DUniv Middx 1993; hon fell Humberside Coll 1983, companion Br Business Graduates Soc 1984; CIMgt 1990, FRSA 1980; author of various articles on education, business education and management; *Recreations* biography, hill walking, squash; *Clubs* Reform; *Style—* John Stoddart, Esq, CBE; ✉ 58 Riverdale Rd, Sheffield S10 3FB (☎ 0114 268 3636); Sheffield Hallam University, Pond Street, Sheffield (☎ 0114 253 2050)

STODDART, Sir Kenneth Maxwell; KCVO (1989), AE (1942), JP (Liverpool 1952); s of Wilfrid Bowring Stoddart (d 1935), of Liverpool, and Mary Hyslop Maxwell; *b* 26 May 1914; *Educ* Sedbergh, Clare Coll Cambridge; *m* 5 Sept 1940, Jean Roberta Benson, da of late Dr John Benson Young; 2 da (Jennifer Jean Maxwell (Mrs J B Jackson) b 1941, Charlotte Maxwell (Mrs Simon Edington) b 1949); *Career* served RAuxAF 1936–45, cmd W Lancs wing ATC 1946–54, vice chm (Air) W Lancs T&AFA 1954–64; Lord Lt Merseyside 1979–89 (DL Lancs then Merseyside 1958–79), High Sheriff Merseyside 1974; chm: Cearns & Brown 1973–84, United Mersey Supply Co 1978–81; chm Liverpool Child Welfare Assoc 1965–81; Hon LLD Liverpool, hon fell Liverpool John Moores Univ (formerly Liverpool Poly) 1989; KStJ 1979; *Clubs* Liverpool Racquet; *Style—* Sir Kenneth Stoddart, KCVO, AE, JP, DL; ✉ The Spinney, Overdale Rd, Willaston, S Wirral L64 1SY (☎ 0151 327 5183)

STODDART, Michael Craig; s of Frank Ogle Boyd Stoddart, of Westbourne, Hants, and Barbara Vincent, *née* Craig; *b* 27 March 1932; *Educ* Marlborough; *m* 15 April 1961, (Susan) Brigid, da of late Capt Denis North-East O'Halloran, RA, of IOW; 2 s (James b 1965, Edward b 1973), 2 da (Phillipa b 1963, Lucinda b 1970); *Career* jt chief exec Singer & Friedlander Ltd 1955–73; chm Electra Investment Trust plc 1986– (dep chm and chief exec 1974–86); chm Electra Kingsway Group 1989–95; non-exec chm: BSG International PLC, Sphere Drake PLC; non-exec dir numerous private and public cos incl Bullough PLC and Next PLC; memb: London Cncl Ironbridge Gorge Museum Tst, London Business Sch Devpt Bd; tstee All Hallows Church; memb Worshipful Co of Chartered Accountants in England and Wales; FCA 1955; *Recreations* country pursuits, shooting, golf, tennis, theatre, travel; *Clubs* Boodle's; *Style—* Michael Stoddart Esq; ✉ Compton House, Kinver, Worcs DY7 5LY; Warwick Lodge, 42 St George's Drive, London SW1V 4BT; Electra Investment Trust plc, 65 Kingsway, London WC2B 6QT (☎ 0171 831 6464, telex 265525 ELECG, fax 0171 404 5388)

STODDART, Patrick Thomas; s of Thomas Stoddart (d 1987), of Leith, Scotland, and Anne Theresa Power (d 1979); *b* 23 Nov 1944; *Educ* Watford Boys' GS; *m* Nicolette, da of Gp Capt A D Murray, RAF (ret); *Career* jr reporter Watford Observer 1962, Evening Echo Herts 1967–72, TV columnist London Evening News 1975–80 (joined as reporter 1972); freelance 1980–85 (various TV series as writer/presenter at TVS and Anglia), TV critic Channel 4 Daily 1989–91, broadcasting ed and TV critic Sunday Times 1986–92, freelance writer on broadcasting affrs The Times and Daily Telegraph, conslt ed Broadcast magazine, script conslt various TV cos; ptnr Keighley Stoddart media consultancy; media conslt to: Rory Bremner, London Radio, Yorkshire Television, Domaine Productions, Virgin Television, Bronson Knight, LWT and Reuters Television 1993–; *Recreations* rugby, cricket; *Clubs* Fullerians RFC (chm), Fleet Street Strollers Cricket; *Style—* Patrick Stoddart, Esq; ✉ Keighley Stoddart, 31 Kingly Court, Kingly Street, London W1 (☎ 0171 494 1289, fax 0171 494 1287)

STODDART, Peter Laurence Bowring; s of Laurence Bowring Stoddart, JP (d 1973), of Cheddington Manor, Leighton Buzzard, Beds, and Gwendolen Mary, *née* Russell; *b* 24 June 1934; *Educ* Sandroyd Sch, Eton, Trinity Coll Oxford; *m* 29 May 1957, Joanna, da of Thomas Adams; 1 s (Clive Laurence Bowring), 2 da (Fiona Gwendolen Jane, Belinda May); *Career* Nat Serv 2 Lt 14/20 King's Hussars 1952–54; with C T Bowring Group 1955–80; dir: C T Bowring & Co Ltd 1967–80, Singer & Friedlander, Crusader Insurance Co Ltd 1967–80, English & American Insurance Co Ltd 1967–80, Fleming Mercantile Investment Trust plc 1976–97; chm: Greenfriar Investment Co Ltd 1977–, Robert Fleming Insurance Brokers 1980–96 (dir 1996–); Capt Bucks CCC 1957–66; Master: Whaddon Chase Hunt 1969–83, Heythrop Hunt 1988–97; memb Ct of Assts Worshipful Co of Salters (Master 1986–87); memb Lloyd's; *Recreations* field sports and countryside, travel; *Clubs* White's, Pratt's, Cavalry and Guards', MCC; *Style—* Peter Stoddart, Esq; ✉ North Rye House, Moreton-in-Marsh, Glos GL56 0XU (☎ 01451 830 636); Robert Fleming Insurance Brokers Ltd, Staple Hall, Stone House Ct, London EC3A 7AX (☎ 0171 621 1263, fax 0171 623 6175, telex 883 735/6)

STODDART OF SWINDON, Baron (Life Peer UK 1983), of Reading in the Royal Co of Berkshire; David Leonard Stoddart; s of late Arthur Leonard Stoddart, and Queenie Victoria, *née* Price; *b* 4 May 1926; *Educ* St Clement Danes GS, Henley GS; *m* 1, 1946 (m dis 1960), Doreen M Maynard; 1 da (Hon Janet Victoria (Hon Mrs Pudney) b 1947); m 2, 1961, Jennifer, adopted da of late Mrs Lois Percival-Alwyn, of Battle, Sussex; 2 s (Hon Howard David b 1966, Hon Mathwyn Hugh b 1969); *Career* clerical offr CEGB 1957–70 (previous employment in PO Telephones, railways and hosp service); ldr Lab Gp Reading Cncl 1964–72 (ldr Cncl 1967–71), memb Reading County Borough Cncl 1954–72; Parly candidate (Lab): Newbury 1959 and 1964, Swindon by-election 1969; MP (Lab) Swindon 1970–83; PPS to Min of Housing and Construction 1974–75, asst Govt whip 1975, Lord Cmmr of the Treasury 1976–77, oppn spokesman on Industry 1982–83, oppn spokesman on Energy (Lords) 1983–88, oppn whip (Lords) 1983–88; trade unions: EETPU 1953–, NALGO 1951–70; memb Nat Jt Cncl Electricity Supply Industry 1967–70; vice pres Assoc of District Cncls 1994–, chm Campaign for an Independent Britain 1991–; *Style—* The Rt Hon the Lord Stoddart of Swindon; ✉ Sintra, 37a Bath Rd, Reading, Berks (☎ 0118 957 6726); House of Lords, London SW1

STOESSL, Susanne Eugenie (Sue); da of Edmund Stoessl (d 1964), of Berkhamsted, Herts, and Olga, *née* Sinreich (d 1945); *b* 28 March 1937; *Educ* Berkhamsted Sch for Girls, Univ of Nottingham; *m* 1968 (sep), Geoffrey William Cleaver; *Career* work study factory mangr C & J Clark 1958–62, prodn mangr British Shoe Corporation 1962–66, statistician Television Audience Measurement 1966–68, head of research and mgmnt servs London Weekend Television 1968–82, head of mktg Channel Four Television 1982–89, freelance media conslt 1989–92, dir gen Market Research Soc 1992–93, head of bdcast research BBC 1993–; non-exec dir: Nuclear Electric plc 1990–96, Ealing NHS Trust 1992–, Magnox Electric plc 1996–; memb Duke of Edinburgh Cwlth Study Conf 1962, pres Women's Advtg Club of London 1981–82, chm Find Your Feet 1989–; memb: Market Research Soc 1973, RTS 1976, Mktg Soc 1982, Mktg Gp of GB 1982; *Recreations* reading, travel, swimming, farming, tapestry; *Clubs* Reform; *Style—* Ms Sue Stoessl; ✉ Broadcast Research, BBC, Woodlands, 80 Wood Lane, London W12 0TT (☎ 0181 576 7475, fax 0181 743 0906)

STOFFBERG, Leon Dutoit; s of William Dutoit Stoffberg, and Yvonne Mei, *née* Robinson; *b* 11 Feb 1951; *Educ* Rondesbosch Boys' Sch, Cape Town Univ (CTA); *children* 1 da (Lisa), 2 s (William, Henry); *Career* fin dir: Fin Div Great Universal Stores Group 1980–85, HSBC Insurance Holdings Ltd 1985–90; chm Premium Credit Ltd 1988–; memb Inst of South African CAs; *Style—* Leon Stoffberg, Esq; ✉ Kirkgate, 19–31 Church Street, Epsom, Surrey KT17 4PF (☎ 01372 748833)

STOKELY, Guy Robert; *b* 30 Oct 1943; *Educ* Forest Sch, Oxford Univ (MA); *m* 4 Oct 1968, Wendy Anne; 3 s (Robert b 1970, Tom b 1979, Tim b 1983), 1 da (Sarah b 1973); *Career* fin vice-pres Manufacturers Life Insur Co 1966–78, gen mangr Saudi Int Bank 1978–91, dir Barclays de Zoete Wedd 1991–; *Recreations* golf, water sports, gardening; *Clubs* RAC; *Style—* Guy Stokely, Esq; ✉ Terleys, Molehill Green, Felsted, Dunmow, Essex CM6 3JP (☎ 01245 361392); Barclays de Zoete Wedd, Ebbgate House, 2 Swan Lane, London EC4R 3TS (☎ 0171 956 4027, fax 0171 956 4591)

STOKER, Dr Dennis James; s of Dr George Morris Stoker (d 1949), of Mitcham, Surrey, and Elsie Margaret, *née* Macqueen (d 1986); *b* 22 March 1928; *Educ* Oundle, Guy's Hosp Med Sch Univ of London (MB BS); *m* 22 Sept 1951, Anne Sylvia Nelson, da of Norman Forster (d 1962), of Haywards Heath, Sussex; 2 s (Philip b 1954, Neil b 1956), 2 da (Claire b 1952, Catherine b 1958); *Career* cmmnd Med Branch RAF 1952: RAF Brampton 1952–53, RAF Bridgnorth 1953–55, RAF Hosp W Kirby 1955–56, Med Div RAF Hosp Wroughton 1956–58, i/c Med Div RAF Hosp Akrotiri Cyprus 1958–61, physician i/c Chest Unit RAF Hosp Wroughton 1961–64, Metabolic Unit St Mary's Hosp London 1964–65, i/c Med Div RAF Hosp Steamer Point Aden 1965–67, i/c Med Div RAF Hosp Cosford Staffs 1967–68, ret Wing Cdr 1968; conslt radiologist: St George's Hosp 1972–87, Royal Nat Orthopaedic Hosp 1972–93; dean Inst of Orthopaedics 1987–91 (dir of radiological studies 1975–93); ed Skeletal Radiology 1984–96, dean Faculty of Clinical Radiology, vice pres Royal Coll of Radiologists 1990–91 (memb Faculty Bd 1983–85, memb Cncl 1985–88); FRSM 1958, FRCP 1976, FRCR 1975, FRCS 1992; *Books* Knee Arthrography (1980), Orthopaedics: self assessment in radiology (jtly, 1988), Radiology of Skeletal Disorders (jtly, 3 edn 1990); *Recreations* medical history, gardening, genealogy, philology; *Clubs* RAF; *Style—* Dr Dennis Stoker; ✉ 18 Llangar Grove, Crowthorne, Berks RG45 6EA (☎ and fax 01344 777948); 25 Wimpole Street, London W1M 7AD (☎ 0171 935 4747, fax 0171 323 0140)

STOKER, John Francis; s of Francis Charles Stoker, of Birmingham, and Joyce, *née* Barnwell; *b* 11 Sept 1950; *Educ* King Edward's Sch Birmingham, Brasenose Coll Oxford

(BA); *m* 1982, Julie Mary, *née* Puddicombe; *Career* DOE: admin trainee 1973–76, private sec to Parly Under Sec of State for Housing and Construction 1976–78, princ 1978–85 (posts incl Tenant's Right to Buy 1979–81, Alternatives to Domestic Rates 1981–83, Cabinet Office 1983–85), asst sec 1985–92, Establishments (Organisation) Div 1985–87, Estate Action and Housing Co-op and Tenant's Choice Div 1987–89, project mangr Property Holdings 1989–90, Environment White Paper Div/Environmental Protection Central Div 1990–91, Fin (Housing and General) Div 1992, under sec 1992–; dir Merseyside Task Force 1992–94, regional dir Government Office for Merseyside 1994–97, dep dir gen National Lottery 1997–; *Recreations* music, books, gardening, food, drink; *Clubs* Athenaeum (Liverpool), MCCC; *Style*— John Stoker, Esq; ✉ c/o Department of National Heritage, 2–4 Cockspur Street, London SW1Y 5DH

STOKER, Linda Beryl; da of Bernard Alistar Dow, and Beryl Georgina Edith, *née* Taylor; *b* 10 July 1954; *Educ* Goffs GS, NE London Poly; *m* 27 Dec 1993, Gordon Smith; 2 step s (Richard b 1982, Alexander b 1983), 2 da from prev alliance (Emma Kate b 1983, Kimberley Frances b 1984); *Career* publicity offr The Rank Orgn, trg offr Guy's Health Dist 1975, trg mangr EMI Leisure 1977, trg advsr Hotel and Catering Indust Trg Bd 1979, field organiser Manpower Servs Cmmn 1981, md Dow-Stoker Ltd 1983–, fndr Women Returners Ltd 1990–; a Woman of the Year 1990, runner-up Price Waterhouse Rising Stars of 1993 Awards; MIPM, MInstD, FRSA; *Books* Women into Training (1990), Having it All (1991), Women Returners Year Book (1991); *Recreations* gym, tennis, sailing, netball; *Style*— Linda Stoker; ✉ Dow-Stoker House, Priors Court, London Road, Bishop's Stortford, Herts CM23 5ED (☎ 01279 466660, fax 01279 466633)

STOKER, Sir Michael George Parke; kt (1980), CBE (1974); *b* 4 July 1918; *Career* former lectr in pathology Cambridge Univ, fell and dir of med studies Clare Coll Cambridge and prof of virology Glasgow Univ, dir Imperial Cancer Research Fund Laboratories 1968–79; former foreign sec and vice-pres Royal Soc 1976–81, former pres Clare Hall Cambridge 1980–87; FRSE 1960, FRS 1968, FRCP; *Style*— Sir Michael Stoker, CBE, FRSE, FRS; ✉ 3 Barrington House, South Acre Drive, Cambridge CB2 2TY

STOKER, Richard; JP (Inner London 1995); s of Capt Bower Morrell Stoker (d 1983), of Scarborough, Yorks, and Winifred *née* Harling; *b* 8 Nov 1938; *Educ* Bredalbane House Sch Castleford, Huddersfield Sch of Music & Sch of Art, RAM (with Sir Lennox Berkeley), Nadia Boulanger Paris; *m* 1, (m dis 1985), Jacqueline Margaret Trelfer; m 2, 10 July 1986, Dr Gillian Patricia Watson, da of Kenneth Walter Watson, of Littleover, Derby; *Career* composer and author; prof RAM 1963–86 (tutor 1970–80); compositions incl: Johnson Preserv'd (Opera in 3 acts), Three String Quartets, Three Piano Trios, Partita, Music that Brings Sweet Sleep, Aspects 1 in 3, Aspects of Flight, Canticle of the Rose, Make me a Willow Cabin, Chinese Canticle, A Little Organ Book, Three Improvisations, Organ Symphony, Three Pieces, Organ Partita, Contemporary Organ Technique, Variants, Piano Concerto, Piano Variations, Two Piano Sonatas, A York Suite, A Poet's Notebook, Five Nocturnes, Duologue, Diversions, Portait of a Town, Assemblages, Partita for Mandolin and Harp, Two Overtures, Benedictus, Three Violin Sonatas, (Guitar) Sonatina, Improvisation, Diversions, Pastoral, Sonata, Concerto; featured festival composer at: Buxton 1962, Harlow 1965 and 1968, Camden 1965, Farnham 1965, Cheltenham 1966, 1970 and 1973, Denmark 1980; film and stage credits incl: Troilus and Cressida (Old Vic), Portrait of a Town (Standard), End of the Line (Nat Film Sch), Garden Party (Coliseum), My Friend-My Enemy (The Place), In Control (Movie-craft); recordings incl: Sonatina for clarinet and piano (Chandos), 3 string quartets and string trio (Gaudeamus), Aspects of Flight (Gaudeamus), Piano Variations, Sonata, concerto (2 guitars, Gaudeamus), Improvisation (Fonal), Chorale for Strings (Saydisc), Fine and Mellow (JSO), two preludes (Royal); as artist exhibited at: Lewisham Soc of Arts Summer Exhibition 1992, Lewisham Arts Festival 1992, Laurence House (one-man show) 1992; editor Composer Magazine 1969–80, memb and treas Steering Ctee Lewisham Arts Festival 1990; memb RAM Guild Ctee 1994– (hon treas 1995–); Mendelssohn scholar 1962, PRS 1962, MCPS 1970, APC 1977 (memb Promotions Ctee 1995), BASCA 1980 (professional memb), exec memb Composers' Guild 1962 (memb Exec Ctee 1969–80); memb: RSM 1984, Blackheath Art Soc 1988, Lewisham Soc of Arts 1991, Poetry Soc 1992, European-Atlantic Gp 1993, Byron Soc 1993, Magistrates Assoc 1995–; fndr memb Atlantic Cncl 1993; finalist Int Poetry Competition Nat Lib of Poetry Maryland USA, Editors Choice Award; ARCM 1962, FRAM 1978 (ARAM 1971); *Books* Portrait of a Town (1974), Words Without Music (1974), Strolling Players (1978), Open Window-Open Door (1985), Tanglewood (1990), Between the Lines (1991), Diva (1992), Collected Short Stories (1993), Compositions on the Internet (http://cdj.cerbernet.co.UK/CDJ/INART/STOKER.HTM); plays: Take Five, Super-Mark, Harry Halleluyah (with Hon Dominick Browne); *Recreations* squash, skiing, tennis, swimming; *Clubs* RAM Guild; *Style*— Richard Stoker, Esq, JP; ✉ c/o Ricordi & Co (London) Ltd, Kiln House, 5 Floor, 210 New King's Road, London SW6 4NZ (☎ 0171 371 7501, fax 0171 371 7270)

STOKES, Dr Adrian Victor; OBE (1983); s of Alfred Samuel Stokes, of Mill Hill, London, and Edna, *née* Kerrison; *b* 25 June 1945; *Educ* Orange Hill GS, UCL (BSc, PhD); *m* 3 Oct 1970 (m dis 1978), Caroline Therese, da of Arthur Campbell Miles, of London; *Career* res programmer GEC Computers Ltd 1969–71, res asst/res fell Inst of Computer Sci/Dept of Statistics and Computer Sci UCL 1971–77, sr res fell and sr lectr Sch of Info Sci The Hatfield Poly 1977–81, dir computing St Thomas' Hosp 1981–88 (King's Fund fell 1981–84), hon res fell Dept of Computer Sci UCL 1988–90, princ conslt NHS Info Mgmnt Centre 1989–; visiting prof of information mgmnt Nene Coll 1994–96; chm: Euro Workshop for Open Systems Expert Gp Healthcare 1991–, Disabled Drivers' Motor Club 1972–82 and 1991–94; vice pres Disabled Drivers' Motor Club 1982–, chm Exec Ctee Royal Assoc for Disability and Rehabilitation 1985–92, govr and memb Cncl of Mgmnt Motability 1977–, memb Fin and Gen Purposes Ctee Assoc for Spina Bifida and Hydrocephalus 1983–91, tstee and memb Cncl of Mgmnt PHAB 1982–90; memb: DHSS Working Party on Mobility Allowance 1975, DHSS Working Party on the Invalid Tricycle Repair Serv 1976–80, DHSS Silver Jubilee Ctee On Improving Access for Disabled People 1977–78, DHSS Ctee on Restrictions Against Disabled People 1979–81, Social Security Advsy Ctee 1980–, Dept of Tport Panel of Advsrs on Disability 1983–85, Disabled Persons' Tport Advsy Ctee 1986–89, Disability Appeal Tbnl 1993–; pres Hendon North Lib Assoc, 1981–83, candidate for London Borough of Barnet Cncl Mill Hill Ward 1968, 1971, 1974 and 1978; Hon DSc Univ of Hertfordshire 1994; Freeman City of London 1988, Liveryman Worshipful Co of Info Technologists 1992 (Freeman 1988); FBCS 1979, FInstD 1986, CChem 1976, CEng 1990, MRSC 1976, MIMgt 1986; *Books* An Introduction to Data Processing Networks (1978), Viewdata: A Public Information Utility (2 edn 1980), The Concise Encyclopaedia of Computer Terminology (1981), Networks (1981), What to Read in Microcomputing (with C Saiady, 1982), A Concise Encyclopaedia of Information Technology (3 edn 1986), Integrated Office Systems (1982), Computer Networks: Fundamentals and Practice (with M D and J M Bacon, 1984), Overview of Data Communications (1985), Communications Standards (1986), The A-Z of Business Computing (1986), OSI Standards and Acronyms (3 edn 1991), The BJHC Abbreviary (with H de Glanville, 1995); *Recreations* philately, science fiction, computer programming; *Style*— Dr Adrian V Stokes, OBE; ✉ 97 Millway, Mill Hill, London NW7 3JL (☎ 0181 959 6665, mobile 0385 502766, fax 0181 906 4137); NHS Information Management Centre, 15 Frederick Road, Birmingham B15 1JD (☎ 0121 625 1992, fax 0121 625 1999)

STOKES, Dr Alistair; *b* 22 July 1948; *Educ* Univ of Wales (BSc, PhD), Univ of Oxford (SRC res fellowship); *m* 22 Aug 1970, Stephanie Mary, da of B H Garland, of Fordingbridge, Hants; 2 da (Charlotte, Samantha); *Career* commercial dir Monsato Co St Louis Missouri USA 1980–82 (joined 1976); Glaxo Pharmaceuticals Ltd: int product mangr 1982–83, mktg and sales dir Duncan Flockhart Ltd 1983–85; gen mangr Yorks Regnl Health Authy 1985–87; Glaxo Pharmaceuticals Ltd: dir business devpt 1987–88, md Glaxo Labs Ltd 1988–89, regnl dir Glaxo Holdings plc 1989–90; dir and chief operating offr Porton International 1990–94, chief exec offr Speywood Pharmaceuticals Ltd 1994–; chm E Berks Community Health Tst 1992–; *Books* Plasma Proteins (1977); *Recreations* reading, walking, music; *Clubs* Naval and Military; *Style*— Dr Alistair Stokes; ✉ Speywood Pharmaceuticals Ltd, 1 Bath Road, Maidenhead, Berkshire SL6 4UH (☎ 01628 770009)

STOKES, (Harold) Beverley (Bev); *b* 12 April 1936, Keighley, Yorkshire; *Educ* Huddersfield Coll, Huddersfield Tech Coll, Liverpool Coll of Commerce; *m* 1963, Patricia, *née* Hewitt; 1 s (Neil Andrew b 9 June 1967), 1 da (Gillian Elizabeth b 25 June 1968); *Career* personnel and trg mangr Kraft Foods Ltd 1967–74, prodn dir Meccano Ltd 1974–79, gp personnel dir GEO Bassett Holdings plc 1979–80, md GEO Bassett & Co Ltd 1980–82, chm & chief exec Bassett Foods plc 1982–89; currently non-exec dir: Portfolio Foods Ltd, Beaumont Industrial Holdings; chm Northern General NHS Trust 1991–; chm Abbeydale Golf Club Ltd; pres Sheffield C of C 1986; formerly: memb Governing Body Sheffield Poly, chm Sheffield Business Sch, memb Ctee Yorkshire CC; visiting speaker Br Inst of Mgmnt, Sheffield Business Sch and IOD; FIPD, CInstM; *Style*— Bev Stokes, Esq; ✉ Northern General NHS Trust, Herries Road, Sheffield S5 7AU (☎ 0114 243 4343, fax 0114 256 0472)

STOKES, David Mayhew Allen; QC (1989); s of Henry Pauntley Allen Stokes (d 1965), and Marjorie Joan, *née* Mollison; *b* 12 Feb 1944; *Educ* Radley, Inst de Touraine (Tours), Churchill Coll Cambridge (MA); *m* 1970, Ruth Elizabeth, da of Charles Tunstall Evans, CMG, of Sussex; 1 s (Harry b 1974), 1 da (Jennifer b 1978); *Career* called to the Bar Gray's Inn 1968, recorder of the Crown Ct 1985–, memb Gen Cncl of the Bar 1989–91 (additional memb 1992–); vice chm Professional Conduct Ctee 1994–96; chm Cambridge Bar Mess 1991–; chm SE Circuit Liaison Ctee: Cambs, Herts, Beds 1991–92, Norfolk, Suffolk 1992–; guest instr/team ldr Nat Inst of Trial Advocacy Workshop York Univ Toronto Canada 1986–; tstee London Suzuki Gp 1988–94; *Recreations* amateur dramatics, madrigals; *Clubs* Norfolk (Norwich); *Style*— David M A Stokes, Esq, QC; ✉ 5 Paper Buildings Temple EC4Y 7HB (☎ 0171 583 6117)

STOKES, Baron (Life Peer UK 1969), of Leyland, Co Palatine of Lancaster; Sir Donald Gresham Stokes; kt (1965), TD (1945), DL (Lancs 1968); s of Harry Potts Stokes (d 1954), of Looe, Cornwall, and Mary Elizabeth Gresham, *née* Yates (d 1969); *b* 22 March 1914; *Educ* Blundell's, Harris Inst of Technol Preston; *m* 25 May 1939, Laura Elizabeth Courteney (d 1995), da of late Frederick C Lamb; 1 s (Hon Michael Donald Gresham b 13 June 1947); *Career* cmmnd Royal N Lancs Regt 1938, transferred to REME and served WWII with 8 Army in Middle East and Italy with rank of Lt-Col; student apprentice Leyland Motors Ltd 1930 (export mangr 1946, gen sales and service mangr 1950, dir 1954), md and dep chm Leyland Motor Corp 1963, chm and md British Leyland Motor Corp 1967, chm and chief exec British Leyland Ltd 1973, pres 1975, conslt to Leyland Vehicles 1980, chm and dir The Dutton-Forshaw Motor Group Ltd 1980–90, pres Jack Barclay Ltd 1989–90; dir: Suits 1980–92, The Dovercourt Motor Co 1982–90, KBH Communications 1985–95 (non-exec chm until 1995); pres: CBI 1962, Univ of Manchester Inst of Science and Technol 1972–75, EEF 1967–75; dir: District Bank 1964–69, National Westminster Bank 1969–81, IRC (dep chm 1969–71), EDC for Electronics Industry 1966–68 (chm), London Weekend TV 1967–71; chm: Two Counties Radio 1979–84 (pres 1984–90, chm 1990–94, pres 1994–), GWR Group 1990–94; Cdre Royal Motor Yacht Club 1979–81; Freeman City of London, Liveryman Worshipful Co of Carmen 1964; hon fell Keble Coll Oxford 1968; Hon LLD Lancaster 1967, Hon DTech Loughborough 1968, Hon DSc Southampton 1969, Hon DSc Salford 1971; FIMI (pres 1962), FIRTE (pres 1982–84), MIRA (pres 1966), FIMechE (pres 1972), SAE (USA), FEng 1976 (CEng 1933), FICE 1984; Officier de l'Ordre de la Couronne (Belgium) 1964, Commandeur de l'Ordre de Leopold II (Belgium) 1972; *Recreations* yachting; *Clubs* Royal Motor Yacht, Army and Navy; *Style*— The Rt Hon the Lord Stokes, TD, DL, FEng; ✉ Branksome Cliff, Westminster Rd, Poole, Dorset BH13 6JW (☎ 01202 763088)

STOKES, Sir John Heydon Romaine; kt (1988); s of late Victor Romaine Stokes, of Hitchin, Herts; *b* 23 July 1917; *Educ* Haileybury, Queen's Coll Oxford; *m* 1, 1939, Barbara Esmee (d 1988), da of late R E Yorke, of Wellingborough, Northants; 1 s, 2 da; m 2, 21 Jan 1989, Mrs E F Plowman (d 1990), wid of John Plowman; m 3, 26 Jan 1991 (m dis), Ruth Bligh, wid of Sir Timothy Bligh, KBE, DSO, DSC; m 4, 4 May 1996, Mrs Frances J S Packham, widow of Lt Cdr Donald Packham, RN; *Career* army 1939–46: Dakar expedition 1940, wounded N Africa 1943, mil asst to HM Min Beirut and Damascus 1944–46, Maj; personnel offr ICI 1946–51, personnel mangr Br Celanese 1951–59, dep personnel mangr Courtaulds 1957–59, ptnr Clive and Stokes Personnel Conslts 1959–80; Parly candidate (C): Gloucester 1964, Hitchin 1966; MP (C): Oldbury and Halesowen 1970–74, Halesowen and Stourbridge 1974–92; delegate to Cncl of Europe and WEU 1983–92; elected to House of Laity Gen Synod of C of E 1985–90, chm Gen Purposes Ctee Primrose League 1971–85, vice-pres Royal Stuart Soc, chm of tstees Battlefields Tst, vice chm Oxford Soc; *Clubs* Buck's; *Style*— Sir John Stokes; ✉ 4 The Bradburys, Stratton Audley, Nr Bicester OX6 9BW

STOKES, Leslie James; s of William James Stokes, and Peggy Florence, *née* Blunsom; *b* 22 May 1951; *Educ* Abbs Cross Tech HS, Sir John Cass Coll, Newcastle upon Tyne Poly (DipAD, RSA travelling bursary prize), RCA (MDes, Braun prize); *m* 1973, Janet Barbara, da of Alfred Johns Victor Hayes; 1 s (William James b 1987), 1 da (Kathryn Louise b 1982); *Career* lectr in 3D design Herts Coll of Art and Design 1976–79, industl design conslt London and Upjohn 1976–81, ptnr London Associates (Industl Design and Product Devpt) 1981–; Br Design Award 1990; memb various jury panels for Design Cncl Design awards; memb Design Business Associates 1986; FCSD 1989 (MCSD 1981); *Style*— Leslie Stokes, Esq; ✉ London Associates, 105 High St, Berkhamsted, Hertfordshire HP4 2DG (☎ 01442 862631, fax 01442 874354)

STOKES, Michael George Thomas; QC (1994); s of Michael Philip Stokes (d 1988); *b* 30 May 1948; *Educ* Preston Catholic Coll, Univ of Leeds (LLB); *m* 9 July 1994, Alison H Pollock; 1 da (Anna Elizabeth Hamilton b 19 July 1995); *Career* called to the Bar Gray's Inn 1971; asst lectr Univ of Nottingham 1970–72, in practice Midland and Oxford circuit 1973–, recorder of the Crown Ct 1990– (asst recorder 1986–90, circuit rep), memb Fees and Legal Aid Ctee Bar Cncl 1996–; *Recreations* horses; *Clubs* Northampton and County (Northampton); *Style*— Michael Stokes, Esq, QC; ✉ Washbrook Farm, Cold Ashby Road, Naseby, Northants NN6 6DW (☎ 01604 740881); 36 Bedford Row, London WC1R 4JH (☎ 0171 421 8000, fax 0171 421 8080)

STOKES, Simon George Garbutt; s of Rev George Smithson Garbutt Stokes, of Charlbury, Oxon, and Constance Betty, *née* Mitchell; *b* 22 Oct 1950; *Educ* Barnard Castle Sch Co Durham, St Peter's Coll Oxford, Bristol Old Vic Theatre Sch; *Career* theatre director; actor/stage mangr Village Tour (Theatre Centre) 1972; asst stage mangr: 69 Theatre Co Manchester 1974, Liverpool Playhouse 1975; artistic dir Bush Theatre 1975–87: Juvenalia (with Simon Callow) 1976, Only Men Shave 1977, Runners 1978, The Transfiguration of Benno Blimpie (with Robbie Coltrane) 1978, Amabel 1979, Viaduct 1980, Lone Star and Private Wars 1980, Golden Leaf Strut 1981, The Miss Firecracker

Contest 1982, Devour The Snow 1982, The Double Man 1982, Crimes of the Heart 1983, Topokana Martyrs' Day 1983, When I Was A Girl, I Used To Scream And Shout 1984, Copperhead 1985, Kiss of the Spider Woman (with Simon Callow) 1985, China (with Natasha Richardson) 1986, The Garden Girls 1986, More Light 1987, Love Field 1987, Dreams of San Francisco 1987; dir of project devpt The Turnstyle Group 1990–92 (artistic assoc 1988–92); other work incl: Juvenalia Omnibus BBC TV (with Simon Callow) 1983, When I Was A Girl...(Lyceum Theatre Edinburgh) 1985 (Whitehall Theatre 1986/87), The Miss Firecracker Contest (Greenwich Theatre) 1986, Boys' Life (Staatstheater Stuttgart) 1988, The Brave (Bush Theatre) 1988, The Glass Menagerie (Cambridge Theatre Co, with Sian Phillips) 1989, When I Was A Girl... (South Coast Repertory Calif) 1989, The Debutant Ball (Hampstead) 1989, The Heidi Chronicles (Staatstheater Stuttgart) 1990, Les Liaisons Dangereuses (Cameri Theatre Tel Aviv) 1990, A Slip Of The Tongue (Steppenwolf Theater Chicago) 1992 (Shaftesbury Theatre 1992); appeared in Blood Sports (Bush Theatre), The Ploughman's Lunch (Channel 4); memb: Directors' Guild of GB, Br Actors' Equity Assoc; *Style*— Simon Stokes, Esq; ✉ c/o Curtis Brown Group Ltd, 28–29 Haymarket, London SW1Y 4SP (☎ 0171 396 6600, fax 0171 396 0110)

STOLLAR, Derek Arthur; s of Harry Stollar (d 1960), and Grace Elizabeth, *née* Rhodes (d 1975); *b* 18 April 1930; *Educ* City of London Sch, Brixton Sch of Bldg, Architectural Assoc Sch (AADipl); *m* 1, 1962 (m dis 1971), Carol, da of Flt Lt Hugh Grehan; 1 s (Mark b 9 March 1964); m 2, 18 July 1970, Dawn Virginia, da of Capt Anthony Paul Reiss; 1 da (Abigail b 31 March 1971), 2 step da (Tabitha b 19 Feb 1961, Rachel b 16 May 1963); *Career* Nat Serv writer RN 1948–50; architect 1957–95, ret; assoc: Stillman & Eastwick - Field 1960–62, Jan Farber & Bartholomew 1968–72; ptnr David Brian & Stollar 1972–74, princ Derek Stollar 1974–75, ptnr Hugh Roberts Graham & Stollar (later Graham & Stollar) 1975–80, sr dir Graham & Stollar Associates Ltd 1980–89, dir and chm Stollar WRM Associates Ltd 1989–90; architectural corr: Bath Evening Chronicle 1991–94, Bath Leader 1994; ed English Historic Towns Forum Newsletter 1991–94; Cambridge/RSA Cert TEFL 1991; fndr memb Social and Lib Democrats, memb and Bath ldr Lib Democrats; Freeman City of London 1971; memb AA 1956, FRIBA 1969 (ARIBA 1958); *Recreations* travel, talk, early music (recorder), water colour painting, reading, history; *Style*— Derek Stollar, Esq; ✉ 6 Princes Building Bath BA1 2ED (☎ 01225 312801); Rue Mandrière, Alet Les Bains, 11580, Aude, France (☎ 00 33 68 69 90 22)

STOLLER, Anthony David (Tony); s of Louis Stoller (d 1973), and Pearl, *née* Poster (d 1992); *b* 14 May 1947; *Educ* Hendon Co GS, Gonville and Caius Coll Cambridge (MA, LLB); *m* 1969, Andrea (Andy), *née* Lewisohn; 1 da (Juliette Louise b 1975), 1 s (Timothy b 1976); *Career* grad trainee Thomson Regnl Newspapers 1969–72, mktg mangr Liverpool Daily Post and Echo Ltd 1972–74, sr offr radio then head radio programming IBA 1974–79, dir AIRC 1979–81, md Thames Valley Broadcasting Plc 1981–85, md Tyrrell & Green John Lewis Partnership 1985–95, chief exec Radio Authority 1995–; *Recreations* music, cricket, sailing; *Clubs* Penn, Island Sailing; *Style*— Tony Stoller, Esq; ✉ The Radio Authority, Holbrook House, 14 Great Queen St, London WC2B 5DG (☎ 0171 430 2724)

STOLLER, Norman Kelvin; MBE (1976), DL (1995); s of Ivor Stoller (d 1992), of Springhill, Florida, USA, and Sally, *née* Fox (d 1940); *b* 6 Sept 1934; *Educ* Eccles HS; *m* 6 June 1960, Diane, da of Leo Morris (d 1977); 1 s (Martin Jeremy b 1964), 1 da (Linzi Sara b 1962); *Career* RAF 1952–55; chief exec Seton Products Ltd 1960–84 (dir 1959); non-exec chm: Seton Healthcare Group plc 1990– (exec chm 1984–90), Mountain Goat Ltd; county pres Gtr Manchester St John Ambulance 1985–, fndr chm Oldham TEC 1990, dep chm Oldham C of C, Trg and Enterprise 1995–; CBI/Daily Telegraph NW Businessman of the Year 1991; Hon MSc Univ of Salford 1993; CStJ 1995 (OStJ 1987); *Recreations* sailing, malt whisky; *Clubs* St James's, Mark's; *Style*— Norman K Stoller, Esq, MBE, DL; ✉ Seton Healthcare Group plc, Tubiton House, Oldham, Greater Manchester OL1 3HS (☎ 0161 652 2222, fax 0161 628 0831, car 0831 171396)

STOLLERY, Prof John Leslie; CBE (1994); s of Edgar George Stollery, and Emma Stollery; *b* 21 April 1930; *Educ* E Barnet GS, Imp Coll of Sci and Technol London (BScEng, MScEng, DScEng, DIC); *m* 1956, Jane Elizabeth, da of Walter Reynolds; 4 s; *Career* Aerodynamics Dept De Havilland Aircraft Co 1952–56, reader Aeronautics Dept Imp Coll London 1962 (lectr 1956); Cranfield Univ (formerly Cranfield Inst of Technol): prof of aerodynamics 1973–95 (emeritus prof 1995–), head Coll of Aeronautics 1976–86 and 1992–95, pro vice-chllr Faculty of Engrg 1982–85 (dean 1976–79); chm: Aerospace Technol Bd MOD 1986–89, Aviation Ctee DTI 1986–94; pres RAeS 1987–88; memb Airworthiness Requirements Bd 1990–; visiting prof: Cornell Aeronautical Labs Buffalo USA 1964, Aeronautical Res Lab Wright Patterson Air Force Base 1971, Nat Aeronautical Lab Bangalore India 1977, Peking Inst of Aeronautics and Astronautics 1979, Univ of Queensland 1983; FRAeS 1975, FCGI 1984, FAIAA 1988, FEng 1992; *Publications* Shock Tube Research (chief ed, 1971); author of papers in Journal of Fluid Mechanics and other aeronautical jls; *Recreations* watching football, travelling; *Style*— Prof John Stollery, CBE, FEng; ✉ College of Aeronautics, Cranfield University, Cranfield, Bedford MK43 0AL (☎ 01234 754743, fax 01234 752149)

STOLLIDAY, Ivor Robert; s of Robert Stolliday, and Marie, *née* Winter; *b* 14 Sept 1946; *Educ* Palmers Sch Grays Essex, Univ of E Anglia (BA, MA); *m* 1972, Alicia Elizabeth, *née* Bennett; 3 s (Hugh Robert Leslie b 1977, John Ivor b 1981, Martin Francis Arthur b 1986); *Career* Dept of Employment 1969–70, British American Tobacco 1970–72, Cmmn on Indust Relations 1972–75, head Human Resources Dept Anglian Mgmnt Centre 1975–80, sec of ITVA 1982–88 (indust relations advsr 1980–88); Television South West: dir of personnel, dep md and co sec 1988–92; sec and chief exec Dartington Hall Trust 1993–; chm: Gemini Radio Ltd 1993–95, South West Film and Television Archive 1993–; dir South West Media Development Agency 1995–; visiting prof California State Univ Sacramento 1979, tstee Dartington Summer Sch Fndn 1991–; FRSA 1991; *Recreations* writing, walking; *Style*— Ivor Stolliday, Esq; ✉ The Courtyard, Tristford, Harberton, Totnes, Devon TQ9 7RZ (☎ 01803 867372); Dartington Hall Trust, Dartington Hall, Totnes, Devon TQ9 6EJ (☎ 01803 866688)

STONE, Sir Alexander; kt (1994), OBE (1988); s of Morris Stone (d 1945), and Rebecca Levi (d 1954); *b* 21 April 1907; *Educ* Hutcheson Boys GS Glasgow, Univ of Glasgow; *m* 26 May 1988, (Phyllis) Bette; *Career* lawyer and banker; settlor The Alexander Stone Fndn; Hon LLD Univ of Glasgow 1986, Hon DLitt Univ of Strathclyde 1989; hon memb Royal Glasgow Inst of the Fine Arts; elected MCIBS 1991; *Style*— Sir Alexander Stone, OBE; ✉ 69 St Andrews Drive, Pollokshields, Glasgow (☎ 0141 423 7223); 36 Renfield St, Glasgow G2 1LU (☎ 0141 226 4431, fax 0141 226 5150)

STONE, Maj Gen Anthony Charles Peter; CB (1994); s of Maj (ret) Charles Cecil Stone, of Somerton, Somerset, and Kathleen Mons, *née* Grogan; *b* 25 March 1939; *Educ* St Joseph's Coll, RMA Sandhurst, Staff Coll Camberley; *m* 29 July 1967, (Elizabeth) Mary Eirlys, da of Rev Canon Gideon Davies (d 1987), of Little Comberton, Worcs; 2 s (Guy b 1972, Mark b 1979); *Career* RA: cmmnd 1960, serv in Far East, Middle East, BAOR and UK (light, field, medium, heavy, locating and air def artillery), Battery Cdr Q (Sanna's Post) Battery and 2 i/c 5 Regt RA 1974–75, GSO 2 DASD MOD 1976, DS RMCS 1977, CO 5 Regt RA 1980; founded Special OP Troop 1982, Col GS Def Progs Staff MOD 1983, Mil Dir of Studies RMCS 1985, Dir of Operational Requirements (Land) MOD 1986, Dir Light Weapons Projects MOD 1989, DG Policy and Special Projects MOD 1990, DG Land Fighting Systems MOD 1992, DG Land Systems MOD 1994–95, ret Army; Hon Col 5 Regt RA 1990–, Col Cmdt Royal Regt of Artillery 1993–; chm Nash Partnership Ltd 1996–; visiting research fell Dept of Def Studies Univ of York 1996–; *Recreations* shooting, skiing, country pursuits, family; *Clubs* Army & Navy; *Style*— Maj Gen Anthony Stone, CB

STONE, Arthur Edward; OBE; s of Samuel Stone, MM (d 1936), and Clara Marsden (d 1968); *b* 10 Dec 1930; *Educ* City of Leeds Sch; *m* Oct 1961, Beryl, da of John Robert Hodson (d 1962); 1 da (Alison Jane b March 1967); *Career* Leeds Permanent Building Society: branch mangr Huddersfield 1961, branch mangr Peterborough 1961–64, branch mangr Leicester 1964–65, branch mangr London (City) 1965–69, southern regnl mangr 1969–71, branch devpt mangr Head Office 1971–75, asst gen mangr Head Office 1975–79; dir and chief exec Leeds and Holbeck Building Society 1980–95; former memb Cncl: BSA, CBSI (nat pres 1983–84); vice pres Northern Assoc of Building Socs (former chm and memb Exec Ctee); memb Ct and treas Univ of Leeds 1995–, special tstee St James Univ Hosp Leeds; Freeman City of London 1967, Liveryman Worshipful Co of Chartered Secretaries and Administrators 1977; FCIB 1961, FCISA 1962; *Clubs* Pannal Golf, Langbourn Ward, Cripplegate Ward, Leeds Rotary; *Style*— Arthur Stone, Esq, OBE; ✉ Daleside Close, Harrogate, N Yorks HG2 9JF (☎ and fax 01423 872780)

STONE, Dr Barry Leonard; *b* 19 Feb 1948; *Educ* Univ of London (BSc), St Bartholomew's Med Sch (MB BS, LRCP, MRCS); *m* 1973, Barbara Mary Deane; 1 s (Andrew b 25 Dec 1984); *Career* house surgn Frimley Park Hosp 1978 (house physician 1977–78), sr house offr Bethlem Royal Hosp 1978–79, registrar Maudsley Hosp 1979–81, lectr in psychiatry Faculty of Med Univ of Southampton 1981–83, med advsr Upjohn Ltd Michigan USA 1983; locum conslt psychiatrist: Warlingham Park Hosp 1983, Luton and Dunstable Hosp 1983–84, Professorial Unit St Mary's Hosp and Drug Dependency Unit London 1984, advsr and cnsllr in alcohol and drug abuse Youth Servs Hampshire CC 1985–86, physician BUPA Med Centres (Portsmouth and Croydon) 1986–87, visiting physician BUPA Med Centre London 1989–91, conslt psychiatrist: Lynbrook Clinic and Windsor Clinic 1990–92, Hampshire Sex Offenders Prog Hampshire Probation Service 1994–; in private practice Harley Street London and in Fleet; hon psychotherapist Heathlands NHS Mental Health Tst 1994–, supervisory membership Consultation Centre Register of Systemic Psychotherapists Kensington; memb: Br Assoc of Psychopharmacology 1983, Assoc of Pharmaceutical Physicians 1983, Soc for the Study of Addiction 1986–, UK Cncl for Psychotherapy 1995; *Recreations* oil painting, walking, travel; *Style*— Dr Barry Stone; ✉ Acorns, Forest Dean, Fleet, Hampshire GU13 8TT (☎ 01252 620667)

STONE, Brian Lance Dawson; s of Lance Browning Stone (d 1966), of Hong Kong and Suffolk, and Susan Caroline, *née* Dawson (d 1962); *b* 9 Sept 1936; *Educ* Charterhouse, ChCh Coll Oxford; *Career* Nat Serv 7 QOH Subalt 1956–57; Mktg Div Sunday Times 1963–66, film indust 1966–67, dir Hamish Hamilton Ltd 1971–76; Hughes Massie Ltd: dir 1977–84, co-owner 1984–86, chm 1988–; dir and co-owner Aitken & Stone Ltd 1986–; *Recreations* travel, opera, current affairs; *Clubs* Garrick; *Style*— Brian Stone, Esq; ✉ Aitken & Stone Ltd, 29 Fernshaw Rd, London SW10 0TG (☎ 0171 351 7561, fax 0171 376 3594)

STONE, Carole; da of Harry A Stone (d 1976), and Kathleen Jacques, *née* Conroy (d 1993); *b* 30 May 1942; *Educ* Ashford County GS for Girls, Southampton Tech Coll; *Career* joined BBC in 1963 as copytypist in Newsroom BBC South, asst prodr BBC Radio Brighton 1967–70, gen talks prodr BBC Radio 4 1970, prodr BBC Radio 4's Any Questions? programme 1977–89, freelance TV broadcaster/media conslt 1990–; dir Lindley Stone Ltd (independent TV prodn co); *Clubs* Reform; *Style*— Miss Carole Stone; ✉ Flat 4, The Coach House, 17a Floral St, London WC2E 9DS (☎ 0171 379 8664, fax 0171 240 3078)

STONE, Clive Graham; s of late Charles Thomas Stone and Frances Lilian Stone; *b* 7 July 1936; *Educ* Northampton Coll of Advanced Technol, City Univ London; *m* 1957, Pamela Mary; 3 s; *Career* chm and chief exec Dollond & Aitchison Group plc 1980–93 (gen mgmnt 1968, md 1973, dep chm 1978); dir: Gallaher Ltd 1981–93, Gallaher Pensions Ltd 1984–93, British Retail Consortium 1985–93, Keeler Ltd 1986–93; chm Theodore Hamblin Ltd 1981–93; govr Royal Nat Coll for the Blind 1985–95, chm Fight for Sight; Freeman City of London, Master Worshipful Co of Spectacle Makers; fell Br Coll of Optometrists; *Recreations* sailing, real tennis, golf; *Clubs* Leamington Tennis Court, Stoneleigh Golf, Island Sailing; *Style*— Clive G Stone, Esq; ✉ Abbey Meads, Forrest Road, Kenilworth, Warwickshire CV8 1LT (☎ and fax 01926 854553)

STONE, Evan David Robert; QC (1979); s of Laurence George Stone (d 1952), and Lillian Stone (d 1955); *b* 26 Aug 1928; *Educ* Berkhamsted Sch, Worcester Coll Oxford (MA); *m* 19 Aug 1959, Gisela Bridget; 1 s (Michael David George b 1960); *Career* Nat Serv cmmnd Army, served UK and ME 1947–49; called to the Bar Inner Temple 1954, recorder of Crown Cts 1979–, bencher Inner Temple 1985–, memb Senate of Inns of Court and the Bar 1985–86, currently head of chambers; former HM dep coroner Inner W London W Middx and City of London; cncllr then alderman London Borough of Islington (dep ldr then ldr of oppn) 1969–74; govr: Moorfields Eye Hosp 1970–79, Highbury Grove Sch 1971–82 (chm Govrs 1978–82); chm City and Hackney Health Authority 1984–92; memb Criminal Injuries Compensation Bd 1989–, memb Ctee of Tstees Country Houses Assoc 1994–; Freeman City of London 1990; *Books* Forensic Medicine (jtly with late Prof Hugh Johnson, 1987); *Recreations* reading, writing, listening to music, sport and games; *Clubs* Garrick, MCC; *Style*— Evan Stone, Esq, QC; ✉ 29 Bedford Row Chambers, 29 Bedford Row, Gray's Inn, London WC1R 4HE (☎ 0171 831 2626, fax 0171 831 0626)

STONE, Dr Gerald Charles; s of Albert Leslie Stone (d 1981), and Grace Madeline, *née* Varndell (d 1980); *b* 22 Aug 1932; *Educ* Windsor GS, SSEES (BA, PhD); m 1, 1953 (m dis 1973), Charlotte Johanna, *née* Steinbach; 2 s (Peter Bernhard b 1953, David Albert b 1961), 1 da (Christine Anne b 1955); m 2, 1974, Vera Fedorovna, da of Fedor Alekseevich Konnov; 1 da (Lydia Grace b 1976); *Career* Nat Serv 1951–53; Metropolitan Police 1953–64, asst master Bexhill Boys' GS 1964–65, lectr Univ of Nottingham 1968–71 (asst lectr 1966–68), asst dir of res Dept of Slavonic Studies Univ of Cambridge 1971–72, lectr in non-Russian Slavonic languages and fell Hertford Coll Oxford 1972–; memb: Philological Soc 1967– (memb Cncl 1981–86), Soc for Slovene Studies 1973–; FBA 1992; *Books* The Smallest Slavonic Nation: The Sorbs of Lusatia (1972), The Russian Language since the Revolution (with Bernard Comrie, 1978), An Introduction to Polish (1980), The Formation of the Slavonic Literary Languages (ed with Dean Worth, 1985); *Recreations* walking, gardening, visiting pubs; *Style*— Dr Gerald Stone, FBA; ✉ 6 Lathbury Road, Oxford OX2 7AU (☎ 01865 558227); Hertford College, Oxford OX1 3BW (☎ 01865 279435)

STONE, Prof (Francis) Gordon Albert; CBE (1990); s of late Sidney Charles Stone and late Florence, *née* Coles; *b* 19 May 1925; *Educ* Exeter Sch, Christ's Coll Cambridge (MA, PhD, ScD), Univ of Southern California (Fulbright scholar); *m* 28 June 1956, Judith Maureen, da of late James Hislop, of Sydney, Australia; 3 s (James Francis b 1957, Peter Gordon b 1961, Derek Charles b 1963); *Career* instr then asst prof Harvard Univ 1954–62, reader in inorganic chemistry Queen Mary Coll London 1962–63, prof of inorganic chemistry and head of dept Univ of Bristol 1963–90, Robert A Welch distinguished prof of chemistry Baylor Univ Texas 1990–; visiting prof: Monash Univ Aust 1966, Princeton Univ 1967, Pennsylvania State Univ 1968, Univ of Arizona 1970, Carnegie Mellon Univ 1972, Rhodes Univ 1976; lectures: Boomer Univ of Alberta 1965, Firestone Univ of Wisconsin 1970, Tilden Chemical Soc 1971, Ludwig Mond RSC 1982,

Reilly Univ of Notre Dame 1983, Waddington Univ of Durham 1984, Sir Edward Frankland prize lecturership RSC 1987, G W Watt Univ of Texas (Austin) 1988; Royal Soc of Chemistry: memb Cncl 1967–70 and 1981–83, pres Dalton Div 1981–83 (vice pres 1983–85); SERC: memb Chemistry Ctee 1972–74 and 1982–85, chm Inorganic Chemistry Panel 1982–85, Royal Soc assessor on Science Bd 1986–88; chm: 4th Int Conf on Organometallic Chemistry Bristol 1969, Royal Soc of Chemistry Conf on the Chemistry of Platinum Metals Bristol 1981, UGC Review of Chemistry in UK Univs 1988; Awards: Organometallic Chemistry medal 1972, Transition Metal Chemistry medal RSC 1979, Chugaev medal Inst of Inorganic Chemistry USSR Acad of Scis 1978, American Chemistry Soc award in Inorganic Chemistry 1985, Davy medal Royal Soc 1989, Longstaff medal RSC 1990; Hon DSc: Exeter 1992, Waterloo (Canada) 1992, Durham 1993, Salford 1993, Zaragoza (Spain) 1994; FRSC 1970, FRS 1976; *Publications* Inorganic Polymers (ed 1962), Hydrogen Compounds of the Group IV Elements (1962), Advances in Organometallic Chemistry (co-ed 1964–89, now in 40 volumes), Comprehensive Organometallic Chemistry I and II (ed, 1984 and 1995), Leaving No Stone Unturned (autobiog, 1993); *Recreations* travel; *Style*— Prof Gordon Stone, CBE, FRS; ✉ 60 Coombe Lane, Bristol BS9 2AY; 88 Hackberry Avenue, Waco, Texas 76706 USA (☎ 817 752 3517); Department of Chemistry, Baylor University, Box 7348, Waco, Texas 76798–7348 (☎ 817 755 3311, fax 817 755 2403)

STONE, Dr Gordon Victor; s of Victor John Stone (d 1972), of Aberdeen, and Madeleine O'Brien, *née* Imlach; *b* 4 Oct 1945; *Educ* Aberdeen GS, Univ of Aberdeen (MB ChB, union sec), Univ of Edinburgh (DCM); *m* 16 July 1969, Aileen Susanna, da of James Manson Wilson; 1 da (Joanna Carol b 17 March 1972), 1 s (Euan James Gordon b 10 Dec 1973); *Career* med offr RAF 1970–75, Scottish Health Serv fell in community med 1975–78, specialist in community med Grampian Health Bd Aberdeen 1978–89, sr lectr Univ of Aberdeen 1984–89, gen mangr Highland Health Bd Inverness 1994– (chief admin offr and dir of public health 1989–94); FFPHM 1987 (MFCM 1977, MFCM Ireland 1990); *Recreations* hill walking, climbing, golf, motor cycling, modern literature; *Style*— Dr Gordon V Stone; ✉ Highland Health Board, Beechwood Park, Iverness IV2 3HG (☎ 01463 717123, fax 01463 235189)

STONE, Gregory; QC (1994); s of Frederick Albert Leslie Stone, of Bromley, Kent, and Marion Gerda, *née* Heller; *b* 12 Dec 1946; *Educ* Chislehurst and Sidcup GS, L'Université de Rennes, Queen's Coll Oxford (MA), Univ of Manchester (DipEcon, MA(Econ)); *Children*; 3 da (Rebecca Anne b 18 March 1978, Catherine Marion b 24 Feb 1980, Alexandra Grace b 26 April 1991); *Career* sr economist Morgan Grenfell & Co 1974–76, called to the Bar Inner Temple 1976, standing counsel to DTI 1989–90, practising barr S Eastern Circuit; *Books* The Law of Defective Premises (co-author, 1982), The Architect's Journal (co-ed, 2–5 edns); *Recreations* travel, walking, music, reading; *Style*— Gregory Stone, Esq, QC; ✉ 4–5 Gray's Inn Square, Gray's Inn, London WC1R 5AY (☎ 0171 404 5252, fax 0171 242 7803)

STONE, John Michael; MBE (1991); s of Robert Alfred Stone (d 1983), and Josephine Margery, *née* Sheen; *b* 26 April 1941; *Educ* Framlingham Coll; *m* 2 May 1964, Maxine Campbell, da of John Campbell-Lemon, of The Grange, Aylesbury Rd, Wendover, Bucks; 1 s (Timothy b 1974), 3 da (Karen b 1965, Paula b 1966, Nicola b 1970); *Career* md E Russell (West Country) Ltd 1971; chm: E Russell Ltd 1983 (dir 1962), Russell Meats Ltd 1984, Donald Russell Ltd 1984, Sims Food Group plc 1990–96 (chief exec 1988, jt chm 1989); dir Meat Training Council Ltd 1994–96; Freeman City of London 1964, Renter Asst Worshipful Co of Butchers (Liveryman 1965); fell Inst of Meat; *Books* Meat Buyers' Guide for Caterers (1983), Poultry and Game Buyers' Guide (1995); *Recreations* shooting, golf, cricket; *Clubs* MCC; *Style*— John Stone, Esq, MBE; ✉ Courtil a Gots, La Rue de la Porte, Castel, Guernsey GY5 7JR; Russell Meats Limited, Russell House, St Peter Technical Park, St Peter, Jersey JE3 7ZN (☎ 01534 483810, fax 01534 483960)

STONE, Sheriff Marcus; s of Morris Stone (d 1945), of Glasgow, and Reva Stone (d 1954); *b* 22 March 1921; *Educ* HS of Glasgow, Univ of Glasgow (MA, LLB); *m* 1956, Jacqueline, da of Paul Barnoin (d 1967), of France; 3 s (Patrick, William, Donald), 2 da (Cynthia, Martine); *Career* WWII served 1939–45, RASC W Africa; advocate 1965; sheriff: Dumbarton 1971–76, Glasgow 1976–84, Lothian and Borders at Linlithgow 1984–93; accredited mediator; memb Judicial Appraisal Panel Scotland Centre for Dispute Resolution; pres Assoc of Mediators, princ The Mediation Bureau; MIMgt; *Books* Proof of Fact in Criminal Trials (1984), Cross-examination in Criminal Trials (1988, 2 edn 1995), Fact-finding for Magistrates (1990), Representing Clients in Mediation (1997); *Recreations* music, swimming; *Style*— Sheriff Marcus Stone; ✉ Faculty of Advocates, Advocates Library, Parliament House, Edinburgh EH1 1RF (☎ 0131 226 5071)

STONE, Martin; s of Abraham Stone (d 1971), of Cardiff, S Wales, and Eva Priscilla, *née* Anstee (d 1988); *b* 28 Feb 1945; *Educ* The Cathedral Sch Llandaff Cardiff, Canton HS Cardiff, Univ of Liverpool (MB ChB, MD); *m* 4 July 1970, Jane, da of Tudor Lloyd-Williams (d 1978), of Mold, N Wales; 2 s (Andrew Martin b 1971, Robert Charles b 1975), 1 da (Louise Jane b 1980); *Career* jr doctor Liverpool Hosps 1968–72, sr house offr Torbay Hosp 1972–73, registrar Charing Cross Hosp 1973–75, res registrar MRC 1975–76; sr registrar: St George's Hosp 1976–77, Southampton Hosp 1977–80; conslt gynaecologist Gwent AHA 1980–; memb: Gwent Med Soc (chm 1994), London Obstetric and Gynaecological Soc (chm 1990), Med Advsy Ctee BUPA Hosp Cardiff (chm 1989), Welsh Obstetric and Gynaecological Soc (treas 1981–92); pres Caerleon Rotary Club 1991–92; memb BMA, MRCOG 1973, FRCOG 1986; *Recreations* skiing, red wine, theatre, golf; *Clubs* Celtic Manor Golf and Country, St Pierre Golf and Country; *Style*— Martin Stone, Esq; ✉ Ye Olde Forge, Llanmartin, Newport, Gwent NP6 2EB (☎ 01633 413073); St Joseph's Private Hospital, Harding Ave, Malpas, Newport, Gwent NPT 6QS (☎ 01633 858203); BUPA Hospital, Croescadarn Rd, Pentwyn, Cardiff, S Glamorgan CF2 7XL (☎ 01222 735515)

STONE, Michael John Christopher; s of Henry Frederick Stone (d 1979), and Joan Barbara, *née* Da Silva; *b* 10 May 1936; *Educ* Bradfield, Hamburg (Language Course); *m* 8 Jan 1966, Louisa, da of Robert Dyson, of Hawaii; 2 s (Charles b 9 Oct 1966, Andrew b 21 Nov 1970), 1 da (Nicola (Mrs Edward Farquhar) b 11 Jan 1968); *Career* cmmnd RHA 1955–57, served Germany, cmmnd HAC 1957–63; gp chm E D & F Man 1983– (commodity broker 1957); chm: E D & F Man Sugar Ltd, London Sugar Futures Market 1981–84; dir: Standard Bank Jersey Ltd 1992–95, Alistair Sampson Antiques 1991–, Calcot Manor Hotel 1993–, Redhill Aerodrome Ventures Ltd 1995–; chm: Nat Hosp for Neurology and Neurosurgery Devpt Fndn 1993–, Bradfield Fndn 1991–; govr Bradfield Coll; *Recreations* shooting, fishing, skiing; *Clubs* Brooks's; *Style*— Michael Stone, Esq; ✉ Ozleworth Park, Wotton-under-Edge, Gloucestershire GL12 7QA (☎ 01453 845591); E D & F Man Ltd, Sugar Quay, Lower Thames Street, London EC3R 6DU (direct ☎ 0171 285 3174)

STONE, Prof Norman; s of Flt Lt Norman Stone, RAF (ka 1942), and Mary Robertson, *née* Pettigrew (d 1991); *b* 8 March 1941; *Educ* Glasgow Acad, Gonville and Caius Coll Cambridge (BA, MA); *m* 1, 2 July 1966 (m dis 1977), Marie Nicole Aubry; 2 s (Nicholas b 1966, Sebastian b 1972); m 2, 11 Aug 1982, Christine Margaret Booker, *née* Verity; 1 s (Rupert b 1983); *Career* Univ of Cambridge: fell Gonville and Caius Coll 1965–71, lectr in Russian history 1968–84, fell Jesus Coll 1971–79, fell Trinity Coll 1979–84; Univ of Oxford: prof of modern history 1984–, fell Worcester Coll 1984–; *Books* The Eastern Front 1914–1917 (1975, Wolfson Prize 1976), Hitler (1980), Europe Transformed 1878–1919 (1983), The Other Russia (with Michael Glenny, 1990); *Recreations* Eastern Europe, music; *Clubs* Garrick, Beefsteak; *Style*— Prof Norman Stone; ✉ 22 St Margarets Rd, Oxford OX2 6RX (☎ 01865 510457); Worcester College, University of Oxford, Oxford OX1 2HB

STONE, Maj-Gen Patrick Philip Dennant; CB (1992), CBE (1984, OBE 1981, MBE 1976); s of Dr Philip Hartley Stone (d 1947), and Elsie Maude, *née* Dennant (d 1993); *b* 7 Feb 1939; *Educ* Christ's Hosp; *m* 5 June 1967, Christine Iredale, da of Gp Capt Leonard Henry Trent, VC (d 1986); 2 s (Edward Patrick Dennant b 1969, Robert Michael b 1972), 1 da (Celia Elizabeth b 1974); *Career* cmmnd East Anglian Regt 1959, King's African Rifles (Tanzania) 1959–61, Regimental Serv Guyana and S Arabia 1962–64, ADC Governor W Aust 1965–67, Regt Serv UK W Germany and NI 1967–72, RAF Staff Coll 1972, CO 2 Bn Royal Anglian Regt 1977–80, Chief of Staff 1 Armd Div 1981–84, Cdr Berlin Brigade 1985–87, dir gen Personnel (Army) 1988, ret 1991; Col The Royal Anglian Regt 1991–; *Recreations* country pursuits; *Clubs* Army & Navy; *Style*— Maj-Gen Patrick Stone, CB, CBE; ✉ Regimental HQ, The Royal Anglian Regiment, Bury St Edmunds, Suffolk IP33 3RN

STONE, Peter Charles Gray; s of Charles Edwin Stone (d 1993), and Blodwyn, *née* Griffiths (d 1985); *b* 28 April 1943; *Educ* Trevelyan Secdy Sch Windsor Berks; *m* Janet; 1 s (Lee Martin Gray b 21 April 1968), 1 da (Alexandra Bonnie b 9 March 1973); *Career* photographer; indentured photographer Maidenhead Advertiser 1958, Birmingham Planet Newspaper 1964, Daily Mirror 1964–88; numerous assignments incl: Trans-African Hovercraft Expedition (through West and Central Africa) 1969, overland expedition NY to Argentina World Cup Finals 1978, extensive war coverage, comprehensive coverage of showbiz personalities, photographs of Bob Geldof and the Boomtown Rats in USA, Japan and UK 1978–80, various features; freelance photographer for numerous magazines and newspapers 1988–; awarded Ilford Photographer of the Year for coverage of the Vietnam War 1973; *Books* Having Their Picture Taken - The Boomtown Rats (1980); *Recreations* golf, wining and dining, watching sport in general; *Style*— Peter Stone, Esq; ✉ Peter Stone Photography, 59 Welley Road, Wraysbury, Staines, Middx TW19 5ER (☎ and fax 01784 482914, mobile 0585 346005)

STONE, Peter John; s of late Dr Thomas Scott Stone; *b* 24 June 1946; *Educ* King's Sch Canterbury, Christ's Coll Cambridge; *m* 1972, Alison, da of Robert Smith Moffett; 2 s, 2 da; *Career* slr, ptnr Clintons 1972–75; banker Close Brothers Ltd 1975–; dir: Close Brothers Group plc, Close Brothers Holdings Ltd, Close Brothers Ltd, Close Invoice Finance Ltd, Close Brothers Trust Ltd, Close Brothers Securities Ltd, Close Brothers Merchant Securities Ltd, Close Nominees Ltd, Close Investmt Mgmnt Ltd, Air & General Finance Ltd, Safeguard Investmts Ltd, Business Advisory Services Ltd, Prompt Fin Inc (US Co), non exec conslt Thomas Miller & Co (mngrs insur mutuals) 1993–; *Recreations* travel, cricket, tennis, sailing, golf, gardening, music; *Style*— Peter Stone, Esq; ✉ Close Brothers Ltd, 12 Appold Street, London EC2A 2AA (☎ 0171 426 4000, fax 0171 426 4044)

STONE, Philippa Jane; da of Vivian Harry George Stubbs, of Duston, Northampton, and Merle Josephine Mure McKerrell, *née* Carver (d 1992); *Educ* Notre Dame HS Northampton, Univ of St Andrews, Univ of Oxford (BSc); *m* (m dis), David Robert Stone, s of Robert Charles Stone; 1 da; *Career* business conslt; dir: P J Stone Ltd 1984–, Sharepoint Ltd 1984–88, City Child Ltd (chm 1985–86), Children of High Intelligence Ltd 1991–94; tstee Self Esteem Network 1992– (chm 1994–95); memb: Redbridge Health Authy 1989–91, European Union of Women (chm London E 1991–, hon sec Gtr London Area 1992–95), Assoc of Eurotunnel Shareholders (chm 1995–); FMS; *Recreations* art, opera, skiing, tennis; *Clubs* St Andrews Univ Club London (chm 1993–); *Style*— Mrs Philippa Stone; ✉ 5 Harman Avenue, Woodford Green, Essex IG8 9DS

STONE, Rex; s of Hiram Stone, of Belper, Derbyshire, and Elsie Lorraine, *née* Taylor; *b* 13 Aug 1938; *Educ* Herbert Strutt GS; *m* 16 Oct 1965, Anita Kay, da of Albert Arthur Hammond (d 1974), of London; 1 s (Alistair b 7 May 1971), 1 da (Rachel b 23 March 1969); *Career* CA; audit mangr Peat Marwick Mitchell & Co (Jamaica) 1961–65, co sec RB MacMillan Ltd 1965–69; chm: Firestone Investments Ltd 1972–, Alida Holdings plc 1974– (fin dir 1969–72, jt md 1972–74), Chevin Holdings Ltd 1975–; dep chm: Derbyshire Building Society 1985–, British Polythene Industries plc 1989–; FCA 1961; *Recreations* wine, travel, game shooting, golf; *Style*— Rex Stone, Esq; ✉ Firestone Investments Ltd, 29 Bridge Street, Belper, Derby DE56 1AY (☎ 01773 827151, fax 01773 829843)

STONE, Richard Anthony; s of Jack Stone (d 1990), and Margaret Elizabeth, *née* Baraclough (d 1983); *b* 3 March 1943; *Educ* Univ of Cambridge (MA); *m* 26 Jan 1975, Susan Joan, da of Ronald James; 2 da (Natasha Louise b 4 Oct 1980, Katrina Elizabeth b 27 June 1984); *Career* Corp Fin Dept Outwich Ltd 1969–72 (dir venture capital subsid 1980), fin dir Regional Properties Ltd 1972–74; W H Cork Gully & Co (merged with Coopers & Lybrand 1980): articled clerk 1965–68, rejoined 1974, ptnr 1977–, head Insolvency Practice for the Midlands (Birmingham Office) 1982–86; Coopers & Lybrand: head Corp Fin Div 1987, chm Euro and UK Corp Fin Div 1994–95, dep chm 1995–; memb Ct of Assts Worshipful Co of Glaziers (Freeman 1973), Freeman Worshipful Co of CAs; memb City Livery; FCA; *Recreations* opera, ballet, golf, horse racing, travel, gardening; *Clubs* Carlton; *Style*— Richard A Stone, Esq; ✉ Coopers & Lybrand, Plumtree Court, London EC4A 4HT (☎ 0171 213 1062, fax 0171 213 1330)

STONE, Richard Frederick; QC (1968); s of Sir Leonard Stone, OBE, QC (d 1978), and Madeleine Marie, *née* Scheffler; *b* 11 March 1928; *Educ* Lakefield Coll Ontario Canada, Rugby, Univ of Cambridge (MA); *m* 1, 1957, Georgina Maxwell, *née* Morris (decd); 2 da (Victoria b 1958, Diana b 1960); m 2, 1964, Susan, *née* Van Heel; 2 da (Georgina b 1965, Amelia b 1967); *Career* Lt Worcester Regt 1946–48; called to the Bar Gray's Inn 1952; memb: Panel of Lloyd's Arbitrators in Salvage 1968, Panel of Wreck Cmmn 1968; bencher Gray's Inn 1974– (treas 1992); *Recreations* sailing, windsurfing, diving; *Clubs* Hayling Island Sailing; *Style*— Richard Stone, Esq, QC; ✉ 5 Raymond Buildings, Gray's Inn, London WC1R 5BP (☎ 0171 242 2697); 4 Field Court, Gray's Inn, London WC1R 5EA (☎ 0171 440 6900, fax 0171 242 0197, telex 262762 MEMG); 18 Wittering Rd, Hayling Island, Hants PO11 9SP (☎ 01705 463645)

STONE, Terence Reginald Stewart; s of Harry Victor Stone, of Grey Stones, Dawlish, Devon, and Hilda Mary, *née* Western; *b* 18 Aug 1928; *Educ* Willesden Coll of Technol, Coll of Architecture, Regent St Poly; *m* 1952, Beryl Joan, da of Douglas Bramwell Stewart; 4 s, 2 da; *Career* sr architect RAF Air Works Sqdn Air Miny 1947–49; chief architect Costain (W Africa) Ltd 1956–60, chm Terence Stone Gp of Companies 1970–, sr ptnr Stewart Stone Design Conslts 1988–; md: Terence Stone (Devpt) Ltd 1962–, Terence Stone (Construction) Ltd 1975–; Lord of the Manor Earl Stone Hants; FIAS, FRSH, FFB, FIMgt; *Recreations* swimming, tennis, badminton, running, motor rallying, skiing, sponsorship and promotion of sport, travel, arts; *Clubs* Rolls Royce Enthusiasts, RROC, RAC; *Style*— Terence Stone, Esq; ✉ Treston House, Earlstone Place, Dawlish, Devon (☎ 01626 863160); Treston Court, Dawlish, Devon (☎ 01626 862732); Terence Stone Group, Company House, Dawlish, Devon (☎ 01626 863543)

STONE, Prof Trevor William; s of Thomas William Stone, and Alice, *née* Reynolds; *b* 7 Oct 1947; *Educ* Mexborough GS, Univ of London (BPharm), Univ of Aberdeen (PhD); *m* 1971, Anne, da of Dr Lewis Corina; *Career* lectr in physiology Univ of Aberdeen 1970–77; Univ of London: sr lectr in neurosciences 1977–83, reader 1983–86, prof of neurosciences 1986–88; prof of pharmacology Univ of Glasgow 1989–; research fell Nat Inst Mental Health Washington DC 1974 and 1977; *Books* Microiontophoresis (1985), Purines: Basic & Clinical (1991), Adenosine in the Nervous System (1991),

Neuropharmacology (1995); *Recreations* snooker, photography, painting, music; *Style—* Prof T W Stone; ✉ Institute of Biomedical and Life Sciences, West Medical Building, University of Glasgow, Glasgow G12 8QQ (☎ 0141 330 4481)

STONEFROST, Maurice Frank; CBE (1983), DL (1986); s of Arthur Stonefrost (d 1980), of Bristol, and Anne, *née* Williams; *b* 1 Sept 1927; *Educ* Merrywood GS Bristol; *m* June 1953, Audrey Jean, da of Charles Fishlock (d 1986); 1 s (Mark), 1 da (Hilary, m William James Gregory Keegan, *qv*); *Career* Nat Serv RAF 1948–51; local govt: Bristol 1951–54, Slough 1954–56, Coventry 1956–61, W Sussex 1961–64; sec Chartered Inst of Public Fin and Accountancy 1964–73, controller of fin GLC 1973–84, dir gen and clerk GLC and ILEA 1984–85, dir and chief exec BR Pension Fund 1986–90, chm Municipal Insurance Group 1990–93, chm CLF Municipal Bank 1992–; pres Soc of Co Treasurers 1982–83, centenary pres Chartered Inst of Public Fin 1984–85; memb: Layfield Ctee on Local Govt Fin 1974–76, Ctee on the Future of the Legal Profession 1987–88, Cncl Architectural Heritage Fund 1987–; chm: Public Sector Liaison Ctee of the Accountancy Profession 1987–90, Speakers Cmmn of Citizenship 1988–90; memb Review of the Finances of the Church Cmmrs 1993, memb London Pension Fund Authy 1995–; dep pro-chllr City Univ 1992–; chm Dolphin Square Tst 1993–; tstee Harry Simpson Meml Library 1995–; Hon DSc City Univ 1987; DPA 1953, CIPIA 1955; *Books* Capital Accounting (1958); *Recreations* walking, gardening; *Style—* Maurice Stonefrost, Esq, CBE, DL; ✉ 611 Hood House, Dolphin Square, London SW1V 3LX (☎ 0171 798 8247)

STONEHAM, Prof (Arthur) Marshall; s of Garth Rivers Stoneham (d 1985), and Nancy Wooler, *née* Leslie; *b* 18 May 1940; *Educ* Barrow-in-Furness GS for Boys, Univ of Bristol (Merchant Venturers' scholar, BSc, PhD); *m* 25 Aug 1962, Doreen, da of John Montgomery (d 1974), of Barrow-in-Furness; 2 da ((Vanessa) Elise b 2 Sept 1963, (Karen) Nicola b 27 Jan 1966); *Career* Harwell Laboratory UKAEA: res fell Theoretical Physics Div 1964–66, sr scientific offr 1966–70, princ scientific offr 1970–74, gp leader Solid State Materials Gp (later Solid State and Quantum Physics Gp) 1974–89, individual merit promotion to Sr Staff Level 1979 (Band Level 1974), head Tech Area Gen Nuclear Safety Res Prog (Core and Fuel Studies) 1988–89, div head Materials Physics and Metallurgy Div 1989–90, dir Res AEA Industrial Technol 1990–, AEA chief scientist 1993–, Massey prof of physics and dir Centre for Materials Research Univ Coll London 1995–; visiting prof Univ of Illinois 1969, Wolfson Industrial fell Wolfson Coll Oxford 1985–89 (fell Governing Body 1989–95); visiting prof of chemistry Univ of Keele 1988–, visiting prof of physics Univ of Salford 1992–; memb Cncl Royal Instn 1992–95; Inst of Physics: ed Jl of Physics C - Solid State Physics 1984–88 (dep ed 1982–84), memb Exec Editorial Bd Jl of Physics - Condensed Matter 1989–, memb Editorial Bd Semiconductor Sci and Technol 1986–87, chm Books Editorial Advsy Ctee 1988–, dir of publishing 1988–, memb Cncl 1994–; memb Cncl Royal Soc 1994–; chm Hooke Ctee Royal Soc 1992–; divnl assoc ed Physical Review Letters (jl of American Inst of Physics) 1992–; memb Polar Solids Gp Ctee RSC; FInstP 1980, FRS 1989; *Books* Theory of Defects in Solids (1975, Russian edn 1978, reprinted 1985), Defects and Defect Processes in Non-Metallic Solids (with W Hayes, 1985), Reliability of Non-Destructive Inspection (with M G Silk and J A G Temple, 1987), Current Issues in Solid State Science (various), Ionic Solids at High Temperatures (1989), Ge Si Strained Layers and their Applications (1995); *Recreations* music scholarship, orchestral horn playing, reading; *Style—* Prof Marshall Stoneham, FRS; ✉ Riding Mill, Bridge End, Dorchester-on-Thames, Wallingford, Oxford OX10 7JP (☎ 01865 340066); Physics Department, University College London, Gower Street, London WC1E 6BT (☎ 0171 391 1377 (direct), 0171 391 1308, fax 0171 391 1360 and 0171 380 7145, e-mail ucapams@ucl.ac.uk or a.stoneham@ucl.ac.uk)

STONHOUSE, Rev Sir Michael Philip; 19 (E 1628) and 16 Bt (E 1670), of Radley, Berkshire; s of Sir Philip Allan Stonhouse, 18 and 15 Bt (d 1993), and (Winnifred) Emily, *née* Shield (d 1989); *b* 4 Sept 1948; *Educ* Medicine Hat Coll, Univ of Alberta (BA), Wycliffe Coll (MDiv); *m* 1977, (The Rev) Colleen Eleanor, da of James Albert Coucill (d 1969), of Toronto, Ontario, Canada; 3 s (Allan James b 1981, David Michael b 1983, Philip Radley b 1987); *Heir* s, Allan James Stonhouse b 20 March 1981; *Career* ordained: deacon 1977, priest 1978 (both Diocese of Calgary, Canada); asst curate St Peter's Calgary Alberta 1977–80; rector and incumbent: Parkland Parish Alberta 1980–87, St Mark's Innisfail and St Matthew's Bowden Alberta 1987–92, St James Saskatoon Saskatchewan 1992–; *Style—* The Rev Sir Michael Stonhouse, Bt; ✉ 3413–Balfour Street, Saskatoon, Saskatchewan S7H 3Z3, Canada (☎ 306 374 4157)

STONIER, George; *b* 12 Oct 1946; *m* 14 Feb 1976, Christine Mary; 1 s (Adam b 1982), 1 da (Anna May b 1978); *Career* fin accountant then co sec and industl rels dir Wedgwood Ltd (joined 1969), human resources dir Waterford Wedgwood UK plc 1988– (co sec 1986–); dir Wedgwood Museum Tst Ltd; chm Staffs LEN, memb Mgmnt Bd Staffs Enterprise Agency, vice pres Pottery and Glass Trades Benevolent Inst; FRSA, ACIS, ACMA; *Recreations* piano and fishing; *Style—* George Stonier, Esq; ✉ Waterford Wedgwood UK plc, Barlaston, Stoke-on-Trent, Staffs (☎ 01782 204141, fax 01782 204433, telex 36170, car 0589 046266)

STONOR, Air Marshal Sir Thomas Henry; KCB (1989); s of Alphonsus Stonor (d 1959), and Ann Stonor; *b* 5 March 1936; *Educ* St Cuthberts HS Newcastle-upon-Tyne, Kings Coll Univ of Durham (BSc); *m* 31 March 1964, Robin Antoinette, da of Wilfrid Budd (d 1980); 2 s (Jeremy Thomas b 1966, Giles Wilfrid b 1969), 1 da (Alexandra Clare b 1965); *Career* cmmnd RAF 1959, No 3 Sqdn 2 ATAF 1961–64, CFS, No 6 FTS, RAF Coll Cranwell 1964–67, No 231 OCU 1967–69, RAF Staff Coll 1970, HQ RAF Germany 1971–73, OC 31 Sqdn 1974–76, MA to VCDS 1976–78, OC RAF Coltishall 1978–80, RCDS 1981, Inspr Flight Safety 1982–84, Dir of Control (Airspace Policy) 1985–86, Dep Controller Nat Air Traffic Servs 1987–88, Gp Dir CAA and Controller Nat Air Traffic Servs 1988–91; aviation conslt 1991–; non exec dir: Parity plc 1994–, Siemens Plessey Electronic Systems 1995–; FRAeS, FCIT, FRSA; *Recreations* music, gardening; *Clubs* RAF; *Style—* Sir Thomas Stonor, KCB; ✉ 213 Woodstock Road, Oxford OX2 7AD (☎ 01865 516374); 82190 Lacour de Visa, France (☎ 00 33 6395 2709)

STOPFORD, Maj-Gen Stephen Robert Anthony; CB (1989), MBE (1971); s of Cdr Robert Maurice Stopford, DSC, RN (d 1977), and Elsie, *née* Lawson (d 1967); *b* 1 April 1934; *Educ* Downside, Millfield, RMA Sandhurst; *m* 8 Feb 1963, Vanessa, da of Theodore Baron (d 1982); *Career* cmmnd Scots Greys 1954 (Regtl Serv 1954–70), OC D Sqdn Scots DG 1970–72, MOD Central Staff 1972–74, CO Scots DG 1974–77, project mangr MBT 80 1977–79, Col OR 1/10 1979–83, mil attaché Washington 1983–85, dir gen Fighting Vehicles and Engr Equipment (DGFVE) 1985–89; dir David Brown Defence Equipment 1990–; AMIEE; *Recreations* shooting, electronics, sailing, diving; *Style—* Maj-Gen Stephen Stopford, CB, MBE

STOPFORD SACKVILLE, Lionel Geoffrey; only s of Lt-Col Nigel Stopford Sackville, CBE, TD, JP, DL, by his 1 w, Beatrix (d 1990), da of Col Hercules Pakenham, CMG (gn of 2 Earl of Longford); Col Stopford Sackville was gs of William Bruce Stopford (whose f Richard was 4 s of 2 Earl of Courtown), by William's wife Caroline, da of Hon George Germain and niece and heir of 5 and last Duke of Dorset; *b* 4 Nov 1932; *Educ* Eton; *m* 1, 1960, Susan, da of Jenkin Coles, of the Abbey, Knaresborough; 2 s (Charles b 1961, Thomas b 1968), 1 da (Lucinda b 1963, d 1992); m 2, 1980, Hon (Mary) Teresa, *née* Pearson, da of 3 Viscount Cowdray (d 1995); 1 da (Camilla b 1981); *Career* late Lt Northants Yeo, former Lt 14/20 Hussars, served Libya; chm: Nelson Gold Corporation, Lowick Manor Farms Ltd, Goedhuis & Co Ltd; dir: Dartmoor Investment Trust plc, Pantheon International Participations plc, Mercury World Mining Trust plc, Ranger Oil (North Sea) Ltd; former dir Charter Consolidated; High Sheriff Northants 1976–77; FCA; *Clubs* White's, Pratt's, MCC; *Style—* Lionel Stopford Sackville, Esq; ✉ Drayton House, Lowick, Kettering, Northants NN14 3BB (☎ 01832 733202); Flat 10, 43–44 Rutland Gate, London SW7 1PB (☎ 0171 584 7419)

STOPPARD, Dr Miriam; da of Sydney Stern, and Jenny Stern; *b* 12 May 1937; *Educ* Newcastle upon Tyne Central HS, Royal Free Hosp Sch of Med London (prize for experimental physiology), King's Coll Med Sch Univ of Durham (MB BS), Univ of Newcastle (MD, MRCP); *m* 1972 (m dis 1992), Tom Stoppard, s of late Eugene Straussler; 2 s, 2 step s; *Career* Royal Victorian Infirmary King's Coll Hosp Newcastle upon Tyne: house surgn 1961, house physician 1962, sr house offr in med 1962–63; Univ of Bristol: res fell Dept of Chemical Pathology 1963–65 (MRC scholar in chemical pathology 1963–65), registrar in dermatology 1965–66 (MRC scholar in dermatology), sr registrar in dermatology 1966–68; Syntex Pharmaceuticals Ltd: assoc med dir 1968–71, dep med dir 1971–74, med dir 1974–76, dep md 1976, md 1977–81, dir Syntex Corp 1991–; TV series: Where There's Life (5 series) 1981–, Baby and Co (2 series) 1984–, Woman to Woman 1985, Miriam Stoppard's Health and Beauty Show 1988 and 1992, Dear Miriam 1989, People Today 1991 and 1992; hon clinical lectr to the Inst of Dermatology Univ of London; memb: Heberden Soc, Br Assoc of Rheumatology and Rehabilitation; memb RSM; *Books* Miriam Stoppard's Book of Baby Care (1977), My Medical School (contrib, 1978), Miriam Stoppard's Book of Health Care (1979), The Face and Body Book (1980), Everywoman's Lifeguide (1982), Your Baby (1982), Fifty Plus Lifeguide (1982), Your Growing Child (1983), Baby Care Book (1983), Pregnancy and Birth Book (1984), Baby and Child Medical Handbook (1986), Everygirl's Lifeguide (1987), Feeding Your Family (1987), Miriam Stoppard's Health and Beauty Book (1988), Every Woman's Medical Handbook (1988), 7 lbs in 7 days (1991), Test Your Child (1991), The Magic of Sex (1991), Conception, Pregnancy and Birth (1992), Menopause (1994), A Woman's Body (1994), Complete Baby and Childcare (1995); over 40 publications in med jls; *Recreations* family, skiing, gardening; *Style—* Dr Miriam Stoppard; ✉ Iver Grove, Iver, Bucks

STOPS, Leigh Warwick; s of Dr Denis Warwick Stops, of Kingston, Surrey, and Patricia, *née* Hill; *b* 29 May 1946; *Educ* Latymer Upper Sch, Univ of Sussex (BSc), Univ of Lancaster (MA); *m* 3 Dec 1976, Patricia Jane, da of F H J Terry; 2 s (Caspar b 1986, Galen b 1988); *Career* advertising exec; dir: Colman RSCG & Ptnrs 1984–85, res and planning Allen Brady & Marsh Ltd 1985–90, planning Yellowhammer Advertising Ltd 1991–92; conslt The Business Development Group 1992–, sr lectr Univ of Bournemouth 1992–95, dir Publicis Ltd 1994–; *Recreations* sailing, theatre, media, advertisements; *Style—* Leigh W Stops, Esq; ✉ 5 Foster Rd, Chiswick, London W4 4NY; The Business Development Group, 20–22 Wellington Street, London WC2E 7DD (☎ 0171 497 3314, fax 0171 497 3312); Publicis Ltd, 82 Baker Street, London W1M 2AE (☎ 0171 935 4426, fax 0171 487 5351, e-mail leigh.stops@publicis.co.uk)

STORER, Prof Roy; s of Harry Storer (d 1980), of Wallasey, and Jessie, *née* Topham (d 1978); *b* 21 Feb 1928; *Educ* Wallasey GS, Univ of Liverpool (LDS, MSc, FDS, DRD); *m* 16 May 1953, Kathleen Mary Frances Pitman, da of Francis Charles Green; 1 s (Michael b 10 March 1961), 2 da (Sheila b 26 Feb 1956, Carolyn b 6 May 1958); *Career* Capt RADC 1951–52 (Lt 1950–51); sr lectr in dental prosthetics Univ of Liverpool 1962–67 (lectr 1954–61), visiting assoc prof Northwestern Univ Chicago 1961–62, hon conslt dental surgn Utd Liverpool Hosps 1962–67; Univ of Newcastle upon Tyne: prof of prosthodontics 1968–92, clinical sub-dean Dental Sch 1970–77, dean of dentistry 1977–92; sec and cncl memb Br Soc for the Study of Prosthetic Dentistry 1960–69; memb: Gen Dental Cncl 1977–92 (chm Educn Ctee 1986–90), Dental Educn Advsy Cncl (UK) 1978–92, Bd of Faculty of Dental Surgery RCS 1982–90, dental sub-ctee of Univ Grants Ctee 1982–89, med sub-ctee of Univ Funding Cncl 1989–91, EEC Dental Ctee Trg of Dental Practitioners 1986–92; Univ of Newcastle upon Tyne: previously memb Senate, Cncl and Court, chm Physical Recreation Ctee; memb Northern Sports Cncl; memb BDA 1950; *Recreations* Rugby football, cricket, gardening; *Clubs* East India, Athenaeum, MCC; *Style—* Prof Roy Storer; ✉ 164 Eastern Way, Darras Hall, Ponteland, Newcastle upon Tyne NE20 9RH (☎ and fax 01161 823286)

STOREY, Brian; s of Frederick Stalker (Eric) Storey, of Low Dubwath Farm, Kirklinton, and Lily, *née* Armstrong; *Educ* Irthins Valley Comp Sch Brampton Cumbria; *m* 16 July 1986, Diane Margaret, da of Frances Digby Coulthard; 3 s (Stuart b 11 Nov 1987, Andrew b 14 June 1989, Philip b 29 Aug 1991); *Career* national hunt jockey; former showjumper: began aged 11, northern jr champion 4 times, qualified for Jr Championships Hickstead and Wembley on Mystic Star 1978; professional nat hunt jockey 1983– (amateur 1981–83), first jockey to win Scot Champion Hurdle (Pat's Jester) and Scot National (Mighty Mark) in same season 1988–89; runs family farm with father; *Recreations* racing; *Style—* Brian Storey, Esq; ✉ Woodland View, Kirklinton, Carlisle, Cumbria CA6 6EF (☎ 01228 376); Low Dubwath Farm, Kirklinton (☎ 01228 331)

STOREY, Christopher Thomas; QC (1995); s of Leslie Hall Storey (d 1974), and Joan, *née* Walsh; *b* 13 Feb 1945; *Educ* Rugby; *m* 1968, Hilary Enid, da of Robert Cushing Johnston; 2 s (Stephen Douglas Edward b 1976, Peter Stuart Desmond b 1978); *Career* chartered accountant 1967–81, barr NE Circuit 1982–; ACA 1967–85; memb Hon Soc Lincoln's Inn 1977; *Recreations* music, motoring, instructor light aeroplanes, cricket, reading; *Style—* Christopher Storey, Esq, QC; ✉ Pearl Chambers, 22 East Parade, Leeds LS1 5BU (☎ 01132 452702)

STOREY, George Anthony (Tony); OBE (1990); s of George William Storey (d 1956), of Haltwhistle, Northumberland, and Edna Mary, *née* Bell; *b* 20 Feb 1939; *Educ* Queen Elizabeth GS Hexham, Univ of Nottingham (BA), Univ of Exeter (DipEd); *m* (m dis), Pamela May, *née* Trapnell; 1 s (Guy Keith b 30 May 1971), 1 da (Anne-Louise b 30 Oct 1972); *Career* Wallasey GS Cheshire 1961–64, tutor Dept of Educn Univ of Oxford 1964–68, curriculum devpt Bicester Sch Oxon 1964–68, warden Cwlth Lodge 1964–68, visiting lectr in education Univ of Botswana Lesotho and Swaziland 1967, asst dir of educn Westmoreland LEA (Kendal) 1968–71, headmaster The Hayfield Sch Doncaster 1971–; memb SHA; *Books* Haltwhistle and South Tynedale (1972); *Recreations* local history, theatre, watching rugby union, Northumberland; *Clubs* The Hayfield Sch; *Style—* Tony Storey, Esq, OBE; ✉ 9 The Paddocks, Lound, Retford, Notts DN22 8RR (☎ 01777 818627); The Hayfield School, Hurst Lane, Auckley, Doncaster DN9 3HG (☎ 01302 770589)

STOREY, Graham; s of Stanley Runton Storey (d 1971), of Meldreth, Cambs, and Winifred Graham (d 1975); *b* 8 Nov 1920; *Educ* St Edward's Sch Oxford, Trinity Hall Cambridge (MA); *Career* WWII 1941–45 served UK France and Germany, Lt 1942 (despatches); called to the Bar Middle Temple 1950; Trinity Hall Cambridge: fell 1949–88 (emeritus fell 1988, hon fell 1996), sr tutor 1958–68, vice master 1970–74, univ reader in English 1981–88 (lectr 1965–81, chm Faculty Bd 1972–74); visiting fell All Souls Coll Oxford 1968; lectr for Br Cncl Overseas, Warton lectr Br Acad 1984, Leverhulme emeritus fellowship, syndic CUP 1983, gen ed Cambridge English Prose Texts 1980–; vice pres G M Hopkins Soc 1971, pres Dickens Soc of America 1983–84; govr: St Edward's Sch Oxford 1959–69, Eastbourne Coll 1965–69; *Books* Reuters' Century (1951), Journals and Papers of G M Hopkins (jt ed, 1959), Angel with Horns (ed 1961), Selected Verse and Prose of G M Hopkins (ed, 1966), Letters of Dickens (jt ed, 1965–), A Preface to Hopkins (1981), Revolutionary Prose of the English Civil War (jt ed, 1983), Bleak House A Critical Study (1987), David Copperfield A Critical Study (1991); *Recreations* gardening, theatre, travel; *Style—* Graham Storey, Esq; ✉ Crown House, Caxton, Cambs (☎ 01954 719316); Trinity Hall, Cambridge (☎ 01223 332500)

STOREY, Helen (Mrs Ron Brinkers); da of David Storey, and Barbara, *née* Hamilton; *b* 16 Aug 1959; *Educ* Kingston Poly; *m* 27 Sept 1985, Ron Brinkers, s of Jan Brinkers; 1 s (Luke Dylan Storey-Brinkers); *Career* fashion designer; involved in design studio/publicity coordination and licensing: Valentino (Rome) 1981–82, Lancetti (Rome) 1982–83; own label launched 1984, estab shop Boyd & Storey (with Karen Boyd and Caroline Coates) London 1987, collections since shown as part of Fashion Week, first catalogue produced 1989, produced 'designer' collection for Jigsaw 1990 and subsequently for other clients incl Knickerbox, Sony, Cellnet and Alpa Romeo, opened flagship store Kings Road Chelsea 1992 and has since exported to 200 stores in 27 countries; work frequently featured in Vogue, Elle and Marie Claire magazines; a pioneer of designer sponsorship; fashion and style spokesperson, numerous interviews on TV and radio at home and abroad; nominated Young Designer of the Year Award and Best Eveningwear Designer Award BFC 1989; winner: British Apparel Export Award 1989, Most Innovative Designer Award Br Fashion Awards 1990 (nominated 1991); *Style—* Ms Helen Storey

STOREY, Jeremy Brian; QC (1994); s of Capt James Mackie Storey (d 1976), of Harrogate, N Yorks, and Veronica, *née* Walmsley (d 1978); *b* 21 Oct 1952; *Educ* Uppingham, Downing Coll Cambridge (MA); *m* 19 September 1981, Carolyn, da of Eric Raymond Ansell (d 1996), of Edenbridge, Kent; 2 da (Alexis Erica b 1991, Sasha Louise b 1994); *Career* called to the Bar Inner Temple 1974; recorder of the Crown Court (Western Circuit) 1995– (asst recorder 1990–95), dep official referee 1995–; *Recreations* travel, theatre, cricket; *Clubs* MCC, Glamorgan CCC; *Style—* Jeremy Storey, Esq, QC; ✉ 56 Westbere Rd, London NW2 3RU (☎ and fax 0171 435 4227); 4 Pump Court, Temple, London EC4Y 7AN (☎ 0171 353 2656, fax 0171 583 2036)

STOREY, Kenelm; s and h of Sir Richard Storey, 2 Bt, CBE, and Virginia Anne, *née* Cayley; *b* 4 Jan 1963; *Educ* Winchester, George Washington Univ USA; *Career* gen mangr Int Publishing Dept Guardian Newspapers Ltd, non-exec dir Portsmouth and Sunderland Newspapers plc; *Recreations* sport, art, theatre, architecture; *Clubs* I Zingari, MCC; *Style—* Kenelm Storey, Esq; ✉ The Grange, Settrington, Malton, Yorkshire YO17 8NU (☎ 01944 768369); 87 Lexham Gardens, London W8 6JN (☎ 0171 370 4862)

STOREY, Maude; CBE (1987); da of Henry Storey (d 1971), and Sarah Farrimond, *née* Davies (d 1981); *b* 24 March 1930; *Educ* Wigan and Dist Mining and Tech Coll, St Mary's Hosp Manchester, Lancaster Royal Infirmary, Paddington Gen Hosp, Royal Coll of Nursing Edinburgh (RN, RM, RCNT), Queen Elizabeth Coll Univ of London (RNT); *Career* domicillary midwife Wigan Co Borough 1953–56, midwifery sister St Mary's Hosp Manchester 1956–59, head nurse Intensive Therapy Unit Mayo Clinic USA 1957–59, theatre sister, clinical instr and nurse tutor Royal Albert Edward Infirmary Wigan 1959–68, lectr in community nursing Univ of Manchester 1968–71, asst and subsequently princ regnl nursing offr Liverpool Regnl Hosp Bd 1971–73, regnl nursing offr Mersey RHA 1973–77, registrar Gen Nursing Cncl for England and Wales 1977–81, chief exec UK Central Cncl for Nursing Midwifery and Health Visiting (UKCC) 1981–87; memb W Berks Health Authy 1977–90, chm Local Research Ethics Ctee W Berks 1993–96; non-exec dir: Berks Health Authy 1990–94, Berks Health Cmmn 1994–96; memb Cncl Univ of Reading 1989–; pres Royal Coll of Nursing of the UK 1986–90 (life vice pres 1990); CStJ 1988; FRCN 1996; *Recreations* theatre, travel; *Style—* Miss Maude Storey, CBE; ✉ 14 Conifer Drive, Tilehurst, Reading, Berks RG31 6YU (☎ 0118 941 2082)

STOREY, Michael Gerald; *b* 8 Oct 1941; *Educ* Queen Elizabeth GS Wakefield Yorks, Hosp Admin Staff Coll King Edward's Hosp Fund London, Univ of Chicago (MBA); *m*; 2 c; *Career* admin trainee Pinderfields Hosp 1958–61, dep admin York Co Hosp 1961–63, dep admin Royal Orthopaedic Gp of Hosps and admin W Heath Hosp Birmingham 1963–64; vice pres/int mgmnt conslt Booz Allen 1968–83; City Centre Communications Ltd (cable TV co): co-fndr 1983, variously gen mangr, md and dep chm, fndr and md Westminster Cable Ltd; gp dir of corp strategy and public affrs Videotron Corporation Ltd (following takeover of City Centre Communications) 1990–92, md MFS Communications Ltd 1993–95, pres and chief exec offr MFS Europe 1995–; co-fndr and chm: Rewind Productions (ind radio prodn co), TV Choice Ltd; non-exec dir: Hammersmith Royal Post Graduate Teaching Hosp 1981–83, Central Blood Laboratories Authy 1982–84, NW Thames RHA 1983–92; chm NW London Mental Health NHS Trust 1993–; past chm Cable TV Assoc (and past chm Telecommunications Ctee); MHSM 1963, MIPM 1966; *Style—* Michael G Storey, Esq; ✉ 4 St Mark's Crescent, London NW1 7TS (☎ 0171 482 2836)

STOREY, Michael John William; s of Jack Storey, and Pamela Jessamine, *née* Helmore; *b* 30 Dec 1947; *Educ* Wells Cathedral Sch, Central Sch of Speech and Drama; *m* 3 Sept 1976, Virginia, da of Havelock Clive-Smith (d 1964); 2 s (Daniel b 1 Feb 1978, d 1985, Alec b 26 April 1983), 1 da (Florence b 8 March 1987); *Career* composer of music for numerous films incl: Gertler, Another Country, Every Picture tells a Story, The Dress, Coming Up Roses, Hidden City, A Perfect Spy; nominated for a BAFTA Award for A Perfect Spy, winner Ivor Novello Award for theme music for Civies 1993; active memb Greenpeace; *Recreations* tennis, squash, snooker; *Style—* Michael Storey, Esq

STOREY, Hon Sir Richard; 2 Bt (UK 1960) of Settrington, Co York; CBE (1996); s of Baron Buckton (Life Peer, d 1978), and Elisabeth (d 1951), da of late Brig-Gen W J Woodcock, DSO; *b* 23 Jan 1937; *Educ* Winchester, Trinity Coll Cambridge (BA, LLB); *m* 1961, Virginia Anne, da of late Sir Kenelm Henry Ernest Cayley, 10 Bt; 1 s, 2 da; *Heir* s, Kenelm Storey, *qv*; *Career* Nat Serv RNVR 1956; called to Bar Inner Temple 1962, practised until 1969; chm Portsmouth and Sunderland Newspapers plc 1973– (joined bd 1962, chief exec 1973–86); contested (C) Don Valley 1966 and Huddersfield West 1970; dir: One Stop Community Stores Ltd 1971–, Reuters Holdings Plc 1986–92, The Fleming Enterprise Investment Trust Plc 1989– (chm 1996–), Press Association Ltd 1986–95 (chm 1991–95), Foreign & Colonial Smaller Companies PLC 1993–; memb: Newspaper Soc Cncl 1980– (pres 1990–91), Press Cncl 1980–86, Regnl Cncl Yorkshire and Humberside CBI 1974–79, Nat Cncl and Exec Ctee CLA 1980–84 (chm Yorkshire Exec 1974–76), Cncl INCA-FIEJ Res Assoc 1983–88, CBI Employment Policy Ctee 1984–88; fndr chm Regnl Daily Advertising Cncl 1988–90 (dir 1988–91), chm Sir Harold Hillier Gardens and Arboretum Mgmnt Ctee 1989–; tstee The Royal Botanic Gardens Kew Fndn 1990–; chm York Health Services NHS Trust 1991–; rep European Newspaper Publishers' Assoc 1990–96; farms and administers land and woodland; High Sheriff N Yorks 1992–93; Liveryman Worshipful Co of Stationers and Newspapermakers; hon fell Univ of Portsmouth, Hon DLitt Univ of Sunderland; FRSA; *Recreations* sport, silviculture; *Style—* The Hon Sir Richard Storey, Bt, CBE; ✉ 7 Douro Place, London W8 5PH (☎ 0171 937 8823); Settrington House, Malton, N Yorks YO17 8NP (☎ 01944 768400); Portsmouth & Sunderland Newspapers plc, Buckton House, 39 Abingdon Rd, London W8 6AH (☎ 0171 938 1066, fax 0171 937 2779)

STOREY, Richard Alec; s of Edwin Alexander Storey, of Mundesley-on-Sea, and Minnie Florence, *née* Trundle (d 1988); *b* 2 June 1937; *Educ* Hertford GS, Downing Coll Cambridge; *m* 14 Jan 1961, Jennifer, da of James Clare (d 1990), of Ware; 2 s (Daniel b 1966, Lawrence b 1968), 1 da (Emma b 1969); *Career* Nat Serv RAEC 1959–61; local govt admin 1961–3, archivist Historical Manuscripts Cmmn 1963–73, sr archivist Modern Records Centre Univ of Warwick Library 1973–; ed Business Archives 1969–73 and 1975–78; memb Nat Cncl on Archives 1988–95; co-proprietor Odibourne Press; *Books* Primary Sources for Victorian Studies (1977, updated 1987); contrib: Ambit (poetry), Dictionary of Labour Biography, Dictionary of Business Biography, New DNB; *Recreations* literature, biography, cinema, local and transport history, archaeology; *Style—* Richard Storey, Esq; ✉ 32 High St, Kenilworth, Warwicks CV8 1LZ (☎ 01926 857409)

STOREY, Stuart Ellis; s of Charles Ellis Storey (d 1995), of Holbeach, Lincs, and Kathleen Mary Storey (d 1982); *b* 16 Sept 1942; *Educ* Spalding GS, Loughborough Coll (Dip PE), Western Kentucky Univ USA (MA); *m* 28 Nov 1970, Shirley, da of Donald Hugh Godfrey Gardner; 2 s (Benjamin Ellis b 24 Feb 1974, James Stuart b 26 Nov 1976); *Career* TV sports commentator (athletics); teacher PE and maths Dr Challoner's GS Amersham 1965–67, graduate asst coach (swimming, judo, volleyball) Western Univ Kentucky 1967–68, supply teacher in PE Kitwood Sch Boston Lincs 1968–69, head of PE Loughton Coll of Further Educn 1969–73 (also dep warden Debden Community Assoc), head of PE Thames Poly 1973 (dir of PE until 1989); with BBC Sports Dept 1974– (currently freelance); covered 6 Olympic Games, 5 World Championships, 4 Cwlth Games and 6 Euro Championships; athletics career: winner All Eng Schs 100m Hurdles 1959, winner All Eng Schs 110m Hurdles 1961 (runner up 1960), first sr int Eng vs GDR (110m Hurdles) 1965, memb GB team Olympics Mexico 1968 and Euro Championships 1969, memb Eng team Cwlth Games 1970 (all at 110m Hurdles); also sometime coach to Geoff Capes (former Shot Putt champion); *Recreations* golf, running; *Style—* Stuart Storey, Esq; ✉ c/o BBC Sport & Events Group, BBC Television Centre, Wood Lane, Shepherds Bush, London W12 7RJ

STORIE-PUGH, Col Peter David; CBE (1981, MBE 1945), MC (1940), TD (1945), DL (1963); s of late Prof Leslie Pugh, CBE, and Paula Storie; *b* 1 Nov 1919; *Educ* Malvern Coll, Queens' Coll Cambridge (MA, PhD), Royal Veterinary Coll Univ of London FRCVS; *m* 1, 1946 (m dis 1971), Alison, da of late Sir Oliver Lyle, OBE; 1 s, 2 da; m 2, 1971, Leslie Helen, da of Earl Striegel; 3 s, 1 da; *Career* served WWII, Queen's Own Royal W Kent Regt (escaped from Spangenberg and Colditz), cmd 1 Bn Cambs Regt, Suffolk and Cambs Regt, Col Dep Cdr 161 Inf Bde, ACF Co Cmdt; lectr Univ of Cambridge 1953–82, UK del EEC Vet Liaison Ctee 1962–75 (pres 1973–75), UK rep Fedn of Veterinarians of EEC 1975–83 (pres 1975–79); chm: Nat Sheepbreeders' Assoc 1964–68, Eurovet 1971–73; pres: Cambridge Soc for Study of Comparative Med 1966–67, Int Pig Vet Soc 1967–69 (life pres 1969), Br Vet Assoc 1968–69 and 1970–71, 1 Euro Vet Congress Wiesbaden 1972, RCVS 1977–78; memb: Econ and Social Consultative Assembly of the Euro Communities 1982–89, Parly and Sci Ctee 1962–67, Home Sec's Advsy Ctee 1963–80, Nat Agric Centre Advsy Bd 1966–69, Miny of Agric Farm Animal Advsy Ctee 1970–73; fell Wolfson Coll Cambridge; CChem, FRSC; *Books* Eurovet: an Anatomy of Veterinary Europe (1972), Eurovet 2 (1975); *Style—* Col Peter Storie-Pugh, CBE, MC, TD, DL; ✉ 16 Pentlands Court, Cambridge CB4 1JN (☎ 01223 354693, fax 01223 327656)

STORMONT, Viscount; Alexander David Mungo; s and h of 8 Earl of Mansfield and Mansfield; *b* 17 Oct 1956; *Educ* Eton; *m* 1985, Sophia Mary Veronica, only da of (Philip) Biden Derwent Ashbrooke (d 1993), of St John, Jersey, CI; 1 s (Hon William Philip David Mungo, Master of Stormont b 1 Nov 1988), 2 da (Hon Isabella Mary Alexandra Murray b 1987, Hon Iona Margaret Sophia Murray b 1992); *Clubs* White's, Pratt's, Perth; *Style—* Viscount Stormont; ✉ Scone Palace, Perth, Perthshire PH2 6BD

STORMONTH DARLING, Sir James Carlisle (Jamie); kt (1982), CBE (1972), MC (1945), TD, WS (1949); s of Robert Stormonth Darling, WS (d 1956), and Beryl Madeleine, *née* Sayer (d 1955); *b* 18 July 1918; *Educ* Winchester, ChCh Oxford (MA), Univ of Edinburgh (LLB); *m* 1948, Mary Finella, BEM (1945), DL (E Lothian), da of Lt-Gen Sir James Gammell, KCB, DSO, MC (d 1975); 1 s (Angus), 2 da (Caroline, Priscilla); *Career* served WWII KOSB and 52 (Lowland) Div Reconnaissance Regt RAC, Lt-Col 1945; memb Queen's Body Guard for Scotland (Royal Co of Archers) 1958–; dir: Scottish Widows' Fund and Life Assur Soc 1981–89, Nat Tst for Scot (chief exec and dir 1949–83, vice pres emeritus 1985–); Scot's Gardens Scheme: exec ctee 1951–, vice pres 1983–; memb Ancient Monuments Bd for Scot 1983–93; a vice pres Scot Conservation Projects Tst (former pres); Edinburgh Old Town Charitable Tst: chm 1987–90, tstee 1987–; tstee Scot Churches Architectural Heritage Tst, tstee and vice chm Scotland's Churches Scheme; patron: The Edinburgh Green Belt Tst, The Woodland Tst, The Dynamic Earth (fndr); Hon DUniv Stirling 1983, Hon LLD Univ of Aberdeen 1984; Hon FRIAS 1982; *Recreations* hill walking, gardening, countryside pursuits; *Clubs* New (Edinburgh), Hon Co of Edinburgh Golfers; *Style—* Sir Jamie Stormonth Darling, CBE, MC, TD, WS; ✉ Chapelhill House, Dirleton, N Berwick, East Lothian EH39 5HG (☎ 01620 850296)

STORMONTH DARLING, Peter; s of Patrick Stormonth Darling (d 1960), and Edith, *née* Lamb (d 1980); *b* 29 Sept 1932; *Educ* Winchester, New Coll Oxford (MA); *m* 1, 1958 (m dis), Candis Hitzig; 3 da (Candis Christa b 1959, Elizabeth Iona b 1960, Arabella b 1962); m 2, 1970, Maureen O'Leary; *Career* 2 Lt Black Watch 1950–53, served Korean War, Flying Offr RAFVR 1953–56; dir Mercury Asset Management Group plc (chm 1979–92); chm: Mercury International Investment Trust, Mercury European Privatisation Trust, Deltec International SA; dep chm: Scottish Equitable plc, Mercury Selected Trust; dir: Scottish Hydro-Electric plc, Mercury Keystone Investment Co, The Europe Fund Inc, The United Kingdom Fund Inc, Greenwich Associates; memb: Int Markets Bd Nat Assoc of Securities Dealers, Investmt Ctee UN Jt Staff Pension Fund, Investmt and Fin Ctee Int Inst of Strategic Studies; *Style—* Peter Stormonth Darling, Esq; ✉ Mercury Asset Management Group plc, 33 King William Street, London EC4R 9AS

STORR, Dr (Charles) Anthony; s of The Rev Vernon Faithfull Storr (d 1940), of Westminster, and Katherine Cecilia Storr (d 1954); ggf Paul Storr (1771–1844) was the Regency Silversmith and also ggf to Laurence and Rex Whistler; *b* 18 May 1920; *Educ* Winchester, Christ's Coll Cambridge (MB BChir, MA); *m* 1, 1942, Catherine, da of late Arthur Cole, of Lincoln's Inn; 3 da (Sophia, Polly, Emma); m 2, 1970, Catherine, da of late A D Peters; *Career* hon conslt psychiatrist Oxford Health Authy, formerly clinical lectr in psychiatry Univ of Oxford, fell Green Coll Oxford 1979 (emeritus fell 1984); FRCPsych, FRCP, FRSL; *Books* The Integrity of the Personality (1960), Sexual Deviation (1964), Human Aggression (1968), Human Destructiveness (1972), The Dynamics of Creation (1972), Jung (1973), The Art of Psychotherapy (1979), Jung: Selected Writings (ed, 1983), Solitude: A Return to the Self (1988), Churchill's Black Dog and Other Phenomena of the Human Mind (1989), Freud (1989), Music and the Mind (1992), Feet of Clay (1996); *Recreations* music, journalism, broadcasting; *Clubs* Savile; *Style—* Dr Anthony Storr, FRSL; ✉ 45 Chalfont Rd, Oxford OX2 6TJ (☎ and fax 01865 553348)

STORR, Catherine; *see:* Balogh, Baroness; Catherine

STORRS, Dr John Alastair; s of Francis Cecil Storrs, of Badwell Ash, Suffolk, and Constance Mary, *née* Budd (d 1990); *b* 27 May 1940; *Educ* St Benedict's Abbey Sch Ealing London, Univ of London (MRCS, LRCP, MB BS, FFARCS, DA); *m* 30 May 1964 (m dis 1989), Maureen Anne, da of late Harry M Hewett; 1 s (Jonathan Amery b 5 March 1965), 1 da (Jacqueline Louise b 8 June 1967); m 2, 8 Sept 1990, Sheila Bowen, da of Albert Hands; *Career* registrar and sr registrar anaesthetist UCH 1967–70, conslt anaesthetist Royal Victoria Infirmary and assoc hosps Newcastle 1971–95, lectr in anaesthesia Univ of Newcastle upon Tyne 1971–95; dep dir Anaesthesia Servs Royal Women's Hosp Victoria Australia 1995–; invitation lectr Univ of Amsterdam 1974; overseas sec Obstetric Anaesthetists Assoc 1990–93, former chm Div of Anaesthesia Newcastle DHA, warden Eustace Percy Hall Univ of Newcastle 1989–93; *Books* Epidural Analgesia in Obstetrics (1974), Current Research on Enflurane: Obstetric Anaesthesia

(1981), Controversies in Obstetric Anaesthesia (contrib, 1990); *Recreations* rowing, sailing, music, photography, travel; *Style—* Dr John Storrs; ✉ 6 Aquarius Court, Donvale, Victoria 3111, Australia (☎ and fax 00 61 03 9873 5039); Royal Women's Hospital, 132 Gratton Street, Carlton, Victoria 3053, Australia (☎ 00 61 03 9344 2100, fax 00 61 03 9347 2464)

STORY, Mark Trafford; s of John Story (d 1991), of Co Kildare, and Elaine Story; *b* 10 May 1955; *Educ* Dublin HS, Sch of Law Trinity Coll Dublin (BA, LLB); *Career* prodr RTE Radio 1978–83; sr prodr: Capital Radio 1983–88, BBC Radio 1 1988–90; prog dir: Piccadilly Radio 1990–95, Virgin Radio 1995–; Sony Award nominee, New York Radio Gold Medal, Premios Ondos Gold winner; *Recreations* collecting Oriental art; *Style—* Mark Story, Esq; ✉ Virgin Radio, 1 Golden Square, London W1 3AB (☎ 0171 434 1215, fax 0171 434 1197)

STOTHARD, Peter Michael; s of Wilfred Max Stothard, and Patricia Jean, *née* Savage; *b* 28 Feb 1951; *Educ* Brentwood Sch Essex, Trinity Coll Oxford (MA); *m* 1980, Sally Ceris, *née*, Emerson; 1 da (Anna Ceris b 22 Nov 1983), 1 s (Michael Peter b 20 Dec 1987); *Career* journalist BBC 1974–77, Shell International Petroleum 1977–79, business and political writer Sunday Times 1979–80; The Times: features ed and leader writer 1980–85, dep ed 1985–92, ed 1992–; *Recreations* ancient and modern literature; *Clubs* Reform; *Style—* Peter Stothard, Esq; ✉ The Times, 1 Pennington Street, London E1 9XN (☎ 0171 782 5145/6)

STOTHER, Ian George; s of John Stother, of Lytham, Lancs, and Joan Lilian, *née* Jones; *b* 12 Feb 1945; *Educ* King Edward VII Sch Lytham, King's Coll Cambridge (MA, MB BChir); *m* 7 April 1969, Jacqueline, da of Alan B Mott, of Heslington, York; 2 da (Lindsay Anne b 21 April 1972, Clare Jennifer (twin) b 21 April 1972); *Career* clinical dir Orthopaedic Dept Glasgow Royal Infirmary Univ NHS Tst 1995–; hon clinical sr lectr in orthopaedics Univ of Glasgow, hon lectr Biological Engrg Unit Univ of Strathclyde, orthopaedic advsr Dance Sch for Scotland; fell: Br Assoc for Surgery of the Knee, Int Arthroscopy Assoc, Assoc of Surgns of E Africa; FRCSEd 1974 (Glasgow 1981), FBOA; *Recreations* classic cars, ballet; *Style—* Ian Stother, Esq; ✉ Glasgow Nuffield Hospital, 25 Beaconsfield Rd, Glasgow G12 OPJ (☎ 0141 334 9441, fax 0141 339 1352); Glasgow Royal Infirmary, Glasgow G4 OSF ☎ 0141 211 4000)

STOTT, Sir Adrian George Ellingham; 4 Bt (UK 1920), of Stanton, Co Gloucester; s of Sir Philip Sidney Stott, 3 Bt (d 1979), and Cicely Florence, *née* Ellingham (d 1996); *b* 7 Oct 1948; *Educ* Univ of British Columbia (BSc, MSc), Univ of Waterloo Ontario (MMaths); *Heir* bro, Vyvyan Philip Stott, *qv*; *Career* dir of planning (county) 1974–77, town planning conslt 1977–80, real estate portfolio mangr 1980–85, mangr of conservation agency 1985, of marketing co 1986–88; mgmnt conslt 1989–; memb: Assoc for Computing Machinery, Canadian Inst of Planners; *Recreations* music, inland waterways, politics; *Clubs* Inland Waterways Assoc; *Style—* Sir Adrian Stott, Bt; ✉ The Downs, Little Amwell, Hertfordshire SG13 7SA (☎ 0956 299966); The Downs, Little Amwell, Hertfordshire SG13 7SA

STOTT, (Robert Thomas) Dursley; OBE (1997), JP (1977); s of Robert Leonard Stott (d 1991), of Onchan, IOM, and Winifrede Anna, *née* Halsall (d 1989); *b* 13 Feb 1935; *Educ* King William's Coll IOM, Magdalene Coll Cambridge (MA); *m* 15 June 1959, Margot, da of George Donald Winston Ashton; 1 s (Paul b 1962), 1 da (Mandy b 1960); *Career* Nat Serv cmmnd 2 Lt 1 Bn The Loyal Regt 1955; non-exec dir: Isle of Man Steam Packet Co Ltd, Sefton Hotel Ltd; pres: IOM Central Cncl Branch British Red Cross Soc, IOM Cwlth Games Assoc; hon pres IOM Shooting Cncl, tstee Manx National Heritage; conslt Messrs Hargreave Hale & Co Stockbrokers; MSI (memb Stock Exchange 1962), FRSA 1988; *Recreations* shooting, walking, reading; *Clubs* MCC, Hawks, Ellan Vannin; *Style—* Dursley Stott, Esq, OBE, JP; ✉ Ivydene, Little Switzerland, Douglas, Isle of Man (☎ 01624 621711); Hargreave Hale & Co (☎ 01624 620909)

STOTT, Rt Hon Lord; George Gordon Stott; PC (1964); s of late Rev Dr G Gordon Stott, and late Flora Corsar Stott; *b* 22 Dec 1909; *Educ* Cramond Sch, Edinburgh Acad, Univ of Edinburgh (MA, LLB, DipEd); *m* 1947, Nancy Deverell, da of late A D Braggins; 1 s, 1 da; *Career* Scottish advocate 1936, advocate-depute 1947–51, KC 1950, sheriff of Roxburgh, Berwick and Selkirk 1961–64, lord advocate 1964–67; a Lord of Session 1967–84; *Publications* Lord Advocate's Diary, Judge's Diary; *Style—* The Rt Hon Lord Stott; ✉ 12 Midmar Gdns, Edinburgh (☎ 0131 447 4251)

STOTT, Ian Hood; s of Alan James Stott, and Mae, *née* Hood; *b* 29 Jan 1934; *Educ* Shrewsbury (1st XV rugby, capt fives); *m* 1, 1957, Gabrielle Mary, da of Rev W S Tuke; 2 s (Robert Ian b 1958, Simon Andrew b 1960 d 1989); m 2, 1979, Patricia Mary, da of Dr M Wynroe; 2 da (Ailsa Jane b 1980, Catherine Mally b 1982); *Career* Nat Serv Green Jackets and Lancs Fus (Lt) 1952–54; James Stott Ltd cotton spinners and weavers Oldham 1954–57, John Bright & Sons Ltd Rochdale 1957–62, proprietor garage gp/caravan park/hotels/property 1962–86, chm and md Oldham Athletic AFC 1986– (chm 1982–); memb: FA Cncl 1986–, Football League Mgmnt Ctee 1986–92, FA Exec 1992–94; *Recreations* cooking, food and drink, bridge, music; *Style—* Ian Stott, Esq; ✉ Oldham Athletic FC, Boundary Park, Oldham, Lancs OL1 2PA (☎ 0161 624 4972, fax 0161 627 5915)

STOTT, Kathryn; da of Desmond Stott, of Nelson, Lancs, and Elsie, *née* Cheetham; *b* 10 Dec 1958; *Educ* Yehudi Menuhin Sch, Royal Coll of Music (ARCM, Tagore Golden Medal); *children* 1 da (Lucy b 9 Nov 1984); *Career* pianist; studied under Vlado Perlemuter, Louis Kentner and Kendall Taylor; fifth place Leeds Int Piano Competition 1978, awarded Churchill scholarship 1979; recent recitals incl: Int Piano Series Wigmore Hall, Michael Nyman Festival South Bank, Poulenc Concerto with Radio Symphony Orch Utrecht, Gabriel Fauré Festival (artistic leader) Manchester 1995, Britten Concerto with Netherlands Philharmonic Orch Concertgebouw 1995, Beethoven Triple concerto with BBC Scottish Symphony Orch BBC Proms 1995; also played in Germany, Italy, Spain, Czech Republic, Poland, France, Switzerland, Hong Kong, Singapore, Japan, Saudi Arabia, Zimbabwe (USA with Yo-Yo Ma); *Recordings* solo recordings incl: works by Chabrier, Debussy, Liszt, Rachmaninov, Frank Bridge, Fauré complete piano works, Chopin complete Nocturnes; other recordings incl: John Ireland Concerto and Walton Sinfonia Concertante with RPO and Vernon Handley, George Lloyd Concerto No 3 with BBC Philharmonic, Herbert Howells Concerto No 2 with Royal Liverpool Philharmonic Orch and Vernon Handley, Michael Nyman Piano Concerto, Fauré Orchestral Works with Yan Pascal Tortelier and BBC Philharmonic; *Recreations* horse riding, travel; *Style—* Ms Kathryn Stott; ✉ c/o Charlie de la Cousine, Interartists Holland BV, Vondelstr 47, 1054 GJ Amsterdam, Holland (☎ 00 31 20 618 0842, fax 00 31 20 689 6384)

STOTT, Prof Nigel Clement Halley; s of Maj Halley Harwin Stott, of Natal, and Joyce, *née* Greathead; *b* 27 Nov 1939; *Educ* Univ of Edinburgh (BSc, MB ChB, MRCP); *m* 7 April 1965, (Eleanor) Mary, da of (Townroe) Stephen Collingwood, of Shaftesbury; 2 s (Philip b 19 April 1969, Howard b 25 Nov 1971), 1 da (Paula b 4 June 1967); *Career* registrar Epidemiology Res Unit MRC 1969–70, med offr St Lucy's Hosp Transkei 1970–71, sr lectr Welsh Nat Sch of Med 1972–79, prof of primary med care Southampton 1979–80, prof of gen practice Univ of Wales Coll of Med 1986–; author of numerous chapters and papers; memb: Jt Med Advsy Ctee of the Higher Educn Funding Cncls for UK, Cncl Univ of Wales Coll of Med; chair MRC: Gen Practice Research Framework, Topic Review on Research in Gen Practice 1996; FRCPE 1980, FRCGP 1985 (MRCGP 1979); *Books* Primary Health Care: Bridging the Gap between Theory and Practice (1983), Care of the Dying (1984), Health Checks in General Practice (1988), Making Changes (1990), Research in Practice (1993), The Nature of General Medical Practice (1995); *Recreations* sailing, gardening; *Clubs* Professional & Academic; *Style—* Prof Nigel Stott; ✉ Department of General Practice, University of Wales College of Medicine, Heath Park, Cardiff CF4 4XN (☎ 01222 541133)

STOTT, Richard Keith; s of Fred Brookes Stott (d 1964), and Bertha, *née* Pickford (d 1995); *b* 17 Aug 1943; *Educ* Clifton; *m* 1970, Penelope Anne Stott, JP, yr da of Air Vice-Marshal Sir Colin Scragg, KBE, CB, AFC and bar (d 1989); 1 s (Christopher b 1978), 2 da (Emily b 1972, Hannah b 1975); *Career* journalist; jr reporter Bucks Herald Aylesbury 1963–65, Ferrari News Agency Dartford 1965–68, reporter Daily Mirror 1968–79 (features ed 1979–81, asst ed 1981–84); ed: Sunday People 1984–85, Daily Mirror 1985–89, The People 1990–91, Daily Mirror 1991–92, Today 1993–95; Br Press Award for Reporter of the Year 1977, What the Papers Say Ed of the Year 1993; *Recreations* theatre, reading; *Style—* Richard Stott

STOTT, Roger; CBE (1979), MP (Lab) Wigan (majority 21,842); s of Richard Stott; *b* 7 Aug 1943; *Educ* Rochdale Tech Coll, Ruskin Coll; *m* 1969 (m dis 1982), Irene Mills; 2 s; m 2, Gillian, *née* Pye; 1 s; *Career* former merchant seaman and PO telephone engr; cncllr Rochdale 1970–74 (sometime chm Housing Ctee), Parly candidate (Lab) Cheadle 1970; MP (Lab, NCU sponsored): Westhoughton May 1973–83, Wigan 1983–; PPS to: Indust Sec 1975–76, Rt Hon James Callaghan as PM 1976–79 and as ldr of oppn 1979–1980; vice-chm NW area PLP, memb Select Ctee on Agric 1980–; oppn front bench spokesman on: tport 1981–83, trade and indust 1983–89, Northern Ireland 1989–; *Style—* Roger Stott, Esq, CBE, MP; ✉ House of Commons, London SW1A 0AA

STOTT, Vyvyan Philip; s of Sir Philip Sidney Stott, 3 Bt (d 1979), and Lady Stott; hp of bro, Sir Adrian Stott, 4 Bt; *b* 5 Aug 1952; *Career* organic farm mangr 1992–; office bearer British-Israel World Fedn Australia 1989–,; *Recreations* history, singing; *Style—* Vyvyan Stott, Esq; ✉ Post Office Box 629, Byron Bay 2481, New South Wales, Australia

STOUGHTON-HARRIS, Anthony Geoffrey (Tony); CBE (1989), DL (1994); s of Geoffrey Stoughton-Harris (d 1966), and Kathleen Mary, *née* Baker Brown; *b* 5 June 1932; *Educ* Sherborne; *m* 1959, Elizabeth Thackery, da of Joseph Brian White, of Ramsgate; 1 s (Peter), 2 da (Sarah, Helen); *Career* RTR 1956–58; CA 1956; Maidenhead and Berkshire Building Society (renamed South of England Building Society 1980, merged with Anglia Building Society 1983, merged to become Nationwide Anglia Building Society 1987, renamed Nationwide Building Society 1992): dir 1967–95, md 1975, exec vice chm 1987–90, dep chm 1990–95; dir: Guardian Royal Exchange 1990–95, Southern Electric plc 1990– (dep chm 1993–); pt/t treas W Herts Main Drainage Authy 1964–70; chm: Met Assoc of Bldg Socs 1979–80, Northamptonshire Trg and Enterprise Cncl 1990–; gen cmmr Inland Revenue 1982–; memb Cncl Bldg Socs Assoc 1979–90 (chm 1987–89), pt/t memb Southern Electricity Bd 1981–90; dir and chm Electronic Funds Transfer Ltd 1984–89; FCA; *Recreations* sport, gardening, DIY; *Style—* Tony Stoughton-Harris, Esq, CBE, DL; ✉ Old Farm House, Blackmile Lane, Grendon, Northants NN7 1JR (☎ 01933 664235); Southern Electric plc, Littlewick Green, Maidenhead, Berkshire SL6 3QB (☎ 01628 822166)

STOURTON, Edward John Ivo; s of Nigel John Ivo Stourton, OBE, of N Yorks, and Rosemary Jennifer Rushworth Abbott, JP; *b* 24 Nov 1957; *Educ* Ampleforth, Trinity Coll Cambridge (MA, pres Cambridge Union); *m* 5 July 1980, Margaret, da of late Sir James Napier Finney McEwen Bt; 2 s (Ivo b 11 June 1982, Thomas b 28 Sept 1987), 1 da (Eleanor b 1 June 1984); *Career* TV journalist 1979–; Washington corr Channel Four News 1986 (fndr memb 1982), Paris corr BBC TV 1988, diplomatic ed ITN 1990–93, presenter BBC One O'Clock News and presenter radio and television documentaries BBC 1993–; Knight of Honour and Devotion SMOM; *Recreations* reading; *Clubs* Travellers', Hurlingham,; *Style—* Edward Stourton, Esq; ✉ c/o BBC TV, Television Centre, Wood Lane, London W12 7RJ

STOURTON, Hon Edward William Stephen; s and h of 26 Baron Mowbray, 27 Segrave and 23 Stourton; *b* 17 April 1953; *Educ* Ampleforth; *m* 1980, Penelope (Nell) Lucy, da of Dr Peter Brunet, of Jesus Coll, Oxford; 1 s (James Charles Peter b 12 Dec 1991), 4 da (Sarah Louise b 1982, Isabel b 1983, Camilla b 1987, Francesca b 1988); *Style—* The Hon Edward Stourton; ✉ The Estate Office, Allerton Park, Knaresborough, N Yorks HG5 0SE

STOURTON, Hon James Alastair; s of 26 Baron Mowbray, 27 Segrave and 23 Stourton, CBE, and Jane Faith, *née* de Yarburgh-Bateson, da of Stephen 5 Baron Deramore; *b* 3 July 1956; *Educ* Ampleforth, Magdalene Coll Cambridge (MA); *m* 9 Oct 1993, Hon Sophia Ulla Stonor, yst da of 7 Baron Camoys; *Career* Sotheby's: Picture Dept 1979, dir Sotheby's London 1987, dir European Valuations Dept 1990, dir of Euro business devpt 1993, dir Euro Bd 1994; proprietor The Stourton Press; Knight of Honour and Devotion SMO Malta; *Clubs* Pratt's, White's, Beefsteak; *Style—* The Hon James Stourton; ✉ 21 Moreton Place, London SW1V 2NL (☎ 0171 821 1101); Sotheby's, 34–35 New Bond St, London W1A 2AA (☎ 0171 408 5435, fax 0171 408 5957)

STOUT, Prof David Ker; s of Prof Alan Stout (d 1983), of Sandy Bay, Hobart, Tasmania, and Evelyn Stout (d 1987); *b* 27 Jan 1932; *Educ* Sydney HS Sydney NSW, Univ of Sydney (BA), Magdalen Coll Oxford (BA, Rhodes scholar); *m* 31 July 1956, Margaret, da of William Sugden (d 1951); 2 s (Nigel b 1957, Rowland b 1959), 2 da (Lucy b 1961, Eleanor b 1963); *Career* Mynors fell and lectr in economics Univ Coll Oxford 1959–76, econ advsr to various govts (Syria, New Hebrides, Aust, Canada) 1965–76, econ dir NEDO 1970–72 and 1976–80, Tyler prof of econs Univ of Leicester 1980–82, head of Econ Dept Unilever 1982–92, dir Centre for Business Strategy London Business Sch 1992–; author of various papers in books and jls on taxation, growth, inflation and industrial policy, ed Business Strategy Review 1993–; memb: ESRC (chm Indust Economics and Environment Gp) 1989–92, Advsy Ctee Cambridge DAE, Biological Sci Res Cncl Technol Interoction Bd 1994–, Mfrg Technol Foresight Panel 1994–; govr and memb Exec Ctee Nat Inst of Economic and Social Res 1972; *Recreations* chess, bivalves, words; *Style—* Prof David Stout; ✉ Nutlands, Ightham, Kent TN15 9DB (☎ and fax 01732 780904); LBS, Sussex Place, Regent's Park, London NW1 4SA (☎ 0171 262 5050)

STOUT, Prof Kenneth John; s of John Ernest William Stout (d 1954), of Potters Bar, Hertfordshire, and Florence Stout (d 1987); *b* 3 Aug 1941; *Educ* Mount Grace Comp Sch Potters Bar, Cranfield (MSc), CNAA (PhD, DSc); *m* 30 Nov 1963, Doreen Margaret, da of Francis Hunter (d 1948), of Hull; 2 s (John Hunter b 1965, Steven Charles Hunter b 1969); *Career* reader in precision engrg Leicester Poly 1978–81, head Dept of Mfrg Systems Coventry Poly 1981–87, head Sch of Mfrg and Mech Engrg Univ of Birmingham 1989– (Lucas prof 1988–); former memb: SERC Ctees Applied Mechanics jt Rolls Royce/SERC and ACME, DTI Advanced Mfrg Technol Ctee; chm Consortium Heads of Prodn Engrg 1988–, memb of Continuing Educn CEI Steering Ctee; FIEE; *Books* Quality Control in Automation (1985), An Atlas of Surface Topography (1990), Precision Machine Design (contrib, 1991), 3D Topography - A Monograph (1994); *Clubs* Nuneaton Golf; *Style—* Prof Kenneth Stout; ✉ 252 Lutterworth Road, Whitestone Nuneaton, Warwickshire CV11 6PQ (☎ 01203 387571); School of Manufacturing and Mechanical Engineering, University of Birmingham, PO Box 363, Birmingham B15 2TT (☎ 0121 414 6882, fax 0121 414 3958, telex 333762 UOBHAM G)

STOUT, Prof Robert William; s of William Ferguson Stout, CB, of Belfast, and Muriel Stout, *née* Kilner; *b* 6 March 1942; *Educ* Campbell Coll Belfast (scholar), Queen's Univ Belfast (MD DSc); *m* 31 Dec 1969, Helena Patricia, da of Frederick William Willis (d

1959), of Comber, Co Down; 2 s (Brian b 1971, Alan b 1972), 1 da (Caroline b 1974); *Career* MRC Eli Lilly Foreign Educn fell Univ of Washington Seattle USA 1971–73, sr res fell British Heart Fndn 1974–75; Queen's Univ Belfast: sr lectr Dept of Med 1975–76, prof of geriatric med Dept of Geriatric Med 1976–, dir Sch of Clinical Med 1991–93, dean Faculty of Med 1991–, provost for Health Sciences 1993–; conslt physician Belfast City Hosp 1975–; vice pres: Res Into Ageing, Age Concern NI; memb: Bd of Govrs Methodist Coll Belfast (hon lay sec 1988–91, chm 1994–), Southern Health and Social Services Bd 1982–91, Eastern Health and Social Services Bd 1992–; memb GMC; FRCP 1979, FRCPEd 1988, FRCPI 1989, FRCPS 1995; *Books* Hormones and Atherosclerosis (1982), Arterial Disease in the Elderly (ed, 1984), Diabetes and Atherosclerosis (ed, 1992); *Recreations* golf, gardening, reading; *Clubs* Royal Belfast Golf, Royal Soc of Medicine; *Style*— Prof Robert Stout; ✉ 3 Larch Hill Drive, Craigavad, Co Down BT18 0JS (☎ 01232 422253, fax 01232 428478); Queen's University, Department of Geriatric Medicine, Whitla Medical Building, 97 Lisburn Road, Belfast BT9 7BL (☎ 01232 335777, fax 01232 325839)

STOUTE, Michael Ronald; s of Maj Ronald Audley Stoute, OBE, of Barbados, and late Mildred Dorothy, *née* Bowen; *b* 22 Oct 1945; *Educ* Harrison Coll Barbados; *children* 1 s (James Robert Michael b 6 June 1974), 1 da (Caroline Elizabeth b 23 Jan 1972); *Career* racehorse trainer 1972–, leading flat racing trainer 1981, 1986, 1989 and 1994; trained Derby winners: Shergar 1981, Shahrastani 1986; Irish Derby winners: Shergar 1981, Shareef Dancer 1983, Shahrastani 1986; *Recreations* cricket, hunting, skiing; *Style*— Michael Stoute, Esq; ✉ Freemason Lodge, Bury Road, Newmarket, Suffolk CB8 7BT (☎ 01638 663801, fax 01638 667276)

STOUTZKER, Ian; OBE (1993); s of Aron Stoutzker (d 1968), and Dora Stoutzker (d 1968); *b* 21 Jan 1929; *Educ* Berkhamstead Sch, RCM (ARCM), LSE (BSc); *m* 3 Sept 1958, Mercedes; 1 s (Robert b 1962), 1 da (Riquita (Mrs Wade Newmark) b 1960); *Career* Samuel Montagu 1952–56, A Keyser and Co (tutor Keyser Ullmann Ltd) 1956–75, chm London Interstate Bank 1971–75, chm Dawnay Day International 1985–; pres Philharmonia Orch 1976–79 (chm 1972–76); chm Advsy Ctee London Symphony Orch 1992–; memb: Exec Ctee RCM 1968–, Musicians' Benevolent Fund 1980–; chm Live Music Now 1980–, co-chm Voices Fndn 1994–; FRCM; *Recreations* music, cross country walking; *Clubs* Carlton; *Style*— Ian Stoutzker, Esq, OBE; ✉ 33 Wilton Crescent, London SW1X 8RX; Dawnay Day & Co Ltd, 15 Grosvenor Gardens, London SW1W OBD (☎ 0171 834 8060, fax 0171 828 1984)

STOW, Sir John Montague; GCMG (1966, KCMG 1959, CMG 1950), KCVO (1966); s of Sir Alexander Stow, KCIE, OBE (d 1936), of Netherwood, Newbury, Berks; *b* 1911; *Educ* Harrow, Pembroke Coll Cambridge; *m* 1939, Beatrice, da of late Capt Tryhorne; *Career* entered Colonial Serv (Nigeria) 1934, asst colonial sec Gambia 1938, chief sec Windward Is 1944, admin St Lucia 1947, dir of estab Kenya 1952–55, colonial sec Jamaica 1955–59, govr and C-in-C Barbados 1959–66, govr-gen Barbados 1966–67; Stewart Wrightson 1967–77; special rep to Sec of State for Foreign and Cwlth Affairs 1977–91; chm Cwlth Soc for the Deaf 1981–84; KStJ 1959; *Clubs* Caledonian, MCC; *Style*— Sir John Stow, GCMG, KCVO; ✉ 26a Tregunter Rd, London SW10 9LH (☎ 0171 370 1921)

STOW, Mary Frances; da of Montague James Lindsay Stow, of Hill End, Newbury, and Colina Mary, *née* Mackintosh; *b* 9 Feb 1960; *Educ* St Bartholomew's Sch Newbury, Univ of Exeter (BA); *Career* advtg exec; sales and mktg mangr Morris & Verdin wine merchants 1985–88, account planner J Walter Thompson 1989–93, gp planning dir McCann Erickson 1993–95, head of planning/planning dir Collett Dickenson Pearce & Partners March-Aug 1995, sr planner HHCL and Partners 1995–; The Charles Channon Award IPA Advtg Effectiveness Awards 1992 (for Andrex); memb: Account Planning Gp, Market Research Soc; *Recreations* Grands Prix, Grands Crus, photography; *Style*— Ms Mary Stow; ✉ HHCL and Partners, Kent House, 14–17 Market Place, Great Titchfield Street, London W1N 7AJ (☎ 0171 915 7575)

STOW, Timothy Montague Fenwick; QC (1989); s of Geoffrey Montague Fenwick Stow, LVO (d 1990), of Azenha, Lugar Do Foro, Pinheiro De Loures, Portugal, and Joan Fortescue, *née* Flannery (d 1984); *b* 31 Jan 1943; *Educ* Eton; *m* 29 May 1965, Alisoun Mary Francis, da of Paul Walter Homberger, OBE (d 1978); 1 s (Richard Montague Fenwick b 15 Dec 1968), 1 da (Emma Mary b 15 Dec 1972); *Career* called to the Bar 1965, recorder and Queen's counsel 1989–; memb Bar Cncl 1982–85; *Recreations* looking after our country property, tennis, foreign travel, skiing; *Clubs* Travellers'; *Style*— Timothy Stow, Esq, QC; ✉ 12 King's Bench Walk, Temple, London EC4Y 7EL (☎ 0171 583 0811, fax 0171 583 7228)

STOW, William Llewelyn (Bill); s of Alfred Frank Stow, of Eastbourne, E Sussex, and Elizabeth Mary Stow; *b* 11 Jan 1948; *Educ* Eastbourne GS, Churchill Coll Cambridge (MA); *m* 1976, Rosemary Ellen, da of Ernest Burrows (d 1976); 2 s (Daniel William b 24 Sept 1976, Richard Ivan b 28 Nov 1978); *Career* HM Civil Serv: graduate trainee DTI 1971–75, princ Consumer Affrs Div Dept of Prices and Consumer Protection 1975–78, Marine Div Dept of Trade 1978–80, first sec UK Delgn to OECD Paris 1980–83, Int Trade Policy Div DTI 1983–85, first sec UK Perm Rep to EC Brussels 1985–88, Internal Euro Policy Div DTI (i/c policy of the EC single market and Euro economic area) 1988–91, Fin and Resource Mgmnt Div DTI (i/c DTI's budget and negotiations with Treasy) 1991–94, head Euro Community and Trade Rels Div DTI (i/c co-ordination of DTI policy on the EC and for bilateral trade policy rels with all UK's maj trading ptnrs) 1994–96, dep dir gen Trade Policy and Europe DTI 1996–; *Recreations* cricket, hill and coastal walking, birdwatching, reading; *Clubs* Mandarins' Cricket; *Style*— Bill Stow, Esq; ✉ Department of Trade and Industry, Room 220, Kingsgate House, 66–74 Victoria Street, London SW1E 6SW (☎ 0171 215 4443, fax 0171 215 4215)

STOWE, Grahame Conway; s of Harry Stowe (d 1968), and Evelyn, *née* Pester (d 1990); *b* 22 May 1949; *Educ* Allerton Grange Sch Leeds, Univ of Leeds (LLB); *m* 27 Dec 1981, Marilyn Joyce, da of Arnold Morris; 1 s (Benjamin Harry George b 21 May 1988); *Career* admitted slr 1974, commenced own practice 1981, currently sr ptnr Grahame Stowe Bateson; gained Higher Rights of Audience (Criminal Proceedings) qualification 1996; chm Benefit Appeal Tbnl 1985, pres Mental Health Tbnl 1987, dep regnl chm Mental Health Tbnl 1991; memb Law Soc, FCIArb 1979; *Recreations* squash; *Style*— Grahame Stowe, Esq; ✉ Woodley Chase, Wigton Lane, Leeds 17; Two Willows, 4 Sandmoor Drive, Leeds LS17 7DG; Grahame Stowe Bateson, 5 and 7 Portland Street, Leeds LS1 3DR (☎ 0113 246 8163, fax 0113 242 6682)

STOWE, Sir Kenneth Ronald; GCB (1986, KCB 1980, CB 1977), CVO (1979); s of Arthur Stowe (d 1965), and Emily Stowe; *b* 17 July 1927; *Educ* Dagenham County HS, Exeter Coll Oxford (hon fell 1989); *m* 1949, Joan Frances Cullen (d 1995); 2 s (Timothy, Richard), 1 da (Janet); *Career* formerly with: DHSS, UNO, Cabinet Office; princ private sec to PM 1975–79, PUS NI Office 1979–81, perm sec DHSS 1981–87, perm sec Cabinet Office 1987; chm Inst of Cancer Res 1987–; UK and Cwlth advisor on Public Service reform 1987–, memb Pres's Cmmn to Review the S Africa Public Serv 1996; life tstee Carnegie UK Tst; *Clubs* Athenaeum; *Style*— Sir Kenneth Stowe, GCB, CVO; ✉ c/o Athenaeum, Pall Mall, London SW1

STOWELL, Dr Michael James; s of Albert James Stowell (d 1986), of Cardiff, and Kathleen Maud, *née* Poole (d 1996); *b* 10 July 1935; *Educ* St Julian's HS Newport Gwent, Univ of Bristol (BSc, PhD); *m* 3 March 1962 (m dis 1990), Rosemary, da of Albert William Allen (d 1962); 1 s (George b 1964), 1 da (Heather b 1966); m 2, 23 Nov 1995, Kerry, da of Edward Taif Kern, of Pittsford, NY, USA; *Career* res mangr TI Res 1978 (res scientist 1960, gp ldr 1968), res dir Alcan International Ltd 1990–94 (princ conslt scientist 1989–90); hon visiting prof Materials Science Centre UMIST 1994–; FInstP 1970, FIM, CEng 1981, FRS 1984; *Recreations* music, amateur operatics; *Style*— Dr Michael Stowell, FRS; ✉ 1 Chalklands, Saffron Walden, Essex CB10 2ER (☎ and fax 01799 526486, e-mail mjs@mezzo.demon.co.uk)

STRABOLGI, 11 Baron (E 1318); David Montague de Burgh Kenworthy; s of 10 Baron (d 1953), by his 1 w, Doris Whitley (d 1988), only da of Sir Frederick Whitley-Thomson, JP, MP; co-heir to Baronies of Cobham and Burgh; *b* 1 Nov 1914; *Educ* Gresham's Sch Holt, Chelsea Sch of Art, Académie Scandinave Paris; *m* 1961, Doreen Margaret, er da of late Alexander Morgan, of Ashton-under-Lyne, Lancs; *Heir* nephew, Andrew David Whitley Kenworthy b 1967; *Career* Maj and Actg Lt-Col RAOC WWII; PPS to Ldr of House of Lords and Lord Privy Seal 1969–70, asst oppn whip House of Lords 1970–74, dep chief Govt Whip 1974–79; oppn spokesman on Arts and Libraries 1979–86; dep speaker House of Lords 1986–; memb: Select Ctee for Privileges 1987, Jt Ctee (with Commons) on Consolidation Bills 1987, Ecclesiastical Ctee 1991, Select Ctee on Procedure of the House 1993; hon treas Franco-British Parly Relations Ctee 1991–96; memb Br Section Franco-British Cncl 1981; vice-pres Franco-British Soc, memb Cncl Alliance-Française in GB; chm Bolton Building Society 1986–87 (dep chm 1983–86); Capt Queen's Bodyguard of Yeomen of the Guard 1974–79; Offr de la Légion d'Honneur 1981; *Clubs* Reform; *Style*— The Rt Hon The Lord Strabolgi; ✉ House of Lords, London SW1A 0PW

STRACEY, Sir John Simon; 9 Bt (UK 1818), of Rackheath, Norfolk; s of Capt Algernon Augustus Henry Stracey (d 1940), and Olive Beryl Stracey (d 1972); Sir John Stracey, 1 Bt, was a Recorder of The City of London; suc cous, Sir Michael George Motley Stracey, 8 Bt, 1971; *b* 30 Nov 1938; *Educ* Wellington, McGill Univ Montreal; *m* 1968, Martha Maria, da of Johann Egger (d 1936), of Innsbruck, Austria; 2 da; *Heir* cous, Henry Mounteney Stracey; *Career* conslt and designer; *Clubs* Royal St Lawrence Yacht; *Style*— Sir John Stracey, Bt

STRACHAN, Alan Lockhart Thomson; s of Roualeyn Robert Scott Strachan (d 1970), and Ellen, *née* Graham (d 1989); *b* 3 Sept 1946; *Educ* Morgan Acad Dundee, Univ of St Andrews (MA), Merton Coll Oxford (BLitt); *m* 2 March 1977, Jennifer Piercey (stage name), da of Leslie Thompson (d 1980); *Career* theatre director and producer; assoc dir Mermaid Theatre London 1970–75; prodns incl: John Bull's Other Island, Children, Cowardy Custard (co-devised), Cole (co-devised and dir); freelance dir 1975–78; West End prodns incl: Confusions, A Family and a Fortune, Yahoo (co-author), Just Between Ourselves; artistic dir of many new plays and revivals Greenwich Theatre London (incl West End transfers) 1978–88: Private Lives, A Streetcar Named Desire, How The Other Half Loves; freelance dir 1988–91; prodns incl: The Deep Blue Sea, Re:Joyce!, Noël and Gertie, Taking Steps (New York); artistic dir Theatre of Comedy Company 1991–; prodr or co-prodr: The Pocket Dream, Six Degrees of Separation, June Moon (also dir), Hay Fever (also dir), Happy Families, Hysteria, Under Their Hats (also devised), The Prime of Miss Jean Brodie (also dir), Make Way for Lucia (also dir), Loot (also dir), Love on a Branch Line (exec prodr for TV); *Recreations* tennis, gardening, travel; *Style*— Alan Strachan, Esq; ✉ c/o Theatre of Comedy Company Ltd, Shaftesbury Theatre, Shaftesbury Ave, London WC2 (☎ 0171 379 3345, fax 0171 836 0466)

STRACHAN, Maj Benjamin Leckie (Ben); CMG (1978); s of Charles Gordon Strachan, MC (d 1957), of Crieff, Perthshire, and Annie Primrose, *née* Leckie (d 1972); *b* 4 Jan 1924; *Educ* Rossall Sch Fleetwood Lancs; *m* 1, 5 Dec 1946 (m dis 1957), Ellen, *née* Braasch; 1 s (Christian b 1949); m 2, 29 Nov 1958, Lize, da of Tage Lund (d 1985), of Copenhagen; 2 s (Robert b 1960, James b 1963); *Career* enlisted 1942, Univ of Durham 1942–43, OCTU Sandhurst 1943–44, 2 Lt Royal Dragoons 1944, Lt served France and Germany (despatches, wounded, POW) 1944–45, Capt instr OCTU 1946–48, Lt 4 QOH serv Malaya (wounded) 1948–51, Capt MECAS 1951–53, Maj GSO2 (int) HQ BT Egypt 1954–55, Capt Sqdn 2 i/c 4 QOH Germany 1955–56 RMSC Shrivenham 1956–58, Maj Sqdn Ldr 10 Royal Hussars 1958–60, GSO2 (int) WO 1960–61, ret to join HM Foreign Serv; FO: first sec Info Res Dept 1961–62, info advsr to Govt of Aden 1962–63, asst head of dept Scientific Relations Dept 1964–66, commercial sec Kuwait 1966–69, cnsllr and chargé d'affaires Amman (Jordan) 1969–71, trade cmmr Toronto 1971–74, consul gen Vancouver 1974–76; HM ambass: Sana'a and Djibouti 1977–78, Beirut 1978–81, Algiers 1981–84; special advsr FCO 1990–91; chm Kincardine and W Aberdeenshire Lib Dems; Citoyen D'Honneur Grimaud France 1987; *Recreations* sailing, crofting, writing; *Clubs* Lansdowne; *Style*— Maj Ben Strachan, CMG; ✉ Mill of Strachan, Strachan, Banchory, Kincardineshire AB31 6NS (☎ and fax 01330 850663)

STRACHAN, Douglas Frederick; s of the Hon Lord Strachan (James Frederick Strachan, d 1978), of Edinburgh, and Irene Louise, *née* Warren (d 1980); *b* 26 July 1933; *Educ* Rugby, Corpus Christi Coll Oxford (MA); *m* 1, 1956, Mary (d 1976), da of Lt-Col Alan Scott Hardie, of Berwickshire; 4 s (Mark Douglas Ashley b 11 Sept 1958, Andrew Bruce b 15 Oct 1961, James Hardie b 31 July 1967, Robert Alan b 5 Aug 1969), 1 da (Sarah Louise b 5 May 1960); m 2, 1980, Norah Jennifer Jane Corden-Lloyd, da of Charles Ernest Sherwin, of Romsey, Hants; *Career* various prodn, mktg and gen mgmnt appts Guinness Ireland 1957–72; Allied-Lyons plc: dir/chm various subsids incl Harveys of Bristol, Showerings of Shepton Mallet, Vine Products and Britvic, chief exec Allied Breweries Ltd and gp main bd dir 1977–85; chief exec Pro Ned 1985–89, professional company dir 1989–; currently: vice chm Cheltenham & Gloucester Building Society, chm Pascoe's Group plc (petfoods prodr), chm Dartington Foods (UK) Ltd, chm Minsterstone (Wharf Lane) Ltd; *Recreations* music, shooting, gardening, travel; *Style*— Douglas Strachan, Esq; ✉ c/o Cheltenham & Gloucester plc, Barnett Way, Gloucester GL4 3RL (☎ 01452 372372)

STRACHAN, Prof Hew Francis Anthony; s of Michael Francis Strachan, CBE, FRSE, *qv*, and Iris Winifred, *née* Hemingway; *b* 1 Sept 1949; *Educ* Rugby, Corpus Christi Coll Cambridge (MA, PhD); *m* 1, 26 June 1971 (m dis 1980), Catherine Blackburn; 2 da (Emily b 1973, Olivia b 1976); m 2, 12 July 1982, Pamela Dorothy Tennant, da of Felix Rowley Symes; 1 s (Mungo b 1990), 1 step s (Jack b 1973), 1 step da (Olivia b 1975); *Career* shipping trainee The Ben Line Steamers Ltd 1971–72; res fell Corpus Christi Coll Cambridge 1975–78, sr lectr Dept of War Studies and Int Affairs RMA Sandhurst 1978–79; Corpus Christi Coll Cambridge: fell 1979– (life fell 1992–), dean of coll 1981–86, tutor for admissions 1981–88, sr tutor 1987 and 1989–92, dir of studies in history 1986–92; prof of modern history Univ of Glasgow 1992–; cncllr Army Records Soc 1990–94, jt ed War in History jl 1994–; memb Cncl: Soc for Army Historical Res 1980–95, Lancing Coll 1982–90, Nat Army Museum 1994–; govr: Wellesley House Sch 1983–92, Rugby Sch 1985–, Stowe Sch 1990–; FRHistS; *Books* British Military Uniforms 1768–1796 (1975), History of the Cambridge University Officers Training Corps (1976), European Armies and the Conduct of War (1983), Wellington's Legacy: The Reform of the British Army 1830–54 (1984), From Waterloo to Balaclava: Tactics, Technology and the British Army (1985, Templer Medal 1986); *Recreations* shooting, rugby football (now spectating), rugby fives (still playing); *Clubs* Hawks (Cambridge); *Style*— Prof Hew Strachan; ✉ Department of Modern History, University of Glasgow, Glasgow G12 8QQ (☎ 0141 339 8855)

STRACHAN, Ian Charles; s of Dr Charles Strachan, of Wilmslow, Cheshire, and Margaret, *née* Craig; *b* 7 April 1943; *Educ* Fettes, Christ's Coll Cambridge (BA, MA), Princeton Univ (MPA), Harvard Univ; *m* 1, 29 July 1967 (m dis 1987), Diane Shafer, da of Raymond P Shafer, of Washington DC, USA; 1 da (Shona Elizabeth b 15 Feb 1970);

m 2, 28 Nov 1987, Margaret, da of Dr Hugh Auchincloss, of New Jersey, USA; *Career* assoc Ford Fndn Malaysia 1967–69, various positions Exxon Corporation 1970–86, fin dir Gen Sekiyu Tokyo Japan 1979–82, chm and chief exec Esso Hong Kong and Esso China 1982–83, corp strategy mangr Exxon Corpn NY 1984–86, chief fin offr and sr vice pres Johnson and Higgins NY 1986–87, dep chief exec RTZ Corporation plc London 1991–95 (fin dir 1987–91); BTR plc: dir April 1995–, md July-Dec 1995, chief exec 1996–; non-exec dir Commercial Union plc 1992–Dec 1995; *Recreations* tennis, reading, oriental antiques; *Style*— Ian Strachan; ✉ BTR plc, Silvertown House, Vincent Square, London SW1P 2PL (☎ 0171 834 3848)

STRACHAN, John Charles Haggart; s of late Charles George Strachan, and Elsie Strachan; *b* 2 Oct 1936; *Educ* Univ of London, St Mary's Hosp (MB BS); *m* Caroline Mary, da of John William Parks, MBE, of London; 1 s (James b 1971), 3 da (Alexandra b 1969, Elisabeth b 1972, Cressida b 1983); *Career* conslt orthopaedic surgn New Charing Cross Hosp 1971, surgn to Royal Ballet 1971, surgn Chelsea and Westminster Hosp 1992; Liveryman Worshipful Soc of Apothecaries; FBOA, FRSM, FRCSEng, FRCSEd; *Recreations* fishing, sailing; *Clubs* Royal Thames Yacht, Royal Southern Yacht, Flyfishers', Garrick; *Style*— John Strachan, Esq; ✉ 28 Chalcot Square, London NW1 (☎ 0171 586 1278); 126 Harley Street, London W1N 1AH (☎ 0171 935 0142)

STRACHAN, (Douglas) Mark Arthur; QC (1987); s of Flt Lt William Arthur Watkin Strachan, of Wembley, Middx, and Joyce, *née* Smith; *b* 25 Sept 1946; *Educ* Orange Hill GS Edgware, St Catherine's Coll Oxford (BCL, MA), Nancy Univ France; *Career* called to the Bar Inner Temple 1969; head of chambers; recorder 1990– (asst recorder 1987–90), dep High Court Judge 1993–; contrib to legal jls: Modern Law Review, New Law Journal, Solicitors Journal; *Recreations* France, food, antiques; *Style*— Mark Strachan, Esq, QC; ✉ 1 Crown Office Row, Temple, London EC4Y 7HH (☎ 0171 583 9292)

STRACHAN, Michael Francis; CBE (1980, MBE Mil 1945); s of Francis William Strachan (d 1958), and Violet Maude Blackwell, *née* Palmer (d 1927); *b* 23 Oct 1919; *Educ* Rugby, CCC Cambridge (MA); *m* 9 June 1948, Iris, *née* Hemingway; 2 s (Hew Strachan, *qv*, b 1949, Gavin b 1952), 2 da (Harriet b 1955, Lucy b 1958); *Career* Army 1939–46, Lt-Col 1945; chm and chief exec: Ben Line Steamers Ltd 1970–82 (ptnr Wm Thomson & Co mangrs Ben Line Steamers Ltd 1950–64, jt md 1964–70), chm Ben Line Containers Ltd 1970–82; chm Assoc Container Transportation Ltd 1971–75; dir: Bank of Scotland 1973–90, EG Thomson (Shipping) Ltd 1982–96; tstee: Nat Galleries of Scotland 1972–74, Nat Library of Scotland 1974– (chm 1974–90); memb Queen's Body Guard for Scotland (The Royal Co of Archers) 1966–; FRSE 1979; *Books* The Life and Adventures of Thomas Coryate (1962), Sir Thomas Roe 1581–1644 A Life (1989, reprinted 1991), The Ben Line 1825–1982 (1992), Esmond de Beer (1895–90), Scholar and Benefactor, A Personal Memoir (with a bibliography by J S G Simmons, 1995); *Recreations* country pursuits, silviculture; *Clubs* New (Edinburgh); *Style*— Michael Strachan, Esq, CBE, FRSE

STRACHAN, Michaela; *b* 7 April 1966; *Educ* Claremont Sch Surrey, Arts Educnl London; *m* July 1996, Duncan Chard; *Career* television presenter; progs incl: The Wide Awake Club, Wacaday, Hey Hey It's Saturday, Michaela, Cool Cube (BSkyB), Go Getters (3 series), Owl TV (ITV/Channel Four), Really Wild Show (four series to date), The Really Wild Guide (BBC), Michaela's Map (12 progs), The Hitman and Her (with Pete Waterman), Disneytime (BBC/Buena Vista); numerous guest appearances on TV; pantomime incl: The Wizard of Oz, Aladdin, Cinderella, Peter Pan; released two singles: Happy Radio 1989, Take Good Care of My Heart 1990; weekly column for Radio Times; involved with environment and wildlife charities; *Style*— Miss Michaela Strachan; ✉ c/o Michael Ladkin Personal Management, Suite 1, Ground Floor, 1 Duchess Street, London W1N 3DE (☎ 0171 436 4626, fax 0171 436 4627)

STRACHAN, Robert Blackwood; s of Robert Blackwood Strachan, and Helen Walker, *née* Boyd; *b* 21 Feb 1926; *Educ* Dumbarton Acad, Univ of Glasgow (MA, LLB); *m* 27 June 1952, Iris Anne, *née* Logan; 2 s (Steven Murray Blackwood b 1961, Douglas George b 1964), 2 da (Helen Ann b 1955, Carol Iris b 1959); *Career* admin asst British Petroleum 1953–57, co sec Playtex Ltd 1957–61, md Hargreaves Group plc 1978–87 (co sec and dir 1961–78); dir The Football Assoc Ltd 1975–89, non-exec dir The Ward Group plc 1988–92, non-exec vice pres Leeds Permanent Building Society 1989–94 (non-exec dir 1986–94); FCIS, CIMgt; *Style*— Robert Strachan, Esq; ✉ Glen Fruin, Welburn, York YO6 7DX

STRACHAN, Valerie Patricia Marie; CB (1991); *b* 10 Jan 1940; *Educ* Newland HS, Hull Univ, Manchester Univ; *m* John Strachan; *Career* Customs and Excise: joined as asst princ 1961, seconded to Dept of Economic Affairs, Home Office and Treasury, princ 1966–74, asst sec 1974–80, cmmr (under sec) 1980–87 (also head Treasy/Cabinet Office Jt Mgmnt Unit), dep chm (dep sec) 1987–93, dir gen Internal Taxation and Customs Gp 1989–93, chm of the Bd 1993–; CIMgt; *Style*— Mrs Valerie Strachan, CB; ✉ c/o Customs & Excise, New King's Beam House, 22 Upper Ground, London SE1 9PJ (☎ 0171 620 1313)

STRACHEY, (Sir) Charles; 6 Bt (UK 1801), of Sutton Court, Somerset, but does not use title; s of Rt Hon Evelyn John St Loe Strachey (d 1963), and cous of 2 Baron Strachie (d 1973); *b* 20 June 1934; *Educ* Westminster, Magdalen Coll Oxford; *m* 1973, Janet Megan, da of Alexander Miller; 1 da; *Heir* kinsman, Henry Leofric Benvenuto Strachey, b 17 April 1947; *Career* district dealer rep mangr Ford Motor Co Ltd 1972–75, local govt offr (ret 1993); *Style*— Charles Strachey, Esq; ✉ 31 Northchurch Terrace, London N1 4EB (☎ and fax 0171 249 1055)

STRADBROKE, 6 Earl of (UK 1821); Sir (Robert) Keith Rous; 11 Bt (E 1660); also Viscount Dunwich (UK 1821) and Baron Rous (GB 1796); s of 5 Earl of Stradbroke (d 1983, shortly after his brother, 4 Earl) and (1 w) Pamela Catherine Mabell (who d 1972, having obtained a divorce 1941), da of late Capt the Hon Edward James Kay-Shuttleworth (s of 1 Baron Shuttleworth); *b* 25 March 1937; *Educ* Harrow; *m* 1, 1960 (m dis 1977), Dawn Antoinette, da of Thomas Edward Beverley, of Brisbane; 2 s (Viscount Dunwich b 1961, Hon Wesley Alexander b 1972), 5 da (Lady Ingrid Arnel b 1963, Lady Sophia Rayner b 1964, Lady Heidi Simone b 1966, Lady Pamela Keri b 1968, Lady Brigitte Aylena b 1970); m 2, 1977, Roseanna Mary Blanche, da of Francis Reitman, MD (d 1955), and Susan, *née* Vernon; 6 s (Hon Hektor Fraser b 1978, Hon Maximilian Otho b 1981, Hon Henham Mowbray b 1983, Hon Winston Walberswick b 1986, Hon Yoxford Ulysses Uluru b 1989, Hon Ramsar Fyans b 1992), 2 da (Lady Zea Katherina b 1979, Lady Minsmere Matilda b 1988); *Heir* s, Viscount Dunwich, *qv*; *Career* grazier; dir Sutuse Pty Ltd; landowner (16,000 acres); *Recreations* making babies; *Style*— The Rt Hon the Earl of Stradbroke; ✉ Mount Fyans, RSD Darlington, Victoria 3271, Australia (☎ 00 61 55 901 294, fax 00 61 55 901 298)

STRADLING, Prof Richard Anthony; s of Harry Wood Stradling (d 1970), of Solihull, and Jessie Holroyde (d 1978); *b* 19 April 1937; *Educ* Solihull Sch, BNC Oxford (MA, DPhil); *m* 10 Jan 1975, Pamela Mary; 1 s (James b 1976); *Career* offical student tutor and lectr ChCh Oxford 1968–78, prof of natural philosophy and chm Physics Dept Univ of St Andrews 1978–84, prof of physics Imperial Coll London 1984–, dep dir London Univ Interdisciplinary Res Centre 1989–; FRSE 1981; *Style*— Prof Richard Stradling, FRSE; ✉ St David's, 5 Elsfield Way, Oxford OX2 8EW (☎ 01865 515601); Blackett Laboratory, Prince Consort Rd, Imperial College, London SW7 2BZ (☎ 0171 589 5111)

STRAFFORD, 8 Earl of (UK 1847); Thomas Edmund Byng; also Baron Strafford (UK 1835), Viscount Enfield (UK 1847); s of 7 Earl of Strafford (d 1984) and his 1 w, Maria Magdalena Elizabeth, da of late Henry Cloete, CMG, of Alpha, S Africa; *b* 26 Sept 1936; *Educ* Eton, Clare Coll Cambridge; *m* 1, 1963 (m dis), Jennifer Mary Denise (she m, 1982, Sir Christopher Bland), da of late Rt Hon William Morrison May, MP; 2 s (Viscount Enfield b 1964, Hon James b 1969), 2 da (Lady Georgia b 1965, Lady Tara b 1967); m 2, 1981, Mrs Judy (Julia Mary) Howard, yr da of Sir (Charlie) Dennis Pilcher, CBE (d 1994); *Heir* s, Viscount Enfield; *Style*— The Rt Hon the Earl of Strafford; ✉ Apple Tree Cottage, Easton, Winchester, Hants SO21 1EF (☎ and fax 01962 779467)

STRAKER, Sir Michael Ian Bowstead; kt (1984), CBE (1973), JP (Northumberland 1962), DL (Northumberland 1989); yr and only surv s of Edward Charles Straker (d 1943), of Hexham, Northumberland, and Margaret Alice Bridget Straker; *b* 10 March 1928; *Educ* Eton; *Career* Coldstream Gds 1946–49; farmer; former chm Newcastle and Gateshead Water Co; chm: Newcastle upon Tyne AHA (teaching) 1973–81, Aycliffe and Peterlee Devpt Corp 1980–88, Northumbrian Water Authy 1980–93; High Sheriff of Northumberland 1977; chm: Northern Area Cons Assoc 1969–72, Bd of Port of Tyne Authy, Go-Ahead Group plc 1987–; Hon DCL Univ of Newcastle upon Tyne 1987; *Style*— Sir Michael Straker, CBE, JP, DL; ✉ High Warden, Hexham, Northumberland NE46 4SR (☎ 01434 602083)

STRAKER, Nicholas David Barclay; s of Hugh Charles Straker (d 1993), and Elaine Felicia, *née* Peat; *b* 6 May 1952; *Educ* Eton, Durham Agric Coll, Lakeland Agric Coll Alberta Canada; *m* 6 Sept 1980, Victoria Eyre, *née* Gray; 2 da (Jacquetta Lucy Eyre, Chloë Victoria Piffard), 1 s (Sam Charles Barclay); *Career* 9/12 Royal Lancers 1971–75; farmer Little Hutton Farms 1975–76, Durham Agric Coll 1976–77, Lakeland Agric Coll Alberta Canada 1977–78, conslt Towry Law & Co 1978–80; dir: Whitehouse Financial Services Ltd 1980–82, Lycetts Insurance Brokers and Financial Services 1982–; High Sheriff for Co of Durham 1994–95; ACII, MIMgt; *Recreations* golf, riding, country sports, tennis, gardening; *Clubs* Northern Counties, Eton Vikings; *Style*— Nicholas Straker, Esq; ✉ Lycetts, Milburn House, Dean Street, Newcastle upon Tyne NE1 1PP (☎ 0191 232 1151, fax 0191 232 1873)

STRAKER, Timothy Derrick; QC (1996); s of Derrick Straker (d 1976), of Bickley, Kent, and Dorothy Elizabeth, *née* Rogers; *b* 25 May 1955; *Educ* Malvern, Downing Coll Cambridge (MA); *m* 17 April 1982, Ann, da of Michael Horton Baylis, of Highgate, London; 2 (Rosemary Elizabeth b 1985, Penelope Ann b 1987); *Career* called to the Bar Gray's Inn 1977, Lincoln's Inn ad eundem 1979; memb: Local Govt and Planning Bar Assoc, Admin Law Bar Assoc; *Recreations* cricket, reading; *Clubs* Highgate Irregular Cricket; *Style*— Timothy Straker, Esq, QC; ✉ 11 Southwood Lawn Rd, Highgate, London N6 5SD (☎ 0181 341 0413, fax 0181 341 4158); 2–3 Gray's Inn Square, Gray's Inn, London WC1R 5JH (☎ 0171 242 4986, fax 0171 405 1166)

STRANG, 2 Baron (UK 1954); Colin Strang; s of 1 Baron Strang, GCB, GCMG, MBE (d 1978), and Elsie Wynne Jones (d 1974); mother's ancestor, Col John Jones, signed Charles I's death warrant; *b* 12 June 1922; *Educ* Merchant Taylors', St John's Coll Oxford (MA, BPhil); *m* 1, 1948, Patricia Marie, da of Meiert C Avis, of Johannesburg, S Africa; m 2, 1955, Barbara Mary Hope (d 1982), da of Frederick Albert Carr, of Wimbledon; 1 da (Caroline b 1957); m 3, 1984, Mary Shewell, da of Richard Miles, of Thornaby-on-Tees; *Heir* none; *Career* prof of philosophy Univ of Newcastle, ret 1982; *Style*— The Rt Hon the Lord Strang; ✉ Stansfield Cottage West, Hole Bottom, Todmorden OL14 8DD

STRANG, Gavin Steel; MP (Lab) Edinburgh East (majority 7,211); s of James Steel Strang, of Perthshire; *b* 10 July 1943; *Educ* Morrison's Acad Crieff, Univ of Edinburgh (PhD), Univ of Cambridge (Dip Agric Sci); *m* 1973, Bettina Smith; 1 s; 2 step s; *Career* memb Tayside Econ Planning Gp 1966–68, scientist with ARC 1968–70; MP (Lab) Edinburgh E 1970–, Parly under sec of state for energy March-Oct 1974, Parly sec to Min for Agric 1974–79; oppn front bench spokesman on: agric 1981–82, employment 1987–89; memb Select Ctee on Science and Technol 1992, memb Shadow Cabinet, chief oppn spokesperson on food, agric and rural affairs 1992–; *Style*— Dr Gavin Strang, Esq, MP; ✉ House of Commons, London SW1A OAA (☎ 0171 219 5155, fax 0171 219 5815)

STRANG, Prof John Stanley; s of William John Strang, CBE, FRS, of Castle Combe, Wilts, and Margaret Nicholas Strang; *b* 12 May 1950; *Educ* Bryanston, Guy's Hosp Med Sch Univ of London (MB BS); *m* 21 April 1984, Jennifer, da of Edwin Austin Campbell Abbey (d 1975); 2 s (Samuel John b 1985, Robert Luke b 1988), 1 da (Jasmine Rebecca b 1991); *Career* regnl conslt in drug dependence Manchester 1982–86; Maudsley Bethlem Royal Hosp: conslt psychiatrist in drug dependence 1986–, prof of addiction behaviour and dir of Addiction Research Unit 1995–; conslt advsr on drug dependence to Dept of Health 1986–; former conslt WHO, involvement in various nat and local drug orgns; FRCPsych 1994 (MRCPsych 1977); *Books* AIDS and Drug Misuse: the challenge for policy and practice in the 1990s (ed with G Stimson, 1990), Drugs, Alcohol and Tobacco: the science and policy connections (ed with G Edwards and J Jaffe, 1993), Heroin Addiction and Drug Policy: the British system (ed with M Gossop, 1994); *Recreations* windsurfing; *Style*— Prof John Strang; ✉ National Addiction Centre, The Maudsley/Institute of Psychiatry, Denmark Hill, London SE5 8AF (☎ 0171 703 5411)

STRANG, Richard William; s of Gordon William Strang, of Lymedale, Milford-on-Sea, Hants, and Elizabeth Piercy, *née* Bernard (d 1981); *b* 19 June 1950; *Educ* Radley, CCC Oxford (MA); *m* 1990, Victoria Jane Gibson; 2 da (Emily Louise b 6 May 1992, Serena Rose b 5 Aug 1994); *Career* CA with Peat Marwick Mitchell London 1971–78, dir Morgan Grenfell & Co Ltd 1986– (joined 1978), non-exec dir Morgan Grenfell Aust (Hldgs) Ltd 1987–91; FCA 1974; *Recreations* opera, skiing, sailing, tennis, bridge; *Style*— Richard Strang, Esq; ✉ Morgan Grenfell & Co Limited, 23 Great Winchester Street, London EC2P 2AX (☎ 0171 826 6827)

STRANG STEEL, Colin Brodie; yr s of Maj Sir (Fiennes) William Strang Steel, 2 Bt (d 1992), of Philiphaugh, Selkirk, and Joan Ella Brodie, *née* Henderson (d 1982); *b* 2 June 1945; *Educ* Eton, RAC Cirencester; *m* 24 Oct 1970, April Eileen, da of Aubrey Fairfax Studd, of Ramsey, IoM; 3 s (James b 1973, Alistair b 1975, Peter b 1977); *Career* chartered surveyor; ptnr Knight Frank & Rutley (now Knight Frank) 1974–; FRICS; *Recreations* cricket, football, squash, tennis, wildlife; *Clubs* MCC, Scottish Cricket Union, New (Edinburgh); *Style*— Colin Strang Steel, Esq; ✉ Threepwood, Blainslie, Galashiels, Selkirkshire TD1 2PY (☎ 01896 860321); Knight Frank, 2 North Charlotte St, Edinburgh EH2 4HR (☎ 0131 225 8171, fax 0131 225 4151)

STRANG STEEL, Malcolm Graham; WS (1973); s of Jock Wykeham Strang Steel (d 1991), of Logie, Kirriemuir, Angus, and Lesley, *née* Graham; *b* 24 Nov 1946; *Educ* Eton, Trinity Coll Cambridge (BA), Univ of Edinburgh (LLB); *m* 21 Oct 1972, Margaret Philippa, da of William Patrick Scott, OBE, TD, DL (d 1989), of Kierfiold, Stromness, Orkney; 1 s (Patrick Reginald b 1975), 1 da (Laura b 1977); *Career* admitted slr 1973; managing ptnr W & J Burness WS; sec Standing Cncl of Scot Chiefs 1973–83, memb Cncl Law Soc of Scotland 1984–90, tstee Scot Dyslexia Tst; memb Queen's Body Guard for Scotland (Royal Co of Archers); FRSA; *Recreations* shooting, fishing, skiing, tennis, reading; *Clubs* New (Edinburgh), MCC; *Style*— Malcolm G Strang Steel, Esq, WS; ✉ Barrowmore, Mawcarse, Kinross KY13 7SL (☎ 01577 863225); W & J Burness, 16 Hope St, Edinburgh EH2 4DD (☎ 0131 226 2561, telex 72405, fax 0131 225 3964)

STRANG STEEL, Maj Sir (Fiennes) Michael; 3 Bt (UK 1938), of Philiphaugh, Co Selkirk, DL; s of Maj Sir (Fiennes) William Strang Steel, 2 Bt, JP, DL (d 1992), and Joan Ella Brodie, *née* Henderson (d 1982); *b* 22 Feb 1943; *m* 1977, Sarah Jane, da of late J A S Russell, of Mayfield, Lochmaben, Dumfriesshire; 2 s (Fiennes Edward b 1978, Sam Arthur b 1983), 1 da (Tara Diana b 1980); *Heir* s, Fiennes Edward Strang Steel b 8 Nov

1978; *Career* Maj 17/21 Lancers, ret; forestry cmmr 1988–; *Style*— Sir Michael Strang Steel, Bt, DL; ✉ Philiphaugh, Selkirk TD7 5LX

STRANGE, Lady (16 Holder of Title, E 1628) (Jean) Cherry Drummond of Megginch; sr heir-general of 17 Earl of Oxford, Hereditary Great Chamberlain of England, through his da Lady Elizabeth de Vere, mother of 1 Baron Strange; eldest da of 15 Baron Strange (d 1982), and Violet Margaret Florence (d 1975), o da of Sir Robert William Buchanan-Jardine, 2 Bt; suc as 16 holder of the peerage when the abeyance between her and her two sisters was terminated after petition to HM The Queen 1986; *b* 17 Dec 1928; *Educ* Univ of St Andrews (MA), Univ of Cambridge; *m* 2 June 1952, Capt Humphrey ap Evans, MC, who assumed the name of Drummond of Megginch by decree of Lord Lyon 1966 (*see* Humphrey Drummond of Megginch), s of Maj James John Pugh Evans, MBE, MC, JP, DL, of Lovegrove, Aberystwyth; 3 s (Maj Hon Adam Humphrey, Dr the Hon Humphrey John Jardine b 11 March 1961, Hon John Humphrey Hugo b 26 June 1966), 3 da (Hon Charlotte Cherry b 14 May 1955, Hon Amélie Margaret Mary b 2 July 1963 (m 1990, Philippe de MacMahon, Duc de Magenta), Hon Catherine Star Violetta b 15 Dec 1967); *Heir* s, Maj Hon Adam Humphrey Drummond of Megginch b 20 April 1953; *Career* pres War Widows Assoc of GB; memb All Party Parly Def Study Gp Exec Ctee of ACP 1990–93; *Books* Love from Belinda, Lalage in Love, Creatures Great and Small, Love is for Ever (poems), The Remarkable Life of Victoria Drummond Marine Engineer (1994); *Style*— The Rt Hon Lady Strange; ✉ Megginch Castle, Errol, Perthshire PH2 7SW; 160 Kennington Rd, London SE11 6QR

STRANGE, Eric Dawson; s of Stanley Arthur Strange (d 1959), and Doris Phoebe, *née* Hewett; *b* 3 June 1943; *Educ* Maldon GS, Regent St Poly Sch of Photography (Coll Dip); *m* 25 Sept 1965, Gillian Georgina, yst da of George Edward Read (d 1971), of Burnham-on-Crouch, Essex; 2 s (David Stanley b 16 May 1966, Jason Leigh b 4 April 1970); *Career* photographic technician Dynacolour Pty Melbourne Aust 1963, Ilford Ltd Ilford Essex 1964; industl photographer Calor Gas Ltd Slough Berks 1964–68, self employed proprietor Dawson Strange Photography Ltd Cobham Surrey 1968–, fndr md Parasol Portrait Photography Ltd Cobham 1977–93; pres British Inst of Professional Photography 1995–96, chm Photography and Photographic Processing Indust Trg Orgn; govr Feltonfleet Sch Cobham; FBIPP 1965, ARPS 1991; *Clubs* Stoics Cricket, West End Esher Cricket, Cobham FC (chm); *Style*— Eric Strange; ✉ Tilt House Cottage, 28 Stoke Road, Cobham, Surrey KT11 3BD (☎ 01932 863316); Dawson Strange Photography Ltd, 15 Between Streets, Cobham, Surrey KT11 1AA (☎ 01932 867161, fax 01932 868941, mobile 0831 117755)

STRANGE, Prof Susan (Mrs Clifford Selly); da of Lt-Col Louis Arbon Strange, DSO, OBE, MC, DFC (d 1966), and Marjorie, *née* Beath (d 1968); *b* 9 June 1923; *Educ* Royal Sch Bath, LSE (BSc); *m* 1 Sept 1945 (m dis 1955), Denis McVicar Merritt, s of Sidney Merritt (d 1967); 1 s (Giles b 20 Nov 1943), 1 da (Jane (Mrs Streatfeild) b 5 March 1948); m 2, 14 Dec 1955, Clifford Selly; 3 s (Mark b 28 Aug 1957 d 1991, Roger b 21 April 1960, Adam b 22 Oct 1963), 1 da (Kate b 24 Oct 1961); *Career* The Economist 1944–46, Washington and UN corr The Observer 1946–48 (econ corr 1951–57), lectr in int relations UCL 1949–64, res fell RIIA 1965–76, German Marshall Fund fell 1976–78, visiting prof Univ of S California 1978, Montague Burton prof of int relations LSE 1978–88; prof of int relations: Euro Univ Inst Florence 1989–92, Univ of Warwick 1993–; *Books* Sterling and British Policy (1971), International Monetary Relations (1976), The International Politics of Surplus Capacity (co ed with R Tooze, 1981), Paths to International Political Economy (ed, 1984), Casino Capitalism (1986), States and Markets (1988), Rival States, Rival Firms (with John Stopford, 1991), The Retreat of the State (1996); *Recreations* cooking, gardening, tennis; *Style*— Prof Susan Strange; ✉ Weedon Hill House, Aylesbury, Bucks HP22 YDP (☎ 01296 27772, fax 01296 399771); Department of Politics And International Studies, University of Warwick, Coventry CV4 7AL (☎ 01203 3523 523)

STRANGER-JONES, Anthony John; s of Leonard Ivan Stranger-Jones (d 1983), and Iris Christine, *née* Truscott (d 1991); *b* 30 Dec 1944; *Educ* Westminster, Christ Church Oxford (MA); *m* 19 June 1976, Kazumi, da of Kazuo Matsuo, of 4500–97 Fukuma-Machi, Munakata-Gun, Fukuoka Pref 811–32, Japan; 1 s (David b 1983), 2 da (Amiko b 1977, Yukiko b 1980); *Career* md Amex Finance (Hong Kong) Ltd 1974–76; dir: Amex Bank Ltd 1976–79, Korea Merchant Banking Corporation 1979–82, Barclays Merchant Bank Ltd 1979–86, Barclays de Zoete Wedd Ltd 1986–; ACIB 1971; *Clubs* MCC; *Style*— Anthony Stranger-Jones, Esq; ✉ 33 Randolph Crescent, London W9 1DP (☎ 0171 286 7342); Barclays de Zoete Wedd Ltd, Ebbgate House, 2 Swan Lane, London EC4R 3TS (☎ 0171 623 2323, fax 0171 623 6075, telex 8950851)

STRANRAER-MULL, Rev Gerald Hugh; s of Capt Gerald Stranraer-Mull (d 1955), and Dolena Mackenzie, *née* Workman (d 1986); *b* 24 Nov 1942; *Educ* Woodhouse Grove Sch, King's Coll London (AKC); *m* 30 Dec 1967, Glynis Mary, da of Capt David Kempe, of Iden Green, Kent; 2 s (Michael Paul b and d 1974, Jamie b 1977), 1 da (Clare b 1970); *Career* journalist 1960–66; curate: Hexham Abbey 1970–72, Corbridge 1972; rector Ellon and Cruden Bay 1972–, canon Aberdeen Cathedral 1981–, dean of Aberdeen and Orkney 1988–; chm: Ellon Schs Cncl 1982–86, Gordon Health Cncl 1982–86; *Books* A Turbulent House - The Augustinians at Hexham (1970), View of the Diocese of Aberdeen and Orkney (1977); *Style*— The Very Rev the Dean of Aberdeen and Orkney; ✉ The Rectory, Ellon, Aberdeenshire AB41 9NP (☎ 01358 720366)

STRATFORD, (Howard) Muir; JP (1978); s of Dr Martin Gould Stratford, VRD (d 1993), of Bryanston Square, London, and Dr Mavis Winifred Muir Stratford, JP, *née* Beddall (d 1993); *b* 6 June 1936; *Educ* Marlborough; *m* 8 July 1961, Margaret Reid, da of Robert Linton Roderick Ballantine (d 1957); 1 s (Duncan b 1971), 2 da (Gail b 1964, Fiona b 1967); *Career* insur broker, memb Lloyd's; dir Bowring London Ltd 1980–85 and 1986–91, chief exec Bowring M K Ltd 1985–86; dir Watford FC 1971–90; Liveryman Worshipful Company of Haberdashers 1959, Liveryman Worshipful Company of Insurers 1986; *Recreations* golf, watching football and cricket; *Clubs* MCC, Moor Park Golf; *Style*— Muir Stratford, Esq, JP; ✉ Nobles, Church Lane, Sarratt, Herts (☎ 01923 260475, car 0836 219412)

STRATFORD, Neil Martin; s of Dr Martin Gould Stratford, VRD (d July 1993), of Bryanston Square, London, and Dr Mavis Winifred Muir Stratford, JP, *née* Beddall (d Sept 1993); *b* 26 April 1938; *Educ* Marlborough, Magdalene Coll Cambridge (BA, MA), Courtauld Inst (BA); *m* 28 Sept 1966, Anita Jennifer (Jenny), da of Peter Edwin Lewis (d 1980); 2 da (Jemima b 1968, Rebecca b 1971); *Career* Coldstream Gds 1956, 2 Lt 1957–58, Lt 1958; trainee Kleinwort Benson Lonsdale 1961–63, lectr Westfield Coll Univ of London 1969–75, Keeper of Medieval and Later Antiquities British Museum 1975–; chm St Albans Cathedral Fabric Advsy Ctee 1995–; Liveryman Worshipful Co of Haberdashers 1959–; hon memb Académie de Dijon 1975, foreign memb Soc Nat des Antiquaires de France 1985; FSA 1976; *Books* La Sculpture Oubliée de Vézelay (1984), Catalogue of Medieval Enamels in the British Museum, II. Northern Romanesque Enamel (1993); *Recreations* cricket and football, food and wine, music, particularly opera; *Clubs* Garrick, Beefsteak, MCC, IZ, Cambridge Univ, Pitt, Hawks; *Style*— Neil Stratford, Esq, FSA; ✉ 17 Church Row, London NW3 6UP; Keeper of Medieval and Later Antiquities, The British Museum, London WC1B 3DG (☎ 0171 323 8217)

STRATHALLAN, Viscount; John Eric Drummond; s and h of 17 Earl of Perth, PC, *qv*; *b* 7 July 1935; *Educ* Trinity Coll Cambridge (BA), Harvard Univ (MBA); *m* 1, 1963 (m dis 1972), Margaret Ann, da of Robert Gordon; 2 s (Hon James b 24 Oct 1965, Hon Robert b 7 May 1967); m 2, 6 Oct 1988, Mrs Marion Elliot; *Heir* s, Hon James David Drummond b 24 Oct 1965; *Clubs* Boodle's; *Style*— Viscount Strathallan; ✉ 46 Tite Street, London SW3 4JA

STRATHALMOND, 3 Baron (UK 1955); William Roberton Fraser; o s of 2 Baron Strathalmond, CMG, OBE, TD (d 1976), and Letitia, *née* Krementz; *b* 22 July 1947; *Educ* Loretto; *m* 1973, Amanda Rose, da of Rev Gordon Clifford Taylor, of St Giles-in-the-Fields Rectory, Gower St, London; 2 s (Hon William b 24 Sept 1976, Hon George b 10 March 1979), 1 da (Hon Virginia b 22 Dec 1982); *Heir* s, Hon William Gordon Fraser b 24 Sept 1976; *Career* md London Wall Members Agency Ltd 1986–91, dir London Wall Holdings plc 1986–91, chm R W Sturge Ltd 1991–94; fin dir Owen & Wilby Underwriting Agency Ltd 1995–; chm tstees RSAS 1989–; Liveryman Worshipful Co of Girdlers; MICAS 1972; *Style*— The Rt Hon The Lord Strathalmond; ✉ Holt House, Elstead, Godalming, Surrey GU8 6LF

STRATHCARRON, 2 Baron (UK 1936); Sir David William Anthony Blyth Macpherson; 2 Bt (UK 1933); s of 1 Baron, KC, PC (d 1937), and Jill, da of Sir George Wood Rhodes, 1 Bt, JP; *b* 23 Jan 1924; *Educ* Eton, Jesus Coll Cambridge; *m* 1, 1947 (m dis 1947), Valerie Cole; m 2, 1948, Diana Hawtry (d 1973), da of late Cdr R H Deane and formerly w of J N O Curle; 2 s; m 3, 1974, Mary Eve, da of late John Comyn Higgins, CIE, and formerly w of Hon Anthony Gerald Samuel; *Heir* s, Hon Ian Macpherson, *qv*; *Career* formerly Flt Lt RAFVR, motoring correspondent of The Field, ptnr Strathcarron & Co; dir: Kirchoffs (London) Ltd, Seabourne World Express Group PLC, Kent Int Airport Ltd; pres: Driving Instrs Assoc, Nat Breakdown Recovery Club, Guild of Motor Writers, Vehicle Builders and Repairers Assoc, Inst of Road Tport Engineers, Fellowship of the Motor Industry; chm: The Order of the Road, All Pty Parly Motor Cycle Gp, House of Lords Motor Club; Liveryman Worshipful Co of Coachmakers & Coach Harness Makers; fell Inst of Advanced Motorists, FIMI, FCIT; *Books* Motoring for Pleasure; *Style*— The Rt Hon Lord Strathcarron; ✉ 22 Rutland Gate, London SW7 1BB (☎ 0171 584 1240); Otterwood, Beaulieu, Hants (☎ 01590 612334)

STRATHCLYDE, 2 Baron (UK 1955); Thomas Galloway Dunlop du Roy de Blicquy Galbraith; PC (1995); er s of Hon Sir Thomas Galbraith, KBE, MP (C & Unionist) Glasgow Hillhead 1948–82 (d 1982), by his w, Simone Clothilde Fernande Marie Ghislaine (d 1991), eldest da of late Jean du Roy de Blicquy, of Bois d'Hautmont, Brabant, whose marriage with Sir Thomas was dissolved 1974; suc gf, 1 Baron Strathclyde, PC, JP (d 1985); *b* 22 Feb 1960; *Educ* Sussex House London, Wellington Coll, Univ of East Anglia (BA), Univ of Aix-en-Provence; *m* 27 June 1992, Jane, er da of John Skinner, of Chenies, Herts; 2 da (Hon Elizabeth Ida Skinner b 1 Dec 1993, another b 15 May 1996); *Career* insurance broker Bain Clarkson Ltd (formerly Bain Dawes) 1982–88; Lord in Waiting (Govt Whip House of Lords) 1988–89; spokesman for DTI; Parly under sec of state: Dept of Employment (and min for tourism) 1989–90, DOE July-Sept 1990, Scottish Office (min for agric, fish, Highlands and Islands) 1990–92, DOE 1992, DTI 1993; Min of State DTI 1994; Capt HM Body Guard of Hon Corps of Gentlemen at Arms (Chief Govt Whip) 1994–; Cons candidate Euro election Merseyside East 1984; *Style*— The Rt Hon Lord Strathclyde, PC; ✉ House of Lords, Westminster, London SW1A 0PW (☎ 0171 219 5353)

STRATHCONA AND MOUNT ROYAL, 4 Baron (UK 1900); Donald Euan Palmer Howard; s of 3 Baron Strathcona and Mount Royal (d 1959), and Hon Diana, *née* Loder (d 1985), da of 1 Baron Wakehurst; *b* 26 Nov 1923; *Educ* Eton, Trinity Coll Cambridge, McGill Univ Montreal; *m* 1, 1954 (m dis 1977), Lady Jane Mary, da of 12 Earl Waldegrave, KG, GCVO, TD (*see* Howard, Lady Jane); 2 s, 4 da; m 2, 1978, Patricia, da of late Harvey Evelyn Thomas and wid of John Middleton; *Heir* s, Hon Donald Alexander Howard; *Career* sits as Cons in Lords; late Lt RNVR; pres Steamboat Assoc of GB, a Lord in Waiting to HM (Govt Whip) 1973–74, parly under sec of state for RAF 1974, jt dep leader of oppn House of Lords 1976–79, min of state MOD 1979–81; dir: UK Falklands Island Tst, Royal Naval Museum, Coastal Forces Heritage Tst; Warden Worshipful Co of Fishmongers; *Recreations* gardening, sailing; *Clubs* Brooks's, Pratt's, RYS, Air Squadron; *Style*— The Rt Hon the Lord Strathcona and Mount Royal; ✉ 16 Henning Street, Battersea, London SW11 (☎ 0171 223 2885); House of Lords, London SW1; Kiloran, Isle of Colonsay, Argyll, Scotland (☎ 0195 1200301)

STRATHEDEN AND CAMPBELL, 6 Baron (UK 1836 and 1841 respectively); Donald Campbell; o s of 5 Baron Stratheden and Campbell (d 1987), and Evelyn Mary Austen, *née* Smith (d 1989); *b* 4 April 1934; *Educ* Eton; *m* 8 Nov 1957, Hilary Ann Holland (d 1991), da of Lt-Col William Derington Turner (d 1988), of Simonstown, S Africa; 1 s (Hon David Anthony b 13 Feb 1963), 3 da (Hon Tania Ann b 19 Sept 1960, Hon Wendy Meriel b 27 Jan 1969, Hon Joyce Margaret b 25 Feb 1971); *Heir* s, Hon David Anthony Campbell, *qv*; *Style*— The Rt Hon the Lord Stratheden and Campbell; ✉ Ridgewood, MS 401, Cooroy, Queensland 4563, Australia

STRATHERN, Prof Andrew Jamieson; s of Robert Strathern (d 1972), and Mary, *née* Sharp; *b* 19 Jan 1939; *Educ* Colchester Royal GS, Trinity Coll Cambridge (major entrance scholar, BA, MA, PhD); *m* 1, 20 July 1973 (m dis 1986), Ann Marilyn Evans; 2 s (Alan Leiper b 1975, Hugh Thomas b 1975), 1 da (Barbara Helen Mary b 1969); m 2, 12 July 1990 (m dis 1996), Gabriele, da of Dr Peter Stürzenhofecker of Bad Neustadt an der Saale, Germany; *Career* res fell Trinity Coll Cambridge 1965–68, fell Res Sch of Paufic Studies ANU 1970–72 (res fell 1969–70), prof of social anthropology Univ of Papua New Guinea 1973–76, prof and head of Dept of Anthropology UCL 1976–83, dir Inst of PNG Studies Port Moresby PNG 1981–86, emeritus prof Univ of London 1987–, Andrew W Mellon Distinguished prof of anthropology Univ of Pittsburgh 1987–, dir Center for Pacific Studies James Cook Univ Townsville 1996–; memb Cncl RAI 1977–80, vice chm Social Anthropology Ctee SSRC 1979–81 (memb 1977–81); Rivers Meml Medal 1976, PNG 10 Anniversary of Ind Medal 1987; memb: Assoc of Social Anthropologists of GB and the Cwlth 1967, Assoc for Social Anthropology in Oceania 1987, European Assoc of Soc Anthropologists 1989, Euro Soc of Oceanists 1993; fell American Anthropological Assoc 1983, FRAI; *Books* The Rope of Moka (1971), One Father, One Blood (1972), Self - Decoration in Mt Hagen (jtly 1971), Ongka (1979), Inequality in Highlands New Guinea Societies (ed, 1982), A Line of Power (1984), The Mi-Culture of the Mt Hagen People (co-ed, 1990), Landmarks (1993), Ru (1993), Voices of Conflict (1993), Migration and Transformations (co-ed, 1994), Body Thoughts (1996); *Recreations* travel, poetry; *Style*— Prof Andrew Strathern; ✉ 1103 Winterton St, Pittsburgh, PA 15206, USA (☎ 00 1 412 441 5778); Department of Anthropology, University of Pittsburgh, Pittsburgh PA 15260, USA (☎ 00 1 412 648 7519, fax 00 1 412 648 5911, e-mail strathert@pitt.edu)

STRATHMORE AND KINGHORNE, 18 Earl of (S 1606 and 1677) Michael Fergus Bowes Lyon; also Lord Glamis (S 1445), Earl of Kinghorne (S 1606), Lord Glamis, Tannadyce, Sidlaw and Strathdichtie, Viscount Lyon and Earl of Strathmore and Kinghorne by special charter (S 1677), Baron Bowes (UK 1887), Earl of Strathmore and Kinghorne (UK 1937); s of 17 Earl of Strathmore and Kinghorne (d 1987), and Mary Pamela, *née* McCorquodale; *b* 7 June 1957; *Educ* Univ of Aberdeen (B Land Econ); *m* 14 Nov 1984, Isobel Charlotte, da of Capt Anthony Weatherall, of Cowhill, Dumfries; 3 s (Simon Patrick (Lord Glamis) b 1986, Hon John Fergus b 1988, Hon George Norman b 1991); *Heir* s, Lord Glamis; *Career* a Page of Honour to HM Queen Elizabeth the Queen Mother (his great aunt) 1971–73; Capt Scots Gds; a Lord in Waiting 1989–91; Capt The Queen's Bodyguard of the Yeomen of the Guard (Dep Chief Whip, House of Lords) 1991–94; *Clubs* White's, Turf, Pratt's, Perth; *Style*— The Rt Hon the Earl of Strathmore and Kinghorne, DL; ✉ Glamis Castle, Forfar, Angus

STRATHNAVER, Lord; Alistair Charles St Clair Sutherland; also Master of Sutherland; s (twin) and h of Countess of Sutherland, *qv*; *b* 7 Jan 1947; *Educ* Eton, Christ Church Oxford (BA); *m* 1, 1968, Eileen Elizabeth, o da of Richard Wheeler Baker, of Princeton, USA; 2 da (Hon Rachel b 1970, Hon Rosemary b 1972); *m* 2, 1980, Gillian Margaret St Clair, da of Robert Murray, of Gourock, Renfrewshire; 1 s, 1 da (Hon Elizabeth b 1984); *Heir* s, Hon Alexander Charles Robert Sutherland b 1 Oct 1981; *Career* constable Met Police 1969–74, IBM UK Ltd 1975–78, Sutherland Estates 1979–; Vice Lord Lieut of Sutherland 1993–; *Style*— Lord Strathnaver; ✉ Sutherland Estates Office, Duke Street, Golspie, Sutherland KW10 6RP (☎ 01408 633268)

STRATHSPEY, 6 Baron (UK 1884); Sir James Patrick Trevor Grant of Grant; 17 Bt (NS 1625); 33 Chief of the Clan Grant; s of 5 Baron Strathspey (d 1992), and his 1 w, Alice, *née* Bowe; *b* 9 Sept 1943; *Educ* abroad, RAC Cirencester; *m* 1, 1966 (m dis 1984), Linda, da of David Piggott, of Forfar; 3 da (Hon Carolyn Anne Maclean b 1967, Hon Philippa Jane b 1971, Hon Victoria Louise b 1976); m 2, 1985 (m dis 1993), Margaret, da of Robert Drummond, of Fife; *Heir* half-bro, Hon Michael Patrick Francis Grant of Grant, *qv*; *Career* pres Clan Grant Soc; *Style*— The Rt Hon the Lord Strathspey; ✉ The School House, Lochbuie, Isle of Mull, Argyllshire PA62 6AA

STRATTON, David; s of Lawrence James William Stratton (d 1989), and Muriel Elizabeth, *née* Hunt; *b* 16 May 1947; *Educ* Altrincham GS for Boys, Colwyn Bay GS, Univ of Leeds (LLB); *m* 29 May 1971, Ruth Hazel, da of John Eric Delhanty; 3 s (James Anthony b 1 March 1976, Charles Edward b 21 April 1978, Oliver John b 26 Nov 1979), 3 da (Rachael Joanna b 6 May 1981, Rebecca Alice b 30 March 1987, Jessica Rose b 17 June 1990); *Career* admitted slr 1971; articled clerk to Town Clerk Warrington 1969–71, asst rising to princ asst slr Warrington Borough Cncl 1971–72, gp slr Christian Salvesen Properties Limited 1975–79 (asst gp slr 1972–75), head Commercial Property Dept and dep sr ptnr Halliwell Landau Solicitors Manchester 1979–95, ptnr Field Cunningham & Co Solicitors Manchester 1995–; *Clubs* St James's, IOD; *Style*— David Stratton, Esq; ✉ Field Cunningham & Co, St John's Court, 70 Quay Street, Manchester M3 3JF (☎ 0161 834 4734, fax 0161 834 1772)

STRAUS, Peter Quentin; s of Dr Ronnie Straus, and Graziella Straus, of Wimbledon; *b* 10 Sept 1960; *Educ* King's Coll Sch Wimbledon, Christ's Coll Cambridge (MA, capt squash and tennis teams); *Career* publisher; Hodder and Stoughton Publishers: graduate trainee 1982–84, sales and marketing asst 1984–86, ed then New English Library later jr ed, ed then sr ed Hodder and Stoughton Paperbacks 1986–88; editorial dir Hamish Hamilton 1990 (sr ed 1988–90); Macmillan Publishers Ltd: publishing dir and publisher Picador 1990–94, gp literary publisher Macmillan, Picador and Papermac 1994–95, ed-in-chief Macmillan, Pan, Picador, Papermac and Sidgwick & Jackson 1995–; memb Booker Prize Mgmnt Ctee Booker plc 1991–; *Books* 20 Under 35 (ed, 1988); *Recreations* sport, film, theatre, reading; *Clubs* Beerhunters Club (Player of the Year 1992), The House, Peg's; *Style*— Peter Straus, Esq; ✉ 6 Golborne Mews, London W10 5SB (☎ 0181 968 6242); Macmillan General Books, 25 Eccleston Place, London SW1W 9NF (☎ 0171 881 8000, fax 0171 881 8001)

STRAUSS, Derek Ronald; s of Ronald Strauss (d 1990), and Theodora, *née* Instone; *b* 16 May 1939; *Educ* Eton; *m* 26 April 1967, Nicola Mary, da of Gp Capt William Blackwood, OBE, DFC; 2 s (James Digby Ronald b 2 July 1969, Toby Anthony Lavery b 21 Sept 1970); *Career* Lt Cdr RNR (ret); Brown Bros Harriman New York 1961–62, Strauss Turnbull (now SGST Securities Ltd) 1962– (currently dep chm); *Recreations* fishing, shooting, skiing; *Clubs* White's, City of London, Pratt's; *Style*— Derek Strauss; ✉ Société Generale Strauss Turnbull Securities, Exchange House, Primrose St, Broadgate, London EC2A 2DD (☎ 0171 638 5966, fax 0171 588 1437, telex 883201)

STRAW, John Whitaker (Jack); MP (Lab) Blackburn (majority 7,027); s of Walter Straw, and Joan Straw; *b* 3 Aug 1946; *Educ* Brentwood Sch Essex, Univ of Leeds, Inns of Court Sch of Law; *m* 1, 1968 (m dis 1978), Anthea Weston; 1 da (decd); m 2, 1978, Alice Elizabeth Perkins, *qv*; 1 s, 1 da; *Career* called to the Bar Inner Temple 1972, barrister 1972–74; pres NUS 1969–71, memb Islington Cncl 1971–78, dep ldr ILEA 1973–74, memb Lab Nat Exec Sub-Ctee Educn and Science 1970, contested (Lab) Tonbridge and Malling 1974; political advsr to Sec of State for: Social Servs 1974–76, Environment 1976–77, Granada TV (World in Action) 1977–79; oppn front bench spokesman on: Treasy and econ affrs 1981–83, environment 1983–87; elected to Shadow Cabinet 1987; chief oppn spokesman on: educn 1987–92, environment and local govt 1992–93, local govt 1993–94, home affrs 1994–; visiting fell Nuffield Coll Oxford 1990–; FRSS 1995; *Style*— Jack Straw, MP; ✉ House of Commons, London SW1A 0AA

STRAWSON, Maj-Gen John Michael; CB (1975), OBE (1964); s of Cyril Walter Strawson (d 1937), of London, and Nellie Dora, *née* Jewell (d 1975); *b* 1 Jan 1921; *Educ* Christ's Coll Finchley; *m* 29 Dec 1960, Baroness Wilfried Marie, da of Baron Harold von Schellersheim (d 1986), of Rittergut Eisbergen, Germany; 2 da (Viola (Mrs David Lambert) b 1961, Carolin b 1963); *Career* cmmnd 1941, 4 Queen's Own Hussars 1942; served: Middle East, Italy, Germany, Malaya; Staff Coll Camberley 1950, Bde Maj 1951–52, directing staff Camberley 1958–60 (master of Staff Coll Drag Hounds), GSO1 and Col GS WO (later MOD) 1961–62 and 1965–66, cmd The Queen's Royal Irish Hussars 1963–65, cmd Inf Bde 1967–68, Imperial Def Coll 1969; chief of staff: SHAPE 1970–72, HQ UKLF 1972–76; ret 1976; Col The Queen's Royal Irish Hussars 1975–85; mil advsr Westland plc 1976–85; chm The Friends of Boyton Church, vice pres The Royal Br Legion (Codford); US Bronze Star 1945; *Books* The Battle for North Africa (1969), Hitler as Military Commander (1971), The Battle for the Ardennes (1972), The Battle for Berlin (1974), El Alamein (1981), A History of the SAS Regiment (1984), The Italian Campaign (1987), The Third World War (jtly, 2 vols 1978 and 1982), Gentlemen in Khaki (1989), Beggars in Red (1991), The Duke and the Emperor: Wellington and Napoleon (1994); *Recreations* equitation, shooting, tennis, reading; *Clubs* Cavalry and Guards' (chm 1984–87); *Style*— Maj-Gen John Strawson, CB, OBE; ✉ c/o Cavalry and Guards' Club, 127 Piccadilly, London W1

STRAWSON, Sir Peter Frederick; kt (1977); s of late Cyril Walter and Nellie Dora Strawson; *Educ* Christ's Coll Finchley, St John's Coll Oxford; *m* 1945, Grace Hall Martin; 2 s, 2 da; *Career* fell Univ Coll Oxford 1948–68 (hon fell 1979–), Waynflete prof of metaphysical philosophy Univ of Oxford 1968–87, fell Magdalen Coll Oxford 1968–87 (hon fell 1989–), hon fell St John's Coll Oxford 1973–, foreign hon memb American Acad of Arts and Sciences 1971, memb Academia Europaea 1990; FBA 1960; *Clubs* Athenaeum; *Style*— Sir Peter Strawson, FBA; ✉ 25 Farndon Road, Oxford OX2 6RT (☎ 01865 515026)

STREATHER, Bruce Godfrey; s of William Godfrey Streather, of Staffs, and Pamela Mary, *née* Revell (d 1993); *b* 3 June 1946; *Educ* Malvern, Univ of Oxford (MA); *m* 15 Dec 1973, Geraldine Susan, da of Colin Herbert Clout, of San Franciso, USA; 3 da (Charlotte, Annabel, Miranda); *Career* admitted slr 1971; sr ptnr Streathers; memb Law Soc; *Recreations* family, golf; *Clubs* R & A, Sunningdale Golf, Vincent's, Little Aston Golf, Littlestone Golf, Moor Hall Golf; *Style*— Bruce Streather, Esq; ✉ Streathers, Sackville House, 40 Piccadilly, London W1V 9PA (☎ 0171 734 4363, fax 0171 734 7539)

STREATOR, Hon Edward; s of Edward Streator (d 1955), of NY, and Ella, *née* Stout (d 1980); *b* 12 Dec 1930; *Educ* Princeton Univ (AB); *m* 16 Feb 1957, Priscilla, da of W John Kenney, of Washington; 1 s (Edward b 1958), 2 da (Elinor b 1960, Abigail b 1965); *Career* Lt (jg) USNR 1952–56; joined US Foreign Service 1956, third sec US Embassy Addis Ababa 1958–60, second sec US Embassy Lome 1960–62, Office of Intelligence & Res Dept of State 1962–64, staff asst to Sec of State 1984–66, first sec US Mission to NATO (Paris, Brussels) 1966–69, dep dir rising to dir Office of Nato Affairs Dept of State 1969–75, dep US permanent rep to Nato (Brussels) 1975–77, min US Embassy (London) 1977–84, ambass and US rep OECD (Paris) 1984–87; dir The South Bank (London) 1988–; govr: Ditchley Fndn (UK) 1980–, RUSI 1988–91, British-American Arts Assoc 1989–, ESU 1988–94; pres American C of C 1989–94, chm European Cncl of American Cs of C 1992–95; memb: Exec Ctee Int Inst Strategic Studies (London) 1988–, Exec Ctee The Pilgrims (London) 1981–, Bd Inst of US Studies Univ of London 1993–, Cncl Oxford Inst for American Studies 1993–; recipient Benjamin Franklin Medal RSA 1992; *Recreations* swimming; *Clubs* Metropolitan (Washington), Beefsteak, Garrick, White's, Mill Reef (Antigua); *Style*— Hon Edward Streator; ✉ 9 St Albans Mansions, Kensington Court Place, London W8 5QH (☎ 0171 937 4772, fax 0171 937 7396); Château de St Aignan, 32480 La Romieu, France (☎ 00 33 62 28 80 35, fax 00 33 62 28 80 53)

STREET, Dr Andrew Maurice; s of Harry Maurice Street, of Swadlincote, Derbys, and Patricia, *née* Wilson; *b* 30 Sept 1961; *Educ* Burton-on-Trent GS, St Hild and St Bede Coll Univ of Durham (BSc theoretical physics, Univ Prize), Lady Margaret Hall Oxford (DPhil); *Career* pt/t researcher AERE Harwell 1986, analyst Baring Brothers & Co Ltd 1986–88, options trader then sr trader Paribas Capital Markets Ltd 1988–91, head of equity derivatives trading Nomura International plc 1991–92, head of equity and commodity risk mgmnt and bd dir Mitsubishi Finance International plc 1992–95, md Value Consultants Ltd 1995–; head of market risk mgmnt and asst dir SFA 1995–; MInstP 1986, MSI; *Publications* Methods of Calculation of Cross Sections for Nuclear Reactors (DPhil thesis, 1987); articles in Nuclear Science & Engineering magazine and Risk magazine; *Recreations* flying (PPL), theatre, cinema, sailing, reading, tinkering with computers; *Style*— Dr Andrew Street; ✉ Value Consultants Ltd, 2 Stonewold Court, Ealing, London W5 2ER (☎ 0181 998 3743, fax 0181 998 3743, e-mail compuserve 100643,1166)

STREET, Brian Frederick; s of Frederick Street, and Ellen, *née* Hollis; *b* 2 June 1927; *Educ* St Philip's GS Edgbaston, Univ of Birmingham (BSc), Harvard Business Sch (AMP); *m* 1951, Margaret Patricia, da of Alderman John William Carleton, JP (d 1951); 1 s (decd), 5 da (Teresa b 1952, Veronica b 1954, Amanda b 1957, Rebecca b 1959, Francesca b 1965); *Career* chartered engr; chief technologist Shell Chemicals UK Ltd 1964–68, dir BCL Group 1972–75, md Air Products Ltd 1975–80 (chm 1981–93); chm: NMC Management Consultants 1989–93, NMC & Kay Management 1994–95; visiting prof Univ of Bath 1988–93; Univ of Surrey: visiting prof 1985–90, hon prof and chm 1991–94, memb Cncl 1985–, pro-chllr 1995–; pres Instn of Chem Engrs 1983–84; memb: Cncl CBI Cncl 1983–93 (chm SE Regnl Cncl 1987–89); Engrg Bd SERC 1985–87; Royal Academy of Engineering: vice pres 1991–92, sr vice pres 1992–94; chm NEDC Specialised Organics Sector Gp 1990–92; Hon DUniv Surrey 1988; FEng 1983, FIChemE, FRSA; *Recreations* golf, oil painting; *Style*— Brian Street, Esq, FEng; ✉ University of Surrey, Guildford, Surrey GU2 5XH (☎ 01483 300800, fax 01483 300803)

STREET, Roger William; s Gordon Harold Street (d 1978), and Mary Joan, *née* Cable; *b* 2 Feb 1944; *Educ* Buckhurst Hill Co HS For Boys, London Bible Coll (BD), Open Univ (MA); *m* 1964, Heather Diane, da of Leonard Owen Spencer; 2 s (Jonathan Philip b 29 April 1967, Simon Michael b 1 Jan 1969), 1 da (Angela Wendy b 21 Sept 1973); *Career* teacher Brooke House Sch Hackney ILEA 1965–74, headteacher Stewards Sch Harlow Essex Educn Authy 1978–90 (dep headteacher 1974–78), headteacher The Helena Romanes Sch Great Dunmow Essex Educn Authy 1990–; memb NAHT 1978–; *Books* Focus on Faiths (1974); *Recreations* active member of the church, lay preacher, running; *Style*— Roger Street, Esq; ✉ The Helena Romanes School, Parsonage Downs, Great Dunmow, Essex CM6 2AU (☎ 01371 872560, fax 01371 874632)

STREET-PORTER, Janet; *b* 27 Dec 1946; *Educ* Lady Margaret GS, Architectural Assoc; *m* 1, 1979 (m dis 1988), Frank Cvitanovich (d 1995); m 2, 1996, David Sorkin; *Career* columnist and fashion writer: Petticoat Magazine 1968, Daily Mail 1969–71, Evening Standard 1971–73, also contrib to Queen, Vogue, etc; own show LBC Radio 1973, entered TV 1975 presenting London Weekend Show (LWT); presenter: Saturday Night People with Clive James and Russell Harty, The Six O'Clock Show with Michael Aspel, Around Midnight 1976–80; series prodr 1980; devised: Twentieth Century Box (for LWT), Get Fresh (for ITV), Bliss (for Channel 4), Network 7 (for Channel 4); BBC TV: joined 1988, head of Youth and Entertainment Features until 1994, head of Independent Production for Entertainment 1994; md cable channel Live TV for Mirror Group 1994–95, dir and co-fndr Screaming Productions 1996–; winner BAFTA award for originality 1988, Prix Italia for opera The Vampyr 1993; pres Ramblers' Assoc 1994–; FRTS 1994; *Recreations* walking, modern art; *Style*— Ms Janet Street-Porter; ✉ c/o Robert Storer, Harbottle & Lewis, Hanover House, 14 Hanover Square, London W1R 0BE (☎ 0171 629 7633)

STREETEN, Reginald Hawkins (Frank); CBE (1991); s of Reginald Craufurd Streeten (d 1944), and Olive Gladys, *née* Palmer (d 1974); *b* 19 March 1928; *Educ* Grey Coll SA, Rhodes Univ Coll SA (BA, LLB); *m* 28 July 1962, Bodile, da of Albin Gustin Westergren (d 1964), of Lycksele, Sweden; 2 s (Mark David b 1967, (James) Peter b 1971); *Career* called to the Bar S Rhodesia 1959; crown counsel and legal draftsman S Rhodesia and Fedn of Rhodesia and Nyasaland 1952–63, jr counsel for fed govt at inquiry into aircraft accident involving late Dag Hammarskjöld 1961, parly draftsman Zambia 1964–66; Law Commission London: joined legal staff 1967, head of statute law revision 1978–93, sec 1981–82; *Recreations* church organist; *Style*— Frank Streeten, Esq, CBE; ✉ 32 Holme Chase, St George's Avenue, Weybridge, Surrey KT13 0BZ

STREETER, David Thomas; s of Reginald David Streeter (d 1976), of East Grinstead, Sussex, and Dorothy Alice, *née* Fairhurst (d 1994); *b* 20 May 1937; *Educ* Cranbrook Sch, Queen Mary Coll London (BSc); *m* 1, 9 Sept 1967 (m dis 1979), Althea Elizabeth, da of Andrew Haig, of Waldringfield, Suffolk; 1 s (James b 1970); m 2, 5 Jan 1980, Penelope Sheila Dale, da of Gordon Kippax, of Netherfield, Sussex; 2 da (Katharine b 1981, Olivia b 1987); *Career* Univ of Sussex: lectr in ecology 1965–76, reader in ecology 1976–, dean Sch of Biological Scis 1984–88, pro vice chllr 1989–; lectr and broadcaster; memb: Gen Advsy Cncl BBC 1975–80, Cncl RSNC 1963–83, Advsy Ctee for England Nature Conservancy Cncl 1973–83, Countryside Cmmn 1978–84, SE Regnl Ctee Nat Tst 1989–, Nat Park Review Panel 1990–91, Sussex Downs Conservation Bd 1992–, Cncl Botanical Soc Br Isles 1994–, Governing Body Hurstpierpoint Coll 1994–; dep pres Sussex Wildlife Tst 1981–; FIBiol 1986, FLS 1996; *Books* Discovering Hedgerows (with R Richardson, 1982), The Wild Flowers of The British Isles (with I Garrard, 1983), The Natural History of the Oak Tree (with R Lewington, 1993); *Recreations* natural history, visiting other people's gardens; *Style*— David Streeter, Esq; ✉ The Holt, Sheepsetting Lane, Heathfield, East Sussex TN21 0UY (☎ 01435 862849), The University of Sussex, Sussex House, Falmer, Brighton BN1 9RH (☎ 01273 678212, fax 01273 678335, telex UNISEX 887159)

STREETER, Gary; MP (C) Plymouth Sutton (majority 11,950); *Career* MP (C) Plymouth Sutton 1992–; asst Govt whip 1995–96, Parly sec Lord Chancellor's Department 1996–; *Style*— Gary Streeter, Esq, MP; ✉ House of Commons, London SW1A 0AA (☎ 0171 219 3000)

STREETON, Sir Terence George; KBE (1989, MBE 1969), CMG (1981); s of Alfred Victor Streeton, of Northampton, and Edith, *née* Deiton; *b* 12 Jan 1930; *Educ* Wellingborough GS; *m* 1962, Molly, da of Oliver Garley (d 1967), of Leicester; 2 s (Matthew, Simon), 2 da (Sarah, Catherine); *Career* HM Diplomatic Serv, first sec Bonn 1966, FCO 1970, first sec and head of chancery Bombay 1972, cncllr Brussels 1975, FCO

1979, asst under sec of state 1982, Br High Cmmr to Bangladesh 1983–89, ret; dir: Contact International (PVT) Ltd Zimbabwe; chm HealthCo (PVT) Ltd Zimbabwe; pres Bangladesh-British Chamber of Commerce; *Recreations* walking, golf; *Clubs* Oriental; *Style—* Sir Terence Streeton, KBE, CMG; ✉ The Langtons, Olney, Bucks MK46 5AE (☎ 01234 711761)

STRETTON, Graham Roy; *b* 22 Oct 1949; *Educ* Leicester Coll of Art, Trent Poly (dip ID); *m* Susan Marie, chartered designer; *Career* designer; asst designer Carter Deign Group Ltd 1971–72, designer Howard Sant Partnership 1972–73, designer Lennon and Partners 1973–77, head of interior design section Carter Design Group Ltd 1977–78, co-fndr (with wife) Design & Co 1978, dir Design & Co Consultants Ltd 1987–93, design mangr under contract Interior Consultancy Services Ltd 1989–94; BIID (merged with CSD 1988): memb Gen Cncl 1981–86, fell 1982–, chm Midland district 1983–84, chm Publications Ctee to 1986, liaison offr with SIAD, jr vice pres 1987, bronze medal 1988; memb Advsy Bd for Interior Design Trent Poly, special project visiting lectr De Montfort Univ (formerly Leicester Poly); FCSD 1980, FRSA 1987; *Recreations* advanced fencing coach (dip foil, dip épée, fencing coach); *Style—* Graham Stretton, Esq; ✉ Design & Co, 39 High Street, Market Harborough, Leicestershire LE16 7HQ (☎ 01858 462507, fax 01858 467204)

STRETTON, James; *b* 16 Dec 1943; *Educ* Laxton GS, Oundle, Worcester Coll Oxford (BA); *m* 20 July 1968, Isobel Christine; *née* Robertson; 2 da (Lynne b 1970, Gillian b 1973); *Career* chief exec UK operations Standard Life Assurance Co 1994– (dep md 1988–94); FFA 1970; *Style—* James Stretton, Esq; ✉ Standard Life Assurance Company, 3 George St, Edinburgh EH2 2XZ (☎ 0131 225 2552, fax 0131 245 6010, telex 72539)

STRETTON, His Hon Judge; Peter John; s of William Frank Stretton (d 1978), and Ella Mary Stretton (d 1987); *b* 14 June 1938; *Educ* Bedford Mod Sch; *m* 6 Sept 1973, Annie Stretton; 3 s (Thomas Michael b 15 March 1977, James Peter b 25 Sept 1981, Philip John b 6 Feb 1987), 1 da (Catherine Anne b 8 March 1979); *Career* called to the Bar 1963, recorder 1982–86, circuit judge (Midland & Oxford Circuit) 1986–; *Recreations* squash, running, gardening, family; *Style—* His Hon Judge Stretton; ✉ Derby Crown Court, Morledge, Derby

STREVENS, Peter Alan Dawson; s of Stanley Dawson Strevens (d 1966), and Dorothy Victoria, *née* Compson (d 1987); *b* 18 April 1938; *Educ* Eltham Coll Mottingham London; *m* April 1969, Janet Hyde, da of Lees Hyde Marland (d 1974); 2 s (Nigel Jeremy b 1971, Timothy Maxwell b 1974); *Career* franchise mangr Hertz Int Ltd NY 1963–67; md: United Serv Tport Co Ltd (Hertz Truck Rental) 1969–72 (operations mangr 1967–69), Chatfields-Martin Walter Ltd 1972–91; chm Ford and Slater (Leyland DAF) Ltd 1991–; MIMI; *Recreations* tennis, golf, gardening; *Clubs* RAC; *Style—* Peter Strevens, Esq; ✉ Ford and Slater (Leyland DAF) Ltd, Hazel Drive, Narborough Road South, Leicester LE3 2JG (☎ 0116 263 0630, fax 0116 263 0042)

STREVENS, Peter Jeffrey; s of Alfred John Strevens (d 1980), of London, and Lilian Ellen, *née* Wiggins (d 1970); *b* 3 Dec 1945; *Educ* Barnsbury Sch; *m* 27 April 1968, Janet Linda, da of George Daniels (d 1982), of Hereford; 1 s (Richard b 1971), 1 da (Emma b 1970); *Career* CA 1968; ptnr: Sydenham & Co 1974, Hodgson Harris 1980, Hodgson Impey 1985, Kidsons Impey 1990; reader Hereford Diocese; memb: Centre for Mgmnt in Agric, Ramblers' Assoc; FCA 1968, ACIArb 1989; *Recreations* hill walking, music, wildlife & conservation; *Style—* Peter Strevens, Esq; ✉ 9 Hither Bush, Lyde, Hereford HR4 8EF (☎ 01432 268 585); Kidsons Impey, Elgar House, Holmer Rd, Hereford HR4 9SF (☎ 01432 352 222, fax 01432 269 367)

STRICKLAND, Benjamin Vincent Michael; s of Maj-Gen Eugene Vincent Michael Strickland, CMG, DSO, OBE, MM (d 1982), and Barbara Mary Farquharson Meares Lamb; *b* 20 Sept 1939; *Educ* Mayfield Coll, Univ Coll Oxford (MA), Harvard Business Sch (Dip AMP); *m* 1965, Tessa Mary Edwina Grant, da of Rear-Adm John Grant, CB, DSO (d 1996); 1 s (Benjamin Michael John b 1968), 1 da (Columbine Mary Grizel b 1971); *Career* Lt 17/21 Lancers BAOR 1959–60; jr mangr Price Waterhouse & Co 1963–68, dir corp fin J Henry Schroder Wagg & Co 1974–91, chm and chief exec Schroders Australia 1978–82, gp md Schroders plc 1983–91; non-exec dir Oakley Investments (subsid of Chelsea Land) 1991–92; chm Iron Trades Insurance Group 1996–; led review of nat mission and finances of Westminster Cathedral 1991, chm Planning and Finance Ctee Westminster Cathedral 1991–96; memb Steering Gp for Vision for London 1991–; advsr on strategy to City law firm 1992–95 and to maj media gp 1993, advsr to fin instns 1994, 1995 and 1996; FCA, FRSA; *Recreations* travel, military and general history, shooting, films, theatre; *Clubs* Boodle's, Hurlingham; *Style—* Benjamin Strickland, Esq; ✉ 23 Juer Street, London SW11 4RE (☎ 0171 585 2970)

STRICKLAND, John E; s of William Strickland, and Ninon Strickland; *b* 23 Oct 1939; *Educ* Univ of Cambridge (MA); *m* 1963, Anthea; 3 s (Andrew b 1964, Neil b 1966, Gerald b 1970); *Career* IBM UK 1963–66, The Hongkong and Shanghai Banking Corp Hong Kong 1966–69, Control Data Corp USA 1969–71, rejoined The Hongkong and Shanghai Banking Corp 1971, in Hong Kong 1971–92, exec dir services HSBC Holdings plc 1989–, chm Hongkong and Shanghai Banking Corporation May 1996–; dir Hang Seng Bank Ltd, chm HonKong Bank Malaysia Bhd; memb Cncl Outward Bound Tst of Hong Kong; *Recreations* mountain walking; *Style—* John Strickland, Esq; ✉ The Hong Kong and Shanghai Banking Corporation Ltd, 1 Queens Road C L/34, Hong Kong

STRICKLAND, (Peel Richard) Jon; s of Douglas Alfred Peel, of Cheltenham, Glos, and Marjory Olive, *née* Hill (d 1996); *b* 3 Dec 1952; *Educ* Cheltenham GS, Univ of Wales (BA); *Career* actor; *Theatre* Scarborough world premieres incl: Douglas Beechey in Man of the Moment 1988, Panaurov in The Parasol 1988, Henry Bell in The Revenger's Comedies 1989; Br premieres incl: Benny in June Moon 1989, Bourdon in Wolf at the Door 1989; other credits incl: Steerpike in Gormenghast (world premiere, nat tour), Jesus in The Passion (Theatr Clwyd), Yossarian in Catch 22 (Euro premiere, nat tour), Norman in The Dresser (Duke's Theatre Lancaster), Beralde in The Hypochondriac (Leicester Haymarket), Ned Weeks in The Normal Heart (Nottingham) 1988, Atticus in To Kill A Mocking Bird (Euro premiere, Contact Theatre Manchester) 1987, Scrouge in a Christmas Carol (Young Vic) 1989, Fagin in Oliver Twist (world premiere, Bristol Old Vic) 1990, Mr Kipps in The Woman in Black (world premiere Fortune Theatre) 1990–91, Man in Full Moon (Br premiere, Theatr Clwyd) 1993–94, Ackroyd in Rough Justice (world premiere, Apollo Theatre) 1994, Full Moon (Young Vic) 1995, Jack in A Going Concern, Norris in It Could be Anyone of Us (Scarborough) 1996; *Television* incl: Jarvis in Coronation Street (Granada) 1987, Watson in Diary of Rita Patel (BBC) 1988, Taylor in She's Been Away (BBC) 1988, Desmond in London's Burning (LWT) 1989, Stephenson in This Is David Harper (Channel 4) 1990, Sex Politics and Alan Ayckbourn (Landseer/Omnibus) 1990, Popeye in Gone To The Dogs (Central Films) 1991, Batman in Gone to Seed (Central Films) 1992, Balderstone in Dalziel & Pascoe (BBC) 1996; *BBC Radio* incl: Giles Winterbourne in The Woodlanders, Derek Meadle in Quartermaine's Terms, Mr Venus in Our Mutual Friend, Guthrie in Night and Day, Tom in The Norman Conquests, Douglas Beechey in Man of the Moment, Elj Nielsen in Il Trovarsi, Ulfheim in When We Dead Awaken; BBC Radio Drama Co 1985–86; *Recreations* writing, tennis; *Style—* Jon Strickland, Esq; ✉ c/o Sally Long-Innes, ICM Ltd, Oxford House, 76 Oxford Street, London W1N 0AX (☎ 0171 636 6565, fax 0171 323 0101)

STRICKLAND-CONSTABLE, Sir Frederic; 12 Bt (E 1641), of Boynton, Yorkshire; s of Sir Robert Frederick Strickland-Constable, 11 Bt (d 1994), and his 2 w Lettice, *née* Strickland; *b* 21 Oct 1944; *Educ* Westminster, CCC Cambridge (BA), London Business Sch (MSc); *m* 1981, Pauline Margaret, *née* Harding; 1 s (Charles b 1985), 1 da (Rose b 1983); *Heir* s, Charles Strickland-Constable b 1985; *Style—* Sir Frederic Strickland-Constable, Bt; ✉ Beech House, Haxby Moor, York YO3 3LH

STRIESSNIG, Herbert; s of Karl Striessnig (d 1938), of Waiern-Feldkirchen, Carinthia, Austria, and Margaret, *née* Steiner (d 1976); *b* 29 Aug 1929; *Educ* Hotel Mgmnt Sch Bad Gleichenberg Styria Austria; *m* 19 March 1956, Davida Eileen, da of David Hunter Williamson; 1 s (Karl b 22 Aug 1957), 1 da (Suzanne b 18 June 1960); *Career* varied hotel trg/experience Switzerland and Mayfair Hotel London 1949–59, reservations mangr Westbury Hotel London 1959–61, asst gen mangr The Carlton Tower Hotel London 1961–63, co-ordinator devpt of Esso (then Standard Oil of New Jersey) motor hotel chain 1963–64; Metropolitan Hotels London: joined as gen mangr Rembrandt Hotel 1964–66, gen mangr St Ermin's Hotel 1967–68, gen mangr Piccadily Hotel 1968, gen mangr Europa Hotel 1969–72, gen mangr Mayfair Hotel 1972–83; resident mangr The Churchill Hotel 1984–88, dir and gen mangr The Savoy Hotel 1989–95, ret; Master Innholder; memb: West One Hotel Mangrs' Assoc, Confrerie de la Chaine des Rotisseurs, Conseil Culinaire Francais; FHCIMA; *Recreations* swimming, skiing, jogging, watching soccer; *Clubs* Skal; *Style—* Herbert Striessnig, Esq; ✉ The Savoy Hotel, The Strand, London WC2R 0EU (☎ 0171 836 4343, fax 0171 240 6040)

STRINGER, Prof Christopher Brian; s of George Albert Stringer, and Evelyn Beatrice, *née* Brien, of Horsham; *b* 31 Dec 1947; *Educ* East Ham GS for Boys, UCL (BSc), Univ of Bristol (PhD, DSc); *m* 2 April 1977, Rosemary Susan Margaret, da of late Leonard Peter Frank Lee; 1 da (Katherine Ann b 25 July 1979), 2 s (Paul Nicholas David b 21 Oct 1981, Thomas Peter b 9 April 1986); *Career* temp secdy sch teacher London Borough of Newham 1966; The Natural History Museum (formerly Br Museum (Natural History)): temp scientific offr 1969–70, sr res fell 1973–76, sr scientific offr 1976–86, princ scientific offr (Grade 7) 1986–, head Human Origins Gp 1990–93, individual merit promotion (Grade 6) 1993–; visiting lectr Dept of Anthropology Harvard Univ 1979, visiting prof Royal Holloway Coll London 1995–; Br rep Int Assoc for Human Palaeontology 1986–; assoc ed: Journal of Human Evolution 1986–, Antiquity 1993, Quaternary Science Reviews 1995; memb: The Primate Soc 1975–, The Quaternary Res Assoc 1975–, The Assoc for Environmental Archaeology 1988–; hon res fell UCL, Lyell lectureship Br Assoc for the Advancement of Science 1988; *Books* Our Fossil Relatives (with A Gray, 1983), Human Evolution - An Illustrated Guide (with P Andrews, 1989), In Search of the Neanderthals (with C Gamble, 1993), African Exodus (with R McKie, 1996); *Recreations* listening to music, soccer, astronomy, current affairs, travel; *Style—* Prof Christopher Stringer; ✉ Human Origins Programme, Department of Palaeontology, The Natural History Museum, London SW7 5BD (☎ 0171 938 9270, fax 0171 938 9277)

STRONACH, Prof David Brian; OBE (1975); s of Ian David Stronach (d 1955), of Newstead Abbey, Notts, and Marjorie Jessie Duncan, *née* Minto; *b* 10 June 1931; *Educ* Gordonstoun, St John's Coll Cambridge (MA); *m* 30 June 1966, Ruth Vaadia; 2 da (Keren b 1967, Tami b 1972); *Career* Nat Serv Lt 1 Bn Duke of Wellington's Regt 1950–51; Br Acad archaeological attaché Iran 1960–61, dir Br Inst of Persian Studies 1961–80, prof of Near Eastern archaeology Univ of Calif Berkeley 1981–, curator of Near Eastern archaeology Hearst Museum of Anthropology Univ of Calif Berkeley 1983–; fell: Br Sch of Archaeology in Iraq 1957–59, Br Inst of Archaeology at Ankara 1958–59; lectureships incl: Hagop Kevorkian visiting lectr in Iranian art and archaeology Univ of Pennsylvania 1967, Rhind lectr Univ of Edinburgh 1973, Charles Eliot Norton lectr American Inst of Archaeology 1980, visiting prof of archaeology and Iranian studies Univ of Arizona 1980–81, Columbia lectr in Iranian studies Columbia Univ 1986, Charles K Wilkinson lectr Metropolitan Museum of Art NY 1990, Victor M Leventritt lectr in art history Harvard Univ 1991; dir of excavations at: Ras al 'Amiya Iraq 1960, Yarim Tepe Iran 1960–62, Pasargadae Iran 1961–63, Tepe Nush-i Jan Iran 1967–78, Shahr-i Qumis/Hecatompylos Iran 1967–78, Nineveh Iraq 1987–90, Horom Armenia 1992–; advsy ed: Iran 1975–, The Jl of Mithraic Studies 1976–79, Iranica Antiqua 1985–, Bulletin of the Asia Institute 1987–, American Journal of Archaeology 1989–; corr memb German Archaeological Inst 1966–73; first hon vice pres Br Inst of Persian Studies 1981–; assoc memb Royal Belgian Acad 1988; fell: German Archaeological Inst 1973, Explorers Club NY 1980; FSA 1963; *Awards* Ghirshman Prize of Acad des Inscriptions et Belles Lettres Paris 1979, Sir Percy Sykes Medal Royal Soc for Asian Affrs 1980; *Books* Pasargadae A Report On The Excavations Conducted By The British Institute of Persian Studies from 1961 to 1963 (1978); *Recreations* tribal carpets; *Clubs* Hawks (Cambridge), Explorers (NY); *Style—* Prof David Stronach, OBE, FSA; ✉ Department of Near Eastern Studies, University of California, Berkeley, Calif 94720, USA (☎ 00 1 510 642 3757, fax 00 1 510 643 8430)

STRONG, Air Cdre David Malcolm; CB (1964), AFC (1941); s of Theophilus Edgar Strong (d 1952), of Llanishen, Glam, and Margaret, *née* McGregor (d 1955); *b* 30 Sept 1913; *Educ* Cardiff HS; *m* 29 March 1941, Daphne Irene, da of Frederick Arthur Brown (d 1922), of Dover Ct; 2 s (Simon David McGregor b 3 March 1946, Christopher Richard b 14 Aug 1947), 1 da (Carolyn Irene Jane b 7 July 1949); *Career* under trg as pilot 1936, No 166 (B) Sqdn 1936–39, No 10 Operation Trg Unit Abingdon 1940–41, No 104 (B) Sqdn 1941 (POW Germany 1941–45), Co No 5 Air Nav Sch Jurby 1945–46, Co No 10 Air Nav Sch Driffield 1946–47, Air Miny P Staff 1947–48, RAF Staff Coll Bracknell (psa) 1948–49, Air HQ Rhodesian Air Trg Gp 1949–51, directing staff RAF Staff Coll 1952–55, Flying Coll Manby 1956, Co RAF Coningsby 1957–58, Air Miny D of P (A) 1959–61, SASO RAF Germany 1961–63, Cmdt RAF Halton 1963–66; chm RAF RFU 1954–55, chm RAF Golf Soc 1962–63; *Recreations* golf, walking; *Clubs* RAF, Ashridge Golf; *Style—* Air Cdre David Strong, CB, AFC; ✉ Old Coach House, Wendover, Bucks HP22 6EB (☎ 01296 624 724)

STRONG, Gwyneth; *Career* actress; *Theatre* Royal Court: Carol in Sugar and Spice, Wilya in Glad Hand, Sally in Live Like Pigs, Cheryl in Care; Lyric Hammersmith: Sarah in Favourite Nights, Maria in Woyzech, Masha in The Three Sisters; other roles incl: Christine in Shout Across the River (RSC/Warehouse), Crystal in Loving Women (Arts Theatre), Betty Forrest in A Piece of Mind (Nuffield/Apollo); *Television* BBC: Linda Thompson in Nice Town, Cynthia in Clothes in the Wardrobe, Cassandra in Only Fools and Horses (3 series), Linda in Rainy Day Women, Sadie in King of the Ghetto, WPC McHoan in The Missing Postman; also Mary Shelley in The Life of Mary Shelley (Channel 4), Charlotte Raynor in 99–1 (Zenith); *Films* incl: Afraid of the Dark, Bloody Kids, Nothing But the Night, Cry Freedom, Crimetime; *Style—* Ms Gwyneth Strong; ✉ c/o William Morris Agency (UK) Ltd, 31/32 Soho Square, London W1V 5DG (☎ 0171 434 2191, fax 0171 437 0238)

STRONG, Liam; *Career* various mktg positions with Reckitt & Colman plc and Procter & Gamble, former dir of mktg and ops British Airways plc, currently chief exec Sears plc; non-exec dir Inchcape plc 1993–; *Style—* Liam Strong, Esq; ✉ Sears plc, 40 Duke Street, London W1A 2HP (☎ 0171 200 5999)

STRONG, Michael John; s of Frank James Strong (d 1987), and Ivy Rose, *née* Fruin (d 1964); *b* 27 Dec 1947; *Educ* Rutlish Sch Merton, Coll of Estate Mgmnt; *m* 25 April 1970, Anne Mary, da of Rev William Hurst Nightingale, of Wimbledon, London; 1 s (Jonathan Alexander b 1977); *Career* chartered surveyor, ptnr Richard Ellis; Freeman: City of London 1981, Worshipful Co of Plumbers 1982; FRICS; memb: Royal Acad, Royal Hort Soc, Arts Club; *Recreations* golf, tennis, music, travel, gardens; *Style—* Michael Strong, Esq; ✉ The Coolins, Manor House Lane, Little Bookham, Surrey (☎ 01372 52196); La Borna, Satuna, Begur, Spain; Richard Ellis, Berkeley Square House, Berkeley Square, London W1 (☎ 0171 629 6290, fax 0171 493 3734)

STRONG, Richard James; s of John Paterson Strong, OBE, of Tilford, Tilbrook, Huntingdon, and Margaret St Claire, *née* Ford (d 1981); *b* 5 July 1936; *Educ* Sherborne, Nat Leather Sellers Coll; *m* 1 May 1963, Camilla Lucretia, da of Maj William Walter Dowding (d 1981); 1 s (James b 30 May 1977), 3 da (Melissa b 30 Dec 1965, Amanda b 13 Nov 1968, Samantha b 28 March 1972); *Career* Nat Serv 10 Royal Hussars (PWO); Tanner Strong & Fisher Ltd 1960, md Strong & Fisher (Holdings) plc 1972–91, chm Strong International Ltd 1992–, chm Turn Leather Ltd 1994–; govr Bilton Grange Sch Tst; hon treas Oakley Hunt, memb Bletsoe Church PCC; Liveryman Worshipful Co of Grocers; *Recreations* fox hunting, farming, sailing, tennis; *Clubs* Royal Thames Yacht; *Style*— Richard Strong, Esq; ✉ Bletsoe Castle, Bletsoe, Beds MK44 1QE

STRONG, Sir Roy Colin; kt (1981); s of G E C Strong; *b* 23 Aug 1935; *Educ* Edmonton Co GS, Queen Mary Coll London (fell 1975), Warburg Inst (PhD); *m* 1971, Julia Trevelyan Oman, CBE, *qv*; *Career* writer, historian, critic (radio, TV and lectures in England and America); Nat Portrait Gallery: asst keeper 1959, dir, keeper and sec 1967–73; dir and sec V & A 1974–87; Ferens prof of fine art Univ of Hull 1972, Walls lectures Pierpont Morgan Library 1974; vice chm South Bank Bd 1986–90; memb: Arts Cncl of GB 1983–87 (chm Arts Panel 1983–87), Fine Arts Advsy Ctee Br Cncl 1974–87, Craft Advsy Cncl, RCA Cncl 1979–87, Br Film Inst Archive Advsy Ctee, Westminster Abbey Architectural Panel 1975–89, Historic Bldgs Cncl Historic Houses Ctee; former tstee: Arundel Castle, Chevening; Shakespeare Prize FVS Fndn Hamburg 1980; Hon DLitt: Leeds 1983, Keele 1984; sr fell RCA 1983; Liveryman Worshipful Company of Goldsmiths; FSA; *Television* Royal Gardens (BBC) 1992; *Publications* Portraits of Queen Elizabeth I (1963), Leicester's Triumph (with J A van Dorsten, 1964), Holbein and Henry VIII (1967), Tudor and Jacobean Portraits (1969), The English Icon: Elizabethan and Jacobean Portraiture (1969), Elizabeth R (with Julia Trevelyan Oman, 1971), Van Dyck - Charles I on Horseback (1972), Mary Queen of Scots (with Julia Trevelyan Oman, 1972), Inigo Jones - The Theatre of the Stuart Court (with Stephen Orgel, 1973), Splendour at Court - Renaissance Spectacle and Illusion (1973), An Early Victorian Album, The Hill/Adamson Collection (with Colin Ford, 1974), Nicholas Hilliard (1975), The Cult of Elizabeth: Elizabethan Portraiture and Pageantry (1977), And When Did You Last See Your Father? The Victorian Painter and the British Past (1978), The Renaissance Garden in England (1979), Britannia Triumphans: Inigo Jones, Rubens and Whitehall Palace (1980), Designing for the Dancer (contrib, 1981), The English Miniature (contrib, 1981), The New Pelican Guide to English Literature (contrib, 1982), The English Year (with Julia Trevelyan Oman, 1982), The English Renaissance Miniature (1983), Artists of the Tudor Court (catalogue 1983), Art and Power: Renaissance Festivals 1450–1650 (1984), Glyndebourne - A Celebration (contrib, 1984), Strong Points (1985), Henry Prince of Wales (1986), For Veronica Wedgewood These (contrib, 1986), Creating Small Gardens (1986), Gloriana (1987), A Small Garden Designer's Handbook (1987), Cecil Beaton The Royal Portraits (1988), Creating Small Formal Gardens (1989), British Theatre Arts Design (contrib, 1989), Lost Treasures of Britain (1990), England and the Continental Renaissance (contrib, 1990), Sir Philip Sidney's Achievements (contrib, 1990), A Celebration of Gardens (1991), The Garden Trellis (1991), The British Portrait (contrib, 1991), Versace Il Teatro (1991), Small Period Gardens (1992), Royal Gardens (1992), The Art of the Emblem (contrib, 1993), William Larkin (1994), A Country Life (1994), Successful Small Gardens (1994), The Tudor and Stuart Monarchy (1995, 2 edn 1997), The Story of Britain (1996), Country Life 1897–1997 - The English Vision (1996); *Recreations* gardening, weight training; *Clubs* Garrick, Beefsteak, Arts; *Style*— Sir Roy Strong, FSA; ✉ The Laskett, Much Birch, Herefordshire HR2 8HZ

STRONGE, Sir James Anselan Maxwell; 10 Bt (UK 1803), of Tynan, Co Armagh; s of late Maxwell Du Pre James Stronge, and 2 cousin of Capt Sir James Matthew Stronge, 9 Bt (assas 1981); *b* 17 July 1946; *Educ* privately; *Style*— Sir James Stronge, Bt

STROSS, Katherine Elizabeth; da of Peter Sigmund Stross, of Co Durham, and Lillian Isobel, *née* Jeary; *b* 25 Jan 1956; *Educ* Hertford Coll Oxford (Coll scholar biochemistry and law, BA Jurisprudence), UCLA (Fulbright scholar, Henry Ford scholar, Edward Carter fell, MBA); *m* 27 Sept 1991, Craig Monroe Imrie, s of Clifton Monroe Imrie; *Career* operator and analyst Supply and Distribution Dept Mobil Oil Co Ltd London and New York 1978–82, mangr The Boston Consulting Group Ltd London 1988–89 (conslt 1984–88); Granada Television Ltd: fin dir 1989–92, commercial dir 1992–, commercial dir LWT (following takeover by Granada) and Television Div Granada Group plc 1994–96, commercial and media devpt dir Granada Media Group 1996–; *Style*— Ms Katherine Stross; ✉ Granada Media Group Ltd, Quay Street, Manchester M60 9EA (☎ 0161 832 7211, 0161 827 2345 direct, fax 0161 953 0282)

STROUD, Prof Sir (Charles) Eric; kt (1988); s of Frank Edmund Stroud (d 1973), of Marlow on Thames, Bucks, and Lavinia May, *née* Noakes (d 1988); *b* 15 May 1924; *Educ* Cardiff HS, Welsh Nat Sch of Med (BSc, MB, BCH, DCH); *m* 15 April 1950, June Mary, da of Harold Dockerill Neep (d 1984), of Bridgend, Mid Glamorgan; 1 s (David b 1961), 2 da (Diana b 1956, Amanda b 1958); *Career* RAF Med Br, Flying Offr 1950–51, Sqdn Ldr 1951–52; sr registrar Hosp for Sick Children Gt Ormond St 1956–61, paediatrician Uganda Govt 1958–60, asst to dir Paediatric Dept Guy's Hosp 1961–62, conslt paediatrician King's Coll Hosp 1962–68, prof and dir Paediatric Dept King's 1968–88; dir Variety Club Children's Hosp King's 1984–88, emeritus prof of paediatrics Univ of London and King's Coll Hosp 1989; currently hon med dir Children's Nationwide Medical Research Fund; chm Standing Medical Advsy Ctee to Sec of State 1986–89; civil conslt in paediatrics RAF; chm Overseas Ctee, tstee Save the Children Fund; second vice pres Royal Coll of Physicians London 1989–90; Hans Sloane fell and dir Overseas Dept Royal Coll of Physicians London; Liveryman Worshipful Soc of Apothecaries; FRCP 1968 (MRCP 1955); FKC 1989; *Recreations* fishing, golf, cricket; *Style*— Prof Sir Eric Stroud; ✉ c/o Children's Nationwide Medical Research Fund, Nicholas House, 181 Union St, London SE1 0LN (☎ 0171 928 2425)

STROUD, Ven Ernest Charles Frederick; s of Charles Henry Stroud (d 1975), of Bristol, and Irene Doris, *née* Venn (d 1975); *b* 20 May 1931; *Educ* Merrywood GS Bristol, Merchant Venturers Tech Coll, Univ of Durham (BA, DipTheol), Luton Industl Coll (Dip); *m* 15 Aug 1959, Jeanne Marquerite, da of Alfred Henry Evans (d 1966), of Bristol; 2 da (Teresa b 1961, Bridget b 1963); *Career* ordained: deacon 1960, priest 1961; curate All Saints S Kirkby Pontefract 1960–63, priest i/c St Ninian Whitby 1963–66; incumbent of: All Saints Chelmsford 1966–75, St Margaret Leigh on Sea 1975–83; rural dean Hadleigh 1979–83, hon canon Chelmsford 1982–83, archdeacon of Colchester 1983–; proctor Gen Synod 1980–, memb Standing Ctee Convocation of Canterbury 1990–96; chm: Additional Curates Soc, Church Union 1989–96; memb: C of E Pensions Bd 1984–96 (vice chm Investment and Fin Ctee 1990–96), Essex CC Libraries and Museums Ctee 1993–96; chm Rev Dr George Richards' Charity; memb The Ecclesiastical Law Soc; *Recreations* travel, theatre, gardening; *Style*— The Ven the Archdeacon of Colchester; ✉ Archdeacon's House, 63 Powers Hall End, Witham, Essex CM8 1NH (☎ 01376 513130, fax 01376 500789)

STROUD, Dr Michael (Mike); OBE (1993); s of Victor Stroud, of Ridley, Kent, and Vivienne Richardson, *née* Zelegman; *Educ* Trinity Sch Croydon, UCL (BSc), St George's Hosp Med Sch (MB BS), Univ of London (MD); *m* 1987, Thea, *née* de Moel; 1 s (Callan b 2 Dec 1987), 1 da (Tarn b 17 April 1990); *Career* various NHS trg posts 1979–85, Footsteps of Scott Antarctic expdn 1985–86, NHS registrar in med 1987–89, research in human performance 1989–95 (latterly chief scientist in physiology Defence Research Agency Centre for Human Scis), research fell in nutrition and sr registrar in gastroenterology Southampton Univ Hosps NHS Tst 1995–; 5 North Pole expdns 1986–90, crossed Antarctic with Sir Ranulph Fiennes 1992–93 (first unsupported crossing in history); Polar Medal 1995; MRCP (UK) 1984, FRCP (London and Edinburgh) 1995; memb: Physiology Soc 1994, FRGS 1994; *Recreations* Polar travel, ultra distance running; *Style*— Dr Mike Stroud, OBE; ✉ c/o Fox Artist Management, Concorde House, 101 Shepherd's Bush Road, London W6 7LP (☎ 0171 602 8822, fax 0171 603 2352)

STROVER, Richard Guy (Dick); *b* 3 July 1941; *Educ* Dragon Sch Oxford, Marlborough; *m* Collette Mary; 1 da (Sara Louise); *Career* articled clerk RF Fraser & Co 1960–65, Harmood Banner & Co 1965–74; ptnr Deloitte Haskins & Sells (following merger) then Coopers & Lybrand (following merger) 1975–96; pres Croydon Dist Soc of Chartered Accountants 1990–91, memb Cncl ICAEW and memb Bd ICAEW Faculty of Fin and Mgmnt until 1996; FCA (ACA 1965), MBCS; *Recreations* squash, tennis, sailing, golf, bridge; *Clubs* RAC; *Style*— Dick Strover, Esq; ✉ The Old Chapel House, Rectory Hill, East Bergholt, Suffolk CO7 6TG (☎ 01206 298243, fax 01206 299243)

STROWGER, Clive; s of Gaston Jack Strowger, CBE, and Kathleen, *née* Gilbert; *b* 4 July 1941; *Educ* Univ Coll Sch Hampstead; *m* 23 Jan 1965, Deirdre Majorie, da of Col Bertram Stuart Trevelyan Archer, GC, OBE; 3 s (Timothy b 26 Aug 1968, Andrew b 18 Dec 1969, Stephen b 29 Sept 1980), 1 da (Louise b 2 June 1975); *Career* various managerial positions Ford Motor Co 1966–71, sr fin mgmnt positions then fin dir BL Int British Leyland Corp 1971–77; Grand Metropolitan 1977–90: md brewing, chief exec consumer servs, chm and chief exec foods, gp fin dir and chief exec retail and property; chief exec Mountleigh Group plc 1990–91, mgmnt conslt 1991–92, chief exec APV plc 1992–94; currently non-exec dir Powell Duffryn plc; Freeman Worshipful Co of Brewers; FCA 1965, ATII 1965, CIMgt 1990; *Recreations* choral singing, family, tennis, skiing; *Style*— Clive Strowger, Esq; ✉ c/o Powell Duffryn plc, Powell Duffryn House, London Road, Bracknell, Berks RG12 2AQ (☎ 01344 53101)

STROYAN, His Hon Judge; (Ronald) Angus Ropner; QC (1972); eld s of Ronald Strathearn Stroyan (d 1957), of Boreland, and Mary Enid, *née* Ropner (d 1985); *b* 27 Nov 1924; *Educ* Harrow, Trinity Coll Cambridge (BA); *m* 1, 2 June 1952 (m dis 1965), Elisabeth Anna, da of Col J P Grant, MC (d 1964), of Rothiemurchus; 2 da (Victoria b 1953, Julia b 1958), 1 s (John b 1955); m 2, 22 Sept 1967, Jill Annette Johnston, da of Sir Douglas Marshall (d 1976), of Hatt House, Saltash; 1 s (Mark b 1969), 2 step s (Robert b 1952, William b 1963), 2 step da (Lucy b 1954, Henrietta b 1959); *Career* Nat Serv Black Watch (RHR) NW Europe 1943–45, attached Argyll and Sutherland Highlanders Palestine 1945–47, Capt (despatches), serv TA; called to the Bar Inner Temple 1950; dep chm N Riding of Yorks QS 1962–70, chm 1970–71, recorder Crown Ct 1972–75; memb Gen Cncl of Bar 1963–67, 1969–73 and 1975; circuit judge 1975–, sr circuit judge and hon recorder of the City of Newcastle-upon-Tyne 1993–; chm West Rannoch Deer Mgmnt Gp 1987–; *Recreations* country sports; *Clubs* Caledonian; *Style*— His Hon Judge Stroyan, QC; ✉ Boreland, Killin, Perthshire (☎ 01567 820252); Chapel Cottage, Whashton, Richmond, North Yorks

STRUTHERS, Prof Allan David; s of Dr David Struthers (d 1987), of Glasgow, and Margaret Thompson, *née* Adams (d 1989); *b* 14 Aug 1952; *Educ* Hutcheson's Boys' GS Glasgow, Univ of Glasgow (BSc, MB ChB, MD); *m* Julia Elizabeth Anne, da of Robert Diggens (d 1993); 1 da (Kate Lisa b 1980), 1 s (Gordon Allan Benjamin b 1982); *Career* jr then sr house offr Glasgow Teaching Hosps 1977–80, registrar then res fell Dept of Materia Medica Stobhill Hosp Glasgow 1980–82, sr med registrar Royal Postgraduate Med Sch and Hammersmith Hosp London 1982–85, sr lectr, reader then prof Dept of Clinical Pharmacology Ninewells Hosp and Med Sch Dundee 1985–; awarded personal chair Univ of Dundee 1992; SKB Prize for Res in Clinical Pharmacology (Br Pharmacological Soc) 1990; memb Assoc of Physicians of GB and I 1992; FRCP, FRCPE, FRCPG, FESC 1994; *Books* Atrial Natriuretic Factor (1990); *Recreations* swimming, cycling; *Style*— Prof Allan Struthers; ✉ Department of Clinical Pharmacology, Ninewells Hospital and Medical School, Ninewells, Dundee DD1 9SY (☎ 01382 660111 ext 3181, fax 01382 644972)

STRUTT, Sir Nigel Edward; kt (1972), TD, DL (Essex 1954); s of Edward Jolliffe Strutt (d 1964); *b* 18 Jan 1916; *Educ* Winchester, Wye Agric Coll; *Career* Essex Yeo (Maj) 1937–56, served WWII Capt 104 Essex Yeo RHA (TA) ME 1939–45; former chm and md Strutt & Parker (Farms) Ltd, md Lord Rayleigh's Farms Inc, memb Eastern Electricity Bd 1964–76, chm Advsy Cncl for Agric and Hort 1973–80; pres: CLA 1967–69, Br Friesian Cattle Soc 1974–75; High Sheriff of Essex 1966; fell Wye Agric Coll 1970; Hon FRASE 1971 (pres 1983); Master Worshipful Co of Farmers 1976; Johann Heinrich von Thunen Gold medal (Univ of Kiel) 1974, Massey-Ferguson Nat award for Servs to UK Agric 1976; Hon DSc Cranfield 1979, Hon DUniv Essex 1981, Hon DPhil Anglia Poly Univ 1993; *Recreations* shooting, travelling; *Clubs* Brooks's, Farmers'; *Style*— Sir Nigel Strutt, TD, DL; ✉ Sparrows, Terling, Chelmsford, Essex (☎ 01245 233213); office: Whitelands, Hatfield Peverel, Chelmsford, Essex (☎ 01245 382224)

STRUTT, Hon Richard Henry; s and h of 4 Baron Belper, *qv*; *b* 24 Oct 1941; *Educ* Harrow; *m* 1, 1966 (m dis), Jennifer Vivian, *née* Winser; 1 s, 1 da; m 2, 1980, Mrs Judith Mary de Jonge, da of James Twynam; *Style*— The Hon Richard Strutt; ✉ Slaughter Farm, Bourton-on-the-Water, Glos GL54 2HJ

STUART, Alexander Charles; s of Alfred William Noble Stuart, of Sussex, and Eileen Lucy, *née* Winter; *b* 27 Jan 1955; *Educ* Bexley GS; *m* Ann Totterdell (m dis); 1 s (Joe Buffalo b 15 Aug 1983 d 1989); *Career* writer; author of film criticism and various screenplays; exec prodr Insignificance (film, dir Nicolas Roeg) 1985, screenwriter Agatha Christie's Ordeal By Innocence (film, dir Desmond Davis) 1985; prof of film Univ of Miami 1994–; *Books* novels: Glory B (1983), The War Zone (1989, short-listed Whitbread award 1989), Tribes (1992); children's books: Joe, Jo-Jo and the Monkey Masks (1988), Henry and the Sea (with Joe Buffalo Stuart, 1989); non-fiction: Five and a Half Times Three: The Short Life and Death of Joe Buffalo Stuart (with Ann Totterdell, 1990), Life on Mars: Gangsters, Runaways, Exiles, Drag Queens and Other Aliens in Florida (1996); *Recreations* swimming, running, cycling, peace; *Style*— Alexander Stuart, Esq; ✉ c/o Charles Walker, Peters Fraser & Dunlop Ltd, 503 The Chambers, Chelsea Harbour, Lots Road, London SW10 0XF (☎ 0171 344 1000, fax 0171 352 7356)

STUART, Andrew Christopher; CMG (1979), CPM (1961); s of Rt Rev Cyril Stuart, Bishop of Uganda (d 1981), and Mary Stuart, OBE, *née* Summerhayes; *b* 30 Nov 1928; *Educ* Bryanston, Clare Coll Cambridge (MA); *m* 18 July 1959, Patricia Moira, da of Robert Douglas Kelly (d 1953), of Uganda; 2 s (James b 11 March 1962, Charles b 17 May 1967), 1 da (Fiona Mary (Mrs Farrelly) b 12 Nov 1960); *Career* called to the Bar Middle Temple; HMOCS Uganda 1952–64 (ret judicial advsr); FCO: head of Chancery Helsinki 1968–71, asst S Asian Dept 1971–72, cnsllr and head Hong Kong and India Ocean Dept 1972–75, head of Chancery Jakarta 1975–78, Br resident cmmr New Hebrides 1978–80, HM ambass Finland 1980–83; princ Utd World Coll of the Atlantic 1983–90, conslt VSO 1990–, chm Centre for Br Teachers 1991–; govr ESU, memb Cncl Lancing Coll; pres Anglo-Finnish Soc; Order of the Lion of Finland; *Recreations* sailing, gliding, mountaineering; *Clubs* Utd Oxford and Cambridge Univ, Alpine, Jesters; *Style*— Andrew Stuart, Esq, CMG, CPM; ✉ Long Hall, North Street, Wareham, Dorset BH20 4AG (☎ 01929 551658, fax 01929 551712)

STUART, Viscount; Andrew Richard Charles Stuart; s and h of 8 Earl Castle Stewart; *b* 7 Oct 1953; *Educ* Millfield, Univ of Exeter; *m* 1973, Annie Yvette, da of Robert le Poulain, of Paris; 1 da (Hon Celia b 1976); *Career* farmer; *Style*— Viscount Stuart; ✉ Combehayes Farm, Buckerell, Honiton, Devon EX14 0ET (☎ 01404 850349)

STUART, Lady Arabella; *née* Stuart; da of 18 Earl of Moray (d 1943); *b* 11 July 1934; *m* 1956 (m dis), (Charles) Mark Edward Boxer (Marc the cartoonist, d 1988); 1 s, 1 da; *Career* author, professional name Arabella Boxer; fndr memb Guild of Food Writers; Glenfiddich Food Writer of the Year 1975 and 1977; Andre Simon Award, Michael Smith Award, Glenfiddich Special Award 1992; *Books* First Slice Your Cookbook, Arabella Boxer's Garden Cookbook, Mediterranean Cookbook, The Sunday Times Complete Cookbook, A Visual Feast, Arabella Boxer's Book of English Food, The Hamlyn Book of Herbs and Others; *Style*— The Lady Arabella Stuart; ✉ 44 Elm Park Rd, London SW3 6AX

STUART, Hon (James) Dominic; s (by 1 m) and h of 2 Viscount Stuart of Findhorn, *qv*; *b* 25 March 1948; *Educ* Eton, Thames Poly (Dip in Estate Mgmnt); *m* 1979, Yvonne Lucienne, da of Edgar Desprès, of Ottawa; *Career* business conslt and cnsllr; ARICS; *Recreations* metaphysics, psychology, walking; *Style*— The Hon Dominic Stuart; ✉ 15 Stowe Rd, London W12

STUART, Duncan; CMG (1989); s of Ian Cameron Stuart (d 1987), of Burton in Kendal, Lancs, and Patricia Forbes, *née* Hardy (d 1988); *b* 1 July 1934; *Educ* Rugby, BNC Oxford (classical scholar, MA); *m* 29 July 1961, Leonore Luise, da of Dr Carl Liederwald (d 1976), of Berlin; 1 s (James Alexander Cameron b 1965), 1 da (Arabella Mary b 1963); *Career* Nat Serv 2 Lt 1 Bn Oxfordshire and Buckinghamshire LI, served BAOR and Cyprus; joined HM Foreign (later Dip) Serv 1959, Office of Political Advsr Berlin 1960–61, FO 1961–64, second sec Helsinki 1964–66, head Chancery Dar-es-Salaam 1966–69, FCO 1969–70, first sec Helsinki 1970–74, FCO 1974–80, cnsllr Bonn 1980–83, FCO 1983–86, cnsllr Washington 1986–88, FCO 1989–92; chm and chief exec Cyrus International 1994–95, special ops exec advsr to FCO 1996–; govr St Clare's Oxford 1992–; *Clubs* Boodle's, United Oxford and Cambridge Univ, MCC; *Style*— Duncan Stuart, Esq, CMG; ✉ c/o C Hoare & Co, 37 Fleet Street, London EC4P 4DQ

STUART, Sir (James) Keith; kt (1986); s of James and Marjorie Stuart; *b* 4 March 1940; *Educ* King George V Sch Southport, Gonville and Caius Coll Cambridge (MA); *m* 1966, Kathleen Anne Pinder, *née* Woodman; 3 s, 1 da; *Career* dist mangr S Western Electricity Bd 1970–72; sec British Transport Docks Bd 1972–75, gen mangr 1976–77, md 1977–82, dep chm 1980–82, chm 1982–83; chm: Associated British Ports Holdings PLC 1983–, Seeboard plc 1992–; dir Int Assoc of Ports and Harbours 1983, vice pres 1985–87; chm Ctee on Int Port Devpt 1979–85; pres Inst of Freight Forwarders 1983–84; dir: Royal Ordnance Factories 1983–85, BAA plc 1986–92; memb Cncl Chartered Inst of Transport 1979–88 (vice pres 1982–83, pres 1985–86); govr Trinity Coll of Music 1991–; Liveryman Worshipful Co of Clockmakers 1987; FCIT, CIMgt, FRSA; *Recreations* music; *Clubs* Brooks's, United Oxford and Cambridge Univ; *Style*— Sir Keith Stuart; ✉ Associated British Ports Holdings PLC, 150 Holborn, London EC1N 2LR (☎ 0171 430 1177)

STUART, Prof Sir Kenneth Lamonte; kt (1977); *b* 16 June 1920; *Educ* Harrison Coll Barbados, McGill Univ Montreal (BA), Queen's Univ Belfast (MB BCh, BAO); *m* 1958, Barbara Cecille; 1 s, 2 da; *Career* Univ of the WI: dean of Med Faculty 1969–71, head Dept of Med 1972–76; med advsr Cwlth Secretariat 1976–85, chm Cwlth Caribbean Med Res Cncl 1989–94, hon med and scientific advsr Barbados High Cmmn 1991–; chm Ct of Govrs LSHTM 1983–86, conslt advsr The Wellcome Tst 1984–90, memb Bd of Govrs Int Devpt Res Centre of Canada 1985–89, chm Errol Barrow Meml Tst, memb Bd of Govrs Liverpool Sch of Tropical Med; Gresham prof of physic Gresham Coll London 1988–92; tstee Schs Partnership Worldwide 1988–, memb Governing Cncl UMDS Guy's and St Thomas's Hosps London 1994–, memb Cncl and tstee London Lighthouse 1994–, memb Cncl Royal Over-Seas League 1994–; Freeman City of London 1994; Hon DSc; MD, FRCP, FRCPE, FACP, FFPM, FFPHM, DTM&H; *Recreations* tennis; *Clubs* Walton Lawn Tennis, Royal Over-Seas League, RSM; *Style*— Prof Sir Kenneth Stuart; ✉ 3 The Garth, Cobham, Surrey KT11 2DZ (☎ 01932 863826, fax 01932 860427); Barbados High Commission, 1 Great Russell St, London WC1B 3JY (☎ 0171 631 4975, fax 0171 323 6872)

STUART, Marian Elizabeth; *b* 17 July 1944; *Educ* Univ of Leicester (MA); *children* 1 s (Alexander b 1982), 1 da (Julia b 1985); *Career* Civil Serv: joined 1967, dep chief inspr Social Servs Inspectorate Dept of Health 1988–89, head of Fin Div Dept of Health 1989–93, resident chm Civil Serv Selection Bd 1993–; *Recreations* bridge, skiing, theatre; *Style*— Ms Marian Stuart; ✉ 24 Whitehall, London SW1A 2ED (☎ 0171 210 6666)

STUART, (Charles) Murray; CBE; s of Charles Maitland Stuart (d 1984), and Grace Forrester, *née* Kerr (d 1990); *b* 28 July 1933; *Educ* Glasgow Acad, Univ of Glasgow (MA, LLB); *m* 10 April 1963, Netta Caroline, da of Robert Thomson (d 1981); 1 s (David Charles Thomson b 19 Oct 1970), 1 da (Caroline Alison b 29 Dec 1972); *Career* CA 1961; chief accountant and co sec P & W McLellan (now Haden McLellan) 1961–62, internal auditor and analyst Ford Motor Company 1962–65, fin dir and sec Sheffield Twist Drill & Steel Co Ltd 1965–69, fin dir and asst md Unicorn Industries Ltd (now Foseco Minsep) 1969–73, fin dir Hepworths Limited (now Next) 1973–74, dep md ICL plc (now part of STC) 1977–81 (fin dir 1974–77); MB Group PLC (formerly Metal Box): fin dir 1981–83, dir fin planning and admin 1983–86, gp md 1986–87, gp chief exec 1988–89, chm 1989–90; dir and chief fin offr Berisford International plc 1990–91; non-exec chm: Scottish Power plc 1992– (dir 1990), Intermediate Capital Group Ltd 1993–, Hill Samuel Bank Scotland Ltd 1993–94; exec dir and a vice chm Hill Samuel Bank Ltd 1992–93; non-exec dir: Hunter Saphir plc 1991–92, Clerical Medical & General Life Assurance Society 1993–; dir St Andrew's Management Institute Ltd 1993–96; dep chm Audit Cmmn 1991–95 (memb 1986–95); memb W Surrey and NE Hants Health Authy 1990–93; memb Law Soc Scotland 1957; FCT 1984, CIMgt 1986, FRSA 1988; *Recreations* ballet, theatre, tennis; *Clubs* Western; *Style*— Murray Stuart, Esq, CBE; ✉ Longacre, Guildford Road, Chobham, Woking, Surrey GU24 8EA; Scottish Power PLC, 1 Atlantic Quay, Glasgow G2 8SP (☎ 0141 248 8200, fax 0141 636 4580)

STUART, Nicholas Willoughby; CB (1990); s of Douglas Willoughby Stuart, of Long Melford, nr Sudbury, Suffolk, and Margaret Eileen, *née* Holms; *b* 2 Oct 1942; *Educ* Harrow, Christ Church Oxford (MA); *m* 1, July 1963 (m dis 1974), Sarah, *née* Mustard; 1 s (Sebastian b 26 Dec 1963, d 8 Dec 1976), 1 da (Henrietta b 21 March 1965); m 2, 29 Dec 1975, Susan Jane Fletcher, *qv*; 1 da (Emily Fletcher b 12 Sept 1983), 1 s (Alexander Fletcher b 1 Feb 1989); *Career* asst princ DES 1964–68, private sec to Min of Arts 1968–69, princ DES 1969–73; private sec to: Head of Civil Serv 1973, PM 1973–76; asst sec DES 1976–79, memb Cabinet of Pres of Euro Cmmn 1979–81, under sec DES 1981–87, dep sec DES 1987–92, dir of resources and strategy Dept of Employment 1992–95, dir gen for Employment and Lifetime Learning Dept for Educn and Employment 1995–; *Style*— Nicholas Stuart, Esq, CB; ✉ Department for Education and Employment, Sanctuary Buildings, 20 Great Smith Street, London SW1P 3BT

STUART, Sir Phillip Luttrell; 9 Bt (E 1660), of Hartley Mauduit, Hants; s of late Luttrell Hamilton Stuart and nephew of 8 Bt (d 1959); Sir Philip's name does not, at time of going to press, appear on the Official Roll of Baronets; *b* 7 Sept 1937; *m* 1, 1962 (m dis 1968), Marlene Rose, da of Otto Muth; 1 da; m 2, 1969, Beverley Claire Pieri; 1 s, 1 da; *Heir* s, Geoffrey Phillip Stuart b 5 July 1973; *Career* Flying Offr RCAF 1957–62; pres Agassiz Industs Ltd; *Style*— Sir Phillip Stuart, Bt; ✉ Apt 50, 10980 Westdowne Road, RR2, Ladysmith, BC, Canada V0R 2E0 (☎ 001 604 245 0569, fax 001 604 245 0568)

STUART-FORBES, Sir William Daniel; 13 Bt (NS 1626), of Pitsligo, and Monymusk, Aberdeenshire; s of William Kenneth Stuart-Forbes (d 1946, 3 s of 10 Bt), and Marjory, *née* Gilchrist; suc uncle, Sir Charles Edward Stuart-Forbes, 12 Bt, 1985; *b* 21 Aug 1935; *m* 1956, Jannette, da of Hori Toki George MacDonald (d 1946), of Marlborough, NZ; 3 s (Kenneth Charles b 26 Dec 1956, Daniel Dawson b 1 April 1962, Reginald MacDonald b 3 Oct 1964), 2 da (Catherine Florence (Mrs William Paraha) b 1958, Eileen Jane (Mrs Neil Bertram Brown) b 1960); *Heir* s, Kenneth Charles Stuart-Forbes b 26 Dec 1956; *Style*— Sir William Stuart-Forbes, Bt; ✉ 9 Church Street, Blenheim, Marlborough, New Zealand

STUART-MENTETH, Charles Greaves; s and h of Sir James Wallace Stuart-Menteth, 6 Bt, *qv*, and (Dorothy) Patricia, *née* Warburton; *b* 25 Nov 1950; *Educ* Trinity Coll Oxford; *m* 1976, Nicola Mary Jane, da of Vincent Charles Raleigh St Lawrence, of 102 Exeter Street, Salisbury; 1 s (Alastair, decd), 4 da (Alice Clare b 1977, Celia Jane b 1978, Sarah Harriet b 1982, Sophie Emily Flora b 1995); *Career* md Datavault plc; *Style*— Charles Stuart-Menteth Esq; ✉ Hillend House, Dalry, Ayrshire (☎ 0129 483 3871); work: PO Box 270, Glasgow G51 3LJ (☎ 0141 425 1885)

STUART-MENTETH, Sir James Wallace; 6 Bt (UK 1838), of Closeburn, Dumfriesshire, and Mansfield, Ayrshire; s of Sir William Frederick Stuart-Menteth, 5 Bt (d 1952); *b* 13 Nov 1922; *Educ* Fettes, Univ of St Andrews, Trinity Coll Oxford (MA); *m* 23 April 1949, (Dorothy) Patricia, da of late Frank Greaves Warburton, of Thorrington, Stirling; 2 s (Charles Greaves b 1950, (William) Jeremy b 1953); *Heir* s, Charles Greaves Stuart-Menteth, *qv*; *Career* served WWII Lt Scots Gds (wounded); sometime md Alkali and Paints Div ICI Ltd; memb: Br Limbless Ex-Service Men's Assoc, Royal British Legion (Scotland); *Style*— Sir James Stuart-Menteth, Bt; ✉ Nutwood, Auchencairn, Castle Douglas, Kirkcudbrightshire DG7 1QZ

STUART-MOORE, Michael; QC (1990); s of Kenneth Basil Moore (d 1987), and Marjorie Elizabeth, *née* Hodges; *b* 7 July 1944; *Educ* Cranleigh Sch; *m* 8 Dec 1973, Katherine Ann, da of Kenneth William and Ruth Scott; 1 s (James b 1976),1 da (Zoe-Olivia b 1978)); *Career* called to the Bar Middle Temple 1966, recorder of the Crown Ct 1985–, judge of the High Ct Hong Kong 1993–; *Recreations* photography, flute, tennis, travel; *Style*— Michael Stuart-Moore, Esq, QC; ✉ 1 Hare Ct, Temple, London EC4Y 7BE (☎ 0171 353 5324, fax 0171 353 0667)

STUART OF FINDHORN, 2 Viscount (UK 1959); David Randolph Moray Stuart; s of 1 Viscount, CH, MVO, MC, PC (d 1971), and Lady Rachel, *née* Cavendish, OBE, da of 9 Duke of Devonshire; *b* 20 June 1924; *Educ* Eton; *m* 1, 1945, Grizel Mary Wilfreda (d 1948), da of late Theodore Fyfe and widow of Michael Gillilan; 1 s; m 2, 1951 (m dis 1979), Marian, da of late Gerald Wilson; 1 s, 3 da; m 3, 1979, Margaret Anne, da of Cdr Peter Du Cane, CBE, RN, and Victoria, sis of Sir John Gawen Carew Pole, 12 Bt, DSO, TD; *Heir* s, Hon (James) Dominic Stuart, *qv*; *Career* late Lt KRRC, Maj 6/7 Royal Welch Fus (TA), FRICS, Page of Honour to HM 1938–40, DL of Caerns 1963–68, land agent; *Style*— The Rt Hon the Viscount Stuart of Findhorn; ✉ 38 Findhorn, nr Forres, Morayshire

STUART-PAUL, Air Marshal Sir Ronald; KBE (1990, MBE 1967); s of James Grey Stuart-Paul (d 1984), and Isobel Mary McDonald (d 1939); *b* 7 Nov 1934; *Educ* Dollar Acad; *m* 9 Nov 1963, Priscilla Frances, da of George Kay (d 1975); 1 s (Craig b 14 April 1965), 1 da (Rowena b 20 Nov 1969); *Career* RAF Coll Cranwell 1953–56, served various fighter sqdns 1957–71, DA Saudi 1974–75, Cmd RAF Lossiemouth 1976–78, RCDS 1979, NATO 1980–82, MOD 1982–83, AOT 1984–85, DG Project Al Yamamah 1985–92; *Clubs* RAF; *Style*— Air Marshal Sir Ronald Stuart-Paul, KBE, RAF (Ret); ✉ Sycamore House, Gaunts Common, Wimborne, Dorset BH21 4JP (☎ 01258 840430)

STUART-SMITH, Elizabeth; *b* 3 Oct 1961; *Educ* Watford GS for Girls, Queens Coll Harley St, Cordwainers Coll London (travelling scholar); *m* 27 Jan 1990, Adam Beck; 1 s; *Career* shoe designer; worked with John Galliano and Jasper Conran; winner Design Cncl awards 1989; *Recreations* travel, food, walking; *Style*— Ms Elizabeth Stuart-Smith; ✉ Elizabeth Stuart Smith, 16 Upper Addison Gardens, W14 8AP (☎ 0171 603 9574, fax 0171 603 2607)

STUART-SMITH, James; CB (1986), QC (1988); s of James Stuart-Smith (d 1937), of Brighton, Sussex, and Florence Emma, *née* Armfield (d 1952); *b* 13 Sept 1919; *Educ* Brighton Coll, London Hosp Med Sch; *m* 28 Dec 1957, Jean Marie Therese, da of Hubert Young Groundsell, of Newport, IOW; 1 s (James b 24 Nov 1959), 1 da (Mary b 11 Nov 1958); *Career* served WWII 1939–47, cmmnd 2 Lt KRRC 1940, served Middle E and Italy 1940–45, staff appts UK 1945–47, demobbed as Actg Lt-Col 1947; called to the Bar Middle Temple 1948, in practice London 1948–55, legal asst to Office of Judge Adv-Gen 1955, dep judge advocate 1957, asst judge adv-gen 1968, vice judge adv-gen 1979, judge adv-gen 1984–91; served: Germany 1959–62, 1971–74 and 1976–79 (as dep judge adv-gen), ME Cmd Aden 1964–65 (as dep judge advocate); recorder Crown Ct 1985–92; hon life pres Int Soc for Mil Law and the Law of War 1991– (vice pres 1979–85, pres 1985–91); *Recreations* writing letters, mowing lawns; *Clubs* RAF; *Style*— James Stuart-Smith, Esq, CB, QC; ✉ The Firs, Copthorne, Sussex, RH10 4HH

STUART-SMITH, Lady; Joan Elizabeth Mary; *née* Motion; JP, DL (Herts 1987); da of Maj T A Motion, and Lady Elizabeth Grimston; *b* 14 Feb 1929; *Educ* Univ of Oxford (MA); *m* Rt Hon Lord Justice Stuart-Smith, *qv*; 3 s, 3 da; *Career* High Sheriff (and first woman sheriff) Herts 1983; chm: Bd of Govrs Abbots Hill Sch 1992–, Herts Garden Tst 1991–; pres Herts Victims Support Scheme; *Recreations* book-binding, music, propagating plants, building; *Style*— Lady Stuart-Smith, JP, DL

STUART-SMITH, Rt Hon Lord Justice; Rt Hon Sir Murray Stuart-Smith; kt (1981), PC (1988); s of Edward Stuart-Smith, and Doris, *née* Laughland; *b* 18 Nov 1927; *Educ* Radley, CCC Cambridge; *m* 1953, Joan Stuart-Smith, *qv*; 3 s, 3 da; *Career* called to the Bar Gray's Inn 1952, vice treas 1996; recorder of the Crown Court 1972–81, QC 1970, master of the Bench Gray's Inn 1978, judge of the High Court of Justice (Queen's Bench Div) 1981–87, presiding judge Western Circuit 1982–86, a Lord Justice of Appeal 1987–; cmmr for Security Service 1989, cmmr for Intelligence Services 1994, memb Criminal Injuries Compensation Bd 1979–81; hon fell CCC Cambridge 1994; *Recreations* playing cello, shooting, building, playing bridge; *Style*— The Rt Hon Lord Justice Stuart-Smith; ✉ Royal Courts of Justice, Strand, London WC2A 2LL

STUART-SMITH, Stephen James Adrian; s of D M Stuart-Smith, of Leics; *b* 18 Aug 1954; *Educ* Denstone Coll, King's Coll London (BA), Univ of London Inst of Educn (PGCE), Univ of Reading (MA); *Career* bookseller 1977–78, teacher 1978–85; head History Dept: Lord Wandsworth Coll Long Sutton 1985–88, Ditcham Park Sch Petersfield 1988–89; md Enitharmon Press 1987–, administrator Ben Nicholson, David Hockney and Aubrey Beardsley exhibitions for Japan 1992–98; literature assessor London Arts Bd 1994–96, memb Literature Advsy Gp London Arts Bd 1996–; memb Ctee Edward Thomas Fellowship 1986–94; FRSA 1990; *Books* Poems from Three Counties (1982, 2 vol 1985), An Enitharmon Anthology (1990); *Recreations* music, theatre, travel; *Style*— Stephen Stuart-Smith, Esq; ✉ Enitharmon Press, 36 St George's Avenue, London N7 0HD (☎ 0171 607 7194, fax 0171 607 8694)

STUART TAYLOR, Sir Nicholas Richard; 4 Bt (UK 1917), of Kennington, Co London; s of Sir Richard Laurence Stuart Taylor, 3 Bt (d 1978), and Lady Stuart Taylor; Sir Frederick Taylor, 1 Bt was pres of RCP; *b* 14 Jan 1952; *Educ* Bradfield; *m* 1984, Malvena Elizabeth, o da of Daniel David Charles Sullivan; 2 da (Virginia Caterina b 1989, Olivia Malvena b 1991); *Heir* none; *Career* slr 1977; *Recreations* skiing and other sports; *Style*— Sir Nicholas Stuart Taylor, Bt; ✉ 3 Horseshoe Drive, Romsey, Hampshire SO51 7TP

STUART-WHITE, Hon Mr Justice; Hon Sir Christopher Stuart; kt (1993); s of Reginald Stuart-White (d 1963), and Catherine Mary Wigmore, *née* Higginson; *b* 18 Dec 1933; *Educ* Winchester, Trinity Coll Oxford (BA); *m* 1957, Pamela, da of late Dr Robert Grant; 1 s (Rev William Stuart-White b 21 Jan 1959), 2 da (Lucy (Mrs Mockett) b 22 Sept 1961, Fiona (Mrs Nixon-Hill) b 31 Aug 1963); *Career* called to the Bar Inner Temple 1957, in practice Midland & Oxford Circuit 1957–78, recorder of the Crown Court 1974–78, circuit judge (Midland & Oxford Circuit) 1978–93, judge of the High Court of Justice (Family Div) 1993–; bencher Inner Temple 1993; *Style—* The Hon Mr Justice Stuart-White; ✉ Royal Courts of Justice, Strand, London WC2A 2LL

STUBBLEFIELD, Sir (Cyril) James; kt (1965); s of James Stubblefield (d 1926), of Cambridge, and Jane Stubblefield; *b* 6 Sept 1901; *Educ* The Perse Sch Cambridge, Chelsea Poly, RCS Univ of London (DSc); *m* 11 June 1932, Emily Muriel Elizabeth, da of late L R Yakchee, of Calcutta and Jersey, CI; 2 s; *Career* geology demonstrator Imperial Coll London 1923–28, memb Geological Survey of GB 1928, chief palaeontologist 1947–53, asst dir 1953–60, dir 1960–66; dir: Geological Survey of NI 1960–66, Museum of Practical Geology 1960–66; pres: Geological Soc London 1958–60, Palaeontographical Soc 1966–71, 8 Int Congress Carboniferous Stratigraphy and Geology 1967; foreign memb: Geological Soc of France, Geological Fndn Stockholm; fell: Chelsea Coll, Imperial Coll, King's Coll London; FRS, FGS, FZS, ARCS; *Style—* Sir James Stubblefield, FRS; ✉ 35 Kent Ave, Ealing, London W13 8BE (☎ 0181 997 5051)

STUBBS, Dawne Alison; da of William Thomas Telford, of Thrapston, Northamptonshire, and Janet Christine, *née* Smith; *b* 8 June 1967; *Educ* Prince William Sch Oundle, Tresham Coll Kettering, Huddersfield Poly (BSc, awards for design in knitwear); *m* 6 July 1996, Philip Michael Stubbs; *Career* asst designer Lister & Co plc colour yarn spinners 1987–88, designer Pierre Sangan Leicester and CI 1989–92, head of design John Smedley Ltd knitwear design 1992–; *Recreations* dressmaking, crafts, aerobics, swimming; *Style—* Mrs Philip Stubbs; ✉ John Smedley Ltd, Lea Mill, Matlock, Derbyshire DE4 5AG (☎ 01629 534571, fax 01629 534691)

STUBBS, Imogen Mary; da of Robin Desmond Scrivener Stubbs (d 1974), and Heather Mary, *née* McCracken (d 1986); *b* 20 Feb 1961; *Educ* St Paul's Girls', Westminster, Exeter Coll Oxford (scholar, BA), RADA (Silver medallist, John Barton Award in Stagefighting); *m* 1994, Trevor Nunn, *qv*; 1 da (Ellie b 1991), 1 s (Jesse b 1996); *Career* actress; numerous contrib book reviews and interviews (incl: The Times, The Observer, The Guardian); *Theatre* incl: Sally Bowles in Cabaret (Ipswich) 1985, Polly Brown in The Boyfriend (Ipswich) 1985, The Gaoler's Daughter in Two Noble Kinsmen (RSC) 1986–87, Helena in The Rover (RSC) 1986–87, Queen Isabel in Richard II (RSC) 1986–87, Desdemona in Othello (RSC 1989, BBC 1990), Heartbreak House (Yvonne Arnaud Guildford and Haymarket) 1992, title role in St Joan (Strand), Yelena in Uncle Vanya (Chichester and Albery); *Television* incl: Romy in Deadline (BBC) 1987, Ursula Brangwen in The Rainbow (BBC) 1988, Ginnie in Relatively Speaking (BBC) 1989, Anna Lee in Anna Lee (ITV), Helen in After The Dance (BBC), Ellie Dunn in Heartbreak House; *Radio* incl: Private Lives, No Way Out, Il Cid, La Bête Humaine, When the Dead Awaken; *Film* incl: Nanou in Nanou (Umbrella Films) 1985, Megan in A Summer Story (ITC Films) 1987, Aud in Erik The Viking (Viking Films) 1988, Sarah in Fellow Traveller (BBC/HBO) 1989, Diana in True Colors (Paramount) 1990, Marie in Sandra C'est la Vie (Gaumont Raubur), Zina in A Pin for the Butterfly (British Screen), Jack and Sarah 1995, Lucy in Sense and Sensibility (Columbia Films) 1995, Viola in Twelth Night (Renaissance/New Line Films) 1996; *Awards* Critics' Award for Most Promising Newcomer (for RSC) 1986–87, Gold Medal Best Actress in a Series Chicago Film Festival (for The Rainbow); nominations incl: Olivier Award for Best Newcomer (for RSC) 1987, Best Actress Evening Standard Film Awards (for A Summer Story) 1988, Best Actress Royal Variety Television Awards (for The Rainbow) 1989; *Style—* Miss Imogen Stubbs; ✉ c/o Michael Foster, ICM Ltd, Oxford House, 76 Oxford Street, London W1N 0AX (☎ 0171 636 6565, fax 0171 323 0101)

STUBBS, Sir James Wilfrid; KCVO (1979), TD (1946); eld s of Rev Wilfrid Thomas Stubbs (d 1968), and Muriel Elizabeth, *née* Pope (d 1966); *b* 13 Aug 1910; *Educ* Charterhouse, Brasenose Coll Oxford (MA); *m* 1938, Richenda Katherine Theodora (d 1995), da of Rt Rev William Champion Streatfeild, Bishop of Lewes (d 1929); 1 s, 1 da (decd); *Career* serv WWII Royal Signals, Lt-Col 1946; asst master St Paul's Sch 1934–46; United Grand Lodge of England: asst grand sec 1948–54, dep grand sec 1954–58, grand sec 1958–80; *Books* The Four Corners (1983), Freemasons' Hall, The Home and Heritage of The Craft (jtly, 1984), Freemasonry in my Life (1985); *Recreations* travel, family history; *Clubs* Athenaeum; *Style—* Sir James Stubbs, KCVO, TD; ✉ 5 Pensioners Court, The Charterhouse, London EC1M 6AU (☎ 0171 253 1982)

STUBBS, Prof Michael Wesley; s of Leonard Garforth Stubbs (d 1987), and Isabella Wardrop, *née* McGavin (d 1991); *b* 23 Dec 1947; *Educ* Glasgow HS for Boys, Kings Coll Cambridge (MA), Univ of Edinburgh (PhD); *Career* lectr in linguistics Univ of Nottingham 1974–85, prof of English in educn Inst of Educn Univ of London 1985–90, prof of English linguistics Univ of Trier Germany 1990–, hon sr res fell Univ of Birmingham 1994–; chm BAAL 1988–91; *Books* Language, Schools and Classrooms (1976), Language and Literacy (1980), Discourse Analysis (1983), Educational Linguistics (1986), Text and Corpus Analysis (1996); *Recreations* walking; *Style—* Prof Michael Stubbs; ✉ FB2 Anglistik, Universität Trier, D-54286 Trier, Germany (☎ 00 49 651 201 2278, fax 00 49 651 201 3928)

STUBBS, Una; da of Clarence Stubbs, of London, and Kathleen Angela Stubbs; *b* 1 May 1937; *Educ* Baylis Court Secdy Modern Sch Slough, La Roche Dancing Sch Slough; *m* 1, March 1960 (m dis), Peter Gilmor; 1 s (Jason); m 2, Oct 1969 (m dis), Nicky Henson; 2 s (Christian, Joe); *Career* actress; *Theatre* Theatre Royal Windsor incl: A Midsummer Night's Dream 1952, Quadrille 1953, The Sun and I 1953, Goody Two Shoes 1953; other credits incl: London Palladium Revue 1954, London Royal Variety Show 1954, 1972 and 1982, Folies Bergères (Prince of Wales) 1955, Star Maker (Manchester Hippodrome) 1956, Grab Me A Gondola (Lyric) 1957, On The Brighter Side (Phoenix) 1960, Aladdin (London Palladium) 1964, A Taste of Honey and The Diary of Anne Frank (Westcliffe) 1966, A Soldier's Tale (Edinburgh Festival and The Young Vic) 1967, The Knack (Golders Green Hippodrome) 1967, Jane Eyre (Adelee Genee Theatre) 1968, Little Malcolm and His Struggle Against The Eunuchs (Young Vic) 1968, Cowardy Custard (Mermaid) 1972, Cole (Mermaid) 1974, Irma La Douce (Watford) 1975, Aladdin (Richmond) 1976, Cinderella (Bromley) 1978, Oh Mr Porter (Mermaid) 1979, Dick Whittington (Richmond) 1979, Baggage (Adelphi) 1980, Worzel Gummidge (Birmingham Rep 1981, Cambridge Theatre London 1982), The Secret Life of Cartoons (Aldwych) 1986, Bless The Bride (Sadlers Wells) 1987, It Runs in The Family (Yvonne Arnaud Theatre Guildford) 1988, Run for Your Wife (Criterion) 1988, She Stoops to Conquer (Royal Exchange) 1989, Rumours (Chichester) 1990, Days of Hope (Hampstead) 1991, An Ideal Husband (Royal Exchange Manchester) 1992, Big Night Out At Little Sands Picture Palace (Nottingham Playhouse) 1993, Peter Pan (West Yorkshire Playhouse) 1996, Philadelphia Story (Royal Exchange) 1996, Deep Blue Sea (Mercury Theatre Colchester) 1996; *Television* BBC incl: Compact, Wayne and Shuster, Boy Meets Girl, Cliff in Scandinavia, Cole, Roy Castle Show, The Rivals of Sherlock Holmes, Morecambe and Wise, The Harry Secombe Show, Happy Families, Fawlty Towers, The Dick Emery Show, It's Cliff Richard, Till Death Us Do Part, In Sickness And In Health, Morris Minar's Marvellous Motors, Tricky Business, Keeping Up Appearances, Wings; other credits incl: Cool for Cats (Rediffusion), Worzel Gummidge (Southern ITV), Worzel Gummidge Down Under (Channel 4), Give Us A Clue (Thames ITV), Woolcraft This Morning (Granada), Off the Cuff (Granada), Threads (Granada), Heartbeat (YTV); *Films* incl: Summer Holiday, 3 Hats for Lisa, Wonderful Life, Till Death Us Do Part; *Books* In Stitches, A Stitch In Time, Una's Fairy Stories; *Recreations* embroidery, dressmaking, cycling; *Style—* Ms Una Stubbs; ✉ c/o The Richard Stone Partnership, 25 Whitehall, London SW1A 2BS (☎ 0171 839 6421, fax 0171 839 5002)

STUBBS, Sir William Hamilton; kt (1994); s of Joseph Stubbs, and Mary, *née* McNicol; *b* 5 Nov 1937; *Educ* Workington GS Cumberland, St Aloysius Coll Glasgow, Univ of Glasgow (BSc, PhD), Univ of Arizona; *m* 19 Sept 1963, Marie Margaret, da of Joseph Pierce; 3 da (Nadine Ann b 1964, Hilary Jo b 1966, Fiona Mairi b 1967); *Career* Shell Oil Co California 1964–67, teacher in Glasgow 1967–72, asst dir of educn Carlisle 1972–73 and Cumbria 1973–76, dep dir of educn 1976–77, dep educn offr ILEA 1977–82, educn offr and chief exec ILEA 1982–88, chief exec Polytechnics and Colleges Funding Cncl 1988–92, chief exec FE Funding Cncl 1992–96, rector London Inst 1996–; Hon Prof Univ of Warwick, Hon Doctorate Open Univ, Hon Dr Sheffield Hallam Univ, Hon Dr Univ of Exeter; *Style—* Sir William Stubbs; ✉ Locke's Cottage, Manor Road, Adderbury, Oxon OX17 3EL; The London Institute Higher Education Corporation, 65 Davies street, London W1Y 2DA (☎ 0171 514 6000)

STUBLEY, Trevor Hugh; s of Frank Stubley (d 1988), of Leeds, and Marie, *née* Ellis; *b* 27 March 1932; *Educ* Leeds Coll of Art, Edinburgh Coll of Art (DA, post dip scholar); *m* 1963, Valerie Ann, *née* Churm; 4 s (Adam b 1964, Justin b 1966, Gabriel b 1970, Nathan b 1974); *Career* artist; *Portraits* Archbishop of York, Dame Janet Baker, Lord Boyle of Handsworth, Lord Briggs, Lord Bullock, Sir Zelman Cowen, Lord Dainton of Hallam Moors, Dame Judi Dench, Prof Sir Fred Hoyle, Lord Morris of Grasmere, Sir Patrick Nairne, Lord Porter, J B Priestley, Dorothy Tutin, Lord Wolfenden, HM The Queen 1986, Lord Hailsham 1992; *Work in Collections* National Portrait Gall, Palace of Westminster, British Library, Cranwell RAF Coll, MOD, Royal Inst, IEE, Tower of London, Windsor Castle; illustrator of over 400 children's books 1960–80; *Awards* Andrew Grant Major travelling scholar 1955, William Hoffman Wood Gold Medal for Painting 1955, Yorkshire TV Fine Art fell 1981–82, Arts Cncl Award 1982, Hunting Group Art Prize 1986, H & J Quick Award Manchester Acad of Fine Art 1989, Singer and Friedlander/Sunday Times Prize 1990; vice pres Royal Soc of Portrait Painters 1994–; memb: Soc of Industl Artists and Designers 1976–85, Manchester Acad of Fine Art 1984–90; RP 1974, RSW 1990, RWS 1995, RBA 1991; *Recreations* painting out of doors in hot countries; *Clubs* The Arts; *Style—* Trevor Stubley, Esq, RP; ✉ The Royal Society of Portrait Painters, Federation of British Artists, 17 Carlton House Terrace, London SW1Y 5BD (☎ 0171 930 6844)

STUCLEY, Sir Hugh George Coplestone Bampfylde; 6 Bt (UK 1859), of Affeton Castle, Devon; s of Sir Dennis Frederic Bankes Stucley, 5 Bt (d 1983), and Hon Sheila Margaret Warwick Bampfylde (d 1996), da of 4 Baron Poltimore; *b* 8 Jan 1945; *Educ* RAC Cirencester; *m* 1969, Angela Caroline, er da of Richard Toller, of Theale, Berks; 2 s, 2 da; *Heir* s, George Dennis Bampfylde Stucley b 26 Dec 1970; *Career* Lt RHG; chm Devon Branch CLA 1995; *Clubs* Sloane; *Style—* Sir Hugh Stucley, Bt; ✉ Affeton Castle, Worlington, Crediton, Devon

STUDD, Sir Edward Fairfax; 4 Bt (UK 1929), of Netheravon, Wilts; s of Sir Eric Studd, 2 Bt, OBE, and Kathleen Stephana, da of Lydstone Joseph Langmead; suc bro, Sir (Robert) Kynaston Studd, 3 Bt, 1977; *b* 3 May 1929; *Educ* Winchester; *m* 1960, Prudence Janet, da of Alastair Douglas Fyfe, OBE, of Grey Court, Riding Mill, Northumberland; 2 s, 1 da; *Heir* s, Philip Alastair Fairfax (b 1961); *Career* Subaltern Coldstream Gds, serv Malaya 1948–49; Macneill & Barry Ltd Calcutta 1951–62, Inchcape & Co Ltd 1962–86 (dir 1974–86), chm Gray Dawes Travel Ltd 1987–96; memb Ct of Assts Worshipful Co of Merchant Taylors (Master 1987–88, 1993–94); *Recreations* rural activities; *Clubs* Boodle's, Pratt's; *Style—* Sir Edward Studd, Bt

STUDD, Dr John William Winston; s of Eric Dacombe Studd (d 1941), and Elsie Elizabeth, *née* Kirby; *b* 4 March 1940; *Educ* Royal Hosp Sch Ipswich, Univ of Birmingham (MB BS, MD); *m* 7 May 1980, Dr Margaret Ann Johnson, da of Dr Frederick Johnson, of Hinton Priory, Hinton Charterhouse, Bath, Avon; 1 s (Thomas b 16 Oct 1981), 2 da (Sarah b 7 Dec 1985, Josephine b 18 Feb 1992); *Career* res fell Univ of Birmingham, lectr in obstetrics and gynaecology Univ Coll of Rhodesia 1972, conslt and sr lectr Univ of Nottingham 1974–75, subsequently consIt obstetrician and gynaecologist King's Coll Hosp and Dulwich Hosp London, currently consIt obstetrician and gynaecologist Chelsea and Westminster Hosp London; author of papers on: labour, menopause, osteoporosis, premenstrual syndrome, post natal depression, depression in women and infertility, HIV infection in women; ed: Menopause Digest, The Diplomate; memb Editorial Bd: Jl of RSM, British Journal of Obstetrics and Gynaecology, Br Jl of Hosp Med, Int Jl of Gynaecological Endocrinology; memb Cncl and pubns offr RCOG, memb Cncl RSM, chm Nat Osteoporosis Soc, pres Section of Obstetrics and Gynaecology RSM, pres Int Soc of Reproductive Med, chm PMS and Menopause Tst, memb Hosp Consits and Specialists Assoc; Hon DSc Univ of Birmingham 1994; memb BMA 1962, FRCOG 1982 (MRCOG 1967); *Books* Management of Labour (ed, 1985), Management of the Menopause (ed, 1988), Progress in Obstetrics and Gynaecology (volumes 1–10), Self Assessment in Obstetrics and Gynaecology, The Menopause and Hormone Replacement Therapy (1993), Annual Progress in Reproductive Medicine (1993–94), RCOG Yearbook (1993 and 1994–95), other undergraduate and postgraduate textbooks; *Recreations* tennis, theatre, music, opera, history of medicine; *Style—* Dr John Studd; ✉ 27 Blomfield Rd, London W9 1AA (☎ 0171 266 0058, fax 0171 266 2663, car 0374 774999); 120 Harley St, London W1 (☎ 0171 486 0497, fax 0171 224 4190); Fertility & Endocrinology Centre, Lister Hospital, Chelsea Bridge Road, London SW1W 8RH (☎ 0171 730 5433, fax 0171 823 6108, telex 21283 LISTER G)

STUDD, Sir Peter Malden; GBE (1971), KCVO (1979), kt (1969), DL (Wilts 1983); s of late Brig Malden Studd, DSO, MC, and late Netta, *née* Cramsie; *b* 15 Sept 1916, Dublin; *Educ* Harrow, Clare Coll Cambridge (MA); *m* 1943, Angela, *née* Garnier; 2 s; *Career* RA 1939–45, serv Middle E and Euro Campaigns; De La Rue Co plc 1939–74, dir Lloyds of Scottish plc 1973–84; UK pres Chiropractic Advancement Assoc 1987–90; tstee: Royal Jubilee Tsts 1980–95, Arts Educnl Schs 1984–; capt of cricket Harrow and Cambridge Univ; Lord Mayor London 1970–71 (Alderman 1959, Sheriff 1967); KStJ; Past Master Worshipful Co of Merchant Taylors, Hon Liveryman Worshipful Co of Fruiterers and Plaisterers; Hon DSc City Univ; *Recreations* fishing, shooting, gardening, saving St Paul's, lighting up the Thames; *Clubs* I Zingari, MCC, Houghton; *Style—* Sir Peter Studd, GBE, KCVO, DL; ✉ c/o Hoare & Co, 37 Fleet St, London EC4

STUDHOLME, Sir Henry William; 3 Bt (UK 1956), of Perridge, Co Devon; er s of Sir Paul Henry William Studholme, 2 Bt, DL (d 1990), and Virginia Katherine, *née* Palmer (d 1990); *b* 31 Jan 1958; *Educ* Eton, Trinity Hall Cambridge (MA); *m* 1 Oct 1988, (Sarah) Lucy Rosita Deans-Chrystall, o da of late Richard S Deans, of Christchurch, NZ, and late Jane R M Deans, of West Wellow, Hants; 2 s (Joshua Henry Paul b 2 Feb 1992, Jacob William Richard b 11 June 1993), 1 da (Lorna Jane b 1 June 1990); *Heir* s, Joshua Henry Paul Studholme b 2 Feb 1992; *Style—* Sir Henry Studholme, Bt

STUDHOLME, Joseph Gilfred; s of Sir Henry Gray Studholme, 1 Bt, CVO (d 1987), of Wembury House, Wembury, Plymouth, Devon, and Judith Joan Mary, *née* Whitbread; *b* 14 Jan 1936; *Educ* Eton, Magdalen Coll Oxford (MA); *m* 5 Sept 1959, Rachel, yr da of Sir William Albemarle Fellowes, KCVO (d 1986), of Flitcham House, Kings Lynn, Norfolk; 3 s (Andrew Gilfred b 1962, (Henry) Alexander b 1967, Hugo William Robert b 1968); *Career* Nat Serv cmmnd 2 Lt 60 Rifles (KRRC) 1954–56; md King & Shaxson Ltd 1961–63, chm and md Editions Alecto gp 1963–; chm: Cncl of Mgmnt Byam Shaw Sch of Art 1988–94 (memb 1963–94), Wessex Regnl Ctee National Trust 1996– (memb 1993–); FRSA; *Clubs* Garrick, MCC; *Style*— Joseph Studholme, Esq; ✉ The Court House, Lower Woodford, Salisbury, Wilts SP4 6NQ (☎ 01722 782237, fax 01722 782669); Editions Alecto Ltd, Sackville House, 40 Piccadilly, London W1V 9PA (☎ 0171 439 6611, fax 0171 434 3514)

STULTIENS, (Alan) Jeffrey; s of Thomas Stultiens (d 1980), of Syresham, Northants, and Kate, *née* Whittaker; *b* 12 Sept 1944; *Educ* Hutton GS, Tiffin Boys' Sch, Kingston Sch of Art, Camberwell Sch of Art and Crafts (DipAD); *m* 4 July 1992, Catherine, da of Martin Knowelden; *Career* fine artist; lectr City of London Poly Sir John Cass Sch of Art 1967–73, sr lectr and leader Fndn Course Hertfordshire Coll of Art & Design 1983–87 (sr lectr 1974–83), visiting tutor Heatherley Sch of Fine Art Dip in Portraiture 1994–; RP 1991 (hon sec 1993–96); *Exhibitions* John Player Portrait Award (Nat Portrait Gallery) 1984 and 1985, British Portraiture 1980–85 1985–86, Portraits for the '80s 1986, Royal Soc of Portrait Painters 1990, Women on Canvas 1991, Hunting/Observer Art Prizes 1992, The Portrait Award 1980–89 (Nat Portrait Gallery) 1992, Oriel Ynys Môn 1992, Nikkei Exhibition Tokyo 1993, Royal Coll of Pathologists 1995–96; *Commissions and Collections* Nat Portrait Gallery, Merton and Oriel Colls Oxford, Nat Heart and Lung Inst, Servite Houses, Royal Nat Lifeboat Inst, Royal Med Fndn, Royal Acad of Music, Royal Coll of Pathologists, numerous private cmmns; *Awards* Commendation Drawings for All Gainsborough House Soc 1984, first prize John Player Portrait Award Nat Portrait Gallery 1985; *Clubs* Arts; *Style*— Jeffrey Stultiens, Esq, RP; ✉ 26 St George's Close, Toddington, Bedfordshire LU5 6AT (☎ and fax 01525 874120)

STUNELL, (Robert) Andrew; OBE (1995); s of late Robert George Stunell, of Powick, nr Worcester, and Trixie Stunell; *b* 24 Nov 1942; *Educ* Surbiton GS, Univ of Manchester, Liverpool Poly; *m* 29 July 1967, Gillian Mary Stunell; 3 s (Peter b 1973, Mark b 1974, Daniel b 1979), 2 da (Judith b 1969, Kari b 1970); *Career* architectural asst: various posts 1965–81, freelance 1981–85; cncllrs offr Assoc of Liberal Cncllrs 1985–88, political sec Assoc of Lib Dem Cncllrs 1989–; cncllr: Chester City Cncl 1979–90, Cheshire CC 1981–91, Stockport MB 1994–; memb Assoc of CCs 1985–90 (ldr SLD Gp 1985–90); Parly candidate: Chester 1979–87, Hazel Grove 1992; *Books* Guide to Local Government Finance (1985), Success on Balanced Councils (1985), Parish Finance (1986), Success on the Council (1988), Running a Successful Council Group (1990), Budgeting For Real (1991), Open, Active and Effective (1994); *Style*— Andrew Stunell, Esq, OBE; ✉ 84 Lyme Grove, Romiley, Stockport, Cheshire SK6 4DJ; Association of Liberal Democrat Councillors, Birchcliffe Centre, Hebden Bridge, W Yorks HX7 8DG (☎ 01422 843785, fax 01422 843036)

STURDEE, Dr David William; s of Cdr Peter Doveton Sturdee, OBE, of Moray House, Priestlands, Sherborne, Dorset, and Daphne, *née* Langdon; *b* 13 May 1945; *Educ* Sherborne, St Thomas' Hosp Med Sch Univ of London (MB BS, DA) MD (Birm); *m* 4 Sept 1971, Elizabeth Morton, da of Dr John Morton Muir (d 1973); 1 s (Simon William b 1973), 1 da (Claire b 1975); *Career* sr registrar W Midlands Rotation 1978–81, conslt obstetrician and gynaecologist Solihull 1981– (past clinical dir), sr clinical lectr Univ of Birmingham 1981– (res fell Dept of Obstetrics and Gynaecology 1975–77); author of many papers in jls, chapters and a book on hormone replacement therapy for menopausal symptoms; past chm Solihull Div BMA, past memb Cncl Birmingham and Midlands Obstetric and Gynaecological Soc, fndr memb Int Menopause Soc, chm Br Menopause Soc; past memb Higher Training and Sub-Specialty Bd Ctees RCOG; ed The Diplomate, Int Med Editorial Bd Menopause Digest; FRCOG 1988; *Recreations* singing, golf; *Clubs* Copt Heath Golf; *Style*— Dr David Sturdee; ✉ 44 Mirfield Rd, Solihull, West Midlands B91 1JD (☎ 0121 705 1759, fax 0121 711 2865); Department of Obstetrics & Gynaecology, Solihull Hosp, Lode Lane, Solihull B91 2JL (☎ 0121 711 4455, fax 0121 709 0409)

STURDY, Robert William; MEP (Cons) Cambridgeshire (majority 3,942); s of Gordon Sturdy (d 1989), and Kathleen, *née* Wells; *b* 22 June 1944; *Educ* Ashville Coll Harrogate; *m* 12 July 1969, Elizabeth Truus, da of John Hommes; 1 s (Julian), 1 da (Joanna); *Career* accountant; ptnr: G E Sturdy and Son, North Deighton Farms; MEP (C) Cambridgeshire 1994–; *Recreations* fishing, tennis, skiing, cricket; *Style*— Robert Sturdy, Esq, MEP; ✉ 153 St Neot's Road, Hardwick, Cambridge CB3 7QJ (☎ 01954 211790, fax 01954 211786)

STURGE, Maj-Gen (Henry Arthur) John; CB (1978); s of Henry George Arthur Sturge (d 1955), and Lilian Beatrice, *née* Goodale (d 1978); *b* 27 April 1925; *Educ* Wilsons GS Camberwell, QMC London; *m* 18 July 1953, Jean Ailsa, da of John Alfred Mountain (d 1969); 2 s (Simon John b 1959, James Henry b 1962), 1 da (Susan Jean b 1954); *Career* RCS 1945–80; served in UK, Egypt, Malaya, Hong Kong, BAOR; Army Staff Coll 1955, Jt Servs Staff Coll 1962, regt cmd BAOR 1967–69, Brig cmd UK 1971–73, Chief Signal Offr BAOR 1975–77, ACDS (signals) MOD 1977–80; gen mangr Marconi Space and Def Systems 1981–84 (asst dir 1980), md Marconi Secure Radio Systems 1984–86, princ conslt Logica Space and Def Systems 1986–91; *Clubs* Army and Navy; *Style*— Maj-Gen John Sturge, CB

STURGEON, Dr David Alexander; s of Flt Lt Alexander Rodger Sturgeon, of Worcs, and Jean, *née* Stansfield; *b* 3 July 1947; *Educ* Hipperholme GS, Univ of Oxford, UCH (BA, MA, BM BCh); *m* 6 Dec 1975, Elizabeth, da of Eric Kurt Lederman, of London; 2 da (Kate b 28 April 1977, Natasha b 29 Aug 1979); *Career* UCH London: Leverhulme jr res fell med sch 1974–75, sr clinical lectr Dept of Mental Health 1977–86, acting head Dept of Mental Health 1981–84, tutor Faculty of Clinical Sciences 1985–87, conslt psychiatrist Camden and Islington NHS Tst and hon sr lectr UCL Hosps 1986–; author of various papers on family treatment of schizophrenia, psychophysiology of schizophrenia and psychotherapy; psychiatric advsr to: Br Assoc of Cancer United Patients, Breast Cancer Care; hon psychiatric advsr to Brandon Centre of Counselling and Psychotherapy for Young People; fell and treas Int Coll of Psychosomatic Med; FRCPsych 1986 (memb 1976); *Books* UCH Textbook of Psychiatry (co-ed, 1990); *Recreations* writing; *Style*— Dr David Sturgeon; ✉ Department of Psychological Medicine, University College Hospital, Gower Street, London WC1 (☎ 0171 387 9300 ext 8585, fax 0171 387 1710)

STURGESS, Colin Andrew; s of Alan Paul Sturgess, and Margaret Ann, *née* Crawley; *b* 15 Dec 1968; *Educ* Marian Coll Johannesburg SA, Loughborough Univ; *Career* cyclist; memb Team Haverhill; nat champion: 1985 (5 jr titles), 1986 (3 jr titles), 1987 (4000m individual pursuit), 1988 (3 titles), 1989 (5000m individual pursuit), 1990 (5000m individual pursuit and 125 miles road race), 1991 (5000m individual pursuit); winner 5000m individual pursuit World Championships 1989 (third place 1991), competed at Cwlth Games 1986 and Olympic Games 1988; holder of world 5000m competition record (5:35:12) 1991; memb Professional Cycling Assoc; *Recreations* the writings of William Seward Burroughs, and a general interest in all Beat Generation literature; *Style*— Colin Sturgess, Esq; ✉ c/o 63 Percy Road, Aylestone, Leicester LE2 8FQ

STURGIS, Ann Elisabeth; da of Maj Peter Sturgis, of Dauntsey Park, Chippenham, Wilts (d 1986), and Rachel Sybil, *née* Borthwick; *b* 23 Oct 1945; *Educ* N Foreland Lodge; *Career* estate agent; chm and md Malverns Estate Agents; dir: Whitburgh Investments Ltd, R H K Seelig Ltd, K A L, Moontron Ltd; FCEA 1988; *Recreations* gardening, riding; *Style*— Miss Ann Sturgis; ✉ 24 South Eaton Place, London SW1W 9JA (☎ 0171 824 8802); Garden Cottage, Dauntsey Park, Chippenham, Wilts; Malverns, Malvern Court, Onslow Square, London SW7 3HU (☎ 0171 589 8122, fax 0171 589 4403)

STURRIDGE, Charles; s of Dr Jerome Sturridge (d 1996), and Alyson Bowman Vaughan, *née* Burke; *b* 24 June 1951; *Educ* Beaumont Coll Windsor, Stonyhurst Coll Lancs, Univ Coll Oxford (BA); *m* 6 July 1985, Phoebe Nicholls, the actress, da of Anthony Nicholls; 3 c; *Career* director and writer; memb BECTU; *Theatre* Hard Times (Belgrade Coventry) 1974, The Seagull (Queens) 1985; *Television* incl: World in Action (4 episodes), Coronation Street (16 episodes), Brideshead Revisited (Granada) 1981, Soft Targets (BBC) 1982, The Story Teller - A Story Short 1987, Troubles (writer only, LWT) 1987, A Foreign Field (BBC) 1993, Gullivers Travels (Channel 4) 1996; *Films* Runners (debut) 1983, Aria (contrib) 1986, A Handful of Dust (co-adaptor) 1988, Where Angels Fear to Tread (co-adaptor) 1991, Illumination (co-writer) 1997; *Awards* for Brideshead Revisited: 17 Awards incl BAFTA for Best Series and Best Actor (Anthony Andrews), two Goldern Globe Awards, The Grand Award (NY Film & TV Festival), Emmy for Best Supporting Actor (Laurence Olivier); for Runners: Best Film at the Karlovy-Vary Festival, Special Prize Venice Film Festival; for Gullivers Travels: 5 Emmy's incl Best Series and Best Special Effects; *Publications* The Seagull (trans with Tania Alexander, Amber Lane Press, 1983); *Clubs* Groucho; *Style*— Charles Sturridge, Esq; ✉ c/o Peters Fraser & Dunlop Ltd, 503 The Chambers, Chelsea Harbour, Lots Road, London SW10 0XF (☎ 0171 344 1000, fax 0171 352 7356)

STURROCK, Philip James; s of James Cars Sturrock, of Brighouse, W Yorks, and Joyce, *née* Knowles; *b* 5 Oct 1947; *Educ* Queen Mary's GS Walsall, Trinity Coll Oxford (MA), Manchester Business Sch (MBA); *m* 5 Aug 1972 (m dis 1995), Susan, da of (William) Horace Haycock, of Walsall, West Midlands; 1 s (Hugh b 5 May 1981), 2 da (Anna b 23 June 1977, Jane b 3 Jan 1983); *Career* md: IBIS Information Services 1972–80, Pitman Books 1980–83; gp md Routledge and Kegan Paul plc 1983–85, chm and md Cassell plc 1986–; Liveryman Worshipful Co of Glaziers; FRSA; *Recreations* walking, reading, travel; *Clubs* Athenaeum; *Style*— Philip Sturrock, Esq; ✉ Flat 14, 11 Avenue Road, St Albans, Hertfordshire AL1 3QG (☎ 01727 832469), Cassell plc, Wellington House, 125 Strand, London WC2R 0BB (☎ 0171 420 5555, fax 0171 240 7261)

STURROCK, Prof Roger Davidson; *b* 20 Oct 1946; *Educ* Llanelli Boys' GS, Queen Mary's Sch Basingstoke, King's Coll and Westminster Med Sch London (MB BS, AKC, MRCS LRCP, FRCPGlas 1984, FRCP (London) 1985, MD); *m*; 3 c; *Career* jt recipient Allessandro Robecchi International Prize in Rheumatology (Euro League Against Rheumatism) 1975, Arthritis and Rheumatism Cncl Anglo-US travelling fell to the USA 1984, currently holds McLeod/ARC chair of rheumatology Univ of Glasgow; currently pres Br Soc for Rheumatology; *Publications* author of numerous articles in learned jls; *Style*— Prof Roger Sturrock; ✉ University Department of Medicine, Queen Elizabeth Building, Royal Infirmary, 10 Alexandra Parade, Glasgow G31 2ER

STURT, Richard Harry Brooke; s of Horace Holford Sturt (d 1962), of Wimborne, Dorset, and Eveline Frances, *née* Brooke; *b* 14 Nov 1939; *Educ* Marlborough, Peterhouse Cambridge (BA, MA); *m* 3 March 1962, Ann Lesley, da of Brig Charles Leslie Morgan, OBE (d 1982), of Walmer, Kent; 4 s ((Richard) Michael Villiers b 1964, Charles (Patrick) Holford b 1966, (Alexander) Fitzgerald Brooke b 1969, Nicholas (Julian) Holford b 1972); *Career* admitted slr 1966, sr ptnr Mowll & Mowll 1984– (ptnr 1967–84); slr: Dover Harbour Bd 1979–, Ind Schs Action Ctee 1980–82; slr and clerk to govrs King's Sch Canterbury 1979–91; registrar of Canterbury Dio and legal sec to Bishop in Canterbury 1996–; dep coroner E Kent 1972–79, HM Coroner for Kent (E Kent) 1979–, conducted inquests into Herald of Free Enterprise disaster 1987 and M2 coach crash 1994; lectr Police Staff Coll 1990–; bd memb CAA 1990–96 (memb Safety Regulation Policy Ctee 1994–96, memb Nat Air Traffic Servs Policy Ctee 1995–96); dir: Dover & Folkestone Building Society 1978–84, Waldershare Park Farms Ltd 1989–, Rubie Estates Ltd 1995–, National Air Traffic Services Ltd 1996, Grosvenor Lifestyle Plc 1996–; chm: Gateway Broadcasting Ltd 1982–84, Invicta Sound plc 1984–91, Mellow 1557 Ltd 1990–91; fndr and chm E Kent Holiday Music Tst 1979–; govr: Betteshanger Sch 1978–80, Northbourne Park Sch 1980–85 and 1993–, The King's Sch Canterbury 1991–, Cumnor House Sch 1996–; tstee: Kent Branch Br Red Cross, All Saints Waldershare Tst, Cicely Stockmann Memorial Fund; memb: SE England Coroners' Soc (pres 1981–82), Coroners' Soc England and Wales 1972–; FRSA 1990; *Books* Fishery Protection and Foreign Sea Fishing Boats (1973), contrib section on Fisheries, Ports and Harbours, European Communities in Halsbury's Laws of England (4 edn), contrib Fisheries section in Vaughan on The Law of the European Communities (2 edn, 1993), The Collision Regulations (3 edn, 1991), The Role of the Coroner in Major Disasters (1988); *Recreations* cricket, singing, bridge, genealogy, fly-fishing; *Clubs* Athenaeum, Flyfishers'; *Style*— Richard Sturt, Esq; ✉ Kent Cottage, 7 Granville Rd, Walmer, Deal, Kent CT14 7LU (☎ 01304 240250); Mowll & Mowll, 34 and 36 Castle Street, Dover, Kent CT16 1PN (☎ 01304 240250, fax 01304 240040)

STURZAKER, Hugh Gerard; s of George Gerard Sturzaker (d 1971), of Chandlers Ford, Hants, and Gladys Maude, *née* French (d 1990); *Educ* W Buckland Sch Barnstaple Devon, Hertford Coll Oxford (MA), Guy's Hosp Med Sch (BM BCh); *m* 30 March 1968, Ann Elizabeth, da of Ernest Philip Featherstone, of South Croydon, Surrey; 3 s (Robert b 1970, John b 1971, James b 1980), 1 da (Nicola b 1973); *Career* house physician and surgn Guy's Hosp 1966–67, jr lectr in anatomy Guy's Hosp Med Sch 1987–68, surgical registrar Guildford and Guy's Hosps 1968–73, res fell St Mark's Hosp London 1973–74, sr surgical registrar Guy's Hosp and Gt Ormond St Hosp for Children, conslt gen surgn James Paget Hosp NHS Tst Great Yarmouth 1979–, clinical teacher Univ of Cambridge; regnl advsr and examiner RCS Edinburgh; past pres: Oxford Univ Med Soc, Br Med Students' Assoc, E Anglian Surgical Club, Gt Yarmouth and Waveney Div BMA; memb: BMA 1966, RSM 1967; FRCSEd 1971, FRCS 1972; *Recreations* windsurfing, gardening, wine and beer making; *Style*— Hugh Sturzaker, Esq; ✉ Hobland House, Hobland, Great Yarmouth, Norfolk NR31 9AR (☎ 01493 665287), James Paget Hospital, Gorleston, Great Yarmouth, Norfolk NR31 6LA (☎ 01493 452452)

STUTTAFORD, Dr (Irving) Thomas; OBE (1996); s of Dr William Joseph Edward Stuttaford, MC (d 1956), of Horning, Norfolk, and Mary Marjorie Dean, *née* Royden (d 1976); *b* 4 May 1931; *Educ* Gresham's, BNC Oxford, W London Hosp (MRCS, LRCP, DObstRCOG); *m* 1 June 1957, Pamela Christine, da of Lt-Col Richard Ropner, TD (d 1975), of Aldie, Tain, Ross-shire; 3 s (Andrew b 1958, Thomas b 1961, Hugo b 1964); *Career* 2 Lt 10 Royal Hussars (PWO) 1953–55, Lt Scottish Horse TA 1955–59; jr hosp appts 1959–60, gen practice 1960–70, visiting physician BUPA 1970– (asst clincial dir 1979–81); clinical asst in venereology: The London Hosp 1974–93, Queen Mary's Hosp for the East End 1974–79, Moorfields Eye Hosp 1975–79; sr med advsr The Rank Orgn 1980–85; private practice in occupational health 1986–; med columnist: The Times 1990– (med corr 1982–90), formerly of ELLE magazine; med advsr: Barclays Bank, Standard Chartered Bank, Rank Hotels and other cos; memb: Blofield and Flegg RDC 1964–66, Norwich City Cncl 1969–71; MP (C) Norwich S 1970–74, Parly candidate (C) Isle of Ely 1974 and 1979, sec Cons Health and Social Servs Ctee; memb: Cncl Res Def Soc 1970–79, Built Control Campaign 1970–79, Select Ctee on Sci and Technol; *Books* A Birth Control Plan for Britain (with Mr Alistair Service and Dr John Dunwoody, 1972); author of chapters in: Drinking to Your Health (1989), Which Wine Guide (1991); *Recreations* living in the country, conservation of old buildings; *Clubs* Beefsteak, Athenaeum, Reform, Cavalry and Guards', Norfolk (Norwich); *Style*— Dr Thomas Stuttaford, OBE;

✉ Houghton St Giles, Walsingham, Norfolk NR22 6AQ (☎ 01328 820947); 8 Devonshire Place, London W1N 1PB (☎ 0171 935 5011)

STUTTAFORD, Sir William Royden; kt (1995), CBE (1989, OBE 1983); s of Dr William Joseph Edward Stuttaford, MC (d 1956), of Horning, Norfolk, and Mary Marjorie Dean, *née* Royden (d 1975); *b* 21 Nov 1928; *Educ* Gresham's, Trinity Coll Oxford (MA); *m* 1, 1958 (m dis), Sarah Jane, da of Philip Legge; 2 s (William Julian b 1962, Dominic Charles b 1964), 2 da (Clare Lucinda b 1960, Melanie Mary b 1964); m 2, 1974, Susan d'Esterre, da of Capt Sir Gerald Curteis, KCVO, RN (d 1972), Broomwood, Sevenoaks, Kent; *Career* Nat Serv 2 Lt 10 Royal Hussars (PWO); memb Stock Exchange 1959–92, chm Framlington Group plc 1983–89, sr ptnr Laurence Prust & Co (stockbrokers) 1983–86, dir Brown Shipley Holdings 1990–93, dir Invesco 1993–; chm: Cons Political Centre 1978–81, East of England Cons Pty 1986–89, Unit Tst Assoc 1987–89; pres Nat Union of Cons Assocs 1994–95; *Clubs* Cavalry and Guards'; *Style*— Sir William Stuttaford, CBE; ✉ Moulshams Manor, Great Wigborough, Colchester, Essex CO5 7RL (☎ 01206 735330)

STUTTARD, Arthur Rupert Davies; s of Harold Stuttard, and Annie Constance, *née* Davies (d 1966); *b* 16 July 1943; *Educ* Accrington GS, ChCh Oxford (MA, pres Univ of Oxford Law Soc); *m* 10 Aug 1972, Margaret Evelyn, da of Reginald Wall Sykes; *Career* called to the Bar Middle Temple (Harmsworth scholar) 1967, practises Northern Circuit; *Books* English Law Notebook (1969), author of various articles on Lancs Witchcraft trials; *Recreations* local history, Egyptian and Minoan archaeology; *Style*— Arthur Stuttard, Esq; ✉ Acre House, Fence, Near Burnley, Lancs; Manchester House Chambers, 18–22 Bridge Street, Manchester 3 (☎ 0161 834 7007)

STUTTARD, John Boothman; s of Thomas Boothman Stuttard (d 1969), and Helena, *née* Teasdale (d 1969); *b* 6 Feb 1945; *Educ* Shrewsbury, Churchill Coll Cambridge (MA); *m* 26 Sept 1970, Lesley Sylvia, da of Thomas Geoffrey Daish, of Kenilworth; 2 s (Thomas Henry Boothman (Tom) b 20 Jan 1975, James Midgley (Jamie) b 21 Aug 1976); *Career* VSO teacher SOAS Brunei 1966–67; Coopers & Lybrand (formerly Cooper Brothers & Co): trainee accountant 1967–70, CA 1970, ptnr 1975–, currently chm and chief exec Coopers & Lybrand China and sr audit and corp finance ptnr, dir of corp mktg and chm of Scandinavian mkt gp 1986–94; accounting advsr to CPRS Cabinet Office Whitehall 1982–83; memb Cambridge Univ Appts Bd 1977–81, dir Totteridge Manor Assoc; Freeman City of London 1994, Freeman Worshipful Co of Glaziers and Painters of Glass 1996; Knight (First Class) Order of the Lion of Finland 1995; FCA, FRSA; *Recreations* travel, Rolls-Royce vintage cars, veteran cars, theatre, opera, tennis; *Clubs* Naval & Military Club, China Club, Rolls-Royce Enthusiasts' Club, 20 Ghost Club, Automobile Club de Monaco, Veteran Car Club of GB; *Style*— John B Stuttard, Esq; ✉ West End House, 56 Totteridge Common, London N20 8LZ (☎ 0181 959 1692, fax 0181 959 8058); Coopers & Lybrand, 1 Embankment Place, London WC2N 6NN (☎ 0171 213 4590, fax 0171 213 2416)

STYLE, Capt Charles Rodney; s of Lt Cdr Sir Godfrey Style, CBE, DSC, RN, *qv*, and Sigrid Elisabeth, *née* Carlberg (d 1985); *b* 15 Jan 1954; *Educ* Eton, Univ of Cambridge (exhibitioner, MA); *m* 31 Jan 1981, Charlotte Amanda, da of Lt Timothy Martin Woodford, RN (d 1966), and Eila Mary, *née* Stirling-Hamilton, step da of George Rudolph Wratislaw Walker; 3 da (Amanda Clare b 24 Nov 1981, Annabel Daisy b 21 Dec 1983, Elizabeth Sigrid b 2 Jan 1990); *Career* joined Royal Navy 1974, trg BRNC Dartmouth (Queen's Sword); served: Antarctic patrol ship HMS Endurance 1977–78, HMS Bacchante 1978–79, HM Yacht Britannia 1980–81, HMS Sandpiper 1981–82 (cmd), HMS Wotton 1982–83 (cmd), HMS Arethusa 1984–85; Flag Lt to C-in-C Fleet, Channel and Eastern Atlantic 1985–87, Cdr 1988, cmd frigate HMS Andromeda 1988–89, Directorate of Naval Plans MOD 1989–92, Staff Offr Ops to Cdr UK Task Gp 1992–93 (incl serv in Adriatic), Capt 1993, cmd frigate HMS Campbeltown 1993–95, Chief Staff Offr (Ops and Trg) to Flag Offr Sea Trg (FOST) 1995–; Yr Bro Trinity House 1991; *Recreations* fishing, reading, sailing; *Style*— Capt Charles Style, RN

STYLE, Christopher John David; s of Maj David Carlyle Willoughby Style, MC, TD (d 1978), of Loweswater, Cumbria, and Dr Anne Marion, *née* Phillips; *b* 13 April 1955; *Educ* St Bees Sch Cumbria, Trinity Hall Cambridge (MA), City of London Poly; *m* 7 April 1990, Victoria Jane, *née* Miles; 3 s (George Alexander b 2 Aug 1991, Charles David b 8 Aug 1993, Peter John b 12 May 1995); *Career* Linklaters & Paines 1977–: articled clerk 1977–79, slr 1979, asst slr 1979–85, ptnr 1985–; seconded to Sullivan & Cromwell NY 1983; memb London Slrs Litigation Assoc; Freeman City of London 1985, memb City of London Slrs Co; *Books* Documentary Evidence (5 edn, 1995); *Recreations* fell walking, rock climbing; *Style*— Christopher Style, Esq; ✉ 45 Rudall Crescent, London NW3 1RR (☎ 0171 435 5711); Linklaters & Paines, Barrington House, 59–67 Gresham St, London EC2V 7JA (☎ 0171 606 7080, fax 0171 606 5113, telex 884349)

STYLE, Lt Cdr Sir Godfrey William; kt (1973), CBE (1961), DSC (1942); er s of Brig-Gen Rodney Style (d 1957; 4 s of Sir William Style, 9 Bt), of Wierton Grange, Boughton-Monchelsea, Kent, and Hélène (d 1975), 2 da of Herman Kleinwort; *b* 3 April 1915; *Educ* Eton; *m* 1, 1942 (m dis 1951), Jill Elizabeth, da of George Bellis Caruth, of Ballymena; 1 s (Montague Style, *qv*), 2 da (Helen, Marieka); m 2, 1951, Sigrid Elisabeth Julin (d 1985), da of Per Stellan Carlberg, of Jönköping, Sweden; 1 s (Capt Charles Style, RN, *qv*); m 3, 1986, Valerie Beauclerk, da of Cdr Cecil Henry Hulton-Sams, RN, and widow of William Duncan McClure; *Career* joined RN 1933, serv HM Yacht Victoria and Albert 1938, Flag Lt to C-in-C Home Fleet 1939–41, Med 1941–42 (Malta convoys), (wounded 1942, despatches 1940 and 1943), thereafter HQ 4 Gp Bomber Cmd (despatches) and Admty, invalided from RN 1946; Lloyd's Name 1944–; chm Nat Advsy Cncl Employment Disabled People 1963–74, dir Star Centre for Youth Cheltenham 1971–, govr Queen Elizabeth's Fndn 1975–, memb Cncl Sir Oswald Stoll Fndn 1975–84; *Recreations* field sports, horticulture, lapidary work; *Clubs* Naval and Military; *Style*— Lt Cdr Sir Godfrey Style, CBE, DSC, RN; ✉ 30 Carlyle Court, Chelsea Harbour, London SW10 0UQ (☎ 0171 352 6512)

STYLE, Montague; s of Cdr Sir Godfrey Style, CBE, DSC, RN, *qv*, and Jill Elizabeth, *née* Caruth; *b* 9 Oct 1943; *Educ* Eton, Ecole des Hautes Etudes Commerciales Paris, INSEAD (MBA), Columbia Univ Graduate Sch of Business (Mktg Mgmnt Prog); *m* 18 July 1970, Susan Jennifer, da of Peter Wrightson, OBE; 1 da (Sophie Elizabeth b 20 June 1974), 1 s (Oliver Rodney b 6 May 1976); *Career* apprentice Kaufhof AG Cologne 1963–64, freelance teacher and translator Madrid 1964–65, advtg sales Morgan Grampian Ltd London 1965–69, advtg sales Continental Europe The Economist Newspaper Ltd 1969–72; Pharmaceutical Div Ciba-Geigy: joined 1973, Head Office Basel Switzerland 1973–75, mktg dir Ciba-Geigy Mexicana Mexico City 1975–81, Head Office Basel 1982–, strategic planning regnl mktg staff (USA, Canada, UK and Scandinavia) 1982–84, head of international mktg support 1984–88, region head Western Europe 1988–91, head of Eastern Europe Business Area 1991–94, head Pharma Overseas 1994–, dep dir Ciba-Geigy Ltd Basel 1992–; chm: Br & Cwlth Soc Mexico 1978–80, Bd International Sch of Basel 1982–85; memb Church Cncl Anglican Church of Basel; Freeman Worshipful Co of Grocers; *Recreations* organist, pianist, walking, fly-fishing, designing and building house and garden in Southern Alsace; *Clubs* Rye Golf, Golf du Rhin Chalampe France; *Style*— Montague Style, Esq; ✉ 27 rue des Romains, Bettlach 68480, France (☎ 00 33 89 07 30 34, fax 00 33 89 07 30 81); Ciba-Geigy AG, Klybeckstrasse PH 5.9, 4002 Basel, Switzerland (☎ 00 41 61 696 1847, fax 00 41 61 696 9350)

STYLE, Rodney Hill; s of Col (Rodney) Gerald Style, of Runfold, Farnham, Surrey, and Barbara Hill Style; *b* 25 March 1956; *Educ* Eton; *m* 24 April 1982, Georgina Eve, da of late John Kinloch Kerr of Abbottrule, of Frocester, Glos; 2 s (George b 1985, Hugo b 1985), 1 da (Elizabeth b 1989); *Career* CA; Spicer and Pegler 1976–85, ptnr Haines Watts 1985–, md Haines Watts Fin Servs Ltd 1987–; Freeman City of London 1981, Liveryman Worshipful Co of Grocers 1991; ACA 1981, ATII 1983; *Recreations* skiing; *Style*— Rodney Style, Esq; ✉ Greenacre, Steeple Aston, Oxfordshire; Sterling House, 19/23 High St, Kidlington, Oxon OX5 2DH (☎ 01865 378282, fax 01865 377518)

STYLE, Sir William Frederick; 13 Bt (E 1627), of Wateringbury, Kent; s of Sir William Montague Style, 12 Bt (d 1981), and La Verne, Lady Style; *b* 13 May 1945; *Educ* (BSc, MEd); *m* 1, 1968, Wendy Gay, da of Gene and Marjory Wittenberger, of Hartford, Wisconsin, USA; 2 da (Shannon b 1969, Erin b 1973); m 2, 1986, Linnea Lorna, da of Donn and Elizabeth Erickson, of Sussex, Wisconsin, USA; 1 s (William Colin b 1995), 2 da (McKenna b 1987, McKayla b 1990); *Heir* s, William Colin Style b 1995; *Career* public sch teacher; *Recreations* yacht (Summer Style); *Clubs* Fond du Lac Yacht; *Style*— Sir William Style, Bt

STYLER, His Hon Judge; Granville Charles; s of Samuel Charles Styler (d 1996), of Shipston-on-Stour, Warwicks, and Frances Joan, *née* Clifford; *b* 9 Jan 1947; *Educ* King Edward VI Sch Stratford-upon-Avon; *m* 11 Sept 1971, Penelope, da of William Arnold Darbyshire, of Lytham St Annes, Lancs; 3 da (Katie b 1974, Sophie b 1977, Emily b 1979); *Career* called to the Bar Gray's Inn 1970, recorder 1988, circuit judge (Midland and Oxford Circuit) 1992–; *Recreations* tennis, carriage driving, horse racing; *Style*— His Hon Judge Styler; ✉ 5 Fountain Ct, Steelhouse Lane, Birmingham 4 (☎ 0121 606 0500)

STYLES, Dr John Trevor; s of Capt Sydney Hubert Styles (d 1989), of Rugby, Warks, and Kathleen Joyce, *née* Hutchen (d 1995); *b* 18 Nov 1939; *Educ* The GS Enfield, UCL (BSc), UCH Med Sch (MB BS); *m* 5 Feb 1966, Hilary Frances, da of Lawrence Rider Simmons (d 1988), of Ringwood, Hants; 1 s (Neville John b 1970), 3 da (Aileen Clare b 1967, Diane Caroline b 1968, Suzanne Catherine b 1971); *Career* registrar anaesthetist: UCH 1967–68, Hosp for Sick Children Gt Ormond St 1968; sr registrar anaesthetist Birmingham Teaching Hosps and Univ of Birmingham 1969–70, hon lectr Dept of Anaesthetics Univ of Birmingham 1970; Wolverhampton Hosp: conslt anaesthetist 1970–, clinical dir Dept of Anaesthetics 1993–96; memb Wolverhampton Health Authy 1982–85; memb Assoc of Anaesthetists of GB and Ireland, fell Royal Coll of Anaesthetists, memb BMA; *Recreations* woodworking and renovation of listed building; *Style*— Dr John Styles; ✉ Lower Mitton Farm, Penkridge, Stafford ST19 5QW (☎ 01785 780507)

SUBAK-SHARPE, Prof John Herbert; CBE (1991); s of Robert Subak (killed in the Holocaust 1942), of Vienna, and Nelly, *née* Bruell (killed in the Holocaust 1942); *b* 14 Feb 1924; *Educ* Humanistisches Gymnasium Vienna, Univ of Birmingham (BSc, PhD); *m* 22 Aug 1953, Barbara Naomi, da of late Ernest Harold Morris; 2 s (Robert John b 1956, Ian David b 1970), 1 da (Anne Barbara (Mrs Morton) b 1959); *Career* HM Forces Parachute Regt 1944–47; memb ARC scientific staff Animal Virus Res Inst Pirbright 1956–61, visiting fell California Inst of Technol USA 1961, memb scientific staff MRC Experimental Virus Research Unit Glasgow 1961–68, visiting prof NIH Bethesda USA 1967–68, prof of virology Univ of Glasgow 1968–94 (asst lectr 1954–56), hon dir MRC Virology Unit Univ of Glasgow 1968–94, prof emeritus 1994; hon sr research fell Univ of Glasgow 1994–; visiting prof: USUHS Bethesda USA 1985, Clare Hall Cambridge 1986; articles in scientific jls on genetic and molecular studies with viruses and cells; tstee Genetical Soc 1971– (sec 1966–72, vice pres 1972–75); memb: Governing Body W Scotland Oncology Orgn 1974–, Genetic Manipulation Advsy Gp 1976–80, BRC SHHD Chief Scientist's Orgn 1979–84, Governing Body AVRI Pribright 1986–88; chm MRC Tap 1986–89; memb: Scientific Advsy Gp Equine Virology Res Fndn 1987–, Cell Biology and Disorders Bd MRC 1988–92; CIBA Medal and Prize Biochem Soc 1994; memb EMBO 1969, FIBiol 1969, FRSE 1970; *Recreations* travel, bridge; *Clubs* Athenaeum; *Style*— Prof John Subak-Sharpe, CBE, FRSE; ✉ 63 Kelvin Court, Great Western Road, Glasgow G12 0AG (☎ 0141 334 1863); Institute of Virology, University of Glasgow, Church St, Glasgow G12 8QQ (☎ 0141 334 9555, fax 0141 330 4808, telex 777070 UNIGLA)

SUBBA ROW, Raman; CBE (1991); s of Panguluri Venkata Subba Row (d 1954), of Croydon, and Doris Mildred, *née* Pinner (d 1972); *b* 29 Jan 1932; *Educ* Whitgift Sch, Trinity Hall Cambridge (MA, Cricket blue); *m* 1960, Anne Dorothy, da of Ronald Harrison; 2 s (Christopher Gordon b 7 March 1961, Alistair Patrick b 9 May 1965), 1 da (Michele Anne (Mrs Wilson) b 10 Dec 1962); *Career* Nat Serv Pilot Offr RAF 1956–57; W S Crawford Advertising Ltd 1963–69, md Management Public Relations Ltd 1969–92; cricket player: Surrey CCC 1953–54, Cwlth tour India 1953–54, Northants CCC 1955–61 (capt 1958–61), RAF 1956–57, represented England 1958–61 (Aust tour 1958 and W Indies 1959); chm Ctee Surrey CCC 1974–79 (memb 1966–), chm TCCB 1985–90 (chm Mktg Ctee 1968–73), chm Cricket Cncl 1985–90; Int Cricket Cncl match referee 1992–97: W Indies, Australia, New Zealand, India, Pakistan, South Africa and Sharjah; *Recreations* golf, rugby football; *Clubs* MCC, Surrey, RAF, IOD; *Style*— Raman Subba Row, Esq, CBE; ✉ Leeward, Manor Way, South Croydon, Surrey CR2 7BT (☎ and fax 0181 688 2991)

SUBHEDAR, Vasant Yadav; s of Yadav Mahadeo Subhedar, of India, and Vatsala, *née* Nulkar; *b* 10 June 1936; *Educ* Univ of Bombay (BM BS, MS), FRCS (Edin), FRCS (London), FFAEM (London); *m* 27 Nov 1960, Dr Manisha, da of Vishnu Jaganath Sabnis (d 1975), of Bombay; 1 s (Dr Nimish b 23 Jan 1965), 1 da (Sangeeta (Mrs Ganvir) b 18 April 1962); *Career* conslt surgn Accident and Emergency Dept Dudley Rd Hosp 1978–; memb Exec Ctee Casualty Surgeons Assoc London 1985–88; RCS advsr in Accident and Emergency Med 1993–, assoc advsr in higher specialist trg Postgrad Inst of Birmingham 1993–; chm: Accident and Emergency Serv Ctee W Midlands RHA 1985–89, W Midlands Regnl Casualty Surgeons Assoc 1985–88, Sub-Ctee for Accident and Emergency Med 1994–; pres Birmingham Indian Med Assoc 1991–93 (vice pres 1988–89), current memb Birmingham Branch Exec Ctee for Overseas Doctors, memb Exec Ctee CSA 1985–89; memb: BMA, Overseas Doctors Assoc, Br Indian Med Assoc, Birmingham Medico-Legal Soc; *Recreations* photography, music, walking; *Style*— Vasant Subhedar, Esq; ✉ Sankey House, 60 Oakham Road, Dudley DY2 7TF (☎ 01384 54849); City Hospital NHS Trust, Winson Green, Dudley Rd, Birmingham B18 7QH (☎ 0121 554 3801)

SUCH, Peter Mark; s of John Henry Such, of East Leake, nr Loughborough, and Margaret June, *née* Mason; *b* 12 June 1964; *Educ* Harry Carlton Comp Sch East Leake; *Career* professional cricketer; Nottinghamshire CCC 1982–86, Leicestershire CCC 1987–89, Essex CCC 1990– (awarded county cap 1991); rep: Young Eng v Young Aust 1983, TCCB XI v NZ 1986, Eng A v Sri Lanka 1991, Eng A tour to Aust 1993, Eng A tour to S Africa 1993–94, Eng debut v Aust (Ashes series) 1993, 3 tests v New Zealand 1994; overseas teams: Kempton Park SA 1982–83, Bathurst Aust 1985–86, Matabeleland Zimbabwe 1989–90; advanced cricket coach; *Recreations* golf, reading, music, movies, following most sports; *Style*— Peter Such, Esq; ✉ c/o Essex CCC, County Cricket Ground, New Writtle Street, Chelmsford, Essex CM2 0PG (☎ 01245 252420, fax 01245 491607)

SUCHET, David; 2 s of Jack Suchet, and Joan, *née* Jarché (d 1992); *b* 2 May 1946; *Educ* Wellington, LAMDA; *m* 1976, Sheila Anne, da of William Ferris (d 1986), of Stratford-upon-Avon; 1 s (Robert b 10 May 1981), 1 da (Katherine b 21 July 1983); *Career*

actor; began professional career Gateway Theatre Chester 1969; repertory theatres incl: Exeter, Worthing, Birmingham; dir Canvasback Ltd, assoc artiste RSC, memb Cncl LAMDA, visiting prof of theatre Univ of Nebraska 1975; *Theatre* incl: Estragon in Waiting for Godot, John Aubrey in Brief Lives, Timon of Athens (Young Vic), This Story of Yours (Hampstead), Separation (Hampstead then Comedy Theatre), Oleanna (Royal Court then Duke of York's Theatre) 1993; RSC incl: Shylock in Merchant of Venice, Achilles in Troilus and Cressida, Bolingbroke in Richard II, Iago in Othello, Mercutio in Romeo & Juliet, Fool in King Lear, Caliban in The Tempest, Lucio in Measure for Measure, Mole in Toad of Toad Hall, Sid Field in What a Performance, George in Who's Afraid of Virginia Woolf; *Television* incl: Edward Teller in Oppenheimer (NNC), Freud in The Life of Freud (BBC), Blott in Blott on the Landscape (BBC), Judge O'Connor in Cause Celebre (Anglia TV), Glougauer in Once in a Lifetime (BBC), Carver in Nobody Here But Us Chickens (Channel 4), Hercule Poirot in Agatha Christie's Poirot (LWT), Joe in Separation (BBC), Verloc in The Secret Agent (BBC); *BBC Radio* incl: Ironhand, The Kreuzer Sonata, First Night Impressions, The Shout, Rosenburg in The Trenches, Debusssy, Anton Chekov, The Willows in Winter, Letters from Prison, Alpha Course (radio premiere); *Films* incl: Trouillfou in Hunchback of Notre Dame, Okana in Falcon and The Snowman, Beria in Red Monarch (for Channel 4), Dyer in Song for Europe, Inspector Japp in Thirteen to Dinner, Lafleur in Bigfoot & The Hendersons, Wil in When the Whales Came, Muller in A World Apart, Nagi Hassan in Executive Decision, Vlachos in Deadly Voyage, Oliver in Sunday; *Awards* nominations for Best Actor incl: Evening Standard Award for Merchant of Venice 1978, SWET Award for The Merchant of Venice 1981, BAFTA Award for Hercule Poirot 1990, 1991 and 1992, Evening Standard Awards for Timon of Athens 1991, Olivier Award for Oleanna 1994, RTA Award for What a Performance 1995; nominations for Best Supporting Actor incl: SWET Award for Once in a Lifetime 1980 and Richard II 1981, ACE Award for The Last Innocent Man 1987; others nominations incl: Actor of the Year in a New Play Award for Separation 1989, Olivier Award 1989, BAFTA Best Actor in a Supporting Role for A World Apart 1989; winner for Best Actor incl: Marseilles Film Festival for Red Monarch 1983, Brit Industry/Scientific Film Assoc Craft Award for Stress 1986; winner 1986 Royal TV Soc Performance Awards for Song for Europe, Freud, Blott on the Landscape; also winner Best Radio Actor Award for Kreutzer Sonata (one man show) 1979 and Variety Club Award for Best Actor for Oleanna; *Publications* author of essays in Players of Shakespeare (on Caliban, Shylock and Iago); *Recreations* photography, clarinet, ornithology; *Style*— David Suchet, Esq; ✉ ICM Ltd, Oxford House, 76 Oxford Street, London W1N 0AX (☎ 0171 636 6565, fax 0171 323 0101)

SUCHET, John Aleck; eldest s of Jack Suchet, and Joan, *née* Jarché (d 1992); *b* 29 March 1944; *Educ* Uppingham, Univ of St Andrews (MA); *m* 1, 1968 (m dis), Moya; 3 s; m 2, 1985, Bonnie Lee; *Career* Reuters News Agency 1967–71, BBC TV News 1971–72, ITN 1972– (reporter, corr, newscaster); TV Journalist of the Year RTS 1986, Newscaster of the Year TRIC 1996; *Books* TV News - The Inside Story (1989), The Last Master - Life of Beethoven (Vol 1, 1996); *Recreations* classical music, photography; *Style*— John Suchet, Esq; ✉ ITN Ltd, 200 Gray's Inn Rd, London, WC1X 8XZ (☎ 0171 833 3000)

SUCKLING, Prof Colin James; s of Charles Walter Suckling, FRS, of Tewin, Herts, and Eleanor Margaret, *née* Watterson; *b* 24 March 1947; *Educ* Quarry Bank HS, Univ of Liverpool (PhD, DSc, Leblanc medal); *m* 19 Aug 1972, Catherine Mary, da of Desmond Patrick Faulkner; 2 s (Christopher Andrew b 5 Nov 1974, Martin Charles b 23 Nov 1981), 1 da (Barbara Janet b 17 May 1977); *Career* Ciba-Geigy res fell Eidgenossiche Technische Hochschule Zürich 1970–72; Univ of Strathclyde: lectr in chemistry 1972–80, Royal Soc Smith & Nephew sr res fell 1980–84, personal prof 1984–89, Freeland prof of chemistry 1989–, dean Faculty of Science 1992–96, dep princ 1996–; chm Bd West of Scotland Sch Symphony Orch, memb Bd City of Glasgow Philharmonic Fndn; Wolfson Res Award 1989–91; FRSC 1980, FRSE 1987, FRSA 1991; author of over 130 research pubns; *Books* Chemistry Through Models (1974), Enzyme Chemistry Impact and Applications (1990); *Recreations* music, horn playing and conducting; *Style*— Prof Colin Suckling, FRSE; ✉ 62 North Grange Road, Bearsden, Glasgow G61 3AF (☎ 0141 942 6984); Department of Pure and Applied Chemistry, University of Strathclyde, 295 Cathedral Street, Glasgow G1 1XL (☎ 0141 552 4400, fax 0141 552 5664)

SUDBURY, Archdeaon of; *see:* Cox, Ven John Stuart

SUDDABY, Dr Arthur; CBE (1980); s of George Suddaby (d 1950), of Kingston upon Hull, and Alice May, *née* Holmes (d 1970); *b* 26 Feb 1919; *Educ* Riley HS Hull, Hull Tech Coll (BSc), Chelsea Coll (BSc, MSc), QMC London (PhD); *m* 23 Dec 1944, Elizabeth Bullin (d 1965), da of the late Charles Vyse, of Cheyne Row, Chelsea; 2 s (John b 1946, Anthony b 1947); *Career* chemist/chem engr 1937–47, sr lectr in chem engrg West Ham Coll of Technol 1947–50; Sir John Cass Coll: sr lectr in physics 1950–61, head of dept 1961–66, princ 1966–70; provost City of London Poly 1970–81; scientific conslt on the carriage of goods by sea until 1990; on various CNAA ctees 1969–81; memb: London and Home Cos Regnl Advsy Ctee on Higher Educn 1971–81, Ct of City Univ 1967–81; chm: Ctee of Dirs of Polys 1976–78, Assoc of Navigation Schs 1972; MIChemE 1944, FRSC 1980; *Recreations* country sports, music; *Clubs* Athenaeum; *Style*— Dr Arthur Suddaby, CBE; ✉ Castle Hill House, Godshill Wood, Fordingbridge, Hants SP6 2LU (☎ 01425 652234); Flat 3, 16 Elm Park Gardens, Chelsea, London SW10 9NY (☎ 0171 352 9164)

SUDELEY, 7 Baron (UK 1838); Merlin Charles Sainthill Hanbury-Tracy; s of Capt David Hanbury-Tracy (gs of 4 Baron) and Colline (d 1985), da of Lt-Col Collis St Hill; the 1 Baron was chm of the Cmmn for the Rebuilding of the new Houses of Parliament 1835; suc kinsman (6 Baron) 1941; *b* 17 June 1939; *Educ* Eton, Worcester Coll Oxford; *m* 1980 (m dis 1988), Hon Mrs Elizabeth Villiers, da of late Viscount Bury (s of 9 Earl of Albemarle) and formerly w of Alastair Villiers; *Heir* kinsman, (Desmond) Andrew John Hanbury-Tracy, *qv*; *Career* former chm Human Rights Soc (founded by Lord St John of Fawsley to oppose legalisation of euthanasia); introduced debates in the House of Lords on: export of manuscripts 1973, cathedral finance 1980, teaching and use of the Prayer Book in theological colls 1987; cleared the Prayer Book (Protection) Bill on second reading in House of Lords 1981; patron: Prayer Book Soc, Bankruptcy Assoc of GB and Ireland, Anglican Assoc, St Peter's (Petersham); memb Governing Cncl Manorial Soc of GB, chm Monday Club, past pres Montgomeryshire Soc, vice chllr Monarchist League; occasional lectr: Extra-Mural Dept Univ of Bristol, ESU; contrib to: Contemporary Review, Family History, London Magazine, Monday World, Quarterly Review, Vogue, The Universe, John Pudney's Pick of Today's Short Stories, Montgomeryshire Collections, Salisbury Review, Transactions of the Bristol and Gloucs Archaeological Soc, Die Waage (Zeitschrift der Chemie Grünenthal); FSA 1989; *Books* The Sudeleys - Lords of Toddington (jt author); *Recreations* conversation; *Clubs* Brooks's; *Style*— The Rt Hon the Lord Sudeley, FSA; ✉ c/o House of Lords, London SW1A 0PW

SUDJIC, Deyan; s of Miša J Sudjic (d 1996), of London, and Ceja, *née* Pavlović; *b* 6 Sept 1952; *Educ* Latymer Upper Sch London, Univ of Edinburgh (DipArch); *m* Sarah, *née* Miller; 1 da (Olivia Katarina b 22 Dec 1988); *Career* architecture corr Sunday Times 1980–85, subsequently critic London Daily News, critic Sunday Correspondent 1989–90, architecture critic The Guardian 1991–; visiting prof Höchschule fur Angewandte Kunst (Vienna) 1993–, dir Glasgow's Year of Architecture and Design (scheduled 1999); *Books* Cult Objects (1985), New British Architecture (1986), Ron Arad (1989), Rei Kawakubo/Comme des Garçons (1990), Cult Heroes (1990), The Hundred Mile City (1992); *Clubs* Groucho; *Style*— Deyan Sudjic, Esq; ✉ c/o Glasgow 1999, The Terrace, Princes Square, 48 Buchanan Street, Glasgow G1 3JX (☎ 0141 227 1999, fax 0141 248 8754)

SUFFIELD, 11 Baron (GB 1786); Sir Anthony Philip Harbord-Hamond; 12 Bt (GB 1745), MC (1950); s of 10 Baron (d 1951), and Nina Annette Mary Crawfuird (d 1955), da of John William Hutchison, of Lauriston Hall, and Edlingham, Kirkcudbrightshire; *b* 19 June 1922; *Educ* Eton; *m* 1952, (Elizabeth) Eve (d 1995), da of late Judge (Samuel Richard) Edgedale, QC, of Field Lodge, Crowthorne, Berks; 3 s, 1 da; *Heir* s, Hon Charles Harbord-Hamond; *Career* Maj Coldstream Gds (ret); served: WWII N Africa and Italy, Malaya 1948–50; memb Hon Corps of Gentlemen-at-Arms 1973–92, Harbinger 1990–92; *Clubs* Army and Navy, Pratt's; *Style*— The Rt Hon the Lord Suffield, MC; ✉ Gardeners Cottage, Gunton Park, Hanworth, Norfolk NR11 7HL (☎ 01263 768 423)

SUFFIELD, Sir Henry John Lester; kt (1973); *b* 28 April 1911; *Educ* Camberwell Central Sch; *m* 1940, Elizabeth Mary White; 1 s, 1 da; *Career* serv WWII Maj RASC, with LNER 1926–35, Morris Motor Corpn Canada and USA 1952–64, dep manager and dir Br Motor Corpn Birmingham 1964–68, sales dir BL Motor Corpn 1968–69, head of defence sales MOD 1969–76; Liveryman Worshipful Co of Coachmakers & Coach Harness Makers; *Clubs* RAC; *Style*— Sir Henry Suffield; ✉ 16 Glebe Court, Fleet, Hants GU13 8NJ (☎ 01252 616861)

SUFFOLK, Archdeacon of; *see:* Arrand, Ven Geoffrey William

SUFFOLK AND BERKSHIRE, Earl of, 21 of Suffolk (E 1603), 14 of Berkshire (E 1626); Michael John James George Robert Howard; also Viscount Andover and Baron Howard of Charlton (E 1622); s of 20 Earl (k on active serv 1941); the 1 Earl was 2 s of 4 Duke of Norfolk; the 9 Earl's w was mistress of George II, who built Marble Hill House, on the Thames between Twickenham and Richmond, for her (the style is Palladian, designed by Lord Pembroke); *b* 27 March 1935; *Educ* Winchester; Nat Serv: Navy; *m* 1, 1960 (m dis 1967), Mme Simone Paulmier, da of Georges Litman, of Paris; m 2, 1973 (m dis 1980), Anita Robsahm, da of Robin Robsahm Fuglesang (d 1991), of Cuckfield, Sussex; 1 s, 1 da (Lady Katharine b 9 April 1976); m 3, 1983, Linda Jacqueline, da of Col Vincent Paravicini and former w of 4 Viscount Bridport; 2 da (Lady Philippa b 1985, Lady Natasha b 28 March 1987); *Heir* s, Viscount Andover; *Style*— The Rt Hon the Earl of Suffolk and Berkshire; ✉ Charlton Park, Malmesbury, Wilts SN16 9DG (☎ 01666 822206/823200)

SUGAR, Alan Michael; *b* 24 March 1947; *m*; 2 s, 1 da; *Career* Amstrad PLC: fndr 1968, currently chm and md; chm Tottenham Hotspur plc 1991–; dir BETACOM 1996–; *Style*— Alan Sugar, Esq; ✉ Amstrad PLC, Brentwood House, 169 Kings Road, Brentwood, Essex CM14 4EF (☎ 01277 228888, fax 01277 211350)

SUGAR, Steven Charles; *Educ* St Peter's Sch York, Peterhouse Cambridge (BA), LSE (MSc), Coll of Law; *married*; *Career* lectr in economics Univ of Bristol 1972–73, research asst Lib Party 1973–74, tutor LSE 1974–76; Frere Cholmeley Bischoff: articled clerk 1976–78, asst slr 1978–81, ptnr Company & Commercial Dept 1981– (head of Dept 1990–93), managing ptnr Frere Cholmeley Bischoff 1993–96; *Style*— Steven Sugar, Esq; ✉ Frere Cholmeley Bischoff, 4 John Carpenter Street, London EC4Y 0NH (☎ 0171 615 8000, fax 0171 615 8080)

SUGDEN, Sir Arthur; kt (1978); s of Arthur Sugden (d 1940), of Manchester, and Elizabeth Ann Sugden (d 1952); *b* 12 Sept 1918; *Educ* Thomas St Sch W Gorton, HS of Commerce Manchester; *m* 1946, Agnes, da of Francis Grayston (d 1930); 2 s; *Career* serv WWII Maj RA, UK and India; certified accountant and chartered sec; chief exec Co-operative Wholesale Society Ltd 1973–80, chm Co-operative Bank 1973–80; FIB; *Recreations* reading, walking, travel; *Style*— Sir Arthur Sugden; ✉ 56 Old Wool Lane, Cheadle Hulme, Cheadle, Cheshire SK8 5JA

SUGDEN, David Arnold; *b* 12 July 1951; *Educ* Imperial Coll London (BSc); *m* Janet; 2 s (twins b 17 April 1978); *Career* mathematics teacher Jamaica 1973–74, articled clerk then chartered accountant Arthur Young London 1974–78, gp accountant Thomas Tilling plc 1978–80, gp fin dir Spear & Jackson International plc 1983–86 (gp financial accountant 1980–83), chief exec Geest PLC 1990–96 (gp fin dir 1986–89); CIMgt; *Style*— David Sugden, Esq

SUGDEN, Prof David Edward; s of John Cyril Gouldie Sugden (d 1963), and Patricia, *née* Backhouse; *b* 5 March 1941; *Educ* Warwick Sch, Univ of Oxford (BA, DPhil); *m* 9 Aug 1966, Britta Valborg, da of Harald Stridsberg, of Sweden; 2 s (John Peter, Michael Edward), 1 da (Pauline Charlotta); *Career* scientific offr Br Antarctic Survey 1965–66, lectr then reader Univ of Aberdeen 1966–87, prof Geography Dept Univ of Edinburgh 1987–; visiting prof Arctic and Alpine Inst USA; pres Inst of Br Geographers 1995; memb: Royal Scot Geographical Soc, Royal Geographical Soc, Royal Soc (Edinburgh); FRSE 1990; *Books* Glaciers and Landscape (with B S John, 1976), Arctic and Antarctic (1982), Geomorphology (with S Schumm and R J Chorley, 1986); *Recreations* hillwalking, gardening, skiing; *Style*— Prof David Sugden, FRSE; ✉ Dept of Geography, University of Edinburgh, Drummond St EH8 9XP (☎ 0131 650 2521, fax 0131 556 2524, telex 727442 UNIVEDG)

SUGDEN, Prof Robert; s of Frank Gerald Sugden (d 1987), and Kathleen, *née* Buckley; *b* 26 Aug 1949; *Educ* Eston GS, Univ of York (BA, DLitt), Univ Coll Cardiff (MSc); *m* 26 March 1982, Christine Margaret, da of Leslie Kenneth Upton, of Woking, Surrey; 1 s (Joe b 1984), 1 da (Jane b 1986); *Career* lectr in economics Univ of York 1971–78, reader in economics Univ of Newcastle upon Tyne 1978–85, prof of economics UEA 1985–; FBA 1996; *Books* The Principles of Practical Cost-Benefit Analysis (with A Williams, 1978), The Political Economy of Public Choice (1981), The Economics of Rights, Cooperation and Welfare (1986); *Recreations* walking, gardening; *Style*— Prof Robert Sugden, FBA; ✉ School of Economic and Social Studies, University of East Anglia, Norwich NR4 7TJ (☎ 01603 593423, fax 01603 250434, telex 975197)

SUGGETT, Gavin Robert; s of Kenneth Frederick Suggett (d 1984), of Weybridge, Surrey, and Nancy, *née* Voss-Bark; *b* 11 May 1944; *Educ* Felsted Sch, Christ's Coll Cambridge (MA), London Business Sch (MSc); *m* 11 Sept 1971, Louise, da of Hon Lord Migdale (d 1983), of Edinburgh and Sutherland; 1 s (Gordon b 1977), 2 da (Clare b 1975, Katie b 1980); *Career* articled clerk Deloittes CAs 1962–66, fin mangr Weir Group Ltd 1971–73; Alliance Trust plc: co sec 1973–89, dir 1987–, md 1994–; FCA 1971; *Recreations* skiing, gardening, hill walking; *Clubs* New (Edinburgh), Royal Perth Golf; *Style*— Gavin Suggett, Esq; ✉ The Alliance Trust plc, 64 Reform St, Dundee DD1 1TJ (☎ 01382 201700, fax 01382 225133, telex 76195)

SUIRDALE, Viscount; John Michael James Hely-Hutchinson; er s and h of 8 Earl of Donoughmore; *b* 7 Aug 1952; *Educ* Harrow; *m* 1977, Marie-Claire, da of Gerard van den Driessche (d 1985); 1 s (Hon Richard Gregory b 1980), 2 da (Hon Marie-Pierre Joanna b 1978, Hon Tatiana Louise b 1985); *Heir* s, Hon Richard Gregory Hely-Hutchinson b 1980; *Career* co dir, Burberrys Ltd 1993–; *Recreations* golf, fishing; *Style*— Viscount Suirdale; ✉ 38 Thornton Avenue, Chiswick, London W4 1QG (☎ 0181 742 1405)

SULLIVAN, David Dimitri; s of late Walter Terence Sullivan, of Southend-on-Sea, Essex, and Xenia Anastasia Sullivan; *b* 19 March 1943; *Educ* Mayfield Coll; *m* 17 June 1967, Lesley June, da of Robert George Berks (d 1968); 1 s (Martyn David b 17 June 1970), 1 da (Karen Susan b 14 Aug 1968); *Career* Herbert Hill & Co (now Stoy Hayward) 1959–65, Clark Battams & Co (now Clark Whitehill) 1965–67, md N M Rothschild & Sons Ltd 1988– (joined 1967, dir 1982–); FCA 1965, ATII 1965; *Recreations* golf, skiing,

Marathon running; *Style*— David Sullivan, Esq; ✉ N M Rothschild & Sons Ltd, New Court, St Swithin's Lane, London EC4P 4DU (☎ 0171 280 5000, fax 0171 929 1643)

SULLIVAN, Jeremy Mirth; QC (1982); s of late Arthur Brian Sullivan, and Pamela Jean, *née* Kendall; *b* 17 Sept 1945; *Educ* Framlingham Coll, King's Coll London (LLB, LLM); *m* 1, 1970 (m dis), Ursula Klara Marie, da of late Benno August Friederich Hildenbrock; 2 s (Richard b 1974, Geoffrey b 1976); m 2, Dr Sandra Jean Farmer, da of Allan Stuart Fisher; *Career* 2 Lt Suffolk & Cambs Regt (TA) 1963–65; called to the Bar Inner Temple 1968, bencher 1993, lectr in law City of London Poly 1968–71; in practice Planning & Local Govt Bar 1971–, recorder 1989–, dep High Ct judge 1993–, attorney-gen to the Prince of Wales 1994–; memb Parly Bar 1990–; memb Cncl RTPI 1983–87, memb Exec Ctee Georgian Gp 1985–89, govr Highgate Sch 1990–; LAMRTPI 1970, LMRTPI 1976; *Recreations* walking, railways, canals, reading history; *Style*— Jeremy Sullivan, Esq, QC; ✉ 4–5 Gray's Inn Square, London WC1R 5JA (☎ 0171 404 5252, telex 895 3743 GRAYLAW)

SULLIVAN, Michael Francis; s of Sir Richard Benjamin Magniac Sullivan, 8 Bt (d 1977), and Muriel Mary Paget Pineo (d 1988); *b* 4 April 1936; *Educ* St Andrew Coll SA, Clare Coll Cambridge (MA, MB BChir), St Mary's Hosp Univ of London; *m* 1, 22 Aug 1957 (m dis 1978), Inger, da of Arne Mathieson (d 1984); 1 s (Richard b 9 Jan 1961), 1 da (Nicola b 20 Aug 1965); m 2, 22 Dec 1978, Caroline Mary, da of Maj Christopher Griffin (d 1994); 1 da (Lucy b 22 Nov 1980); *Career* spinal surgn Royal Nat Orthopaedic Hosp London 1971–; sec Int Lumbar Spine Surgns 1975–78; pres European Spinal Surgns 1990–91; visiting lectr in spinal surgery: Australia 1985, S Africa 1981, USA 1980, Canada 1982, Japan 1989; author of numerous articles on spinal surgery; FRCS 1966; *Recreations* cricket, sailing, shooting; *Clubs* MCC, Royal Harwich Yacht; *Style*— Michael Sullivan, Esq; ✉ 12 Gloucester Crescent, London NW1 7DS (☎ 0171 485 4473); The Old Hall, Worlington, Suffolk (☎ 01638 716664); 95 Harley Street, London W1N 1DF (☎ 0171 486 4970, fax 0171 935 5467)

SULLIVAN, (Sir) Richard Arthur; 9 Bt (UK 1804); does not use title; s of Sir Richard Benjamin Magniac Sullivan, 8 Bt (d 1977), and Muriel Mary Paget (d 1988); *b* 9 Aug 1931; *Educ* Univ of Cape Town (BSc), MIT (MS); *m* 1962, Elenor Mary, da of Kenneth Merson Thorpe, of Somerset W, S Africa; 1 s, 3 da; *Heir* s, Charles Merson Sullivan, b 15 Dec 1962; *Career* civil engr; mangr Woodward Clyde Oceaneering; *Recreations* tennis; *Clubs* Houston Racquet; *Style*— Richard Sullivan, Esq

SULLMAN, Tony Frederick; s of Bernard Frederick Sullman, of Stafford, and Joan, *née* Wells; *b* 7 Sept 1954; *m* 23 Aug 1985, Freddie, *née* Roberts; 1 s (Andrew Frederick b 13 Nov 1990); *Career* RAF 1971–76, property devpt business 1975–77, serv Sultan of Oman's Air Force (decorated 3 times) 1977–81, franchisee Intacab Ltd 1982–87, purchased KLM Ltd 1987–89, resided Spain 1989–90, fndr franchise gp Somerford Claims PLC 1990 (incorporating Claims Direct 1995), currently chief exec Somerford Group; *Recreations* reading law, playing poker, avoiding tax; *Style*— Tony Sullman, Esq; ✉ Chief Executive, Somerford Group, Somerford Hall, Stafford ST19 9DQ (☎ 01902 850721, fax 01902 850922)

SULTOON, Jeffrey Alan; s of Maurice Sultoon, of London, and Babette, *née* Braun; *b* 8 Oct 1953; *Educ* Haberdashers' Aske's, St Edmund Hall Oxford; *m* 11 May 1985, Vivien Caryl, da of Peter Woodbridge, of Guildford, Surrey; 1 s (Hugh); *Career* admitted slr 1978; slr Freshfields 1978–81, ptnr Ashurst Morris Crisp 1986– (slr 1981–86); memb Company Law Ctee Law Soc; *Books* Tolley's Company Law (contrib); *Style*— Jeffrey Sultoon, Esq; ✉ Ashurst, Morris, Crisp, Broadwalk House, 5 Appold St, London EC2A 2HA (☎ 0171 638 1111, fax 0171 972 7990, telex 387067)

SUMBERG, David Anthony Gerald; MP (C) Bury South (majority 788); s of late Joshua Sumberg, and Lorna Sumberg; *b* 2 June 1941; *Educ* Tettenhall Coll Wolverhampton, Coll of Law London; *m* 1972, Carolyn Franks; 1 s, 1 da; *Career* formerly slr; Parly candidate (C) Manchester Wythenshawe 1979, MP (C) Bury S 1983–, PPS to Sir Patrick Mayhew as Attorney-Gen 1986–90; memb Select Ctee: on Home Affairs 1991–92, on Foreign Affrs 1992–; memb Lord Chllr's Advsy Ctee on Public Records 1992–; cncllr Manchester City Cncl 1982–84; *Recreations* family and friends; *Style*— David Sumberg, Esq, MP; ✉ House of Commons, London SW1A 0AA (☎ 0171 219 4459)

SUMMERFIELD, Gordon Caleb; s of Donald Caleb Summerfield (d 1994), and Mary, *née* Ritson (d 1989); *b* 16 Dec 1939; *Educ* Wellingborough GS; *m* 23 Sept 1961, (Margaret) Anita, da of William Lewis Williams; 1 s (Mark Caleb b 21 Aug 1962), 1 da (Kay b 31 Oct 1964); *Career* mgmnt trainee rising to md Dale Farm Foods Northern Foods plc 1960–86, prodn dir St Ivel plc 1986–89, md Unigate Dairies 1989–91; Unigate plc: md Dairy Gp 1991–94, chief exec Unigate European Foods 1994–; pres Dairy Indust Fedn, memb Cncl Inst of Grocery Distribution; *Recreations* aviation, walking, reading; *Style*— Gordon Summerfield, Esq; ✉ Unigate European Food, St Ivel House, Interface Business Park, Wootton Bassett, Swindon, Wilts SN4 8QE (☎ 01793 843397, fax 01793 843117)

SUMMERFIELD, Sir John Crampton Summerfield; kt (1973), CBE (1966, OBE 1961), QC (Bermuda 1963); s of Arthur Frederick Summerfield (d 1941), and Lilian Winifred, *née* Staas (d 1958); *b* 20 Sept 1920; *Educ* Lucton Sch Herefordshire; *m* 11 Aug 1945, Patricia Sandra, da of John Geoffrey Musgrave (d 1926), of Salisbury, Rhodesia; 2 s (John b 1946, Michael b 1948), 2 da (Rosemary b 1955, Margaret (Mrs Goodwin) b 1960); *Career* served WWII, E Africa NFD, Ethiopia and Madagascar, Capt Royal Signals; called to the Bar Gray's Inn 1949; Tanganyika crown counsel/legal draftsman 1949–58, dep legal sec E Africa High Cmmn 1958–62; AG Bermuda 1962–72; chief justice: Bermuda 1972–77, Cayman Islands 1977–87; justice of appeal Court of Appeal Bermuda 1980–88, pres Court of Appeal Belize 1981–82; memb Exec Cncl and MLC Bermuda until 1966; *Recreations* photography, chess; *Clubs* Cwlth Trust, Royal Over-Seas League; *Style*— Sir John Summerfield, CBE, QC; ✉ 3 The Corniche, Sandgate, Folkestone, Kent CT20 3TA (☎ 01303 249479)

SUMMERFIELD, Linda Victoria (Lin); da of Henry Conrad Fullbrook (d 1952), and Rose Iris, *née* Hollings (d 1991); *b* 24 Feb 1952; *Educ* Sudbury HS for Girls; *children* 1 da (Fiona Ruth); *Career* author; works published incl: Count the Days (1989, shortlisted for John Creasey prize), Never Walk Behind Me (1990), Taken by a Stranger (US, 1995); various short stories; *Recreations* reading, walking, sketching, opera, worrying; *Style*— Ms Lin Summerfield; ✉ 24 Butt Road, Great Cornard, nr Sudbury, Suffolk CO10 0DS; c/o Heather Jeeves, 9 Dryden Place, Edinburgh EH9 1RP (☎ and fax 0131 668 3859)

SUMMERFIELD, Peter William; s of Frank Summerfield (d 1984), and Margot Summerfield; *b* 3 June 1933; *Educ* William Ellis Sch, Pembroke Coll Oxford (MA); *m* 1, 15 July 1962, Susan Evelyn (d 1990) da of late Willy Wharton, of Ealing, London; 2 s (Mark Steven b 1965, David Michael b 1968), 1 da (Amanda Deborah b 1965); m 2, 5 July 1973, Marianne Dorothee, da of Hans Granby (d 1993), of Hendon, London; *Career* Nat Serv, Egypt and Malta 1952–54; admitted slr 1960; ptnr: Oppenheimer Nathan and Vandyk 1965–88 (articled clerk 1957–60, asst slr 1960–65), Nabarro Nathanson 1988–; slr in UK to: Austrian Govt and Embassy 1986–, Swiss Govt and Embassy 1988–; chm London Chapter Br-Swiss C of C 1992–95; chm Int Bd of Advrs Univ of the Pacific McGeorge Sch of Law (visiting prof 1987); memb: Law Soc of Eng and Wales, Euro Gp of Law Soc, Int Bar Assoc, American Bar Assoc, Br-German Jurists' Assoc, IOD, RIIA, Bd of Visitors McGeorge Sch of Law Univ of the Pacific USA, Soc of Eng and American Lawyers, American C of C UK, Anglo-Austrian Soc, Anglo-German, Anglo-Swiss Soc, Br-Swiss C of C, Br C of C in Germany, German-Br Chamber of Indust and Commerce UK, Franco-Br Chamber of Indust and Commerce, Japan Assoc, Finnish-Br Trade Guild, Norwegian C of C, Swedish C of C; *Books* Dispute Resolution for the International Commercial Lawyer (co-ed, 1988); *Recreations* tennis; *Style*— Peter Summerfield, Esq; ✉ Nabarro Nathanson, 50 Stratton St, London W1X 6NX (☎ 0171 493 9933, fax 0171 629 7900, telex 8813144 NABARO G)

SUMMERHAYES, Gerald Victor; CMG (1979), OBE (1969); s of Victor Samuel Summerhayes, OBE (d 1977), and Florence Ann Victoria Summerhayes (d 1978); *b* 28 Jan 1928; *Educ* Kings' Sch Ely, BNC Oxford; *Career* admin offr Col Serv 1952–60, Overseas Civil Serv 1960–83, permenant sec Sokoto State Nigeria 1970–81, various ministries including Cabinet Office, Health and Local Govt, ret 1983; *Style*— Gerald Summerhayes, Esq, CMG, OBE; ✉ Bridge Cottage, Bridge St, Sidbury, Devon EX10 0RU (☎ 01395 597311); Box 172, Sokoto, Nigeria

SUMMERS, Andrew William Graham; s of Basil Summers (d 1988), and Margaret, *née* Hunt; *b* 19 June 1946; *Educ* Mill Hill Sch (exhibitioner), Fitzwilliam Coll Cambridge, Harvard Business Sch (ISMP); *m* 1971, Frances, *née* Halestrap; 2 da (Sarah b 1974, Kate b 1976), 1 s (Bennet b 1979); *Career* economist CBC Bank Sydney 1968, salesman rising to brand mangr Ranks Hovis McDougall plc 1968–75, md J A Sharwood & Co 1980–85 (mktg mangr then mktg dir 1975–80), md RHM Foods Ltd 1987–90 (commercial dir 1986–87), chief exec Management Charter Initiative 1991–94, chief exec Design Council 1995–; non-exec dir S Daniels PLC 1991–; memb Food from Britain Export Cncl 1982–86, chm France Country Gp Euro Trade Ctee DTI 1986–; FRSA 1991; *Recreations* tennis, fives, theatre; *Style*— Andrew Summers, Esq; ✉ Design Council, Haymarket House, 1 Oxendon St, London SW1Y 4EE (☎ 0171 208 2121, fax 0171 930 6483)

SUMMERS, Brian; *b* 1945; *m* Janet; 1 da; *Career* trainee then public finance accountant W Bromwich County Cncl 1964–73, asst county treas W Midlands County Cncl 1975–84 (chief accountant 1973–75); Birmingham International Airport: joined as commercial dir 1984, financial dir (following company formation) 1987–90, dep md 1990–94, md 1994–; chm Eurohub (Birmingham) Ltd; memb Cncl/Ctee: Airport Operators' Assoc (UK), Birmingham C of C, Birmingham Marketing Partnership, Birmingham and Midlands Soc of Finance, West Midlands Regional Cncl CBI; vice chm Heart of England Tourist Bd; *Recreations* West Bromwich Albion FC, sport generally; *Style*— Brian Summers, Esq; ✉ Birmingham International Airport plc, Birmingham B26 3QJ (☎ 0121 767 7100, fax 0121 767 7310)

SUMMERS, David Lewis; s of Maj Lewis Summers (d 1948), and Beatrice, *née* Greenaway; *b* 25 Nov 1941; *Educ* Mundella Sch Nottingham, St Edmund Hall Oxford (MA); *m* 24 Dec 1966, Veronica Yvonne Elizabeth, da of Cyril Clarence King (d 1970); 2 s (Jonathan b 1971, Benjamin b 1973); *Career* RN Lt 1963–66; Longmans 1966–69, dep chm Butterworth & Co Publishers Ltd 1991– (joined 1969), chief exec Butterworths UK 1986–96, dir Reed Elsevier (UK) Ltd 1996–; contrib various chapters to professional pubns; memb: Harvard Business Club, Soc of Bookmen, Anglo-Finnish Soc; govr St Bede's Sch Sussex; Freeman City of London 1988, Liveryman Worshipful Co of Stationers & Newspaper Makers 1989; *Recreations* tennis; *Clubs* Garrick; *Style*— David Summers, Esq; ✉ Fir Tree Farm, Golford Road, Cranbrook, Kent TN17 3NW (☎ 01580 713377); Butterworth & Co Publishers Ltd, 35 Chancery Lane, London WC2A 1EL (☎ 0171 400 2505, fax 0171 400 2506)

SUMMERS, Jonathan; *b* 2 Oct 1946; *Educ* Macleod HS Melbourne Aust, Prahan Tech Coll Melbourne; *m* 29 March 1969, Lesley; 3 c; *Career* baritone; professional debut singing title role in Rigoletto (Kent Opera under Roger Norrington, dir Jonathan Miller) 1975, ENO debut as Tonio in I Pagliacci 1976, Royal Opera House debut as Killian in Der Freischütz 1977; princ Royal Opera Co 1976–86; has performed with: Orchestre de Paris, Berlin Philharmonic, Orchestre Symphonie de Montreal, Sydney Symphony Orch, Melbourne Symphony Orch, most leading Br orchs; Green Room Theatre award for leading male artist (Melbourne Australia) 1988; *Performances* recent roles incl: title role in Macbeth (ENO) 1990, Figaro in Le Nozze di Figaro (Bavarian Staatsoper) 1990, Marcello in La Bohème (Covent Garden 1990, Chicago Lyric Opera 1993, Nat Theatre Munich 1993, Théâtre du Capitole Toulouse 1995), Grand Prêtre in Samson and Dalila (Covent Garden) 1991 and 1992, Balstrode in Peter Grimes (ENO) 1991, Iago in Otello (Australian Opera Sydney) 1991, Ford in Falstaff (Théâtre du Capitole Toulouse 1991 and 1995, Théâtre Municipale Lausanne 1995), Rodrigo in Don Carlos (ENO) 1992, Don Carlos in The Force of Destiny (ENO) 1992 and 1995, title role in Rigoletto (ENO and Bergen Festival) 1993, Anckarstroem in Un Ballo in Maschera (Australian Opera Melbourne) 1993, Zurga in The Pearl Fishers (ENO) 1994, De Siriex in Fedora (Covent Garden and Chicago Lyric Opera) 1994, Père Germont in La Traviata (Australian Opera Sydney) 1994, Michele in Il Tabarro (Australian Opera Sydney) 1995, title role in Nabucco (WNO) 1995, Kurwenal in Tristan und Isolde (ENO) 1996; concert repertoire incl: Mendelssohn Elijah, Faure Requiem, Brahms Requiem, Elgar The Kingdom, The Apostles and The Dream of Gerontius, Orff Carmina Burana, Vaughan Williams Sea Symphony, Mahler Das Knaben Wunderhorn, Delius A Mass of Life, Berlioz L'enfance du Christ, Britten War Requiem; *Recordings* incl: Peter Grimes (Grammy Award 1979), Samson et Dalila, La Bohème (as Leoncavallo), The Bohemian Girl, Carmina Burana, Sea Symphony, Gloriana 1993; videos incl: Samson et Dalila, Der Rosenkavalier, Il Trovatore; *Style*— Jonathan Summers, Esq; ✉ c/o Patricia Greenan, 19b Belsize Park, London NW3 4DU (☎ 0171 794 5954, fax 0171 431 3503)

SUMMERS, (Robert) Michael; s of Leslie Summers, and Sophie, *née* Joel; *b* 4 May 1940; *Educ* Haberdashers' Aske's Hampstead Sch; *m* Cilla; 1 s (Raphael b 1979), 3 da (Gaye b 1966, Dawn b 1969, Coral b 1984); *Career* fin dir London City & Westcliff Properties Ltd 1966–77; md: Sterling Publishing Group plc 1978–96, Debrett's Peerage Ltd 1988–96; FCA; *Recreations* family, music, literature, Scrabble; *Clubs* Old Haberdashers' Assoc; *Style*— Michael Summers, Esq; ✉ 6 Woodtree Close, Hendon, London NW4 1HQ (☎ 0181 203 3351)

SUMMERS, Nicholas; s of Henry Forbes Summers, CB, of Tunbridge Wells, and Rosemary, *née* Roberts; *b* 11 July 1939; *Educ* Tonbridge, CCC Oxford (BA, MA); *m* 3 April 1965, Marian Elizabeth (Mandy), da of Stanley George Ottley, of Fairlight; 4 s (Timothy b 1966, William b 1968, Michael b 1973, Stephen b 1977); *Career* Civil Serv; Dept for Educn and Employment (formerly Dept for Educn): asst princ 1961–66, princ 1966–74, asst sec 1976–81, under sec 1981–96; asst sec Cabinet Office 1975–76 (princ 1974–75); FRSA 1993; *Recreations* music; *Style*— Nicholas Summers, Esq

SUMMERS, Sue; da of David Summers, of Monte Carlo, and Honey Beatrice, *née* Phillips; *Educ* Queen's Coll London, Univ of Bristol (BA); *m* 1, 1979 (m dis 1989), Rod Allen; m 2, Philip Norman; 1 da (Jessica Rose b 22 Nov 1990); *Career* journalist; trainee Thomson Regional Newspapers, trainee reporter Reading Evening Post, TV and film corr Screen International, TV ed London Evening Standard, ed screen pages Sunday Times, arts ed London Daily News, ed 7 Days Sunday Telegraph; freelance writer and broadcaster: The Daily/Sunday Telegraph, You Magazine, BBC Radio 4 and others; memb: Broadcasting Press Guild, Thames TV Theatre Writers' Award Scheme, Ctee Edinburgh TV Festival 1990; judge Sony Radio Awards 1991; *Recreations* opera, telephoning; *Style*— Ms Sue Summers; ✉ c/o The Daily Telegraph, 1 Canada Square, Canary Wharf, London E14 5DT (☎ 0171 538 5000)

SUMMERS, William Hamilton; LVO (1990, MVO 1974); s of Dr Maxwell Hamilton Summers, DSO, OBE (d 1989), and Evelyne Elizabeth, *née* Baird (d 1992); *b* 4 Oct 1930; *Educ* King's Sch Bruton Somerset; *m* 1959, Rosemarie Jean, da of Thomas Norman Hutchison (d 1982), of Chile; 1 s (John b 1964), 2 da (Alison Jane b 1961, Catherine b 1969); *Career* jeweller; dir Garrard & Co Ltd 1972–91, ret; conslt and lectr on Crown

Jewels, jewellery and silver; fell Gemologists Assoc; FGA; *Recreations* walking, reading; *Style*— William H Summers, Esq, LVO; ✉ Tollgate House, 18 Hadlow Road, Tonbridge, Kent TN9 1NY (☎ and fax 01732 364107)

SUMMERSCALE, David Michael; s of Noel Tynwald Summerscale (d 1960), and Beatrice French, *née* Wilson (d 1993); *b* 22 April 1937; *Educ* Sherborne, Trinity Hall Cambridge; *m* 19 July 1975, Pauline Gabrielle Marie-Thérèse, da of Prof Michel Fleury; 1 s (Tristan Edward Fleury b 1985), 1 da (Emily Noelle Fleury b 1982); *Career* lectr in English Literature and tutor St Stephen's Coll Univ of Delhi 1959–63, head of English and housemaster Charterhouse 1963–75, Master of Haileybury 1976–86, Head Master of Westminster Sch 1986–; memb: Managing Ctee Cambridge Mission to Delhi 1965, CF Andrews Centenary Appeal Ctee 1970, Headmasters' Conf Academic Policy Sub-Ctee 1982–86, Cncl Charing Cross & Westminster Med Sch 1986–; vice chm English Speaking Union Scholarship Ctee 1982–92; govr: The Hall Sch Hampstead 1986–, Arnold House Sch St John's Wood 1988–, King's House Sch 1991–; Merchant Taylors' Co: nominated memb Sch Ctee 1988–96, memb Governing Body 1996–; staff advsr Governing Body Westminster Abbey Choir Sch 1989–, conslt and govr Assam Valley Sch India 1990–, govr Hellenic Coll of London, awarder and reviser in English Oxford & Cambridge Schs Examination Bd; dir: Namdang Tea Company (India) Ltd 1991–95, The Education Group Ltd 1996–; memb: Cncl Queen's Coll London 1991–, Cncl Book Aid Int 1992–, Advsy Bd Criterion Theatre 1992–; FRSA 1984; *Publications* articles on English and Indian literature; dramatisations of novels and verse; *Recreations* music, play production, reading, mountaineering, squash, golf, cricket, tennis, rackets; *Clubs* Athenaeum, I Zingari, Free Foresters, Jesters, Alpin Suisse; *Style*— D M Summerscale, Esq; ✉ Westminster School, 17 Dean's Yard, Westminster, London SW1P 3PB (☎ 0171 963 1042, fax 0171 963 1043)

SUMMERSCALE, John Nelson (Jack); s of Sir John Percival Sumerscale, KBE (d 1980), and Nelle Blossom, *née* Stogsdall (d 1977); *b* 27 July 1944; *Educ* Bryanston Sch, Pembroke Coll Cambridge (BA); *m* 1, 15 March 1969, Cordelia Isobel, da of Sir Alexander Lees Mayall, KCVO, GCMG, of Sturford Mead, Walminster, Wilts; 2 s (Aaron b 26 Aug 1969, Gideon b 24 Dec 1970); m 2, 25 July 1981, Lynda Susan, da of Eric Stewart, of 36 Allbrook House, Roehampton, London; *Career* CA, Coopers & Lybrand 1965–69, Market Investigations Ltd 1969–70, de Zoete & Bevan 1970–86, dir Barclays de Zoete Wedd Securities 1986–91, head UK res Barclays de Zoete Wedd 1989–91, fndr JNS Consultancy 1991–, dir Cambridge Training and Development Ltd 1992–; treas Fulham Parents and Children 1995–; FCA 1968; *Style*— Jack Summerscale, Esq; ✉ JNS Consultancy, 10 Ruvigny Mansions, The Embankment, London SW15 1LE (☎ and fax 0181 789 6920)

SUMMERTON, Dr Neil William; s of Hila Summerton (d 1975), and Nancy Summerton (d 1975); *b* 5 April 1942; *Educ* King's Coll London (BA, PhD); *m* 1965, Pauline, *née* Webb; 2 s (Ian b 1968, Matthew b 1970); *Career* asst princ Miny of Tport 1966–69, asst sec King's Coll London 1971–74 (PA to Princ 1969–71); DOE: princ 1974–78, asst sec 1978–85, under sec Land Use Planning 1985–88, under sec Local Govt Fin Policy 1988–91, under sec Water Directorate 1991–95, dir Water and Land 1996–; dir and tstee various Christian charities, ldr local Christian congregation; *Books* A Noble Task: Eldership and Ministry in the Local Church (rev edn 1994); various articles on historical, ethical and theological subjects; *Style*— Dr Neil Summerton; ✉ Department of the Environment, Romney House, 43 Marsham Street, London SW1P 3PY (☎ 0171 276 8259, fax 0171 276 8639)

SUMNER, Dr Ann Beatrice; da of Tim, and Rita, Sumner, of Lansdown, Bath; *b* 15 July 1960; *Educ* The Royal Sch Bath, Kingswood Sch Bath, Courtauld Inst London (BA), Newnham Coll Cambridge (PhD); *m* 2 da; *Career* archive asst Nat Portrait Gallery London 1984–85, asst curator Holburne of Menstrie Museum Univ of Bath 1985–88, res asst Whitworth Art Gallery Univ of Manchester 1988–89, freelance writing and lecturing Milan 1989–91, curator Museum of Farnham 1991–92, successively keeper then research fell Dulwich Picture Gallery 1992; AMA; *Exhibition Catalogues* Italian Treasures - Victorian and Edwardian Taste in Italian Art (1987), Men, Birds, Beasts and Flowers - Seventeenth Century Needlework Pictures (1987), Gainsborough in Bath - A Bicentenary Exhibition (1988), Ruskin and the English Watercolour (1989), Sir William Waller and the Civil War in the Farnham Area (1992), Painting in Context IV - Rembrandt's Girl at a Window (1993); author of numerous art historical articles and pamphlets; *Recreations* reading, swimming, tennis, skiing and walking, parenthood, collecting Houbraken engravings and crested china; *Style*— Dr Ann Sumner; ✉ c/o Dulwich Picture Gallery, College Road, London SE21 7AD

SUMNER, Bernard; *b* 4 Jan 1956; *Educ* Salford GS; *Career* fndr memb and guitarist Joy Division 1978–79 (albums Unknown Pleasures (1978), Closer (1979)); New Order: formed (after death of Joy Division singer Ian Curtis) 1980, debut performance The Beach Club Manchester 1980, major tours of the USA 1986, 1987 and 1989; completed solo project alongside Johnny Marr and the Pet Shop Boys with release of album Electronic 1991 (gold UK, debut performance Electronic 1990); currently involved with Electronic; gold albums: Power Corruption and Lies (UK), Low-life (UK), Brotherhood (UK), Technique (UK, USA), Republic (UK) 1993; platinum album Substance (UK, USA); Blue Monday best selling 12 inch single of all time; *Recreations* skiing, yachting, clubs; *Style*— Bernard Sumner, Esq; ✉ c/o Gainwest, 11 Whitworth Street, Manchester M1 5WG (☎ 0161 237 5957)

SUMNER, Hon Mr Justice; Hon Sir Christopher John; kt (1996); s of His Hon (William) Donald Massey Sumner, OBE, QC (d 1990), of High Halden, Kent, and Muriel Kathleen, *née* Wilson (d 1992); *b* 28 Aug 1939; *Educ* Charterhouse, Sidney Sussex Coll Cambridge (MA); *m* 24 Sept 1970, Carole Ashley, da of John Ashley Mann (d 1985), and Alison Mann; 1 s (William Mark b 30 Nov 1978), 2 da (Claire Louise b 6 Sept 1972, Emma Jane b 29 Oct 1974); *Career* called to the Bar Inner Temple 1961 (bencher 1994), recorder 1986–87 (asst recorder 1983–86), circuit judge (SE Circuit) 1987–96, judge of the High Court of Justice (Family Div) 1996–; memb Judicial Studies Bd 1991–96; *Recreations* reading, theatre, sport; *Clubs* Hurlingham; *Style*— The Hon Mr Justice Sumner; ✉ The Royal Courts of Justice, Strand, London WC2A 2LL

SUMNER, Christopher Kent; s of George Tomlinson Sumner (d 1979), and Alice Mary Bettley Sumner, *née* Brown (d 1989); *b* 28 Sept 1943; *Educ* The King's Sch Chester, Univ of Durham (BA, MA); *m* 3 Aug 1967, Marjorie, da of George Prince (d 1994); 2 s (Stuart b 1970, Edward b 1974); *Career* slr; currently sr ptnr Goffeys (Southport); chm: Social Security Appeal Tbnls 1984–, Disability Appeal Tbnls 1992–; Parly candidate (Lib) Runcorn 1970; pres Southport and Ormskirk Law Soc 1994; *Recreations* squash, scouting; *Clubs* Rotary; *Style*— Christopher K Sumner, Esq; ✉ 4 Mossgiel Ave, Ainsdale, Southport (☎ 01704 573153); Goffeys, 1 London St, Southport PR9 0UF (☎ 01704 531755, fax 01704 536646)

SUMNER, Francis Ian; s of Guy Chadwick Sumner (d 1986), and Margaret Hilliard, *née* Wilson (d 1995); *b* 25 Oct 1942; *Educ* Tonbridge; *m* 29 Dec 1978, Diana Harriman, da of John Ernest Newman; 2 s (Edward John b 18 Nov 1979, Richard William b 12 May 1981), 1 da (Nicola Margaret b 6 Dec 1983); *Career* asst slr Slaughter & May 1966–72 (articled clerk 1961–66); Norton Rose: asst slr 1972–73, ptnr 1973–, currently ptnr Corp & Fin Dept; Freeman City of London Solicitors' Co; memb Law Soc; *Recreations* golf, gardening, fishing, shooting; *Style*— Francis Sumner, Esq; ✉ Norton Rose, Kempson House, Camomile Street, London EC3A 7AN (☎ 0171 283 6000, fax 0171 283 6500)

SUMNER, Hazel Mary; da of Charles Fox Cullwick, of Sheriffhales, Shropshire, and Enid May, *née* Rogers, of Gresford, Clwyd; *b* 17 April 1930; *Educ* Priory GS Shrewsbury, Leicester Coll of Domestic Sci, Univ of Birmingham, LSE (BScEcon, MSc); *m* 14 Aug 1954, Herbert Sumner; 1 da (Katherine b 25 March 1960); *Career* teacher 1951–61, lectr in educn 1961–71, sr res offr Univ of Liverpool 1971–74, teacher educn co-ordinator BBC 1975–88, chief asst to controller BBC Educn 1988–92; educnl media conslt 1992–; hon sec BBC Pensioner's Assoc 1993–95, OFSTED inspector of primary schs 1993–; author of various papers on bdcasting and educn; *Recreations* grandchildren, conversation, entertaining, biographies, music, gardens; *Style*— Ms Hazel Sumner; ✉ The Ark, St Weonards, Hereford HR2 8QL

SUMNERS, Dr David George; s of George William Sumners, of London, and Irene Florence, *née* Kelly; *b* 23 Sept 1952; *Educ* William Ellis Sch, UCL (BSc, MB BS, MRCPsych); *m* 12 June 1976, Susan Mary, da of late Thomas Arthur Bourn; 1 s (William David b 28 Feb 1985), 1 da (Emily Mary b 23 March 1982); *Career* conslt psychiatrist: Edgware Gen Hosp and Napsbury Hosp 1988–92, Grovelands Priory Hosp 1988–; dir NW Thames RHA Brain Injury Rehabilitation Unit 1988–92, med dir Barnet Healthcare NHS Trust 1992–, conslt forensic psychiatrist Kneesworth House Hosp 1992–94, conslt Brain Injury Rehabilitation Tst 1994–; MRCPsych 1983; *Style*— Dr David Sumners; ✉ West Herts Community NHS Trust, St Albans, Herts AL3 5JF (☎ 01727 834330, fax 01727 834182)

SUMPTION, Jonathan Philip Chadwick; QC (1986); s of Anthony James Sumption, DSC, and Hedy, *née* Hedigan; *b* 9 Dec 1948; *Educ* Eton, Magdalen Coll Oxford (MA); *m* 26 June 1971, Teresa Mary, da of Jerome Bernard Whelan; 1 s (Bernard b 1981), 2 da (Frederique b 1979, Madeleine b 1983); *Career* fell Magdalen Coll Oxford 1971–75, called to the Bar Inner Temple 1975, bencher 1990, recorder 1993–, judge Cts of Appeal Jersey and Guernsey 1995–; *Books* Pilgrimage An Image of Medieval Religion (1975), The Albigensian Crusade (1978), The Hundred Years War (vol 1, 1990); *Recreations* music, history; *Style*— Jonathan Sumption, Esq, QC; ✉ 34 Crooms Hill, London SE10 (☎ 0181 858 4444); 1 Brick Court, Temple, London EC4 (☎ 0171 583 0777, fax 0171 583 9401 (Group 3), telex 892687 IBRICK G)

SUMSION, John Walbridge; OBE (1991); s of Dr Herbert Whitton Sumsion, CBE (d 1995), sometime organist of Gloucester Cathedral, composer and Prof Royal Coll of Music, and Alice Hartley, *née* Garlichs; *b* 16 Aug 1928; *Educ* Rendcomb Coll, Clare Coll Cambridge (MA), Yale Univ (MA), Cornell Univ; *m* 1, 1961 (m dis 1979), Annette Dorothea, *née* Wilson; 2 s (Christopher b 1965, Michael b 1968), 2 da (Bridget b 1963, Kate b 1970); m 2, 1979, Hazel Mary, *née* English; *Career* dir K Shoemakers Ltd 1962–81, registrar of Public Lending Right 1981–91; Univ of Loughborough: dir Library & Info Statistics Unit 1991–96, sr fell Dept of Info and Library Studies 1996–; hon fell Library Assoc 1990; non-exec dir Tele Ordering Ltd 1991–94; chm Statistics Ctee Int Fedn of Library Assocs 1995–; *Books* PLR In Practice (1988 and 1991); also author of various reports and jl articles; *Recreations* music (singing, flute), walking, tennis; *Clubs* United Oxford and Cambridge Univ; *Style*— John Sumsion, Esq, OBE; ✉ The Granary, 29 Main Street, Rotherby, Melton Mowbray, Leics LE14 2LP (☎ 01664 434 485); Department of Information and Library Studies, University of Loughborough, Leics LE11 3TU (☎ 01509 223050, fax 01509 223053, e-mail j.w.sumsion@lboro.ac.uk)

SUNDERLAND, Adam Philip Rothwell; s of Henry Sunderland, of Doncaster, and Marjorie, *née* Rothwell (d 1990); *b* 13 Dec 1958; *Educ* Oundle, Doncaster GS, Queen's Coll Oxford (MA); *Career* Ogilvy & Mather Advertising: account exec London 1980–81, account exec NY 1981–84, account supr NY 1984–85, vice pres/account supr NY 1985–86; vice pres and memb Exec Ctee Saunders Lubinski and White Advertising Dallas 1986–87, vice pres/mgmnt supr Ogilvy & Mather Advertising UK 1987–90; Woollams Moira Gaskin O'Malley: bd account dir 1990–92, client servs dir 1992–94, dep md 1994–95; *Recreations* golf, tennis, skiing, travel; *Clubs* RAC; *Style*— Adam Sunderland, Esq

SUNDERLAND, Alistair John; s of Dr Robert Slater Sunderland, and Marion, *née* Wilson; *b* 24 March 1949; *Educ* Lewis' Sch for Boys, Liverpool Poly; *m* Glenys, da of Gwylim Thomas; 2 s (Adam Thomas, Geraint John), 2 da (Sian Marion, Rhian Alice); *Career* ptnr Austin-Smith: Lord 1974–; memb RIBA 1978, ARCUK; *Recreations* jogging, sailing; *Clubs* Liverpool Architectural Soc; *Style*— Alistair Sunderland, Esq; ✉ Austin-Smith: Lord, 5–6 Bowood Court, Calver Rd, Warrington, Cheshire WA2 8QZ

SUNDERLAND, Prof Eric; s of Leonard Sunderland (d 1990), of Ammanford, Dyfed, and Mary Agnes, *née* Davies; *b* 18 March 1930; *Educ* Amman Valley GS, Univ Coll Wales Aberystwyth (BA, MA), UCL (PhD); *m* 19 Oct 1957, (Jean) Patricia, da of George Albert Watson (d 1972), of Cardiff; 2 da (Rowena, Frances); *Career* res scientist NCB 1957–58; Univ of Durham: lectr in anthropology 1958–66, sr lectr 1966–71, prof 1971–84, pro vice-chllr 1979–84; princ Univ Coll of N Wales Bangor 1984–95, vice-chllr Univ of Wales 1989–91 (emeritus prof 1995–); sec gen Int Union of Anthropological and Ethnological Scis 1978–; chm: Local Govt Boundary Cmmn of Wales 1994–, Environment Agency's Advsy Ctee for Wales 1996–; Br Cncl: memb Welsh Advsy Ctee 1990–, chm Welsh Advsy Ctee 1996–, memb Main Bd 1996–; chm Welsh Language Educn Devpt Ctee 1987–94; memb: Welsh Language Bd 1988–93, Ct of Govrs Nat Museum of Wales 1991–94, Bdcasting Cncl for Wales (BBC) 1996–; patron Schizophrenia Assoc GB 1985–, vice pres Gwynedd Branch Gt Ormond St Hosp Appeal 1988, chm Gregynog Press Bd 1991–; Hrdlička Medal for Anthropological Res 1976, The Mahatma Gandhi Freedom Award (Coll of William & Mary Virginia) 1989; hon memb Gorsedd of Bards Royal Nat Eisteddfod of Wales 1985; hon fell: Croatian Anthropological Soc (Gorjanovic-Krambergeri Medal), Univ of Wales Lampeter 1995, Univ of Wales Bangor 1996; memb: RAI (hon treas 1985–89, pres 1989–91), SSHB, Biosocial Soc; FIBiol 1975; *Books* Genetic Variation in Britain (1973), The Operation of Intelligence: Biological Preconditions for Operation of Intelligence (1980), Genetic and Population Studies in Wales (1986); *Recreations* book collecting, watercolours, gardening, music, travelling; *Clubs* Athenaeum; *Style*— Prof Eric Sunderland; ✉ Bryn, Ffriddoedd Rd, Bangor, Gwynedd LL57 2EH; Faculty of Health Studies, University College of North Wales, Fron Heulog, Ffriddoedd Road, Bangor, Gwynedd LL57 2EF (☎ 01248 354036, fax 01248 355830)

SUNDERLAND, (Frank) Graham; *b* 13 June 1932; *Educ* Elland GS; *m* 8 June 1957, Sheila; *Career* chief exec and dir Yorkshire Bank 1978–92 (joined 1948), cmmr Building Socs Cmmn 1992–; FCIB (dep chm 1987–89), ACIS 1956; *Style*— Graham Sunderland, Esq; ✉ The Building Societies Commission, 15 Great Marlborough Street, London W1V 2AX (☎ 0171 494 6602, fax 0171 494 6652)

SUNDERLAND, John Michael; s of Harry Sunderland, and Joyce Eileen, *née* Farnish; *b* 24 Aug 1945; *Educ* King Edward VII Lytham, Univ of St Andrews (MA); *m* Sept 1965, Jean Margaret, da of Col Alexander Grieve (d 1975); 3 s (Jonothan b 1969, Robin b 1972, Ben Alexander b 1978), 1 da (Corianne b 1966); *Career* Cadbury Schweppes plc: joined 1968, main bd dir 1993–, md Confectionery Stream 1993–96, chief exec 1996–; *Style*— John Sunderland, Esq; ✉ Woodlands, Penn St, Bucks HP7 0PX (☎ 01494 713235); Cadbury Schweppes plc, 25 Berkeley Square, London W1X 6HT (☎ 0171 409 1313, fax 0171 830 5200)

SUNNUCKS, James Horrace George; DL (Essex 1990); s of Stanley Lloyd Sunnucks (d 1953), and Edith Vera Constance, *née* Sendell (d 1979); *b* 20 Sept 1925; *Educ* Wellington, Trinity Hall Cambridge (MA); *m* 1 Oct 1955, Rosemary Ann (Tessa), da of Col J W Borradaile (d 1946); 4 s (William b 2 Aug 1956, John b 4 March 1959, David b

4 April 1961, Andrew b 3 May 1965); *Career* RNVR 1943–46; called to the Bar Lincoln's Inn 1950, bencher 1980, head of chambers, memb Senate Inns of Ct and Bar; memb Parole Review Ctee Chelmsford Prison (later chm) 1970–82, asst Parly boundary cmmr (Wandsworth, Camden, Wilts) 1975–85; Freeman: City of London 1986, Worshipful Co of Gardeners 1986; licensed reader diocese of Chelmsford 1954, pres County of Essex (Eastern Area) Order of St John 1990, pres Essex Club 1995; memb Inst of Conveyancers 1974 (pres 1988–89); *Books* Williams, Mortimer and Sunnucks on Executors (ed), Halsbury's Laws of England (ed); *Recreations* gardening, local history, sailing; *Clubs* United Oxford and Cambridge Univ, Garrick, Norfolk; *Style*— James Sunnucks, Esq, DL; ✉ East Mersea Hall, Colchester, Essex CO5 8TJ (☎ 01206 383 215); 19 Old Buildings, Lincoln's Inn, London WC2; 5 New Square, Lincoln's Inn, London WC2A 3RJ (☎ 0171 404 0404, fax 0171 831 6016); Octagon House, Colegate, Norwich

SUNNUCKS, John Lloyd; s of James Sunnucks, and Rosemary Ann, *née* Borradaile; *b* 4 March 1959; *Educ* Wellington, Lincoln Coll Oxford, RMA Sandhurst; *m* Lucinda Jane Frances, *née* Davies; 2 da (Isabel, Miranda); *Career* served HM Forces 1981–87, Life Gds; City and Commercial Communications 1987–89, Brunswick Public Relations 1989– (currently ptnr); *Clubs* Turf; *Style*— John Sunnucks, Esq; ✉ 40 Bassingham Road, London SW18 3AG; Brunswick Public Relations Ltd, 15–17 Lincoln's Inn Fields, London WC2A 3ED (☎ 0171 404 5959)

SUPER, Dr Maurice; s of Eric Simon Super, MM (d 1979), of Johannesburg, and Aida, *née* Marsden (d 1980); *b* 17 Oct 1936; *Educ* King Edward VII Sch Johannesburg, Univ of the Witwatersrand (MB BCh), Univ of Cape Town (MD), Univ of Edinburgh (MSc), DCH; *m* 16 Dec 1958, Anne Monica, da of Jan Gliksman; 2 s (Michael b 18 March 1960, Jonathan b 21 Oct 1966), 1 da (Beth b 4 April 1969); *Career* paediatric trg Baragwanath Hosp Johannesburg 1959–67, conslt paediatrician to SW African Admin and SW African Railways and Harbours 1967–78, conslt paediatric geneticist Royal Manchester Children's Hosp 1979–, postgrad tutor 1991–96; author of numerous articles on cystic fibrosis; fndr SA Cystic Fibrosis Assoc; FRCPE 1977, FRCP 1992; *Books* Cystic Fibrosis: The Facts (1987, 3 edn, 1995); *Recreations* cricket, tennis, bridge; *Clubs* Northern Lawn Tennis, Manchester Bridge, Salford District Hospitals Cricket (chm); *Style*— Dr Maurice Super; ✉ Dept of Clinical Genetics, Royal Manchester Children's Hospital, Manchester M27 4HA (☎ 0161 727 2335, fax 0161 727 2328)

SUPPERSTONE, Michael Alan; QC (1991); s of Harold Bernard Supperstone (d 1992), of London, and Muriel, *née* Weinstein (d 1978); *b* 30 March 1950; *Educ* St Paul's, Lincoln Coll Oxford (MA, BCL), Harvard Law Sch (visiting scholar); *m* 18 April 1985, Dianne, da of Abe Jaffe, of Surrey; 1 s (Daniel b 1986), 1 da (Laura b 1988); *Career* called to the Bar Middle Temple 1973, recorder 1996– (asst recorder 1992–96); visiting lectr Nat Univ of Singapore 1981 and 1982; vice chm Administrative Law Bar Assoc 1994– (sec 1986–90, treas 1991–94), tstee Int Centre for Public Law; *Books* Judicial Review (1992), Halsbury's Laws of England - Administrative Law Title (4 edn, 1989), Immigration - The Law and Practice (1983, 1988 and 1994), Brownlie's Law of Public Order and National Security (2 edn, 1981); *Recreations* tennis; *Clubs* Garrick, RAC, Roehampton; *Style*— Michael Supperstone, Esq, QC; ✉ 11 King's Bench Walk, Temple, London EC4Y 7EQ (☎ 0171 583 0610, fax 0171 583 9123, telex 884620 BARLEX)

SURATGAR, David; s of Prof Lotfali Suratgar (d 1969), of Tehran, and Prof Edith Olive, *née* Hepburn (d 1985); *b* 23 Oct 1938; *Educ* Silcoates Sch Yorks, New Coll Oxford (BA, MA), Columbia Univ NYC (MIA); *m* 1, 6 Aug 1962, Barbara Lita (d 1990), da of Donald Telfer Low, of Wytham Abbey, Wytham, Oxford; 1 s (Karim Donald Hepburn b 4 Aug 1966), 1 da (Roxanne Christina Noelle b 25 Dec 1964); m 2, 29 Aug 1994, Wandra Edith, da of Senator Ike Smalley, of Deming, New Mexico; *Career* Legal Dept UN Secretariat 1961–62, Sullivan & Cromwell (lawyers) NYC 1963–64, legal counsel World Bank 1964–73, adjunct prof of law Univ of Georgetown 1966–73; Morgan Grenfell & Co Ltd: dir 1973–88, gp dir 1988–, dep chm International 1992–; legal counsel Bank of England and Nat Water Cncl 1976, counsel Le Boeuf Lamb Green & MacRae 1995–; dir: Société Internationale Financiere Pour Investissements et le Developpement en Afrique 1981–95, Banque Marocain du Commerce Exterieur 1995–, Oxford Playhouse Tst 1989–, Garsington Opera Co 1991–; chm: West India Ctee (Royal Charter) 1987–89 (vice pres 1989–), Caribbean Cncl for Europe 1994–; hon treas Worldaware 1992–; memb Bd Major Projects Assoc Templeton Coll Oxford, Bodleian Library Appeal 1987–; memb Cncl: Royal Inst of Int Affrs 1993–, Federal Tst 1992–96, Br Exec Serv Overseas 1993–; sr res fell Int Law Inst Washington DC; memb: Gray's Inn, Int Bar Assoc, Br Inst of Int and Comparative Law; *Books* Default and Rescheduling - Sovereign and Corporate Borrowers in Difficulty (1984), International Financial Law (jlty, 1980); *Recreations* shooting, book collecting, theatre, travelling; *Clubs* Travellers', Chelsea Arts; *Style*— David Suratgar, Esq; ✉ 2 Inverness Gardens, London W8 4RN; Morgan Grenfell & Co Ltd, 23 Gt Winchester St, London EC2P 2AX (☎ 0171 588 4545, fax 0171 826 6155, telex 893511)

SURMAN, Martyn Charles; s of Leslie Charles Surman (d 1970), of Brighton, and Irene Grace, *née* Rogers; *b* 21 Nov 1944; *Educ* Varndean GS for Boys, Brighton Coll of Technol, Coll of Estate Mgmnt; *m* 1, 1 Oct 1966 (m dis); 1 s (David Keith b 20 Jan 1968), 1 da (Tracey Deborah (twin) b 20 Jan 1968); m 2, 13 March 1976 (m dis); m 3, 14 Sept 1990, Irene Florence, da of Sidney William Hart (d 1986); *Career* trainee bldg surveyor Watney Mann Brewers 1963–69, sr architectural asst and dep to Borough Architect Architect's Dept Hove BC 1974–78 (joined 1969); PSA Services: troubleshooter Bldg Advsy Branch Croydon 1978, area design mangr Portsmouth 1984, gp planning mangr Portsmouth 1986, gp bldg surveyor 1989, PSA dep head of profession bldg surveyors Jan 1990, superintending bldg surveyor July 1990, PSA head of profession bldg surveyors Oct 1990–91; dir: of Bldg Surveying PSA Specialist Services 1991–92, of Bldg Surveying Servs SpS Surveying Dec 1992–93; div dir TBV Consult Ltd 1993–94, div dir TBV Surveying 1995–96, seconded to Buffon Binnie Int Johannesburg March 1996 - Aug 1996 (ldr int team for devpt of strategy policy for future maintenance of state-owned properties in SA), dir of mktg Schal Property Services 1996–; RICS: memb Bldg Surveyors Divnl Exec 1987–91, memb Gen Cncl 1988–91, chm Health and Safety Working Gp 1989–90, memb Bldg Surveyors Divnl Cncl 1987–, pres Bldg Surveyors Div 1990–91; memb Sussex Branch Bldg Surveyors 1991– (chm 1992–93); ABE: memb Gen Cncl 1994–, memb Devpt and Monitoring Ctee 1994–; memb numerous BSI Cmmns; author and presenter of numerous papers on bldg surveying and construction technol at nat confs seminars and BSI launch, co-author PSA tech guides, extenal examiner BSc Hons Building Surveying Univ of Brighton 1995–98; external examiner BSc Hons Building Surveying De Montfort Univ 1993–97; observer memb Bldg Regulations Advsy Ctee (BRAC) 1992–, memb Buxted PC 1993–; FRICS 1986 (ARICS 1975), FIAS 1993, FBEng 1993; *Recreations* photography, sport, travelling, angling, theatre; *Style*— Martyn Surman, Esq; ✉ Bramblehurst, Limes Lane, Potters Green, Buxted, E Sussex TN22 4PB (☎ 01825 733111); Schal Property Services, The Lansdowne Building, 2 Lansdowne Road, Croydon, Surrey CR0 2BX (☎ 0181 256 4631, fax 0181 256 4579)

SURREY, Archdeacon of; *see:* Reiss, Ven Robert Paul

SURREY, Christopher Durden (Kit); s of Stephen James Surrey, of Southampton, Hampshire, and Frances Vera Talbot, *née* Durden, of Bishopsteignton, Devon; *b* 23 June 1946; *Educ* Tauntons GS Southampton, Southampton Art Coll, Wimbledon Sch of Art (DipAD); *m* 19 July 1969, Margaret Jullian, da of Leslie Arnold Grealey; 1 s (Thomas Hamo b 7 May 1973), 1 da (Charlotte Sarah b 18 Sept 1975); *Career* theatre designer and artist; asst designer: Citizens Theatre Glasgow 1968–69, London fringe 1970–72; designer: York Theatre Royal 1972–74, Northcott Theatre Exeter 1974–76; freelance 1976–; GB rep Int Orgn of Scenographers and Theatre Technicians E Berlin 1981 and Moscow 1982; memb Soc of Br Theatre Designers; *Theatre* incl: The Master Builder, Jumpers, Death of a Salesman, Toad of Toad Hall (all Theatr Clwyd), One Flew Over the Cuckoo's Nest, Shades of Brown, The Wizard of Oz, Alice in Wonderland, The Turn of the Screw, The Merchant of Venice, The Taming of the Shrew, The Last Yankee, Amadeus (all Northcott) Rosmersholm (Royal Exchange Manchester), Turkey Time, John Bull, The Secret Rapture (all Bristol Old Vic), Peter Grimes, The Queen of Spades (both New Sussex Opera), Troilus and Cressida (Shakespeare Theatre Washington DC 1992), Othello, Volpone, The Servant, Divine Right (all Birmingham Rep), Blue Remembered Hills (Crucible Sheffield); prodns for RSC incl: Dingo, Captain Swing, Sore Throats, A Doll's House, The Accrington Pals, Men's Beano, The Suicide, Bond's, Lear, Golden Girls, The Comedy of Errors, The Merchant of Venice, Twelfth Night, Cymbeline, The Churchill Play, Playing with Trains, Much Ado About Nothing, The Bright and Bold Design; *Exhibitions* Soc of Br Theatre Designers incl: Central Sch of Art 1976, The Roundhouse 1979, Riverside Studios 1983 and 1987; also exhibited at: Cleveland International Drawing Biennale 1991, 1st Malvern Open Drawing Competition 1992, Gordon Hepworth Gallery Newton St Cyres 1991, Devon & Exeter Arts Centre 1992, Coopers Gallery Bristol 1992, RA Summer Exhbn 1993, Stansell Gallery Taunton 1994, Hawkings Gallery Salisbury 1994, Cheltenham Drawing Competition 1994, Unit 10 Gallery 1995; *Books* Artswest (contrib 1988), British Theatre Design - The Modern Age (contrib 1989); *Recreations* walking and climbing; *Style*— Kit Surrey, Esq; ✉ 77 Queens Road, St Thomas, Exeter, Devon EX2 9EW (☎ 01392 270240)

SURTEES, John; MBE (1959); *b* 11 Feb 1934; *m* Jane; 1 s (Henry b 1991), 2 da (Edwina b 1987, Leonora b 1989); *Career* motorcycle and racing car driver; apprentice Vincent HRD Co Stevenage; won first race Vincent Grey Flash (built by himself) 1951, competed in first int world championship 1952, raced on maj Br Circuits 1952–54, Br champion 1954–55, commenced riding in world championships 1956; world champion: 1958–60 (350cc), 1956 and 1958–60 (500cc); driving racing cars 1960–68, Formula 1 world champion 1964; winner: Canadian American Championship Sports Car Series 1966, Japanese Grand Prix 1972, Imola Shell Formula 2 championship 1972; car constructor 1968– (Formula 2 Euro champion car constructor 1972); currently motor sport and engrg conslt and property developer; Freeman City of London 1990, Liveryman Worshipful Co of Carmen 1990; *Style*— John Surtees, Esq, MBE; ✉ Monza House, Fircroft Way, Edenbridge, Kent TN8 6EJ (☎ 01732 865496, fax 01732 866945)

SURTEES, Maj John Freville Henry; OBE (1975), MC (1940); s of Maj Robert Lambton Surtees, OBE, JP (d 1968), of Littlestone, Kent, and Anne Olive Marguerite, da of Col Charles Edward Beck, 12 Lancers (d 1944); *b* 26 Jan 1919; *Educ* Eton, RMC Sandhurst; *m* 1, 1946 (m dis 1967), Audrey, da of Maj Basil Baillie Falkner (d 1964); 2 da (Anna, Christian); m 2, 1969 (m dis 1985), Anne, da of Sir Edward Denham, GCVO, KBE (d 1938); m 3, 1996, Marian, da of Brig Reginald Andrews, DSO, MC (d 1978); *Career* 2 Lt 1 Bn The Rifle Bde 1939, POW (wounded Calais 1940) 1940–45, 2 Bn Rifle Bde 1945–46, GSO 2 Allied Liaison Branch BAOR 1946–47, ret 1948; md: Percy Fox & Co (Wine Importers) 1962 (chm 1970–73), Garvey (London) Ltd 1973–84; memb Inst of Masters of Wine 1956; memb Ct of Assts Worshipful Co of Grocers (Master 1966–67); *Recreations* fishing, racing, music; *Clubs* Boodle's, Green Jackets, White's; *Style*— Maj John Surtees, OBE, MC; ✉ Down House, Wylye, Warminster, Wiltshire BA12 0QN (☎ 01985 248387)

SUSCHITZKY, (John) Peter; s of Wolfgang Suschitzky, and Ilona, *née* Donath; *b* 6 April 1940; *Educ* Mountgrace Sch, Inst des Hautes Etudes Cinématographiques Paris; *m* June 1964 (m dis 1982), Johanna Roeber; 1 s (Adam b 1972), 2 da (Anya b 1969, Rebecca b 1974); m 2, July 1992, Ilona Guinsberg; *Career* dir of photography; memb: Br Soc of Cinematographers, Dirs' Guild of America; *Films* incl: Charlie Bubbles 1966, Leo The Last 1967, The Rocky Horror Picture Show 1974, The Empire Strikes Back 1978, Falling in Love 1984, Dead Ringers 1988, Where the Heart Is (Nat Soc of Film Critics Award USA for Best Cinematography), Naked Lunch 1991, The Public Eye 1991, The Vanishing 1992, M Butterfly 1993, Crash 1995, Mars Attacks 1996; *Recreations* music, playing the transverse flute, history, cooking; *Style*— Peter Suschitzky, Esq; ✉ 13 Priory Rd, London NW6 4NN (☎ 0171 624 3734, fax 0171 625 6863)

SUSSKIND, Prof Richard Eric; s of Dr Werner Susskind, of Glasgow, and Shirley, *née* Banks; *b* 28 March 1961; *Educ* Hutchesons' GS Glasgow, Univ of Glasgow (LLB, Dip in Legal Practice), Balliol Coll Oxford (Snell exhibitioner, DPhil); *m* 11 Aug 1985, Michelle Dawn, da of Harvey Saul Latter (d 1991); 2 s (Daniel Rex b 10 Oct 1987, Jamie Ross b 28 June 1989), 1 da (Alexandra Lee b 5 Feb 1995); *Career* tutor in law Univ of Oxford 1984–86, head Expert Systems Ernst & Young 1986–89, memb Mgmnt Bd Masons 1994– (special advsr 1989–94); visiting prof The Law Sch Univ of Strathclyde 1990–; hon memb Soc for Computers and Law 1992 (chm 1990–92); gen ed Int Jl of Law and IT 1992–; conslt Lord Woolf's inquiry into civil justice system 1995–96; Freeman City of London 1992; Worshipful Co of Info Technologists: Freeman 1992, Liveryman 1993, memb Court 1994; FRSA 1992; *Books* Expert Systems in Law (1987), Latent Damage Law - The Expert System (1988), Essays on Law and Artificial Intelligence (1993), The Future of Law (1996); *Recreations* running, reading; *Style*— Prof Richard Susskind; ✉ Masons, 30 Aylesbury Street, London EC1R 0ER (☎ 0171 490 4000, fax 0171 490 2545)

SUSSMAN, Norman Frederick; CBE (1988, OBE 1981); s of Samuel Sussman (d 1941), of London, and Miriam, *née* Eisen; *b* 19 Jan 1925; *Educ* Univ Coll Sch Hampstead; *m* 8 Feb 1953, Iris (d 1993), da of Maurice Williams; 1 da (Valerie b 21 March 1958); *Career* WWII Capt RA 1943–47; currently chm of family co L S & J Sussman Ltd (joined 1941); memb Clothing Econ Devpt Cncl 1968–88, chm Shirt, Collar & Tie Manufacturers' Fedn 1968 and 1972 (memb Exec Ctee 1962), pres Appeal Textile Benevolent Assoc 1974–75, chm Br Clothing Industry's Jr Cncl 1977–80, fndr chm/Br memb Clothing Indust Assoc 1980–87 (pres 1987–), BCIA rep CBI Cncl 1987–; memb: Devon and Cornwall Trg and Enterprise Cncl 1989– (chm North Devon Bd), Bd CAPITB Tst 1990, Cncl Apparel, Knitting and Textile Alliance, Clothing Manufacturers Wages Cncl 1990–, Cncl Br Knitting and Clothing Confederation 1991–, Cncl Br Apparel and Textile Confedn; chm: Bill Cole Meml Tst, Br Clothing Indust Assoc Pension Fund Mgmnt Ctee, One in Twelve Appeal, Tstees Action against Breast Cancer; formerly: pres Clothing and Footwear Inst 1980–81, memb Cncl WIRA, chm Shirley Inst Clothing Ctee, memb Bd Clothing Industry's Productivity Resources Agency, memb Bd Br Clothing Centre, memb Shirt Making Wages Cncl; Univ of Bradford: hon visiting fell, chm Steering Ctee for Clothing Degree Course, memb Advsy Ctee Dept of Industl Technol 1991–; patron Renaissance Maritime Charitable Tst Ltd; memb Cons Pty (ward chm Hendon South Constituency); Hon DLitt Univ of Bradford 1995; *Style*— Norman Sussman, Esq, CBE; ✉ Montana, Winnington Rd, Finchley, London N2 0TX (☎ 0181 455 9394); L S & J Sussman Limited, 17/18 Radford Crescent, Billericay, Essex CM12 0DG (☎ 01277 652165, fax 01277 651921)

SUTCH, Andrew Lang; s of Rev Canon Christopher Lang Sutch, of Henleaze, Bristol, and Gladys Ethelwyn, *née* Larrington; *b* 10 July 1952; *Educ* Haileybury Coll, Oriel Coll Oxford (MA); *m* 22 May 1982, Shirley Anne, da of Gordon Alger Teichmann, of Wimbledon; 2 s (James b 12 Dec 1983, Francis b 24 Aug 1986); *Career* Lt Intelligence Corps TA 1976–86; admitted slr 1979, ptnr Stephenson Harwood 1984– (joined 1977); memb Law Soc 1979; *Recreations* theatre, running; *Style*— Andrew Sutch, Esq;

✉ Stephenson Harwood, One St Paul's Churchyard, London EC4M 8SH (☎ 0171 329 4422, fax 0171 606 0822)

SUTCH, Rev Dom Antony; s of Ronald Antony Sutch (d 1994), and Kathleen, *née* Roden; *b* 19 June 1950; *Educ* Downside, Univ of Exeter (BA), Univ of Oxford (MA); *Career* former CA London; Downside Abbey: Benedictine monk 1975, solemnly professed 1980, ordained 1981; Downside Sch: housemaster 1985–91, dir of admissions 1991–95, headmaster 1995–; memb Cncl Univ of Bath; author various articles in newspapers incl the Spectator, also sometime presenter Thought for the Day (BBC Radio 4); memb Order of Malta Volunteers; FRSA 1992; *Recreations* gardening, horse racing, cricket (pres Stratton on the Fosse CC); *Clubs* East India; *Style—* Dom Antony Sutch, OSB; ✉ Downside School, Stratton on the Fosse, Bath, Somerset BA3 4RJ (☎ 01761 232206/513, fax 01761 233575, e-mail downside@rmple.co.uk)

SUTCLIFFE, Prof Charles Martin Sydenham; s of Gordon Edward Sutcliffe, and Florence Lillian, *née* Cole; *b* 5 Jan 1948; *Educ* KCS Wimbledon, Univ of Reading (BA); *Career* International Computers Ltd 1965–68, Unilever 1971–73, lectr Univ of Reading 1973–86, Northern Soc prof of accounting and fin Univ of Newcastle 1986–90, prof of finance and accounting Univ of Southampton 1990–; memb Berkshire CC 1981–85; ACMA 1985, AT11 1968, MInstAM 1968; *Books* The Dangers of Low Level Radiation (1987), Stock Index Futures (1993, 2 edn 1997), Banks and Bad Debts (1995), Management Accounting in Healthcare (1996); *Recreations* cycling; *Style—* Prof Charles Sutcliffe; ✉ Department of Accounting and Management Science, The University, Southampton SO17 1BJ (☎ 01703 595000)

SUTCLIFFE, (Charles Wilfred) David; OBE (1995), DL (W Yorks 1991); s of Max Sutcliffe (d 1976), of Shipley, W Yorks, and Mary Doreen Sutcliffe (d 1977); *b* 21 June 1936; *Educ* Uppingham, Univ of Leeds (BA); *m* 6 May 1960, Hanne, da of Carl Olaf Carlsen (d 1967), of Copenhagen, Denmark; 2 s (Charles Peter David b 1961, John Mark Benson b 1963); *Career* Lt 4 Royal Tank Regt; Benson Turner Ltd: jt md 1968–, chm 1978–; chm Benson Turner (Dyers) Ltd 1976–78; dir: Bradford Microfirms Ltd 1981–88, A N Vevers Ltd 1983–, Bradford Breakthrough Ltd 1990–, Bradford Training & Enterprise Cncl 1991– (dep chm 1994); fndr chm Bradford Enterprise Agency 1983–89, pres Bradford C of C 1983–85, memb Cncl Lazards West Riding Tst 1985–93; memb High Steward's Cncl York Minster 1980– (tstee York Minster Fund 1987–); pres Bradford Textile Soc 1987–88; High Sheriff for Co of W Yorks 1994–95; memb Co of Merchants of the Staple of England 1979, Freeman City of London, Liveryman Guild of Framework Knitters 1983; hon fell Bradford & Ilkley Community Coll 1985; CText, FTI; *Recreations* golf, shooting, tennis, skiing, sailing; *Clubs* Brooks's; *Style—* David Sutcliffe, Esq, OBE, DL; ✉ Ivy House Farm, Kettlesing, nr Harrogate, N Yorks HG3 2LR (☎ 01423 770561); Dakota, The Boat Pool, Rhosneigr, Anglesey LL64 5YZ (☎ 01407 811080); Benson Turner Ltd, Station Mills, Wyke, Bradford, West Yorks BD12 8LA (☎ 01274 696220, fax 01274 691170)

SUTCLIFFE, Gerard (Gerry); MP (Lab) Bradford S (majority 9,664); s of Henry (Harry) Sutcliffe (d 1985), of Bradford, and Margaret, *née* McCann; *b* 13 May 1953; *Educ* Cardinal Hinsley GS, Bradford Coll; *m* 14 Oct 1972, Maria, da of Eric Holgate; 3 s (Craig Anthony b 17 Aug 1973, Adrian John b 26 Aug 1975, Christopher James 14 May 1989), 1 da (Mary b 29 Dec 1982 d 1983); *Career* retail trainee Brown Muffs dept store, advtg clerk Bradford T&A, printing dept Field Printers; MP (Lab) Bradford S 1994–; Bradford Met Cncl: cnclIr 1982–88 and 1990–, dep ldr 1986–88, ldr 1992–94; dep sec: SOGAT 1982, GPMU (memb); *Recreations* music, sport, politics; *Style—* Gerry Sutcliffe, Esq, MP; ✉ 1st Floor, Jacobs Well Building, Bradford (☎ 01274 754972); House of Commons, London SW1A 0AA (☎ 0171 219 3000)

SUTCLIFFE, James Harry (Jim); *Educ* Univ of Cape Town (BSc); *Career* Prudential Corporation plc: joined 1976, chief operating offr subsid Jackson National Life 1989–92, dep md Home Service Div 1992–, main bd dir 1994–, chief exec Prudential UK 1995–; FIA; *Clubs* Pinner Hill Golf; *Style—* Jim Sutcliffe, Esq; ✉ Prudential Corporation plc, 142 Holborn Bars, London EC1N 2NH (☎ 0171 405 9222)

SUTCLIFFE, James Stocks; s of Peter Stocks Sutcliffe (d 1991), and Hon Mrs (Dora) Valerie Patricia, *née* Canning; *b* 9 March 1953; *Educ* Stowe, Grimsby Tech Coll (HND); *m* 18 June 1988, Susan Diana, da of John Beaumont, of Legbourne, Louth, Lincs; 1 s (William George b Oct 1989), 1 da by previous m (Hannah Elizabeth b 20 April 1983); *Career* chm and dir: John Sutcliffe & Son (Holdings) Ltd, John Sutcliffe & Son (Grimsby) Ltd, Confill (UK) Ltd, Sutcliffe Solloway & Co Ltd, Sutcliffe Solloway (Life & Pensions) Ltd, Solloway Group Pensions Schemes Ltd; md Port of Boston (1992) Ltd; MInstD; *Recreations* motor sport; *Style—* James Sutcliffe, Esq; ✉ John Sutcliffe & Son (Holdings) Ltd, Sutcliffe House, Market St, Grimsby, S Humberside DN31 1QT (☎ 01472 359101, telex 52502 SUTGBY G, fax 01472 241935)

SUTCLIFFE, John Harold Vick; CBE (1994), DL (North Yorkshire 1996); s of Sir Harold Sutcliffe, sometime MP (d 1958), and Emily Theodora, *née* Cochrane (d 1981); *b* 30 April 1931; *Educ* Winchester (Princess Elizabeth Cup winner Henley Royal Regatta 1949), New Coll Oxford (MA); *m* 25 July 1959, Cecilia Mary, da of Ralph Meredyth Turton, DL (d 1988), of Kildale Hall, Whitby, N Yorks; 3 s (Andrew Harold Wentworth b 1960, John Ralph Beaumont b 1964, Mark David Chetwynd b 1967), 1 da (Henrietta Cecilia b 1961); *Career* Nat Serv 2 Lt RA 1950–51, later served HAC (TA); called to the Bar Inner Temple 1956, in practice Midland Circuit; Capricorn Africa Soc and African Med & Research Fndn Kenya 1960–61; chm Great Fosters (1931) Ltd 1958–; dir: Allied Investors Trusts Ltd 1958–69, Norton Junction Sand & Gravel Ltd 1958–64, Tyne Tees Waste Disposal Ltd 1964–71; Parly candidate (C): Oldham W 1959, Chorley Lancs 1964, Middlesbrough W 1966; MP (C) Middlesbrough W 1970–Feb 1974, Parly candidate (C) Teesside Thornaby Oct 1974; DL Cleveland 1983–96, High Sheriff N Yorks 1987–88; chm: Northern Heritage Tst 1981–88, N Housing Assoc Ltd 1986–94 (dir 1977–86), NE Civic Tst 1988–93 (dir 1976–88), Bow Street Project Ltd 1988–; former chm: Zebra Trust Ltd, County Endeavour; memb: N York Moors Nat Park Ctee 1982–88, Bd Housing Corp 1982–88, Bd Teesside Devpt Corp 1987–; past chm and pres Youth Clubs N Yorks; *Recreations* growing trees, shooting, travel; *Clubs* Leander, MCC; *Style—* John Sutcliffe, Esq, CBE, DL; ✉ Chapelgarth, Great Broughton, Middlesbrough, N Yorks TS9 7ET (☎ 01642 712228); Great Fosters (1931) Ltd, Egham, Surrey TW20 9UR (☎ 01784 433822)

SUTCLIFFE, Her Hon Judge; Linda; da of James Loftus Woodward (d 1967), and Florence, *née* Brown (d 1990); *b* 2 Dec 1946; *Educ* Eccles GS, LSE (LLB); *m* 1 (m dis); m 2, 3 Oct 1987, Peter Brian Walker; *Career* lectr in law Univ of Sheffield 1968–81 (pt/t 1976–81); called to the Bar Gray's Inn 1975, practising barr 1976–93, circuit judge (NE Circuit) 1993–; pt/t chm Industrial Tbnls 1983–92; FRSA; *Recreations* music, gardening; *Style—* Her Hon Judge Sutcliffe; ✉ c/o North-Eastern Circuit Office, Lord Chancellor's Department, 17th Floor, West Riding House, Albion Street, Leeds LS1 5AA

SUTCLIFFE, Martin Rhodes; s of John Sutcliffe, JP, DL, of Oldham, Lancashire, and the Hon Helen, *née* Rhodes; gs of late Lord Rhodes of Saddleworth, KG, DFC, PC, DL; *b* 21 Sept 1955; *Educ* Hulme GS (house capt, represented sch in swimming & athletics), Univ of Sheffield (BA, DipArch); *m* 26 July 1980, Gillian Margaret, da of Arthur Price, of Rochdale, Lancashire; 1 s (Henry Ellis b 16 April 1987), 1 da (Hannah Sarah Rhodes b 19 April 1982); *Career* architect; Skidmore Owings and Merrill Chicago 1977–78, Montague Assocs Derby 1980–81, Derek Latham and Assocs Derby 1981–85 (assoc 1983–85); projects incl: St Michaels Derby, Veterinary Hospital Derby, Heights of Abraham Cable Car Project and Wirksworth Heritage Centre (Civic Tst award commendations); Building Design Partnership (BDP): joined 1985, assoc 1988–90, ptnr 1990–; projects incl: PowerGen HQ Annexe Coventry, City of Leeds Coll of Music, Carbrook Hall Office Park Sheffield, Grimsby Auditorium (RIBA White Rose Regnl Commendation 1996), Sheffield Hallam Univ 'Campus 21' redevelopment programme (RIBA White Rose Regnl Award 1994); registered architect 1981, RIBA 1981; *Recreations* family and home, visual and performing arts, the built and natural environment, dinghy sailing, Derbyshire well dressing; *Style—* Martin Sutcliffe, Esq; ✉ Building Design Partnership, 38 Carver Street, Sheffield S1 4FY (☎ 0114 273 1641, fax 0114 270 1878, car 0831 476116)

SUTCLIFFE, Col Patrick Malcolm Brogden; CBE (1983, MBE 1966), TD, DL (Hants 1973); s of William Francis Sutcliffe, MRCS, LRCP (d 1959), and Edna Mary, *née* Brogden (d 1978); *b* 21 Oct 1922; *Educ* Marlborough Coll, Pembroke Coll Cambridge (MA); *m* 1950, Dorothy Anne Daly, da of Arnold Daly Briscoe, TD, MB BChir, of Woodbridge, Suffolk; 2 s, 1 da; *Career* Berks Yeo 1942–60, Berks & Westminster Dragoons 1961–67, Lt-Col Royal Berks Territorials 1967–69, Col TA & VR E and SE District 1969–74, vice-chm (Hants) Eastern Wessex TA & VRA 1974 (chm 1975–84 and vice-chm Cncl 1981–84); ADC to HM The Queen 1970; ptnr: Sutcliffe & Son Chartered Surveyors 1956–88, Smiths Gore Chartered Surveyors 1981–85 (conslt 1985–88); FRICS; *Clubs* Army and Navy; *Style—* Col Patrick Sutcliffe, CBE, TD, DL; ✉ Burntwood Farm, Winchester, Hants SO21 1AF (☎ 01962 882384, fax 01962 886788)

SUTCLIFFE, Serena; *b* 1945; *m* David Peppercorn, *qv*; *Career* translator UNESCO; author, conslt and expert on wine; dir Peppercorn and Sutcliffe 1988–91, sr dir Sotheby's London and head of Int Wine Dept Sotheby's 1991–; memb Académie Internationale du Vin; Chevalier dans L'Ordre des Arts et des Lettres; chm Inst Masters of Wine 1994–95; *Books* Wines of The World, Great Vineyards and Winemakers, The Wine Drinker's Handbook, A Celebration of Champagne (Decanter book of the year award 1988), Bollinger (1994), The Wines of Burgundy (1995); *Style—* Serena Sutcliffe; ✉ Sotheby's, 34 & 35 New Bond Street, London W1A 2AA

SUTHERLAND, Alasdair Douglas Scott; s of R W Sutherland (d Colombo Ceylon 1946), and Audrie, *née* Finch Noyes; *b* 13 Oct 1945; *Educ* Tonbridge, Trinity Coll Dublin; *m* 1984, Felicity Bosanquet, *née* Fearnley-Whittingstall; *Career* Publicity Dept Metal Box Co 1966–67, Lexington International PR 1967–68, Burson-Marsteller London 1968–72, ptnr in family restaurant business (Small's Cafe, Maunkberry's, etc) 1972–76, vice pres and divnl dir of mktg communications Burson-Marsteller Hong Kong 1980–82 (joined 1976), dir Good Relations plc and md Good Relations Consumer Ltd 1982–83, jt md Kingsway PR (later Kingsway Rowland, now The Rowland Company) 1983–90; Manning Selvage & Lee: md London and business devpt dir Europe 1990–94, chm London and dir of Euro strategic devpt 1994–; MIPRA 1984 (memb Cncl 1992–, tstee Int PR Fndn 1992–), MIPR 1985 (memb Int Ctee 1988–90); *Recreations* sailing; *Clubs* Foreign Correspondents' (Hong Kong); *Style—* Alasdair Sutherland, Esq; ✉ Manning Selvage & Lee Ltd, 123 Buckingham Palace Road, London SW1W 9SH (☎ 0171 878 3000, fax 0171 878 3030)

SUTHERLAND, Colin John MacLean; QC (Scot 1990); s of Eric Alexander Cruickshank Sutherland, and Mary, *née* Macaulay; *b* 20 May 1954; *Educ* Edinburgh Acad, Univ of Edinburgh (LLB); *m* 1988, Jane Alexander Turnbull; 2 s; *Career* admitted to Faculty of Advocates 1977, advocate depute 1986–89, treas Faculty of Advocates 1994–; *Clubs* Scottish Arts (Edinburgh); *Style—* C J M Sutherland, Esq, QC; ✉ Advocates' Library, Parliament House, Edinburgh EH1 1RF (☎ 0131 226 5071, fax 0131 225 5341)

SUTHERLAND, David George Carr; CBE (1974), MC (1942, and bar 1943), TD, DL (Tweeddale 1974); s of Lt-Col Arthur Henry Carr Sutherland, OBE, MC (d 1962), of Cringletie, Peebles, Scotland, and Ruby, *née* Miller (d 1982); *b* 28 Oct 1920; *Educ* Eton, Sandhurst RMA; *m* 1, Sept 1945, Jean Beatrice (d 1963), da of Evelyn Henderson, of Sedgwick Park, Nr Horsham, Sussex; 1 s (Michael b 1946), 2 da (Sarah (twin) b 1946, Fiona b 1953); m 2, May 1964, Christine Alexandra Hotchkiss, author, of New York; *Career* served WWII Black Watch and SAS: Dunkirk, Western Desert, Aegean, Adriatic (wounded, despatches); various cmd and staff appts 1945–55 incl: Br Mil Mission to Greece, instr Sandhurst, Gold Staff Offr at HM The Queen's Coronation; ret 1955, Cdr 21 SAS Regt (Artists Rifles) TA 1956–60; MOD 1955–80; landowner and farmer 1962–, non-exec dir Asset Protection International Ltd 1981–85, conslt Control Risks Group Ltd 1985–; memb Queen's Body Guard for Scotland (Royal Co of Archers) 1949–; FRGS; awarded Greek War Cross 1944 and 1945, Commemorative medal for distinguished service during liberation of Greece 1991; *Recreations* fishing, shooting, walking; *Clubs* Brooks's, Special Forces; *Style—* David Sutherland, Esq, CBE, MC, TD, DL; ✉ 51 Victoria Rd, London W8; Ferniehaugh, Dolphinton, Tweeddale

SUTHERLAND, Donald Gilmour; s of Robert Brayton Sutherland (d 1973), of Edinburgh, and Annie Brown, *née* Gilmour (d 1988); *b* 15 April 1940; *Educ* George Watsons Coll; *m* 1970, Linda, *née* Malone; 2 s (Hamish b 3 April 1971, Neil b 27 March 1973), 1 da (Polly b 31 Jan 1979); *Career* CA; apprentice W M Home Cook & Coy 1958–63; Whinney Murray: sr accountant 1963–68 (Glasgow 1966–68), ptnr 1968–73; managing ptnr (Edinburgh) Ernst & Whinney 1985–88 (ptnr 1973–95), regnl managing ptnr (South) Ernst & Young 1990–95 (North 1988–90); dir: Standard Life 1990–, CALA plc 1995–, Murray Smaller Markets Tst plc 1995–, Alexander Russell plc 1995–, Quayle Munro Holdings plc 1995–; *Recreations* antique clocks, conservation, golf; *Clubs* New; *Style—* Donald Sutherland, Esq; ✉ Woodside House, Gladsmuir, East Lothian EH33 2AL (☎ 01875 852327)

SUTHERLAND, (Ian) Douglas; s of Col Francis Ian Sinclair Sutherland, OBE, MC, ED (d 1962), of Moffat and Ceylon, and Helen Myrtle Sutherland (d 1988); *b* 23 Oct 1945; *Educ* St Bees Sch Cumberland; *m* 11 Oct 1975, Kathyrn, da of John Henry Wallace (d 1989), of Haltwhistle, Northumberland; 1 s (Jonathan b 6 Nov 1976), 1 da (Iseabail b 13 July 1972); *Career* D M Hall & Son: joined as trainee surveyor 1965, ptnr 1975–, managing ptnr 1994–; memb Co of Merchants of the City of Edinburgh; FRICS 1980; *Clubs* New (Edinburgh), Royal Scots (Edinburgh); *Style—* Douglas Sutherland, Esq; ✉ 2 Ormidale Terrace, Edinburgh EH12 6EQ (☎ 0131 337 5584); D M Hall & Son, Chartered Surveyors, 36 Melville Street, Edinburgh EH3 7HA (☎ 0131 477 6000, fax 0131 477 6029, car tel 0378 330330)

SUTHERLAND, Countess of (24 in line, S circa 1235); Elizabeth Millicent Sutherland; also Lady Strathnaver (strictly speaking a territorial style, but treated as a Lordship for purposes of use as courtesy title for heir to Earldom since the end of the sixteenth century); adopted surname of Sutherland under Scots law 1963; Chief of Clan Sutherland; o da of Lord Alistair St Clair Sutherland-Leveson-Gower, MC (d 1921, s of 4 Duke of Sutherland, KG, and Lady Millicent St Clair-Erskine, da of 4 Earl of Rosslyn), and Elizabeth Hélène, *née* Demarest (d 1931); suc to Earldom of Sutherland held by unc, 5 Duke of Sutherland, KT, PC, 1963 (thus came about precisely the contingency that might have caused objection to be made when the Dukedom was so named on its creation 130 years earlier in 1833, *viz* that because the latter was heritable in tail male while the Earldom not only could be held by a female but actually was (by the 1 Duke's wife) at the time of the cr, the two might become separated; the then Countess of Sutherland in her own right (gggg mother of present Countess) was known as the 'Duchess-Countess' in a style analogous to that of the Spanish Count-Duke Olivares of the seventeenth century; *b* 30 March 1921; *Educ* Queen's Coll Harley St, abroad; *m* 5 Jan 1946, Charles Noel Janson, eldest s of late Charles Wilfrid Janson, of

16 Wilton Crescent, London SW1; 2 s (Alistair, Martin (twins)), 1 s (Matthew decd), 1 da (Annabel); *Heir* s, Lord Strathnaver; *Career* serv Land Army 1939–41; hosp laboratory technician: Raigmore Hosp Inverness, St Thomas's Hosp London; chm: Northern Times 1963–88, Dunrobin Sch Ltd 1965–72, Dunrobin Castle Ltd 1972–; *Recreations* reading, swimming; *Style*— The Rt Hon the Countess of Sutherland; ✉ 39 Edwardes Sq, London W8; Dunrobin Castle, Golspie, Sutherland; House of Tongue, by Lairg, Sutherland

SUTHERLAND, Euan Ross; CB (1993); s of Dr Alister Sutherland (d 1983), and Margaret Louisa, *née* Carter (d 1994); *b* 24 Nov 1943; *Educ* Kingswood Sch Bath, Balliol Coll Oxford (BA); *m* 1967 (m dis 1995), Katharine Mary, da of Dr Daniel Jenkins; 1 s (Daniel b 1974), 1 da (Eleanor b 1978); *Career* practised at the Bar 1970–74; Office of the Parly Counsel: joined 1974, seconded to Law Cmmn 1979–80, seconded to Govt of Solomon Islands 1980–81, seconded to Law Cmmn 1986–88, currently Parly counsel; *Recreations* music, gardening, hill walking; *Style*— Euan Sutherland, Esq, CB; ✉ Office of the Parliamentary Counsel, 36 Whitehall, London SW1A 2AY (☎ 0171 210 6636)

SUTHERLAND, Dr George Roberton (Roy); s of George Roberton Sutherland (d 1993), of Milngavie, Glasgow, and Barbara Barnett, *née* Smith; *b* 15 Dec 1931; *Educ* George Heriot's Sch Edinburgh, Univ of Edinburgh (MB ChB); *m* 22 March 1963, Lorna Hunter, da of Dr Thomas Rodger Murray (d 1989), of Glasgow; 2 da (Fiona b 1965, Karen b 1968); *Career* Flt Lt RAF 1957–58 (Flying Offr 1956–57); Univ of Edinburgh: lectr Dept of Med 1959–64, hon clinical lectr Dept of Radiology 1966–68; conslt radiologist: S Gen Hosp Glasgow 1968–77, (i/c) Stobhill Gen Hosp Glasgow 1977–87, (i/c) Royal Infirmary and Stobhill Gen Hosp Glasgow 1987–92, ret; hon clinical sr lectr Dept of Radiology Univ of Glasgow 1972–92, ret; conslt radiologist Nuffield Hosp and Bon Secours Hosp Glasgow 1983–; former: pres Scottish Radiological Soc, chm Standing Scot Ctee, memb Faculty Bd and chm Computer Ctee RCR, memb Governing Body The Queen's Coll Glasgow; memb: BMA, RSGB; elder St George's-Tron Church Glasgow; FRCR 1968, FRCPE 1973, FRCPG 1986; *Books* Textbook of Radiology by Sutton (contrib chapter on Eye and Orbit); *Recreations* golf, classic cars, electronics, boating; *Clubs* Royal Air Force; *Style*— Dr Roy Sutherland; ✉ 22 Montrose Drive, Bearsden, Glasgow G61 3LG (☎ 0141 9427802), Tigh Na Lachan, Stuckrioch, by Strachur Strathlachlan, Argyllshire PA27 8BZ (☎ 01369 860605); Nuffield Hospital, Beaconsfield Rd, Glasgow (☎ 0141 334 9441)

SUTHERLAND, Dr James; CBE (1974); s of James Sutherland, JP (d 1951), and Agnes, *née* Walker; *b* 15 Feb 1920; *Educ* Queen's Park Secdy Sch Glasgow, Glasgow Univ (MA, LLB, LLD); *m* 1, 6 Sept 1948, Elizabeth Kelly Barr; 2 s (David b 1949, Malcolm b 1952, d 1975); m 2, 27 Sept 1984, Grace Williamson Dawson; *Career* Royal Signals 1940–46; ptnr McClure Naismith Anderson & Gardiner (solicitors) Glasgow Edinburgh and London 1951–87 (conslt 1987–90); examiner Univ of Glasgow: in Scot law 1951–55, in mercantile and industrial law 1968–69; chm Glasgow South Nat Insurance Tribunal 1964–66; memb Law Soc of Scotland Cncl 1959–77 (vice pres 1969–70, pres 1972–74), memb Int Bar Assoc Cncl 1972– (chm Gen Practices Section 1978–80, sec gen 1980–84, pres 1984–86); chm Glasgow Maternity and Women's Hosps 1966–74, vice chm Glasgow Eastern Health Cncl 1975–77, dean of Royal Faculty of Procurators in Glasgow 1977–80; memb: Gen Dental Cncl 1975–89, Ct of Strathclyde Univ 1977–92; Deacon Incorporation of Barbers Glasgow 1962–63; Hon LLD Glasgow 1985; *Recreations* golf; *Clubs* Royal and Ancient, Western (Glasgow); *Style*— Dr James Sutherland, CBE; ✉ Greenacres, 20/1 Easter Belmont Road, Edinburgh EH12 6EX (☎ 0131 337 1888, fax 0131 346 0067); Johnston Court, St Andrews, Fife

SUTHERLAND, (Robert) James Mackay; s of James Fleming Sutherland (d 1932), of Knockbrex, Kirkcudbright, Scot, and Edith Mary, *née* Meredith (d 1964); *b* 3 Nov 1922; *Educ* Stowe, Trinity Coll Cambridge (BA); *m* 7 June 1947, Anthea, da of John Christopher Hyland (d 1961), of Donegal, Ireland; 2 da (Chloe Helena Meredith b 15 Sept 1952, Sabina Rachel b 20 Nov 1954); *Career* RNVR 1943–46, Lt; asst civil engr: Sir William Halcrow & Partners 1946–56, A J Harris 1956–58; Harris & Sutherland: ptnr 1958–87, active conslt 1987–; author of various chapters and papers on engineering and engineering history; memb Royal Fine Art Cmmn 1986–96, former pres Newcomen Soc for the Study of Hist of Sci and Technol 1987–89; memb various ctees incl: Br Standards Inst, English Heritage; FEng 1986, FICE, FIStructE (vice pres 1980–82); *Recreations* engineering history, architectural travel and photography; *Clubs* Travellers'; *Style*— James Sutherland, Esq, FEng; ✉ 4 Pitt St, London W8 4NX (☎ 0171 938 1169, fax 0171 938 4939)

SUTHERLAND, Dame Joan; OM (1991), AC (1975), DBE (1979, CBE 1961); da of William Sutherland, of Sydney; *b* 7 Nov 1926; *Educ* St Catherine's Waverley; *m* 1954, Richard Bonynge, *qv*; 1 s; *Career* opera singer; debut Sydney 1947, Royal Opera House Covent Garden 1952; performed in operas at: Glyndebourne, La Scala Milan, Vienna State Opera, Metropolitan Opera NY; has made numerous recordings; *Style*— Dame Joan Sutherland, OM, AC, DBE; ✉ c/o Ingpen & Williams, 14 Kensington Court, London, W8 5DN (☎ 0171 937 5158, fax 0171 938 4175)

SUTHERLAND, 6 Duke of (UK 1833); Sir John Sutherland Egerton; 13 Bt (E 1620), TD, DL (Berwicks); also 5 Earl of Ellesmere (UK 1846), which known as 1944–63 (when he inherited the Dukedom); also Baron Gower (GB 1703), Earl Gower and Viscount Trentham (GB 1746), Marquess of Stafford (GB 1786), Viscount Brackley (UK 1846); s of 4 Earl of Ellesmere (d 1944), and Lady Violet Lambton, da of 4 Earl of Durham; *b* 10 May 1915; *Educ* Eton, Trinity Coll Cambridge; *m* 1, 1939, Lady Diana Percy (d 1978), da of 8 Duke of Northumberland; m 2, 1979, Evelyn, da of late Maj Robert Moubray (whose w Claire was gda of Sir Charles Morrison-Bell, 1 Bt); *Heir* kinsman, Francis Ronald Egerton b 18 Feb 1940; *Career* late Capt RAC (TA), serv WWII (POW); *Style*— His Grace the Duke of; ✉ Mertoun, St Boswell's, Melrose, Roxburghshire; Lingay Cottage, Hall Farm, Newmarket, Suffolk

SUTHERLAND, Dr Mackenzie Stewart; s of Sinclair Millar Sutherland (d 1969), of Carluke, Scot, and Elsie, *née* Shand; *b* 31 March 1933; *Educ* Univ of Aberdeen (MB ChB, DPM, Dip in Psychotherapy); *m* 20 June 1962, Una Marguerite, da of John George Weir (d 1982), of Aberdeen; 1 s (Grant b 1969), 1 da (Shona b 1963); *Career* RAC 5th Royal Tank Regt Korea 1952–54; jr med posts 1962–72; N Tees Gen Hosp: conslt psychiatrist 1972–94, sr conslt 1987–94, chm Div of Psychiatry 1988–90; MRCPsych 1972; *Recreations* squash, golf, philately; *Style*— Dr Mackenzie Sutherland; ✉ 70 Chestnut Drive, Marton, Cleveland (☎ 01642 315712)

SUTHERLAND, Sir Maurice; kt (1976); s of Thomas Daniel Sutherland (d 1953); *b* 12 July 1915; *Educ* Stockton Secdy Sch; *m* 1, 1941, Beatrice Skinner; 1 s; m 2, 1960, Jane Ellen; 1 step da; m 3, 1984, Ellen Margaret; 1 step s; *Career* slr; ldr Teesside County BC 1968–74 (mayor 1972–73), ldr Cleveland CC 1974–77 and 1981–85 (ldr of oppn 1977–81); *Style*— Sir Maurice Sutherland; ✉ 8 Manor Close, Low Worsall, Yarm, Cleveland

SUTHERLAND, (John Alexander) Muir; s of John Alexander Sutherland (d 1988), and Eleanor, *née* Muir (d 1936); *b* 5 April 1933; *Educ* Trinity Coll Glenalmond, Hertford Coll Oxford (MA); *m* 26 March 1970, Mercedes Gonzalez; 2 s (Alejandro b 1 July 1971, Stuart b 2 May 1974); *Career* Nat Serv 2 Lt Highland Light Infantry 1951–53; head of presentation and planning Border Television 1963–66, prog coordinator ABC Television 1966–68; Thames Television: prog coordinator 1968–72, controller int sales 1973–74, md Thames TV International 1975–82, dir of progs 1982–86; dir Celtic Films Ltd 1986–; *Recreations* golf; *Clubs* Club De Campo (Madrid); *Style*— Muir Sutherland, Esq; ✉ Celtic Films Ltd, 1/2 Bromley Place, London W1P 5HB (☎ 0171 637 7651, fax 0171 436 5387, telex 264639)

SUTHERLAND, Peter Denis William; s of William George Sutherland, of Dublin, and Barbara, *née* Nealon; *b* 25 April 1946; *Educ* Gonzaga Coll, Univ Coll Dublin (BCL), Hon Soc of the King's Inns; *m* 18 Sept 1971, Maruja Cabria Valcarcel, da of Paulino Cabria Garcia, of Reinosa, Santander, Spain; 2 s (Shane b 1972, Ian b 1974), 1 da (Natalia b 1979); *Career* called to the Bar: King's Inns 1968, Middle Temple 1976; attorney of New York Bar, admitted to practice before the Supreme Ct of the US, practising memb of Irish Bar 1968–81 (sr counsel 1980); tutor in law Univ Coll Dublin 1969–71, memb Cncl of State of Ireland and attorney-gen of Ireland 1981–Aug 1982 and Dec 1982–84; Cmmr of EC for Competition and Relations with Euro Parl 1985–89; visiting fell Kennedy Sch of Govt Univ of Harvard 1989, visiting prof Univ Coll Dublin 1989–93; chm Allied Irish Banks 1989–93 (non-exec dir 1995–), dir gen GATT 1993–95, dir gen World Trade Organisation 1995; dep chm British Petroleum plc 1995– (non-exec dir 1990–93 and 1995–); head Euro ops Goldman Sachs Ltd 1995–, chm and md Goldman Sachs International Nov 1995–; dir: Investor 1995–, Delta Airlines 1995–, Asea Brown Boveri (ABB) 1996–, L M Ericsson 1996–; chm Bd of Govrs Euro Inst of Public Admin Maastricht; Bencher Hon Soc of King's Inns Dublin; Hon LLD: St Louis Univ 1985, Nat Univ of Ireland, Dublin City Univ, Holy Cross Univ, Trinity Coll Dublin, The Open Univ, Suffolk Univ Mass, Univ of Bath; Grand Cross Order of Leopold II (Belgium), Grand Cross of Civil Merit (Spain), Chevalier of the Legion d'Honneur (France), Centenary Medal (NZ), Euro Parl Gold Medal, Commandeur du Wissam (Morocco), Order of Rio Branco (Brazil); *Books* 1er Janvier 1993 - çe qui va changer en Europe (1988); *Recreations* tennis, reading; *Clubs* FitzWilliam Lawn Tennis (Dublin), Lansdowne Rugby Football, Royal Irish Yacht, Milltown Golf; *Style*— Peter Sutherland, SC; ✉ Goldman Sachs International, Peterborough Court, 133 Fleet Street, London EC4A 2BB (☎ 0171 774 1000, fax 0171 774 4001)

SUTHERLAND, Dr Sheena (Lady Sutherland); da of John William Robertson (d 1975), and Christina, *née* McLeman; *b* 4 Dec 1938; *Educ* Fraserburgh Acad, Univ of Aberdeen (MB ChB); *m* 1 Aug 1964, Prof Sir Stewart Ross Sutherland, *qv*, 1 s (Duncan Stewart b 1970), 2 da (Fiona Mair b 1966, Kirsten Ann b 1968); *Career* registrar Inst of Virology Glasgow 1975–77, lectr Middx Hosp Med Sch 1978–84, conslt virologist Public Health Laboratory Dulwich 1985–94, hon sr lectr King's Coll Sch of Med and Dentistry 1985–94, hon conslt Camberwell Health Authy 1985–94, sr lectr in med microbiology Univ of Edinburgh 1995–; MRCPath 1982; *Recreations* weaving, gardening, crafts, theatre; *Clubs* Royal Soc of Med; *Style*— Dr Sheena Sutherland; ✉ 14 Heriot Row, Edinburgh EH3 6HP (work ☎ 0131 650 3151)

SUTHERLAND, Stephen William; s of John Stuart Sutherland, of Salisbury, Wilts, and Sylvia Florence, *née* Lock; *b* 15 Feb 1956; *Educ* Bishop Wordsworth's GS Salisbury, Christ Church Oxford (BA); *Career* Melody Maker: reporter/feature writer 1981–84, reviews ed 1984–86, features ed 1986–88, asst ed 1988–92; ed New Musical Express 1992–, ed Vox Magazine 1995–; *Books* 10 Imaginary Years (with Robert James Smith, *qv* of The Cure, 1988); *Recreations* football; *Clubs* Mortons; *Style*— Steve Sutherland, Esq; ✉ IPC Magazines, New Musical Express, 25th Floor, King's Reach Tower, Stamford Street, London SE1 9LS (☎ 0171 261 6471, fax 0171 261 5185)

SUTHERLAND, Prof Sir Stewart Ross; kt (1995); s of George Arthur Caswell Sutherland (d 1974), of Aberdeen, and Ethel, *née* Masson; *b* 25 Feb 1941; *Educ* Robert Gordon's Coll Aberdeen, Univ of Aberdeen (MA), Corpus Christi Coll Cambridge (MA); *m* 1 Aug 1964, Dr Sheena Sutherland, *qv*, da of John Robertson (d 1975), of Fraserburgh; 1 s (Duncan Stewart b 9 March 1970), 2 da (Fiona Mair b 11 Dec 1966, Kirsten Ann b 20 Aug 1968); *Career* asst lectr UCNW 1965–68; Univ of Stirling: lectr 1968, sr lectr 1972, reader 1976–77; King's Coll London: prof of history and philosophy of religion 1977–85, fell 1983, vice princ 1981–85, princ 1985–90; vice chancellor Univ of London 1990–94, princ and vice-chllr Univ of Edinburgh 1994–; HM chief inspector of schools HM Inspectorate 1992–94; memb: C of E Bd of Educn 1980–84, UGC Arts Sub-Ctee 1983–85, City Parochial Fndn 1988–90, NW Thames Health Authy 1992–94, Hong Kong Cncl for Academic Accreditation 1992–95, Cncl for Science and Technol 1993–, Humanities Res Bd 1994–95, Hong Kong VGC 1995–; chm: Br Acad Postgrad Studentships Ctee 1987–94, Ethiopian Gemini Tst 1987–92, CVCP Academic Standards Gp 1988–92, Cncl Royal Inst of Philosophy 1988–, London Conf on Overseas Students 1989–93, Ctee of Review Scottish Appeals 1994–96; vice chm Ctee of Vice Chancellors and Principals 1989–92; ed Religious Studies 1984–90; memb Editorial Bd: Scottish Journal of Religious Studies 1980–, Modern Theology 1984–91; pres Soc for the Study of Theology 1985 and 1986, assoc fell Centre for Philosphy and Literature Univ of Warwick 1986–94; Liveryman Worshipful Co of Goldsmiths 1991 (Freeman 1986); Hon LHD: Coll of Wooster Ohio USA, Cwlth Univ of Virginia 1992, New York Univ 1996; Hon LLD: Univ of Aberdeen, Nat Univ of Ireland 1992; Hon DUniv Univ of Stirling 1993; Hon DLitt: Richmond Coll 1995, Univ of Wales 1996; Dr hc Uppsala 1995; hon fell: CCC Cambridge 1989, UC Bangor 1991, Coll of Preceptors 1994; FRSA 1986, FBA 1992, FRSE 1995; *Books* Atheism and Rejection of God (1977, 2 edn 1980), The Philosophical Frontiers of Christian Theology (ed with B L Hebblethwaite, 1983), God, Jesus and Belief (1984), Faith and Ambiguity (1984), The World's Religions (ed, 1988); author of numerous articles in books and learned jls; *Recreations* Tassie medallions, jazz, theatre; *Clubs* Athenaeum; *Style*— Prof Sir Stewart Sutherland, FRSE, FBA; ✉ University of Edinburgh, Old College, South Bridge, Edinburgh EH8 9YL (☎ 0131 650 2150)

SUTHERLAND, Prof (Norman) Stuart; s of Norman McCleod Sutherland (d 1979), and Cecelia Dickson, *née* Jackson; *b* 26 March 1927; *Educ* King Edward's HS Birmingham, Univ of Oxford (MA, DPhil); *m* 3 July 1954, Jose Louise, da of Michael Fogden; 2 da (Gay b 3 March 1959, Julia Claire b 7 Aug 1961); *Career* Sergeant RAF 1949–51; Univ of Oxford: fell Magdalen Coll 1954–58, res dir in experimental psychology 1956–64, fell Merton Coll 1959–64; prof Mass Inst of Technol USA 1960–61 and 1962–63; Univ of Sussex: prof of experimental psychology 1964–92 (prof emeritus 1992), dir Centre for Res in Perception and Cognition 1969–92; ed Quarterly Jl Experimental Psychology 1970–72; dir: William Schlackman Ltd 1978–88, Deedland Ltd 1987–; memb Int Brain Soc; hon fell Experimental Psychology Soc 1994 (pres 1975–77); *Books* Quarterly Jl Experimental Psychology Monograph (1961), Animal Discrimination Learning (ed with R M Gilbert, 1969), Mechanisms of Animal Discrimination Learning (with N J Mackintosh, 1971), Brain and Behaviour (with O Wolthuis, 1972), National Attitudes held by European Executives (with V Selwyn, 1974), Breakdown: A Personal Crisis and a Medical Dilemma (1976, revised 1987), Tutorial Essays in Psychology (ed Vol 1 1977, Vol 2 1979), Prestel and the User (1980), Discovering the Human Mind (1982), Men Change Too (1987), Macmillan Dictionary of Psychology (1989), Irrationality: The Enemy Within (1992); *Recreations* buildings; *Style*— Prof Stuart Sutherland; ✉ Department of Experimental Psychology, University of Sussex, Falmer, Brighton (☎ 01273 678304)

SUTHERLAND, HE Veronica Evelyn; CMG (1988); da of Lt-Col M G Beckett, KOYLI (d 1949), and Constance Mary, *née* Cavenagh-Mainwaring; *b* 25 April 1939; *Educ* Royal Sch Bath, Univ of London (BA), Univ of Southampton (MA); *m* 29 Dec 1981, Alex James, s of James Sutherland (d 1969); *Career* third later second sec FCO 1965, second sec Copenhagen 1967, first sec FCO 1970, first sec (Devpt) New Delhi 1975, FCO 1978, cnsllr and perm UK del UNESCO 1981, cnsllr FCO 1984, HM ambassador Abidjan 1987, asst under sec of State (Personnel) FCO 1990–95, HM ambass Dublin 1995–; *Recreations* painting; *Style*— HE Mrs Veronica E Sutherland, CMG; ✉ c/o FCO (Dublin), King Charles Street, London SW1A 2AH

SUTHERLAND, Sir William George MacKenzie; kt (1988), QPM; *b* 12 Nov 1933; *Educ* Inverness Technical HS; *m* Jennie; 2 da; *Career* Cheshire Police 1954–73, Surrey Police 1973–75, Hertfordshire Police 1975–79; chief constable: Bedfordshire Police 1979–83, Lothian and Borders Police 1983–96; HM Chief Inspr of Constabulary for Scotland 1996–; FRSA; *Recreations* squash, hill-walking; *Style*— Sir William Sutherland, QPM; ✉ HM Inspectorate of Constabulary, 2 Greenside Lane, Edinburgh EH1 3AH (☎ 0131 244 5614)

SUTHERS, Martin William; OBE (1988); s of Rev Canon George Suthers (d 1965), of Newcastle upon Tyne, and Susie Mary, *née* Jobson (d 1984); *b* 27 June 1940; *Educ* Dulwich, Christ's Coll Cambridge (Harvey exhibitioner, MA); *m* 1, April 1970 (m dis 1988), Daphne Joan, da of Stuart Glanville Oxland; m 2, March 1990, Philippa Leah, da of Denis Ray Melville De La Borde; *Career* articled clerk then asst slr Wells & Hind slrs Nottingham 1961–66, conveyancing asst Clerk's Dept Notts County Council 1966–69, asst slr Fishers Burton-on-Trent 1969–70; Messrs J A Simpson, Coulby: asst slr 1970–71, ptnr 1971–, sr ptnr 1992–; chm Queen's Med Centre Nottingham Univ NHS Tst 1993–; cncllr (C) Nottingham City Cncl 1967–69 and 1976–95 (Lord Mayor 1988–89), Parly candidate (C) W Nottingham gen election 1970; chm: W Nottingham Cons Assoc 1974–77, City of Nottingham Cons Fedn 1983–87, Notts Valuation Tbnl 1990– (memb Notts Local Valuation Panel 1976–90); memb Cncl Univ of Nottingham 1987–; vice pres (designate) Notts Law Soc 1996 (Parly liaison offr 1989–); hon sec Notts Wildlife Tst 1983–; memb Law Soc 1965; *Recreations* ornithology; *Style*— Martin Suthers, Esq, OBE; ✉ Messrs J A Simpson, Coulby, 27 Regent St, Nottingham NG1 5DE (☎ 0115 941 1357, fax 0115 948 3476)

SUTRO, Joan Maud; da of Arthur Bertram Colyer (d 1976), and Florence Maud, *née* Maycroft (d 1982); *Educ* Farnborough Hill Convent, Bedford HS, Coll De Jeunes Filles Dreux; *m* 29 March 1941, Edward Leopold, MC (d 1978), s of Leopold Sutro (d 1943); 1 s (decd), 2 da (Caroline Alexandra b 1943, Rosemary Jane b 1945); *Career* WWII served Balkans 1939–41; memb: Godstone Rural Dist Cncl 1948–52, Surrey Div Exec for Educn; chm Int Social Service Spring Fair 1974–79 (patron 1980–); Women's Cncl: chm 1980–84, chm Delgn to China 1982, diplomatic liaison offr 1990–; translated and adapted play Auguste by Raymond Castans (produced by BBC Radio and for the stage in S Africa), made various bdcasts on theatre and travel in UK and abroad, also appeared on Australian TV; memb Royal Inst of Int Affrs 1944–; memb Bd: Open Space Theatre 1973–77, Round House Theatre 1977–83; vice pres Anglo-Turkish Soc 1983–, vice chm London Central Branch European Union of Women 1991–92; govr: Oxted Co Sch 1950–71, Central Sch of Speech & Drama 1956–; *Recreations* travel to remote places, theatre; *Style*— Mrs Edward Sutro; ✉ 12 South Eaton Place, London SW1W 9JA

SUTTIE, Ian Alexander; *b* 8 June 1945; *Educ* Robert Gordons Coll Aberdeen, Univ of Aberdeen (CA); *m* 1 Dec 1971, Dorothy Elizabeth, *née* Small; 1 s (Martin b 1978), 2 da (Julia b 1974, Fiona b 1976); *Career* chm and md: Wellserv plc, Tank Rentals plc, Harran Engineering Ltd, Marischal Industrial Services Ltd, Offshore Rentals Ltd, Offshore Rentals Norge AS, Fishing Services Ltd, Downhole Technology Ltd, Oilwell Production Services Ltd, Mid Europe Supply Ltd, Quality Commissioning Ltd, International Petroleum Equipment Ltd; chm: Orwell Group plc, Enaco plc, Pump Systems Ltd; dir: Elbora Ltd, Handling Equipment Services Ltd, IDJ Properties Ltd, Pump Rentals (International) Ltd, Integrated Well Services Ltd, Tripos Ltd; MICAS; *Recreations* golf, curling; *Clubs* Aberdeen Petroleum, Royal Northern & Univ; *Style*— Ian A Suttie, Esq; ✉ Parklea, North Deeside Rd, Pitfodels, Aberdeen AB15 9PB (☎ 01224 861389, fax 01224 869541); Orwell House, Souterhead Rd, Altens, Aberdeen

SUTTON, Alan John; s of William Clifford Sutton (d 1964), of Abertillery, and Emily, *née* Batten (d 1992); *b* 16 March 1936; *Educ* Hafod-Y-Ddôl GS, Bristol Univ (BSc); *m* 7 Sept 1957, Glenis, da of George Henry (d 1986), of Ebbw Vale; 1 s (Andrew Jonathan b 1964), 1 da (Lisa Jayne b 1963); *Career* chief engr English Electric 1957–62, sales mangr Solartron 1962–69, md AB Connectors 1969–76, industl dir Welsh Office 1976–79, exec dir Welsh Devpt Agency 1979–88, chm and chief exec Anglolink Ltd 1988–; MIEE 1962; *Recreations* golf, walking; *Style*— Alan Sutton, Esq; ✉ Brockton House, Heol-y-Delyn, Lisvane, Cardiff CF4 5SR (☎ 01222 753194, fax 01222 747037)

SUTTON, Andrew; s of William Stanley Sutton, of Birkenhead, Wirral, and Evelyn Margaret, *née* Kitchin; *b* 27 Aug 1947; *Educ* Jesus Coll Cambridge (MA); *Career* ptnr Price Waterhouse London 1978–; vice pres Opportunities for the Disabled, memb Cncl Bede House Assoc; Freeman City of London 1988; FCA 1979; *Recreations* walking, opera, music, reading; *Clubs* United Oxford and Cambridge Univ; *Style*— Andrew Sutton, Esq; ✉ 82 New Crane Wharf, Wapping High Street, London E1 9TU (☎ 0171 481 1872); Price Waterhouse, Southwark Towers, 32 London Bridge St, London SE1 9SY (☎ 0171 939 3000, fax 0171 939 2655)

SUTTON, Andrew Waugh; s of Edward James Sutton, of Leamington Spa, and Joyce Christine, *née* Plant; *b* 6 July 1945; *Educ* Leamington Coll for Boys, RCA (MDes, Leverhulme scholarship); *Career* design conslt and lectr; ctee memb: Design and Industs Assoc, CSD; external examiner London Guildhall Univ; *Style*— Andrew Sutton, Esq; ✉ 136 Coldharbour Lane, Camberwell, London SE5 9PZ (☎ 0171 274 6345)

SUTTON, Andrew William; *b* 4 Oct 1939; *Educ* Brentwood Sch, Univ of Birmingham, Aston Univ; *m* 13 July 1964, Kay, da of Lionel Edge, of Birmingham; 1 s (Benjamin b 21 Feb 1969), 1 da (Rebecca b 6 April 1967); *Career* psychologist: Newport (Mon) 1965–67, Birmingham 1968–84; Univ of Birmingham: hon lectr in educnl psychology 1970–84, assoc Centre for Russian & E Euro Studies 1980–, hon res fell Dept of Psychology 1984–; chief exec Fndn for Conductive Educn 1986–; hon conductor Peto Inst Budapest 1990; ed The Conductor magazine; *Books* jtly: Home, School and Leisure in the Soviet Union (1980), Reconstructing Psychological Practice (1981), Conductive Education (1985); *Recreations* gardening, garden-railways, postcards; *Style*— Andrew Sutton, Esq; ✉ 78 Clarendon St, Leamington Spa, Warwicks CV32 4PE (☎ and fax 01926 311966); The Foundation For Conductive Education, Cannon Hill House Russell Road, Birmingham B13 8RD (☎ 0121 449 1569, fax 0121 449 1611)

SUTTON, Barry Bridge; JP (Taunton); s of Albert Sutton (d 1976), of Taunton, and Ethel Ada, *née* Bridge; *b* 21 Jan 1937; *Educ* Eltham Coll, Peterhouse Coll Cambridge (MA), Univ of Bristol (DipEd); *m* 12 Aug 1961, Margaret Helen, da of (Edward) Thomas Palmer (d 1986); 1 s (Mark b 1964), 2 da (Clare b 1965, Jane b 1968); *Career* housemaster and sr history master Wycliffe Coll Stonehouse Glos 1961–75; headmaster: Hereford Cathedral Sch 1975–87, Taunton Sch 1987–; chm: Ctee of the Cncl of Scout Assoc, Somerset Scout Cncl; memb: HMC, Historical Assoc; *Recreations* mountain walking; *Clubs* East India, Devonshire, Sports, Public Schools; *Style*— Barry Sutton, Esq, JP; ✉ Headmaster's House, Private Road, Staplegrove, Taunton TA2 6AJ (☎ 01823 272 588); Taunton School, Taunton TA2 6AD (☎ 01823 349224)

SUTTON, Chris Roy; *b* 10 March 1973; *m* 31 Jan 1995, Samantha, *née* Williamson; *Career* professional footballer; Norwich City 1989–94; Blackburn Rovers: transferred for fee of £5m 1994, winners FA Premier League 1994/95; former England under-21 player; *Style*— Chris Sutton, Esq; ✉ c/o Blackburn Rovers FC, Ewood Park, Blackburn BB2 4JF (☎ 01254 55432)

SUTTON, Dr George Christopher; *b* 4 Feb 1934; *Educ* Rugby, Corpus Christi Coll Cambridge (MD, MA), UCH Med Sch London; *m* 7 Feb 1959, Angela Elizabeth, *née* Dornan-Fox; 3 da (Sarah-Jane b 1962, Caroline b 1965, Rachel b 1967); *Career* med registrar St George's Hosp London 1963–67 (Addenbrooke's Hosp Cambridge 1962–63), fell in cardiology Univ of N Carolina Chapel Hill Med Sch 1965–66, sr registrar in cardiology Brompton Hosp London 1967–71, conslt cardiologist Hillingdon Hosp Middx 1972–, hon conslt Harefield Hosp Middx 1972–, sr lectr in cardiology Nat Heart and Lung Inst London 1972–, hon conslt Royal Brompton and Nat Heart and Lung Hosp London 1972–; author of various scientific papers on cardiology; memb: Br Cardiac Soc (Cncl 1982–86), Euro Soc of Cardiology; FRCP 1977, FACC 1977; *Books* Physiological and Clinical Aspects of Cardiac Auscultation, an audio-visual programme (1967), Slide Atlas of Cardiology (1978), An Introduction to Echocardiography (1978), Clinical and Investigatory Features of Cardiac Pathology (1988); *Recreations* watching cricket, golf, music, photography; *Clubs* MCC; *Style*— Dr George Sutton; ✉ Cardiology Dept, Hillingdon Hospital, Pield Heath Rd, Uxbridge, Middx UB8 3NN (☎ 01895 256509, fax 01895 256509)

SUTTON, Graham Charles; s of Charles James Sutton (d 1975), and Ruby Ethel, *née* Moorecroft (d 1984); *b* 29 Aug 1942; *Educ* Brentwood Sch, Coll of Estate Mgmnt; *m* 12 March 1966, Elizabeth Anne, da of Robert Woodman, of Gidea Park, Essex; 2 s (Matthew b 1968, Christopher b 1971); *Career* articled pupil asst Stanley Hicks & Son 1959–66, asst surveyor DTZ Debenham Thorpe 1966–68, sr ptnr Freeth Melhuish 1982– (asst surveyor 1969–72, ptnr 1972–82); Freeman City of London 1982, Liveryman Worshipful Co of Coopers; FRICS 1965, IRRV 1971; *Recreations* shooting, windsurfing, flying; *Clubs* City Livery, Surveyors 1894, Soc of Old Brentwoods, St Stephen's Constitutional; *Style*— Graham Sutton, Esq; ✉ 24 Holywell Hill, St Albans, Herts AL1 1BZ (☎ 01727 848680, fax 01727 851745)

SUTTON, Prof John; s of John Sutton, and Marie, *née* Hammond; *b* 10 Aug 1948; *Educ* Univ Coll Dublin (BSc), Trinity Coll Dublin (MSc(Econ)), Univ of Sheffield (PhD); *m* 1974, Jean, da of Frank Drechsler; 2 da (Gillian b 4 Sept 1979, Katherine b 23 Nov 1981), 1 s (Christopher b 2 Nov 1984); *Career* lectr Univ of Sheffield 1973–77; LSE: lectr 1977–84, reader 1984–88, prof 1988–; visiting prof: Univ of Tokyo 1981, Univ of California at San Diego 1986; Marvin Bower fell Harvard Business Sch 1990–91; memb Advsy Cncl Access to Japanese Markets (JETRO/MITI) Tokyo 1995–; Franqui medal 1992; fell Econometric Soc 1991, FBA 1996; *Books* Protection and Industrial Policy in Europe (jtly, 1986), Sunk Costs and Market Structure (1991); *Style*— Prof John Sutton, FBA; ✉ London School of Economics and Political Science, Houghton Street, London WC2A 2AE (☎ 0171 955 7716)

SUTTON, Air Marshal Sir John Matthias Dobson; KCB (1986, CB 1980); s of Harry Rowston Sutton (d 1990), of Alford, Lincs, and Gertrude, *née* Dobson (d 1979); *b* 9 July 1932; *Educ* Queen Elizabeth GS Alford Lincs; *m* 1, 25 Sept 1954 (m dis 1968), Delia Eleanor, *née* Woodward; 1 s (Shaun b 13 Feb 1961), 1 da (Shenagh b 22 Jan 1957); m 2, 23 May 1969, Angela Faith, da of Wing Cdr G J Gray, DFC, of Fowey, Cornwall; 2 s (Mark b 13 April 1971, Stephen b 8 Oct 1972); *Career* joined RAF 1950, pilot trg (cmmnd) 1951, Fighter Sqdns UK and Germany 1952–61, Staff Coll 1963, CO 249 Sqdn 1964–66, asst sec Chief of Staff's Ctee 1966–69, OC 14 Sqdn 1970–71, asst chief of staff (plans and policy) HQ 2 ATAF 1971–73, staff chief of def staff 1973–74, RCDS 1975, cmdt Central Flying Sch 1976–77, asst chief of air staff (policy) 1977–79, dep Cdr RAF Germany 1980–82, asst chief of def staff (commitments) 1982–84, asst chief of def staff (overseas) 1985, AOC-in-C RAF Support Command 1986–89; Lt-Govr and C-in-C Jersey 1990–95; govr Nene Coll of HE 1996–; KStJ 1990; *Recreations* golf, skiing; *Clubs* RAF, Luffenham Heath Golf; *Style*— Air Marshal Sir John Sutton, KCB

SUTTON, John Sydney; CBE (1996); s of Sydney Sutton, of Lordswood, Southampton, and Mabel Bessie Sutton; *b* 9 June 1936; *Educ* King Edward VI Sch Southampton, Univ of Keele (BA, MA); *m* 23 Aug 1961, Carmen Grandoso Martinez, da of Matias Grandoso Astorga (d 1970), and Maria Luisa Martinez Gonzalez (d 1996); 3 s (John Anthony b 1963, Robert Michael b 1964, Alexander Matthew Sydney b 1967); *Career* asst teacher Christopher Wren Sch London 1958–60, asst master then head of history Bemrose Sch Derby 1960–68, head Social Studies Dept Sir Wilfrid Martineau Sch Birmingham 1968–73; headmaster: Corby GS 1973, Southwood Sch Corby 1973–82, Queen Elizabeth Sch Corby 1982–88; gen sec Secdy Heads Assoc 1988–; memb: Cncl Hansard Soc for Parly Govt, Geddington Volunteer Fire Bde; fell Politics Assoc 1994; FIMgt 1988, FRSA 1989; *Books* American Government (1974), Understanding Politics in Modern Britain (1977), People and Politics in Britain (jtly, 1985), School Management in Practice (jtly, 1985); *Recreations* gardening, wine appreciation; *Style*— John Sutton, Esq, CBE; ✉ 24 Bright Trees Road, Geddington, Kettering, Northants NN14 1BS; Secondary Heads Association, 130 Regent Rd, Leicester LE1 7PG (☎ 0116 247 1797, fax 0116 247 1152, mobile 0585 582294)

SUTTON, Rt Rev Keith Norman; *see:* Lichfield, Bishop of

SUTTON, Linda; *b* 14 Dec 1947; *Educ* Southend Coll of Technol, Winchester Sch of Art, RCA (MA); *Career* artist; *Solo Exhibitions* Galerij de Zwarte Panter Antwerp 1971, Bedford House Gallery London 1974, L'Agrifoglio Milan 1975, World's End Gallery London 1978, Ikon Gallery Birmingham 1979, Chenil Gallery London 1980, Royal Festival Hall London 1984, Stephen Bartley Gallery London 1986, Beecroft Gallery Westcliff-on-Sea (with Carel Weight, CBE, RA) 1987, Jersey Arts Centre St Helier Channel Islands 1988, Christopher Hull Gallery London 1988, Beaux Arts Bath 1988, Austin/Desmond Fine Art Bloomsbury 1989, Isis Gallery Leigh-on-Sea 1993, Lamont Gallery London 1993 and 1996, Pump House Gallery Battersea Park 1994, Sutton House Hackney 1994, Chappel Galleries Essex 1995, Bromham Mill Bedford Arts Festival 1995, Piers Feetham Gallery Fulham London 1995, Emscote Lawn Gallery 1996; *Group Exhibitions* incl: Royal Acad Summer Exhibitions 1972–96, British Painting 1952–77 (Royal Acad) 1977, Bath Festival 1985 and 1988, Jonleigh Gallery Guildford 1987, The Lefevre Gallery London 1988, Business Art Centre Islington 1991–95, Int Art Fair Olympia 1990 and 1991, Directors Choice (New Academy Gallery) 1990, Academia Italia 1990, On Line Gallery Southampton 1992–94, Isis Gallery Leigh-on-Sea 1992, Lamont Gallery London 1992–95, Chappel Galleries Essex 1993, Fosse Galleries Stow-on-the-Wold 1992–94, One Line Gallery 1993–94, Royal Museum and Art Gallery Canterbury 1993–94; *Awards* prizewinner GLC Spirit of London (Royal Festival Hall) 1979, 1980 and 1981, first prize Contemporary Arts Soc 1981, third prize Nat Portrait Gallery 1982, prizewinner Royal Acad Summer Exhibition 1987; *Clubs* Chelsea Arts, Colony Rooms, Arts; *Style*— Miss Linda Sutton; ✉ 192 Battersea Bridge Road, London SW11 3AE

SUTTON, Michael Phillip; s of Charles Phillip Sutton, of Worksop, Notts, and Maisie, *née* Kelsey; *b* 25 Feb 1946; *Educ* Haileybury and ISC; *m* 24 July 1971, Susan Margaret, da of John Turner, JP, DL, of Lound, Notts; *Career* chartered accountant 1970; Old Broad Street Securities Ltd 1970–71, md Singer and Friedlander Ltd 1983– (joined 1971), dir Creighton's Naturally plc 1994–; Freeman: City of London 1978, Worshipful Co of Pipe Tobacco Makers and Blenders (memb Ct of Assts 1982); FCA 1976; *Recreations* shooting, fishing, national hunt racing, gardening; *Clubs* Turf, MCC; *Style*— Michael Sutton, Esq; ✉ West Bank, Gamston, Retford, Notts DN22 0QD (☎ 0177 783 8387); Singer and Friedlander Ltd, 31 Park Square, Leeds LS1 2PF (☎ 0113 243 5000)

SUTTON, Capt Oliver Peter; CBE (1978); s of Albert Bernard Sutton (d 1961), of Chile, and Joan Firth, *née* Brewster (d 1981); *b* 17 Jan 1926; *Educ* RNC Dartmouth; *m* 16 Dec 1962, Gay, da of Charles Owen (d 1949); 2 s (Matthew b 5 Feb 1964, Simon b 31 Oct 1968); *Career* RN: Cadet 1939, Cdre 1978, specialist in navigation, ret as COS to Flag

Offr Plymouth; dir Br Radio and Electronic Equipment Mfrs Assoc 1978–91, sec Euro Assoc of Consumer Electronics Mfrs (EACEM) 1987–90, chm JRS Associates EMC Consultancy 1991–94; FIMgt; *Recreations* fishing, tennis, gardening; *Style—* Capt Oliver Sutton, CBE, RN; ✉ Lindisfarne Two, Amport, Hants SP11 8AQ (☎ 01264 710999)

SUTTON, Peter John; s of Charles James Sutton (d 1975), and Ruby Ethel, *née* Moorecroft (d 1984); *b* 29 Aug 1942; *Educ* Brentwood Sch, Clare Coll Cambridge; *m* 12 April 1969, Marjorie, da of Robert Howe; 1 s (David Robert b 22 May 1973), 1 da (Catherine Fiona b 19 Oct 1970); *Career* sr accountant and mangr Deloitte Plender Griffiths & Co 1967–73 (articled clerk 1964–67), mangr Black Geoghegan & Till 1973–74; Spicer and Pegler (name changed to Spicer & Oppenheim 1988, merged to become part of Touche Ross 1990, now Deloitte & Touche): mangr 1974–76, ptnr 1976–; pres Cambridge Soc of CAs 1991–92; hon treas Cambridgeshire Lawn Tennis Assoc; FCA 1968; *Style—* Peter Sutton, Esq; ✉ 2 West Hill Rd, Foxton, Cambridge CB2 6SZ (☎ 01223 870721); Deloitte & Touche, Leda House, Station Rd, Cambridge CB1 2RN (☎ 01223 460222, fax 01223 350839)

SUTTON, Philip John; s of Louis Sutton (d 1976), and Ann, *née* Lazarus (d 1980); *b* 20 Oct 1928; *Educ* Slade Sch of Fine Art UCL; *m* 11 July 1953, Heather Minifie Ellis, da of Arthur Owen Ellis Cooke; 1 s (Jacob b 11 May 1954), 3 da (Imogen b 21 Feb 1956, Saskia b 19 Jan 1958, Rebekah b 30 Sept 1960); *Career* artist; RA 1976 (ARA 1971); *Recreations* running, swimming; *Style—* Philip Sutton, Esq, RA; ✉ 3 Morfa Terr, Manorbier, Tenby, Dyfed SA70 7TH (☎ 01834 871 474, fax 01834 871 665)

SUTTON, Dr Richard; s of Dick Brasnett Sutton (d 1981), of Newport, Gwent, and Greta Mary, *née* Leadbeter; *b* 1 Sept 1940; *Educ* Gresham's, King's Coll London, King's Coll Hosp London (MB BS); *m* 28 Nov 1964, (Anna) Gunilla, da of Carl-Axel Cassö (d 1976), of Stockholm, Sweden; 1 s (Edmund b 24 April 1967); *Career* house offr: Plymouth Gen Hosp 1964–65, King's Coll Hosp 1965, St Stephen's Hosp 1966, London Chest Hosp 1966–67; registrar St George's Hosp 1967–68, fell in cardiology Univ of N Carolina USA 1968–69, registrar then sr registrar and temporary conslt Nat Heart Hosp 1970–76, conslt cardiologist Chelsea & Westminster (formerly Westminster Hosp) 1976–, conslt cardiologist Royal Brompton Hosp 1993–; hon conslt cardiologist St Luke's Hosp for the Clergy 1980–; chm Cardiology Ctee and chm Specialty Trg Ctee Cardiology N Thames (West) RHA; ed European Journal of Cardiac Pacing and Electrophysiology; Govr's award American Coll of Cardiology 1979 and 1982; co fndr and former pres and sec Br Pacing and Electrophysiology Gp, co-chm Euro Working Gp on Cardiac Pacing Euro Soc of Cardiology; DSc(Med) Univ of London 1988; FRCP 1982 (MRCP 1967); memb: BMA, RSM, Br Cardiac Soc, American Coll of Cardiology, American Heart Assoc, Euro Soc of Cardiology; *Books* Pacemakers (chapter in Oxford Textbook of Medicine, 1987), Foundations of Cardiac Pacing (Pt 1 1991, Pt 2 1996); *Recreations* opera, tennis, cross-country skiing; *Style—* Dr Richard Sutton; ✉ 149 Harley St, London W1N 1HG (☎ 0171 935 4444, fax 0171 935 6718, telex 263250)

SUTTON, Sir Richard Lexington; 9 Bt (GB 1772), of Norwood Park, Nottinghamshire; s of Sir Robert Lexington Sutton, 8 Bt (d 1981); *b* 27 April 1937; *Educ* Stowe; *m* 1959, Fiamma, da of Giuseppe Marzio Ferrari, of Via S Giacomo 28, Rome; 1 s (David Robert b 1960), 1 da (Caroline Victoria (Mrs Alexander Gibbs) b 1965); *Heir* s, David Robert Sutton, b 26 Feb 1960; *Style—* Sir Richard Sutton, Bt; ✉ Moor Hill, Langham, Gillingham, Dorset

SUTTON, Richard Manners; s of John Charles Ludlow Manners Sutton, of Willerby Lodge, Staxton, Scarborough, North Yorks, and Daphne Agnes, *née* Wormald (d 1961); *b* 5 May 1947; *Educ* Charterhouse; *m* 1, 1972 (m dis 1979), Mary, *née* Diebold; m 2, 1979, Penelope Jane, *née* Quinlan; 2 s (William b 1980, Thomas b 1982); *Career* slr i/c intellectual property Dibb Lupton Broomhead; *Style—* Richard Sutton, Esq; ✉ Dibb Lupton Broomhead, 117 The Headrow, Leeds LS1 5JX

SUTTON, Robert Hiles; s of John Ormerod Sutton, of The Old School House, Tichborne, Hants, and Margaret Patricia, *née* Buckland; *b* 19 Jan 1954; *Educ* Winchester, Magdalen Coll Oxford (BA); *m* 8 Aug 1981, Carola Jane (Tiggy), da of Sir Anthony Dewey, 3 Bt, of The Rag, Galhampton, Yeovil, Somerset; 2 s (Patrick William b 1984, Jonathan David Ormerod b 1990), 1 da (Joanna Kate b 1987); *Career* Macfarlanes Slrs: joined 1976, ptnr 1983–, currently in charge Japanese prac; memb Law Soc; *Recreations* rackets, poker; *Clubs* City; *Style—* Robert Sutton, Esq; ✉ Macfarlanes, 10 Norwich Street, London EC4A 1BD (☎ 0171 831 9222, fax 0171 831 9607)

SUTTON, Timothy Patrick; s of William Arthur Sutton, of Derby, and Maria Ephigenia, *née* Macronopoulou; *b* 19 June 1958; *Educ* Queen Elizabeth's GS Ashbourne Derbys, Magdalen Coll Oxford (MA PPE); *Career* currently chief exec Charles Barker plc (memb MBO team 1992); campaigns incl: long term repositioning prog for British Midland since 1989 (for which recipient PR Week Grand Prix 1991 and IPR Sword of Excellence 1994), defence of brewing indust against MMC recommendations 1989, campaign by independent gas cos to end British Gas plc's domestic monopoly 1993–95, advising int oil indust on the decommissioning of North Sea platforms (current); speaker at PR indust confs and events; memb Amnesty Int; MIPR 1992, FRSA 1996; *Recreations* flying, cinema, poetry, Derby Co FC; *Style—* Timothy Sutton, Esq; ✉ 34 Kensington Place, London W8 7PR (☎ 0171 792 3604); Charles Barker plc, 56 Dean Street, London W1V 6HX (☎ 0171 830 8400, fax 0171 439 1071, pager 0941 117004, e-mail tims@cbarker.co.uk)

SUZMAN, Janet; da of Saul Suzman, of Johannesburg, SA, and Betty, *née* Sonnenberg; *b* 9 Feb 1939; *Educ* Kingsmead Coll Johannesburg, Univ of the Witwatersrand (BA), LAMDA; *m* 1969 (m dis 1986), Trevor Robert Nunn, *qv*; 1 s (Joshua b 1980); *Career* actress and director; performances incl: The Wars of the Roses 1964, The Relapse 1967, The Taming of the Shrew 1967, A Day in the Death of Joe Egg 1970, Nicholas and Alexandra (Acad Award nomination) 1971, Antony and Cleopatra 1972, Hello and Goodbye (Evening Standard Award) 1973, Three Sisters (Evening Standard Award) 1976, Hedda Gabler 1978, The Greeks 1980, The Draughtsman's Contract 1981, Vassa 1985, Mountbatten-Viceroy of India 1986, The Singing Detective 1987, Andromache 1988, A Dry White Season 1989, Another Time 1989–90, Hippolytos 1991, Nuns on the Run 1991, Leon the Pig Farmer 1992, The Sisters Rosensweig (Greenwich and The Old Vic) 1994–95; directed: Othello (Market Theatre Johannesburg 1987, TV 1988), A Dream of People (RSC, The Pit) 1990, No Flies on Mr Hunter (Chelsea Centre) 1992, Death of a Salesman 1993, The Deep Blue Sea (both Theatr Clwyd) 1996, The Good Woman of Sackville (Market Theatre Johannesberg) 1996; vice chm LAMDA Cncl 1992–; lectr Tanner Lectures Brasenose Coll Oxford 1995; Hon MA Open Univ 1986, Hon DLitt Univ of Warwick 1990, Hon DLitt Univ of Leicester 1992; *Recreations* yacht 'Chicken Sloop'; *Style—* Miss Janet Suzman; ✉ c/o William Morris Agency (UK) Ltd, 31/32 Soho Square, London W1V 6DG (☎ 0171 434 2191, fax 0171 437 0238)

SVENDSEN, Dr Elisabeth Doreen; MBE (1980); da of Vincent Aubrey Knowles (d 1976), of Elland, Yorkshire, and Ileene Hughan, *née* Gowling (d 1978); *b* 23 Jan 1930; *Educ* Brighouse GS, Rachel McMillen Trg Coll; *m* 20 Oct 1954 (m dis 1982), Niels Denis Svendsen, step s of Svend Iversen; 4 c (Diana Lise b 13 Oct 1955, Paul Andrew b 30 March 1957, Clive Niels b 3 May 1961, Sarah Anna b 28 Jan 1968); *Career* teacher West Vale Sch 1951–53, co sec W T Knowles & Sons Ltd 1953–55; dir: Modern Equipment Co Ltd 1955–61, Branch Thorn Industries 1961–63; business conslt 1963–66 (incl dir Ponsharden Shipyard), dir Salston Hotel Ltd 1966–82; administrator: The Donkey Sanctuary 1977– (fndr and hon administrator 1969–77), Int Donkey Protection Tst 1985– (fndr and chm of tstees 1976–85); fndr and hon administrator: The Slade Centre 1975–, The Elisabeth Svendsen Tst 1989–; memb Br Assoc of Veterinary Parasitology, pres Colaton Raleigh & Dist Ploughing Assoc; Science Pioneer Prize Egyptian Veterinary Assoc 1992; Hon DVMS Univ of Glasgow 1992; *Books* adult: Down Among the Donkeys (1981), Twelve of My Favourite Donkeys (1982), In Defence of Donkeys (1985), The Professional Handbook of the Donkey (1986), Donkey's Years (1986), A Week in the Life of the Donkey Sanctuary (1988), A Passion for Donkeys (1988), Travels for a Donkey (1990), The Bumper Book of Donkeys (1991), For the Love of Donkeys (1993), Donkey Tales (1995); for children: The Story of Eeyore - the Naughtiest Donkey in the Sanctuary (1976), Suey the Beach Donkey (1977), More Adventures of Eeyore (1978), Eeyore Helps the Children (1981), The Great Escape (1981), Jacko the Hurricane Donkey (1982), Eeyore and Christmas Crackers (1984), Eeyore Meets a Giant! (1987), The Champion Donkeys (1989), The Story of Blackie and Beauty (1993), The Tale of Naughty Mal and Other Donkey Stories (1994), The Story of Dusty, The Little Ethiopian Donkey (1996); *Recreations* sailing, gold panning, antique collecting, keeping birds, cookery; *Clubs* Royal Western Yacht, Variety Club of GB (barker); *Style—* Dr Elisabeth Svendsen, MBE; ✉ Administrator, The Donkey Sanctuary, Sidmouth, Devon EX10 0NU (☎ 01395 578222, fax 01395 579266, car 0860 604167)

SWAAB, Richard Laing; s of Jack Swaab, of London, and Zena, *née* Urquhart; *b* 7 May 1955; *Educ* King's Coll Sch Wimbledon, Christ's Coll Cambridge (scholar, MA); *Career* carpenter Harvey Nichols dept store 1976–77; Lintas advtg: prodn controller 1977–79, account exec 1979–82, account dir 1982; planner Benton & Bowles 1982–83, planning ptnr Chester Morgenthau 1983–87; planner: Ayer Barker 1987, Ogilvy & Mather 1987–90; head of planning Collett Dickenson Pearce 1990–92, strategy dir Wight Collins Rutherford Scott 1996– (head of planning 1992–96); *Recreations* football, swimming, cricket, socialising; *Style—* Richard Swaab, Esq; ✉ Wight Collins Rutherford Scott, 41–44 Great Queen Street, London WC2 (☎ 0171 242 2800, mobile 0860 482475)

SWAAB, Roger Henry; s of Cyril Henry Swaab, of Shrewsbury, and Betty Joan, *née* Moore; *b* 6 June 1944; *Educ* Brewood GS, Birmingham Sch of Arch (Dip Arch); *m* 12 July 1968, Elizabeth Kay, da of William Edward Smith Penlon, of Staffs; 1 s (Christian b 1973), 1 da (Beth b 1973); *Career* architect; sr ptnr Hickton Madeley & Partners; dir: Hickton Madeley Interiors Ltd 1986, Hickton Madeley Landscape Ltd 1989–, Hickton Madeley Project Management Ltd 1988–, Hickton Madeley Property Services 1991–; ARIBA, ACIArb; *Recreations* golf; *Clubs* Hawkstone Park Golf, Nefyn and Dist Golf, The New Golf (St Andrews); *Style—* Roger H Swaab, Esq; ✉ Ashley House, Euston Way, Telford TF3 4LT (☎ 01952 200002, fax 01952 200001)

SWADLING, Prof Sidney John; *b* 21 Aug 1935; *Educ* Imperial Coll London (BSc), London Inst (City and Guilds); *m*, 2 c; *Career* British Aerospace Airbus Ltd: joined 1956, gp ldr (air intakes and engine nacelle structures on Concorde) 1961–66, designer i/c Concorde powerplant 1966–68, asst chief structures engr 1968, seconded to Working Gp 1968–69, chief Advanced Technol 1970–77, divnl res co-ordinator (Manufacturing) 1975–77, chief Advanced Manufacturing Technol 1977–80, chief structures engr Bristol 1980–84, chief designer Airbus Industrie A320 Aircraft 1984–85, dir of engrg 1985–93 (ret 1993); visiting prof Sch of Mechanical Engrg Univ of Bath 1994–; FEng 1993, FRAeS (pres Bristol Branch 1993) 1992; author of numerous pubns and papers; *Recreations* gardening, music, singing, playing the viola, sailing, walking; *Style—* Prof Sidney Swadling, FEng; ✉ 86 Wotton Road, Charfield, Wotton-under-Edge, Glos GL12 8SR (☎ 01453 843116)

SWAEBE, Barry James; s of Albert Victor Swaebe (d 1967), and Sophy Estlin Hancock, *née* Grundy (d 1982); *b* 12 May 1923; *m* 28 May 1966, Miriam Isobel, da of Robert Owen Morgans; 2 da (Sophy Anna b 1 Jan 1967, Clare Isobel b 9 Jan 1968); *Career* WWII RAF; social and portrait photographer; photographs in numerous pubns incl Harpers and Queen; exhibition: photographs of Barbados (Harrods) 1965, Portraits, Parties and People (Sports Bar Gallery Grosvenor House) 1994; *Style—* Barry Swaebe, Esq; ✉ Flat 2a, 1 North Grove, Highgate Village, London N6 4SH (☎ 0181 348 6010)

SWAFFIELD, David Richard; s of Sir James Chesebrough Swaffield, CBE, DL, RD, *qv*; *b* 11 Nov 1951; *Educ* Dulwich, Downing Coll Cambridge (MA); *m* 20 Oct 1979, (Barbara) Dianne, da of Albert Ernest Pilkington, JP (d 1988), of Wilmslow, Cheshire; 2 s (James b 1983, Robin b 1988); *Career* investment analysis Rowe & Pitman 1973–75, admitted slr 1979, ptnr Hill Dickinson & Co 1982–89 (slr 1979–82), dir Grayhill Ltd 1984–85, ptnr Hill Dickinson Davis Campbell 1989–, dir Liverpool Law Society Ltd 1991–, mangr Liverpool & London War Risks Insurance Association Ltd 1994– (jt mangr 1992–94); govr Birkenhead Sch 1994–; *Style—* David Swaffield, Esq; ✉ Brentwood, 12 Meols Drive, Hoylake, Wirral L47 4AQ (☎ 0151 6321389); Hill Dickinson Davis Campbell, Pearl Assurance House, Derby Street, Liverpool L2 9UB (0151 236 5400, fax 0151 227 1352)

SWAFFIELD, Sir James Chesebrough; kt (1976), CBE (1971), RD (1967), DL (Greater London 1978); s of Frederick Swaffield (d 1970); *b* 1924; *Educ* Cheltenham GS, Haberdashers' Aske's Sch, Univ of London (LLB), MA (Oxon); *m* 1950, Elizabeth Margaret Ellen, da of Albert Victor Maunder (d 1965); 2 s (one of whom David Richard Swaffield, *qv*), 2 da; *Career* WWII RNVR Atlantic and NW Europe, Lt-Cdr; admitted slr 1949; asst slr: Norwich Corp 1949–52, Cheltenham Corp 1952–53, Southend-on-Sea Corp 1953–56; town clerk Blackpool 1961–62 (dep town clerk 1956–61), sec Assoc of Municipal Corps 1962–73, dir-gen and clerk GLC 1973–84, clerk to ILEA 1973–84, clerk of Lieutenancy for Gtr London 1973–84; chm: BR Property Bd 1984–91, Ct of Advsrs St Paul's Cathedral, London Marathon Charitable Tst; vice pres: Royal Soc for Nature Conservation, Age Concern London; patron Age Resource; tstee: Civic Tst, Outward Bound Tst, Silver Jubilee Walkway Tst, Tudor Tst; govr Dulwich Coll, pres Beckenham and Bromley Centre Nat Tst; Distinguished Service Award Int City Mgmnt Assoc 1984; hon fell Inst Local Govt Studies Birmingham Univ; OStJ; FRSA; *Clubs* Reform, Naval; *Style—* Sir James Swaffield, CBE, RD, DL; ✉ 10 Kelsey Way, Beckenham, Kent BR3 3LL

SWAIN, Ann; da of Owen Morris, of Buxton, Derbyshire, and Joan Elaine, *née* Collinson; *b* 12 Sept 1944; *Educ* Eggars GS Alton, Oxford Poly; *m* 17 Sept 1965, David Russell Swain, s of Joseph Swain; 1 da (Pamela Mary b 1 Feb 1973), 1 s (Martin James b 4 Dec 1975); *Career* Radiobiological Laboratory Wantage ARC 1963–65, Rutherford High Energy Laboratory Harwell SRC 1965–68, Forest Sch 1969–71, head of science and technol Farlington Sch Horsham 1979–91, fndr Links Consultancy 1991–; non-exec dir S Thames Regnl Health Authy 1994–96, chm W Sussex Family Health Services Authy 1992–96, ind memb Sussex Polic Authy; nat pres UK Fedn of Business and Professional Women 1991–93, exec memb Women's Nat Cmmn 1991–93; memb: Women's Advsy Panel RSA 1991–93, Women's Advsy Panel Opportunity 2000 1992–93; chm The 300 Group 1996–; govr Tanbridge House Sch 1993–, chm of Govrs Arunside Sch; licentiate RSC; FRSA 1991; *Recreations* swimming; *Clubs* Westminster Dining; *Style—* Mrs Ann Swain; ✉ Links Consultancy, 9 Hillside, Horsham, W Sussex RH12 1NE (☎ 01403 266164, fax 01403 251165)

SWAIN, Marilyn Janice; da of Percival Harold Swain (d 1994), and Alice Maud, *née* George (d 1969); *b* 3 May 1931; *Educ* Berkhamsted Sch for Girls, Bartlett Sch of Architecture, Univ Coll London; *Career* Phillips auctioneers London 1960–70, Bonhams 1970–73, freelance valuer and lectr 1973–78, head of dept Neales of Nottingham 1978–82, md Fine Art Div William H Brown 1982–92, dir Marilyn Swain Auctions 1992–; memb Furniture and Works of Art Ctee RICS 1984–95, fndr memb and hon sec Derby Porcelain

Int Soc, hon sec Soc of Fine Art Auctioneers 1985–; fell Gemmological Assoc of GB 1967–91, FRSA 1972, FRICS 1981, FSVA 1992–95; *Recreations* fair weather sailing and walking, embroidery, giving and receiving dinner parties; *Style*— Miss Marilyn Swain; ✉ The Old Barracks, Sandon Road, Grantham, Lincolnshire NG31 9AS (☎ 01476 568861, fax 01476 576100)

SWAINE, Anthony Wells; s of Albert Victor Alexander Swaine (d 1972), of Cornwall, and Hilda May Allen (d 1983); *b* 25 Aug 1913; *Educ* Chatham House, Ramsgate; *Career* architect; in private practice specialising in architectural conservation and repair of historic bldgs; del to int conferences: ICOMOS, Confrontation E of Cncl of Europe Avignon 1966, Europa Nostra, Int Conference for Stone Conservation Athens and European Architectural Heritage Year Zurich and Amsterdam; patron Venice in Peril, author of conservation report to UNESCO Il Problema di Venezia; architectural advsr Friends of Friendless Churches and memb Panel of Hon Conslt Architects to Historic Churches Preservation Tst, past memb of panel of Architects The Churches Conservation Tst (formerly The Redundant Churches Fund); memb Panel of Architects of the Almshouses Assoc, former architectural advsr to Faversham Town Cncl within the Swale Borough Cncl (responsible for the restoration of historic Faversham, author of Faversham Conserved), conslt architect for historic bldgs to Thanet Dist Cncl (responsible for restoration of Margate Old Town, author of conservation report entitled Margate Old Town, responsible for the administering of the Town Scheme Grants), conslt architect for historic buildings Tenterden Town Cncl, conslt to other dist cncls; past pt/t listing of historic bldgs Ministry of Housing and Local Govt Dept of the Environment; memb: Cncl and Technical Panel Ancient Monuments Soc representing the Soc on the Int Cncl of Monuments and Sites, Soc for the Protection of Ancient Bldgs, Georgian Gp, Victorian Soc, Kent and Canterbury Archaeological Socs; fndr memb Canterbury Soc and other amenity socs; responsible during last war for the Cathedral, the Precincts and King's Sch to the Dean and Chapter of Canterbury; past pt/t teacher of history of architecture and bldg construction Canterbury and Margate Colls of Art; FRIBA, FSA, FASI; *Recreations* travelling, languages, lecturing (as memb of panel of speakers of Civic Tst), history as applied to architecture, drawing, painting, photography; *Style*— Anthony Swaine, Esq; ✉ 19 Farrier Street, Deal, Kent (☎ 01304 366369); Latchmere House, Watling Street, Canterbury, Kent (☎ 01277 462680)

SWAINSON, Dr Charles Patrick; s of John Edward Swainson, of Winchcombe, Glos, and Diana Patricia, *née* O'Rorke; *b* 18 May 1948; *Educ* White Friars Sch Cheltenham, Univ of Edinburgh (MB ChB); *m* 3 July 1981, Marie Adele, da of Charleton Irwin; 1 s (Andrew b 1983); *Career* sr lectr Univ of Otago NZ 1981–86, conslt physician Royal Infirmary 1986–, pt/t sr lectr dept of med Univ of Edinburgh 1986–, med dir Royal Infirmary 1996–; FRCP 1984; *Recreations* wine, singing, skiing, mountaineering; *Style*— Dr Charles Swainson; ✉ Department of Renal Medicine, Royal Infirmary of Edinburgh NHS Trust, Edinburgh EH3 9YW (☎ 0131 536 1000, fax 0131 536 2340)

SWAINSON, Eric; CBE (1981); *b* 5 Dec 1926; *Educ* Univ of Sheffield (BMet); *m* 1953, Betty Irene; 2 da; *Career* md IMI plc (metals fabricating and gen engrg) 1974–86, dir Birmingham Broadcasting Ltd 1973–92, dir Midlands Radio Holdings plc 1988–90, chm Lloyds Bank (Birmingham & W Mids Regnl Bd) 1985–91 (memb 1979–91), dir Amec plc 1987–95; vice chm: Fairey Group plc 1987–, Lloyds Bank plc 1992–96 (dir 1986–); dir Cheltenham & Glocester plc 1996–; memb Review Bd for Govt Contracts 1978–93, chm W Mids Indust Devpt Bd 1985–90; pro-chllr Aston Univ 1981–86; Hon DSc Aston 1986; *Style*— Eric Swainson Esq, CBE; ✉ Paddox Hollow, Norton Lindsey, Warwick CV35 8JA (☎ 0192 684 3190); c/o Lloyds Bank plc, 71 Lombard Street, London EC3P 3BS (☎ 0171 626 1500)

SWALES, Prof John Douglas; s of Frank Swales (d 1969), of Leicester, and Doris Agnes, *née* Flude (d 1959); *b* 19 Oct 1935; *Educ* Wyggeston GS Leicester, Univ of Cambridge (MA, MD); *m* 7 Oct 1967, Kathleen Patricia, da of Cdr Edward Townsend (d 1986), of Dublin; 1 s (Philip Patrick Richard b 1972), 1 da (Charlotte Rachel b 1975); *Career* sr lectr in med Univ of Manchester 1970–74, prof of med Univ of Leicester 1974–96, dir of R&D Dept of Health 1996–; ed: Clinical Sci 1980–82, Jl of Hypertension 1982–87, Jl of Royal Soc of Med 1994–; pres Br Hypertension Soc 1984–86, censor RCP 1985–87; chm: Assoc Clinical Profs of Med 1987–, Fedn of Assoc Clinical Profs 1987–; FRCP; *Books* Sodium Metabolism in Disease (1975), Clinical Hypertension (1979), Platt versus Pickering - an Episode in Medical History (1985), Hypertension Illustrated (1990), Hypertension Textbook (1994); *Recreations* bibliophile; *Clubs* Athenaeum; *Style*— Prof John Swales; ✉ 21 Morland Avenue, Leicester LE2 2PF (☎ 0116 270 7161); Department of Health, Richmond House, 79 Whitehall, London SW1A 2NS (☎ 0171 210 5556, fax 0171 210 5868)

SWALES, Prof Martin William; s of Peter John Swales (d 1978), and Doris, *née* Davies (d 1989); *b* 3 Nov 1940; *Educ* King Edward's Sch Birmingham, Christ's Coll Cambridge, Univ of Birmingham; *m* 23 Sept 1966, Erika Marta, da of Ernst Meier (d 1988), of Basel, Switzerland; 1 s (Christopher b 1970), 1 da (Catherine b 1973); *Career* lectr in German Univ of Birmingham 1964–70, reader in German King's Coll London 1972–75, prof of German Univ of Toronto 1975–76 (assoc prof 1970–72), prof of German UCL 1976– (dean of arts 1982–85), hon dir Inst of Germanic Studies Univ of London 1989–93; *Books* Arthur Schnitzler (1971), The German Novelle (1977), The German Bildungsroman (1978), Thomas Mann (1980), Adalbert Stifter (with E M Swales, 1984), Goethe - The Sorrows of Young Werther (1987), Buddenbrooks - Family Life as the Mirror of Social Change (1991), Studies of German Prose Fiction in the Age of European Realism (1995); *Recreations* music, theatre, film, amateur dramatics, travel; *Style*— Prof Martin Swales; ✉ 11 De Freville Avenue, Cambridge CB4 1HW (☎ 01223 352510); Dept of German, University College, Gower St, London WC1E 6BT (☎ 0171 380 7120)

SWALLOW, Sir William; kt (1967); s of late W T Swallow; *b* 2 Jan 1905; *m* 1929, Kathleen Lucy, *née* Smith; *Career* chm and md: General Motors Ltd 1953–61, Vauxhall Motors Ltd 1961–66; *Recreations* golf; *Style*— Sir William Swallow; ✉ Alderton Lodge, Ashridge Park, Berkhamsted, Herts (☎ 01442 842284)

SWAN, Dr Charles Henry James; s of Matthew Charles Swan, of Wolverhampton, and Kathleen, *née* Downie (d 1992); *b* 5 Oct 1937; *Educ* Wolverhampton Municipal GS, Univ of Birmingham (MB ChB, MD); *m* 17 June 1961, Ann, da of Robert O'Connor, of Wolverhampton; 1 da (Lindsay Ann b 25 Oct 1967), 1 s (Edward D'Arcy b 12 March 1969); *Career* research fell: Birmingham Gen Hosp 1967–69, NY Med Coll 1969–70; conslt physician N Staffs Hosp 1972–; memb: Br Soc of Gastroenterology 1967 (pres (endoscopy) 1991–93), Assoc of Physicians 1985; holder President's Medal Br Soc of Gastroenterology 1996; FRCP 1969 (memb Cncl), FRCPEd 1994; *Books* Gastrointestinal Endoscopy (1984); *Recreations* golf, horticulture, fell walking, languages; *Clubs* Trentham Golf, Royal St David's Golf; *Style*— Dr Charles Swan; ✉ 9 Sutherland Drive, Westlands, Newcastle, Staffs ST5 3NA (☎ 01782 616897); 11 King Street, Newcastle-under-Lyme, Staffs ST5 1EH (☎ 01782 614174); North Staffordshire Hospital, Stoke-on-Trent ST5 6QG (☎ 01782 714565)

SWAN, Sir Conrad Marshall John Fisher; KCVO (1994, CVO 1986, LVO 1978); s of Dr Henry Swan (*né* Swenciski or Swiecicki), of Vancouver (whose f, Paul, emigrated from Poland, where the family had long been landed proprietors and from time to time represented in the Senate of pre-Partition Poland); *b* 13 May 1924; *Educ* St George's Coll Weybridge, SOAS Univ of London, Univ of Western Ontario, Peterhouse Cambridge; *m* 1957, Lady Hilda Susan Mary Northcote (d 1995), da of 3 Earl of Iddesleigh; 1 s, 4 da; *Career* Rouge Dragon Pursuivant 1962–68, York Herald of Arms 1968–92, Registrar and Sr Herald-in-Waiting Coll of Arms 1982–92, Garter Principal King of Arms 1992–95, inspr Regtl Colours (UK) 1993–95; lectr; genealogist of Order of Bath 1972–95; KStJ (genealogist of Grand Priory, Order of St John 1976–95), hon genealogist Order of St Michael & St George 1989–95; memb Ct of Assts Worshipful Co of Gunmakers; Knight of Honour & Devotion SMO Malta 1979, cdr Royal Norwegian Order of Merit with Star 1995, cdr Order of Merit Republic Poland 1995; FSA; *Books* Canada: Symbols of Sovereignty (1977), The Chapel of the Order of Bath (1978), Blood of the Martyrs (with Peter Drummond Murray of Mastrick, Slains Pursuivant of Arms, 1993); *Video* The Aboriginal in Heraldry (1996); *Style*— Sir Conrad Swan, KCVO, PhD, FSA; ✉ Boxford House, Suffolk CO10 5JT (☎ and fax 01787 210208, fax 01787 211626)

SWAN, Francis Joseph (Frank); s of Robert Ernest Swan, and Margaret Ann, *née* Burg; *b* 26 Sept 1940; *Educ* De La Salle Sch Marrickville Sydney, Univ of New South Wales (BSc); *m* 5 Aug 1967, Helen Margaret, da of Clarence Murphy; 3 s (David 14 Aug 1968, Jeffrey, Stephen (twins) b 14 Feb 1971), 1 da (Lianne b 17 March 1974); *Career* Cadbury Schweppes: chief chemist Schweppes New Zealand Auckland 1964–73, prodn mangr Beverage Div Cadbury Schweppes Australia Melbourne 1973–77, gen mangr CSAL Beverage Div NE Region Melbourne 1977–79, md CSAL Beverage Div Melbourne 1979–88, chief exec CSAL Melbourne 1988–91, md Beverages Stream Cadbury Schweppes plc London 1991–96, ret; dir Fosters Brewing Group Ltd 1996; memb Business Cncl of Australia 1988–91; Fndn fell Australian Inst of Company Dirs 1990, FInstD 1992; *Recreations* tennis; *Clubs* Hawthorn; *Style*— Frank Swan, Esq; ✉ 58–60 Old Warrandyte Road, Donvale, Victoria 3111, Australia

SWAN, Richard Roland Seymour; s of Capt Seymour Lankester Swan, RM (d 1988), and Ethel Hayward, *née* Drew; *b* 21 April 1937; *Educ* Cranleigh, Sidney Sussex Coll Cambridge (MA); *m* 1, 16 Sept 1961 (m dis 1967), Penelope Ann, da of Anthony Urling Clark, of Gwelhale, Rock, nr Wadebridge, Cornwall; 2 s (Mark b 1963, Rupert b 1965); m 2, 14 Oct 1967 (m dis 1990), Hedwig Erna Lydia, da of Dr Franz Pesendorfer (d 1944), of Vienna, Austria; 1 s (Michael b 1969), 2 da (Caroline b 1968, Olivia b 1970); *Career* Nat Serv Royal Sussex Regt, 2 Lt 1956, Lt 1959 East Surrey Regt; admitted slr 1963; Notary Public; sr ptnr Heald Nickinson (Milton Keynes) 1979–; non-exec dir Scantronic Holdings plc; dir: Southern Arts, Milton Keynes and N Bucks C of C Trg and Enterprise, Milton Keynes City Orch; memb Norman Hawes Educnl Tst; chm BABC Clubs for Young People 1986–, memb Cncl NABC Clubs for Young People; memb Law Soc 1963; *Recreations* book collecting, reading, walking; *Clubs* Naval and Military, Woburn Golf and Country; *Style*— Richard Swan, Esq; ✉ Five Pines, Wood Lane, Aspley Guise, Milton Keynes MK17 8EL (☎ 01908 583495); Heald Nickinson, Chancery House, 199 Silbury Boulevard, Grafton Gate East, Central Milton Keynes MK9 1LN (☎ 01908 662277, fax 01908 675667, car tel 0836 742932)

SWANN, Dr Ian Lonsdale; s of Dr Geoffrey Swann, and Ida, *née* Lonsdale; *b* 13 March 1947; *Educ* Liverpool Coll, Univ of St Andrews (MB ChB, DCH); *m* 4 Aug 1973, Alison Gleave, da of Charles Edward Brownlow, of Burnley, Lancs; 1 s (Alexander David b 1977), 1 da (Gayle Penelope b 1980); *Career* sr house offr in paediatrics to Prof R G Mitchell Dundee 1973; registrar: Chalmers Unit Edinburgh Royal Infirmary 1973–74, Royal Hosp for Sick Children Edinburgh 1975–77; sr registrar and clinical tutor Univ Hosp of Wales 1978–80; Burnley Health Care Tst: conslt paediatrician 1980–, clinical dir of child health 1992–; MRCP 1974, FRCPE 1985, memb Br Paediatric Assoc; *Books* The Asthmatic Child in Play and Sport (contrib); *Recreations* walking, skiing, music, oil painting; *Style*— Dr Ian Swann; ✉ Burnley General Hospital, Casterton Ave, Burnley, Lancs (☎ 01282 425071)

SWANN, Dr James Cyprian; s of Ven Cecil Gordon Aldersey Swann (d 1969), and Hilda, *née* McMahon (d 1978); *b* 10 July 1931; *Educ* Gosfield Sch, The London Hosp Med Coll (MB BS, DMRD); *m* 28 Jan 1961, Josephine Margaret, da of Joseph Winston Ellis (d 1975); 3 da (Rachel b 1963, Laura b 1965, Clare b 1972); *Career* 2 Lt RA; conslt radiologist: The London Hosp 1968–76, The Royal Masonic Hosp 1970–84, Bromley Hosps NHS Tst 1976–; chm Bromley Health Dist CAT Scanner Appeal; FFR, memb Br Inst Radiology 1965, FRCR 1975; *Recreations* painting in oils, photography, gardening; *Clubs* BMA; *Style*— Dr James Swann; ✉ 104 Hayes Way, Beckenham, Kent BR3 6RT (☎ 0181 650 3673); Department of Diagnostic Imaging, Farnborough Hospital, Farnborough Common, Orpington, Kent BR6 8ND (☎ 01689 814141)

SWANN, Sir Michael Christopher; 4 Bt (UK 1906), of Prince's Gardens, Royal Borough of Kensington, TD; s of Sir Anthony Charles Christopher Swann, 3 Bt, CMG, OBE (d 1991), and Jean Margaret, *née* Niblock-Stuart; *b* 23 Sept 1941; *Educ* Eton; *m* 1, 1965 (m dis 1985), Hon Lydia Mary Hewitt, da of 8 Viscount Lifford; 2 s (Jonathan Christopher b 1966, Toby Charles b 1971), 1 da (Tessa Margaret b 1969); m 2, 1988, Marilyn Ann, da of Leslie Charles Tobitt, of Montevideo, Uruguay; *Heir* s, Jonathan Christopher Swann b 1966; *Career* late 60 Rifles; ptnr Smith Swann & Co; vice chm Gabbitas Truman and Thring Educnl Tst, gen cmmr of Income Tax; *Style*— Sir Michael Swann, Bt, TD; ✉ 100 Hurlingham Rd, London SW6 3NR

SWANNELL, John; *b* 27 Dec 1946; *Career* professional photographer; began career as photographic asst Vogue Studios, former asst to David Bailey, fashion photographer (Vogue, Harpers & Queen, Tatler, Ritz newspaper); exhibitions incl: several at the Nat Portrait Gallery London (which holds 40 Swannell photographs in their Permanent Collection), fashion photography since 1974 (Royal Photographic Soc Bath) July-Sept 1990; photographer of set of 26 portraits for The Prince Charles Tst 1991 (incl Sir John Gielgud, Lord King, Bernard Weatherill, Harvey Goldsmith and David Hockney); other personalities photographed incl: HRH The Princess Royal, Joan Collins, George Michael, Grace Jones, Jane Seymour, Shakira Caine, Yasmin Le Bon, Brian Ferry, Patsy Kensit, Pete Townsend, HRH The Princess of Wales with her children (private commission); dir over 50 commercials since 1984 specialising in high fashion and beauty; awards incl: Gold award for Best Commercial of the Year 1984 (Boots No 7), Silver award at Cannes for Best 40 Second Commercial (Rimmel Cosmetics), Best Commercial NY 1990 (Johnsons); *Books* Fine Line (1982), Naked Landscape (1982); *Style*— John Swannell, Esq; ✉ John Swannell Studios, 10a Belmont St, Chalk Farm, London NW1 8HH (☎ 0171 284 3644, fax 0171 267 4882)

SWANNELL, Robert William Ashburnham; s of Maj David William Ashburnham Swannell, MBE (d 1992), and Pamela Mary, *née* Woods; *b* 18 Nov 1950; *Educ* Rugby; *m* Jan 1982, Patricia Ann, da of John Ward; 1 s (William), 1 da (Alicia); *Career* CA 1973; Peat Marwick Mitchell & Co 1969–73, Inns of Ct Sch of Law 1973–76, called to the Bar Lincoln's Inn 1976, dir J Henry Schroder & Co Ltd 1985–; *Style*— Robert Swannell, Esq; ✉ J Henry Schroder & Co Ltd, 120 Cheapside, London EC2 6DS (☎ 0171 382 6000, fax 0171 382 6459)

SWANSEA, 4 Baron (UK 1893); Sir John Hussey Hamilton; 4 Bt (UK 1882), DL (Powys 1962); s of 3 Baron Swansea, DSO, MVO, TD (d 1934), and Hon Winifred Hamilton (d 1944), da of 1 Baron HolmPatrick; *b* 1 Jan 1925; *Educ* Eton, Trinity Coll Cambridge; *m* 1, 1956 (m dis 1973), Miriam (d 1975), da of Anthony Caccia-Birch, MC; 1 s, 2 da; m 2, 1982, Mrs Lucy Temple-Richards, da of Rt Rev Hugh Gough and Hon Mrs (M E) Gough; *Heir* s, Hon Richard Anthony Hussey Vivian, *qv*; *Career* vice pres and former vice chm Cncl Nat Rifle Assoc; pres: Shooting Sports Tst, Welsh Rifle Assoc, Br Shooting Sports Cncl; Liveryman Worshipful Co of Gunmakers; CStJ; *Recreations* shooting, fishing, rifle shooting; *Clubs* Carlton; *Style*— The Rt Hon the Lord Swansea, DL; ✉ 16 Cheyne Gardens, London SW3 5QT (☎ 0171 352 7455)

SWANSEA AND BRECON, Bishop of 1988–; Rt Rev Dewi Morris Bridges; s of Harold Davies Bridges (d 1970), and Elsie Margaret, *née* Morris (d 1986); *b* 1933; *Educ* St David's Univ Coll Lampeter (BA), CCC Cambridge (exhibitioner, MA, Purvis prize), Westcott House Cambridge; *m* 1959, Rhiannon, *née* Williams; 1 da (Sian Rhian (Mrs John Cammack)), 1 s (Jonathan Huw); *Career* ordained: deacon 1957, priest 1958; curate: Rhymney 1957–60, Chepstow 1960–63; vicar Tredegar St James 1963–65, gen licence to officiate Dio of Worcester 1965–68, sr lectr Summerfield Coll of Educn Kidderminster 1968–69 (lectr 1965–68), vicar Kempsey 1969–79, rural dean of Upton-on-Severn 1974–79, rector of Tenby with Gumfreston 1979–85, rector Rectorial Benefice of Tenby with Penally and Gumfreston 1985–88, rural dean of Narberth 1980–82, archdeacon of St David's 1982–88; memb: Ct of Govrs UCW Swanswea 1989–, Cncl St David's Univ Coll Lampeter 1992–; chm Div for Educn Bd of Mission of the Church in Wales 1992; *Recreations* music, walking, gardening; *Style*— The Rt Rev the Bishop of Swansea and Brecon; ✉ Ely Tower, Brecon, Powys LD3 9DE (☎ and fax 01874 622008)

SWANSON, Magnus P; *b* 25 April 1958; *Educ* Univ of Edinburgh (LLB Hons); *Career* lawyer and qualified insolvency practitioner; legal apprenticeship Steedman Ramage & Co WS Edinburgh 1980–82, foreign attorney Corp Dept Paul Weiss Rifkind Wharton & Garrison New York 1986–87, ptnr and head of Company Dept Maclay Murray & Spens Glasgow 1987– (slr 1982–86); memb: Law Soc of Scotland, Int Bar Assoc; *Publications* Aircraft Finance (co-author Scottish Chapter); *Style*— Magnus P Swanson, Esq; ✉ Maclay Murray & Spens, 151 St Vincent Street, Glasgow G2 5NJ (☎ 0141 248 5011, fax 0141 248 5819, e-mail mps@maclaymurrayspens.co.uk)

SWANSON, Peter Richard; JP; *Educ* Harrow, Wolverhampton Coll of FE, Staffordshire Agricultural Coll; *m*; 2 c; *Career* farmer (600 acres mixed farming), property developer; joined Ansells Brewery Birmingham as mgmnt trainee 1960, seconded to Threlfalls Brewery Liverpool 1961–63, divnl dir of catering Ansells 1967–70 (various supervisory positions 1963–67); farmer 1973–; dir Farmore Farmers (Co-op Farm Requisite Soc) 1973–79; formerly: dir Welsh Quality Lamb Ltd, chm Montgomery Quality Livestock (Mktg Co-operative), ptnr in co mktg animal foodstuffs 1987–92; chm: Coleg Powys 1990–95 (govr 1987–), Powys Health Authy 1993–96, Dyfed Powys Health Authy 1996–; memb: Wales Agricultural Trg Bd 1990–92 (chm Powys Ctee 1980–92), Bd Powys TEC 1990–, NFU (memb Montgomery Co Exec Ctee); *Recreations* scuba diving, cricket, skiing, shooting, wildlife; *Style*— Peter R Swanson, Esq, JP; ✉ Middle Aston, Montgomery, Powys SY15 6TA (☎ 01588 638246, fax 01588 630076)

SWANSTON, Andrew Roger; s of James Alexander Swanston (d 1988), and Olive Dora, *née* May, of Great Yarmouth, Norfolk; *b* 15 Nov 1948; *Educ* Great Yarmouth GS, Brunel Univ (BTech), St Bartholomew's Hosp Med Coll Univ of London (MB BS, MRCS, LRCP); *m* 11 March 1978, Dorothy Jean, da of John Gibson Robson; 1 s (James Andrew b 4 July 1979), 1 da (Kathryn Elizabeth b 18 Jan 1982); *Career* sr registrar in ENT Surgery Royal Nat Throat Nose and Ear Hosp (also Great Ormond Street Hosp for Sick Children, Royal Berkshire Hosp Reading) 1984–87, Janet Nash res fellowship Univ of Zurich 1987, conslt ENT surgn St Bartholomew's Hosp 1987–93, currently conslt ENT surgn and dir The London Otological Centre; VSO Cameroun West Africa 1967–68, memb Cncl Br Assoc of Otolaryngologists 1990–93; FRSM 1980, FRCS in otolaryngology (Eng) 1983; *Books* Otolaryngology volume 4 Rhinology (contrib, 5 edn 1987); *Recreations* trout fishing, classic car restoration; *Style*— Andrew Swanston, Esq; ✉ The London Otological Centre, 66 New Cavendish Street, London W1N 7LD

SWANSTON, Roy; s of Robert Trotter Swanston, of Lincoln, and Margaret Anne, *née* Paxton; *b* 31 Oct 1940; *Educ* Berwick upon Tweed GS, Coll of Estate Mgmnt; *m* Doreen, da of late John William Edmundson; 1 s (Philip b 17 Oct 1968), 1 da (Heather b 1 Dec 1966); *Career* various quantity surveying posts Sunderland CBC 1958–67, sr quantity surveyor CLASP Development Group Nottingham 1967–71, asst chief quantity surveyor Nottinghamshire CC 1971–74, directing surveyor Durham CC 1974–75, dir of Building Economics Cheshire CC 1975–82, dir Dept of Architecture Cheshire CC 1982–87, mgmnt conslt Peat Marwick McLintock 1987–88, dir Bucknall Austin plc 1988–90; English Heritage: dir Properties in Care 1990–93, dir Research and Professional Services 1993–95; chm Local Govt Residuary Body (England) 1995–; RICS: pres Quantity Surveyors Div 1982–83, hon treas 1986–90, chm Educn and Membership Ctee 1990–93, chm Mgmnt Bd 1993–, pres 1994– (vice pres 1990–94), chm Jt Contracts Tribunal 1995–; Barnardos: memb Nat Cncl 1987–, memb Investment Ctee 1995–; Liveryman Worshipful Co of Chartered Surveyors; DSc (hc) Univ of Salford 1994; FRICS; *Recreations* fell walking, watching soccer (supporter of Sunderland AFC), lay preacher with Methodist Church; *Style*— Roy Swanston, Esq

SWANTON, Ernest William (Jim); CBE (1994, OBE 1965); s of William Swanton (d 1966), of Malvern, Worcs, and Lillian Emily, *née* Walters (d 1953); *b* 11 Feb 1907; *Educ* Cranleigh Sch; *m* 11 Feb 1958, Ann Marion Carbutt, da of R H de Montmorency (d 1938), of Wentworth, Surrey; *Career* served WWII 1939–45, Actg Maj 148 Field Regt Bedfordshire Yeo RA (captured Singapore POW 1942–45); journalist author and bdcaster 1924–; journalist Evening Standard 1927–39; Daily Telegraph: cricket corr 1946–75, rugby corr 1948–64; played cricket for Middx 1937–38; managed own X1: W Indies 1956 and 1961, Malaya and Far East 1964; life vice pres MCC 1990 (memb Ctee 1975–85); memb Ctee Kent CCC 1971–91; pres: Cricket Soc 1976–83, Sandwich Town CC 1977–, Forty Club 1983–86, The Cricketer 1988–; *Books* A History of Cricket (with HS Altham, 1938), Denis Compton a Cricket Sketch (1948), Elusive Victory (1951), Cricket and the Clock (1952), Best Cricket Stories (1953), West Indian Adventure (1954), Victory in Australia 1954/55 (1955), Report from South Africa (1957), West Indies Revisited (1960), The Ashes in Suspense (1963), World of Cricket (ed, 1966, 1980, 1986), Cricket from All Angles (1968), Sort of a Cricket Person (1972), Swanton in Australia (1975), Follow On (1985), As I Said at the Time (anthology, 1984), Kent Cricket a Photographic History 1744–1984 (with CH Taylor, 1985), Back Page Cricket (1987), The Anglican Church: A Layman's Sketch (1988), The Essential E W Swanton (anthology, 1990), Arabs in Aspic (1993), Last Over (1996); *Recreations* golf, watching cricket; *Clubs* MCC, Vincent's (Oxford), Army and Navy, I Zingari; *Style*— E W Swanton, Esq, CBE; ✉ Delf House, Sandwich, Kent CT13 9HB

SWANTON, Dr (Robert) Howard; s of Robert Neil Swanton (d 1976), and Susanne, *née* Baldwin; *b* 30 Sept 1944; *Educ* Monkton Combe Sch, Queen's Coll Cambridge (fndn scholar, MA, MB BChir, MD), St Thomas's Hosp Med Sch (exhibitioner, Mead medal in med, Bristowe medal in pathology); *m* Lindsay Ann, da of Arnold Jepson, of Blackburn, Lancashire; 1 s (Robert Charles b 24 Feb 1972), 1 da (Josephine Kate b 23 Jan 1975); *Career* house physician St Thomas's Hosp 1969, house surgn St Peter's Hosp Chertsey 1970; sr house offr: Hammersmith Hosp 1970–71, Nat Heart Hosp 1971; med registrar Poole Hosp 1971–72, sr med registrar St Thomas's Hosp London 1975–77 (cardiac registrar 1972–74), sr registrar in cardiology Nat Heart Hosp 1977–79; conslt cardiologist Middlesex Hosp 1979–, King Edward VII Hosp for Offrs 1984–; Br Cardiac Soc: memb 1979–, asst sec 1986–88, sec 1988–; fell Euro Soc of Cardiology 1994; FRCP 1984 (MRCP 1971); *Books* Pocket Consultant in Cardiology (1984, 3 edn 1993); *Recreations* music, photography; *Clubs* St Albans Medical; *Style*— Dr Howard Swanton; ✉ Kent Lodge, 10 Dover Park Drive, Roehampton, London SW15 5BG (☎ 0181 788 6920); Dept of Cardiology, Middlesex Hospital, Mortimer St, London W1N 8AA (☎ 0171 380 9055); 81 Harley Street, London W1N 1DE (☎ 0171 486 7416)

SWANWICK, Sir Graham Russell; kt (1966), MBE (Mil 1944); s of Eric Drayton Swanwick (d 1955), of Whittington House, Chesterfield, and Margery Eleanor, *née* Norton (d 1959); *b* 24 Aug 1906; *Educ* Winchester, Univ Coll Oxford; *m* 1, 1933 (m dis 1945), Helen Barbara Reid (d 1970); 2 s (Richard (decd), Anthony); m 2, 1952, Mrs Audrey Celia Parkinson (d 1987), da of H C Hextall of Ford, Ashurst, Steyning, Sussex (d 1987); 2 step s (Richard, Dale (decd)); *Career* WWII Wing Cdr RAFVR 1940–45 (despatches); called to the Bar Inner Temple 1930, QC 1956, bencher 1962; recorder of: Lincoln 1957–59, Leicester 1959–66; dep chm Lincs QS (parts of Kesteven) 1960–63, chm Derbyshire QS 1963–66 (dep chm 1966–71), judge Jersey and Guernsey Cts of Appeal 1964–66, judge of High Ct of Justice (Queen's Bench Div) 1966–80, presiding judge Midland and Oxford circuit 1975–78; *Recreations* country pursuits; *Clubs* RAF; *Style*— Sir Graham Swanwick, MBE; ✉ Burnett's School Lane, Ashurst, Steyning, West Sussex BN44 3AY (☎ 01403 710241)

SWARBRICK, David William; s of Rev John W Swarbrick (d 1973), of Nottingham, and Lydia, *née* Rains (d 1984); *b* 17 Jan 1927; *Educ* Kingswood Sch Bath, Merton Coll Oxford (MA); *m* 1956, (Joyce Elaine) Margaret; 1 da (Jane Elizabeth b 1957); *Career* ICI plc UK, Europe and SA 1949–85 (latterly chm of cos in SA and dir of others cos); chm: Hillingdon DHA 1986–90, Mount Vernon Hosp NHS Tst 1991–94, Mount Vernon & Watford Hosps NHS Tst 1994–; pres Merton Soc 1989–92, memb Cncl Brunel Univ 1992–; former rugby player Oxford Univ, Blackheath, Barbarians and England; FInstD; *Clubs* Vincent's, British Sportsman's, Johannesburg CC; *Style*— David Swarbrick, Esq; ✉ Kenwith, Orchehill Avenue, Gerrards Cross, Bucks SL9 8QL (☎ 01753 883307); Mount Vernon & Watford Hospitals NHS Trust, Rickmansworth Road, Northwood, Middx HA6 2RN (☎ 01923 844132)

SWARBRICK, Dr Edwin Thornton; s of Richard Thornton Swarbrick, and Mary Elizabeth, *née* Cooper; *b* 29 April 1945; *Educ* Pocklington Sch Yorks, Wilbraham Acad Mass USA, St George's Med Sch London (MB BS, MD, FRCP); *m* 3 March 1984, (Angela) Corinne, da of Kenneth Hamer; 2 s (Benjamin Thornton b 8 Jan 1985, Matthew Thornton b 9 Feb 1987), 1 da (Kate Hannah b 31 March 1993); *Career* house physician and surgn St George's Hosp London 1968–69, sr house offr Brompton Hosp 1970–71, registrar The London Hosp 1971–72, registrar St Mark's Hosp 1972–74, res fell Inst of Child Health London 1974–76, lectr in gastroenterology Bart's 1976–80, conslt physician Wolverhampton 1980–, hon reader in gastroenterology Univ of Wolverhampton 1995; memb Br Soc for Gastroenterology, memb BMA, FRCP; *Recreations* equestrian sports, skiing, music, the arts; *Style*— Dr Edwin Swarbrick; ✉ Coppice Green, Shifnal, Shropshire (☎ 01952 462226); Nuffield Hospital, Wood Rd, Tettenhall, Wolverhampton (☎ 01902 754177)

SWARBRICK, Prof James; s of George Winston Swarbrick, and Edith, *née* Cooper; *b* 8 May 1934; *Educ* Sloane GS, Chelsea Coll London (BPharm, PhD, DSc); *m* 1960, Pamela Margaret Oliver; *Career* lectr Chelsea Coll 1964 (asst lectr 1962), visiting asst prof Purdue Univ 1964; Univ of Conn: assoc prof 1966, prof and chm Dept of Pharmaceutics 1969, asst dean 1970; dir product devpt Sterling-Winthrop Res Inst NY 1972–75, first prof of pharmaceutics Univ of Sydney 1975–76, dean Sch of Pharmacy Univ of London 1976–78, prof of pharmacy Univ of South Calif LA 1978–81, chm Div Pharmaceutics and prof of pharmaceutics Univ of North Carolina 1981–93, vice pres R&D AAI Inc 1993–; visiting scientist Astra Laboratories Sweden 1971, indust conslt 1965–72 and 1975–93, conslt Aust Dept of Health 1975–76, memb Ctee on Specifications Nat Formulary 1970–75, chm Jt US Pharmacopoeia Nat Formulary Panel on Disintegration 1971–75; memb: Ctee on Graduate Programs American Assoc Colls of Pharmacy 1969–71, Practice Trg Ctee Pharmaceutical Soc of NSW 1975–76, Academic Bd Univ of Sydney 1975–76, Collegiate Cncl 1976–78, Educn Ctee Royal Pharmaceutical Soc GB 1976–78, Working Pty on Pre-Registration Training 1977–78; Pharmaceutical Mfrs Assoc Fndn: memb Basic Pharmacology Advsy Ctee 1982–91, chm Pharmaceutics Advsy Ctee 1986–, memb Sci Advsy Ctee 1986–; chm Generic Drugs Advsy Ctee Food and Drug Admin 1995– (memb 1992–); memb Editorial Bd: Jl of Biopharmaceutics and Pharmacokinetics 1973–79, Drug Devpt Communications 1974–82, Pharmaceutical Technol 1978–, Biopharmaceutics and Drug Disposition 1979–; series ed: Current Concepts in the Pharmaceutical Sciences, Drugs and the Pharmaceutical Sciences; CChem, FRSC, FAAS 1966, FRIC 1970; fell: Acad of Pharmaceutical Sciences, Royal Pharmaceutical Society of GB 1978 (memb 1961), American Assoc of Pharmaceutical Scientists 1987; *Publications* Physical Pharmacy (with A N Martin and A Cammarata, 2 edn, 1969, 3 edn, 1983), Encyclopedia of Pharmaceutical Technology (jt ed), Drugs and the Pharmaceutical Sciences (series ed), contrib to various pharmaceutical books and jls; *Recreations* woodwork, listening to music, golf; *Style*— Prof James Swarbrick; ✉ AAI Inc, 1206 N 23rd Street, Wilmington, North Carolina 28405, USA (☎ 00 1 910 251 6433, fax 00 1 910 763 9633)

SWASH, Prof Michael; s of Edwin Frank Swash, of Milford on Sea, Hants, and Kathleen, *née* Burton; *b* 29 Jan 1939; *Educ* Forest Sch Snaresbrook London, London Hosp Med Coll London (MD), Univ of Virginia Med Sch Charlottesville Virginia USA; *m* 22 Jan 1966, Caroline Mary, da of Edward Payne, of Box, Nr Stroud, Glos; 3 s (Jesse Edward, Thomas Henry, (Edmond) Joseph); *Career* current positions held: conslt neurologist The Royal London Hosp 1972–, hon conslt neurologist St Mark's Hosp London and St Luke's Hosp for the Clergy London, sr lectr in neuropathology The London Hosp Med Coll 1981–, chief med offr Swiss Reinsurance (UK) Ltd 1985–, prof of neurology The London Hosp and St Bartholomew's Hosp Med Colls Univ of London 1995–; neurologist-adjunct Cleveland Clinic Fndn Ohio USA 1980–, med dir The Royal London Hosp and Assoc Community Servs NHS Tst 1991–94; hon sec Section of Neurology RSM 1974–77, hon sec NETRHA Advsy Ctee for Neurology and Neurosurgery 1975–78, hon sec Assoc of Br Neurologists 1979–84, chm Southwark and Camberwell Multiple Sclerosis Soc 1985–, memb Neuroscience Bd MRC 1986–91; memb: NY Acad of Scis, Br Neuropathological Soc, RSM, Br Soc of Clinical Neurophysiology, Assoc of Br Neurologists, American Acad of Neurology, American Neurological Assoc, Australian Neurological Assoc, Pathological Soc of GB, Br Soc of Gastroenterology; membre d'honneur de la Société Nationale Française de Colo-Proctologie; Liveryman Worshipful Soc of Apothecaries 1989; FRCPath, FRCP 1977 (MRCP 1972); *Books* incl: Clinical Neuropathology (jtly, 1982), Muscle Biopsy Pathology (jtly, 1984, 2 edn 1984), Scientific Basis of Clinical Neurology (jtly, 1985), Hierarchies in Neurology (jtly, 1989), Neurology: a concise clinical text (jtly, 1989), Clinical Neurology (2 vols, jtly, 1991), Neuromuscular Diseases (jtly, 3 edn 1995), Hutchison's Clinical Methods (20 edn 1995); *Recreations* walking, music, rowing, theatre, opera; *Clubs* London Rowing, Athenaeum, Royal Over-Seas League; *Style*— Prof Michael Swash; ✉ Department of Neurology, The Royal London Hospital, London E1 1BB (☎ 0171 377 7472, fax 0171 377 7008/7949, mobile 0468 242335, e-mail M.Swash@mds.qmw.ac.uk)

SWATMAN, Philip Hilary; s of Philip Stenning Swatman Parkstone Dorset and Patricia Meeson; *b* 1 Dec 1949; *Educ* St Edwards Sch Oxford, ChCh Oxford (BA); *m* Rosemary Anne; 1 s (Richard Oliver b 14 Oct 1981,), 2 da (Elizabeth Harriet b 16 Aug 1978, Rowena Jane b 16 April 1984); *Career* KPMG Peat Marwick Mclintock 1971–77, National Enterprise Board 1977–79; dir: NM Rothschild & Sons 1986–87 (joined 1979), of corp fin Chase Property Holdings plc 1987–88, NM Rothschild & Sons Ltd 1988–; FCA; *Recreations* sailing, squash, shooting, opera, theatre; *Style*— Philip Swatman, Esq; ✉ Hamblings, Church Rd, Ham Common, Surrey TW10 5HG; NM Rothschild & Sons Ltd, New Court, St Swithin's Lane, London EC4P 4DU (☎ 0171 280 5000)

SWAYNE, Giles Oliver Cairnes; s of Sir Ronald Oliver Carless Swayne, MC (d 1991), and Charmian, *née* Cairnes (d 1984); *b* 30 June 1946; *Educ* Ampleforth Coll York, Trinity Coll Cambridge; *m* 1, 1972 (m dis 1983), Camilla, *née* Rumbold; 1 s (Orlando b 1974); m 2, 1984, Naa Otua, *née* Codjoe; 1 da (Ophelia b 1996); *Career* composer; studied at RAM 1968–71, répétiteur Glyndebourne 1972–74, dir of music St Paul's Girls' Sch 1976, composer in residence London Borough of Hounslow 1980–83; Hon ARAM 1988; *Works* incl: Chamber Music for Strings (1970), String Quartet no 1 (1972, GLAA Young Composers prize), Orlando's Music (1974, first performed 1976 by Royal Liverpool Philharmonic Orch, conducted by Sir Charles Groves), Pentecost Music (1977, first performed 1981 by BBC Northern Symphony Orch, conducted by Nicholas Cleobury), CRY for 28 amplified voices and electronics (1979, BBC cmmn, first performed at St John's Smith Square 1980, first full realisation at Concertgebouw Amsterdam 1982), Symphony for small orchestra (1984), Le Nozze di Cherubino (two-act opera with libretto by the composer, 1984), Naaotwa Lala (1984, cmmnd and first performed by BBC Philharmonic Orch), godsong (1985–86), Songlines (1987), Harmonies of Hell (1988, Harrogate Festival), The Song of Leviathan (1988, cmmnd by Salomon Orch), No quiet place (1990), No man's land (1990), Circle of Silence (cmmnd by The King's Singers, first performed Boston Symphony Hall 1991), The Song of the Tortoise (1992, cmmnd by the Bournemouth Sinfonietta Orch), The Owl and the Pussycat (1993, for narrator and small ensemble), String Quartet no 3 (cmmnd by Lord Harewood, first performed Harewood House 1993), Squeezy (1994), All about Henry (1995), The Tiger (1995, Strasbourg Festival "Musica"), A Convocation of Worms (1995), The Silent Land (1996, cmmnd by Clare Coll Cambridge), Ophelia Drowning (1996), Wormes Meate (1996); *Recordings* CRY (BBC Singers, conducted by John Poole, 1985), Magnificat; *Style—* Giles Swayne, Esq; ✉ c/o Performing Arts, 6 Windmill Street, London W1P 1HF (☎ 0171 255 1362, fax 0171 631 4631)

SWAYTHLING, 4 Baron (UK 1907) David Charles Samuel Montagu; 4 Bt (UK 1894); s of 3 Baron Swaythling, OBE (d 1990), and his 1 w, Mary Violet, *née* Levy; *b* 6 Aug 1928; *Educ* Eton, Trinity Coll Cambridge (BA); *m* 14 Dec 1951, Christiane Françoise (Ninette), yr da of Edgar Dreyfus (d 1976), of Paris; 1 s (Hon Charles Edgar Samuel b 1954), 2 da (Fiona Yvonne b 1952 (d 1982), Hon Nicole Mary (Hon Mrs Campbell) b 1956); *Heir* s, Hon Charles Edgar Samuel Montagu b 20 Feb 1954; *Career* chm Samuel Montagu & Co Ltd 1970–73, chm and chief exec Orion Bank Ltd 1974–79, chm Ailsa Investment Trust plc 1981–87, dir (later dep chm) J Rothschild Holdings plc 1981–89, chm Rothmans International 1988–; dir: Chelsfield PLC 1993–, The British Horseracing Board; hon prof European Business Sch; *Recreations* shooting, racing, theatre; *Clubs* White's, Pratt's, Portland, Union (Sydney); *Style—* The Rt Hon the Lord Swaythling; ✉ 14 Craven Hill Mews, Devonshire Terrace, London W2 3DY (☎ 0171 724 7860); Rothmans International, 15 Hill St, London W1X 7FB (☎ 0171 491 4366, telex 24764)

SWEENEY, Edward (Ed); s of William Sweeney (d 1988), and Louise, *née* Cawley; *b* 6 Aug 1954; *m* 3 Jan 1987, Janet, da of Cliff Roydhouse; *Career* BIFU: research offr 1976–79, negotiating offr TSB 1979–86, national offr Scotland 1986–89, nat offr insurance 1989–91, dep gen sec 1991–96, gen sec 1996–; memb Bd City and Inner London North Training and Enterprise Cncl (CILNTEC); *Recreations* sport of all kinds, reading, egyptology; *Style—* Ed Sweeney, Esq; ✉ General Secretary, Banking Insurance Finance Union, Sheffield House, 1b Amity Grove, London SW20 0LG (☎ 0181 946 9151, 0181 879 7916)

SWEENEY, Jeremy Michael; s of Terence Ernest Michael Sweeney, and Dawn Yvonne, *née* Franklin; *b* 3 June 1963; *Educ* Epsom Coll, Univ of Southampton; *m* Philippa Sara, da of Maj (ret) Patrick Garway-Templeman; *Career* product devpt Wessex Medical Ltd Midhurst W Sussex 1982–85, resort mangr Bladon Lines Risoul France 1986–87, first mate Schooner Fleurtje Hamilton Bermuda 1987–88, with Mercury Communications 1988–89, subsequently md Ian Greer Associates public affrs conslts until 1996 (joined 1989), with A S Biss & Co 1996–; *Recreations* shooting, rugby, dogs; *Clubs* Naval and Military, Cavalry and Guards', Carlton; *Style—* Jeremy Sweeney, Esq; ✉ A S Biss & Co, 8 Wilfred Street, London SW1E 6PL (☎ 0171 828 3030)

SWEENEY, Matthew Gerard; s of Clement Sweeney, of Co Donegal, and Josephine, *née* Lavelle; *b* 6 Oct 1952; *Educ* Franciscan Coll Gormanstown Co Meath, Univ Coll Dublin, Univ of Freiburg (yr abroad), Poly of N London (BA); *m* 14 Sept 1979, Rosemary, da of Benjamin Barber (d 1967); 1 da (Nico Sara b 3 Aug 1980), 1 s (Malvin Leigh b 11 April 1983); *Career* writer; writer in residence Farnham Coll 1984 and 1985, Henfield writing fell UEA 1986, events and publicity asst The Poetry Soc 1988–90, poet in residence Hereford & Worcester 1991, writer in residence The South Bank Centre 1994–95, other residencies incl Birmingham Readers & Writers Festival 1993, Salisbury Festival 1994; memb Aosdána 1990; gives regular readings throughout UK and abroad, has reviewed for Telegraph, Sunday Times, Times supplements and Poetry Review; featured regularly on BBC Radio; awards: Prudence Farmer Prize 1984, Cholmondely Award 1987, Arts Cncl bursary 1992; *Poetry* A Dream of Maps (1981), A Round House (1983), The Lame Waltzer (1985), Blue Shoes (1989), Cacti (1992), The Blue Taps (limited edn pamphlet, 1994), Emergency Kit: Poems For Strange Times (anthology, co-ed with Jo Shapcott, 1996); for children: The Flying Spring Onion (1992), Fatso in the Red Suit (1995); *Fiction* for children: The Snow Vulture (1992 and 1994), The Chinese Dressing Gown (1987); *Style—* Matthew Sweeney, Esq; ✉ Rogers, Coleridge & White, 20 Powis Mews, London W11 1JN (☎ 0171 221 3717)

SWEENEY, Michael Anthony (Mike); s of Michael Dominick Sweeney (d 1969), of Nottingham, and Madaleine, *née* Beatty; *b* 14 Oct 1944; *Educ* Becket Sch, St John's Coll Cambridge (rowing blue); *m* 3 August 1968, Tina, *née* Marson; 1 s (Paul Michael b 29 Nov 1971), 1 da (Claire Helena 15 April 1970); *Career* Boat Race: stroke 1965, stroke and pres 1966, umpire 1984, 1986, 1988, 1990 and 1996; GB eights Euro championships 1967, GB coxless pairs World championships 1970, chm GB Selection Bd 1972–76; team mangr: GB rowing teams 1973–79, Olympic rowing teams 1980 and 1984; elected Henley steward 1974, int (FISA) umpire 1982–, chm of Regattas Cmmn World Rowing (FISA) Cncl 1990–; chm Henley Royal Regatta 1993–; Henley medals: Ladies' Plate 1966, Visitors' 1966, Wyfold 1967, Stewards' 1968; civil engr construction indust 1967–70, district mangr Severn Trent Water Ltd 1987–95 (river engr 1970–86), customer servs dir The Data Base (Nottingham) Ltd 1995–; *Recreations* squash, tennis, skiing, golf; *Style—* Mike Sweeney, Esq; ✉ 36 The Ropewalk, Nottingham NG1 5DW (☎ 0115 947 4690, fax 0115 947 4691)

SWEENEY, Walter E; MP (C) Vale of Glamorgan (majority 19); *b* 23 April 1949; *Educ* Lawrence Sheriff Sch Rugby, Darwin Coll Cambridge, Univ of Hull; *m* 29 Dec 1992, Dr Nuala Kennan; 2 da (Siobhan, Lucy); *Career* admitted slr 1976, in private practice Barry until 1992 (now consit); Parly candidate (C) Stretford 1983, MP (C) Vale of Glamorgan 1992–; memb: Welsh Select Ctee 1992–, Home Affrs Select Ctee 1995–; vice chm Legal Affrs Ctee 1994– (sec 1992–94); sec: Cons Backbench Home Affrs Ctee 1994–, Legal Affrs Ctees 1994–96 (vice chm 1995–); former pt/t lectr in law, former memb Vale of Glamorgan Community Health Cncl; former cncllr: Rugby BC, Bedfordshire CC; former chm: Rugby YCs, Rugby CPC, Hull Univ FCS; *Recreations* theatre, rugby; *Style—* Walter Sweeney, Esq, MP; ✉ House of Commons, London SW1A 0AA

SWEETBAUM, Henry Alan; s of Irving Sweetbaum (d 1985), and Bertha Sweetbaum (d 1952); *b* 22 Nov 1937; *Educ* Wharton Sch Univ of Pennsylvania (BSc); *m* 1, 29 May 1960, late Suzanne, *née* Milburn; m 2, 8 Nov 1971, Anne Betty Leonie, *née* de Vigier; 4 s (Jeffrey Alan b 15 Aug 1961, Barry Jay b 31 March 1964, Peter Mark b 13 Dec 1967, James William Mark b 21 Nov 1974); *Career* mangr cost accounting Mohican Corporation 1959–60, sales rep Underwood Corp 1960–62, exec vice pres and dir Leasco Corporation (Reliance Group) 1962–69, exec dir Plessey Company Ltd 1970–71, fndr chm Huntington Securities Limited 1971–, pt/t chm Data Recording Instrument Company Ltd 1976–82 (non-exec dir 1973–76); non-exec dir: Decision Data Corporation 1980–83, Ashton-Tate Corporation 1986–91, Silicon Systems Inc 1988–89; chm Wickes International Corporation 1982–87, chm and chief exec Wickes plc 1986–96; dir: Centre for Strategic Mgmnt Studies Wharton Sch Univ of Pennsylvania, Bd of Overseers Wharton Sch Univ of Pennsylvania; FIMgt; *Books* Restructuring: The Management Challenge (contrib, 1990); *Recreations* shooting, swimming; *Clubs* Reform, University (NY), Penn (NY); *Style—* Henry Sweetbaum, Esq

SWEETING, Adam Raymond Charles; s of Raymond Ernest William Sweeting (d 1966), and Vera Christine, *née* Potts; *b* 3 Jan 1955; *Educ* Brentwood Sch Essex, Univ of York (BA, MA); *partner* Gillian Harvey; *Career* feature writer TV & Home Video magazine 1979–80, sub-ed Titbits magazine 1980–81, features ed Melody Maker magazine 1984–86 (feature writer 1981–84), freelance writer 1986; currently: arts and culture feature writer The Guardian (formerly rock critic), ptnr Do It productions (video-makers); regular contributor: Esquire, GQ, BBC Radio 2 Arts Prog, Radio Times; sometime contributor: Elle (UK and USA), Vogue, Q, You magazine (The Mail on Sunday), The Times, Sunday Times, The Daily Telegraph, Radio 4, London News Radio; *Books* Springsteen - Visions of America (IPC, 1985), Simple Minds (Sidgwick & Jackson, 1988); *Recreations* cricket (playing and watching), cycling, The Caribbean, movies, opera, Formula 1; *Style—* Adam Sweeting, Esq; ✉ The Guardian, 119 Farringdon Road, London EC1R 3ER

SWEETMAN, Mrs Ronald; Jennifer Joan; *see:* Dickson, Jennifer

SWEETMAN, John Francis; CB (1990), TD (1964); s of Thomas Nelson Sweetman (d 1982), and Mary Monica, *née* D'Arcy-Reddy (d 1994); *b* 31 Oct 1930; *Educ* Cardinal Vaughan Sch, St Catharine's Coll Cambridge (MA); *m* 1, 1959, Susan Manley, da of Lt-Col Manley (d 1986); 1 s (Edward John D'Arcy b 4 March 1969), 1 da (Jane Frances b 17 Jan 1960; m 2, 1983, Celia Elizabeth, da of Sir William Nield (d 1994); 2 s (Thomas William b 27 Aug 1984, James Benedict b 24 Sept 1987); *Career* 2 Lt RA, served in Gibraltar and Med 1949–51, TA (City of London RA) and AER 1951–65; House of Commons: clerk 1954–95, clerk of Select Ctees on Nationalised Industs and on Sci and Technol 1962–65 and 1970–73, second clerk Select Ctees 1979–83, clerk of Overseas Office 1983–87, clerk asst 1987–90, Clerk of Ctees 1990–95, clerk of Select Ctee on Sittings of the House 1991–92; memb Assoc of Secretaries-Gen of Parls (IPU) 1987–95; memb Oxford and Cambridge Catholic Educn Bd 1964–84; *Books* contrib to: Erskine May's Parliamentary Practice, Halsbury's Laws of England (4 edn); ed Cncl of Europe Procedure and Practice of the Parliamentary Assembly (9 edn, 1990); *Clubs* Garrick, MCC; *Style—* John Sweetman, Esq, CB, TD; ✉ 41 Creffield Road, London W5 3RR (☎ 0181 992 2456)

SWEETNAM, Sir (David) Rodney; KCVO (1992), CBE (1990); s of Dr William Sweetnam (d 1970), of Broadlands Ave, Shepperton, Middx, and Irene, *née* Black (d 1967); *b* 5 Feb 1927; *Educ* Clayesmore, Peterhouse Cambridge, Middlesex Hosp Med Sch (MA, MB BChir), FRCS; *m* 23 May 1959, Patricia Ann Staveley, da of A Staveley Gough, OBE; 1 s (David Ian Staveley b 9 May 1963), 1 da (Sarah Ann Staveley (Mrs Dawidek) b 20 March 1961); *Career* Surgn Lt RNVR 1950–52; conslt orthopaedic surgn: Middx Hosp 1960–92, King Edward VII Hosp for Offrs 1964–97; hon conslt orthopaedic surgn: Royal Hosp Chelsea 1974–92, Royal Nat Orthopaedic Hosp 1983–92; hon civil conslt in orthopaedic surgery to the Army 1974–92, orthopaedic surgn to HM the Queen 1982–92, conslt advsr in orthopaedic surgery to DHSS 1981–90; Hunterian prof RCS 1967, Gordon Taylor Meml lectr 1982, Stamford Cade Meml lectr 1986, Bradshaw lectr 1992, Robert Jones lectr 1993; chm MRC Working Pty on Bone Sarcoma 1980–85, dir Medical Sickness Annuity and Life Assurance Society 1982–, dir and dep chm Permanent Assurance Co 1988–95; tstee: Devpt Tst Queen Elizabeth Fndn for the Disabled 1984–96, Smith & Nephew Charitable Tst 1988–, Newman Fndn 1989–; memb Cncl Royal Surgical Aid Soc 1994–95; chm Br Editorial Soc of Bone and Joint Surgery 1992–95 (sec and treas 1975–92); fell Br Orthopaedic Assoc 1960 (pres 1985–86), memb Combined Servs Orthopaedic Soc 1983 (past pres), pres Royal Coll of Surgns of England 1995– (memb Cncl 1985–, vice pres 1992–94); Hon Freeman Worshipful Co of Barbers; *Books* The Basis and Practice of Orthopaedic Surgery (jt ed), Essentials of Orthopaedics (1970), Osteosarcoma (British Medical Journal, 1979); also author of papers on bone tumours and gen orthopaedic surgery and fractures; *Recreations* garden labouring; *Style—* Sir Rodney Sweetnam, KCVO, CBE, PRCS; ✉ 23 Wimpole St, London W1M 7AD

SWENSEN, Joseph; s of Anton Swensen, of Pearl River, NY, USA, and Kikue Okamoto Swensen; *b* 4 Aug 1960; *Educ* Juilliard Sch of Music; *Children* 1 s (David Noah b 17 Aug 1988); *Career* conductor, composer, violinist and pianist; debut as pianist 1967, debut as violinist 1968, debut as conductor Juilliard Sch 1975, violin recital debut NY 1982, London debut Sibelius Concerto with Royal Philharmonic Orch 1984; violin soloist 1984–88 with orchs incl: The Philharmonia, Cleveland Orch, LA Philharmonic, Pittsburgh Symphony, Bavarian and Stuttgart Radio Symphony Orchs, City of Birmingham Symphony, Bournemouth Symphony; conductor 1988– with orchs incl: Royal Danish Symphony Orch, Stockholm Philharmonic, Finnish Radio Symphony Orch, Scottish Chamber Orch (princ conductor 1995–), Swedish Radio Symphony Orch (premier of composition 1995), Jerusalem Symphony, Minnesota Orch, Rochester Philharmonic, Kansas City Symphony, Bergen Philharmonic, Bournemouth Symphony, Bournemouth Sinfonietta, London Mozart Players, Stockholm Chamber Orch (princ guest conductor 1995–), Helsinki Chamber Orch, Israel Chamber Orch, Aalborg Symphony, New World Symphony, Lahti Symphony Orch Finland (princ guest conductor 1995–), Royal Liverpool Symphony Orch, BBC Symphony Orch, Toronto Symphony Orch, BBC Scottish Symphony Orch; premier of composition Shizue Fantasy for Shakuhachi and String Orch 1995; Leventritt sponsorship award 1978, Avery Fisher career award 1982; *Recordings* as conductor incl: Shostakovich Symphony No 14 (Tapiola Sinfonietta (Helsinki)); as violinist incl: Beethoven Violin Concerto (with André Previn and the Royal Philharmonic Orch), Schubert complete violin and piano works, Bach complete violin and harpsichord works, Beethoven works (with James Galway), Sibelius Violin Concerto Humoresques and Serenades (with Jukka-Pekka Saraste and the Finnish Radio Symphony Orch); *Compositions* incl: Ghazal (for cello, orch and five female voices, premiere Helsinki Choral Orch Inkoo Finland 1993), Seven Last Words (for violin, cello, piano and percussion, premiere March 1993), Mantram (for string orch and amplified chimes, premiere Stockholm Chamber Orch Aug 1994), Elegy (for oboe and orch, premiere Finnish Radio Orch Nov 1994), Latif (for solo cello and low strings, premiere Israel Chamber Orch Dec 1994), Shizue Fantasy for Shakuhachi and String Orch (premiere Swedish Radio Orch Aug 1995); *Style—* Joseph Swensen, Esq; ✉ c/o Van Walsum Management, 26 Wadham Road, London SW15 2LR (☎ 0181 874 6344, fax 0181 877 0077)

SWETENHAM, (John) Foster; s of Brig John Edmund Swetenham, DSO (d 1982), and Alison Ann, yst da of Col the Hon Guy Greville Wilson, CMG, DSO; descended from Elias de Swetenham living in the reigns of Richard I, John and Henry III. Family received land at the Somerford Booths 1298, land sold 1930's; *b* 16 Jan 1939; *Educ* Eton, Sandhurst; *m* 1964, Marion Sylvia, yr da of George Alfred Parker (d 1982); 1 s, 1 da; *Career* Mil Serv 1957–70, tt 1964, Adjutant Royal Scots Greys 1965–67, Capt, ret 1970;

memb Stock Exchange 1973–, currently with Williams de Broe plc; MSI(Dip); *Recreations* sailing, country pursuits; *Clubs* Royal Yacht Squadron, Royal Ocean Racing, Pratt's, Essex; *Style*— Foster Swetenham, Esq; ✉ Pound Farmhouse, Rayne, Braintree, Essex CM7 5DJ (☎ 01376 326738); Williams de Broe plc, 6 Broadgate, London EC2 (☎ 0171 588 7511)

SWIFT, Prof Cameron Graham; s of Rev Graham Swift (d 1973), and Victoria, *née* Williamson (d 1996); *b* 5 April 1946; *Educ* Lawrence Sheriff Sch Rugby, Univ of London (MB BS), Univ of Dundee (PhD); *m* Margaret Rosemary, da of Henry K Vernon; *Career* MRC res fell in clinical pharmacology Univ of Dundee 1977–80, conslt physician Dept of Med for the elderly N Humberside 1980–84, dir of postgraduate med educn N Humberside 1982–84, conslt physician and sr lectr Dept of Geriatric Med Univ of Wales Coll of Med 1984–86; prof of health care of the elderly: Univ of London 1986–, Univ of Kent 1986–; conslt physician: King's Coll Hosp, Dulwich Hosp 1986–; sec Specialist Advsy Ctee in Geriatric Med Jt Ctee on Higher Med Trg 1992–94; visiting prof Christchurch Sch of Medicine New Zealand 1994; Br Geriatrics Soc: chm Trg Ctee 1989–91, chm Pharmacology and Therapeutics Section 1989–93, memb Scientific Ctee 1995–; bd memb: Age Concern, King's Coll Inst of Gerontology; memb Cncl Int Assoc of Gerontology (Europe) 1995–; memb: Sub Ctee on Efficacy and Adverse Reactions, Ctee on Safety of Meds 1987–92, Br Pharmacological Soc, Br Geriatrics Soc; FRCP 1988; *Books* Clinical Pharmacology in the Elderly (ed, 1987); *Recreations* music, ornithology, hill walking, scuba diving; *Style*— Prof Cameron Swift; ✉ King's College School of Medicine and Dentistry, King's College Hospital, Denmark Hill, London SE5 9RS (☎ 0171 737 4000 ext 6076, fax 0171 346 6476)

SWIFT, Caroline Jane (Mrs C P L Openshaw); QC (1993); da of Vincent Seymour Swift (d 1979), and Amy Ruth, *née* Johnson; *b* 30 May 1955; *Educ* Lancaster Girls' GS, Univ of Durham (BA, pres Union Soc); *m* 15 Dec 1979, Charles Peter Lawford Openshaw, *qv*, s of late Judge William Harrison Openshaw; 1 da (Alexandra Caroline b 17 July 1984), 1 s (William Henry b 31 Aug 1986); *Career* called to the Bar 1977, in practice Northern Circuit 1978–, recorder of the Crown Court 1995– (asst recorder 1992–95); *Recreations* home and family, participating in parish affairs, riding; *Style*— Miss Caroline Swift, QC; ✉ 25 Byrom St, Manchester M3 4PF (☎ 0161 829 2100, fax 0161 829 2101); 61 Fleet St, London E4Y 7JU (☎ 0171 353 4363, fax 0171 583 1491)

SWIFT, Clive Walter; *b* 1936; *Educ* Clifton Coll Bristol, Caius Coll Cambridge (MA); *m* 1960 (m dis 1975), Margaret Drabble, CBE, *qv*; 3 c; *Career* actor, author, initiator The Actors' Centre; *Theatre* debut Notts Playhouse 1959, RSC original long-contract artist 1960–68; Prospect prodns 1963 and 1966, Chichester 1966 and 1971; freelance credits London incl: Man and Superman, The Young Churchill, Dear Antoine, Dirty Linen, Inadmissable Evidence, The Potsdam Quartet, Roll on Four O'Clock, Messiah, The Genius, An Enemy of the People, Othello, Mr and Mrs Nobody; An Old Man's Love 1996; dir: LAMDA and RADA 1970's; currently poetry-speaking at The Actor's Centre; *Television* numerous single plays and series; serials incl: Dombey and Son, Dig This Rhubarb!, Waugh On Crime, South Riding, Clayhanger, The Barchester Chronicles, Churchill - The Wilderness Years, The Pickwick Papers, First Among Equals, Keeping Up Appearances (5 series); *Radio* debut reading Fielding's Tom Jones 1962, memb BBC Radio Rep 1973; recent credits incl: The Double Dealer, Happy Days, People Like Us, Everyone Comes to Shicklgrubers; *Films* incl: Catch Us If You Can, Frenzy, The National Health, Deathline, Excalibur, A Passage to India, Gaston's War 1996; *Books* The Job of Acting (1976), The Performing World of the Actor (1981), All Together Now (play, co-author with Peter Buckman, 1981); numerous reviews, articles, poems for Theatre Quarterly, World Medecine, BBC World Service, part-adaptor with Michael Napier Brown & Wilma Holingbery of Anthony Trollope's An Old Mans Love 1996; *Audio Books* incl: The Moonstone, The Canterbury Tales, The History of Mr Polly, The Witch of Exmoor; *Recreations* watching cricket and soccer, playing piano; *Clubs* Actors' Centre, London Library, Middlesex CC; *Style*— Clive Swift, Esq; ✉ c/o agent, Roxanne Vacca Management, 73 Beak Street, London W1R 3LF (☎ 0171 734 8085, fax 0171 734 8086)

SWIFT, Graham Colin; s of Lionel Allan Stanley Swift, and Sheila Irene, *née* Bourne; *b* 4 May 1949; *Educ* Dulwich, Queens' Coll Cambridge, Univ of York; *Career* author; *Awards* Geoffrey Faber Meml prize, Guardian Fiction prize, RSL Winifred Holtby award 1983, Booker McConnell prize nominee 1983, Premio Grinzane Cavour Italy 1987, Prix du Meilleur Livre Étranger France 1994, Booker prize 1996 (for Last Orders); FRSL 1984; *Books* novels: The Sweet Shop Owner (1980), Shuttlecock (1981), Waterland (1983), Out of this World (1988), Ever After (1992), Last Orders (1996); others: Learning to Swim (short stories, 1982, reissued 1993), The Magic Wheel (anthology, ed with David Profumo, 1986); *Recreations* fishing; *Style*— Graham Swift, Esq, FRSL

SWIFT, Lionel; QC (1975); s of Harris Swift (d 1971), and Bessie Swift (d 1991); *b* 3 Oct 1931; *Educ* UC London (LLB), Brasenose Coll Oxford (BCL), Univ of Chicago Law Sch (JD); *m* 1966, Elizabeth, da of Max Herzig, of Montreal; 1 da (Allison (Mrs Jeremy Kanter) b 1968); *Career* called to the Bar Inner Temple 1959, recorder 1979–, bencher Inner Temple 1984, head of chambers; jr counsel to Treasy in Probate 1974; chm Institute of Laryngology and Otology 1985–86; *Style*— Lionel Swift, QC; ✉ 4 Paper Buildings, Temple, London EC4Y 7EX (☎ 0171 583 0816, fax 0171 353 4979)

SWIFT, Malcolm Robin Farquhar; QC (1988); s of late Willie Swift, of Huddersfield, W Yorks, and Heather May Farquhar Swift, OBE, *née* Nield (d 1996); *b* 19 Jan 1948; *Educ* Colne Valley HS W Yorks, King's Coll London (LLB); *m* 20 Sept 1969 (m dis 1993), (Anne) Rachael, da of Ernest Rothery Ayre, of Bolton-by-Bowland, Lancs; 1 s (Daniel b 1977), 2 da (Joanna b 1972, Catherine b 1975); *Career* called to the Bar Gray's Inn 1970, in practice NE Circuit, recorder Crown Ct 1987; Bar Cncl: co-opted memb Remuneration Ctee 1978–89, elected memb Public Affrs Ctee 1995–; *Recreations* fitness, cycling, music (lead singer Count One and the TIC's); *Style*— Malcolm Swift, Esq, QC; ✉ Park Court Chambers, 40 Park Cross St, Leeds LS1 2QH (☎ 0113 243 3277, fax 0113 242 1285, telex 666135, dx Leeds 26401); 6 Gray's Inn Square, Gray's Inn, London WC1R 5EZ (☎ 0171 242 1052, fax 0171 405 4934, dx LDE 224 Chancery Lane)

SWIFT, Dr Peter George Furmston; s of Herbert Swift (d 1988), and Catherine Nell, *née* Edwards (d 1977); *b* 22 Jan 1943; *Educ* Wyggeston GS for Boys, Downing Coll Cambridge (MA, MB BChir), Guy's Hosp London; MRCP, DCH, FRCP; *m* 19 Sept 1970, Heather, da of Douglas Hillhouse (d 1970); 3 da (Kate b 1973, Lucy Jane b 1974, Elizabeth Anne b 1976); *Career* sr house offr neonatal paediatrics UCH 1971, registrar in paediatrics Sheffield Children's Hosp 1972–74; sr registrar: Royal Hosp for Sick Children Bristol 1974–77, Exeter Hosps 1977–78; conslt paediatrician with special interest in endocrinology and diabetes Leicester Hosps 1979–, conslt paediatrician Children's Hosp Leicester Royal Infirmary (clinical dir until 1996); chm: Children and Young Persons' Advsy Ctee Br Diabetic Assoc 1983–86, Working Pty on Servs for Diabetic Children Br Paediatric Assoc 1987–89; sec Br Soc of Paediatric Endocrinology 1990–93; memb: Br Paediatric Assoc, BDA, GMC, ESPE, ISPAD; *Recreations* sports; *Clubs* Leicester Squash, Leicester Univ Sports; *Style*— Dr Peter Swift; ✉ The Children's Hospital, Leicester Royal Infirmary, Leicester LE1 5WW (☎ 0116 254 1414, fax 0116 258 6912)

SWIFT, Robert; s of Max Swift (d 1960), and Leah, *née* Seigle (d 1978); *b* 13 Aug 1941; *Educ* John Marshall HS Los Angeles, Univ of London (LLB), Coll of Law; *m* 25 Aug 1963, Hilary, da of Simon Bernard Casson (d 1971); 2 s (Mark b 1969, Simon b 1972); 1 da (Miranda b 1976); *Career* slr; Patent & Trademark Dept EMI Ltd 1967–71, Linklaters & Paines 1971–75, legal asst White and Case NY 1975, ptnr Linklaters & Paines 1976– (head Intellectual Property Dept 1981–94); vice chm Intellectual Property Sub-ctee City of London Law Soc; memb: Jt Bar/Law Soc Working Pty on Intellectual Property Law 1986–90, Commercial and Consumer Law Ctee and Intellectual Property Law Sub-ctee Law Soc; Freeman Worshipful Co of Slrs 1976; memb: Law Soc 1967, Patent Slrs' Assoc, Computer Law Gp; *Recreations* music, books, walking; *Style*— Robert Swift, Esq; ✉ Linklaters & Paines, Barrington House, 59/67 Gresham Street, London EC2V 7JA (☎ 0171 606 7080, fax 0171 606 5113)

SWINBURN, Brig David Henry Amyatt; CBE (1989); s of Maj-Gen Henry Robinson Swinburn, CB, OBE, MC (d 1981), and Naomi Barbara, *née* Hull (d 1992); bro of Sir Richard Swinburn, KCB, *qv*; *b* 15 July 1934; *Educ* Wellington, Peterhouse Cambridge (MA), RMA Sandhurst; *m* 1, 7 Jan 1961, Belinda Marion (d 1961), da of Vernon Stainton, ICS (d 1945), and Mrs Stainton, of Crowborough; m 2, 17 Sept 1966, Gillian Adair, MVO, da of Col Adair (d 1994) and Mrs Murray, of Winchester; 2 s (Jonathan b 1969, Christopher b 1970), 1 da (Joanna b 1970); *Career* cmmnd RE 1954, Lt-Col and CO 26 Engr Regt 1974, Brig and cmd RE of Corps 1979, RCDS course 1981; MOD: dir NATO 1982, dir Engr Servs 1984, dir Exams and Courses 1986, ADC to HM The Queen 1986–89, ret 1989; gp trg mangr Mott MacDonald Consltg Engrs 1989–94, dir Strategic Management Solutions Ltd 1994–; FIPD, FIMgt, Companion of Inst of Civil Engrs; *Recreations* squash, skiing, tennis, fishing, gardening; *Style*— Brig David Swinburn, CBE; ✉ Lower Eashing Farmhouse, Godalming, Surrey GU7 2QF (☎ and fax 01483 421436)

SWINBURN, Sir Richard Hull; KCB (1991); s of Maj-Gen Henry Robinson Swinburn, CB, OBE, MC (d 1981), and Naomi Barbara, *née* Hull (d 1992); bro of Brig D H A Swinburn, CBE, *qv*; *b* 30 Oct 1937; *Educ* Wellington, RMA Sandhurst; *m* 29 Aug 1964, Jane Elise, da of A B Brodie (ka 1942); *Career* cmmnd 1957, CO 17/21 Lancers 1979–82, cmmnd 7 Armoured Bde 1983–85, GOC 1 Armoured Div 1987–89, Asst Chief of Gen Staff MOD 1989–90, GOC SE District 1990–92, GOC Southern District 1992–94, Dep C-in-C, Cdr UK Field Army and Inspr Gen TA 1994–95, Lt-Gen, ret 1995; farmer 1993–; huntsman RMA Sandhurst Beagles 1956–57, master and huntsman Dheklia Draghounds 1971, memb Hampshire Hunt 1974–, master and huntsman Staff Coll Draghounds 1985–86, chm Army Beagling Assoc 1988–94; dir Glancal Property Co 1990–96, dir Friarsgrove Management Services Ltd 1995–; govr Duke of York Sch Dover 1990–94, memb Cncl RUSI 1991–95; Hon Col Exeter Univ OTC 1994–, Col The Queen's Royal Lancers 1995–; *Recreations* hunting; *Clubs* Cavalry and Guards'; *Style*— Sir Richard Swinburn, KCB; ✉ Stone, Exford, Somerset TA24 7NX

SWINBURNE, Prof Richard Granville; s of William Henry Swinburne, OBE (d 1994), of Colchester, and Gladys Edith Swinburne (d 1988); *b* 26 Dec 1934; *Educ* Exeter Coll Oxford (BA, MA, BPhil); *m* 1960 (sep 1985), Monica; 2 da (Caroline (Mrs David Cope) b 1961, Nicola b 1962); *Career* Fereday fell St John's Coll Oxford 1958–61, Leverhulme res fell Univ of Leeds 1961–63, lectr Univ of Hull 1963–69 (sr lectr 1969–72), visiting assoc prof of philosophy Maryland Univ 1969–70, prof of philosophy Keele Univ 1972–84, Nolloth prof of philosophy of the Christian religion Univ of Oxford 1985–; visiting lectureships: Wilde lectr Univ of Oxford 1975–78, Marrett Meml lectr Exeter Coll Oxford 1980, Gifford lectr Univ of Aberdeen 1982–83 and 1983–84, Edward Cadbury lectr Univ of Birmingham 1987, Wade Meml lectr St Louis Univ 1990, Dotterer lectr Penn State Univ 1992; distinguished visiting scholar Univ of Adelaide 1982, visiting prof of philosophy Syracuse Univ 1987; FBA; *Books* Space and Time (1968, 1981), The Concept of Miracle (1971), An Introduction to Confirmation Theory (1973), The Coherence of Theism (1977, 1993), The Existence of God (1979, 1991), Faith and Reason (1981), Personal Identity (with Sydney Shoemaker 1984), The Evolution of the Soul (1986), Responsibility and Atonement (1989), Revelation (1991), The Christian God (1994), Is There a God? (1996); ed: The Justification of Induction (1974), Space, Time and Causality (1983), Miracles (1988); *Style*— Prof Richard Swinburne, FBA; ✉ Oriel College, Oxford OX1 4EW (☎ 01865 276589, fax 01865 791823)

SWINBURNE, Prof Terence Reginald; s of Reginald Swinburne, of Gravesend, Kent, and Gladys Hannah, *née* Shrubsall; *b* 17 July 1936; *Educ* Kent Co GS for Boys Gravesend, Imperial Coll of Sci and Technol Univ of London (BSc, PhD, DSc); *m* 23 Aug 1958, Valerie Mary, da of Daniel Parkes; 2 s (Julian Edward b 25 Sept 1965, Nigel David b 17 Jan 1968); *Career* reader Faculty of Agric Queen's Univ of Belfast 1977 (joined 1960), sr princ sci offr Plant Pathology Res Div Dept of Agric NI 1979–80, head of Crop Protection Div E Malling Res Station 1980–85, dir AFRC Inst of Hort Res 1985–90, prof of hort devpt and sr res fell Wye Coll Univ of London 1990–; memb: Br Mycological Soc, Assoc of Applied Biologists, Inst of Biol; FIHort; *Books* Iron, Siderophores and Plant Diseases; *Recreations* sailing; *Clubs* Farmers'; *Style*— Prof Terence Swinburne; ✉ Tan House, Frog Lane, West Malling, Kent (☎ 01732 846 090); Wye College, University of London, Kent (☎ 01233 812410)

SWINDELLS, Maj-Gen (George) Michael Geoffrey; CB (1985); s of George Martyn Swindells (d 1960), and Marjorie, *née* Leigh (d 1991); *b* 15 Jan 1930; *Educ* Rugby; *m* 8 July 1955, Prudence Bridget Barbara, da of William Scarth Carlisle Tully, CBE (d 1987); 1 s (Adam George Carlisle b 1975, d 1995), 2 da (Diana Harris b 1956, Georgina b 1961); *Career* cmmnd 5 Royal Inniskilling Dragoon Gds 1949, cmd 9/12 Royal Lancers 1968–71, Cdr 11 Armd Bde 1975–76, RCDS 1977, chief Jt Servs Liaison Orgn Bonn 1980–83, dir Mgmnt and Support of Intelligence 1983–85, Col 9/12 Royal Lancers 1990–94; controller Army Benevolent Fund 1987–; chm: Governing Body Royal Sch Hampstead 1985–89, Servs Liaison Variety Club of GB 1986–, Br Limbless Ex-Servicemans Assoc 1991–96; *Recreations* country life; *Clubs* Cavalry and Guards'; *Style*— Maj-Gen Michael Swindells, CB; ✉ Wilcot Lodge, Pewsey, Wilts SN9 5NS (☎ 01672 563465); Army Benevolent Fund, 41 Queen's Gate, London SW7 5HR (☎ 0171 584 5232)

SWINDEN, (Thomas) Alan; CBE (1971); s of Dr Thomas Swinden (d 1944), of Sheffield, and Ethel Taylor, *née* Thompson (d 1974); *b* 27 Aug 1915; *Educ* Rydal Sch, Univ of Sheffield (BEng); *m* 21 June 1941, Brenda Elise, da of Frederick John Roe (d 1961), of Epsom; 1 da (Gail b 1950); *Career* Rolls Royce Ltd 1937–55 (seconded armd fighting vehicle div Miny of Supply 1941–45); dir: Engrg Employers' Fedn 1964–65 (joined 1955), Engrg Indust Trg Bd 1965–70; dep DG CBI 1970–78, chm Inst of Manpower Studies 1977–86, dir Kingston Regnl Mgmnt Centre 1980–84; memb: Cncl ACAS 1974–84, Consultative Gp on Industl and Business Affrs BBC 1977–83; chm Derby No 1 Hosp Mgmnt Ctee 1953–55; govr: NE Surrey Coll of Technol 1973–91 (chm Bd of Govrs 1986–91), Box Hill Sch 1996–; *Recreations* gardening, golf, reading; *Clubs* RAC; *Style*— Alan Swinden, Esq, CBE; ✉ 85 College Rd, Epsom, Surrey KT17 4HH (☎ 01372 720848)

SWINDON, Archdeacon of; *see:* Middleton, Ven Michael John

SWINDON, Bishop of 1994–; Rt Rev Michael Doe; s of Albert Henry Doe (d 1977), of Lymington, Hants, and Violet Nellie, *née* Curtis; *b* 24 Dec 1947; *Educ* Brockenhurst GS, Univ of Durham, Ripon Hall Theol Coll Oxford; *Career* hon curate St Peter St Helier Morden Surrey 1976–81 (asst curate 1972–76), youth sec Br Cncl of Churches 1976–81, vicar Blackbird Leys (local ecumenical project) Oxford 1988–89 (priest-missioner 1981–88), rural dean of Cowley 1986–89, social responsibility advsr to Anglican Dio of Portsmouth and canon residentiary Portsmouth Cathedral 1989–94, memb C of E Gen Synod 1990–94; *Recreations* travel, radio and TV; *Style*— The Rt Rev the Bishop of Swindon; ✉ Mark House, Field Rise, Swindon (☎ 01793 538654)

SWINFEN, Prof David Berridge; s of Thomas Berridge Swinfen (d 1973), and Freda Mary Swinfen (d 1990); *b* 8 Nov 1936; *Educ* Fettes, Hertford Coll Oxford (MA, DPhil); *m* 1960, Ann, da of A B Pettit; 2 s (Michael and Richard), 3 da (Tanya, Katrina and

Nicola); *Career* 2 Lt KOSB (Malaya) 1955–57; lectr in modern history Queen's Coll (later Univ of Dundee) 1963–75; Univ of Dundee: sr lectr 1975–90, prof of Cwlth history 1990–, dean Faculty of Arts and Social Scis 1984–88, head Dept of Modern History 1988–92, dep princ 1992–94, vice princ 1994–; FRHistS; *Books* Imperial Control of Colonial Legislation (1970), Ruggles' Regiment - The 122nd New York Volunteers in the American Civil War (1982), Imperial Appeal - The Debate on the Right of Appeal to the Privy Council (1987), The Life and Times of Dundee (1993), The Fall of the Tay Bridge (1994); *Recreations* music, gardening; *Style*— Prof David Swinfen; ✉ 14 Cedar Road, Broughty Ferry, Dundee DD5 3BB; University of Dundee, Dundee DD1 4HN (☎ 01382 345557, fax 01382 229948)

SWINFEN, 3 Baron (UK 1919); Roger Mynors Swinfen Eady; s of 2 Baron Swinfen (d 1977), and his 1 w, Mary Aline (*see* Wesley, Mary Aline), da of late Col Harold Mynors Farmar, CMG, DSO; *b* 14 Dec 1938; *Educ* Westminster, RMA Sandhurst; *m* 24 Oct 1962, Patricia Anne, o da of Frank D Blackmore (d 1968), of Dublin; 1 s, 3 da (Hon Georgina (Hon Mrs Liley) b 1964, Hon Katherine (Hon Mrs Davies) b 1966, Hon Arabella (Hon Mrs Mayo) b 1969); *Heir* s, Hon Charles Roger Peregrine Swinfen Eady b 8 March 1971; *Career* Lt The Royal Scots; memb Direct Mail Services Standards Bd 1983–96; chm Parly Gp Video Enquiry Working Party 1983–85, memb Sub-ctee C House of Lords Euro Communities Ctee 1990–94; fell Indust and Parly Tst 1983; pres SE Region Br Sports Assoc for the Disabled 1986–; hon pres Britain Bangladesh Friendship Soc 1996–; patron: Disablement Income Gp 1995–, 1 in 8 Gp 1996–, Labrador Rescue SE 1996–; JP Kent 1983–85; Liveryman Worshipful Co of Drapers; ARICS 1970; *Style*— The Rt Hon the Lord Swinfen; ✉ House of Lords, London SW1A 0PW

SWINGLAND, Owen Merlin Webb; QC (1974); s of Charles Swingland (d 1941), of Kent, and Maggie Eveline, *née* Webb (d 1961); family moved from Worcestershire ca 1680 to parish of St Margaret Pattens, Eastcheap, London, lived in Kent about 200 years; *b* 26 Sept 1919; *Educ* Haberdashers' Aske's, King's Coll London; *m* 1941, Kathleen Joan Eason, da of late Frederick William Parry; 1 s (Charles), 2 da (Diana, Carole); *Career* barr; bencher of Gray's Inn, gen cmmr of income tax; a church cmmr for England 1982–90; Master Worshipful Co of Haberdashers 1987 (memb Ct of Assts); memb Lincoln's Inn 1978; *Recreations* reading, music, theatre, gardening; *Style*— Owen Swingland, Esq, QC; ✉ Redwings House, Bayleys Hill, Weald, Sevenoaks, Kent TN14 (☎ 01732 451667)

SWINGLER, Raymond John Peter; s of Raymond Joseph Swingler (d 1942), of Christchurch, NZ, and Mary Elizabeth, *née* Alexander (d 1975); *b* 8 Oct 1933; *Educ* St Thomas's Acad Oamaru NZ, St Bede's Coll Christchurch NZ, Univ of Canterbury NZ; *m* 11 July 1960, Shirley (d 1980), da of Frederick Wilkinson (d 1962), of Plymouth; 2 da (Elisabeth-jane b 1 July 1961, Claire-louise b 6 Oct 1963); *Career* journalist: The Press (NZ) 1956–57, Marlborough Express 1957–59, Nelson Mail 1959–61, freelance Middle East 1961–62, Cambridge Evening News 1962–79; memb: Press Cncl 1975–78, Press Cncl Complaints Ctee 1976–78, Nat Exec Cncl NUJ 1973–75 and 1978–79, Prov Newspapers Indust Cncl 1976–79; chm Gen Purposes Ctee 1974–75, sec Press Cncl 1980–89 (asst dir 1989–90), asst dir The Press Complaints Cmmn 1991, charitiy advsr 1992–; *Recreations* travel; *Style*— Raymond Swingler, Esq; ✉ 11A Church Path, London E17 9RQ (☎ 0181 520 7538, fax 0181 509 0589, e-mail 100622.2753@compuserve.com)

SWINLEY, Margaret Albinia Joanna; OBE (1980); da of Capt Casper Silas Balfour Swinley, DSO, DSC, RN (d 1983), and Sylvia Jocosa, *née* Carnegie; *b* 30 Sept 1935; *Educ* Southover Manor Sch Lewes Sussex, Univ of Edinburgh (MA); *Career* English teacher/sec United Paper Mills Ltd Jämsänkoski Finland 1958–60; British Cncl 1960–89: Birmingham Area Office 1960–63, Tel Aviv 1963, Lagos 1963–66, seconded to London HQ of VSO 1966–67, New Delhi 1967–70, dep rep Lagos 1970–73, dir Tech Cooperation Trg Dept 1973–76, rep Israel 1976–80, asst (later dep) controller Educn Med & Sci Div 1980–82, controller Africa and Middle East Div 1982–86 and Home Div 1986–89, ret 1989; memb Soroptimist Int of Greater London (pres 1988–89), tstee Lloyd Fndn, advsr overseas projects HelpAge Int; govr: Westbury-on-Severn C of E Primary Sch (chm 1990–96), Int Students House London, Hosting for Overseas Students; *Recreations* theatre going, country life, keeping dogs and shire horses; *Clubs* Cwlth Tst, Soroptimist Int of Greater London; *Style*— Miss M A J Swinley, OBE

SWINNERTON-DYER, *see:* Dyer

SWINSON, Christopher; s of Arthur Montagu Swinson, of 52 Green Moor Link, Winchmore Hill, London, and Jean, *née* Dudley; *b* 27 Jan 1948; *Educ* Wadham Coll Oxford (BA, MA); *m* 9 Sept 1972, Christine Margaret, da of Walter Yeats Hallam (d 1973); 1 s (Timothy b 1987); *Career* mangr Price Waterhouse 1970–78, nat managing ptnr BDO Binder Hamlyn 1989–92 (sr mangr 1978–81, ptnr 1981–92), ptnr BDO Stoy Hayward 1993–; memb Cncl and Exec Ctee ICAEW (vice-pres 1996–97), memb Financial Reporting Cncl 1990–, memb Financial Reporting Review Panel 1992–; hon treas NCVO; Freeman City of London 1985, memb Worshipful Co of CAs; FCA 1974; *Clubs* Athenaeum; *Style*— Christopher Swinson, Esq; ✉ 2 Seymour Close, Hatch End, Pinner, Middx HA5 4SB (☎ 0181 421 0951, fax 0181 421 3344)

SWINSON, Sir John Henry Alan; kt (1984), OBE (1973); s of Edward Alexander Swinson (d 1944), of Knock, Belfast, and Mary Margaret, *née* McLeod (d 1966); *b* 12 July 1922; *Educ* Royal Belfast Acad Inst; *m* 1944, da of John Gallagher (d 1958), of Castlereagh, Belfast; 2 s (Alan, Peter); *Career* commercial dir Ireland Trusthouse Forte plc (now Forte plc) 1962–94, dir various subsid cos until 1994, ret; chm: NI Tourist Bd 1980–88 (memb 1970–80), Livestock Mktg Cmmn 1970–85, Catering Indust Trg Bd (NI) 1966–75, NI Trg Exec 1975–83; *Recreations* sailing; *Clubs* Royal NI Yacht; *Style*— Sir John H A Swinson, OBE; ✉ 10 Circular Road East, Cultra, Co Down BT18 0HA, N Ireland (☎ 01232 422494)

SWINTON, 2 Earl of (UK 1955); David Yarburgh Cunliffe-Lister; JP (N Yorks 1971), DL (1978); also Viscount Swinton (UK 1935), Baron Masham (UK 1955); s of late Maj the Hon John Yarburgh Cunliffe-Lister, eldest s of 1 Earl, GBE, CH, MC, MP; suc gf 1972; *b* 21 March 1937; *Educ* Winchester, RAC Cirencester; *m* 1959, Susan Lilian Primrose (Baroness Masham of Ilton, *qv*), da of late Sir Ronald Norman John Charles Udny Sinclair, 8 Bt (cr 1704); 1 s, 1 da (both adopted); *Heir* bro, Hon Nicholas Cunliffe-Lister; *Career* sits as Cons in House of Lords, Capt HM's Body Guard of Yeomen of the Guard (dep govt chief whip in Lords) 1982–86; co cncllr: N Riding Yorks 1961–74, N Yorks 1973–77; countryside cmmr 1987–93; FRSA 1993; *Clubs* Whites's, Pratt's, Leyburn Market; *Style*— The Rt Hon the Earl of Swinton, JP, DL; ✉ Dykes Hill House, Masham, N Yorks HG4 4NS (☎ 01765 689241); 46 Westminster Gdns, Marsham St, London SW1P 4JG (☎ 0171 834 0700)

SWINTON, Maj-Gen Sir John; KCVO (1979), OBE (1969), JP (Berwicks 1989); the family of Swinton of that Ilk, now represented by the Kimmerghame branch, has owned land in the Swinton area of Berwickshire since the eleventh century; s of Brig A H C Swinton, MC (d 1972), of Kimmerghame, Duns, Berwicks, and Mrs I D Erskine (d 1996), of Swinton, Berwickshire; *b* 21 April 1925; *Educ* Harrow; *m* 1954, Judith Balfour, da of Harold Killen, of Merribee, NSW; 3 s (James Christopher b 12 Nov 1955, Alexander Harold b 6 Nov 1958, Maj William H C b 1 July 1965), 1 da (Katherine Matilda b 5 Nov 1960, actress as Tilda Swinton); *Career* served Scots Gds 1943–71, Lt-Col Cmdg 1970–71, cmd 4 Gds Armd Bde 1972–73, Brig Lowlands 1975–76, GOC London Dist and Maj-Gen cmdg The Household Div 1976–79, ret 1979; Ensign Queen's Body Guard for Scotland (Royal Co of Archers), Hon Col 2 Bn 52 Lowland Volunteers 1983–90; nat chm Royal Br Legion Scotland 1986–89 (vice chm 1984–86); chm Scottish Ex-Serv Charitable Orgns (SESCO) 1988–89; chm of tstees Scottish Nat War Meml 1996– (tstee 1984–); tstee: Army Museums Ogilby Tst 1978–90, Berwick Military Tattoo 1996–; memb Centl Advsy Ctee on War Pensions 1986–89; chm: Thirlestane Castle Tst 1984–90, Jt Mgmnt Ctee St Abbs Head Nat Nature Reserve 1991–; pres: Lowland TA & VRA 1992–96, Royal Highland & Agricultural Soc of Scotland 1993–94, Borders Branch SSAFA 1993–, Berwickshire Naturalists' Club 1996–, Berwickshire Civic Soc (chm 1982–96); Lord Lt Berwicks 1989– (DL 1980–89); *Clubs* New (Edinburgh); *Style*— Maj-Gen Sir John Swinton, KCVO, OBE, JP; ✉ Kimmerghame, Duns, Berwicks TD11 3LU (☎ and fax 01361 883277)

SWIRE, Sir Adrian Christopher; kt (1982), DL (Oxon 1989); yr s of John Kidston Swire, DL (d 1983), of Hubbards Hall, Old Harlow, Essex, by his w Juliet Richenda (d 1981), da of Charles Barclay, bro of Sir John A Swire, CBE, *qv*; *b* 15 Feb 1932; *Educ* Eton, Univ Coll Oxford (MA); *m* 1970, Lady Judith Compton, da of 6 Marquess of Northampton, DSO (d 1978); 2 s, 1 da; *Career* Nat Service Coldstream Gds 1950–52, RAFVR and Royal Hong Kong AAF 1953–61; joined Butterfield & Swire Far East 1956; John Swire & Sons Ltd: dir 1961–66, dep chm 1966–87, chm 1987–; dir: Swire Pacific Ltd, Cathay Pacific Airways, HSBC Holdings plc 1995–; memb Int Advsy Cncl China International Trust & Investment Corporation Beijing 1995–; dir: Brooke Bond Group 1972–82, NAAFI 1972–86 (dep chm 1982–85); pres Gen Cncl of Br Shipping 1980–81, chm Int Chamber of Shipping 1982–87; memb Gen Ctee Lloyd's Register 1967–; visiting fell Nuffield Coll Oxford 1981–89; pro-chllr Univ of Southampton 1995–; Hon Air Cdre RAuxAF 1987–, tstee RAF Museum 1983–91, chm RAF Benevolent Fund 1996–, pres Spitfire Soc 1996–; memb Cncl Wycombe Abbey Sch 1988–95; Elder Brother Trinity House 1990; Liveryman: Worshipful Co of Fishmongers 1962, Guild of Air Pilots and Air Navigators 1986; Hon DSc Cranfield Univ 1995; Hon CRAeS 1991; *Clubs* White's, Brooks's, Pratt's, Hong Kong; *Style*— Sir Adrian Swire, DL; ✉ John Swire & Sons Ltd, Swire House, 59 Buckingham Gate, London SW1E 6AJ (☎ 0171 834 7717)

SWIRE, Hugo George William; s of Humphrey Roger Swire, and Philippa Sophia Montgomerie, da of late Col George Jardine Kidston-Montgomerie of Southannan, DSO, MC, DL; *b* 30 Nov 1959; *Educ* Eton, Univ of St Andrews, RMA Sandhurst; *m* 12 Dec 1996, Alexandra (Sasha) M P, o da of Rt Hon Sir John William Frederic Nott, KCB; *Career* Lt 1 Bn Grenadier Guards 1980–83; head Nat Gallery Devpt Office 1988–92, dep dir Sotheby's 1996– (joined 1992); prospective parly candidate (Scottish Cons and Unionist) Greenock & Inverclyde; FRSA 1993; *Clubs* White's, Pratt's, Beefsteak; *Style*— Hugo Swire, Esq; ✉ 38 Evelyn Gardens, London SW7 3BJ (☎ 0171 244 0496); Sotheby's, 34–35 New Bond Street, London W1A 2AA (☎ 0171 408 5484, fax 0171 408 5941)

SWIRE, Sir John Anthony; kt (1990), CBE (1977), DL (1996); er s of John Kidston Swire (d 1983); bro of Sir Adrian Swire, DL, *qv*; *b* 28 Feb 1927; *Educ* Eton, Univ Coll Oxford; *m* 1961, Moira Ducharne; 2 s, 1 da; *Career* served Irish Gds (UK and Palestine) 1945–48; joined Butterfield & Swire Hong Kong 1950; hon pres John Swire & Sons Ltd 1987– (dir 1955–, chm 1966–87); former dir: Royal Insurance Co, British Bank of the Middle East, Ocean Transport & Trading Ltd, James Finlay & Co plc, Shell Transport & Trading Co plc; memb: London Advsy Ctee Hongkong and Shanghai Banking Corp 1969–89, Euro-Asia Centre Advsy Bd 1980–91, Advsy Cncl Sch of Business Stanford Univ 1981–90; dep pro-chllr Univ of Kent at Canterbury 1993– (memb Cncl 1989–); hon fell St Antony's & Univ Colls Oxford; Hon DL Hong Kong 1989, Hon DCL Univ of Kent at Canterbury 1995; Liveryman Worshipful Co of Fishmongers; *Style*— Sir John Swire, CBE, DL; ✉ Swire House, 59 Buckingham Gate, London SW1E 6AJ (☎ 0171 834 7717)

SWIRE, Rhoderick Martin; s of Patrick Douglas Swire, (d 1960), of Shropshire, and Joan Mary, *née* Allison (d 1970); *b* 27 March 1951; *Educ* Eton, Univ of Birmingham (BSc); *m* 11 June 1977, Georgina Mary, da of Christopher Ronald Thompson, of Shropshire; 1 s (Hugh b 1979), 2 da (Henrietta b 1981, Camilla b 1985); *Career* Peat Marwick Mitchell 1972–76; John Swire & Sons Ltd: gp accountant Hong Kong 1976–79, asst to chm Aust 1979–81, London 1981; GT Management plc: mangr unquoted investmt 1981–88, main bd dir 1987–; md Pantheon Holdings, chm Pantheon Ventures Ltd; FCA 1980 (ACA 1975); *Recreations* shooting, tennis, gardening; *Clubs* Boodle's; *Style*— Rhoderick Swire, Esq; ✉ Aldenham Park, Bridgnorth, Shropshire; Pantheon Ventures Ltd, 43/44 Albemarle St, London W1X 3FF (☎ 0171 493 5685, fax 0171 629 0844)

SWITHENBANK, Prof Joshua (Jim); s of Joshua Swithenbank (d 1971), and Ethel Eva, *née* Foster (d 1992); *b* 19 Oct 1931; *Educ* Friend's Sch Wigton Cumberland, Univ of Birmingham (BSc), Univ of Sheffield (PhD); *m* 29 March 1958, Margaret Elizabeth Anderson, da of Rev James Herbert Manson; 1 s (Joshua Ross b 11 July 1962), 3 da (Elizabeth b 7 May 1960, Christine b 28 March 1965, Shirley Joyce b 20 May 1966); *Career* engr Res and Devpt Dept Rolls Royce Ltd 1953–58, engr Design Dept Canadair 1958, assoc prof Mechanical Engrg McGill Univ Canada 1958–61, prof Dept of Mechanical and Process Engrg Univ of Sheffield 1961–; author of over 200 articles in scientific jls and books; fndr memb Watt Ctee on Energy Ltd 1975–, memb ACORD 1988–90, gen superintendent res Int Flame Res Fndn 1989–91; memb: American Inst of Chemical Engrg, American Inst of Astronautics and Aeronautics; FEng 1978, FInstE (pres 1987–88), FIChemE; *Recreations* scuba diving, photography, travel; *Clubs* British Sub Aqua; *Style*— Prof Jim Swithenbank, FEng; ✉ Department of Mechanical and Process Engineering, Sheffield University, Western Bank, Sheffield S10 2TN (☎ 0114 222 7502, fax 0114 278 0611, e-mail j.swithenbank@sheffield.ac.uk)

SWITZER, Barbara; da of Albert McMinn (d 1981), of Manchester, and Edith, *née* Hughes (d 1986); *b* 26 Nov 1940; *Educ* Chorlton Central Sch, Stretford Tech Coll, Wythenshawe Tech Coll, N Cheshire Tech Coll (City & Guilds' Electrical Technician Cert); *m* 18 Aug 1973, (John) Michael Switzer (d 1994), s of Jack Switzer (d 1989), of Mississauga, Canada; *Career* engrg apprentice Metropolitan Vickers Trafford Park 1957–62, electrical engrg draughtswoman 1962–76 (AEI/GEC, Cableform, Mather & Platt); Manufacturing Science and Finance Union: regnl offr 1976–80, nat offr 1980–83, asst gen sec 1983–; memb: Gen Cncl TUC 1993–94, Exec Ctee Inst of Employment Rights 1993–, Employment Appeal Tbnl 1996–, NEC Lab Pty; assoc memb Women's Engrg Soc; pres Confedn of Shipbuilding and Engrg Unions (CSEU) 1995–; TUC Women's Gold Badge for Servs to Trade Unionism 1976; *Style*— Mrs Barbara Switzer; ✉ Manufacturing Science and Finance Union, MSF Centre, 33–37 Moreland Street, London EC1V 8BB (☎ 0171 505 3000, fax 0171 505 3030)

SWORN, Dr Michael John; s of Ernest James Sworn (d 1942), and Clarice, *née* Heath; *b* 12 April 1942; *Educ* All Saints Sch Bloxham, London Hosp Med Coll, Univ of London (MB BS, LLB); *m* 9 Sept 1967, Bridget Mary, da of John Shanahan (d 1991), of Somerville, New Jersey, USA; 1 da (Sarah Louise b 1973); *Career* jr lectr in morbid anatomy Inst of Pathology The London Hosp 1967–69, sr registrar in morbid anatomy United Sheffield Hosps 1969–70, lectr in pathology Univ of Sheffield 1970–73, conslt pathologist The Royal Hampshire Co Hosp 1974–; examiner for the primary fellowship RCS England 1983–89, examiner FRCS applied basic science examination RCS England, examiner in pathology The Examining Bd England 1983–89, tutor in pathology Royal Coll of Pathologists to Winchester and Eastleigh NHS Tst 1995–; asst sec then sec Winchester Div BMA 1976–82, liaison offr Assoc of Clinical Pathologists for Winchester 1983–; memb: Ctee on Histopathology Assoc of Clinical Pathologists 1994–, Cytopathology Sub Ctee of the Specialist Advsy Ctee on Histopathology Royal Coll of Pathologists 1995–; author of pubns on histopathology; Cert BA Univ of Warwick; memb: Pathological Soc 1972, Assoc of Clinical Pathologists 1973, Br Soc of Clinical Cytology 1975; MRCS, LRCP, FRCPath; *Recreations* golf; *Style*— Dr Michael Sworn; ✉ Barncliffe, 28 Chilbolton Ave, Winchester, Hants SO22 5HD (☎ 01962 853558); Royal

Hampshire County Hospital, Romsey Rd, Winchester, Hants SO22 5DG (☎ 01962 824454)

SWYNNERTON, Sir Roger John Massy; kt (1976), CMG (1959), OBE (1951), MC (1941); s of Charles Francis Massy Swynnerton, CMG (d 1938), and Norah Aimee Geraldine Smyth (d 1963); *b* 16 Jan 1911; *Educ* Lancing, Gonville and Caius Cambridge (BA, DipAgric), Imperial Coll of Tropical Agric Trinidad (AICTA); *m* 1943, Grizel Beryl, da of Ralph William Richardson Miller, CMG (d 1958), of Lushoto, Tanganyika; 2 s (John, Charles); *Career* 2 Lt OC CUOTC Artillery Batty 1932–33, TARO 1933–60, served with 1/6 KAR (Kenya, Italian Somaliland, Abyssinia) 1939–42, temp Capt; Colonial Agric Serv Tanganyika 1934–51, seconded to agric duties Malta 1942–43, Kenya 1951–63 (asst dir of agric 1951, dep dir 1954, dir 1956–60, perm sec Miny of Agric 1960–62, temp min 1961, MLC 1956–61, ret 1963); memb Advsy Ctee on Devpt of Economic Resources of Southern Rhodesia 1961–62, agric advsr and memb Exec Mgmnt Bd Cwlth Devpt Corpn 1962–76, self-employed conslt in tropical agric and devpt 1976–85; dir Booker Agriculture International Ltd 1976–88; Univ of Southampton: visiting lectr 1977–88, memb Advsy Bd on Irrigation Studies 1980–88; pres Swynnerton Family Soc 1982–93, Tropical Agric Assoc 1983–89; *Publications* All About KNCU Coffee (1948), A Plan to Intensify the Development of African Agriculture in Kenya (1954); *Clubs* Royal Over-Seas League, Royal Cwlth Soc; *Style—* Sir Roger Swynnerton, CMG, OBE, MC; ✉ Cherry House, 2 Vincent Rd, Stoke D'Abernon, Cobham, Surrey KT11 3JB

SYCAMORE, Phillip; s of Frank Sycamore, of Lancaster, Lancs, and Evelyn Martin, *née* Burley; *b* 9 March 1951; *Educ* Lancaster Royal GS, Univ of London (LLB); *m* 22 June 1974, Sandra, da of Peter Frederick Cooper (d 1986), of Morecambe, Lancs; 2 s (Thomas b 1980, Jonathan b 1983), 1 da (Hannah b 1978); *Career* admitted slr 1975, asst recorder; ptnr with Lonsdales slrs Blackpool Lancs; Law Soc: memb Cncl 1991–, vice pres 1996–97; *Clubs* Royal Lytham and St Annes Golf, Athenaeum; *Style—* Phillip Sycamore, Esq; ✉ 213 Clifton Drive South, Lytham St Annes FY8 1ES (☎ 01253 728532); 342 Lytham Road, South Shore, Blackpool, Lancs FY4 1DW (☎ 01253 345258, fax 01253 348943)

SYDENHAM, Colin Peter; s of Herbert Willmott Sydenham (d 1975), of Croydon, Surrey, and Veronica Margery, *née* Denny (d 1988); *b* 13 Dec 1937; *Educ* Eton, King's Coll Cambridge (MA); *m* 15 Sept 1964, (Priscilla) Angela, da of Anthony Tannett, of Aldeburgh, Suffolk; 2 s (Simon b 1 Jan 1967, Rupert b 16 July 1968), 1 da (Katharine b 9 July 1969); *Career* Nat Serv RA 1956–58 (2 Lt 1958); called to the Bar 1963, in practice at Chancery Bar 1964–, pt/t chm of industl tbnls 1975–81; FIDE master of chess compositions 1990 (int judge for chess compostions 1991); memb: Br Chess Problem Soc (memb Ctee 1976–, vice-pres 1986, pres 1989–91), Horatian Soc (hon sec 1980–), Cncl Classical Assoc 1995–; *Recreations* chess problems, the odes of Horace, medieval sculpture and architecture, sailing; *Clubs* MCC; *Style—* Colin Sydenham, Esq; ✉ 4 Breams Buildings, London EC4A 1AQ (☎ 0171 353 5835, fax 0171 430 1677)

SYKES, Allen; s of Jack Sykes, of Slaithewaite, Yorks, and Dorothy, *née* Main (d 1956); *b* 26 Dec 1931; *Educ* Texas Country Day Sch Dallas, Selhurst GS, LSE (BScEcon); *m* 1959, Dorothy June; 1 s (Jeremy Jonathan Nicholas), 1 da (Caroline Emma Jane (Mrs James D G Morris)); *Career* Nat Serv cmmnd Sub Lt Exec Branch RN 1953–55, Lt RNVR 1951–65; economist and mgmnt trainee Econs Dept Unilever 1955–60, head project evaluation RTZ 1960–70, md RTZ Devpt Enterprises (in charge of Channel Tunnel Project for RTZ and Br Channel Tunnel Co) 1970–72, dir Willis Faber plc 1972–86 (advsr to govts, banks, utilities, mining and oil cos on major int projects), md Consolidated Gold Fields plc 1986–89 (responsible for devpt Britain and part of N America); non-exec dir: Willis Corroon plc 1986–, Lawson Mardon Group Ltd 1990–94; chm: Economic Insurance Co Ltd 1994–96, TEG Environment plc, GSB (Holdings) plc; fndr and memb Cncl Br Major Projects Assoc 1981–95 (fndr Canadian Assoc 1984); chm Peer Review Panel Venice Lagoon Project 1993; *Publications* Finance & Analysis of Capital Projects (with A J Merrett, 1963 and 1972), Successful Accomplishment of Giant Projects (1979), Privatise Coal (with Colin Robinson, 1987), Current Choices - Ways to Privatise Electricity (with Colin Robinson, 1987), Corporate Takeovers - The Need for Fundamental Rethinking (1990), Competitive Coal (1991); *Recreations* tennis, chess, opera; *Clubs* ESU, RAC; *Style—* Allen Sykes, Esq; ✉ Mallington, 29 The Mount, Fetcham, Leatherhead, Surrey KT22 9EB (☎ 01372 375851, fax 01372 362693)

SYKES, David Michael; s of Michael le Gallais Sykes (d 1981; yr s of Capt Stanley Edgar Sykes, who was yr s of Sir Charles Sykes, 1 Bt, KBE), and his 1 w, Joan, *née* Groome; hp of unc, Sir John Charles Anthony le Gallais Sykes, 3 Bt; *b* 10 June 1954; *m* 1974 (m dis 1987), Susan Elizabeth, 3 da of G W Hall; 1 s (Stephen David b 1978); m 2, 1987, Margaret Lynne, da of J T McGreavy; 1 da (Joanna Lauren b 1986); *Style—* David Sykes, Esq; ✉ The Chesnuts, Middle Lane, Nether Broughton, Melton Mowbray, Leics LE14 3HD

SYKES, Prof Elizabeth Ann Bowen; da of Sir Francis Godfrey Sykes, 9 Bt (d 1990), and Eira Betty, *née* Badcock (d 1970); *b* 17 Sept 1936; *Educ* Howell's Sch Denbigh, Bedford Coll London (BSc, Gamble Scholar, MSc), Univ of Edinburgh (PhD); *Career* res staff Nat Inst of Industl Psychology 1959–62, res assoc Dept of Psychological Med Univ of Edinburgh 1962–65, lectr Dept of Psychology Univ Coll N Wales 1965–74; Middx Univ: sr lectr in psychology 1974–87, princ lectr 1987–90, reader 1990–92, prof 1992–, head Sch of Psychology 1993– (acting head 1991–93); memb Ctee Assoc of Heads of Psychology Depts 1993–; Univ Coll London: hon res fell Dept of Pharmacology 1977–79, hon res fell Dept of Psychology 1979–92; articles and chapters on psychopharmacology, physical exercise and mental health in books and learned jls; memb Assoc for Study of Animal Behaviour 1963, sci fell Zoological Soc of London 1975, memb Br Assoc for Psychopharmacology 1978, fndr memb European Behavioural Pharmacology Soc 1986, assoc fell Br Psychological Soc 1988, memb European Health Psychology Soc 1992; CPsychol 1990; *Style—* Prof Elizabeth A Sykes; ✉ 19 Torriano Cottages, off Leighton Road, London NW5 2TA; School of Psychology, Middlesex University, Queensway, Enfield, Middlesex EN3 4SF (☎ 0181 362 5466, fax 0181 362 5343, e-mail eas@mdx.ac.uk)

SYKES, Eric; OBE; s of Vernon Sykes, and Harriet Sykes; *b* 4 May 1923; *m* 14 Feb 1952, Edith Eleanore, da of Bruno Milbrandt; 1 s (David Kurt b 2 June 1959), 3 da (Katherine Lee b 6 Sept 1952, Susan Jane b 20 Sep 1953, Julie Louise b 2 July 1958); *Career* comic actor, writer and director; wireless operator Mobile Signals Unit RAF 1941–47; varied TV and film career (20 feature films); numerous TV appearances incl writing and lead role in Sykes and A... Show for 21 years; silent film writer and dir: The Plank (V), Rhubarb, Mr H is Late, It's Your Move, The Big Freeze; Freeman City of London; *Recreations* golf; *Clubs* Royal and Ancient Golf; *Style—* Eric Sykes, Esq, OBE; ✉ 9 Orme Court, Bayswater, London W2 4RL (☎ 0171 727 1544)

SYKES, Gerard William; s of William Joshua Sykes (d 1987), and Dorothy Lily, *née* Freeman; *b* 3 Dec 1944; *Educ* Sir Roger Manwoods Sandwich Kent; *m* 1974, Rosalind Mary Louise, da of S Peter Meneaugh; *Career* articled clerk Percy Gore & Co Margate, qualified chartered accountant 1966, mangr Hurdman and Cranstoun 1968–71, ptnr Thornton Baker (now Grant Thornton) 1973– (int mangr 1971–73); Freeman City of London 1977; ACA 1966; *Recreations* vintage cars, skiing; *Clubs* RAC; *Style—* Gerard Sykes, Esq; ✉ Grant Thornton, Grant Thornton House, 22 Melton St, London NW1 2EP (☎ 0171 383 5100)

SYKES, John; MP (C) Scarborough (majority 11,734); s of Malcolm Sykes, and Angela Sykes; *b* 24 Aug 1956; *Educ* Giggleswick Sch N Yorks; *m* 29 Aug 1981, Jane, *née* Aspinall; 1 s, 2 da; *Career* dir family businesses (estab 1845) involved in property, agric, plastics mfrg and petrol retailing; Parly candidate (C) Sheffield Hillsborough 1987, MP (C) Scarborough 1992–; memb: Backbench Tourism Ctee, De-regulation Select Ctee; PPS to Viscount Cranborne, PC as Lord Privy Seal and Leader of the House of Lords 1995–; cncllr Kirklees MBC 1987–91, former dir Leeds/Bradford Airport; chm Dewsbury Cons Assoc 1988–89, memb Fin and Gen Purposes Ctee Yorks Area Cons Assoc, former vice chm Yorks Area CPC; *Recreations* travel, walking, history, reading, photography, music, rugby union; *Style—* John Sykes, Esq, MP; ✉ House of Commons, London SW1A 0AA

SYKES, Sir (Francis) John Badcock; 10 Bt (GB 1781), of Basildon, Berks; o s of Sir Francis Godfrey Sykes, 9 Bt (d 1990), and his 1 w, Eira Betty, *née* Badcock (d 1970); *b* 7 June 1942; *Educ* Shrewsbury, Worcester Coll Oxford (MA); *m* 1966, Susan Alexandra, da of Adm of the Fleet Sir Edward Ashmore, GCB, DSC, by his w Elizabeth, da of Sir Lionel Sturdee, 2 and last Bt, CBE; 3 s (Francis Charles b 1968, Edward William b 1970, Alexander Henry Ashmore b 1974); *Heir* s, Francis Charles Sykes b 18 June 1968; *Career* admitted slr 1968, ptnr in legal firm of Townsends, Swindon and Newbury 1972; pres Swindon Chamber of Commerce 1981; govr: Swindon Coll 1982–90, Swindon Enterprise Tst 1982–89; tstee: Roman Research Tst 1990–, Merchant's House (Marlborough) Tst 1991–, Wilts Community Fndn 1994–; memb: Soc of Trusts and Estates Practitioners (STEP), HAC; *Style—* Sir John Sykes, Bt; ✉ Kingsbury Croft, Kingsbury St, Marlborough, Wilts SN8 1HU

SYKES, Sir John Charles Anthony le Gallais; 3 Bt (UK 1921), of Kingsknowes, Galashiels, Co Selkirk; er s of Capt Stanley Sykes (yr s of Sir Charles Sykes, 1 Bt, KBE, JP, MP Huddersfield), and Florence Anaïse, da of François le Gallais, of Jersey; suc unc, Sir Hugh Sykes, 2 Bt, 1974; *b* 19 April 1928; *Educ* Churchers' Coll; *m* 1954 (m dis 1969), Aitha Isobel, da of Lionel Dean, of Huddersfield; *Heir* nephew, David Sykes; *Recreations* wine, food, travel, bridge; *Style—* Sir John Sykes, Bt

SYKES, Prof Sir (Malcolm) Keith; kt (1991); s of Prof Joseph Sykes, OBE, (d 1967), and Phyllis Mary Sykes (d 1972); *b* 13 Sept 1925; *Educ* Magdalene Coll Cambridge (MA, MB BChir), Univ Coll Hosp London (DA); *m* 14 Jan 1956, Michelle June, da of William Ewart Ratcliffe (d 1951); 1 s (Jonathan b 1964), 3 da (Karen b 1957, Virginia b 1958, Susan b 1967); *Career* cmmnd RAMC 1950–52, Capt, served BAOR; prof of clinical anaesthesia Royal Postgraduate Med Sch London 1970–80 (lectr, sr lectr then reader 1958–70); Nuffield prof of anaesthetics and fell Pembroke Coll Oxford 1980–91 (emeritus prof and supernumerary fell 1991–, hon fell 1996); Rickman Godlee travelling scholar and fell in anaesthetics Massachusetts Gen Hosp Boston USA 1954–55; pres Section of Anaesthetics Royal Soc of Med 1989–90, vice pres Assoc of Anaesthetists 1990–92, former vice pres and senator Euro Acad of Anaesthesiology; FRCA 1953, Hon FANZCA 1978, Hon FCA (SA) 1989; memb: BMA, RSM; *Books* Respiratory Failure (1965, 1976), Principles of Measurement for Anaesthetists (1970), Principles of Clinical Measurement (1981), Principles of Measurement and Monitoring in Anaesthesia and Intensive Care (1991), Respiratory Support (1995); *Recreations* walking, sailing, birdwatching, gardening; *Style—* Prof Sir Keith Sykes; ✉ 10 Fitzherbert Close, Iffley, Oxford OX4 4EN (☎ 01865 771152)

SYKES, Peter; s of Percy Sykes (d 1947), of Bedford, and Alexa Mary, *née* Kirkland (d 1984); *b* 30 May 1924; *Educ* Burton-upon-Trent GS, King's Sch Peterborough, Bedford Sch, Guy's Hosp Med Sch (LDS RCS, Fencing blue); *m* 6 Sept 1952, Nancy Elizabeth Norah, da of Charles Henry Shelton Cox; 3 s (David Gerald b 2 Feb 1953, Andrew Peter b 14 March 1955, Hugh Shelton b 11 Oct 1959), 1 da (Elizabeth Mary b 13 Aug 1966); *Career* locum conslt dental surgn Bedford Gen Hosp 1958–59, gen dental practitioner 1952–70; Surgn Lt Cdr (D) RNR, ret 1960; hon scientific advsr Br Dental Jl 1976–92, chm Editorial Bd Dental Practice 1993– (memb 1962–); memb GDC 1984–86 and 1991–96; sec gen Int Fedn of Dental Anesthesiology Socs 1982–94 (treas 1994–), vice pres Aust Soc of Dental Anaesthesiology 1984–, pres Soc for the Advancement of Anaesthesia in Dentistry 1983–86 and 1990–94 (memb 1962–); Heidbrink Award (American Dental Soc of Anesthesiology), Horace Wells Award (Int Fedn of Dental Anesthesiology Socs); DGDP (UK) 1992; FRSM 1980; *Books* Dental Sedation and Anaesthesia (1979); *Clubs* Rotary; *Style—* Peter Sykes, Esq; ✉ Hawthorns, The Avenue, Ampthill, Beds MK45 2NR (☎ and fax 01525 405008)

SYKES, Philip John; s of Herbert Cartman Sykes (d 1989), of Fleetwood, Lancs, and Alice, *née* Forrest (d 1985); *b* 1 Dec 1939; *Educ* Rossall Sch, Univ of Cambridge (MA, MB BChir); *m* 1967, (Evelyn) Christina, da of George Kenneth D Sharples; 2 da (Anna K F b 14 Dec 1967, Charlotte Helen b 15 March 1971); *Career* registrar then sr registrar in gen surgery Northampton 1967–70, sr registrar in plastic surgery Stoke Mandeville Hosp and Churchill Hosp Oxford 1970–74, Nuffield res fell in microsurgery St Vincent's Hosp Melbourne Aust 1974–75, sr conslt plastic surgn Welsh Regnl Unit for Plastic, Maxillo-Facial and Burns Surgery Morriston Hosp Swansea 1975–; chm London Implementation Gp Plastic Surgery Review (Dept of Health) 1993, plastic surgical advsr to Chief Med Offr 1993–96; visiting plastic surgn: Muscat Oman during 1980's, Addis Ababa 1990, Sarajevo 1994; Thackeray Prize for Microsurgery; memb: Br Burns Assoc, RSM, Br Soc for Surgery of the Hand (pres 1992), Br Microsurgical Soc, Br Assoc of Plastic Surgns (pres 1994); hon memb South African Assoc of Plastic Surgns; FRCS 1970; *Publications* author of numerous book chapters and papers on aspects of plastic surgery, hand surgery and burns; *Recreations* squash, hill walking, food and drink; *Style—* Philip Sykes, Esq; ✉ Plastic Surgery Unit, Morriston Hospital, Swansea, W Glamorgan

SYKES, Phillip Rodney; s of Sir Richard Adam Sykes, KCMG, MC (d 1979), and Ann Georgina, *née* Fisher; *b* 17 March 1955; *Educ* Winchester, ChCh Oxford (MA); *m* 26 June 1982, Caroline Frances Gordon, da of Michael Dawson Miller, of Scarsdale Villas, London; 2 s (Richard b 1985, Christopher b 1988), 1 da (Marina b 1991); *Career* Binder Hamlyn: joined 1976, seconded fin services section Nat West Bank plc 1985–86, ptnr 1986–94, head Insolvency and Recovery Servs 1991–94; ptnr Corporate Financial Servs Arthur Andersen 1994–; ACA 1986, MSPI 1991; *Recreations* field sports, tennis, reading, theatre; *Clubs* Hurlingham; *Style—* Phillip Sykes, Esq; ✉ Arthur Andersen, 1 Surrey Street, London WC2R 2NT (☎ 0171 438 3000, fax 0171 438 3771)

SYKES, (James) Richard; QC (1981); s of Philip James Sykes (d 1985), and Lucy Barbara, *née* Cowper (d 1981); *b* 28 May 1934; *Educ* Charterhouse, Pembroke Coll Cambridge (MA); *m* 27 Aug 1959, Susan Ethne Patricia, da of Lt Col John Manchester Allen (ka 1941); 1 s (Christopher James b 1965), 3 da (Annabel Mary b 1961, Camilla Jane b 1963, Rosemary Anne b 1969); *Career* RASC 1952–54, 2 Lt 1953; called to the Bar Lincoln's Inn 1958, bencher 1989, head of chambers; memb: Law Soc Standing Ctee on Co Law 1973–, City Co Law Ctee 1974–79, City Capital Markets Ctee 1980–94, Mgmnt Ctee International Exhibition Cooperative Society Ltd 1986–, Exec Ctee VSO 1987–93; chm Judging Panel: Accountant and Stock Exchange Annual Awards 1982–89, Int Stock Exchange and Inst of Chartered Accountants Annual Awards for Published Accounts 1990–; *Books* Gore-Browne on Companies (conslt ed, 42 edn 1972, 43 edn 1977, 44 edn 1986), The Conduct of Meetings (jt ed, 20 edn 1966, 21 edn 1975); *Style—* Richard Sykes, Esq, QC; ✉ Erskine Chambers, 30 Lincoln's Inn Fields, London WC2A 3PF (☎ 0171 242 5532, fax 0171 831 0125)

SYKES, Sir Richard Brook; kt (1994); *b* 7 Aug 1942; *Educ* Royds Hall GS Huddersfield, Paddington Tech Coll, Chelsea Coll, Queen Elizabeth Coll Univ of London, Univ of Bristol (PhD), Univ of London (DSc); *m*; 2 c; *Career* head Antibiotic Res Unit Glaxo Research UK 1972–77; Squibb Inst for Medical Research: asst dir Dept of Microbiology

1977–79, dir Microbiology 1979–83, assoc dir Inst 1981–86, vice pres Infectious Diseases and Metabolic Diseases 1983–86; Glaxo plc: rejoined as dep chief exec Glaxo Group Research Ltd 1986–87, gp R & D dir Glaxo plc and chm and chief exec Glaxo Group Research Ltd 1987–93, dep chm and chief exec Glaxo plc 1993– (Glaxo Wellcome plc since 1995); chm: Business Ldr Gp Br Lung Fndn 1993–, Br Red Cross Corporate Patrons 1994–, Task Force Inward Investmt in UK Pharmaceutical Industry 1994–, Br Pharma Gp 1996–; vice pres Nat Soc for Epilepsy 1995–; memb: Bd of Govrs Univ of Hertfordshire (formerly Hatfield Poly) 1988–, Centre for Exploitation of Science and Technol 1990–, Int Advsy Panel Nat Science and Technol Bd 1991–, Central Research and Devpt Ctee NHS 1991–93, Cncl for Science and Technol 1993–, Advsy Ctee on Human Genome Research 1993–, Advsy Cncl Save British Science 1993–, Fndn for Science and Technol Cncl 1994–, Bd of Mgmnt Ct of Govrs LSHTM 1994–, Cncl for Industry and HE 1995–, Pres's Ctee CBI 1995–, Trade Policy Forum 1995–, Econ Devpt Bd Int Advsy Cncl 1995–, Bd of Tstees Natural History Museum 1996–, Nat Ctee of Inquiry into Higher Educn 1996–; visiting prof King's Coll London; author of over 100 scientific articles and lecture papers; Hon DSc: Brunel Univ, Univ of Bristol, Univ of Hertfordshire, Univ of Hull, Univ of Newcastle upon Tyne, Univ of Huddersfield, Univ of Westminster; Hon MD Univ of Birmingham, Hon Dr in Pharmacy Univ of Madrid; Hon FRCP, MInstD 1995; *Style*— Sir Richard Sykes; ✉ Glaxo Wellcome plc, Lansdowne House, Berkeley Square, London W1X 6BQ (☎ 0171 408 8606, fax 0171 408 8767)

SYKES, Richard Hugh; s of John George Sykes (d 1971), of York, and Dorothy Eleanor Chamberlin, *née* Chilman; *b* 11 April 1943; *Educ* Winchester, Trinity Coll Oxford (scholar, MA); *m* 26 April 1969, Linda, da of Richard Saxby-Soffe; 2 s (Thomas Richard b 1 April 1971, John Nicholas b 1 Jan 1975), 1 da (Eleanor Mary b 30 Sept 1977); *Career* teacher St Joseph's Coll Chidya in Masasi Diocese Tanzania 1964–65; Allen & Overy: articled clerk, asst slr 1969–74, ptnr 1974– (currently head of Int Capital Markets Dept); memb Co of Merchant Adventurers of City of York; memb: Law Soc, City of London Solicitors Co; *Recreations* reading, walking; *Clubs* Brooks's; *Style*— Richard Sykes, Esq; ✉ Allen & Overy, One New Change, London EC4M 9QQ (☎ 0171 330 3000, fax 0171 330 9999)

SYKES, Robert Lacy Tatton; s of late Geoffrey Percy Frederick Sykes, of Kirribilli, NSW, and Margaret Rose, *née* White; *b* 28 April 1943; *Educ* Brighton, Hove and Sussex GS, Jesus Coll Oxford (Open exhibitioner, MA); *m* 1981, Hon Laura Catherine James, da of late Baron Saint Brides, PC, GCMG, CVO, MBE; *Career* British Council: joined 1964, various positions in Nigeria, Pakistan and London 1965–73, seconded as first sec Br High Commission Jamaica 1973–77, asst dir Educnl Contracts 1977–79, dir Drama and Dance 1979–87, Henley Mgmnt Coll 1987, dir Calcutta 1987–90, cnsllr Br Cncl Div Br High Commission New Delhi 1990–93, dir Tanzania 1993–; *Clubs* Tollygunge (Calcutta), Delhi Gymkhana, Dar es Salaam Gymkhana, United Oxford and Cambridge Univs, Dar es Salaam Yacht; *Style*— Robert Sykes, Esq; ✉ The Old House, Ibthorpe, Andover, Hants SP11 0BJ; 6 Hans Crescent, London SW1X 0LJ; c/o Foreign and Commonwealth Office (Dar es Salaam), King Charles Street, London SW1A 2AH

SYKES, Rt Rev Stephen Whitefield; *see:* Ely, Bishop of

SYKES, Sir Tatton Christopher Mark; 8 Bt (GB 1783), of Sledmere, Yorkshire; s of Lt-Col Sir (Mark Tatton) Richard Tatton-Sykes, 7 Bt (d 1978; assumed additional surname of Tatton by deed poll 1977, discontinued at his demise); *b* 24 Dec 1943; *Educ* Eton, Université d'Aix Marseilles, RAC Cirencester; *Heir* bro, Jeremy John Sykes; *Clubs* Brooks's; *Style*— Sir Tatton Sykes, Bt; ✉ Sledmere, Driffield, Yorkshire

SYME, Dr James; s of James Wilson Syme (d 1988), of Edinburgh, and Christina Kay, *née* Marshall; *b* 25 Aug 1930; *Educ* Beath HS, Univ of Edinburgh (MB ChB); *m* 15 Dec 1956, Mary Pamela, da of Peter McCormick (d 1957), of Bolton, Lancs; 1 s (Peter James b 1959), 1 da (Victoria Claire b 1961); *Career* Capt RAMC in W Africa 1955–57; conslt paediatrician Edinburgh 1965–94, hon sr lectr Univ of Edinburgh 1965–; vice pres RCPEd 1985–89 (cncl memb 1976–81), chm and memb several ctees and working parties of med profession; FRCPE 1968 (memb 1958), FRCPG 1978, FRCP 1991; *Publications* approx 30 articles in medical press, three contributions to textbooks; *Recreations* walking, church history and architecture; *Clubs* New (Edinburgh); *Style*— Dr James Syme; ✉ Holme Barn, Airton, by Skipton, N Yorks BD23 4AL (☎ 01729 830579)

SYMES, Dr David Millman; s of Henry Millman Symes (d 1978), and Harvey Gwendoline, *née* Davies (d 1975); *b* 20 June 1936; *Educ* Hove Co GS, St Mary's Hosp London, Univ of London (MB BS, MRCS, LRCP), Univ of Wales (dip dermatology); *m* (m dis) Jose Ann Symes; 2 da (Kathryn Ann b 6 June 1960, Tiffany Jane b 19 Sept 1964); *Career* princ and sr ptnr in gen practice 1960–91, visiting MO Morgan Crucible Co 1961–62, MO Columbia Pictures 1964, ship surgn Blue Star Line 1965, euro med conslt Whittaker Int 1976–84; med advsr: John Brown Engrg 1978–83, Tate & Lyle Group 1982–90; examining med practitioner DHSS 1978–; hon clinical tutor in dermatology St George's Hosp London, hon hosp practitioner in dermatology Kingston Univ Hosp Surrey; yacht master (ocean) 1982; Chevalier De L'Ordre de Coteaux de Champagne 1988, Freeman City of London 1971, Liveryman Worshipful Soc of Apothecaries 1972; memb: Soc of Occupational Med 1983, BMA 1990; *Recreations* tennis, sailing; *Clubs* Cruising Assoc, Royal Yachting Assoc, Emsworth Slipper Sailing, City Livery Yacht; *Style*— Dr David Symes; ✉ 3 Ditton Reach, Thames Ditton, Surrey KT7 OXB (☎ 0181 398 0958)

SYMES, Prof Martin Spencer; s of Oliver Edward Symes, of Burcombe, Salisbury, Wilts, and Beatrice Mary, *née* Spencer; *b* 19 Aug 1941; *Educ* Dauntsey's Sch, Univ of Cambridge (BA, MA, DipArch), Architectural Assoc (PlanDip), Univ of London (PhD); *m* 23 June 1964, Valerie Joy, da of Harold James Willcox (d 1979); 1 s (Benedick b 1967), 1 da (Francesca b 1971); *Career* architectural asst: London CC 1963, Eero Saarinen Assocs 1964, Yorke Rosenberg Mardall 1965–67; architect Arup Assocs 1968–73, conslt Duffy Eley Giffone Worthington 1975–82, visiting fell Princeton Univ 1980, sr lectr UCL 1983–89 (lectr 1973–83), res fell Univ of Melbourne 1985, British Gas chair of urban renewal Univ of Manchester 1989– (head Dept of Architecture 1991–93); visiting prof Tokyo Univ 1990; sec IAPS Int Assoc for the Study of People and their Physical Surroundings 1984–88, chm RIBA Professional Literature Ctee 1988–93; Freeman City of London 1995; RIBA 1967, FRSA 1990; jt ed Journal of Architectural and Planning Research 1984–93; *Books* Architects Journal Handbook on the Reuse of Redundant Industrial Buildings (jt ed, 1978), Urban Waterside Regeneration (jt ed, 1993), The Urban Experience (jt ed, 1994), Architects and their Practices (jt author, 1995); *Style*— Prof Martin Symes; ✉ 2 Corner Green, Blackheath, London SE3 9JJ (☎ 0181 852 6834); Department of Architecture, The University, Manchester M13 9PL (☎ 0161 275 6912, fax 0161 275 6935)

SYMES, Robert Alexander (Bob); Robert Alexander Baron Symes-Schutzmann von Schutzmannsdorff (cr Austria 1407); s of Dr Herbert Paul Schutzmann von Schutzmannsdorff (d 1937), of Vienna, and Lolabeth (Elizabeth), *née* Bruce Zipser; *b* 6 May 1924; *Educ* Realgymnasium Vienna, Institut am Rosenberg St Gallen Switzerland, Regent St Poly; *m* 4 Dec 1946, Monica, da of Harold Byron James Chapman (ka 1917); 1 da (Roberta Anne b 4 May 1953); *Career* Br Colonial Serv 1940–41, cmmnd RN 1942, acting Lt Cdr 1942–46 (despatches); freelance broadcaster, writer, film dir, experimental engr, lectr; UK press offr Royal Dutch Airlines 1950–53, BBC Overseas Serv 1953–56, dist offr i/c bdcasting Eastern Region Colonial Office Nigeria 1956–57; BBC: prodr Overseas Servs 1957–58, prog asst German Serv 1958–59, sci prodr and prog co-ordinator Tomorrow's World 1968–74, sci prodr and presenter 1974–80; lectured to orgns incl: Br Assoc of Young Scientists, IEE, Chartered Inst of Surveyors, Inst of Engrs, numerous schs and engrg socs, Southern Electric on Tomorrow's World Today; ptnr S H Radio Independent Producers; former dir County Sound Radio Network plc, formerly chm Border Union Railway; voluntary helper Lockwood Centre for the Disabled, formerly Special Constable Thames Div and Surrey (long service medal and bar), formerly memb E Horsley PC, formerly prospective Euro Parly candidate (Cons); hon pres Surrey Soc, patron Southern Vintage Agricultural Club, life memb Anglo-Austrian Soc, memb Br Deer Soc; Knights Cross (First Class) Republic of Austria; assoc Royal Aeronautical Soc, pres Inst of Patentees and Inventors 1991– (formerly chm); *Broadcasts* radio work incl: History of Flying (series, prodr, 1958), History of Surgery (series, prodr, 1958), The Ad Hoc Cook (series of cookery progs, 1982), Ad Hoc Living (series, 1983), series of progs on sci for China BBC English by Radio 1987, regular progs on BFBS, LBC and BBC German Serv (in German), regular contributor to Pick of the Week BBC Radio 4, currently Radio 4 quiz show panellist, sci corr Talk Radio 1995–; film and television work incl: A Bit of an Experience (documentary on brain surgery, prodr, 1963), Model World (series, presenter, 1978), The Model World of Robert Symes (1979), The Line That Refused to Die (documentary, presenter, 1980), The Danube Power Game (documentary, researcher and presenter in Eng and German, 1981), A Lineside Look at Model Railways (presenter, 1984, Silver award Int Film & TV Festival NY), The Strange Affair of... (series, 1985), Bob's Your Uncle (children's TV series, 1985–88), Tomorrow's World (regular contributor to series, 1986–94), The House That Bob Built (documentary in QED series, presenter), Making Tracks (series on railways, presenter, 1993), series of bi-lingual railway films (produced in Austria) 1995; *Publications* Powered Flight (1958), Crikey it Works - Technology for the Young (1992), Young Engineer's Handbook (1993), Eureka - The Book of Inventing (1994), numerous articles in model railway press and on travel and food; *Recreations* model railways, shooting, cooking, travelling, running own steam power station, industrial archaeology, preserved trains, trams and steam cars, history and geopolitics; *Style*— Bob Symes, Esq; ✉ Green Dene Cottage, Honeysuckle Bottom, East Horsley, Surrey KT24 5TD (☎ 01483 283223)

SYMINGTON, Prof Sir Thomas; kt (1978); s of James Symington (d 1919), of Muirkirk, Ayrshire, and Margaret Steven Symington (d 1967); *b* 1 April 1915; *Educ* Cumnock Acad, Glasgow Univ (BSc, MB ChB, MD); *m* 1943, Esther Margaret, da of John Forsyth, of Bellshill (d 1951); 1 s (decd), 1 da; *Career* Maj RAMC, served Malaya 1947–49; prof of Pathology Univ of Glasgow 1954–70, prof of Pathology Univ of London 1971–77, dir Inst of Cancer Res Royal Cancer Hosp London 1970–77; visiting prof of Pathology Stanford Univ 1965–66; Hon Dr of Med Szeged Univ Hungary (1971), Hon DSc McGill Univ Canada 1983; FRSE 1956; *Recreations* golf, gardening; *Clubs* Roy Troon Golf; *Style*— Prof Sir Thomas Symington, FRSE; ✉ Greenbriar, 2 Lady Margaret Drive, Troon KA10 7AL (☎ 315 707)

SYMON, Prof Lindsay; CBE (1994), TD (1967); s of William Lindsay Symon (d 1972), of Innellan, Argyllshire, and Isabel, *née* Shaw (d 1967); *b* 4 Nov 1929; *Educ* Aberdeen GS, Univ of Aberdeen (MB ChB); *m* 14 Aug 1953, Pauline Barbara, da of William Rowland (d 1970), of Liverpool; 1 s (Lindsay b 17 March 1955), 2 da (Barbara Rosemary b 6 July 1956, Fiona Margaret b 12 May 1959); *Career* Capt RAMC 1953–55, Maj RAMC TA 1955–69; emeritus prof of neurological surgery, sr neurological surgn Nat Hosp for Nervous Diseases Queen Square and Maida Vale; hon conslt neurological surgn: St Thomas' Hosp, Hammersmith Hosp, Royal Nat Nose Throat and Ear Hosp; civilian advsr in neurological surgery to the RN 1979–95, chief ed Advances and Technical Standards in Neurosurgery 1984–94; pres World Fedn of Neurosurgical Socs 1989–93; Freeman City of London 1982; FRCSEd 1957, FRCS 1959, Hon FACS 1994; *Books* Operative Surgery (Neurosurgery) (1989); *Recreations* golf; *Clubs* Caledonian, Royal and Ancient, Rye, Hadley Wood, Tidworth; *Style*— Prof Lindsay Symon, CBE, TD; ✉ Maple Lodge, Rivar Road, Shalbourne, Nr Marlborough, Wiltshire SN8 3QE (☎ and fax 01672 870501)

SYMONDS, Graham John; s of Henry Herbert Symonds, of Ludlow, and Mildred, *née* Tristram; *b* 28 Aug 1949; *m* Judith, da of late Robert William Mann; 2 da (Louise Jane b 31 Oct 1974, Kate Marie b 5 May 1977); *Career* md: South Shropshire Communications Ltd, Sunshine Radio; *Style*— Graham Symonds, Esq; ✉ South Shropshire Communications Ltd, Sunshine House, Waterside, Ludlow, Shropshire SY8 1PE (☎ 01584 873795, fax 01584 875900)

SYMONDS, Prof (Edwin) Malcolm; s of Edwin Joseph Truman Symonds, MBE (d 1985), of Adelaide, S Aust, and Eugene Mary Symonds; *b* 6 Nov 1934; *Educ* St Peter's Coll Adelaide, Univ of Adelaide (MB BS, MD); *m* 1, 26 April 1958 (m dis 1992), (Beverley) Sue, da of Rex Bertram Martin, of Adelaide, S Aust; 4 s (Ian Martin b 1959, David Malcolm b 1963, Thomas Rex b 1967, Matthew Richard Edwin b 1973); m 2, 1993, Chlöe Woolcott, da of Michael Charles Reginald Simpson, of East Keal, Lincs; *Career* sr registrar and clinical lectr Liverpool 1963–66, sr lectr and reader Univ of Adelaide 1967–71; Univ of Nottingham: fndn prof of obstetrics and gynaecology 1972–, dean of the Faculty of Med 1993–; non-exec dir Queen's Med Centre Nottingham Univ Hosp NHS Tst 1992–94, cmmr Cwlth Scholarships Cmmn; memb: Cncl RCOG, GMC; hon fell: American Gynaecological and Obstetrical Soc, American Coll of Obstetrics and Gynaecology, Polish Gynaecological Soc, Hungarian Gynaecological Soc, Italian Perinatal Soc; former memb: Nottingham Dist Health Authy, Trent RHA; FRCOG, FFPHM; *Books* Hypertension in Pregnancy (1985), In Vitro Fertilization Past, Present Future (1987), Essential Obstetrics and Gynaecology (1987, 2 edn 1992), Chorion Villus Sampling (1987), Current Obstetrics and Gynaecology (ed, 1993), Gamete and Embryo Micromanipulation in Human Reproduction (with Simon Fishel, 1993), Magnetic Resonance in Obstetrics and Gynaecology (with M C Powell and B S Worthington, 1994), A Color Atlas of Obstetrics and Gynaecology (with M B A Macpherson, 1994); *Recreations* cricket, golf, classical music and travel; *Style*— Prof Malcolm Symonds; ✉ Department of Obstetrics and Gynaecology, D Floor, East Block, University Hospital, Queen's Medical Centre, Nottingham NG7 2UH (☎ 0115 970 9240, fax 0115 970 9234)

SYMONDS, Dr Michael Anthony Edward; s of Edward Samuel Symonds (d 1983), of Chingford, London E4, and Marjorie Symonds (d 1960); *b* 1 April 1929; *Educ* Trent Coll Derbyshire, St Thomas's Hosp Med Sch; *m* 6 Nov 1957, Rowena, da of Fred Thornley (d 1980), of Walton-on-the-Naze, Essex; 2 s (William b 1958, James b 1961), 1 da (Joanna b 1964); *Career* house appts 1958–60, conslt physician in genito-urinary med City and Hackney Health Authy 1969–93, conslt physician in genito-urinary med Herts and Essex Hosp Bishop's Stortford (also physician i/c) 1974–96, hon conslt physician in genito-urinary med St Thomas's Hosp London 1976–, conslt advsr in genito-urinary med BUPA Med Centre London 1981–96, physician i/c genito-urinary med Bart's 1982–93; examiner in genito-urinary med Soc of Apothecaries of London 1980–94 (convenor 1987–92); govr: St Aubyn's Sch Woodford Green Essex 1982–, Bart's Med Coll 1994–; MRCP 1968, FRCP 1981; *Recreations* people, jogging, wine; *Clubs* RSM; *Style*— Dr Michael Symonds; ✉ 9 Beulah Road, Epping, Essex CM16 6RH (☎ 01992 572614)

SYMONDS, (John) Richard Charters; s of Air Vice-Marshal Sir Charles Symonds, MD (d 1978), and Janet, *née* Poulton (d 1919); *b* 2 Oct 1918; *Educ* Rugby, Corpus Christi Coll Oxford (MA); *m* Ann Spokes; *Career* Friends Ambulance Unit 1939–44, Govt of Bengal 1944–45, UN 1946–63 and 1968–79; sr res offr Oxford Univ Inst of Cwlth Studies 1963–65, professorial fell Inst of Devpt Studies Univ of Sussex 1966–69, sr assoc memb St Antony's Coll Oxford 1979–92, hon dir UN Career Records Project 1989–92, sr res assoc Queen Elizabeth House Oxford 1979–; conslt: UNESCO, WHO, Cwlth Fndn; *Books* The Making of Pakistan (1950), The British and Their Successors (1966), International Targets for Development (ed, 1970), The United Nations and the Population Question (with M Carder, 1973), Oxford and Empire (1986), Alternative Saints (1988), Far Above Rubies (1993); *Recreations* walking, travel; *Clubs* Royal Commonwealth Society, Royal Over-Seas League; *Style*— Richard Symonds, Esq; ✉ 43 Davenant Rd, Oxford OX2 8BU (☎ 01865 515661)

SYMONS, Christopher John Maurice; QC (1989); s of Clifford Louis Symons, and Pamela Constance, *née* Vos; *b* 5 Feb 1949; *Educ* Clifton Coll, Univ of Kent (BA); *m* 13 July 1974, Susan Mary, da of Gordon Teichmann; 1 s (Nicholas b 1978), 1 da (Samantha b 1980); *Career* called to the Bar Middle Temple 1972; memb Supplemental Panel of Jr Counsel to The Crown (common law) 1982–85, called to the Gibraltar Bar 1985, jr counsel to The Crown Common Law 1985–89, called to the Irish Bar 1988, called to the Northern Ireland Bar 1990, recorder 1993– (asst recorder 1990–93); *Recreations* hitting balls; *Clubs* Hurlingham, Berkshire, Woking, Royal Tennis Court, Sotogrande; *Style*— Christopher Symons, Esq, QC; ✉ 3 Verulam Buildings, Gray's Inn, London WC1R 5NT (☎ 0171 831 8441, fax 0171 831 8479, telex 295119 LEXCOL G)

SYMONS, Dr John Charles; s of Dr Percy Symons (d 1969), of Reading, Berks, and Constance Mary, *née* Dyer (d 1982); *b* 13 May 1938; *Educ* Oratory Sch, Trinity Coll Cambridge (BA, MA), St Thomas' Med Sch (MB BChir); *m* 3 Aug 1968, Louisa Beverley McKenzie, da of Dr S G M Francis, lately of Edinburgh; 1 s (James b 1977), 2 da (Emma b 1970, Rebecca b 1973); *Career* house offr: surgery (later med) Burton on Trent 1962–63, obstetrics St Thomas' Hosp 1963–64; sr house offr (later registrar) paediatrics Royal Berks Hosp 1964–67, paediatric specialist Corner Brook Newfoundland 1967–68, princ gen practice Wonersh Guildford 1968–69, med registrar Prospect Park Hosp Reading 1969–71; sr registrar: Jenny Lind Hosp Norwich 1971–73, Brompton Hosp 1973–75; conslt paediatrician Colchester 1975–, hon clinical tutor Guy's Hosp Med Sch 1985–, clinical dir Essex Rivers Healthcare Trust 1992–; memb Colchester Med Soc 1975; chm: Colchester Action for Epilepsy, Colchester Branch Liver Fndn; med advsr local branches Asthma Soc & Diabetic Assoc, aeromedical advsr St John, churchwarden and parish cncllr Assington; RCOG 1964, DCH 1967; memb: BMA 1962, Br Paediatric Assoc 1968; FRCP 1987; *Recreations* fishing, cricket; *Style*— Dr John Symons; ✉ Moors Farm, Assington, Suffolk CO10 5NE (☎ 01787 227 379); Colchester General Hospital, Turner Rd, Colchester, Essex (☎ 01206 853535); Rooms: Oaks Hospital, Mile End Road, Colchester, Essex

SYMONS, Prof Leslie John; *b* 8 Nov 1926; *Educ* LSE, Queen's Univ of Belfast (PhD); *m* 24 March 1954, Gloria Lola Colville; 2 da (Alison b 28 Feb 1956, Jennifer b 16 Oct 1962); *Career* asst and lectr Queen's Univ of Belfast 1953–62, sr lectr Univ of Canterbury NZ 1962–70 (visiting lectr 1960), Univ of Wales Swansea 1970– (sr lectr, reader, prof of geography, emeritus prof); Simon sr res fell Univ of Manchester 1967–68, Leverhulme emeritus fell 1993–95; *Books* Land Use in Northern Ireland (ed, 1963), Agricultural Geography (1967), Northern Ireland, A Geographical Introduction (with L Hanna, 1967 and 1978), Russian Agriculture, A Geographical Survey (1972), Russian Transport, An Historical and Geographical Survey (ed with C White, 1975), The Soviet Union, A Systematic Geography (ed, 1982, 1990 and 1992), Soviet and East European Transport Problems (ed with J Ambler and D Shaw, 1985), Transport and Economic Development, Soviet Union and Eastern Europe (ed with J Ambler and J Tismer, 1987), Highway Meteorology (ed with A Perry, 1991); *Recreations* mountain walking, flying, landscape painting; *Style*— Prof Leslie Symons; ✉ Squirrels' Jump, 17 Wychwood Close, Langland, Swansea SA3 4PH (☎ 01792 369675); Ard Tigh an t'Sruthain, Laggan Bridge, Newtonmore, Inverness-shire; Dept of Geography, University of Wales Swansea, Swansea SA2 8PP (☎ 01792 205678, fax 01792 205556, telex 48358)

SYMONS, Prof Martyn Christian Raymond; s of Stephen White Symons (d 1972), and Marjorie, *née* Le Brassuer (d 1958); *b* 12 Nov 1925; *Educ* John Fisher Sch Purley Surrey, Battersea Poly London (BSc, PhD, DSc); *m* 1, Joy Lendon (d 1963); 1 s (Richard b 1957), 1 da (Susan b 1954); m 2, 12 Jan 1972, Janice (Jan) Olive (d 1995), da of George O'Connor; *Career* Army 1946–49, Actg Capt 1948; lectr in chemistry Battersea Poly 1949–53, lectr in organic chemistry Univ of Southampton 1953–60, prof of physical chemistry Univ of Leicester 1960–89, res prof of chemistry and dir Career Res Campaign Electric Spin Resonance Gp Univ of Leicester 1989–93, res prof of chemistry Univ of Essex 1993–95, sr visiting res prof of chemistry De Montfort Univ Leicester 1993–, also hon prof of chemical biology Univ of London; author of 3 books and over 1000 original sci papers; FRSC 1949, FRSA 1965, FRS 1985; *Recreations* water colour painting, piano playing; *Style*— Prof Martyn Symons, FRS; ✉ 324 Old Heath Road, Colchester, Essex CO2 8BW (☎ 01206 790137); Department of Chemistry, De Montfort University, Leicester LE1 9BH (☎ 0116 257 7102); The Inflammation Research Group, ARC Building, The London Hospital Medical College, London E1 2AD (☎ 0171 377 7765)

SYMONS, Mitchell Paul; s of Alan Stanley Symons, and Louise, *née* Yager; *b* 11 Feb 1957; *Educ* Mill Hill Sch, LSE (LLB); *m* 1984, Penny Chorlton, da of William Moss; 2 s (Jack b 1987, Charles b 1989); *Career* writer and broadcaster; researcher then dir BBC TV 1980–82 (progs incl Friday Night...Saturday Morning, In My Fashion, Film 81), TV prodr 1982– (progs incl An Evening for Nicaragua 1983, Everybody's Equal 1987–, Your Number Please 1992); a princ writer British & Cwlth edns Trivial Pursuit 1985–86; regular contrib/columnist: Hello! 1988–, Punch 1989–92, Sunday Magazine 1990–, Evening Standard 1993–94; conslt Daily Mirror; also contrib: New Society, The Observer, The Sun, The People, The Sunday Times, The Times, The Guardian, Sunday Express; numerous TV appearances (incl What the Papers Say), regular radio broadcaster; *Books* Forfeit! (1986), The Equation Book of Sports Crosswords (1988), The Equation Book of Movie Crosswords (1988), Journolists 1–4 (with John Koski, 1989–92), Movielists (with John Koski, 1992), Hello! Book of Crosswords (1992), Sunday Book of Crosswords (1992), The Chip & Fry Diet (with Penny Symons, 1992), Hello! Crossword Books 1, 2 and 3 (1994), The Book of Criminal Records (1994); *Recreations* tennis, poker, cricket, bridge, cinema and listening to Steely Dan; *Clubs* Old Millhillians, Angmering Lawn Tennis, Rustington Golf; *Style*— Mitchell Symons, Esq; ✉ Willow House, 24 Angmering Lane, Angmering-on-Sea, West Sussex BN16 2TA (☎ 01903 771458, fax 01903 786548)

SYMONS, Rex Herbert Moss; CBE (1993); s of Herbert Thomas Symons, OBE (d 1959), and Winifred May Symons; *b* 10 May 1934; *Educ* Bournemouth Sch, Univ of Southampton (BSc, fencing colours, pres univ theatre gp); *m* Margaret Gwendoline, da of Henry Charles Everett; 1 s (Paul Rex Charles b 1964); *Career* sales controller phenol Heavy Organic Chemicals Div ICI 1958–61; with British Drug Houses Ltd 1961–68; BDH Ltd (initially subsid of Glaxo, sold to E Merck AG 1973): mktg dir 1968–81, md 1981–89; dep chm Merck Holding Ltd (UK subsid holding co of Merck AG) 1989–91; memb Health and Safety Cmmn 1989–, chm Occupational Health and Safety Lead Body 1992–, chm CBI Health and Safety Consultative Ctee, chm E Dorset Health Authy 1989–91, chm Poole Hosp NHS Trust 1991–; also chm: Dorset Trg and Enterprise Cncl 1991–, Dorset Enterprise Agency, Bournemouth Transport Ltd 1989–, Dorset Travel Ltd 1989–; pres Dorset C of C and Industry 1986, govr Bournemouth and Poole Coll of Art and Design; FRSA, MCIM, FIMgt; *Recreations* theatre, opera, books, gardening, travel; *Style*— Rex Symons, Esq, CBE; ✉ Poole Hospital NHS Trust, Longfleet Road, Poole, Dorset BH15 2JB (☎ 01202 665511)

SYMONS OF VERNHAM DEAN, Baroness (Life Peer UK 1996), of Vernham Dean in the County of Hampshire; Elizabeth Conway Symons; da of Ernest Vize Symons (d 1990), of Richmond, and Elizabeth Megan, *née* Jenkins; *b* 14 April 1951; *Educ* Putney HS for Girls, Girton Coll Cambridge (MA); *partner* Philip Alan Bassett, industrial ed The Times; 1 s (James Alexander Bassett Symons b 1985); *Career* res Girton Coll Cambridge 1972–74, admin trainee DOE 1974–77, dep gen sec Inland Revenue Staff Fedn (ISRF) 1988–89 (asst sec 1977–88), gen sec Assoc of First Div Civil Servants 1989–96; sits as Labour peer in House of Lords 1996–; memb: Gen Cncl TUC, Civil Serv Coll Advsy Cncl, Cncl Hansard Soc, Exec Cncl Campaign for Freedom of Information, Cncl The Industrial Soc, Cncl Open Univ; cmmr Equal Opportunities Cmmn 1995–, govr London Business Sch, tstee Inst of Public Policy Research; hon assoc Nat Cncl of Women; FRSA; *Recreations* reading, gardening, entertaining friends; *Style*— The Rt Hon Lady Symons of Vernham Dean; ✉ c/o House of Lords, Westminster, London SW1A 0PW (☎ 0171 219 3000)

SYNGE, Sir Robert Carson; 8 Bt (UK 1801), of Kiltrough; s of late Neale Hutchinson Synge and n of 7 Bt (d 1942); *b* 4 May 1922; *m* 1944, Dorothy Jean, da of Theodore Johnson, of Cloverdale, BC, Canada; 2 da; *Heir* cousin, Neale Francis Synge, b 28 Feb 1917; *Style*— Sir Robert Synge, Bt; ✉ 19364 Fraser Valley Highway, RR4, Langley, BC, Canada

SYNNOTT, Hilary Nicholas Hugh; CMG (1997); s of Cdr J N N Synnott, DSC, RN (d 1978), and Florence England, *née* Hillary (d 1971); *b* 20 March 1945; *Educ* Beaumont Coll, BRNC Dartmouth (scholar), Peterhouse Cambridge (MA), RN Engrg Coll Manadon; *m* 28 April 1973, Anne Penelope, *née* Clarke; 1 s (b 1975 (decd)); *Career* served RN 1962–73 (HM Submarines 1968–73); HM Dip Serv: joined 1973, UK Delgn to OECD Paris 1975–78, Br Embassy Bonn 1978–81, FCO 1981–85, head of chancery Amman 1985–89, head Western Euro Dept FCO 1989–91, head Security Co-ordination Dept FCO 1991–93, min and dep high cmmr New Delhi 1993–96, director (S and SE Asia) FCO 1996–; CEng, MIEE; *Clubs* United Oxford and Cambridge Univ; *Style*— Hilary Synnott, Esq, CMG; ✉ Foreign and Commonwealth Office, King Charles Street, London SW1A 2AH

SYRUS, David; s of William Henry Syrus (d 1978), and Amie Sills (d 1987); *b* 13 Oct 1946; *Educ* Hastings GS, Queen's Coll Oxford (MA); *m* 27 July 1972, Lorna, da of Stanley Miller, of Kinross, Scotland; 2 s (Daniel b 15 Jan 1976, Oliver b 25 May 1977), 1 da (Emma b 30 July 1979); *Career* head of music Royal Opera House Covent Garden 1993– (joined staff 1971); asst conductor: Bayreuth Festival 1977–84, Salzburg Festival 1991–; accompanist Carnegie Hall 1985 (also London, Montreal, Chicago, Paris, Munich, Vienna), continuo player (Monte Carlo, Munich, London, Paris, Cologne, Stuttgart, Salzburg Festival); *Performances* conductor Royal Opera House: Ariadne auf Naxos 1985, Die Zauberflöte 1993, Le Nozze di Figaro 1995, The Midsummer Marriage 1996, Don Giovani 1996, world premieres of The Tailor of Gloucester and Pig Organ, British premieres of Menotti The Boy Who Grew Too Fast and Henze Pollicino; *Recordings* various for EMI, Phonogram, Decca and BMG, also various television prodns; *Recreations* swimming, walking, reading; *Style*— David Syrus, Esq; ✉ 95 Alric Avenue, New Malden, Surrey KT3 4JP (☎ 0181 949 2432); Royal Opera House, London WC2 (☎ 0171 240 1200 ext 140)

SYSON, William Watson Cockburn; s of William Cockburn Syson (d 1939), of Edinburgh, and Mary Jane, *née* Watson (d 1983); *b* 12 Sept 1930; *Educ* Broughton; *Career* Nat Serv Army 1949–51, TA 1951–58; joined Bank of Scotland 1947, sr managerial positions Edinburgh 1969–81, chief mangr Head Office 1981–90, asst gen mangr 1987–90; chm Bank of Scotland Edinburgh & District Mangrs and Officials Circle 1978; dir: Great Western Resources Inc 1990–94, The British Real Estate Group plc 1990–96, First International Leasing Corporation Ltd 1990–94, Regent Investment Trust Ltd 1991–94, Scottish Value Trust plc; chm: City Site Estates plc 1991–, Johnson Fry Second Utilities Trust plc 1993–, Wiggins Group plc 1993–, Aitken Dott Limited (t/a The Scottish Gallery); former lectr Heriot-Watt Coll and Univ, former examiner and moderator Inst of Bankers Scotland; world sen Jr Chamber Int 1970, sr vice-pres Edinburgh and Midlothian Bn Boys' Bde 1970–90 (actg pres 1987–88); chm: City Centre Christian Outreach 1981–82, British Olympic Appeal Scotland 1992–93; hon treas: East of Scotland Branch Br Red Cross 1974–82 (memb Scottish Fin Ctee 1976–81), Scottish Branch Soldiers Sailors and Airmen's Families Assoc 1974–82, Victoria League Scotland 1969–75, Scottish Churches Architectural Heritage Tst 1980–84; treas and memb Cncl The Prince's Tst East of Scotland and Borders Area 1978–84; FCIBS 1979 (memb 1954); *Books* Interpretation of Balance Sheets (1957), Sources of Finance (1973), Forestry (1985); *Recreations* art, music, reading, hill walking, sport; *Clubs* New (Edinburgh), Cronies, Edinburgh Academicals Sports; *Style*— William Syson, Esq; ✉ Kilrymont, 6A Easter Belmont Road, Edinburgh EH12 6EX (☎ 0131 337 1321); Business: 116/4 Hanover Street, Edinburgh EH2 1DR (☎ 0131 225 5312, fax 0131 225 5787)

SYSONBY, 3 Baron (UK 1935); John Frederick Ponsonby; s of 2 Baron, DSO (d 1956); *b* 5 Aug 1945; *Heir* none; *Style*— The Rt Hon the Lord Sysonby

SZÉLL, Patrick John; s of János Sandor Széll, and Vera, *née* Beckett (d 1987); *b* 10 Feb 1942; *Educ* Reading Sch, Trinity Coll Dublin (MA, LLB, Julian prize); *m* 1967, Olivia, *née* Brain; 2 s (Redmond b 1969, Thaddeus b 1976), 1 da (Benedicta b 1975); *Career* called to the bar Inner Temple 1966, legal asst Miny of Housing and Local Govt 1969–70; DOE: legal asst 1970–73, sr legal asst 1973–85, asst slr 1985–92, under sec (legal) 1992–; head of the Int Environmental Law Div 1985–, legal advsr to UK Delgns at int environmental negotiations 1974–; memb: Int Cncl Environmental Law Bonn 1982–, IUCN Cmmn on Environmental Law 1994–; UNEP Global Ozone Award 1995, Elizabeth Haub Prize, Free Univ of Brussels 1995; *Recreations* travel, hockey, butterflies; *Style*— Patrick Széll, Esq; ✉ Legal Directorate, DOE, Eland House, Bressenden Place, London SW1E 5DU

SZIRTES, George Gábor Nicholas; s of László Szirtes, of Budapest, now of Pinner, Middx, and Magdalena Kardos Nussbacher (d 1975); *b* 29 Nov 1948; *Educ* Kingsbury Co GS, Harrow Sch of Art, Leeds Coll of Art (history of art prize, BA, travelling scholarship), Goldsmiths' Coll London; *m* 11 July 1970, Clarissa, da of Rev W S Upchurch; 1 s (Thomas Andrew b 31 Dec 1973), 1 da (Helen Magdalena b 13 Jan 1976); *Career* poet and translator; pt/t teaching jobs until 1975, head of art Hitchin Girls' Sch 1975–80, dir of art and history of art St Christopher Sch Letchworth 1980–89 (pt/t 1989–92), sr lectr in poetry Norfolk Inst of Art and Design 1992–; memb Int PEN 1980–; Br Cncl scholar 1985 and 1989 (latter spent in Budapest); FRSL 1982; *Awards* Geoffrey Faber Meml Prize 1980, Cholmondeley Award 1986, shortlisted for Whitbread Prize 1992; for translation: Déry Prize 1991, Gold Medal of Hungarian Republic 1991, Euro Poetry Translation Prize 1995; *Poetry* The Slant Door (1979), November and May (1981), Short Wave (1984), The Photographer in Winter (1986), Metro (1988), Bridge Passages (1991), Blind Field (1994), Selected Poems (1996); work incl in various anthologies of modern verse incl British Poetry Since 1945, and the New Poetry; ed: The Collected Poems of Freda Downie (1995), The Colonnade of Teeth, Twentieth Century Hungarian Poetry (jtly with George Gömöri, also trans 1996); *Translations* The Tragedy of Man (by Imre Madách, 1989), Through the Smoke (by István Vas, 1989), Anna Édes (by Dezsó Kosztolányi, 1992), The Blood of the Walsungs (by Ottó Orbán, 1993), New Life (by Zsuzsa Rakovszky, 1994); *Recreations* playing piano, writing and producing plays for children, proprietor of Starwheel Press 1976–; *Style*— George Szirtes, Esq, FRSL;

✉ 16 Damgate Street, Wymondham, Norfolk NR18 0BQ (☎ 01935 603533); Oxford University Press, Walton Street, Oxford

SZPIRO, Richard David; *b* 11 Aug 1944; *Educ* St Paul's Sch, Churchill Coll Cambridge (MA); *m* annulled; 2 s (Toby b 1971, Jamie b 1973); *Career* merchant banker; Wintrust plc: md 1969–, chm 1995–; md Wintrust Securities Ltd; *Recreations* golf, tennis; *Clubs* Mark's, Vanderbilt, Hurlingham; *Style*— Richard Szpiro, Esq; ✉ Wintrust plc, 21 College Hill, London EC4R 2RP (☎ 0171 236 2360)

T

TABAKSBLAT, Morris; *Educ* Leiden Univ (Law degree); *m*; 2 s, 1 da; *Career* Unilever: joined 1964, various mktg, sales and gen mgmnt positions in Spain, Brazil and the Netherlands until 1984, joined main Unilever NV and Unilever PLC Bds 1984–, personal products coordinator 1984–87, regnl dir N America and chm and chief exec Unilever US Inc 1987–90, chm Foods Exec 1990–93, chm and chief exec Unilever 1994– (chief exec 1992–), also tstee Conf Bd; memb Supervisory Bd: AEGON NV, Royal PTT Nederland NV; memb Euro Round Table of Industrialists; chm Mauritshuis Museum; *Style*— Morris Tabaksblat, Esq; ✉ Unilever NV, Weena 455, 3013 AL Rotterdam, The Netherlands; Unilever plc, Unilever House, London EC4P 4BQ (☎ 0171 822 5252, fax 0171 822 5898)

TABNER, Leonard (Len); s of Arthur Leonard Tabner (d 1984), and Thelma, *née* Morten; *b* 20 Sept 1946; *Educ* Victoria St Co Modern Boys South Bank Middlesbrough, Eston GS, Middlesbrough Art Coll, Bath Acad of Art (DipAD), Univ of Reading (MA); *m* 15 May 1971, Helen Lilian, da of Thomas Pitt de Paravicini, and Lillian, *née* Horrocks; 4 s (Isaac Thomas Tabner 22 April 1973, Samuel Leonard 7 Aug 1975, Reuben Frederick b 17 July 1980, Edward Arthur b 24 Jan 1983), 1 da (Kathleen Ella b 6 April 1985); *Career* artist; working on NE coast with British Steel Corp, Cleveland potash mine, Tees & Hartlepool Port Authy and Smith's Dock Shipbuilders 1976–87, offshore oil and gas indust 1987–88; cmmnd by Conoco/DOE/V&A to work in N York Moors Nat Park 1987–88, three month sea voyage to Falkland Islands and S Georgia as guest of RN 1990, two voyages on HMS Exeter N Atlantic 1992 and 1993, cmmnd by Gifu Prefectural Govt to work in the Haku-San Mountains Japan 1995; Northern Arts prodn award 1974, Northern Arts Printmaking bursary 1975, prize winner Singer & Friedlander Watercolour Competition 1989; vice pres Cleveland Wildlife Trust; *Solo Exhibitions* Middlesbrough Museum and Art Gallery 1973, Stockton Municipal Gallery 1975, Response to the Earth (N Arts Gallery Newcastle and Univ of Durham) 1976, Guisborough, Chapel Beck Museum and Art Gallery and touring 1977, Washington Tyne & Wear 1980, Cleveland and touring 1981, Moira Kelly Gallery London 1982, Univ of Durham 1982, 1985–96 and 1987, Oldham City Art Gallery 1985–86, Cleveland Potash Mine (Sunderland Museum and Art Gallery) 1987, Paintings and Drawings 1970–89 (Agnew's) 1989, Cowbar Breakwater (Vanessa Devereux Gallery London) 1989, A Voyage to the South London (Broadgate) 1992, Retrospective Exhibition (Laing Art Gallery Newcastle 1992, tour of Scotland and Ulster Museum Belfast 1993), Paintings From Recent Sea Voyages (Agnew's London) 1993, New Paintings (Agnew's London) 1995; *Two Man Exhibitions* Redcar Blast Furnace (with Ian Macdonald) 1983–85, Smiths Docks (with Ian Macdonald, Smiths Docks and touring) 1986–87, V Fields (with Ian Macdonald, touring) 1988, Images of the Tees (with Ian Macdonald, touring) 1989, From the Land and the Sea (with Peter Prendergast, Scarborough Art Gallery and Glynn Vivian Art Gallery Swansea) 1991–92; *Group Exhibitions* numerous since 1970, incl: Artists' Parish Maps (organised by Common Ground, touring) 1986, Artists in National Parks (V & A, and touring UK and USA) 1988–89, Salute to Turner (Agnew's) 1989, The Broad Horizon (Agnew's) 1990, The New Patrons (Christie's London) 1992, Centenary Exhbn (Christie's London) 1994; work in numerous public and private collections in UK and abroad; *Books* Len Tabner Drawings · Response to the Earth (1976), Smiths Dock Shipbuilders (with Ian Macdonald, 1987), Images of the Tees (with Ian Macdonald, 1989), Len Tabner · Paintings and Drawings 1970–89 (1989), Inspiration of Landscape (1989), From the Land and the Sea (with Peter Prendergast, 1991), A Voyage to the South (1992); *Recreations* building, farming/conservation; *Clubs* Royal Over-Seas League; *Style*— Len Tabner, Esq; ✉ High Boulby, Easington, Saltburn by the Sea, North Riding, Yorks TS13 4UT (☎ 01287 640948); Thos Agnew & Sons Ltd, 43 Old Bond Street, London (☎ 0171 629 6176, fax 0171 629 4359)

TABOR, Charles James; er s of Robert Charles Tabor (d 1985), of Shalford, nr Braintree, Essex, and Beryl Nora, *née* Lewis; *b* 15 March 1946; *Educ* Summerfields Sch Oxford, Cokethorpe Sch Witney Oxon, RAC Cirencester (NCA); *m* 23 Oct 1968, Gillian, da of John Buckley (d 1966), of Hartsmead, Ashton Keynes, Wilts; 2 s (Christopher Charles Robert b 26 Sept 1970, Oliver Charles John b 7 Oct 1978), 1 da ((Sarah) Claire Buckley b 26 Jan 1973); *Career* dir Tabor Farms Ltd; memb: Essex Farming and Wildlife Advsy Gp, Essex Farmers' Union, Essex CLA; dir Rolls Royce Enthusiasts' Club, tstee The Sir Henry Royce Meml Fndn; *Clubs* Farmers', Essex; *Style*— Charles Tabor, Esq; ✉ Sutton Hall, Rochford, Essex SS4 1LQ (☎ 01702 545730)

TABOR, Maj-Gen David John St Maur; CB (1977), MC (1944); yst s of Harry Ernest Tabor; *b* 5 Oct 1922; *Educ* Eton, RMA Sandhurst; *m* 1, 27 July 1955, Hon Pamela Roxane Nivison (d 1987), 2 da of 2 Baron Glendyne (d 1967); 2 s; m 2, 4 Oct 1989, Marguerite, widow of Col Peter Arkwright; *Career* 2 Lt RHG 1942, served NW Europe WWII (wounded), Lt-Col cmdg Household Cavalry and Silver Stick in Waiting 1964, Brig 1966, Cdr Berlin Inf Bde 1966, Cdr Br Army Staff and mil attaché Washington 1968, RCDS 1971, Maj-Gen 1972, defence attaché Paris 1972–74, GOC Eastern Dist 1975–77; vice chm ACFA 1979; Liveryman Worshipful Co of Grocers; *Recreations* shooting, fishing, gardening; *Clubs* MCC, Turf, RAC; *Style*— Maj-Gen David Tabor, CB, MC; ✉ Lower Farm, Compton Abdale, Glos GL54 4DS

TACK, David; s of Raphael Tack (d 1992), and Laura, *née* Irving; *b* 5 Dec 1943; *m* 1, 1963 (m dis 1968), Gaynor; 1 da (Nicola b 1964), 1 s (Paul b 1966); m 2, 1978, Carol; 3 s (Joe b 1976, James b 1978, Robbie b 1980), 1 da (Holly b 1981); *Career* asst to various fashion photographers 1960–66, in own studio (specialising in fashion and advtg photography) 1968–; one-man exhbns incl Impressions of Spain (RPS and touring) 1990; cmmnd by British govt to produce exhbn for central feature in British Pavillion Expo 92 Spain (calendar won Kodak Int Calendar of the Year Award 1993), Burma '94 calendar (runner-up Kodak Int Calendar of the Year Award 1994); Int Award RPS 1990; Assoc of Photographers: 4 Awards 1991, 3 Awards 1993, 1 Award 1994, 2 Awards 1995 (judge 1992 Awards); dir of commercials 1995–; *Books* Impressions of Spain (forward by V S Pritchett, 1991); *Recreations* pilot (aeroplane and glider), mountain biking; *Clubs* Chelsea Arts, Groucho's; *Style*— David Tack, Esq; ✉ The Clockhouse, Henley Park, Henley on Thames, Oxon (☎ 0941 119911, mobile 0860 300900)

TACKABERRY, John Antony; QC (1982); s of Thomas Raphael Tackaberry (d 1971), and Mary Catherine, *née* Geoghegan (d 1985); *b* 13 Nov 1939; *Educ* Downside, Trinity Coll Dublin, Downing Coll Cambridge (MA, LLM); *m* Penelope (d 1994), da of Seth Holt (d 1971); 2 s (Christopher b 1966, Antony b 1968); *Career* lectr: Chinese Miny of Further Educn 1963–64, Poly of Central London 1965–67; called to the Bar Gray's Inn 1967 (Republic of Ireland Bar 1987, Californian Bar 1988), recorder of the Crown Ct 1988–, currently head of chambers; HM Counsel NSW Aust 1990; pres: Soc of Construction Law 1987–85, Euro Soc of Construction Law 1985–87; memb: Arbitral Panels of Los Angeles Center for Commercial Arbitration 1987–, Int Arbitrators Panel Indian Cncl of Arbitration 1991–, Singapore Int Arbitration Cncl, Indian Cncl of Arbitration (panel of int arbitrators); chm Chartered Inst of Arbitrators 1990 (vice pres 1988); author of numerous articles; FCIArb, FFB; *Recreations* good food, good wine, good company, windsurfing, photography; *Clubs* Athenaeum; *Style*— John Tackaberry, Esq, QC; ✉ Arbitration Chambers, 22 Willes Road, London NW5 3DS (☎ 0171 267 2137, fax 0171 482 1018)

TAFROV, HE Stefan Lyubomirov; *b* 11 Feb 1958, Sofia Bulgaria; *Educ* French Language Sch Sofia, Clement of Ohrid Univ of Sofia (degree in journalism); *m* (m dis); *Career* Bulgarian diplomat; ed and head of dept ABC literary weekly 1983–87, head of dept Suvremennik (Contemporary) magazine 1987–89, head Int Information Dept Democracy newspaper, head Int Dept Union of Democratic Forces and foreign political advsr to Pres of Bulgaria 1990–91, first dep min of foreign affrs 1991–92, ambass to Italy and non-resident ambass to Malta 1992–95, ambass to the Ct of St James's 1995–; *Style*— HE Mr Stefan Tafrov; ✉ Embassy of the Republic of Bulgaria, 186–188 Queen's Gate, London SW7 5HL (☎ 0171 584 9400, fax 0171 584 4948)

TAGER, Romie; QC (1995); s of Osias Tager, of London, and Minnie Tager (d 1974); *b* 19 July 1947; *Educ* Hasmonean GS Hendon London, UCL (LLB); *m* 29 Aug 1971, Esther Marianne, da of Rev Leo Sichel, of London; 2 s (Joseph and Simon (twins) b 23 Oct 1980); *Career* called to the Bar Middle Temple 1970; practising barrister specialising in commercial, professional negligence and property law; memb Hon Socs of: Lincoln's Inn, Middle Temple, Inner Temple, Int Bar Assoc; *Recreations* opera, theatre, travel; *Clubs* Peak; *Style*— Romie Tager, Esq, QC; ✉ Hardwicke Building, New Square, Lincoln's Inn, London WC2A 3SB (☎ 0171 242 2523, fax 0171 831 6968)

TAGG, Alan; s of Thomas Bertram Tagg, and Annie, *née* Hufton; *b* 13 April 1928; *Educ* Mansfield Coll of Art, Old Vic Theatre Sch; *Career* freelance theatre designer; asst to Cecil Beaton, Oliver Messel, first play Charles Morgan's The River Line 1952, worked for H M Tennent Ltd, fndr memb English Stage Co 1956; designed: first prodn Look Back in Anger 1956, The Entertainer (with Lawrence Olivier) 1957, fifteen other prodns at Royal Court Theatre, four prodns for RSC incl Graham Greene's The Return of A J Raffles 1975, twelve prodns at Chichester Festival Theatre incl Dear Antoine (with Edith Evans) 1971 and Waters of the Moon (with Ingrid Bergman) 1977, prodns of nine plays by Alan Ayckbourn, ten prodns for NT, 93 West End prodns (incl Billy Liar 1959, How the Other Half Loves 1970, The Constant Wife 1973, Alphabetical Order 1975, Donkey's Years 1976, The Kingfisher 1977, Candida 1977, The Millionairess 1978, Peter Shaffer's Lettice and Lovage (with Maggie Smith) 1987, eleven prodns on Broadway incl Peter Shaffer's Black Comedy 1967 and Lettice and Lovage (with Maggie Smith) 1990, prodn of Look Back in Anger Moscow Arts Theatre 1961, Taking Steps in Copenhagen and Sleuth in Berlin, redesigned Lettice and Lovage (American nat tour, starring Julie Harris) 1992; worked with dirs incl: Lindsay Anderson, Michael Blakemore, John Dexter, John Gielgud, Tony Richardson and Michael Rudman; exhbns designed incl: Shakespeare Stratford-upon-Avon 1964, Hector Berlioz 1969, 25 Years of Covent Garden, V & A Museum 1971, Byron 1974; *Recreations* living in France; *Clubs* Groucho; *Style*— Alan Tagg, Esq; ✉ Chemin de Masmolène, 30700 Vallabrix, France (☎ 00 33 466 22 63 93); 19 Parsons Green, London SW6 4UL (☎ 0171 731 2787)

TAGG, David Edward; *Educ* Alleyns Sch Dulwich, Pembroke Coll Oxford (MA), Dip Public and Social Admin; *Career* main bd dir Grand Metropolitan plc 1988– (joined Watney Mann & Truman Brewers as personnel dir 1980); chm Grand Metropolitan Community Servs and Gp Pension Fund; non-exec dir Storehouse plc; dir various charitable and other orgns; FIPM; *Style*— David Tagg, Esq; ✉ Grand Metropolitan plc, 8 Henrietta Place, London W1M 9AG (☎ 0171 518 5200, fax 0171 518 4641)

TAGGART, Dr Hugh McAllister; s of Dr James Taggart (d 1994), of Belfast, and Margaret Helen, *née* Thompson; *b* 29 Nov 1949; *Educ* Campbell Coll Belfast, Queen's Univ of Belfast (MB, MD); *m* 5 July 1974, Grace Ann Margretta, da of James Campbell (d 1982); 1 s (Christopher b 24 Oct 1978), 1 da (Kathryn b 19 July 1981); *Career* sr post doctoral res fell Univ of Washington Seattle USA 1979–80, sr lectr in geriatric med Queen's Univ of Belfast 1980–92, conslt physician Belfast City Hosp 1980– (sr registrar in geriatric med 1977–79); memb Med Advsy Bd Nat Osteoporosis Soc; memb BMA, fell Ulster Med Soc, FRCP; *Recreations* golf, skiing, swimming, tennis; *Clubs* Royal Belfast Golf; *Style*— Dr Hugh Taggart; ✉ 1 Crawfordsburn Wood, Crawfordsburn, Bangor, Co Down BT19 1XB; Health Care for the Elderly, Belfast City Hospital, Lisburn Road, Belfast BT9 7AB (☎ 01232 329241 ext 2907, fax 01232 263946)

TAIT, Andrew Wilson; OBE (1967); s of Dr Adam Tait (d 1934), of Fife, and Jenny Tait (d 1925); *b* 25 Sept 1922; *Educ* George Watson's Coll Edinburgh, Univ of Edinburgh; *m* 1954, Betty Isobel, da of Finlay Maclennan (d 1960); 3 da (Jane, Susan, Christine); *Career* ldr writer The Scotsman 1947–48, Scottish Office 1948–64, dir gen Nat Housebuilding Cncl and Housing Res Fndn 1964–87 (chm 1985–87), non-exec dep chm: Barratt Developments plc, Home Buyers Advsy Serv; advsr on housing in USA, Canada and Aust 1973–81; chm: New Homes Environmental Group, World Housing and Home Warranty Conf 1987–; *Recreations* golf, tennis; *Clubs* Caledonian; *Style*— Andrew Tait, Esq, OBE; ✉ Orchard Croft, Grimmshill, Great Missenden, Bucks

TAIT, Arthur Gordon; s of George Aidan Drury Tait (d 1970), and Margaret Evelyn (Peggy), *née* Gray (d 1981); *b* 28 July 1934; *Educ* Eton, St John's Coll Cambridge (MA); *m* 20 Sept 1958, Ann Sutcliffe, da of late Stuart Kendrick Gilbert; 3 s (Charles William b 5 April 1960 d 1961, Gordon Peter b 8 Feb 1962, Michael George b 15 Nov 1966), 2 da (Clare Penelope (twin) b 8 Feb 1962, Celia Helen Gilbert b 30 March 1964); *Career* Nat Serv 2 Lt KRRC 1953–54; ICI plc: staff offr 1957–59, staff offr Alkali Div 1961–63 (labour offr 1959–60), works personnel mangr Agric Div 1963–68, industl relations mangr Dyestuffs Div 1968–71, dir Mond Div 1976–82 (personnel mangr 1971–76), head office project mangr and int personnel mangr 1983–91; sec-gen Inst of Actuaries 1991–; FIPD (MIPD 1965), FRSA; *Recreations* family, swimming, travel, following sports, friends who visit; *Clubs* Hurlingham, Holmes Health; *Style*— Arthur Tait, Esq; ✉ 39 Hollywood Road, London SW10 9HT (☎ 0171 352 5127, fax 0171 351 2149); Institute of Actuaries, Staple Inn Hall, High Holborn, London WC1V 7QJ (☎ 0171 242 0106, fax 0171 405 2482)

TAIT, Eric; MBE (Mil 1980); s of William Johnston Tait (d 1959), and Sarah, *née* Jones; *b* 10 Jan 1945; *Educ* George Heriot's Sch, RMA Sandhurst, Univ of London (BSc), Univ of Cambridge (MPhil); *m* 29 March 1967, Agnes Jane Boag, da of Capt Henry George Anderson (d 1958); 1 s (Michael b 1969), 1 da (Eva b 1973); *Career* Lt-Col RE, served BAOR, Middle East, Caribbean, N Ireland (despatches 1976); dir Euro ops Pannell Kerr Forster 1989–, exec dir Pannell Kerr Forster Worldwide 1992–; ed in chief The Accountant's Magazine; sec Inst of CAs of Scotland 1984–89; memb Exec Scottish Cncl for Devpt and Indust 1984–89, chm Univ of Nottingham and Trent Euro Advsy Forum 1993–; *Recreations* hillwalking, swimming, reading, writing; *Style—* Eric Tait, Esq, MBE; ✉ Pannell Kerr Forster Worldwide, 78 Hatton Garden, London EC1N 8JA (☎ 0171 831 7393, fax 0171 405 6736, telex 295998)

TAIT, Ivan Ballantyne; TD (1967); s of Ivan Tait (d 1976), and Elise Alexander, *née* Forsyth (d 1972); *b* 14 Sept 1928; *Educ* Glasgow Acad, Daniel Stewart's Coll, Univ of Edinburgh (MB ChB); *m* 3 July 1965, Jocelyn Mary Connel, da of Lt-Col William Michael Leggatt, DSO (d 1946); 1 s ((Ivan) Alexander Leggatt b 12 June 1974), 1 da (Arabella Elizabeth b 24 Oct 1968); *Career* Nat Serv PMO Gurkha Rifles, RAMC 1952–54 (despatches 1953), Col L RAMC (Vol) TA 1955–, hon surgn (TA) to HM The Queen; Edinburgh Royal Infirmary and St Mary's Hosp London 1951–64, Univ of Kentucky 1965–67, conslt surgn Tayside Health Bd 1967–72, conslt dept of genitourinary med Edinburgh 1973–82, conslt in admin charge of genitourinary med services West of Scot 1982–94; memb: business ctee of Gen Cncl Univ of Edinburgh, Scot Priory Chapter Order of St John; Liveryman Worshipful Soc of Apothecaries 1959, Hammerman Glasgow 1986; FRCS, FRCSE, FRCSG; UN Cyprus Medal 1984; KStJ 1982; *Recreations* TA, charitable societies; *Clubs* New (Edinburgh); *Style—* Ivan B Tait, Esq, TD; ✉ 6 Lennox Row, Edinburgh EH5 3HN (☎ 0131 552 9329)

TAIT, Prof James Francis; s of Herbert Tait (d 1935), and Constance Levinia, *née* Brotherton (d 1974); *b* 1 Dec 1925; *Educ* Darlington GS, Univ of Leeds (BSc, PhD); *m* 1 Sept 1956, Sylvia Agnes Sophia, da of James W Wardropper (d 1947); *Career* Dept of Physics Middx Hosp Med Sch: lectr 1948–55, external sci staff MRC 1955–58, Joel prof and head of dept 1970–82, jt head of Biophysical Endocrinology Unit 1970–86; sr scientist Worcester Fndn for Experimental Biology Mass USA 1958–70 (chm Sci Cncl 1968–70), emeritus prof Univ of London 1982–; memb at large Howard Florey Inst of Experimental Physiology and Med Melbourne 1980–; sec Laurentian Hormone Ctee; memb: Gen Med Bd US PHS Study Section USA 1967–70, Editorial Bd Clinical Endocrinology USA, Cncl Soc for Endocrinology 1971–74, Grant in Aid Ctee Royal Soc 1979–82, Steroid Reference Ctee MRC 1972–79; hon memb Faculty of Radiology UK; *Awards* Soc of Endocrinology medal 1969, Tadeus Reichstein award Int Endocrine Soc 1976, Gregory Pincus Meml medal 1977, CIBA award Cncl for High Blood Pressure 1977, Dale medal Soc for Endocrinology 1979, Res Career award United Public Health Serv 1962–70; gave Douglas Wright Lecture Melbourne Aust 1989; elected to American Acad of Arts and Scis 1958–70; Hon DSc Univ of Hull; FRS 1959, FRSM 1971; *Publications* many chapters in books, 200 scientific papers; *Recreations* photography, gardening, walking the dog, chess; *Clubs* Royal Society, RSM; *Style—* Prof James Tait, FRS; ✉ Moorlands, Main Road, East Boldre, Nr Brockenhurst, Hants SO42 7WT (☎ and fax 01590 626312)

TAIT, Sir James Sharp; kt (1969); s of William Blyth Tait; *b* 13 June 1912; *Educ* Royal Tech Coll Glasgow, Univ of Glasgow (BSc, PhD); *m* 1939, Mary Cassidy, da of Archibald Linton, of Kilmaurs, Ayrshire; 2 s, 1 da; *Career* princ: Woolwich Poly 1951–56, Northampton Coll of Advanced Technol London 1956–66; vice chllr and princ The City Univ 1966–74; Liveryman Worshipful Co of Scientific Instrument Makers; Hon LLD Univ of Strathclyde, Hon DSc City Univ; *Style—* Sir James Tait; ✉ 23 Trowlock Avenue, Teddington, Middx

TAIT, Marion Hooper (Mrs Marion Morse); OBE (1992); da of Charles Arnold Browell Tait, OBE (d 1962), of London, and Betty Maude, *née* Hooper; *b* 7 Oct 1950; *Educ* Royal Acad of Dancing, Royal Ballet Sch; *m* 9 Oct 1971, David Thomas Morse, s of Thomas Walter Morse (d 1984); *Career* princ dancer with Sadler's Wells Royal Ballet (now The Birmingham Royal Ballet); ballet mistress Birmingham Royal Ballet 1995; worked with leading choreographers and had roles created by: Sir Kenneth MacMillan, Sir Frederick Ashton, David Bintley, Christopher Bruce, Joe Layton; danced all maj classical roles; guest dancer: The Houston Ballet, Munich Ballet, Japan, Aust, Poland (Polich Ballet's Bicentenial medal of Honour); nominated Olivier Award (for Romeo and Juliet) 1994, winner Dancer of the Year (Dance and Dancers magazine) 1994, winner The Evening Standard Ballet Award (for outstanding performance) 1994, nominated Olivier Award for Outstanding Achievement in Dance (for Pillar of Fire) 1996; *Recreations* needlework; *Style—* Ms Marion Tait, OBE; ✉ c/o Birmingham Royal Ballet, Hippodrome Theatre, Thorp Street, Birmingham B5 4AU

TAIT, Michael Logan; CMG (1987), LVO (1972); s of William Tait, and Dorothea Tait; *b* 27 Sept 1936; *Educ* Calday Grange GS, New Coll Oxford (BA, MA); *m* 1968 (m dis 1990); 2 s, 1 da; *Career* Nat Serv 2 Lt Royal Signals 1955–57; joined FO 1961, MECAS 1961, Bahrain 1963, asst political agent Dubai Trucial States 1963, FO 1966, private sec to Min of State FO (later FCO) 1968, first sec and head of Chancery Belgrade 1970, first sec (political), head of Chancery and consul Amman 1972, FCO 1975, cnsllr and head of Chancery Baghdad 1977, cnsllr FCO 1978, dep head of delgn CSCE Madrid 1980, dep head of delgn and cnsllr (econ and fin) OECD Paris 1982, head Economic Rels Dept FCO 1984, ambass UAE 1986–89, asst under sec of state (i/c Soviet Union and Eastern Europe) 1990–92, ambass Tunisia 1992–Oct 1995, resigned; chm Oxford and Edinburgh Conslts 1995–; *Clubs* Garrick, Vanderbilt, Wimbleball Sailing (Brompton Regis); *Style—* M L Tait, Esq, CMG, LVO; ✉ 8 Chalcot Crescent, London NW1 8YD

TAIT, Simon John Anderson; s of William Anderson Tait (d 1973), and Alice Mary, *née* Crowther; *b* 30 Jan 1948; *Educ* Hawes Down Secdy Modern Sch; *m* 1979, Ann Sandra, da of George William Hugh Williams (d 1990); 1 s (Adam Anderson b 1988); *Career* journalist; Croydon Advertiser 1966–70, Brighton Evening Argus 1970, Newham Recorder 1971, Manchester Evening News 1972, writer Government Info Serv 1975, head of PR servs V & A 1980, Telegraph Sunday Magazine 1984, freelance writer 1985, The Times 1988, freelance 1992–; author of many newspaper and magazine articles on the arts and heritage; *Books* Palaces of Discovery (The Story of British Museums) (1989), Times Guide to Museums and Galleries 1989–90 and 1990–91, London Philharmonic Yearbook 1996–97 (ed); *Recreations* finding out; *Clubs* Reform; *Style—* Simon Tait; ✉ 12 Derwent Grove, London SE22 8EA (☎ 0181 693 5672, fax 0181 299 9818)

TALBOT, Vice Adm Sir (Arthur Allison) FitzRoy; KBE (1964), CB (1961), DSO (1940 and bar 1942), DL (Somerset 1973); s of Capt Henry FitzRoy George Talbot, DSO, RN (gs of Rev Henry Talbot by his w Mary, da of Maj-Gen Hon Sir William Ponsonby, KCB (ka Waterloo 1815, 2 s of 1 Baron Ponsonby of Imokilly, cr 1806 & extinct 1866) by his w Georgiana, da of 1 Baron Southampton. The Rev Henry Talbot was eldest s of Very Rev Charles Talbot, Dean of Salisbury, by his w Lady Elizabeth Somerset, da of 5 Duke of Beaufort. The Dean was 2 s of Rev and Hon George Talbot, 3 s of 1 Baron Talbot (cr 1833) and unc of 1 Earl Talbot (of the 1784 cr); *b* 22 Oct 1909; *Educ* RNC Dartmouth; *m* 1, 1940, Joyce Gertrude, er da of late Frank Edwin Linley, of Fowey, Cornwall; 2 da (Anthea Jane (Mrs James Charrington) b 1944, Elizabeth Ann (Mrs Michael Shuttleworth) b 1945); m 2, 1983, Elizabeth Mary (d 1995), da of Rupert Charles Ensor, of Co Armagh; *Career* served RN 1922–67: Channel, East Coast UK, Mediterranean, Atlantic, Western Isles during WWII, Staff Offr Ops to C-in-C Br Pacific Fleet & Far East Station 1947–48, Capt 1950, Naval Attaché Moscow & Helsinki 1951–53, IDC 1954, Cdre RN Barracks Portsmouth 1957–59, Rear Adm 1960, Flag Offr Arabian Seas & Persian Gulf 1960–61, ME 1961–62, Vice Adm 1962, C-in-C S Atlantic & S America 1963–65, C-in-C Plymouth 1965–67; *Style—* Vice Adm Sir FitzRoy Talbot, KBE, CB, DSO*, DL; ✉ Wootton Fitzpaine Manor, Bridport, Dorset DT6 6NF (☎ 01297 560455)

TALBOT, Sir Hilary Gwynne; kt (1968); s of Rev Prebendary A Talbot, RD; *b* 22 Jan 1912; *Educ* Haileybury, Worcester Coll Oxford; *m* 1963, Jean Whitworth, JP, da of Kenneth Fisher; *Career* served WWII RA; barr 1935, dep chm Northants Quarter Sessions 1948–62, chm Derbyshire Quarter Sessions 1958–63, judge of County Cts 1962–68, dep chm Hants Quarter Sessions 1964–71, High Court judge Queen's Bench Div 1968–83, judge Employment Appeals Tbnl 1978–81, memb Parole Bd 1980–83, dep chm Boundary Cmmn Wales 1980–83; memb Rule Ctee Supreme Ct until Nov 1981; *Style—* Sir Hilary Talbot; ✉ Old Chapel House, Little Ashley, Bradford on Avon, Wilts BA15 2PN (☎ 01225 862182)

TALBOT, John Andrew; s of Robert Talbot and Lucy Eileen, *née* Jarvis; *b* 2 Aug 1949; *Educ* Queen's Sch Wisbech; *m* 1 (m dis), Susan Anne, *née* Hollingberry; 1 s (Martin b 5 March 1969), 1 da (Helen b 28 Dec 1970); m 2, Jennifer Anne, *née* Crouch; 1 s (George b 25 March 1991), 2 da (Hannah b 7 April 1982, Bethany b 7 Aug 1984); *Career* articled clerk Larking, Larking and Whiting Wisbech 1966 (transferred to Stevenson Smart & Co Peterborough), qualified 1971, various accounting posts 1971–75, joined Spicer and Pegler Nottingham 1975 (ptnr specialising in insolvency and investigation work 1980); Arthur Andersen & Co: ptnr establishing Corp Recovery Practice Birmingham 1983, currently ptnr responsible for worldwide corp recovery and corp fin serv line; hon treas English Nat Ballet; FCA 1971; *Recreations* contemporary art, modern and classic dance, antiquarian books, natural history; *Clubs* RAC; *Style—* John Talbot, Esq; ✉ Arthur Andersen & Co, 1 Surrey Street, London WC2R 2PS (☎ 0171 438 3739)

TALBOT, John Michael Arthur; s of John Edward Lightfoot Talbot (Capt WWI and WWII, d 1974), of 22 Chepstow Place, London, and Muriel Emily Mary, *née* Horsley; *b* 29 Dec 1934; *Educ* Sherborne, Trinity Hall Cambridge (MA); *m* 9 Sept 1961, Adrienne Mary, da of Capt R F T Stannard, CBE, DSC, RN (d 1969), of Little Barley Mow, Headley, Hants; 1 s (Michael b 1962), 1 da (Claire b 1964); *Career* Nat Serv 2 Lt Middx Regt; sr ptnr Bower Cotton & Bower 1982– (ptnr 1964–); clerk to govrs Highgate Sch; vice pres Blackheath FC; memb Law Soc; *Recreations* swimming, walking, wine, history; *Clubs* Blackheath FC, Teddington CC; *Style—* John Talbot, Esq; ✉ 51 Culmington Rd, Ealing, London W13 9NJ (☎ 0181 567 4905); 36 Whitefriars St, London EC4Y 8BH (☎ 0171 353 3040)

TALBOT, Prof Michael Owen; s of Prof Alan Talbot (d 1981), and Dr Annelise Talbot, *née* Tømmerup; *b* 4 Jan 1943; *Educ* Welwyn Garden City GS, RCM (ARCM), Clare Coll Cambridge (open scholar, BA, MusB, PhD); *m* 26 Sept 1970, Shirley Ellen Mashiane-Talbot, da of Jacob Mashiane (d 1975), of SA; 1 s (Stephen b 1975), 1 da (Natasha b 1982); *Career* Univ of Liverpool: asst lectr then lectr in music 1968–79, sr lectr in music 1979–83, reader in music 1983–86, Alsop prof of music 1986–; memb: Standing Ctee Nat Assoc of Univ Music Staff, Royal Musical Assoc, Società Italiana di Musicologia; memb Editorial Bd: Music and Letters, Istituto Italiano Antonio Vivaldi; corresponding memb Ateneo Veneto 1986, FBA 1990; Cavaliere dell' Ordine Al Merito della Repubblica Italiana 1980; *Books* Vivaldi (Dent, 1978), Vivaldi (BBC, 1979), Albinoni: Leben und Werk (1980), Antonio Vivaldi: A Guide to Research (1988), Tomaso Albinoni: The Venetian Composer and His World (1990), Benedetto Vinaccesi: A Musician in Brescia and Venice in the Age of Corelli (1994), The Sacred Vocal Music of Antonio Vivaldi (1995); *Recreations* chess, reading novels, travel; *Style—* Prof Michael Talbot, FBA; ✉ 36 Montclair Drive, Liverpool L18 0HA (☎ 0151 722 3328); Department of Music, University of Liverpool, PO Box 147, Liverpool L69 3BX (☎ 0151 794 3096, fax 0151 794 3141)

TALBOT, Patrick John; QC (1990); s of John Bentley Talbot, MC, of Farnham, Surrey, and Marguerite Maxwell, *née* Townley (d 1995); *b* 28 July 1946; *Educ* Charterhouse, Univ Coll Oxford (MA); *m* 8 May 1976, Judith Anne, da of David Percival Urwin; 1 s (William Patrick Charles b 2 June 1983), 2 da (Sophie Camilla b 28 Nov 1977, Alexandra Claire Maxwell b 8 Nov 1979); *Career* called to the Bar Lincoln's Inn 1969 (bencher 1996), in practice Chancery Bar 1970–; memb: Senate of Inns of Court and the Bar 1974–77, Cncl of Legal Educn 1977–95 (vice chm 1992–95), Gen Cncl of the Bar 1993; *Recreations* cricket, skiing, bridge, collecting old toys; *Clubs* MCC, Wimbledon Wanderers Cricket; *Style—* Patrick Talbot, Esq, QC; ✉ 22 West Park Rd, Kew, Richmond, Surrey TW9 4DA (☎ 0181 878 3516, fax 0181 876 2669); 31 Farm Lane, Great Bedwyn, Marlborough, Wilts SN8 3LU (☎ 01672 870974); 13 Old Square, Lincoln's Inn, London WC2A 3UA (☎ 0171 242 6105, fax 0171 405 4004)

TALBOT, Paul Darius; s of William Ernest Talbot (d 1970), and Winifred May, *née* Mason (d 1991); *b* 9 Jan 1947; *Educ* Gordons Sch W End Woking Surrey; *m* May 1970, Pamela; 1 s (Darren William b 12 Feb 1971); *Career* with Hill Samuel 1964–81, sales dir Wardley Unit Trust Managers 1981–83; md: Brown Shipley Unit Trust Managers Ltd 1983–92, Brown Shipley Asset Management Ltd 1989–92; exec dir Fidelity Investment Services Ltd 1992–; memb Exec Ctee Assoc of Unit Tsts and Investment Funds 1987–90 and 1994–95; *Recreations* golf, bridge; *Style—* Paul D Talbot, Esq; ✉ Green Courts, 148 Ember Lane, Esher, Surrey KT10 8EJ (☎ 0181 398 4603); Fidelity Investment Services Ltd, Oakhill House, 130 Tonbridge Road, Hildenborough, Tonbridge, Kent TN11 9DZ (☎ 01737 777397, fax 01737 833886, car 0836 214852)

TALBOT OF MALAHIDE, 10 Baron (I 1831); Reginald John Richard Arundell; DL (Wilts); also Hereditary Lord Adm of Malahide and the Adjacent Seas (a distinction dating by charter from 5 March in the 15 year of the reign of Edward IV). The mother of the 2 and 3 Barons, who was the first holder of the title, was, to use the full designation, cr Baroness Talbot of Malahide and Lady Malahide of Malahide; s of Reginald John Arthur Arundell (changed his surname to Arundell 1945, s of Reginald Aloysius Talbot, ggs of Baroness Talbot of Malahide), and Mabile Arundell, gda of 9 Baron Arundell of Wardour; suc kinsman 9 Baron Talbot of Malahide (d 1987); *b* 9 Jan 1931; *Educ* Stonyhurst, RMA Sandhurst; *m* 1, 1955, Laura Duff (d 1989), yr da of Gp Capt Edward Tennant, DSO, MC, JP (n of 1 Baron Glenconner), and his 2 w, Victoria Duff, MBE, o da of Sir Robert Duff, 2 Bt; 1 s (Hon Richard John Tennant b 1957), 4 da (Hon Juliet Anne Tennant (Hon Mrs Teakle) b 1959, Hon Catherine Mary Tennant (Hon Mrs Allwood) b 1960, Hon Caroline Rose Tennant b 1962, Hon Lucy Veronica Tennant (Hon Mrs Daniel) b 1965); m 2, 1992, Patricia Mary, eldest da of late John Cuthbert Widdrington Riddell, OBE, of Felton Park, and Swinburne Castle, Northumberland, and formerly w of late Maj Geoffrey Thomas Blundell-Brown, MBE; *Heir* s, Hon Richard John Tennant Arundell, JP, b 1957; *Career* Vice Lord-Lieut for Wilts 1996–; chm St John Cncl for Wilts; memb Chapter Gen 1993–, KStJ 1988 (CStJ 1983, OStJ 1978); Kt of Honour and Devotion SMOM 1977; hon citizen of State of Maryland; *Style—* The Rt Hon Lord Talbot of Malahide, DL; ✉ Park Gate, Donhead St Andrew, Shaftesbury, Dorset (☎ 01747 828270)

TALBOT-PONSONBY, Nigel Edward Charles; s of Edward Fitzroy Talbot-Ponsonby (d 1996; ggs of Adm Sir Charles Talbot, KCB, who was s of Very Rev Charles Talbot, Dean of Salisbury, by Lady Elizabeth Somerset, da of 5 Duke of

Beaufort; the Dean was n of 3 Baron and 1 Earl Talbot, which two dignities are now held by the Earl of Shrewsbury); *b* 24 Sept 1946; *Educ* Harrow; *m* 1977, Robina, da of Lt Cdr Henry Bruce, JP, DL, RN, Ret (gs of 9 Earl of Elgin & 13 of Kincardine), of Barley Down House, Alresford; 3 s (Henry b 1981, James b 1986, Alexander b 1987); *Career* chartered surveyor; chm Humberts Leisure chartered surveyors and leisure property specialists; firm handled sale of Highgrove to HRH The Prince of Wales 1981; former memb Recreation and Leisure Mgmnt Ctee RICS, memb Land Decade Cncl; FRICS; *Recreations* sailing, field sports; *Clubs* Royal Thames Yacht; *Style*— Nigel Talbot-Ponsonby, Esq; ✉ Langrish Lodge, Langrish, Petersfield, Hants GU32 1RB (☎ 01730 63374); Humberts Leisure, 12 Bolton Street, Mayfair, London W1Y 7PA (☎ 0171 629 6700, fax 0171 409 0475)

TALBOT-RICE, Nigel; s of Mervyn Gurney Talbot-Rice (d 1979), and Eleanor Butler Adair, *née* Williamson (d 1965); *b* 14 May 1938; *Educ* Charterhouse, ChCh Oxford (MA, DipEd); *m* 20 July 1968, (Rosfrith) Joanna Sarah, da of Air-Cdr F J Manning, CB, CBE, RAF (d 1988); 1 s (Samuel b 17 March 1982), 4 da (Sarah b 24 Oct 1969, Caroline (Mrs Jonathan Bewes) b 26 Sept 1971, Rebecca b 2 Sept 1973, Helena b 28 Jan 1977); *Career* Nat Serv Coldstream Gds 1957–58; asst master Papplewick Sch Ascot 1961–64, headmaster Summer Fields Sch Oxford 1975– (asst master 1965–71, asst headmaster 1971–75); memb IAPS 1971; *Books* Survey of Religion in Preparatory Schools (1965); *Recreations* golf, gardening; *Style*— Nigel Talbot-Rice, Esq; ✉ Beech House, Mayfield Rd, Oxford; Cool Bawn, Thurlestone, Devon; Summer Fields, Oxford OX2 7EN (☎ 01865 54433)

TALLBOYS, Richard Gilbert; CMG, OBE; s of Harry Tallboys (d 1963), and Doris Gilbert (d 1967); *b* 25 April 1931; *Educ* Palmers Sch, Univ of London (LLB), Univ of Tasmania (BCom); *m* 1954, Margaret Evelyn, da of Brig Horace William Strutt DSO, ED (d 1985), of Tasmania; 2 s (Roger, Peter), 2 da (Prudence, Sarah); *Career* Lt Cdr RANR (ret 1991); Merchant Navy 1947–55, accountant in Aust 1955–62, Aust Govt Trade Cmmn 1962–68 (served in Johannesburg, Singapore and Jakarta); HM Dip Serv 1968–88: served in Brasilia and Phnom Penh, commercial cnsllr Seoul 1976–80, HM consul-gen Houston 1980–85, HM ambass Hanoi 1985–87; chief exec World Coal Inst 1988–93; currently int trade advsr and lectr on Asia; memb Cncl: London C of C and Industry 1990–93 and 1995–, RIIA 1995–; Freeman City of London 1985; FCA, FCIS, FCPA, FAIOD; *Books* Doing Business with Indonesia (1968), Fifty Years of Business in Indonesia (jtly, 1995), Developing Vietnam (ed, 1995); *Recreations* skiing; *Clubs* Travellers', Little Ship, Tasmanian; *Style*— Richard G Tallboys, Esq, CMG, OBE; ✉ 7 Chapel Side, Bayswater, London W2 4LG (☎ and fax 0171 727 2441)

TALLON, David Seymour; s of Claude Reginald Tallon, of London, and Blanche Mary, *née* Mahony (d 1984); *b* 7 Oct 1940; *Educ* Rugby; *children* 2 s (Alastair James b 14 May 1965, Timothy Paul b 6 July 1967), 3 da (Victoria Kate Rebecca b 1 March 1969, Elizabeth Jane Biddy b 16 May 1970, Sarah Georgina b 18 Oct 1994); *Career* CA 1964; Deloitte Plender Griffiths 1958–67, ptnr Dearden Harper Miller 1969, sr ptnr Dearden Farrow 1986–87, managing ptnr Bristol office BDO Binder Hamlyn 1990–92 (dep sr ptnr nat firm 1987–90), ptnr Sharp Parsons Tallon 1992–; chm Children with AIDS Charity 1994–; Liveryman Worshipful Co of Needlemakers; FCA; *Books* Capital Transfer Tax Planning (2 edn 1976, 3 edn 1978), Inland Revenue Practices & Concessions (1980); *Recreations* golf; *Clubs* Wig and Pen; *Style*— David Tallon, Esq; ✉ Sharp Parsons Tallon, 167 Fleet Street, London EC4A 2EA (☎ 0171 353 1053, fax 0171 815 0126)

TAMBUNTING, HE Jesus P; s of Antonio Tambunting, of Makati, Manila, and Aurora, *née* Paraiso; *b* 21 Dec 1937; *Educ* Culver Military Acad Indiana, Univ of Maryland (BSBA); *m* 9 July, Margarita, da of José Ansaldo, and Mary Whitaker; 2 da (Angela b 10 Oct 1968, Victoria b 20 Jan 1975), 2 s (Tomas b 11 May 1973, Steven b 2 Aug 1976); *Career* Philippine diplomat; sr exec trg prog Chemical Bank NYC 196?, Philippine ambass to the Ct of St James's (concurrently non-resident ambass to Ireland) 1993–; currently: perm rep to Int Maritime Orgn, chm Planters Development Bank, chm Planters DB Leasing Corp, chm Fin Ctee Small and Medium Enterprise Div Philippines Chamber of Commerce and Indust, memb Bd of Tstees Philippines Agro-Industrial Fund, vice chm Review Ctee Cottage Enterprise Fin Project; former positions incl: dir Guarantee Fund for Small & Medium Enterprise, chm Hambrecht & Quist Philippine Ventures, memb Bd of Tstees Philippine Business for Social Progress, dir, sr vice pres and treas The Manila Banking Corp; pres Mgmnt Assoc of the Philippines 1988, dir then vice chm Makati Business Club 1987–97, pres Devpt Bankers Assoc of the Philippines 1978–80, pres Chambers of Thrift Bank 1980, memb Bishop-Businessmen's Conf for Human Devpt; *Recreations* tennis; *Clubs* Manila Polo; *Style*— HE Mr Jesus P Tambunting; ✉ Embassy of the Philippines, 9 Palace Green, London W8 4QE (☎ 0171 937 1600, fax 0171 937 2925)

TAMLIN, Keith Maxwell; s of Sydney Thomas Tamlin (d 1946), and Madeline Isabel, *née* Prowse; *b* 19 July 1928; *Educ* Ruthin Sch, Univ of Wales (LLB); *m* 21 June 1954, Marian, da of Thomas Roberts; 2 da (Helen Susan b 25 May 1955, Karen Michele b 26 April 1958); *Career* Nat Serv King's (Liverpool) Regt RASC 1947–49 (cmmnd 1948, served ME); slr Supreme Ct of Judicature 1954, ptnr North Kirk & Co Slrs Liverpool 1959 (joined 1954), currently conslt Cuff Roberts Slrs Liverpool; dir: Everton Football Club Co Ltd 1974–, H Samuel plc 1979– (and other cos within H Samuel Group incl Watches of Switzerland plc), several cos within distributive sector, various cos dealing with racehorses, publications and breeding; pres: Liverpool Jr C of C 1960, Liverpool Round Table 1965; chm Jt Ctees organising Charity Gala Performances at Liverpool Playhouse 1964–65 (to raise funds for Liverpool Central Boys' Club, Liverpool Maternity Hosp and the Br Red Cross and Women's Hosp), memb and slr Ctee Liverpool and Dist Family Servs Unit 1963–82, memb The Mail Order Traders' Assoc of GB (sec 1967, dir 1974); memb: PO Users' Nat Cncl 1970–90, Trg Ctee Distributive Indust Bd 1971–, Mgmnt Ctee and Cncl Retail Consortium 1973–, Cncl Advtg Assoc 1982–, Cncl CBI 1988–; nominated by HM Govt as a Gp 1 Employers' Rep to Econ and Social Ctee Brussels 1983, memb Ctee for Commerce and Distribution Euro Cmmn; memb: Liverpool Law Soc, The Law Soc (pres 1984); *Recreations* walking, swimming, golf, watching football and professional golf; *Clubs* Athenaeum (Liverpool), East India; *Style*— Keith Tamlin, Esq; ✉ Cuff Roberts, 100 Old Hall, Liverpool L3 9TD (☎ 0151 227 4181, fax 0151 051 227 2584)

TAMM, Mary; da of Endel Tamm, of Tauinn, and Raissa, *née* Kisseliev (d 1989); *b* 22 March 1950; *Educ* Bradford, RADA; *m* 14 Jan 1978, Marcus Jonathan Hardman Ringrose, s of Wing Cdr Richard Ringrose, DFC (d 1973), of London; 1 da (Lauren Zoe b 18 Nov 1979); *Career* actress, journalist, drama teacher, director and freelance writer; assoc of RADA (and memb Assocs' Ctee); *Theatre* incl: Oedipus, Macbeth, Mother Earth, Action Replay, The Bitter Tears of Petra Von Kant, Cards on the Table, Good Morning Bill, Swimming Pools at War, Present Laughter, Why is Here There Everywhere Now?, Later Leonardo, The Maintenance Man, The Lover; *Television* incl: : Donati Conspiracy, Warship, Girls of Slender Means, Not the Nine O'Clock News, The Assassination Run, The Treachery Game, Hunter's Walk, Jane Eyre, Bergerac, The Hello Goodbye Man, Coronation Street, A Raging Calm, Public Eye, Whodunnit, The Inheritors, Dr Who, Only When I Laugh, Quest for Love, Return of the Saint, Worlds Beyond, Hercule Poirot, Casualty, The Bill, Scarlet Woman, Perfect Scoundrels, Crosswits, Pressing Engagement (TV film), Brookside, Darkside (TV film), The New Adventures of Robin Hood; *Films* incl: Witness Madness, Odessa File, The Likely Lads, The Doubt, Rampage, Three Kinds of Heat, Night Swimming; *Recreations* riding, piano, reading, theatre, opera, computer scrabble,skiing, painting; *Style*— Ms Mary Tamm; ✉ c/o Barry Langford Associates, 17 Westfields Avenue, London SW13 0AT (☎ 0181 878 7148)

TAMS, Gerald Raymond; s of Peter Tams (d 1977), and Olive Margaret, *née* Simmons; *b* 11 Sept 1939; *Educ* Ratcliffe Coll Leicester, N Staffs Coll of Technol; *m* Angela Margaret, da of Alan Gibbons Weston, RE; 2 s (Robert William b June 1967 d 1968, Stephen Charles b 4 Dec 1969), 1 da (Catherine Monica b 11 Aug 1971); *Career* currently chm John Tams Group plc (manufacturer of earthenware and fine bone china); former pres Br Ceramic Mfrs Fedn, memb Nat Jt Cncl Br Ceramic Indust; MInstD, FIM; *Recreations* golf, garden, Jaguars; *Clubs* Jaguar Drivers', Alvis Owners', Trentham Golf; *Style*— Gerald Tams, Esq; ✉ Fradswell Hall, Stafford ST18 0EX; John Tams Group plc, Longton, Stoke-on-Trent (☎ 01782 599226, fax 01782 593579, telex 367162 TAMS G)

TAMWORTH, Viscount; Robert William Saswalo Shirley; s and h of 13 Earl Ferrers, *qv*; *b* 29 Dec 1952; *Educ* Ampleforth; *m* 21 June 1980, Susannah Mary, da of late Charles Edward William Sheepshanks (d 1991), of Arthington Hall, Otley, W Yorks; 2 s (Hon William Robert Charles b 10 Dec 1984, Hon Frederick James Walter b 2 June 1990), 1 da (Hon Hermione Mary Annabel b 11 Dec 1982); *Heir* s, Hon William Shirley; *Career* teaching in Kenya under CMS Youth Service Abroad Scheme 1971–72; articled to Whinney Murray & Co (chartered accountants) 1972–76, asst mangr Ernst & Whinney (now Ernst & Young) 1976–82, gp auditor and sr treasy analyst with BICC plc 1982–86, gp fin controller Viking Property Gp Ltd 1986; dir: Viking Property Gp Ltd 1987–88, Norseman Holdings Ltd (formerly Ashby Securities Ltd) 1987–92 (and assoc cos 1988–92), Ruffer Investment Management Ltd 1994–; FCA; *Recreations* the British countryside and related activities, the garden; *Clubs* Boodle's; *Style*— Viscount Tamworth; ✉ The Old Vicarage, Shirley, Ashbourne, Derbyshire DE6 3AZ (☎ 01335 360815, fax 01335 361032)

TAN, Melvyn; s of Tan Keng Hian, of Singapore, and Wong Sou Yuen; *b* 13 Oct 1956; *Educ* Yehudi Menuhin Sch Surrey, Royal Coll of Music; *Career* fortepianist and harpsichord player; interpreter of Baroque, classical and early Romantic works; debut Wigmore Hall 1977, played in all major UK venues; repertoire incl: Weber, Mendelssohn, Chopin; performed with orchs and ensembles incl: Acad of Ancient Music, Eng Chamber Orch, RPO, London Classical Players; US tour playing Beethoven 1985, concert series with Roger Norrington and London Classical Players 1987 and 1988; festivals in 1989 incl: The Beethoven Experience (Purchase NY, with Roger Norrington and London Classical Players), Midsummer Mozart Festival in San Francisco (also Aldeburgh, Bath, Holland and Helsinki); performed in 1990: San Francisco, toured France and Japan, Queen Elizabeth Hall; involved in bringing Beethoven's own fortepiano from Budapest to England for European tour 1992; *Recordings* incl: Beethoven's Waldstein, Appassionata and Les Adieux sonatas, Schubert Impromptus, Beethoven Piano Concertos (with Roger Norrington and the London Classical Players), Salonkonzert (with Eric Hoeprich, Michel Garcin-Marrou and Konrad Hünteler; also numerous Mozart Piano Concertos (with London Classical Players and own group The New Mozart Ensemble); *Style*— Melvyn Tan, Esq; ✉ c/o Valerie Barber, Fifth Floor, 24 Chancery Lane, London WC2A 1LS (☎ 0171 404 2266/2277, fax 0171 831 2724)

TANCRED, Dr William Raymond (Bill); MBE (1992); s of Adrian Nicholas Tancred, of Ipswich, Suffolk, and Elsie Catherine Jane, *née* Donovan; *b* 6 Aug 1942; *Educ* Army Sch of Physical Training, Loughborough Coll of Education (CertEd), Loughborough Univ (MSc), West Virginia Univ (NATO scholar, PhD); *m* 12 Sept 1970, Angela Joyce, da of John Lloyd Moore; 3 da (Nicola Anne b 27 March 1972, Andrea Sacha b 4 Nov 1973, Joanna Louise b 20 July 1975); *Career* former athlete; represented GB: Euro Championships (discus) 1966, 1969 and 1974, Cwlth Games (discus) 1966 and 1970 (Bronze medal) and 1974 (Silver medal), discus event 1968/72 Olympic Games; AAA Champion discus 1966, 1967, 1968, 1969, 1970, 1972 and 1973, AAA Champion shot (indoors) 1969 and 1973, current UK discus record holder 64.32m (1974), represented GB in 54 full Internationals; physical trg and recreation instr attached to 1 E Anglian Regt 1961–63, physical trg instructor Br Mil Garrison in Aden 1964–65, physical trg and recreation staff instr RMA Sandhurst 1965–68, head Physical Educn Dept Tower Ramparts Sch Ipswich 1970–71, lectr and head Dept of Physical Educn and Recreation W Bridgeford Coll of Further Educn 1973–75, sr lectr Nottingham Coll of Educn/Trent Poly 1975–78, dir of physical educn and recreation The Univ of Sheffield 1980–93, princ lectr in leisure mgmnt The Buckinghamshire Coll of HE 1993–; Winston Churchill fell 1989, fell Br Assoc of Physical Trg 1986, memb Inst of Leisure and Amenity Mgmnt 1988, sr memb Br Inst of Sports Coaches; *Books* Weight Training For Sport (1984), Olympic Games (1984), Health Related Fitness (1987), Leisure Management (1992); *Recreations* walking in the Peak District and SW England coastal paths, watching all sports (particularly Sheffield United FC and Ipswich Town FC), keeping fit; *Clubs* The International Athletes (chm); *Style*— Dr Bill Tancred, MBE; ✉ Buckinghamshire College of Higher Education, Faculty of Leisure and Tourism, Queen Alexandra Road, High Wycombe, Bucks HP11 2JZ (☎ 01494 522141)

TANDY, Michael John; s of Donald Alfred Tandy, of Stourbridge, Worcestershire, and Irene Dorothy, *née* Hardiman (d 1976); *b* 11 May 1939; *Educ* Chigwell House Sch, Halesowen GS (Hereford & Worcs Co Rugby XV, Worcs Co Cricket Schs XI); *m* 10 Sept 1965, Julia Ann, da of Charlton William Jasper Chinner (d 1975), of Staffordshire; 1 s (Jonathan David b 31 March 1967), 1 da (Emma Kathryn b 30 June 1969); *Career* CA; articled clerk Felton & Co 1957–62, with GKN PLC 1963–76, Glynwed PLC 1977–80, Bloxwich Engineering Ltd 1980–83; ptnr: Arthur Young (now Ernst & Young) 1984–90, Tandy & Co 1991–93, Bentley Jennison (following merger) 1993–96; pres: Shropshire C of C and Indust 1992–94, W Mercia C of C and Indust 1992–94; govr Univ of Wolverhampton (formerly Wolverhampton Poly) 1990–93; FCA; *Recreations* cricket, rugby, horse racing; *Clubs* MCC, Gentlemen of Staffordshire CC; *Style*— Michael J Tandy, Esq; ✉ Hatton Hill House, Shifnal, Shropshire TF11 9HU (☎ and fax 01952 461867)

TANFIELD, Jennifer Bridget; da of Doylah Ernst Thomas Tanfield, of Bridgnorth, Shropshire, and Phoebe Phyllis, *née* Hickman; *b* 19 July 1941; *Educ* Sch of St Mary and St Anne, LSE (BSc(Econ)); *Career* House of Commons Library: worked in Research Div 1963–87, head of Parly Div 1987–91, dep librarian 1991–93, librarian 1993–; *Books* In Parliament 1939–50 (1991); *Recreations* opera, theatre, travel, squash; *Clubs* RSA; *Style*— Ms Jennifer Tanfield; ✉ House of Commons Library, London SW1A 0AA (☎ 0171 219 3635)

TANKEL, Henry Isidore; OBE (1991); s of Hyman William Tankel (d 1946), of Glasgow, and Bertha, *née* Sacks (d 1968); *b* 14 Jan 1926; *Educ* Glasgow HS, Univ of Glasgow (MB ChB, MD); *m* 2 Oct 1956, Judith Benita, da of Edward Woolfson (d 1982), of Glasgow; 2 s (Jeremy b 1957, Alan b 1961), 2 da (Belinda b 1964, Laura b 1968); *Career* Capt: RAMC 1950–51 (Lt 1949–50), TA 1951–54; Fulbright scholar Mount Sinai Hosp NY 1954–55, conslt surgn Southern Gen Hosp Glasgow 1962–91; memb: Cncl RCPSGlas 1977–82, Nat Panel Specialists 1978–82 and 1987–90; treas Scot Ctee Hosp Med Servs 1978–90, invited to address Gen Assembly Church of Scotland 1984; chm: Surgery Ctee W of Scotland Ctee Postgrad Med Educn 1985–89, Scot Jt Conslts Ctee 1989–92; memb Scot Health Serv Advsy Cncl 1989–93, non-exec dir Southern Gen Hosp NHS Tst 1993–; former pres Glasgow Jewish Rep Cncl, jt chm Christian Jewish Consultation Gp Church of Scotland; occasional bdcaster; FRCSE 1954, FRCSGlas 1962; *Books* Gastroenterology - An Integrated Course (contrib, 1983), Cancer in the Elderly (contrib, 1990); *Recreations* walking, making model boats; *Style*— Henry I Tankel, Esq, OBE; ✉ 26 Dalziel Drive, Glasgow G41 4PU (☎ 0141 423 5830, fax 0141 424 3648)

TANKERVILLE, Countess of; Georgiana Lilian Maude; *née* Wilson; da of late Gilbert Wilson, DD, PhD of Vancouver, BC,; *Educ* Univ of Br Columbia (BA), BLS Univ of Toronto; *m* 1954, as his 2 w, 9 Earl of Tankerville (d 1980); *Career* WRCNS 1944–46; librarian: BC Provincial Library, Victoria Public Library, The Hamlin School San Francisco, UNICEF, San Francisco; *Style*— The Rt Hon the Countess of Tankerville; ✉ 139 Olympia Way, San Francisco, CA 94131, USA

TANKERVILLE, 10 Earl of (GB 1714); Peter Grey Bennet; also Baron Ossulston (E 1682); s of 9 Earl of Tankerville (d 1980), and Georgiana Lilian Maude, *née* Wilson; *b* 18 Oct 1956; *Educ* Grace Cathedral Sch San Francisco (chorister), Oberlin Conservatory Ohio (BMus), San Francisco State Univ (MA); *Heir* uncle, Rev the Hon George Arthur Grey Bennet, *qv*; *Career* musician San Francisco; *Style*— The Rt Hon the Earl of Tankerville; ✉ 139 Olympia Way, San Francisco, Calif 94131, USA (☎ 415 826 6639)

TANLAW, Baron (Life Peer UK 1971), of Tanlawhill, Co Dumfries; Hon Simon Brooke Mackay; yst s of 2 Earl of Inchcape (d 1939), and Leonora Margaret Brooke (d 1996), da of HH the 3 Rajah of Sarawak (Sir Charles Vyner Brooke (d 1963)); *b* 30 March 1934; *Educ* Eton, Trinity Coll Cambridge (MA); *m* 1, 1959, Joanna Susan, o da of Maj John Henry Hirsch (d 1983), of Sungrove Lodge, Newbury, Berks; 1 s (Hon James Brooke b 1961) (and 1 s decd), 2 da (Hon Iona Héloïse b 1960, Hon Rebecca Alexandra (Hon Mrs Ayre-Smith) b 1967); m 2, 1976, Rina Siew Yong, yst da of late Tiong Cha Tan, of Kuala Lumpur, Malaysia; 1 s (Hon Brooke Brooke b 1982), 1 da (Hon Asia Brooke b 1980); *Career* sits as Ind (formerly Lib) in House of Lords; 2 Lt 12 Royal Lancers 1952–54; chm Fandstan Gp of private cos, former dir Inchcape plc, pres Sarawak Assoc 1972–75; memb of govrs LSE 1980–96, hon fell Univ of Buckingham 1981; Hon DUniv Buckingham 1983; nat appeal chm of the Elizabeth FitzRoy Homes for the Mentally Handicapped 1985–; Liveryman: Worshipful Co of Fishmongers, Worshipful Co of Clockmakers; *Clubs* White's, Oriental, Buck's, Puffin's; *Style*— The Rt Hon the Lord Tanlaw; ✉ Tanlawhill, Eskadalemuir, By Langholm, Dumfriesshire; 31 Brompton Square, London SW3; work: 36 Ennismore Gardens, London SW7

TANN, Prof Jennifer; da of Alfred John and Frances Booth, of Birmingham; *b* 25 Feb 1939; *Educ* Badminton Sch Bristol, Univ of Manchester (BA), Univ of Leicester (PhD); *m* 12 Oct 1963, Roger William Tann, s of Richard Henry Tann; 2 s (Edmund John b 8 March 1966, Oliver Richard b 4 June 1974); *Career* research asst Historic Towns Project Oxford 1964–66, pt/t tutor Univ of Hull 1966–69, lectr Aston Univ 1969–73, reader Aston Univ Business Sch 1973–86, dir Centre for Continuing Educn Univ of Newcastle 1986–89, prof of innovation studies Univ of Birmingham 1989– (dean Faculty of Educn and Continuing Studies 1993–96); visiting prof Dept of Economics Univ of Queensland Australia 1985, visiting prof of mgmnt Univ of Newcastle 1989–94; ministerial appointee Standing Ctee for Pharmacy Educn (SCOPE); memb: Br Acad of Mgmnt, Business Archives Cncl, Newcomen Soc, Church of England Theological Colleges Inspection Bd; *Books* Development of the Factory (1971), Selected Papers of Boulton and Watt (1981), Children at Work (1981), Short History of the Stock Exchange Birmingham (1983), Birmingham Assay Office (1993); *Recreations* reading, music, laughter; *Style*— Prof Jennifer Tann; ✉ Faculty of Education and Continuing Studies, University of Birmingham, Edgbaston, Birmingham B15 2TT (☎ 0121 414 5609, fax 0121 414 5619)

TANNAHILL, Dr Andrew James; s of Andrew Leckie Tannahill, of Inchinnan, Renfrewshire, and late Elizabeth Johnstone, *née* Preston; *b* 28 April 1954; *Educ* John Neilson Inst Paisley, Univ of Glasgow (MB ChB, Brunton meml prize), Univ of Edinburgh (MSc); *m* Dr Carol Elizabeth Tannahill, *née* Fyfe; *Career* lectr in pathology Univ of Glasgow and hon registrar in pathology Western Infirmary Glasgow 1981–82, registrar then sr registrar in community med Lothian Health Bd 1982–85, hon clinical tutor Univ of Edinburgh 1984–85, regional specialist in community med E Anglian RHA 1985–88, assoc lectr Univ of Cambridge 1988, sr lectr in public health med Univ of Glasgow and hon conslt in public health med Gtr Glasgow Health Bd 1988–91, gen mangr Health Educn Bd for Scotland 1991–, hon sr lectr Univ of Dundee 1993–, hon fell Univ of Edinburgh 1994–, hon sr lectr Univ of Glasgow 1996–; FFPHM 1992 (MFPHM 1985), MHSM 1993, FRCPEd 1996; *Books* Health Promotion: Models and Values (1990, 2 edn 1996); *Recreations* photography, painting, music, theatre, birdwatching, countryside, reading (especially humour); *Style*— Dr Andrew Tannahill; ✉ Health Education Board for Scotland, Woodburn House, Canaan Lane, Edinburgh EH10 4SG (☎ 0131 447 8044)

TANNAHILL, Reay; da of James Cowan Tannahill (d 1961), of Glasgow, and Olive Margery, *née* Reay (d 1973); *Educ* Shawlands Sr Secdy Sch Glasgow, Univ of Glasgow (MA, CSS); *m* 1958 (m dis 1983), Michael Edwardes (d 1990); *Career* writer; probation offr, advtg copywriter, reporter, historical researcher and graphic designer; *Non-Fiction* Paris in the Revolution (1966), The Fine Art of Food (1968), Food in History (1973, revised and updated edn 1988, Premio Letterario Internazionale: Chianti Ruffino Antico Fattore), Flesh and Blood (1975, revised and updated edn 1996), Sex in History (1980, revised and updated edn 1989); *Novels* A Dark and Distant Shore (1983), The World, the Flesh and the Devil (1985), Passing Glory (1989, Romantic Novel of the Year Award), In Still and Stormy Waters (1992), Return of the Stranger (1995); *Recreations* work; *Clubs* Authors'; *Style*— Ms Reay Tannahill; ✉ c/o Rogers, Coleridge & White Ltd, 20 Powis Mews, London W11 1JN (☎ 0171 221 3717, fax 0171 229 9084)

TANNER, Adrian Christopher; s of Alfred Charles Tanner, and Betty Margaret Tanner; *b* 13 Oct 1946; *Educ* Skinners Sch Tunbridge Wells; *m* 1969, Anna Margaret, *née* Shepherd; 2 da; *Career* marine insur broker; dir: Alexander Howden Insurance Brokers Ltd 1978–81, Robert Fleming Marine Ltd 1982–, RFIB Europe Ltd 1992–, Robert Fleming Insurance Brokers Ltd 1993–; memb Lloyd's; *Style*— Adrian Tanner, Esq; ✉ Wallington House, Smarden, Kent TN27 8NN

TANNER, Bruce Winton; DL (W Midlands 1995); s of Denis Frank Winton Tanner, MC, and Gladys, *née* Colegrove; *b* 21 Feb 1931; *Educ* King Edward's Sch Birmingham, St Catherine's Coll Oxford (BA); *m* 4 April 1960, Alma, da of Harold Athur Stoddard; 3 da (Jane b 1963, Ruth b 1965, Judith b 1968); *Career* 2 Lt RASC 1950; md Horizon Midlands Ltd 1965–74, chm and chief exec Horizon Travel Ltd 1974–85, chm Horizon Travel plc 1985–87, chm Chimes Restaurants (UK) plc 1987–91, dir Birmingham Cable Corp 1988–; pres Int Fedn of Tour Operators 1980–83, memb Cncl Birmingham Chamber of Indust and Commerce 1984–94; dep chm: Birmingham Cons Assoc 1987–89, Birmingham Hippodrome Theatre Tst 1990–; chm: Birmingham Civic Soc 1994– (dep chm 1993–94), Aston Univ Audit Ctte 1994–; govr Schs of King Edward VI Fndn Birmingham 1995–96; High Sheriff of W Midlands 1991–92; Hon DSc Aston Univ 1996; *Recreations* theatre, tennis, hill walking; *Style*— Bruce Tanner, Esq, DL; ✉ 37 St Agnes Rd, Moseley, Birmingham B13 9PJ (☎ 0121 449 3953); Flat 10, 4 Hans Place, London SW1X 0EY

TANNER, Dr John Ian; CBE (1979); s of R A Tanner, and I D M Tanner, *née* Manners; *b* 2 Jan 1927; *Educ* Switzerland, City of London Library Sch, Univ of London (BA), Univ of Nottingham (MA, PhD), Univ of Oxford (MA); *m* 1953 (m dis 1972 in law and by RC Tbnl), April, *née* Rothery; m 2, 1991, Andrea, *née* Duncan; *Career* archivist and librarian Kensington Library 1950–51, curator Leighton House Art Gallery and Museum 1951–53, curator librarian and tutor RAF Coll 1953–63, extra-mural lectr in history of art Univ of Nottingham 1959–63; founding dir: RAF Museum 1963–87, Battle of Britain Museum 1978–87, Cosford Aero-Space Museum 1978–87, Bomber Cmd Museum 1982–87; sr res fell Pembroke Coll Oxford 1982–96 (hon archivist 1980–, supernumary fell 1996); Walmsley lectr City Univ 1980, visiting fell Wolfson Coll Cambridge 1983–; prof Univ of Poland 1988–95 (emeritus prof 1995); chm Int Air Museum Ctee; pres: Anglo-American Ecumenical Assoc, Bd of Advsrs Battle Harbour Fndn's Anglican Serv, Trg and Religious Orgn, USAF Euro Meml Fndn; founding tstee Manchester Air and Space Museum, memb Founding Ctee All England Lawn Tennis Museum, memb Advsy Cncl Inst of Heraldic and Genealogical Studies, hon sec Old Cranwellian Assoc 1956–64; Hon DLitt City Univ, Hon LLD Univ of Poland, Convocation lectr and Hon DCL Assumption Coll Worcester Mass 1993; Freeman City of London 1966; Liveryman: Worshipful Co of Gold and Silver Wyre Drawers 1966, Worshipful Co of Scriveners 1978; Freeman Guild of Air Pilots and Air Navigators 1979; FLA, FMA, FRHistS, FRAeS, FSA; hon memb Collegio Araldico of Rome 1963, Tissandier Award Fedn Aeronautique Int 1977; OStJ 1964, KStJ 1978, St John Serv Medal 1985, KCSG 1977 (star 1985), Cross of Merit Order of Malta 1978, Nile Gold Medal Egypt 1987, Grand Cdr OM Holy Sepulchre Vatican, Constantinian Order 1988; *Books* List of Cranwell Graduates (ed second edn 1963), Encyclopaedic Dictionary of Heraldry (jtly, 1968), How to Trace Your Ancestors (1971), Man in Flight (1973), The Royal Air Force Museum: one hundred years of aviation history (1973), Badges and Insignia of the British Armed Forces (with W E May and W Y Carmen, 1974), Charles I (1974), Who's Famous in Your Family (second edn 1979), Wings of the Eagle (exhibition catalogue, 1976), They Fell in the Battle (1980), Sir William Rothenstein (exhibition catalogue, 1985), RAF Museum - a combined guide (1987); gen ed: Museums and Librarians, Studies in Air History; *Recreations* cricket, opera, reading; *Clubs* Athenaeum, Reform, MCC; *Style*— Dr John Tanner, CBE; ✉ Flat One, 57 Drayton Gardens, London SW10 9RU

TANNER, Prof Paul Antony (Tony); *b* 18 March 1935; *Educ* Raynes Park County GS, Jesus Coll Cambridge (BA), Univ of Calif Berkeley; *Career* Intelligence Corps 1953–55; dir English Studies King's Coll Cambridge 1961– (fell 1960–), ACLS fell Univ of Calif Berkeley 1962–63, lectr Univ of Cambridge 1966– (asst lectr 1964–66), visiting Concora lectr Northwestern Univ 1967, visiting prof Univ of Venice 1969; lectr: Kyoto Seminar Japan 1972, Salzburg Seminar Austria 1973; visiting fell Center for Twentieth Century Studies Univ of Wisconsin 1974, fell Center for Advanced Study in the Behavioral Sciences Stanford Calif 1974–75, univ lectr Univ of Cambridge 1975–76, prof Johns Hopkins Univ, univ lectr with responsibility for American lit Univ of Cambridge 1977–80, reader Univ of Cambridge 1980–89, prof of Eng and American lit Univ of Cambridge 1989–; *Publications* Lord Jim (1963), Henry James, Subjective Adventurer (Essays and Studies, 1963), Saul Bellow (1965), Robert Musil (London Magazine, 1965), Malamud's New Life (Critical Quarterly, 1968), City of Words: American Fiction 1950–70 (1970), My Life in American Literature (Tri Quarterly, 1974), Adultery in the Novel (1979), The Ever-Dying, Ever-Living Novel (Lugano Review, 1981), Thomas Pynchon (1982), Jane Austen (1986), Conrad and the Last Gentleman (Critical Quarterly, 1986), Venice Desired (1992); *Style*— Prof Tony Tanner; ✉ King's College, Cambridge (☎ 01223 331319)

TANQUERAY, David Andrew; s of David Yeo Bartholemew Tanqueray (d 1944), and Majorie Edith, *née* Macdonald; *b* 23 May 1939; *Educ* Rugby, Clare Coll Cambridge (MA), Univ of California Berkeley; *m* 20 Aug 1966, Tamsin Mary, da of Air Cdre Cyril Montague Heard; 1 s (David b 1981), 2 da (Venetia b 1974, Tabitha b 1977); *Career* conslt Control Data Ltd 1969–84, Floating Point Systems UK Ltd 1985–91, Cray Research UK Ltd 1992–; awarded Harkness Fellowship 1966; *Recreations* music, amateur dramatics; *Style*— David Tanqueray, Esq; ✉ 27 Cheriton Ave, Twyford, Berks RG10 9DB (☎ 0118 934 1544); Cray Research UK Ltd, 1530 Arlington Business Park, Theale, Berks RG7 4SB (☎ 0118 925 7020)

TANSEY, Rock Benedict; QC (1990); *b* 22 July 1939; *Educ* Univ of Bristol (LLB, Dip in Social Studies); *m* 10 Oct 1964, Wendy Jennifer Ann Tansey; 3 c; *Career* called to the Bar Lincoln's Inn 1966, recorder of the Crown Court, head of chambers 3 Gray's Inn Sq; memb: Bar Cncl, Criminal Bar Assoc; *Recreations* theatre, golf, travel; *Style*— Rock Tansey, Esq, QC; ✉ 3 Gray's Inn Square, Gray's Inn, London WC1R 5AH (☎ 0171 831 2311, fax 0171 404 4939)

TANT, Russell Byron; s of Melvyn John Tant (d 1970), and Sadie Jacobs (d 1989); *b* 20 March 1949; *Educ* Orange Hill Co GS, UCH London (BDS, capt UCH CC); *m* 1, 1981 (m dis 1990), Elizabeth Mary Lorimer; 2 s (Radleigh Lewis Byron b 6 Oct 1983, Sebastian Charles Russell b 5 July 1985); m 2, 29 Oct 1994, Katrina Rushton; 2 da (Emily Charlotte Maris b 3 April 1992, Mollie Bryony b 11 March 1996); *Career* gen dental practice Knightsbridge 1972–76, commenced practice Harpenden Herts 1978, fully private practice Wimpole Street 1985; pres London Dental Study Club 1983; *Recreations* cricket, golf, skiing, squash, music; *Clubs* MCC, Royal Cinque Ports Golf, Harpenden Golf; *Style*— Russell Tant, Esq; ✉ 22 Wimpole Street, London, W1 (☎ 0171 935 0087)

TANTAM, Prof Digby John Howard; s of Donald Harry Tantam (d 1993), of Cheam, Surrey, and Daphne, *née* Winterbone; *b* 15 March 1948; *Educ* St Paul's, Univ of Oxford (MA, BM BCh), Univ of Harvard (MPH), Univ of London (PhD), Open Univ (BA); *m* 6 July 1974, Sheila Jean, da of Richard Geoffrey Hunt Salkeld; 1 s (Robert John Geoffrey b 1978), 1 da (Grace Ruth b 1980); *Career* St George's Hosp 1974–75, Harvard Med Sch 1976–77, Maudsley Hosp 1977–83, Dept of Psychiatry Univ of Manchester 1983–90, prof of psychotherapy Univ of Warwick 1990–95, clinical prof of psychotherapy Univ of Sheffield 1995–; memb Inst of Group Analysis; FRCPsych; *Books* Making Sense of Psychiatric Cases (with M Greenberg and G Szmukler, 1986), A Mind of One's Own (1988, 2 edn 1991), Public Health Impact of Mental Disorder (with D Goldberg, 1990), College Seminars in Psychology and Social Science (with M Birchwood); *Recreations* cycling, reading, cooking, gardening, philosophy; *Style*— Prof Digby Tantam; ✉ Centre for Psychotherapeutic Studies, University of Sheffield, 16 Claremont Crescent, Sheffield

TAPLEY, (David) Mark; s of John Randolph Tapley (d 1972), of Stafford, and Nancy Doris Rathbone (d 1986); *b* 24 March 1946; *Educ* King Edward VI Sch Stafford, Oriel Coll Oxford (BA), London Business Sch (MBA); *m* April 1970, Judith Ann, da of Basil Wilford, of Stafford; 1 s (Richard Paul b March 1979), 1 da (Charlotte Emily b June 1977); *Career* systems engr ICL 1969–72, investmt analyst and portfolio mangr JP Morgan 1974–84 (vice pres 1982), dir of equities American Express Asset Management (later Shearson Lehman Global Asset Management and Posthorn Global Asset Management) 1984–90, chief investmt offr and md Quorum Capital Management Ltd 1991–; regular speaker at conferences seminars and trg courses on devpts in investmt mgmnt indust; memb NY Soc of Investmt Analysts 1974, Chartered Fin Analyst 1980; AIIMR 1976; *Books* International Portfolio Management (ed and contrib 1986); *Recreations* running, theatre, music; *Style*— Mark Tapley, Esq; ✉ Quorum Capital Management Ltd, Bastion House, 140 London Wall, London EC2Y 5DN (☎ 0171 457 3600, fax 0171 457 3699)

TAPPER, Prof Colin Frederick Herbert; s of Herbert Frederick Tapper (d 1977), and Florence, *née* Lambard (d 1976); *b* 13 Oct 1934; *Educ* Bishopshalt GS, Magdalen Coll Oxford (Vinerian scholar); *m* 1 April 1961, Margaret, da of Harold White (d 1978); 1 da (Lucy b 22 Jan 1973); *Career* called to the Bar Gray's Inn 1961; lectr LSE 1959–65; Univ of Oxford: fell Magdalen Coll 1965– (vice pres 1991–92), reader in law All Souls 1979–92, univ prof of law 1992–; visiting prof: Univ of Alabama and Univ of NY 1970, Stanford Univ 1976, Monash Univ 1984, Univ of Northern Kentucky 1986, Univ of Sydney 1989, Univ of Western Aust 1991; dir: Butterworth 1979–85, Butterworth Telepublishing 1979–90; conslt: Butterworths 1968–90, Masons (Solicitors) 1990–; *Books*

Computers and The Law (1973), Computer Law (1978, 4 edn 1990), Cross and Tapper on Evidence (8 edn 1995); *Recreations* reading, writing, computing; *Style*— Prof Colin Tapper; ✉ Corner Cottage, Woodstock Road, Stonesfield, Witney, Oxon OX8 8QA (☎ 01993 891284); Magdalen College, Oxford OX1 4AU (☎ 01865 276055, fax 01865 276103)

TAPPIN, Andrew Brice; s of Walter Philip Tappin, of Bridport, Dorset, and Daphne Mary, *née* Brice; *b* 27 Jan 1945; *Educ* Willington Sch, Stamford Sch, Tiffin Sch; *m* 4 Sept 1971, Barbara Jane, da of late Clive Edward Midwinter; 1 s (Rupert Clive b 22 Feb 1972), 1 da (Laura Rachel b 22 Oct 1974); *Career* chartered accountant; Annan Dexter & Co 1967–71 (articled clerk 1963–67); ptnr: Dearden Lord Annan Morrish 1972, Dearden Farrow (after merger) 1977, BDO Binder Hamlyn (after merger) 1987–94, conslt Binder Hamlyn 1994–; memb Soc of Tst and Estate Practitioners; tstee and dir Suzy Lamplugh Tst; govr E Sheen Primary Sch; FCA 1977 (ACA 1967); *Books* Capital Transfer Tax Planning (jtly, 1975), Financial Planning for Clients (jtly, 1979); *Recreations* squash, running, education; *Style*— Andrew Tappin, Esq; ✉ Binder Hamlyn, 20 Old Bailey, London EC4M 7BH (☎ 0171 489 6428, fax 0171 489 6490)

TAPPIN, Michael; MEP (Lab) Staffordshire W and Congleton (majority 40,277); s of Thomas Ernest Tappin, of Hendon, and Eileen Sarah, *née* Kitson; *b* 22 Dec 1946; *Educ* Moat Mount Secdy Modern, Harrow Tech Coll, Univ of Essex, LSE, Univ of Strathclyde; *m* Oct 1971, Angela Florence, da of Douglas Murray Reed; 1 s (Thomas Edward Michael b 7 Jan 1984), 1 da (Abigail Sarah b 3 September 1977); *Career* lectr in American studies Univ of Keele 1974–94 (pt/t lectr 1994–); MEP (Lab) Staffordshire W and Congleton 1994–; Staffordshire CC: memb 1981–, chm Planning Ctee 1985–89, chm Enterprise and Econ Devpt Ctee 1989–94; dep chm Staffordshire Devpt Assoc 1989–94, chm W Midlands Forum of Local Authys 1993–94; memb American Political Science Assoc 1974–; *Books* American Politics Today (jtly, 1981, 1985, 1989, revised edn 1991); *Recreations* squash, walking, theatre, cinema, reading, music, guitar; *Clubs* Potters; *Style*— Michael Tappin, Esq, MEP; ✉ Europa House, 28–30 Hartshill Road, Stoke-on-Trent, Staffordshire ST4 7QU (☎ 01782 414771, fax 01782 414805)

TAPPS-GERVIS-MEYRICK, Ann, Lady; Ann; *née* Miller; yr da of Edward Clive Miller (d 1956), of Melbourne, Aust; *m* 20 March 1940, Sir George David Eliott Tapps-Gervis-Meyrick, 6 Bt, MC (d 1988); 1 s (Sir George, 7 Bt, *qv*), 1 da (Caroline Susan Joan (Mrs Hulse) b 30 April 1942); *Style*— Ann, Lady Tapps-Gervis-Meyrick; ✉ Waterditch House, Bransgore, Christchurch, Dorset

TAPPS-GERVIS-MEYRICK, Sir George Christopher Cadafael; 7 Bt (GB 1791), of Hinton Admiral, Hampshire; o s of Lt-Col Sir George David Eliott Tapps-Gervis-Meyrick, 6 Bt, MC (d 1988), and Ann, *née* Miller; *b* 10 March 1941; *Educ* Eton, Trinity Coll Cambridge; *m* 14 March 1968, Jean Louise, yst da of Lord William Walter Montagu Douglas Scott, MC (d 1958), 2 s of 7 Duke of Buccleuch; 2 s (George William Owen b 1970, Charles Valentine Llewelyn b 1972), 1 da (Suzannah Daisy b 1978); *Heir* s, George William Owen Tapps-Gervis-Meyrick b 1970; *Style*— Sir George Meyrick, Bt; ✉ Hinton Admiral, Christchurch, Dorset

TAPSELL, Sir Peter Hannay Bailey; kt (1985), MP (C) Lindsey East (majority 11,846); s of late Eustace Tapsell, and late Jessie Tapsell; *b* 1 Feb 1930; *Educ* Tonbridge, Merton Coll Oxford (MA); *m* 1, 1963 (m dis 1971), Hon Cecilia, 3 da of 9 Baron Hawke; 1 s (decd); m 2, 1974, Gabrielle, da of late Jean Mahieu, of Normandy, France; *Career* Nat Serv Subaltern The Royal Sussex Regt Middle East 1948–50, hon life memb 6 Sqdn RAF 1971; librarian Oxford Union 1953 (rep on debating tour of USA 1954); Cons Res Dept (Social Servs and Agric) 1954–57 (PA to PM Anthony Eden 1955 Gen Election Campaign), memb London Stock Exchange 1957–90, int investmt advsr to several central banks, foreign banks and trading cos; Parly candidate (C) Wednesbury by-election 1957; MP (C): Nottingham W 1959–64, Horncastle 1966–83, Lindsey E 1983–; oppn front bench spokesman on: foreign and Cwlth affrs 1976–77, Treasy and econ affrs 1977–78; chm Coningsby Club 1957–58, jt chm Br Caribbean Assoc 1963–64; memb: Cncl Inst for Fiscal Studies, Trilateral Cmmn 1979–, Organising Ctee Zaire River Expedition 1974–75, Ct Univ of Nottingham 1959–64, Ct Univ of Hull 1966–; hon memb Investmt Advsy Bd Brunei Govt 1976–83, Brunei Dato 1971; vice pres Tennyson Soc 1966–, hon dep chm Mitsubishi Tst Oxford Fndn 1988–, hon fell Merton Coll Oxford 1989; *Recreations* travel, walking in mountains, reading history; *Clubs* Athenaeum, Carlton, Hurlingham; *Style*— Sir Peter Tapsell, MP; ✉ c/o House of Commons, London SW1 (☎ 0171 219 3000)

TARBUCK, Jimmy; OBE (1994); *b* 6 Feb 1940; *Career* comedian, entertainer and after-dinner speaker; started work as garage mechanic, Butlin's Redcoat, TV debut Comedy Box 1962, resident compere Sunday Night at the London Palladium Sept 1965 (following earlier guest appearances), London cabaret debut Talk of the Town, numerous pantomimes and summer seasons; *Television* incl: The Jimmy Tarbuck Show (ATV), Tarbuck's Back (ATV), It's Tarbuck (ATV), Tarbuck's Luck (BBC), Winner Takes All (Yorkshire) 1975–86, Tarby's Frame Game (Yorkshire), reg guest The Parkinson Show, Live From Her Majesty's (LWT) 1983–85, Tarby and Friends (LWT) 1984–86, Live From The Piccadilly (LWT) 1986, Live From The London Palladium (LWT) 1987–88, Tarby After Ten (LWT) 1988, An Audience With Jimmy Tarbuck (LWT) 1994, Tarbuck Late (LWT) 1995; fndr Jimmy Tarbuck Golf Classic (held annually); Variety Club of Great Britain Award Show Business Personality of the Year; OStJ; *Books* Tarbuck on Golf, Tarbuck on Showbiz; *Recreations* golf, supporter Liverpool Football Club; *Style*— Jimmy Tarbuck, Esq, OBE; ✉ c/o Peter Prichard Ltd, Mezzanine Floor, 235 Regent Street, London W1R 8AX (☎ 0171 352 6417, fax 0171 409 2070)

TARGETT, Jocelyn; s of Peter John Targett, of Fordham, Cambridgeshire, and Joan Valerie, *née* Baker; *b* 7 Dec 1965; *Educ* Southgate Comprehensive Sch, Girton Coll Cambridge (exhibitioner, BA, winner Guardian/NUS Student Media Award); *partner* since 1989, Judy Rumbold; 1 da (Lola Faye b 17 April 1992), 1 s (Ted Joshua b 23 June 1995); *Career* The Guardian: joined as feature writer 1988, dep ed Weekend Guardian 1989–92, arts ed The Guardian 1992–93; managing ed Sunday Times Culture, Books and Style & Travel sections 1993, ed Night & Day Mail on Sunday 1993–96, dir Mail on Sunday 1995–96, dep ed (features) The Observer 1996–; series ed First Reaction (Channel 4) 1991–; winner British Press Awards Young Journalist of the Year 1989; *Recreations* Judy, Lola and Ted, hedge cutting, horse racing; *Style*— Jocelyn Targett, Esq; ✉ The Observer, 119 Farringdon Road, London EC1R 3ER (☎ 0171 278 2332)

TARLETON, Ray Bernard; s of Bernard Tarleton, of Bradford, and Ethel, *née* Atkinson; *b* 4 Oct 1950; *Educ* Belle Vue Boys' GS Bradford, Univ Coll Durham (BA, PGCE), UEA (MA); *m* Jacqueline Claire, da of Rev Dr Keith Cripps; 1 da (Alice Emily b 18 Sept 1980), 1 s (Edmund Keith b 2 June 1982); *Career* teacher Overseas Devpt Admin/Christians Abroad Zambia 1973–75, English teacher Sir Roger Manwood's GS Sandwich Kent 1976–79, second in English N Walsham Girls' HS 1979–80, head of English and drama N Walsham HS 1980–86, dep headmaster Marshland HS Wisbech Norfolk 1986–89, princ South Dartmoor Community Coll Devon 1989–; memb SHA; lectr and teachers' workshop organizer LEAS; addressed HMI and RES confs; nat recognition for work on oracy during 1980's; FRSA; *Books* Learning and Talking - A Practical Guide to Oracy Across the Curriculum (1988); *Recreations* travel, reading, swimming, walking, camping, theatre and amateur dramatics; *Style*— Ray Tarleton, Esq; ✉ South Dartmoor Community College, Balland Lane, Ashburton, Devon TQ13 7EW (☎ 01364 652230, fax 01364 654069)

TARLING, Nikolas Daniel; s of Keith Ellis Tarling (d 1993), formerly of Yarlet, Stafford, and Ethel Marjorie Joy, *née* Harris (d 1967); *b* 1 May 1941; *Educ* Repton, Jesus Coll Oxford (MA); *m* 14 Feb 1969, Elizabeth Helen Margaret, da of Maj Alexander David Duncan Lawson, MBE (d 1991), formerly of Blinkbonny, Newburgh, Fife; 3 da (Rebecca b 1 Jan 1971, Camilla b 10 March 1973, Serena b 14 August 1976); *Career* admitted slr 1966; Freshfields: ptnr 1974–96, managing ptnr Paris 1974–75 and Frankfurt 1994–96; chm The Yarlet Tst 1992–; *Recreations* fishing, skiing, music, old master drawings; *Clubs* City of London, Hurlingham; *Style*— Nikolas Tarling, Esq; ✉ 13 Markham Sq, London SW3 4UY; Yarlet House, Stafford ST18 9SU

TARLOW, Dr Michael Jacob; s of Dr Samuel Tarlow, of London, and Fanny, *née* Young (d 1987); *b* 27 Dec 1939; *Educ* Haberdashers' Aske's, Guy's Hosp Med Sch London (MB BS), Univ Coll London (MSc); *m* Olwynne, da of Harry Frank (d 1963), of Darlington; 3 c (Sarah b 1967, Joanna b 1969, Ben b 1973); *Career* various jr hosp appts 1962–68, house physician and registrar Hosp for Sick Children Gt Ormond St 1968–70, fell Mayo Clinic Rochester USA 1970–72, sr registrar Royal Aberdeen Hosp for Sick Children 1972–74, sr lectr in paediatrics and hon conslt paediatrician Univ of Birmingham Med Sch 1974–; pres Euro Soc for Paediatric Infectious Disease 1994–95; memb Editorial Bd: Archives of Disease in Childhood 1984–90, British Journal of Hospital Medicine 1984–94; FRCP 1982; *Books* Paediatric Revision (with Dr K C Chin, 1989); *Recreations* chess, squash, hillwalking; *Style*— Dr Michael Tarlow; ✉ 43 Silhill Hall Rd, Solihull, W Midlands B91 1JX (☎ 0121 681 9656); Department of Paediatrics, Birmingham Heartlands Hospital, Bordesley Green East, Birmingham B9 5SS (☎ 0121 766 6611, fax 0121 753 2743, e-mail m.j.tarlow@bham.ac.uk)

TARN, Prof John Nelson; OBE (1992); s of Percival Nelson Tarn (d 1976), and Mary Isabell, *née* Purvis (d 1972); *b* 23 Nov 1934; *Educ* Royal GS Newcastle upon Tyne, King's Coll Newcastle (BArch), Gonville and Caius Coll Cambridge (PhD); *Career* architectural asst W B Edwards and Ptnrs Newcastle 1960–63, sr lectr in architecture Univ of Sheffield 1970 (lectr 1963–70), prof of architecture and head of dept Univ of Nottingham 1970–73, Roscoe prof of architecture 1974–95 and head of Liverpool Sch of Architecture 1974–86, head of Liverpool Sch of Architecture and Building Engrg 1986–90, pro-vice-chllr Liverpool Univ 1988–91 and 1994– (actg vice-chllr 1991–92); memb Peak Park Planning Bd 1973–86: chm Planning Control Ctee 1979–, vice chm of Bd 1981–86, co-opted memb Planning Control Ctee 1986–; RIBA: chm Examinations Sub Ctee 1975–, memb Professional Literature Ctee 1968–77, memb Educn and Professional Devpt Ctee 1978–; memb: Countryside Cmmn Review Ctee on Nat Parks 1989–90, Technol Ctee UGC 1974–84, Architecture Ctee CNAA 1981–86, Built Environment Ctee 1986–89, Bd Riverside Housing Assoc 1992–, Liverpool Cathedral Fabric Advsy Ctee, Patrimony Sub-Ctee Catholic Bishops' Conference of England and Wales 1994, Historic Churches Ctee for RC Diocese of Lancaster, Liverpool, Salford & Shrewsbury 1994; ARCUK: chm Bd of Educn 1983–86, vice chm Cncl 1985–86, chm 1987–90; chm: Art and Architecture Dept Liverpool Archdiocese Liturgy Cmmn 1980–, Liverpool Architecture and Design Tst 1996; tstee Nat Museums and Galleries on Merseyside 1996; FRIBA, FRHistS, FSA, FRSA; *Books* Working Class Housing in Nineteenth Century Britain (1971), Five Per Cent Philanthropy (1973), The Peak District, Its Architecture (1973); *Clubs* Athenaeum; *Style*— Prof John Tarn, OBE, FSA; ✉ Liverpool School of Architecture and Building Engineering, Liverpool University, PO Box 147, Liverpool L69 3BX (☎ 0151 794 2602, fax 0151 794 2605, telex 627095 UNILPL G)

TARRANT, Christopher John (Chris); s of Maj B A Tarrant, MC, and Joan Ellen, *née* Cox; *b* 10 Oct 1946; *Educ* King's Sch Worcester, Univ of Birmingham (BA); *m* 1, 1977 (m dis 1982), Sheila Margaret, da of Maj Ralph Roberton (d 1982); 2 da (Helen Victoria, Jennifer Mary); m 2, May 1991, Ingrid, da of Frederick Henry (Jimmy) Dupré de St Maur (d 1996); 1 da (Samantha Charlotte), 1 s (Toby Charles); *Career* prodr/writer/presenter of TV progs incl: ATV Today 1972, Tiswas 1974, OTT 1981, Everybody's Equal 1989, Tarrant on Television 1989–, The Main Event 1993, Lose a Million 1993, Pop Quiz 1994, Man O Man (ITV) 1996; presenter of Capital Radio's Breakfast Show 1987–; patron: Headway Battle Hosp Berks, Phoenix Centre for Physically Handicapped; *Awards* incl: Best On-Air Personality Int Radio Festival of NY 1987, TV and Radio Industries Club Radio Personality of the Year 1989, Sony Radio Awards Radio Personality of the Year 1990, Variety Club of GB Independent Radio Personality of the Year 1991, Sony Radio Awards Silver Medal 1992 and 1993, Sony Radio Awards Best Breakfast Show 1995, New York World Awards Best Breakfast Show 1996; *Books* Ken's Furry Friends (1986), Fishfriar's Hall Revisited (1987), Ready Steady Go (1990), Rebel, Rebel (1991); *Recreations* fishing, cricket; *Clubs* White Swan Piscatorials, Lord's Taverners; *Style*— Chris Tarrant, Esq; ✉ c/o Paul Vaughan, PVA Management Ltd, Hallow Park, Worcester WR2 6PG (☎ 01905 640663, fax 01905 641842)

TARRANT, Prof John Rex; *b* 12 Nov 1941; *Educ* Marling GS Stoud, Univ of Hull (BSc, PhD); *m* Biddy, *née* Fisher; *Career* asst lectr Univ Coll Dublin 1966–68; UEA: lectr 1968–74, dean Sch of Environmental Scis 1974–77 and 1981–84, sr lectr 1974–82, reader 1982–94, pro vice-chllr 1985–88, dep vice-chllr 1989–95, prof 1994–95; vice-chllr Univ of Huddersfield 1995–; visiting prof Dept of Geography Univ of Nebraska USA 1970, visiting lectr Dept of Geography Univ of Canterbury NZ 1973, visiting research assoc Int Food Policy Research Inst Washington DC 1977–78, visiting scholar Food Research Inst Stanford Univ USA 1978, Harris visiting prof Coll of Geoscis Texas A and M Univ USA 1989; memb Assoc of American Geographers 1991; hon fell UEA 1996; FRGS 1965; *Books* Agricultural Geography (1974), Food Policies (1980), Food and Farming (1991); also author of 16 book chapters and over 40 articles in professional publications; *Recreations* gliding, motor cycling; *Style*— Prof John Tarrant; ✉ University of Huddersfield, Queensgate, Huddersfield, W Yorkshire HD1 3DH (☎ 01484 472214/5, fax 01484 539467, e-mail j.r.tarrant@hud.ac.uk)

TARRANT, Peter Elliot; s of Cuthbert Easton Tarrant (d 1985), of Auckland, NZ, and Maud, *née* Dotchin (d 1989); *b* 19 May 1925; *Educ* Takapuna GS, Auckland Univ Coll, Univ of NZ (Dip Journ); *m* July 1951, Noeline Margaret Anne, *née* Harris; 1 s (Richard Peter b 1955), 1 da (Robyn Penelope Anne (Mrs Bailey) b 1953); *Career* ed various NZ Magazines 1948–50, dir Cuthbert E Tarrant Ltd NZ 1952–58, press offr Colonial Office London 1959–61 (info offr 1951–52), press and info offr The De La Rue Group 1961–63, PR mangr International Computers Ltd 1963–69; md: Tarrant Wilkinson and Partners Ltd 1970–71, Peter Tarrant & Associates Ltd UK 1972–88; dir A Plus Group Ltd UK 1988–92, freelance conslt 1992–; awarded: Dip CAM, Pres's Prize Inst of PR 1977, IPR Sword of Excellence 1988; memb Chartered Inst of Journalists 1950, MIPR 1963; *Books* British Dependencies in the Caribbean and the North Atlantic (co-author, 1952), Handbook of Consumer Sales Promotion (exec ed, 1974), Clean Up - It's Good Business (1986); *Recreations* golf, reading; *Clubs* United Oxford and Cambridge Univ, Burhill Golf; *Style*— Peter Tarrant, Esq; ✉ Aotea, 17 Woodland Grove, Weybridge, Surrey KT13 9EF (☎ 01932 847850)

TARRING, Trevor John; MBE; s of Leslie Herbert Tarring (d 1964), of Cobham, Surrey, and Ethel Anne (d 1976), *née* Rosser; *b* 5 July 1932; *Educ* Brentwood Sch, Brasenose Coll Oxford (MA); *m* 21 March 1959, Marjorie Jane, da of John Henry Colbert (d 1966), of Malvern, Worcs; 1 da (Emma Jane b 1964); *Career* dir Metal Information Bureau Ltd 1964, chm Metal Bulletin plc 1990– (jt ed 1968, md 1978); Freeman Worshipful Co of Stationers & Newspaper Makers; MInstMet 1963; *Books* Trading in Metals (1996), Nonferrous Metal Works of the World (ed, 1974); *Recreations* vintage car competitions;

Clubs Vintage Sports Car; *Style*— Trevor Tarring, Esq, MBE; ✉ Metal Bulletin plc, PO Box 28E, Worcester Park, London KT4 7HY (☎ 0171 827 9977, fax 0181 337 8943, telex 21 383)

TARSEM, (Tarsem Singh Dhandwar); s of Sohan Singh Dhandwar, of Tehran, Iran, and Harbhans Ekaur, *née* Dhillon; *b* 26 May 1961; *Educ* Bishop Cotton Sch Simla India, Modern Sch Dehli, Hansraj Coll Dehli (BComm), City Coll Los Angeles, Arts Centre Coll of Design Pasadena (BA); *Career* music video dir with The A & R Group Los Angeles 1990–91 (directed REM's 'Losing My Religion' video, winner 6 MTV Awards and Grammy Award for Best Video), commercials dir with Spots Films London 1991–96 (directed Levi's 'Swimmer' 1991, 'Cinderella' 1992 and 'Washroom' 1995, Smirnoff 'Message in the Bottle' 1992, McKewans 'Love and Hate' 1992, Vauxhall 'Supermodels' 1993, Nike 'Forces of Darkness'), commercials dir with @radical.media 1996–; awards incl: Gold and Silver Lions and Grand Prix de la Presse (int advtg awards Cannes) 1992 and 1993, Best Commercial of the Year (for Swimmer) and 3 Gold and 2 Silver Arrows (British TV Advtg Awards) 1992, numerous other awards in USA, France, Germany, etc; *Recreations* cricket, squash; *Style*— Tarsem; ✉ @radical.media, 44 Earlham Street, London WC2H 9LA (☎ 0171 497 5777)

TARUSCHIO, Franco Vittorio; s of Giuseppe Taruschio (d 1974), of Italy, and Apina Cecati (d 1988); *b* 29 March 1938; *Educ* GS Osimo, Hotel Sch, Bellagio Como Italy; *m* 9 Nov 1963, Emily Ann Dunant, da Dr Gerald Owen Forester, 1 da (Sasha Dunant b and d 1976), 1 adopted da (Pavinee Mia b 27 Feb 1977); *Career* restaurateur; formerly at: Hotel Splendide Lugano, Restaurant La Belle Meunière Clermont-Ferrand, Three Horse Shoes Hotel Rugby; Walnut Tree Inn Gwent 1963–; Gold medal for services to tourism in Wales 1985, Egon Ronay Restaurant of the Year award 1987, Premio Portonovo for excellence in Italian gastronomy 1995, 4/5 Good Food Guide 1996; *Books* Leaves from The Walnut Tree - Recipes of a Lifetime (1993), Bruschetta, Crostoni and Crostini (1995), Pasta Al Forno (1997); *Recreations* swimming and walking; *Style*— Franco Taruschio, Esq; ✉ Walnut Tree Inn, Llandewi Skirrid, Abergavenny, Gwent, Wales NP7 8AW (☎ 01873 852797)

TATCH, Brian; s of David Tatch, of London and formerly of Glasgow (d 1958), and Gertrude Tatch (now Gertrude Alper); *b* 24 April 1943; *Educ* Central Fndn Grammar, UCL (BSc); *m* 1965, Denise Ann, da of William Eugene Puckett (d 1979), of London and formerly of Louisville, Kentucky; 2 s, 1 da; *Career* consulting actuary; ptnr Clay & Partners 1975–91, chief exec Buck Paterson Consultants Ltd 1991–92, proprietor Brian Tatch & Co 1992–; fndr memb Assoc of Pensioneer Tstees (chm 1981–85); chm: Clay Clark Whitehill Ltd 1987–91 (jt chm 1985–87), The Bridford Group Ltd 1987–91, MCP Pension Tstees Ltd (tstee Maxwell Communication Works Pension Scheme) 1992–96; FIA, FPMI; *Style*— Brian Tatch, Esq; ✉ Brian Tatch & Co, Consulting Actuaries and Trustees, 11 Elm Park Road, London N21 2HP (☎ 0181 364 3738, fax 0181 364 3141)

TATE, David Read; s of Maurice Tate, of Penarth, S Glam, and Florence, *née* Read; *b* 10 Feb 1955; *Educ* Penarth GS, Jesus Coll Oxford (MA), UCL (MSc); *Career* Deloitte Haskins & Sells CAs 1977–80 (Mgmnt Consultancy Div 1980–83), Barclays de Zoete Wedd Ltd 1983–90 (dir 1987–90), dir Corporate Fin Div West Merchant Bank Ltd (formerly Chartered WestLB) 1990–; FCA 1992 (ACA 1980); *Recreations* golf, hillwalking, opera, theatre; *Clubs* Royal Porthcawl Golf, United Oxford and Cambridge; *Style*— David R Tate, Esq; ✉ West Merchant Bank, 33–36 Gracechurch St, London EC3V 0AX (☎ 0171 623 8711, fax 0171 626 5262, telex 884689)

TATE, Dr Jeffrey Philip; CBE (1990); s of Cyril Henry Tate, of Odiham, Hants, and Ivy Ellen, *née* Naylor; *b* 28 April 1943; *Educ* Farnham GS, Christ's Coll Cambridge (MA, MB BChir), St Thomas's Hosp London; *Career* trained as doctor of med St Thomas's Hosp London 1961–67, left medicine to join London Opera Centre 1969, joined Covent Garden staff 1970, assisted conductors incl Kempe, Krips, Solti, Davies and Kleiber 1973–77; later assisted: Boulez (Bayreuth Ring) 1976–81, Sir John Pritchard (Cologne Opera) 1977; conducted Gothenberg Opera Sweden 1978–80; NY Met Opera debut USA 1979, Covent Garden debut 1982, Salzburg Festival debut 1985; princ conductor English Chamber Orch 1985–; princ guest conductor: French Nat Radio Orch 1989–, Royal Opera House Covent Garden 1991–94 (princ conductor 1986–91); music dir Rotterdam Philharmonic Orch 1991–94; pres: Assoc for Spina Bifida and Hydrocephalus, Music Space; patron Br Lung Fndn, tstee Firebird Tst; hon fell Christ's Coll Cambridge 1989, hon fell St Thomas' and Guy's Hosp Med Sch 1994; Hon DMus Univ of Leicester 1993; Chev Ordre des Arts et des Lettres France 1990; *Recreations* reading, looking at the world going by, a bit of gastronomy; *Style*— Dr Jeffrey Tate, CBE; ✉ c/o English Chamber Orchestra, 2 Coningsby Road, London W5 4HR (☎ 0181 840 6565, fax 0181 567 7198)

TATE, Dr (Edward) Nicholas; s of Joseph Edwin Tate, of Kirklevington, Cleveland, and Eva Elsie, *née* Hopkinson (d 1987); *b* 18 Dec 1943; *Educ* Huddersfield New Coll, Balliol Coll Oxford (MA), Univ of Liverpool (MA, PhD), Univ of Bristol (PGCE); *m* 1973, Nadya, da of George Grove; 2 da (Emily Sarah b 1974, Harriet Louisa b 1976), 1 s (Oliver Lucian b 1985); *Career* asst master De La Salle Coll Sheffield 1966–71, lectr City of Birmingham Coll of Educn 1972–74, sr lectr Moray House Coll of Educn Edinburgh (joined as lectr) 1974–88, professional offr Nat Curriculum Cncl 1989–91, asst chief exec Sch Examinations and Assessment Cncl 1991–93, chief exec Sch Curriculum and Assessment Authy 1994– (asst chief exec 1993–94); *Books* Pizarro and the Incas (1982), Modern World History (1988), People and Events in the Modern World (1988), A History of the Modern World (1994); *Style*— Dr Nicholas Tate; ✉ School Curriculum and Assessment Authority, Newcombe House, 45 Notting Hill Gate, London W11 3JB (☎ 0171 243 9362, fax 0171 243 1060)

TATE, Sir (Henry) Saxon; 5 Bt (UK 1989), of Park Hill, Streatham, Co London; CBE (1991); s of Lt-Col Sir Henry Tate, 4 Bt, TD, DL (d 1994), and his 1 w, Lilian Nairne, *née* Gregson-Ellis (d 1984); *b* 28 Nov 1931; *Educ* Eton, Ch Ch Oxford; *m* 1, 3 Sept 1953 (m dis 1975), Sheila Ann, da of Duncan Robertson; 4 s (Edward Nicholas b 1966, Duncan Saxon b 1968, John William b 1969, Paul Henry (twin) b 1969); m 2, 31 Jan 1975, Virginia Joan Sturm; *Heir* s, Edward Nicolas Tate b 1966; *Career* Nat Serv 2 Lt Life Guards 1949–51 (Lt Special Reserve 1951–); Tate & Lyle plc: prodn trainee Liverpool 1952, dir 1956–, chm Exec Ctee 1973–78, md 1978–80, vice chm 1980–82; chief exec offr Redpath Industries Ltd Canada 1965–73; also dir: Tate Appointments Ltd 1982– (chm 1991–), A E Staley Manufacturing Inc; chief exec Industl Devpt Bd for NI 1982–85, chm and chief exec London Future and Options Exchange (London FOX) 1985–91; FIMgt 1975; *Style*— Sir Saxon Tate, Bt, CBE; ✉ 26 Cleaver Square, London SE11 4BA (☎ 0171 582 6507)

TATE, Simon Neil (*né* Tattersall); s of Dr Robert Edward Neil Tattersall (d 1982), and Margaret, *née* Wood; *b* 30 May 1956; *Educ* Blackpool Coll of Technol and Art; *m* 1 Dec 1984, Alexandra, da of Leslie Barker Rawcliffe; 1 da (Samantha Louise b 24 Nov 1987), 2 s (Nicholas Simon b 10 Nov 1989, James Alexander b 26 Jan 1991); *Career* presenter: Radio Victory Portsmouth 1979, Radio City Liverpool 1979–83, Red Rose Radio Preston 1983–92; prog dir and head of music Radio Wave Blackpool 1992–; Sony Radio Awards 1993: Radio Wave programming awarded Sony Gold Award for Best Newcomer, commended Station of the Year Award; *Style*— Simon Tate, Esq; ✉ Radio Wave, 965 Mowbray Drive, Blackpool, Lancs FY3 7JR (☎ 01253 304965, fax 01253 301965)

TATHAM, Amanda Jane; da of Christopher Trevor Caton Tatham, MW, of Winchester, and Regine Marien, *née* Legge; *b* 13 March 1953; *Educ* St Paul's Girls' Sch, London Coll of Printing (BA); *Career* graphic design asst Pentagram Design 1975–79, designer SMS Design 1979–80, fndr and proprietor Amanda Tatham Design Ltd 1980–84, fndr ptnr Lambton Place Design 1984–87, co fndr and ptnr Tatham Pearce Ltd 1987–96, fndr Amanda Tatham 1996; corporate brochure, print and annual report accounts worked on incl: Graseby (formerly Cambridge Electronic Industries) 1980–, George Wimpey 1981–91, Woolworths 1983, Reckitt & Colman 1983 and 1984, Lloyds Bank 1985–93, Dalgety 1986 and 1987, Hepworth/Next 1984–88, WCRS 1987, Asda 1989, The Broadgate Club 1989, Eurotherm 1989, Ratners Group 1990–92, Seagram Europe 1990, Mitsubishi Finance International 1990–94, Dept of Employment 1992–94, Barclays 1993–; corporate indentity accounts worked on incl: Framlington 1982–87, Lloyds Bank 1985, Healey & Baker 1989, The Broadgate Club 1989, LWT and TVS (sales merger) 1990, Graseby 1991, Eurotherm 1992, Inst of Masters of Wine 1993, Portfolio Fund Management 1994, Signet Group (formally Ratners Group) 1993; awarded: Communication Arts Award for Design Excellence 1979, Spicer & Oppenheim Effective Finance Communications Award 1988, Stock Exchange & Chartered Accountants' Annual Award for smaller companies' published accounts (Graseby plc) 1995; memb: Design Business Assoc (Cncl of Mgmnt 1988–90), D&AD 1978; FCSD 1986 (memb Cncl 1990–93), FRSA 1992; *Recreations* food, wine, classical and contemporary music, the visual arts; *Clubs* Blacks; *Style*— Ms Amanda Tatham

TATTERSALL, Geoffrey Frank; QC (1992); s of Frank Tattersall, of Ashton-under-Lyne, and Margaret, *née* Hassall; *b* 22 Sept 1947; *Educ* Manchester GS, Christ Church Oxford (MA, exhibitioner), Lincoln's Inn (Tancred studentship in common law); *m* 7 Aug 1971, Hazel, da of late Harold Shaw, and Alice Shaw; 1 s (Mark b 13 Sept 1976), 2 da (Victoria Louise b 5 April 1979, Hannah Jayne b 12 Nov 1984); *Career* called to the Bar Lincoln's Inn 1970, in practice N Circuit 1970–, recorder 1989–, called to the Bar New South Wales 1992; lay chm Bolton Deanery Synod 1993–, chm House of Laity and vice pres Manchester Diocesan Synod 1994–, memb Gen Synod 1995–; *Recreations* family, music, travel; *Style*— Geoffrey Tattersall, QC; ✉ 25 Byrom Street, Manchester M3 4PF (☎ 0161 829 2100); 61 Fleet Street, London EC4Y 1JU (☎ 0171 353 4363)

TATTERSALL, John Hartley; s of Robert Herman Tattersall (d 1958), of Roewen, Conwy, Gwynedd, and Jean, *née* Stevens (d 1995); *b* 5 April 1952; *Educ* Shrewsbury, Christ's Coll Cambridge (MA); *m* 8 Sept 1984, Madeleine Virginia, da of Robert Edward Hugh Coles, of Caversham, Berks; 2 s (Robert b 1985, Luke 1987), 1 da (Clare b 1990); *Career* ptnr Coopers & Lybrand 1985– (joined 1975); memb: Banking Sub Ctee ICAEW 1989–, Capital Ctee Securities and Futures Authy 1993–; dir London City Ballet Trust Ltd 1987–96 (dep chm 1995–96); advsy govr St Augustine's Priory Ealing 1995–; Freeman Worshipful Co of Horners 1980; FCA 1989 (ACA 1978); *Books* Towards a Welfare World (jtly, 1973), The Investment Business - Compliance with the Rules (1990), Current Issues in Auditing (contrib, 1991); *Recreations* walking, opera, ballet; *Style*— John Tattersall, Esq; ✉ 3 St Ann's Villas, Holland Park, London W11 4RU (☎ 0171 603 1053); Coopers & Lybrand, 1 Embankment Place, London WC2N 6NN (☎ 0171 212 4689, fax 0171 822 4652, telex 887470 COLYLN G)

TATTERSFIELD, Prof Brian; s of Norman Tattersfield (d 1959), and Marian, *née* Rogers; *b* 12 April 1936; *Educ* Heckmondwike GS, Batley Sch of Art (NDD), RCA (ARCA); *m* 20 April 1963, (Elizabeth) Mary Tindall, da of Richard Newton Wakelin (d 1964), of Richmond, Surrey; 2 da (Jane Charlotte Wakelin b 1964, Emma Louisa Wakelin b 1972); *Career* art dir Young and Rubicam Ltd 1962–63, designer Fletcher Forbes Gill 1963, co-fndr, ptnr and creative head Minale Tattersfield 1964–95, ret; visiting lectr RCA 1978, visiting prof in design Univ of Brighton 1988–; govr: Norwich Sch of Art, The London Inst; design awards incl: Typomundus Canada 1964, creativity on paper NY 1966, Silver award D&AD 1968 (1970 and 1974–84), Gold award Art Dir Club NY 1975, Poster award Warsaw Biennale 1969, Br Poster Design award 1970, Liderman Gold award for graphic design Madrid 1983, Civic Tst award 1985, D&AD president's award for outstanding contrib to Br design 1987; exhibitions: Museum of Modern Art NY 1978, London Design Centre 1981, Glasgow Design Centre 1981, Museum of Modern Art Milan 1983, Cultural Centre of Madrid 1985, Axis Gallery Tokyo 1988; various articles in Br and int jls; memb D&AD; hon fell RCA, FCSD, FRSA; *Style*— Prof Brian Tattersfield; ✉ Sarisberie Cottage, The Street, W Clandon, Surrey GU4 7ST (☎ 01483 222908); 178 High St, Aldeburgh, Suffolk; c/o Minale Tattersfield & Partners Ltd, The Courtyard, 37 Sheen Rd, Richmond, Surrey TW9 1AJ (☎ 0181 948 7999, fax 0181 948 2435, tlx 22397 MINTAT G)

TATUM, Kelvin Martin; s of Martin Tatum, of Coolham, W Sussex, and Janet, *née* Reeve; *b* 8 Feb 1964; *Educ* Brighton Coll; *m* 12 March 1988, Deborah Ann, da of David Edward Rule, of Hedge End, Hants; 1 s (Oliver b 17 March 1991), 1 da (Emma b 28 Feb 1993); *Career* 3 times Br schoolboy scramble champion; speedway rider; debut Wimbledon British League 1983, Young Rider of the Year 1983 and 1985, third place Individual World Final Poland Katowice 1986, Br and Cwlth champion 1987 and 1988, Eng Capt 1989 (winners of World Team Cup Final 1989), Inter-Continental champion 1989, Br and Cwlth champion 1990, Cwlth champion 1992, Euro Grasstrack champion 1995, fastest man in the world record holder, World Longtrack champion 1995; *Recreations* golf; *Style*— Kelvin Tatum, Esq; ✉ London Speedway, Hackney Stadium, London

TAUBER, Peter; s of Nandor Tauber, and Ilona, *née* Tibor (d 1990); *b* 13 Jan 1927; *Educ* Univ of Budapest, Univ of Zürich, St Andrews Univ; *m* 18 Oct 1952, Martha, da of Emeric Balazs; 1 s (Robert John Michael b 9 Nov 1956); *Career* fndr and proprietor Peter Tauber Press Agency 1950– (major literary and syndication agency placing books about and by the famous worldwide); *Recreations* reading, travel, art, antiques, music; *Style*— Peter Tauber, Esq; ✉ Peter Tauber Press Agency, 94 East End Rd, London N3 2SX

TAUNTON, Archdeacon of; *see:* Frith, Ven Richard Michael Cokayne

TAUNTON, Terence Grosvenor; s of Hugh Grosvenor Taunton (d 1986), of Whitstable, Kent, and Dorothy Edna, *née* Fulcher; *b* 16 Aug 1938; *Educ* Faversham GS; *m* Kay, da of late James Herbert Rochester; 2 s (Kevin James b 21 April 1967, Toby Edwin b 20 July 1969); *Career* Nat Serv RN 1956–58; insur broker Bland Payne (later Sedgwicks) 1958–82 (dir Bland Payne International 1978–), Fenchurch Insurance Brokers Ltd 1982–92 (md 1984–92), dir Fenchurch Construction Brokers 1982–92, exec chm James Hunt Dix (Insurance) Ltd May 1993–96 (dir Feb 1993–96), chm Kay International plc 1996–, conslt Hammond Suddards Solicitors 1996–; ACII 1968; *Recreations* sailing, golfing, gardening, walking; *Clubs* Hampton Pier Yacht, Herne Bay Golf; *Style*— Terence Taunton, Esq; ✉ 15 Spenser Rd, Herne Bay, Kent CT6 5QL (☎ 01227 361823); Kay International plc, 29/30 Margaret Street, London W1N 7LB (☎ 0171 323 2021, fax 0171 323 0304); Hammond Suddards Solicitors, Moor House, 119 London Wall, London EC2Y 5ET (☎ 0171 448 1000, fax 0171 448 1001)

TAUSCHER, Hans; s of Friedrich Tauscher (d 1983), and Margarete, *née* Doellinger (d 1968); *b* 16 June 1932, Cologne; *Educ* Helmholzschule Leipzig, Wirtschaftsoberschule Leipzig; *m* 3 Sept 1972, Eileen, da of Robert Hammond; 1 da (Petra b 27 August 1973), 1 s (Robert b 16 Oct 1977); *Career* Daimler-Benz: apprentice at former Daimler-Benz works Leipzig (until escape from Russian-occupied E Germany) 1948–50, Cologne 1950–63; Ford Motor Co: Cologne 1963–68 (involved in mgmnt of Ford Transit project), various sr mgmnt posts Ford of Europe Brentwood Essex 1968–73, rejoined Ford of Germany 1973; Mercedes-Benz (United Kingdom) Ltd: truck sales mangr 1974–76, gen mangr commercial vehicles 1976–77, dir of ops 1977–83, md 1983–; memb: Exec Ctee and Cncl Soc of Motor Manufacturers and Traders 1989–, Cncl German-British C of C;

Recreations skiing, tennis, walking, spending time with the family; *Style*— Mr Hans Tauscher; ✉ Mercedes-Benz (United Kingdom) Ltd, Mercedes-Benz Centre, Delaware Drive, Tongwell, Milton Keynes, Bucks MK15 8BA (☎ 01908 245000, fax 01908 664351)

TAUSIG, Peter; s of Dr Walter Charles Tausig (d 1969), and Judith, *née* Morris (d 1995); *b* 15 Aug 1943; *Educ* Battersea GS, UCL (BSc); *m* 28 June 1987, Geraldine Angharad Alice, da of Leslie Stanley, of Chelsea, London; 2 da (Eva Lily Ibolya b 3 April 1988, Katja Francesca b 30 Dec 1990); *Career* economist: Aust Bureau of Census and Statistics 1965–69, CBI 1969, Bank of London and S America 1970–74, International Marine Banking Co 1974–76, S G Warburg/Warburg Securities 1976–88 (dir 1983); exec dir UBS Phillips & Drew 1989–91, dir Crédit Lyonnais Securities and Crédit Lyonnais Capital Markets 1992–; chm: Kateva Sch 1992–, Ladbroke Square Montessori Sch 1992–, Annemount Sch 1993–; *Recreations* theatre, literature, music, walking, skiing, travel; *Clubs* Groucho, Oriental; *Style*— Peter Tausig, Esq; ✉ 11 Downshire Hill, Hampstead, London NW3 1NR (☎ 0171 435 7099); Crédit Lyonnais Securities, Broadwalk House, 5 Appold St, London EC2A 2DA (☎ 0171 214 5072, fax 0171 214 5002)

TAUSKY, Vilem; CBE (1981); s of Dr Emil Tausky (d 1945), of Czechoslovakia, and Josephine, *née* Ascher (d 1935); *b* 20 July 1910; *Educ* Janacek Conservatoire Brno Czechoslovakia, Meisterschule Prague Czechoslovakia; *m* 1 Jan 1948, Margaret Helen, *née* Powell (d 1982); *Career* Czechoslovak Army; served: France 1939–40, England 1940–45; conductor Brno Opera House 1929–39, musical dir Carl Rosa Opera 1945–49; guest conductor: Royal Opera House 1951–, Sadler's Wells 1953–; dir of opera Guildhall Sch of Music 1977–87; Freeman: City of London, Worshipful Co of Musicians; FGSM 1979; Czechoslovakia Military Cross 1944, Czechoslovakia Order of Merit 1945; *Books* Vilem Tausky Tells His Story (1979), Leos Janacek - Leaves from his Life (1982), Concerto (1957), Concertino for Harmonica and Orchestra (1963), Soho Scherzo for Orchestra (1966), Divertimento for Strings (1966); *Style*— Vilem Tausky, Esq, CBE; ✉ 44 Haven Green Court, Ealing, London W5 2UY (☎ 0181 997 6512)

TAVARÉ, Sir John; kt (1989), CBE (1983); s of Leon Alfred Tavaré (d 1976), and Grace Tavaré (d 1976); *b* 12 July 1920; *Educ* Chatham House Ramsgate, King's Coll London Univ (BSc); *m* 1949, Margaret Daphne Wray; 3 s; *Career* PA Managment Consultants 1948–58, Unilever plc 1958–70, chm and md Whitecroft plc 1970–85, chm Luxonic Lighting plc 1986–; chm: Mersey Basin Campaign Dept of Environment 1985–92, Professional Access Project Br Cncl 1993–95, Tstees of Flying Start Prog Granada TV 1993–; memb: Nat Rivers Authy (NW) Rivers Advsy Bd 1990–92, Olympic Bid Ctee 1991–93; CEng, MIMechE, FIWEM; *Recreations* golf; *Clubs* Prestbury Golf; *Style*— Sir John Tavaré, CBE; ✉ The Gables, 4 Macclesfield Road, Prestbury, Cheshire SK10 4BN (☎ 01625 829778)

TAVENER, Prof John Kenneth; s of Charles Kenneth Tavener (d 1996), and Muriel Evelyn, *née* Brown (d 1985); *b* 28 Jan 1944; *Educ* Highgate Sch, RAM (scholarship); *m* 1, 17 Nov 1974 (m dis 1980), Victoria, da of Dr Costas Marangopoulos, of Athens; m 2, 8 Sept 1991, Maryanna Elizabeth Malecka, da of Prof Glen Schaefer (d 1986), of Cranfield, Beds; 1 da (Theodora Alexandra b 26 Aug 1993); *Career* composer; organist St John's Church London 1960–75, prof of composition Trinity Coll of Music 1968–; memb Russian Orthodox Church; Hon FRAM, Hon FTCL, Hon FRSCM, Hon DMus New Delhi Univ India for services to the Sacred in Art 1990, Hon DMus City Univ London 1995; Apollo Prize Friends of Greek Nat Opera 1993; *Compositions* incl: Cain and Abel (first prize Prince Rainier of Monaco 1965) 1965, The Whale (London) 1968, Celtic Requiem, Ultimos Ritos (Holland Festival) 1974, Akhmatova Requiem 1980 (Edinburgh Festival), Antigone, Thérèse (Covent Garden) 1979, Palintropos (Moscow) 1989, Sappho Fragments, Towards the Son, Mandelion, A Gentle Spirit, Ikon of Light (Tallis Scholars) 1984, Liturgy of St John Chrysostom, Risen!, In Memory of Cats, Let Not the Prince be Silent, Requiem for Father Malachy, Two Hymns to the Mother of God, Kyklike Kinesis, Collegium Regale (King's Coll Cambridge) 1987, Hymn to the Holy Spirit, Acclamation for His All Holiness the Ecumenical Patriarch Demetrios I (Canterbury Cathedral) 1988, Akathist of Thanksgiving (Westminster Abbey) 1988, Ikon of St Seraphim (Truro Cathedral) 1988, The Protecting Veil (Royal Albert Hall) 1989 (The Gramophone award 1992), Resurrection (Glasgow Cathedral) 1990, Apocalypse (BBC Proms cmmn) 1990–92, The Hidden Treasure 1990, The Repentant Thief (LSO cmmn, Barbican) 1991, Mary of Egypt 1992, We Shall See Him as He is 1992, Eternal Memory 1992, Last Sleep of the Virgin 1992, The World is Burning (Monteverdi Choir cmmn) 1994, The Myrrh-Bearer (London Symphony Chorus cmmn) 1994, Melina 1994, Innocence 1994, Agraphon 1995, Three Antiphons 1995, Let's Begin Again 1993–95, Svyatuiee 1995, Vlepontas (Delphi cmmn) 1996, Wake Up and Die (Sony cmmn) 1996, The Toll Houses (opera) 1996; subject of many TV progs incl: Art and Belief, A Week in the Life of, Making Out, Ultimos Ritos, Celtic Requiem, Glimpses of Paradise 1992; subject of book by Geoffrey Haydon John Tavener: Glimpses of Paradise (1995); *Recreations* travelling in Greece, house in Greece, collecting ikons; *Style*— Prof John Tavener; ✉ c/o Chester Music Ltd, 8/9 Frith St, London W1V 5TZ (☎ 0171 434 0066, fax 0171 287 6329)

TAVERNE, Baron (Life Peer UK 1996), of Pimlico in the City of Westminster; Dick Taverne; QC (1965); s of Dr Nicolaas Jacobus Marie Taverne (d 1966), and Louise Victoria, *née* Koch; *b* 18 Oct 1928; *Educ* Charterhouse, Balliol Coll Oxford; *m* 6 Aug 1955, Janice, da of late Dr Robert Samuel Fleming Hennessey; 2 da (Hon Suzanna b 1960, Hon Caroline b 1963); *Career* called to the Bar 1954; MP (Lab) Lincoln 1962–72: Parly sec Home Office 1966–68, min of state Treasy 1968–69, fin sec 1969–70, resigned Labour Party 1972; re-elected Independent Social Democrat MP Lincoln 1973–74; first dir Inst for Fiscal Studies 1971 (chm 1979–83), chm Public Policy Centre 1984–87, Br memb Spierenburg Ctee to examine working of Euro Cmmn 1979; PRIMA Europe: dir 1987–, chm 1991–94, pres 1994–; dir: AXA Equity & Law Life Assurance Society plc 1972–, BOC Group plc 1975–95; chm OLIM Convertible Trust 1989–, dep chm Central European Growth Fund; *Books* The Future of the Left (1974); *Recreations* sailing, marathon running; *Style*— The Rt Hon Lord Taverne, QC; ✉ 60 Cambridge Street, London SW1V 4QQ (☎ 0171 828 0166); PRIMA Europe Ltd, 14 Soho Square, London W1V 5FB (☎ 0171 287 6676)

TAVISTOCK, Marquess of; Henry Robin Ian Russell; DL (Beds 1985); s and h of 13 Duke of Bedford, *qv*; *b* 21 Jan 1940; *Educ* Le Rosey Switzerland, Harvard; *m* 20 June 1961, Henrietta Joan, da of Henry Frederic Tiarks (d 1995); 3 s; *Heir* s, Lord Howland, *qv*; *Career* chm: Berkeley Development Capital Ltd 1984–92, Kennedy Memorial Trust 1985–90; dir: United Racecourses (Holdings) Ltd 1977–94, Trafalgar House plc 1977–91, TR Property Investment Trust plc 1982–91 (chm 1982–89), Berkeley Govett & Co Ltd 1985–95, London Pacific Group Ltd 1996–; pres Woburn Golf and Country Club; *Clubs* White's, Jockey Club Rooms, The Brook (NY); *Style*— Marquess of Tavistock, DL; ✉ Woburn Abbey, Woburn, Bedfordshire MK43 0TP (☎ 01525 290 666)

TAYAR, Graham Joseph; s of Robert Alfred Victor Tayar (d 1958), of Birmingham, and Muriel Sara, *née* Aaron (d 1977); *b* 5 March 1933; *Educ* King Edward's Sch Birmingham, Jesus Coll Cambridge (BA, MA); *m* 1, 7 July 1956 (m dis 1966), (Alice) Meriel, da of Clarendon Monsell (d 1936); 2 da (Penelope (Mrs Simon Vevers) b 1957, Imogen (Dr Bloor) b 1958); m 2, July 1969 (m dis 1983), Lynn Hilary, da of J Kramer; 1 step s (Daryl Leon b 1966); m 3, Dec 1983 (m dis 1991), Christina Elizabeth, da of Darsie Rawlins; *Career* schoolmaster Birmingham 1956–59, schoolmaster (later dep head and sec Nat Curriculum Ctee) Addis Ababa Ethiopia 1959–64; extra mural univ lectr: Haile Selassie Univ Addis Ababa 1960–63, London Univ 1968–71, Univ of Manchester; freelance journalist and broadcaster 1962–65 (BBC, Observer, Daily Telegraph, AFP, NBC (NY)); BBC radio: prodr Birmingham 1965–66, prodr Bush House (African and World Serv) 1966–69, sr radio prodr 1969–80, exec prodr Broadcasting House 1980–89; freelance prodr and broadcasting conslt 1989–; head of radio/audio SAGE 1989–90, Br Cncl and ODA conslt to Ethiopia 1990–91, conslt FE Unit (DFE) 1990–95, conslt Cwlth Secretariat/AIBD Seminar Sri Lanka 1993, conslt dir radio skills course Univ of Cambridge Exams Bd 1994; fndr ldr and pianist Crouch End Allstars New Orleans Jazz Band 1971–, prodr various records incl Sunday Best (Jazzology US) 1985, organizer of jazz festivals and jazz band balls; literary ed New Middle East 1970–73; poetry published: Tribune, Birmingham Post, Extra Verse, Envoi, Poetry and Audience, etc 1985–95; memb: Kentish Town Police and Community Crime Panel (chm 1991–94), Advsy Ctee W Sussex Inst Maths Centre 1986–89, Media Studies Ctees BTEC and C & G; hon memb CGLI 1991; FRSA 1989; *Books* Personality and Power (ed, 1971), Education at Home and Abroad (with Prof J Lauwerys, 1972), Living Decisions (1973); *Recreations* playing jazz, tennis, writing occasional verses; *Clubs* BBC, The Academy, RSA, Cambridge Union; *Style*— Graham Tayar, Esq; ✉ 25 Fortess Rd, Kentish Town, London NW5 1AD (☎ 0171 485 0578); 17 Middle St, Port Isaac, Cornwall PL29 3RH (☎ 01208 880658)

TAYAR, Dr René Benedict; s of Oscar Tayar, of Sliema, Malta, and Violet, *née* Riccardi; *b* 3 Oct 1945; *Educ* St Aloysius' Coll Malta, Royal Univ of Malta (MD), Royal Coll of Radiologists London (FRCR); *m* 25 Jan 1971, Margaret Rose, da of Louis Francis Tortell, of Sliema, Malta; 1 s (Benjamin b 8 Sept 1978); *Career* sr registrar in radiology Bristol Royal Infirmary 1977–81 (registrar in radiology 1974–77); conslt radiologist: St Helier Hosp Carshalton 1981–, Nelson Hosp Raynes Park London 1981–, Parkside Hosp Wimbledon 1984–, St Helier Hosp NHS Trust (also sec Med Staff Ctee), Atkinson Morley Imaging Centre Wimbledon 1992–, St Anthony's Hosp N Cheam Surrey 1995–; hon sr lectr St George's Hosp Med Sch 1988–; fndr memb: Sir Harry Secombe Scanner Appeal, Secombe Magnet Appeal; *Recreations* tennis, music, literature; *Clubs* RAC, Pall Mall; *Style*— Dr René Tayar; ✉ 45 Epsom Lane South, Tadworth, Surrey KT20 5TA (☎ 01737 813582); Department of Radiodiagnosis, St Helier Hospital, Wrythe Lane, Carshalton, Surrey SM5 1AA (☎ 0181 644 4343)

TAYLOR, His Hon Judge Alan Broughton; s of Valentine James Broughton Taylor (d 1992), of Birmingham, and Gladys Maud, *née* Williams (d 1988); *b* 23 Jan 1939; *Educ* Malvern, Univ of Geneva, Univ of Birmingham (LLB), BNC Oxford (MLitt); *m* 15 Aug 1964, Diana, da of Dr James Robson Hindmarsh (d 1970), of Peach Cottage, Lytchett Matravers, Dorset; 2 s (Stephen James b 30 Nov 1965, Robert David b 21 Feb 1968); *Career* called to the Bar Gray's Inn 1961, in practice 1962–91, recorder 1979–91, circuit judge (Midland and Oxford Circuit) 1991–; govr St Matthew's Sch Smethwick W Mids 1988–92; FCIArb 1994; *Books* A Practical Guide to the Care of the Injured (by P S London, contrib 1964); *Recreations* philately, fell walking; *Style*— His Hon Judge Alan Taylor; ✉ c/o Circuit Administrator's Office, The Priory Courts, 33 Bull Street, Birmingham B4 6DW

TAYLOR, Dr Alexander James; s of James Torrie Taylor (d 1973), and Agnes Neil, *née* Bowman; *b* 16 Jan 1928; *Educ* George Heriot's Sch Edinburgh, Robert Gordon's Coll Aberdeen, Banchory Acad, Univ of Aberdeen Med Sch (MB ChB); *m* 6 Sept 1951, Renee Myles, da of David Humble; 2 s (Alistair James b 28 Dec 1952, David John b 4 July 1954), 1 da (Margaret Helen b 8 Dec 1955); *Career* trainee med asst Gen Practice Kirkwall and Balfour Hosp Kirkwall 1950–52; princ in NHS practice: Wigan 1952–55, Flotta Orkney 1955–56, Shapinsay Orkney 1957–60, Fyvie Aberdeenshire 1960–93; med offr House of Daviot Inverurie 1973–93, med examiner to CAA 1974–; lectr in gen practice Univ of Aberdeen 1974–93, hon sr lectr Univ of Aberdeen 1993–; chm Area Gen Practice Sub Ctee Grampian 1975–78, chm Grampian Area Med Ctee 1978–81, memb Grampian Health Bd 1985–90, chm Grampian Healthcare NHS Tst 1993–; pres Grampian Div BMA 1981–82; pres Rotary Club of Turriff 1979–80; FRCGP 1978 (MRCGP 1963); *Recreations* private flying, sailing, golf; *Clubs* Royal Northern and Univ (Aberdeen); *Style*— Dr Alexander Taylor; ✉ Beechwood, Fyvie, Turriff AB53 8PB (☎ 01651 891349); Grampian Healthcare NHS Trust, Westholme, Woodend Hospital, Aberdeen AB2 6LR (☎ 01224 663131 ext 56552, fax 01224 840790, mobile 0374 104562)

TAYLOR, Alexandra; da of Kenneth Taylor, and Maureen, *née* Bell; *b* 17 Feb 1959; *Educ* Blaydon Comp, Newcastle upon Tyne Sch of Art (HND, DipAD); *Career* art dir: BBD&O advtg 1981–83, Saatchi & Saatchi 1983–89; sr art dir, gp head and bd dir WCRS 1989, head of art Saatchi & Saatchi 1992– (rejoined as gp head and bd dir 1989); memb D&AD; *Awards* 9 Silver Campaign Press Awards, 1 Gold Campaign Poster Award, 6 Silver Campaign Poster Awards, 3 Silver Br TV Awards, 1 ITVA Award, 2 Gold, 1 Silver and 2 Bronze Cannes, 115 entries accepted in Design and Art Direction Annual, 3 Silver nominations D&AD; *Style*— Ms Alexandra Taylor; ✉ Saatchi & Saatchi, 80 Charlotte Street, London W1A 1AQ (☎ 0171 636 5060, fax 0171 580 9249)

TAYLOR, Andrew John Robert; s of Rev Arthur John Taylor, of Monmouth, and Hilda Mary, *née* Haines; *b* 14 Oct 1951; *Educ* The King's Sch Ely, Woodbridge Sch Suffolk, Emmanuel Coll Cambridge (BA), UCL (MA); *m* 8 Sept 1979, Caroline Jane, da of Ian George Silverwood; 1 s (William John Alexander b 6 March 1989), 1 da (Sarah Jessica b 9 June 1986); *Career* writer; various jobs ranging from boatbuilding to teaching 1973–76, freelance sub ed for London publishers 1975–84, library asst then asst librarian London Borough of Brent 1976–81, self-employed writer 1981–; memb: Soc of Authors, Crime Writers' Assoc; *Awards* John Creasey Meml Award Crime Writers' Assoc 1982 and Edgar nomination from Mystery Writers of America for Caroline Minuscule, Our Fathers' Lies shortlisted for Gold Dagger of Crime Writers Assoc 1985, Snapshot shortlisted for NatWest Children's Book of the Year award 1989; *Books* for children incl: Hairline Cracks (1988), Private Nose (1989), Snapshot (1989), Double Exposure (1990), Negative Image (1992), The Invader (1994); for adults incl: Caroline Minuscule (1982), Waiting for the End of the World (1984), Our Fathers' Lies (1985), An Old School Tie (1986), Freelance Death (1987), The Second Midnight (1988), Blacklist (1988), Blood Relation (1990), Toyshop (1990), The Raven on the Water (1991), The Sleeping Policeman (1992), The Barred Window (1993), Odd Man Out (1993), An Air That Kills (1994), The Mortal Sickness (1995), The Four Last Things (1996); *Style*— Andrew Taylor, Esq; ✉ The Carriage House, 13 Lords Hill, Coleford, Gloucestershire GL16 8BG (☎ 01594 833923, fax 01594 833203); Richard Scott Simon Ltd, 43 Doughty St, London WC1N 2LF

TAYLOR, (Winifred) Ann; MP (Lab) Dewsbury (majority 634); *b* 2 July 1947; *Educ* Bolton Sch, Univ of Bradford, Univ of Sheffield; *m*; 1 s (b 1982), 1 da (b 1983); *Career* MP (Lab) Bolton W Oct 1974–83 (also contested Feb 1974), Parly candidate Bolton NE 1983, MP (Lab) Dewsbury 1987–; PPS to: Sec of State for Defence 1976–77, Sec of State DES 1975–76; Govt whip 1977–79; oppn front bench spokesman: on educn 1979–81, on housing 1981–83, on home affrs 1987–88; memb Shadow Cabinet 1988–; chief oppn spokesman: on environmental protection 1988–92, on educn 1992–94, on Citizen's Charter 1994–95; shadow ldr House of Commons 1994–, memb Select Ctee on Standards in Public Life (Nolan Select Ctee) 1995, memb Standards and Privileges Ctee 1995–; former teacher, pt/t tutor Open Univ; *Books* Political Action (with Jim Firth, 1978), Choosing Our Future (1992); *Style*— Mrs Ann Taylor, MP; ✉ House of Commons, London SW1A 0AA

TAYLOR, Annita; da of Romola Piapan (d 1967), of Switzerland, and Rosalia Smak Piapan (d 1984); *b* 21 Sept 1925; *Educ* Avviamento Professionale Tecnico di Monfalcone Italy; *m* 10 Nov 1946, Alfred Oakley Taylor, s of George Oakley Taylor; 1 da (Ligmoi

Hannah b 18 Oct 1947); *Career* md ABBA DG Co Ltd 1983–90 (dir 1978–90); dir: Liglets Co Ltd 1982–, Rosalia Management Services Co Ltd 1989–90; involved with: Riding for the Disabled, Red Cross; *Recreations* racing, polo, shooting; *Clubs* Guards' Polo, Jockey, Racehorse Owners' Assoc; *Style*— Mrs Annita Taylor; ✉ Wadley Manor, Faringdon, Oxon (☎ 01367 20556); 19 Millers Court, Chiswick Mall, London W4 (☎ 0181 748 2997)

TAYLOR, Dr Arnold Joseph; CBE (1971); s of Dr John George Taylor (d 1942), of Battersea, and Mary Matilda, *née* Riley (d 1965); *b* 24 July 1911; *Educ* Sir Walter St John's Sch Battersea, Merchant Taylors', St John's Coll Oxford (MA); *m* 19 April 1940, Patricia Katharine, da of Samuel Arthur Guilbride (d 1950), of Victoria, BC; 1 s, 1 da; *Career* RAF Intelligence served UK, N Africa and Italy 1942–46; asst master Chard Sch Somerset 1934–35, HM Office of Works Inspectorate of Ancient Monuments 1935, chief inspr of ancient monuments and historic bldgs MPBW 1961, ret 1972; pres Soc of Antiquaries 1975–78 (gold medal 1988); hon vice pres: Royal Archaeological Inst, Surrey Archaeological Soc; memb: Ancient Monuments Bds for Eng Wales & Scotland 1973–81, Cathedrals Advsy Ctee 1964–80, Advsy Bd for Redundant Churches 1973–81 (chm 1975–77), Westminster Abbey Architectural Advsy Panel 1979–92; cmmr Royal Cmmns on Historic Monuments Wales 1956–83 (Eng 1963–78); Freeman: City of London, Worshipful Co of Merchant Taylors; Hon DLitt Wales 1969, Hon DUniv Caen 1980; FSA 1942, FBA 1972; *Recreations* observing the built environment, music; *Style*— Dr Arnold Taylor, CBE, FSA, FBA; ✉ Rose Cottage, Lincoln's Hill, Chiddingfold, Surrey (☎ 0142 868 2069)

TAYLOR, Baz; s of Alfred William Taylor, of Tankerton, Whitstable, Kent, and Marjorie, *née* Steventon; *b* 30 Aug 1944; *Educ* Simon Langton GS Canterbury, Queen's Coll Oxford (MA); *m* 16 May 1970, (Marianne) Valerie, da of Eiddfryn James (d 1957), of Caemorgan, Cardigan, Dyfed; 2 da (Alice Jane b 28 May 1971, Katharine Elizabeth b 4 Nov 1972); *Career* prodr World in Action Granada TV 1968, dir The Christians 1975 (NY Film and TV Festival Award); memb: Friends of the Earth, Nat Tst, BAFTA 1975; elected memb Cncl Dirs' Guild of GB 1990, memb Advsy Cncl Directors' and Producers' Rights Soc (DPRS) 1995; *Television* dir, prodr and exec prodr numerous series incl: Talent with Julie Walters (NY Film and TV Award), Auf Wiedersehen Pet (Br Press and Broadcasting Award 1983, Drama of the Decade Award 1989), Shine on Harvey Moon, Young Charlie Chaplin (Thames TV 1989, Emmy nomination), Minder (Euston Films 1992–93); *Films* Near Mrs (1991), Shooting Elizabeth (1992), Tattle Tale (1992), Jusqu'a la Lie (Canal Plus Paris 1996); *Books* Cash and Carrie (1986), Love Me, Love My Dog (1987); *Recreations* sailing, golf, walking, skiing; *Clubs* BAFTA, The Stage Golfing Soc; *Style*— Baz Taylor, Esq; ✉ 17 Alexander St, London W2 5NT (☎ 0171 727 1191, fax 0171 229 1256, telex 263361, mobile 0973 320447)

TAYLOR, Bernard David; CBE (1993); s of late Thomas Taylor, of Coventry, and Winifred, *née* Smith; *b* 17 Oct 1935; *Educ* John Gulson GS Coventry, Univ of Wales Bangor (BSc), London Business Sch; *m* 5 Sept 1959, Nadine Barbara, da of Ben Maile, of Devoran, Cornwall; 2 s (Jonathan b 5 Oct 1964, Michael b 5 Nov 1966), 2 da (Sian b 30 Sept 1960, Sarah b 10 Oct 1962); *Career* md Glaxo Aust 1972–83, md Glaxo Pharmaceuticals UK 1984–86, chief exec Glaxo Holdings plc 1985–89, exec chm Medeva PLC 1990–April 1996; cncllr Victorian Coll of Pharmacy 1976–82; memb: CBI Europe Ctee 1987–89, BOTB 1987–; fell London Business Sch 1988; CIMgt 1986; *Style*— Bernard Taylor, Esq, CBE; ✉ c/o Medeva PLC, 10 St James's Street, London SW1A 1EF (☎ 0171 839 3888, fax 0171 930 1514)

TAYLOR, Bernard Irvin; s of Albert Ernest Taylor (d 1965), of Swindon, Wilts, and Edna Marion, *née* Tanner; *b* 2 Oct 1934; *Educ* Swindon Sch of Art, Chelsea Sch of Art (Chelsea Dip, Nat Dip in Design), Univ of Birmingham (BA, Art Teacher's Dip); *Career* author and playwright; teacher and book illustrator London 1960–63, teacher and painter of portraits and landscapes, actor New York 1963–70, writer and actor UK 1970–; memb: Actors' Equity, Soc of Authors; *Plays* Daughter of the Apachés (1973), Mice on the First Floor (1974, Thames TV most promising playwright award 1974), Maggie it's Me! (BBC TV 1975); *Novels* The Godsend (1976, translated into 17 languages and filmed), Sweetheart Sweetheart (1977), The Reaping (1980), The Moorstone Sickness (1982), The Kindness of Strangers (1986), Madeleine (1987), Mother's Boys (1988), Saddle the Wind (under pseudonym Kate Irvine, 1989), Charmed Life (1991), Evil Intent (1994); *Non-Fiction* Cruelly Murdered (1979), Perfect Murder (with Stephen Knight, 1987, Crime Writers' Assoc Gold Dagger award), Murder at the Priory (with Kate Clarke, 1988); has also published numerous short stories; *Style*— Bernard Taylor, Esq; ✉ c/o A M Heath & Co Ltd, 79 St Martin's Lane, London WC2N 4AA (☎ 0171 836 4271)

TAYLOR, Bernard John; s of John Taylor (d 1962), and Evelyn Frances Taylor (d 1995); *b* 2 Nov 1956; *Educ* Cheltenham, St John's Coll Oxford (scholar, MA); *m* 16 June 1984, Sarah Jane, da of John Paskin Taylor, of Paris; 1 s (Henry Bernard Charles b 22 Sept 1992); *Career* dir Med Div Smiths Industries plc 1983–85 (business planning and acquisitions 1979–82); exec dir: Baring Bros & Co Ltd 1985–94 (mangr and asst dir Corp Fin Dept), Robert Fleming & Co Ltd 1994–, Robert Fleming Holdings Ltd 1995–; non-exec dir New Focus Healthcare 1986; LRPS (memb 1971), FRSC (memb 1972), CChem; *Books* Photosensitive Film Formation on Copper (I) (1974), Photosensitive Film Formation on Copper (II) (1976), Oxidation of Alcohols to Carbonyl Compounds, Synthesis (1979); *Recreations* photography, gardening, wine; *Clubs* United Oxford and Cambridge Univ; *Style*— Bernard Taylor, Esq; ✉ Robert Fleming & Co Ltd, 25 Copthall Avenue, London EC2R 7DR (☎ 0171 638 5858)

TAYLOR, Prof Brent William; s of Robert Ernest Taylor (d 1971), of Christchurch, NZ, and Norma Gertrude, *née* Collett; *b* 21 Nov 1941; *Educ* Christchurch Boys' HS, Otago Univ (MB ChB), Univ of Bristol (PhD); *m* 17 Jan 1970, Moira Elizabeth, da of Thomas Richard Hall (d 1983), of Palmerston North, NZ; 1 s (Samuel b 1973), 1 da (Katherine b 1975); *Career* jr med posts Christchurch NZ 1967–71, res and trg posts Great Ormond Street and Inst of Child Health London 1971–74, sr lectr in paediatrics Christchurch NZ 1975–81, conslt sr lectr in social paediatrics and epidemiology Univ of Bristol and visiting paediatrician and epidemiologist Riyadh Mil Hosp 1981–84, conslt sr lectr in child health St Mary's Hosp Med Sch London 1985–88, prof of community child health Royal Free Hosp Sch of Med Univ of London 1988–; FRCP 1985 (MRCP 1971), FRACP 1981 (MRACP 1970); *Recreations* opera, walking, Macintosh computing; *Style*— Prof Brent Taylor; ✉ 42 Oakley Rd, London N1 3LS (☎ 0171 354 8442); Department of Child Health, Royal Free Hospital/School of Medicine, London NW3 2QG (☎ 0171 794 0500, fax 0171 830 2003)

TAYLOR, Brian Arthur Edward; s of Arthur Frederick Taylor (d 1979), of Barnes, London, and Gertrude Maclean, *née* Campbell (d 1992); *b* 10 Jan 1942; *Educ* St Benedict's Sch Ealing, Corpus Christi Coll Oxford (MA); *m* 22 April 1967, Carole Ann, da of Albert James Smith; 3 s (Daniel Andrew Edward b 2 March 1968, Christopher Brian b 15 Feb 1970, William James Arthur b 7 Nov 1973), 1 da (Katharine Helen b 5 Nov 1978); *Career* MOD: asst princ 1965–69, asst private sec to Sec of State for Def 1969–70, private sec to CAS 1973–75, sec to MOD Mgmnt Review 1975–77, head of MOD Mgmnt Services Div 1977–79, head of Naval Personnel Div 1979–81, RCDS 1982; CPRS Cabinet Office 1983; MOD: Re-orgn Secretariat 1984, head of Civilian Mgmnt Div 1984–86, asst under sec (quartermaster) 1986–88, asst under sec (Air) PE 1988–92; under sec Personnel Policy Gp HM Treasy 1992–95, AUS (CM) (Policy) MOD 1995–; *Recreations* sport, music, reading; *Style*— Brian Taylor, Esq; ✉ Ministry of Defence, Room 319, Northumberland House, Northumberland Avenue, London WC2N 5BP

TAYLOR, Brian William (Bill); s of Alan Stuart Taylor (d 1975), of Chatham, Kent, and Dora Frances Mary, *née* Betts (d 1969); *b* 29 April 1933; *Educ* Emanuel Sch Wandsworth; *m* 15 Aug 1959, Mary Evelyn, da of William Henry Buckley (d 1976), of Great Bookham, Surrey; 2 s (Jeffrey William b 16 Feb 1967, Michael John b 20 Jan 1972), 2 da (Helen Mary (Mrs Compston) b 28 Jan 1963, Gillian Elizabeth (Mrs Cooksley) b 30 Oct 1964); *Career* Miny of Nat Insur: exec offr 1952, higher exec offr 1963, princ 1968, asst sec 1976, under sec 1982; on secondment from Dept of Social Security; Civil Service Cmmn 1990–95 (full-time 1990–93, pt/t 1993–95), ret; *Recreations* grandchildren, music, theatre, literature, tennis; *Style*— Bill Taylor, Esq; ✉ c/o Civil Service Commission, 24 Whitehall, London SW1A 2ED (☎ 0171 210 6674, fax 0171 210 6793)

TAYLOR, Cavan; s of Albert William Taylor (d 1993), and Muriel, *née* Horncastle (d 1985); *b* 23 Feb 1935; *Educ* King's Coll Sch Wimbledon, Emmanuel Cambridge (MA, LLM); *m* 1962, Helen, da of late Everard Tinling; 1 s (Sean b 1965), 2 da (Karen b 1963, Camilla b 1970); *Career* Nat Serv 2 Lt RASC 1953–55; admitted slr 1961; ptnr: Piesse & Sons 1966–73, Durrant Piesse 1973–88; sr ptnr Lovell White Durrant 1991–96 (ptnr 1988–96); dir Ludorum Management Ltd 1996–; memb Panel of Adjudicators of the Investment Ombudsman 1996–; memb Governing Body KCS Wimbledon 1970– (chm 1973–90); Liveryman City of London Solicitors' Co; memb: Law Soc, Int Bar Assoc; *Recreations* conversation with my children, reading, sailing, gardening; *Clubs* Travellers', KCS Old Boys RFC (pres 1996–); *Style*— Cavan Taylor, Esq; ✉ Covenham House, 10 Broad Highway, Cobham, Surrey KT11 2RP (☎ 01932 864258, fax 01932 865705)

TAYLOR, Charles Spencer; s of Leonard Taylor (d 1991), and Phyllis Rose, *née* Emerson (d 1982); *b* 18 Jan 1952; *Educ* William Fletcher Sch Bognor Regis, Univ of Hull (LLB); *m* 7 Sept 1973, Elizabeth Mary (Liz), da of Ernest Richard Stephens; 2 s (Leo John Julius b 5 June 1987, Jack Michael Marius b 10 Feb 1990); *Career* called to the Bar Middle Temple 1974, in practice SE Circuit; memb Hon Soc of the Middle Temple 1969; *Recreations* gardening; *Style*— Charles Taylor, Esq; ✉ 3 East Pallant, Chichester, Sussex PO19 1TR (☎ 01243 784538, fax 01243 780861)

TAYLOR, Prof Christopher Malcolm; *b* 15 Jan 1943; *Educ* KCL (William Siemens prize, Engrg Centenary prize, Jelf medal, BSc Eng), Univ of Leeds (MSc, PhD, DEng); *Career* res engr Lubrication Labs English Electric Co Ltd Whetstone Leics 1967–68; Univ of Leeds: sr engr Industrial Unit of Tribology 1968–71, lectr in mechanical engrg 1971–80, sr lectr in mechanical engrg 1980–86, reader in tribology Dept of Mechanical Engrg 1986–90, dir Inst of Tribology 1987–, prof of tribology Dept of Mechanical Engrg 1990–, head Dept of Mechanical Engrg 1992–96, dean Faculty of Engrg 1996–; conf organizer and jt ed Proceedings series of Leeds-Lyon Symposia on Tribology annually since 1974, memb Editorial Bd: Tribology International, Proceedings of Inst of Mechanical Engrs 1990–; referee SERC and NSF res grants and reports 1986–; sr res assoc Nat Res Cncl of America at NASA Res Center Cleveland Ohio 1976–77; author of numerous articles in scientific jls and pubns; awards: Tribology Silver Medal 1992, IMechE Tribology Gp Donald Julius Groen Prize 1993; CEng, FIMechE, FEng 1995; *Style*— Prof Christopher Taylor, FEng; ✉ Department of Mechanical Engineering, University of Leeds, Leeds LS2 9JT (☎ 0113 233 2156, fax 0113 242 4611, e-mail C.M.TAYLOR@leeds.ac.uk)

TAYLOR, Dr Christopher Michael; s of Harry Taylor (d 1983), and Margaret Elizabeth, *née* Leigh; *b* 27 July 1952; *Educ* Hutton GS, Christ's Coll Cambridge (MA), King's Coll Hosp Med Sch Univ of London (MB BChir); *m* 4 Nov 1978, Soopamah, da of Arnasalon Munisami (d 1991), of Mauritius; 2 s (Michael Khrisnen b 1983, Andrew James Silven b 1987), 1 da (Rachel Kevina b 1980); *Career* conslt psychiatrist Leeds Eastern Health Authy 1986– (area mangr Gen Psychiatry 1991–95); MRCPsych; *Style*— Dr Christopher Taylor; ✉ St James's University Hospital, Beckett St, Leeds, W Yorks LS9 7TF (☎ 0113 2 433 144)

TAYLOR, Christopher Skidmore; s of S E W Taylor (d 1963), and D Skidmore-Jones; *b* 28 May 1941; *Educ* Clifton Coll, Clare Coll Cambridge (exhibitioner, MA), Graduate Sch of Business Stanford Univ California (MBA); *m* 1971, Alexandra Nancy, da of Maj Roger Alexander Howard; 1 s (Charles Argentine Weston b 1981), 2 da (Emily Clare b 1973, Alexia Lucy b 1975); *Career* Harkness fell Cwlth Fund 1963–65, sr fell then lectr Coll of Aeronautics Cranfield (now Cranfield Inst of Technol) 1965–67, visiting lectr Graduate Sch of Business Harvard Univ 1967–68, corp financier then head of venture capital Hill Samuel & Co Ltd 1968–76, gp treas then asst fin dir Tarmac plc 1976–86; fin dir: Babcock International plc 1986–87, William Collins plc 1988–89, Smiths Industries plc 1989–95; dir The Economist Group 1995–; non-exec dir: JBA Holdings plc 1994–, Hayes plc 1995–; FCT 1980; *Recreations* golf, sailing, skiing, opera; *Clubs* RAC, Royal Western; *Style*— Christopher Taylor, Esq; ✉ 67 Abbotsbury Road, London W14 8EL (☎ 0171 603 6430)

TAYLOR, Sir Cyril Julian Hebden; kt (1989); s of Rev Cyril Eustace Taylor (d 1935), and Marjory Victoria, *née* Hebden; *b* 14 May 1935; *Educ* St Marylebone GS London, Roundhay Sch Leeds, Trinity Hall Cambridge (MA), Harvard Business Sch (MBA); *m* 5 June 1965, June Judith (Judy), da of Earl Denman (d 1970); 1 da (Kirsten Livia Hebden b 1970); *Career* Nat Serv 1954–56 (cmmn with E Surrey Regt seconded to 3 Bn King's African Rifles in Kenya during Mau Mau emergency); brand mangr Procter & Gamble Cincinnati Ohio 1961–64; fndr chm AIFS Inc 1964– (cos incl American Inst for Foreign Study, Camp America, Au Pair in America, Richmond Coll, American International Univ London, American Cncl for Int Studies); chm Technology Colleges Trust 1987–, advsr to Sec of State for Educn and Employment 1987–; Parly Candidate (C) Huddersfield E Feb 1974 and Keighley Oct 1974; Gtr London Cncl for Ruislip Northwood: memb 1977–86, chm Profession and Gen Servs Ctee 1978–81, opposition spokesman for tport, policy and resources 1981–86, dep ldr of the opposition 1983–86; memb Bd of Dirs Centre for Policy Studies 1984–; pres: Ruislip Northwood Cons Assoc 1986–, Harvard Business Sch Club of London 1990–93; vice pres Alumni Cncl Harvard Business Sch 1994–96; chm Lexham Gdns Residents' Assoc; High Sheriff of Greater London 1996–97; Hon PhD New England 1991; FRSA; *Books and Pamphlets* The Guide to Study Abroad (with Prof John Garraty and Lily von Klemperer), Peace has its Price (1972), No More Tick (1974), The Elected Member's Guide to Reducing Public Expenditure (1980), A Realistic Plan for London Transport (1982), Reforming London's Government (1984), Qualgoes Just Grow (1985), London Preserv'd (1985), Bringing Accountability Back to Local Government (1985), Employment Examined: The Right Approach to More Jobs (1986), Raising Educational Standards (1990), The Future of Britain's Universities (jtly, 1996); *Recreations* keen tennis player, swimmer, gardener and theatre goer; *Clubs* Carlton, Chelsea Arts, Hurlingham, Harvard (New York), Racquet and Tennis (New York); *Style*— Sir Cyril Taylor; ✉ 1 Lexham Walk, London W8 5JD (☎ 0171 370 2081); American Institute for Foreign Study, 37 Queen's Gate, London SW7 5HR (☎ 0171 581 7391, fax 0171 581 7388)

TAYLOR, David George Pendleton; CBE (1993); s of George James Pendleton Taylor (d 1972), and Dorothy May Taylor, *née* Williams (d 1978); *b* 5 July 1933; *Educ* Clifton, Clare Coll Cambridge (MA); *Career* Sub Lt (Special) RNVR 1952–54; dist offr and subsequently sr local govt offr Tanganyika (now Tanzania) 1958–63; with Booker plc 1964–89 (sr mgmnt post and dir, chm and chief exec Booker (Malawi) 1976–77); seconded as chief exec Falkland Islands Govt 1983–87 and 1988–89 (on an interim basis), govr Montserrat 1990–93; memb: Cwlth Tst, RIIA RGS, Royal African Soc; *Recreations* painting, reading; *Clubs* Br Sportsman's, MCC, United Oxford and Cambridge; *Style—* David Taylor, Esq, CBE; ✉ 53 Lillian Road, London SW13 9JF

TAYLOR, David John; s of Charles Stanley Taylor (d 1980), of Bath, and Eileen Florence Taylor (d 1980); *b* 7 July 1943; *Educ* The King's Sch Ottery St Mary, Kingswood GS Bristol; *m* Dianna Rose, *née* Forman; 3 da (Penelope Jane b 26 April 1971, Melanie Claire b 25 March 1973, Anna Elizabeth Kate b 20 Nov 1978); *Career* CA 1967; articled clerk Ricketts Cooper & Co 1961–67; Cooper Bros & Co (now Coopers & Lybrand: audit sr Bristol office 1967, audit sr Accra office Ghana 1967, audit mangr Accra office 1969, secondments to Monrovia Liberia, memb of World Bank funded mgmnt consultancy (working on project for Electricity Corp of Ghana); founding ptnr Robson Taylor 1969–90, chm Team Services plc 1994–; non-exec dir various other cos; chm Fin Ctee and memb Cncl of Mgmnt Bath Festival Soc Ltd 1984–90, pres W of Eng Soc of CAs 1990–91; vice chm Bath Mental Healthcare NHS Tst 1991–; FCA 1974; *Recreations* skiing, horse riding, wine, travel, theatre; *Clubs* MCC, Lansdown, Bath RFU, Landsdown CC, Forty Club; *Style—* David Taylor, Esq; ✉ 31 Sion Hill, Bath BA1 2UW (☎ 01225 424509, office ☎ 01225 420808, fax 01225 420808, mobile 0374 641560)

TAYLOR, David John; s of John Robert George Taylor, of Norwich, and Elizabeth Anne Castell, *née* Spalding; *b* 22 Aug 1960; *Educ* King Edward VI Sch Norwich, St John's Coll Oxford (BA); *m* 22 June 1990, Rachel Elizabeth, da of Richard Paul Hore; 2 s (Felix John Richard b 29 Oct 1992, Benjamin Anthony b 17 Jan 1996); *Career* writer; contrib various papers incl: The Independent, Night and Day (Mail on Sunday Review), TLS, The Spectator, Private Eye, New Statesman & Society, The Oldie; *Books* Great Eastern Land (novel, 1986), A Vain Conceit - British Fiction in the 1980s (1989), Other People - Portraits From the 90s (with Marcus Berkmann, 1990), Real Life (novel, 1992), After The War: The Novel and England Since 1945 (1993), W M Thackeray - A Shabby-Genteel Story and other sketches (ed, 1993), W M Thackeray - The Newcomer (ed, 1994), English Settlement (novel, 1996), George Gissing - New Grub Street (ed, 1997); *Recreations* reading, following Norwich City FC; *Style—* D J Taylor, Esq; ✉ c/o Rogers, Coleridge & White Ltd, 20 Powis Mews, London W11 1JN (☎ 0171 221 3717, fax 0171 229 9084)

TAYLOR, David Mills; s of Donald Charles Taylor (d 1940), and Elsa Marjorie Taylor (d 1967); *b* 22 Dec 1935; *Educ* Royal Commercial Travellers' Schs; *m* 1960, Gillian Irene, da of George Edward Washford; 4 da; *Career* gp fin dir: Brooke Bond Oxo Ltd 1968–71, The Guthrie Corporation Ltd 1971–79, Trafalgar House plc 1979–87; fin dir The Fitzroy Robinson Partnership 1987–90, dep dir and dir of fin and servs WWF UK (World Wide Fund For Nature) 1991–96, independent charity conslt 1996–; dep chm Royal Pinner Sch Fndn; FCA; *Recreations* golf, travel, Oriental cooking; *Style—* David M Taylor, Esq; ✉ Appin Cottage, 2 Beechwood Drive, Cobham, Surrey KT11 2DX (☎ 01372 843697)

TAYLOR, David Samuel Irving; s of Samuel Donald Taylor (d 1970), of Pulborough, Sussex, and Winifred Alice May, *née* Marker; *b* 6 June 1942; *Educ* Dauntsey's Sch, Univ of Liverpool (MB ChB); *m* 5 July 1969, Anna, da of Air Cdre John Rhys-Jones (d 1972), of Nutbourne Manor, Pulborough, Sussex; 2 s (Matthew Samuel b 1970, Nicholas James b 1972); *Career* res surgn Moorfields Eye Hosp 1971–74, fell in neurophthalmology Univ of California San Francisco 1976–77, conslt ophthalmologist Nat Hosp for Nervous Diseases London 1976–89, conslt paediatric ophthalmologist Hosp for Sick Children Gt Ormond St London 1976–, hon sr lectr Inst Child Health London 1976–; memb Cncl Royal London Soc for the Blind, fndr and organiser Help a Child to See; memb: BMA 1970, RSM 1974, American Acad of Ophthalmology 1976; FRCS 1973, FRCP 1984, FCOphth 1988; *Books* Pediatric Ophthalmology (1990, 1997), Practical Paediatric Ophthalmology (jtly, 1996); *Recreations* sailing, tennis, skiing, forestry; *Style—* David Taylor, Esq; ✉ 23 Church Road, Barnes, London SW13 9HE (☎ 0181 878 0305); 234 Great Portland Street, London W1N 5PH (☎ 0171 935 7916, fax 0171 323 5430)

TAYLOR, Prof David William; s of Leslie David Taylor (d 1973), of Erith, Kent, and Doris Evelyn, *née* Jarvis; *b* 23 Feb 1949; *Educ* Picardy Secdy Modern Sch for Boys Erith Kent, Bromley Tech Coll Bromley Kent, Univ of Southampton (BSc), Univ of Cambridge (PhD); *m* Susan Miriam, da of Donald Robert Baggett; *Career* lab technician Wellcome Labs for Tropical Med The Wellcome Fndn Langley Ct 1967–70, undergraduate Univ of Southampton 1970–73, postgraduate Univ of Cambridge 1973–77, Nat Acad of Scis (USA) post doctoral fell Nat Naval Med Center Bethesda Maryland 1977–79; Dept of Pathology Univ of Cambridge: research assoc 1979–82, sr research assoc 1982–86, lectr in parasitology 1986–94; prof of tropical animal health and dir Centre for Tropical Veterinary Med Univ of Edinburgh 1994–; memb: French Soc for Parasitology, Scandinavian Soc for Parasitology, Br Soc for Parasitology, Br Soc for Immunology, Zoological Soc of London, Royal Zoological Soc of Edinburgh; *Recreations* birdwatching, painting, cooking, gardening, living in France, DIY; *Style—* Prof David W Taylor; ✉ Centre for Tropical Veterinary Medicine, Royal (Dick) School of Veterinary Studies, The University of Edinburgh, Easter Bush, Roslin, Midlothian EH25 9RG (☎ 0131 650 6289, fax 0131 650 6289, e-mail DAVID.W.TAYLOR@ED.AC.UK)

TAYLOR, Denise Marilyn; *Educ* Belvedere Sch Liverpool, Liverpool Sch of Dental Surgery Univ of Liverpool (BDS), DipOrth RCS, Cert of Specialist Training in Orthodontics for EC purposes, Cert of Accreditation of Br Soc of Med and Dental Hypnosis; *Career* house offr Liverpool Dental Hosp and Liverpool Royal Infirmary; sr house offr: in oral and maxillofacial surgery Walton Hosp and Liverpool Dental Hosp, in children's dentistry and orthodontics St George's Hosp and Royal Dental Hosp; registrar in orthodontics Southampton Gen Hosp, clinical orthodontist Middx Hosp London and Whipps Cross Hosp Leytonstone, currently specialist in orthodontics Wexham Park Hosp Slough; memb Cncl Section of Hypnosis and Psychosomatic Medicine RSM; memb: Br Assoc of Orthodontists, BDA, RSM, Br Soc of Med and Dental Hypnosis; *Recreations* ice skating, skiing, tennis, riding, photography, art; *Style—* Ms Denise Taylor; ✉ Wexham Park Hospital, Slough, Berks SL2 4HL (☎ 01753 633000)

TAYLOR, Dennis James; s of Thomas Taylor, of Coalisland, Co Tyrone, NI, and Annie, *née* Donnelly (d 1984); *b* 19 Jan 1949; *Educ* Prima Dixon Sch; *m* 1970 (m dis 1994), Patricia Ann, *née* Burrows; 2 s (Damian Thomas b 26 June 1973, Brendon Martin b 21 Oct 1976), 1 da (Denise Ann b 27 April 1971); *partner* Louise Parr; *Career* snooker player; turned professional 1971; winner: Rothmans Grand Prix 1984, Embassy World Championship 1985, BCE Canadian Masters 1985, Kit Kat Break for World Champions 1985, Carlsberg Challenge 1986, Benson & Hedges Masters 1987, Carling Champions 1987, Labatts Canadian Masters 1987, Matchroom Championship 1987, Tokyo Masters champion 1987, Aust Masters champion 1987, World Team Championships (with Ireland) 1985–87; Irish Professional Champion 1982, 1985, 1986 and 1987; currently snooker commentator BBC; involved with the Snooker Golf Soc; *Style—* Dennis Taylor, Esq; ✉ c/o Ian Doyle, Cuemasters Ltd, Kerse Road, Stirling, Scotland (☎ 01786 462634)

TAYLOR, Donald Leslie; s of Frank St Armand Taylor, of Villeneuve Sur Lot, France, and Elizabeth Richmond, *née* Turnbull; *b* 20 Sept 1948; *Educ* Tollington GS London, Royal Agric Coll (DipAgSci, NDA, MRAC); *Career* journalist; trainee Mgmnt Devpt Prog Barclays Bank 1970–73, head office advsr Beechams 1973–74, markets and business corr British Farmer and Stockbreeder 1974–80, dep business ed Farmers Weekly 1980–82, business ed Farming News 1982–91 (also asst ed 1984–91); ed: Farming News 1991–, Whats new in Farming 1992–; tstee Morgan Grampian plc Pension Fund 1984–90; memb Guild of Agric Journalists 1974– (memb Cncl 1988–); *Recreations* stalking, wildfowling, rough shooting, game shooting, gardening, walking; *Clubs* Br Deer Soc, Br Assoc for Shooting and Conservation, East Barnet Shooting, Farmer's; *Style—* Donald Taylor, Esq; ✉ 14 Friary Way, London N12 9PH

TAYLOR, Dr Douglas Hugh Charles; s of Richard Hugh Taylor (d 1987), of Lichfield, Staffs, and Alice Mary, *née* Davis; *b* 4 April 1938; *Educ* King Edward VI GS Lichfield, Univ of Loughborough (BTech, PhD); *m* 25 July 1970, Janet Elizabeth, da of Ernest William Scott; 2 da (Emily Clare b 15 Jan 1973, Jane Victoria b 21 July 1975); *Career* research mangr Ruston & Hornsby Lincoln 1970–72 (graduate apprentice 1962); Ricardo Consulting Engineers: mangr 1972–77, dir 1977–85, md 1985–87, chm and md 1987–90; gp md Ricardo Group 1990–91; ind conslt 1991–; visiting prof Dept of Mech Engrg Loughborough Univ of Technol 1994–; memb Soc of Automotive Engrs, FIMechE, FEng 1987; *Recreations* flying, campanology; *Style—* Dr Douglas Taylor, FEng; ✉ 20 Coombe Drove, Bramber, Steyning, West Sussex BN44 3PW (☎ 01903 813566)

TAYLOR, Sir Edward Macmillan (Teddy); kt (1991), MP (C) Southend East (majority 13,111); s of Edward Taylor (d 1962), and Minnie Hamilton Taylor; *b* 18 April 1937; *Educ* Glasgow HS, Univ of Glasgow (MA); *m* 1970, Sheila, da of late Alex Duncan, of Southend-on-Sea; 2 s, 1 da; *Career* journalist with Glasgow Herald 1958–59, industl rels offr with Clyde Shipbuilders' Assoc 1959–64; MP (C): Glasgow Cathcart 1964–79, Southend E 1980– (by-election); Parly under-sec Scottish Office 1970–71 and 1974; opposition spokesman on: trade 1977, Scottish affrs 1977–79; vice chm Cons Parly Trade Ctee 1981–83, sec Cons Parly Home Affrs Ctee 1983–95; lost Cons Pty whip over extra Euro funding (one of eight) 1995; *Recreations* golf, chess; *Style—* Sir Teddy Taylor, MP; ✉ 12 Lynton Road, Thorpe Bay, Southend, Essex (☎ 01702 586282); House of Commons, London SW1A 0AA (☎ 0171 219 3476)

TAYLOR, Eric; s of Sydney Taylor (d 1979), of Wigan, Lancs, and Sarah Helen, *née* Lea (d 1982); *b* 22 Jan 1931; *Educ* Wigan GS, Univ of Manchester (LLB, LLM); *m* 7 April 1958, (Margaret) Jessie Taylor, *qv*, da of Thomas Brown Gowland (d 1951); *Career* admitted slr 1955, ptnr Temperley Taylor Chadwick 1957–, recorder of the Crown Ct 1978–; pt/t lectr in law Univ of Manchester 1958–80 (hon special lectr in law 1981–), examiner Law Soc Final Exam 1968–81 (chief examiner 1978–83); chm: Manchester Young Slrs Gp 1963, Manchester Nat Insur Appeal Tbnl 1967–73, NE Cheshire Drag Hunt 1987–; pres Oldham Law Assoc 1970–72; Law Soc: memb Cncl 1972–91, chm Educn and Trg Ctee 1980–83, chm Criminal Law Ctee 1984–87, memb Common Professional Exam (CPE) Bd 1990–; govr Coll of Law 1984–; memb: CNAA Legal Studies Bd 1975–84, Lord Chancellor's Advsy Ctee on Trg of Magistrates 1974–79; memb Law Soc 1955; *Books* Modern Conveyancy Precedents (2 edn, 1989), Modern Wills Precedents (1969, 3 edn 1996); *Recreations* horse riding, dressage; *Clubs* Farmers'; *Style—* Eric Taylor, Esq; ✉ 10 Mercers Rd, Heywood, Lancs OL10 2NP (☎ 01706 366630); Suffield House, Middleton, Manchester M24 4EL (☎ 0161 643 2411, fax 0161 655 3015)

TAYLOR, Prof Eric Andrew; s of Dr Jack Andrew Taylor, of Bruton, Somerset, and Grace, *née* Longley; *b* 22 Dec 1944; *Educ* Clifton, Univ of Cambridge (MA, MB BChir), Harvard Univ, Middx Hosp Med Sch; *m* Dr Anne Patricia Roberts, da of Edgar Roberts, of St Albans; 2 s (Thomas b 1976, Paul b 1980); *Career* prof of developmental neuropsychiatry Univ of London 1993– (reader 1987–93); ed Journal of Child Psychology and Psychiatry 1983–; memb scientific staff MRC 1990–; hon conslt child and adolescent psychiatry 1978–: Bethlem Royal Hosp, Maudsley Hosp, KCH; memb Cncl Assoc of Child Psychology and Psychiatry; FRCP 1986, FRCPsych 1988; *Books* The Overactive Child: Clinics in Developmental Medicine No 97 (1986), The Hyperactive Child: A Parent's Guide (1986), The Epidemiology of Childhood Hyperactivity (1991), Child and Adolescent Psychiatry: Modern Approaches (ed jtly, 1993); *Style—* Prof Eric Taylor; ✉ Institute of Psychiatry, De Crespigny Park, London SE5 (☎ 0171 703 5411)

TAYLOR, Chief Constable Francis William (Frank); QPM (1989), DL (Durham 1990); *b* 27 March 1933; *m* 17 Dec 1955, Sylvia; 2 s (Andrew b 17 Nov 1959, John b 6 June 1965), 1 da (Julie b 18 Feb 1957); *Career* chief superintendent Gtr Manchester Police 1958–82 (previously constable Manchester City Police), asst chief constable Lincolnshire Police 1982–85; Durham Constabulary: dep chief constable 1985–88, chief constable 1988–; chm Northern Police Convalescent Home, vice chm Home Office Standing Advsy Ctee on Police Dogs, memb and vice pres Upper Teesdale and Weardale Fell Rescue Assoc; CIMgt 1994; *Recreations* reading, music, swimming, walking; *Style—* Frank Taylor, Esq, QPM, DL; ✉ Durham Constabulary, Chief Constable's Office, Aykley Heads, Durham DH1 5TT (☎ 0191 386 4929, telex Durpol 53530, fax 0191 375 2210)

TAYLOR, Frank William; s of Frank Taylor (d 1963), and Mary Gibson, *née* Steward; *b* 7 Oct 1937; *Educ* Birkenhead Inst; *m* 3 Aug 1963, Ann; 1 s (Michael b 13 Oct 1965), 1 da (Steffanie b 28 April 1968); *Career* former ptnr Ernst & Young CAs, ret; non-exec dir: Mersey Docks and Harbour Co, Royal Liverpool Children's Hospital NHS Trust; chm Burke Ford Insurance Group; pres Insolvency Practitioners' Assoc 1973; FCA; *Recreations* golf; *Clubs* Heswall, Nefyn; *Style—* Frank Taylor, Esq; ✉ Stableford, Brook Lane, Parkgate, Wirral, Cheshire

TAYLOR, Prof Fredric William; s of William Taylor, of Swindon, Wilts, and Ena Lloyd, *née* Burns (d 1993); *b* 24 Sept 1944; *Educ* Duke's Sch, Univ of Liverpool (BSc), Univ of Oxford (DPhil); *m* 28 June 1970, Doris Jean, da of Iver Buer; *Career* sr scientist Jet Propulsion Laboratory California Inst of Technol 1970–79, head Dept of Atmospheric, Oceanic and Planetary Physics and fell Jesus Coll Univ of Oxford 1979–; medal for exceptional scientific achievement Nat Aeronautics and Space Admin 1981, Rank prize for opto-electronics 1989, special award Worshipful Co of Scientific Instrument Makers 1990; FRMS, FRAS; *Books* Cambridge Atlas of the Planets (1982 and 1986), Remote Sensing of Atmospheres (1984); *Recreations* walking, gardening, history, literature, theatre, sport, gastronomy, railways, poker; *Clubs* Meteorological; *Style—* Prof Fredric Taylor; ✉ Department of Atmospheric, Oceanic and Planetary Physics, University of Oxford, Clarendon Laboratory, Parks Road, Oxford OX1 3PU

TAYLOR, Geoffrey Newton (Geoff); s of William Henry Taylor, of Bovingdon Green, Bucks, and Elsie May Taylor; *b* 25 April 1938; *Educ* Royal GS High Wycombe, Oxford Univ (MA); *m* 1, 1963, Julia Nora Barnes; 2 s (Scott Geoffrey b 1967, Jon Michael b 1970); m 2, 1976, Janice Darleen Swett; *Career* chm and pres 3i Corp 1989–91 (dir 1985–90); dir: 3i plc 1985–90, Rodime plc 1981–89, LSI Logic (Europe) 1985–94; gen ptnr Newton Capital 1992–; *Recreations* music, tennis, pilot; *Clubs* IOD, Sloane; *Style—* Geoff Taylor; ✉ 21 South Meadow Ridge, Concord, MA 01742, USA (☎ 00 1 508 371 9293)

TAYLOR, Geoffrey William; s of Joseph William (d 1980), of Heckmondwike, Yorks, and Doris, *née* Parr (d 1984); *b* 4 Feb 1927; *Educ* Heckmondwike GS, Univ of London (BCom); *m* 21 July 1951, Joyce, da of George Clifford Walker, (d 1952), of Liversedge, Yorks; 3 s (Nigel b 1954, Christopher b 1957, Julian b 1959), 1 da (Ruth b 1966); *Career* RN 1945–47; Midland Bank 1943–87: md Midland Bank Fin Corp 1967–72, gp treas 1972–73, asst chief gen mangr 1974–80, dep gp chief exec 1980–81, gp chief exec 1982–86, vice chm 1986–87; chm: Daiwa Europe Bank plc 1987–93, Foster Menswear Ltd 1992–, Atkins Holdings Ltd 1993–, EFIS Ltd 1993–94; memb Banking Servs Law Review Ctee 1987–88, dir Y J Lovell Holdings plc 1987–, Daiwa Europe Bank plc 1987–94; Freeman City of London 1984; FCIOB 1975, FIMgt 1979; *Recreations* golf, reading, music; *Clubs* Burhill Golf; *Style—* Geoffrey Taylor, Esq; ✉ Thornlea, Stokesheath Road, Oxshott, Surrey KT22 0PS

TAYLOR, Dr George Browne; s of John Taylor, of Sunderland, and Doreen, *née* Browne; *b* 11 May 1949; *Educ* St Aidan's Sch Sunderland, Univ of Newcastle upon Tyne Med Sch (MB BS); *m* Penelope Rose Anne, *née* Stanford; 2 da (Sarah b 2 Dec 1972, Ruth b 4 May 1979), 2 s (Matthew b 15 Dec 1975, James b 13 Nov 1981); *Career* princ in gen practice Guide Post Northumberland 1976–; assoc regnl advsr in gen practice Univ of Newcastle upon Tyne 1986–; RCGP: memb Examination Bd 1982–89, memb Cncl 1992–94 and 1996–, chm Quality Network 1995–; visitor Jt Ctee on Postgrad Trg in Gen Practice 1990–; fndr Northumberland Young Practitioner Educnl Gp 1977; Nuffield visiting scholar Fiji Sch of Med 1970, RCGP visiting scholar The Netherlands 1984; FRCGP 1986 (MRCGP 1976); *Recreations* family, travel, France, wine; *Style*— Dr George Taylor; ✉ 41 Clayton Road, Newcastle upon Tyne NE2 4RQ (☎ 0191 281 1728, fax 0191 281 8268); The Royal College of General Practitioners, 14 Princes Gate, Hyde Park, London SW7 1PU (☎ 0171 581 3232, fax 0171 225 3047)

TAYLOR, Sir (Arthur) Godfrey; kt (1980), DL (Gtr London 1988); *b* 3 Aug 1925; *Career* formerly: borough cncllr, alderman, chm London Borough Assoc; chm Assoc of Met Authorities 1978–80, managing tstee Municipal Mutual Insurance Ltd 1979–86; chm: Southern Water Authy 1981–85, London Residuary Body 1985–96; Liveryman Worshipful Co of Needlemakers; *Style*— Sir Godfrey Taylor, DL; ✉ 23 Somerhill Lodge, Somerhill Rd, Hove, E Sussex BN3 1RU

TAYLOR, Gordon; s of Alec Taylor (d 1980), of Ashton under Lyne, Lancs, and Mary, *née* Walsh; *b* 28 Dec 1944; *Educ* Ashton under Lyne GS, Bolton Tech Coll, Univ of London (BSc Econ); *m* 27 July 1968, Catharine Margaret, da of Frederick Johnston, of Bury, Lancs; 2 s (Simon Mark b 1970, Jonathan Peter b 1973); *Career* professional footballer: Bolton Wanderers 1960–70, Birmingham City 1970–76, Blackburn Rovers 1976–78, Vancouver Whitecaps (N American Soccer League) 1977, Bury 1978–80; sec and chief exec Professional Footballers Assoc 1981– (chm 1978–80), pres Int Body Professional Footballers Assoc (FIF-PRO) 1994–; Hon MA Loughborough Univ; *Recreations* theatre, music, reading, watching sport; *Style*— Gordon Taylor, Esq; ✉ Professional Footballers Association, 2 Oxford Court, Bishopsgate, Manchester M2 3WQ (☎ 0161 236 0575, fax 0161 228 7229)

TAYLOR, Graham John; s of John Stanley Bennett Taylor (d 1988), of Johannesburg, SA, and Shona, *née* Fulton; *b* 20 Oct 1960; *Educ* Johannesburg Sch of Art, Ballet and Music, Pretoria Technikon (Nat Dip in Art & Design); *m* 4 Feb 1989, Gaile Margaret, da of Frederick Cosmo Dudding; *Career* graphic designer Grapplegroup Design (Pty) Ltd Johannesburg SA 1985–93 (dep creative dir 1992–93), design dir Trademark Design Ltd London 1994–; major clients incl: Ciba Geigy, Smithkline Beecham, South African Airways, Wooltru Group, Delta Motor Corporation, Capespan International, Argus Group; S African Designer of the Yr Award 1992, numerous other S African and int design awards for projects incl packaging, pubn design, corp and promotional design and typography; *Recreations* jazz, cycling; *Style*— Graham Taylor, Esq; ✉ Trademark Design Ltd, Riverside Three, 22 Hester Road, Battersea, London SW11 4AN (☎ 0171 924 2888, fax 0171 924 5207)

TAYLOR, Dr Howard Peter John; s of Ronald Taylor (d 1988), and Winifred Enid, *née* Hedge; *b* 17 April 1940; *Educ* The GS Frome Somerset, Univ of Manchester (BScTech), City Univ (PhD); *m* Eleanor Stewart, da of Stewart Maloch, of Riverside, California; 2 s (James b 8 Aug 1973, Robert b 24 June 1980); *Career* Sir Alexander Gibb & Partners: grad engr 1961–64, dep head (formerly res engr) Design Res Dept 1964–78; chief engr Downmac Concrete Ltd 1978–, currently dir of Tarmac Precast Concrete Ltd; FICE (memb 1968), FIStructE (memb 1971, pres 1993–94), FEng 1993, FRSA 1994; *Awards* for published work: American Soc of Civil Engrs, Permanent Way Inst, Inst of Structural Engrs; *Books* Precast Concrete Cladding (1992); *Recreations* tennis, walking, books; *Style*— Dr Howard Taylor, FEng; ✉ Tarmac Precast Concrete Ltd, Tallington, Stamford, Lincs PE9 4RL (☎ 01778 381000, fax 01778 348041)

TAYLOR, Hugh Henderson; s of Leslie Henderson Taylor (d 1982), and Alison, *née* Brown; *b* 22 March 1950; *Educ* Brentwood Sch, Emmanuel Coll Cambridge (BA); *m* 13 May 1989, Diane Heather, da of Idwal George Bacon; 2 da (Alice Joy b 25 Sept 1991, Madeleine Louise b 6 May 1993); *Career* Home Office: admin trainee 1972–77, private sec to Min of State 1976–77, princ Criminal Policy Dept 1981–83 (Radio Regulatory Dept 1977–81), princ private sec to Home Sec 1983–85, asst sec 1984, head of Parole and Lifer Div 1985–88, seconded to Cabinet Office 1988–91, head of Personnel Div Prison Service 1992–93, under sec 1993–, seconded as head of Civil Service Employer Gp Cabinet Office (OPS) 1993–96 and dir of Top Mgmnt Prog 1994–96, dir of servs Prison Service 1996–; *Recreations* reading, watching cricket, rugby and football, music and opera, visiting galleries; *Style*— Hugh Taylor, Esq; ✉ Cabinet Office, Horseguards Parade, London SW1

TAYLOR, Rt Rev Humphrey; *see:* Selby, Bishop of

TAYLOR, Iain Scott; OBE (1991), TD; s of John Ross Taylor (d 1963), of Kerryston House, Kellas, by Dundee, Angus, and Annie, *née* Scott Paterson (d 1982); *b* 1 June 1931; *Educ* Dundee HS, Merchiston Castle Sch; *m* 8 Aug 1956, Nancy Christine, da of Dr William Allison (d 1979), of Dundee; 2 s (Alastair b 1958, Andrew b 1964), 2 da (Shirley b 1960, Sandra b 1962); *Career* Nat Serv RAF Regt 1950–52 (Pilot Offr 1951, Sqdn Adj 23 LAA Sqdn 1951–52, Flt Cdr 1952); TA 1953–75: Fife and Forfar Yeomanry 1953–56, FFY Scottish Horse 1956–66, Maj Sqdn Cdr 1966–71, 2 i/c 1971, OC Highland Yeo at disbandment 1975; Army Cadet Force: Lt-Col Cmdt Angus-Dundee Bn 1976–79, Col 1979–89, cadet Force Medal 1988, Brig 1989, Cmdt Scotland 1989–94; WS Taylor & Co Ltd 1952–56, sole ptnr A Watson & Co 1956–63, jt ptnr Taylor Stewart Ltd 1961–66, fin dir John Cooper & Sons Ltd; non-exec dir: Century Aluminium Co Ltd 1969–77, Kinnes Oilfield Services Ltd 1974–80; schs liaison offr Tayside Region Dundee Chamber of Commerce 1983; chm Lord Armitstead Tst, tstee and memb exec and Scottish Veterans Residences (chm Ctee Rosendael House), chm Dundee Dist Scottish Veterans' Garden City Assoc, hon treas (formerly founding chm) Murroes & Wellbank Community Cncl, elder Murroes Parish Church, vice pres ACF Assoc (Scotland) 1994–, memb Ctee ABF (Scotland) 1994–, chm Angus St John Assoc 1994–; SBStJ 1993, OStJ 1995; curling: memb RCCC Cncl 1981–84, memb Scottish Team in Switzerland 1980; *Recreations* shooting, curling, swimming, sailing, philately, militaria; *Clubs* Army and Navy; *Style*— Iain S Taylor, Esq, OBE, TD; ✉ Tigh-Na-Torr, Kellas, Dundee DD5 3PD (☎ 01382 350327)

TAYLOR, Ian Charles Boucher; s of Leslie Charles Taylor, of Kidderminster, Worcs, and Freda May, *née* Bell; *b* 24 Sept 1954; *Educ* Queen Elizabeth GS Hartlebury Worcs, Borough Road Coll, West London Inst of Higher Educn Univ of London (BEd, CertEd); *m* 25 Oct 1980, Julie Ann, da of James William Whitehead, of Whitestone, Nuneaton, Warwicks; 2 s (Simon Christopher b 16 Nov 1984, Oliver Sebastian b 9 Nov 1986); *Career* former hockey goalkeeper; England hockey career: World Cup Buenos Aires 1978, Euro Cup Hanover 1979 (Bronze), World Cup Bombay 1982–83, Euro Cup Amsterdam 1983, World Cup London 1986 (Silver), Euro Cup Moscow 1987 (Silver); GB career Champion's Trophy: Lahore 1978, Karachi 1981, 1982, 1984 (Bronze), Perth 1985 (Silver), Lahore 1986, Amsterdam 1987, Lahore 1988; Los Angeles Olympics 1984 (Bronze), Seoul Olympics 1988 (Gold), voted best goalkeeper for 11 consecutive years, captained World XI 12 times; memb Exec Mgmnt Ctee and Tech Ctee Hockey Assoc, minister's nominee on Regnl Sports Cncl; company managing dir; *Books* Taylor On Hockey (1988), Behind The Mask (1989); *Recreations* golf, antiques; *Style*— Ian Taylor, Esq; ✉ Simol House, 42 Stamford Road, Oakham, Rutland LE15 6JA

TAYLOR, Ian Colin; MBE (1974), MP (C) Esher (majority 20,371); s of late Horace Stanley Taylor, and late Beryl, *née* Harper; *b* 18 April 1945; *Educ* Whitley Abbey Sch Coventry, Univ of Keele (BA), LSE; *m* 17 June 1974, Hon Carole Alport, da of Baron Alport (Life Peer), *qv*; 2 s (Arthur b 1977, Ralph b 1980); *Career* MP (C) Esher 1987–, memb Foreign Affrs Select Ctee 1987–90, PPS to Rt Hon William Waldegrave MP 1990–94, Parly under-sec DTI 1994–; memb Cons Nat Union Exec Ctee 1967–75 and 1990–95, nat chm Fedn of Cons Students 1968–69, chm Euro Union of Christian Democratic and Cons Students 1969–70, hon sec Br Cons Assoc in France 1976–78; chm: Cons Gp for Europe 1985–88, Cwlth Youth Exchange Cncl 1980–84 (vice-pres 1984–), Cons Back Bench Euro Affrs Ctee 1988–89, Cons Foreign and Cwlth Cncl 1990–95; patron UK Centre for Euro Educn 1991–94; dir Mathercourt Securities Ltd 1980–91, consIt Commercial Union plc 1988–94, consIt BZW Investment Management Ltd 1991–94; AIIMR 1972; *Publications* pamphlets: Under Some Delusion (1975), Fair Shares for all the Workers (1988), Releasing the Community Spirit (1990), A Community of Employee Shareholders (1992), The Positive Europe (1993), Networking (1996); *Recreations* playing cricket, opera, shooting; *Clubs* Carlton; *Style*— Ian Taylor, Esq, MBE, MP; ✉ House of Commons, London SW1A 0AA (☎ 0171 219 5221, fax 0171 219 5492)

TAYLOR, Ian Stuart; s of Alan Taylor, of Horsforth, Leeds, and Phyllis, *née* Hutchinson; *b* 21 June 1951; *Educ* Bradford GS, Univ Coll Durham (BA); *m* 1 May 1976, Ann Lynda, da of Harold Sydney Foley; 2 da (Emma Elizabeth b 22 Sept 1980, Katherine Victoria b 11 May 1983); *Career* library asst Shrewsbury BC 1973–74, museum asst Shrewsbuy & Atcham BC 1974–76, dep curator Castle Museum York 1976–81, dir Big Pit Mining Museum Blaenavon Gwent 1981–86, dir NW Museums Serv 1986–; convenor Gp of Area Museum Cncl Dirs 1990–; served bds of mgmnt: NW Tourist Bd, NW Arts Bd; FMA; *Books* Forward Planning - A Handbook to Business (contrib, 1992); *Style*— Ian Taylor, Esq; ✉ 5 Brett Close, Clitheroe, Lancs BB7 1LN (☎ 01200 423001): North West Museums Service, Griffin Lodge, Cavendish Place, Blackburn, Lancs BB2 2PN (☎ 01254 670211, fax 01254 681995)

TAYLOR, Prof Irving; s of Samuel Taylor (d 1982), and Fay, *née* Valcovitch; *b* 7 Jan 1945; *Educ* Roundhay Sch Leeds, Univ of Sheffield Med Sch (MB ChB, MD, ChM); *m* 31 Aug 1969, Berenice Penelope, da of Dr Henry Brunner, of Slough; 3 da (Justine Samantha b 20 Oct 1971, Tamara Zoe b 5 June 1973, Gabrielle Rivka b 31 Aug 1983); *Career* sr registrar surgery Sheffield 1973–77 (registrar surgery 1971–73, res registrar 1973), sr lectr in surgery Liverpool 1977–81, prof of surgery and head Dept of Surgery Univ of Southampton 1981–93, head Dept of Surgery and chm Bd of Surgery UCL 1993–; Hunterian prof RCS 1981; sec: Surgical Res Soc 1985–87, Assoc of Profs of Surgery 1988; ed sec Assoc of Surgns 1987, ed-in-chief Euro Jl of Surgical Oncology; pres Br Assoc Surgical Oncology; chm MRC Colorectal Working Party; FRCS 1972, memb RSM 1982; *Books* Complications of Surgery of Lower Gastrointestinal Tract (1985), Progress in Surgery 1 (1985), Progress in Surgery 2 (1987), Progress in Surgery 3 (1989), Benign Breast Disease (1989), Recent Advances in Surgery 14–18 (1990, 1992, 1993, 1994 and 1995); *Recreations* swimming, golf, tennis; *Clubs* RSM; *Style*— Prof Irving Taylor; ✉ Department of Surgery, UCL Medical School, 67–73 Riding House Street, London W1P 7LD (☎ 0171 380 9312, fax 0171 636 5176)

TAYLOR, His Hon Ivor Ralph; QC (1973); s of late Abraham Taylor, and late Ruth Taylor; *b* 26 Oct 1927; *Educ* Stand GS Whitefield, Univ of Manchester; *m* 1, 1954 (m dis 1974), Ruth Cassel; 1 s, 1 da; m 2 (m dis); m 3, 1984, (Audrey) Joyce Goldman, *née* Wayne; *Career* AC2 RAF 1945; called to the Bar Gray's Inn 1951; standing counsel to Inland Revenue Northern Circuit 1969–73, recorder of the Crown Ct 1972–76, circuit judge 1976–94; govr Royal Manchester Children's Hosp 1967–70, memb Mgmnt Ctee Salford Hosp Mgmnt Ctee 1967–70, pres Manchester and Dist Medico Legal Soc 1974–75; *Style*— His Hon Ivor R Taylor, QC; ✉ 5 Eagle Lodge, 19 Harrop Road, Hale, Altrincham, Cheshire WA15 9DA

TAYLOR, James Alastair; s of Alastair Robert Taylor (d 1983), of Nairn, and Margaret Robertson Fraser; *b* 21 Feb 1951; *Educ* Nairn Acad, Univ of Aberdeen (BSc, LLB); *m* 1 Nov 1980, Lesley Doig MacLeod; 2 s (Andrew James b May 1983, Robbie MacLeod b June 1985); *Career* apprentice to Brander & Cruickshank and Lefevre & Co Aberdeen 1975–77, asst then ptnr A C Morrison & Richards Aberdeen 1978–86; McGrigor Donald: joined 1987, ptnr 1988–, currently head Litigation Dept; slr advocate (practising in Court of Session) 1993–; convenor Rights of Audience Trg Course 1995–; memb Indust Law Gp Law Soc 1979–87, memb Law Soc of Scotland; *Recreations* golf, swimming, music, food and wine; *Clubs* Pollok Golf, Royal Aberdeen Golf, Nairn Golf; *Style*— James Taylor, Esq; ✉ McGrigor Donald, Erskine House, 68–73 Queen Street, Edinburgh EH2 4NF (☎ 0131 226 7777, fax 0131 226 7700)

TAYLOR, Prof James Allan (Jim); s of John William Taylor (d 1949), of St Helens, Merseyside, and Ethel, *née* Middlehurst (d 1972); *b* 20 June 1925; *Educ* Prescot GS, Univ of Liverpool (BA, MA, DipEd); *m* 31 March 1962, Sylvia Brenda, da of William Reginald Parr (d 1963), of Christleton, Chester; 1 s (Marcus b 31 Aug 1966), 1 da (Amanda b 29 March 1964); *Career* geography master: Pudsey GS Yorks 1946–47, Farnworth GS Bolton Lancs 1947–49; successively lectr, sr lectr, reader then prof Dept of Geography UCW Aberystwyth 1950–91; moderator for geography A-level with ULEAC 1978–93, environmental consIt 1980–88, dir and sec Environmental Consultants Ltd (incl nine assoc consIts and Bracken Control Advsy Service) 1989–; chm: Int Bracken Gp 1986–, Prescot GS Old Boys' Annual Reunions 1981–; memb: Geographical Assoc 1948–90, Inst Br Geographers 1950, Assoc of Br Climatologists 1970, Biogeography Research Gp 1976, Royal Geographical Soc 1990; *Books* incl: British Weather in Maps (with R A Yates, 1958), Weather and Agriculture (ed, 1967), Weather Economics (ed, 1970), Climatic Resources and Economic Activity (ed, 1974), Culture and Environment in Prehistoric Wales (ed, 1980), Themes in Biogeography (ed, 1984), Integrated Physical Geography (1994), Bracken: An Environmental Issue (jt ed, 1995); Proceedings of an International Bracken Conference (1994); *Recreations* contributions on environmental issues to radio and television, golf, jazz piano, walking; *Style*— Prof Jim Taylor; ✉ Glyn Ceiro, Dole, Bow Street, Aberystwyth, Dyfed, Wales SY24 5AE (☎ 01970 828436, fax 01970 622455)

TAYLOR, Dr James Francis Nuttall; s of Evan Nuttall Taylor (d 1994), of Bromley, Kent, and Margaret Susie, *née* Howes (d 1979); *b* 19 Oct 1938; *Educ* Sherborne, Queens' Coll Cambridge (MA, MB BChir, MD), St Thomas's Hosp Med Sch; *m* 18 Sept 1965, Ann, da of Ernest Ensor (d 1985); 4 s (Jonathan James Nuttall b 30 May 1969, Andrew David Nuttall b 10 Aug 1970, Richard Paul Nuttall b 31 Jan 1973, Michael Christopher Nuttall b 14 June 1974); *Career* res fell: Yale Univ Sch of Med New Haven Conn 1971–72, Br Heart Assoc 1972–75; consIt paediatric cardiologist Gt Ormond St Hosp for Children 1975–, sr lectr Inst of Child Health 1975–, hon consIt paediatric cardiologist E Anglian RHA 1978–; memb Bd of Govrs Gt Ormond St Hosp 1982–84 and 1985–90; memb: Br Paediatric Assoc 1970, Br Cardiac Soc 1971, Assoc Euro Paediatrics Cardiologists 1975; FRCP 1978, FACC 1979, FRSM 1985; Knight Order of Falcon (Iceland) 1981; *Recreations* music, photography, walking; *Style*— Dr James Taylor; ✉ 1 Bolton Gardens, Bromley, Kent BR1 4ES (☎ 0181 464 8027); Cardiac Wing, Great Ormond Street Hospital for Children, London WC1N 3JH (☎ 0171 430 2987, fax 0171 430 2995)

TAYLOR, (Margaret) Jessie; OBE (1989); da of Thomas Brown Gowland (d 1951), of Middleton, Manchester, and Ann Goldie, *née* Brighouse (d 1962); *b* 30 Nov 1924; *Educ* Queen Elizabeth GS Middleton, Univ of Manchester (BA, DipEd); *m* 7 April 1958, Eric Taylor, *qv*, s of Sydney Taylor (d 1979), of Wigan; *Career* jr classics teacher Cheadle Hulme Sch 1946–49; N Manchester GS for Girls: sr classics teacher 1950, sr mistress 1963, actg headmistress 1967; dep headteacher Wright Robinson HS 1967–75, headmistress Whalley Range HS for Girls 1976–88, chm Manchester HS Heads 1982–88; dir Piccadilly Radio 1980–; memb Cncl Examining Ctee Assoc Lancs Schs Examining

Bd 1976–89, conslt course tutor NW Educn Mgmnt Centre 1980–82; memb: Nurse Educn Ctee S Manchester Area 1976–88, Williams Ctee (Home Office Ctee on Obscenity and Censorship) 1977–79, Ct of Univ of Salford 1982–88, Northern Examining Assoc (NEA) Examinations Ctee 1988–92, UNICEF 1988 (schs links organiser and memb Nat Exec Ctee), British Horse Soc (riding and equitation jumping judge, stable mgmnt examiner) Northern Dressage Gp, Middleton Musical Soc, Cheshire Drag Hunt, Middleton Parish Church; FRSA 1979; *Recreations* music, riding; *Clubs* Leigh Riding, Rochdale Riding; *Style*— Mrs M Jessie Taylor, OBE; ✉ 10 Mercers Rd, Hopwood, Heywood, Lancs OL10 2NP (☎ 01706 366630)

TAYLOR, Hon (Joan Evelyn); *née* Underhill; da of Baron Underhill, CBE (Life Peer; d 1993), and Flora Janet, *née* Philbrick; *b* 11 April 1944; *Educ* Warren Farm Secdy Sch Birmingham, Brooklyn Tech Coll Birmingham, Open Univ; *m* 1, 9 Oct 1965 (m dis 1973), Edwin Fennell; 1 s (Adrian b 5 July 1969); m 2, 28 July 1973 (m dis 1989), Ian Robert Taylor; 2 s (Patrick b 11 May 1975, David b 1 Nov 1979); m 3, 24 Oct 1993, John Robert Stocks; *Career* private sec Labour Party HQ 1960–64; cncllr: Nottingham City Cncl 1972–74, Nottinghamshire CC 1973–77 and 1985– (chm Social Servs Ctee 1985–94, sec Lab Gp 1995–), Selston PC 1983–87 and 1990– (chm 1986–87); Assoc of CCs: memb 1987–, sec Lab Gp 1987–95, chm Social Servs Ctee 1993–94, ldr Lab Gp 1995–, chm Policy Ctee 1996–, vice chm 1996–; Local Govt Assoc: memb Policy Ctee 1996–, memb Exec Ctee 1996–, chief whip Labour Gp 1996–; active memb and office holder GMB/APEX (TU); chm Regnl Exec Ctee Labour Party; memb GMB's Parly Panel; Lab Parly candidate 1992; tstee Child Migrants Tst; *Recreations* politics, bobbin lace making, gardening, golf; *Style*— The Hon Joan Taylor; ✉ 88 Mansfield Rd, Selston, Notts NG16 6ER (☎ 01773 812655, fax 01773 811770); County Hall, West Bridgford, Nottingham NG2 7QP (☎ 0115 977 3204, fax 0115 982 2432)

TAYLOR, Sir Jock (John) Lang; KCMG (1979, CMG 1974); s of Sir John William Taylor, KBE, CMG; *b* 3 Aug 1924; *Educ* Prague, Vienna, ISC Windsor; *m* 1952, Molly, only da of James Rushworth; 5 s; *Career* RAFVR 1944–47, Flt Lt 1946; joined HM Foreign Serv 1949; served: FO 1949–50 and 1957–60, Saigon 1950–52, Hanoi 1951, Beirut 1952–55, Prague 1955–57, Montevideo 1960–64, Bonn 1964–69; min Buenos Aires 1969–71, RCDS 1972, head of Indust Science and Energy Dept FCO 1972–73, asst under-sec of state FCO 1973–74, under-sec Dept of Energy 1974–75; ambass to: Venezuela 1975–79, the Netherlands 1979–81; chm Latin American Trade Advsy Gp BOTB 1986–89, vice chm Hispanic and Luso-Brazilian Cncls 1987, tstee Anglo-American Fndn for the Study of Industl Soc 1988; *Style*— Sir Jock Taylor, KCMG; ✉ The Old Flint, Boxgrove, nr Chichester, West Sussex

TAYLOR, John; MBE (1981); s of Percival Henry Taylor (d 1969), and Florence, *née* Jeffries (d 1981); *b* 4 March 1928; *Educ* Peter Symonds, Winchester; *m* 1, 1949, Joyce, da of Harold Hodson (d 1970); 3 s (Patrick b 1950, Ian b 1953, Andrew b 1964), 2 da (Janet b 1956, Jillian b 1960); m 2, 1980, Christiane, da of Capt Edouard Jean Talou (d 1947); *Career* cmmnd RE 1947; chartered architect and designer; fndr: Taylor & Crowther (princ) 1952, John Taylor Architects (sole princ) 1963, Marshman Warren Taylor (jt princ) 1968, MWT Architects (chm) 1972, MWT Planning 1975, MWT Landscapes 1982, MWT Design 1986; fndr and chm The Co of Designers plc 1986–90, fndr and sole princ John Taylor Architects 1991–95, sr ptnr Kensington Taylor Architects 1995–; 7 times Gold medallist DOE Housing Award, 5 times Civic Tst Award; FRIBA, FCSD; *Recreations* sailing, travel; *Style*— John Taylor, Esq, MBE; ✉ Milbury Barton, Exminster, Exeter (☎ 01392 824151); Kensington Taylor Architects (☎ 01392 4200081)

TAYLOR, Rt Rev John Bernard; s of George Ernest Taylor and Gwendoline Irene Taylor; *b* 6 May 1929; *Educ* Watford GS, Christ's Coll Cambridge, Jesus Coll Cambridge (MA); *m* 1956, Linda Courtenay, da of Allan Dearden Barnes (d 1976); 1 s, 2 da; *Career* former examining chaplain to Bishop of Chelmsford, archdeacon of W Ham 1975–80, bishop of St Albans 1980–95, Lord High Almoner to HM the Queen 1988–; took seat House of Lords 1985; author; Hon LLD Univ of Herefordshire 1995; *Books* A Christian's Guide to the Old Testament, Tyndale Commentary on Ezekiel, Understanding the Old Testament: the Minor Prophets, Preaching through the Prophets, Preaching on God's Justice; *Style*— The Rt Rev John Taylor; ✉ 22 Conduit Head Road, Cambridge CB3 0EY (☎ 01223 313783)

TAYLOR, Prof John Bryan; s of Frank Herbert Taylor (d 1978), and Ada, *née* Stinton (d 1973); *b* 26 Dec 1928; *Educ* Oldbury GS, Univ of Birmingham (BSc, PhD); *m* 18 Aug 1951, Joan Margaret, da of Ivor William Hargest (d 1957); 1 s (Paul Robert John b 1961), 1 da (Helen Margaret b 1957); *Career* Flying Officer RAF 1950–52; head of Theoretical Physics Div and chief physicist UK AEA Culham Laboratory 1962–89, chm Plasma Physics Div Inst of Physics 1972–73, Fondren fndn prof of plasma theory Univ of Texas at Austin 1989–94; numerous contribs to jls; FInstP 1969, FRS 1970, fell American Physical Soc 1984; *Recreations* model engineering, gliding; *Style*— Prof J B Taylor, FRS; ✉ Radwinter, Winterbrook Lane, Wallingford, Oxon OX10 9EJ (☎ 01491 837269, fax 01235 463435)

TAYLOR, John Charles; QC (1984); s of Sidney Herbert Taylor (d 1977), of St Ives, Cambridgeshire, and Gertrude Florence, *née* Law; *b* 22 April 1931; *Educ* Palmer's Sch Essex, Queens' Coll Cambridge (MA, LLB), Harvard Univ (LLM); *m* 1964, Jean Aimée, da of William Rankin Monteith (d 1976), late of Purston Manor, Brackley, Northants; 1 da (Victoria Mary Aimée (Mrs Stephen Wolfe-Brown) b 1967); *Career* memb Stevens Ctee on Minerals Planning Control 1972–74; chm EIP Panel for Leics and Rutland Structure Plan 1985; apptd inspr by Sec of State for the Environment for County Hall London Inquiries 1990 and 1991; *Recreations* country pursuits, boardsailing, skiing, sailing; *Clubs* Athenaeum, Travellers', Royal Ocean Racing; *Style*— John Taylor, Esq, QC; ✉ Clifton Grange, Clifton, Shefford, Beds; 2 Mitre Court Buildings, Temple, London EC4Y 7BX (☎ 0171 583 1380)

TAYLOR, Rt Hon John David; PC (NI 1970), MP (UU) Strangford (majority 8,911); s of George David Taylor, of Armagh (d 1979), and Georgina, *née* Baird (d 1986); *b* 24 Dec 1937; *Educ* Royal Sch Armagh, Queen's Univ Belfast (BSc); *m* 1970, Mary Frances, da of Ernest Leslie Todd (d 1985); 1 s (Jonathan), 5 da (Jane, Rachel, Rowena, Alex, Hannah); *Career* memb (UU): NI Parliament Stormont (memb for S Tyrone) 1965–73 (min of state Miny of Home Affrs 1970–72), NI Assembly (memb for Fermanagh and S Tyrone) 1973–75, NI Constitutional Convention (memb for N Down) 1975–76, NI Assembly (memb for N Down) 1982–86; MEP NI 1979–89, MP (UU) Strangford 1983–; chartered engr; dir: West Ulster Estates Ltd 1968–, Bramley Apple Restaurant Ltd 1974–, Ulster Gazette (Armagh) Ltd 1983–, Gosford Housing Assoc (Armagh) Ltd 1978–, Cerdac Print (Belfast) Ltd, Tyrone Printing Ltd, Tyrone Courier Ltd, Sovereign Properties (NI) Ltd, Tontine Rooms Holding Co Ltd; *Clubs* Armagh County, Armagh City, Farmers' (Whitehall London); *Style*— The Rt Hon John D Taylor, MP; ✉ Mullinure, Armagh, N Ireland BT61 9EL (☎ 01861 522409)

TAYLOR, Prof John Gerald; s of Dr William Taylor (d 1984), and Elsie, *née* Boyd (d 1986); *b* 18 Aug 1931; *Educ* Lancaster GS, Blackburn GS, Chelmsford GS, Mid Essex Tech Coll (BSc), Christ's Coll Cambridge (BSc, BA, MA, PhD); *m* 1 (m dis); m 2, Pamela Nancy, da of late Matthew Cutmore; 2 s (Geoffrey, Robin), 3 da (Frances, Susan, Elizabeth); *Career* Cwlth fell Inst for Advanced Study Princeton NJ USA 1956–58, res fell Christ's Coll Cambridge 1958–60 (asst lectr Faculty of Mathematics 1959–60); memb: Inst Hautes Études Scientifiques Paris 1960–61, Inst for Advanced Study Princeton 1961–63; sr res fell Churchill Coll Cambridge 1963–64, prof of physics Rutger Univ NJ USA 1964–66, lectr in Mathematics Inst and fell Hertford Coll Oxford 1966–67, lectr and reader QMC London 1967–69, prof of physics Univ of Southampton 1969–71, prof of mathematics King's Coll London 1971–, dir Centre for Neural Networks King's Coll 1990–; chm: Mathematics and Physics Gp Inst of Physics 1981–86 (vice chm 1988–91), Jt Euro Neural Networks Initiative Cncl 1990–91; Euro ed in chief Neural Networks 1990–; convenor Br Neural Network Soc 1988–92; vice pres European Neural Network Soc 1991–93 and 1994– (pres 1993–94), pres Int Neural Network Soc 1995 (memb Governing Bd 1992–), dir NEURONET EC Network of Excellence 1994; fell Cambridge Philosophy Soc; FInstP; *Books* Quantum Mechanics (1969), The Shape of Minds to Come (1971), The New Physics (1972), Black Holes: The End of the Universe? (1973), Superminds (1975), Special Relativity (1975), Science and the Supernatural (1980), The Horizons of Knowledge (1982), Finite Superstrings (1992), The Promise of Neural Networks (1993), When the Clock Struck Zero (1993); over 400 sci papers, ed 14 books and numerous radio and TV programmes on popular science; *Recreations* travelling, listening to music, theatre, reading; *Style*— Prof John Taylor; ✉ 33 Meredyth Rd, Barnes, London SW13 0DS (☎ 0181 876 3391); Dept of Mathematics, King's Coll, Strand, London WC2R 2LS (☎ 0171 873 2214, fax 0171 873 2017)

TAYLOR, John Hilton; s of Charles Ronald Taylor, of St Helens, Merseyside, and Brenda, *née* Hilton; *b* 7 May 1958; *Educ* Grange Park Secdy Sch St Helens, Cowley Boys Sch St Helens, Univ of Birmingham (BA, PhD); *m* 24 Sept 1988, Rhona Margaret, da of James Henry Minshull; 1 da (Katherine Sarah Minshull Taylor b 29 Aug 1991), 1 s (James Nicholas Minshull b 26 Oct 1994); *Career* Egyptologist; memb Egypt Exploration Soc expedition to Amarna 1981, lectr in Egyptology: Workers Educnl Assoc 1981 and 1985–86, Dept of Extramural Studies Univ of Birmingham 1985–87; curator Dept of Egyptian Antiquities British Museum 1988–; specialist conslt to Gold of the Pharaohs exhbn City Art Centre Edinburgh 1987–88, exhbn organiser Howard Carter - Before Tutankhamun Br Museum 1992–93; ctee memb Egypt Exploration Soc 1988–91 and 1993–95 (hon librarian 1993–), reviews ed jl of Egyptian Archaeology 1993–, ed Egyptian Archaeology 1994–96; hon fell Inst for Advanced Res in the Humanities Univ of Birmingham 1987–89; *Books* Egyptian Coffins (1989), Egypt and Nubia (1991), Howard Carter - Before Tutankhamun (with Nicholas Reeves, 1992), Unwrapping a Mummy (1995); *Recreations* genealogy, English literature, music; *Style*— John Taylor, Esq; ✉ Department of Egyptian Antiquities, The British Museum, Great Russell Street, London WC1B 3DG (☎ 0171 323 8330)

TAYLOR, John Leonard; s of Leonard William Taylor, and Kathleen, *née* Markey; *b* 21 June 1957; *Educ* St Peter's Sch Southbourne; *m* Moyra; 1 da (Verity b 5 Sept 1989), 1 s (Sean b 22 Jan 1992); *Career* media planner/buyer Allen Brady & Marsh Ltd 1975–78; FCB Advertising Ltd: media mangr 1978–86, media dir 1986–90, dep md 1990–92; md Optimedia UK 1992–96, dir of Euro ops Optimedia International Ltd 1996–; *Recreations* marathon running, motorcycling, golf, skiing; *Style*— John Taylor, Esq; ✉ Optimedia International Ltd, 84–86 Baker Street, London W1M 1DL (☎ 0171 935 0040, fax 0171 486 1985)

TAYLOR, John Mark; MP (C) Solihull (majority 25,146); s of Wilfred Taylor and Eileen Taylor; *b* 19 Aug 1941; *Educ* Bromsgrove, Coll of Law; *Career* admitted slr 1966; memb: Solihull Cncl 1971–74, W Mids CC 1973–86 (ldr 1977–79); Parly candidate (C) Dudley E Feb and Oct 1974; MEP (EDG) Mids E 1979–84, dep chm Cons Gp Euro Parl 1981–82; MP (C) Solihull 1983–, memb House of Commons Environment Select Ctee 1983–87, PPS to Chllr of the Duchy of Lancaster 1987–88, asst Govt whip 1988–89, Lord Cmmr of the Treasy (Govt whip) 1989–90, Vice-Chamberlain of HM Household (sr Govt whip) 1990–92, Parly sec Lord Chllr's Dept 1992–95, Parly under sec of state DTI 1995–; govr Univ of Birmingham 1977–81; *Recreations* cricket, golf and reading; *Clubs* Carlton, MCC; *Style*— John Taylor, Esq, MP; ✉ Northampton House, Poplar Road, Solihull, West Midlands B91 3AW (☎ 0121 704 3071)

TAYLOR, Dr John Michael; OBE (1994); s of Eric John Taylor (d 1979), and Dorothy Irene, *née* Spring; *b* 15 Feb 1943; *Educ* King Edward's Sch Birmingham, Emmanuel Coll Cambridge (MA, PhD); *m* 14 Aug 1965, Judith, da of Maurice Moyle; 2 s (Michael James b 21 April 1967, David Charles b 13 April 1971), 2 da (Miranda Elizabeth b 14 Feb 1969, Lydia Jane b 7 March 1976); *Career* res engr GEC Hirst Res Centre 1965–66; UK Govt 1969–84: supt Computer Applications Div RSRE Malvern 1979–81, head of Command Systems Div Admiralty Surface Weapons Estab 1981–82, head of Command Control and Communications Dept Admiralty Res Estab 1982–84; dir Info Systems Laboratory Hewlett-Packard Laboratories 1984–86, dir Bristol Res Centre 1986–90, dir Hewlett-Packard Laboratories Europe 1990–, memb Bd of Dirs Hewlett Packard Ltd 1992–; visiting industl prof Univ of Bristol 1985–, visiting prof Imperial Coll of Sci Technol and Med Univ of London 1990–; memb Technol and Innovation Ctee CBI 1988–, chm ITEC Panel UK OST Technology Foresight Prog 1994–, dep pres UK IEE 1996–; FEng 1986, FIEE, FBCS, FRSA, MInstD 1992; *Recreations* family, music, theatre, photography, sailing; *Style*— Dr John M Taylor, OBE, FEng; ✉ Hewlett-Packard Laboratories, Filton Rd, Stoke Gifford, Bristol BS12 6QZ (☎ 0117 922 8052, fax 0117 922 8923, e-mail jmt@hplb.hpl.hp.com)

TAYLOR, Rt Rev John Mitchell; *see:* Glasgow and Galloway, Bishop of

TAYLOR, John Richard Creighton; s of Richard Henry Chase Taylor (d 1987), and Rachel Loveday, *née* Creighton; *b* 17 Dec 1942; *Educ* Malvern Coll, Ecole des Hautes Etudes Commerciales Paris; *m* 7 Feb 1970, Sarah Barbour, da of Peter Thomas Simon Brown; 2 s (Oliver b 1973, Humphrey b 1981), 2 da (Eliza b 1972, Sophie b 1976); *Career* dir: Vine Products and Whiteways 1981–84, Grants of St James's 1984–94, London Wine Bars 1984–, Trouncer Wine and Spirit Merchants 1985–90; chm and md Hatch, Mansfield and Co 1984–94; Liveryman Worshipful Co of Distillers 1980, memb Inst of Masters of Wine 1972; *Recreations* opera, theatre, walking, foreign interests, all sports; *Clubs* RAC; *Style*— John Taylor, Esq; ✉ The Coach House, South Wanborough, nr Basingstoke, Hants RG25 1RR (☎ 01256 862782)

TAYLOR, John Russell; s of Arthur Russell Taylor (d 1966), of Dover, Kent, and Kathleen Mary, *née* Picker (d 1991); *b* 19 June 1935; *Educ* Dover GS, Jesus Coll Cambridge (MA), Courtauld Inst of Art London; *Career* The Times: sub-ed Educnl Supplement 1959–60, ed asst Literary Supplement 1960–62, film critic 1962–73, art critic 1978–; prof of Cinema Div Univ of Southern California 1972–78, ed Films and Filming 1983–90; memb: Critics' Circle 1962, Private Libraries Assoc 1967 (pres 1986–88), Assoc Art Historians 1985; AICA 1978; *Books* incl: Anger and After (1962), Cinema Eye Cinema Ear (1964), The Art Nouveau Book in Britain (1966), The Rise and Fall of the Well-Made Play (1967), The Art Dealers (1969), The Hollywood Musical (1971), The Second Wave (1971), Graham Greene on Film (ed 1972), Directors and Directions (1975), Hitch (1978), Impressionism (1981), Strangers in Paradise (1983), Alec Guinness (1984), Edward Wolfe (1986), Orson Welles (1986), Bernard Meninsky (1990), Impressionist Dreams (1990), Ricardo Cinalli (1992), Muriel Pemberton (1993), Igor Mitoraj (1994), Claude Monet (1995), Michael Parkes (1996), Bill Jacklin (1997), Tne Sun is God (1997); *Recreations* buying books, talking to strange dogs; *Style*— John Russell Taylor, Esq; ✉ The Times, 1 Pennington Street, London E1 9XN (☎ 0171 782 5000, fax 0171 782 5748)

TAYLOR, John Stephen; s of Maj Gerald Howard Taylor (d 1963), and Helen Mary Rivett, *née* Harrington (d 1993); *b* 26 Dec 1928; *Educ* Stowe, Trinity Coll Cambridge (MA), Architectural Assoc London (AADipl); *m* 1, 1956 (m dis 1963), Tye Pagan, da of Tully Grigg, of Biot, France; 1 s (Fred b 1963), 1 da (Nona b 1960); m 2, 1965, Susan Marriott Sweet; *Career* joined Irish Gds 1947, served GHQ FARELF Singapore RE, Capt Cheshire Yeo 1949–58; former sr ptnr Chapman Taylor Ptnrs whose London bldgs incl:

Caxton House DOE, One Drummond Gate (Metropolitan Police), Lansdowne House Berkeley Square; planning conslts and princ architects to Crown Cmmrs Millbank Estate; govr Stowe Sch 1962–90 (chm 1975–81), chm Allied Schs Cncl 1982–88, memb Cncl of Mgmnt Ruthin Sch 1994–; Freeman Worshipful Co of Chartered Architects; FRIBA, FRAIA; *Recreations* gardens, boats; *Clubs* Royal Thames Yacht; *Style—* J S Taylor, Esq; ✉ Castell Gyrn, Llanbedr, Ruthin, Denbighshire, N Wales LL15 1YE; 9 Kinnerton Yard, London SW1X 8ED; 11 Capri Close, Clareville, NSW 2107, Australia; Isle of Scalpay, Harris, Western Isles, Scotland PA84 3YB

TAYLOR, Dr John William Ransom; OBE (1991); s of Victor Charles Taylor (d 1976), of Ely, Cambs, and Florence Hilda, *née* Ransom (d 1969); *b* 8 June 1922; *Educ* Ely Cathedral Choir Sch, Soham GS Cambs; *m* 7 Sept 1946, Doris Alice, da of George Arthur Haddrick (d 1933), of London; 1 s (Michael John Haddrick b 1949), 1 da (Susan Hilda Haddrick b 1947); *Career* design engr Hawker Aircraft Ltd Kingston upon Thames 1941–47, air corr Meccano Magazine 1943–71, publicity offr Fairey Aviation Group 1947–55, ed Air BP Magazine Br Petroleum 1956–72; ed, ed-in-chief and ed emeritus Jane's All the World's Aircraft 1959–, contrib ed Air Force Magazine (US) 1971–, specialist corr Jane's Intelligence Review 1989–, jt ed Guinness Book of Air Facts and Feats 1974–83; dist cmmr Surbiton Scout Assoc 1965–69, dep warden and warden Christ Church Surbiton Hill 1971–80; pres: Chiltern Aviation Soc Ruislip, Aerosociety Kingston Univ; govr Horse Rangers Assoc; vice pres: Guild of Aviation Artists, Croydon Airport Soc, Surbiton Scout Assoc; hon memb Central Flying Sch Assoc; awards: C P Robertson Meml Trophy Air PR Assoc MOD 1959, Paul Tissandier Diploma Fédération Aéronautique Internationale 1990, Lauren D Lyman award Aviation/Space Writers Assoc USA 1990; Freeman City of London 1987, Liveryman Guild Air Pilots and Air Navigators 1987 (Freeman 1983); memb assoc étranger Académie Nationale de l'Air et de l'Espace (France) 1985–; Hon DEng; FRAeS, FRHistS; *Books* 231 incl: Spitfire (1946), Aircraft Annual (1949–75), Civil Aircraft Markings (1950–78), Picture History of Flight (1955), CFS Birthplace of Air Power (1958, revised 1987), Combat Aircraft of the World (1969), Westland 50 (1965), Encyclopaedia of World Aircraft (with M J H Taylor 1966), Pictorial History of the Royal Air Force (3 vols 1968–71, revised 1980), Aircraft Aircraft (1967), The Lore of Flight (1971), Spies in the Sky (with D Mondey 1972), History of Aviation (with K Munson 1973), Soviet Wings (1991), The de Havilland Aircraft Company (with M Allward, 1996); *Recreations* historical studies, travel, philately; *Clubs* City Livery, RAF (hon life memb), RAeC, Avro 504 (Manchester), Int Order of Characters (USA); *Style—* Dr John W R Taylor, OBE; ✉ 36 Alexandra Drive, Surbiton, Surrey KT5 9AF (☎ 0181 399 5435)

TAYLOR, Jonathan Francis; s of Sir Reginald William Taylor (d 1971), of Great Haseley, Oxford, and Lady (Sarah) Ruth, *née* Tyson (d 1993); *b* 12 Aug 1935; *Educ* Winchester, CCC Oxford (BA, MA); *m* 8 April 1965, (Anthea) Gail, da of Robert Vergette Proctor (d 1985), of Sheffield; 3 s (Luke b 1968, Matthew b 1970, James b 1972); *Career* Nat Serv 2 Lt KAR 1954–56; Booker plc: joined 1959, chm Agric Div 1976–80, dir 1980, chief exec 1984–93, chm 1993–, chm Booker Prize Mgmnt Ctee; non-exec dir: Tate & Lyle plc 1988–, MEPC plc 1992–, The Equitable Life Assurance Society 1995–; chm Ellis & Everard 1993–; pres IBEC Inc (USA) 1980–84, dir Arbor Acres Farm Inc USA 1996– (dir 1991–96); dir Int Agribusiness Mgmnt Assoc 1990–, Winrock International (USA) 1991–; dir and chm Fndn for the Devpt of Polish Agriculture 1991–; memb Advsy Cncl UNIDO 1986, govr SOAS 1988–, curator Bodleian Library 1989–, govr RAC Cirencester; CIMgt 1984, FRSA 1990; *Recreations* travel, skiing, collecting watercolours; *Clubs* Travellers', Knickerbocker (NY); *Style—* Jonathan Taylor, Esq; ✉ Booker plc, Portland House, Stag Place, London SW1E 5AY (☎ 0171 828 9850, fax 0171 630 8029)

TAYLOR, Jonathan Jeremy Kirwan; s of Sir Charles Stuart Taylor, TD, DL; *b* 12 Oct 1943; *Educ* Eton, St Edmund Hall Oxford (MA); *m* 1966, Victoria Mary Caroline, da of Hon John Francis McLaren (d 1953); 4 da (Arabella b 1969, Lucinda b 1972, Caroline b 1976, Katherine b 1979); *Career* called to the Bar Middle Temple 1968; dir Baring Asset 1989– (formerly Baring International Investment Management Ltd) and other Baring Investmt Gp Cos, md Onyx Country Estates Ltd; *Recreations* skiing (Br Olympic Team 1964), tennis, boating; *Clubs* Turf, Royal Thames Yacht, Hong Kong; *Style—* Jonathan Taylor, Esq; ✉ 42 Addison Rd, London W14 8JH (☎ 0171 603 7853); Baring Asset Management Ltd, 155 Bishopsgate, London EC2M 3XY (☎ 0171 628 6000, fax 0171 638 7928, telex 885888 BAMUK G)

TAYLOR, Judy Julia Marie (Mrs Richard Hough); MBE (1971); adopted da of Gladys Spicer Taylor; *b* 12 Aug 1932; *Educ* St Paul's Girls' Sch; *m* 1980, Richard Hough; *Career* writer and publisher; The Bodley Head: joined (specialising in children's books) 1951, dep md 1971–80, dir 1967–84; Chatto, Bodley Head & Jonathan Cape Ltd 1973–80, Chatto, Bodley Head & Jonathan Cape Australia Pty Ltd 1977–80; Publishers' Assoc: chm Children's Book Gp 1969–72, memb Cncl 1972–78; memb: Book Devpt Cncl 1973–76, UNICEF Int Art Ctee 1968–70, 1976 and 1982–83, UNICEF Greeting Card Ctee 1982–85; conslt to Penguin (formerly to Frederick Warne) on Beatrix Potter 1981–87 and 1989–92; assoc dir Weston Woods Inst USA 1984–, consulting ed Reinhardt Books 1988–93; chm Beatrix Potter Soc 1990–, memb London Ctee Volunteer Reading Help 1993–; FRSA 1991; *Books* Sophie and Jack (1982), Sophie and Jack Help Out (1983), My First Year: a Beatrix Potter Baby Book (1983), Sophie and Jack in the Snow (1984), Beatrix Potter: Artist, Storyteller and Countrywoman (1986), Dudley and the Monster (1986), Dudley Goes Flying (1986), Dudley in a Jam (1986), Dudley and the Strawberry Shake (1986), That Naughty Rabbit: Beatrix Potter and Peter Rabbit (1987), My Dog (1987), My Cat (1987), Dudley Bakes a Cake (1988), Beatrix Potter and Hawkshead (1988), Sophie and Jack in the Rain (1989), Beatrix Potter and Hill Top (1989), Beatrix Potter's Letters: a Selection (1989), The Adventures of Dudley Doormouse (1990), Letters to Children from Beatrix Potter (ed, 1992), So I Shall Tell You a Story - Encounters with Beatrix Potter (ed, 1993); Beatrix (play, with Patrick Garland, 1996); author of numerous articles; *Recreations* collecting early children's books, gardening; *Style—* Ms Judy Taylor, MBE; ✉ 31 Meadowbank, Primrose Hill Road, London NW3 3AY (☎ 0171 722 5663, fax 0171 722 7750)

TAYLOR, Dr Keith Henry; s of George Henry Philip Taylor (d 1980), and Vera May, *née* Jones; *b* 25 Oct 1938; *Educ* King Edward VI Sch Stratford-upon-Avon, Univ of Birmingham (BSc, PhD); *m* 28 Sept 1964, Adelaide; 1 s (Mark b 1969), 1 da (Karen b 1966); *Career* various positions Esso Petroleum Co Ltd 1964–80, div ops mangr Exxon USA New Orleans, exec asst to chm Exxon Corporation NY 1984–85, md Esso Exploration & Production UK Ltd 1985–93 (prodn mangr 1982–84), chm and chief exec Esso UK plc 1993–; pres UK Offshore Operators' Assoc 1988 and 1989, memb Offshore Indust Advsy Bd 1989–; non-exec dir Lloyd's Register of Shipping; CIMgt 1985, MInstD 1986, memb Soc of Petroleum Engrs 1987, FRSA, FIChemE (pres 1996), FInstPet, FEng 1994; *Recreations* opera, walking, fishing, watching rugby and golf; *Style—* Dr Keith Taylor, FEng; ✉ Esso UK plc, Esso House, 96 Victoria St, London SW1E 5JW (☎ 0171 245 3294, fax 0171 245 3541)

TAYLOR, Kenneth; JP (1983); s of Kenneth Warburton Taylor (d 1989) and Kathleen, *née* Dilworth; *b* 26 Jan 1941; *Educ* Accrington Tech Sch, Burnley Coll (HNC), Openshaw Coll (IHVE); *m* 10 June 1960, Jean, da of Dr Staff (d 1956); 1 s (John b 1961), 1 da (Jeanette b 1962); *Career* design engr Burnley Co Borough 1963–71, princ Taylor Marren and Haslam (consltg engrs) 1971–85, chief building serv engr Oldham Met Borough 1985–88, chm Taylor Associates Ltd (consltg engrs) 1988–; expert witness; many pubns in professional jls on legal matters; memb Magistrates Assoc, past chm CIBSE North West; memb: Soc of Construction Law, American Soc of Heating Refrigerating and Air Conditioning Engrs; CEng, FCIBSE, FIPlantE, FIHospE, FSE, FIOP, FIMgt, FRSA, ACIArb, MConsE, MBAE; *Books* Plant Engineers Reference Book (jt author); *Recreations* church activities, lectures on legal matters; *Clubs* Foreign Travel; *Style—* Eur Ing Kenneth Taylor, JP; ✉ 40 Wilkie Ave, Glen View, Burnley, Lancs BB11 3QE (☎ 01282 433872); Taylor Associates Ltd, 1 Manchester Rd, Burnley, Lancs BB11 1HQ (☎ 01282 452111, fax 01282 424217, DX 23880 Burnley, car 0421 300449)

TAYLOR, Dr Kenneth George; s of George Edward Taylor (d 1990), of Twickenham, Middx, and Kathleen Anne, *née* Weaver (d 1989); *b* 9 Dec 1944; *Educ* Latymer Upper Sch Hammersmith, St Bartholomew's Hosp Med Sch (MB BS, MD); *m* 5 July 1969, Gwendoline, da of Thomas Edward Wilson (d 1979), of Mitton, nr Clitheroe, Lancashire; *Career* res fell and hon sr registrar Bart's London 1975–78, sr registrar in med The Gen Hosp Birmingham 1978–81, hon sr clinical lectr Univ of Birmingham 1981–, conslt physician City Hosp Birmingham 1981–; former sec Birmingham Div BMA, chm Birmingham Conslts for the Rescue of the NHS 1988–90; memb Cruising Assoc, FRCP 1988; *Books* Diabetic Eye Disease (jtly, 1984), Diabetes and the Heart (ed, 1987); *Recreations* coastal cruising, classical music; *Clubs* Walton and Frinton Yacht; *Style—* Dr Kenneth Taylor; ✉ City Hospital, Dudley Road, Birmingham B18 7QH (☎ 0121 554 3801)

TAYLOR, Kenneth Heywood (Ken); s of Edgar Mason Taylor (d 1931), of Bolton, and Helen Agnes, *née* Higgin (d 1978); *b* 10 Nov 1922; *Educ* Gresham's; *m* 1, 1946 (m dis 1951), Elizabeth Jane, *née* Tillotson; 1 da (Pamela b 1948); m 2, 28 March 1953, Gillian Dorothea, da of Harry Erskine Black (d 1971), of Sidmouth; 2 s (Matthew Taylor, *qv* b 1963, Simon b 1964), 1 da (Victoria b 1956); *Career* TV dramatist; TV plays incl: China Doll, Into the Dark, The Long Distance Blue, The Slaughtermen, The Devil and John Brown, The Seekers, Shoulder to Shoulder, The Poisoning of Charles Bravo; TV adaptions incl: The Melancholy Hussar, The Girls of Slender Means, The Birds Fall Down, Mansfield Park, The Jewel in the Crown, Cause Celebre, The Camomile Lawn, The Peacock Spring, Midnight's Children; BAFTA Writer of the Year Award 1964, Writers' Guild Best Original Teleplay Award 1964, Royal TV Soc Writers' Award (for The Jewel in the Crown) 1984; memb Writers' Guild of GB; *Recreations* walking, music; *Style—* Ken Taylor, Esq; ✉ Churchtown House, Gwithian, Hayle, Cornwall (☎ 01736 752287, fax 01736 752536)

TAYLOR, Prof Kenneth MacDonald (Ken); s of Hugh Baird Taylor (d 1996), of Crail, Fife, and Mary, *née* MacDonald (d 1978); *b* 20 Oct 1947; *Educ* Jordanhill Coll Sch Glasgow, Univ of Glasgow (MB ChB, MD); *m* 14 May 1971, Christine Elizabeth, da of John Buchanan (d 1986), of Ullapool, Ross-shire, Scotland; 1 s (Iain b 1972), 1 da (Kirstin b 1975); *Career* Hall fell in surgery Western Infirmary Glasgow 1971–72, sr lectr in cardiac surgery Royal Infirmary Glasgow 1980–83 (lectr 1974–79), prof of cardiac surgery Royal Post Grad Med Sch Hammersmith Hosp 1983–; memb: Assoc of Profs of Surgery, Specialist Advsy Ctee in Cardiothoracic Surgery (chm 1992–95), Dept of Health Working Pty on Waiting Times for Coronary Artery Disease 1994–95; chm: Database Ctee Euro Assoc for Cardiac Surgery 1994–, UK Central Cardiac Audit Steering Ctee 1995–; pres Soc of Perfusionists GB and Ireland 1989–; dir Sch of Perfusion Sciences, govr Drayton Manor HS London 1989–94; memb Editorial Bd: Annals of Thoracic Surgery 1990–, Jl of Cardiothoracic and Vascular Anaesthesia 1993–, Jl of Heart Valve Disease 1992–; hon memb American Acad of Cardiovascular Perfusion; memb: Surgical Res Soc 1977, Soc of Cardiothoracic Surgns of GB and Ireland 1979, British Cardiac Soc 1983, Soc of Thoracic Surgns of America 1986, Euro Assoc for Cardiothoracic Surgery 1988, American Assoc for Thoracic Surgery 1989; FRCS (Eng), FRCS (Glasgow), FESC; *Books* Pulsatile Perfusion (1982), Handbook of Intensive Care (1984), Perfusion (ed, 1984–), Cardiopulmonary Bypass - Principles and Management (1986), Principles of Surgical Research (1989, 2 edn 1995), Cardiac Surgery and the Brain (1992); *Recreations* family, church, music; *Style—* Prof Ken Taylor; ✉ 129 Argyle Rd, Ealing, London W13 0DB; Cardiac Surgery Unit, Royal Postgrad Medical School, Hammersmith Hospital, Ducane Rd, London W12 01NN (☎ 0181 740 3214, fax 0181 740 7019)

TAYLOR, Prof Laurence John (Laurie); s of Stanley Douglas Taylor, and Winifred Agnes, *née* Cooper; *Educ* St Mary's Coll Liverpool, Rose Bruford Coll, Birkbeck Univ of London (BA), Univ of Leicester (MA); *m* 1; 1 s (Matthew b 5 Dec 1960); m 2, 16 Dec 1988, Catherine, da of Harold Francis Mahoney; *Career* librarian Liverpool City Cncl 1952–54, salesman British Enka Ltd 1954–57, teacher Forest Hill Comp 1961–64, actor Theatre Workshop Stratford 1960–61; Univ of York: lectr 1965–70, sr lectr 1970–73, reader 1973–75, prof 1975–94; visiting prof Birkbeck Coll Univ of London 1994–; Hon DLitt Univ of Nottingham 1992; fell Birkbeck Coll; *Books* Psychological Survival (1972), Escape Attempts (1976), In The Underworld (1984), Professor Lapping Sends His Apologies (1986), The Tuesday Afternoon Time Immemorial Committee (1989), Escape Attempts Revisited (1992), Laurie Taylor's Guide to Higher Education (1994); *Recreations* football, jazz; *Clubs* Groucho's; *Style—* Prof Laurie Taylor

TAYLOR, Margaret Cecilia (Maggie); da of John Marcus Kisch (d 1992), of Dunsfold, Surrey, and Gillian May, *née* Poyser; *b* 31 March 1955; *Educ* Godolphin Sch, St Hilda's Coll Oxford (BA); *m* 30 June 1984, Lee Taylor, s of Edward Thomas Taylor; 1 da (Chloë May b 9 March 1992), 1 s (Henry Thomas b 1 July 1994); *Career* res exec Br Market Res Bureau 1978–80, sr res exec Market Behaviour Ltd 1980–83; Saatchi & Saatchi Advertising: account planner 1983–87, bd dir 1987–90, divnl planning dir 1990; fndr planning ptnr Cowan Kemsley Taylor Ltd 1990–; memb: Market Res Soc 1978, Assoc of Qualitative Res Practitioners 1982, Account Planning Gp 1983; MIPA 1990; *Recreations* riding, walking, croquet, bridge; *Style—* Mrs Maggie Taylor; ✉ The Old Fox, Winkfield Row, Berkshire RG42 6NG; Cowan Kemsley Taylor Ltd, 37 Dean Street, London W1V 5AP (☎ 0171 734 9090, fax 0171 734 9097)

TAYLOR, Mark Christopher; s of Joseph Norman Taylor, and June Taylor; *b* 24 Nov 1958; *Educ* Loughborough GS, Univ of Birmingham (BA), Leeds Poly (post grad dip in hotel mgmnt); *m* 24 June 1989, Debra June, da of Alan Howes; 2 s (Jack b 1990, Liam b 1994), 1 da (Eleanor b 1991); *Career* hotel mangr Norfolk Capital Hotels 1981–84; dir Museums Assoc 1989– (conf mangr 1984–89); memb Cncl Nat Campaign for the Arts; *Recreations* sport, film, food; *Style—* Mark Taylor, Esq; ✉ Museums Association, 42 Clerkenwell Close, London EC1R 0PA (☎ 0171 250 1789 fax 0171 250 1929)

TAYLOR, Mark R F; *b* 6 Dec 1943; *Educ* Oriel Coll Oxford (MA), Univ of Manchester (NHS UK Admin Trg Scheme), Canadian Coll of Health Serv Execs (Certified Health Exec); *m*; *Career* lectr/tutor Dip Course in Health Servs Admin Aston Univ Birmingham 1968–70, admin The Aga Khan Hosp Kenya 1971–74 (asst admin 1970), conslt Peat Marwick & Partners Canada 1974–79, exec sec The Aga Khan Fndn Kenya 1979–81, princ Woods Gordon (Ernst & Young) Management Consultants Canada 1981–84, chief exec Toronto Western Hosp Canada 1984–86, chief exec Cromwell Hosp London 1986–89, pres Addiction Res Fndn Toronto Canada 1989–94; chief exec: Royal Devon & Exeter Healthcare NHS Tst 1994–96, Royal Brompton Hosp NHS Tst 1996–; memb Bd Ind Hosps Assoc 1988–89, fndr memb Bd Crossmatch Health Personnel Agency Ltd 1988–89, chm Toronto Academic Health Scis Cncl 1990–94, hon vice pres Int Cncl on Alcohol and Addictions 1991– (chair Fin Panel 1992–); contrib various learned jls and other pubns; *Recreations* sailing, travel, reading; *Style—* Mark R F Taylor, Esq; ✉ Royal Brompton Hospital NHS Trust, Sydney Street, London SW3 6NP (☎ 0171 352 8121)

TAYLOR, (John) Martin; *Career* chm and chief exec Courtaulds Textiles plc until 1993, chief exec Barclays plc 1994– (dir 1993–); non-exec dir W H Smith Group plc; *Style—* Martin Taylor, Esq; ✉ Barclays plc, 54 Lombard Street, London EC3P 3AH (☎ 0171 699 5000)

TAYLOR, Martin Francis (Frank); s of Dr Albert William Taylor (d 1982), of Lamberhurst, Kent, and Margaret Oyston (d 1989); *b* 19 Jan 1944; *Educ* Sidcot Sch, Queen Mary Coll Univ of London; *m* 8 Aug 1970, Margaret Anne, da of Frederick William Harris (d 1975), of Beckenham, Kent; 1 s (Jeremy b 1975), 1 da (Claire b 1972); *Career* town planner, ptnr T P Bennett Partnership 1979– (joined 1966, assoc 1970–79); MRTPI; *Recreations* travel, gardening, choral singing, family life; *Style—* Frank Taylor, Esq; ✉ T P Bennett Partnership, 262 High Holborn, London WC1V 7DU (☎ 0171 405 9277, fax 0171 208 2406)

TAYLOR, Martin Gibbeson; CBE (1993); s of Roy Gibbeson Taylor (d 1955), of Worthing, Sussex, and Vera Constance, *née* Farmer (d 1993); *b* 30 Jan 1935; *Educ* Haileybury, St Catharine's Coll Cambridge (MA); *m* 18 June 1960, Gunilla Chatarina, da of Nils Bryner (d 1962), of Stockholm, Sweden; 2 s (Thomas b 1963, Seth b 1967); *Career* 2 Lt RA 1953–55; with Mann Judd & Co (CA) 1958–62, co sec Dow Chemical UK 1963–69; Hanson plc: joined 1969, dir 1976–95, vice chm 1988–95, advsr 1995–; chm National Westminster Life Assurance Ltd 1992–; non-exec dir: Vickers plc, National Westminster Bank PLC 1990–, Charter PlC 1995–; memb: Panel on Takeovers and Mergers until 1995, Cncl CBI, Companies Ctee CBI (chm 1990–94); govr The Mall Sch; FCA 1961; *Recreations* pictures, books, theatre, sport; *Clubs* MCC; *Style—* Martin G Taylor, Esq, CBE; ✉ Hanson plc, 1 Grosvenor Place, London SW1X 7JH (☎ 0171 245 1245, fax 0171 235 2721, telex 917698)

TAYLOR, Prof Martin John; s of John Maurice Taylor, of Leicester, and Sheila Mary Barbara, *née* Camacho; *b* 18 Feb 1952; *Educ* Wyggeston GS, Pembroke Coll Oxford (MA), King's Coll London (PhD); *m* 1 Dec 1973, Sharon Lynn, da of Harold Marlow; 2 s (Andrew b 19 March 1981, James b 3 July 1983), 2 da (Rebecca b 28 July 1977, Deborah b 9 May 1979); *Career* res asst King's Coll London 1976–77, jr lectr Oxford 1977–78, lectr QMC 1978–81, professeur associé Besançon 1979–80, fell Trinity Coll Cambridge 1981–85, chair in pure mathematics UMIST 1985–; Royal Soc Leverhulme sr res fell 1991–92; chm Bramhall Cncl of Churches; memb Cncl London Mathematics Soc: jr Whitehead prize 1982, Adams prize 1983; FRS 1996; *Books* Classgroups of Group Rings (1983), Elliptic Functions and Rings of Integers (with P Cassou-Noguès), Algebraic Number Theory (with A Fröhlich), L-functions and Arithmetic (with J Coates), Group Rings and Class Groups (with K Roggenkamp); *Style—* Prof Martin Taylor, FRS; ✉ Dept of Mathematics, UMIST, PO Box 88, Manchester M60 1QD (☎ 0161 200 3640)

TAYLOR, Martyn Graeme; s of John William Havelock Taylor (d 1977), of Calne, Wilts, and Betty Evelyn, *née* Clarke; *b* 8 June 1938; *Educ* Marlborough, Pembroke Coll Oxford (MA); *m* 23 May 1964, Jean, da of Thomas Topping (d 1983), of Churchill, Somerset; 2 s (Jeremy b 1966, Bruce b 1968), 1 da (Kirsty b 1972); *Career* CA; Coopers & Lybrand (and predecessor firms): joined 1959, ptnr 1972–, compliance ptnr 1994–; reader C of E 1979–, memb Winchester Diocesan Bd of Fin 1984–; FCA; *Books* Financial Times World Survey of Bank Annual Reports (jtly, 1982), Banks: An Accounting and Auditing Guide (jtly, 1983 and 1993); *Recreations* hill walking, history and statistics of cricket; *Clubs* MCC, National Liberal, Sloane; *Style—* Martyn Taylor, Esq; ✉ Coopers & Lybrand, 1 Embankment Place, London WC2N 6NN (☎ 0171 583 5000)

TAYLOR, Matthew Owen John; MP (Lib Dem) Truro (majority 7,570); s of Kenneth Heywood (Ken) Taylor, *qv*, and Gillian Dorothea, *née* Black; *b* 3 Jan 1963; *Educ* St Paul's, Tremorvah Sch, Treliske Sch, Univ Coll Sch, Lady Margaret Hall Oxford (BA); *Career* pres Oxford Univ Students' Union 1985–86, econ res asst Parly Lib Pty 1986–87 (attached to late David Penhaligon, MP for Truro), MP (Lib until 1988, now Lib Dem) Truro March 1987– (by-election); Parly spokesman on: energy 1987–88, local govt, housing and tport 1988–89, trade and indust 1989–90, educn 1990–92, Citizens' Charter and youth issues 1992–94, the environment 1994–; chm: Lib Dem Communications Ctee 1989–92, Lib Dem Campaigns & Communications Ctee 1992–94; *Style—* Matthew Taylor, Esq, MP; ✉ House of Commons, London SW1A 0AA (☎ 0171 219 6686)

TAYLOR, Rt Rev Maurice; *see:* Galloway, Bishop of (RC)

TAYLOR, Rev Michael Hugh; s of Albert Taylor and Gwendoline Taylor; *b* 8 Sept 1936; *Educ* Northampton GS, Univ of Manchester (BD, MA), Union Theological Seminary NY (STM); *m* 1960, Adele May, *née* Dixon; 2 s, 1 da; *Career* Baptist min 1960–69 (North Shields Northumberland, Hall Green Birmingham), princ Northern Baptist Coll Manchester 1970–85, lectr in theology and ethics Univ of Manchester 1970–85, examining chaplain to Bishop of Manchester 1975–85; chm Tstees Audenshaw Fndn 1979–92, dir Christian Aid 1985–, memb Cncl VSO 1986–94, memb Cncl Overseas Devpt Inst 1987–, chm Assoc of Protestant Devpt Orgns in Europe (APRODEV) 1991–95; memb WCC Cmmns 1976–91 and 1991–; Fulbright travel award 1969; *Books* Variations on a Theme (1973), Learning to Care (1983), Good for the Poor (1990), Christianity and the Persistence of Poverty (1991), Not Angels but Agencies (1995); *Recreations* walking, theatre, cooking; *Style—* The Rev Michael H Taylor; ✉ 53 Woodland Rise, London N10 3UN (☎ 0181 883 7217); Christian Aid, PO Box 100, London SE1 7RT (☎ 0171 620 4444, fax 0171 620 0179)

TAYLOR, Michael Paul Gordon; s of Gordon Taylor, and Stella, *née* Marsh; *b* 2 March 1949; *Educ* Altrincham GS, St John's Coll Cambridge; *Career* ptnr Norton Rose 1979– (head Energy Gp 1987–); Freeman City of London Slrs Co; memb: Int Bar Assoc, Law Soc; *Recreations* sport, theatre, reading; *Clubs* RAC; *Style—* Michael Taylor, Esq; ✉ Norton Rose, Kempson House, Camomile Street, London EC3A 7AN (☎ 0171 283 6000, fax 0171 283 6500)

TAYLOR, Neil Frederick; *b* 25 May 1951; *Educ* Batley GS, Univ of Sheffield (BA, Dip in Architecture); *Career* architect; ptnr FaulknerBrowns; commissions incl: The Dome Doncaster, Civic Offices Chester-le-Street, Claremont Sports Hall, Blackburn Leisure Pool, Perth Waters, Leeds Pedestrianisation; contrib various publications incl: Architects Jl, Architects Review, Domus, Design, Beven Wohnen, Architekt, Architecture d'Aujourdhui, Sunday Times, Financial Times, Guardian, Telegraph, Economist, Building Design; Summer Exhibition RA (rep UK World Expo Brisbane 1988); *Awards* incl: Civic Tst, RIBA, Europa Nostra, IAKS, Structural Steel, Financial Times; visiting prof Univ of Newcastle 1992–, external examiner Liverpool John Moores Univ (previously for Univ of Newcastle), visiting critic Univ of Sheffield; memb: Urban Design Gp, Validation Ctee Liverpool John Moores Univ, RIBA Visiting Bd of Educn, Higher Educn Funding Cncl Validation Bd, ARCUK; RIBA, MIMgt; *Recreations* involved in local education, architectural history, social evolution of history, football, cricket, riding; *Style—* Neil Taylor, Esq; ✉ FaulknerBrowns, Dobson House, Northumbrian Way, Killingworth, Newcastle upon Tyne NE12 0QW (☎ 0191 268 3007, fax 0191 268 5227, car 0860 665498)

TAYLOR, Neville; CB (1989); s of late Frederick Herbert Taylor, and late Lottie, *née* London; *b* 17 Nov 1930; *Educ* Sir Joseph Williamson's Mathematical Sch Rochester, Coll of Commerce Gillingham; *m* 4 Sept 1954, Margaret Ann, da of late Thomas Bainbridge Vickers; 2 s (Andrew b 1956, Martin b 1958); *Career* RCS 1948–50; journalist 1950–58; press offr Admty 1958–63, fleet info offr Far E Fleet Singapore Malaysia 1963–65, chief press offr MOD 1966–68, info advsr NEDO/NEDC London 1968–70, dep dir of PR RN 1970, head of info MAFF 1971–72, dir of info DOE 1974–79 (dep dir 1972), DHSS 1979–82, chief of PR MOD 1982–85, dir gen COI and head of Govt Info Serv 1985–88, princ assoc Europac Group Ltd and Defence Public Affairs Consultants Ltd 1989–; *Recreations* fishing, bird watching; *Clubs* Castle (Rochester); *Style—* Neville Taylor, Esq, CB; ✉ Crow Lane House, Crow Lane, Rochester, Kent (☎ 01634 842 990)

TAYLOR, (John) Patrick Enfield; s of Arthur Hugh Enfield Taylor, RNVR (d 1983), of Midhurst, W Sussex, and Monica Soames, *née* Cooke; *b* 3 April 1948; *Educ* Eton; *m* 1972, Heather Diana, da of Col Roger Barratt, of Haverthwaite, nr Ulverston, Cumbria; 1 s (Rupert b 1979), 3 da (Melissa b 1976, Pippa b 1980, Hermione b 1983); *Career* ptnr Coopers & Lybrand 1980–86 (qualified 1972), fin dir Langdale Group plc 1986–88, dir of fin and business devpt Capital Radio plc 1989–96, dep chief exec and fin dir GWR Group plc 1996– (non-exec dir 1994–96); also dir: Satellite Media Services Ltd (chm), Independent Radio News Ltd; FCA; *Recreations* tennis, swimming, sailing, skiing; *Style—* Patrick Taylor, Esq; ✉ GWR Group plc, 382 Westlea, Swindon, Wilts SN5 7HF (☎ 01793 422778, fax 01793 422771)

TAYLOR, Paul Duncan; JP (1969); s of Edward Duncan Taylor (d 1984), and Mary Edith Thornton, *née* Laxton (d 1966); *b* 25 April 1936; *Educ* Mill Hill Sch; *m* 16 April 1964, Lindsay Veronica Moncrieff, da of late Ronald Irvine Smith; 2 s (Nicholas Charles Duncan b 18 Aug 1965, Christopher Paul Irvine b 26 July 1967); *Career* chartered accountant 1959; ptnr Touche Ross (now Deloitte & Touche) 1961–; dir: Wagon Industrial Holdings plc 1968– (chm 1986–), John Foster & Son plc 1982–93, Leeds and Holbeck Building Society 1987– (pres 1991–93); FCA 1959, AInstT; *Clubs* The Leeds; *Style—* Paul Taylor, Esq, JP; ✉ Deloitte & Touche, 10–12 East Parade, Leeds LS1 2AJ (☎ 0113 243 9021, fax 0113 244 5580)

TAYLOR, Peter Cranbourne; s of Maurice Ewan Taylor, OBE, of St Andrews, and Mary Ann, *née* Gorst (d 1993); *b* 11 Aug 1938; *Educ* Univ of Edinburgh (MA); *m* 27 June 1970, Lois Mary, da of Anthony Godard Templeton, TD (d 1986), of St Andrews; 1 s (Christopher b 13 Nov 1975), 1 da (Kerrie b 18 Dec 1972); *Career* CA 1962; ptnr: Romanes & Munro Edinburgh 1964–74, Deloitte Haskins & Sells (now Coopers & Lybrand) 1974–95; convenor ICAS, memb Servs Ctee 1984–90, memb Scot Dental Practice Bd 1991–; non-exec dir Joint Insolvency Monitoring Unit Ltd 1994–; chm Scottish Nat Blood Transfusion Assoc 1995– (sec and treas 1981–95); *Recreations* shooting, country pursuits; *Clubs* New (Edinburgh), Lansdowne; *Style—* Peter Taylor, Esq; ✉ Totleywells House, Winchburgh, West Lothian EH52 6QJ (☎ and fax 0131 319 2155)

TAYLOR, Peter Duncan; s of Capt Arthur Gilbert Taylor (d 1967), of Manchester, and Amy Margaret, *née* Duncan (d 1958); *b* 4 May 1925; *Educ* Oakham Sch, Univ of St Andrews; *m* 20 June 1956, Barbara, da of Daniel Greenaway (d 1968); 1 s (John); *Career* Pilot RAF; Simon Engrg plc, dir Simon-Carves Ltd and Lodge-Cottell Ltd 1951–72, dir and sec Turriff Corp plc 1972–91, dir Horton's Estate Ltd 1992–; FCA 1951; *Recreations* golf, antiques, bridge; *Style—* Peter Taylor, Esq; ✉ Tanglewood, 6 Woodside Way, Solihull, W Mids B91 1HB

TAYLOR, (Louis) Philip Chetwynd; s of Philip Hugh Taylor, of Newcastle under Lyme, Staffs, and Mable Doreen, *née* Bladen (d 1986); *b* 9 Oct 1950; *Educ* Malvern Coll; *m* 22 May 1976, Odette, da of Thomas Demajo; 2 da (Ruth Doreen Theresa b 21 Nov 1980, Harriet Charlotte Christina b 6 May 1984); *Career* Price Waterhouse: London 1970–75, Johannesburg 1975–78, London 1978–85, ptnr 1985–, joined Channel Islands firm 1985, sr ptnr 1993–; chm Jersey Branch IOD 1990–93; FCA (ACA 1973); *Recreations* cricket, gardening; *Clubs* United (St Helier); *Style—* Philip Taylor, Esq; ✉ Price Waterhouse, Eagle House, Don Road, St Helier, Jersey, Channel Islands JE2 4QB (☎ 01534 815000, fax 01534 36790)

TAYLOR, Philippe Arthur; s of Arthur Peach Taylor, (d 1974), of St Andrews, Fife, and Simone, *née* Vacquin; *b* 9 Feb 1937; *Educ* Trinity Coll Glenalmond, Univ of St Andrews; *m* 10 Feb 1973, Margaret Nancy, da of Arnold Frederick Wilkins, OBE (d 1985), of Framlingham, Suffolk; 2 s (Rupert Arthur James b 1975, Charles Philip b 1976); *Career* Proctor and Gamble 1961–66, Masius Int 1966–70, Br Tourist Authy 1970–75; chief exec: Scottish Tourist Bd 1975–81, Birmingham Convention Bureau 1982–93; chm Br Assoc of Conference Towns 1988–91, vice chm Ikon Gallery 1988–, Chevalier de L'Ordre des Coteaux de Champagne 1985; FTS 1975; *Books* Captain Crossjack and the Lost Penguin (1969); *Recreations* sailing, painting, tourism, making things; *Clubs* Royal Northumberland YC, Orford Sailing; *Style—* Philippe Taylor, Esq

TAYLOR, Phillip; s of Harry Sidney Taylor, of Newcastle, and Elisabeth, *née* Telford; *b* 27 Sept 1948; *Educ* Anfield Palin Boys' Sch, Newcastle Coll; *m* 30 Sept 1972, Iris, da of John Harland (d 1979); 2 s (Christopher b 29 June 1977, Michael James b 16 Aug 1978), 1 da (Leigh b 21 Oct 1974); *Career* Minories Garages Ltd: gen mangr 1974–78, dir 1978, chm 1990–; gp dir Appleyard Group plc 1990–; *Recreations* golf, sailing, skiing; *Clubs* Slaley Golf, Seahouses Golf, Fontburn Ski, Beadnell Yacht; *Style—* Phillip Taylor, Esq; ✉ 63 Cornmoor Road, Whickham, Newcastle upon Tyne NE16 4PU (☎ 0191 488 4192); Appelyard Group plc, Windsor House, Cornwall Road, Harrogate HG1 2PW (☎ 01423 531999, fax 01423 530949)

TAYLOR, Richard; *b* 6 Feb 1945; *Educ* Corpus Christi Coll Oxford (MA); *Career* admitted slr 1969; McKenna & Co: articled clerk 1967–69, asst slr 1969–74, on secondment to lawyers' cos in Germany, France and Holland 1973, ptnr 1974–, currently head of Euro Practice, estab (and currently jtly responsible for) Brussels office 1988; specialist in competition law and EEC law, has pleaded before Euro Ct of Justice Luxembourg; author of various articles on competition and EEC law, ed McKenna & Co bulletin on EEC law; past chm Solicitors' Euro Gp; *Style—* Richard Taylor, Esq; ✉ McKenna & Co, Mitre House, 160 Aldersgate Street, London EC1A 4DD (☎ 0171 606 9000, fax 0171 606 9100)

TAYLOR, Richard; s of Horace Christopher Taylor (d 1933), of Hampstead Garden Suburb, and Dulcie Muriel, *née* Marriott; *b* 16 June 1929; *Educ* UCS London, Univ Coll Oxford (exhibitioner, BA, MA); *Career* Larkins Studio: animation trainee 1953, dir i/c prodn 1957, md 1959–66; fndr Richard Taylor Cartoon Films Ltd 1966; RCA: animation course dir RCA 1989–94, head of Animation Dept 1986, prof of animation 1992–94; currently independent prodr of animation material; producer designer and/or dir: Mr Finley's Feelings (Metropolitan Life, US) 1956, commercials for Barclay's Bank (winner Grand Prix SAWA and Coppa di Venezia) 1956–66, industl films 1966–76, educnl material BBC TV 1976–85, Muzzy in Gondoland (BBC) 1985, Muzzy Comes Back (BBC) 1988; pres ASIFA UK 1986–; memb BAFTA; *Books* The Encyclopedia of Animation Techniques (1996); *Style—* Richard Taylor, Esq; ✉ River View, Waterloo Drive, Clun, Craven Arms, Shropshire SY7 8JD

TAYLOR, Richard John; s of William Taylor, of Northwich, Cheshire (d 1993), and Florence Littler, *née* Hough (d 1986); *b* 15 April 1951; *Educ* North Cestrian GS Altrincham Cheshire, Univ of St Andrews (BSc, capt rowing and United Colls Rugby 1st XV); *m* 2 June 1979, Kay Vivienne, da of Edward Jack Haddon; 1 s (Samuel James b 29 Jan 1983), 1 da (Alice Edwina b 22 Jan 1986); *Career* Spicer and Pegler CAs Manchester 1973–78 (qualified 1976), ptnr Murray Smith & Co CAs 1980– (joined 1978); govr: The Grange Sch Hartford Ltd 1983–, Mid-Cheshire Coll of FE 1993–; chm Chester and N Wales Soc of CAs 1991–92; FCA 1983; *Recreations* sailing (racing a Dart 18 catamaran), golf, waterskiing; *Clubs* Dee Sailing, Sandiway Golf; *Style—* Richard J Taylor, Esq; ✉ Pool Bank, Oulton, Tarporley, Cheshire CW6 9BH (☎ 01829 760680); Murray Smith & Co, Chartered Accountants, Grange House, Winsford, Cheshire CW7 2BP (☎ 01606 551238, fax 01606 861174, car 0836 646113)

TAYLOR, His Hon Judge Robert Carruthers; s of John Houston Taylor, CBE (d 1983), and Barbara Mary, *née* Carruthers (d 1994); *b* 6 Jan 1939; *Educ* Wycliffe Coll, St John's Coll Oxford (MA); *m* 16 April 1968, Jacqueline Marjorie, da of Nigel Geoffrey Randall Chambers, of West Yorks; 1 s (John b 1972), 1 da (Susannah b 1969); *Career* called to the Bar Middle Temple 1961, practised NE Circuit 1962–84, recorder 1976–84, circuit judge (NE Circuit) 1984–, designated family judge Leeds 1995–; chm Agric Land Tbnl (Lancs/Yorks/Humberside) 1979–; *Recreations* reading, music, gardening; *Style*— His Hon Judge Robert Taylor; ✉ The Courthouse, 1 Oxford Row, Leeds LS1 3BE

TAYLOR, Robert Richard (Bob); OBE (1989, MBE 1972), JP (1994); s of Sydney Arthur Taylor (d 1969), and Edith Alice, *née* Shepherd (d 1961); *b* 14 June 1932; *Educ* Yardley GS Birmingham; *m* 1957, Sheila, *née* Welch; *Career* RAF: joined as trainee pilot 1950, served in Egypt, Germany and Singapore, ret as Sqdn Ldr 1973; worked for a Midlands Property Co 1973; Birmingham Airport: asst dir (Admin) 1974–76, airport dir 1976–87, md 1987–94 (ret); dir: Maersk Air (UK) Ltd, Capital Radio PLC; chm: Birmingham Broadcasting Ltd, Airport Operators' Assoc 1987–88, Disabled Persons Tport Advsy Ctee Dept of Tport; pres: Warwicks and Birmingham Wing ATC, 2030 Sqdn ATC, Birmingham branch Air Crew Assoc, W Midlands central branch SSAFA, St John Cncl for the W Midlands, Solihull Operatic Soc; vice pres: TAVR Assoc, Warwickshire CCC; tstee: RAF and Dependents Disabled Holiday Tst, Warwickshire Private Hosp Tst; patron: CCHA Extra Care Ltd, Midlands branch British Lung Fndn, Birmingham Sports Club for the Disabled, Empathy Ltd, Midland Air Museum, Nat Assoc of Special Needs Providers, Midlands Branch Red Cross, Disability W Midlands, Pulse Tst; vice patron Missing Persons Helpline; Lord Lieutenant for Co of W Midlands 1993 (DL 1985); memb Ct and Cncl Univ of Warwick; Hon Col Univ of Birmingham OTC, hoon chm Co Air Ambulance Tst; Hon DUniv Univ of Central England 1993; Midlander of the Year 1989, QCVSA 1966, Inst of Mgmnt Silver Medal 1992, Airport Operators' Assoc Silver Medal 1995, Aston Univ Centennial Medal 1995; KStJ 1994; *Recreations* people, books, countryside; *Clubs* RAF; *Style*— Bob Taylor, Esq, OBE, JP; ✉ Lieutenancy Office, The Coach House, Wood Lane, Barston, Solihull, West Midlands B92 0JL (☎ 01675 442921, fax 01675 442934)

TAYLOR, Dr Robert Thomas; CBE (1990); s of George Taylor (d 1973), of Derwent Rd, Warrington, Lancs, and Marie Louise, *née* Fidler (d 1986); *b* 21 March 1933; *Educ* Boteler GS, Univ of Oxford (BA, MA, DPhil); *m* 1, 20 Aug 1954 (m dis 1965), Ina, *née* Wilson; 1 s (Timothy b 1959); m 2, 25 Sept 1965, Rosemary Janet, da of Charles Leonard Boileau, of 36 Ryders Bolt, Bexhill on Sea, Sussex; 2 s (Aubrey b 1967, Christopher 1968), 1 da (Alison b 1973); *Career* res assoc in Randall laboratory physics Univ of Michigan USA 1957–58, lectr in physics Univ of Liverpool 1959–61 (ICI res fell 1958–59); The Br Cncl: asst regnl rep Madras 1961–64, sci offr Spain 1964–69, dir staff recruitment 1969–73, regnl rep Bombay 1973–77, rep Mexico 1977–81, personnel controller London 1981–86, rep Greece 1986–90, ADG 1990–93; Manchester Business Sch: visiting sr fell 1993–, chm Mgmnt Interviewing and Research Inst (MIRI) 1993–; examiner in physics: Oxford Local Bd 1956–61, Oxford and Cambridge Bd 1957; chief examiner physics NUJMB 1961 (examiner 1960), lay team memb for sch inspections OFSTED 1993–; *Books* contrib Chambers Encyclopaedia (1967); *Recreations* war games, computers, theatre; *Style*— Dr Robert T Taylor; ✉ Mark Haven, High St, Cranbrook, Kent TN17 3EW (☎ 01580 714212); MIRI, Manchester Business School, Booth Street, Manchester M15 6PB

TAYLOR, Roger Meddows; s of Michael Meddows Taylor, and Winifred Taylor; *b* 26 July 1949; *Educ* Truro Public Sch, London Hosp Med Coll, N London Poly (BSc); *m*; 2 s (Felix Luther, Rufus Tiger), 2 da (Rory Eleanor, Tigerlily); *Career* drummer, vocalist and songwriter; co-fndr: Smile 1968, Queen 1970– (with Freddie Mercury (d 1991), Brian May, *qv*, John Deacon, *qv*), The Cross 1987–; Queen albums: Queen (1973, Platinum), Queen II (1974, Platinum), Sheer Heart Attack (1974, Platinum), A Night at the Opera (1975, Platinum), A Day at the Races (1976, Platinum), News of the World (1977, Platinum), Jazz (1978, Gold), Live Killers (1979, Gold), The Game (1980, Platinum), Flash Gordon Original Soundtrack (1980, Gold), Greatest Hits (1981, 12 times Platinum), Hot Space (1982, Gold), The Works (1984, double Platinum), A Kind of Magic (1986, double Platinum), Live Magic (1986, Platinum), The Miracle (1989, Platinum), Queen at the Beeb (1989), Innuendo (1991, Platinum), Greatest Hits Two (1991, 8 times Platinum), Made in Heaven (1995, 4 times Platinum); The Cross albums: Shove It (1988), Mad Bad and Dangerous to Know (1990), Blue Rock (1991); other albums: Gettin' Smile (earlier recordings of Smile, 1982), Fun In Space (solo, 1981), Strange Frontier (solo, 1984), Happiness (solo, 1994); number 1 singles: Bohemian Rhapsody 1975 and 1991 (with days of Our Lives), Under Pressure 1981, Innuendo 1991, Somebody to Love (with George Michael); produced 1st hit by Jimmy Nail (Love Don't Live Here Any More); numerous tours worldwide, performed at Live Aid Concert Wembley Stadium 1985; voted Best Band of the Eighties ITV/TV Times 1990, Br Phonographic Indust award for Outstanding Contribution to Br Music 1990; *Recreations* fast cars, travel, reading, renovating, working, boating, skiing; *Style*— Roger Taylor, Esq; ✉ Nightjar Productions Ltd, PO Box 159, Godalming, Surrey GU8 6YJ (☎ 01428 682426, fax 01428 685965)

TAYLOR, Roger Miles Whitworth; s of Richard Taylor (d 1965), of Stafford, and Joan Elizabeth, *née* Whitworth; *b* 18 May 1944; *Educ* Repton, Univ of Birmingham (LLB); *m* 26 July 1969, Georgina Lucy, da of Francis Tonks (d 1973), of Sark, CI; 2 s (Richard Francis Miles b 1971, Matthew William Roger b 1976), 2 da (Sarah Elizabeth May b 1981, Lucy Emily Jane (twin) b 1981); *Career* admitted slr 1968; asst slr: Staffordshire CC 1968–69, Cheshire CC 1969–71; asst co clerk Lincs parts of Lindsey 1971–73, dep co sec Northants CC 1971–73, town clerk and chief exec City of Manchester 1985–88 (dep town clerk 1979–85), chief exec Birmingham City Cncl and sec W Midlands Jt Ctee 1988–94, dir Local Govt Newchurch and Company Strategic Mgmnt Consits 1994–; memb Farrand Ctee on Conveyancing 1983–84, clerk Gtr Manchester Passenger Tport Authy 1986–88; dir Birmingham Training and Enterprise Cncl 1990–93; Mancunian of the Year Manchester Jr C of C 1988; *Recreations* sailing, walking; *Style*— Roger Taylor, Esq; ✉ Newchurch and Company, 24 Britton Street, London EC1M 5NQ (☎ 0171 566 6666, fax 0171 566 6650)

TAYLOR, Ronald George (Ron); CBE (1988); s of Ernest Noel Taylor (d 1978), of Bristol, and May Elizabeth, *née* Besant (d 1955); *b* 12 Dec 1935; *Educ* Cotham GS Bristol, Jesus Coll Oxford (BA); *m* 14 June 1960, Patricia, da of Septon Stoker, of Hemingbrough; 1 s (David Robert b 1963), 2 da (Gillian Mary b 1961, Alison Catherine b 1965); *Career* Nat Serv 2 Lt Royal Signals 1957–59; dir Leeds C of C and Indust 1974 (joined 1959), dir-gen Br C of C 1984–; *Recreations* bridge, rugby union football; *Style*— Ron Taylor, Esq, CBE; ✉ 2 Holly Bush Lane, Harpenden, Herts (☎ 01582 712139); British Chambers of Commerce, 22 Carlisle Place, London SW1P 1JA (☎ 0171 565 2000, fax 0171 565 2049)

TAYLOR, (Robert Murray) Ross; s of Dr George Ross Taylor (d 1940), and Helen Bailey, *née* Murray (d 1989); *b* 10 Dec 1932; *Educ* Coatbridge Secondary Sch, Univ of Glasgow (MB ChB, ChM); *m* 7 Jan 1959, Margaret Rose, da of Capt Albert Henry Cutland (d 1975); 1 s (Bill b 1965), 3 da (Linda b 1960, Jill b 1962, Anne b 1964); *Career* Capt RAMC 23 Para Field Ambulance and 2 Bn Parachute Regt 1957–59; registrar Bishop Auckland Gen Hosp 1959–62, res fell Univ of Newcastle upon Tyne 1964–65, conslt surgn Royal Victoria Infirmary Newcastle 1970–95 (registrar in surgery 1962–64, sr registrar 1965–70), ret; chm and tstee: Transplant Patients' Tst of GB, Transplant Sports Assoc of GB 1984–; fndr memb: Euro Soc for Organ Transplantation, Int Transplantation Soc, Br Transplantation Soc (pres 1986–89); pres N of England Surgical Soc 1990–91; tstee: Great North Run Tst 1984–, Northern Counties Kidney Res Fund; hon memb: Br Transplantation Soc, Durham CCC; *Recreations* golf, gardening, charity fundraising; *Clubs* Northumberland Golf; *Style*— R M R Taylor, Esq; ✉ Croft House, Slaley, Hexham, Northumberland NE47 0AA (☎ and fax 01434 673322)

TAYLOR, Russell Colin; s of Cyril Wilfred Taylor (d 1971), and Ruby Phillis Taylor (d 1977); *b* 27 Sept 1945; *Educ* City of Oxford GS, Birmingham Coll of Commerce; *m* 29 July 1967, Sheila Mary (d 1994); 2 s (Adrian Keith b 25 July 1975, Philip Russell b 17 June 1978); *Career* asst prod mangr Cadbury Schweppes (formerly Cadbury Brothers Ltd) 1968–70 (mgmnt trainee 1964–68), brand mangr CWS Ltd Manchester 1970–72; Anglia Canners: mktg mangr 1972–73, sales and mktg mangr 1973–75, mktg dir 1975–77, sales and mktg dir 1977–79, dep md 1979–81, md 1981–87; chief exec Armitage Brothers plc 1987–; memb ICSA; *Recreations* sport, music, current affrs, card games, quizzes, amateur dramatics; *Style*— Russell Taylor, Esq; ✉ 8 The Banks, Bingham, Nottingham NG13 8BL (☎ 01949 837577); Armitage Brothers plc, Armitage House, Colwick, Nottingham NG4 2BA (☎ 0115 961 4984, fax 0115 961 7496)

TAYLOR, Prof Samuel Sorby Brittain; s of late Samuel Stephen Taylor, and Elsie Irene, *née* Chappell (d 1992); *b* 20 Sept 1930; *Educ* High Storrs GS Sheffield, Univ of Birmingham (MA, PhD); *m* 15 Aug 1956, (Agnes) Nan McCreadie, da of late Peter Ewan, of Dundee; 2 da (Moira Elizabeth b 13 Aug 1959, Dorothy Frances b 1 Feb 1962); *Career* Nat Serv 1956–58, Sub Lt RNVR 1957–; personnel res offr Dunlop Rubber Co 1958–60, res fell (for Voltaire's correspondence vols 66–98, under Theodore Besterman) Institut et Musée Voltaire Geneva 1960–63; Univ of St Andrews: asst 1963, lectr 1964, reader 1972, personal chair 1977–95, prof emeritus 1995–; dir Nuffield Fndn Project on French for Science and Technol 1991–96; author of studies of Voltaire, memb Editorial Ctee Voltaire's Complete Works 1967–91; sec gen Soc for Eighteenth Century Studies 1967–68; memb Nat Cncl for Modern Languages 1979– (chm 1981–85), chm Scottish Nat Working Pty on Standard Grade; memb Examinations Bd Inst of Linguists 1986–91; hon sec Scottish Univs French Language Res Assoc 1985–; Officier dans l'Ordre des Palmes Académiques 1986; *Publications* contrib to: Voltaire's Correspondence (1953–63), Rousseau's Contemporary Reputation in France (1963), New Cambridge Bibliography of English Literature Vol 2 (1971), The Definitive Text of Voltaire's Works: The Leningrad Encadrée (1974), Voltaire's Humour (1979), Re-appraisals of Rousseau: Studies in Honour of R A Leigh (1980), Modern Swiss Literature: Unity and Diversity (1985); Initiator Le Français en Faculté (jtly, 1980), En Fin de Compte (jtly, 1988), Definitive Iconography of Voltaire (1996); *Recreations* grade 1 SAF timekeeper for athletics, photography; *Clubs* Fife Athletic, Paris University, Hallamshire Harriers; *Style*— Prof Samuel Taylor; ✉ 11 Irvine Crescent, St Andrews, Fife KY16 8LG (☎ 01334 472588)

TAYLOR, Hon Mrs (Sarah Lovell); *née* Rippon; 2 da of Baron Rippon of Hexham, PC, QC (Life Peer); *b* 10 March 1950; *Educ* Sherborne Sch for Girls Dorset, St Paul's Girls' Sch London, St Anne's Coll Oxford (MA); *m* 1978 (m dis 1988), Michael Taylor; 2 s (James Geoffrey Bethune b 1979, Alexander Edward Yorke b 1982); *Career* admitted slr 1978; called to the NY Bar 1980; Theodore Goddard Solicitors 1974–77, Nixon Hargraves Devans & Doyle NY (Lawyers) 1980–84; dir: Robert Fraser Group Ltd 1986–91, Robert Fraser & Partners Ltd and subsid 1986–91; subsequently ptnr Penningtons, currently ptnr Woodroffes; *Style*— The Hon Mrs Taylor; ✉ Woodroffes, 36 Ebury Street, London SW1W 0LU (☎ 0171 730 0001)

TAYLOR, Selwyn Francis; s of Alfred Petre Taylor (d 1958), of Combe, Malborough, S Devon, and Emily, *née* Edwards (d 1965); *b* 16 Sept 1913; *Educ* Keble Coll Oxford (MA), King's Coll Hosp London, Stockholm, Harvard, DM MCh; *m* 14 Oct 1939, Ruth Margaret, da of Sir Alfred Bakewell Howitt, CVO, MP (d 1950), of Wolfhall Manor, Burbage, Wilts; 1 s (Simon b 8 Sept 1945), 1 da (Jane b 18 Nov 1950); *Career* served RNVR 1940–45, Surgn Lt Cdr 1944; surgical specialist: Kintyre, E Africa, Mobile Surgical Unit Malaya, Sydney; univ lectr and conslt surgn: RPMS 1947–78 (dean 1965–75), KCH 1951–65; Rockefeller travelling fell Harvard 1948–49; visiting prof: Duke Univ, UCLA, Cincinnati, Chapel Hill, Hong Kong, SA; memb: Gen Med Cncl, Senate Univ of London, Euro Thyroid Assoc (fndr memb), Cncl RCS 1965 (vice pres 1976–78); pres: Harveian Soc, Med Educn Soc, RSM (ed Proceedings); first pres Int Assoc Endocrine Surgns 1978–81; chm London Thyroid Club, corresponding fell American Thyroid Assoc; Gold Staff Offr Coronation 1953; Freeman City of London, Liveryman Worshipful Soc of Apothecaries; Hon FRCSEd, Hon FCM South Africa; FRCS, fell RPMS; *Books* Recent Advances in Surgery (edns 5–10, 1959–80), Short Text Book of Surgery (edns 1–7,1960–80), Surgical Management (1984); *Recreations* sailing, tennis, gardening, wine; *Clubs* Garrick, Hurlingham, RN Sailing Assoc, Bosham Sailing, Saintsbury; *Style*— Selwyn Taylor, Esq; ✉ Trippets, Bosham, Chichester PO18 8JE (☎ 01243 573387)

TAYLOR, Simon John; s of John Kenneth Taylor, of Chesterfield, and Ruth Marjorie, *née* Standeven; *b* 28 Dec 1950; *Educ* Repton, St Peter's Coll Oxford (BA, MA); *m* 25 April 1992, Elizabeth Ann, da of Grant and Patricia Gerrard, of Vancouver, Canada; 1 s (Guy Grant b 4 Sept 1993); *Career* articled clerk Gordon Dadds & Co 1975–77, admitted slr 1977, ptnr Sinclair Roche & Temperley 1983– (asst slr 1977–83); memb Law Soc; *Recreations* fishing, sailing, riding, theatre; *Style*— Simon Taylor, Esq; ✉ Sinclair Roche & Temperley, Royex House, 5 Aldermanbury Square, London EC2V 7LE (☎ 0171 452 4000, fax 0171 452 4001)

TAYLOR, Stanley Thomas; s of Charles Taylor (d 1948), and Eleanor Marion, *née* North (d 1969); *b* 26 Sept 1923; *Educ* Archbishop Tenisons's GS; *m* 12 Feb 1955, Valerie Mary, da of Ernest Whitmarsh-Everiss (d 1972), of Bristol; 1 s (Stephen Charles b 1960), 1 da (Helen Frances b 1956); *Career* war serv cmmnd RAFVR; admin of Hertfordshire Health Authy until 1979, chief exec and sec Children's Film & Television Fndn 1980–; Freeman City of London, fndr memb Worshipful Co Chartered Secretaries and Administrators; FHSM 1968, FCIS 1970; *Recreations* golf, reading (biographies), walking; *Clubs* RAF; *Style*— Stanley T Taylor, Esq; ✉ 22 Stakers Ct, Milton Rd, Harpenden, Herts AL5 5PA (☎ 01582 715287); Children's Film & Television Foundation Ltd, Elstree Studios, Borehamwood, Herts WD6 1JG (☎ 0181 953 0844, fax 0181 207 0860)

TAYLOR, Wendy Ann (Mrs Bruce Robertson); CBE (1988); da of Edward Philip Taylor, and Lilian Maude, *née* Wright; *b* 29 Jan 1945; *Educ* St Martin's Sch of Art (LDAD); *m* 1982, Bruce Robertson, s of Maurice Robertson; 1 s (Matthew Thomas b 1984); *Career* sculptor; examiner Univ of London 1982–83, memb Ct RCA 1982–, memb Cncl Morley Coll 1985–88, conslt New Town Cmmn Basildon (formerly Basildon Devpt Corp) 1985–88, specialist advsr Fine Art Bd CNAA 1985–93 (memb 1980–85, memb Ctee for Art Design 1987–91), memb Royal Fine Art Cmmn 1981–, design conslt London Borough of Barking and Dagenham 1989–93; memb London Docklands Design Advsy Bd 1989–; tstee LAMA 1993–; memb PCFC 1989–90; fell Queen Mary and Westfield Coll Univ of London 1993; FZS 1989, FRBS 1994; *Solo Exhibitions* Axiom Gallery London 1970, Angela Flowers Gallery London 1972, 24 King's Lynn Festival Norfolk and World Trade Centre London 1974, Annely Juda Fine Art London 1975, Oxford Gallery Oxford 1976, Oliver Dowling Gallery Dublin 1976 and 1979, Building Art The Process (Building Centre Gallery) 1986, Austin Desmond & Phipps 1992; shown in over 100 gp exhibitions 1964–82; represented in collections in: GB, USA, Repub of Ireland, NZ, Germany, Sweden, Qatar, Switzerland, Seychelles; *Major Commissions* The Travellers London 1969, Gazebo (edn of 4 London, NY, Oxford, Suffolk) 1970–72, Triad

Oxford 1971, Timepiece London 1973, Calthae Leics 1977, Octo Milton Keynes 1979, Counterpoise Birmingham 1980, Compass Bowl Basildon 1980, Sentinel Reigate 1982, Bronze Relief Canterbury 1981, Equatorial Sundial Bletchley 1982, Essence Milton Keynes 1982, Opus Morley Coll 1983, Gazebo Golder's Hill Park London 1983, Network London 1984, Geo I and Geo II Stratford-upon-Avon 1985, Landscape and Tree of the Wood Fenhurst Surrey 1986, Pharos Peel Park E Kilbride 1986, Ceres Fenhurst Surrey 1986, Nexus Corby Northants 1986, Globe Sundial Swansea Maritime Quarter 1987, Spirit of Enterprise Isle of Dogs London 1987, Silver Fountain Guildford Surrey 1988, The Whirlies E Kilbride 1988, Pilot Kites Norwich Airport 1988, Fire Flow Hamilton Scotland 1988, Armillary Sundial Basildon Essex 1989, Pharos II E Kilbride 1989, Phoenix E Kilbride 1990, Globe Sundial London Zoological Gardens, Continuum Guildford, Sundial Sheffield 1991, Anchorage Salford Quays Manchester, Square Piece Plano Illinois USA, Wyvern Leicestershire 1992, Railings Univ of Sheffield 1993, Stained Glass Window St George's Church Sheffield 1994, Jester Emmanuel Coll Cambridge 1994, Challenge Stockley Park Middlesex, Equilibrium London 1995, Spirit Vann Surrey; *Awards* Walter Neurath 1964, Pratt 1965, Sainsbury 1966, Arts Cncl 1977, Duais Na Riochta (Kingdom prize), Gold medal Repub of Ireland 1977; winner silk screen Barcham Green Print Competition 1978; *Recreations* gardening; *Style—* Ms Wendy Taylor, CBE; ✉ 73 Bow Road, Bow, London EC3 2AN (☎ 0181 981 2037, fax 0181 980 3153)

TAYLOR, Prof Sir William; kt (1990), CBE (1982); s of Herbert Taylor (d 1969), and Maud Ethel, *née* Peyto (d 1972); *b* 31 May 1930; *Educ* Erith GS, LSE (BScEcon), Westminster Coll London (PGCE), Univ of London Inst of Educn (DipEd, PhD); *m* 30 Dec 1954, Rita, da of Ronald Hague (d 1957); 1 s (Dr Richard William James b 27 July 1964), 2 da (Anne Catherine (Mrs Mitchell) b 12 April 1958, Rosemary Caroline (Dr Williams) b 11 March 1960); *Career* Nat Serv Royal West Kent Regt 1948–49, Intelligence Corps 1950–53, 135 Field Security Section TA; teacher in Kent 1953–59, dep head Slade Green Secdy Sch 1956–59, sr lectr St Luke's Coll Exeter 1959–61, princ lectr and head of Educn Dept Bede Coll Durham 1961–64, tutor and lectr in educn Univ of Oxford 1964–66, prof of educn Univ of Bristol 1966–73, dir Univ of London Inst of Educn 1973–83, princ Univ of London 1983–85, vice-chllr Univ of Hull 1985–91, hon fell Green Coll and visiting prof Univ of Oxford 1991–, vice-chllr Univ of Huddersfield 1994–95, Leverhulme emeritus fell Univ of London Inst of Educn 1995–; chm of convocation Univ of London 1994–97; chm: Educnl Advsy Cncl of the IBA 1977–83, Univs Cncl for the Educn of Teachers 1976–79, Ctee for Educnl Res Cncl of Europe 1968–71, Nat Fndn for Educnl Res 1984–88, Cncl for the Accreditation of Teacher Educn (CATE) 1984–93, Univs Cncl for Adult and Continuing Educn 1986–90, NFER/Nelson Publishing Co 1988–, NI Teacher Educn Ctee 1994–; dir Fenner plc 1988–93; pres: Cncl for Educn in World Citizenship 1980–90, Assoc of Colls of Further and Higher Educn 1985–88, Soc for Research in HE 1996–; vice pres Cncl for International Educn 1992–; Freeman City of London 1986, Liveryman Worshipful Soc of Apothecaries 1986; Hon DSc Aston Univ 1977, Hon LittD Univ of Leeds 1979, Hon DCL Univ of Kent 1981, Hon DUniv Open Univ 1983, Hon DLitt Loughborough Univ 1984, Hon LLD Univ of Hull 1992; Hon DEd: Univ of Kingston 1993, Univ of Plymouth 1993, Oxford Brookes Univ 1993, Univ of the West of England 1994; hon fell Westminster Coll Oxford 1990, centenary fell Thames Poly 1991; FCP 1977, FCCEA 1978, FWACEA 1979; *Books* The Secondary Modern School (1963), Educational Administration and the Social Sciences (ed jtly 1969, Japanese edn 1970), Society and the Education of Teachers (1969), Towards a Policy for the Education of Teachers (ed, 1969), Policy and Planning in Post Secondary Education (1971), Theory into Practice (1972), Heading for Change (1973), Research Perspectives in Education (ed, 1973), Perspectives and Plans for Graduate Studies (with Downey, Daniels and Baker, 1973), Educational Administration in Australia and Abroad (jt ed with Thomas and Farquhar, 1975), Research and Reform in Teacher Education (1978), Education for the Eighties - the Central Issues (ed with Simon, 1981), New Zealand - OECD Reviews of National Policies for Education (with P H Karmel and Ingrid Eide, 1983), Metaphors of Education (ed, 1984), Universities under Scrutiny (1987); *Recreations* books, music; *Style—* Prof Sir William Taylor, CBE; ✉ 26 Woburn Square, London WC1H 0AL (☎ 01304 362086, fax 01304 362086, e-mail w.taylor@ioe.ac.uk)

TAYLOR, William; s of Abraham Taylor (d 1962), of Newcastle upon Tyne, and Isabella Oliver, *née* Franks (d 1983); *b* 31 Dec 1921; *Educ* Rutherford Coll Newcastle upon Tyne, AA Sch of Architecture (AADipl, SADG); *m* 1, 16 April 1949, Stella (d 1984), da of Edwin George Wilkins (d 1954), of Marnhull, Dorset; 1 s (Randolph b 1960); m 2, 15 Dec 1992, Jean Graham, of Harrogate; *Career* lectr in architecture Univ of Durham 1945–47, private practice 1947–52, RIBA bursar Br Sch of Archaeology Athens 1957, Fulbright scholar and visiting prof Sch of Architecture Univ of Virginia USA 1959–60, princ lectr Sch of Architecture Oxford 1964– (sr lectr 1952–), sr tutor Dept of Architecture Oxford Poly 1970–81, assoc architect Br Sch of Archaeology at Knossos Crete 1977–; ARIBA 1945, FRIBA 1970; *Books* A Bibliography on Romanesque Architecture (1960), Greek Architecture (1971), History of Architecture (contrib 18 edn, 1975), The Worlds Great Architecture (contrib, 1980), The Bronze Age Palace at Knossos (jtly, 1981); *Recreations* music, ancient history, archaeology; *Style—* William Taylor, Esq; ✉ 23 Callerton Court, Ponteland, Northumberland NE20 9EN (☎ 01661 872588)

TAYLOR, William; QPM; *b* 25 March 1947; *m*, 2 step-s; *Career* constable 1966, subsequently sergeant then inspr London 1966–74, detective chief inspr i/c Divisional CID London 1974–76, Community Relations Branch New Scotland Yard 1976–78, detective superintendent Central Drugs Squad 1978–79, detective chief superintendent and staff offr to Cmmr of Police 1980–82, cdr No 9 Regnl Crime and Robbery Squad (Area HQ 1982–85) 1985, dep to Cmmr City of London Police 1985–89, dep to the Chief Constable of Thames Valley Police 1989–90, asst cmmr Specialist Ops New Scotland Yard 1990–94, cmmr City of London Police 1994–; ACPO rep for EUROPOL discussions; chm: ACPO Crime Ctee, Nat User Gp Regnl Crime Squad, User Gp Nat Criminal Intelligence Service, Euro Ctee of Interpol; memb: Home Office Regnl Crime Squads Standing Ctee, NCIS Standing Ctee, Crime Ctee of Central Conference, ACPO Terrorism Ctee, ACPO Int Affairs Advsy Ctee, Home Office Working Gp on Confiscation, SFO Mgmnt Bd; *Recreations* reading, hill walking, horse riding; *Style—* William Taylor, Esq, QPM; ✉ Commissioner, City of London Police, 26 Old Jewry, London EC2R 8DJ (☎ 0171 601 2004)

TAYLOR, William Bernard (Bill); s of Francis Augustus Taylor (d 1956), of Swansea, and Mary Elizabeth, *née* George; *b* 13 Dec 1930; *Educ* Dynevor Sch Swansea, Univ of Kent (MA); *m* 26 April 1956, Rachel May, da of Daniel Brynmor Davies (d 1959), of Godre Rhiw, Morriston, Swansea; 1 s (Simon b 1965), 2 da (Kim b 1959, Deborah b 1961); *Career* Nat Serv 1949–51, cmmnd RNVR 1950, Sub Lt RNVR 1951–53; Dist Audit Serv 1951–61, treas Llwchwr UDC 1967–68 (dep treas 1961–67), asst educn offr Fin and Mgmnt Manchester Corp 1969–72, co treas Kent 1980–87 (asst co treas 1972–73, dep co treas 1973–80); specialist local authy advsr: Arthur Young Management Consultants 1987–89, Lombard North Central plc 1987–92, Invesco 1987–96, Sedgwick (UK) Ltd 1987–95, Baronsmead PLC 1993–96; dir Interlake DRC Ltd 1989–94, non-exec memb Medway Health Authy 1990–94 (chm Fin and Review Ctee 1990–94), vice chm Medway Nat Health Tst 1994– (chm Audit Ctee, chm Performance Review Ctee); author of numerous articles for learned magazines; memb Exec Ctee Soc of Co Treas 1983–86, fin advsr to Social Servs Ctee of Assoc of CCs 1983–86, Lloyd's underwriter 1988–96; memb: Maidstone Rotary Club (pres 1995–96), Union St Methodist Church; life memb W Kent Speakers Club, hon treas SE Eng Tourist Bd 1980–87, govr Kent Inst of Art and Design (chm Fin Ctee 1989–95); FRSA, CIPFA; *Books* Terotechnology & The Pursuit of Life Cycle Costs (1980), The Financial Management of Local Authorities (report to Council of Europe, 1993); *Recreations* public speaking, tennis, cricket, watching rugby, golf; *Style—* Bill Taylor, Esq; ✉ Selby Shaw, Heath Rd, Boughton Monchelsea, Maidstone, Kent ME17 4JE (☎ 01622 7450 22, fax 01622 741259)

TAYLOR, (Peter) William Edward; QC (1981); s of Peter Taylor (d 1963), and Julia Anne, *née* North (d 1989); *b* 27 July 1917; *Educ* Peter Symonds' Sch Winchester, Christ's Coll Cambridge (MA); *m* 2 Jan 1948, Julia Mary, da of Air Cdre Sir Vernon Brown, CB (d 1986), of Chelsea, London SW3; 2 s (Malcolm b 1950, Nigel b 1952); *Career* cmmd TA 1937; served RA 1939–46: France and Belgium 1939–40, N Africa 1942–43, N W Europe 1944–45 (despatches), acting Lt-Col 1945; Hon Maj TARO 1946; called to the Bar Inner Temple 1946, Lincoln's Inn 1953, in practice 1947–94, lectr in construction of documents Cncl of Legal Educn 1952–70, Conveyancing Counsel of the Ct 1974–81, bencher Lincoln's Inn 1976–; memb: Gen Cncl of the Bar 1971–74, Senate of the Inns of Ct and the Bar 1974–75, Inter-professional Ctee on Retirement Provision 1974–92, Land Registration Rule Ctee 1976–81, Standing Ctee on Conveyancing 1985–87, Inc Cncl of Law Reporting 1977–87 (vice chm 1987–91); *Recreations* sailing, music; *Style—* William Taylor, Esq, QC; ✉ 46 Onslow Sq, London SW7 3NX (☎ 0171 589 1301); Carey Sconce, Yarmouth, Isle of Wight, PO41 OSB

TAYLOR, William Gibson (Bill); s of John Taylor (d 1983), and Brenda Louise, *née* Gibson; *b* 27 Jan 1957; *Educ* Rushcliffe Comprehensive Sch Nottingham, Univ of Sheffield (RIBA Nat Students prize, MA, Dip in Architecture); *m* 1982, Denise, da of George Roper; 2 s (Robert John Gibson b 1987, Andrew George Gibson b 1989); *Career* worked with Mervyn Awon (architect) on Central Bank of Barbados 1979–80; Michael Hopkins and Partners: architect 1982–88, project architect Mound Stand Lord's Cricket Ground 1985–87, ptnr 1988–; visiting tutor Univ of Sheffield; RIBA; *Style—* Bill Taylor, Esq; ✉ Michael Hopkins and Partners, 27 Broadley Terrace, London NW1 6LG (☎ 0171 724 1751, fax 0171 723 0932)

TAYLOR, Lt Cdr William Horace; GC (1941), MBE (1973); s of William Arthur Taylor (d 1945), and Hilda Jane, *née* Nicholson; *b* 23 Oct 1908; *Educ* Manchester GS; *m* 19 Sept 1946, Joan Isabel, da of John Skaife D'Ingerthorpe; 1 s (William Norman b 1949), 3 da (Susan Rosemary b 1948, Jane Elizabeth b 1951, Belinda Mary b 1954); *Career* Dept of Torpedoes and Mines Admty (despatches and commendation for brave conduct 1941), fndr memb Naval Clearance Divers, HMS Vernon 1944; travelling cmmr Sea Scouts UK 1946, field cmmr SW Eng Scout Assoc 1952–74, estate mangr 1975–84; *Recreations* scouting, boating, music; *Clubs* Banchory Branch Royal British Legion of Scotland, Banchory Ternan Probus; *Style—* Lt Cdr William Horace Taylor, Esq, GC, MBE, RNR (ret); ✉ 3 Hanover Court, Banchory AB31 3ZA (☎ 01330 824038)

TAYLOR, William James; QC (Scot 1986); s of Cecil Taylor, of 15 Drumblair Crescent, Inverness, and Ellen, *née* Daubney; *b* 13 Sept 1944; *Educ* Robert Gordon's Coll, Univ of Aberdeen (MA, LLB); *Career* admitted Faculty of Advocates 1971, standing jr DHSS 1978–79, standing jr counsel FCO 1979–86, called to the Bar Inner Temple 1990; *Recreations* sailing, skiing, hillwalking, theatre, opera, music; *Style—* William Taylor, Esq, QC; ✉ Hill House, Dirleton Avenue, North Berwick, East Lothian EH39 4QL (☎ 01620 895111, fax 01620 894570); Parliament House, Parliament Square, Edinburgh, EH1 1RF (☎ 0131 226 2881); 3 Gray's Inn Square, London WC1R 5AH (☎ 0171 831 2311, fax 0171 404 4939)

TAYLOR BRADFORD, Barbara; *see:* Bradford, Barbara Taylor

TAYLOR OF BLACKBURN, Baron (Life Peer UK 1978), of Blackburn, Co Lancaster; Thomas Taylor; CBE (1974, OBE 1969), JP (Blackburn 1960), DL (Lancs 1994); s of James Taylor; *b* 10 June 1929; *Educ* Blakey Moor Higher Grade Sch; *m* 1950, Kathleen, da of John Edward Nurton; 1 s (Hon Paul Nurton b 1953); *Career* memb Blackburn Town Cncl 1954–76 (ldr, and chm Policy and Resources Ctee 1972–76), dep pro chllr Lancaster Univ 1974–95, chm Govt Ctee of Enquiry into Mgmnt and Govt of Schs, past chm Juvenile Bench, pres Free Church Cncl 1962–68, former memb Norweb Bd, former memb Select Ctee on Sci and Technol, memb Cwlth Parly Assoc; chm: Canatxx Energy Ventures Ltd, Grove Properties Ltd, Chameleon Educational Systems Ltd; conslt to serveral other cos; LLD Univ of Lancaster 1996; FRGS 1994; *Style—* The Rt Hon the Lord Taylor of Blackburn, CBE, JP, DL; ✉ 9 Woodview, Cherry Tree, Blackburn, Lancs BB2 5LL

TAYLOR OF GOSFORTH, Baron (Life Peer UK 1992), of Embleton in the County of Northumberland; Sir Peter Murray Taylor; kt (1980), PC (1988); s of Herman Louis Taylor (d 1966), of Newcastle upon Tyne, and Raie Helena, *née* Shockett; *b* 1 May 1930; *Educ* Newcastle Royal GS, Pembroke Coll Cambridge; *m* 1956, Irene Shirley (d 1995), da of Lionel Harris, of Newcastle; 1 s (Hon David Louis), 3 da (Hon Ruth Diana b 4 June 1958, Hon Deborah Frances (Hon Mrs Stevenson) b 18 Dec 1959, Hon Judith Claire (Hon Mrs Bridge) b 22 Dec 1961); *Career* called to the Bar Inner Temple 1954; recorder of Huddersfield 1969, dep chm Northumberland QS 1970; recorder of: Teesside 1970–71, Crown Court 1972–80; QC 1967, bencher 1975, chm of the Bar 1980, judge of the High Court of Justice (Queen's Bench Div) 1980–87, presiding judge North Eastern Circuit 1984–87 (ldr 1975–80), a Lord Justice of Appeal 1987–92, Lord Chief Justice of England 1992–96; hon master of the bench Middle Temple 1995; pres Inns of Ct Cncl 1991–92; chm Hillsborough Disaster Inquiry 1989 (leading to Taylor Report); controller Royal Opera House Devpt Land Tst 1990–, chm Trinity Coll of Music 1991–92; hon fell Pembroke Coll Cambridge 1992; Hon LLD: Univ of Newcastle, Univ of Northumbria, Univ of Liverpool, Univ of Nottingham, Univ of Leeds, City Univ of London; *Style—* The Rt Hon Lord Taylor of Gosforth, PC; ✉ c/o Royal Courts of Justice, The Strand, London WC2A 2LL

TAYLOR OF GRYFE, Baron (Life Peer UK 1968), of Bridge of Weir, Renfrewshire; Thomas Johnston Taylor; DL (Renfrewshire 1970); s of John Sharp Taylor, of Glasgow; *b* 27 April 1912; *Educ* Bellahouston Acad Glasgow; *m* 1943, Isobel, da of William Wands; 2 da (Hon Jill (Hon Mrs Waber) b 1945, Hon Joyce (Hon Mrs Richards) b 1948); *Career* sits as Lab Peer in House of Lords; chm: The Forestry Cmmn 1970–76, Econ Forestry Gp 1976–82, Morgan Grenfell (Scotland) Ltd 1973–86, Scottish Railways Bd 1971–80, Scottish Peers Assoc 1987–, Parly All-Pty Forestry Gp; memb: BR Bd 1968–80, Bd Scottish Television Ltd 1968–82; dir: Scottish Civic Tst, Whiteaway Laidlaw & Co Ltd (Bankers) 1971–90, Friends' Provident Life Office 1972–82, Scottish Metropolitan Property Co Ltd 1972–90, BR Property Bd 1972–82; Hon LLD Strathclyde 1974; tstee The Dulverton Tst 1980–, vice chm Scot Cncl Devpt and Indust; Cdr's Cross Order of Merit (FRG); FRSE 1977; *Clubs* Caledonian, Royal and Ancient (St Andrews); *Style—* The Rt Hon the Lord Taylor of Gryfe, DL, FRSE; ✉ 33 Seagate, Kingsbarns, St Andrews, Fife KY16 8SC (☎ 0133 488 430)

TAYLOR-SMITH, John Roderick; s of Harold Wilfred Taylor-Smith (d 1990), and Kathleen, *née* MacDonald; *b* 14 July 1959; *Educ* Rongotai Coll Wellington NZ, Univ of Otago (BDS); *m* 16 Jan 1988, Janice Wendy, da of Stewart Withell (d 1991); 1 s (Max Stewart b 24 April 1993), 1 da (Megan Kate b 28 Jan 1995); *Career* house surgeon Wellington Public Hosp NZ 1983–84, sr house surgeon Plastics and Maxillo-Facial Unit Lower Hutt Hosp NZ 1984–85, proprietor dental practice Wimpole St 1990– (dental surgeon London 1985–); memb: BDA, Br Soc for Occlusal Studies 1988; *Recreations* cricket, rugby, golf, squash, tennis, skiing, scuba diving, riding; *Clubs* Roehampton, London New Zealand Cricket, Wellington Golf (NZ); *Style—* John Taylor-Smith, Esq; ✉ 30A Wimpole St, London W1M 7AE (☎ 0171 224 4432)

TAYLOR THOMPSON, (John) Derek; CB (1985); s of John Taylor Thompson (d 1964), of Herts, and Marjorie Bligh, *née* Westcott (d 1993); *b* 6 Aug 1927; *Educ* St Peter's Sch York, Balliol Coll Oxford (MA); *m* 2 Oct 1954, Helen Margaret, da of George Laurie Walker (d 1934), of Wimbledon; 2 da (Catherine b 1957, Bopha b 1960); *Career* memb Bd Inland Revenue 1973–87; chm Fiscal Affrs Ctee OECD 1984–89; sec Churches Main Ctee 1990–, churchwarden St James the Less Nutley, memb Chichester Diocesan and Uckfield Deanery Synods; *Recreations* rural pursuits, reading, historical writing; *Clubs* United Oxford and Cambridge Univ; *Style—* Derek Taylor Thompson, Esq, CB; ✉ Jessops, Nutley, E Sussex TN22 3PD

TAYLORSON, John Brown; s of John Brown Taylorson (d 1945), and Edith Maria Taylorson (d 1981); *b* 5 March 1931; *Educ* Forest Sch Snares Brook Essex; *m* 1, 1960 (m dis), Barbara June Hagg; 2 s (Jonathan, James), 1 da (Sally); m 2, 1985, Helen Anne; *Career* Flying Offr RAF 1959–61; md: Int Div Gardner Merchant Food Services 1974–77, Fedics Food Services Pty 1977–80; chief exec Civil Serv Catering Orgn 1980–81, head of catering BA plc 1981–89; md: John Taylorson Associates 1990–, Inflight Marketing Services 1990–; chm International Service Industry Search 1990–95, dir Berkeley Scott Ltd 1992–95; pres International Flight Catering Assoc 1983–86; *Recreations* golf, walking, theatre, crosswords; *Clubs* Escorts, Jesters, Burhill Golf; *Style—* John Taylorson, Esq; ✉ Deer Pond Cottage, Highfields, East Horsley, Surrey KT24 5AA; John Taylorson Group of Companies (☎ 01483 283577)

TE ATAIRANGIKAAHU, Te Arikinui Dame Arikinui; DBE (1970); da of Koroki Te Rata Mahuta V (d 1966); *b* 23 July 1931; *Educ* Waikato Diocesan Secdy Sch for Girls Hamilton; *m* 1952, Whatumoana Paki, QSO; 2 s, 5 da; *Career* Hon Doctorate (Waikato); The Maori Queen 1966–; Te Atairangikaahu (the soaring bird of the dawn); ONZ (1988), OStJ (1986); *Style—* Te Arikinui Dame Te Atairangikaahu, ONZ, DBE; ✉ Turangawaewae Marae, Turongo House, Ngaruawahia, NZ

TE KANAWA, Dame Kiri Janette; DBE (1982, OBE 1973), ONZ (1995), AC; da of Thomas Te Kanawa, of Auckland, NZ, and late Elanor Te Kanawa; *b* 6 March 1944, Gisborne, NZ; *Educ* St Mary's Coll Auckland, London Opera Centre; *m* 1967, Desmond Stephen Park, s of Joseph Frank Park, of Brisbane, Aust; 1 s, 1 da; *Career* opera singer; studied singing under Dame Sister Mary Leo 1959–65; has sung major roles at: Royal Opera House (Covent Garden), Metropolitan Opera (New York), Paris Opera, San Francisco Opera, Sydney Opera, Cologne Opera, La Scala (Milan); sang at Royal Wedding of HRH Prince of Wales to Lady Diana Spencer 1981; Hon LLD Dundee; Hon DMus: Durham 1982, Oxford 1983; *Style—* Dame Kiri Te Kanawa, DBE, ONZ, AC

TEACHER, (Rosemary) Chloe; da of Sir Henry d'Avigdor-Goldsmid, Bt (d 1976), and Rosemary, *née* Nicholl; *b* 25 Jan 1945; *Educ* Southover Manor Sch, UCL; *m* 26 April 1969, (Anthony) James Moreton Teacher; 1 s (Harry Donald Macdonald b 14 Oct 1970); 3 da (Laura Poppy Macnaghten b 30 May 1973, Petra Rose Macnaghten b 8 June 1980, Sarah Cordelia Macnaghten b 23 March 1983); *Career* worked at Granada Television 1966–67, asst London Magazine & Alan Ross Ltd 1967–69; High Sheriff for Co of Kent 1994–95; chm: Country Landowners' Assoc 1986–88 and 1990–91 (memb Cncl 1988–92), Weald and W Kent Economic Forum, Rural Interest Gp; memb Cncl: Wildfowl and Wetlands Tst 1984–90, Game Conservancy Tst 1988–; memb Ctee Tonbridge and Malling District CPRE 1992–96; pres Tonbridge Cottage Hosp; tstee: Southover Manor Educnl Tst, Capel Community Tst; govr: Capel County Primary Sch (chm of Govrs 1988–93), Hadlow Coll of Agric and Horticulture 1985–; *Style—* Mrs James Teacher; ✉ Hadlow Place, Tonbridge, Kent TN11 0BW (☎ 01732 851722, fax 01732 850904)

TEAGUE, Alan Richard; *b* 11 July 1947; *Career* co sec British Vita plc; FCCA 1980; *Style—* Alan Teague, Esq; ✉ British Vita plc, Oldham Road, Middleton, Manchester M24 2DB (☎ 0161 643 1133, fax 0161 653 5411)

TEAGUE, (Edward) Thomas Henry; s of Harry John Teague, and Anne Elizabeth, *née* Hunt; *b* 21 May 1954, Weymouth, Dorset; *Educ* St Francis Xavier's Coll Liverpool, Christ's Coll Cambridge (MA); *m* 8 Aug 1980, Helen Mary Bernadette, da of Daniel Matthew Howard (d 1974); 2 s (Michael b 1983, Dominic b 1985); *Career* called to the Bar Inner Temple 1977, in practice Wales and Chester Circuit 1978–, asst recorder 1993–; author of various astronomical papers; FRAS; *Style—* Thomas Teague, Esq; ✉ Campion House, Becketts Lane, Chester CH3 5RW (☎ 01244 311520); 40 King St, Chester CH1 2AH (☎ 01244 323886/349591, fax 01244 347732)

TEALL OF TEALLACH, Dr (Dennistoun) Gordon; s of Bernard John Teall (d 1966), Baron of Huntly, of Radford Semele, formerly of the County of Dunbarton, and Agnes Mary, *née* Cottrell (d 1977); *b* 8 Aug 1924; *Educ* Warwick Sch, Cooper's Hill Coll (Ed Cert), Univ of Leicester (MEd, PhD), Coll of Preceptors (LCP); *m* 4 Oct 1946, Eleanor Joan, da of John Thomas Ackland (d 1967), of Quadring; 2 s (David b 1947, Richard b 1962), 2 da (Maryon b 1950, Christine b 1956); *Career* serv WWII despatch rider Civil Defence 1940–43, radio offr Merchant Navy 1945–46 (cadet 1943–44); works chemist Colas Products Ltd 1946–47; headmaster: Yarwell Sch 1952–60, Priory Prep Sch 1960–62, princ Priory Coll 1962–84; chm: Midlands area Independent Schs Assoc 1982–85, NE England and Scotland Independent Schs Assoc 1982–85, Scottish Tartans Museum Tst; hon exec pres Scottish Tartans Soc 1983– (patron 1978–, chm 1979–83), hon pres: Highland Heritage Museum Tst; registrar Register of All Publicly Known Tartans; memb: Manorial Soc of GB, Royal Scottish Country Dance Assoc, Caledonian Soc Edinburgh, Scottish Railways Preservation Soc, Scottish Landowners Assoc; chm bd of tstees Scottish Tartans Museum N Carolina USA 1988–; memb Lloyd's of London; cncllr: Oundle and Thrapston RDC 1961–67, Barnack RDC 1965–68, Nassington Parish Cncl 1958–66, St Martin's Without Parish Cncl 1965–68; hon memb Clan Grant, memb House of Gordon, life memb Saltire Soc; Lord of the Manor of Croyland; feudal superior Gordon Schs Huntly Aberdeenshire; coastal skipper RYA; Royal Humane Soc's Award for Gallantry in Saving Life, certificate of honour California State Senate 1990; MInstD, FCS 1945, FSA Scot 1978, FSTS 1981; Hon Lt-Col Militia of the State of Georgia 1987; *Books* May Festivals (1963), The Tradesmen and Corporation of Stamford 1485–1750 (1975), The Manx Tartans (1981), A Brief History of The Scottish Tartans Society (1988), The District Tartans of Scotland (jtly, 1992); *Recreations* sailing in strong winds, windsurfing in light airs, horse riding, Scottish dancing, cross country skiing, mountain walking, swimming in warm waters; *Clubs* Univ Centre (Cambridge), Manx Soc; *Style—* Dr Gordon Teall of Teallach, Baron of Huntly; ✉ Cornaa House, Maughold, IOM (☎ 01624 813580); Scottish Tartans Society, Port-na-Craig, Pitlochry, Perthshire PH16 5ND (☎ 01796 474079, car tel 0860 640 234)

TEAR, Robert; CBE (1984); s of Thomas Arthur Tear, of Barry, S Glam, and Edith Marion Tear; *b* 8 March 1939; *Educ* Barry GS, King's Coll Cambridge (MA); *m* 10 Jan 1961, Hilary, da of William Thomas, of Cwmbran, Gwent; 2 da (Rebecca b 22 Nov 1961, Elizabeth b 11 Feb 1966); *Career* opera/concert singer and conductor; regular appearances: throughout America, Covent Garden, Munich, Park, Salzburg, Brussels and Geneva; holder of Chair of Int Vocal Studies at RAM; hon fell King's Coll Cambridge 1988; RAM, RCM; *Books* Tear Here (1990), Singer Beware (1995); *Recreations* anything interesting; *Style—* Robert Tear, Esq, CBE; ✉ Harold Holt Ltd, 31 Sinclair Rd, London W14 0NS (☎ 0171 603 4600)

TEARE, (Eleanor) Christine; da of James Ralph Teare (d 1990), of the Isle of Man, and Kathleen Mona, *née* Duggan; *b* 21 March 1956; *Educ* Castle Rushen HS Isle of Man, Royal Acad of Music (two scholarships from Countess of Munster Fndn, DipRAM); *Career* soprano; princ soprano WNO 1985–89, freelance 1989–; ARCM, FTCL, Hon ARAM; *Roles* with WNO incl: Donna Anna in Don Giovanni (debut) 1982, Empress in Die Frau ohne Schatten, Amelia in Un Ballo in Maschera, Countess Almaviva in The Marriage of Figaro, Berta in The Barber of Seville, Musetta in La Bohème, Helmwige in Die Walküre, Third Norn in Götterdämmerung, Flower Maiden in Parsifal; others incl: Donna Anna (Opera North) 1986, First Lady in The Magic Flute (ENO) 1986, Helmwig in Die Walküre (Royal Opera House Covent Garden debut) 1988 (also Helmwig and Third Norn in full Ring Cycle 1991), Berta in The Barber of Seville (ENO) 1992; also appeared in Julian Mitchell's play After Aida (Old Vic) 1986; *Recordings* incl: Flower Maiden in Parsifal (WNO under Reginald Goodall) 1984, Janacek's Osud (under Sir Charles Mackerras) 1989; *Recreations* theatre, golf, Manx history and culture; *Style—* Miss Christine Teare; ✉ Stafford Law Associates, 6 Barnham Close, Weybridge, Surrey KT13 9PR (☎ 01932 854489, fax 01932 858521)

TEARE, Nigel John Martin; QC (1991); s of Eric John Teare (d 1980), and Mary Rackham, *née* Faragher (d 1985); *b* 8 Jan 1952; *Educ* King William's Coll Castletown IOM, St Peter's Coll Oxford (BA, MA); *m* 16 Aug 1975, (Elizabeth) Jane, da of Alan James Pentecost, of Beaulieu, Derby Rd, Nottingham; 2 s (Roland b 1981, David b 1984), 1 da (Charlotte b 1982); *Career* called to the Bar Lincoln's Inn 1974, junior counsel to treasy in Admty matters 1989–91, asst recorder 1993; memb Panel Lloyd's Salvage Arbitrators 1994; *Recreations* collecting Manx paintings, golf, squash, tennis; *Clubs* RAC; *Style—* Nigel Teare, Esq, QC; ✉ The Towers, Hawkshill Place, Portsmouth Rd, Esher, Surrey KT10 9HY (☎ 01372 464552); 4 Essex Ct, Temple, London EC4 (☎ 0171 797 7970, fax 0171 353 0998, telex 8812528 ADROIT)

TEARE, Richard Maxwell (Max); s of Arthur Hubert Teare, and Rosalind Margaret, *née* Baker; *b* 29 Jan 1946; *Educ* Kingswood Sch Bath, UCL (BScEcon); *m* 30 Oct 1971, Margaret Hamilton, da of William Joseph Bell; 2 s (Henry Hamilton b 9 July 1977, George Hamilton b 12 Aug 1983), 2 da (Sarah Margaret b 24 June 1973, Hannah Rosalind b 15 June 1975); *Career* Binder Hamlyn & Co CAs London until 1972; Deloitte Haskins & Sells CAs: Sydney 1972–75, Nottingham 1975–; ptnr Audit Investigations Coopers & Lybrand 1980–; dir Nottingham Playhouse; FCA 1979 (ACA 1970); *Recreations* skiing, singing, swimming, golf, family; *Style—* Max Teare, Esq; ✉ Coopers & Lybrand, Cumberland House, 35 Park Row, Nottingham NG1 6FY (☎ 0115 950 3500, fax 0115 950 2747, car 0378 337764)

TEASDALE, Anthony Laurence; s of John S Teasdale, of Beverley, N Humberside, and Pauline, *née* Tomlinson (d 1983); *b* 4 June 1957; *Educ* Slough GS, Balliol Coll Oxford (MA), Nuffield Coll Oxford (MPhil); *Career* lectr in politics Corpus Christi and Magdalen Colls Oxford 1980–82, policy advsr Euro Democratic Gp in Euro Parliament Brussels and London 1982–86, asst to Dir Gen for Econ and Fin Affrs EC Cncl of Mins Brussels 1986–88; special advsr: to Sec of State for Foreign and Commonwealth Affairs 1988–89, to Lord President of the Council and Leader of House of Commons 1989–90; res fell Nuffield Coll Oxford 1992–93, head London office and policy advsr EPP Gp in Euro Parl 1993–96, special advsr to Chllr of the Exchequer 1996–; *Books* Penguin Companion to European Union (1995); various articles; *Recreations* music, reading, travel; *Clubs* RAC; *Style—* Anthony Teasdale, Esq; ✉ HM Treasury, Parliament Street, London SW1 3AG (☎ 0171 270 5051)

TEBBIT, Sir Donald Claude; GCMG (1980, KCMG 1975, CMG 1965); s of Richard Claude Tebbit (d 1967), of Toft, Cambridge; *b* 4 May 1920; *Educ* Perse Sch Cambridge, Trinity Hall Cambridge (MA); *m* 1947, Barbara, da of Rev Norman Matheson (d 1952), of Beauly, Inverness-shire; 1 s, 3 da; *Career* Nat Serv WWII RNVR; entered FO 1946, min Br Embassy Washington 1970–72, chief clerk FCO 1972–76, high cmmr Aust 1976–80, ret; chm Dip Appeals Bd 1980–87, dir gen British Property Federation 1980–85, dir RTZ 1980–90; pres: (UK) Australian-British C of C 1980–90, Old Persean Soc 1981–82; govr Nuffield Hosps 1980–90 (dep chm); chm Marshall Aid Commemoration Cmmn 1985–95, memb Appeals Bd Cncl of Europe 1981–91; chm: ESU of the Cwlth 1983–87, Jt Cwlth Socs Cncl 1987–93; *Clubs* Travellers', Gog Magog Golf; *Style—* Sir Donald Tebbit, GCMG; ✉ Priory Cottage, Toft, Cambridge CB3 7RH

TEBBIT, Baron (Life Peer UK 1992), of Chingford in the London Borough of Waltham Forest; Norman Beresford Tebbit; CH (1987), PC (1981); 2 s of Leonard Albert and Edith Tebbit, of Enfield, Middx; *b* 29 March 1931; *Educ* Edmonton Co GS; *m* 1956, Margaret Elizabeth, da of Stanley Daines, of Chatteris; 2 s (Hon John Beresford b 1958, Hon William Mark b 1965), 1 da (Hon Alison Mary (Hon Mrs Shakespear-Smith) b 1960); *Career* RAF 1949–51, RAuxAF 1952–55; journalist 1947–49, in publishing and advertising 1951–53, airline pilot 1953–70 (memb BALPA and former lay official); MP (C): Epping 1970–74, Chingford 1974–92; formerly: memb Select Ctee Science and Technol, chm Cons Aviation Ctee, vice chm and sec Cons Housing and Construction Ctee, sec New Town MPs; PPS to Min of State for Employment 1972–73, Parly under sec of state for trade 1979–81, min of state for indust 1981, sec of state for employment 1981–Oct 1983, sec of state for trade and indust Oct 1983–85, chllr of Duchy of Lancaster 1985–87, chm Cons Pty 1985–87; political commentator BSkyB television 1989–; columnist Sun newspaper 1995–; dir: BET plc 1987–96, BT plc 1987–96, Sears plc 1987–; Liveryman Guild of Air Pilots and Air Navigators; *Books* Upwardly Mobile, An Autobiography (1988), Unfinished Business (1991); *Style—* The Rt Hon Lord Tebbit, PC, CH; ✉ c/o House of Lords, London SW1A 0PW

TEDDER, John Anthony; s of Ronald Sidney Tedder, RAF (ka 1943), and Florence Eva, *née* Buist; *b* 15 Sept 1943; *Educ* St Dunstan's Coll London, Ravensbourne Coll of Art, Birmingham Coll of Art and Design (BA); *m* 22 Dec 1970, Vera Jean, da of Douglas Osmonde; 2 da (Germaine b 23 March 1974, Lauren b 28 Dec 1977); *Career* asst design mangr John Harper & Co Ltd 1968–70, designer Taylor Law & Co Stourbridge 1970–71, ideas progressor Frido Div Friedland Doggart Ltd Stockport; sr indust designer: Corning (UK) Ltd Sunderland 1973–78, Rank Radio Int Plymouth 1978–81; product design assoc TACP Architects Liverpool 1981–84, owner Tedder Associates (industrial designers) 1984–, assoc lectr in product design N Staffs Univ 1987–; licenciate memb CSD 1967 (past chm various regions, former hon sec), FCSD 1976; *Recreations* photography, videography, getting away from England; *Style—* John Tedder, Esq; ✉ Tedder Associates, 37 Westbourne Rd, West Kirby, Wirral L48 4DQ (☎ 0151 625 1498, fax 0151 625 2548)

TEDDER, Philip Anthony; s of Arthur Henry Tedder (d 1988), and Winifred May, *née* Marshall; *b* 3 Sept 1945; *Educ* Sutton Co GS, Univ Coll of Wales; *m* 6 July 1968, Pauline, da of William Richarson, of Manchester; 1 s (Richard b 1977); *Career* Coopers & Lybrand (formerly Deloitte Haskins & Sells): joined 1968, Panel on Take-Overs and Mergers 1979–81, ptnr CA's 1981–; FCA; *Recreations* tennis, swimming, walking, photography; *Clubs* MCC, RAC; *Style—* Philip A Tedder, Esq; ✉ Coopers & Lybrand, 1 Embankment Place, London WC2N 6NN (☎ 0171 583 5000, fax 0171 213 5379, telex 887470)

TEDDER, 3 Baron (UK 1946); Robin John Tedder; s of 2 Baron Tedder (d 1994), and Peggy Eileen, *née* Growcott; *b* 6 April 1955; *m* 1, 1977, Jennifer Peggy (d 1978), da of John Mangan, of Christchurch, NZ; m 2, 1980, (Rita) Aristea, yr da of John Frangidis, of Sydney, NSW, Australia; 2 s (Hon Benjamin John, b 1985, Hon Christopher Arthur b 1986), 1 da (Hon Jacqueline Christina b 1988); *Heir* s, Hon Benjamin John Tedder b 1985; *Career* merchant banker and investor; dir of various cos; *Recreations* sailing, golf; *Clubs* Royal Sydney Yacht Squadron, Royal & Ancient Golf (St Andrews), The Australian Golf; *Style—* The Rt Hon the Lord Tedder

TEDDY, Peter Julian; s of Francis Gerald Teddy, of Te Awamutu, NZ, and Beryl Dorothy Fogg; *b* 2 Nov 1944; *Educ* Rhyl GS, Univ of Wales (BSc), Univ of Oxford (MA, DPhil, BM BCh); *m* 1, 1 June 1974 (m dis 1988), Fiona Margaret, da of Richard Edward

Millard, CBE, JP; 2 s (Alexander Francis b 1982, William Peter b 1986); m 2, 1989, Rosalee Margaret Elliott; 1 s (Timothy James Elliott b 1990); *Career* conslt neurological surgn: Radcliffe Infirmary Oxford (clinical dir Dept of Neurological Surgery), Nat Spinal Injuries Centre, Dept of Spinal Neurosurgery Univ of Oxford, Stoke Mandeville Hosp 1981–; sr res fell St Peter's Coll Oxford 1983, clinical lectr (formerly dir of clinical studies) Univ of Oxford Med Sch; asst ed British Jl of Neurosurgery; *Recreations* tennis, dinghy sailing, foreign travel; *Style—* Peter Teddy, Esq; ✉ Department of Neurological Surgery, Radcliffe Infirmary, Oxford OX2 6HE (☎ 01865 224941)

TEED, Roy Norman; s of Thomas Westcott Teed (d 1983), and Jeannette Sutton (d 1956); *b* 18 May 1928; *Educ* King's Coll Sch Wimbledon, RAM; *m* 30 Dec 1981, Jennifer Ann, da of Frederick Perry, of Colchester, Essex; 1 s (Paul Lennox Perry b 26 Oct 1982), 2 da (Lucy Charlotte Emily b 16 Sept 1985, Trudy Sarah Jane b 4 March 1988); *Career* composer; Nat Serv RAF 1946–49; prof RAM 1966–92, pt/t teacher Colchester Sixth Form Coll, pt/t piano teacher Music Sch Colchester Inst 1966–79; author of articles in RAM magazine 1983 and 1985, numerous concert programme notes; memb: Performing Right Soc, Composers' guild of GB, Incorporated Soc of Musicians, NATFHE, Royal Soc of Musicians; FRAM 1977; *Compositions* incl: Fanfares and March, Piano Trio, Serenade for 10 Winds, Concertino for Treble Recorder and Strings, Piece for a Special Occasion, A Celebration Overture, Scena for Clarinet and Piano, Toccata for Organ, Elegy and Tarantella for Violin and Piano, Sextet Variations, Overture for Organ, Overture, The Overcoat - An Opera in One Act, Music Fills The Air, Music of the Seasons, Te Deum, Music for a Ballet, A Trip to the Zoo, Elegy Scherzo and Trio, The Pardoner's Tale, Five Funny Songs, Five Epitaphs, Rondo with Variations for Violin and Piano, Two Song Cycles, Sonata for Violin and Piano, Fanfare and Wedding March for Organ, words and music for Jack and the Beanstalk, Theme and Variations for Chamber Orch, Concerto-in-One-Movement for Tenor Trombone and Chamber Orch, Siciliano for Oboe and Piano, The Solitary Reaper for High Voice and Piano, Concert Piece for Tenor Trombone and Piano; *Recreations* walking, reading, theatre, swimming, playing with my children; *Clubs* RAM; *Style—* Roy Teed, Esq; ✉ 63 Egret Crescent, Longridge Park, Colchester, Essex CO4 3FP (☎ 01206 870839)

TEELING SMITH, Prof George; OBE (1983); s of Herbert Teeling Smith, of Edinburgh, and Jessie Sybil, *née* Dickson (d 1983); *b* 20 March 1928; *Educ* Bryanston, Clare Coll Cambridge (BA), Heriot-Watt Coll; *m* 6 Sept 1967, Diana, *née* St John Stevas; *Career* Nat Serv 1946–48; various pharmaceutical indust appts rising to dep md Winthrop Laboratories 1960–62, dir Office of Health Economics 1962–92, assoc prof Health Economics Res Gp Brunel Univ 1980–94; memb NEDO Pharmaceutical Working Party 1975–77, chm Int Sci Policy Fndn 1988–91, advsr Parly Health Ctee 1993–94; chm BUPA Medical Research and Development Ltd 1992–; MPharm Univ of Bradford 1977; FRPharmS 1978; *Books* How to use the NHS (1970), Health Economics, Prospects for the Future (1987), Measuring Health: A Practical Approach (1989); *Recreations* swimming, collecting prints; *Style—* Prof George Teeling Smith, OBE; ✉ 65 Castelnau, London SW13 9RT (☎ 0181 748 4254)

TEGNER, Ian Nicol; s of Sven Stuart Tegner, OBE (d 1971); *b* 11 July 1933; *Educ* Rugby; *m* 1961, Meriel Helen, da of Maurice Stanley Lush, CB, CBE, MC; 1 s, 1 da; *Career* CA (Scotland) 1957; Clarkson Gordon & Co Toronto Canada 1958–59, Barton Mayhew & Co 1959–71 (ptnr 1965–71), fin dir Bowater Industries plc 1971–86, dir gp fin Midland Bank plc 1987–90; chm: Control Risks Group Ltd 1992– (dir 1990–), Crest Packaging plc 1993–; dir: Arjo Wiggins Appleton plc 1990–, English Touring Opera 1991–, TIP Europe plc 1992–93, Teesside Power Ltd 1992–, Coutts & Co 1996–; chm The 100 Gp of Fin Dirs 1988–90, pres Inst of CAs of Scotland 1991–92; *Recreations* book collecting, walking, choral singing, family life, travel; *Style—* Ian Tegner, Esq; ✉ 44 Norland Square, London W11 4PZ (☎ 0171 229 8604); Keepers Cottage, Kilninver, Argyll

TELFER, Dr Robert Gilmour Jamieson (Rab); CBE (1985); s of James Telfer (d 1987), of Edinburgh, and Helen Lamble, *née* Jamieson (d 1977); *b* 22 April 1928; *Educ* Bathgate Acad, Univ of Edinburgh (BSc, PhD); *m* 8 July 1953, Joan Audrey, da of George William Gunning (d 1964), of Swansea; 3 s (James Gilmour b 26 June 1957, Robin Gunning b 26 Jan 1959, John Telfer b 26 July 1961); *Career* shift chemist AEA 1953–54; ICI 1954–81 (R&D dir Petrochemical Div, dep chm 1975–76, chm 1976–81); dir: Phillips Imperial Petroleum Ltd 1976–81, Manchester Business Sch 1984–88, Renold plc 1984–, Volex Group plc 1985–; chm and md Mather and Platt Ltd 1981–84, chm European Industrial Services Ltd 1988–89, exec chm BSI Standards 1989–92 (ret); chm Advsy Cncl on Energy Conservation 1982–84, personal advsr to Sec of State for Energy 1984–87; memb: Advsy Cncl on R&D for Fuel and Power 1981–87, Civil Serv Coll Advsy Cncl 1985–90, Higher Educn Funding Cncl for England 1992–; chm Bd of Govrs Univ of Teesside 1992–; sr visiting fellow Manchester Business Sch Univ of Manchester; Hon MBA Univ of Manchester; CIMgt; *Recreations* poetry, gardening, walking, swimming, supporting Middlesbrough FC; *Clubs* Caledonian; *Style—* Dr Rab Telfer, CBE; ✉ Downings, Upleatham Village, Redcar, Cleveland TS11 8AG (fax 01287 623993)

TELFER BRUNTON, Dr (William) Andrew; JP; s of Robert Brunton (d 1973), and Sarah Hamilton, *née* Telfer (d 1961); *b* 23 Feb 1948; *Educ* Edinburgh Acad, Strathallan Sch, Univ of Edinburgh (BSc, MB ChB); *m* 9 Dec 1977, Patricia, da of Leslie Noble, of Broadstairs; 3 da (Lisa b 1981, Anne b 1984, Fiona b 1985); *Career* lectr in bacteriology Univ of Edinburgh, conslt med microbiologist, dir Truro Public Health Laboratory; memb: Assoc of Medical Microbiologists, The Br Soc for the Study of Infection, The Pathological Soc; memb Cncl Assoc of Clinical Pathologists, dep Wines and Spirits Educn Tst, memb The Grand Antiquity Soc Glasgow; Freeman Burgess of Incorporation of Gardeners Glasgow; FRCPath 1991 (MRCPath 1980); *Recreations* gardening, wine (WSET Diploma in Wine); *Style—* Dr Andrew Telfer Brunton, JP; ✉ Public Health Laboratory, Penventinnie Lane, Truro, Cornwall TR1 3LQ (☎ 01872 254940)

TELFORD, Sir Robert; kt (1978), CBE (1967), DL (Essex 1981); s of Robert Telford; *b* 1 Oct 1915; *Educ* Quarry Bank HS Liverpool, Queen Elizabeth GS Tamworth, Christ's Coll Cambridge (MA); *m* 1, 1941 (m dis 1950); 1 s; m 2, 1958, Elizabeth Mary, da of F W Shelley; 3 da; *Career* md: Marconi Co 1965–81 (previously md and mangr various Marconi subsids), GEC-Marconi Electronics Ltd 1968–84; dir: GEC plc 1973–84, Ericsson Radio Systems Sweden 1969–83, Canadian Marconi Co Canada 1968–83; chm: The Marconi Co Ltd 1981–84 (hon life pres 1984–), Marconi Avionics Ltd 1981–85, Prelude Technology Investments Ltd 1984–91, CTP Investments Ltd 1987–90; pres Marconi Italiana (Italy) 1983–85; advsr to Comett Prog of Euro Community 1987–94; memb: Electronics Econ Devpt Ctee 1964–67 and 1980–85, Engrg Indust Trg Bd 1968–82, Cncl Univ of Essex 1980–88, Ct Univ of Essex 1980–, Cncl Industl Soc 1982–86, Cncl Fellowship of Engrg 1983–86, Business and Technician Educn Cncl 1984–86, Engrg Bd SERC 1985–88, Info Technol Advsy Gp DTI 1985–88, Engrg Cncl 1985–89, Industl Res and Devpt Advsy Ctee to Euro Community 1987–91, Chllr's Cncl Anglia Poly Univ 1992–; chm: Electronics Avionics Requirements Bd of DOI 1981–85, Alvey Steering Gp 1983–88, Teaching Co Mgmnt Cmmn 1984–88, Cwlth Engrs Cncl 1989–93; pres: Electronic Engrg Assoc 1963–64, Instn of Prodn Engrs 1982–83; visitor to Hatfield Poly 1986–91; Freeman City of London 1984; Hon DSc: Salford 1981, Cranfield Inst of Technol 1982, Bath 1984, Aston 1985; Hon DEng: Bradford 1986, Birmingham 1986; Hon DTech Anglia Inst 1989, hon fell Univ of Hertfordshire (formerly Hatfield Poly) 1991; Hon FIMechE 1983, Hon FIEE 1986, Hon FICE 1992; FEng 1978, FIProdE, FRSA, CIMgt; *Clubs* RAF; *Style—* Sir Robert Telford, CBE, DL, FEng; ✉ Rettendon House, Rettendon, Chelmsford, Essex CM3 8DW (☎ 01268 733131)

TELTSCHER, Bernard Louis; s of Felix Teltscher (d 1978), of Kingston Upon Thames, and Lillie, *née* Knoepfmacher (d 1961); *b* 18 Feb 1923; *Educ* Czech GS Breclav, UCL (BSc), Trinity Coll Cambridge (MA); *m* 1, 1963 (m dis), Irene Gladys Valerie, da of George Nathaniel Hotten, of Carshalton, Surrey; 1 da (Lisa (decd)); m 2, 1978 (m dis), Jill Patricia, da of Ivor Cooper, of Cornwall Gardens, London; 1 s (Mark b 1980), 1 da (Natalie b 1981); m 3, 11 March 1991, Catherine Ann, da of Leslie Frankl (d 1965); *Career* wine importer and property developer; chm: Teltscher Bros Ltd 1978–95 (dir 1958–95), chm Teltscher Estates Ltd 1987–; dir: St James's Bridge Club Ltd 1982–92, Wine & Spirit Assoc of GB & NI 1985–86, Wine Devpt Bd 1985–86, Telco Estates Ltd 1989–, C Hotsu Ltd 1989–; Yugoslav Flag with Gold Star; *Recreations* bridge; *Clubs* Hurlingham, Crockfords, Aspinalls, Les Ambassadeurs; *Style—* Bernard Teltscher, Esq; ✉ 17 Carlyle Square, London SW3 6EX (☎ 0171 351 5091, fax 0171 376 7687); Lutomer House, West India Dock, Prestons Road, London E14 9SB (☎ 0171 987 5020, fax 0171 537 2428)

TEMIRKANOV, Yuri; *Career* conductor; artistic dir and chief conductor Kirov Opera until 1988, music dir and princ conductor St Petersburg Philharmonic Orch 1988–92, princ conductor Royal Philharmonic Orch 1992– (London debut 1977, princ guest conductor 1979–92); other orchs conducted incl: Berlin Philharmonic, Vienna Philharmonic, Dresden Staatskapelle, l'Orchestre de Paris, Royal Concertgebouw Orch, all major American orchs; exclusive recording contract with BMG/RCA 1988–; *Style—* Yuri Temirkanov, Esq; ✉ c/o Elizabeth Collins, IMG Artists, Media House, 3 Burlington Lane, London W4 2TH (☎ 0181 233 5800, fax 0181 233 5801)

TEMKIN, Prof Jennifer (Mrs Graham Zellick); da of late Michael Temkin, of London, and late Minnie, *née* Levy; *b* 6 June 1948; *Educ* South Hampstead HS for Girls, LSE, Univ of London (LLB, LLM); *m* 18 Sept 1975, Prof Graham John Zellick, s of Reginald H Zellick, of Windsor, Berks; 1 s (Adam b 1977), 1 da (Lara b 1980); *Career* called to the Bar Middle Temple 1971, lectr in law LSE 1971–89, visiting prof of law Univ of Toronto 1978–79, prof of law and dean Sch of Law Univ of Buckingham 1989–92, prof of law Univ of Sussex 1992– (dir Centre for Legal Studies 1994–97); memb: Editorial Advsy Gp Howard Jl of Criminal Justice 1984–, Scrutiny Ctee on Draft Criminal Code Old Bailey 1985–86, Editorial Bd Jl of Criminal Law 1986–, Home Sec's Advsy Gp on Use of Video Recordings in Criminal Proceedings 1988–89, Ctee of Heads Univ Law Schs 1989–92 and 1994–97, Nat Children's Home Ctee on Children who Abuse other Children 1990–92; govr S Hampstead HS for Girls 1991–; FRSA 1989; *Books* Rape and the Legal Process (1987), Rape and Criminal Justice (1996); *Style—* Prof Jennifer Temkin; ✉ Centre for Legal Studies, Arts Building, University of Sussex, Falmer, Brighton BN1 9QN (☎ 01273 606755, fax 01273 678466)

TEMPERLEY, Prof Howard Reed; s of Fred Temperley (d 1972), of Sunderland, and Eva May Temperley (d 1965); *b* 16 Nov 1932; *Educ* Newcastle Royal GS, Magdalen Coll Oxford, Yale Univ; *m* 1, 1957 (m dis 1966), Jane Mary, da of William Flambert (d 1993), of Hampshire; 1 da (Alison b 1962); m 2, 1966, Rachel Stephanie (d 1990), da of Rowley S Hooper (d 1951), of Toronto; 1 s (Nicholas b 1971), 1 da (Rebecca b 1969); *Career* Nat Serv 2 Lt Armoured Corps 1951–53; asst lectr Univ Coll of Wales Aberystwyth 1960–61, lectr Univ of Manchester 1961–67, prof Univ of East Anglia 1981– (sr lectr 1967–81); chm Br Assoc for American Studies 1986–89; *Books* British Antislavery 1833–1870 (1972), Lieut Colonel Joseph Gubbins's New Brunswick Journals of 1811 and 1813 (ed), Introduction to American Studies (ed jtly, 2 edn 1989), White Dreams, Black Africa: The Antislavery Expedition to the Niger 1841 to 1842 (1991); *Recreations* jogging; *Clubs* Norfolk; *Style—* Prof Howard Temperley; ✉ Arlington House, Arlington Lane, Norwich NR2 2DB (☎ 01603 628497); School of English and American Studies, University of East Anglia, Norwich NR4 7TJ (☎ 01603 592811, fax 01603 507728, telex 976197)

TEMPERLEY, Eur Ing Dr Tom Groome; OBE (1970); s of Thomas Temperley (d 1960), of Bolton, and Mabel Alberta (d 1971); *b* 22 Nov 1930; *Educ* Bolton Co GS, Bolton Coll of Technol, Etude Universitaires Luxemburg; *m* 11 Jan 1961, Edith, da of Edmund Kay, of Bolton; 1 s (Tom Gaskell b 10 Dec 1961), 1 da (Elizabeth Katherine b 1 June 1967); *Career* chemist Br Electricity Authy 1948–54, chief chemist and tech advsr Kuwait Miny of Electricity and Water 1954–70, princ Temperley & Associates 1957–, pres Conam Servs Inc 1970–79, advsr to and authority on Middle E; past pres Euro Desalination Assoc, fndr bd memb Int Desalination Assoc, patron fndr memb and former chm Continental Sch Jeddah, fndr Temperley Awards (encouraging handicapped to improve themselves physically), vice pres Oscar Heidenstam Tst Fund; life memb: Nat Amateur Body-Builders' Assoc, Assoc of Strength Athletes; fndr memb Br Business Gp Jeddah Saudi Arabia, elected Desalination Engr of Year by Int Desalination & Environmental Assoc in Tokyo 1978; life patron Continental Sch Jeddah; life memb: AWWA, ACE, AACE; CEng, FIE, FINucE, Fell Inst of Corrosion, FInstD, MAChemE, FRSH, FInstPet; *Recreations* weight training, swimming; *Clubs* RAC; *Style—* Eur Ing Dr Tom Temperley, OBE; ✉ Lovely Hall, Salesbury, Blackburn, Lancashire BB1 9EQ (☎ 01254 48630, fax 01254 248091); 213 Darwen Rd, Bromley Cross, Bolton, Lancashire; PO Box 82, Muttrah-114, Muscat, Sultanate of Oman; PO Box 3240, Jeddah, Saudi Arabia

TEMPEST, Henry Roger; DL (N Yorks 1981); yr but only surviving s of Brig-Gen Roger Tempest, CMG, DSO, JP, DL; inherited Broughton Hall Estate on death of elder bro in 1970; *b* 2 April 1924; *Educ* The Oratory, Ch Ch Oxford; *m* 1957, Janet Evelyn Mary, da of Harold Longton, of Johannesburg; 2 s (Roger Henry b 1963, Piers b 1973), 3 da (Bridget Mary b 1957, Anne Valerie (Mrs James McConnel) b 1959, Mary Hazel (Mrs Geoffrey Stocker) b 1961); *Career* Scots Gds 1943–47, serv NW Europe (wounded 1945), apptd to Q Staff HQ Gds Div 1945, Staff Capt 1946; Britannia Rubber Co Ltd 1947–51; emigrated to Lusaka (then in Northern Rhodesia) 1952, incorporated cost accountant (AACWA) S Africa 1959; returned to UK 1961, fin offr Univ of Oxford Dept of Nuclear Physics 1962–72; memb: N Yorks Co Cncl 1973–85, Skipton Rural Dist Cncl 1973–74, Br Computer Soc 1973, Exec Ctee CLA Yorks 1973–87, Cncl Order of St John N Yorks 1977–87, pres Skipton Branch Royal Br Legion 1974–91; govr: Craven Coll of Further Educn 1974–85, Skipton Girls' HS 1976–85; Lord of the Manors of Broughton, Coleby, Burnsall and Thorpe; ACIS 1958, FCIS 1971; Knight of Malta; *Clubs* Lansdowne, Pratt's; *Style—* Henry Tempest, Esq, DL; ✉ Broughton Hall, Skipton, N Yorks BD23 3AE (☎ 01756 792267, fax 01756 792362)

TEMPEST, (Albert) John; MBE (1994); s of Allan Tempest (d 1969), and Ruth, *née* Kettlewell (d 1974); *b* 7 Oct 1938; *Educ* Giggleswick Sch, Leeds Coll of Art (DipArch, DipTP); *m* 29 Aug 1969, Susan Dorothea, da of Arthur Rooke (d 1983); 1 s (Matthew b 20 Jan 1973), 1 da (Caroline b 31 Aug 1975); *Career* chartered architect and town planner; Woodhall Planning & Conservation; former projects incl: John Brunton Plc, British Rail, GLC Town Development; pres Br Architectural Students Assoc 1961–62, memb Cncl TCPA 1973–76; RIBA: memb Cncl 1982–85, vice pres 1985–87, chm architectural competitions RIBA 1989–95; RIBA, MRTPI; *Recreations* arts, literature, architectural history, design, photography; *Style—* John Tempest, Esq, MBE; ✉ Woodhall Planning & Conservation, Woodhall, Woodhall Lane, Calverley, Leeds LS28 5NY (☎ 01132 554660, fax 01132 569688)

TEMPEST-MOGG, Dr Brenden Dayne; s of Alan Reginald Mogg, JP (NSW) (d 1994), Capt RAAF, and Ethyl Mavis Tempest-Hay; *b* 10 April 1945; *Educ* The Scots Coll Sydney, Univ of NSW (BA), Essex Univ (MA), Hertford Coll Oxford (MLitt), George Washington Univ Washington DC (EdD); *m* 27 May 1984 (m dis 1990), Galina, da of Ivan Mikhailovich Kobzev (d 1995), of Frunze, Russia; 1 da (Gloria Dela Hay b 27 Feb 1987); *Career* pres Warnborough Coll (The American Coll in Oxford) 1973–96; visiting lectr in Aust, India and USA 1976–; guest ed Sociological Perspectives 1982–; conslt on int educn 1988–; JP (NSW) 1967; FRSA 1994; *Recreations* sailing, polo, travel, tennis; *Clubs* The Victoria League for Cwlth Friendship, Cowdray Park Polo, Cirencester Park Polo; *Style*— Dr Brenden D Tempest-Mogg; ✉ GPO Box 1055, Sydney, Australia 2001

TEMPLE, Anthony Dominic Afamado; QC; s of Sir Rawden John Afamado Temple, CBE, QC, *qv*, and Margaret, *née* Gunson (d 1980); bro of Victor Bevis Afoumado Temple, QC, *qv*; *b* 21 Sept 1945; *Educ* Haileybury and ISC, Worcester Coll Oxford (MA); *m* 28 May 1983, Susan Elizabeth, s of Ernst Bodansky (d 1990), of Millmead, Broadbridge Heath, Sussex; 2 da (Jessica Elizabeth b 11 Dec 1985, Alexandra Louise b 21 Aug 1988); *Career* called to the Bar Inner Temple 1968; Crown Law Office W Aust 1968–69; in practice UK 1970–, recorder of the Crown Court 1989– (asst recorder 1982), dep High Ct judge 1995–; *Recreations* modern pentathlon, travel; *Style*— Anthony Temple, QC; ✉ 4 Pump Court, London EC4 (☎ 0171 353 2656, fax 0171 583 2036)

TEMPLE, Prof John Graham; s of Joseph Henry Temple, and Norah, *née* Selby (d 1987); *b* 14 March 1942; *Educ* William Hulme's GS Manchester, Univ of Liverpool (MB ChB, ChM); *m* 11 April 1966, (Margaret) Jillian Leighton, da of Robert Leighton Hartley (d 1966), of Wigan; 2 s (Robert b 27 Oct 1967, Christopher b 5 July 1972), 1 da (Caroline b 29 Dec 1969); *Career* conslt surgn Queen Elizabeth Hosp Birmingham 1979–; postgrad dean Univ of Birmingham 1991– (hon sr clinical lectr 1979–); regnl advsr in surgery RCS England 1990–94, memb Cncl RCS Edinburgh 1995–, special advsr to CMO (Calman Training) 1995–; memb: BMA 1965, Assoc of Surgns of GB 1974; FRCSEd, FRCS; *Recreations* skiing, sailing; *Style*— Prof John Temple; ✉ Wharncliffe, 24 Westfield Rd, Edgbaston, Birmingham B15 3QG (☎ 0121 454 2445); Queen Elizabeth Hospital, Edgbaston, Birmingham B15 2TH (☎ 0121 472 1311)

TEMPLE, Nicholas John; s of Leonard Temple (d 1990), and Lilly Irene, *née* Thornton; *b* 2 Oct 1947; *Educ* Kings Sch Gloucester; *m* 28 March 1970, Janet, *née* Perry; 1 s (Alexander James b 10 Jan 1975), 2 da (Charlotte Elizabeth b 22 July 1977, Rosanna Louise b 12 July 1980); *Career* IBM: joined as systems engr 1965, conslt on R&D 1981, estab banking industry products lab Germany 1983, vice pres systems and product mgmnt IBM Europe 1985–91, chief exec IBM UK Ltd 1991–95, chm IBM UK Ltd 1995–96, mgmnt conslt 1996–; dep chm Business in the Community 1993–; *Recreations* rowing, opera, cooking; *Style*— Nicholas Temple, Esq; ✉ 10 Coulson Street, Chelsea, London SW3 3NG (☎ 0171 581 2181, fax 0171 584 0644)

TEMPLE, Nina Claire; da of Landon Royce Temple, and Barbara Joan Temple; *b* 21 April 1956; *Educ* Imperial Coll London (BSc); *partner* John Davies, s of Stanley Davies; 1 s (Oliver b 1988), 1 da (Rebecca 1986); *Career* former full time worker Communist Party, nat sec Communist Party GB 1990–91, sec Democratic Left Organisation (formerly Democratic Left Party) 1991–; ARSM; *Recreations* rambling, swimming, gardening, movies; *Style*— Ms Nina Temple; ✉ Democratic Left Organisation, 6 Cynthia Street, London N1 9JF (☎ 0171 278 4443)

TEMPLE, Ralph; s of Harry Temple (ka 1941), and Julia, *née* Glassman; *b* 15 Nov 1933; *Educ* Hackney Downs GS; *m* 22 May 1955, Patricia Yvonne, da of Samuel Gould (d 1975), of London; 2 s (Graham Robin b 23 April 1958, Howard Jeremy b 28 March 1960); *Career* managing clerk Wilson Wright and Co CAs 1955–61; Tesco plc: sr exec 1961–73, gp fin dir 1973–83, jt gp md 1983–86; md Temple Consultants (business conslts) 1986–; Freeman City Of London, Liveryman Worshipful Co of Chartered Accountants; FCA 1956; *Recreations* golf, travel, bridge, keep fit; *Style*— Ralph Temple, Esq; ✉ 2 Culverlands Close, Stanmore, Middx HA7 3AG

TEMPLE, Sir Rawden John Afamado; kt (1980), CBE (1964), QC (1951); *b* 1908; *Educ* King Edward's Sch Birmingham, Queen's Coll Oxford (MA, BCL); *m* 1936, Margaret (d 1980), da of Sir James Gunson, CMG, CBE; 2 s (Victor Bevis Afoumado Temple, QC, *qv*, Anthony Dominic Afamado Temple, QC, *qv*); *Career* barr 1931, master of Bench Inner Temple 1960 (treas 1983); chief social security cmmr 1975–81, child benefit referee 1976–; vice chm Gen Cncl of the Bar 1960–64, memb Industl Injuries Advsy Cncl; Liveryman Worshipful Co of Pattenmakers; *Recreations* fishing; *Style*— Sir Rawden Temple, CBE, QC; ✉ 3 North King's Bench Walk, Temple, London EC4Y 7DQ (☎ 0171 353 6420)

TEMPLE, Richard; s and h of Sir Richard Antony Purbeck Temple, 4 Bt, MC, *qv*; *b* 17 Aug 1937; *m* 1964, Emma Rose, da of late Maj-Gen Sir Robert Edward Laycock, KCMG, CB, DSO; 3 da; *Style*— Richard Temple, Esq; ✉ The Temple Gallery, 6 Clarendon Cross, London W11 4AP

TEMPLE, Sir Richard Anthony Purbeck; 4 Bt (UK 1876), MC (1941); s of Sir Richard Durand Temple, 3 Bt, DSO (d 1962); *b* 19 Jan 1913; *Educ* Stowe, Trinity Hall Cambridge; *m* 1, 1936 (m dis 1946), Lucy Geils, da of late Alain Joly de Lotbiniere, of Montreal; 2 s; m 2, 1950, Jean, da of late James T Finnie, and widow of Oliver P Croom-Johnson; 1 da; *Heir* s, Richard Temple, *qv*; *Career* serv WWII (wounded), former Maj KRRC; *Clubs* Army and Navy; *Style*— Sir Richard Temple, Bt, MC

TEMPLE, His Hon Sir (Ernest) Sanderson; kt (1988), MBE (1946), QC (1969); s of Ernest Temple (d 1957); *b* 23 May 1921; *Educ* Kendal Sch, Queen's Coll Oxford; *m* 1, 1946, June Debonnaire, *née* Saunders (d 1995); 1 s (Simon), 2 da (Cecilia, Sarah); m 2, 1996, Patricia Margaret Shrubsole, wid of Paul Patrick Shrubsole, 2 da of the Late J B Smalley, of Birkby Hall, Cark-in-Cartmel; *Career* served Army, India and Burma, Temp Lt-Col (despatches); called to the Bar Gray's Inn 1943; chm Westmorland QS 1968–71 (dep chm 1967–68), former asst recorder Salford and Blackburn, recorder of the Crown Court 1971–77, hon recorder of Kendal 1972, circuit judge and recorder of Liverpool 1977–91, hon recorder Lancaster 1987; former memb Bar Cncl, dep chm Agric Land Tbnl, jt master Vale of Lune Harriers 1963–85, pres Br Harness Racing Club, pres Cumbria Bridleways Soc; pres: Royal Lancs Agric Soc 1991, NW Driving Club; hon fell Clerks of Works Soc, hon citizen of Kendal 1992; *Recreations* farming and horses; *Clubs* Racquet (Liverpool); *Style*— His Hon Sir Sanderson Temple, MBE, QC; ✉ Yealand Hall, Yealand Redmayne, nr Carnforth LA5 9TD (☎ 01524 781200)

TEMPLE, Victor Bevis Afoumado; QC (1993); s of Sir Rawden Temple, QC, CBE, *qv*, and Margaret, *née* Gunson (d 1980); bro of Anthony Dominic Afamado Temple, QC, *qv*; *b* 23 Feb 1941; *Educ* Shrewsbury, Inns of Ct Sch of Law; *m* 1974, Richenda, *née* Penn-Bull; 2 s (Benjamin, Samuel); *Career* mktg exec: S H Benson 1960–63, J Lyons 1964–65, Beecham Group 1965–68, Alcan Aluminium 1968; called to the Bar 1971, sr prosecuting counsel to the Crown 1991–93 (jr prosecuting counsel 1985–91), recorder 1989–; DTI inspr into National Westminster Bank 1992, a chm Police Discipline Appeals Tbnls 1993; *Recreations* rowing, carpentry; *Clubs* Thames Rowing; *Style*— Victor Temple, Esq, QC; ✉ 6 King's Bench Walk, Temple, London EC4Y 7DR (☎ 0171 583 0410)

TEMPLE-MORRIS, Peter; MP (C) Leominster (majority 16,680); s of His Honour Sir Owen Temple-Morris (d 1985), and Vera, *née* Thompson (d 1986); *b* 12 Feb 1938; *Educ* Malvern, St Catharine's Coll Cambridge; *m* 1964, Taheré, er da of H E Senator Khozeimé Alam, of Teheran; 2 s, 2 da; *Career* called to the Bar Inner Temple 1962, Hampstead Cons Political Centre 1971–73, second prosecuting counsel Inland Revenue SE Circuit 1971–74; MP (C) Leominster Feb 1974–, PPS to Sec of State for Tport 1979; chm: Br Iranian Parly Gp, Br Spanish and Br Netherlands Parly Gps, Br Gp Inter-Parly Union 1982–85 (exec 1976–); vice chm: Cons Parly Foreign Affrs Ctee 1982–90, Cons Parly N Ireland Ctee 1990–92, UK-Argentine and Lebanese Parly Gps, Cons Euro Affrs Ctee 1990–; chm All Pty Southern Africa Gp 1992–94, vice chm S Africa Gp 1995– (chm 1994–95), vice pres UN Assoc Cncl, vice chm GB-Russia Centre, memb Commons Select Ctee on Foreign Affrs 1987–90, first Br co-chm Br-Irish Inter-Parly Body 1990–, exec Commonwealth Parly Assoc (UK Branch) 1993– (vice chm 1994–95); admitted slr 1989; memb Academic Cncl Wilton Park (FCO) 1990–; memb Cncl Malvern Coll 1977–, pres Iran Soc 1995–, vice chm and chm exec Soc of Cons Lawyers 1995– (exec 1968–71 and 1990–95); Liveryman Worshipful Co of Basketmakers, Freeman Worshipful Co of Barbers; Chevalier du Tastevin (Chateau de Clos de Vougeot); *Recreations* shooting, wine, food, travel; *Clubs* Carlton, Cardiff and County; *Style*— Peter Temple-Morris, Esq, MP; ✉ House of Commons, London SW1A 0AA (☎ 0171 219 4181, fax 0171 219 3801)

TEMPLE OF STOWE, 8 Earl (UK 1822); (Walter) Grenville Algernon Temple-Gore-Langton; o s of Cdr Hon Evelyn Arthur Grenville Temple-Gore-Langton, DSO, RN (d 1972; yst s of 4 Earl), and Irene, *née* Gartside-Spaight (d 1967); suc his cousin 7 Earl Temple of Stowe 1988; *b* 2 Oct 1924; *Educ* Nautical Coll Pangbourne; *m* 1, 24 July 1954, Zillah Ray (d 1966), da of James Boxall, of Fir Grove, Tillington, Petworth, Sussex; 2 s (James Grenville, Lord Langton b 1955, Hon Robert Chandos b 1957), 1 da (Lady Anna Clare b 1960); m 2, 1 June 1968, (Margaret) Elizabeth Graham, o da of Col Henry William Scarth of Breckness, of Skaill House, Orkney; *Heir* s, Lord Langton, *qv*; *Style*— The Rt Hon the Earl Temple of Stowe; ✉ The Cottage, Easton, Winchester, Hants; Garth, Outertown, Stromness, Orkney

TEMPLEMAN, Michael; s of Geoffrey Templeman CBE (d 1988), and Dorothy May, *née* Heathcote (d 1996); *b* 6 May 1943; *Educ* King Edward's Sch Birmingham, Selwyn Coll Cambridge (MA); *m* 5 Dec 1970, Jane Margaret Willmer, da of Capt John Kenneth Lee; 4 da (Kathryn Alexandra Joan b 14 Oct 1971, Charlotte Heathcote Mary b 31 Aug 1973, Judith Margaret Elizabeth b 26 Jan 1977, Rosalind Sarah May b 20 June 1981); *Career* Inland Revenue 1965–94: inspr of taxes Maidstone 1965–67 then Canterbury 1967–70, district inspr Cannock 1971–72, tech specialist Oil Taxation 1972–78, district inspr Luton 1978–81, tech specialist Co Taxation 1981–84 then Fin Instns 1984–89, controller Oil Taxation Office 1989–91, dir Fin Instns Div 1992–94; dir Taxation Dept J Henry Schroder 1994–; *Recreations* running, music; *Style*— Michael Templeman, Esq; ✉ J Henry Schroder, 120 Cheapside, London EC2 (☎ 0171 483 6000)

TEMPLEMAN, Miles Howard; s of Robert James Templeman (d 1990), of London, and Margot Elizabeth, *née* Charlton; *b* 4 Oct 1947; *Educ* Jesus Coll Cambridge (MA Econs, Capt Rugby first XV), Columbia Univ (Dip Mktg); *m* Janet Elizabeth, da of Lionel James Strang; 2 s (Mark b 1977, James b 1979), 1 da (Sara b 1984); *Career* Young & Rubicam: trainee account mangr Daz 1970–73, product mangr/mktg mangr Lucozade, Ribena and others 1973–78; gen merchandise mangr and mktg dir N Europe Levi Strauss 1978–84; Whitbread plc: md Thresher 1985–87, gp mktg dir 1988–89, md Whitbread Beer Co 1989–, main bd dir 1991–; dir Soft Drinks Ltd/Britvic Holdings Ltd 1991–, non-exec dir The Albert Fisher Group PLC 1994–; dir Portman Gp; memb Ct of Assts Worshipful Co of Brewers; *Recreations* tennis, bridge, cinema; *Style*— Miles Templeman, Esq; ✉ Whitbread Beer Company, Porter Tun House, Capability Green, Luton, Beds LU1 3LS (☎ 01582 391166, fax 01582 397397); Whitmore Farm, Church Road, Windlesham, Surrey GU20 6BH (☎ 01276 472723)

TEMPLEMAN, Baron (Life Peer 1982), of White Lackington, Co Somerset; Sydney William Templeman; kt (1972), MBE (1946), PC (1978); s of Herbert William Templeman; *b* 3 March 1920; *Educ* Southall GS, St John's Coll Cambridge; *m* 1946, Margaret Joan (d 1988), da of Morton Rowles; 2 s (Rev Hon Peter Morton b 1949, Hon Michael Richard b 1951); *Career* called to the Bar 1947, QC 1964, memb Middle Temple & Lincoln's Inn, memb Bar Cncl 1961–65, bencher Middle Temple 1969 (treas 1987), High Ct judge (Chancery) 1972–78, Lord Justice of Appeal 1978–82, Lord of Appeal in Ordinary 1982–94; attorney-gen Duchy Lancaster 1970–72; pres Bar Assoc for Commerce Fin & Indust 1982–86; hon fell St John's Coll Cambridge 1982; Hon DLitt Reading 1980; Hon LLD: Univ of Birmingham 1986, CNAA Huddersfield Poly 1990, Univ of Exeter 1991; Hon LLD Nat Law Sch of India Univ Bangalore 1993; visitor Univ of Essex 1990–96; hon memb Canadian & American Bar Assocs; former pres Senate of Inns of Ct & Bar; *Style*— The Rt Hon Lord Templeman, MBE, PC; ✉ Manor Heath, Knowl Hill, Woking, Surrey (☎ 01483 761930)

TEMPLER, Maj-Gen James Robert; CB (1989), OBE (1978, MBE 1973); s of Brig Cecil Robert Templer, DSO (d 1986), and Angela Mary, *née* Henderson; *b* 8 Jan 1936; *Educ* Charterhouse, RMA Sandhurst; *m* 1, 1963 (m dis 1979); 2 s (William b 1964, Tristram b 1969), 1 da (Sophie b 1966); m 2, 18 July 1981, Sarah Ann (Sally), o da of Capt W K Rogers, DSC, RM, of Nether Wallop; *Career* 2 Lt 41 and 4 Regt BAOR 1956–59, Lt King's Troop RHA 1960–63, Capt 6 Regt Borneo 1964–66, Staff Coll 1967, Maj GSO2 3 Div UK 1968–69, BC 5 and 3 Regt NI 1970–72, GSO2 Sch of Artillery 1973, Lt-Col instr Staff Coll 1974–75, CO 42 Regt 1976, CO 5 Regt 1977, GSO1 MOD 1978, Col (later Brig) CRA 2 Armd Div 1979–81, Study Artillery in 90s 1982, RCDS 1983, ACOS Trg HQ UKLF 1984–86, Maj-Gen ACDS MOD 1986–89, ret 1990; Br Nat Cross Country Ski Champion 1958; riding, winner of: Euro Individual Championship 3 day event 1962, RA Gold Cup Sandown 1962 and 1963, Burghley 1962, Munich 1963, Badminton 1964; memb Br Olympic 3 day event team Tokyo; FIMgt 1988; *Recreations* riding, sailing, skiing, gardening, shooting, fishing; *Style*— Maj-Gen James Templer, CB, OBE; ✉ c/o Lloyds Bank Ltd, Crediton, Devon

TEMPLETON, Prof (Alexander) Allan; s of Richard Templeton (d 1968), of Aberdeen, and Minnie, *née* Whitfield; *b* 28 June 1946; *Educ* Aberdeen GS, Univ of Aberdeen (MB ChB, MD); *m* 17 Dec 1980, Gillian Constance, da of Geoffrey William John Penney, of Eastbourne; 3 s (Richard b 1981, Robert b 1983, Peter b 1987), 1 da (Katherine b 1985); *Career* lectr then sr lectr Univ of Edinburgh 1976–85; regius prof of obstetrics and gynaecology Univ of Aberdeen 1985–; author of various pubns on Human Infertility and Gynaecological Endocrinology; MRCOG 1974, FRCOG 1987; *Books* The Early Days of Pregnancy (1987), Reproduction and the Law (1990), Infertility (1992); *Recreations* mountaineering; *Clubs* Royal Northern and Univ; *Style*— Prof Allan Templeton; ✉ Department of Obstetrics and Gynaecology, University of Aberdeen, Foresterhill, Aberdeen AB25 2ZN (☎ 01224 681818)

TEMPLETON, Allan; JP (1982); s of Harry Templeton (d 1993), and Sarah, *née* Blackburn (d 1968); *b* 8 Feb 1933; *Educ* Batley Boys' GS; *m* Jennifer Sylvia, da of Stanley Thornber; 2 s (Andrew Miles b 13 Aug 1961, Howard Mark b 2 Nov 1963), 2 da (Louise Margaret (Mrs Thompson) b 28 Sept 1962, Sally Elizabeth (Mrs Smallman) b 28 Nov 1966); *Career* trainee Norwich Union Insurance Soc 1949–54, local mangr Commercial Union Assurance Co Ltd 1954–59, chief exec The Pennine Insurance Co Ltd 1963–66 (agency mangr 1959–63), md Halifax Insurance Co Ltd 1966–83, jt md West Yorkshire Insurance Company Ltd 1983–95, chm White Rose Motor Policies Ltd 1985–95; chm: Calderdale AHA 1979–82 (memb 1974–82, vice chm 1977–79), Calderdale DHA 1982–93, Calderdale Healthcare NHS Tst 1993–96, Calderdale and Kirlees HA 1996–; ACCI 1963, chartered insurer 1989; *Recreations* bowling, fell walking, gardening; *Clubs* Rotary; *Style*— Allan Templeton, Esq, JP; ✉ Calderdale and Kirklees Health Authority, St Luke's House, Blackmoorfoot Road, Huddersfield, W Yorks HD4 5RH (☎ 01484 466000, fax 01484 466111)

TEMPLETON, (William) Berry; s of Douglas Joseph Templeton (d 1948), and Elizabeth Jane, *née* Caton (d 1964); *b* 13 Sept 1925; *Educ* Birkenhead Sch, Univ of Liverpool; *m* 2, 3 April 1962, Adele Monica, da of late Louis Arthur Westley; *Career* chm W Berry Templeton Ltd 1963–, vice chm Gateway Building Soc 1985–88; dir: Woolwich Building Soc 1988–92, Town & Country Home Builders Ltd 1992–95, Woolwich Homes 1988–95, Woolwich Assured Homes (1987) Ltd 1989–95; KStJ;

Freeman City of London, memb Guild of Freemen; memb AMInstBE, MCIOB, FFB; *Recreations* horse racing, polo, music, ballet; *Clubs* Oriental, Guards' Polo; *Style*— Berry Templeton, Esq; ✉ 39 York Terrace East, Regent's Park, London NW1 4PT (☎ 0171 486 2209)

TEMPLETON, Sir John; kt (1987); s of late Harvey Maxwell Templeton, and late Vella, *née* Handly; *b* 29 Nov 1912; *Educ* Yale (BA), Balliol Coll Oxford (Rhodes scholar, MA); *m* 1, 17 April 1937, Judith Dudley Folk (d 1951); 2 s (John Marks b 1939, Christopher Winston b 1947), 1 da (Anne Dudley (Mrs Zimmerman) b 1941); m 2, 31 Dec 1958, Irene Reynolds (d 1993); *Career* vice pres National Geophysical Co 1937–40; pres: Templeton Dobbrow and Vance Inc 1940–60, Templeton Growth Fund Ltd 1954–85, Templeton Investment Counsel Ltd Edinburgh 1976–83, Templeton World Fund Inc 1978–87; chm Templeton Galbraith and Hansberger Ltd 1986–92; sec Templeton Fndn 1960–; fndr: Templeton Prizes for Progress in Religion 1972, Templeton UK Project Tst 1984; pres Bd of Tstees Princeton Theol Seminary 1967–73 and 1976–85, memb Cncl Templeton Coll (formerly Oxford Centre for Mgmnt Studies) 1983–95, tstee Westminster Abbey Restoration 1993–; hon rector Dubuque Univ 1982–92, hon chllr Florida Southern Coll 1992–93; Hon LLD: Beaver Coll 1968, Marquette Univ 1980, Jamestown Coll 1983, Maryville Coll 1984; Hon DLitt Wilson Coll 1974, Hon DD Buena Vista Coll 1979, Hon DCL Univ of the South 1984, Hon DLitt Manhattan Coll 1990, Hon DLit Florida Southern Coll 1992; Hon LLD: Babson Coll 1992, Rhodes Coll 1992, Univ of Dubuque 1992, Louisiana Coll 1993, Stonehill Coll 1995, Notre Dame Univ 1996; Hon DHL Campbell Coll 1993; Benjamin Franklin Prize RSA 1995, Robert E Lee Award 1996; KStJ 1994; charterd fin analyst 1965, memb Soc of Security Analysts; *Books* The Humble Approach (1981), The Templeton Touch (jtly, 1985), The Templeton Plan (1987), Global Investing (1988), The God Who Would be Known (1989), Riches for the Mind and Spirit (1990), Discovering the Laws of Life (1994), Is There Any Reality Except God? (1994), Evidence of Purpose (1994); *Clubs* White's, Athenaeum, Lansdowne, Royal Over-Seas League, United Oxford and Cambridge Univ, Royal Institution, Royal Society of Arts; *Style*— Sir John Templeton; ✉ First Trust Bank Ltd, Lyford Cay, PO Box N-7776, Nassau, Bahamas (☎ 00 1 242 362 4904, fax 00 1 242 362 4880)

TEMPLETON, Richard; s of Capt John Templeton (d 1953), of Radyr, Cardiff, and Janet, *née* Morgan; *b* 11 April 1945; *Educ* Clifton Coll, Univ of Reading (BA), Univ of Bradford (MSc); *m* Belinda Susan, da of Tim Timlin, of Hook Norton, Oxon; 2 da (b 1992, b 1994); *Career* trainee analyst Philips & Drew stockbrokers 1969–71, dir Robert Fleming & Co Ltd 1980– (joined 1971); Freeman Town of Llantrisant; chm West of England Tst Ltd 1993; ASIA 1972; *Recreations* beagling, reading; *Clubs* Turf, MCC; *Style*— Richard Templeton, Esq; ✉ Robert Fleming & Co Ltd, 25 Copthall Ave, London EC2R 7DR (☎ 0171 638 5858, 0171 638 8742)

TENBY, 3 Viscount (UK 1957) William Lloyd George; JP (Hants); s of 1 Viscount Tenby, TD, PC (d 1967), s of 1 Earl Lloyd George; suc bro, 2 Viscount 1983; *b* 7 Nov 1927; *Educ* Eastbourne Coll, St Catharine's Coll Cambridge (BA); *m* 1955, Ursula, da of late Lt-Col Henry Edward Medlicott, DSO (d 1948); 1 s (Hon Timothy Henry Gwilym b 1962), 2 da (Hon Sara Gwenfron b 1957, Hon Clare Mair b 1961); *Heir* s, Timothy Henry Gwilym Lloyd George, *qv*; *Career* editorial asst Herbert Jenkins Ltd 1951–54, Advtg Dept Associated Newspapers 1954–57, gp advtg mangr United Dominions Trust Ltd 1957–74, PR advsr to Chm Kleinwort Benson Ltd 1974–87; dir Ugland International plc; Capt RWF (TA) 1951–61; *Style*— The Rt Hon the Viscount Tenby, JP; ✉ Triggs, Crondall, nr Farnham, Surrey GU10 5RU (☎ 01252 850592, fax 01252 850913)

TENCH, David Edward; OBE (1987); s of Henry George Tench (d 1971), and Emma Rose, *née* Orsborn (d 1980); *b* 14 June 1929; *Educ* Merchant Taylors'; *m* 1, 17 Aug 1957, Judith April Seaton Gurney (d 1986); 2 s (Matthew David Gurney b 1960, Daniel John Gurney b 1966), 1 da (Emma Rose Caroline (Mrs Reid) b 1962); m 2, 2 April 1988, Elizabeth Ann Irvine Macdonald; *Career* slr 1952; in private practice 1954–58, slr Inland Revenue 1958–69; Consumers' Assoc (publishers of Which?): legal advsr 1969–94, head Legal Dept 1988–94, dir of legal affairs 1991–94; conslt on public policy 1994–; broadcaster on consumer affairs 1964–; chm Domestic Coal Consumers' Cncl 1976–87, energy cmmr 1977–79; *Books* The Law for Consumers (1962), The Legal Side of Buying a House (1965), Wills and Probate (1968), Towards a Middle System of Law (1981); *Recreations* gardening, music; *Style*— David Tench, Esq, OBE; ✉ Pleasant View, The Platt, Amersham, Bucks HP7 0HZ (☎ 01494 724974)

TENNANT, Sir Anthony John; kt (1992); s of Maj John Tennant, TD (d 1967), and Hon Antonia Mary Roby Benson (later Viscountess Radcliffe, d 1982), da of 1 Baron Charnwood; *b* 5 Nov 1930; *Educ* Eton, Trinity Coll Cambridge (BA); *m* 1954, Rosemary Violet, da of Col Henry Charles Minshull Stockdale (d 1982); 2 s (Christopher, Patrick); *Career* cmmnd Scots Guards, served in Malaya; account exec Ogilvy & Mather 1953, dir Mather & Crowther 1960–66, dir Tennant & Sturge 1966–70, dir Watney Mann & Truman 1970–76, md International Distillers & Vintners Ltd 1977–83 (dep md 1976), md Grand Metropolitan plc 1977–87, chm International Distillers & Vintners Ltd 1983–87, gp chief exec Guinness plc 1987–89; chm: Guinness plc 1990–92, Christie's International plc 1993–96 (dir 1993–), Royal Academy Tst 1996–; dep chm: Forte plc 1992–96, Wellcome plc 1994–95, Arjo Wiggins Appleton plc 1996–; dir: Guardian Royal Exchange plc 1989–, Guardian Royal Exchange Assurance plc 1989–94, BNP UK Holdings Ltd 1991–, International Stock Exchange of the UK and Ireland Ltd 1990–94, Savoy Hotel plc 1995–96; sr advsr Morgan Stanley UK Gp 1993–, tstee Cambridge Fndn, tstee Royal Acad Tst, tstee Southampton Univ Devpt Tst 1992– (chm 1996–); memb Cncl Food From Britain 1983–86; *Clubs* Boodle's; *Style*— Sir Anthony Tennant; ✉ Morgan Stanley, 9 Upper Grosvenor Street, London W1X 9PA (☎ 0171 425 5902, fax 0171 499 1524)

TENNANT, Bernard; *b* 14 Oct 1930; *Educ* Farnworth GS, Open Univ (BA); *m* 17 Nov 1956, Marie, *née* Tonge; 2 s (Simon Richard b 1960, Philip David b 1963), 1 da (Sarah Elizabeth b 1970); *Career* Nat Serv RAF 1949; admin Worsley UDC and Bolton BC until 1955, vol admin Walkden Chamber of Trade Manchester 1957; sec: Bolton Chamber of Trade 1960–74, Bolton Chamber of Commerce and Indust 1968–74, numerous trade assocs; dir gen Nat Chamber of Trade 1987–92 (sec 1975–87), dir of retail Assoc of British Cs of C 1992–95, ret; fndr sec Moorside Gp of charitable housing assocs 1968; JP: Bolton 1968–75, Reading 1975–78; *Recreations* music, film musicals, photography, collating historical chronology; *Style*— Bernard Tennant, Esq

TENNANT, Hon Mrs Emma Christina; *née* Tennant; da of late 2 Baron Glenconner by his 2 w; *b* 20 Oct 1937; *Educ* St Paul's Girls' Sch; *m* 1, 1957 (m dis 1962), Sebastian, s of Henry Yorke and Hon Mrs (Adelaide) Yorke, da of 2 Baron Biddulph; m 2, 1963 (m dis), Christopher Booker, *qv*; m 3, 1968 (m dis 1973), Alexander Cockburn; *Career* novelist (as Emma Tennant); founder ed literary newspaper Bananas; FRSL; *Books* The Bad Sister, Wild Nights, The House of Hospitalities (1983), Sisters' Strangers (1989), Frankenstein's Baby (BBC film), Faustine (1992), ABC of Writing (1992), Tess (1993), Pemberley (1994), An Unequal Marriage (1994), Elinor and Marianne (1995), Emma in Love (1996); *Recreations* exploring, walking in Dorset; *Style*— The Hon Mrs Emma Tennant; ✉ c/o Carys Thomas, Hodder Headline plc, 338 Euston Road, London NW1 3BH (☎ 0171 873 6000)

TENNANT, Sir Iain Mark; KT (1986), JP (Morayshire 1961); s of Lt-Col John Edward Tennant, DSO, MC (ka 1942; gs of Sir Charles Tennant, 1 Bt, and n of 1 Baron Glenconner), of Innes House, Elgin, and his 1 w, Georgina Helen, da of Sir George Kirkpatrick, KCB, KCSI; *b* 11 March 1919; *Educ* Eton, Magdalene Coll Cambridge; *m* 11 July 1946, Lady Margaret Helen Isla Marion, *née* Ogilvy; 2 s (Mark Edward Tennant, *qv*, b 1947, Christopher b 1950), 1 da (Emma (Mrs Cheape) b 1954); *Career* Capt Scots Gds 1941, served N Africa 1940–42; memb Royal Co of Archers (Queen's Body Guard for Scotland) and Ensign 1981, Lt 1988; HM Lord-Lt for Morayshire 1963–94 (DL 1954); chm: Bd of Govrs of Gordonstoun Sch 1957–72, Glenlivet Distillers 1964–84, Scottish Northern Investmt Tst 1964–84, Grampian TV 1967–89, Seagram Distillers 1979–84; Crown Estate Cmmr 1970–90; Lord High Cmmr to Gen Assembly of the Church of Scotland 1988 and 1989; dir: Clydesdale Bank 1968–89, Abbey National Building Society 1981–89 (chm Scottish Advsy Bd 1981–89, memb 1968–89); former dir Times Publishing Co Ltd, memb Newspaper Panel Monopolies and Mergers Cmmn; Hon LLD Univ of Aberdeen 1990; Freeman of Moray 1994; FRSA 1971, CIMgt 1983; *Recreations* country pursuits; *Style*— Sir Iain Tennant, KT, JP; ✉ Lochnabo House, Lhanbryde, Morayshire (☎ 01343 84 2228)

TENNANT, Mark Edward; s of Sir Iain Tennant, KT, JP, *qv*, and the Lady Margaret Tennant; *b* 9 May 1947; *Educ* Eton; *m* 16 Oct 1971, Hermione Rosamond, da of Lt-Col Maurice Howe, OBE; 2 da (Miranda Rosamond Hermione b 15 June 1974, Clementina Margaret Georgina b 21 Nov 1977), 1 s (Edward Iain b 12 May 1983); *Career* vol serv Ockenden Venture India 1965–66, Capt Scots Gds 1966–73; Hambros Bank Ltd: trainee 1973–74, mangr Banking Control Dept 1973–76, mangr International Fixed Interest Dept 1976–81, md Hambro Pacific Ltd Hong Kong 1981–83; dir Fidelity International Ltd 1983–86, chm Bell Laurie White & Co Ltd 1986–91, chm Hill Samuel Unit Trust Managers Ltd and dir Hill Samuel Investment Services Group Ltd 1986–91, md Chase Global Securities Services (Scotland) 1991–; non-exec dir: Quality Street Ltd 1993–, Scotland International 1994–; head of youth leadership St John Ambulance 1973–83, cncllr Surrey Heath DC 1977–79, treas Scottish Cons Pty 1991–; Parly candidate (C) Dunfermline E 1992, Euro Parly candidate (C) Highlands and Islands 1994; *Recreations* golf, field sports, Scottish music, politics, opera, playing the bagpipes; *Clubs* Boodle's, Swinley Forest Golf; *Style*— Mark Tennant, Esq; ✉ The Hill House, Dunfermline, Fife KY11 3DQ (☎ 01383 722853); Chase Manhattan Bank NA, 91 George St, Edinburgh EH2 3ES (☎ 0131 225 7776, fax 0131 225 9445)

TENNANT, Maj Gen Michael Trenchard (Mike); CB (1994); s of Lt Col Hugh Trenchard Tennant, MC (d 1989), of Jersey, and Mary Isobel, *née* Wilkie (d 1986); *b* 3 Sept 1941; *Educ* Wellington Coll, RMA Sandhurst, Army Staff Coll; *m* 1, 28 Nov 1964, Susan Daphne (d 1993), da of Lt-Col Frank Maurice Beale, LVO; 3 s (Mark David Trenchard b 27 Aug 1966, Paul Philip b 15 June 1968, Toby Michael James b 21 March 1973); m 2, 8 June 1996, Jacqueline Mary, *née* ap Ellis, wid of David Parish; *Career* Subaltern 7 RHA 1962–67 (served Aden, Bahrain and UK), Adj 32 Regt BAOR 1967–69, Capt 25 Regt 1969–71 (served Hong Kong and Ulster), RMCS 1972, psc 1973, staff offr Mil Ops MOD 1974–75, Battery Cdr 49 Regt BAOR 1976–78, Directing Staff Army Staff Coll 1978–80, CO 1 RHA 1980–83, Cdr BR Trg Team Nigeria 1983–85, Cdr 3 Div RA 1985–87, Cdr RA UKLF 1988–91, Dir Royal Artillery 1991–94, Hon Regt Col 1 RHA 1994–, Col Cmdt RA 1994–, head of external communications Royal Ordnance Div British Aerospace 1994–; chm CCF's Assoc 1996–; *Recreations* tennis, golf, bridge; *Clubs* Army & Navy, Fadeaways, Denham Golf, Rye Golf; *Style*— Maj-Gen Mike Tennant, CB; ✉ Royal Ordnance Public Affairs, Lancaster House, PO Box 87, Aerospace Centre, Farnborough, Hants GU14 6YU (direct ☎ 01252 384886, fax 01252 384703)

TENNANT OF BALFLUIG, Mark Iain; Baron of Balfluig; s of Maj John Tennant, TD (d 1967), of Budds Farm, Wittersham, Kent, and Hon Antonia Mary Roby Benson (later Viscountess Radcliffe; d 1982), da of 1 Baron Charnwood; *b* 4 Dec 1932; *Educ* Eton, New Coll Oxford (MA); *m* 11 Dec 1965, Lady Harriot Pleydell-Bouverie, da of 7 Earl of Radnor, KG, KCVO, JP, DL (d 1968); 1 s (Lysander Philip Roby b 1968), 1 da (Sophia Roby b 1967); *Career* Lt The Rifle Bde (SRO); called to the Bar Inner Temple 1958, master of the Bench 1984, recorder Crown Ct 1987, master of the Supreme Ct Queen's Bench Div 1988; restored Balfluig Castle (dated 1556) in 1967; memb Royal Orchestral Soc for Amateur Musicians 1989; *Recreations* music, architecture, books, shooting; *Clubs* Brooks's; *Style*— M I Tennant, Esq; ✉ Balfluig Castle, Aberdeenshire AB33 8EJ; Royal Courts of Justice, Strand, London WC2A 2LL

TENNYSON, 5 Baron (UK 1884); Mark Aubrey Tennyson; DSC (1943); s of 3 Baron Tennyson (d 1951), and his 1 w, Hon Clarissa Tennant (d 1960), da of 1 Baron Glenconner; suc bro 4 Baron Tennyson 1991; *b* 28 March 1920; *Educ* RNC Dartmouth; *m* 1964, Deline Celeste (d 1995), da of Arthur Harold Budler, of Cradock, S Africa; *Heir* kinsman, Lt Cdr James Alfred Tennyson, DSC, RN b 26 Nov 1913; *Career* 1939–45 War (DSC and despatches), Cdr RN 1954; *Clubs* White's, RAC; *Style*— Cdr The Rt Hon Lord Tennyson, DSC; ✉ 304 Grosvenor Square, Duke Road, Rondebosch, Cape Town 7700, South Africa (☎ 00 27 021 686 1464)

TENNYSON-d'EYNCOURT, Sir Mark Gervais; 5 Bt (UK 1930), of Carter's Corner Farm, Parish of Herstmonceux, Co Sussex; o s of Sir Giles Gervais Tennyson-d'Eyncourt, 4 Bt (d 1989), and Juanita, *née* Borromeo; *b* 12 March 1967; *Educ* Charterhouse, Kingston Poly (BA); *Heir* none; *Career* fashion designer; Freeman City of London 1989; *Style*— Sir Mark Tennyson-d'Eyncourt, Bt; ✉ 404 Alaska Building, 61 Grange Road, London SE1 3BH

TEPER, Carl Wolf; s of Joseph Elliot Teper, of Kenton Harrow, and Pauline, *née* Mercado (d 1992); *b* 15 June 1955; *Educ* Aylestone Sch, Univ of Warwick (LLB), Cncl of Legal Educn; *Career* called to the Bar Middle Temple 1980, pupillage in chambers of Lord Boston of Faversham, QC 1980–81, head of chambers 1 Gray's Inn Sq 1990– (dep head 1988–90); Cncl of Legal Educn: assessor and examiner 1987–, memb Bd of Examiners 1990–, memb Bd of Studies 1992–; pt/t chm of Industrial Tbnls 1992–, memb Social Security Appeal Tbnl 1992; memb: Middle Temple 1980, Gray's Inn 1990; *Recreations* running; *Style*— Carl Teper, Esq; ✉ The Chambers of Jocelyn Gibbs and Carl Teper, 1 Gray's Inn Square, Gray's Inn, London WC1R 5AA (☎ 0171 405 8946, fax 0171 405 1617)

TER HAAR, Roger Eduard Lound; QC (1992); s of Dr Dirk ter Haar, and Christine Janet ter Haar; *b* 14 June 1952; *Educ* Felsted, Magdalen Coll Oxford (BA); *m* 10 Sept 1977, Sarah Anne, da of Peter Leyshon Martyn; 2 s (James b 1978, Harry b 1983), 1 da (Camilla b 1980); *Career* called to the Bar Inner Temple 1974, bencher 1993; *Recreations* gardening, golf; *Clubs* Brooks's; *Style*— Roger ter Haar, Esq, QC; ✉ 2 Crown Office Row, Temple, London EC4Y 7HJ (☎ 0171 797 8100, fax 0171 797 8101)

TERFEL, Bryn; *né* Bryn Terfel Jones; s of Hefin Jones, of Garndolbenmaen, Gwynedd, and Nesta, *née* Jones; *Educ* Ysgol Dyffryn Nantlle Gwynedd, Guildhall Sch of Music & Drama (Kathleen Ferrier scholar, Gold Award); *m* 22 August 1987, Lesley, da of George Winston Halliday; 1 s (Tomos b 1 July 1994); *Career* bass baritone; pres: Nat Youth Choir of Wales, Festival of Wales; vice pres: Cymru A'r Byd, Llangollen Int Eisteddfod; patron: Mid Wales Opera, Taunton Choral Soc, Hope House, Cor Meibion Hart, Criccieth Memorial Hall; hon fell Univ of Wales Aberystwyth, hon fell Welsh Coll of Music and Drama, hon Dr Univ of Glamorgan, white robe Gorsedd Eisteddfod Genedlaethol Frenhinol Cymru; *Roles* incl: Guglielmo in Cosi Fan Tutte (WNO) 1990, Figaro in Le Nozze di Figaro (WNO) 1990, Sprecher in Die Zauberflöte (La Monaie de Brussels) 1991, Figaro in Figaro's Wedding (ENO) 1991, Spirit Messenger in Die Frau ohne Schatten (Salzburg Easter Festival) 1992, Masetto in Don Giovanni (Covent Garden) 1992, Figaro in Le Nozze di Figaro (Santa Fe) 1992, Jochanaan in Salome (Salzburg Festival) 1993, Donner in Das Rheingold (Lyric Opera of Chicago) 1993, Ford in Falstaff (WNO) 1993, 4 Male Roles in Les Contes d'Hoffmann (Vienna State Opera) 1994, Leporello in Don

Giovanni (Salzburg Festival) 1994, 1995 and 1996, Figaro in Le Nozze di Figaro (Metropolitan Opera NY) 1994, Balstrode in Peter Grimes (Covent Garden) 1995, Leporello (Metropolitan Opera and Lyric Opera of Chicago) 1995, Nick Shadow in The Rake's Progress (WNO) 1996, Sharpless in Madame Butterfly (New Japan Philharmonic) 1996; *Recordings* on Decca, Deutsche Grammophon, L'Oiseau-Lyre, Archiv, Sony Classical, Philips, RCA, Chandos, Hyperion, EMI Classics, BMG Classics, Sain; *Awards* Lieder Prize Cardiff Singer of the World 1989, first winner Br Critics Circle Award (for most outstanding contribution to musical life in GB) 1992, Gramophone Magazine Young Singer of the Year 1992, Newcomer of the Year Int Classic Music Award 1993, Caecillia Prize (for recording of Vagabond) 1995; *Recreations* golf, supporting Manchester United, collecting Fob watches; *Style*— Bryn Terfel, Esq; ✉ c/o Harlequin Agency Ltd, 203 Fidlas Road, Llanishen, Cardiff CF4 5NA (☎ 01222 750821, fax 01222 755971)

TERRAINE, John Alfred; s of Charles William Terraine, and Eveline, *née* Holmes; *b* 15 Jan 1921; *Educ* Stamford Sch, Keble Coll Oxford; *m* 1945, Joyce Elizabeth; 1 da (Carola Louise (Mrs Attwater)); *Career* historian and author; BBC: joined 1944, Pacific and S African prog organiser 1953–63, assoc prodr and chief scriptwriter The Great War (BBC TV) 1963–64; freelance historian 1964–; scriptwriter: The Lost Peace (BBC, jtly) 1965, The Life and Times of Lord Mountbatten (Rediffusion/Thames TV) 1966–68, The Mighty Continent (BBC, also narrator) 1974–75; memb RUSI 1961– (memb Cncl 1976–84), hon pres Western Front Assoc 1981–; hon fell Keble Coll Oxford 1986; Documentary Script award Screenwriters' Guild 1964, Script award SFTA 1969, Chesney Gold medal RUSI 1982, C P Robertson Meml Trophy Air PR Assoc 1985; FRHistS 1987; *Books* Mons: the Retreat to Victory (1960), Douglas Haig: the Educated Soldier (1963), The Western Front (1964), General Jack's Diary (ed, 1964), The Great War: an Illustrated History (1965), The Life & Times of Lord Mountbatten (1968), Impacts of War 1914 and 1918 (1970), The Mighty Continent (1974), Trafalgar (1976), The Road to Passchendaele (1977), To Win a War: 1918 The Year of Victory (1978), The Smoke and the Fire: Myths and Anti-Myths of War 1861–1945 (1980), White Heat: the New Warfare 1914–18 (1982), The Right of the Line: The RAF in the European War 1939–45 (1985, Yorkshire Post Book of the Year), Business in Great Waters: the U-Boat Wars 1916–45 (1989); *Style*— John Terraine, Esq; ✉ 77 Sirdar Road, London W11 4EQ (☎ 0171 229 8152)

TERRAS, (Christopher) Richard; s of Frederick Richard Terras (d 1976), and Katherine Joan, *née* Anning; *b* 17 Oct 1937; *Educ* Uppingham, Univ Coll Oxford (MA); *m* 27 Oct 1962, Janet Esther May, da of Leslie Harold Sydney Baxter (d 1980); 1 s (Nicholas b 1965), 3 da (Clare b 1964, Penelope b 1968, Joanna b 1971); *Career* CA; ptnr: Swanwick Terras & Co 1963–65, Abbott & Son 1963–65, Arthur Andersen 1971–; *Recreations* cricket (played for Cheshire); *Clubs* Free Foresters, Cheshire Gentlemen, Leicestershire Gentlemen, Vincent's, Forty, St James's (Manchester); *Style*— Richard Terras, Esq; ✉ Arthur Andersen, Bank House, 9 Charlotte Street, Manchester M1 4EU (☎ 0161 228 2121)

TERRINGTON, Derek Humphrey; s of late Douglas Jack, of Newmarket, and Jean Mary, *née* Humphrey; *b* 25 Jan 1949; *Educ* Sea Point Boys' HS, Univ of Cape Town (MA); *m* 15 July 1978, Jennifer Mary, da of late Leslie Vernon Jones; 1 da (Sarah b 29 Sept 1984); *Career* assoc ptnr Grieveson Grant 1984, exec dir Phillips & Drew 1991 (asst dir 1987, dir 1988), dir Kleinwort Benson Securities 1991–96, dir and head of equity research Teather & Greenwood 1996–; AIIMR, MSI, FRSA; *Style*— Derek Terrington, Esq; ✉ 16 St Winifred's Road, Teddington, Middlesex TW11 9JR; Teather & Greenwood, 12–20 Camomile Street, London EC3A 7NN

TERRINGTON, 4 Baron (UK 1918); James Allen David Woodhouse; s of 3 Baron Terrington, KBE (d 1961); *b* 30 Dec 1915; *Educ* Winchester, RMC Sandhurst; *m* 1942, Suzanne, da of Col T S Irwin, JP, DL, late Royal Dragoons, of Justicetown, Carlisle, and Mill House, Holton, Suffolk; 3 da (Hon Mrs Bolton, Hon Mrs Leatham, Countess Alexander of Tunis); *Heir* bro, Hon Christopher Montague Woodhouse, DSO, OBE; *Career* Staff Coll Haifa 1944, psc 1944, served WWII in India, N Africa and Middle East (wounded); sits as Independent Peer in House of Lords; Maj (ret) Royal Norfolk Regt and Queen's Westminster Rifles (King's Royal Rifle Corps) TA, an ADC to GOC Madras 1940; former memb Stock Exchange, ptnr Sheppards and Chase 1952–80, dep chm of Ctees House of Lords 1961–63; exec memb Nat Listening Library (talking books for the disabled); vice pres Small Farmers Assoc; memb: Ecclesiastical Ctee since 1979, Int Advsy Bd of the American Univ Washington DC USA; former exec memb and dep chm Wider Share Ownership Cncl; *Recreations* fishing, gardening; *Clubs* Boodle's; *Style*— The Rt Hon the Lord Terrington; ✉ 3 Whitelands House, Cheltenham Terrace, London SW3 4QX

TERRY, *see also:* Imbert-Terry

TERRY, Prof Arthur Hubert; s of Arthur Terry (d 1962), of York, and Beatrice, *née* Hardisty (d 1983); *b* 17 Feb 1927; *Educ* St Peter's Sch York, Trinity Hall Cambridge (BA, MA); *m* 25 June 1955, Mary (Molly) Gordon, da of Dr John Sellar (d 1963), of Markinch, Fife; 2 s (Richard, Philip), 1 da (Sally); *Career* Nat Serv 1947–49, Sgt-Instr RAEC; prof of Spanish Queen's Univ of Belfast 1962–72 (asst lectr 1950–54, lectr 1954–60, sr lectr 1960–62), prof of lit Univ of Essex 1973–93, special prof Univ of Nottingham 1990–93, visiting prof Queen Mary and Westfield Coll 1993–, sr res fell Inst of Romance Studies 1990–; pres: Int Catalan Studies Assoc 1982–88, Br Comparative Lit Assoc 1986–92; Cross of St George 1982 (awarded by Catalan Govt for work as critic and historian of Catalan lit and services to Catalan culture), Int Ramon Llull Prize (awarded by Catalan Govt and Inst of Catalan Studies for work as critic of Catalan lit) 1995; corresponding memb Inst of Catalan Studies 1992; *Books* La Poesia de Joan Maragall (1963), An Anthology of Spanish Poetry 1500–1700 (2 vols, 1965 and 1968), Catalan Literature (1972), Antonio Machado: Campos de Castilla (1973), Selected Poems of Ausiàs March (1976), Joan Maragall, Antologia Poètica (1981), Sobre poesia catalana contemporània: Riba, Foix, Espriu (1985), Quatre poetes catalans: Ferrater, Brossa, Gimferrer, Xirau (1991), Seventeenth-Century Spanish Poetry: the Power of Artifice (1993); *Recreations* music; *Style*— Prof Arthur Terry; ✉ 11 Braiswick, Colchester CO4 5AU (☎ 01206 851807); Department of Literature, The University of Essex, Wivenhoe Park, Colchester CO4 3SQ (☎ 01206 873333, fax 01206 873598, telex 98440 UNILIB G)

TERRY, Air Vice-Marshal Colin George; CB (1995), OBE (1984); s of George Albert Terry, of Shropshire, and Edna Joan, *née* Purslow; *b* 8 Aug 1943; *Educ* Bridgnorth GS, RAF Colls Henlow and Cranwell, Imperial Coll London (BSc, ACGI, hockey colours); *m* 12 March 1966, Gillian, da of late Conrad Glendor Grindley; 2 s (Sarn Conrad b 22 May 1969, Leon Alexander b 24 Jan 1974), 1 da (Adrienne Miya b 24 Nov 1976); *Career* tech cadet RAF Tech Coll Henlow 1961, cmmnd engrg offr 1962, various engrg and instructing appts at tport, trg and fighter stations 1962–69, trg as serv pilot 1969–71, promoted Sqdn Ldr 1971, aircraft project offr Royal Navy Belfast 1971–74, sr engrg offr RAF Phantom sqdns Germany 1974–77, engrg authy for Vulcan, Victor and VC10 propulsion systems HQ Strike Cmd 1977–79, attended RAF Staff Coll Bracknell 1979, promoted Wing Cdr 1979, CO Engrg Wing RAF Coltishall (Jaguars and Sea Kings) 1979–81, engrg authy Lightnings and Phantoms HQ Strike Cmd 1981–82, sr RAF engr and OC Engrg Wing RAF Stanley Falkland Is 1982, promoted Gp Capt 1984, engrg authy Cmd Staff, OC RAF Abingdon (Jaguars, Hawks and Buccaneers), RCDS 1989, promoted Air Cdre 1989, Dir of Support Mgmnt 1989–93, promoted Air Vice-Marshal 1993, DG Support Mgmnt (RAF) 1993–95, Chief of Staff 1995–; vice cdre RAF Sailing Assoc; *Recreations* sailing, flying, skiing, cooking, modern languages, music; *Clubs* RAF; *Style*— Air Vice-Marshal Colin Terry, CB, OBE; ✉ Chief of Staff, HQ Logistics Command, RAF Brampton, Huntingdon, Cambs PE18 8QL (☎ 01480 52151, fax 01480 413563)

TERRY, David Robins; s of Joseph Robins Terry (d 1977), of Little Hall, Heslington, York, and Mary Patricia Colston, *née* Douty; *b* 11 Nov 1942; *Educ* Rishworth Sch Halifax; *m* 19 Nov 1966, Katharine Ruth, da of Amos Eastham, of Selby; 2 s (Nigel Joseph Douty b 15 June 1970, Oliver Stuart Robins b 6 May 1972); *Career* Army Serv 4 and 7 Royal Dragoon Gds 1961; CA 1968; John Gordon Walton & Co Leeds 1962–67; Price Waterhouse: joined Leeds Office 1969, ptnr 1980, transferred to Birmingham 1980, specialist in business servs 1986–, gp ldr 1986–92, seconded to Budapest office as sr audit ptnr 1992–95, transferred to Sofia office as ptnr i/c 1995–; pres Cncl of Dudley and Dist C of C 1989–90 (memb 1985–), chm Mgmnt Ctee Dudley Nat Pianoforte Competition 1987–92, govr St Richards Hospice Worcester 1991–92; Merchant Adventurer of Co of Merchant Adventurers of City of York; ATII 1971, FCA 1978; *Recreations* golf, music, family, travel, assistant church organist; *Clubs* Lansdowne; *Style*— David Terry, Esq; ✉ Tapenhall House, Porters Mill, Droitwich, Worcester WR9 OAN; Price Waterhouse, Sophia 1000, 10 Stefan Karadja Street, Bulgaria (☎ 00 359 2 4920060, fax 00 359 2 872461)

TERRY, (Robert) Jeffrey; s of Robert James Terry (d 1996), of Stockport, and Emily, *née* Davison (d 1975); *b* 10 Sept 1952; *Educ* William Hulme's GS Manchester, King's Coll London (LLB), City of London Poly (MA Business Law); *m* 15 July 1978, Susan, da of Reginald Trevor Kingston Gregory, of Bath; 2 da (Sarah Louise b 7 Aug 1983, Anna May Emily b 7 May 1987); *Career* called to the Bar 1976, community lawyer Southend CAB 1976–78; in private practice: London 1978–, Manchester 1989– (chm 8 King St Chambers Commercial Gp); memb: Hon Soc of Lincoln's Inn 1975, Northern Chancery Bar Assoc, Professional Negligence Assoc; fndr memb Northern Circuit Commercial Bar Assoc, assoc memb American Bar Assoc; *Recreations* walking, photography, reading, smallholding husbandry; *Style*— Jeffrey Terry, Esq; ✉ Hall Stones Green Farm, Hey Head Lane, Cross Stone, Todmorden, W Yorks (fax 01706 817936); 8 King St, Manchester M2 6AQ (☎ 0161 834 9560, fax 0161 834 2733); Lamb Building, Temple, London EC4 (☎ 0171 353 6701, fax 0171 353 4686); clerk: Peter Whitman (☎ 0161 834 9560)

TERRY, John Victor; s of Norman Victor Terry (d 1981), and Mary Josephine Terry; *b* 6 Sept 1942; *Educ* Leys Sch Cambridge, Jesus Coll Cambridge (MA), Harvard Business Sch (MBA); *m* 3 April 1965, Jane Gillian, da of Donald Pearson, of Cambridge; 2 s (Nicholas b 11 Jan 1969, Simon b 6 May 1971); *Career* gen mangr Herbert Terry and Sons Ltd 1971–75; Anglepoise Lighting Ltd: purchased and formed as independent co 1975, md 1975–88, chm 1988–; pres: Harvard Business Sch Assoc of Midlands 1983–85, Lighting Indust Fedn 1988–89; Freeman Worshipful Co of Lightmongers 1985; sec Frazer Nash Section Vintage Sports Car Club 1990–94; *Recreations* windsurfing, cars, sailing, real tennis; *Clubs* Royal London Yacht, Leamington Tennis, British Racing Drivers; *Style*— John Terry, Esq; ✉ Wasperton House, Warwick CV35 8EB (☎ 01926 624264); Anglepoise Lighting, Redditch B97 8DR (☎ 01527 63771, fax 01527 61232)

TERRY, Nicholas John; s of John Edmund Terry (d 1978), of Nottingham, and Winifred Nina, *née* White (d 1970); *b* 12 Nov 1947; *Educ* Peveril Sch Nottingham, Bilborough GS Nottingham, Univ of Bath Sch of Architecture (BSc, BArch); *m* 27 June 1970, Dorothy, da of Leslie Atkins; 1 da (Alexandra Louise Terry b 31 Dec 1977); *Career* architect; Terry Associates Bath 1970; Building Design Partnership Manchester: architect (work incl Manchester Museum, Durham Millburngate and Albert Dock Liverpool) 1972–75, conslt design architect 1978, architect ptnr (work incl Cribbs Causeway Regnl Shipping Centre Bristol, Longavia Building Lisbon) 1990–, dir Dixon Jones BPP (work incl Royal Opera House) 1995; Arthur Erickson Architects Canada (Provincial Law Courts Vancouver BC) 1975–77, John S Bonnington Partnership St Albans (Cyprus Govt Centre and Kuwait Stock Exchange) 1978–81, dir of architecture and md Heery Architects and Engineers London 1983–89 (architect for Citibank HQs London and Frankfurt 1981–83); design awards for Durham Millburngate (Building Design Partnership): RIBA award 1977, Civic Trust award 1978, Europa Nostra award 1978; Honour award for Robson Square Law Courts (Arthur Erickson Architects) 1980; *Exhibitions* Durham Millburngate: Royal Acad Summer Exhibition 1974, Museum of Modern Art NY 1979; Albert Dock Royal Acad Summer Exhibition 1975, Kuwait Stock Exchange RIBA 1982; MRIBA 1973; memb: RAIC 1976, Architectural Inst of BC 1976, Soc of American Mil Engrs 1976; MInstD 1988; *Recreations* swimming, walking, gardening, architecture, reading; *Style*— Nicholas Terry, Esq; ✉ Building Design Partnership, PO Box 4WD, 16 Gresse St, London W1A 4WD (☎ 0171 631 4733, fax 0171 631 0393); Dixon Jones BDP, 41 Shelton Street, London WC2H 9HJ (☎ 0171 240 9585, fax 0171 240 7114)

TERRY, Air Chief Marshal Sir Peter David George; GCB (1983, KCB 1978, CB 1975), AFC (1959); s of (James) George Terry (d 1968), and Laura Chilton, *née* Powell (d 1980); *b* 18 Oct 1926; *Educ* Chatham House Sch Ramsgate; *m* 1946, Betty Martha Louisa, da of Arthur Thompson; 2 s (Stephen, David (decd)), 1 da (Elizabeth); *Career* RAF 1945–84, cmmnd 1946, dir Air Staff Briefing MOD 1970–71, dir Forward Policy RAF 1971–75, ACOS Policy and Plans 1975–77, Vice Chief of Air Staff 1977–79, C-in-C RAF Germany and Cdr 2 Allied Tactical Air Force 1979–81, dep C-in-C AFCENT 1981, Dep Supreme Allied Cdr Europe 1981–84; Govr and C-in-C Gibraltar 1985–89; QCVSA 1959 and 1962; *Recreations* golf; *Clubs* RAF; *Style*— Air Chief Marshal Sir Peter Terry, GCB, AFC

TERRY, (John) Quinlan; s of Philip John Terry, of Suffolk, and Phyllis May Whiteman; *b* 24 July 1937; *Educ* Bryanston, Architectural Assoc; *m* 9 Sept 1961, Christina Marie-Therese, da of Joachin Tadeusz de Ruttié (d 1968); 1 s (Francis Nathanael b 1969), 4 da (Elizabeth b 1964, Anna b 1965, Martha b 1979, Sophia b 1982); *Career* architect in private practice; works incl: country houses in the classical style, Richmond Riverside Devpt, New Howard Bldg Downing Coll Cambridge, New Brentwood Cathedral, three villas in Regent's Park for the Crown Estate Cmmrs, New Library Downing Coll, restoration of St Helen's Bishopsgate, restoration of the three state rooms No 10 Downing St; memb Royal Fine Art Cmmn; FRIBA 1962; *Recreations* the Pauline Epistles; *Style*— Quinlan Terry, Esq; ✉ Old Exchange, High Street, Dedham, Colchester CO7 6HA

TERRY, Simon Duncan; s of Michael Terry, and Janice Mary, *née* McKenzie; *b* 27 March 1974; *Educ* Aveland Sch; *Career* target archer; memb Lincoln Archery Club; first competition win 1982, competed in Jr World Championships Norway 1991; Bronze medals individual and team event Olympic Games Barcelona 1992; nat records: Bristol IV (1234) Coventry 1987, Portsmouth indoor (594) Coventry 1991, short metric (691) Chester 1992; *Recreations* shooting, fishing; *Style*— Simon Terry, Esq; ✉ 15 Mareham Lane, Sleaford, Lincs NG34 7JP (☎ 01529 306214)

TESLER, Brian; CBE; s of David Tesler (d 1972), and Esther Tesler; *b* 19 Feb 1929; *Educ* Chiswick Co Sch for Boys, Exeter Coll Oxford (MA); *m* 1959, Audrey Mary; 1 s; *Career* former TV prodr/dir; dir of progs: ABC 1963–68, Thames TV 1968–74; London Weekend Television: dep chief exec 1974–76, md 1976–90, chm and md 1984–90, chm 1990–92, chm LWT International Ltd 1990–92, chm The London Studios Ltd 1990–92, dep chm LWT (Holdings) plc 1990–94; chm ITV Superchannel Ltd 1986–88, chm The Magazine Business Ltd 1992–96; dir: ITN 1979–90, Channel 4 1980–84, Oracle Teletext Ltd 1980–92, Services Sound and Vision Corp 1980; ret; govr: Nat Film and TV Sch

1977, BFI 1986 (dep chm 1994); memb Br Screen Advsy Cncl 1977–94; chm: ITCA Cncl 1980–82, ITV Film Purchase Ctee 1988–90, Lord Chllr's Advsy Ctee on JPs Inner London 1994– (memb 1991–); *Recreations* books, theatre, cinema, music; *Style*— Brian Tesler, Esq, CBE

TESORIERE, HE (Harcourt) Andrew Pretorius; s of Maj Pieter Ivan Tesoriere, GPR (ret), and Joyce Margaret, *née* Baxter; *b* 2 Nov 1950; *Educ* Nautical Coll Pangbourne, Britannia Royal Naval Coll Dartmouth, Univ Coll Wales Aberystwyth (BSc(Econ)), Ecole Nationale d'Administration Paris, SOAS Univ of London; *m* 14 Feb 1987, Dr Alma Gloria Vasquez, da of Joseph and Eva Vasquez, of Harlingen, Texas; *Career* RNR 1964–68, Royal Naval Offr 1969–73; HM Dip Serv: FCO 1974, Persian language student SOAS and Iran 1975, Oriental sec Kabul 1976–79, third sec Nairobi 1980–81, second sec Abidjan (also accredited to Ouagadougou and Niamey) 1982–84, FCO 1985–87, first sec and head of chancery Br Interests Section Damascus 1987–91 (chargé d'affaires when UK/Syria rels restored 1990), FCO 1991–94 (sec to Ministerial UK Dependent Territories Gp 1993–94), seconded as head of field ops UN Office for Humanitarian Assistance to Afghanistan 1994–95, HM ambass Albania 1996–; FRGS 1993; *Recreations* travel, sport, foreign languages, countryside, art; *Style*— HE Mr Andrew Tesoriere; ✉ 35 Hamilton Gardens, St Johns Wood, London NW8 9PX (☎ 0171 289 6734); c/o Foreign & Commonwealth Office (Tirana), King Charles Street, London SW1A 2AH (☎ and fax 00 355 42 34973/4/5)

TESTA, Dr Humberto Juan; s of Orestes Miguel Angel Testa (d 1956), of Buenos Aires, Argentina, and Victoria Juana, *née* Vidal; *b* 11 Dec 1936; *Educ* Sch of Med Buenos Aires Univ (MD, PhD); *m* 18 Dec 1964, Nydia Esther Testa, *qv*, da of Victor Anibal D Garcia (d 1982), of Neuquen, Argentina; 1 s (Fernando Julio b 31 Dec 1965), 2 da (Cecilia b 27 Nov 1973, Paula b 2 May 1982); *Career* Manchester Royal Infirmary: res offr 1967–68, res registrar 1968–70, fell nuclear med 1970–73, conslt nuclear med 1974–; pt/t lectr diagnostic radiology and nuclear med Univ of Manchester 1977–; fell: Manchester Med Soc, Br Nuclear Med Soc; miembro honorario nacional Academia De Medicina de Buenos Aires 1988; FRCP 1980, FRCR 1989; *Books* Nuclear Medicine in Urology and Nephrology (ed with O'Reilly and Shields, 1986), Adult Dementias (jtly, 1994); *Recreations* squash, music and reading; *Style*— Dr Humberto Testa; ✉ 27 Barcheston Rd, Cheadle, Cheshire SK8 1LJ (☎ 0161 428 6873); Department of Nuclear Medicine, Royal Infirmary, Oxford Road, Manchester M13 9WL (☎ 0161 276 4820)

TESTA, Dr Nydia Esther Garcia; da of Victor Anibal Garcia (d 1981), and Manuela, *née* Barreiros; *b* 15 Feb 1938; *Educ* Univ of Buenos Aires, Univ of Manchester (PhD); *m* 18 Dec 1964, Humberto Juan Testa, *qv*, s of Orestes Testa (d 1955); 1 s (Fernando b 1965), 2 da (Cecilia b 1973, Paula b 1981); *Career* res fell Cncl of Scientific and Tech Investigations Buenos Aires 1963–67, visiting res fell Paterson Laboratories 1967–74, scientist and sr scientist Paterson Inst for Cancer Res 1974–; author numerous scientific pubns in jls and books; *Style*— Dr Nydia Testa; ✉ Paterson Institute for Cancer Research, Christie Hospital (☎ 0161 446 3237, fax 0161 446 3033)

TETLEY, Brian; s of Herbert Tetley (d 1957), of Little Gomersal, and Gladys, *née* Holliday (d 1985); *b* 5 Sept 1937; *Educ* Heckmondwike GS; *m* 29 Aug 1959, Winifred Mary, da of William Sylvester O'Neill (d 1981), of Birkenshaw, Bradford; 2 s (Mark Richard b 1963, Neil Jon b 1966); *Career* CA; dir The Bradford Property Tst plc; dir: Margrave Estates Ltd, Faside Estates Ltd, Ashday Property Co Ltd, Sydenham Estates Ltd, and dir of various other cos; FCA; *Recreations* Rotary, golf; *Clubs* The Bradford; *Style*— Brian Tetley, Esq; ✉ Reighton, 123 Huddersfield Rd, Liversedge, W Yorks WF15 7DA; The Bradford Property Trust plc, 3 Commercial Street, Bradford BD1 4AN (☎ 01274 723181)

TETLEY, Glen; s of Glenford Andrew Tetley (d 1985), and Mary Eleanor Byrne (d 1986); *b* 3 Feb 1926; *Educ* Franklin and Marshall Coll, NY Univ (BSc); *Career* choreographer; ballets incl: Pierrot Lunaire 1962, The Anatomy Lesson 1964, Mythical Hunters 1965, Ricercare 1966, Ziggurat 1967, Circles 1968, Embrace Tiger and Return to Mountain 1968, Arena 1968, Field Figures 1971, Laborintus 1972, Gemini 1973, Voluntaries 1973, Sacre du Printemps 1974, Greening 1975, Sphinx 1978, The Tempest 1979, The Firebird 1981, Revelation and Fall 1984, Alice 1986, Orpheus 1987, La Ronde 1987, Tagore 1989, Dialogues 1991, Oracle 1994; choreographer for: Royal Ballet Covent Garden, Ballet Rambert, Festival Ballet, American Ballet Theatre, Nat Ballet of Canada, Royal Danish Ballet, Royal Swedish Ballet, Nat Ballet of Norway, Australian Ballet, Stuttgart Ballet, Paris Opera, La Scala Milan, Ater Balletto; dir Glen Tetley Dance Co 1962–69, co dir Nederlands Dans Theater 1969–71, dir Stuttgart Ballet 1972–74, artistic associate National Ballet of Canada 1987–90; *Awards* Queen Elizabeth II Coronation Award 1981, Prix Italia 1982, Tennant Caledonian Award Edinburgh Festival 1983, Ohioana Career Medal 1986, New York University Achievement Award 1988; *Style*— Glen Tetley, Esq; ✉ Christine Dobush, Suite 17F, 215 East 95th Street, New York, NY (☎ and fax 010 1 212 860 7699)

TETLEY, Sir Herbert; KBE (1965), CB (1958); s of Albert Tetley (d 1926), of Leeds, and Mary Tetley (d 1947); *b* 23 April 1908; *Educ* Leeds GS, Queen's Coll Oxford (MA); *m* 1941, (Nancy) Agnes MacLean MacFarlane, da of John Macphee of Glasgow; 1 s; *Career* jt actuary Nat Provident Inst 1946–53, govt actuary 1958–73 (dep govt actuary 1953–58); chm: Civil Serv Insur Soc and assoc socs 1961–73, Ctee on Econs Road Res Bd 1962–65; pres Inst of Actuaries 1964–66, memb Res Ctee on Road Traffic 1966–72; *Style*— Sir Herbert Tetley, KBE, CB; ✉ 37 Upper Brighton Rd, Surbiton, Surrey KT6 6QX (☎ 0181 399 3001)

TETLOW, His Hon Judge; Christopher Bruce; s of George Wilfred Tetlow and Betty Tetlow; *b* 27 Feb 1943; *Educ* Stowe, Magdalene Coll Cambridge (MA); *m* 1981, Rosalind Jane Cope; 2 s, 1 da; *Career* called to the Bar Middle Temple 1969, circuit judge (Northern Circuit) 1992–; *Clubs* St James's (Manchester); *Style*— His Hon Judge Tetlow

TETLOW, District Judge Raymond Charles; s of Charles Thomas Tetlow (d 1968), of Pinner, and Rosa Emily, *née* Milton (d 1972); *b* 15 July 1939; *Educ* Harrow Co GS for Boys; *m* 14 June 1985, Gillian Margaret Simmonite, da of late Wallace Frederick Thomas Aries; 2 step s (Derek Andrew Simmonite b 6 July 1965, Neil James Simmonite b 17 Feb 1968); *Career* articled to David Pritchard town clerk Borough of Harrow, Law Soc finals 1965, admitted slr 1966, asst slr London Borough of Harrow, slr to the council Bletchley UDC 1967–73, ptnr Andrew Marchant Solicitors Newport Pagnell 1973–77, sole practitioner in own name Newport Pagnell 1977–92, district judge 1992–; hon legal advsr Bucks Assoc of Parish Cncls 1970–91, fndr memb and legal advsr Milton Keynes CAB until 1991; memb Law Soc 1966–, memb Assoc of District Judges 1992–; memb, treasurer, sec and pres Milton Keynes Dist Law Soc 1970–91; *Clubs* Castle Baynard Ward - City of London; *Style*— District Judge Tetlow; ✉ The Manor House, Broughton Village, Milton Keynes, Bucks MK10 9AA (☎ 01908 675074); Milton Keynes County Court, 351 Silbury Boulevard, Central Milton Keynes, Bucks MK9 2DT

TETT, Sir Hugh Charles; kt (1966); s of James Charles Tett (d 1955); *b* 28 Oct 1906; *Educ* Hele's Sch Exeter, Univ Coll Exeter, RCS (BSc, DIC, ARCS); *m* 1, 1931, Katie Sargent (d 1948); 1 da; m 2, 1949, Joyce Lilian, *née* Mansell (d 1979); 1 da; m 3, 1980, Barbara Mary, *née* Mackenzie; *Career* Esso Petroleum Co: joined 1928, dir 1951, chm 1959–67; chm Cncl Inst of Petroleum 1947–48; memb: CSIR 1961–64, Advsy Cncl Miny of Technol 1964–67; chm Econ Devpt Ctee for Motor Mfrg Indust 1967–69; pro chllr Univ of Southampton 1967–79; fell Imperial Coll of Sci and Technol 1964; Hon DSc: Southampton 1965, Exeter 1970; *Style*— Sir Hugh Tett; ✉ Primrose Cottage, Bosham, Chichester, W Sussex PO18 8HZ (☎ 01243 572705)

TEVERSON, Robin; MEP (Lib Dem) Cornwall and Plymouth W (majority 29,498); *b* 31 March 1952; *Educ* Chigwell Sch, Waltham Forest Tech Coll, Univ of Exeter (BA); *Career* BRS Western: gen mangr Yate Distribution Centre 1983–86, dir 1986–89; md (and devpt dir of contract distribution) SPD Ltd 1987–89, dir Exel Logistics 1987–89, md Supply Chain Consultancy (Rationale Ltd) 1989–94; MEP (Lib Dem) Cornwall and Plymouth W 1994–; memb Inst of Logistics Management; *Style*— Robin Teverson, Esq, MEP; ✉ Office Address: Newton Farm, Metherell, Callington, Cornwall PL17 8DQ (☎ 01579 351234, fax 01579 351321)

TEVIOT, 2 Baron (UK 1940); Charles John Kerr; s of 1 Baron Teviot, DSO, MC (d 1968, himself ggs of 6 Marquess of Lothian), by his 2 w Angela (d 1979), da of Lt-Col Charles Villiers, CBE, DSO (ggn of 4 Earl of Clarendon) by his w Lady Kathleen Cole (2 da of 4 Earl of Enniskillen); *b* 16 Dec 1934; *Educ* Eton; *m* 1965, Patricia Mary, da of late Alexander Harris; 1 s, 1 da (Hon Catherine b 1976); *Heir* s, Hon Charles Robert Kerr b 19 Sept 1971; *Career* genealogist; memb Advsy Cncl on Public Records 1974–82; dir: Debrett's Peerage Ltd 1977–83, Burke's Peerage Research 1983–85, Burke's Peerage Ltd 1984–85; FSG 1975; *Recreations* genealogy, walking; *Style*— The Rt Hon the Lord Teviot; (☎ 01444 811654, fax 01444 811379)

TEWKESBURY, Bishop of 1996–; Rt Rev John Stewart Went; s of Douglas Norman Went (d 1970), and Barbara Adelaide, *née* Rand; *b* 11 March 1944; *Educ* Colchester Royal GS, Corpus Christi Coll Cambridge (MA); *m* 31 Aug 1968, Rosemary Evelyn Amy, da of late Peter Dunn; 3 s (Simon Charles b 28 June 1970, David James b 12 August 1972, Matthew John b 2 June 1975); *Career* asst curate Emmanuel Northwood Middx 1969–75, vicar Holy Trinity Margate Kent 1975–83, vice princ Wycliffe Hall Theol Coll Oxford 1983–89, archdeacon of Surrey 1989–96; memb Ecclesiastical Law Soc 1989; *Recreations* music, photography, swimming; *Style*— The Right Rev the Bishop of Tewkesbury; ✉ Green Acre, 166 Hempsted Lane, Gloucester GL2 5LG (☎ 01452 521824, fax 01452 505554)

TEWSON, Jane; da of Dr Tim Tewson, of Oxford, and Dr Blue Johnston; *b* 9 Jan 1958; *Educ* Headington Sch Oxford, Lord William's Sch Thame; *m* 16 May 1992, Dr Charles Lane; 2 s (Charlie, Sam); *Career* project co-ordinator MENCAP 1979–83, fndr and chief exec Charity Projects and Comic Relief 1984–96, fndr PilotLight 1996–; tstee: Oxfam, The Media Tst; *Recreations* travel, walking, gardening, sport, reading; *Style*— Ms Jane Tewson; ✉ The Manor Barn, Little Ickford, Ickford, Aylesbury, Bucks HP18 9HS (fax 01844 338319)

TEYNHAM, 20 Baron (E 1616); John Christopher Ingham Roper-Curzon; s of 19 Baron Teynham, DSO, DSC (d 1972), by his 1 w Elspeth (m dis 1956, she d 1976, having m 2, 1958, 6 Marquess of Northampton, DSO); *b* 25 Dec 1928; *Educ* Eton; *m* 1964, Elizabeth, da of Lt-Col the Hon David Scrymgeour-Wedderburn, DSO (ka 1944) 2 s of 10 Earl of Dundee; 5 s (Hon David, Hon Jonathan b (twin) 27 April 1973, Hon Peter b 20 Nov 1977, Hon William b 27 July 1980, Hon Benjamin b 15 Sept 1982), 5 da (Hon Emma (Hon Mrs Murphy) b 19 Sept 1966, Hon Sophie b 30 Nov 1967, Hon Lucy (Hon Mrs Fraser) b 23 July 1969, Hon Hermione b (twin) 27 April 1973, Hon Alice b 18 Dec 1983); *Heir* s, Hon David John Henry Ingham Roper-Curzon, b 5 Oct 1965; *Career* late Capt The Buffs (TA) and 2 Lt Coldstream Gds, active serv Palestine 1948, ADC to Govr of Bermuda 1953 and 1955, ADC to Gov of Leeward Islands 1955 (also private sec 1956), ADC to govr of Jamaica 1962; pres Inst of Commerce 1972–, vice-pres Inst of Export, memb Cncl Sail Training Assoc 1964; memb Cncl of l'Orchestra du Monde 1987–; land agent; OStJ; *Clubs* Turf, House of Lords Yacht, Ocean Cruising, Beaulieu River Sailing, Puffin's (Edinburgh); *Style*— The Rt Hon the Lord Teynham; ✉ Pylewell Park, Lymington, Hants

THACKARA, John Alexander; s of Alexander Daniel Thackara, of Bath, and Eleanor Hazel, *née* Miller; *b* 6 Aug 1951; *Educ* Marlborough, Univ of Kent (BA), Univ of Wales (Dip in Journalism); *m* 20 April 1989, Hilary Mary, da of late Bowyer Arnold, DFC; 1 da (Kate Eleanor b 1989); *Career* commissioning ed Granada Publishing 1975–79, managing ed NSW Univ Press 1979–80, ed Design Magazine 1981–85, freelance design critic 1985–87, fndr and dir Design Analysis Int 1987, special advsr RCA 1991– (dir of research 1989–91), currently dir Netherlands Design Inst and chm European Design Industry Summit (EDIS); FRSA 1987; *Books* New British Design (1987), Design after Modernism (1988); *Recreations* writing; *Clubs* Groucho; *Style*— John Thackara, Esq; ✉ The Netherlands Design Institute, Keizergracht 609, 1017 DS Amsterdam, The Netherlands (☎ 00 31 20 551 6508, e-mail thack@design-inst.NL)

THACKER, David Thomas; s of Thomas Richard Thacker, and Alice May, *née* Beaumont; *b* 21 Dec 1950; *Educ* Wellingborough GS, Univ of York (BA, MA); *m* Margot Elizabeth, *née* Leicester; 3 s (Thomas David b 1984, William Charles b 1986, Edward Arthur b 1989), 1 da (Elizabeth Grace b 1992); *Career* theatre director; York Theatre Royal: asst stage mangr, dep stage mangr then stage mangr 1974–75, asst dir 1975–76; Chester Gateway Theatre: Arts Cncl asst dir 1976–77, assoc dir 1977–78; Duke's Playhouse Lancaster: Arts Cncl assoc dir 1978–79, dir 1980–84; dir Young Vic 1984–93; dir in residence RSC 1993–95; *Theatre* prodns incl: nine plays by Arthur Miller, Ghosts (Young Vic and West End, London Fringe Award for Best Dir and Olivier Award nomination for Outstanding Achievement 1987), Who's Afraid of Virginia Woolf (Young Vic, London Fringe Award for Best Prodn 1987), A Touch of the Poet (Young Vic and West End), An Enemy of the People (Young Vic and West End, Olivier Award for Best Dir 1989), The Last Yankee (Young Vic and West End) 1993, Broken Glass (RNT and West End), A View From The Bridge (West End) 1994, Death of a Salesman (RNT) 1996; RSC prodns incl: Pericles (Olivier Award Best Dir and Best Rival of a Play 1991), The Two Gentlemen of Verona (also West End), As You Like It, The Merchant of Venice, Julius Caesar, Coriolanus, The Tempest; *Television* BBC prodns incl: A Doll's House (BAFTA Best Single Drama nomination), Measure for Measure, Death of a Salesman, Broken Glass; *Recreations* sport, family; *Style*— David Thacker; ✉ 55 Onslow Gardens, Muswell Hill, London N10 3JY (☎ 0181 444 8436)

THAIN, Gregory Neil David; *b* 12 Feb 1954; *Career* chief exec International Communication and Data Ltd until 1993, chm Russian Market Research Company 1993–; memb N London Ctee for the Employment of People with Disabilities (CEPD), dir Grant-Maintained Schools Centre Ltd, chm Books for Poland, chm Conservatives Abroad Russia; *Recreations* gliding, tennis, cricket; *Clubs* Carlton; *Style*— Gregory Thain, Esq; ✉ Suite 2, First Floor, 7 Telegraphniy Per, Moscow 101000, Russia (☎ 00 7 095 926 4346, fax 00 7 095 926 4353)

THATCHER, Anthony Neville; s of Edwin Neville Thatcher (d 1978), and Elsie May, *née* Webster; *b* 10 Sept 1939; *Educ* Sir John Lawes Sch Harpenden, Luton Tech Coll, Univ of Manchester (MSc); *m* 20 Oct 1968, Sally Margaret, da of Henry Joseph Clark, of Norfolk; *Career* Ultra Electronics 1967–77, md Dowty Electronics Controls Ltd 1978–82, gp chief exec Dowty Group plc 1986–91 (md Electronics Div 1982–86, memb Bd 1983), vice chm Thyssen Bornemiza Group SAM Monaco 1991–; memb: Cncl Electronics Engrg Assoc 1983–91 (pres 1986), Cncl Soc of Br Aerospace Cos 1986–91, Bd SW Electricity Bd 1989–91, Engrg Cncl 1989–91, RARDE Mgmnt Bd (industl) 1986–91, Mgmnt Bd Engrg Employers Fedn 1988–91 (vice pres 1990), Electronics and Avionics Requirements Bd of DTI 1981–85, Innovation Advsy Bd DTI 1988–91, Engrg Mkts Advsy Ctee DTI 1988–90; memb Cncl The Cheltenham Ladies Coll 1989–91; Liveryman Worshipful Co of Glass Sellers; CEng, FIMechE; *Recreations* art, jazz piano, opera, fishing, gardening, bird watching; *Style*— Anthony Thatcher, Esq; ✉ 12 Gayfere St, London SW1P 3HP

THATCHER, Sir Denis; 1 Bt (UK 1991), of Scotney, Co Kent, MBE (1944), TD (1948); s of Thomas Herbert Thatcher, of Uffington, Oxfordshire, and Lillian Kathleen, da of Thomas Bird; *b* 10 May 1915; *Educ* Mill Hill; *m* 1, 1942 (m dis 1946), Margaret Doris (d 1996) (who m 2, 1948, Sir (Alfred) Howard Whitby Hickman, 3 Bt (d 1979)), o da of Leonard Kempson, of Potters Bar, Middx; m 2, 13 Dec 1951, Baroness Thatcher, LG, OM, PC, FRS, *qv*, yr da of late Alfred Roberts, of Grantham, Lincs; 1 s (Hon Mark), 1 da (Hon Carol b (twin) 15 Aug 1953); *Heir* s, Hon Mark Thatcher b 15 Aug 1953; *Career* served WWII as Maj RA; vice-chm Attwoods plc 1983–94; dir: Quinton Hazell plc 1968–, Halfords Ltd 1968–92, Burmah Castrol 1970–75; conslt: Amec plc, CSX Corp (US) 1988–96; *Recreations* golf; *Clubs* East India, Bucks, Pratt's; *Style*— Sir Denis Thatcher, Bt, MBE, TD; ✉ 73 Chester Square, London SW1W 9DU

THATCHER, Grant Ashley; s of Stephen Thatcher, of Llandudno, North Wales, and Doreen, *née* Lambton; *b* 24 Nov 1962; *Educ* Rodway Comp, Filton Tech Coll, RADA; *Career* actor; *Theatre* incl: Jacques and Phoebe in As You Like It (Cherub Co), Valentine in Twelfth Night (Sheffield Crucible), Marchbanks in Candida (West End), Rt Hon Alan Howard in French Without Tears (Leicester Haymarket); RSC 1990–92: Anfriso in The Last Days of Don Juan, Diomedes in Troilus and Cressida, Gaveston in Edward II, Molina in Kiss of the Spider Woman (Bolton, Octagon), Septimus Hodge in Arcadia (RNT tour); *Television* incl: Peter Wessel in The Diary of Anne Frank (BBC), Bond in Aliens in the Family (BBC), Hannay (Thames), Lovejoy (BBC), Sir Guy Willard in Poirot (BBC), Thomas Hunt in Revelations (Granada); *Film* work incl: Strapless, Mark Members in A Dance to the Music of Time (for Channel Four); *Style*— Grant Thatcher, Esq; ✉ c/o Roger Carey Associates, 31 Kensington Church Street, London W8 4LL (☎ 0171 937 6200, fax 0171 937 0444)

THATCHER, Baroness (Life Peer UK 1992), of Kesteven in the County of Lincolnshire; Margaret Hilda Thatcher; LG (1995), OM (1990), PC (1970); yr da of Alfred Roberts (d 1970), grocer, of Grantham, Lincs, sometime borough cncllr, alderman and mayor of Grantham, and Beatrice Ethel, *née* Stephenson (d 1960); *b* 13 Oct 1925; *Educ* Huntingtower Primary Sch Grantham, Kesteven and Grantham Girls' Sch, Somerville Coll Oxford (MA, BSc, hon fell 1970); *m* 13 Dec 1951, as his 2 w, Sir Denis Thatcher, 1 Bt, *qv*; 1 s (Hon Mark b 15 Aug 1953), 1 da (Hon Carol (twin) b 15 Aug 1953, freelance radio journalist and presenter); *Career* former research chemist; called to the Bar Lincoln's Inn 1954 (hon bencher 1975); Parly candidate (C) Dartford 1950 and 1951, MP (C) Finchley 1959–92, jt Parly sec Miny of Pensions and National Insurance 1961–64, memb Shadow Cabinet 1967–70 (spokesman on tport, power, Treasury matters, housing and pensions), chief oppn spokesman on educn 1969–70, sec of state for educn and science (and co-chm Women's National Cmmn) 1970–74, chief oppn spokesman on the environment 1974–75, leader of the Opposition Feb 1975–79, prime minister and First Lord of the Treasury (first woman to hold this office) 4 May 1979–28 Nov 1990; minister for the Civil Service Jan 1981–Nov 1990; chllr: Buckingham Univ 1992–, William and Mary Coll USA 1994–; Freedom of Borough of Barnet 1980; Hon Freeman: Worshipful Co of Grocers 1980, Worshipful Co of Poulters; Freedom of Falkland Islands 1983; Donovan Award USA 1981, US Medal of Freedom 1991; FRS 1983; *Books* The Downing Street Years (1993), The Path to Power (1995); *Style*— The Rt Hon Baroness Thatcher, LG, OM, PC, FRS; ✉ House of Lords, London SW1A 0PW

THAYER, Pamela Patricia; OBE (1993), ISO; da of Albert Harold Thayer (d 1969), of Ibstone Common, Bucks, and Kathleen, *née* Holloway (d 1984); *Educ* Notting Hill and Ealing High Sch GPDST, Girton Coll Cambridge (MA), Bedford Coll London (Social Science Cert), LSE (Child Care Cert); *Career* Children's Dept Inspectorate Home Office 1954–70, asst chief inspector Social Servs Inspectorate DHSS 1970–85, child care conslt 1985–; govt advsr Gibraltar 1970 and 1978 (Thayer Report 1970), dir Comparative Study of Child Care Cncl of Europe 1986–87, pres Pre-Sch Learning Alliance, hon memb NSPCC Cncl, chm Oxford Region Girtonians, memb Roll Ctee Girton Coll; FRSA; *Books* Forms of Child Care (1988); *Recreations* politics, writing, theatre, music; *Clubs* Oriental; *Style*— Miss Pamela Thayer, OBE, ISO; ✉ Great Wood Cottage, Ibstone Common, Buckinghamshire HP14 3XU; 60 Lord's View, London NW8 7HQ

THELWELL, Norman; s of Christopher Thelwell (d 1974), and Emily, *née* Vick (d 1964); *b* 3 May 1923; *Educ* Rock Ferry HS, Liverpool Coll of Art (ATD); *m* 1949, Rhona Evelyn, da of Harold Clyde Ladbury (d 1961); 1 s (David), 1 da (Penelope); *Career* artist & cartoonist; lectr Wolverhampton Coll of Art 1950–56; regular contributor to Punch 1952–77, cartoonist to News Chronicle, Sunday Express, Sunday Dispatch, and many other publications; *Books* Angels on Horseback (1957), Thelwell Country (1959), Thelwell in Orbit (1961), A Place of Your Own, A Leg at Each Corner, Thelwell's Riding Academy, Top Dog, Up the Garden Path, The Compleat Tangler (1967), Thelwell's Book of Leisure (1968), This Desirable Plot (1970), The Effluent Society (1971), Penelope (1972), Three Sheets in the Wind, Belt Up (1974), Thelwell Goes West (1975), Thelwell's Brat Race (1977), Thelwell's Gymkhana, A Plank Bridge by a Pool (1978), A Millstone Round My Neck (1981), Pony Cavalcade (1981), Some Damn Fool's Signed the Rubens Again (1982), Thelwell's Magnificat (1983), Thelwell's Sporting Prints (1984), Wrestling with a Pencil (autobiography, 1986), Play It As It Lies (1987), Thelwell's Pony Panorama (1988), Penelope Rides Again (1989), The Cat's Pyjamas (1992); *Recreations* trout fishing; *Style*— Norman Thelwell, Esq; ✉ Herons Mead, Timsbury, Romsey, Hants SO51 0NE (☎ 01794 368238)

THEMEN, Arthur Edward George; s of Dr Lambert Christian Joseph Themen (d 1945), of Oldham, Lancs, and Ethel Elizabeth, *née* Nadin; *b* 26 Nov 1939; *Educ* Manchester GS, St Catharine's Coll Cambridge (MA), St Mary's Hosp Med Sch Univ of London; *m* 8 Jan 1968 (m dis 1979), Judith Frances Anquetil, da of Frank Alexander Arrowsmith, OBE, of Oxford; 2 s (Daniel b 1971, Benjamin b 1972), 1 da (Justine b 1969); *Career* former house surgn St Mary's Hosp, RPMS; surgical registrar Royal Northern Hosp 1969, sr registrar St Mary's and Royal Nat Orthopaedic Hosps 1971–74, currently conslt orthopaedic surgn Royal Berks Hosp and assoc surgn Nuffield Orthopaedic Centre Oxford; special interest incl spinal and jt replacement surgery; various articles on joint replacement in professional jls; musical career as jazz musician; memb prize winning Cambridge Univ Jazz Gp 1958 (best soloist 1959), involved with early Br Blues movement; worked with: Mick Jagger, Rod Stewart, Georgie Fame; UK rep in Int Jazz Orch Festival Zurich 1965; began long assoc with Stan Tracey 1974; toured and recorded with: Charlie Parker alumni, Al Haig, Red Rodney; most recent tours incl Chicago and NY Jazz Festivals; records incl: Captain Adventure 1975, Under Milk Wood 1976, Expressly Ellington 1978 (with Al Haig), Spectrum 1982, Playing in the Yard 1986, Genesis 1987 (with Stan Tracey); memb Contemporary Music Ctee Arts Cncl; FBOA 1974, FRSM; *Recreations* skiing, sailing; *Clubs* Ronnie Scott's; *Style*— Arthur Themen, Esq; ✉ 6 The Blades, Lower Mall, Hammersmith, London W6 (☎ 0181 741 7066); Orthopaedic Department, Royal Berkshire Hospital, London Rd, Reading, Berks (☎ 0118 958 4711)

THEOBALD, Prof Michael Francis; s of George Charles Theobald (d 1994), of Sanderstead, Surrey, and Dorothy, *née* Baker; *b* 1 Sept 1946; *Educ* King's Coll London, Univ of Manchester (BSc, MA, PhD); *m* 26 Oct 1972, Pauline Florence, da of Capt Christopher Herbert Harman (d 1989), of St Leonards, nr Ringwood; 1 s (Jonathan Harman b 3 Sept 1978), 1 da (Sarah Pauline b 5 June 1981); *Career* CA; Price Waterhouse & Co: London 1968–72, Buenos Aires 1972–74; Univ of Manchester 1974–85; KPMG prof Univ of Birmingham 1985– (sometime head Dept of Accounting and Finance); chm Market Analytical Techniques; memb: Research Bd ICAEW, Trg and Qualifications Cmmn Euro Fedn of Financial Analysts' Socs, various ctees Inst of Investmt Mgmnt and Research, Cncl on Educn and Research of the Assoc for Investmt Mgmnt and Research USA; conslt to the ESRC and Accounting Standards Bd; tstee Chartered Financial Analysts Research Fndn USA; FCA 1972, hon memb Inst of Investmt Mgmnt and Research 1994; *Publications* Research Method and Methodology (co-author); articles published in: Journal of Finance, Journal of Financial and Quantitive Analysis, Journal of Banking and Finance, Journal of Portfolio Management, Journal of Futures Markets; *Recreations* sport, literature, travel, maintaining equilibrium; *Style*— Prof Michael Theobald; ✉ Deparment of Accounting and Finance, University of Birmingham, PO Box 363, Birmingham B15 2TT (☎ 0121 414 6540)

THEOBALD, (George) Peter; JP (1974); s of George Oswald Theobald (d 1952), of Surrey, and Helen, *née* Moore (d 1972); *b* 5 Aug 1931; *Educ* Betteshanger Sch, Harrow; *m* 1955, Josephine Mary, da of Wilfrid Andrew Carmichael Boodle (d 1961); 2 s (Carmichael, Christopher), 3 da (Caroline, Jane, Kate); *Career* cmmnd 5 Regt RHA 1950–52, Lt 290 City of London Regt RA (TA) 1953–59; gp chief exec Robert Warner plc 1953–74; dir: Moran Holdings plc 1977– (chm 1992–), Moran Tea Co (India) plc 1981– (chm 1992–); memb: Tport Users Consultative Ctee for London 1969–84 (dep chm 1978–79), London Regnl Passengers Ctee 1984–90; church cmmr for England 1978–79, licensed asst diocese of Guildford 1970–; Alderman City of London 1974–79 (common councilman 1968–74); govr: Bridewell Royal Hosp 1974–93, Christ's Hosp 1976–91, King Edward's Sch Witley 1974–93 (tstee Educn Tst 1977–95), St Leonards Mayfield Sch 1982–88; chm S John's Sch Northwood 1990–; tstee: Harrow Club W10 1978–, Nat Flood and Tempest Distress Fund 1977–; memb Ct of Assts Worshipful Co of Merchant Taylors 1983– (Master 1989–90 and 1991–92); *Recreations* gardening, transport, walking; *Clubs* Oriental, MCC; *Style*— Peter Theobald, Esq, JP; ✉ Towerhill Manor, Gomshall, Guildford, Surrey GU5 9LP (☎ 01483 202381, fax 01483 203200)

THEOCHAROUS, The Most Rev Archbishop Gregorios; s of Theocharis Hadjittofi, and Maria, *née* Koronou; *b* 2 Jan 1929; *Educ* HS Lefkonikon Famagusta Cyprus, Pan-Cyprian Gymnasium Nicosia Cyprus, Theol Faculty Univ of Athens Greece; *Career* monk Monastery of Stavrovounion Cyprus 1951; ordained deacon 1953, priest 1959; asst priest then parish priest All Saints' Church Camden Town London 1959–69; consecrated bishop of Tropaeou 1970; Archdiocese of Thyateira and GB: chllr 1965–79, asst bishop 1970–88, archbishop of Thateira and GB 1988–; orthodox pres: Anglican and Eastern Churches' Assoc, Fellowship of St Alban and St Sergius; co-pres: Soc of St John Chrysostom, Cncl of Christians and Jews; co-patron Religious Educn and Environment Prog; Hon Doctorate Univ of N London 1993; *Recreations* walking, gardening, reading; *Style*— The Most Rev Archbishop Gregorios; ✉ Archdiocese of Thyateira and Great Britain, 5 Craven Hill, London W2 3EN (☎ 0171 723 4787, fax 0171 224 9301)

THEODOROU, Skevos Gregory; s of Gregory Alfred Theodorou (d 1970), and Irene, *née* Alakouzos (both of shipping families); *b* 12 Oct 1939; *Educ* Le Rosey Switzerland, Neuchâtel Univ (Dip Business Admin); *m* 1, 1968 (m dis), Gillian Geraldine Anne, da of Maj-Gen Sir (Harold) John Crossley Hildreth, KBE (d 1992), and sis of Jan Hildreth (sometime dir gen of IOD); 1 s (Alexander John (Skevos) Hildreth b 11 May 1976), 1 da (Charlotte Amanda Joanna Hildreth b 26 Oct 1978); m 2, Antonia Henriette de Galard Brassac de Béarn, eldest da of Count Jean de Béarn; 1 s (Gregory b 23 Oct 1986), 1 da (Clementine Eléonore b 6 Sept 1990); *Career* shipping; memb Baltic Exchange 1964–, md Transmarine SA Paris 1967–79, dir Clarkson & Co Ltd 1975–91, chm and chief exec Theodorou Shipping Ltd 1991–; *Recreations* shooting, sailing; *Clubs* Royal Thames Yacht, Royal Hellenic Yacht (Athens); *Style*— Skevos Theodorou, Esq; ✉ 58d Blomfield Rd, London W9 2PA

THESIGER, Hon Frederic Corin Piers (Kim); s and h of 3 Viscount Chelmsford, *qv*; *b* 6 March 1962; *Career* television production; *Style*— The Hon Kim Thesiger; ✉ 4/4 Hampstead Hill Gardens, London NW3 2PL

THESIGER, Sir Wilfred Patrick; KBE (1995, CBE 1968), DSO (1941); eld s of Capt the Hon Wilfred Gilbert Thesiger, DSO (d 1920), and Kathleen Mary, *née* Vigors, CBE (d 1973); *b* 3 June 1910; *Educ* Eton, Magdalen Coll Oxford (MA); *Career* hon attaché Duke of Gloucester's Mission to Haile Selassie's Coronation 1930; explored Danakil Country and Aussa Sultanate of Abyssinia 1933–34; Sudan Political Serv Darfur 1935–37, and Upper Nile 1938–40, Sudan Def Force Abyssinian Campaign 1940–41, Maj SOE Syria 1941–42, SAS Regt W Desert 1942–43, advsr to the Crown Prince in Ethiopia 1944; explored in Southern Arabia 1945–50 (twice crossed the Empty Quarter by camel), lived with the Madan in the marshes of Southern Iraq 1950–58; awarded Back Grant RGS 1936, Founder's Medal RGS 1948, Lawrence of Arabia Medal RCAS 1955, Livingstone Medal RSGS 1962, W H Heinemann Bequest RSL 1964, Burton Meml Medal Royal Asiatic Soc 1966; hon vice pres Royal Soc Asian Affrs 1991; hon memb Explorers Club (NYC) 1991; hon fell: Magdalen Coll Oxford 1982, Br Acad 1982; Hon DLitt: Univ of Leicester 1967, Univ of Bath 1992; FRSL 1966; Star of Ethiopia third class 1930; *Books* Arabian Sands (1959), The Marsh Arabs (1964), Desert, Marsh and Mountain (1979), The Life of My Choice (1987), Visions of a Nomad (1987), My Kenya Days (1994); *Recreations* travel in remote areas, photography; *Clubs* Travellers' (special memb 1993), Beefsteak (hon memb 1993); *Style*— Sir Wilfred Thesiger, KBE, DSO, FBA; ✉ 15 Shelley Court, Tite St, London SW3 4JB (☎ 0171 352 7213)

THETFORD, Bishop of 1992–; Rt Rev Hugo Ferdinand de Waal; s of Bernard Hendrik de Waal, of Taunton, and Albertine Felice, *née* Castens; *b* 16 March 1935; *Educ* Tonbridge, Pembroke Coll Cambridge (MA), Munster Univ Germany, Ridley Hall Cambridge; *m* 4 April 1961, Brigit Elizabeth Townsend, da of Rev John Massingberd-Mundy, of Newport Pagnell; 1 s (Bernard b 1967), 3 da (Katharine b 1962, Joanna b 1964, Penelope b 1966); *Career* curate St Martin's-in-the-Bull-Ring Birmingham 1960, chaplain Pembroke Coll Cambridge 1964, priest i/c Dry Drayton Diocese of Ely (rector 1967), anglican minister Ecumenical Church Bar Hill Cambs, vicar Blackpool Parish Church 1974, princ Ridley Hall 1978–92; hon canon Ely Cathedral 1985; *Recreations* music, squash, fly fishing, walking; *Style*— The Rt Rev the Bishop of Thetford; ✉ Rectory Meadow, Bramerton, Norwich NR14 7DW

THEWLIS, David; s of Alec Raymond Wheeler, of Blackpool, and Maureen, *née* Thewlis; *b* 20 March 1963; *Educ* Highfield HS Blackpool, St Anne's Coll of FE, Guildhall Sch of Music and Drama; *m* 10 April 1992, Sara Jocelyn, da of Paul Sugarman; *Career* actor; *Theatre* incl: Buddy Holly at the Regal (Greenwich), Ice Cream (Royal Court), Lady and the Clarinet (Netherbow Edinburgh, winner Fringe First, also at King's Head Islington), The Sea (NT); *Television* incl: Dandelion Dead, Valentine Park, Road, Singing Detective, Bit of a Do, Scullduggery, Journey to Knock (Best Actor Rheims Film Festival 1992), Filipina Dreamgirls, Frank Stubbs Promotes, Prime Suspect 3, *Films* incl: Short and Curlies, Vroom, Resurrected (1989), Afraid of the Dark, Life is Sweet, Damage, The Trial, Naked (Best Actor Cannes Film Festival 1993), Black Beauty; *Recreations* painting; *Style*— David Thewlis, Esq; ✉ c/o ICM Ltd, Oxford House, 76 Oxford Street, London W1N 0AX (☎ 0171 636 6565, fax 0171 323 0101)

THIAN, Robert Peter; s of Clifford Peter Thian, of Jersey, and Frances Elizabeth, *née* Stafford-Bird (d 1980); *b* 1 Aug 1943; *Educ* Kenton Coll Nairobi, Oundle, Univ of Geneva; *m* 24 Oct 1964, Liselotte, da of Wilhelm Von Borges; 2 da (Stéfanie b 15 Sept 1967, Samantha b 15 March 1970); *Career* called to the Bar Gray's Inn, legal advsr Glaxo

Group Ltd 1968–69, project devpt exec Glaxo Allenburys Export Ltd 1969–72, md Glaxo Farmaceutica 1972–80, regnl dir (Europe) Abbott Laboratories 1984–87 (business devpt dir Europe 1980–84), vice pres international ops Pharmaceutical Div Novo Industri AS 1987–89, chief exec North West Water Group Plc 1989–93, dir Celltech Group plc 1992–, chief exec The Stationery Office Ltd 1996–; *Clubs* East India Sports (London); *Style*— Robert Thian, Esq; ✉ c/o TSO Group Ltd, St Crispins, Duke Street, Norwich NR3 1PD (☎ 01603 622211)

THIMBLEBY, Prof Harold William; s of Peter Thimbleby, of Rugby, Warwicks, and Angela Marion, *née* Hodson; *b* 19 July 1955; *Educ* Rugby, Univ of London (BSc, MSc, PhD); *m* 16 Feb 1980, Prudence Mary (Prue), da of Rev Capt Arundel Charles Barker, of Matlock, Derbyshire; 3 s (William, Samuel, Isaac), 1 da (Jemima b 1987); *Career* lectr in computer sci: Queen Mary Coll 1980–82, Univ of York 1982–88; prof of info technol Univ of Stirling (in Dept of Computing 1988–93, Dept of Psychology 1993–94); Univ of Middx: prof of computing research 1994–, dir of research Faculty of Technol 1995–; co-inventor of Liveware (technique for exploiting computer viruses) 1989; Br Computer Soc Wilkes Medal 1987, Toshiba Year of Invention Award; CEng, AM, FIEE, FRSA; *Books* author of over 200 pubns incl: Formal Methods In Human-Computer Interaction (ed with M D Harrison, 1989), User Interface Design (1990), Hyperprogramming (with G F Coulouris, 1993); *Recreations* hill walking, woodwork, electronics; *Style*— Prof Harold Thimbleby; ✉ Computing Science, University of Middlesex, Bounds Green Road, London N11 2NQ (☎ 0181 362 6061, fax 0181 362 6411, e-mail harold@mdx.ac.uk, World Wide Web http://www.cs.mdx.ac.uk/harold)

THIN, Dr (Robert) Nicol Traquair; OBE (1995); s of Robert Traquair Thin (d 1990), of Bromley, Kent, and Annie Dempster, *née* Snowball; *b* 21 Sept 1935; *Educ* Loretto, Univ of Edinburgh Med Sch (MB ChB, MD); *m* 1962, (Agnes) Ann, da of Alexander William Graham, OBE (d 1964), of Inverness; 2 s (Sandy b 1964, Iain b 1968); *Career* cmmnd into RAMC 1964, Malaya, Singapore and UK, ret Maj; Maj TA 1974–76; venereologist BMH Singapore 1969–71, conslt venereologist Edinburgh Royal Infirmary 1971–73, conslt in genitourinary med St Bartholomew's Hosp London 1973–81, conslt venereologist St Peter's Hosps London 1975–94 (emeritus conslt Univ Coll London Hosps 1994–), civilian conslt in genitourinary Med to the Army 1981–, hon sr lectr Inst of Urology and conslt in genitourinary med St Thomas' Hosp London 1982–, personal conslt advsr in genitourinary med to The CMO at The Dept of Health 1994–; ed British Journal of Venereal Diseases 1975–80, contrib specialist and general textbooks incl Lecture Notes on Sexually Transmitted Diseases; pres Med Soc of Venereal Diseases 1987–89 (memb 1968–), chm Specialist Advsy Ctee on Genitourinary Medicine of the Jt Ctee on Higher Med Training 1982–83 (memb 1976–81, sec 1981–82), examiner for Dip in Genitourinary Med for The Soc of Apothecaries of London 1981–, pres Soc of Health Advsrs in Sexually Transmitted Diseases 1983–86, memb Expert Advsy Gp on AIDS 1985–87, external examiner of Dip in Venereology for Univ of Liverpool 1987–89, memb Genitourinary Med Sub Ctee of RCP 1987–95 (chm 1995–), founding chm Assoc for Genitourinary Med 1992–; memb Nat Tst; former: postgrad dean St Bartholomew's Hosp Med Coll, pres Edinburgh Univ Boat Club; vice pres St Thomas' Hosp Boat Club; memb: BMA 1960, Med Soc of Venereal Diseases 1968; FRSM 1988, FRCP, FRCPE; *Recreations* music, reading, overseas travel; *Clubs* City Volunteer Officers; *Style*— Dr Nicol Thin, OBE; ✉ Teratak, 13 Park Ave, Bromley, Kent BR1 4EF (☎ 0181 464 9278); Department of Genitourinary Medicine, St Thomas' Hospital, London SE1 7EH (☎ 0171 928 9292 ext 2429, fax 0171 620 0903, telex 27913 STHLDN G)

THIRLWALL, Prof Anthony Philip; s of Isaac Thirlwall (d 1960), and Ivy, *née* Ticehurst (d 1988); *b* 21 April 1941; *Educ* Clark Univ USA (MA), Univ of Leeds (BA, PhD); *m* 26 March 1966 (sep 1986), Gianna, da of Bruno Paoletti (d 1985), of Trieste; 2 s (Lawrence b 1967, Adrian b and d 1975), 1 da (Alexandra 1974); *Career* asst lectr in economics Univ of Leeds 1964, Univ of Kent: lectr in economics 1966, prof of applied economics 1976–; econ advsr Dept of Employment 1968–70; memb: Action Aid, Royal Economic Soc 1964; *Books* Growth and Development: With Special Reference to Developing Economies (1972, 5 edn 1994), Inflation, Saving and Growth in Developing Economies (1974), Regional Growth and Unemployment in the United Kingdom (with R Dixon, 1975), Financing Economic Development (1976), Keynes and International Monetary Relations (ed, 1976), Keynes and Laissez Faire (ed, 1978), Keynes and the Bloomsbury Group (ed with D Crabtree, 1980), Balance of Payments Theory and the United Kingdom Experience (1980, 4 edn 1991), Keynes on a Policy Adviser (ed, 1982), Keynes and Economic Development (ed, 1987), Nicholas Kaldor (1987), Collected Essays of Nicholas Kaldor Volume 9 (ed with F Targetti, 1989), The Essential Kaldor (ed with F Targetti, 1989), European Factor Mobility: Trends and Consequences (ed with I Gordon, 1989), Deindustrialisation (with S Bazen, 1989, 2 edn), Keynes and the Role of the State (ed, 1993), Economic Growth and the Balance of Payments Constraint (with J McCombie, 1994), The Economics of Growth and Development: Selected Essays of A P Thirlwall (1995); *Recreations* athletics, tennis, travel; *Clubs* Royal Over-Seas League; *Style*— Prof Anthony Thirlwall; ✉ 14 Moorfield, Canterbury, Kent (☎ 01227 769904); Keynes College, University of Kent, Canterbury, Kent (☎ 01227 764000, fax 01227 827850)

THISELTON, Prof Rev Canon Anthony Charles; s of Eric Charles Thiselton (d 1979), of Woking, Surrey, and Hilda Winifred, *née* Kevan (d 1969); *b* 13 July 1937; *Educ* City of London, King's Coll London (BD, MTh), Univ of Sheffield (PhD), Univ of Durham (DD); *m* 21 Sept 1963, Rosemary Stella, da of Ernest Walter Harman (d 1979), of Eastbourne, Sussex; 2 s (Stephen b 1964, Martin b 1969), 1 da (Linda b 1966); *Career* curate Holy Trinity Sydenham 1960–63, chaplain Tyndale Hall Bristol 1963–67, recognised teacher in theology Univ of Bristol 1965–70, sr tutor Tyndale Hall 1967–70, lectr in biblical studies Univ of Sheffield 1970–79 (sr lectr 1979–85), visiting prof and fell Calvin Coll Grand Rapids 1982–83; princ: St John's Coll Nottingham 1985–88, St John's Coll Univ of Durham 1988–92 (hon prof in theology 1992); prof of Christian theology and head of Dept of Theology Univ of Nottingham 1992–; canon theologian of Leicester Cathedral 1995–; memb: C of E Doctrine Cmmn 1976–91 (vice chm 1987–91), C of E Faith and Order Advsy Gp 1971–81 and 1986–91, CNAA Ctee for Arts and Humanities 1983–87, CNAA Ctee for Humanities 1987–90, Revised Catechism Working Pty 1988–89, C of E Initial Ministerial Educn Ctee 1990–92, Cncl Lincoln Theological Coll 1992–, Cncl of St John's Nottingham 1992–, Human Fertilisation and Embryology Authy 1995–, C of E Gen Synod (rep northern univs) 1995–, Studiorum Novi Testamenti Societas, Soc for the Study of Theology, American Acad of Religion; memb Editorial Bd: Biblical Interpretation (Leiden) 1992–, Ex Auditu (Princeton) 1988–, Int Jl for Anglican Studies; examining chaplain to: Bishop of Sheffield 1976–80, Bishop of Leicester 1979–86 and 1993–; Br Acad Research Award 1995–96; *Books* Language, Liturgy and Meaning (1975), The Two Horizons: New Testament Hermeneutics and Philosophical Description (1980, reprinted 1993, trans into Korean 1990), The Responsibility of Hermeneutics (jtly, 1985), New Horizons in Hermeneutics (1992), Interpreting God and the Post-Modern Self (1995); contrib: Believing in the Church, We Believe in God, Their Lord and Ours; *Recreations* organ, choral music, opera; *Style*— Prof the Rev Canon Anthony C Thiselton; ✉ Department of Theology, University of Nottingham, University Park, Nottingham NG7 2RD (☎ 0115 951 5852, fax 0115 951 5887)

THISTLETHWAITE, Prof Frank; CBE (1979); s of Lee Thistlethwaite (d 1973), of Bibury, Glos, and Florence Nightingale, *née* Thornber (d 1982); *b* 24 July 1915; *Educ* Bootham Sch York, St John's Coll Cambridge (MA), Univ of Minnesota USA; *m* 11 Aug 1940, Jane (d 1992), da of Harry Lindley Hosford (d 1946), of Lyme, Connecticut, USA; 2 s (Stephen Lee b 1944 d 1951, Miles b 1949), 3 da (Jill (Mrs Pellew) b 1942, Harriet b 1953, Sarah Lee (Mrs More) b 1956); *Career* RAF 1941–45, seconded to Offices of War Cabinet 1942–45; Br Press Serv NY 1940–41; fell St John's Coll Cambridge 1945–61, lectr Faculty of Econs and Politics Univ of Cambridge 1949–61, Inst for Advanced Study Princeton Univ 1954; founding chm Br Assoc for American Studies 1955–59, founding vice chllr UEA 1961–80; visiting fell Henry E Huntingdon Library California 1973, chm Ctee of Mgmnt Inst of US Studies Univ of London (Leverhulme emeritus fell 1980), Hill visiting prof Univ of Minnesota 1986; memb: Inter-Univ Cncl for Higher Educn Overseas 1962–81 (chm 1977–81), Marshall Aid Commoration Cmmn 1964–80, Bd (formerly Exec Ctee) Br Cncl 1971–82; pres Friends of Cambridge Univ Library 1983–; Hon LHD Univ of Colorado 1972, hon fell St John's Coll Cambridge 1974, Hon DCL UEA 1980, hon prof of history Univ of Mauritius; Hon DSc Univ of Minnesota 1994; Hon FRIBA 1985, FRHistS 1963; *Books* The Great Experiment: An Introduction to the History of the American People (1955), The Anglo-American Connection in the Early Nineteenth Century (1958), Dorset Pilgrims: The Story of West Country Puritans who went to New England in the 17th Century (1989); *Recreations* playing the piano, historical writing; *Clubs* Athenaeum; *Style*— Prof Frank Thistlethwaite, CBE; ✉ 15 Park Parade, Cambridge CB5 8AL (☎ 01223 352680); Island Cottage, Winson, Glos

THOM, Timothy Ritchie; s of David Ritchie Thom (d 1957), and Edna Beryl, *née* May (d 1986); *b* 20 May 1940; *Educ* Bedford Sch; *m* 8 Feb 1964, Diana Monica Mae, da of Edward James Morrow Tait (d 1973); 2 da (Fiona b 1965, Belinda b 1967); *Career* CA; managing ptnr Gulf Offices Price Waterhouse; tstee Bristol Old Vic Theatre Sch; formerly JP; FCA 1964; *Recreations* golf, fishing, gardening; *Clubs* Clifton, Burnham and Berrow Golf; *Style*— Timothy Thom, Esq; ✉ The Forge, Lower Langford, Bristol BS18 7HU (☎ 01934 862356)

THOMANECK, Prof Jürgen Karl Albert; JP; *b* 12 June 1941; *Educ* Altes Gymnasium Flenburg, Univ of Kiel (DPhil), Univ of Tübingen, Univ of Aberdeen (MEd); *m* 3 Aug 1964, Guinevere, *née* Ronald; 2 da (Yasmin Helene b 6 Dec 1964, Naomi Morwenna b 20 May 1977); *Career* Dept of German Univ of Aberdeen: lectr 1969–87, sr lectr 1987–92, dept head 1984–88 and 1989–, prof 1992–; pres Aberdeen Trades Cncl, Grampian regnl cncllr 1983–96, city cncllr Aberdeen 1995–; *Books* Deutsches Abiturienten Lexikon (4 edn jtly, 1974), Fremdsprachenunterricht und Soziolinguistik (1981), Police and Public Order in Europe (1984), Ulrich Plenzdorf's Die neuen Leiden des jungen W (1988), The German Democratic Republic: Politics, Government and Society: Basic Documents (1989); *Recreations* reading, soccer; *Clubs* Aberdeen Trades Council; *Style*— Prof Jurgen Thomaneck, JP; ✉ 17 Elm Place, Aberdeen AB25 3SN (☎ 01224 637744); Department of German, University of Aberdeen, Taylor Buildings, King's College, Old Aberdeen AB9 2UB (☎ 01224 272487)

THOMAS, Dr Adrian Mark Kynaston; s of Prof Peter Kynaston Thomas, of Highgate, London, and Mary Truscott Cox (d 1977); *b* 1 April 1954; *Educ* Christ Coll Finchley, UCL (MB BS, BSc, FRCR, FRCP 1996); *m* 8 July 1978, Susan Margaret, da of Arthur Oliver Viney, of Amersham, Bucks; 2 s (Gareth Kynaston b 1985, Owen Matthew Truscott b 7 July 1990), 1 da (Charlotte Mary Truscott b 1988); *Career* sr registrar Hammersmith Hosp 1981–87; conslt radiologist 1987–: Bromley Hosps NHS Trust Hosp, Sloane Hosp; clinical dir of diagnostic imaging Bromley Hosps NHS Trust 1995–; chm Bromley Div BMA 1995–96; memb: Radiology History and Heritage Charitable Tst, Bromley MENCAP, Milton Soc of America, Charles Williams Soc, Blackheath Harriers; memb: BMA 1976, RSM 1981, Br Inst of Radiology 1981, RCR 1982, Christian Med Fellowship 1989; *Books* Self Assessment in Radiology and Imaging: Nuclear Medicine (jt ed, 1989), The Invisible Light, 100 Years of Medical Radiology (jt ed, 1995); *Recreations* music, bonsai, life and works of John Milton and Charles Williams; *Style*— Dr Adrian Thomas

THOMAS, Adrian Peter; OBE (1995); s of George Lynn Thomas, of Holland-on-Sea, Essex, and Glady Ella Grace, *née* Webster (d 1992); *b* 19 Feb 1945; *Educ* Forest Sch, Wadham Coll Oxford (MA); *m* 1977, Robyn Alycon, da of Prof J Laurence Malcolm; 1 da (Clare Sally b 1978), 2 s (Hugh Robert and Neil Malcolm (twins) b 1980); *Career* VSO teacher Ihungo Sedy Sch Tanzania 1967–68, various jobs in market res and accountancy 1969–70; British Council: asst rep Sierra Leone 1970–73, regnl offr N Africa 1973–75, Overseas Educnl Appointments Dept 1975–77, Univ of London 1977–78, regnl dir Isfahan 1978–80, asst and dep dir Tech Cooperation Trg Dept 1980–84, regnl rep E Malaysia 1984–88, dep dir Nigeria 1988–91, dir Sudan 1991–95, dir E India 1995–; memb: Amnesty Int, Friends of the Earth; Hon PhD Univ of Gezira Sudan 1995; *Recreations* running, hill walking, sailing, archaeology, history, poetry, bird watching; *Clubs* Calcutta, Tollygunge; *Style*— Adrian Thomas, Esq, OBE; ✉ The British Council, 5 Shakespeare Sarani, Calcutta 700071, India (☎ 00 91 33 242 5378/9, fax 00 91 33 242 4804)

THOMAS, Prof Adrian Tregerthen; s of Rev Owen George Thomas, of Cardiff, and Jean Tregerthen, *née* Short; *b* 11 June 1947; *Educ* Kingswood Sch Bath, Univ of Nottingham (BMus), Univ Coll Cardiff (MA), Conservatory of Music Kraków Poland; *Career* Queen's Univ Belfast: lectr in music 1972–82, sr lectr 1982–85, Hamilton Harty prof of music 1985–90 and 1993–96; prof of music Cardiff Univ of Wales 1996–; head of music BBC Radio 3 1990–93; conductor Br première Lutoslawski's Trois Poèmes d'Henri Michaux 1969, medal Polish Composers' Union for outstanding servs to contemporary Polish music 1989, Order of Merit for Polish Culture 1996; chm Music Ctee Arts Cncl of NI 1986–90, chm BBC Central Music Advsy Ctee 1987–89, memb BBC Gen Advsy Cncl 1988–90; memb Royal Musical Assoc, memb Composers' Guild of GB, FRSA 1988; *Compositions* Intrada (orchestra, 1981), Elegy (violin and piano, 1983), Rau (string octet, 1985), Black Rainbow (a cappella choir, BBC cmmn, 1989); *Books* Grażyna Bacewicz: Chamber and Orchestral Music (1985), Górecki (1996); *Recreations* hill walking, poetry, Oriental arts; *Style*— Prof Adrian Thomas; ✉ Department of Music, University of Wales, Cardiff CF1 3EB (☎ 01222 874816)

THOMAS, Sir (John) Alan; kt (1993); s of Idris Thomas, of Langland, Swansea, and Ellen Constance, *née* Noakes; *b* 4 Jan 1943; *Educ* Dynevor Sch Swansea, Univ of Nottingham (Richard Thomas & Baldwins Industl scholar, BSc); *m* 1966, Angela, da of Kathleen Taylor; 2 s (Andrew James b 1971, Alexander Michael b 1974); *Career* chief exec Data Logic Ltd 1973–85, pres and chief exec offr Raytheon Europe 1985–89, vice pres Raytheon Co (US), dir various Raytheon subsid cos 1978–89, seconded to MOD as head of Defence Export Servs Orgn 1989–94; chm Firth Holdings plc 1994–; Univ of Westminster (formerly Poly of Central London): visiting prof 1982, govr 1989–, dep chm Ct of Govrs 1995–; dir: PowerGen plc 1996–, Centre for Policy Studies 1996–; memb: Defence Industries Cncl 1990–94, Engrg Cncl 1994–96; pres Computing Servs & Software Assoc 1980–81; Liveryman Co of Info Technologists 1988–; CEng, FIEE, FCMA (1st prizewinner); *Recreations* music, sport; *Clubs* Athenaeum; *Style*— Sir Alan Thomas; ✉ 40 Catherine Place, London SW1E 6HL (☎ 0171 828 9989)

THOMAS, Anthony Charles (Tony); s of Charles Derek Thomas (d 1990), and Rosina Miriam, *née* Dukes; *b* 27 May 1952; *Educ* Leamington Coll Leamington Spa, Univ of Manchester (LLB); *m* June 1976, Penelope Bebbington; 2 s (Oliver b 7 Sept 1981, Nicholas b 9 Jan 1987), 1 da (Rebecca b 12 Sept 1983); *Career* Clyde & Co: joined as articled clerk 1974–76, slr 1976–80, ptnr 1980–, also currently head Shipping Department; memb Law Soc; *Recreations* squash, tennis, cricket, rugby (now as spectator), theatre, motor cars;

Clubs Guildford & Godalming Rugby (vice pres); *Style*— Tony Thomas, Esq; ✉ Clyde & Co, 51 Eastcheap, London EC3M 1JP (☎ 0171 623 1244, fax 0171 623 5427, mobile 0831 866839)

THOMAS, Hon Barbara S; *b* 28 Dec 1946; *Educ* Univ of Pennsylvania (BA), New York Univ Law Sch (ed NYU Law Review, John Norton Pomeroy Scholar, Jefferson Davis Prize in Public Law, seventeen other prizes in various subjects, JD); *m*; 1 s; *Career* assoc Paul Weiss Rifkind Wharton & Garrison (law firm) 1969–73, ptnr Kaye Scholer Fierman Hays & Handler 1978–80 (joined as assoc 1973), cmmr US Securities and Exchange Cmmn 1980–83 (fndr Int Ctee of Securities Regulators), regnl dir Hong Kong Samuel Montagu & Co Ltd 1984–86, sr vice pres and head of Int Private Banking Gp Bankers Trust Co 1986–90, md mktg and international Cramer Rosenthal McGlynn Inc 1990–93, exec dir business and legal affrs News International plc 1993–94, chm Scotia Haven Food Group 1995–; non-exec dir: Allders plc, Watson & Philip plc, Friends' Provident Life Assurance, United Asset Management Corp (US parent of Murray Johnstone Ltd and others); memb: US-Hong Kong Econ Assistance Ctee, Cncl on Foreign Relations, Young Pres's Orgn (London, Hong Kong and Gotham NY chapters), Advsy Cncl Women's Economic Round Table, Forum UK, London and NY chapters Women's Forum, Bd of Govrs Lauder Inst of Mgmnt and Int Studies Wharton Sch Univ of Pennsylvania 1985–, Bd Int Salzburg Assoc (organisers of Salzburg Festival) 1987–92, Advsy Ctee LSO 1993–, Special Projects Advsy Ctee Royal Acad of Art 1994–; *Clubs* Reform, Cosmopolitan Club of NY, Economic Club of NY, River Club of NY; *Style*— The Honorable Barbara S Thomas; ✉ 4 John Carpenter Street, London EC4Y 0NH (☎ 0171 615 8207, fax 0171 615 8209)

THOMAS, Capt (John Anthony) Bruce; s of John Haydn Thomas (d 1987), of Crowborough and Hove, Sussex, and Barbara Ann, *née* Jones (d 1974); *b* 15 Nov 1929; *Educ* Warden House, RNC Dartmouth and Greenwich; *m* 30 Nov 1957, Genevieve Margaret, da of Walter Frederick Whiting (d 1985), of Felixstowe; 1 da (Rachel (Mrs Michael Vaughan Johns)); *Career* RNC Dartmouth 1943, Lt Cdr 1960, Cdr 1964, in cmd HMS Houghton and Sr Offr 6 M Sqdn 1964–66, JSSC 1966/67, MOD (N) 1967–68, 2 i/c HMS Albion 1968–71, Dir of Serv Intelligence FE Cmd 1971–72, Capt 1972, in cmd HMS Phoebe 1973–74, ACOS (Ops) NAVSOUTH 1974–76, in cmd HMS Hermione and Capt 5 Frigate Sqdn 1977–78, Cdre 1978, Cdre Naval Ship Acceptance and Dir of Naval Equipment 1978–82; ADC to HM The Queen 1981–82; bd memb Br Marine Equipment Cncl 1987– (vice pres 1990–92, pres 1992–), chm Br Naval Equipment Assoc; currently conslt BAe Defence; *Recreations* golf; *Clubs* Army & Navy, Lansdown Golf, XL Club, Anchorites; *Style*— Capt Bruce Thomas, RN; ✉ Church End, Hawkesbury Upton, Badminton GL9 1AU (☎ 01454 238707)

THOMAS, Dr Cedric Marshall; CBE (1991, OBE 1983); s of David John Thomas (d 1958), of Birmingham, and Evis Margaret, *née* Field (d 1946); *b* 26 May 1930; *Educ* King Edward's Sch Birmingham, Univ of Birmingham (BSc, PhD); *m* 1, 12 June 1954, (Dora) Ann (d 1975), da of Walter Pritchard (d 1975), of N Wales; 1 s (Nicholas b 1955), 1 da (Sarah b 1957); m 2, 19 Sept 1976, Margaret Elizabeth, *née* Shirley; 1 step s (Michael b 1954), 3 step da (Carolyn b 1952, Beth b 1959, Helen b 1961); *Career* NCB 1954–59, Morgan Crucible Co Ltd 1960–61, chief exec Johnson Progress Group 1970–77 (joined 1961), business conslt 1977–80, chief exec Benjamin Priest Group 1983–84 (joined 1980), dir and chief exec Engineering Employers W Midlands Assoc 1984–91, chm Jesse Shirley 1991–, dep chm Thomas William Lench Ltd 1991–, non-exec dir Poplars Resource Management Co Ltd 1992–, non-exec dir Staffs Ambulance Service NHS Tst 1995–; EEF: memb Mgmnt Bd 1972–80 and 1981–84, chm Health and Saftey Ctee 1981–84, memb Cncl and Pres's Ctee 1992–95, chm Health Safety and Environment Policy Ctee 1992–95; govr N Staffs Poly 1973–80, pres Engineering Employers W Midlands Assoc 1976–78, chm Special Programmes Area Bd 1978–83; memb: Health and Safety Cmmn 1980–90, CBI Health and Safety Policy Ctee 1983–93; chm Area Manpower Bd 1986–88; CEng, FIMinE, FMES, CIMgt, Hon FFOM, FRSA; *Recreations* tennis, walking; *Style*— Dr Cedric Thomas, CBE; ✉ Parkfields House, Tittensor, Staffs ST12 9HQ (☎ and fax 01782 373677)

THOMAS, Prof (Antony) Charles; CBE (1991), DL (Cornwall 1988); s of Donald Woodroffe Thomas (d 1959), of Lowenac, Camborne, Cornwall, and Viva Warrington, *née* Holman (d 1980); *b* 26 April 1928; *Educ* Winchester, CCC Oxford (MA, DLitt), Inst of Archaeology (Dip Prehistoric Archaeology); *m* 1 July 1959, Jessica Dorothea Esther, da of Prof Frederick Alexander Mann (d 1991); 2 s (Richard b 1961, Martin b 1963), 2 da (Susanna b 1966, Lavinia b 1971); *Career* Army Serv 1946–48; lectr in archaeology Univ of Edinburgh 1957–67, prof of archaeology Univ of Leicester 1967–71, prof of Cornish studies Univ of Exeter 1972–91 (emeritus 1993); pres: CBA 1970–73, Royal Inst of Cornwall 1970–72, Soc for Medieval Archaeology 1986–89, Cornwall Archaeological Soc 1984–88, Soc for Landscape Studies 1993–; chm: Cornwall Ctee for Rescue Archaeology 1974–88, BBC's SW Regnl Advsy Cncl 1975–80, DOE Area Archaeology Ctee Devon and Cornwall 1975–79, Soc for Church Archaeology 1996; acting chm Royal Cmmn on the Hist Monuments of Eng 1988–91 (memb 1983–97); Frend Medal London Soc 1982, Hon DLitt NUI 1996; hon memb Royal Irish Acad 1973, hon fell Royal Soc of Antiquaries of Ireland 1975, hon fell St David's Univ Coll Lampeter 1992, Leverhulme emeritus fell 1992, fell Univ Coll London 1993; FSA (Scot) 1957, FSA 1960, FRHistS 1982, FBA 1989; *Books* Christian Antiquities of Camborne (1967), The Early Christian Archaeology of North Britain (1971), Britain and Ireland in Early Christian Times (1971), St Ninian's Isle and its Treasure (with A Small and D M Wilson, 1973), Military Insignia of Cornwall (with D Ivall, 1974), Christianity in Roman Britain to AD 500 (1981), Exploration of a Drowned Landscape (1985), Celtic Britain (1986), Views and Likenesses: Photographers in Cornwall and Scilly 1939–70 (1988), Tintagel (1993), And Shall These Mute Stones Speak (1994); *Recreations* military history, bibliophily, archaeological fieldwork; *Style*— Prof Charles Thomas, CBE, FSA, FBA; ✉ Lambessow, St Clement, Truro, Cornwall TR1 1TB

THOMAS, Christopher (Chris); s of Neofitos Theophilou, of London, and Mary, *née* Mouzouris; *b* 1 Sept 1963; *Educ* Highgate Wood Sch London; *Career* bd dir MJP Carat International 1989–92 (joined as trainee media exec 1980), bd dir MCW Ltd 1992–; dir Int Advertising Assoc (UK Chapter) 1990–95 (joined 1981); memb Br Mensa 1988–; FRGS 1992; *Style*— Chris Thomas, Esq; ✉ MCW Ltd, 22 Peters Lane, London EC1M 6DS (☎ 0171 490 2626, fax 0171 490 2684, e-mail ct@mcw.co.uk)

THOMAS, Christopher Peter (Chris); s of Cecil Stevens Thomas, of Highcliffe, Dorset, and Ruth Ela, *née* Roberts; *b* 13 Jan 1947; *Educ* Upper Latimer, RAM (jr exhibitioner); *m* (m dis); 1 s (Jan Stevens b 29 Sept 1970), 1 da (Carla b 22 Nov 1971); *partner*, Tine Steincke; 1 s (Michael James b 15 May 1988), 1 da (Mia b 1 Feb 1991); *Career* pop music producer; credits incl: Climax Blues Band (Climax Chicago Blues Band, The Climax Blues Band Plays On, A Lot of Bottle, Tightly Knit), Nirvana (Dedicated to Markos III), Procol Harum (Home, Broken Barricades, Live with The Edmonton Symphony Orchestra, Grand Hotel, Exotic Birds and Fruit), Mick Abrahams Band (Mick Abrahams Band, At Last), Christopher Milk (Some People Will Drink Anything), John Cale (Paris 1919), Roxy Music (For Your Pleasure, Stranded, Siren, Viva Roxy Music), Badfinger (Ass, Badfinger, Wish You Were Here), Sadistic Mika Band (Black Ship, Hot! Menu), Kokomo (Kokomo), Bryan Ferry (Let's Stick Together), Krazy Kat (China Seas), Eno (Here Comes The Warm Jets), The Sex Pistols (Never Mind the Bollocks, Filthy Lucre Live), Frankie Miller (Full House), Chris Spedding (Hurt), Tom Robinson Band (Power in the Darkness), Wings (Back to The Egg), The Pretenders (Pretenders, Pretenders II, Learning to Crawl), Pete Townshend (Empty Glass, All The Best Cowboys Have Chinese Eyes, White City), Elton John (The Fox, Jump Up, Too Low For Zero, Breaking Hearts, Reg Strikes Back, Sleeping With the Past, The One, tracks on The Lion King soundtrack album, Live Like Horses (with Luciano Pavarotti)), INXS (Listen Like Thieves, Kick, X), Dave Stewart & The Spiritual Cowboys, Shakespear's Sister (Goodbye Cruel World (prodr), Stay (co-prodr)), Miss World debut album, Marcella Detroit (Jewel), Bryan Adams, Sting and Rod Stewart (All for Love), Pulp (Different Class); mixing credits incl: Pink Floyd (Dark Side of the Moon, The Division Bell (jtly)), Roxy Music (Country Life), Ronnie Lane (One for the Road); 24 albums produced went silver, gold, platinum; winner: Rolling Stone Critics' Award 1980, Best Single Prodr Billboards 1988, Best Prodr BRIT Awards 1990; *Recreations* travelling, meeting people; *Style*— Chris Thomas, Esq; ✉ c/o Steve O'Rourke, 43 Portland Road, London W11 4LJ (☎ 0171 221 2046, fax 0171 229 5445)

THOMAS, Dr Christopher Sydney; QC (1989); s of John Raymond Thomas (d 1982), and Daphne May, *née* Thomas; *b* 17 March 1950; *Educ* King's Sch Worcester, Univ of Kent at Canterbury (BA), Faculté International de Droit Comparé (Diplome de Droit Comparé), King's Coll London (PhD); *m* 28 May 1979, Patricia Jane, da of Leslie Heath, of Gillingham, Kent; 1 s (Alexander), 1 da (Felicity); *Career* called to the Bar Lincoln's Inn 1973 (Hardwick and Jenkins scholarships); counsel and arbitrator in building and civil engrg disputes, asst recorder 1993; FCIArb 1994; *Recreations* farming; *Style*— Dr Christopher Thomas, QC; ✉ Keating Chambers, 10 Essex St, London WC2R 3AA (☎ 0171 240 6981, fax 0171 240 7722)

THOMAS, Christopher Wilson; CBE; *b* 29 April 1927; *Educ* Sherborne, Pembroke Coll Cambridge; *Career* currently: chm Bristol Development Corporation, non-exec dep chm Bristol Waterworks Company; non-exec dep chm Bristol & West Building Society; *Style*— Christopher Thomas, Esq, CBE; ✉ Bristol Development Corporation, Techno House, Redcliffe Way, Bristol BS1 6NX (☎ 0117 925 5222, fax 0117 925 2666)

THOMAS, (David) Craig Owen; s of John Brinley George Thomas, of Cardiff, S Wales, and Gwendoline Megan, *née* Owen (d 1984); *b* 24 Nov 1942; *Educ* Cardiff HS, Univ Coll Cardiff (BA, MA); *m* 28 July 1967, Jill Lesley, da of Wilfrid Ebenezer White (d 1987); *Career* asst Eng master King Edward VI Sch Stafford 1966–68, second Eng master King Edward VI Sch Lichfield 1968–73, sr Eng master Shire Oak Sch 1973–77; professional novelist 1977–; memb Soc of Authors 1988, bd memb Lichfield Int Arts Festival; *Books* Rat Trap (1976), Firefox (1977), Wolfsbane (1978), Snow Falcon (1979), Sea Leopard (1981), Jade Tiger (1982), Firefox Down (1983), The Bear's Tears (1985), Winter Hawk (1987), All The Grey Cats (1988), The Last Raven (1990), There to Here - Ideas of Political Society (1991), A Hooded Crow (1992), Playing with Cobras (1993), A Wild Justice (1995); as David Grant: Moscow 5000 (1979), Emerald Decision (1980); *Recreations* history, philosophy, music (jazz, classical), gardening, cricket; *Style*— Craig Thomas, Esq

THOMAS, Prof David; s of William Thomas, and Florence Grace Thomas; *b* 16 Feb 1931; *Educ* Bridgend GS, UCW Aberystwyth (BA, MA), Univ of London (PhD); *m* 1955, Daphne Elizabeth Berry; 1 s, 1 da; *Career* Nat Serv RAF 1949–51; UCL 1957–70: asst lectr, lectr, reader, sec AUT 1963–65, convenor non-professorial staff 1968–70, chm Arts and Laws Library Ctee 1969–70; Saint David's Univ Coll 1970–78: prof and head of Dept, dean Faculty of Arts 1971–73, chm Computer Users' Ctee 1971–75, memb Cncl Univ of Wales 1971–74, chm Student Health and Welfare Ctee 1977–78 (also Safety Ctee), dep princ 1977–78; Univ of Birmingham 1978–: prof and head of Dept 1978–86 and 1991–93, prof of geography 1987–91 and 1993–95, emeritus prof 1995–; chm Field Course & Vacation Grants Ctee 1983–86, pro vice chllr 1984–89, univ rep on Jt Matriculation Bd 1989–92, chm Jt Safety Advsy Ctee 1990–95; visiting prof: Federal Sch in Euro Geography Minnesota 1968, Univ of Minnesota 1975, Hubert H Humphrey and Fulbright prof Macalester Coll St Paul 1982; memb: Field Studies Cncl 1972–74 and 1978–95, Br Nat Ctee for Geography of the Royal Soc 1972–74 and 1976–78, W Midlands Cncl for Further Educn 1984–86; memb: Cncl RGS 1987–91, Cncl Inst of Br Geographers 1972–74 (hon sec 1976–78, jr vice pres 1986, sr vice pres 1987, pres 1988); sec and convenor Conf of Geography Heads of Depts 1972–74, chm 18+ Ctee for Geography of Secondary Examinations Cncl 1983–89, vice chm Nat Curriculum Geography Working Gp 1989–90, auditor CVCP Academic Audit Unit 1991–93, teaching quality assessor HEFCE 1994–95; dir NHS Tst 1994–; *Books* Agriculture in Wales during the Napoleonic Wars (1963), London's Green Belt (1970), Man and His World: an Introduction to Human Geography (with J A Dawson, 1975), Wales, The Shaping of a Nation (with P Morgan, 1984); *Recreations* music, wine; *Style*— Prof David Thomas; ✉ 6 Plymouth Drive, Barnt Green, Birmingham B45 8JB (☎ 0121 445 3295); School of Geography, University of Birmingham, Edgbaston, Birmingham B15 2TT

THOMAS, Rev Canon David; s of Rt Rev John James Absalom Thomas, DD, of Tenby, and Elizabeth Louise, *née* James (d 1991); *b* 22 July 1942; *Educ* Christ Coll Brecon, Keble Coll Oxford, St Stephen's House Oxford (BA, MA); *m* 1 April 1967, Rosemary Christine, da of Arthur Louis Calton, of Southampton; 1 s (John Dyfrig b 1971), 1 da (Felicity Jane b 1968); *Career* curate Hawarden 1967–69, chaplain St Michael's Coll Llandaff 1970–75 (tutor 1969), princ St Stephen's House Oxford 1982–87 (vice princ 1975–79), vicar of Chepstow 1979–82, vicar of Newton 1987–, residentiary canon of Brecon Cathedral 1994–, rural dean of Clyne 1996–; memb: Church in Wales Liturgical Cmmn 1969 (sec 1970–75), Church in Wales Doctrinal Cmmn 1975–93, Church in Wales Standing Liturgical Advsy Ctee 1987–, Working Gp on Authy 1987–88, Working Gp on Healing 1987–88, Working Gp on Children and Holy Communion 1991–93; managing tstee St Michael's Coll Llandaff 1988–, memb Governing Body of the Church in Wales 1972–75, 1980–82 and 1989–; *Books* The Ministry of the Word (contrib, 1979); *Recreations* music, history, travel in Europe, walking, anything to do with the sea; *Style*— The Rev Canon David Thomas; ✉ The Vicarage, Mary Twill Lane, Newton, Swansea SA3 4RB (☎ 01792 368348)

THOMAS, David; MEP (Lab) Suffolk and Norfolk South West (majority 12,535); *Career* MEP (Lab) Suffolk and Norfolk SW 1994–; *Style*— David Thomas, Esq, MEP; ✉ European Constituency Office, 6 St Mary's Street, Bungay, Suffolk NR35 1AX

THOMAS, David; s of Harold Bushell Thomas, of Bebington, Wirral, and Margaret, *née* Browne (decd); *b* 7 Nov 1945; *Educ* St Anselm's Coll Birkenhead, Univ of Liverpool (LLB); *m* (m dis); 1 da (Rachel Elenore b 27 Aug 1974), 3 s (Mark Aidan b 10 July 1976, James Matthew b 28 Feb 1980, Neil William (twin) b 1980); partner, Jane Bibby; *Career* F S Moore & Price Birkenhead: slr 1969–71, ptnr 1971–85, managing ptnr 1984–85; managing ptnr: Lees Moore & Price Birkenhead 1985–88, Lees Lloyd Whitley Liverpool 1988–93; chm Lees Lloyd Whitley Liverpool and London 1993–96; the Banking Ombudsman Jan 1997–; pres Liverpool Law Soc 1987–88; The Law Soc: memb Cncl 1987–96, chm Specialisation Ctee 1989–92, Practice Devpt Ctee 1992–95, Quality Standards Working Party 1995–96, Research Sub-Ctee 1991–96; *Recreations* theatre, modern history, walking; *Style*— David Thomas, Esq; ✉ Office of the Banking Ombudsman, 70 Gray's Inn Road, London WC1X 8NB (☎ 0171 404 9944, fax 0171 405 5052, e-mail banking.ombudsman@obo.org.uk)

THOMAS, David Arthur; s of David Martell Thomas (d 1960), of Hampton, Middx, and Sybil Elizabeth, *née* Perry; *b* 7 April 1938; *Educ* DES RCA; *m* 1, 8 Aug 1976 (m dis 1986), Georgina Anne Caroline, da of Dr Joseph Linhart, of London; 1 s (Edward b 14 Feb 1977); m 2, 12 Sept 1987, Gillian Mary, da of Norman Duncan Mussett (d 1983); 1 da (Jessica b 5 Jan 1988); *Career* md David Thomas Design Ltd 1965– (designing and producing fine jewellery and silver); one man exhibitions: St Louis and NY USA, Sydney Aust, Tokyo Japan, Goldsmiths' Hall London, Florence Italy; jewellery in perm collections: Worshipful Co of Goldsmiths, De Beers Diamonds, V & A; chm Goldsmiths' Craft Cncl 1986–88; Freeman City of London 1964, Liveryman Worshipful Co of Goldsmiths 1985; FRSA 1964; *Style*— David Thomas, Esq; ✉ 65 Pimlico Rd, London SW1 (☎ 0171 730 7710, fax 0171 730 5532)

THOMAS, David Emrys; s of Emrys Thomas (d 1979), of Guildford, and Elsie Florence, *née* Brown (d 1994); *b* 9 July 1935; *Educ* Tiffin GS Kingston upon Thames; *m* 1 June 1957, Rosemary, da of Alexander De'Ath, of Hampton, Middlesex; 2 s (Guy b 1963, Mark b 1964), 1 da (Caroline b 1967); *Career* local govt admin 1951–63, chief admin offr Local Govt Trg Bd 1968–69, county personnel offr Surrey CC 1970–77 (dep estab offr 1969–70), under sec for manpower Assoc of Met Authys 1977–81, sec LACSAB 1987–91 (indust rels offr 1963–68, dep sec 1981–87), employers' sec Nat Jt Negotiating Cncls in Local Govt 1987–91, management and personnel conslt 1991–, memb Local Govt Cmmn for England 1992–, fndr pres Soc of Chief Personnel Offrs in Local Govt; Dip in Municipal Admin; FIPD; *Recreations* unskilled gardening, the musical theatre; *Style*— David Thomas, Esq; ✉ The White House, Three Pears Rd, Merrow, Guildford, Surrey GU1 2XU (☎ 01483 569588)

THOMAS, David Gavin; s of Cecil Goring Thomas (d 1974), of Penarth, and Vera Winifred, *née* Wilson; *b* 30 Jan 1943; *Educ* Wycliffe; *m* 14 Aug 1971, Jane Annette, da of John Edward Verdon (d 1984); 1 s (William David b 24 Dec 1976), 2 da (Joanna Louise b 10 April 1975, Laura Anne b 6 July 1979); *Career* qualified CA Peat Marwick Mitchell 1966–68 (articled clerk 1960–66), fin accountant GKN (S Wales) Ltd 1972–73 (mgmnt accountant 1968–72), chief accountant Nova Jersey Knit Ltd 1973–74; Golley Slater & Partners Ltd: co sec 1974–75, fin dir 1976–87, gp fin dir 1987–; FCA; *Recreations* golf, sailing, bridge; *Clubs* Cardiff and County, Glamorganshire Golf, Penarth Yacht, Royal Porthcawl Golf; *Style*— David G Thomas, Esq; ✉ 20 Clinton Road, Penarth, South Glamorgan CF64 3JD (☎ 01222 705677); Golley Slater Group, 9/11 The Hayes, Cardiff, South Glamorgan CF1 1NU (☎ 01222 388621, fax 01222 238729)

THOMAS, David Glyndor Treharne; s of Dr John Glyndor Treharne Thomas, MC (Capt RAMC, d 1955), of Cambridge, and Ellen, *née* Geldart (d 1970); *b* 14 May 1941; *Educ* Perse Sch Cambridge, Gonville and Caius Coll Cambridge (BA, MA, MB BChir); *m* 29 Dec 1970, Hazel Agnes Christina, da of William John Cockburn (d 1977), of Paisley, Renfrewshire; 1 s (William b 1972); *Career* St Mary's Hosp London: house surgn 1966, asst lectr in anatomy 1967–68, sr house offr in neurology 1969, casualty offr 1969; Royal Post Grad Med Sch Hammersmith Hosp London: sr house offr in surgery 1970, registrar in cardio-thoracic surgery 1970–71; Inst of Neurological Scis Southern Gen Hosp Glasgow: registrar, sr registrar and lectr in neurosurgery 1972–76; conslt neurosurgn Nat Hosp for Neurology and Neurosurgery and Northwick Park Hosp Harrow 1976–, prof of neurosurgery Inst of Neurology 1992– (sr lectr 1976–92), conslt neurosurgn St Mary's Hosp London 1994–; memb: Med Acad Staff Ctee BMA 1981–82, Jt Hosp Med Servs Ctee 1981–82; chm EORTC Experimental Neuro-Oncology Gp 1986–88; chm MRC Brain Tumour Working Pty 1989–; vice pres: Euro Assoc of Neurosurgical Socs 1991–95, Euro Soc for Stereotactic and Functional Neurosurgery 1994–; Freeman City of London 1969, Liveryman Worshipful Soc of Apothecaries 1971; MRCS 1966, MRCP 1970, FRCS (Edinburgh) 1972, FRCPG 1985, FRCP (London) 1994; *Books* Brain Tumours: Scientific Basis, Clinical Investigation and Current Therapy (ed with D I Graham, 1980), Biology of Brain Tumour (ed with M D Walker, 1986), Neuro-oncology: Primary Brain Tumours (ed, 1989), Stereotactic and Image Directed Surgery of Brain Tumours (ed, 1993), Handbook of Stereotaxy Using the CRW Apparatus (ed with M F Pell, 1994); numerous invited lectures and visiting professorships worldwide; *Recreations* military and naval history; *Clubs* Athenaeum, RSM; *Style*— Prof David Thomas; ✉ 34 Oppidans Rd, Primrose Hill, London NW3 3AG (☎ 0171 586 2262); The National Hospital, Queen Square, London WC1 3BG (☎ 0171 837 3611 ext 3154/0171 829 8755, fax 0171 278 7894)

THOMAS, David Graeme; s of Edgar Henry Edwin Thomas (d 1974), and late Freda Dorothy Thomas; *b* 22 Oct 1925; *Educ* St Paul's; *m* 1, 23 Aug 1961, (Annie) Muriel (d 1988); m 2, 15 April 1992, (Margaret) Jean, widow of Walter (Wally) Clark; *Career* Scots Gds 1943–47, cmmnd 1944; Whinney Murray CAs 1951–56, sec Hill Samuel & Co 1956–63, dir Robert Fleming & Co 1963–86, chm Aberdare Holdings 1971–74; dep chm: HAT Holdings 1974–86, Robert Fleming Holdings 1981–86, chm Fleming Enterprise Investment Trust plc 1986–94, Interface Inc USA 1990–96; *Recreations* golf; *Clubs* Pratt's, Naval and Military; *Style*— David Thomas, Esq; ✉ Bubblewell House, Minchinhampton, Gloucestershire GL6 9AT (☎ 01453 882531, fax 01453 886925)

THOMAS, Dr David John (Dafydd); s of Jack Lloyd Thomas, of Fulmer, Bucks and Rachel, *née* Hunt; *b* 7 Dec 1943; *Educ* Alleyn's Sch Dulwich, Clare Coll Cambridge (MA, MB BChir), Univ of Birmingham Med Sch (Arthur Thompson scholar, MD); *m* 1966, Celia Margaret, da of Sir Charles Barratt (d 1971), of Kenilworth, Warwicks; 3 da (Dr Rachel Thomas b 25 Jan 1970, Eleanor b 13 July 1980, Laura b 3 April 1983), 2 s (Dr Charles Lloyd b 18 Aug 1971, George Llewellyn b 26 Jan 1973); *Career* neurological registrar then sr registrar Queen Elizabeth Hosp and Midland Centre for Neurology and Neurosurgery 1972–76, MRC research fell Inst of Neurology and St Thomas' Hosp 1976–78 (Queen Square prize), conslt neurologist and head of dept St Mary's Hosp and E Berkshire Hosps 1978–, sr lectr in neurology and hon conslt neurologist Inst of Neurology and Nat Hosps for Neurology and Neurosurgery 1980–; chm Special Advsy Ctee on Neurology to Royal Colls, princ neurological investigator MRC Asymptomatic Carotid Surgery Trial 1994–; memb Cncl Stroke Assoc 1992–; memb: Assoc of Br Neurologists 1978, Stroke Cncl (American Heart Assoc) 1991, Euro Stroke Cncl 1994; FRCP 1985 (MRCP 1972); *Books* Strokes and their Prevention (1988), Neurology, What Shall I Do? (1989), The Eye in Systemic Disease (1990); *Recreations* photography, lecturing; *Style*— Dr Dafydd Thomas; ✉ Woolletts, Fulmer, Bucks SL3 6JE (☎ 01753 662147, fax 01753 664023); Neurology Deparment, St Mary's Hospital, Praed Street, London W2 1NY (☎ 0171 725 1361)

THOMAS, David John Godfrey; s and h of Sir Godfrey Michael Thomas, 11 Bt; *b* 11 June 1961; *Educ* Harrow; *Career* dir; *Recreations* squash (Eng int), tennis; *Clubs* Hurlingham, MCC, Jesters, Escorts; *Style*— David Thomas, Esq; ✉ 23 Branksea Street, London SW6 6TT (☎ and fax 0171 381 4078)

THOMAS, Hon David William Penrose; o s of David Churchill Thomas, CMG, and Susan Petronella Thomas, OBE, *née* Arrow (*see* Baroness Thomas of Walliswood); *b* 17 Jan 1959; *Educ* Eton, King's Coll Cambridge (BA); *m* 28 June 1986, Clare Elizabeth, da of John Jeremy, MBE; 2 da (Holly b 1988, Lucy b 1989); *Career* Young Journalist of the Year Br Press Awards 1983–84; ed: The Magazine 1984–85, Sunday Today Magazine 1986; chief feature writer You Magazine 1986–88 (formerly asst ed), ed Punch 1989–92; Columnist of the Year Magazine Publishing Awards 1989; features incl: Sunday Times, Observer, Daily Mail, Tatler, The Face, Rolling Stone, GQ (US); *Books* Bilko, the Fort Baxter Story (1984), Fame & Fortune (1988), Sex and Shopping (1988), Great Sporting Moments (1989), Not Guilty: Men, The Case for the Defence (1993), Girl (1995); *Clubs* Groucho, Goodwood; *Style*— The Hon David Thomas; ✉ c/o Patrick Walsh, Christopher Little, 48 Walham Grove, London SW6 1QR (☎ 0171 386 1800)

THOMAS, Sir Derek Morison David; KCMG (1987, CMG 1977); s of Kenneth Peter David Thomas (d 1982), of Hill House, Hempstead, Saffron Walden, Essex, and Mali McLeod, *née* Morison (d 1972); *b* 31 Oct 1929; *Educ* Radley, Trinity Hall Cambridge (MA); *m* 1956, Lineke, da of Thijs Van der Mast (d 1988), of Eindhoven, Netherlands; 1 s (Matthew b 1967), 1 da (Caroline b 1963); *Career* Sub Lt RNVR 1955 (Midshipman 1953–55); articled apprentice Dolphin Industry Developments Ltd 1947; entered Dip Serv 1953; served in: Moscow, Manila, Brussels, Sofia, Ottawa, Paris, Washington; dep under sec of state for Europe and political dir FCO 1984–87, Br ambass to Italy 1987–89; Euro advsr NM Rothschild & Sons 1990–; dir: NM Rothschild & Sons 1991–, Rothschild Italia 1990–, Rothschild Europe 1991–, Christow Consultants 1990–, CDP Nexus 1991–92 (assoc 1990); memb Export Guarantees Advsy Cncl 1991–96, chm Ctee of Liberalisation of Trade in Servs (Br Invisibles); memb Cncl: SOSSAHEL, Univ of Reading 1991–, RIIA 1994–; *Style*— Sir Derek Thomas, KCMG; ✉ 12 Lower Sloane Street, London SW1W 8BJ

THOMAS, Donald Michael; s of Harold Redvers Thomas, and Amy, *née* Moyle; *b* 27 Jan 1935; *Educ* New Coll Oxford (BA, MA); 2 s (Sean, Ross), 1 da (Caitlin); *Career* poet and novelist; teacher Teignmough GS 1959–63, head of English Dept Hereford Coll of Educn 1973–75 (lectr 1964–78); full time author 1978–; *Novels* The Flute-Player (1978), Birthstone (1979), The White Hotel (1981), Russian Nights, a quintet (Ararat 1983, Swallow 1984, Eating Pavlova (1984), Sphinx 1986, Summit 1987, Lying Together 1990), Flying in to Love (1992), Pictures at an Exhibition (1993), Eating Pavlolva (1994); *Memoirs* Memories and Hallucinations (autobiography, 1988); *Poetry* Penguin Modern Poets 11 (1968), Two Voices (1968), Logan Stone (1971), Love and Other Deaths (1975), The Honeymoon Voyage (1978), Dreaming in Bronze (1979), Selected Poems (1982), The Puberty Tree (1992); *Translations* Requiem and Poem Without a Hero (Akhmatova, 1976), Way of All the Earth (Akhmatova, 1979), Bronze Horseman (Pushkin, 1982), The Puberty Tree (New and Selected, 1992); *Style*— D M Thomas, Esq; ✉ The Coach House, Rashleigh Vale, Truro, Cornwall TR1 1TJ (☎ 01872 78885)

THOMAS, Prof (James) Edward; s of James Edward Thomas (ka 1941), of Portfield, Haverfordwest, Pembrokeshire, and Margaret Elizabeth, *née* Absalom (d 1981); *b* 20 Dec 1933; *Educ* Haverfordwest GS, Univ of Oxford, Univ of London, Univ of York, Univ of Nottingham (DLitt); *m* 24 Aug 1957, Olwen, da of John Yolland (d 1980), of Colby, Wiston, Pembrokeshire; 2 s (Simon b 24 Oct 1958, Philip b 6 June 1961); *Career* Nat Serv RA 1952–54; admin offr Govt of N Rhodesia 1957–60, govr HM Prison Serv 1960–67, lectr and sr lectr Univ of Hull 1967–78; Univ of Nottingham: joined as reader 1978, now prof Dept of Adult Educn, also dean of educn, pro vice chllr; bursar Imp Rels Tst 1970, fell Japan Soc for Promotion of Sci, former chm Standing Conf on Univ Teaching and Res in Educn of Adults, vice chm Univ Cncl on Adult and Continuing Educn; FRSA; *Books* The English Prison Officer since 1950: A Study in Conflict (1972), Imprisonment in Western Australia: Evolution Theory and Practice (with A Stewart, 1978), The Exploding Prison: Prison Riots and the Case of Hull (with R Pooley, 1980), Radical Adult Education: Theory and Practice (1982), International Biography of Adult Education (with B Elsey, 1985), Learning Democracy in Japan: The Social Education of Japanese Adults (1986), House of Care: Prisons and Prisoners in England 1500–1800 (1988), A Select Biography of Adult Continuing Education (with J H Davis, 5 edn 1988), Radical Agendas? The Politics of Adult Education (with Sallie Westwood, 1991), Making Japan Work (1993), Modern Japan: A Social History since 1868; *Recreations* music, walking, cinema; *Style*— Prof J E Thomas; ✉ University of Nottingham, University Park, Nottingham NG7 2RD (☎ 0115 951 4396, fax 0115 942 0825, telex 37346 UNINOT 2)

THOMAS, Prof Edward John; s of John Henry Thomas (d 1958), of Plymouth, Devon, and Lily Elizabeth Jane Thomas; *b* 25 Nov 1937; *Educ* Devonport HS, Keble Coll Oxford (MA), Univ of London (MSc), Univ of Manchester (PhD); *m* 12 Sep 1964, Erica Jean, da of Eric Distin (d 1977), of Salcombe, Devon; 1 s (Gerard William b 1969), 1 da (Katherine Grace b 1965); *Career* res scientist GEC plc 1962–64, lectr Univ of Manchester 1964–68; Univ of Bristol: staff tutor 1968–80, sr lectr 1980–81, prof of adult educn 1981–92, prof of continuing educn 1992–, formerly head of Dept for Continuing Educn; sec gen Euro Univs Continuing Educn Network; MInstP 1972, FRSA 1983; *Books* Type II Superconductivity (1969), From Quarks to Quasars (1977); *Recreations* reading, writing, eating, drinking, talking; *Style*— Prof Edward Thomas; ✉ Department for Continuing Education, University of Bristol, Bristol BS8 1HH (☎ 0117 928 7138, fax 0117 925 4975, e-mail E.J.Thomas @ uk.ac.bristol)

THOMAS, Dr Gareth; s of Rev Evan George Thomas, and Nina Mary, *née* Clargo; step s of Olwen Elizabeth, *née* Jones; *b* 3 Nov 1945; *Educ* Merchant Taylors', St Mary's Hosp Med Sch (MB BS), Univ of London (MD), LLM (Univ of Wales), MRCS, MRCOG, FRCOG 1987; *m* 20 Sept 1969, Alison Muir, da of late David Muir Kelly, of Haile, Cumbria; 3 s (Mark b 1971, Robert b 1973, James b 1976), 2 da (Anna b 1980, Abigail b 1982); *Career* obstetrician and gynaecologist; house physician St Mary's Hosp London 1969; resident med offr: Queen Charlotte's Hosp London 1970–71, Samaritan Hosp London 1971–72; lectr and hon registrar UCL 1972–75, hon lectr Univ of Oxford 1975–77, sr registrar Oxfordshire RHA 1975–79, conslt Ipswich and East Suffolk 1979–, clinical dir Dept of Gynaecological and Maternity Servs 1991–, chm Med Staff Ctee The Ipswich Hosp 1996–; memb Bd Christchurch Park Hosp Ipswich, examiner Univ of London 1988–; Law Soc expert; *Recreations* sailing; *Clubs* Association Broadcasting Doctors; *Style*— Dr Gareth Thomas; ✉ Boxbush, 243 Rushmere Road, Suffolk IP4 3LU (☎ 01473 232718)

THOMAS, Dr Geoffrey Price; s of Richard Lewis Thomas (d 1983), of Maesteg, Mid-Glamorgan, and Aerona, *née* Price (d 1969); *b* 3 July 1941; *Educ* Maesteg GS, Univ Coll of Swansea (BSc), Churchill Coll Cambridge (PhD); *m* 1965, Judith Vaughan, da of Arsul John Williams; 2 da (Susannah Judith b 1965, Rachel Louise b 1967); *Career* res assoc Cavendish Laboratory 1966–67, staff tutor Univ Coll of Swansea 1967–78; Univ of Oxford: dep dir Dept of External Studies 1978–86, dir Dept for Continuing Educn 1986–, founding pres Kellogg Coll Oxford (formerly Rewley House) 1990–; visiting scholar: Smithsonian Inst, Harvard Univ, Univ of Washington, Univ of Calif Berkeley, Northern Illinois Univ; hon fell Linacre Coll Oxford 1990– (fell 1978–90); *Books* The Nuclear Arms Race (jt ed with C F Barnaby, 1982), Science and Sporting Performance (jt ed with B Davies, 1982); *Clubs* Athenaeum; *Style*— Dr Geoffrey Thomas; ✉ Kellogg College, 1 Wellington Square, Oxford OX1 2JA (☎ 01865 270376, fax 01865 270309)

THOMAS, Graham Stuart; OBE (1975); s of William Richard Thomas (d 1947), of 169 Hills Rd, Cambridge, and Lilian, *née* Hays (d 1951); *b* 3 April 1909; *Educ* Botanic Garden Univ of Cambridge; *Career* foreman then mangr T Hilling & Co 1931, assoc dir Sunningdale Nurseries Windlesham Surrey 1968–71 (mangr 1956), gardens conslt Nat Tst 1974– (advsr 1954–74); vice patron Royal Nat Rose Soc; vice pres: Garden History Soc, Br Hosta and Hemerocallis Soc, RHS 1990 (Veitch Meml Medal 1966, Victoria Medal of Hon 1968); Dean Hole Medal Royal Nat Rose Soc 1976, hon memb Irish Garden Plant Soc 1983, hon pres Historic Roses Gp Royal Nat Rose Soc; *Books* The Old Shrub Roses (1955), Colour in the Winter Garden (1957), Shrub Roses of Today (1962), Climbing Roses Old and New (1965), Plants for Ground Cover (1970), Perennial Garden Plants (1976), Gardens of the National Trust (1979), Three Gardens (1983), Trees in the Landscape (1983), Recreating the Period Garden (ed, 1984), A Garden of Roses (1987), The Complete Paintings and Drawings of Graham Stuart Thomas (1987), The Rock Garden and its Plants (1989), An English Rose Garden (1991), Ornamental Shrubs, Climbers and Bamboos (1992), The Graham Stuart Thomas Rose Book (1994); *Recreations* music, painting flowers, reading; *Style*— Graham Thomas, Esq, OBE; ✉ Briar Cottage, 21 Kettlewell Close, Horsell, Woking, Surrey

THOMAS, (John) Harvey Noake; CBE (1990); s of Col John Humphrey Kenneth Thomas (d 1984), of Leamington Spa, and Olga Rosina, *née* Noake; *b* 10 April 1939; *Educ* Westminster, Univ of Minnesota, Univ of Hawaii, Northwestern Bible Coll Minnesota; *m* 22 Dec 1978, Marlies, da of Erich Kram, of Wölmersen, Germany; 2 da (Leah Elisabeth b 1984, Lani Christine b 1986); *Career* Billy Graham Evangelistic Assoc 1960–75, int PR conslt 1976–, dir presentation and promotion Cons Party 1985–91, field dir PM's Election Tour 1987, dir The London Cremation Co 1984–; memb: Oakwood Baptist Church N London, Salvation Army UK Advsy Bd; fell: Inst of PR, Chartered Inst of Journalists; *Books* In The Face Of Fear (1985), Making an Impact (1989), If They Haven't Heard It, You Haven't Said It! (1995); *Recreations* family, travel; *Clubs* IOD; *Style—* Harvey Thomas, Esq, CBE; ✉ 23 The Service Road, Potters Bar, Herts EN6 1QA (☎ 01707 649910, fax 01707 662653)

THOMAS, Dr Hilary; da of John Dewi Thomas, of Barnet, Herts, and Maureen Edith, *née* Thomas; *b* 12 Nov 1959; *Educ* Bishop's Hatfield Girls' Sch, New Hall Cambridge (MA), UCH London (MB BS, MRCP); *m* 23 April 1992, Nicholas James Braithwaite, s of Roderick Clive Braithwaite; 2 da (Isobel Angharad Thomas b 18 Feb 1990, Phoebe Clara Thomas b 13 Feb 1993); *Career* formerly house offr: in med Whittington Hosp, in surgery Hillingdon Hosp; SHO: in med Chase Farm Hosp 1985–86, in cardiology Middx Hosp 1986, in med Hammersmith Hosp 1986–87, in neurology Royal Free Hosp 1987; registrar in clinical oncology Hammersmith Hosp 1987–90, clinical res fell Imperial Cancer Research Fund 1990–94, sr lectr in clinical oncology Hammersmith Hosp 1994–; hon sec Med Women's Fedn, memb Cncl Women's Nationwide Cancer Control Campaign, memb GMC 1994–; MRCP 1987, FRCR 1991; *Books* Fight Cancer (with Karol Sikora, 1989), Cancer: A Positive Approach (with Karol Sikora, 1995); *Clubs* Bloomsbury; *Style—* Dr Hilary Thomas; ✉ Department of Clinical Oncology, Hammersmith Hospital, Du Cane Road, London W12 0HS (☎ 0181 740 3059, fax 0181 743 8766);

THOMAS, Prof Howard Christopher; s of Harold Thomas (d 1986), and Hilda, *née* Pickering (d 1980); *b* 31 July 1945; *Educ* Thornbury GS, Univ of Newcastle upon Tyne (BSc, MB BS, Phillipson prize in med), Univ of Glasgow (PhD); *m* 31 May 1975, Dilys, da of John Andrew Ferguson (d 1979); 2 s (Robin James b 4 Oct 1978, Oliver b 11 July 1992), 1 da (Lucy b 18 Feb 1980); *Career* lectr in immunology Univ of Glasgow 1971–74; Royal Free Hosp Med Sch London: lectr in med 1974–78, sr Wellcome Fell in Clinical Sci 1978–83, reader in med 1983–84, prof of med 1984–87; prof and chm of med: St Mary's Hosp Med Sch, Imp Coll, Univ of London; conslt physician and hepatologist St Mary's Hosp 1987–; memb Cncl Educn Ctee Euro Soc for Study of Liver Disease; Br Liver Tst: memb Med Advsy Ctee 1990–, tstee 1993–; ed Jl of Viral Hepatitis 1993–; Humphry Davy Rolleston lectr RCP 1986, Bushell lectr Aust Soc of Gastroenterology 1990; British Soc of Gastroenterology Res medal 1984, Hans Popper Int prize for Distinction in Hepatology 1989; FRCP, FRCPS, FRCPath; *Books* Clinical Gastrointestinal Immunology (1979), Recent Advances in Hepatology (jt ed Vol 1 1983, Vol 2 1986), Viral Hepatitis (ed, 1993); author of various publications on Hepatology; *Recreations* tennis and golf; *Style—* Prof Howard Thomas; ✉ Department of Medicine, St Mary's Hospital Medical School, Praed Street, London W2 1PG (☎ 0171 725 1606)

THOMAS, (David) Hugh; CBE (1992); s of David Rogers Thomas (d 1980), of Ammanford, Dyfed, and Mary, *née* Jones; *b* 1 April 1937; *Educ* Amman Valley GS, Univ Coll of Wales; *m* 22 Aug 1963, Beryl Dorothy, da of David Garth Williams (d 1951), of Penrhyndeudraeth, Gwynedd; 1 da (Nia b 29 May 1971); *Career* slr; asst slr: Carmarthenshire CC 1961–64, Llanelli RDC 1964–65; dep town clerk Port Talbot 1965–74, dep county clerk W Glamorgan CC 1974–80, co clerk and co-ordinator Mid Glamorgan CC 1980–90, chief exec Mid Glamorgan CC 1990–95, ret; hon sec Court of the Royal Nat Eisteddfod 1975–, chm St Johns Cncl Mid Glamorgan 1984–90, hon sec Welsh Counties Ctee 1985–90, memb Welsh Arts Cncl 1986–92 (chm of Arts Ctee), sec Assembly of Welsh Counties 1992–, chm Morgannwg Health Authority 1995–; OStJ 1986; Cross of the Order of Merit Federal Republic of Germany 1990; *Recreations* rugby, bowls, music, art; *Style—* Hugh Thomas, Esq, CBE

THOMAS, Hugh; *see:* Thomas of Swynnerton, Baron

THOMAS, (Edward) Hugh Gwynne; s of Edward Gwynne Thomas, OBE, VRD (d 1976), and Lisbeth Helen Mair, *née* Thomas (d 1950); *b* 12 Dec 1938; *Educ* Canford; *m* 1 Dec 1973, Annemary Perry, da of Lawrence Walter Dixon, of Poole, Dorset; 3 da (Juliet b 16 Oct 1974, Annabel b 15 May 1977, Louisa b 30 July 1979); *Career* slr 1963, ptnr Keene Marsland 1966–; Freeman: City of London 1966, Worshipful Co of Slrs 1966; memb Law Soc 1963; *Recreations* golf, sailing; *Clubs* Beaconsfield Golf; *Style—* Hugh Thomas, Esq; ✉ Orchard Corner, Curzon Ave, Beaconsfield, Bucks HP9 2NN (☎ 01494 671056); Dragoon House, 37 Artillery Lane, Bishopsgate, London E1 7LT (☎ 0171 375 1581, fax 0171 375 0318)

THOMAS, Hugh Miles; OBE (1995); s of Dr Gwilym Dorrien Thomas, of 47 Ty Rhŷs, The Parade, nr Camarthen, and late Dorothy Gertrude, *née* Jones; *b* 14 Oct 1944; *Educ* Clifton, Univ of Southampton (BSc); *m* 10 Sept 1966, Alison Mary, da of Lt-Col Richard Ryder Davies (d 1968); 2 s (Simon b 1 July 1970, Ryder b 24 May 1973); *Career* CA 1969; Price Waterhouse: articled clerk 1966, ptnr 1978–, ptnr in charge Wales 1983–; pres S Wales Inst of CAs 1987–88; treas Univ Coll of Wales Cardiff 1991–95; memb: Cncl UWIST 1983–88, Cncl UCW Cardiff 1988 and 1991–95, Mgmnt Ctee Cardiff Business Sch, Sports Cncl for Wales 1991–95, Prince of Wales' Ctee (chm Fin and Gen Purposes Ctee) 1984–96; vice pres: Cardiff Business Club, The Welsh Inst of Int Affrs; FCA 1979; *Recreations* sailing, farming; *Clubs* Cardiff Co; *Style—* Hugh Thomas, Esq, OBE; ✉ The Court, Carrow Hill, St Brides Netherwent, Monmouthshire NP6 3AU (☎ 01633 400134, fax 01633 400031); Price Waterhouse, Haywood House, Dumfries Place, Cardiff CF1 4BA (☎ 01222 376255, fax 01222 374124)

THOMAS, Huw Owen; s of Goronwy Evan Thomas (d 1984), and Morfydd Owen, *née* Jones (d 1993); *b* 11 May 1941; *Educ* Liverpool Coll, Welsh Nat Sch of Med (MB BCh), Univ of Liverpool (MChOrth); *m* 25 Oct 1975, Judith Audrey; 2 s (Tom Owen b 11 March 1977, Tristan Goronwy b 26 Jan 1979); *Career* Capt TA RAMC 1970–73; house surgn Cardiff Royal Infirmary 1966, sr house offr Liverpool 1967–69, prosecutor RCS 1967, sr registrar Liverpool & Wrightington Hosp for Hip Surgery 1974–78, sr conslt orthopaedic surgn Wirral Hosps 1978–96; memb Regnl Sub Ctee Orthopaedic Surgery (also memb Post Grad Advsy Panel); memb: Medical Appeals Tbnl, LFA Soc, BMA; FRCSEd 1971, FRCS 1972, MChOrth 1973, FRSM, FBOA; *Publications* author of articles on: Metallic Implants from Crematoria, Isolated Dislocation of Scaphoid, Recurrent Dislocation of Patella; *Recreations* family, fishing, shooting, railways and industrial archaeology, music; *Style—* Huw Thomas, Esq; ✉ Pinwydden, 18 Pine Walks, Prenton, Wirral L42 8NE (☎ 0151 608 3909); 31 Rodney Street, Liverpool; Bupa Murrayfield Hospital, Wirral (☎ 0151 648 7000)

THOMAS, Ian Mitchell; s of John Bythell Thomas (d 1977), of Connah's Quay, and Gladys Ethel, *née* Miller (d 1994); *b* 17 May 1933; *Educ* Liverpool Coll, Selwyn Coll Cambridge (MA); *m* 1, 1960 (m dis 1976), Jenifer Diana, da of Dr George Thomas Lance Fletcher Morris, of Coggeshall, Essex; 2 s (James b 1961, Mark b 1965), 2 da (Emma b 1963, Victoria b 1969); m 2, 24 Oct 1977, Diana Lesley Kathryn, wid of Nicholas Thorne (d 1976), and da of Donald William Leslie (d 1984), of Wimbledon; 1 step s (Alexander b 1972), 1 step da (Camilla b 1976); *Career* Nat Serv 4 KORR 1952–54 (2 Lt 1953), PA to COS Br Cwlth Forces Korea 1953, Capt The Liverpool Scottish Queen's Own Cameron Highlanders TA; asst md Hobson Bates and Partners 1965 (dir 1963), jt md Cavenham Foods Ltd 1965–67, md Fabbri and Partners Ltd 1968–70, chm and md Culpeper Ltd 1972–; cncllr (C) Islington Cncl 1968–70, vice pres Herb Soc 1986–87 (memb Cncl 1978–87); *Books* Culpeper's Book of Birth (1985), How to Grow Herbs (1988), Culpeper Herbal Notebook (1991); *Recreations* running, sailing, skiing, gardening; *Style—* Ian Thomas, Esq; ✉ 10 Rathmore Road, Cambridge CB1 4AD (☎ 01223 245293); Culpeper Ltd, Hadstock Rd, Linton, Cambridge CB1 6NJ (☎ 01223 891196, fax 01223 893104, e-mail culpeper@dial.pipex.com)

THOMAS, Irene; da of Edmund Roberts Ready (d 1956), and Ethel, *née* Crapnell (d 1970); *b* 28 June 1920; *Educ* The County Sch Ashford Middx; *m* 1, 1940 (m dis 1949), Wesley J C Baldry; m 2, 23 Jan 1950, Edward Kenfig Thomas, s of Walter Thomas, of Porth, Rhondda; *Career* NFS 1940–45, Covent Garden Opera 1946–49, freelance singer 1950–68; broadcaster; progs incl: Brain of Britain 1961, Brain of Brains 1962, Round Britain Quiz 1967 and 1973–95, Round Europe Quiz, Transatlantic Quiz, Desert Island Discs 1979, With Great Pleasure 1986, Hoax! 1987, The Gardening Quiz 1988–93, Full Score 1995, Private Passions 1995; TV progs incl: The 60–70–80 show (with Roy Hudd) 1974–80, About Face 1986, Did You See...? 1993; regular contrib Woman & Home Magazine; a vice pres Hearing Research Tst 1993–; Hon MUniv Open Univ 1987; *Books* The Bandsman's Daughter (1979), The Almost Impossible Quiz Book (1982); *Recreations* watching cats, thinking; *Style—* Mrs Irene Thomas; ✉ c/o BBC, Broadcasting House, London W1A 1AA

THOMAS, James; CBE (1992); s of late David Thomas, of Llysnewydd, Llanybydder, and late Hannah, *née* Morgans; *b* 3 Jan 1933; *m* 3 Aug 1957, Ann, *née* Roberts; 1 s (David Richard b 24 Aug 1958), 2 da (Dorothy Anna b 12 Jan 1960, Catrin Margaret b 2 July 1967); *Career* farmer; vice chm RAC 1984– (memb Bd of Mgmnt), dep chm Royal Agric Soc of the Cwlth (hon treas 1971–, memb Advsy Ctee 1971, chm 1990, hon fell 1991); memb: Nat Agric and Countryside Forum, Cncl Royal Assoc of British Dairy Farmers, Cncl NFU; chm Co Branch British Food and Farming 1988–89; chm E Dyfed Health Authy 1984–95 ret, vice chm Health Promotion Authy of Wales 1987–, memb Welsh Health Devpt Int 1991– (chm Jt Staff Consultative Cncl Mgmnt Div); memb Cncl Welsh Sch of Med 1985–88 and 1990–92, fndr memb Standing Ctee Inst of Health Infomatics UC Aberystwyth, chm Welsh Health Authorities' Chairmen; govr: Coleg Ceredigion, Llanwenog Primary Sch; mangr Highmead Residential Sch; sec PCC; *Recreations* photography; *Clubs* Farmers'; *Style—* James Thomas, Esq, CBE

THOMAS, James Alfred; s of Robert Thomas (d 1962), of Shrewsbury, Shrops, and Margarett, *née* Griffiths (d 1989); *b* 31 March 1927; *Educ* Univ of Sussex (MPhil), Brighton Univ Sch of Architecture (Dip Arch); *m* 21 March 1951, Cynthia, da of John Rance Goddard (d 1984), of Brighton, Sussex; 1 s (James Matthew b 21 Feb 1968); *Career* Royal Signals 1st Air Support Troops Central Med 1945–48, cmmnd RAF(VR) 1948–52; electricity bds 1950–63, Electricity Cncl scholar 1960–63, univ architect and engr Univ of Sussex 1964–81 (responsible for tech planning and devpt of univ campus and bldgs 1981–, conslt architect to the univ 1981–92), sr lectr Sch of Architecture and Interior Design Brighton Univ (formerly Brighton Poly); in private practice with James Thomas Architects & Environmental Consultants 1981–; energy convenor for SE England Construction Industry Cncl; ARIBA 1964, CEng 1972, fell Inst of Energy 1972, FCIBSE 1974; *Recreations* looking at mostly old buildings; *Style—* James Thomas, Esq; ✉ 3 Lewes Crescent, Brighton, Sussex (☎ 01273 607100)

THOMAS, James Robert Graham; s of Cyril John Thomas (d 1987), and Hilary Allcroft, *née* Palins (d 1976); *b* 19 March 1934; *Educ* Whitgift Sch, UCL (State scholar, Bartlett exhibitioner, BA (Arch)), Univ of Westminster (DipTP); *m* 4 Aug 1963, Anne Margaret, da of Thomas Arthur Pawsey (d 1982); 2 da (Joanna Susan b 1965, Catherine Sara (Mrs Flett) b 1966), 1 s (James William Pawsey b 1968); *Career* architect and town planner; asst architect: with Sir Basil Spence 1957, with Jorn Utzon 1960, with Sir Denys Lasdun 1964–66; dep gp ldr GLC 1966–68, gp planner London Borough of Lewisham 1968–70, princ architect-planner GLC 1972–79 (dep surveyor of historic buildings 1970–72), dep city architect and planning offr City of London 1979–81, dir of devpt London Borough of Tower Hamlets 1981–85, dir of planning and transportation City of Westminster 1985–87, princ Rothermel Thomas 1987–; memb Structural Advsy Gp Athenaeum 1993–96; pres Soc of Architects Cities of London and Westminster 1986–88; RIBA: memb Cncl, vice pres 1995–, hon librarian, chm Library Bd, memb Policy Mgmnt Bd; ARCUK: memb Cncl, memb Bd of Architectural Educn, memb Discipline Ctee; tstee Br Architectural Library Tst; memb: Ctee Soc of Chief Architects in Local Authy 1979–81, Assoc of London Borough Architects 1979–87, Assoc of London Borough Engrs and Surveyors 1985–, Assoc of London Borough Planning Offrs 1979–87, Met Planning Offrs Soc 1979–87; govr Collingwood Sch Wallington, parish clerk St John the Evangelist, memb Southwark Diocesan Advsy Ctee for the Care of Churches 1970–73; Freeman City of London 1979, fndr memb and Liveryman Worshipful Co of Chartered Architects (Master 1987–88); brother: Worshipful Co of Parish Clerks 1991, Ct Worshipful Co of Fanmakers 1992; FRIBA 1968, FRTPI 1974, FIMgt 1978, FRSA 1980; *Books* Battle of the Styles (1974), Salisbury Cathedral Close: Conservation and Management (1990); *Recreations* theatre, reading, walking, family, wine; *Clubs* Athenaeum; *Style—* James R G Thomas, Esq; ✉ Brook Cottage, 22A Lower Camden, Chislehurst, Kent BR7 5HX (☎ 0181 467 3662); Rothermel Thomas, 14–16 Cowcross Street, London EC1M 6DR (☎ 0171 490 4255, fax 0171 490 1251)

THOMAS, Jeremy Jack; s of Maj Ralph Thomas, MC, and Joy Eveleyn, *née* Spanjer; *b* 26 July 1949; *Educ* Millfield; *m* 1, (m dis 1977), Claudia Frolich; 1 da (Jessica Emily); m 2, 1982, Vivien Patricia, da of Adolph Coughman; 2 s (Jack Felix, Joshua Kit),; *Career* film producer; chm British Film Inst 1993–; *Films* credits incl: Mad Dog Morgan 1976, The Shout 1977, The Great Rock 'n Roll Swindle 1979, Bad Timing 1979, Eureka 1982, Merry Christmas Mr Lawrence 1982, The Hit 1983, Insignificance 1984, The Last Emperor (winner of nine Academy awards incl Best Picture) 1988, Everybody Wins 1989, The Sheltering Sky 1990, Let Him Have It (exec prodr) 1991, Naked Lunch 1991, Little Buddha 1993, Victory (exec prodr) 1994, Stealing Beauty 1995, Blood and Wine 1996, The Ogre (exec prodr) 1996; *Style—* Jeremy Thomas, Esq; ✉ The Recorded Picture Co, 24 Hanway Street, London W1P 9DD (☎ 0171 636 2251, fax 0171 636 2261)

THOMAS, Jessica D E; *see:* Mann, Jessica D E

THOMAS, Prof (William) John; s of Trevor Roylance Thomas (d 1975), of Dinas Powys, S Glam, Swansea and Carmarthen, and Gwendoline Novello, *née* Williams (d 1984); *b* 13 July 1929; *Educ* Dynevor GS Swansea, Univ Coll Swansea, Univ of Wales (BSc, DSc), Imperial Coll London (PhD); *m* 11 June 1955, Pamela Heather, da of Clifford Rees; 1 s (Mark b 1959), 1 da (Clare b 1963); *Career* scientific offr Int Nickel Co 1954–55, lectr Univ Coll Swansea 1955–58 and 1960–68, sr scientific offr Atomic Energy Authy Harwell 1958–60, prof of chem engrg Univ of Bath 1968–95 (now emeritus), pro vice chllr Univ of Bath 1987–93; vice pres Inst of Chem Engrg 1987–90; FIChemE 1970, FEng 1995; *Books* Introduction to the Principles of Heterogeneous Catalysis (1968), Heterogeneous Catalysis: Principles and Practice (1996); extensive contribs to scientific books and papers; *Recreations* former Welsh Rugby Union (WRU) referee, assistant organist at Bathampton Parish church; *Style—* Prof John Thomas, FEng; ✉ School of Chemical Engineering, University of Bath, Claverton Down, Bath BA2 7AY (☎ 01225 826575, fax 01225 826894, telex 449097)

THOMAS, Dr John Anthony Griffiths; s of William Thomas (d 1991), of Rhyl, Clwyd, and Bernice Margaret, *née* Griffiths; *b* 28 Aug 1943; *Educ* Alun GS Clwyd, Univ of Leeds (BSc), Univ of Keele (PhD); *m* 16 Aug 1965, Sylvia Jean, da of Robert Norman (d 1983); 2 da (Rachel b 1971, Emily b 1974); *Career* Reed Business Publishing Ltd: dir

1970–86, dep md IPC Science and Technology Press Ltd 1977–78, publishing dir IPC Business Press Ltd 1978–84, md Update Gp Ltd 1984–85, md Update-Siebert Ltd 1985–86; BBC Worldwide Ltd (formerly BBC Enterprises Ltd): dir of magazines 1986–93, md 1993–94, md BBC Worldwide Television 1994–95, md BBC Worldwide Learning 1995–97; memb BBC Bd of Mgmnt 1993–95; chm: Redwood Publishing Ltd 1986–93, BBC Frontline Ltd; formerly dir Periodical Publishers Assoc Ltd; FRSA; *Books* Energy Today (1977), The Quest for Fuel (1978), Energy Analysis (ed, 1978); *Recreations* jogging, swimming, reading; *Style*— Dr John Thomas; ✉ BBC Worldwide Learning, 80 Wood Lane, London W12 0TT (☎ 0181 743 5588)

THOMAS, Hon Mr Justice; Hon Sir (Roger) John Laugharne; kt (1996); s of Roger Edward Laugharne Thomas (d 1970), of Ystradgynlais, and Dinah Agnes, *née* Jones (d 1994); *b* 22 Oct 1947; *Educ* Rugby, Trinity Hall Cambridge (BA), Univ of Chicago Law Sch (JD); *m* 6 Jan 1973, Elizabeth Ann, da of Stephen James Buchanan (d 1984), of Ohio; 1 s (David b 1978), 1 da (Alison b 1980); *Career* teaching asst Mayo Coll India 1965–66; called to the Bar Gray's Inn 1969, QC 1984, QC Eastern Caribbean Supreme Ct 1986, recorder of the Crown Ct 1987–96, bencher Gray's Inn 1992, judge of the High Ct of Justice (Queen's Bench Div Commercial Ct) 1996–; DTI inspr Mirror Group Newspapers plc 1992; faculty fell Univ of Southampton 1990–96; *Recreations* gardens, travel, walking; *Style*— The Hon Mr Justice Thomas; ✉ Royal Courts of Justice, Strand, London WC2A 2LL

THOMAS, Prof Sir John Meurig; kt (1991); *b* 15 Dec 1932; *Educ* Univ Coll Swansea (BSc), Univ of Wales/Queen Mary Coll London (PhD), Univ of Wales (DSc), Univ of Cambridge (MA, ScD); *m*, Margaret; 2 da (Lisa Marged (Mrs Oliver Graham) and Eden Naomi Fflur); *Career* tech asst Safety in Mines Research Estab Sheffield 1953, scientific offr UKAEA Aldermaston 1957–58; UCNW Bangor: asst lectr in chemistry 1958–59, lectr in physical chemistry 1959–65, reader in chemistry 1965–69; prof of chemistry and head Edward Davies Chemical Lab UCW Aberystwyth 1969–78, head Dept of Physical Chemistry and professorial fell King's Coll Cambridge 1978–86; The Royal Instn of GB: dir 1986–91, dir Davy Faraday Research Lab 1986–91, resident prof of chemistry 1986–88, Fullerian prof of chemistry 1988–; dep pro-chllr Univ of Wales 1991–94, master Peterhouse Cambridge 1993–; visiting scientist: Dept of Physics Technol Univ of Eindhoven 1962, Technische Hochshule Karlsruhe 1966, Dept of Organic Chemistry Univ of Florence 1972, IBM Research Lab San José 1977; visiting scholar Pennsylvania State Univ: Dept of Fuel Sci 1963, Coll of Mineral Industs 1967; visiting prof: Dept of Structural Chemistry Weizmann Inst of Sci Israel 1969 (memb Governing Body 1981–), Dept of Chemistry Univ of Western Ontario 1971, Centre for Materials Sci McMaster Univ Ontario 1978; distinguished visiting prof: The American Univ Cairo 1973, École Nationale Superieure de Chemie de Paris 1991, Jawaharal Nehru Centre for Advanced Scientific Research Bangalore 1991; distinguished visiting lectr Univ of London 1980; hon visiting prof: Imperial Coll London 1986–91, Queen Mary and Westfield Coll London 1986–; pres: Chemistry Section BAAS 1988–89, London Int Youth Sci Fortnight 1989–93; numerous named lectureships worldwide 1978–; hon fell: UMIST 1984, Univ Coll Swansea 1985, UCNW Bangor 1988, Queen Mary and Westfield Coll London 1990, Royal Soc of Edinburgh 1993 (Bruce-Preller Prize lectr 1989); hon professorial fell Academia Sinica 1985, sesquicentenary hon fell Royal Microscopical Soc 1989, hon bencher Gray's Inn London 1986, foreign hon memb US Acad of Arts and Scis Boston 1990, hon foreign assoc Engrg Acad Japan 1991, hon foreign fell American Philosophical Soc 1993, hon foreign memb Russian Acad of Scis 1994, hon foreign corr memb Nat Acad of Scis Venezuela 1994, hon assoc Third World Acad of Scis 1995; Royal Soc of Chemistry: Solid State Chemistry Medal 1978, Hugo Muller Medal 1989, Faraday Medal 1989, vice pres Faraday Div 1989; Chemical Soc London: Corday Medal 1969, Tilden Medal 1973; Messel Prize Soc of Chemical Indust 1992, Willard Gibbs Medal American Chemical Soc 1995; Hon LLD: Univ of Wales 1984, CNAA 1987; Hon DSc: Heriot-Watt Univ 1989, Univ of Birmingham 1991, Univ of Lyon 1994, Univ of Western Ontario 1995, Univ of Glamorgan 1995; Hon DUniv Open Univ 1991, Dr(hc) Universidad Complutense 1994; memb Editorial Bd Int Review of Physical Chemistry 1989–; memb Bd of Tstees: Nat History Museum 1987–91, Sci Museum 1990–; memb: Advsy Cncl of Applied Research and Devpt Cabinet Office 1982–85, Governing Body Sci Centre Alexandria Univ Egypt 1982–88, Main Ctee UK SERC 1986–90, Chemrawn Ctee Int Union of Pure and Applied Chemistry 1988– (chm 1988–91), Academia Europaea 1989; fndr memb Ctee on the Popularisation of Sci Royal Soc Royal Instn and Br Assoc 1986–91; ind memb Radioactive Waste Mgmnt Advsy Ctee 1980–82; fell: Indian Acad Bangalore 1981, Indian Nat Acad New Dehli 1985; FRS 1977 (Bakerian lectr and Prize 1990, Davy Medal 1994); *Publications* Introduction to the Principles of Heterogeneous Catalysis (with W J Thomas, 1967, Russian edn, 1969), Surface and Defect Properties of Solids (vols 1–6, contrib and co-ed with M W Roberts, 1972–77), Chemical Physics of Solids and their Surfaces (vol 7 and 8, contrib and co-ed with M W Roberts, 1978–80), Pan Edrychwyf Ar Y Nefoedd, Annual BBC Welsh Lecture (1978), Characterization of Catalysts (contrib and co-ed with R M Lambert, 1980), Proceedings of the Royal Institution of Great Britain (vols 58–63, 1986–91), The Microstructure and Properties of Catalysts (contrib and co-ed with M M J Treacy and J M White, 1988), Michael Faraday and his Contemporaries, National Portrait Gallery handlist booklet (with Sir Brian Pippard, 1991), Michael Faraday and the Royal Institution: The Genius of Man and Place (1991, Japanese edn 1994), The Legacy of Sir Lawrence Bragg (contrib and co-ed with Sir David Phillips, 1991), Perspectives in Catalysis: Theory and Practice (contrib and co-ed with K I Zamaraev, 1992), New Methods of Modelling Processes Within Solids and on their Surfaces (co-ed with C R A Catlow and A M Stoneham, 1993), Heterogeneous Catalysis: Theory and Practice (with W J Thomas, 1995); *Style*— Prof Sir John Meurig Thomas, FRS; ✉ The Master's Lodge, Peterhouse, Cambridge CB2 1RD (☎ 01223 338202, fax 01223 337578); Davy Faraday Research Laboratory, Royal Institution of Great Britain, 21 Albemarle Street, London W1X 4BS (☎ 0171 409 2992, fax 0171 629 3569)

THOMAS, Judyth Jacqueline; da of Ernest Vivian Mason (d 1954), of Stockton-on-Tees, and Grace Helen Mason, JP, *née* White (d 1991); *b* 14 Sept 1939; *Educ* Harrogate Coll; *m* 1, 4 April 1964, Anthony Robert Graham-Bowman (d 1988), s of Lt-Col Gerald Wilberforce Graham-Bowman, OBE, MC, DL (d 1968), of Carlisle; 1 da (Vanessa Elizabeth b 29 May 1965); m 2, 3 April 1995, (David) Michael Harries Thomas, s of David Gwilym Thomas, of Cardigan; *Career* fndr memb North Tees Community Health Cncl 1974–81, memb Cleveland FPC 1982–85, nat chm Nat Assoc for Welfare of Children in Hosp 1987–89 (memb Exec Ctee 1985–89), vice chm North Tees DHA 1989–91 (memb 1981–91), chm North Tees Health NHS Tst 1991–, memb Bd of Mgmnt Children's Fndn (Newcastle upon Tyne) 1990–91, govr Univ of Teesside 1994–, Home Sec's rep Selection Panel Independent Membs of Cleveland Police Authy 1994–; JP Teesside Bench 1984–93; *Recreations* opera-going, collecting antique maps, needlepoint, reading; *Style*— Mrs Michael Thomas; ✉ 84 Wimpole Road, Fairfield Park, Stockton-on-Tees, Cleveland TS19 7LR (☎ 01642 580122)

THOMAS, Kate; JP, DL (Mid Glamorgan 1989); da of Dillwyn Evans (d 1974), of Cardiff, and Dorothy Nelle, *née* Bullock; *b* 20 May 1944; *Educ* Cheltenham Ladies' Coll, Sorbonne; *m* 21 Jan 1967, Edward Vaughan Thomas, s of Edward Thomas; 2 s (Richard Edward b 7 Feb 1969, Robert Dillwyn b 12 Jan 1971); *Career* dir Penywaun Farms Ltd Nelson Mid Glamorgan; Prince's Tst: chm S Wales 1988–95, currently chm Bro area and memb Advsy Cncl; currently memb: HRH Prince of Wales Co-ordinating Ctee, Welsh Bd Business in the Community, S Wales Bd Prince's Youth Business Tst; chm: Mid Glamorgan HA 1994–96, Mid Glamorgan FHSA 1990–94; currently chm Bro Taf HA; dep pres Mid Glamorgan Red Cross 1983–85, memb Mid Glamorgan War Pensions Ctee 1984–90; High Sheriff of Mid Glamorgan 1986–87, currently Vice Lord Lt Mid Glamorgan; *Recreations* farming and reading; *Style*— Mrs Edward Thomas, JP, DL; ✉ Gelli Hir, Nelson, Treharris CF46 6PL; Bro Taf Health Authority, Churchill House, Churchill Way, Cardiff CF1 4TW (☎ 01222 226216, fax 01222 222307)

THOMAS, Keith Henry Westcott; CB (1982), OBE (1962); s of Henry Westcott Thomas (d 1957), and Norah Dorothy, *née* Stone (d 1985); *b* 20 May 1923; *Educ* Southern Secdy Sch for Boys Portsmouth, Royal Dockyard Sch Portsmouth, RN Engrg Coll Manadon, RNC Greenwich; *m* 31 Aug 1946, Brenda Jeanette, da of William Royston Crofton (d 1964); 2 s (Michael b 1948, David b 1951); *Career* RCNC: asst constructor Admty Experiment Works Haslar 1946–49, professional sec to Dir of Naval Construction Admty 1949–52, constructor Admty (HM Yacht Britannia) 1952–53, constructor on staff of Dir Tactical and Staff Requirements Div Admty 1953–56, constructor large carrier design Admty Bath 1956–60, constructor HM Dockyard Portsmouth 1960–63, chief constructor 1963–66, dep planning mangr HM Dockyard Devonport 1966–68 (project mangr 1968–70), dir gen Naval Design Canberra Aust 1970–73, planning mangr HM Dockyard Rosyth 1973–75 (gen mangr 1975–77), gen mangr HM Dockyard Devonport 1977–79, chief exec Royal Dockyards (head RCNC) 1979–83, ret 1983; chm Portsmouth Royal Dockyard Historical Tst; FEng 1981, FRINA 1970, FIMgt 1981; *Recreations* painting, music, lapidary; *Style*— Keith Thomas, Esq, CB, OBE, FEng; ✉ 6 Wyborn Close, Hayling Island, Hants PO11 9HY (☎ 01705 463 435)

THOMAS, Sir Keith Vivian; kt (1988); s of Vivian Jones Thomas (d 1987), and Hilda Janet Eirene, *née* Davies (d 1979); *b* 2 Jan 1933; *Educ* Barry Co GS, Balliol Coll Oxford (MA, hon fell 1984); *m* 16 Aug 1961, Valerie June, da of Eric Charles Little, of Beaconsfield, Bucks; 1 s (Edmund b 1965), 1 da (Emily b 1963); *Career* fell: All Souls Coll Oxford 1955–57, St John's Coll Oxford 1957–86 (hon fell 1986), prof of modern history Univ of Oxford 1986 (reader 1978–85), pres CCC Oxford 1986–, pro vice chllr Univ of Oxford 1988–; del OUP 1980–; memb: ESRC 1985–90, Reviewing Ctee on Exports of Works of Art 1990–93, Royal Cmmn on Historical MSS 1992–; tstee Nat Gallery 1991–; Hon DLitt: Univ of Kent 1983, Univ of Wales 1987, Univ of Hull 1995, Univ of Leicester 1996, Univ of Sussex 1996; Hon LLD Williams Coll Mass 1988; Hon LittD: Univ of Sheffield 1992, Univ of Cambridge 1995; hon fell Univ of Wales Cardiff 1995; foreign hon memb American Acad of Arts and Sci 1983; FRHistS 1970 (jt literary dir 1970–74, memb Cncl 1975–78, vice pres 1980–84), FBA 1979 (memb Cncl 1985–88, pres 1993–), memb Academia Europaea 1993; Cavaliere Ufficiale Ordine al Merito della Repubblica Italiana 1991; *Books* Religion and the Decline of Magic (1971), Man and the Natural World (1983); *Recreations* visiting secondhand bookshops; *Style*— Sir Keith Thomas, PBA; ✉ The President's Lodgings, Corpus Christi College, Oxford OX1 4JE (☎ 01865 250738); Corpus Christi College, Oxford OX1 4JF (☎ 01865 276739, fax 01865 793121)

THOMAS, Leslie John; s of David James Thomas, MN (ka 1943), and Dorothy Hilda Court (d 1943); *b* 22 March 1931; *Educ* Dr Barnardo's Kingston-on-Thames, Kingston Tech Sch; *m* 1, 1956 (m dis 1970), Maureen, da of Charles Crane; 2 s (Mark, Gareth), 1 da (Lois); m 2, Nov 1971, Diana Miles; 1 s (Matthew); *Career* Nat Serv Singapore, Malaya 1949–51; journalist 1951–63: Exchange Telegraph 1955–57, London Evening News 1957–63; many radio and TV appearances; Hon MA Univ of Wales 1995; *Television Plays and Documentaries* incl: Great British Isles (C4 series, also presented, 1989); *Novels* The Virgin Soldiers (1966), Orange Wednesday (1967), The Love Beach (1968), Come to the War (1969), His Lordship (1970), Onward Virgin Soldiers (1971), Arthur McCann and All His Women (1972), The Man with Power (1973), Tropic of Ruislip (1974), Stand Up Virgin Soldiers (1975), Dangerous Davies (1976), Bare Nell (1977), Ormerod's Landing (1978), That Old Gang of Mine (1979), The Magic Army (1981), The Dearest and the Best (1984), The Adventures of Goodnight and Loving (1986), Dangerous in Love (1987), Orders for New York (1989), The Loves and Journeys of Revolving Jones (1991), Arrivals and Departures (1992), Dangerous By Moonlight (1993), Running Away (1994), Kensington Heights (1995); *Non-Fiction* Some Lovely Islands (1968), The Hidden Places of Britain (1981), A World of Islands (1983); *Autobiographies* This Time Next Week (1964), In My Wildest Dreams (1984); *Recreations* cricket, music, antiques, stamp collecting; *Clubs* MCC, Lord's Taverners, Wig and Pen; *Style*— Leslie Thomas, Esq

THOMAS, Prof Lyn Carey; s of William Carey Thomas (d 1994), of Mid Glamorgan, and Eunice, *née* Morgan (d 1968); *b* 10 Aug 1946; *Educ* The Lewis Sch, Jesus Coll Oxford (Dip in Mathematics, MA, DPhil); *m* 30 July 1970, Margery Wynn, da of Frederick James Bright; 2 s (Matthew James Carey b 22 June 1974, Stephen Daniel Adam b 10 April 1980), 1 da (Elizabeth Angharad b 29 Sept 1976); *Career* Pilcher sr res fell Dept of Mathematics Univ Coll Swansea 1973–74 (res fell 1971–73), lectr then sr lectr in decision theory Univ of Manchester 1974–85, prof of mgmnt science Univ of Edinburgh 1985–; NRC sr res assoc Naval Postgrad Sch Montery 1982–83; memb: Operational Res Soc 1974 (pres 1994 and 1995), Operations Res Soc of America 1979, Edinburgh Mathematical Soc 1985; FRSE 1989, FIMA 1989; *Books* Games, Theory and Applications (1984), Operational Research Techniques (1986), Credit Scoring and Credit Control (1992); *Recreations* reading, walking, rugby; *Style*— Prof Lyn Thomas, FRSE; ✉ 8 Fernielaw Avenue, Edinburgh EH13 0EE (☎ 0131 441 1202); Department of Business Studies, University of Edinburgh EH8 9JY (☎ 0131 650 3798, fax 0131 668 3053)

THOMAS, Sir (John) Maldwyn; kt (1984); s of Daniel Thomas (d 1930), and Gwladys Thomas Davies (d 1954); *b* 17 June 1918; *Educ* Porth Glamorgan GS; *m* 1975, Maureen Elizabeth; *Career* called to the Bar Gray's Inn 1954 (re-admitted 1986), admitted slr 1965; chm Rank Xerox Ltd 1972–79 (co sec 1964, md 1970), dir Xerox Corporation 1974–79, non-exec dir Int Military Servs 1978–84; non-exec dep chm John Brown plc 1984–86, non-exec dir Westland plc 1985–94; pres London Welsh Assoc 1994–, vice pres London Welsh Rugby FC, tstee London Welsh Sch 1989–; FCIS 1947 (ACIS 1943); *Clubs* Reform, National Liberal; *Style*— Sir Maldwyn Thomas; ✉ 9 Chester Terrace, Regent's Park, London NW1 4ND (☎ 0171 486 4368)

THOMAS, Margaret; da of Francis Stewart Thomas (d 1971), of London, and Grace Darling, *née* Whetherly (d 1978); *b* 26 Sept 1916; *Educ* Slade, Royal Acad Schs; *Career* artist and painter; solo shows: Leicester Galleries London (1949 and 1951), five shows at Aitken Dotts and Scot Gallery Edinburgh (1952–82), Howard Roberts Cardiff, Canaletto Gallery London, Minories Colchester, Mall Galleries London, Octagon Gallery Belfast, Sally Hunter Fine Arts (1988, 1991 and 1995), Maltings Concert Hall Gallery Snape; work in numerous public collections incl: Chantrey Bequest, Miny of Educn, Robert Fleming Holdings Ltd, Lloyd's of London, Exeter Coll Oxford, Univ of Bath, Scot Nat Orchestra, Edinburgh City Corp, Mitsukshi Ltd Tokyo, Warburg & Co; regular exhibitor at Royal Acad and Royal Scot Acad (painting purchased by HRH Prince Philip), winner Hunting Gp award Oil Painting of the Year 1981; memb: Royal W of Eng Acad, RBA, NEAC; *Recreations* gardening, dogs, vintage cars; *Style*— Miss Margaret Thomas; ✉ 8 North Bank St, Edinburgh (☎ 0131 225 3343); Ellingham Mill, Bungay, Suffolk (☎ 01508 518656); 13a North Road, Highgate Village, London N6 4BD (☎ 0181 340 2527)

THOMAS, Martin Robert; s of Philip Anthony Thomas, of Warmington, Oxon, and Joan, *née* Edwards; *b* 2 July 1964; *Educ* N Leamington Sch, Jesus Coll Oxford (BA); *m* 1 April 1995, Alison, da of Derek Field; *Career* account mangr Paragon Communications 1987–89, exec Brunswick Public Relations 1989–90; Cohn & Wolfe: account dir 1990–93, bd dir 1993–94, jt md 1994–; *Recreations* rugby, beer and other cultural activities; *Style—* Martin Thomas, Esq; ✉ Cohn & Wolfe Ltd, Communications House, 48 Leicester Square, London WC2H 7LJ (☎ 0171 331 5300, fax 0171 331 9083)

THOMAS, Meyric Leslie; OBE (1987), DL (W Glamorgan 1993); s of Lt-Col Charles Leslie Thomas (d 1979), of Horton, Gower, Glamorgan, and Edith Annie Thomas (d 1983); *b* 17 Nov 1928; *Educ* Clifton, Jesus Coll Oxford (MA); *m* 2 March 1956, Jillian Hamilton, da of Lt-Col Robert William Armstrong (d 1975), of Oxford; 2 s (Peter Leslie b 1956, Charles Leslie b 1958), 1 da (Clare Leslie b 1960); *Career* Nat Serv 2 Lt Glos Regt 1947–49; admitted slr 1953, ptnr LC Thomas & Son 1953–91 (conslt 1991–); clerk Neath Harbour Cmmrs' Neath Div Income Tax Cmmrs; Oxford Rowing blue 1952 and 1953, pres OUBC 1953, former pres and chm Neath RFC; pres: Neath Br Legion, Neath Cons Assoc; *Clubs* Vincent's, Neath Constitutional; *Style—* Meyric Thomas, Esq, OBE, DL; ✉ 13 Westernmoor Rd, Neath, SA11 1BJ (☎ 01639 643322); L C Thomas & Son, 19 London Rd, Neath, SA11 1LF (☎ 01639 645061, fax 01639 646792)

THOMAS, Sir (Godfrey) Michael David; 11 Bt (E 1694), of Wenvoe, Glamorganshire; s of Rt Hon Sir Godfrey John Vignoles, 10 Bt, PC, GCVO, KCB, CSI (d 1968); *b* 10 Oct 1925; *Educ* Harrow; *m* 1956, Margaret Greta, da of John Cleland, of Stormont Court, Godden Green, Sevenoaks; 1 s, 2 da (of whom 1 s and 1 da are twins); *Heir* s, David John Godfrey Thomas; *Career* Capt The Rifle Bde 1944–56; memb Stock Exchange 1959–88; *Clubs* MCC, Hurlingham; *Style—* Sir Michael Thomas, Bt; ✉ 2 Napier Avenue, London SW6 3PS (☎ 0171 736 6896)

THOMAS, Michael David; CMG (1985), QC (1973); s of D Cardigan Thomas and Kathleen Thomas; *b* 8 Sept 1933; *Educ* Chigwell Sch Essex, LSE; *m* 1, 1958 (m dis 1978), Jane Lena Mary, eldest da of late Francis Neate; 2 s, 2 da; m 2, 1981 (m dis 1986), Mrs Gabrielle Blakemore; m 3, 1988, Baroness Dunn (Life Peeress), *qv*; *Career* called to the Bar Middle Temple 1955 (bencher 1982), jr counsel to Treasury in admiralty matters 1966–73, wreck cmmr and salvage arbitrator Lloyd's 1974–83, attorney-gen Hong Kong 1983–88; memb of Exec and Legislative Cncls Hong Kong 1983–88; *Style—* Michael Thomas, Esq, CMG, QC

THOMAS, Prof Michael Frederic; s of Hugh Frederic Thomas (d 1987), and Kathleen Helena Doris, *née* Phelps (d 1981); *b* 15 Sept 1933; *Educ* Royal GS Guildford, Univ of Reading (BA, MA), Univ of London (PhD); *m* 29 Dec 1956, (Elizabeth) Anne (d 1992), da of Harry Guest Dadley (d 1955); 1 s (Graham Hugh b 31 Oct 1959), 1 da (Gillian Anne b 31 March 1965); *Career* asst lectr Magee Univ Coll Londonderry NI 1957–60, lectr Univ of Ibadan 1960–64, sr lectr in geography Univ of St Andrews 1974–79 (lectr 1964–74), fndn prof of environmental sci Univ of Stirling 1980–; memb: Cncl Royal Scot Geographical Soc (and convener Research Ctee), Bd of Dirs Scot Environmental Educn Cncl, Scottish Examinations Bd 1992–, Exec Scottish Cncl for Nat Parks 1994–; FGS 1985, FRSE 1988; *Books* Environment & Land Use in Africa (jtly and jt ed, 1969), Tropical Geomorphology (1974), Land Assessment in Scotland (jt ed, 1980), Evaluation of Land Resources in Scotland (jtly and jt ed, 1990), Geomorphology in the Tropics (1994); jt ed Catena (int jl) 1994–; *Recreations* listening to classical music, jazz, hill walking, travel; *Style—* Prof Michael Thomas, FRSE; ✉ Department of Environmental Science, University of Stirling, Stirling FK9 4LA (☎ 01786 467840, fax 01786 467843)

THOMAS, Prof Michael James; *b* 15 July 1933; *Educ* King Edward's Sch Birmingham, UCL (BSc), Graduate Sch of Business Indiana Univ (MBA); *m* Nancy, *née* Yeoman; 1 s (Huw), 1 da (Helen); *Career* cmmnd Br Army 1952, served Royal Warwickshire Regt, seconded W African Frontier Force Nigeria Regt 1952–53, army res offr 1953–56; market res mangr The Metal Box Co Ltd London 1957–60, Faculty Sch of Mgmnt Syracuse Univ 1960–71 (assoc prof); Univ of Lancaster 1971–86: head Dept of Mktg 1972–77, dep chm Sch of Mgmnt 1975–79, memb Univ Cncl 1979–85; prof Univ of Strathclyde 1987– (head Dept of Mktg 1988–92); visiting prof: Syracuse Univ 1977, Univ of Nigeria 1979, Temple Univ Philadelphia 1980, Univ of Gdansk 1977, Georgetown Univ Washington 1996, Helsinki Sch of Economics 1996; ldr Strathclyde Consortium (Polish Know-How Fund) 1991–; md Silverdale Ltd (editorial prints); memb Bd CFM Technologies; sr consIt: Silverdale Marketing Consultants, International, Alliance of Univs for Democracy, American Marketing Assoc; dep chm Gas Consumers' Cncl for the Northwest 1977–86; chm of mktg: Educn Bd Inst of Mktg 1979–86, Mktg Educn Gp of GB and Ireland 1986–90; nat chm Chartered Inst of Mktg 1995, bd dir Chartered Institute of Marketing Charitable Trust; ed Mktg Intelligence and Planning Jl; memb Editorial Bd: Jl of Marketing Mgmnt, Jl of Int Marketing, Jl of East-West Business, Jl of Brand Mgmnt, Jl of Mktg Practice; chm Jt Parish Ctee Arnside-Silverdale Area of Outstanding Nat Beauty 1975–85; OM (Poland) 1995; FRSA, FCIM; *Books* International Marketing Management (1969), International Marketing (1971), Modern Marketing Management (1970–73), Management Sales and Marketing Training (contrib, 1984), The Pocket Guide to Marketing (1986), The Marketing Book (contrib, 1987), The Marketing Digest (1988), The Marketing Handbook (4 edn, 1995); *Recreations* book collecting, bird watching, the study of Polish politics; *Clubs* Scottish Ornithologists, Indiana Univ Int Business Forum; *Style—* Prof Michael Thomas; ✉ Department of Marketing, University of Strathclyde, Stenhouse Building, 173 Cathedral St, Glasgow G4 0RQ (☎ 0141 552 4400, fax 0141 552 2802, telex 77472 UNSLIB G)

THOMAS, Col Michael John Glyn; s of Glyn Pritchard Thomas (d 1985), and Mary, *née* Moseley (d 1987); *b* 14 Feb 1938; *Educ* Haileybury and ISC, Univ of Cambridge (MA, MB BChir), Bart's; *m* 23 May 1969, (Sheelagh) Jane, da of Harold Thorpe (d 1979); 1 da (Fleur b 1970); *Career* RMO 2 Bn Para Regt 1964–67, trainee in pathology BMH Singapore 1967–71; specialist in pathology: Colchester MH 1971–74, Singapore 1974–76; sr specialist in pathology and 2 i/c Army Blood Supply Depot (ABSD) 1977–82, exchange fell Walter Reed Army Medical Centre Washington DC 1982–83, offr i/c Leishman Lab 1984–87, CO ABSD 1987–94; private consIt in transfusion medicine and clinical dir The Blood Care Foundation 1995–; memb BMA: Cncl 1973–74 and 1977–82, Central Ethical Ctee 1976–82 (chm 1977–82), Armed Forces Ctee 1971–82 and 1988–93, Jr Membs Forum 1971–78 (chm 1974), Bd of Sci and Educn 1987–93, Rep Body 1972–82 and 1987–93, Expert Ctee on AIDS 1986–, EEC Ctee 1989–93; expert witness on gene mapping ESC, jt patent holder of new method of freezing blood together with special bag in which it is frozen; memb: Br Blood Transfusion Soc 1987 (fndr chm Autologous Transfusion Special Interest Group 1992–), Int Soc of Blood Transfusion 1988, Inst of Medical Ethics 1987, Euro Sch of Transfusion Med (faculty memb) 1993 (faculty memb Slovenia 1997); LMSSA, DTM & H; *Books* co-author: Control of Infection (1989), Nuclear Attack, Ethics and Casualty Selection (1988), Handbook of Medical Ethics (1979 and subsequent edns), Our Genetic Future, Medicine Betrayed, A Code of Practice for the Safe Use and Disposal of Sharps · Dictionary of Medical Ethics (contrib), AIDS and Human Rights a UK Perspective (contrib), Wylie and Churchill Davidson's A Practice of Anaesthesia (contrib chapter on Autologous Transfusion), Cryopreservation and Freeze-Drying Protocols (contrib chapter on Cryopreservation of Human Red Blood Cells), Transfusion in Europe (contrib); *Recreations* DIY, photography, philately; *Clubs* Tanglin (Singapore); *Style—* Dr Michael J G Thomas; ✉ The White Cottage, Warren Corner, Farnham, Surrey GU10 5AT (☎ 01252 850389, fax 01252 851828, e-mail 101621.343@compuserve.com)

THOMAS, Sir (William) Michael Marsh; 3 Bt (UK 1918), of Garreglwyd, Anglesey; s of Major Sir William Eustace Rhyddlad Thomas, 2 Bt, MBE (d 1958), and Enid Helena Marsh (d 1982); *b* 4 Dec 1930; *Educ* Oundle; *m* 1957, Geraldine, da of Robert Drysdale, of Trearddur Bay, Anglesey; 3 da; *Heir* none; *Career* formerly md Gors Nurseries Ltd; *Style—* Sir Michael Thomas, Bt; ✉ Belan Fawr, Rhosneigr, Anglesey, Gwynedd LL64 5JE (☎ 01407 810541)

THOMAS, Michael Stuart (Mike); s of Arthur Edward Thomas, and Mona, *née* Parker; *b* 24 May 1944; *Educ* Latymer Upper Sch, King's Sch Macclesfield, Univ of Liverpool (BA); *m* 31 July 1975, Maureen Theresa, da of Denis Kelly; 1 s by previous m (Paul b 1973); *Career* pres Liverpool Univ Guild of Undergrads 1965, formerly memb Nat Exec NUS, head Res Dept Co-op Pty 1966–68, sr res assoc Policy Studies Inst 1968–73, dir The Volunteer Centre 1973–74; MP (Lab and Co-op 1974–81, SDP 1981–83) Newcastle upon Tyne East 1974–83; PPS to Rt Hon Roy Hattersley MP 1974–76, memb Commons Select Ctee on Nationalised Industs 1975–79, chm PLP Trade Gp 1979–81, SDP spokesman on Health and Social Security 1981–83; Parly candidate (SDP): Newcastle upon Tyne East 1983, Exeter 1987; memb: SDP Policy Ctee 1981–83 and 1984–90, SDP Nat Ctee 1981–90; chm SDP: Orgn Ctee 1981–88, Fin Ctee 1988–89; communications mgmnt consIt 1978–; chm Burnaby Communications and Information Services Ltd 1978–; dir: Dewe Rogerson Ltd 1984–88, BR Western Region 1985–92; md Corporate Communications Strategy 1988–; chm: Media Audits Ltd 1990–, Fotorama Ltd 1995–; dir Education 2000 1991–94; fndr Parliament's weekly jl The House Magazine 1976, ed The BBC Guide to Parliament 1979 and 1983, author of various articles, reviews and pamphlets; memb USDAW; *Recreations* collecting election pottery and medals, gardening, walking, countryside, music, opera, theatre, fine arts and architecture; *Style—* Mike Thomas, Esq; ✉ Media Audits Ltd, 16 Dufours Place, London W1V 1FE (☎ 0171 734 4080, fax 0171 439 2455)

THOMAS, Michael Tilson; *b* 21 Dec 1944; *Educ* Univ of Southern California; *Career* conductor; studied under Ingolf Dahl, John Crown and Alice Ehlers; music dir Young Musicians' Foundation Debut Orch 1963, asst conductor then principal guest conductor Boston Symphony Orch 1969–74, conductor New York Philharmonic Young People's Concerts 1971–77, music dir Buffalo Philharmonic 1971–79, princ guest conductor Los Angeles Philharmonic 1981–85, fndr New World Symphony (trg orchestra for young musicians USA) 1988, princ conductor LSO 1988–95 (princ guest conductor 1995–), music dir San Francisco Symphony Orch 1995–; recordings incl: Copland orchestral works 1986, Tchaikovsky, Liszt and Rachmaninov Piano Concertos 1986, Mahler Symphony No 3 1987, Kurt Weill Seven Deadly Sins and Little Threepenny Opera 1987, Ravel orchestral works 1988, John McLaughlin Guitar Concerto 1988, Prokofiev Piano Concertos Nos 1 and 2 1988, Steve Reich The Four Sections 1988, Brahms Serenades 1989, Haydn Variations 1989, Tchaikovsky Swan Lake 1990, Janacek Glagolitic Mass 1990, Debussy orchestral works 1991, Tavener Dance Lament of the Repentent Thief 1991, Ives Three Places in New England 1992, Bernstein On the Town 1992, Strauss Lieder 1993, Schumann and Grieg Piano Concertos 1993, Shostakovich Concertos Nos 1 and 2 1993, Bartok Violin Concerto No 2 1993, Copland Quiet City and Emily Dickinson Songs 1994, Barber orchestral works 1994; television: Discovery concerts with LSO (BBC), On the Town 1993 (winner of Gramophone Award for Best Musical Recording), Concerto! (with Dudley Moore, Channel 4/BMG 1993); festivals with LSO (Barbican Centre): The Gershwin Years 1987, The Flight of the Firebird 1989, Steve Reich Series 1989, Childhood 1991, Takemitsu Festival 1991, The Mahler Festival 1994 and 1995; opera (with LSO): Rimsky-Korsakov Mlada 1989, L'Enfant et Les Sortilèges 1991, Bernstein On the Town 1992, La Bohème 1994; Robin Holloway Concerto No 3 (world première) 1996; tours with LSO incl: Shell LSO UK Tour 1986, Salzburg Summer Festival 1988 and 1991, USA, Japan 1989, 1991 and 1992, Canary Islands 1989, Pacific Music Festival Sapporo Japan 1990, Israel and Salzburg Whitsun Festival 1991, USA and several Euro visits 1992, Austria, Germany and USA 1993, Italy, Spain 1994, Japan, Vienna 1995; *Style—* Michael Tilson Thomas, Esq; ✉ c/o Columbia Artists Management Ltd, 28 Cheverton Road, London N19 3AY (☎ 0171 272 8020, fax 0171 272 8991)

THOMAS, Neil Philip; s of Simon David Thomas, of 149 Stanmore Hill, Stanmore, Middx, and Jessie, *née* Blagborough; *b* 29 April 1950; *Educ* Stowe, Univ of London (BSc); *m* 1, 25 Jan 1974, Mary Josephine Christian (d 1977), da of A V M Patrick Joseph O'Connor, CB, OBE; 1 da (Joanna b 19 June 1977); m 2, 29 April 1979, Julia Vera, da of J J Ashken; 1 s (James b 17 March 1981), 1 da (Gemma b 15 Oct 1982); *Career* late sr registrar in orthopaedics: Royal Nat Orthopaedic Hosp, UCH and the Westminster Hosp; consIt orthopaedic surgn N Hampshire Hosp; memb: Int Knee Soc, Euro Soc of Knee and Arthroscopic Surgery; sec Br Assoc of Surgery of the Knee 1993–; RCS rep Engrg in Med Gp Ctee; Sir Herbert Seddon Prize and Medal 1986, President's Medal Br Assoc of Surgery of the Knee 1985–86; FRCS 1978, FRSM, fell Br Orthopaedic Assoc; *Recreations* golf, horticulture, wine; *Style—* Neil Thomas, Esq; ✉ Little Bullington House, Bullington, Sutton Scotney, Winchester, Hampshire SO21 3QQ (☎ 01962 760233); The Hampshire Clinic, Basing Rd, Basingstoke, Hampshire (☎ 01256 819222)

THOMAS, Neil Roderick; MBE (1995); s of Christopher George Thomas, of Welshampton, Shrops, and Gladys, *née* Havers; *b* 6 April 1968; *Educ* Adams Sch Wem Shrops, John Moores Univ Liverpool; *Career* gymnast; with N Staffs Gymnastics Club 1978–86; full-time trg: Liverpool Sch of PE 1986–89, Lilleshall Nat Sports Centre 1989–; achievements incl: debut int for English Schs Gymnastics Assoc aged 12, nat age gp under 12 and 13 champion, memb Eng and Br sch squads, memb GB squad Jr Euro Championships 1984 and 1986, debut sr int Moscow News Tournament 1986, nat all around champion 1990–91 and 1992–93 (holder of all 6 apparatus titles), Bronze medal vault Euro Championships 1990 (first GB medal for 32 years), first Britain to compete in World Cup (Brussels 1990), Gold medal floor and Silver medal team Cwlth Games 1990, first Britain to compete in a World Championship final (floor event 1991), GB rep Olympic Games 1992, Silver medal floor exercise World Chamionships Birmingham 1993 (first ever Br world championship medal), Silver medal floor exercise World Championships Brisbane 1994, Gold medal floor exercise and Gold medal all-round event Cwlth Games 1994; awarded Federation International de Gymnastique World Class Pin 1989; *Recreations* true crime stories; *Style—* Neil Thomas, Esq, MBE; ✉ 10 Welsh View, Welshampton, Ellesmere, Shropshire SY12 0PZ (☎ 0194 875 478); Lilleshall National Sports Centre, Ford Hall, nr Newport, Shropshire TF10 9NG (☎ 01952 677137, fax 01952 820326)

THOMAS, Lt Cdr Neil Ronald Lindley; RD (1969, and Clasp 1980); s of Henry Ronald Thomas (d 1989), and Edith Lindley (d 1992); *b* 31 Jan 1934; *Educ* Wallasey GS, Jesus Coll Cambridge; *Career* Nat Serv RN 1953–55, Sub Lt RNR 1955, Lt RNR 1958, Lt Cdr RNR 1966, ret 1985; mgmnt trainee N Greening and Sons Warrington (wire weavers and metal perforators) 1957, various mgmnt posts in sales 1959–76, fund raiser Voluntary and Christian Serv (Help the Aged) 1977–78, dir Serve Wirral (youth trg) 1979, sec and chief exec Serve Wirral Tst Co Ltd (charitable co providing vocational trg to young and unemployed) 1985–; Lib cncllr: Wallasey Borough Cncl 1971–74, Wirral Met Cncl (dep gp leader) 1973–79; Lib/Lib Dem Parly candidate: Ellesmere Port and Bebington 1974, Wallasey 1979 and 1992; chm Wallasey Constituency Lib Dems 1994–; dist commissioner for scouts Wallasey Dist 1973–79; capt: Wallasey GS Boat Club 1952–53, Liverpool Victoria Rowing Club (14 times) 1959–85; chm: Merseyside Regatta Ctee 1959–85, NW Rowing Cncl 1967–85 (former sec); memb Exec Amateur Rowing Assoc Cncl 1969–85 (divnl rep 1968–85), int rowing umpire 1972–, chm Nat Umpires' Commission 1976–, pres Amateur Rowing Assoc 1985–93 (hon life vice pres 1993–), chm Nat Assoc of Trg Agencies 1987–90, memb Exec Ctee NCVO 1992–93, sec Nat Trg Fedn 1993–96 (chm 1990–91); *Recreations* rowing, music, politics; *Clubs* Leander,

Liverpool Victoria Rowing (pres 1993–), Hollingworth Lake Rowing; *Style*— Lt Cdr Neil Thomas, RD; ✉ 7 Marine Terrace, Wallasey, Merseyside L45 7RE (☎ 0151 630 2533); Serve Wirral Trust Co Ltd, Liscard Hall, Central Park, Wallasey, Merseyside L44 0BT (☎ 0151 691 2070, fax 0151 691 1073)

THOMAS, (Robert) Neville; QC (1975); s of Robert Derfel Thomas (d 1983), of Clwyd, and Enid Anne, *née* Edwards (d 1990); *b* 31 March 1936; *Educ* Ruthin Sch, Univ of Oxford (MA, BCL); *m* 28 March 1970, Jennifer Anne, da of Philip Henry Akerman Brownrigg, CMG, DSO, OBE, TD, *qv*; 1 s (Gerran b 19 March 1973), 1 da (Meriel b 21 Aug 1975); *Career* Lt Intelligence Corps 1955–57; called to the Bar Inner Temple 1962, recorder of the Crown Ct 1975–82, master of the Bench Inner Temple 1985, head of chambers; *Recreations* fishing, walking, gardening; *Clubs* Garrick; *Style*— Neville Thomas, Esq, QC; ✉ Glansevern, Berriew, Welshpool, Powys; 38 Courtfield Gardens, London SW5; 3 Verulam Buildings, Gray's Inn, London WC1R 5NT (☎ 0171 831 8441, fax 0171 831 8479, telex 295119 LEXCOL G)

THOMAS, Nicholas Andrew; s of Stanley Thomas (d 1971), of Plymouth, Devon, and Phyllis Doreen, *née* Larman (d 1990); *b* 14 April 1953; *Educ* Kelly Coll Tavistock Devon, Exeter Coll Oxford (BA); *Career* admitted slr 1977; Macfarlanes: articled clerk 1975–77, asst slr 1977–82, ptnr 1982–95; memb: City of London Slrs Co, Law Soc; *Recreations* golf, walking, classical music, opera; *Style*— Nicholas Thomas, Esq; ✉ 10 Magnolia Wharf, Strand-on-the-Green, Chiswick, London W4 (☎ 0181 995 6921)

THOMAS, (James) Nigel; s of Charles Walter Thomas (d 1956), of Bradford, Yorks, and Kathleen, *née* Lister; *b* 11 May 1944; *Educ* Bradford GS, St Edmund Hall Oxford (MA), Univ of Oxford Med Sch (BM, BCh); *m* 1 April 1968, Gerda, da of Gustav Oelgeklaus (d 1967), of Lengerich, Westphalia, Germany; 1 s ((Charles Walter) Christian b 31 May 1978), 2 da ((Julia Elizabeth) Kirsten b 22 Sept 1970, (Heide Alicia) Katrin b 28 Aug 1972); *Career* conslt ENT specialist Groote Schuur Hosp Capetown SA 1974–76, first asst Radcliffe Infirmary Oxford 1976–79, conslt ENT surgn King's Coll 1979–; George Herbert Hunt fellowship Univ of Oxford 1978; memb Camberwell Health Authy, pres Osler House Club 1967–68; FRCS 1972; *Books* Mawson's Diseases of the Ear (contrib, 1988); *Recreations* rugby, squash, music; *Style*— Nigel Thomas, Esq; ✉ King's College Hospital, Denmark Hill, Camberwell, London SE5 9RS (☎ 0171 346 6130)

THOMAS, Prof Noel L'Estrange; s of Richard Gratton Thomas (d 1971), of Sale, Manchester, and Gladys L'Estrange (d 1978); *b* 5 Dec 1929; *Educ* Sale Co GS for Boys, Univ of Manchester (BA), Univ of Liverpool (MA), Univ of Salford (PhD); *m* 20 Feb 1954, Norma, da of Robert Brown (d 1950), of Manchester; 2 da (Katharine b 1962, Ruth b 1965); *Career* master Das erste Bundesrealgymnasium Graz 1951–52, asst master German Canon Slade GS Bolton 1959–64 (Holt HS for Boys Liverpool 1953–59); Univ of Salford Dept of Modern Languages: lectr in German 1964–73, sr lectr 1973–83, prof 1983–, chm 1984–89; visiting lectr Pädagogische Hochschule Erfurt 1993–94; dir Services for Export and Language; memb Conf of Univ Teachers of German, memb Assoc for Study of German Politics, memb AUT; *Books* Modern Prose Passages for Translation into German (with G Weischedel, 1968), Modern German Prose Passages (with G Weischedel, 1972), The Narrative Works of Günter Grass - a critical interpretation (1983), Interpreting as a Language Teaching Technique (ed with Richard Towell, 1985), Grass: Die Blechtrommel (1985), Grass: Katz und Maus (1992); *Recreations* fell walking, choral singing; *Style*— Prof Noel Thomas; ✉ 4 Forest Way, Bromley Cross, Bolton, Lancashire BL7 9YE (☎ 01204 591682); Department of Modern Languages, University of Salford, Salford M5 4WT (☎ 0161 745 5614, fax 0161 745 59999, telex 668680)

THOMAS, Norman; CBE; s of Bowen Thomas (d 1961), of Edmonton, London, and Ada, *née* Redding (d 1987); *b* 1 June 1921; *Educ* Latymer's Sch Edmonton, Camden Trg Coll; *m* 24 Dec 1942, Rose Matilda, da of Jack Henshaw (d 1954), of Islington, London; 1 s (Paul b 1955), 1 da (Jill (Mrs Singer) b 1947); *Career* various posts in commerce and indust 1936–47, primary sch teacher London and Herts 1948–56, primary sch head teacher Stevenage Herts 1956–61, HM inspr of schs Lincs and SE 1962–69, HM staff inspr of primary educn 1969–73, HM chief inspector of primary educn 1973–81, chm ILEA enquiry into primary educn in central London with report published 1985, advsr House of Commons Select Ctee 1984–86 and 1994–, memb Task Gp on Assessment and Testing in the Nat Curriculum 1987–88; hon prof Univ of Warwick 1987–94, visiting prof Univ of Hertfordshire (formerly Hatfield Poly) 1991–; contrib to various books on primary educn; *Books* Handbook of Primary Education in Europe (contrib 1989), Primary Education from Plowden to the 1990's (1990), Breadth and Balance in the Primary Curriculum (contrib, 1993); *Recreations* photography, reading; *Style*— Norman Thomas, Esq, CBE; ✉ 19 Langley Way, Watford, Herts WD1 3EJ (☎ 01923 223766)

THOMAS, Patricia Eileen; da of Ieuan Gwynn Thomas (d 1989), and Lovice Eileen, *née* Phillips; *b* 3 June 1949; *Educ* St Joseph's Convent Reading, St Hugh's Coll Oxford (MA); *Career* slr; ptnr: Denton Hall Burgin & Warrens (formerly Denton Hall & Burgin) 1982–88, S J Berwin & Co 1988–; former chm Environmental Law Ctee Int Bar Assoc; memb: Section on Business Law Int Bar Assoc, Planning Law Ctee and Environmental Law Sub Ctee Law Soc; memb Worshipful Co of Slrs; *Books* Surveyors Factbook (contrib 1990), Planning Factbook (ed and contrib 1991); *Recreations* architecture, fly-fishing, flying; *Style*— Miss Patricia Thomas; ✉ S J Berwin & Co, 222 Gray's Inn Rd, London WC1X 8HB (☎ 0171 533 2222, fax 0171 533 2000)

THOMAS, Pauline Ann; da of Rupert Augustus Thomas, of Georgia, USA, and Beryl Leone Thomas; *b* 6 Feb 1956; *Educ* Saker Baptist Coll and CCAST W Cameroon, LSE (LLB); *m* 19 April 1986, Stephen Neil Mobbs, s of Noel Edward Henry Mobbs, of Norwich, Norfolk; 3 c (Sarah Elizabeth b 31 Oct 1988, David Peter b 22 April 1991, Andrew Michael (twin) b 22 April 1991); *Career* mgmnt conslt Intermatrix Ltd 1984–86, practice devpt mangr Lovell White & King 1986–88, nat mktg mangr Grant Thornton 1989–95, writer/marketing conslt 1995–; *Recreations* travel, theatre, reading, classical music; *Style*— Ms Pauline Thomas; (☎ and fax 0171 794 2773)

THOMAS, Prof Peter David Garner; s of David Thomas (d 1967), and Doris, *née* Davies (d 1965); *b* 1 May 1930; *Educ* St Bees Sch Cumberland, Univ Coll of N Wales (BA, MA), UCL (PhD); *m* 1963 (m dis 1992), Sheila; 2 s (Alan b 1963, Michael b 1965, d 1983), 1 da (Sally b 1970); *Career* lectr Univ of Glasgow 1959–65 (asst lectr 1956–59); Univ Coll Wales: lectr 1965–68, sr lectr 1968–71, reader 1971–75, prof 1976–; chm: Dyfed LTA 1981–, Aberystwyth Lib Democrats 1988–; awarded Soc of Cincinnati Book Prize 1992; FRHistS 1971; *Books* The House of Commons in the Eighteenth Century (1971), British Politics and the Stamp Act Crisis (1975), Lord North (1976), The American Revolution (1986), The Townshend Duties Crisis (1987), Tea Party to Independence (1991), Revolution in America - Britain and the Colonies 1763–76 (1992), John Wilkes: A Friend to Liberty (1996); *Recreations* lawn tennis; *Style*— Prof Peter Thomas; ✉ 16 Pen-Y-Craig, Aberystwyth, Dyfed SY23 2JA (☎ 01970 612053); History Department, University College of Wales, Aberystwyth, Dyfed SY23 3DY (☎ 01970 622663)

THOMAS, Prof Peter Kynaston; CBE; *b* 28 June 1926; *Educ* UCL (scholar, BSc, Trotter medal in clinical surgery), Univ of London (MB BS, MRCP, MD, DSc); *m* 1977, Anita Elizabeth Harding (prof of clinical neurology Inst of Neurology Queen Square London; d 1995); *Career* Nat Serv RAMC 1952–54 (sec to Mil Personnel Research Ctee, graded specialist in physiology); jr hosp appts 1950–52 and 1954–61 (UCH, Middx and Nat Hosp Queen Square), asst prof of neurology McGill Univ Montreal, neurologist Montreal Gen Hosp and physician i/c EMG Dept Montreal Neurological Inst 1961–62; conslt neurologist (now hon conslt neurologist): Royal Free Hosp 1962–91, Nat Hosp for Neurology and Neurosurgery 1963–91, Royal Nat Orthopaedic Hosp 1965–74; pt/t sr lectr Univ Dept of Clinical Neurology Inst of Neurology Queen Square 1963–74, prof of neurology (now emeritus prof) Royal Free Hosp Sch of Med and Inst of Neurology Queen Square 1974–91; ed Jl of Anatomy, formerly ed Brain; memb: Assoc of Br Neurologists (past pres), Anatomical Soc of GB and Ireland (memb Cncl), American Neurological Assoc (hon memb), Australian Neurological Soc (hon memb), Canadian Neuroligcal Soc (hon memb), Euro Neurological Soc (past pres), Spanish Neurological Soc (hon memb), Polish Neurological Soc (hon memb), Austrian Soc of Neurology and Psychiatry (hon memb); Doctor (hc) Mil Med Acad Lódz Poland 1991; fell UCL; FRCP 1967, FRCPath 1990; *Style*— Prof P K Thomas, CBE; ✉ Consultant Neurologist, Royal Free Hospital, Pond Street, London NW3 3QG

THOMAS, Peter Roy; *b* 29 March 1946; *Career* Garland Compton Advertising 1968–70, Lyons Marketing 1970–72; chief exec: Purchasepoint 1972–90, Lopex plc 1990–; *Style*— Peter Thomas, Esq; ✉ Lopex plc, Wimbledon Bridge House, Hartfield Road, London SW19 3RU (☎ 0181 254 1790, fax 0181 254 1792)

THOMAS, Philip Owain; s of Prof James Edward Thomas, and Olwen, *née* Yolland; *b* 6 June 1961; *Educ* Hymers Coll Hull, Plymouth Art Coll; partner Colleen Teresa McDonnell, da of Joseph McDonnell; 1 s (Joseph Matthew McDonnell Thomas b 29 Oct 1991); *Career* photographic asst 1982–84, freelance photographer 1984, writer and features ed Practical Photography magazine 1984–87, features ed then asst ed SLR Photography 1987–88, freelance writer 1988–90, asst ed then ed Empire magazine 1990–93, managing ed Empire and Premier magazines 1994–96, publishing dir 1996–; writer of the yr PTC 1988, shortlisted for writer of the year PPA 1988 and 1992, eight awards won with EMAP PLC, shortlisted for ed of the year Br Soc of Magazine Editors 1992 and 1993; *Books* Photography in a Week (1992); *Recreations* cooking, talking, drinking wine, attempting to bring up a young family; *Style*— Philip Thomas, Esq; ✉ Empire Magazine, EMAP Metro, Mappin House, 4 Winsley Street, London W1N 7AR (☎ 0171 436 1515)

THOMAS, Prof Phillip Charles; s of William Charles Thomas (d 1984), of Abersychan, Gwent, and Gwendolen, *née* Emery (d 1986); *b* 17 June 1942; *Educ* Abersychan GS, Gwent, UCNW Bangor (BSc, PhD); *m* 1967, Pamela Mary, da of Leonard Hirst, of Huddersfield, W Yorks; 1 s (Adam James b 18 Nov 1975), 1 da (Rachel Louise b 9 Aug 1973); *Career* lectr Dept of Nutrition and Physiology Univ of Leeds 1966–71, head of Animal Nutrition and Prodn Dept Hannah Res Inst Ayr 1974–87 (res nutritionist 1971–74), prof of agric Univ of Glasgow 1987–, princ West of Scotland Coll 1987–90, princ and chief exec Scottish Agric Coll Edinburgh 1990–; hon prof Univ of Edinburgh 1991; memb: Nutrition Soc 1969, Biochemical Soc 1970, Br Soc for Animal Prodn 1981; FIBiol 1983 (MIBiol 1981), FRSE 1993; *Books* Silage for Milk Production (with J A F Rook, 1982), Nutritional Physiology of Farm Animals (with J A F Rook, 1983); *Recreations* watching rugby (formerly rep Caernarfonshire and N Wales); *Clubs* Farmers'; *Style*— Prof Phillip Thomas, FRSE; ✉ Scottish Agricultural College, Central Office, West Mains Road, Edinburgh EH9 3JG (☎ 0131 535 4001, fax 0131 535 4242)

THOMAS, Ralph Philip; MC (1942); *Educ* Telisford Sch Clifton; *m* 1944, Joy, *née* Spanjer; 1 s, 2 da; *Career* film director; WWII 1939–44 Maj 9 Lancers, Instr RMC 1944–46; film industry 1932–39 (all prodn depts incl editing), Rank Organisation Trailer Dept 1946–48, Gainsborough Pictures 1948–; dir: Once Upon a Dream, Travellers Joy; dir at Pinewood Studios: The Clouded Yellow, Appointment with Venus, The Venetian Bird, A Day To Remember, Doctor In The House, Mad About Men, Above Us The Waves, Doctor At Sea, The Iron Petticoat, Checkpoint, Doctor at Large, Campbell's Kingdom, A Tale of Two Cities, The Wind Cannot Read, The 39 Steps, Upstairs and Downstairs, Conspiracy of Hearts, Doctor In Love, No My Darling Daughter, No Love for Johnnie, The Wild and the Willing, Doctor In Distress, Hot Enough for June, The High Bright Sun, Doctor in Clover, Deadlier Than The Male, Nobody Runs Forever, Some Girls Do, Doctor In Trouble, Quest, Percy, It's a 2 foot 6 inch Above The Ground World, Percy's Progress, A Nightingale Sang in Berkeley Square, Doctor's Daughters, Pop Pirates; *Clubs* Garrick; *Style*— Ralph Thomas, Esq, MC

THOMAS, Dr Raymond Tudor; OBE (1994); s of Edgar William Thomas (d 1959), and Lilian Phylis, *née* Clift (d 1975); *b* 19 May 1946; *Educ* King's Sch Macclesfield, Jesus Coll Oxford (Meyricke exhibitioner, MA), Univ of the West Indies (Dip in Int Relations), Univ of Sussex (DPhil); *m* 23 April 1973, Gloria, da of Bernard Anthony Forsyth; 2 s (Max Richard b 23 July 1975, James Matthew b 28 April 1978); *Career* lectr Inst of Int Relations Trinidad 1970–71; British Council: asst rep Morocco 1974–77, Islamabad 1977–80 and Kuala Lumpur 1980–82, regnl rep Sabah 1982–84, projects offr Science, Technol and Educn Div 1984–86, dir Educnl Contracts Dept 1988–90 (dep dir 1986–88), dir EC Relations 1990–95, regnl dir Middle E and N Africa 1995–; dir and treas Lingua Assoc 1990–95, exec sec Euro Fndn for Educnl Capacity Transfer 1993–95, treas Office for Cooperation in Educn 1993–95, memb Euro Assoc for Int Educn; *Books* Britain and Vichy: The Dilemma of Anglo-French Relations 1940–42 (1979); *Recreations* family life, travel, reading, fly fishing; *Style*— Dr Raymond Thomas, OBE; ✉ The British Council, 10 Spring Gardens, London SW1A 2BN

THOMAS, HE Richard; CMG (1990); s of Anthony Hugh Thomas, JP, of Stone-In-Oxney, Tenterden, Kent and Molly, *née* Bourne, MBE; *b* 18 Feb 1938; *Educ* Leighton Park, Merton Coll Oxford (MA); *m* 12 Feb 1966, Catherine Jane, da of Daniel Hayes (d 1969), of Richmond, NSW; 1 s (Alexander James b 1969), 2 da (Phoebe Elizabeth b 1967, Corinna Jane b 1971); *Career* Nat Serv 2 Lt RASC 1959–61; HM Diplomatic Serv: asst princ CRO 1961, private sec to Parly Under Sec 1962–63; second sec: Accra 1963–65, Lomé 1965–66; second later first sec: UK Delgn NATO Paris and Brussels 1966–69, FCO 1969–72, New Delhi 1972–75, FCO (asst head of Dept) 1976–78; FCO visiting res fell RIIA 1978–79, cnsllr Prague 1979–83, ambass Iceland 1983–86, overseas inspr 1986–89, ambass Bulgaria 1989–94, high cmmr Eastern Caribbean 1994–; *Books* India's Emergence as an Industrial Power: Middle Eastern Contracts (1982); *Recreations* foreign parts, gardening, skiing; *Clubs* Royal Over-Seas League; *Style*— HE Mr Richard Thomas, CMG; ✉ c/o Foreign and Commonwealth Office (Bridgetown), King Charles St, London SW1A 2AH

THOMAS, HE (Anthony) Richard; CMG; s of Frederick James Thomas (d 1992), and Winifred Apthorpe, *née* Webb; *b* 11 July 1939; *Educ* Ampleforth, Peterhouse Cambridge (scholar); *m* 5 June 1976, Ricky Parks, da of Hugo Parks, of Lima, Peru; 1 da (Frances b 16 Dec 1980), 1 s (Paul b 12 May 1982); *Career* HM Dip Serv: FCO 1961–62, third sec Caracas 1962–64, UN Dept FCO 1964–66, second sec Budapest 1966–68, first sec Washington 1968–72, News Dept FCO 1972–75, first sec Madrid 1975–79, EEC Dept FCO 1979–81, dep consul gen and cnsllr Johannesburg 1981–86, min cnsllr Brasilia 1986–89, head S Pacific Dept FCO 1989–93, ambass Luanda 1993–95, high cmmr Kingston Jamaica 1995–; *Recreations* tennis, food, listening to music (jazz and classical), visual arts; *Style*— HE Mr Richard Thomas, CMG; ✉ c/o Foreign and Commonwealth Office (Kingston), King Charles Street, London SW1A 2AH

THOMAS, Richard James; s of Daniel Lewis Thomas, JP, of Southend on Sea, Essex, and Norah Mary, *née* James; *b* 18 June 1949; *Educ* Bishop's Stortford Coll, Univ of Southampton (LLB), Coll of Law Guildford; *m* 18 May 1974, Julia Delicia Thomas, da of Dr Edward Granville Woodchurch Clarke, MC, of Shurlock Row, Berks; 2 s (Andrew b 1977, Christopher b 1983), 1 da (Gemma b 1979); *Career* articled clerk and asst slr Freshfields 1971–74, slr CAB Legal Serv 1974–79, legal offr and head of resources gp Nat Consumer Cncl 1979–86, dir Consumer Affairs Office of Fair Trading 1986–92, dir

Public Policy Gp Clifford Chance 1992–; author of reports, articles and broadcasts on a range of legal and consumer issues; tstee W London Fair Housing Gp 1976–79; memb: Mgmnt Ctee Gtr London CAB Serv 1977–79, Lord Chllr's Advsy Ctee on Civil Justice Review 1985–88, Cncl Banking Ombudsman Scheme 1992–, Mgmnt Ctee Royal Courts of Justice CAB 1992–, Advsy Ctee Oftel 1995–, Advtg Advsy Ctee ITC 1996–; memb Law Soc, FRSA; *Recreations* family, maintenance of home and garden, travel, sailing; *Style*— Richard Thomas, Esq; ✉ Clifford Chance, 200 Aldersgate Street, London EC1A 4JJ (☎ 0171 600 1000)

THOMAS, Adm Sir (William) Richard Scott; KCB (1987), KCVO (1995), OBE (1974); s of Cdr William Scott Thomas, DSC, RN (d 1983), and Mary Hilda Bertha, *née* Hemelryk (d 1990); *b* 22 March 1932; *Educ* Downside; *m* 1959, Patricia Margaret, da of Dr John Henry Cullinan (d 1957), of Fressingfield, Suffolk; 4 s (Gavin (decd), Dominic b 1962, Gareth b 1967, George b 1973), 4 da (Victoria b 1960, Emma (Mrs Guy Tillyard) b 1964, Harriet b 1968, Jemima b 1970); *Career* Naval Offr; CO HM Ships: Buttress 1958, Wolverton 1960–61, Greetham 1962, Torquay 1965, Troubridge 1966–68, Fearless 1977–78; Naval Sec 1983–85, Flag Offr Second Flotilla 1985–87, Dep SACLANT 1987–89, Adm 1989, UK mil rep of NATO 1989–92; Gentleman Usher of the Black Rod, Serjeant-at-Arms to the Lord Chllr and Sec to the Lord Great Chamberlain 1992–95; student of Naval Staff Coll, Jt Servs Staff Coll and RCDS; memb: Cncl Stroke Assoc 1996–, Ctee Royal Humane Soc; Knight Cdr with Star of the Order of Pius IX 1995, Liveryman (hc) of the Worshipful Co of Haberdashers; *Recreations* family and gardening; *Style*— Adm Sir Richard Thomas, KCB, KCVO, OBE

THOMAS, Richard Stephen; s of Richard Thomas (d 1979), and Leah Mary, *née* Bowen (d 1988); *b* 13 June 1943; *Educ* Pentre GS, UWIST; *m* 23 Sept 1967, Sandra, da of Norman Bishop (d 1990); 1 s (Christopher Richard b 11 Sept 1969), 1 da (Sarah Elizabeth b 7 Sept 1973); *Career* Welsh Hosp Bd 1961–63, admin Cardiff N Hosp Mgmnt Ctee 1963–65, admin Cardiff Royal Infirmary 1965–69, commissioning offr Univ Hosp of Wales 1969–71, commissioning mangr Prince Charles Hosp Merthyr Tydfil 1971–73, project mangr Welsh Health Tech Servs Orgn Cardiff 1974–75, personnel offr West Glamorgan Health Authy 1975–78, area personnel offr Dyfed Health Authy 1978–85, asst gen mangr E Dyfed Health Authy 1986–87, unit gen mangr Carmarthen/Dinefwr Health Unit 1987–92, chief exec Carmarthen & Dist NHS Tst 1993–; past hon sec Welsh Assoc of Health Authorities 1986–88, past chm SW Wales Branch IHSM; MHSM 1966 (DipHSM), MIPD 1971; *Recreations* golf, walking, music, sport spectating; *Clubs* Carmarthen Round Table (past chm), Carmarthen Ex Round Tablers (vice pres, past chm), Towy Carmarthen Rotary (past pres); *Style*— Richard Stephen Thomas, Esq; ✉ 7 Llygad-Yr-Haul, Llangunnor, Carmarthen, Dyfed SA31 2LB (☎ 01267 231635); Carmarthen and District NHS Trust, West Wales General Hospital, Glanwili, Carmarthen, Dyfed (☎ 01267 235151, fax 01267 237662)

THOMAS, Sir Robert Evan; kt (1967), JP (Manchester 1948), DL (County Palatine of Greater Manchester 1974); s of Jesse Thomas, of Leigh, Lancs; *b* 8 Oct 1901; *Educ* St Peter's Leigh, Univ of Manchester (MA) 1974; *m* 1924, Edna, da of William Isherwood, of Leigh; 1 s, 1 da; *Career* former bus driver and trade union official; Lord Mayor of Manchester 1962–63, DL County Palatine of Lancaster 1967–73, dep chm Manchester Ship Canal until 1974, ldr Greater Manchester Met CC 1973–77, chm Assoc of Met Authorities 1974–77; *Books* Sir Bob; *Style*— Sir Robert Thomas, JP, DL; ✉ 29 Milwain Road, Manchester M19 2PX

THOMAS, Roger Geraint; s of Geraint Phillips Thomas (d 1989), and Doreen Augusta, *née* Cooke (d 1975); *b* 22 July 1945; *Educ* Penarth Co Sch, Leighton Park Sch Reading, Univ of Birmingham (LLB); *m* 23 Oct 1971, Rhian Elisabeth Kenyon, da of Erith Kenyon Thomas (d 1975), of Cardigan; *Career* ptnr Eversheds (formerly Phillips & Buck slrs) 1969–; memb: Ct Nat Museum of Wales 1983– (cncl memb 1985–), Welsh Cncl CBI 1987–, Cncl CBI 1991–, Gen Advsy Cncl BBC 1992–95, Bd Wales Millenium Centre 1996–; vice chm Techniquest Cardiff; govr Univ of Glamorgan 1994–; memb Law Soc 1969, CIMgt 1984 (chm Cardiff Branch 1988–90); *Recreations* hill walking; *Clubs* Cardiff and County, Penarth Yacht; *Style*— Roger G Thomas, Esq; ✉ Eversheds, Fitzalan House, Fitzalan Rd, Cardiff CF2 1XZ (☎ 01222 471147, fax 01222 464347)

THOMAS, Roger Lloyd; QC (1994); s of David Eyron Thomas, CBE, of Cardiff, and Mary Lloyd James; *b* 7 Feb 1947; *Educ* Cathays HS Cardiff, Univ Coll of Wales Aberystwyth (LLB); *m* 10 Aug 1974, Susan Nicola, da of Stuart Ernest Orchard; 1 s (Adam Nicholas Lloyd b 22 Nov 1978), 1 da (Kirsty Nicola Claire b 15 Jan 1981); *Career* called to the Bar Gray's Inn 1969, recorder of the Crown Court 1987–; specialises in criminal law; memb Criminal Bar Assoc; *Recreations* tennis, music, reading; *Clubs* Cardiff Lawn Tennis; *Style*— Roger Thomas, Esq, QC; ✉ 9 Park Place, Cardiff CF1 3DP (☎ 01222 382731, fax 01222 222542)

THOMAS, Rosalind Mary; da of John Wyndham Pain (d 1963), of Howey Hall, Llandrindod Wells, Powys, and Nina Owena, *née* Lankester (d 1980); *b* 28 May 1921; *Educ* RCM; *m* 1, 16 Dec 1941, Lt John Stewart Hallam, KRRC (ka 1943); 1 da (Nina b 7 March 1943); m 2, 21 March 1952, Edward Llewelyn Thomas (d 1963), s of Capt Edward Aubrey Thomas (d 1952), of Cefndyrys, Builth Wells, Powys; 1 s (Evan David b 19 Jan 1953), 1 da (Celia b 22 April 1954); *Career* Powys CC: memb Cncl 1973–96, chm 1987–88; co cncllr Radnor 1964–73; memb: Radnor LEA 1964–73, Powys LEA 1973–96; memb Brecon & Radnor HMC 1956, memb Powys Health Authy 1973–91, chm Adoption Panel Powys Social Servs 1974–87, chm Govrs Llandrindod Wells HS 1980–91, former pres Radnor Fedn of YFCs, former pres Brecon & Radnor CLA (memb Exec Ctee and Cncl 1987), chm SE Wales Arts Cncl, High Sheriff of Powys 1987–88, memb Gen Advsy Cncl BBC 1988–91; OStJ 1995; *Style*— Mrs Edward L Thomas; ✉ Pengraig, Cefndyrys, Builth Wells, Powys LD2 3TF (☎ 01982 552726)

THOMAS, Roydon Urquhart; QC (1985); s of Rowland Donald Thomas (d 1957), and Jean Milne, *née* Leslie (d 1993); *b* 17 May 1936; *Educ* Fettes, Sidney Sussex Coll Cambridge (BA); *m* (dis); 2 s (Peter Urquhart Milne b and d 1960, Guy Roydon Patrick b 1984), 1 da (Rosemary Urquhart (Mrs Justin Paines) b 1964); *Career* called to Bar Middle Temple, practising barr SE Circuit, recorder 1986–; bencher Middle Temple 1993–; *Recreations* golf, fishing, skiing; *Clubs* High Post, Hurlingham; *Style*— Roydon Thomas, Esq, QC; ✉ 1 Essex Court, Temple, London EC4Y 9AR (☎ 0171 583 2000, fax 0171 583 0118/353 8958)

THOMAS, Simon; *b* 3 Feb 1960; *Educ* Plymouth Coll of Art & Design (fndn course), Ravensbourne Coll of Art & Design (BA), RCA (MA); *Career* sculptor; asst to: John Maine for Arena on S Bank London 1983–84, Philip King on Docklands Sculpture Project Canary Wharf 1984; Kemijarvi Int Wood Carving Symposium Kemijarvi Finnish Lapland 1987, Peterborough festival of carving 1988, lecture tour Finnish Lapland centering on Art and Soc Symposium Sarestoniemi Art Museum (for Lappish Summer Univ) 1989, Tir Saile Sculpture Symposium Co Mayo 1993, Tachana Int Sculpture Symposium Lebanon 1995; solo exhibition Albermarle Gallery London 1989; *Gp Exhibitions* Toute Quarry Portland Sculpture Park Dorset 1983, Quarries (Camden Arts Centre London) 1983, Landscape Work in Snowdonia National Park, Llandudno Art Gallery 1984, RCA Final Year Show 1988, Sculptors of Fame and Promise (Chichester Cathedral) 1988, New Milestones (Dorchester Co Musem) 1988, Concept 88 - Reality 89 (Univ of Essex) 1989, Dartmoor (Plymouth City Art Gallery) 1989, Trees Woods and the Green Man (Craft Cncl Gallery and tour) 1989, Art at Your Fingertips (St Mary Tradescant Museum of Garden History Lambeth) 1990, London Art Fair 1991, 20th C Art Fair (RCA) 1991, British Art Fair (RCA) 1992, Out of Italy (Eagle Gallery London) 1992, Touch Milton Keynes Exhbn Centre 1994, Cabinet Pieces Jason Rhodes Gallery London 1995; *Cmmns* New Milestones (Common Ground on Coastal Walk Durdle Moor Dorset) 1985, Three Large Wood Carvings (London Wildlife Tst) 1986, Burning Bush (Louisville Kentucky USA) 1990, Belhus Pole (Essex) 1991, Dryad (Rhinefield House) 1991, two large stone carvings (Louise Steinman Von Hess Museum Penn USA) 1993, three large wood carvings for Leicester Square model farm Norfolk 1994; Madame Tussauds award 1988; pt/t research fell and artist in residence Physics Dept Univ of Bristol 1995–; *Style*— Simon Thomas, Esq; ✉ Jason and Rhodes Gallery, 4 New Burlington Place, London W1X 1FB (☎ 0171 434 1768)

THOMAS, Stephen Richard; s of Maj Norman Arthur Thomas (d 1974), of E Horsley, and Norah Margaret, *née* Cooke; *b* 9 June 1947; *Educ* Elizabeth Coll Guernsey; *m* 17 July 1971, Felicity Ruth, da of Harold Arthur George Quaintance (d 1992), of Rowlstone; 2 s (Daniel b 1973, Peter b 1979), 2 da (Hannah b 1975, Elizabeth b and d 1977); *Career* Deloitte Haskins & Sells: mangr and staff accountant 1965–81, sr accounting advsr seconded to HM Treasy 1981–83, fin servs sector ptnr and Japanese liaison ptnr 1983–90; ptnr and chm Building Socs and Mortgage Lenders Indust Gp Coopers and Lybrand 1990–94; tech advsr Nat Audit Office 1995–96, head Jt Monitoring Unit of the three Insts of CAs 1996–; memb Alton Evangelical Free Church; FCA 1969; *Recreations* golf, skiing and tennis with family; *Clubs* Alton Golf; *Style*— Stephen Thomas, Esq; ✉ Hawthorn House, Tunnel Lane, North Warnborough, Hook, Hants RG29 1JT (☎ 01256 703254)

THOMAS, Rt Hon Lord Justice; Rt Hon Sir Swinton Barclay; kt (1985), PC (1994); s of Brig William Bain Thomas, CBE, DSO (d 1967), and Mary Georgina Thomas (d 1986); *b* 12 Jan 1931; *Educ* Ampleforth, Lincoln Coll Oxford (MA, hon fell 1995); *m* 1967, Angela Rose Elizabeth, wid of Sir Anthony Cope, 15 Bt, da of James Alfred Snarey Wright (d 1975); 1 s (Dominic), 1 da (Melissa); *Career* Lt Cameronians (Scottish Rifles) 1950–51; called to the Bar Inner Temple 1955, QC 1975, bencher Inner Temple 1983, recorder of the Crown Court 1975–85, presiding judge Western Circuit 1987–90, judge of the High Court of Justice (Queen's Bench Div) 1990–94 (Family Division 1985–90), Lord Justice of Appeal 1994–; memb: Gen Cncl of the Bar 1970–74, Criminal Injuries Compensation Bd 1984–85, Parole Bd 1992–94 (vice chm 1994); *Recreations* reading, travel; *Clubs* Garrick; *Style*— The Rt Hon Lord Justice Swinton Thomas, PC; ✉ Royal Courts of Justice, Strand, London WC2A 2LL

THOMAS, Terence James (Terry); s of William Emrys (d 1993), of Carmarthen, Dyfed, and Mildred Evelyn Thomas, of Ammanford, Dyfed; *b* 19 Oct 1937; *Educ* Queen Elizabeth 1 GS Carmarthen, Univ of Bath Sch of Mgmnt (Postgrad Dip), INSEAD (Advanced Mgmnt Prog); *m* 27 July 1963, Lynda, da of William John Stevens; 3 s (Justin b 12 July 1965, Neil b 2 May 1967, Brendan b 9 Jan 1969); *Career* banker; various positions rising to mangr National Provincial Bank then National Westminster Bank, seconded as research mangr then national sales mangr Joint Credit Card Co (Access) 1971–72; Co-operative Bank plc: joined as mktg mangr 1973, subsequently asst gen mangr, jt gen mangr then dir of gp devpt, md 1988–; former pres Int Co-operative anking Assoc (currently vice pres ICBA European Regn), memb Cncl Chartered Inst of Bankers (chief examiner in Mktg of Financial Servs 1983–85); visiting prof Univ of Stirling 1988–91; chm: North West Partnership, Venture Technic (Cheshire) Ltd; former chm: Vector Investments, East Manchester Partnership; vice chm North West Business Leadership Team Ltd; alternate dir Manchester Ringway Developments, non-exec dir Stanley Leisure Organisation; memb Bd of Tstees Campaign to Promote the University of Salford (CAMPUS); author of various articles in banking and financial jls, has addressed various financial seminars and conventions on banking issues; Hon DLitt Univ of Salford 1996; FCIB, FCIM, FIMgt, FRSA 1992; *Style*— Terry Thomas, Esq; ✉ The Co-operative Bank plc, 1 Balloon Street, Manchester M60 4EP (☎ 0161 832 3456, fax 0161 832 9707)

THOMAS, Dr Trevor Anthony; s of Arthur William Thomas (d 1981), and Gladys Mary Gwendoline, *née* Hulin (d 1986); *b* 16 March 1939; *Educ* Bristol GS, Univ of St Andrews (MB ChB); *m* 10 July 1965, Yvonne Mary Louise, da of Percival Charles Branch (d 1946); 1 s (Jeremy Simon b 1969); *Career* sr conslt anaesthetist Bristol Maternity Hosp 1975–, chm Anaesthesia Div United Bristol Hosp 1977–80 (conslt anaesthetist 1972), South Western regnl assessor in anaesthesia for confidential enquiries into maternal deaths 1978–, hon clinical lectr Univ of Bristol 1980–, chm Hosp Med Ctee Bristol and Weston Health Dist 1988–90, chm Med Audit Ctee United Bristol Healthcare NHS Tst 1991–94, special tstee United Bristol Hosps 1992–96, med vice chm Regnl Distinction Awards Ctee 1991–93, dep chm Part 1 Examination for Fellowship of the Royal Coll of Anaesthetists 1991–96 (examiner 1985–96), vice chm SW Regnl Hosp Med Advsy Ctee 1991–93 (memb 1989–95); ed Anaesthesia Points West 1976–80; pres: Obstetric Anaesthetists Assoc 1996–, Soc of Anaesthetists of the South Western Region 1996–97 (hon sec 1985–88); hon sec: Obstetric Anaesthetists Assoc 1981–84 (memb Ctee 1979–81 and 1994–97), Section of Anaesthetics RSM 1993–95; memb Cncl Section of Anaesthetics RSM 1989–96, chm Obstetric Anaesthesia and Analgesia Sub-Ctee World Fedn of Socs of Anaesthesiology 1992–96 (memb Ctee 1988–92); FFARCS 1969, FRCA 1989; *Books* chapters in: Prescribing in Pregnancy (ed by Gordon M Stirrat and Linda Beeley in Clinics in Obstetrics and Gynaecology, 1986), Problems in Obstetrics Anaesthesia (ed by B M Morgan, 1987), Cardiopulmonary Resuscitation (ed by P J F Baskett, 1989), Controversies in Obstetric Anaesthesia 1 & 2 (ed by B M Morgan, 1990 and 1992), Handbook of Obstetric Analgesia and Anaesthesia (ed by Graham H McMorland and Gertie F Marx, 1992), International Practice of Anaesthesia (ed C Prys-Roberts and B R Brown, 1996); *Recreations* scuba diving, swimming, shooting, music, theatre; *Style*— Dr Trevor A Thomas; ✉ 14 Cleeve Lawns, Downend, Bristol BS16 6HJ (☎ 0117 956 7620, fax 0117 970 2378); Sir Humphry Davy Department of Anaesthesia, Bristol Royal Infirmary, Maudlin Steet, Bristol BS2 8HW (☎ 0117 928 2163)

THOMAS, Dr Tudor Ewart; s of William Ewart Thomas (d 1980), and Phyllis, *née* Bevan (d 1986); *b* 27 Nov 1944; *Educ* Amman Valley GS, UCW Aberystwyth (BSc), Univ of Salford (PhD); *m* 27 July 1968, Brenda, da of Emlyn Davies; 1 s (Huw Glyn b 14 April 1972), 1 da (Carys Wyn b 3 Oct 1973); *Career* Unilever: mgmnt trainee 1968–70, area prodn mangr Unichema Chemicals Ltd 1970–74 (co prodn mangr 1974–78), divnl head Unichema International West Germany 1978–82, tech dir Vinyl Products Ltd 1982–85; unit gen mangr Mid Surrey Health Authy 1986–90, chief exec Epsom Health Care NHS Tst 1991–; magistrate Epsom 1988–, elder United Reform Church 1986–, pres Dorking St John Ambulance Div (Adult); FRSC 1982, CChem 1982, FRSA 1994; *Recreations* gardening, rugby; *Clubs* Surrey Magistrates; *Style*— Dr Tudor Thomas; ✉ Epsom Health Care NHS Trust, Epsom General Hospital, Dorking Road, Epsom, Surrey KT18 7EG (☎ 01372 735200 fax 01372 735310)

THOMAS, (Gwyn Edward) Ward; CBE (1973), DFC; s of William John Thomas (d 1941), and Constance, *née* Daborn; *b* 1 Aug 1923; *Educ* Bloxham, Rouen Lycée; *m* 1, 1945, Patricia, da of Cecil Cornelius; 1 da; m 2, 1991, Janice; 1 s; *Career* served WWII Flt Lt RAF Bomber and Tport Cmd Europe and India; Granada Television 1955–61; md: Grampian Television 1961–67, Yorkshire Television 1967–73; Trident Television: md 1970–84, chm 1973–84; pres Trident Independent Television SA 1969–82; chm and chief exec Yorkshire-Tyne Tees Television Holdings plc 1993–; former chm: Castlewood Investments Ltd, Don Robinson Holdings Ltd, Watts & Corry Ltd, Trident Casinos, United Cable Programmes Ltd, British Cable Services, Scarborough Zoo and Marineland, Trident International, Trident Holdings Pty, Trident Films Ltd; former dir Survival

Anglia Ltd; Br Bureau of TV Advtg: dir 1966, chm 1968–70; memb Cncl ITCA 1961–76 (chm Labour Rels Ctee 1967, chm Network Prog Ctee 1971), memb Br Screen Advsy Cncl 1985–; Croix de Guerre; *Clubs* British Racing Drivers'; *Style*— G E Ward Thomas, Esq, CBE, DFC; ✉ Yorkshire-Tyne Tees Television Holdings plc, 15–16 Bloomsbury Square, London WC1A 2LJ (☎ 0171 312 3700, fax 0171 312 3720); La Gamberge, Les Hauts de St Paul, 06570 France (☎ 00 33 4 93 32 86 45)

THOMAS, William Ernest Ghinn; s of Kenneth Dawson Thomas, of Sheffield, and Monica Isobel, *née* Markham; *b* 13 Feb 1948; *Educ* Dulwich, King's Coll London (BSc), St George's Hosp Med Sch (MB BS); *m* 30 June 1973, Grace Violet, da of Alfred Henry Samways (d 1979), of London; 2 s (Christopher b 1977, Benjamin b 1985), 3 da (Nicola b 1974, Jacqueline b 1979, Hannah b 1983); *Career* Hunterian prof RCS 1987 (Arris and Gale lectr 1982, Bernard Sunley fell 1977), tutor in surgical skills 1995–, Moynihan fell Assoc of Surgns 1982, conslt surgn and clinical dir Royal Hallamshire Hosp Sheffield 1986–; exec ed Current Practice in Surgery 1988–; memb Ed Bd: Hospital Update, Surgery; memb Ct of Examiners Royal Coll of Surgns, memb Intercollegiate Court of Examiners, vice pres Surgical Section Royal Soc of Med; memb: BMA 1974, BSG 1980, SRS 1981, Assoc of Surgns 1986; nat pres Gideons Int 1996– (nat pres 1987–90, vice pres 1994–96); Royal Humane Soc Award for Bravery 1974, Dr of the Year Award 1985, European Soc Prize for Surgical Res 1981, Med Mangr of the Year Award 1995; FRCS 1976, MS 1980; *Books* Preparation and Revision for the FRCS (1986), Self-assessment Exercises in Surgery (1986), Nuclear Medicine: Applications to Surgery (1988), Colour Guide to Surgical Pathology (1992); *Recreations* skiing, photography, oil painting; *Style*— William Thomas, Esq; ✉ Ash Lodge, 65 Whirlow Park Rd, Whirlow, Sheffield, S Yorks S11 9NN (☎ and fax 0114 262 0852); Royal Hallamshire Hospital, Glossop Rd, Sheffield, S Yorks S10 2JF (☎ 0114 271 3142, fax 0114 271 3512)

THOMAS, His Hon Judge; William Fremlyn Cotter; *b* 18 March 1935; *Career* called to the Bar 1961, circuit judge (SE Circuit) 1990–; *Style*— His Hon Judge Thomas; ✉ Kingston Crown Court, Canbury Park Road, Kingston upon Thames, Surrey KT2 6JU

THOMAS, Sir William James Cooper; 2 Bt (UK 1919), of Ynyshir, Co Glamorgan, TD, JP (Monmouthshire 1958), DL (1973); s of Sir (William) James Thomas, 1 Bt (d 1945); *b* 7 May 1919; *Educ* Harrow, Downing Coll Cambridge; *m* 1947, Freida Dunbar (d 1990), da of late F A Whyte, of Montcoffer, Banff; 2 s, 1 da; *Heir* s, William Michael Thomas; *Career* served RA WWII; called to the Bar Inner Temple 1948; High Sheriff Co Monmouthshire 1973–74; *Style*— Sir William Thomas, Bt, TD, JP, DL; ✉ Tump House, Llanrothal, Monmouth, Gwent (☎ 01600 712757)

THOMAS, Prof (Meurig) Wynn; s of William John Thomas (d 1962), and Tydfil, *née* Rees (d 1983); *b* 12 Sept 1944; *Educ* Gowerton Boys' GS (major state scholar, prize for best arts A-Levels), Univ Coll Swansea (Coll scholar, E A Williams jr and sr prizes, major state studentship, BA); *m* 20 Sept 1975, Karen Elizabeth, da of W A Manahan; 1 da (Elin Manahan b 26 Aug 1977); *Career* Univ Coll Swansea: asst lectr 1966–69, lectr in English 1969–88, sr lectr 1988–94, prof of English 1994–; visiting prof: Harvard Univ 1991–92 (Harvard Summer Sch 1989), Univ of Tübingen 1994–95; Obermann fell Center for Advanced Studies Univ of Iowa 1992; presenter arts progs (BBC Radio Cymru) 1985–88; vice-chm: Yr Academi Gymreig (Welsh Acad, Welsh language section) 1996– (memb 1986–), Friends of Welsh Books Cncl 1996–; sec Univ of Wales Assoc for the Study of Welsh Writing in English 1983–96; memb Welsh Arts Cncl and chm Literature Ctee 1985–91, trust memb UK Year of Literature; memb Bd Seren Books, memb Ed Bd Walt Whitman Quarterly Review, assoc ed Welsh Writing in English: a Yearbok of Critical Essays; nominator The Arts Fndn 1993, adjudicator David Cohen Prize 1996–97; FBA 1996; *Books* Morgan Llwyd (1984), The Lunar Light of Whitman's Poetry (1987), Llyfr y Tri Aderyn (ed, 1988), A Toy Epic (ed, 1989), Emyr Humphreys (1989), R S Thomas: Y Cawr Awenydd (ed, 1990), Morgan Llwyd: ei gyfeillion a'i gyfnod (1991, Welsh Arts Cncl prize, Vernam Hull Meml prize, Ellis Griffith Meml prize), Wrenching Times: Whitman's Civil War Poetry (ed, 1991), Internal Difference: literature in twentieth-century Wales (1992), The Page's Drift: R S Thomas at Eighty (ed, 1993), Walt Whitman, Dail Glaswellt (trans, 1995), DiFfinio Dwy Lenyddiaeth Cymru (ed, 1995), Walt Whitman and the World (ed British Isles Section, 1996), Annotated Bibliography of English Studies (ed Welsh Studies Section, 1996); also author of numerous book chapters and articles in learned jls; *Recreations* reading, music, sport (couch-potato style); *Style*— Prof M Wynn Thomas, FBA; ✉ Department of English, University of Wales Swansea, Singleton Park, Swansea SA2 8PP (☎ 01792 295306, fax 01792 295761)

THOMAS ELLIS, Alice; *see:* Haycraft, Anna Margaret

THOMAS-EVERARD, Christopher Philip; s of Maj Charles Richard Thomas, MA (ka 1944), and Prunella Peel Lewin-Harris, *née* Bentley-Taylor (d 1979); *see* Burke's Landed Gentry, 18 edn, vol 1, 1965; *b* 19 March 1941; *Educ* Stowe, RAC; *m* 1966, Rohaise Harriet Julia, da of Maj Eudo Tonson Rye; 1 s (Guy Richard), 2 da; *Career* farmer, landowner, chartered surveyor, mangr of Miltons Estate and Broford Farm 1966–; chm: W Somerset NFU 1978–80, Somerset NFU Hill Farming Ctee 1981–82, Devon and Somerset Exmoor Hill Farming Ctee 1985–88; memb of MAFF SW Regnl Panel 1977–83, SW rep on MAFF Hill Farming Advsy Ctee 1979–; underwriting memb of Lloyd's 1973–93; High Sheriff of Somerset 1996–97; *Recreations* sailing, hunting; *Style*— Christopher Thomas-Everard, Esq

THOMAS OF GRESFORD, Baron (Life Peer UK 1996), of Gresford in the County Borough of Wrexham; (Donald) Martin Thomas; OBE (1982), QC (1979); s of Hywel Thomas (d 1961), and Olwen, *née* Jones; *b* 13 March 1937; *Educ* Grove Park GS Wrexham, Peterhouse Cambridge (MA, LLB); *m* 22 July 1961, Nan, da of John Kerr; 3 s (Hon Andrew b 18 Oct 1965, Hon Gavin b 9 April 1969, Hon Jamie b 18 March 1975), 1 da (Hon Claire b 15 July 1964); *Career* admitted slr 1961, lectr 1966–68, called to the Bar Gray's Inn 1967, jr counsel Wales and Chester Circuit 1968–79, recorder of the Crown Ct 1976, bencher Gray's Inn 1989, dep High Ct judge 1985, head of chambers; memb Criminal Injuries Compensation Bd 1985–93; chm Marcher Sound Ltd (ind local radio for N Wales and Chester) 1992– (vice chm 1985–92); Parly candidate (Lib): W Flint 1964, 1968 and 1970, Wrexham 1974, 1979, 1983 and 1987; pres Welsh Lib Pty 1978 (chm 1969–71), pres Welsh Lib Dems 1993–; *Recreations* rugby football, rowing, fishing, music making; *Clubs* Reform, Western, Wrexham RFC; *Style*— The Rt Hon Lord Thomas of Gresford, OBE, QC; ✉ Glasfryn, Gresford, Clwyd LL12 8RG (☎ 01978 852205, fax 01978 855078); Ground Floor, 1 Dr Johnson's Bldgs, Temple, London EC4Y 7AX (☎ 0171 353 9328, fax 0171 353 4410)

THOMAS OF GWYDIR, Baron (Life Peer UK 1987), of Llanrwst, Co Gwynedd; Peter John Mitchell Thomas; PC (1964), QC (1965); o s of late David Thomas, Slr, of Llanrwst, Denbighshire, and Anne Gwendoline, *née* Mitchell; *b* 31 July 1920; *Educ* Epworth Coll Rhyl, Jesus Coll Oxford (MA); *m* 1947, Frances Elizabeth Tessa (d 1985), o da of late Basil Dean, CBE, the theatrical prodr, by his 2 w, Lady Mercy Greville, 2 da of 5 Earl of Warwick; 2 s (Hon David Nigel Mitchell b 1950, Hon Huw Basil Maynard Mitchell b 1953), 2 da (Hon Frances Jane Mitchell (Hon Mrs Clargo) b 1954, Hon Catherine Clare Mitchell (Hon Mrs Howe) b 1958); *Career* served WWII Bomber Cmd RAF (POW); called to the Bar Middle Temple 1947; memb Wales and Chester Circuit, dep chm Cheshire Quarter Sessions 1966–70, Denbighshire Quarter Sessions 1968–70, Master of the Bench Middle Temple 1971 (Master Emeritus 1991), recorder Crown Court 1974–88, arbitrator ICC Ct of Arbitration Paris 1974–88; MP (C): Conway 1951–66, Hendon S 1970–87; PPS to Solicitor Gen 1954–59, parly sec Miny of Labour 1959–61, parly under sec of state for Foreign Affrs 1961–63, min of state for Foreign Affrs 1963–64, oppn front bench spokesman on Foreign Affrs and Law 1964–66; chm Cons Pty 1970–72, sec of state for Wales 1970–74; pres Nat Union of Cons and Unionist Assocs 1974–76; *Clubs* Carlton; *Style*— The Rt Hon Lord Thomas of Gwydir, PC, QC; ✉ Millicent Cottage, Elstead, Surrey (☎ 01252 702052); 37 Chester Way, London SE11 (☎ 0171 735 6047)

THOMAS OF SWYNNERTON, Baron (Life Peer UK 1981), of Notting Hill in Greater London; Hugh Swynnerton Thomas; s of Hugh Whitelegge Thomas, CMG (d 1960; s of Rev T W Thomas and sometime of the Colonial Serv, sec for Native Affairs in the Gold Coast; chief commissioner Ashanti 1932 and UK rep to League of Nations *re* Togoland Mandate Report 1931 & 1934), and Margery Angelo Augusta, *née* Swynnerton; *b* 21 Oct 1931; *Educ* Sherborne, Queens' Coll Cambridge (MA); *m* 1962, Hon Vanessa Mary Jebb, da of 1 Baron Gladwyn (d 1996); 2 s (Hon Charles Inigo Gladwyn b 1962, Hon (Henry) Isambard Tobias b 1964), 1 da (Hon Isabella Pandora b 1966); *Career* sits as Conservative in House of Lords; historian; with Foreign Office 1954–57, sec to UK Delgn to UN Disarmament Sub-ctee 1955–56, lectr RMA Sandhurst 1957, prof of history Reading Univ 1966–76; chm Centre for Policy Studies 1979–91; King Juan Carlos I prof of Spanish civilisation NY Univ 1995–96, univ prof Boston Univ 1996; co pres Hispano-British Tertulias 1987–93; Somerset Maugham Prize 1962, Arts Cncl Prize for History (first Nat Book Awards) 1980; Cdr Order of Isabel la Católica (Spain) 1987; *Publications* as Hugh Thomas: The World's Game (1957), The Spanish Civil War (1961, revised edn 1977, revised and illustrated edn Spain 1979), The Story of Sandhurst (1961), The Suez Affair (1967), Cuba, or the Pursuit of Freedom (1971), The Selected Writings of José Antonio Primo de Rivera (ed, 1972), Goya and the Third of May 1808 (1972), Europe, the Radical Challenge (1973), John Strachey (1973), The Cuban Revolution (1977), An Unfinished History of the World (1979, revised edn 1989, published in the US as A History of the World 1979), The Case for the Round Reading Room (1983), Havannah (novel, 1984), Armed Truce (1986), A Traveller's Companion to Madrid (1988), Klara (novel, 1988), The Conquest of Mexico (1993, US title Conquest 1994); *Style*— The Rt Hon Lord Thomas of Swynnerton; ✉ 29 Ladbroke Grove, London W11 3BB (☎ 0171 727 2288)

THOMAS OF WALLISWOOD, Baroness (Life Peer UK 1994); Susan Petronella Thomas; OBE (1989), DL (Surrey 1996); da of John Arrow, and Ebba Fordham, *née* Roll; *b* 20 Dec 1935; *Educ* Univ of Oxford; *m* 1958, David Churchill Thomas, CMG, o s of late David Bernard Thomas; 1 s (Hon David William Penrose, *qv*), 2 da; *Career* Parly candidate (Lib Dem) Mole Valley 1983 and 1987, Euro Parly candidate Surrey constituency 1994; recent past pres Women Lib Dems; Surrey CC: memb 1985–, served on various ctees, vice-chair Cncl and chair Highways and Tport Ctee 1993–; Surrey CC rep on Assoc of CCs, Airports Policy Consortium and SERPLAN; former memb E Surrey Community Health Cncl, currently non-exec dir E Surrey Hosp and Community Healthcare Tst; former memb Mole Valley Access for the Disabled Gp; a sch govr 1985–, former chair Mole Valley Youth Ctee; *Recreations* gardening, reading, ballet, theatre, travel; *Style*— The Rt Hon Baroness Thomas of Walliswood, OBE, DL; ✉ c/o House of Lords, London SW1

THOMASON, Prof George Frederick; CBE (1982); s of George Frederick Thomason (d 1967), of Hawkshead, Lancs, and Eva Elizabeth, *née* Walker (d 1977); *b* 27 Nov 1927; *Educ* Kelsick GS Ambleside, Univ of Sheffield (BA), Univ of Toronto (MA), Univ of Wales (PhD); *m* 5 Sept 1953, Jean Elizabeth, da of Henry Horsley (d 1982), of Montreal, Canada; 1 s (Geraint b 25 Nov 1960), 1 da (Sian b 1 March 1957); *Career* RASC 1946–48; Univ Coll Cardiff: res asst 1953–54, asst lectr 1954–56, res assoc 1956–59, lectr 1959–60, sr lectr 1963–69, head of dept 1966–84, reader 1969, prof 1969–84, prof emeritus 1984–; asst to md Flex Fasteners Ltd 1960–62; dir: Enterprise Training and Development Ltd 1989–93; vice pres (Employee Rels) Inst of Personnel Mgmnt 1991–93; chm Prosthetic and Orthotic Worldwide Education and Relief 1996–; memb: Ct and Cncl Univ of Wales Coll of Cardiff, ACAS Panel of Industl Rels Arbitrators; CIPM 1975, FIMgt 1975, FCIT 1989; *Books* Textbook of Human Resource Management (1988), Textbook of Industrial Relations Management (1984), Professional Approach to Community Work (1969); *Recreations* gardening; *Style*— Prof George Thomason, CBE; ✉ 149 Lake Rd West, Cardiff CF2 5PJ (☎ and fax 01222 754236)

THOMASON, Prof Harry; s of (Joseph) Alfred Thomason (d 1982), of Croston, and Edna, *née* Penwarden (d 1994); *b* 29 Feb 1940; *Educ* Hutton GS, Chester Coll, Loughborough Univ of Technol (DLC, PhD), Univ of Salford (MSc); *m* 3 Aug 1966, Marie, da of Herbert Flintoff (d 1975), of Newburgh; 1 s (Timothy Simon b 26 Jan 1968); *Career* lectr Royal Coll of Advanced Technol Salford 1963–66, sr lectr Univ of Salford 1974–77 (lectr 1966–74); Loughborough Univ of Technol: founding prof and head Dept of Physical Educn and Sports Sci 1977–87, pro vice chllr 1985–87, sr pro vice chllr 1987–90, pro vice chllr External Rels 1990–; dir Nat Inst of Sport and Med 1991–; Br Assoc of Sport and Med: memb Cncl and treas, memb Exec Ctee 1964–80 and 1987–; memb Med Sub-Ctee of BOA, assessor Assoc of Cwlth Univs Scholarship Scheme 1984–, dir Loughborough Consultants Ltd 1989–, advsr to: Miny of Educn Singapore 1983–87 and 1990–, BAe plc, Telekom Malaysia, Min of Educn Malaysia; dir Ford Design Inst; Miny of Sports rep E Midlands Region 1983–89; govr Leicester GS; FRSM 1970, FRSA 1990; *Books* Sports Medicine (contrib, 1976), Basic Book of Sports Medicine (contrib, 1978), Science and Sporting Performance (contrib, 1982); *Recreations* skiing, hill walking, learning to sail, golf; *Clubs* Athenaeum, Royal Windemere Yacht, Royal Dornoch Golf; *Style*— Prof Harry Thomason; ✉ Loughborough University of Technology, Loughborough, Leics LE11 3TU (☎ 01509 263171, fax 01509 610813)

THOMASON, (Kenneth) Roy; OBE (1986), MP (C) Bromsgrove (majority 13,702); s of Thomas Roger Thomason (d 1989) of Ringwood, Hants, and Constance Dora, *née* Wilcox; *b* 14 Dec 1944; *Educ* Cheney Sch Oxford, Univ of London (LLB); *m* 6 Sept 1969, Christine Ann, da of William Richard Parsons (d 1985), of Queen's Park, Bournemouth; 2 s (Richard b 1972, Edward b 1974); 2 da (Julia b 1978, Emily b 1981); *Career* admitted slr 1969, sr ptnr Horden & George Bournemouth 1979–91; MP (Cons) Bromsgrove 1992–, Cons ldr Environment Select Ctee 1994–; vice chm Cons Environment Ctee 1992–, jt chm All Pty Export Gp 1995–, Cons Pty: constituency chm Bournemouth West 1981–82, chm Wessex Area Local Govt Advsy Ctee 1981–83, memb Nat Local Govt Advsy Ctee 1981– (vice chm 1989–91), memb Nat Union Exec 1989–91; ldr Bournemouth Borough Cncl 1974–82 (memb 1970–92); Assoc of Dist Cncls: memb Cncl 1979–91, Cons gp ldr 1981–87, chm Housing and Environmental Health Ctee 1983–87, chm 1987–91; FRSA; *Recreations* family, sailing, architectural history; *Style*— Roy Thomason, Esq, OBE, MP; ✉ House of Commons, London SW1 0AA (☎ 0171 222 9458/4214)

THOMPSON, Adrian Richard; s of Harold Albert Thompson, of London, and Daphne Yvonne, *née* Shrimpton (d 1990); *b* 28 July 1954; *Educ* Wandsworth Sch, Guildhall Sch of Music & Drama; *m* 30 July 1977, Judith Mary, da of John William Panes (decd); 2 s (George Harold Gwilym b 16 Oct 1982, Samuel John b 17 June 1985); *Career* tenor; roles at Glyndebourne Festival: Snout and Flute in A Midsummer Night's Dream, Pedrillo in Die Entführung Aus Dem Serail, Mayor in Albert Herring, Ferrando in Cosi Fan Tutte; roles with Netherlands Opera: Narraboth in Salome, Pedrillo, Iro in Ullyses; roles with Opera London: Arnalta in Coronation of Poppea, Flute in A Midsummer Night's Dream; other prodns incl Orfeo (ENO) 1996; worked with orchs incl: LSO, London Philharmonic, The Philharmonia, London Mozart Players, Eng Chamber Orch, BBC Symphony Orch, Northern Sinfonia, RTE Symphonia Orch; worked with conductors incl: Jane Glover,

Bernard Haitinck, Hartmut Hänchen, Richard Hickox, Jean-Bernard Pommier, Gennadi Rozhdestvensky; *Recordings* incl: Die Schöne Mullerin, On Wenlock Edge, Coronation of Poppea, A Midsummer Night's Dream, Schubert Songs, Geoffrey Bush - Summer Serenade, Master Peter's Puppet Show; *Recreations* walking, trams, touring; *Style*— Adrian Thompson, Esq; ✉ c/o Ron Gonsalves Personal Artists & Concert Management, 7 Old Town, Clapham, London SW4 0JT (☎ 0171 622 2244, fax 0171 622 2288)

THOMPSON, Prof Alan Eric; s of Eric Joseph Thompson (d 1956), and Florence, *née* Holmes (d 1974); *b* 16 Sept 1924; *Educ* Univ of Edinburgh (MA, PhD); *m* 3 Dec 1960, da of Frank Long (d 1963); 3 s (Matthew b 1962, Andrew b 1967, Hamish b 1971); *Career* WWII (served with Infantry, Army Educn, and Br Forces Network in Centl Med Forces, Italy and Austria); lectr in economics Univ of Edinburgh 1953–59 and 1964–71, A J Balfour prof of economics Heriot Watt Univ 1972–87; visiting prof: Stanford Univ USA 1966 and 1968, Istanbul 1988; Parly advsr: Scottish TV 1966–76, Pharmaceutical Gen Cncl Scotland 1985–; pres Edinburgh Amenity and Port Assoc 1970–75, hon vice pres Assoc of Nazi War Camp Survivors 1960–; chm: Northern Offshore (Maritime) Resources Study 1974–84, Newbattle Abbey Coll, Edinburgh Ctee Peace Through NATO 1984–; govr: BBC and chm Broadcasting Cncl for Scotland 1976–79, Leith Nautical Coll 1981–84; memb: Royal Fine Art Cmmn for Scotland 1975–80, Local Govt Boundaries Cmmn (Scotland) 1975–82, Jt Military Educn Ctee Edinburgh and Heriot-Watt Univs 1975–, Scottish Cncl for Adult Educn in HM Forces 1973–; MP (Lab) Dunfermline 1959–64, Parly candidate (Lab) Galloway 1950 and 1951, memb Parly delgn to USA 1962; FRSA 1972; *Books* Development of Economic Doctrine (jtly, 1980); *Recreations* bridge, croquet, writing children's stories, plays; *Clubs* New (Edinburgh), Edinburgh University Staff, Loch Earn Sailing; *Style*— Prof Alan Thompson; ✉ 11 Upper Gray Street, Edinburgh EH9 1SN; Ardtrostan Cottage, St Fillan's, Perthshire PH6 2NL (☎ 0131 667 2140, 01764 485275)

THOMPSON, Ann Frances (Fran); da of Kenneth Charles Thompson, of Binsted, Hampshire, and Mary Philomena, *née* Rex; *b* 3 Feb 1955; *Educ* Farnborough Hill Convent Sch, UCW Aberystwyth (BA); *partner*, Patrick Nils Connellan, s of Michael Anthony Connellan; 1 s (Ruari Svend b 20 Jan 1991); *Career* theatrical designer; assoc designer: Wolsey Theatre Ipswich (Saved, Peer Gynt) 1980–81, Nuffield Theatre Southampton (A Midsummer Night's Dream, Summer and Smoke, Dead Men, Adventures of Alice, Working Class Hero, Just a Kick in the Grass, The Dealer) 1981–83, Wilde Theatre Bracknell (The Importance of Being Earnest (opening show)) 1984; head of design Palace Theatre Watford (Trumpets and Raspberries, Chance Visitor (premiere), Lulu) 1984; freelance: Comedians (Everyman Liverpool) 1987, All's Well That Ends Well (Leeds Playhouse) 1987, Julius Caesar (Young Vic) 1987, Romeo and Juliet 1987, Enemy of the People (transferred to London Playhouse) 1988, Measure for Measure 1989, Passion Play (Liverpool Playhouse) 1988, Picture Palace (premiere, Women's Theatre Group) 1988, Twelfth Night (Theatre Royal Stratford East) 1988, A Winters Tale (Regent's Park) 1988, La Traviata (WNO) 1989, The Price (Young Vic) 1990, Pericles (RSC, Swan, Pit Barbican (Olivier Award for Best Revival 1991)) 1989–90, Safe In Our Hands (W Yorkshire Playhouse) 1990, All My Sons (Birmingham Repertory) 1990, My Mother Said I Never Should (Birmingham Repertory) 1992, Memoirs of a Survivor (Salisbury Playhouse Studio) 1992, Jane Eyre (Crucible Sheffield) 1992, Julius Caesar (RSC, The Other Place, regnl and int tour) 1993–94, Coriolanus (RSC, Swan and Barbican) 1994–95, Death of a Salesman (RNT and Price Guthrie Theatre Minneapolis 1997) 1996; *Style*— Ms Fran Thompson; ✉ c/o Curtis Brown Group Ltd, 28–29 Haymarket, London SW1Y 4SP (☎ 0171 396 6600, fax 0171 396 0110)

THOMPSON, His Hon Judge; Anthony Arthur Richard; QC (1980); s of William Frank McGregor Thompson (d 1934), and Doris Louise, *née* Hill (d 1988); *b* 4 July 1932; *Educ* Latymer Upper Sch, Univ Coll Oxford (MA), Sorbonne; *m* 1958, Francoise Alix Marie, da of Joseph Justin Reynier (d 1981); 2 s (Richard, Mark), 1 s decd, 1 da (Melissa); *Career* called to the Bar Inner Temple 1957; chm Bar Euro Gp 1984–86, recorder of the Crown Ct 1985–92, bencher Inner Temple 1986; avocat of the Paris Bar 1988; circuit judge 1992– (S Eastern Circuit 1992, Western Circuit 1993–), liaison judge for Cornwall 1993–, resident judge for Cornwall 1996–; vice pres Cornwall Magistrates' Assoc 1994–; FCIArb 1991; *Publications* The Second Banking Directive of the European Community (1991); *Recreations* food and wine, theatre, cinema, lawn tennis; *Clubs* Roehampton; *Style*— His Hon Judge Thompson, QC; ✉ Coln Manor, Coln St Aldwyns, Gloucestershire GL7 5AD; Combined Court Centre, Edward Street, Truro, Cornwall TR1 2PB

THOMPSON, Dr Catriona; da of John MacIntosh (d 1938), and Kate Ann, *née* Mackinnon (d 1975); *b* 29 May 1937; *Educ* Portree HS Isle of Skye, Univ of Edinburgh (MB ChB); *m* 16 July 1964, Douglas Theophilus Thompson, s of George Batchin Thompson, MBE (d 1958); 2 s (Hal b 1 Sept 1968, Andrew b 20 Jan 1975); *Career* hon lectr Dept of Anaesthetics Univ of Zimbabwe 1972–76; conslt anaesthetist: Harare Central Hosp Zimbabwe 1967–77, Parirenyatwa Gp of Hosps Harare Zimbabwe 1970–82, Ayrshire and Arran Health Bd Crosshouse Hosp 1988–; first nat pres Zimbabwe Assoc of Univ Women 1980–82, pres Glasgow Assoc of Women Graduates 1995–, memb Br Fedn of Women Graduates 1986–, pre convener Membership Ctee Int Fedn of Univ Women 1989–92, procedural advsr 79 and 80 Cncls 25 Conf of Int Fedn of Univ Women Japan 1995; memb NW Regnl Pain Soc 1986–; FFARCS 1970; *Recreations* golf, badminton, walking, bridge; *Style*— Dr Catriona Thompson; ✉ Crosshouse Hospital, Crosshouse, Kilmarnock, Ayrshire KA2 0BE (☎ 01563 521133)

THOMPSON, Sir Christopher Peile; 6 Bt (UK 1890), of Park Gate, Guiseley, Yorks; s of Lt-Col Sir Peile Thompson, OBE, 5 Bt (d 1985), and his wife, Barbara Johnson (d 1993), da of late Horace Johnson Rampling; *b* 21 Dec 1944; *Educ* Marlborough, RMA Sandhurst, Staff Coll; *m* 22 Nov 1969, Anna Elizabeth, da of late Maj Arthur George Callander, of Avebury, Wilts; 1 s (Peile Richard b 1975), 1 da (Alexandra Lucy (Hon Mrs Piers Portman) b 1973); *Heir* s, Peile Richard Thompson b 3 March 1975; *Career* 11 Hussars (PAO), then Royal Hussars (PWO), cmmnd 1965, CO Royal Hussars 1985–87, ret 1990; private sec to HRH Prince Michael of Kent 1990–92 (equerry 1989–); dir: The Hyde Park Appeal, Nuclear Decommissioning Ltd 1994– (non-exec chm 1995–), Logical Security Limited 1995–; tstee: Tusk, The Queen Elizabeth Gate Appeal, Bike Aid, Antigua and Barbuda Heritage Tst (UK); *Recreations* shooting, fishing, sailing, skiing, golf, tennis, reading, vegetable gardening, Cresta; *Clubs* Cavalry and Guards', St Moritz Toboganning, Mill Reef (Antigua); *Style*— Sir Christopher Thompson, Bt; ✉ c/o Barclays Bank PLC, PO Box 8, 13 Library Place, St Helier, Jersey

THOMPSON, Clive Hepworth; s of Sidney Hepworth Thompson (d 1956), and Vera, *née* Wynne (d 1981); *b* 9 July 1937; *Educ* Holywell GS, Univ of Manchester (BSc, MSc), Harvard Univ (Mgmnt Dip); *m* 1962, Joan Mary, da of Henry Kershaw; 2 s (David Stuart b 28 Aug 1965, Graham John b 1 Feb 1969); *Career* British Resin Products (pt of BP Chemicals): trainee 1961, various positions rising to gen mangr Barry 1975–78, gen mangr Baglan Bay 1978–83; dir Petrochemicals and Mfrg BP Chemicals 1983–90, vice pres Ops and Supply ARCO Chemical Europe 1990–95, conslt 1995–; sec of state for Wales nominee Welsh Water Authy 1980–82, memb IMMAC DTI 1986–88; Audit Cmmn: memb 1991–, dep chm 1995–, acting chm 1995; chm various industl reorganisation initiatives; author various articles for chemical indust; memb Ct of Assts Worshipful Co of Horners 1995 (Liveryman 1989); *Recreations* hill walking (mainly Scotland), opera, watching cricket and rugby, golf, reading; *Clubs* Harvard Business, Windlesham Golf; *Style*— Clive Thompson, Esq; ✉ Dwr Golau, 13 Herons Court, Lightwater, Surrey GU18 5SW (☎ 01276 476410, mobile 0836 787602); The Audit Commission, 1 Vincent Square, London SW1P 2PN (☎ 0171 828 1212, fax 0171 976 6187)

THOMPSON, Sir Clive Malcolm; kt (1996); *b* 4 April 1943; *Educ* Clifton Coll, Univ of Birmingham (BSc); *Career* formerly exec Royal Dutch Shell Group, Boots Co plc and Cadbury Schweppes plc; gp chief exec Rentokil Group plc 1982–; non-exec dir: BAT Industries PLC, J Sainsbury PLC 1995–, Farepak plc; vice pres Chartered Inst of Mktg; *Style*— Sir Clive Thompson; ✉ Rentokil Group plc, Felcourt, East Grinstead, W Sussex RH19 2JY (☎ 01342 833022, fax 01342 326229)

THOMPSON, Damian Mark; s of Leonard Gilbert Thompson (d 1985), and Pamela Mary, *née* Benbow; *b* 24 Jan 1962; *Educ* Presentation Coll Reading, Mansfield Coll Oxford (MA); *Career* reporter The Reading Chronicle 1984–88; religious affairs correspondent The Daily Telegraph 1991–95 (diarist Peterborough Column 1988–91), currently freelance; author of reviews and articles in: The Daily and Sunday Telegraphs, The Spectator, Harpers & Queen, The Literary Review; *Recreations* playing the piano, recent American crime fiction; *Clubs* The Academy, Savile; *Style*— Damian Thompson, Esq

THOMPSON, (John) Daniel; DL (Co Armagh); s of Eric McCrea Thompson (d 1987), of Portadown, and Betty Georgina, *née* Brown (d 1986); *b* 31 Aug 1944; *Educ* Portadown Coll, Trinity Coll Dublin (MA); *m* 15 March 1973, Joan Evelyn, da of Ernest Elkin; 2 s (Hugo Charles Daniel b 10 April 1975, Rory James William b 18 June 1977); *Career* slr of the Supreme Ct NI 1970–, NP 1975–, HM coroner for S Down 1987– (dep coroner 1982–87); chm: Southern Health and Social Servs Bd 1990–94, Eastern Health and Social Servs Bd 1994–; vice chm Nat Appeal Panel 1990–; pt/t chm: Med Appeal Tbnl, Social Security Appeal Tbnl, Disability Appeal Tbnl; memb: NI Advsy Ctee on Telecommunications 1989–95, Post Office Users' Cncl NI 1989–, Historic Bldgs Cncl NI 1991– (vice chm 1995–), Senate of Queen's Univ of Belfast Equal Opportunities Ctee 1994–; patron Newry Hospice; High Sheriff Co Armagh 1991; memb: Law Soc of NI 1970, Coroners' Assoc of NI 1982 (chm 1992–94), NI Medico-Legal Soc (former cncl memb) 1984, Coll of Notaries NI 1987, Coroners' Soc of England and Wales (corresponding memb) 1993; ACIArb; *Recreations* pétanque (Irish International 1990 and 1991 and Irish Doubles 1993), maritime activities; *Clubs* Royal Over-Seas League, The Armagh (tstee and sec), Tynan and Armagh Hunt, Loughgall Tennis; *Style*— J Daniel Thompson, Esq, DL; ✉ Ardress Cottage, Portadown, Co Armagh, N Ireland BT62 1SQ (☎ 01762 851347); Green Cottage, Greencastle, Co Down, N Ireland BT34 4LR (☎ 016937 63503); Eric McCrea Thompson & Son, Solicitors & Notary Public, 74 & 107 Church Street, Portadown, Co Armagh, N Ireland BT62 (☎ 01762 350227/332485, fax 01762 851347)

THOMPSON, David; s of Bernard Thompson, of Castleford, and Violet, *née* Laidler; *b* 28 Oct 1944; *Educ* King's Sch Pontefract; *m* 24 Oct 1970, Glenys, da of Harry Colley, of Badsworth, nr Pontefract; 2 s (Anthony David b 24 Aug 1972, Richard Martin b 17 Feb 1976); *Career* John Gordon Walton CAs until 1967, sr ptnr Buckle Barton 1981– (ptnr 1978–81); fin dir: Bradford City AFC (1983) Ltd 1986– (vice chm 1990–), European Concert Orchestra Ltd 1991–, Campbells Leisure (Bradford) Ltd 1996–; chm: Omnis Associates Ltd 1986–95, DT Financial Consultants Ltd 1986–, Buckle Barton Pensioneer Trustees Ltd 1988–; dep songster ldr Castleford Corps Salvation Army; FCA 1979 (ACA 1969); *Recreations* football, most sports; *Clubs* Regency (Leeds), Napoleon's (Bradford); *Style*— David Thompson, Esq; ✉ Stone Lea, Badsworth Court, Badsworth, Pontefract, W Yorks WF9 1NW (☎ 01977 645467); Buckle Barton, Sanderson House, Station Rd, Horsforth, Leeds LS18 5NT (☎ 0113 258 8216/258 1640, fax 0113 239 0270, car tel 0836 265 365)

THOMPSON, David Anthony Roland; *Career* The Boots Company plc: joined 1966, fin dir Retail Div 1980–89, gp fin controller 1989–90, gp fin dir 1990–; non-exec dir East Midlands Electricity plc; FCA; *Style*— David Thompson, Esq; ✉ The Boots Company plc, Nottingham NG2 3AA (☎ 0115 968 7005, fax 0115 968 7156)

THOMPSON, Derek Paul; s of Stanley Moorhouse Thompson (d 1985), and Lilian, *née* Forster; *b* 31 July 1950; *Educ* Fyling Hall, Guisborough GS; *m* 1996, Julie; 2 s from previous m (Alexander McLaren b 5 June 1982, James Gordon b 5 Nov 1984); *Career* sports commentator and presenter; BBC Radio Sport 1972–81, ITV Sport 1981–85, Channel 4 Racing 1985–; racecourse commentator UK and Dubai Racing Club; *Recreations* tennis, golf, jogging; *Style*— Derek Thompson, Esq; ✉ Channel Four Racing, Hawley Lane, Farnborough, Hants (☎ 01252 517467)

THOMPSON, (Ila) Dianne; da of Ronald Wood, of Thornhill Lees, Dewsbury, W Yorks, and Joan, *née* Pinder (d 1985); *b* 31 Dec 1950; *Educ* Batley Girls' GS, Manchester Poly (Univ of London external BA), Inst of Mktg (sr exec dip); *m* 9 Aug 1972 (m dis 1992), Roger Paul Thompson, s of William Thompson; 1 da (Joanna Rachel b 29 Aug 1984); *Career* product and gp product mangr Cooperative Wholesale Soc 1972–74, export and UK mktg mangr ICI Paints Div 1974–79, md Thompson Maud Jones (Advertising) Ltd 1981–86, mktg dir Sterling Roncraft 1986–88, md Sandvik Saws & Tools Ltd 1988–92, dir of mktg Woolworths plc 1992–94, mktg dir Signet Group plc (formerly Ratners) 1994–96, commercial ops dir Camelot Group plc 1996–; sr lectr in strategic planning and marketing Manchester Poly 1979–86, sr conslt Business & Technol Centre 1985–86; memb: Inst of Mktg, Mktg Soc, Mktg Gp, Women's Advtg Club of London; *Recreations* theatre, cooking, dining out, reading; *Style*— Mrs Dianne Thompson; ✉ Adam Cottage, Hammersley Lane, Penn, Bucks HP10 8HB; Camelot Group plc, Tolpits Lane, Watford, Herts WD1 8RN (☎ 01923 425000)

THOMPSON, Sir Donald; kt (1992), MP (C) Calder Valley (majority 4,878); s of Geoffrey Thompson; *b* 13 Nov 1931; *Educ* Hipperholme GS; *m* 1957, Patricia Hopkins; 2 s; *Career* farmer; md Armadillo Plastics; memb: West Riding and West Yorkshire CC, Calderdale DC 1967–79; chm Cons Candidates' Assoc 1972–74; Parly candidate (C): Batley and Morley 1970, Sowerby Feb and Oct 1974; MP (C): Sowerby 1979–1983, Calder Valley 1983–; asst Govt whip 1981–83, Lord Cmmr of the Treasy (Govt whip) 1983–86, Parly sec MAFF 1986–89, Govt whip Cncl of Europe and WEU 1990–95; Liveryman Worshipful Co of Butchers; *Style*— Sir Donald Thompson, MP; ✉ Moravian House, Lightcliffe, nr Halifax, W Yorks (☎ 01422 202920, fax 0171 219 3614); House of Commons, London SW1A 0AA

THOMPSON, Dr Dorothy Joan; da of Frank William Walbank, and Mary Woodward, *née* Fox (d 1987); *b* 31 May 1939; *Educ* Birkenhead High Sch GPDST, Girton Coll Cambridge (William Menzies exhibitioner in classics, Thérèse Montefiore and Alfred Zimmern prizes, BA, MA, PhD), Univ of Bristol (CertEd), Br Sch of Archaeology Athens; *m* 1, (m dis 1979), Michael Hewson Crawford; m 2, 1982, John Alexander Thompson; *Career* Henry Carrington and Bentham Dumont Koe studentship Univ of Cambridge 1962–64; Girton Coll Cambridge: Eugénie Strong research fell and lectr in classics 1965–68, official fell and lectr in classics and history 1968–, graduate tutor (arts) 1971–81 and 1995–96, sr tutor 1981–92, dir of studies in classics 1983–; lectr in classics Clare Coll Cambridge 1973–, Isaac Newton Tst lectr in classics Univ of Cambridge 1992–; visiting memb Inst for Advanced Study Princeton NJ (Fulbright Travel award and scholarship, Volkswagenstiftung award) 1982–83; Princeton Univ USA: visiting prof Dept of Classics 1986, visiting sr fell Cncl of the Humanities and Old Dominion fell 1986; Josephus Daniels fell Research Triangle Fndn Nat Humanities Center N Carolina 1993–94; memb: Classical Assoc 1961, Hellenic Soc 1963, Fondation Égyptologique Reine Elisabeth Bruxelles 1964, Roman Soc 1977, American Soc of Papyrologists; Br Cncl and Flemish Nationaal Fonds voor Wetenschappelijk Onderzoek award (jtly) 1993–94; FBA 1996; *Books* Kerkeosiris: an Egyptian village in the Ptolemaic period (1971), Studies on

Ptolemaic Memphis (jtly, 1980), Classics. CRAC Degree Course Guide (jtly, 1988), Memphis under the Ptolemies (1988, James H Breasted prize American Historical Assoc 1989); also author of numerous book chapters and articles in learned jls; *Recreations* reading, walking; *Style—* Dr Dorothy J Thompson, FBA; ✉ Girton College, Cambridge CB3 0JG (☎ 01223 338999, fax 01223 338896, e-mail djt17@cam.ac.uk)

THOMPSON, Dudley Stuart; s of Joel Percy Thompson (d 1964), and Joan Evelyn, *née* Anstey (d 1984); *b* 4 Nov 1942; *Educ* Whitgift Sch; *m* 27 June 1970, Anne Elizabeth, da of John Egerton Coope (d 1964); 1 s (Paul Dudley Fitzgerald b April 1975), 2 da (Karen Juliette b July 1973, Hazel Joan b Sept 1978); *Career* sr mangr Touche Ross & Co 1969–78, gp chief accountant Imperial Continental Gas Association 1978–87, gp fin dir Goode Durrant plc 1988–; dir: Northgate Motor Holdings Ltd 1988–, Rawlings Brothers Ltd 1989–95, Ravenstock Tam (Holdings) Ltd 1991–; chm Merstham Village Tst, pres Merstham Village Club; FCA 1965, FCT 1982, MIMgt 1985; *Recreations* golf, theatre, gardening; *Clubs* Walton Heath Golf, Hunstanton Golf; *Style—* Dudley Thompson, Esq; ✉ The Georgian House, Rockshaw Rd, Merstham, Surrey RH1 3DB; Goode Durrant plc, Belgrave House, Station Way, Crawley, West Sussex RH10 1HP (☎ 01293 615615, fax 01293 616888)

THOMPSON, Eric John; CB (1995); s of Herbert William Thompson (d 1990), of Beverley, E Yorks, and Florence, *née* Brewer (d 1937); *b* 26 Sept 1934; *Educ* Beverley GS, LSE (BScEcon); *Career* Pilot Offr RAF 1956–58; statistician in: computer indust 1958–60, oil indust 1960–65, Gen Register Office 1965–67, GLC 1967–74; chief statistican Central Statistical Office 1975–80; dir of statistics Dept of Tport 1980–89, Office of Population Censuses and Surveys 1989–94; *Style—* Eric J Thompson, Esq, CB

THOMPSON, Ernest Gerald (Tommy); OBE (1973); s of Joseph Thompson (d 1943), of Goodmayes, Essex, and Rhoda Annie, *née* Messenger (d 1970); *b* 22 Nov 1925; *Educ* Brentwood Sch, Trinity Coll Cambridge; *m* 14 Sept 1968, Janet Muriel, da of Philip Andrew Smith (d 1977), of Blackmore, Essex; 1 s (Richard Michael b 1971); *Career* Flt Lt navigator and bomb aimer RAF 1943–47; Int Secretariat of the Euro Movement Paris 1951–55, joined Baird & Tatlock Ltd 1955 (instrument sales mangr 1962–68), dir Dannatt SA Paris 1963–68, chm and md Chemlab Instruments Ltd 1968–86, chm Chemlab Manufacturing Ltd, chm Chemlab Scientific Products Ltd 1986–; memb Hon Lecturing Faculty Inst of Mktg 1966–78, hon sec Britain in Europe 1958–68, vice chm Cons Gp for Europe 1967–75; memb: Gen Cncl of Cons Gp for Europe 1975–, Nat Exec of the Euro Movement 1969–83, Nat Cncl of Euro Movement 1983–94, Int Fed Ctee of Union Européenne des Fédéralistes 1974–94; Honorary Senator of the Belgian Movement for the Utd States of Europe; Freeman City of London 1979, Liveryman Worshipful Co of Scientific Instrument Makers; LRSC 1968, FInstD; *Recreations* music, swimming, travel, gardening; *Style—* Tommy Thompson, Esq, OBE; ✉ Yew Tree House, Morgan Crescent, Theydon Bois, Essex (☎ 01992 812486); Chemlab Scientific Products Ltd, Construction House, Grenfell Ave, Hornchurch, Essex RM12 4EH (☎ 01708 476162, fax 01708 707778)

THOMPSON, Ernest Victor; s of Ernest Arthur Thompson (d 1964), and Victoria, *née* Harrup (d 1949); *b* 14 July 1931; *Educ* Burford GS Oxon; *m* 1, 1952 (m dis 1972), Elizabeth Spiller; 2 da (Carol b 1954, Virginia b 1957); *m* 2, 1972, Celia Carole, da of Nelson Burton; 2 s (Nathan Wyatt b 1977, Luke Adam b 1980); *Career* RN 1947–56; Bristol Constabulary 1956–63, investigator BOAC 1963–64, chief security offr Dept of Civil Aviation Rhodesia 1964–70, various Civil Serv appts 1970–75, author 1975–; regnl vice pres RDA; vice pres: Three Spires Festival, West Country Writers' Assoc; pres Cornwall Drama Assoc; memb: Royal Inst of Cornwall 1977, Royal Soc of Literature 1992, Missouri Supreme Ct Historical Assoc 1983, Soc of Authors 1986; *Books* incl: Chase the Wind (1977, Best Historical Novel Macmillan, Pan, Coward McCann and Geoghegan), Harvest of the Sun (1978), Music Makers (1979), Ben Retallick (1980), The Dream Traders (1981), Singing Spears (1982), The Restless Sea (1983), Cry Once Alone (1984), Polrudden (1985), The Stricken Land (1986), Becky (1988), God's Highlander (1989), Lottie Trago (1990), Cassie (1991), Homeland (as James Munro, 1991), Wychwood (1992), Blue Dress Girl (1992), Mistress of Polrudden (1993), The Tolpuddle Woman (1994), Ruddlemoor (1995), Lewin's Mead, Moontide (1996); *Recreations* travel, historical research, music; *Clubs* Royal Over-Seas League; *Style—* E V Thompson, Esq; ✉ Parc Franton, Pentewan, St Austell, Cornwall PL26 6EH (☎ and fax 01726 843417)

THOMPSON, Estelle Margaret; *b* 8 June 1960; *Educ* Sheffield City Poly (BA), RCA (MA); *Career* artist; pt/t lectr: St Martin's Sch of Art, Christie's Fine Art Course, Ruskin Sch of Art, RCA, Slade Sch UCL, sr research fell De Montfort Univ 1995–97; *Solo Exhbns* incl: Pomeroy Purdy (now Purdy Hicks) Gallery 1989, 1991, 1992, 1993 and 1996, Eastbourne Clarke Gallery Florida 1989 and 1990, Castlefield Gallery Manchester 1992, Purdy Hicks Gallery London touring to Winchester Gallery Winchester Sch of Art, Towner Art Gallery Eastbourne and Darlington Arts Centre 1993, Galerie Helmut Pabst Frankfurt 1996; *Gp Exhbns* incl: Three Painters from the RCA Paton Gall 1985, Women and Water Odette Gilbert Gallery 1988, Homage to the Square Flaxman Gallery 1989 and 1990, The Theory and Practice of the Small Painting Anderson O'Day Gallery 1990, Whitechapel Open 1990 and 1992, Art in Worship Worcester Cathedral and Tewkesbury Abbey 1991, (dis)parities Mappin Art Gallery Sheffield and Pomeroy Purdy Gallery 1992, Bruise - Paintings for the 90's Ikon Gallery Birmingham 1992, BDO Binder Hamlyn Art Collection London 1993, Moving into View: Recent British Painting Royal Festival Hall London touring to Darlington Arts Centre, Chapter Cardiff, Oriel Gallery Mold, Newlyn Orion Gallery Penzance, Univ of Northumbria Newcastle upon Tyne, Drumcroon Arts Centre Wigan, Harrogate Museum and Art Gallery and Victoria Art Gallery Bath 1993–96, Castlefield Gallery 10th Anniversary Whitworth Art Gallery Univ of Manchester 1994, Six British Painters Galerie Helmut Pabst Frankfurt, Shadow of Life Art 97 The Printshow Flowers Graphics; awards: Royal Over-Seas League Travel Award 1988, Prudential awards for the arts/Arts Cncl special award 1990; work in the collections of: Arts Cncl, Br Cncl, Br Museum, Towner Art Gallery Sussex, Arthur Andersen Collection, The Contemporary Art Soc, County NatWest, Reed International, Unilever, Coopers & Lybrand, De Beers, Pearl Assurance, New Hall Cambridge, Oldham Art Gallery Greater Manchester, Univ of Warwick, Chelsea & Westminster Hosp, Ferens Art Gallery Hull, Deutsche Bank, Economist Gp, Reynolds Porter Chamberlain, TI Group Plc; *Books* A Year of Art for London Lighthouse; British Painting (1993); *Style—* Ms Estelle Thompson; ✉ c/o Purdy Hicks Gallery, 65 Hopton Street, London SE1 9GZ (☎ 0171 237 6062)

THOMPSON, Frank Robert; s of Corpl Arthur Robert Thompson (d 1964), of Newark, Notts, and Margaret Ellen, *née* Fordham; *b* 1 Jan 1938; *Educ* Magnus GS Newark, Univ of Hull (BA, DipEd); *m* 21 Dec 1963, (Janet) Deirdre, da of Robert Fraser Skinner, of Melton Mowbray, Leicestershire; 1 s (Alastair b 1966), 1 da (Virginia b 1965); *Career* dep head Park FE Centre Swindon 1969–70, head Westbourne FE Centre Swindon 1971–72; Pontypool Coll: head gen studies 1975–82, sr lectr Dept of Arts and Gen Studies 1982–90; Parly candidate (Lab): S Norfolk 1964, Wells 1970, Monmouth 1974; memb Univ of Bristol Ct 1981–86; Glos CC: cncllr (Lab) Coleford 1981–, dep ldr Lab Gp 1982–85, Lab gp ldr 1985–93, chm of Cncl 1993–, rep on Assoc of CCs 1985–, memb ACC Planning and Transportation Ctee (now Environment Ctee) 1985–, dep spokesman Lab Gp ACC Environment Ctee 1990–, vice chm Cncl 1992–93, chm Strategy and Resource Ctee 1992–93 (chm Ctee's Performance Review Bd 1992–93); vice chm Environment Ctee Assoc of County Cncls 1993–, memb Nat Planning Forum 1993–; rep Assembly of Euro Regions 1993– (memb Environment Ctee 1994–); Staunton Parish Cncl: memb 1979–87 (chm 1981–87), rep Forest of Dean CAB Mgmnt Ctee 1979–87; chm Govrs: Royal Forest of Dean GS 1982–85, Lakers Sch 1985–91; hon vice pres Three Choirs Festival 1994–; memb NATFHE 1973–; *Recreations* long-distance walking, swimming, chess, listening to music; *Style—* Frank Thompson, Esq; ✉ Steep Meadow, Staunton, Coleford, Gloucestershire GL16 8PD (☎ 01594 833873, fax 01594 810039); Shire Hall, Gloucester (☎ 01452 425008, fax 01452 425850)

THOMPSON, Gabriel Piers; s of James Thompson, of King's Norton, Birmingham, and Mary Josephine, *née* McAndrew; *b* 8 March 1962; *Educ* The Reading Bluecoat Sch Sonning-on-Thames Berkshire; *m* 20 Aug 1982, Martina Josephine, da of Francis Joseph Devlin; *Career* Reading Evening Post: trainee reporter 1981, sub-ed 1982, passed NCTJ proficiency test 1983, sr reporter 1983; sub-ed: Middlesbrough Evening Gazette 1984, Newcastle Journal 1985; The Independent: layout sub-ed 1986, foreign sub-ed 1987, foreign prodn ed 1989; prodn ed The Independent on Sunday 1990 (chief sub-ed 1990), currently dep night ed The Independent; *Recreations* smoking, drinking, eating, falling in love, walking on desks; *Clubs* The Irish National Foresters (County Tyrone); *Style—* Gabriel Thompson, Esq; ✉ The Independent, 1 Canada Square, Canary Wharf, London E14 5AP (☎ 0171 293 2000, fax 0171 293 2435)

THOMPSON, (Alec) Geoffrey; OBE (1983), DL (1993); s of Alexander William Thompson (d 1968), and Edna May Thompson (d 1980); *b* 25 April 1926; *Educ* Preston GS, Manchester GS, Univ of Manchester (BSc); *m* 1949, Irene Lilian, da of James Eatock; 2 s (John, Peter); *Career* J Bibby & Sons plc: dir 1977–87, md 1979–82, vice chm 1982–87; vice chm: Petranol plc 1980–83, Fothergill-Harvey plc 1980–85; chm: Westmorland Smoked Foods Ltd 1985–95, Gilbert Gilks & Gordon Ltd 1989–, Glentarret Ltd 1994–, Blue Thane Ltd 1994–, The East Lancashire Paper Mill Co Ltd 1994–; dir: Majorfinch Ltd 1984–, Lancord Ltd 1991–93, NHS Trust Federation Ltd 1992–93; chm Lancaster University Residences I, II and III plcs 1993–; hon treas and memb Cncl Univ of Lancaster 1983–93; tstee: Francis Scott Charitable Tst 1985–95, Dowager Lady Shuttleworth Tst 1989–; chm Lancaster & Dist Health Authy 1985–91, chm Lancaster Acute Hosp NHS Tst 1991–; Hon LLD Univ of Lancaster 1994; CIMgt, FRSA; *Recreations* fishing, shooting, travel; *Style—* Geoffrey Thompson Esq, OBE, DL; ✉ Barcaldene, Leighton Drive, Beetham, Milnthorpe, Cumbria LA7 7BE (☎ 01539 562276, fax 01539 562453)

THOMPSON, Dr Geoffrey Stuart; s of Frank Vincent Thompson (d 1975), of Oldham, Lancashire, and Maud Partington, *née* Hague (d 1989); *b* 26 June 1926; *Educ* Manchester GS, Trinity Coll Cambridge (MA, MD); *m* 28 April 1962, Angela Mary Stewart, da of Dr David Brown, CBE (d 1973), of Bootle, Lancashire; 1 s (Jonathan Richard b 1967), 1 da (Jane Elizabeth b 1969); *Career* Nat Serv Flt Lt RAF 1952–54; house surgn UCH 1951, house physician then registrar then sr registrar Liverpool Teaching Hosps 1954–65, conslt physician S Manchester DHA 1965–91 (hon conslt physician 1991–); memb Med and Scientific Section Br Diabetic Assoc, fell Manchester Med Soc; memb BMA, FRCP 1974; *Recreations* cycling, walking, swimming; *Style—* Dr Geoffrey Thompson; ✉ 41 The Downs, Altrincham WA14 2QG (☎ 0161 928 2471, fax 0161 927 9175)

THOMPSON, Prof Gilbert Richard; s of Lt-Col Richard Louis Thompson (d 1976), and Violet Mary, *née* Harrison (d 1955); *b* 20 Nov 1932; *Educ* Downside, St Thomas's Hosp Med Sch (MB BS, MRCP), Univ of London (MD); *m* 14 June 1958, Sheila Jacqueline Mary, da of Melchior Deurvorst (d 1977); 2 s (Mark b 1961, Philip b 1971), 2 da (Anna b 1959, Jennifer b 1977); *Career* Lt RAMC Royal Army Med Coll Millbank 1957–58; Capt RAMC mil hosp: Accra Ghana 1959–61, Millbank 1961–63; registrar and sr registrar in med Hammersmith Hosp 1963–66, res fell Harvard Med Sch and Mass Gen Hosp Boston 1966–67, lectr in med Royal Postgrad Med Sch and conslt physician Hammersmith Hosp 1967–72, asst prof Baylor Coll of Med and Methodist Hosp Houston 1972–73, sr lectr in med Royal Postgrad Med Sch 1972–74, conslt MRC Lipid Metabolism Unit Hammersmith Hosp 1975–83, visiting prof Royal Victoria Hosp Montreal 1981–82, currently prof of clinical lipidology Lipoprotein Team MRC Clinical Sciences Centre Hammersmith Hosp; former chm Br Hyperlipidaemia Assoc; FRCP 1973; *Books* A Handbook of Hyperlipidaemia (1989 and 1994), Coronary Risk Factors and their Detection (1992); *Recreations* running, skiing, fly-fishing; *Style—* Prof Gilbert Thompson; ✉ Lipoprotein Team, MRC Clinical Sciences Centre, Hammersmith Hospital, Ducane Rd, London W12 0NN (☎ 0181 383 3262, fax 0181 383 2077)

THOMPSON, Guy Charles Wallace; s of Cdr John Lionel Wallace Thompson (d 1987), and Patricia June, *née* Etchells; *b* 23 Nov 1952; *Educ* Sutton Valence, Univ of Newcastle upon Tyne (BA, BArch); *m* 2 Aug 1975, Gillian Edna, da of P R Brown; 1 da (Amy Charlotte b 21 Nov 1982), 1 s (Joel Henry Xavier b 31 Dec 1991); *Career* architectural asst PSA Edinburgh 1974–75, design conslt Planning Dept Tyne and Wear Cncl (Highways and Environmental Works Team Section) 1977; Norman & Dawbarn: architectural asst 1977, assoc 1983, ptnr/dir 1988–, md 1994–; projects incl: operating theatres RAF Hosp Ely 1978, Mil Works Force accommodation Chilwell 1984, Southwood Business Park Farnborough, Consulate and Cultural Centre Queensgate Kensington, Wembley Community Care Centre; dir The Wren Insurance Association Ltd 1990; chm W Surrey Branch RIBA 1994–96, vice chm SE Regn RIBA 1995; pres Guildford and Dist C of C 1995, dir and vice pres Thames Valley C of C and Indust 1995–96; memb ARCUK 1978, ARIBA 1978, Ordre des Architectes 1993; *Awards* Northern Brick Fedn Design Award 1977, competition winner Hawth Centre for the Performing Arts 1986, Civic Design Award Best Office Building 1991; *Recreations* squash, walking, architecture; *Clubs* Reform; *Style—* Guy Thompson, Esq; ✉ 53 Wodeland Ave, Guildford, Surrey GU2 5JZ (☎ 01483 31097); Norman & Dawbarn, Studio 7, Riverside Business Centre, Walnut Tree Close, Guildford GU2 4UG (☎ 01483 33551, fax 01483 506459)

THOMPSON, Harry William; s of Gordon William Thompson, of Llandovery, Dyfed, and Brenda, *née* Houghton; *b* 6 Feb 1960; *Educ* Highgate, BNC Oxford (MA); *m* 1993, Fiona Duff; 1 da, 1 s; *Career* BBC TV: researcher (Chronicle, Newsnight, Not the 9 O'Clock News) 1981–82, dir (Film 83, Destination D Day, Nationwide) 1982–84; script ed and sr prodr BBC radio comedy (incl The News Quiz, Weekending, The Mary Whitehouse Experience, Lenin of The Rovers, Beachcomber.....by the Way, The Crusader Chronicles, Memoirs of the Forgotten) 1985–91; writer of TV documentaries incl: Decibels of the Decade, The Man in the Iron Mask; presenter: Opening Shot - Tintin' (TV documentary), If I Ruled the World (BBC Radio 5 series); TV prodr: Have I Got News For You (also writer) 1990– (winner 9 awards), Beethoven's Not Dead 1992, Newman and Baddiel in Pieces 1993, Bore of the Year Awards 1993, Harry Enfield and Chums 1994, They Think it's all Over 1995–; contrib to: Spitting Image, Not The Nine O'Clock News, Private Eye, The Independent, The Evening Standard, The Observer, Mail on Sunday, The Times, Time Out, The Listener, The Daily Telegraph, The Daily Mirror; reg columnist The Guardian 1996–; prodr Private Eye Floppy Records; nominated Travel Writer of the Year 1995; *Books* The Prejudice Library (1986), The Man in the Iron Mask (1987), The News Quiz Book (1987), The Spitting Image Book (contrib, 1988), Tintin - Hergé and his Creation (1991), Richard Ingrams - Lord of the Gnomes (1994), The Have I Got News For You Book (contrib, 1994); *Recreations* cricket, long-distance travel; *Clubs* Black's, Captain Scott; *Style—* Harry Thompson, Esq; ✉ 37 Craven Hill Gardens, London W2 3EA

THOMPSON, (Geoffrey) Hewlett; *see:* Exeter, Bishop of

THOMPSON, (James) Howard; OBE (1985); s of James Alan Thompson (d 1982), and Edna, *née* Perkins; *b* 26 March 1942; *Educ* Northampton GS, Magdalene Coll Cambridge (BA), Stanford Univ (MA); *m* 11 Sept 1965, Claire Marguerite, da of Thomas Hayes Dockrell, TD (d 1970), of Northampton; 1 s (Hayes Benedict b 1972), 1 da (Catherine Frances b 1967); *Career* English language offr Br Cncl Yugoslavia 1965–69, assoc prof of English Regnl Inst of English Chandigarh India 1970–73, dep rep (British Cncl) Kenya 1974–78, advsr Schs and Further Educn Br Cncl London 1978–80, educn attaché Br Embassy Washington 1980–84; Br Cncl: dep controller Sci Technol and Educn Div London 1984–87, controller Educn and Sci Div London 1987–89, dir Indonesia 1989–92, dir Egypt 1993–; chm Educn and Trg Export Ctee 1987–89; *Books* Teaching English; *Recreations* travel, photography; *Style*— Howard Thompson, Esq, OBE; ✉ British Council, 192 Sharia El Nil, Agouza, Cairo, Egypt (☎ 00 20 2 340 2095, fax 00 20 2 344 3076, telex 21534 BRICO UN)

THOMPSON, James Craig; s of Alfred Thompson, of Newcastle upon Tyne, and Eleanor, *née* Craig; *b* 27 Oct 1933; *Educ* Heaton GS, Rutherford Coll Newcastle; *m* 4 Sept 1957, Catherine, da of James Warburton, of Newcastle upon Tyne; 1 s (Roderic b 1959), 1 da (Fiona b 1963); *Career* commercial exec 1960–76: Belfast Telegraph, Newcastle Chronicle and Journal, Scotsman Publications, Liverpool Post and Echo; advtg and mktg mangr Kent Messenger Gp 1976–79 (dir 1972–79), md South Eastern Newspapers 1975–79, chm and md Adverkit International Ltd 1979–90, chm and md Maidstone United Football Club Ltd 1970–92, chm and md Harvest Publications 1983–95, chm North Kent Land Holdings Ltd 1992–94; chief exec Maidstone and District C of C and Indust 1994–; md: Dartford Football Club plc 1991–93, Maidstone Invicta FC Ltd 1993–94; pres: Maidstone Minor League 1976–, Eastern Professional Floodlight League 1976–94, Kent League 1984–89, Football Conf 1989–; chm: Southern Football League 1977–79 (life memb 1985–), Alliance Premier Football League 1979–89; life govr Kent County Agric Soc, hon life memb Kent County CC; memb: MCC, Catenian Assoc (pres Maidstone Circle 1974–75); Liveryman Worshipful Co of Stationers & Newspaper Makers; MCIM, MIMgt, FInstD; *Recreations* walking, Northumbrian history; *Clubs* Maidstone, Wig and Pen; *Style*— James Thompson, Esq; ✉ Prescott House, Otham, nr Maidstone, Kent (☎ 01622 861606)

THOMPSON, James Francis (Paddy); s of John Cherry Watson Thompson (d 1967), and Gladys Jessie, *née* Taylor (d 1989); *b* 11 March 1939; *Educ* Loretto; *m* 30 March 1967, Alison Margaret, da of John Burnet Maitland Cowan; 3 da (Heather Alison b 5 Oct 1970, Jennifer Isabel b 11 July 1972, Patricia Jean b 13 Oct 1975); *Career* stockbroking trainee Glasgow 1957–62, journalist Financial Times 1962–65, business ed Glasgow Herald 1965–70, dir Portfolio Management (Scotland) Ltd 1970–75, local dir Singer and Friedlander 1975–81; dir: James Finlay Investment Management Ltd 1981–96, James Finlay Nominees Ltd 1981–96, James Finlay Bank Ltd 1986–96, Bell Lawrie Investment Management 1996–; *Recreations* golf, reading; *Clubs* West of Scotland FC, Buchanan Castle Golf; *Style*— Paddy Thompson, Esq; ✉ Bell Lawrie Investment Management, 10 West Nile Street, Glasgow G1 2PP (☎ 0141 226 9990, fax 0141 226 9991)

THOMPSON, Rt Rev James Lawton; *see:* Bath and Wells, Bishop of

THOMPSON, Prof (John) Jeffrey; CBE (1989); s of John Thompson (d 1968), of Southport, Lancs, and Elsie May, *née* Wright; *b* 13 July 1938; *Educ* King George V Sch Southport, St John's Coll Cambridge (MA), Balliol Coll Oxford (MA), Hatfield Poly (PhD); *m* 6 April 1963, Kathleen Audrey, da of Francis Arthur Gough (d 1989), of Southport, Lancs; 3 da (Karen b 1965, Alison b 1966, Lynda 1971); *Career* schoolmaster Blundell's Sch Tiverton 1961–65, head of chemistry Watford GS 1965–69, lectr KCL 1968–69, Shell fell UCL 1969–70, lectr and tutor Dept of Educnl Studies Oxford 1970–79, lectr in chemistry Keble Coll Oxford 1970–76, prof of educn Univ of Bath 1979– (pro vice-chllr 1986–89); dep chm Sch Examinations and Assessment Cncl 1988–92, vice pres and gen sec Br Assoc for the Advancement of Sci 1984–91 (chm Cncl 1991–96, vice pres 1996–); chm: Assoc for Sci Educn 1981, Examining Bd Int Baccalaureate 1984–89; memb: Cncl Wildfowl and Wetlands Tst, Royal Soc Educn Ctee, Assoc for Sci Educn, Nat Cmmn for Educn, English Nat Bd for Nursing Midwifery and Health Visiting 1993–; Liveryman of the Worshipful Co of Goldsmiths 1992, Freeman of the City of London 1992; FRSC, FRSA 1984; *Books* An Introduction to Chemical Energetics (1967), Study of Chemistry Programmes (1972), Modern Physical Chemistry (1982), A Foundation Course in Chemistry (1982), Dimensions of Science (ed, 1986), The Chemistry Dimension (1987); *Recreations* N country art and music, collecting sugar wrappers; *Style*— Prof Jeffrey Thompson, CBE; ✉ School of Education, University of Bath, Claverton Down, Bath BA2 7AY

THOMPSON, Jeremy Gordon; s of Gordon Alfred Thompson, and Elizabeth Betty, *née* Illman; *b* 23 Sept 1947; *Educ* Sevenoaks Sch Kent, King's Sch Worcester; *m* 1, 1970 (m dis 1980), Nichola Wood; 2 s (James Spencer b 1971, Adam Redvers b 1972); *m* 2, 1986, Lynn Patricia Bowland; *Career* foreign affairs correspondent; trainee chartered surveyor then trainee account exec with advtg agency London 1965–67; reporter: Cambridge Evening News 1967–71, BBC Radio Sheffield 1971–74, Look North (BBC TV Leeds) 1974–77; N of England corr BBC TV News 1977–82; ITN: chief sports corr 1982–86, Asia corr (setting up new bureau in Hong Kong) 1987–90, corr covering Gulf War and Yugoslavia 1990–91, Africa corr 1991; currently Washington corr Sky Television PLC; major assignments with ITN: *Sporting* Olympic Games LA 1984 and Seoul 1988, England cricket tours to Aust, W Indies, India and Pakistan, football World Cup Spain 1982, numerous other sporting events; *News* assassination of Indira Ghandi 1984, Bhopal tragedy India 1984, student political uprising Tianamen Square China 1989, democracy riots in S Korea, Benazir Bhutto's election in Pakistan, child labour scandal in India, Sri Lankan war, Phillipine and Fiji coups, Vietnamese pull out from Cambodia, famine in Somalia; memb: NUJ 1967–, Sports Writers Assoc 1982–, Hong Kong Foreign Correspondents Assoc; winner Outstanding Coverage of a Single Breaking News Story EMMY for report on Bisho massacre S Africa 1992 (first EMMY won by a British network); *Recreations* cricket, golf, swimming, walking, game and bird watching; *Style*— Jeremy Thompson, Esq

THOMPSON, Jeremy Sinclair; s of Norman Sinclair Thompson, CBE, of Burton Bradstock, Dorset, and Peggy, *née* Sivil; *b* 6 April 1954; *Educ* Durham Sch, Keble Coll Oxford (MA); *m* 12 June 1982, Lucy Jane Thompson, da of Peter Joseph Wagner (d 1983); 2 da (Victoria b 1986, Poppy b 1989), 1 s (Samuel b 1995); *Career* Peat Marwick Mitchell 1976–80, dir accounting servs Air Florida Europe Ltd 1980–82, conslt Coopers & Lybrand Associates 1982–84; md: Sinclair Thompson Associates 1985–86, Tranwood Earl & Co Ltd 1986–91; dir: Tranwood plc 1987–91, Filofax Group plc 1990–92; gp md Vaile Sinclair Ltd 1991–; ACA 1980; *Recreations* rowing, sailing; *Clubs* Leander, Royal Ocean Racing; *Style*— Jeremy Thompson, Esq; ✉ Milton Manor, Milton Abbas, Dorset DT11 0AZ (☎ 01258 880857); Vaile Sinclair Ltd, Hazelbury Bryan, Dorset (☎ 01258 817177, fax 01258 817666)

THOMPSON, (Thomas d'Eyncourt) John; s and h of Sir Lionel Tennyson Thompson, 5 Bt; *b* 22 Dec 1956; *Educ* Eton, King's Coll London; *Career* investment surveyor Weatherall Green & Smith; professional associate RICS; *Style*— John Thompson, Esq; ✉ Doctor Castelo 30, 8B, 28009 Madrid, Spain (☎ 00 34 1 504 6386); Weatherall Green & Smith, Torres de Colón 1.8, Plaza de Colón, 28046 Madrid, Spain (☎ 00 34 1 310 1016)

THOMPSON, John; MBE (1975); s of late Arthur Thompson, and late Josephine, *née* Brooke; *b* 28 May 1945; *Educ* St Nicholas GS, Central London Poly (DMS); *m* 9 July 1966, Barbara, da of late Ernest Hopper; 1 da (Ailsa b 1967); *Career* FCO: vice consul Dusseldorf 1966–69, Abu Dhabi 1969–72, Phnom Penh 1972–74; DTI 1975–77; FCO: first sec consul and head of chancery, Luanda 1979–82; consul São Paulo 1982–85; asst head: South Pacific Dept, Aid Policy Dept; high cmmr Vanuatu 1988–92, dep consul gen and dir of trade NYC 1992; *Recreations* philately, reading, walking, bridge; *Clubs* Commonwealth Tst; *Style*— John Thompson, Esq, MBE; ✉ c/o Foreign and Cwlth Office, London SW1A 2AH

THOMPSON, John Brian; CBE (1980); s of Jack Thompson (d 1985), of Chilton, Bucks, and Lilian Elizabeth, *née* Sutton (d 1981); *b* 8 June 1928; *Educ* St Paul's, Pembroke Coll Oxford (MA), LSE; *m* 12 Dec 1957, Sylvia Gough (Sally), da of Thomas Waterhouse, CBE (d 1961), of Holywell, N Wales; 2 s (Piers b 1959, Barnaby b 1961), 1 da (Eliza b 1963); *Career* ed Observer Colour Mag 1966–70, sr advsr (radio) to Min of Posts and Telecom 1971, dir of radio IBA 1972–87, vice chm (radio) Euro Broadcasting Union 1986–88, judge Booker Fiction prize 1987, ed The Viewer 1988–90, independent dir The Observer 1989–93; *Clubs* Garrick, Groucho; *Style*— John Thompson, Esq, CBE; ✉ 1 Bedwyn Common, Great Bedwyn, Marlborough, Wilts SN8 3HZ (☎ 01672 870641)

THOMPSON, Dr John Handby; CB (1988), CVO (1994); s of Rev John Thomas Thompson (d 1931), and Clara, *née* Handby (d 1974); *b* 21 Feb 1929; *Educ* Silcoates Sch Wakefield, St John's Coll Oxford (MA), Univ of Sheffield (PhD) 1991); *Career* Intelligence Corps 1947–49; HM Civil Serv: joined 1953, Inland Revenue 1953–64, Dept of Educn and Sci 1964–88 (under sec 1978, dir of establishments 1984), Cabinet Office 1988–94 (ceremonial offr 1988–94, sec Political Honours Scrutiny Ctee 1988–94); govr Univ of North London; memb Ctee The Chapels Soc; *Publications* The Free Church Army Chaplain 1830–1930 (thesis), The History of the Coward Trust; *Recreations* reading nonconformist history; *Clubs* Reform; *Style*— Dr John Thompson, CB, CVO

THOMPSON, John (Jack); MP (Lab) Wansbeck (majority 18,174); s of Nicholas Thompson, of Ashington, Northumberland (d 1966), and Lilian Thompson; *b* 27 Aug 1928; *Educ* Bothal Sch; *m* 1952, Margaret, da of John Robert Clarke (d 1974), of Newbiggin-by-Sea, Northumberland; 1 s, 1 da; *Career* electrical engineer 1966–83; dist cncllr 1970–79, co cncllr 1974–85, ldr and vice chm Northumberland Co Cncl 1974–83, memb Bd Northumbrian Water Authority 1981–83; MP (Lab) Wansbeck 1983–, alternate memb Parly Assembly Cncl of Europe and W Euro Union 1987– (full memb 1991–), oppn whip Northern Region, foreign affrs and Europe 1991–; chm W Euro Union Rules and Privileges Ctee 1991–, chm Cncl of Euro Fisheries Sub Ctee 1995–; *Recreations* caravanning, listening; *Style*— Jack Thompson, Esq, MP; ✉ House of Commons, London SW1A 0AA (☎ 0171 219 4048); 20 Falstone Crescent, Ashington, Northumberland (☎ 01670 817830, fax 01670 521005)

THOMPSON, John Michael; s of Arthur Leslie Thompson (d 1972), of Eastbourne, E Sussex, and Hilda Maud, *née* Shapland; *b* 15 July 1944; *Educ* Stationers' Co's Sch, London Business Sch; *m* 21 Dec 1968, Farzie; 1 s (Neil John b 23 May 1974), 1 da (Sarah Elizabeth b 1 Jan 1973); *Career* articled clerk Wilkins Kennedy & Co CAs London 1961–66, Thornton Baker & Co London 1966–68; Coopers & Lybrand: Tehran 1968–72, London 1972–73, ptnr Tehran 1974–79, ptnr London 1980–, ptnr i/c Insolvency Div London 1987–96, ptnr i/c IT 1988–96, managing ptnr Business Recovery and Insovency 1996–; memb Ctee for Middle E Trade (COMET) 1992–93, memb Insolvency Licensing Ctee ICAEW 1991–; memb: Insolvency Practitioners' Assoc 1986, Soc of Practitioners in Insolvency 1990; FCA 1966; *Recreations* music, piano, travel, theatre, walking, tennis; *Style*— John Thompson, Esq; ✉ 68 Dennis Lane, Stanmore, Middx HA7 4JW (☎ 0181 954 5859); Coopers & Lybrand, Plumtree Court, London EC4A 4HT (☎ 0171 583 5000, fax 0171 822 4652)

THOMPSON, John Michael Anthony; s of George Edward Thompson (d 1982), of Deganwy, Gwynedd, N Wales, and Joan, *née* Smith; *b* 3 Feb 1941; *Educ* William Hulme's GS Manchester, Univ of Manchester (BA, MA); *m* 24 July 1965, Alison Sara, da of Walter Bowers, of Cheadle Hulme, Greater Manchester; 2 da (Hannah Jane b 19 March 1973, Harriet Mary b 13 Feb 1976); *Career* res asst Whitworth Art Gallery 1964–66, keeper Rutherston Collection Manchester City Art Gallery 1966–68; dir: NW Museum and Gallery Serv 1968–70, Arts and Museums Bradford 1970–75, Tyne and Wear Co Museums and Galleries 1975–86, Tyne and Wear Jt Museums Serv 1986–91; museums and heritage conslt 1991–, dir Museums and Galleries Consultancy 1992–95; fndr memb and hon sec Gp of Dirs of Museums in Br Isles, pres Museums North 1990–91; advsr Assoc of Met Authorities 1983–91; memb Standards Steering Ctee Museums Trg Inst 1990–93 (chair Curatorship Gp 1990–93), chm Gosforth Adult Educn Assoc 1993–, tstee Jarrow 700AD Ltd 1993–, govr Gosforth HS 1993–, tech advsr Heritage Lottery Fund 1996–; memb: Assoc of Independent Museums, American Assoc of Museums; FMA 1977 (AMA 1970), MIMgt 1994; *Books* Manual of Curatorship, A Guide to Museum Practice (ed, new edn 1992); *Recreations* running, travel, visiting exhibitions; *Style*— John Thompson, Esq; ✉ 21 Linden Rd, Gosforth, Newcastle upon Tyne (☎ and fax 0191 284 2797)

THOMPSON, Prof John Quentin Warburton; s of Frederick John Warburton Thompson (d 1951), of Highgate and Ealing, London, and Ethel Georgina Eleanor, *née* Wade, of Buenos Aires (d 1966); *b* 7 Nov 1924; *Educ* City of London Sch (Temple choir), London Hosp and Univ of London (MB BS, PhD); *m* 3 Oct 1969, Judith Russell, da of Harry Hick, of Wakefield, Yorks; 1 s (Jonathan b 29 March 1972), 1 da (Georgina b 13 Feb 1974); *Career* Nat Serv Flt Lt RAF Med Branch 1949–51; res asst Dept of Applied Pharmacology Med Unit Univ Coll Hosp and Dept of Pharmacology UCL 1952–54, lectr Dept of Pharmacology Inst of Basic Med Sciences RCS 1954–64, sr lectr in pharmacology Med Unit St George's Hosp London 1961–64, prof of pharmacology Dept of Pharmacological Sciences Med Sch Newcastle 1964–90, conslt clinical pharmacologist Royal Victoria Infirmary 1964–90 (conslt in charge pain relief clinic 1979–90); dir of studies St Oswald's Hospice 1989–94, currently hon physician and hon conslt in med studies St Oswald's Hospice; emeritus prof of pharmacology Univ of Newcastle upon Tyne, emeritus conslt clinical pharmacologist Newcastle Health Authy; memb: Br Pharmacological Soc 1958, The Pain Soc of GB and Ireland 1978, Int Assoc for the Study of Pain 1981, Br Med Acupuncture Soc, Assoc for Palliative Med 1985; past pres Tyne and Wear Branch Nat Back Pain Assoc; Hon Master of Chinese Med China Acad Taiwan; memb BMA 1948, FRCP 1981; *Books* Textbook of Dental Pharmacology and Therapeutics (jtly, 1994); also chapters in medical works of reference and papers in learned scientific and medical jls; *Recreations* music, photography, DIY; *Style*— Prof John W Thompson; ✉ 1 Hackwood Park, Hexham, Northumberland NE46 1AX (☎ and fax 01434 608552)

THOMPSON, Rear Adm John Yelverton; CB (1960); s of Sir John Perronet Thompson, KCSI, KCIE, ICS (d 1935), and Ada Lucia, *née* Tyrrell (d 1957); *b* 25 May 1909; *Educ* Mourne Grange, Kilkeel Co Down, RNC Dartmouth (psc 1946); *m* 15 Dec 1934, Barbara Helen Mary Aston (d 1996), da of Dr Benjamin William Martin Aston Key, OBE (d 1961), of Southsea; 2 s (Richard b 1935, Martin b 1939); *Career* Lt Cdr HMS Anson N Atlantic 1941–43, Cdr Naval Ordnance Dept Admty 1943–45, US 5 Fleet 1946, Liverpool 1947, Newcastle 1948; Capt Ordnance Bd 1948–50, Unicorn (Korean War) 1951–52 (despatches), dir Gunnery Div, Naval Staff 1952–54, idc 1955; Cdre RN Barracks Portsmouth 1956–57; ADC to HM The Queen 1957–58; Rear Adm Admty Interview Bd 1958, Adm Supt HM Dockyard Chatham 1958–61 (ret); naval advsr Elliott-Automation

1961–66; govr Aldenham Sch 1967–75; chm Herts Scout Cncl 1962–71; DL Hertfordshire 1966–73, Cornwall 1973–88; American Legion of Merit 1953; *Style*— Rear Adm J Y Thompson, CB; ✉ Rydons, 104 Ridgway, Wimbledon SW19 4RD (☎ 0181 947 7514)

THOMPSON, (Charles Arthur) Jonathan; s of William Arthur Lisle Thompson, of Liverpool and Anglesey, and Margaret Elizabeth; *b* 27 May 1954; *Educ* Liverpool Coll, Blackpool Coll (HND); *m* 4 Oct 1986, Caroline Jane, da of John Albert Howard; 2 da (Elizabeth Jane b 3 March 1989, Emily Louise b 25 Sept 1990); *Career* dep gen mangr The Compleat Angler Hotel Marlow 1978–81, gen mangr Stratton House Hotel Cirencester 1981–83; Historic House Hotels 1983– (gen mangr Bodysgallen Hall 1983–88, dir and gen mangr Hartwell House 1989–); past memb Overseas Mktg Intelligence Ctee; chm Thames and Chilterns Div BHA; memb: Hotel Catering and Institutional Mgmnt Assoc, Restaurateurs Assoc of GB, Confrerie des Chevalliers de Tastevin; Master Innholder 1990–; AA Red Stars 1983–, RAC Blue Ribbons 1988, Hotel of the Year Andrew Hayer's Hideaway Report 1985–87 and 1992, Welsh Tourist Bd award for services to tourism 1986–, Queen's award for export achievement 1987, Good Hotel Guide Cesar award for outstanding restoration and first class hotel mgmnt 1988–, Good Food Guide Buckinghamshire County Restaurant of the Year 1989, Which? Hotel Guide Buckinghamshire County Hotel of the Year 1996; MHCIMA; *Recreations* sailing, history and heritage, my family; *Style*— Jonathan Thompson, Esq; ✉ Awelfor, Ffordd Llechi, Rhosneigr, Isle of Anglesey, Gwynedd LL64 5JY (☎ 01407 810289); Historic House Hotels, Hartwell House, Oxford Rd, nr Aylesbury, Buckinghamshire HP17 8NL (☎ 01296 747444, fax 01296 747450)

THOMPSON, (Rupert) Julian de la Mare; s of Rupert Spens Thompson (d 1952), and Florence Elizabeth de la Mare; *b* 23 July 1941; *Educ* Eton, King's Coll Cambridge (MA); *m* 6 March 1965, Jacqueline Mary, da of John William Linnell Ivimy; 3 da (Rebecca b 1966, Sophia b 1968, Cecilia b 1971); *Career* Sothebys: dir 1969–, chm 1982–86, chm Sotheby's Asia 1992–; *Style*— Julian Thompson, Esq; ✉ 43 Clarendon Rd, London W11 4JD (☎ 0171 727 6039); Crossington Farm, Upton Bishop, Ross-on-Wye, Hereford HR9 7UE (☎ 01989 780363); Sotheby's 34–45 New Bond St, London W1A 2AA (☎ 0171 408 5371)

THOMPSON, Maj Gen Julian Howard Atherden; CB (1982), OBE (1978); s of Maj A J Thompson, DSO, MC (d 1966), of Cornwall, and Mary Stearns, *née* Krause (d 1978); *b* 7 Oct 1934; *Educ* Sherborne; *m* 1960, Janet Avery, da of Richard Robinson Rodd, of Devon; 1 s (David), 1 da (Henrietta); *Career* CO 40 Commando RM 1975–78; Cdr 3 Commando Bde 1981–83, including Falklands Campaign 1982, Maj Gen cmd Training and Special Forces Royal Marines; sr research fell King's Coll London; pres Br Assoc of Physical Trg; Liveryman Worshipful Co of Carpenters; *Books* No Picnic (1985), Ready for Anything: The Parachute Regiment at War 1940–82 (1989), The Lifeblood of War: Logistics in Armed Conflict (1991), Military Strategy in a Changing Europe (contrib Command and Control in the Falklands War, 1991), Fallen Stars (contrib John Lucas and Anzio, 1991), Iraq, the Gulf War and the World Community (contrib The Military Coalition, 1993), Victory in Europe: The North-West European Campaign 1944–45 (1994), The War at Sea: The Royal Navy in the Second World War (1996); *Recreations* sailing, stalking, cross-country, skiing, ballet, opera, jazz; *Clubs* Army and Navy; *Style*— Maj Gen Julian Thompson, CB, OBE; ✉ Lloyds Bank plc, 8 Royal Parade, Plymouth

THOMPSON, Dr (Malcolm) Keith; s of Ralph Whittier Thompson (d 1962), of London, and Ethel Eva, *née* Smith (d 1972); *b* 30 June 1921; *Educ* Trinity Sch of John Whitgift, Univ of St Andrews (MB ChB), Univ of London (DObst); *m* 24 Oct 1953, Jeanne Sophie Auguste, da of Jean Bernard Struys (d 1971), of Brussels; 1 da (Chantal (Mrs Blake-Milton) b 18 July 1957); *Career* Friends Ambulance Unit 1943–45; house physician to Sir Ian Hill 1952–53, house surgn in obstetrics and gynaecology Wanstead Hosp 1953, princ GP Woodside Health Centre London SE25 1955–86; conslt in geriatric med American Univ of Beirut 1993, visiting prof Ain Wazein Hosp Lebanon 1994; examiner for MRCGP examination 1976–86, examiner for RCP diploma in geriatric med 1984–92; Nuffield travelling fell 1970, Med Gilliland travelling fell 1984; fndr assoc memb RCGP 1953; med ed: Medical Opinion 1978–79, Geriatric Medicine 1984–86; med corr Yours newspaper 1974–, lectr Coll of GP Hong Kong 1987; advsr: WHO Copenhagen 1979, DHSS 1980; distinctions: Butterworth Gold medal 1967, Hunterian Soc Gold medal 1968; med advsr Help the Aged; memb: Governing Body Age Concern, Med Advsy Panel Parkinsons Disease Soc of GB (pres Croydon Branch), BMA, Br Geriatrics Soc 1971; MRCOG 1954, MRCGP 1965, FRCGP 1977, FRSM; *Books* Geriatrics and the General Practitioner Team (1969), Geriatrie Voor Die Huisarts (1971), The Care of the Elderly in General Practice (1984), Caring for an Elderly Relative (1986), Commonsense Geriatrics (1990); *Recreations* swimming, golf, music, theatre, walking; *Style*— Dr Keith Thompson; ✉ 28 Steep Hill, Stanhope Rd, Croydon CR0 5QS (☎ 0181 686 7489)

THOMPSON, Keith Bruce; s of Charles Bruce Thompson (d 1982), and Eva Elizabeth, *née* Vidler (d 1966); *b* 13 Sept 1932; *Educ* Bishopshalt Sch Hillingdon, New Coll Oxford (MA), Oxford Dept of Educn (DipEd), Univ of Bristol (MEd); *m* 17 Aug 1956, Kathleen Anne, da of Sydney Reeves, OBE (d 1982); 1 s (Bruce b 1959), 1 da (Fiona b 1961); *Career* RAOC 1950–52; schoolmaster City of Bath Boys' Sch 1956–62, lectr Newton Park Coll Bath 1962–67, head of dept Philippa Fawcett Coll Streatham 1967–72, princ Madeley Coll Staffs 1972–78, vice-chancellor Staffordshire Univ 1992–95 (dep dir (N) Staffs Poly 1978–86, dir 1986–92); chm: Standing Conf on Studies in Educn 1980–82, Undergraduate Initial Trg Bd (Educn) CNAA 1981–85, Polys Central Admissions System (PCAS) 1989–93; dep chm Univs and Colls Admissions Serv 1993–95; memb Nat Advsy Body for Public Sector Higher Educn 1983–88 (chm Teacher Educn Gp 1983–85); ed Education for Teaching jl 1968–74; *Books* Education and Philosophy (1972), Curriculum Development (jtly, 1974); *Recreations* sport, music; *Style*— Keith Thompson, Esq; ✉ Hawthorn House, Little Tixall Lane, Great Haywood, Stafford ST18 0SE (☎ 01889 881874)

THOMPSON, Sir (Thomas) Lionel Tennyson; 5 Bt (UK 1806), of Hartsbourne Manor, Hertfordshire; s of Lt-Col Sir Thomas Raikes Lovett Thompson, 4 Bt, MC (d 1964), and of late Millicent Ellen Jean, da of late Edmund Charles Tennyson-d'Eyncourt, of Bayons Manor, Lincs; *b* 19 June 1921; *Educ* Eton; *m* 1955 (m dis 1962), Mrs Margaret van Beers, da of late Walter Herbert Browne; 1 s, 1 da; *Heir* s, Thomas d'Eyncourt John Thompson; *Career* WWII Flying Offr RAFVR (invalided), and subsequently Able Seaman Royal Fleet Auxiliary (1939–45, and Aircrew (Europe) stars, Defence and Victory Medals); called to the Bar Lincoln's Inn 1952; *Style*— Sir Lionel Thompson, Bt

THOMPSON, Dr (Ian) McKim; s of John William Thompson (d 1976), of Solihull, and Dr Elizabeth Maria, *née* Williams; *b* 19 Aug 1938; *Educ* Epsom Coll, Univ of Birmingham (MB ChB); *m* 8 Sept 1962, Dr (Veronica) Jane, da of John Dent Richards (d 1987), of Fladbury; 2 s (David b 1966, Peter b 1969), 1 da (Suzanne b 1972); *Career* lectr in pathology Univ of Birmingham 1964–67, conslt forensic pathologist to HM Coroner City of Birmingham 1966–, dep sec BMA 1969–, lectr Dept of Adult Educn Keele Univ 1985–; fndr memb AMEC, memb GMC 1979–95; hon memb Collegiate Med Coll of Spain 1975; BMA 1961, FRSM 1988; *Books* The Hospital Gazeteer (ed, 1972), BMA Handbook for Trainee Doctors in General Practice (ed 1985), BMA Handbook for Hospital Junior Doctors (ed, 1985); *Recreations* inland waterways, rambling; *Style*— Dr McKim Thompson; ✉ Weir Cottage, Fladbury, Pershore, Worcs WR10 2QA (☎ 01386 860 668); BMA House, Tavistock Square, London WC1H 9JP (☎ 0171 383 6005, fax 0171 383 6220)

THOMPSON, Mark; s of Owen Edgar Thompson, of Dorset, and Barbara Adele, *née* Lister; *b* 12 April 1957; *Educ* Radley Coll, Univ of Birmingham; *partner* Anthony Ward, *qv*; *Career* set and costume designer; *Theatre* rep incl: Worcester, Exeter, Sheffield, Leeds; for Royal Manchester Exchange credits incl: Jumpers, The Country Wife, Mumbo Jumbo (also Hammersmith Lyric), The School for Scandal; for Almeida credits incl: Volpone, Betrayal, Party Time, Butterfly Kiss; for RSC credits incl: Measure for Measure, The Wizard of Oz, Much Ado About Nothing, The Comedy of Errors; for RNT credits incl: The Wind in the Willows, The Madness of George III, Arcadia (also Haymarket West End, Lincoln Centre New York), Pericles, What the Butler Saw; other credits incl: Owners (Old Vic), Good (Brussels), The Scarlet Pimpernel (Chichester and Her Majesty's), Cabaret (Strand), The Sneeze (Aldwych), Ivanov, Much Ado About Nothing (both Strand), A Little Night Music (Piccadilly), Shadowlands (Queen's and Broadway), Joseph and the Amazing Technicolor Dreamcoat (Palladium and Canadian/Aust/USA tours), Six Degrees of Separation (Royal Court and Comedy Theatre), Hysteria (Royal Court and Mark Taper Forum LA), The Kitchen (Royal Court), Insignificance, Company (both Donmar Warehouse and Albery); *Opera* credits incl: Falstaff (Scottish Opera), Peter Grimes (Opera North), Ariadne Auf Naxos (Salzburg), Il Viaggio A Reims (ROH), Hansel and Gretal (Sydney Opera House), The Two Widows (ENO); costume design credits incl: Montag Aus Licht (La Scala, Milan), Queen of Spades (Met, New York); *Ballet* Don Quixote (Royal Ballet); *Films* costumes for The Madness of King George; *Awards* for Wind in the Willows awards incl: Olivier Award 1991, Plays and Players Award 1991, Critics' Circle Award 1991; other awards incl: Olivier Award for Set Design and Costume Design for Joseph and the Amazing Technicolor Dreamcoat and The Comedy of Errors 1992, Olivier Award for Set Design for Hysteria 1994, Critics' Circle Award for The Kitchen 1995; *Style*— Mark Thompson; ✉ c/o Simpson Fox Associates Ltd, 52 Shaftesbury Avenue, London W1V 7DE (☎ 0171 434 9167, fax 0171 494 2887)

THOMPSON, Mark John Thompson; s of Duncan John Thompson Thompson (d 1986), of Preston, and Sydney Columba, *née* Corduff; *b* 31 July 1957; *Educ* Stonyhurst (scholar), Merton Coll Oxford (postmaster, BA, Violet Vaughan Morgan English prize, ed Isis); *m* 20 Sept 1987, Jane Emilie, da of Prof Baruch Samuel Blumberg, *qv*; 1 s (Caleb John Thompson Thompson b 23 Sept 1991), 1 da (Emilie Grainne Corduff b 8 Jan 1994); *Career* BBC TV: joined as res asst trainee 1979, researcher Everyman and Nationwide 1979–80, asst prodr Nationwide 1980–82, prodr Breakfast Time 1982–84, output ed London Plus 1984–85, output ed Newsnight 1985–87, ed Nine O'Clock News 1988–90, ed Panorama 1990–92, head of Features Dept 1992–94, head of Factual Progs 1994–96, controller of BBC2 1996–; chair Edinburgh Int TV Festival 1996; Monte Carlo TV Festival Golden Nymph Award for Panorama film Drowning in Blood 1991, RTS Home Current Affrs Award for Panorama film The Max Factor 1992; *Recreations* walking, cooking; *Style*— Mark Thompson, Esq; ✉ BBC Television, Television Centre, Wood Lane, London W12 7RJ (☎ 0181 743 8000)

THOMPSON, Martin William; s of John William Thompson (d 1968); *b* 8 May 1946; *Educ* Deacons Sch Peterborough, Goldsmiths' Sch of Art (DipAD); *m* 1972, Lynda Mia Minka, da of Sir John Peel; 3 s (Ansel b 7 Feb 1977, Robbie b 5 Jan 1980, Murray b 24 July 1982); *Career* photographer; asst to John S Clarke 1969–72, freelance 1972–74, carpenter and gen builder 1974–78, advtg photography 1978–; campaigns incl: Volvo, Sainsbury's, Benson & Hedges, Sherwoods, COI; winner 4 Campaign Silver Awards; *Recreations* sailing, keeping a small flock of sheep; *Clubs* Haven Ports, Cruising Assoc; *Style*— Martin Thompson, Esq

THOMPSON, Michael; s of Eric Thompson, of Menston, and Mary, *née* Shuttleworth; *b* 18 June 1954; *Educ* Bradford GS, Trinity Coll Cambridge (MA); *m* Linda, *née* Adapoe; 1 s (Christopher), 1 da (Bethany); *Career* RAF Reservist 1973–76; Freshfields: articled clerk 1977–79, asst slr 1979–85, ptnr Corporate Tax Dept 1985–; chm Law Soc's Revenue Law Sub Ctee on Petroleum Taxation; Freeman Worshipful Co of Slrs 1987; memb Law Soc; *Recreations* sailing, fell walking; *Style*— Michael Thompson, Esq; ✉ Freshfields, 65 Fleet Street, London EC4Y 1HS (☎ 0171 936 4000, fax 0171 832 7001)

THOMPSON, Prof (Francis) Michael Longstreth; CBE (1992); s of Francis Longstreth-Thompson, OBE (d 1973), of Little Waltham, Essex, and Mildred Grace, *née* Corder (d 1963); *b* 13 Aug 1925; *Educ* Bootham Sch York, Queen's Coll Oxford (MA, DPhil), Merton Coll Oxford; *m* 11 Aug 1951, Anne Longstreth, da of Maj John Lovibond Challoner, TA, of Northumberland (d 1970); 2 s ((Francis) Jonathan Longstreth b 1958, Matthew Longstreth b 1964), 1 da (Suzanna Jane Longstreth b 1959); *Career* WWII 1943–47, Lt 1944, 7 Indian Field Regt RIA India and Sumatra 1945–46, Staff Capt 26 Indian Div E Bengal 1946–47, Capt 1946–47; reader in economic history UCL 1963–68 (lectr in history 1951–63), prof of modern history Bedford Coll London 1968–77, dir Inst of Historical Res and prof of history Univ of London 1977–90 (emeritus prof of history 1990), Ford's lectr in history Univ of Oxford 1994; pres: Economic History Soc 1984–87, Royal Historical Soc 1988–92, Br Agric History Soc 1989–92; sec Br Nat Ctee of Historians 1977–93, Br Acad rep Humanities Ctee Euro Sci Fndn 1983–94, hon treas Int Econ History Assoc 1986–94; ed Econ History Review 1968–80; hon fell Royal Holloway and Bedford New Coll 1992; Hon DUniv York 1995; FRHistS 1963, ARICS 1968, FBA 1979; *Books* English Landed Society in the Nineteenth Century (1963), Victorian England: The Horse Drawn Society (1970), Chartered Surveyors: The Growth of a Profession (1968), Hampstead: Building a Borough (1974), The Rise of Suburbia (ed, 1982), Horses in European Economic History (ed, 1983), The Rise of Respectable Society (1988), The Cambridge Social History of Britain 1750–1950 (3 vols, ed, 1990), The University of London and the World of Learning, 1836–1986 (ed, 1990), Landowners, Capitalists and Entrepreneurs: Essays for Sir John Habakkuk (ed, 1994); *Recreations* gardening, walking, carpentry; *Style*— Prof Michael Thompson, CBE, FBA; ✉ Institute of Historical Research, University of London, Senate House, London WC1E 7HU (☎ 0171 636 0272)

THOMPSON, Michael Reginald; s of Frederick John Thompson, of Bramcote, Notts, and Dorothy, *née* Greensmith (d 1987); *b* 19 July 1943; *Educ* High Pavement GS, Univ of Sheffield (MB ChB, MD); *m* 3 Jan 1970, Judith Ann, da of John Hatchett Glover (d 1987), of Stratford-upon-Avon; 3 da (Hannah Louise b 28 April 1972, Emma Judith b 14 Nov 1975, Victoria Jillian b 24 March 1977); *Career* Nuffield travelling fell 1963, lectr in surgery Univ of Manchester Med Sch 1972–75, Harkness fell Dept of Physiology Univ of Michigan Ann Arbour and VA Centre Wadsworth UCLA 1973–75, sr registrar Bristol Hosps 1975–81, conslt surgn Portsmouth and SE Hants 1981–; treas Assoc of Coloproctology of GB and I, sec Cncl Coloproctology Section RSM 1996–, sec Surgical Sub-section Ctee Br Soc of Gastroenterology, pres Portsmouth and SE Hants Div BMA 1995–96; memb: Br Soc of Gastroenterology, Assoc of Surgns of GB and I, BMA (treas 1984–), RSM; FRCS 1971; *Recreations* sailing, theatre; *Clubs* 83 Surgical Travelling (sec); *Style*— Michael Thompson, Esq; ✉ St Andrews, 9 Eastern Parade, Southsea, Hants PO4 9RA (☎ 01705 756938; 31 Mill Lane, Sheet, Petersfield; Queen Alexandra Hospital, Cosham, Portsmouth (☎ 01705 379451); BUPA Hospital, Havant, Portsmouth (☎ 01705 454511)

THOMPSON, (John) Michael Strutt; s of John Thompson (d 1951), of Dale Farm, Weald, Sevenoaks, Kent, and Donnie Agnes Beatrice, *née* Strutt (d 1979); *b* 14 Dec 1931; *Educ* Felsted; *m* 24 Oct 1959, Fiona Mary, da of Wing Cdr Malcolm Glassford Begg, MC (d 1969), of Armsworth Park Farm, Alresford, Hants; 1 s (Marcus Peter Strutt b 1961), 1 da (Julia Mariette (Mrs Gallagher) b 1963); *Career* Nat Serv 2 Lt cmmnd Rifle Bde 1956–58; res sub agent RH & RW Clutton Hursley Estate Hants 1958–65, agent and sec Ernest Cook Tst Fairford Glos 1965–73, chief agent Fitzwilliam Estates Milton Park Peterborough Cambs 1974–; pres local Cons branch 1981–, gen cmmr Income Tax Peterborough 1981–, pres Land Agency and Agric Div RICS 1985–86; chm Landowners Gp 1987–91, pres Cambs CLA 1994–96; FRICS 1956, FAAV 1986; *Recreations* fishing, shooting, sailing; *Clubs* Farmers; *Style—* Michael Thompson, Esq; ✉ Stibbington House, Wansford, Peterborough, Cambs PE8 6JS (☎ 01780 782043); Estate Office, Milton Park, Peterborough, Cambs PE6 7AH (☎ 01733 267740, fax 01733 331200)

THOMPSON, Sir Michael Warwick; kt (1991); s of Kelvin Warwick Thompson (d 1985), of Cotherstone, Co Durham, and Madeleine, *née* Walford; *b* 1 June 1931; *Educ* Rydal Sch, Univ of Liverpool (BSc, DSc, Oliver Lodge prizewinner); *m* 1954, Sybil Noreen, da of John Rosser Spooner (d 1959); 2 s (Andrew Warwick b 5 Dec 1957, Dr Paul WARWICK THOMPSON, *qv*, b 9 Aug 1959); *Career* res scientist AERE Harwell 1953–65, prof of experimental physics Univ of Sussex 1965–80 (pro vice chllr 1972–78), vice chllr Univ of E Anglia 1980–86, vice chllr and princ Univ of Birmingham 1987–96; tstee Barber Inst of Fine Art 1987–; non-exec dir: Alliance & Leicester Building Society 1979– (dep chm 1995–), Cobuild Ltd 1987–96, W Midlands RHA 1990–96 (memb 1987–90, dep chm 1995–96); author of one book, edited works and numerous papers in sci jls; scientific intrests incl atomic collisions in solids, nuclear power and its applications and energy policy; Inst of Physics C V Boys prizewinner 1972; memb: E Sussex Educn Ctee 1973–78, E Sussex Area Health Authy 1973–80, Physics Ctee SRC 1972–79 (sometime chm), Cncl Ctee of Vice-Chllrs and Principals 1989–93 and 1994–96, Cncl Assoc of Commonwealth Univs 1990–95, Cncl Queen Mary and Westfield Coll Univ of London 1996–; FInstP 1964, FRSA 1994; *Recreations* the arts, navigating small ships offshore; *Clubs* Athenaeum, Royal Fowey Yacht, Royal Over-Seas League; *Style—* Sir Michael Thompson; ✉ Stoneacre, The Warren, Polperro, Cornwall PL13 2RD (☎ 01503 272821, fax 01503 272875)

THOMPSON, Nicholas; s of Eric Thompson (d 1975), of Kilmington, Devon, and Dorothy, *née* Lake (d 1982); *b* 25 Feb 1936; *Educ* Christ's Hosp, Oxford Sch of Architecture (DipArch, 4th Year Travel bursary), Architects Journal Travel bursary, RIBA Goodwin & Wimperis bursary and medal; *m* Alice Clare, da of Rev Canon Heneage Ferraby; 2 s (Mark b 1968, Paul b 1971); *Career* architect; with Norman and Dawbarn architects 1957–59; 2 Lt RE Hong Kong and Sabah 1960–61; joined Andrew Renton & Assocs, ptnr RHWL (Renton Howard Wood Levin) Ptnrship 1974–; specialises in building design for the performing arts incl: Crucible Theatre Sheffield (Civic Tst & RIBA awards) 1971, Univ of Warwick Arts Centre (RIBA award) 1973, Theatre Royal and Royal Concert Hall Nottingham (both RIBA awards) 1978–82, Duke of York's Theatre London 1979, The Old Vic London (RIBA commendation, Civic Tst award) 1984, Alhambra Theatre Bradford (RIBA regnl award) 1986, Towngate Theatre Basildon 1987, Theatre Royal Newcastle (RIBA regnl award) 1988, New Theatre Cardiff (Civic Tst commendation) 1988, Lyceum Theatre Sheffield (RIBA regnl award and Sheffield City Cncl design award) 1990, New Victoria Theatre Woking 1992, Donmar Warehouse 1992, BBC Radio Drama Studio 1992, Prince Edward Theatre London 1993, Haymarket Theatre Basingstoke 1993, Anvil Concert Hall Basingstoke (RIBA Regnl award) 1994, Chicken Shed Children's Theatre N London 1994, auditorium Musik Theater Stuttgart 1994, Duisberg 1995, Camberley Hall 1995, Bridgewater Concert Hall Manchester 1996, Sadler's Wells Theatre redevelopment, refurbishment of Palladium Theatre London, Malvern Festival Theatre, The Dome Concert Hall and Museum Brighton, Greshams Sch Theatre, study for Opera North and Grand Theatre Leeds, study for RSC Stratford, Collins Theatre Islington; overseas projects incl: theatre consultancy to Shah of Iran, design of Concert Hall and Acad of Music for Sultan of Oman, Nat Theatre Damascus (int competition winner), TV studios for Hutchvision Hong Kong 1991, design concept St James Theatre Wellington NZ 1995, design concept Theatre Royal Sydney 1996, Crown Theatre Melbourne 1996, design conslt Lazaristes Theatre Thessalonika 1996; ARIBA 1961; *Recreations* outdoors and active by day (travel, sailing, gardening), watching performances by night; *Clubs* Garrick; *Style—* Nicholas Thompson, Esq; ✉ Renton Wood Howard Levin Partnership, 77 Endell Street, London WC2H 9AJ (☎ 0171 379 7900, fax 0171 836 4881)

THOMPSON, Nicholas Annesley Marler; s and h of Sir Richard Hilton Marler Thompson, 1 Bt, *qv*; *b* 19 March 1947; *m* 1982, Venetia Catherine, yr da of John Horace Broke Heathcote, of Conington House, nr Peterborough; 3 s (Simon William b 1985, Charles Frederick b 1986, David Jonathan b 1990), 1 da (Emma Louise b 1991); *Career* admitted slr 1973, currently asst slr Denton Hall; memb Westminster City Cncl 1978–86, dep Lord Mayor of Westminster 1983–84; Parly candidate (C) Newham South 1983; *Recreations* foreign travel, skiing, riding, walking, theatre, reading; *Clubs* Carlton; *Style—* Nicholas Thompson, Esq; ✉ Maxgate, George Rd, Kingston upon Thames, Surrey KT2 7NR (☎ 0181 942 7251); Denton Hall, 5 Chancery Lane, Clifford's Inn, London EC4A 1BU (☎ 0171 242 1212)

THOMPSON, Brig Nicholas Herbert; CBE (1990); s of Brig Guy Owen Netterville Thompson, DSO, OBE (d 1974), and Doreen Gertrude Helen Thompson (d 1994); *b* 4 Dec 1937; *Educ* Eastbourne Coll, Welbeck Coll, RMA Sandurst, RMC of Science Shrivenham (BSc(Eng)); *m* 1968, Mary Penelope Say; 2 da (Alexandra b 1971, Helen b 1974); *Career* cmmnd RE 1957; cmd ind construction troop Belize 1962–63, ADC to GOC NW Dist 1963–65, served Cyprus 1965–67, civil engrg 1967–70, Pakistan Staff Coll and staff appts 1971–75, OC 52 Field Sqdn (Airfields) 1975–77, CO 38 Engr Regt Ripon (Lt Col) 1977–79, memb directing staff RMC of Science 1979–82, cmd Engrs 1 Br Corps (Brig) 1982–84, RCDS 1985, Dir of Manning (Army) 1986–89, ADC 1987–91, Dir Engr Servs 1989–91, ret 1991; bursar Headington Sch Oxford 1991–; Liveryman Worshipful Co of Tallow Chandlers (currently Renter Warden), Freeman City of London (by redemption); FICE 1983 (MICE 1969); *Recreations* riding, DIY, Shetland sheep, stonewalling, sailing, Scottish country dancing, travel; *Style—* Brig Nicholas Thompson, CBE; ✉ c/o Headington School, Oxford, Oxon OX3 0BL (☎ 01865 61144, fax 01865 60268)

THOMPSON, Nicolas de la Mare; s of Rupert Spens Thompson (d 1951), and Florence Elizabeth, *née* de la Mare (d 1990); *b* 4 June 1928; *Educ* Eton, Christ Church Oxford (MA); *m* 13 Sept 1956, (Fenella Mary) Erica (d 1993), da of Powlett Pennell (d 1970); 2 s (Rupert b 1962, Simon b 1964), 1 da (Sarah (Mrs James Maclean) b 1960); *Career* RAF 1949–51; md George Weidenfeld & Nicolson Ltd 1956–70, publishing dir Pitman plc 1976–84, md Heinemann Group of Publishers Ltd 1985–87; dir: Octopus Publishing Group plc 1985–89, Reed International Books Ltd 1989–93, International Book Development Ltd 1992–, Copyright Licensing Agency Ltd 1992–96, Almeida Theatre Company Ltd; chm Book Devpt Cncl 1984–86; *Style—* Nicolas Thompson, Esq; ✉ Flat A, 8 Ennismore Gardens, London SW7 (☎ 0171 584 9769)

THOMPSON, Prof Noel Brentnall Watson; s of George Watson Thompson (d 1980), and Mary Henrietta, *née* Gibson (d 1944); *b* 11 Dec 1932; *Educ* Manchester GS, Univ of Cambridge (MA), Imperial Coll London (MSc, PhD); *m* Jan 1957, Margaret Angela Elizabeth, da of Ernest William Baston (d 1967), of Bristol; 1 s (Gareth b 1972); *Career* Sub Lt RN 1951–53; sec Nat Libraries Ctee 1967–69, lectr Univ of Birmingham 1961–65, under sec Dept of Educn and Sci 1980–88, Cabinet Office Secretariat 1977–79, chief exec Nat Cncl for Educnl Technol 1988–92; conslt 1992–, visiting prof of educnl devpt Luton Univ 1993–; chief exec English Folk Song and Dance Society 1995–; CEng, MBCS; *Recreations* railways of all sizes, electronics, mechanics, music, photography, walking; *Style—* Prof Noel B W Thompson; ✉ 101 Woodcock Hill, Kenton, Harrow HA3 0JJ (☎ and fax 0181 907 1716)

THOMPSON, (Charles) Norman; CBE (1978); s of Robert Norman Thompson (d n962), of Prenton, Birkenhead, Cheshire, and Evelyn Tivendale, *née* Woods (d 1956); *b* 23 Oct 1922; *Educ* Birkenhead Inst, Univ of Liverpool (BSc); *m* 8 June 1946, Pamela Margaret, da of Alfred Christopher Francis Wicks, MBE (d 1971), of Liverpool; 1 da (Fiona Jane b 1954); *Career* res chemist Shell UK Ltd 1943, personnel supt Shell International Petroleum Ltd 1958–61, dir res admin Shell Research Ltd 1961–78, head of R&D and Health Safety & Environment Shell UK Ltd 1978–82; chm Res Advsy Ctee Inst of Petroleum 1961–78, Tech Educn Cncl 1974–81, Ct Univ of Surrey 1978–; pres RIC 1976–78 (memb Cncl 1972–80); memb Bd Thames Water Authy 1980–87, chm Professional Affrs Bd RSC 1980–84; CSTI: memb Bd 1974–83, chm 1981–83, chm Health Care Sci Advsy Ctee 1986–94; CChem, FRSC 1971; *Recreations* golf, travel, theatre-going, bridge, bowls, photography; *Clubs* West Byfleet Golf, Wey Valley Indoor Bowling (Guildford); *Style—* Norman Thompson, Esq, CBE; ✉ Delamere, Horsell Park, Woking, Surrey GU21 4LW (☎ 01483 714939)

THOMPSON, (Hugh) Patrick; MP (C) Norwich North (majority 266); s of Gerald Leopold Thompson (d 1993), of 11 Gretton Court, Girton, Cambridge, and Kathleen Mary Landsdown Thompson; *b* 21 Oct 1935; *Educ* Felsted, Emmanuel Coll Cambridge (MA); *m* 1 Sept 1962, Kathleen, da of Thomas Falkingham Howson (d 1963); *Career* Nat Serv 2 Lt KOYLI 1957–59; TA 1959–65; jr engr English Electric Valve Co Chelmsford 1959–60; physics master: The Manchester GS 1960–65, Gresham's Sch Holt 1965–83 (Maj CCF, Cadet Force); Parly candidate (C): Bradford North Feb and Oct 1974, Barrow-in-Furness 1979; MP (C) Norwich N 1983–; PPS: to Min of State for Transport 1987–88, to Min of State for Social Security and the Disabled 1988–89, PPS to Min of State for Health 1992–93; fndr memb All Pty Gp for Engrg Devpt 1985–; memb Select Ctee on: Educn, Science and the Arts 1991–92, Science and Technology 1995–; memb Commons Chairmen's Panel 1994–; MInstP; *Recreations* travel, music, gardening; *Clubs* The Norfolk; *Style—* Patrick Thompson, Esq, MP; ✉ House of Commons, London SW1A 0AA (☎ 0171 219 6398)

THOMPSON, Paul; *see:* Warwick Thompson, Dr Paul

THOMPSON, Sir Paul Anthony; 2 Bt (UK 1963), of Walton-on-the-Hill, City of Liverpool; s of Sir Kenneth Pugh Thompson, 1 Bt (d 1984), MP (C) for Walton Liverpool 1950–64, Asst PMG 1957–59, and Nanne, Lady Thompson, JP (d 1994), *née* Broome; *b* 6 Oct 1939; *m* 1971, Pauline Dorothy, da of Robert Orrell Spencer, of Tippett House, Smithills, Bolton, Lancs; 2 s (Richard, David), 2 da (Karena, Nicola); *Heir* s, Richard Kenneth Spencer Thompson, *qv*; *Career* co dir; *Style—* Sir Paul Thompson, Bt; ✉ The Old Vicarage, Church Road, Bickerstaffe, Lancashire L39 0EB

THOMPSON, Prof Paul Richard; *b* 1935; *Educ* Bishop's Stortford Coll, Corpus Christi Coll Oxford, Queen's Coll Oxford (MA, DPhil); *m* 1, Thea, *née* Vigne; 1 s, 1 da; m 2, Natasha Burchardt; 1 da; *Career* jr res fell Queen's Coll Oxford 1961–64; Univ of Essex: lectr in sociology 1964–69, sr lectr 1969–71, reader 1971–88, res prof of social history 1988–; sr res fell Nuffield Coll Oxford 1968–89, visiting prof of art history Johns Hopkins Univ 1972, Hoffman Wood prof of architecture Univ of Leeds 1977–78, Benjamin Meaker prof Univ of Bristol 1987; dir Nat Life Story Collection 1987–; ed: Victorial Soc Conf Reports 1965–67, Oral History 1970–, Life Stories 1985–89, Int Yearbook of Oral History and Life Stories 1992–96, Memory and Narrative 1996–; *Books* History of English Architecture (jtly, 1965, 2 edn 1979), The Work of William Morris (1967, new edns 1977 and 1991), Socialists Liberal and Labour: The Struggle for London 1880–1914 (1967), William Butterfield (1971), The Edwardians: The Remaking of British Society (1975, new edn 1992), Living the Fishing (1983), The Voice of the Past: Oral History (2 edn, 1988), I Don't Feel Old (1990), The Myths We Live By (1990), The Nineties: Personal Recollections of the 20th Century (1993), Listening for a Change: Oral Testimony and Development (1993), Between Generations: Family Models, Myths and Memories (1993), City Lives (1996); *Recreations* cycling, drawing, music, friendship, travel; *Style—* Prof Paul Thompson; ✉ 18 Lonsdale Rd, Oxford OX2 7EW (☎ 01865 510840)

THOMPSON, Sir Peter Anthony; kt (1984); s of late Herbert Thompson and Sarah Jane (Jean) Thompson (d 1993); *b* 14 April 1928; *Educ* Bradford GS, Univ of Leeds (BA Econ); *m* 1, 1958, Patricia Anne Norcott (d 1983); 1 s (Michael), 2 da (Gail, Manndy); m 2, 1986, Lydia Mary Kite, *née* Hodding; 2 da (Emma Elizabeth, Harriet Claire); *Career* formerly with: Unilever, GKN, Rank Organisation, British Steel Corp, British Road Services; chief exec and dep chm National Freight Company 1977–82 (exec vice chm National Freight Corp 1976–77), chm and chief exec National Freight Consortium (NFC) plc 1982–90, hon pres NFC plc 1990–93; chm: Community Hospitals Group plc until 1996, FI Group, Child Base Ltd, M-31 Ltd, Douglas Stewart Ltd; dir: Smiths Industries plc (non-exec) 1986–, Aegis plc, Brewin Dophin plc 1994–; pres Pro Share Ltd; former dir: Wembley plc, Pilkington plc; former pres: Inst of Freight Forwarders, Inst of Logistics and Distribution Mgmnt; chm Milton Keynes Fndn for the Arts 1992–; Hon Doctorates: Univs of Leeds and Bradford, Cranfield Business Sch, Nottingham Poly; Hambros Business Man of the Year 1984; FCIT, CIMgt (Gold medallist 1991); *Publications* Sharing the Success (1990); *Recreations* golf, walking, music; *Clubs* RAC; *Style—* Sir Peter Thompson; ✉ Tickford House, Silver Street, Newport Pagnell, Bucks MK16 0EX (☎ 01908 216660, fax 01908 211698)

THOMPSON, Dr Peter John; s of George Kenneth Thompson (d 1982), of Fazeley, Staffs, and Gladys Pamela, *née* Partington (d 1987); *b* 17 April 1937; *Educ* Chance Tech Coll, Aston Univ (BSc, MSc), CNAA (DTech); *m* 9 Sept 1964, (Dorothy) Ann, da of Frank Smith (d 1969), of Holly Hall, Dudley; 1 s (Mark b 1965), 2 da (Nicola b 1968, Louise b 1988); *Career* student apprentice Tube Investments Birmingham 1953–61, lectr and sr lectr Harris Coll Preston 1961–65 and 1968–70, sr sci offr UKAEE Preston 1965–68, princ lectr in prodn engrg Sheffield City Poly 1970–77, dean and head Dept of Engrg Trent Poly Nottingham 1977–83, chief exec Nat Cncl Vocational Qualifications 1986–91, educn and training conslt 1991–; visiting prof Open Business Sch 1992–96; conslt City & Guilds Sr Awards 1992–94; memb: Mfrg Mech and Prodn Engrg Bd CNAA 1978–85, Ctee for Engrg in Polys 1981–85, Engrg Scis Divnl Bd IMechE 1982–84, Further Educn Unit 1989–91, Cncl Open Coll 1987–89; CEng, FIEE 1979, FIPD 1987; *Recreations* golf, genealogy; *Style—* Dr Peter Thompson; ✉ Berkhamsted, Hertfordshire (☎ 01442 865127)

THOMPSON, Peter John Stuart (Nimble); s of late Douglas Stuart Thompson, and Irene Agnes, *née* Laird, OBE; *b* 28 Sept 1946; *Educ* Rossall Sch, Univ of Leeds; *m* 18 July 1970, Morven Mary, da of late Guy Hanscombe; 2 s (Angus Iain Stuart b 1973 d 1988, Archibald Fergus Stuart b 1992), 1 da (Siona Catherine Stuart b 1975); *Career* admitted slr 1971; Eversheds (formerly Eversheds Hepworth and Chadwick): ptnr 1973–, managing ptnr 1989–94, sr ptnr Leeds and Manchester 1994–, vice-chm 1995–; dir TEP Stores Ltd, Eversheds, non-exec dir S Lyles plc; former chm CIArb NE Branch, chm Royal Armouries Business Partnership; govr Leeds Metropolitan Univ, tstee Yorkshire Childrens Hosp Fund; memb Law Soc; ACIArb, FID; *Recreations* fishing, walking and talking; *Clubs* RAC, Leeds; *Style—* Nimble Thompson, Esq; ✉ The Grange, Kirkby Malzeard, Ripon, N Yorks (☎ 01765 658398); Eversheds, Cloth Hall Court, Infirmary St, Leeds LS1 2JB (☎ 0113 243 0391, fax 0113 245 6188); London Scottish House, 24 Mount Street, Manchester M2 3DB (☎ 0161 832 6666)

THOMPSON, Peter Kenneth James; s of Rt Rev Kenneth George Thompson (first Bishop of Sherwood, d 1976), and Doreen May Latchford; *b* 30 July 1937; *Educ* Worksop

Coll, Christ's Coll Cambridge (MA, LLB); *m* 10 Aug 1970, Sandy Lynne, da of Wallace Harper (d 1970); 2 da (Helena b 1978, Gemma b 1981); *Career* called to the Bar Lincoln's Inn 1961, practised at Common Law Bar 1961–73, lawyer in Government Serv 1973–, slr to Depts of Health and Social Security 1989–; *Recreations* writing; *Style*— Peter K J Thompson, Esq; ✉ Room 401, New Court, Carey Street, London WC2A 2LS (☎ 0171 412 1404)

THOMPSON, (William) Pratt; s of Phillip Amos Thompson, and Regina Beatrice, *née* Kirby; *b* 9 Feb 1933; *Educ* Princeton, Columbia Univ (BA), Univ of Geneva (MBA); *m* 1963, Jenny Frances Styles; 2 da; *Career* vice pres AMF Incorporated 1958–73 (exec assignments in NY, Geneva, Tokyo, Hong Kong and London 1959–68), dep md Bowthorpe Holdings plc 1973–78, md Jaguar Rover Triumph Ltd 1978–79, chm BL International Ltd 1979–81, dir Metalurgica de Santa Ana SA Madrid 1978–81, vice chm Colbert Group Geneva 1981–84, chm: AIDCOM International plc 1983–86 (dir 1982–86), AIDCOM Technology Ltd 1982–86, Husky Computers Ltd 1982–86; md Unitech plc 1989–93 (dir 1987–93), memb: Cncl SMMT 1978–81, Cncl on Foreign Rels USA 1980–89; currently dir various cos; *Clubs* Brooks's; *Style*— Pratt Thompson, Esq; ✉ Trinity Hall, Castle Hedingham, Essex CO9 3EY

THOMPSON, Dr Raymond; CBE (1988); s of William Edward Thompson (d 1946), and Hilda, *née* Rowley (d 1990); *b* 4 April 1925; *Educ* Longton HS, Univ of Nottingham (MSc, PhD), Imperial Coll London (DIC); *Career* dir Borax Holdings Ltd 1969–87, md Borax Research Ltd 1980–86 (dep chm 1986–90), dir Boride Ceramics and Composites Ltd 1988–92, dir Azmat Ltd 1993–; conslt to: Borax Consolidated Ltd, Rhone-Poulenc Chemicals, CRA Ltd 1988–92; special prof of inorganic chemistry Univ of Nottingham 1975–96, hon prof of chemistry Univ of Warwick 1975–95; govr Kingston-upon-Thames Poly 1978–88; Freeman City of London; Liveryman: Worshipful Co of Glass Sellers 1983, Worshipful Co of Engineers 1987; FEng 1985, FRSC 1957, FIMM 1972; *Books* Mellor's Comprehensive Treatise, Boron Supplement (1979), The Modern Inorganic Chemicals Industry (1977), Speciality Inorganic Chemicals (1980), Energy and Chemistry (1981), Trace Metal Removal from Aqueous Solution (1986), The Chemistry of Wood Preservation (1991), Industrial Inorganic Chemicals - Production and Uses (1995); *Recreations* gardening; *Style*— Dr Raymond Thompson, CBE, FEng; ✉ The Garth, 7 Winchester Close, Esher Place, Esher, Surrey KT10 8QH (☎ 01372 464428)

THOMPSON, Richard Henry; s of Lt-Col Richard Louis Thompson (d 1976), and Violet Mary, *née* Harrison (d 1955); *b* 6 Aug 1936; *Educ* Downside, St Catharine's Coll Cambridge (County Major scholarship, MA); *m* 14 July 1962, Cynthia Joan, da of Col Robert Nicholas Hurst, MC; 2 da (Emma Catharine b 16 April 1963, Lucinda Mary b 20 Aug 1966); *Career* Nat Serv cmmnd RE 1954–56; qualified with Sir Alexander Gibb & Partners 1959–63, exec dir P E Consulting Group Limited 1964–75, chief exec New Court & Partners Limited 1976–77, co-fndr and chm Thompson Clive & Partners Ltd 1978–; pt/t chm: Medicom International Ltd, Pantheon International Ltd, Phonic Ear Holdings Inc; pt/t dir: Aenix Informatique SA, Quintiles Transnational Corporation; CEng, MICE 1963, FIMC 1975; *Recreations* literature, music, fishing, tennis, golf; *Clubs* Brooks's, Hawks', RAC, Roehampton; *Style*— Richard Thompson, Esq; ✉ Thompson Clive & Partners Ltd, 24 Old Bond Street, London W1X 4JD (☎ 0171 409 2062, fax 0171 493 9172)

THOMPSON, Sir Richard Hilton Marler; 1 Bt (UK 1963), of Reculver, Co Kent; s of Richard Smith Thompson (d 1952), and Kathleen Hilda, *née* Marler (d 1916), of London and Calcutta; *b* 5 Oct 1912; *Educ* Malvern; *m* 9 Aug 1939, Anne Christabel de Vere, da of late Philip de Vere Annesley (bro of 13 Viscount Valentia); 1 s; *Heir* s, Nicholas Annesley Marler Thompson, *qv*; *Career* RNVR 1940–46, cmmnd 1941 (despatches 1942), Lt Cdr 1944; publishing business in India 1930–39; MP (C) Croydon West 1950–55, asst-govt whip 1952, Lord Cmmr of the Treasy 1954, MP (C) Croydon South 1955–66 and 1970–74, vice chamberlain of HM Household 1956, Parly sec Mlny of Health 1957–59, under-sec of state CRO 1959–60, Parly sec Miny of Works 1960–62; tstee Br Museum 1951–84, Br Museum's rep on Cncl Nat Tst 1978–84; dir: Rediffusion TV Ltd and Rediffusion Holdings Ltd 1966–83; fndr memb and first elected pres Br Museum Soc 1970–74, chm Capital Counties Property Co Ltd 1971–77; pres Br Property Fedn 1976–77; *Recreations* gardening, country pursuits, reading; *Clubs* Carlton, Army and Navy; *Style*— Sir Richard Thompson, Bt; ✉ Rhodes House, Sellindge, Ashford, Kent TN25 6JA

THOMPSON, Richard Kenneth Spencer; s and h of Sir Paul Thompson, 2 Bt, *qv*, of Walton-on-the-Hill, City of Liverpool; *b* 27 Jan 1976; *Style*— Richard Thompson, Esq

THOMPSON, Dr Richard Paul Hepworth; s of Stanley Henry Thompson (d 1966), and Winifred Lilian Collier; *b* 14 April 1940; *Educ* Epsom Coll, Univ of Oxford (MA, DM), St Thomas's Hosp Med Sch; *m* 1974, Eleanor Mary, da of Timothy Noel Joseph Hughes (d 1979); *Career* conslt physician: St Thomas's Hosp 1972–, King Edward VII Hosp for Offrs 1982–; physician to the Royal Household 1982–93, physician to HM The Queen 1993–; examiner in med Soc of Apothecaries 1976–80, examiner Faculty of Dental Surgery RCS 1980–87, govr Guy's Hosp Med Sch 1980–82, memb Mgmnt Ctee Inst of Psychiatry 1981–95, memb Mgmnt Ctee King Edward VII's Fund for London 1985–89 and 1992–96; Liveryman Worshipful Soc of Apothecaries; FRCP; *Recreations* gardening; *Style*— Dr Richard Thompson; ✉ 36 Dealtry Rd, London SW15 6NL (☎ 0181 789 3839); St Thomas' Hospital, London SE1 7EH (☎ 0171 928 9292, ext 2650)

THOMPSON, (Peter) Robin; s of Robert Leslie Thompson (d 1967), of Bristol, and Ellen Mabel, *née* Gibbons (d 1966); *b* 30 Sept 1941; *Educ* Farmor's Sch Gloucestershire, Hinckley Sch Leicestershire; *m* 27 March 1965, Pauline Ann, da of Frederick Box; 2 s (Julian Guy b 25 July 1967, Dominic Giles b 23 Jan 1971); *Career* chief reporter Wilts and Gloucestershire Standard 1963 (joined 1958), sr journalist Bristol Evening Post 1967–73 (acted as corr for most nat media, subsequently specialised in Gloucestershire region), first PR offr Reading Borough Cncl 1973–78 (work incl promotion of the Hexagon Centre), PR mangr to six cos under Vickers Ltd 1978–80, sr practitioner design consultancy 1980–81, founding ptnr Contact Marketing Services (now Earl & Thompson Marketing Ltd) 1981 (chm and jt md until 1996), dep chm The Marketing Services Group plc 1996–; memb SW Regnl Cncl CBI, chm Glos Prince's Tst, presented with commemorative certificate by HRH The Prince of Wales in appreciation of work for the Prince's Tst and Volunteers, chm Glos Crimestoppers 1995; MIPR 1979, memb PRCA 1989; *Recreations* Prince's Trust, Pied Piper Appeal work, travel, reading, football, my business; *Clubs* Cirencester Rotary; *Style*— Robin Thompson, Esq; ✉ Birch Cottage, Park Way, Upper Siddington, Cirencester, Gloucestershire GL7 6HH (☎ 01285 654106); The Marketing Services Group plc, 34 Imperial Square, Cheltenham GL50 1QZ (☎ 01242 253323, fax 01242 253214)

THOMPSON, (David) Robin Bibby; CBE (1997), TD (1987); s of Noel Denis Thompson (d 1967), of Sansaw Hall, Clive, Shrewsbury, and Cynthia Joan, *née* Bibby (d 1971); *b* 23 July 1946; *Educ* Uppingham; *m* 21 July 1971, Caroline Ann, da of Lt-Col O H J Foster, of Ardraccan House, Navan, Co Meath, Ireland; 1 s (James Peter Bibby b 1975), 1 da (Alexandra Jane b 1976); *Career* Mons OCS 1964–65, cmmnd QRIH 1965–71, ADC to HE Govr Victoria 1970–71, cmd Queen's Own Yeo TA 1984–87 (cmmnd 1984), Col TA 1987, ADC to HM The Queen 1988; farmer and landowner 1971–, dir Bibby Line Ltd 1974–87; chm S Shropshire Housing Assoc 1991–; memb: Rural Devpt Cmmn 1986– (dep chm 1992–96), Bd Housing Corpn 1989–, Cncl RASE 1985–91; High Sheriff of Shropshire 1989–90; Liveryman Worshipful Co of Gardeners; *Recreations* skiing, gardening, conservation, horses; *Clubs* Cavalry and Guards'; *Style*— Robin Thompson, Esq, CBE, TD; ✉ Sansaw Hall, Clive, Shrewsbury, Shropshire SY4 3JR; Harwicke Estate Office, Black Birches, Shrewsbury SY4 3DH (☎ 01939 210226)

THOMPSON, Prof Ronald Augustine; MBE (1962), TD (1982); s of Lionel Wellesley Thompson, MBE (d 1989), of Surrey, and Eileen Charlotte, *née* Byrne (d 1978); *b* 28 Aug 1933; *Educ* Karachi GS, Univ Coll Hosp London (BSc, MB BS); *m* 8 Sept 1962, Anthea Georgina Erica, da of Eric George Midwinter (d 1981), of Whitton; 1 s (Richard b 1968), 2 da (Juliet b 1963, Suzanne b 1965); *Career* Nat Serv RAMC, seconded to Ghana AMC 1960–62, TA RAMC (vol) 1967–88, Col RAMC, CO 202 Midland Gen Hosp RAMC (vol) 1985–88; med registrar Univ Coll Hosp London 1963–65, sr registrar Univ of Birmingham Med Sch 1965–68, lectr in immunology Univ of Birmingham 1968–69, conslt immunologist and dir Regnl Immunology Laboratory E Birmingham Hosp 1969–; hon prof Dept of Immunology Univ of Birmingham 1993–; memb: E Birmingham DHA 1978–82, Cncl RCPath 1977–80; treas Br Soc for Immunology 1979–85; FRCP 1979, FRCPath 1981; *Books* Practice of Clinical Immunology (1974), Techniques in Clinical Immunology (1977), Clinical and Experimental Immunology (ed, 1989); *Recreations* squash, tennis, music; *Clubs* Edgbaston Priory; *Style*— Prof Ronald Thompson, MBE, TD; ✉ Regional Immunology Department, Birmingham Heartlands Hospital, Birmingham B9 5SS (☎ 0121 766 6611, fax 0121 766 6879)

THOMPSON, Stephen (Steve); s of Harold Thompson (d 1992), of Burnley, Lancs, and Nora, *née* Gavaghan; *b* 30 April 1950; *Educ* Rosegrove Secdy Modern, Burnley Coll of HE; *m* (m dis); 1 da (Lindsey Carol b 9 Dec 1973); *partner* Hilary Ann Slater; *Career* apprentice mill tackler rising to motor mechanic 1965–73, self-employed in garage partnership 1975–87; amateur photographer 1980–87, professional advtg photographer 1987–; asst to Alan Brooking and Geoff Smith 1987–91, in own studio 1991–; clients incl top advtg agencies in UK, Europe and USA; *Exhibitions* Rhythms of Landscape (solo exhbn sponsored by NW Arts) 1982, Best of North West (gp exhbns) 1983 and 1984; prints in both private and public collections; recipient Assoc of Photographers awards 1989, 1991 and 1992, work included in British Jl of Photography Annual 1994; lectr Nelson Coll Lancs 1982–84; memb Assoc of Photgraphers 1988; *Recreations* fly-fishing, football; *Style*— Steve Thompson, Esq

THOMPSON, Suki Frances Allison; da of Barry Martin Owen Bunker, of Cardiff, and Alison Marjorie, *née* Hayman; *b* 7 March 1967; *Educ* Truro HS Cornwall, Univ of Leeds (BA (Drama)), Kingston Univ (MA (Marketing)); 1995, Alan Vaughan Thompson, s of Gordon Thompson; *Career* advtg exec; account exec BMP Young Clark Craig 1989–91, mktg mangr The Rapp Collins Partnership (after merger with BMP Young Clark Craig) 1991–92, mktg dir Impact FCA! 1992–95, business devpt dir TBWA 1995–; *Recreations* sailing, surfing, lepidopterist, cooking; *Clubs* IOD, Kingston Business Sch Alumni; *Style*— Mrs Suki Thompson; ✉ TBWA, 8 Crinan Street, Battle Bridge Basin, London N1 9UF (☎ 0171 833 5544, fax 0171 833 8751, car 0385 391573)

THOMPSON, Terence James; s of James Andrew Thompson (d 1984), of Burton upon Trent, and Irene, *née* Smith (d 1974); *b* 19 Jan 1928; *Educ* Birmingham Sch of Music; *m* 18 Aug 1951 (m dis 1957); *Career* Band of 1 Bn S Staffs Regt 1946–48; music master W Bromwich Tech HS 1950–59, clarinet teacher Sch of St Mary and St Anne Abbots Bromley 1957–95, head of music March End Sch Wednesfield 1960–66, lectr W Midlands Coll of Higher Educn 1965–89, sr teacher Wolverhampton Music Sch 1968–93; professional clarinettist and saxophonist, numerous published works; memb: Composers Guild of GB, Schs Music Assoc, Clarinet and Saxophone Soc, Central Composer's Alliance, Black Country Soc, Performing Rights Soc, Mechanical Copyright Protection Soc; *Recreations* motoring, philately, the canal scene; *Style*— Terence Thompson, Esq; ✉ 58 Willenhall Rd, Bilston, W Midlands WV14 6NW (☎ 01902 495646)

THOMPSON, Prof William; s of William Thompson (d 1969), and Amelia Thompson; *b* 2 Feb 1937; *Educ* Wallace HS Lisburn Co Antrim NI, Queen's Univ Belfast (BSc, MB BCh, BAO, MD); *m* 8 July 1961, Anne Elizabeth, da of Professor James Morrison, OBE (d 1987); 1 s (Andrew James b 1964), 3 da (Christine Louise (Mrs Gordon) b 1963, Gillian Claire (Mrs Gordon) b 1967, Karen Anne b 1968); *Career* lectr in obstetrics and gynaecology Univ of Singapore 1968–69, sr lectr and conslt obstetrician and gynaecologist Royal Maternity Hosp Belfast 1970–80, prof and head Dept of Obstetrics and Gynaecology Queen's Univ of Belfast 1980–, conslt obstetrician and gynaecologist Royal Maternity and Royal Victoria Hosps Belfast 1980–; treas Int Fedn of Fertility Socs, chm Med Staff Ctee Royal Maternity Hosp Belfast; memb: Br Med Soc, Gynaecological Visiting Soc; FRCOG; *Books* Fertility and Sterility (1986), Perinatal Medicine (1988); *Recreations* gardening, travelling, photography; *Style*— Prof William Thompson; ✉ Institute of Clinical Science, Dept of Obstetrics and Gynaecology, Grosvenor Rd, Belfast, Northern Ireland BT12 6BJ (☎ 01232 894600, fax 01232 328247, telex 74487)

THOMSON, *see:* Hyde-Thomson, White-Thomson

THOMSON, Sir Adam; kt (1983), CBE (1976); s of Frank Thomson and Jemima Roger; *b* 7 July 1926; *Educ* Rutherglen Academy, Coatbridge Coll, Royal Tech Coll (Univ of Strathclyde) Glasgow; *m* 1948, Dawn Elizabeth Burt; 2 s (Scott, Anthony); *Career* dep chm Martin Currie Pacific Tst 1985; non-exec dir: Royal Bank of Scotland Group 1982–89, Metropolitan Estates Property Co 1982–89; dir: Br Caledonian Hotel Management Ltd until 1988, Br Caledonian Helicopters Ltd until 1988, Bachelors Abroad Ltd, The Royal Bank of Scotland Group plc; chm Gold Stag Ltd 1988–, chm and chief exec British Caledonian Group (formerly The Caledonian Aviation Group plc) 1970–88 (chm and md 1964–70), chm and chief exec British Caledonian Airways 1970–88; sr dir Stanford Research International until 1989, chm Assoc of Euro Airlines 1977–78, winner Scottish Free Enterprise Award Aims for Freedom and Enterprise 1976, Businessman of the Year 1971; Hon LLD: Univ of Glasgow 1979, Univ of Sussex 1984, Univ of Strathclyde 1986; FRAeS; *Recreations* golf, sailing; *Clubs* Caledonian, Walton Heath Golf, Royal and Ancient Golf St Andrews; *Style*— Sir Adam Thomson, CBE

THOMSON, Alan Matthew; s of George Kerr Thomson (d 1991), and Jean Lees, *née* Gemmell, of Renfrewshire; *b* 6 Sept 1946; *Educ* Eastwood HS Renfrewshire (capt Scottish Schs football team), Univ of Glasgow (MA); *m* 8 Aug 1973, Linda Mary, da of Peter Hamilton, of W Lothian; 2 da (Jennifer b 5 March 1976, Victoria b 27 June 1987), 2 s (Paul b 26 Sept 1977, Richard b 2 Aug 1983); *Career* professional footballer Glasgow Rangers FC 1962–66, trainee chartered accountant Fleming and Wilson Glasgow 1967–70, auditor Arthur Andersen & Co Glasgow 1970–71, audit mangr Price Waterhouse 1971–75; Rockwell International: fin dir Paris 1975–78, treasy mangr Pittsburgh 1978–79, fin dir UK 1979–82; chief financial offr Raychem Ltd Swindon 1982–84, financial controller Courtaulds Textiles plc 1984–87; fin dir: Courtaulds Coatings 1987–92, The Rugby Group plc 1992–95, Smiths Industries plc 1995–; non-exec dir Laporte plc 1996–; MICAS 1970; *Recreations* golf, tennis; *Clubs* Copt Heath Golf; *Style*— Alan Thomson, Esq; ✉ Smiths Industries plc, 765 Finchley Road, London NW11 8DS (☎ 0181 458 3232, fax 0181 458 5285)

THOMSON, Dr Allan David; s of Reginald William Thomson (d 1953), of Ascot, and Florence, *née* Pestell (d 1984), of London; *b* 22 Dec 1936; *Educ* Univ of Edinburgh Med Sch (BSc, MB ChB, PhD); *m* 1, 28 Dec 1963 (m dis 1987), Jocelyn, da of F Price, of Sedgley, Dudley; 2 s (Simon Bruce b 28 Feb 1964, Jeremy Alexander b 14 June 1976); m 2, 12 May 1988, Wendy Phyllis Nesbit Howard, *née* Evans; *Career* asst prof of med Coll of Med & Dentistry New Jersey USA 1970, conslt physician and gastroenterologist Greenwich Dist Hosp London 1974–, hon sec lectr KCH London 1975–, recognised teacher Univ of London 1983–; emeritus ed in chief of res jl of Med Cncl on Alcoholism

- Alcohol and Alcoholism, memb Med Advsy Bd Brain Damage Res Tst; pres Greenwich & Bexley BMA 1974; Freeman City of London; Liveryman: Worshipful Co of Basketmakers, Worshipful Soc of Apothecaries; memb: American Assoc for Study of Liver Disease, Med Cncl on Alcoholism, RCPE, Euro Assoc for Study of the Liver; FRCPE 1984, FRCP 1993 (MRCP 1973); *Books* over 140 res articles and books relating to gen gastroenterology and alcoholic brain damage; *Recreations* music, reading, walking, photography; *Clubs* Brooks's; *Style—* Dr Allan Thomson; ✉ The Blackheath Hospital, 40–42 Lee Terrace, London SE3 9UD (☎ 0181 318 7722)

THOMSON, Andrew Edward; s of Andrew Thomson, of Leven Fife, Scotland, and Margaret Gordon Cairns, *née* Trainer; *b* 26 Nov 1955; *Educ* Kirkland HS; *m* 18 Sept 1982, Linda June, da of Tony Gerald Leeves; 2 s (Edward Thomas b 24 Aug 1986, David Andrew b 27 Sept 1990); *Career* bowls player; memb Cyphers Indoor Bowling Club, first tournament win Buckhaven Bowls Club Championship 1972; titles: Thames Cockney Classic 1986, Ely Masters Singles 1988 and 1991, Tennants Welsh Classic 1989, UK Singles 1991 and 1992, World Indoor Pairs champion 1993, World Indoor Singles champion 1994 and 1995, Mazda International Singles winner 1994, Woolwich Scottish Master winner 1994, World Outdoor Fours champion 1996; represented Scotland 1979; represented England 1981–: sixth place singles Cwlth Games Edinburgh 1986, fifth place pairs Cwlth Games Auckland 1990, bronze medal pairs Cwlth Games Victoria 1994; records: nat singles indoor 1989, 1990 and 1991 (outdoor 1981), pairs indoor 1986 and 1991, triples indoor 1981, fours indoor 1983, 1984, 1988, 1989 and 1990; *Recreations* football, cricket; *Style—* Andrew Thomson, Esq; ✉ 71 Gerda Road, New Eltham, London SE9 3SJ (☎ 0181 850 4798); Cyphers Indoor Bowling Club, Kingshall Rd, Beckenham, Kent BR3 1LP (☎ 0181 778 3889)

THOMSON, Andrew Gordon; s of James Thomson (d 1981), of Cromarty, Scotland, and Anne, *née* Skinner (d 1981); *b* 20 July 1928; *Educ* Nigg Sch, Tain Royal Acad Scotland; *m* 27 March 1954, Jean Ann, da of Leonard Walter Collison, MBE (d 1974), of Edgware, Middx; 1 s (Stuart), 1 da (Susan); *Career* Nat Serv 1946–48; Waterman Partnership Ltd (formerly H L Waterman and Partners): engr, sr engr 1959, assoc 1961, ptnr 1962, sr ptnr 1983, chm 1988–; memb Worshipful Co of Fletchers, Freeman City of London 1982; MSocIS France (memb Société des Ingenieurs et Scientifiques de France); *Recreations* golf; *Clubs* St Stephen's, City Livery, St George's Hill Golf; *Style—* Andrew Thomson, Esq; ✉ Waterman Partnership, 46–47 Blackfriars Rd, London SE1 8PN (☎ 0171 928 7888, fax 0171 928 3033, telex 24157)

THOMSON, Prof Andrew James; s of Andrew Henderson Thomson, of Shoreham-by-Sea, Sussex, and Eva Frances Annie Thomson (d 1979); *b* 31 July 1940; *Educ* Steyning GS, Wadham Coll Oxford (State scholar, BA), Univ of Oxford (DPhil, MA); *m* Anne, da of Jack Marsden; 2 s (Mark Andrew b 29 May 1967, Neil Henderson b 25 March 1969); *Career* research asst prof Dept of Biophysics Michigan State Univ 1965–67; Sch of Chemical Sciences Univ of E Anglia: sr demonstrator 1967–68, lectr 1968–77, sr lectr 1977–83, reader 1983–84, head Inorganic Chemistry Sector 1984–93, prof of chemistry 1985–; jt dir UK Centre for Metallobiology 1988–; Silver Medal for analytical spectroscopy RSC 1991; memb: British Biophysical Soc, Biochemical Soc; FRS 1993; *Recreations* hill walking; *Style—* Prof Andrew Thomson, FRS; ✉ 12 Armitage Close, Cringleford, Norwich NR4 6XZ (☎ 01603 504623); School of Chemical Sciences, University of East Anglia, Norwich NR4 7TJ (☎ 01603 592023, fax 01603 592710, e-mail a.thomson@uea.ac.uk)

THOMSON, Caroline Agnes Morgan; da of Lord Thomson of Monifieth, KT, *qv*, and Grace, *née* Jenkins; *b* 15 May 1954; *Educ* Mary Datchelor Girls' Sch Camberwell London, Univ of York (BA); *m* 1, 12 Nov 1977 (m dis 1981), Ian Campbell Bradley; m 2, 30 July 1983, Roger John Liddle; 1 s (Andrew b 29 Oct 1989); *Career* BBC: trainee BBC News 1975–77, parly reporter 1977–78, sr prodr various radio and TV progs incl Analysis and Panorama 1978–82; political asst to Rt Hon Roy Jenkins MP 1982–83; Channel 4 TV: commissioning ed 1984–90, head of corp affrs 1990–95; dir of strategy and corp affairs BBC World Service 1995–; dir Edinburgh Film Festival, memb Edinburgh Film and Television Festivals 1994–95; memb: RTS 1985, BAFTA 1988; FRSA 1992; *Recreations* domesticity; *Style—* Miss Caroline Thomson; ✉ BBC World Service, Bush House, The Strand, London WC2B 4PH (☎ 0171 240 3456, fax 0171 257 8258)

THOMSON, Charles Grant; s of William Eddie Spalding Thomson, of Bearsden, Glasgow, and Helen Donaldson, *née* Campbell (d 1994); *b* 23 Sept 1948; *Educ* Jordanhill Coll Sch, Univ of Glasgow (BSc); *m* 11 July 1970, Pamela Anne, da of Frederick Simpson Mackay (d 1987), of Bearsden, Glasgow; 1 s (Richard b 1979), 1 da (Susan b 1975); *Career* Scottish Mutual Assurance plc (t/o by Abbey National plc 1992): joined 1969, various official and exec appts from 1974, actuary 1990, dir and dep chief exec Scottish Mutual Group 1992–94, dir and actuary Abbey National Life plc 1993–95, dir and actuary Scottish Mutual Assurance plc 1994–95; exec bd dir and appointed actuary Scottish Widows Fund and Life Assurance Society 1995–; Faculty of Actuaries: memb Cncl 1983–86 and 1989–92, chm Faculty Examinations Bd 1989–92 (memb 1982–92, sec 1985–89); FFA 1973; *Recreations* golf, swimming; *Clubs* Glasgow Golf, Windyhill Golf; *Style—* Charles Thomson, Esq; ✉ St Fillans, Ralston Rd, Bearsden, Glasgow; Scottish Widows Fund and Life Assurance Society, 15 Dalkeith Road, Edinburgh EH16 5BU (☎ 0131 655 6000, fax 0131 662 4053, telex 72654)

THOMSON, Clive Benjamin; JP (Gloucester 1985); s of Benjamin Alfred Thomson, of Brighton, and Ivy Grace, *née* Smith; *b* 29 May 1935; *Educ* Westminster City; *m* 11 Jan 1959, Mary Lilian (Molly), da of Eric Clements (d 1985); 1 s (Michael Clive b and d 1963), 2 da (Deborah Jane b 1962, Victoria Louise b 1965); *Career* Nat Serv 2 Lt Royal Berks Regt 1953–55, Capt Royal Berks Regt (TA) 1955–65, HAC 1980; chm East Gloucestershire NHS Tst; JP Richmond 1975–85; formerly chm: Westbury Cons Assoc, Twickenham Cons Assoc, London SW Euro Cons Assoc; former dep chm Gtr London Cons Assoc, former pres Surbiton Griffins FC; vice pres Nat Assoc of Voluntary Hostels, chm Safe Home Income Plans; dir: Sandford Park Lido, Allchurches Life Assurance Ltd; patron Kambia Hosp; Freeman City of London 1980; Liveryman Worshipful Co of: Insurers 1980, Marketors 1991; FCIM 1988; *Recreations* walking, politics, tennis, racing; *Clubs* Army and Navy, United, Cecil; *Style—* Clive Thomson, Esq, JP; ✉ Chota Koti, Oakley Rd, Cheltenham, Glos GL52 6PA (☎ 01242 582 936); East Gloucestershire NHS Trust, Burlington House, Lypiatt Road, Cheltenham, Glos GL53 7AN (☎ 01242 221188)

THOMSON, Sir (Frederick Douglas) David; 3 Bt (UK 1929), of Glendarroch, Co Midlothian; s of Sir (James) Douglas Wishart, 2 Bt (d 1972), and Bettina, er da of late Lt Cdr David William Shafto Douglas, RN; *b* 14 Feb 1940; *Educ* Eton, Univ Coll Oxford (BA); *m* 1967 (m dis 1994), Caroline Anne, da of Maj Timothy Stuart Lewis, Royal Scots Greys; 2 s, 1 da; *Heir* s, Simon Douglas Charles Thomson b 16 June 1969; *Career* dir Ben Line Steamers Ltd 1964–89; chm: Jove Investment Trust plc 1983–, Britannia Steamship Insurance Assoc Ltd (dir 1965–), Through Transport Mutual Insurance Assoc Ltd (dir 1973–), Abtrust Index European Index Investment Trust plc 1990–, Ptarmigan International Capital Trust plc 1990–, Laurence J Smith Ltd 1993, Wright & Jobson (Galashiels) Ltd 1996; dir: Martin Currie Pacific Trust plc 1985–, Danae Investment Trust plc 1979–, Cairn Energy plc 1971–, Kynoch Group plc 1990–, James Fisher and Sons plc 1993–, Asset Management Investment Co PLC 1994, Ionian Group Ltd 1994, Asset Management Investment Co Securities Ltd 1996; memb Royal Co of Archers (Queen's Body Guard for Scotland); *Style—* Sir David Thomson, Bt; ✉ Holylee, Walkerburn, Peebleshire EH43 6BD (☎ 01896 870673, fax 01896 870461)

THOMSON, Hon David Kenneth Roy; s and h of 2 Baron Thomson of Fleet; *b* 12 June 1957; *Style—* The Hon David Thomson

THOMSON, David Paget; s of late Sir George Thomson, FRS, Nobel Laureate; *b* 19 March 1931; *Educ* Rugby, Trinity Coll Cambridge; *m* 1959, Patience Mary, da of late Sir Lawrence Bragg, CH, MC, FRS, Nobel Laureate; 2 s, 2 da; *Career* Lt Cdr RNR, joined Lazard Bros & Co Ltd 1956, md 1966, seconded HM Foreign Service 1971–73, economic counsellor Bonn, Lazards 1973–86; chm: Jufcrest Ltd 1985–88, F & C German Investment Tst PLC 1990–, Kleinwort Emerging Markets Trust PLC 1993–; memb Monopolies and Mergers Cmmn 1984–, dir gen Br Invisible Exports Cncl 1987–89; cncl chm The Royal Instn 1985–87, chm Portsmouth Naval Base Property Tst 1992–, tstee Lucy Cavendish Coll Cambridge 1987, chm Fitzwilliam Museum Tst Cambridge 1988–, dir Med Sickness Soc 1990; *Clubs* Athenaeum; *Style—* David Thomson, Esq; ✉ Little Stoke House, Wallingford, Oxon OX10 6AX (☎ 01491 837161)

THOMSON, Maj-Gen David Phillips; CB (1993), CBE (1989), MC (1965); s of Cyril Robert William Thomson (d 1957), and Louise Mary, *née* Phillips (d 1984); *b* 30 Jan 1942; *Educ* Eastbourne Coll, RMA Sandhurst (Earl Wavell Meml Prize, Brian Philpott Mil History Prize); *Career* cmmnd Argyll and Sutherland Highlanders 1962, Bde Maj 6th Armoured Bde 1975, instr Staff Coll 1980, CO 1st Bn The Argyll and Sutherland Highlanders 1982, COS RMCS 1985, COS 1st Armoured Div 1986, Cdr 1st Infantry Bde/UK Mobile Force 1987, sr Army memb RCDS 1992–95; Col The Argyll and Sutherland Highlanders, Capt of the Royal Castle of Tarbert; despatches 1968 and 1992; FRGS; *Recreations* golf, historical research; *Clubs* Caledonian (London); *Style—* Maj-Gen D P Thomson, CB, CBE, MC; ✉ c/o Regimental Headquarters, The Argyll and Sutherland, Highlanders, The Castle, Stirling FK8 1EH (☎ 01786 475165)

THOMSON, Prof Derick S; s of James Thomson (d 1971), and Christina, *née* Smith (d 1968); *b* 5 Aug 1921; *Educ* Nicolson Inst Stornoway, Univ of Aberdeen (MA), Emmanuel Coll Cambridge (BA), UCNW Bangor; *m* 31 March 1952, Carol MacMichael, da of Daniel Galbraith (d 1943); 5 s (Dòmhnall Ruaraidh b 1954, Daniel (James) b 1956, Ranald b 1963, Roderick b 1969, Calum b 1974), 1 da (Tia b 1960); *Career* WWII serv RAF 1942–45; asst in Celtic Univ of Edinburgh 1948–49, lectr in Welsh Univ of Glasgow 1949–56, reader in Celtic Univ of Aberdeen 1956–63, prof of Celtic Univ of Glasgow 1963–91; former memb Scottish Arts Cncl; chm: Gaelic Books Cncl 1968–91, Catherine McCaig Tst; pres Scottish Gaelic Texts Soc; Ossian Prize FVS Fndn Hamburg 1974; Hon DLitt: Univ of Wales 1987, Univ of Aberdeen 1994; FRSE 1977, FBA 1992; *Books* Gairm (ed, 1952–), Creachadh na Clàrsaich/Plundering the Harp (collected poems, 1982), The Companion to Gaelic Scotland (1983), An Introduction to Gaelic Poetry (1989), European Poetry in Gaelic (1990), The McDiarmid Manuscript Anthology (1992), Smeur an Dòchais/Bramble of Hope (poems, 1992), Meall Garbh/The Rugged Mountain (poems, 1995), Alasdair Mac/Mhaighstir Alasdair, Selected Poems (1996); *Recreations* publishing, travel; *Clubs* Glasgow Arts, Town and Gown; *Style—* Prof Derick Thomson, FRSE, FBA; ✉ 15 Struan Road, Glasgow G44 3AT (☎ 0141 637 3704)

THOMSON, Dr Duncan; s of Duncan Murdoch Thomson (d 1958), and Jane McFarlane, *née* Wilson (d 1982); *b* 2 Oct 1934; *Educ* Airdrie Acad, Univ of Edinburgh (MA, PhD), Edinburgh Coll of Art; *m* 15 July 1964, Julia Jane, da of Donald Campbell MacPhail (d 1962); 1 da (Rebecca b 1974); *Career* art teacher 1959–67, keeper Scottish Nat Portrait Gallery 1982– (asst keeper 1967–82); *Recreations* literature; *Style—* Dr Duncan Thomson; ✉ 3 Eglinton Crescent, Edinburgh EH12 5DH (☎ 0131 225 6430); Scottish National Portrait Gallery, 1 Queen Street, Edinburgh EH2 1JD (☎ 0131 556 8921)

THOMSON, Grant Hugh; s of Albert Edward Thomson (d 1976), of Toronto, Canada, and Muriel Frances, *née* Craggs (d 1986); *b* 11 Nov 1935; *m* 1, 1959 (m dis), Vera Anne, da of H Cibula; 1 da; m 2, 1985, Mary Rayleigh, da of Harold Stanfield Strutt; *Career* served HM Forces RAF photographer II 1954–60, photographer Guided Weapons and Aircraft Divs BAC 1960–64, photographic mangr BKS Surveys Ltd 1964–67, tech servs product specialist (aerial) Ilford Ltd 1967–72, lectr Int Inst for Aerospace Survey and Earth Scis (ITC) Enschede The Netherlands 1972–74; photographic mangr: Hunting Technical Services Ltd, Hunting Surveys and Consultants Ltd 1974–95; convener RPS Aerospace Imaging Section 1992–, UK corr to Ctee I ISPRS; independent conslt to commercial and govt remote sensing orgns in the UK and overseas; author of numerous pubns relating to aerospace photography in various photographic jls; FRPS 1985, FBIPP 1987; *Style—* Grant H Thomson, Esq; ✉ 57 Winslow Field, Great Missenden, Buckinghamshire HP16 9AR

THOMSON, Sir Ian Sutherland; KBE (1985, MBE mil 1945), kt (1985), CMG (1968); s of William Sutherland Thomson (d 1966), of Glasgow, and Jessie McCaig, *née* Malloch (d 1982); *b* 8 Jan 1920; *Educ* Glasgow HS, Univ of Glasgow (MA); *m* 1 Sept 1945, Nancy Marguerite (d 1988), da of William Kearsley (d 1956), of Suva, Fiji; 7 s (Andrew b 1947, Peter b 1948, John K Thomson, *qv*, b 1950, David b 1953, Richard b 1954, Mark b 1956, Douglas b 1960), 1 da (Sally b 1958); m 2, 1989, Nancy Caldwell, da of Robert Smyth McColl, of Glasgow; *Career* The Royal Highland Regt The Black Watch 1940, Fiji Mil Forces, ret Capt 1945; HM Colonial Admin Serv Fiji 1946–54, seconded to W Africa Dept and Civil Aviation Dept Colonial Office 1954–56, chm Native Lands and Fisheries Cmmn Fiji 1957–63 (cmmr for native reserves), cmmr Western Div Fiji 1963–66, actg chief sec and ldr of govt business Fiji Legislative Cncl 1966, admin Br Virgin Is 1966–70, independent chm Fiji Sugar Indust 1971–84; chm: Fiji Econ Devpt Bd 1981–86, Air Pacific Ltd 1984–87, Sedgwick (Fiji) Ltd 1984–87; Freeman City of Glasgow 1946; FBIM 1984–87; *Books* Fiji in the Forties and Fifties; *Recreations* golf, gardening; *Style—* Sir Ian Thomson, KBE, CMG; ✉ 1/4 Fettes Rise, Inverleith, Edinburgh EH4 1QH (☎ 0131 552 6421)

THOMSON, Lt-Col James Currie; MBE (Mil 1945), TD (1946), JP (Hertfordshire 1956), DL (1975); s of James Thomson (d 1961), of Leith, Edinburgh, and Nell Gertrude, *née* Hutt (d 1943); *b* 4 Feb 1911; *Educ* Marlborough, Pembroke Coll Cambridge (MA); *m* 12 May 1945, Letitia Blanche, wid of Capt M V Fleming (POW, d of wounds 1940), and da of Hon Malcolm Algernon Borthwick (d 1941), of Woodcote House, Oxon; 1 s (James Borthwick b 9 Feb 1946), 1 da (Clare Nell (Hon Mrs R C Denison-Pender) b 9 Feb 1946 (twin)), 3 step s (Valentine Patrick b 1 Aug 1935, Christopher Michael b 8 May 1937, David Algernon b 24 Nov 1938 d 1975), 1 step da (Gillian (Mrs N C Newbery) b 28 Jan 1940); *Career* London Scottish Regt: joined 1936, cmmnd 2 Lt 1938, Adj 1 Bn 1940 serv UK and PAIFORCE 1939–42, on staff N Africa and Italy 1943–44 (despatches), 2 i/c then CO 2 Bn Queen's Own Cameron Highlanders (wounded) serv Italy Greece Austria 1944–45, hon rank Lt-Col; Charles Mackinlay & Co Ltd: apprentice 1932, dir then chm 1970–76; cncllr Hertford RDC 1948–66, chm Stevenage Bench 1980; High Sheriff 1971–72; chm Herts Soc 1974–80; Liveryman Worshipful Co of Distillers; Hon Asst Worshipful Co of Founders (Master 1964–65); *Clubs* Boodle's; *Style—* Lt-Col James Thomson, MBE, TD, JP, DL; ✉ Stable Court, Walkern, nr Stevenage, Herts SG2 7JA

THOMSON, James Philips Spalding; s of Dr James Laing Spalding Thomson, and Peggy Marion, *née* Phillips; *b* 2 Oct 1939; *Educ* Haileybury and Imperial Serv Coll, Middx Hosp Med Sch London (MB BS, LRCP, DObstRCOG, FRCS 1969, MS); *m* 1968, Dr Anne Katharine Thomson, da of Richard Derek Richards; 1 s (James Richards Philips b 2 Feb 1971), 3 da (Rebecca Jane Katharine b 21 Aug 1973, Sally Anne Charlotte b 9 Feb 1979, Georgina Mary Caroline b 22 Jan 1985); *Career* jr med and surgical appts: Kettering Gen Hosp 1962, Middx Hosp 1963, 1968, 1969 and 1971–74, Cheltenham Gen Hosp 1966–67, Central Middx Hosp 1970, St Mark's Hosp 1970–71; demonstrator Dept of Anatomy Middx Hosp Med Sch 1964–66, pt/t hon conslt surgn St John's Hosp for

Diseases of the Skin 1973–75; conslt surgn: St Mark's Hosp 1974– (clinical dir 1990–), Royal Northern Hosp 1975–77, Hackney and Homerton Hosps 1977–90; hon conslt surgn St Luke's Hosp for the Clergy 1976– (vice chm Cncl), civil conslt in surgery RAF 1984–, civilian conslt in colorectal surgery RN 1986–, hon conslt advsr in surgery Ileostomy Assoc of GB and Ireland 1986–, hon sr lectr in surgery Bart's Med Coll 1977–94, hon sr clinical lectr in surgery St Mary's Hosp Med Sch Imperial Coll 1994–; Liveryman: Worshipful Soc of Apothecaries, Worshipful Co of Barbers; memb: Travelling Surgical Soc (sec 1982–90), Surgical Research Soc, Br Soc of Gastroenterology (memb Ctee Surgical Section 1986–88), Assoc of Coloproctology of GB and Ireland (sec 1989–90), NE Thames Metropolitan Surgical Soc, BMA, Med Soc for the Study of Venereal Disease, RN Med Club, Military Surgical Soc; associate memb Br Assoc of Clinical Anatomists; Section of Coloproctology RSM: memb Cncl 1983–, vice pres 1986–88 and 1990–94, hon sec 1988–90, pres 1994–95; DM (Lambeth) 1987; fell Assoc of Surgns of GB and Ireland (memb Cncl 1983–86), fell Hunterian Soc (memb Cncl 1994–); *Books* Colorectal Disease - An Introduction for Surgeons and Physicians (jtly, 1981), Frontiers in Colorectal Disease (jtly, 1986), Updates in Coloproctology (jtly, 1992), Familial Adenomatous Polyposis (jtly, 1994); also author of pubns and chapter contribs to books mainly on colon and rectal surgery; *Recreations* church music, railways and canals; *Clubs* RSM; *Style—* James P S Thomson, Esq; ✉ 1 Seaforth Gardens, Winchmore Hill, London N21 3BT (☎ 0181 886 3960); St Mark's Hospital, Northwick Park and St Mark's NHS Trust, Watford Road, Harrow, Middlesex HA1 3UJ (☎ 0181 239 4000/4002, fax 0181 235 4001); St Luke's Hospital for the Clergy, 14 Fitzroy Square, London W1P 6AH (☎ 0171 388 4954); secretary (☎ 01223 413500)

THOMSON, Sir John; KBE (1972), TD (1944); s of late Guy Thomson, JP; *b* 3 April 1908; *Educ* Winchester, Magdalen Coll Oxford; *m* 1, 1935, Elizabeth, *née* Brotherhood, JP (d 1977); m 2, 1979, Eva Elizabeth Dreaper, *née* Russell; *Career* Lt-Col Cmd Oxfordshire Yeo Regt RA 1942–44 and 1947–50, Brevet-Col; dir Union Discount Co of London Ltd 1960–74; chm: Barclays Bank Ltd 1962–73 (dir 1947–78), Morland and Co Ltd 1979–83; pres Br Bankers' Assoc 1964–66; memb: Royal Cmmn on Trade Unions and Employees Assocs 1965–68, BR Nat Export Cncl 1968; steward Jockey Club 1974–77, dep steward Univ of Oxford, curator Univ of Oxford Chest 1949–74, chm Nuffield Med Tstees 1951–82; High Sheriff Oxon 1957, DL Oxon 1947–57, Vice Lord-Lt Oxon 1957–63, Lord-Lt Oxon 1963–79; Freeman City of Oxford; Hon DCL Oxford 1957, hon fell St Catherine's Coll Oxford; FIB; KStJ (1973); *Recreations* steeplechase horse owner and breeder; *Clubs* Cavalry and Guards', Jockey, Overseas Bankers' (pres 1968–69, currently vice pres); *Style—* Sir John Thomson, KBE, TD; ✉ Manor Farm House, Spelsbury, Oxford OX7 3LG (☎ 01608 810266)

THOMSON, Sir John Adam; GCMG (1985, KCMG 1978, CMG 1972); s of Sir George Paget Thomson, FRS (d 1975), sometime Master CCC Cambridge, and Kathleen Buchanan, *née* Smith (d 1941); *b* 27 April 1927; *Educ* Phillips Exeter Acad USA, Univ of Aberdeen, Trinity Coll Cambridge; *m* 1, 1953, Elizabeth Anne McClure (d 1988); 3 s, 1 da; m 2, 1992, Judith Ogden Bullitt; *Career* joined FO 1950, head of Planning Staff FO 1967, on secondment to Cabinet Office as chief of Assessments Staff 1968–71, min and dep perm rep N Atlantic Cncl 1972–73, head UK Delgn MBFR Exploratory Talks in Vienna 1973, asst under sec FCO 1973–76, high cmmr India 1977–82, UK perm rep UNO NY and UK rep Security Cncl (with personal rank of ambass) 1982–87, chm CSCE rapporteur mission to Bosnia-Hercegovina 1992, memb CSCE mission to Albania 1994; dir ANZ Grindlays Bank 1987–96 (int advsr 1996–), chm Fleming Emerging Markets Investment Trust plc 1991–; princ dir 21 Century Trust London 1987–90, memb Howie Ctee on Sch Educn in Scot, tstee Nat Museums of Scot 1990–, memb Cncl Int Inst of Strategic Studies 1987–96, chm Minority Rights Gp International 1991–; tstee: Univ of Aberdeen Devpt Tst 1989–, Indian Nat Tst for Art and Cultural Heritage (UK) 1989–, Inst for Advanced Studies in the Humanities Edinburgh 1991–; memb Governing Body: Inst of Devpt Studies, Overseas Devpt Inst, 21 Century Tst; dir's visitor Inst for Advanced Study Princeton USA 1995–96; assoc memb Nuffield Coll Oxford 1987–91; *Books* Crusader Castles (co-author with R Fedden, 1956); *Recreations* hill walking; *Clubs* Athenaeum, Century (New York); *Style—* Sir John Thomson, GCMG; ✉ c/o Heads of Mission Section, Foreign and Commonwealth Office, King Charles Street, London SW1A 2AH

THOMSON, John K; s of Sir Ian Thomson, KBE, CMG, *qv*, of Edinburgh, and Nancy, *née* Kearsley (d 1988); *b* 17 Feb 1950; *Educ* St Kentigern Coll Auckland, Edinburgh Acad, Univ of Strathclyde (BA), Univ of Oxford (Dip in Econ Devpt); *m* July 1973, Lorna, da of Allan White; 1 s (Alastair b Aug 1991); *Career* research economist South Pacific Bureau for Economic Co-operation Fiji 1973–75, research offr Scottish Cncl (Devpt and Indust) Edinburgh 1976–80, analyst Scottish Investment Trust Edinburgh 1980–82; Standard Life: investmt mangr 1982–94, asst gen mangr (Devpt) 1994–96, chief investmt mangr 1996–; memb Exec Ctee Institutional Fund Mangrs Assoc; MSI 1993; *Recreations* gardening, walking; *Style—* John K Thomson; ✉ Standard Life Assurance Company, 30 Lothian Road, Edinburgh EH1 2DH (☎ 0131 245 6800, fax 0131 245 1296)

THOMSON, John Murray; s of John Wilson Thomson, and Catherine, *née* Murray Phillips; *b* 30 Jan 1928; *Educ* Falkirk HS, Univ of Edinburgh (MA); *m* Ingrid, Erich Haugas; 1 s (Ian b 24 June 1961), 1 da (Clare b 1 Sept 1964); *Career* Lazard Bros & Co Ltd 1950–59, Manufacturers Hanover Trust Company 1959–66, dep chief exec Brook Bond Group plc 1966–84; non-exec chm: Borthwicks plc until 1995, Compass Group plc, Wellington Underwriting plc; also former non-exec chm London & Manchester Group plc; non-exec dir: Thames Water plc, Scottish & Newcastle Breweries plc, J Bibby & Sons plc (vice chm), C Czarnikow Holdings Ltd; *Recreations* reading, walking, theatre, foreign travel; *Style—* John Thomson, Esq; ✉ Compass Group plc, Cowley House, Guildford Street, Chertsey, Surrey KT16 9BA (☎ 01932 573000)

THOMSON, Prof Joseph McGeachy; s of James Thomson, of Campbeltown, and Catherine Morrans, *née* McGeachy; *b* 6 May 1948; *Educ* Keil Sch Dumbarton, Univ of Edinburgh (LLB); *Career* lectr: Univ of Birmingham 1970–74, King's Coll London 1974–84; prof of law Univ of Strathclyde 1984–90, Regius prof of law Univ of Glasgow 1991–, dep gen ed Stair Meml Encyclopaedia of the Laws of Scotland 1985–96; FRSE 1996; *Books* Family Law in Scotland (3 edn, 1996), Delictual Liability (1994); *Recreations* opera, ballet, food and wine; *Style—* Prof Joseph Thomson, FRSE; ✉ 2 Kew Terrace, Glasgow G12 (☎ 0141 334 6682); The Law School, Stair Building, University of Glasgow G12 8QQ (☎ 0141 339 8855, fax 0141 330 4900

THOMSON, June Valerie; da of Alfred Manders (d 1974), of Norfolk, and Lily, *née* Marshall (d 1988); *b* 24 June 1930; *Educ* Chelmsford HS for Girls, Bedford Coll London (BA); *m* 1952 (m dis 1973), Alan Thomson; 2 s (Garrett Oliver b 3 June 1956, Paul Michael b 22 Feb 1962); *Career* writer; taught full time and pt/t time various schs in Stoke-on-Trent, London and St Albans; memb Crime Writers' Assoc (former Ctee Memb), memb and cncl memb Soc of Women Writers and Journalists; *Books* Not One of Us (1972), Case Closed (1977), Deadly Relations (1979), Shadow of a Doubt (1981, Prix du Roman d'Adventures 1983), No Flowers by Request (1987), Rosemary for Remembrance (1988), The Secret Files of Sherlock Holmes (1990), The Secret Chronicles of Sherlock Holmes (1992), Flowers for the Dead (short stories, 1992), The Secret Journals of Sherlock Holmes (1993), Holmes and Watson: A Study in Friendship (1995), Burden of Innocence (1996); writer of over twenty novels (18 featuring Det Insp Finch); *Recreations* gardening, theatre; *Clubs* Detection; *Style—* Ms June Thomson; ✉ c/o Curtis Brown, 4th Floor, Haymarket House, 28–29 Haymarket, London SW1Y 4SP (☎ 0171 396 6600)

THOMSON, Malcolm George; QC (Scot 1987); s of George Robert Thomson, OBE (d 1987), and Daphne Ethel, *née* Daniels; *b* 6 April 1950; *Educ* The Edinburgh Acad, Univ of Edinburgh (LLB); *m* 18 March 1978, Susan Gordon, da of Gordon Aitken, of Bath; 2 da (Victoria b 1982, Jacqueline b 1989); *Career* advocate at the Scottish Bar 1974, barr Lincoln's Inn 1991; standing jr counsel 1982–87: Dept of Agriculture and Fisheries for Scotland, The Forestry Cmmn Scotland; Scottish case ed Current Law 1977–96, ed Scots Law Times Reports 1989–, chm National Health Service Tribunal (Scotland) 1995–; *Recreations* sailing, skiing; *Clubs* New (Edinburgh); *Style—* Malcolm Thomson, Esq, QC; ✉ 2 Gamekeeper's Park, Edinburgh EH4 6PA (☎ 0131 336 5261); Advocates Library, Parliament House, Edinburgh EH1 1RF (☎ 0131 226 5071)

THOMSON, Sir Mark Wilfrid Home; 3 Bt (UK 1925), of Old Nunthorpe, Co York; s of Sir Ivo Wilfrid Home Thomson, 2 Bt (d 1991), and his 1 w, Sybil Marguerite, *née* Thompson; *b* 29 Dec 1939; *m* 1976, Lady Jacqueline Rosemary Margot Rufus Isaacs, o da of 3 Marquess of Reading; 3 s (Albert Mark Home b 1979, Jake Michael Alfred b 1983, Luke Ivo Charles b (twin) 1983), 1 da (Daisy Jacqueline Carol b 1977); *Heir* s, Albert Mark Home Thomson b 3 Aug 1979; *Style—* Sir Mark Thomson, Bt; ✉ 49 Hays Mews, London W1X 7RT (☎ 0171 408 1592)

THOMSON, Michael Brown; s of David Gordon Thomson, and Margaret Brown, *née* Walker; *b* 25 April 1957; *Educ* Bangor GS, Ulster Poly Jordanstown, Belfast Coll of Art and Design (BA, Johnson Matthey Metals student award), Fachhochschüle für Gestaltung Schwäbisch Gmünd Germany (King Edward VII British/German Fndn scholar for postgrad design studies), Ulster Poly (ATD); *Career* head Dept of Art and Design Donaghadee HS Co Down 1985–87 (teacher 1981–84), sr educn offr Design Cncl NI 1992–94 (educn offr 1987–92), asst dir Industry Matters Ltd NI 1994–95, princ Design Connect (int design promotion consultancy) 1995–; fndr memb Int Forum for Learning through Design (IFLTD) Vienna 1994–; CSD: memb Cncl London 1992–, chm NI Regnl Cncl 1993–; MSCD, FRSA; *Recreations* Anglican choral singing, cooking, travel; *Style—* Michael Thomson; ✉ Design Connect, 89b St John's Way, London N19 3QU (☎ and fax 0171 281 7949, mobile 0385 996203, e-mail designconnect@unite.co.uk, www http://www.unite.co.uk/customers/designconnect)

THOMSON, Prof Neil Campbell; s of Prof Adam Simpson Turnbull Thomson, of Ayr, and Margaret Campbell, *née* Templeton; *b* 3 April 1948; *Educ* Spiers Sch Beith, Univ of Glasgow (MB ChB, MD); *m* 16 Aug 1973, Lorna Jean, da of William Sim Walker Fraser, of Perth; 2 s (David Fraser b 10 July 1976, Andrew Campbell b 8 May 1978), 1 da (Jennifer Lorna b 22 May 1985); *Career* jr hosp doctor Glasgow Teaching Hosps 1972–80, res fell McMaster Univ Hamilton Ontario Canada 1980–81, conslt physician Western Infirmary Glasgow 1982–; hon prof Univ of Glasgow 1996–; former memb Res Ctees: Br Lung Fndn, The Nat Asthma Campaign; memb: Assoc of Physicians, Br Thoracic Soc (former hon sec), American Thoracic Soc, Scot Soc of Physicians, Br Soc for Allergy and Clinical Immunology; FRCP; *Books* Handbook of Clinical Allergy (1990), Asthma: Basic Mechanisms and Clinical Management (1988, 2 edn 1992), Manual of Asthma Management (1995); *Recreations* fishing, gardening, hill walking; *Style—* Prof Neil Thomson; ✉ Department of Respiratory Medicine, West Glasgow Hospitals University NHS Trust, Glasgow G12 0YN (☎ 0141 211 3241, fax 0141 211 3464)

THOMSON, Sheriff Nigel Ernest Drummond; CBE (1993); s of Rev James Kyd Thomson (d 1939), of Edinburgh, and Joan Drummond (d 1929); *b* 19 June 1926; *Educ* George Watson's Boys' Coll Edinburgh, Univ of St Andrews (MA), Univ of Edinburgh (LLB); *m* 1964, Snjólaug, da of Consul Gen Sigursteinn Magnússon (d 1982), of Edinburgh; 1 s (Diggi b 1969), 1 da (Ingalo b 1967); *Career* Lt Indian Grenadiers; advocate; sheriff at: Hamilton 1966–1976, Edinburgh 1976–96; hon Texas ranger 1995; chm: Music Ctee Scottish Arts Cncl 1979–84, Edinburgh Youth Orchestra 1986–92; convenor Cncl for Music in Hospitals in Scotland 1992–; hon pres: Scottish Assoc for Counselling 1984–88, Strathaven Arts Guild 1976–, Tenovus-Edinburgh 1985–; vice pres Br Assoc for Counselling 1992–; *Recreations* music, woodwork, golf; *Clubs* New (Edinburgh), Bruntsfield Golf, Strathaven Arts; *Style—* Sheriff Nigel Thomson, CBE; ✉ 50 Grange Rd, Edinburgh (☎ 0131 667 2166)

THOMSON, Dr Oliver Campbell Watt; s of (James) Oliver Thomson OBE (d 1972), of Milngavie, and Linda Marie, *née* Kelly; *b* 28 Feb 1936; *Educ* King Edward VI Sch Birmingham, Trinity Coll Cambridge (MA), Univ of Glasgow (PhD); *m* 10 Sept 1960, Jean Patricia Dawson, da of James Sellar Christie, CBE (d 1986), of Glasgow; 2 s (Calum b 1961, Iain b 1964), 1 da (Margaret b 1967); *Career* RN 1954–56, Lt RNR 1964–70; dir McCallum Advertising 1972–75, md Charles Barker Scotland 1975–85, mktg dir Holmes McDougall 1985–86, md Levy McCallum Ltd 1986–; chm: Four Acres Charitable Tst, Kilmory Tst; MCAM, FIMgt, FIPA; *Books* The Romans in Scotland (1965), Mass Persuasion in History (1970), History of Sin (1993); *Plays* Dapifer (1994); *Recreations* sailing, hillwalking; *Clubs* RSAC; *Style—* Dr Oliver Thomson; ✉ 3 Kirklee Terrace, Glasgow G12 0TQ (☎ 0141 339 7453); Levy McCallum Advertising Agency, 203 St Vincent St, Glasgow G2 5NH (☎ 0141 248 7977, fax 0141 221 5803)

THOMSON, HE Peter Alexander Bremner; CVO (1986); s of Alexander Bremner Thomson (d 1976), and Dorothy Davison, *née* Scurr; *b* 16 Jan 1938; *Educ* Canford, RNC Dartmouth, SOAS (BA, MPhil, MA); *m* 31 July 1965, Lucinda Coleman, da of Colin Sellar (d 1965), of Morayshire; 3 s (Philip b 1970, Nicholas b 1972, Christopher b 1978); *Career* RN 1954–75; Sub Lt and Lt in HM Ships: Albion, Plover, Tiger, Ark Royal, Eagle; Lt Cdr ashore Hong Kong and Taiwan; Dip Serv 1975–; first sec: FCO 1975–77, Lagos 1977–79, Hong Kong 1979–82, FCO 1982–84; cnsllr and head of chancery Peking 1984–87, high cmmr Belize 1987, cnsllr FCO 1991–95, high cmmr Seychelles (Victoria) 1995–; *Recreations* sailing, walking, 19th century fiction; *Clubs* Travellers', Thames Barge Sailing, Hong Kong; *Style—* HE Peter Thomson, CVO; ✉ c/o FCO (Victoria), King Charles Street, London SW1; private address: Mr Peter Thomson, The Red House, Charlton Horethorne, Sherborne, Dorset

THOMSON, Stanley; CBE (1989); s of William Ingram Thomson (d 1971), and Annie Blanche Thomson (d 1975); *b* 23 June 1926; *Educ* Robert Gordon's Coll Aberdeen; *m* 8 June 1956, Elizabeth Wright, da of Eric Knox Wilson, of Scotland; 1 s (David Bruce b 1960); *Career* certified accountant; exec dir Ford Motor Co Ltd 1980–90 (dir of fin 1967–90), chm Wivenhoe Enterprises Ltd 1991–; non-exec dir Ford Credit Europe plc 1993–; pres Chartered Assoc of CAs 1987–88 (fell 1952, memb Cncl 1974–92); memb: Industl Devpt Advsy Bd 1978–86, Bd Int Accounting Standards Ctee 1990–92, Fin Reporting Cncl 1990–93; vice chm Accounting Standards Ctee (memb 1982–85); treas Univ of Essex 1994– (memb Cncl 1988–); FCCA, CIMgt; *Recreations* gardening, reading; *Style—* Stanley Thomson, Esq, CBE; ✉ 6 Belvedere Rd, Brentwood, Essex (☎ 01277 226111)

THOMSON, Sir Thomas James; kt (1991), CBE (1983, OBE 1978); s of Thomas Thomson (d 1949), of Airdrie, Scotland, and Annie Jane, *née* Grant (d 1968); *b* 8 April 1923; *Educ* Airdrie Acad, Univ of Glasgow (MB ChB); *m* 10 Jan 1948, Jessie Smith, da of George Edward Shotbolt (d 1955), of Ardrossan, Scotland, and Mary Brown, *née* White (d 1978); 2 s (Ian b 1954, Alan b 1960), 1 da (Shona b 1955); *Career* Flt-Lt RAF 1946–48; conslt physician and gastroenterologist Stobhill Gen Hosp Glasgow 1961–87; Dept of Materia Medica Univ of Glasgow: lectr 1953–61, hon lectr 1961–87; postgrad advsr to Glasgow Northern Hosps 1961–80, sec Specialist Advsy Ctee for Gen Internal Med UK 1970–74; chm: Medica - Pharmaceutical Forum 1978–80 (chm Educn Advsy

Bd 1979–84), Conf of Royal Colls and Faculties in Scotland 1982–84, Nat Med Consultative Ctee for Scotland 1982–87; pres RCPSGlas 1982–84 (hon sec 1965–73), active in postgrad med educn ctees locally, nationally and in EC; chm Greater Glasgow Health Bd 1987–93 (memb 1985–93); Univ of Strathclyde: memb Court 1993–, chm Staff Ctee 1994–; Hon Fell American Coll of Physicians 1983, Hon LLD Univ of Glasgow 1988; FRCP (Glasgow) 1964, FRCP (London) 1969, FRCP (Edin) 1982, FRCP (Ireland) 1983; *Books* Dilling's Pharmacology (jt ed 1969), Gastroenterology - an integrated course (1972, 3 edn 1983); *Recreations* swimming, golfing; *Clubs* RAF London, RSAC (Glasgow); *Style*— Sir Thomas J Thomson, CBE; ✉ 1 Varna Rd, Glasgow G14 9NE (☎ 0141 959 5930)

THOMSON, Dr Wendy; da of Shirley Basil Thomson (d 1970), and Grace, *née* Frazer; *b* 28 Oct 1953; *Educ* Verdun HS, McGill Univ Montreal (Dip Collegial Studies, Batchelor of Social Work, Master of Social Work), Univ of Bristol (PhD); *Career* pt/t sessional lectr McGill Univ 1977–81; exec dir: Head and Hands (Montreal) 1976–80, West Island Association for People with Learning Disabilities (Quebec) 1981–82; sr programmes offr GLC 1985–86, head of fin and programmes London Strategic Policy Unit (LSPU) 1986–87, asst chief exec Islington Cncl 1987–93; chief exec: Turning Point (charity) 1993–96, London Borough of Newham 1996–; *Books* incl: Bureaucracy and Community (contrib, 1990), Citizen's Rights in a Modern Welfare System (contrib, 1992), Management for Quality in Local Government (contrib, 1992), Fitness for Purpose: Shaping new Patterns for Organisations and Management (co-author, 1993); also contrib to various other publications and author numerous conf papers; *Recreations* tennis, reading, gardening; *Style*— Dr Wendy Thomson; ✉ London Borough of Newham, Town Hall, Barking Road, E Ham, London E6 2RP (☎ 0181 472 1430)

THOMSON OF FLEET, 2 Baron (UK 1964), of Northbridge in the City of Edinburgh; Kenneth Roy Thomson; s of 1 Baron Thomson of Fleet, GBE (d 1976), fndr of the Thomson newspapers; *b* 1 Sept 1923; *Educ* Upper Canada Coll Toronto, Univ of Cambridge (MA); *m* 1956, Nora Marilyn, da of Albert Vernard Lavis, of Toronto; 2 s (David Kenneth Roy, Peter John), 1 da (Lesley Lynne); *Heir* s, Hon David Kenneth Roy Thomson; *Career* serv WWII RCAF; newspaper proprietor; began in editorial dept Timmins Daily Press 1947, with Advtg Dept Cambridge (Galt) Reporter 1948–50 (gen mangr 1950–53); chm: The Thomson Corporation Ltd, The Thomson Organisation Plc, The Woodbridge Company Limited, Thomson US Inc; pres and dir Thomson Works of Art Limited; dir Markborough Properties Inc; *Recreations* collecting paintings and works of art, walking; *Clubs* National, Hunt, Granite, York Downs, York, Toronto; *Style*— The Rt Hon Lord Thomson of Fleet; ✉ 8 Castle Frank Rd, Toronto, Ontario M4W 2Z4, Canada; 8 Kensington Palace Gardens, London W8; offices: The Thomson Corporation, 65 Queen Street West, Toronto, Ontario M5H 2M8, Canada; The Thomson Corporation Plc, The Quadrangle, PO Box 4YG, 180 Wardour St, London W1A 4YG (☎ 0171 437 9787)

THOMSON OF MONIFIETH, Baron (Life Peer UK 1977), of Monifieth in the District of the City of Dundee; George Morgan Thomson; KT (1981), PC (1966), DL (1992); s of late James Thomson, of Monifieth, Angus; *b* 16 Jan 1921; *Educ* Grove Acad Dundee; *m* 1948, Grace, da of Cunningham Jenkins, of Glasgow; 2 da (Hon Caroline Agnes Morgan (Hon Mrs Liddle) b 1954, Hon Ailsa Ballantine b 1956); *Career* on staff of Dandy rising to chief sub-ed 1930s; asst ed then ed Forward 1946–53; MP (Lab) Dundee East 1952–72, min of State FO 1964–66, chllr of Duchy of Lancaster 1966–67 and 1969–70, joint min of State FO 1967, sec of State for Cwlth Affrs 1967–68, min without portfolio 1968–69, shadow def min 1970–72; EEC cmmr 1973–77; chm: Euro Movement in Br 1977–80, Advertising Standards Authy 1977–80; dir: ICI plc 1977–90, Woolwich Equitable Building Soc 1979–91, Royal Bank of Scotland Group 1977–90, English National Opera 1987–93, Value and Income Tst 1986–; First Crown Estate cmmr 1978–80, chm IBA 1981–88, vice-pres Royal TV Soc 1982–88, vice chm Euro Inst of Media 1989–94; pres: History of Advertising Tst 1985–, Voice of Listener and Viewer 1990–; chllr Heriot Watt Univ 1977–91; tstee: Pilgrim Tst, Thomson Fndn; chm of tstees Leeds Castle Fndn 1994–; memb Nolan Ctee 1994–; Lib Dem spokesman foreign affrs and broadcasting House of Lords; Gold medal Euro Assoc of Advtg Agencies 1994; Hon LLD Dundee 1967, Hon DLitt Heriot-Watt 1973, Hon DSc Aston 1976, Hon DLitt New Univ of Ulster 1984, Hon DCL Kent 1989, FRSE 1985; *Style*— The Rt Hon the Lord Thomson of Monifieth, KT, PC, DL, FRSE; ✉ House of Lords, London SW1A 0PW (☎ 0171 219 6718, 01622 880656, fax 01622 880545)

THORBEK, Erik; s of Kai Birch (d 1988), and Dr Agro Grete Thorbek; *b* 10 Jan 1941; *Educ* Billum Coll Denmark; *m* 6 April 1963, Susan Margaret, da of Sidney Gair (d 1977); 2 s (Alexander b 1964 m Alexandra Hindley, Nikolas b 1973), 2 da (Francesca (Mrs Jonathan Brunton) b 1966, Natasha b 1975); *Career* chm and chief exec Anglo Viking Corporation Ltd 1977– (dir 1964–, md 1972–77); *Recreations* travel, skiing, golf, horse racing, shooting, sailing; *Clubs* Turf, Helford River Sailing, Moatlands Golf, Farm; *Style*— Erik Thorbek; ✉ Maynards, Matfield, Kent TN12 7DU (☎ 01892 723966); Anglo Viking Corporation Ltd, Produce House, Matfield, Kent TN12 7JP (☎ 01892 723232, fax 01892 723131)

THORBURN, Andrew; s of James Beresford Thorburn (d 1972), and Marjorie Clara Thorburn (d 1987); *b* 20 March 1934; *Educ* Univ of Southampton (BSc); *m* 1957, Margaret Anne, da of Reginald Crack (d 1964); 1 s (Edward), 2 da (Jenny, Anna); *Career* dir Notts/Derbys Sub-Regnl Study 1968–70, county planning offr of E Sussex 1973–83, chief exec English Tourist Bd 1983–85, head of tourism and leisure Grant Thornton 1986–90, chm Thorburns (leisure planning consultancy) 1990–; dir: Sussex Heritage Tst, Stanmer House Preservation Tst; pres Royal Town Planning Inst 1982; memb: Int Soc of City and Regnl Planners, Town and Country Planning Assoc; fell Tourism Soc; FRTPI; *Books* Planning Villages (1971); *Recreations* sailing; *Style*— Andrew Thorburn, Esq; ✉ Hyde Manor, Kingston, Lewes, E Sussex BN7 3PB (☎ 01273 476019)

THORBURN, Paul Huw; s of Geoffrey George Thorburn, and Pauline Hughes, *née* Jenkins; *b* 24 Nov 1962; *Educ* Hereford Cathedral Sch, Univ Coll Swansea; *m* 5 Oct 1987, Sharon Elizabeth Ann, da of Thomas Conlin; 1 da (Kelly Elizabeth Ann b 17 March 1990), 1 s (Rory George Thomas b 15 March 1992); *Career* rugby union full back Neath RFC and Wales (37 caps); clubs: Ebbw Vale RFC, Neath RFC 1984– (299 appearances), Welsh Universities, UAU RFC, capped Wales B 1984; Wales: debut v France 1985, scored record 52 points Five Nations Championship 1986, Triple Crown winners 1988, capt 9 times, third place World Cup 1987, kicked 70 yard penalty v Scotland (longest in int match) 1986; dir 1999 Rugby World Cup 1996–; *Recreations* waterskiing, squash, golf; *Style*— Paul Thorburn, Esq; ✉ 2 Mandinam Park, Gower Road, Sketty, Swansea SA4 7AA

THORBURN, Dr Samuel; OBE (1987); s of Samuel Thorburn, MBE (d 1984), of Strathclyde, and Isabella Thorburn (d 1983); *b* 15 Oct 1930; *Educ* Hamilton Acad, Royal Technical Coll (now Univ of Strathclyde); *m* 1953, Margaret Elizabeth May; 1 s (David John b 1958), 1 da (Lynne Margaret b 1967); *Career* design and construction engr Colvilles Limited 1951–58, chief engr Whatlings Foundations Ltd 1958–61; engrg dir: Caledonian Foundations Limited 1961–64, GKN Foundations Limited 1964–66; Thorburn Group: fndr 1966, dir Thorburn Associates 1966–90, dir Thorburn PLC 1990–92, gp conslt 1992–; visiting prof Univ of Strathclyde; chm: Certification Advsy Cncl for the Service Sector, Int Ctee on Professional Practice Int Soc of Soil Mechanics and Fndn Engrg, Structural Engineering Trading Organization Ltd; memb: Tech Sector Bd BSI, Cncl and Exec Ctee ICE, Football Licensing Authy; conslt Dept of Energy, specialist advsr to Home Office and Defence Ctees House of Commons, advsr Br design and construction of bridge fndns; former memb Tech Advsy Ctee: BSI, CIRIA, Science and Res Cncl, DOE, Dept of Energy; former chm of Tech Ctee: IStructE, ICE; Oscar Faber award IStructE 1970, Eur Ing; Freeman of the City of Glasgow; FICE 1967, FIStructE 1970, FASCE 1971, FEng 1985; *Books* Underpinning (1985), Underpinning and Retention (1992), author of numerous papers and contribs to publications on engrg; *Recreations* golf, painting, public speaking; *Style*— Dr Sam Thorburn, OBE, FEng; ✉ 32 Lochbroom Drive, Newton Mearns, Eastwood, Strathclyde, Scotland G77 5PF (☎ 0141 639 2724); Thorburn Colquhoun, Kinneil House, 243 West George St, Glasgow G2 4QE (☎ 0141 226 3611, fax 0141 248 3773)

THORLEY, Simon Joe; QC (1989); s of Sir Gerald Bowers Thorley, TD (d 1988), and Beryl Preston, *née* Rhodes (who m 2, Sir David Lancaster Nicolson (d 1996)); *b* 22 May 1950; *Educ* Rugby, Keble Coll Oxford (MA); *m* 7 May 1983, Jane Elizabeth, da of Frank Cockcroft, of Saltburn by Sea, Cleveland; 2 s (Matthew b 1984, Nicholas b 1985), 1 da (Francesca b 1988); *Career* called to the Bar Inner Temple 1972, barr specialising in patent matters; chm IP Bar Assoc (formerly Patent Bar Assoc) 1995–, memb Bar Cncl 1995–; *Books* Terrell on Patents (jt ed, 13 and 14 edn); *Recreations* family, shooting, opera; *Style*— Simon Thorley, Esq, QC; ✉ 3 New Square, Lincoln's Inn, London WC2A 3RS (☎ 0171 405 1111, fax 0171 405 7800)

THORN, Jeremy Gordon; s of James Douglas Thorn, of Appleton, nr Warrington, Cheshire, and Daphne Elizabeth, *née* Robinson; *b* 23 March 1948; *Educ* Mill Hill Sch, Univ of Leeds (BSc), European Coll of Marketing (Dip), Cranfield Sch of Mgmnt, London Business Sch; *m* 24 July 1971, Éilis Anne, da of Christopher Maurice Coffey, of Street, Somerset; 4 da (Jessica b 1977, Rachel b 1982, Alicen b 1984, Stephanie b 1987); *Career* dir of sales and mktg: Baugh & Weedon Ltd 1978–81, Bradley & Foster Ltd 1981–83, Spear & Jackson Ltd 1984–86, British Ropes Ltd 1986–89, Bridon Fishing Ltd 1989–93; chm Bristol Wire Rope Ltd 1988–93, md Bridon Ropes Ltd 1989–93; Bridon Ropes Ltd awarded Investor in People Award 1992 and 1993, Design Award 1993, Prince Michael of Kent Award for Road Safety 1993, Queen's Award for Technol 1993; chm Fedn of Wire Rope Manufacturers of GB 1989–92, UK spokesman Euro Wire Rope Info Serv 1986–93; chm Quantum Enterprise Development 1993–; dir: Barnsley/Doncaster Trg and Enterprise Cncl (dep chm) 1989–93, Thorn Hinton Ltd 1993–, Quantum Generation Ltd 1993–95; pres Doncaster Branch Inst of Mgmnt 1989–, memb Judging Panel Nat Trg Awards 1993–; CEng, MIM, CIMgt; *Books* How to Negotiate Better Deals (1989), The First Time Sales Manager (1990), Developing Your Career in Management (1992); *Recreations* music, sport (former chm W Midlands Region Amateur Fencing Assoc, sometime fencing team capt Univ of Leeds, Warwickshire, W Midlands and Yorkshire, former Warwickshire épée and sabre champion and W Midlands and Yorkshire sabre champion); *Style*— Jeremy Thorn, Esq; ✉ 239 Graham Road, Sheffield, S Yorks S10 3GS (☎ 0114 230 6506, fax 0114 230 8422)

THORN, Roger Eric; QC (1990); s of James Douglas (Pat) Thorn, of Appleton, Cheshire, and Daphne Elizabeth, *née* Robinson; *b* 23 March 1948; *Educ* Mill Hill Sch London, Univ of Newcastle upon Tyne (LLB); *Career* called to the Bar Middle Temple 1970 (Harmsworth scholar and Major exhibitioner); in practice NE Circuit, asst recorder; memb Bd Faculty of Law Univ of Newcastle upon Tyne 1990–94, life govr Mill Hill Sch; *Books* A Practical Guide to Road Traffic Accident Claims (1987), Road Traffic Accident Claims (1990), Negotiating Better Deals (legal contrib, 1988); *Recreations* theatre, music, walking, bridge, learning patience; *Clubs* National Liberal, Durham County, Old Millhillians; *Style*— Roger Thorn, Esq, QC; ✉ Whitton Grange, Rothbury, via Morpeth, Northumberland NE65 7RL; 199 Strand, London WC2R 1DR; New Court Chambers, 3 Broad Chare, Quayside, Newcastle upon Tyne NE1 3DQ

THORN, Air Cdre Timothy Gane; AFC (1983); s of Jack Gane Thorn (d 1985), of Little Blakenham, nr Ipswich, Suffolk, and Ivy May, *née* Chaplin (d 1985); *b* 21 Sept 1942; *Educ* Ipswich Sch, RAF Coll Cranwell; *m* 2 Oct 1971, (Elisabeth) Rosemary, da of Donald Garmon Meredith (d 1969); 1 s (Christopher b 18 Oct 1974), 1 da (Jennifer b 2 Oct 1976); *Career* won minor counties cricket championship with Suffolk 1960, offr trg RAF Coll 1961–64, Pilot Offr 1964, played rugby for RAF 1964–66, Flying Offr 1965, played for Blackheath RFC 1965, ejected from aircraft after mid-air collision 1966, Flt Lt 1967, bronze medal at Euro bobsleigh championships 1968, GB rep in bobsleigh at Grenoble Winter Olympics 1968, Sqdn Ldr 1972, landed without parachute from 500 feet at night 1973, Indian Def Servs Staff Coll 1975, Flt Cdr number 41 (F) Sqdn 1976–79, Wing Cdr 1979, QCVSA 1979, CO number II (AC) Sqdn 1980–83, Operational Requirements Div MOD 1983–86, Gp Capt 1986, CO RAF Cranwell 1986–88, Gp Capt Flying Trg HQ RAF Support Command 1988–89, attended RCDS 1990; Air Cdre 1990, Sr Air Staff Offr RAF Germany 1991–93, Cmdt Gen RAF Regiment HQ RAF Strike Cmd 1993–95, ret 1995; head of security CSO Valuations AG (De Beers) 1995–; chm: Aircrew Assoc 1994, RAF Regt Assoc 1995–; qualified parachutist with 150 descents, qualified mil and civil flying instr with 7000 hrs; chm Inter-Services Bobsleigh 1985–93; FRAeS 1993 (MRAeS 1986); *Clubs* Royal Aeronautical, Royal Air Force, Adastrian CC; *Style*— T G Thorn, AFC; ✉ Nell House, Hannington, Highworth, Swindon, Wilts SN6 7RU (☎ 01793 765209)

THORNBER, Iain; JP (1988), DL (Lochaber, Inverness and Badenoch and Strathspey); s of James Thornber (d 1982), of Morvern, Argyll, and Jeannie Easton Campbell, *née* Stenhouse; *b* 3 Feb 1948; *Educ* Glenhurich Public Sch; *Career* company factor Glensanda Estate Morvern (Foster Yeoman Ltd) 1980; dir: Highland Opportunity Ltd 1992–, Nevis Community Radio Ltd 1992–; life memb and tstee W Highland Museum Fort William; memb: Forestry Cmmn local advsy panel, Morvern Red Deer Mgmnt Gp, Inverness Prison Visiting Ctee, Country Life Museums Tst; tstee Glenfinnan Station Museum Tst 1992; rep memb Royal Soc for Nature Conservation Rahoy Hills Nature Res; memb Lochaber DC for Ardgour Sunart and Morvern (vice chm 1992, chm Resources and Gen Purposes Ctee 1992), chm Lochaber District Licensing Bd; FSA Scot 1973, FRSA 1987, FSA 1990; *Books* The Castles of Morvern, Argyll (1975), The Sculptured Stones of Cill Choluimchille Morvern, Argyll (1975), The Gaelic Bards of Morvern (1985), Rats (1989), Bronze Age Cairns in the Aline Valley, Morvern, Argyll (in Proceedings of the Society of Antiquaries of Scotland Vol 106, jt author, 1974–75), The Gaelic Bards of Morvern (1985), Cairn 3, Acharn, Morvern, Argyll (in Proceedings of the Society of Antiquaries of Scotland Vol 118, jt author, 1988), Moidart, or Among the Clanranalds (ed 1989 edn), 1793–1993 - The Story of the 79th Cameron Highlanders (Seaforth & Camerons) (1993); *Recreations* deer stalking, photography, local history research; *Style*— Iain Thornber, Esq, FSA, JP, DL; ✉ Knock House, Morvern, Oban, Argyll PA34 5UU (☎ 01967 421651, fax 01967 421638); Glensanda Estate, Morvern, Argyll (☎ 0163 173 415, fax 0163 173 460, telex 777792); Lochaber House, Fort William, Inverness-shire (☎ 01397 703881, fax 01397 704016)

THORNE, Angela Margaret Leslie; da of Lt-Col Dr William Herbert Alfred Thorne, OBE (d 1982), and (Leslie) Sylvia (May) Thorne; *b* 25 Jan 1939; *Educ* Farlington House Horsham Sussex; *m* 22 Sept 1967, Peter David Penry-Jones, s of Rev David Penry-Jones; 2 s (Rupert William b 22 Sept 1970, Laurence David b 18 Aug 1977); *Career* actress; theatre credits incl: Gloria Claudon in You Never Can Tell (Theatre Royal) 1966, Julia in The Rivals (Theatre Royal) 1966, Portia in The Merchant of Venice (Theatre Royal) 1967, Io in Prometheus Bound (Mermaid Theatre) 1971, Vanessa in Yahoo (Queens Theatre) 1976, Mrs Thatcher in Anyone for Dennis (Whitehall Theatre) 1981, Lady Gay Spanker in London Assurance (Theatre Royal) 1989, Body and Soul (Albery) 1992, The

Weekend (Strand) 1994, Communicating Doors (Savoy) 1996; film credits: Betty Smith in Oh! What a Lovely War 1968; TV credits incl: Marjorie Frobisher in To the Manor Born, Daphne in Three Up Two Down; memb: The Actors' Charitable Tst, The Theatrical Ladies Guild; *Style—* Miss Angela Thorne; ✉ c/o Michael Whitehall Ltd, 125 Gloucester Road, London SW7 4TE (☎ 0171 244 8466, fax 0171 244 9060)

THORNE, Clive Duncan; s of Desmond Clive Thorne, of Eastbourne, and May, *née* Davey; *b* 21 Jan 1952; *Educ* Eastbourne GS, Trinity Hall Cambridge (BA, MA); *m* 1, 11 Oct 1975 (m dis 1982), Catherine Sykes; m 2, 12 July 1986, Alison Mary Healy, da of Cdr Michael Healy, of Beaulieu Sur Mer, France; *Career* articled clerk Clifford Turner 1975–77, slr England 1977–84, slr Hong Kong 1984–87, barr and slr Victoria Aust 1985, currently ptnr Intellectual Property Gp Denton Hall; author of numerous articles on intellectual property and various articles in Euro Intellectual Property Review and other jls; memb: Cons and U party, Law Soc; Assoc: Inst of Trade Mark Agents, Chartered Inst of Patent Agents; FCIArb; *Books* Sony Guide to Home Taping (contrib 1983), Intellectual Property - The New Law (1989); *Recreations* English music, reading, walking, flute playing; *Style—* Clive Thorne, Esq; ✉ Denton Hall, Five Chancery Lane, Cliffords Inn, London EC4A 1BU (☎ 0171 242 1212, fax 0171 404 0087)

THORNE, Maj-Gen Sir David Calthrop; KBE (1983, CBE 1979, OBE 1975), CVO (1995); s of Richard Everard Thorne (d 1957), and Audrey Ursula, *née* Bone (d 1994); identical twin bro of Brig Michael Thorne, CBE; *b* 13 Dec 1933; *Educ* St Edward's Sch Oxford, RMA Sandhurst; *m* 1962, Suzan Anne, da of Edward Eaton Goldsmith; 1 s, 2 da; *Career* cmmnd Royal Norfolk Regt 1952, cmd 1 Bn Royal Anglian Regt 1972–74, Bde Cdr 3 Infantry Bde NI 1977–79, Maj-Gen 1981, Vice QMG 1981–82, Cdr British Forces Falkland Islands 1982–83, cmd 1 Armd Div 1983–85; Dep Col Royal Anglian Regt 1981–87, dir of Infantry 1986–88, Col Cmdt Queen's Div 1986–88; dir gen Cwlth Tst 1989–; non-exec dir W Suffolk Hosps NHS Tst 1992–, pres Norfolk CCC 1993–95; tstee Falklands Conservation, govr Langley Sch; *Recreations* family, cricket, butterfly collecting; *Clubs* Army and Navy, MCC, I Zingari, Free Foresters, Jesters; *Style—* Maj-Gen Sir David Thorne, KBE, CVO; ✉ c/o Barclays Bank, 52 Abbeygate St, Bury St Edmunds, Suffolk IP33 1LL

THORNE, Maj George; MC (1945), ERD, DL (Oxfordshire 1961); 2 s of Gen Sir (Augustus Francis) Andrew Nicol Thorne, KCB, CMG, DSO, DL (d 1970), of Knowl Hill House, nr Reading (*see* Burke's Landed Gentry, 18 edn, vol II, 1969), and Hon Margaret Douglas-Pennant (d 1967), 10 da of 2 Baron Penrhyn; *b* 1 July 1912; *Educ* Eton, Trinity Coll Oxford; *m* 18 April 1942, Juliet Agnes, o da of Hon (Arthur) George Villiers Peel, JP, DL (d 1956), 2 s of 1 Viscount Peel, and Lady Agnes Lygon, da of 6 Earl Beauchamp; 2 s (Robert George (Robin), m Sarah, *née* Priestley, wid of Brian Bond, Ian David Peel, m Paula, *née* Endwezoh), 1 da (Viola Georgina Juliet (Mrs Nicholas Halsey)); *Career* Maj late Grenadier Guards (SR), serv WWII, ADC to GOC 1 Div (Maj-Gen Hon Harold Alexander) 1939–40, OC No 3 Co 1 Bn Gren Gds 1941–45, Capt The King's Co 1 Bn Gren Gds 1945 (despatches); memb sales staff McVitie & Price Ltd 1934–39 and 1946–67; farmer 1950–; pres: Royal Br Legion (Peppard), Dunkirk Veterans Assoc (Henley); *Recreations* country pursuits; *Clubs* Farmers; *Style—* Maj George Thorne, MC, ERD, DL; ✉ 24 Swallowfield Park, Reading, Berks RG7 1TG (☎ 0118 988 5983)

THORNE, Ian David Peel; s of Maj George Thorne, MC, ERD, DL, *qv*; *b* 14 Oct 1944; *Educ* Eton, RMA Sandhurst, Trinity Coll Oxford (MA); *m* 1992, Paula Enwezoh; 1 da (Davina b 1992), 1 step-s (Du'aine Ladejo b 1971, *qv*), 1 step-da (Alison Thorne-Enwezoh b 1972); *Career* served in Grenadier Gds 1965–73 (ret as Capt), Cons Research Dept 1973–74; country landowner 1974–; chm Promise (Film) Production Co 1990–93; pres Newark and Notts Agric Soc 1989–90, vice pres Notts Assoc of Boys' and Keystone Clubs 1986–93, jt chm Notts Macmillan Nurse Appeal 1993–95, chm Cancer Relief Macmillan Fund in Notts 1996–; High Sheriff of Notts 1986–87; *Publications* Purple Patches; *Recreations* shooting, travel, golf; *Clubs* I Zingari; *Style—* I D P Thorne, Esq

THORNE, Matthew Wadman John; s of Robin Horton John Thorne, CMG, OBE, of Old Heathfield, E Sussex, and Joan Helen, *née* Wadman; *b* 27 June 1952; *Educ* Dragon Sch, King's Sch Canterbury, Trinity Coll Oxford (MA); *m* 1978, (Sheila) Leigh, da of Col Hon Robert George Hugh Phillimore, OBE (d 1984), 3 s of 2 Baron Phillimore, MC, DL; 3 s (Robin b 15 Feb 1983, Andrew b 27 Feb 1986, Edward b 16 July 1989), 2 da (Aelene b 17 June 1981, Marini b 4 Aug 1992); *Career* Price Waterhouse 1975–78, County Natwest 1978–83, Beazer plc 1983–91 (dir 1984–91); dir: Ricardo International PLC 1991–92, McCarthy & Stone plc 1993–; non-exec dir: BM Group PLC 1991–93, UMECO plc 1992–; FCA 1978; *Style—* Matthew Thorne, Esq; ✉ The Mount, Bannerdown Rd, Batheaston, Bath BA1 8EG

THORNE, Dr Napier Arnold; s of Arnold Thorne (d 1959), of Kenilworth, Cape Town, SA, and Wilhelmina Rosa, *née* Ayson (d 1970); *b* 26 Dec 1920; *Educ* Eastbourne Coll, St Bartholomew's Hosp Med Coll London (MB BS, MD); *m* 16 May 1953, Pamela Joan, da of Robert Thomas Frederick Houchin, of Turves, Ruckinge, Kent; 1 s (Robert Napier b 1959), 3 da (Susan b 1954, Jane b 1957, Katherine b 1959); *Career* conslt dermatologist: Prince of Wales Hosp 1955–85, Royal London Hosp 1968–81; hon conslt dermatologist: Italian Hosp London 1969–89, Hosp of St John and St Elizabeth 1976–; sen Univ of London 1970–80, pres Inst of Trichologists 1972–, tstee and chm Philological Fndn 1982–95; Freeman City of London; Liveryman: Worshipful Co of Farriers 1965, Worshipful Soc of Apothecaries 1978; MRCS 1945, LRCP 1945, memb BMA 1945, fell Hunterian Soc 1947, MRCP 1949, FRSM 1949, fell Br Assoc of Dermatologists 1959, fell Med Soc of London 1961, FRCP 1972, FRSA 1983; *Recreations* gardening, music, sailing, travelling; *Clubs* RSM; *Style—* Dr Napier Thorne; ✉ 106 Orchard Rd, Tewin, Herts AL6 0LZ (☎ 01438 798294, mobile 0468 583220)

THORNE, Sir Neil Gordon; kt (1992), OBE (1980), TD (1969), DL (Greater London 1991); s of Henry Frederick Thorne (d 1964); *b* 8 Aug 1932; *Educ* City of London Sch, Univ of London; *Career* TA 1952–82, Lt-Col RA, CO London Univ OTC 1976–80; memb Metropolitan Special Constabulary (HAC) 1983–92; chartered surveyor 1961–, sr ptnr Hull & Co 1962–77; Borough of Redbridge: cnclir 1965–68, alderman 1975–78; memb GLC and chm Central Area Bd 1967–73; MP (C) Ilford S 1979–92; chm: Nat Cncl for Civil Def 1982–86, Armed Forces Parly Scheme 1987–, Lord Mayor's Appeal for St Paul's Cathedral 1993–94, Police Serv Parly Scheme 1994–; memb Military Educn Ctee and Court Univ of Leeds 1994–; pres: London Dist St John Ambulance 1992–, Redbridge Age Concern 1993, Inst of Fire Defence and Disaster Studies 1996–; chm Cons One Nation Forum 1995–; memb Ct of Referees 1987–92; memb Ct of Assts Worshipful Co of Blacksmiths 1992, almoner Order of St John 1995–; Silver Jubilee Medal 1977; KStJ 1995 (OStJ 1988, CStJ 1992); *Publications* A study of pedestrian shopping streets (1973), Highway Robbery in the Twentieth Century - policy reform for compulsory purchase (1990); *Recreations* tennis, mountain walking, riding and music; *Clubs* St John House, Ilford Conservative, Hon Artillery Co; *Style—* Sir Neil Thorne, OBE, TD, DL; ✉ 60 Gyllyngdune Gardens, Seven Kings, Ilford, Essex IG3 9HY (☎ 0181 590 3262 and 0181 554 1449); 13 Cowley Street, London SW1P 3LZ (☎ 0171 222 0480)

THORNE, Sir Peter Francis; KCVO (1981), CBE (1966), ERD; s of Gen Sir (Augustus Francis) Andrew Nicol Thorne, KCB, CMG, DSO (d 1970); *b* 6 Aug 1914; *Educ* Eton, Trinity Coll Oxford; *m* 16 May 1959, Lady Anne Patricia Pery, da of 5 Earl of Limerick, GBE, CH, KCB, DSO (d 1967); 1 s (Andrew Henry b 1965), 3 da (Bridget Iolanthe (Mrs Peter Sychta) b 1961, Meriel Patricia b 1963, Janet Melinda b 1968); *Career* Hon Lt-Col Grenadier Guards 1945 (serv WWII France and SE Asia); with ICI Ltd 1946–48; asst serjeant at arms House of Commons 1948–57, dep serjeant at arms 1957–76, serjeant at arms 1976–82; Liveryman Worshipful Co of Cordwainers; *Publications* The Royal Mace in the House of Commons (1990); *Clubs* Cavalry and Guards', Royal Yacht Sqdn; *Style—* Sir Peter Thorne, KCVO, CBE, ERD; ✉ Chiddinglye Farmhouse, West Hoathly, East Grinstead, W Sussex RH19 4QS (☎ 01342 810338)

THORNE, Peter Geoffrey; s of Ernest Geoffrey Thorne (d 1976), of Duncliffe, Saunton, N Devon, and Edwina Mary, *née* Wilkinson; *b* 2 June 1948; *Educ* Clifton; *m* Jane Frances, da of John David Henson, MC, OBE; 1 s (Benjamin David Geoffrey b 11 July 1981), 1 da (Lucy Frances Alice b 18 Jan 1984); *Career* articles Messrs Sargent & Probert Slrs of Exeter 1965–70, admitted slr 1971 (Sir George Fowler prize for best qualifier from Devon); Norton Rose (formerly Norton Rose Botterell & Roche): joined 1971, specialist in asset fin (particularly ship and aircraft), ptnr 1977–, Hong Kong office 1981–83; memb: City of London Slrs Co, Law Soc, Int Bar Assoc; MRAeS; *Recreations* flying, fishing, philately, skiing; *Style—* Peter Thorne, Esq; ✉ Norton Rose, Kempson House, Camomile St, London EC3A 7AN (☎ 0171 283 6000, fax 0171 283 6500)

THORNE, Robert George; s of Maj George Thorne, MC, DL; *b* 7 Feb 1943; *Educ* Eton, RAC Cirencester; *m* Feb 1990, Sarah, da of J F Priestley; *Career* local dir Barclays Bank Ltd: Bristol 1973–76, Newcastle upon Tyne 1977–80, London Northern 1980–83, Pall Mall 1983–94; dir Phillips Auctioneers and Valuers; *Recreations* country pursuits; *Clubs* Brooks's, Pratt's; *Style—* Robert Thorne, Esq; ✉ Ovington House, Ovington, Alresford, Hants

THORNE, Robin Horton John; CMG (1966), OBE (1963); s of Sir John Anderson Thorne, KCIE, CSI (d 1964), and Lady Dorothy Thorne, *née* Horton (d 1944); *b* 13 July 1917; *Educ* Dragon Sch Oxford, Rugby, Exeter Coll Oxford (MA); *m* 18 May 1946, Joan Helen, da of Edwin Trangmar Wadman, OBE, JP (d 1972), of Priesthawes, Polegate, E Sussex; 1 s (Matthew b 27 June 1952); *Career* WWII Devonshire Regt and King's African Rifles; served: E Africa, Abyssinia, Madagascar, ME, Burma; Capt 1939–46; Colonial Admin Serv and HM Overseas Serv 1946–67: Tanganyika 1946–58, Aden 1958–67, asst chief sec (Colony) MLC and memb Govrs Exec Cncl 1959–63, ministerial sec to Chief Min 1963–65, asst high cmmr 1966–67; tstee Aden Port Tst 1959–66, officer of Ctee of Vice Chllrs and Princs of UK Univs (CVCP) 1967–77 (asst sec 1968–77), pt/t admin vice chllr's office Univ of Sussex 1978–81; chm Staines Tst 1979–86 (tstee 1976–86), memb Mgmnt Ctee Sussex Housing Assoc for Aged 1983–88; *Recreations* travel, ornithology, gardening, books; *Clubs* Commonwealth Trust; *Style—* Robin Thorne, Esq, CMG, OBE; ✉ The Old Vicarage, Old Heathfield, Heathfield, E Sussex TN21 9AD (☎ 01435 863160)

THORNE, Rosemary Prudence; da of Arnold Rex Bishop, of Clevedon, Avon, and Brenda Prudence, *née* Withers; *b* 12 Feb 1952; *Educ* Univ of Warwick (BSc); *Career* accountant BOC Limited 1974–77, chief accountant Mothercare plc 1977–82, gp financial controller Habitat Mothercare plc 1982–85, gp fin controller Storehouse plc Jan-Sept 1986, fin dir and co sec House of Fraser plc (Harrods Ltd) 1986–90; gp fin controller Grand Metropolitan plc 1990–92, fin dir J Sainsbury plc 1992–; hon treas Prince's Youth Business Tst; FCMA, FCT, CIMgt; *Style—* Miss Rosemary P Thorne; ✉ J Sainsbury plc, Stamford House, Stamford Street, London SE1 9LL (☎ 0171 921 6025, fax 0171 921 6644)

THORNE, William Joseph (Willie); s of Joseph William Thorne, of Leicester, and Nancy Sybil, *née* Causon; *b* 4 March 1954; *Educ* Anstey Martin Sch, Thomas Rawlins GS Quorn; *m* 8 May 1985, Fiona Walker; 2 s (Tristan b 25 July 1985, Kieron (twin) b 25 July 1985), 1 da (Tahli b 24 Aug 1988); *Career* snooker professional; amateur record incl: Br under 16 champion 1970, Br under 19 champion 1973, runner-up English Amateur Championship 1975; turned professional 1975; achievements incl: winner Pontins Open 1980, Pontins Professional champion 1984, winner Mercantile Credit Classic 1985, runner-up Coral UK Open 1985, runner-up Dulux Br Open 1986, runner-up Benson & Hedges Irish Masters 1986 and 1987, winner Camus Hong Kong Masters 1986, winner Matchroom Trophy 1986 (runner-up 1987), winner Kent China Cup Peking 1987, winner Lion Brown Masters NZ 1989; currently ranked world number 25; tournament 147 at Tennents UK Open 1987; *Recreations* golf, football; *Style—* Willie Thorne, Esq

THORNEYCROFT, Hon John Hamo; LVO (1992); s of Baron Thorneycroft, CH, PC (Life Peer; d 1994), and his 1 w Sheila Wells, *née* Page; *b* 24 March 1940; *Educ* Eton, Cambridge, Univ of Wales Inst of Science and Technology (DipArch); *m* 1971, Delia, da of Arthur William Lloyd (d 1977), of Penallt, Monmouth; 1 s (Richard b 1977), 1 da (Eleanor b 1974); *Career* head of Central Govt and Palaces Branch London Region English Heritage; currently head of Government Historic Buildings Advisory Unit London Region English Heritage 1996–; memb: Irish Georgian Soc, Soc for the Protection of Ancient Buildings, Soc of Architectural Historians of GB; memb Order of Orange Nassau 1982; RIBA; *Style—* The Hon John Thorneycroft, LVO; ✉ 21 St Peters St, Islington, London N1 8JD

THORNEYCROFT, John Patrick; s of Gerald Hamo Thorneycroft (d 1967), of Codsall Wood, Wolverhampton, and Kathleen Mary, *née* Wilson (d 1985); *b* 9 Dec 1939; *Educ* Wellington, Pembroke Coll Cambridge (MA); *m* 16 Oct 1965, Rev Philippa Hazel Jeanetta (Pippa), da of Philip Fitzgerald Mander (d 1972), of The Folley, Bridgnorth, Shropshire; 2 s (Hugh b 1967, Martin b 1977), 2 da (Veryan b 1971, Naomi b 1975); *Career* slr; sr ptnr Manby & Steward; registrar Dio of Lichfield, legal sec to Bishop of Lichfield 1988; dir Staffordshire Building Society 1992; chm Kaleidoscope Theatre 1988–94; *Recreations* tennis, squash, walking; *Style—* John Thorneycroft, Esq; ✉ The Vicarage, 11 Brookhouse Lane, Featherstone, Wolverhampton WV10 7AW (☎ 01902 727579); Manby & Steward, 9th Floor, Mander House, Wolverhampton, West Midlands WV1 3NE (☎ 01902 772711, fax 01902 713564)

THORNEYCROFT, Dr Malcolm; s of Alec Charles Thorneycroft (d 1974); *b* 7 June 1936; *Educ* Wellingborough GS, Univ of Nottingham; *m* 1960, Margaret Rose, *née* Fisher; 1 s, 2 da; *Career* chartered electrical engr, engrg dir TI Churchill Ltd 1976–85, TI Machine Tools Ltd 1985–87, Matrix Churchill Ltd 1987–92, BSA Tools Ltd 1992–; *Recreations* swimming, walking; *Clubs* 41 Club, Coventry; *Style—* Dr Malcolm Thorneycroft; ✉ 1 Riverford Croft, Kenilworth Grange, Coventry

THORNHILL, Andrew Robert; QC (1985); s of Edward Percy Thornhill, of Bristol, and Amelia Joy Thornhill; *b* 4 Aug 1943; *Educ* Clifton, CCC Oxford; *m* 5 Aug 1971, Helen Mary, da of George William Livingston, of Gainsborough; 2 s (George Percy b 1 Dec 1973, Henry Robert b 26 May 1977), 2 da (Emily Mary b 12 June 1972, Eleanor Clare b 19 June 1980); *Career* called to the Bar Middle Temple 1969, joined chambers of H H Monroe 1969, bencher 1995, head of chambers; *Recreations* sailing, walking, education; *Clubs* Oxford and Cambridge, Tamesis, Bristol Avon Sailing; *Style—* Andrew Thornhill, Esq, QC; ✉ Pump Court Tax Chambers, 16 Bedford Row, London WC1R 4EB (☎ 0171 414 8080, fax 0171 414 8099)

THORNHILL, (George Edmund) Peter; s of Lt-Col Edmund Basil Thornhill, MC, of Manor House, Boxworth, Cambs, and Diana Pearl Day, *née* Beales (d 1983); descendant in unbroken male line of the family of Thornhill of Thornhill, Yorkshire (landowners); *b* 13 April 1935; *Educ* Cheam Sch, Eton, Trinity Coll Cambridge (MA); *m* 12 Sept 1959, Margaret Daughne, o da of Cdr William Geoffrey Barnard Hartley (d 1983), of Houghton Hill House, Huntingdon; 1 s (Edmund George William b 1969), 3 da (Vanessa (Mrs John Fairhead) b 1960, Claire (Mrs Christopher Hill) b 1962, Harriet b 1965); *Career* Nat Serv 1953–55, 2 Lt RA; landowner, patron of 2 livings; former ptnr Smith-Woolley and Co chartered surveyors and chartered land agents, resigned 1975; dir Thornhill Yorkshire Estates Co; chm Huntingdon/Peterborough Branch CLA 1983–85, Nottinghamshire

Branch 1993–94 (memb Legal Ctee 1977–81 and 1990–94, memb Taxation Ctee 1984–88); memb Landowners Panel Agric Land Tribunal (Midlands Area) 1995–; High Sheriff of Nottinghamshire 1995–96; FRICS, formerly FLAS; *Recreations* shooting; *Clubs* Boodle's, Farmers', Cambridge County, Eton Vikings; *Style*— Peter Thornhill, Esq; ✉ The Grove, Winthorpe, Newark, Notts NG24 2NR (☎ 01636 703577, fax 01636 640609); Estate Office, The Gardens, Diddington, Huntingdon, Cambs PE18 9XU (☎ 01480 810240)

THORNHILL, Richard John; s of Richard Norwood Thornhill, and Eleanor Louise, *née* Hoey; *b* 13 Nov 1954; *Educ* Malvern, St John's Coll Oxford (MA); *m* 30 Aug 1980, Nicola, da of Peter John Dyke, of Derby; 2 s (Hugo b 1989, Frederick b 1992); *Career* admitted slr 1979, admitted slr of the Supreme Court Hong Kong 1982; Slaughter & May: articled clerk 1977–79, asst slr Hong Kong Office 1982–84, ptnr 1986–, sr ptnr Slaughter & May Hong Kong 1993–; memb Law Soc; *Recreations* walking, water skiing, theatre, opera; *Style*— Richard Thornhill, Esq; ✉ Slaughter and May, 27th Floor, Two Exchange Square, Hong Kong (☎ 00 852 252 10551)

THORNTON, His Hon Judge; Anthony Christopher Lawrence; QC (1988); s of Maj Richard Thornton (d 1983), and Margery Alice Clerk, CBE (d 1993); *b* 18 Aug 1947; *Educ* Eton, Keble Coll Oxford (MA, BCL); *m* 18 Feb 1983, Lyn Christine, da of Laurence Thurlby, of Cambridge; 1 s (Matthew James b 12 June 1983); *Career* called to the Bar Middle Temple 1970, bencher 1992, recorder 1992–94, official referee and circuit judge 1994–; memb Gen Cncl of the Bar 1988–94 (treas 1990–92, chm Professional Standards Ctee 1992–93); Freeman: City of London 1976, Worshipful Co of Leathersellers 1976; assoc Inst of Arbitrators 1987; *Books* Halsbury's Laws Vol 4: Building Contracts (jt ed and contrib, 1972, reissue 1992), Construction Law Review (jt ed), Burns - The Expert Witness (contrib, 1989), Fay & Thornton - Official Referees' Business (3rd edn 1997); *Recreations* opera, cricket, legal history; *Clubs* RAC; *Style*— His Hon Judge Thornton, QC; ✉ Official Referees' Courts, St Dunstan's House, 133–137 Fetter Lane, London EC4A 1HD (☎ 0171 936 6022)

THORNTON, Clive Edward Ian; CBE (1983); s of Albert Thornton (d 1963), of Newcastle upon Tyne, and Margaret, *née* Coil; *b* 12 Dec 1929; *Educ* St Anthony's Newcastle upon Tyne, Coll of Commerce Newcastle upon Tyne, Univ of London (LLB, BA); *m* 17 March 1956, Maureen Carmine, da of Michael Crane (d 1975), of London; 1 s (Richard b 1963), 1 da (Elizabeth b 1957); *Career* admitted slr 1962, slr to First National Finance Corp 1964–67, chief exec Abbey National Building Soc 1979–83 (chief slr 1967–78, dep chief exec 1978), ptnr Stoneham Langton and Passmore Solicitors 1985–87; dir: The Housing Corporation 1980–86, Investment Data Services Ltd 1986–90, Mirror Group Newspapers 1983–84; chm: Financial Weekly 1983–87, Thamesmead Town Ltd 1986–90, Universe Publications 1986–96, Independent Radio Thamesmead Ltd 1989–90, Melton Mowbray Building Society 1988–, Armstrong Capital Holdings Ltd 1988–, Burgin Hall Ltd 1988–92, Thorndale Benedict Ltd 1988–96, The Catholic Times 1993–96; Liveryman Worshipful Co of Bakers; FCIB; *Recreations* breeding Devon, Sussex and Lincoln Red cattle; *Style*— Clive Thornton, Esq, CBE; ✉ Keythorpe Grange, East Norton, Leicestershire LE7 9XL (☎ 0116 259 8201); Armstrong Capital Holdings Ltd, 3 St Mary's Place, Stamford, Lincs

THORNTON, Ian Charles; s of Charles William Thornton (d 1977), and Fay, *née* Eastwood (d 1992); *b* 23 March 1934; *Educ* Manchester GS, Schs of Architecture/Civic Design Univ of Liverpool (BArch, MCD); *m* 1 Oct 1959, Mary Doreen, da of Robert Thomas Evans (d 1956); 2 da (Jacqueline b 1960, Jennifer b 1962); *Career* asst architect Morter & Dobie 1956–59, ptnr Bruxby & Evans 1959–61, assoc and ptnr Ronald Fielding Ptnrship 1961–70, ptnr and dir Alec French Partnership 1970–84; fndr dir Thornton Hartnell 1985–91, princ in own consulancy 1991–; nat pres: Faculty of Bldg 1982–84, Concrete Soc 1985–86; RIBA: memb Cncl 1984–87, vice-pres (practice) 1986–87; vice-pres Bristol FC (Rugby); Freeman Worshipful Co of Chartered Architects; FRIBA, FFB, MAE 1991 (QDR 1996), ACIArb 1992, fell Concrete Soc 1995, hon fell Inst of Clerks of Works 1996; *Recreations* rugby, cricket, golf, snooker, walking; *Clubs* MCC, Royal Western Yacht; *Style*— Ian Thornton, Esq; ✉ Ian Thornton Chartered Architect, 8 Home Farm Way, Easter Compton, Bristol BS12 3SE (☎ and fax 01454 632137, home ☎ 01454 632353)

THORNTON, Katy Louise; da of Dennis Thornton, and Sandra, *née* Parker; *b* 7 Feb 1973; *Career* feature writer/entertainment columnist Sunday Mirror 1992–95, entertainment columnist Daily Mirror 1995, ed Smash Hits 1996–; *Recreations* music; *Style*— Ms Katy Thornton; ✉ Smash Hits, Emap Metro, Mappin House, 4 Winsley Street, London W1N 7AR (☎ 0171 312 8719, fax 0171 636 5792)

THORNTON, Prof (Robert) Kelsey Rought; s of Harold Thornton (d 1975), and Mildred, *née* Brooks (d 1995); *b* 12 Aug 1938; *Educ* Burnley GS, Univ of Manchester (BA, MA, PhD); *m* 1, 3 Aug 1961 (m dis 1976), Sarah Elizabeth Ann, da of Hendri Griffiths; 2 s (Jason b 1965, Ben b 1968); m 2, 22 Sept 1989, Eileen Valerie, da of Maurice Davison; 1 da (Amy b 1979), 1 s (Thomas b 1982); *Career* prof Univ of Newcastle upon Tyne 1984–89 (lectr 1965–75, sr lectr 1975–84), prof Sch of Eng Univ of Birmingham 1989– (head of Sch 1989–96); chm John Clare Soc 1987–90; *Books* incl: The Decadent Dilemma (1983), Gerard Manley Hopkins: The Poems (1973), All My Eyes See: The Visual World of Gerard Manley Hopkins (1975), Ivor Gurney Collected Letters (1991); *Recreations* water colour painting, book collecting; *Style*— Prof Kelsey Thornton; ✉ School of English, The University of Birmingham, Edgbaston, Birmingham B15 2TT (☎ 0121 414 5667, fax 0121 414 5668)

THORNTON, Sir (George) Malcolm; kt (1992), MP (C) Crosby (majority 14,806); s of George Edmund Thornton by his w Ethel; *b* 3 April 1939; *Educ* Wallasey GS, Liverpool Nautical Coll; *m* 1, 1962; 1 s; m 2, 1972, Sue Banton (d 1989); m 3, 1990, Rosemary, *née* Hewitt; *Career* former River Mersey pilot; memb: Wallasey County Borough Cncl 1965–74, Wirral Metropolitan Cncl 1973–79 (ldr 1974–77); chm Merseyside Dists Liaison Ctee 1975–77; vice-pres: Assoc of Met Authys, Burnham Ctee 1978–79; chm: AMA Educn Ctee 1978–79, Cncl of Local Educn Authys 1978–79; MP (C): Liverpool Garston 1979–83, Crosby 1983–; PPS to Rt Hon Patrick Jenkin: as Indust Sec 1981–83, as Environment Sec 1983–84; memb Select Ctee on Environment 1979–81, chm Select Ctee on Educn and Employment; sec: Cons Parly Shipping and Shipbuilding Ctee 1979–81, Cons Parly Educn Ctee; fell Industry and Parliament Tst; Hon DEd De Montfort Univ; FRSA; *Style*— Sir Malcolm Thornton, MP; ✉ House of Commons, London SW1A 0AA (☎ 0171 219 4489)

THORNTON, Margaret Barbara; da of Cyril Arthur Wales (d 1983), and Anna Margaret Wales, MBE, *née* Chang; *b* 28 Jan 1940; *Educ* Burgess Hill PNEU Sussex, Mary Wray Secretarial Coll Sussex; *m* 1972, Adrian Heber Thornton, s of Nigel Heber Thornton, Croix de Guerre (d 1941); 2 da (Emily Harriet b 1973, Rebecca Louise b 1980), 1 s (Jasper Hamilton b 1975); *Career* md Redfern Gallery; artists represented: Sarah Armstrong-Jones, Frank Avray Wilson, Paul Emsley, Paul Feiler, Annabel Gault, William Gear RA, Dann Markey, Margaret Mellis, Brendan Neiland RA, Bryan Organ, Patrick Procktor, David Tindle RA, Marc Vaux, Paul Wunderlich; *Recreations* visiting galleries, museums and antique markets; *Style*— Mrs Margaret Thornton; ✉ The Redfern Gallery, 20 Cork Street, London W1 (☎ 0171 734 1732, 0171 734 0578, fax 0171 494 2908)

THORNTON, Michael Stanley; OBE (1995); s of (Joseph) Stanley Thornton (d 1992), and Jeanetta, *née* Jamieson (d 1982); *b* 1 Aug 1936; *Educ* Uppingham; *m* 1, 3 Sept 1960 (m dis 1977), Marie Margaret, *née* Pepper; 2 da (Jill Susan b 18 Aug 1961, Sally-Ann Margaret b 6 March 1964); m 2, 1977, Jane Susan Hinckley, *née* Bourne; 1 s (Matthew Michael b 11 Sept 1978); *Career* Nat Serv, cmmnd RASC 1955, Lt 1956; currently dep chm and co sec Thorntons plc (joined family business JW Thornton Ltd 1957, subsequently dir and chief exec); hon memb NSPCC Cncl, memb Mgmnt Bd Prince's Tst (former chm Derbyshire Ctee), vice pres The Arkwright Soc, pres Business Environment Assoc (Midlands) 1993; former pres: Matlock Rugby Club, Ashbourne Shire Horse Soc, Midlands Co Show; chm Derbyshire Children's Hosp Appeal 1994–; tstee: The Bishop of Derby's Urban Fund, The Spirit of Normandy Tst 1996–; patron: Derby Normandy Veterans' Assoc 1992–, Village Aid 1992–; memb Governing Body Belper Sch 1994–, treas St Mary's Lower Slaughter PCC 1994–; former chieftan Ashbourne Highland Gathering; FInstD 1970, FCIS 1977 (Assoc 1963), FRSA 1994; *Recreations* rugby football, community work, the church; *Clubs* Caledonian; *Style*— Michael Thornton, Esq, OBE; ✉ Thorntons plc, Thornton Park, Somercotes, Derbyshire DE55 4XJ (☎ 01773 540550, fax 01773 540842)

THORNTON, Peter Anthony; s of Robert Thornton (d 1990), and Freda, *née* Willey; *b* 8 May 1944; *Educ* Bradford GS, Univ of Manchester (BSc); *m* 1969 (m dis 1987); 1 s (James William b 1976), 2 da (Victoria Jane b 1973, Charlotte Sarah b 1974); *Career* chartered surveyor and engineer; chief exec Greycoat plc; Liveryman Worshipful Co of Chartered Surveyors; FRICS, FICE, FCIOB; *Recreations* tennis, water skiing, cars; *Clubs* RAC, Riverside, Prince's; *Style*— Peter Thornton, Esq; ✉ Van Buren Cottage, Queen's Ride, Barnes Common, London SW13 0JF (☎ 0181 788 1969); Greycoat plc, 9 Savoy Street, London WC2E 7EG (☎ 0171 379 1000, car 0468 152584)

THORNTON, Sir Peter Eustace; KCB (1974); s of D O Thornton; *b* 28 Aug 1917; *Educ* Charterhouse, Gonville and Caius Cambridge; *m* 1946, Rosamond Hobart Myers, US Medal of Freedom; 2 s, 1 da; *Career* BOT 1946, asst under-sec of State Dept of Economic Affrs 1964–67, under-sec Cabinet Office 1967–70, dep sec 1970–72, dep sec DTI 1972–74, second perm sec Dept of Trade 1974, perm sec 1974–77; dir: Laird Gp 1978–91, Courtaulds, Rolls Royce, Hill Samuel Gp 1977–87; pro-chllr Open Univ 1979–83; *Style*— Sir Peter Thornton, KCB

THORNTON, Peter Kai; CBE (1996); s of Sir Gerard Thornton (d 1977), of Kingsthorpe Hall, Northampton, and Gerda Nørregaard, of Copenhagen; *b* 8 April 1925; *Educ* Bryanston, De Havilland Aeronautical Tech Sch, Trinity Hall Cambridge (BA); *m* 22 Aug 1950, Mary Ann Rosamund, da of Arthur Helps (d 1976), of Cregane, Rosscarbery, Co Cork; 3 da; *Career* served Intelligence Corps Austria 1945–48; asst keeper V & A: Dept of Textiles 1954–62, Dept of Furniture and Woodwork 1962–84 (keeper 1966–84), also keeper-in-charge Ham House and Osterley Park; curator Sir John Soane's Museum 1984–95; memb: Cncl Nat Tst 1983–84, London Advsy Ctee Eng Heritage 1986–88; chm Furniture History Soc 1974–84; FSA 1976; *Books* Baroque and Rococo Silks (1965), Musical Instruments as Works of Art (1968, 2 edn 1982), Seventeenth Century Decoration in England, France and Holland (1978), The Furnishing and Decoration of Ham House (with M Tomlin), Authentic Decor - The Domestic Interior 1620–1920 (1984), The Italian Renaissance Interior 1400–1600 (1991), A Miscellany of Objects from Sir John Soane's Museum (with Helen Dorey, 1992), Form and Ornament: Innovation in the Decorative Arts, 1470–1870 (1997); *Style*— Peter Thornton, Esq, CBE, FSA; ✉ 102 West Kensington Court, London W14 9AB (☎ and fax 0171 603 6031); Ballycahane, Castletownshend, Co Cork, Eire

THORNTON, Peter Norman; s of William Norman Thornton (d 1984), and Muriel Thornton (d 1995); *b* 5 May 1933; *Educ* Repton; *m* Julia Emma Thornton; 1 s (Miles b 1968), 3 da (Sarah b 1962, Samantha b 1965, Rebecca b 1996); *Career* Royal Signals Malaya 1951–53, Hallamshire Bn (Maj) 1955–61, GSM; dir (ret as chm) J W Thornton Ltd 1962–87, chm Peter Thornton Assocs (venture capital and mgmnt consultancy); dir Buxton International Festival Soc 1983–91; chm: Midland Asthma & Allergy Res Assoc 1976–79, Confectioners Benevolent Fund 1990–; fndr Sheffield Asthma Soc 1977; fndr memb SDP; FIIM 1976, FInstD 1981; *Recreations* offshore sailing, skiing, music, flying helicopters; *Clubs* IOD, Ogston Sailing, Helicopter Club of GB; *Style*— Peter Thornton, Esq; ✉ Field Farm, Wensley, Matlock, Derbyshire DE4 2LL (☎ 01629 732598); Peter Thornton Associates, The Archway, Crown Square, Matlock, Derbyshire DE4 3AT (☎ 01629 584422, fax 01629 580678, car 0836 212713)

THORNTON, Peter Ribblesdale; QC (1992); s of Robert Ribblesdale Thornton, of Winterborne Whitechurch, Dorset, and Ruth Eleanor, *née* Tuckson; *b* 17 Oct 1946; *Educ* Clifton Coll Bristol, St John's Coll Cambridge (BA); *m* 13 June 1981, Susan Margaret, da of Maneck Ardeshir Dalal; 1 s (Daniel Richard Dalal b 14 July 1990), 1 da (Amy Christina Dalal b 30 June 1992); *Career* called to the Bar Middle Temple 1969, asst recorder 1994–; fndr memb and dep head Doughty Street Chambers 1990–; chm: Nat Cncl for Civil Liberties 1981–83, Civil Liberties Tst 1991–95; *Books* Public Order Law (1987), Decade of Decline: Civil Liberties in the Thatcher Years (1989), The Penguin Civil Liberty Guide (co-ed, 1989), Archbold: Criminal Pleading, Evidence and Practice (contrib ed, 1992–); *Style*— Peter Thornton, Esq, QC; ✉ Doughty Street Chambers, 11 Doughty Street, London WC1N 2PG (☎ 0171 404 1313, fax 0171 404 2283)

THORNTON, Richard Chicheley; s of Capt Edward Chicheley Thornton, DSC, RN (d 1959), of Titchfield, Hants, and Margaret Noel, *née* Terry (d 1970); *b* 5 July 1931; *Educ* Stowe, Keble Coll Oxford; *m* 1, 1958 (m dis 1987), Jennifer Mary, da of Col Leo Dominic Gleeson, DSO (d 1976); 1 s (Henry Dominic Chicheley b 1963), 2 da (Mary Virginia Chicheley (Mrs Woodhouse) b 1959, Lucy Margaret Chicheley (Mrs Torrington) b 1960); m 2, 4 March 1989, Susan Joy, da of Dudley Middleton (d 1986), of Melbourne, Aust; *Career* Nat Serv cmmnd 2 Lt Royal Signals 1950; Capt Royal Signals TA 1952–58; called to the Bar Gray's Inn 1957; co-fndr GT Management 1969, fndr Thornton & Co 1985 (pres 1991–94); chm The Establishment Tst 1991–; hon fell Keble Coll Oxford 1986; a vice pres The Marine Soc 1992; memb Worshipful Co of Watermen and Lightermen 1987, Freeman City of London 1987; *Recreations* sailing, golf, opera; *Clubs* The Garrick, Royal Thames Yacht, Hong Kong, Royal Bermuda Yacht, Mid Ocean Golf; *Style*— Richard Thornton, Esq; ✉ Bay House, 4 Old Slip Lane, Hamilton HM 06, Bermuda (☎ 00 1 441 295 3357, fax 00 1 441 292 5772)

THORNTON, Richard Eustace; OBE (1980), JP (1972); s of Eustace Edward Thornton (d 1948), of Hampton Lodge, Seale, and Myrtle Estelle, *née* Bellamy; *b* 10 Oct 1922; *Educ* Eton, Trinity Coll Cambridge (MA); *m* 11 Sept 1954, Gabrielle Elizabeth, da of William Henry Sharpe (d 1948), of Culverlands, Farnham; 4 da (Sarah Elizabeth b 1955, Louise Mary b 1958, Bridget Jane b 1960, Emma Frances b 1963); *Career* farmer and landowner; memb: Thames Conservancy 1968–74, Royal Cmmn on Environmental Pollution 1970–84, Thames Water Authy 1974–80, Governing Body Charterhouse Sch (chm 1981–90); chm: Govrs Bishop Reindorp Sch 1985–, Hosp Mgmnt Bd Mt Alvernia Hosp 1992–; High Sheriff 1978–79, HM Lord Lt of Surrey 1986–; KStJ 1986; *Style*— Richard E Thornton, Esq, OBE, JP; ✉ Hampton Lodge, Seale, nr Farnham, Surrey GU10 1JF (☎ 01483 810208)

THORNTON, Dr Robert Luke Grant (Bob); BEM (1992); er s of Rev Canon Cecil Grant Thornton, of Leicester, and Winifred Dorothy, *née* Fawkes; *b* 22 Dec 1923; *Educ* Bromsgrove; *m* 1953, Helen, da of Rev C B Hodson; 3 s (James, John, Peter), 1 da (Catherine); *Career* Capt RIASC 1942–45, India 1942–43, 36 Br Div in N Burma 1944, with 3 Commando Bde Hong Kong 1945; combined dental med course Guy's Hosp 1946, orthodontic house surgn Royal Dental Hosp 1952, gen dental practitioner Salisbury 1952, dental surgn WDHO Wills Bristol 1953–79, gen dental practitioner Almondsbury 1978–; hon treas (and life memb) Assoc of Industl Dental Surgns 1968–78; fndr JOGLE Club raising £160,000 in aid of the Nat Star Centre for Disabled Youth Cheltenham having walked 3 times and cycled 3 times between John O'Groats and Lands End since 1972; *Recreations* amateur potter, foreign travel, gardening, reading about Sir Winston Churchill, raising money for the Star Centre; *Style*— Dr Bob Thornton, BEM; ✉ 3 Red House Lane, Almondsbury, Bristol BS12 4BB (☎ 01454 612300)

THORNTON, Robert Thomas; s of Tom Devlin, of California, and Ethel Thornton, *née* Conroy; *b* 8 July 1951; *Educ* Sharston Secdy Sch, Hollings Coll Manchester (City & Guilds), Westminster Coll (City & Guilds); *m* 12 July 1981, Susan Elizabeth, da of Brian Steer; 2 da (Rachel b 28 Oct 1983, Jennifer b 30 Sept 1985); *Career* apprentice chef Grosvenor House Park Lane 1969–71, commis saucier Bayerischerhof Hotel München 1971–72, garde mangr Hotel Schweizerhof Davos Platz Schweiz 1972–73, fndr Moss Nook 1973, sous chef Montreux Palace 1974–76, head chef Moss Nook 1976–90, exec chef Underscar Manor Cumbria 1990–; appeared on Kios in the Kitchen 1993; fndr memb Culinary Circle of NW England; fundraiser for various charities; *Awards* Cheshire Life Restaurant of the Year (Moss Nook) 1992, Lancashire Life Magazine Top Twelve Chefs of NW 1992, Underscar Manor recommended in various pubns 1992–, Lancashire Life Magazine Small Hotel of the Year (Underscar Manor) 1993, Harpers & Queen 100 Best Restaurants 1996; *Recreations* marathons, cricket, football, golf, swimming, fell walking, guitar playing; *Clubs* Keswick Golf; *Style*— Robert Thornton, Esq; ✉ Underscar Manor, Applethwaite, Nr Keswick, Cumbria CA12 4PH (☎ 017687 75000, fax 017687 74904)

THORNTON, Timothy Kenneth; s of Kenneth Thornton, of Windsor Forest, Berks, and Angela, *née* Brett; *b* 7 March 1935; *Educ* Sunningdale Sch, Eton; *m* 17 May 1966, Jacqueline Green, da of David Hillman; 1 s (Daniel b 7 April 1968), 1 da (Katharine 5 Oct 1970); *Career* Nat Serv Lt Coldstream Gds 1953–55; ptnr Joseph Sebag 1957–82, memb Stock Exchange 1959–95, ptnr Grieveson Grant 1982–86, dir Kleinwort Benson Securities 1986–95; non-exec dir: Moorgate Investment Trust 1994–, Siebe plc 1995–; dir John Field Meml Ballet Seminars; *Recreations* gardening; *Clubs* White's, Pratt's; *Style*— Timothy Thornton, Esq; ✉ Juthware Hall, Halstock, Yeovil, Somerset BA22 9SG (☎ 01935 891644)

THOROGOOD, Alfreda; da of Edward Thorogood (d 1966), and Alfreda, *née* Langham; *b* 17 Aug 1942; *Educ* Lady Eden's Sch, Royal Ballet Sch (Jr and Upper); *m* 1 Aug 1967, David Richard Wall, CBE, *qv*, s of Charles Wall; 1 s (Daniel b 12 Dec 1974), 1 da (Annaliese b 15 Oct 1971); *Career* Royal Ballet Co: joined 1960, soloist 1966, princ dancer Touring Section 1968, transferred to resident co 1970, left 1980; danced all leading roles in major classical ballets; roles cr for her by: Sir Frederick Ashton, Sir Kenneth MacMillan, Anthony Tudor, Geoffrey Cauley; danced roles choreographed by: Dame Ninette de Valois, Glen Tetley, Jerome Robins, Rudolf Nureyev, Leonide Massine, John Cranko, John Neumier, David Bintley, André Howard; Bush Davies Sch: sr teacher 1982–85, dep ballet princ 1985–88, dir 1988–89; artistic advsr Royal Acad of Dancing 1989–92, artistic dir Elmhurst Ballet Sch 1994– (sr ballet teacher 1992–94); ARAD, PDTC; *Style*— Miss Alfreda Thorogood

THOROLD, Capt Sir Anthony Henry; 15 Bt (E 1642), OBE (1942), DSC (1942, and bar 1945); s of Sir James Ernest Thorold, 14 Bt (d 1965), and Katharine (d 1959), eldest da of Rev William Rolfe Tindal-Atkinson, formerly vicar of St Andrew's, Burgess Hill; *b* 7 Sept 1903; *Educ* RNC Osborne and Dartmouth; *m* 1939, Jocelyn Elaine Laura (d 1993), da of Sir Clifford Edward Heathcote-Smith, KBE, CMG (d 1963); 1 s, 2 da; *Heir* s, (Anthony) Oliver Thorold, *qv*; *Career* RN 1917, served WWII in Home and Med Fleets as SO, ops in Force H and Western Approaches, Capt 1946, Cdre in Charge Hong Kong 1953–55, ADC to The Queen 1955–56, ret 1956; memb Kesteven CC 1958–74, ldr Lincs CC 1973–81; DL Lincs 1959–95, JP Lincs 1961, High Sheriff Lincs 1968; chm: Grantham Hosp Mgmnt Ctee 1963–74, Lincoln Diocesan Tst and Bd of Fin 1966–71; *Recreations* shooting; *Clubs* Army and Navy; *Style*— Capt Sir Anthony Thorold, Bt, OBE, DSC; ✉ Syston Old Hall, Grantham, Lincs NG32 2BX (☎ 01400 250270)

THOROLD, (Anthony) Oliver; s and h of Sir Anthony Thorold, 15 Bt, OBE, DSC, *qv*; *b* 15 April 1945; *Educ* Winchester, Lincoln Coll Oxford; *m* 1977, Genevra, da of John L Richardson, of Broadshaw, W Calder, W Lothian; 1 s (Henry b 1981), 1 da (Lydia b 1985); *Career* barr Inner Temple 1971; *Style*— Oliver Thorold, Esq; ✉ 8 Richmond Cres, London N1 (☎ 0171 609 0437); 11 Doughty Street, London WC1N 2PG (☎ 0171 404 1313)

THORP, James Noble; s of Arthur Thorp (d 1953), and Annie, *née* Rollinson (d 1975); *b* 27 Oct 1934; *Educ* Rothwell GS, Leeds Coll of Art Sch of Architecture (DipArch); *m* 18 Jan 1958, Jean, da of Arthur Brown (d 1972); 2 s (Ian James b 1958, Julian Alexander b 1969), 2 da (Sally Ann b 1961, Jayne Stella b 1964); *Career* architect, estab private practice 1961 (specialised in ecclesiastical design); lectr in design 1964–87: Leeds Coll of Art, Leeds Poly, Sheffield Univ; Civic Tst assessor; awards: Leeds Gold medal 1964, DOE Award for Design 1976, Civic Tst Commendation 1987, Wakefield MDC Design Award 1996; ARIBA; *Recreations* skiing, amateur theatre, scenic design, music; *Style*— James Thorp, Esq; ✉ 73 Church St, Woodlesford, Leeds 26 (☎ 0113 282 6303); James Thorp & Partners, The Studio, 73 Church Street, Woodlesford, Leeds LS24 8RE (☎ and fax 0113 288 0048)

THORP, Jeremy Walter; s of Walter Thorp (d 1977), of Dublin, and Dorothy Bliss (d 1989); *b* 12 Dec 1941; *Educ* King Edward VII Sch Sheffield, CCC Oxford (MA); *m* 15 Sept 1973, Estela Maria, da of Alberto Lessa (d 1968), of Montevideo, Uruguay; *Career* HM Treasy 1963–78: asst private sec to Sec of State for Econ Affrs 1967–69, financial attaché HM Embassy Washington 1971–73; FCO 1978–: first sec head of Chancery and consul gen HM Embassy Lima Peru 1982–86, dep head of mission HM Embassy Dublin 1988–92, head Res and Fin Dept FCO 1993–; *Recreations* music, buying and looking at paintings, walking, swimming, travel, reading; *Clubs* Kildare Street and Univ (Dublin); *Style*— Jeremy Thorp, Esq; ✉ Foreign and Commonwealth Office, London SW1A 2AH

THORPE, *see:* Gardner-Thorpe

THORPE, Adam Naylor; s of Bernard Naylor Thorpe, and Sheila Grace, *née* Greenlees; *b* 5 Dec 1956; *Educ* Marlborough, Magdalen Coll Oxford (BA); *m* 23 Nov 1985, Joanna Louise Wistreich; 2 s (Joshua, Sacha), 1 da (Anastasia); *Career* co fndr Equinox Travelling Theatre 1980, drama and mime teacher City and E London Coll Stepney 1983–87, lectr in English PCL 1987–90, poetry critic the Observer 1989–95, currently poetry critic Poetry Review; author and poet; *Publications* Mornings in the Baltic (1988, shortlisted Whitbread Prize for Poetry 1988), Meeting Montaigne (poetry, 1990), The Fen Story (Monday Play Radio 4, 1991), Ulverton (novel, 1992, winner Winifred Holtby Prize for best regional novel), Offa's Daughter (Sunday Play Radio 3, 1993), Still (novel, 1995), Couch Grass and Ribbon (stage play, 1996); winner: Eric Gregory award 1985, second prize Nat Poetry Competition 1986; *Recreations* walking, swimming, music, theatre; *Style*— Adam Thorpe; ✉ c/o A M Heath Ltd, 79 St Martin's Lane, London WC2N 4AA (☎ 0171 836 4271)

THORPE, HE Adrian Charles; CMG (1994); s of Prof Lewis Guy Melville Thorpe (d 1977), and (Eva Mary) Barbara, da of Alfred Reynolds; *b* 29 July 1942; *Educ* The Leys Sch, Christ's Coll Cambridge (BA, MA); *m* 26 Oct 1968, Miyoko, da of Taketaro Kosugi (d 1950), of Japan; *Career* HM Dip Serv: entered 1965, Tokyo 1965–70, FCO 1970–73, Beirut 1973–76 (head of Chancery 1975–76), FCO 1976, Tokyo 1976–81, FCO 1981–85 (cnsllr and head of Info Technol Dept 1982–85), econ cnsllr Bonn 1985–89, dep high cmmr Kuala Lumpur 1989–91, min Tokyo 1991–95, HM ambass to the Philippines 1995–; FRSA; *Recreations* opera, travel, bookshops, comfort; *Clubs* Tokyo (Japan), Foreign Correspondents' (Japan), Polo (Philippines); *Style*— HE Mr Adrian Thorpe, CMG; ✉ c/o Foreign and Commonwealth Office (Manila), King Charles Street, London SW1A 2AH; Philippines (☎ 00 63 2 816 7116, fax 00 63 2 819 7206)

THORPE, Amelia Jane; da of Robert Barrie Thorpe, of Boxford, Suffolk, and Margaret, *née* Davenport; *b* 1 July 1961; *Educ* Beaconsfield HS; *m* 23 Dec 1991, Adam Russell, s of Peter Caton Russell; 2 da (Evelina Kathleen Rose b 28 March 1994, Edie Celeste b 4 May 1996); *Career* publishing dir Merehurst Ltd 1983–89, md Ebury Press (responsible for Ebury Press, Vermilion, Barrie & Jenkins, Condé Nast Books, Rider, Ebury Press Stationery, Studio Editions, Leopard, Cresset and Rider, Fodor's and Ebury Press New Media) 1989–; main bd dir Random House UK Ltd; memb Women in Mgmnt in Publishing; *Recreations* food and wine, art and antiques; *Style*— Ms Amelia Thorpe; ✉ Ebury Press, Random House, 20 Vauxhall Bridge Road, London SW1V 2SA (☎ 0171 973 9690, fax 0171 233 6057)

THORPE, His Hon Judge; Anthony Geoffrey Younghusband; s of Lt Cdr G J Y Thorpe, MBE; *b* 21 Aug 1941; *Educ* Highgate Sch, BRNC Dartmouth, Inns of Ct Sch of Law (Treas's prize for Inner Temple), King's Coll London; *m* 15 Jan 1966, Janet Patricia; 1 s (Simon Francis Younghusband b 27 Sept 1969), 1 da (Madeleine Louise b 12 Dec 1967); *Career* RN: Cdr 1978, served HMS Hermes, Ark Royal, Vidal and Blake, Capt and Chief Naval Judge Advocate 1984, sec to Adm Sir John Woodward, GBE, KCB (C in C Naval Home Cmd) 1987, ret 1990; called to the Bar Inner Temple 1972, recorder Crown Ct 1989–90 (asst recorder 1984–89), circuit judge (SE Circuit) 1990–; pres: Social Security Appeal Tribunals, Medical Appeal Tribunals and Disability Appeal Tribunals 1992–94, Vaccine Damage Appeal Tribunals 1992–94, Child Support Appeal Tribunals 1992–94; memb: Probation Ctees, Judicial Standing Ctee on IT; author of treatise Mine Warfare at Sea (Ocean Devpt and Int Law, 1987); *Recreations* sailing; *Style*— His Hon Judge Thorpe; ✉ The Crown Court, Southgate, Chichester, W Sussex PO19 1SX (☎ 01243 787590)

THORPE, Denis; s of Thomas Thorpe (d 1995), of Mansfield, Notts, and Laura Thorpe (d 1995); *b* 6 Aug 1932; *Educ* High Oakham Sch Mansfield; *m* 30 March 1959, Patricia Ann, *née* Fiddes; 3 da (Josephine Mary b 8 May 1960, Jane Elizabeth b 17 Oct 1961, Lucy Ann b 28 Aug 1964), 3 s (Peter John b 11 Feb 1963, Robert James b 18 Nov 1966, David Gerard b 23 Aug 1971); *Career* photographer; Nat Serv RAF 1950–52; Mansfield Reporter (weekly newspaper) 1948, Northampton Chronicle & Echo 1954–55, Lincolnshire Echo 1955, Birmingham Gazette & Dispatch 1955–56, Daily Mail 1956–74, The Guardian 1974–96; subject of BBC TV Film Worth A Thousand Words 1983; Hon MA Univ of Manchester 1995; life memb NUJ 1996; FRPS 1990 (ARPS 1974), FBIPP 1994 (ABIPP 1992); *Exhbns* The World of Denis Thorpe (Portico Gallery Manchester) 1982, Russia Through the Lens (Barbican) 1986, Denis Thorpe - Guardian Photographer (Victoria Theatre Stoke-on-Trent) 1990; *Awards* Br Press Pictures Awards: Br Regnl Press Photographer of the Year 1971, Picture Essay of the Year 1975–77; Photokina Obelisk (Cologne) 1974, FIAP Medals 1974–76, UN Special Award 1976, Worlds Press Photo Fndn Gold Medal 1979, Ilford Photographer of the Year 1988, UK Picture Ed's Guild Business and Indust Photographer of the Year 1995; *Books* The Shepherds Year 1979, Pictorial Group Monograph 1994; *Recreations* hill walking, skiing, playing ragtime piano, learning the Italian language; *Style*— Denis Thorpe, Esq; ✉ c/o The Guardian, Editorial Department, 164 Deansgate, Manchester M60 2RR

THORPE, Geoffrey Digby; s of late Gordon Digby Thorpe, of Scotland, and Agnes Joyce Saville, *née* Haines; *b* 24 Sept 1949; *Educ* Windsor GS for Boys, Architectural Assoc Sch of Architecture (AA Dip); *m* 29 Sept 1973, Jane Florence, da of James Hay McElwee, of Havant, Hampshire; 1 da (Holly b 1980); *Career* indust gp architect; Milton Keynes Devpt Corp 1974–78, asst co architect East Sussex 1978–80, chm Thorpe Architecture Ltd 1980–, princ Thorpe Architecture Partnership 1993–; dir Prospace Ltd; memb Br Cncl for Offices; RIBA 1975; memb: ARCUK 1975, AA; *Recreations* fly and game fishing, boating; *Style*— Geoffrey Thorpe, Esq; ✉ Lower Farm, Madehurst, Arundel, West Sussex BN18 0NU (☎ 01243 814531, fax 01243 814505); The Bridge House, 14th Street, Key Colony Beach, Florida Keys, Florida 33050, USA (☎ 00 1 305 743 3938, fax 00 1 305 743 0326); Thorpe Architecture, Sparks Yard Tarrant St, Arundel, West Sussex BN18 9SB (☎ 01903 883500, fax 01903 882188, car tel 0385 366095)

THORPE, Rt Hon (John) Jeremy; PC (1967); s of Capt John Henry Thorpe, OBE, KC, JP (d 1944), sometime MP (C) for Rusholme and dep chm Middx QS (eldest s of Ven John Thorpe, Archdeacon of Macclesfield), and Ursula, JP (d 1992), er da of Sir John Norton-Griffiths, 1 Bt, KCB, DSO, sometime MP for Wednesbury and Wandsworth Central; *b* 29 April 1929; *Educ* Rectory Sch Pomfret, Eton, Trinity Coll Oxford (pres Oxford Union 1951); *m* 1, 1968, Caroline (d 1970), da of Warwick Allpass, of Kingswood, Surrey; 1 s; m 2, 1973, Marion, Countess of Harewood (*see* Harewood, Earl of), da of Erwin Stein (d 1958); *Career* called to the Bar Inner Temple 1954; MP (Lib) N Devon 1959–79, ldr Lib Pty 1967–76 (hon treas 1965–67); chm Jeremy Thorpe Associates Ltd (Devpt Conslts), conslt Stramit Ltd; exec chm UN Assoc 1976–80; memb Devon Sessions; hon fell Trinity Coll Oxford, Hon LLD Univ of Exeter; FRSA; *Clubs* Nat Lib; *Style*— The Rt Hon Jeremy Thorpe; ✉ 2 Orme Square, London W2 4RS

THORPE, John Frederick; s of Thomas Alfred Thorpe (d 1983), of Blisworth, Northants, and Edith Rosamund, *née* Ashby; *b* 17 Oct 1939; *Educ* Oundle, Law Soc Sch of Law; *m* 4 May 1963, Susan Margaret, da of Andrew Roy Banham; 1 da (Joanna Margaret b 8 Sept 1967), 2 s (Michael Jonathan b 6 Nov 1968, Roger James Thomas b 19 June 1975); *Career* solicitor; articles with Phipps & Troup Northampton 1957–62, admitted as slr 1963, slr Boyes, Turner & Burrows Reading 1963–64; Shoosmiths & Harrison: joined as ptnr 1964, managing ptnr 1986–89, sr ptnr 1989–; pres Northampton Law Soc 1984–85; chm: Northamptonshire C of C Trg & Enterprise Cncl, Nene Fndn; govr Moulton Coll; *Recreations* cricket, tennis, walking, rugby supporter; *Style*— John Thorpe, Esq; ✉ The Manor House, Everdon, Daventry, Northants NN11 6BN (☎ 01327 361286); Shoosmiths & Harrison, Compton House, Abington Street, Northampton NN1 2LR (☎ 01604 29977, fax 01604 20229)

THORPE, John Grafton; s of Grafton Gould Thorpe (d 1963), of Epsom, Surrey, and Ivy Dorothy, *née* Locks (d 1984); *b* 29 Oct 1932; *Educ* St John's Sch Leatherhead, City of London Freemen's Sch; *m* 30 March 1957, Pamela, da of Thomas Francis Faithfull, of Leatherhead, Surrey; 1 s (Martin John Richard b 9 Sept 1958), 1 da (Caroline Jane b 31 May 1960); *Career* underwriter: Lloyd's 1963–, St Quintin Syndicate 1979–85, Coster Syndicate 1986–90; dir Alexander Howden Underwriting 1979–84; Freeman City of London 1955; Liveryman Worshipful Co of Glass Sellers 1955 (apprentice 1950–55, memb Ct 1989, Renter Warden 1993, Prime Warden 1994, Master 1995–96), Liveryman Worshipful Co of Makers of Playing Cards 1979 (Steward 1984–86, elected to Ct 1986, Junior Warden 1988, Sr Warden 1989, Master 1990–91); *Books* The Playing Cards of the Worshipful Company of Makers of Playing Cards (1980); *Recreations* playing cards, watching cricket; *Clubs* MCC; *Style*— John Thorpe, Esq; ✉ Pinehurst, Epsom Rd, Leatherhead, Surrey

THORPE, Rt Hon Lord Justice; Rt Hon Sir Mathew Alexander; kt (1988); yr s of late Michael Alexander Thorpe, of Petworth, Sussex, and Dorothea Margaret, *née* Lambert; *b* 30 July 1938; *Educ* Stowe, Balliol Coll Oxford; *m* 1, 30 Dec 1966, Lavinia Hermione, da of Maj Robert James Buxton (d 1968); 3 s (Gervase b 1967, Alexander b 1969, Marcus b 1971); m 2, 3 Aug 1989, Mrs Carola Millar; *Career* called to the Bar Inner Temple 1961, QC 1980, recorder of the Crown Court 1982, judge of the High Court of Justice (Family Div) 1988–95, a Lord Justice of Appeal 1995–; memb Matrimonial Causes Rule Ctee 1978–83, memb Family Proceedings Rules Ctee 1988–94, pres Nat Cncl for Family Proceedings 1995–; bencher Inner Temple 1985; *Style*— The Rt Hon Lord Justice Thorpe; ✉ Royal Courts of Justice, Strand, London WC2A 2LL

THORPE, Nigel James; CVO (1991); s of Ronald James Thorpe, of Seaford, and Glenys, *née* Robilliard; *b* 3 Oct 1945; *Educ* East Grinstead GS, Univ of Wales (BA); *m* Susan Diane, *née* Barnforth; 3 da (Victoria Jane b 1985, Jessica Clare b 1985, Sophie Virginia b 1991); *Career* FO (now FCO): joined 1969, third then second sec Warsaw 1970–72, second then first sec Dacca 1973–74, London 1974–79, first sec Ottowa 1979–81, London 1981–85, Cnsllr and head of Chancery Warsaw 1985–88, dep high cmmr Harare 1989–92, head of Central European Dept 1992–; *Style*— Nigel J Thorpe, Esq, CVO; ✉ Central European Department, FCO, King Charles Street, London SW1H 2AH (☎ 0171 270 2368)

THORPE, Phillip A; *Career* barr and slr Wellington NZ 1976–79, public prosecutor Republic of Nauru 1979–81, various appts Securities Cmmn Hong Kong 1981–87, chief exec Hong Kong Futures Exchange 1987–89, chief exec Assoc of Futures Brokers and Dealers (AFBD) UK 1989–91, dep chief exec Securities and Futures Authy (SFA) following merger of AFBD and Securities Assoc 1991–93 (seconded as chief exec London Commodity Exchange Ltd 1991–92, seconded to SIB working on review of Financial Services Act regulatory system 1992–93), chief exec Investment Management Regulatory Organisation Ltd (IMRO) 1993–; *Style*— Phillip Thorpe, Esq; ✉ IMRO Ltd, Lloyds Chambers, 1 Portsoken Street, London E1 8BT (☎ 0171 390 5000, fax 0171 680 0550)

THORPE-TRACEY, Maj Stephen Frederick; s of Rev Julian Stephen Victor Thorpe-Tracey (d 1949), of The Rectory, Monkokehampton, Devon, and Faith Catherine Gwendoline, *née* Powell; *b* 27 Dec 1929; *Educ* Plymouth Coll; *m* 1 Jan 1955, Shirley, da of Lt-Col George Frederick Byles (d 1951), and Kathleen Mary, *née* Walker (d 1987), of Tiverton, Devon; 1 s (Jeremy), 2 da (Catherine, Barbara); *Career* emergency cmmn 1948, short serv cmmn 1950, regular cmmn DLI 1952, Staff Coll Camberley 1960 (psc), GSO2 Def Operational Res Estab 1961–63, Trg Maj 8 DLI TA 1964–65, Maj 1 DLI 1965–66, GSO2 MOD 1966–70; direct entry Civil Serv: princ 1970–77, asst sec 1977–86, under sec and controller Newcastle Central Office DHSS 1986–89; independent mgmnt conslt 1990–95, assoc conslt Royal Inst of Public Admin 1990–92; memb Prescription Pricing Authy 1990–93, hon sec Civil Serv Chess Assoc 1974–77, cdre Goring Thames SC 1981–82, chm Northern Gp Royal Inst of Public Admin 1988–89, hon sec Mid Devon Div SSAFA 1992–, chm Grantlands Residents' Assoc 1993–, chm Tiverton Chess Club 1994–, chm Uffculme Soc 1994–, memb Uffculme Parish Cncl 1995–, chm Tstees Coldharbour Mill 1996– (hon sec 1994–96); *Recreations* chess, golf, fell walking; *Clubs* Tiverton Golf; *Style*— Maj Stephen Thorpe-Tracey; ✉ 9 Grantlands, Uffculme, Cullompton, Devon EX15 3ED (☎ 01884 841864)

THOURON, Sir John Rupert Hunt; KBE (1976, CBE 1967); s of John Longstreth Thouron, and Amelia Thouron; *b* 10 May 1908; *Educ* Sherborne; *m* 1 (m dis); 1 s; m 2, 1953, Esther duPont, da of Lammot duPont; *Career* Br Army Offr, served WWII Major Black Watch; (with Lady Thouron) fndr Thouron Univ of Pennsylvania Fund for British-American Student Exchange 1960; *Recreations* horticulture, racing, hunting, fishing, golf; *Clubs* Vicmead, Seminole, Jupiter Island, The Brook (all US), White's, Sunningdale, Royal St George's; *Style*— Sir John Thouron, KBE; ✉ Summer: DOE RUN, Unionville, Chester County, Pa 19375, USA (☎ 00 1 610 384 5542); Winter: 416 South Beach Rd, Hobe Sound, Florida 33455, USA (☎ 00 1 407 546 3577); office: 5801 Kennett Pike, Greenville, Delaware 19807, USA (☎ 00 1 302 652 6350)

THREADGOLD, Andrew Richard; s of Stanley Dennis Threadgold, of Brentwood, Essex, and the late Phyllis Ethel, *née* Marsh; *b* 8 Feb 1944; *Educ* Brentwood Sch, Nottingham Univ (BA), Melbourne Univ (PhD); *m* 1, 1966 (m dis), Rosalind; 2 s (Richard b 1967, Matthew b 1971); m 2, 1994, Deirdre; 1 da (Zoe b 1995); *Career* mangr econ info Int Wool Secretariat 1971–74, advsr Econ Div Bank of England 1974–84, on secondment chief economist Postel Investment Management Ltd 1984–86, head fin supervision Gen Div Bank of England 1986–87; chief exec and dir securities investmnt Postel Investment Management Ltd 1987–93, chief gen mangr AMP Society Sydney 1993–, dir AMP Asset Management plc; *Style*— Andrew Threadgold, Esq; ✉ AMP Society, AMP Building, 33 Alfred Street, Sydney Cove, NSW 2000, Australia (☎ 00 612 257 7100, fax 00 612 257 7106)

THRELFALL, (John) Peter; s of William Emmett Threlfall (d 1976), of Yorks, and Edith, *née* Jackson; *b* 11 Oct 1936; *Educ* Ilkley GS; *m* 16 Sept 1967, Karin Hedda, da of Gerhard Johannes Rothkamn, of Halle; 2 s (Jörn Peter, Axel Christopher (twins) b 11 Sept 1968); *Career* Nat Serv 2 Lt RAPC 1960–62, trainee accountant 1954–59, CA Cooper Brothers & Co London 1962–71, ptnr Coopers & Lybrand 1971–95 (conslt 1995–); FCA 1969 (ACA 1959); *Recreations* travel, theatre, music; *Clubs* Naval and Military; *Style*— Peter Threlfall, Esq; ✉ Wynyates, The Drive, Hook Heath, Woking, Surrey GU22 0JS (☎ and fax 01483 773633)

THRING, Jeremy John; DL (Avon); o s of late Christopher William Thring, MBE, TD, of King Meadow, Upton Lovell, Warminster, Wilts, and Joan Evelyn, *née* Graham; *b* 11 May 1936; *Educ* Winchester; *m* 30 June 1962, Cynthia Kay, da of late Gilbert Kirkpatrick Smith, of Bath; 2 da (Lucinda Katharine b 8 Aug 1963, Candida Sara b 11 May 1965); *Career* Nat Serv cmmnd 3 Kings Own Hussars 1955; admitted slr 1962, NP 1962, in practice Thrings & Long Bath; local dir Coutts Bank 1989; chm: Royal Nat Hosp for Rheumatic Diseases NHS Trust, Cncl Univ of Bath 1994–; govr Bath HS; tstee: Bath Inst for Research into Care of the Elderly, Bath Unit for Research into Paediatrics, Nat Eye Research Centre; memb: Law Soc, Soc of Provincial Notaries; *Recreations* stalking, shooting, fishing; *Clubs* Bath and Co; *Style*— Jeremy Thring, Esq, DL; ✉ Belcombe House, Bradford-on-Avon, Wilts (☎ 01225 862295); Thrings & Long, Midland Bridge, Bath BA1 2HQ (☎ 01225 448494, fax 01225 319735)

THRING, Prof Meredith Wooldridge; s of Capt W H Thring, CBE, RN (d 1949), and Dorothy Wooldridge (d 1922); *b* 17 Dec 1915; *Educ* Malvern, Trinity Coll Cambridge (BA, ScD); *m* 14 Dec 1940, (Alice) Margaret (d 1986), da of Robert Hooley (d 1949), of London; 2 s (John b 1944, Robert b 1949), 1 da (Susan (Mrs Kalaugher) b 1942); *Career* HG 1941–45; scientific offr Br Coal Utilisation Res Assoc 1937–46, head Physics Dept Br Iron & Steel Res Assoc 1946–53 (asst dir 1953), prof of fuel technol and chem engrg Univ of Sheffield 1953–64, prof of mechanical engrg QMC London 1964–81; lectured in Aust, Canada, USA, France, Holland, Italy, Russia, Argentina, Mexico, W Germany, Bulgaria, Hungary, Czechoslavakia and Poland; Hadfield medal Iron and Steel Inst 1949; jt fndr Int Flame Res Fndn 1949; memb: Clean Air Cncl 1957–62, Advsy Cncl R & D Miny of Power 1960–66, Fire Res Bd 1961–64, Educn Ctee RAF 1968–76, UNESCO Cmmn to Bangladesh 1979; Hon DUniv Open Univ 1982; memb Royal Norwegian Scientific Soc 1974, corr memb Nat Acad of Engrg Mexico 1977, memb NY Acad of Sciences 1994; FInstP 1944, SFInstFuel 1951 (pres 1962–63), FIMechE 1968, FIEE 1968, FIChemE 1972, FEng 1976; *Books* The Science of Flames and Furnaces (1952, 2 edn 1962), Machines - Masters or Slaves of Man? (1973), Man, Machines and Tomorrow (1973), How to Invent (1975), The Engineer's Conscience (1980), Robots and Telechirs (1983); *Recreations* wood carving, arboriculture; *Clubs* Athenaeum; *Style*— Prof Meredith Thring, FEng; ✉ Bell Farm, Brundish, Suffolk IP13 8BL (☎ 01379 384296)

THROWER, Keith Rex; OBE (1986); s of Stanley Frank Thrower (d 1966), of London, and Ellen Amelia Thrower (d 1963); *b* 26 Dec 1934; *Educ* St Dunstan's Coll London, Reading Coll of Advanced Technol (HNC Electronic Engrg, HNC Endorsements); *m* 1, 1958, Janice Barbara, *née* Brooks; 3 da (Sarah Jane b 10 Nov 1959, Marianne Judith b 7 March 1965, Margaret Louise b 17 July 1966); m 2, 1984, Alma, *née* Heath; *Career* technician: Cinema Television Ltd 1955–56, New Electronics Products 1956–58; electronic engr Dynatron Radio Ltd 1958–60; Racal Electronics plc: sr electronic engr 1960–64, princ electronic engr 1964–66, chief engr/gen mangr Radio Div 1966–68, tech dir Racal Instruments Ltd 1968–73, dir of advanced devpt 1973–78, dep chm Racal Research Ltd 1985–95 (md 1978–85), tech dir Racal Chubb Ltd 1985–91, res dir Racal Radio Group Ltd 1985–95; fndr Kalma Ltd 1995–; FIERE 1984 (MIERE 1964, pres 1986–87), FIEE 1988, FEng 1992; *Books* History of the British Radio Valve to 1940 (1992); *Recreations* reading, writing, philately, history of science and technology; *Style*— Keith Thrower, Esq, OBE, FEng; ✉ Kalma Ltd, 12 Wychcotes, Caversham, Reading, Berks RG4 7DA (☎ 0118 947 4813)

THROWER, (James) Simeon; s of Derek Bert Thrower, MBE, of Woldingham, Surrey, and Mary, *née* O'Connor; *b* 24 May 1950; *Educ* Royal GS High Wycombe, Univ of Leeds (LLB); *m* 21 June 1980, Alexandra Mary Elizabeth, da of late George Reginald Lanning, MC; 3 da (Justine Victoria b 15 Aug 1982, Catherine Georgina b 22 April 1985, Eleanor Juliet b 19 Nov 1990); *Career* called to the Bar Middle Temple 1973 (ad eundem Lincoln's Inn 1983), head of chambers 1985–; *Recreations* golf, sailing, travel; *Clubs* Wentworth Golf, Wig & Pen, Rosslyn Park RFC; *Style*— Simeon Thrower, Esq; ✉ 11 Old Square, Lincoln's Inn, London WC2A 3TS (☎ 0171 242 5022, fax 0171 404 0445)

THRUSH, Prof Brian Arthur; s of Arthur Albert Thrush (d 1963), of Hampstead, London, and Dorothy Charlotte, *née* Money (d 1982); *b* 23 July 1928; *Educ* Haberdashers' Aske's, Emmanuel Coll Cambridge (BA, MA, PhD, ScD); *m* 31 May 1958, Rosemary Catherine, da of George Henry Terry (d 1970), of Ottawa, Canada; 1 s (Basil Mark Brian b 1965), 1 da (Felicity Elizabeth b 1967); *Career* conslt to US Nat Bureau of Standards 1957–58; Univ of Cambridge: demonstrator in physical chemistry 1953–58, asst dir of res 1959–64, lectr 1964–69, reader 1969–78, prof of physical chemistry 1978–95, head of Chemistry Dept 1988–93, vice master Emmanuel Coll 1986–90 (fell 1960–); visiting prof Chinese Acad of Sci 1980–; memb: Lawes Agric Tst Ctee 1979–89, Natural Environment Res Cncl 1985–90, Cncl of the Royal Soc 1990–92, Cncl of Academia Europaea 1992–; Tilden lectr of Chemical Soc 1965, Michael Polanyi medallist Royal Soc of Chemistry 1980, awarded Rank Prize for Opto-Electronics 1992; memb Academia Europaea 1990 (memb Cncl 1992–); FRS 1976, FRSC 1977; *Recreations* wine, walking; *Style*— Prof Brian Thrush, FRS; ✉ Brook Cottage, Pemberton Terrace, Cambridge CB2 1JA (☎ 01223 357 637); University of Cambridge, Department of Chemistry, Lensfield Road, Cambridge CB2 1EW (☎ 01223 336 458, fax 01223 336 362, telex 81240); Emmanuel College, Cambridge CB2 3AP

THUBRON, Colin Gerald Dryden; s of Brig Gerald Ernest Thubron, DSO, OBE (d 1992), of Pheasants Hatch, Piltdown, Uckfield, Sussex, and Evelyn Kate Mary, *née* Dryden; *b* 14 June 1939; *Educ* Eton; *Career* on editorial staff: Hutchinson & Co 1959–62, Macmillan Co NY 1964–65; freelance filmmaker 1962–64; author; *Books* Mirror to Damascus (1967), The Hills of Adonis (1968), Jerusalem (1969), Journey Into Cyprus (1975), The God in the Mountain (1977), Emperor (1978), Among the Russians (1983), A Cruel Madness (1984, Silver Pen Award), Behind the Wall (1987, Hawthornden Prize, Thomas Cook Award), Falling (1989), Turning Back the Sun (1991), The Lost Heart of Asia (1994), Distance (1996); FRSL 1969; *Style*— Colin Thubron, Esq, FRSL; ✉ Garden Cottage, 27 St Ann's Villas, London W11 4RT (☎ 0171 602 2522)

THUM, Maximilien John Alexandre (Max); s of Maximilien Francois Thum (d 1972), of Geneva, Switzerland, and Kathleen Isabel, *née* Crouch (d 1972); *b* 15 Feb 1933; *Educ* Ecole Internationale de Genéve, Chigwell Sch Essex, Law Socs Coll of Law; *m* 1, 15 Feb 1958 (m dis 1981), Freda, *née* Wray; 2 s (Nicolas Charles Maximilien b 3 Feb 1959, Jonathan Richard Alexandre b 25 March 1962), 1 da (Annabel Maxine Elizabeth b 26 Nov 1963); m 2, 25 Feb 1982, Valerie, *née* Kay; *Career* RAF 1955–57, cmmnd Pilot Offr 1956; admitted slr of Supreme Court 1955, asst slr Lewis and Lewis and Gisborne 1955, slr Rodyk and Davidson Singapore 1957–60, called to Singapore Bar 1958, Professional Purposes Dept Law Soc 1961, ptnr Sharpe Pritchard and Co London 1962–66, sr litigation ptnr Ashurst Morris Crisp London 1967–93 (conslt 1993–95), sr conslt Davies Arnold Cooper London 1995–; memb: Int Bar Assoc, American Bar Assoc, Int Assoc of Defense Counsel; FCIArb; *Recreations* photography, opera, swimming, tennis, shooting; *Clubs* RAC; *Style*— Max Thum, Esq; ✉ Fosters, Mattingley, Hants; 24 Stanhope Gardens, London SW7; Davies Arnold Cooper, 6–8 Bouverie Street, London EC4Y 8DD (☎ 0171 936 2222, fax 0171 936 2020, telex 262894)

THURLEY, Dr Simon John; s of Thomas Manley Thurley, of Godmanchester and Madras, and Rachel, *née* House; *b* 29 Aug 1962; *Educ* Kimbolton Sch Cambs, Bedford Coll London (BA), Courtauld Inst (MA, PhD); *Career* inspector of ancient monuments Crown Bldgs and Monuments Gp English Heritage 1981–89, curator of the Historic Royal Palaces 1989–; *Books* Henry VIII - Images of a Tudor King (1989), The Royal Palaces of Tudor England - Architecture and Court Life 1460–1547 (1993); contrib many volumes, magazines and jls; *Style*— Dr Simon Thurley; ✉ Historic Royal Palaces, Hampton Court Palace, East Molesey, Surrey KT8 9AU (☎ 0181 781 9781, fax 0181 781 9782)

THURLOW, Dr Alexander Cresswell; s of Maurice Cresswell Thurlow (d 1940), and Despina Alexandra, *née* Evangelinou; *b* 13 April 1940; *Educ* Brighton Hove E Sussex GS, St Mary's Hosp Med Sch (MB BS); *m* 29 June 1963, Joanna, da of Stefan Woycicki, of Wiltshire; 2 da (Susan Kristina b 1965, Jane b 1966); *Career* sr registrar in anaesthesia St Thomas' Hosp and Hosp For Sick Children 1969–72; conslt anaesthetist: St George's Hosp 1972–, Royal Dental Hosp 1972–82; asst prof of anaesthesia Stanford Univ California USA 1975–76, tutor and lectr in anaesthesia Royal Coll of Anaesthetists 1977–; chm Southern Soc of Anaesthetists, memb Assoc of Anaesthetists, memb Assoc of Dental Anaesthetists; memb BMA, FRCA 1968; *Books* contrib: Clinics In Anaesthesiology (1983), A Practice of Anaesthesia (1984), Anaesthesia and Sedation in Dentistry (1983); *Recreations* swimming, travel, opera, theatre; *Style*— Dr Alexander Thurlow; ✉ Dept of Anaesthesia, St George's Hospital, Blackshaw Rd, London SW17 (☎ 0181 672 1255)

THURLOW, Prof David George; OBE (1987); s of Frederick Charles Thurlow (d 1986), of Bury St Edmunds, and Audrey Isabel Mary, *née* Farrow; *b* 31 March 1939; *Educ* King Edward VI Sch Bury St Edmunds, Dept of Architecture Cambridge Coll of Art, Sch of Architecture Canterbury Coll of Art, Univ of Cambridge (MA); *m* 19 Dec 1959, Pamela Ann, da of Percy Adolphous Rumbelow; 3 da (Suzanne Elizabeth, Jane Ann, Emma Louise); *Career* architect; fndr ptnr: Cambridge Design Group 1970, Cambridge Design Architects 1975, Design Group Cambridge 1988, Thurlow, Carnell & Thornburrow 1991–; Faculty of Architecture Univ of Cambridge 1970–77, Sch of Architecture Univ of Nottingham 1991–96, prof of architecture South Bank Univ 1996–; exhibitor Royal Acad Summer Exhibition 1983–; awards incl: RIBA Award 1976, 1984, 1986 and 1990, Civic Tst Award 1978 and 1986, DOE Housing Award 1985; fndr memb: Granta Housing Soc, Cambridge Forum for the Construction Indust 1981 (chm 1985–86); pres Assoc of Conslt Architects (ACA) 1991–93; assessor: RIBA Awards 1979, 1984, 1986 and 1990, Civic Tst Awards 1979–; memb PSA Design Panel 1987–89; ARIBA 1965; *Recreations* cricket, golf, food; *Clubs* Athenaeum; *Style*— Prof David Thurlow, OBE; ✉ 1 Old Pound Yard, High Street, Great Shelford, Cambridge CB2 5EH (☎ 01223 842888, fax 01223 566267)

THURLOW, 8 Baron (GB 1792); Francis Edward Hovell-Thurlow-Cumming-Bruce; KCMG (1961, CMG 1957); 2 s of Rev 6 Baron Thurlow (d 1952), and Grace Catherine, *née* Trotter (d 1959); suc bro, 7 Baron Thurlow,

CB, CBE, DSO (d 1971); *b* 9 March 1912; *Educ* Shrewsbury, Trinity Coll Cambridge (MA); *m* 13 Aug 1949, Yvonne Diana (d 1990), da of late Aubyn Harold Raymond Wilson, of Westerlee, St Andrews, Fife, and formerly w of Mandell Creighton Dormehl; 2 s, 2 da; *Heir* s, Hon Roualeyn Robert Hovell-Thurlow-Cumming-Bruce, *qv*; *Career* Dept of Agric for Scotland 1935–37, sec British High Cmmn in NZ 1939–44 and Canada 1944–45, private sec to Sec of State for Commonwealth Relations 1947–49, cnsllr British High Cmmn in New Delhi 1949–52, advsr to Govr of Gold Coast 1955, dep high cmmr in Ghana 1957 and Canada 1958, high cmmr for UK in NZ 1959–63 and Nigeria 1963–66, dep under sec FCO 1964, govr and C-in-C of Bahamas 1968–72; KStJ; *Recreations* gardening; *Clubs* Travellers'; *Style*— The Rt Hon the Lord Thurlow, KCMG; ✉ 102 Leith Mansions, Grantully Road, London W9 1LJ (☎ 0171 289 9664); Philham Water, Hartland, Bideford, Devon EX39 6E2 (☎ 01237 441433)

THURNHAM, Peter Giles; MP (C until Oct 1996, whereafter Lib Dem) Bolton North East (majority 185); s of Giles Rymer Thurnham (d 1975), and Marjorie May, *née* Preston (d 1994); *b* 21 Aug 1938; *Educ* Oundle Sch, Peterhouse Cambridge, Harvard Business Sch, Cranfield Inst of Tech; *m* 1963, Sarah Janet, da of Harold Keenlyside Stroude (d 1974); 1 s, 3 da, 1 s adopted; *Career* professional engr running own business 1972–; memb S Lakeland Dist Cncl 1982–84; MP (C until Oct 1996, whereafter Lib Dem) Bolton NE 1983–, vice chm Cons Small Business Ctee 1985–87, sec Cons Employment Ctee 1986–87, vice chm All Party Parly Gp for Children 1987–, vice chm All Pty Parly Gp for Disability 1992–; PPS to: Rt Hon Norman Fowler as Sec of State for Employment 1987–90, Eric Forth and Robert Jackson as jt Parly Under-Secs of State Dept of Employment 1991–92, Rt Hon Michael Howard as Sec of State DOE 1992–93; chm Cons Disability Gp, memb Social Security Select Ctee 1993–95, memb Public Accounts Ctee 1995–; pres Campaign for Inter Country Adoption; FIMechE; *Recreations* Lake District, family life; *Style*— Peter Thurnham, Esq, MP; ✉ Hollin Hall, Crook, Kendal, Cumbria LA8 9HP (☎ 01539 821 382); House of Commons, London SW1A 0AA (☎ 0171 219 3000)

THURSBY-PELHAM, Brig (Mervyn) Christopher; OBE (1986); s of Nevill Cressett Thursby-Pelham (d 1950), of Danyrallt Park, Carmarthenshire, and Yseulte, *née* Peel (d 1982); *b* 23 March 1921; *Educ* Wellington, Merton Coll Oxford; *m* 16 Jan 1943, Rachel Mary Latimer, da of Sir Walter Stuart James Willson (d 1952), of Kenward, Kent; 1 s (David Thomas Cressett b 1948), 1 da (Philippa Rachel Mary b 1943); *Career* cmmnd Welsh Gds 1941, serv 3 Bn N Africa, Italy and Austria 1943–45, serv 1 Bn Palestine and Egypt, graduate Staff Coll Camberley 1950, GSO2 (Ops) 6 Armd Div BAOR 1951–53, Regtl Adj Welsh Gds 1956–57, DS Staff Coll Camberley 1957–60, Cmdt Gds Depot Pirbright 1960–63, GSO1 (Ops) Allied Staff Berlin 1963–64, Regtl Lt-Col cmdg WG 1964–67, COS Br Forces Gulf 1967–69, COS London Dist 1969–72, Dep Fortress Cdr Gibraltar 1972–74, Dep Cdr Midwest Dist UK 1974–76; ADC to HM The Queen 1972–76; dir gen Br Heart Fndn 1976–86 and 1988–90 (memb Cncl 1990–93), co pres Royal Br Legion Berks 1985–91 (vice pres 1991–), pres Welsh Gds Assoc Monmouthshire branch 1987–, Gds Assoc Reading branch 1991–; *Recreations* fishing, sailing, travel; *Clubs* Cavalry and Guards', Royal Yacht Sqdn; *Style*— Brig Christopher Thursby-Pelham, OBE; ✉ Ridgeland House, Finchampstead, Berks RG40 3TA; King's Quay, Whippingham, IOW PO32 6NU

THURSBY-PELHAM, Douglas Thomas Harvey; s of Col Donald Hervey Thursby-Pelham, of Bagshot, Surrey, and Chantal Jeanne Marie Anne, *née* Walsh de Serrant; *b* 27 Sept 1956; *Educ* Wellington, KCL (BA); *m* 9 Aug 1986, Zoë Anne, da of late David Stanley Joseph Moseley; 2 da (Alexandra Anne b 10 Aug 1988, Victoria Alice b 26 July 1993), 1 s (Charles David Harvey b 13 Dec 1989); *Career* Lonsdale Advertising Ltd: grad trainee 1979–81, account exec 1981–83, account mangr 1983–84; account dir Allen Brady and Marsh Ltd 1985–86 (joined 1984), bd dir BMP DDB Needham (formerly known as Reeves Robertshaw Needham then DDB Needham Worldwide) 1988–89 (joined 1986), client servs dir Publicis Ltd 1994– (gp account dir 1990–94); IPA Advertising Effectiveness Award 1992, Advtg and Mktg Effectiveness Award New York Festival 1995; *Recreations* cricket, Everton FC, the Rolling Stones; *Style*— Douglas Thursby-Pelham, Esq; ✉ Littledean, Bramdean, Alresford, Hampshire SO24 0JU (☎ 01962 771358)

THURSFIELD, John Richard; s of Maj Rupert MacNaghten Cecil Thursfield (d 1979), and Elizabeth Margaret Mary, *née* Gunning; *b* 2 Oct 1937; *Educ* Rugby Sch; *m* 29 April 1961, Sarah, da of Charles Clinton Dawkins (d 1985); 2 s (Peter John b 1964, Robert Charles b 1967), 2 da (Mary Elizabeth b 1963, Rachel Sarah b 1969); *Career* dir Union Fund Management London and Guernsey; *Recreations* skiing; *Style*— John Thursfield, Esq; ✉ Hodges Farm, Lower Froyle, Alton, Hants, GU34 4LL (☎ 01420 23294); Union plc, 39 Cornhill, London EC3V 3NU (☎ 0171 623 1020)

THURSO, 3 Viscount (UK 1952); Sir John Archibald Sinclair; 6 Bt (GB 1786); s of 2 Viscount Thurso (d 1995), and Margaret Beaumont, *née* Robertson; *b* 10 Sept 1953; *Educ* Eton, Westminster Tech Coll; *m* 12 June 1976, Marion Ticknor, da of Louis D Sage, of Connecticut, USA, and Constance Cluett Ward, *qv*, of Dunkeld, Perthshire; 2 s (Hon James Alexander Robin b 14 Jan 1984, Hon George Henry MacDonald b 29 Oct 1989), 1 da (Hon Louisa Ticknor Beaumont b 15 March 1980); *Heir* s, Hon James Alexander Robin Sinclair, yr of Ulbster, b 14 Jan 1984; *Career* mgmnt trainee Savoy Hotel plc 1972–77, reception mangr Claridge's 1978–81, gen mangr Hotel Lancaster Paris (part of the Savoy Gp) 1981–85, dir SA Lancaster 1982–85, vice-chm Prestige Hotels 1984–89, fndr gen mangr Cliveden Bucks for Blakeney Hotels 1985–92; dir: Cliveden House Ltd 1987–, Savoy Hotel plc (non-exec) 1993–; chief exec Granfel Holdings Ltd 1992–95; md Fitness and Leisure Holdings Ltd 1995–; non-exec chm: Lochdhu Hotels Ltd, Thurso Fisheries Ltd, Sinclair Family Trust Ltd; vice chm Prestige Hotels 1983–90; chm: Game Conservancy Bucks 1990–92, Clubs Panel BHA 1992–95, Scrabster Harbour Tst 1996–; sits as Lib Dem in House of Lords; Freeman City of London 1991; FHCIMA 1991, Master Innholder 1991 (chm 1995–); *Recreations* fishing, shooting, food, wine; *Clubs* New (Edinburgh); *Style*— The Rt Hon the Viscount Thurso; ✉ Thurso East Mains, Thurso, Caithness KW14 8HW (☎ 01847 892600)

THURSTON, Dr John Gavin Bourdas; s of Gavin Leonard Bourdas Thurston (d 1980), and Ione Witham, *née* Barber (d 1967); *b* 8 April 1937; *Educ* Haileybury Coll, Guy's Hosp Med Sch London (MB BS); *m* 1, Felicity, *née* Neal; 1 s (Gavin b 1962), 1 da (Georgette Margaret (Mrs McCready) b 1959); m 2, Joy Elizabeth, *née* Leech; 3 s (Gareth b 1966, John b 1969, Andrew b 1972); m 3, 25 July 1986, Stephanie Sarah, da of John Henry Mayo; *Career* house physician and surgn: Guy's 1961–62, Lewisham Hosp 1962; house physician Brompton Hosp 1962–63, registrar Westminster Hosp 1964–66, res sr registrar Br Heart Fndn 1967–68, sr cardiology registrar Westminster Hosp 1968–78, conslt Accident and Emergency Dept Queen Mary's Univ Hosp Roehampton 1979–; disaster doctor RFU Twickenham; med offr: Surrey Co RFC, Rosslyn Park RFC; med companion Grand Order of Water Rats; pres A/E Section RSM 1988–90, hon sec Br Assoc of A/E Med 1984–90; Freeman City of London 1965, Liveryman Worshipful Soc of Apothecaries 1963; memb: BMA 1962, Br Assoc of A/E Med 1979; FRSM 1986, FRCP 1992, FFAEM (fndr fell and hon registrar); *Books* Hyperbaric Medicine (co-author, 1977), Scientific Foundations of Anaesthesia (co-author, 1976); *Recreations* eating, drinking, rugby, humour, after-dinner speaking, study of good English; *Clubs* Snowball, Rosslyn Park RFC, Grand Order of Water Rats; *Style*— Dr John Thurston; ✉ 164 Upper Richmond Rd West, East Sheen, London SW14 8AW (☎ 0181 878 9875); Queen Marys University Hospital, Roehampton, London SW15 5PN (☎ 0181 789 6611)

THURSTON, Julian Paul; s of Ronald Thurston, of Dunstable, Beds, and Eileen Joyce Thurston, *née* Salmon; *b* 11 May 1955; *Educ* Bedford Sch, Merton Coll Oxford (MA); *m* 11 July 1981, Julia Sarah, da of Thomas George Kerslake (d 1966); 1 s (Thomas b 1989), 1 da (Sarah b 1987); *Career* admitted slr 1979; ptnr McKenna & Co 1986–; *Style*— Julian Thurston, Esq; ✉ McKenna & Co, Mitre House, 160 Aldersgate Street, London EC1A 4DD (☎ 0171 606 9000, fax 0171 606 9100, telex 27251)

THUYSBAERT, HE Jonkheer Prosper; s of Prosper Thuysbaert (d 1965), and Marguerite, *née* Levie (d 1979); *b* 7 Dec 1931; *Educ* LLB, BA (Thomistic Philosophy); *m* 1957, Marie-Claire Vuylsteke; 2 s (Prosper Reginald b 16 Jan 1959, Alexis Dominique b 29 July 1961); *Career* Belgian diplomat; joined Diplomatic Serv 1957, attaché Luxembourg 1960–61, economic attaché Paris 1961–62, first sec Tel Aviv 1963–64, advsr to Belgian Min for Foreign Trade 1964–65, cnsllr Perm Representation to the EC 1965–70, Euro advsr to Belgian Min for Foreign Affrs 1970–77, Euro advsr to Belgian PM 1977–80, dir Euro orgns Miny for Foreign Affrs 1980–81, chef de cabinet Belgian Min for External Rels 1981–83, political dir Miny for Foreign Affrs 1983–85; ambass Perm Representation: to the UN Geneva 1985–87, to NATO Brussels 1987–93; EC conslt Euro Stability Pact 1993–94, Belgian ambass to the Ct of St James's 1994–; prof Univ of Leuven Belgium 1992–; *Publications* La Diplomatie Multilatérale (1991), Multilateraal Kunst en Vliegwerk (1991), Het Belgisch Buitenlamse Beleid (1995); *Recreations* art, tennis, skiing, swimming; *Clubs* Army and Navy, Anglo-Belgian; *Style*— HE Jonkheer Prosper Thuysbaert; ✉ Belgian Embassy, 103 Eaton Square, London SW1W 9AB (☎ 0171 470 3700, fax 0171 259 6213)

THWAITE, Ann Barbara; da of A J Harrop (d 1963), and Hilda Mary, *née* Valentine (d 1990); *b* 4 Oct 1932; *Educ* Marsden Sch Wellington NZ, Queen Elizabeth Girls' GS Barnet, St Hilda's Coll Oxford (MA); *m* 4 Aug 1955, Anthony Thwaite, OBE, FRSL, *qv*; 4 da (Emily b 1957, Caroline b 1959, Lucy b 1961, Alice b 1965); *Career* writer; occasional reviewer of children's books: TLS 1963–85, The Guardian, TES, Washington Post, Daily Telegraph; Churchill fell 1993; govr: St Mary's Middle Sch Long Stratton 1990–, Hapton VC Primary Sch 1994–; FRSL; *Books* children's books incl: The Camelthorn Papers (1969), Tracks (1978), Allsorts 1–7 (ed, 1968–75), Allsorts of Poems (1978), The Ashton Affair (1995), The Horse at Hilly Fields (1996); other publications: Waiting for the Party: The Life of Frances Hodgson Burnett (1974, reissued 1994), My Oxford (ed, 1977), Edmund Gosse: A Literary Landscape (1984, winner Duff Cooper Meml Award 1985), A A Milne: His Life (1990, winner Whitbread Biography Prize 1990), Portraits from Life: Essays by Edmund Gosse (ed, 1991), The Brilliant Career of Winnie-the-Pooh (1992), Emily Tennyson, the Poet's Wife; *Recreations* other people's lives, punting on the Tas; *Clubs* PEN, Soc of Authors, Royal Over-Seas League, Children's Books History Soc; *Style*— Ann Thwaite; ✉ The Mill House, Low Tharston, Norfolk NR15 2YN (☎ 01508 489569); c/o Curtis Brown, 162 Regent St, London W1R 5TB (☎ 0171 872 0332)

THWAITE, Anthony Simon; OBE (1990); s of Hartley Thwaite, JP (d 1978), of Yorks, and Alice Evelyn, *née* Mallinson; *b* 23 June 1930; *Educ* Kingswood Sch Bath, ChCh Oxford (MA); *m* 4 Aug 1955, Ann Barbara Thwaite, *qv*, da of Angus John Harrop (d 1963), of NZ and London; 4 da (Emily b 1957, Caroline b 1959, Lucy b 1961, Alice b 1965); *Career* Nat Serv Sgt Instr Rifle Bde and RAEC 1949–51; lectr English lit Univ of Tokyo 1955–57, prodr BBC radio 1957–62, literary ed The Listener 1962–65, asst prof English Univ of Libya Benghazi 1965–67, literary ed New Statesman 1968–72, co-ed Encounter 1973–85, dir Andre Deutsch Ltd 1986–92 (editorial conslt 1992–95), writer in residence Vanderbilt Univ Nashville USA 1992; Richard Hillary Meml Prize 1968, Cholmondeley Award for Poetry 1983, chm of judges Booker Prize 1986; former memb: Ctee of Mgmnt Soc of Authors, Cncl RSL, Lit Panel Arts Cncl of GB; current memb: Lit Advsy Ctee Br Cncl, Ctee RLF; Hon LittD Univ of Hull 1989; FRSL 1978; *Books* Poems 1953–83 (1984), Six Centuries of Verse (1984), Poetry Today (1985, revised edn 1996), Letter From Tokyo (1987), Philip Larkin: Collected Poems (ed, 1988), Poems 1953–88 (1989), Philip Larkin: Selected Letters 1940–1985 (ed, 1992), The Dust of the World (1994); *Recreations* archaeology, travel; *Style*— Anthony Thwaite, OBE, FRSL; ✉ The Mill House, Low Tharston, Norfolk (☎ 01508 489569)

THWAITES, Prof Sir Bryan; kt (1986); s of Ernest James Thwaites (d 1978), and Dorothy Marguerite, *née* Dickeson; *b* 6 Dec 1923; *Educ* Dulwich, Winchester, Clare Coll Cambridge (MA, PhD); *m* 11 Sept 1948, Katharine Mary (d 1991), da of H R Harries (d 1946); 4 s (Barnaby Christopher b 1953, Quentin Mark b 1956, Dominic John b 1958, Jacoby Michael b 1963), 2 da (Eleanor Jane b 1951, Matilda Bridget b 1966); *Career* sci offr Nat Physical Lab 1944–47, lectr Imperial Coll London 1947–51, asst master Winchester Coll 1951–59, prof of mathematics Univ of Southampton 1959–66, princ Westfield Coll Univ of London 1966–83; fndr Sch Mathematics Project (SMP) 1961 (chm of Tstees 1968–83, life pres 1984); co-fndr Education 2000 1982; JP 1963–66; chm: Mgmnt Ctee Northwick Park Hosp 1970–74, Brent and Harrow AHA 1973–82, Wessex RHA 1982–88; tstee Forbes Tst 1986–, memb City Technol Colls Tst 1987–, pres Inst of Mathematics and its Applications 1967 (life fell); chm: Br False Memory Soc 1993, More House Sch 1993–96; hon prof Univ of Southampton 1983–; FIMA (pres 1966); *Books* Incompressible Aerodynamics (1960), On Teaching Mathematics (1961), The SMP: The First Ten Years (1973), Education 2000 (1983); *Recreations* sailing, music; *Clubs* Royal Over-Seas League; *Style*— Prof Sir Bryan Thwaites; ✉ Milnthorpe, Winchester, Hampshire SO22 4NF (☎ and fax 01962 852394)

THWAITES, (John Gilbert) Hugh; s of Dr John Gilbert Thwaites (d 1990), and Enid Joan, *née* Baker; *b* 24 Sept 1935; *Educ* St Andrew's Sch Eastbourne, Winchester; *m* 17 Nov 1961, Valerie Norwood, da of Norman Oscar Wright; 2 s (James Nicholas Gilbert b 30 Aug 1962, Peter Hugh b 11 Dec 1968), 1 da (Louise Catherine b 4 March 1964); *Career* Nat Serv as 2 Lt RA 1954–56; mangr Harrisons & Crosfield Ltd in India and Indonesia 1956–64; Brooke Bond Group plc: mangr Calcutta 1964–67, dir Brooke Bond Ceylon 1967–72, gen mangr Brooke Bond Kenya 1972–77, md Brooke Bond Pakistan 1977–80, dir Brooke Bond Oxo Ltd 1981–85; chm Lipton Ltd (subsid of Unilever plc) 1986–95; non-exec dir Croydon Health Authy 1990–92, chm Mayday Healthcare NHS Trust Croydon 1993–; pres UK Tea Buyers' Assoc 1983, chm UK Tea Assoc 1988–89; *Recreations* music, history, golf, sailing; *Clubs* Oriental, MCC; *Style*— Hugh Thwaites, Esq; ✉ Chailey End, Newick, E Sussex BN8 4RA (☎ 01825 722933, fax 01825 722062); Mayday Healthcare NHS Trust, Mayday Road, Croydon, Surrey CR7 7YE (☎ 0181 401 3347)

THWAITES, Ronald; QC (1987); s of Stanley Thwaites, of Stockton-on-Tees, and Aviva, *née* Cohen; *b* 21 Jan 1946; *Educ* Richard Hind Secdy Tech Sch Stockton, Grangefield GS Stockton, Kingston Coll of Technol (LLB); *m* 7 Aug 1972, Judith Adelaide Foley, da of Barry Baron Myers, of Surbiton; 3 s (George b 1973, David b 1976, Richard b 1981), 1 da (Stephanie b 1980); *Career* called to the Bar Gray's Inn 1970 (ad eundem Inner Temple 1981); *Recreations* swimming, squash, lighting bonfires; *Style*— Ronald Thwaites, Esq, QC; ✉ 10 King's Bench Walk, Temple, London EC4Y 7EB (☎ 0171 353 2501, fax 0171 353 0658)

THYKIER, Hans; s of Svend Thykier (d 1986), and Emilie Marie Johansen (d 1980); *b* 22 April 1931; *Educ* Ostre Borgerdyd Skole Copenhagen, Univ of Copenhagen; *m* 1971, Gertrud Ilona Birgitta, da of Baron Oscar Didrik Staël von Holstein (d 1969); 3 s (Lars Peter b 1958, Svend Kristoffer b 1972, Jens Caspar b 1974), 1 da (Alette Louise b 1965); *Career* A H Riise Copenhagen Denmark 1957–66, Mobil Europe Inc (in Denmark, Austria, Switzerland and the UK) 1966–71, mktg dir in Europe for Occidental

International Oil Inc 1971–74, exec dir Int Planned Parenthood Fedn (IPPF) 1974–76, American Express Co 1976–85, vice pres American Express Bank (in Europe, ME and Africa) 1983–85; dir: Foreign & Colonial Management (Jersey) Ltd 1985–88, John Govett & Co Management (Jersey) Ltd 1988–95 (now tstee), Global Stock Investments Ltd; md Nordic CIE Ltd 1996–; tstee The Help Charitable Trust; *Recreations* tennis, yachting; *Clubs* Brooks's, Oriental, Queen's, Royal Thames Yacht, Royal Danish Yacht, Danish; *Style*— Hans Thykier, Esq; ✉ 15 Abingdon Court, Abingdon Villas, London W8 (☎ 0171 937 6787); La Vielle Verrerie, F-83440 Tourettes, France

THYNE, Malcolm Tod; s of Andrew Tod Thyne (d 1982), and Margaret Melrose, *née* Davidson (d 1984); *b* 6 Nov 1942; *Educ* Leys Sch Cambridge, Clare Coll Cambridge (MA); *m* 31 July 1969, Eleanor Christine, da of James Fleming Scott (d 1995), of Edinburgh; 2 s (Douglas b 1973, Iain b 1976); *Career* asst master: Edinburgh Acad 1965–69, Oundle Sch 1969–80 (housemaster 1972–80); headmaster: St Bees Sch Cumbria 1980–88, Fettes Coll 1988–; HMC 1980; FRSE; *Books* Periodicity, Atomic Structure and Bonding (1976), contribs to Nuffield Chemistry pubns; *Recreations* mountaineering; *Style*— Malcolm Thyne, Esq, FRSE; ✉ The Lodge, Fettes College, Edinburgh EH4 1QX (☎ 0131 332 2281)

THYNNE, Jane Catherine; da of John Francis Thynne, of Wimbledon, and Rosemary Annette, *née* Carey; *b* 5 April 1961; *Educ* Lady Eleanor Holles Sch Hampton, St Anne's Coll Oxford (MA); *m* 6 April 1991, Philip Ballantyne Kerr, s of late William Kerr; 2 s (William, Charles); *Career* prodn trainee BBC TV 1985–87 (researcher BBC South 1984), news reporter Sunday Times 1987–88, media corr Daily Telegraph 1988– (joined on Peterborough diary 1988); contrib to various magazines, various radio and TV bdcasts incl newspaper reviews BBC TV, GMTV, The News Quiz and Start the Week; memb Bdcasting Press Guild 1988; fndr memb Women's Press Club 1990; *Recreations* writing, gardening; *Style*— Ms Jane Thynne; ✉ The Daily Telegraph, 1 Canada Square, Canary Wharf, London E14 5DT (☎ 0171 538 6462, fax 0171 538 7842)

TIBBER, His Hon Judge Anthony Harris; s of Maurice Tibber (d 1969), and Priscilla, *née* Deyong (d 1970); *b* 23 June 1926; *Educ* Univ Coll Sch Hampstead, Magdalen Coll Sch Brackley; *m* 1954, Rhona Ann, da of Julius Salter, and Marjorie Salter; 3 s (Peter, Clifford, Andrew); *Career* recorder Crown Court 1976, circuit judge (SE Circuit) 1977–; *Style*— His Hon Judge Tibber; ✉ c/o Edmonton County Court, Fore St, London N18 2TN (☎ 0181 807 1666, fax 0181 803 0564)

TIBBITS, Capt Sir David Stanley; kt (1976), DSC (1943); s of Hubert Tibbits (d 1933), of Warwick, and Edith Lucy, *née* Harman (d 1965); *b* 11 April 1911; *Educ* Wells House Sch Malvern Wells, RNC Dartmouth; *m* 1938, Mary Florence, da of Harry St George Butterfield, of Bermuda; 2 da; *Career* joined RN 1925, served WWII, Navigating Offr HMS York, Devonshire and Anson, started RN Radar Plotting Sch 1943, Cdr 1946, Capt 1953, Dir Radio Equipment Dept Admty 1953–56, i/c HMS Manxman, Dryad and Hermes 1956–61, ret 1961; elder bro of Trinity House 1961 (dep master and chm of Bd 1972–76), fndr chm The Pilots' Nat Pension Fund 1967–76, tstee Nat Maritime Museum 1973–77, govr Pangbourne Coll 1973–78, lay vice pres Missions to Seamen 1973–, nat hon sec King George's Fund for Sailors 1974–80, memb Bermuda Port Authy & chm Pilotage Ctee 1978–92, pres Bermuda Soc for the Blind 1978–, lay memb BDA Diocesan Synod and Cathedral Vestry 1982–88; Liveryman Worshipful Co of Shipwrights 1973 (memb Ct 1976); memb Cncl Order of St John Bermuda 1977–; CStJ 1993; FNI 1979 (fndr memb 1972); *Recreations* sailing, photography, music; *Clubs* Army and Navy, Royal Yacht Sqdn, Hurlingham, Royal Bermuda Yacht, Royal Hamilton Amateur Dinghy; *Style*— Capt Sir David Tibbits, DSC, RN; ✉ Harting Hill, PO Box HM 1419, Hamilton, Bermuda HM FX (☎ 00 1 441 295 4394, Fax 00 1 441 296 4834)

TIBBUTT, Dr David Arthur; s of Sidney Arthur William Tibbutt (d 1955), of Wadhurst, Sussex, and Dorothy Ellen, *née* Lay (d 1994); *b* 8 March 1941; *Educ* The Skinners' GS Tunbridge Wells, St Peter's Coll Oxford (MA, BM BCh, DM); *m* 26 Nov 1966, Jane, da of Air Vice-Marshal Sir George David Harvey, KBE, CB, DFC (d 1969), of Over Worton, Oxon; 2 s (Mark David b 1968, William George b 1970); *Career* jr hosp doctor United Oxford Hosp 1968–76; Worcester Royal Infirmary NHS Tst: conslt physician 1976–, med dir 1994–96; various pubns on thromboembolic disease 1974–, visiting lectr and external examiner Makerere Univ Med Sch Kampala Uganda 1965–96, post grad clinical tutor (Worcester Dist) 1987–92, RCP tutor for Worcester Dist 1987–93; memb Local Exec Ctee BMA, pres Worcester Dist Br Heart Fndn, tstee Worcestershire Hosp Charitable Tst; memb: BMA 1968, W Midlands Physicians Assoc 1976, Br Cardiac Soc 1993; FRCP 1983 (MRCP 1971), FRSM 1992; *Books* Pulmonary Embolism: Current Therapeutic Concepts (1977); *Recreations* watercolour painting, gardening, philately, enjoying Scotland; *Style*— Dr David Tibbutt; ✉ Perry Point, 4 Whittington Rd, Worcester WR5 2JU (☎ 01905 355451); Keeper's Cottage, East Kinnauld, Rogart, Sutherland; Worcester Royal Infirmary, Worcester (☎ 01905 763333)

TICKELL, Sir Crispin Charles Cervantes; GCMG (1989), KCVO (1983, MVO 1958); s of Jerrard Tickell (d 1966), and Renée Oriana, *née* Haynes (d 1992); *b* 25 Aug 1930; *Educ* Westminster (King's scholar), Christ Church Oxford (Hinchliffe and hon scholar, Gladstone Meml exhibitioner, MA); *m* 1, 1954 (m dis 1976), Chloë, da of Sir James Gunn, RA; 2 s, 1 da; m 2, 1977, Penelope Thorne Thorne, da of Dr Vernon Thorne Thorne; *Career* Coldstream Gds 1952–54; joined British Dip Serv 1954, served FO 1954–55, The Hague 1955–58, Mexico 1958–61, FO Planning Staff 1961–64, Paris 1964–70; private sec to Mins responsible for British entry into Euro Community 1970–72, head Western Orgns Dept FCO 1972–75, fell Center for Int Affairs Harvard Univ 1975–76, chef de cabinet to Pres of Cmmn of Euro Community 1977–81, visiting fell All Souls Coll Oxford 1981, British ambass to Mexico 1981–83, dep under sec of state (Economic) FCO 1983–84, permanent sec Overseas Devpt Admin 1984–87, British permanent rep to UN 1987–90; warden Green Coll Oxford 1990–, dir Green Coll Centre for Environmental Policy and Understanding 1992–; dir BOC Foundation; non-exec dir: IBM UK Holdings Ltd 1990–95 (memb Advsy Bd 1995–), Govett Mexican Horizons Investment Co Ltd 1992–96, Govett American Smaller Companies Trust 1996–; chm: Climate Inst Washington DC 1990–, Int Inst for Environment and Devpt 1990–94, Earthwatch Europe 1991–, Advsy Ctee Darwin Initiative for the Survival of Species 1992–; pres: Royal Geographical Soc 1990–93 (vice pres 1993–), Marine Biological Assoc 1990–; tstee: Natural History Museum 1992–, WWF (UK) 1993–; convenor of the Govt Panel on Sustainable Devpt 1994–; Chllr Univ of Kent at Canterbury 1996–; Hon LLD: Univ of Massachusetts USA 1990, Univ of Birmingham 1991, Univ of Bristol 1991; Hon DUniv Stirling 1990; Hon DSc: UEA 1990, Univ of Sussex 1991, Cranfield Univ 1992, Univ of Loughborough 1995, Sheffield Hallam Univ 1996; Hon DLitt Poly of Central London (now Univ of Westminster) 1990; hon fell Westminster Sch 1993; hon memb: Academia Mexicana de Derecho Internacional 1983, Orden Academica de Derecho, de la Cultura, y de la Paz 1989; Offr Order of Orange Nassau (Netherlands) 1958, Order of the Aztec Eagle with sash (Mexico) 1994; *Books* Climatic Change and World Affairs (Harvard Univ 1977, Pergamon 1978, jt revised edn 1986), The Evacuees (contrib, 1968), Life After Death (1976), The United Kingdom-The United Nations (1990), Sustaining Earth (1990), Science for the Earth (contrib, 1995); *Recreations* climatology, palaeohistory, art (especially pre Columbiana), mountains; *Clubs* Brooks's; *Style*— Sir Crispin Tickell, GCMG, KCVO; ✉ Warden's Lodgings, Green College at the Radcliffe Observatory, Oxford OX2 6HG

TICKELL, Maj-Gen Marston Eustace; CBE (1973, MBE 1955), MC (1945); s of Maj-Gen Sir Eustace Francis Tickell, KBE, CB, MC (d 1972), and Mary Violet, *née* Buszard (d 1996); *b* 18 Nov 1923; *Educ* Wellington, Peterhouse Cambridge (MA); *m* 1961, Pamela Vere, da of Vice Adm Arthur Duncan Read, CB (d 1976); *Career* RE 1944, Engr-in-Chief (Army) 1972–75, Cmdt RMCS 1975–78, ret as Maj-Gen 1978; Col-Cmdt RE, pres RE Inst 1979–82, Hon Col Engr and Tport Staff Corps 1983–88; memb Lord Chllr's Panel of Insprs 1979–93; FICE; *Recreations* sailing; *Clubs* Royal Ocean Racing, Army and Navy; *Style*— Maj-Gen Marston Tickell, CBE, MC; ✉ The Old Vicarage, Branscombe, Seaton, Devon EX12 3DW

TICKLE, Brian Percival; CB (1985); s of William Tickle, and Lucy, *née* Percival; *b* 31 Oct 1921; *Educ* The Judd Sch Tonbridge; *m* 3 March 1945, Margaret Alice (d 1994); 1 s (John b 1948), 1 da (Margaret (Mrs Schofield) b 1949); *Career* WWII RCS 1941–46; Civil Serv 1938–70; sr registrar (now called sr district judge) Family Div High Court of Justice 1982–88 (registrar 1970–82), ret 1988; co-chm Independent Schools Tbnl 1988–93; capt Nevill Golf Club 1975 (tstee 1974–); *Books* Rees Divorce Handbook (ed 1963), Atkins Court Forms and Precedents Probate (2 edn, vol 32 in 1974 and 1984 issues); *Recreations* golf, watching cricket, rugby football and other sports; *Clubs* Nevill Golf; *Style*— B P Tickle, Esq, CB; ✉ 1A Royal Chase, Tunbridge Wells, Kent, TN4 8AX

TICKTIN, Dr Stephen Jan; s of Benjamin Isaac Ticktin, of Toronto, Canada, and Syme Rebecca, *née* Slavner; *b* 30 March 1946; *Educ* Vaughan Rd Collegiate Toronto Canada, Univ of Toronto (MA, MD); *m* 2 Sept 1988, Olga Evaldovna, da of Evalid Moiseyevich Dvorkin, of Leningrad, USSR; *Career* drug dependence unit UCH 1985–89, dept of child psychiatry Central Middx Hosp 1987–91, private practice (primarily psychotherapy) 1991–; visiting lectr Regent's Coll Sch for Psychotheraphy and Counselling 1993–; London ed of Asylum magazine for democratic psychiatry; assoc memb Philadelphia Assoc; memb Soc for Existential Analysis; MRCPsych; *Recreations* American folk music, badminton; *Style*— Dr Stephen Ticktin; ✉ Flat 29, Church Garth, Pemberton Gardens, London N19 5RN (☎ 0171 272 2474); work (☎ 0171 272 9214)

TIDBURY, Sir Charles Henderson; kt (1989), DL (Hants 1989); s of late Brig O H Tidbury, MC, and Beryl, *née* Pearce; *b* 26 Jan 1926; *Educ* Eton; *m* 1950, Anne, da of late Brig Hugh Edward Russell, DSO, and Dorothy (d 1989) (who m 2, 1963, Gen Sir Richard Nugent O'Connor, KT, GCB, DSO, MC, d 1981); 2 s, 3 da; *Career* served KRRC 1944–52, Palestine 1946–48 (despatches), Queen's Westminster TA 1952–60; chm: Whitbread & Co 1978–84, Brickwoods Brewery Ltd 1966–71; dir: Whitbread & Co plc 1959–88, Whitbread Investment Co plc 1978–94, Barclays Bank plc 1978–91, Nabisco Gp Ltd 1985–88, Mercantile Credit Co Ltd 1985–91, Vaux Gp plc 1985–91, ICL Europe 1985–93, Pearl Group plc 1986–94, George Gale & Co Ltd 1991–96; dep chm INSPEC Group plc 1994–; pres: Shire Horse Soc 1986–88, Inst of Brewing 1976–78 (vice pres 1978–), Br Inst of Innkeeping 1985–92; chm: Brewers' Soc 1982–84 (vice pres 1985–), Brewing Res Fndn 1985–96, Mary Rose Tst 1980–93, William & Mary Tercentenary Tst 1985–93, Exec Bd Hampshire Enterprise Partnership 1992–; tstee Nat Maritime Museum 1984–96, memb Royal Naval Museum Devpt Ctee; govr: The Nat Heart & Chest Hosps 1988–90, Univ of Portsmouth 1988–96; memb: Centre for Policy Studies 1984–93, Portsmouth and SE Hants Health Authy and Cmmn 1992–96; chm of govrs Portsmouth HS 1992–96; Hon Asst Worshipful Co of Brewers (Master 1988–89); *Recreations* family, sailing, shooting, countryside, the sea; *Clubs* Brooks's, Royal Yacht Sqdn, Bembridge Sailing; *Style*— Sir Charles Tidbury, DL; ✉ Crocker Hill Farm, Forest Lane, Wickham, Hants PO17 5DW (☎ and fax 01329 833229)

TIDMARSH, John Alan; s of Charles Frederick Tidmarsh (d 1962), and Violet Beatrice, *née* Bishopp (d 1984); *b* 13 Aug 1928; *Educ* Cotham; *m* 29 March 1955, Patricia Charlotte, da of Gp Capt Norman Charles Pleasance (d 1943); 1 s (Patrick Charles Holden b 19 April 1962), 1 da (Emma Charlotte b 16 Nov 1960); *Career* Nat Serv RAF 1946–48, sports reporter Western Daily Press 1948–53; BBC: reporter Western Region 1953–55, TV news reporter and reader 1955–66; freelance news reporter 1966–68, presenter BBC World Service Outlook programme 1966–; memb: Geese Theatre Co of GB, Windsor Community Arts Centre; *Recreations* cricket, gardening, cooking, travel; *Clubs* MCC, BBC Bushmen Cricket; *Style*— John Tidmarsh, Esq; ✉ c/o Outlook, BBC World Service, Bush House, Strand, London WC2B 4PH (☎ 0171 257 2767)

TIDY, William Edward (Bill); *b* 9 Oct 1933; *m* 1960, Rosa; 2 s (Nick, Robert), 1 da (Sylvia); *Career* Mil Serv RE 1952–56, worked within advtg agency 1956–57, professional cartoonist 1957–; cartoon strips incl: Chelm of Tryg (Punch) 1966–67, The Cloggies (Private Eye) 1967–81, (The Listener) 1985–86, Doctor Whittle (General Practitioner) 1970–, Grimbledon Down (New Scientist) 1970–94, The Fosdyke Saga (The Daily Mirror) 1971–85, Kegbuster (What's Brewing) 1976–, The Sporting Spagthorpes (Titbits) 1976–79, Intergalatic Mirror (The Mirror Group) 1979–81, The Last Chip Shop (Private Eye) 1981–85, The Crudgingtons (Today) 1986–87, Billy Bucket (Private Eye) 1988–89, Savage Sports (The Mail On Sunday) 1988–89, God's Own County (Yorkshire Post) 1989–90; TV presenter: Weekend (Granada), Three Days Last Summer (BBC 2), Tidy Up Walsall (BBC 1), Tidy Up Naples (BBC 2), It's My City (BBC 1), Draw Me (BBC 2); numerous radio and TV guest appearances incl This Is Your Life 1975; radio presenter Tidy Answers (BBC Radio 4), several radio guest appearances; after-dinner speaker for numerous orgns incl pub cos and charities; designer of stage sets and costumes; fndr (with Sylvia Tidy) Tidy Publications Ltd 1988 (producing range of greetings and christmas cards); Granada TV's What The Papers Say Cartoonist of the Year 1974, The Soc of Strip Illustrators Award 1980; *Publications* playwright: The Great Eric Ackroyd Disaster (Oldham Coliseum), The Cloggies (Theatre Clwyd), The Fosdyke Saga (Bush Theatre and Arts Cncl tour); writer and illustrator: Laugh with Bill Tidy, Tidy's World, The Fosdyke Saga (15 vols), The World's Worst Golf Club, Robbie And The Blobbies, A Day At Cringemound School, The Incredible Bed, Draw Me 387 Baked Beans, Save Daring Waring with a Pencil?, Is There Any News of the Iceberg? (autobiog, 1995); illustrator: The Exploding Present (by John Wells), Napoleon's Retreat From Wigan (by Mike Harding), The Book of Heroic Failures (by Stephen Pile), Everbody's Doing It (by Max Hodes), Fisherman's Friend (by Bill Tidy and Derrick Geer), Rosa Tidy's Pasta Book (by Rosa Tidy), Fine Glances (by Mike Seabrook), Golfing Anthology (by Mike Seabrook), Food For All The Family (by Magnus Pike), Service Banking (by Michael Hanson), Justices of the Peace Guide to Procedure, Improving Relationships Between the Public and Civil Servants (COI), EEC Hygiene Rules on the Preparation and Serving of Foodstuffs; *Recreations* supporting Everton FC, cultivating peas and beans, watching ships and aircraft, playing cricket, looking after various dependants, furry friends and masses of goldfish; *Clubs* Cartoonists' Club of GB, Lord's Taverners, Armed Forces Benevolent Fund; *Style*— Bill Tidy, Esq; ✉ The Yews, 59 High Street, Kegworth, Derby DE74 2DA (☎ 01509 673939, fax 01509 674763)

TIERNAN, John Patrick; s of Joseph Anthony Tiernan, of Dublin, and Bridget, *née* Keogh; *b* 30 April 1958; *Educ* Trinity Coll Dublin (BDSc, BA, Sheldon Friel meml prize), RCS (Dip in Gen Practice); *m* 27 Oct 1978, Maire Eilis, da of Lt Col Alphonsis Igoe; 2 s (Mark John b 5 April 1979, David Raymond b 23 March 1982); *Career* asst in dental practice Sheerness Kent 1980–81; princ in practice: Waterlooville Hants 1981–84, Portsmouth 1983–94; clinical asst Queen Alexandra Hosp Porsmouth 1988–90; dento-legal advsr Dental Protection 1994– (pt/t 1993–94); conslt John Thompson Production 1985–94; dir: Petrie Tucker Ltd 1991–93, Domas Ltd 1992–94; GDC: memb 1991–, memb Professional Conduct Ctee 1991–93, memb Special Purposes Ctee 1991–94, memb Oral Health Educn Ctee 1991–94, memb Dental Auxiliaries Ctee 1994–95, chm Specialist Review Gp 1995–, memb Educn Ctee 1995–, memb Postgraduate Educn Ctee 1995–; BDA: memb 1981–, memb Representative Bd 1990–94, memb Cncl 1992–94, memb Wessex Branch Cncl 1990–94; Br Dental Health Fndn: memb 1983–, memb Cncl 1985–95, chm 1986, media spokesperson 1986–, dir of PR 1989–91; pres London Irish Dental Soc 1985–87 (vice pres 1984–85), chm Caring Dental Gp 1992–93; lectures extensively in the UK and internationally on both dental and after-dinner occasions; *Recreations* skiing, swimming, golf, formerly running (rep Ireland cross-country); *Style*— John Tiernan, Esq; ✉ Dental Protection, 50 Hallam Street, London W1N 6DE (☎ 0171 323 6555)

TIERNEY, Sydney; JP (1965); s of James Tierney (d 1977), and Eleanor, *née* Mould (d 1979); *b* 16 Sept 1923; *Educ* Dearne Secondary Modern Sch, Plater Coll Oxford; *m* 5 Sept 1957, Audrey (d 1981), da of Alfred Duffield; 2 da (Susan b 14 Sept 1958, Patricia b 17 April 1960); m 2, 5 Dec 1985, Margaret Olive, *née* Hannah; *Career* WWII RAF 1942–46 (served SE Asia Command, SA, Pakistan, India, Bangladesh); Trade Union organiser US DAW 1953–74, Labour MP Yardley Birmingham 1974–79, pres USDAW 1977– (nat offr 1979–87); memb Nat Exec Ctee Labour Party 1978–90, chm Labour Party 1987; *Recreations* fell walking, natural history, sport; *Style*— Sydney Tierney, Esq, JP; ✉ 56 Priory Lane, Grange Over Sands, Cumbria LA11 7BJ (☎ 05395 34935); Oakley, 188 Wilsmlow Rd, Manchester M14 6LJ (☎ 061 224 2804, fax 061 257 2566)

TIGHE, Anthony Rodger; s of Brian Anthony Michael Tighe, of Bickerstaff, Lancs, and Paula Angela, *née* Capper; *b* 9 March 1951; *Educ* St Edward's Coll Liverpool, Univ of Greenwich; *m* 1991, Rachel Suzanne, *née* Pearson; 1 c; *Career* with Berger Paints 1972–74, in family business 1974–76; Wilsons Brewery Manchester: sales force 1976–78, area sales mangr 1978–80, sales promotion mangr 1980–82, PR mangr 1982–83; head of PR Grand Metropolitan Brewing North 1983–84; Greenwood Tighe Public Relations (now part of Euro RSCG Group): fndr md 1984–88, chief exec 1988–93; fndr Mere Communication Ltd 1993–; MIPR 1984, MInstD 1988; *Awards* first winner Inst of PR Sword of Excellence for product relations 1984; *Recreations* golf, Everton FC; *Clubs* Mere Golf and Country, RAC; *Style*— Anthony Tighe, Esq; ✉ Wyecroft, Toft Road, Knutsford, Cheshire (☎ 01565 633767); Mere Communication Ltd, Tatton House, 20–22 Tipping Street, Altrincham, Cheshire WA14 2EZ (☎ 0161 928 8700)

TIKARAM, Hon Justice Sir Moti; KBE (1980), CF (1996); s of Tikaram and Singari; *b* 18 March 1925; *Educ* Marist Bros HS Suva, Victoria Univ Wellington NZ (LLB); *m* 1944, Satyawati (d 1981); 2 s, 1 da; *Career* started law practice 1954, stipendiary magistrate 1960, puisne judge 1968; acted as chief justice 1971, 1990 and 1995, ombudsman Fiji 1972–87; Court of Appeal judge 1988, pres Fiji Court of Appeal 1994–; patron: Fiji Lawn Tennis Assoc, Fiji Library Assoc, Fiji Chess Fedn; *Publications* articles in The Pacific Way, Recent Law 131, Fiji Library Assoc Jl and Commonwealth Law Bulletin; *Recreations* tennis; *Clubs* Fiji, Fiji Golf (Suva); *Style*— The Hon Justice Sir Moti Tikaram, KBE, CF; ✉ PO Box 514, 45 Domain Road, Suva, Fiji; office: PO Box 2215, Government Buildings, Suva (☎ 00 679 211489)

TILBURY, Alan George; CBE (1966, OBE 1962); s of George Tilbury (d 1945); *b* 9 Dec 1925; *Educ* Sutton Co GS, schs in Pietermaritzburg, LLB (London, external), Advocate (S Rhodesia); *m* 1949, Jean-Mary McInnes, *née* Pinkerton; 3 da; *Career* Palestine Police 1946–48, Colonial Police Serv (Kenya, Bechuanaland) 1948–54; entered Colonial Legal Serv (Bechuanaland) 1954; attorney-gen Botswana (formerly known as Bechuanaland) 1963–69; The Brewers Soc London: head Legal Dept 1970–72, dep sec 1972–82, sec 1982–90, dir 1990–92; *Recreations* sailing (yacht Arabella), listening to music, visiting France; *Clubs* UK Botswana Soc (chm), Tollesbury Cruising; *Style*— Alan Tilbury, Esq, CBE; ✉ Oakwood, Tolleshunt Major, Essex CM9 8LL (☎ 01621 860656)

TILEY, Prof John; s of William Arthur Tiley (d 1965), Audrey Ellen Tiley (d 1974); *b* 25 Feb 1941; *Educ* Winchester, Lincoln Coll Oxford (Winter Williams law scholar, MA, BCL), LLD (Cantab) 1995; *m* 1964, Jillinda Millicent, da of William Bryan Draper; 2 s (Nicholas John b 19 Dec 1966, Christopher George b 17 June 1968), 1 da (Mary Isobel b 13 Aug 1971); *Career* lectr Lincoln Coll Oxford 1963–64, lectr in law Univ of Birmingham 1964–67; Univ of Cambridge: fell Queens' Coll 1967– (vice pres 1988–96), asst lectr in law 1967–72, lectr 1972–87, reader in law of taxation 1987–90, prof of law of taxation 1990–, chm Faculty Bd of Law 1992–95; visiting prof: Dalhousie Univ 1972–73, Univ of Auckland 1973, Univ of Western Ontario 1978–79, Case Western Reserve Univ 1985–86, 1987 and 1988, Univ of Paris IX 1992–96; sr scholar Univ of Melbourne 1979; called to the Bar Inner Temple 1964, hon bencher 1993; recorder 1989– (asst recorder 1984–88); gen ed Butterworth's UK Tax Guide 1982–; author of numerous articles in pubns; *Books* A Casebook on Equity and Succession (1968), Beattie's Elements of Estate Duty (ed, 7 edn 1970, 8 edn 1974), Elements of Capital Transfer Tax (with Hayton, 1975, 2 edn 1978), Revenue Law (1976, 3 edn 1981); *Recreations* walking, listening to music, travel, visiting art galleries and museums; *Style*— Prof John Tiley; ✉ Queens' College, Cambridge CB3 9ET (☎ 01223 335511)

TILEY, Timothy Francis Thornhill; s of Rev George Edward Tiley (d 1985), and Cecilia Frances Mystica Thornhill (d 1982); descended from ancient family of Thornhill, of Thornhill in Yorkshire, which can trace continuous line of descent from saxon theign Eisulf de Thornhill (1080–1165), membs of the family of Jordan de Thornhill (s of Eisulf) are portrayed in a group of the most famous of the 13th century miracle windows in the Trinity chapel of Canterbury Cathedral; *b* 6 June 1949; *Educ* Malvern, St Peter's Coll Oxford (MA); *m* 12 Oct 1990, Margaret Reid; *Career* fndr and md Tim Tiley Ltd (publishers of philosophical and religious prints) 1978–; co-fndr of Brass Rubbing Centres: Oxford 1973, Bristol 1974, Stratford upon Avon 1974, London 1975, Edinburgh 1976, Bath 1976, Glastonbury 1977, Washington DC 1977; FInstD 1992; *Recreations* piano, reading, cycling, travelling, historical studies; *Clubs* Royal Cwlth Soc; *Style*— Timothy Tiley, Esq; ✉ 12 Salisbury Road, Redland, Bristol BS6 7AW (☎ 0117 942 3397)

TILL, David Richard; s of Henry Rheid Till, and Dorothy, *née* Smith (d 1975); *b* 27 April 1942; *Educ* Univ of Oxford (BA), Univ of London (MSc); *m* Elizabeth Mary, da of Ralph Ambrose Kekwick, FRS; 2 da (Corinna Ruth b 1970, and Isabel Sarah b 1973); *Career* maths teacher Latymer Upper Sch Hammersmith 1964–68, lectr then sr lectr in computer sci Westfield Coll then King's Coll Univ of London 1970–89; City Univ: sr lectr then reader 1989–, head of Computer Sci Dept 1991–95; *Books* Principles of Functional Programming (jtly, 1984), An Introduction to Formal Specification and Z (jtly, 1991, 2 edn 1996); *Recreations* music a consuming passion, playing piano and violin, singing in and conducting choirs, composing a little, languages (Spanish and German); *Style*— David Till, Esq; ✉ Department of Computer Science, City University, Northampton Square, London EC1V 0HB (☎ 0171 477 8552, 0171 477 8587, e-mail till@cs.city.ac.uk)

TILL, Ian Jeremy; s of Francis Oughtred Till (d 1992), of Ilkley, Yorks, and Kathleen Emily, *née* Munt; *b* 6 Sept 1938; *Educ* Ghyll Royd Sch Ilkley, The Leys Sch (scholar); *m* 25 July 1964, Caroline Elizabeth Minden, da of Ronald Minden Wilson (d 1987), of Capetown, SA; 2 s (Rodger, Rupert); *Career* CA; formerly with: Robson Rhodes, Deloitte Haskins & Sells, Crompton Parkinson, Courtaulds, Air Products; gp chief accountant Shepherd Building Group Ltd 1975–; dir The Centre for Software Engineering Ltd, dir The Shepherd Group Pension Trust Ltd; cncl memb ICAEW 1985–91, memb Jt Tax Ctee Bldg Employers' Confedn, memb Financial Reporting Panel CBI; tstee N Yorks Scanner Appeal, hon auditor Barbarians FC, govr Univ Coll of Ripon and York St John, treas St Paul's Church Holgate, memb Old Leysian Lodge, memb Ct Guild of Scriveners City of York; JDipMA, FCA; *Recreations* chess, rambling, music, financial markets; *Style*— Ian Till, Esq; ✉ 21 Hamilton Way, Acomb, York, N Yorks; Shepherd Building Group Ltd, Blue Bridge Lane, York, N Yorks

TILL, Very Rev Michael Stanley; s of Maj Stanley Brierley Till (d 1985), of Sunderland, and Charlotte Mary, *née* Pearse; *b* 19 Nov 1935; *Educ* Brighton Hove and Sussex GS, Lincoln Coll Oxford (BA), Westcott House Cambridge; *m* 1965, Theresa Sybil Henriette (Tessa), da of Capt Stephen Wentworth Roskill, CBE, DSC, RN (d 1982), of Cambridge; 1 s (Tobias b 21 April 1969), 1 da (Sophie Elizabeth b 18 May 1971); *Career* Nat Serv 2 Lt RASC HQ NID 1955–57; asst curate St Johns Wood Parish Church 1964–67, dean and fell King's Coll Cambridge 1970–81 (chaplain 1967–70), vicar All Saints Fulham 1981–86, rural dean Hammersmith and Fulham 1982–86, archdeacon of Canterbury 1986–96, dean of Winchester 1996–; memb: ABM (chm) 1975–95, General Synod 1986–96; govr: The Pilgrims' Sch Winchester, St Swithun's Sch Winchester; tstee Hosp of St Cross Winchester; *Recreations* painting, walking, art and music appreciation, building; *Style*— The Very Rev the Dean of Winchester; ✉ The Deanery, Winchester S023 9LS

TILLARD, Andrew John; s of Maj Gen Philip Blencowe Tillard, CBE (d 1994), and Patricia Susan, *née* Robertson (d 1988); *b* 19 Oct 1956; *Educ* Bradfield Coll; *m* 7 June 1986, Sarah-Jane Clare, da of Christopher Wysock-Wright; 2 da (Katie b 22 Feb 1988, Natasha b 18 Oct 1989); *Career* Sandhurst 1976, 1318 Royal Hussars 1976–80; sales and mktg exec Procter and Gamble 1980–82, sr exec International Marketing and Promotions 1982–83, md The Decisions Group 1983–; dir: Mitre plc 1992–, Telephone Preference Service Ltd 1994–96, WWAV Teleservices Ltd 1994–; memb: Br Direct Mktg Assoc, Inst of Direct Mktg; *Recreations* tennis, fishing, shooting; *Style*— Andrew Tillard, Esq; ✉ 54 Elmfield Rd, Balham, London SW17 (☎ 0181 675 9347, fax 0181 784 1001); Church House, Chailey, Sussex; The Decisions Group, Mitre House, Canbury Park Road, Kingston, Surrey KT2 6LZ (☎ 0181 784 1000, fax 0181 784 1001)

TILLER, Rev John; s of Harry Maurice Tiller (d 1992), and Lucille Tiller; *b* 22 June 1938; *Educ* St Albans Sch, ChCh Oxford (MA), Univ of Bristol (MLitt); *m* 5 Aug 1961, Ruth Alison, da of Charles Arthur Watson (d 1966); 2 s (Andrew b 1964, Jonathan b 1967), 1 da (Rachel b 1965); *Career* lectr Trinity Coll Bristol 1967–73, priest in charge Christ Church Bedford 1973–78, chief sec Advsy Cncl for the Church's Miny 1978–84, chllr and canon residentiary of Hereford Cathedral 1984–, dir of trg Diocese of Hereford 1991–; *Books* A Strategy for the Church's Ministry (1983), The Gospel Community (1987); *Style*— The Rev Canon John Tiller; ✉ Canon's House, 3 St John St, Hereford HR1 2NB (☎ 01432 265 659)

TILLETT, Michael Burn; QC (1996); s of Cyril Vernon Tillett, of Warwicks, and Norah Phyllis Tillett (d 1986); *b* 3 Sept 1942; *Educ* Marlborough, Queens' Coll Cambridge (MA); *m* 2 April 1977, Kathryn Ann, da of Dr J K Samuel; 2 da (Alexandra b 15 Nov 1978, Kirstey b 12 Aug 1980); *Career* called to the Bar Inner Temple 1965, recorder of the Crown Ct 1989–; *Recreations* riding, mountaineering, skiing, sailing; *Clubs* Hurlingham, RAC, Downhill Only, Seaview Yacht; *Style*— Michael Tillett, Esq, QC; ✉ 39 Essex Street, London WC2R 3AT (☎ 0171 583 1111, fax 0171 353 3978)

TILLEY, Andrew Raymond; s of Raymond Hugh Tilley, of Tettenhall, Wolverhampton, and Carrie, *née* Lucas; *b* 22 Sept 1956; *Educ* Regis Comp Tettenhall, Univ of Southampton (BSc, PhD); *m* 16 Nov 1990, Olwen Mary, da of James Anthony Rice, of Rugeley, Staffs; 1 da (Grace Elizabeth b 27 June 1995); 2 c from prev m (Laura Anne b 18 Sept 1983, Mark Thomas b 14 Aug 1985); *Career* water quality controller Essex Water Co 1978–79, postgrad res 1979–82; Boase Massimi Pollitt advtg: joined as trainee media planner 1982, assoc dir 1984–86, bd dir 1986–89, md BMP Solutions in Media (subsid) 1987–89; Delaney Fletcher Slaymaker Delaney & Bozell (formerly Delaney Fletcher Delaney): media planning dir Feb-Sept 1989, exec media dir Sept 1989–91, dep md Jan-Oct 1991; Zenith Media: dir of strategic planning Oct 1991–94, dep md 1994–95, md 1995–; memb Media Circle Exec 1990, MIPA 1990; *Recreations* football, cricket, photography, horse racing, collecting old maps; *Style*— Andrew Tilley, Esq; ✉ Zenith Media, Bridge House, 63–65 North Wharf Road, London W2 1LA (☎ 0171 224 8500, fax 0171 706 2650)

TILLEY, Clifford James; CBE (1981); s of Henry James Tilley (d 1952), of Burnham on Sea, Somerset, and Zenobia Ruth Tilley (d 1959); *b* 23 Oct 1911; *Educ* Wycliffe Coll, St John's Coll Oxford (BA); *m* 1936, Ingeborg Hildegard Erna, da of Dr Heinrich Hoepker (d 1958), of Berlin; 2 s (Christopher, Stephen); *Career* WWII Maj RA AA Cmd 1939–44, Staff Coll Camberley 1944, HQ Allied Land Forces Norway 1945; chm Willett & Son (Corn Merchants) Ltd Bristol 1962–88; pres: Grain & Feed Trade Assoc London 1976–77 and 1988–89, Bourse de Commerce Européenne Strasbourg 1976–78, Comité du Commerce des Céréales et des Aliments du Bétail de la Communauté Européenne Brussels 1978–79 and 1981–83 (hon pres 1983); *Recreations* travel; *Style*— Clifford Tilley, Esq, CBE; ✉ 17 Dennyview Rd, Abbots Leigh, Bristol BS8 3RD (☎ 01275 372307)

TILLEY, John Vincent; *b* 1941; *Career* former memb Wandsworth Borough Cncl; contested (Lab): Kensington & Chelsea Feb and Oct 1974, Southwark and Bermondsey 1983; MP (Lab) Lambeth Central 1978–83; memb Lambeth Police Monitoring Gp 1981–82; oppn front bench spokesman Home Affrs 1981–82 (sacked for opposing official Lab policy on Falklands crisis); chief economic advsr London Borough of Hackney 1983–88, parly sec Co-operative Union 1988–; memb: NUJ, Co-Op Pty, Fabian Soc; *Style*— John Tilley, Esq

TILLEY, Robert Alfred (Bob); s of George Edward Alfred Tilley (d 1983), and Grace Maud, *née* Payne (d 1992); *b* 29 June 1941; *Educ* Latymer Upper Sch Hammersmith, UCW Aberystwyth (BA); *m* 5 Aug 1963, Roberta Elaine, da of late Gwyn Harry; 2 da (Fiona Jane b 13 May 1967, Helen Susan b 10 July 1968); *Career* Arthur Andersen: articled clerk and CA London 1962–66, Manchester 1966–85 (ptnr 1977, managing ptnr 1980–85), managing ptnr Newcastle 1985–89; dir and chief exec The Wearside Opportunity 1989–91, regnl managing ptnr (Yorkshire) Baker Tilly 1991–94, regnl md (NE England) Understanding Industry 1994–; co cncllr (Lib) Greater Manchester Cncl 1973–77, pres The Manchester Club 1984–85 (chm 1977–78), chm W Yorks Professional Firms Gp, dir Northern Sinfonia Orch; FCA, FIMgt; *Recreations* walking, music, community affairs; *Clubs* Leeds; *Style*— Bob Tilley, Esq; ✉ High Mead, Ben Rhydding Drive, Ilkley, W Yorks LS29 8BD (☎ 01943 607582)

TILLYER, William; *b* 25 Sept 1938; *Educ* Middlesbrough Coll of Art, Slade Sch of Fine Art, Atelier 17 Paris; *Career* artist and lectr; Central Sch of Art 1964–70, Bath Acad of Art 1964–72, Watford Sch of Art 1970–73, Goldsmiths' Coll 1975–76, Loughborough Sch of Art 1975–76; visiting prof Rhode Island Sch of Brown Univ 1975–76; visiting lectr: Reading Coll of Art 1975–76, St Martin's Sch of Art 1980; artist in residence Univ of Melbourne Aust 1981–82; *Solo Exhibitions* incl: Arnolfini Gallery Bristol 1970–73, Serpentine Gallery 1971, Galerie Theodor Hoss Stuttgart 1974, Museum of Contemporary Art Utrecht 1975, ICA 1975, Sunderland Arts Centre 1975–79, Melbourne Univ Gallery Aust 1982, Jan Turner Gallery LA 1987, Smith Anderson Gallery Calif 1989, Bernard Jacobson Gallery 1989, 1991 and 1993, Wildenstein & Co 1991 and 1994, Adelson Galleries NY 1993, Andre Emmerich Gallery NY 1994, Galerie Miya Tokyo 1995, The Fluxion Paintings (Bernard Jacobson Gallery) 1996, William Tillyer 1956–1996 (The Cleveland Gallery Middlesbrough 1996 and Whitworth Art Gallery Manchester 1997); *Group Exhibitions* incl: Young Contemporaries (ICA) 1959 and 1961, Forty Christmas Trees (Arnolfini Gallery) 1972, Recent Acquisitions (V & A) 1973, Le Jeune Gravure Contemporaine (Musée d'Art Madame Paris) 1974, British Painting 1952–77

(RA, New Dehli, touring) 1977, British Art since 1960 (Kunsthalle, Lund Univ Sweden) 1979, Eight British Artists (Bernard Jacobson Gallery NY) 1980, Four British Artists (Jan Turner Gallery LA) 1988, Cleveland Gallery 1994; *Work in Collections* V & A, Arts Cncl of GB, The Br Cncl, Tate, Manchester City Art Gallery, Reading of Univ, MOMA NY, Brooklyn Art Museum NY, Boston Museum of Art, Fort Worth Art Museum Texas, Northern Arts Assoc, Museum of Contemporary Art Friedrickstad Norway, Museum of Art Lodz Poland, Museum of Contemporary Art Ultrecht Holland, Westminster Bank London, Bank of America, Univ of Melbourne, Federal Savings Bank LA, The Art Gallery of Western Aust; *Style—* William Tillyer, Esq; ✉ Bernard Jacobson Gallery, 14A Clifford Street, London W1X 1RF (☎ 0171 495 8575)

TILNEY, Dame Guinevere (Lady Tilney); DBE (1984); yst da of Sir Alfred Hamilton Grant, 12 Bt, KCSI, KCIE (d 1937); *b* 8 Sept 1916; *Educ* Westonbirt Girls Sch; *m* 1, 19 Feb 1944, Capt K Lionel Hunter, Royal Canadian Dragoons (d 1947); 1 s; m 2, 3 June 1954, Sir John Dudley Robert Tarleton Tilney, TD, JP (d 1994); *Career* former 2 Offr WRNS; former DL Lancs (later Merseyside); memb BBC Gen Advsy Cncl 1967–75, pres Nat Cncl of Women of GB 1968–70, chm Women's Nat Cmmn 1969–71, Br rep of UN Status of Women Cmmn 1970–73, co-chm Women Caring Tst 1972–75; served in private and political office of Rt Hon Margaret Thatcher 1975–83; *Recreations* writing, reading, making soup; *Style—* Dame Guinevere Tilney, DBE; ✉ 3 Victoria Sq, London SW1W 0QY

TILSON, Jake; s of Joe Tilson, of Wiltshire, and Jos, *née* Morton; *b* 14 Feb 1958; *Educ* Holland Park Sch, Chippenham GS, Chelsea Sch of Art (BA), Royal Coll of Art (MA); *m* Jennifer Elizabeth Lee, *qv*, da of Ernest McLean Bovelle Lee; 1 da (Hannah Lee Tilson b 26 May 1995); *Career* artist; lectr in communication design RCA, lectr Painting Dept Ruskin Sch of Art Oxford; Erna Plachte artist in residence The Laboratory Ruskin Sch of Drawing and Fine Art 1994–96; ed and publisher: Cipher magazine 1979–81, Atlas magazine 1985–; *Exhibitions* solo exhibitions: Xerographies 1977–83 (Galerie J et J Donguy Paris) 1983, Excavator-Barcelona-Excavador (Nigel Greenwood Gallery) 1986, One World (Warehouse London & Liverpool) 1987, Collages 1986–89 (Stylt Goteborg Sweden) 1989, How Far is an Hour (Nigel Greenwood Gallery) 1989, How Far is an Hour (Galleria Cavalino Venice Italy) 1990, The Terminator Line (Nigel Greenwood Gallery) 1990, The Terminator Line Outtakes (Printed Matter at Dia, NY) 1991; *group exhibitions* Northern Young Contemporaries (Whitworth Gallery Manchester) 1977, Ecritures (Fondation National des Arts Graphiques et Plastiques Paris) 1980, Ars Machina (La Maison de la Culture de Rennes) 1982, Paris Bienale 1982, New Media 2 (Malmo Konsthall Sweden) 1984, Copyart Biennale Barcelona 1985, Br Art & Design (Vienna) 1986, Artist as Publisher (Crafts Cncl) 1986, Rencontres Autour de la Revue Luna-Park (Centre Georges Pompidou) 1987, Br Artists' Books (Centre for the Book Arts NY) 1987, Art in Production (Manchester City Art Gallery) 1988 and 1989, Exhibition Road - 150 Years (RCA) 1988, 20 Years of Br Art from the Sackner Archive (BASS Museum Miami Florida) 1988, Atlas 3 (Nigel Greenwood Gallery) 1988, Echtzeit (Kasseler Kunstverein) 1988, Paper (Amics Tokyo) 1988, Original Copies (MOMA Kyoto Tokyo, RCA) 1990, Self Image (Design Museum) 1991, Langu(im)age (Nigel Greenwood Gallery) 1992, John Moores Exhbn Liverpool 1992, Work and Turn (Tokyo and Sweden) 1992, Stylt Germany 1993, John Moores 18 Liverpool 1993, Whitechapel Open London 1994, Looking At Words Reading Pictures London 1994, tidsvag Goteborg 1994, Artists Books Tate Gallery 1995, Networks 95; *Film and Video* Jour et Nuit (Atlas Films, 1989), Jeff and Jake Get Married (Atlas Films 1990), Put the Message in the Box (World Party, Ensign Records, 1990), Thankyou World (World Party, Ensign Records, 1991), Outtakes (Atlas Films, 1991), Dry Signals (Atlas Films, 1992); Gate 23 (Atlas audio) 1993, Foundsounds CD (Atlas) 1994, The Cooker www site 1994 *Awards* London Arts Assoc Literature grant 1980, Art Cncl Arts Publishing subsidy 1981, Unilever prize 1983, Major Travelling scholarship RCA 1983, first prize Royal Over-Seas League Exhibition 1988; *Books* artists' books incl: Light and Dark (1979), Exposure (1980), 8 Views of Paris (1980), The V Agents (1980), Excavator-Barcelona-Excavador (1986), Breakfast Special (1989), The Terminator Line (1991), Wallphone (1994); *Style—* Jake Tilson, Esq

TILSON, Joseph Charles (Joe); s of Frederick Arthur Edward Tilson (d 1973), and Ethel Stapeley Louise, *née* Saunders (d 1982); *b* 24 Aug 1928; *Educ* St Martin's Sch of Art, RCA, Br Sch at Rome; *m* 2 Aug 1956, Joslyn, da of Alistair Morton (d 1963); 1 s (Jake b 1958), 2 da (Anna Jesse b 1959, Sophy Jane b 1965); *Career* RAF 1946–49; painter, sculptor, printmaker; worked in Italy and Spain 1955–57; visiting lectr 1962–63: Slade Sch of Art, King's Coll London, Univ of Durham; teacher Sch of Visual Arts NY 1966, visiting lectr Staatliche Hochschule für Bildende Kunste Hamburg 1971–72; memb Arts Panel and Cncl 1966–71; exhibitions incl Venice Biennale 1964; work at: Marlborough Gallery 1966, Waddington Galleries; retrospective exhibitions: Boymans Van Beuningen Museum Rotterdam 1973, Vancouver Art Gallery 1979, Volterra 1983; Biennale prizes Krakow 1974 and Ljubljana 1985, subject of TV films 1963, 1968 and 1974; ARCA 1955, RA 1991 (ARA 1985); *Recreations* planting trees; *Style—* Joe Tilson, Esq, RA; ✉ c/o Theo Waddington Fine Art Ltd, 5a Cork Street, London W1X 1PB (☎ 0171 494 1584, fax 0171 287 0926); Alan Cristea Gallery, 31 Cork Street, Lonson W1X 2NU (☎ 0171 439 1866, fax 0171 734 1549)

TILT, (Robin) Richard; s of Francis Arthur Tilt (d 1988), of Malvern, Worcs, and Mary Elizabeth, *née* Ashworth; *b* 11 March 1944; *Educ* King's Sch Worcester, Univ of Nottingham (BA), Open Univ (Dip); *m* 22 Oct 1966, Kate, da of Thomas Henry and Mabel Busby; 2 s (Jonathan Richard b 12 Nov 1967, Matthew Edward b 3 Jan 1970), 1 da (Rachel Gwynedd b 20 June 1974); *Career* with HM Prison Service; asst govr HM Borstal Wellingborough 1968–71, tutor Prison Serv Staff Coll Wakefield 1971–74, govr HM Borstal Pollington 1974–75; dep govr: HM Prison Ranby 1975–78, HM Prison Gartree 1978–80; govr HM Prison Bedford 1980–82, head Manpower Section HQ 1982–84, govr HM Prison Gartree 1984–88, dep regnl dir Midlands 1988–89, head of industl rels HQ 1989–92, head of fin Police Dept 1992–94, dir of security Prison Serv 1994– (dir of servs 1994); Churchill fell 1991; *Recreations* theatre, reading, walking; *Style—* Richard Tilt; ✉ HM Prison Service Agency, Room 538, Cleland House, Page Street, London SW1P 4LN (☎ 0171 217 6703)

TIMBERS, John; s of Wilfrid Charles Timbers (d 1973), of Eastbourne, E Sussex, and Florence Majorie, *née* Clarke (d 1969); *b* 27 Jan 1933; *Educ* Monmouth Sch, St Alban's Sch, Regent St Poly Sch of Photography; *m* 1975, Belinda, da of Patrick Barr; 2 s (William b 6 Oct 1977, Thomas b 16 Oct 1980); *Career* photographer; asst to Tony Armstrong-Jones (later Lord Snowdon) 1955–60, in shared studio with Zoë Dominic 1960–85, in own studio 1985–; projects incl: film and TV work for Radio Times and other mags, corp and annual report photography for design gps; theatre work spanning 35 years starting with Orson Welles and Laurence Olivier at The Royal Court Theatre in 1960, continuing with many West End prodns and over fifty plays for the Chichester Festival Theatre; solo exhbns: Familiar Faces (Olympus Gallery) 1981, Dame Edna and Friends (RPS Bath) 1988; memb Assoc of Photographers 1971 (memb Cncl 1973–76, chm 1979–80 and 1983–84); *Books* contrib numerous books incl: Sloane Rangers Handbook (1982), Inside BBC TV (1983), A Bite Between the Teeth (Molly Parkin, 1985), various stage and TV biographies; *Recreations* cricket and conversation; *Clubs* Chelsea Arts, Invalids' Cricket; *Style—* John Timbers, Esq; ✉ John Timbers Studio, 61 St James's Drive, London SW17 7RW (☎ 0181 767 8386)

TIMBERS, Brig Kenneth Alan; s of Capt Arthur Robert Timbers (d 1942), of Woodbridge, Suffolk, and Nancy Gwendoline, *née* Smith (d 1985); *b* 11 July 1935; *Educ* Harvey GS Folkestone, RMA Sandhurst; *m* 21 Sept 1957, (Ursula) Bridget, da of Canon Eric Arthur Newman (d 1970); 2 s (Stephen b 1961, Michael b 1962), 1 da (Tricia b 1959); *Career* cmmnd RA 1956, gunnery staff course 1963–64, army staff course 1966–68, promoted Maj 1967, Lt-Col 1974, cmd 47 Field Regt RA 1976–78, GSO1 (W) HQDRA 1978–81, promoted Col 1981, project mangr 155mm Systems 1981–85, promoted Brig 1985, dir Quality Assurance 1985–88, ret 1988; hist sec of the RA Inst; dir: RA Museum, Museum of Artillery in The Rotunda, RA Medal Collection, RA Library 1988; FIMgt 1985; *Recreations* fine arts; *Style—* Brig K A Timbers; ✉ Royal Artillery Institution, Old Royal Military Academy, Woolwich, London SE18 4DN (☎ 0181 781 5623)

TIMBRELL, Christopher John; s of Sidney Benjamin Timbrell (d 1973), of Kings Heath, Birmingham, and Marion Leah, *née* Bailey (d 1976); *b* 17 July 1941; *Educ* Kings Coll Taunton; *m* 12 Sept 1967, Margaret Joy, da of Phillips William Doleman Winkley; 1 s (Philip Benjamin Christopher b 2 June 1973), 1 da (Kerstin Margaret Leah b 9 Feb 1970); *Career* articled clerk Charlton & Co CAs Birmingham 1960, mangr Newman Biggs Charlton & Co Birmingham 1972, ptnr BDO Binder Hamlyn Birmingham (formerly Josolyne Layton-Bennett & Co Birmingham) 1976 (became ptnr i/c Trust and Executorship), currently ptnr Deloitte & Touche (formerly Touche Ross) Birmingham; sr churchwarden St Philips Cathedral Birmingham 1992–; govr St John's Sch Sparkhill Birmingham 1987–, trustee various Birmingham charities; treas: The Birmingham Foundation, Birmingham Cathedral Admin Chapter 1996; memb Lunar Soc; FCA 1979 (ACA 1969), memb Soc of Tst and Estate Practitioners 1993; *Recreations* listening to music, genealogy, amateur radio licensee; *Clubs* Old Aluredian; *Style—* Christopher Timbrell, Esq; ✉ 92 Honeyborne Rd, Sutton Coldfield, West Midlands B75 6BN (☎ 0121 378 0731); Deloitte & Touche, Colmore Gate, 2 Colmore Row, Birmingham B3 2BN (☎ 0121 200 2211, fax 0121 236 1513)

TIMBURY, Dr Morag Crichton; da of William McCulloch (d 1975), of Glasgow, Scotland, and Dr Esther Sinclair, *née* Hood (d 1981); *b* 29 Sept 1930; *Educ* St Bride's Sch Helensburgh, Univ of Glasgow (MB, MD, PhD); *m* 5 Oct 1954, Dr Gerald Charles Timbury (d 1985), s of Montague Timbury (d 1980), of Glasgow; 1 da (Judith Susan (Ms McCulloch) b 16 Nov 1959); *Career* sr lectr and reader in virology Inst of Virology Glasgow, prof of bacteriology Univ of Glasgow Royal Infirmary 1978–88, head Regnl Virus Laboratory Ruchill Hosp Glasgow 1983–88, dir Central Public Health Laboratory Colindale London 1988–95; FRSE 1979, FRCP (London), FRCPath, FRCPG; memb: BMA, Soc for Gen Microbiology; *Books* Notes on Medical Virology (10 edn, 1994), Notes on Medical Bacteriology (4 edn, 1994); *Recreations* reading, theatre, military history; *Clubs* RSM; *Style—* Dr Morag Timbury, FRSE; ✉ 22 Monckton Court, Strangways Terrace, London W14 8NF (☎ 0171 602 3345)

TIMMINS, Derek John; s of Ronald Timmins (d 1979), and Ann, *née* Mulville; *b* 7 Oct 1953; *Educ* UP Holland GS, Univ of Liverpool (BM, MB BS, ChB); *Career* appointed conslt physician Liverpool Health Authy 1988; FRCP, MRCGP, DRCOG; *Recreations* music, gardening, sports, walking, photography; *Style—* Derek Timmins, Esq; ✉ The Royal Liverpool Hospital, Prescot St, Liverpool L7 8XP (☎ 0151 709 0141 ext 2088)

TIMMINS, Col John Bradford; OBE (1973), TD (1968 and bar 1974), JP (1987); s of Capt John James Timmins (d 1972); *b* 23 June 1932; *Educ* Dudley GS, Aston Univ Birmingham (MSc); *m* 1956, Jean, *née* Edwards; 5 s, 1 da; *Career* Col TA; ADC to HM The Queen 1975–80; Cdr 75 Engr Regt 1971–73, Dep Cdr 30 Engr Brigade 1973–75; Hon Col: 75 Engr Regt 1980–90, Manchester & Salford UOTC 1990–, Gtr Manchester ACF 1991–; former civil engr and chartered builder, chm Warburton Properties Ltd 1973–; pres TA & VRA for NW England and IOM 1994– (vice pres 1987–94); co pres Order of St John 1988–, Lord Lt of Gtr Manchester 1987– (High Sheriff 1986–87), Hon DSc Salford 1990; KStJ 1988; Hon RNCM 1994; *Recreations* gardening, sailing (yacht Jemma Louise); *Clubs* Army and Navy, Manchester Literary and Philosophical; *Style—* Col John Timmins, OBE, TD, JP; ✉ The Old Rectory, Warburton, Lymm, Cheshire

TIMMIS, Fiona Christine; da of David Hugh Cameron (d 1981), of Feock, Cornwall, and Irene Dorothy, *née* Simmons; *b* 9 April 1944; *Educ* Truro HS, Philippa Fawcett Coll (Univ of London CertEd); *m* 20 July 1968, William Nicholas Timmis; 2 s (William Hugh Cameron b 31 Oct 1970, Alexander James Hinchcliffe b 1 April 1973), 1 da (Leonora Charlotte Grace b 13 Oct 1976); *Career* maths teacher and form mistress Westminster City Sch 1965–70; Unicorn Sch (ind 3–11 yr olds trust sch): pt/t teacher 1971–74 and 1975–84, acting headmistress 1984–85, dep headmistress 1985–88, headmistress 1988–; memb IAPS 1988–; *Recreations* sailing, skiing, theatre, opera; *Style—* Mrs Fiona Timmis; ✉ Unicorn School, 238 Kew Road, Richmond, Surrey TW9 3JX (☎ 0181 948 3926)

TIMMS, Richard Brian; OBE (1994); s of Leslie George Timms (d 1977), of East Dean, E Sussex, and Ethel May, *née* Woolford (d 1994); *b* 2 May 1936; *Educ* Bancroft's Sch, St John's Coll Oxford (MA); *m* 1, 1964, Anne-Karin (d 1988), da of Hans Berg; 1 da (Ragnhild Katharine b 1967), 2 s (Anders Michael Berg b 1969, Eirik Richard b 1971); m 2, 1993, (Julienne) Bronwen Earle, da of Laurence Bands; *Career* Nat Serv 2 Lt Royal Artillery 1954–56; school master Westminster Sch 1960–68; British Council: asst rep Tanzania 1968–72, dir Istanbul 1972–76, rep Romania and cultural attaché Bucharest 1976–78, dir Staff Trg Dept 1978–83, rep Zambia 1983–88, dep controller Africa and ME Div 1988–91, dir S Africa 1991–94; memb: Philharmonia Chorus 1961–68, 1978–83 and 1988–91, S Africa Broadcasting Corp Choir 1992–94, Symphony Choir of Cape Town 1994–; memb Rotary Clubs: Maluba Lusaka 1983–88, Westminster West 1988–91, Johannesburg 1991–94, Hout Bay 1994–, Paul Harris fell Rotary Int 1988; S African tstee Buskaid; *Recreations* music, walking, wildlife conservation, cabinet-making, travelling, reading; *Style—* Richard Timms, Esq, OBE; ✉ 6 Leeuloop, Kein Leeukop Estate, Hout Bay, Cape Town 7800, South Africa (☎ and fax 00 27 21 790 3089)

TIMMS, Stephen Creswell; MP (Lab) Newham NE (majority 11,818); s of Ronald James Timms (d 1991), and Margaret Joyce, *née* Johnson; *b* 29 July 1955; *Educ* Farnborough GS, Emmanuel Coll Cambridge (exhibitioner, sr scholar, MA, MPhil); *m* 26 July 1986, Hui-Leng, da of C C Lim; *Career* conslt Logica Ltd 1978–86, mangr telecommunications reports Ovum Ltd 1994 (princ conslt 1986–94); MP (Lab) Newham NE 1994–, memb Treasy Select Ctee 1995–; sec: Little Ilford branch Lab Pty 1979–81, Newham NE CLP 1981–84; London Borough of Newham: cncllr 1984–, chm Planning Ctee 1987–90, ldr 1990–94; memb: E London Partnership Newham Area Bd 1990–, Stratford Devpt Partnership Bd 1992–94; hon pres Telecommunications Users' Assoc 1995–; vice chm Christian Socialist Movement; memb: Ramblers' Assoc, Plaistow Christian Fellowship, Inst of Mathematics and its Applications; *Books* Broadband Communications: The Commercial Impact (with Richard Kee, 1986), ISDN: Customer Premises Equipment (with Richard Kee, 1988), Broadband Communications: Market Strategies (with Iain Stevenson, 1992); *Recreations* walking; *Style—* Stephen Timms, Esq, MP; ✉ House of Commons, London SW1A OAA (☎ 0171 219 3000)

TIMNEY, Janet Susan Patricia (Sue); da of Maj A L Carruthers, of Dumfries, Scotland, and late Jetta Hutton; *b* 9 July 1950; *Educ* Jarrow GS, Univ of Newcastle (BA), Heriot Watt Univ, RCA (MA), RCA (MA); *m* 1, 1968 (m dis), late John Timney, s of Jack Timney, of Workington, Cumberland; 1 da (Alix b 1974); m 2, 1981, Grahame Fowler; 3 s (Louis b 1980, Max b 1984, Todd b 1986); *Career* photography and graphics 1967–71, estab Timney-Fowler partnership with Grahame Fowler 1979– (developing range of prods, retail outlets and contracts in Japan, USA and Europe); perm collections: V & A, Cooper-Hewitt Museum NY, Art Inst of Chicago; visiting lectr RCA 1979–; memb:

Textile Ctee Design Cncl, Ctee for Young Designers into Indust RSA, Scot Devpt Cncl; Roscoe award (USA) Surface Decoration Category 1988 and 1989, Textile Inst Design medal 1991; memb Interior Designers' and Decorators' Assoc 1986, FCSD 1989; *Clubs* Chelsea Arts; *Style*— Sue Timney; ✉ Timney Fowler Ltd, 388 King's Road, London SW3 5UZ (☎ 0171 352 2263, fax 0171 352 0351)

TIMOTHY, Christopher Hugh; s of Eifion Andrew Comber Timothy (d 1990), and Gwladys Marian, *née* Hailstone; *b* 14 Oct 1940; *Educ* Priory GS, Central Sch of Speech and Drama (John Gielgud scholar, Laurence Olivier Award); *m* 1; 4 s (Simon Jon, Nicholas Eifion, Robin James, David), 2 da (Tabitha Jane, Kate Elizabeth); m 2; 1 da (Grace Jane); *Career* actor; other work incl various radio plays and voice-overs for both radio and TV; *Theatre* weekly rep Worthing, 3 years with NT; roles incl: MP in Chips with Eveyrything (NY), Petruchio in Taming of the Shrew (Farnham), Brian in A Day in the Death of Joe Egg (Haymarket Leicester), Fanny in Charlie's Aunt (Theatre Royal Plymouth), Rassendyl and The King in The Prisoner of Zenda (Bromley and Chichester), Trofimov in The Cherry Orchard (Festival Theatre Chichester); West End incl: Chesney Allen in Underneath the Arches, Hibbert in Journey's End, Bernard in Happy Birthday, Rosencrantz in Rosencrantz and Guildenstern Are Dead, Walter Plinge in The Actor's Nightmare, Clive in See How They Run, Dangerous Corner; nat tours incl: The Cure For Love, The Real Thing, Moment of Weakness, Confusions, Darling Buds of May; various pantomime roles incl Robinson Crusoe (also prodr/dir, Theatre Royal Brighton) 1990–91; *Television* James Herriot in All Creatures Great and Small (series, BBC), Murder Must Advertise (Lord Peter Wimsey series, BBC), Julius Caesar, Much Ado About Nothing, Twelfth Night, Ladykillers, Galton and Simpson Playhouse, The Ronnie Barker Playhouse, Murder Most English (Flaxborough Chronicles), The Moon Shines Bright on Charlie Chaplin, Take Three Girls, Take Three Women, The Fenn Street Gang, Z-Cars, The Liver Birds, Return of the Saint; other appearances incl: Celebrity Squares, Give Us a Clue, The Two Ronnies, Call My Bluff; *Films* Othello, Here We Go Round The Mulberry Bush, The Virgin Soldiers, Alfred the Great, The Mind of Mr Soames, Spring and Port Wine, Up the Chastity Belt; co-produced and presented James Herriot's Yorkshire...the film (available on video, 1993); *Awards* Outstanding Male Personality of the Year Screenwriters' Guild 1978, BBC Personality of the Year Variety Club of GB (jtly) 1979; *Style*— Christopher Timothy, Esq; ✉ c/o Peter Froggatt, Markham & Froggatt, 4 Windmill Street, London W1T 1HF (☎ 0171 636 4412, fax 0171 637 5233)

TIMPERLEY, Dr Walter Richard; s of Capt Walter Alonzo Timperley, RAMC (d 1965), and Rosalie Mary, *née* Randles (d 1967); *b* 16 June 1936; *Educ* Oundle, Univ of Oxford (MA, BM BCh, DM); *m* 1 April 1961, Rosalind Marjorie, da of late Frederick Norman Baron; 2 da (Jane Clare b 8 Feb 1964, Anne Louise b 29 June 1965); *Career* lectr in neuropathology Univ of Manchester 1967–71, conslt neuropathologist Sheffield Health Authy 1971–, hon clinical lectr Univ of Sheffield 1971–; sec-gen World Assoc of Socs of Pathology 1993– (sometime chm Constitution and Byelaws Ctee), pres Assoc of Clinical Pathologists 1994 (memb Cncl 1984–, chm Cncl 1990–93), pres N of England Neurological Assoc 1994–95, cncl memb RCPath 1987–90 and 1993–; memb: BMA, Br Neuropathological Assoc, Int Neuropathological Soc, World Assoc of Socs of Pathology, Assoc of Br Neurologists; *Books* Neurological Complications in Clinical Haematology (1980); *Recreations* walking, photography, reading, ornithology; *Style*— Dr Walter Timperley; ✉ Department of Neuropathology, Royal Hallamshire Hospital, Glossop Road, Sheffield S10 2JF (☎ 0114 276 6222 ext 2038)

TIMPSON, John Harry Robert; OBE (1987); s of John Hubert Victor Timpson (d 1955), and Caroline Willson (d 1970); *b* 2 July 1928; *Educ* Merchant Taylors'; *m* 1951, Muriel Patricia, da of Albert Edward Whale (d 1962); 2 s (Jeremy, Nicholas); *Career* reporter Eastern Daily Press 1951–59, radio and TV reporter BBC News 1959–70, co-presenter Today programme Radio 4 1970–86, chm Any Questions? Radio 4 1984–87; Hon MA UEA 1991; *Books* Today and Yesterday (1976), The Lighter Side of Today (1983), The John Timpson Early Morning Book (1986), Timpson's England - A Look Beyond The Obvious (1987), Norwich - A Fine City (1988), Paper Trail (1989), Requiem For a Red Box (1989), Timpson's Towns of England and Wales (1989), Timpson's Travels in East Anglia (1990), Sound Track (1991), Timpson's English Eccentrics (1991), Little Trains of Britain (1992), Timpson's English Villages (1992), Timpson's Other England (1993), Timpson's Timepaths (1994), Timpson's English Country Inns (1995), Timpson's Book of Curious Days (1996); *Recreations* enjoying Norfolk; *Style*— John Timpson, Esq, OBE; ✉ Kennel House, The Green, Weasenham St Peter, King's Lynn, Norfolk PE32 2TD

TIMSON, Mrs Rodney; Penelope Anne Constance; *see:* Keith, Penelope Anne Constance

TIMSON, (Christopher) Rodney Grosvenor; s of late Albert Ernest Timson, and Mary Clare, *née* Elliott; *b* 6 July 1942; *Educ* Dean Close Sch Cheltenham; *m* Angela Susan, da of John Charles Kift; *Career* md Abbey Dropforgings Ltd 1974–82, non-exec dir T L Elliott & Co Ltd 1979–91, chm and md Tom Smith Gp 1989–96, chm Afterfield Ltd 1989–96; ind memb Parole Review Ctee Stafford Prison 1978–82, memb Br Pyrotechnists Assoc 1987–96, Royal Warrant Holder 1989–96; *Recreations* fishing, shooting, restoration of steam traction engines; *Style*— Rodney Timson, Esq; ✉ Rose Cottage, Wramplingham, Norfolk NR18 0RZ

TINDALE, Gordon Anthony; OBE (1983); s of late George Augustus Tindale, and late Olive Sarah, *née* Collier; *b* 17 March 1938; *Educ* Highgate Sch, Trinity Coll Oxford (BA), Birkbeck Coll London (MA); *m* June 1960, Sonia Mary, da of late Arthur Bertram Spencer Soper; 1 s (Stephen Christopher b March 1963), 1 da (Helen Frances b Nov 1960); *Career* Nat Serv 1956–58, 2 Lt Royal Signals, Lt reserve serv 23 SAS; language training MECAS serv in Amman Baghdad London 1961–71, Br Cncl rep Lesotho, Botswana and Swaziland 1975–78, dir Middle East Dept 1978, Br Cncl rep Lusaka Zambia 1979–83, head Mgmnt Div 1983–87, Br Cncl rep Cairo Egypt 1987–89 (asst cultural attaché 1971–74), cultural cnsllr Washington DC USA 1989–94, dir Govt and Public Affairs W H Smith (USA) Inc 1994–; *Recreations* golf, music, theatre; *Clubs* Hendon Golf, West Heath Tennis, Brooke Manor Golf (Washington DC), Washington Conversation (Washington DC); *Style*— Gordon Tindale, Esq, OBE; ✉ 23 Heath Hurst Rd, London NW3 2RU; 4450 South Park Avenue, 1619 Chevy Chase, MD 20815, USA (☎ 00 1 301 215 7132)

TINDALE, Patricia Randall; da of Thomas John Tindale (d 1986), and Princess May, *née* Uttin (d 1986); *b* 11 March 1926; *Educ* Blatchington Ct Sch, Architectural Assoc Sch of Architecture (AA Dip); *Career* architect; Miny of Educn: Welsh Dept 1949–50, Devpt Gp 1951–61; Miny of Housing and Local Govt R & D Gp 1961–72; DOE: head of Bldg Regulations Professional Div 1972–74, head Housing Devpt Directorate, dir Central Unit of the Built Environment 1980–81, chief architect 1982–86; architectural conslt 1986–, chair: Housing Design Awards 1986–93, Anchor London Housing Trust 1995–; ARIBA 1950; *Books* Housebuilding in the USA (1965), Designing Housing for Frail Elderly People (1992); *Recreations* weaving, textiles; *Clubs* Reform; *Style*— Miss Patricia Tindale; ✉ 34 Crescent Grove, London SW4 7AH (☎ 0171 622 1926)

TINDALL, Gillian Elizabeth; da of D H Tindall; *b* 4 May 1938; *Educ* Univ of Oxford (BA, MA); *m* 1963, Richard G Lansdown; 1 s; *Career* novelist/biographer/historian; freelance journalist; occasional articles and reviews for: The Observer, Guardian, New Statesman and Society, London Evening Standard, The Times, Encounter, Sunday Times, The Independent, The Telegraph, occasional broadcaster BBC; FRSL, FRSA; *Books* novels: No Name in the Street (1959), The Water and the Sound (1961), The Edge of the Paper (1963), The Youngest (1967), Someone Else (1969, 2 edn 1975), Fly Away Home (1971, Somerset Maugham Award 1972), The Traveller and His Child (1975), The Intruder (1979), Looking Forward (1983), To the City (1987), Give Them All My Love (1989), Spirit Weddings (1992); short stories: Dances of Death (1973), The China Egg and Other Stories (1981), Journey of a Lifetime (1990); biography: The Born Exile (George Gissing, 1974); other non-fiction: A Handbook on Witchcraft (1965), The Fields Beneath (1977), City of Gold: the biography of Bombay (1981), Rosamond Lehmann: an Appreciation (1985), Architecture of the British Empire (contrib, 1986), Countries of the Mind: the meaning of place to writers (1991), Célestine: Voices from a French Village (1995, Enid McLeod Prize); *Recreations* keeping house, foreign travel; *Style*— Ms Gillian Tindall, FRSL; ✉ c/o Curtis Brown Ltd, 4th Floor, Haymarket House, 28–29 Haymarket, London SW1Y 4SP (☎ 0171 396 6600, fax 0171 396 6600)

TINDLE, David; s of Ernest Edwin Cook (d 1975), and Dorothy, *née* Smith (who m 2, 1946, William Tindle, and d 1974); assumed surname of Tindle 1946; *b* 29 April 1932; *Educ* Coventry Secdy Mod Sch, Coventry Sch of Art; *m* 3 Jan 1969 (m dis 1992); 1 s, 2 da; *Career* artist: visiting tutor many art schs 1956–, tutor RCA 1972–83; Ruskin Master of Drawing and Fine Art Oxford 1985–87 (MA 1985); many one man exhibitions incl: Piccadilly Gallery 1954–83, Coventry City Art Gallery 1957, Galerie du Tours San Francisco 1964, Northern Art Gallery 1972, Fischer Fine Art 1985, 1989 and 1992, Gallery XX Hamburg 1974, 1977, 1980 and 1985, Redfern Gallery 1994 and 1996, St Edmund Hall Univ of Oxford 1994; represented in exhibitions: Royal Acad 1954, 1968 and 1970–83 (winner Johnson Wax Award 1983), Salon de la Jeune Peinture (Paris) 1967, Internationale Biennale of Realist Art (Bologna) 1967, Eros in Albion - Six English Painters (Florence) 1989; work represented at: The Tate Gallery, The Arts Cncl, Chantrey Bequest DOE, London Museum, De Beers Collection, Royal Acad, Nat Portrait Gallery; designed stage set for Tchaikovsky's Iolanta (Aldeburgh Festival) 1988; hon fell St Edmund Hall Oxford 1988; ARA 1973, RA 1979, FRCA 1981, Hon FRCA 1983; *Style*— David Tindle, Esq, RA; ✉ c/o The Royal Academy, Burlington House, Piccadilly, London W1V 0DS; Fischer Fine Art, 49 Carlton Hill, London NW8 0EL; The Redfern Gallery, 20 Cork St, London W1X 2HL

TINDLE, Sir Ray Stanley; kt (1994), CBE (1987, OBE 1974), DL (Surrey); s of John Robert Tindle (d 1975), and Maud, *née* Bilney (d 1952); *b* 8 Oct 1926; *Educ* Torquay GS, Strand Sch; *m* 8 Oct 1949, Beryl Julia, da of David Charles Ellis (d 1968); 1 s (Owen Charles b 1956); *Career* Capt Devonshire Regt 1944–47, served Far East; chm: Farnham Castle Newspapers Ltd 1969–, Tindle Newspapers Ltd, Surrey Advertiser Newspaper Holdings Ltd, Farnham Herald, Cornish Times, Cornish & Devon Post, Mid Devon Advertiser, Tenby Observer, Belfast News Letter, Abergavenny Chronicle and 100 other titles; dir Guardian & Manchester Evening News Ltd and 36 other newspaper cos; fndr Tindle Enterprise Centres for the Unemployed 1984, treas Newspaper Soc (pres 1971–72); memb Cncl Cwlth Press Union, vice pres Newspaper Press Fund, memb MMC Newspaper Panel 1987–93; chm Project Planning Sub Ctee Univ of Surrey 1964–69; life patron Small Business Bureau 1995; memb Ct of Assts Worshipful Co of Stationers and Newspaper Makers (Master 1985–86); FCIS, FCIArb; *Style*— Sir Ray Tindle, CBE, DL; ✉ Tindle Newspapers Ltd, 114–115 West St, Farnham, Surrey GU9 7HL (☎ 01252 735667, fax 01252 734007)

TINER, John Ivan; s of Kenneth Ivan Tiner, of Surrey, and Joan, *née* Benham; *b* 25 Feb 1957; *Educ* St Peter's Sch Guildford, Kingston Poly (accountancy fndn course); *m* 1978, Geraldine Marion Alison, da of James Henry Kassell; 2 s (Mark Andrew James b 1981, Matthew Paul Ivan b 1984), 1 da (Annabelle Elizabeth Mary b 1987); *Career* chartered accountant Tansley Witt (merged with Arthur Andersen) 1976–79; Arthur Andersen: joined 1979, mangr 1982, ptnr 1988–, head of fin markets 1993–, managing ptnr UK Financial Markets 1995–; ACA 1980; *Books* Accounting for Treasury Products (jtly, 1988, 2 edn 1991); *Recreations* tennis, golf, sailing; *Clubs* Mosimann's, Dear Old; *Style*— John Tiner, Esq; ✉ Arthur Andersen, 1 Surrey Street, London WC2R 2PS (☎ 0171 438 3120, fax 0171 438 2054)

TINKER, Prof Anthea Margaret; da of James Collins (d 1991), and Margaret, *née* Herring; *b* 24 Oct 1932; *Educ* Convent of Our Lady of Compassion Olton Solihull, Univ of Birmingham (BCom, William Morton meml prize), City Univ London (PhD); *m* 29 Dec 1956, Rev Prebendary Eric Tinker, OBE, *qv*, s of Frank Stanley Tinker (d 1923); 2 s (Jonathan Hugh b 27 March 1959, Andrew Michael b 14 May 1960), 1 da (Rachel Mary b 4 May 1964); *Career* asst then buyer Boxfoldia Ltd Birmingham 1953–54, HM inspr of factories 1954–58; pt/t lectr and res: Univ of Birmingham and Birmingham Sch of Planning 1958–65, Dept of Extra Mural Studies Univ of London and other London colls 1965–75 (full time res Royal Cmmn on Local Govt 1967); res fell City Univ London 1975–77, sr then princ res offr DOE 1977–88, dir Age Concern Inst of Gerontology King's Coll London 1988–, prof of social gerontology Univ of London 1989–; memb C of E Synod Working Pty on Ageing 1987–90, govr Centre for Policy on Ageing 1988–94, conslt OECD Paris 1989–94, memb Joseph Rowntree Fndn Inquiry into the Costs of Continuing Care 1994–96, expert Euro Union 1996–; memb various nat advsy ctees on ageing, scientific advsr to various Govt Depts; cncl memb Section Gerontology/Geriatrics RSM; memb: Br Soc of Gerontology, Social Res Assoc, Social Policy Assoc, Assoc for Educnl Gerontology, Royal Soc of Arts, Br Assoc; FRSM; *Books* The Non-Specialist Graduate in Industry (1954), The Inner London Education Authority (1968), Housing the Elderly: How Successful are Granny Annexes? (1976), Housing the Elderly near Relatives: Moving and Other Options (1980), Women in Housing: Access and Influence (with Marion Brion, 1980), Elderly People in Modern Society (1981, 2 edn 1984, 3 edn 1992), Families in Flats (with Judith Littlewood, 1981), Staying at Home: Helping Elderly People (1984), The Telecommunication Needs of Disabled and Elderly People (1989), An Evaluation of Very Sheltered Housing (1989), A Review of Research on Falls Among Elderly People (jtly, 1990), Falls and Elderly People: a Study of Current Professional Practice in England and Innovations Abroad (jtly, 1991), Medication in Sheltered Housing (jtly, 1992), Caring: The Importance of Third Age Carers (jtly, 1992), Life after Sixty - A Profile of Britain's Older Population (jtly, 1992), Homes and Travel: Local Life in the Third Age (jtly, 1992), The Information Needs of Elderly People (jtly, 1993), Loneliness in Old Age (ed, 1993), The Care of Frail Elderly People in the UK (jtly, 1994), Difficult to Let Sheltered Housing (jtly, 1995), Getting Around After Sixty (1996); *Recreations* social policy, family, visiting France; *Style*— Prof Anthea Tinker; ✉ 35 Theberton St, London N1 0QY (☎ 0171 359 4750); Age Concern Institute of Gerontology, King's College London, Cornwall House Annex, Waterloo Rd, London SE1 8WA (☎ 0171 872 3033, fax 0171 872 3235)

TINKER, Dr (Philip) Bernard Hague; s of Philip Tinker (d 1978), and Gertrude, *née* Hague (d 1977); *b* 1 Feb 1930; *Educ* Rochdale HS, Univ of Sheffield (BSc, PhD), Univ of Oxford (MA, DSc); *m* 27 Aug 1955, Maureen, da of Joseph Ellis (d 1952); 1 s (John Philip b 1956), 1 da (Amanda Jane b 1960); *Career* Overseas Res Serv 1955–62, Rothamsted Experimental Station 1962–65, lectr in soil sci Univ of Oxford 1965–71, prof of agric botany Univ of Leeds 1971–77, head of Soils Div and dep dir Rothamsted Experimental Station 1977–85, dir of sci NERC 1985–92, sr research assoc Plant Sci Dept Univ of Oxford 1992–; sr res fell St Cross Coll Oxford 1987–95, visiting prof Imperial Coll of Sci and Technol 1992–95; Francis New medal Fertilizer Soc 1991, Busk medal RGS 1994; FIBiol 1976, FRSC 1985, memb Norwegian Acad of Sci 1987, Hon FRAgS 1990; *Publications* Ninth Symposium of British Ecological Society (1969), Solute Movement in the Soil-Root System (1977), Endomycorrhizas (1977), Soil and Agriculture: Critical Reviews (1980), Advances in Plant Nutrition (vol I 1984, vol II 1985, vol III 1988);

Recreations gardening, map collecting; *Clubs* Farmers'; *Style—* Dr Bernard Tinker; ✉ The Glebe House, Broadwell, nr Lechlade, Glos GL7 3QS (☎ 01367 860436); Plant Science Department, University of Oxford, South Parks Rd, Oxford OX1 3RB (☎ 01865 275000, fax 01865 275060)

TINKER, Rev Prebendary Eric Franklin; OBE (1989); s of Frank Stanley Tinker (d 1923), and Margaret Louise, *née* Wiseman (d 1981); *b* 29 June 1920; *Educ* Lambrook, Radley, Exeter Coll Oxford (BA, MA), Lincoln Theol Coll; *m* 29 Dec 1956, Prof Anthea Margaret Tinker, *qv*, da of Lt Cdr James Collins, RN (d 1991), of Melton Mowbray; 2 s (Jonathan b 1959, Andrew b 1960), 1 da (Rachel b 1964); *Career* curate: Great Berkhamsted 1944, Rugby Parish Church 1946; chaplain to the Forces 1948, London sec Student Christian Movement 1949, chaplain Univ of London 1951; vicar: St James Handsworth 1955, Enfield Parish Church 1965; sr chaplain Univs and Polys in London 1969–90, dir of educn Dioceses of London and Southwark 1972–80, prebendary St Paul's Cathedral London 1969–90 (emeritus 1990); memb Middx Univ Ecumenical Chaplaincy Tst 1981– (chm 1982–94), vice chm All Saints Educnl Tst 1983–, vice chm Nikaean Ecumenical Tst 1992–, chm Islington Age Concern 1992–, memb Ctee Friends of the the Guildhall Sch of Music and Drama 1992–, memb Ct Middlesex Univ 1995–; Hon DD City Univ 1987, Hon DD Univ of London 1989, Hon DUniv Middx Univ 1993; Freeman City of London 1980; *Style—* The Rev Prebendary Eric Tinker, OBE; ✉ 35 Theberton Street, London N1 0QY (☎ 0171 359 4750)

TINKER, Dr Jack; s of Lawrence Schofield Tinker (d 1980), and Jessie, *née* Keenesmith (d 1957); *b* 20 Jan 1936; *Educ* Eccles GS, Univ of Manchester (MB ChB, BSc), Imperial Coll London (DIC); *m* 26 July 1961, Maureen Ann, da of Capt Wilfred Crawford (d 1963); 2 s (Andrew b 1963, Alastair b 1964); *Career* Middx Hosp: dir in intensive therapy 1974–88, postgrad sub-dean Med Sch 1979–85, hon conslt physician 1988–96; dean of postgrad med Univ of London 1988–96, hon sr clinical lectr UCL and Middx Sch of Med 1988–96, emeritus conslt physician UCHL 1996; sr med conslt Sun Life of Canada 1981–, med conslt RTZ Corporation 1985–, ed in chief Br Jl of Hosp Med 1985–; hon sub dean RSM 1996; FRCP, FRCS(Glas); *Books* A Course in Intensive Therapy Nursing (1980), Care of the Critically Ill Patient (1985, 2 edn 1991), A Pocket Book for Intensive Care (1986, 2 edn 1989), Critical Care: Standards, Audit, Ethics (1996); *Recreations* watching cricket, road running; *Clubs* RAC, Scarborough Cricket, MCC; *Style—* Dr Jack Tinker; ✉ 1 Rectory Road, Barnes, London SW13 9HH

TINNISWOOD, Peter; s of Thomas Henry Bismark Tinniswood (d 1985), and May, *née* Broley (d 1995); *b* 21 Dec 1936; *Educ* Sale Co GS for Boys, Univ of Manchester (BA); *m* 1981, Liz Goulding, da of James Callaghan; 2 s (Stephen, David), 2 da (Victoria, Beth); *Career* journalist: Sheffield Star, Liverpool Echo, Western Mail; writer; winner: Winifred Holtby Prize, Sony Award, Giles Cooper Award, Writers' Guild Comedy Award; memb: Writers' Guild, Soc of Authors; FRSL; *Books* novels incl: A Touch of Daniel, Mog, The Stirk of Stirk, I Didn't Know You Cared, Tales From a Long Room, Except You're A Bird, Hayballs, Winston, Tales From A Long Room, Witney Scrotum, Pen Pals, The Wireless Lady; *Radio Plays* incl: The Village Fete, The Sitter, A Small Union, Winston (series), The Governor's Consort; *Radio Documentaries* Tinniswood About, Tinniswood's Sporting Lives, Tinniswood's Authorised History of MCC; *Stage Plays* incl: Wilfred, The Day War Broke Out, You Should See Us Now, The Investiture, At the End of the Day, The Village Feter, Napolia Milionarie; *TV Plays* incl: The Day War Broke Out, Stoker Leishman's Diaries, The Home Front (series); *TV Comedy Series* incl: I Didn't Know You Cared, Tales from a Long Room, South of the Border; *TV Drama Documentary* Tinniswood's North Country; *Recreations* watching cricket, travel; *Style—* Peter Tinniswood, Esq; ✉ c/o Jonathan Clowes, Iron Bridge House, Bridge Approach, London NW1 8BD (☎ 0171 722 7674, fax 0171 722 7677)

TINSTON, Robert Sydney; s of Sydney James Tinston (d 1985), of Margaret Hester, *née* Jardine; *b* 29 March 1951; *Educ* Stockport Sch, Univ of Edinburgh (BSc); *m* 1975, Catherine Mary, da of John Joseph Somers; 1 da (Helen Catherine b 8 Feb 1978), 1 s (James Robert b 11 Sept 1979); *Career* asst sector admin: Withington Hosp Manchester 1976–78, KCH London 1978–79; hosp sec Cookridge Hosp Leeds 1979–83, gen mangr General Infirmary Leeds 1986–89 (commissioning offr 1983–86), chief exec Royal Liverpoool Univ Hosp 1989–91, dep chief exec Mersey RHA 1991–93, chief exec NW RHA 1993–96, regnl dir NHS Exec North West 1996–; visiting prof Univ of Manchester; MHSM (DipHSM) 1979; FRSA 1994; *Recreations* astronomy, genealogy, Stockport County FC; *Style—* Robert Tinston, Esq; ✉ The Thatched Cottage, Utkinton, Tarporley, Cheshire CW6 0LL; North Western Regional Health Authority, Birchwood Boulevard, Millenium Park, Warrington WA3 7QN (☎ 01925 704000)

TINTON, Stephen Christopher Ben (Steve); s of Ben Howard Tinton, and Joan Wanda Tinton; *b* 19 July 1948; *Educ* Royal GS High Wycombe, St Catharine's Coll Cambridge (BA); *m* 9 Dec 1972, Dr Marilyn Margaret, da of John Reginald St George Stead, FRCS, of Highcliffe, Dorset; 1 s (Paul b 27 May 1980), 1 da (Sarah b 24 June 1978); *Career* teacher Dehra Dun India 1967; audit and business advsy ptnr Price Waterhouse 1982– (audit mangr 1976–82); *Recreations* sport, music, theatre; *Clubs* RAC; *Style—* Steve Tinton, Esq; ✉ Price Waterhouse, Thames Court, Victoria Street, Windsor SL4 1HB (☎ 01753 752000)

TIPPET, Vice Adm Sir Anthony Sanders; KCB (1984); s of W Tippet and H W Kitley, *née* Sanders; *b* 2 Oct 1928; *Educ* W Buckland Sch Devon; *m* 1950, Lola, *née* Bassett; 2 s (1 s decd), 1 da; *Career* RN 1946, Rear Adm 1979, Asst Chief of Fleet Support MOD 1979–81, Chief Naval Supply and Secretariat Offr 1981–83, Flag Offr and Port Adm Portsmouth 1981–83, Vice Adm 1983, Chief of Fleet Support 1983–87; called to the Bar Gray's Inn 1958; gen mangr Hosps for Sick Children London 1987, chief exec Great Ormond Street Hosp for Children NHS Tst 1994–95; chm: Bd of Govrs W Buckland Sch 1989–95, Nat Appeal for Music Therapy 1995–96, Children in Hospital, Write Away, RN Benevolent Soc; memb: RN Sailing Assoc, Anchorites, RN Assoc; hon fell: Inst of Child Health, Univ of the S Bank; CIMgt; *Style—* Vice Adm Sir Anthony Tippet, KCB; ✉ c/o Barclays Bank, 46 North St, Taunton TA1 1LZ

TIPPETT, Sir Michael Kemp; KBE (1966, CBE 1959), OM (1983), CH (1979); s of late Henry William Tippett; *b* 2 Jan 1905; *Educ* Stamford Sch, RCM; *Career* composer; RCM 1923–28, private lessons with RO Morris 1930, dir of music Morley Coll London 1940–51, artistic dir Bath Festival 1969–74, pres London Coll of Music 1983–; imprisoned for 3 months as conscientious objector Wormwood Scrubs 1943, pres Peace Pledge Union, hon pres Bath CND; works incl: String Quartets 1–5, Piano Sonatas 1–4, Symphonies 1–4, The Rose Lake 1991–93; operas: The Midsummer Marriage 1947–52, King Priam 1958–61, The Knot Garden 1966–70, The Ice Break 1973–76, New Year 1985–88; choral works incl: A Child of Our Time 1939–41, The Vision of St Augustine 1965, The Mask of Time 1980–82, Byzantium 1988–89; chamber works: Sonata for Four Horns 1955, The Blue Guitar 1982; brass: Festal Brass with Blues 1983; hon pres Nat Music Cncl; Hon DMus: Univ of Cambridge 1964, Trinity Coll Dublin 1964, Univ of Leeds 1965, Univ of Oxford 1967, Univ of Leicester 1968, Univ of Wales 1968, Univ of Bristol 1970, Univ of London 1975, Univ of Sheffield 1976, Univ of Birmingham 1976, Univ of Lancaster 1977, Univ of Liverpool 1981, RCM 1982, Melbourne Univ 1984, Univ of Keele 1986, Univ of Aberdeen 1987, Univ of Hartford USA 1989, Univ of Western Australia 1990; Hon DHL Albany USA 1991; memb: Akademie der Künste Berlin 1976, American Acad of Arts and Letters 1976; Gold Medal Royal Philharmonic Soc 1976, Prix de Composition (Monaco) 1984, Lifetime Achievement Gramophone Award 1995, Lifetime Achievement Award Assoc of Br Orchestras 1996; Cdr de l'Ordre des Arts et des Lettres (France) 1988; Hon Freeman Worshipful Co of Musicians; FRCM 1991; *Books* Moving into Aquarius (1974), Music of the Angels (1980), Those Twentieth Century Blues (1991), Tippett on Music (1995); *Style—* Sir Michael Tippett, KBE, OM, CH; ✉ 5 Thirsk Road, London SW11 5SU (☎ 0171 228 0465, fax 0171 738 2790, e-mail knot.garden@argonet.co.uk)

TIPPING, Simon Patrick (Paddy); MP (Lab) Sherwood (majority 2,910); s of late John Tipping, and late Joan Tipping; *b* 24 Oct 1949; *Educ* Hipperholme GS W Yorks, Univ of Nottingham (BA, MA); *m* 8 Jan 1970, Irene Margaret, *née* Quinn; 2 da; *Career* social worker Notts 1972–79, project ldr Church of England Children's Soc Nottingham 1979–83, cncllr Notts CC 1981–93 (sometime chm Fin Ctee); Parly candidate (Lab) Rushcliffe 1987, MP (Lab) Sherwood 1992–; dir: Notts Co-operative Devpt Agency 1983–93, Nottingham Devpt Enterprise; memb: UNISON, Co-op Pty; *Recreations* family, gardening, running; *Clubs* Clipstone Miners' Welfare; *Style—* Paddy Tipping, Esq, MP; ✉ House of Commons, London SW1A 0AA

TIPTAFT, David Howard Palmer; CBE (1992), JP (1972); s of C Paxman Tiptaft, MC, JP (d 1984), of Wentworth, S Yorks, and Irene, *née* Palmer (d 1968); *b* 6 Jan 1938; *Educ* Goldsborough Hall N Yorks, Shrewsbury; *m* 1 June 1963, Jennifer Cherry, da of Gerald Richard Millward (d 1967); 2 s (Justyn b 30 Sept 1965, Quintin b 19 June 1970), 2 da (Elgiva b 10 March 1964, Genovefa b 20 Dec 1966); *Career* qualified CA 1962, Arthur Young 1961–64, princ Tiptaft Smith & Co 1966–; chm Don Valley Cons Assoc 1964–75, treas Rother Valley Cons Assoc 1976–83, chm Wentworth Cons Assoc 1983–92, chm Yorks Area Conservatives 1993–96 (treas 1988–93); memb Redundant Churches Uses Ctee Sheffield Diocese; FCA 1973; *Recreations* flying, tennis, opera, Wagner, horticulture; *Clubs* Carlton; *Style—* David Tiptaft, Esq, CBE, JP; ✉ Ashcroft House, Wentworth, nr Rotherham, S Yorks (☎ 01226 742972); Tiptaft Smith and Co, Montagu Chambers, Montagu Square, Mexborough, S Yorks (☎ 01709 582991)

TISHLER, Gillian; da of Harry Tishler, of Ponteland, Northumberland, and Joyce, *née* Andrews; *b* 27 March 1958; *Educ* St Anne's Coll Oxford (BA); *m* 8 June 1991, Richard Wood; *Career* fast stream trainee rising to private sec to Junior Min MAFF 1979–87, Parly offr rising to head of public affrs RNIB 1987–93, chief exec YWCA of GB 1993–; *Style—* Ms Gillian Tishler; ✉ YWCA of Great Britain, Clarendon House, 52 Cornmarket Street, Oxford OX1 3EJ (☎ 01865 726110)

TITCHELL, John; s of Arthur Titchell (d 1980), and Elsie, *née* Catt (d 1970); *b* 6 Aug 1926; *Educ* Sidcup Sch of Art, RCA (ARCA); *m* 1947, Audrey, da of Victor Ward; 1 s (Timothy b 18 April 1948), 1 da (Joanna b 20 May 1954); *Career* artist; RA 1993 (ARA 1986); *Recreations* music and books; *Style—* John Titchell, Esq, RA; ✉ c/o Royal Academy of Arts, Burlington House, Piccadilly, London W1V 0DS

TITCHMARSH, Alan Fred; s of Alan Titchmarsh (d 1986), of Ilkley, Yorkshire, and Bessie, *née* Hardisty; *b* 2 May 1949; *Educ* Shipley Art and Tech Inst, Hertfordshire Coll of Agriculture and Horticulture (Nat Cert Horticulture), Royal Botanic Gardens Kew (Dip in Horticulture, Sir Joseph Hooker prize, Keith Jones Cup for public speaking); *m* 1975, Alison Margaret, da of Geoffrey Herbert Needs; 2 da (Polly Alexandra b 1980, Camilla Rose b 1982); *Career* apprentice gardener Parks Dept Ilkley Urban District Cncl 1964–68, staff training supervisor Royal Botanic Gardens Kew 1972–74, asst ed Gardening Books Hamlyn Publishing Group 1974–76, dep ed Amateur Gardening magazine 1978–79 (asst ed 1976–78); freelance writer, presenter, interviewer and broadcaster 1979–; BBC Radio progs: You and Yours 1975–82, Down to Earth 1982–89, A House In A Garden 1987–91, Radio 2 Arts Prog 1990–; presenter BBC TV progs: Nationwide (gardening expert) 1980–83, Breakfast Time (gardening expert) 1983–86, The Chelsea Flower Show 1983–, Open Air 1986–87, Daytime Live 1987–90, Grow Biz Quiz 1989, Songs of Praise 1989–94, More Than Meets The Eye 1990, Scene Today 1990, Pebble Mill 1991–96, Titchmarsh's Travels 1991, Titchmarsh On Song 1992, Sweet Inspiration 1993–94, Gardeners' World 1996–; presenter Down by the River (Meridian) 1994–95; gardening corr: Woman's Own 1982–85, Daily Mail 1986–, Radio Times 1996–; gardening ed Homes and Gardens 1985–89; winner of: Gardening Writer of the Year 1980 and 1983, Royal Horticultural Soc's Gold Medal Chelsea Flower Show 1985; pres Gardening for Disabled Tst 1989–, pres Telephones for the Blind 1993–, vice pres Wessex Cancer Tst 1988–, patron Rainbow Tst 1993–; Freeman City of London 1989, Liveryman Worshipful Co of Gardeners 1989; MIHort; *Books* incl: Gardening Under Cover (1979), Climbers and Wall Plants (1980), Gardening Techniques (1981), The Allotment Gardener's Handbook (1982), The Rock Gardener's Handbook (1983), Supergardener (1983), Alan Titchmarsh's Avant-Gardening (1984 and 1994), Daytime Live Gardening Book (1990), The English River (1993), Alan Titchmarsh's Favourite Gardens (1995); *Recreations* theatre, reading, gardening, boating, riding; *Clubs* Lord's Taverners, Birmingham Press; *Style—* Alan Titchmarsh, Esq; ✉ c/o Arlington Enterprises, 1–3 Charlotte St, London W1P 1HD (☎ 0171 580 0702)

TITCOMB, (Simon) James; s of Geoffrey Cowley Baden Titcomb (d 1960), of Brighton, and Molly Gwendolyn Titcomb (d 1985); *b* 10 July 1931; *Educ* Brighton Coll; *m* 1957, Ann Constance, da of Gerald Bernard Vokins (d 1987); 2 s (Clive b 1958, Mark b 1962), 1 da (Clarissa b 1965); *Career* Lt Nat Serv 1955–57; memb Stock Exchange 1962, ptnr de Zoete & Bevan (Stockbrokers) 1962–86 (sr ptnr 1976–86); dir of various public and private companies; FCA, CIMgt; *Recreations* golf, bridge, travel, wildlife; *Clubs* Brooks's, City of London, Piltdown Golf, E Sussex National Golf; *Style—* James Titcomb, Esq; ✉ Plummerden House, Lindfield, W Sussex RH16 2QS (☎ 01444 482117)

TITE, Prof Michael Stanley; s of Arthur Robert Tite (d 1985), and Evelyn Francis Violet, *née* Endersby (d 1971); *b* 9 Nov 1938; *Educ* Trinity Sch of John Whitgift Croydon, ChCh Oxford (exhibitioner, MA, DPhil); *m* 10 June 1967, Virgina Byng, da of Rear Adm Gambier John Byng Noel, CB (d 1995), of Woodpeckers, Church Lane, Haslemere, Surrey; 2 da (Sarah Beatrice b 1970, Alice Evelyn Byng b 1972); *Career* ICI res fell Univ of Leeds 1964–67, lectr Univ of Essex 1967–75, keeper Res Laboratory British Museum 1975–89, Edward Hall prof of archaeological sci Univ of Oxford 1989–; fell Linacre Coll Oxford; fell Int Inst for Conservation (FIIC) 1990, FSA 1977; *Books* Methods of Physical Examination in Archaeology (1972); *Recreations* walking, gardening, travel; *Style—* Prof Michael Tite, FSA; ✉ Research Laboratory for Archaeology and the History of Art, 6 Keble Rd, Oxford OX1 3QJ (☎ 01865 515211)

TITE, Nicholas William Spencer (Nick); s of William Timpson Tite (d 1970), and Stephanie Frances, *née* Spencer; *b* 29 July 1950; *Educ* Wellingborough Sch, Northampton Sch of Art (travelling scholar), Winchester Sch of Art (DipAD, first year painting prize); *Career* Studio Prints Queen's Crescent London 1974–76, etching technician Central Sch of Art 1976–78, Editions Alecto (working on Tom Phillips's Dante's Inferno) 1978, creation of Talfourd Press (prodn controller Tom Phillips's Dante's Inferno) 1980–83, ed RA Magazine 1983–; responsible for exhibitions in Friends' Room at Royal Acad incl: Ghika, Bryan Kneale, Carel Weight, S W Hayter, Leonard McComb, RAs Through the Lens, Etchings by Academicians 1988–; *Recreations* cricket; *Clubs* Groucho; *Style—* Nick Tite, Esq; ✉ RA Magazine, Royal Academy of Arts, Burlington House, London W1V 0DS (☎ 0171 494 5659, fax 0171 287 9023)

TITHERIDGE, Roger Noel; QC; s of Jack George Ralph Titheridge (d 1959), of Havant, Hants, and Mabel, *née* Steains (d 1964); *b* 21 Dec 1928; *Educ* Midhurst GS, Merton Coll Oxford (exhibitioner, MA); *m* 30 May 1963, Annabel Maureen (Ann), da of Cyril Digby Scott-Fisher (d 1961), of Chelsea, London; 2 da (Lucinda Ann b 22 May 1964, Jane Emma b 7 April 1966); *Career* called to the Bar Gray's Inn 1954, bencher 1985, head of chambers; asst/dep recorder Southampton Quarter Sessions 1967–71, recorder of the

Crown Court 1972–, dep High Court judge 1984–, ldr Western Circuit 1989–92; *Recreations* sailing, tennis; *Style—* Roger Titheridge, Esq, QC; ✉ 13 The Moat, Traps Lane, New Malden, Surrey KT3 4SB (☎ 0181 942 2747); 1 Paper Buildings, Temple, London EC4Y 7EP (☎ 0171 353 3728, fax 0171 353 2911)

TITLEY, Gary; MEP (Lab) Gtr Manchester West (majority 56,635); s of Wilfred James Titley, and Joyce Lillian Titley; *b* 19 Jan 1950; *Educ* Univ of York (BA, PGCE); *m* 1975, Maria (Charo) Rosario; 1 s (Adam), 1 da (Samantha); *Career* various positions until 1973 incl: bus conductor, delivery driver, postman, security guard, labourer and barman; TEFL Bilbao 1973–75, history teacher Earls High Sch Halesowen 1976–84; campaign mangr to Terry Pitt MEP (and later John Bird MEP) 1983–89; Parly candidate (Lab): Bromsgrove 1983, Dudley West 1987; memb Bolton West CLP; memb West Midlands CC 1981–86: vice chm Econ Devpt Ctee 1981–84, vice chm Consumer Servs Ctee 1984–86; MEP (Lab) Greater Manchester West 1989–; Euro Parliament activities: memb External Rels Ctee, memb Foreign Affrs Ctee, memb S American Delgn, memb Delgn for Rels with Finland, Socialist Group spokesman on EFTA rels, pres European Economic Area Jt Parly Assembly; dir W Midlands Enterprise Bd 1982–89, vice-chair Euro Parly Delgn for Rels with Czech Republic, rapportuer on Finland's accession to EU 1995; chm: W Midlands Co-op Finance Co 1982–89, Black Country Co-op Development Agency 1982–88; Cdr Order of the White Rose of Finland; *Recreations* family, reading, sport; *Clubs* Halesowen Lab (W Midlands), Springvale Sports and Social (Bilston), Little Lever (Bolton); *Style—* Gary Titley, Esq, MEP; ✉ 16 Spring Lane, Radcliffe, Manchester M26 9TQ (☎ 0161 724 4008)

TITMAN, Sir John Edward Powis; KCVO (1991, CVO 1982, LVO 1966, MVO 1957), JP (Surrey 1971), DL (Surrey 1991); s of Sir George Alfred Titman, CBE, MVO (d 1980), and Eva Ellen, *née* Comfort (d 1987); *b* 23 May 1926; *Educ* City of London Sch; *m* 1953, Annabel Clare, da of late C F Naylor; 2 s; *Career* sec The Lord Chamberlain's Office 1978–91, Serjeant at Arms to HM The Queen 1982–91; Liveryman Worshipful Co of Wax Chandlers (Master 1984); *Clubs* RAC, MCC; *Style—* Sir John Titman, KCVO, JP, DL; ✉ Friars Garth, The Parade, Epsom, Surrey (☎ 0137 272 2302)

TITTERINGTON, David Michael; s of Geoffrey Bridge Titterington, of Beverley, East Yorks, and Claire Elizabeth, *née* Parsons; *b* 10 Jan 1958; *Educ* Northern Sch of Music, Pembroke Coll Oxford (MA, organ scholar), Conservatoire Rueil-Malmaison Paris; *Career* organist; debut Royal Festival Hall 1986; concert and concerto performances at major festivals and venues worldwide incl: Bicentennial Festival of Sydney 1988 and festivals of Hong Kong, New Zealand, Istanbul, Schleswig-Holstein, Cheltenham, Adelaide and Israel; prom debut 1990; orchestras played with incl: BBC Scottish Symphony, Bournemouth Sinfonietta, English Sinfonia, Berlin Symphony, Lahti Symphony; has given masterclasses internationally; numerous recordings made incl complete works of César Franck (for BBC), also recorded for Hyperion Records, Multisonic and ASV; world premiere performances incl: Petr Eben's Job 1986, Naji Hakim's Rubaiyat 1990, Diana Burrell's Arched Forms with Bells (Proms cmmn) 1990; artistic dir Euro Organ Festival 1992; Royal Acad of Music: prof of organ 1990–, head of organ studies 1996–; gen ed organ repertoire series United Music Publishers London 1987–; Ian Fleming award 1983, French Government Scholarship 1983–84, Arts Council Bursary 1984, Premier Prix 1984, Prix d'Excellence 1985 (Rueil-Malmaison Conservatoire, Paris); memb: Royal Philharmonic Soc 1992, Royal Soc of Musicians of GB 1996; hon fell Bolton Inst of HE 1992; Hon ARAM 1994; *Style—* David Titterington, Esq; ✉ c/o Denny Lyster Artists' Management, 25 Courthope Road, London NW3 2LE (☎ 0171 485 5932, fax 0171 267 0179)

TIZARD, Prof Barbara Patricia; *née* Parker; da of Herbert Parker, and Elsie, *née* Kirk, sis to His Honour Judge Michael Clynes Parker, *qv*; *b* 16 April 1926; *Educ* St Paul's, Somerville Coll Oxford (BA), Inst of Psychiatry London (PhD); *m* 15 Dec 1947, Prof Jack Tizard (d 1979), s of John Marsh Tizard, of Stratford, NZ; 3 s (William b 3 Jan 1951, John b 10 Dec 1952, d 1983, Martin b 17 Nov 1966, d 1975), 2 da (Jenny b 17 Dec 1955, Lucy b 26 Jan 1968); *Career* co ed Br Jl of Psychology 1975–, memb Editorial Bd Jl of Child Psychology and Psychiatry, reader in educn Inst of Educn London 1978–80, dir Thomas Coram Res Unit 1980–90, prof of educn Univ of London 1982–90 (emeritus prof 1990); former chm Assoc of Child Psychology and Psychiatry; FBPsS; *Publications* Early Childhood Education (1975), Adoption - A Second Chance (1977), Involving Parents in Nursery and Infant Schools (1981), Young Children Learning (with M Hughes, 1984), Young Children at School in the Inner City (with P Blatchford, J Burke, C Farquhar, I Plewis 1988), Black, White or Mixed Race? (with Ann Phoenix, 1993); *Style—* Prof Barbara Tizard; ✉ Institute of Education, 27 Woburn Square, London WC1H OAA (☎ 0171 612 6957, fax 0171 612 6927)

TIZARD, Dame Catherine Anne; GCMG (1990), GCVO (1995), DBE (1985); da of Neil Maclean, and Helen Maclean; *b* 4 April 1931; *Educ* Matamata Coll, Univ of Auckland (BA); *m* 1951 (m dis 1983), Rt Hon Robert James Tizard; 1 s (Nigel Robert), 3 da (Anne Frances, Linda Catherine, Judith Ngaire); *Career* sr tutor in zoology Univ of Auckland 1963–83; JP 1980; memb Auckland City Cncl 1971–83, Mayor of Auckland 1983–90, Govr Gen NZ 1990–96; occasional radio, TV and newspaper commentator; Winston Churchill fell 1981; former memb: Cncl of Auckland War Meml Museum and Inst, Auckland City Art Gallery Bd of Mgmnt, Auckland Theatre Tst, ASB Community Tsts, Auckland Maritime Museum Tst, Eastern Secdy Schs Bd of Govrs, Auckland Teachers Coll Cncl, Univ of Auckland Cncl; Hon Freeman Worshipful Co of Butchers; Hon LLD Univ of Auckland 1992; Prior OStJ (NZ) 1990, NZ 1990 medal; *Style—* Dame Catherine Tizard, GCMG, GCVO, DBE; ✉ 12A Wallace Street, Herne Bay, Auckland, New Zealand

TOALSTER, John Raymond; s of Chief Petty Offr John Edward Toalster, RNVR (ka 1944), and Adeline Enid, *née* Smith; *b* 12 March 1941; *Educ* Kingston HS Hull N Humberside, LSE (BSc); *m* 21 Sept 1963, Christine Anne, da of Edward Percy Paget (d 1970); 1 s (Quentin Simon Edward b 1966), 2 da (Rachel Jane b 1969, Bethan Claire b 1981); *Career* lectr in economics Univ of Sierra Leone 1964–67, corp planner Mobil Oil 1967–69, sr analyst (oils) stockbroking 1970–77, corporate fin mangr Kuwait International Investment Co 1977–81, energy specialist stockbroking 1982–90; dir: Hoare Govett 1982–90, Security Pacific, Société General Strauss Turnbull 1990–; FInstPet 1988; private circulation to clients; *Recreations* swimming, sailing, badminton; *Style—* John Toalster, Esq; ✉ Fig St Farm, Sevenoaks, Kent (☎ 01732 453357); Société General Strauss Turnbull, Exchange House, Primrose St, London EC2A (☎ 0171 638 5699, fax 0171 588 1437)

TOBIAS, Dr Jeffrey Stewart; s of Gerald Joseph Tobias, of Bournemouth, and Sylvia, *née* Pearlberg; *b* 4 Dec 1946; *Educ* Hendon GS, Gonville and Caius Coll Cambridge (MA, MD), St Bartholomew's Hosp Med Sch; *m* 16 Nov 1973, Dr Gabriela Jill Jaecker, da of Hans Jaecker, of Crowborough, Sussex; 2 s (Benjamin Alexander b 1980, Max William Solomon b 1983), 1 da (Katharine Deborah b 1978); *Career* sr house offr Bart's, UCH and Hammersmith Hosp 1972–73, fell in med (oncology) Harvard Med Sch 1974–75, sr registrar Royal Marsden Hosp and Inst of Cancer Research 1976–80, conslt clinical oncology UCH and Middlesex Hosps London 1981–, clinical dir Meyerstein Inst of Oncology 1992–; hon sec Br Oncological Assoc 1985–90, chm UK Co-ordinating Ctee for Cancer Research Head and Neck Working Pty 1989–, pres elect Assoc of Head and Neck Oncologists of Great Britain 1995–; memb: MRC Working Pty in Gynaecological and Brain Tumors, Cancer Research Campaign Working Pty in Breast Cancer (chm New Studies Sub-Gp), Cncl Royal Coll of Radiologists 1991–; fell American Soc for Therapeutic Radiology; FRCP, FRCR; *Books* Primary Management of Breast Cancer (1985), Cancer and its Management (with R L Souhami, 1986, 2 edn 1994), Cancer - A Colour Atlas (1990), Cancer: What Every Patient Needs to Know (1995); author of features and editorials in BMJ and The Lancet; *Recreations* music, writing, theatre, cycling, walking; *Clubs* Albatross Wind and Water, RSM; *Style—* Dr Jeffrey Tobias; ✉ 48 Northchurch Rd, London N1 (☎ 0171 249 2326); The Green, 34 The Kymin, Monmouth, Gwent; Meyerstein Institute of Oncology, Middlesex Hospital, London W1 (☎ 0171 637 1214, fax 0171 637 1201)

TOBIN, Julian Jacob; OBE (1992); s of John Tobin (d 1966), and Georgina Tobin (d 1972); *b* 13 Aug 1927; *Educ* Great Yarmouth GS, Cambridge and Co HS, Magdalene Coll Cambridge (MA, LLM); *m* 6 Dec 1959, Jocelyne, da of Bernard Prevezer (d 1958), of 30 Green St, London W1; 1 s (Rupert b 1963), 2 da (Sasha b 1965, Annabel b 1968); *Career* admitted slr 1953; sr ptnr Pritchard Englefield & Tobin 1973–92, London sr ptnr Pannone & Partners 1992–94, sr ptnr Pritchard Englefield 1995–; admitted slr Hong Kong, ptnr Robert W H Wang & Co and Pritchard Englefield & Wang 1983–; cncllr: Hampstead Borough Cncl 1956–65, Camden Borough Cncl 1964– (ldr Cons Gp 1979–81); vice chm Covent Garden Area Tst 1994–; tstee: Athlone Tst 1979–, Lib Jewish Synagogue 1989– (treas 1984–89); special tstee: London Hosps 1981–88, Univ Coll Hosps 1986–94; govr Univ Coll Sch 1981–87, former chm Hampstead Cons Assoc (now sr tstee); *Recreations* reading, watching cricket, opera, music generally; *Clubs* Carlton, City of London, Garrick; *Style—* Julian Tobin, Esq, OBE; ✉ 18 Eton Villas, Hampstead, London NW3 (☎ 0171 722 8000); Orchard Cottage, Thicket Rd, Houghton, Huntingdon, Cambs; Pritchard Englefield, 14 New St, London EC2 (☎ 0171 972 9720, fax 0171 972 9721)

TOBIN, Capt Nicholas John; DSC (1982); s of Lt-Col P A Tobin, MBE, of Haslemere, Surrey, and Rosemary Nicoll, *née* Armitage; *b* 1 Jan 1945; *Educ* Duke of York Sch Nairobi Kenya, Britannia RNC Dartmouth; *m* 7 Aug 1976, Josephine Anne, da of Lt-Col J G Fisher, OBE (d 1976); 1 da (Naomi b 1983); *Career* naval offr HM ships 1963–74: Glasserton, Victorious, Aisne, London, Dryad; CO HMS Beachampton and HMS Wolverton 1974, HMS Ark Royal 1976, dir staff RN Staff Coll 1979, CO HMS Antelope 1981, naval and def staff MOD 1982, defence and naval attache Tokyo 1987, dir of naval manning 1994–95, Domus bursar Magdalene Coll Cambridge 1997; *Recreations* sailing, golf, walking; *Clubs* Royal Navy; *Style—* Capt N J Tobin, DSC, RN; ✉ Hillside House, Trudoxhill, Frome, Somerset BA11 5DP (☎ and fax 01373 836831)

TODD, Dr (William Taylor) Andrew; s of James McArthur Todd, of Edinburgh, and Jean Morley, *née* Smith; *b* 14 July 1953; *Educ* George Heriot's Sch, Univ of Edinburgh (BSc, MB ChB); *m* 1 July 1978, Morag Jennifer, da of Trevor John Ransley, of Edinburgh; 3 da (Jennifer b 1980, Rachel b 1983, Anna b 1987); *Career* Royal Infirmary Edinburgh: res house offr 1972, SHO in med 1978, registrar 1979–82, sr registrar 1985; sr registrar City Hosp Edinburgh 1984 (registrar 1979–81); visiting lectr Univ of Zimbabwe 1983, conslt physician and postgrad tutor Monklands Dist Gen Hosp (now Monklands and Bellshill Hosps NHS Tst) 1985–; elder Church of Scotland; memb Cncl and chm Clinical Servs Sub-Ctee Br Soc for Study of Infection; FRCPE, FRCPG; *Recreations* curling, hill walking; *Style—* Dr Andrew Todd; ✉ 17 Crosshill Drive, Rutherglen, Glasgow G73 3QT (☎ 0141 647 7288); Infectious Diseases Unit, Monklands and Bellshill Hospitals NHS Trust, Airdrie, Lanarkshire, Scotland ML6 0JS (☎ 01236 748748)

TODD, Colin; s of John James Todd (d 1964), of Chester-le-Street, and Ruby, *née* Irwin; *b* 12 Dec 1948; *m* 7 July 1970, Jennifer, da of Jack Renshaw; 2 s (Stephen b 4 Feb 1970, Andrew John James b 21 Sept 1974); *Career* professional football manager; player: debut Sunderland 1967, Derby County, Everton, Birmingham City, Nottingham Forest, Oxford Utd, Luton Town; England: 14 under 23 caps, 27 full caps 1972–77; mangr Middlesbrough 1990–91 (formerly coach); asst mangr Bradford City 1991–92, mangr Bolton Wanderers FC 1995– (asst mangr 1992–95); Professional Footballers' Assoc Player of the Year 1975; *Recreations* golf, gardening; *Style—* Colin Todd, Esq; ✉ Bolton Wanderers FC, Burnden Park, Manchester Rd, Bolton, Lancs BL3 2QR (☎ 01204 389200)

TODD, Daphne Jane; da of Frank Todd (d 1976), of Whitstable, and Annie Mary, *née* Lord; *b* 27 March 1947; *Educ* Simon Langton GS for Girls Canterbury, Slade Sch of Fine Art (DFA, Higher Dip in Fine Art); *m* 31 Aug 1984, Lt-Col (Patrick Robert) Terence Driscoll; 1 da (Mary Jane b 12 Nov 1977); *Career* artist; dir of studies Heatherley Sch of Art 1980–86; govr: Thomas Heatherley Educnl Tst 1986–, Fedn of Br Artists 1994–; pres Royal Soc of Portrait Painters 1994– (hon sec 1990–91); hon memb Soc of Women Artists 1995; NEAC 1984, RP 1985, FRSA; *Exhibitions* incl retrospective exhibition Morley Gallery 1989; *Collections* work in numerous collections incl: Royal Acad (Chantrey Bequest), Regtl HQ Irish Guards, London, Cambridge, Oxford, Wales and De Montfort Univs, Royal Holloway Museum and Art Gallery, Bishop's Palace Hereford, BMA, Instn of Civil Engrs, Ondaatje Hall, Nat Portrait Gallery, Science Museum; *Awards* David Murray Award for Landscape Painting 1971, Br Inst Award for Figurative Painting 1972, second prize John Player Portrait Award Nat Portrait Gallery 1983, first prize Oil Painting of the Year Hunting Group Nat Art Prize Competition 1984, GLC Prize 1984; *Clubs* Arts, Chelsea Arts; *Style—* Miss Daphne Todd, PRP; ✉ Salters Green Farm, Mayfield, East Sussex TN20 6NP (☎ and fax 01892 852472)

TODD, Dr Gillian Bees; da of Dr David Joseph Davies, MBE (d 1987), of Johnston, Pembrokeshire, and Beti Mary Davies (d 1977); *b* 29 Sept 1942; *Educ* Taskers Sch for Girls, Welsh Nat Sch of Med (Elizabeth Pipe prize in med); *m* 1981, Dr John Neild Todd; 2 s; *Career* med GP 1967–70, trainee in public health med 1970–79, conslt in public health med Trent Regnl Health Authy 1979–83, district gen mangr Central Nottinghamshire 1983–91; chief exec: S Birmingham Acute Unit 1991–94, S Glamorgan Health Authy 1994–96, Bro-Taf Health Authy 1996–; memb BMA, MIMgt, MHSM, FFPHM 1987; *Recreations* walking, embroidery, knitting; *Style—* Dr Gillian Todd; ✉ 20 Highfields, Llandaff, Cardiff CF5 2QA (☎ 01222 578244); Bro-Taf Health Authority, Churchill House, Churchill Way, Cardiff CF1 4TW (☎ 01222 226216)

TODD, Sir Ian Pelham; KBE (1989); s of late Alan Herapath Todd, MS, FRCS, and late Constance Edwards; *b* 23 March 1921; *Educ* Sherborne, Bart's Med Coll, Toronto Univ (MRCS, LRCP, FRCS, MD, MS, DCH); *m* 25 July 1946, Jean Audrey Ann, da of late James Morton Noble; 2 s (Neil b 1947, Steuart b 1957), 3 da (Jocelyn b 1948, Jane b 1952, Caroline b 1955); *Career* Maj RAMC; consltg surgn King Edward VII Hosp for Offrs, hon consltg surgn Bart's and St Mark's Hosps; former civilian conslt RN; former pres RCS, former vice pres Imperial Cancer Res Fund, former pres Med Soc of London, vice pres Int Fedn of Surgical Colleges 1990–93; Hon Freeman Worshipful Co of Barbers; hon memb: Academie de Chirurgie de Paris, Assoc of Surgns of India, Hellenic Surgical Assoc, American Soc of Coloproctology, Brazilian Soc of Coloproctology, RACS (sec Coloproctology), Acad of Med Malaysia; Hon: FCS (SA) 1986, FACS 1988, FRACS 1988, FRCS (Canada) 1989, FRCPS (Glasgow) 1989, FCPS (Bangladesh) 1993; Star of Jordan 1973; *Recreations* music, travel, philately, skiing; *Clubs* RSM; *Style—* Sir Ian P Todd, KBE; ✉ 4 Longmead Close, Farleigh Road, Norton St Philip, Bath BA3 6NS (☎ 01373 834081)

TODD, (Thomas) Keith; s of Thomas William Todd, and Cecilie Olive Francis, *née* Hefti; *b* 22 June 1953; *m* 19 May 1979, Anne Elizabeth, da of Hilson Adam Hendrie, of Edinburgh; 2 s ((Thomas) Christopher b 1984, Andrew Adam Paul b 1986), 2 da (Fiona Elizabeth b 1980, Nicola Anne b 1982); *Career* chief fin offr Cincinnati Electronics 1981–86, fin dir The Marconi Co 1986–87, chief exec ICL plc 1996– (fin dir 1987–96); memb Bd Camelot plc 1993; hon treas Open University 1992; FCMA; *Recreations* golf, swimming; *Style—* Keith Todd, Esq; ✉ ICL plc, 1 High St, Putney, London SW15 1SW (☎ 0181 788 7272)

TODD, Prof Malcolm; s of Wilfrid Todd (d 1980), of Durham, and Rose Evelyn, *née* Johnson; *b* 27 Nov 1939; *Educ* Henry Smith Sch, Univ of Wales (BA, DLitt), BNC Oxford (Dip); *m* 2 Sept 1964, Molly, da of Alexander John Tanner (d 1987), of London; 1 s (Malcolm Richard b 1966), 1 da (Katharine Grace b 1965); *Career* res asst Rheinisches Landesmuseum Bonn 1963–65, reader Univ of Nottingham 1977–79 (lectr 1965–74, sr lectr 1974–77), prof of archaeology Univ of Exeter 1979–96, princ Trevelyan Coll Univ of Durham 1996–; visiting fell: All Souls Coll Oxford 1984, BNC Oxford 1990–91; sr res fell Br Acad 1990–91; vice pres Roman Soc 1984–, tstee Roman Res Tst 1994–; memb: Royal Cmmn on Historical Monuments 1986–93, Cncl Nat Tst 1986–92, German Archaeological Inst 1977; FSA 1970; *Books* The Northern Barbarians (1975, 2 edn 1987), Roman Britain (1981 and 1985), The South-West To AD 1000 (1987), Britannia (ed, 1984–89), Research on Roman Britain: 1960–89 (ed 1989), Les Germains aux Frontières de l'Empire Romain (1990), The Early Germans (1992); *Recreations* reading, writing; *Style—* Prof Malcolm Todd, FSA; ✉ Trevelyan College, University of Durham, Durham DH1 3LN (☎ 0191 374 3760)

TODD, Mark James; CBE (1994, MBE 1984); s of Norman Edward Todd, of Cambridge, NZ, and Lenore Adele Todd, *née* Nickle; *b* 1 March 1956; *Educ* Cambridge HS, Waikato Tech Inst (DipAg); *m* 29 Nov 1986, Carolyn Faye; 1 da (Lauren b 1988), 1 s (James b 9 April 1993); *Career* equestrian; winner Badminton Horse Trials 1980, Gold medal winner LA Olympics 1984, Br Open Champion 1985, 1988 and 1989, winner of the German championship at Luhmuhlen 1986; Burghley Horse Trials: winner and runner-up 1987, winner 1990 and 1991, winner 3 Day Event 1991; Gold medal winner and team Bronze medal winner Seoul Olympics 1988, winner of Int Three Day Events Stockholm Achelswang and Boekelo 1989, Scot Champion 1989, team Gold medalist World Three Day Event Championships 1990, winner World Cup Qualifying Round Helsinki (CS10) 1991, winner Badminton Horse Trials 1994 and 1996; number one in the world 1984, 1988 and 1989; *Books* Charisma (1989), One Day Eventing (1996); *Recreations* swimming, skiing, tennis, squash; *Style—* Mark Todd, Esq, CBE

TODD, Paul Rodney; s of Tom Robert Todd (d 1977), of Spalding, and Gladys, *née* Blyth; *b* 17 Nov 1952; *Educ* Spalding GS, Bretton Hall Coll, Univ of Leeds (BEd, DipEd); *Career* composer, scriptwriter, lyricist and music dir: Leeds Playhouse 1974–75 and 1978, Newcastle Univ Theatre 1976, Backworth Drama Centre 1977, Stephen Joseph Theatre Scarborough 1978–88, Royal NT 1985–88; now freelance writer of musical theatre; memb: Musicians' Union, Equity, Performing Rights Soc, Br Acad of Songwriters, Composers and Authors; *Books* Suburban Strains (with Alan Ayckbourn, 1982); *Recreations* cricket, crosswords; *Style—* Paul Todd, Esq; ✉ 3 Rosehart Mews, 165A Westbourne Grove, London W11 3JN (☎ 0171 229 9776)

TODD, Richard Andrew Palethorpe; OBE (1993); s of Maj Andrew William Palethorpe Todd, MC (d 1941), Wimborne, Dorset, and Marvilla Rose, *née* Agar-Daly; *b* 11 June 1919; *Educ* Norwood Sch Exeter, Shrewsbury, Queen Elizabeth's Wimborne, and privately; *m* 1, 13 Aug 1949 (m dis 1970), Catherine Stewart Crawford, da of William Grant-Bogle (d 1967); 1 s (Peter Grant Palethorpe b 1952), 1 da (Fiona Margaret Palethorpe b 1956); m 2, 1970 (m dis 1992), Virginia Anne Rollo, da of Colin Cotterill Rollo Mailer; 2 s (Andrew Richard Palethorpe b 1973, Seumas Alexander Palethorpe b 1977); *Career* actor, producer and director 1937–; WWII Serv: RMC Sandhurst 1940, cmmnd KOYLI 1941, seconded Parachute Regt 1943, D Day with 7 (LI) Para Bn Normandy, GSO3 (ops) 6 Airborne Div 1944, served Battle of the Bulge, Ardennes and Rhine crossing, 2 i/c 3 Para Bde Def Co Palestine 1945–46; former Grand Steward and Worshipful Master Lodge of Emulation no 21; pres: Henley and Dist Agric Assoc 1963, Thames Valley Branch Save The Children Fund 1958–64, Grantham Branch Inst of Advanced Motorists; life pres Friends of Smith Hosp Henley, pres Birmingham Age Concern 1989–; *Theatre* returned to theatre 1965 in An Ideal Husband, fndr dir Truimph Theatre Prodns 1970, led RSC N American tour of The Hollow Crown 1975; subsequent appearances incl: The Business of Murder (London) 1981–88, The Woman In Black (Sydney Opera House) 1991; *Television* incl: Heathcliff in Wuthering Heights (BBC) 1953, H G Wells in Beautiful Lies (BBC) 1992; *Films* entered indust 1948 making many Br and American films incl: The Hasty Heart (with Ronald Reagan), Disney's Robin Hood, Rob Roy, The Dam Busters, The Virgin Queen, A Man Called Peter, Yantze Incident, Chase a Crooked Shadow, D Day the 6th of June, The Longest Day; *Awards* Brit Nat Film Award, Oscar nomination and Hollywood Golden Globe (for The Hasty Heart) 1950; *Books* Caught In The Act (1986), In Camera (1989); *Recreations* shooting, fishing, working; *Clubs* Army & Navy; *Style—* Richard Todd, Esq, OBE; ✉ Chinham Farm, Faringdon, Oxfordshire SN7 8EZ

TODD, Rev Dr (Andrew) Stewart; s of William Stewart Todd (d 1977), of Alloa, Clackmannanshire, and Robina Victoria, *née* Fraser (d 1988); *b* 26 May 1926; *Educ* Stirling HS, Univ of Edinburgh (MA, BD), Univ of Basel; *m* 17 Sept 1953, Janet Agnes Brown, da of John Smith, JP, DL, of Symington, Lanarkshire; 2 s (David b 1956, Philip b 1960), 2 da (Diana b 1955, Jane b 1958); *Career* asst min St Cuthbert's Edinburgh 1951–52; min: Symington Lanarkshire 1952–60, N Leith 1960–67, St Machar's Cathedral Old Aberdeen 1967–93; memb Church Hymnary Revision Ctee 1963–73, convener Gen Assembly's Ctee on Public Worship and Aids to Devotion 1974–78, moderator Aberdeen Presbytery 1980–81, convener Gen Assembly's Panel on Doctrine 1990–95; chaplain to HM The Queen in Scotland 1991–96 (extra chaplain 1996); Hon DD Univ of Aberdeen 1982; hon pres: Church Serv Soc, Scottish Church Soc; memb Societas Liturgica; *Recreations* music, gardening; *Style—* The Rev Dr Stewart Todd; ✉ Culearn, Balquhidder, Lochearnhead, Perthshire FK19 8PB (☎ 01877 384662)

TODHUNTER, Michael John Benjamin; s of Brig Edward Joseph Todhunter (d 1976), and Agnes Mary, *née* Swire (d 1975); *b* 25 March 1935; *Educ* Eton, Magdalen Coll Oxford (MA); *m* 1959, Caroline Francesca, da of Maj William Walter Dowding (d 1980); 1 s (Charles), 2 da (Nicola (Mrs James Denoon Duncan), Emily (Mrs E J (Manoli) Olympitis)); *Career* 2 Lt 11 Hussars (PAO); banker; London advsr Yasuda Trust and Banking Co Ltd, chm Clyde Shipping Co Ltd; dir: James Finlay plc, Kleinwort Development Fund plc, Newbury Racecourse plc; special tstee Great Ormond Street Hosp, tstee The Gift of Thomas Pocklington; hon fell Inst of Child Health; *Recreations* travel, shooting; *Clubs* White's, Pratt's, City of London, Western (Glasgow); *Style—* Michael Todhunter, Esq; ✉ The Old Rectory, Farnborough, Wantage, Oxon OX12 8NX (☎ 01488 638298); The Studio, 4 Lowndes St, London SW1 (☎ 0171 235 6421); office: 12 Cock Lane, London EC1A 9BU (☎ 0171 489 9259)

TOFT, Dr Anthony Douglas; CBE (1995); s of William Vincent Toft (d 1982), of Newport, Salop, and Anne, *née* Laing; *b* 29 Oct 1944; *Educ* Perth Acad, Univ of Edinburgh (BSc, MB ChB, MD); *m* 23 July 1968, Maureen Margaret, da of John Darling (d 1986), of Perth; 1 s (Neil b 1970), 1 da (Gillian b 1972); *Career* conslt physician gen med and endocrinology Royal Infirmary Edinburgh 1978–, chief MO Scottish Equitable Life Assurance Society 1988–; Royal Coll of Physicians of Edinburgh: memb Cncl 1985–88, vice pres 1990–91, pres 1991–94; memb Assoc of Physicians of GB and I 1984, chm Scottish Royal Colleges 1992–94, vice chm UK Conf of Med Royal Colleges 1993–94, chm Jt Ctee on Higher Med Trg 1994–96, memb Health Advsy Appts Ctee 1994–; memb GMC; physician to HM The Queen in Scotland 1996–; FRCPEd 1980, FRCP 1992, FRCPGlas 1993, FRCPI 1993, FRCSEd ad hominem 1994; Hon: FCPS (Pakistan) 1990, FRACP 1993, FACP 1993, FRCP (Canada) 1994, FRCGP 1994, FCPS (Bangladesh) 1994, FFPM 1994, FAM (Singapore) 1994; *Books* Diagnosis and Management of Endocrine Diseases (1982); *Recreations* golf, gardening, hill walking; *Clubs* New (Edinburgh); *Style—* Dr Anthony Toft, CBE; ✉ 41 Hermitage Gardens, Edinburgh EH10 6AZ (☎ 0131 447 2221); Department of Medicine, Royal Infirmary, Edinburgh EH3 9YW (☎ 0131 536 2093)

TOGHILL, Dr Peter James; s of John Walter Toghill (d 1991), of Bushey, Hertfordshire, and Lena Mary, *née* Jow (d 1985); *b* 16 June 1932; *Educ* Watford GS, Univ Coll Hosp Med Sch (MB BS), Univ of London (MD); *m* 25 April 1964, Rosemary Anne, da of Alfred Samuel Cash, of Whatton, Nottinghamshire; 3 da (Claire Elizabeth b 1966, Helen Louise b 1969, Joanna Mary b 1972); *Career* Capt RAMC 1956–58; British Empire Cancer Campaign res fell and med registrar Univ Coll Hosp London 1960–64, sr med registrar King's Coll Hosp 1964–68, conslt physician Gen Hosp Nottingham and Univ Hosp Nottingham 1968–93, clinical dean Univ of Nottingham Med Sch 1977–80, currently dir of educn RCP London; pres: Nottingham Med/Chirurgical Soc 1987–88, Nottinghamshire Medico-Legal Soc 1990–91; cncllr, pro-censor and censor RCP London 1990–93; Simms lectr RCP 1994, Samuel Gee lectr RCP 1996; memb Assoc of Physicians of GB and I, FRCP, FRCPE, MRCS; *Books* Examining Patients (1990), Essential Medical Procedures (1996); author of numerous pubns on diseases of the liver and spleen; *Recreations* Nottinghamshire cricket, growing roses; *Style—* Dr Peter Toghill; ✉ 119 Lambley Lane, Burton Joyce, Nottingham NG14 5BL (☎ 0115 931 2446); Department of CME, Royal College of Physicians, London NW1 4LE (☎ 0171 935 1174, fax 0171 487 5218)

TOKSVIG, Sandi Birgitte; da of Claus Bertel Toksvig (d 1988), and Julie Anne, *née* Brett, of Surrey; *b* 3 May 1958; *Educ* Mamaroneck HS NY, Tormead Sch Guildford, Girton Coll Cambridge (MA, Therese Montifiore Meml Award); *Career* actress, comedienne and writer; *Theatre* Nottingham Rep 1980–81, New Shakespeare Co (Open Air Theatre Regents Park) 1981, with The Comedy Store Players 1987–93; plays incl: The Pocket Dream (co-writer with Elly Brewer, Nottingham Playhouse then Albery Theatre) 1991–92, Big Night Out At The Little Sands Picture Palace (writer, Nottingham Playhouse) 1993; *Television* incl: Number 73 (co-writer) 1982–87, Toksvig (co-writer), Whose Line Is It Anyway?, Behind The Headlines, The Big One, Sindy Hits Thirty, The Talking Show; *Films* Paris By Night, Sweet Nothings; *Radio* reg contrib to Loose Ends (BBC Radio 4), Pick of the Week (BBC Radio 4) 1993, presenter Sound Company (BBC Radio 4) 1995, host Darling You Were Marvellous (BBC Radio 4) 1996; also co-writer: Kin of the Castle, Cat's Whiskers; *Books* Island Race: Improbable Voyage Round the Coast of Britain (with John McCarthy, 1996); *Recreations* skiing, arboreal activities; *Clubs* 2 Brydges Place; *Style—* Ms Sandi Toksvig; ✉ c/o Peters Fraser & Dunlop Ltd, 5th Floor, The Chambers, Chelsea Harbour, London SW10 0XF (☎ 0171 352 4446, fax 0171 352 8135)

TOLAN, Peter Graham; s of Daniel Tolan (d 1954), and Marjorie, *née* Goode; *b* 9 Sept 1944; *Educ* Ullathorne GS Coventry, Birmingham Coll of Commerce; *m* 26 Oct 1968, Christine Elizabeth, da of Kenneth Murray; 1 s (Mark Damien b 30 Jan 1971), 1 da (Danielle Elizabeth b 6 Oct 1972); *Career* trainee reporter Warwick and Warwickshire Advertiser 1961–67, sr reporter Nuneaton Evening Tribune 1967–68, freelance journalist and broadcaster 1968–75, press and PR offr TI Machines (Int) 1975–77, PR conslt Harrison Cowley Public Relations (Birmingham) 1978–85 (dep md 1983), dir of PR Rex Stewart (Bristol) 1985, md Rex Stewart PR Ltd 1988, chief exec Rex Stewart Grayling Group Ltd 1990–94, business devpt dir Grayling International 1994 (bd dir 1990–94), md Golley Slater Brooker PR Birmingham 1995–; MIPR 1988; *Recreations* rugby union (chm Warwickshire Soc of Referees); *Style—* Peter Tolan, Esq; ✉ 7 Gloster Drive, Mount Royal, Kenilworth CV8 2TU (☎ 01926 512349); Golley Slater Brooker PR, 23 Highfield Road, Birmingham B15 3DP (☎ 0121 693 3233, fax 0121 693 3243)

TOLER, Maj-Gen David Arthur Hodges; OBE (1963), MC (1945), DL (1982); s of Maj Thomas Clayton Toler, JP, DL (d 1940), of Swettenham Hall, Congleton, Cheshire, and Gertrude Marianna, *née* Wilkinson (d 1962); *b* 13 Sept 1920; *Educ* Stowe, Ch Ch Oxford (MA); *m* 11 Sept 1951, Judith Mary, da of late Maj James William Garden, DSO, of Aberdeen; 1 s (Hugh b 1953), 1 da (Jane b 1955); *Career* WWII 2 Lt Coldstream Gds 1940; served in WWII in N Africa and Italy 1942–45; Adj RMA Sandhurst 1958–60, Br liaison offr US Continental Army Cmd (Col) 1960–62, cmd 2 Bn Coldstream Gds 1962–64, cmd Coldstream Gds 1964–65, cmd 4 Gds Bde 1965–68, Brig 1966, dep cmdt Staff Coll Camberley 1968–69, Maj-Gen 1969, GOC E Midland Dist 1970–73; Dep Hon Col Lincs Royal Anglian Regt 1979–84; co emergency planning offr Lincs 1974–77; chm Lincoln Diocesan Advsy Ctee 1981–86; hon clerk to the Lieutenancy (Co of Lincoln) 1983–90; pres Lincs Branch SSAFA 1978–, chm Lincs TA & VR Ctee 1984–86; *Recreations* gardening; *Clubs* Army and Navy; *Style—* Maj-Gen David Toler, OBE, MC, DL; ✉ Rutland Farm, Fulbeck, Grantham, Lincs NG32 3LG

TOLKIEN, Faith Lucy Tilly; da of Frank Thomas Faulconbridge (d 1973), and Gladys Lilian, *née* Tilly (d 1946); *b* 9 June 1928; *Educ* St Felix Sch Southwold, St Anne's Coll Oxford (MA), Oxford City Art Sch; *m* 1, 2 April 1951 (m dis 1967), Christopher Reuel Tolkien, s of John Ronald Reuel Tolkien (d 1973); 1 s (Simon Mario Reuel b 12 Jan 1959), m 2, Tracy Steinberg; 1 s (Nicholas Faulconbridge Reuel b 20 Aug 1990)); *Career* sculptor; teacher 1964–79; portrait heads incl: The Rt Hon Lord Jenkins of Hillhead, Sir Richard Doll, C S Lewis, J R R Tolkien, Dame Iris Murdoch, DBE, Sir Michael Oppenheimer, Bt, Lady Oppenheimer; has exhibited in the Royal Acad exhibition; church works incl: Madonna and Child in Univ of Birmingham RC Chapel, Stations of the Cross in Corpus Christi Church Oxford and bronze relief Shrine of St John Wall in St Mary's Church Harvington Worcs, crucifixion sculpture Chapel of the Sacred Heart St John's Seminary Wonersh Surrey, high relief frieze Church of Sacred Heart Four Oaks Sutton Coldfield, high relief sculpture Church of Blessed Dominic Barberi Littlemore Oxon (to mark 150th anniversary of Newman's reception into the Catholic Church 1995), plaque in high relief St George and the Dragon, St George's Church Worcester; *Recreations* novels, poetry, biography, scripture and theology, bird watching, walking, travelling, visiting pubs; *Style—* Mrs Faith Tolkien; ✉ 28 Church St, Watlington, Oxford OX9 5QR (☎ 01491 612514)

TOLLEMACHE, Sir Lyonel Humphry John; 7 Bt (GB 1793), JP (Leics), DL (Leics); s of Maj-Gen Sir Humphry Thomas Tollemache 6 Bt, CB, CBE, DL (d 30 March 1990), and Nora Priscilla, *née* Taylor (d 24 Oct 1990); *b* 10 July 1931; *Educ* Uppingham, RAC Cirencester; *m* 6 Feb 1960, Mary Joscelyne, da of Col William Henry Whitbread, TD; 2 s (Lyonel Thomas b 23 Jan 1963, d 22 Aug 1996, Richard John b 4 May 1966), 2 da (Katheryne Mary b 1960, Henrietta Joscelyne (Mrs David Chubb) b 1970); *Heir* s, Richard John Tollemache b 4 May 1966; *Career* cmmnd Coldstream Gds, Maj; High Sheriff of Leicestershire 1978–79, co cncllr Leicestershire 1985–; Liveryman Worshipful Co of Grocers; FRICS; *Style—* Sir Lyonel Tollemache, Bt, JP, DL; ✉ Buckminster Park, Grantham NG33 5RU (☎ 01476 860 349; office 01476 860 297)

TOLLEMACHE, Hon Michael David Douglas; s of 4 Baron Tollemache (d 1975); *b* 23 Aug 1944; *Educ* Eton, Trinity Coll Cambridge (MA); *m* 5 Feb 1969, Thérèsa, da of Peter Bowring; 2 s (twins), 1 da; *Career* dir: Michael Tollemache Ltd 1967–, David Carritt Ltd 1983–93, Artemis Fine Arts Ltd 1983–93; chm Soc of London Art Dealers 1995–; *Clubs* White's; *Style—* The Hon Michael Tollemache; ✉ Framsden Hall, Helmingham, Stowmarket, Suffolk (☎ 0171 930 9883)

TOLLEMACHE, 5 Baron (UK 1876); Timothy John Edward Tollemache; DL (Suffolk 1984); s of 4 Baron Tollemache, MC, DL (d 1975); *b* 13 Dec 1939; *Educ* Eton; *m* 1970, Alexandra Dorothy Jean, da of Col Hugo Meynell, MC, JP, DL (d 1960); 2 s (Hon Edward, Hon James b 1980), 1 da (Hon Selina b 1973); *Heir* s, Hon Edward John

Hugo Tollemache b 12 May 1976; *Career* cmmnd Coldstream Gds 1959–62; dir Fortis (UK) Ltd 1980–, and other companies; farmer and landowner; pres: Suffolk Assoc of Local Cncls 1978–96, Friends of Ipswich Museums 1980–96, Northwest Agronomy 1983–, Suffolk Family History Soc 1988–, Suffolk Agric Assoc 1988, Suffolk Historic Churches Tst 1996–, SSAFA (Suffolk) 1996–; chm: HHA (E Anglia) 1979–83, Cncl St John (Suffolk) 1982–89, St Edmundsbury Cathedral Appeal 1986–90, Suffolk Branch CLA 1990–93; vice pres: Cheshire BRCS 1980–, Suffolk Preservation Soc; patron Suffolk Accident Rescue Services 1983–; Vice Lord-Lt of Suffolk 1994–; CStJ 1988; *Recreations* shooting, fishing; *Clubs* White's, Pratt's; *Style*— The Rt Hon Lord Tollemache, DL; ✉ Helmingham Hall, Stowmarket, Suffolk IP14 6EF

TOLLEY, David Anthony; s of Frank Stanley Tolley, of Sale, Cheshire, and Elizabeth, *née* Dean; *b* 29 Nov 1947; *Educ* Manchester GS, King's Coll Hosp Med Sch (MB BS); *m* 4 July 1970, Judith Anne, da of Wing Cdr Dennis Martin Finn, DFC (d 1983), of Salisbury; 3 s (Nicholas, Christopher, Jeremy), 1 da (Felicity Jane); *Career* conslt urological surgeon: Royal Infirmary Edinburgh 1980–91, Western General Hospital 1991–; dir the Scottish Lithotriptor Centre Western Gen Hosp Edinburgh 1991–; examiner Intercollegiate Bd in Urology; memb: Urological Cancer Working Pty MRC, Bd Minimal Access Therapy Trg Unit Scotland, various ctees Br Assoc of Urological Surgns (also memb Cncl), various ctees Royal Coll of Surgns Edinburgh, Editorial Bd Br Jl of Urology, Editorial Ctee Jl of Endourology; pres Br Soc of Endourology; FRCS 1974, FRCSEd 1983; *Recreations* golf, motor racing, music; *Clubs* New (Edinburgh), Luffness New Golf; *Style*— David Tolley, Esq; ✉ Murrayfield Hospital, Corstorphine Road, Edinburgh (☎ 0131 334 0363)

TOLLEY, Rev Canon George; s of George Enoch Frederick Tolley (d 1971), of Old Hill, Staffs, and Elsie, *née* Billingham (d 1977); *b* 24 May 1925; *Educ* Halesowen GS Worcs, Birmingham Central Tech Coll, Princeton Univ, Lincoln Theol Coll, Univ of London (BSc, MSc, PhD), Univ of Sheffield (MA); *m* 21 June 1947, Joan Amelia, da of Isaac Grosvenor (d 1984), of Blackheath, Worcs; 2 s (Christopher b 1951, Martin b 1952), 1 da (Jane b 1955); *Career* chief chemist Metallisation Ltd 1947–51, Chemistry Dept Birmingham Coll of Advanced Technol 1951–58 (head of dept 1954–58), head of research Allied Ironfounders Ltd 1958–61, princ Worcester Tech Coll 1961–65, sr dir of studies RAF Coll Cranwell 1965–66, princ Sheffield Poly 1966–82; Manpower Services Cmmn: dir of Open Tech, head of Quality Branch, chief offr Review of Vocational Qualifications 1987, conslt in educn and training 1988–91; ordained priest C of E 1968, hon canon Sheffield 1976; one of twelve Capital Burgesses and Commonality of Sheffield 1980–; memb Yorks and Humberside Economic Planning Cncl 1974–79, hon sec Assoc of Colls of Higher and Further Educn 1974–83; pres Inst of Home Econs 1987–90; chm: Cncl Plastics Inst 1959–61, Further Educn Unit 1977–83, Cncl Selly Oak Colls 1983–92, Educn-Industry Forum Industry Matters 1984–88, Central Sheffield Univ Hosps NHS Trust 1991–; memb: CNAA 1973–82, Cncl RSA 1985–92, Cncl S Yorks Fndn 1986–90; Hon DSc: Univ of Sheffield 1983, Open Univ 1983, CNAA 1986; hon fell: City and Guilds of London, Sheffield Poly, Coll of Preceptors, Columbia Pacific Univ, Inst of Trg and Devpt, Selly Oak Colls; FRSC 1954, fell Plastics and Rubber Inst 1973, CIMgt 1978; *Books* Meaning and Purpose in Higher Education (1976); *Recreations* music, hill walking, bird watching; *Clubs* Athenaeum; *Style*— The Rev Canon George Tolley; ✉ 74 Furniss Ave, Dore Sheffield S17 3QP (☎ 0114 2 360 538)

TOLMAN, Jeffery Alexander Spencer; s of Gerald James Spencer, of Cornwall, and Doris Rosaline, *née* Lane (d 1966); *b* 12 July 1950; *Educ* St Clement Danes GS, Univ of Wales Sch of Int Politics; *Career* product mangr Birds Eye Foods (Unilever) 1971–73, account exec Ogilvy & Mather 1973–74; McCann Erickson 1974–79: account supervisor, account dir, assoc dir then dir; fndr ptnr Grandfield Rork Collins 1979–85; Saatchi & Saatchi Advertising: gp account dir 1985–86, dep chm 1987–91, chief exec (strategy) 1987–91, non-exec dep chm 1991–93; chm Tolman Cunard Ltd (corp and strategic communication advsrs); non-exec dep chm Forward Publishing, non-exec dir The Royal Automobile Club Ltd; *Recreations* walking, eating, drinking, politics; *Clubs* RAC, Groucho; *Style*— Jeffery Tolman, Esq; ✉ 12 Stonor Rd, London W14 8RZ (☎ 0171 603 6697, fax 0171 603 3100); Lushers, Whitsbury, Hampshire; Tolman Cunard Ltd, 10 Yeoman's Row, London SW3 2AH (☎ 0171 589 9500, fax 0171 589 9100)

TOLOND, Avril Louise; da of Idwal Johns (d 1950), of Bargoed, S Wales; *b* 24 April 1951; *Educ* Lewis' Sch for Girls Ystrad Mynach, Univ of London (BA, external); *m* (m dis); 1 da (Lucy Victoria b 16 Sept 1978); *Career* formerly trainee in health serv mgmnt Nottingham, dep mangr and commissioning offr Queen's Med Centre Univ Hosp Nottingham until 1988, gen mangr Chesterfield and N Derbyshire Royal Hosp 1988–93, chief exec Chesterfield and N Derbyshire Royal Hosp NHS Tst 1993–; non-exec dir N Derbyshire TEC, govr NE Derbyshire Tertiary Coll; MHSM; *Style*— Mrs Avril Tolond; ✉ Chesterfield & North Derbyshire Royal Hospital, Calow, Chesterfield, Derby S44 5BL (☎ 01246 277271, fax 01246 550171)

TOLSTOY-MILOSLAVSKY, Count Andrei; s of (Count) Dimitry Tolstoy, QC, and Natalie; half-bro of Count Nikolai Tolstoy-Miloslavsky, *qv*; *b* 12 May 1949; *Educ* French Lycée, Wellington Coll, Univ of Surrey; *m* 1976, Carolinda Beatrice Catherine, da of Maj Ralph Pilcher, Welsh Gds, of Hay Place, Binsted, Hants; 2 s (Igor b 1985, Oleg b 1986), 1 da (Liubov b 1979); *Career* businessman; *Recreations* tennis, swimming, running, reading; *Clubs* Beefsteak; *Style*— Count Andrei Tolstoy-Miloslavsky; ✉ c/o National Westminster Bank plc, 34 Sloane Square, London SW1W 8AW

TOLSTOY-MILOSLAVSKY, Count Nikolai Dmitrievich; s of (Count) Dimitry Tolstoy, QC; half-bro of Count Andrei Tolstoy-Miloslavsky, *qv*; *b* 23 June 1935; *Educ* Wellington, Trinity Coll Dublin (MA); *m* 1971, Georgina Katherine, da of Maj Peter Brown, of Southmoor, Berkshire; 1 s (Dmitri b 1978), 3 da (Alexandra b 1973, Anastasia b 1975, Xenia b 1980); *Heir* (Count) Dmitri Nikolaevich Tolstoy-Miloslavsky; *Career* author, historian, biographer; has appeared on numerous TV and radio progs and delivered lectures at univs and int academic confs worldwide; Int Freedom Award US Industl Cncl Educnl Fndn 1987; appointed Capt in the Cossack Army 1993; chllr Monarchist League, hon memb Russian Heraldry Soc; life memb: Royal Stuart Soc, Royal Martyr Church Union, Forty-Five Assoc; memb: Cncl for Christians and Jews, Irish Texts Soc, Roman Soc, Int Arthurian Soc; FRSL; *Books* The Founding of Evil Hold School (1968), Night of The Long Knives (1972), Victims of Yalta (1978), The Half-Mad Lord (biography of Thomas Pitt, 1978), Stalin's Secret War (1981), The Tolstoys - Twenty-Four Generations of Russian History (1983), The Quest for Merlin (1985), The Minister and the Massacres (1986), States, Countries, Provinces (1986), The Coming of the King - The First Book of Merlin (1988); author of numerous articles and reviews on Celtic studies in learned jls; *Recreations* second-hand and academic bookshops, walking, tennis, drinking in inns; *Style*— Count Nikolai Tolstoy-Miloslavsky; ✉ Court Close, Southmoor, Abingdon, Berks (☎ 01865 820186)

TOM, Peter William Gregory; s of John Gregory Tom, of Bardon House, Bardon Hill, Leicester, and Barbara, *née* Lambden; *b* 26 July 1940; *Educ* Hinckley GS; *children* 1 s (decd), 2 da (Saffron b 1972, Layla b 1975) by first m; *Career* chief exec Bardon Group plc; CIMgt; *Recreations* tennis, theatre, golf; *Style*— Peter W G Tom, Esq; ✉ Bardon Group plc, Radcliffe House, Blenheim Court, Lode Lane, Solihull, W Midlands B91 2SS (☎ 0121 711 1717)

TOMALIN, Claire; da of Emile Delavenay, and Muriel Emily, *née* Herbert (d 1984); *b* 20 June 1933; *Educ* Lycée Français de Londres, Girls GS Hitchin, Dartington Hall Sch, Newnham Coll Cambridge (BA, MA); *m* 1, 17 Sept 1955, Nicholas Osborne Tomalin (d 1973), s of Miles Ridley Tomalin (d 1983); 2 s (Daniel b and d 1960, Thomas Nicholas Ronald b 1970), 3 da (Josephine Sarah b 1956, Susanna Lucy b 1958 d 1980, Emily Claire Elizabeth b 1961); m 2, 5 June 1993, Michael Frayn, *qv*; *Career* writer; publishers ed, reader, journalist 1953–67; literary ed: New Statesman 1974–78 (dep literary ed 1968–70), Sunday Times 1980–86; registrar Royal Literary Fund 1984– (tstee 1975), tstee Nat Portrait Gallery 1992–; FRSL 1974; *Books* Life and Death of Mary Wollstonecraft (1974, reissued 1993), Shelley and His World (1980), Katherine Mansfield: A Secret Life (1987), The Invisible Woman: The Story of Nelly Ternan and Charles Dickens (1990), Mrs Jordan's Profession (1994); play: The Winter Wife (1991); *Style*— Mrs Claire Tomalin, FRSL

TOMALSKI, Bob; s of Felix Stanislaus Tomalski (d 1964), and Gladys Nora, *née* Russell (d 1988); *b* 7 Feb 1953; *Educ* Holy Family Sch Morden, Carshalton Tech Coll, Merton Tech Coll; *Career* shop asst Davis Photographic New Malden 1971–78, tech sales mangr Unilet HiFi New Malden 1978–87, tech ed CD Review and ed Making Better Movies 1987–90, gp tech ed WV Publications (publishers of What Video magazine and others) 1990–; freelance bdcaster on technology and sci incl BBC Radio 5 (Five Aside, Formula Five, AM Alternative, The Big Byte), BBC Radio 4 (The Parts, You and Yours), London News Radio phone-ins, Talk UK, BBC TV (Homewise, People Today, Breakfast News, 9 O'Clock News), ITV (Video View, Amazing Science), Channel Four (The Big Breakfast); regular writer for: What Video, What Satellite, What Camcorder, Camcorder User, What Cellphone, Home Cinema Choice, World Radio and TV Handbook, Theatre Living Tokyo; *Recreations* amateur radio (call sign G6CQF), internet, videography, computing, reading, homebrew real ale; *Clubs* British Amateur TV; *Style*— Bob Tomalski, Esq; ✉ WV Publications, 57–59 Rochester Place, London NW1 9JU (☎ 0171 485 0011, fax 0181 687 0453)

TOMBS, Brian John; s of Herbert James Tombs, of Rustington, W Sussex, and Aliviné Helena Tombs (d 1991); *b* 19 Nov 1935; *Educ* Glyn GS Epsom Surrey; *m* 5 Aug 1961, Diana Rosemary, *née* Oulton; 4 s (Nicholas John b 25 Feb 1964, David John b 25 Nov 1965, Andrew John b 31 July 1967, Robin John b 17 April 1969), 1 da (Jacqueline Rosemary b 15 Aug 1974); *Career* articled clerk Neville Russell CAs London 1951–57, Nat Serv RAF 1957–59, trainee mgmnt accountant British Steel Corp 1959–61, budgetary control accountant Radio Rentals 1961–63, ptnr John Craggs & Co CAs London 1965–71 (joined 1963); Neville Russell CAs: ptnr London Office (following merger with John Craggs & Co) 1971–86, sr ptnr Sutton Office 1986–, managing ptnr Provincial Offices 1990–94; chm Fin Ctee Shaftesbury Housing Assoc; memb ESU; ACA 1957; *Recreations* tennis, hockey, travelling; *Style*— Brian Tombs, Esq; ✉ Neville Russell, Chartered Accountants, 2/4 Sutton Court Road, Sutton, Surrey SM1 4TN (☎ 0181 661 1826, fax 0181 643 5058)

TOMBS, Baron (Life Peer UK 1990), of Brailes in the County of Warwickshire; Sir Francis Leonard Tombs; kt (1978); s of Joseph Tombs; *b* 17 May 1924; *Educ* Elmore Green Sch Walsall, Birmingham Coll of Technol, Univ of London (BSc); *m* 1949, Marjorie Evans; 3 da (Hon Catherine Barbara b 22 April 1950, Hon Elisabeth Jane b 18 Dec 1952, Hon Margaret Clare b 25 Nov 1958); *Career* trained with: GEC Ltd Birmingham 1939–45, Birmingham Corp Electricity Supply Dept 1946–47, Br Electricity Authy 1948–57; gen mangr GEC Ltd Kent 1958–67, dir and gen mangr James Howden & Co Glasgow 1967–68; South of Scotland Electricity Bd: dir of engrg 1969–73, dep chm 1973–74, chm 1974–77; chm: Electricity Cncl for England and Wales 1977–80, Weir Group plc 1981–83, Turner & Newall plc 1982–89, Rolls-Royce plc 1985–92, The Engineering Cncl 1985–88, The Advsy Cncl on Sci and Technol 1987–90, Molecule Theatre Co 1985–92; dir: N M Rothschild & Sons Ltd 1981–94, Rolls-Royce Ltd 1982–92, Turner & Newall International Ltd 1982–89, Turner & Newall Welfare Trust Ltd 1982–89, Shell-UK Ltd 1983–94; pro chllr and chm Cncl Cranfield Inst of Technol 1985–91, chllr Univ of Strathclyde 1991–; vice pres Engrs for Disaster Relief 1985–93; Liveryman and Prime Warden Worshipful Co of Goldsmiths 1994–95, Freeman City of London; Hon DUniv and Hon LLD Univ of Strathclyde; Hon DSc: Aston Univ, Lodz Univ (Poland), Cranfield Inst of Technol, The City Univ London, Univ of Bradford, Queen's Univ Belfast, Univ of Surrey, Univ of Nottingham, Univ of Cambridge, Univ of Warwick; Hon DTech Loughborough Univ of Technol, Hon DEd CNAA; FEng 1977 (past vice pres), Hon FIEE (past pres), Hon FIMechE, Hon FICE, Hon FIChemE, Hon FRSE 1996; hon memb Br Nuclear Energy Soc; *Style*— The Rt Hon the Lord Tombs, FEng; ✉ Honington Lodge, Honington, Shipston-upon-Stour, Warwickshire CV36 5AA

TOMBS, Sebastian; s of David Martineau Tombs (d 1986), of Sussex, and Jane Burns, *née* Parley; *b* 11 Oct 1949; *Educ* Bryanston, Corpus Christi Coll Cambridge (choral exhibitioner, DipArch); *m* Eva, da of Leo Heirman (d 1983), of Soest, Holland; 2 s (Michael b 1985, Leonardo b 1988), 1 da (Rowena b 1987); *Career* on staff in architectural/planning office N Philadelphia USA 1972–73 (yr practical trg from CCC Cambridge), RMJM Partnership Edinburgh 1975–76, Roland Wedgwood Associates Edinburgh 1976–77, Fountainbridge Housing Assoc 1977–78, area architect Housing Corp 1978–81, private sector work Housing Dept Edinburgh DC 1981–86, sec and treas RIAS 1995– (dep sec and dir of practice 1986–94); chm: Edinburgh Gp Anthroposophical Soc 1986–89, Scottish Ecological Design Assoc (co-fndr) 1994–, Assoc of Planning Suprs 1995–; ARCUK 1977, FRIAS 1990 (ARIAS 1978), ACIArb 1991; *Recreations* sketching, composing songs and doggerel; *Style*— Sebastian Tombs, Esq; ✉ Royal Incorporation of Architects in Scotland, 15 Rutland Square, Edinburgh EH1 2BE (☎ 0131 229 7545, fax 0131 228 2188)

TOMKINS, Prof Cyril Robert; s of Charles Albert Tomkins (d 1955), of Southampton, and Gladys Rose Sylvester; *b* 27 May 1939; *Educ* Price's Sch, Univ of Bristol (BA), LSE (MSc); *m* 10 Aug 1963, Dorothy, da of Sydney Parker (d 1988), of Portsmouth; 2 s (Neil b 1967, Stephen b 1969); *Career* accountant for four years, lectr Univ of Hull 1969–70, sr res offr and lectr Univ Coll of N Wales 1970–73, sr lectr Univ of Strathclyde 1973–75, prof of accounting and finance Univ of Bath 1975– (pro-vice chllr 1993–96); dir of several univ based cos; funded res projects incl work on local govt financial control, comparison of investment decision making in UK and German cos, developing financial mgmnt in central govt and fin control in the construction indust; memb Editorial Bd: Accounting and Business Research, Auditing and Accountability, Journal of Accounting and Business Finance, Financial Management and Accountability; chm Br Accounting Assoc 1989; CIPFA 1967, FCCA; *Books* incl: Financial Planning in Divisionalised Companies (1974), Achieving Economy Efficiency and Effectiveness in the Public Sector (1987), Corporate Resources Allocation - Strategy and Finance (1991), Strategic Investment Decisions: a comparison of UK and German investments in the motor components industry (1994); numerous journal articles, govt reports and other papers incl: The Development of Relevant Accounting Reports (1969), The Everyday Accountant and Researching his Reality (1983), Changing Attitudes to Innovation in the Civil Service (1989), Making Sense of Cost-Plus Transfer Prices (1990); various reviews; *Recreations* travel, gardening, reading, rugby, walking; *Style*— Prof Cyril Tomkins; ✉ University of Bath, School of Management, Bath BA2 7AY (☎ 01225 826683)

TOMKINS, Sir Edward Emile; GCMG (1975, KCMG 1969, CMG 1960), CVO (1957); s of Lt-Col Ernest Leith Tomkins; *b* 16 Nov 1915; *Educ* Ampleforth, Trinity Coll Cambridge; *m* 15 Nov 1955, Gillian, da of Air Cdre Constantine Evelyn Benson, CBE, DSO (yr bro of late Sir Rex Benson), by his w Lady Morvyth, *née* Ward (2 da of 2 Earl of Dudley and sis of 1 Viscount Ward of Witley); 1 s (Julian b 1956), 2 da (Sarah b

1958, Rosemary-Louise b 1961); *Career* served WWII 1940–43 (liaised with French Free Forces); diplomat, joined Foreign Service 1939; served: Moscow 1944–46, FO 1946–51, Washington 1951–54, cnsllr (Information) Paris 1954–59, FO 1959–63, min Bonn 1963–67, min Washington 1967–69; ambass: Netherlands 1970–72, France 1972–75, ret; memb Bucks CC 1977–85, pres Friends of Univ Coll of Buckingham 1977; Croix de Guerre, Grand Officer Légion d'Honneur 1984; *Style*— Sir Edward Tomkins, GCMG, CVO; ✉ Winslow Hall, Winslow, Buckingham MK18 3HL (☎ 01296 712323)

TOMKINS, Dr Peter Maurice; s of Rowland Maurice Tomkins, of Leeds, Yorks, and Gwendoline Mary, *née* Dunkley; *b* 29 Nov 1941; *Educ* Leeds Modern Sch, Univ of Bradford (BTech), Univ of Leeds (PhD); *m* 14 May 1988, Rosemary Anne, da of John Gale Harrison, of Stockport, Cheshire; 1 da (Amber Lauren b 17 Oct 1990); *Career* R & D scientist Albright & Wilson plc 1963–64, univ demonstrator then fell Univ of Leeds 1964–67, dept mangr (mfrg, R & D devpt, brands) Mars Confectionery Ltd 1967–69, mangr then princ conslt Arthur Young & Co 1969–71, vice pres and gen mangr Encyclopaedia Britannica International Ltd 1971–73, chief exec and dir D M Management Consultants Ltd (strategic direct mktg consultancy) 1973–; chm Community Indust Bd (Nat Assoc of Youth Clubs) 1975–78, vice pres Youth Clubs UK 1982– (former dep chm), fndr tstee CAF Cert 1984–, memb SW Thames RHA 1986–90, tstee Bd Volunteer Centre UK 1992–96; author of mgmnt and mktg articles in various jls; memb Lloyd's 1978–; memb: Bd BDMA 1979–91, Cncl Inst of Mgmnt Conslts 1986– (pres 1995–96); memb RSC 1968, CChem 1970, FIMgt 1972, FInstD 1980, FIMC 1982, memb DMA 1992 (fndr memb), MCIM 1992, MIDM 1994; *Recreations* squash, skiing, jogging, yoga, charity work; *Clubs* IOD, Roehampton; *Style*— Dr Peter Tomkins; ✉ D M Management Consultants Ltd, 19 Clarges St, London W1Y 7PG (☎ 0171 499 8030, fax 0181 948 6306, mobile 0802 484789)

TOMKINSON, Robert Charles; s of William Robert Tomkinson (d 1980), and Helen Mary Tomkinson, MBE, *née* Blane; *b* 14 July 1941; *Educ* Marlborough, Univ of Oxford (MA); *m* 15 June 1968, Joanna Sally, da of Maj William Philip Stuart Hastings; 2 s (James Robert b 1970, Simon William b 1972); *Career* mangr Peat Marwick Mitchell & Co 1966–75, dep md Scrimgeour Hardcastle & Co Ltd 1975–79, fin dir Intercontinental Fuels Ltd 1979–81; gp fin dir: Automotive Products plc 1982–86, Electrocomponents plc 1986–; non-exec dep chm Lloyd Thompson Gp plc 1987–; FCA 1966, FCT 1985; *Recreations* salmon fishing, riding, skiing; *Clubs* Boodle's; *Style*— Robert Tomkinson, Esq; ✉ Home Farm, Wappenham, Towcester, Northants NN12 8SJ (☎ 01327 860439, fax 01327 860839); Electrocomponents plc, Broadoak, Bakewell Road, Orton, Peterborough PE2 6YS (☎ 01733 361234, fax 01733 363800)

TOMKYS, Sir (William) Roger; KCMG (1991, CMG 1984), DL (Cambs 1996); s of William Arthur Tomkys (d 1973), of Harden, Yorks, and Edith Tomkys (d 1984); *b* 15 March 1937; *Educ* Bradford GS, Balliol Coll Oxford (MA); *m* 1963, Margaret Jean, da of Norman Beilby Abbey (d 1964), of Barrow-in-Furness; 1 s, 1 da; *Career* HM Foreign Serv 1960–92; seconded to Cabinet Office 1975, head Near East and N Africa Dept FCO 1977–80, head chancery and cnsllr Rome 1980–81, ambass and consul gen to Bahrain 1981–84, ambass to Syria 1984–86, princ fin offr FCO 1986–89, dep under sec of state 1989–90, high cmmr Nairobi 1990–92; also served: Athens, Benghazi, Amman; studied MECAS; master Pembroke Coll Cambridge 1992–; Commendatore Dell'Ordine Al Merito Italy 1980, Order of Bahrain (first class) 1984; *Style*— Sir Roger Tomkys, KCMG, DL; ✉ Pembroke College, Cambridge CB2 1RF

TOMLINS, Christopher David Corbett; s of Maj David Corbett Tomlins, of Bosham, West Sussex, and Pamela Gertrude, *née* Steele; *b* 15 Aug 1940; *Educ* Bradfield, Guy's Hosp Med and Dental Sch BDS, MB BS (London), LRCP, MRCS, FDSRCS; *m* 28 Oct 1972, Gillian Joan, da of Spencer Charles Cawthorn (d 1974); 4 s (David b 1974, Julian b 1976, Roger b 1976 (twin), Michael b 1979); *Career* dental house surgn Edgware Gen Hosp and Guy's Hosp 1964, orthopaedic house surgn Guy's Hosp 1970, house physician St Luke's Hosp Guildford 1970; registrar: Eastman Dental Hosp 1971–72, Westminster and Queen Mary's Roehampton 1972–73; sr registrar Westminster, Queen Mary's and Univ Coll Hosp 1973–76, visiting registrar Univ of Witswatersrand Johannesburg 1976, conslt oral and maxillofacial surgn Royal Berks Hosp Reading 1976–; hon treas BMA 1988 (chm 1984, vice chm W Berkshire dist 1986), chm Reading Section BDA 1986, chm Oxford Regnl Ctee Hosp Dental Servs 1991; memb: Central Ctee Hosp Dental Servs 1991, Central Manpower Ctee (Dental) 1991, regional advsr in oral surgery 1996–, Reading Pathological Soc; fell BAOMS 1976; *Recreations* sailing, skiing, walking, photography; *Style*— Christopher Tomlins, Esq; ✉ Silbury, 50 Shinfield Rd, Reading, Berkshire RG2 7BW (☎ 0118 987 1566); 13 Bath Rd, Reading, Berkshire RG1 6HH (☎ 0118 958 4711)

TOMLINSON, Sir Bernard Evans; kt (1988), CBE (1981), DL (1989); s of James Arthur Tomlinson (d 1980), and Doris Mary, *née* Evans (d 1985); *b* 13 July 1920; *Educ* Brunts Sch Mansfield Notts, UCL (MB BS), UCH (MD); *m* 9 Aug 1944, Betty, da of Edgar Oxley (d 1941); 1 s (David Andrew b 1945), 1 da (Elizabeth Oxley (Mrs Peerless) b 1950); *Career* Maj RAMC specialist pathologist 1947–49; trainee pathologist (EMS) 1943–47, conslt neuropathologist Gen Hosp Newcastle upon Tyne 1972–85 (conslt pathologist 1949–55, sr conslt pathologist 1955–82), prof emeritus pathology Univ of Newcastle 1985– (hon prof of pathology 1972–85); chm Jt Planning Advsy Ctee Dept of Health 1985–90; leader of recently published enquiry into Health Servs, Med Educn and Research in Inner London; pres Br Neuropathological Soc (Dorothy Russell Meml lectr 1989); memb and vice chm Newcastle Health Authy 1975–80, chm Northern RHA Sci and Research Cmmn 1976–82, chm Northern RHA 1982–90, non-exec dir Newcastle upon Tyne City Health NHS Tst 1994–95; pres Northern Alzheimer Disease Soc 1986–89; chm Friends of Durham Cathedral 1991–94; Privy Cncl nominee memb Royal Pharmaceutical Soc Cncl 1990–95; author of numerous book chapters and articles on the pathology of the brain in old age and the pathology of dementia; Gold medallist for res into Alzheimer's disease at 3rd Int Conf on Alzheimer's Disease and Related Disorders Padua 1992; FRCP, FRCPath; *Recreations* golf, gardening, walking, music; *Clubs* Army & Navy, Pall Mall; *Style*— Sir Bernard Tomlinson, CBE, DL; ✉ Greyholme, Wynbury Rd, Low Fell, Gateshead, Tyne & Wear NE9 6TS

TOMLINSON, Prof (Alfred) Charles; s of Alfred Tomlinson, DCM (d 1973), of Stoke-on-Trent, and May, *née* Lucas (d 1972); *b* 8 Jan 1927; *Educ* Longton HS, Queens' Coll Cambridge (BA, MA), Univ of London (MA); *m* 23 Oct 1948, Brenda, da of Edwin Albert Raybould (d 1977), of Stoke-on-Trent; 2 da (Justine, Juliet); *Career* visiting prof Univ of New Mexico 1962–63, O'Connor prof Colgate Univ NY 1967–68 and 1989–90, visiting fell of humanities Princeton Univ 1981, prof of Eng lit Univ of Bristol 1982–92 (lectr 1956–68, reader 1968–82, prof emeritus 1992), Lamont prof Union Coll NY 1987; numerous public lectures and poetry readings throughout the world 1960–; graphics exhibited at Gimpel Fils and Leicester Galleries, one man shows at OUP London 1972 and Clare Coll Cambridge 1975, Arts Cncl touring exhibition The Graphics and Poetry of Charles Tomlinson opened at the Hayward Gallery London then toured England, Canada and the USA 1978; hon fell Queens' Coll Cambridge 1976; Hon DLitt: Univ of Keele 1981, Colgate Univ NY 1981, Univ of New Mexico 1986; hon prof Univ of Keele 1989–92, hon fell Royal Holloway and Bedford New Coll 1991; FRSL 1975; *Books* incl: Selected W C Williams (ed, 1976), Selected Octavio Paz (ed, 1979), Oxford Book of Verse in English Translation (ed, 1980), Some Americans (1981), Poetry and Metamorphosis (1983), Collected Poems (1987), The Return (1987), Annunciations (1989), Renga and Airborn (with Octavio Paz), Selected George Oppen (ed, 1990), The Door in the Wall (1992), Eros English'd, Erotic Classical Poems (ed, 1992), Selected Attilio Bertolucci (ed and trans, 1993), Jubilation (1995); *Graphics* incl: Eden (1985); *Recreations* music, gardening, walking, travel; *Style*— Prof Charles Tomlinson; ✉ c/o Oxford University Press, Walton Street, Oxford OX2 6DP

TOMLINSON, Claire Janet; da of Lascelles Arthur Lucas (d 1988), of Woolmers Park, nr Hertford, Herts, and Ethel Barbara, *née* Daer; *b* 14 Feb 1944; *Educ* Wycombe Abbey, Millfield, Somerville Coll Oxford (MA); *m* 16 March 1968, (George) Simon Tomlinson, s of George Antony Tomlinson (d 1954); 2 s (Luke b 27 Jan 1977, Mark b 25 March 1982), 1 da (Emma b 30 Oct 1974); *Career* polo player; Oxford half blue 1964–66, first woman to play against Cambridge, capt Oxford Univ team 1966, pioneered breakthrough for women to be allowed in high-goal polo 1978, memb winning team Queen's Cup 1979, capt English Team who were winners of the first worldwide Ladies' Int Polo Tournament 1991; highest rated woman polo player in the World, has achieved higher handicap than any other woman (5 goals in 1986, currently 2 goals); fencing: Oxford half blue 1963–66, capt Oxford ladies' team 1965–66, memb England under-21 team 1962–63; squash: Oxford half blue 1964–66; *Style*— Mrs Claire Tomlinson; ✉ Down Farm, Westonbirt, nr Tetbury, Glos (☎ 01666 880214)

TOMLINSON, David Cecil MacAlister; s of Clarence Samuel Tomlinson (d 1978), slr, of London Folkestone, and Florence Elizabeth Sinclair Thomson (d 1968); maternal uncle Albert Borlase Armitage (1864–43) was second in cmd on Capt Scott's first Antarctic Expedition 1901–04; uncle Sir Cecil Hamilton Armitage (1867–1933) was Govr of Gambia 1924–30; *b* 7 May 1917; *Educ* Tonbridge; *m* 1953, Audrey, da of Walter Redvers Freeman, of S Yorks; 4 s (David, James, William, Henry); *Career* actor and director; Grenadier Gds 1935–36, WWII Flt Lt RAF (pilot), demobbed 1946; princ roles incl: Henry in The Little Hut (Lyric) 1950–53, Clive in All Mary (Duke of Yorks) 1954–55, David in Dear Delinquent (Westminster and Aldwych) 1957–58, Tom in The Ring of Truth (Savoy) July 1959, Robert in Boeing-Boeing (Apollo) 1962; acted in and directed: Mother's Boy (Globe) 1964, A Friend Indeed (Cambridge) 1966, On the Rocks (Dublin Festival) 1969, A Friend Indeed and A Song at Twilight (SA) 1973–74, The Turning Point (Duke of Yorks) 1974; first appeared in films 1939, since then appeared in leading roles in over 50 films; *Books* Luckier Than Most (autobiography, 1990); *Recreations* putting my feet up; *Clubs* Boodle's; *Style*— David Tomlinson, Esq; ✉ Brook Cottage, Mursley, Bucks MK17 0RS (☎ 01296 720 213); 610 Chelsea Cloisters, Sloane Ave, London SW3 (☎ 0171 589 7303)

TOMLINSON, John; s of Frank Tomlinson, of Ashbourne, Derbys, and Barbara, *née* Mayer (d 1986); *b* 30 Jan 1941; *Educ* Lawton Hall, Alsager; *m* 31 March 1962, Christine Ann, da of Thomas Evan Jones, of Clifton Drive, Stafford; 2 s (Nicholas John b 1963, David Nigel b 1964), 1 da (Lisa Ann b 1969); *Career* dep chief exec London Scottish Bank plc; dir: London Scottish Bank plc and subsidiaries, Reliance Guarantee Co Ltd, Robinson Way & Co Ltd, Glengall Est Ltd; MIMgt 1972, fell Inst of Fin Accountants 1975; *Recreations* shooting, fishing; *Style*— John Tomlinson, Esq; ✉ London Scottish Bank plc, London Scottish House, Mount Street, Manchester M2 3LS (☎ 0161 834 2861)

TOMLINSON, John; MEP (Lab/Co-op) Birmingham West (majority 39,350); *Career* MP (Lab) Meriden 1974–79, PPS to PM Harold Wilson 1975–76, Parly under sec of state FCO 1976–79; MEP (Lab/Co-op) Birmingham W 1984–; currently vice chm Hansard Soc for Parliamentary Government, tstee Industry and Parliament Tst; *Style*— John Tomlinson, Esq, MEP; ✉ c/o European Parliament, 93–113 Rue Belliard, 1040 Brussels, Belgium

TOMLINSON, Prof John Race Godfrey; CBE (1983); s of John Angell Tomlinson (d 1968), and Beatrice Elizabeth Race, *née* Godfrey (d 1992); *b* 24 April 1932; *Educ* Stretford GS, Univ of Manchester (BA, MA), Univ of London; *m* 27 March 1954, Audrey Mavis, da of John Barrett (d 1935); 2 s (John b 1958, Graham b 1962), 2 da (Susan b 1959, Janet b 1960); *Career* Flt Lt RAF 1955–58; teacher 1958–60; educn offr: Shropshire LEA 1960–63, Lancs LEA 1963–67; dir of educn Cheshire LEA 1972–84 (dep dir 1967–71), prof of education and dir Inst of Educn Univ of Warwick 1985–; pres Soc Educn Offrs 1982–83; chm: Further Educn Curriculum Devpt Unit 1976–78, Schs Cncl 1978–82, Tstees Schs Curriculum Award 1982–95, RSA Examinations Bd 1985–89, Cncl RSA 1989–91 (memb Cncl 1980–), Gen Teaching Cncl 1990–, Ctee on Special Educn Further Educn Funding Cncl (FEFC) 1993–96, Cncl Policy Studies Inst 1994–; Freeman City of London 1988; Liveryman Worshipful Co of Goldsmiths; fell Coll of Preceptors, memb Royal Northern Coll of Music, FBIM 1977, FRSA 1976; *Books* Additional Grenville Papers (ed 1962), The Changing Government of Education (ed with S Ranson, 1986), Teacher Appraisal: A Nationwide Approach (ed with A Evans, 1989), The Control of Education (1993), School Cooperation: New Forms of Local Government (ed with S Ranson, 1994); *Recreations* walking, music, gardening; *Clubs* Athenaeum, Army and Navy; *Style*— Prof John Tomlinson, CBE; ✉ Institute of Education, University of Warwick, Westwood, Coventry CV4 7AL (☎ 01203 523830, fax 01203 524177, telex 317472 UN IREG)

TOMLINSON, John Rowland; CBE (1997); s of Rowland Tomlinson, of and Ellen Tomlinson, *née* Greenwood (d 1969); *b* 22 Sept 1946; *Educ* Accrington GS, Univ of Manchester (BSc), Royal Manchester Coll of Music; *m* 9 Aug 1969, Moya, da of William Joel (d 1978); 1 s (Joseph b 3 March 1976), 2 da (Abigail 27 Aug 1971, Ellen Tamasine 15 Feb 1973); *Career* bass; princ opera singer: Glyndebourne festival 1971–74, English Nat Opera 1974–80; numerous appearances at international venues incl Royal Opera House Covent Garden (debut 1976), Paris Opera, Berlin, Vienna, Amsterdam, Geneva, New York, Tokyo, Salzburg and San Francisco; major roles incl Wotan/The Wanderer in The Ring (Bayreuth) 1988–92 and 1994–95, Hans Sachs in Die Meistersinger (Covent Garden) 1993, Gurnemanz in Parsifal (Staatsoper Berlin) 1992–94, King Fisher in Midsummer Marriage (Covent Garden) 1996; awards incl Royal Philharmonic Soc singing award 1992; *Recreations* tennis; *Style*— John Tomlinson, Esq, CBE; ✉ c/o Music International, 13 Ardilaun Rd, Highbury, London N5 2QR (☎ 0171 359 5183)

TOMLINSON, Lindsay; *Educ* Univ of Cambridge (MA); *m*; 1 da, 4 s; *Career* with Commercial Union plc 1974–76, conslt pensions actuary 1976–81, sr investmt mangr Provident Mutual 1981–87; BZW Investment Management Ltd: joined 1987, md UK business 1990–92, dep chief exec 1992–94, chief exec 1994–; *Style*— Lindsay Tomlinson, Esq; ✉ BZW Investment Management Ltd, Seal House, 1 Swan Lane, London EC4R 3UD (☎ 0171 623 7777, fax 0171 621 9411)

TOMLINSON, Maj-Gen Michael John; CB (1981), OBE (1973, MBE 1964); s of Sidney Cyril Tomlinson (d 1983), and Emily Rose, *née* Hodges (d 1986); *b* 20 May 1929; *Educ* The Skinners' Sch Tunbridge Wells, RMA Sandhurst; *m* 24 June 1955, Lily Patricia, da of Lt-Col A Rowland, OBE, MC (d 1971); 1 s (Peter b 1958), 1 da (Jane (Mrs Wallis) b 1962); *Career* cmmnd RA 1949, served Tripoli, Canal Zone, Jordan and Germany 1950–60, GSO2 ops to dir of ops Brunei 1962–64 (despatches); dep asst mil sec 1966–68, instr Staff Coll Camberley 1968–70, CO 2 Field Regt RA 1970–72, Col GS Staff Coll Camberley 1972–73, CRA 3 Div 1973–75, dep mil sec 1976–78, dir of manning (Army) 1978–79, Vice Adj Gen 1979–81, DRA 1981–84, ret May 1984; Col Cmdt RA 1982–91, Hon Col 104 Regt RA (V) 1985–87, Hon Regt Col 2 Field Regt RA 1985–89; vice pres Nat Artillery Assoc 1984–91, pres Central Branch RA Assoc 1988–90; sec The Dulverton Tst 1984–94; FIMgt 1984, FRSA 1985; *Recreations* gardening, music; *Clubs* Army and Navy; *Style*— Maj-Gen Michael Tomlinson, CB, OBE; ✉ c/o Lloyds Bank, 82 Mount Pleasant Road, Tunbridge Wells, Kent TN1 1RP

TOMLINSON, Michael John; s of Jack Tomlinson (d 1993), of Rotherham, Yorkshire, and Edith, *née* Cresswell (d 1988); *b* 17 Oct 1942; *Educ* Oakwood Tech HS Rotherham, Bournemouth Sch, Univ of Durham (BSc), Univ of Nottingham (PGCE); *m* 17 July 1965, Maureen Janet, da of Wilfred Ernest Tupling; 1 s (Philip John b 3 Jan 1968), 1 da (Jane Louise 23 March 1970); *Career* chemistry teacher Henry Mellish GS Nottingham 1965–69, head of chemistry Ashby-de-la-Zouch GS Leics 1969–78, schs/indust liaison offr ICI Ltd 1977, chief inspr of schools HM Inspectorate of Schools 1989–92 (joined 1978), dir of inspection OFSTED 1995– (dep dir 1992–94); Chemical Society Education Bronze Medal 1975; author of various pubns for BP Ltd 1974–78; *Books* New Movements in the Study and Teaching of Chemistry (1975), Organic Chemistry: A Problem-Solving Approach (1977), Mechanisms in Organic Chemistry: Case Studies (1978); *Recreations* gardening, reading, food and drink; *Style*— Michael Tomlinson, Esq; ✉ Office for Standards in Education, Alexandra House, 29–33 Kingsway, London WC2B 6SE (☎ 0171 421 6786, fax 0171 925 6707)

TOMLINSON, Prof Richard Allan; s of James Edward Tomlinson (d 1963), and Dorothea Mary, *née* Grellier (d 1983); *b* 25 April 1932; *Educ* King Edward's Sch Birmingham, St John's Coll Cambridge (BA, MA); *m* 14 Dec 1957, Heather Margaret, da of Ernest Fraser Murphy (d 1965); 3 s (Nicholas John b 1959, Peter Brian b 1962, Edward James b 1965), 1 da (Penelope Ann b 1961); *Career* asst Dept of Greek Univ of Edinburgh 1957–58; Univ of Birmingham: asst lectr 1958–61, lectr 1961–69, sr lectr 1969–71, prof of ancient history and archaeology 1971–95; dir Br Sch at Athens 1995–96; memb: Victorian Soc, Hellenic Soc; FSA; *Books* Argos and the Argolid (1972), Greek Sanctuaries (1976), Epidauros (1980), Greek Architecture (1989), The Athens of Alma Tadema (1991), From Mycenae to Constantinople (1992), Greek and Roman Architecture (1994); *Recreations* walking; *Style*— Prof Richard Tomlinson, FSA; ✉ c/o Department of Ancient History and Archaeology, University of Birmingham, Birmingham B15 2TT (☎ 0121 515 5497, fax 0121 414 3595)

TOMLINSON, Prof Sally; da of Clifford Gilmore Entwistle (d 1966), and Alice Nora, *née* Stubbs (d 1974); *b* 22 Aug 1936; *Educ* Macclesfield HS, Univ of Liverpool (BA), Univ of Birmingham (MSocSci), Univ of Warwick (PhD); *m* 31 Aug 1957, Sqdn Ldr Brian Joseph Tomlinson (RAF ret); 1 s (Simon b 1962), 2 da (Susan b 1960, Joanna b 1963); *Career* lectr and sr lectr W Midlands Coll of Educn 1969–73, sr res fell Univ of Warwick 1974–77, prof of educn Univ of Lancaster 1984–91 (lectr and sr lectr 1978–84), prof of educn Univ Coll Swansea 1991–92, Goldsmith prof of policy and mgmnt in educn Goldsmiths' Coll Univ of London 1992– (dean Faculty of Educn 1993–95, pro-warden 1994–); sr assoc memb St Antony's Coll Oxford 1984–85; memb Univ Cncl for Educn of Teachers 1984–, res assoc Inst for Public Policy Res 1990–92; *Books* Colonial Immigrants in a British City - A Class Analysis (with John Rex, 1979), Education Subnormality - A Study in Decision Making (1981), Special Education: Policy Practices and Social Issues (jt ed, 1981), A Sociology of Special Education (1982), Ethnic Minorites in British Schools: A Review of the Literature 1960–1982 (1983), Home and School in Multicultural Britain (1984), Special Education and Social Interests (ed with Len Barton, 1984), Affirmative Action and Positive Policies in the Education of Ethnic Minorities (ed with Abraham Yogev, 1989), The School Effect: A Study of Multi-Racial Comprehensives (with David Smith, 1989), Multi-Cultural Education in White Schools (1990), The Assessment of Special Educational Needs: Whose Problem? (with David Galloway and Derrick Armstrong, 1994), Educational Reform and its Consequences (1994), Ethnic Relations and Schooling (ed with Maurice Craft, 1995); *Style*— Prof Sally Tomlinson; ✉ Goldsmiths' College, University of London, New Cross, London SE14 6NW (☎ 0181 692 7171, fax 0181 691 9504)

TOMLINSON, Prof Stephen; s of Frank Tomlinson, of Bolton, Lancs, and Elsie, *née* Towler; *b* 20 Dec 1944; *Educ* Hayward GS Bolton, Univ of Sheffield (MB ChB, MD); *m* 14 Oct 1970, Christine Margaret, da of George Hope, of Sheffield, Yorks; 2 da (Rebecca b 1974, Sarah b 1977); *Career* Wellcome Tst sr lectr in clinical sci 1980–85 (sr res fell 1977–80), reader in med Univ of Sheffield 1982–85; Univ of Manchester Med Sch: prof of med 1985–, chm Sch of Med Scis 1990–93, dean Med Sch and Faculty of Med Dentistry and Nursing 1993–; author of pubns on mechanisms of hormone action, and intracellular signalling and orgn of health care in diabetes; chm Assoc of Clinical Profs of Med 1996– (sec 1994–96), exec sec Cncl of Deans of Med Schs & their Faculties in UK 1997–; treas Assoc of Physicians of GB and I 1993– (sec 1988–93); FRCP; *Style*— Prof Stephen Tomlinson; ✉ Makants Farm, Blackburn Rd, Eagley Bank, Bolton, Lancs BL1 7LH (☎ 01204 304765, fax 01204 300535); The Medical School, Stopford Building, Oxford Road, Manchester M13 9PT (☎ 0161 275 5027, fax 0161 275 5584)

TOMLINSON, Stephen Miles; QC (1988); s of Capt Enoch Tomlinson, of Winslow, Bucks, and Mary Marjorie Cecelia, *née* Miles; *b* 29 March 1952; *Educ* King's Sch Worcester, Worcester Coll Oxford (MA); *m* 15 March 1980, Joanna Kathleen, da of Ian Joseph Greig; 1 s, 1 da; *Career* called to the Bar Inner Temple 1974, bencher 1990, currently recorder of the Crown Court; *Recreations* cricket, gardening, walking, family; *Clubs* MCC; *Style*— Stephen Tomlinson, Esq, QC; ✉ 7 King's Bench Walk, Temple, London EC4Y 7DS (☎ 0171 583 0404, fax 0171 583 0950, telex 887491)

TOMS, Carl; OBE (1969); s of Bernard Toms (d 1947), of Mansfield, Notts, and Edith Toms; *b* 29 May 1927; *Educ* Sch of Art Mansfield, RCA, Old Vic Sch; *Career* asst to Oliver Messel 1953–59, theatre designer 1960–; first design cmmn Suzanna's Secret (Glyndebourne) 1960, designed interior for Theatre Royal Bath, design conslt for investiture of Prince of Wales at Caernarvon Castle 1969, head of design Young Vic Theatre until 1980 (dir); Tony award for prodn of Sherlock Holmes (RSC) 1975, Olivier award for the Provoked Wife (NT) 1981; worked on: 14 prodns for the NT, 10 prodns for the Burg Theatre and Staatsoper Vienna, NY City Opera, Metropolitan Opera, San Francisco Opera, many West End prodns; active in charitable work; FRSA; *Recreations* work, theatre, art, architecture, gardens; *Clubs* Groucho; *Style*— Carl Toms, Esq, OBE; ✉ The White House, Beaumont, nr Wormley, Broxbourne, Herts EN10 7QJ (☎ 01992 463961)

TOMS, Dr Rhinedd Margaret; da of David Peregrine Jones (d 1983), of Llanelli, Dyfed, and Margaret Edith, *née* Davies (d 1996); *b* 18 June 1942; *Educ* Howells Sch Denbigh, Girton Coll Cambridge (MA), Westminster Med Sch (MB BChir); *m* 19 Oct 1968, Brian Frank Toms (d 1985), s of Harold Frank Toms (d 1989), of Rushden, Northamptonshire; 1 s (David b 1971), 1 da (Eleanor b 1969); *Career* clinical med offr London Borough of Southwark 1968–71, sr med offr Lambeth Lewisham and Southwark AHA 1973–75, trg posts in psychiatry 1976–84, conslt psychiatrist NE Essex Mental Health Services 1984–; hon conslt St Luke's Hosp for the Clergy 1990–, clinical tutor in psychiatry Br Postgrad Med Fedn 1988–92, tst med advsr 1993–; hon conslt: Colchester and Ipswich branches Relate, Colchester branch MIND; memb Exec Ctee Phoenix Gp Homes; memb BMA; *Recreations* gardening, music, choral singing; *Style*— Dr Rhinedd Toms; ✉ 45 Oaks Drive, Colchester, Essex CO3 3PS (☎ 01206 549547); The Lakes Unit, Colchester General Hospital, Colchester, Essex CO4 5JL (☎ 01206 853535)

TOMSETT, Alan Jeffrey; OBE (1974); s of Maurice Jeffrey Tomsett (d 1987), and Edith Sarah, *née* Mackelworth (d 1953); *b* 3 May 1922; *Educ* Trinity Sch of John Whitgift Croydon, Univ of London (BCom); *m* 1948, Joyce May, da of Walter Albert Hill (d 1959); 1 s (Ian), 1 da (Ann); *Career* served WWII 1941–46 with RAF (Middle East 1942–45); Hodgson Harris & Co Chartered Accountants London 1938, Smallfield Rawlins & Co 1951, Northern Mercantile & Investment Corporation 1955, William Baird & Co Ltd 1962–63; fin dir British Transport Docks Board 1974–83 (chief accountant and fin controller 1964–73), dir Associated British Ports Holdings plc 1983–92 (fin dir 1983–87); churchwarden St John's Shirley 1988–92; FCA, FCMA, CPFA, JDipMA, FCIS, FCIT (vice pres 1981–82, hon treas 1982–88), FRSA; *Recreations* gardening; *Style*— Alan Jeffrey Tomsett, Esq, OBE; ✉ 102 Ballards Way, Croydon, Surrey CR0 5RG

TONBRIDGE, Bishop of 1993–; Rt Rev Brian Arthur Smith; s of Arthur Smith (d 1992), of Edinburgh, and Doris Marion, *née* Henderson; *b* 15 Aug 1943; *Educ* George Heriot's Sch Edinburgh, Univ of Edinburgh (MA), Univ of Cambridge (MA, MLitt); *m* 1 Aug 1970, Elizabeth Berring, da of Lt-Col Charles Francis Hutchinson (d 1980), of Longframlington, Northumberland; 2 da (Tessa b 1974, Alice b 1978); *Career* ordained: deacon 1972, priest 1973; curate of Cuddesdon 1972–79, tutor in doctrine Cuddesdon Coll Oxford 1972–75, dir of studies Ripon Coll Oxford 1975–78 (sr tutor 1978–79), dir of ministerial trg Diocese of Wakefield 1979–87; priest i/c Cragg Vale 1978–86, warden of readers Diocese of Wakefield 1981–87, hon canon of Wakefield Cathedral 1981–87, archdeacon of Craven 1987–93; vice chm Northern Ordination Course 1986–93; *Recreations* reading, music, walking, browsing in junk shops, short-wave radio listening, snorkling; *Clubs* National Liberal; *Style*— The Rt Rev the Bishop of Tonbridge; ✉ Bishop's Lodge, 48 St Botolph's Road, Sevenoaks, Kent TN13 3AG (☎ 01732 456070, fax 01732 741449)

TONGEMAN, Rev Peter Henry Kelway; s of Henry Tongeman (d 1975), and Irene Winifred Kelway, *née* Bamber; *b* 21 Nov 1929; *Educ* Palmers Sch Grays Essex, Spurgeons Theol Coll London; *m* 26 July 1958, Ruth Linda, da of Harold Eccles; 2 s (David Kelway b 13 June 1964, Christopher Kelway b 23 Nov 1965); *Career* Nat Serv RASC 1948–50; Spurgeons Coll London 1950–54; min: Ramridge Baptist Church Luton Beds 1954–60, Broadmead Baptist Church Northampton 1960–65; dir Youth Dept Baptist Union of GB 1965–71, min Ashley Baptist Church New Milton Hants 1972–86, SE Area gen superintendent (Kent, Sussex, Surrey and NE Hants) 1986–94, pres Baptist Union of GB 1995–96; *Books* Thirteen Plus (1974), A Silence and a Murmuring (poetry, 1993); *Recreations* swimming, cycling (tandem), gardening, poetry, violin; *Style*— The Rev Peter Tongeman; ✉ 3 Budds Lane, Romsey, Hants SO51 0HA (☎ 01794 524166)

TONGUE, Carole; MEP (Lab) London East (majority 57,389); da of Walter Archer Tongue, of Lausanne, Switzerland, and Muriel Esther, *née* Lambert; *b* 14 Oct 1955; *Educ* Brentwood Co HS, Loughborough Univ of Technol (BA); *m* 28 Dec 1990, Chris Pond; 1 da (Eleanore Christabel b 20 Dec 1992); *Career* asst ed Laboratory Practice 1977–78, courier for Sunsites Ltd in France 1978–79, Robert Schumann scholarship for res in social affrs Euro Parliament 1979–80, sec and admin asst in Socialist Gp Secretariat of Euro Parliament 1980–84; MEP (Lab) London East 1984–; spokesperson on media/culture policy for Pty of the Gp of Euro Socialists Euro Parliament 1995– (memb Temporary Ctee on Employment and Industry, memb Youth, Media and Culture Ctee, substitute memb Social Affairs Ctee); sr visiting fell Dept of Euro Studies Loughborough Univ; vice chm: AMA, SERA; memb: RIIA, MSF, GMB, CND, END, One World, Friends of the Earth, Greenpeace, Fabian Soc; *Recreations* piano, cello, tennis, squash, riding, cinema, theatre, opera; *Style*— Ms Carole Tongue, MEP; ✉ London East European Constituency Office, 97a Ilford Lane, Ilford, Essex IG1 2RJ (☎ 0181 514 0198, fax 0181 553 4764)

TONKIN, Derek; CMG (1982); s of Henry James Tonkin (d 1947), and Norah, *née* Wearing (d 1994); *b* 30 Dec 1929; *Educ* High Pavement GS Nottingham, St Catherine's Coll Oxford (MA); *m* 1953, Doreen, da of Horace Samuel Rooke (d 1967); 2 s (Christopher (decd), Jeremy), 2 da (Caroline, Susan); *Career* HM Diplomatic Service 1952–89; ambass to Vietnam 1980–82, min to S Africa 1983–85, ambass to Thailand and Laos 1986–89 (ret); chm: Gen Ctee Ockenden Venture, Beta Viet Nam Fund Ltd, Beta Mekong Fund Ltd; dir: AsiaInvest Fund Management Ltd, Indochina Consultants Ltd; *Recreations* tennis, music; *Clubs* Royal Over-Seas League; *Style*— Derek Tonkin, Esq, CMG; ✉ Heathfields, Berry Lane, Worplesdon, Guildford, Surrey GU3 3PU (☎ 01483 232955, fax 01483 233161); Beta Mekong Fund Ltd, Canada Court, St Peter Port, Guernsey, Channel Islands GY1 3BQ (☎ 01481 723021, fax 01481 723524)

TONKING, (Russel) Simon William Ferguson; s of Lt-Col John Wilson Tonking, MBE, TD (d 1992), and Mary Oldham, *née* Ferguson (d 1971); *b* 25 March 1952; *Educ* The King's Sch Canterbury, Emmanuel Coll Cambridge (MA); *m* 10 July 1976, (Sylvia) Mithra, da of Colin Ian McIntyre; 1 s (William b 1988), 1 da (Flora b 1984); *Career* called to the Bar Inner Temple 1975, recorder Midland and Oxford Circuit 1994–; steward Lichfield Cathedral (head steward 1984–86); *Recreations* music, old motor cars, watercolour painting; *Clubs* Vintage Sports Car; *Style*— Simon Tonking, Esq; ✉ 4 Fountain Court, Steelhouse Lane, Birmingham B4 6DR (☎ 0121 236 3476)

TONKS, Dr Clive Malcolm; s of Clarence Tonks (d 1989), of York, and Annie, *née* Holt (d 1992); *b* 21 March 1932; *Educ* Normanton GS, Univ of Leeds (MB ChB); *m* 25 Oct 1958, Dr Joyce Margaret Handby, da of Clarence Handby (d 1983); 1 s (David b 1964), 2 da (Susan b 1960, Alison b 1962); *Career* conslt psychiatrist St Mary's Hosp and Med Sch London 1969–91, sr lectr in psychiatry Univ of Leeds 1963–69, assoc prof of psychiatry Yale 1969–70, currently conslt psychiatrist Stamford Wing Royal Masonic Hosp London; chm Med Staff Paddington & North Kensington Health Authy 1983–87; author of papers and chapters on psychiatric topics; memb various standing ctees Royal Coll of Psychiatry; memb Parole Bd 1989–95; FRCP, FRCPsych, DPM Univ of London; *Recreations* geology, opera, walking; *Style*— Dr Clive M Tonks; ✉ 10 Anselm Rd, Pinner, Middlesex HA5 4LJ (☎ 0181 428 3894); Stamford Wing, The Royal Masonic Hospital, Ravenscourt Park, London W6 0TN (☎ 0181 741 9000)

TONKS, John; s of late John Henry Tonks, of Brewood, Staffs, and late Gladys Mary, *née* Maddocks; *b* 14 Aug 1927; *Educ* Dudley GS, Birmingham Coll of Art (maj scholar, NDD Sculpture, art teacher's Dip); *m* 14 July 1951, Sylvia Irene, da of Thomas William Taylor; 1 s (Julian Matthew John b 19 April 1953), 1 da (Caroline Louise Sylvia Mary b 12 April 1956); *Career* specialist art teacher in secdy schs 1952–65, lectr rising to sr lectr and princ lectr in sculpture W Midlands Coll of Higher Educn 1965–82, freelance sculptor 1982–; solo exhibitions incl: V B Gallery St Louis USA 1981, Oriel 31 Welshpool 1983, Ombersley Gallery Worcs 1983, Britain Salutes New York (Poole Willis Gallery NY) 1983, Helias Gallery Birmingham 1984, Univ of Birmingham 1984, Liverpool Int Garden Festival 1984, Garden Festival Wales 1992; public cmmns: Statue of Virgin Mary (St Mary's Church, Enville, Staffs), Sculpture of the Risen Christ (Wombourne Parish Church Staffs), The Family (Alexander Hosp, Redditch, Worcs), St Cecilia (Gardens of Penrell Hall, Staffs), Girl Awakening (Gretna Museum/Tourist Centre), Roman Woman (Birmingham Botanical Gardens), The Runaway Lovers (Gretna Museum/Tourist Centre); fell RSBS 1978 (assoc 1967, vice pres 1990); *Recreations* walking and work; *Style*— John Tonks, Esq; ✉ Downshill Cottage, Comhampton, Stourport-on-Severn, Worcester DY13 9ST (☎ 01905 620718)

TONKS, Julian Matthew John; s of John Tonks, of Comhampton, Worcs, and Sylvia Irene, *née* Taylor; *b* 19 April 1953; *Educ* Dudley GS, Trinity Coll Oxford (MA, MLitt); *m* 14 Aug 1980, Ann Miles, da of James Miles Henderson, of Granite City, Illinois; 1 s (Henry Miles James); *Career* admitted slr 1982; asst slr Freshfields 1982–86; Pinsent Curtis (formerly Pinsent & Co): tax ptnr 1987–, dep sr ptnr 1993–94, sr ptnr 1994–; chm Birmingham Common Purpose 1994–, tstee Birmingham Royal Ballet Tst 1996–; *Recreations* reading modern novels and medieval history, swimming, Castles, collecting photographs, cricket, wine; *Clubs* Worcestershire CC; *Style*— Julian Tonks, Esq; ✉ 17 Ampton Road, Edgbaston, Birmingham B15 2UJ; Pinsent Curtis, Solicitors, 3 Colmore Circus, Birmingham B4 6BH (☎ 0121 200 1050, fax 0121 626 1040)

TONYPANDY, 1 Viscount (UK 1983), of Rhondda, Co Mid Glamorgan; Rt Hon (Thomas) George Thomas; PC (1968); s of Zachariah Thomas (d 1925), of Tonypandy, S Wales, and Emma Jane Thomas; *b* 29 Jan 1909, Port Talbot; *Educ* Tonypandy GS, Univ Coll Southampton; *Career* former schoolmaster and vice pres Methodist Conference 1959–60; MP (Lab): Cardiff Central 1945–50, Cardiff W 1950–83; PPS to Min of Civil Aviation 1951, chm Welsh Labour Party 1950–51, parly under sec Home Office 1964–66, first chm Welsh Parly Grand Ctee, min of state Welsh Office 1966–67, Cwlth Office 1967–68, sec of state for Wales 1968–70, Speaker of House of Commons 1976–83 (Dep Speaker and chm Ways and Means Ctee 1974–76); hon master bencher Gray's Inn 1982–; pres: Nat Children's Home 1990–95 (formerly chm), Br Heart Fndn 1983–88; vice pres: Cancer Relief Macmillan Fund 1993–, Imperial Cancer Research 1993–; patron: Royal Coll of Radiologists 1993–, Royal Coll of Radiology 1996–, Coll of Preceptors 1996– (pres 1983–87); Freeman: Rhondda 1970, City of Cardiff 1974, City of London 1987, Paphos (Cyprus) 1988, Port Talbot 1990; hon memb Worshipful Co of Blacksmiths 1977; hon life memb: Cambridge Students Union 1982, NUT 1977; hon fell: Univ Coll Cardiff 1982, Poly of Wales 1982, St Hugh's Coll Oxford 1983, Hertford Coll Oxford 1983, Pembrokeshire Coll 1990, Westminster Coll Oxford 1990; hon companion Leicester Poly 1988; hon pres Guideposts Tst 1976; Hon LLD: Asbury Coll Kentucky, Univ of Southampton, Univ of Wales, Birmingham, Oklahoma USA, Liverpool, Leeds, Open Univ, Warwick 1984, Keele 1984; Hon DCL Oxford 1983, Hon DD Shreveport Louisiana 1982; Dato Setia Negara Brunei 1971, Grand Cross of Peruvian Congress 1980, Gold Award for Work of Democracy (State of Carinthia) Austria 1982; *Books* Christian Heritage in Politics (1960), Memoirs of Mr Speaker (1985), My Wales (1986); *Recreations* travel; *Clubs* Travellers' (hon life memb), Reform (hon life memb), United Oxford and Cambridge Univ (hon life memb), County Club (Cardiff, hon life memb); *Style*— The Rt Hon the Viscount Tonypandy, PC; ✉ House of Lords, London SW1A 0PW

TOOBY, Michael Bowen; s of Leslie and Jill Tooby, of Long Itchington, Warwicks; *b* 20 Dec 1956; *Educ* King Henry VIII Sch Coventry, Magdalene Coll Cambridge; *Career* asst curator Kettles Yard Cambridge 1978–80, exhbns organiser Third Eye Centre Glasgow 1980–84, keeper Mappin Art Gall Sheffield 1984–92, curator Tate Gall St Ives 1992–; *Style*— Michael Tooby, Esq; ✉ The Tate Gallery St Ives, Porthmeor Beach, St Ives, Cornwall TR26 1TG (☎ 01736 796226, fax 01736 794480)

TOOGOOD, James Anthony Gordon; s of Maj Leonard Gordon Toogood (d 1988), of St Albans, Herts, and Muriel Frances Georgina, *née* Robinson (d 1987); *b* 12 July 1932; *Educ* Aldenham, St John's Coll Cambridge (MA); *m* 12 Oct 1963, (Anne) Margaret, da of Charles Wilfred Robbins (d 1977), of St Albans, Herts; 3 s (Michael b 1964, Paul b 1967, Oliver b 1970); *Career* Nat Serv RA 1951–53, Capt Herts Yeo 1953–59; admitted slr 1959; sr ptnr Forrester & Forrester 1977–; Mayor of Malmesbury 1978; chm Bd of Govrs Malmesbury Sch 1970–75 and 1988–93; pres Gloucester and Wiltshire Incorporated Law Soc 1996–97; memb Law Soc; *Recreations* music, country pursuits, chairing ctees; *Style*— James Toogood, Esq; ✉ Riversdale, Malmesbury, Wiltshire (☎ 01666 822120); Forrester & Forrester, 59 High Street, Malmesbury, Wiltshire (☎ 01666 822671)

TOOGOOD, John; QPM (1977); s of James Waller Giddings Toogood (d 1964), of Chippenham, Wilts, and Katherine Mary, *née* Winter (d 1956); *b* 19 Aug 1924; *Educ* Chippenham GS, King's Coll London (LLB, LLM); *m* 1, 19 Oct 1946 (m dis 1949), June, da of Leslie Llewellyn Rowlands (d 1970), of Plymouth, Devon; m 2, 20 Dec 1951, Josephine, *née* Curran (d 1984); 1 da (Katherine b 3 Sept 1962); m 3, 23 July 1986 (remarried), June Martin (Rowlands); *Career* RM 1942–46; Met Police 1946–83 (ret as Cdr); called to the Bar Gray's Inn 1957, in practice 1983–; memb Medico-Legal Soc 1955; SBStJ 1984; *Recreations* family; *Style*— John Toogood, Esq, QPM; ✉ 4 King's Bench Walk, Temple, London EC4V 7DL (☎ 0171 353 0478)

TOOK, Barry; s of Charles William Took (d 1961), of Worthing, and Kate Louie Rose, *née* Cox (d 1969); *b* 19 June 1928; *Educ* Stationers' Cos' Sch; *m* 1, 10 Aug 1950 (m dis 1965), Dorothy Bird, da of Richard Bird (d 1965), of Lincoln; 2 s (Barry b 1951, David b 1961), 1 da (Susan b 1956); m 2, 29 Oct 1965, Lynden L, da of Mark Leonard (d 1967), of Scunthorpe; 1 da (Elinor b 1968); *Career* Nat Serv RAF 1946–49; broadcaster: Late Extra 1959–60, Bootsie and Snudge 1960–63, Round the Horne 1964–68, Marty 1968–69, Rowan and Martin's Laugh In (NBC) 1969–70, On the Move (BBC adult literacy project) 1975–79, Points of View (BBC1) 1979–86, The News Quiz (Radio 4) 1979–; conslt Comedy Dept Thames TV 1968–69, advsr BBC TV 1969–70, head of light entertainment LWT 1971–72; hon cncllr NSPCC; *Books* Laughter in the Air (1976), Tooks Eye View (1983), Comedy Greats (1989), A Point of View (autobiography, 1990), Star Turns (1992); *Recreations* golf, travel; *Clubs* MCC; *Style*— Barry Took, Esq; ✉ 17 Hanover House, St John's Wood, London NW8 7DX (☎ 0171 722 8049, fax 0171 483 2834)

TOOKE, Brian Cecil; CBE (1983); s of Cecil George Tooke (d 1982), and Violet Mabel, *née* Rolfe (d 1988); *b* 29 Dec 1933; *Educ* St Joseph's Coll Ipswich; *m* 4 July 1959 (m dis 1988), Patricia Ann, *née* Sadler (d 1993); 2 s (Robert James b 1964, Julian Charles George b 1968), 2 da (Clarissa Jane b 1961, Melissa Mary b 1972); *Career* chm: Sadler Holdings Ltd until 1991, Local Bd Commercial Union Assurance plc 1983–91; JP Suffolk 1965–95; chm East of England Area Young Cons 1962–64; memb: Cons Party Nat Union Exec 1962–64 and 1975–84, Nat Union GP Ctee 1980–83, Cons Party Nat Advsy Ctee for Local Govt 1968–77, Ipswich CBC 1959–74; pres East of England Area Cons Assoc 1987–90 (chm 1980–83), chm Ipswich and Suffolk Industl Advsy Cncl 1985–88 (fndr memb 1972–), pres, tstee, former chm and fndr Suffolk Cncl Nat Assoc of Boys Clubs 1962–92, memb Cncl East Anglian TAVR Assoc 1985–91 (memb Suffolk Ctee TAVR 1980–91); chm: Ipswich and Dist Appeal Ctee Suffolk Tst for Nature Conservations 1983–85, East Anglian Region C of C 1984–87, Suffolk Podiatric Clinic Appeal 1989–93; govr St Joseph's Gp Coll Ipswich 1963–88; *Recreations* theatre, bridge, architecture; *Style*— Brian Tooke, Esq, CBE; ✉ Chattisham Hall, Suffolk IP8 3PX

TOOKEY, Christopher David; s of Alan Oliver Tookey, and Winifreda, *née* Marsh; *b* 9 April 1950; *Educ* Tonbridge, Exeter Coll Oxford (MA, ed of Isis, pres Oxford Union); *m* 2 Sept 1989, Frances Anne, da of Henry Robert Heasman; 1 s (Daniel b 12 April 1991); *Career* writer, broadcaster, director, producer and composer of musicals; prodns incl: Hard Times 1973, Room with A Revue 1974, Retrogrim's Progress 1974, Hanky Park 1975, Dick Whittington 1975 and 1976, An Evening with Noel and Gertie 1975 and 1976, The Resurrection of the British Musical 1977, Him 'n' Her 1979, Ladies and Jurgen 1980; asst theatre dir Belgrade Theatre Co 1973–74, Haymarket and Phoenix Theatre Leicester 1974–75, TV prodr and dir Associated Television 1975–82, weekend ed and assoc features ed TV-am 1982–83, freelance TV dir 1983–; credits incl: After Dark, Network 7, various rock videos; as freelance journalist: Books and Bookmen 1983–86, film critic Sunday Telegraph 1989–92 (freelance feature writer 1986, TV critic 1987–89), film critic Daily Telegraph 1993– (feature writer Daily Telegraph 1986–93, TV critic 1989–90), film critic, feature writer and occasional theatre critic Daily Mail 1993–, theatre critic Mail on Sunday 1993; also freelance journalist for Prospect, Applause, The Sunday Times, The Observer, The European, The Literary Review, Drama, National Review (US); freelance broadcaster 1989– (progs incl Sky News, The Arts Prog (BBC Radio 2), What the Papers Say (BBC2), Book Choice (Channel 4), Meridian (BBC) and First Edition (BSB); presenter ALFS Awards Ceremony (London Film Critics) 1994–; chm Film Critics' Circle 1994–; *Books* The Critics' Film Guide (1994); *Recreations* workaholicism; *Style*— Christopher Tookey, Esq; ✉ Chris Tookey Productions, 4 Alwyne Villas, London N1 2HQ (☎ 0171 226 2726, fax 0171 354 2574)

TOOLEY, Alan Hunter; s of Henry Hunter Tooley (d 1972), of Middlesbrough, and Josephine; *b* 13 May 1930; *Educ* Falmouth and East Ham GS, Univ of London (MB BS); *m* 1, 1 March 1958 (m dis 1976), Mary Josephine, *née* Aitken; 1 s (Timothy Hunter b 13 June 1964), 2 da (Elizabeth Mary b 29 Oct 1958, Fiona Margaret (twin)); m 2, 3 June 1977, Barbara Elizabeth, da of William Miller (d 1960), of Coventry; *Career* Surgn Cdr RN Med Serv 1955–68; conslt surgn South Tees Health Dist 1968–; examiner in anatomy for Primary FRCS 1978–84, regnl advsr in surgery RCS 1983; memb: Darlington Health Authy 1983–, Ct of Examiners in Surgery Final RCS 1985–, pres N of Eng Surgical Soc 1987–88, chm Regnl Sub Ctee in Surgery Northern Region 1989; memb Vasular Soc, fell Assoc of Surgns; LRCP, FRCS, AKC; *Recreations* music, woodturning; *Clubs* Army and Navy; *Style*— Alan Tooley, Esq; ✉ 26 The Avenue, Linthorpe, Middlesbrough, Cleveland TS5 6PD (☎ 01642 818750); South Cleveland Hospital, Marton Road, Middlesbrough, Cleveland TS4 3BW (☎ 01642 850850)

TOOLEY, Sir John; kt (1979); yr s of late H R Tooley; *b* 1 June 1924; *Educ* Repton, Magdalene Coll Cambridge; *m* 1, 1951 (m dis 1965), Judith Craig Morris; 3 da; m 2, 1968 (m dis 1990), Patricia Janet Norah, 2 da of late G W Bagshawe; 1 s; m 3, 1995, Jennifer Anne Shannon; *Career* served Rifle Bde 1943–47; sec Guildhall Sch of Music and Drama 1952–55; Royal Opera House: asst to gen administrator 1955–60, asst gen admin 1960–70, gen admin 1970–80, gen dir 1980–88; arts conslt 1988–, chm Almeida Theatre 1990–, chm Rudolf Nureyev Foundation 1995–; govr Repton Sch 1984–94; Commendatore della Repubblica Italiana 1976; DUniv Univ of Central England (UCE); Hon FRAM, Hon GSM, Hon RNCM; *Recreations* walking, theatre; *Clubs* Arts; *Style*— Sir John Tooley; ✉ 2 Leinster Mews, London W2 3EY (☎ 0171 262 5038, fax 0171 262 4425)

TOOLEY, Dr Peter John Hocart; s of Dr Patrick Hocart Tooley (d 1991), of Vale, Guernsey, and Brenda Margaret, *née* Williams (d 1939); *b* 28 Feb 1939; *Educ* Elizabeth Coll Guernsey, St George's Sch Harpenden, Univ of London, London Hosp Med Coll London Univ (MB BS, DObst RCOG, DMJ), LLM 1995; *m* 1, 22 Sept 1966 (m dis 1983), Elizabeth Monica, da of Percy Roche (d 1991), of Twyford, Berks; 1 s (Patrick b 1969), 2 da (Lucy b 1967, Josephine b 1971); m 2, 1987, Diana Edith, *née* Sturdy; *Career* sr ptnr gen med practice Twyford Berks 1974–90 (princ 1966, trainer 1977–81), asst dep coroner Borough of Reading 1984–89; Janssen-Cilag Ltd (formerly Janssen Pharmaceutical Ltd): med conslt gen practice affrs 1986–90, sr med advsr 1990–93, head of med affrs 1993–, med dir Ireland 1996–; MO: Oxfordshire RFU 1970–, Marks & Spencer plc Reading 1980–90, Wasps RFC; memb: Berks Local Med Ctee 1978–86, Reading Pathological Soc; chm Reading Med Club 1980–83 and 1987–90 (fndr memb), vice chm Polehampton Charities 1986–90 (tstee 1975); Freeman City of London, Liveryman Worshipful Soc of Apothecaries 1965; MRCS, LRCP 1963, MRCGP 1971; memb: BMA, Br Acad of Forensic Scis, Br Assoc of Pharmaceutical Physicians; FRSM; *Recreations* sports, gardening, travel; *Style*— Dr Peter Tooley; ✉ Siplak House, Station Rd, Lower Shiplake, Henley on Thames, Oxon RG9 3NY (☎ and fax 0118 940 3545); Janssen-Cilag Ltd, Saunderton, High Wycombe, Bucks HP14 (☎ 01494 567627, fax 01494 567445, mobile 0831 161178)

TOONE, Dr Brian Kenneth; s of Donald Freer Thomas (d 1979), and Mary Mable Ethel, *née* Downing; *b* 1 July 1937; *Educ* St Laurence Coll Ramsgate, King's Coll and St George's Hosp Med Sch London (MB BS, MPhil); *m* 28 Sept 1965 (m dis 1979), Megan Reece; *Career* conslt: Dept of Psychological Med KCH 1980–, The Maudsley and Bethlem Royal Hosp 1991–; hon sr lectr Inst of Psychiatry London 1986– (sub-dean 1984–87), currently recognised teacher Univ of London; author of chapters and scientific articles on organic psychiatry and psychiatric aspects of epilepsy; MRCP 1967, MRCPsych 1973, FRCP 1988, FRCPsych 1988; *Recreations* tennis, squash; *Style*— Dr Brian Toone; ✉ King's College Hospital, Department of Psychological Medicine, Denmark Hill, London SE5 9RS (☎ 0171 346 3228/3226, fax 0171 346 3445)

TOOP, Alan James; s of James Cecil Toop (d 1973), of Clephane Rd, London, and Elsie Ada, *née* Lavers (d 1993); *b* 25 Feb 1934; *Educ* Highbury GS, UCL (BA); *m* 12 Sept 1964, Tessa Peggy Elaine, da of Richard Eric Widdis (d 1966), of Kenton, Middx; 1 s (Adam b 1965), 2 da (Annie b 1968, Rosie b 1972); *Career* brand mangr Wall's Ice Cream 1958–61, mktg mangr Lever Bros 1961–65, account dir J Walter Thompson 1967–70, chm The Sales Machine International Ltd 1970–; FCIM, FISP; *Books* Choosing The Right Sales Promotion (1966), Crackingjack! Sales Promotion Techniques (1991), European Sales Promotion (1992), Sales Promotion in Postmodern Marketing (1994); *Recreations* exercise; *Clubs* IOD; *Style*— Alan Toop, Esq; ✉ 93 Riverview Gardens, London SW13 9RA; The Sales Machine International Ltd, 5 Dolphin Square, Edensor Road, London W4 2RG (☎ 0181 995 1949, fax 0181 742 3679)

TOOP, David; s of Leslie John Toop, of Waltham Cross, Herts, and Doris Ada May, *née* Purver; *b* 5 May 1949; *Educ* Broxbourne GS, Hornsey Coll of Art, Watford Coll of Art; *m* 30 May 1987, Kimberley (d 1995), da of Les Leston; 1 da (Juliette Angelica b 13 Feb 1990); *Career* music journalist and musician; played with Paul Burwell 1970–80, gave three illustrated music talks BBC Radio 3 1971–75, recorded three pieces for The Obscure Label 1975, launched record label Quartz 1978, recorded with Flying Lizards 1979, publisher and co-ed Collusion magazine 1981–83, pop music critic The Sunday Times Newspaper 1986–88; currently: monthly music columnist and feature writer The Face 1984–, music critic The Times; contrib to Arena, Wire, GQ and various books; *Recordings* Buried Dreams (with Max Eastley) 1994, Screen Ceremonies (solo album) 1995, Pink Noir (solo album) 1996; *Books* The Rap Attack (1984), The Rap Attack 2 (1991), Ocean of Sound (1995); *Style*— David Toop, Esq

TOOTAL, Christopher Peter; s of Charles Stanley Albert Tootal, of Plaxtol, Kent, and Patricia Mary, *née* Swanson; *b* 10 March 1936; *Educ* Repton, Queen's Coll Oxford (Robert Styring scholar, BA, BSc); *m* 20 April 1968, Alison Jane, da of late Archibald James Forbes; 1 s (Alastair James David b 22 April 1970), 1 da (Joanna Helen Natacha b 13 March 1974); *Career* tech asst Frank B Dehn & Co 1958–60, chartered patent agent Gill Jennings & Every 1962–64 (tech asst 1960–62); Herbert Smith: articled clerk 1964–67, asst slr 1967–68, ptnr 1968–; Liveryman Worshipful Co of Tallow Chandlers 1965–; *Books* The Law of Industrial Design - Registered Designs, Copyright and Design Right (1990); *Recreations* music, sailing, photography; *Clubs* Royal Harwich Yacht; *Style*— Christopher Tootal, Esq; ✉ Herbert Smith, Exchange House, Primrose Street, London EC2A 2HS (☎ 0171 374 8000, fax 0171 496 0043)

TOPE, Baron (Life Peer UK 1994), of Sutton in the London Borough of Sutton; Graham Norman; CBE (1991); s of Leslie Norman Tope (d 1983), of Sutton, and Winifred Sophia, *née* Merrick (d 1972); *b* 30 Nov 1943; *Educ* Whitgift Sch; *m* 22 July 1972, Margaret, da of Frank East; 2 s (Hon Andrew b 3 July 1974, Hon David b 21 June 1976); *Career* with Unilever Group 1961–69, insur mangr Air Products Ltd 1970–72, MP (Lib) Sutton and Cheam 1972–74, dep gen sec Voluntary Action Camden 1975–90; London Borough of Sutton: cncllr (Lib/Lib Dem) 1974–, ldr 1986–; pres London Lib Dems 1991–; UK memb EU Ctee of the Regions 1994–; spokesperson on educn House of Lords 1994–; *Recreations* politics, history, reading, walking, gardening; *Style*— The Rt Hon the Lord Tope, CBE; ✉ 88 The Gallop, Sutton, Surrey SM2 5SA (☎ and fax 0181 770 7269); Leadership Office, London Borough of Sutton, Civic Offices, St Nicholas Way, Sutton, Surrey SM1 1EA (☎ 0181 770 5406, fax 0181 770 5414)

TOPLIS, Philip John; s of Ivor Toplis (d 1991), of Penarth, Glamorgan, and Theresa Mary, *née* Williams (d 1986); *b* 6 March 1950; *Educ* Christ's Coll Brecon, Univ of Bristol (MB ChB); *m* 12 March 1983, Catherine Diana Suzanne, da of Robert Pierre Marcel

Lassalle; 2 s (Gareth b 1983, Alexander b 1989), 1 da (Laura (twin) b 1983); *Career* W Surrey and NE Hants HA: conslt obstetrician and gynaecologist 1986–, chm Div of Obstetrics Gynaecology and Paediatrics; memb BMA 1973, FRCS 1979, FRSM 1984, FRCOG 1993 (MRCOG 1980); *Books* Alcohol and Coffee Consumption in Pregnancy (1982), Colposcopy and the Postmenopausal Woman (1986); *Recreations* golf, skiing, pianoforte; *Clubs* RSM; *Style*— Philip Toplis, Esq; ✉ Windmill House, Hagley Rd, Fleet, Hants GU13 8LH (☎ 01252 615886); Frimley Park Hospital, Camberley, Surrey (☎ 01276 69277)

TOPOL, Chaim; s of Jacob and Rela Topol; *b* 9 Sept 1935; *Educ* Tachkemoni, La Salle HS; *m* 23 Oct 1956, Galia, da of Joseph Finkelstein; 1 s (Omer b 1962), 2 da (Anat b 1958, Adi b 1966); *Career* actor; began acting career 1954 during army serv; fndr Haifa Theatre 1960, film debut in I Like Mike; dir Popular Theatre of Israel; *Theatre* incl: Tevye in Fiddler on the Roof (Tel Aviv and London prodns, Broadway 1991); Chichester Festival Theatre: The Caucasian Chalk Circle, Romanoff and Juliet, Othello; A View from the Bridge (Palace Theatre Manchester) 1985; *Television* incl: It's Topol (BBC), Topol's Israel (BBC); *Films* incl: Sallah, Tevye in Fiddler on the Roof (Golden Globe Award, Oscar nomination) 1970, Before Winter Comes, A Talent for Loving, The Publc Eye, Galileo, The House on Garibaldi Street, Flash Gordon, For Your Eyes Only, The Winds of War, War and Remembrance, Queenie, A Dime Novel; *Awards* Golden Gate Award, Golden Globe Award (twice), David Donatello Award; *Books* Topol by Topol, To Life; *Recreations* drawing; *Style*— Topol; ✉ c/o Brian Eagles, Hammond Suddards, Moor House, 119 London Wall, London EC2Y 5ET (☎ 0171 448 1000, fax 0171 448 1001)

TOPOLSKI, Daniel; s of Feliks Topolski (d 1989), the artist, of London, and Marion Everall Topolski (d 1985); *b* 4 June 1945; *Educ* French Lycée London, Westminster, New Coll Oxford; *partner*, Susan Gilmore, da of James Gilbert; 2 da (Emma Sheridan b 30 Jan 1987, Tamsin Lucy Gilbert b 17 Nov 1990); *Career* prodr BBC TV 1969–73, expedition leader Iran and Turkey 1973–74; writer on travel and sport, TV and radio presenter, journalist, photographer; memb: London Rowing Club 1964–, Morton's 1975–, Leander Club 1965–, Upper Thames Rowing Club 1986–; participant Oxford v Cambridge Boat Race 1967 (winner) and 1968; Henley Royal Regatta: competitor 1962–93, winner 1969–70 and 1976–77, Henley steward 1991–; maj championships: 5 place VIIIs N American Championships (St Catherine's, Canada) 1967, 12 place Coxless IVs Euro Championships (Klagenfurt, Austria) 1969, 7 place Lightweight Coxless IVs World Championships (Lucerne) 1974, 2 place Lightweight Coxless IVs World Championships (Nottingham) 1975, winner Coxed IVs Home International (Cork) 1976, Gold medallist Lightweight VIIIs World Championships (Amsterdam) 1977, 7 place Lightweight Double Sculls World Championships (Copenhagen) 1978; chief coach to Oxford Univ for Boat Race 1973–87 (won 12, longest ever Oxford winning sequence (10), 3 course records 1974, 1976 and 1984 (16mins 45secs)), coach to Nat Women's Rowing Squad 1978–80, coaching dir Oxford Univ Boat Club 1994–; maj championships as coach: 8 place Women's VIIIs World Championships (Bled, Yugoslavia) 1979, 5 place Women's VIIIs Olympics (Moscow) 1980, 12 place Men's Pair and 10 place Women's Pair World Championships (Lucerne) 1982, 12 place Men's Pair Olympics (Los Angeles) 1984; winner Travel Radio Prog of Yr Award 1994; Churchill fell, FRGS; *Books* Muzungu: One Man's Africa (1976), Travels with My Father (1983), Boat Race (1985), True Blue (1989, sports book of the year, filmed 1996), Henley the Regatta (1989); *Style*— Daniel Topolski, Esq; ✉ 69 Randolph Avenue, London W9 1DW (☎ 0171 289 8939, fax 0171 266 1884)

TOPP, Air Cdre Roger Leslie; AFC (1950, and 2 Bars 1955 and 1957); s of Horace William Topp (d 1972), and Kathleen, *née* Peters; *b* 14 May 1923; *Educ* North Mundham Sch, RAF Cranwell; *m* 21 April 1945, Audrey Jane, da of Arther Stanley Jeffery (d 1969); 1 s (Jeffery b 12 Aug 1950), 1 da (Marilyn b 24 March 1946); *Career* WWII: cmmnd RAF 1944, Glider Pilot Regt E Sqdn Rhine Crossing Operation Varisity 1945; pilot Nos 107 and 98 Mosquito Sqdns BAFO Germany 1947–50, Empire Test Pilots Sch Farnborough 1950; lead test pilot: Armament and Structures flights Farnborough, Comet Flight tests after disasters 1951–55; OC No 111 Fighter Sqdn, formed and led Black Arrows aerobatic team 1955–58; ops staff: HQ AAFCE Fontainebleau 1959, HQ Brockzetel Sector Control Germany 1960–61; jssc Latimer 1961; OC: Fighter Test Sqdn Boscombe Down 1952–64, RAF Coltishall 1964–66; Canadian Nat Def Coll Ontario 1966–67; Staff Ops Requirements MOD (air) 1966–67, Cmdt Aeroplane & Armament Experimental Estab Boscombe Down 1970–72, dep gen mangr NATO Multi-role Combat Aircraft Mgmnt Agency Munich 1972–78 (head mil factors 1969–70), ret RAF 1978; conslt: Ferranti Defence Systems Edinburgh 1978–88, Br Indust for mil aviation, avionic and gen equipment 1988–; *Recreations* golf, yachting; *Clubs* RAF; *Style*— Air Cdre Roger Topp, AFC; ✉ Cedar Lodge, Meadow Drive, Hoveton St John, Norfolk (☎ 01603 783887)

TOPPING, Rev Francis (Frank); s of Francis Bede Topping (d 1982), of Birkenhead, and Dorothy Veronica, *née* Kelly (d 1985); *b* 30 March 1937; *Educ* St Anselm's Coll Birkenhead, North West Sch of Speech and Drama Southport, Didsbury Coll Bristol; *m* 15 April 1958, June, da of Alfred Sydney Berry; 2 s (Simon b 1961, Mark b 1963), 1 da (Anne b 1959); *Career* Nat Serv RAF Cyprus 1955–57; stage mangr and actor Leatherhead Repertory Co 1957–58, stage mangr and actor Wolverhampton Grand Theatre 1959–60, played Krishna in Dear Augustine (Royal Court) 1959, actor and stage mangr Touring Co 1960–; Granada TV: stage hand/TV floormangr 1960, first asst film dir 1962–64; freelance bdcaster BBC Radio Brighton 1967–70, prodr BBC Radio 1970–80; author or radio plays; presenter: Sunday Best (ITV), Topping on Sunday (ITV) 1982–84, The 5 Minute Show (TVS) 1989; partnership with Donald Swann 1973–81 (wrote songs and sketches for Radio and TV as Swann with Topping (Ambassadors) 1980), co-dir Topping Theatre 1986–, currently touring UK with two one-man plays; Theological Coll 1964–67, probationer Methodist min Woodingdean Brighton and univ chaplin Univ of Sussex 1967–70, ordained Methodist min 1970, temp officiating chaplain RSME Regt 1983–84, nat chaplain Toch 1984–86 (hon chaplain 1985–), chaplain Kent Coll 1988–93; Grace Wyndham Goldie Award 1975; *Books* Lord of the Morning (1977), Lord of the Evening (1979), Lord of my Days (1980), Working at Prayer (1981), Pause for Thought - with Frank Topping (1981), Lord of Life (1982), The Words of Christ, 40 Meditations (1983), God Bless You Spoonbill (1984), Lord of Time (1985), An Impossible God (1985, recorded 1995), Wings of the Morning (1987), Act Your Age (1989), Laughing in my Sleep (autobiog, 1993), All The Days of my Life (1994), Bunyan's Pilgrim's Progress (audio book) 1995; *Recreations* sailing, sketching, watercolours; *Clubs* Naval, Hurst Castle Sailing; *Style*— The Rev Frank Topping; ✉ 34 Eastland Road, Thornbury, Bristol BS12 1DS (☎ and fax 01454 418722)

TORA, Brian Roberto; adopted s of Ernest Carlo Tora, and Betty Lilian, *née* Squires (d 1971); *b* 21 Sept 1945; *Educ* Bancroft's Sch Woodford Green Essex; *m* 4 July 1975 (m dis 1988), Jennifer, da of (Julius) Dennis Israel Blanckensee (d 1951); 2 s (Matthew b 26 Dec 1977, Thomas b 5 June 1979); m 2, 20 Oct 1989, Elizabeth Mary, *née* Edgecombe; *Career* Grieveson Grant 1963–74, investmt mangr Singer & Friedlander 1974–79; investmt dir: van Cutsem & Assocs 1979–82, Touche Remnant Fin Mgmnt 1982–85; head of retail mktg James Capel & Co 1985–91, mktg dir Greig Middleton 1991–; regular bdcaster; MSI; *Publications* The Second Financial Services Revolution (Rushmere Wynne, 1995); contrib articles on investment to several jls; *Recreations* bridge, reading, food and wine; *Style*— Brian Tora, Esq; ✉ Enniskillen Lodge, Little Waldingfield, Suffolk C010 0SU (☎ 01787 247783); Greig Middleton & Co Ltd, 66 Wilson Street, London EC2A 2BL (☎ 0171 392 4000, fax 0171 392 4200)

TORDOFF, Baron (Life Peer UK 1981), of Knutsford, Co Cheshire; Geoffrey Johnson Tordoff; s of late Stanley Acomb Tordoff, of Marple, Cheshire; *b* 11 Oct 1928; *Educ* Manchester GS, Univ of Manchester; *m* 1953, Mary Patricia, da of Thomas Swarbrick, of Leeds; 2 s (Hon Nicholas Gregory b 1958, Hon Mark Edmund b 1962), 3 da (Hon Mary Catherine b 1954, Hon Frances Jane b 1956, Hon Paula Mary b 1960); *Career* contested (Lib) Northwich 1964, Knutsford 1966 and 1970; Lib Party: chm Assembly Ctee 1974–76, memb Nat Exec 1975–84, chm 1976–79, pres 1983–84, chm Campaigns and Elections Ctee 1980 and 1981; Lib Democrat Chief Whip House of Lords 1988–94 (dep Lib Chief Whip 1983–84, Lib Chief Whip 1984–88), princ dep chm of ctees House of Lords and chm House of Lords Select Ctee on the Euro Communities 1994–; memb Press Complaints Cmmn 1995–; *Clubs* National Liberal; *Style*— The Rt Hon the Lord Tordoff; ✉ House of Lords, London SW1A 0PW

TOREN, Amikam; s of Benjamin Toren and Alisa Toren; *b* 18 May 1945; *m* 1972, Christina, da of Ian Camden Pratt; 1 s (Manuel b 5 Nov 1973); *Career* artist; lectr Univ of Brighton (formerly Brighton Poly) 1990–, visiting lectr: Byam Shaw Sch of Art, Dep of Fine Art Goldsmiths' Coll; individual exhibitions incl: Annely Juda Fine Art London 1973, Serpentine Gallery London 1976, Replacing (ICA London) 1979, If Painting then... (Riverside Studios London) 1981, Actualities (Matt's Gallery London) 1984, unnamed exhibitions Anthony Reynolds Gallery London 1985 and 1991, Pidgin Paintings 1987, Stacks 1989; Ikon Gallery Birmingham 1990, Arnolfini Gallery Bristol 1991, Gabrielle Maubrie Paris 1991, Chisenhale Gallery London 1991; particpated in numerous gp exhibitions 1967–; *Style*— Amikam Toren; ✉ c/o Anthony Reynolds Galleries, 5 Dering Street, London W1R 9AB (☎ 0171 491 0621)

TORNBOHM, (Peter) Noel; s of Eric Anthony Tornbohm (d 1986), of Darlington, and May, *née* Barrow (d 1969); *b* 11 Jan 1943; *Educ* Queen Elizabeth GS Darlington, UCL (LLB); *m* 1, 29 May 1965 (m dis 1982), Yvonne Hamilton (Mrs Way), da of Wilfred Vincent Miller, of Darlington; 1 s (Paul b 28 March 1971), 1 da (Catherine b 16 June 1969); m 2, 1983, Maureen Roberta (Mo), da of Frank Griffin, of Mickleover, Derby; *Career* admitted slr 1967; ptnr Smith Roddam & Co 1968–71 (joined 1967), sr ptnr Gadsby Coxon & Copestake 1973 (joined 1971); former memb City of Derby 126 Round Table, chm Derby 41 Club 1990–91 (memb); memb Law Soc, Slrs Benevolent Assoc; *Recreations* playing & listening to music, keeping dogs; *Style*— Noel Tornbohm, Esq; ✉ Hillbank House, 2 The Common, Quarndon, Derby DE22 5JY (☎ 01332 553376); Gadsby Coxon & Copestake, Sterne House, Lodge Lane, Derby (☎ 01332 372372, fax 01332 365715)

TORODE, John Arthur; s of Alfred Charles Torode (gen sec Sign and Display Trades Union, d 1980), and Dorothy Amelia Torode (d 1966); *b* 4 Jan 1939; *Educ* Lincoln Coll Oxford (BA), Cornell Univ Ithaca NY; *m* 1974, Naseem Fatima, da of Dr Abdul Wasl Khan (d 1977); 1 s from previous marriage (Jonathan b 22 Jan 1970), 1 s (George b 6 Dec 1976), 1 da (Amelia b 21 Jan 1975); *Career* political leader writer and columnist The Guardian 1977–86 (labour ed 1967–72, diary ed 1974–77), policy ed and chief leader writer The Independent 1986–94, currently freelance broadcaster and also political commentator Daily Mail 1995–; memb Younger Ctee on Privacy 1969–72, memb editorial bd New Statesman 1969–72, jt presenter Weekend World 1972, conslt India for UN World Food Programme 1982, chm Labour and Industl Corrs Gp 1969–72; Parly candidate: (Lab) Kingston on Thames 1979, (SDP) Saffron Walden 1983; memb Exec Ctee Friends of Cyprus 1982–; hon citizen Huntsville Alabama; *Recreations* swimming, travel, amateur archaeology; *Clubs* Reform, Zoological Society of London; *Style*— John Arthur Torode, Esq; ✉ 25 Platt's Lane, Hampstead, London NW3 7NP (☎ 0171 435 6105, fax 0171 431 6073)

TORPHICHEN, Master of; Douglas Robert Alexander Sandilands; s of late Hon Walter Alexander Sandilands (s of 12 Lord Torphichen, d 1966), and hp of cous, 15 Lord Torphichen, *qv*; *b* 31 Aug 1926; *m* 1, 1949, Ethel Louise Burkitt; 1 s (Robert Powell b 1950); m 2, Suzette Vera, *née* Pernet; 2 s (Bruno Charles b 1977, Edward Louis b 1979); *Style*— The Master of Torphichen; ✉ 109 Royal George Road, Burgess Hill, W Sussex

TORPHICHEN, 15 Lord (S 1564); James Andrew Douglas Sandilands; s of 14 Lord Torphichen (d 1975); *see also* Sir Francis Sandilands; *b* 27 Aug 1946; *Educ* King's Sch Canterbury, Univ of Birmingham, Napier Coll Edinburgh; *m* 1976, Margaret Elizabeth, da of William Alfred Beale (d 1967), of Boston, Mass; 4 da (Margaret b 1979, Mary b 1981, Anne b 1985, Alison b 1990); *Heir* Master of Torphichen, *qv* (first cous once removed); *Career* electronics engr; *Style*— The Rt Hon the Lord Torphichen; ✉ Calder House, Mid-Calder, West Lothian EH53 0HN

TORRANCE, (David) Andrew; s of James Torrance, of Blundellsands, Liverpool, and Gladys, *née* Riley (d 1995); *b* 18 May 1953; *Educ* Merchant Taylors' Sch Crosby, Emmanuel Coll Cambridge (MA), London Business Sch (MSc); *m* 30 Dec 1983, Ann Lesley, da of George Tasker (d 1972), of Bebington, Wirral; 1 s (James b 1987), 1 da (Lucy b 1984); *Career* The Boston Consulting Group Ltd: joined 1976, mangr 1981, vice pres and dir until 1992; chm and chief exec ITT London & Edinburgh Insurance Group 1995– (joined 1992); *Recreations* cars, tennis, food, wine; *Style*— Andrew Torrance, Esq; ✉ 117 Lansdowne Rd, London W11 2LF (☎ 0171 727 9019); ITT London & Edinburgh Insurance Group, The Warren, Worthing, W Sussex BN14 9QD (☎ 01903 820820, fax 01903 273920, telex 87412)

TORRANCE, Prof John Steele (Jack); s of Robert Torrance (d 1941), of Belfast, NI, and Charlotte Robinson Torrance (d 1982); *b* 11 Jan 1926; *Educ* Belfast Coll of Technol (MBA); *m* 8 Sept 1948, Rosetta Fitz-Simons, da of Thomas Patterson Shepherd (d 1980), of Donaghadee, NI; 4 da (Sharon Rose b 1952, Cheryl Sara b 1954, Candida Eleanor b 1956, Dara Rosetta b 1960); *Career* trainee Harland & Wolfe Belfast 1941–50 (seconded DNC Bath 1946), sr engr G N Haden and J R W Murland 1950–60, sr ptnr Steensen Varming Mulcahy & Partners Edinburgh 1972–85 (associate then ptnr 1960–72); involved in design for major projects incl: hosps, univs, banks, insur cos, commercial offices, swimming and leisure complexes; ret, now specialises in litigation, arbitration and adjudication matters, currently memb Dispute Resolution Gp Chek Lap Kok Int Airport HK; visiting prof: Univ of Strathclyde 1988–94, Caledonian Univ 1994–; industl prof Heriot-Watt Univ 1989–; contrib numerous articles in tech jls; CEng, Hon FCIBSE (nat pres 1985–86), Hon FRIAS, FCIArb, MAE, MConsE; *Recreations* music, reading, golf; *Clubs* Sloane; *Style*— Prof Jack Torrance; ✉ 1 Southbank Ct, Easter Park Drive, Edinburgh EH4 6JR (☎ 0131 312 6923, fax 0131 539 7038)

TORRANCE, Samuel Robert (Sam); MBE (1990); s of Robert Torrance, of Largs, Ayrshire, and June Torrance; *b* 24 Aug 1953; *m* Suzanne Danielle; 1 s (Daniel b 4 Aug 1988), 2 da (Phoebe b 29 June 1992, Anouska b 19 June 1995); *Career* professional golfer; *Tournament Victories* under 25 Match Play Radici Open 1972, Zambian Open 1975, Piccadilly medal Martini Int 1976, Scottish PGA Championship 1980, 1985, 1991 and 1993, Australian PGA Championship 1980, Irish Open 1981 and 1995, Spanish Open 1982, Portuguese Open 1982 and 1983, Scandinavian Open 1983, Tunisian Open 1984, Benson & Hedges Int 1984, Sanyo Open 1984, Monte Carlo Open 1985, Italian Open 1987 and 1995, German Masters 1990, Jersey Open 1991, Kronenbourg Open 1993, Catalan Open 1993, Honda Open 1993; capt Asahi Glass Four Tours 1991 (winners); memb Ryder Cup team: 1981, 1983, 1985 (winners), 1987 (winners), 1989 (winners), 1991, 1993 and 1995 (winners); memb Dunhill Cup team: 1976, 1978, 1982, 1984, 1985, 1987,

1989, 1990, 1991, 1993 and 1995 (winners); memb World Cup team: 1976, 1978, 1982, 1984, 1985, 1987, 1989, 1990, 1991, 1993 and 1995; memb Hennessy Cognac Cup: 1976, 1978, 1980, 1982 and 1984; memb Double Diamond team: 1973, 1976 and 1977; finished 2nd Order of Merit 1995 (3rd 1993); *Recreations* tennis, snooker; *Style*— Sam Torrance, Esq, MBE; ✉ c/o Katrina Johnston, Carnegie Sports International, 4th Floor, The Glasshouse, 1 Battersea Bridge Road, London SW11 3BZ (☎ 0171 924 4882, fax 0171 924 4883)

TORRANCE, Very Rev Prof Thomas Forsyth; MBE (1944); s of Rev Thomas Torrance (d 1959), of Edinburgh, and Annie Elizabeth, *née* Sharpe; *b* 30 Aug 1913; *Educ* Canadian Sch Chengdu, Bellshill Acad Scotland, Univ of Edinburgh (MA, BD, DLitt), Univ of Basel (DTheol), Oriel Coll Oxford; *m* 2 Oct 1946, Margaret Edith, da of George Frederick Spear (d 1946), of Combe Down, Bath; 2 s (Thomas Spear b 3 July 1947, Iain Richard b 13 Jan 1949), 1 da (Alison Meta Elizabeth b 15 April 1951); *Career* Chaplain Church of Scotland MEF and CMF 1943–45, Combined Ops and 10 Indian Div, Emergency Serv Palestine Police Force May 1936; prof of systematic theol Auburn NY 1938–39, minister Alyth Barony Parish Perthshire 1940–47, minister Beechgrove Parish Church Aberdeen 1947–50, prof of church history New Coll Univ of Edinburgh 1950–52, prof of christian dogmatics Univ of Edinburgh 1952–79, moderator of the Gen Assembly of the Church of Scotland 1976–77; fndr and co-ed Scottish Journal of Theology 1948–82; memb: Academie Internationale de Philosophie des Sciences 1976–, Kuratorium Das Deutsche Inst für Bildung and Wissen Paderborn and Berlin, Europaeische Akademie für Umweltfragen Tübingen, Cmmn of Faith and Order of the World Cncl of Churches 1952–62, Bd Center of Theological Inquiry Princeton 1979–; pres Académie Internationale des Sciences Religieuses 1972–81; Hon DD Presbyterian Coll Montreal 1950, Hon DTheol Univ of Geneva 1959, DTheol Faculté Libre Paris 1959, Hon DD St Andrews 1960, Hon DTheol Oslo 1961, Hon DSc Heriot-Watt Univ 1983, Hon DTheol Debrecen Reformed Coll Hungary 1988, Hon DD Univ of Edinburgh 1996; FRSE 1977, FBA 1982; Cross of St Mark Patriarchate of Alexandria 1973, Proto-Presbyter of the Greek Orthodox Church Patriarchate of Alexandria 1973, Cross of Thyateira 1977; *Books* incl: The Doctrine in the Apostolic Fathers (1946 and 1948), Kingdom and Church (1956), When Christ Comes and Comes Again (1957), The Mystery of the Lord's Supper (1958), The School of Faith (1959), Conflict and Agreement in the Church, Vol 1 Order and Disorder (1959), The Apocalypse Today (1959), Conflict and Agreement in the Church, Vol II The Ministry and the Sacraments of the Gospel (1960), Theology in Reconstruction (1965), Theological Science (1969), Space Time and Incarnation (1969), God and Rationality (1971), Theology in Reconciliation (1975), Space, Time and Resurrection (1976), The Ground and Grammar of Theology (1980), Christian Theology and Scientific Culture (1980), Divine and Contingent Order (1981), Reality and Evangelical Theology (1982), Juridical Law and Physical Law (1982), The Mediation of Christ (1983 and 1992), Transformation and Convergence in the Frame of Knowledge (1984), The Christian Frame of Mind (1985, 2 edn 1989), Reality and Scientific Theology (1985), The Trinitarian Faith (1988, 2 edn 1993), The Hermeneutics of John Calvin (1988), Karl Barth Biblical and Evangelical Theologian (1990), Royal Priesthood - A Theology of Ordained Ministry (1993), Trinitarian Perspectives, Toward Doctrinal Agreement (1994), Preaching Christ Today (1994), Divine Meaning - Studies in Patristic Hermeneutics (1995), The Christian Doctrine of God - One Being Three Persons (1996), Scottish Theology from John Knox to James McLeod Campbell (1996); works edited: Karl Barth Church Dogmatics (with G Bromiley, 1956–77), Calvin's Tracts and Treatises (1959), Calvin's New Testament Commentaries (with D W Torrance, 1959–73), Belief in Science and the Christian Life (1980), Christian Theology and Scientific Culture (1980–83), James Clerk Maxwell, A Dynamical Theory of the Electromagnetic Field (1982), Theology and Science at the Frontiers of Knowledge (1985–90), Theological Dialogue between Orthodox and Reformed Churches (Vol I 1985, Vol II 1993); *Recreations* walking; *Clubs* Edinburgh Univ Staff, New (Edinburgh); *Style*— The Very Rev Prof Thomas F Torrance, FRSE, FBA; ✉ 37 Braid Farm Road, Edinburgh EH10 6LE (☎ 0131 447 3224)

TORRANCE, Prof Victor Brownlie; CBE (1991); s of Thomas Brownlie Torrance (d 1969), and Mary King Torrance, MBE, *née* Miller (1992); *b* 24 Feb 1937; *Educ* Wisham High Sch, Heriot-Watt Univ (BSc, MSc), Univ of Edinburgh (PhD); *m* 1 (m dis 1982), Mary McFarland; 1 s (Andrew Brownlie b 19 March 1968), 2 da (Adrienne Joan b 20 Sept 1964, Deirdrie Ann b 15 March 1967); m 2, (m dis 1992); *Career* sr lectr i/c Bldg Div Sch of Architecture and Bldg Singapore Poly Singapore 1966–68, assoc prof and head Dept of Bldg and Estate Mgmnt Faculty of Architecture and Bldg Nat Univ of Singapore 1968–72, William Watson prof of bldg Dept of Bldg Engrg and Surveying Heriot-Watt Univ 1972–91, prof of bldg Dept of Civil Engrg Loughborough Univ 1991–93, London Master Builders' prof of bldg Bartlett Sch of the Built Environment UCL 1993–; ptnr Building and Design Consultants 1976–91; memb: Bd of Govrs Edinburgh Coll of Art 1973–88, Civil Engrg and Transport Ctee and Bldg Sub-Ctee Science Res Cncl 1975–78, CNAA Bldg Bd 1978–81, CNAA Technol Res Ctee 1982–85, Scot Bldg Standards Advsy Ctee Res Sub-Ctee 1982–85; chm RIAS Res Steering Ctee 1982–85, memb Panel of Visitors to the Bldg Res Estab 1985–89, co-ordinator CIB Working Cmmn 71 1986–92, conslt of Bldg Investigation Centre 1987–91, dir Lloyds Surveyors 1989–; chm Cncl of Profs of Bldg 1987–92, pres Chartered Inst of Bldg 1988–89; chm: Advsy Bd of Wimlas Testing Servs, Geo Wimpey Laboratories 1988–; chm CIOB Environment Cmmn 1990–; FCIOB 1972, FBIM 1972, FRSA 1973, Hon ARICS 1986; *Style*— Prof Victor Torrance, CBE; ✉ The Bartlett School of the Built Environment, University College London, Wates House, 22 Gordon Street, London WC1H 0QB (direct ☎ 0171 380 7509, fax 0171 380 7517, e-mail UCLFT 710@uclasu.k.)

TORRE DIAZ, 7 Conde (Count; cr of 1846 by Queen Isabel II of Spain); Paul Gerald de Zulueta; only s of Maj Peter Paul John de Zulueta (Welsh Gds, d 1982; whose mother, Dora, m as her 2 husband, 5 Marquess of Bristol), by his w Tessa, who m as 2 husb, 2 Viscount Montgomery of Alamein, er da of late Lt-Gen Sir Frederick Browning, GCVO, KBE, CB, DSO, and Daphne du Maurier, the novelist; *b* 12 April 1956; *Educ* Ampleforth, RMA Sandhurst; *m* 18 June 1988, Susan, o da of Dr G J Pritchard, of The Old Mill House, Stanwell Moor; 2 s (Guy Peter b 26 Aug 1990, Hugh Philip b 1 Aug 1993); *Career* Maj Welsh Gds 1979, Adj 1983–85; Robert Fleming & Co 1987–89, ptnr MaST International plc 1990–, md MaST Americas 1996–; Kt of Honour and Devotion SMOM; *Recreations* reading, family and fitness; *Clubs* Royal Fowey Yacht, Pratt's, Bath and Racquets, Anglo-Chilean, Anglo-Argentine; *Style*— P G de Zulueta; ✉ 24 Anhalt Road, London SW11 4NX

TORRINGTON, 11 Viscount (GB 1721); Sir Timothy Howard St George Byng; 11 Bt (GB 1715); Baron Byng of Southill (GB 1721); s of Hon George Byng, RN (d on active service 1944, himself s of 10 Viscount, whom present Viscount suc 1961), and Anne Yvonne Bostock, *née* Wood; *b* 13 July 1943; *Educ* Harrow, St Edmund Hall Oxford (BA); *m* 1973, Susan Honor, da of Michael George Thomas Webster, of Little Manor Farm, Dummer, Hants; 3 da (Hon Henrietta Rose b 1977, Hon Georgina Isabel b 1980, Hon Malaika Anne b 13 April 1982); *Heir* kinsman, John Cranmer-Byng, MC; *Career* dir Conrad plc, md Heritage Oil & Gas Ltd; former memb House of Lords Select Ctee on Euro Community; *Recreations* travel and field sports; *Clubs* White's, Pratt's, Muthaiga (Nairobi); *Style*— The Rt Hon the Viscount Torrington; ✉ Great Hunts Place, Owslebury, Winchester, Hants (☎ 01962 777234); London office: (☎ 0171 351 5555)

TORVILL, Jayne; MBE (1981); da of George Henry Torvill, of Nottingham, and Betty, *née* Smart; *b* 7 Oct 1957; *Educ* Clifton Hall GS for Girls Nottingham; *m* 21 Sept 1990, Philip Christensen, s of Douglas A Christensen, of USA; *Career* ice skater; with Michael Hutchinson: Br Jr Pairs champions 1970, Br Sr Pairs champions 1971; partnership with Christopher Dean, *qv*, 1975–; achievements incl: first int win St Gervais 1976, Br champions 1978, 1979, 1980, 1981, 1982, 1983 and 1994; Euro champions: Innsbruck 1981, Lyon 1982, Budapest 1984, Copenhagen 1994; World champions: Hartford USA 1981, Copenhagen 1982, Helsinki 1983, Ottawa 1984; Gold medal Olympic Games Sarajevo 1984 (fifth place Lake Placid 1980), Bronze medal Olympic Games Lillehammer 1994; World Professional Ice Dance champions 1984, 1985 and 1990; first professional tour 1984, co-fndr skating co with Christopher Dean (tour Eng, Aust, USA and Canada) 1985, TV special Fire & Ice (LWT) 1986, tour IceCapades USA 1987, fndr co of Soviet skaters (tour UK, USSR, Aust, USA and Canada) 1988, recorded Bladerunners (Omnibus, BBC) 1991, tour Aust with Soviet co 1991, Torvill and Dean Face the Music world tour 1994; re-entered int competition 1994; world record holders for most number of perfect 6.0 scores in skating competition (Olympic Games 1984), only couple to attain Gold Star Ice Dance Test 1983, BBC Sports Personality and Team awards 1983, 1984 and 1986, awarded Jacques Favart Trophy Int Skating Union; Hon MA Nottingham Trent Univ 1993; *Recreations* theatre, cinema, ballet, contemporary dance; *Style*— Ms Jayne Torvill, MBE; ✉ c/o Debbie Turner, PO Box 32, Heathfield, East Sussex TN21 0BW (☎ 01435 867825, fax 01435 867826)

TORY, Sir Geofroy William; KCMG (1958, CMG 1956); s of William Frank Tory, of Sheffield, and Edith Wreghitt; *b* 31 July 1912; *Educ* King Edward VII Sch Sheffield, Queens' Coll Cambridge; *m* 1, 1938, Emilia Strickland; 2 s, 1 da; m 2, 1950, Florence Hazel (d 1985), da of Arthur William Thomas, of Halifax, Nova Scotia; *Career* IDC, WWII serv RA; entered Dominions Office 1935, PPS to Sec State Dominion Affrs 1945–46, sr sec Office of UK High Cmmr Canada 1946–49, cnsllr Br Embassy Dublin 1950–51; dep UK high cmmr: Pakistan (Peshawar) 1953–54, Australia 1954–57; asst under sec state Cwlth Rels Office 1957, UK high cmmr Fedn of Malaya 1957–63, Br ambass Eire 1963–66, UK high cmmr Malta 1967–70, ret 1970; PMN (Malaysia) 1963; *Style*— Sir Geofroy Tory, KCMG; ✉ Cliff Top, Harbour View, Kilbrittain, Co Cork, Eire

TOSSWILL, (Timothy Maurice) Stephen; s of Timothy Dymond Tosswill (d 1991), and Sigrid, *née* Bohn (d 1985); *b* 28 April 1949; *Educ* Rugby, St Paul's, Univ of London (LLB, LLM); *Career* criminal lawyer, admitted slr 1976; ptnr Tosswill & Co 1976–, author of articles in legal periodicals; MRIN; *Recreations* masterly inactivity; *Clubs* Little Ship; *Style*— Stephen Tosswill, Esq; ✉ 260 Brixton Hill, London SW2 1HP (☎ 0181 674 9494, fax 0181 671 8987)

TOTMAN, Edward Bartram; s of Edward Bartram Totman (d 1989), of Sutton, Surrey, and Joan Cecilia Mary, *née* McCamley; *b* 28 June 1942; *Educ* Wimbledon Coll, King's Coll London (LLB); *m* 25 July 1970, Colette Maria, da of Vincent Aloysius Jackson (d 1962), of Cheam, Surrey; 1 s (Julian b 1971), 3 da (Marissa b 1973, Siobhan b 1976, Carmel b 1979); *Career* admitted slr 1970; articled clerk then slr GLC 1965–72, Abbey National Building Society 1972–74, Mercantile Credit Co Ltd 1974–79, ptnr D J Freeman 1981– (joined 1979); memb Law Soc 1970; *Recreations* tennis, swimming, photography, reading; *Style*— Edward Totman, Esq; ✉ 91 The Green, Ewell, Epsom, Surrey KT17 3JX (☎ 0181 393 3530); D J Freeman, 1 Fetter Lane, London EC4A 1BR (☎ 0171 583 5555, fax 0171 583 3232, telex 913434)

TOTNES, Archdeacon of; *see:* Tremlett, Ven Anthony Frank (Tony)

TOUCHE, Sir Rodney Gordon; 2 Bt (UK 1962), of Dorking, Surrey; s of Rt Hon Sir Gordon Cosmo Touche, 1 Bt (d 1972); *b* 5 Dec 1928; *Educ* Marlborough, Univ Coll Oxford; *m* 30 April 1955, Ouida Ann, er da of late Frederick Gerald MacLellan, of Moncton, New Brunswick, Canada; 1 s, 3 da; *Heir* s, Eric MacLellan Touche; *Style*— Sir Rodney Touche, Bt; ✉ 1100 8th Ave (Apt 2403), Calgary, Alberta T2P 3T9, Canada (☎ 00 1 403 233 8800, fax 00 1 403 233 8801)

TOUHIG, James Donnelly (Don); MP (Lab) Islwyn (majority 13,097); s of Michael Touhig (d 1982), and Agnes Catherine, *née* Corten; *b* 5 Dec 1947; *Educ* St Francis Sch, East Monmouth Coll; *m* 21 Sept 1968, Jennifer, da of Clifford Hughes; 2 s (Matthew b 24 Jan 1972, James b 19 April 1978), 2 da (Charlotte b 3 May 1975, Katie b 27 Sept 1983); *Career* apprentice radio and TV engr, journalist then ed; gen mangr: newspaper gp, business devpt gp, printing company; MP (Lab) Islwyn 1995–; sec Welsh Groups PLP; memb: Welsh Select Ctee, Leadership Campaign Team (responsible for devolution campaign in Wales); *Recreations* reading, cooking for family and friends; *Style*— Don Touhig, Esq, MP; ✉ The Mount, Greenhill Road, Griffithstown, Pontypool, Gwent NP4 5BE; Constituency Office, The Institute, Crumlin, Gwent NP1 4QB (☎ 01495 244699, fax 01495 245109); House of Commons, London SW1A 0AA (☎ 0171 219 6435)

TOULMIN, John Kelvin; CMG (1994), QC (1980); s of Arthur Heaton (Mike) Toulmin (d 1994), of Reigate, and late B Toulmin, *née* Fraser; *b* 14 Feb 1941; *Educ* Winchester, Trinity Hall Cambridge (MA), Univ of Michigan Law Sch (LLM); *m* 13 May 1967, Carolyn Merton, da of Merton Gullick (d 1953); 1 s (Geoffrey b 1969), 2 da (Alison b 1972, Hilary b 1975); *Career* called to the Bar Middle Temple 1965, bencher 1986; memb Bar Cncl/Senate 1971–77, 1978–81 and 1986–, memb Supreme Court Rules Ctee 1976–80, recorder Crown Ct 1984–, called to the Bar NI 1989, called to the Bar Irish Republic 1991; govr The Maudsley and Bethlem Royal Hosps 1979–87, memb Ctee of Mgmnt Inst of Psychiatry 1982–, chm Young Barrs' Ctee 1973–75, chm Bar Int Practice Ctee 1987, UK delegation to Cncl of the Bars and Law Socs of Europe (CCBE) 1983–90 (ldr of the UK delegation 1987–90), vice pres CCBE 1991–92, pres 1993; tstee: ProCorda 1992–, Europaeische Rechtsakademie Trier 1993– (vice chm 1994); memb CPR Int Arbitration and Conciliation Panel New York 1993–; Univ of Michigan Law Sch: W W Bishop fell 1993, memb Bd of Visitors 1996–; hon memb Law Soc of England and Wales 1994; Austrian Great Decoration for Merit 1995; *Books* DHSS report into Unnecessary Dental Treatment in NHS (co author, 1986), author of articles on rights of estab and recognition of diplomas in Europe, Butterworths Banking Encyclopaedia (ed Euro Law Section), Butterworths European Legal Systems (conslt ed, 1992), EFTA Legal Systems (conslt ed, 1993); *Recreations* cricket, listening to music, theatre; *Clubs* MCC, Pilgrims; *Style*— John Toulmin, Esq, CMG, QC; ✉ 3 Verulam Buildings, Gray's Inn, London WC1R 5NT (☎ 0171 831 8441, fax 0171 831 8479)

TOULSON, Alan Kilsha; s of Stanley Kilsha Toulson (d 1992), of Redhill, and Lilian Mary, *née* Picknell (d 1985); *b* 27 Aug 1942; *Educ* Mill Hill Sch, KCL (LLB); *m* 28 June 1969, Sarah, da of Noel Stanley Farrow; 2 da (Katie b 5 June 1971, Bonnie b 2 March 1980), 2 s (Sam b 27 Jan 1973, Luke b 17 Oct 1976); *Career* slr; Reynolds Porter Chamberlain: articled clerk 1964–66, ptnr 1966–, sr ptnr 1991–; memb Law Soc 1966–; chm Swedish C of C for UK 1996–; chm Govrs St Clement Danes Sch 1985–95; AKC; *Recreations* skiing, sailing, walking, school management; *Style*— Alan Toulson, Esq; ✉ Doggetts, Chipperfield, Herts WD4 9DJ (☎ 01923 263413); Reynolds Porter Chamberlain, Chichester House, 278–282 High Holborn, London WC1V 7HA (☎ 0171 242 2877, fax 0171 242 1431)

TOULSON, Lady; Elizabeth; da of Henry Bertram Chrimes, and Suzanne Corbett-Lowe; *b* 10 Nov 1948; *Educ* Univ of Liverpool (LLB), Univ of Cambridge (Dip in comparitive law); *m* April 1973, Roger Grenfell Toulson, *qv*, s of Stanley Kilsha Toulson; 2 da (Susanna Jane b 4 Feb 1975, Rachel Elizabeth b 26 Feb 1977), 2 s (Henry Alexander b 4 Nov 1979, Thomas Grenfell b 8 April 1984); *Career* called to the bar 1974; WRVS: tstee 1981, vice chair 1989–93, chm 1993–; tstee Nat Listening Library;

Recreations skiing, tennis, walking, swimming, classical music; *Style*— Lady Toulson; ✉ Women's Royal Voluntary Service, 234–244 Stockwell Road, Brixton, London SW9 9SP (☎ 0171 416 0146, fax 0171 416 0148)

TOULSON, Hon Mr Justice; Hon Sir Roger Grenfell; kt (1996); s of Stanley Kilsha Toulson (d 1992), of Redhill, Surrey, and Lilian Mary Toulson (d 1985); *b* 23 Sept 1946; *Educ* Mill Hill Sch, Jesus Coll Cambridge (MA, LLB); *m* 28 April 1973, Elizabeth, *qv*, da of Henry Bertram Chrimes, of Wirral, Merseyside; 2 s (Henry b 1979, Thomas b 1984), 2 da (Susanna b 1975, Rachel b 1977); *Career* called to the Bar Inner Temple 1969, QC 1986, bencher 1995, recorder of the Crown Court 1987–96, judge of the High Court of Justice (Queen's Bench Div) 1996–; *Books* Confidentiality (with C M Phipps, 1996); *Recreations* skiing, tennis, gardening; *Style*— The Hon Mr Justice Toulson; ✉ Billhurst Farm, Wood St Village, nr Guildford, Surrey GU3 3DZ (☎ 01483 235 246, fax 01483 235 347); Royal Courts of Justice, Strand, London WC2A 2LL

TOUZIN, François Robert; s of Robert Touzin (d 1981), and Suzanne, *née* Dupont; *b* 1 Jan 1952; *Educ* Lycée Technique Tananarive Madagascar, L'Académie de Poitiers France, Institute Int of Glion Switzerland (Dip in Advanced Hotel Mgmnt); *m* 13 Aug 1977, Mia, da of Göran Leffler; 2 da (Sophie b 8 July 1983, Anna b 23 Jan 1990), 1 s (Philippe b 2 Nov 1987); *Career* hotelier; practical trg: Hotel des Bergues Geneva 1974, The Hilton Athens 1975; London InterContinental Hotel Hyde Park Corner: coffee house mangr 1976–79, exec chief steward 1979–80; materials mangr Portman InterContinental Hotel Portman Square London 1981–83; food and beverage mangr: Britannia InterContinental Hotel Grosvenor Square London 1983–84, Mayfair InterContinental Hotel Stratton Street London 1984–86; food and beverage dir Sydney InterContinental Hotel Sydney Aust 1986–88, asst to Gen Mangr Claridge's Brook Street London 1989–90, dir and gen mangr Hotel Lancaster rue de Berri Paris 1990–94, gen mangr Claridge's London 1994–; *Recreations* wine collecting, antiques, fly fishing, waterskiing, swimming, gardening, windsurfing, tennis and jogging; *Style*— François Touzin, Esq; ✉ Claridge's, Brook Street, Mayfair, London W1A 2JQ (☎ 0171 629 8860, fax 0171 499 2210)

TOVEY, Sir Brian John Maynard; KCMG (1980); s of Rev Collett John Tovey (d 1967), and Kathleen Edith Maud Maynard (d 1972); *b* 15 April 1926; *Educ* St Edward's Sch Oxford, St Edmund Hall Oxford, Sch of Oriental and African Studies London (BA); *m* 1989, Mary Helen, *née* Lane; *Career* dir Govt Communications Headquarters (GCHQ) Cheltenham 1978–83; Plessey Electronics Systems Ltd: defence systems conslt 1983–85, defence and political advsr 1985–88; chm: Cresswell Associates Ltd 1988–, Fujitsu Europe Telecom R & D Centre Ltd 1990–, IES plc 1993–, Advanced Media Group PLC 1995–96 (dep chm 1994–95); vice pres Info and Communications Technol Fedn of the Electronics Indust 1995–; *Recreations* music, walking, 16th Century Italian art; *Clubs* Naval & Military (vice pres 1995–); *Style*— Sir Brian Tovey, KCMG; ✉ 8 Cresswell Gardens, London SW5 OBJ

TOVEY, Dr Geoffrey Harold; CBE (1974); s of Harold John Tovey (d 1976), of Midsomer Norton, and Gertrude, *née* Taylor (d 1936); *b* 29 May 1916; *Educ* Wycliffe Coll, Univ of Bristol (MB ChB, MD); *m* 6 Sept 1941, Margaret Beryl, da of Frederick Charles Davies (d 1941), of Abertysswg; 2 s (Charles b 1943, d 1973, Stuart b 1946); *Career* RAMC 1941–46, 8 Field Ambulance 1941–42, Army Blood Transfusion Serv 1942–46, OC No 3 Base Transfusion Unit India Cmd 1945–46; conslt physician Southmead Hosp Bristol 1946–79, dir SW Regnl Blood Transfusion Serv 1946–79, clinical lectr in haematology Univ of Bristol 1947–79, fndr and dir UK Transplant Serv 1969–79, conslt advsr in blood transfusion DHSS 1978–81, hon conslt in blood transfusion MOD 1978–82; pres: Int Soc of Blood Transfusion 1973–76, Br Soc for Haematology 1977–78; Hellenic Soc for Transplantation award 1976, Oliver Memorial award 1977, Alwyn Zoutendyk Meml Award medal SA Inst for Med Res 1979; memb: Select Ctee of Experts on Histocompatability Cncl of Europe 1970–79, Select Ctee of Experts on Immunohaematology 1978–81; fndr Rehabilitation at Home Serv for Adult Brain Damaged Eastbourne 1989, memb Eastbourne Dist Med Soc; FRCPath 1963, FRCP 1968; *Books* Technique of Fluid Balance (1957); *Recreations* helping the disabled, foreign travel, croquet; *Style*— Dr Geoffrey Tovey, CBE; ✉ 23 Westfield House, Cote Lane, Westbury on Trym, Bristol BS9 3UN (☎ 0117 949 4823)

TOVEY, John Joseph; s of Arthur Tovey (d 1970), and Minnie, *née* Hewetson (d 1990); *b* 19 May 1933; *Career* with Colonial Office 1950, with Her Majesty's Theatre Barrow in Furness 1959, appts in various English Lakes hotels 1961–71, proprietor and chef Miller Howe hotel/restaurant Windermere 1971–, proprietor Uplands hotel/restaurant Cumbria; numerous appearances on BBC TV, currently food corr Radio Times; elected to Acad of Gastronomes (amongst first Br) 1986; hon citizen: Bath, Dallas, Houston; *Books* Eating Out with Tovey (1988), BBC Radio Times Cookbook (1990), Entertaining on a Plate (1991); *Clubs* RAC; *Style*— John Tovey, Esq; ✉ Miller Howe, Rayrigg Rd, Windermere, Cumbria LA23 1EY (☎ 01539 442536, fax 01539 445664)

TOWERS, Dr David Anthony; s of George Thomas Towers (d 1970), of Winsford, Cheshire, and Joyce Leigh, *née* Sadler; *b* 27 May 1947; *Educ* Verdin GS Winsford Cheshire, Univ of Newcastle upon Tyne (BSc), Univ of Leeds (PhD); *m* 1, 8 Sept 1973 (m dis 1991), Lorna Mary, da of Samuel Hoole (d 1954), of Winsford, Cheshire; 2 s (Martin b 1968, Timothy b 1974), 1 da (Ailsa b 1976); m 2, 22 Oct 1994, Sandra Marie, da of Hubert Bott, of Ravensthorpe, Northamptonshire; *Career* temp lectr Univ of Sheffield 1973–74 (jr res fell 1971–73); Univ of Lancaster: lectr 1974–88, sr lectr 1988–, head of mathematics 1989–95; res assoc Univ of California Berkeley 1978–79, various papers on algebra and mathematical educn; ed: Proceedings of Undergraduate Mathematics Teaching Conf Univ of Nottingham, Macmillan Guides Series in Mathematics; memb London Mathematical Soc 1972; *Books* Guide to Linear Algebra (1988); *Recreations* singing, opera, theatre, reading, DIY; *Style*— Dr David Towers; ✉ Department of Mathematics, Lancaster University, Lancaster LA1 4YF (☎ 01524 65201 ext 3944, fax 01524 841710, telex 65111 LANCUL G)

TOWERS, John; CBE (1995); *b* 30 March 1948; *Educ* Durham Johnston Sch, Univ of Bradford (BTech(MechEng)); *m* Bethanie, *née* Williams; 1 da (Laura b 23 Sept 1980), 1 s (Michael b 30 Aug 1982); *Career* gen mangr Perkins Engines Ltd Peterborough 1985–86 (joined 1970), vice pres Varity Corporation Ltd Toronto (formerly Massey-Ferguson, parent co of Perkins Engines) 1986–87, md Massey-Ferguson Tractors Ltd Coventry 1987–88; Rover Group 1988–96: dir of mfrg and acting md Land Rover Ltd Solihull 1988–89, dir of product devpt Rover Group Ltd Coventry 1989–91, md product supply 1991–92, gp md 1992–94, chief exec 1994–96; chief exec Concentric plc 1996–, fndr dir HatWel Ltd (mgmnt conslts) 1996–; non-exec dir: Honda UK Ltd 1989–94, Midland Bank plc 1994–96, B Elliott plc 1996–; FIMechE, CEng, FIIM, FEng 1992; *Recreations* golf, squash, tennis, music; *Style*— John Towers, Esq, CBE, FEng; ✉ Concentric plc, Coleshill Road, Sutton Coldfield, W Midlands B75 7AZ (☎ 0121 378 4229, fax 0121 378 4941)

TOWERS, Jonathan Henry Nicholson; s of John Richard Hugh Towers, of Lund House, Lund House Green, Harrogate, North Yorkshire, and Gwyneth Helen Marshall, *née* Nicholson; *b* 5 April 1939; *Educ* Radley, Clare Coll Cambridge (MA); *m* 29 Sept 1979, Vanessa Catherine, da of Francis John Milward, of Barlow Woodseats Hall, Nr Chesterfield, Derbyshire; 2 s (Edward b 1982, Harry b 1988); *Career* ptnr Grays slrs York 1967–; under sheriff Yorkshire and Hallamshire 1988–, hon sec The Shrievalty Assoc 1995–; past chm York Area Appeals Ctee for Mental Health; pres The Yorkshire Law Soc 1996–97; memb Law Soc 1966; *Recreations* golf, shooting, walking, reading, skiing; *Clubs* Leander (assoc), Alwoodley (Leeds); *Style*— Jonathan Towers, Esq; ✉ Grays, Solicitors, Duncombe Place, York YO1 2DY (☎ 01904 634771, fax 01904 610711)

TOWERS, (William) Lennox; s of John Maxwell Towers, of Peebles, and Elizabeth Torrance Aitchison, *née* Moodie (d 1977); *b* 24 Sept 1946; *Educ* Hutchesons' Boys' GS Glasgow, Leeds GS, Univ of Exeter (LLB); *m* 23 Sept 1972, Jan Elaine, da of Frank Morrill, of Menston, W Yorks; 2 s (Alexander b 1977, Edmund b 1985), 1 da (Francesca b 1980); *Career* ptnr Booth & Co Slrs Leeds 1974– (managing ptnr 1990–92), chm H Foster & Co (Stearines) Ltd Group 1978–, dir M 5 Ltd 1988–89; memb Law Soc 1971; *Recreations* family pursuits; *Style*— Lennox Towers, Esq

TOWILL, Prof Denis Royston; *b* 28 April 1933; *Educ* Univ of Bristol (BSc), Univ of Birmingham (MSc, DSc); *m* 27 March 1961, Christine Ann Forrester; 2 s (Jonathan b 2 Dec 1964, Edwin b 17 May 1970), 1 da (Rachel b 22 Dec 1962); *Career* engr; dynamic analyst Br Aerospace Weston/Filton 1957–59, conslt Norris Consultants Bristol 1959–62; subsequently: sr lectr RMCS Shrivenham, prof and head of dept UWIST Cardiff (reader 1966–69, prof 1970–81); prof and head of Sch of Electrical, Electronic and Systems Engrg Univ of Wales Coll of Cardiff 1988–92, Univ of Wales Lucas research prof 1992–; memb Exec Cmmn to oversee formation of Univ of Wales Coll of Cardiff 1987–88; served on various SERC, IFAC and Royal Acad of Engrg ctees, memb IEE Cncl (chm IEE Mgmnt and Design Bd 1990–91); distinguished overseas scientist fell of Eta Kapa Nu 1978; awarded Clerk Maxwell Langham Thompson and McMichael Premiums by IERE; MIProdE 1964, FIEE 1972, FEng 1988; *Books* Transfer Function Techniques for Control Engineers (1970), Coefficient Plane Models for Control System Analysis and Design (1981), Systems Approach to AMT Deployment (1993); *Recreations* music, sport; *Clubs* Bristol Rovers Presidents, Radyr CC (vice pres); *Style*— Prof Denis R Towill, FEng; ✉ Director, Logistics Systems Dynamics Group, Department of Maritime Studies and International Transportation, Faculty of Engineering and Environmental Design, University of Wales Cardiff, PO Box 924, Cardiff CF1 3TS (☎ 01222 874635, fax 01222 842292)

TOWLER, Peter Jeremy Hamilton; s of Stuart Hamilton-Towler, MBE, and Betty Irene, *née* Hardwidge; *b* 21 March 1952; *Educ* Peter Symonds Sch Winchester, Clare Coll Cambridge (BA, MA); *m* 15 Sept 1979, Dr Martha Crellin, da of Norman Langdon-Down (d 1991), of Shepperton-on-Thames, Middx; 1 s, 1 da; *Career* called to the Bar Middle Temple 1974 (Harmsworth scholar); memb: Western Circuit 1976– (Circuit and Wine Ctee 1990–96), Admin Law Bar Assoc 1987–, Planning and Environment Bar Assoc 1988–; legal examiner Diocese of Winchester 1994–; fndr memb and chm Ampfield Conservation Tst 1988–92 (pres 1992–); memb Romsey Deanery Synod 1985–88, churchwarden 1988–93, chm Stroud Sch Assoc 1993–95; Liveryman Worshipful Co of Weavers 1982, Freeman City of London 1982; FCIArb 1994 (ACIArb 1984); *Recreations* cricket, tennis, skiing, conservation; *Clubs* MCC; *Style*— Peter Towler, Esq; ✉ 17 Carlton Crescent, Southampton SO15 2XR (☎ 01703 320320, fax 01703 320321)

TOWNELEY, Sir Simon Peter Edmund Cosmo William; KCVO (1994), JP (Lancs 1956); f assumed surname of Worsthorne by deed poll in 1921, but reverted to Koch de Gooreynd in 1937; Simon (Towneley) discontinued by deed poll the name of Worsthorne, and assumed by Royal Licence of 1955 the arms of Towneley, by reason of descent from the eldest da and sr co-heiress of Col Charles Towneley of Towneley; ancestors of the Towneley family were Lay Deans of Whalley Abbey and were granted lands near Burnley by Roger de Lacy, Earl of Lincoln, c 1200; s of Alexander Koch de Gooreynd, OBE, late Irish Gds (s of Manuela, da of Alexandre de Laski, and Joaquina, Marquessa de Souza Lisboa, herself da of José Marques Lisboa, sometime min Plenipotentiary of Emperor of Brazil to Court of St James), and Priscilla, later Baroness Norman (d 1991); er bro of Sir Peregrine Worsthorne, *qv*; *b* 14 Dec 1921; *Educ* Stowe, Worcester Coll Oxford (MA, DPhil); *m* 30 June 1955, Mary, 2 da of Cuthbert Fitzherbert (d 1987); 1 s (Peregrine b 1962), 6 da (Alice b 1956, Charlotte b 1957, Katharine b 1958, Victoria b 1964, Cosima b 1967, Frances b 1969); *Career* served KRRC Italy 1941–46; lectr in history of music Worcester Coll Oxford 1949–55; cncllr Lancs 1961–66, High Sheriff Lancs 1971–72, HM Lord-Lt and Custos Rotulorum Lancs 1976–96, Hon Col Duke of Lancaster's Own Yeomanry 1979–88; non-exec dir Granada TV 1981–92, life pres Northern Ballet Theatre; memb Bd of Govrs Royal Northern Coll of Music; memb Cncl Duchy of Lancaster 1986–96, tstee Br Museum 1988–93; companion Royal Northern Coll of Music, hon fell Univ of Central Lancashire; Hon DMus Lancaster; KStJ 1976, KCSG (Papal decoration); *Books* Venetian Opera in the Seventeenth Century; *Clubs* Beefsteak, Pratt's, Boodle's; *Style*— Sir Simon Towneley, KCVO, JP; ✉ Dyneley, Burnley, Lancs (☎ 01282 423322)

TOWNELEY STRACHEY, Hon Richard; s of Hon (Thomas) Anthony Edward Towneley Strachey (d 1955), by his w (now Lady Mary Gore); hp of bro Baron O'Hagan, *qv*; *b* 29 Dec 1950; *Educ* Eton, Bath Acad of Art Corsham; *m* 1983, Sally Anne, yr da of Frederick Cecil Cross, of Upcompton, Compton Bishop, Somerset; 1 s (Columba O'Hagan b 28 Feb 1985), 1 da (Amy Lauren b 27 Jan 1989); *Style*— Hon Richard Towneley Strachey; ✉ Lower House Farm, Godney, Wells, Somerset BA5 1RX

TOWNEND, James Barrie Stanley; QC (1978); s of Frederick Stanley Townend (d 1967), of Deal, Kent, and Marjorie Elizabeth, *née* Arnold (d 1991); *b* 21 Feb 1938; *Educ* Tonbridge, Lincoln Coll Oxford (MA); *m* 20 June 1970, Airelle Claire, da of Hermann Dail Nies, of Wimbledon; 1 step da (Pascale Jéhanne Lucie Stagnell-Howe); *Career* Nat Serv in BAOR and UK 1955–57, Lt RA; called to the Bar Middle Temple 1962, recorder of the Crown Court 1979–, bencher Middle Temple 1987, head of chambers; memb: Kingston and Esher DHA 1983–86, Senate of the Inns of Court and Bar 1984–86, Gen Cncl of the Bar 1984–88; chm: Family Law Bar Assoc 1986–88, Supreme Ct Procedure Ctee 1986–88; *Recreations* fishing, sailing, writing verse; *Clubs* Bar Yacht; *Style*— James Barrie Stanley Townend, QC; ✉ 1 King's Bench Walk, Temple, London EC4Y 7DB (☎ 0171 583 6266, fax 0171 583 2068)

TOWNEND, John Coupe; s of Harry Norman Townend (d 1988), of Sherborne, Dorset, and Joyce Dentith, *née* Coupe; *b* 24 Aug 1947; *Educ* Liverpool Inst, LSE (BSc Econ, MSc); *m* 15 March 1969, Dorothy, da of David William Allister (d 1971); 3 s (Andrew, Jonathan, Christopher); *Career* Bank of England: joined 1968, head of Wholesale Mkts Supervision Div 1986–90, head Gilt-Edged and Money Mkts Div 1990–94, dep dir 1994–; contrib articles to various economic jls; *Recreations* running, fell walking, opera, birds; *Style*— John Townend, Esq; ✉ Bank of England, Threadneedle St, London EC2R 8AH

TOWNEND, John Ernest; MP (C) Bridlington (majority 16,358); s of Charles Hope, and Dorothy Townend; *b* 12 June 1934; *Educ* Hymers Coll Hull; *m* 1963, Jennifer Ann; 2 s, 2 da; *Career* served RAF 1957–59; CA 1951–56; chm: J Townend & Sons (Hull) Ltd 1977– (dir and sec 1959–67, md 1967–77), Humber Bridge Bd 1969–71, Willerby Manor Hotels Ltd, Merchant Vintners Ltd, dir: AAH Holdings PLC until taken over by GEHE 1995, Surrey Building Society until taken over by Northern Rock Building Society 1993 (latterly vice chm); cncllr (C): Hull City Cncl 1966–74, Humberside CC 1973–79 (ldr of oppn 1973–77, ldr of Cncl 1977–79); Parly candidate (C) Kingston upon Hull North 1970, MP (C) Bridlington 1979–, PPS to Hugh Rossi (Min of State for the Disabled) 1981–83; vice chm Backbench Fin Ctee 1983–92, chm Cons Small Business Ctee 1983–92, memb Treasy and Civil Service Select Ctee 1983–92, chm Cons Backbench Fin Ctee 1992–; memb 1922 Exec 1992–; memb Parly Assembly: Cncl of Europe 1993–, Western European Union 1993–; divnl chm Haltemprice and Beverley Young Conservatives 1952–54; govr Hymers Coll; memb Lloyd's; Liveryman Worshipful Co of Woolmen; FCA;

Clubs Carlton; *Style*— John Townend, Esq, MP; ✉ Sigglesthorne Hall, Sigglesthorne, Hull, N Humberside HU11 5QA

TOWNEND, Richard Frank Stuart; s of Col H Stuart Townend, *qv*, and Beatrice May, *née* Lord; *b* 15 July 1942; *Educ* Westminster, Univ of Lausanne, Royal Coll of Music, Academie d'Orgue Romainmôtier Switzerland; *m* 1970, Janet Elaine, da of James Gibson; 2 s (William b 19 Jan 1974, Edmund b 4 March 1977); *Career* organist; resident recitalist St Margaret Lothbury, specialises in Renaissance and Baroque repertoire; given recitals throughout Europe incl Int Organ Festival Switzerland (first English musician so invited), numerous bdcasts and recordings; sometime visiting lectr Int Organ Acad St Vith Belgium, Fachakademie für Evangelische Kirchenmusik Bayreuth Germany; *Style*— Richard Townend, Esq; ✉ Hill House, 17 Hans Place, London SW1X 0EP (☎ 0171 589 1206, fax 0171 589 5925)

TOWNEND, Lt-Col (Henry) Stuart; OBE (1948); s of Rev Frederick William Townend (d 1915), of Withleigh, Tiverton, Devon, and Florence Stewart, *née* Henry (d 1963); *b* 24 April 1909; *Educ* St Edmund's Sch Canterbury, Brasenose Coll Oxford (MA, pres univ athletic club), Rosenberg Coll St Gallen Switzerland, Staff Coll Camberley (psc); *m* 1936, Beatrice, *née* Lord (d 1984); 1 s (Richard Townend, *qv*, b 15 July 1942); *Career* Offr RA 1931–47, cmd field artillery battery NW Europe Campaign (despatches) 1939–45; Staff Appts: Adj, Bde Maj RA, GSOI RA War Office, Asst-Adj-Gen World Wide Air Movements WO; headmaster Hill House Int Jr Sch 1951– (six London sites and Swiss annex, 1050 3–13 yr old pupils); chm Housing Ctee Olympic Games London 1948; chm Anglo-Swiss Soc, Chelsea memb London Co Cncl; gold medal Br Cwlth Games 1930; Freeman City of London 1987; FRSA 1951; *Recreations* mountain climbing, skiing, swimming; *Clubs* Achilles; *Style*— Col H Stuart Townend; ✉ Hill House School, Hans Place, London SW1X 0EP (☎ 0171 584 1331)

TOWNS, Robin Peter; s of Harold George Towns, and Mildred, *née* Evans; *b* 3 Nov 1943; *Educ* Ilford Co HS, UCL (LLB); *m* 10 Aug 1968, (Isabel) Susan, da of Albert Partington (d 1966), of Bolton, Lancs; 3 da (Emma b 1971, Sarah b 1973, Rebecca b 1976); *Career* admitted slr 1968, memb Legal Section Private Banking and Fin Servs Lloyds Bank plc 1968– (sr legal advsr 1980–); govr Harlands Primary Sch Haywards Heath 1988–93 (chm 1989–93), govr Haywards Heath Sixth Form Coll 1988–93 (vice chm 1991–93) chm Friends of Haywards Heath Coll 1988–90, independent memb Corp of Haywards Heath Coll 1992– (vice chm 1992–), memb Govrs' Forum W Sussex 1991–93; *Recreations* listening to music, collecting Vanity Fair prints, watching cricket; *Style*— Robin P Towns, Esq; ✉ Llechwedd, 65 Lincoln Wood, Haywards Heath, W Sussex RH16 1LJ (☎ 01444 412393); Capital House, 1–5 Perrymount Rd, Haywards Heath, W Sussex RH16 3SP

TOWNSEND, Andy David; s of Donald Edward Townsend, and Thelma, *née* Leaver; *b* 23 July 1963; *Educ* Upton Co Primary Sch, Bexleyheath Secdy Sch; *m* Jacqueline Sheila, da of Norman Evans; 1 s (Daniel Andrew b 19 June 1986), 1 da (Kelly Louise b 10 July 1989); *Career* professional footballer; debut Southampton v Aston Villa 1985, 101 appearances Southampton 1985–88, 85 appearances Norwich City 1988–90, transferred for £1.2m to Chelsea 1990–93, with Aston Villa 1993– (currently capt, winners Coca Cola Cup 1994 and 1996); Republic of Ireland: over 35 full caps, 3 goals, played in World Cup Italy 1990 (scored penalty v Romania), memb World Cup squad 1994; transferred from Welling Utd to Weymouth for record non-league fee at time (£13,500); *Recreations* snooker, golf, playing guitar; *Style*— Andy Townsend; ✉ Aston Villa FC, Villa Park, Trinity Road, Birmingham B6 6HE (☎ 0121 327 2299)

TOWNSEND, (John) Anthony Victor; s of John Richard Christopher Townsend (d 1996), of Kintbury, Berks, and Carla Hillerns, *née* Lehmann (d 1990); *b* 24 Jan 1948; *Educ* Harrow, Selwyn Coll Cambridge (MA); *m* 16 April 1971, Carolyn Ann, da of Sir Walter Salomon (d 1987); 1 s (Christopher b 26 Feb 1974), 1 da (Alexandra b 26 Feb 1976); *Career* with Brown Shipley & Co Ltd bankers 1969–74, Rea Brothers Ltd bankers 1974–78, John Townsend & Co (Holdings) Ltd 1979–87, Finsbury Asset Management Ltd (investment banking) 1988–; dir: Rea Brothers Group plc, Finsbury Technology Trust PLC, Finsbury Underwriting Investment Trust plc, Finsbury Worldwide Pharmaceutical Trust plc, Blue Ridge Real Estate Co (USA), Immuno International A G (Switzerland); memb Lloyd's 1972–; chm Adam & Harvey Group PLC; govr Cranleigh Sch 1989–, tstee Harrow Mission 1989–; Master Worshipful Co of Pattenmakers; FRSA; *Recreations* tennis, shooting, skiing; *Clubs* City of London, RAC, Doubles (New York); *Style*— Anthony Townsend, Esq; ✉ The Coach House, Winterfold, Barhatch Lane, Cranleigh, Surrey GU6 7NH (☎ 01483 271366); Rea Brothers Group plc, Alderman's House, Alderman's Walk, London EC2M 3XR (☎ 0171 623 1155, fax 0171 626 3446)

TOWNSEND, Bruce Arnold; s of James Townsend (d 1978), of Rugby, and Hilda Norah, *née* Parker; *b* 25 July 1929; *Educ* Rugby, UCL (BSc); *m* 7 July 1956, Gillian Rosina, da of Norman Powell; 2 s (Matthew Gavin Bruce b 27 Sept 1958, Adam Robert James b 4 July 1962), 1 da (Hannah Gillian Ruth b 23 March, 1966); *Career* Lt Royal Warwicks Regt 1949–54 (seconded to 3 Battalion Nigeria Regt Royal W African Frontier Force 1949–51); Chemical Engrg Dept Courtaulds Coventry 1954–69 (head of dept 1967–69), chm Accrington Brick and Tile 1969–76, md Ashton Brothers Hyde 1969–75, chm Talbot Weaving Chorley 1972–76, md Robert Usher Drogheda 1975–76, chm Processing Div Courtaulds Nuneaton 1976–79, chief exec Courtaulds Research Coventry 1986–92 (gen mangr 1980–86, ret 1992); dir: Biwater Desalination 1983–87, Usutu Pulp Co Ltd Swaziland 1985–90, SAICCOR Natal SA 1987–89; Queen's award for technol 1989; FIChemE 1968 (memb Cncl 1982–85), FEng 1984 (memb Cncl 1987–90); *Recreations* art, history, wine-making, cycling; *Style*— Bruce Townsend, Esq, FEng; ✉ Long Lea, Castle Lane, Woolscott, Rugby, Coventry CV23 8DE (☎ 01788 810348)

TOWNSEND, Bryan Sydney; CBE (1994); s of Sydney Townsend, of Derbyshire, and Gladys Clara, *née* Russel; *b* 2 April 1930; *Educ* Wolverton Tech Coll; *m* Betty Eileen; 1 s (Nicholas), 2 da (Lynn Jane (Mrs Punter), Sally (Mrs Carmichael)); *Career* Royal Marines 1950–52; Southern Electricity: dist engr 1964–66, dist mangr 1966–68, area engr 1968–70, asst chief engr plant and design 1970–73; dep chief engr SE Electricity 1973–76, chief engr S Wales Electricity 1976–78, dep chm SW Electricity 1978–86, chm Midlands Electricity plc 1986–; chm Cncl W Midlands Region CBI, memb Birmingham C of C and Indust; FIEE; *Recreations* golf; *Clubs* Labrook Park Golf; *Style*— Bryan Townsend, Esq, CBE; ✉ Midlands Electricity plc, Mucklow Hill, Halesowen, W Midlands B62 8BP (☎ 0121 423 2345, fax 0121 422 2777, telex 338092)

TOWNSEND, Sir Cyril David; kt (1997), MP (C) Bexleyheath (majority 14,086); s of Lt-Col Cyril Moseley Townsend, and Lois, *née* Henderson; *b* 21 Dec 1937, Woking; *Educ* Bradfield, RMA Sandhurst; *m* 1976, Anita Sarah Weldon, da of late Lt-Col F G W Walshe, MC; 2 s (Hugh, John); *Career* cmmnd Durham LI 1958; served: Berlin, UK, Cyprus, Borneo; Adj IDLI 1966–68, ADC to Govr and C-in-C Hong Kong (Sir David Trench, GCMG, MC) 1964–66; PA to Lord Plummer (former ldr GLC) and the Rt Hon Edward Heath, MBE, MP (then ldr of the Oppn) 1968–70, memb CRD 1970–74; MP (C) Bexleyheath 1974–; memb Select Ctees on: Violence in the Family 1975, Foreign Affrs 1982–83, Armed Forces Bill (chm) 1981; PPS to Rt Hon Reg Prentice as Min of State DHSS 1979, sponsor of Protection of Children Act 1978; chm Br-Cyprus CPA Gp 1980–92, chm Organising Ctee First Argentine-Br Conf 1988–90, former chm All-Pty Freedom for Rudolph Hess Campaign, chm Bow Gp Standing Ctee on Foreign Affrs 1977–84, former vice chm (previously jt sec) Cons Parly Def Ctee, vice chm Friends of Cyprus 1980–92, memb Exec Ctee UK Branch Cwlth Parly Assoc 1992–93, memb SE London Industl Consultative Gp 1975–83; chm UN Parly Gp 1992–, chm Cons ME Cncl 1992– (hon sec 1980–88, jt vice chm 1988–92), co-fndr and first chm S Atlantic Cncl 1983–; vice chm: Cons Parly Foreign and Cwlth Affrs Ctee 1991–, Hansard Soc 1988–; tstee Lord Caradon Lecture Tst, fell Indust and Parl Tst, memb Nat Ctee Br-Arab Univ Assoc, Br Parly observer Presidential Election Lebanon 1982; ldr Parly delgn: to the Argentine 1984, to Iran 1988; pres Bexley Arthritis Care; *Publications* Helping Others To Help Themselves: Voluntary Action in the Eighties (1981), Cyprus and NATO's Southern Flank (1986); contrib to Contemporary Review, political jls and a Middle East newspaper (Al Hayat); *Recreations* books, music, exercise, exploring Cornwall; *Style*— Sir Cyril Townsend, MP; ✉ House of Commons, London SW1A 0AA (☎ 0171 219 3553, fax 0171 839 3509)

TOWNSEND, Gregor Peter John; s of Peter Bowers Townsend, of Galashiels, and Janette, *née* Burt; *b* 26 April 1973; *Educ* Galashiels Acad, Univ of Edinburgh (MA (Hons)); *Career* Rugby Union outside-half; debut Gala RFC 1990; Scotland: memb B team 1991, 19 full caps (int debut v England 1993, capt v Barbarians 1996), memb tours to Aust 1992, S Seas 1993, Argentina 1994 and New Zealand 1996, also Irish Wolfhounds and Barbarians; joined Northampton RFC 1995; *Recreations* tennis, squash, athletics, golf (yst qualifier Daily Record Masters 1988), travel, early 20th century art, reading classical novels, history, poetry, theatre, cinema; *Style*— Gregor Townsend, Esq; ✉ Hollymount, Elm Row, Galashiels, Borders Region TD1 3HT (☎ 01896 55843); c/o Northampton RFC, Trinity Pavilion, Abbey Street, St James, Northampton NN5 5LN (☎ 01604 755149)

TOWNSEND, Brig Ian Glen; s of Kenneth Townsend, of Leamington Spa, Warwickshire, and Irene Dorothy, *née* Singleton; *b* 7 Feb 1941; *Educ* Dulwich, RMA Sandhurst, Staff Coll; *m* 1, 19 Sept 1964 (m dis 1988), Loraine Jean, da of William A H Birnie (d 1978), of USA; 2 da (Lucie b 1966, Helen (twin) b 1966); m 2, 17 Feb 1989, Susan Natalie, da of Cdr Frank A L Heron-Watson (d 1990), of Dalbeattie, Scotland; 2 step s (Anthony b 1965, Ben b 1969); *Career* regtl and staff appts in UK, Germany, NI, Belgium 1961–91 incl: mil asst to UK Mil Rep NATO HQ 1979–81, CO 27 Field Regt RA 1981–83, Col operational requirements MOD 1983–86, Cdr artillery 1 Armoured Div 1986–88, asst chief of staff trg HQ UKLF 1988–91, ret 1991; dir mktg and sales VSEL 1991–93, md Townsend Associates 1993–96, sec gen Royal Br Legion 1996–; FIMgt 1988; *Recreations* skiing, golf, painting, music; *Clubs* Army and Navy; *Style*— Brig Ian Townsend; ✉ Royal British Legion, 48 Pall Mall, London SW1Y 5JY (☎ 0171 973 7218, fax 0171 973 7399)

TOWNSEND, Joan; da of Emlyn Davies (d 1971), of Shotton, North Wales, and Amelia Mary, *née* Tyrer (d 1987); *b* 7 Dec 1936; *Educ* Wigan Girls' HS, Hawarden GS, Somerville Coll Oxford (Beilby scholarship, BA, MA), Univ Coll of Swansea (MSc); *m* 23 April 1960, Prof (William) Godfrey Townsend, s of William Hughes Townsend (d 1976), of Swansea; 2 da (Frances Mary (Mrs Walker) b 1965, Helen Louise (Mrs Wray) b 1967); *Career* various sch teaching and lecturing appts incl: tutor Open Univ 1971–75, pt/t lectr Oxford Poly 1975–76, head of mathematics Sch of St Helen and St Katharine Abingdon 1976–81, headmistress Oxford HS GPDST 1981–96; tstee Westminster Centre Oxford; FRSA; *Publications* paper in Quarterly Journal of Mathematics and Applied Mechanics 1965, various articles on education; *Recreations* music (singing and piano), walking, skiing, dressmaking, reading; *Style*— Mrs Joan Townsend; ✉ Silver Howe, 62 Iffley Turn, Oxford OX4 4HN (☎ 01865 715807)

TOWNSEND, Dr John; s of George Townsend (d 1978), of Stoke-on-Trent, and Irene, *née* Hirst (d 1973); *b* 17 May 1935; *Educ* Whitehaven GS, St Bartholomew's Hosp Med Coll Univ of London (BSc, MBBS, DObstRCOG), Capernwray Hall (theological study); *m* 28 May 1960, Rev Dr Anne Jennifer Townsend, da of Rev Henry Howarth Cawthorne; 1 da (Janet Ruth b 6 Nov 1961), 2 s (David Hugh b 22 Feb 1964, Christopher John b 13 June 1966); *Career* house surgn and house doctor St Bartholomew's Hosp 1960, casualty sr house offr and casualty registrar Southend Gen Hosp 1961, obstetrics house offr Rochford Hosp 1961–62, staff doctor Manorom Christian Hosp Thailand 1964–67, house surgn N Staffs Royal Infirmary 1968–69, surgn then supt Manorom Christian Hosp 1969–79, medical and health care conslt to Tear Fund UK in S America, Africa and Asia 1979–86, medical dir ECHO International Health Services Ltd consulting for Africa, Central and South America and Asia 1988–95 (dep med dir 1986–88), trg mangr Tear Fund UK 1995–96, interchange progs advsr Church Mission Soc 1996–; chm Christian Leprosy Fndn of Thailand 1971–79; preacher and lectr; FRSM 1980–86, FRCSEd 1969; *Recreations* fencing, photography, walking; *Style*— John Townsend, Esq; ✉ Church Mission Society, Partnership House, 157 Waterloo Road, London SE1 8UU (☎ 0171 928 8681, fax 0171 401 3215)

TOWNSEND, Jonathan Richard Arthur; s of David Charles Humphrey Townsend, and Honor Stobart, *née* Hancock (d 1967); *b* 30 Nov 1942; *Educ* Winchester, Corpus Christi Coll Oxford (BA); *m* Sarah Elizabeth, da of Cdr Gordon Chalmers Fortin, RN, of Lavenham, Suffolk; 2 da (Honor Sarah b 2 Sept 1968, Louise Rosamond b 12 March 1971); *Career* prodn mangr DRG plc 1961–62 and 1965–68, ptnr Laing and Cruickshank 1972–73 (joined 1969), ptnr de Zoete and Bevan 1973–86, md Barclays de Zoete Securities 1986–90, dir in charge of business devpt Kleinwort Benson 1990–93, vice chm ABN AMRO Hoare Govett Corporate Finance Ltd 1993–; *Recreations* my girls, Italy, cricket, shooting, bridge; *Clubs* Brooks's, MCC, Vincent's (Oxford); *Style*— Jonathan Townsend, Esq; ✉ Villa Il Bacchino, Via Bobolino, Torreone 126, Cortona (Arezzo), Italy; 18 Eaton Square, London SW1W 9DD (☎ and fax 0171 235 8324); ABN AMRO Hoare Govett Ltd, 4 Broadgate, London EC2M 7LE (☎ 0171 601 0101, fax 0171 374 7635)

TOWNSEND, Lady Juliet Margaret; *née* Smith; LVO (1981), DL (Northamptonshire 1990); da of 2 Earl of Birkenhead, TD (d 1975); *b* 9 Sept 1941; *Educ* Westonbirt, Somerville Coll Oxford; *m* 1970, John Richard Townsend, s of Lt-Col Clarence Henry Southgate Townsend, OBE, MC, TD, MRCVS (d 1953); 3 da; *Career* lady-in-waiting to HRH The Princess Margaret, Countess of Snowdon 1965–71, extra lady-in-waiting 1971–; High Sheriff of Northamptonshire 1991–92; *Style*— The Lady Juliet Townsend, LVO, DL; ✉ Newbottle Manor, Banbury, Oxon (☎ 01295 811295)

TOWNSEND, Rear Adm Sir Leslie William; KCVO (1981), CBE (1973); s of William Bligh Townsend and Ellen, *née* Alford; *b* 22 Feb 1924; *Educ* Regent's Park Sch Southampton; *m* 1947, Marjorie Bennett; 1 s, 3 da; *Career* joined RN 1942, cmmnd 1943; sec to: Vice-Chief of Naval Staff 1967–70, First Sea Lord and Chief of Naval Staff 1970–71; mil asst to: Chief Def Staff 1971–74, chm NATO Military Ctee 1974–76; dir Naval and WRNS Appointments 1976, Rear Adm 1979, Defence Services sec 1979–82, ret 1982; memb: Lord Chllr's Panel of Independent Inspectors 1982–94, Services Pensions Appeals Tbnl 1985–96; *Clubs* Army and Navy, RN and Royal Albert Yacht; *Style*— Rear Adm Sir Leslie Townsend, KCVO, CBE; ✉ 8 King Charles Street, Old Portsmouth PO1 2BS (☎ 01705 877508)

TOWNSEND, Michael; s of Edgar Maurice Townsend (d 1985), and Agnes, *née* Pearson (d 1988); *b* 10 June 1941; *Educ* Harrogate GS, Sidney Sussex Coll Cambridge (minor scholar, MA); *m* 1966, Gillian Maryska, da of Wilfred Dorrien Wickson (d 1992); 3 s (Alistair John b 3 Sept 1970, Christopher James b 1 Dec 1972, Jonathan Mark b 13 Nov 1975); *Career* articled clerk Blackburns Robson Coates CAs (now Robson Rhodes) Leeds 1963–69, various posts rising to fin controller Sperry Gyroscope Ltd Bracknell 1969–75, fin controller Plessey Radar Ltd 1975–79, gp fin controller Smiths Industries plc 1988–90 (fin controller Smiths Industries Aerospace Defence Systems 1979–88); Rolls-Royce plc: gp fin controller 1990–91, fin dir 1991–; non-exec dir Northern Electric plc 1994–; FCA 1976 (ACA 1966), FRSA 1992; *Recreations* cricket, all ball games, dogs, canals; *Clubs* Kennel; *Style—* Michael Townsend, Esq; ✉ Rolls-Royce plc, 65 Buckingham Gate, London SW1E 6AT (☎ 0171 222 9020, fax 0171 227 9183)

TOWNSEND, Prof Peter Brereton; s of Flt Lt Philip Brereton Townsend (d 1991), of Scotton, Knaresborough, Yorks, and Alice Mary, *née* Southcote (d 1995); *b* 6 April 1928; *Educ* Univ Coll Sch, St John's Coll Cambridge (BA), Free Univ Berlin; *m* 1, 18 June 1949 (m dis 1974), Ruth, *née* Pearce; 4 s (Matthew b 1952, Adam b 1953, Christian b 1957, Benjamin b 1962); m 2, 14 June 1976 (m dis 1980), Joy, *née* Skegg; 1 da (Lucy b 1976); m 3, 4 Jan 1985, Jean Ann Corston, MP, *qv*, da of Laurie Parkin, of Yeovil; *Career* RASC and RAEC 1946–48; res sec Political and Econ Planning 1952–54, res offr Inst of Community Studies Bethnal Green 1954–57, res fell (later lectr) LSE 1957–63, prof of sociology Univ of Essex 1963–81 (pro vice chllr 1975–78), prof of social policy Univ of Bristol 1982–93 (emeritus 1993); distinguished visiting Michael Harrington prof of social science (International Poverty) City Univ of NY 1991–92; conslt: to the UN 1993, to the UN Devpt Prog 1994–96; chm: Child Poverty Action Gp 1969–89 (pres 1989–), Disability Alliance 1974–, Channel 4 Poverty Cmmn 1996; former pres Psychiatric Rehabilitation Assoc 1967–85, pres Mencap SW region 1990–93, pt/t govt advsr and conslt; memb: Exec Ctee Fabian Soc 1958–89 (chm 1965–66, vice pres 1989–), Chief Scientist's Ctee DHSS 1976–79, Res Working Gp on Inequalities in Health 1977–80, Br Sociological Assoc 1961–, Social Policy Assoc 1978–; Hon DUniv Essex 1990, Hon DLitt Univ of Teesside 1994, Hon D Open Univ 1995, Hon DSci Univ of Edinburgh 1996; *Books* incl: Cambridge Anthology (ed, 1952), The Family Life of Old People (1957), The Last Refuge: A Survey of Residential Institutions and Homes for the Aged in England and Wales (1962), The Poor and Poorest (with Brian Abel-Smith, 1965), The Aged in the Welfare State (with Dorothy Wedderburn, 1965), Old People in Three Industrial Societies (with Ethel Shanas and others, 1968), The Concept of Poverty (ed, 1970), The Social Minority (1973), Disability Rights Handbook (jtly, 1976–84), Sociology and Social Policy (1975), Poverty in the United Kingdom (1979), Inequalities in Health (with Sir Douglas Black and others, 1980), Disability in Britain (with Alan Walker, 1982), Responses to Poverty: Lessons from Europe (with Roger Lawson and Robert Walker, 1984), Health and Deprivation: Inequality and the North (with Peter Phillimore and Alastair Beattie 1987), Poverty and Labour in London (with Paul Corrigan and Ute Kowarzik, 1987), Inequalities in Health: The Black Report and the Health Divide (ed with Margaret Whitehead and Nick Davidson, 1982, revised 1988 and 1992), The International Analysis of Poverty (1993); *Recreations* athletics, gardening; *Style—* Prof Peter Townsend; ✉ c/o School of Policy Studies, University of Bristol, 8 Woodland Road, Bristol BS8 1TN (☎ 0117 928 8533)

TOWNSEND, Susan (Sue); *b* 2 April 1946; *Educ* South Wigston Girls' HS; *Career* author and playwright; joined Writers Group Phoenix Arts Centre 1978 (winner Thames Television Bursary as writer in residence for Womberang); FRSL 1993; *Books* The Secret Diary of Adrian Mole aged 13 3/4, The Growing Pains of Adrian Mole, The True Confessions of Adrian Albert Mole, Margaret Hilda Roberts and Susan Lilian Townsend (1989), Rebuilding Coventry (1988), The Secret Diary of Adrian Mole aged 13 3/4 - The Play, Bazaar and Rummage, Groping for Words, Womberang: Three Plays by Sue Townsend, Great Celestial Cow (1984), Mr Bevan's Dream, The Queen and I (1992), Adrian Mole: The Wilderness Years (1994); *Plays* Womberang (Soho Poly) 1979, The Ghost of Daniel Lambert (Phoenix Arts Centre and Leicester Haymarket Theatre) 1981, Dayroom (Croydon Warehouse Theatre) 1981, Captain Christmas and the Evil Adults (Phoenix Arts Centre) 1982, Bazaar and Rummage (Royal Court Theatre Upstairs) 1982, Groping for Words (Croydon Warehouse Theatre) 1983, The Great Celestial Cow (Royal Court Theatre and tour) 1984, Ten Tiny Fingers, Nine Tiny Toes (Library Theatre Manchester) 1989, Ear Nose and Throat (Arts Theatre Cambridge) 1988, Disneyland it Ain't (Royal Court Theatre Upstairs) 1989, Queen and I (Vaudeville Theatre London) 1994; *Television* incl: contrib Revolting Women (BBC, 1981), Bazaar and Rummage (BBC, 1983), The Secret Diary of Adrian Mole (Thames TV, 1985), The Growing Pains of Adrian Mole (Thames TV, 1987), The Refuge (Channel 4, 1987); *Recreations* reading, looking at pictures, canoeing; *Style—* Ms Sue Townsend, FRSL; ✉ Tessa Sayle Agency, 11 Jubilee Place, London SW3 3TE; Curtis Brown Group Ltd, 28–29 Haymarket, London SW1Y 4SP (☎ 0171 396 6600, fax 0171 396 0110); Sheil Land Associates Ltd, 43 Doughty Street, London WC1N 2LF

TOWNSHEND, Prof Alan; s of Stanley Charles Townshend, of Ammanford, Carms, and Betsy, *née* Roberts; *b* 20 June 1939; *Educ* Pontadawe GS, Univ of Birmingham (BSc, PhD, DSc); *m* 11 Aug 1962, Enid, da of Harold Horton (d 1990), of S Kirkby, Pontefract, W Yorks; 3 s (Robert Michael b 1966, Peter Charles b 1967, Gareth Richard b 1970); *Career* lectr in chemistry Univ of Birmingham 1964–80; Univ of Hull: sr lectr then reader in analytical chemistry 1980–84, prof 1984–, dean Sch of Chemistry 1989–92, dir Inst for Chemistry in Indust 1993–; Royal Soc of Chemistry Silver medal 1975 (Gold medal 1991), AnalaR Gold medal 1987, Theophilus Redwood lectr 1988; memb Analytical Div Ctee Int Union of Pure and Applied Chemistry 1991–95, pres Analytical Div Royal Soc of Chemistry 1996–98; CChem, FRSC 1978; *Books* Inorganic Reaction Chemistry: Systematic Chemical Separation (1980), Inorganic Reaction Chemistry: Reactions of the Elements and their Compounds Part A: Alkali Metals to Nitrogen (1981), Inorganic Reaction Chemistry: Reactions of the Elements and their Compounds Part B: Osmium to Zirconium (1981), Dictionary of Analytical Reagents (1993), Flame Chemiluminescence Analysis by Molecular Emission Cavity Detection (1994), Encyclopedia of Analytical Science (10 vols, ed-in-chief, 1995); *Recreations* walking, food and wine; *Style—* Prof Alan Townshend; ✉ School of Chemistry, University of Hull, Hull HU6 7RX (☎ 01482 465027, fax 01482 466410)

TOWNSHEND, Lady Carolyn Elizabeth Ann; has resumed surname Townshend; da of 7 Marquess Townshend; *b* 27 Sept 1940; *Educ* Univ of Florence Italy; *m* 13 Oct 1962 (m dis 1971), Antonio Capellini; 1 s (Vincenzo Charles Capellini Townshend); *Career* international special event mgmnt and promotions; md Carolyn Townshend & Associates; FRSA; *Recreations* theatre, painting, skiing and music; *Style—* The Lady Carolyn Townshend; ✉ 89 Elizabeth Street, London SW1W 9PG (☎ 0171 730 9190)

TOWNSHEND, 7 Marquess (GB 1787); Sir George John Patrick Dominic Townshend; 11 Bt (E 1617); also Baron Townshend of Lynn Regis (E 1661) and Viscount Townshend of Raynham (E 1682); s of 6 Marquess (d 1921) whose forebear, 1 Marquess and Field Marshal commanded the field of Quebec after the death of Gen Wolfe; *b* 13 May 1916; *Educ* Harrow; *m* 1, 1939 (m dis 1960), Elizabeth Pamela Audrey (d 1989), da of Maj Thomas Luby; 1 s, 2 da; m 2, 1960, Ann Frances (d 1988), da of late Arthur Pellew Darlow; 1 s, 1 da; *Heir* s, Viscount Raynham; *Career* Norfolk Yeomanry 1936–40, Scots Gds 1940–45; chm: Anglia TV Ltd 1958–86, Anglia TV Group plc 1976–86, Survival Anglia Ltd 1971–86, AP Bank Ltd 1975–87, London Merchant Securities plc 1964–95, Raynham Farm Co Ltd 1957–, Norfolk Agric Station 1973–87 (pres 1987–); dir: Norwich Union Life Insurance Society Ltd 1950–86 (vice chm 1973–86), Norwich Union Fire Insurance Society Ltd 1950–86 (vice chm 1975–86), Riggs National Corporation 1987–89; DL Norfolk 1951–61; Hon DCL UEA 1989, FRSA 1990; *Clubs* White's, MCC, Norfolk, Pilgrim's; *Style—* The Most Hon the Marquess Townshend; ✉ Raynham Hall, Fakenham, Norfolk NR21 7EP (☎ 01328 862133)

TOWNSHEND, Peter (Pete); s of Cliff Townshend; *b* 19 May 1945; *Educ* Acton Co GS; *Career* musician; memb: The Detours 1961–63, The High Numbers (released single I'm The Face 1964) 1963–64, The Who 1964–89; albums with The Who: My Generation (1965, reached UK no 5), A Quick one (1966, UK no 4), The Who Sell Out (1968, UK no 13), Tommy (1969, UK no 2, Broadway musical 1993, winner 5 Tony awards, revived London 1996), Live At Leeds (live, 1970, UK no 3), Who's Next (1971, UK no 1), Meaty Beaty Big And Bouncy (compilation, 1971, UK no 9), Quadrophenia (1973, UK no 2), Odds And Sods (compilation, 1974, UK no 10), Tommy (soundtrack, 1975, UK no 14), The Who By Numbers (1975, UK no 7), The Story Of The Who (compilation, 1976, UK no 2), Who Are You? (1978, UK no 6), The Kids Are Alright (compilation, 1979, UK no 26), Quadrophenia (soundtrack, 1979, UK no 23), Face Dances (1981, UK no 2), It's Hard (1982, UK no 11), Who's Last (1984, UK no 48), Who's Better, Who's Best (1988, UK no 10); solo albums: Who Came First (1972, UK no 30), Rough Mix (with Ronnie Lane, 1977, UK no 44), Empty Glass (1980, UK no 11), All The Best Cowboys Have Chinese Eyes (1982, UK no 32), Scoop (1983), White City (1985, UK no 70), Scoop II (1987), The Iron Man (1989, London musical at Old Vic 1993); final Who tour 1989; *Books* Horses Neck (1985); *Style—* Pete Townshend, Esq; ✉ c/o Atlantic Records, 35–38 Portman Square, London W1H 0EU (☎ 0171 467 2550, fax 0171 467 2555)

TOWNSHEND, Timothy John Hume; s of late Canon Horace Lyle Hume Townshend, of Norwich, and Lorna Ethel, *née* Lutton; *see Burke's Irish Family Records, 1976*; *b* 20 May 1949; *Educ* Ipswich Sch, Pembroke Coll Cambridge (BA, MA); *Career* called to the Bar Lincoln's Inn 1972, in practice SE Circuit; pt/t chm Mental Health Review Tbnl 1996–; memb Bd Broadland Housing Assoc; *Recreations* choir (Norwich Philharmonic Society), sailing, skiing, gardening; *Clubs* Norfolk (Norwich); *Style—* Timothy Townshend, Esq; ✉ 24 Newmarket Rd, Norwich, Norfolk NR2 2LA (☎ 01603 661519); Octagon House, 19 Colegate, Norwich, Norfolk (☎ 01603 623186, fax 01603 760519)

TOWNSIN, Michael Farndon; s of Reginald Townsin, and Mary, *née* Tebbs; *b* 7 April 1940; *Educ* Kings Sch Peterborough; *m* 1, 17 June 1967 (m dis 1977), Denise Margaret, da of George Ellicott (d 1972), of Peterborough; 1 s (Luke William), 3 da (Tara Sophie, Talitha Lucy, Georgina Sarah); m 2, 3 Jan 1981, Christine Noelle, da of Leonard Barker (d 1969), of Perth, W Aust; *Career* exec offr DHSS 1960–64, jt md and dep chm Young & Rubicam 1980–83 (media exec 1964–74, media dir and bd dir 1974–80), chm and chief exec offr Havas Conseil Marsteller 1983–86, advertising and mktg conslt 1986, subsequently chm and chief exec offr GGK London until 1993, int media dir i/c global BAT business Grey London (Mediacom) 1995–; FIPA; *Recreations* swimming, reading, films; *Clubs* Annabel's, Mark's, Harry's Bar; *Style—* Michael Townsin, Esq; ✉ MediaCom UK Ltd, 1–7 Livonia Street, London W1V 3PT (☎ 0171 872 9928)

TOWNSLEY, Barry Stephen; s of Dr William Townsley; *b* 14 Oct 1946; *Educ* Hasmonean GS; *m* 3 Nov 1975, Hon Laura Helen, da of Lord Wolfson of Marylebone (Life Peer); 1 s (Charles Ralph Wolfson b 2 June 1984), 3 da (Alexandra Jane Wolfson b 3 May 1977, Georgina Kate Wolfson b 26 May 1979, Isabella Edith Wolfson b 22 June 1994); *Career* W Greenwell & Co 1964–69; dir Astaire & Co 1969–76; fndr and sr ptnr Jacobson Townsley & Co 1976– (co now called Townsley & Co); vice chm and tstee Serpentine Gallery London; MSI; *Recreations* contemporary art; *Style—* Barry Townsley, Esq; ✉ Townsley & Co, 44 Worship St, London EC2A 2JT (☎ 0171 377 6161, fax 0171 375 1380)

TOY, Rev Canon John; s of Sidney Toy (d 1967), of London, and Violet Mary, *née* Doudney (d 1952); *b* 25 Nov 1930; *Educ* Epsom Co GS, Hatfield Coll Durham (BA, MA), Univ of Leeds (PhD); *m* 1963, Mollie, da of Eric Tilbury (d 1987), of Ross-on-Wye; 1 s (Paul Bernard James b 1964), 1 da (Katherine Violet b 1966); *Career* priest C of E 1956, curacy in London 1955–58, travelling sec with Student Christian Movement 1958–60, chaplain and lectr Ely Theol Coll 1960–64, chaplain St Andrew's Gothenburg Sweden 1965–69, lectr, sr lectr and princ lectr in theol St John's Coll York 1969–83, canon residentiary and chllr York Minster 1983–; *Publications* Cathedral Booklets; Jesus: Man for God (1988); *Recreations* music, architecture, travel; *Style—* The Rev Canon John Toy; ✉ 4 Minster Yard, York YO1 2JF (☎ 01904 620877)

TOYE, Bryan Edward; JP; s of Herbert Graham Donovan Toye (d 1969), and Marion Alberta, *née* Montignani; *b* 17 March 1938; *Educ* Stowe; *m* 8 Oct 1982, Fiona Ann, da of Gordon Henry James Hogg, of Wellington, NZ; 2 s (Charles Edward Graham b 16 Dec 1983, Frederick b 6 Jan 1988), 1 da (Elisabeth Fiona Ann b 27 July 1985); *Career* Hon Col 124 Havering Petroleum Sqdn (V) RLC; joined Toye & Co 1956, dir Toye Kenning & Spencer 1962–, dir Toye & Co 1966, chm Toye and Co plc and 23 assoc subsid cos 1969–; non-exec dir: Futurama Signs Ltd (dep chm), Trehaven Trust Ltd; govr: Bridewell Royal Hosp, Christ's Hosp; estates and sch govr King Edward's Sch Witley 1988–93; tstee: Queen Elizabeth Scholarship Tst, Britain-Australia Bicentennial Tst, Black Country Museum (London Gp), British Red Cross (London Branch, vice pres); steward Henley Royal Regatta 1980; alderman The Ward of Lime St 1983 (pres Lime St Ward Club), pres City Livery Club 1988–89; memb Ct of Assts: Worshipful Co of Gold & Silver Wyre Drawers (Master 1984), Worshipful Co of Broderers (Renter Warden 1994–95, Warden 1995–96), Guild of Freemen of the City of London, Worshipful Co of Goldsmiths 1992 (Liveryman 1985–92); hon memb Ct of Assts Hon Artillery Co, pres Royal Warrant Holders Assoc 1991–92 (memb Cncl 1982–); FInstD 1966, FIMgt 1983, FRSA; memb Lloyd's; OStJ 1980; *Recreations* swimming, tennis, gardening, music, entertaining; *Clubs* Leander, Wig and Pen, RAC, Middx Co RFC, Wasps FC (tstee and vice pres, chm Exec Ctee 1992–93); *Style—* Bryan Toye, Esq, JP; ✉ Toye & Co plc, 19–21 Great Queen St, London WC2B 5BE (☎ 0171 242 0471, fax 0171 831 8692)

TOYE, Col (Claude) Hugh; OBE (1962, MBE 1947); s of Rev Percy Sheffield Toye (d 1968), and Sarah, *née* Griffiths (d 1966); *b* 28 March 1917; *Educ* Kingswood Sch Bath, Queens' Coll Cambridge (BA, MA); *m* 28 April 1958, Betty, da of Lionel Hayne (d 1932), of Oulton Broad, Suffolk; 1 s (decd); *Career* enlisted Private RAMC (TA) 1938, Field Ambulance France 1940 (despatches), cmmnd RA 1941, Maj CSDIC (India) 1944–46, GSO 11 (Intelligence) HQ ALFSEA 1946–47, Staff Coll Camberley 1948, 14 Fd Regt RA Hong Kong 1949–51 (Adj), DAA and QMG HQ 56 Armd Div (TA) 1951–53, GSO II Political Office MEF Cyprus 1956–58, Cmd 36 Battery RA Cyprus 1958 (UK 1959), Lt-Col Mil Attaché Vientiane 1960–62, GSO I (SD) SHAPE Paris 1962–64, Gwilym Gibbon res fell Nuffield Coll Oxford (DPhil) 1964–66, Col UK mil advsr's rep HQ SEATO Bangkok 1966–68, def advsr UK Mission to UN NY 1969–70, Dep Cdr Br Army Staff Washington 1970–72, ret 1972; treas Cuddesdon Coll 1974–75, local SSAFA rep 1975–85; reviewer of books on Indo-China; *Books* The Springing Tiger, a study of Subhas Chandra Bose (1959, revised 1996), Laos: Buffer State or Battleground (1968); *Recreations* gardening, music; *Clubs* Army and Navy; *Style—* Col Hugh Toye, OBE; ✉ 5 Farm Close Lane, Wheatley, Oxford OX33 1UG

TOYE, Prof John Francis Joseph; s of John Redmond Toye, of Lewes, E Sussex, and Adele, *née* Francis (d 1972); *b* 7 Oct 1942; *Educ* Christ's Coll Finchley, Jesus Coll Cambridge (BA, MA), Harvard, SOAS (MSc, PhD); *m* 18 March 1967, Janet, da of late Richard Henry Reason, of Harrow, London; 1 s (Richard b 1973), 1 da (Eleanor b 1970); *Career* asst princ HM Treasy 1965–68, res fell SOAS London 1970–72, fell (later tutor) Wolfson Coll Cambridge 1972–80 (asst dir of devpt studies 1977–80); dir: Commodities Research Unit Ltd 1980–82, Centre for Devpt Studies Univ Coll Swansea 1982–87, Inst of Devpt Studies Univ of Sussex (professorial fell) 1987–; memb: Wandsworth Community Rels Cncl 1968–72, Cambridge Cncl of Community Rels 1972–80, W Glamorgan Equal Opportunities Gp 1983–87; pres Devpt Studies Assoc of GB and I 1994; *Books* Taxation and Economic Development (1978), Trade and Poor Countries (1979), Public Expenditure and Indian Development Policy (1981), Dilemmas of Development (1987), Does Aid Work in India? (1990), Aid and Power (1991); *Recreations* music, walking, theatre; *Style*— Prof John Toye; ✉ Institute of Development Studies, University of Sussex, Falmer, Brighton, Sussex BN1 9RE

TOYE, Wendy; CBE (1992); da of Ernest Walter Toye and Jessie Crichton, *née* Ramsay; *b* 1 May 1917; *Educ* privately; *m* Edward Selwyn Sharp (m dis); *Career* choreographer, actress, director and dancer; studied dancing as a child and first appeared at the Royal Albert Hall in 1921, winner numerous dancing awards incl the Charlston championship (Albert Hall) 1929, produced a ballet at the Palladium when only ten years of age, made her first professional appearance on the stage at the Old Vic as Cobweb in a Midsummer Night's Dream 1929, Marigold in Toad of Toad Hall, choreographer Mother Earth (Savoy) 1929, numerous roles with Ninette de Valois Vic-Wells Ballet Co 1930, princ dancer in The Golden Toy, toured with Anton Dolin 1934–35; choreographed and princ dancer: Markora Dolin Co, Rambert Ballet Co; arranged the dances for George Black's prodns 1937–44 (incl Black and Blue, Black Velvet, Black Vanities, Strike a New Note and Strike It Again), Gay Rosalinda (Palace) 1945–48, starred opposite Arthur Askey in Follow the Girls (Her Majesty's) 1945; directed prodns of Big Ben, Bless the Bride and Tough at the Top for Sir Charles B Cochran (Adelphi) 1946, played princ girl in the pantomime Simple Simon (Birmingham) 1947, Winnie Tate in Annie Get Your Gun (London Coliseum), sent her co Ballet-Hoo de Wendy Toye to Paris for a season 1948; dir numerous prodns incl: Virtue in Danger, Robert & Elizabeth, On The Level, As You Like It, Show Boat, She Stoops to Conquer, Soldiers Tale (Young Vic), The Great Waltz and Cowardy Custard, Follow the Star (Chichester), The Mikado (Opera House Ankara Turkey); more recent prodns incl: This Thing Called Love (Ambassadors) 1984, Noel and Gertie (Princess Grace Theatre Monte Carlo) 1984, assoc prodr Barnum (Victoria Palace) and Singin' in the Rain (London Palladium), Gala tribute to Joyce Grenfell 1985; Shaw Festival Theatre Canada: Celemare, Mad Woman of Chaillot; assoc prodr Torvill & Dean Ice Show World Tour 1985, dir and choreographer Kiss Me Kate (Copenhagen) and Unholy Trinity (Stephenville Festival) 1986, Laburnham Grove (Watford Palace) 1987, Miranda (Chichester Festival Theatre) 1987, Songbook (Watermill Theatre) 1988, Ziegfeld (London Palladium) 1988, Mrs Dot (Watford Palace) 1988, Family and Friends (Sadler's Wells) 1988, When That I Was (Manitoba Theatre Center) 1988, Oh (Coward Playhouse Hong Kong) 1989, Cinderella (Palace Waterford), Till We Meet Again Concert (Festival Hall) 1989, Retrospective Season of Films Directed by Wendy Toye (Festival de Films des Femmes International, Paris) 1990, Penny Black (Wavendon) 1990, Moll Flanders (Watermill Theatre) 1990, Captain Beaky's Heavens Up (Playhouse) 1990, 2 Operas (Aix en Provence Festival) 1991, The Drummer (Watermill Theatre) 1991, Sound of Music (pre London Nat Tour and Sadler's Wells) 1992/93, See How They Run (Watermill Theatre), The Kingfisher (Vienna's Eng Theatre) 1993, Under Their Hats (King's Head) 1994, Anastasia File (Watermill Theatre) 1994, Lloyd George knew my Father (Watermill Theatre) 1995, Warts and All, Rogues to Riches (Watermill Theatre) 1996, Under Their Hats (Northcott Exeter, Yvonne Arnard Theatre and London) 1996; ENO prodns incl: Bluebeards Castle, The Telephone, Russalka, La Vie Parisienne, Orpheus In The Underworld, Italian Girl in Algiers, Fledermaus; Opera de Chambre Menton prodns incl: Der Apothoker 1994, Serva Padrona 1994; Seraglio, The Impresario For Yehudi Menuhin's Bath Festival (with Menuhin conducting); dir films: The Stranger Left No Card (first prize Cannes Film Festival), On The Twentieth Day, Raising A Riot, We Joined The Navy, Three Cases of Murder, The Teckman Mystery, All For Mary, True As A Turtle, The King's Breakfast; Br Film Inst: A Restrospective (NFT) 1995; lectured in Australia 1977, memb Cncl LAMDA, original memb Accreditation Bd instigated by NCDT for Acting Courses 1981–84, served Equity Cncl as first dirs rep 1974 (dirs sub ctee 1971); examiner LAMDA, guest of hon Tokyo Int Film Festival 1992; memb: Grand Cncl Royal Acad of Dancing, Ctee for Wavenden All Music Scheme, Vivian Ellis Award Scheme, Richard Stillgoe Award Scheme; Queen's Silver Jubilee Medal 1977; Hon DLitt City Univ 1996; *Recreations* embroidery, gardening; *Style*— Dr Wendy Toye, CBE; ✉ c/o Jay Benning & Co, Canberra House, 315 Regent St, London W1R 7YB

TOYN, His Hon (Richard) John; s of Richard Thomas Millington Toyn (d 1961), of Leamington Spa, Warwicks, and Ethel, *née* Crimp (d 1981); *b* 24 Jan 1927; *Educ* Solihull Sch, Bristol GS, Univ of Bristol (LLB); *m* 20 Aug 1955, Joyce Evelyn, da of Harold Llewelyn Goodwin (d 1970), of Solihull, W Midlands; 2 s (Andrew b 1956, Richard b 1960), 2 da (Julia b 1958, Louise b 1964); *Career* RASC 1948–50; called to the Bar Gray's Inn 1950; circuit judge 1972–92; memb Parole Bd for England and Wales 1978–80; *Publications* Butterworths County Court Precedents and Pleading (contributing ed, 1985); *Style*— His Hon John Toyn

TOYNBEE, Mary Louisa (Polly); da of Philip Toynbee (d 1981), and Anne Barbara Denise, *née* Powell; *b* 27 Dec 1946; *Educ* Badminton Sch Bristol, Holland Park Comprehensive, St Anne's Coll Oxford (John Gamble scholar); *m* 28 Dec 1970, Peter George James Jenkins (d 1992), s of Kenneth E Jenkins, of Norfolk; 1 s (Nathaniel b 10 Jan 1985), 2 da (Millicent (Milly) b 5 Dec 1971, Flora b 17 Dec 1975), 1 step da (Amy b 29 Oct 1967); *Career* journalist; reporter The Observer 1968–71, ed The Washington Monthly USA 1971–72, feature writer The Observer 1972–77, columnist The Guardian 1977–88, social affrs ed BBC 1988–95, assoc ed and columnist The Independent 1995–; Parly candidate (SDP) Lewisham East 1983; Catherine Pakenham Award for Journalism 1975, Columnist of the Year British Press Awards 1986; memb NUJ; *Books* Leftovers (1966), A Working Life (1972), Hospital (1979), The Way We Live Now (1981), Lost Children (1985); *Recreations* children; *Style*— Ms Polly Toynbee; ✉ The Independent, 1 Canada Square, Canary Wharf, London E14 5DL (☎ 0171 293 2000)

TOYNBEE, Simon Victor; yst s of Ralph Victor Toynbee (d 1970), and Bridget, *née* Monins; *b* 30 Jan 1944; *Educ* Winchester; *m* 12 Aug 1967, Antoinette Mary, da of John Walter Devonshire, of Santa Monica, California, USA; 3 da (Georgina, Elizabeth, Susannah); *Career* 2 Lt The RB 1963–65; Jessel Toynbee and Co Ltd 1966–72, Singer and Friedlander Ltd 1973–82 (dir Investment Dept 1977–82), Henderson Administration Ltd 1982–90 (dir 1986–90), investment dir Mercury Fund Managers Ltd 1990–92, head of investment Principal Investment Management Ltd 1992–94, sr investment mangr Majedie Investments plc 1995–, dir Majedie Investment Trust Ltd 1995–; hon investment advsr Royal Green Jackets Funds and Church Army, memb Cncl W Heath Sch Sevenoaks; *Recreations* gardening, golf; *Clubs* Royal Green Jackets, MCC; *Style*— S V Toynbee, Esq; ✉ Old Tong Farm, Brenchley, Kent TN12 7HT (☎ 01892 723552); Majedie Investments plc, 1 Minster Court, Mincing Lane, London EC3R 7ZZ (☎ 0171 626 1243, fax 0171 929 0904)

TOYNE, Prof Peter; DL (Merseyside 1990); s of Harold Toyne, and Lavinia Doris, *née* Smith (d 1968); *b* 3 Dec 1939; *Educ* Ripon GS, Univ of Bristol (BA); *m* 2 Aug 1969, Angela, da of Rev John Alroy Wedderburn; 1 s (Simon b 1970); *Career* Univ of Exeter: lectr in geography 1965–75, sr lectr 1975–80, sub dean of social studies 1976–79; dir Dept of Educn and Sci Educnl Credit Transfer Feasibility Study 1977–80, dep dir W Sussex Inst of HE 1980–83, dep rector NE London Poly 1983–86, rector The Liverpool Poly 1986–92, vice chllr Liverpool John Moores Univ (formerly Liverpool Poly) 1992–; fell Eton Coll 1996–; chm: Liverpool St George's Hall Tstees, Liverpool Compact, Rodolfus Choir Tstees; memb Bd: HEQC, Assoc of Cwlth Universities, Royal Liverpool Philharmonic Soc, Liverpool Architecture Bd, Liverpool City of Learning Bd, Euro Lifelong Learning Initiative, Rover Learning Business; vice chm Ctee for Int cooperation in HE Br Cncl, chm ECCTIS 2000 Advsy Ctee, Theological Coll inspr House of Bishops; Hon DEd CNAA 1992; CIMgt; FRSA; *Books* World Problems (1969), Techniques in Human Geography (1971), Recreation and Environment (1974), Organisation, Location and Behaviour (1974), Toyne Report on Credit Transfer (1979), Toyne Report on Environmental Responsibility (1993), and numerous articles in various professional jls; *Recreations* music (orchestral and church), railways; *Clubs* Liverpool Athenaeum; *Style*— Prof Peter Toyne, DL; ✉ Liverpool John Moores University, Egerton Court, 2 Rodney St, Liverpool L3 5UX (☎ 0151 709 3676, fax 0151 709 9864)

TOYNE SEWELL, Maj-Gen Timothy Patrick; s of Brig Edgar Patrick Sewell, CBE (d 1956), and Elizabeth Cecily Mease, *née* Toyne, MBE; *b* 7 July 1941; *Educ* Bedford Sch, RMA Sandhurst; *m* 7 Aug 1965; 1 s (Patrick b 1967), 1 da (Melanie b 1969); *Career* cmmnd King's Own Scottish Borderers 1961; served: Aden, Malaysia, BAOR, NI; Staff Coll 1973, CO 1 KOSB 1981–83, COS HQ British Forces Falkland Island 1983–84, Cdr 19 Inf Bde 1985–87, RCDS 1988, Cdr BMATT Zimbabwe 1989–91, Cmdt RMA Sandhurst 1991–94, head Recruiting Implementation Team 1994–95; dir The London Goodenough Trust for Overseas Graduates 1995–; govr Haileybury, memb Cncl Queen Mary and Westfield Coll; *Recreations* rackets, tennis, squash, golf, fishing; *Clubs* Caledonian, Royal Over-Seas League; *Style*— Maj-Gen Timothy Toyne Sewell; ✉ The London Goodenough Trust, London House, Mecklenburgh Square, London WC1N 2AB (☎ 0171 837 8888)

TRACEY, Eric Frank; s of Allan Lewis Tracey, of Auckland, NZ, and late Marcelle Frances, *née* Petrie; *b* 3 July 1948; *Educ* Mount Albert GS Auckland NZ, Univ of Auckland (BCom, MCom); *m* 16 May 1970, Patricia, da of late G S (Bill) Gamble, of Hatch End, Middx; *Career* Inland Revenue NZ 1965, lectr Univ of Auckland 1970–72, Touche Ross (now Deloitte & Touche) London 1973– (ptnr 1980–); FCA 1975 (ACA 1970), ACIS 1972; *Recreations* walking, rugby, cricket, cooking, creative gardening, NZ plants; *Style*— Eric Tracey, Esq; ✉ 6 De Beauvoir Square, De Beauvoir Town, London N1 4LG (☎ and fax 0171 254 6057); Deloitte & Touche, Hill House, 1 Little New Street, London EC4A 3TR (☎ 0171 303 3233, fax 0171 936 3190)

TRACEY, Prof Ian Graham; s of William Tracey (d 1994), and Helene Mignon, *née* Harris; *b* 27 May 1955; *Educ* Trinity Coll of Music, St Katharine's Coll Liverpool (PGCE); *Career* organist and master of the choristers Liverpool Cathedral 1980–; prof, fell and organist Liverpool John Moores Univ (formerly Liverpool Poly) 1988–; chorus master Royal Liverpool Philharmonic Soc 1985–, organist City of Liverpool (formerly conslt organist) 1986–, organist titulaire of Father Willis Organ Alexandra Palace 1995–; memb: Jospice Int, Cambridge Soc of Musicians, Int Contemporary Music Awards; Award for Classical Music NW Arts 1994; FTCL, FRSA 1988; *Recreations* cookery, fine wines, canal boating, fell walking; *Clubs* Artists' (Liverpool); *Style*— Prof Ian Tracey; ✉ 6 Cathedral Close, Liverpool L1 7BR (☎ 0151 708 8471, fax 0151 708 0378)

TRACEY, Richard Patrick; JP (1977), MP (C) Surbiton (majority 9,639); s of P H (Dick) Tracey (d 1959), of Stratford upon Avon, and Hilda, *née* Timms; *b* 8 Feb 1943; *Educ* King Edward VI Sch Stratford upon Avon, Univ of Birmingham (LLB); *m* Katharine R, da of John Gardner (d 1969), of Ealing; 1 s, 3 da; *Career* ldr writer Daily Express 1964–66, presenter of current affrs programmes BBC Radio and TV 1966–78, documentaries BBC 1974–76, dep chm Gtr London Cons Pty 1981–83; MP (C) Surbiton 1983–, Parly under sec of state for Environment and min for Sport 1985–87; memb: Select Ctee on Televising the House of Commons 1988–91, Ctee of Selection 1992–94, Public Accounts Ctee 1994–; chm London Cons MPs 1990–; Cons London election coordinator 1989–93; vice chm Special Olympics UK 1989–93; fell Industry and Parliament Tst 1985; Freeman City of London 1984; *Books* The World of Motor Sport (with R Hudson-Evans), Hickstead - The First Twelve Years (with M Clayton); *Recreations* boating, riding, wildlife conservation; *Clubs* Wig and Pen; *Style*— Richard Tracey, Esq, JP, MP; ✉ House of Commons, London SW1A 0AA (☎ 0171 219 5196)

TRACEY, Stanley William; OBE (1986); s of Stanley Clark Tracey (d 1957), and Florence Louise, *née* Guest (d 1984); *b* 30 Dec 1926; *m* 1, 1946 (m dis), Joan Lower; m 2, 1957 (m dis 1960), Jean Richards; m 3, 24 Dec 1960, Florence Mary (Jackie), da of Douglas Richard Buckland (d 1970), of London; 1 s (Clark b 1961), 1 da (Sarah b 1962); *Career* served RAF 1946–48; composer of over 300 titles incl: Under Milkwood Suite 1965, Genesis and some 40 albums; resident pianist Ronnie Scotts Club London 1960–66, ptnr (with wife) Steam Record Co 1975–91; toured ME 1982, S America 1980 with own quartet, pianist/leader quartet, quintet, sextet (Hexad), octet and 15 piece orchestra, signed to Blue Note record label 1992; winner: piano section Br Jazz Awards 1992, composer/arranger Br Jazz Awards 1993 and 1995, composer/arranger BBC Radio 2 Award 1993, Octet album Portraits Plus shortlisted for Mercury Music Prize 1993, small gp Br Jazz Awards 1995; hon RAM; memb RSM & JB, fell City of Leeds Coll of Music; *Style*— Stanley Tracey, Esq, OBE; ✉ 12 Cotlandswick, London Colney, Herts, AL2 1EE (☎ 01727 823286)

TRAFFORD, Edward Willoughby; s of Maj S W Trafford (d 1953), of Wroxham Hall, Norwich, Norfolk, and Lady Elizabeth, *née* Bertie, OBE (d 1987); *b* 2 July 1924; *Educ* Harrow, Downside, RAC Cirencester; *m* 3 April 1952, June Imelda, da of Richard Harding, of Echo Valley, Springbrook, Queensland, Aust; 3 s (Michael Francis b 1953, Bernard Edward b 1955, Andrew Martin b 1960), 1 da (Amanda Gabriel Mary b 1959); *Career* served Scots Gds 1942–47; memb: St Faith and Aylsham RDC 1966–74, Norfolk Local Valuation Panel 1967 (chm 1984, dep chm 1979), Broadland DC 1974–88 (chm 1983–86); pres Valuation and Community Charge Tribunal 1989–95; Knight of Honour and Devotion Sovereign Military Order of Malta; *Recreations* shooting, opera; *Clubs* Brooks's, Royal Automobile; *Style*— Edward Trafford, Esq; ✉ Broad House, Wroxham, Norwich NR12 8TS (☎ 01603 782616)

TRAFFORD, Ian Colton; OBE (1967); s of Dr Harold Trafford (d 1993), of Warlingham, Surrey, and Laura Dorothy, *née* Porteous (d 1965); bro of Baron Trafford (Life Peer, d 1989); *b* 8 July 1928; *Educ* Charterhouse, St John's Coll Oxford (BA); *m* 20 July 1949 (m dis 1964), Nella, da of Petros Georgara (d 1958), of Athens, Greece; m 2, 12 Dec 1972, Jacqueline Carole, *née* Trenque; *Career* Intelligence Corps 1946–48, cmmnd 1947, Actg Capt 1948, GSO3 Br Mil Mission to Greece 1948; feature writer (subsequently features ed and industl corr) The Financial Times 1951–58, UK corr Barrons Weekly NY 1954–60, md Industrial and Trade Fairs Holdings 1966–71 (dir 1958); DG Br Trade Fairs: Peking 1964, Moscow 1966, Bucharest 1968, Sao Paolo 1969, Buenos Aires 1970; md The Economist Newspaper Ltd 1971–81, chm The Economist Intelligence Unit Ltd 1971–79, local dir W London Branch Commercial Union Insurance 1974–83; publisher 1981–88: The Times Educational Supplement, The Times Higher Educational Supplement, The Times Literary Supplement; ret 1988; *Recreations* gardening; *Style*— Ian Trafford, Esq, OBE; ✉ Grafton House, Westhall Rd, Warlingham, Surrey CR6 9HF (☎ 01883 622048)

TRAFFORD, Roger Samuel; s of Jack Trafford, of St Cleer, Liskeard, Cornwall, and Sylvia, *née* Holmwood (d 1979); *b* 12 Feb 1939; *Educ* Forest Sch London, Hertford Coll Oxford (MA); *m* 24 July 1971, Cheryl Anne, da of Gordon Robert Ellis Norbrook, of Barnes, London; 2 s (James Richard Ellis b 11 Nov 1973, George Roger Ellis b 21 April 1976); *Career* Eng teacher The Fessenden Sch Boston Mass 1962–65, housemaster and head of Eng St Paul's Prep Sch London 1965–73; headmaster: King's Coll Prep Sch Taunton Somerset 1973–82, Clifton Coll Prep Sch Bristol 1982–93, Dragon Sch Oxford 1993–; Walter Hines Page scholarship to USA 1987; vice chm ISIS South and West 1977–82, chm Nat ISIS 1996–; memb Cncl IAPS 1982–84, 1987–89, 1990–92 and 1994– (chm 1991–92); govr: Cheam Sch, Cheltenham Coll, Sch Fees Insurance Agency; memb: IAPS, NAHT, Oxford Soc; *Books* The Heads Guide (1989); *Recreations* rackets, real tennis, skiing, education, rugby; *Clubs* Lansdowne, Boasters, Unicorn; *Style*— Roger Trafford, Esq; ✉ 6 Chadlington Road, Oxford OX2 6SY (☎ 01865 315445); Dragon School, Bardwell Road, Oxford OX2 6SS (☎ 01865 315400, fax 01865 315429)

TRAILL, Sir Alan; GBE (1984), QSO (1990); s of George Traill, and Margaret Eleanor, *née* Matthews; *b* 7 May 1935; *Educ* St Andrew's Sch Eastbourne, Charterhouse, Jesus Coll Cambridge (MA); *m* 1964, Sarah Jane, *née* Hutt; 1 s (Philip); *Career* dir Morice Tozer & Beck 1960–73; chm: Traill Attenborough Ltd 1973–81, Lyon Holdings 1981–86; dir: Lyon Traill Attenborough (Lloyd's Brokers) 1981–86, PWS Holdings 1986–87, Aegis Insurance Brokers 1987–89; md: Colburn Traill Ltd 1989–96, Colburn French & Keen Ltd 1994–96; div dir First City Insurance Brokers 1996–; md: Grandactual Ltd (t/a Texas Embassy Cantina) 1993–, Medex Assistance (Europe) plc 1993–; memb: Lloyd's 1964–89, Ct of Common Cncl City of London 1970–, London Ct of Int Arbitration 1981–86; memb Cncl Br Insur Brokers' Assoc 1978–79 (chm Reinsurance Brokers' Ctee 1978); Alderman Langbourn Ward 1975–, Sheriff 1982–83, Lord Mayor of London 1984–85; dir City Arts Tst 1980–, almoner Christ's Hosp Fndn 1980–; govr: King Edward's Sch Witley 1980–, St Paul's Cathedral Choir Sch 1987–95; Lord Mayor Treloar Coll 1987–; tstee RSC 1982–94, chllr City of London Univ 1984–85 (DMus 1984); chm: UK-NZ 1990 Ctee, Bd of Tstees Waitangi Fndn; memb Ct of Assts Worshipful Co of Cutlers (Master 1979–80), Liveryman Worshipful Co of Musicians 1990; ACIArb; *Recreations* shooting, DIY, music and opera, assisting education; *Style*— Sir Alan Traill, GBE, QSO; ✉ First City Insurance Brokers, 13–15 Folgate Street, London E1 6BX (☎ 0171 247 6595, fax 0171 410 4818)

TRAIN, Andrew John; s of David Walter Train, of Glen Villa, Fladbury, Worcs, and Eileen, *née* Dobbing; *b* 21 Sept 1963; *Educ* Pershore HS, Univ of Birmingham (LLB); *m* 30 July 1988, Alison Ann, da of Arthur Patrick Peters, of Wickhamford, Evesham, Worcs; 2 da (Hannah Catherine b 10 Oct 1990, Joanna Michelle b 27 Feb 1993); *Career* pairs canoeist with brother Stephen Train: memb GB team Olympic Games 1984, 1988, and 1996 (6th place 1992 and 1996), Silver Medal World Sprint Championships 1985, Bronze Medal World Sprint Championships 1987, Gold Medal World Cup Marathon 1989, World Marathon Champion 1988–89, Bronze Medal World Sprint Championships 1991, Gold Medal World Cup Marathon 1991 and 1995; Silver Medal World Sprint Championships 1993, Silver Medal World Marathon Championships 1994, Gold Medal World Marathon Championships 1996; singles canoeist Bronze Medal World Sprint Championships 1991; slr; *Recreations* canoe coaching, swimming, family; *Clubs* Fladbury Paddle; *Style*— Andrew Train, Esq; ✉ 16 Chestnut Close, Lower Moor, Pershore, Worcs WR10 2RE

TRANCHELL, Christopher Peter John (Chris); s of Allan George Small, of Southampton, and Irene Rose Kathleen, *née* Trowbridge; *b* 13 April 1941; *Educ* Portswood Rd Secdy Modern, Southampton Tech Coll, Bristol Old Vic Theatre Sch; *m* 1 s (Benedick George b 21 March 1969), 2 da (Sophi b 22 Aug 1964, Imogen Lucy b 24 Aug 1967); *Career* actor; fndr memb Margate Stage Company 1962; memb Bd of DITS Lyric Theatre Hammersmith 1983–89 (currently hon patron), fndr memb Arts for Labour 1981; *Theatre* incl: Romeo in Romeo and Juliet (Lincoln), Sergius in Arms and the Man (Margate), Biff in Death of a Salesman (Worcester), Frank in Forget-me-not Lane by Peter Nichols (Worcester), Nathan in Guys and Dolls by Frank Loesser (Worcester), Aydak in Caucasian Chalk Circle by Brecht (Orange Tree), Shamrock Wombs in All Walks of Leg by John Lennon, Friar Lawrence in Romeo and Juliet, The Real Inspector Hound by Tom Stoppard (Young Vic), Ken in Whose Life is it Anyway (Salisbury), Houst in Bent (for Theatr Clwyd), Not Just a War, Ten Years of Freedom (Lyric Studio Hammersmith) 1989, Merlin in Morte D'Arthur by David Freeman 1990; *Television* BBC: Dr Who, Play School, The Survivors, The Bill, Casualty; LWT: London's Burning (1992 series); *Films* incl: Oh What a Lovely War! The Battle of Britain, The Hiding Place; *Recreations* singing, sailing, travel in Europe, the USA and South America; *Clubs* West London Trades, Actor Centre; *Style*— Chris Tranchell, Esq; ✉ 52 Dewhurst Road, Hammersmith, London W14 OES (☎ 0171 603 6493); c/o Ken McReddie Ltd, 91 Regent Street, London W1 7TB (☎ 0171 439 1456, fax 0171 734 6530)

TRANGMAR, Donald George; s of George Edward Trangmar (d 1975), of Barrow-in-Furness, and Mabel Winifred, *née* Rose (d 1994); *b* 16 Nov 1939; *Educ* Barrow-in-Furness GS; *m* 1, 1968 (m dis 1986), Norma, *née* Denison; 1 da (Natalie Jane b 26 Dec 1981); m 2, 14 Oct 1988, Christabelle Jane, *née* Emerson; *Career* joined Marks and Spencer 1965 (dir 1983–); tstee Sick Children's Tst; *Recreations* cricket, reading; *Style*— Donald Trangmar, Esq; ✉ Marks and Spencer plc, Michael House, 47–67 Baker Street, London W1A 1DN (☎ 0171 935 4422)

TRANT, Gen Sir Richard Brooking; KCB (1982, CB 1979); s of Richard Brooking Trant, and Dora Rodney, *née* Lancaster; *b* 28 March 1928; *m* 1957, Diana, da of Rev Stephen Zachary Edwards; 1 s (Richard b 1967), 2 da (Diana b 1962, Sarah b 1965); *Career* cmmnd RA 1947, Def Servs Staff Coll India 1962–63, Brig Maj Aden Protectorate Levies FRA 1963–65, Cmd 3 RHA 1968–71, sr instr Army Staff Coll 1971–72, cmd 5 Air Portable Bde 1972–74, cmd Landforces NI 1977–79, Dir Army Staff Duties 1979–81, GOC SE Dist 1982–83, Land Dep C-in-C Falklands 1982, QMG and Gen 1983–86, Col Cmdt RAEC 1979–86, RA 1982–87, RAOC 1984–88, HAC 1984–92, cmmr Duke of York's Royal Mil Sch 1987–93; sr def advsr Short Bros Belfast, conslt Peat Marwick McLintock 1986–88, dep chm Wilson's Hogg Robinson 1988–96; chm: Hunting Engrg Ltd 1988–93, Def Div Hunting plc 1988–96, Irvin Aerospace 1992–96; cmmr Royal Hosp Chelsea 1988–94, memb Armed Forces Pay Review Body 1988–94, memb Cncl Soc of Br Aerospace Cos 1988–96, vice pres Defence Manufacturers Assoc 1987–96; dir S Beds Community Health Tst 1991–95; pres Bedfordshire C of C 1992–96, tstee Cornwall Heritage Tst 1987– (chm 1995–), chm Royal Artillery Museums Ltd 1990–96; offr Order of Saudi Arabia 1965; Freeman City of London 1984; Hon DSc Cranfield Univ 1995; CRAeS 1995; *Recreations* field sports, sailing, golf; *Clubs* Army and Navy, Royal Fowey Yacht; *Style*— Gen Sir Richard Trant, KCB; ✉ c/o Lloyds Bank, Newquay, Cornwall TR7 1JB

TRANTER, Jane; da of Donald Tranter, and Joan, *née* Gay; *b* 17 March 1963; *Educ* Kingswood Sch Bath, King's Coll London (BA English Lit); *partner* David Attwood; *Career* asst floor mangr BBC 1986–88, script ed Casualty BBC Drama Dept 1988, script ed BBC Films Dept 1989–92 (TV credits incl award-winning Alive and Kicking, The Last Romantics, The Kremlin Farewell and Bad Girl, feature films credits The Hour of the Pig and Sarafina); Carlton TV: commissioning ed Drama 1992–93, head of drama 1993–95; exec prodr Carlton UK Productions 1995– (credits incl Bramwell, Body and Soul, Bliss, Frank Stubbs, Moving Story, Sharman, A Village Affair, Bodyguards, Wilderness and London Bridge); memb Lab Pty; *Style*— Ms Jane Tranter; ✉ Carlton UK Productions, 35–38 Portman Square, London W1H 0NU (☎ 0171 612 7270, fax 0171 487 5043)

TRANTER, Nigel Godwin; OBE (1983); s of Gilbert Tredgold Tranter (d 1929), of Edinburgh, and Eleanor Annie Cass (d 1933); *b* 23 Nov 1909; *Educ* George Heriot's Sch Edinburgh; *m* 1933, May Jean Campbell (d 1979), da of Thomas Douglas Grieve (d 1925), of Edinburgh; 1 s (Philip, d 1966), 1 da (Frances-May); *Career* author and novelist; published over 100 books, fiction and non-fiction; hon pres Scottish Pen Club; former chm: Soc of Authors Scotland, Nat Book League Scotland, Nat Forth Rd Bridge Ctee 1953–57, E Lothian Lib Assoc 1960–70; currently chm St Andrew Soc of E Lothian; hon pres Saltire Soc; BBC Scot of the Year 1989; Hon MA Univ of Edinburgh 1971, Hon DLitt Univ of Strathclyde 1990; *Books include* Robert the Bruce Trilogy (1965–69), The Fortified House in Scotland (5 vols, 1962–71), The Queen's Scotland (4 vols 1971–77), Nigel Tranter's Scotland (1981), Columba (1987), The Story of Scotland (1987), Flowers of Chivalry (1988), Mail Royal (1989), Warden of The Queen's March (1989), Kenneth (1990), Crusader (1991), Children of the Mist (1992), Druid Sacrifice (1993), Tapestry of the Boar (1993), Price of A Princess (1994), Lord in Waiting (1994), Highness in Hiding (1995), A Rage of Regents (1996); *Recreations* walking, historical research, castle-restoration; *Clubs* PEN; *Style*— Nigel Tranter, Esq, OBE; ✉ Quarry House, Aberlady, East Lothian, Scotland EH32 0QB (☎ 01875 870258)

TRAPNELL, Rev Canon Stephen Hallam; s of Hallam Trapnell (d 1982), of Clifton, Bristol, and Ruth, *née* Walker; *b* 10 June 1930; *Educ* Clifton Coll, Gonville and Caius Coll Cambridge (MA), Ridley Hall Cambridge, Virginia Theological Seminary Alexandria Va USA (MDiv); *m* 6 May 1961, Ann Mary Hensleigh, da of Lt-Col Eric H L H Walter, of Chaldon, Surrey; 2 s (Andrew b 1964, Mark b 1967), 2 da (Rachel b 1962, Lydia b 1965); *Career* 2 Lt RASC 1949; ordained priest 1957; curate of: St Matthias Upper Tulse Hill London 1956–59, St Mary's Reigate 1959–61; vicar of: Christ Church Richmond Surrey 1961–72, Holy Trinity Sydenham London 1972–80; rector of Worting Basingstoke Hants 1980–92, field offr Decade of Evangelism Dio of Winchester 1992–96, canon of Shyogwe Dio Rwanda and commissary to the Bishop of Shyogwe, ret 1996; *Publications* Teaching The Families (contrib, 1973), More for all the Family (contrib, 1990); *Recreations* the study of wild flowers (especially orchids); *Clubs* The Co of All Faithful People (life memb); *Style*— The Rev Canon Stephen Trapnell; ✉ Downs Cottage, Rivar Road, Shalbourne, Marlborough, Wilts SN8 3QE (☎ 01672 870514)

TRAPP, Prof Joseph Burney; CBE (1990); s of Henry Mansfield Burney Trapp (d 1957), and Frances Melanie, *née* Wolters (d 1950); *b* 16 July 1925; *Educ* Dannevirke HS, Victoria Univ NZ (MA); *m* 9 June 1953, Elayne Margaret, da of Sir Robert Alexander Falla, KCMG, of Days Bay, Wellington, NZ (d 1979); 2 s (Michael b 1957, James b 1959); *Career* asst librarian Alexander Turnbull Library Wellington 1946–50; asst lectr: Victoria Univ Coll 1950–51, Univ of Reading 1951–53; Warburg Inst Univ of London: asst librarian 1953–66, librarian 1966–76, dir 1976–90; British Academy: vice-pres 1983–85, foreign sec 1985–95; foreign memb Royal Swedish Academy of Letters, History and Antiquities 1995–; FSA 1978, FRSA 1978–90, FBA 1980; *Books* The Apology of Sir Thomas More (ed 1979), Essays on the Renaissance and the Classical Tradition (1990), Erasmus, Colet and More: The Early Tudor Humanists and their Books (1991); *Style*— Prof J B Trapp, CBE, FBA, FSA

TRASLER, Prof Gordon Blair; JP (Hants 1978); s of Frank Ferrier Trasler (d 1978), and Marian, *née* Blair (d 1940); *b* 7 March 1929; *Educ* Bryanston, Univ Coll Exeter (MA), Univ of London (BSc, PhD); *m* 19 Sept 1953, Kathleen Patricia, da of Gerald Richard Fitzarthur Fegan (d 1955); *Career* Nat Serv Royal Fusiliers and RCS 1947–49; asst in statistics Univ Coll Exeter 1952–53, psychologist HM Prison Winchester 1956–57 (HM Prison Wandsworth 1955–56); Univ of Southampton: lectr 1957–64, prof of psychology 1964–94 (emeritus prof 1994–), Leverhulme research fell 1995–, dean of social sciences 1970–73; ed in chief British Journal of Criminology 1981–86, memb Winchester Health Authy 1982–90, vice pres Inst for the Study and Treatment of Delinquency 1987– (chm 1982–87); Sellin-Glueck award for outstanding contributions to criminology American Society of Criminology 1990; FBPsS 1964, CPsychol 1988; *Books* In Place of Parents (1960), The Explanation of Criminality (1962), The Shaping of Social Behaviour (1967), The Formative Years (jtly, 1968), Behaviour Modification with Offenders (with DP Farrington, 1980); *Recreations* writing, photography, reading, music; *Style*— Prof Gordon Trasler, JP; ✉ Fox Croft, Old Kennels Lane, Oliver's Battery, Winchester, Hants SO22 4JT (☎ 01962 852345); Department of Psychology, The University, Southampton SO9 5NH (☎ 01703 594582, fax 01703 593939, telex 47661)

TRAVERS, Andrew Keith Buchanan; *b* 3 Jan 1962; *Educ* BSc (Physics); *Career* well-logging engr 1982–83, IC design engr National Semi Conductor, ASIC design engr/conslt Dectroswiss Switzerland 1986–89, sr design engr/conslt IBB PC Company UK 1989–94, dir CIPD (IBM) UK 1994–96, chief exec offr Scottish Design Ltd 1996–; *Recreations* rugby, tennis, sailing, skiing; *Clubs* Hillhead Sports; *Style*— Andrew Travers, Esq; ✉ Scottish Design Ltd, Stock Exchange House, 7 Nelson Mandela Place, Glasgow G2 7JN (☎ 0141 221 6121, fax 0141 221 8799, e-mail scot.design@scotent.co.uk)

TRAVERS, David; s of George Bowes Travers (d 1966), and Gertrude Colbert, *née* Churnside; *b* 19 March 1957; *Educ* Spennymoor Secdy Sch, King's Coll London (LLB, AKC, LLM), Inns of Court Sch of Law; *m* 13 Oct 1984, Sheila Mary, da of Martin Killoran, CBE, QFSM; 1 s (James David b 28 July 1992), 2 da (Rosamond b 11 Oct 1988, Jennifer Claire b 15 April 1991); *Career* called to the Bar Middle Temple 1981 (Harmsworth scholar), formerly in practice Northern Circuit (memb Exec 1985–87), in practice Midland and Oxford Circuit 1988–; pt/t lectr Accountancy Tuition Centre Manchester and Liverpool until 1983, occasional lectr Dept of Mgmnt Scis UMIST 1986–87, occasional libel reader Express newspapers 1987–88, occasional tutor Dept of Biomedical Sci and Biomedical Ethics Univ of Birmingham 1995–; exec ed King's Counsel 1979 (ed 1978); joined chambers Birmingham 1988, Royal Inst sci scholar 1975, memb Delegacy Governing Body King's Coll London 1977–78, sabbatical pres King's Coll London Union of Students 1979–80 (hon life memb 1980), pres Middle Temple Students' Assoc 1980–81; participant Warwick Int Workshop on Corporate Control and Accountability 1991, occasional lectr professional conferences; memb: Soc for Computers and Law, Family Law Bar Assoc, Food Law Soc, Hon Soc of the Middle Temple 1978, Bar Cncl 1995–, Birmingham Law Soc IT Ctee 1995–, Law Reform Ctee Bar Cncl 1996–, Bar Services & IT Ctee Bar Cncl 1996–; *Recreations* language, music, running; *Clubs* The Last Slursh; *Style*— David Travers, Esq; ✉ 3 Fountain Ct, Steelhouse Lane, Birmingham B4 6DR (☎ 0121 236 5854 and 0121 236 2286, fax 0121 236 7008, document exchange DX 16079)

TRAVERSE-HEALY, Annette Susan; da of Evan André Preece, and Margery, *née* Phillips; *b* 30 July 1956; *Educ* Univ of Liverpool (BSc); *Career* press offr RSPB 1983–86 (ed Birdlife 1980–83), head of pubns and ed-in-chief Birds Magazine 1986–93, currently head Communications Servs RSPB; *Recreations* gardening, painting, birdwatching; *Style*— Mrs Annette Traverse-Healy; ✉ Royal Society for the Protection of Birds, The Lodge, Sandy, Beds SG19 2DL (☎ 01767 680551, fax 01767 692365, telex 82469 RSPB G)

TRAVERSE-HEALY, Kevin Timothy; s of Prof Tim Traverse-Healy, OBE *qv*, and Joan, *née* Thompson; *b* 30 Nov 1949; *Educ* Xavarian Coll Brighton, Redrice Coll Hampshire, Lewes Tech Coll Sussex, Coll of Law London; *m* 12 Jan 1974, Sarah-Jane (Sally), *née* Magill; 1 s (James Timothy Brendan b 16 May 1983), 1 da (Alexia Claire b 9 Aug 1979); *Career* articled clerk Duchin & Co and Berwin & Co 1969–72; exhibitions offr (later PR exec) British Oxygen Co and PR exec BOC International (Southern Africa) 1972–76, dir Traverse-Healy Ltd 1976–92, fndr md Traverse-Healy & Regester Ltd 1980–87, md Charles Barker Traverse-Healy Ltd 1987–91, chief exec (ops) Charles Barker Ltd 1991–92, md Centre for Public Affairs Studies Ltd 1992–, ind mgmnt conslt 1992–, advsr National Commercial Bank of Saudi Arabia 1995–96, dir e.g. Limited 1996–; ptnr: Traverse-Healy Consult 1996–, Everden Gordon 1996–; dir Rainbow Rovers Ltd (charity) 1989–; lectr and contrib to various PR handbooks; first recipient CERP (Centre European de Relations Publique) medal for contrib to Euro PR 1985; memb Foreign Press Assoc; FIPR (pres 1985); *Recreations* sailing, French farm; *Clubs* Savile, Guards' Polo, London Flotilla; *Style*— Kevin Traverse-Healy, Esq; ✉ Traverse-Healy Consult,

78 Royal Hospital Road, Chelsea, London SW3 4HN (☎ 0171 351 2757, fax 0171 351 2677, mobile 0378 021720, e-mail kevin@traverse-healy.com)

TRAVERSE-HEALY, Prof Tim; OBE (1989); s of John Healy, MBE, and Gladys, *née* Traverse; *b* 25 March 1923; *Educ* Stonyhurst, St Mary's Hosp London Univ (DipCAM); *m* 8 March 1946, Joan, da of Sidney Thompson (d 1968), of London and Sussex; 2 s (Sean b 1947, Kevin, *qv*, b 1949), 3 da (Sharon (Mrs Butterfield) b 1951, Corinne (Mrs Russell) b 1953, Jeannine b 1954); *Career* WWII RA Territorial Res, RM Commandos and Special Forces 1941–46; memb Public and Social Policy Ctee Nat Westminster Bank 1952–92, sr ptnr Traverse-Healy Ltd Corporate Affrs Counsel 1947–93, dir Centre for Public Affrs Studies 1969–; chm (UK) PR Educn Tst 1990–92; visiting prof: Univ of Stirling, Univ of Wales; hon prof Baylor Univ Texas USA; vice pres Euro PR Confedn 1965–69, memb Professional Practices Ctee (UK) PR Conslts Assoc 1988–92; Int PR Assoc: fndr sec 1950–61, cncl memb 1961–68, pres 1968–73, emeritus memb 1982, Presidential Gold medal 1985, pres World PR congress Tel Aviv 1970 and Geneva 1973; PR congress fndr lectures: Boston 1976, Bombay 1982, Melbourne 1988; pres: Int Fndn for PR Res and Educn 1983–85, Int Fndn for PR Studies 1986–87 (tstee 1987–88); memb (US) Public Affairs Cncl 1975–; PR News award 1983, PR Week award 1987, (US) Page Soc award 1990; Hon FIPR 1988 (Tallents Gold medal 1985); memb: RM Officers' Assoc, Commandos Assoc, London Flotilla; MIPR 1948, FIPR 1956 (pres 1967–68), FIPA 1957, FRSA 1953; *Recreations* Irish Soc, French politics; *Clubs* Athenaeum, Philippics; *Style*— Prof Tim Traverse-Healy, OBE; ✉ PO Box 810, London SE24 9NQ; Griffoul, 82150 Montaigu de Quercy, Tarn et Garonne, France (fax 00 33 63 95 26 56)

TRAVIS, (Ernest Raymond) Anthony; s of Ernest Raymond Travis, and Constance Mary Travis; *b* 18 May 1943; *Educ* Harrow; *m* 1, 1967 (m dis 1977), Hon Rosemary Gail, da of Baron Pritchard, of Haddon; m 2, 1978, Jean Heather, da of John MacDonald (d 1983); m 3, 1987, Peta Jane, da of Sir Peter Foster; *Career* called to the Bar Inner Temple 1965; chm Travis Perkins plc; *Style*— Anthony Travis, Esq; ✉ 86 Drayton Gardens, London SW10; Pitters Farm, Naish Hill, Chippenham, Wilts; Travis Perkins plc, Lodge Way House, Harlestone Road, Northampton NN5 7UG (☎ 01604 752424)

TRAVIS, Dave Lee; *b* 25 May 1945; *Educ* Manchester Central GS; *m* June 1971, Marianne; *Career* radio presenter; Radio Caroline South 1964–1966, Radio Caroline North 1966, Radio One 1967–93, commercial radio 1993–; currently The World Service (A Jolly Good Show), GWR Classic Gold Network, Great North Radio; patron DIAL UK - Disablement Charity; Assoc of the Royal Photographic Society; *Television* incl: The Golden Oldie Picture Show, Top of The Pops, Photo Assignment Week, The British Rock and Pop Awards, Saturday Night Affair, Archive Jive; appearances incl: Blankety Blank, Celebrity Squares, What's My Line, Ask No Questions, Give Us A Clue; *Awards* incl: Carl-Allan Award for Most Popular DJ 1978 and 1979, Pipeman of the Year, Head of the Year; *Books* A Bit of A Star (1985); *Recreations* classic cars, photography, old books; *Style*— Dave Lee Travis, Esq; ✉ c/o PO Box 800, Hemel Hempstead, Herts HP3 0DQ (☎ 01296 661600, fax 01296 661688)

TRAVIS, John Anthony; s of Leonard Kirkbride Travis, of Brighton, Sussex, and Elsie Travis (d 1961); *b* 18 Aug 1945; *Educ* Brighton Sch of Music & Drama, Doris Isaacs Sch of Dancing, Royal Ballet Sch, Univ of Manchester (Dip in Theatre Archives); *Career* dancer Covent Garden Opera Ballet; London Festival Ballet: dancer then leading soloist 1966–77, created London Festival Ballet Archive 1979, prog presenter and head Educn Dept 1980–87; on secondment to study at V&A 1977, studied at Lincoln Centre NY 1978; teaching: annually at Nat Festivals of Youth Dance classes and repertoire at all levels, at community centres, theatres, schs; five Brazilian Cities 1982 and first Summer Sch in Dominica 1990; teacher of classical ballet and coordinator for all performances and projects Northern Sch of Contemporary Dance Leeds 1989–95; guest teacher Northern Ballet Sch Manchester 1985–88; lectr on history of dance; artistic co-ordinator Dance Advance 1988–89 (touring mangr for China visit 1989), dir of 3 Youth Dance Spectaculars for Greater London Arts and Opening Gala of Northern Sch of Contemporary Dance 1988; dir Bd Phoenix Dance Co 1985–93, dir British Ballet Organization 1995–; patron: East London Regnl Dance Cncl, Harehills Dance Umbrella; memb: Exec Ctee Nat Organization for Dance and Mime (Dance UK) 1984–89, Cncl of Mgmnt Br Ballet Orgn 1991–95, Bd Northern Ballet Theatre (chm Educn Ctee) 1990–93, memb Dance Panel: SE Arts 1982–87, Eastern Arts 1983–87, Greater London Arts Assocs 1980–86; *Style*— John Travis, Esq; ✉ The British Ballet Organization, Woolborough House, 39 Lonsdale Road, London SW13 9JP (☎ 0181 748 1241, fax 0181 748 1301)

TRAYHURN, Prof Paul; s of William George Trayhurn (d 1975), and Eileen Ella, *née* Morphew (d 1986); *b* 6 May 1948; *Educ* Colyton GS, Univ of Reading (BSc), Univ of Oxford (DPhil, DSc); *m* 12 July 1969, Deborah Hartland, *née* Gigg; 3 s (Theo William b 24 Dec 1977, Hanno Edmund b 9 March 1983, Felix Timothy b 13 May 1985), 1 da (Venetia Harriet b 24 Aug 1980); *Career* NATO Euro res fell Centre de Neurochimie CNRS 1972–73, post-doctoral fell Univ of Oxford 1973–75, MRC scientific staff Dunn Nutrition Laboratory 1975–86, prof and heritage scholar Nutrition and Metabolism Res Gp Univ of Alberta 1986–88; head Div of Biochemical Sciences Rowett Research Inst 1988–, hon prof Depts of Biomedical Sciences and Molecular and Cell Biology Univ of Aberdeen 1992–; Evelyn Williams visiting prof Univ of Sydney 1992; chm: Human Nutrition Advsy Panel BBSRC 1994–, Mgmnt Ctee BBSRC Food Directorate, Scientific Ctee 8th Euro Congress on Obesity (Dublin); author of over 250 scientific pubns; memb: Biochemical Soc 1970, Nutrition Soc 1975 (chm Scottish section 1993–95), Physiological Soc 1993; FIBiol 1992; *Recreations* listening to classical music, bemoaning the decline of British scientific culture and the standards of public life; *Style*— Prof Paul Trayhurn; ✉ Division of Biochemical Sciences, Rowett Research Institute, Bucksburn, Aberdeen AB21 9SB (☎ 01224 716610, fax 01224 716622)

TREACHER, Adm Sir John Devereux; KCB (1975); s of late Frank Charles Treacher, of Bentley Grove, Suffolk; *b* 23 Sept 1924, Chile; *Educ* St Paul's; *m* 1, 1953 (m dis 1968), Patcie, da of Dr F McGrath, of Evanston, Illinois; 1 s, 1 da; m 2, 1969, Kirsteen Forbes, da of D F Landale, of Dumfries; 1 s, 1 da; *Career* RN 1941–77: qualified pilot 1946, Capt 1962, Rear Adm 1970, Vice Adm 1972, Vice Chief Naval Staff 1973–75, Adm 1975, C-in-C Fleet & Allied C-in-C Channel & E Atlantic 1975–77; non-press memb Press Cncl 1978–81, chief exec Nat Car Parks 1977–81 (dir 1977–85); dir: Westland Group plc 1978–89 (vice chm 1984, dep chm 1986), Meggitt plc 1989–95; chm Interoute Telecommunications PLC 1996–; FRAeS 1973; *Clubs* Boodle's; *Style*— Sir John Treacher; ✉ 22 Newton Rd, London W2 5LT

TREACHER, William Charles (Bill); s of William Charles Treacher (d 1960), and Minnie, *née* Chapal; *b* 4 June 1930; *Educ* The Webber Douglas Drama Acad; *m* 1 Dec 1971, Katherine, da of Glyn Kessey (d 1986), of Perth, Western Aust; 1 s (Jamie b 6 Nov 1974), 1 da (Sophie b 24 Oct 1978); *Career* actor; LAC RAF 1948–50; MN 1951–55; extensive theatre and TV experience incl: Brian Rix Theatre of Laughter Garrick Theatre 1966–69, Murder at the Vicarage (Fortune Theatre) 1977–79, Arthur Fowler in EastEnders (BBC) 1985–96; memb Br Actor's Equity; *Recreations* sailing, reading; *Style*— William Treacher, Esq; ✉ c/o Glyn Management, The Old School House, Brettenham, Ipswich IP7 7QP (☎ 01449 737695, fax 01449 736117)

TREACY, Colman Maurice; QC (1990); s of Dr Maurice Colman Treacy, and Mary Teresa, *née* Frisby; *b* 28 July 1949; *Educ* Stonyhurst, Jesus Coll Cambridge (open scholar, MA); *children* 1 s, 1 da; *Career* called to the Bar Middle Temple 1971, in practice Midlands and Oxford Circuit, recorder of the Crown Ct Midland and Oxford Circuit 1991–, head of chambers; *Style*— Colman Treacy, Esq, QC; ✉ 3 Fountain Court, Steelhouse Lane, Birmingham B4 6DR (☎ 0121 236 5854, fax 0121 236 7008)

TREACY, Philip Anthony; s of James Vincent Treacy (d 1978), and Katie Agnes Treacy (d 1993); *b* 26 May 1967; *Educ* St Cuan's Coll Castle Blakeney Co Galway, Regional Tech Coll Galway, Nat Coll of Art and Design Dublin (BA), RCA (MDes); *Career* milliner; estab Philip Treacy Ltd (backed by Right Impression hat mfrs) 1990; hat mfr to: Karl Lagerfeld at Chanel (Paris), Gianni Versace (Milan), Valentino (Rome), Rifat Ozbek (London); Accessory Designer of the Year (British Fashion Awards) 1991, 1992, 1993 and 1996; *Style*— Philip Treacy, Esq; ✉ Philip Treacy Ltd, 69 Elizabeth Street, London SW1W 9PJ (☎ 0171 259 9605, fax 0171 824 8559); Ahascragh, Ballinasloe, Co Galway, Ireland

TREADGOLD, Very Rev John David; LVO (1990); s of Oscar Treadgold (d 1943), of Nottingham, and Sybil, *née* Baker (d 1975); *b* 30 Dec 1931; *Educ* West Bridgford GS, Univ of Nottingham (BA), Wells Theol Coll; *m* Hazel Rhona Treadgold, JP; 2 s (Marcus Edward Newton b 1961, Simon John Newton b 1964), 1 da (Joanna Clare b 1968); *Career* deacon 1959, priest 1960, vicar choral of Southwell Minster 1959–64, CF (TA) 1962–67, rector of Wollaton Nottingham 1964–74, CF (TAVR) 1974–78, vicar of Darlington 1974–81, surrogate 1976–81, canon of Windsor and chaplain of The Royal Chapel Windsor Great Park 1981–89, chaplain to HM The Queen 1981–89, dean of Chichester 1989–; memb NSPCC 1974–81, fell Woodard Corpn 1989–95, memb Chichester Cathedral Tst 1989–, tstee Chichester Festival Theatre 1989–, vice pres Chichester Festivities 1989–, chm of govrs Prebendal Sch Chichester; govr: Slindon Coll 1994–, Wycombe Abbey Sch 1995–; chaplain Worshipful Co of Drapers 1995–96; FRSA 1991; *Recreations* cricket, church architecture, listening to music; *Clubs* Sussex; *Style*— The Very Rev John Treadgold, LVO; ✉ The Deanery, Chichester, W Sussex PO19 1PX (☎ 01243 783286, fax 01243 536190)

TREASE, (Robert) Geoffrey; s of George Albert Trease (d 1932), of Nottingham, and Florence, *née* Dale; *b* 11 Aug 1909; *Educ* Nottingham HS, Queen's Coll Oxford (open classical scholar); *m* 1933, Marian Haselden Granger Boyer (changed name to Boyer by deed poll) d 1989, da of Henry Haselden Granger; 1 da (Jocelyn Heather (Mrs Norman Payne) b 1936); *Career* served WWII KORR, AEC; freelance writer 1933–, author of 106 books, published in 20 languages, 16 for adults and 90 for older children; Welwyn Drama Festival New Play prize 1938 (for After The Tempest published in Best One Act Plays of 1938), New York Herald Tribune Book award 1966 (for This Is Your Century); chm Soc of Authors 1972–73 (perm memb Cncl 1974–), fndr chm Children's Writers' Group; fell PEN, FRSL 1979; *Books* incl: Bows Against the Barons (1934), Such Divinity (1939), Cue for Treason (1940), Only Natural (1940), Tales Out of School (1949), Snared Nightingale (1958), The Red Towers of Granada (1966), The Condottieri (1970), A Whiff of Burnt Boats (autobiography, 1971), Laughter At The Door (autobiography, 1974), Portrait of a Cavalier: William Cavendish, first Duke of Newcastle (biography, 1979), Tomorrow Is A Stranger (1987), The Arpino Assignment (1988), Shadow Under The Sea (1990), Calabrian Quest (1990), Aunt Augusta's Elephant (1991), Song for a Tattered Flag (1992), Fire on the Wind (1993), No Horn at Midnight (1994), Bring out the Banners (1994), Curse on the Sea (1996); *Recreations* walking, theatre; *Clubs* Royal Over-Seas League; *Style*— Geoffrey Trease, Esq, FRSL; ✉ c/o David Higham Associates, 5–8 Lower John Street, Golden Square, London W1R 4HA (☎ 0171 437 7888, fax 0171 437 1072)

TREASURE, Prof John Albert Penberthy; s of Harold Paul Treasure (d 1969), and Constance Frances, *née* Shapland (d 1987); *b* 20 June 1924; *Educ* Cardiff HS, Univ of Wales (BA), Univ of Cambridge (PhD); *m* 30 March 1954, Valerie Ellen, da of Lawrence Bell (d 1981); 2 s (Julian Paul b 1958, Simon John Richard b 1960), 1 step s (Jonathan Edward b 1948); *Career* md British Market Research Bureau Ltd 1957–60; marketing dir J Walter Thompson Co London 1960–66 (chm 1967–77); dean City Univ Business Sch 1978–81; vice chm Saatchi & Saatchi London 1983–89; tstee Charities Aid Fndn 1983–88; chm History of Advtg Tst 1985–90; Freeman City of London 1981, chm Taylor Nelson AGB plc 1992–; memb Ct of Assts Worshipful Co of Marketors (Liveryman 1981); CIMgt 1980, FIPA 1967; *Recreations* golf, tennis; *Clubs* Queen's, Hurlingham, Royal Mid-Surrey; *Style*— Prof John Treasure; ✉ 20 Queensberry House, Friars Lane, Richmond, Surrey TW9 1NT (☎ 0181 967 4132)

TREASURE, Prof Tom; s of Wilfrid Samuel Treasure, of Cheltenham, and Rita, *née* Luanaig (d 1991); *b* 12 Aug 1947; *Educ* St Boniface's Coll Plymouth, Guy's Hosp Med Sch Univ of London (MB BS, MRCS, LRCP, MS, MD); *m* 25 June 1977, Dr Janet Linda Treasure, da of Peter Burden; 1 s (Samuel Wilfrid b 17 Dec 1981), 1 da (Jean Dorothy b 6 Nov 1983); *Career* surgical trg Addenbrooke's Hosp, Hammersmith Hosp, Charing Cross Hosp, St Thomas's Hosp and Kent & Canterbury Hosp 1972–77, specialist trg The London Chest Hosp, The Brompton Hosp and Univ of Alabama 1978–81; res trg: Anatomy Dept Univ of Newcastle upon Tyne 1971–72, Sherrington Sch of Physiology St Thomas's Hosp Med Sch 1976–77, Dept of Surgery Univ of Alabama 1981; currently: prof of cardiothoracic surgery St George's Hosp Med Sch London, conslt in private practice Wimpole St London; Editorial Bds incl: Br Heart Jl, Int Jl of Cardiology; Hunterian prof RCS 1983; memb: Cncl Br Cardiac Soc 1986–90, Specialist Advsy Ctee in Cardiothoracic Surgery RCS 1989–96, Cncl Euro Assoc of Cardiothoracic Surgery 1989–92, Br Cardiac Soc, Br Assoc of Clinical Anatomists, BMA, Br Thoracic Soc, Euro Assoc for Cardiothoracic Surgery, MRS, RSM, Soc of Thoracic and Cardiovascular Surgns of GB and I, Surgical Res Soc; FRCS 1975, fell Fellowship of Postgrad Med 1991; *Books* A Pocket Examiner in Surgery (with J M A Northover, 1984), Belcher's Thoracic Surgical Management (5 edn with M F Sturridge, 1985), Current Surgical Practice Vol 5 (ed with J Hadfield and M Hobsley, 1990), Current Surgical Practice Vols 6 & 7 (ed with M Hobsley and A Johnson, 1993), Disorders of the Cardiovascular System (with David Patterson, 1994); *Style*— Prof Tom Treasure; ✉ 19 Wimpole Street, London W1M 7AD (☎ 0181 725 3288, fax 0171 701 8737)

TREDINNICK, David; MP (C) Bosworth (majority 19,094); s of Stephen Victor Tredinnick (d 1995) and Evelyn Mabel, *née* Wates; *b* 19 Jan 1950; *Educ* Eton, Mons Offr Cadet Sch, Graduate Business Sch, Cape Town Univ (MBA), St John's Coll Oxford (MLitt); *m* 7 July 1983, Rebecca, da of Roland Shott (Thomas b 6 July 1989), 1 da (Sophie b 22 Feb 1987); *Career* Grenadier Gds 1968–71; sales and mktg computer indust 1976–79; MP (C) Bosworth 1987–, jt sec Cons Backbench Defence and Foreign Affrs Ctees 1990, PPS to Rt Hon Sir Wyn Roberts as Min of State for Wales 1990–94; chm: Anglo-East Euro Trading Co, Br Atlantic Gp of Young Politicians 1989–91, Future of Europe Tst 1991–95, Ukraine Business Agency 1992–; *Recreations* golf, skiing, shooting, windsurfing, tennis, travel; *Style*— David Tredinnick, Esq, MP; ✉ House of Commons, London SW1A 0AA (☎ 0171 219 4514)

TREDINNICK, Noël Harwood; s of Harold James Tredinnick, of Beckenham, Kent, and Nola Frewin, *née* Harwood; *b* 9 March 1949; *Educ* St Olave's GS for Boys, Southwark Cathedral, Guildhall Sch of Music and Drama, Inst of Educn Univ of London (Dip Ed); *m* 3 July 1976, Fiona Jean, da of James Malcolm Couper-Johnston, of Beckenham, Kent; 1 s (James Alexander Johnston b 24 Aug 1994), 1 da (Isabel Jane b 1983); *Career* school master Langley Park Sch for Boys Beckenham 1971–75, prof and memb Acad Bd Guildhall Sch 1975–, organist and dir of music All Souls Church Langham Place London 1972–, artistic dir Langham Arts 1987–; composer, orchestrator and conductor: Beckenham Chorale 1971–72, All Souls Orch 1972–, BBC Concert Orch 1985–89, BBC Radio Orch 1988–90; musical dir: BBC Radio (Religious Dept), Songs of

Praise BBC TV; writer and broadcaster radio series; fndr and conductor Prom Praise, conductor Palm Beach Opera Orch 1994–95, musical dir Billy Graham Mission Toronto 1995; numerous recordings and performances incl Cliff Richard, Mary O'Hara and Wendy Craig; memb: Archbishop's Cmmn on Church Music, Cncl Music in Worship Tst; *Recreations* theatre, architecture, country-walking; *Clubs* ACG; *Style*— Noël Tredinnick, Esq; ✉ 2 All Souls Place, London WIN 3DB (☎ 0171 935 7246, fax 0171 224 6087)

TREDRE, Roger Ford; s of Alec Ford Tredre, and Angela Joyce, *née* Morris; *b* 9 March 1962; *Educ* Epsom Coll, Sidney Sussex Coll Cambridge (scholar, MA); *Career* journalist; staff writer The Bulletin Brussels 1984–86, dep ed Fashion Weekly 1989 (news ed 1987–88), fashion and design corr The Independent 1989–93, news and features writer The Observer 1993–; freelance work for magazines, radio and TV; *Recreations* travel, walking; *Style*— Roger Tredre, Esq; ✉ 101 Haberdasher Street, London N1 6EH (☎ 0171 253 0230); The Observer, 119 Farringdon Road, London EC1R 3DA (☎ 0171 713 4267)

TREDWELL, Paul Philippe; s of Ronald Jean Tredwell, of Dudley, W Midlands, and Rita May, *née* Pugh; *b* 23 Feb 1956; *Educ* Queen Mary's GS, Queens' Coll Cambridge (MA, LLB); *m* 31 Oct 1987, Melanie Barbara Alice, da of Robin Stuart Brown; 1 da (Rosanna Elise b 4 Nov 1989), 1 s (Rory Luc b 11 Nov 1992); *Career* account mangr Young & Rubicam advtg 1980–83 (joined as graduate trainee 1979); Abbott Mead Vickers BBDO Ltd: joined 1983, account dir 1984–93, bd dir 1987–93; client gp dir Euro RSCG Ltd (now Euro RSCG Wnek Gosper) 1993–96, bd account dir Leagas Delaney Partnership 1996–; *Recreations* Rugby Union, golf; *Style*— Paul Tredwell, Esq; ✉ Leagas Delaney Partnership Ltd, 233 Shaftesbury Avenue, London WC2H 8EL (☎ 0171 836 4455)

TREFFRY, David Charles; OBE (1966), DL (Cornwall 1995); yr s of Col Roger Carpenter Treffry, MC, TD, RA (d 1945), and Dorothy Emma, *née* Gundry Mills (d 1970); descended from an old Cornish family which acquired the manor of Fowey and the house of Place by marriage with an heiress *ca* 1300 (*see* Burke's Landed Gentry, 18 edn, vol I, 1965); *b* 7 Oct 1926; *Educ* Marlborough, Magdalen Coll Oxford (MA); *Career* Capt Frontier Force Regt IA 1945–48; joined HM Overseas Serv 1952, political offr S Arabia 1952, asst chief sec Aden 1959, perm sec Miny of Finance S Arabian Fedn 1963, cabinet sec S Arabian Fedn 1966, ret 1968; Int Monetary Fund 1968–87 (fin advsr Indonesia 1971–73); pres: Royal Inst of Cornwall 1992–94, Campaign for Cornwall 1994; dep chm Regnl Ctee Nat Tst Devon and Cornwall, govr Falmouth Coll of Art; High Sheriff of Cornwall 1991; *Clubs* Travellers'; *Style*— David Treffry, Esq, OBE, DL; ✉ Place, Fowey, Cornwall PL23 1BS; 1684 32nd Street NW, Washington DC 20007, USA

TREFGARNE, 2 Baron (UK 1947); David Garro Trefgarne; PC (1989); s of 1 Baron Trefgarne (d 1960), and Elizabeth (who m 2, 1962 (m dis 1966), Cdr Anthony Tosswill Courtney, OBE (d 1988); and 3, 1971, Hugh Cecil Howat Ker (d 1987)), da of late Charles Edward Churchill, of Ashton Keynes, Wilts; *b* 31 March 1941; *Educ* Haileybury, Princeton Univ USA; *m* 1968, Rosalie Lane, er da of Baron Lane of Horsell (Life Peer); 2 s (Hon George, Hon Justin b 1973), 1 da (Hon Rebecca b 1976); *Heir* s, Hon George Garro Trefgarne b 4 Jan 1970; *Career* oppn whip House of Lords 1977–79, a Lord in Waiting (Government whip) 1979–81; under sec of state: Dept of Trade 1981, FCO 1981–82, DHSS 1982–83, Miny of Def (for armed forces) 1983–85; min of state for def support 1985–86, min of state for def procurement 1986–89, min for trade DTI 1989–90; dir and conslt various cos; non-exec dir Siebe plc 1991–; pres: Mech and Metal Trades Confedn 1990–, Popular Flying Assoc 1992–; life govr Haileybury 1992–, govr Guildford Sch of Acting 1992–, tstee Mary Rose Tst 1994–, chm Engrg Trg Authy 1994–; pres British Assoc of Aviation Consultants 1995–; awarded Royal Aero Club Bronze medal (jtly) for flight from UK to Aust and back in light aircraft 1963; *Recreations* flying, photography; *Style*— The Rt Hon the Lord Trefgarne, PC; ✉ House of Lords, London SW1A 0PW

TREFGARNE, Hon Trevor Garro; 2 s of 1 Baron Trefgarne (d 1960), and Elizabeth, *née* Churchill; *b* 18 Jan 1944; *Educ* Cheltenham, Cranfield Sch of Mgmnt; *m* 1, 1967 (m dis 1979), Diana Elizabeth, da of late Michael Gibb, of Forge House, Taynton, Oxon, by his w Ursula; 2 s (Rupert b 1972, Oliver b 1974), 1 da (Susannah Julia b 1976); m 2, 1979, Caroline France, da of Michael Gosschalk, of Monte Carlo; 1 s (Mark b 1982), 1 da (Camilla b 1988); *Career* dir Pentos plc 1972–75, chm Nesco Investments plc 1976–87, EFG plc 1992–94; dir: Garro Securities Ltd, Templeton Emerging Markets Investment Trust plc, Templeton Central & Eastern European Investment Co; *Style*— The Hon Trevor Trefgarne; ✉ 30 Kimbell Gardens, London SW6 6QQ

TREGLOWN, Prof Jeremy Dickinson; s of late Rev Geoffrey Leonard Treglown, MBE, Hon CF, of Cheltenham, Glos, and Beryl Miriam Treglown; *b* 24 May 1946; *Educ* Bristol GS, St Peter's Coll Saltley Birmingham, St Peter's Coll Oxford (MA, BLitt), UCL (PhD); *m* 1970 (m dis 1982), Rona Mary Bower; 1 s, 2 da; m 2, 1984, Holly Mary Belinda Eley, *née* Urquhart; *Career* lectr in English Lincoln Coll Oxford 1973–76, lectr UCL 1976–79, ed Times Literary Supplement 1982–90 (asst ed 1980–82), prof of English Univ of Warwick 1993–; contrib to: Sunday Times, Observer, Independent on Sunday, TLS, London Review of Books, New Yorker and many other jls; visiting fell All Souls Coll Oxford 1986, Mellon visiting assoc California Inst of Technol, fell Huntington Library California 1988, fell and memb Cncl RSL 1989–, hon res fell UCL 1991–, Ferris prof Princeton Univ 1992; chm of judges Booker Prize 1991; *Publications* (ed) The Letters of John Wilmot, Earl of Rochester (1980), Spirit of Wit (1982), The Lantern-Bearers: Essays by Robert Louis Stevenson (1988); general ed Plays in Performance series 1981–85; Roald Dahl: A Biography (1994); author of various articles and introductions on poetry, drama and literary history; *Style*— Prof Jeremy Treglown; ✉ 102 Savernake Rd, London NW3

TREGONING, Christopher William Courtenay; 3 and yst s of Lt-Col John Langford Tregoning, MBE, TD (d 1976), of Windrush House, Inkpen, Newbury, and Sioned Georgina Courtenay, *née* Strick (d 1994); bro of Julian George Tregoning, *qv*; *b* 15 June 1948; *Educ* Harrow, Fitzwilliam Coll Cambridge (MA); *m* 15 Sept 1973, Antonia Isabella Mary, da of Maj John Albert Miles Critchley-Salmonson, of The Manor House, Great Barton, Bury St Edmunds; 3 s (Harry John William b 28 Jan 1976, Daniel Christopher Leonard b 30 Dec 1977, Thomas Anthony Cecil b 26 Jan 1982); *Career* Thomson McLintock & Co 1970–74, Barclays Bank Ltd 1974–79, dep md Den Norske Bank plc (formerly Nordic Bank plc) 1986– (joined 1979); FCA 1974; *Recreations* field sports, racing; *Style*— Christopher Tregoning, Esq; ✉ Den Norse Bank plc, 20 St Dunstan's Hill, London EC3R 8HY (☎ 0171 621 1111, fax 0171 626 7400)

TREGONING, Julian George; 2 s of Lt-Col John Langford Tregoning, MBE, TD (d 1976), of Windrush House, Inkpen, Newbury, Berks, and Sioned Georgina Courtenay, *née* Strick (d 1994); bro of Christopher William Courtenay Tregoning, *qv*; *b* 24 Oct 1946; *Educ* Harrow, BRNC Dartmouth; *m* Tessa Jane, da of Cdr Norman Lanyon, DSC** (d 1982); 2 s (Oliver b 1973, Guy b 1975); *Career* RN 1965–68; dir Save & Prosper Group Ltd 1985–95 (joined 1968), dir Robert Fleming & Co Ltd 1995–; chm Assoc of Unit Tst and Investmt Funds 1993–95 (int rep 1993–), vice pres Fédération Européene des Fonds et Sociétés d'Investissement (FEFSI), former ex-officio memb Panel on Takeovers and Mergers; treas Royal UK Beneficent Assoc (Rukba), dep chm City of London Club; memb Ct of Assts Worshipful Co of Grocers; *Recreations* tennis, 'messing about in boats', skiing, watercolours, wine; *Clubs* Boodle's, City of London, MCC, St Moritz Tobogganing; *Style*— Julian Tregoning, Esq; ✉ Robert Fleming & Co Ltd, 25 Copthall Avenue, London EC2R 7DR (☎ 0171 638 5858, fax 0171 282 4330)

TREHANE, Sir (Walter) Richard; kt (1967); s of James Trehane (d 1949), of Wimborne, Dorset, and Muriel Yeoman Cowl; *b* 14 July 1913; *Educ* Monkton Combe Sch, Univ of Reading; *m* 1948, Elizabeth Mitchell, da of Martin Shaw, MC; 2 s; *Career* mangr Hampreston Manor Farm 1936–79, chm Hampreston Manor Farm Ltd 1955–; dir: Rivers Estate Co 1964–88, Southern TV 1968–81, Rank Orgn 1971–84; former memb: Dorset War Agric Exec Ctee, Milk Mktg Bd 1947–77 (chm 1958–77), Dorset CC; former chm: English Country Cheese Cncl 1955–77, UK Dairy Assoc; pres: Int Dairy Fedn 1968–72, Euro Assoc Animal Prodn 1961–67 (hon pres 1967–95); chm Alfa-Laval Co 1982–85 (dir 1977–85); govr Monkton Combe Sch 1957–83; Hon DSc Univ of Reading; FRAgS; Cdr Order of Merit (France) 1964; *Style*— Sir Richard Trehane; ✉ Hampreston Manor Farm, Wimborne, Dorset BH21 7LX

TREITEL, Prof Sir Guenter Heinz; kt (1997), QC (1983); s of Theodor Treitel (d 1973), and Hanna, *née* Levy (d 1951); *b* 26 Oct 1928; *Educ* Kilburn GS, Magdalen Coll Oxford (BA, MA, BCL, DCL); *m* 1 Jan 1957, Phyllis Margaret, da of Ronald Cook; 2 s (Richard James b 1958, Henry Marcus b 1960); *Career* called to the Bar Gray's Inn 1952, hon bencher 1982; asst lectr LSE 1951–53; Univ of Oxford: lectr Univ Coll 1953–54, fell Magdalen Coll 1954–79 (hon fell 1979), All Souls reader in Eng law 1964–79, Vinerian prof of Eng law 1979–96 (hon prof 1996), fell All Souls Coll 1979–96 (hon fell 1996); visiting lectr/prof 1963–94 Univs of: Chicago, Houston, Southern Methodist, Virginia, Santa Clara, W Aust; visiting scholar Ernst von Caemmerer Stiftung 1990; tstee Br Museum 1983–, memb Cncl Nat Tst 1984–93; FBA 1977; *Books* The Law of Contract (1962, 9 edn 1995), An Outline of the Law of Contract (1975, 5 edn 1995), Remedies for Breach of Contract, A Comparative Account (1988), Unmöglichkeit, 'Impracticability' und 'Frustration' im anglo-amerikanischen Recht (1991), Frustration and Force Majeure (1994); jt ed of: Benjamin's Sale of Goods (1975, 4 edn 1992), Chitty on Contracts (23 edn 1968 - 27 edn 1994), Dicey (& Morris) Conflict of Laws (7 edn 1958, 8 edn 1967); *Recreations* reading, music; *Style*— Prof Sir Guenter Treitel, QC, FBA; ✉ All Souls College, Oxford OX1 4AL (☎ 01865 279379, fax 01865 279299)

TRELAWNY, Sir John Barry; *see:* Salusbury-Trelawny, Sir John Barry

TRELFORD, Donald Gilchrist; s of Thomas Staplin Trelford, of Coventry, and Doris, *née* Gilchrist; *b* 9 Nov 1937; *Educ* Bablake Sch Coventry, Selwyn Coll Cambridge (MA); *m* 1, Janice; 2 s, 1 da; m 2, 1978, Katherine Louise, da of John Mark, of Guernsey; 1 da; *Career* ed Times of Malawi 1963–66; corr in Africa: The Observer, The Times, BBC; The Observer: dep ed 1969–75, ed and dir 1975–93, chief exec 1992–93; sports columnist Daily Telegraph 1993–, prof of journalism studies Univ of Sheffield 1993–; regular bdcasts on radio and TV, regular speaker at int media confs; vice pres Br Sports Tst; memb: Br Exec Ctee Int Press Inst, Defence Press and Bdcasting Ctee 1984–93, Olivier Awards Ctee 1985–93, MCC Ctee 1988–91, Advsy Bd London Choral Soc; chm Soc of Gentlemen Lovers of Musick 1995–; Hon DLitt Univ of Sheffield; Freeman City of London, Liveryman Worshipful Co of tationers & Newspaper Makers; FRSA; *Publications* County Champions (contrib, 1982), Sunday Best (annual anthology, ed, 1981–83), Siege (jt author, 1980), Snookered (1986), Child of Change (with Garry Kasparov, 1987), Saturday's Boys (contrib, 1990), Fine Glances (contrib, 1990), Len Hutton Remembered (1992), The Observer at 200 (ed, 1992); *Recreations* golf, tennis, snooker; *Clubs* Garrick, Beefsteak, RAF, MCC; *Style*— Donald Trelford, Esq; ✉ 20 Richmond Crescent, London N1 0LZ (☎ and fax 0171 607 5346)

TREMAIN, Rose; da of Keith Nicholas Thomson, and Viola Mabel, *née* Dudley; *b* 2 Aug 1943; *Educ* Sorbonne, Univ of East Anglia (BA); *m* 1, 7 May 1971 (m dis 1976), Jon Tremain; 1 da (Eleanor Rachel b 16 July 1972); m 2, 2 Aug 1982 (m dis 1991), Jonathan Dudley; *Career* author; FRSL 1983; *Awards* winner: Dylan Thomas Prize 1984, Giles Cooper Award 1985, Angel Prize 1985 and 1989, Sunday Express Book of the Year Award 1989, James Tait Black Meml Prize 1992, Prix Femina Etranger 1994; *Books* Sadlers Birthday (1975), Letter to Sister Benedicta (1978), The Cupboard (1980), The Colonel's Daughter (1982), The Swimming Pool Season (1984), The Garden of The Villa Mollini (1986), Restoration (1989), Sacred Country (1992), Evangelista's Fan (1994), Collected Short Stories (1996), The Way I Found Her (1997); *Recreations* gardening, yoga; *Style*— Ms Rose Tremain; ✉ 2 High House, South Avenue, Thorpe St Andrew, Norwich NR7 0EZ (☎ 01603 439682, fax 01603 434234)

TREMLETT, Ven Anthony Frank (Tony); s of Frank Tremlett and Sally Tremlett; *b* 25 Aug 1937; *Educ* Plymouth Coll; *m* 1958, Patricia Lapthorn; 2 s, 1 da; *Career* British Rail 1953–68; Nat Freight Corpn 1968–80: posts incl depot services mangr, traffic mangr London, dist mangr Devon and Cornwall, ret as ops dir Bristol; ordained: deacon 1981, priest 1982; vicar Southway 1984–88 (curate 1981–82, priest i/c 1982–84), rural dean Moorside 1986–88; archdeacon of: Totnes 1988–94, Exeter 1994–; fell Cheltenham and Gloucester Coll of HE Tst; govr: Dartington Coll of Arts; MIMgt; *Style*— The Ven the Archdeacon of Exeter; ✉ St Matthew's House, 45 Spicer Road, Exeter, Devon EX1 1TA (☎ 01392 425432, fax 01392 425783)

TREMLETT, Timothy Maurice (Tim); s of Maurice Fletcher Tremlett (d 1984), of Southampton, and Melina Mae, *née* Cousins; *b* 26 July 1956; *Educ* Bellemoor Secdy Modern, Richard Taunton Sixth Form Coll; *m* 28 Sept 1979, Carolyn Patricia, da of Terence Michael Hickley; 3 s (Christopher Timothy b 2 Sept 1981, Alastair Jonathan b 1 Feb 1983, Benjamin Paul b 2 May 1984); *Career* dir of cricket and coaching; represented W of England under 15; Hampshire CCC: debut v Sussex 1976, awarded county cap 1983, 200 first class appearances, county coach 1992–; tours: England B to Sri Lanka 1986, English Cos to Zimbabwe 1984–85; former sales asst in furriers; *Recreations* golf, table tennis, most sports; *Style*— Tim Tremlett, Esq; ✉ Hampshire CCC, Northlands Rd, Southampton, Hampshire SO9 2TY (☎ 01703 333788, fax 01703 330121)

TRENCH, Sir Peter Edward; kt (1979), CBE (1964, OBE (Mil) 1945), TD (1949); s of James Trench; *b* 16 June 1918; *Educ* privately, Univ of London and Cambridge; *m* 1940, Mary St Clair Morford; 1 s, 1 da; *Career* served WWII Queen's Royal Regt; formerly: md Bovis Ltd, chm Y J Lovell Holdings, dir Capital & Counties plc, dir LEP Group plc, dir Nationwide Building Society, dir Crendon Concrete, dir The Builder Group plc, dir Haden plc, dir Trench & Ptnrs Ltd, chm Construction & Housing Res Advsy Cncl, chm Nat House Bldg Cncl, memb Cncl CBI and RSA, memb Ct of Govrs LSE, hon treas St Mary's Hosp Med Sch; visiting prof of construction mgmnt Univ of Reading 1981–88, vice pres Bldg Centre, hon memb Architectural Assoc; JP Inner London 1963–71; Hon DSc; FCIArb, FRSA, CIMgt, Hon FCIOB, Hon FRIBA; *Style*— Sir Peter Trench, CBE, TD; ✉ 4 Napier Close, Napier Rd, London W14 8LG (☎ 0171 602 3936)

TRENCHARD, 3 Viscount (UK 1936); Sir Hugh Trenchard; 3 Bt (UK 1919); also Baron Trenchard (UK 1930); s of 2 Viscount Trenchard, MC (d 1987), and of Patricia, da of Adm Sir Sidney Bailey, KBE, CB, DSO; *b* 12 March 1951; *Educ* Eton, Trinity Coll Cambridge; *m* 1975, Fiona Elizabeth, da of Maj 2 Baron Margadale, TD, DL, *qv*; 2 s (Hon Alexander Thomas b 1978, Hon William James b 1986), 2 da (Hon Katherine Clare b 1980, Hon Laura Mary b 1987); *Heir* s, Hon Alexander Thomas Trenchard b 1978; *Career* Capt 4 Royal Green Jackets, TA 1973–80; Kleinwort Benson Ltd: joined 1973, chief rep in Japan 1980–85, dir 1986–96; Kleinwort Benson International Inc: gen mangr Tokyo 1985–88, pres 1988–95, dep chm 1995–96; rep in Japan of Kleinwort Benson Group plc 1993–95; dir: Dover Japan Inc 1985–87, ACP Holdings Ltd 1990–94, Japan Securities Dealers Assoc 1994–95, Bond Underwriters Assoc of Japan 1994–95; European

Business Community in Japan: chm Securities Ctee 1993–95, vice chm Cncl 1995; memb: Japan Assoc of Corp Execs 1987–95, Cncl Japan Soc 1992–93 and 1995– (vice chm 1996–); hon treas House of Lords All Pty Defence Study Gp 1992–93, memb Cncl RAF Benevolent Fund 1991–; *Style—* The Rt Hon the Viscount Trenchard; ✉ Standon Lordship, Ware, Hertfordshire SG11 1PR (☎ 01920 823785)

TREND, Hon Michael St John; MP (C) Windsor and Maidenhead (majority 12,928); er s of Baron Trend, GCB, CVO, PC (Life Peer, d 1987), and Patricia Charlotte, *née* Shaw; *b* 1952; *Educ* Westminster, Oriel Coll Oxford, in Athens (Greek Govt scholarship); *m* 28 Feb 1987, Jill E, er da of L A Kershaw; 1 s, 2 da; *Career* journalist, editor and broadcaster; ed: History Today 1981–84, House of Commons Magazine 1984–86; home ed The Spectator 1986–, latterly chief leader writer Daily Telegraph; MP (C) Windsor and Maidenhead 1992–, memb Select Ctee on Health 1992–93; PPS: Dept of Environment 1993–94, Dept of Health 1994, Dept of Tport 1994–95; dep chm Cons Party 1995–; *Style—* The Hon Michael Trend, MP; ✉ House of Commons, London SW1A 0AA

TRENDELL, Derek; s of Clifford Trendell, of Chew Magna, Somerset, and Joyce Mabel, *née* Hunt; *b* 7 May 1945; *Educ* Keynsham GS; *m* 7 Sept 1968, Diane Pamela, 2 da (Joanna Catherine b 19 Nov 1969, Sarah Louise b 1 March 1973); *Career* trainee Grace Derbyshire & Todd of Bristol 1962–68; Price Waterhouse: Kingston Jamaica 1969–73, London 1973–79, Nottingham 1979–88, sr ptnr Leicester 1988–90, sr ptnr East Midlands 1991–93, nat dir Price Waterhouse Meyernel S Africa 1993–; FCA 1967; *Recreations* golf, walking, ornithology, wine; *Clubs* Riviera, Sherwood Forest Golf; *Style—* Derek Trendell, Esq; ✉ Price Waterhouse Meyernel, PO Box 783027, Sandton 2146, South Africa (☎ 00 27 11 780 2000)

TRENOUTH, Dr Michael John; s of John Trenouth, of Grange-over-Sands, and Marjorie Trenouth; *b* 2 June 1946; *Educ* Friend's Sch Lancaster, Univ of Manchester (BSc, BDS, MDS, PhD, DOrth, DDO, FDS, RCPS); *Career* Manchester Dental Hosp: house offr 1971–72, lectr in oral surgery 1972–75, lectr in dental anatomy and hon registrar orthodontics 1975–78, lectr in orthodontics and hon sr registrar orthodontics 1978–85; consIt orthodontist Preston Royal Hosp 1985–, dental post graduate tutor Lancaster, Preston, Chorley and Blackpool Dists 1991–; treas Manchester and Region Orthodontic Study Gp 1980–85; *Recreations* skiing, sailing, fell walking, ice skating; *Style—* Dr Michael Trenouth; ✉ Royal Preston Hospital, PO Box 66, Sharoe Green Lane, Preston PR2 4HT (☎ 01772 710597)

TRESS, Dr Ronald Charles; CBE (1968); s of Stephen Charles Tress (d 1953), and Emma Jane, *née* Blewitt (d 1975); *b* 11 Jan 1915; *Educ* Gillingham Co Sch, Univ Coll Southampton, Univ of London (BSc), St Deiniol's Library Hawarden, Univ of Manchester; *m* 25 July 1942, Josephine Kelly (d 1993), da of Hubert James Medland (d 1968); 1 s (Thomas b 1949), 2 da (Sarah b 1944, Janet b 1946); *Career* asst lectr economics Univ Coll of the SW Exeter 1938–41, econ asst War Cabinet Offices 1941–45, econ advsr Cabinet Sec 1945–47, reader in public fin Univ of London 1947–51, prof of political economy Univ of Bristol 1951–68, master Birkbeck Coll London 1968–77; dir The Leverhulme Tst 1977–84, chm SW Econ Planning Cncl 1965–68, devpt cmmr 1959–81, tstee City Parochial Fndn 1974–77 and 1979–89, govr Christ Church Coll Canterbury 1975–91, memb Cncl Univ of Kent Canterbury 1977–92, vice pres Royal Econ Soc 1979– (sec gen 1975–79), chm Lord Chllr's Advsy Ctee on Legal Aid 1979–84; Hon DSc Bristol 1968, Hon LLD Furman S Carolina 1973, Hon DUniv Open Univ 1974, Hon LLD Exeter 1976, Hon DSc Southampton 1978, Hon DCL Univ of Kent at Canterbury 1984; *Clubs* Athenaeum; *Style—* Dr R C Tress, CBE; ✉ The Red House, 29 Palace Road, East Molesey, Surrey KT8 9DJ (☎ 0181 979 0605)

TRETHOWAN, (Henry) Brock; s of Michael Trethowan, OBE (d 1968), of Hampshire, and Phyllis Franklin, *née* Miles (d 1981); *b* 22 June 1937; *Educ* Sherborne; *m* 11 April 1970, Virginia, da of Lt-Col Geoffrey Charles Lee, of Farnham, Surrey; 2 da (Rebecca b 1966, Henrietta b 1977); *Career* solicitor; consIt Trethowans of Salisbury; recorder County and Crown Court; pt/t immigration adjudicator; pres Wilts Valuation Tbnl 1989–, vice pres Enham Tst; tstee Salisbury Hospice Care Tst 1981– (vice chm 1988–, hon treas 1993–); *Recreations* family, gardening, food and wine; *Style—* Brock Trethowan, Esq; ✉ 32 Pilgrims Mead, Bishopdown, Salisbury, Wilts SP1 3GX (☎ and fax 01722 332017); College Chambers, New Street, Salisbury, Wilts SP1 2LY (☎ 01722 412512, fax 01722 411300)

TREUHERZ, Julian Benjamin; s of Werner Treuherz and Irmgard, *née* Amberg; *b* 12 March 1947; *Educ* Manchester GS, ChCh Oxford (MA), Univ of East Anglia (MA); *Career* Manchester City Art Gallery: trainee 1971, asst keeper of fine art 1972, keeper of fine art 1974; keeper of art galleries (Walker Art Gallery, Liverpool, Sudley House, Liverpool and Lady Lever Art Gallery, Port Sunlight) 1989–; memb: Museums Assoc 1971, Victorian Soc 1971 (hon sec Manchester Group 1972–79, chm Manchester Group 1980–83); memb Ctee: Contemporary Art Soc 1990–94, Liverpool Univ Fine Arts Sub-Gp 1990–, NACF Merseyside Gp 1991–, Whitworth Art Gallery 1993–; *Publications* Pre-Raphaelite Paintings from the Manchester City Art Gallery (1981), Hard Times - Social Realism in Victorian Art (1987), Country Houses of Cheshire (jtly with Peter de Figueiredo, 1988), Victorian Painting (1993); various articles in art-historical jls; *Recreations* playing the piano, cooking, opera; *Style—* Julian Treuherz, Esq; ✉ Walker Art Gallery, William Brown St, Liverpool L3 8EL (☎ 0151 207 0001)

TREVAIL, Charles; s of Donald Charles Trevail (d 1986), and Lois Mary, *née* Rowse; *b* 22 Aug 1960; *Educ* Plymouth Coll, Univ of Durham (BA Modern History), Postgrad Dip in Mktg; *m* 1995, Imelda Primrose; 1 da (Florence Lois Kate b 15 Sept 1996); *Career* formerly: various mktg posts LDDC and Acco Rexel, business consIt Strategy International; Sampson Tyrrell Enterprise: account dir 1988–91, bd dir 1991–95, dep chief exec 1995–; advsr on identity and branding issues for clients incl: Avis, EMI, Financial Times Group, Dun & Bradstreet, KPMG, Barclays, Saab; reg speaker at confs on branding, identity and mktg; *Style—* Charles Trevail, Esq; ✉ Sampson Tyrrell Enterprise, 6 Mercer Street, London WC2H 9QA (☎ 0171 574 4000, fax 0171 574 4100)

TREVELYAN, Dennis John; CB (1981); s of John Henry Trevelyan (d 1982), and Eliza Trevelyan; *b* 21 July 1929; *Educ* Enfield GS, Univ Coll Oxford (scholar); *m* 1960, Carol, da of John Coombes (d 1944); 1 s, 1 da; *Career* entered Home Office 1950, princ private sec to Lord Pres and Ldr of House 1964–67, asst under sec of state NI Office 1972–76, asst under sec of state Home Office Broadcasting Dept 1976–77, dep under sec of state Home Office and dir-gen Prison Serv 1978–83, first Civil Serv cmmr 1983–89 (responsible to the Queen and the Privy Cncl for keeping unqualified persons out of the Civil Service); princ Mansfield College Oxford 1989–96, govr Oxford Centre for Postgrad Hebrew Studies 1992–; memb: Bd Euro Inst of Public Mgmnt 1985–89, City of London Univ Business Sch Cncl 1986–89; vice pres Industl Participation Assoc 1987–; govr: Ashridge Mgmnt Coll 1985–89, London Contemporary Dance Tst 1986–89; *Recreations* music; *Clubs* Athenaeum, MCC, Vincent's (Oxford); *Style—* Dennis Trevelyan, Esq, CB; ✉ Lindfield, 1 Begbroke Lane, Begbroke, Oxford OX5 1RN

TREVELYAN, Sir Edward Norman; 11 Bt (E 1662), of Nettlecombe, Somerset; s of Sir Norman Irving Trevelyan, 10 Bt (d 1996), and Jennifer Mary, *née* Riddett; *b* 14 Aug 1955; *Educ* Univ of California Santa Barbara (PhD political science 1997); *m* 10 Aug 1993, Debbie J, da of Robert A Mullin, of Corpus Christi, Texas, USA; 1 s (Reed Edward b Oct 1996); *Heir* s, Reed Edward Trevelyan b Oct 1996; *Style—* Sir Edward Trevelyan, Bt

TREVELYAN, Sir Geoffrey Washington; 5 Bt (UK 1874), of Wallington, Northumberland; s of Rt Hon Sir Charles Philips Trevelyan, 3 Bt (d 1958); s bro, Sir George Lowthian Trevelyan, 4 Bt (d 1996); *b* 4 July 1920; *Educ* Oundle, Trin Coll Camb (MA); *m* 3 May 1947, Gillian Isabel, eldest da of late Alexander Louis Sandison Wood, OBE, of Spencer's Farm, Whelpley Hill, Chesham, Bucks; 1 s (Peter John b 11 Sept 1948), 1 da (Sandra Mary (Mrs David Bradley) b 5 Aug 1951); *Heir* s, Peter John Trevelyan b 11 Sept 1948; *Career* de Havilland AC Co Ltd 1941–61; dir: Chatto & Windus Ltd, Hogarth Press Ltd 1962–78, Chatto, Bodley Head and Jonathan Cape Ltd 1970–78; chm Thames North Region of Abbeyfield Soc 1985–94, hon treas Family Planning Assoc 1975–90; dir: Family Planning Sales Ltd 1985–90, The Lake Hunts Ltd; *Style—* Sir Greoffrey Trevelyan, Bt; ✉ Lower Silkstead, 3 Abbey Mill End, St Albans, Herts AL3 4HN (☎ 01727 864866)

TREVELYAN, (Walter) Raleigh; s of Col Walter Raleigh Fetherstonhaugh Trevelyan (d 1953), and Olive Beatrice, *née* Frost (d 1976); *b* 6 July 1923, Andaman Islands; *Educ* Winchester; *Career* Nat Serv WWII, Capt Rifle Bde (Italian campaign, despatches, mil mission to Italian Army); publisher 1948–88: Collins, Hutchinson, Michael Joseph (as editorial dir), Hamish Hamilton, Jonathan Cape, Bloomsbury; translator from Italian (John Florio Prize 1967), reviewer; contrib: various National Trust publications, Apollo, Connoisseur, John Rylands Bulletin; chm Anglo-Italian Soc for the Protection of Animals; memb PEN (memb Ctee); FRSL, FRGS; *Books* The Fortress (1956), A Hermit Disclosed (1960), Italian Short Stories: Penguin Parallel Texts (ed 1965), The Big Tomato (1966), Italian Writing Today (ed 1967), Princes Under The Volcano (1972), The Shadow of Vesuvius (1976), A Pre-Raphaelite Circle (1978), Rome' 44 (1982), Shades of the Alhambra (1984), The Golden Oriole (1987), La Storia dei Whitaker (1988), Grand Dukes and Diamonds (1991), A Clear Premonition (1995), The Companion Guide to Sicily (1996); *Recreations* travel, gardening; *Clubs* Brooks's, Lansdowne, Groucho; *Style—* Raleigh Trevelyan, Esq, FRSL; ✉ 18 Hertford St, London W1Y 7DB (☎ and fax 0171 629 5879); St Cadix, St Veep, Lostwithiel, Cornwall PL22 0PB (☎ 01208 872313)

TREVELYAN KEE, Hon Mrs (Catherine Mary); OBE (1977); da of Baron Trevelyan (Life Peer, d 1985), and Violet Margaret, *née* Bartholomew; *b* 1943; *Educ* St Mary's Sch Calne Wilts, Univ of St Andrews; *m* 10 Dec 1990, Robert Kee; *Career* exec dir New York City Cultural Cncl and Cultural Cncl Fndn 1969–73, admin Windsor Festival 1974–76, dep sec-gen London Celebrations Ctee for the Queen's Silver Jubilee 1976–77, exhibition organiser 1978–80, gen mangr and dir The Burlington Magazine 1980–; govr Int Students House Univ of London, memb Cncl Br Museum Soc; *Style—* The Hon Mrs Trevelyan Kee, OBE

TREVERTON-JONES, Ronald; s of Dennis Ford Treverton-Jones (d 1950), of Newport, Gwent, and Alison Joy Bielski, *née* Morris-Prosser; *b* 1 Aug 1949; *Educ* Malvern, Univ of Wales Swansea (BSc); *m* 1, 31 July 1970 (m dis 1985), Margaret Jean, da of Donald John Purser, of Northfield, Birmingham; 2 s (Peter b 1976, Michael b 1978); m 2, 17 Oct 1987, Jacqueline Diane, da of James Leslie Beckingham Welch (d 1974), of Quinton, Birmingham; *Career* graduate trainee National Westminster Bank 1970–72, trainee N Lea Barham & Brooks 1970–74, sr ptnr Harris Allday Lea & Brooks 1992– (ptnr 1976–); vice chm The Bow Group London 1979–80, chm Birmingham Bow Group 1979–80; chm Birmingham Stock Exchange Assoc 1995–; memb Stock Exchange 1975; *Books* Financing our Cities (with Edwina Currie and Peter McGauley, 1976), Right Wheel - A Conservative Policy for the Motor Industry (1977); *Recreations* country pursuits, woodland management, travel; *Style—* Ronald Treverton-Jones, Esq; ✉ Ravenhill Court, Lulsley, Knightwick, Worcs WR6 5QW (☎ 01886 821242); La Bartelle Basse, Pont De Russac, 46170, Castelnau-Montratier, France; Harris Allday Lea & Brooks, 33 Great Charles St, Birmingham B3 3JN (☎ 0121 233 1222, fax 0121 236 2587)

TREVES, Vanni Emanuele; s of Giuliano Treves (ka 1944), and Marianna, *née* Baer; *b* 3 Nov 1940; *Educ* St Paul's, Univ of Oxford (MA), Univ of Illinois (LLM); *m* 7 Jan 1971, Angela Veronica, da of Lt-Gen Sir Richard Fyffe, DSO, OBE, MC (d 1971); 2 s (Alexander b 1973, William b 1975), 1 da (Louise b 1983); *Career* slr; sr ptnr Macfarlanes 1987– (ptnr 1970–); dir: Oceonics Group plc 1984–95, Saatchi & Saatchi Co plc 1987–90, Fiskars Ltd 1989–; chm: BBA Group plc 1989– (dir 1987–), McKechnie plc 1991– (dir 1990–), Trinity Holdings plc 1996–; tstee: J Paul Getty Jr Charitable Tst, 29th May 1961 Charitable Tst, Fledgeling Equity and Bond Funds (chm 1992–); vice pres London Fedn of Boys' Clubs, chm Devpt Ctee Nat Portrait Gallery, govr London Business Sch, slr to the Royal Acad of Arts; *Recreations* walking, eating, watercolours; *Clubs* Boodle's, City of London; *Style—* Vanni Treves, Esq; ✉ Macfarlanes, 10 Norwich Street, London EC4A 1BD (☎ 0171 831 9222, fax 0171 831 9607)

TREVETHIN, Baron *see:* Oaksey, Baron

TREVETT, Peter George; QC (1992); s of George Albert Trevett, of 56 Berrylands, Surbiton, Surrey, and Janet, *née* Ayling; *b* 25 Nov 1947; *Educ* Kingston GS, Queens' Coll Cambridge (MA, LLM); *m* 8 July 1972, Vera Lucia; 2 s (Thomas b 1973, Philip b 1978), 1 da (Jessica b 1982); *Career* called to the Bar Lincoln's Inn 1971, practising revenue barr 1973–; memb Hon Soc of Lincoln's Inn; author of various articles in professional jls; *Recreations* golf, collecting cactaceae, gardening, book collecting, reading; *Clubs* Woking Golf; *Style—* Peter Trevett, Esq, QC; ✉ 11 New Square, Lincoln's Inn, London WC2A 3QB (☎ 0171 242 4017, fax 0171 831 2391)

TREVITT, William James Piper; s of William John Maskell Trevitt, of Hereford, and Jane Valerie, *née* Piper; *b* 8 April 1969; *Educ* Royal Ballet Schools; *m* 9 Aug 1992, Rebecca, *née* Holmes; 2 s (Joseph Zebulon b 15 April 1994, Zachary George b 25 Aug 1996); *Career* Royal Ballet: joined 1987, first artist 1989–90, soloist 1990–93, first soloist 1993–94, princ 1994–; performances incl: Mercutio in Romeo and Juliet, Siegfried in Swan Lake, Solor in La Bayadere, Florimund in Sleeping Beauty, Messenger of Death in Song of the Earth, Oberon in The Dream, pas de deux in Scenes de Ballet; *Recreations* photography, cinema; *Style—* William Trevitt, Esq; ✉ The Royal Ballet, Royal Opera House, Covent Garden, London WC2E 9DD (☎ 0171 240 1200)

TREVOR, John Clyfford; s of Clyfford Trevor (d 1970), and Louisa Ryder, *née* Airey; *b* 16 Aug 1932; *Educ* USA, Millfield; *m* 14 Sept 1957, Jane Carolyn, da of Capt Charles Houstoun-Boswall (d 1946), Royal Scots Greys (*see* Baronetage); 2 s (Mark b 1961, Richard b 1969), 2 da (Carolyn b 1959, Emma b 1963); *Career* Nat Serv 2 Lt First Bn East Surrey Regt 1952–53, serv Libya and Egypt; J Trevor and Sons: sr ptnr 1972–88, chm 1988–96, sr exec 1996–; chm J Trevor Mortleman and Poland Ltd Lloyd's brokers 1985–88; RICS: chm Gen Practice Div of the Central London Branch 1973–74, chm Central London Branch 1978–79, chm Working Pty on Conveyancing 1986–92; memb Gen Practice Divisional Gen Cncl 1985–91; FRICS, ACIArb; *Recreations* furniture restoration, gardening; *Clubs* Naval and Military, MCC; *Style—* John Trevor, Esq; ✉ J Trevor & Webster, 58 Grosvenor St, London W1X 0DD (☎ 0171 629 8151, fax 0171 499 5555)

TREVOR, William; CBE (1977); *b* 24 May 1928; *Educ* St Columba's Coll Dublin, Trinity Coll Dublin; *m* 1952, Jane, da of C N Ryan; 2 s; *Career* writer; winner Allied Irish Banks' Prize 1976; Hon DLitt: Univ of Exeter 1984, Trinity Coll Dublin 1986, Queen's Univ Belfast 1989, Nat Univ of Ireland (Cork) 1990; memb Irish Acad of Letters; CLit 1994; *Books* The Old Boys (1964), The Boarding House (Hawthornden Prize, 1965), The Love Department (1966), The Day We Got Drunk on Cake (1967), Mrs Eckdorf in O'Neill's Hotel (1969), Miss Gomez and the Brethren (1971), The Ballroom of Romance (1972), Elizabeth Alone (1973), Angels at the Ritz (1975, Royal Soc of Lit Award), The Children of Dynmouth (1976, Whitbread Award), Lovers of Their Time (1978), The Distant Past (1979), Other People's Worlds (1980), Beyond the Pale (1981), Fools of Fortune (1983, Whitbread Award), A Writer's Ireland (1984), The News from Ireland (1986), The Silence in the Garden (1989, Yorkshire Post Book of the Year Award), Family Sins (1990), Two Lives (1991), Excursions in the Real World (1993), Felicia's Journey (1994, Sunday Express Book of the Year, Whitbread Book of the Year), After Rain (1996); *Style*— William Trevor, Esq, CBE; ✉ c/o Peters Fraser & Dunlop Ltd, 503 The Chambers, Chelsea Harbour, Lots Road, London SW10 0XF (☎ 0171 352 4446, fax 0171 352 7356)

TREW, Anthony Leslie Gwynn; s of Howel Douglas Gwynne Trew, of Burwash, E Sussex, and Madeline Louisa, *née* Daniel (d 1987); *b* 20 March 1942; *Educ* Haileybury and Imperial Service Coll; *m* 24 April 1976 (m dis 1994), Angela Rosalind Drury, da of late Gerald Drury Culverwell; 1 s (Charles b 1989), 3 da (Cressida b 1981, Annabel b 1985, Felicity b 1987); *Career* admitted slr 1968, ptnr Richards Butler 1974– (resident ptnr Abu Dhabi 1978–); govr Al Khubairat Community Sch, chm Br Business Gp Abu Dhabi 1996–; Freeman City of London 1977; memb Law Soc; *Recreations* swimming, walking, talking, reading, sailing a Drascombe Lugger; *Clubs* Reform, Al Falah (Abu Dhabi), Law Soc; *Style*— Anthony Trew, Esq; ✉ PO Box 46904, Abu Dhabi, UAE (☎ 00 971 2 778600, fax 00 971 2 778630, telex 22261 RBLAW EM); Richards Butler, Beaufort House, 15 St Botolph Street, London EC3A 7EE (☎ 0171 247 6555, fax 0171 247 5091, telex 949494 RBLAW G); Pleasure House, Ashburnham, Battle, E Sussex TN33 9PE (☎ 01435 830524)

TREWAVAS, Prof Anthony James; s of Clifford John Trewavas (d 1986), of Penzance, and Phyllis Mary, *née* Timms (d 1993); *b* 17 June 1939; *Educ* Roan GS, UCL (BSc, PhD); *m* 29 Aug 1963, Valerie, da of Ivor John Leng; 2 da (Seren Angharad b 6 Jan 1969, Eira Siobhan b 14 Feb 1970), 1 s (Joseph Jonathan Christopher b 16 July 1979); *Career* post doctoral fell Univ of E Anglia; prof of plant biochemistry Univ of Edinburgh 1990– (lectr 1970–84, reader 1984–90); visiting prof: Michigan State Univ 1973, Nat Acad of Sciences Poland 1979, Univ of Illinois 1980, Univ of Alberta 1983, Univ of California Davis 1985, Univ of Bonn 1987, Univ of N Carolina 1988, Nat Univ of Mexico 1989, Univ of Milau 1996; memb Editorial Bd Plant Physiology 1989–; FRSE 1993, FRSA 1995; *Recreations* music, reading, bonsai growing; *Style*— Prof Anthony Trewavas, FRSE; ✉ Institute of Cell and Molecular Biology, King's Buildings, University of Edinburgh, Edinburgh EH9 3JH (☎ 0131 650 5328, fax 0131 650 5392)

TREWBY, Vice Adm Sir (George Francis) Allan; KCB (1974); s of Vice Adm George Trewby, CMG, DSO (d 1953), of Richmond, Surrey; *b* 8 July 1917; *Educ* RNC Dartmouth, RNEC Keyham, RNC Greenwich; *m* 1942, Sandra Coleridge, da of late G C Stedham, of Kenya; 2 s; *Career* joined RN 1931, Cdr 1950, Capt 1959, Rear Adm 1968, asst controller (Polaris) MOD 1968–71, Vice Adm 1971, Chief of Fleet Support and memb of Admty Bd 1971–74, ret 1974; mangr Messrs Foster Wheeler Ltd 1975–77, conslt 1977–87, ret 1987; author of various papers on naval marine engrg published in UK, USA, Italy and Sweden; FEng 1978, FIMechE, FIMarE, CIMgt; *Style*— Vice Adm Sir Allan Trewby, KCB, FEng; ✉ 2 Radnor Close, Henley-on-Thames, Oxon RG9 2DA

TREWIN, Ion Courtenay Gill; s of John Courtenay Trewin, OBE (d 1990), the theatre critic and author, and Wendy Elizabeth, *née* Monk; *b* 13 July 1943; *Educ* Highgate; *m* 7 Aug 1965, Susan Harriet, da of Walter Harry Merry (d 1953), of 48 Cholmeley Cres, Highgate, London; 1 s (Simon b 1966), 1 da (Maria b 1971); *Career* reporter: The Independent & South Devon Times Plymouth 1960–63, The Sunday Telegraph 1963–67; The Times: ed staff 1967–79, ed The Times Diary 1969–72, literary ed 1972–79; ed Drama Magazine 1979–81; publisher: Hodder & Stoughton 1979–92 (sr ed 1979–85, editorial dir 1985–91, publishing dir 1991–92), Orion Publishing Group 1992– (dir 1994–, publishing dir Weidenfeld & Nicolson imprint 1992–96, md Weidenfeld & Nicolson div 1996–); chm: Library Ctee Highgate Literary & Scientific Inst 1974–90, Soc of Bookmen 1986–88; chm of judges Booker Prize for Fiction 1974; memb: Arts and Library Ctee MCC 1988–, Lit Panel Arts Cncl of GB 1975–78, Mgmnt Ctee Booker Prize 1989–; author of introductions to new edns of classic thrillers (for Leslie Charteris, Sapper and Dornford Yates); *Books* Journalism (1975), Norfolk Cottage (1977); *Recreations* indulging grandson, restoring clocks, watching cricket, gossip; *Clubs* Garrick, MCC; *Style*— Ion Trewin, Esq; ✉ 48 Cholmeley Cres, Highgate, London N6 5HA (☎ 0181 348 2130, fax 0181 348 9405); Bank Cottage, Surrey St, Wiggenhall St Germans, King's Lynn, Norfolk PE34 3EX (☎ 01553 617389); Weidenfeld & Nicolson, Orion House, 5 Upper St Martin's Lane, London WC1H 9EA (☎ 0171 240 3444, fax 0171 240 4822)

TRIBBLE, Norman Reginald; s of Frederick John Tribble (d 1972), of Exeter, and Alice Maud, *née* Hooper (d 1980); *b* 17 Feb 1927; *Educ* St Luke's Coll Sch Exeter, Univ of London (BSc); *m* 20 July 1946, Christine Mary, da of Stuart Allan Moore (d 1960), of Folkestone; 1 da (Hilary b 1953); *Career* Lt 1 Bn Devonshire Regt 1945–48, served Singapore 1946 and Hong Kong 1947; accountant Inst of Prodn Engrs 1948–53; mgmnt accountant Shell-Mex and BP Ltd 1953–60, dir and proprietor Manchester Exchange and Investment Bank Ltd 1960–89; chm Varne Court Management Ltd; memb London Advsy Bd Bank Julius Baer & Co Ltd; hon life pres ACT (fndn chm 1979); memb Ct Worshipful Co of Musicians; FCCA 1953; *Recreations* opera, travel; *Clubs* Naval and Military; *Style*— Norman Tribble, Esq; ✉ 6 Varne Court, The Riviera, Sandgate, Folkestone, Kent CT20 3SU (☎ 01303 255388, fax 01303 255488)

TRIBE, John Edward; s of George Edward Tribe, of March, Cambs, and Gwendoline, *née* Morton; *b* 24 March 1946; *Educ* Oundle, Univ of Reading (BSc); *Career* in family farming businesses 1969–; dir Marcam & MDS Supplies Ltd 1978–, chm United Farmers Trading Agency 1990–95 (dir 1989–95); first chm March and Chatteris Training Group 1978–80; chm: March Branch NFU 1985–86, Agric Trg Bd Cambridgeshire Area Trg Ctee 1987–90, Fenland Crime Prevention Panel 1988–89, Cambridgeshire Co NFU 1990, E of England Agric Soc Safety Ctee 1990–93 (memb Cncl 1990–); memb Bd ATB West Anglia (LATB9) 1990–93, dir CambsTEC (Central and Southern Cambs Trg and Enterprise Cncl) 1990–, first chm Consortium of Rural TEC's 1991–; *Recreations* shooting (game and target), flying; *Style*— John Edward Tribe, Esq; ✉ Stapleford Grange, Stapleford, Cambridge CB2 5ED (☎ 01223 843098); G E Tribe Ltd, 59 Elwyn Rd, March, Cambs PE15 9BY (☎ 01354 653180, fax 01354 654457, mobile 0585 439693)

TRICKETT, Jon; MP (Lab) Hemsworth (majority 13,875); s of Laurence Thomas Trickett, of Leeds, and Rose Trickett; *b* 2 July 1950; *Educ* Univ of Hull (BA), Univ of Leeds (MA); *m* 1994, Sarah, da of Thomas Balfour, of Carlisle; 1 s (Daniel Paul b 1975), 1 da (Emma Rachel b 1975); *Career* leader Leeds City Cncl 1989–96 (cncllr 1984–96); MP (Lab) Hemsworth 1996–; *Recreations* cycling; *Style*— Jon Trickett, Esq, MP; ✉ House of Commons, London SW1A 0AA (☎ 0171 219 5074)

TRICKETT, Lynn; da of Dr Jack Fishman, of London, and Eileen, *née* Slonims; *b* 19 May 1945; *Educ* St Martin in the Fields HS for Girls, Chelsea Coll of Art; *m* 8 March 1968, Terence Wilden Trickett; 1 s (Alexander Wilden b 9 Aug 1973), 2 da (Polly Kate b 4 Nov 1977, Rosey Anna b 22 Dec 1983); *Career* designer: Planning Unit 1966–67, Wiggins Teape 1967–69, FFS Advertising Agency NY 1969–70; fndr ptnr Trickett & Webb 1971–; work exhibited and published throughout the world, winner of numerous awards in UK and USA; regular jury memb D&ADA and RSA Bursaries, external examiner various BA and MA graphic design courses, memb Graphic Design Ctee CNAA 1986–87, memb Cncl Chartered Soc of Designers, chm Nat Graphic Design & Print Awards 1990, fndr memb of Donside Student Awards; FCSD, FRSA; *Recreations* 20th Century English and American literature, Russian avant garde art, British art of the 1930s-1950s, poster design of the 1940s; *Style*— Ms Lynn Trickett; ✉ 9 Hamilton Terrace, London NW8 9RE (☎ 0171 286 5209); Trickett & Webb Limited, The Factory, 84 Marchmont St, London WC1 (☎ 0171 388 5832, fax 0171 387 4287)

TRICKETT, (Mabel) Rachel; da of James Trickett, and Margaret, *née* Hesketh; *b* 20 Dec 1923; *Educ* Lady Margaret Hall Oxford (BA, MA); *Career* asst to curator Manchester City Art Galleries 1945–46, lectr Univ of Hull 1946–49 and 1950–54, Cwlth Fund fell Yale 1949–50; St Hugh's Coll Oxford: fell and tutor in English 1954–73, princ 1973–91; *Books* The Return Home (1952), The Course of Love (1954), Point of Honour (1958), A Changing Place (1952), The Elders (1966), The Honest Muse (1967), A Visit to Timon (1970); *Style*— Miss Rachel Trickett

TRIER, Peter Eugene; CBE (1980); s of Ernst Joseph Trier (d 1938), and Nellie Marie, *née* Bender (d 1979); *b* 12 Sept 1919; *Educ* Mill Hill Sch, Trinity Hall Cambridge (Mathematical Wrangler, MA); *m* 1946, Margaret Nora, da of Frederick James Holloway (d 1964), of Shoreham-by-Sea; 3 s (Michael b 1949, Colin b 1951, Nicholas b 1953); *Career* RN Scientific Serv 1941–50; dir: Mullard Research Labs 1953–69, Philips Electronics 1969–85; chm Def Sci Advsy Cncl 1981–85, pro chllr Brunel Univ 1980– (chm Cncl 1973–79), pres Inst of Mathematics 1982 and 1983; Liveryman Worshipful Co of Scientific Instrument Makers; memb Mgmnt Ctee The Wine Soc 1977–92; Hon DTech Brunel 1975; Glazebrook medal and prize Inst of Physics 1984; FEng 1978, FIEE, FInstP, FIMA; *Recreations* travel, mathematics, railway history, Trier family history; *Clubs* Old Millhillians; *Style*— Peter Trier, Esq, CBE, FEng; ✉ Yew Tree House, Bredon, Tewkesbury, Glos GL20 7HF (☎ 01684 772200)

TRIESMAN, David Maxim; s of Michael Triesman (d 1992), of London, and Rita, *née* Lubran (d 1986); *b* 30 Oct 1943; *Educ* Stationers' Company's Sch London, Univ of Essex (BA, MA), King's Coll Cambridge; *partner* Michelene Dinah Wandor; *Career* research offr in addictions Inst of Psychiatry Univ of London 1970–74, seconded to ASTMS 1974–75, sr lectr and co-ordinator of postgraduate research in social scis South Bank Poly (now Univ of the South Bank) 1975–84, dep gen sec Nat Assoc of Teachers in Further and Higher Educn 1984–93, gen sec Assoc of Univ Teachers 1993–; visiting prof in social economics S Lawrence Univ 1977; chm Teacher's Panel Burnham FHE Ctee 1980–84; memb: Kensington, Chelsea and Westminster AHA 1976–82, Univ Entrance and Schs Examinations Bd for social sci 1980–84, Home Office Consultative Ctee on Prison Educn 1980–83, Greater London Manpower Bd (additional memb GLC) 1981–86, TUC Public Servs Ctee 1984–; memb: Highgate Literary and Scientific Inst 1990, Charles Rennie MacKintosh Soc; FSS 1984, FRSA 1992; *Books* The Medical and Non-Medical Use of Drugs (1970), Football Mania (with G Vinai, 1972), Football in London (1985), College Administration (1988), Managing Change (1991); *Recreations* football (memb Tottenham youth team 1961–63), walking, fine art and print collecting, blues guitar; *Clubs* Tottenham Hotspur Supporters', Middlesex CCC, Reform; *Style*— David Triesman, Esq; ✉ Association of University Teachers, United House, 9 Pembridge Road, London W11 3JY (☎ 0171 221 4370, fax 0171 727 6547)

TRIGG, John Anthony FitzGerald (Tony); *b* 8 July 1940; *Career* Allied Domecq plc (Allied-Lyons plc until 1994): joined 1965, dir 1991–, md Ind Coope Ltd 1989–91, md Allied Breweries 1991, chief exec Allied Domecq Retailing 1992–95, fin dir Allied Domecq plc 1995–; FCMA; *Style*— J A F Trigg, Esq; ✉ Allied Domecq plc, 24 Portland Place, London W1N 4BB (☎ 0171 323 9000)

TRIGG, Prof Roger Hugh; s of The Rev Ivor Trigg, of Taunton, Somerset, and Muriel Grace, *née* Collins; *b* 14 Aug 1941; *Educ* Bristol GS, New Coll Oxford (MA, DPhil); *m* 12 July 1972, Julia, da of Wilfred Gibbs, of Taunton, Somerset; 1 s (Nicholas b 10 May 1973, d 1990), 1 da (Alison b 26 Jan 1977); *Career* Univ of Warwick: lectr 1966–74, sr lectr 1974–78, reader 1978–87, chm Dept of Philosophy 1984–91 and 1994–95, founding dir Centre for Res in Philosophy and Literature 1985–91, prof of philosophy 1987–; visiting fell: St Cross Coll Oxford 1986–87 and 1991–92, Harris Manchester Coll Oxford 1996; Stanton lectr in philosophy of religion Univ of Cambridge 1997; pres: British Soc for the Philosophy of Religion 1993–96, Mind Assoc 1997–98; JP Warwickshire 1981–91; *Books* Pain and Emotion (1970), Reason and Commitment (1973), Reality at Risk (1980, revised edn 1989), The Shaping of Man (1982), Understanding Social Science (1985), Ideas of Human Nature (1988), Rationality and Science (1993); *Clubs* Worcestershire CCC; *Style*— Prof Roger Trigg; ✉ Department of Philosophy, University of Warwick, Coventry CV4 7AL (☎ 01203 523421, fax 01203 523019)

TRIGGER, His Hon Judge; Ian James Campbell; s of Lt Walter James Trigger (d 1961), and Mary Elizabeth, *née* Roberts (d 1984); *b* 16 Nov 1943; *Educ* Ruthin Sch Wales, Univ Coll of Wales Aberystwyth (LLB), Downing Coll Cambridge (MA, LLM); *m* 28 Aug 1971, Jennifer Ann, da of Harry Colin Downs (d 1986); 2 s (Ieuan Mungo Campbell b 12 Oct 1973, Simon Huw Campbell b 21 April 1977); *Career* lectr in law UWIST 1967–70, called to the Bar Inner Temple 1970 (major scholar 1968), in practice Northern Circuit 1970–93, asst recorder 1986–90, recorder 1990–93, circuit judge (Northern Circuit) 1993–; pres Mental Health Appeal Trbl 1995–; pt/t chm: Social Security Appeal Tbnl 1983–93, Med Appeal Tbnl 1989–93, Disability Appeal Tbnl 1992–93; churchwarden St Saviour's Church Oxton 1986–88; chm: Vale of Clwyd Alliance 1993–, Denbighshire branch Campaign for the Protection of Rural Wales 1996–; *Recreations* preserving the countryside from the ravages of greed and the Church from mediocrity; *Style*— His Hon Judge Trigger; ✉ Queen Elizabeth II Law Courts, Derby Square, Liverpool L2 1XA (☎ 0151 473 7373)

TRIGGS, Helen Lois; da of Robert Roy Triggs, of Hull, and Ethel, *née* Pettican (d 1974); *b* 16 Nov 1950; *Educ* Beverley HS Yorkshire, Univ of Leicester (BA), Hull Coll of Commerce (LCC private sec's Dip); *Career* editorial asst Orbis Publishing 1973, account exec Bell Capper Assoc 1975; Leslie Bishop Co: account exec 1978, dir 1981, jt md 1985, md 1988; dep chm Shandwick PR Ltd 1990–92 (acquired Leslie Bishop Co 1990), dir Cameron Choat and Partners 1992–; FIPR, memb Mktg Soc; *Recreations* dressage, travel; *Clubs* British Horse Soc Dressage Group; *Style*— Ms Helen Triggs; ✉ Cameron Choat and Partners, Bury House, 126 Cromwell Road, London SW7 (☎ 0171 373 4537)

TRIMBLE, (William) David; MP (UU) Upper Bann (majority 16,163); s of William Trimble (d 1968), and Ivy, *née* Jack; *b* 15 Oct 1944; *Educ* Bangor GS, Queen's Univ Belfast (LLB); *m* 1978, Daphne Elizabeth, da of Gerald Montgomery Orr (d 1981); 2 s (Richard David b 1982, Nicholas James b 1986), 2 da (Victoria Claire b 1984, Sarah Elizabeth b 1992); *Career* called to the Bar of NI 1969; sr lectr Faculty of Law Queen's Univ Belfast 1977–90 (lectr 1968–77), ed NI Law Reports 1975–90; MP (UU) Upper Bann 1990–, ldr UU 1995–; *Books* Housing Law in Northern Ireland (co-author, 1984), Human Rights and Responsibilities in Britain and Ireland (co-author, 1986); *Style*— David Trimble, Esq, MP; ✉ 2 Queen St, Lurgan, Northern Ireland BT66 8BQ (☎ 01762 328088, fax 01762 322343)

TRIMLESTOWN, 20 Baron (I 1461); Anthony Edward Barnewall; s of 19 Baron Trimlestown (d 1990), and his 1 w, Muriel, *née* Schneider (d 1937); *b* 2 Feb 1928; *Educ* Ampleforth; *m* 1, 1963 (m dis 1973), Lorna Margaret Marion (d 1988), da of late Charles Douglas Ramsay; m 2, 1977, Mary Wonderly, er da of late Judge Thomas F McAllister, of Grand Rapids, Michigan, USA; *Heir* bro, Hon Raymond Charles Barnewall b 29 Dec 1930; *Career* late Irish Gds; yacht designer with late Jack Jones; shipbroker; sales exec P & O Shipping Co; *Style*— The Rt Hon the Lord Trimlestown; ✉ Ada, Michigan 49301, USA

TRINGHAM, David Lawrence; s of George William Tringham (d 1986), of Grasse, France, and Madeleine Joyce, *née* De Courcy (d 1987); *b* 13 March 1935; *Educ* Bedford Modern, Preston Manor GS; *m* 24 Oct 1962, Annette Alberte, da of Raymond Andre Schmitt (d 1987), of Paris; 2 da (Andréa Fréderique b 18 March 1966, Gaia Frances b 3 April 1970); *Career* Nat Serv Bombardier 39 Heavy Field Regt 1953–55; entered film indust under Sir Michael Balcon at Ealing Studios 1955, asst dir Lawrence of Arabia 1961–62; first asst dir working with: David Lean, Joseph Losey, Richard Lester, Sidney Lumet, Don Siegel, John Schlesinger amongst others; writer of numerous screenplays, adaptor and dir The Last Chapter; *Recreations* painting and drawing, reading and writing in the sun; *Style*— David Tringham, Esq; ✉ 40 Langthorne St, London SW6 6JY

TRINICK, Anthony Graham Kyle (Tony); s of Alexander Leslie Trinick (d 1983), and Jean Edna Kyle, *née* Ferrier (d 1983); *b* 26 Oct 1943; *Educ* St Dunstan's Coll Catford, Borough Poly London (ONC, Dip in H & V Engrg, HNC); *m* 1967, Clare Elisabeth, da of Dr Paul Freeman; 2 s (Mark David Kyle b 21 Sept 1973, Andrew Timothy Kyle b 5 April 1977); *Career* Haden Young Ltd: apprentice 1962–66, engr 1966–73, design mangr Lloyds Computer Centre 1973–77, project mangr Haden International 1977–81, project dir Torness NPS 1981–84, project dir Aldermaston AWRE 90 Building 1984–87, HQ dir 1987–91, dir Haden Young Ltd 1987, dir Haden Building Services Ltd and Haden International Ltd 1992–95; princ Tritone Partnership 1995–, visiting prof Dept of Architecture and Building Technol Univ of Nottingham 1995–, devpt dir Fox Linton Assoc (interior design and architecture) 1996–; memb: American Soc for Heating, Refrigeration and AC Engrs 1970, Assoc of Project Mangrs 1979; Freeman City of London, Liveryman Worshipful Co of Fan Makers; CEng 1990; FCIBSE 1989, FEng 1994; *Recreations* sailing, swimming, walking, bee keeping (memb Kent Beekeepers' Assoc); *Clubs* Portcullis, IOD; *Style*— Tony Trinick, Esq, FEng; ✉ Tritone Partnership, 64 Towncourt Crescent, Pettswood, Orpington, Kent BR5 1PJ (☎ 01689 820838, fax 01689 890488)

TRIPP, Rt Rev Howard George; s of Basil Howard Tripp (d 1981), and Alice Emily, *née* Haslett (d 1985); *b* 3 July 1927; *Educ* The John Fisher Sch Purley, St John's Seminary Wonersh Guildford; *Career* asst priest: St Mary's Blackheath SE3 1953–56, Our Lady Queen of Peace E Sheen 1956–62; asst fin sec RC Diocese of Southwark 1962–68, parish priest Our Lady Queen of Peace E Sheen 1965–71, dir Southwark Catholic Children's Soc 1971–80, auxiliary bishop Southwark and titular bishop of Newport 1980–; chm: London Churches Gp 1992–, Churches' Ctee for Hosp Chaplains 1993–; *Recreations* vegetable gardening; *Style*— The Rt Rev Howard Tripp; ✉ 8 Arterberry Road, London SW20 8AJ (☎ 0181 946 4609, fax 0181 947 9117)

TRIPPIER, Sir David; kt (1992), RD, JP (Rochdale 1975), DL (Lancashire 1994); s of Maj Austin Wilkinson Trippier, MC (d 1993), of Norden, Rochdale, Greater Manchester, and Mary Trippier (d 1974); *b* 15 May 1946; *Educ* Bury GS; *m* 1975, Ruth Worthington; 3 s; *Career* cmmnd Offr Royal Marines Reserve 1968; MP (Cons): Rossendale 1979–83, Rossendale and Darwen 1983–92; PPS to Kenneth Clarke as min of state for health DHSS 1982–83; Parly under sec of state: for trade and indust 1983–85, Dept of Employment 1985–87, Dept of the Environment 1987–89; min of state DOE 1989–92; sec Cons Parly Def Ctee; ldr Cons Gp Rochdale Cncl 1974–76 (cncllr 1969–78); nat vice chm Assoc of Cons Clubs 1980, dep chm Cons Pty May-Dec 1990; chm: Vector Investments Ltd, W H Ireland Ltd Stockbrokers, Murray V C T PLC, Sir David Trippier & Associates Ltd; dir: St Modwen Properties plc, Dunlop Heywood Ltd, Murray Income Investment Trust PLC, Inter Lotto Ltd; conslt: Halliwell Landau slrs, Halliday Meecham architects, Waste Management Ltd; govr Manchester GS 1993–; fndr: Rossendale Enterprise Trust, Rossendale Groundwork Trust; Hon Col Royal Marines Reserve Merseyside 1996–; memb Stock Exchange 1968–; *Style*— Sir David Trippier, RD, JP, DL

TRISTEM, (Cyril Edward) Rossiter (Ross); *b* 26 Aug 1939; *Educ* Henley Royal GS, Univ of Nottingham (BSc), Univ of Warwick (PhD); *Career* res asst Atomic Weapon Res Establishment 1961–66, asst Police Res and Planning Branch Home Office 1966–70; Operational Res Unit DHSS: mangr 1970–73, head Strategic Studies Div 1973–77; head Policy Analysis Div HM Treasy 1977–83, seconded to Fin Mgmnt Unit Cabinet Office 1982–83; Audit Cmmn: dir of local govt studies 1983–89, dir of health and personal social servs studies 1989–94; seconded as dir NHS Trust Fedn 1994–96; hon prof Warwick Business Sch (memb bd 1990–); author of numerous papers; *Style*— Ross Tristem, Esq; ✉ Watermans, Harpsden Way, Henley-on-Thames, Oxon RG9 1NX (☎ 01491 578741)

TRITTON, Alan George; DL (Essex 1993); s of George Henton Tritton, of Lyons Hall, Essex, and Iris Mary, *née* Baillie; *b* 2 Oct 1931; *Educ* Eton; *m* 1, 1958 (m dis), Elizabeth Clare Tritton, QC, *qv*, *née* d'Abreu; 2 s, 1 da; m 2, 1972, Diana Marion Spencer; *Career* memb Br Schs Exploring Soc Expedition Arctic Norway 1949, served 1 Bn Seaforth Highlanders Malaya 1950–52 (wounded in action Pahang), ldr S Orkneys Falkland Island Dependencies Survey Base 1952–54; dir: Barclays Bank 1974–91 (joined 1954), Mercantiile Credit 1973–90; vice pres Equitable Life Assurance Society 1983– (dir 1976–); chm: University Life Assurance Society 1994–, Plantation & General Investments PLC 1994–, Permanent Insurance Co Ltd 1995–; advsr to Barclays Bank for India 1991–; Royal Geographical Soc: memb Cncl 1975–, a vice pres 1983–86, hon treas 1984–; chm: Westminster Abbey Investment Ctee 1976–94, Calcutta Tercentenary Tst 1989–; memb: Ctee Br Trans Arctic Expedition 1966–69, Ctee Br Everest SW Face Expedition 1974–75, Mgmnt Ctee Mount Everest Fndn 1976–81, Ctee Scott Polar Research Inst 1976–80, Cncl Fndn for Aviation and Tourism New Delhi 1993–; High Sheriff of Essex 1992–93; *Clubs* Boodle's, Pratt's, Antarctic, Geographical, Essex, Tollygunge, Calcutta; *Style*— Alan Tritton, Esq, DL; ✉ c/o Directors' Office, Royal Geographical Society, 1 Kensington Gore, London SW7 2AR (☎ 0171 589 0648)

TRITTON, Maj Sir Anthony John Ernest; 4 Bt (UK 1905); s of Maj Sir Geoffrey Ernest Tritton, 3 Bt, CBE (d 1976); *b* 4 March 1927; *Educ* Eton; *m* 1957, Diana, da of Rear Adm St John Aldrich Micklethwait, CB, DSO; 1 s, 1 da (Clarissa); *Heir* s, Jeremy Ernest Tritton; *Career* Maj (ret) The Queen's Own Hussars; farmer; *Recreations* shooting, fishing; *Clubs* Cavalry and Guards'; *Style*— Maj Sir Anthony Tritton, Bt; ✉ River House, Heytesbury, Warminster, Wilts BA12 0EE

TRITTON, (Elizabeth) Clare (Mrs McLaren-Throckmorton); QC (1988); da of Prof A L d'Abreu, CBE (d 1976), of Coughton, Warwickshire, and Elizabeth Throckmorton (d 1970); *b* 18 Aug 1935; *Educ* Convent of The Holy Child, Mayfield St Leonards, Univ of Birmingham (BA); *m* 1 (m dis 1971), Alan George Tritton, DL, *qv*; 2 s (Guy b 18 Nov 1963, Charles b 12 May 1965), 1 da (Christina Margaret (Mrs Williams) b 24 Sept 1960); m 2, 21 Dec 1973, Andrew McLaren; *Career* called to the Bar 1968; chm The Bar European Group 1982–84, UK rapporteur to FIDE Sept 1988, vice chm Int Practice Ctee Bar Cncl 1988–90; non-exec dir Severn Trent plc 1991–; memb Cmmn on the Legislative Process of the Hansard Soc for Parly Govt 1991–93, fndr Bar European News, author of numerous legal articles; memb Euro Ctee Br Invisible Exports Cncl, independent dir FIMBRA 1991–, cmmr Monopolies and Mergers Cmmn 1993–; tstee dir Birmingham Royal Ballet 1996–; *Books* Towards A Community Air Transport Policy (contrib, 1989); *Recreations* travelling, gardening, reading; *Style*— Mrs Clare Tritton, QC; ✉ Coughton Court, Alcester, Warwickshire B49 5JA (☎ 01789 400777); The Manor, Molland, S Molton, N Devon EX36 3ND (☎ 01769 550325, car 0860 564320)

TRITTON, Jeremy Ernest; s and h of Sir Anthony Tritton, 4 Bt; *b* 6 Oct 1961; *Style*— Jeremy Tritton, Esq; ✉ 6 St Stephen's Terrace, London SW8 1DH (☎ 0171 582 9326)

TRITTON, Peter Robert Jolliffe; s of Lt-Col J H Tritton, MBE (d 1988), and Pamela, *née* Skewes-Cox; *b* 22 May 1951; *Educ* Charterhouse; *m* 9 Sept 1975, Hon Sally Louise Nelson, yr da of 2 Baron Nelson of Stafford (d 1995); 1 s (Jonathan James Hedley b 1981), 1 da (Emma Pamela Louise b 1986); *Career* dir Alexander Howden Insurance Brokers 1980–85; dir of PR: Alexander Howden Group 1985–, Alexander & Alexander Services UK plc 1988–; *Recreations* shooting, organ music, good food; *Style*— Peter Tritton, Esq; ✉ Weasel Cottage, Brent Pelham, Herts SG9 0HH (☎ 01279 777584); Alexander Howden Group Ltd, 8 Devonshire Square, London EC2M 4PL (☎ 0171 623 5500, fax 0171 626 1178, telex 882171 HOWDEN G, car tel 0831 111619)

TROLLOPE, Andrew David Hedderwick; QC (1991); s of Arthur George Cecil Trollope, of Overton, Hants, and Rosemary, *née* Hodson; *b* 6 Nov 1948; *Educ* Charterhouse, Univ of Nancy; *m* 1978, Anne Forbes; 2 s (Harvey Evelyn b 16 Jan 1980, Francis Henry b 2 Nov 1981); *Career* called to the Bar Inner Temple 1971, recorder of the Crown Court 1989– (asst recorder 1984), jt head of chambers; memb: Criminal Bar Assoc Ctee 1991–, SE Circuit Ctee 1990–93 and 1994–; *Recreations* opera, jazz, travel, tennis, sailing; *Clubs* Hurlingham; *Style*— Andrew Trollope, Esq, QC; ✉ 1st Floor, 1 Middle Temple Lane, Temple, London EC4Y 9AA (☎ 0171 583 0659, fax 0171 353 0652)

TROLLOPE, Sir Anthony Simon; 17 Bt (E 1642), of Casewick, Co Lincoln; o s of Sir Anthony Owen Clavering Trollope, 16 Bt (d 1987), and Joan Mary Alexis, *née* Gibbes; *b* 31 Aug 1945; *Educ* Sydney Univ (BA); *m* 1969, Denise, da of Trevern Thompson, of N Sydney, NSW, Australia; 2 da (Kellie Yvette b 1970, Analese Christine b 1972); *Heir* bro, Hugh Irwin Trollope, *qv*; *Style*— Sir Anthony Trollope, Bt; ✉ Churinga Lodge, 28 Midson Rd, Oakville, NSW 2765, Australia

TROLLOPE, Hugh Irwin; yr s of Sir Anthony Owen Clavering Trollope, 16 Bt (d 1987); bro and hp of Sir Anthony Simon Trollope, 17 Bt, *qv*; *b* 31 March 1947; *m* 1971, Barbara Anne, da of William Ian Jamieson, of Lawley Crescent, Pymble, NSW, Australia: 1 s (Andrew Ian b 1978), 2 da (Edwina Anne b 1976, Jennifer Kate b 1980); *Style*— Hugh Trollope, Esq; ✉ Casewick Cottage, 26 Bayswater Road, Lindfield, NSW 2070, Australia

TROLLOPE, Joanna (Mrs Curteis); OBE (1996); da of Arthur George Cecil Trollope, of Overton, Hampshire, and Rosemary, *née* Hodson; *b* 9 Dec 1943; *Educ* Reigate Co Sch For Girls, St Hugh's Coll Oxford (MA); *m* 1, 14 May 1966 (m dis 1984), David Roger William Potter, *qv*, s of William Edward Potter, of Durweston, Dorset; 2 da (Louise (Mrs Paul Ansdell) b 15 Jan 1969, Antonia (Mrs Jonathan Prentice) b 23 Oct 1971); m 2, 12 April 1985, Ian Bayley Curteis, *qv*, s of John Richard Jones, of Lydd, Romney Marsh; *Career* writer; Info Res Dept FO 1965–67, English teacher in various schs, feature writer Harpers and Queen, freelance work for maj newspapers; patron Co of Glos Community Fndn; fndr and co-tstee Joanna Trollope Charitable Tst; memb: Soc of Authors, PEN, Trollope Soc, Romantic Novelists' Assoc, West Country Writers' Assoc; *Books* Parson Harding's Daughter (Historical Novel of the Year, 1980), The Taverners' Place (1986), Britannia's Daughters (1983), The Choir (1988), A Village Affair (1989), A Passionate Man (1990), The Rector's Wife (1991), The Men and the Girls (1992), A Spanish Lover (1993), The Best of Friends (1995), A Country Habit - An Anthology (ed and introduction, 1993), Next of Kin (1996); under pseudonym Caroline Harvey: Legacy of Love (1992), A Second Legacy (1993), A Castle in Italy (1993), Parson Harding's Daughter (reissue, Corgi, 1995), The Steps of the Sun (1996); *Style*— Miss Joanna Trollope, OBE; ✉ c/o Peters, Fraser and Dunlop, Fifth Floor, The Chambers, Chelsea Harbour, London SW10 0XF

TROMANS, District Judge Christopher John; s of Percy Tromans (d 1979), and Phyllis Eileen, *née* Berryman (d 1991); *b* 25 Nov 1942; *Educ* Truro Sch, St Edmund Hall Oxford (MA); *m* 31 May 1969, Gillian, da of John Delbridge Roberts (d 1966); 1 s (Andrew b 1972), 1 da (Sarah b 1970); *Career* admitted slr 1968; ptnr: Sitwell Money and Murdoch Truro 1971–79, Murdoch Tromans and Hoskin Truro and Redruth 1979–88, Murdoch Tromans Truro 1988–92; NP 1970; memb No 4 SW Legal Aid Area Ctee and Appeals Panel 1982–92, dep High Ct and County Ct registrar W Circuit 1987–90, dep district judge 1991–92, jt district judge Plymouth District Registry of High Ct and Plymouth Co Ct 1992–, nominated care district judge 1996; visitng lectr Univ of Plymouth 1995–; memb Lions Club of Tavistock, govr Truro Sch (dep chm 1978–91), memb Royal Inst of Cornwall; hon memb W Circuit 1992; ACIArb 1978, FRSA 1990; *Recreations* country life, travel, military history; *Clubs* East India, Plymouth Athenaeum, West Devon (Tavistock); *Style*— District Judge Christopher Tromans; ✉ The Law Courts, Armada Way, Plymouth, Devon PL1 2ER (☎ 01752 674808, fax 01752 661447)

TROMPETER, Dr Richard Simon; s of Nysen Trompeter, and Betty, *née* Rubin; *b* 27 Jan 1946; *Educ* Orange Hill Co GS for Boys London, Guy's Hosp Med Sch (MB BS); *m* 26 March 1978, Barbara Ann, da of Ervin Blum; 2 s (Alexander b 1979, Nicholas b 1981), 1 da (Rebecca b 1986), 1 step da (Sara b 1973); *Career* house surgn Guy's Hosp and house physician St Mary Abbots Hosp 1970–71; sr house offr 1971–74: Renal Unit Royal Free Hosp, paediatrics Guy's Hosp and The London Hosp, neonatal paediatrics John Radcliffe Hosp, Gt Ormond St Hosp; registrar Hosp for Sick Children Gt Ormond St 1975–77, res fell Dept of Immunology Inst of Child Health 1977–78, hon sr registrar and lectr in paediatrics Guy's Hosp Med Sch 1979–84, sr lectr in paediatrics Royal Free Hosp Sch of Med 1984–87, conslt paediatric nephrologist The Royal Free Hosp 1986–89 (hon sr lectr Sch of Med), conslt paediatric nephrologist Hosp for Sick Children Gt Ormond St 1986–89 (princ appt 1989–, clinical dir Medical Unit and Urology Directorate 1991–); ed Guy's Hosp Gazette 1969–70, memb RCP Standing Ctee of Membs 1976–78, jr staff rep Br Paediatric Assoc Cncl 1982–83, clinical rep Conf of Med Academic Reps 1982–83, govr ILEA Royal Free Hosp Sch 1985–89; memb: Bd of Studies in Med Univ of London 1986–89, Div of Physicians Hosp for Sick Children Gt Ormond St 1987–; chm Div of Child Health Hampstead Authy 1987–89 (memb Div of Physicians 1984–89, memb Exec Ctee 1988–89); Royal Free Sch of Med Univ of London: memb Academic Staff Assoc 1984–87, memb Educn Cncl 1984–89, memb Sch Cncl 1986–87, memb Library Ctee 1988–89; memb Exec Ctee and Cncl Renal Assoc 1989; FRCP 1989 (MRCP 1973); *Recreations* literature, theatre; *Style*— Dr Richard Trompeter; ✉ 1 Holt Close, London N10 3HW (☎ 0181 444 8985); Hospital for Sick Children, Great Ormond St, London WC1 3JH (☎ 0171 405 9200, fax 0171 829 8841)

TROOSTWYK, David Koos; s of Joseph Koos Troostwyk (d 1976), and Beatrice Isobel, *née* Thornborough (d 1978); *b* 5 Aug 1929; *Educ* Royal Coll of Art (travelling scholar, ARCA); *Career* artist; head of painting Winchester Sch of Art 1964–67, head of sculpture Sydney Coll of Arts 1977–79, former visiting lectr Slade and Chelsea Sch of Arts; work in collections incl: Arts Cncl, Tate Gallery; *Solo Exhibitions* Univ of Southampton 1966, Gulbenkian Gallery 1969, Kasmin Ltd 1971, ICA 1974, Felicity Samuel Gallery 1977, Inst of Modern Art Brisbane 1979, Matt's Gallery 1979, Akumulatory Gallery Poznan 1980, Matt's Gallery 1981, 1984 and 1994; *Gp Exhibitions* incl: Kursaal Ostende 1968, Galerie 20 Amsterdam 1968, Annely Juda Gallery 1969, Axiom Gallery 1970, Alfred Schmela Dusseldorf 1972, Int Poezie Rotterdam 1974, Int Art Fair Basle 1975, Biannual Sydney 1976, ICA LA 1978, Tate Gallery (books) 1982, Barcelona (books) 1983, Artspace Sydney 1984; *Style*— David Troostwyk, Esq; ✉ Apartment 4, 3 Chester Way, London SE11 4UT (☎ and fax 0171 735 9278); Agent: Matt's Gallery, 42–44 Copperfield Road, London E3 4RR (☎ 0181 983 1771, fax 0181 983 1435)

TROSS, Jonathan Edward Simon; s of Francis Gisbert Tross, and Audrey, *née* Payne; *b* 21 Jan 1949; *Educ* Chislehurst and Sidcup GS, UC Oxford (BA); *m* 17 June 1972, Ann Elizabeth, da of John Leslie Humphries; 1 s (David Edward b 29 Dec 1978), 1 da (Ruth Ellen b 22 Aug 1981); *Career* teacher in Kenya 1971; DHSS: grad trainee 1972–77, princ 1977–84, asst sec Supp Benefit Review 1984–87; asst dir Corp Div Barclays Bank 1987–90, head Pharmaceutical Indust Branch Dept of Health 1990–91, head Fin Div DSS (formerly DHSS) 1991–94, dir Corp Mgmnt Gp 1994–; *Recreations* football, theatre, books, allotment; *Clubs* Fulham FC; *Style—* Jonathan Tross, Esq; ✉ DSS, Richmond House, 79 Whitehall, London SW1A 2NS (☎ 0171 238 0706)

TROTMAN, Palma Noreen Sarah; da of Algernon Bernard Harcourt (d 1941), of Jersey, and Irene Priscilla, *née* McFarling (d 1951); *Educ* Jersey Ladies Coll, St Anne's Coll Oxford (MA); *m* 1945, Jack Harry Walter Trotman, s of Harry Walter Trotman (d 1964); *Career* novelist; formerly with British FO, sometime tutor Queen's Univ Kingston Ontario and magazine ed; author of 20 diplomatic thrillers under Palma Harcourt pseudonym, novels published in UK, USA and translated into numerous languages; most recent books: Double Deceit (1990), The Reluctant Defector (1991), Cue for Conspiracy (1992), Bitter Betrayal (1993), The Vermont Myth (1994), Shadows of the Past (1996); *Recreations* reading and writing; *Style—* Ms Palma Harcourt; ✉ Murray Pollinger Literary Agency, 222 Old Brompton Rd, London SW5 01BZ (☎ 0171 373 3711, fax 0171 373 3775)

TROTMAN-DICKENSON, Sir Aubrey Fiennes; kt (1989); s of Edward Newton Trotman-Dickenson, MC (d 1977), of Alresford, and Violet Murray, *née* Nicoll (d 1989); *b* 12 Feb 1926; *Educ* Winchester, Balliol Coll Oxford (MA, BSc), Univ of Manchester (PhD), Univ of Edinburgh (DSc); *m* 11 Aug 1953, Danusia Irena, da of Maj Eugeniusz Karel Hewell (d 1955), of Warsaw; 2 s (Casimir b 1955, Dominic b 1961), 1 da (Beatrice b 1957); *Career* tech offr EI Pont de Nemours USA 1953–54, lectr Univ of Edinburgh 1954–60, prof of chemistry Univ Coll of Wales Aberystwyth 1960–68; princ: UWIST 1968–88, Univ Coll Cardiff 1987–88, Univ of Wales Coll of Cardiff 1988–93; vice chllr Univ of Wales 1975–77, 1983–85 and 1991–93; memb Wales Gas Bd 1966–72, chm Job Creation Scheme 1975–78, govr Christ Coll Brecon 1985–88, chm Kingswood Cons Assoc 1996; Hon LLD Univ of Wales 1995; *Style—* Sir Aubrey Trotman-Dickenson; ✉ Syston Court, Mangotsfield, Bristol BS17 3LU (☎ 0117 937 2109)

TROTT, John Francis Henry; s of Francis Herbert Trott (d 1969), of Coulsdon, Surrey, and Ellen Jane, *née* Tilbury; *b* 23 Jan 1938; *Educ* Whitgift Sch, Merton Coll Oxford (BA); *m* 24 April 1965, Averil Margaret, da of Harold Charles Milestone, of Caterham, Surrey; 2 s (Christopher John b 1966, Jeremy Charles b 1973), 1 da (Nicola Margaret b 1968); *Career* merchant banker; dir Kleinwort Benson Ltd 1972–86, chm and chief exec Kleinwort Benson International Investment Ltd 1986–92, exec vice-pres Bessemer Trust Co NA 1992–; dep chm Standard Life Assurance Co (dir 1974–), dir Brunner Investment Trust 1978–; *Recreations* golf, tennis; *Clubs* Union, New York; *Style—* John Trott, Esq; ✉ Odstock, Castle Square, Bletchingley, Surrey RH1 4LB (☎ 01883 743100); Bessemer Trust Co NA, 1 Angel Court, London EC2R 7HJ

TROTT, Philip David Anthony; s of Sqdn Ldr Sydney Harold Trott (d 1985), of Fareham, and Ruth, *née* Neubauer; *b* 5 June 1952; *Educ* Oxford Poly, UCL (LLB); *Career* admitted slr 1979; Dale Parkinson & Co 1977–78; Lawford & Co: articles 1978–79, asst slr 1979–82, ptnr 1982–89; ptnr: Thomson Snell & Passmore 1989–92, Bates Wells & Braithwaite 1992–; lectr and speaker at various legal conferences and seminars; memb: Industl Law Soc 1978–89, Law Soc, Employment Lawyers' Assoc 1993–, American Immigration Lawyers' Assoc 1993–; hon legal advsr Holborn Cross CAB 1979–96, advsr to Art Law 1983–84, chm Immigration Law Practitioners' Assoc 1986–88 (memb Exec 1984–90 and 1994–95); occasional author of legal articles on immigration and employment law, occasional speaker on immigration issues on radio and TV; lectr Univ of the West of England; *Recreations* sailing, swimming, playing squash, hill walking, flying, travel; *Style—* Philip Trott, Esq; ✉ Bates Wells & Braithwaite, 61 Charterhouse Street, London EC1M 6HA (☎ 0171 251 1122, fax 0171 251 2061)

TROTTER, Alexander Richard; DL (Berwicks 1987); s of Maj H R Trotter (d 1962), of Charterhall, Duns, Berwickshire, and Rona M, *née* Murray; *b* 20 Feb 1939; *Educ* Eton, City of London Tech Coll; *m* 1 June 1970, Julia Henrietta, da of Sir Peter McClintock Greenwell, 3 Bt (d 1979); 3 s (Henry b 1972, Edward b 1973, Rupert b 1977); *Career* served Royal Scots Greys 1958–68; mangr Charterhall Estate and Farm 1969, chm Meadowhead Ltd (formerly Mortonhall Park Ltd) 1973–, memb Cncl Scot Landowners' Fedn 1975– (convener 1982–85, vice pres 1986–96, pres 1996–), dir Timber Growers GB Ltd 1977–82, vice chm Border Grain Ltd 1984–; memb Berwickshire CC 1969–75 (chm Roads Ctee 1974–75), memb Dept of Agric Working Party on the Agric Holding (Scotland) Legislation 1981–82, chm Scottish Ctee of Nature Conservancy Cncl 1985–90, memb UK Ctee for Euro Year of the Environment 1986–88; memb Royal Co of Archers (Queen's Body Guard for Scotland); FRSA 1987; *Recreations* skiing, hunting, shooting; *Clubs* New (Edinburgh), Pratt's; *Style—* Alexander Trotter, Esq, DL; ✉ Charterhall, Duns, Berwickshire TD11 3RE (☎ 01890 84210, office ☎ 01890 84301, fax 01890 84651)

TROTTER, Colin John Richard; s of Maj Frederick Liddel (d 1961), and Evelyn Grace, *née* Oxley; *b* 12 Sept 1932; *Educ* Eton, RAC Cirencester; *m* 10 July 1964, Elizabeth Mary, da of Richard Joseph Stallard, (d 1986), of Monte Carlo; 1 s (Rupert Alexander John b 1965); *Career* Nat Serv 2 Lt KRRC; asst to Messrs Rylands & Co Cirencester 1956–60, res agent Wherwell Estate Andover 1961–64; owner-mangr: Mells Park Estate Frome 1964–79, Attington Stud Oxford 1979–; chm: Bristol Bd Commercial Union Assur Gp 1977–84, EDECO Holdings Ltd 1985–89; High Sheriff of Somerset 1972; memb: Co Agric Ctee Somerset 1968–74, Cncl Royal Bath and W Agric Soc 1970–82, Panel Agric Lands Tbnl 1970–89; FRICS 1970, FIMgt; *Recreations* racing, shooting; *Style—* C J R Trotter, Esq; ✉ Attington Stud, Tetsworth, Oxfordshire OX9 7BY (☎ 01844 281206)

TROTTER, Janet Olive; OBE (1991); da of Anthony George Trotter, of Canterbury, and Joyce Edith, *née* Patrick; *b* 29 Oct 1943; *Educ* Tech HS for Girls Maidstone, Derby Diocesan Coll of Educn, Univ of London (BD, MA), Brunel Univ (MSc); *Career* teacher: Hythe Secdy Sch Kent 1965–67, Chartham Secdy Sch Kent 1967–69, Rochester GS for Girls 1969–73; lectr: King Alfred's Coll of HE Winchester 1973–85, St Martin's Coll of HE Lancaster 1985–86; dir Cheltenham and Gloucester Coll of HE 1986– (following merger with Coll of St Paul and St Mary); memb: HE Funding Cncl 1992–, Teacher Trg Agency 1994–; memb and chair Gloucester Health 1993–96, chair S and West NHS Exec 1996–; contrib to various pubns on religious educn and curriculum devpt; involvement with various church orgns incl inspr of theol courses, chair Winston's Wish (charity for bereaved children); Hon DTech PECS Univ Hungary; FRSA 1988; *Recreations* walking, cycling and music; *Style—* Miss Janet Trotter, OBE; ✉ Cheltenham and Gloucester College of Higher Education, PO Box 220, The Park, Cheltenham GL50 2QF (☎ 01242 532701, fax 01242 532879); South and West NHS Executive, Westward House, Lime Kiln Lane, Bristol B12 6SR

TROTTER, John Geoffrey; *b* 13 July 1951; *Educ* Lancing, Worcester Coll Oxford (Open exhibitioner, BA English), Coll of Law London; *Career* Lovell White Durrant: articled clerk 1974–77, based New York 1980–82, ptnr London 1983–; co-chm Professional Indemnity Sub-Ctee Int Bar Assoc; memb: Law Soc, London Slrs' Litigation Assoc, City of London Slrs' Co; *Books* Liability of Lawyers and Indemnity Insurance (co-ed); *Recreations* golf, tennis, ornithology, theatre, gardening; *Clubs* Roehampton; *Style—* J G Trotter, Esq; ✉ Lovell White Durrant, 65 Holborn Viaduct, London EC1A 2DY (☎ 0171 236 0066, fax 0171 236 0084)

TROTTER, Neville Guthrie; JP (Newcastle upon Tyne 1973), MP (C) Tynemouth (majority 597); s of Capt Alexander Trotter (d 1941), and Elizabeth, *née* Guthrie (d 1992); *b* 27 Jan 1932; *Educ* Shrewsbury, Univ of Durham (BCom); *m* 1983, Caroline, da of Capt John Darley Farrow, OBE, RN, and Oona, *née* Hall; 1 da (Sophie b 1985); *Career* RAF 1955–58; CA, ptnr Thornton Baker & Co 1962–74 (now conslt Grant Thornton); MP (C) Tynemouth 1974–, chm Cons Parly Shipping and Shipbuilding Ctee 1979–85 (vice chm 1976–79); memb: Select Ctee on Defence, US Naval Inst, RUSI; former memb: Select Ctee on Tport, Trade & Indust Sub-Ctee of Expenditure Ctee, House of Commons Armed Forces Parly Scheme; conslt to: Br Marine Equipment Cncl, Go Ahead Gp, British Transport Police Federation, Bowrings plc; dir Romag plc; private bills passed on Consumer Safety, Licensing Law, Glue Sniffing; memb Newcastle City Cncl 1963–74 (Alderman 1970–74, chm Fin Ctee); formerly: memb Tyne & Wear Met Cncl, memb CAA Airline Users Ctee, vice chm Northumberland Police Authy, mil sec Cons Parly Aviation Ctee; memb: Northern Econ Planning Cncl, Tyne Improvement Cmmn, Tyneside Passenger Tport Authy, UK Atlantic Cncl; Liveryman Worshipful Co of Chartered Accountants; memb Cncl RUSI; FCA; *Recreations* aviation, military history, gardening, fell walking; *Clubs* RAF, Northern Counties, Newcastle upon Tyne, Whitley Bay, Tynemouth Cons; *Style—* Neville Trotter, Esq, JP, MP; ✉ House of Commons, London SW1A 0AA

TROTTER, Thomas Andrew; s of His Hon Richard Stanley Trotter (d 1974), of Heswall, Merseyside, and Ruth Elizabeth, *née* Pierce (d 1982); *b* 4 April 1957; *Educ* Malvern, RCM, Univ of Cambridge (MA); *Career* concert organist; scholar RCM 1974; organ scholar: St George's Chapel Windsor 1975–76, King's Coll Cambridge 1976–79; organist: St Margaret's Church Westminster 1982–, to the City of Birmingham 1983–; debut Royal Festival Hall 1980, Prom Royal Albert Hall 1986, festival performances in UK and Europe; tours to: USA, Aust, and the Far East; recording artist for Decca 1989–; first prize winner: Bach Prize, St Albans Int Organ Competition 1979, Prix de Virtuosité, Conservatoire Rueil-Malmaison Paris 1981, Franz Liszt Grand Prix du Disque 1995; ARCM, FRCO; *Style—* Thomas Trotter, Esq; ✉ c/o The Town Hall, Birmingham B3 3DQ (☎ 0121 605 5006)

TROTTER, Timothy Hugh Southcombe; s of Antony Stuart Trotter (d 1976), of Brandsby, North Yorkshire, and Marie Louise, *née* Brook; *b* 7 Jan 1959; *Educ* Wellington, Ealing Coll London (BA, capt of Tennis, capt of Rugby); *m* 31 May 1986, Caroline, da of Peter Edney Brewer; 2 s (Alexander Antony Stuart b 16 May 1989, Oliver Peter Hugh b 3 Sept 1991); *Career* marketing mangr: Lanier Business Products Inc 1980–83, Fraser Henderson Limited 1983–85; ptnr and dep md Hill Murray Limited 1985–91, fndr and chm Ludgate Communications Limited 1991–, md Ludgate Group Ltd 1991–; MCIM 1984, MIPR 1986, MInstD 1993; *Recreations* tennis, skiing, shooting, backgammon, equestrianism, theatre; *Clubs* City of London, Queen's, Harlequins RFC, O W Tennis; *Style—* Timothy Trotter, Esq; ✉ Ludgate Communications Limited, 111 Charterhouse St, London EC1M 6AA (☎ 0171 253 2252)

TROTTER, Maj William Kemp; CBE (1989), DL (Co Durham 1990); s of Lt-Col William Dale Chaytor Trotter (d 1983), of Gorst Hall, Staindrop, Darlington, Durham, and Gladys Mona, *née* Brendon (d 1996); *b* 4 Sept 1929; *Educ* Canford; *m* 6 Aug 1960, (Mary) Virginia, da of Maj Sir Reginald Culcheth Holcroft, 2 Bt (d 1978); 3 s (James William Dale b 1964, Henry Edward Dale b 1966, Philip George Dale b 1969), 1 da (Victoria Mary (Mrs Nicholas James Thomas) b 1962); *Career* cmmnd 11 Hussars (PAO) 1948, Capt 1956, Maj 1963, serv Malaya, NI, Aden, BAOR; ret 1972; chm: Bishops Auckland Constituency Cons Assoc 1974–79 and 1992–96, Northern Area Cons Assoc 1987–90; High Sheriff Co Durham 1977; *Recreations* field sports; *Clubs* Army and Navy; *Style—* Maj William Trotter, CBE, DL; ✉ The Deanery, Staindrop, Darlington, Co Durham DL2 3LD (☎ 01833 60253)

TROUBRIDGE, Sir Thomas Richard; 7 Bt (GB 1799); s of Sir Peter Troubridge, 6 Bt (d 1988), and Hon Venetia (now Hon Mrs (Derick) Forbes), da of 1 Baron Weeks; *b* 23 Jan 1955; *Educ* Eton, Univ Coll Durham; *m* 1984, Hon Rosemary Douglas-Pennant, da of 6 Baron Penrhyn, DSO, MBE, *qv*; 2 s (Edward Peter b 1989, Nicholas Douglas St Vincent b 1993), 1 da (Emily Rose b 1987); *Heir* s, Edward Peter Troubridge b 10 Aug 1989; *Career* ptnr Price Waterhouse; FCA; *Recreations* sailing ('Spreadeagle'), skiing; *Clubs* Hurlingham, Itchenor Sailing; *Style—* Sir Thomas Troubridge, Bt; ✉ 28 Lilyville Rd, London SW6 5DW; Price Waterhouse, Southwark Towers, 32 London Bridge St, London SE1 9SY

TROUGHTON, Alistair Anthony James Lionel; s of Capt James Cecil Martin Troughton, of High Wych, Sawbridgeworth, Herts, and Georgina Mary, *née* Madell; *b* 8 Jan 1954; *Educ* Wellington Coll; *m* 24 April 1976, (Helen) Mary Claire, da of George Xenophon Constantinidi, of Henley-on-Thames, Oxon; 2 s (James Anthony George Lionel b 16 May 1980, Albert Henry William (Bertie) b 19 Aug 1987), 2 da (Sarah Emily Jane b 22 May 1978, Lucy Mary b 16 July 1982); *Career* Bland Welch and Sedgwick Payne 1973–79, Seascope Insurance Services 1979–82 (dir 1981), Steel Burrill Jones Group plc 1983–93 (dir 1988), Troughton Bell Ltd 1993–96, md IMG Insurance Co Ltd London Contact Office 1996–; Liveryman Worshipful Co of Gold & Silver Wyre Drawers; *Recreations* shooting, racing, fishing, cricket, golf; *Clubs* Boodle's, City, MCC, Huntercombe Golf; *Style—* Alistair Troughton, Esq; ✉ The Old Rectory, Boothby Pagnell, nr Grantham, Lincs NG33 4DG (☎ 01476 585538, office 0171 626 6001, mobile 0468 876651)

TROULLIDES, Andrew John (Andy); s of Joannis Panayis Troullides, of London, and Mirianthi, *née* Stylianou; *b* 1 Sept 1957; *Educ* Archbishop Tenison's GS London; *m* Sept 1991, Clare Jane, da of Richard E Little; 1 da (Lydia b 29 July 1993), 1 s (William b 21 Aug 1995); *Career* Ulster TV 1974–77, Anglia TV 1978–79, J Walter Thompson 1979–82, dir Lowe Howard-Spink 1982–90, media dir Burkitt Weinreich Bryant 1990–93, md MediaCom UK Ltd (part of Grey Communications Group) 1994– (gen mangr 1993–94); fndr chm Blandford St Soc; MIPA 1993; *Style—* Andy Troullides, Esq; ✉ MediaCom UK Ltd, 1 Livonia Street, London W1V 3PG (☎ 0171 413 2274, fax 0171 413 2276, mobile 0374 105768)

TROUP, His Hon Alistair Mewburn; s of William Annandale Troup, MC, and Margaret Lois, *née* Mewburn (d 1966); *b* 23 Nov 1927; *Educ* Merchant Taylors', New Coll Oxford; *m* 1969, Marjorie Cynthia, da of Francis Graham Hutchinson (d 1976); by previous marriages, 1 s (Alistair b 1964), 3 da (Victoria b 1953, Rosalind b 1955, Claudia b 1956); *Career* called to the Bar Lincoln's Inn 1952, crown counsel Tanganyika 1955–62, sr counsel 1962–64, dep circuit judge 1975–77, recorder Crown Ct 1977–80, circuit judge (SE Circuit) 1980–95 (pt/t judge 1995–96); *Recreations* walking, gardening, golf; *Clubs* Seaford Golf; *Style—* His Hon Alistair Troup

TROUP, Vice Adm Sir (John) Anthony Rose; KCB (1975), DSC (1943, and bar 1945); s of Capt H R Troup, RN; *b* 18 July 1921; *Educ* RNC Dartmouth; *m* 1, 1943 (m dis 1952), Joy Gordon-Smith; 2 s, 1 da; *m* 2, 1953, Cordelia Mary, da of W K T Hope, of Newbury, Berks; 2 s, 1 da; *Career* joined RN HMS Worcester and RNC Britannia 1934–38, HMS Cornwall 1939–40, submarine specialist 1941, wartime serv in Submarines Turbulent H32 and Strongbow (despatches 1943), Capt 1959, Rear Adm 1969, Flag Offr Sea Trg 1969–71, Cdr Far E Fleet 1971–72, Flag Offr Submarines and NATO Cdr Submarines E Atlantic Area 1972–74, Flag Offr Scotland and N Ireland and NATO Cdr N Atlantic 1974–77; *Recreations* sailing, shooting, golf, gardening; *Clubs* Army and Navy, Royal Yacht Sqdn; *Style—* Vice Adm Sir Anthony Troup, KCB, DSC*; ✉ Bridge Gardens, Hungerford, Berks RG17 0DL

TROUP, Donald Alexander Gordon; OBE (1988); s of Francis Gordon Troup (d 1984), of Haslemere, and Olive Mary Katharine, *née* Mosse (d 1959); *b* 20 Dec 1927; *Educ* Radley, Corpus Christi Coll Cambridge; *m* 1, 22 May 1954, Alison Joyce (d 1985), da of Dr Clement Neve (d 1939), of Croydon; 3 s (Robert James b 1955, Andrew Richard b 1957, Nigel Francis b 1960); m 2, 20 Dec 1986, Anne Hanson Barnes, wid of Brian Dearden Barnes (d 1982), da of Walter Hanson Freeman, MC, TD (d 1949); *Career* ptnr Porter & Cobb 1963–85, dir Cobbs 1985–86, exec conslt G A Property Servs 1986–90, conslt Caxtons 1990–; memb Cncl RURAL 1984–95, pres RICS 1986–87; tstee Richard Watts and City of Rochester Almhouse Charities 1969–, memb Gp Bd Hanover Housing Assoc 1994– (chm South Regnl Bd 1995–); Freeman Worshipful Co of Chartered Surveyors 1978; FRICS 1954, FAAV 1970; *Books* Agricultural Holdings Act (1984); *Style—* Donald Troup, Esq, OBE; ✉ Lees Lodge, Yalding, Kent (☎ 01622 814169, office ☎ 01622 812064)

TROUP, (John) Edward Astley; s of Vice Adm Sir Anthony Troup, KCB, DSC, and Lady Cordelia Mary; *b* 26 Jan 1955; *Educ* Oundle, CCC Oxford (MA, MSc); *m* 16 Dec 1978, Siriol Jane, da of Lt-Col John Samuel Martin, OBE; 3 s (Lawrence 18 May 1985, Madoc 19 May 1989, Galen b 23 Feb 1991), 1 da (Mabyn 9 April 1987); *Career* admitted slr 1981; ptnr Simmons and Simmons 1984–95, special advsr (on tax matters) HM Treasury 1995–; memb Cncl Inst for Fiscal Studies; Freeman Worshipful Co of Grocers, Freeman City of London 1980; ATII; *Recreations* cinema, Anglo-Saxon studies, reading Moby Dick, sleep; *Style—* Edward Troup, Esq; ✉ HM Treasury, Parliament Street, London SW1P 3AG (☎ 0171 270 4300)

TROUP, Prof Malcolm; s of William John Troup (d 1971), of Toronto, and Wendela Mary, *née* Seymour Conway (d 1960); *b* 22 Feb 1930; *Educ* Royal Conservatory of Music Toronto (ARCT), Saarlandisches Konservatorium, Univ of York (DPhil Mus), Guildhall Sch of Music and Drama (FGSM); *m* 24 Feb 1962, Carmen Lamarca-Bello Subercaseaux, da of Arturo Lamarca-Bello (d 1963), of Paris, Santiago and San Francisco; 1 da (Wendela (Mrs Christopher Lumley) b 1963); *Career* concert pianist 1954–70; toured worldwide; int festivals incl: Prague, Berlin, York, Belfast, Montreal Expo, CBC Toronto, Halifax, Cwlth Arts Festival London; played with leading orchestras incl: LSO, Hallé, Berliner-Sinfonie, Hamburg, Bucharest, Warsaw, Oslo Philharmonic, Bergen Harmonien, Toronto, Winnipeg, Sao Paulo, Lima, Santiago; first performances of important modern works, numerous recordings; dir music Guildhall Sch of Music and Drama 1970–75, prof of music and head of dept City Univ London 1975–93, emeritus prof 1995; judge: CBC Nat Talent Competition, Chopin Competition of Aust 1988, Eckhard-Grammaté Piano Competition, Young Musicians of the Year; vice pres Nat PowerWorld Piano Competition, fndr and vice pres Asociacion Latinoamericana de Profesores de Piano (ALAPP/Chile), govr Music Therapy Charity Tst, chm Euro Piano Teachers Assoc, chm Beethoven Piano Soc of Europe, ed Piano Journal 1987–; external examiner: King's Coll London, Univ of York, Univ of Keele; music advsr: Royal Netherlands Govt, Br Cncl, Canada Cncl; Cwlth medal 1955, Harriet Cohen Int award; Freeman City of London 1971, Liveryman Worshipful Co of Musicians 1973 (memb Ct 1991–); hon prof Univ of Chile 1966, Hon LLD Meml Univ of Newfoundland Canada 1985, Hon DMus City Univ London 1995; FRSA 1986, memb RSM 1988; *Books* Serial Strawinsky in 20 Century Music, Orchestral Music of the 1950s and 1960s in The Messiaen Companion (1994); author of various articles in: Composer, Music and Musicians, Music Teacher, Piano Journal, Revista Universitaria de Chile; *Style—* Prof Malcolm Troup; ✉ Department of Music, The City University, Northampton Square, London EC1V 0HB (☎ 0171 477 8284, fax 0171 477 8576)

TROWBRIDGE, Martin Edward O'Keeffe; CBE (1987); s of Edward Stanley Trowbridge (d 1962), of London, and Ida, *née* O'Keeffe (d 1981); *b* 9 May 1925; *Educ* Royal Coll of Sci, City and Guilds Coll (ACGI), Imperial Coll London (BSc), American Mgmnt Assoc Coll NY (Dip Business Studies); *m* 1946, Valerie Ann, da of Royden Glazebrook (d 1948), of Eastbourne, Sussex; 1 s (Sean); *Career* dir (later gp md) Pennwalt International Corporation Philadelphia USA 1953–72, gp md Pegler Hattersley Ltd 1972–73, chm and md Martin Trowbridge Ltd 1972–; dir gen Chem Industs Assoc 1973–87; dir: Nat Radiological Protection Bd 1987–91, Investmt Mangrs Regulatory Orgn 1987–95; memb: Conseil d'Administration CEFIC Brussels 1973–87 (later chm), Advsy Ctee Euro Business Inst 1985–90; tstee Catalyst Nat Chem Museum 1986–90; Hinchley medal Inst of Chem Engrs, Int medal Soc of Chem Indust; CEng, FIChemE, ACGI, FCGI, MSCI; *Books* incl: Poems (1953), Collected Poems, Exhibiting for Profit, Centrifugation, Solid-Liquid Separation, Economics of the Process Plant Industry, The Purification of Marine Oils; *Recreations* shooting, painting, intaglio and relief printing, mineralogy, Italian literature, containers; *Clubs* Old Siberians, Frensham Gun, Boffles (NYC); *Style—* Martin Trowbridge, Esq, CBE; ✉ 51A Moreton Terrace, London SW1V 2NS

TROWBRIDGE, Rear Adm Sir Richard John; KCVO (1975); s of Albert George Trowbridge (d 1970); *b* 21 Jan 1920; *Educ* Andover GS; *m* 1955, Anne Mildred, da of Francis W Perceval; 2 s; *Career* joined RN 1935, serv WWII (despatches), Cdr 1953 (destroyer Carysfort 1956–58); exec offr: HMS Bermuda 1958–59, HMS Excellent 1959–60; Capt 1960, cmd Fishery Protection Sqdn 1962–64, Rear Adm 1970, Flag Offr Royal Yachts 1970–75; extra equerry to HM the Queen 1970–; yr bro Trinity House 1972; govr Western Australia 1980–83; KStJ 1980; *Recreations* sailing, golf, fishing; *Clubs* Army and Navy; *Style—* Rear Adm Sir Richard Trowbridge, KCVO; ✉ Old Idsworth Garden, Waterlooville, Portsmouth, Hants (☎ 0170 541 2714)

TROWELL, Dr Joan Mary; da of Gordon Watson Trowell (d 1984), and Vera, *née* Kilham (d 1969); *b* 2 Jan 1941; *Educ* Walthamstow Hall Sevenoaks, Royal Free Hosp Med Sch London (MB BS), MRCP; *m* 31 Oct 1970, John Percy Perry (d 1985), s of Percy Perry (d 1964); 1 s (Mark b 1972), 1 da (Helen b 1974); *Career* house physician London: Royal Free Hosp 1964, Royal Northern Hosp 1965, Brompton Hosp 1967, Hammersmith Hosp 1967; med registrar: Addenbrooke's Hosp Cambridge 1968, Hammersmith Hosp 1969; lectr in med Nuffield Dept of Clinical Med Oxford 1971, hon conslt physician John Radcliffe Hosp Oxford 1981, dep dir of Clinical Studies Oxford 1995–; exec of Oxon Cncl for Alcohol and Drug Use, memb Alcohol Concern; Med Cncl on Alcoholism: regnl and univ rep, memb Educn Ctee; memb and vice chm Bd of Visitors Oxford Prison until 1996, memb Bd of Visitors HMP Grendon & Springhill 1996–; memb local review ctee Parole Bd; Hon MA Oxford 1971; FRCP 1987; memb: BMA (pres Oxford Div 1992–93), Med Women's Fedn (pres Oxford Region 1991–93, Nat Cncl 1993–, Nat Exec Ctee 1994–); *Books* Topics in Gastroenterology (1975), Oxford Textbook of Medicine (contrib, 1986), Oxford Textbook of Pathology (contrib, 1991); *Style—* Dr Joan Trowell; ✉ John Radcliffe Hospital, Headington, Oxford OX3 9DU (☎ 01865 741166)

TROWER, John; s of Geoffrey Arthur Owen Trower, of Lewes, E Sussex, and Lillian Helen, *née* Watts; *b* 6 Feb 1956; *Educ* Chailey Co Secdy Sch, Lewes Priory Comp, Loughborough Univ (BSc); *ptnr* Karen Angela, da of Graham Peter Dawson; 1 s (Thomas George b 19 June 1986), 2 da (Sophie Lily b 24 May 1985, Harriet Daisy b 11 April 1990); *Career* athletics coach; competitive career (javelin): joined Brighton & Hove Athletics Club 1970, participated in English Sch Championships 1970–75 (winner 1972 with schs record), B int England v France 1978, 6 full int appearances for England 1979–83 (debut v USSR), ret from competitive athletics through injury 1983; sr nat javelin coach Amateur Athletic Assoc 1987–; played cricket, soccer and rugby at under 19 county level; recreation offr Telford Devpt Corp 1980–85; Wrekin Cncl: dep mangr 1985–87, mangr 1987–89, area mangr 1989–, business mangr Leisure 1992–; Post Office Counters Coach of the Month Oct 1989, Coach of the Year Nat Coaching Fndn 1991, Panasonic/ITV Coach of the Year 1994; *Recreations* my family, athletics; *Style—* John Trower, Esq; ✉ Rose Cottage, 58 Pave Lane, Chetwynd Aston, Newport, Shropshire TF10 9LQ (☎ and fax 01952 811802)

TRUBSHAW, (Ernest) Brian; CBE (1970, OBE 1964), MVO (1948); s of Maj Harold Ernest Trubshaw, JP, DL (d 1952), of Pembrey, Carmarthenshire, and Lumley Victoria, *née* Carter (d 1980); *b* 29 Jan 1924; *Educ* Winchester; *m* 21 April 1973, Yvonne Patricia, wid of R H Edmondson, and da of late John Arthur Clapham, of Harrogate, Yorks; *Career* RAF 1942–50, Bomber Cmd 1944, Tport Cmd 1945, The King's Flt 1946–48, Empire Flying Sch 1949, RAF Flying Coll 1949–50; Vickers-Armstrong: experimental test pilot 1950–53, dep chief test pilot 1953–60, chief test pilot 1960–66; dir of flt test and chief test pilot BAC/BAE 1966–80, dir and gen mangr Br Aerospace Filton 1980–86, pt/t memb CAA Bd 1986–93, dir A J Walker (Aviation) Ltd 1986–96, aviation conslt 1986–; Freeman City of London, Liveryman Guild of Air Pilots and Air Navigators (Warden 1958–61), memb Worshipful Co of Coachmakers and Coach Harness Makers; Derry and Richards Memorial Medal 1961 and 1964, Richard Hansford Burroughs Memorial Trophy (USA) 1964, R P Alston Medal 1964, Seagrave Trophy 1970, Air League founders Medal 1971, Iven C Kincheloe Award (USA) 1971, Harmon Trophy 1971, Bluebird Trophy 1973, French Aeronautical Medal 1976; Hon DTech Loughborough 1986; FRAeS, fell Soc of Experimental Test Pilots; *Clubs* RAF, MCC; *Style—* Brian Trubshaw, Esq, CBE, MVO; ✉ The Walled Garden, Cherington, nr Tetbury, South Gloucestershire GL8 8SN (☎ 01285 841423, fax 01285 841484)

TRUDGILL, Prof Peter John; s of John Trudgill (d 1986), of Norwich, and Hettie Jean, *née* Gooch; *b* 7 Nov 1943; *Educ* City of Norwich Sch, King's Coll Cambridge (MA), Univ of Edinburgh (MA, PhD); *m* 15 Feb 1980, Jean Marie, da of Wade F Hannah; *Career* successively lectr, reader then prof Univ of Reading 1970–86, reader then prof Univ of Essex 1986–92, prof of English language and linguistics Univ of Lausanne Switzerland 1993–; Dr(hc) Uppsala Univ Sweden 1995, fell Norwegian Acad of Arts and Scis 1995, FBA 1989; *Books* academic: The Social differentiation of English in Norwich (1974), Sociolinguistics: an introduction (1974, reprinted 17 times, 3 edn, 1995), Accent dialect and the school (1975), Sociolinguistic patterns in British English (ed, 1978), English accents and dialects: an introduction to social and regional varieties of British English (with A Hughes, 1979, 3 edn 1996), Dialectology (with J K Chambers, 1980), International English: a guide to varieties of Standard English (with J Hannah, 1982), On dialect: social and geographical perspectives (1982), Language in the British Isles (ed, 1984), Applied sociolinguistics (ed, 1984), A grammar of English dialect (with V Edwards and B Weltens, 1984), Dialects in contact (1986), Dialects of England (1990), Bad language (with L G Andersson, 1990), English dialects: studies in grammatical variation (ed with J K Chambers, 1991), Introducing language and society (1992), Dialects (1994); non academic: Coping with America: a beginners guide to the USA (1982, shortlisted for the Thomas Cook Travel Book Prize 1983, 2 edn 1985); *Style—* Prof Peter J Trudgill, FBA; ✉ Section D'Anglais, Université de Lausanne, BFSH 2, 1015 Lausanne, Switzerland (☎ 00 41 21 692 2994, fax 00 41 21 692 2935)

TRUE, Nicholas Edward; CBE (1992); s of Edward Thomas True (d 1991), and Kathleen Louise; *b* 31 July 1951; *Educ* Nottingham HS, Peterhouse Cambridge (MA); *m* 7 July 1979, Anne-Marie Elena Kathleen Blanco, da of Robin Adrian Hood (d 1993); 2 s (James Alexios Edward b 26 Aug 1981, Thomas-Leo Richard b 30 May 1984), 1 da (Sophia Miriam Marie-Louise Blanco b 10 Aug 1992); *Career* memb Cons Res Dept 1976–82, PA to Lord Whitelaw 1978–82, special advsr to Sec of State DHSS 1982–86, dir of Public Policy Unit Ltd 1986–90, dep head Prime Minister's Policy Unit 1990–95; cncllr Richmond-upon-Thames 1986–90; ministerial nominee English Sports Cncl 1996–, tstee Sir Harold Hood's Charitable Tst 1996–; *Recreations* books, Italy, opera, Byzantium; *Clubs* Travellers', Beefsteak; *Style—* Nicholas True, Esq, CBE; ✉ 114 Palewell Park, London SW14 8JH (☎ 0181 876 9628, fax 0181 876 9628)

TRUEMAN, Frederick Sewards; OBE; s of Alan Thomas Trueman (d 1970), of Maltby, S Yorks, and Ethel Bennett, *née* Stimpson (d 1992); *b* 6 Feb 1931; *Educ* Stainton Cncl Sch, Maltby Hall Mod Sch; *m* 1, (m dis 1972), Enid Elizabeth, *née* Chapman; 1 s (Rodney Fredrick Bennett b 1965), 2 da (Karen (Mrs Slight) b 1960, Rebecca Elizabeth Jane b 1965); m 2, 28 Feb 1973, Veronica; *Career* former cricket player: Yorkshire CCC 1949–68 (took 2304 first class wickets), England 1952–65 (took 307 test wickets), world record holder Christchurch NZ 1963 (243 test wickets), first man to reach 300 test wickets at Oval v Aust 1964, ret 1968; writer and broadcaster; journalist Sunday People 1957–, cricket commentator BBC, after dinner speaker; memb: Lord's Taverners, Variety Club of GB; *Books* incl: Fast Fury (1961), The Freddie Trueman Story (1966), Ball of Fire (autobiography, 1976), On Cricket (with John Arlott, 1977), You Nearly Had Him That Time (with Frank Hardy, 1978), From Larwood to Lillee (with Trevor Bailey, 1983), Fred Trueman's Yorkshire (with Don Mosey, 1984), Fred Trueman's Cricket Masterpieces (with Peter Grosvenor, 1990), Champion Times (with Don Mosey, 1994); *Recreations* golf, wildlife (chiefly birds); *Style—* Fredrick Trueman, Esq, OBE; ✉ Bay Tree Cottage, Flasby, Gargrave, Skipton, N Yorks BD23 3PU (fax 01756 748235)

TRUEMAN, John Francis; *b* 14 Feb 1943; *Career* chm S G Warburg & Co Ltd; *Style—* John Trueman, Esq; ✉ S G Warburg & Co Ltd, 2 Finsbury Avenue, London EC2M 2PA (☎ 0171 860 0494)

TRUESDALE, Geoffrey Ashworth; OBE (1995); s of Reginald Truesdale (d 1934), and Ellen, *née* Ashworth (d 1974); *b* 16 March 1927; *Educ* King Edward's HS Birmingham, Bishop Vesey's Sch Sutton Coldfield, Univ of London (BSc); *m* 5 May 1951, Beryl, da of Leslie Charles Hathaway (d 1988); 1 s (David Geoffrey b 1953), 1 da (Carolyn (Mrs Mitchell) b 1957); *Career* Water Pollution Res Laboratory (now Water Res Centre) 1947–68, chemical inspr DOE 1968–70; Balfours Consulting Engrs: joined 1970, ptnr 1976–88, conslt 1988–92; chm Consultants in Environmental Sciences Ltd 1982–92 (conslt 1992–95); pres: Euro Water Pollution Control Assoc 1984–87, Chartered Instn of Water and Environment Mgmnt (UK) 1988–89; Freeman City of London 1989; memb Co of Water Conservators (Master of Guild 1991–92); FCIWEM 1987 (predecessor bodies FIWPC 1959, FIPHE 1966, FIWES 1979–87); *Recreations* music, gardening; *Style—* Geoffrey Truesdale, Esq, OBE; ✉ Bracebridge, Oast Rd, Oxted, Surrey RH8 9DX (☎ 01883 717473)

TRUETT, Philip Arthur; s of William Arthur Truett (d 1945), of Croydon, Surrey, and Nancy, *née* Reid; *b* 14 Oct 1942; *Educ* Cranleigh Sch, Grenoble Univ; *m* 29 Dec 1973, Juliet Anne, da of Joseph Desmond Macadam, MBE, of Buenos Aires, Argentina; 2 da (Emma b 1977, Victoria b 1981); *Career* Lloyd's underwriting agent; Lloyd's 1961, dir Furness-Houlder (Reinsurance) Ltd and dir Furness-Houlder (Overseas Insurance Services) Ltd 1971–80, MWE Underwriting Agencies Ltd 1980–83, dir Minories Underwriting Agencies Ltd 1983–; memb Lloyd's 1973–; formerly capt Old Cranleighan Golf Soc, pres SE Junior Golf Soc, fndr memb Ctee Br Golf Collectors' Soc (capt 1992–93), hon librarian The Truett Golf Library, memb Ctee Annual Nat Serv for Seafarers, memb Ephemera Soc, memb Private Libraries Assoc; *Recreations* golf, golf history, golf book collecting, skiing; *Clubs* Royal and Ancient Golf, Walton Heath Golf (capt 1993), Rye Golf, W Sussex Golf, Royal Cinque Ports Golf, Lloyd's Golf (hon sec 1985–95, capt 1996), Kandahar Ski; *Style—* Philip Truett, Esq; ✉ Woodbine House, 12 Spencer Road, South Croydon, Surrey CR2 7EH (☎ 0181 686 1080); Minories Underwriting Agencies Ltd, 18 Mansell Street, London E1 8AA (☎ 0171 264 7031, fax 0171 488 2789)

TRUMAN, Prof Aubrey; s of Edwin Truman (d 1966), of Wolstanton, Newcastle-under-Lyme, Staffs, and Nellie, *née* Nixon (d 1972); *b* 9 Dec 1943; *Educ* Wolstan CGS, Univ Coll Oxford (MA, DPhil); *m* 24 July 1965, Jane, da of Harold Pratt; 2 da (Rachel b 12 Nov 1968, Emma b 26 July 1970), 1 s (Thomas b 29 Aug 1977); *Career* sr lectr Dept of Maths Heriot-Watt Univ 1978–82 (lectr 1969–78); Univ of Wales Swansea: prof of maths 1982–, head Dept of Maths, dean Faculty of Sci 1989–92, chm IT Ctee 1984–90, chm Library Ctee 1992–; sec Int Assoc of Mathematical Physics 1991–; organiser IX Int Congress on Mathematical Physics 1988 (memb Sci Advsy Ctee); ed books on stochastic processes and applications, mathematical physics ed Proceedings of the Royal Soc of Edinburgh; FRSE 1983, FIMA; *Recreations* walking and bridge; *Style*— Prof Aubrey Truman, FRSE; ✉ Department of Maths and Computer Science, University of Wales Swansea, Singleton Park, Swansea SA2 8PP (☎ 01792 205678, fax 01792 295618)

TRUMPINGTON, Baroness (Life Peer UK 1980), of Sandwich, Co Kent; Jean Alys Barker; PC (1992); da of late Maj Arthur Edward Campbell-Harris, MC, and Doris Marie, *née* Robson; *b* 23 Oct 1922; *Educ* privately in England and France; *m* 1954, William Alan Barker (d 1988); 1 s (Hon Adam Campbell Barker, *qv* b 1955); *Career* sits as Cons peer in House of Lords; Cons cncllr Cambridge City Cncl Trumpington Ward 1963–73 (Mayor of Cambridge 1971–72, Dep Mayor 1972–73), Cons co cncllr Cambs Trumpington Ward 1973–75, hon cncllr City of Cambridge 1975–; JP: Cambridge 1972–75, S Westminster 1976–82; UK delegate to UN Status of Women Cmmn 1979–81; Baroness in Waiting to HM The Queen 1983–85; Parly under-sec of state: DHSS 1985–87, MAFF 1987–89; min of state MAFF 1989–92; Baroness in Waiting 1992–; hon fell Lucy Cavendish Coll Cambridge 1980, Hon FRCPath, Hon ARCVS; *Recreations* bridge, racing, golf, antique hunting; *Style*— The Rt Hon the Baroness Trumpington; ✉ House of Lords, London SW1

TRUSCOTT, Sir George James Irving; 3 Bt (UK 1909), of Oakleigh, East Grinstead, Sussex; s of Sir Eric Homewood Stanham Truscott, 2 Bt (d 1973); *b* 24 Oct 1929; *Educ* Sherborne; *m* 1, 1954 (m dis 1958), Irene Marion Craig Barr Brown; m 2, 1962, Yvonne Dora, da of late Frank Edward Nicholson; 1 s, 1 da; *Heir* s, Ralph Eric Nicholson Truscott b 21 Feb 1966; *Style*— Sir George Truscott, Bt; ✉ BM QUILL, London WC1N 3XX

TRUSCOTT, Peter; MEP (Lab) Hertfordshire (majority 10,304); *Career* MEP (Lab) Hertfordshire 1994–; *Style*— Dr Peter Truscott, MEP; ✉ c/o European Parliament, 93–113 Rue Belliard, 1040 Brussels, Belgium

TRUSCOTT, Ralph Eric Nicholson; s and h of Sir George James Irving Truscott, 3 Bt, *qv*; *b* 21 Feb 1966; *Style*— Ralph Truscott, Esq

TRUSCOTT, Prof Terence George; s of Leonard Truscott (d 1979), of Bargoed, and Doris, *née* Lloyd (d 1994); *b* 8 May 1939; *Educ* Bargoed GS, Univ of Wales Swansea (BSc, PhD, DSc); *m* 1962, Marylin, da of Idris Evans; 1 da (Caroline Siân b 1971); *Career* post-doctoral research fell Univ of Minnesota 1964–65, sr scientist J Lyons & Co 1965–66, lectr in chemistry Univ of Bradford 1966–71, project ldr International Nickel Company of Canada 1971–73, prof and head of chemistry Univ of Paisley 1974–90, head Dept of Chemistry and Sch of Sci Univ of Keele 1993– (prof of physical chemistry 1990–93); The Dr Lee's visiting fell Christ Church Coll Oxford 1993–94; fndr pres Euro Soc of Photobiology; FRSC 1974, FRSE 1988; *Books* Flash Photolysis and Pulse Radiolysis: Chemistry of Biology and Medicine (contrib, 1983, Russian edn 1987), Excited States and Free Radicals in Biology and Medicine (1993), also ed of three text-books; *Recreations* golf, bridge; *Clubs* Trentham Golf; *Style*— Prof Terence Truscott, FRSE; ✉ Department of Chemistry, University of Keele, Staffs ST5 5BG (☎ 01782 583038, fax 01782 712378)

TRUSLER, Colin Harold; s of Harold Sidney Trusler (d 1973), and Alice Joan, *née* Angell; *b* 11 July 1942; *Educ* Loughborough GS, Wadham Coll Oxford (scholar, MA), Harvard Business Sch; *m* 1, 1965, Jill Vivienne, *née* Bullen; 2 s (Rupert Charles b 1969, Simon Edward b 1973), 1 da (Phillipa Sarah b 1971); m 2, 1982, Fiona Innes, *née* Parsons; 2 s (Felix Colin Innes b 1986, Barnaby Colin Innes b 1991); *Career* graduate trainee Public Relations Partnership 1963–66, conslt Brook Hart Ruder & Finn International 1966–69; Lloyds Bank: PR advsr 1969–72, mktg mangr 1972–78, head of mktg 1978–86; Shandwick Consultants: dir 1986–88, md 1988–90, chm and chief exec 1990–93, chm 1993–; md Shandwick UK 1993–; tstee Devpt Tst Natural History Museum 1994–; FRSA 1992, MIPR 1994; *Recreations* astronomy, family life; *Style*— Colin Trusler, Esq; ✉ Shandwick International plc, 18 Dering Street, London W1R 9AF (☎ 0171 355 1908, fax 0171 499 1926)

TRUST, Howard Bailey; *b* 6 Oct 1954; *Educ* Gonville & Caius Coll Cambridge (MA); *m* 1982, Jennifer Marshall; 2 c; *Career* slr: Lovell, White & King London 1980–85, Morgan Grenfell & Co Ltd London 1985–87; co sec Morgan Grenfell plc London 1987–89, gp legal dir Barclays de Zoete Wedd Holdings Ltd London 1989–95, gp gen counsel and sec Barclays plc 1995–; memb: Int Bar Assoc, Law Soc, City of London Slrs' Co; *Style*— Howard Trust, Esq; ✉ Barclays plc, 54 Lombard Street, London EC3P 3AH (☎ 0171 699 5000, fax 0171 699 3414)

TRUST, Peter; s of Ernest Jones Travis (d 1979), and Lillian Varley, *née* Pearson; *b* 1 March 1936; *Educ* Salford GS, Salford Royal Tech Coll, art apprenticeship Spain; *m* 7 April 1970, Doreen, MBE, da of Ernest Duckett Runcorn (d 1973); *Career* artist and illustrator; charity fndr and chm; originator Childfriend (art projects for improved hosp environments); 31 one man shows; Art into Industry; murals; public portraits and commissions; paintings in public and private collections worldwide; creator 'Art Constructions' (pre-cursor to concrete poetry); lectr on disfigurement and guidance; memb Soc of Authors; *Recreations* detective novels, walking dog; *Style*— Peter Trust, Esq; ✉ Hillview, Wester Kinsleith, Luthrie, Fife KY15 4NX (☎ 01337 870281, fax 01337 870310); Disfigurement Guidance Centre, Laserfair, PO Box 7, Cupar, Fife KY15 4PF (☎ 01334 839084, fax 01334 839105)

TRYON, 3 Baron (UK 1940); Anthony George Merrik Tryon; DL (Wilts 1992); s of 2 Baron Tryon, GCVO, KCB, DSO, PC (d 1976), and Ethelreda (da of Sir Merrik Burrell, 7 Bt, CBE); *b* 26 May 1940; *Educ* Eton; *m* 1973, Dale Elizabeth, da of Barry Harper, of Melbourne, Aust; 2 s (Hon Charles b 1976, Hon Edward b (twin) 1979), 2 da (Hon Zöe b 1974, Hon Victoria b (twin) 1979); *Heir* s, Hon Charles George Barrington Tryon, b 15 May 1976; *Career* page of honour to HM The Queen 1954–56; Capt Royal Wilts Yeo; dir Lazard Bros & Co Ltd 1976–83, chm English & Scottish Investors Ltd 1977–87; Liveryman Worshipful Co of Gunmakers; *Recreations* fishing, shooting; *Clubs* White's, Pratt's; *Style*— The Rt Hon the Lord Tryon, DL; ✉ The Manor House, Great Durnford, Salisbury (☎ 01722 782225, fax 01722 782242)

TRYTHALL, Maj-Gen Anthony John (Tony); CB (1983); s of late Eric Stewart Trythall, and late Irene, *née* Hollingham; *b* 30 March 1927; *Educ* Lawrence Sheriff Sch Rugby, St Edmund Hall Oxford (BA, DipEd), King's Coll London (MA); *m* 2 Aug 1952, Celia, da of Sidney Richard Haddon, of Rugby; 2 s (Timothy b 1960, Peter b 1961), 1 da (Susan b 1967); *Career* Royal Army Educnl Corps Offr 1948–49 and 1953–84, serv Egypt, Transjordan, Malaya, W Germany, UK, Chief Inspr and Col Research 1973–74, Chief Educn Offr UK Land Forces 1976–80, Dir Army Educn 1980–84; md Brassey's Defence Publishers 1984–87, dir Brassey's (UK) Ltd 1984– (exec dep chm 1988–95), dir Brassey's (US) Inc 1987–95 (vice chm 1994–95); memb: Cncl Royal Utd Services Inst 1978–84, Bd of War Studies London Univ 1983–94, Gallipoli Meml Lecture Tst 1984– (chm 1986–89), Bd Br Mil Studies Gp; publisher to Int Inst for Strategic Studies 1989–94, Centre for Euro Policy Studies 1990–94, Centre for Defence Studies 1990–95; First Prize Trench Gascoigne Essay 1969; govr Selwyn Sch Glos 1996–; *Books* Boney Fuller: The Intellectual General 1878–1966 (1977), The Downfall of Leslie Hore-Belisha in the Second World War (1982), articles in military and historical journals; *Recreations* garden, family, good food and wine, military thoughts; *Clubs* Naval and Military; *Style*— Maj-Gen Anthony Trythall, CB; ✉ c/o Holts Farnborough Branch, Royal Bank of Scotland, Lawrie House, Victoria Road, Farnborough GU14 7NR; Brassey (UK) Ltd, Brassey House, 33 John Street, London WC1N 2AT (☎ 0171 753 7771, fax 0171 753 7794)

TSUNEMATSU, Samuel Ikuo (Sammy); s of Takashi Tsunematsu (d 1966), of Satsuma, Japan, and Toyono, *née* Nakanoue; *b* 4 Oct 1951; *Educ* Obirin Univ Tokyo Japan (BA); *m* 15 Feb 1985, Yoshiko, da of Dr Kiyoshi Yorifuji, of Hokkaido, Japan; *Career* dir Gendai Travel Ltd 1980, md Soseki Museum London 1984, dir Y & S Co; fndr Anglo Satsuma Soc London; *Books* Soseki in London (1985), The World of Yoshio Markino (1989), Yoshio Markino - A Japanese Artist in London (1990), Chuzo Matsuyama - A Japanese Artist in London (1991), The Color of London-Markino Yoshio Gashu (1992), Alone in this World (1992), My Fair London (1993), Kochira London Soseki Kinenkan (1994); Japanese translations: Watashino London Paris Rome Inshoki (1990), Waga Riso no Eikokujosei Tachi (1990), Kirino London (1991), Jutsukai Nishi (1991), Seiyo to Toyo no Hikaku Shisoron (1992); other translations: Un artista japonés en Londres (Spanish, 1993), Un artiste japonais à Londres (French, 1993); *Recreations* reading the ancient Chinese Latin and Greek classics in order to forget the modern civilisation; *Clubs* National Liberal; *Style*— Sammy Tsunematsu, Esq; ✉ 48 Elliott Road, Croydon, Surrey CR4 7QA (☎ 0181 664 8215, e-mail khb13403@niftyserve.or.jp); 80 The Chase, London SW4 ONG (☎ 0171 720 8718, fax 0181 684 9925); Urbanisation La Colina 35, Calle Eucaliptus 15, Buzon 2824, 03734 Moraira, Alicante, Spain (☎ and fax 00 1 34 6574 4682)

TUAM, KILLALA AND ACHONRY, Bishop of 1986–; Rt Rev John Robert Winder Neill; *b* 17 Dec 1945; *m* 24 Aug 1968, Betty Anne, da of Norman Cox; 3 s (Stephen Neill b 18 June 1969, Andrew Mark b 18 Dec 1971, Peter John Norman b 26 Oct 1978); *Career* curate asst St Paul's Glenageary Dublin 1969–71, bishop's vicar and librarian St Canice's Cathedral Kilkenny 1971–74, rector of Abbeystrewry Cork 1974–78, vicar of St Bartholomew's with Christ Church Leeson Park Dublin 1978–84, examining chaplain to Archbishop of Dublin 1982–84, lectr in pastoral liturgy Church of Ireland Theol Coll 1982–84, dean of Waterford 1984–86; sec Irish House of Bishops 1988–95, memb Central Ctee World Cncl of Churches 1994–; memb: Gen Synod Church of Ireland 1976–, Governing Body Univ Coll Galway 1986–; *Recreations* travel, photography; *Style*— The Rt Rev the Bishop of Tuam, Killala and Achonry; ✉ Bishop's House, Crossmolina, Co Mayo, Ireland (☎ 00 353 96 31317, fax 00 353 96 31775, e-mail peterne@iol.ie)

TUBY, John; OBE; s of Joseph Tuby (d 1983), and Georgette, *née* Ismalun (d 1970); *b* 17 June 1923; *Educ* Private; *m* 29 May 1958, Edith Joan Redmayne, da of Col William Eric Walker, CBE, TD (d 1949); *Career* WWII Army 1941–47: Western Desert, Eritrea, Palestine, Syria and Three Force; sr exec Feeds Sales Div Quaker Oats Ltd 1953–63, exec dir of subsidiary of Thomas Tilling Gp 1963–83, dir gen Franco-Br C of C and Indust 1988–89 (pres 1982–84), dep chm Br Sch of Paris 1985–, pres The Br Luncheon Club (1916) of Paris 1981; *Style*— John Tuby, Esq, OBE; ✉ 60850 Le Coudray Saint Germer (Oise), France (☎ 00 33 44 81 62 18)

TUCK, Prof (John) Anthony; s of Prof John Philip Tuck, of Cambridge, and Jane Adelaide, *née* Wall; *b* 14 Nov 1940; *Educ* Royal GS Newcastle upon Tyne, Jesus Coll Cambridge (BA, MA, PhD); *m* 17 July 1976, Amanda Jane, da of Dr Lawrence John Cawley, of Thirsk, Yorks; 2 s (Robert James b 1979, Michael Richard b 1982); *Career* sr lectr in history Univ of Lancaster 1975–87 (lectr 1965), master Collingwood Coll Univ of Durham 1978; Univ of Bristol: reader 1987–90, prof of medieval history 1990–93, emeritus prof 1993; FRHistS 1987; *Books* Richard II and the English Nobility (1973), Crown and Nobility 1272–1461 (1985), Royal Grammar School, Newcastle Upon Tyne (with B Mains and others, 1986); *Style*— Prof Anthony Tuck; ✉ 26 Church Street, Stapleford, Cambridge CB2 5DS

TUCK, Brian Peter; *b* 16 July 1950; *Educ* Minchenden GS Southgate London; *m* Jennifer; 1 s (Michael Henry James b 12 June 1985), 1 da (Laura May b 10 Nov 1986); *Career* chief exec PaineWebber International Bank Ltd; FCA (ACA 1973); *Style*— Brian Tuck, Esq; ✉ PaineWebber International Bank Ltd, 1 Finsbury Avenue, London EC2M 2PA (☎ 0171 422 2000, fax 0171 247 2050)

TUCK, Sir Bruce Adolph Reginald; 3 Bt (UK 1910), of Park Crescent, St Marylebone; s of Major Sir (William) Reginald Tuck, 2 Bt (d 1954, s of Sir Adolph Tuck, 1 Bt, who was gs of Raphael Tuck, fine art publisher and chm and md of Raphael Tuck and Sons); *b* 29 June 1926; *Educ* Canford; *m* 1, 1949 (m dis in Jamaica 1964), Luise, da of John C Renfro, of San Angelo, Texas, USA; 2 s; m 2, 1968, Pamela Dorothy, da of Alfred Michael Nicholson, of London; 1 da; *Heir* s, Richard Bruce Tuck; *Career* Lt Scots Gds 1945–47; with Miller-Carnegie; *Clubs* Lansdowne; *Style*— Sir Bruce Tuck, Bt; ✉ Montego Bay, PO Box 274, Jamaica

TUCKER, Alistair John James; s of James Charles Henry Tucker (d 1982), and Mary Hannah, *née* Featherstonehaugh (d 1975); *b* 17 Feb 1936; *Educ* Southend HS, Keble Coll Oxford (BA, MA); *m* 2 Sept 1967, Deirdre Ann Forster, da of George Moore, of Amersham, Bucks; 1 s (Alistair b 1976), 1 da (Hannah b 1972); *Career* Subaltern The Green Howards 1958–60; exec dir within Transport Holding Co 1967–70, md Alistair Tucker Halcrow and Assoc 1970–91, dir Air Tport Practice Price Waterhouse Management Consultants 1991–95, md Alistair Tucker Ltd 1995–; special advsr UK House of Commons Tport Ctee 1992–; visiting prof Univ of Surrey 1987–; MCIT 1972, MRAeS 1980; *Recreations* walking, travel, archaeology; *Clubs* Athenaeum; *Style*— Alistair Tucker, Esq; ✉ 50 Primrose Gardens, London NW3 4TP (☎ 0171 586 0027, ☎ and fax 0171 722 7718)

TUCKER, Christopher Robey; s of Lt Leslie Freeman Tucker, JP (d 1991), of Kemsing, Kent, and Leila Annie, *née* Ison; *b* 23 March 1941; *Educ* Eversley Sch Southwold Suffolk, Elizabeth Coll Guernsey CI, Guildhall Sch of Music and Drama London; *m* 29 July 1971 (m dis 1977), Marion Edith, da of Philip John Flint, of Wellingborough; *Career* princ special effects make-up artist; active involvement in local history, archaeology, natural history; Freeman City of London 1962, Freeman Worshipful Co of Haberdashers 1962; memb: BFI, BAFTA, HHA, NPA; *Theatre* incl: Richard III 1984, Cyrano de Bergerac 1984, Phantom of the Opera 1986; *Television* I Claudius 1975, Holocaust 1976, Lillie Langtry 1979, Prince Regent 1980, War and Remembrance 1986; *Films* Star Wars 1976, The Boys from Brazil 1978, The Elephant Man 1979, Quest for Fire 1980, The Company of Wolves 1983, High Spirits 1988, Spider's Web 1990; *Recreations* antiquarian books, opera, antiquities; *Style*— Christopher Tucker, Esq; ✉ Bere Court, Pangbourne, Berks RH8 8HT (☎ 0118 984 2393, fax 0118 984 5190)

TUCKER, Colin Patrick; s of Douglas Edwin Allen Tucker (d 1981), and Bridget Tucker (d 1969); *Educ* Prior Park Coll Bath, Univ of Cambridge (BA); *m* 18 June 1966, Sarah Madeline, da of Stanley Owen Fisher (d 1986); 3 da (Rebecca Jane b 1969, Abigail b 1971, Hannah Matilda b 1976); *Career* fell Univ of Manchester 1964–65, BBC Radio Drama Dept 1969–74, script ed BBC TV Play for Today 1975–77; prodr for BBC TV: Prince Regent 1978, Fair Stood the Wind for France 1979, Shadow of the Noose 1988–89, Portrait of a Marriage 1989–90, The Secret Agent 1991, Henri 1993, Rocking the Boat 1993, Amongst Women 1995; prodr for LWT Drummonds 1984–85; memb: BAFTA, PACT; *Style*— Colin Tucker, Esq; ✉ 86 Church Rd, Richmond, Surrey TW10 6LW (☎ 0181 940 4561)

TUCKER, (Allan) James; s of Wiliam Arthur Tucker (d 1983), of Cardiff, and Violet Irene, *née* Bushen; *b* 15 Aug 1929; *Educ* Grange Cncl Cardiff, Cardiff HS, Univ of Wales (MA); *m* 17 July 1954, Marian Roberta, da of Sqdn Ldr Samuel Edward Craig; 3 s (Patrick James b 1955, Guy William b 1959, David Craig b 1962), 1 da (Catherine Marian b 1957); *Career* writer; Flying Offr RAF 1951–53; journalism in newspapers, broadcasting and magazines 1954–, pt/t univ teaching 1968–; various radio plays; memb:

Crime Writers' Assoc, Mystery Writers of America, Soc of Authors; *Books* as James Tucker: Equal Partners (1960), The Right Hand Man (1961), Burster (1966), Honourable Estates (documentary, 1966), The Novels of Anthony Powell (literary criticism, 1976), Blaze of Riot (1979), The King's Friends (1982, reissued as by Bill James 1995); as David Craig: The Alias Man (1968), Message Ends (1969), Contact Lost (1970), Young Men May Die (1970), A Walk at Night (1971), Up From the Grave (1971), Double Take (1972), Bolthole (1973), Whose Little Girl Are You? (filmed as The Squeeze, 1974), A Dead Liberty (1974), The Albion Case (1975), Faith, Hope and Death (1976), Forget It (1995); as Bill James: You'd Better Believe It (1985), The Lolita Man (1986), Halo Parade (1987), Protection (1988, televised 1996), Come Clean (1989), Take (1990), Club (1991), Astride a Grave (1991), Gospel (1992), Roses, Roses (1993), In Good Hands (1994), The Detective Is Dead (1995), Top Banana (1996), The Last Enemy (1996); *Recreations* walking; *Clubs* RAF, Druidstone; *Style—* James Tucker, Esq; ✉ c/o Curtis Brown, 28/29 Haymarket, London SW1Y 4SP

TUCKER, Prof John Barry; *b* 17 March 1941; *Educ* Queen Elizabeth GS Atherstone Warwickshire, Peterhouse Cambridge (state scholar, Kitchener Nat Meml scholar, MA, PhD); *m* 1975, Janet, *née* Murray; 2 c; *Career* Fulbright scholar and research assoc Dept of Zoology Indiana Univ 1966–68, SRC post-doctoral research fell Dept of Zoology Univ of Cambridge 1968–69; Univ of St Andrews: lectr in Zoology 1969–78, reader 1978–90, prof of cell biology 1990–, memb Ct (Senate assessor 1993–97); memb Ed Bd Development (formerly Jl of Embryology and Experimental Morphology) 1979–88; FRSE 1996; *Publications* author of numerous book chapters, papers and articles in learned jls; *Style—* Prof John Tucker, FRSE; ✉ School of Biological and Medical Sciences, Bute Medical Building, University of St Andrews, St Andrews, Fife KY16 9TS (☎ 01334 463560, fax 01334 463600, e-mail jbt@st-and.ac.uk)

TUCKER, (John) Keith; s of Reginald John Tucker (d 1976), and Nancy, *née* Harker (d 1993); *b* 24 March 1945; *Educ* Haberdashers' Aske's, Charing Cross Hosp Med Sch (MB BS); *m* 4 Oct 1975, Jill Margaret, da of Dr Thomas Oliphant McKane (d 1972), of Gtr Easton Essex; 3 s (Timothy b 1977, Alexander b 1979, Ian b 1981); *Career* house surgn Charing Cross Hosp 1969, registrar Addenbrooke's Hosp Cambridge 1971–73, sr registrar St Bartholomew's Higher Orthopaedic Training Scheme 1973–77, conslt orthopaedic surgn Norfolk and Norwich Hosp 1977–; hon clinical tutor in med Univ of Cambridge; author of various scientific papers, co-designer of Hip Replacements System 1982–; examiner for the Intercollegiate Bd in Orthopaedic Surgery 1989, external examiner in surgery Univ of Cambridge 1994–; memb: The Br Hip Soc, Br Orthopaedic Assoc (memb Cncl 1993–96); hon MD Univ of Murcia Spain 1985; memb: BMA, RSM; MRCS, FRCS, LRCP; *Recreations* family; *Style—* Keith Tucker, Esq; ✉ 77 Newmarket Rd, Norwich (☎ 01603 614016, fax 01603 766469)

TUCKER, Louis Newton; s of Sidney Tucker (d 1968), of Aust, and Elsie Louise Marion, *née* Newton (d 1971); *b* 3 Aug 1925; *Educ* Christ's Hosp Horsham; *m* 1, Nov 1949 (m dis 1963), Beryl, da of Reginald White, of Epsom; 1 s (Nicholas b 6 July 1951); m 2, 19 Oct 1966, Vera Catherine Watkins, da of George Frederick Goodwin; 1 s (Marcus Newton b 12 July 1967), 1 da (Sarah b 6 March 1969); *Career* Maj N Staffs Regt 1942–46, serv Middle E; slr 1953, formerly sr ptnr Helder Roberts & Co; dir: New Estates Ltd 1950–, Estates Property Investmt Co plc 1961–88, PSIT plc 1961–; govr Christ's Hosp; Freeman Worshipful Co of Merchant Taylors 1950; memb Law Soc, MInstD; *Recreations* tennis, gardening; *Style—* Louis Newton Tucker, Esq

TUCKER, His Hon Judge; (Henry John) Martin; QC (1975), DL (Hampshire 1996); s of Percival Albert Tucker (d 1959), of Bournemouth, and Dorothy Effie Mary, *née* Hobbs (d 1990); *b* 8 April 1930; *Educ* Downside, ChCh Oxford (MA); *m* 17 Aug 1957, Sheila Helen, da of Hugh Thomas Wateridge (d 1988), of Dovercourt, Essex; 1 s (Adrian Mark b 1958), 4 da (Helen Mary b 1959, Elizabeth Frances b 1963, Catharine Clare b 1964, Philippa Rose b 1968); *Career* called to the Bar Inner Temple 1954, dep chm Somerset QS 1971, recorder 1972–81, judge Western Circuit 1981–, resident judge Winchester Combined Court Centre 1994–; pres Cncl of HM Circuit Judges 1993; *Recreations* walking occasionally, gardening gently, listening to music; *Style—* His Hon Judge Tucker, QC, DL

TUCKER, Ravenna Michele; da of John William Tucker, MBE, of Malaysia, and Valerie Saw, *née* Hong Bee; *Educ* King George V Sch Hong Kong; *m* 8 July 1995, Timothy Quentin Leon; *Career* ballet dancer with: The Royal Ballet 1979–90, Birmingham Royal Ballet (formerly Sadler's Wells Royal Ballet); first role as soloist Pas de Trois in Swan Lake 1980; other roles incl: title role in Requiem, Juliet in Romeo and Juliet, title role in Ondine, Aurora in Sleeping Beauty, Nikiya in La Bayadere, Odette and Odile in Swan Lake, title roles in Giselle, Cinderella and Coppelia, Sugar Plum Fairy in Nutcracker, title role in The Snow Queen, Rhapsody, Afternoon of A Faun; involved with: Action Aid, Royal Ballet educn projects for schs and hosps, teaching projects; *Recreations* painting, swimming, reading, travel, needlepoint; *Style—* Miss Ravenna Tucker; ✉ c/o Birmingham Royal Ballet, Thorp Street, Birmingham B5 4AU (☎ 0121 622 5118)

TUCKER, Hon Mr Justice; Hon Sir Richard Howard; kt (1985); s of His Hon Judge Howard Archibald Tucker (d 1963), and Margaret Minton, *née* Thacker (d 1976); *b* 9 July 1930; *Educ* Shrewsbury, Queen's Coll Oxford (MA, hon fell 1992); *m* 1, 1958 (m dis 1974), Paula Mary Bennett Frost; 1 s (Stephen), 2 da (Anneli, Gemma); m 2, 1975, Wendy Kate Standbrook (d 1988); m 3, 16 Sept 1989, Mrs Jacqueline S R Thomson, wid of William Thomson; *Career* called to the bar Lincoln's Inn 1954, bencher 1979, QC 1972, recorder 1972–85, judge of the High Court of Justice (Queen's Bench Div) 1985–, presiding judge Midland and Oxford Circuit 1986–90; memb: Employment Appeal Tbnl 1986–, Parole Bd 1996–; *Recreations* gardening, shooting, sailing; *Clubs* Garrick, Leander, Bar Yacht; *Style—* The Hon Mr Justice Tucker; ✉ Royal Courts of Justice, Strand, London WC2A 2LL

TUCKER, Dr Sam Michael; s of Harry Tucker (d 1970), and Ray Tucker (d 1982); *b* 15 Oct 1926; *Educ* Benoni HS SA, Witwatersrand Univ (MB BCh); *m* 13 Dec 1953, Barbara Helen, da of M Kaplan; 2 s (Mark b 1957, Trevor b 1962), 1 da (Dana b 1956); *Career* conslt paediatrician Hillingdon Hosp Uxbridge and 152 Harley St London, clinical tutor and examiner RCP; memb Hillingdon Dist Health Authy, pres Section of Paediatrics RSM 1987–88, chm Med Advsy Ctee Portland Hosp 1987–88; assoc prof Brunel Univ Uxbridge 1988–; memb Cncl RSM 1996; *Recreations* football, golf; *Clubs* RSM; *Style—* Dr Sam Tucker; ✉ 65 Uphill Rd, Mill Hill, London NW7 4PT; 152 Harley St, London W1

TUCKEY, Andrew Marmaduke Lane; s of Henry Lane Tuckey (d 1982), and Aileen Rosemary, *née* Newsom-Davis; *b* 28 Aug 1943; *Educ* Plumtree Sch Zimbabwe; *m* 24 June 1967, Margaret Louise, da of Dr Clive Barnes (d 1979); 1 s (Jonathan b 1970), 2 da (Clara b 1972, Anna b 1982); *Career* chm Baring Bros & Co Ltd and dir various Baring subsids until April 1995, conslt ING Barings 1995–96, conslt Phoenix Securities Limited 1996–; dir Friends of Covent Garden, tstee Esmee Fairbairn Charitable Tst, tstee Classic FM Charitable Tst; *Recreations* music, tennis; *Clubs* White's, Roehampton, City of London; *Style—* Andrew Tuckey, Esq; ✉ Flat 4, 13 Cornwall Gardens, London SW7 4AN (☎ 0171 581 5710); Phoenix Securities Limited, One Laurence Pountney Hill, London EC4R 0EU

TUCKEY, Hon Mr Justice; Hon Sir Simon Lane Tuckey; kt (1992); s of Henry Lane Tuckey (d 1982), and Aileen Rosemary, *née* Newsom-Davis; *b* 17 Oct 1941; *Educ* Plumtree Sch Zimbabwe; *m* 1964, Jennifer Rosemary, da of Sir Charles Edgar Matthews Hardie, of Henley-on-Thames; 1 s (William b 1966), 2 da (Camilla (Mrs Richard Parsons) b 1965, Kate b 1970); *Career* called to the Bar Lincoln's Inn 1964, QC 1981, recorder of the Crown Court 1984, chm Review Panel Fin Reporting Cncl 1990, judge of the High Court of Justice (Queen's Bench Division) 1992–, presiding judge Western Circuit 1995–; co-chm Civil and Family Ctee Judicial Studies Bd 1993–95; *Recreations* sailing, tennis; *Style—* The Hon Mr Justice Tuckey; ✉ Royal Courts of Justice, Strand, London WC2

TUCKWELL, Barry Emmanuel; AC (1992), OBE (1963); s of Charles Robert Tuckwell (d 1986), and Elizabeth Jane, *née* Hill (d 1991); *b* 5 March 1931; *Educ* Sydney Conservatorium; *m* 1, 1958 (m dis 1970); 2 s (David Michael, Thomas James), 1 da (Jane Madeleine); m 2, 1970 (m dis 1988); m 3, 1992; *Career* princ horn LSO 1955–68, princ conductor Tasmanian Symphony Orch 1980–83, music dir and conductor Maryland Symphony Orch 1982–; final London performance Oliver Knussen's Horn Concerto (London premiere BBC Proms 1996); Hon RAM, Hon GSM; FRSA, FRCM; *Clubs* Athenaeum; *Style—* Barry Tuckwell, Esq, AC, OBE; ✉ 13140 Fountain Head Road, Hagerstown, MD 21742, USA

TUCKWELL, Dr Gareth David; s of Sir Edward Tuckwell, KCVO (d 1988), and Phyllis Courthope, *née* Regester (d 1970); *b* 3 Dec 1946; *Educ* Charterhouse, Univ of London and St Bartholomew's Hosp Med Coll (MB BS, DObstRCOG); *m* 4 Aug 1973, (Susan) Mary, da of Dr Hugh Wilfred Sansom, OBE, of Langton Green, Kent; 2 s (Jonathan b 1977, Paul b 1984), 1 da (Deborah b 1976), 1 adopted da (Alexandria b 1984); *Career* princ in gen practice 1974–86, clinical tutor in gen practice St Bartholomew's Hosp Med Coll 1976–86; dir Dorothy Kerin Tst 1986–, med dir of Burrswood Tunbridge Wells 1986–, vice pres Phyllis Tuckwell Memorial Hosp Farnham; memb Christians in Caring Professions, tstee The Burrswood Endowment Tst, memb Christian Med Fellowship; editorial advsr Healing and Wholeness magazine; Freeman City of London, Liveryman Worshipful Soc of Apothecaries 1971; MRCS LRCP 1971, MRCGP 1977, Dip Palliative Med Univ of Wales 1992; memb: Assoc of Palliative Medicine, BMA, Br Assoc of Medical Mangrs; fell Royal Soc of Med; *Books* A Question of Healing (with D Flagg, 1995); *Recreations* photography, walking, gardening; *Style—* Dr Gareth Tuckwell; ✉ St Luke's House, Burrswood, Groombridge, Tunbridge Wells, Kent TN3 9PY (☎ 01892 864349); Burrswood, Groombridge, Tunbridge Wells, Kent TN3 9PY (☎ 01892 863637, fax 01892 862597)

TUDOR, Rev Dr (Richard) John; s of Rev Charles Leonard Tudor (d 1986), and Ellen, *née* Clay (d 1981); *b* 8 Feb 1930; *Educ* Clee GS Grimsby, Queen Elizabeth's Barnet, Univ of Manchester (BA); *m* 21 July 1956, Cynthia Campbell, da of Richard Anderson (d 1951); 1 s (Peter b 1964), 1 da (Helen b 1967); *Career* RAF 1948–51; jr Methodist minister East Ham London 1954–57, ordained Newark 1957, minister Thornton Cleveleys Blackpool 1957–60; supt minister: Derby Methodist Mission 1960–71, Coventry Methodist Mission 1971–75, Brighton Dome Mission 1975–81, Westminster Methodist Central Hall 1981–95; hon devpt offr Harris Manchester Coll Oxford 1995–; Free Church chaplain Westminster Hosp 1982–93, chm Westminster Christian Cncl 1988–90; chaplain to: Int Charity Stewards Ancient Order of Foresters Friendly Soc, Lord Mayor of Westminster 1993; Hon Texan 1965, Freeman Fort Worth Texas 1970, Freeman Arkansas 1987; Hon DD Texas Wesleyan Univ Fort Worth Texas 1981; *Books* A Word For All Seasons (1991); *Recreations* motoring, cooking, photography, the delights of family life; *Style—* The Rev Dr R John Tudor; ✉ c/o Harris Manchester College, Mansfield Road, Oxford OX1 3TD (☎ 01865 271006)

TUDOR-CRAIG, Dr Pamela (Pamela, Lady Wedgwood); *née* Wynn Reeves; da of Herbert Wynn Reeves, of London, and Madeleine Marian, *née* Brows; *Educ* Courtauld Inst; *m* 1, (Algernon) James Riccarton Tudor-Craig, FSA (d 1969), o s of Maj Sir Algernon Tudor Tudor-Craig, KBE, FSA (d 1943); 1 da (Elisabeth Jocelyn); m 2, 1982, as his 2 w, Sir John Hamilton Wedgwood, 2 Bt, TD (d 1989); *Career* art historian; prof of art history: Univ of Evansville at Harlaxton Coll 1979–89 (fndr Annual Int Symposium on Inter-disciplinary Eng Medieval Studies 1984), Grinnell London 1990–; speaker in confs at Poitiers and Regensburg; lecture tours of America: Kalamazoo, Smithsonian and Nat Gallery Washington, Harvard Univ, Metropolitan Museum NY (twice), Univ Museum in Philadelphia, Stanford Univ; TV work: Richard III with Barlow and Watt 1976, Light of Experience 1976, Round Table at Winchester (Horizon) 1977, Richard III for Timewatch 1983, The Trial of Richard III for ITV (nominated as programme of the year) 1984, The Secret Life of Paintings BBC2 1986; many radio progs; ctee memb to advise on conservation: West Front at Wells Cathedral 1973–85, Exeter Cathedral 1979–86; vice chm Paintings Ctee Cncl for the Care of Churches; memb: Cathedrals Advsy Cmmn for Eng 1976–91, Architectural Advsy Panel Westminster Abbey, Cncl Soc of Antiquaries 1989–92, Cultural Affrs Ctee ESU 1991–, Ctee Fabric Peterborough Cathedral, Fabric Ctee Southwell Minster, fndr Cambridgeshire Historic Churches Tst; FSA; *Publications* incl: Richard III (1973), The Secret Life of Paintings (with Richard Foster, 1986), New Bell's Cathedral Guide to Westminster Abbey (jtly, 1986), Harlaxton Symposium Volumes; reg contributor to Arts Page of Church Times, History Today and Resurgence; *Recreations* being with animals, walking; *Style—* Dr Pamela Tudor-Craig, FSA; ✉ 9 St Anne's Crescent, Lewes, East Sussex BN7 1SB (☎ 01273 479564)

TUDOR EVANS, Hon Sir Haydn; kt (1974); s of John Edgar Evans by his w, Ellen Stringer; *b* 20 June 1920; *Educ* Cardiff HS, W Monmouth Sch, Lincoln Coll Oxford; *m* 1947, Sheilagh Isabella, *née* Pilkington; 1 s; *Career* served WWII RNVR; called to the Bar 1947, QC 1962, bencher Lincoln's Inn 1970, recorder Crown Ct 1972–74, High Ct judge Family Div 1974–78, Queen's Bench Div 1978–94, judge Employment Appeal Tbnl 1982–94; *Clubs* Garrick, MCC, RAC; *Style—* The Hon Sir Haydn Tudor Evans; ✉ c/o Royal Courts of Justice, Strand, London WC2A 2LL

TUDOR JOHN, William; s of Tudor John, of Castle House, Llantrisant, Mid Glamorgan, and Gwen, *née* Griffiths (d 1969); *b* 26 April 1944; *Educ* Cowbridge Sch, Downing Coll Cambridge; *m* 25 Feb 1967, Jane, da of Peter Clark, of Cowbridge, Mid Glam; 3 da (Rebecca (Mrs Adrian Riggs) b 1971, Katherine b 1974, Elizabeth b 1980); *Career* Allen & Overy: articled clerk 1967–69, asst slr 1969–70, ptnr 1972–, managing ptnr 1992–94, sr ptnr 1994–; banker Orion Bank Ltd 1970–72; non-exec chm: Suttons Seeds Ltd 1978–93, Horticultural and Botanical Holdings Ltd 1985–93; appeal steward Br Boxing Bd of Control 1980–; assoc fell Downing Coll Cambridge 1986–92; Freeman City of London, memb City of London Slrs' Co 1972, Liveryman Worshipful Co of Gunmakers 1994; memb: Law Soc 1969, Int Bar Assoc 1976; *Recreations* shooting, rugby football, reading, music; *Clubs* The Justinians, Cardiff and County, Bankers'; *Style—* William Tudor John, Esq; ✉ Willian Bury, Willian, Herts SG6 2AF (☎ 01462 683532); Allen & Overy, One New Change, London EC4M 9QQ (☎ 0171 330 3000, fax 0171 330 9999, car 0836 730128)

TUDOR-POLE, Edward Felix; s of David Wellesly Tudor-Pole, of Southern France, and Shirley Cecila, *née* Brown; *b* 6 Dec 1955; *Educ* KESW, RADA; *Career* actor, also singer; toured northern hemisphere with rock and roll band Tenpole Tudor; *Theatre* roles incl: Scullery in Road (Royal Ct) 1986, Churchill in Sink The Belgrano 1987, The Hon Ernest Wooley in The Admirable Crichton (Theatre Royal) 1988, Riff Raff in Rocky Horror Show (Piccadilly) 1990, Jackie Jackson in The Deep Blue Sea (Apollo); *Television* presenter The Crystal Maze (Channel 4) 1994–96; *Films* incl: The Great Rock and Roll Swindle, Absolute Beginners, Straight to Hell, Walker, White Hunter Black Heart, Horse Opera, Kull the Conqueror; *Recreations* long distance running, equestrianism, playing the guitar; *Style*— Edward Tudor-Pole, Esq; ✉ c/o ICM Ltd, Oxford House, 76 Oxford Street, London W1N 0AX (☎ 0171 636 6565, fax 0171 323 0101)

TUDOR-WILLIAMS, Dr Robert; s of David Tudor-Williams (d 1990), of Cleddau Lodge, Haverfordwest, and Nanette *née* Llewellin; *b* 4 Nov 1945; *Educ* Haverfordwest GS, Guy's Hosp (BDS, LDS, RCS); *m* 1971, Margaret Ann, da of Alfred Hector Morris; 2 s (Laurence b 6 April 1973, Dylan b 8 April 1974), 1 da (Rebecca b 16 Jan 1979); *Career* asst house surgn Guy's Hosp 1970, house surgn King's Coll Hosp 1970–71, sr hosp dental offr Eastman Dental Hosp 1972, gen practice in City and West End 1970–72, princ of gp practice Fulham 1972–80, clinical asst in oral surgery Charing Cross Hosp 1974–87; in private practice: Fulham and Esher Surrey 1980–88, Harley St 1988–; special interests: cosmetic and restorative dentistry, headaches, migraines and disorders of the TMJ 1988–; lectr Hammersmith and W London Coll: to med secs 1978–87, to dental surgery assts 1977–88; lectr and course dir to dental surgery assts BDA 1988–94; radio dentist: LBC 1989–94, London Newstalk 1152 AM 1994–; memb Panel of Examiners: RCS (Edinburgh) 1988–, Examining Bd for Dental Surgery Assts 1982–94; external examiner Royal Coll of Surgns England 1991–93; memb: BDA 1970– (chm Kingston and Dist Section 1983–84), Ealing Hammersmith and Hounslow LDC 1975–90, Br Soc of Periodontology 1985–, L D Pankey Assoc 1985–, Br Dental Migraine Study Gp 1985–, Br Soc of Gen Dental Surgery 1986–, Br Dental Health Fndn 1988–, Fedn Dentair Int 1990–, Faculty of General Dental Practice UK 1992–, American Equilibration Soc 1996–, Exec Ctee Central London Private Practitioners' Forum; MGDS RCSEd 1986, FRSM 1986; *Recreations* sailing, gardening, theatre, swimming, cycling, shooting, fishing; *Clubs* Royal Soc of Med, IOD, Esher 41; *Style*— Dr Robert Tudor-Williams; ✉ 73 Harley Street, London W1N 2ES (☎ 0171 224 3848, fax 0171 224 1706, mobile 0831 293763, e-mail 100441.441@compuserve.com); The Birches, 50 Grove Way, Esher, Surrey KT10 8HL

TUDWAY QUILTER, David Cuthbert; *b* 26 March 1921, "; *see:* Quilter, David Cuthbert

TUFFIN, Alan David; CBE (1993); *b* 2 Aug 1933; *Career* former postal and telegraph worker; Union of Communication Workers: elected to Exec Cncl 1966, full time offr 1969, dep gen sec 1979, gen sec 1982–93; TUC: memb Gen Cncl 1982–93, former memb Fin and Gen Purposes Ctee, Econ and Int Ctee, chm Social Insurance and Industl Welfare Ctee, pres 1992–93; memb Health and Safety Cmmn 1978–96; dir Trade Union Unit Trust; memb: Exec Ctee Duke of Edinburgh Cwlth Study Conf, Industl Appeal Tbnl 1995–; FRSA; *Recreations* reading, squash, West Ham Utd FC; *Style*— Alan Tuffin, Esq, CBE; ✉ c/o TUFM Ltd, Congress House, Great Russell Street, London WC1B 3LQ

TUFNELL, Col Greville Wyndham; DL (Glos 1994); s of Maj K E M Tufnell, MC (d 1976); *b* 7 April 1932; *Educ* Eton, RMA Sandhurst; *m* 1, 1962, Hon Anne Rosemary Trench (d 1992), da of 5 Baron Ashtown, OBE (d 1979), and widow of Capt Timothy Patrick Arnold Gosselin, Scots Guards (d 1961); 3 da (Caroline, Belinda (Mrs Benjamin Wright), Georgina (Mrs Edward Way)), 1 step da (Nicola (Mrs Angus Ward)); m 2, 1994, Susan Arnot, da of Edward Gordon Heath, and formerly w of David Burrows; *Career* 2 Lt Grenadier Gds 1952, Adj 2 Bn 1959–61, GSO 3 WO (MO2) 1962–63, Staff Coll 1964, Maj 1965, DAQMG London Dist 1966–67, GSO 2 HQ Div 1969–71, Lt-Col 1971, cmdg 1 Bn Grenadier Gds 1971–73 (despatches 1972), Bde Maj Household Div 1974–76, Col 1976, cmdg Grenadier Gds 1976–78, Yeoman of the Guard Exon 1979, Ensign 1985, Clerk to the Cheque and Adjutant 1987, Lieutenant 1993; devpt offr Nat Star Centre for Disabled Youth 1982–94; Liveryman Worshipful Co of Grocers', Freeman City of London; *Clubs* Cavalry and Guards', MCC; *Style*— Col G W Tufnell, DL; ✉ The Manor House, Ampney St Peters, Cirencester, Glos GL7 5SH (☎ 01285 851065, fax 01285 850314)

TUFNELL, Philip Clive Roderick (Phil); *b* 29 April 1966; *Educ* Highgate Sch, Southgate Sch; *Career* professional cricketer; Middlesex CCC: debut 1986, awarded county cap 1990, winners County Championship 1990; England: test debut v Aust Melbourne 1990, 22 test matches (taking 65 wickets), 19 one day Ints, memb tour Aust 1991 and NZ 1992, memb World Cup squad Aust 1992, memb tour India and Sri Lanka 1992/93, memb team touring W Indies 1993/94 and Aust 1994/95, memb team touring Zimbabwe and New Zealand 1996–97; best bowling figures in test matches: 6 for 25 Fifth Test v W Indies Oval 1991, 7 for 47 First Test v NZ Christchurch 1992 (took 11 wickets in match, winner Man of the Match award), 5 wickets in an innings 4 times, 10 wickets in a match once; *Recreations* sleeping, sports cars, American football, Arsenal FC; *Style*— Phil Tufnell, Esq; ✉ Middlesex County Cricket Club, Lord's Cricket Ground, London NW8 8QN (☎ 0171 289 1300)

TUGENDHAT, Baron (Life Peer UK 1993), of Widdington in the County of Essex; Sir Christopher Samuel Tugendhat; kt (1990); er s of Dr Georg Tugendhat (d 1973), of London, and Máire, *née* Littledale (d 1994); bro of Michael George Tugendhat, QC, *qv*; *b* 23 Feb 1937; *Educ* Ampleforth, Gonville and Caius Coll Cambridge; *m* 1967, Julia Lissant, da of Kenneth D Dobson, of Keston, Kent; 2 s (Hon James Walter b 1971, Hon Angus George Harry b 1974); *Career* leader and feature writer Financial Times 1960–70; MP (C): Cities of London and Westminster 1970–74, City of London and Westminster South 1974–76; dir Sunningdale Oils 1971–76, conslt Phillips Petroleum International Ltd 1972–1976, former conslt to Wood Mackenzie & Co Stockbrokers; Br EEC cmmr (responsible for budget, fin control, personnel and admin) 1977–81, vice pres Cmmn of Euro Communities (responsible for budget, fin control, fin insts and taxation) 1981–85; chm: CAA 1986–91, Royal Inst of Int Affrs Chatham House 1986–95, Abbey National plc 1991–, Blue Circle Industries plc 1996–; dep chm Nat Westminster Bank 1990–91 (dir 1985–91); also non-exec dir: The BOC Group plc 1985–96, Commercial Union Assurance Co plc 1988–91, LWT (Holdings) plc 1991–94, Eurotunnel PLC 1991–; *Publications* books incl: Oil: The Biggest Business (1968), The Multinationals (1971), Making Sense of Europe (1986), Options for British Foreign Policy in the 1990's (with William Wallace, 1988); pamphlets incl: Britain, Europe and the Third World (1976), Conservatives in Europe (1979), Is Reform Possible? (1981); *Recreations* conversation, reading, being with my family; *Clubs* Buck's, Anglo-Belgian; *Style*— The Rt Hon Lord Tugendhat; ✉ 35 Westbourne Park Rd, London W2 5QD; Chairman, Abbey National plc, Abbey House, 215 Baker Street, London NW1 6XL (☎ 0171 612 4000)

TUGENDHAT, Michael George; QC (1986); s of Dr Georg Tugendhat (d 1973), and Máire, *née* Littledale (d 1994); bro of The Rt Hon Lord Tugendhat, *qv*; *b* 21 Oct 1944; *Educ* Ampleforth, Gonville & Caius Coll Cambridge (MA), Yale; *m* 6 June 1970, Blandine Marie, da of Comte Pierre-Charles Menche de Loisne, of France, 4 s (Charles b 1972, Thomas b 1973, Gregory b 1977, Henry b 1986); *Career* called to the Bar Inner Temple 1969, Midlands & Oxford Circuit, bencher Inner Temple, recorder Crown Ct; *Clubs* Brooks's; *Style*— Michael Tugendhat, Esq, QC; ✉ 5 Raymond Buildings, Gray's Inn, London WC1R 5BP (☎ 0171 242 2902)

TUITE, Sir Christopher Hugh; 14 Bt (I 1622), of Sonnagh, Westmeath; s of Sir Dennis George Harmsworth Tuite, 13 Bt, MBE (d 1981, descended from the Sir Richard de Tuite or Tuitt, who was one of Strongbow's followers in his invasion of Ireland in 1172); *b* 3 Nov 1949; *Educ* Wellington Coll, Liverpool Univ (BSc), Bristol Univ (PhD); *m* 1976, Deborah Ann, da of A E Martz, of Punxutawny, USA; 2 s (Thomas Livingstone b 1977, Jonathan Christopher Hannington b 1981); *Heir* s, Thomas Livingstone Tuite; *Career* res offr The Wildfowl Tst 1978–81; pres Spirutec Inc (Arizona) 1982–86, controller Nature Conservancy Washington DC 1987–; *Style*— Sir Christopher Tuite, Bt

TUITE, Margaret, Lady; Margaret Essie; da of Col Walter Leslie Dundas, DSO, of Farnham; *m* 1947, Sir Dennis Tuite, 13 Bt, MBE (d 1981); 3 s; *Style*— Margaret, Lady Tuite; ✉ 7 Vicarage Gardens, Grayshott, Hindhead, Surrey GU26 6NH (☎ 01428 605026)

TUIVAGA, Hon Chief Justice; Hon Sir Timoci Uluiburotu; kt (1981); s of Isimeli Siga Tuivaga and Jessie Hill; *b* 1931; *Educ* Univ of Auckland (BA); *m* 1958, Vilimaina Leba Parrott Tuivaga; 3 s, 1 da; *Career* called to the Bar Gray's Inn, acting chief justice of Fiji 1974–80, chief justice 1980–87 and 1988–; *Style*— Hon Chief Justice Sir Tuivaga; ✉ 228 Ratu Sukuna Rd, Suva, Fiji

TUKE, Sir Anthony Favill; kt (1979); s of Anthony Tuke; *b* 22 Aug 1920; *Educ* Winchester, Magdalene Coll Cambridge; *m* 1946, Emilia Mila Antic; 1 s, 1 da; *Career* chm: Savoy Hotel plc 1984–94 (dir 1982–94), RTZ Corporation 1981–85 (dir 1980–91); dir: Barclays Bank 1965–90 (chm 1973–81), Barclays Bank UK 1971–81, Barclays Bank International 1965–87 (chm 1972–79), Urban Foundation 1980–86, Merchants Trust 1969–94, Royal Insurance 1978–92 (dep chm 1985–92), Whitbread Investment Co plc 1984–94; memb Trilateral Cmmn 1973–90; govr Motability 1978–84, former vice pres Inst of Bankers and Br Bankers Assoc; Liveryman Worshipful Co of Mercers; *Clubs* MCC (pres 1982–83, memb ctee, chm fin ctee 1983–90); *Style*— Sir Anthony Tuke; ✉ Freelands, Wherwell, Andover, Hants

TUKE, Peter Godfrey; s of Dr Reginald Godfrey Tuke (d 1973), of Bournemouth, and Dorothy Beatrice, *née* Underwood (d 1948); *b* 14 June 1944; *Educ* Radley, Keble Coll Oxford (MA, Rowing blue), Poly of Central London (DipArch); *m* 21 June 1975, Susan, da of Edward Albert Hamilton Lawrence (d 1978), of Handcross, Sussex; 2 s (Edward b 1978, William b 1980); *Career* corporate planning BP 1967–71, architect and ptnr Prior Manton Tuke Ptnrship 1981–; pres Radley Mariners 1993–96; RIBA 1979; *Recreations* theatre, sailing, walking; *Clubs* Vincents, Leander, Newport (Pembs) Boat; *Style*— Peter Tuke, Esq; ✉ 48 Brodrick Rd, London SW17 7DY (☎ 0181 672 8678); Prior Manton Tuke Partnership, 20 Prescott Place, London SW4 6BT(☎ 0171 627 8085, fax 0171 627 2658)

TULLO, Carol Anne; da of Edward Alan Dodgson, of Woolton, Liverpool, and Patricia, *née* Masterson; *b* 9 Jan 1956; *Educ* Holly Lodge, Univ of Hull (LLB); *m* 5 May 1979, Robin Brownrigg Tullo, s of James Francis Swanzy Tullo, of Highgate, London; 1 s (Luke Edward Swanzy b 1991), 1 da (Alice Sophia b 1986); *Career* called to the Bar Inner Temple 1977; dir Stevens 1985–96, publishing dir Sweet & Maxwell Ltd 1988–96, dir ESC Publishing Ltd 1990–96, publishing conslt 1996–, dir Legal Information Resources Ltd 1994–96, chm Law Publishers' Exec Publishers' Assoc 1995–; *Recreations* motherhood, France; *Style*— Mrs Carol Tullo; ✉ 38 Friern Park, London N12 9DA (☎ 0181 445 9689)

TULLOCH, Alastair Robert Clifford; s of James Richard Moore Tulloch, and Heather Netta (d 1989); *b* 1 Oct 1955; *Educ* St Andrew's Coll SA, Magdalen Coll Oxford; *m* 15 Aug 1987, Hilary, da of Rev Alisdair MacDonell, of St Mary's Haddington, Scotland; 1 da (Emma Heather b 1988), 4 s (Robin b and d 1989, Hugh Gordon b 1991, Iain Alastair and Angus James (twins) b 1992); *Career* asst slr: Lovell White and King 1980–82 (articled 1978–80), McNeil and Co Dubai 1982–84, Clifford Turner 1984–86; ptnr Frere Cholmeley Bischoff 1987–; memb Law Society; *Recreations* DIY, skiing, sailing, hill-walking; *Style*— Alastair Tulloch, Esq; ✉ 46 Laurier Road, London NW5 1SJ (☎ 0171 482 0820); Frere Cholmeley Bischoff, 4 John Carpenter Street, London EC4Y 0NH (☎ 0171 615 8000, fax 0171 615 8080)

TULLOCH, Clive William; s of Ewan William Tulloch, of Richmond, Surrey, and Sylvia Phoebe, *née* Mott; *b* 21 June 1948; *Educ* Winchester; *m* Tessa Celia Geraldine, da of Prof Harry Frederick Trewman; 1 s (James Harry William b 23 Aug 1985), 1 da (Caroline Sylvia Geraldine b 2 Dec 1982); *Career* Coopers & Lybrand 1967–79, ptnr Morison Stoneham & Co 1980–81 (joined 1979), re-joined Coopers & Lybrand 1981 (ptnr 1983–), specialist in tax treatment of remuneration and financial affairs of directors and sr execs; chm Taxation Ctee London C of C 1994; govr St Nicholas Primary Sch Chislehurst 1989–95; memb Guild of Tax Advsrs; FCA 1976 (ACA 1971), FTII 1994; *Books* The CCH Company Car Tax Guide 1996–97 (jt author and princ ed (and on previous edns)), Car or Cash? (CCH, 2 edn 1994), Employee Share Schemes in Practice; *Recreations* choral singing (The Bach Choir), walking; *Clubs* Lansdowne, RSA, National Liberal, Aldrich Catch; *Style*— Clive Tulloch, Esq; ✉ Lamorna, Sleeper's Hill, Winchester, Hampshire SO22 4NB; Coopers & Lybrand, Hill House, Richmond Hill, Bournemouth BH2 6HR

TULLOCH, Iain William Patrick; s of Maj William Alexander Tulloch, (d 1988), of Southwood House, Monkton, Ayrshire, and Margaret Edith Phyllis, *née* Farquhar (d 1968); *b* 12 Dec 1940; *Educ* Rugby, Brown Univ Providence Rhode Island USA; *m* 5 Oct 1967, Charmian Mary, da of Michael Anthony Callender, of Gaston Cottage, Alton, Hants; 1 s (Gillem b 1971), 1 da (Leesa b 1969); *Career* Lt Ayrshire Yeomanry 1966; qualified CA 1966; exec dir: Murray Johnstone Ltd 1987–, Murray Ventures PLC 1992–, Murray VCT PLC 1995–, Mining Scotland Ltd 1995–; non-exec dir: American Opportunity Trust 1989, IFC Group 1990–92; memb Cncl Br Venture Capital Assoc 1988–94; *Recreations* royal tennis, squash, golf, gardening; *Clubs* Prestwick Golf, Western; *Style*— Iain Tulloch, Esq; ✉ Swallow Ha', Symington, Ayrshire KA1 5PN; Murray Johnstone Ltd, 7 West Nile St, Glasgow (☎ 0141 226 3131, fax 0141 248 5636, telex 778667)

TULLOCH, Jean Douglas; *b* 19 Jan 1941; *m* 1, 1961, William David Jack (decd); 3 s (Alister b 1963, Douglas b 1965, James b 1972); m 2, 1985, John Glen Alexander Tulloch; *Career* memb Bd and chm Dumfries and Galloway Health Bd 1995–; vice chm Dumfries and Galloway Care Tst, memb Bd Dumfries Town Centre Management Co; *Recreations* riding, skiing, fishing; *Style*— Mrs Jean Tulloch; ✉ Courance, Lockerbie DG11 1TP; Dumfries and Galloway Health Board, Nithbank, Dumfries DG1 2SD (☎ 01387 241803, fax 01387 252375)

TULLOCH, William Paul; s of William Andrew Tulloch, of Sydney, Australia, and Ada Imelda, *née* Ratcliffe; *b* 26 Sept 1956; *Educ* Marcellin Coll Randwick Sydney, Univ of NSW (BSc, BArch); *m* 28 Sept 1985, Melanie Susan, da of James Sutherland Oag McKay; 2 s (William David b 30 Jan 1989, Harry James b 1 Oct 1993); *Career* architect; dir Fitzroy Robinson International, exec dir Fitzroy Robinson Ltd 1994–; projects incl parliamentary complex Muscat 1992; RIBA, ARCUK; *Recreations* sailing, skiing, rugby; *Style*— William Tulloch, Esq; ✉ Fitzroy Robinson Ltd, 77 Portland Place, London W1N 4EP (☎ 0171 636 8033)

TULLY, David John; s of William Scarth Carlisle Tully, CBE (d 1987), and Patience Treby, *née* Betts; *b* 13 March 1942; *Educ* Twyford, Sherborne; *m* 7 May 1965, Susan Patricia, da of (James) Geoffrey Arnott; 1 s (James Herbert b 1967), 2 da (Louise Patience b 1969, Clare Jane b 1972); *Career* slr; sr ptnr Addleshaw Sons & Latham Manchester 1994– (ptnr 1969–); dir Joseph Holt plc; formerly chm: Manchester Young Slrs, Nat Young Slrs, The St James's Club, Cransley Sch; formerly pres Manchester Law Soc; govr Manchester GS; *Recreations* shooting, fishing, golf; *Clubs* St James's (Manchester); *Style*— David Tully, Esq; ✉ 2 Warwick Drive, Hale, Altrincham, Cheshire WA15 9EA (☎ 0161 928 3029); Addleshaw Sons & Latham, Dennis House, Marsden St, Manchester M2 1JD (☎ 0161 832 5994, fax 0161 832 2250)

TULLY, (William) Mark; OBE (1985); s of late William Scarth Carlisle Tully, CBE, and Patience Treby, *née* Betts; *b* 24 Oct 1935; *Educ* New Sch Darjeeling India, Twyford Sch Winchester Hants, Marlborough, Trinity Hall Cambridge (MA); *m* 13 Aug 1960,

(Frances) Margaret, da of late Frank Howard Butler; 2 s (Sam b 1965, Patrick b 1967), 2 da (Sarah b 1961, Emma b 1963); *Career* Nat Serv 2 Lt 1 Royal Dragoons 1954–56; regnl dir Abbeyfield Soc for housing old people 1960–64; BBC: Personnel Dept 1964–65, asst then acting rep BBC Delhi 1965–69, Hindi prog organiser External Servs London 1969–70, chief talks writer External Servs 1970–71, chief of Delhi Bureau 1972–93, S Asia corr 1993–94 (resigned from the BBC); currently freelance journalist and bdcaster, presenter Something Understood (Unique Broadcasting Ltd for BBC Radio 4) 1995–; hon fell Trinity Hall Cambridge 1994; *Awards* Dimbleby Award BAFTA 1984, Radio and Critics Broadcasting Press Guild Radio Award 1984, Sony Award for Radio Documentary 1994; *Books* Amritsar Mrs Gandhi's Last Battle (with Satish Jacob, 1985), Raj to Rajiv (with Zareer Masani, 1988), No Fullstops in India (Viking, 1991); *Recreations* reading, fishing, bird watching; *Clubs* Oriental, Press and Gymkhana (Delhi); *Style*— Mark Tully, Esq, OBE; ✉ 1 Nizamuddin East, New Delhi 110013, India (☎ 00 964 11 4628697)

TUMIM, His Hon Sir Stephen; kt (1996); s of Joseph Tumim, CBE (d 1957), and Renée, *née* Davis (d 1941); *b* 15 Aug 1930; *Educ* St Edward's Sch Oxford, Worcester Coll Oxford (Open scholar); *m* 1962, Winifred Letitia Tumim, OBE, JP, *qv*, da of Lt-Col Algernon Borthwick (d 1975), of Essex; 3 da (Matilda b 1963, Emma b 1964, Olivia b 1968); *Career* called to the Bar Middle Temple 1955, bencher 1990; recorder of the Crown Ct 1977–78, circuit judge (SE Circuit) 1978–96; HM chief inspr of prisons for England and Wales 1987–95; princ St Edmund Hall Oxford 1996–; chm: Friends of Tate Gallery 1983–90, British Art Market Standing Ctee 1990–95, Koestler Award Tst 1993–; pres Royal Literary Fund 1990–; hon fell: LSE 1993, Worcester Coll Oxford 1994, UEA 1994, The Royal Philanthropic Soc 1994, Law Sch Grand Cayman 1994, Oxford Brookes Univ 1995; Hon Doctorate Univ of Stirling 1993; Hon LLD: Univ of Leicester 1994, Univ of the West of England 1994, Univ of Essex 1995, Univ of Birmingham 1995, Univ of Southampton 1995, Univ of Keele 1996, Univ of Exeter 1996; Hon FRCP 1993; *Books* Great Legal Disasters (1983), Great Legal Fiascos (1985); *Recreations* books and pictures; *Clubs* Garrick, Beefsteak; *Style*— His Hon Sir Stephen Tumim; ✉ St Edmund Hall, Oxford OX1 4AR

TUMIM, Lady; Winifred Letitia; OBE (1992), JP; da of Lt-Col Algernon Malcolm Borthwick, MC (d 1975), of Braintree, Essex, and Edith Wilde, *née* Addison (d 1975); *b* 3 June 1936; *Educ* North Foreland Lodge Sch, Lady Margaret Hall Oxford (BA, MA), Univ of London (Dip Social Admin, Dip Linguistics); *m* 1962, His Hon Sir Stephen Tumim, *qv*, s of Joseph Tumim, CBE (d 1957), of Headington, Oxford; 3 da (Matilda Edith (Mrs Prendergast), Emma Renee (Mrs Iliffe), Olivia Blanche); *Career* Parly candidate (SDP) Wantage 1983 and 1987; memb: Govt Ctee of Enquiry on Educn of Handicapped Children (Warnock Ctee) 1974–78, Mgmnt Ctee Family Housing Assoc 1981–89 (vice chm 1983–88), Hammersmith and Fulham Health Authy 1982–85, Nat Advsy Cncl on the Employment of Disabled People 1986–91, Marks & Spencer HealthPlus Ethics Advsy Gp 1993–, Advsy Ctee on Tsteeship Charity Cmmn 1993–; non-exec dir Parkside Health (NHS Community Tst) 1991– (chm Audit Ctee and Quality Steering Gp); chm: RNID 1985–92 (tstee 1982–93), Independent Living Fund 1988–91 (tstee until 1992), NCVO/Charity Cmmn Working Party on Tstee Trg 1991–92, Sec of State's Youth Treatment Service Gp 1991–, Carer's Impact Gp (King's Fund) 1993–95, Cncl for the Advancement of Communication with Deaf People 1994–; chm designate NCVO 1996; govr: Mary Hare GS for the Deaf 1974–90, City Literary Inst 1991–95; tstee: City Parochial Fndn 1989–, National Portrait Gallery 1992–, Carlton TV Tst 1993–96, Charity Appointments 1993–96; lay memb GMC 1996–; FRSA; *Publications* Weekly Boarding - Why & How (1974), Parents as Partners (1980), A Pre-School Service of Deaf Children and their Parents (1981), Bibliography for and about Young People with Special Needs (1981), International Year of the Child - Notebook for School Leavers with Special Needs (1985); also author of articles and reviews in TES, Nursing, Where?, Education Today, Higher Education, The British Journal of Audiology, Jl of the Royal Soc of Arts and The Times; *Recreations* walking, talking, gardening, opera, watercolour painting; *Style*— Lady Tumim, OBE, JP; ✉ 18 Stafford Place, London SW1E 6NP

TUNBRIDGE, Dr (William) Michael Gregg; s of Sir Ronald Ernest Tunbridge, OBE (d 1984), of Leeds, and Dorothy, *née* Gregg; *b* 13 June 1940; *Educ* Kingswood Sch Bath, Queens' Coll Cambridge (MA, MD), UCH; *m* 28 Aug 1965, Felicity Katherine Edith, da of Arthur Myers Parrish (d 1987), of Bangor; 2 da (Clare b 1968, Anne b 1970); *Career* conslt physician Newcastle Gen Hosp 1977–94, sr lectr in med Univ of Newcastle upon Tyne until 1994, dir of postgrad med educn and trg Univ of Oxford and Region 1994–, hon conslt physician John Radcliffe Hosp and The Radcliffe Infirmary Oxford 1994–, professorial fell Wadham Coll Oxford 1994–; memb Br Diabetic Assoc; FRCP 1979; *Recreations* walking; *Clubs* Athenaeum; *Style*— Dr Michael Tunbridge; ✉ Department of Postgraduate Medical Education, Medical School Offices, John Radcliffe Hospital, Oxford, Oxon OX3 9DU (☎ 01865 221517, fax 01865 750750)

TUNNELL, George Edmund; s of Osmond Tunnell (d 1973), of Stratton on the Fosse, Somerset, and Iris Gabrielle, *née* Sharvelle; *b* 19 Sept 1941; *Educ* Millfield Sch, Brasenose Coll Oxford (MA, cross-country and athletics blue), UCSW (Dip in Personnel Mgmnt), UCNW (DipEd), Univ of Essex (MA); *m* 3 Dec 1988, Maria Marcela, da of Manuel Gonzalez; 2 s (Sebastian Gabriel b 25 March 1990, Juan Felipe b 18 Dec 1991); *Career* lectr in English Univ of Libya 1968–70, teacher of English Gymnasium Wesermunde Bremerhaven 1971–72, lectr in English Institut de la Technologie de L'Education Algiers 1972–75; British Council: lectr Madrid 1975–80, asst dir of studies Valenica 1980–83; lectr in English language and applied linguistics Univ of Bucharest 1983–84, dir of studies Br Cncl Bogota 1984–86, head of studies Euroschools 1986–87, dir Br Cncl Palma de Mallorca 1988–92, dir Br Cncl Bilbao 1992–; memb IATEFL 1968–; *Recreations* running and racing in veterans' athletic competitions; *Style*— George Tunnell, Esq; ✉ The British Council, Av Lehendakari Aguirre 29, 48014 Bilbao, Spain

TUNNELL, Hugh James Oliver Redvers; s of Oliver Tunnell, and Heather Vera Audrey Tunnell (d 1980); *b* 31 Dec 1935; *Educ* Chatham House GS Ramsgate; *m* 26 June 1979, Margaret Louise, da of Sir Richard Randall, KB (d 1982); 2 da (Camilla Zoe b 7 June 1984, Olivia Rose b 28 April 1988); *Career* Nat Serv RA 1954–56; HM Dip Serv: commercial sec Amman 1959–62, MECAS 1962, 2 sec Aden 1964–65, Damascus 1966–67, UK rep EEC Brussels 1968–70, FCO 1970–72, 1 sec Kuwait 1972–76, FCO 1976–79, head of Chancery Muscat 1979–83, consul gen Brisbane 1983–88, cmmr gen Br participation at Expo '88 1988, consul gen Jedda 1989–92, HM ambassador Bahrain 1992–96, ret; *Recreations* tennis, water sports; *Clubs* Brisbane, Royal Over-Seas League; *Style*— Hugh Tunnell, Esq; ✉ 37 Parsons Green, London SW6 4UJ (☎ 0171 736 6213)

TUNNEY, Kieran Patrick; s of Patrick Adam Tunney, and Julia O'Callaghan, *née* Clancy; *b* 14 Oct 1922; *Educ* Repub of Ireland, England and France; *Career* offr cadet Grenadier Gds 1942; theatre corr, playwright, author; theatre critic: Daily Sketch, Queen Magazine, News Chronicle, Tatler, Truth Ballet; memb Dramatisis Guild NY; *Plays* The Patriot (Cork Ireland) 1938, Day After Tomorrow (Q Theatre and Fortune Theatre) 1946, The Marriage Playground (Q Theatre) 1946, A Priest in the Family (Observer Play of the Season, Family Westminster Theatre) 1951, The Wedding Ring (Manchester Opera House) 1952, Royal Exit (Cambridge) 1953, God and Kate Murphy (Broadway) 1959 (Best Record of the Theatrical Year), A House of Glass (London) 1963; *Screenplays* The Rasputin Yousoupoff Affair, The Red Prophet, Justice Deferred; *Books* Tallulah Darling of the Gods, Interupted Autobiography & Aurora (1990); *Recreations* walking, tennis, reading; *Style*— Kieran Tunney, Esq; ✉ 510 Beatty House, Dolphin Square, London SW1V 3PL (☎ 0171 798 8285)

TUNNICLIFFE, Denis; CBE (1993); *b* 17 Jan 1943; *Educ* Henry Cavendish Sch Derby, UCL (State scholar, BSc), Coll of Air Trg Hamble; *m* 1968, Susan, *née* Dale; 2 s (Alan Dale b 29 Sept 1971, Richard Dale b 1 March 1973); *Career* British Airways: co-pilot VC10 then B747 1966–72, various personnel and industl rels roles BOAC (latterly Overseas Div BA) 1972–77, head of planning Flight Ops 1977–80, controller of fuel 1980–82, gen mangr Caribbean 1982, head of consultancy servs 1982–83, sr gen mangr Market Centres 1983–84, dir of marketplace performance 1984–86; chief exec Aviation Div International Leisure Group 1986–88, md London Underground Ltd 1988–; memb Bd London Transport 1993–; cncllr: New Windsor BC 1971–75, Berks CC 1974–77, Bracknell DC 1979–83; FCIT 1990, CIMgt 1991, FRSA 1992; *Recreations* boating, church, helicopter flying; *Clubs* RAF, RAC; *Style*— Denis Tunnicliffe, Esq, CBE; ✉ London Underground Ltd, 55 Broadway, London SW1H 0BD (☎ 0171 918 3440)

TUNNICLIFFE, Prof Jonathan Frederick; s of William Frederick Tunnicliffe (d 1979), of Grassington, Skipton, N Yorks, and Doris, *née* Thompson (d 1966); *b* 20 Sept 1929; *Educ* Chesterfield GS, Queen Elizabeth GS Wakefield, Univ of Leeds (BSc, ICI Mining prize); *m* 1 Sept 1951, Enid Barbara, da of Edward Richardson; 2 s (William Richard b 3 Feb 1952, Jonathan Edward b 4 May 1965), 2 da (Susan Carol b 21 April 1953, Anne Elizabeth b 1 May 1957); *Career* mine underofficial NCB 1956–57 (mgmnt trainee 1954–56); colliery mangr: Snydale Colliery 1959–64, Newmarket Silkstone Colliery 1964–68 (colliery undermangr 1957–59); area safety engr N Yorks Area NCB 1973–75; colliery gen mangr: Prince of Wales Colliery 1968–73, Lofthouse Colliery 1975–78, Selby Coalfield 1978–82; Milburn prof of mining engrg and head of Dept of Mining Engrg Univ of Newcastle 1982–90, prof of mining engrg and head of Dept of Mining and Mineral Engrg Univ of Leeds 1990–91 (emeritus 1991); pres Midland Inst of Mining Engrs 1978–79 (awarded Thomas Adam Medal 1983 and Peake Medal 1995), nat pres Inst of Mining Engrs 1987–88 (Eimco-McArthur award 1983, Sir Andrew Bryan award 1989); tstee Panasonic Tst Royal Acad of Engrg 1992–95; FIMinE, FEng 1989; *Recreations* walking, reading, Gilbert and Sullivan Soc, sport; *Style*— Prof Jonathan Tunnicliffe, FEng; ✉ 10 The Russets, Sandal, Wakefield, W Yorks WF2 6JF (☎ 01924 256675)

TUNNICLIFFE, Michael John (Mike); s of Brian Tunnicliffe, of London, and Dorothy Anne Baxendale, *née* Richardson; *b* 19 Jan 1961; *Educ* Bramhall HS; *m* 24 Aug 1990, Elaine Clare, *née* Jackson; 1 da (Ava Talullah Grace b 14 Jan 1994); *Career* advtg sales exec Link House Publications 1979–80, advtg sales mangr Burke House Periodicals 1980–81, media exec, media mangr then dep gp dir Saatchi and Saatchi Advertising 1981–83, media mangr Leagas Delaney Partnership 1983–84, media mangr, assoc dir then dir HDM: Horner Collis and Kirvan 1984–90; CIA Group plc: dir CIA Media UK 1990, dep md CIA Media UK 1993, dir CIA UK Holdings 1994–, md CIA Medianetwork UK 1994–, dir CIA Medianetwork Europe Holdings 1995–; IPA Advertising Effectiveness Award 1988; memb: Media Circle 1981, Mktg Soc 1994; *Recreations* sailing, golf, tennis; *Clubs* RAC, Little Ship; *Style*— Mike Tunnicliffe, Esq; ✉ CIA Medianetwork UK, 1 Paris Garden, London SE1 8NU (☎ 0171 633 9999, fax 0171 401 9015)

TUNSTALL-PEDOE, Prof Hugh David; s of Prof Dan Pedoe, of Minneapolis, USA, and (Bessie Maude) Mary, *née* Tunstall (d 1965); *b* 30 Dec 1939; *Educ* Haberdashers' Aske's, Dulwich Coll, Hampstead Sch, King's Coll Cambridge, Guy's Hosp Med Sch (MB BChir, MA, MD); *m* 24 June 1967, Jacqueline Helen, da of Kenneth B Burbidge (d 1991), of Felmersham, Bedfordshire; 2 s (William b 1969, Oliver b 1973), 1 da (Susan b 1971); *Career* house physician 1964–66: Guy's, Brompton Hosp, Nat Hosp for Nervous Diseases; jr registrar Guy's 1967, clinical scientific staff Social Med Unit MRC 1969–71, lectr in med London Hosp 1971–74 (registrar in gen med 1968–69); St Mary's Hosp 1974–81: sr lectr in epidemiology, conslt physician, hon community physician; Univ of Dundee Ninewells Med Sch 1981–: dir Cardiovascular Epidemiology Unit, prof of cardiovascular epidemiology, sr lectr in med; conslt cardiologist and specialist in public health med Tayside Health Bd 1981; various pubns in jls; chm Working Gp on Epidemiology and Prevention Euro Soc of Cardiology 1983–85, memb Resuscitation Cncl of UK; FRCP 1981, FFPHM 1981, FRCPE 1985, FESC 1988; *Inventions* Dundee Coronary Risk-Disk (Toshiba Year of Invention award 1991); *Books* Multiple Choice Questions in Epidemiology and Community Medicine (with W C S Smith, 1987); *Recreations* golf, bee-keeping, jogging; *Clubs* RSM; *Style*— Prof Hugh Tunstall-Pedoe; ✉ 4 Hill Street, Broughty Ferry, Dundee DD5 2JL (☎ 01382 477358); Cardiovascular Epidemiology Unit, Ninewells Hosp and Medical Sch, Dundee DD1 9SY (☎ 01382 644255, fax 01382 641095)

TUOHY, Denis John; s of John Vincent Tuohy (d 1976), of Scariff, Co Clare, and Anne Mary, *née* Doody; *b* 2 April 1937; *Educ* Clongowes Wood Coll Ireland, Queen's Univ Belfast (BA, Blayney exhibition prize, Peel prize, debating medal); *m* 1960 (m dis 1988), Eleanor Moya, da of Felix Charles McCann; 2 s (Mark b 12 June 1962, Christopher b 3 April 1964), 2 da (Eleanor b 14 July 1969, Catherine b 21 Oct 1974); *Career* TV reporter, presenter and writer; presenter and reporter: BBC NI 1960–64 (also actor), 24 Hours (BBC 1) 1967–71 (also prodr), Panorama (BBC 1) 1974–75, TV Eye (Thames) 1979–86; presenter: Late Night Line Up (BBC 2) 1964–67, People and Politics (Thames) 1973, Midweek (BBC 1) 1974, Tonight (BBC 1) 1975–79, Reporting London (Thames) 1981–82, The Garden Party (BBC 1) 1990–91, Central Weekend (Central) 1993, Classic FM 1993, Something Understood (BBC Radio 4) 1995, The Jimmy Young Programme (guest presenter) 1996; reporter: Man Alive (BBC 2) 1971–72, This Week (Thames) 1972–74 and 1987–92; prodr Southern Eye (BBC South) 1993, newscaster ITN 1994–; special documentaries as presenter, writer and narrator: Lord of the Rings (BBC 1) 1974, A Life of O'Reilly (BBC 1) 1974, Mr Truman Why Did You Drop the Second Bomb? (BBC 1) 1975, Do You Know Where Jimmy Carter Lives? (BBC 1) 1977, To Us a Child (Thames, UNICEF) 1986, The Blitz (Thames) 1990, The Longest Walk (BBC 2) 1994, Dispatches (Channel 4), various Channel 4 documentaries 1994–; Eisenhower travelling fellow (survey of public TV in USA) 1967, special prize for documentary To Us a Child (Third World film/TV festival Algiers) 1987; contrib: The Independent, New Statesman, The Scotsman, The Listener, British Poetry Review 1993; memb NUJ 1970–; *Recreations* watching rugby and cricket, theatre, cinema, walking; *Clubs* Harlequins RFC, London Irish RFC; *Style*— Denis Tuohy, Esq; ✉ c/o The Roseman Organisation, 46 Sutton Court Road, London W4 4NL (☎ 0181 742 0552, fax 0181 742 0554)

TUOHY, John Francis (Frank); s of Patrick Gerald Tuohy (d 1958), and Dorothy Marion, *née* Annandale (d 1964); *b* 2 July 1925; *Educ* Stowe, King's Coll Cambridge (MA); *Career* novelist and short story writer; prof of English Univ of Sao Paulo Brazil 1950–56; visiting prof: Jagiellonian Univ Krakow Poland 1958–60, Waseda Univ Tokyo 1964–67, Rikkyo Univ Tokyo 1983–89; writer in res Purdue Univ Indiana USA 1970, 1976 and 1980; winner Bennett award (Hudson Review) 1994; Hon DLitt Purdue Univ 1986; FRSL 1963; *Books* The Animal Game (1957), The Warm Nights of January (1960), The Ice Saints (1964, James Tait Black Meml prize, Geoffrey Faber Meml prize), Portugal (1970), Yeats: a biographical study (1976); short stories: The Admiral and the Nuns (1962, Katherine Mansfield Meml prize), Fingers in the Door (1970, E M Forster Meml award), Live Bait (1978, Heinemann award), Collected Stories (1984); *Recreations* travel; *Style*— Frank Tuohy, Esq; ✉ Shatwell Cottage, Yarlington, nr Wincanton, Somerset BA9 8DL (☎ 01963 440264)

TUPPER, Sir Charles Hibbert; 5 Bt (UK 1888), of Armdale, Halifax, Nova Scotia; s of Sir James Macdonald Tupper, 4 Bt (d 1967), and Mary Agnes Jean, *née* Collins; Sir

Charles, 1 Bt (d 1915), was PM of Nova Scotia 1864–67 (encompassing date of Union), PM of Canada 1896, ldr of oppn 1896–1900; *b* 4 July 1930; *m* 1959 (m dis 1975); 1 s (Charles Hibbert b 1964); *Heir* s, Charles Hibbert Tupper, *qv* b 10 July 1964; *Career* ret; *Style*— Sir Charles Tupper, Bt; ✉ Suite 1101, 955 Marine Drive, W Vancouver, British Columbia V7T 1A9, Canada (☎ 001 604 926 5734)

TUPPER, Charles Hibbert; s of h of Sir Charles Hibbert Tupper, 5 Bt, *qv*; *b* 10 July 1964; *m* 1987, (Elizabeth) Ann Heaslip; 1 da (Cara-Lyn Ann b 1991); *Style*— Charles Tupper, Esq; ✉ PO Box 2064, 641 Wallace Place, Ladysmith, Vancouver Island, British Columbia V0R 2E0, Canada (☎ 00 1 604 245 4760)

TURBERFIELD, Alan Frank; CBE (1990); s of Frank Turberfield (d 1993), and Agnes, *née* Jackson (d 1970); *b* 24 Sept 1930; *Educ* Ashby de la Zouch Boys' GS, St John's Coll Oxford (Open scholar, MA); *m* 4 Aug 1956, Gillian Doris, da of Leonard William George Markwell (d 1973), of Bexhill, and Doris, *née* Stone (d 1990); 1 s (Paul b 1961), 1 da (Alison b 1963); *Career* RAEC 1952–54; asst master: King Edward VII Sch Sheffield 1954–58, Birkenhead Sch 1958–63; head of classics Portsmouth GS 1963–68, HM Inspectorate of Schs 1968–90, staff inspr for secdy educn 1977–90 (with classics 1977–83), official visits to Sweden, Holland, Austria, Bonn, Strasbourg, China and Malaysia, dir sch and coll awards Royal Anniversary Tst 1990–91, DPhil res student in church history Harris Manchester Coll Oxford 1992–; Methodist local preacher 1953–, circuit sec and tutor; memb: 20 Club (DES), Assoc HMI, Jt Assoc of Classical Teachers, Virgil Soc, Br Sch of Athens; *Books* Voyage of Aeneas (BCP/Macmillan, with D A S John, 1968); *Recreations* theatre, travel, theology, Methodism and Ecumenism, watching cricket; *Style*— Alan Turberfield, Esq, CBE; ✉ 75 Hurst Rise Rd, Cumnor Hill, Oxford OX2 9HF (☎ 01865 864450)

TURBOTT, Sir Ian Graham; kt (1968), CMG (1962), CVO (1966), JP (1971); s of Thomas Turbott (d 1956), of Auckland, NZ; *b* 9 March 1922; *Educ* Takapuna GS, Auckland Univ, Jesus Coll Cambridge, LSE; *m* 1952, Nancy, da of Lyman Lantz (d 1935), of Sacramento, California; 3 da; *Career* Capt 2 NZEF (W Pacific and Italy) WWII, 1939–45 Star, Pacific Star, Italy Star, War Medal, Def Medal, NZ Medal; entered Colonial Serv 1947, admin offr Gilbert and Ellice Islands 1947–56, seconded Colonial Office 1956–58; admin and HM The Queen's rep: Antigua 1958–64, Grenada 1964–67; govr Assoc State of Grenada 1967–68; chm: Chloride Batteries Australia Ltd 1974–84, Advsy Bd American Int Underwriters (Aust) Pty Ltd 1976–89, TNT Security Pty Ltd 1976–93, The Triple M Broadcasting Group Pty Ltd 1976–93, Penrith Lakes Developement Corporation Pty Ltd 1980–, Essington Ltd 1984–89, Spencer Stuart & Assoc Pty Ltd 1970–82, I T Graham Investments plc 1980–, Hoyts Media Ltd 1987–93; dir: Capita Financial Group 1977–89, Standard Chartered Bank Ltd 1980–91, Hoyts Entertainment Ltd 1990–93; chm: Sydney Int Piano Competition 1977–86, Duke of Edinburgh's Award Scheme (NSW) 1984–95, Trade Mission Japan 1982, Trade Mission Yugoslavia 1986, Japan Entrepreneurs and Presidents Assoc Aust (JEPA) 1996; tstee: Australian Cancer Research Fndn for Med Research, World Wildlife Fund Australia; fndn chllr Univ of S Sydney 1989–; govr NSW Conservatory of Music 1976–90, hon memb Japanese Diet 1972; Father of the Year award 1986; Hon DLitt Univ of Western Sydney 1993; CStJ 1964; FRSA, FInstD; *Recreations* fishing, tennis, cricket; *Clubs* Australia (Sydney), Royal Sydney Yacht Sqdn; *Style*— Sir Ian Turbott, CMG, CVO, JP; ✉ 8/8 Lauderdale Ave, Fairlight, NSW 2094, Australia

TURCAN, Henry Watson; s of Henry Hutchison Turcan, TD (d 1977), of Newburgh, Fife, and Lilias Cheyne (d 1975); *b* 22 Aug 1941; *Educ* Rugby, Trinity Coll Oxford (MA); *m* 18 April 1969, Jane, da of Arthur Woodman Blair, WS, of Dunbar, E Lothian; 1 s (Henry b 1974), 1 da (Chloë b 1972); *Career* called to the Bar Inner Temple 1965, bencher 1992; legal assessor Gen Optical Cncl 1982–; recorder Crown Ct 1985–; *Recreations* hunting, shooting, fishing, golf; *Clubs* Royal and Ancient Golf (St Andrews), Hon Co of Edinburgh Golfers (Muirfield); *Style*— Henry Turcan, Esq; ✉ 4 Paper Buildings Temple, London EC4 (☎ 0171 353 3420)

TURCAN, Robert Cheyne; s of H H Turcan (d 1977), of Lindores, Fife, and Lilias, *née* Cheyne (d 1975); *b* 28 May 1947; *Educ* Rugby, Trinity Coll Oxford, Univ of Edinburgh; *m* 1974, Elizabeth Catherine, da of John Carslake, DL, of Preston Bagot, Warwicks; *Career* apprentice Shepherd & Wedderburn 1970–72; Dundas & Wilson: joined 1973, ptnr 1973–, head of Private Client Dept 1989–; dir of several private cos; chm Law Parly Ctee Scottish Landowners' Fedn; jt master Fife Foxhounds; *Recreations* foxhunting, gardening, stalking; *Clubs* New (Edinburgh), Royal & Ancient Golf; *Style*— Robert Turcan, Esq; ✉ Lindores House, Cupar, Fife (☎ 01337 840369); Dundas & Wilson, Saltire Court, 20 Castle Terrace, Edinburgh EH1 2EN (☎ 0131 228 8000, fax 0131 228 8888)

TURCAN, William James; *b* 4 Jan 1943; *Educ* Rugby, Trinity Coll Oxford (MA); *Career* Binder Hamlyn 1965–70, Pauls Malt Ltd 1970–86, fin dir Pauls plc 1986–88, chief exec Harrisons & Crosfield plc 1994– (fin dir 1988–94); memb Bd Glenrothes Devpt Corp 1983–86; ACA; *Style*— William Turcan, Esq; ✉ Harrisons & Crosfield plc, One Great Tower St, London EC3R 5AH (☎ 0171 711 1400, fax 0171 711 1401, telex 885636)

TURI, Joseph (Joe); *b* 18 Nov 1955; *Career* showjumper; memb Seoul Olympic team (riding Vital and Kruger) 1988, winner Hickstead Jumping Derby (riding Vital) 1990, memb Euro Gold Medal winning team; *Recreations* watching other sports, fishing; *Style*— Joe Turi, Esq; ✉ Bennetts Farm, Wardington, Oxfordshire (☎ 01295 758231)

TURING, Sir John Dermot; 12 Bt (NS 1638), of Foveran, Aberdeenshire; s of John Ferrier Turing (d 1983), and his 2 w, Beryl Mary Ada, *née* Hann; suc kinsman Sir John Leslie Turing, 11 Bt, MC (d 1987); *b* 26 Feb 1961; *Educ* Sherborne, King's Coll Cambridge (MA), New Coll Oxford (DPhil); *m* 26 July 1986, (Dr) Nicola Jane, da of Malcolm Douglas Simmonds, of Wimborne Minster, Dorset; 2 s (John Malcolm Ferrier b 5 Sept 1988, James Robert Edward b 6 Jan 1991); *Heir* s, John Malcolm Ferrier Turing b 5 Sept 1988; *Career* admitted slr 1991; *Style*— Sir John Dermot Turing, Bt; ✉ 55 Shirley Avenue, Southampton, Hants SO15 5NH

TURL, Philip Austin; s of Lt-Col Henry William Turl, RAOC (d 1988), of North Finchley, London, and Clara, *née* Pinnell (d 1980); *b* 23 May 1932; *Educ* City of London Sch, Jesus Coll Cambridge (MA); *m* 5 April 1969, Wendy Rosemary, da of Rev Frank Jones, of Dereham, Norfolk; 2 s (Graham b 1970, Andrew b 1977), 1 da (Catherine b 1973); *Career* Lt RAOC (res); called to the Bar Middle Temple 1959; Freeman: City of London 1952, Worshipful Co of Glass Sellers; memb Methodist Church, Christian youth worker; *Books* Praises in Sorrow and Praises in Faith, fifth book of Psalms (1962); *Clubs* Wig and Pen; *Style*— Philip Turl, Esq; ✉ 22 Wolstonbury, Woodside Park, London N12 7BA; 5 Bell Yard, London WC2A 2JR

TURLIK, Piotr (Peter) Zbigniew Vincent de Paulo; s of Zbigniew Tomasz Turlik (d 1943 in Majdanek Concentration Camp), of Warsaw, Poland, and Teresa Zofia, *née* Majewska; *b* 15 Jan 1943; *Educ* The John Fisher Sch Purley Surrey, Coll of Estate Mgmnt Kensington London; *m* 9 Sept 1967, Marie-Madeleine, da of Theodor Radosky (d 1947), of Beauvoir sur Niort, France; *Career* asst dir Gtr London Cncl (Docklands Jt Ctee) 1978–80, asst sec seconded to Dept of Environment 1980–81, dir of strategic affairs London Docklands Devpt Corp 1989– (dir of industrial devpt 1981–84, dir of business devpt 1984–89); vice pres Docklands Business Club 1989 (jt chm 1984–89), govr Hackney Coll 1984–90, memb Working Party on Urban Regeneration RICS 1988–; ARICS 1971; *Recreations* travel, reading (biographies, history), small scale gardening; *Clubs* East India, Ognisko (Polish Hearth); *Style*— Peter Turlik, Esq; ✉ 12 Wincott St, Kennington, London SE11 4NT (☎ 0171 5823045), 4 Chemin du College, Clavette-la Jarrie, France 17220; London Docklands Development Corporation, Thames Quay, 191 Marsh Wall, London E14 9TJ (☎ 0171 512 3000, fax 0171 512 0777, telex 894041 LDDC G)

TURMEAU, Prof William Arthur; CBE; s of Frank Richard Turmeau (d 1972), of Stromness, Orkney, and Catherine Lyon, *née* Linklater; *b* 19 Sept 1929; *Educ* Stromness Acad, Univ of Edinburgh (BSc), Moray House Coll of Educn, Heriot-Watt Univ (PhD); *m* 4 April 1957, Margaret Moar, da of Arthur Burnett; 1 da (Rachel Margaret b 1967); *Career* Nat Serv RCS 1947–49; res engr Northern Electric Co Ltd Montreal 1952–54, mechanical engr USAF Goose Bay Labrador 1954–56, contracts mangr Godfrey Engineering Co Ltd Montreal 1956–61, lectr Bristo Tech Inst Edinburgh 1962–64; Napier Univ (formerly Napier Poly): lectr and sr lectr 1964–68, head Dept of Mechanical Engrg 1968–75, asst princ and dean Faculty of Technol 1975–82, princ 1982–94, vice chllr 1992–94; chm Scottish Environment Protection Agency 1995–; memb: Br Cncl Ctee for Cooperation in Higher Educn, IMechE Standing Ctee for Degree Accreditation, Scot Action on Smoking and Health; Dr (hc) Univ of Edinburgh, Hon DEd Napier Univ; FIMechE, CEng, FRSE 1990; *Recreations* study of Leonardo da Vinci, modern jazz; *Clubs* Caledonian; *Style*— Prof William Turmeau, CBE, FRSE; ✉ 71 Morningside Park, Edinburgh EH10 5EZ (☎ 0131 447 4639)

TURNAGE, Mark-Anthony; *b* 10 June 1960; *Educ* RCM, Tanglewood USA (Mendelssohn scholar); *Career* composer; studied with Oliver Knussen, John Lambert, Gunther Schuller, Hans Werner Henze; composer in assoc CBSO 1989–93, currently composer in assoc ENO, artistic conslt Contemporary Opera Studio; subject of retrospective Birmingham Contemporary Music Gp 1994; *Compositions* orchestral works incl: Night Dances 1981, Three Screaming Popes 1989, Momentum 1991, Drowned Out 1993; voice and ensemble: Lament for a Hanging Man 1983, Greek Suite 1989, Some Days 1989, Her Anxiety (cmmnd by Nash Ensemble) 1991, Killing Time (cmmnd by BBC Television) 1991, Your Rockaby 1993, Twice Through the Heart (Aldeburgh) 1997; various ensembles: On All Fours 1985, Release 1987, Three Farewells 1990, This Silence 1993, Blood on the Floor (cmmnd by Ensemble Modern) 1994, Four-Horned Fandango (CBSO) 1995–96; other: Entranced (solo piano) 1982, Sarabande (soprano saxophone and piano) 1985, Greek (opera, televised 1990) 1988, Kai (solo cello and ensemble) 1990, Sleep On (cello and piano) 1992, Two Elegies Framing a Shout (soprano saxophone and piano) 1994, Dispelling the Fears (2 trumpets and orch, cmmnd by Philharmonia Orch) 1995; *Recordings* labels: EMI Classical, Argo, NMC Recordings; currently signed exclusively to Decca; *Awards* winner Yorkshire Arts Young Composers' Competition (Entranced) 1982, RPS/Charles Heidsieck Music Award for best television prog (Greek) 1990; *Style*— Mark-Anthony Turnage, Esq; ✉ c/o Schott & Co, 48 Great Marlborough Street, London W1V 2BN (☎ 0171 494 1487, fax 0171 287 1529, e-mail 101627,166@compuserve.com)

TURNBERG, Prof Sir Leslie Arnold; kt (1994); s of Hyman Turnberg (d 1985), and Dora, *née* Bloomfield; *b* 22 March 1934; *Educ* Stand GS, Univ of Manchester (MB ChB, MD); *m* 30 Jan 1968, Edna, da of Berthold Barme (d 1981); 1 s (Daniel b 1970), 1 da (Helen b 1971); *Career* lectr Royal Free Hosp 1966–67, res fell Univ of Texas Dallas 1967–68, prof of med Univ of Manchester 1973– (sr lectr 1968–73, dean of Faculty of Med 1986–89); pres RCP 1992–; former memb: GMC, Med Advsy Ctee of Ctee of Vice Chllrs and Principals, MRC; currently memb: Br Soc of Gastroenterology, Assoc of Physicians of GB; FRCP 1973; *Books* Intestinal Transport (1981), Electrolyte and Water Transport Across Gastro-Intestinal Epithelia (1982), Clinical Gastroenterology (1989); *Recreations* reading, painting, walking; *Style*— Prof Sir Leslie Turnberg; ✉ Department of Medicine, University of Manchester School of Medicine, Hope Hospital, Salford M6 8HD (☎ 0161 789 7373, fax 0161 787 7432)

TURNBULL, Andrew; CB (1990), CVO (1992); s of Anthony Turnbull (d 1984), and Mary, *née* Williams; *b* 21 Jan 1945; *Educ* Enfield GS, Christ's Coll Cambridge (BA); *m* 8 Sept 1967, Diane Elizabeth, da of Roland Clarke; 2 s (Adam b 1974, Benet b 1977); *Career* economist Govt of Zambia 1968–70; HM Treasy: asst princ 1970–72, princ 1972–76, seconded to IMF Washington 1976–78, asst sec 1978–83, under sec 1985–88; private sec of econ affrs to the PM 1983–85, princ private sec to the PM 1988–92; HM Treasy: dep sec of public fin 1992–93, second perm sec of public expenditure 1993–94; perm sec DOE 1994–; *Recreations* walking, running, opera; *Style*— Andrew Turnbull, Esq, CB, CVO; ✉ Department of Environment, 2 Marsham Street, London SW1P 3EB

TURNBULL, (Charles Colin) Andrew; s of Charles Elliot Turnbull, of Ilkley, Yorkshire, and Vera Mavis, *née* Clarke; *b* 10 May 1950; *Educ* Leeds GS, Coll of Estate Management Univ of Reading, Univ of Liverpool (BA Econ), Univ of Birmingham (MSc); *m* 31 July 1976, Una Jane, da of Arnold Raymond Humphrey; 3 da (Hannah Elizabeth b 24 Sept 1981, Holly Katherine b 13 March 1984, Lydia Helen b 13 June 1988); *Career* British Airways: joined 1973, cargo marketing offr 1974, passenger traffic forecasts offr 1975, sr forecasts offr 1977–78; project work in: Ecuador, Venezuela, USA, Ghana, Ivory Coast, Sudan, SA, Saudi Arabia, Abu Dhabi, Dubai; Poulter plc: joined as res mangr 1979, head of res 1981, dir of res and planning 1983–, ptnr 1985–, dep md 1992–; awarded Communications, Advertising and Marketing Dip 1979, Kelliher Cup (Communications Advertising and Marketing Fndn) for paper on int advtg 1979; memb: Market Res Soc 1980–, Account Planning Group 1989–; *Recreations* sailing, tennis, music, three young daughters; *Style*— Andrew Turnbull, Esq; ✉ Low Rigg, 15 Clifton Road, Ben Rhydding, Ilkley, West Yorkshire LS29 8TU (☎ 01943 609367); Poulter plc, Poulter House, 2 Burley Rd, Leeds LS3 1NJ (☎ 0113 246 9611, fax 0113 244 8796)

TURNBULL, (George) Anthony Twentyman; s of Stuart John Twentyman Turnbull (d 1991), and Hilda Joyce, *née* Taylor (d 1983); *b* 26 June 1938; *Educ* Charterhouse, ChCh Oxford (MA); *m* 14 June 1962, Petronel Jonette Rene Turnbull, JP, da of Maj James Williams Thursby Dunn (d 1969), of St Leonards Lodge, Clewer, Windsor, Berks; 2 s (Robert Edward Twentyman b 1965, Timothy William John b 1970), 1 da (Victoria Jonette b 1963); *Career* called to the Bar 1962; Debenham Tewson & Chinnocks: joined 1962, ptnr 1965, chief exec 1987; chief exec DTZ Debenham Thorpe 1993–95 (int conslt 1995–96); non-exec dir: Greycoat plc 1996–, Property Intelligence plc 1996–, Oriental Restaurants plc 1996–; Freeman Worshipful Co of Fruiterers (hon asst 1992); FRICS; *Recreations* theatre, conversation, playing games; *Clubs* Savile; *Style*— Anthony Turnbull, Esq; ✉ Beachfield, Beachfield Road, Sandown, Isle of Wight PO36 8LT (☎ 01983 403533); Greycoat plc, 9 Savoy Street, London WC2E 7EG

TURNBULL, Christopher James; s of Rev Capt James Turnbull, of Glastonbury, and Rosemary Erskine Turnbull; *b* 15 April 1950; *Educ* Haileybury, Queens' Coll Cambridge (MA, MB BChir), Westminster Med Sch; *m* 5 Jan 1974, Susan Mary, da of Roger Avery Lovelock, Horsell, Woking; 2 s (James Edward b 1979, Luke Christopher b 1985), 1 da (Claire Elizabeth b 1982); *Career* GP vocational trainee Sandhurst Berks 1976–79, registrar in med Wellington Hosp NZ 1979–81, sr registrar in geriatric med Liverpool rotations 1981–83, conslt physician geriatric med Wirral 1983–, clinical dir for the elderly 1988–89 and 1995–96; author of articles on: glaucoma in the elderly, postural hypotension in the elderly, Parkinsons Disease in the elderly, diabetes in the elderly, fractures in the elderly; chm: Wirral Assoc for Care of the Elderly 1983–91, Wirral Planning GP for the Elderly 1988–91, Special Interest Gp in Diabetes 1992–95; memb: Br Geriatrics Soc, Br Assoc for Serv to the Elderly; FRCP, MRCGP; *Recreations* dinghy sailing, windsurfing, renaissance music; *Style*— Christopher Turnbull, Esq; ✉ Arrowe Park Hospital, Arrowe Park Road, Upton, Wirral, Merseyside L49 5PE (☎ 0151 6785111 ext 2134)

TURNBULL, Ven David Charles; *b* 16 March 1944; *Educ* King James I GS Bishop Auckland, Univ of Leeds (BA), Chichester Theol Coll, Univ of Sheffield (MEd); *m* 16

April 1971, (Margaret) Elaine, *née* Sutton; 1 da (Rachel Clare b 27 Nov 1973), 1 s (John Norman Charles b 23 Dec 1976); *Career* asst master Old Buckenham Hall Sch Brettenham Suffolk 1965–67, asst curate Jarrow 1969–74, vicar of Carlinghow 1974–83, vicar of Penistone 1983–86, priest i/c Thurlstone 1985–86, team rector of Penistone and Thurlstone 1986–93, rural dean of Barnsley 1988–93, hon canon of Wakefield 1993, archdeacon of Carlisle and canon residentiary 1993–; *Style*— The Ven the Archdeacon of Carlisle; ✉ 2 The Abbey, Carlisle, Cumbria CA1 8TZ (☎ 01228 23026, fax 01228 594899)

TURNBULL, Jeffrey Alan; CBE (1991); s of Alan Edward Turnbull (d 1986), of Monkseaton and Carlisle, and Alice May, *née* Slee (d 1940); *b* 14 Aug 1934; *Educ* Newcastle upon Tyne Royal GS, Liverpool Coll of Technol (DipTE); *m* 7 Aug 1957, Beryl, da of Walter Griffith (d 1974), of Crewe; 2 s (Martin John b 1964, Andrew Malcolm b 1972), 1 da (Alison Denise b 1962); *Career* Nat Serv Corpl RE 1956–58; jr engr Cheshire CC 1951–55, engr Herefordshire CC 1955–59, res engr Berks CC 1959–66; Mott Hay & Anderson: dep chief designer (roads) 1966–68, chief designer (roads) 1968–78, assoc 1973–78, dir (int) 1975–89, dir 1978–89, chief exec Mott Hay & Anderson (Holdings) 1987–89, (dir 1983–89); chm and dir Mott MacDonald Group Ltd 1989–94 (conslt 1994–96); chm Br Nat Ctee PIARC 1991–95, memb Editorial Bd New Civil Engineer 1979–82; CEng 1959, FIHT 1966, FICE 1973, FEng 1992; *Books* Civil Engineers Reference Book (contrib 4 edn, 1988), numerous papers to PIARC and IRF confs; *Recreations* cruising, visiting France, walking; *Clubs* RAC; *Style*— Jeffrey Turnbull, Esq, CBE, FEng; ✉ 63 Higher Drive, Banstead, Surrey SM7 1PW (☎ 0181 393 1054)

TURNBULL, John Neil; s of John Smith Turnbull (d 1941), of South Shields, and Kathleen Bernadette Higgins; *b* 13 Feb 1940; *Educ* St Cuthbert GS Newcastle upon Tyne, King's Coll Univ of Durham (BSc); *m* 1966, Aloysia, *née* Lindemann; 2 s (John Michael b 13 Oct 1968, David Stephen b 11 Dec 1970); *Career* British Petroleum: technologist BP Research Centre 1961–64, commissioning engr BP refinery Dinslaken W Germany 1964–66, project ldr BP Res Centre 1966–70, commissioning engr BP Chemicals Baglan Bay W Glamorgan 1970–74, prodn control mangr BP Baglan Bay 1974–76, tech devpt mangr BP Baglan Bay 1976–77, asst works mangr BP Baglan Bay 1977–79, gen mangr polyethylene BP Chemicals Geneva 1979–84, dir polymers BP Chemicals London 1984–86, dir technol petrochemicals and polymers BP Chemicals London 1986–89, dep chief exec nitrogen/nitriles BP Chemicals America 1989–91, dep chief exec mfrg technol BP Chemicals London 1991–93, ret; conslt 1994–, dir International Forum Stowe Vermont USA 1995–; chm Tech Policy Bd Inst of Chem Engrs 1992–96; FIChemE, FEng 1992; *Recreations* skiing, music, reading, walking, theatre; *Style*— John Turnbull, Esq, FEng; ✉ Mulberry House, Vineyard Drive, Bourne End, Bucks SL8 5PD (☎ 01628 850768, fax 01628 530062, e-mail @compuserve100577.253)

TURNBULL, (Wilson) Mark; *b* 1 April 1943; *Educ* George Watson Coll, Edinburgh Coll of Art Sch of Architecture (DipArch with Distinction in Design), Univ of Pennsylvania (MLA); *Career* teaching asst Dept of Landscape Architecture and Regional Planning Univ of Pennsylvania 1968–70, asst prof of architecture Univ of Southern Calif 1970–74, assoc then ptnr W J Cairns and Partners environmental consltss 1974–82, ptnr Design Innovations Research 1978–82, princ Turnbull Jeffrey Partnership 1982–; external examiner Dept of Landscape Architecture Heriot Watt Univ 1984–88; Edinburgh Corp Medal for Civic Design 1968, Andrew Grant scholarships Edinburgh Coll of Art Sch of Archtecture 1964, 1965, 1967 and 1968, Fulbright travel scholarship 1968, faculty medal Dept of Landscape Architecture Univ of Pennsylvania 1970; memb: Cncl Cockburn Assoc 1986–95, Countryside Cmmn for Scotland 1988–92, Royal Fine Art Cmmn for Scotland 1996–; chm Edinburgh Green Belt Initiative 1988–91, dir and vice chm Edinburgh Green Belt Tst 1991–; RIBA 1977, MBCS 1986, FLI 1989 (ALI 1975), FRIAS 1991 (ARIAS 1977); *Recreations* sailing; *Style*— Mark Turnbull, Esq; ✉ Turnbull Jeffrey Partnership, Sandeman House, 55 High Street, Edinburgh EH1 1SR (☎ 0131 557 5050, fax 0131 557 5064, mobile 0374 685970, e-mail tjp@tjp.co.uk)

TURNBULL, Rt Rev Michael; *see:* Durham, Bishop of

TURNBULL, Nicholas Stahel (Nick); s of John James Turnbull (d 1994), and Joyce Auberon, *née* Sparks (d 1990); *b* 6 Sept 1936; *Educ* Univ Coll Sch London, Harvard Business Sch (AMP Dip); *m* 1960, Ann Elizabeth, da of George Mark Anderson; 2 s (Mark John b 19 Jan 1963, Guy Michael b 9 Sept 1965), 1 da (Susannah Elizabeth b 19 Dec 1971); *Career* Nat Serv 2 Lt KAR (Kenya) 1955–57 (Kenya Medal 1956); trainee/account exec S H Benson Ltd then account exec Smith Warden Ltd 1957–63, gp advtg mangr Harveys of Bristol 1963–65, sr account supr Ogilvy & Mather Ltd 1965–66; Bass Charrington Vintners Ltd: sales mangr Evans Marshall & Co 1966–70, mktg mangr 1970–72, sales and mktg dir (concurrently chm Hedges & Butler (Ireland) Ltd) 1972–78; mktg dir European Wine & Spirit Agencies Ltd 1978–80, mktg and sales dir Cinzano (UK) Ltd 1980–84, mktg servs conslt 1984–88, dir of mktg Nat Cncl for Voluntary Qualifications 1988–89, mktg and sales dir Mondial Wine Ltd 1989–93, mktg conslt 1993–95, DG Marketing Soc 1995–; MIPA 1965, memb Marketing Soc 1995; *Recreations* golf, gardening, reading, walking, travel; *Style*— Nick Turnbull, Esq; ✉ 43 Detillens Lane, Limpsfield, Surrey RH8 0DH (☎ 01883 715329); The Marketing Society, St George's House, 3/5 Pepys Road, London SW20 8NJ (☎ 0181 879 3464, fax 0181 879 0362)

TURNBULL, (Stephen) Paul; s of Norman Ellis Swift Turnbull (d 1990), of Liverpool, and Joan, *née* Rashbrook; *b* 11 Dec 1952; *Educ* Quarry Bank HS Liverpool, Corpus Christi Coll Oxford (exhibitioner, BA); *Career* economist; res exec British Market Research Bureau Ltd 1976–77; economist: The Building Societies' Assoc 1977–79, L Messel & Co stockbrokers 1979–84; chief economist and strategist Scott Goff Layton & Co stockbrokers 1984–86, chief economist Smith New Court plc 1986–95, chief UK economist Merrill Lynch (following takeover of Smith New Court plc) 1995–; *Awards* winner Best UK Economic Forecast Independent on Sunday Golden Guru Award (1991), topped FT survey to find best forecaster of UK economy during period 1990–92 (1992), ranked first in the Extel survey of UK fund mangrs (1996); *Recreations* backgammon (Irish Open Champion 1995, top-ranked UK player Br Isles Backgammon Assoc 1995), tennis, piano; *Style*— Paul Turnbull, Esq; ✉ Merrill Lynch, 20 Farringdon Road, London EC1M 3NH (☎ 0171 772 1574, fax 0171 772 2284)

TURNBULL, Peter John; s of John Colin Turnbull, of Rotherham, S Yorks, and Patricia, *née* O'Brien; *b* 23 Oct 1950; *Educ* Oakwood Secdy Modern Sch Rotherham, Richmond Coll of FE, Cambs Coll of Arts & Technol (BA), UC Cardiff (CQSW); *Career* offr Regnl Cncl Public Serv of Strathclyde 1978–92, Leeds City Cncl 1992–95; crime writer 1981–; *Books* Deep and Crisp and Even (1981), Dead Knock (1982), Fair Friday (1983), Big Money (1983), The Claws of the Gryphon (1986), Two Way Cut (1988), Condition Purple (1989), The Justice Game (1990), And Did Murder Him (1991), Long Day Monday (1992), The Killing Floor (1994), The Killer Who Never Was (1996), Embracing Skeletons (1996); *Recreations* relaxing in the company of good friends; *Style*— Peter Turnbull, Esq; ✉ c/o Charles Walker, Peters Fraser & Dunlop, The Chambers, Chelsea Harbour, Lots Rd, London (☎ 0171 376 7676)

TURNBULL, Sir Richard Gordon; GCMG (1962, KCMG 1958, CMG 1953); s of Richard Francis Turnbull (d 1963); *b* 1909; *Educ* Univ Coll Sch, UCL, Magdalene Coll Cambridge; *m* 1939, Beatrice, da of John Wilson (d 1986); 2 s, 1 da; *Career* entered Colonial Admin Serv 1931, dist offr Kenya 1931, provincial cmmr 1948, provincial cmmr Northern Frontier Province 1948–53, min for Internal Security and Def 1954, chief sec and govr's dep Kenya 1955–58, govr and c-in-c Tanganyika Territory 1958–61 (govr gen and c-in-c 1961–62), chm Central Land Bd Kenya 1963–64, high cmmr for Aden and Protectorates of South Arabia 1965–67; fell UCL, hon fell Magdalene Coll Cambridge; KStJ 1958; *Style*— Sir Richard Turnbull, GCMG

TURNBULL, Steven Michael; s of Philip Peveril Turnbull (d 1987), of Rock, Cornwall, and Dorothy June Turnbull; *b* 24 Oct 1952; *Educ* Monkton Combe Sch, Univ Coll Oxford (BA); *m* 22 Sept 1985, Mary Ann, da of David M Colyer, of Cheltenham, Glos; 1 s (Matthew b 11 July 1987), 1 da (Clare b 21 Aug 1988); *Career* Linklaters & Paines: joined 1975, slr 1978, joined Corporate Dept, ptnr 1985; memb Law Soc, memb City of London Slrs Co; *Recreations* golf, tennis, family; *Clubs* Oxford and Cambridge Golfing Soc, Royal Wimbledon Golf; *Style*— Steven Turnbull, Esq; ✉ Linklaters & Paines, Barrington House, 59–67 Gresham St, London EC2V 7JA (☎ 0171 606 7080)

TURNBULL, William; *b* 11 Jan 1922; *Educ* Slade Sch of Art; *Career* artist; solo exhibitions: Hanover Gallery 1950 and 1952, ICA 1957, Molton Gallery 1960 and 1961, Marlborough-Gerson Gallery NY 1963, Art Inst Detroit 1963, Bennington Coll Vermont 1965, Galeric Muller Stuttgart 1965 and 1974, Pavilion Gallery Balboa Calif 1966, Waddington Galleries 1967, 1969, 1970, 1976, 1981, 1982, 1985, 1987 and 1991, IX Bienal Sao Paolo Brazil touring 1967–68, Hayward Gallery 1968, Tate Gallery 1973, Scottish Arts Cncl 1974, Waddington and Tooth Galleries 1978, The Scottish Gallery Edinburgh 1981, Galerie Kutter Luxembourg 1983, Nat Museum Art Gallery Singapore 1984, Galerie Folker Skulima W Berlin 1987, Terry Dintenfass Inc NY 1988, John Berggruen Gallery San Francisco 1988–89, Arnold Herstand Gallery NY 1989, Sculpture on the Close (Jesus Coll Cambridge) 1990, Galeria Freites Caracas 1992, Galerie Michael Haas Berlin 1992, Galerie Neuman Düsseldorf 1993, Galerie Von Braunbehrens Munich 1993, Serpentine Gallery 1995; selected group exhibitions: Venice Biennale (Br Pavilion, Venice) 1952, Pittsburgh Int (Carnegie Inst Pittsburg Pa) 1958, 1961 and 1962, Situation (RBA Galleries) 1960, Second Int Exhibition of Sculpture (Musee Rodin Paris) 1961, Hirshhorn Collection (Guggenheim Museum NY) 1962, Seventh Int Art Exhibition Tokyo 1963, Guggenheim Int NY 1964, Br Sculpture in the Sixties (Tate Gallery) 1965, First Int Exhibition of Modern Sculpture (Hakone Open Air Museum Japan) 1969, McAlpine Collection (Tate Gallery) 1971, Art Inglese Oggie (Palazzo Reale Milan), Tate 79 (Tate Gallery) 1979, Br Sculpture in the twentieth century: part 2 symbol and imagination 1951–80 (Whitechapel Art Gallery 1982, Forty Years of Modern Art 1945–85 (Tate Gallery) 1986, Br Art in the Twentieth Century: The Modern Movement (Royal Acad and touring) 1987, Britannica: Trente Ans de Sculpture 1960–88 (Musee de Beaux Arts, Le Havre) 1988, Modern Br Sculpture from the Collection (Tate Liverpool) 1988, Scottish Art Since 1900 (Scottish Nat Gallery of Modern Art Edinburgh and Barbican Art Gallery) 1989, The Independent Group: Postwar Britain and the Aesthetics of Plenty (ICA) 1990–91; works in the collections of: Albright - Knox Art Gallery Buffalo, Arts Cncl of GB, Art Gallery of Ontario, Br Cncl, Contemporary Arts Soc, Dundee Museum and Art Gallery, Franklin P Murphy Sculpture Garden UCLA, Glasgow Museum and Art Gallery, Hirshhorn Museum and Sculpture (Smithsonian Inst) Washington DC, Univ of Hull, McCrory Corp NY, Museum of Contemporary Art Tehran, Nat Gallery of Art Washington DC, Scottish Nat Gallery of Modern Art Edinburgh, Stadtisches Museum Leverkusen Germany, Sydney Opera House, Tate Gallery, V & A, Westfalisches Landesmuseum Munster; *Style*— William Turnbull, Esq; ✉ c/o Waddington Galleries Ltd, 11 Cork Street, London W1X 1PD (☎ 0171 437 8611, fax 0171 734 4146)

TURNER, (Jonathan) Adair; s of Geoffrey Vincent Turner, and Kathleen Margaret, *née* Broadhurst (d 1977); *Educ* Hutcheson's GS Glasgow, Trinity Coll Glenalmond, Gonville & Caius Coll Cambridge (scholar, MA, chm Cambridge Univ Cons Assoc, pres Cambridge Univ Union Soc); *m* 5 May 1985, Orna Ni Chionna; 2 da (Eleonar Catherine b 18 Nov 1988, Julia Christine b 1 Sept 1991); *Career* Corp Planning Dept BP 1979, Chase Manhattan Bank NA 1979–82; McKinsey & Co (strategic consltss): joined 1982, princ (ptnr) 1988, dir (sr ptnr) 1994; dir-gen CBI 1995–; ESU debating tour of USA 1979; memb: RIIA, Nat Advsy Cncl on Educn and Training Targets (NACETT); *Recreations* theatre, opera, skiing; *Style*— Adair Turner, Esq; ✉ Confederation of British Industry, Centre Point, 103 New Oxford Street, London WC1A 1DU (☎ 0171 379 7400)

TURNER, Adrian Geoffrey Leslie; LVO (1986); er s of Leslie Bertram Turner, MBE (d 1979), and Lillian Augusta, *née* Broad (d 1995); *b* 28 April 1927; *Educ* Highgate, Clayesmore, Univ of London; *Career* HM Dip Serv: entered 1948, Lahore Pakistan 1955–57 (also broadcaster western music Radio Pakistan and external examiner Univ of the Punjab), Colombo Sri Lanka 1960–63 (also broadcaster Radio Ceylon), Asuncion Paraguay 1969–71, Holy See 1971–73; memb Br delegation: Int Lab Conf Geneva 1959, UN Gen Assembly New York 1965, UN Conf on the Law of Treaties Vienna 1969; head Hons Section FCO 1979–87, ret; memb: Cncl Heraldry Soc 1947–86 (hon fell 1954, vice pres 1996), Hon Cncl of Mgmnt The Royal Philharmonic Soc 1981–86 (fell 1951), Cncl St John Historical Soc 1985–90, Conslt False Orders Ctee Orders of St John of Jerusalem 1987; Freeman City of London 1978, Liveryman Worshipful Co of Scriveners; Sovereign Mil Order of Malta 1972, Knight of Obedience 1981; memb Grand Priory of England 1981; OStJ 1988; FRSA 1987–92; *Recreations* music, heraldry, genealogy, reading, the study of the Orders of St John and the promotion of the legality of Roman Catholic territorial titles; *Clubs* Royal Over-Seas League; *Style*— Adrian Turner, Esq, LVO; ✉ Shelsley, 135 Cranley Gdns, Muswell Hill, London N10 3AG

TURNER, Alan Charles; s of Edwin Charles Turner (d 1986), and Mary Bettina, *née* Poncia; *b* 21 Aug 1941; *Educ* Marlborough, Univ of Birmingham (LLB); *m* 4 Sept 1971, Rosemary Ann, da of Graham John Hartman Johnson; 3 da (Josephine Mary b 22 Oct 1974 d 1992, Amy Jane b 5 Sept 1977, Frances Bettina b 10 Dec 1983); *Career* articled clerk Howard Smith Thompson & Co (merged with Price Waterhouse 1963) 1963, ptnr 1978, regnl sr tax ptnr 1990, dir Regnl Offices 1992; FCA 1966; *Recreations* dry fly fishing, theatre; *Clubs* Lansdowne, Birmingham; *Style*— Alan Turner, Esq; ✉ Price Waterhouse, Southwark Towers, 32 London Bridge Street, London SE1 9SY (☎ 0171 939 3000, fax 0171 378 0647); Price Waterhouse, Cornwall Court, 19 Cornwall Street, Birmingham B3 2DT (☎ 0121 200 3000, fax 0121 200 2464)

TURNER, Amédée Edward; QC (1976); s of Frederick William Turner (d 1945), and Ruth Hempson (d 1970); mother's side Huguenot Swiss; *b* 26 March 1929; *Educ* ChCh Oxford; *m* 1960, Deborah Dudley, da of Dr Philip Owen; 1 s, 1 da; *Career* called to the Bar Inner Temple 1954; practised Patent Bar 1954–57, assoc Kenyon & Kenyon patent attorneys NY 1957–60, in practice London 1960–; Parly candidate (C) Norwich N gen elections 1964, 1966 and 1970; MEP (EDG 1979–92, EPP 1992–94): Suffolk and Harwich 1979–84, Suffolk and SE Cambridgeshire 1984–94; vice chm Legal Ctee 1979–84; memb: Econ and Monetary Ctee 1979–84, Tport Ctee 1981–84, Energy Ctee 1983–89, ACP Jt Assembly 1989–94; chief whip Euro Democratic Gp 1989–92, chm Ctee on Int Affrs and Civil Rights 1992–94; hon memb Euro Parl 1994–, memb Exec Ctee Euro League for Economic Co-operation 1996–; sr counsel to: Oppenheimer, Wolff & Donnelly (US lawyers) 1995–, APCO Europe (Brussels) 1995–; *Books* The Law of Trade Secrets (1962, supplement 1968), The Law of the New European Patent (1979), author of many Cons Pty study papers on defence, oil and Middle East; *Recreations* garden designs, painting; *Clubs* Carlton, Coningsby, United and Cecil; *Style*— Amédée Turner, Esq, QC; ✉ 3 Montrose Place, London SW1X 7DU; The Barn, Westleton, Saxmundham, Suffolk; La Combe de la Boissière, St Maximin, Uzès, France

TURNER, Andrew Charles; s of Ralph Turner, of Leeds, and Jean, *née* Belcher; *b* 3 July 1956; *Educ* Leeds GS, Christ's Coll Cambridge (MA); *m* 4 Sept 1982, Janice Helen, da of Albert Charles Minker; 3 s (Nicholas Ralph Charles b 4 June 1987, William George Leonard b 5 Sept 1990, Jonathan Robert Lawrence (twin) b 5 Sept 1990); *Career* Coopers & Lybrand: sr mangr Audit 1977–85, mangr CHUO Audit Corporation Tokyo 1985–86, dir Fin Servs Div CHUO Coopers & Lybrand Consulting Co Ltd 1986–88, managing conslt Fin Servs Div Mgmnt Consulting Servs 1988–89, audit ptnr 1990–, liaison ptnr Vietnam/Indo-China, chm Korean and Taiwan Market Sector Gps, memb Japan Market Sector Gp; FCA 1990 (ACA 1980); *Recreations* house renovation, golf, photography; *Style—* Andrew Turner, Esq; ✉ Coopers & Lybrand, 1 Embankment Place, London WC2N 6NN (☎ 0171 583 5000, fax 0171 822 4652)

TURNER, Anthea; da of Brian Turner, of Stoke-on-Trent, and Jean, *née* Walker; *b* 25 May 1960; *Educ* St Dominic's GS for Girls; *m* 31 Jan 1990, Peter James Powell, *qv*; *Career* television personality; presenter live music progs Sky Television 1986–89; presenter for BBC 1987–96: But First This 1987, Up2U, Best of Magic 1989–91, Top of the Pops 1988–91, Blue Peter 1992–94, The Good Health Show 1994, live opening of Channel Tunnel 1994, Children's Royal Variety Performance 1995, National Lottery Live 1994–96; presenter GMTV 1994–96; under exclusive contract to Carlton TV 1996–; host All You Need Is Love 1996–; voted Best Dressed Woman on TV and Head of the Year 1995, Variety Club Show Business Star of the Year 1995, BBC Personality of the Year 1996; patron: Born Free Fndn, Anti Bullying Campaign, Humane Research Tst, Elizabeth Tst Refuge for Women and Children, St Tiggywinkle's; ambass Prince's Tst, memb Tidy Britain Gp; *Style—* Miss Anthea Turner; ✉ c/o James Grant Media Group, Syon Lodge, London Road, Syon Park, Middx TW7 5BH (☎ 0181 232 4100, fax 0181 232 4101)

TURNER, Ven Antony Hubert Michael (Tony); s of Frederick George Turner (d 1960), and Winifred Frances Turner (d 1956); *b* 17 June 1930; *Educ* Royal Liberty Sch Romford, Univ of London (Dip Theol); *m* 5 July 1956, Margaret Kathleen, da of Reginald McKenzie Phillips, of Essex; 2 da (Ruth b 1958, Susan b 1960), 1 s (Michael b 1961),; *Career* ordained deacon 1956, curate St Ann's Nottingham 1956–59, curate in charge St Cuthbert's Cheadle Diocese of Chester 1959–62, vicar Christ Church Macclesfield 1962–68, home sec Bible Churchmen's Missionary Soc 1968–74, vicar St Jude's Southsea 1974–86, rural dean Portsmouth 1979–84, archdeacon of the IOW 1986–96 (archdeacon emeritus 1996–); church cmmr 1983–93; vice chm C of E Pensions Bd; ACA 1952, FCA 1962; *Recreations* photography, caravanning; *Style—* The Ven Tony Turner

TURNER, Brian James; s of Lawrence Turner, of Morley, Leeds, and late Lily, *née* Riley; *b* 7 May 1946; *Educ* Morley GS, Leeds Coll of Food Technol, Borough Poly, Ealing Hotel Sch; *m* Denise, da of Alan Parker, of Rothwell, Leeds, Yorks; 2 s (Simeon James b 18 Nov 1974, Benjamin Jon b 5 July 1977); *Career* chef/restaurateur; Simpsons on the Strand London 1964–66, Savoy Hotel London 1966–69, Beau-Rivage Palace Lausanne-Ouchy Switzerland 1969–70, Claridges Hotel London 1970–71, Capital Hotel London 1971–86, Turners of Walton Street London 1986–; chm Acadèmie Culinaire 1993–; Good Food Guide Special Award 1996; FHCIMA 1988 (MHCIMA 1980–88); *Books* Ready Steady Cook (with Antony Worrall-Thompson, 1996); *Style—* Brian Turner, Esq; ✉ Turner's, 87–89 Walton Street, London SW3 2HP (☎ 0171 584 6711, 0171 584 4441)

TURNER, Prof Cedric Edward; CBE (1987); s of Charles Turner (d 1949), and Mabel Evelyn, *née* Berry (d 1962); *b* 5 Aug 1926; *Educ* Brockenhurst Co GS, Univ of Southampton (BSc), Univ of London (PhD, DSc); *m* 29 Aug 1953, Margaret (Peggy) Dorothy, da of Edward Percy Davies (d 1976), of Merrow, Guildford; 1 s (Jeffrey b 1961), 2 da (Hazel b 1956, Gillian b 1959); *Career* Imperial Coll: lectr 1951–66, asst dir 1966–73, reader 1966–75, prof of materials in mechanical engrg 1975–91 (ret), seconded to Nat Physical Laboratory 1976–78, seconded to British Aerospace 1978–79; memb UK Ctee on Structural Integrity; Silver medal Plastics Inst 1963, James Clayton Prize Inst of Mech Engrs 1981, hon prof Shenyang Inst of Aeronautical Engrg People's Republic of China 1986, Leverhulme sr res fell 1990–92; FIMechE 1976, FEng 1989; *Books* Introduction to Plate & Shell Theory (1967), Post-Yield Fracture Mechanics (jtly 2 edn, 1985); *Recreations* walking, gardening, fracture mechanics; *Style—* Prof Cedric Turner, CBE, FEng

TURNER, Sir Colin William Carstairs; kt (1993), CBE (1984), DFC (1944); s of Colin Carstairs William Turner (d 1963), of Enfield, Middx, and Phebe Marianne Miller (d 1945); *b* 4 Jan 1922; *Educ* Highgate Sch; *m* 7 May 1949, Evelyn Mary, da of Claude Horatio Buckard (d 1966), of Enfield; 3 s (Anthony b 18 Feb 1954, Nigel b 7 Jan 1956, Christopher b 1 Aug 1964), 1 da (Susan b 23 Aug 1951); *Career* air observer RAFVR, volunteered 1940, ITW Torquay 1941, 47 Air Sch Queenstown SA 1941, 31 Air Sch E London SA 1941, 70 OTU Nakuru Kenya 1942, 223 Sqdn Baltimores Desert Air Force Egypt 1942 (cmmnd 1943), Tunisia 1943, Malta 1943, Sicily 1943, Italy 1943, returned UK 1944, 527 Sqdn Digby Lincs (crashed 1944), RAF Hosp Northallerton and Rehabilitation Centre Loughborough 1944–45, invalided out as Flying Offr 1946; Colin Turner Group of Cos (family co): joined 1940, dir 1945–, md 1964–84, chm 1985–87, life pres 1988–; Overseas Press and Media Assoc: fndr pres 1965–67, hon treas 1974–82, life pres 1983–; ed Overseas Media Guide 1968–74; Cwlth Press Union: assoc memb 1963–, chm PR Ctee 1970–87, memb Fin Ctee 1972–87, Exec Ctee 1988–93; memb Nat Exec Cons Pty 1946–53, 1968–73 and 1976–82; chm Cons Cwlth and Overseas Cncl 1976–82 (vice-pres 1984–94); Parly candidate (C) Enfield East 1950 and 1951, MP (C) West Woolwich 1959–64; RAFA: memb 1945–, pres Enfield Branch 1947–58 and 1966–93, chm Sheringham and Dist Branch 1994–; chm 223 Sqdn Assoc 1947–93; pres Old Cholmeleian Assoc (Highgate Sch Old Boys) 1985–86, ed The Cholmeleian 1982–95; *Recreations* DIY, gardening, sailing, fishing; *Clubs* Cromer Conservative; *Style—* Sir Colin Turner, CBE, DFC; ✉ The Thatched House, Balfour Road, West Runton, Norfolk NR27 9QJ (☎ and fax 01263 837229)

TURNER, David Andrew; QC (1991); s of James Turner (d 1986), and Phyllis, *née* Molyneux; *b* 6 March 1947; *Educ* King George V Sch Southport, Queens' Coll Cambridge (MA, LLM); *m* 18 March 1978, Mary Christine, da of Eric Herbert Moffatt, of Douglas, IOM; 2 s (James b 1981, Charles b 1982), 1 da (Helen b 1984); *Career* called to the Bar Gray's Inn 1971, recorder of the Crown Ct 1990–; *Recreations* squash, music; *Clubs* Liverpool Racquet; *Style—* David Turner, Esq, QC; ✉ Exchange Chambers, Pearl Assurance House, Derby Square, Liverpool L2 9XX (☎ 0151 236 7747)

TURNER, David George Patrick; s of George Patrick Turner (d 1988), of Londonderry, and Elsie Bamford, *née* McClure; *b* 11 July 1954; *Educ* Foyle Coll Londonderry, King's Coll London (LLB, AKC), Coll of Law London; *m* 4 March 1978, Jean Patricia, da of Gerald William Hewett, of Carleton Rode, Norfolk; 2 s (Robert b 7 Oct 1980, Richard b 30 Oct 1982); *Career* called to the Bar Gray's Inn 1976, S Eastern Circuit; dir Society of Wildlife Art of the Nations Ltd; churchwarden and lay reader All Souls' Langham Place; tstee: Langham Tst, St Paul's Tst (Portman Square); memb: Family Law Bar Assoc, Criminal Bar Assoc, Ecclesiastical Law Soc, Assoc of Lawyers for Children, Intercountry Adoption Lawyers' Assoc; *Recreations* reading, swimming, family; *Style—* David Turner, Esq; ✉ 32 Allerton Rd, London N16 5UJ (☎ 0181 802 3805); 14 Gray's Inn Square, Gray's Inn, London WC1R 5JP (☎ 0171 242 0858, fax 0171 242 5434)

TURNER, David John; s of Frederick Turner, of Prenton, Birkenhead, Merseyside, and Sheila Margaret, *née* Collinson; *b* 7 Feb 1945; *Educ* Birkenhead Sch; *m* Julia Anne, *née* Thompson; 1 s (Jonathon Frederick b 22 March 1978), 2 da (Sarah Frances b 28 Feb 1970, Catherine Margaret b 19 Feb 1974); *Career* CA: Cook & Co Liverpool 1963–67, Touche Ross & Co London 1967–69; mgmnt auditor Mobil Oil Corpn 1969–71, chief accountant Mobil Servs Ltd 1971–73, special projects co-ordinator Mobil Europe Inc 1973–74; fin dir: Booker Agriculture 1975–84, Booker plc (formerly Booker McConnell Ltd) 1984–93, GKN plc 1993–; non-exec dir Iron Trades Insurance Co Ltd; memb Quotations Ctee London Int Stock Exchange; FCA; *Recreations* tennis, skiing; *Clubs* Boodles, Roehampton; *Style—* David J Turner, Esq; ✉ GKN plc, Ipsley Church Lane, Redditch, Worcs B98 0TL (☎ 01527 517715, fax 01527 517700)

TURNER, Dr David John; s of Edward John Versey Turner, and Maud Beatrice, *née* Fisher; *b* 13 Feb 1935; *Educ* Felixstowe County GS, Univ of Edinburgh (MB ChB); *m* 25 July 1959, Jill, da of John Walter Lewis; 2 s (John b 1962, Scott b 1964); *Career* sr house offr and registrar in anaesthetics Ipswich Hosp and E Suffolk Hosp 1963–66, registrar and sr registrar in anaesthetics Royal Infirmary Edinburgh 1966–69, conslt anaesthetist to Gt Yarmouth and Waveney Dist at James Paget Hosp 1969–96, ret (hon conslt 1996–); memb: BMA, E Anglia Assoc of Anaesthetics; FFARCS; *Recreations* sailing, birdwatching, squash; *Clubs* Royal Norfolk and Suffolk Yacht, Waveney and Oulton Broad Yacht, Gunton Park Squash; *Style—* Dr David J Turner; ✉ Gosford House, 3 Noel Rd, Oulton Broad, Lowestoft, Suffolk NR32 3JS (☎ 01502 564263); Department of Anaesthesia, James Paget Hospital, Lowestoft Rd, Gorleston, Gt Yarmouth, Norfolk (☎ 01493 452452)

TURNER, Prof David Robert; s of Harry James Turner (d 1963), of Sevenoaks, Kent, and Vera May, *née* Jackson; *b* 26 Feb 1939; *Educ* Chislehurst and Sidcup GS for Boys, Guy's Hosp Med Sch (MB BS, PhD); *m* 1, (m dis); 3 da (Karen Mary b 1963, Sarah Ann b 1973, Judith Dawn b 1975), 1 s (Ian Keith b 1965); m 2, 1981, Dr Juliet Mary Heaton; *Career* Guy's Hosp: various house appointments 1962–63, demonstrator and lectr in anatomy 1963–69, sr lectr and laterly reader in pathology 1969–80, prof of histopathology 1980–81; conslt histopathologist Musgrove Park Hosp 1981–83, prof of pathology Nottingham Med Sch 1983– (vice dean 1985–88); memb WHO Ctee for histological classification of renal disease 1976–; chm: Assoc of Profs of Pathology 1992–, Fedn of Assocs of Clinical Profs 1993–; FRCPath 1985 (MRCPath 1973); *Books* Atlas of Renal Pathology (1981); *Recreations* long distance running, reading, organising a smallholding; *Style—* Prof David Turner; ✉ Department of Pathology, University Hospital, Queen's Medical Centre, Nottingham NG7 2UH (☎ 0115 970 9169, fax 0115 970 4852)

TURNER, Prof David Warren; s of Robert Cecil Turner (d 1983), of Leigh on Sea, Essex, and Constance Margaret, *née* Bonner (d 1969); *b* 16 July 1927; *Educ* Westcliff HS, Univ of Exeter (BSc), Imperial Coll Univ of London (PhD, DIC); *m* 11 Sept 1954, Barbara Marion, da of Cyril Fisher (d 1982), of Oxford; 1 s (Paul b 1958), 1 da (Susan b 1963); *Career* reader in organic chemistry Imperial Coll Univ of London 1965 (lectr 1958); Univ of Oxford: fell and tutor Balliol Coll 1967, lectr in physical chemistry 1968, reader in physical chemistry 1978, prof of electron spectroscopy 1984–94, emeritus prof 1994–; memb IUPAC Cmmn on Molecular Spectroscopy; Hon DTech Royal Tech Inst Stockholm 1971, Hon DPhil Univ of Basel 1980; FRS 1973; *Books* Molecular Photoelectron Spectroscopy (1970); *Recreations* music, gardening, tinkering with gadgets; *Style—* Prof David Turner, FRS; ✉ Balliol College, Oxford

TURNER, Dennis; MP (Lab/Co-op) Wolverhampton South East (majority 10,240); s of Thomas Herbert Turner (d 1981), and Mary Elizabeth, *née* Peasley (d 1974); *b* 26 Aug 1942; *Educ* Stonefield Secdy Sch Bilston W Mids, Bilston Coll of Further Educn; *m* 19 June 1976, Patricia Mary, da of Joseph Henry Narroway (d 1984), of Bilston; 1 s (Brendon Robert b 1977), 1 da (Jenny Mary b 1980); *Career* chm: Springvale Co-op Ltd Bilston, Springvale Enterprises Ltd Bilston; dep ldr Wolverhampton MDC 1979–86 (sometime chm Social Servs, Housing Further Educn and Econ Devpt Ctees), cncllr W Midlands CC 1975–; MP (Lab) Wolverhampton SE 1987–, Lab whip for Defence and W Midlands; chm: Co-operative Parly Gp, All Pty Parly FE Colls Gp, All Pty Parly Housing Co-op Gp; pres: Bilston Community Assoc, Bradley Community Assoc, Ettingshall Darts League, Bradley and Wultrun Corps of Drums; sec and tstee Bradley and Dist Sr Citizens' Centre; *Recreations* compereing, beer tasting, all card games; *Clubs* New Springvale Sports & Social (Bilston); *Style—* Dennis Turner, Esq, MP; ✉ Ambleside, King St, Bradley, Bilston, W Midlands (☎ 01902 41822); Springvale House, Millfields Rd, Bilston, W Midlands (01902 42364); House of Commons, London SW1A 0AA (☎ 0171 219 3000)

TURNER, Donald; s of Frederick Henry Turner (d 1959), of Enfield, Middx, and Doris Primrose, *née* Gilbertson (d 1980); *b* 26 July 1932; *Educ* Enfield GS, City of London Coll; *m* 8 Sept 1956, Jean Shirley, da of Percival McEntire; 1 s (Craig b 21 Sept 1957), 1 da (Nicola Diane b 26 March 1960); *Career* Nat Serv RAF 1950–52, with Chartered Bank 1948–50 and 1952–69; Butler Till Ltd: dir 1972–87, dep md 1979–82, chm 1982–87; non-exec dir: Guardian Building Society 1987–90, Cheltenham & Gloucester Building Society 1990–, Cheltenham & Gloucester PLC 1995, Cheltenham & Gloucester (Channel Islands) PLC 1995; ACIB 1963; *Recreations* golf, woodwork; *Style—* Donald Turner, Esq; ✉ Cheltenham & Gloucester Building Society, Barnett Way, Gloucester GL4 7RL (☎ 01452 372372)

TURNER, Donald Ian; s of John Moncrieff Turner (d 1991), of Kilmarnock, and Ann Grant, *née* Henderson; *b* 20 Sept 1944; *Educ* Strathallan Sch; *m* 22 Oct 1971, Patricia Anne Lindsay, da of late John Lindsay Hardie; 1 s (Alastair John b 25 Nov 1974), 1 da (Katharine Jane b 10 Sept 1976); *Career* apprentice McClelland Moores & Co CAs Glasgow 1962–67, CA Paris Office Peat Marwick 1967–69, ptnr Turner Hutton & Lawson CAs Glasgow 1971–81 (joined 1969), ptnr Arthur Young McClelland Moores & Co Glasgow 1981, regnl managing ptnr Arthur Young Scotland 1986, regnl managing ptnr North Region and memb UK Exec Ernst & Young 1990–95, regnl managing ptnr Scotland and NI and managing ptnr Regions Ernst & Young 1995–; memb: Exec Cncl Scottish Devpt and Indust, Cncl Inst of Directors, Cncl Scottish Economic Cncl 1995–; MICM, MSPI; *Recreations* golf, fishing, shooting, rugby (capt British Rugby Club of Paris); *Clubs* Western, Caledonian, Prestwick Golf, Royal and Ancient Golf (St Andrews); *Style—* Donald I Turner, Esq; ✉ Ernst and Young, George House, 50 George Square, Glasgow G2 1RR (☎ 0141 553 4363, fax 0141 552 4119)

TURNER, Frank; s of Frank Turner (d 1977), of Earby, Yorkshire, and Marion, *née* Robinson; *b* 7 June 1943; *Educ* Keighley Tech Coll, Univ of Salford (BSc), Columbia Univ Business Sch NY (long distance running trophy); *m* 1967, Byrnece, da of Jack Crawshaw; 1 s (Julian Mark b 4 July 1977), 1 da (Suzanne Nicola b 5 Feb 1972); *Career* Rolls-Royce Ltd: apprentice 1959, graduate apprentice 1963–67, machine tool devpt engr 1967–69, tech asst and prog mangr RB211 1969–72, fin controller Rolls Royce 1971 Ltd Barnoldswick 1972–73, prodn products mangr Barnoldswick 1973–75, product centre mangr Derby 1975–78, gen mangr prodn 1978–80, dir mfrg 1980–83, dir mfrg engrg 1983–85, dir industl and marine Ansty 1985–87, chm Cooper Rolls Inc 1985–87, dir Civil Engines Rolls-Royce plc 1987–92, dir International Aero Engines AG 1987–, appointed to Main Bd Rolls-Royce plc 1988, memb Bd Rolls-Royce Inc 1987–90, chm Sawley Packaging Co 1990–92; md Aerospace Lucas Industries plc 1992–96, chief exec BM Aviation Services Ltd 1996–; non-exec dir: ASW plc 1995–, Wagon Industrial Holdings plc 1996–; pres engrg Br Assoc for Advancement of Science 1993–, pres Aviation Trg Assoc 1994–; prof Univ of Warwick 1993–; *Awards* Mensforth Gold Medal of Inst of Prodn Engrs (for contrib to Br mfrg technol) 1985, James Clayton Award Inst of Mechanical Engrs (for contrib to design, devpt and mfr of aero gas turbines); FEng 1986, FIProdE 1986, FIMechE 1986, FRAeS 1989; *Recreations* family, sailing, running, windsurfing, keep fit, music; *Style—* Frank Turner, Esq, FEng; ✉ BM Aviation Services, Donington Hall, Derby (☎ 01332 854820)

TURNER, Geoffrey Howard; s of Charles William Turner (d 1990), of Willaston-in-Wirral, and Evelyn Doris, *née* Harris; *b* 23 July 1945; *Educ* The Kings's Sch Chester, St Edmund Hall Oxford (BA, MA); *m* 31 May 1975, Margaret Linda, da of John Aitken Donaldson (d 1996), of Sedgley, West Midlands; 2 da (Katherine b 1978, Charlotte b 1981); *Career* Stock Exchange: mangr Membership Dept 1975–78 (asst mangr 1973–75), sec Wilson Evidence Ctee 1978, sec Planning Ctee 1977–78, sec Restrictive Practices Case Ctee 1978–83, head of membership 1983–86; dir of membership Int Stock Exchange 1986–90, dir of public affairs Securities and Futures Authy Ltd 1993–94 (dir of membership 1986–92), chief exec Assoc of Private Client Investment Managers and Stockbrokers 1994–; chm Bd of Govrs Wood End Sch Harpenden 1988–91; Freeman City of London 1980; *Recreations* visiting country churches, collecting books and prints; *Clubs* Vincents (Oxford), Leander; *Style—* Geoffrey Turner, Esq; ✉ 44 Roundwood Lane, Harpenden, Herts (☎ 01582 769882); Association of Private Client Investment Managers and Stockbrokers, 112 Middlesex Street, London E1 7HY (☎ 0171 247 7080, fax 0171 377 0939)

TURNER, Geoffrey Martin (Geoff); *see:* Stockport, Bishop of

TURNER, Prof Grenville; s of Arnold Turner, of Todmorden, and Florence Turner; *b* 1 Nov 1936; *Educ* Todmorden GS, St John's Coll Cambridge (BA, MA), Balliol Coll Oxford (DPhil); *m* 8 April 1961, Kathleen, da of William Morris (d 1986), of Rochdale; 1 s (Patrick b 1968), 1 da (Charlotte b 1966); *Career* asst prof Univ of California Berkeley 1962–64, res assoc California Inst of Technol 1970–71, prof of physics Univ of Sheffield 1980–88 (lectr 1964–74, sr lectr 1974–79, reader 1979–80), prof of isotope geochemistry Univ of Manchester 1988–; memb Ctees: SERC, Br Nat Space Centre; winner Rumford Medal Royal Soc 1996; geochemistry fell Geochemical Soc and Euro Assoc of Geochemistry 1996, fell Meteoritical Soc 1980; FRS 1980 (memb Cncl 1990–92); *Recreations* photography, walking, theatre; *Style—* Prof Grenville Turner, FRS; ✉ 42 Edgehill Road, Sheffield S7 1SP; Department of Geology, The University of Manchester M13 9PL (☎ 0161 275 3800, fax 0161 275 3947, e-mail grenville.turner@man.ac.uk)

TURNER, Harry Edward; s of Harry Turner (d 1967), of London, and Bessie Marguerite Jay (d 1984); *b* 28 Feb 1935; *Educ* Sloane Sch Chelsea; *m* 2 June 1956, Carolyn Louie, da of Frank Bird (d 1958), of Guernsey; 1 s (Gregory Alexander b 1957), 1 da (Jane Louie b 1959); *Career* RA 1953–55, cmmnd 2 Lt 1 Bn Middx Regt 1934; Westward TV: sales exec 1962, gen sales mangr 1966, head of sales 1970, dir of sales 1972; md Television South West PLC 1985–92 (joined 1981), dir ITN 1987–92, chm Amcom Resources PLC 1992–; dir Prince of Wales Tst 1988–92; vice chm The Advertising Assoc, pres NABS 1997–; FRSA 1986; *Books* The Man Who Could Hear Fishes Scream (1978), The Gentle Art of Salesmanship (1985), So You Want to be a Sales Manager (1986), The Salesman's Bedside Trilogy (1992); *Recreations* skiing, riding, tennis, writing; *Clubs* English Speaking Union, Tramp, Mannheim (NY); *Style—* Harry Turner, Esq; ✉ Four Acres, Lake Road, Deepcut, Surrey GU16 6RB

TURNER, (Robert) Ian; s of Major Lewis John Turner, of Grove House, Singleton, nr Chichester, W Sussex, and Jean Cleghorn, *née* Dashwood; *b* 22 Oct 1940; *Educ* Eton; *m* 4 May 1974, Alexandra Susan, da of Brig Peter Chambré Hinde, DSO (d 1983); 1 s (Peter b 1975), 1 da (Katharine b 1977); *Career* dir Fuller, Smith & Turner plc 1967–; Master Worshipful Co of Brewers 1995–96; FCA; *Recreations* shooting, skiing; *Style—* Ian Turner, Esq; ✉ Weston Mark, Upton Grey, Basingstoke, Hants RG25 2RJ (☎ 01256 862429)

TURNER, James; s of James Gordon Melville Turner, GC (d 1967), and Peggy Pamela, *née* Masters; *b* 23 Nov 1952; *Educ* Bexhill GS, Univ of Hull (LLB); *m* 7 July 1979, Sheila, da of John Barclay Green, OBE, of Woking, Surrey (d 1994); 3 s (George b 27 Jan 1981, Roderick b 1 Nov 1986, Felix b 31 Jan 1991), 2 da (Phoebe b 23 Nov 1983, Poppy b 11 Nov 1992); *Career* called to Bar Inner Temple 1976; *Publications* Archbold's Criminal Pleading, Evidence & Practice (jt ed); *Recreations* eating, drinking, reading, law; *Style—* James Turner, Esq; ✉ 1 King's Bench Walk, Temple, London EC4Y 7DB (☎ 0171 583 6266, fax 0171 583 2068)

TURNER, Janet Mary; QC (1996); da of Cecil Sidney Turner, and Gwendoline Joyce, *née* Loseby; *b* 16 Nov 1957; *Educ* Wycombe Abbey Sch, Univ of Bristol (LLB); *m* 16 April 1983, Paul Griffin, s of Reginald Stuart Griffin; 1 da (Leonie Sabrina b 20 May 1991), 1 s (Alexander Jake b 25 Sept 1994); *Career* called to the Bar Middle Temple 1979 (Harmsworth scholar), practising barr; sec of London Common Law and Commercial Bar Assoc, memb Commercial Bar Assoc; *Recreations* collecting art, books, antique furniture and ephemera, travel, music, wine, gardening, skiing; *Style—* Miss Janet Turner, QC; ✉ 3 Verulam Buildings, Gray's Inn, London WC1R 5NT (☎ 0171 831 8441, fax 0171 831 8479, DX: LDE 331)

TURNER, John; s of William Cecil Turner, and Hilda Margaret Turner; *b* 22 April 1946; *Educ* Northwood Hills GS; *m* 1971, Susan Georgina, *née* Kennedy; 2 s, 1 da; *Career* joined Civil Serv 1967, princ DTI 1979, MSC 1981–84, asst sec Dept of Employment 1985–86, princ private sec to Rt Hon Norman Fowler and Rt Hon Lord Young 1986–87, head of Small Firms and Tourism Div Dept of Employment 1987–89, under sec Employment Dept Gp (formerly Dept for Employment) 1988, dep chief exec Employment Serv 1989–94, Govt regional dir for Eastern Regn 1994–; *Style—* John Turner, Esq; ✉ Government Office for Eastern Region, Unit 7, Enterprise House, Vision Park, Chivers Way, Histon, Cambs CB4 4ZR (☎ 01223 202000)

TURNER, John; s of Arnold Turner, of Thorpe Willoughby, nr Selby, Yorks, and Winifred Mary, *née* Goodrum; *b* 4 April 1945; *Educ* Otago Boys's HS NZ, King's Sch Pontefract, Leeds Coll of Technol; *m* 1, Joy Mary Cousins; 1 da (Mary Elizabeth b 13 Feb 1974); m 2, Jennifer Anne, da of late William Shakespeare Clark; 1 da (Eve b 13 Dec 1980); *Career* advtg photographer specialising in still-life and automotive photography; asst to Gene Vernier and Peter Alexander 1964–67, freelance 1967–; pictures featured in Campaign Press & Poster, AFAEP, D&AD, Clio, Creative Circle and other related awards; memb AFAEP (judge The Tenth Awards); *Recreations* photography; *Style—* John Turner, Esq; ✉ 3/6 Kensal Road, London W10 5BZ (☎ 0181 968 0344, fax 0181 968 0791, mobile 0385 232465)

TURNER, Prof John Derfel; s of Joseph Turner (d 1962), of Manchester and Southport, and Dorothy Winifred, *née* Derfel (d 1979); *b* 27 Feb 1928; *Educ* Manchester GS, The Univ of Manchester (BA, MA, DipEd); *m* 6 June 1951, Susan Broady, da of Robert Baldwin Hovey, MC, OBE (d 1974), of Wheelock, Cheshire; 2 s (Stephen b 1953, Leigh b 1959); *Career* Educn Offr RAF 1948–50; teacher Prince Henry's GS Evesham 1951–53, sr lectr in educn Nigerian Coll of Arts Sci and Technol 1956–61 (lectr in English 1953–56), lectr in educn Inst of Educn Univ of Exeter 1961–64, prof of educn and dir Sch of Educn Univ of Botswana Lesotho and Swaziland 1964–70 (pro vice chllr 1966–70, emeritus prof 1970), prof of adult and higher educn Univ of Manchester 1976–85 (prof of educn and dir Sch of Educn 1970–76), rector Univ Coll of Botswana Univ of Botswana and Swaziland 1981–82 (vice chllr 1982–84); Univ of Manchester: dir Sch of Educn, dean Faculty of Educn 1985–91, pro vice chllr 1991–94, emeritus prof of educn 1994; pres Coll of Preceptors 1994–; memb: UK Nat Cmmn UNESCO 1975–81, IUC Working Parties on E and Central Africa and on Rural Devpt 1975–81, Educn Sub-ctee UGC 1980–81, Working Pty on Academic Devpt of Univ of Juba 1977–78; chm: Cncl Social Studies Advsy Ctee Selly Oak Colls 1975–81, Univ's Cncl for Educn of Teachers 1979–81 and 1988–91 (vice-chm 1976–79), Bd Govrs Abbotsholme Sch 1980–, Cncl of Validating Univs 1990–94, Pres's Cmmn on HE in Namibia 1991–92; chm Editorial Bd Int Journal of Educn and Devpt 1978–81, ed Jl of Practice in Educn for Devpt 1994–; methodist local preacher; Hon LLD Ohio Univ 1982, Hon DLitt Univ of Botswana 1995; Hon FCP 1985, hon fell Bolton Inst of Technol 1988; *Recreations* reading, music, theatre, walking; *Clubs* Royal Cwlth Soc; *Style—* Prof John Turner; ✉ 13 Firswood Mount, Gatley, Cheadle, Cheshire SK8 4JY (☎ 0161 283 8429); School of Education, University of Manchester, Oxford Rd, Manchester M13 9PL (☎ 0161 275 3458, fax 0161 275 3932)

TURNER, John Frayn; s of late George Francis Turner, and late Daisy Louise, *née* Frayn; *b* 9 Aug 1923; *Educ* Royal GS Guildford; *m* 9 Aug 1945, Joyce Isabelle, da of late Wilfred Ernest Howson; 1 da (Francesca Lynn b 1947); *Career* served Admty and RN 1941–47; journalist; writer and ed 1948–63, responsible for RAF publicity MOD 1963–73, sr ed pubns COI 1973–83; managing ed 1984–85: Art and Artists, Dance and Dancers, Films and Filming, Music and Musicians, Plays and Players; *Books* Service Most Silent (1955), VCs of the Royal Navy (1956), Prisoner at Large (1957), Hovering Angels (1957), Periscope Patrol (1958), Invasion '44 (1959), VCs of the Air (1960), Battle Stations (1960), Highly Explosive (1961), The Blinding Flash (1962), VCs of the Army (1962), A Girl Called Johnnie (1963), Famous Air Battles (1963), Fight for the Sky (with Douglas Bader, 1973), Destination Berchtesgaden (1975), British Aircraft of World War 2 (1975), Famous Flights (1978), The Bader Wing (1981), The Yanks Are Coming (1983), Frank Sinatra (1983), The Bader Tapes (1986), The Good Spy Guide (1988), Rupert Brooke - The Splendour and the Pain (1992), Douglas Bader - the biography (1995); *Recreations* music, theatre, films, art; *Style—* John Frayn Turner, Esq; ✉ Apartment 302, The Metropole, Folkestone, Kent (☎ 01303 250144)

TURNER, John R; s of Walter George Turner (d 1985), and Sarah Leonora, *née* Radley (d 1967); *b* 28 Jan 1939; *Educ* Rugby, Univ of Cambridge (MA, MusB); *Career* asst master Cheltenham Coll 1961–65, organist and dir of music Glasgow Cathedral, lectr Royal Scot Acad of Music and Drama, organist Univ of Strathclyde 1965–; has made various recordings and toured in Italy and USA; Hon MA Univ of Strathclyde 1990; FRCO 1960; *Recreations* motor-caravaning, gardening; *Style—* Mr John R Turner; ✉ Binchester, 1 Cathkin Road, Rutherglen, Glasgow G73 4SE (☎ 0141 634 7775)

TURNER, Prof John Richard George; s of George Hugh Turner (d 1983), of Liverpool, and Elsie Ellen, *née* Booth; *b* 11 Sept 1940, Liverpool; *Educ* Quarry Bank HS Liverpool, Univ of Liverpool (BSc), Univ of Oxford (DPhil, DSc); *m* 3 April 1967, Sandra Fordyce, da of Alexander Thomson Millar (d 1994), of Dundee; 1 s (Richard b 1970), 1 da (Lois b 1977); *Career* lectr in biology Univ of York 1965–72, assoc prof of biology Stony Brook Campus NY State Univ 1971–77, princ scientific offr Rothamsted Experimental Station Harpenden 1977–78, prof of evolutionary genetics Univ of Leeds 1987– (lectr 1978–81, reader in evolutionary genetics 1981–87); various radio and TV appearances, exhibition of drawings Fairbairn House Leeds 1991; fndr memb Conservation Soc, jt sec Cncl for Academic Autonomy; memb: Soc for Study of Evolution, Assoc for Tropical Biology, Lepidopterists' Soc, British Ecological Soc, Genetical Soc; Yorkshire Wildlife Tst, Yorkshire Naturalists Union, Br Dragonfly Soc, Plantlife, American Soc of Naturalists 1971; FRES 1962, FRSA 1993; *Publications* incl: Rimbaud Translations in Poetry and Audience (1989); author of over 100 papers in scientific jls and book reviews for TLS; contrib to books on: evolution, ecology, genetics, butterflies, history of science; *Recreations* opera, swimming, philately, wildlife, drawing, translating poetry, spoonerising; *Style—* Prof John Turner; ✉ Department of Biology, University of Leeds, Leeds LS2 9JT (☎ 0113 233 3095, fax 0113 244 1175, telex 556473 UNILDS G, e-mail j.r.g.Turner@leeds.ac.uk)

TURNER, John Warren; CBE (1988); s of Thomas Henry Huxley Turner, CBE (d 1973), of Cardiff, and Phebe Elvira, *née* Evans; *b* 12 Oct 1935; *Educ* Shrewsbury, St John's Coll Cambridge; *m* 8 Oct 1966, Jillian Fiona Geraldine, da of Thomas Ouchterlony Turton Hart (d 1995); 1 s (Gavin b 1972); *Career* 2 Lt RE Middle East 1957–59, TA 1959–66, ret Capt; construction conslt; former chm and md E Turner and Sons Ltd (dir 1964–89), dir Principality Building Society 1985–, dir Peter Alan Ltd 1991–, chm Principality Property Sales Ltd 1991–, dir BSI 1994–; chm: Bldg Regulations Advsy Ctee BRAC 1985–91 (memb 1971–91), Cncl Bldg and Civil Engrg BSI 1985–91, Technical Sector Bd Building and Civil Engrg BSI 1991–; perm UK rep Technical Sector Bd Construction Comité Européen de Normalisation (CEN) 1990–; memb: Wales Cncl CBI 1980–86, Cncl Br Bd of Agrément BBA 1980–; pres: Concrete Soc 1976–77, Wales Div IOD 1981–86 (memb Employment Ctee IOD 1982–), Bldg Employers' Confedn 1985–86; memb Nat Jt Cncl for the Building Indust (ldr Employers' Side 1981–84) 1980–, UK del XII and XIII Construction Indust Confs ILO Geneva 1983 and 1987; memb TAVR Assoc for Wales 1974–91; govr Christ Coll Brecon 1981–84; IAAS Peter Stone Award (for contrib to devpt of building regulations) 1985; JP 1979–85; CIMgt, FCIOB; *Recreations* golf; *Clubs* Cardiff and County, Leander, Royal Porthcawl Golf, Royal and Ancient Golf; *Style—* John Turner, Esq, CBE; ✉ 38 Victoria Rd, Penarth, S Glamorgan CF64 3HX (☎ 01222 707924)

TURNER, Jon Lys; s of Edward Turner (d 1976), and Anne, *née* Telfer; *b* 14 June 1959; *Educ* Felsted Sch Essex, Newport Art Sch (BA), RCA (MA); *Career* trained as graphic designer; proprietor Jon Lys Turner Ltd 1984–88 (clients incl Liberty and Virgin), divnl dir (retail) Fitch RS 1988–90 (clients incl Dillons the Bookstore), gp creative head Imagination Ltd 1990–94 (clients incl MTV and Ford), head of global design The Body Shop International plc 1994–; other design projects incl murals for Soho Soho Restaurant and Royal Nat Theatre London; contrib TV progs: Business Matter (BBC) 1994, Winning by Design (BBC) 1995; FCSD 1995; *Books* The Retail Future (creator and designer, 1990); *Style—* Jon Turner, Esq; ✉ The Body Shop International plc, Elsey Court, 20–22 Great Titchfield Street, London W1P 7AD (☎ 0171 208 7600, fax 0171 436 7166)

TURNER, Jonathan David Chattyn; s of Maxwell Turner, and Naomi, *née* Myers; *b* 13 May 1958; *Educ* Rugby, Corpus Christi Coll Cambridge (BA, MA), Université Libre de Bruxelles (Lic Sp Dr Eur), Queen Mary Coll Univ of London; *m* 23 Nov 1986, Caroline Frances Esther, da of Lawrence Sam Berman, CB; 2 s (Jacob b 1988, Gabriel b 1992), 1 da (Camilla b 1990); *Career* called to the Bar Gray's Inn 1982, pupillage in chambers of Leonard Hoffmann QC, Robin Jacob QC and Alastair Wilson QC 1982–83, in private practice as barr specialising in intellectual property and competition law 1983–95, princ Coopers and Lybrand Legal Servs London 1995–; assoc memb Chartered Inst of Patent Agents, FRSA; *Books* Halsbury's Laws of England, EC Competition Law (1986), European Patent Office Reports (1986–1995), Forms and Agreements on Intellectual Property and International Licensing (1979–89), Law of the European Communities (1986–96); *Recreations* walking, theatre, music; *Style—* Jonathan D C Turner, Esq; ✉ Coopers and Lybrand, 1 Embankment Place, London WC2N 6NN (☎ 0171 583 5000)

TURNER, Prof Kenneth John; s of Graham Leslie Turner (d 1970), of Glasgow, and Christina McInnes, *née* Fraser; *b* 21 Feb 1949; *Educ* Hutchesons Boys' GS, Univ of Glasgow (BSc), Univ of Edinburgh (PhD); *m* 15 Sept 1973, Elizabeth Mary Christina, da of Rev William James Hutton, of Glasgow; 2 s (Duncan b 1979, Robin b 1981); *Career* data communications conslt 1980–86, prof of computing sci Univ of Stirling 1986–; memb: Int Fedn for Info Processing, BSI; *Books* Formal Description Techniques (ed 1988), Using Formal Description Techniques (ed 1993); *Recreations* choral activities, handicrafts, sailing; *Style—* Prof Kenneth Turner; ✉ Department of Computing Science, University of Stirling, Stirling FK9 4LA (☎ 01786 467420, fax 01786 464551)

TURNER, Lawrence Frederick; OBE (1982); s of Frederick Thomas Turner (d 1967), of Warwicks, and Edith Elizabeth Turner (d 1975); *b* 28 Jan 1929; *Educ* Moseley GS, Univ of Aston (BSc, CEng); *m* 5 June 1954, Jeanette, da of Wilfred Edwin Clements (d 1967), of Warwicks; 2 s (Adrian Richard Lawrence b 1957, (Anthony) Christopher b

1959), 1 da (Susan Kathryn b 1965); *Career* chartered electrical engr; chm Static Systems Group plc 1964–; dep chm Dudley Health Tst 1994–; pres Inst of Hosp Engrg 1979–81; Freeman City of London 1986; memb Ct of Assts Worshipful Co of Fanmakers, past Master Worshipful Co of Engineers; FIEE, FCIBSE; *Recreations* sailing (yacht Green Gavotte), music, opera, rowing; *Clubs* Athenaeum, Royal Dart Yacht; *Style*— Lawrence Turner, Esq, OBE; ✉ Harborough Hall, Blakedown, Worcs DY10 3LQ (☎ 01562 700129); 381 Shakespeare Tower, Barbican, London EC2Y 8NJ (☎ 0171 638 5393); Static Systems Group plc, Heath Mill Rd, Wombourn, Staffs (☎ 01902 895551)

TURNER, Lowri; da of Merfyn Lloyd Turner, of London, and Shirley Elizabeth, *née* Davis; *b* 31 Dec 1964; *Educ* Greycoat Hospital Westminster, Camden Sch for Girls, St Martin's Sch of Art, Newcastle upon Tyne Poly; *Career* fashion asst Observer 1987–90, fashion ed Evening Standard and fashion dir ES Magazine 1990–94, columnist Sunday Mirror 1994–; *Recreations* champagne lifestyle; *Style*— Ms Lowri Turner; ✉ The Sunday Mirror, 1 Canada Square, Canary Wharf, London E14 5AP (☎ 0171 293 3000)

TURNER, Mark George; s of Jeffrey Farrar Turner, of Kendal, Cumbria, and Joyce, *née* Barkas; *b* 27 Aug 1959; *Educ* Sedbergh, Queen's Coll Oxford (BA); *m* 23 Jan 1988, Caroline Sophia, da of George Haydn Bullock, of Richmond, Surrey; 3 da (Alice Elizabeth b 29 Oct 1989, Fiona Maud b 6 June 1991, Lydia Sophia b 20 May 1993); *Career* called to the Bar Gray's Inn 1981, tenant Deans Ct Chambers Manchester 1982–, called to the Bar Northern Circuit 1982; memb: Manchester and District Medico-Legal Soc, Hon Soc of Gray's Inn, Union Internationale des Avocats; *Recreations* classical music, history, general knowledge quizzes; *Clubs* Mastermind (semi finalist 1988); *Style*— Mark Turner, Esq; ✉ The Oaks, 17 Hollins Lane, Marple Brdge, Cheshire; 1 Deans Court, Cumberland House, Crown Square, Manchester M3 3HA (☎ 0161 834 4097)

TURNER, Martin Paul; s of Fredrick William Harold Turner, of Llanfoist, Abergavenny, Gwent, and Magaret Mary, *née* Downey; *b* 28 Feb 1951; *Educ* Tredegar RC GS; *m* 8 Aug 1970, Elizabeth Jane, da of Haydn Hedworth Houlding; 2 da (Kathryn Louise b 17 Aug 1976, Carys Elizabeth b 1 Nov 1987), 2 s (David Martyn b 15 Jan 1980, Peter John b 17 Aug 1990); *Career* finance trainee N Monmouthshire Health Authy 1969, chief internal auditor Hosp Mgmnt Ctee 1974; Gwent Health Authy: asst treas 1976–77, finance offr 1977–81, sr asst treas 1981–, dep treas 1982–86, gen mangr Community Servs 1986–90, gen mangr (Hosp Servs) 1990–92; chief exec Glan Hafren NHS Tst 1992–; FCCA, MHSM, MIMgt; *Recreations* golf, travel, gardening; *Style*— Martin Turner, Esq; ✉ Maescoed, Bettws Newydd, Usk, Gwent NP5 1EQ (☎ 01873 880841); Glan Hafren NHS Trust, Management Centre, Friars Field, Royal Gwent Hospital, Newport, Gwent NP9 2UB (☎ 01633 238000, fax 01633 221217)

TURNER, (Francis) Michael; MBE (1994); s of Francis Richard Turner (d 1978), of Leicester, and Rosalie, *née* Gudger; *b* 8 Aug 1934; *Educ* City of Leicester Boys GS, Leicester Colls of Art and Technol; *m* Patricia Irene, da of Sidney James Coley; 1 s (Michael James b 2 July 1958), 2 da (Helen Louise b 23 April 1962, Susan Jane b 25 Feb 1964); *Career* cricket administrator; Leicestershire CCC: player 1951–58, asst sec 1959–60, sec 1960–69, sec and mangr 1969–85, chief exec 1985–93; TCCB: memb Exec Ctee 1968–93, memb Cricket Cncl 1968–94, conslt 1993–; Hon MA Univ of Leicester 1986; hon life memb MCC 1993; *Style*— Michael Turner, Esq, MBE; ✉ c/o Test and County Cricket Board, Lord's Cricket Ground, London NW8 8QZ (☎ 0171 286 4405); Leicester (direct ☎ 0116 283 1615)

TURNER, Michael James; s of James Henry Turner (d 1966), and Doris May, *née* Daniels (d 1983); *b* 8 July 1939; *Educ* BEC GS London, Imperial Coll London (BSc, ARCS), London Business Sch, Harvard Business Sch; *m* 29 Dec 1962, Elizabeth Joyce, da of George Edward Hanselman (d 1969); 1 s (David b 1964), 1 da (Anne b 1966); *Career* gen mangr Sun Life Assurance Society plc 1989–91 (joined 1960), md Woolwich Life Assurance Co Ltd 1991–; Liveryman Worshipful Co of Actuaries; elder Redland Park Utd Reformed Church; *Recreations* Rotary, rambling, overseas travel; *Style*— Michael Turner, Esq; ✉ Woolwich Life Assurance Co Ltd, Regent House, 1–3 Queensway, Redhill, Surrey RH1 1NH (☎ and fax 01737 767810)

TURNER, Michael John; s of Gerald Mortimer Turner, of Ashtead, Surrey, and Joyce Isobel Marguerite, *née* Healy; *b* 12 June 1951; *Educ* Eton; *m* 17 July 1982, Diana Mary St Clair, da of David Michael St Clair Weir; 4 s (Freddie b 1985, George b 1987, Harry b 1989, Tom b 1992); *Career* dir: Fuller Smith and Turner Estates Ltd 1985–, Ringwoods Ltd 1985–, Griffin Inns Ltd 1992–; chm Leonard Tong 1986–87 (dir 1982–91), md Fuller Smith & Turner plc 1992– (dir 1985–); Liveryman Worshipful Co of Vintners; FCA; *Recreations* skiing, shooting, golf, tennis, motor racing, travel; *Clubs* Aldeburgh Golf, Eton Vikings, Wine Trade Sports, Hurlingham; *Style*— Michael Turner, Esq; ✉ 5 Bowerdean St, London SW6 3TN; Fuller Smith & Turner plc, Griffin Brewery, Chiswick, London W4 2QB

TURNER, Hon Mr Justice; Hon Sir Michael John; kt (1985); s of Theodore Francis Turner, QC (d 1986), and Elizabeth Alice, *née* Schuster (d 1983); *b* 31 May 1931; *Educ* Winchester, Magdalene Coll Cambridge (BA); *m* 1, 26 July 1956 (m dis 1965), Hon Susan Money-Coutts, da of 7 Baron Latymer (d 1987); 1 s (Mark b 1958), 1 da (Louise b 1959); m 2, 1965 (m dis 1994), Frances Deborah, da of The Rt Hon Sir David Powell Croom-Johnson; 2 s (James b 1967, David b 1968); m 3, 4 Feb 1995, Mrs Ingrid Fear; *Career* called to the Bar Inner Temple 1955, recorder of the Crown Court 1970, QC 1973, chm E Midlands Agric Lands Tribunal 1972, judge of the High Court of Justice (Queen's Bench Div) 1985–; memb Judicial Studies Bd 1988–93, co-chm Civil & Family Ctee Judicial Studies Bd 1988–93; *Recreations* listening to music, horses; *Clubs* Army & Navy; *Style*— The Hon Mr Justice Turner; ✉ Royal Courts of Justice, Strand, London WC2A 2LL

TURNER, Michael John; s of Geoffrey Maurice Turner (d 1993), and Peggy Patricia Dora, *née* Brookes; *b* 8 Feb 1950; *Educ* King Edward VI Sch Southampton; *m* 7 Jul 1975, Kazue, da of Goro Shimada; 2 da (Anna-Marie Namie b 2 Jan 1977, Louisa-Jane Kei b 4 March 1981); *Career* articled clerk Hamilton and Rowland CA's Southampton 1968–72; Touche Ross (now Deloitte & Touche): joined 1972, ptnr 1979–, ptnr i/c Japanese Business 1983, gp ptnr Audit Dept London 1984–94, ptnr Chinese Business 1992–94; chm European Japanese Ctee for Deloitte Touche Tohmatsu; FCA 1980 (ACA 1972); *Recreations* golf, hockey, tennis; *Clubs* Teddington Hockey (vice pres), Burhill Golf; *Style*— Michael Turner, Esq; ✉ Miyabi, 92 Burwood Road, Walton on Thames, Surrey KT12 4AP (☎ 01932 223679, fax 01932 223679); Deloitte & Touche, Hill House, 1 Little New Street, London EC4A 3TR (☎ 0171 936 3000, fax 0171 583 8517)

TURNER, Michael John (Mike); s of Thomas Albert Turner, of Stockport, Cheshire, and Hilda, *née* Pendlebury; *b* 5 Aug 1948; *Educ* Didsbury Tech HS Manchester, Manchester Poly (BA); *m* 1, 1972 (m dis 1984), Rosalind, *née* Thomas; 2 s (Andrew Richard b 14 Sept 1976, Nicholas James b 5 July 1978); m 2, 1985, Jean Crotty; 2 step da (Johanna Crotty b 17 Jan 1969, Victoria Crotty b 25 May 1971); *Career* British Aerospace plc (and predecessor cos): contracts officer Hawker Siddeley Aviation Manchester 1970 (undergrad apprentice 1966–70), contracts mangr (military) Manchester Div British Aerospace Aircraft Gp 1978–80, admin mangr 1980–81, exec dir admin 1981–82, divnl admin dir 1982–84 (concurrently ldr Advanced Turboprop Project), divnl dir and gen mangr Kingston 1984–86, dir and gen mangr Weybridge, Kingston and Dunsfold 1986–87, dir of mktg and product support Mil Aircraft Div 1987–88, exec vice pres defence mktg 1988–92, chm and md British Aerospace Regional Aircraft Ltd and chm Jetstream Aircraft 1992–94, chm British Aerospace Airbus Ltd 1994–, chm Commercial Aerospace and main bd dir British Aerospace plc 1994–; pres Soc of Br Aerospace Cos 1996 (vice pres 1995–96); Br Inst of Mgmnt Young Mangr of the Year 1973; ACIS 1973, FRAeS 1991; *Recreations* golf, cricket, rugby, Manchester United; *Style*— Mike Turner, Esq; ✉ British Aerospace plc, PO Box 87, Farnborough, Hants GU14 6YU (☎ 01252 383928, fax 01252 383906)

TURNER, Michael Ralph; *b* 26 Jan 1929; *Educ* Univ of Cambridge (BA); *Career* gp md and chief exec Associated Book Publishers plc 1982–88, chm Methuen Inc New York 1981–88, sr vice-pres publishing/information gp Int Thomson Organisation Ltd 1988–89; pres Publishers' Assoc 1987–89, chm Book Tst 1990–92 (dep chm 1992–93); FRSA; *Books* with Antony Miall: Parlour Poetry (1967), The Parlour Song Book (1972), Just a Song at Twilight (1975), The Edwardian Song Book (1982), Victorian Parlour Poetry (1992); others incl: The Bluffer's Guide to the Theatre (1967), Gluttony, Pride and Lust and Other Sins for the World of Books (with Michael Geare, 1984), translation of Tintin books (with Leslie Lonsdale-Cooper, 1958–); *Recreations* theatre, writing, maritime art; *Clubs* Garrick; *Style*— Michael Turner, Esq; ✉ Paradise House, Boscastle, Cornwall PL35 0BL (☎ 01840 250250)

TURNER, Dr Michael Skinner; s of Sir Michael William Turner, CBE (d 1980), of London, and Lady Wendy, *née* Stranack; *b* 12 Aug 1947; *Educ* Dragon Sch, Marlborough, Univ of London and St Thomas's Hosp (MB BS, MRCS, LRCP), Washington (MD); *children* 4 da (Lucinda b 6 Dec 1974, Nara b 9 Oct 1976, Camilla b 3 July 1980, Alexia b 29 Jan 1984); *Career* chief med advsr: Jockey Club, Lawn Tennis Assoc, British Ski Fedn; dir of med services British Olympic Assoc 1992–94; med advsr: P & O, Vickers, Barclays de Zoete Wedd, ANZ/Grindlays Bank, Hongkong & Shanghai Banking Group, Hoare Govett; British Team doctor: Winter Olympics Calgary 1988, Albertville 1992 and Lillehammer 1994; Freeman City of London 1971, Liveryman Worshipful Co of Skinners; Desborough Award for Services to Olympic Sport 1994; *Recreations* skiing, racing, tennis; *Style*— Dr Michael Turner; ✉ City Medical Services Ltd, 17 St Helen's Place, London EC3A 6DE (☎ 0171 588 5477, fax 0171 256 5295)

TURNER, Hon (Edward) Neil; s of 1 Baron Netherthorpe (d 1980), and Margaret Lucy, *née* Mattock; *b* 27 Jan 1941; *Educ* Rugby, RAC Cirencester, Univ of London; *m* 12 Oct 1963, Gillian Mary, da of Christopher John King (d 1963); 1 s (Charles b 3 May 1966), 1 da (Sara b 4 Feb 1971); *Career* chm: Edward Turner and Son Ltd 1971–, Lazard Smaller Equities Investment Tst PLC 1994–; pres Sheffield Chamber of Commerce 1996–97; vice-chm Yorks and Humberside Devpt Assoc 1989–92; memb: Yorks and Humberside Econ Planning Cncl 1975–79, Residuary Body for S Yorks 1985–89, Cncl BIM 1976–81 and 1982–88, Regnl Cncl CBI 1989–, Nat Cncl CBI 1993–; gen cmmr of Taxes 1973–; High Sheriff S Yorks 1983–84, memb Co of Cutlers in Hallamshire; FRICS, QALAS, Dip FBA (Lond), FIMgt, FRSA; *Recreations* shooting, golf; *Clubs* Lindrick Golf, Farmers'; *Style*— The Hon Neil Turner; ✉ The Limes, Crowgate, South Anston, nr Sheffield, S Yorks S31 7AL; 312 Petre St, Sheffield S4 8LT (☎ 01909 550097)

TURNER, Prof Raymond; s of Mrs Winifred Howe; *b* 28 April 1947; *Career* prof of computer sci Univ of Essex 1985– (lectr 1973–85); Sloan fell in cognitive sci Univ of Mass USA 1982 (sr res fell 1986 and 1989), visiting prof Univ of Rochester NY 1982, visiting fell Centre for Study of Language and Information Stanford Univ Calif 1984 (conslt in sci 1982), visiting prof Univ of Texas Austin 1987; *Books* Logics for Artificial Intelligence (1984), Truth and Modality for Knowledge Representation (1990), Constructive Foundations for Functional Languages; *Style*— Prof Raymond Turner; ✉ Department of Computer Science, University of Essex, Colchester, Essex

TURNER, Raymond Edward; *b* 3 Aug 1946; *Educ* Fairfax HS Southend, Braintree and Chelmsford Tech Coll (HNC), Leeds Coll of Art (BA); *m* 16 Aug 1969, Sandra Rosemary; 2 da (Alice b 27 Feb 1971, Coral b 6 April 1973); *Career* sr creative designer Gillette Industries 1974–77; Kilkenny Design - Nat Design Authy of Ireland: ind design mangr 1978–80, mangr of design 1980–83, head of design consultancy and asst chief exec 1983–85; design dir London Regnl Transport 1985–88; Wolff Olins: divnl md 1988–90, dir and princ 1990–92; design mgmnt conslt to Eurotunnel and IBM-UK; gp design dir BAA plc 1995– (design dir 1993–95); advsr to Design Mgmnt Inst of Finland; memb Design Mgmnt Inst Boston; FCSD, FRSA; *Recreations* outdoor pursuits and the arts; *Style*— Raymond Turner, Esq; ✉ Group Design Director, BAA plc, Jubilee House, Gatwick Airport, West Sussex RH6 0JN (☎ 01293 595499, fax 01293 3595710)

TURNER, Richard Timmis; OBE (1978); s of Dr John Richard Timmis Turner, and Alison Elizabeth, *née* Bythell; *b* 17 Aug 1942; *Educ* Shrewsbury, Univ of Manchester (BA); *m* 11 Sept 1982, Margaret Rose Mary, da of Dr Ivor Corbett (d 1982); 2 da (Catherine b 1983, Rebecca b 1985); *Career* joined Rolls-Royce Ltd 1965, commercial mangr Rolls-Royce Inc NY 1971–74, mktg exec civil engines Rolls-Royce Ltd 1977, commercial dir civil engines Rolls-Royce plc 1986–88, dir STC plc 1989–91 (gp mktg dir 1988–91), dir Rolls-Royce plc 1992– (re-joined as gp mktg dir 1991); non-exec dir: British Steel plc 1994–, Senior Engineering Group plc 1996–; memb Cncl Soc of Br Aerospace Companies (pres 1994–95); MInstD, FRAeS; *Recreations* opera, music, rugby, farming; *Clubs* Athenaeum; *Style*— Richard Turner, Esq, OBE; ✉ 45 Clarendon Road, London W11 4JD (☎ 0171 727 7697); Rolls-Royce plc, 65 Buckingham Gate, London SW1E 6AT (☎ 0171 222 9020, fax 0171 976 8548)

TURNER, Robert Lockley; s of Capt James Lockley-Turner, OBE (d 1954), of Purley, Berks, and Maud Beatrice, *née* Hillyard (d 1993); *b* 2 Sept 1935; *Educ* Clifton, St Catharine's Coll Cambridge (MA); *m* 5 Oct 1963, Jennifer Mary, da of Alan Guy Fishwick Leather, TD, of Tarporley; 1 s (Guy Lockley b 1967), 1 da (Claire Henrietta b 1969); *Career* barr; cmmnd Gloucestershire Regt 1959, Army Legal Serv 1959–66 (Maj 1962); practised Midland and Oxford Circuit 1967–84, recorder of the Crown Ct 1981–84, Senior Master Queen's Bench Div of High Ct 1996– (Master 1984–), Queen's Remembrancer 1996–; assessor Access to Justice Inquiry 1994–96; hon steward Westminster Abbey 1985–; *Publications* The Office and Functions of Queen's Bench Masters (1990), Chitty and Jacobs Queen's Bench Forms (ed jtly, 1992), High Court Litigation Manual (conslt ed, 1992), The Annual Practice (ed, 1995), Supreme Court Practice (ed jtly, 1997); *Recreations* painting, gardening; *Clubs* Royal Fowey Yacht, Army and Navy; *Style*— Robert Turner, Esq; ✉ Royal Courts of Justice, Strand, London WC2A 2LL

TURNER, Prof (James Charles) Robin; s of Dr James William Cecil Turner, MC (d 1968), of Cambridge, and Beatrice Maude, *née* Stooke (d 1987); *b* 14 July 1930; *Educ* Greshams, Trinity Coll Cambridge (ScD, MA, PhD); *m* 20 Dec 1958, (Margaret) Anne, da of George Binford Sellwood (d 1937), of Cullompton; 1 s (Michael b 1962), 2 da (Julia b 1960, Caroline b 1962); *Career* Nat Serv RAEC 1948–49; lectr Univ of Cambridge 1955–79, fell Pembroke Coll Cambridge 1962–79; Univ of Exeter: prof of chemical engrg 1979–95, dean Faculty of Engrg 1980–85 and 1993–95, emeritus prof 1995–; visiting prof: Austin Texas 1965, Sydney 1970, Seattle 1975, Christchurch NZ 1978, Bahia Blanca 1980, Tufts USA 1992; former chm SW Branch Inst Chemical Engrs; memb: Engrg Profs Conf Ctee 1990–95, Tst Panel of CIBA and Farringdon Tst; FIChemE; *Books* Chemical Reactor Theory (with K G Denbigh, 1971); *Recreations* watching sport, playing golf, choral singing, gardening, philately and antiques; *Style*— Prof Robin Turner; ✉ School of Engineering, University of Exeter, Exeter, Devon (☎ 01392 263623, fax 01392 217965, telex 42894 EXUNIV G)

TURNER, Ven (Peter) Robin; QHC; s of late Ronald James Turner, OBE (d 1989), and Irene Bertha, *née* Stocker; *b* 8 March 1942; *Educ* Dulwich, KCL (AKC), St Luke's Coll Exeter (PGCE), Open Univ (BA); *m* 5 Aug 1967, Elizabeth Mary, da of late Rev Harry Kennen, DSC; 2 s (Christopher Michael b 10 June 1968, Jonathan Richard b 11 March 1972); *Career* ordained (Exeter) deacon 1966, priest 1967; asst curate Crediton Devon

1966–69; RAF Chaplains Dept: chaplain 1970, asst chaplain-in-chief 1989–95, chaplain-in-chief and archdeacon 1995–; non-residentiary canon and prebendary Lincoln Cathedral 1995–; ex-officio memb Gen Synod C of E 1995–; memb Bereavement Research Forum; *Recreations* choral singing, classical music, armchair cricket, wine appreciation; *Clubs* RAF; *Style*— The Ven Robin Turner, QHC; ✉ Ministry of Defence, RAF Innsworth, Gloucester GL3 1EZ (☎ 01452 712612 ext 5030, fax 01452 510828)

TURNER, Roger Burton; s of late Jack Burton Turner, of Soham, Cambridgeshire, and Jean, *née* Trevor; *b* 28 July 1947; *Educ* Hawes Down Co Secdy Sch, King's Coll London (BD, MTh), Univ of London Inst of Educn (PGCE), Univ of Kent (MA), Inns of Ct Sch of Law; *Career* asst master Ashford GS 1972–77, lectr in New Testament studies La Sainte Union Coll of Higher Educn Southampton 1977–80, called to the Bar Gray's Inn 1982, in practice SE Circuit 1983–; visiting research fell Inst of Historical Research Univ of London 1995–96; memb Ecclesiastical Law Soc, contrib Ecclesiastical Law Jl; contrib symposium The Earl of Burlington and His Politics 1995; reviews ed: Royal Stuart Review, New DNB; memb Cncl Royal Stuart Soc; Manchester and the '45: a study of Jacobitism in context (1996); *Recreations* watercolour painting, church history (esp 17th and 18th Century) and doctrine, reading, Bristol cars; *Clubs* Sion Coll; *Style*— Roger Turner, Esq; ✉ Mitre Court Chambers, Temple, London EC4Y 7BP (☎ 0171 353 9394, fax 0171 353 1488)

TURNER, Ronald Frederick; s of Frederick Turner (d 1942), of Sheffield, and Dorothy May, *née* Williams; *b* 8 May 1941; *Educ* Stacey Rd Secdy Modern Sch Roath Cardiff; *m* 23 March 1963, Barbara Miriam, da of Harold Geoffrey Hoare; 3 s (Martin Jason b 4 May 1968, Simon John b 11 May 1975, Matthew David b 24 Jan 1978), 1 da (Tracy Hazel b 3 Nov 1965); *Career* craft apprenticeship as tinsmith British Steel Corp 1956–61; portrait photographer 1970–; masterclasses for Kodak (10 per year) 1987– and in numerous Euro countries, Scandinavia and USA; work accepted in the Loan Collection of Professional Photographers of America and selected for Kodak exhibit (Walt Disney's Epcot Centre Disney World Florida) 1990 and 1991; Best Creative Use of Colour Nat Print Awards 1986; BIPP: Nat Wedding Photographer of the Year 1985, 1988 and 1989, Nat Portrait Photographer of the Year 1987 and 1988; Int Wedding Photographer of the Year 1989, Kodak Portrait Photographer of the Year 1989 (and 7 Kodak Gold awards); fndr memb Br Guild of Portrait Photographers, FBIPP 1989 (assoc in Portrait and Wedding Photography 1974, memb 1971), FRSA; *Books* contrib photographs: Decade of Golden Images (Kodak, 1991), Loan Collection Book (Professional Photographers of America, 1991); *Recreations* researching Impressionist painters, water gardening, natural history, classical music; *Style*— Ronald Turner, Esq

TURNER, Simon Andrew; s of Ernest Neville Turner (d 1982), of Grimsby, Lincs, and Joyce, *née* Frow; *b* 9 Oct 1954; *Educ* Brigg GS, Sidney Sussex Coll Cambridge (BA, dep pres Student Union, Cncl of the Senate student rep); *m* 9 June 1984, Nancy Katherine, da of James Baird, of Tuscaloosa, Alabama; 2 s (Christopher James b 15 April 1985, John Michael b 10 Sept 1986), 1 da (Lindsay Katherine b 4 May 1990); *Career* trainee accountant George Angus Ltd fluid seals factory Wallsend 1978–79; Procter & Gamble: brand asst UK 1979–82, brand mangr Switzerland 1982–84, brand mangr Holland 1985–86, assoc advtg mangr Belgium 1986–87; bd mktg dir Coca-Cola GB 1988–90, mangr New Product Devpt The Coca-Cola Co Atlanta 1990–93, mktg dir Van Den Bergh Foods Ltd 1993–; *Recreations* family, church, creative writing (none published); *Style*— Simon Turner, Esq; ✉ Marketing Director, Van Den Berghs Foods Ltd, Brooke House, Crawley Business Centre, Manor Royal, Crawley, West Sussex RH10 2PY (☎ 01293 648000)

TURNER, Simon John Edward; DL (Lincs 1993); s of Ronald Edward Streatfeild Turner (d 1981), and Evelyn Frances, *née* Ingram (d 1984); *b* 7 June 1935; *Educ* Malvern Coll, RMA Sandhurst; *m* 12 Oct 1962, Helen Annetta, da of Gordon Ian Brand Dick; 3 da (Lucy Helen b 21 Aug 1963, Celia Frances b 29 Dec 1965, Diana Mary b 28 April 1971), 1 s (Philip Ronald William b 9 July 1968); *Career* offr Scots Guards 1956–67, GSO III (L) HQ 16th Para Bde Gp 1961–62, ret as Maj 1967; dir: Wherry & Sons Ltd 1967–74, Stowpark Feeds Ltd 1974–77; md RW & F Money Ltd 1977–; High Sheriff for Co of Lincolnshire 1994–95; *Recreations* gardening, shooting, stamp collecting; *Clubs* Army & Navy; *Style*— Simon Turner, Esq, DL; ✉ Willow Holt, Folkingham, Lincolnshire NG34 0SA (☎ 01529 497215); RW & F Money Ltd, The Old School, Folkingham, Lincolnshire NG34 0SE (☎ 01529 497457, fax 01529 497417, car 0402 669018)

TURNER, Wilfred; CMG (1977), CVO (1979); s of Allen Turner (d 1966), and Eliza, *née* Leech (d 1955); *b* 10 Oct 1921; *Educ* Heywood GS, Univ of London (BSc); *m* 26 March 1947, June Gladys, da of Leonard Ham Tite, MBE (d 1983); 2 s (Nicholas Hugh b 1950, Matthew Julian b 1955), 1 da (Harriet Louise Macrae b 1960); *Career* ret diplomat; REME: cmmnd 2 Lt 1942, Capt 1945, demobbed 1947; Miny of Lab 1938–60 (asst lab advsr India 1955–59, sr wages inspr 1959–69), Miny of Health 1960–66 (sec Ctee on Safety of Drugs 1963–66), HM Dip Serv 1966–81 (Br high cmmr Botswana 1977–81), chief exec Southern Africa Assoc 1983–88, non-exec dir Transmark (BR) 1987–90; memb: Royal Inst of Int Affrs, Royal African Soc; *Recreations* hill walking; *Clubs* Royal Cwlth Soc; *Style*— Wilfred Turner, Esq, CMG, CVO; ✉ 44 Tower Rd, Twickenham, Middlesex TW1 4PE (☎ 0181 892 1593)

TURNER-SAMUELS, David Jessel; QC (1972); s of late Moss Turner-Samuels, QC, MP, of London, and Gladys Deborah, *née* Belcher; *b* 5 April 1918; *Educ* Westminster; *m* 5 Nov 1939 (m dis 1976), Norma, da of Philip Verstone, of Worthing (d 1971); 1 s (Michael b 17 Aug 1946), 1 da (Elizabeth b 28 March 1958); m 2, 10 April 1977, Norma Florence (Her Hon Judge Negus, *qv*), da of George David Shellabear (d 1973), of Devon; *Career* WWII RA 1939–46; called to the Bar Middle Temple 1939, bencher Middle Temple, attorney at law Trinidad and Tobago; *Style*— David Turner-Samuels, Esq, QC; ✉ Cherry Tree Cottage, Petworth Rd, Haslemere, Surrey GU27 3BG; New Court, Temple, London EC4Y 9BE; Cloisters, Temple, London EC4Y 7AA (☎ 0171 583 0303, fax 0171 583 2254)

TURNER-WARWICK, Prof Dame Margaret Elizabeth Harvey; DBE (1991); da of William Harvey Moore, QC (d 1965), and Maud Kirkdale, *née* Baden-Powell; *b* 19 Nov 1924; *Educ* City of London, Maynard, St Paul's Sch for Girls, Lady Margaret Hall Oxford (scholar, MA, DM), UCH Univ of London (PhD); *m* 21 Jan 1950, Dr Richard Trevor Turner-Warwick, CBE, *qv*, s of William Turner-Warwick (d 1949); 2 da (Gillian (Mrs Bathe) b 1953, Lynne (Dr Turner-Stokes) b 1955); *Career* conslt physician Elizabeth Garrett Anderson Hosp 1960–67, conslt physician London Chest Hosp and Brompton Hosp 1967–72, dean Cardiothoracic Inst 1984–87 (sr lectr 1963–72, prof 1972–87); emeritus prof of med Univ of London; chm Royal Devon and Exeter NHS Trust 1992–95; pres Br Thoracic Soc 1982–83, chm Asthma Res Cncl 1988–89, chm UKCCCR 1991–; memb: Bd National Asthma Campaign 1970–, Bd of Govrs Nat Heart and Chest Hosps 1971–88, Systems Bd MRC 1982–85, Senate Univ of London 1983–87, Med Advsy Ctee CORDA 1985–88, Imperial Cancer Res Fund Cncl 1988–92, NW Thames RHA 1988–90, SHA 1990–93, Mgmnt Ctee Cardiothoracic Inst, Nuffield Bioethics Cncl 1992–; Osler Meml Medal Univ of Oxford 1995; Hon DSc Univ of Exeter, Univ of London, New York Univ, Univ of Hull, Univ of Oxford, Univ of Sussex, Univ of Cambridge; RCP: fell 1969, second vice pres 1988, pres 1989–92; memb Alpha Omega Alpha (USA) 1988, hon bencher Middle temple 1991; hon fell: Lady Margaret Hall Oxford 1991, Girton Coll Cambridge 1993; fell Imperial Coll London 1996; memb Assoc of Physicians; FRACP 1983, FRCPE 1988, FACP 1988, FRCP Canada 1989, FRCSPhys (Glas) 1991, FRCGP 1990, FRCAnaes 1991, FRCPath 1992, FFOM, FFPHM 1990, Hon FRCS 1993, Hon FRCR 1994; *Recreations* family and their hobbies, classical music, violin playing, watercolour painting, gardening; *Style*— Prof Dame Margaret Turner-Warwick, DBE; ✉ Pynes House, Thorverton, Exeter, Devon EX5 5LT (☎ 01392 861173, fax 01392 860940)

TURNER-WARWICK, Dr Richard Trevor; CBE (1991); s of William Turner-Warwick, FRCS (d 1949), and Dr Joan Margaret Warwick (d 1990); *b* 21 Feb 1925; *Educ* Bedales, Oriel Coll Oxford (pres Oxford Univ Boat Club and 1946 Crew), Middlesex Hosp (Broderip scholarship); *m* 21 Jan 1950, Prof Dame Margaret Turner-Warwick, DBE, *qv*, da of W Harvey Moore, QC (d 1965); 2 da (Gillian (Mrs Bathe) b 1953, Lynne (Dr Turner-Stokes) b 1955); *Career* surgn; Hunterian prof RCS 1957 and 1977; conslt surgn Middlesex Hosp 1960, conslt urologist Royal Nat Orthopaedic Hosp 1962, St Peter's Hosp 1964, King Edward VII Hosp for Officers 1964, Royal Prince Alfred Hosp Sydney 1978, Robert Luff Fndn fell in reconstructive urology 1990–, numerous scientific pubns and contrib to urological texts; memb: Cncl RCS 1978–92, Cncl RCOG 1990–92; Freeman City of London, Liveryman Worshipful Soc of Apothecaries; Hon DSc NY 1985, Hon FRACS 1986; memb American Assoc of Genito-Urinary Surgns 1978, fell Aust Urological Soc 1987; FRCS 1957, FACS 1978, FRCP 1987, FRCOG 1990; *Recreations* family, fishing, gardening; *Clubs* Vincent's (Oxford), Leander, The Houghton; *Style*— Dr Richard Turner-Warwick, CBE; ✉ Pynes House, Thorverton, Exeter EX5 5LT (☎ 01392 861173)

TURNEY, Alan Harry; CB; s of Harry Landrey Turney (d 1951), and Alice Theresa, *née* Bailey (d 1995); *b* 20 Aug 1932; *Educ* St Albans GS, LSE (BSc Econ); *m* 22 June 1957, Ann Mary, da of George William Dollimore (d 1988); *Career* Home Office 1961–92: private sec to Home Sec (Henry Brooke) 1962–64, princ Police, Prison and Gen Depts 1964–76, asst sec Broadcasting Dept 1976–81, Rayner Review of Forensic Sci Service 1981, Criminal and Prison Depts 1981–86, asst under sec of state Fire and Emergency Planning Dept 1986–92; sec Hertfordshire RFU 1969–77; *Recreations* rugby union football (now spectating!); *Style*— Alan Turney, Esq, CB; ✉ Brookfield Cottage, Bury End, Nuthampstead, Royston, Herts SG8 8NG (☎ 01763 848935)

TURNOR, Maj Anthony Richard; CBE (1973), DL (Wiltshire 1982–); s of Lt-Col Algernon Turnor, MC (d 1930), and Beatrice Mildred Denison (d 1981); *b* 4 Feb 1914; *Educ* Eton, RMC Sandhurst; *m* 6 Oct 1952, Joyce Winifred, da of William James Osborn, of Spinney Green, Little Over, Derby; 1 s (Richard b 1956), 1 da (Carey b 1954); *Career* Kings Royal Rifle Corps 1934, Palestine medal 1936–37, WWII Italy 1943–44, No 2 Army Commando Italy Yugoslavia Albania, wounded 1945, retired 1947; memb Wiltshire CC 1974–81, High Sheriff Wiltshire 1977–78, farmer at Foxley; chm: Malmesbury RDC 1964–69, Chippenham Cons Assoc 1962–65, Wessex Area Cons 1969–72, chm Wilts Community Cncl 1973–75 (vice chm 1966–72); pres Royal Br Legion Wilts Co 1985–89; *Recreations* shooting, fishing, skiing; *Clubs* Army and Navy; *Style*— Maj Anthony Turnor, CBE, DL; ✉ Foxley Manor, Malmesbury, Wiltshire (☎ 01666 824607)

TURNOR, Richard William Corbet; s of Maj Anthony Richard Turnor, CBE, DL, and Joyce Winnifred, *née* Osborn; *b* 15 March 1956; *Educ* Maidwell Hall Sch, Eton, Keble Coll Oxford (BA); *m* 31 Dec 1985, Louisa Mary, da of Andrew Garden Duff Forbes; 1 s (William Michael Francis b 1988), 2 da (Elizabeth Beatrice b 1990, Rosalind Mary b 1993); *Career* admitted slr 1980; Allen & Overy: joined 1979, ptnr 1985–, memb Private Client Dept and Professional Partnerships Gp; memb Law Soc 1981; *Recreations* conservation, growing trees, field sports, skiing; *Style*— Richard Turnor, Esq; ✉ Allen & Overy, One New Change, London EC4M 9QQ (☎ 0171 330 3000, fax 0171 330 9999)

TURPIN, (James) Alexander; CMG (1966); s of Samuel Alexander Turpin (d 1944), of Dublin, and Marie Louise, *née* Mitchell (d 1921); *b* 7 Jan 1917; *Educ* The King's Hospital Dublin, Trinity Coll Dublin (MA); *m* 1942, Kathleen Iris, da of Thomas Tait Eadie (d 1968), of Co Kerry; 1 da (Alexa); *Career* Royal Irish Fus 1942–46, Capt; HM Foreign (later Dip) Serv 1947; served: Paris, Warsaw, Tokyo, The Hague, New Delhi, Manila (ambass Manila 1972–76); chm Br Philippine Soc 1986–88; *Publications* New Society's Challenge in the Philippines (1980), The Philippines: Problems of the Ageing New Society (1984); *Recreations* music, cookery, wine, tennis, swimming; *Style*— Alexander Turpin, Esq, CMG; ✉ 12 Grimwood Rd, Twickenham, Middlesex

TURRELL, Michael Frederick; *Educ* Milton Sch; *Career* Reckitt & Colman plc: joined as finance trainee Colman's of Norwich 1963, various appts in S and E Africa 1967–72, gen mangr Portuguese W Africa 1972–74, regnl mangr then regnl dir Latin America (based London) 1974–77, md Household Business Brazil 1977–81, pres and gen mangr Colombia and Ecuador 1981–84, gen mangr Reckitt & Colman Household Products S Africa 1984–89, md Colman's of Norwich 1989–91, main bd dir Reckitt & Colman plc 1991–, chief exec Reckitt & Colman Inc 1991–94, chm Reckitt & Colman Inc 1991–, gp dir with responsibility for N America 1991–94, gp dir with responsibility for The Americas and Europe 1994–96, gp dir Global Ops 1996–; FCA, FIMgt; *Style*— Michael Turrell, Esq; ✉ Reckitt & Colman plc, One Burlington Lane, London W4 2RW (☎ 0181 994 6464)

TURTLE, Dr Mark Jonathan; s of Edgar Ernest Turtle, MBE, of 97 Charlton Lane, Cheltenham, Gloucs, and Kathleen, *née* Furlong; *b* 28 Jan 1952; *Educ* Surbiton Co GS, Guy's Hosp and Univ of London (MB BS, MRCS, LRCP); *m* 26 May 1979, Lynette Caryn, da of Lewis Malcolm Llewelyn, of Parc Yr Onen, Llwyn Meredydd, Camarthen; *Career* conslt anaesthetist and specialist in chronic pain relief, previously sr registrar Bristol and SW Region and registrar Salford Manchester; memb: Assoc of Anaesthetists, Pain Soc, Intensive Care Soc, Soc Anaesthetists of Wales, BMA; FRCA 1981; *Style*— Dr Mark Turtle; ✉ Nant-Y-Grove, Llangynog, Carmarthen, Dyfed SA33 5DE (☎ 01267 211 391); West Wales General Hospital, Camarthen, Dyfed SA31 2AF (☎ 01267 235151)

TURTON, Eugenie Christine (Genie); CB (1996); da of Arthur Turton (d 1973), and Georgina, *née* Fairhurst; *b* 19 Feb 1946; *Educ* Nottingham Girls HS (GPDST), Girton Coll Cambridge (MA); *m* 1, 20 July 1968 (m dis 1972), Richard Lindsay Gordon; m 2, 14 June 1974 (m dis 1978), Gerrard Flanagan; *Career* princ private sec to Sec of State for Tport 1978–80, memb Channel Link Financing Group Midland Bank 1981–82, head Machinery of Govt Div Cabinet Office 1982–85, dep sec DOE 1991–94 (under sec 1986–91), dir Citizen's Charter Unit Cabinet Office 1994–; non-exec dir Woolwich Building Soc 1987–91; tstee Pilgrim Tst 1991–; FRSA 1986; *Recreations* music, books; *Style*— Miss Genie Turton, CB; ✉ Cabinet Office, Horseguards Road, London SW1 (☎ 0171 270 5786)

TURTON, Richard Charles; s of Charles Ernest Turton (d 1978), of Epperstone, Notts, and Aline Audrey Turton (d 1983); *b* 17 Dec 1936; *Educ* Uppingham; *m* 1, 15 Aug 1961 (m dis 1969), Rosemary Margaret, da of Arthur J C Moore, of Uppingham, Rutland; 2 s (Andrew b 20 June 1962, Philip b 6 Feb 1965); m 2, Susan Katharine, da of Capt Edward Norman Allan (d 1944); 1 s (Paul b 29 May 1970); *Career* qualified CA 1961; ptnr: Turton Ross & Co 1961–63, Chamberlain Turton & Dunn 1963–75, Spicer & Oppenheim (formerly Spicer & Pegler) 1975–90, Touche Ross & Co (following merger) 1990–92; insolvency conslt 1992–; chm Insolvency Practitioners Assoc 1975–76, pres Insol International 1985–89, memb Cncl ICAEW 1986–90, exec dir Assoc Europeéne des Praticiens des Procedures Collectives 1991–; memb Nottingham District Health Authy 1992–; sec Nottingham Glyndebourne Assoc 1967–, memb Fin Ctee Glyndebourne 1980–92, dir Welsh National Opera 1994–; pres Nottingham Hockey Club 1975–80; Freeman: City of London, Worshipful Co of CAs; FCA 1966, FIPA, FSPI, MICM; *Books* Meet the Receiver (1985); *Recreations* singing, violin, listening to classical music, gardening, golf, tennis, walking; *Clubs* Nottingham and Notts United Services; *Style*—

Richard Turton, Esq; ✉ Insol Studio, 7 Russell Place, Nottingham NG1 5HJ (☎ 0115 924 0175, fax 0115 924 0272, car 0802 655918)

TURVEY, Garry; CBE (1991); s of Henry Oxley Turvey (d 1981), and Annie Maude, *née* Braley; *b* 11 Oct 1934; *Educ* Morecambe GS, Manchester Business Sch; *m* 11 June 1960, Hilary Margaret, da of Walter Saines; 3 s (Ian Michael b 1961, Peter Geoffrey b 1964, David Mark b 1965); *Career* Nat Serv RAF 1954–56; sec Traders Road Transport Association 1966–68 (asst sec 1960–66); Freight Transport Association Ltd: sec 1969–74, dep dir gen 1974–83, dir gen 1984–93; Liveryman Worshipful Co of Carmen 1993; FCIS 1959, FCIT 1983; *Recreations* cricket, fly-fishing, gardening; *Clubs* RAC, MCC; *Style*— Garry Turvey, Esq, CBE; ✉ 139 Imberhorne Lane, E Grinstead, W Sussex RH19 1RP (☎ 01342 325829)

TURVEY, Peter James; s of late Douglas Ronald Turvey, of Croydon, and Kathleen Mildred, *née* Smith; *b* 9 May 1943; *Educ* Whitgift Sch, BNC Oxford (MA); *m* 23 Oct 1965, (Norah) Louise, da of Dr Peter O'Flynn, of Croydon; 1 s (Andrew b 1968), 3 da (Marie-Louise b 1967, Caroline b 1972, Fiona b 1975); *Career* asst gen mangr Swiss Re (UK) 1972–87, princ William M Mercer 1987–94, md Gerling Global Re 1995–; vice pres Inst of Actuaries 1988–91 (hon sec 1984–86), chm Staple Inn Actuarial Soc 1988–90; memb Ct of Assts Worshipful Co of Actuaries (Master 1990–91); FIA 1968; *Recreations* jogging, skiing, windsurfing, cycling, bridge; *Style*— Peter Turvey, Esq; ✉ Gerling Global Re, 50 Fenchurch Street, London EC3M 3JY (☎ 0171 696 8103, fax 0171 696 8126)

TURZYNSKI, Gregory Michael Stefan (Greg); s of Leon Dominik Turzynski, of Crowborough, E Sussex, and Olivia Lilian, *née* Ball; *b* 16 June 1959; *Educ* St Mary's RC Sch, St Ignatius Coll, Bedford Coll London (BSc); *m* 25 June 1993, Kim, da of Sidney Burgess; *Career* Young & Rubicam advtg: joined 1982, gp buying mangr 1986–90, bdcast dir 1990–92, dep media dir 1992–94, media dir 1994–96; managing ptnr Optimedia 1996–; *Style*— Greg Turzynski, Esq; ✉ Optimedia, 84–86 Baker Street, London W1M 1DL (☎ 0171 935 0040)

TUSA, John; s of John Tusa, OBE (d 1994), of Dorset, and Lydia, *née* Sklenarova; *b* 2 March 1936; *Educ* Gresham's, Trinity Coll Cambridge (BA); *m* 1960, Ann Hilary, da of Stanley Dowson, of Lancs; 2 s (Sash, Francis); *Career* BBC: presenter Newsnight (BBC 2) 1980–86, presenter Timewatch (BBC 2) 1982–84, md BBC World Service 1986–92, presenter One O'Clock News 1993–95; md Barbican Centre 1995–; pres Wolfson Coll Cambridge 1993; chm Advsy Ctee Govt Art Collection, a vice chm London Int String Quartet Competition 1995–, chm BBC MDM Tst; bd memb: Public Radio International, English National Opera 1994–; tstee Nat Portrait Gallery 1988–; former tstee: Thomson Fndn, Wigmore Hall Tst; Hon DUniv Heriot Watt 1994, Hon LLD London 1993; *Awards* RTS Journalist of the Year 1984, BAFTA Richard Dimbleby Award 1984, Harvey Lee Award BPG TV and Radio Awards 1992, RTS Presenter of the Year 1995; *Books* The Nuremberg Trial (co-author with Ann Tusa, 1984), The Berlin Blockade (co-author with Ann Tusa, 1988), Conversations with the World (1990), A World in Your Ear (1992); *Recreations* tennis, opera, listening; *Style*— John Tusa, Esq; ✉ 21 Christchurch Hill, London NW3 1JY (☎ 0171 435 9495); Barbican Arts Centre, Silk Street, London EC2Y 8DS (☎ 0171 382 7011)

TUSHINGHAM, Rita; da of John Tushingham, of Liverpool, and Enid Ellen, *née* Lott; *b* 14 March 1942; *Educ* La Sagesse Convent Liverpool; *m* 1, 1 Dec 1962 (m dis 1976), Terence William Bicknell; 2 da (Dodonna b 1 May 1964, Aisha b 16 June 1971); m 2, 27 Aug 1981 (m dis 1996), Ousama Rawi, s of Najib El-Rawi, of Geneva, Switzerland; *Career* actress; began career Liverpool Repertory Theatre 1958; *Television* incl: Bread 1988, Dante and Beatrice in Liverpool 1989, Sunday Pursuit 1990, Dieter Gütt ein Journalist 1991, Hamburg Poison (TV film) 1992; *Films* A Taste of Honey (first film) 1961, The Girl with Green Eyes 1965, The Knack 1965, Doctor Zhivago 1966, The Trap 1967, The Guru 1968, Bedsitting Room 1969, A Judgement in Stone 1986, Resurrected 1988, Hard Days Hard Nights 1989, Paper Marriage 1991, The Rapture of Deceit 1991, Desert Lunch 1992, An Awfully Big Adventure 1994, The Boy From Mercury 1995, Under the Skin 1996; *Awards* incl: Cannes Film Festival Award for Best Actress, New York Film Critics' Award, Golden Globe Award (for A Taste of Honey); Variety Club of GB Best Actress Award (for The Girl with Green Eyes), Mexican Film Festival Award for Best Actress (for The Knack); *Recreations* incl care and protection of animals, cooking, painting, gardening; *Style*— Miss Rita Tushingham; ✉ c/o Grizelda Burgess, London Management, 2–4 Noel Street, London W1V 3RB (☎ 0171 287 9000, fax 0171 287 3036)

TUSTIN, Rt Rev David; *see:* Grimsby, Bishop of

TUTIN, Dorothy; CBE (1967); da of late Dr John Tutin, and Adie Evelyn, *née* Fryers (d 1992); *b* 8 April 1930; *Educ* St Catherine's Bramley, RADA (Dip); *m* 1964, Derek Barton-Chapple (stage name Derek Waring), s of Wing Cdr Harry John Barton-Chapple; 1 s (Nicholas b 1966), 1 da (Amanda b 1964); *Career* stage and film actress; began stage career 1959; Hon DLitt Reading; *Theatre* many Shakespearian parts, Sally Bowles in I Am A Camera, Peter Pan; *Films* Polly Peachum in The Beggar's Opera, Cecily in The Importance of Being Earnest, Lucie Manette in A Tale of Two Cities, Sophie Breska in Savage Messiah, The Shooting Party; *Awards* Variety Club of GB Film Actress Award 1972, twice winner Evening Standard Best Actress Award, twice winner Olivier Award; *Style*— Miss Dorothy Tutin, CBE; ✉ c/o Michael Whitehall Ltd, 125 Gloucester Road, London SW7 4TE (☎ 0171 244 8466, fax 0171 244 9060)

TUTSSEL, Mark Christopher; s of Stanley Ernest Tutssel, of Barry, S Wales, and Mavis, *née* Jones; *b* 31 Aug 1958; *Educ* Barry Boys' Comp Sch, Cardiff Coll of Art & Design (DipAD, Harrison Cowley advtg fell); *m* 16 May 1987, Julie Elizabeth, da of Dennis James Cripps; 1 s (Lewis James b 5 Jan 1991); *Career* jr art dir Saatchi & Saatchi advtg 1980, art dir MWK/Aspect 1981–85; Leo Burnett: art dir 1986–89, creative gp head 1989–91, assoc creative dir 1992–93, bd creative dir 1994–; winner various advtg indust awards incl: two Cannes Gold Lions, Grand Prix Eurobest Poster Awards; MSIAD 1980; *Recreations* modern art, sport (former Welsh schoolboys champion football and basketball), music, my son; *Clubs* Cannons Health; *Style*— Mark Tutssel, Esq; ✉ Leo Burnett Ltd, The Leo Burnett Building, 60 Sloane Avenue, London SW3 3XB (☎ 0171 591 9111, fax 0171 591 9126/7)

TUTT, Leo Edward; s of Leo Edward Tutt (d 1975), of Sydney, NSW, Australia, and Dorothy, *née* M C Adam (d 1988); *b* 6 April 1938; *Educ* Knox GS NSW Aust; *m* 26 May 1961, Heather Elphinstone, da of Charles Walter Coombe (d 1965), of Sydney, NSW, Australia; 2 s (Leo, James), 1 da (Katie); *Career* CA in public practice 1966–73; chm Tutt Bryant Ltd 1973–96 (jt md 1973–74), dir and chief exec Escor Ltd 1974–78, chm and chief exec Bowater Industries Australia 1974–96, dir and chief exec Australia and Far East Rexam plc (formerly Bowater plc) 1978–96; non-exec dep chm Bundaberg Sugar Company Limited (Aust Listed Co) 1984–91, non-exec dir Friends Provident Life Office 1987–93; dir: State Rail Authy NSW 1989–94, MIM Holdings Ltd (Aust Listed Co) 1991–, Metway Bank Ltd (Aust Listed Co) 1992–; chm: Sun Alliance and Royal Insurance Australia Ltd 1996–, Detroit Diesel-Allison Australia Pty Ltd 1996–; dir The Graduate Sch of Business Univ of Sydney 1989–; hon fell Univ of Sydney 1996; FCA 1966, FAIM 1966, FCPA 1994; *Recreations* sailing, golf; *Clubs* American, Avondale Golf, Elanora Country, Royal Motor Yacht, Royal Prince Alfred Yacht, Royal Sydney Yacht Squadron; *Style*— Leo Tutt, Esq; ✉ Sedlescombe, 58 Prince Alfred Parade, Newport, NSW 2106, Australia (☎ 00 61 2 9979 5744); Suite 1802, 18th Floor, 52 Martin Place, Sydney, NSW 2000, Australia (☎ 00 61 2 9221 1966, fax 00 61 2 9235 2585)

TUTT, Dr Leslie William Godfrey; s of Charles Leslie Tutt, of London, and Emily Ditcham, *née* Wiseman; *b* 13 Oct 1921; *Educ* RMC of Sci (pac), Univ of London (MSc, PhD); *Career* RA 1940–46, Maj SO 1944; actuary and mathematical statistician in private practice, lectr and writer; contrib numerous res papers and tech articles to actuarial, statistical and fin jls 1950–; Inst of Statisticians: memb Cncl 1968–74 and 1975–81, vice chm 1981–84, chm 1984–87, vice pres 1987–93; memb: Exec Ctee Pensions Res Accountants Gp 1976–85, Cncl Nat Assoc Pension Funds 1979–83; Faculty of Actuaries: memb Cncl 1975–78, memb Bd of Examiners 1980–90; examinations assessor CII 1980–; Liveryman: Worshipful Co of Loriners 1975, Worshipful Co of Actuaries 1979; FFA 1949, FSS 1951, FIS 1951, assoc Soc of Actuaries USA 1968, FPMI 1976; *Books* Private Pension Scheme Finance (1970), Pensions and Employee Benefits (contrib, 1973), Pension Schemes, Investment, Communications and Overseas Aspects (1977), Pension Law and Taxation (1985), Financial Aspects of Pension Business (1986), Financial Aspects of Life Business (1987), Financial Services Marketing and Investor Protection (1988), Life Assurance (1988), Pensions (1988), Financial Advisers' Competence Test (jtly, 1989), Taxation and Trusts (1990), Personal Investment Planning (1990), Corporate Investment Planning (1991), Pensions and Insurance Administration (1992), Personal Financial Planning (1995); *Recreations* running, bobsleighing, riding the Cresta Run, golf; *Clubs* Athenaeum, City Livery, New (Edinburgh); *Style*— Dr L W G Tutt; ✉ 21 Sandilands, Croydon, Surrey CR0 5DF (☎ 0181 654 2995)

TUTT, Prof Norman Sydney; s of Sydney Robert Tutt (d 1968), and Stella May, *née* Curtis (d 1993); *b* 8 June 1944; *Educ* Chislehurst & Sidcup GS, Univ of Keele (BA), Univ of Leeds (MSc), Univ of Nottingham (PhD); *m* 10 Sept 1966, Diana Patricia, da of Stanley Hewitt (d 1944); 2 s (Karl b 1969, Keir b 1970); *Career* clinical psychologist Nottingham Area Psychological Serv 1966–69, res psychologist St Gilbert's Boys' Approved Sch 1969–73, professional advsr Northamptonshire Social Servs 1973–74, sr devpt offr London Boroughs Children's Regnl Planning Ctee 1974–75, princ social work servs offr DHSS 1975–79, prof of applied social studies Univ of Lancaster 1979–89, dir of social servs Leeds City Cncl 1989–92, exec dir Social Information Systems Ltd 1992–; memb Assoc of Dirs of Social Servs, memb Cncl ASA 1996–; memb Br Psychological Soc; *Books* Care or Custody (1975), Violence (ed, 1975), Alternative Strategies for Coping with Crime (ed, 1978), A Way of Life for the Handicapped (ed with Glenys Jones, 1983), Children in Custody (with Gillian Stewart, 1987); *Style*— Prof Norman Tutt; ✉ Styche Hall, Market Drayton, Shropshire TF9 3RB (☎ 01630 658985); Le Grand Margantinet, 61300 Torchamp, France; Social Information Systems Ltd, 19 King St, Knutsford, Cheshire WA16 6DW (☎ 01565 750511)

TUTT, Sylvia Irene Maud; da of Charles Leslie Tutt, of London, and Emily Ditcham, *née* Wiseman; *Career* chartered sec and administrator in private practice; author of numerous technical articles in professional and financial journals 1956–; Inst of Chartered Secs and Administrators: memb Benevolent Fund Mgmnt Ctee 1975–90, memb Cncl 1975–76 and 1980–82, memb Educn Ctee 1980–82, memb Pubns and PR Ctee 1980–82, rep memb Crossways Tst 1977–, pres Women's Soc 1975–76 (memb Ctee 1968–71 and 1976–87, hon sec 1971–74, vice pres 1973–75), chm London Branch 1984–85 (memb Ctee 1974–82 and 1985–87, vice chm 1982–84); sr examiner CII 1975–; pres Soroptimist Int of Central London 1976–78 (vice pres 1974–76); vice-pres United Wards Club of the City of London 1996, Liveryman Worshipful Co of Scriveners 1978, Freeman Guild of Freemen City of London 1976; Worshipful Co of Chartered Secs and Administrators: Liveryman 1977, memb Ct of Assts 1977–, Jr Warden 1981–82, Sr Warden 1982–83, Master 1983–84, managing tstee Charitable Tst 1978–, memb Fin and Gen Purposes Ctee 1995–; FCIS 1956, FRSA 1983, FSS 1996; *Books* Private Pension Scheme Finance (jtly, 1970), Pensions and Employee Benefits (contrib, 1973), Pension Law and Taxation (jtly, 1985), Financial Aspects of Pension Business (jtly, 1986), Financial Aspects of Life Business (jtly, 1987), A Mastership of a Livery Company (1988), Financial Aspects of Long Term Business (1991); *Recreations* horse riding, golf, winter sports; *Clubs* City Livery, Royal Over-Seas League; *Style*— Sylvia I M Tutt; ✉ 21 Sandilands, Croydon, Surrey CR0 5DF(☎ 0181 654 2995)

TUZO, Gen Sir Harry Craufurd; GCB (1973, KCB 1971), OBE (1961), MC (1945); s of John Tuzo, and Annie, *née* Craufurd; *b* 26 Aug 1917; *Educ* Wellington, Oriel Coll Oxford (MA); *m* 1943, Monica Salter; 1 da; *Career* WWII RA, on staff Far East 1946–49, RHA, Staff Sch Inf, GSO1 WO, Cdr 51 Gurkha Bde, IDC, COS BAOR 1967–69, dir RA 1969–71, GOC and dir of ops NI 1971–73, Gen 1973, Cdr N Army Gp and C-in-C BAOR 1973–76, Dep Supreme Allied Cdr Europe 1976–78, ADC Gen to HM The Queen 1974–77; Col Cmdt RA 1971–83, and RHA 1976–83; chm: RUSI 1980–83, Marconi Space and Defence Systems 1979–83; Master Gunner St James's Park 1977–83; hon fell Oriel Coll Oxford; govr Wellington Coll 1977–87; chm: King's Lynn Festival and Fermoy Centre 1982–87, Pensthorpe Wildfowl Tst 1986–96; pres Norfolk Soc 1987–92; DL Norfolk 1983–96; *Clubs* Army and Navy; *Style*— Gen Sir Harry Tuzo, GCB, OBE, MC; ✉ c/o Army and Navy Club, Pall Mall, London SW1 1JJ

TWEED, Jill (Mrs Hicks); da of late Maj Jack Robert Lowrie Tweed, and Kathleen Janie, *née* Freeth; *b* 7 Dec 1935; *Educ* Slade Sch of Art (BA); *m* Philip Lionel Sholto Hicks, s of Brig P Hicks; 1 s (David b 1971), 1 da (Nicola b 1960); *Career* sculptor; solo and gp exhibitions incl: Royal Acad 1979, Poole-Willis Gallery NYC 1984, Barbican Centre 1990, Flowers East Gallery 1991, Bruton Street Gallery 1992, The McHardy Sculpture Co 1995; cmmns incl: HM Queen Elizabeth Queen Mother 1980, HRH Prince Charles and Lady Diana Spencer 1981, HE The Governor of Guernsey, Hampshire Sculpture Tst 1991; 4m bronze purchased by Hants CC for Caen Normandy (D-Day Remembrance) 1994, other work incl 3m high bronze (The Railwayman) Eastleigh 1995, 3m high bronze (The Bargeman) Sittingbourne Kent 1996; FRBS, FRSA; *Recreations* horse riding; *Style*— Ms Jill Tweed; (☎ 01993 850347)

TWEED, (David) John; s of William Tweed (d 1989), and Margaret, *née* Gittus (d 1984); *b* 14 Dec 1946; *Educ* The King's Sch Chester, Univ of Manchester (BA, BArch); *m* 26 April 1980, Helen Elspeth Hamilton, da of Dr Frank Hamilton-Leckie, MC, TD, of Monklands, Uddingston, Glasgow; 2 da (Hilary b 1986, Anna b 1994); *Career* founded John Tweed Assocs Architects Chester; memb Cncl: RIBA NW Region 1983–87 and 1994–, Chester Sports and Leisure Assoc 1984–; chm Mgmnt Ctee Claverton Ct Chester 1985–89, pres Cheshire Soc of Architects 1985–86; memb Cncl The Architects Benevolent Soc 1986–, memb RIBA NW Educn Ctee 1987–, chm RIBA NW Practice Ctee 1994–, chm Chester Historic Bldgs Preservation Tst 1991–92; current cmmns incl masterplanning phase 1 Old Port of Chester Regeneration Programme; RIBA 1974, ACIArb 1983, FRSA 1995; *Recreations* family, rowing, sailing, gardening, boatbuilding; *Clubs* Royal Chester Rowing; *Style*— John Tweed, Esq; ✉ Ivy House, Hob Hill, Tilston, nr Malpas, Cheshire SY14 7DU (☎ 01829 250301); Duncraig House, Salen, Argyll; Tweed Nuttall Warburton Chartered Architects, Chapel House, City Road, Chester CH1 3AE (☎ 01244 310388, fax 01244 325643)

TWEEDIE, Prof Sir David Philip; kt (1994); s of Aidrian Ian Tweedie, of Doncaster, and Marie Patricia, *née* Phillips; *b* 7 July 1944; *Educ* Grangemouth HS, Univ of Edinburgh (BCom, PhD); *m* 6 June 1970, Janice Christine, da of George Haddow Brown; 2 s (Ross Steven b 10 June 1976, Mark David b 25 May 1977); *Career* apprentice Mann Judd Gordon & Co Chartered Accountants Glasgow 1969–72, CA 1972; Univ of Edinburgh: lectr Dept of Accounting and Business Methods 1973–78, dir of studies 1973–75, assoc dean Faculty of Social Scis 1975–78; tech dir Inst of Chartered Accountants of Scotland 1978–81, nat res ptnr KMG Thomson McLintock 1982–87, nat tech ptnr KPMG Peat Marwick McLintock 1987–90; chm Accounting Standards Bd 1990– (ex officio memb Fin Reporting Cncl), chm Urgent Issues Task Force; Univ of Lancaster: visiting prof of accounting Int Centre for Res in Accounting (ICRA) 1978–88, tstee ICRA 1982–93, dep chm Bd of Tstees ICRA 1986–93; visiting prof of accounting Dept of Economics Univ of Bristol 1988–; memb Cncl ICAEW 1989–91 (memb Auditing Res Fndn 1988–90), chm CCAB Auditing Practices Ctee 1989–90 (vice chm 1986–88, memb 1985–90), UK and Irish rep Int Auditing Practices Ctee 1983–88, UK and Irish rep International Accounting Standards Ctee 1995–; Hon DSc(Econ) Univ of Hull 1993, Hon LLD Univ of Lancaster 1993, Hon DLitt Heriot-Watt Univ 1996; *Books* The Private Shareholder & The Corporate Report (with T A Lee, 1977), Financial Reporting Inflation and The Capital Maintenance Concept (1979), The Institutional Investor & Financial Information (with T A Lee, 1981), The Debate on Inflation Accounting (with G Whittington, 1984); *Style—* Prof Sir David Tweedie; ✉ Accounting Standards Board, Holborn Hall, 100 Gray's Inn Rd, London WC1X 8AL (☎ 0171 404 8818, fax 0171 404 4497)

TWEEDIE, James Hamilton; s of George Carrick Tweedie (FRCS, d 1978), of Little Ellingham, Norfolk, and Gladys Mary, *née* Telford; *b* 31 March 1950; *Educ* Loughborough Coll, Bart's (BSc, MB BS, MS); *m* 17 Feb 1973, Julia Evelyn, da of Eric Raymond Workman, of Gloucester; 1 s (George b 1973), 1 da (Juliette b 1975); *Career* conslt surgn Stoke Mandeville Hosp; memb: BMA, RSM; FRCSEd, FRCS; *Recreations* golf, skiing; *Clubs* Grey Turner Surgical, Ashridge Golf; *Style—* James Tweedie, Esq; ✉ Loosley House, Loosley Row, Bucks HP27 0PF (☎ 01844 346819); Stoke Mandeville Hospital, Aylesbury, Bucks (☎ 01296 315000)

TWEEDSMUIR, 3 Baron (UK 1935), of Elsfield, Co Oxford; William James de l'Aigle Buchan; s of 1 Baron Tweedsmuir, GCMG, GCVO, CH, PC (d 1940; the author John Buchan), and Susan Charlotte (d 1977), da of Capt Hon Norman de l'Aigle Grosvenor; suc bro, 2 Baron Tweedsmuir, CBE, CD (d 1996); *b* 10 Jan 1916; *Educ* Eton, New Coll Oxford; *m* 1, 1939 (m dis 1946), Nesta Irene, da of Lt-Col C D Crozier; 1 da (Hon Perdita Caroline (Hon Mrs Connolly) b 1940); m 2, 1946 (m dis 1960), Barbara Howard (d 1969), da of Ernest Nash Ensor, of Wimbledon; 3 s (Hon John William Howard de l'Aigle (Toby) b 1950, Hon (Charles Walter) Edward Ralph) b 1951, Hon James Ernest b 1954), 3 da (Hon Deborah Charlotte (Baroness Stewartby) b 1947, Hon Laura Mary Clare (Hon Mrs Chanter) b 1953, Hon Ursula Margaret Bridget (Hon Mrs Wide) b (twin) 1953); m 3, 1960, Sauré Cynthia Mary, da of late Maj G E Tatchell, Royal Lincs Regt; 1 s (Hon Alexander Edward b 1961); *Career* Sqdn Ldr RAF Vol Reserve; *Books* John Buchan, a Memoir (biography of father, 1982), The Rags of Time (autobiography), three novels; *Clubs* Travellers'; *Style—* The Rt Hon the Lord Tweedsmuir; ✉ West End House, Hornton, Banbury, Oxon OX15 6DA

TWEEDY, Colin David; s of Clifford Harry Tweedy, of Abbotsbury, Dorset, and Kitty Audrey, *née* Matthews; *b* 26 Oct 1953; *Educ* City of Bath Boys' Sch, St Catherine's Coll Oxford (MA); *Career* mangr Thorndike Theatre Leatherhead 1976–78, corp fin offr Guinness Mahon 1978–80, asst dir Streets Financial PR 1980–83, DG Assoc for Business Sponsorship of the Arts (ABSA) 1983–; dir ABSA Consulting, vice chm Comité Européen pour le Rapprochement de l'Economie et de la Culture (CEREC); memb: UK Nat Ctee Euro Cinema and TV Year 1988–89, Cncl Japan Festival 1991, Nat Cinema Centenary Ctee, Cncl for Charitable Support; tstee Serpentine Gallery; dir: Oxford Stage Co, Covent Garden Int Festival, Crusaid; Freeman City of London 1978; MInstD, FRSA; *Books* A Celebration of Ten Years' Business Sponsorship of the Arts (1987); *Style—* Colin Tweedy, Esq; ✉ ABSA, 60 Gainsford St, Butlers Wharf, London SE1 2NY (☎ 0171 378 8143, fax 0171 407 7527)

TWEEDY, (Oliver) Robert; s of Cdr G J D Tweedy, OBE, RN (d 1969), and V E Maurice (d 1984); *b* 4 Feb 1930; *Educ* Sedbergh, RMA Sandhurst; *m* 11 Aug 1956, April Dawn, da of E T Berrangé; 2 s (Christopher b 1962, Andrew b 1964), 1 da (Sareth (Mrs J C Nainby-Luxmoore) b 1959); *Career* cmmnd The Black Watch 1949; CO 1 BW Scotland, N Ireland and Hong Kong 1971–73; cdr British Advsy Team Nigeria 1980–82; cdr 51 Highland Brigade 1982–84; ADC to HM The Queen 1983–85, ret Brig 1985; Cmdt Queen Victoria Sch Dunblane 1985–91; chm: Perth Branch Scottish Veterans Garden City Assoc 1990–, The Black Watch Assoc 1992–; memb Cncl Scottish Conservation Projects Tst 1995–; *Recreations* golf, country pursuits; *Clubs* Royal and Ancient (St Andrews), Royal Perth; *Style—* Robert Tweedy, Esq; ✉ Inverbraan, Little Dunkeld, Perthshire PH8 0AD

TWEMLOW, William Antony (Tony); s of Richard Lawrence Twemlow (d 1994), of West Kirby, Wirral, and Sylvia Doreen Twemlow (d 1991); *b* 2 Dec 1943; *Educ* Calday Grange GS, Downing Coll Cambridge (MA); *m* 12 Oct 1968, Margaret, da of William Thompson Scollay (d 1979); 2 s (Roy William b 15 Dec 1971, James Antony b 28 Sept 1982), 1 da (Laura Jane b 6 July 1973); *Career* Cuff Roberts: articled clerk 1965–68, asst slr 1968–71, ptnr 1971–, managing ptnr 1986–93; licensed insolvency practitioner 1987; chm: Liverpool Young Slrs Gp 1969–70, Young Slrs Gp Law Soc 1978–79, Liverpool Bd of Legal Studies 1988–91; dir Slrs' Benevolent Assoc 1980–91, memb Remuneration and Practice Devpt Ctee Law Soc 1980–92, pres Liverpool Law Soc 1994–95; memb Royal Liverpool Philharmonic Choir 1965–94, dep vice chm Royal Liverpool Philharmonic Soc 1988–91 (memb Bd 1986–93); dir Hoylake Cottage Hosp Tst Ltd 1989–92; memb: Law Soc 1968, Liverpool Law Soc 1968, Insolvency Lawyers Assoc 1989, Insolvency Practitioners Assoc 1990; *Recreations* music, tennis; *Style—* Tony Twemlow, Esq; ✉ Cuff Roberts, 100 Old Hall Street, Liverpool L3 9TD (☎ 0151 227 4181, fax 0151 227 2584)

TWIGG, David Joseph; s of John Twigg (d 1960), of Lincs, and Edith Mary, *née* Waterfield (d 1982); *b* 7 March 1934; *Educ* Queen Elizabeth's Sch Lincs; *m* 1, 9 May 1970 (m dis 1987), Hilary Ann, da of Maj Ronald Hedley Vickers (d 1977), of Gloucester; m 2, 15 July 1988, Nina, da of Ivan Prokopenko, of Moscow; *Career* Nat Serv RE 1958–60, serving Mil Engrg Experimental Estab Christchurch and No 1 Bomb Disposal Unit; civil engr Lincs and Bucks CC 1953–62, sr civil engr Huntingdonshire CC 1962–65, sr appts with consulting engrs 1965–70; ptnr: Donovan H Lee and Partners Consulting Engineers 1970–79, The Henderson Busby Partnership Consulting Engineers (winners of Queen's award for export achievement 1982) 1979–82; fndr and sr ptnr: David Twigg Associates 1983–, DTA Transportation Consulting Engineers and Planners 1987–; co-fndr Twigg Graham Rail; chm Merton Community Rels Cncl 1983; various offices Kingston Lib Assoc 1976–88, Lib Dem cncllr Kingston upon Thames 1990, mayor Royal Borough of Kingston upon Thames 1995–96; Parly candididate Wimbledon: (Lib) 1979, (Alliance) 1983; contested London SW Euro Seat 1984; CEng 1963, FICE 1973, FIHT 1968, MConsE 1986; *Recreations* tennis, cricket, history; *Style—* David Twigg, Esq; ✉ 87 Blenheim Gardens, Kingston upon Thames, Surrey KT2 7BJ (☎ 0181 549 3690); David Twigg Associates, 101 East Hill, Wandsworth, London SW18 2QB (☎ 0181 874 0834/3291, fax 0181 333 1453)

TWIGG, Patrick Alan; QC (1986); s of Alan Oswald Twigg (d 1994), of W Linton, Scotland, and Gwendoline Mary (Molly), *née* Slocock; *b* 19 May 1943; *Educ* Repton, Sorbonne, Perugia Univ Italy, Univ of Bristol (LLB), Univ of Virginia (scholar, LLM); *m* 24 July 1974, Gabrielle Madeline Bay, da of Anthony Green; 1 s (Harry Matthew Edmund b 25 July 1984), 1 da (Venetia Madeline (twin) b 25 July 1984); *Career* called to the Bar Inner Temple (maj scholar) 1967, recorder of the Crown Court 1987–, in practice specialising in commercial and construction law UK and abroad 1987–; memb Western Circuit; memb: Old Stagers 1970–, Bd of the Canterbury Festival; pres Bishopsbourne CC; *Recreations* family, house, planting trees, music, composition, amateur dramatics, piano, landscape gardening; *Clubs* Delta Theta Phi Fraternity; *Style—* Patrick Twigg, Esq, QC; ✉ 2 Temple Gardens, Temple, London EC4Y 9AY (☎ 0171 583 6041, fax 0171 583 2094)

TWIGGY, *see:* Lawson, Lesley

TWINCH, Richard William; s of Richard Herbert Twinch, of Whitchurch, Salop, and Roma Bayliss, *née* Silver; *b* 29 Oct 1950; *Educ* Wellington, Clare Coll Cambridge (MA), Architectural Assoc (AADipl); *m* Hazel Cecilia, da of James Herbert Merrison (d 1987); 1 s (Oliver b 1975), 2 da (Jemila b 1977, Anna b 1981); *Career* architect and special technol conslt; lectr and tutor Prince of Wales's Inst of Architecture 1992–95, lectr in architecture Oxford Brookes Univ 1996–; author of tech software for architects incl: Condensation Control 1981–92, Heat Loss Performance 1983–91; dir: Richard Twinch Design, Chisholme Inst Beshara Sch of Esoteric Educn; commentator to Beshara Magazine 1986–90, lectr and conslt in CAD; MA external examiner Visual and Traditional Arts Unit RCA 1990 and 1991; computer columnist to Building Design magazine 1985–92, author of numerous articles on CAD in architectural press, papers incl Thermal Insulation and Condensation and Building Materials (1988); RIBA; *Recreations* listening to music, walking, tennis; *Style—* Richard Twinch, Esq; ✉ 7 Hill Top Road, Oxford OX4 1PB (☎ 01865 246775/202108)

TWINE, Derek Milton; s of Edward Montague Twine (d 1976), of Horley, Surrey, and Winifred May, *née* Milton (d 1993); *b* 1 May 1951; *Educ* The GS Reigate Surrey, Univ Coll of N Wales Bangor (BA Educn (1st class)); *m* 7 Sept 1974, Rhoda, da of Very Rev R J N Lockhart; 1 da (Nicola b 11 April 1977), 1 s (Paul b 12 Jan 1979); *Career* lectr Univ of Wales 1975–76 (researcher 1973–75); The Scout Association: dir Venture Scout Trg 1976–79, dir of Programme 1979–85, exec cmmr (Programme and Trg) 1985–96, chief exec 1996–; currently: chm Trg Mangrs' Gp Nat Cncl for Voluntary Youth Servs (NCVYS), conslt London Fedn of Clubs for Young People, memb Voluntary Sector Panel Royal Soc for the Arts; memb Mgmnt Ctee and chm Educn and Standards Nat Youth Agency (NYA) 1991–95, memb Exec Ctee and chm Devpt Project NCVYS 1979–82, memb Youth Panel Nat Tst 1978–85; tstee: Whitechapel Fndn, Croatia Sunrise City Support; govr Davenant Fndn Sch; author of various articles in youthwork and educnl press; FITD 1987, FIPD 1994; *Recreations* church activities, theatre, cooking, cross-country running; *Style—* Derek Twine, Esq; ✉ The Scout Association, Baden-Powell House, Queen's Gate, London SW7 5JS (☎ 0171 590 5110, fax 0171 590 5112)

TWINING, Prof William Lawrence; s of Baron Twining (Life Peer, d 1967); *b* 1934; *Educ* Charterhouse, BNC Oxford (DCL), Chicago Univ (JD); *m* 1957, Penelope Elizabeth, da of Richard Wall Morris; 1 s, 1 da; *Career* prof of jurisprudence Queen's Univ Belfast 1965–72, prof of law Univ of Warwick 1972–82, Quain prof of jurisprudence UCL 1983–; pres Soc of Public Teachers of Law 1978–79, chm Cwlth Legal Educn Assoc 1983–93; Hon LLD: Victoria Univ BC Canada 1980, Univ of Edinburgh 1994; *Books* Karl Llewellyn and the Realist Movement (1973), How to do Things with Rules (3 edn, with David Miers, 1991), Theories of Evidence - Bentham & Wigmore (1985), Rethinking Evidence (1990), Analysis of Evidence (with Terence Anderson, 1991), Legal Records in the Commonwealth (with Emma Quick), Blackstone's Tower: The English Law School (1994); *Style—* Prof William Twining; ✉ 10 Mill Lane, Iffley, Oxford OX4 4EJ; University College London, Faculty of Law, Bentham House, 4 Endsleigh Gardens, London WC1H 0EG

TWINN, Dr Ian David; MP (C) Edmonton (majority 593); s of David Twinn, of Cambridge, and Gwynneth Irene, *née* Ellis; *b* 26 April 1950; *Educ* Netherhall Secdy Mod Sch Cambridge, Cambridge GS, Univ Coll of Wales Aberystwyth (BA), Univ of Reading (PhD); *m* 28 July 1973, Frances Elizabeth, da of Godfrey Nall Holtby (d 1988), of Poltesco, Cornwall; 2 s (David b 1983, John b 1986); *Career* sr lectr in town planning Poly of the South Bank 1975–83; MP (C) Edmonton 1983–; PPS to: Rt Hon Sir Peter Morrison 1985–90, David Trippier as Min of State DOE 1990–92, Sir John Cope as Paymaster-Gen at the Treasy 1992–94; jt chm Br Parly Lighting Gp, chm All-Pty Parly Greek Ctee, vice chm Parly Cyprus Ctee; Freeman of City of London 1981; MIBG 1972, FRSA 1989; *Recreations* antique furniture restoration, collecting second-hand books, bookcase building; *Style—* Dr Ian Twinn, MP; ✉ House of Commons, London SW1A 0AA (☎ 0171 219 3000)

TWISK, Russell Godfrey; s of K Y Twisk, of Twisk, Holland, and Joyce, *née* Brunning; *b* 24 Aug 1941; *Educ* Salesian Coll Farnborough; *m* 1965, Ellen Elizabeth Bambury; 2 da; *Career* Harmsworth Press: dep ed Golf Illustrated 1960, sub ed Sphere; freelance journalist 1962; BBC: joined Editorial Staff Radio Times 1966, dep ed Radio Times 1971, devpt mangr 1975, ed The Listener 1981–87, ed numerous BBC pubns; ed-in-chief British Reader's Digest 1988–; dir: The Reader's Digest Assoc Ltd 1989–, Berkeley Magazines Ltd 1990–; radio critic The Observer 1989–94, publisher BBC Adult Literacy Project, deviser Radio Times Drama Awards; govr London Coll of Printing 1967–87 (chm 1974 and 1978); chm: The Reader's Digest Tst 1988, Br Soc of Magazine Eds 1989, Nat Leadership Ctee Charities Aid Fndn 1991; memb Advsy Cncl ASH 1989–, pres Media Soc 1993–95; *Recreations* running, map reading; *Clubs* Reform, Groucho; *Style—* Russell Twisk, Esq; ✉ c/o Reader's Digest, Berkeley Square House, Berkeley Square, London W1X 6AB

TWISLETON-WYKEHAM-FIENNES, *see also:* Fiennes

TWISS, (Lionel) Peter; OBE (1956), DSC (1942, and bar 1943); s of Col Dudley Cyril Twiss, South Staffordshire Regt (d 1964), of Lindfield, Sussex, and Laura Georgina Smith, *née* Chapman (d 1980); *b* 23 July 1921; *Educ* Sherborne; *m* 1, Oct 1944; m 2, 1949; 2 da (Joanna d 1954, Sarah b 1954); m 3, 1960; 1 da (Miranda b 1961); m 4, 4 Nov 1964, Heather Linda (d 1988), da of Strachan Goldingham (d 1981), of Palmerston North, NI, New Zealand; *Career* fleet air arm 804 sqdn 1939–46, Med Convoys 807 Sqdn, Nightfighters 1 Seafire Sqdn N Africa Op Torch, NFIU, Br Air Cmmn Patuxent River USA, A & AEE Boscombe Down Empire Test Pilots Sch, Naval Test Sqdn A & AEE Lt RNVR; Fairey Aviation test pilot 1946–60 (chief test pilot 1957); world absolute air speed record 1956; Fairey Marine sales mangr; dir: Fairey Marine, Fairey Yacht Harbours; gen mangr and dir Hamble Point Marina; marine conslt; *Recreations* ornithology, yachting, gliding, gardening; *Clubs* Royal Southern Yacht, Surrey & Hampshire Gliding, Lasham Gliding Soc; *Style—* Peter Twiss, Esq, OBE, DSC; ✉ Nettleworth, 33 South St, Titchfield, Hampshire PO14 4DL

TWIST, Stephen John; s of late James Twist, of Darlington, Co Durham, and Kathleen Marion, *née* Gamble; *b* 26 Sept 1950; *Educ* Queen Elizabeth GS Darlington, Univ of Liverpool (LLB); *m* 4 May 1990, Ann, *née* Stockburn; 1 s (Miles Henry b 16 March 1993); *Career* with Metropolitan Police 1974–78; called to the Bar Middle Temple 1979; memb: Hon Soc of Middle Temple, Hon Soc Gray's Inn, North Eastern Circuit; *Style—* Stephen Twist, Esq; ✉ York Chambers, 14 Toft Green, York YO1 1JT (☎ 01904 620048, fax 01904 619956)

TWISTON-DAVIES, Audley William; s of William Anthony Twiston-Davies, DL (d 1989), of Much Dewchurch, Herefordshire, and Rosemary, *née* Archdale; *b* 13 Nov 1950; *Educ* Radley; *m* 9 Feb 1985, Hon Caroline Harbord-Hamond, da of 11 Baron Suffield, MC; 1 s (Thomas Audley b 31 Oct 1994), 3 da (Antonia Rose b 22 Oct 1987, Sophie Louise b 13 Feb 1990, Zoe Caroline b 24 Oct 1992); *Career* md Foreign & Colonial Emerging Markets Ltd; chm Foreign & Colonial Emerging Middle East Fund Inc (NY); dir: Foreign & Colonial Management Ltd, Foreign & Colonial Emerging Markets Trust

PLC, Latin American Management Ltd, Latin American Investment Trust plc, Latin American Extra Yield Fund Ltd, Brazilian Investment Trust plc, Brazilian Investment Co, Argentinian Investment Co Sicav, Mexican Investment Co Sicav, Colombian Investment Sicav, Indian Investment Co Sicav (Lux), Peruvian Investment Co Sicav (Lux); dir: Inst of Latin American Studies Univ of London, Hereford Cathedral Tst; Liveryman Haberdashers' Co; *Clubs* Boodle's, City, White's; *Style—* Audley Twiston-Davies, Esq; ✉ 43 Chester Square, London SW1; Exchange House, Primrose Street, London EC2A 2NY (☎ 0171 628 1234, fax 0171 628 2281)

TWISTON DAVIES, David James; s of Mervyn Peter Twiston Davies, of Somerset, and Isabel Anne, *née* Fox; *b* 23 March 1945; *Educ* Downside; *m* 10 June 1970, Margaret Anne (Rita), da of Francis Gerard Montgomery (d 1978); 3 s (Benedict, James, Huw), 1 da (Bess); *Career* journalist; East Anglian Daily Times 1966–68, Winnipeg Free Press 1968–70; The Daily Telegraph: news sub ed 1970–77, asst literary ed 1977–86, dep obituaries ed 1986–88, ed Peterborough column 1988–89, letters ed 1989–; Freeman City of London; *Books* Canada from Afar: The Daily Telegraph Book of Canadian Obituaries (ed, 1997); *Recreations* defending reputation of the British Empire; *Clubs* Travellers'; *Style—* David Twiston Davies, Esq; ✉ 20 Warwick Park, Tunbridge Wells, Kent (☎ 01892 528292); The Daily Telegraph, 1 Canada Square, Canary Wharf, London E14 5DT (☎ 0171 538 6458, fax 0171 538 6455)

TWITCHETT, John Anthony Murray; s of Joseph Ernest James Twitchett (d 1959), of Chigwell, Essex, and Olive Jessie, *née* Lidford (d 1986); *b* 26 July 1932; *Educ* Chigwell Sch Essex; *m* 1, 30 March 1960, Doricka Edith (d 1963), da of late Henry Edmund Palfreman, of London; m 2, 25 Jan 1964 (m dis 1972), Rosemary, da of Joseph Hallam, of Torquay, S Devon; 2 da (Elizabeth Anne b 23 Nov 1964, Caroline Mary b 11 June 1966); *Career* former landowner Woodeaton Oxon; ptnr David John Ceramics 1970–, curator Royal Crown Derby Museum 1972–; int lectr; venues incl: V&A, Canadian Nat Gallery Ottawa, Royal Ontario Museum Toronto, Musée des Beaux Arts Montréal; first Charles Norman lecture 1996; dir The Antique Ceramic Bureau 1996–; memb Cncl Derby Porcelain Int Soc, memb Ctee Burford and Dist Refugee Aid Soc; memb: Nat Tst, NFU; life tstee The Royal Crown Derby Museum Trust 1988, tstee The Raven Mason Bd Keele Univ; FRSA 1975; *Books* Royal Crown Derby (1976), Derby Porcelain (1980), Landscapes on Derby and Worcester (with Henry Sandon, 1984), Painters and the Derby China Works (with John Murdoch, 1987), London - World City 1800–1840 (contrib exhbn catalogue Essen, 1992), In Account (with Sampson Hancock, 1996), Derby Porcelain: The Dictionary (1997); *Recreations* golf; *Style—* John Twitchett, Esq; ✉ 5 Swan Lane Close, Burford, Oxford OX18 4SP

TWIVY, Paul Christopher Barstow; s of Dr Samuel Barstow Twivy, of Dunstable, and Sheila, *née* Webster (d 1993); *b* 19 Oct 1958; *Educ* Haberdashers' Aske's Sch, Magdalen Coll Oxford (BA); *m* 1, 31 July 1982 (m dis), Martha Mary Sladden; 2 s (Samuel b 1985, Joshua b 1988); m 2, 27 Oct 1991, Gabrielle Ruth Guz; 1 s (Max b 1994), 1 da (Eve b 1995); *Career* bd dir Hedger Mitchell Stark 1982–83, md Still Price Court Twivy D'Souza Lintas 1985–92, dep chm J Walter Thompson 1992–93, gp chief exec Bates Dorland 1994–96; memb: Steering Ctee Comic Relief, IPA Cncl, President's Ctee CPRE; spokesman for advtg indust; memb Mktg Soc; FIPA; *Recreations* freelance comedy writer, playwright, poetry, reading, swimming, music (guitar and piano); *Clubs* Oxford Union, Groucho's; *Style—* Paul Twivy, Esq; ✉ 46 Pattison Road, London NW2 2HJ

TWOSE, Roger Graham; s of Paul Francis Worth Twose, of NZ, and Patricia Ann, *née* Tolchard; *b* 17 April 1968; *Educ* King's Coll Taunton; *Career* professional cricketer; Warwickshire CCC: debut 1989, Benson & Hedges Cup winners 1994 and 1995, Britannic Assurance County Championship winners 1994 and 1995, Axa Equity & Law League Champions 1994, NatWest Trophy winners 1995 (runners-up 1994); off-seasons: Northern Districts NZ 1989–90, Central Districts NZ 1991–; highest score 277 v Glamorgan 1994, best bowling 6–28 v Surrey 1994; *Recreations* water and snow skiing, keeping fit, fishing; *Style—* Roger Twose, Esq; ✉ Warwickshire CCC, County Ground, Edgbaston, Birmingham B5 7QU (☎ 0121 446 4422)

TWYFORD, Donald Henry; CB (1990); s of Henry John Twyford (d 1982), of Ferring and Crowborough, Sussex, and Lily Hilda, *née* Ridler (d 1977); *b* 4 Feb 1931; *Educ* Wembley Co Sch; *Career* Nat Serv RAF Educn Branch 1949–51; Export Credits Guarantee Dept: joined 1949, sr princ (chief underwriter) 1968, asst sec 1972, estab offr 1976, under sec 1979–89, chm EC Policy Co-ordination Gp 1981, dir and chm Project Gp 1981–89; *Recreations* growing citrus fruit in Spain, travel, music; *Style—* Donald Twyford, Esq, CB; ✉ Cansala Lluca 16, Javea 03730, Alicante, Spain (☎ 00 34 6 597 4015)

TWYMAN, Prof Michael Loton; s of Lawrence Alfred Twyman (d 1980), and Gladys Mary, *née* Williams; *b* 15 July 1934; *Educ* Sir George Monoux GS, Univ of Reading (BA, PhD), Trinity Coll Cambridge; *m* 31 July 1958, Pauline Mary, da of Edward Frank Andrews; 2 s (Jeremy James b 9 Oct 1960, Daniel John Soulby b 9 Oct 1966), 1 da (Nicola Clare b 25 Jan 1963); *Career* Univ of Reading: asst lectr in typography & graphic art 1959–62, lectr 1962–71, sr lectr in typography & graphic communication 1971–76, professor and head Dept of Typography & Graphic Communication 1976–, dir Centre for Ephemera Studies 1993–; visiting fell Mellon Center for British Art Yale 1981; chm: Icograda (Int Cncl of Graphic Design Assocs) Working Gp on Graphic Design History 1984–88, Curatorium Int Inst for Information Design Vienna 1989–; Assoc Typographique Internationale: chm Ctee for Educn in Letterforms 1974–77, chm Res and Educn Ctee 1991–, memb Bd of Dirs 1994–; Printing Historical Soc: memb Ctee 1964–, asst ed Jl 1969–84, chm 1991–; memb Graphic Design Panel Nat Cncl for Diplomas in Art & Design 1971–74; Cncl for Nat Academic Awards: memb Ctee of Art & Design 1978–81, vice chm Graphic Design Bd 1972–80, memb Sub-ctee for Res Degrees 1978–83; tstee: Fndn for Ephemera Studies, Printing Heritage Tst; Samuel Pepys medal for Outstanding Contribution to Ephemera Studies 1983; fell Inst of Printing (FIOP); *Books* John Soulby, printer, Ulverston (1966), Lithography 1800–1850: the techniques of drawing on stone in England and France and their application in works of topography (1970), Printing 1770–1970: an illustrated history of its development and uses in England (1970), A Directory of London Lithographic Printers 1800–1850 (1976), Henry Bankes's Treatise on Lithography (1976), The Landscape Alphabet (1986), Early Lithographed Books (1990), Early Lithographed Music (1996); numerous articles in professional jls; *Style—* Prof Michael Twyman; ✉ Department of Typography & Graphic Communication, The University of Reading, 2 Earley Gate, Whiteknights, Reading, Berks RG6 6AU (☎ 0118 931 8081, fax 0118 935 1680)

TWYMAN, Paul Hadleigh; s of late Lawrence Alfred Twyman, and Gladys Mary, *née* Williams; *Educ* Chatham House Sch Ramsgate, Univ of Sheffield (BA(Econ)), LSE (MSc(Econ)); *Career* schoolmaster 1963–64; Civil Serv: asst princ Bd of Trade 1967–71, memb Secretariat Cmmn on the Third London Airport 1969–71, private sec to Sec of State for Trade and Indust 1971–73, princ Anti-Dumping Unit DTI 1976–78, asst sec and head Overseas Projects Gp DTI 1978–81, Civil Aviation Div 1981–83, Dept of Tport 1983, Cabinet Office 1984, under sec and dir Enterprise and Deregulation Unit Dept of Employment 1985–87; econ advsr to Chm of Cons Pty and head Econ Section Cons Res Dept 1987, exec chm Political Strategy Ltd 1988–; non-exec dir: Nationwide Building Society 1987– (dir Anglia Building Society 1983 until merger 1987), D'Arcy Masius Benton and Bowles (DMB&B) 1990–96; corp strategy dir Bates Dorland Ltd 1996–; Euro Parly candidate Greater Manchester West 1989, chm N Thanet Cons Assoc 1989–91, cncllr Thanet DC 1991–95; FIMgt, MCIT, FRSA; *Recreations* hill walking, gardening, observing gorillas; *Style—* Paul Twyman, Esq; ✉ Bates Dorland Ltd, 121–141 Westbourne Terrace, London W2 6JR (☎ 0171 262 5077); Nationwide Building Society, Pipers Way, Swindon SN38 1NW

TYACKE, Maj-Gen David Noel Hugh; CB (1970), OBE (1957); s of Capt Charles Noel Walker Tyacke (ka 1918), and Phoebe Coulthard (d 1969); *b* 18 Nov 1915; *Educ* Malvern, RMC Sandhurst; *m* 1940, Diana, da of Aubrey Hare Duke (d 1972); 1 s (Nicholas); *Career* cmmnd DCLI 1935 RA, cmd 1 Bn DCLI 1957–59, cmd 130 Inf Bde (TA) 1961–63, GOC Singapore Dist 1966–70; *Recreations* walking, motoring, bird watching; *Style—* Maj-Gen David Tyacke, CB, OBE; ✉ c/o Lloyds Bank, 7 Pall Mall, London SW1Y 5NA

TYDEMAN, John Peter; s of George Alfred Tydeman (d 1960), of Cheshunt, Herts, and Gladys Florence Beatrice, *née* Brown (d 1982); *b* 30 March 1936; *Educ* Hertford GS, Trinity Coll Cambridge (MA); *Career* 2 Lt 1 Singapore Regt RA 1954–56, served Malaya; drama director; head of drama radio BBC 1986–94 (radio drama prodr 1960–79, asst head radio drama 1979–86); awarded: Prix Italia 1970, Prix Futura 1979 and 1983, Bdcasting Press Guild Award for outstanding radio prodn 1983, Sony Special Award for Servs to Radio 1994; stage prodns incl: Objection to Sex and Violence (Royal Ct) 1975, The Bells of Hell (Garrick Theatre) 1977, Falstaff (Fortune Theatre) 1984; *Recreations* swimming, foreign places, theatre; *Clubs* Garrick, Rugby; *Style—* John Tydeman, Esq; ✉ 88 Great Titchfield St, London W1P 7AG (☎ and 0171 636 3886)

TYDEMAN, Prof William Marcus; s of Henry Marcus Tydeman, MBE (d 1975), of East Malling, Kent, and Elizabeth Mary, *née* Shepherd (d 1988); *b* 29 Aug 1935; *Educ* Maidstone GS, Univ Coll Oxford (BA, MA, MLitt); *m* 29 July 1961, Jacqueline Barbara Anne, da of Robert Lewis Jennison (d 1957); 2 da (Josephine b 1963, Rosalind b 1966); *Career* RCS 1954–56, cmmnd 2 Lt 1955; Univ Coll of N Wales Bangor: asst lectr in English 1961–64, lectr 1964–70, sr lectr 1970–83, reader 1983–86, prof 1986–, head Dept of English 1983–89, head Sch of English and Linguistics 1989–92; *Books* English Poetry 1400–1580 (ed, 1970), The Theatre in the Middle Ages (1978), Four Tudor Comedies (ed, 1984), Dr Faustus: Text and Performance (1984), English Medieval Theatre 1400–1500 (1986), The Welsh Connection (ed, 1986), The State of the Art: Christopher Marlowe (jtly, 1989), Two Tudor Tragedies (ed, 1992), Christopher Marlowe: the plays and their sources (jtly, 1994), The Bancrofts at the Prince of Wales's Theatre (1996), Oscar Wile: Salome (1996); *Recreations* theatre, local history; *Style—* Prof William Tydeman; ✉ School of English & Linguistics, University of Wales, Bangor, Gwynedd LL57 2DG (☎ 01248 382101)

TYE, Alan Peter; *b* 18 Sept 1933; *Educ* Regent St Poly Sch of Architecture (DipArch); *m* 1, 1960; 1 da (Helen Elna b 1962), 1 s (Martin Anders b 1964); m 2, 1966, Anita Birgitta Goethe-Tye; 1 da (Madeleine b 1967), 2 s (Nicolas b 1969, Kevin b 1973); *Career* Alan Tye Design 1962–, assoc dir Advanced Workplace Associates Ltd 1993–; memb Selection Ctee Cncl of Industl Design 1967, Civic Tst Award assessor 1968 and 1969, visiting tutor RCA 1978–83 (external assessor 1987–), specialist advsr on ind design CNAA 1980, London regnl assessor RIBA 1981, RSA Bursary judge 1983–, chm Product Liability Seminar CSD 1987, awards assessor RIBA 1988, external assessor RCA degrees 1989, chm RSA New for Old EEC Bursary 1993; RIBA; *Awards* Int Design Prize Rome 1962, Cncl of Ind Design Award 1965, 1966 and 1981, Br Aluminium Design Award 1966, first prize GAI Award 1969, Observer (London) Design Award 1969, Ringling Museum of Art (Fla) Award 1969, Gold Medal Graphic Design 1970, first prize GAI Award Int Bldg Exhibition 1971, British Aluminium Eros Trophy 1973, 4 awards for design excellence Aust 1973, commendation for architecture 1977, IBD Int Award (NY) 1982, Int Bldg Exhibits top design award 1983 (1985), Royal Designer for Indust 1986, ROSCOE Design Award NY 1988, finalist Prince Philip Designer of the Year award 1993, RIBA Regnl Design Award 1995; *Recreations* tai chi, aikido, badminton, fly dressing; *Style—* Alan Tye, Esq; ✉ Great West Plantation, Tring, Herts HP23 6DA (☎ 0144282 5353, fax 0144282 7723)

TYERS, Anthony Gordon; s of Arthur Tyers, of Sunbury on Thames, Surrey, and Marion Joan, *née* Cheal; *b* 14 Sept 1944; *Educ* Hampton Sch, Charing Cross Hosp Univ of London (MB BS); *m* 7 Oct 1983, Renée Constance Barbara, da of Frits De Waard, of Waalre, Netherlands; 2 s (Jonathan Richard Duncan b 30 July 1986, Richard Christopher James b 30 April 1989), 2 da (Johanna Rachel Caroline b 19 May 1991, Rebecca Charlotte Louise b 9 Nov 1993); *Career* registrar Univ Coll Hosp London 1973–76, sr registrar Moorfields Eye Hosp 1978–81, fell Massachusetts Eye and Ear Infirmary Boston USA 1981–82, sr registrar Moorfields Eye Hosp and Middx Hosp London 1982–86, conslt ophthalmic surgn Salisbury Gen Hosps 1986–; tstee Salisbury Hosps Fndn, sec Wessex Regnl Advsy Ctee for Ophthalmology; memb: BMA, RSM, Euro Soc of Ophthalmic Plastic and Reconstructive Surgery, Southern Ophthalmological Soc; FRCS 1974, FRCSEd 1980, FRCOphth 1989; *Books* Basic Clinical Ophthalmology (contrib, 1984), Colour Atlas of Ophthalmic Plastic Surgery (jtly, 1994); *Recreations* squash, skiing, golf, campanology; *Style—* Anthony Tyers, Esq; ✉ Salisbury District Hospital, Salisbury SP2 8BJ (☎ 01722 336262, fax 01722 322871); New Hall Hospital, Salisbury SP5 4EY (☎ and fax 01722 331021)

TYLER, Maj-Gen Christopher; CB (1989); s of Maj-Gen Sir Leslie Norman Tyler, KBE, CB (d 1992), and his 1 w, Louie Teresa, *née* Franklin (d 1950); *b* 9 July 1934; *Educ* Beaumont Coll Old Windsor, RMA Sandhurst, Trinity Coll Cambridge (MA); *m* 12 July 1958, Suzanne, da of (Hubert John) Patrick Whitcomb (d 1962); 1 s (William b 1959), 3 da (Catherine b 1961, Louisa b 1965, Sophie b 1967); *Career* cmmnd REME 1954, Army Staff Coll 1966–67, Lt-Col CO 1 Parachute Logistic Regt 1974–76, Asst Mil Sec (MS6) 1976–77, Col Asst Adj Gen (AG21) 1977–80, Chief Aircraft Engr Army Air Corps 1980–82, Brig Dir EME Mgmnt Servs 1982–83, Cdr Maintenance 1 (BR) Corps 1983–85, Dep Cmdt Royal Mil Coll of Sci 1985–87, Maj-Gen Dep Chief of Staff (Support) HQ AFNORTH 1987–89, Col Comdt REME 1989–94, Hon Col REME (V) 1994–, PARA Regt Cncl 1993–; Resident Govr and Keeper of the Jewel House HM Tower of London 1989–94; dir of fundraising Airborne Forces Charities 1995, sec Royal Humane Soc 1995–; tstee: Tower Hill Imp Tst 1990–, Ulysses Tst 1992–94; govr St Mary's Sch Ascot 1995–; hon sec RFU Referee Advsy Panel 1979–83; Liveryman Worshipful Co of Turners 1979 (memb Ct of Assts 1991, chm Educn Ctee 1994–); CEng 1964, FRAeS 1981, FIMechE 1982, FIMgt 1982; *Recreations* most sports but especially Rugby Union Football; *Clubs* Hawks' (Cambridge), Br Sportsman's; *Style—* Maj-Gen Christopher Tyler, CB; ✉ Oak Cottage, Stratfield Saye, Reading, Berks RG7 2AB (☎ 0118 933 2562)

TYLER, John William; s of Joseph Thomas Tyler (d 1975), of Newark, Notts, and Clara Gertrude, *née* Martin (d 1979); *b* 21 Nov 1931; *Educ* The Magnus Sch Newark Notts, Univ of Nottingham (BA), Coll of Law; *m* 8 Jan 1955, Patricia, da of John Reginald Neal (d 1966), of Hove, E Sussex; 2 s (Timothy John Neal b 30 Oct 1957 d 1978, Gavin Thomas b 6 Dec 1960), 1 da (Nicola Patricia (Mrs Hulm) b 3 March 1965); *Career* Flt Lt Adjs Branch RAF 1952–58; dir and co sec Atcost Gp of Co's 1958–69; admitted slr 1973; ptnr Cripps Harries Hall 1974–94 (joined 1970); NP; chm Jones Clifton Gp of Co's 1985 (dir 1975–); govr Sandown Court Community Coll Tunbridge Wells; Freeman City of London, Liveryman Worshipful Co of Carmen 1977–93; memb Law Soc; pres Tunbridge Wells and Dist Law Soc 1993–94; *Recreations* golf, skiing, gardening; *Style—* John Tyler, Esq; ✉ 19 Bishop's Court, Bishop's Down Road, Tunbridge Wells, Kent TN4 8XL (☎ 01892 527822)

TYLER, Leonard Charles; s of Sydney James Tyler, and Elsie May, *née* Reeve; *b* 14 Nov 1951; *Educ* Southend HS, Jesus Coll Oxford (Open exhibitioner, MA), City Univ (MSc); *m* 22 Sept 1984, Ann Wyn, da of William Evans; 1 s (Thomas Huw b 11 Oct

1985), 1 da (Catrin Victoria b 13 Feb 1987); *Career* DOE 1975–78; British Council: asst rep Malaysia 1978–81, asst rep Sudan 1981–84, regnl offr S E Asia 1984–86, trg City Univ 1986–87, Information Technology Gp 1987–93, dir Nordic Countries Copenhagen 1993–; memb Mensa; *Recreations* skiing, hill walking, reading; *Style*— Leonard Tyler, Esq; ✉ Sortedam Dossering 63B 1, 2100 Copenhagen Ø, Denmark; The British Council, Gammel Mont 12, 1117 Copenhagen K, Denmark

TYLER, Paul Archer; CBE (1985), MP (Lib Dem) Cornwall N (maj 1,921); s of Oliver Walter Tyler (d 1957), of Elm Park, Broadhempston, Totnes, Devon, and (Ursula) Grace Gibbons, *née* May; *b* 29 Oct 1941; *Educ* Mount House Sch Tavistock, Sherborne, Exeter Coll Oxford (MA); *m* 27 June 1970, Nicola Mary (Nicky), da of Michael Warren Ingram, OBE, of the Manor House, S Cerney, Cirencester, Glos; 1 s (Dominick b 1975), 1 da (Sophie b 1972); *Career* dep dir then dir of public affrs RIBA 1966–73, regnl organiser and bd memb Shelter 1975–76, md Courier Newspaper Group 1976–81, dir then sr conslt Good Relations Ltd 1982–92, dir Western Approaches PR Ltd 1987–; Parly candidate (Lib) Totnes 1966, MP (Lib) Bodmin Feb-Sept 1974 (also contested 1970, Oct 1974 and 1979), Euro Parly candidate Cornwall and Plymouth 1989, chm Lib Pty NEC 1983–86, MP (Lib Dem) Cornwall N 1992–; Lib Dem Parly spokesman on agriculture and rural affrs 1992–, memb Select Ctee on Procedure 1992–, chm All Pty Coastal Gp, hon treas All Pty Tourism Gp, hon sec All Pty Water Gp; cncllr Devon CC 1964–70, memb Devon and Cornwall Police Authy 1965–70, vice chm Dartmoor Nat Park 1965–70, vice pres Assoc of County Cncls, vice pres Action for Communities in Rural England (ACRE); MIPR 1987; *Recreations* sailing, walking, cornish ancestry; *Clubs* Nat Lib; *Style*— Paul Tyler, Esq, CBE, MP; ✉ House of Commons, London SW1A 0AA (☎ 0171 219 6355); Constituency Office, Church Stile, Launceston, Cornwall PL15 8AT (☎ 01566 777123, fax 01566 772122)

TYLOR, John Edward; s of Maj Vyvian Alfred Tylor, MC (d 1968), and M S Tylor; *b* 1 July 1942; *Educ* Eton, Trinity Coll Dublin (MA); *m* 18 Oct 1975, Heather Catherine, da of Richard Alan Budgett, of Kirtlington, Oxon; 2 s (Sam Vyvian b 1980, Hugo Alexander b 1985); *Career* slr Herbert Smith & Co 1967–73; Samuel Montagu & Co: joined 1973, exec dir Corp Fin Dept 1981–95, conslt 1995–; *Recreations* field sports, polo; *Style*— John Tylor, Esq; ✉ Stud Farm, Chesterton, Bicester, Oxon OX6 8TF; Samuel Montagu & Co, 10 Lower Thames St, London EC3R 6AE (☎ 0171 260 9000)

TYNAN, Prof Michael John; s of Sqdn Ldr Jerry Joseph Tynan, MBE (d 1990), and Florence Ann (d 1964); *Educ* Bedford Modern Sch, London Hosp Med Coll (FRCP); *m* Eirlys Pugh, da of Ernest Williams; *Career* sr resident Children's Hospital Boston Mass, teaching fell Harvard Med Sch 1961, lectr Inst of Child Health London 1968–71; conslt paediatric cardiologist: Newcastle Gen Hosp 1971–77, Guy's Hosp 1977–82; prof of paediatric cardiology Guy's Hosp 1982–, hon conslt paediatric cardiologist Cambridge Mil Hosp; memb Physiological Soc; Freeman Worshipful Soc of Apothecaries; *Books* Paediatric Cardiology (jtly 1988); *Clubs* Athenaeum; *Style*— Prof Michael Tynan; ✉ 5 Ravensden Street, London SE11 4AQ (☎ 0171 735 7119); Guy's Hospital, St Thomas Street, London SE1 9RT (☎ 0171 378 7351)

TYREE, Sir (Alfred) William; kt (1975), OBE (1971); s of J V Tyree; *b* 4 Nov 1921; *Educ* Auckland GS, Sydney Tech Coll (Dip Electrical Engrg); *m* 3 Jan 1946, Joyce, da of F Lyndon; 2 s, 1 da; *Career* fndr Tyree Industries and Westralian Transformers and Subsids 1956; chm and fndr: Alpha Air (Sydney) P/L, Technical Components P/L, Tycan Australia P/L, Tyree Holdings P/L, A W Tyree Transformers P/L, Wirex P/L, A W Tyree Fndn; awards: James N Kirby Gold Medal Instn of Prodn Engrs Aust 1980, Honour Medal Instn of Electrical & Electronic Engrs Inc NY USA 1984, Peter Nicol Russell Meml Medal Instn of Engrs Aust 1984; memb Cncl and Nat Exec Metal Trades Industries Assoc; hon fell Univ of Sydney 1985, hon life govr Aust Post Graduate Fedn of Med 1985, Hon DSc Univ of NSW 1986; fell Instn of Engrs Aust 1968 (memb 1966), FIEE 1983; *Recreations* skiing, yachting, tennis, computers, music, golf, photography, sail boarding; *Clubs* American, Aust Golf, Kosiusko Alpine, Royal Prince Alfred Yacht, Cruising Yacht of Aust, RAC, Royal Motor Yacht; *Style*— Sir William Tyree, OBE; ✉ 60 Martin Place, Sydney NSW 2000, Australia

TYRER, His Hon Judge; Christopher John Meese; s of late Jack Meese Tyrer, of Rhiwbina, Cardiff, and Margaret Joan, *née* Wyatt; *b* 22 May 1944; *Educ* Wellington Coll, Univ of Bristol (LLB); *m* 9 Feb 1974, (Monica) Jane Tyrer, JP, da of Peter Beckett, of Pontefract, Yorkshire; 1 s (David b 1981), 1 da (Rebecca b 1979); *Career* called to the Bar Inner Temple 1968; dep judiciary 1979 (dep judge 1979–82), asst recorder 1982–83, recorder 1983–89, circuit judge (SE Circuit) 1989–; vice chm St John's Sch Lacey Green 1989–90 (govr 1984–92), chm Speen Sch 1989–90 and 1995–96 (govr 1984–96), memb Bucks Assoc of Govrs of Primary Schs 1989–90 (chm High Wycombe Div 1989–90), govr The Misbourne Sch 1993–; *Recreations* music, reading, photography, growing things; *Style*— His Hon Judge Christopher Tyrer; ✉ Randalls Cottage, Loosley Row, Princes Risborough, Aylesbury, Bucks HP27 0NU (☎ 01844 344650); Milton Keynes County Court, 351 Silbury Boulevard, Wilton Gate East, Central Milton Keynes MK9 2DT (☎ 01908 668855)

TYRONE, Earl of; Henry Nicholas de la Poer Beresford; s and h of 8 Marquess of Waterford by his w Lady Caroline Wyndham-Quin, da of 6 Earl of Dunraven and Mount-Earl; *b* 23 March 1958; *Educ* Harrow; *m* 1986, Amanda, da of Norman Thompson, of The Castle, Boris in Ossory, Co Laois; 2 s (Baron le Poer, Hon Marcus Patrick b 23 April 1990), 1 da (Lady Camilla Juliet b 25 July 1995); *Heir* s, Richard John, Baron le Poer b 19 Aug 1987; *Recreations* polo; *Clubs* Cirencester Park Polo; *Style*— Earl of Tyrone

TYRRELL, Alan Rupert; QC (1976); *b* 27 June 1933; *m* 1960, Elaine Eleanor, *née* Ware; 1 s, 1 da; *Career* called to the Bar Gray's Inn 1956 (bencher 1986), recorder of the Crown Ct 1972–, head of chambers; MEP (EDG) London East 1979–84, chm Bar European Gp 1986–88; chm Int Practice Ctee Bar Cncl 1988, Lord Chancellor's legal visitor 1990–; memb Cncl Medical Protection Soc 1990–, dir Papworth Hosp NHS Tst 1993–; FCIArb 1993; *Books* The Legal Professions in the New Europe (ed, 1992, 2 edn 1996); *Style*— Alan Tyrrell, Esq, QC; ✉ 15 Willifield Way, Hampstead Garden Suburb, London NW11 7XU; 205 Boulevard St Germain, Paris 75007, France; Francis Taylor Building, Temple, London EC4Y 7BY (☎ 0171 797 7250, fax 0171 797 7299)

TYRRELL, Dr David Arthur John; CBE (1980); s of late Lt-Col Sidney Charles Tyrrell, of Stalham, Norfolk, and Agnes Kate, *née* Blewett (d 1990); *b* 19 June 1925; *Educ* Ashford Co Sch Middx, King Edward VII Sch Sheffield, Univ of Sheffield (MB ChB, MD); *m* 15 April 1950, (Betty) Moyra, da of Dr John Wylie, MC, of Woodlands, Doncaster, Yorks; 1 s (Stephen b 1955 d 1979), 2 da (Frances b 1951, Susan b 1953); *Career* res registrar Sheffield Utd Hosps 1950–51, asst physician and res asst Rockefeller Inst Hosp NY 1951–54; memb: MRC scientific staff Virus Res Laboratory Univ of Sheffield 1954, Common Cold Unit Salisbury 1957 (head 1962); dir of WHO Virus Reference Laboratory 1962–90, head Div of Communicable Diseases Clinical Res Centre Harrow 1967–84 (dep dir 1970–84); hon conslt physician: West Hendon Hosp 1967–70, Northwick Park Hosp Harrow 1970–85, Wessex RHA 1985–90; dir MRC Common Cold Unit Salisbury 1982–90; chm Advsy Ctee on Dangerous Pathogens until 1991, memb Governing Body Animal Virus Disease Res Inst Pirbright, hon chm Biological Prods Sub Ctee of Ctee on Safety of Med until 1993, tstee Nuffield Fndn until 1992, memb Steering Ctee MRC AIDS Directed Prog until 1994; chm: Spongiform Encephalopathy Advsy Ctee 1990–95, Nat Task Force on CFS/PVFS/ME 1993–, Nuffield Inquiry into the Educn and Trg of Dental Auxiliaries until 1994; lectures: The Rock Carling lecture 1982, The Leewenhoek lecture, The Jenner lectr (St George's), Jack Pepys meml lectr; author of numerous scientific pubns; Hon DSc Univ of Sheffield 1979; Hon DM Univ of Southampton 1990; FRCP 1965, FRS 1970, FRCPath 1971, memb Assoc of Physicians; hon memb: Infectious Disease Soc of America, Australian Soc of Infectious Diseases, American Assoc of Physicians; *Books* Common Colds and Related Diseases (1965), Interferon and its Clinical Potential (1976), The Abolition of Infection: Hope or Illusion (1982); *Recreations* music, gardening, walking, various Christian organisations; *Style*— Dr David Tyrrell, CBE, FRS; ✉ Ash Lodge, Dean Lane, Whiteparish, Salisbury SP5 2RN (☎ and fax 01794 884352); Centre for Applied Microbiology and Research, Porton Down, Salisbury SP4 0JG (☎ 01980 612682, fax 01980 611384)

TYRRELL, Jean Margaret; OBE (1982), DL (W Yorks 1983); da of Fredrick Harrap (d 1960), of Wakefield, and Bertha Harrap (d 1977); *b* 1 July 1918; *Educ* St Leonards St Andrews Fife, Univ of Geneva; *m* 15 July 1944, James Hall Tyrrell (d 1992), s of Robert Tyrrell (d 1942); 3 da (Susan Gay (Mrs Ainslie), Anne Maureen (Mrs Upsdell), Carolyn Jane (Mrs Tobin)); *Career* served WWII with Mechanised Tport Corps; joined Harrap Bros (Sirdar Wools) Ltd 1939; Sirdar plc: exec dir 1953–93, jt md 1959, chm and md 1960–93, non-exec dir 1993–; The Times/Veuve Cliquot Business Woman of the Year 1980; former memb: local MSC, Advsy Ctee on Women's Employment (Dept of Employment); former gen cmmr of taxes; Hon LLD Univ of Leeds 1988; MInstD; *Recreations* golf, sailing, bridge; *Clubs* Wakefield Golf; *Style*— Mrs Jean Tyrrell, OBE, DL; ✉ Sirdar plc, Flanshaw Lane, Alverthorpe, Wakefield, W Yorks (☎ 01924 371501, fax 01924 290506, telex 557426); Invermor, 23 Woodthorpe Lane, Wakefield, W Yorks WF2 6JC (☎ 01924 255468); Keewaydin, Golf Rd, Abersoch, Gwynedd, N Wales

TYRRELL, Prof Robert James; *b* 6 June 1951; *Educ* Univ of Oxford (MA PPE), LSE (MSc Social Philosophy); *Clubs* chm The Henley Centre 1995– (chief exec 1986–95); visiting prof City Univ Business Sch 1994–; memb Advsy Cncl Demos 1993–; *Style*— Prof Robert Tyrrell; ✉ The Henley Centre, 9 Bridewell Place, London EC4V 6AY (☎ 0171 955 1800, fax 0171 353 2899)

TYRWHITT, Brig Dame Mary Joan Caroline; DBE (1949, OBE 1946), TD; er da of late Adm of the Fleet Sir Reginald Tyrwhitt, 1 Bt, GCB, DSO; *b* 27 Dec 1903; *Career* sr controller ATS (dir 1946–49), Brig WRAC 1949–50; Hon ADC to George VI 1949–50, asst admin WRVS Southern Region 1953–72; *Style*— Brig Dame Mary Tyrwhitt, DBE, TD

TYRWHITT, Sir Reginald Thomas Newman; 3 Bt (UK 1919), of Terschelling, and of Oxford; s of Adm Sir St John Reginald Joseph Tyrwhitt, 2 Bt, KCB, DSO, DSC (d 1961), and Nancy Veronica, da of Charles Newman Gilbey (gn of Sir Walter Gilbey, 1 Bt); gs of 1 Bt Adm of the Fleet Sir Reginald York Tyrwhitt, GCB, DSO; Sir St John's gf's gf, Richard, was 3 s of Capt John Tyrwhitt, RN (d 1812), of Netherclay House, Somerset, by his w Katherine (paternal gda of Lady Susan Clinton, da of 6 Earl of Lincoln (a dignity now subsumed in the Duchy of Newcastle); Richard's er bro was (Sir) Thomas, *née* Tyrwhitt, who assumed (1790) the name of Jones (although subsequent holders of the Btcy appear to have been known as Tyrwhitt) & was cr a Bt 1808; Sir Thomas's ggs, Sir Raymond Tyrwhitt, 4 Bt, inherited his mother's Barony of Berners, the Btcy becoming extinct 1950; John Tyrwhitt of Netherclay was seventh in descent from Marmaduke Tyrwhitt, yr s of Sir William Tyrwhitt, of Kettilby; *b* 21 Feb 1947; *Educ* Downside; *m* 1, 1972 (m dis 1980 and annulled 1984), Sheila Gail, da of late William Alistair Crawford Nicoll, of Liphook, Hants; m 2, 1984, Charlotte, o da of Capt Angus Jeremy Christopher Hildyard, DL, RA (d 1995); 1 s (Robert St John Hildyard b 1987), 1 da (Letitia Mary Hildyard b 1988); *Heir* s, Robert St John Hildyard b 1987; *Career* 2 Lt RA 1966, Lt 1969, RARO 1969; *Style*— Sir Reginald Tyrwhitt, Bt; ✉ 51 Whitecross Street, Barton-on-Humber, South Humberside DN18 5EU

TYSON, Dr Alan Walker; CBE (1989); s of Henry Alan Maurice Tyson (d 1975), of Edinburgh, and Dorothy Allan, *née* Walker (d 1959); *b* 27 Oct 1926; *Educ* Rugby, Magdalen Coll Oxford (BA, MA), Univ Coll London and Univ Coll Hosp Med Sch (MB BS); *Career* sr research fell All Souls Coll Oxford 1971–94 (fell 1952–94), on editorial staff standard edn of Freud's works 1952–74, visiting lectr in psychiatry Montefiore Hosp NY 1967–68, lectr in psychopathology and developmental psychology Oxford Univ 1968–70, visiting prof of music Columbia Univ NY 1969, James P R Lyell reader in bibliography Oxford Univ 1973–74, Ernest Bloch prof of music Univ of California Berkeley 1977–78, memb Inst for Advanced Studies Princeton 1983–84, visiting prof of music Graduate Center City Univ of NY 1985; assoc memb Br Psychoanalytical Soc 1957, MRCPsych 1972, FBA 1978; *Books* The Authentic English Editions of Beethoven (1963), English Music Publishers' Plate Numbers (with O W Neighbour, 1965), Selected Letters of Beethoven (ed, 1967), Thematic Catalogue of the Works of Muzio Clementi (1967), Beethoven Studies (ed Vol 1 1973, Vol 2 1977, Vol 3 1982), The Beethoven Sketchbooks (with D Johnson and R Winter, 1985), Mozart: Studies of the Autograph Scores (1987), Mozart's Thematic Catalogue: A Facsimile (with A Rosenthal, 1990); *Style*— Dr Alan Tyson, CBE, FBA; ✉ 7 Southcote Road, London N19 5BJ (☎ 0171 609 2981)

TYZACK, David Ian Heslop; s of Ernest Rudolf Tyzack, MBE (d 1973), and Joan Mary, *née* Palmer (d 1993); *b* 21 March 1946; *Educ* Allhallows Sch, St Catharine's Coll Cambridge (MA); *m* 27 Jan 1973, Elizabeth Anne, da of Maj Henry Frank Cubitt, TD (d 1991); 1 s (William b 12 June 1983), 1 da (Anna b 6 April 1981); *Career* called to the Bar Inner Temple 1970, in practice Western Circuit, head of chambers 1988–, asst recorder of the Crown Court 1995–; chm Devon & Cornwall Branch Family Law Barristers' Assoc, memb The Hon Soc of the Inner Temple 1970; *Recreations* gardening, walking, skiing, church; *Style*— David Tyzack, Esq; ✉ 33 Southernhay East, Exeter, Devon (☎ 01392 55777, fax 01392 412021, car 0860 649686)

TYZACK, Margaret; OBE (1970); da of Thomas Edward Tyzack, and Doris, *née* Moseley; *Educ* St Angela's Ursuline Convent, RADA; *m* 26 March 1958, Alan Stephenson, s of Thomas Stephenson; 1 s (Matthew b 10 Aug 1964); *Career* actress; *Theatre* Royal Court: Progress to the Park, The Ginger Man, Tom and Viv (also Public Theatre NY, nominated for US Drama Desk Award); RSC: Coriolanus, Julius Caesar, Titus Andronicus, Summerfolk (also NY, Stratford, Ontario), Ghosts, Richard III, All's Well that End's Well (also NY), Lower Depths (Arts); other theatre work incl: The Cherry Orchard and Sisters (Exeter and UK tour), A Man for All Seasons and Macbeth (Nottingham and European tour), Find your Way Home, Open Space, Vivat Vivat Regina (Piccadilly), People are Living There (Royal Exchange Manchester), Veronica's Room (Palace Watford), Mornings at Seven (Westminster), An Inspector Calls and Night Must Fall (Greenwich), The Importance of Being Earnest (Aldwych) 1993, Martha in Who's Afraid of Virginia Woolf? (NT (SWET Best Actress Award)), the Countess in All's Well that Ends Well (Tony nomination), Lettice and Lovage (Globe (Variety Club Best Actress Award)), An Inspector Calls (Aldwych), Indian Ink (Aldwych) 1995; *Television* incl: The Forsythe Saga, The First Churchills (BAFTA Best Actress Award), Cousin Bette (US Emmy Nomination), A Winter's Tale, I Claudius, The Reason of Things, Another Man's Life, Waters of the Moon, The Silver Box, Dear Octopus, Amelia Edwards, The Flowering Cherry, An Inspector Calls, Thacker, Chronicles of Young Indiana Jones, Inspector Alleyn Mysteries; *Films* incl: Prick Up Your Ears, 2001, A Clockwork Orange, A Touch of Love, The Whisperers, Ring of Spies, The Wars, Mr Love; *Style*— Ms Margaret Tyzack, OBE; ✉ c/o Joyce Edwards, 275 Kennington Road, London SE11 (☎ 0171 735 5736)

U

UBOGU, Victor Eriakpo; s of Stephen Ubogu, of Lagos, Nigeria, and Florence Ubogu; *b* 8 Sept 1964; *Educ* West Buckland Sch, Univ of Birmingham, Univ of Oxford; *Career* gby union player (prop); former clubs: Moseley, Richmond; currently with Bath RFC (winners Pilkington Cup 1990, 1992 and 1994, winners Courage League Div 1 1991, 1992, 1993, and 1994); rep: South West Div, England schools under 18, England Students; England: memb tour Argentina 1990, tour to S Africa 1994, 4 B caps, currently memb full England squad, 4th place World Cup S Africa 1995, 21 full caps; devpt dir Cobrawatch Ltd security co, owner Shoeless Joe's King's Road London; *Style*— Victor Ubogu, Esq; ✉ Bath RFC, Recreation Ground, Bath (☎ 01225 425192)

UCHIDA, Mitsuko; da of Fujio Uchida, of Tokyo, and Yasuko Uchida; *b* 20 Dec 1948; *Educ* Hochschule für Musik und Davstellende Kunst Wien; *Career* pianist; performed complete Mozart piano sonatas in London, Tokyo, Germany and NY; extensive work with English Chamber Orchestra incl complete Mozart piano concertos, has played with most major int orchs (repertoir ranges from J S Bach to Schönberg Méssiaen and Birtwhistle); *Recordings* incl: complete Mozart piano sonatas, all Mozart piano concertos, Mozart quintet for piano and winds, Chopin Piano Sonatas 2 and 3, Debussy 12 Ětudes, R Schumann Carnaval; *Awards* first prize Int Beethoven Competition Wien, second prize Int Chopin Competition Warsaw; numerous record prizes incl: The Gramaphone prize, Edison prize (Holland); *Recreations* music; *Style*— Ms Mitsuko Uchida; ✉ Van Walsum Management, 26 Wadham Road, London SW15 2LR (☎ 0181 874 6344, fax 0181 877 0077)

UDAL, John Oliver; s of Nicholas Robin Udal, CBE (d 1964), of Tunbridge Wells, and Margaret Ruth, *née* Oliver (d 1969); *b* 2 May 1926; *Educ* Winchester, New Coll Oxford (MA); *m* 1, 27 June 1959 (m dis 1979), Ann Leone Murray, *née* Hopkins; 2 s (Nicholas b 1960, Adrian b 1960), 1 da (Joanna b 1964); m 2, 17 May 1979, Ann Marie, da of Albert Edward Bridges Webb (d 1970); *Career* Irish Guards BAOR and Palestine 1944–48 (2 Lt 1945, Lt 1946); Sudan Political Serv 1950–55, asst dist cmmr Khartoum and Upper Nile, MECAS 1951, first class magistrate 1953; Cons Res Dept 1955–66 (head cwlth affrs); shipbroker 1966–76, princ Baltic Mercantile and Shipping Exchange 1970–79, dir Eggar Forrester Hldgs Ltd 1970–79 (md Eggar Forrester Ltd, chm Terminal Operators Ltd); shipping conslt 1980–84 (UNCTAD Roster 1983–85), vice pres Jebsens UK Ltd 1980–82; liaison dir Central Cncl Econ League 1984–89 (ret 1989); chm London Voluntary Sector Resource Centre 1992–; memb S Kensington Div LCC 1961–65, Parly candidate Leeds South (by-election) 1963, alderman GLC 1967–73, dep chm W London Magistrates Div 1992–95, chm Trg Advsy Ctee 1992–94; memb: City Parochial Fndn 1973– (chm Estates Ctee 1977–87), Tst for London 1988–, Exec Gordon Sch Fndn 1967– (govr 1969–81 and 1989–95); JP W London 1966–96; Freeman City of London, Liveryman Worshipful Co of Girdlers; *Books* Paying for Schooling (with T E Utley 1975); *Recreations* lower fell walking; *Clubs* Athenaeum; *Style*— John Udal, Esq, JP; ✉ 5 Soudan Rd, London SW11 4HH (☎ 0171 627 1887)

UDAL, Shaun David; s of Robin Francis Udal, of Cove, Farnborough, Hants, and Mary Elizabeth, *née* Halpin; *b* 18 March 1969; *Educ* Cove Co Secdy Sch; *m* Emma Jane, da of Graham Joblin; 2 da (Katherine Mary b 26 Aug 1992, Rebecca Jane b 17 Nov 1995); *Career* professional cricketer; former rep Hants Colts under 13, under 15, under 17 and under 19; Hampshire CCC: joined 1988, debut 1989, over 100 appearances, took 100 wickets in a season 1992; taken two hat-tricks and scored a double century in club cricket; England: memb team touring Aust 1994/95, A team Pakistan 1995; *Recreations* Aldershot Town FC, all sports; *Style*— Shaun Udal, Esq; ✉ Hampshire CCC, County Ground, Northlands Rd, Southampton SO9 2TY (☎ 01703 333788)

UDELL, Peter Laurence; s of Laurence Cecil Udell, of London, and Emma, *née* Neesham; *b* 28 Feb 1941; *Educ* King Edward's Sch Birmingham, Haberdashers' Aske's, Keble Coll Oxford (BA, Rugby Fives half blue); *children* 1 s (Hallam b 30 April 1970), 2 da (Sasha b 2 April 1966, Anika b 4 Feb 1968); *Career* BBC: gen trainee 1962–64, external servs prodr Bristol 1964–66, scriptwriter 1966–71, prog organiser Bulgarian Serv 1971–73, asst head of central talks and features 1973–75, asst head E Euro Servs 1975–79, special responsibility for Russian 1977–79, head E Euro Servs 1979–84, head Central Euro Servs 1984–86, controller Euro Servs 1986–88, controller Overseas Servs 1988–92; int broadcasting conslt 1992–; *Recreations* running, swimming; *Style*— Peter Udell, Esq; ✉ 9 Lodge Avenue, E Sheen, London SW14 8PQ (☎ and fax 0181 878 8590)

UDOMA, Hon Sir (Egbert) Udo; kt (1964), CFR (1978); s of Chief Udoma Inam of Ibekwe Ntanaran Akama, Ikot Abasi, Akwa Ibom State, Nigeria, and Adiaha Edem; *b* 21 June 1917; *Educ* Methodist Coll Uzuakoli, Trinity Coll Dublin, St Catherine's Coll Oxford (LLB, MA, PhD); *m* 1950, Grace Bassey; 5 s (and 1 s decd), 1 da; *Career* called to the Bar Gray's Inn 1945, practised as barr and slr Supreme Ct Nigeria 1946–61, MHR Nigeria 1952–59, High Ct judge Lagos 1961–63, govr gen 1963, chief justice of Uganda 1963–69, justice Supreme Ct of Nigeria 1969–82, ret; nat pres Ibibio State Union 1947–61, memb Nigeria Marketing Co 1952–54, mangr ctee W Africa Inst for Oil Palm Research 1953–63, chm Bd of Tstees King George V Memorial Fund 1964–69, patron Nigeria Soc of Int Law 1968, chllr Ahmadu Bello Univ 1972–75, chm Constituent Assembly Nigerian Constitution 1977–78, dir and presiding justice Seminar for Judges Nigeria 1980 and 1981, memb Nigerian Inst of Int Affrs 1979–; awarded title of Obong Ikpa Isong Ibibio 1961, awarded Knight of John Wesley by the Methodist Church Nigeria 1994; Hon LLD: Univ of Ibadan 1967, Ahamadu Bello Univ 1972, Trinity Coll Dublin 1973; *Publications* The Lion and the Oil Palm and other essays (1943), The Human Right to Individual Freedom - a Symposium on World Habeas Corpus (jty 1970), The Story of the Ibibio Union (1987), History and the Law of the Constitution of Nigeria (1994); *Clubs* Metropolitan, Island (both Lagos); *Style*— Hon Sir Udo Udoma, CFR; ✉ Mfut Itiat Enin, 8 Dr Udoma Street, PO Box 47, Ikot Abasi Township, Ikot Abasi LGA, Akwa Ibom State, Nigeria

UFF, Prof John Francis; QC (1983); s of Frederick Uff (d 1981), and Eva Uff (d 1969); *b* 30 Jan 1942; *Educ* Stratton Sch Biggleswade, King's Coll London (BSc, PhD); *m* 29 July 1967, Diana Murial, da of Prof Ronald Graveson, CBE; 2 s (Alexander John b 1973, Christopher Edward b 1975), 1 da (Leonora Meriel b 1977); *Career* civil engr 1966–70, called to the Bar 1970, practised in chambers of Donald Keating QC, head of chambers 1992; bencher of Gray's Inn 1993, asst recorder of Crown Court 1994; appointed arbitrator in many UK and foreign commercial disputes (mostly engrg and construction), chm Ind Cmmn of Inquiry into Yorkshire Water 1996; dir Centre of Construction Law and Mgmnt King's Coll London 1987, Nash prof of engrg law Univ of London 1991–; FICE 1982, FCIArb 1982, FEng 1995; *Books* Construction Law (5 edn, 1991), ICE Arbitration Practice (1985), Construction Contract Policy (1989), International and ICC Arbitration (1991), Legal Obligations in Construction (1992); *Recreations* violin making, farming; *Style*— Prof John Uff, QC, FEng; ✉ 10 Essex Street, Outer Temple, London WC2R 3AA (☎ 0171 240 6981); Ashstead Farm, Selside, Cumbria

UFLAND, Richard Mark; s of Bertram Ufland, and Shirley, *née* Gross; *b* 4 May 1957; *Educ* St Paul's Sch, Downing Coll Cambridge (MA); *m* 20 Oct 1985, Jane Camilla, da of Louis Rapaport; 2 s (James b 1987, William b 1990), 1 da (Olivia b 1994); *Career* ptnr Stephenson Harwood 1986– (articled 1979–81, asst slr 1981–86); Freeman: City of London, Worshipful Co of Solicitors of the City of London; memb Law Soc; *Recreations* opera, bridge, theatre, skiing; *Style*— Richard Ufland, Esq; ✉ Brambers, The Grove, Radlett, Herts WD7 7NF (☎ 01923 854378, fax 01923 854339); Stephenson Harwood, One St Paul's Churchyard, London EC4M 8SH (☎ 0171 329 4422, fax 0171 606 0822, telex 886789 SHSPC G)

UGLOW, Euan Ernest Richard; s of Ernest Uglow, of London, and Elizabeth Jane, *née* Williams; *b* 10 March 1932; *Educ* Strand GS for Boys, UCL, Slade Sch of Fine Art; *Career* artist; work represented in public collections: Tate Gallery, Arts Cncl, Ferens Art Gallery, Cardiff Art Gallery, Govt Art Collection, Australian Nat Gallery, Metropolitan NY USA; fell Univ Coll London; artist tstee National Gallery London 1990–; *Clubs* Garrick; *Style*— Euan Uglow, Esq; ✉ c/o Browse & Darby Ltd, 19 Cork St, London W1X 2LP (☎ 0171 734 7984)

ULLATHORNE, Peter Lindley; JP (SW London 1994); s of Philip Stanley Ullathorne (d 1990), and Mary Lindley, *née* Burland (d 1996); *b* 6 Aug 1948; *Educ* Chesterfield GS, City of Leicester Poly, AA Sch of Architecture (AADipl); *Career* architect; Richard Rogers Partnership 1971–74, Louis De Soissons Partnership 1974–77, GMW Partnership 1977–80, YRM Architects 1980–83, DEGW Architects 1983–86, md First Architecture Group plc 1986–89, gp dir McColl Gp Limited 1989–91, dir Chanin Hartland Ullathorne 1991, dir of architecture Gensler and Associates/Architects; visiting prof Univ of Cincinatti 1985; Freeman City of London 1990, Liveryman Worshipful Co of Chartered Architects; memb AA 1971, RIBA 1974, FRSA 1989, AIA 1995; *Recreations* reading, painting, opera, country life; *Clubs* RAC, London Library; *Style*— Peter Lindley Ullathorne, Esq, JP; ✉ 136 Somerset Road, Wimbledon, London SW19 5HP (☎ 0181 879 1208); Gensler and Associates/Architects, Roman House, Wood Street, London EC2Y 5BA (☎ 0171 256 6060, fax 0171 256 8747)

ULLMAN, Tracey; da of Anthony John Ullman (d 1966), and Dorin, *née* Cleaver; *b* 30 Dec 1959; *Educ* The Italia Conti Stage Sch Brixton; *m* 27 Dec 1983, Allan McKeown, *qv*; 1 da (Mabel Ellen b 2 April 1986), 1 s (John Albert Victor b 6 Aug 1991); *Career* comedy actress and singer; *Dancer* Gigi (Theatre des Westerns Berlin) 1976, Second Generation (Blackpool and Liverpool) 1977; musicals: Elvis (Astoria) 1978, Oh Boy (Astoria) 1978, Rocky Horror Show (Comedy Theatre) 1979; *Theatre* Talent (Everyman Liverpool) 1980, Dracula (Young Vic) 1980, Four in a Million (Royal Court) 1981, She Stoops to Conquer (Lyric Hammersmith) 1982, The Taming of the Shrew (NY Shakespeare Festival Broadway) 1990, The Big Love (one woman show) 1991; *Television* incl: Three of a Kind 1981–83, A Kick up the Eighties 1981 and 1983, The Young Visitors 1984, Girls on Top 1985, The Tracey Ullman Show 1987–90; *Film* Plenty 1984, I Love You to Death 1989; *Recordings* various top ten singles 1981–84, You Broke my Heart in Seventeen Places (album, Gold record); *Awards* Most Promising New Actress London Theatre Critics Award 1981, Best Light Entertainment Performance BAFTA 1983, five American comedy awards 1988–90, Best Female Comedy Performance Golden Globe Awards USA 1988; Emmy Awards (USA): Best Variety Show TV 1989, Best Writing 1990, Best Performance in a Variety or Music Show 1990 and 1994; *Recreations* hiking, riding, finding unspoilt areas of the earth and being quiet; *Style*— Miss Tracey Ullman; ✉ c/o ICM Ltd, Oxford House, 76 Oxford Street, London W1N 0AX (☎ 0171 636 6565, fax 0171 323 0101)

ULLMANN, Prof Julian Richard; s of Richard Edwin Ullmann (d 1988), of West Hoathly, Sussex, and Thelma Beatrice, *née* Ford; *b* 21 June 1936; *Educ* Eastbourne Coll, Pembroke Coll Cambridge (MA), Imperial Coll London (PhD); *m* 7 Nov 1964, Margaret Evelyn, da of Dr Gerald Beeston (d 1968); 1 s (David b 1967), 1 da (Karen b 1969); *Career* princ scientific offr Nat Physical Laboratory 1970 (scientific offr 1959), head Dept of Computer Sci Univ of Sheffield 1980 (prof 1975), head and prof of computer sci Royal Holloway and Bedford New Coll Univ of London 1986, prof and head Dept of Computer Science King's Coll Univ of London 1989–96; chm: British Pattern Recognition Assoc 1976–84, Alvey MMI Pattern Analysis Ctee 1983–87; an assoc ed of the jls Pattern Recognition, and Pattern Recognition Letters; CEng, FBCS; *Books* Pattern Recognition Techniques (1973), Micro Computer Technology (1982), A Pascal Database Book (1986), Compiling in Modula-2 (1994); *Recreations* serious music; *Style*— Prof Julian Ullmann; ✉ Department of Computer Science, King's College London, Strand, London WC2R 2LS (☎ 0171 873 2595)

ULLSTEIN, Augustus Rupert Patrick Anthony; QC (1992); s of Frederick Charles Leopold Ullstein (d 1988), of Chiswick, and Patricia, *née* Guinness; *b* 21 March 1947; *Educ* Bradfield, LSE (LLB); *m* 12 Sept 1970, Pamela Margaret, da of Claude Wells (d 1974), of Woodford, Essex; 2 s (William b 3 July 1980, George b 29 April 1983), 2 da (Elizabeth b 1 June 1977, Caroline b 28 Oct 1978); *Career* called to the Bar Inner Temple 1970, dep registrar Family Div 1987, asst recorder of the Crown Ct 1994; dir Saxon Radio 1980–87; Freeman City of London 1982, Liveryman Worshipful Co of Bowyers 1982; *Books* The Law of Restrictive Trade Practices and Monopolies (second supplement to second edn, 1973), Matrimonial and Domestic Injunctions (1982); *Recreations* after dinner speaking, my children; *Clubs* Farmers', Wig and Pen; *Style*— Augustus Ullstein, Esq, QC; ✉ 74 Duke's Ave, Chiswick, London W4 2AF; 29 Bedford Row, Holborn, London WC1 (☎ 0171 831 2626)

ULLSWATER, 2 Viscount (UK 1921); Nicholas James Christopher Lowther; PC (1994); s of Lt John Arthur Lowther, MVO, RNVR (d 1942); suc ggf, 1 Viscount Ullswater, GCB (s of late Hon William Lowther, bro of late 3 Earl of Lonsdale), 1949; *b* 9 Jan 1942; *Educ* Eton, Trinity Coll Cambridge; *m* 1967, Susan, da of James Howard Weatherby, of Salisbury, Wilts, by his w Mary (4 da of Sir Hereward Wake, 13 Bt, CB, CMG, DSO, JP, DL); 2 s (Hon Benjamin b 1975, Hon Edward b 8 Oct 1981), 2 da (Hon

Emma b 1968, Hon Clare (Hon Mrs Flawn-Thomas) b 1970); *Heir* s, Hon Benjamin James Lowther b 26 Nov 1975; *Career* Capt Royal Wessex Yeo TAVR 1973–78; a Lord in Waiting 1989–90; Parly under-sec of state Dept of Employment 1990–93, Capt HM Body Guard of Hon Corps of Gentlemen at Arms (Chief Govt Whip) 1993–94, min of state DOE 1994–95; *Style*— The Rt Hon the Viscount Ullswater, PC; ✉ The Old Rectory, Docking, King's Lynn, Norfolk PE31 8LJ (☎ 01485 518822)

UNDERHILL, Prof Allan Edward; s of Albert Edward Underhill (d 1977), and Winifred, *née* Bailey (d 1982); *b* 13 Dec 1935; *Educ* Derby Sch Derby, Univ of Hull (BSc, PhD), Univ of Wales (DSc); *m* 13 Aug 1960, Audrey Jean, da of Harry Foster (d 1973); 1 s (David b 1964), 1 da (Ann b 1963); *Career* res chemist ICI Ltd 1961–62, lectr Univ of Loughborough 1962–65; Univ of Wales Bangor: lectr 1965–74, sr lectr 1974–83, prof 1983–, dean Faculty of Science and Engrg 1985–87 and 1994–95, pro vice-chllr 1995–; coordinator initiative on materials for the 21 century SERC 1988–93; FRCS 1972; *Recreations* photography, badminton, theatre; *Style*— Prof Allan Underhill; ✉ Meifod, 46 Ffiddoedd Rd, Bangor, Gwynedd LL57 2TW (☎ 01248 370929); Department of Chemistry, University of Wales, Bangor, Gwynedd LL57 2UW (☎ 01248 382376, fax 01248 370528)

UNDERHILL, Nicholas Edward; QC (1992); s of Michael Thomas Ben Underhill (d 1987), and Rosalie Jean Beaumont, *née* Kinloch; *b* 12 May 1952; *Educ* Winchester, New Coll Oxford (MA); *m* 1987, Nina Charlotte Margarete, *née* Grunfeld; 1 s (b 1987), 2 da (b 1990 and 1992); *Career* called to the Bar Gray's Inn 1976, recorder of the Crown Ct 1994–; *Books* The Lord Chancellor (1976); *Style*— Nicholas Underhill, Esq, QC; ✉ Fountain Court, Temple, London EC4Y 9DH (☎ 0171 583 3335, fax 0171 353 0329)

UNDERHILL, Nicholas Peter; s of Kenneth Underhill, and Evelyn Ellen, *née* Barnard; *b* 15 Jan 1955; *Educ* William Ellis Sch; *m* 28 July 1973, Julie Ann Evelyn, da of Wilfred Augustus Michael Chard, of London; 4 s (Matthew, James, Julian, Oliver), 1 da (Lyndsey); *Career* property advtg mangr Evening Standard 1974–75, ptnr Druce & Co 1978–81, equity ptnr Hampton & Sons 1986–87, md Hamptons (estate agents) 1988–89, chm Underhill Group of Companies 1989–92, dir Keith Cardale Groves 1992–; memb Hampstead and Highgate Cons Assoc; memb Land Inst; *Recreations* shooting, rugby, skiing, opera; *Clubs* Carlton, MCC, Saracens RFC, Lord's Taverners; *Style*— Nicholas Underhill, Esq; ✉ Keith Cardale Groves, 36 North Audley Street, Mayfair, London W1Y 1WG (☎ 0171 495 2494, fax 0171 491 2667); Villa Sous Colline, 5 Rue De L'Occident, Port Grimaud, France

UNDERHILL, Hon Robert; s of Baron Underhill, CBE (Life Peer; d 1993), and Flora Janet, *née* Philbrick; *b* 26 Feb 1948; *Educ* Handsworth GS, Chingford County HS, Queen Mary Coll London (BSc Econ); *m* 1970, Christine Ann, da of Ernest Edward Lawrence Vinsen; 1 s (Bruce), 1 da (Helen); *Career* sr mangr Touche Ross & Co; fin dir and co sec: Ritz Design Gp plc 1986–87, Campbell & Armstrong plc 1987–91, Ritz Design Group plc 1991; dir Stirling Group plc 1992; gp fin dir The Gardiner Group plc 1993–; non-exec chm Unity Brands Ltd 1993–; FCA; *Recreations* most sports especially football, golf, other outdoor pursuits; *Style*— The Hon Robert Underhill

UNDERWOOD, Derek Leslie; MBE (1981); s of Leslie Frank Underwood (d 1978), of Kent, and Evelyn Ann, *née* Wells; *b* 8 June 1945; *Educ* Dulwich Coll Prep Sch, Beckenham and Penge GS; *m* 1973, Dawn, da of Gerald Daniel Sullivan, of Surrey; 2 da (Heather b 1976, Fiona b 1977); *Career* former professional cricketer (left-arm spin bowler); Kent CCC 1962–87 (awarded county cap 1964); England: debut 1966, 86 test matches, 297 test wickets; yst player ever to take 100 wickets in debut season, ret from first class cricket 1987; dir Club Surfaces Ltd (artificial grass surfaces co); pres Met Dist Assoc of Kent CCs; patron The Primary Club; *Style*— Derek Underwood, Esq, MBE; ✉ c/o Kent CCC, St Lawrence Ground, Canterbury, Kent (☎ 01227 456886)

UNDERWOOD, Elaine (Mrs Roberts Grimsey); *b* 19 April 1958; *Educ* Portobello HS, Univ of Edinburgh (MA), Univ of Pennsylvania (exchange prog); *m* 24 June 1994; 1 s (Jamie William b 2 Aug 1995); *Career* RHM Foods Ltd: marketing trainee rising through various positions to sr brand mangr 1980–85, mktg mangr Soft Drinks 1986–87, mktg controller Soft Drinks and Preserves (Robertsons) 1987–88, actg cmmercial dir Soft Drinks June-Oct 1988, business devpt controller Nov 1988–89, commercial dir Soft Drinks and McDougalls Gps 1989–90, commercial dir Soft Drinks 1990–91, mktg dir 1991–94, md subsid J A Sharwood & Co 1994–; *Recreations* skiing, golf, travel; *Style*— Ms Elaine Underwood; ✉ J A Sharwood & Co Ltd, Sharwood House, Church Road, Egham, Surrey TW20 9QG (☎ 01784 473000, fax 01784 437093

UNDERWOOD, Grahame John Taylor; s of Wing Cdr Shirley Taylor Underwood, OBE, of Elston, nr Newark, and Joyce Mary, *née* Smith; *b* 1 July 1944; *Educ* Ashby De La Zouch GS, Poly of N London (DipArch); *m* 4 May 1968, Christine Elva, da of Sqdn Ldr Cecil Reginald Long, MBE, DSM (d 1972); 2 s (Christopher Taylor b 1971, Toby Grahame b 1972), 1 da (Lucy Jane b 1974); *Career* Watkins Gray International: architect and planner 1969–72, assoc 1972–83, ptnr and dir 1983–; dir: Watkins Gray Peter Jones 1983–90, Watkins Gray International Ltd 1983–, Watkins Gray Ho & Partners 1989–; princ designs incl: Royal Masonic Hosp, Nat Heart and Chest Hosps London and Baghdad, Dammam and Unayzah Hosps Saudi Arabia, Bromley Hosp, Orpington Hosp, Ekaterinburg Cardiology Hosp and Oncology Hosp, Togliatti Maternity Hosp, Belfast Children's Hosp, Altnagelvin Hosp, Joyce Green Hosp, health planning for govts of Syria and Indonesia; fndr memb Care Health Planning; chm Edgbaston Round Table 1984; Freeman Guild of Air Pilots and Air Navigators 1993; RIBA 1973; *Books* Architects Jl Handbook of Ironmongery (1979), The Security of Buildings (1984); author of numerous tech articles; *Recreations* flying, gliding; *Style*— Grahame Underwood, Esq; ✉ Watkins Gray International, Alexander House, Spur Road, Orpington, Kent BR6 0QR (☎ 01689 870521, fax 01689 835152)

UNDERWOOD, Rory; MBE (1992); s of James Ashley Underwood (d 1982), and Annie, *née* Tan; *b* 19 June 1963; *Educ* Barnard Castle Sch Durham; *m* 19 Sept 1987, Wendy, da of Laurence Sydney Blanshard; 2 da (Rebecca Jennifer Anne b 25 June 1990, Alexandra Mary Louise b 9 Dec 1991); *Career* rugby union wing threequarter; sr rep rugby debut for Durham 1981, Yorkshire 1982–87, played in Co Championship final for Yorkshire 1983 and 1987 (winners); clubs: Middlesbrough RUFC, Leicester FC (joined 1983), RAF RU, Barbarians RFC; rep: Eng Colts 1982, Eng under 23 tour Italy 1982, Eng B debut 1982; England: debut v Ireland 1984, memb World Cup squad 1987 (3 appearances), tour Aust/Fiji 1988 (2 test appearances), tour Romania 1989, memb Grand Slam winning team 1991 and 1992, tour to S Africa 1994, memb runners-up squad World Cup 1991 (6 appearances), 85 caps, memb World Cup squad S Africa 1995 (fourth place); Eng records: most capped player, most tries in internationals (48), most tries in an international (jtly held, 5 v Fiji 1989), 11 tries in World Cup; memb Br Lions tour Aust 1989 (3 tests) and tour NZ 1993 (3 tests); cmmnd RAF 1983, awarded wings 1985, 360 Sqdn 1986–92, 100 Sqdn 1992–; *Recreations* crosswords, reading, music; *Style*— Rory Underwood, Esq, MBE; ✉ c/o Leicester Football Club, Aylestone Road, Leicester

UNDERWOOD, Susan Lois; da of John Ayton Underwood, of St Andrews, and Sheila Lois, *née* Rankin; *b* 6 Aug 1956; *Educ* Kilgraston Sch, Allhallows Sch, Univ of St Andrews (MA), Univ of Leicester (grad cert mus studies), TEFL; *children* 1 da (Mitya Susan Underwood b 16 July 1983), 1 s (Callum John Underwood b 17 June 1987); *Career* res supvr Yorkshire & Humberside Museums Cncl 1981–82, volunteer Yorkshire Mus of Farming 1982–83, curator Nat Railway Nus York 1983–84, keeper of local history Scunthorpe Mus and Art Gall 1985–88, dir North of England Museums Serv 1990– (dep dir 1988–90); pres Museums North 1992–93, chair Social History Curators Gp 1990–91; Bd memb: Northern Centre for Contemporary Art 1990–92, Northern Arts 1991–, Live Theatre Co Ltd 1992–; examiner Mus Assoc dip 1990–92; FMA 1993 (AMA 1985); *Recreations* tennis, the arts, enjoying time with my children; *Clubs* St Rules Golf (St Andrews); *Style*— Miss Susan Underwood; ✉ North of England Museums Service, House of Recovery, Bath Lane, Newcastle upon Tyne NE4 5SQ (☎ 0191 222 1661, fax 0191 261 4725)

UNDERWOOD, Tony; s of James Ashley Underwood (d 1982), of Barnard Castle, Co Durham, and Annie, *née* Tan; *b* 17 Feb 1969; *Educ* Barnard Castle Sch, Univ of Leicester (BSc), Univ of Cambridge (BA, Rugby blue, Athletics blue); *Career* rugby union player; over 50 appearances Leicester FC 1988–95 (winners Courage Clubs' Championship 1994/95 season), 34 appearances Cambridge Univ 1990–92, transferred to Newcastle RFC 1995; England: memb 18 Gp 1985–87, represented student team 1987–91 (played in inaugural Student World Cup France 1988), 14 B caps 1989–, 21 full caps; memb tour: Argentina 1990, New Zealand 1992, S Africa 1994; memb team World Cup S Africa 1995 (fourth place); represented XV v Barbarians 1990, Barbarians v Scotland 1991, XV v Leicester 1992; memb British Lions' team touring NZ 1993; also represented: Irish Wolfhounds in Hong Kong Sevens 1989, Barbarians v All Blacks 1989 and in Hong Kong Sevens 1991; hon sec Cambridge Univ RUFC 1990–91; fin grad Lehman Bros International 1992–94, Asian Equity sales Crosby Securities (Europe) 1994–95, mktg exec Newcastle Utd Sporting Club 1996–; weekly columnist The Independent; *Recreations* golf, squash, fell walking, reading, playing saxophone, music, family and friends; *Style*— Tony Underwood, Esq; ✉ Newcastle RFC, Kingston Park, Brunton Road, Kenton Bank Foot, Newcastle-upon-Tyne NE13 8AF (☎ 0191 214 0422, fax 0191 214 0488)

UNGER, Michael Ronald; s of Ronald Unger, CBE, of Carvoeiro, Algarve, Portugal, and Joan Maureen Unger; *b* 8 Dec 1943; *Educ* Wirral GS; *m* 1, 20 Aug 1966 (m dis 1991), Eunice; 1 s (Paul b 1973), 1 da (Sarah decd); m 2, Aug 1993, Noorah; *Career* ed: Daily Post Liverpool 1977–82, Liverpool Echo 1982–83, Manchester Evening News 1983–; dir: The Guardian Media Group plc 1983–; tstee The Scott Tst 1986–, chm NW Arts Bd 1991–93; *Books* The Memoirs of Bridget Hitler; *Recreations* reading, walking; *Style*— Michael Unger, Esq; ✉ 164 Deansgate, Manchester (☎ 0161 832 7200)

UNMACK, Timothy Stuart Brooke; s of Randall Carter Unmack (d 1978), and Anne Roberta, *née* Stuart (d 1972); *b* 5 Aug 1937; *Educ* Radley, Christ Church Oxford (MA); *m* 21 May 1966, Eleanor Gillian, da of George Aidan Drury Tait (d 1970); 2 s (Guy Douglas b 13 March 1975, Neil Alexander b 29 July 1977); *Career* Nat Serv RN; admitted slr 1965, sr ptnr Beaumont and Son 1987 (ptnr 1968–); memb Int Law Assoc's Ctee on Legal Aspects of Air Traffic Control; former chm Royal Philanthropic Soc Redhill; memb Worshipful Co of Barbers; memb: Law Soc 1965, Royal Aeronautical Soc 1987, Royal Soc for Asian Affairs 1987; *Recreations* sailing, languages; *Clubs* Utd Oxford & Cambridge Univ, Kingston Rowing; *Style*— Timothy Unmack, Esq; ✉ Beaumont and Son, 1 Portsoken Street, London E1 8AW (☎ 0171 481 3100, fax 0171 481 3353, telex 889018 BOSUN G)

UNSWORTH, Prof Anthony; s of James Unsworth (d 1982), of Astley, Lancs, and Annie, *née* Halliwell; *b* 7 Feb 1945; *Educ* Worsley Coll nr Manchester, Warrington Tech Coll, Univ of Salford (BSc Mechanical Engrg (1st class)), Univ of Leeds (MSc in Tribology, Samuel Denison Prize, PhD, Tribology Silver Medal IMechE, DEng); *m* 22 Dec 1967, Jill, da of late Kenneth Chetwood; *Career* apprentice David Brown Corporation 1961, research engr David Brown Gear Industries 1967–69, ARC lectr in bioengineering Univ of Leeds 1971–76 (ARC research fell 1969–71); Univ of Durham: lectr 1976–79, sr lectr 1979–83 (visiting research scientist Mechanical and Aerospace Engrg Cornell Univ NY 1981), reader 1983–89, prof of engrg and chm Sch of Engrg and Applied Sci 1990–94, prof of engrg, dep dean of sci and dir Centre for Biomedical Engrg 1994–; memb Senate Univ of Durham 1984–87, 1990–94 and 1996– (memb Cncl 1993–96, also memb or chm numerous univ ctees); memb Ctee Engrg in Med Gp IMechE 1984– (chm 1989–92), memb Ctee ACTION Research 1989– (chm Bioengineering Advsy Panel 1992–95); memb Bd of Govrs Univ of Teesside (formerly Poly) 1986–, dir ACTION (charity) 1992–95, memb S Durham Health Authy 1993–96; chm: S Durham Research Ethics Ctee 1993–96, Northern Regnl Research Ethics Ctee 1995–96; memb Editorial Bd: Jl of Orthopaedic Rheumatology 1987–, Current Orthopaedics 1988–; ed Engrg in Med Newsletter IMechE 1988–90, ed Proceedings of Instn of Mech Engrs Part H Engrg in Med 1993– (memb Editorial Bd 1988–); scientific referee for papers submitted to various learned jls; author of over 120 publications; deliverer of over 150 lectures to learned socs (incl 30 overseas); memb Br Orthopaedic Research Soc 1975, memb Br Soc for Rheumatology 1984; FIMechE 1984 (MIMechE 1972), FEng 1996; *Recreations* singing operetta and sacred music; *Style*— Prof Anthony Unsworth, FEng; ✉ School of Engineering, University of Durham, South Road, Durham DH1 3LE (☎ 0191 374 3932, fax 0191 374 7392, e-mail tony.unsworth@durham.ac.uk)

UNSWORTH, Barry Forster; s of Michael Unsworth (d 1949), and Elsie, *née* Forster (d 1954); *b* 10 Aug 1930; *Educ* Stockton-on-Tees GS, Univ of Manchester (BA); *m* 1, 1959 (m dis 1991), Valerie Irene, *née* Moore; 3 da (Madeleine b 1961, Tania b 1964, Thomasina b 1968); m 2, 1992, Aira, *née* Pohjanvaara-Buffa; *Career* novelist; Arts Cncl literary fell Charlotte Mason Coll Ambleside Cumbria 1978–79, Northern Arts literary fell Univs of Durham and Newcastle 1982–84; writer in residence: Univ of Liverpool 1984–85, Lund Univ Sweden 1988–; memb Soc of Authors; FRSL 1974; *Books* The Partnership (1966), The Greeks Have a Word for It (1967), The Hide (1970), Mooncranker's Gift (winner Heinemann prize 1973), The Big Day (1976), Pascali's Island (shortlisted for Booker Prize 1980, filmed 1988), The Rage of the Vulture (1982), Stone Virgin (1985), Sugar and Rum (1988), Sacred Hunger (co-winner Booker Prize 1992), Morality Play (1995), After Hannibal (1996); *Style*— Barry Unsworth, Esq, FRSL; ✉ c/o Giles Gordon, Curtis Brown, Haymarket House, 28–29 Haymarket, London SW1Y 4SP (☎ 0171 396 6600, fax 0171 396 0110)

UNSWORTH, Sir Edgar Ignatius Godfrey; kt (1963), CMG (1954), QC (N Rhodesia, now Zambia, 1951); s of John Unsworth; *b* 18 April 1906; *Educ* Stonyhurst, Univ of Manchester; *m* 1964, Eileen, widow of Raymond Ritzema; *Career* called the the Bar Gray's Inn 1930, Parly candidate (C) Farnworth 1935 gen election, Crown counsel Nigeria 1937, Crown counsel N Rhodesia 1942, slr-gen N Rhodesia 1946, attorney-gen N Rhodesia 1951–56, attorney-gen Nigeria 1956–60, federal justice Supreme Court of Nigeria 1960–62; chief justice: Nyasaland 1962–64, Gibraltar 1965–76; justice of appeal Gibraltar 1976–81; *Style*— Sir Edgar Unsworth, CMG, QC; ✉ Pedro el Grande 9, Sotogrande, (Cadiz), Spain; 12 Brock Street, Bath BA1 2LW

UNSWORTH, Michael Anthony; s of Lt Cdr John Geoffrey Unsworth, MBE, of Hayling Island, Hants, and Joan Rhyllis, *née* Clemes; *b* 29 Oct 1949; *Educ* St John's Coll Southsea Hants, Enfield Coll of Technol (BA); *m* 1 Dec 1973, Masa, da of Prof Zitomir Lozica, of Orebic, Croatia; 2 da (Tania Elizabeth b 10 Oct 1978, Tessa Joanna b 27 June 1981); *Career* res analyst Grieveson Grant & Co 1972–79; Scott Goff Hancock & Co: sr oil analyst 1979–81, ptnr 1981–86, co merged with Smith Bros to form Smith New Court plc 1986, dir i/c energy res 1986–95, dir i/c res 1989–95, Bd dir 1991–95, md Capital Markets 1994–95; dep chief exec Smith New Court Far East Ltd 1995, head of research Asia Pacific Region Merrill Lynch 1995–; MSI, AIIMR, AInstPet; *Recreations* sailing, opera, theatre; *Clubs* China, Little Ship; *Style*— Michael Unsworth, Esq; ✉ 1604 Tower B, Queen's Garden, 9 Old Peak Road, Mid Levels, Hong Kong (☎ 00 852 2801 6147, fax 00 852 2530 5957)

UNSWORTH, Dr Philip Francis; s of Stephen Unsworth (d 1959), of Manchester, and Teresa *née* McElin; *b* 18 Sept 1947; *Educ* St Bede's Coll, Univ of Manchester (BSc, MB ChB); *Career* house surgn and physician Manchester Royal Inf 1971–72; lectr: Middlesex Hosp 1972–75, St Thomas' Hosp 1975–76; microbiologist Colindale 1977–79; conslt microbiologist: Tameside and Glossop DHA 1979–94, Tameside and Glossop Acute Services NHS Tst 1994–; FRCPath; *Recreations* sports and walking, music, reading; *Style*— Dr Philip Unsworth; ✉ 1 Pine Rd, Didsbury, Manchester M20 6UY (☎ 0161 445 6480); Department of Microbiology, Tameside General Hospital, Ashton-under-Lyne, Lancs OL6 9RW (☎ 0161 331 6000, fax 0161 344 6496)

UNSWORTH, Walter (Walt); *b* 16 Dec 1928; *Educ* Wigan Tech Coll, Chester Coll (LCP); *m* 2 June 1952, Dorothy Winstanley; 1 s (Duncan b 1958), 1 da (Gail b 1953); *Career* RA 1947–49; sci teacher 1951–73, editorial dir Cicerone Press 1968, ed Climber and Rambler Magazine 1974–86; hon vice pres Lancashire Mountaineering Club, memb Soc of Authors 1970, pres Outdoor Writers' Guild 1979, memb Br Guild of Travel Writers 1988; *Books* The Young Mountaineer (1959), The English Outcrops (1964), Matterhorn Man (1965), Tiger in the Snow (1966), The Book of Rock Climbing (1968), North Face (1969), Portrait of the River Derwent (1971), High Fells of Lakeland (1972, revised 1992), Encyclopaedia of Mountaineering (1975, revised 1993), Peaks, Passes and Glaciers (1981), Everest (1981, revised 1989), The Pennine Playground (1984), Classic Walks of the World (1985), Savage Snows (1986), Classic Walks in the Lake District (1988), Illustrated Companion into Lakeland (1988), Classic Walks of Europe (1989), Classic Walks in the Yorkshire Dales (1989, ITAS first prize for mountain lit Trento Festival 1992), Hold the Heights (1994); *Recreations* travel, mountain walking, photography; *Clubs* Alpine; *Style*— Walt Unsworth, Esq; ✉ Harmony Hall, Milnthorpe, Cumbria LA7 7QE (☎ 01539 562112); Cicerone Press, 2 Police Square, Milnthorpe, Cumbria LA7 7PY (☎ 01539 562069, fax 01539 563417)

UNWIN, Sir (James) Brian; KCB (1990); s of Reginald Unwin (d 1975), and Winifred Annie, *née* Walthall (d 1989); *b* 21 Sept 1935; *Educ* Chesterfield Sch, New Coll Oxford (MA), Yale Univ (MA); *m* 5 May 1964, Diana Susan, da of Sir David Aubrey Scott, GCMG, *qv*; 3 s (Michael Alexander, Christopher James, Nicholas Edward); *Career* HM Civil Serv: asst princ CRO 1960, second later first sec Br High Cmmn Salisbury Southern Rhodesia 1961–64, first sec Br High Cmmn Accra 1964–65, FCO 1965–68, HM Treasy 1968–81 (asst sec 1972, under sec 1975), dep sec Cabinet Office 1985–87 (under sec 1981–83), dep sec HM Treasy 1983–85, chm of the Bd HM Customs & Excise 1987–93, pres European Investment Bank 1993–, chm Supervisory Bd European Investment Fund 1994–; UK dir Euro Investmt Bank 1983–85, memb Bd of Dirs ENO 1993–94 (hon sec 1987–93); chm: Civil Serv Sports Cncl 1989–93, Customs Cooperation Cncl 1991–92; CIMgt 1988; *Recreations* bird watching, opera, Wellingtoniana, Trollope; *Clubs* Reform, Kingswood Village (Surrey); *Style*— Sir Brian Unwin, KCB; ✉ President European Investment Bank, 100 Boulevard Konrad Adenauer, L-2950 Luxembourg (☎ 00 352 4379–1, fax 00 352 437704)

UNWIN, David Charles; QC (1995); s of Peter Charles Unwin (d 1991), and Rosemary Gwendolen Winifred, *née* Locket; *b* 12 May 1947; *Educ* Clifton, Trinity Coll Oxford (BA); *m* 16 Aug 1969, Lorna, da of Richard Frank Bullivant; 1 s (James b 1978), 1 da (Catherine b 1974); *Career* called to the Bar Lincoln's Inn 1971, Treasy jr counsel in charity matters 1987–95; *Recreations* music, mountaineering, sailing; *Style*— David Unwin, Esq, QC; ✉ 7 Stone Buildings, Lincoln's Inn, London WC2 (☎ 0171 405 3886, fax 0171 242 8502)

UNWIN, David Storr; s of Sir Stanley Unwin, KCMG (d 1968), and Alice Mary Storr (d 1971); *b* 3 Dec 1918; *Educ* Abbotsholme Sch Derbys; *m* 31 July 1945, Bridget Mary Periwinkle, da of Capt E Sydney Jasper Herbert, RN (d 1941); 1 da (Phyllida b 1950), 1 s (Corydon b 1950); *Career* author; *Books include* The Governor's Wife (1954), A View of the Heath (1956), Fifty Years with Father (biography, 1982); books for children: Rick Afire! (1942), Dream Gold (1948), Drumbeats (1953), The Future Took Us (1957), Foxy-Boy (1959), The Girl in the Grove (1974), The Wishing Bone (1977); *Recreations* travel; *Clubs* PEN; *Style*— David S Unwin, Esq; ✉ Garden Flat, 31 Belsize Park, London NW3 4DX (☎ 0171 435 5198)

UNWIN, Eric Geoffrey (Geoff); s of Maurice Doughty Unwin, and Olive Milburn, *née* Watson; *b* 9 Aug 1942; *Educ* Heaton GS Newcastle upon Tyne, Kings Coll Durham (BSc); *m* 1 July 1967, Margaret Bronia (Bron), *née* Element; 1 s (b 1 May 1973), 1 da (b 25 April 1975); *Career* with Cadbury 1963–68; Hoskyns Group plc (computer servs gp): joined John Hoskyns & Co 1968, md Hoskyns Systems Development 1978, dir Hoskyns Group plc 1982–, md 1984–88 (incl Stock Exchange flotation 1986), exec chm 1988–, chief operating offr Cap Gemini Sogeti 1992–, non-exec dir Volmac Software Group NV 1992–, chm Cap Programmator AB 1993–; pres UK Computing Servs Assoc 1987–88, memb Info Technol Advsy Bd 1988–91; Freeman City of London 1987, fndr memb and Liveryman Worshipful Co of Information Technologists 1987; CIMgt 1987 (memb Bd of Companions 1990–93); *Recreations* golf, sailing, skiing, the Arts, theatre, gardening, riding; *Clubs* RAC; *Style*— Geoff Unwin, Esq; ✉ Cap Gemini Sogeti, Hoskyns House, 130 Shaftesbury Avenue, London W1V 8HH (☎ 0171 434 8601, fax 0171 434 8349)

UNWIN, Peter William; CMG (1981); s of Arnold Unwin, and Norah Unwin; *b* 20 May 1932; *Educ* Ampleforth, ChCh Oxford (MA); *m* 1955, Monica Steven; 2 s, 2 da; *Career* army 1954–56; entered Foreign Office 1956, cnsllr (econ) Bonn 1973–75, head Personnel Policy Dept FCO 1976–78, min (econ) Bonn 1980–82, ambass to Hungary 1983–86, ambass to Denmark 1986–88, dep sec gen (economic) of the Commonwealth 1989–93; dir David Davies Meml Inst of Int Studies 1995–; *Books* Voice in the Wilderness. Imre Nagy & the Hungarian Revolution (1991), Baltic Approaches (1996); *Style*— Peter Unwin, Esq, CMG; ✉ 30 Kew Green, Richmond, Surrey TW9 3BH (☎ 0181 940 8037)

UNWIN, Rayner Stephens; CBE; s of Sir Stanley Unwin (d 1968), and Alice Mary Storr (d 1971); *b* 23 Dec 1925; *Educ* Abbotsholme Sch, Trinity Coll Oxford (MA), Harvard (MA); *m* 1952, Carol Margaret, *née* Curwen; 1 s (Merlin b 1954), 3 da (Camilla b 1955, Tamara b 1958, Sharon b 1958); *Career* book publisher; *Recreations* hill walking, birds, gardens; *Clubs* Garrick; *Style*— Rayner Unwin, Esq, CBE; ✉ Limes Cottage, Little Missenden, Nr Amersham, Bucks; 19 New Row, London WC2

UNWIN, Vicky; da of Thomas Michael Unwin, of Milverton, Somerset, and Sheila Margaret Findlay Mills; *b* 3 Nov 1957; *Educ* Wycombe Abbey, Oxford HS, Girton Coll Cambridge (BA); *m* 18 June 1983, Ross Brett Cattell, s of Dr William Ross Cattell, of London; 1 s (Thomas William b 21 Jan 1988), 1 da (Louise Ann b 7 Dec 1989); *Career* dir Heinemann Educnl Boleswa 1987–, publishing dir Heinemann Educnl Books 1987–90 (graduate traineeship 1979–80), md Heinemann International Literature and Textbooks 1990–93, ptnr Specialist Advsy Gp on Africa 1993–96, mangr Telegraph Books 1996–; sec Int Charity Assoc for Teaching Caribbean and African Lit 1984–87; *Recreations* skiing, walking, riding, gardening, reading, diving; *Style*— Ms Vicky Unwin; ✉ 26 Glenmore Road, London NW3 4DB (☎ 0171 722 1697, fax 0171 722 5018)

UPHILL, Paul David Graham; JP (Torbay 1982); s of Clifford Uphill, of Kingsteignton, Devon, and Dorothy, *née* Nutt (d 1990); *b* 16 Nov 1947; *Educ* St Nicholas' Sch Clevedon, St Aldham's Sch Sherborne; *m* (sep); 1 da (Sarah Louise b 14 Feb 1974), 1 s (John Christian b 2 May 1975); *Career* hotelier; trainee mangr The Imperial Hotel Torquay 1963–68, mangr i/c Country Club and Apartment ops Bigwin Island Country Club & Condominium Complex (formerly Bigwin Island Hotel) The Lake of Bays Ontario 1969–71 (asst mangr i/c personnel and food & beverage 1968–69), gen mangr Sherwood Inn Hotel Port Carling Ontario 1971–72, mangr The Orwell Hotel Felixstowe Suffolk June-Aug 1972, gen mangr The Queens Hotel Torquay Aug 1972–73; The Palace Hotel Torquay: gen mangr 1973–76, md 1976–91, md and shareholder 1991–; former memb: Hotel & Catering Advsy Ctee S Devon Tech Coll, Chaine de Rotisseurs; commercial memb: BHRCA, Torbay Tourist Bd, Torquay Hotels' Assoc; fndr memb: Torquay Hotels' Buying Consortium, Devon Tourism Hotels of Distinction; chm Magistrates' Betting & Gaming Licensing Ctee 1993–; Freeman City of London 1993; Master Innholder 1992, FHCIMA; *Recreations* fly fishing, deer stalking, conservation; *Style*— Paul Uphill, Esq, JP; ✉ The Torquay Palace Ltd, The Palace Hotel, Torquay, Devon TQ1 3TG (☎ 01803 200200, fax 01803 299899)

UPSHON, Laurence Marshall (Laurie); s of Lt-Col Hector Llewellyn Marshall Upshon (d 1957), and Hilda Winifred, *née* Southgate; *b* 21 June 1950; *Educ* St Peter's Sch Merrow Guildford Surrey; *m* 18 July 1970, Heide Maria, da of Gustav Hawlin, of Salzburg, Austria; 2 s (Rupert b 1977, Robin b 1979), 1 da (Claire b 1976); *Career* asst gp ed Stratford Express Gp 1974–76, Southern TV 1976–87 (features ed 1980); TVS Televison: exec prodr news and current affairs 1982–84 (sr prodr 1981), ed Coast to Coast 1984–85; controller of news and operations Central Television 1995– (ed Central News 1985, controller of news Central Television 1989–95); memb: RTS, BAFTA, ABE, RTNDA(US); *Recreations* sport (cricket), painting, reading, music; *Style*— Laurie Upshon, Esq; ✉ Whitlenge House, Hartlebury, Worcestershire DY10 4HD (☎ 01299 250567); Central Television plc, Broad St, Birmingham B1 2JP (☎ 0121 643 9898, fax 0121 634 4108)

UPTON, Prof Anthony Frederick; s of C A Upton (d 1936), and S G, *née* McCarthy (d 1980); *b* 13 Oct 1929; *Educ* Windsor Co Boy's Sch, Queen's Coll Oxford (MA), Duke's Univ USA (AM); *m* 12 Aug 1951, Sirkka Rauha, da of Onni Pöllänen, of Helsinki, Finland; 3 s (Nicholas b 3 July 1957, Timothy b 19 Dec 1958, Jeremy b 11 Jan 1963); *Career* asst lectr in modern history Univ of Leeds 1953–56; Univ of St Andrews 1956–95: lectr in modern history 1956, sr lectr 1966, reader 1974, prof of Nordic history 1983, chm Modern History Dept 1987, ret 1995 (hon prof); memb: Lab Pty, Hist Assoc, Socialist Educn Assoc; fell Porthan Soc Univ of Turku Finland; FRHistS; *Books* Sir Arthur Ingram (1961), Finland in Crisis 1940–41 (1964), The Communist Parties of Scandinavia and Finland (1973), Finland 1939–40 (1974), The Finnish Revolution 1917–18 (1980); *Recreations* promoting the demise of capitalism; *Style*— Prof Anthony Upton; ✉ 5 West Acres, St Andrews, Fife (☎ 01334 473358); Department of Modern History, University of St Andrews, St Andrews, Fife KY16 9AL (☎ 01334 476161 ext 2929)

UPTON, Prof Brian Geoffrey Johnson; s of Harry Johnson Upton, and Constance Ethel, *née* Bailey; *b* 2 March 1933; *Educ* Reading Sch, Oxford (BA, MA, DPhil); *m* 13 Sept 1958, Bodil, da of Svend Aalbaek Madsen; 2 s (Peter Lawrence Johnson b 16 Dec 1961, Michael Geoffrey b 12 March 1964), 1 da (Melanie Jane b 15 June 1975); *Career* Geological Survey of Greenland 1958–60, post-doctoral fell California Inst of Technol 1961–62; Univ of Edinburgh: lectr in geology 1962–72, reader in geology 1972–82, prof of petrology 1982–; memb Editorial Bd: Scottish Journal of Geology 1969–73, Transactions RSE Earth Sciences 1983–89, Journal of Petrology (exec ed) 1983–; memb Geological Soc London 1967, FRSE 1974; *Recreations* painting, gardening, wild-life conservation; *Style*— Prof Brian Upton, FRSE; ✉ Department of Geology and Geophysics, West Mains Rd, Edinburgh EH9 3JW (☎ 0131 650 4840, fax 0131 668 3184, telex 727442)

UPTON, Prof Graham; s of late William Upton, of Sydney, Aust, and Edna May, *née* Groves; *b* 30 April 1944; *Educ* Univ of Sydney (MA, DipEd), Univ of NSW (MEd), Univ of Wales (PhD); *m* 1 (m dis 1984), Jennifer Ann; 1 s (Stuart Ingham b 10 Jan 1969), 1 da (Sonja Cape b 13 March 1970); m 2, Elizabeth Mary Hayward, da of Jack Speed; 1 s (James Llewellyn b 20 Dec 1986), 1 da (Hermione Catherine b 19 Jan 1988); *Career* schoolteacher NSW 1966–71, lectr in special educn Leeds Poly 1972–74; Univ Coll Cardiff 1974–88: lectr, sr lectr, reader, head Dept of Educn, dean Faculty of Educn; pro-vice-chllr Univ of Birmingham 1993– (prof of educn and head Sch of Educn 1988–93); memb: Nat Assoc for Special Educn Needs, Assoc of Workers for Maladjusted Children; FBPsS 1996 (assoc 1983); *Books* Physical & Creative Activities for the Mentally Handicapped (1979), Educating Children with Behaviour Problems (1983), Staff Training and Special Education Needs (1991), Special Educational Needs (1992), Emotional and Behavioural Difficulties (1994), Voice of the Child (1996); *Style*— Prof Graham Upton; ✉ Pro-Vice-Chancellor, University of Birmingham, Edgbaston, Birmingham B15 2TT (☎ 0121 414 5940, fax 0121 414 4534)

UPTON, (John Henry) Peter; s of Charles Vivian Upton (d 1977), of Billericay, Essex, and Lynda Winifred, *née* Gracey; *b* 18 May 1949; *Educ* Palmer's Boys' Sch Grays Essex; *m* 1, 4 Aug 1973 (m dis 1989), Heather Mary, da of Philip Edward Stormont; 1 s (Michael Peter b 7 July 1977), 1 da (Rebecca Heather b 11 April 1975); m 2, 27 Oct 1989 (m dis 1996), Tracey Elizabeth, da of Anthony Bruce Coxall; 1 da (Elizabeth Peta b 2 June 1991); *Career* articled clerk Smallfield Fitzhugh Tillett & Co CAs London 1967–71, religious min 1971–79, Coulson & Co CAs Scarborough 1979–80; Hodgson Harris (later Hodgson Impey): London 1980–83, Reading 1983–88; in private practice Maidenhead 1988–; memb Nat Cncl ICAEW (Thames Valley Area rep) 1991–; ACA 1971, memb Inst of Taxation 1982; *Recreations* golf, bridge, racketball, gardening; *Clubs* Castle Royle, Henley Golf; *Style*— Peter Upton, Esq; ✉ 47 Forlease Road, Maidenhead, Berks SL6 1RX (☎ 01628 781636, fax 01628 75705)

UPTON, Robin James; DL (Suffolk 1991); s of Col (Philip) Valentine Upton, MBE, TD, JP, DL (d 1985), of Margaretting, Essex, and (Veronica) Rosemary (d 1993), da of Lt-Col Leslie Heber Thornton, CMG, DSO, of Lewes, Sussex; *b* 18 March 1931; *Educ* Trinity Coll Glenalmond, Trinity Coll Cambridge (MA); *m* 1961, Priscilla Mary, yr da of Dr William Sydney Charles Copeman, CBE, TD, MD, FRCP (d 1970), of London W2; 2 s (Hugo, Simon), 1 da (Victoria); *Career* farmer; dir: R J Upton Farms Ltd 1969–, Reed & Upton Ltd 1971–, Mereacre Farms Ltd 1983–97, Assoc Farmers plc 1983–90; county chm Suffolk Country Landowners Assoc 1981–84, JP 1969–94, High Sheriff of Suffolk 1988–89; Master Worshipful Co of Farmers 1990; *Recreations* conservation, shooting, fishing; *Style*— R J Upton, Esq, DL; ✉ Park Farm, Herringswell, Bury St Edmunds, Suffolk (☎ 01638 750317)

URBAN, Stuart; s of Dr Garri Simonyevich Urban, of Caracas, Venezuela, and Josephine Maureen, *née* Johnson; *b* 11 Sept 1958; *Educ* King's Coll Sch Wimbledon, Balliol Coll Oxford (exhibitioner, MA); *m* 12 July 1987, Dr Dana Bežanov, da of Ilija Bežanov; 1 da (Leah Jessie Rebeccah b 13 Sept 1988), 1 s (David Alexander b 2 March 1991); *Career* writer and director; made two half-hour films as teenager (The Virus of War 1972 and Spaghetti Special 1974) since preserved in Nat Film Archive; writer, prodr and dir The Panther L2 (Channel 4) 1980, professional debut as dir Pocketful of Dreams (BBC Playhouse) 1981, co-writer and dir Off To The Wars (Channel 4) 1985; dir many series incl: Bergerac, The Bill, The Good Guys; dir Our Friends in the North (BBC) 1994/95, writer and dir An Ungentlemanly Act (BBC/Union Pictures); writer Deadly Voyage (HBO/BBC) 1996; writer/prodr/dir Preaching to the Perverted (feature film) 1997; winner BAFTA Award for Best Single Drama 1992, The Indy (best overall prodn) and Best Drama Awards at The Indies Awards 1993; Gold Plaques (best TV movie, best direction) and Silver Plaque (screenplay) at Chicago Film Festival 1992; Bronze Medal (best writing) NY Int Film & TV Festival 1993; nomination Best Single Drama 1992 RTS; memb: BAFTA 1981, Writers' Guild of GB 1982, Directors' Guild of GB 1988; *Recreations* snow and water skiing; *Clubs* Annabel's, Tramp; *Style*— Stuart Urban, Esq; ✉ c/o Seifert Deuch Associates, 24 D'Arblay St, London W1V 3FH (☎ 0171 437 4551, fax 0171 439 1355)

URE, Alan Willis; CBE (1984), RD (1969); s of Colin McGregor Ure (d 1963), and Edith Hannah Eileen Willis Swinburne (d 1945); *b* 30 March 1926; *Educ* Kelvinside Acad, Merchiston Castle Sch, Pembroke Coll Cambridge; *m* 1953, Mary Christine, *née* Henry; 2 da (Fiona b 1954 d 1995, Alison b 1959), 1 s (John b 1956); *Career* RNVR 1944–58, RNR 1958–81 (Lt Cdr); memb Construction Indust Trg Bd 1982–85, pres Nat Fedn of Bldg Trades Employers 1981–82, memb Royal Cmmn on Civil Liability and Compensation for Personal Injury 1974–78; chm Nat Jt Cncl for the Bldg Industry 1989–91, formerly dep md Trollope and Colls Holdings, formerly md Trollope and Colls Ltd and Trollope and Colls Management Ltd; vice pres Fedn Internationale Européenne de Constructon 1982–85; Freeman: City of London, City of Glasgow; Liveryman Worshipful Co of Bakers, memb Incorporation of Bakers; *Recreations* vintage motoring, bell ringing, walking, reading, sailing; *Clubs* Naval, RNSA, RNVR Yacht (Cdre 1992–93); *Style*— Alan Ure, Esq, CBE, RD; ✉ The Shambles, Brettenham, Ipswich, Suffolk IP7 7QP

URE, David; *Career* Reuters Holdings plc: joined Reuters as journalist 1968, i/c ops in Europe 1983–92 (also i/c Middle E and Africa 1989–92), main bd dir 1989–, dir of mktg and technical policy 1992–; *Style*— David Ure, Esq; ✉ Reuters Holdings plc, 85 Fleet Street, London EC4P 4AJ (☎ 0171 250 1122)

URE, Jean Ann; da of William Ure (d 1969), of Croydon, and Vera Primrose, *née* Belsen (d 1988); *b* 1 Jan 1943; *Educ* Croydon HS, Webber-Douglas Acad of Dramatic Art; *m* 12 Aug 1967, Leonard Gregory; *Career* writer; memb Soc of Authors; *Books* Dance for Two (children's book, publ while at sch), See You Thursday (1980), A Proper Little Nooryeff (1981), Hi There, Supermouse (1983), One Green Leaf (1987), Plague 99 (1989, Lancs Book Award 1990), Play Nimrod for Him (1990), Come Lucky April (1992), A Place to Scream (1992), Watchers at the Shrine (1994), Skinny Melon and Me (1996); *Recreations* animal rights, walking, reading, music; *Style*— Ms Jean Ure; ✉ 88 Southbridge Road, Croydon CR0 1AF (☎ 0181 688 6565); Maggie Noach Agency, 21 Redan Street, London W14 0AB (☎ 0171 602 2451)

URE, Sir John Burns; KCMG (1987), LVO (1968); s of Tam Ure, MBE (d 1963), and Mary Jeanie, *née* Bosworth (d 1963); *b* 5 July 1931; *Educ* Uppingham Sch, Magdalene Coll Cambridge (MA), Harvard Business Sch (AMP); *m* 1972, Caroline, da of Charles Allan, of Roxburghshire; 1 s (Alasdair b 1978), 1 da (Arabella b 1981); *Career* 2 Lt Cameronians (Scot Rifles) 1949–51, active serv during Emergency in Malaya; Lt London Scot (Gordon Highlanders) 1951–55 (TA); joined HM Diplomatic Serv 1956, served at Br Embassies in Moscow, Leopoldville, Santiago and in the Foreign and Cwlth Office in London 1956–71, cnsllr and chargé d'affaires Lisbon 1972–77, head of S America Dept FCO 1977–79, ambass to Cuba 1979–81, asst under-sec of state FCO 1981–84, ambass to Brazil 1984–87, ambass to Sweden 1987–91; cmmr-gen for Expo '92 1990–92; dir: Thomas Cook Group 1991–, Sotheby's Scandinavia AB 1991–, CSE Aviation Ltd 1992–94; conslt Robert Flemings (merchant bankers) 1995–; chm: Anglo-Swedish Soc 1992–96, Brazilian C of C 1994–96; tstee Leeds Castle Fndn 1995–; Cdr of Military Order of Christ (Portugal) 1973; *Books* Cucumber Sandwiches in the Andes (1973), The Trail of Tamerlane (1980), The Quest for Captain Morgan (1983), Prince Henry The Navigator (1977), Trespassers on the Amazon (1986), A Bird on the Wing (1992), Diplomatic Bag (1994); book reviews for TLS; *Recreations* travelling uncomfortably in remote places and writing about it comfortably afterwards; *Clubs* White's, Beefsteak, Pilgrims, Royal Geographical Soc; *Style*— Sir John Ure, KCMG, LVO; ✉ Netters Hall, Hawkhurst, Kent TN18 5AT (☎ 01580 752191, fax 01580 754532)

UREN, (John) Michael Leal; s of Arthur Claude Uren (d 1977), of Rickmansworth, Herts, and Doris May, *née* Leal (d 1983); *b* 1 Sept 1923; *Educ* Sherborne, Imperial Coll London (BSc, ACGI); *m* 26 Nov 1955, Serena Anne, da of Edward Raymond Peal, of Salisbury; 2 s (David Richard b 1960, (Robert) Mark b 1962); *Career* RN 1943–46; cmmnd Sub-Lt RNVR, air engr offr Fleet Air Arm; chartered civil engr; Sir Alexander Gibb & Partners Persia 1946–51, The Cementation Company Ltd Scotland 1951–53, Holland & Hannen and Cubitts NZ 1953–55, Industrial Complex for Pressed Steel Co Swindon 1955–56, British European Airways Base Heathrow 1956–58, Dowsett Engineering Construction Ltd (dir 1958, md 1961); currently chm: Civil and Marine Slag Cement Ltd, North East Slag Cement Ltd, The Appleby Group Ltd; memb Cncl Royal London Soc for the Blind 1974–94 (chm 1981–94); Freeman City of London 1958, Master Worshipful Co of Cordwainers 1990–91 (Liveryman 1958, Second Warden 1988, Sr Warden 1989, memb Ct of Assts); CEng, MICE, MIStructE, MCIWEM, FRICS; *Recreations* 15th and 16th century timber framed buildings, country pursuits, farming (pedigree Romney sheep, beef cattle, cereals); *Clubs* Naval and Military; *Style*— Michael Uren, Esq; ✉ Priory Farm, Appledore Road, Tenterden, Kent TN30 7DD (☎ 01580 764161); North East slag Cement Ltd, Croudace House, Godstone Road, Caterham, Surrey CR3 6XQ (☎ 01883 331071, fax 01883 331072)

URQUHART, Sir Brian Edward; KCMG (1986), MBE (1945); s of Murray Urquhart (d 1977), and Bertha Rendall Urquhart (d 1984); *b* 28 Feb 1919; *Educ* Westminster, Ch Ch Oxford; *m* 1, 1944 (m dis 1963), Alfreda, da of Constant Huntington (d 1964), of London; 2 s (Thomas b 1944, Robert b 1948), 1 da (Katherine b 1946); m 2, 1963, Sidney, da of Sidney Howard (d 1939), of USA; 1 s (Charles b 1967), 1 da (Rachel b 1963); *Career* Maj Dorset Regt and Airborne Forces Africa and Europe 1939–45; UN Secretariat 1945–86 (under sec gen special political affrs 1972–86), scholar in residence Ford Fndn 1986–96; Hon DCL Oxford; *Books* Hammarskjold (1972), A Life in Peace and War (1987), Decolonization and World Peace (1989), A World in Need of Leadership - Tomorrow's United Nations (with Erskine Childers, 1990), Ralph Bunche - An American Life (1993), Renewing the United Nations System (with Erskine Childers, 1994); *Recreations* reading, writing; *Clubs* Century (New York); *Style*— Sir Brian Urquhart, KCMG, MBE; ✉ 50 West 29th St, New York 10001; Howard Farm, Tyringham, Massachusetts 01264

URQUHART, James Graham; CVO (1983); s of James Urquhart (d 1982), of Edinburgh, and Mary, *née* Clark (d 1984); *b* 23 April 1925; *Educ* Berwickshire HS; *m* 1 Oct 1949, Margaret, da of Earnest Hutchinson (d 1982), of Rock Ferry; 2 da (Janet b 10 May 1952, Alison b 18 May 1955); *Career* British Rail: mgmnt trainee 1949–52, dist traffic supt Perth 1960–62, divnl mangr Glasgow 1964–67, asst gen mangr York 1967–69, chief operating offr BR HQ 1969–72, personnel dir BRHQ 1972–74, gen mangr London Midlands Region 1975–77, memb Bd Ops and Productivity 1977–85, memb Bd Exports 1985–86, ret; chm: British Transport Police 1977–86, BR Engineering 1982–86, Transmark 1983–86, Freightliner 1983–86, FIOX Ltd 1989–93; dir: Park Air Electronics Ltd 1986–89, Waterslides plc 1987–89, Systems Connection Group 1988–91, CVC Ltd 1989–91; MIT 1978, MIMH 1979, CIMgt 1982, fell Inst of Personnel 1983; *Recreations* golf, reading; *Style*— James Urquhart, Esq, CVO; ✉ 10 Wychcotes, Caversham, Reading, Berks (☎ 0118 947 9071)

URQUHART, Lawrence McAllister; s of Robert Urquhart (d 1993), of Cirencester, Glos, and Josephine McEwan, *née* Bissell (d 1988); *b* 24 Sept 1935; *Educ* Strathallan Sch Perthshire, King's Coll London (LLB); *m* 26 Aug 1961, Elizabeth Catherine, da of William Burns (d 1952); 3 s (Douglas b 1964, Ross b 1965, Guy b 1971), 1 da (Caroline b 1972); *Career* qualified CA; appts: Price Waterhouse 1957–62, Shell International Petroleum 1962–64, PA Management Consultants 1964–68; sr gp exec Charterhouse Group Ltd 1968–74; gp fin dir: Tozer Kemsley and Millbourn Holdings 1974–77, Burmah Oil Co Ltd 1977–82; chief exec Castrol Ltd 1982–85, gp chief exec Burmah Oil plc 1988–90 (gp md 1985–88); currently non-exec chm: Burmah Castrol plc, English China Clays plc, Scottish Widows' Fund and Life Assurance Society; non-exec dir: BAA plc 1993–, Kleinwort Benson plc 1994–; CIMgt, FInstPet; *Recreations* golf, music; *Clubs* Frilford Heath Golf, Sendford Springs Golf; *Style*— Lawrence Urquhart, Esq; ✉ Burmah Castrol plc, Burmah Castrol House, Pipers Way, Swindon, Wiltshire SN3 1RE (☎ 01793 511521)

URQUHART, Peter William; s of Maj-Gen Ronald Walton Urquhart, CB, DSO, DL (d 1968), of Meredith, Tibberton, Gloucestershire, and Jean Margaret, *née* Moir; *b* 10 July 1944; *Educ* Bedford Sch, Pembroke Coll Cambridge (BA, MA); *m* 1 May 1976, The Hon Anne Serena, da of Lord Griffiths, of Kensington, London; 1 s (James b 1980), 3 da (Katherine b 1978, Flora b 1981, Serena b 1984); *Career* RMA Sandhurst 1963–64, Lt RE 1964–69; stockbroker: James Capel 1969–75, Gilbert Elliot 1975–76, Sheppards & Chase 1976–79, Mercury Asset Management (formerly Warburg Investment Management) 1981–96 (dir 1984–96); non-exec dir Phase Eight 1996–; *Recreations* field sports, racing, golf, gardening; *Style*— Peter Urquhart, Esq; ✉ Fisherton de la Mere House, Warminster, Wiltshire BA12 0PZ

URQUHART, His Hon Judge Peter William Gordon; s of Gordon Eldridge Urquhart (d 1983), and Constance Margaret, *née* Taylor (d 1984); *b* 18 March 1934; *Educ* Liverpool Coll, Peterhouse Cambridge (MA, LLB); *m* 5 Sept 1965, Carolyn Hemingway, da of Frank Bristow Hines; 1 s (Nathaniel Gordon Hemingway b 24 July 1967), 1 da (Jessica Mary Hines b 15 May 1970); *Career* articled to J Stuart Crook Peace Darlington, asst slr Lovell White & King, slr and ptnr Bremner Sons & Corlett Liverpool, ptnr Urquhart Knight & Broughton Liverpool, circuit judge (Northern Circuit); memb Lord Cllr's Legal Aid Advsy Ctee, memb Equal Opportunities Cmmn; *Recreations* reading, singing, gardening; *Clubs* Athenaeum (Liverpool); *Style*— His Hon Judge Urquhart; ✉ Queen Elizabeth II Law Courts, Derby Square, Liverpool

URQUHART, Hon Ronald Douglas Lauchlan; yr s of Baron Tayside, OBE (Life Peer, d 1975), and Hilda Gwendoline, *née* Harris; name of Lauchlan derives from ancestor in 1745 rebellion nicknamed 'the Big Sword' or 'Lauchlan'; *b* 20 Feb 1948; *Educ* Fettes, Univ of Edinburgh (LLB); *m* 1975, Dorothy May Jackson; *Career* chartered accountant; fin dir Harris & Dixon Insurance Brokers Ltd 1996–; Liveryman Worshipful Co of Needlemakers; *Recreations* golf, backgammon; *Clubs* Caledonian, Hong Kong, West Surrey Golf; *Style*— The Hon Ronald Urquhart; ✉ The Willows, Hill Close, Wonersh, Guildford, Surrey GU5 0QP

URSELL, Bruce Anthony; s of Stuart Ursell, of Edgware, London, and Nancy, *née* Fallowes; *b* 28 Aug 1942; *Educ* William Ellis Sch Highgate; *m* 19 Feb 1966, Anne Carole, da of John Pitt (d 1970); 1 s (Piers John b 1971), 2 da (Philippa Anne b 1972, Virginia Anne b 1974); *Career* mangr Standard Chartered Bank 1961–68, gen mangr Western American Bank 1968–74, chief exec Guinness Mahon & Co Ltd 1984–87 (dir 1974–84), chm Lockton Developments Plc 1985–95, dir Surrey Broadcasting (USA) 1986–93, chief exec British & Commonwealth Merchant Bank plc 1987–90; dir: British & Commonwealth Holdings plc 1987–90, Oppenheimer Fund Management (USA) 1989–90; chm Mgmnt Bd Pannell Kerr Forster 1994–; *Recreations* tennis, theatre, cinema, reading; *Clubs* East India; *Style*— Bruce Ursell, Esq; ✉ 1 The Crescent, Hartford, Cheshire (☎ 01606 781219, fax 01606 781528); MGR Ltd, PO Box 28, Northwich, Cheshire CW8 1QY

URSELL, Rev Philip Elliott; s of late Clifford Edwin Ursell, of Porthcawl, S Wales, and late Hilda Jane, *née* Tucker; *b* 3 Dec 1942; *Educ* Cathays HS Cardiff, Univ Coll Cardiff (BA), St Stephen's House Oxford (MA); *Career* ordained Llandaff Cathedral: deacon 1968, priest 1969; asst curate Newton Nottage 1968–71, asst chaplain Univ Coll Cardiff 1971–77, chaplain The Poly of Wales 1974–77, fell chaplain and dir of studies in music Emmanuel Coll Cambridge 1977–82, princ Pusey House Oxford 1982–, fell St Cross Coll Oxford 1982–, warden Soc of the Holy and Undivided Trinity Ascot Priory 1985–, examining chaplain to the Bishop of London 1986–; *Style*— The Rev P E Ursell; ✉ Pusey House, Oxford OX1 3LZ (☎ and fax 01865 278415); Ascot Priory, Berks SL5 8RT (☎ 01344 885157); 8 Raglan House, Castle Court, Westgate Street, Cardiff CF1 1DN (☎ and fax 01222 665775)

URWICK, Sir Alan Bedford; KCVO (1984), CMG (1978); s of Col L F Urwick; *b* 2 May 1930; *Educ* The Dragon Sch, Rugby, New Coll Oxford (MA); *m* 1960, Marta Yolanda, da of Adhemar Montagne (formerly Peruvian ambass in London 1969–78); 3 s (Christopher, Richard, Michael); *Career* FO 1952–89; served: Brussels, Moscow, Baghdad, Amman, Washington, Cairo; memb Central Policy Review Staff Cabinet Office 1973–75, head Near East and N Africa Dept FCO 1975–76, min Madrid 1977–79; ambass: Jordan 1979–84, Egypt 1984–87; high cmmr Canada 1987–89, Sgt at Arms House of Commons 1989–95; Liveryman Worshipful Co of Glovers; KStJ 1983; Jordanian Order of Independence 1 Class 1984; *Style*— Sir Alan Urwick, KCVO, CMG; ✉ The Moat House, Slaugham Place, nr Haywards Heath, W Sussex RH17 6AL

URWIN, Rt Rev Lindsay Goodall; *see:* Horsham, Bishop of

URWIN, (Terence) Peter; s of John Robson Urwin, of Durham City, and Nancy, *née* Harrison; *b* 28 Oct 1948; *Educ* Durham Johnston Sch, Univ of Liverpool (LLB); *m* 18 Sept 1971, Mary Theresa, da of Phillip J Smith; 1 da (Katharine Louise Fleur); *Career* Durham CC: articled clerk 1971–73, admitted slr 1973, asst slr 1973–74, asst clerk of the Cncl 1974–86, dep co slr 1986–90; dir of admin and co slr Northumberland CC 1990–; clerk to the Ltcy Northumberland 1990–, sec Northumberland Advsy Ctee JPs 1990–, sec gen Cmmrs of Income Tax Northumberland; memb Law Soc (chm Local Govt Gp 1996–97); *Recreations* rugby, painting, crosswords, walking; *Style*— Peter Urwin, Esq; ✉ Buckburns, Brancepeth Village, Durham DH7 8DT (☎ 0191 378 3086, mobile 0385 294759); Northumberland CC, County Hall, Morpeth, Northumberland NE61 2EF (☎ 01670 533200, fax 01670 533238)

USBORNE, (Thomas) Peter; s of Thomas George Usborne (d 1993), and Gerda, *née* Just; *b* 18 Aug 1937; *Educ* Summerfields Sch, Eton, Balliol Coll Oxford, INSEAD (MBA); *m* 30 Oct 1964, Cornelie, da of Alfred Tüecking, of Munich; 1 s (Martin b 3 May 1973), 1 da (Nicola b 12 Dec 1969); *Career* 2 Lt Rifle Brigade, seconded VI KAR 1956–58; co-fndr and md Private Eye Magazine 1962–65, sr scientist Metra Sigma Martech Management Consultancy, publishing dir Macdonald Educational 1968–73, fndr and md Usborne Publishing Ltd; *Recreations* flying, sailing, France; *Clubs* Garrick, Groucho; *Style*— Peter Usborne, Esq; ✉ Usborne Publishing Ltd, Usborne House, 83–85 Saffron Hill, London EC1 (☎ 0171 430 2800)

USHER, Sir (William) John Tevenar; 7 Bt (UK 1899), of Norton, Ratho, Midlothian, and of Wells, Hobkirk, Roxburghshire; s of William Dove Usher (d 1969), and Christa Elizabeth, da of Bruno von Tevenar; suc his kinsman, Sir Robert Edward Usher, 6 Bt (d 1994); *b* 18 April 1940; *Educ* Uppingham; *m* 1, 6 Jan 1962 (m dis 1990), Rosemary Margaret, da of Col Sir Reginald Douglas Henry Houldsworth, 4 Bt, OBE, TD; 2 s (Andrew John b 1963, Michael William Reginald b 1967), 1 da (Caroline Rosemary (Mrs Britz) b 1966); m 2, 1992, Georgina Elizabeth, da of Charles Manclark; *Heir* s, Andrew John Usher b 8 Feb 1963; *Style*— Sir John Usher, Bt; ✉ 7 Thorngate Road, Scotsville, Pietermaritzburg, South Africa

USHER, (Andrew) Michael; s of Francis George Usher (d 1993); *b* 15 Oct 1938; *Educ* Cheltenham Coll; *m* 1964, Anne, *née* Whittington; 3 s, 1 da; *Career* admitted slr 1964; sec British Investment Trust plc 1979–86, dir The Fleming Fledgeling Investment Trust plc 1978–96, ptnr Baillie Gifford & Co 1986–95; *Recreations* genealogy, music, golf; *Clubs* New (Edinburgh), Hon Co of Edinburgh Golfers (Muirfield); *Style*— Michael Usher, Esq; ✉ 12 Blackford Rd, Edinburgh EH9 2DS

USHER, Peter Joseph; CBE (1990, OBE 1980); s of Philip Usher, of Dymchurch, Kent (d 1960), and Gertrude, *née* Capon (d 1964); *b* 28 July 1926; *Educ* Maidstone Tech Sch,

Royal Naval Coll Greenwich; *m* 31 March 1951, Pamela; 2 s (Martin b 1952, David b 1954); *Career* constructor cdr RN Staff of Flag Offr (submarines) 1960–64, Naval constructor overseer 1964–66; Vosper Thornycroft (UK) Ltd: tech gen mangr 1966–68, tech dir 1968–74, dep md 1974–81, md 1981–89, dep chm 1989–90, chm 1990–95; pres Royal Inst of Naval Architects 1993–96; Hon DSc Univ of Southampton 1995; FEng 1987, FRINA, RCNC; *Recreations* golf, music; *Clubs* Naval and Military; *Style—* Peter Usher, Esq, CBE, FEng; ✉ c/o Vosper Thornycroft Holdings plc, Victoria Road, Woolston, Southampton SO19 9RR (☎ 01703 445144, fax 01703 440596, telex 47682 VT WOOL (G))

USHER, (Thomas) Raymond; s of Thomas Edward Usher (d 1987), of Easington, Co Durham, and Catherine, *née* McGourley; *b* 10 April 1932; *Educ* Ryhope Robert Richardson GS Co Durham, Univ of Sheffield (BA); *m* 1, 11 Feb 1956, Clare (d 1990), da of Antony Wear Elliott, of Durham (d 1976); 1 s (Antony Edward b 1965); m 2, 5 March 1992, Rachel Ann, da of Geoffrey John Stackhouse, of Windermere; *Career* dir: National Employers General Insurance Co Ltd (S Africa) 1972–86, National Employers Life Association Co Ltd (UK) 1976–84, National Underwriters (Reinsurance) Ltd (Bermuda) 1979–85, National Employers' Mutual General Insurance Association (UK) Ltd 1976–88, The Chancellor Group Ltd (Canada) 1986–90, American Family Ltd 1985–90, American Family Health & Sec Co Ltd 1985–90, American Family Life Association Co Ltd 1985–90, East West Insurance Co Ltd 1987–; conslt C E Heath Plc 1990–; chm: Chancellor Insurance Co Ltd (UK) 1985–90, Usher Insurance Services Ltd 1988–, Sino Heath Ltd 1989–, Rodney Smith and Partners Ltd 1988–94, C E Heath Pension Fund Trustees 1989–, Edward Erdman Pension Fund Trustees 1992–; memb Ct of Assts Worshipful Co of Upholders, Liveryman Worshipful Co of Insurers; *Recreations* golf, sailing, horse racing; *Clubs* Royal Thames Yacht, City Livery, Oriental; *Style—* Raymond Usher, Esq; ✉ Parsonage Farmhouse, Church Road, Wanborough, Wiltshire SN4 0BZ (☎ 01793 790818); 12 Stevens Lane, Rotherfield Peppard, Henley-on-Thames, Oxon RG9 5RG (☎ 01491 628069); C E Heath Plc, 133 Houndsditch, London EC3 7AH (☎ 0171 234 4000)

USHER, Shaun David; s of John Gray Usher (d 1988), of Clevedon, Avon, and Judith Usher (d 1986); *b* 18 May 1937; *Educ* Clevedon Secdy Modern Sch; *m* Sylvia May, da of Arthur Joseph White; 1 s (Peter b 19 March 1963); *Career* trainee reporter Clevedon Mercury 1953–54 and 1957–59, Western Daily Press 1954–55, Bristol Evening Post/Western Daily Press 1959–61, entertainments ed Daily Sketch 1970–71 (broadcasting corr 1964–70); Daily Mail: entertainments ed 1971–72, TV critic 1972–78, foreign corr and sr feature writer 1978–83, film critic and video columnist 1983–93, books ed 1993; Best Short Story prize Crime Writers Assoc 1976 and 1977; *Recreations* reading and writing; *Style—* Shaun Usher; ✉ Daily Mail, 2 Derry St, London W8 5TT (☎ 0171 938 6365)

USHERWOOD, Nicholas John; s of Stephen Dean Usherwood, of London and Hazel, *née* Weston (d 1968); *b* 4 June 1943; *Educ* Westminster, Courtauld Inst of Art Univ of London (BA); *m* 1, 1979 (m dis 1990), Henrietta Mahaffy; 1 s (Theodore Patrick John b 1981), 1 da (Constance Hazel Kate b 1985); m 2, 1991, Jilly Szaybo; *Career* lectr in art history Portsmouth and Wimbledon Colls of Art 1965–68, res under Sir Nikolaus Pevsner on Pelican History of Art 1966–68; Royal Acad of Arts: admin 1969–74 (admin Turner Bicentenary Exibition 1974), exhibitions sec 1974–77; dep keeper i/c exhibitions and PR British Museum 1977–78; freelance writer, critic, lectr and exhibition organiser and curator 1978–; curator and cataloguer of exhibitions incl: David Inshaw (Brighton Gallery and Museum) 1978, Algernon Newton RA (Sheffield and Royal Acad of Arts) 1980, The Ruralists (Arnolfini Bristol and Camden Arts Centre) 1981, Tristram Hillier (Bradford and Royal Acad of Arts) 1983, Julian Trevelyan (Watermans Art Centre) 1985, Peter Blake - Commercial Art (Watermans Art Centre Brentford) 1986, Alfred Munnings 1878–1959 (Manchester City Art Galleries) 1986, Mass Observation (Watermans Art Centre Brentford) 1987, Richard Eurich War Paintings (Imperial War Museum) 1991, Sir Sidney Nolan 75th Birthday Retrospective (Terrace Gallery Harewood House) 1992, Richard Eurich Retrospective (Southampton Art Gallery) 1994, David Inshaw (Bristol City Art Gallery) 1995; exhibitions organized: Athena Art Awards 1985–88, Images of Paradise 1989, New Generation (Bonhams London) 1990, Painting Today (Bonhams London) 1991, 1992 and 1993, Endangered Spaces (CPRE/Christies) 1996; regular contrib to: Daily Telegraph, Royal Acad Magazine, Galleries, Modern Painters; regular lectr at regnl art schs; Picker fell and critic in residence Kingston Poly (now Kingston Univ) 1990–91 and 1992–93, memb: CNAA 1976–78, Int Assoc of Art Critics (sec Br section 1995–); Chevalier Order of Leopold II of Belgium 1972; *Recreations* maps (new), music, poetry, new places (town and country), cricket, talking to painters; *Style—* Nicholas Usherwood, Esq; ✉ 17a Abinger Road, Bedford Park, London W4 1EU (☎ 0181 994 2604)

USHERWOOD, Stephen Dean; s of John Frederick Usherwood (d 1964), and Grace Ellen, *née* Crush (d 1966); *b* 14 Sept 1907; *Educ* St Dunstan's Coll London, Oriel Coll Oxford (MA); *m* 1, 27 July 1935, Hazel Doreen, *née* Weston (d 1968); 1 s (Nicholas John b 1943), 1 da (Susan Clare b 1939); m 2, 24 Oct 1970, Elizabeth Ada, *née* Beavington; *Career* Flt Lt RAF attached GCHQ 1941–46; sch master 1931–41; Monitoring Service BBC 1946–56, Education Service BBC 1956–68; author, coll lectr and broadcaster 1968–; *Books* Reign by Reign (1960), The Bible, Book by Book (1962), Shakespeare, Play by Play (1967), History from Familiar Things (1969–71), Britain, Century by Century (1972), Europe, Century by Century (1972), Food, Drink and History (1972), The Great Enterprise, The Story of the Spanish Armada (1982); with Elizabeth Usherwood: Visit Some London Catholic Churches (1982), The Counter Armada 1596: The Journal of the Mary Rose (1983), We Die For The Old Religion (1987), A Saint in the Family (1992); *Recreations* travel, theatre, music; *Clubs* Soc of Authors; *Style—* Stephen Usherwood, Esq; ✉ 24 St Mary's Grove, Canonbury, London N1 2NT (☎ 0171 226 9813)

USTINOV, Sir Peter Alexander; CBE (1975); s of late Iona Ustinov, journalist, and late Nadia Benois, painter (niece of Alexandre Benois, the stage designer); *b* 16 April 1921; *Educ* Westminster, London Theatre Sch; *m* 1, 8 Aug 1940 (m dis 1950), Isolde Denham, actress, da of Reginald Denham, actor (and half-sister of Angela Lansbury, *qv*); 1 da (Tamara b 1945); m 2, 15 Feb 1954 (m dis 1971), Suzanne Cloutier; 1 s (Igor b 1956), 2 da (Pavla b 1954, Andrea b 1959); m 3, 21 June 1972, Hélène du Lau d'Allemans; *Career* actor, producer, director, author and playwright; Nat Serv WWII 1942–46 Royal Sussex Regt, Army Kinematograph Service Directorate of Army Psychiatry; rector Univ of Dundee 1968 and 1971–73, chllr Univ of Durham 1992–; Hon DMus Cleveland Inst of Music 1967, Hon LLD Univ of Dundee 1969, Hon LLD La Salle Coll of Philadelphia 1971, Hon DLitt Lancaster Univ 1972, Hon DLitt Univ of Durham 1992; Hon DUniv: Letherbridge Canada 1974, Univ of Toronto 1984 and 1995, Georgetown Univ Washington DC 1988, Carlton Ottawa 1991, Free Flemish Univ of Brussels 1995; *Television* incl: History of Europe (BBC), Einstein's Universe 1979, The Well Tempered Bach (Emmy nomination) 1984, Thirteen at Dinner 1985, Deadman's Folly 1986, Appointment With Death 1987, Peter Ustinov in China 1987, Peter Ustinov's Russia 1987, Ustinov on the Orient Express 1991–92, Ustinov Meets Pavarotti 1993, Inside The Vatican 1993–94, The Old Curiosity Shop 1994–95, Haydn Gala 1994–95, documentaries on Thailand and Hong Kong 1994–95, An Evening with Sir Peter Ustinov (worldwide TV & video) 1995, Paths of the Gods (documentaray on Greece) 1995–96; *Films* incl: Private Angelo 1949, Odette 1950, Quo Vadis 1950, Beau Brummel 1953), We're No Angels 1955, The Spies 1955, The Sundowners 1960, Spartacus 1960, Romanoff and Juliet 1961, Billy Budd 1962, Topkapi 1963, Blackbeard's Ghost 1967, The Comedians 1967, Hot Millions 1968, Hammersmith Is Out 1971, One of Our Dinosaurs Is Missing 1974, Purple Taxi 1977, Death on the Nile 1977, The Thief of Baghdad 1978, Ashanti 1979, Charlie Chan and the Curse of the Dragon Queen 1980, Evil Under the Sun 1981, Memed My Hawk 1982, The French Revolution 1989, Lorenzo's Oil 1991, The Phoenix and the Magic Carpet 1994; *Operas* dir several operas incl: The Magic Flute (Hamburg) 1968, Les Brigands (Berlin) 1978, The Marriage (Piccola Scala) 1981, Mavra 1982, Katja Kabanowa (Hamburg) 1985, The Marriage of Figaro (Salzburg and Hamburg) 1987, Jolanthe and Francesca da Rimini (Dresden) 1993; *Phonographic recordings* incl: Mock Mozart, Peter and the Wolf, Hary Janos, The Old Man of Lochnagar; *Awards* Benjamin Franklin Medal RSA 1957, UNICEF Award for Distinguished Service 1978, Prix de la Butte (for Dear Me) 1978, Variety Club of GB Best Actor 1979, Commandeur des Arts et des Lettres 1985, elected to Acad of Fine Arts 1988, Britannia Award BAFTA 1992, Critics' Circle Award 1993, Ordem Nacional do Cruzerio do Sul 1994, German Cultural Award 1994, German Bambi 1994, Int Child Survival Award (presented by Jimmy Carter on behalf of UNICEF) 1995, Rudolph Valentino Award (for lifetime achievement in Motion Pictures) 1995, 1995 Norman Cousins Global Governance Award (awarded by The World Federalist Movement); *Books* incl: Add A Dash of Pity (1960), The Loser (1961), Frontiers of the Sea (1966, reissued as God and the State Railways, 1993), Krumnagel (1971), Dear Me (1977), My Russia (1983), Ustinov in Russia (1987), The Disinformer (1989), The Old Man and Mr Smith (1990), Ustinov at Large (1991), and Still at Large (1993, compilations of his columns for the European), Quorable Ustinov (1995, compilation of quotations and witticisms); *Plays* writer of: House of Regrets (1942), Blow Your Own Trumpet (1943), The Banbury Nose (1944), The Indifferent Shepherd (1948), The Man in the Raincoat (1949), The Love of Four Colonels (1951), The Moment of Truth (1951), High Balcony (1952), Romanoff and Juliet (1956), Paris Not So Gay (1958), Photo Finish (1962), Half Way Up the Tree (1967), The Unknown Soldier and His Wife (1967), Overheard (1981), Beethoven's Tenth (1983); *Screenplays* incl: The Way Ahead (1942), School for Secrets (1946), Vice Versa (1947), Private Angelo (1949), Romanoff and Juliet (1961), Billy Budd (1962), The Lady L (1964), Hot Millions (1968), Memed My Hawk (1982); *Recreations* sailing, music, motor cars; *Clubs* Garrick, Arts Theatre, Queens, Royal Automobile; *Style—* Sir Peter Ustinov, CBE; ✉ William Morris Agency (UK) Ltd, 31/32 Soho Square, London W1V 6DG (☎ 0171 434 2191, fax 0171 437 0238)

UTTING, Prof John Edward; JP; s of Henry Alphege Utting (d 1979), of Liverpool, and Theresa Gladys, *née* Mullins (d 1983); *b* 17 March 1932; *Educ* Liverpool Coll, Peterhouse Cambridge (MA, MB BChir); *m* 27 Oct 1958, Dr Jean Oliver (d 1991), da of James Gerrard, JP, of St Andrews, Fife; 1 s (James Henry b 14 Aug 1965), 3 da (Clare Helen (Mrs Sanderson) b 10 Aug 1959, Mary Elizabeth (Mrs White) b 11 Aug 1960, Catherine Emily (Mrs Barton) b 17 Jan 1962); *Career* Univ of Liverpool: sr lectr in anaesthesia 1970–77, prof of anaesthesia 1977–94, pro vice chllr 1987–90, emeritus prof 1994–; vice pres Govrs Liverpool Coll 1995– (chm 1986–90), chm Linacre Centre for Study of Med Ethics 1987–95; memb: Liverpool Med Instn, RSM; *Books* General Anaesthesia (jtly, 4 and 5 edns), various papers on anaesthesia; *Style—* Prof John Utting, JP; ✉ Sanjo, Green Lane, Liverpool L18 2EP (☎ 0151 722 0501); University Department of Anaesthesia, The University, PO Box 147, Liverpool L69 3BX (☎ 0151 709 0141, fax 0151 708 6502, telex 627095 UNILPL G)

UTTING, Sir William Benjamin; kt (1991), CB (1985); s of John William Utting (d 1968), of Great Yarmouth, and Florence Ada Anne, *née* Thompson (d 1961); *b* 13 May 1931; *Educ* Great Yarmouth GS, New Coll Oxford (MA), Barnett House Oxford (Cert Social Work); *m* 27 Dec 1954, Mildred Sadie, da of David Whiteford Jackson (d 1967), of Grantham; 2 s (Andrew John b 1956, Patrick William b 1964), 1 da (Sarah Anne b 1959); *Career* probation offr: Durham 1956–58, Norfolk 1958–61; sr probation offr Durham 1961–64, princ probation offr Newcastle upon Tyne 1964–68, lectr in social studies Univ of Newcastle upon Tyne 1968–70, dir of social servs Royal Borough of Kensington & Chelsea 1970–76, chief inspector Social Servs Inspectorate DHSS 1985–91 (chief social work offr 1976–85), chm Nat Inst for Social Work; dep chm Goldsmith's Coll; tstee: Mental Health Fndn, Joseph Rowntree Fndn, Community Service Volunteers, Family Fund Tst; memb: Assoc of Dirs of Social Servs, Br Assoc of Social Workers, Social Care Assoc, Nolan Ctee 1995; hon fell New Coll 1996, Hon LittD Univ of E Anglia 1992; FRSA; *Recreations* literature, art, music; *Style—* Sir William Utting, CB; ✉ 76 Great Brownings, College Road, Dulwich, London SE21 7HR (☎ 0181 670 1201)

UTTLEY-MOORE, William James (Bill); CBE (1988); s of William Uttley-Moore (d 1973), and Louisa Clara, *née* Ward; *b* 19 July 1944; *Educ* Erith Tech Sch, S E London Tech Coll, Borough Poly (BSc); *m* 4 June 1966, Jennifer, da of late Henry James Benger; 1 s (William Daren b 4 April 1972); *Career* student apprentice and devpt engr Cintel Ltd 1960–68, project ldr Molins Machine Co Ltd 1968–69; Computing Devices Co Ltd: chief engr 1969–75, tech dir 1975–79, md 1979–85, chm and md 1985–; fndr dir: Sussex Trg and Enterprise Cncl, Southern Sound Local Radio; dir: Southdown TV, 1066 Country Devpt Panel, Castleham Industries, Hastings Economic Development Company; chm: Sussex Inst of Dirs, Indust Section Hastings C of C; memb: Chancellor's Advsy Gp Univ of Sussex, Defence Scientific Advsy Cncl; govr William Parker Secdy Sch; CEng, FEng 1993, FIEE, FRAeS; *Recreations* practical engineering, running, walking, nature, classical music, charities; *Style—* Bill Uttley-Moore, Esq, CBE, FEng; ✉ Tilekiln Farm, Ore, Hastings, E Sussex TN35 5EL; Computing Devices Company Ltd, St Leonards-on-Sea, E Sussex TN38 9NJ (☎ 01424 798001, fax 01424 855042, e-mail WUM@mhs.compd.com)

UTTON, Prof Michael Arthur; s of Arthur Leslie Utton (d 1987), and Lucy Eileen, *née* Gepp; *b* 19 Sept 1939; *Educ* Westcliff HS, Univ of Nottingham (BA), Univ of Reading (PhD); *m* 11 Oct 1963, Vera, da of Robert Georg Niebler, of Langenfeld; 3 s (Ralph b 1966, Oliver b 1968, Tim b 1970); *Career* asst Univ of Glasgow 1961–62, res Economist Intelligence Unit 1962–64; conslt: Nat Inst of Economic and Social Res 1970–84, Euro Cmmn 1985–87; prof Dept of Econs Univ of Reading 1986– (lectr 1964–79, reader 1979–86), conslt OECD 1987–88; *Books* Industrial Concentration (1970), Diversification and Competition (1979), The Political Economy of Big Business (1982), The Profits and Stability of Monopoly (1986), The Economics of Regulating Industry (1986), Market Dominance and Antitrust Policy (1995); *Recreations* opera, theatre, cycling; *Style—* Prof Michael Utton; ✉ Department of Economics, University of Reading, Whiteknights, PO Box 218, Reading RG6 2AA (☎ 0118 931 8231, fax 0118 975 0236)

UVAROV, Dame Olga; DBE (1983, CBE 1978); da of Nikolas Uvarov, and Elena Uvarov; *Educ* Royal Veterinary Coll; *Career* private veterinary practice 1934–53, clinical res pharmaceutical indust 1953–70, head of Veterinary Advsy Dept Glaxo Laboratories 1967–70, Br Veterinary Assoc Tech Info Serv 1970–76, worked on MAFF Ctees (under Medicines Act 1968) 1972–77, memb Medicines Cmmn 1978–82; pres: Soc of Women Veterinary Surgeons 1947–49, Central Veterinary Soc 1952–53, Assoc of Veterinary Teachers and Res Workers 1967–68, Comparative Medicine Section RSM 1967–68, Int Affairs Section RSM 1983–, Royal Coll of Veterinary Surgeons 1976–77 (memb Cncl 1968–88), Laboratory Animal Science Assoc 1984– (vice pres 1983–85); vice pres: Res Def Soc 1982 (hon sec 1978–82), Inst of Animal Technicians 1983, Univ Fedn of Animal Welfare 1986–91 (memb Cncl 1983–91, hon life memb 1991–); Hon DSc Guelph Canada 1976; hon life memb The Laboratory Animal Science Assoc 1993; FRCVS 1973 (memb 1934, memb Cncl 1968–88), fell RVC 1979, hon fell RSM 1982, FIBiol 1983; Victory Gold

Medal Central Veterinary Soc 1965; *Books* The Veterinary Annual, Int Encyclopaedia of Veterinary Medicine, many publications in the Veterinary Record and other journals; *Style*— Dame Olga Uvarov, DBE; ✉ Silverlands, 36 Wellington Road, Hatch End, Middx HA5 4NW

UXBRIDGE, Earl of; Charles Alexander Vaughan Paget; s and h of 7 Marquess of Anglesey, DL, *qv*; *b* 13 Nov 1950; *Educ* Eton, Exeter Coll Oxford, Sussex Univ (MA, DPhil); *m* 1986, Georganne Elizabeth Elliott, da of Col John Alfred Downes, MBE, MC, of Tudor Cottage, Whittlesford, Cambs; 1 s (Lord Paget de Beaudesert b 11 April 1986), 1 da (Lady Clara Elizabeth Isis b 12 Sept 1988); *Heir* s, Benedict Dashiel Thomas, Lord Paget de Beaudesert; *Style*— Earl of Uxbridge; ✉ Plas Newydd, Llanfair PG, Anglesey, Wales

UZIELL-HAMILTON, Her Hon Judge; Adrianne Pauline; da of late Dr Marcus Grantham, and Ella Grantham; *b* 14 May 1932; *Educ* Maria Gray's Acad for Girls; *m* 1952, Mario Reginald Uziell-Hamilton; 1 s, 1 da; *Career* called to the Bar Middle Temple 1965 (ad eundem Inner Temple 1976), head of chambers 1976–90, recorder Crown Ct 1985–90, circuit judge (SE Circuit) 1990–; memb: Legal Aid Panel 1969–90, Gen Cncl of the Bar 1970–74 (memb Exec Ctee 1973–74); pres Mental Health Review Tbnl; govr Univ of N London 1986–; former memb Med Ethics Ctee: Nat Hosps Queen Sq, Camden and Islington District; former memb Parole Bd; author of various articles on pre-marriage contracts; FRSA; *Recreations* collecting theatre and ballet costume design, cooking for my friends, conversation; *Style*— Her Hon Judge Uziell-Hamilton; ✉ Wood Green Crown Court, Woodall House, Lordship Lane, London N22 5LF

UZIELLI, (William) John; s of Herbert Rex Uzielli, ICS, CIE, JP (d 1961); *b* 2 March 1937; *Educ* Marlborough, Trinity Coll Oxford (MA); *m* 1968, Angela Mary, *née* Carrick; 1 s, 1 da; *Career* insur broker, memb Lloyd's, conslt Gibbs Hartley Cooper; tstee Jt Educnl Tst, sec Marlburian Club; *Recreations* golf, gardening; *Clubs* Royal and Ancient Golf, Berkshire Golf, Trevose Golf, City of London; *Style*— John Uzielli, Esq; ✉ Buckhurst Park Cottage, Cheapside, Ascot, Berks (☎ 01344 22932, office 0171 247 5433)

V

VADASZ, Dr Imre Mihail; s of Imre Vadasz (d 1944), of Budapest, Hungary, and Renee, *née* Rasko; *b* 8 March 1938; *Educ* Guy's Hosp Med Sch, Univ of London (MB BS); *m* 22 April 1989, Bridget Christine, da of Raymond Joseph Mannion (d 1974); *Career* sr registrar Guy's Hosp 1967–70, conslt physician and rheumatologist Dartford and Gravesend Hosps 1970–, clinical tutor Univ of London 1973–81; cncl memb Nat Assoc of Clinical Tutors 1977–81; FRCP 1972 (MRCP 1966); *Recreations* sailing, flying; *Clubs* Royal Ocean Racing; *Style*— Dr Imre Vadasz; ✉ Silver Birches, Bower Lane, Shoreham, Kent TN15 6XT (☎ 01959 525562)

VADGAMA, Prof Pankaj; s of Maganlal Premji Vadgama (d 1963), of London, and Champaben, *née* Gajjar; *b* 16 Feb 1948; *Educ* King's Sch Harrow, Orange Hill GS, Univ of Newcastle (MB BS, BSc, PhD, MRCPath); *m* 1977, Dixa, da of Mohanlal Bakrania; 1 s (Rooshin b 2 Nov 1979), 2 da (Reena b 10 March 1978, Preeya b 1 May 1988); *Career* house physician Newcastle Gen Hosp 1971–72, demonstrator in histopathology 1972, sr registrar in clinical biochemistry Royal Victoria Infirmary Newcastle 1977–78 (registrar 1973–77), MRC trg fell Univ of Newcastle 1978–81, sr registrar in clinical biochemistry Newcastle Gen Hosp 1981–83; Univ of Newcastle: princ res assoc 1983–87, dir of Biosensor Gp 1987–88; prof of clinical biochemistry Univ of Manchester 1988–, head Dept of Med Hope Hosp 1992– (hon chemical patholgist 1988–); memb: Med Engrg & Sensors Ctee SERC 1987–92, Molecular Sensors Ctee LINK/SERC 1989–96, Project Mgmnt Gp EC Concerted Action on In Vito Sensors 1988–96, MEDLINK 1995–, EPSRC Med Engrg Coll 1994–; memb Editorial Bd: Analyst and Analytical Communications (RSC) 1990–, Medical Engrineering and Physics; sec UK Heads of Academic Depts of Clinical Biochemistry 1992–96; IEE Engineering Sci and Educn Jl Prize 1994, Sandoz lectr Br Geriatrics Soc 1989, invited lectr to numerous other meetings and confs; invited organiser of scientific meetings for: Br Biophysical Soc, IEE, Assoc of Clinical Biochemists, American Chemical Soc, etc; awarded £1m of grants for res into biosensors since 1989; memb: Br Biophysical Soc 1987, Assoc of Clinical Biochemists 1988; FRCPath 1989, FRSC 1996; *Publications* author of numerous original articles and reviews in scientific jls on biosensors; *Recreations* reading, walking, cycling; *Style*— Prof Pankaj Vadgama; ✉ 4 The Sidings, Worsley, Manchester M28 2QD (☎ 0161 793 8504); Department of Medicine, Hope Hospital, Stott Lane, Salford, Manchester M6 8HD (☎ 0161 787 4428, fax 0161 787 4429)

VAES, Baron Robert R L; Hon KCMG 1968; *Educ* Brussels Univ (LLD); *m* 22 July 1947, Anne Albers; 1 da (Corinne (Lady John Wellesley)); *Career* joined Belgian Dip Serv 1946; served: Washington, Paris, Hong Kong, London, Rome Madrid; personal private sec to Min of Foreign Trade 1958–60, dir-gen of political affairs 1964–66, perm under-sec Min of Foreign Affairs (Foreign Trade and Devpt Cooperation 1966–72); ambass: Spain 1972–76, UK 1976–84; dir Sotheby's 1984–; cr Baron (Kingdom of Belgium) 1985; Grand Offr Order of Leopold Belgium, Grand Offr Legion of Honour France, Grand Cross Order of Isabel the Catholic Spain; *Recreations* bridge; *Clubs* White's, Pratt's, Anglo-Belgian; *Style*— Baron Vaes, KCMG; ✉ The Orangery, Langley Park, Bucks SL3 6DW; Sotheby's, 34/35 New Bond St, London W1A 2AA (☎ 0171 408 5378)

VAISEY, David George; CBE (1996); s of William Thomas Vaisey (d 1992), and Minnie, *née* Payne (d 1987); *b* 15 March 1935; *Educ* Rendcomb Coll Glos, Exeter Coll Oxford (BA, MA); *m* 7 Aug 1965, Maureen Anne, da of August Alfred Mansell (d 1939); 2 da (Katharine b 1968, Elizabeth b 1969); *Career* Nat Serv 1954–56, 2 Lt Glos Regt, seconded KAR 1955–56 serv Kenya; archivist Staffs CC 1960–63, asst (later sr asst) librarian Bodleian Library Oxford 1963–75, dep keeper Univ of Oxford Archives 1966–75, keeper of western manuscripts Bodleian Library Oxford 1975–86, Bodley's librarian 1986–96, keeper Univ of Oxford Archives 1995–; professorial fell Exeter Coll Oxford 1975–, visiting prof library studies UCLA 1985, memb Royal Cmmn on Historical Manuscripts 1986–, hon res fell Sch of Library Archive and Info Studies UCL 1987–, chm Nat Cncl on Archives 1988–91; visiting prof Texas Christian Univ Fort Worth Texas 1991; tstee Kraszna Krausz Fndn 1991–; Encomienda Order of Isabel la Católica (Spain) 1989; FRHistS 1973, FSA 1974; *Books* Staffordshire and the Great Rebellion (jtly, 1964), Probate Inventories of Lichfield and District 1568–1680 (1969), Victorian and Edwardian Oxford from Old Photographs (jtly, 1971), Oxford Shops and Shopping (1972), Art for Commerce (jtly, 1973), Oxfordshire, A Handbook for Local Historians (jtly, 1973, 2 edn 1974), The Diary of Thomas Turner 1754–65 (1984, revised 1985 and 1995); *Style*— David Vaisey, Esq, CBE, FSA; ✉ Bodleian Library, Oxford OX1 3BG (☎ 01865 277166, fax 01865 277182)

VAIZEY, Baroness; Marina Alandra; o da of late Lyman Stansky, of New York, USA, and late Ruth Stansky; *b* 16 Jan 1938; *Educ* Brearley Sch New York, Putney Sch Putney Vermont, Radcliffe Coll, Harvard Univ (BA), Girton Coll Cambridge (MA); *m* 1961, Baron Vaizey (Life Peer, d 1984); 2 s (Hon Thomas b 1964, Hon Edward b 1968), 1 da (Hon Polly (Hon Mrs McAndrew) b 1962); *Career* art critic: Financial Times 1970–74, Sunday Times 1974–91; dance critic Now! 1979–81; ed Nat Art Collections Fund Publications 1991–94, conslt Nat Art Collections Fund 1994–; memb Visual Arts Advsy Ctee Br Cncl 1987–; tstee: Arts Cncl 1975–78, Nat Museums and Galleries on Merseyside 1986–, Crafts Cncl 1988–94, Geffrye Museum London 1990–, Imperial War Museum 1991–, South Bank Centre 1993–, 20th Century Soc 1995–; author, broadcaster, exhibition organiser, lecturer, ctee memb; *Books* 100 Masterpieces of Art (1979), Andrew Wyeth (1980), The Artist as Photographer (1982), Peter Blake (1985), Christo (1990), Christiane Kubrick (1990); *Recreations* arts, travel; *Style*— The Lady Vaizey; ✉ 24 Heathfield Terrace, Chiswick, London W4 4JE (☎ 0181 994 7994, fax 0181 995 8057)

VALDINGER, Jan Robin; s of Maj Stefan Valdinger-Vajda, MC, of Chertsey, Surrey, and Peggy, *née* Chadwick; *b* 28 Sept 1945; *Educ* Univ of Newcastle upon Tyne (LLB); *m* 28 Sept 1974, Rosemary Jane, da of Brendan O'Conor Donelan, of Esher, Surrey; 1 s (Stefan b 1975), 2 da (Anna b 1977, Juliet b 1980); *Career* articled clerk Pinsent & Co 1968–70, slr Clifford Turner & Co 1970–74, corp fin exec Morgan Grenfell & Co 1974–79; Standard Chartered Merchant Bank Ltd (now known as West Merchant Bank): chief exec Merchant Banking Div India 1979–83, md Hong Kong 1983–87, dir Advsy Servs London 1987–91; dir of corp servs TI Group plc 1991–92, ptnr Jaques & Lewis 1992–94, md Investment Strategies 1994–95; chief-exec PPF Investment Company 1996–; memb Law Soc; *Clubs* Hong Kong, Royal Hong Kong Jockey, Burhill Golf; *Style*— Jan Valdinger, Esq; ✉ Bechovicka 18, 100 00 Prague 10, Czech Republic (☎ 00 42 2 771142); PPF Investment Company, Oldrichova 15, 128 00 Praha 2, Czech Republic (☎ 00 42 2 692 6649/6107/6134, fax 00 42 2 692 6520)

VALE, Dr (John) Allister; s of John Richard Vale (d 1994), of Grappenhall, Cheshire, and Ellen, *née* Warburton; *b* 13 June 1944; *Educ* Co GS Altrincham, Guy's Hosp London (MB BS, MD); *m* 4 Sept 1971, Elizabeth Margaret Hastings, da of Brig Leonard Walter Jubb (d 1979), of Chislehurst, Kent; 2 da (Fiona b 1974, Katherine b 1975); *Career* clinical pharmacologist and dir Nat Poisons Information Service (Birmingham Centre) and W Midlands Poisons Unit City Hosp Birmingham 1982–, co-dir Centre for Chemical Incidents 1996–; sr clinical lectr Dept of Med Univ of Birmingham 1982–; chm MRCP(UK) Part 1 Examining Bd 1995– (sec 1982–95); examiner: RCP (MRCP(UK) and AFOM), Univ of Birmingham (Med and Toxicology), Univ of London (Clinical Pharmacology); conslt to: DOH, DOT, DOE, MOD, CEC, WHO/IPCS; chm West Midlands RHA Advsy Ctee on Chemical Incidents; assoc ed Clinical Toxicology; memb Editorial Bd: Medicine, Drugs, InPharma, Human and Experimental Toxicology, Drug Safety, Adverse Drug Reactions and Toxicological Reviews; memb: Poisons Bd Home Office, W Birmingham Health Authy 1985–90; pres Euro Assoc of Poisons Centres and Clinical Toxicologists 1992–; memb: Br Pharmacological Soc, Br Toxicology Soc; FRSM, FRCP 1984, fell American Acad of Clinical Toxicology 1988 (tstee 1991–), FFOM (by Distinction) 1992, FRCPEd 1994; *Books* Poisoning - Diagnosis and Treatment (with T J Meredith, 1979), A Concise Guide to the Management of Poisoning (with T J Meredith, 1981); *Recreations* reading, photography; *Clubs* National; *Style*— Dr Allister Vale; ✉ National Poisons Information Service (Birmingham Centre), West Midlands Poisons Unit, City Hospital, Birmingham B18 7QH (☎ 0121 507 4120, fax 0121 507 5580); Royal College of Physicians, St Andrews Place, Regents Park, London NW1 4LE (☎ 0171 935 1174 ext 326)

VALE, Brian; CBE (1994, OBE 1977); s of Leslie Vale, of Headcorn, Kent (d 1986), and May, *née* Knowles (d 1983); *b* 26 May 1938; *Educ* Sir Joseph Williamson's Mathematical Sch Rochester, Univ of Keele (BA, DipEd), King's Coll London (MPhil); *m* 12 Dec 1966, Margaret Mary, da of Thomas Ernest Cookson, of Cockerham, Lancs (d 1983); 2 s (Nicholas b 1970, Jonathan b 1977); *Career* Overseas Civil Serv: Northern Rhodesia 1960–63, asst cmmr N Rhodesia London 1964, educn attaché Zambia High Cmmn London 1964–65; Br Cncl: Rio de Janeiro 1965–68, Appts Div London 1968–71, Educn and Sci Div 1972–75, rep Riyadh Saudi Arabia 1975–78, dep controller Educn and Sci Div London 1978–83, dir gen TETOC 1980–81, controller Sci Technol and Educn Div, rep and cultural cnsllr Cairo Embassy 1983–87, asst dir gen Br Cncl London 1987–91, dir Spain and cultural attaché Madrid Embassy 1991–95, regnl dir ME and N Africa 1995, ret; FRSA; *Books* Independence or Death! British Sailors and Brazilian Independence 1822–5 (1996); *Recreations* reading, talking, naval history; *Style*— Brian Vale, Esq, CBE; ✉ 40 Gloucester Circus, Greenwich, London SE10

VALENTIA, 15 Viscount (I 1642, with precedence of 1622); Sir Richard John Dighton Annesley; Bt (I 1620, Premier Baronet of Ireland); also Baron Mountnorris (I 1628); s of 14 Viscount Valentia (d 1983), and Joan, Viscountess Valentia (d 1986); *b* 15 Aug 1929; *Educ* Marlborough, RMA; *m* 10 Aug 1957, Anita Phyllis, o da of William Arthur Joy, of Bristol; 3 s (1 of whom decd), 1 da; *Heir* s, Hon Francis Annesley, *qv*; *Career* Capt RA (ret); farmer Zimbabwe 1957–; schoolmaster Ruzawi Prep Sch Marondera Zimbabwe 1977–83; *Style*— The Rt Hon the Viscount Valentia

VALENTIN, Dr Friedrich Heinrich Hermann; s of Kurt Heinrich Valentin (d 1940), and Margarete Hedwig Eva, *née* Beermann (d 1957); *b* 10 Jan 1918; *Educ* Grunewald Gymnasium Berlin, Univ of Edinburgh, Univ of Witwatersrand (BSc, MSc, PhD); *m* 31 Jan 1953, Nancy, da of George Henry Hitchin (d 1962), of Bury, Lancs; 2 s (Peter Henry b 1959, Leo Kurt b 1964), 1 da (Claire Marguerite b 1955); *Career* offr S African MOD 1942–45, lectr Univ of Natal 1946–49, chem engr Petrocarbon Ltd 1949–51, sr chem engr British Oxygen Co Ltd 1951–55, sr lectr Univ of Cape Town 1955–56, prof of chem engrg Univ of Natal 1957–62, dep dir (research) Warren Spring Labs 1970–82 (head chem engrg 1962–69), consltg chem and environmental engr 1982– (specialist engr in pollution assessment and control); has served over 300 clients in UK and abroad, has acted as tech expert in over 100 legal cases; over 200 scientific and tech papers published incl 31 given at int confs, 4 patents; memb: Nat Soc Clean Air, Filtration Soc Inst of Environmental Assessment, Int Professional Assoc for Environment Affrs, UK Environmental Law Assoc; Eur Ing, CEng, FIChemE, FCIWEM, MConsE, FAE, FRSA; *Books* Absorption in Gas Liquid Dispersions (1965), Odours, Working Party Reports Parts 1 and 2 (ed, 1974–75), Odour Control - A Concise Guide (1980), Silos - Draft Design Code for Silos, Bins, Bunkers and Hoppers (1987); *Recreations* gardening, yoga, jogging, walking, family, writing computer programs, travel; *Style*— Dr Friedrich Valentin; ✉ Elm Tree House, Letchworth Lane, Letchworth, Herts SG6 3ND (☎ 01462 684940, fax 01462 671436)

VALENTINE, David Aitken; s of David Aitken Valentine (d 1979), of Balgrummo, Perth, and Isabella, *née* Dow (d 1983); *b* 31 Jan 1939; *Educ* Perth Acad, CPU Calif (BA, MBA); *m* 15 Nov 1963, Sheena Mairi, da of John McLean (d 1984), of Perth; 1 da (Janine Lynne b 12 July 1966); *Career* corp planning mangr and lectr in Aust 1972, Airfix Products Ltd 1973–76, BSG International (special and subsids) 1976–80, chief exec Bullers plc and subsids 1983–88, dir Valentine Associates 1988–; investment cmmr Australian Trade Cmmn London High Cmmn 1992–96; FRSA; *Books* Insolvency Prevention (1985); *Recreations* shooting, water colour painting; *Clubs* Phyllis Ct; *Style*— David Valentine, Esq; ✉ Sussex House, Berkeley Gardens, Claygate, Esher, Surrey (☎ 01372 468430, fax 01372 464956); Res Gordon Bennett, Boulevard Gordon Bennett, Beaulieu-sur-Mer, Cote d'Azur, France (☎ 00 33 93 01 10 87)

VALENTINE, Dr Donald Graham; s of Rev Cyril Henry Valentine (d 1957), and Ada Grace, *née* Herington (d 1982); *b* 5 Nov 1929; *Educ* East Grinstead Co GS, Trinity Coll Cambridge (BA, MA, LLB), Utrecht Univ Netherlands (Dr Jur); *m* 25 March 1961, Vera Ruth, da of Robert Klinger (d 1954); 2 da (Tessa, Jill); *Career* asst lectr LSE 1954, called to the Bar Lincoln's Inn 1956, lectr LSE 1957, practising barr 1958–, prof of law Univ of Nigeria 1966–67, reader in law LSE 1967–81; chm London Branch Chartered Inst of Arbitrators 1991–93, memb Cncl CIArb 1994–; Liveryman Worshipful Co of Arbitrators 1994, Freeman City of London 1988; FCIArb; *Books* The Court of Justice of the European Coal and Steel Community (1956), The Court of Justice of the European Communities (2 vols, 1966); *Recreations* greenhouse gardening; *Clubs* Garrick, Royal Over-Seas

League; *Style—* Dr D G Valentine; ✉ 1 Atkin Building, Gray's Inn, London WC1R 5AT (☎ 0171 404 0102, fax 0171 405 7456)

VALENTINE, Ian Balfour; s of Andrew Valentine (d 1977), of Glasgow, and Elizabeth, *née* Balfour; *b* 17 Oct 1940; *Educ* Hutchesons' Boys GS; *m* 7 June 1967, Elaine, da of James Harris; 1 s (Mark Andrew b 16 April 1969), 1 da (Claire Harris b 7 Oct 1971); *Career* trainee chartered accountant J Wylie & Ballantine Glasgow 1958–63, ptnr Wylie Guild & McIntyre 1965, regnl managing ptnr Scotland BDO Stoy Hayward 1985–96, sr ptnr 1996–; memb Ayrshire and Arran Health Bd 1981–93, memb Cncl Inst of Chartered Accountants of Scotland 1989–; MICAS 1963; *Recreations* golf, rugby; *Clubs* Royal Troon Golf (capt); *Style—* Ian Valentine, Esq; ✉ Senior Partner, BDO Stoy Hayward, 64 Dalblair Road, Ayr KA7 1UH (☎ 01292 263277, fax 01292 268852)

VALENTINE, Michael Robert; s of Alfred Buyers Valentine, CB (d 1970), and Violet Elise; *b* 16 Jan 1928; *Educ* Shrewsbury, Corpus Christi Coll Cambridge (MA); *m* 1957, Shirley Josephine, *née* Hall; 1 s (James b 1964), 2 da (Josephine b 1958, Helen b 1960); *Career* Lt RCS; sr mangr Cooper Brothers & Co CAS 1957–60; dir: S G Warburg & Co Ltd 1966–88 (vice-chm 1986–88, non-exec dir 1991–96), Mercury Securities Ltd 1974–86, S G Warburg Group plc 1986–91 (non-exec 1988–91); Croda International plc: non-exec dir 1982–86, vice-chm 1986–89, chm 1989–; non-exec dir Reckitt & Colman plc 1986–; FCA; *Recreations* opera, vintage cars, social life, travel; *Style—* Michael Valentine, Esq; ✉ Croda International plc, 168/173 High Holborn, London WC1V 7AF (☎ 0171 836 7777)

VALIOS, Nicholas Paul; QC (1991); *b* 5 May 1943; *Educ* Stonyhurst; *m* 2 Sept 1967, Cynthia Valerie; 1 s (Mark b 11 Sept 1973), 1 da (Natalie b 6 Aug 1969); *Career* called to the Bar Inner Temple 1964, recorder of the Crown Ct 1986– (asst recorder 1981), head of chambers; *Recreations* windsurfing, computing; *Style—* Nicholas Valios, Esq, QC; ✉ Francis Taylor Building, Temple, London EC4Y 7BY (☎ 0171 353 7768, fax 0171 353 0659)

VALLANCE, Dr Elizabeth Mary (Lady Vallance); JP (Inner London); da of William Henderson McGonnigill, and Hon Jean, da of 1 Baron Kirkwood of Bearsden; *b* 8 April 1945; *Educ* Univ of St Andrews (MA), LSE (MSc), Univ of London (PhD); *m* 5 Aug 1967, Sir Iain Vallance, *qv*; 1 da (Rachel Emma Jane b 1972), 1 s (Edmund William Thomas b 1975); *Career* chm St George's Healthcare NHS Tst; Sloan fell London Business Sch; univ lectr, reader in politics Queen Mary and Westfield Coll Univ of London (head Dept of Political Studies 1985–88); dir: HMV Group, Norwich Union; author; *Books* The State, Society and Self-Destruction (1975), Women in the House (1979), Women of Europe (1985), Member of Parliament (jtly, 1987, 2 edn 1990), Business Ethics in a New Europe (jtly, 1992), Business Ethics at Work (1995); *Style—* Dr Elizabeth Vallance, JP; ✉ St George's Healthcare Trust, St George's Hospital, Blackshaw Road, London SW17 0QT

VALLANCE, Sir Iain David Thomas; kt (1994); s of Edmund Thomas Vallance, CBE, ERD; *b* 20 May 1943; *Educ* Edinburgh Acad, Dulwich Coll, Glasgow Acad, Brasenose Coll Oxford (BA), London Business Sch (MSc); *m* 5 Aug 1967, Dr Elizabeth Mary Vallance, JP, *qv*; 1 da (Rachel Emma Jane b 1972), 1 s (Edmund William Thomas b 1975); *Career* joined GPO 1966; British Telecommunications (BT) plc: dir (following separation from GPO) 1981–, chief of operations 1985–86, chief exec 1986–95, chm 1987–; non-exec vice chm Royal Bank of Scotland Group plc 1994– (dir 1993–); memb: Pres's Ctee CBI, Int Advsy Bd Br-American C of C, Listed Cos Advsy Ctee London Stock Exchange, Pres's Ctee European Fndn for Quality Mgmnt, Pres's Ctee and Advsy Cncl Business in the Community; chm Princess Royal Tst for Carers, tstee Police Fndn; fell and govr London Business Sch, hon govr Glasgow Acad; Liveryman Worshipful Co of Wheelwrights, Freeman City of London; Hon DSc Univ of Ulster, Hon DSc Napier Univ, Hon DTech Loughborough Univ of Technol, Hon DBA Kingston Univ; *Recreations* walking, playing the piano, listening to music; *Style—* Sir Iain Vallance; ✉ British Telecommunications plc, 81 Newgate Street, London EC1A 7AJ (☎ 0171 356 5000)

VALLANCE, Michael Wilson; s of Vivian Victor Wilson Vallance (d 1967), of Wandsworth and Helston, Cornwall, and Kate, *née* Edwards (d 1986); *b* 9 Sept 1933; *Educ* Brighton Coll, St John's Coll Cambridge (MA); *m* 1 April 1970, Mary Winifred Ann, da of John Steele Garnett (d 1969), of Runcorn, Cheshire; 1 s (Vivian b 1974), 2 da (Rachel b 1971, Emma b 1972); *Career* staff memb United Steel Companies Ltd 1952–53; asst master: Abingdon Sch 1957–61, Harrow Sch 1961–72; headmaster: Durham Sch 1972–82, Bloxham Sch 1982–91; conslt to World Challenge Expeditions 1991–, dir World Challenge Expeditions Ltd 1992–97 (chm of Bd 1995–97); ctee chm Northern ISIS 1976–77, tstee Bloxham Project 1988–91 (memb Steering Ctee 1986–91), memb HMC 1972–91 (chm NE Div 1981–82), chm of Tstees Cncl for the Registration of Schs Teaching Dyslexic Pupils 1996– (chm of Cncl 1992–96); *Recreations* books, cricket, the sea, gardens (sitting in); *Clubs* MCC, Jesters; *Style—* Michael Vallance, Esq; ✉ 22 Foxholes Hill, Exmouth, Devon EX8 2DQ (☎ 01395 271633, fax 01395 223418)

VALLANCE, Philip Ian Fergus; QC (1989); s of Aylmer Vallance (d 1955), and Helen, *née* Gosse (d 1952); *b* 20 Dec 1943; *Educ* Bryanston, New Coll Oxford (scholar, BA); *m* 23 June 1973, Wendy Lee, da of J D Alston, CBE, of Diss, Norfolk; 1 s (Henry b 6 Dec 1979), 1 da (Lucy b 10 April 1981); *Career* called to the Bar Inner Temple 1968; *Clubs* Travellers'; *Style—* Philip Vallance, Esq, QC; ✉ 1 Crown Office Row, Temple, London EC4Y 7HH (☎ 0171 797 7500, fax 0171 797 7550)

VALLANCE-OWEN, Dr Andrew John; s of Prof John Vallance-Owen, *qv*, of Cambridge, and Renée, *née* Thornton; *b* 5 Sept 1951; *Educ* Epsom Coll Surrey, Univ of Birmingham Med Sch (MB ChB), Open Univ (MBA); *m* 1977, Frances Mary, da of Albert William Glover (d 1990); 2 s (Anthony Ian b 20 April 1983, Simon Huw b 10 Sept 1985), 1 da (Nicola Louise b 4 July 1988); *Career* surgical trg: Newcastle upon Tyne 1977–80 and 1981–83, Melbourne Aust 1980; BMA: provincial sec N of England 1983–85, Scottish sec 1986–89, head of central servs and int affrs London 1989–94, sec BMA charitable tsts 1989–94; BUPA: med dir BUPA Health Servs Aug 1994–May 1995, group med dir May 1995–; fndn govr and chm Fund-raising Appeal Ctee The Latymer Sch Edmonton; Freeman City of London, Liveryman Worshipful Soc of Apothecaries; memb BMA 1976; FRSCEd 1982, FRSM 1989, FRSA 1992; *Recreations* music, sailing, gardening, photography, family; *Style—* Dr Andrew Vallance-Owen; ✉ 13 Lancaster Avenue, Hadley Wood, Herts EN4 0EP (☎ 0181 440 9503, fax 0181 364 8770); BUPA House, 15–19 Bloomsbury Way, London WC1A 2BA (☎ 0171 656 2037, fax 0171 656 2708, mobile 0836 750252)

VALLANCE-OWEN, Prof John; s of Edwin Augustine Owen (d 1973), of Bangor, N Wales, and Julia May, *née* Vallance (d 1974); *b* 31 Oct 1920; *Educ* Friars Sch Bangor N Wales, Epsom Coll Surrey, St John's Coll Cambridge, The London Hosp (MA, MD); *m* 24 June 1950, Renee, da of Harold Thornton (d 1952), of Stanmore, Middx; 2 s (Andrew, *qv*, b 1951, Colin b 1963), 2 da (Sarah b 1954, Catherine b 1961); *Career* ROC 1939–43; pathology asst and med first asst to Sir Horace Evans London Hosp 1947–51, Rockefeller travelling fell Univ of Pennsylvania Philadelphia USA 1955–56, sr med registrar to Prof Russell Fraser Royal Postgrad Med Sch London Hammersmith Hosp 1951–55 (liaison physician Obstetric Dept 1953–55); Royal Victoria Infirmary Newcastle upon Tyne: conslt physician and lectr in med Univ of Durham 1958–64, conslt physician and reader in med Univ of Newcastle upon Tyne 1964–66; conslt physician and prof of med Queen's Univ Royal Victoria Hosp Belfast NI 1966–82; Prince of Wales Hosp Shatin NT Hong Kong: fndn prof and chm Dept of Med Chinese Univ of Hong Kong 1983–88; assoc dean Faculty Med Chinese Univ of Hong Kong, hon conslt med to Hong Kong Govt 1984–88, hon conslt med Br Army Hong Kong 1985–88, med advsr on clinical complaints NE Thames RHA 1989–96; currently visiting prof Royal Postgrad Med Sch Hammersmith Hosp, conslt physician London Ind Hosp 1988–; memb Northern Health and Social Servs Bd DHSS NI 1973–82 (memb Standing Med Advsy Ctee 1969–73); cncllr: RCP London 1976–79 (regnl advsr NI 1970–75), RCP Ireland 1976–82; memb: RSM, RCPath; *Books* Essentials of Cardiology (1961, 2 edn 1968), Diabetes: Its Physiological & Biochemical Basis (1975); *Recreations* tennis, golf, music; *Clubs* E India, Utd Servs Recreation (Hong Kong); *Style—* Prof John Vallance-Owen; ✉ 17 St Matthews Lodge, Oakley Square, London NW1 1NB (☎ 0171 388 3644); 10 Spinney Drive, Gt Shelford, Cambridge CB2 5LY (☎ 01223 842767); Cuildochart, Killin, Perthshire (☎ 015672 337); London Independent Hospital, Beaumont Sq, London E1 (☎ 0171 790 0990)

VALLANCE WHITE, James Ashton; s of Frank Ashton White, and Dieudonnée, *née* Vallance; *b* 25 Feb 1938; *Educ* Allhallows Sch, Albert Schweitzer Coll Switzerland, St Peter's Coll Oxford (MA); *m* 1987, Anne, *née* O'Donnell; *Career* House of Lords: clerk 1961–71, clerk of ctees 1971–78, chief clerk Public Bill Office 1978–83, princ clerk Judicial Office and Fourth Clerk at the Table 1983–; *Clubs* Brooks's; *Style—* James Vallance White, Esq; ✉ Parliament Office, House of Lords, London SW1A 0PW (☎ 0171 219 3000); 14 Gerald Road, London SW1 (☎ 0171 730 7658); Biniparell, San Luis, Menorca

VALLAT, Prof Sir Francis Aimé; GBE (1981), KCMG (1962, CMG 1955), QC (1961); s of Col Frederick Vallat, OBE (d 1922); *b* 25 May 1912; *Educ* Univ Coll Toronto, Gonville and Caius Coll Cambridge; *m* 1, 1939 (m dis 1973), Mary Alison, da of F H Cockell, of Barnham, Sussex; 1 s, 1 da; m 2, 1988, Patricia Maria (d 1995), da of Capt Hamish Morton Anderson, MB ChB, RAMC; m3, 1996, Joan Olive, wid of Adm Sir F R Parham, GBE, KCB, DSO; *Career* served WWII as Flt Lt RAFVR; called to the Bar Gray's Inn 1935; joined FO 1945, legal advsr Perm UK Delegation to UN 1950–54, dep legal advsr FO 1954–60, legal advsr 1960–68, visiting prof McGill Univ 1965–66; dir Int Law Studies King's Coll London 1968–76, reader Int Law Univ of London 1969–70 (prof 1970–76, prof emeritus 1976–); bencher Gray's Inn 1971–; memb: Int Law Cmmn 1973–81 (chm 1977–78), Permanent Ct of Arbitration 1981–92, Curatorium Hague Acad of Int Law 1982– (vice pres 1993–), Inst of Int Law 1965– (vice pres 1989–91); Dr en dr hc Univ of Lausanne 1979; *Clubs* Hurlingham, Sloane; *Style—* Prof Sir Francis Vallat, GBE, KCMG, QC; ✉ The Old Coach House, Sheeplane, Midhurst, West Sussex GU29 9NT (☎ 01730 813475)

VALLINGS, Vice Adm Sir George Montague Francis; KCB (1986); s of Robert Archibald Vallings, DSC (d 1970), of Perth, Scotland, and Alice Mary Joan, *née* Bramsden (d 1964); *b* 31 May 1932; *Educ* Belhahen Hill Dunbar, RNC Dartmouth; *m* 12 Sept 1964, Tessa Julia, da of Bernard Delacourt Cousins (d 1963), of Haslemere; 3 s (Sam b 10 Jan 1966, Tom b 1 Oct 1968, Andrew b 28 June 1970); *Career* Cdr 1965, CO HMS Defender 1967–68, Exec Offr HMS Bristol 1970–73, Capt 1974, NA Canberra Aust 1974–76, Capt 2 Frigate Sqdn 1977–78, dir Naval Op and Trade 1978–80, Cdre Clyde 1980–82, Rear Adm 1983, Flag Offr Gibraltar 1983–85, Vice Adm 1985, Flag Offr Scotland and NI 1985–87; sec Chartered Inst Mgmnt Accountants 1987–95, non-exec chm Reed Accountancy 1996–; chm Int Sail Trg Assoc 1988–96; memb Cncl: Royal Nat Mission to Deep Sea Fisherman, Bede House Assoc (Bermondsey); FRSA 1992; *Recreations* various sports; *Clubs* Woking Golf, Royal Ocean Racing; *Style—* Vice Adm Sir George Vallings, KCB; ✉ Meadowcroft, 25 St Marys Rd, Long Ditton, Surrey KT6 5EU (☎ 0181 224 2211)

VALLINGS, Robert Ross; s of Lt Cdr Robert Archibald Vallings, DSC, RNVR (d 1969), of Perth, Scotland, and Alice Mary Joan, *née* Bramsdon (d 1964); *b* 18 Nov 1943; *Educ* Rugby; *m* 12 May 1973, Penelope Claire, da of Dr Thomas Parham Lalonde (d 1982), of Romsey, Hants; 1 s (Timothy b 1974), 1 da (Claire b 1975); *Career* admitted slr 1969; ptnr Radcliffes Crossman Block (formerly Radcliffes & Co) 1970–; *Recreations* sport; *Clubs* Naval and Military, Richmond FC, Hurlingham; *Style—* Robert Vallings, Esq; ✉ Radcliffes Crossman Block, 5 Great Coll Street, Westminster, London SW1P 3SJ (☎ 0171 222 7040, fax 0171 222 6208, telex 919302)

VALLIS, Rear-Adm Michael Anthony; CB (1986); s of Ronald William Harvey Vallis (d 1980), of Frome, Somerset, and Sarah Josephine (d 1964); *b* 30 June 1929; *Educ* RNC Dartmouth, RNEC Manadon, RNC Greenwich; *m* 1959, Pauline Dorothy, da of George Abbott (d 1967), of Wymondham, Leics; 3 s, 1 da; *Career* dir Naval Recruiting 1979–82, dir-gen Surface Ships MOD 1983–84, dir-gen Marine Engrg MOD 1984–86 and sr naval rep Bath 1983–86; pres: Inst of Marine Engrs 1991–93, Soc for Underwater Technology 1993–95; memb Cncl (now Senate) Engrg Cncl; FEng 1987; *Recreations* fishing, walking, music, theatre, wine; *Clubs* Royal Over-Seas League; *Style—* Rear-Adm Michael Vallis, CB, FEng; ✉ 4A St Stephen's Close, Bath BA1 5PP (☎ 01225 314286)

VALMAN, Dr (Hyman) Bernard; s of Samuel Valman, and Lillian, *née* Schwoltz; *b* 10 Feb 1934; *Educ* Charterhouse, Univ of Cambridge (MA, MD); *m* 24 May 1964, Thea, da of Maj Weiss (d 1958); 1 s (Martin David b 29 Dec 1969), 1 da (Nadia Deborah b 11 Jan 1968); *Career* Nat Serv Capt RAMC 1959–61; sr registrar The Hosp for Sick Children Gt Ormond St 1969–72, conslt paediatrician Northwick Park Hosp and Clinical Res Centre Harrow 1972–; ed Archives of Disease in Childhood 1982–94; memb Soc of Authors, sec to paediatric ctee of RCP (chm of examining bd for dip in child health); memb: RSM, BPA; FRCP; *Books* Keeping Babies and Children Healthy (1985), 1–7 (3 edn, 1993), The First Year of Life (4 edn, 1994); *Recreations* gardening, editing, writing; *Style—* Dr Bernard Valman; ✉ Northwick Park Hospital, Harrow, Middx HA1 3UJ (☎ 0181 864 3232)

VALNER, Nicholas Edmund (Nick); *b* 14 Sept 1953; *Educ* Stonyhurst, Univ of Oxford (MA); *m*; 3 c; *Career* Frere Cholmeley Bischoff: articled clerk (admitted 1979), ptnr 1985–, currently head of Litigation; chair numerous confs on arbitration law Inst of Arbitrators, frequent speaker IBA, Inst of Civil and Comparative Law and American Bar Assoc; memb: IBA, London Slrs' Litigation Assoc; ACIArb; *Style—* Nick Valner, Esq; ✉ Frere Cholmeley Bischoff, 4 John Carpenter Street, London EC4Y 0NH (☎ 0171 615 8000, fax 0171 615 8080)

VALPY, Peter Francis; s of Kenneth Francis Valpy (d 1986), of Blackheath, London, and Freda Frances, *née* Stone; *b* 4 June 1938; *Educ* King's Canterbury, Univ of Swansea; *m* 13 Jan 1962, Virginia Judith, da of Michael Carter Gower Ringer; 1 s (Edward Francis Ringer b 5 Jan 1970), 2 da (Tessa Frances (Mrs Christopher White) b 23 Oct 1963, Lisa Frances (Mrs Russell Philpott) b 1 Jan 1966); *Career* Nat Serv 2 Lt Royal W Kent Regt Queen's Own Cyprus 1958–60; sr buyer C & A Modes 1967–69 (trainee mangr 1960–67), merchandising mangr Freemans (Liverpool) Ltd 1969–71, merchandising controller Peter Robinson Ltd (part of Burton Group) 1971–74, md Country Casuals Ltd (part of Coats Patons) 1977–86 (gen mangr 1974–77), conslt Textile Market Studies 1986–87, dir Br Knitting & Clothing Export Cncl 1991– (exec dir 1987–91); chm Old King's Scholars Assoc Tst and Bursary Soc; Freeman City of London, Liveryman Worshipful Co of Woolmen; memb Twenty Club; MInsD, FRSA, FIMgt; *Recreations* shooting, wine; *Clubs* Leander, London Rowing, Henley Royal Regatta Stewards; *Style—* Peter Valpy, Esq; ✉ British Knitting & Clothing Export Council, 5 Portland Place, London W1N 3AA (☎ 0171 636 5577, fax 0171 636 7515)

VAN ALLAN, Richard; s of Joseph Arthur Jones, of Mansfield, Notts, and Irene Hannah, *née* Taylor; *b* 28 May 1935; *Educ* Brunts GS Mansfield, Worcester Coll of Educ (Dip Ed), Birmingham Sch of Mus; *m* 1, 1963 (m dis 1974), Elizabeth Mary, da of Bib Peabody (d 1973), of Leamington Spa; 1 s (Guy Richard b 1967); m 2, 31 Dec 1976 (m dis 1987), Elisabeth Rosemary, da of Richard Pickering, DM, of Cape Town, SA; 1 s

(Robert Tristan b 1979), 1 da (Emma Mary b 1983); *Career* operatic bass; former police offr (Sgt Special Investigation Branch, RMP police constable 1953–56) and sch teacher, professional singer 1964–; dir Nat Opera Studio, memb Bd of Dirs ENO 1995–; principal bass at: Glyndebourne, WNO, ENO, Scottish Opera, Royal Opera House Covent Garden, Nice, Bordeaux, Paris, Marseille, Bruxelles, Madrid, San Diego, Miami, Boston, Seattle, Metropolitan NY, Buenos Aires, Victoria State Opera Melbourne; awarded Sir Charles Santley Meml Gift 1995; Hon RAM, fell Birmingham Schs of Music (FBSM); *Recordings* incl: Don Alfonso in Cosi Fan Tutte (Grammy award), Leporello in Don Giovanni (Grammy nomination), Sir Walter Raleigh in Gloriana (Grammy nomination); *Recreations* cricket, golf, shooting; *Style*— Richard Van Allan, Esq; ✉ 18 Octavia Street, London SW11 3DN (☎ 0171 228 8462, fax 0171 228 4367)

VAN CULIN, Rev Canon Samuel; *Educ* Princeton Univ (AB), Virginia Theol Seminary (BD); *Career* curate St Andrew's Cathedral Honolulu 1955–56, canon precenter and rector Hawaiian congregation Honolulu 1956–58, asst rector St John's Washington DC 1958–60, gen sec Lyman Int Washington DC 1960–61, asst sec Overseas Dept Exec Cncl of Episcopal Church USA 1968–76, exec World Mission Episcopal Church USA 1976–83, sec gen Anglican Consultative Cncl 1983–94; hon canon: Canterbury 1983, Jerusalem 1983, Ibadan Nigeria 1984, Cape Town SA 1989, Honolulu 1992; Hon DD Virginia Theol Seminary 1977; *Recreations* music, swimming; *Clubs* Athenaeum, Princeton (NY); *Style*— The Rev Canon Samuel Van Culin; ✉ 16a Burgate, Canterbury, Kent CT1 2HG

van CUTSEM, Geoffrey Neil; yr s of Bernard van Cutsem (d 1975), and Mary (d 1989), da of Capt Edward Compton, JP, DL (s of Lord Alwyne Compton, 2 s of 4 Marquess of Northampton, KG), of Newby Hall, Ripon; yr bro of Hugh van Cutsem, *qv*; *b* 23 Nov 1944; *Educ* Ampleforth; *m* 30 Oct 1969, Sarah, only da of Alastair McCorquodale; 2 da (Sophie b 5 Aug 1975, Zara b 11 Dec 1978); *Career* served RHG (Blues and Royals) 1963–68, Capt 1967; exec dir Savills 1987– (joined 1969); dir Cancer Res Campaign; chm of govrs St Mary's Sch Ascot Berks; FRICS 1973; *Clubs* White's, Pratt's; *Style*— Geoffrey van Cutsem, Esq; ✉ 9a Elm Park Rd, London SW3 6BP (☎ 0171 352 8281); The Old Rectory, Old Somerby, Grantham, Lincs NG33 4AG (☎ 01476 563167); Savills, 20 Grosvenor Hill, London W1X 0HQ (☎ 0171 499 8644)

van CUTSEM, Hugh Bernard Edward; s of Bernard van Cutsem (d 1975), and Mary, da of Capt Edward Compton, JP, DL (himself s of Lord Alwyne Compton, 2 s of 4 Marquess of Northampton, KG), of Newby Hall, Ripon; er bro of Geoffrey van Cutsem, *qv*; *b* 21 July 1941; *Educ* Ampleforth; *m* 1971, Jonkvrouwe Emilie Elise Christine, da of Jonkheer Pieter Quarles van Ufford (Netherlands cr of Willem I 1814), of Westgate House, Hilborough, Thetford; 4 s; *Career* Lt Life Gds; bloodstock breeder, farmer; chm: Kestrel Holdings Inc, Countryside Business Group, Membership and Funding Ctee Game Conservancy Trust; *Clubs* White's, Jockey; *Style*— Hugh van Cutsem, Esq; ✉ Anmer Hall, King's Lynn, Norfolk PE31 6RW (☎ 01485 600508)

van der LEM, Prof Paul Johan; *b* 16 Nov 1943; *Educ* Free Acad The Hague, Rotterdam Acad of Art and Design, Univ State of NY, Municipal Univ of Amsterdam, Leicester Poly; *m* 1971, Martha Thomson Mearns; 2 s (Andrew Cornelis b 1972, Roderic Gerard b 1974); *Career* graphic designer; Erasmus Univ 1967–69, art dir and pubns prodr Excerpta Medica 1969–71; conslt designer 1971–72; film prodr ACT Ltd 1972–73, dir for devpt of educn and trg progs ACT Ltd 1973–77, princ lectr Leicester Poly Sch of Graphic Design 1973–83, head Design Dept London Coll of Printing 1983–89, dean Faculty of Art Media and Design University of the West of England Bristol 1989–; *Style*— Prof Paul van der Lem; ✉ Faculty of Art, Media and Design, University of the West of England, Bower Ashton Campus, Clanage Road, Bristol BS3 2JU (☎ 0117 966 0222, fax 0117 976 3946)

van der MEER, Lydia Anna Petronella; *b* 24 Nov 1962; *Educ* Den Haag Art Acad Holland, Den Haag Sch of Photography; *Career* press photographer; Photoburo 't Sticht (news agency) Utrecht Holland 1986–88, came to UK as freelance photographer 1988–; currently working for Financial Times (since 1988), and European Nat Newspapers and Magazines; *Books* 2 x 24 Hours in the Province of Utrecht, One Day in Belgium; *Style*— Ms Lydia van der Meer; ✉ c/o Picture Desk, Financial Times, Number One Southwark Bridge, London SE1 9HL (☎ 0171 873 3000)

van der WATEREN, Jan Floris; s of Jacob van der Wateren (d 1981), of Pretoria, and Wilhelmina, *née* LaBuschagné; *b* 14 May 1940; *Educ* Univ of Potchefstroon SA (MA), Univ of Sussex, UCL (Dip in Library Studies); *Career* managing librarian RIBA Library 1976–83, dir and Sir Banister Fletcher librarian Br Architectural Library 1984–87, keeper and chief librarian Nat Art Library 1988–; FLA, FRSA, Hon FRIBA 1995; *Clubs* Grolier (NY), Architecture (London); *Style*— Jan Floris van der Wateren, Esq; ✉ 52 Blenheim Crescent, London W11 1NY (☎ and fax 0171 221 6221); National Art Library, Victoria & Albert Museum, London SW7 2RL (☎ 0171 938 8303, fax 0171 938 8275, telex 268831 VICART G, e-mail 100316.3515@COMPUSERVE.COM)

van der WERFF, His Hon Judge; Jonathan Ervine; s of James van der Werff (d 1960), of London, and Clare Poupart, *née* Ervine; *b* 23 June 1935; *Educ* Harrow, RMA Sandhurst; *m* 17 Sept 1968, Katharine Bridget, da of Maj James Colvin (d 1993), of Withypool, Somerset; 2 da (Olivia b 1971, Claudia b 1976); *Career* joined Coldstream Gds 1953, RMA Sandhurst 1954–55, cmmnd 1955, Adj 1 Bn 1962–64, Maj 1967, ret 1968; called to the Bar Inner Temple 1969, recorder 1986, circuit judge (SE Circuit) 1986–, resident judge Croydon Combined Court Centre 1989–93, sr circuit judge 1993, resident judge Inner London Crown Court 1993–; *Clubs* Pratt's, Bembridge Sailing, Something; *Style*— His Hon Judge van der Werff; ✉ Inner London Crown Court, The Sessions House, Newington Causeway, London SE1 6AZ

van der WYCK, Jonkheer Herman Constantyn; s of Jonkheer Hendrik Lodewyk van der Wyck, OBE (d 1986), Col Royal Netherlands Artillery, and Berendina Johanna van Welderen, Baroness Rengers (d 1963); *b* 17 March 1934; *Educ* Inst for Int Studies Univ of Geneva (MA), Rotterdam and Ann Arbour Business Sch (MA); *m* 1, 1959 (m dis 1969), Danielle Mourgue d'Algue; 1 s (Patrick Henri Louis b 5 Dec 1962), 1 da (Edina Nathalie b 8 Aug 1960); m 2, 1977 (m dis 1988), Jonkvrouwe Viviana Olga Paulina van Reigersberg Versluys; 2 s (Edzard Lorillard b 10 Oct 1980, Alexander Lodewyk b 5 Aug 1985); *Career* ret Capt Royal Dutch Cavalry; vice chm and md SBC Warburg; dir: Automobiles Peugeot, Energy International NV; *Recreations* skiing, water skiing, swimming, tennis, reading, music; *Style*— Jonkheer Herman C van der Wyck; ✉ 27 South Terrace, London SW7 2TB (☎ 0171 584 9931); SBC Warburg, 1 Finsbury Avenue, London EC2M 2PP (☎ 0171 395 2268)

van GELDER, Peter Samuel; s of Joseph van Gelder (d 1988), and Sylvia, *née* Cornberg; *b* 12 Aug 1953; *Educ* Westmount HS Montreal, Univ of Aston (BSc), Univ Coll Cardiff (post grad dip in journalism); *m* Mary-Jane, da of Hugh Campbell Drummond; 1 s (Joseph Robert b 22 Jan 1989), 1 da (Katharine Elizabeth b 12 Feb 1992); *Career* news asst BBC Wales Cardiff 1977–78, news prodr and political corr BBC Radio Leeds 1978–81, asst prodr Newsnight BBC TV London 1981–82; TV-am: asst prodr Michael Parkinson Show 1982–84, news reporter 1984–86, prodr Good Morning Britain 1986–88, ed Children's Progs 1988–89, asst managing ed 1989–91, managing ed 1991–93; md Teletext Ltd 1993–; *Books* Offscreen Onscreen (1991); *Recreations* pinball; *Style*— Peter van Gelder, Esq; ✉ Teletext UK, 101 Farm Lane, Fulham, London SW6 1QJ (☎ 0171 386 5000, fax 0171 386 5751)

van HAGEN, Margaret Joan; da of Reginald Howard, of Warley, W Midlands, and Joan Agnes, *née* Davies; *b* 9 Sept 1953; *Educ* Holly Lodge Girls' GS, Univ of Birmingham (LLB); *m* 18 July 1987, Christopher Seymour Nigel, s of Ladislav van Hagen (d 1993), of Christchurch, Dorset; 1 da (Frederika b 15 May 1989); *Career* called to the Bar Middle Temple 1977, lectr law Accountancy Tuition 1978–85, in practice 1985–; memb Bar England and Wales 1977; *Recreations* sailing; *Clubs* Royal Automobile; *Style*— Mrs Margaret van Hagen; ✉ Peter Heppel Chambers, 4 King's Bench Walk, Temple, London EC4Y 7DL (☎ 0171 353 0478, fax 0171 583 3549, car 0836 646478)

VAN HEE, David William; s of Victor George Van Hee (d 1990), of Coventry, Warks, and Vera, *née* Gibson (d 1994); *b* 26 Feb 1949; *Educ* King Henry VIII Sch Coventry, Downing Coll Cambridge (MA, LLB); *Career* called to the Bar Middle Temple 1972, barr SE circuit; *Recreations* gliding; *Clubs* United Oxford and Cambridge, Surrey and Hants Gliding; *Style*— David Van Hee, Esq; ✉ 3 Dr Johnson's Buildings, Temple EC4 (☎ 0171 353 4854, fax 0171 583 8784)

van PRAAG, Lucas; s of Louis van Praag, CBE (d 1993), and Angela, *née* McCorquodale; *b* 12 Jan 1950; *Educ* Frensham Heights Sch, Sch of Navigation Warsash Hants, Univ of Durham (BA); *m* 1996, Miranda, da of Richard Allan; *Career* Bankers Trust Company 1975–85, Sabre International Group Ltd 1986–89, John Brown Publishing Ltd 1989–92, ptnr Brunswick Public Relations Ltd 1992–; *Recreations* reading, sailing, skiing, friends; *Clubs* Groucho; *Style*— Lucas van Praag, Esq; ✉ Brunswick Public Relations Ltd, 16 Lincoln's Inn Fields, London WC2A 3ED (☎ 0171 404 5959, fax 0171 831 2823)

van RIJSBERGEN, Prof Cornelis Joost; s of Jacob Adam van Rijsbergen (d 1987), and Gerritdina, *née* Verheij; *b* 17 Oct 1943; *Educ* Univ of W Aust (BSc), Univ of Cambridge (PhD); *m* 22 May 1965, Juliet Hilary, da of Ernest Arthur Clement Gundry, of Perth, Aust; 1 da (Nicola b 1973); *Career* tutor in mathematics Univ of W Aust 1966–68, lectr Monash Univ 1973–75, Royal Soc res fell Univ of Cambridge 1975–79 (sr res offr King's Coll 1969–72); prof of computer sci: Univ Coll Dublin 1980–86, Univ of Glasgow 1986–; ed-in-chief The Computer Jl 1993–; MBCS 1971, FIEE 1987, FRSE 1994; *Books* Information Retrieval (2 edn, 1979); *Recreations* swimming, cinema, travel, fiction; *Clubs* Utd Oxford & Cambridge Univ; *Style*— Prof Cornelis van Rijsbergen, FRSE; ✉ 14 Park Parade, Cambridge CB5 8AL (☎ 01223 360318); 18A Westbourne Gardens, Glasgow G12 9XD (☎ 0141 339 8331); Department of Computing Science, University of Glasgow, Glasgow G12 8QQ (☎ 0141 330 4463, fax 0141 330 4913, telex 777070 UNIGLA, e-mail keith@dcs.gla.ac.uk)

VAN ROIJEN, HE Jan Herman Robert Dudley; *b* 17 Dec 1936, Tokyo; *Educ* Groton Sch Mass USA, Univ of Utrecht (LLM); *m* Jonkvrouw Carolina, *née* Reuchlin; *Career* Dutch diplomat; Mil Serv Platoon Cdr New Guinea 1962; entered Foreign Serv 1963, third sec Jakarta 1965–67, second sec Perm Mission NATO Paris and Brussels 1967–70, head Recruitment and Trg Section Foreign Serv 1970–73, chargé d'affaires Saigon 1973–75; cnsllr and dep chief of mission: Athens 1975–78, Ottawa 1978–81; min plenipotentiary and dep chief of mission Jakarta 1981–83, dep dir gen of int cooperation Miny of Foreign Affrs 1983–86, ambass to Israel 1986–89, princ dir of personnel, diplomatic budget and bldgs Miny of Foreign Affrs 1989–91; ambass: to Indonesia 1992–94, to the Ct of St James's (concurrently accredited to Reykjavik) 1995–; *Style*— HE Mr J H R D Van Roijen; ✉ Royal Netherlands Embassy, 38 Hyde Park Gate, London SW7 5DP (☎ 0171 584 5040, fax 0171 225 0947)

van STRAUBENZEE, Sir William Radcliffe; kt (1981), MBE (1954); s of late Brig A B van Straubenzee, DSO, MC, and Margaret Joan, da of A N Radcliffe, of Bag Park, Widecombe-in-the-Moor, Newton Abbot, S Devon; *b* 27 Jan 1924; *Educ* Westminster; *Career* serv WWII Maj RA; slr 1952; former memb Gen Synod C of E, chm Dioceses Cmmn 1978–86, church cmmr 1968–87; MP (C) Wokingham 1959–87; PPS to Min Educn 1960–62, jt parly under sec of state Dept of Educn and Sci 1970–72, Min State NI 1972–74, second church estates cmmr 1979–87, chm YCs Nat Advsy Ctee 1951–53; chm: Cons Parly Educn Ctee 1979–83, Select Ctee Assistance to Private Membs 1975–77; memb Exec 1922 Ctee 1979–87; former chm Nat Cncl for Drama Trg; Freeman: of Wokingham 1980, of Bracknell 1994; Hon DEd Univ of E London 1995; *Clubs* Carlton, Garrick; *Style*— Sir William van Straubenzee, MBE; ✉ 36 Ebury Street, London SW1W 0LU (☎ 0171 730 0001)

van WALSUM, Joeske; s of Hans van Walsum, of Amsterdam, Holland, and Lies, *née* Schuurman-Stekhoven; *b* 26 May 1949; *Educ* Robert Gordon's Coll Aberdeen, RCM London; *m* 10 July 1969, Elizabeth Ann, da of Ronald Charles Marsh; 2 da (Georgiana b 27 Feb 1976, Abigail b 16 Dec 1977); *Career* freelance musician and flute teacher 1971–74, md Van Walsum Management (int mangrs of conductors, musicians and orchs and promoters of concert series and tours) 1975–; chm Br Assoc of Concert Agents 1989–92; organiser and chm Musicians for Armenia benefit concert 1988; *Recreations* white water canoeing, long distance walking; *Style*— Joeske van Walsum, Esq; ✉ Van Walsum Management, 26 Wadham Road, London SW15 2LR (☎ 0181 874 6344, fax 0181 877 0077)

VANCE, Charles Ivan; s of E Goldblatt; *b* 1929; *Educ* Royal Sch Dungannon, Queen's Univ Belfast; *m* 1966, Hon Imogen Moynihan, da of 2 Baron Moynihan, OBE, TD (d 1965); 1 da (Jacqueline); *Career* actor, theatrical director, producer, publisher and editor; acting debut with Anew MacMaster Co (Gaiety Dublin) 1949, directing debut The Glass Menagerie (Arts Cambridge) 1960, fndr Civic Theatre Chelmsford 1962, i/c rep cos Tunbridge Wells, Torquay, Whitby and Hastings 1962–, fndr dir Charles Vance Prodns (created Eastbourne Theatre Co 1969), purchased Leas Pavilion Theatre Folkestone 1976 (HQ until 1985); mangr: Floral Hall Theatre Scarborough 1984–86, Beck Theatre Hillingdon 1986–90, Grand Opera House York 1988–89, Summer Theatre Manor Pavilion Sidmouth 1987–; dir and vice chm Festival of Britain Theatre 1975–; numerous prodns as dir incl Witness for the Prosecution (revival) 1979 and 1992; numerous prodns as dir and prodr incl: Daisy Pulls it Off 1991, Gaslight 1991, Time and Time Again 1991, My Cousin Rachel 1992, Witness for the Prosecution 1992, Godspell 1994, Brideshead Revisited 1995, Jane Eyre 1996; fndr Vance Offord (Publications) Ltd (publishers of Br Theatre Directory, Br Theatre Review and Municipal Entertainment) 1971, chm and fndr Platform Publications Ltd 1987–, ed-in-chief Team Publishing 1986–87, ed Amateur Stage 1987–; ed All I Want for Christmas 1995; dir: Theatres Investment Fund 1975–83, Entertainment Investments Ltd 1980–82, International Holiday Investments 1980–87, Southern Counties Television 1980–87, Channel Radio 1981–86, Gateway Broadcasting Ltd 1982; chm Prestige Plays Ltd (dir 1987–93); ops dir Contemporary Theatres Ltd 1992–94, chm Charles Vance Productions 1994–; patron Voluntary Arts Network; Theatrical Mgmnt Assoc: memb Cncl 1969, pres 1971–73 and 1973–76, exec vice pres 1976–; tstee dir Folkestone Theatre Co 1979–85; chm: Provincial Theatre Cncl 1971–87, Standing Advsy Ctee on Local Authy and the Theatre 1977–90 (vice chm 1975–77), Gala and Fund-raising Ctee Br Theatre Assoc 1986–90, Standing Advsy Ctee on Local Authy and the Performing Arts 1990–; vice chm Theatres Advsy Cncl responsible for theatres threatened by devpt 1974–; memb: Theatres Nat Ctee 1971–, Drama Advsy Panel SE Arts Assoc 1974–85, Prince of Wales's Jubilee Entertainments Ctee 1977, Entertainment Exec Ctee Artists' Benevolent Fund 1980–; vice pres E Sussex RSPCA 1975–; memb CBI, FRSA, FInstD; *Books* British Theatre Directory (1972, 1973, 1974 and 1975), Amateur Theatre Yearbook (ed, 1989, 1991, 1992 and 1994), Agatha Christie, the Theatrical Celebration (1990); *Recreations* travel, cooking, sailing (in 1956 single handed crossing Atlantic), dog breeding; *Clubs* RAC, Wig and Pen, Kennel (memb Ctee 1989–), Hurlingham, Groucho, Variety Club of GB, Rotary Club of London, Lord's Taverners'; *Style*— Charles Vance, Esq; ✉ Oak Lodge, Farway, nr Colyton, E Devon EX13 6DH

VANDELINDE, Prof (Vernon) David; *b* 9 Aug 1942; *Educ* Carnegie-Mellon Univ Pittsburgh (BSc, MSc, PhD); *m*; 2 c; *Career* The Johns Hopkins Univ Baltimore: asst prof of electrical engrg 1967–74, sabbatical US Army Ballistic Res Lab Aberdeen Maryland 1974, assoc prof of electrical engrg 1974–77, prof of electrical engrg 1977–92, dean G W C Whiting Sch of Engrg 1978–92; vice-chllr Univ of Bath 1992–; Engrg Deans Cncl Chair of Fed Legislative Ctee 1989–, memb Advsy Ctee Office of Enterprise Devpt 1985–, memb Baltimore Poly HS Bd of Overseers 1983–, Baltimore Economic Devpt Corps memb Inst of Electrical and Electronics Engrs; memb: Tau Beta Pi, Eta Kappa Nu, Omicron Delta Kappa; author of numerous articles and lectures in res jls; *Style*— Prof David VandeLinde; ✉ The University of Bath, Claverton Down, Bath BA2 7AY (☎ 01225 826262, fax 01225 826626)

VANDEN-BEMPDE-JOHNSTONE, *see:* Johnstone

VANDER ELST, Philip Denis Andrew; *b* 25 June 1951; *Educ* Bryanston, Exeter Coll Oxford (MA); *m* 17 Sept 1977, Rachel Jane, *née* Tingle; *Career* Centre for Policy Studies 1977–78, Inst of Econ Affrs 1979–80; ed Freedom Today; *Publications* Freedom and Free Enterprise (US Industl Cncl, 1977), British Collectivism: The Bitter Harvest (American Con Union, 1978), Capitalist Technology for Soviet Survival (Inst of Econ Affrs, 1981), The Future of Freedom (Freedom Assoc, 1987), Idealism Without Illusions: A Foreign Policy for Freedom (Freedom Assoc, 1989), Resisting Leviathan: The Case Against A European State (1991), The Conservative Case Against Libertarianism (1991), Conservatism and Foreign Policy (1992), The Abandonment of Conservatism (1993), Rediscovery the Roots of Liberty (1993); *Recreations* walking, swimming, reading; *Style*— Philip Vander Elst, Esq; ✉ Freedom Association, 35 Westminster Bridge Rd, London SE1 7JB (☎ 0171 928 9925, fax 0171 928 9524)

VANDERFELT, Sir Robin Victor; KBE (1973, OBE 1954); s of Sydney Vanderfelt, OBE; *b* 24 July 1921; *Educ* Haileybury, Peterhouse Cambridge; *m* 1962, Jean Margaret Becker (d 1996), da of John Steward; 2 s (Zach, Tom); *Career* serv WWII Burma and India; Cwlth Parly Assoc: asst sec (UK Branch) 1949–59, sec 1960–61, sec-gen 1961–86; *Recreations* gardening; *Clubs* Royal Cwlth Soc, Royal Over-Seas League; *Style*— Sir Robin Vanderfelt, KBE; ✉ No 6 Saddler's Mead, Wilton, Salisbury, Wilts SP2 0DE

VANDERSTEEN, Martin Hugh; s of William Martin Vandersteen (d 1983), and Dorothy Margaret, *née* Leith (d 1994); *b* 9 Aug 1935; *Educ* Harrow Co GS; *m* 3 April 1967, Catherine Susan Mary, da of John Cansdale Webb; 2 s (Anthony b 1970, William b 1973); *Career* managing ptnr resources & quality Andersen Consulting 1994– (joined 1957, ptnr 1968–, UK managing ptnr 1973–86, managing ptnr rgnl 1989–94); chm UK Mgmnt Consulting Assoc 1981, FCA; *Recreations* sailing, fishing, golf, swimming; *Clubs* Royal Ocean Racing, Royal Southern Yacht, RAC, Royal Wimbledon Golf, Otter Swimming; *Style*— Martin Vandersteen, Esq; ✉ 2 Bristol Gardens, Putney Heath, London SW15 3TG (☎ 0181 788 9026); 2 Arundel St, London WC2R 3LT (☎ 0171 438 3106)

VANDORE, Peter Kerr; QC (Scotland, 1982); s of James Vandore (d 1977), and Janet Kerr Fife; *b* 7 June 1943; *Educ* Berwickshire HS, Univ of Edinburgh (MA, LLB); *m* 5 Sept 1970, Hilary Anne, da of Clement Davies (d 1990), of Huddersfield; 2 da (Emma Mary b 13 March 1975, Sara Elizabeth b 15 Sept 1977); *Career* called to the Scottish Bar 1968, standing counsel to Sec of State for Scotland for private legislation procedure 1975–86; memb: Legal Aid Central Ctee 1972–85, Cncl Cockburn Assoc 1988–; chm Central New Town Assoc (CENTA) 1989–90 (memb 1980–90); *Style*— Peter Vandore, Esq, QC; ✉ Advocates Library, Parliament House, Parliament Square, High Street, Edinburgh (☎ 0131 226 5071)

VANE, Hon Henry Francis Cecil (Harry); s and h of 11 Baron Barnard, TD, JP, *qv*, and Lady Davina, *née* Cecil, da of 6 Marquess of Exeter; *b* 11 March 1959; *Educ* Eton, Univ of Edinburgh (BSc); *Style*— The Hon Harry Vane; ✉ c/o The Rt Hon the Lord Barnard, TD, JP, Raby Castle, PO Box 50, Staindrop, Darlington, Co Durham DL2 3AY

VANE, Sir John Robert; kt (1984); s of Maurice Vane, and Frances Florence, *née* Fisher; *b* 1927; *Educ* King Edward's HS Birmingham, Univ of Birmingham (BSc), St Catherine's Coll Oxford (BSc, DPhil, DSc); *m* 1948, Elizabeth Daphne Page; 2 da; *Career* RCS: sr lectr in pharmacology Inst of Basic Med Scis 1955–61, reader in pharmacology 1961–65, prof of experimental pharmacology 1966–73; gp res and devpt dir The Wellcome Fndn 1973–85; DG The William Harvey Res Inst 1995– (chm 1986–95); tstee: Migraine Tst 1988–91, Imperial Cancer Research Fund 1994–; recipient of numerous int prizes and awards incl: Nobel Prize for Physiology or Med (jtly) 1982, Royal Medal of the Royal Soc 1989; FRS 1974; *Recreations* underwater swimming and photography; *Clubs* Athenaeum, Garrick; *Style*— Sir John Vane, FRS; ✉ The William Harvey Research Institute, St Bartholomew's & Royal London School of Medicine & Dentistry, Queen Mary & Westfield College, University of London, Charterhouse Sq, London EC1M 6BQ (☎ 0171 982 6116, fax 0171 251 1685)

VANE PERCY, Christopher David; s of Kenneth Vane Percy, of Biddenham, Bedfordshire, and Jean Farquharson; *b* 15 March 1945; *Educ* Bedford Sch; *m* 17 May 1973, Hon Linda Denise Grosvenor, da of 5 Baron Ebury, DSO (d 1957); 1 s (Maximilian Egerton b 1979), 2 da (Grace Dorothy Denise b 1981, Tryce Mary Susanne b 1991); *Career* interior designer; *Books* The Glass of Lalique - A Collector's Guide (1977); *Style*— Christopher Vane Percy, Esq; ✉ Island Hall, Godmanchester, Cambs PE18 8BA (☎ 01480 459676); CVP Designs Ltd, 27 Bruton Place, London W1X 7AB (☎ 0171 493 7995, fax 0171 355 4006)

VANEZIS, Prof Peter; s of Savvas Petrou Vanezis, of London, and Efrosini Vanezis (d 1993); *b* 11 Dec 1947; *Educ* Wanstead HS, Univ of Bristol (MB ChB 1972, MD 1985), (Soc of Apothecaries (DMJ (Path) 1976), MRCPath 1978, FRCPath 1990, Univ of London (PhD 1990), MRCPGlas 1996; *m* Maria, da of Stephanos Galatariotis; 2 s (Andrew b 29 May 1984, Frosini b 8 Nov 1986); *Career* jr house offr in pathology St Olaves Hosp 1973–74, sr lectr in forensic med London Hosp Med Coll 1979–90 (jr lectr 1974–75, lectr 1975–79); Charing Cross and Westminster Med Sch: reader and head Dept of Forensic Med and Toxicology 1990–93, dir Facial Identification Centre 1992–93; Univ of Glasgow: Regius prof of forensic med and science 1993–, dir Facial Identification Centre 1994–; conslt pathologist Kenyon Emergency Services 1994–; hon conslt in forensic med: Tower Hamlets Area Health Authy 1982–90, Govt of Rep of Cyprus 1984–, Riverside Area Health Authy 1990–93, Greater Glasgow Health Bd 1993–, Nat Inst of Legal Med Santiago 1994–; hon civilian conslt in forensic med Army 1992–; Br Acad of Forensic Sciences: pres, meetings sec, memb Exec Cncl; memb: Cncl Br Assoc of Forensic Med, Forensic Science Soc, Police Surgeon's Assoc, Medico-Legal Soc, Assoc of Clinical Pathologists, Cncl Int Assoc for Craniofacial Identification, Policy Advsy Gp for Forensic Pathology 1993–94, Euro Cncl of Legal Med; memb Ed Bd: Science and Justice, American Jl of Forensic Med and Pathology, INFORM; *Publications* Pathology of Neck Injury (1989), Suspicious Death-Scene Investigation (1996); author of various articles on forensic med and science in learned jls; *Recreations* painting, golf; *Clubs* RSAC; *Style*— Prof Peter Vanezis; ✉ Department of Forensic Medicine and Science, University of Glasgow, Glasgow G12 8QQ (☎ 0141 330 4573, fax 0141 330 4602, mobile 0850 584617)

VANN JONES, Prof John; s of John Jones (d 1975), and Elizabeth, *née* Kelly; *b* 8 May 1945; *Educ* Hyndland Sch Glasgow, Univ of Glasgow (MB ChB, PhD); *m* 23 Sept 1970, Anne Margaret, da of Andrew Abercrombie, of Glasgow; 2 s (Richard John, Simon Andrew), 2 da (Kerstin Anne, Caroline Patricia); *Career* lectr in cardiology Univ of Glasgow 1972–77 (res fell 1969–72), MRC travelling fell Univ of Gothenburg 1975–76, reader in cardiovascular med Univ of Oxford 1980–81 (lectr 1977–80), conslt cardiologist Bristol 1981–; memb: Br Cardiac Soc, Br Hypertension Soc, Med Res Soc, Physiological Soc; hon prof Univ of Bristol 1993; FRCP 1987; *Books* Scientific Foundations of Cardiology (1983), Outline of Cardiology (1983 and 1992), Essential Medicine (1993); *Recreations* golf, table tennis, swimming; *Clubs* Bristol Clifton Golf; *Style*— Prof John Vann Jones; ✉ Park House, Chew Lane, Chew Magna BS18 8QA (☎ 01275 332164); Cardiology Department, Royal Infirmary, Bristol BS2 8HW (☎ 0117 923 0000)

VANNER, Michael John; s of Walter Geoffrey Vanner (d 1933), of Winkfield, Berks, and Doris Ellen, *née* Hall (d 1977); *b* 6 Dec 1932; *Educ* Blundell's, Sidney Sussex Coll Cambridge (BA, MA); *m* 1 July 1961, Myra, da of William John Sharpe (d 1982), of Fetcham, Surrey; 2 s (Luke b 1967, Guy b 1970); *Career* res engr Electrical Res Assoc 1955–64, chief devpt engr BICC Construction Co Ltd 1964–75, engrg conslt Balfour Beatty Power Construction Ltd 1981–86 (engrg mangr 1975–81), princ Construction and Material Servs (int consulting) 1986–, princ engr Ewbank Preece Ltd 1989–92, transmission engr AMEC Power Ltd 1992–94, OHL engr Merz & McLellan 1994–; chm IEE PG Power Cables and Overhead Lines 1988–91, chm BSI PEL/11 Overhead Lines 1991–, chm CIGRE SC22–07 Overhead Lines 1995–; CEng, FIEE 1994 (MIEE 1984), CPhys, MInstP 1962, MBGS 1961; *Books* The Structure of Soil and A Critical Review of The Mechanisms of Soil Moisture Retention And Migration (1961); *Recreations* walking, sailing; *Style*— Michael Vanner, Esq; ✉ 15 Pensford Court, Newcastle Upon Tyne NE3 2RA (☎ 0191 271 2546); Construction And Material Services, 1 Blanford Rd, Reigate, Surrey RH2 7DP (☎ 01737 222 173)

VANSTONE, Hugh; s of J R B Vanstone, of Exeter, and M L Vanstone; *b* 8 Aug 1965; *Educ* Exeter Sch; *partner* George Stiles, composer, *qv*; *Career* lighting designer; trained Northcott Theatre Exeter 1980–86, conslt Imagination (designers for Millennium Exhbn Greenwich) 1986–, freelance 1989–, assoc to Andrew Bridge, *qv* (lighting designer) 1989–94; memb Assoc of Lighting Designers 1983–; *Theatre* recent credits RSC incl: Richard III, Romeo and Juliet, The Taming of the Shrew, Three Hours After Marriage, Slaughter City, Cymbeline, Hamlet; other recent credits incl: The Homecoming (RNT), Peter Pan, The World Goes Round (both West Yorkshire Playhouse), Miss Julie (Young Vic), Insignificance (Donmar Warehouse), The Cabinet of Doktor Caligari (Nottingham Playhouse), Butterfly Kiss (Almeida), Moll Flanders, Romeo and Juliet, Mrs Warren's Profession (all Lyric Hammersmith); West End credits incl: When we are Married (Savoy), Scrooge (also Aust), Art (Wyndham's); Once on this Island, Copacabana, Leonardo, Moby Dick; *Opera* credits incl: Macbeth (ROH), The Rake's Progress (WNO), La Bohème (ENO), The Barber of Seville (English Touring Opera), Die Fledermaus (Scottish Opera); *Ballet* Alice in Wonderland (English Nat Ballet); *Style*— Hugh Vanstone, Esq; ✉ c/o Jeffrey Cambell, 18 Queen Anne Street, London W1M 0HB (☎ 0171 637 0993, fax 0171 637 0985); Imagination, 25 Store Street, London WC1E 7BL (☎ 0171 323 3300, fax 0171 462 2837)

VARAH, Preb Dr (Edward) Chad; CBE (1995, OBE 1969); s of Canon William Edward Varah (d 1945), of Barton on Humber, and Mary, *née* Atkinson (d 1965); *b* 12 Nov 1911; *Educ* Worksop Coll Notts, Keble Coll Oxford (MA), Lincoln Theological Coll; *m* 1940, (Doris) Susan, OBE (d 1993), da of Harry Whanslaw (d 1961), of Putney; 4 s (Michael, Andrew, David, Charles), 1 da (Felicity (Mrs Harding)); *Career* staff scriptwriter Eagle 1950–62; C of E clerk in holy orders 1935; rector Lord Mayor's Parish Church of St Stephen Walbrook 1953–, prebendary St Paul's Cathedral 1975–; fndr: The Samaritans 1953, Befrienders International 1974, Men Against Genital Mutilation of Girls 1992; chm: The Samaritans Inc 1963–66, Befrienders Int 1974–83 (pres 1983–86); conslt: Forum Magazine 1962–82, Nat Assoc of Crisis Intervention People's Republic of China 1994–; patron: Outsiders Club 1984, Terrence Higgins Tst 1987; pres Ctee Publishing Russian Church Music 1960–80; Albert Schweitzer Gold Medal 1972, Louis Dublin Award American Assoc Suicidology 1974, Prix de l'Inst de la Vie 1977, Romanian Patriarchal Cross 1968; Hon Liveryman Worshipful Cos of Carmen and of Grocers; Hon DSc City Univ; Hon LLD: Univ of Leicester, Univ of St Andrews, Univ of Leeds; hon fell Keble Coll Oxford; *Books* The Samaritans, Befriending the Suicidal (1988), Before I Die Again (autobiog, 1992); *Recreations* reading, music, watching TV nature programmes; *Clubs* Oxford Union; *Style*— Prebendary Dr Chad Varah, CBE; ✉ St Stephen Walbrook, 39 Walbrook, London EC4N 8BN (☎ 0171 283 4444, 0171 626 8242)

VARCOE, Jeremy Richard Lovering Grosvenor; CMG (1989); s of Ronald Arthur Grosvenor Varcoe, TD (d 1993), and Zöe Elizabeth, *née* Lovering (d 1971); *b* 20 Sept 1937; *Educ* Charterhouse, Lincoln Coll Oxford (MA); *m* 1, 30 Dec 1961, Wendy Anne (d 1991), da of Robert F Moss, MBE (d 1973); 2 da (Francesca b 1964, Lucy b 1966); m 2, 8 July 1995, Ruth S Murdoch, *née* Wallis; *Career* Nat Serv 2 Lt 4 RTR 1956–58; dist offr HMOCS Swaziland 1962–65, called to the Bar Gray's Inn 1966, asst legal advsr GKN Ltd 1966–67, lectr in law Univ of Birmingham 1967–70; HM Dip Serv 1970–91: first sec FCO 1970–71, dep sec gen Pearce Cmmn on Rhodesian Opinion 1971–72, first sec (Info) Ankara 1972–74, head of Chancery Lusaka 1974–78, first sec FCO 1978–79, cnsllr (Commercial) Kuala Lumpur 1979–82, head Southern Africa Dept FCO 1982–84, cnsllr Ankara 1984–85, Standard Chartered Bank Istanbul (unpaid leave from FCO) 1985–86, HM ambass Somalia 1987–89, min and dep high cmmr Lagos 1989–90, asst under-sec coordinator London Economic Summit 1991, ret; dir General United World Colleges 1992–94, dep dir Oxford Univ Devpt Office 1995–96, pt/t immigration adjudicator 1995–; *Books* Legal Aid In Criminal Proceedings - A Regional Survey (with Prof G F Borrie, 1970); *Recreations* sailing, public affairs; *Clubs* Royal Cwlth Tst; *Style*— Jeremy Varcoe, Esq, CMG; ✉ Dozmary House, Romsey Road, King's Somborne, Stockbridge, Hants SO20 6PR

VARCOE, (Christopher) Stephen; s of Philip William Varcoe, OBE (d 1980), of Lanescot, Par, Cornwall, and Mary Northwood, *née* Mercier; *b* 19 May 1949; *Educ* King's Sch Canterbury, King's Coll Cambridge (MA), Guildhall Sch of Music; *m* 22 April 1972, Melinda, da of William Arthur Davies; 3 s (Josiah b 6 March 1979, Amyas b 16 Nov 1982, Leander b 26 March 1986 d 1986), 2 da (Flora b 22 Nov 1975, Oriana b 9 April 1988); *Career* baritone; freelance concert and opera singer 1970–; Calouste Gulbenkian Fndn Fellowship 1977; *Recreations* building, painting, gardening; *Style*— Stephen Varcoe, Esq; ✉ c/o Ron Gonsalves, 7 Old Town, Clapham, London SW4 0JT (☎ 0171 622 2244, fax 0171 622 2288)

VARDE, John; s of Shamrao Varde (d 1949), and Helen, *née* Leontzini; *b* 2 Jan 1935; *Educ* Malvern; *m* 1964, Elizabeth Lilian, da of James Hudson Foskett (d 1985); 1 s (Andrew b 1965), 1 da (Nicola b 1967); *Career* mechanical and mfrg engr; md Westland Helicopters Ltd 1987–92; visiting prof Univ of Bath 1994–; vice pres Inst of Prodn Engrs (now merged with IEE) 1989–91; FIMechE 1985; *Recreations* music; *Style*— John Varde Esq; ✉ 32 Richmond Road, Sherborne, Dorset

VAREY, Dr Nicolas Calvert; s of Frederick Joseph Varey (d 1989), and late Edith Varey; *b* 16 Sept 1940; *Educ* Beverley GS, Univ of St Andrews (MB ChB), RCP (FFPM); *m* 28 Sept 1963, Helen, da of Malcolm Pack; 2 da (Catherine b 17 July 1964, Sarah Anne b 7 Feb 1966), 1 s (Nicholas James b 31 May 1972); *Career* med cadet RAMC 1963–66, GD No 28 Field Ambulance 1967, dermatologist Cambridge Mil Hosp Aldershot 1968–71; GP and Howden clinical asst Goole Hosps 1971–78, med dir Reckitt & Colman 1982– (joined 1978); chm: Hull Health Authy 1984–92, Royal Hull Hosps NHS Tst 1992–96; memb Bd of Mgmnt Yorks Cancer Research 1992–; gen cmmr of taxes 1974–; memb BMA; FFPM; *Style*— Dr Nicolas Varey; ✉ Caduceus, Knedlington, Goole, N Humberside DN14 7EU (☎ 01430 430833); Reckitt & Colman, Danson Lane, Hull HU8 7DS

VARLEY, Baron (Life Peer UK 1990), of Chesterfield in the County of Derbyshire; Eric Graham Varley; PC (1974), DL; s of Frank and Eva Varley; *b* 11 Aug 1932; *Educ* Ruskin Coll Oxford; *m* 1955, Marjorie Turner; 1 s; *Career* worked in engineering and mining industry; branch sec NUM 1955–64 (memb Derbys Area Exec Ctee 1956–64); MP (Lab) Chesterfield 1964–84, asst govt whip 1967–68, PPS to Harold Wilson as PM 1968–69, min of state Technology 1969–70; energy sec 1974–75, industry sec 1975–79; chief oppn spokesman Employment 1979–83, treas Lab Pty 1981–83, oppn front bench spokesman Employment 1981–83; chm and chief exec Coalite Gp 1984–89 (dep exec chm 1983–84); non-exec dir: Cathelco Ltd, Laxgate Ltd 1991–92; memb: Thyssen (GB) Advsy Cncl, House of Lords Euro Communities Ctee 1992–96; steward and bailiff of the Manor of Northstead 1984–85; *Style*— The Rt Hon Lord Varley, PC, DL; ✉ House of Lords, London SW1A OPW

VARLEY, Dame Joan Fleetwood; DBE (1985, CBE 1974); da of Fleetwood Ireton Varley (d 1941), of London, and Harriet Elizabeth, *née* Heenan; *b* 22 Feb 1920; *Educ* Cheltenham Ladies' Coll, LSE (BSc); *Career* WAAF Corpl Fighter Cmd radio operator, section offr Fighter Cmd Meteorological Offr; Cons Pty: dep agent Warwick & Leamington Constituency 1949–52, agent Shrewsbury Constituency 1952–56, CPC offr W Midlands Area Cons Central Office 1956–57, dep Central Office agent NW Area 1957–64, dep chief orgn offr Cons Central Office 1965–66, dep dir of orgn Cons Central Office 1966–74, chief asst to Dir Gen and chief woman exec 1974–75, dir of central admin Cons Central Office 1975–76, dir of local govt orgn 1976–84; churchwarden St Clements & St James Norlands Jt Parish; memb Brighter Kensington & Chelsea Scheme Ctee; chm Ct of Govrs Thames Poly 1991–92, pro chllr Univ of Greenwich (formerly Thames Poly) 1992–94 (govr 1980–95, vice-chm 1986–91), pt/t memb VAT Appeals Tbnl 1986–94; Hon DUniv Greenwich; *Recreations* gardening, walking; *Clubs* St Stephen's; *Style*— Dame Joan Varley, DBE; ✉ 9 Queensdale Walk, Holland Park, London W11 4QQ (☎ 0171 727 1292)

VARMA, Dr Alakh Niranjan; s of Phulan Prasad Varma (d 1957), of India, and Karorpati Varma (d 1989); *b* 27 Feb 1932; *Educ* Patna Univ of India (BSc, MB BS, DPM), Univ of Edinburgh (DPM); *m* 17 Nov 1959, Dr Sashi Bala Varma, MD, DCP, da of Anjani Bir Prasad (d 1960), of Lucknow, India; 2 s (Dr Niraj Varma b 1 Oct 1960, Anu Ranjan b 14 June 1964); *Career* asst MO India 1957–60, sr MO Ghana Africa 1961–68, conslt in child and adolescent psychiatry 1973–, psychiatrist BC Canada 1981–82; MRCPsych, FRSH; *Recreations* travelling, photography; *Style*— Dr Alakh Varma; ✉ 149 Grantham Road, Sleaford, Lincs NG34 7NR (☎ 01529 303681); Rauceby Hosp, Sleaford, Lincs NG34 7PP (☎ 01529 488241)

VARNEY, Capt Gordon Sidney; MBE (1992); s of Percy Frederick Varney, of London (d 1971), and Florence Freda, *née* Spence; *b* 13 May 1932; *Educ* St Albans Co GS, Sch of Navigation Univ of Southampton (MN Cadet trg); *m* 1 (m dis 1976), Anna Maria, *née* Frigo; 1 s (Stuart Gordon b 3 March 1955); m 2, 1983, Marlon Roberts, da of Ernest Randle; *Career* Royal Mail Lines Ltd: offr cadet 1949–53, deck offr (concurrently marine supt and CO experience) 1953–64; Port of London Authy (PLA): asst dockmaster 1964–70, Planning Dept 1970–71, asst marine staff offr 1971–76, sr duty offr Thames Navigation Serv 1976–77, marine staff and trg offr 1977–81, princ marine offr (Staff and Admin) 1981–83, chief harbour master 1983–94; chm Nautical Inst Harbour Master Working Gp; Freeman: City of London 1990, Worshipful Co of Watermen and Lightermen 1991, Younger Bro Trinity House 1989; memb London Maritime Assoc 1965 (currently vice-chm), FNI 1985 (MNI 1974); *Recreations* sailing, swimming, walking; *Clubs* Cruising Assoc, Tollesbury Yacht; *Style*— Capt G S Varney, MBE

VARNISH, Peter; OBE (1982); s of John Varnish (d 1985), and Hilary Ilma Ada, *née* Godfrey (d 1982); *b* 30 May 1947; *Educ* Warwick Sch, UCNW (BSc); *m* 10 Aug 1968, Shirley Anne, da of George Bertram Bendelow; 2 s (Jason b 7 March 1973, David b 8 May 1975); *Career* SERL: memb Res Gp on High Power Lasers 1968–70, memb Res Gp on High Power Travelling Wave Tubes 1970–72; head Electron Bombarded Semiconductor Res RSRE 1972–75, scientific advsr to MOD British Embassy Washington 1975–79; MOD: UK electronic warfare coordinator ARE Portsdown 1979–81, head Antenna Section and offr i/c ARE Funtinton 1981–84, head Radar Div ARE Portsdown 1984, head Signature Control Div ARE Funtington 1984–89, head Electronic Warfare and Weapons Dept ARE 1989–90, dir Above Water Warfare ARE 1990, Business Sector dir Above Water Systems DRA 1991–92, RCDS 1992, dir Strategic Defence Initiative Participation Office 1993, dir Science Ballistic Missile Defence 1994–95, dir Int Business Devpt Defence Evaluation and Research Agency (DERA); chm: Stealth Conf 1988, Military Microwaves 1990, Asia DEF EX, IDEX 1995–; vice chm RF Technology 1994–; memb: Sensors Ctee Defence Scientific Advsy Cncl, Stealth Working Pty Defence Scientific Advsy Cncl, Jt MOD Indust Liaison Ctee of Guided Weapons, Mgmnt Bd ARE, Cncl ERA Ltd, Advsy Ctee Dept of Electrical and Electronics Engrg Univ of Surrey; author of numerous scientific papers and patents; SMIEEE 1976, CEng 1988, FIEE 1988, MIMgt 1989, FEng 1995; *Recreations* watching rugby-football, mountain bikes, hill walking, computer engineering, photography, hi-fi; *Style*— Peter Varnish, Esq, OBE, FEng; ✉ Four Corners, 1 Greatfield Way, Rowlands Castle, Hampshire PO9 6AG (☎ 01705 412440); Cody Building, DERA, Ively Road, Farnborough, Hampshire GU14 0LX (☎ 01252 394876, fax 01252 394659)

VARTY, Prof (Ernest) Kenneth Charles; s of Ernest Varty (d 1986), and Doris, *née* Hollingworth (d 1962); *b* 18 Aug 1927; *Educ* Bemrose Sch Derby, Univ of Nottingham (BA, PhD), Univ of Keele (DLitt); *m* 26 Sept 1958, Hedwig Hermine Juliane (Hety), da of Ludwig Beninghoff (d 1966); 2 da (Anne, Catherine); *Career* RAF 1946–48; serv in UK, Egypt, Southern Rhodesia; asst lectr then lectr in French Univ of Keele 1953–56, lectr then sr lectr Univ of Leicester 1961–66; Univ of Glasgow: prof of French 1968–90, dean Faculty of Arts 1979–82; visiting lectr Univ of Warwick 1967, visiting res fell Univ of Oxford 1974, visiting prof Univ of Jerusalem 1977, elected life memb Clare Hall Cambridge 1986 (visiting res fell 1984); jt ed The Bibliographical Bulletin of Int Arthurian Soc 1969–76; chm Bd of Studies for Modern Languages Univ of Glasgow 1974–77, vice pres Br Branch The Int Arthurian Soc 1976– (sec 1969–76), hon pres Int Reynard Soc (pres 1974–87), hon life memb of Hon Soc Phi Kappa Phi 1989; awarded Gold Medal of City of Orléans 1993; Chevalier dans L'Ordre des Palmes Académiques 1988; FSA 1969; *Books* Reynard The Fox - A Study of the Fox in Medieval English Art (1967), A la Recherche du Roman de Renart (1987); *Recreations* photography, travel; *Style*— Prof Kenneth Varty, FSA; ✉ 4 Dundonald Road, Glasgow G12 9LJ (☎ 0141 339 1413); Department of French, University of Glasgow, Glasgow G12 8QL

VARVILL, Michael; s of Robert Varvill, DSC, of W Wittering, W Sussex, and Rachel, *née* Millar; *b* 21 Oct 1950, Calabar, Nigeria; *Educ* Gordonstoun, Schule Schloss Salem Germany, Univ of London (LLB), Coll of Law; *m* 1978 (m dis 1990), Margrete, da of late Per Halfdan Lynner (d 1991); 2 s (Wilfrid Halfdan b 28 Aug 1982, John Fitzadam b 11 April 1987), 1 da (Celia Anemone b 29 June 1984); *Career* admitted slr 1974; ptnr: Lane & Partners London 1981– (asst slr 1974–81), Marks & Murase (formerly Wender, Murase & White) Park Avenue NY 1984–; Freeman City of York; memb Law Soc, ordinary memb Inst of Trade Mark Agents, ACIArb; *Recreations* sport, the arts; *Clubs* Itchenor Sailing, Hurlingham, Royal Thames Yacht; *Style*— Michael Varvill, Esq; ✉ Lane & Partners, 46/47 Bloomsbury Square, London WC1A 2RU (☎ 0171 242 2626, fax 0171 242 0387)

VASARY, Tamas; s of Josef Vasary (d 1975), and Elisabeth, *née* Baltazar (d 1977); *b* 11 Aug 1933; *Educ* Franz Liszt Music Acad Budapest; *m* 30 March 1967, Ildiko (d 1994), da of Lajos Kovács, of Sao Paulo, Brazil; *Career* pianist and conductor; first concert at age of 8, asst prof Budapest Music Acad at 21; London debut 1960, New York debut 1961, debut as conductor 1969; prizes at int competitions: Paris 1955, Warsaw 1955, Brussels 1956, Rio de Janeiro 1957; conducted numerous major orchs incl: Berlin Philharmonic, London Symphony, Royal Philharmonic; music dir Northern Sinfonietta 1979–82; musical dir: Bournemouth Sinfonietta 1989–, Hungarian Radio Orchestra 1993–; Awarded Bach and Paderewski medals 1961; *Recordings* incl works by: Chopin, Liszt, Brahms, Mozart, Rachmaninoff; *Recreations* yoga, writing; *Style*— Tamas Vasary, Esq; ✉ c/o IMG Europe, 3 Burlington Lane, Media House, London W4 2TH (☎ 0181 233 5800, fax 0181 233 5801)

VASQUEZ, The Hon Sir Alfred Joseph; kt (1987), CBE (1974), QC (1986); s of Alfred J Vasquez (d 1971), of Gibraltar, and Maria Josefa, *née* Rugeroni (d 1942); *b* 2 March 1923; *Educ* Mount St Mary's Sch, Millfield, Fitzwilliam Coll Cambridge (MA); *m* 10 April 1950, Carmen, da of Lt-Col Robert Michael Sheppard-Capurro, OBE, JP, of Cloister Ramp, Gibraltar; 3 s (Alfred b 1951, Robert b 1952, Peter b 1953), 1 da (Mrs Maurice Sene b 1958); *Career* served Gibraltar Def Force 1943–45, Gibraltar Regt 1957–64, Capt; called to the Bar Inner Temple 1950, ptnr Triay & Triay barrs and slrs incorporationg Vasquez Benady (of which formerly sr ptnr); speaker Gibraltar House of Assembly 1970–89, Mayor of Gibraltar 1970–76; chm Gibraltar Bursary and Scholarship Bd; memb: Ctee Gibraltar Lawyers Assoc, Ctee Gibraltar Soc for Cancer Relief; *Recreations* golf, shooting, bridge; *Clubs* Royal Gibraltar Yacht, Sotogrande Golf (Cadiz), Mediterranean Racing (Gibraltar), Calpe Rowing; *Style*— The Hon Sir Alfred Vasquez, CBE, QC; ✉ 2 St Bernards Road, Gibraltar (☎ 00 350 73710); 26A St Georges Drive, London SW1 (☎ 0171 821 0987); 28 Irish Town, Gibraltar (☎ 00 350 72020)

VASSAR-SMITH, Sir John Rathborne; 4 Bt (UK 1917), of Charlton Park, Charlton Kings, Co Gloucester; s of Sir Richard Rathborne Vassar-Smith, 3 Bt, TD (d 1995), and Dawn Mary, *née* Woods; *b* 23 July 1936; *Educ* Eton; *m* 1971, Roberta Elaine, da of Wing Cdr Norman Williamson; 2 s (Richard Rathborne b 1975, David Rathborne b 1978); *Heir* s, Richard Rathborne Vassar-Smith b 29 Dec 1975; *Career* runs St Ronan's Prep Sch; *Style*— Sir John Vassar-Smith, Bt; ✉ St Ronan's, Hawkhurst, Kent TN18 5DJ

VASUDEV, Dr Kadaba Srinath; s of Dr Kadaba Vedanta Srinath, and Lalitha Srinath; *b* 5 May 1943; *Educ* Univ of Bangalore India (MB BS); *m* 28 June 1972, Pratibha, da of Mandyam Dhati Narayan; 2 s (Naveen Srinath, Chetan Srinath), 1 da (Archana Srinath); *Career* conslt histopathologist/cytopathologist Dept of Pathology Victoria Hosp Blackpool 1977– (clinical dir Pathology Directorate), undergrad tutor Univ of Manchester 1982–94 (postgrad clinical tutor 1982–93); chm Blackpool Div Overseas Doctors' Assoc, sec Blackpool and Fylde Div BMA; memb: Int Acad of Pathology, Manchester Med Soc, Assoc of Clinical Pathologists; FRCPath 1988; *Recreations* photography, music appreciation, theatre; *Clubs* Rotary Club of Blackpool, Palatine (pres 1995–96, chm Int Cmmn 1992–93 and 1993–94); *Style*— Dr Kadaba Vasudev; ✉ 10 Silverdale Rd, St Annes, Lancs FY8 3RE (☎ 01253 720747, fax 01253 720747); Department of Pathology, Victoria Hospital, Whinney Heys Rd, Blackpool, Lancs FY3 8NR (☎ 01253 300000 ext 3751, fax 01253 303675)

VAUGHAN, Dr Caroline Lesley; da of Frederick Alan Vaughan (d 1970), and Helen Mary, *née* Brackett (d 1983); *b* 5 Feb 1941; *Educ* Croydon HS, Univ of Manchester (BSc), Chelsea Coll London (PhD); *Career* post doctoral fell: MD Anderson Hosp Houston USA 1965–68, King's Coll London 1968–69; fin analyst and mktg mangr WR Grace Euro Consumer Products Div Paris 1969–74, commerical planner Tube Investments (Domestic Appliances Div and Head Office) 1974–78, divnl exec Nat Enterprise Bd 1978–80; dir of business devpt Celltech Ltd 1980–84, chief exec Newmarket Venture Capital Plc 1984–94, dep chm Home Grown Cereals Authy 1994–; non-exec dir Hammersmith Hosps Tst 1994–, memb Ownership Bd Veterinary Labs Agency 1995–; MInstD, FRSA; *Recreations* theatre, opera, travel, viticulture; *Style*— Dr Caroline Vaughan; ✉ 61 Milson Road, London W14 0LH (☎ and fax 0171 603 6365)

VAUGHAN, Prof David John; s of Samuel John Vaughan (d 1982), of Newport, Gwent, and Esther Ruby, *née* Edwards (d 1984); *b* 10 April 1946; *Educ* Newport HS, UCL (BSc), Imperial Coll London (MSc), University Coll Oxford (D Phil, DSc); *m* 31 Dec 1971 (m dis 1993), Heather Elizabeth, da of Alan Marat Ross (d 1979), of Christchurch, Hants; 1 s (Emlyn James b 1979); *Career* res assoc Dept Earth and Planetary Sci Mass Inst of Technol Cambridge USA 1971–74, reader mineralogy Aston Univ 1979–88 (lectr geological scis 1974–79), visiting prof Virginia Poly Inst and State Univ USA 1980, prof mineralogy Univ of Manchester 1988–; pres Mineralogical Soc (GB & Ireland) 1988–89; FIMM 1984, fell Min Soc of America; *Books* Mineral Chemistry of Metal Sulfides (with J Craig, 1978), Ore Microscopy and Ore Petrography (with J Craig, 1981), Resources of The Earth (with J Craig and B Skinner, 1988); *Recreations* painting, walking; *Style*— Prof David Vaughan; ✉ c/o Department of Geology, University of Manchester, Manchester M13 9PL (☎ 0161 275 3935)

VAUGHAN, Viscount; David John Francis Malet Vaughan; s and h of 8 Earl of Lisburne, *qv*; *b* 15 June 1945; *Educ* Ampleforth; *m* 1973, Jennifer Jane (an artist), da of late James Desiré John William Fraser Campbell, of Glengarry, Inverness-shire; 1 s (Hon Digby b 3 Jan 1973 but since b before f's marriage legitimated for all purposes except succession to f's and gf's titles), 1 da (Hon Lucy b 2 Aug 1971); *Career* artist; *Style*— Viscount Vaughan

VAUGHAN, Dr Elizabeth; da of William Jones (d 1974), and Mary Ellen Morris (d 1987); *b* 12 March 1937; *Educ* Llanfylin GS, RAM London; *m* 1, June 1968, Raymond Peter Brown, s of Stanley Kitchener Brown (d 1980); 1 s (Mark b 21 Oct 1970), 1 da (Sarah b 5 Aug 1974); *Career* opera singer; Royal Opera House princ soprano roles: Butterfly, Traviata, Leonora, Gilda, Abigaille, Elettra, Donna Elvira, Teresa, Liu, Musetta, Alice; ENO guest artist: Aida, Butterfly, Fidelio; Scottish Opera, WNO and Opera North: Lady Macbeth, Abigaille, Butterfly, Traviata; performed worldwide incl in: Paris Opera, Metropolitan NY, Florence, Vienna, Japan, S America, Canada, Aust, Miami, Houston, Berlin, Athens; numerous TV and radio performances; prof Royal Northern Coll of Music; Hon DMus Univ of Wales; FRAM (licentiate and assoc); *Recreations* needlepoint, antiques fairs; *Style*— Dr Elizabeth Vaughan; ✉ c/o IMG Artists, Media House, 3 Burlington Lane, London W4 2TH

VAUGHAN, Frankie; CBE (1997, OBE 1965), DL (Bucks 1993); *b* 3 Feb 1928; *m* 1951, Stella; 2 s (David, Andrew), 1 da (Susan); *Career* singer and actor; turned professional 1951; record hits incl: Green Door, Garden of Eden (first Br number 1 1957), Kisses Sweeter than Wine, The Heart of a Man, Tower of Strength (Br number 1 1961), Loop de Loop, Made of Fire, There Must be a Way; theatre concert and cabaret engagements worldwide; venues incl: London Palladium, London's Talk of the Town, Rainbow Grill Copacabana NY, Dunes Hotel Las Vegas; film appearances incl: These Dangerous Years, The Heart of a Man, Wonderful Things, The Lady Is a Square, Let's Make Love (with Marilyn Monroe), The Right Approach and It's All Over Town; portrayed Julian Marsh in 42nd Street (West End); tour of GB with the Syd Lawrence Orchestra 1990; patron Nat Boys' Clubs; past King Rat of the Grand Order of Water Rats 1968; Freeman City of London 1983, Liveryman Worshipful Co of Carmen 1988; hon fell John Moores Univ 1988; *Style*— Frankie Vaughan, Esq, CBE, DL; ✉ Peter Charlesworth Ltd, 2nd Floor, 68 Old Brompton Road, London SW7 3LQ (☎ 0171 581 2478, fax 0171 589 2922)

VAUGHAN, Sir Gerard Folliott; kt (1984), MP (C) Reading East (majority 14,555); s of Leonard A Vaughan, DSO, DFC, by his w Joan, *née* Folliott; *b* 11 June 1923; *Educ* privately, Univ of London, Guy's Hospital (MB BS); *m* 1955, Joyce Thurle, *née* Laver; 1

s, 1 da; *Career* med conslt emeritus Guy's Hosp; lectr and author; Party candidate (C) Poplar 1955; alderman GLC 1966–72 (LCC 1955–64); MP (C): Reading 1970–74, Reading S 1974–83, Reading E 1983–; PPS to NI Sec 1974, oppn whip 1974, oppn spokesman on Health 1975–79; min of state: for health DHSS 1979–82, for trade with responsibility for consumer affrs 1982–83; Hon FFAS; memb Ct of Assts Worshipful Co of Barbers; FRCP, FRCPsych; *Clubs* Carlton, White's; *Style—* Sir Gerard Vaughan, MP; ✉ House of Commons, London SW1A 0AA

VAUGHAN, Oliver John; s of Maj Joseph Herbert Vaughan (d 1972), and Mary Lavender, *née* Holroyd Smith (d 1989); *b* 28 July 1946; *Educ* Dominican Schs of Llanarth & Laxton, Univ of Neuchatel Switzerland; *m* June 1984, Diana Frances Elizabeth (Boo), da of Cdr Philip Richard Martineau, RN, of Moses Hill Farm, Marley Heights, Haslemere, Surrey; 2 s (Jamie Joseph b 12 July 1986, Jeremy Philip b 22 Oct 1988), 1 da (Tara Megan b 1 Aug 1991), 1 foster da (Joanna Eu b 2 Jan 1970); *Career* co fndr Juliana's 1966, subsequently opened offices in London, Hong Kong, Singapore and NY, obtained Stock Exchange listing 1983, sold to Wembley plc 1989; chief exec: Mountcashel plc, Gander Holdings plc; *Recreations* sailing, computer programming, skiing, shooting, fishing; *Clubs* Brooks's, Royal Thames Yacht; *Style—* Oliver Vaughan, Esq; ✉ 20 Phillimore Gardens, London W8 7QE; Blackbrook, Skenfrith, Monmouthshire NP7 8UB

VAUGHAN, Paul William; s of Albert George Vaughan (d 1987), and Ada Rose, *née* Stocks (d 1991); *b* 24 Oct 1925; *Educ* Raynes Park Sch, Wadham Coll Oxford; *m* 1, 11 Aug 1951 (m dis 1988), Barbara, da of Arthur Glyn Prys-Jones, OBE (d 1988); 2 s (Timothy Owain b 1955, Matthew David b 1964), 2 da (Katherine Amanda b 1953, Lucy Elizabeth b 1966); m 2, 12 July 1988, Phillipa Jane, *née* Burston; 2 s (Benedict William b 1985, Thomas Edward b 1988); *Career* asst export mangr Menley & James 1951–56, chief press offr BMA 1960–64 (asst PR offr 1956–60), freelance journalist and broadcaster 1964–, dep ed World Med 1970–73; presenter: Science and Industry, Science in Action, Discovery (BBC World Serv), New Worlds (Radio 4), Kaleidoscope (Radio 4 1973–), Record Review (Radio 3) 1981–88; contrib incl: Today, Woman's Hour, Home This Afternoon (Radio 4); princ narrator Horizon (BBC 2 1970–90); journalist contrib incl: Spectator, Observer, Sunday Times, Truth, Family Doctor, Medical Tribune (NY), Scope Weekly (NY), Medical News, Medical Tribune (London); chm Med Journalists' Assoc 1968–72 (life memb); memb: NUJ, Equity; *Plays* The Conspirators (1996); *Books* Doctors Commons, A Short History of the British Medical Association (1959), Family Planning - The FPA Book of Birth Control (1969), The Pill on Trial (1969), Something in Linoleum (1994), Exciting Times in the Accounts Department (1995); *Recreations* playing the clarinet; *Style—* Paul Vaughan, Esq; ✉ 60 King's Road, Wimbledon, London SW19 8QW (☎ 0181 540 5979, fax 0181 544 1245)

VAUGHAN, Rt Rev Peter St George; *see:* Ramsbury, Bishop of

VAUGHAN, Dr Roger; s of Benjamin Frederick Vaughan, of Longframmlington, Northumberland, and Marjorie, *née* Wallace; *b* 14 June 1944; *Educ* Manchester GS, Univ of Newcastle Upon Tyne (BSc, PhD); *m* 1; 3 s (Adam John b 1973, Benjamin Nicholas Gray b 1974, Thomas Peter b 1976), 2 da (Ellen Kate b 1979, Anna Cecila b 1980); m 2, Valerie; 2 step s (James Maxwell Phillpott b 1973, Jonathan Peter Phillpott b 1975); *Career* student apprentice Vickers Group 1962, shipbuilding devpt engr Swan Hunter Shipbuilders Ltd 1970–71, md A & P Appledore Ltd (joined 1971), dir Performance Improvement and Productivity Br Shipbuilders 1981–86, dir Swan Hunter Ltd, chm and chief exec Swan Hunter Shipbuilders Ltd until 1993, conslt 1993–, chief exec Univ of Newcastle Sch of Mgmnt 1995–; pres Shipbuilders and Shiprepairers Assoc 1991–93; memb Nat Curriculum Council (NCC) 1992–93; Shipbuilding Gold Medal NE Coast Inst of Engrs and Shipbuilders 1969; FRINA (MRINA 1963), FEng 1990, FRSA 1993; *Recreations* music, theatre, ballet, opera, sailing, walking, reading; *Style—* Dr Roger Vaughan, FEng; ✉ Correslaw, Netherwitton, Morpeth, Northumberland NE61 4NW (☎ and fax 01670 772686); Newcastle School of Management, University of Newcastle upon Tyne NE1 7RU (☎ 0191 222 8010)

VAUGHN, James Hurd; *Career* Ensign Supply Corps US Navy 1944–46; pres Vaughn & Blake Inc insur brokers San Francisco 1954–70, chm Frederick S James & Co Inc New York 1975–80 (joined 1970, dir 1973–81), dep chm Hogg Group plc 1993–94 (joined 1981, dir 1983–, chm 1987–93); dir: Kleinwort Benson NA New York 1982–85, Portals Ltd NA New York 1981–85, J F Johnson Bahamas 1986–, BNB Resources plc London 1983–90, International Art and Antique Loss Register Ltd 1993–, Loss Management Group Ltd 1994–; non-exec dir Bain Hogg Group 1994–96; tstee Children's Aid Soc New York 1985–; memb Lloyd's 1973–; *Clubs* River (NY), City, Queen's, Brooks's, Cypress Point (Calif); *Style—* James H Vaughn, Esq; ✉ c/o Chairman's Office, Bain Hogg Group plc, Lloyds Chambers, 1 Portsoken Street, London E1 8DF (☎ 0171 301 4401, fax 0171 301 4388)

VAUX, Marc; s of John Leslie Vaux (d 1979), and Molly Millicent, *née* White (d 1983); *b* 29 Nov 1932; *Educ* Commonweal Secdy GS Swindon, Oxford Poly, Swindon Sch of Art (pre-dip cert), Slade (dip); *m* 1, 1961 (m dis 1983), Tess Jaray, *qv*; 2 da (Anna b 1964, Georgia b 1966); m 2, 1984, Gillian, *née* Parkinson; 1 step s (Benedick b 1971), 1 da (Alexandra b 1985); *Career* artist; Nat Serv RAF 1952–54; scientific asst AERE Harwell Berks 1949–51, asst Jean Pons' lithographic studio Paris 1961; pt/t freelance artist; teacher: Bath Acad of Art Corsham, Hornsey Coll of Art London and others 1962–72; princ lectr in painting Central Sch of Art and Design 1973–86, head of painting Central/St Martins Coll of Art and Design 1986–89; awards incl: Boise Travelling Scholarship 1960, British Arts Cncl Major Award 1977; *Solo Exhibitions* Grabowski Gallery London 1963 (with Tess Jaray), Hamilton Galleries London 1965, Axiom Gallery London 1967, Galerie Wilbrand Cologne 1969, Axiom Gallery 1970, Whitechapel Art Gallery (with Tess Jaray) 1973, Park Gallery Cheltenham 1989, Center for Int Contemporary Arts NYC 1990, Anderson O'Day Gallery London 1990; *Group Exhibitions* incl: 2e Biennale de Paris Musée d'Art Moderne Paris 1961, John Moores Liverpool Exhbn Walker Art Gall 1965, 1967 and 1985, Ninth Int Art Exhbn of Japan Tokyo, Six Artists (V & A) 1967, Soc of Scottish Artists 73rd Exhbn (RSA Galleries Edinburgh) 1967, Fine Art for Industry (RCA) 1969, British Painting '74 (Hayward Gall) 1974, Whitechapel Summer Show '79 London 1979, London Group (RCA) 1984, Thirty London Painters (RA) 1985, Small is Beautiful (Flowers East London) 1991; *Public Collections* Arts Cncl, DOE, UCL, V & A, City Art Gallery Bradford, City Art Gallery Leeds, Leics Educn Authy, Graves Art Gallery Sheffield, Contemporary Arts Soc, Tate Gallery, York Art Gallery, and numerous foreign collections; *Recreations* chess fanatic; *Clubs* Chelsea Arts; *Style—* Marc Vaux, Esq; ✉ 10 Fawe Street Studios, London E14 6NT (☎ 0171 515 9372); Redfern Gallery, Cork Street, London (☎ 0171 734 1732/0578, fax 0171 494 2908)

VAUX, Maj-Gen Nicholas Francis (Nick); CB (1989), DSO (1982); s of Harry Vaux, and Penelope Vaux; *b* 15 April 1936; *Educ* Stonyhurst; *m* 1966, Zoya, da of Gen Sir Peter Hellings, KCB, DSC, MC; 1 s (Piers b 1973), 2 da (Zoya b 1967, Tara b 1969); *Career* cmmnd RM 1954, Suez 1956, Far East 1958–61, frigate W Indies 1962–64, Staff Coll Camberley 1969, MOD (Army) 1975–77, 2 i/c 42 Commando RM 1977–79, Lt Col Special Advsr US Marine Corps 1979–81, CO 42 Commando RM (Operation Corporate) 1981–83, Col 1983, COS to Maj Gen Trg Reserve and Special Forces 1983–85, RCDS 1985, COS Maj-Gen Commando Forces 1986, Maj Gen RM Commando Forces 1987–90; md Secar (Br-Russian Security Co) 1993–; *Books* March to the South Atlantic (1986); *Recreations* skiing, field sports; *Clubs* Farmers'; *Style—* Maj-Gen Nick Vaux, CB, DSO; ✉ c/o National Westminster Bank, 14 Old Town Street, Plymouth PL1 1DG

VAUX OF HARROWDEN, 10 Baron (E 1523); John Hugh Philip Gilbey; s of William Gordon Gilbey (d 1965), and Grace Mary Eleanor, Baroness Vaux of Harrowden (d 1958); suc bro, 9 Baron, 1977; *b* 4 Aug 1915; *Educ* Ampleforth, Ch Ch Oxford; *m* 5 July 1939, his 1 cous Maureen Pamela, eld da of late Hugh Gilbey, of Shellwood Bend, Leigh, Reigate, Surrey; 3 s, 1 da; *Heir* s, Hon Anthony William Gilbey, *qv*; *Career* Maj, Duke of Wellington's Regt, served War of 1939–45; sits as Conservative in House of Lords; Liveryman Worshipful Co of Vintners; *Style—* The Rt Hon the Lord Vaux of Harrowden; ✉ Cholmondeley Cottage, 2 Cholmondeley Walk, Richmond, Surrey TW9 1NS

VAVASOUR, Sir Geoffrey William; 5 Bt (UK 1828), DSC (1943); s of Capt Sir Leonard Pius Vavasour, 4 Bt (d 1961, himself ggs of Hon Sir Edward Vavasour, 1 Bt, né Stourton and 2 surviving s of 17 Baron Stourton, but who changed his name to Vavasour on inheriting the estates of his mother's 1 cous, Sir Thomas Vavasour, 7 & last Bt of the 1628 cr; the 1 Bt of this previous cr was Knight Marshal of the King's Household and ggs through his mother of the 1 Earl of Rutland, while his w Ursula was one of the Giffards of Chillington); *b* 5 Sept 1914; *Educ* RNC Dartmouth; *m* 1, 1940 (m dis 1947), Joan Millicent Kirkland, da of Arthur John Robb; 2 da; m 2, 1971, (m dis 1980), (Marcia) Christine, da of Marshall Shaw Lodge, of Batley, Yorks; *Heir* kinsman, Eric Michel Joseph Marmaduke Vavasour b 3 Jan 1953; *Career* RN (ret); dir W M Still & Sons; *Clubs* All England Lawn Tennis; *Style—* Sir Geoffrey Vavasour, Bt, DSC; ✉ 8 Bede House, Manor Fields, Putney, SW15 (☎ 0181 788 0707)

VAZ, (Nigel) Keith Anthony Standish; MP (Lab) Leicester East (majority 11,316); s of late Tony Vaz, and Merlyn Verona Rosemary, *née* Pereira; *b* 26 Nov 1956; *Educ* Latymer Upper Sch, Gonville & Caius Coll Cambridge (MA); *m* 3 April 1993, Maria Fernandes; 1 s (Luke Swraj b 2 March 1995); *Career* slr Richmond upon Thames Cncl 1982, sr slr London Borough of Islington 1982–85, slr Highfields & Belgrave Law Centre Leicester 1985–87; called to the Bar 1990; contested Euro elections: Richmond & Barnes 1983, Surrey West 1984; MP (Lab) Leicester E 1987–, memb Home Affrs Select Ctee 1987–; memb Standing Ctees on: Immigration Bill 1987–88, Legal Aid Bill 1988, Children Bill 1989, Football Spectators Bill 1989, NHS and Community Care Bill 1989–90, Cts and Legal Servs 1990–, Armed Forces Bill 1991; chm Lab Party Race Action Gp; chair: Parly Nupe Gp, All Party Parly Footwear and Leather Indust Gp; sec: Legal Servs Campaign, Indo-Br Parly Gp, Lab Educn Gp, Parly Lab Party Wool and Textiles Gp; co-ordinator BCCI Parly Gp 1991–, shadow jr min for environment (with responsibilities for inner city and local govt) 1992–94, shadow min for planning and regeneration 1994–; pres: Leicester and S Leicestershire RSPCA 1988–, Hillcroft Football Club 1988–, Thurnby Lodge Boys Club 1987–; govr: Hamilton Community Coll Leicester 1987–91, St Patrick's Sch Leicester 1986–90; columnist: Tribune, Catholic Herald; memb Nat Advsy Bd Crime Concern; memb: UNISON, Lab Party; MCFI 1988; *Style—* Keith Vaz, Esq, MP; ✉ 144 Uppingham Rd, Leicester (☎ 0116 276 8834); House of Commons, London SW1A 0AA

VEAL, Sheriff Kevin Anthony; s of George Algernon Veal (d 1985), of Dundee, and Pauline Grace, *née* Short (d 1992); *b* 16 Sept 1946; *Educ* Lawside Roman Catholic Acad Dundee, Univ of St Andrews (LLB); *m* 29 Oct 1969, Monica, da of James Flynn, and Mary, *née* Breslin; 4 c (Mary Pauline b 8 Sept 1970, Matthew Gerard b 23 April 1974, Dominic Joseph b 18 March 1978, Bridget Ann b 17 July 1987); *Career* apprentice slr Dickie, McDonald, Gray & Fair WS Dundee 1966–68, asst to Gilruth Pollock & Smith Dundee 1968–71, Notary Public 1971, ptnr Burns Veal & Gillan Dundee 1971–93, sheriff of Tayside Central and Fife (at Forfar) 1993– (temp sheriff 1984–93); pt/t tutor Dept of Law Univ of Dundee 1978–85, dean Faculty of Procurators and Solicitors Dundee 1991–93; Kt of Equestrian Order Holy Sepulchre of Jerusalem 1989, Kt of St Gregory the Great 1993; *Recreations* choral and classical music, organ playing, hill walking; *Style—* Sheriff Kevin Veal; ✉ Viewfield, 70 Blackness Avenue, Dundee DD2 1JL (☎ 01382 668633); Sheriff Court House, Market Street, Forfar DD8 3LA (☎ 01307 462186)

VEALE, Sir Alan John Ralph; kt (1984); s of Leslie Henry Veale (d 1971); *b* 2 Feb 1920; *Educ* Exeter Sch, Manchester Coll of Technol; *m* 1946, Muriel, da of John William Edwards; 2 children; *Career* CEng; dir and gen mangr AEI Motor & Control Group 1966–68; md: GEC Diesels Ltd 1968–70, GEC Power Engineering Ltd 1970–85; dir GEC 1973–85; chm: Rossmore Warwick Ltd 1986–89, RFS Industries Ltd 1987–92, Exeter Enterprise Ltd 1989–; pres Inst of Prodn Engrs 1985–86; Hon DSc 1984; FEng 1980, FIMechE, FIEE; *Recreations* sailing, walking; *Style—* Sir Alan Veale, FEng; ✉ 41 Northumberland Rd, Leamington Spa, Warwickshire CV32 6HF (☎ 01926 424349)

VEATS, John Arthur; s of Arthur Ernest Veats (d 1987), of Woking, Surrey, and Grace Alice, *née* Brooks (d 1994); *b* 10 Dec 1929; *Educ* Latymer Sch; *m* 1955, Elizabeth Anne, da of Norman Alexander Stemp; 1 s (James b 26 Aug 1961), 3 da (Elizabeth b 13 Jan 1963, Sophia b 24 Jan 1966, Victoria b 23 Oct 1969); *Career* rowing administrator; oarsman: Lensbury Rowing Club 1950–58 (capt and chm), memb Leander Club, rowed Henley Royal Regatta 1951–58; Amateur Rowing Assoc: hon treas 1965–80, chm 1980–89, exec vice pres 1989–; hon treas World Rowing Championships 1975 (vice chm 1986); memb: Mgmnt Ctee Henley 1987– (steward 1982–), Ctee BOA 1985–90, Exec Ctee CCPR 1989– (vice chm Water Recreation Div 1989–); Shell International Petroleum until 1984, Institute of Directors 1985–93, dir Letheby and Christopher Ltd 1992–; govr Glebelands Sch 1992–; FInstD 1991; Desborough medal 1955, Amateur Rowing Assoc medal of honour 1986; *Style—* John Veats, Esq; ✉ Thorns Brook, Guildford Rd, Cranleigh, Surrey GU6 8PG (☎ 01483 274939)

VEEDER, Van Vechten (Johnny); QC (1986); s of John Van Vechten Veeder (d 1976), and Helen, *née* Townley; *b* 14 Dec 1948; *Educ* Neuilly Paris, Clifton, Jesus Coll Cambridge (MA); *Career* called to the Bar Inner Temple 1971; co-ed Arbitration International; *Publications* The ICCA National Report on England (1988 and 1996), The Final Report on the Independent Inquiry into the Capital Market activities of the London Borough of Hammersmith and Fulham (with Barratt and Reddington, 1991); *Recreations* sailing, reading, travelling; *Clubs* Aldeburgh Yacht, Orford Sailing, Little Ship; *Style—* V V Veeder, Esq, QC; ✉ Essex Court Chambers, 24 Lincoln's Inn Fields, London WC2A 3ED (☎ 0171 813 8000, fax 0171 813 8080)

VEEN, Dr Peter; *b* 20 Oct 1940; *Educ* Univ of Utrecht Holland (PhD cum laude); *m* 1966, Lien, *née* Witteveen; 1 s (Folkert Michiel b 4 Dec 1970), 1 da (Barbara Marije b 2 June 1972); *Career* Reserve Offr Royal Dutch Navy 1966–68; res fell Univ of Utrecht 1968–70, mgmnt conslt with Berenschot Consultants 1970–75, prof of social psychology Univ of Utrecht 1975–77, prof of applied social psychology and head of dept Univ of Groningen 1977–84, md Royal Theodorus Niemeyer BV 1986–90 (dir 1984–85), md Gallaher Tobacco Ltd 1994– (mktg dir 1990–94); *Style—* Dr Peter Veen; ✉ Gallaher Tobacco Ltd, Members Hill, Brooklands Road, Weybridge, Surrey KT13 0QU (☎ 01932 859777, fax 01932 832571)

VEITCH, Andrew David; s of Henry Scribbens Veitch (d 1991), and May, *née* Silver; *b* 15 July 1946; *Educ* Reading Sch, Trinity Coll Dublin (BSocSci); *m* 10 Aug 1968, Elizabeth Mary, da of Rev Charles Bryan; 2 s (Joel Andrew b 28 March 1974, Alexander Charles b 1 Sept 1975); *Career* reporter rising to sub-ed Middlesbrough Evening Gazette 1968–71, sub-ed Daily Express 1971–72, The Guardian 1972–88 (successively sub-ed, theatre critic, feature writer, dep ed Women's Page then medical corr), theatre critic Capital Radio 1986–87, sci corr Channel Four News 1988–; Terence Higgins Trust Award for The Individual Contributing Most to the Understanding of AIDS, RTS Best

Topical Feature 1991, Br Environmental and Media Awards Best National TV News Coverage 1989, 1991, 1992 and 1994, Br Assoc for the Advancement of Sci Award for Outstanding TV Coverage of Sci, NY Film and TV Festivals Finalists' Awards 1991 and 1992 and Silver Award 1992; memb Br and American Assocs for the Advancement of Sci; *Books* The Naked Ape - An Anthology of Sexism 1982–83; *Recreations* computing, gardening, whisky tasting, R&B music; *Clubs* Working Men's (Eccles); *Style*— Andrew Veitch, Esq; ✉ Channel 4 News, ITN Ltd, 200 Gray's Inn Road, London WC1X 8XZ (☎ 0171 430 4673, fax 0171 430 4608)

VEITCH, Prof George Bryan Austin; *b* 18 April 1935; *Educ* Houghton-le-Spring GS, Rutherford Tech Coll (HNC), Sch of Pharmacy Sunderland Tech Coll (Pharmaceutical Chemist Qualifying Exam), Royal Victoria Infirmary Newcastle (MR Pharm S), Univ of London (ext deg, BSc), Univ of Aston (PhD); m, 2 c; *Career* scientific technician NCB 1951–55, res technician Univ of Durham 1955–56, pre-registration student Royal Victoria Infirmary 1959–60, locum pharmacist 1960; Univ of Aston: asst lectr in phytochemistry 1960–64, lectr in medicinal chemistry 1964–76, organiser Continuing Educn Courses 1971–83, sr lectr and course tutor 1976–83; regnl pharmaceutical offr Oxford Regnl Health Authy 1983–87, chief pharmaceutical advsr to Sec of State for Wales Welsh Office 1987–95; visiting sr lectr Univ of Aston 1983–89, visiting prof Univ of Wales 1990–; external examiner: Natural Products Al Faateh Univ Tripoli 1980–83, Clinical Pharmacy to Undergrad Course UWIST 1984–87, res degrees Univ of Bradford, Univ of Wales, Sunderland Poly 1984–87, Univ of Portsmouth 1990–94, Univ of Leeds 1995–; fndr memb Coll of Pharmacy Practice 1981; memb: Soc of Drug Res 1968, Phytochemical Soc Europe 1972, American Soc of Pharmacognosy 1975, UK Clinical Pharmacy Assoc 1981, European Clinical Pharmacy Assoc 1986, W Midlands Region Pharmaceutical Educn Ctee; govr Bd of Coll of Pharmacy Practice 1989; author of books and articles in med jls; CChem 1985, FRSC 1985, FLS 1985, FRPharmS 1988; *Recreations* fell walking, photography, railways, music; *Style*— Prof George Veitch; ✉ Welsh School of Pharmacy, University of Wales College of Cardiff, Cardiff CF1 3XF (☎ 01222 074783, fax 01222 874149)

VELARDE, (Peter) Giles; s of F X Velarde, OBE, FRIBA (d 1960), of Liverpool; *b* 12 Feb 1935; *Educ* Ampleforth, Chelsea Sch of Art; *m* 1966, Celia Mary, *née* Heddy; 1 s, 2 da; *Career* Nat Serv Sub Lt RN; museum and heritage exhbn designer, author of books and articles, lectr in English and French; estab Giles Velarde Associates creative consultancy; maj design projects incl: exhibits for Natural History Museum (British Fossils 1980, Treasures of the Earth 1985, Britain's Offshore Oil and Gas 1988), creative conslt/designer Musee du Marbre Boulogne 1989, designer and conslt for new museum in the 18th century Manor House restoration project Bury St Edmunds 1990–93, design of new Musicology Gallery Horniman Museum and Gardens 1993, concept designer for phase II of Museum of Liverpool Life 1993–, concept designer for phase III - the King's Regiment Galleries Nat Museums and Galleries on Merseyside 1994–, concept for new Ulster/American Gallery on the History of Emigration NI 1994, designer for re-design of Oxfordshire Co Musuem Oxfordshire CC 1995; visiting lectr for annual museum exhbn project Kingston Poly Sch of 3D Design 1985–92; Univ of Humberside: visiting lectr 1985–, outside advsr for Museum and Exhbn Design degree course and external examiner 1991–95; visiting lectr Inst of Archaeology Univ of London 1990–; memb: Bullough Ctee on Graphic Communication Zoological Soc of London 1983, Design Advsy Ctee MOMI 1986–87, Panel of Judges for new Museum of Evolution Natural History Museum Paris 1987; past chm Museum Designers' Gp Museums Assoc; occasional contrib: Design Week, Museums Jl; FCSD 1981, fell Museums Assoc 1983, FRSA 1993; *Books and Publications* Did Britain Make It? Part 1: Exhibition Design (Design Cncl, 1986), Designing Exhibitions (Design Cncl, 1988); Manual of Curatorship (contrib Section 3, 1984), Manual of Heritage Management (contrib, 1995), Manual of Touring Exhibitions (contrib, 1995); *Recreations* cooking, walking, English market towns; *Style*— Giles Velarde, Esq; ✉ Giles Velarde Associates, Fir Trees Studio, Cliff End Lane, Pett Level, E Sussex TN35 4EF (☎ 01424 813777, fax 01424 813266)

VELJANOVSKI, Dr Cento; s of Gavril Veljanovski, of Macedonia, and Margaret, *née* Wagenaar; *b* 19 Feb 1953; *Educ* Monash Univ (BEc, MEc), Univ of Oxford (DPhil); *m* 1990, Annabel, da of Col William Fazakerley, of Sherborne, Dorset; 1 s (Tomas Cento b 6 July 1995), 1 da (Lydia Rose b 17 Oct 1992); *Career* jr res fell Wolfson Coll Oxford 1978–84, visiting prof Univ of Toronto 1980–81, lectr UCL 1984–87, res and ed dir Inst of Econ Affairs 1987–91; dir Lexecon Ltd 1990–94, non-exec dir Flextech plc 1993–; pres and exec dir Waverley International Ltd (Bermuda and Hong Kong); econ advsr Republic of Macedonia 1991–; memb: Royal Economics Soc, Soc of Business Economists, IOD; *Books* The New Law and Economics (1982), Choice by Cable (1983), Selling the State - Privatisation in Britain (1987), Privatisation and Competition - A Market Prospectus (1989), Freedom in Broadcasting (1989), The Media in Britain Today (1990), Regulators and the Market (1991); *Recreations* rowing, art, television, walking; *Clubs* United Oxford and Cambridge Univ, Chelsea Arts, Annabel's; *Style*— Dr Cento Veljanovski

VELLACOTT, Keith David; s of Hugh Douglas Sempill Vellacott (d 1987), of Tavistock, and Lorraine Freda Vellacott; *b* 25 Feb 1948; *Educ* Kelly Coll, The London Hosp Med Coll, DM (Nottingham); *m* 17 March 1973, Jinette, da of Godfrey Herbert Gibbs, of Teignmouth; 2 s (Darren Adrian b 1975, d 1986, Guy Neil b 1977), 1 da (Adele Fiona b 1980); *Career* res fell Univ of Nottingham 1977–81, surgical sr registrar Bristol Royal Infirmary 1981–86, conslt gen surgn Royal Gwent Hosp 1986–; memb: Br Soc of Gastroenterology, Assoc of Surgns of England and Ireland; FRCS 1976; *Style*— Keith Vellacott, Esq; ✉ Glasllwch House, 4 Glasllwch Crescent, Newport, South Wales NP9 3SE (☎ 01633 252303); Royal Gwent Hospital, Cardiff Road, Newport, South Wales NP2 2UB

VELMANS, Marianne H; da of Loet A Velmans, of Sheffield, Mass, and Edith, *née* Van Hessen; *b* 5 July 1950; *Educ* Int Sch of Geneva, Univ of Sussex (BA); *m* Paul A Sidey; 1 s (Jack b 18 Oct 1984), 1 da (Saskia b 23 April 1990); *Career* Penguin Books 1973–80, head of London office Doubleday & Co Inc 1980–87, Doubleday publishing dir Transworld Publishers Ltd (following takeover) 1987–; *Books* Working Mother - A Practical Handbook (with Sarah Litvinoff, 1987, revised edn 1993); *Style*— Ms Marianne Velmans; ✉ Doubleday, 61–63 Uxbridge Road, London W5 5SA (☎ 0181 579 2652, fax 0181 579 5479)

VENABLES, (Harold) David Spenser; CB (1993); s of Maj Cedric Venables TD, of Oatlands, Warborough, Oxford (d 1976), and Gladys, *née* Hall (d 1973); *b* 14 Oct 1932; *Educ* Denstone Coll; *m* 18 July 1964, Teresa Grace, da of James Cornelius Watts (d 1960), of Hove, Sussex; 1 s (Julian b 1967), 1 da (Louise b 1965); *Career* Pilot Offr Central Reconnaissance Estab RAF 1957–58; admitted slr 1956; entered Official Slr's Office 1960, memb Lord Chllr's Ctee on Age of Majority 1965–67, asst official slr 1977–80, official slr to the Supreme Court 1980–93; *Books* A Guide to the Law Affecting Mental Patients (1975), Halsbury's Laws of England (contrib to 4 edn), The Racing Fifteen-Hundreds: A History of Voiturette Racing 1931–40 (1984); *Recreations* vintage motor cars, military and motoring history; *Style*— David Venables, Esq, CB; ✉ 11 Onslow Road, Hove, East Sussex BN3 6TA (☎ 01273 502374)

VENABLES, Robert; QC (1990); s of Walter Edwin Venables, MM, of Wath upon Dearne, Rotherham, and Mildred Daisy Robson, *née* Taylor; *b* 1 Oct 1947; *Educ* Wath upon Dearne Co GS, Merton Coll Oxford (MA), LSE (LLM); *Career* lectr: Merton Coll Oxford 1972–75, UCL 1973–75; Univ of Oxford 1975–80: official fell and tutor in jurisprudence St Edmund Hall (fell by special election 1992), CUF lectr; called to the Bar Middle Temple 1973, in practice 1976–; consltg ed The Offshore Tax Planning Review and Personal Tax Planning Review, chm Advsy Editorial Bd The Charity Law and Practice Review; treas Crusaid 1991–96, dir Yves Guihannec Fndn 1992–; FTII 1983; *Books* Inheritance Tax Planning (3 edn, 1996), Preserving the Family Farm (1989), Lifetime Giving (1989), Tax Planning Through Trusts (1990), National Insurance Contribution Planning (1990), The Company Car (1990), Holdover Relief (1990), Capital Gains Tax Planning for Non UK Residents (2 edn, 1992), Tax Planning and Fundraising for Charities (2 edn, 1994), Non-Resident Trusts (6 edn, 1995); *Recreations* music making; *Clubs* Travellers; *Style*— Robert Venables, Esq, QC; ✉ 61 Harrington Gardens, London SW7 4JZ; Chambers, 24 Old Buildings, Lincoln's Inn, London WC2A 3UJ (☎ 0171 242 2744, fax 0171 831 8095)

VENABLES, Robert Michael Cochrane; s of Cdr Gilbert Henry Venables, DSO, OBE, RN (d 1986), and Muriel Joan, *née* Haes (d 1990); *b* 8 Feb 1939; *Educ* Portsmouth GS; *m* 13 May 1972, Hazel Lesley, da of Wilfred Keith Gowing (d 1990); 2 s (Gilbert b 1974, John b 1977), 2 da (Caroline b 1973, Sarah b 1987); *Career* admitted slr 1962, in private practice London, Petersfield and Portsmouth 1962–70; Treasy Slr's Dept: legal asst 1970–73, sr legal asst 1973–80, asst Treasy slr 1980–89; charity cmmr 1989–; memb: Int Nuclear Law Assoc 1976–91 (memb Bd 1981–83), First Div Assoc (Exec Ctee 1980–82 and 1987–92, chm Legal Section 1981–83), Law Soc (memb Cncl 1993–), City of Westminster Law Soc; *Recreations* opera, theatre, collecting domestic anachronisms; *Style*— Robert Venables, Esq; ✉ The Charity Commission, St Alban's House, 57–60 Haymarket, London SW1Y 4QX (☎ 0171 210 4419)

VENABLES, Terence Frederick (Terry); *b* 6 Jan 1943; *Educ* Dagenham HS; *m* Yvette; 2 da (Nancy, Tracy); *Career* former professional footballer, now coach; clubs as player: Chelsea 1958–66 (capt 1962), Tottenham Hotspur 1966–68 (winners FA Cup 1967), Queens Park Rangers 1968–73; clubs as manager: Crystal Palace 1976–80 (coach 1973–76), Queens Park Rangers 1980–84 (winners Second Div 1980, runners up FA Cup final 1982), Barcelona 1984–87 (winners Spanish Championship 1984, finalists European Cup 1985), Tottenham Hotspur 1987–91 (winners FA Cup 1991); chief exec Tottenham Hotspur plc 1991–93; coach English National Team 1994–96 (left following European Championship finals); dir of football Portsmouth FC 1996–, coach Australian National Soccer Team 1996–; only player to have represented England at all levels; regular appearances on various TV soccer progs; proprietor Scribes West (members dining club Kensington High Street); co-author TV detective series Hazell; *Books* They Used to Play on Grass (1971), Terry Venables: Autobiography (1994), Venables' England (1996), Terry Venables: The Best Game in the World (1996); *Style*— Terry Venables, Esq; ✉ Terence Venables Holdings Ltd, 213 Putney Bridge Road, London SW15 2NY (☎ 0181 874 5001, fax 0181 874 0064)

VENABLES-LLEWELYN, Sir John Michael Dillwyn-; 4 Bt (UK 1890), of Penllergaer, Llangyfelach and Ynis-y-gerwn, Cadoxton juxta Neath, Glamorganshire; s of Brig Sir (Charles) Michael Dillwyn-Venables-Llewelyn, 3 Bt, MVO (d 1976), and Lady Delia Mary Hicks-Beach, sister of 2 Earl St Aldwyn; *b* 12 Aug 1938; *Educ* Eton, Magdalene Coll Cambridge; *m* 1, 1963 (m dis 1972), Nina, da of late J S Hallam; 2 da (Georgina Katherine (Mrs Antony H Mead) b 1964, Emma Susan b 1967); m 2, 1975, Nina Gay Richardson Oliver (d 1995); *Heir* none; *Career* farmer; *Style*— Sir John Venables-Llewelyn, Bt; ✉ Llysdinam, Newbridge-on-Wye, Llandrindod Wells, Powys (☎ 0159 789 351)

VENN, Paul William; s of Capt Christopher Joseph Venn, of Seaford, E Sussex, and Ellen, *née* Kenny; *b* 20 Jan 1958; *Educ* St Boniface's Coll Plymouth, St Olave's GS Orpington, Univ of Sussex Brighton (BA); *m* 19 Sept 1987, Claire Michelle, da of William Brian Charity; 1 s (Oliver William b 16 Oct 1988), 1 da (Imogen Amy b 3 Jan 1991); *Career* Newton and Godin advtg Tunbridge Wells 1980–81, Geers Gross London 1981–84, Foote Cone & Belding 1984–87, dep md Butterfield Day Devito Hockney 1987–94, dir Young & Rubicam 1994–; MIPA; *Recreations* cricket (Abyssinian CC), golf; *Style*— Paul Venn, Esq; ✉ 41 Windermere Road, Muswell Hill, London N10 2RD (☎ 0181 883 6367); Young & Rubicam Ltd, Greater London House, Hampstead Road, London NW1 7QP (☎ 0171 387 9366, fax 0171 611 6570)

VENNER, Rt Rev Stephen Squires; *see:* Middleton, Bishop of

VENNING, Martin John Wentworth; s of Maj Peter Wentworth Venning, of Surrey, and Vera Venning, *née* Heley (d 1956); *b* 30 June 1942; *Educ* Cranleigh Sch Surrey; *m* 1, 5 May 1973, Barbara Lesley; 2 da (Zoe b 1974, Nicola b 1976); m 2, 4 Dec 1982, Marian Kay, da of Ronald Rupert Arthur (d 1994), of Surrey; *Career* CA, licensed insolvency practitioner; sr and managing ptnr Sheffield Office BDO Stoy Hayward; hon treas: Sheffield & Dist Soc of CAs 1984–87, W Yorks Soc of CAs 1981–83; pres Sheffield & Dist Soc of CAs 1993–94 (hon sec 1989–92, vice pres 1991–92, dep pres 1992–93), pres CA Student Soc of Sheffield 1991–92 and 1994–95; dep chm High Peak Cons Assoc 1996– (hon treas 1986–90), dir Sheffield & Dist Chamber of Trade 1996–; dir Hope Valley Tourist Assoc; business govr Dore Infant Sch 1990–; *Recreations* hockey (Yorkshire Co 1972–73), squash, tennis; *Clubs* Purley Hockey, Farsley Hockey, Bamford Tennis; *Style*— Martin J W Venning, Esq; ✉ The Old Vicarage, Church Bank, Hathersage, Sheffield S30 1AB (☎ 01433 651099); Nimrod House, 42 Kingfield Road, Sheffield S11 9AT (☎ 0114 255 6591)

VENNING, Philip Duncombe Riley; s of Roger Riley Venning, MBE (d 1953), and Rosemary Stella Cenzi, *née* Mann; *b* 24 March 1947; *Educ* Sherborne, Principia Coll Illinois USA, Trinity Hall Cambridge (MA); *m* 4 April 1987, Elizabeth Frances Ann, da of late Michael Anthony Robelou Powers; 2 da (Laura Rosemary Ann b 28 May 1993, Grace Merlyn Frances b 14 July 1995); *Career* journalist Times Educnl Supplement 1970–81 (asst ed 1978), freelance writer 1981–84; sec: Soc for the Protection of Ancient Buildings 1984–, William Morris Craft Fellowship Ctee 1986–96; memb: Conf on Trg in Architectural Conservation 1988–, Cncl Nat Tst 1992–; tstee Historic Churches Preservation Tst 1995–; FSA 1989, FRSA 1990; *Recreations* visiting old buildings, book collecting; *Style*— Philip Venning, Esq, FSA; ✉ 17 Highgate High St, London N6 5JT (☎ 0181 341 0925); Society for the Protection of Ancient Buildings, 37 Spital Square, London E1 6DY (☎ 0171 377 1644)

VENNING, Robert William Dawe (Bob); s of Tom William Dawe Venning, of Harrow, Middlesex, and Elsie Lillian, *née* Durdin; *b* 25 July 1946; *Educ* Midhurst Sch W Sussex, Univ of Birmingham (BA); *m* 1969, Jennifer Mei-Ling, o da of Prof Richard Meredith Jackson; 1 da (Camilla Jane b 24 Feb 1976), 1 s (Oliver William Dawe b 16 March 1978); *Career* tutor in philosophy Univ of Birmingham 1968–69, lectr in logic and scientific method Lanchester Poly 1969–70; DHSS: (now Dept of Health) admin trainee 1971–73, private sec to Min for the Disabled 1974–75, princ 1975–81, private sec to Min for Health 1981–82, asst sec 1983–90, under sec and dep dir of NHS Personnel 1990–93; princ estab and fin offr Cabinet Office 1993–; *Recreations* playing classical and flamenco guitar, electronics and computing; *Style*— Bob Venning, Esq; ✉ Establishment Officer's Group, Cabinet Office, Queen Anne's Chambers, 28 Broadway, London SW1H 9JS

VENTON, Peter Charles; OBE (1989); s of Terence Basil Venton, and Joan Jessica, *née* Smith; *b* 22 Dec 1942; *Educ* Hardye's Sch Dorchester, Univ of London (BSc); *m* 23 Sept 1967, Susan Marilyn, da of Harry James (d 1988); 1 s (Darren James b 20 April 1972), 1 da (Michelle Louise b 20 May 1970); *Career* sr scientist UKAEA Harwell 1962–66; Plessey: devpt engr 1966–70, engr 1970–75, project mangr 1970–75; project dir and gen mangr Plessey Defence Systems 1982–85 (tech dir 1979–82), md Plessey Radar (now Siemens Plessey Radar) 1985–91, md Siemens Plessey Electronic Systems 1991–93; md GEC-Marconi Naval Systems Ltd 1994–96; MIEE; *Recreations* skiing, sailing, golf, squash; *Clubs* Royal Ocean Racing; *Style*— Peter Venton, Esq, OBE

VENTRY, 8 Baron (I 1800); Sir Andrew Wesley Daubeny de Moleyns; 8 Bt (1797); assumed by deed poll 1966 the surname of Daubeny de Moleyns; s (by 2nd w) of Hon Francis Alexander Innys Eveleigh-Ross-de-Moleyns (d 1964), s of 6 Baron Ventry, and his 2 w Joan (later Mrs Nigel Springett; d 1993), eldest da of Harold Wesley, of Surrey; suc uncle, 7 Baron, 1987; *b* 28 May 1943; *Educ* Aldenham; *m* 1, 20 Feb 1963 (m dis 1979), Nelly Edouard Renée, da of Abel Chaumillon, of Loma de los Riseos, Villa Angel, Torremolinos, Malaga, Spain; 1 s, 2 da (Hon Elizabeth-Ann b 1964, Hon Brigitte b 1967); m 2, 1983, Jill Rosemary, da of Cecil Walter Oram; 1 da (Hon Lisa b 1985); *Heir* s, Hon Francis Wesley Daubeny de Moleyns b 1 May 1965; *Career* farmer 1961–, in electronics 1986–; dir: Burgie Lodge Farms Ltd 1970–, C & R Briggs Commercials 1986–87, Glenscott Motor Controls Inc 1987–88 (vice-pres), Glenscott Motor Controls Inc 1988–94 (pres); European mktg mangr Unico Internat 1994–; *Recreations* shooting, stalking, photography, sailing, skiing; *Style*— The Rt Hon the Lord Ventry; ✉ Hill of Errol House, Errol, Perthshire PH2 7TQ

VENUGOPAL, Dr Sriramashetty; s of Satyanarayan Sriramashetty (d 1962), and Manikyamma, *née* Akkenapalli; *b* 14 May 1933; *Educ* Osmania Med Coll Hyderabad India (BSc, MB BS), Madras Univ (DMRD); *m* 22 May 1960, Subhadra (Meena), da of Raja Bahadur Sita Ramachander Rao (d 1949); 1 s (Arun b 1964), 1 da (Anu b 1962); *Career* med posts Osmania Hosp, state med servs Hyderabad Singareni Collieries 1959–65, registrar in radiology Selly Oak Hosp Birmingham 1965–66, registrar in chest med Springfield Hosp Grimsby 1966–67, princ in general practice Aston Birmingham 1967–, hosp practitioner in psychiatry All Saints Hosp Birmingham 1972–, contrib jls on medico-political subjects; fndr memb and chm Link House Cncl 1975–92, memb Local Review Ctee for Winson Green Prison 1981–83, fndr memb Osmania Grad Med Assoc in UK 1984–; memb: W Birmingham Health Authy 1984–89, Working Gp DHSS 1984–89 (Local Med Ctee 1975, Dist Med Ctee 1978–93), GMC 1984–, Birmingham Community Liaison Advsy Ctee 1985; vice chm: Hyderabad Charitable Tst 1985, Birmingham Div BMA 1980 (chm 1985–86); Overseas Doctors' Assoc: fndr memb 1975–, dep treas 1975–81, nat vice chm 1981–87, chm info and advsy serv 1981–, nat chm 1987–93, nat pres 1993–; memb and former pres Aston Branch Rotary Club; FRSM 1986, FRIPHH 1988, MRCGP 1990; *Recreations* medical politics, music, gardening; *Clubs* Aston Rotary; *Style*— Dr Sriramashetty Venugopal, OBE; ✉ 24 Melville Road, Edgbaston, Birmingham B16 9JT (☎ 0121 454 1725); Aston Health Centre, 175 Trinity Rd, Aston, Birmingham B6 6JA (☎ 0121 328 3597, fax 0121 327 1674)

VENVILLE, Malcolm Frank; s of Barry Venville (d 1978), of Birmingham, and Catherine Louise, *née* May; *b* 5 Sept 1962; *Educ* Lighthall Comp, Solihull Tech Coll, Poly of Central London (BA); *Career* engrg apprenticeship British Leyland 1980–81, Art and Design foundation course Solihull Tech Coll 1981–83, BA(Hons) in Film, Video and Photographic Arts Poly of Central London 1983–86, photographic asst 1987–90, freelance photographer 1990–; *Awards* Creative Circle Advtg Awards: bronze Most Promising Beginner for Photography 1992, silver Most Promising Beginner for Direction 1993, various gold and silvers; Assoc of Photographers: 3 merits and 1 silver Tenth Awards 1993, 2 silvers and 1 merit Eleventh Awards 1994, 1 merit 1995; 1 silver and inclusions D&AD; *Style*— Malcolm Venville, Esq; ✉ Basement Studio, 23 Nassau Street, London W1N 7RF (☎ 0171 436 5191, fax 0171 637 1707)

VERCO, Sir Walter John George; KCVO (1981, CVO 1970, MVO 1952); s of John Walter Verco (RN, ka 1914); *b* 18 Jan 1907; *m* 1929, Ada Rose (d 1989), da of Bertram Leonard Bennett, of Lymington, Hants; 1 s, 1 da; *Career* served WWII RAFVR; sec to Garter King of Arms 1949–60, sec Order of Garter 1974–88, sec to Earl Marshal 1961–96; Rouge Croix Pursuivant 1954–60, Chester Herald 1960–71, Norroy and Ulster King of Arms 1971–80, Surrey Herald of Arms Extraordinary 1980–; served on Earl Marshal's staff for: State Funeral of King George V 1936, Coronation and Funeral of King George VI 1937 and 1952, Coronation of HM Queen Elizabeth II 1953, Funeral of Sir Winston Churchill 1965, Investiture of the Prince of Wales 1969; hon genealogist: Order of the British Empire 1959–, Royal Victorian Order 1968–88; inspr: RAF Badges 1970–96, RAAF Badges 1971–96; advsr on Naval Heraldry 1970–96; tstee Coll of Arms Tst; OStJ; *Recreations* travel; *Style*— Sir Walter Verco, KCVO, Surrey Herald of Arms Extraordinary; ✉ College of Arms, Queen Victoria St, London EC4 (☎ 0171 248 2762); 8 Park Court, Linkfield Lane, Redhill, Surrey RH1 1JG

VERCOE, David James; s of Henry Frank Vercoe, of Kegworth, nr Derby, and Lillian Joy, *née* Surrage, of Kegworth; *b* 15 Sept 1949; *Educ* Loughborough GS, Univ of Manchester (BA); *m* 26 April 1976 (m dis), Elizabeth Anne, *née* Latta; *Career* head of Music Dept Radio Two 1991–93 (ed progs 1988–90, managing ed 1990–91), managing ed BBC Radio Two 1994–; *Recreations* sailing, skiing; *Style*— David Vercoe, Esq; ✉ BBC Radio Two, Broadcasting House, London W1A 1AA (☎ 0171 765 2123, telex 265781 BBC HQG, fax 0171 765 3416)

VERDIN, Anthony; s of Jack Arthur Verdin, and Doris Hilda; *b* 16 Nov 1932; *Educ* Christ's Hosp, Merton Coll Oxford (MA, MSc); *m* 1, 1958, Greta; 1 s (John b 1965), 2 da (Julia b 1962, Annemarie b 1963); m 2, 1986, Araminta, da of Michael Henry Carlile Morris; 1 s (Arthur b 1987), 2 da (Aurelia b 1986, Agatha b 1991); *Career* managing ptnr Cherwell Boathouse 1968–; dir: Chelart Ltd 1978–, Chelsea Arts Club Ltd 1987–, Morris & Verdin Ltd 1981–; md: Analysis Automation Ltd 1971–90, Verdin Ltd 1990–; chm: first Sch on Process Analytical Instrumentation Warwick Univ 1972, Cncl of Gas Detection Equipment Manufacturers 1987–90; toured USA and W Indies with Golden Oldies and Miami Rugby Club 1977; Freeman City of London 1989, Liveryman Worshipful Co of Scientific Instrument Makers; CEng, MInstMC; *Publications* books incl: Gas Analysis Instrumentation (1973), and numerous articles and lectures on instrumentation techniques and air pollution; *Recreations* family, rugby football, tennis (lawn and real), cricket, music, reading, wine tasting; *Clubs* Chelsea Arts, Henley RFC; *Style*— Anthony Verdin, Esq

VERDIN, Peter Anthony; s of Norman Verdin, of Northwich, Cheshire (d 1985), and Mary Winifred, *née* McCormack (d 1993); *b* 4 March 1934; *Educ* Ushaw Coll Durham, Univ of Durham (LLB); *children* 2 s (Christopher b 1966, Michael b 1971), 2 da (Catherine b 1968, Caroline b 1972); *Career* admitted slr 1957; ptnr Healds (Wigan); pres: Assoc of North West Law Socs 1973–74, Wigan Law Soc 1988–89, chm: Remuneration Ctee Law Soc 1980–84, Contingency Planning Working Party Law Soc 1984–87, Industl Tribunals (pt/t); memb Law Soc (memb Cncl 1974–96); *Recreations* golf; *Clubs* RAC, Lymm Golf (capt 1996–97); *Style*— Peter A Verdin, Esq; ✉ 15 Mill Bank, Lymm, Cheshire, WA13 9DG; Moot Hall Chambers, 8 Wallgate, Wigan WN1 1JE (☎ 01942 241511, fax 01942 826639)

VERE HODGE, Dr (Richard) Anthony; s of Rev Preb Francis Vere Hodge, and Eleanor Mary, *née* Connor; *b* 27 Dec 1943; *Educ* Radley, Trinity Coll Dublin (BA), Worcester Coll Oxford (DPhil); *m*; 1 s, 2 da; *Career* joined Beecham Pharmaceuticals (now SmithKline Beecham Pharmaceuticals) 1969, worked on Inteferon Inducers then Human Interferon (project mangr 1974–76), transferred to Antiviral Chemotherapy Project (which discovered Penciclovir, 1983, and Famiclovir, 1985); princ author of first publicaton with named antiherpesvirus compounds Famciclovir and Penciclovir (1989) and other articles on subject; seconded to Worldwide Strategic Product Devpt SmithKline Beecham 1993, assoc dir Anti-infectives Section Jan 1995–Aug 1996; dir Vere Hodge Antivirals Ltd Sept 1996–; memb: Royal Soc of Chemistry 1968, The Chromotographic Soc 1989, Int Soc for Antiviral Research 1990; *Recreations* bell ringing, gardening, hill walking; *Style*— Dr Anthony Vere Hodge; ✉ Vere Hodge Antivirals Ltd, Leigh, Reigate, Surrey RH2 8RD (☎ 01306 611212)

VERE-LAURIE, Lt-Col George Edward; DL (1993 Notts); o s of Lt-Col George Halliburton Foster Peel Vere-Laurie, JP, DL (d 1981), of Carlton Hall, Notts, and (Caroline) Judith, *née* Francklin (d 1987); Carlton Hall was purchased in 1832 by John Vere (d 1881), descended in an illegitimate line from the de Vere Earls of Oxford, and passed on his death to his niece Clementina Isabella Margaret, Mrs Craig, whose eldest da (by her 1 m to Hon Sydney William Foster-Skeffington (3 s of 10 Viscount Massereene and 3 Viscount Ferrard) Florence Clementina Vere m 1, Lt-Col George Brenton Laurie (ka 1915) and assumed the additional surname of Vere for herself and issue (*see* Burke's Landed Gentry, 18 edn, Vol III, 1972); *b* 3 Sept 1935; *Educ* Eton, RMA Sandhurst, Univ of London (BSc); *Career* cmmnd 9 Lancers 1955, cmd 9/12 Royal Lancers (PWO) 1974–77; md Trackpower Transmissions Ltd 1979–91, chm Central Notts Healthcare (NHS) Tst 1992–; Lord of the Manors of Carlton-on-Trent and Willoughby-in-Norwell Notts; High Sheriff of Nottinghamshire 1991–92; Freeman City of London, memb Ct of Assts Worshipful Co of Saddlers (Master 1989–90); FIMgt 1981; *Recreations* horses, fox hunting, country life; *Style*— Lt-Col George Vere-Laurie, DL; ✉ Carlton Hall, Carlton-on-Trent, Newark, Notts (☎ 01636 821421)

VEREKER, John Michael Medlicott; CB (1992); s of Cdr Charles William Medlicott Vereker (d 1995), and Marjorie Hughes, *née* Whatley (d 1984); *b* 9 Aug 1944; *Educ* Marlborough, Univ of Keele (BA); *m* 7 Nov 1971, Judith, da of Hobart Rowen, of Washington, DC; 1 s (Andrew b 1975), 1 da (Jennifer b 1973); *Career* asst princ: ODM 1967–69, World Bank Washington 1970–72; princ ODM 1972, private sec to successive Mins at ODM, asst sec 1978, PM's Office 1980–83, under sec FCO ODA 1983–88 (princ fin offr 1986–88), dep sec (teachers) DES 1988, dep sec (further and higher educn and science) DES 1988–94, permanent sec ODA 1994–; chm Student Loans Co Ltd 1989–91; *Style*— John Vereker, Esq, CB; ✉ Overseas Development Administration, 94 Victoria Street, London SW1E 5JL

VEREKER, Peter William Medlicott; s of Cdr Charles William Medlicott Vereker (d 1995), of Wylye, Wilts, and Marjorie Hughes, *née* Whatley (d 1984); *b* 13 Oct 1939; *Educ* Marlborough, Trinity Coll Cambridge (MA), Harvard Univ (Henry fellow); *m* 7 April 1967, Susan Elisabeth, da of Maj-Gen A J Dyball, CBE, MC, TD (d 1985); 3 s (Connel b 1971, Toby b 1973, Rory b 1981); *Career* Dip Serv: head of Chancery Athens 1975–78, RCDS 1982, cnsllr and consul-gen HM Embassy Bangkok 1983–86 (chargé d'affaires 1984 and 1986), dep perm rep UK Mission Geneva 1987–90, head Arms Control and Disarmament Dept FCO 1991–94, sr civilian instr RCDS 1994–95, ambass and UK perm rep to OECD Paris 1995–; *Recreations* tennis, sailing, skiing, poetry; *Style*— Peter W M Vereker, Esq; ✉ c/o Foreign & Commonwealth Office (OECD Paris), King Charles Street, London SW1A 2AH

VEREKER, Rupert David Peregrine Medlicott; s of John Stanley Herbert Medlicott Vereker, and Valerie Ann Virginia, *née* Threlfall; *b* 31 July 1957; *Educ* Radley, Univ of Bradford (BA); *m* 9 Aug 1986, Philippa Janet, da of Geoffrey Stocks; 2 s (Frederick James Herbert Medlicott b 30 June 1990, Jack Rupert William Medlicott b 30 Jan 1992); *Career* advertising exec; Benton & Bowles (now DMB & B) 1980–85 (graduate trainee then account mangr), Doyle Dane Bernbach (now BMP DDB Needham) 1985–87 (account mangr then dir), md Barnes Vereker 1987–; *Style*— Rupert Vereker, Esq; ✉ Barnes Vereker, 3 Lloyds Wharf, Mill Street, London SE1 2BA (☎ 0171 231 3100, fax 0171 231 6868)

VEREY, David John; s of Michael John Verey, *qv*, and Sylvia Mary, *née* Wilson; cous of (Henry) Nicholas Verey (d 1996); *b* 8 Dec 1950; *Educ* Eton, Trinity Coll Cambridge (MA); *m* 1, 1974 (m dis 1990), Luise, *née* Jaschke; 2 s, 1 da; m 2, 1990, Emma Katharine Broadhead, da of Sir Christophor Laidlaw, *qv*; *Career* Lazard Brothers & Co: joined 1972, dir 1983–, dep chief exec 1985–90, chief exec 1990–, chm 1992–; dir Pearson plc 1996–; tstee Tate Gallery 1994–; *Recreations* stalking, bridge, gardening, travel; *Style*— David Verey, Esq; ✉ Lazard Brothers & Co, 21 Moorfields, London EC2P 2HT (☎ 0171 588 2721)

VEREY, Michael John; TD (1945); s of Henry Edward Verey, DSO (d 1968), of Bridge House, Twyford, Berks, and Lucy Alice, *née* Longstaffe (d 1968); *b* 12 Oct 1912; *Educ* Eton, Trinity Coll Cambridge (MA); *m* 26 March 1947, Sylvia Mary, da of Lt-Col Denis Wilson, MC (k 1916); 2 s (Geoffrey b 1949, David, *qv*, b 1950), 1 da (Angela b 1948); *Career* joined Warwicks Yeo 1936; served: ME, Iraq, Syria and Persia Campaigns 1941, El Alamein 1942, Italy 1943; Lt-Col 1945; dir: Helbert Wagg & Co Ltd 1948–77 (joined 1934), Australian Mercantile Land & Finance Co 1950–70; chm Invest International SA 1968–90, dep chm Commercial Union Assurance Co 1951–82, vice chm The Boots Co 1962–83; chm: Broadstone Investment Trust 1962–83, Brixton Estate Co 1971–83, Schroders Ltd 1973–77; dir British Petroleum Co 1974–82; memb Covent Garden Mkt Authy 1961–66; chm: Charities Official Investmt Fund 1974–77, Accepting Houses Ctee 1974–77; vice pres Br Bankers' Fedn 1974–77; High Sheriff of Berks 1968; *Recreations* gardening, travel; *Clubs* Boodle's; *Style*— Michael Verey, Esq, TD; ✉ The Lodge, Little Bowden, Pangbourne, Berkshire (☎ 0118 984 2210); 120 Cheapside, London EC2 (☎ 0171 382 6000)

VEREY, Rosemary Isabel Baird; OBE (1996); da of Lt-Col Prescott Sandilands, DSO (d 1956), of London, and Gladys Baird, *née* Murton (d 1964); *b* 21 Dec 1918; *Educ* Eversley Sch Folkestone, UCL; *m* 21 Oct 1939, David Cecil Wynter Verey (d 1984), s of Rev Cecil Henry Verey (d 1958), of Barnsley, Glos; 2 s (Charles b 1940, Christopher b 1942), 2 da (Veronica (Mrs Bidwell) b 1946, Davina (Mrs Wynne-Jones) b 1949); *Career* garden designer and author; jt creator Barnsley House Garden Glos; presenter The English Country Garden (7 pt series, BBC 2) 1996; winner of Christies and HHA Garden of the Year Award 1988; lectured on gardening subjects in UK, America and Aust; *Books* The Englishwoman's Garden (1980), The Scented Garden (1981), The Englishman's Garden (1982), The American Woman's Garden (1983), Classic Garden Design (1984), The New Englishwoman's Garden (1987), The Garden in Winter (1988), The Flower Arranger's Garden (1989), The American Man's Garden (1990), Good Planting (1990), The Garden Gate (1991), A Countrywoman's Notes (1991), A Gardener's Book of Days (1992), Rosemary Verey's Garden Plans (1993), Secret Gardens (with Katherine Lambert, 1994), Rosemary Verey's Making of a Garden (1995), The English Country Garden (1996); *Style*— Mrs Rosemary Verey, OBE; ✉ The Close, Barnsley, Cirencester, Gloucestershire GL7 5EE (☎ 01285 740 281, fax 01285 740281)

VERGETTE, John Francis; s of John Sidney Vergette (d 1971), of Swansea, S Wales, and Ethel May, *née* Cockrill (d 1973); *b* 15 March 1930; *Educ* Dynevor GS Swansea, Univ of Swansea, Sch of Architecture UWIST Cardiff (BArch); *m* 30 March 1956, Mary Elizabeth, da of Geoffrey Edgar Turpin; 3 da (Elizabeth Nicola b 8 March 1957, Sarah Frances b 9 Nov 1959, Emma Mary Louise b 3 Sept 1965); *Career* architect; Vergette and Brooks Cardiff 1952–55; Nat Serv cmmnd RE (served Egypt, Somaliland and Cyprus) 1953–55, TA 1955–61 (ret Maj); Percy Thomas Partnership (Architects) Ltd (formerly Sir Percy Thomas & Son then Percy Thomas Partnership) 1955–96: joined 1955, assoc 1959–68, ptnr 1968–90, chm 1990–93, chm and chief exec 1993–96, ret; fndr pres Soc of Architects in Wales 1971–73, vice pres Birmingham Architecture Assoc 1984–86; chm Univ of Nottingham Architecture Mgmnt Seminar 1990, external examiner

Univ of Central England 1992–95; chm RIBA Regional Awards Jury (SW and NE regions) 1972 and 1974; FRIBA; *Awards* Halls of Residence Univ of Wales Aberystwyth (Civic Tst Award 1969), Great Hall, Students Union and Central Concourse Univ of Wales Aberystwyth (Gold Medal for Architecture Royal Nat Eisteddford of Wales 1971, Civic Tst Award 1971), Hugh Owen Library Univ of Wales Aberystwyth (RIBA Architectural Award 1977, SCONUL (Librarians) Design Award 1978, Gold Medal for Architecture Royal Nat Eisteddford of Wales 1979), Physics and Mathematics Bldg Univ of Swansea (Civic Tst Award 1969, Gold Medal for Architecture Royal Nat Eisteddford of Wales 1970), Parke David Pharmaceutical Plant Pontypool (RIBA Architectural Award 1972, Gold Medal for Architecture Royal Nat Eisteddford of Wales 1976), Dylan Thomas Memorial Shelter Swansea (Silver Jubilee Award 1970, Civic Tst Award 1971), Brynamlwg Univ Club Univ of Wales Aberystwyth (Civic Tst Award 1975, Euro Heritage Yr Award 1975), Guardian Royal Exchange Offices Birmingham (Bldg of the Yr W Midlands Soc of Architects 1990, Birmingham Design Initiative Award 1993), Int Convention Centre and Symphony Hall Birmingham (high commendation Br Construction Indust Awards 1991, Royal Town Planning Inst Jubilee Cup 1992, Birmingham Design Initiative Renaissance Award 1993, RIBA Regional Award 1993, Marche International des Professionnels de l'Immobilier Best Centre for Business in Europe 1994); *Competitions* Brindley Place and Nat Indoor Arena Birmingham 1987, Morrison Street Haymarket Edinburgh 1989; *Recreations* painting, travel; *Clubs* Birmingham; *Style*— John Vergette, Esq

VERITY, Anthony Courtenay Froude; s of Arthur Verity (d 1962), of Bristol, and Alice Kathleen, *née* Froude (d 1980); *b* 25 Feb 1939; *Educ* Queen Elizabeth's Hosp Bristol, Pembroke Coll Cambridge; *m* 3 Nov 1962, Patricia Ann, da of Walter Siddall, of Northampton; 1 s (James Adam b 1965), 1 da (Alice Lucy b 1968); *Career* metal broker Henry Gardner & Son 1961–62; asst master: Dulwich Coll 1962–65, Manchester GS 1965–69; head of classics Bristol GS 1969–76, headmaster Leeds GS 1976–86, master Dulwich Coll 1986–95, educn advsr to HH the Shaikha Mousa (wife of Emir of Qatar) 1995–; govr RGS Guildford 1993–; *Books* Latin as Literature (1969); *Recreations* mountaineering, squash, cricket, theatre and opera-going; *Clubs* Academy; *Style*— Anthony Verity, Esq; ✉ Elm Lawn, Dulwich Common, London SE21 7EW; Park End, Town Head, Stainton, nr Penrith, Cumbria CA11 0EP (☎ and fax 01768 868001)

VERITY, Dr Christopher Michael; s of Rev Harry William Verity (d 1988), of Cambridge, and Gladys, *née* Banks; *b* 18 Feb 1946; *Educ* Merchant Taylors' Sch Crosby, Leeds GS, Keble Coll Oxford (MA, BM BCh), St Thomas' Hosp Med Sch; *m* 5 May 1984, Dorothy Bowes (Kelly), da of Clifford Claud Jupp, of Br Columbia; *Career* MO Save The Children Fund Phnom Penh Cambodia 1974, med registrar St Thomas' Hosp 1974–75, house physician Hosp For Sick Children Gt Ormond St 1977, fell Dept of Paediatric Neurology Univ of Br Columbia Canada 1980–81, lectr Dept of Child Health Bristol Royal Hosp For Sick Children 1982–85, conslt paediatric neurologist Addenbrooke's Hosp Cambridge 1985–, assoc lectr Univ of Cambridge Med Sch 1985–; author papers on: the Polle syndrome, follow up after cerebral hemispherectomy, hereditary sensory neuropathies, febrile convulsions in a nat cohort; memb: Br Paediatric Neurology Assoc, Paediatric Res Soc; FRCP 1990; *Recreations* windsurfing, skiing, tennis, painting; *Style*— Dr Christopher Verity; ✉ Addenbrooke's Hospital, Department of Paediatrics, Hills Road, Cambridge CB2 2QQ (☎ 01223 216662)

VERMES, Prof Geza; s of Ernö Vermes (d 1944), and Terezia, *née* Riesz (d 1944); *b* 22 June 1924; *Educ* Gymnasium of Gyula Hungary, Budapest Univ, Univ of Louvain, Coll St Albert of Louvain; *m* 12 May 1958, (Noreen) Pamela, *née* Hobson (d 1993); *Career* lectr (later sr lectr) in biblical studies Univ of Newcastle 1957–65; Univ of Oxford: prof of Jewish Studies 1989–91 (reader 1965–89, now emeritus prof), professorial fell Wolfson Coll 1965–91 (now emeritus); ed Jl of Jewish Studies 1971–; govr Oxford Centre for Hebrew Studies 1972–91, dir Oxford Forum for Qumran Research 1991–, chm Oxford Cncl of Christians and Jews 1980–86; Hon DD: Edinburgh 1989, Durham 1990; Hon DLitt Univ of Sheffield 1994; FBA 1985; *Books* Discovery in the Judean Desert (1956), Scripture and Tradition in Judaism (1961), Jesus the Jew (1973), Post-Biblical Jewish Studies (1975), Jesus and the World of Judaism (1983), History of the Jewish People in the Age of Jesus by E Schürer (jt reviser, 1973–87), The Religion of Jesus the Jew (1993), The Dead Sea Scrolls - Qumran in Perspective (1994), The Dead Sea Scrolls in English (1995); *Recreations* watching wildlife; *Style*— Prof Geza Vermes, FBA; ✉ West Wood Cottage, Foxcombe Lane, Boars Hill, Oxford OX1 5DH (☎ 01865 735 384, fax 01865 735 034)

VERMONT, David Neville; s of Leon Vermont (d 1949), and Anne MacDonald, *née* Hardy (d 1972); *b* 13 Feb 1931; *Educ* Mercers' Sch, Christ's Coll Cambridge (BA, MA); *m* 1, 16 March 1957, Ann Marion (d 1992), da of late Lloyd Wilson; 2 s (Christopher b 1959, Charles b 1961), 1 da (Rachel b 1964); m 2, Grizelda, da of late Alexander d'Agapeyeff; *Career* Cadet Bn HAC 1947–50, Nat Serv 2 Regt RHA 1950–52 (served Germany BAOR, cmmnd 1951), 1 Regt HAC RHA 1952–62 (cmmnd 1956); Sedgwick Group plc 1955–88: dep chm gp reinsurance subsid E W Payne Cos Ltd 1975–87, dir Sumitomo Marine & Fire Insurance Co (Europe) Ltd 1975–90, dir City Fire Insurance Co Ltd and Bimeh Iran Insurance Co (UK) Ltd, London rep Compagnie de Réassurance d'Ile de France (Corifrance); memb Lloyd's 1969–; chm: Reinsurance Brokers' Assoc 1976–77, Brokers' Reinsurance Ctee 1977–78; chm: Cncl Gresham Coll 1988–93, Anglo-Norse (London) Fund for Disabled; vice pres Argentine Dio Assoc (chm 1973–88), chm London Handel Society Ltd; govr: St Paul's Schs (chm 1981–82), Corp of the Sons of the Clergy and memb Ct; memb: Ct City Univ, Bd Centre for Insurance and Investmnt Studies; tstee Whitechapel Art Gallery Fndn; Freeman City of London 1952, Master Worshipful Co of Mercers 1981–82; FRSA; *Recreations* walking, opera, chamber music; *Clubs* Garrick, MCC, United Oxford & Cambridge Univ, City Livery, Nikaean, Beefsteak; *Style*— David Vermont, Esq; ✉ 3 Morgan House, 127 Long Acre, London WC2E 9AA (☎ 0171 240 0269); 6 Lovat Lane, London EC3R 8DT (☎ 0171 929 2414, fax 0171 626 2099)

VERNER-JEFFREYS, Robert Gerard; s of Lt Robert David Verner-Jeffreys, RN (ka 1942, *see* Burke's Landed Gentry 1969 edn, Jeffreys formerly of Canterton Manor), and Audrey Marion, *née* Bray (*see* Burke's Landed Gentry, 1952 edn); *b* 30 Sept 1937; *Educ* St Aubyns, Marlborough, RNC Dartmouth; *m* 12 Sept 1964, Anne, da of Col Samuel Alexander Holwell Kirkby, MC (ka 1943); 1 s (Robert b 1969), 1 da (Annabel b 1966); *Career* insur broker; dir: various divisions and companies in Bowring Group 1977–96, dir John Broadwood & Sons Ltd 1983–86, Pendlehill Ltd 1986–; tstee: Broadwood Tst, Fullers Almshouses, Neale's Charity; ACII, ABIBA; *Recreations* genealogy, music; *Style*— Robert Verner-Jeffreys, Esq; ✉ 19 High Park Rd, Farnham, Surrey GU9 7JJ (☎ 01252 721676)

VERNEY, Edmund Ralph; s and h of Sir Ralph Verney, 5 Bt, *qv*; *b* 28 June 1950; *Educ* Harrow, York Univ; *m* 1982, Daphne Fausset-Farquhar, of Lovelocks House, Shefford Woodlands, Hungerford; 1 s (Andrew Nicholas b 1983), 1 da (Ella b 1985); *Career* FRICS; *Clubs* Brooks's; *Style*— Edmund Verney, Esq; ✉ Rectory Close, Middle Claydon, Buckingham MK18 2EU

VERNEY, His Hon Judge; Sir Lawrence John; kt (1993), TD (1955), DL (Bucks 1967); 5 s of Sir Harry Verney, 4 Bt (d 1974), by his w Lady Rachel Bruce (d 1964), da of 9 Earl of Elgin and Kincardine, KG; *b* 19 July 1924; *Educ* Harrow, Oriel Coll Oxford; *m* 1972, Zoë Auriel, da of Lt-Col P G Goodeve-Docker; *Career* Capt Grenadier Gds 1943–46, Lt-Col Royal Bucks Yeo TA 1947–68, Hon Col Bucks Army Cadet Force 1975–80; called to the Bar Inner Temple 1952; dep chm QS: Bucks 1962–71, Middx 1971; circuit judge 1972–90, recorder of London 1990–; govr Harrow Sch 1972–87; Liveryman Worshipful Co of Curriers, Past Master Worshipful Co of Pattenmakers; OStJ 1992; *Style*— His Hon Judge Sir Lawrence Verney, TD, DL; ✉ Central Criminal Court, City of London, London EC4M 7EH

VERNEY, Sir Ralph Bruce; 5 Bt (UK 1818), of Claydon House, Buckinghamshire, KBE (1974), JP (Bucks 1954), DL (Bucks); s of Sir Harry Calvert Williams Verney, 4 Bt, DSO (d 1974); *b* 18 Jan 1915; *Educ* Canford, Balliol Coll Oxford (BA); *m* 7 July 1948, Mary, da of late Percy Charles Vestey (3 s of Sir Edmund Vestey, 1 Bt) and 2 cous of the present Lord Vestey; 1 s, 3 da; *Heir* s, Edmund Ralph Verney; *Career* Maj RA Java 1945; Vice Lord-Lt for Bucks 1965–85, High Sheriff 1957, Co cnclr 1952–73, Co alderman 1961–73, chm Nat Ctee for England of Forestry Cmmn 1968–80 (produced plan for Chiltern Hills 1971), pres CLA 1961–63, memb Royal Cmmn on Environmental Pollution 1973–79; tstee: Radcliffe and Chequers Tsts; chm Nature Conservancy Cncl 1980–83; memb Ct of Assts Worshipful Co of Dyers; Hon Doctorate Univ of Buckingham; Hon FRIBA 1977, hon fell Green Coll Oxford; *Clubs* Cavalry and Guards'; *Style*— Sir Ralph Verney, Bt, KBE, JP, DL; ✉ Ballams, Middle Claydon, Buckingham MK18 2ET (☎ 01296 730297); Plas Rhoscolyn, Holyhead LL65 2NZ (☎ 01407 860288)

VERNEY, Rt Rev Stephen Edmund; MBE (Mil 1945); 2 s of Sir Harry Verney, 4 Bt, DSO, by Lady Rachel Bruce, da of 9 Earl of Elgin and Kincardine; *b* 17 April 1919; *Educ* Harrow, Balliol Coll Oxford; *m* 1, 1947, Priscilla (d 1974), da of George Schwerdt, of Alresford; 1 s, 3 da; m 2, 1981, as her 2 husband, Sandra Bailey, of Llandeilo Fawr; 1 s (Harry, decd); *Career* late Lt and Temp Capt Intelligence Corps; canon of Coventry Cathedral 1964–70, canon St George's Chapel Windsor 1970–77, suffragan bishop Repton 1977–85, asst bishop Oxford Diocese 1990–; *Books* Fire in Coventry (1964), People & Cities (1969), Into the New Age (1976), Water into Wine (1985), The Dance of Love (1989); *Recreations* conversation and aloneness, music, gardening, walking; *Clubs* English Speaking Union; *Style*— The Rt Rev Stephen Verney, MBE; ✉ The Charity School House, Church Rd, Blewbury, Didcot, Oxon OX11 9PY

VERNON, Dr Clare Christine; da of Stephen Vernon, 12 Willows Ave, Lytham St Annes, Lancashire, and Mary, *née* Dewhirst; *b* 23 Oct 1951; *Educ* Queen Mary Sch Lytham Lancs, Girton Coll Cambridge (MA, MB BChir), Bart's; *m* 17 July 1976 (m dis 1988), George, s of Herbert Evans (d 1984); *Career* registrar in radiotherapy: Royal Free Hosp 1979, Middx Hosp 1982; sr registrar in radiotherapy Mount Vernon Hosp 1984, conslt clinical oncologist Hammersmith Hosp 1986–; prof in radiation oncology Hong Kong; memb: BMA 1976, GMC 1976, 1951 Club 1986; FRCR 1984, MPS 1989; *Recreations* sports, music, archaeology; *Clubs* 1951; *Style*— Dr Clare C Vernon; ✉ 18 Brookfield Avenue, Ealing, London W5 1LA (☎ 0181 997 1786); Department of Clinical Oncology, Hammersmith Hospital, Du Cane Road, London W12 0HS (☎ 0181 383 3177)

VERNON, (John) Fane; s of Capt John Edward Vernon (d 1951), of Co Cavan, Ireland, and Dolores Arnold (d 1931); *b* 16 Jan 1924; *Educ* Winchester; *m* 1948, Pamela Elizabeth, da of Archibald Evander McIver (d 1962), of Dublin; 1 s (John), 1 da (Katharine); *Career* Nat Serv 1942–46, 820 Naval Air Sqdn, HMS Formidable, HMS Indefatigable, Home Fleet, Med and Pacific, demob Lt (A) RNVR; joined Ash & Lacy plc 1951 (chm 1970–89); chm: British Dredging plc 1980–95, Brooke Tool Engrg (Hldgs) plc 1984–90; dir: Shipton Communications Ltd 1982–86, Hargreaves Gp plc 1984–87, Davenports Brewery (Hldgs) plc 1985–86; *Recreations* golf, bridge; *Style*— Fane Vernon, Esq; ✉ 60 Richmond Hill Rd, Edgbaston, Birmingham B15 3RZ (☎ 0121 454 2047)

VERNON, Hon Jack Leslie; s and h of 6 Baron Lyveden, *qv*; *b* 10 Nov 1938; *m* 1961, Lynette June, da of William Herbert Lilley; 1 s, 2 da; *Style*— The Hon Jack Vernon; ✉ 17 Carlton Street, Te Aroha, New Zealand

VERNON, James William; s and h of Sir Nigel Vernon, 4 Bt, *qv*; *b* 2 April 1949; *Educ* Shrewsbury; *m* 1981, Davinia, da of Christopher David Howard, of Ryton Corner, Ryton, Shrewsbury; 2 s (George William Howard b 1987, Guy Alexander Howard b 1993), 1 da (Harriet Lucy Howard b 1985); *Career* ptnr Wilson de Zouche & Mackenzie; FCA; *Recreations* shooting; *Clubs* Hon Artillery Co, Liverpool Artists'; *Style*— James Vernon, Esq; ✉ The Hall, Lygan-y-Wern, Pentre Halkyn, Holywell, Clwyd

VERNON, 10 Baron (GB 1762); John Lawrance Venables-Vernon; s of 9 Baron Vernon (d 1963); *b* 1 Feb 1923; *Educ* Eton, Magdalen Coll Oxford; *m* 1, 1955 (m dis 1982), Sheila Jean, da of W Marshall Clark, OBE, of Johannesburg, S Africa; 2 da (Hon Georgina Frances b 1963 d 1991, Hon Joanna Elizabeth b 1965); m 2, 1982, Sally June, da of Robin Stratford, QC, and formerly w of (1) Colin Fyfe-Jamieson and (2) Sir (John) Jeremy Eustace Tennyson d'Eyncourt, 3 Bt; *Heir* kinsman, William Ronald Dennis Vernon-Harcourt, OBE, b 1909; *Career* WWII Capt Scots Gds, took Conservative Whip in Lords to 1981, since when has sat as SDP Peer and then Ind Peer; called to the Bar Lincoln's Inn 1949; served: Cabinet Office 1953–57, Colonial Office Kenya 1957–58, Foreign Office 1958–60; JP Derbys 1965–77; chm Population Concern 1985–90; *Style*— The Rt Hon the Lord Vernon; ✉ Sudbury House, Sudbury, Derbyshire DE6 5HT (☎ 01283 585208); 10 Ringmer Ave, Fulham, London SW6 (☎ 0171 736 5900)

VERNON, Sir (William) Michael; kt (1995); s of Sir Wilfred Douglas Vernon (d 1973), of Anningsley Park, Ottershaw, Surrey, and Nancy Elizabeth, *née* Jackson; *b* 17 April 1926; *Educ* Marlborough, Trinity Coll Cambridge (MA); *m* 1, 25 April 1952 (m dis 1977), Rosheen Elizabeth Mary, da of George O'Meara (d 1932), of Johannesburg, S Africa; 1 s (Mark Thornycroft Vernon b 7 March 1958); m 2, 7 Sept 1977, Jane Olivia Colston, da of Denys Kilham-Roberts (d 1975); *Career* Lt RM 1944–46; chm and chief exec Spillers Ltd 1968–80 (joined 1948, dir 1960, jt md 1962); pres: Nat Assoc of Br and Irish Millers 1965, Br Food Export Cncl 1977–80; vice chm Millers' Mutual Assoc 1968–80; dir: EMI Ltd 1973–80, Strong & Fisher (Holdings) plc 1980–91; chm: Granville Meat Co Ltd 1981–94, Famous Names Ltd 1981–85, RNLI 1989–96 (dep chm 1981–89), Politics International Ltd 1996–; CIMgt; *Recreations* sailing (ASSEGAI VII), skiing, shooting; *Clubs* Royal Yacht Sqdn, Royal Ocean Racing (cdre 1964–68); *Style*— Sir Michael Vernon; ✉ Fyfield Manor, Andover, Hants SP11 8EN

VERNON, Sir Nigel John Douglas; 4 Bt (UK 1914), of Shotwick Park, Co Chester; s of Sir (William) Norman Vernon, 3 Bt (d 1967); *b* 2 May 1924; *Educ* Charterhouse; *m* 29 Nov 1947, Margaret Ellen, da of late Robert Lyle Dobell, of The Mount, Waverton, Chester; 2 s (1 s decd), 1 da; *Heir* s, James William Vernon, *qv*; *Career* Lt RNVR 1942–45; dir Bain Hogg Insurance Brokers 1984–; *Recreations* gardening, shooting, golf; *Clubs* Naval, Army and Navy; *Style*— Sir Nigel Vernon, Bt; ✉ Top-y-Fron Hall, Kelsterton, Flint, Flinshire CH6 5TF

VERNON, Richard Evelyn; s of Evelyn Vernon, and Violet Mary Stuart, *née* Foley (d 1974); *b* 7 March 1925; *m* 1955 (m dis 1989), Benedicta Lucia, *née* Hoskyns; 1 s (Thomas b 1958), 1 da (Sarah b 1956); *Career* actor; *Theatre* incl: Stratton (first professional prodn, Mercury) 1949, Pack of Lies (Lyric) 1983, Look No Hans (Strand) 1985, Dry Rot (Lyric) 1988, Hidden Laughter (Vaudeville) 1990; *Television* incl: Upstairs Downstairs 1973, The Duchess of Duke Street 1976, Ripping Yarns 1978, Paradise Postponed 1985, The Camomile Lawn 1992, TV Class Act 1993; *Radio* incl: The Hitchhiker's Guide to the Galaxy, Blandings, The Trial of Lady Chatterley, Uncyclopedia of Rock, The Small House at Allington; *Films* incl: Indiscreet 1958, Goldfinger 1964, A Hard Day's Night 1964, The Pink Panther Strikes Again 1976, Ghandi 1982, A Month in the Country 1986; *Recreations* sailing; *Style*— Richard Vernon, Esq; ✉ c/o Julian Belfrage Associates, 46 Albemarle Street, London W1X 4PP (☎ 0171 491 4400, fax 0171 493 5460)

VERNON, Dr Stephen Andrew; s of Alan Vernon (d 1979), of Alderley Edge, Cheshire, and Phyllis Mary Vernon; *b* 10 Feb 1955; *Educ* King's Sch Macclesfield, Univ of Bristol Med Sch (MB ChB), Univ of Nottingham (DM); *m* 1 Sept 1985, Alison Elizabeth Mary, da of Claude Walton (d 1990), of Mansfield, Notts; 1 da (Olivia Katherine b 2 Dec 1989), 1 s (Simon Alexander Alan b 5 Feb 1992); *Career* house physician Bristol Royal Infirmary 1978–79, house surgn Frenchay Hosp Bristol 1979, demonstrator and lectr in anatomy Bristol Med Sch 1979–80, sr house offr and registrar in ophthalmology Bristol Eye Hosp 1980–83, sr registrar Oxford Eye Hosp 1983–86, sr lectr and founding head Academic Unit of Ophthalmology Univ of Nottingham and hon conslt ophthalmologist Nottingham Health Authy 1986–94, conslt ophthalmologist Univ Hosp NHS Tst Nottingham 1994–; author of academic pubns on ophthalmic epidemiology and glaucoma detection and mgmnt; memb: Euro Glaucoma Soc, UK Eye Study Gp; FRCS 1982, FRCOphth 1989; *Books* Ophthalmology (1988), Passing Postgraduate Examinations in Ophthalmology (1992); *Recreations* golf, skiing, music and drama; *Style—* Dr Stephen Vernon; ✉ Department of Ophthalmology, University Hospital, Nottingham NG7 2UH (☎ 0115 924 9924 ext 43200)

VERRILL, John Rothwell; s of Dr Peter John Verrill, of London, and Christine Mary, *née* Rothwell; *b* 25 March 1954; *Educ* Univ Coll Sch, UCL (LLB); *m* 6 Sept 1980, Katharine Mary, da of Hugh Schofield Spensley; 4 s (William b 27 Aug 1986, Edward b 27 Jan 1989, Henry b 25 April 1992, Nicholas b 25 June 1994); *Career* articled clerk Ward Bowie 1978–82, admitted slr 1981; Lawrence Graham (previously Crane & Hawkins): asst slr 1982–86, ptnr Co Commercial Dept 1986–; Licensed Insolvency Practitioner 1990–; Freeman Worshipful Co of Slrs 1988; memb: Law Soc, City of Westminster Law Soc, Int Bar Assoc (UK Energy Lawyers Gp), Insolvency Practitioners Assoc, Insolvency Lawyers Assoc (memb Cncl), Soc of Practitioners of Insolvency; *Books* Butterworth's Insolvency Meetings Manual (1995); *Recreations* rowing, sailing; *Clubs* Thames Tradesmen's Rowing, Leander, Aldeburgh Yacht, Harlequins FC; *Style—* John Verrill, Esq; ✉ Lawrence Graham, 190 Strand, London WC2R 1JN (☎ 0171 379 0000, fax 0171 379 6854)

VERSCHOYLE, Hamilton Stuart; s of Capt Frederick Hildyard Hawkins Stuart Verschoyle, OBE (d 1958), and Joan Mary, *née* Archbold; *b* 16 June 1937; *Educ* Bloxham Sch Oxon; *m* 26 Aug 1970, Marion Elizabeth, da of Reginald Stanley Taplin; 1 s (James Hildyard Hawkins Stuart b 24 April 1975), 1 step s (Andrew John George b 20 May 1962), 1 step da (Elisabeth Jane Mary b 10 Jan 1964); *Career* estate agent; Hampton & Sons (Collins, Collins and Rawlence until 1966): joined 1957, ptnr 1964, equity ptnr (i/c of London region) 1966, sr ptnr 1985, chm 1988 (Hamptons sold to Abaco 1988, subsequently to Bristol and West); *Recreations* tennis, golf, sailing; *Clubs* Turf, St James's, Annabel's, Hurlingham, St George's Hill Tennis, Burhill Golf, Rock Sailing; *Style—* Hamilton Verschoyle, Esq; ✉ Hamptons, 6 Arlington Street, London SW1 (☎ 0171 493 8222)

VERULAM, 7 Earl of (UK 1815); Sir John Duncan Grimston; 14 Bt (E 1629); also Lord Forrester (S 1633), Baron Dunboyne and Viscount Grimston (I 1719), Baron Verulam (GB 1790), Viscount Grimston (UK 1815); s of 6 Earl of Verulam (d 1973); *b* 21 April 1951; *Educ* Eton, Christ Church Oxford; *m* 1976, Dione Angela, da of Jeremy F E Smith, of Balcombe House, Balcombe, Sussex; 3 s (Viscount Grimston b 1978, Hon Hugo Guy Sylvester b 1979, Hon Sam George b 1983), 1 da (Lady Flora Hermione b 1981); *Heir* s, Viscount Grimston, *qv*; *Career* dir Baring Brothers & Co Ltd; *Recreations* country pursuits; *Clubs* Beefsteak, White's; *Style—* The Rt Hon the Earl of Verulam; ✉ Gorhambury, St Albans, Herts AL3 6AH (☎ 01727 855000)

VESSEY, Prof Martin Paterson; CBE (1994); s of Sydney James Vessey (d 1988), of Mill Hill, London, and Catherine, *née* Thompson; *b* 22 July 1936; *Educ* Univ Coll Sch Hampstead, UCL, Univ Coll Hosp Med Sch (MD, MA Oxon); *m* 21 May 1959, Anne, da of Prof Benjamin Stanley Platt, CMG (d 1969); 2 s (Rupert b 1964, Ben b 1967), 1 da (Alice b 1970); *Career* prof of public health Univ of Oxford 1974–, fell St Cross Coll Oxford 1974–; memb: Oxford Preservation Tst, Nat Tst, Cncl for the Preservation of Rural England, BMA, Soc for Social Medicine; author of 3 books and over 300 scientific papers; FRS 1991; *Recreations* fine arts, motoring, Victorian engineering, conservation; *Style—* Prof Martin Vessey, CBE, FRS; ✉ 8 Warnborough Road, Oxford OX2 6HZ (☎ 01865 552698); Department of Public Health and Primary Care, Radcliffe Infirmary, Oxford (☎ 01865 319107)

VESTEY, Sir (John) Derek; 2 Bt (UK 1921); s of late John Joseph Vestey (eldest s of Sir Edmund Vestey, 1 Bt, the latter being bro of 1 Baron Vestey); suc gf 1953; *b* 4 June 1914; *Educ* The Leys Sch; *m* 21 June 1938, Phyllis Irene, o da of Harry Brewer, of Banstead; 1 s, 1 da; *Heir* s, Paul Edmund Vestey; *Career* WWII Flt Lt RAFVR 1940–45; *Clubs* MCC, RAC; *Style—* Sir Derek Vestey, Bt

VESTEY, Edmund Hoyle; DL (Essex 1978, Suffolk 1991); only s of Ronald Vestey, DL; *b* 1932; *Educ* Eton; *m* 1960, Anne Moubray, yr da of Gen Sir Geoffry Scoones, KCB, KBE, CSI, DSO, MC; 4 s (Timothy b 1961, James b 1962, George b 1964, Robin b 1968); *Career* served as 2 Lt Queen's Bays 1951–52; chm: Albion Insurance Co 1970, Blue Star Line 1971–95, Union International PLC 1988–96, Star Offshore Services PLC 1989–95, Vestey Group Limited 1993–95 (dir 1995–); pres: Gen Cncl Br Shipping 1981–82, Chamber of Shipping 1992–94; jt master Thurlow Foxhounds 1967–, chm MFHA 1992–96; pres: Suffolk Agric Soc 1976, E of England Agric Soc 1995, Essex County Scouts Council 1979–87; High Sheriff Essex 1977–78; Lt City of London Yeomanry 1952–60; Liveryman: Worshipful Co of Butchers, Worshipful Co of Shipwrights, Worshipful Co of Farmers; *Clubs* Cavalry, Carlton; *Style—* Edmund Vestey, Esq, DL; ✉ Iolaire Lodge, Lochinver, Sutherland IV27 4JY; Sunnyside Farmhouse, Hawick, Roxburghshire; Little Thurlow Hall, nr Haverhill, Suffolk CB9 7LQ

VESTEY, Paul Edmund; s and h of Sir (John) Derek Vestey, 2 Bt, *qv*; *b* 15 Feb 1944; *Educ* Radley; *m* 1971, Victoria Anne Scudamore, da of John Salter, of Old Ford House, Tiverton, Devon; 3 da; *Clubs* British Racing Drivers', Farmers', Royal Automobile; *Style—* Paul Vestey Esq; ✉ 53 Cheval Place, London SW7 (☎ 0171 589 0562); Manor House Farm, Bishops Sutton, Hants

VESTEY, 3 Baron (UK 1922); Sir Samuel George Armstrong Vestey; 3 Bt (UK 1913), DL (Glos 1982); s of Capt the Hon William Howarth Vestey, Scots Gds (ka Italy 1944, only s of 2 Baron Vestey), and Pamela, da of George Nesbitt Armstrong, s of Charles Nesbitt Frederick Armstrong and Dame Nellie Melba, the opera singer; suc gf 1954; *b* 19 March 1941; *Educ* Eton; *m* 1, 1970 (m dis 1981), Kathryn Mary, da of John Eccles, of Moor Park, Herts; 2 da (Hon Saffron Alexandra (Hon Mrs Idiens) b 1971, Hon Flora Grace b 1978); m 2, 1981, Celia Elizabeth, yr da of Maj (Hubert) Guy Broughton Knight, MC, of Lockinge Manor, Wantage (d 1993), and Hester, sis of Countess (w of 6 Earl) of Clanwilliam; 2 s (Hon William Guy b 1983, Hon Arthur George b 1985), 1 da (Hon Mary Henrietta b 1992); *Heir* s, Hon William Guy Vestey b 27 Aug 1983; *Career* Lt Scots Gds; dir Vestey Group plc and associated cos; pres: London Meat Trade and Drovers' Benevolent Assoc 1973, Inst of Meat 1978–83, Royal Bath & W of England Soc 1994, Br Horse Soc 1994–; chm: Meat Trg Cncl 1992–95, Steeplechase Co Cheltenham; Liveryman Worshipful Co of Butchers; patron of one living; GCStJ, Lord Prior of the Order of St John 1991–; *Clubs* White's, Jockey (Newmarket), Melbourne (Melbourne); *Style—* The Rt Hon the Lord Vestey, DL; ✉ Stowell Park, Northleach, Glos (☎ 01285720 308, fax 01285720 360)

VICE, (Henry) Anthony; s of S J Vice (d 1981), and L I Vice (d 1992); *b* 24 Dec 1930; *Educ* Hymers Coll Hull, Queen's Coll Oxford (MA); *m* 4 Sept 1954, Elizabeth Joan Spencer, da of Prof J N Wright (d 1982); 1 s (John b 6 Aug 1962), 2 da (Susan b 6 Feb 1961, Philippa b 24 Aug 1965); *Career* dir: N M Rothschild 1972–91, Drummond Group plc 1986–93, Chaucer Estates Ltd 1990–, Dewhirst Group plc 1984–95 (chm 1988–93), CIA Group plc 1993–96; chm: Jeyes Group plc 1996–, Bowthorpe plc 1992– (dir 1978–, dep chm 1991); *Style—* Anthony Vice, Esq; ✉ 76 Wimpole Street, London W1M 7DD (☎ 0171 486 6698)

VICK, Sir (Francis) Arthur; kt (1973), OBE (1945); s of Wallace Devenport Vick (d 1952), of Birmingham, and Clara, *née* Taylor (d 1932); *b* 5 June 1911; *Educ* Waverley GS Birmingham, Univ of Birmingham (BSc, PhD); *m* 1943, Elizabeth Dorothy (d 1989), da of Ernest Story; 1 da; *Career* physicist; lectr UCL 1936–44, asst dir of scientific res Miny of Supply 1939–44, sr lectr Univ of Manchester 1947–50 (lectr 1944–47), physics prof Univ Coll North Staffs (now Univ of Keele) 1950–59 (vice princ 1950–54), dir AERE Harwell 1960–64, memb for res UKAEA 1964–66, pres and vice chllr Queen's Univ Belfast 1966–76, pro chllr Univ of Warwick 1977–92 (chm of Cncl 1977–90); memb UGC 1959–66; Hon DSc: Keele, Nat Univ of Ireland, Birmingham, Warwick; Hon LLD: Dublin, Belfast; Hon DCL Kent; FIEE, FInstP, MRIA; *Recreations* music, gardening, DIY; *Clubs* Athenaeum, Savile; *Style—* Sir Arthur Vick, OBE; ✉ Fieldhead Cottage, Fieldhead Lane, Myton Rd, Warwick CV34 6QF (☎ 01926 491822)

VICK, David John; s of John Howard George Vick (d 1993), of W Drayton, Middx, and Pearl Kathleen, *née* Cast; *b* 15 Dec 1951; *Educ* Latymer Upper Sch, Peterhouse Cambridge (MA); *m* 1, 1 Sept 1973 (m dis 1980), (Anne) Sheena Bowyer; m 2, 15 July 1988, Linda, da of Gordon Hunt, of Northallerton, Yorks; 1 s (Daniel David b 1995); *Career* Radio Authority: IBA res offr 1975–77, radio servs offr 1977–81, sr radio offr 1981–87, princ radio devpt offr 1987–90, head of devpt 1990–, dep chief exec 1995–; memb: Amnesty Int, Br Film Inst, Radio Acad; *Books* The Voice of Kenya: Radio in a Developing African Nation (1985), Radio Research: An Annotated Bibliography 1975–88 (1989); *Recreations* travel, cinema, sports; *Clubs* Barnet, Everton; *Style—* David Vick, Esq; ✉ 4 Woodside Close, Beaconsfield, Bucks HP9 1JQ (☎ 01494 673875); Radio Authority, Holbrook House, 14 Great Queen Street, London WC2B 5DG (☎ 0171 430 2724, fax 0171 405 7062)

VICK, Dr John Alexander Stewart; s of John Oliver Curtis Vick (d 1993), of Hitchin, Herts, and Mary Macfarlane, *née* Stewart (d 1988); *b* 4 April 1937; *Educ* Taunton Sch, The London Hosp Med Coll and Univ of London (MB BS, MRCS, LRCP); *m* 14 Sept 1963, Patricia Anne Marie, da of William Vincent Cassidy (d 1963), of Londonderry; 1 s (Peter John William b 1965), 1 da (Emma Mary Louise b 1969); *Career* receiving room offr London Hosp 1960, obstetric house surgn and house physician Brighton Gen Hosp 1961, med and paediatric registrar Lister Hosp Hitchin 1962–64 (sr house offr surgery 1962), med registrar Queen Elizabeth II Hosp Welwyn Garden City 1964–66, sr ptnr Drs Vick, Tidy, Christie, Ingram, Cooper, Kendell and Pickett 1966–97, paediatric hosp practitioner Lister Hosp Stevenage 1966–92 (hon paediatric hosp practitioner 1993–), med offr William Ransom & Son Hitchin, coroner Hitchin Dist Herts 1992– (dep coroner 1979–92); former: divnl surgn Hitchin St John Ambulance Bde, memb Herts Local Med Ctee, memb Herts Family Practitioner Ctee, chm E Herts Div BMA; memb: BMA, Medico-Legal Soc, RSM; MRCGP, DObstRCOG; *Recreations* bridge, croquet, philately, photography; *Clubs* Hitchin Rotary; *Style—* Dr John Vick; ✉ The Pines, 7 Wymondley Close, Hitchin, Herts SG4 9PW (☎ 01462 432904); The Portmill Surgery, 114 Queen St, Hitchin, Herts SG4 9TH (☎ 01462 434246, fax 01462 441246)

VICK, His Hon Judge (Arnold Oughtred) Russell; QC (1980); yr s of His Honour Judge Sir Godfrey Russell Vick, QC (d 1958), of Seal, and Marjorie, JP, *née* Compston (d 1985); *b* 14 Sept 1933; *Educ* The Leys School, Jesus Coll Cambridge (MA); *m* 5 Sept 1959, Zinnia Mary, da of Thomas Brown Yates (d 1968), of Godalming; 2 s (Philip Godfrey Russell b 1960, Mark Thomas b 1964), 1 da (Tessa Louise (Mrs Hendrikz) b 1963); *Career* Nat Serv RAFVR Flying Offr 1952–54; called to the Bar Inner Temple 1958; practised SE Circuit 1958–82: prosecuting counsel to PO 1964–69, dep recorder Rochester City QS 1971, recorder Crown Ct 1972–82; circuit judge (SE Circuit) 1982–, princ civil judge Kent 1990–, designated family judge Medway Care Centre 1991–; govr New Beacon Sch; Master Worshipful Co of Curriers 1976–77; *Books* A Hundred Years of Golf at Wildernesse 1890–1990; *Recreations* golf, cricket, bridge, gardening; *Clubs* MCC, Hawks (Cambridge), Wildernesse Golf (capt 1978), Band of Brothers, Royal Worlington and Newmarket Golf, Bromley Hockey; *Style—* His Honour Judge Russell Vick, QC; ✉ The Law Courts, Barker Rd, Maidstone, Kent ME16 8EW (☎ 01622 754966, fax 01622 685428)

VICKERMAN, Prof Keith; s of Jack Vickerman, and Mabel, *née* Dyson; *b* 21 March 1933; *Educ* King James GS Almondbury, UCL (BSc, PhD, DSc), Univ of Exeter; *m* 16 Sept 1961, Moira, da of Wilfrid Dutton, MC; 1 da (Louise Charlotte b 1973); *Career* Royal Soc tropical res fell UCL 1963–68 (Wellcome lectr 1958–63); Univ of Glasgow: reader 1968–74, prof 1974–84, Regius prof of zoology 1984–, head of dept 1979–85; Leeuwenhoek lectr Royal Soc 1994, Linnean Soc Gold Medal for Zoology 1996; served on various ctees of WHO, ODA and SERC; fell UCL 1985; FRSE 1970, FRS 1984; *Books* The Protozoa (with F E G Cox, 1967); author numerous articles and res papers in learned jls; *Recreations* sketching, gardening; *Style—* Prof Keith Vickerman, FRS, FRSE; ✉ 16 Mirrlees Drive, Glasgow G12 0SH (☎ 0141 334 2794); Division of Environmental and Evolutionary Biology, University of Glasgow, Glasgow G12 8QQ (☎ 0141 330 4433, fax 0141 330 5973, e-mail k.vickerman@bio.gla.ac.uk)

VICKERS, Adrian Michael; s of Hugh Anthony Vickers (d 1970), of Greasby, Cheshire, and Margaret, *née* Rae (d 1989); *b* 24 Sept 1938; *Educ* Beaumont Coll, Merton Coll Oxford (MA); *m* 1977 (m dis), Andrea Tyminski; 2 s (Matthew b 29 Jan 1979, Dominic b 25 May 1983), 1 da (Sophie b 8 Nov 1981); *Career* trainee S H Benson 1962–63, dir Robert Sharp & Partners 1963–76, dep chm Abbott Mead Vickers BBDO 1976–; FIPA; *Recreations* golf, skiing; *Clubs* Royal Mid-Surrey Golf; *Style—* Adrian Vickers, Esq; ✉ Abbott Mead Vickers BBDO Ltd, 191 Old Marylebone Rd, London NW1 5DW (☎ 0171 402 4100, fax 0171 935 5883)

VICKERS, Dr Anthony Leonard (Tony); s of Leonard Vickers (d 1980), and Denise Oweena, *née* Wastnedge, of Sheffield; *Educ* King Edward VII Sch Sheffield, Univ of Leeds (BSc, PhD); *m* 28 May 1966, Jennifer Mary, da of William Henry Jarratt (d 1978); 1 da (Kathryn Louise b 25 Jan 1968), 1 s (Simon Leonard b 9 Jan 1970); *Career* princ operational research offr British Steel South Wales Group 1967–70, mangr Prodn Control & Mgmnt Servs British Steel Stainless 1970–77, works mangr Coated Products British Steel Shotton Works 1977–80, mangr Ops British Steel Shotton Works 1980–88, dir Tech British Steel Strip Products 1988–94, md British Steel Tinplate 1994–; Freeman City of London 1994, Liveryman Worshipful Co of Tinplate Workers Alias Wireworkers 1995 (Freeman 1994); FIM 1993, FEng 1995; *Publications* The Stability of Diffusion Flames of Gases: The Effect of Partially Enclosing the Flames (jtly, 1968), Galvanising Development in the UK (jtly, 1987), Steel in Automotives (1993); *Recreations* swimming, gardening, rugby and soccer (spectator); *Style—* Dr Tony Vickers, FEng; ✉ 24 Grange Park, St Arvans, Chepstow, Gwent NP6 6EA (☎ 01291 621825, fax 01291 625829); British Steel Tinplate, Group Office, Trostre, Llanelli, Dyfed SA12 9SD (☎ 01554 74111, fax 01554 773264, e-mail GBBS2WQG@IBMMAIL.COM)

VICKERS, Edward Roger; s of Edward Roger Vickers (d 1958), and Winifred Florence Lily, *née* Silva-White; *b* 7 May 1943; *Educ* Duke of York's Mil Sch Dover, privately in Berlin, Archer's Ct Secdy Modern Sch Dover, Sir Roger Manwood's Sch Sandwich Kent, Grey Coll Univ of Durham; *m* Lesley, da of Frederick Collings; 2 da (Kate b 12 May

1976, Anna b 7 Dec 1978); *Career* Capt 5 Bn Royal Greenjackets (TA) with special responsibility for PR in BAOR; reporter and announcer BFBS Cologne W Germany 1966–68, producer and presenter BBC Radio Leicester 1968–73, presenter BBC TV 1973–74, Berlin corr BBC 1974–78, reporter The World Tonight BBC Radio 4 1978–79, actg dep mangr BBC Radio Kent 1979–80, md Severn Sound 1981–90 (prog controller 1980–81); Chiltern Radio: gen mangr Western Div 1991–92, chief exec SuperGold 1991–92; md BroadVision Radio (consits) 1993–, dir BroadVision Communications Ltd 1993–; project dir Central European Broadcasting 1994, country mangr (Austria) GWR Group plc 1996; AIRC: bd dir, chm Labour Relations Ctee, formerly chm Trg Ctee; *Recreations* tennis, badminton, swimming, walking; *Style*— Edward Vickers, Esq; ✉ Longwood House, Bushcombe Lane, Cleeve Hill, Glos GL52 3PN (☎ and fax 01242 672399)

VICKERS, Hugo Ralph; s of Ralph Cecil Vickers, MC (d 1992), and Dulcie, *née* Metcalf (d 1992); nephew of Baroness Vickers, DBE (d 1994); *b* 12 Nov 1951; *Educ* Eton, Strasbourg Univ; *m* 23 Sept 1995, Elizabeth Anne Blyth, yr da of Michael Vickers, of Skelbo, Dornoch, Sutherland, and Montaillac, France; *Career* author, reviewer, broadcaster, lectr; worked with London Celebrations Ctee for Queen's Silver Jubilee 1977, admin Great Children's Pty 1979; literary executor to the late Sir Charles Johnston and the late Sir Cecil Beaton; lay steward St George's Chapel Windsor Castle 1970– (dep vice capt 1996–); Liveryman Worshipful Co of Musicians; *Books* We Want The Queen (1977), Gladys, Duchess of Marlborough (1979, reissued 1987), Debrett's Book of the Royal Wedding (1981), Cocktails and Laughter (ed,1983), Cecil Beaton - The Authorised Biography (1985, reissued 1986 and 1993), Vivien Leigh (1988, reissued 1990), Royal Orders (1994), Loving Garbo (1994), The Private World of the Duke and Duchess of Windsor (1995), The Kiss: The Story of an Obsession (1996); *Recreations* photography, reading, music, travel; *Style*— Hugo Vickers, Esq; ✉ Wyeford, Ramsdell, Hants RG26 5QL; 62 Lexham Gardens, London W8 5JA

VICKERS, Jeffrey; s of Edward Vickers (d 1984), and Rose, *née* Soloman; *b* 3 June 1937; *Educ* Harold Co Sch Stratford; *m* 1 (m dis 1982), Angela Vickers; 1 s (Andrew b 11 Feb 1967), 1 da (Joanne b 1 May 1965); m 2, 22 July 1982, Barbara, da of James Ebury Clair May, DSM, RN (d 1986); *Career* chm: DPM Group of Companies 1959–, Chromacopy 1979– (fndr and ptnr Chromacopy of America 1979–), Helicopter Grafix Ltd 1992–, Genix Imaging Ltd, Cactus Imaging Systems Inc (sole UK & Ireland distributors), Blastech Plant Hire Ltd; non-exec dir Sarner International Ltd; finalist Prince of Wales Award for Industl Innovation and Prodn; memb Fulham Cons Assoc; FInstD 1983; *Recreations* skiing, sailing, swimming, classical music/opera; *Clubs* Hurlingham; *Style*— Jeffrey Vickers, Esq; ✉ DPM Design Consultants Ltd, 32 Broadwick Street, London W1V 1FG (☎ 0171 439 7786, fax 0171 434 1528)

VICKERS, Prof John Stuart; s of Aubrey and Kay Vickers, of Eastbourne, Sussex; *b* 7 July 1958; *Educ* Eastbourne GS, Oriel Coll Oxford (BA), Univ of Oxford (MPhil, DPhil); *m* 1991, Maureen Emily, da of David and Dorothy Freed; 1 s (James Alexander b 19 Oct 1994); *Career* fin analyst Shell UK 1979–81; Univ of Oxford: fell All Souls 1979–84 and 1991–, Roy Harrod fell in the economics of business and public policy Nuffield Coll 1984–90, Drummond prof of political economy 1991–; visiting scholar Princeton Univ 1988, visiting lectr Harvard Univ 1989 and 1990, visiting prof London Business Sch 1996; *Books* Privatization - An Economic Analysis (with George Yarrow, 1988), Regulatory Reform (with Mark Armstrong and Simon Cowan, 1994); author of articles on industl orgn, regulation and competition in jls; *Style*— Prof John Vickers; ✉ All Souls College, Oxford OX1 4AL (☎ 01865 279379, fax 01865 279299)

VICKERS, Prof Michael Douglas Allen; s of George Alexander Vickers (d 1973), and Freda Kathleen Vickers; *b* 11 May 1929; *Educ* Abingdon Sch, Guy's Hosp Med Sch; *m* 16 July 1960, Ann Hazel; 2 s (Andrew b 1958 d 1987, Guy b 1964), 1 da (Charlotte b 1961); *Career* Nat Serv RAMC 1948–49; lectr Royal Postgrad Med Sch 1965–68, conslt in anaesthetics and clinical measurement and hon lectr Univ of Birmingham 1968–76, prof of anaesthetics Coll of Med Cardiff 1976–95 (vice provost Coll of Med 1990–93), med and hosp dir King Khalid Hosp Jeddah Saudi Arabia 1984–85; pres Assoc of Anaesthetists of GB and Ireland 1982–84, former memb Cncl RCS; currently: pres World Fedn of Socs of Anaesthesiologists, chair N Glamorgan NHS Tst; FFARCS 1979, FRCA; *Books* Drugs in Anaesthetic Practice (7 edn, 1991), Medicine for Anaesthetists (3 edn, 1988), Principles of Measurement (3 edn, 1991), Ethical Issues in Anaesthesia (1994), OSCEs in Anaesthesia (1995); *Recreations* music; *Clubs* RSM; *Style*— Prof Michael Vickers; ✉ North Pines, 113 Cyncoed Road, Cardiff CF2 6AF (☎ 01222 753698, fax 01222 763865); Les Treilles Hautes, 24250 Grolejac, France (☎ 53 28 55 00); Department of Anaesthetics, University of Wales College of Medicine, Heath Park, Cardiff CF4 4XN (☎ 01222 743110, fax 01222 747203)

VICKERS, Rt Rev Michael Edwin; s of William Edwin Vickers (d 1967), and Florence Alice, *née* Parsons (d 1975); *b* 13 Jan 1929; *Educ* St Lawrence Coll, Worcester Coll Oxford (MA), Cranmer Hall Durham (DipTheol); *m* 3 Sept 1960, Janet Cynthia, da of Arthur Herbert Croasdale (d 1944), of Rostead, Cark-in-Cartmel, N Lancashire; 3 da (Lorna b 1963, Fiona b 1965, Nicola b 1966); *Career* Military Serv 1947–49, Warrant Offr II RAEC serving with Br Troops in Austria; co sec Hoares (Ceylon) Ltd Colombo 1952–56; refugee admin Br Cncl for Aid to Refugees 1956–57; asst curate Christ Church Bexleyheath 1959–62, sr chaplain Lee Abbey 1962–67, vicar of Newland Hull 1967–81, area dean Central Hull 1972–81, chm York Diocesan House of Clergy 1975–85, canon and prebendary York 1981–88, archdeacon of the East Riding 1981–88, bishop of Colchester 1988–94, hon asst bishop Dio of Blackburn 1994–; Int Rugby Union caps for Ceylon 1954–55; *Recreations* fell walking, photography, gardening; *Style*— The Rt Rev Michael E Vickers; ✉ 2 Collingham Park, Lancaster LA1 4PD (☎ 01524 848492)

VICKERS, Paul Andrew; s of John Frederick Vickers, of Chislehurst, Kent, and Daphne Rosemary, *née* Reed; *b* 20 Jan 1960; *Educ* Alleyn's Sch, Univ of Southampton (LLB); *m* 21 May 1988, Eileen Anne, da of John Danial MacDonald; *Career* called to the Bar Inner Temple 1983, in practice 1983–86, legal mangr London Daily News 1986–87; TV-am plc: co lawyer 1987–88, co sec 1988, exec dir 1991, asst md 1992–93; dir Independent Music Radio Ltd (Virgin Radio Ltd) 1992–93, sec and gp legal dir Mirror Group Newspapers Plc 1992–94, exec dir Mirror Group plc 1994–; *Recreations* food, wine, reading, films; *Style*— Paul Vickers, Esq; ✉ Mirror Group plc, 1 Canada Square, Canary Wharf, London E14 5AP (☎ 0171 293 3358)

VICKERS, Rex Adrian; s of Henry Allen Hamilton Vickers (d 1972), and Gladys May, *née* Hardy (d 1976); *b* 27 July 1934; *Educ* Chingford GS, SW Essex Tech Coll; *m* 23 July 1960, Gillian Elizabeth, da of Leonard Frank Edmonds, of Oxted, Surrey; 4 s (Mark b 1961 d 1975, Andrew b 1963, James b 1965, Nicholas b 1972), 1 da (Lucy b 1976); *Career* Nat Serv RE 1955–57; dir: Mott Hay of Anderson Conslt Engrs 1979–94 (assoc 1978–79, dir overseas ptnrships 1979–94), chm SE Gp Assoc Conslting Engrs 1988, memb Bd of Examiners ICE; pres Chinghoppers Cricket Club; CEng 1962, FICE 1973, FFB 1980, MConsE 1980, Eur Ing; *Recreations* cricket, rugby football, golf, gardening; *Clubs* MCC; *Style*— Rex Vickers, Esq; ✉ Neb Corner, Neb Lane, Old Oxted, Surrey RH8 9JN

VICKERS, Lt-Gen Sir Richard Maurice Hilton; KCB (1982), LVO (1959), OBE (1970, MBE 1964); s of Lt-Gen Wilmot Gordon Hilton Vickers, CB, OBE, DL (d 1987); *b* 21 Aug 1928; *Educ* ISC Haileybury, RMA Sandhurst; *m* 1957, Gaie Bradley, da of Maj-Gen George Philip Bradley Roberts, CB, DSO, MC; 3 da; *Career* Capt Tank Regt 1954, Equerry to HM The Queen 1956–59, Maj 1961, Lt-Col 1967, CO The Blues and Royals 1968–70, Brig 1972, dep dir Army Trg 1975–77, GOC 4 Armd Div 1977–79, Cmdt RMA Sandhurst 1979–82; dir-gen Army Trg 1982–83, Winston Churchill Meml Tst 1983–93; Gentleman Usher to HM The Queen; *Clubs* Cavalry and Guards'; *Style*— Lt-Gen Sir Richard Vickers, KCB, LVO, OBE; ✉ Batcombe Barn, Dorchester, Dorset DT2 7AP

VICKERY, David William; s of William James Vickery (d 1986), of Dulwich, London, and Margaret Edith, *née* Bidwell; *b* 29 April 1948; *Educ* Borough Beaufoy Tech Sch Lambeth, East Ham Coll, High Wycombe Coll of Tech and Art (Dip in Interior Design); *m* 7 Sept 1968, Jean Margaret; 3 s (Benjamin David 15 May 1970, Thomas William b 13 May 1981, Joseph James b 12 Jan 1987), 4 da (Sarah Louise b 28 June 1971, Lucy Hannah b 28 Feb 1976, Holly Claire b 5 Dec 1978, Fay Maryanne b 31 Aug 1983); *Career* jr designer Conran Associates 1973; designer: Dale Keller & Associates 1977, Fitch & Co 1978, Wrenn & Co 1979; assoc dir Conran Associates 1980, assoc Wrenn & Co 1984; The Jenkins Group: design dir 1986–, bd dir 1988–; ptnr Vickery Oldman 1995–; work incl: refurbishment of Victoria Coach Station (Grand Prix winner DBA's Design Effectiveness awards and Sign Design Soc awards 1994), Buchanan Bus Station (DBA Environmental award 1995); external examiner BA (Hons) interior design course Ravensbourne Coll of Design & Communication 1995–, course advsr BA (Hons) interior design Surrey Inst of Art and Design; *Recreations* playing association football for Wandsworth Borough FC in Southern Olympian league; *Style*— David Vickery, Esq; ✉ Vickery Oldman, 9 Tufton St, London SW1P 3QB (☎ 0171 222 3222)

VICKERY, Philip; s of Robert Edmund Vickery, of Densole, Folkestone, and Theresa Mary, *née* Billington; *b* 2 May 1961; *Educ* St Edmund's RC Secdy Sch Dover Kent, S Kent Coll of Technol Folkestone (former memb Int Squad Amateur Judo Assoc); *m* 25 Aug 1990 (m dis), Sarah Ann, da of William Brian Lock; *Career* apprentice chef Burlington Hotel Folkestone 1978–79; chef: Michael's Nook Country House Hotel Grasmere 1979–84, Gravetye Manor E Grinstead 1985–86, Restaurant 74 Winchen Canterbury 1986–87, Gravetye Manor 1987–88, Mount Somerset Country House Hotel Taunton 1989–90, Castle Hotel 1990– (also company dir); awards for Castle Hotel: Michelin star, Egon Ronay star, four out of five Good Food Guide 1996; memb Academie Culinaire de France 1992; *Style*— Philip Vickery, Esq; ✉ Castle Hotel, Castle Green, Taunton, Somerset TA1 1NF (☎ 01823 272671, fax 01823 336066)

VICTOR, Ed; s of Jack Victor (d 1987), of Los Angeles, and Lydia Victor; *b* 9 Sept 1939; *Educ* Dartmouth Coll USA (BA), Pembroke Coll Cambridge (MLitt); *m* 1, 1963, Michelene Dinah, da of Avram Samuels (d 1985); 2 s (Adam b 1964, Ivan b 1966); m 2, 1980, Carol Ryan, da of Clifton Boggs (d 1992), of San Diego, California; 1 s (Ryan b 1984); *Career* editorial dir: Weidenfeld & Nicolson 1965–67, Jonathan Cape Ltd 1967–70; sr ed Alfred A Knopf Inc NY USA 1971–72, dir John Farquharson Ltd 1973–77, chm and md Ed Victor Ltd 1977–; *Recreations* opera, tennis, travel; *Clubs* Beefsteak; *Style*— Ed Victor, Esq; ✉ 10 Cambridge Gate, Regents Park, London NW1 (☎ 0171 224 3030); Ed Victor Ltd, 6 Bayley Street, Bedford Square, London WC1B 3HB (☎ 0171 304 4100, fax 0171 304 4111, e-mail 10447,1046@compuserve.com)

VIDLER, Cedric Graham (Ced); *b* 20 June 1944; *m*; *Career* with Doyle Dane Bernbach advtg NY 1966–67, subsequently with KMP later Davidson Pearce advtg, then fndr of creative consultancy Lippa Newton, fndr ptnr Carl Ally London (became Pincus Vidler Arthur FitzGerald following MBO) 1974–82, creative dir rising to exec creative dir and chm BBDO London (following takeover) 1982–89, exec creative dir Lintas:London 1989, subsequently Euro creative dir Lintas Worldwide until 1996 (currently conslt); chm Annistone Ltd; numerous awards won for creative work throughout career; MIPA; *Recreations* driving a very fast boat, restoring classic cars, Prince's Youth Business Tst; *Style*— Ced Vidler, Esq; ✉ Annistone Ltd, 20 Starrock Road, Coulsdon, Surrey CR5 3EH

VIGARS, Robert Lewis; s of late Francis Henry Vigars, and Susan Laurina May, *née* Lewis; *b* 26 May 1923; *Educ* Truro Cathedral Sch, Univ of London (LLB); *m* 1962, Margaret Ann Christine, yr da of late Sir John Walton, KCIE, CB, MC; 2 da; *Career* WWII, RA and RCS 1942–47, attached Indian Army (Capt) 1944–47, Capt Princess Louise's Kensington Regt TA 1951–54; admitted slr 1948; ptnr Simmons & Simmons London 1951–75; memb Kensington Borough Cncl 1953–59 (memb London and Home Cos Traffic Advsy Ctee 1956–58 and London Roads (Nugent) Ctee 1958–59), memb LCC and GLC Kensington (formerly S Kensington) 1955–86; GLC: chm and memb Environmental Planning Ctee 1967–71, chm and memb Strategic Planning Ctee 1971–73, chm 1979–80; memb Standing Conf on London and SE Regnl Planning and SE Econ Planning Cncl 1968–75, ldr of opposition ILEA 1974–79, memb Ct Univ of London 1977–82; Historic Bldgs and Monuments Cmmn for England: commissioner 1986–89, memb London Advsy Ctee 1986–92 (chm 1986–89); memb Cncl of Mgmnt: Heritage of London Tst 1986–, Historic Chapels Tst 1993–; Liveryman City of London Solicitors' Co; *Recreations* mountain walking; *Clubs* Hurlingham, Carlton; *Style*— Robert Vigars, Esq; ✉ 24 Cope Place, Kensington, London W8 6AA

VIGGERS, Peter John; MP (C) Gosport (majority 16,318); s of John Sidney Viggers (d 1969), of Gosport; *b* 13 March 1938; *Educ* Alverstoke Sch, Portsmouth GS, Trinity Hall Cambridge (MA); *m* 1968, Jennifer Mary, da of Dr R B McMillan (d 1975); 1 da, 2 s; *Career* RAF pilot 1956–58, TA 1963–70; co slr Chrysler (UK) Ltd 1968–70; dir: Edward Bates & Sons Ltd 1970–75, Richardson Smith Ltd (chm), Gough Hotels Ltd and other cos 1970–76, Premier Consolidated Oilfields Ltd 1973–86, Sweetheart International Ltd 1982–86, Nynex Group of Cos 1991–95, Tracer Petroleum Corporation 1996–; MP (C) Gosport Feb 1974–, PPS to Slr Gen 1979–83, delegate to N Atlantic Assembly 1980–86, PPS to Chief Sec to Treasy 1983–85, Parly under sec of state for NI (indust min) 1986–89, chm Brtish-Japanese Parly Gp 1992–, memb Select Ctee on Membs' Interests 1991–93, memb Select Ctee on Defence 1992–; underwriting memb of Lloyd's 1973– (memb Cncl 1992–), chm tstees Lloyd's Pension Fund 1996–; memb Nat Ctee RNLI 1980–90 (vice pres 1990–); *Style*— Peter Viggers, Esq, MP; ✉ House of Commons, London SW1A 0AA

VILLAR, Anthony Sidney Rex; s of Arthur Andrew Sidney Villar (d 1966), and Betty Helen Fyfe-Jamieson, MBE, *née* Cohen; *b* 4 Sept 1934; *Educ* Stowe; *m* 21 Oct 1961, Clare, da of Henry William Pearson-Rogers, CBE; 4 da (Sally b 1962, Francesca b 1965, Caroline b 1968, Alexandra b 1975); *Career* RNVR, ret 1955; farmer; former pres: Racehorse Owners' Assoc (memb Cncl), St Moritz Curling Club; memb Cncl: The Distressed Gentlefolk's Aid Assoc, Animal Health Tst; *Recreations* shooting, fishing, curling, racing; *Clubs* Naval, Jockey Club Rooms, St Moritz Curling; *Style*— Anthony Villar, Esq; ✉ Tostock Old Rectory, Bury St Edmunds, Suffolk IP30 9NU; Little Haugh Farm, Norton, Bury St Edmunds, Suffolk (☎ 01359 230468)

VILLAR, Richard Neville; s of George Roger Villar, DSC, RN, and Diana Mary, *née* Thomas; *b* 24 April 1953; *Educ* Marlborough, St Thomas' Hosp Medical Sch (BSc, MB BS), Univ of Southampton (MS), Coll of Surgns (FRCS); *m* 4 June 1983, (Barbara) Louise Bell, da of Patrick George Arthur Ross Lobban; 2 s (Ruairidh b 1985, Angus b 1988), 1 da (Felicity b 1995); *Career* RAMC 1979–84; conslt Addenbrooke's Hosp Cambridge 1988– (sr registrar 1985–88), clinical dir Cambridge Hip and Knee Unit; overseas liaison offr Br Orthopaedic Assoc, memb World Orthopaedic Concern; memb: Euro Hip Soc, Br Assoc for Surgery of the Knee; fell Br Orthopaedic Assoc 1989; Lord of the Manor of Twineham Benfield; *Recreations* fell running, martial arts, cross country skiing; *Style*— Richard Villar, Esq; ✉ Cambridge Hip and Knee Unit (☎ 01223 235885, fax 01223 235884)

VILLAS-BOAS, Manuel de Magalhães e Menezes; s of Augusto de Magalhães e Menezes Villas-Boas, and Maria Luisa, *née* Ribeiro de Sa Ramos Chaves Bessone Basto;

b 29 May 1945; *Educ* Economics Inst Lisbon Univ (BA); *m* 20 April 1985, Christine Marie Françoise, da of Michael Julien Gudefin, Chev Legion d'Honneur, of Greenwich, Connecticut, USA; 2 s (António b 1986, Alexandre b 1990); *Career* asst mangr Banco Espirito Santo e Comercial de Lisboa Lisbon 1972–76, sr mangr Manufacturers Hanover Ltd London 1976–79; exec dir 1979–83: The Royal Bank of Canada, Orion Royal Bank Ltd London; sr vice pres and London rep Espírito Santo International Holding London 1983–; dir: Espírito Santo Financial Holding SA 1990–, Banco Espírito Santo e Comercial de Lisboa Lisbon 1992–; Knight of Honour and Devotion Sovereign and Military Order of Malta; *Recreations* art, music, sport; *Clubs* IOD, Turf (Lisbon); *Style*— Manuel de Magalhães e Menezes Villas-Boas, Esq; ✉ 73 Harrington Gardens, London SW7 4JZ; Espírito Santo International Holding, 33 Queen Street, London EC4R 1ES (☎ 0171 332 4350, fax 0171 332 4355)

VILLIERS, Charles Nigel; s of Capt Robert Alexander Villiers, CBE, RN (d 1990), and Elizabeth Mary, *née* Friend (d 1985); *b* 25 Jan 1941; *Educ* Winchester, New Coll Oxford (MA); *m* 7 Aug 1970, Sally Priscilla, da of Capt David Henry Magnay, RN (d 1968); 1 s (Christopher b 1976), 1 da (Caroline b 1974); *Career* Arthur Andersen 1963–67, Industrial & Commercial Finance Corporation 1967–72; County Bank (subsid of National Westminster Bank): dir 1974, dep chief exec 1977, chm and chief exec 1984–86; dir National Westminster Bank 1985–88, chm County NatWest 1986–88, chief exec NatWest Investment Bank 1986–88, dir and md corp devpt Abbey National plc 1989–; pres Abbey National France 1993–96, chm First National Bank 1996– (dep chm 1995–96); FCA 1976 (ACA 1966); *Recreations* opera, skiing, tennis; *Style*— Charles Villiers, Esq; ✉ 8 Sutherland St, London SW1V 4LB; Abbey House, Baker St, London NW1 6XL

VILLIERS, George Edward; TD; s of Algernon Edward Villiers (d 1991), of Hayling Island, Hants, and Annie Augusta Merewether, *née* Massy (d 1979); *b* 23 Aug 1931; *Educ* Wellington Coll, Brasenose Coll Oxford (MA); *m* 25 Aug 1962, (Anne) Virginia, da of Cuthbert Raymond Forster Threlfall, MC (d 1965), of Warstone House, Bewdley, Worcs; 2 s (Edward b 1963, Henry b 1965), 1 da (Theresa b 1968); *Career* Nat Serv 2 Lt RHA 1949–51, TA 1951–65 (Maj Berks and Westminster Dragoons); stockjobber Moir & Shand 1956–64, memb Stock Exchange 1960; stockbroker; assoc Sorrell Lamb & Co 1964–65, ptnr H Evans Gordon & Co 1966–70, ptnr Beardsley Bishop & Co 1970–83, assoc Cawood Smithie 1983–96; pres Oxford Univ Athletic Club 1953–54; *Recreations* golf, bridge; *Clubs* Boodle's, Wentworth; *Style*— George Villiers, Esq; ✉ Clyde Villa, 98 Ravenscourt Road, London W6 0UG (☎ 0181 563 1238, fax 0181 563 1382)

VILLIERS, Viscount; George Henry Child Villiers; s and h of 9 Earl of Jersey; *b* 29 Aug 1948; *Educ* Eton, Millfield; *m* 1, 1969 (m dis 1973), Verna, da of K A Stott, of St Mary, Jersey; 1 da (Hon Sophia Georgiana b 25 June 1971); m 2, 1974 (m dis 1988), Sacha Jane Hooper, da of Peter Hooper Valpy, former w of K F Lauder; 1 s, 2 da (Hon Helen Katherine Luisa b 21 Oct 1978, Hon Luciana Dorothea Sacha b 23 July 1981); m 3, 1992, Stephanie Louise, da of John Ian Penman; 1 s (Hon Jamie Charles b 31 May 1994); *Heir* s, Hon George Francis William Child Villiers b 5 Feb 1976; *Career* late 2 Lt 11 Hussars and the Royal Hussars; guitarist and composer of music for TV, radio, video and computer games; dir Lion Eagle Records Ltd (recordings incl: Magical Dance, Dawn and No Dog Required); publisher: Reel Time Music; *Style*— Viscount Villiers; ✉ The Flat, Radier Manor, Longueville, Jersey, CI

VILLIERS, James; *Educ* Wellington Coll, RADA; *Career* actor; worked with Old Vic Co and English Stage Co; *Theatre* West End appearances incl: Toad of Toad Hall (Shakespeare Meml Co), Write Me A Murder, The Burglar, The Happy Apple, Private Lives, The Little Hut, The Doctor's Dilemma, The White Devil (Old Vic), Henry IV, The Ghost Train, The Passion of Dracula, Peter Pan (Shaftesbury), The Last of Mrs Cheyney, The Way of the World (Theatre Royal Haymarket), The Madness of George III (RNT), Oliver; *Television* incl: The First Churchills, Lady Windermere's Fan, The Millionairess, Pygmalion, Unity, Mrs Silly, The Scarlet Pimpernel, The Good Doctor Bodkin Adams, The Dirty Dozen (US TV), Fortunes of War (BBC), Radical Chambers, Hemingway, Anything More Would Be Greedy (ATV), Chelworth (BBC), House of Cards (BBC), The Gravy Train; *Films* King and Country, Children of the Damned, The Nanny, Half a Sixpence, Nothing But the Best, Otley, The Ruling Class, The Amazing Mr Blunden, Seven Nights in Japan, Joseph Andrew, St Jack, For Your Eyes Only, Under the Volcano, Scandal, Mountains of the Moon, Let Him Have It, King Ralph; *Style*— James Villiers, Esq; ✉ c/o ICM Ltd, Oxford House, 76 Oxford Street, London W1N 0AX (☎ 0171 636 6565, fax 0171 323 0101)

VILLIERS, Mary Elizabeth; da of Robert Hugh Swan Corbett (d 1988), and Elizabeth Cavan, *née* Lambart (d 1988); *b* 21 July 1936; *Educ* Beaufront Sch Camberley; *m* 1959, Henry Hyde Villiers, s of Eric Hyde Villiers, DSO; 2 da (Charlotte b 1961, Henrietta b 1962), 3 s (Alexander b and d 1966, Charles b 1967, Robert b 1969); *Career* dep ed Official Report (Hansard) House of Lords 1982–84, ed of debates Official Report (Hansard) House of Lords 1984–; chm: Southern Regn Art Collections Fund, SE Regnl Ctee National Trust; memb Fabric Ctee Canterbury Cathedral; FRSA 1991; *Recreations* gardening, sailing, bridge; *Style*— Mrs Mary Villiers; ✉ Editor of Debates, Hansard, House of Lords, London SW1A 0PW (☎ 0171 219 3397, fax 0171 219 3824, car 0860 120692)

VINCE, Dr Frank Peter; s of Dr Rupert James Vince (d 1987), of Doncaster, and Olive Myra Vince, *née* King (d 1985); *b* 19 June 1937; *Educ* Doncaster GS, Sidney Sussex Coll Cambridge (BA), The London Hosp Med Sch (MB BChir); *m* 7 Jan 1967, Sheila, da of Dr Laurence Cleveland Martin (d 1981), of Cambridge; 1 s (Richard James Martin b 1970), 1 da (Joanna b 1968); *Career* med registrar Addenbrooke's Hosp Cambridge 1964–66, lectr and sr registrar The London Hosp Whitechapel 1967–71 (house offr 1962–63), conslt physician Coventry Hosp 1971–, chief med offr Axa Equity and Law Insurance Soc 1982–, sr lectr in postgrad med Univ of Warwick 1985–; various pubns in med jls on subjects of diabetes, endocrinology and problems of growth and development; examiner for RCP, pres Coventry Branch Br Diabetic Assoc, dep chm Home Farm Tst, former co-opted memb Coventry City Cncl; former memb Coventry Health Authy; memb: Coventry Educn Authy 1981–90, Soc for Endocrinology, Cncl Assurance Med Soc (AMS); FRSM, FRCP 1979; *Recreations* music; *Style*— Dr Frank Vince; ✉ 42 Kenilworth Rd, Coventry CV3 6PG (☎ 01203 410347); Walsgrave Hospital, Coventry (☎ 01203 602020)

VINCENT, Rev Dr John James; s of David Vincent (d 1976), and Ethel Beatrice, *née* Gadd; *b* 29 Dec 1929; *Educ* Manchester GS, Richmond Coll London (BD), Drew Univ NJ USA (STM), Univ of Basel (DTheol); *m* 4 Dec 1958, Grace Johnston, da of Rev Wilfred Stafford; 2 s (Christopher b 1961, James b 1966), 1 da (Faith b 1964); *Career* Sgt RAMC 1947–49; min Manchester and Salford Mission 1956–62; supt min: Rochdale Mission 1962–69, Sheffield Inner City Ecumenical Mission 1970–; dir Urban Theol Unit Sheffield 1970–, supervisor Doctoral Prog in Contextual, Urban and Liberation Theologies Univ of Sheffield 1993–; visiting prof of theol: Univ of Boston Autumn 1969, NY Theol Seminary Spring 1970; visiting prof of theol Drew Univ NJ 1977; chm NW CND 1957–65; founding memb and leader Ashram Community Tst 1967–, chm Urban Mission Training Assoc of GB 1976–77 and 1984–91, memb Cncl Christian Orgns for Social, Political and Economic Change 1981–89, exec Assoc Centres of Adult Theol Educn 1984–90, memb Studiorum Novi Testamenti Societas 1961–, pres Methodist Church GB 1989–90, hon lectr Biblical Studies Dept Univ of Sheffield 1990–, co-ordinator British Liberation Theology Project 1990–; dir Inst for Br Liberation Theology 1994–; *Books* Christ in a Nuclear World (1962), Christ and Methodism (1965), Secular Christ (1968), The Race Race (1970), The Jesus Thing (1973), Alternative Church (1976), Starting All Over Again (1981), OK, Let's be Methodists (1984), Radical Jesus (1986), Britain in the 90's (1989), Discipleship in the 90's (1991), Liberation Theology UK (ed, 1995), Faith From the City (ed, 1996); *Recreations* writing, jogging; *Style*— The Rev Dr John Vincent; ✉ 178 Abbeyfield Rd, Sheffield, S4 7AY (☎ 0114 243 6688); Urban Theology Unit, 210 Abbeyfield Rd, Sheffield S4 7AZ (☎ 0114 243 5342)

VINCENT, Robin Anthony; s of John Kenneth Vincent (d 1991), and Ivy Elizabeth Anne, *née* Grayer (d 1996); *b* 27 Feb 1944; *Educ* King's Sch Worcester; *m* 12 June 1971, Hazel Ruth, da of Frederick John Perkins; 2 s (Mark Christian b 4 Aug 1972, Stephen Peter b 30 June 1974); *Career* clerk Worcestershire Quarter Sessions 1962–70, sr asst then dep clerk to Worcester Co Justices 1970–72; higher exec offr: Worcester Crown Court 1972–76, Worcester Co Court 1976–77; sr exec offr (Personnel) Circuit Administrator's Office Birmingham 1977–80, chief clerk Worcester Crown Court 1980–82, princ chief clerk Manchester Crown Court 1982–86; head of div: Court Serv Devpt Div London 1986–91, Personnel Mgmnt Div London 1991–93, Judicial Appointments Div London 1993; administrator Northern Circuit Manchester 1993–; *Recreations* cricket, soccer, gardening; *Clubs* Eggington CC, Old Vigornians, Stockport Georgians; *Style*— Robin Vincent, Esq; ✉ The Moorings, 33 Grange Road, Bramhall, Stockport SK7 3BD (☎ 0161 440 9526); Circuit Administrator's Office, The Court Service, 15 Quay Street, Manchester M60 9FD (☎ 0161 833 1004/1005, fax 0161 832 8596)

VINCENT, Sir William Percy Maxwell; 3 Bt (UK 1936), of Watton, Co Norfolk; s of Sir Lacey Vincent, 2 Bt (d 1963), and Helen, Lady Vincent; *b* 1 Feb 1945; *Educ* Eton, New York Inst of Finance; *m* 1976, Christine Margaret, da of Rev Edward Gibson Walton (d 1989), of Petersfield; 3 s; *Heir* s, Edward Mark William Vincent b 6 March 1978; *Career* late 2 Lt Irish Gds, served Malaya; dir Save & Prosper Investment Management 1980–85, Touche Remnant & Co 1985, md and investment dir Touche Remnant Co 1986, dir Société Genérale Touche Remnant 1989–92, dir M & G (North America) Ltd 1992–95, md Cambridge Associates (UK) Ltd 1995–; *Recreations* sailing, skiing; *Clubs* Household Div Yacht; *Style*— Sir William Vincent, Bt; ✉ Whistlers, Buriton, Petersfield, Hants (☎ 01730 263532)

VINCENT OF COLESHILL, Field Marshal Baron (Life Peer UK 1996), of Shrivenham in the County of Oxfordshire; Sir Richard Frederick Vincent; GBE (1990), KCB (1984), DSO (1972); s of late Frederick Vincent, and late Frances Elizabeth, *née* Coleshill; *b* 23 Aug 1931; *Educ* Aldenham, RMC of Sci Shrivenham; *m* 1955, Jean Paterson, da of late Kenneth Stewart; 1 s, 1 da (and 1 s decd); *Career* Cmdt RMC of Sci 1980–83, Master Gen of the Ordnance MOD 1983–87, Chief of the Def Staff 1991–92 (Vice Chief 1987–91), chm Mil Ctee NATO 1993–96; Col Cmdt: REME 1983–87, RA 1983; Hon Col: 100 (Yeo) Field Regt RA (Volunteers) TA 1982–91, 12 Air Def Regt 1985–91; Master Gunner St James's Park 1996–; chm Hunting Defence Ltd 1996–; dir: Hunting Engineering Ltd 1996–, Vickers Defence Systems 1996–; vice pres Defence Manufacturers Assoc 1996–; Kermit Roosevelt lectr USA 1988, visiting fell Aust Coll of Def and Strategic Studies; pres: Combined Servs Winter Sports Assoc 1983–90, Army Skiing Assoc 1983–87; memb Ct Cranfield Inst of Technol 1981–83, govr Aldenham Sch 1987–, chm of Govrs Imperial Coll of Sci, Technology and Med 1996– (govr 1995); Jordanian Order of Merit (First Class), USA Legion of Merit (Degree of Cdr); Freeman City of London, memb Guild of Freemen; Hon DSc Cranfield 1985; FIMechE 1990; FRAeS 1990; *Recreations* establishing a second career, seven grandchildren; *Style*— Field Marshal Lord Vincent of Coleshill, GBE, KCB, DSO; ✉ c/o Midland Bank, The Commons, High Street, Shaftesbury, Dorset SP7 8JX

VINCENZI, Penny; da of Stanley George Hannaford (d 1985), of New Milton, Hants, and Mary Blanche, *née* Hawkey (d 1987); *b* 10 April 1939; *Educ* Notting Hill and Ealing HS; *m* 27 May 1960, Paul Robert Vincenzi, s of Dr Julius Vincenzi (d 1996), of Earls Colne, Essex; 4 da (Polly b 1963, Sophie b 1965, Emily b 1975, Claudia b 1979); *Career* freelance journalist and author; work incl: former first fashion ed Nova Magazine; *Books* The Complete Liar (1979), There's One Born Every Minute (1985), Old Sins (1989), Wicked Pleasures (1992), An Outrageous Affair (1993), Another Woman (1994), Forbidden Places (1995), The Dilemma (1996); *Recreations* family life, talking, eating and drinking; *Style*— Mrs Penny Vincenzi

VINCZE, Ernest Anthony; *b* 1942; *Educ* BSc; *Career* director of photography; started in the field of documentaries winning several awards incl: Flaherty Award, Prix Italia, Golden Gate San Francisco, BAFTA; pt/t tutor of Cinematography RCA and Nat Film Sch, nominated Br Acad Award for Best Cinematography 1984 and 1989; features, serials and made-for-TV movies incl: Business As Usual, Shangai Surprise, Biggles, Hitler's SS, A Woman of Substance, Kennedy, Scrubbers, Roseland, Winstanley, A Very British Coup (Emmy Award 1988), Nightmare Years, Jeeves and Wooster, A Perfect Hero, The Camomile Lawn, Grushko, Heavy Weather, Stone Scissors Paper; memb Br Soc of Cinematographers 1978, ACTT; *Style*— Ernest A Vincze, Esq; ✉ 25 Marville Road, London SW6 7BB (☎ 0171 385 3413); c/o CCA Personal Management, 4 Court Lodge, 48 Sloane Square, London SW1 8AT (☎ 0171 730 8857, fax 0171 730 6971)

VINE, Barbara; *see:* Rendell, Ruth Barbara

VINE, Brian John; s of Frank Alexander Vine, of St Leonard's-on-Sea, Sussex, and Edith Ellen, *née* Sharp; *b* 11 July 1932; *Educ* Winton House, St Dunstan's Coll London; *m* 18 Sept 1972, Beverley Jacqueline, da of Dr Alan Wardale, of Alexandra, NZ; 1 s (Alexander Charles b 1979); *Career* Nat Serv RAF (2 yrs) Zimbabwe; home reporter News Chronicle 1956–60; Daily Express 1960–84: William Hickey Column 1960–69, Chief of Bureau New York (This is America columnist) 1969–73, foreign ed 1973–74, asst ed 1974–84; Daily Mail: foreign ed 1985–86, asst ed 1986–87, managing ed 1987–93; memb Press Cncl, judge Br Press Awards; *Books* Zola; *Recreations* racehorse ownership, shooting, tennis; *Clubs* Turf, Scribes, University NY; *Style*— Brian Vine, Esq; ✉ 10 Stafford Terrace, London W8 7BH (☎ 0171 937 1517, fax 0171 937 2854); Lower Farm Cottage, Haywards Bottom, nr Hungerford, Berkshire (☎ 01488 683774)

VINE, Deirdre Ann; da of Paul Ashley Lawrence Vine, of Pulborough, Sussex; *b* 21 Sept 1953; *Educ* UCL (BA); *Career* ed (book publishing) 1976–78, sub ed Woman 1978–79, dep ed In Britain 1979–81, freelance 1981–83, ed dir Publishing Holdings 1983–86, editor 19 Magazine 1986–88, ed in chief Womans Journal 1988–; memb: Br Guild of Travel Writers 1978, Br Soc of Magazine Editors 1986, Cosmetic Executive Women 1993; *Books* Boulogne (1983), Paris and Ile De France (1992); *Recreations* opera, theatre, cinema, riding, wine and food; *Clubs* Oxford and Cambridge; *Style*— Ms Deirdre Vine; ✉ 5 Horbury Crescent, London W11 3NF; IPC Magazines, King's Reach Tower, Stamford Street, London SE1 9LS (☎ 0171 261 6622, fax 0171 261 7028)

VINE, Dennis; s of Harold Edward Vine (d 1966), of Ealing, London, and Mary Maud Vine (now Nicholls); *b* 24 April 1937; *Educ* Penyrenglyn Treherbert S Wales, Drayton Manor GS Ealing W London, Regent St Poly (now Univ of Westminster); *m* 12 June 1965, Anne, da of H S Hawley; 1 s (Richard Edward b 9 March 1967), 1 da Joanna b 6 March 1969); *Career* surveyor; Ealing Borough Cncl 1954, Westminster City Cncl 1960; Vigers Chartered Surveyors (now Grimley): joined 1962, ptnr responsible for Building Surveying 1969, jt sr ptnr 1983, sr ptnr 1990, ptnr of new merged practice 1991–; RICS: memb 1962–, pres Building Surveyors Div 1987–88; chm Advsy Bd Coll of Estate Mgmnt Dip in Building Conservation; memb Bd British Home & Hosp for Incurables (BHHI); external examiner various univs; Freeman City of London 1987, Liveryman Worshipful Co of London Surveyors 1987; *Recreations* tennis, squash, golf; *Clubs* RAC,

West Surrey Golf; *Style*— Dennis Vine, Esq; ✉ Grimley, 10 Stratton Street, London W1X 6JR (☎ 0171 911 2131, fax 0171 911 2426, car 0836 773049)

VINE, Dr (Roland) Stephen; s of Joseph Soutter Vine (d 1944), and Margaret Mary Josephine, *née* Moylan (d 1976); *b* 26 Dec 1910; *Educ* Southend-on-Sea Boys' HS, Univ of London and Guy's Hosp Med Sch (BSc, MRCS, LRCP); *m* 14 Dec 1935, Flora Betty, da of Charles Strutton Brookes, MBE (d 1960), of Dovercourt, Essex; 3 da; *Career* served Regular Army as MO in RAMC 1934–60, sr specialist in pathology 1949, ret as Hon Col 1960; inspr under the Cruelty to Animals Act at the HO 1960 (chief inspr 1962–75); fndr fell Coll of Pathologists 1962; FZS; *Style*— Dr Stephen Vine; ✉ Shola, Fielden Road, Crowborough, East Sussex TN6 1TR (☎ 01892 661381)

VINE-LOTT, Anthony Keith; s of Keith Miles Vine-Lott, of Hyde, Cheshire, and Jessie, *née* Meadowcroft; *b* 24 Oct 1947; *Educ* King Edward VI Macclesfield Cheshire, Sheffield Poly (HND); *m* 1, 13 Dec 1969 (m dis 1980), Barbara Elaine; 1 da (Anne Marie Elizabeth b 4 Jan 1974); m 2, 18 June 1982, Dr Ailsa Vine-Lott, da of Capt Frank Edward Webb, of Singleton, Ashford, Kent; *Career* engrg scholarship Wimpey UK Ltd 1966–70, mktg mangr UK computer software co's 1970–76, md Surlodge Ltd 1976–78, field servs mangr Honeywell Network Information Systems Ltd (taken over by General Electric USA) 1978–81, mktg servs dir WANG UK Ltd 1981–86, chm The Cleaver Co; md Barclays Stockbrokers Ltd 1988–96, dir Barclays Financial Services Ltd 1993–96, chm Barclays Bank Trust Co Ltd 1995–96, chm Barclays Insurance Services Co Ltd 1995–96; currently non-exec dir Webb Carrington (Business Consultants) Ltd; Lord of the Manor of Beckett; FCIM 1990, FRSA 1991; *Recreations* yachting, swimming, gardening, travel; *Clubs* Inst of Directors; *Style*— Anthony Vine-Lott, Esq; ✉ Broom House, Crabtree Lane, Headley, Epsom, Surrey KT18 6PS (☎ 01372 374728)

VINELOTT, Hon Sir John Evelyn Vinelott; kt (1978); s of Frederick George Vine-Lott (d 1984), and Vera Lilian Mockford (d 1957); *b* 15 Oct 1923; *Educ* Queen Elizabeth's GS Faversham, Queens' Coll Cambridge (MA); *m* 1956, Sally Elizabeth, da of His Hon Sir Walker Kelly Carter (decd); 2 s, 1 da; *Career* served WWII Sub-Lt RNVR; called to the Bar Gray's Inn 1953 (Atkin scholar), QC 1968, bencher 1974, High Court judge (Chancery Div) 1978–94; chm: Insolvency Rules Advsy Ctee 1984–90, Tst Law Reform Ctee 1995–; memb City Disputes Panel 1995–; *Clubs* Garrick; *Style*— The Hon Sir John Vinelott; ✉ 22 Portland Rd, London W11 (☎ 0171 727 4778)

VINEN, Prof William Frank; s of Gilbert Vinen (d 1945), and Olive Maud, *née* Roach (d 1971); *b* 15 Feb 1930; *Educ* Watford GS, Clare Coll Cambridge (MA, PhD); *m* 16 Sept 1960, Susan Mary Audrey, da of Lt-Col Reginald Arthur Master (d 1954); 1 s (Richard Charles b 1963), 1 da (Catherine Susanna b 1965); *Career* RAF 1948–49; demonstrator Dept of Physics and fell Pembroke Coll Cambridge 1958–62 (res fell Clare Coll 1955–58), visiting prof Univ of Illinois 1964, Poynting prof of physics Univ of Birmingham 1974– (prof of physics 1962–74); memb: bds and ctees SERC, Visiting Ctee Open Univ, Cncl Royal Soc 1976–77, Governing Body Coventry Poly 1984–89, Cncl Inst of Physics 1980; hon fell Coventry Univ 1989; FRS 1973, FInstP 1980; *Recreations* good food; *Style*— Prof William Vinen, FRS; ✉ 52 Middle Park Road, Birmingham B29 4BJ (☎ 0121 475 1328); School of Physics and Space Research, University of Birmingham, Birmingham B15 2TT (☎ 0121 414 4667, fax 0121 414 4719)

VINER, Gordon; s of Joseph Viner (d 1982), of Liverpool, and Muriel, *née* Sharp (d 1996); *b* 14 Nov 1940; *Educ* Kings Sch Chester; *m* 9 Oct 1966, Helen Frances, da of Philip Waters (d 1990), and Beatrice, *née* Cohen, of London; 3 s (Andrew b 1970, Paul b 1970, Richard b 1974), 1 da (Michelle b 1972); *Career* CA; trainee CA Chester 1957–63, H & J Supplies Ltd Chester 1963, ptnr Lerman Quaile Birkenhead 1966–; chm: Chester and N Wales CAs Students Assoc 1963–64, Merseyside branch Chartered Inst of Taxation 1984–87, Chester Jewish Community 1981–96; memb Mensa; FCA 1963, ATII 1965; *Recreations* golf, bridge; *Clubs* Upton-by-Chester Golf; *Style*— Gordon Viner, Esq; ✉ 5 Nield Court, Upton-By-Chester, Cheshire CH2 1DN (☎ 01244 383745); Lerman Quaile, 56 Hamilton Square, Birkenhead, Merseyside L41 5AS (☎ 0151 647 7171, fax 0151 666 2585); Lerman Quaile, 80 Whitby Road, Ellesmere Port, South Wirral L65 0AA (☎ and fax 0151 356 4148)

VINES, Eric Victor; CMG (1984), OBE (1971); s of late Henry E Vines; *b* 28 May 1929; *Educ* St Dunstan's Coll London, St Catharine's Coll Cambridge (MA); *m* 1953, Ellen-Grethe Ella Küppers; 1 s; *Career* Nat Serv Army 1947–49; joined Cwlth Rels Office 1952, Colombo 1954–55, first sec Singapore 1958–61, Canberra 1961–65, Dip Serv Admin Office 1965–68, first sec (information) Mexico City 1968–70, cnsllr exec sec-gen SEATO conf London 1971, head Cultural Exchange Dept FCO 1971–74, cnsllr (commercial) Tel Aviv 1974–77, Stockholm 1977–80, consul-gen Barcelona 1980–83; ambass: Maputo 1984–85, Montevideo 1986–89; memb Personnel Assessment Staff FCO 1991–94; tstee: Southern African Studies Tst 1990–94, Gemini (Ethiopia) Tst 1990–; chm Brit-Uruguayan Soc 1995–; *Clubs* Cwlth Tst; *Style*— Eric Vines, Esq, CMG, OBE; ✉ 80 Farquhar Road, London SE19 1LT

VINK, *see:* de Vink

VINKEN, Pierre; *b* 25 Nov 1927; *Educ* Univ of Utrecht (MD); *Career* publisher; co-fndr and ed literary jl Tirade 1957–58, ed-in-chief Excerpta Medica Fndn Amsterdam 1958–80, neurosurgeon and sr scientific offr Univ of Amsterdam and conslt neurosurgeon Boerhaave Clinic Amsterdam 1964–70, co-fndr and ed Handbook of Clinical Neurology 1968–; md Elsevier Science Publishers 1971–73; Elsevier NV: exec dir 1972–79, chm 1979–95, chm Supervisory Bd 1995–; Reed Elsevier plc London (following merger with Reed International plc): chm 1992–95, non-exec dir 1995–; also chm: Bank MeesPierson Amsterdam 1982–, Halder Holdings The Hague 1988–, The Lancet 1991–; vice chm Wereldhave The Hague 1988–; dir: Pearson plc 1988–91, The Economist Ltd 1989–93, Logica plc London and Rotterdam 1990–, Aalberts Industries Driebergen 1992–; co-fndr and dep chm European Publishers Cncl 1991–; extraordinary prof of Medical Database Infomatics Univ of Leyden 1975–92; hon corresponding memb Neurological Soc of India, hon foreign memb Société Française de Neurologie, hon memb Peruvian Soc of Psychiatry, Neurology and Neurosurgery; Dr (hc) Univ of Paris 1981; Kt Order of the Netherlands Lion 1983, Cdr Order of Hipolito Unanue (Peru) 1984; *Style*— Pierre Vinken; ✉ c/o Logica plc, Stephenson House, 75 Hampstead Road, London NW1 2PL

VINNICOMBE, John; s of Francis William Vinnicombe (d 1964), of St Saviour, Jersey, CI, and Marjorie Florence, nee Shuff (d 1972); *b* 17 Jan 1930; *Educ* Godalming GS, St John's Coll Cambridge (MA), St Thomas's Hosp Med Sch (MB MChir); *m* 12 July 1958, Diana Mary, da of Maj-Gen Dennis Charles Tarrant Swan, CB, CBE, (d 1992); 3 da (Sarah b 1959, Amanda b 1961, Jane b 1964); *Career* Nat Serv Capt RAEC 1948–49; conslt urological surgn: Portsmouth Dist Hosp 1966–95 (ret), King Edward VII Hosp Midhurst 1970; Br Assoc of Urological Surgns: memb Cncl 1976–79 and 1985–88, hon sec 1981–84, hon treas 1985–86; former pres Portsmouth Div BMA 1981–82; Freeman City of London, Liveryman Worshipful Soc of Apothecaries 1972; FRCS, FRSM (pres Urology section 1987–88); *Recreations* travel, sailing, skiing; *Style*— John Vinnicombe, Esq; ✉ Hindon House, Emsworth, Hants, (☎ 01243 372528)

VINSON, Baron (Life Peer UK 1985), of Roddam Dene, Co Northumberland; Nigel Vinson; LVO (1979), DL (1990); s of Ronald Vinson (d 1976), of Nettlestead Place, Wateringbury, Kent, and his 2 w, Bettina Myra Olivia (d 1966), da of Dr Gerald Southwell-Sander; *b* 27 Jan 1931; *Educ* RNC Pangbourne; *m* 10 June 1972, Yvonne Ann, da of Dr John Olaf Collin, of Forest Row, Sussex; 3 da (Hon Bettina Claire b 1974, Hon Rowena Ann b 1977, Hon Antonia Charlotte b 1979); *Career* Lt Queen's Royal Regt 1949–51; fndn donor Martin Mere Wildfowl Tst; fndr Plastic Coatings Ltd (chm 1952–72); dir: Sugar Bd 1968–75, British Airports Authority 1973–80, Centre for Policy Studies 1974–80; dep chm: Electra Investment Trust 1975–, Barclays Bank UK 1982–88; memb Cncl King George V Jubilee Tst 1974–78, hon dir Queen's Silver Jubilee Tst 1974–78: dep chm CBI Smaller Firms Cncl 1979–84, chm: Cncl for Small Industries in Rural Areas 1980–82, Newcastle Technol Centre 1985–88, Rural Devpt Cmmn 1980–90, Bd of Tstees Inst of Econ Affrs 1989– (memb 1971–); pres Industrial Participation Assoc 1979–90 (chm 1971–78); tstee St George's House Windsor Castle 1990–; FIMgt, FRSA; *Books* Personal and Portable Pensions for All (1985); *Recreations* horses, objets d'art, crafts, farming; *Clubs* Boodle's; *Style*— The Rt Hon Lord Vinson, LVO, DL

VINTCENT, John; s of Nevill Vintcent, OBE, DFC (d 1942), and Pamela Vintcent (d 1993); *b* 13 Nov 1937; *Educ* Winchester; *m* Elizabeth Susan, da of Edward Graham Pank (d 1984); 2 s, 1 da; *Career* Nat Serv 2 Lt 16/5 The Queen's Royal Lancers 1956–58; ptnr Laurence Keen & Gardner 1964–70 (joined 1958); Warburg Investment Management Ltd: dir 1970, dep chm 1979, non-exec dir until 1986; exec dir S G Warburg & Co Ltd 1973–79; md: Hanford Farms Ltd 1979–87, Foster & Braithwaite Ltd 1988–96; chm Foster & Braithwaite Fund Management Ltd 1989–96; pres Nat Pig Breeders' Assoc 1987, chm Pig Res Consultative Ctee 1987–88, Gen Cmmr for Income Tax 1985–, memb Income Tax Advsy Ctee for Dorset 1987–; *Recreations* golf, photography, fishing; *Clubs* Brooks's, Grasshoppers; *Style*— John Vintcent, Esq

VINTER, Graham David; s of Alan James Vinter (d 1993), and Lilian Ann Esther, *née* Brown (d 1985); *b* 4 March 1956; *Educ* Chichester HS for Boys, Brasenose Coll Oxford (BA Jurispurdence), Ludwig-Maximilians-Universität Munich; *m* 22 Sept 1990, Anne Elizabeth, da of Alec Baldock; 1 da (Rebecca Jane Alexandra b 28 July 1991), 1 s (William Oliver James b 9 Sept 1993); *Career* Allen & Overy: articled clerk 1980–82, assoc 1982–88, ptnr 1988–; memb Law Soc 1980; *Books* Project Finance: A Legal Guide (1995); *Recreations* squash, skiing, chess; *Style*— Graham Vinter, Esq; ✉ Allen & Overy, One New Change, London EC4M 9QQ (☎ 0171 330 3000, fax 0171 330 9999)

VINTON, Alfred Merton; *b* 1938, Argentina; *Educ* Choate Sch Connecticut, Harvard Univ (BA); *m* Anna (-Maria) Vinton, *qv*; 1 da (Isabel Anousha b 3 Dec 1985), 1 s (George Oliver b 21 Oct 1987); *Career* J P Morgan: offr Latin American Banking Dept 1964–68, seconded as gen mangr and dir to Banco Frances del Rio de la Plata Argentina 1968–73, responsible for Latin American business 1973–77, seconded as gen mangr to Saudi International Bank London 1977–80, sr vice pres and gen mangr Morgan Guaranty's London Branch 1980–86, vice chm Morgan Guaranty Ltd and chm Morgan Guaranty Sterling Securities Ltd London 1986–87; chief operating offr N M Rothschild & Sons Ltd 1988–92; chief exec offr Enterprises Quilmes SA and Three Cities Holdings Ltd 1992–94; chm Electra Fleming Ltd 1995–; chm American Banks Assoc of London 1984–85, memb Exec Ctee BBA 1984–85; *Style*— Alfred Vinton, Esq; ✉ 37 Thurloe Square, London SW7 2SR (☎ 0171 584 8179, fax 0171 584 7681)

VINTON, Anna (-Maria); da of Charles Dugan-Chapman, and Mary Elizabeth Chapman; *b* 17 Nov 1947; *Educ* Chatelard Sch Les Avants Switzerland, Guildhall Sch of Music and Drama; *m* 1, 1970 (m dis 1982), Anthony Greatrex Hawser; m 2, Alfred Merton Vinton, *qv*; 1 s (George Oliver b 21 Oct 1987), 1 da (Isabel Anusha b 3 Dec 1985); *Career* theatre agent: Cochrane Theatrical Agency 1967–68, Norma Skemp Agency 1969–70; ran private property co 1970–72; fndr and mangr: The Reject Linenshop Beauchamp Place London 1972, The Reject Shops plc 1973 (jt chm 1973–94); non-exec dir: Cadbury Schweppes plc 1991–, Courtaulds Textiles plc, Thomas Jourdan PLC 1996–; tstee Marie Curie Fndn; memb: School Teachers' Review Body 1992–96, Covent Garden Market Authy; *Recreations* skiing, riding, gardening, theatre, reading; *Style*— Mrs Anna Vinton; ✉ Stoke Albany House, nr Market Harborough, Leics; 37 Thurloe Square, London SW7 (☎ 0171 589 7981)

VIRDI, Prof Kuldeep Singh; s of Gurdial Singh Virdi, of Faridabad, India, and Sital Kaur, *née* Hoogan; *b* 19 May 1944; *Educ* Univ of Agra (BSc), IIT Bombay (BTech), Univ of Roorkee (ME), Univ of London (PhD, DIC); *m* 24 March 1975, Anne Margaret, da of Raymond Robert Pope, of Sydney, Aust; 1 da (Nina b 1979); *Career* res fell and scientist Structural Engrg Res Centre Roorkee India 1965, asst engr Engineers India Ltd New Delhi 1970, Constrado res fell Dept of Civil Engrg Imperial Coll London 1973 (res asst 1970), lectr in structural engrg Dept of Civil Engrg Univ of Melbourne Aust 1976; Sch of Engrg City Univ London: lectr in civil engrg 1979, reader 1983, head of dept 1986–91, prof of structural engrg 1988–, dep dean 1988–93, currently dir Structures Res Centre; external examiner: Univ of Wales Coll of Cardiff 1994–, Univ of W Indies; FICE 1982, FIStuctE 1982; *Recreations* theatre, music, badminton, travel; *Style*— Prof Kuldeep S Virdi; ✉ Dept of Civil Engineering, City University, London EC1V OHB (☎ 0171 477 8142, fax 0171 477 8570)

VIRGILS, Katherine Ruth; da of Russell Virgils, of San Marcos, Texas, and Shirley, *née* Koppen; *b* 28 Aug 1954; *Educ* Brighton Art Coll, Ravensbourne Art Coll (BA), RCA (MA); *m* 1989, Peter Raymond Camp, s of Maurice Raymond Camp; 2 s (Louis Elliot Virgils Camp b 4 July 1990, Maurice Emil Camp b 28 Sept 1995); *Career* artist; memb: Royal Coll Soc 1982, Crafts Cncl 1983, Ranthamhore Soc 1989, Tibet Soc 1991; FRGS 1991; *Solo Exhibitions* Head Faces Elevations (Camden Arts Centre) 1983, Spirit Syntax Structure (Thumb Gallery London) 1986, Moguls Myths Minatures (Thumb Gallery) 1988, Ruth Segel Gallery NY 1988, Tales of Tigers and Temples (Jill George Gallery London) 1989, The Latitude of Ruins (Jill George Gallery) 1995; *Group Exhibitions* V&A 1981, Hayward Annual London 1982, LA Int Art Fair 1987–90; important works in the collections of: Contemporary Art Soc, Sainsbury Collection, Crafts Cncl Collection, Merrill Lynch, Arthur Andersen, Calvin Klein, Glaxo Export HQ, IBM, BR, Herbert Smith, Lloyds Bank HQ (Cannons Marsh Bristol), Prudential Insurance Co, Harlech TV, Honeywell, Sir Terence Conran, Mitsui, Burma Oil; *Awards*: Crafts Cncl grant 1982, Oxford Arts Cncl award 1984, Sainsbury prize (Chelsea Fair) 1985; *Books* The Latitude of Ruins (1992); *Recreations* travel in India, exploring Indian forts and wildlife, reading, Mayan architecture and ruins; *Style*— Ms Katherine Virgils; ✉ Flat 8, 35 Cheyne Place, Chelsea, London SW3 5HL (☎ 0171 352 0870)

VITA-FINZI, Prof Claudio; s of Paolo Vita-Finzi (d 1986), of Rome, and Nadia, *née* Touchmalova (d 1952); *b* 21 Nov 1936; *Educ* Univ of Cambridge (BA, MA, PhD, DSc); *m* 1 May 1969, Penelope Jean, da of Robert Lawrence Angus (d 1949), of Prestwick; 1 s (Leo b 1970); *Career* res fell St John's Coll Cambridge 1961–64; UCL: lectr 1964–74, reader 1974–87, prof 1987–; *Books* The Mediterranean Valleys (1969), Recent Earth History (1973), Archaeological Sites (1978), Recent Earth Movements (1986); *Recreations* music; *Style*— Prof Claudio Vita-Finzi; ✉ 22 South Hill Park, London NW3 2SB (☎ 0171 794 4415); University College, Department of Geological Sciences, Gower St, London WC1E 6BT (☎ 0171 387 7050, fax 0171 388 7614, e-mail ucfbcvf@ucl.ac.uk)

VITEZ, Charles Oscar; s of Samuel Thomas Vitez (d 1972), and Suzanne Vitez; *b* 24 Oct 1948; *Educ* Westminster City Sch; *Career* CA 1972, ptnr KPMG 1987–93 (joined as taxation specialist 1973), ptnr Charles Vitez & Co 1993–; *Books* Taxation of UK Life Assurance Business (1986), Taxation of Unit Trusts (1994); *Style*— Charles Vitez, Esq; ✉ 37 Preston Road, Wembley, Middlesex HA9 8JZ (☎ 0181 904 5996, fax 0181 908 3207)

VIVIAN, 6 Baron (UK 1841), of Glynn, and of Truro, Co Cornwall; Sir Nicholas Crespigny Laurence Vivian; 6 Bt (UK 1828); s of 5 Baron Vivian (d 1991), and Victoria Ruth Mary Rosamund, *née* Oliphant (d 1985); *b* 11 Dec 1935; *Educ* Eton, Madrid Univ; *m* 1, 1960 (m dis 1972), Catherine Joyce, yst da of James Kenneth Hope,

CBE, DL; 1 s (Hon Charles Crespigny Hussey b 1966), 1 da (Hon Henrietta Mary (Hon Mrs Hoyland) b 1963); m 2, 1972, Carol, eldest da of F Alan Martineau, MBE, JP, of Valley End House, Chobham, Surrey; 2 da (Hon Natasha Sarah (Hon Mrs Piggott) b 1973, Hon Camilla Harriet b 1976); *Heir* s, Hon Charles Crespigny Hussey Vivian b 1966; *Career* cmmnd 3 Carabiniers (Prince of Wales's Dragoon Gds) 1955, Royal Scots Dragoon Gds (Carabiniers and Greys) 1971, 16/5 The Queen's Royal Lancers 1976, cmd Ind Sqdn The Royal Scots Dragoon Gds 1973–75, Princ Staff Offr to Cdr Br Contingent UNFICYP 1975–76, CO 16/5 The Queen's Royal Lancers 1976–79, MOD Def Intelligence Staff 1979–81, Col/Gen Staff Offr Future Anti Armour Study MOD 1982–84, Chief of Staff and Dep Cdr Land Forces Cyprus 1984–87, Brig/Cdr Br Communication Zone (NW Europe, Netherlands, Belgium and NW France) 1987–90, ret; sits as Cons in House of Lords; hon sec All Pty Def Study Gp; special Parly interests: defence, UN mil aspects, terrorism and drugs, Cyprus, Cornwall; cmmr Royal Hosp Chelsea; tstee Queen's Royal Lancers Assoc; *Clubs* White's, Cavalry and Guards'; *Style*— Brig The Rt Hon The Lord Vivian; ✉ c/o House of Lords, London SW1

VIVIAN, Hon Richard Anthony Hussey; s and h of 4 Baron Swansea, *qv*; *b* 24 Jan 1957; *Educ* Eton, Univ of Durham (BA); *m* 24 August 1996, Anna Clementine, da of Michael Austin; *Career* journalist; memb Wandsworth BC 1994–; *Publications* China's Metals and World Markets (1992); *Style*— The Hon Richard Vivian; ✉ 34 York Mansions, Prince of Wales Drive, London SW11 4DL (☎ 0171 622 0425)

VOADEN, Alistair Harold Conway; s of Richard Philip Ball Voaden (d 1957), and Marjorie, *née* Cowlishaw (d 1966); *b* 28 July 1937; *Educ* Perse Sch Cambridge, Coll of Estate Management; *m* 18 Dec 1961, Rosemary Anne, da of Arnold John Wilson (d 1972); 1 s (Jeremy Richard b 1963), 2 da (Katharine Rosemary b 1965, Tania Juliette b 1967); *Career* chartered auctioneer 1958, chartered surveyor 1959; Nat Serv 3 RHA, Lt 94 Locating Regt RA 1959–61; ptnr Grimley & Son 1964 (asst 1961), chm Trident Housing Soc 1965–69, dir Maybrook Properties plc 1970–87, chm Howle Chapman Raymer Ltd 1980–89; Grimley (formerly Grimley JR Eve) Chartered Surveyors: jt managing ptnr 1988–90, jt sr ptnr 1990–93, sr ptnr 1993–; chm GVA Worldwide Ltd 1994–; RICS: chm W Midlands Branch 1975–76, chm RICS/ISVA Code of Measuring Practice Working Party 1978–82, chm STS 1980–81, chm Surveyors Holdings Ltd 1986–89 (dir 1980–89), chm Annual Conf York 1984, chm Regnl Policy Working Pty 1986–87, chm Commercial Property and Fin Servs Ctee 1991–92; chm Hampstead Wells and Campden Tst 1992–95 (chm Estates and Fin Ctee 1990–92); *Recreations* skiing, sailing, gardening, opera; *Clubs* St Stephen's Constitutional, Anglo-Belgian; *Style*— Alistair Voaden, Esq; ✉ Norman Chapel, Broad Campden, Gloucestershire GL55 6UR (☎ 01386 840343); Grimley Chartered Surveyors, 10 Stratton St, London W1X 6JR (☎ 0171 895 1515, fax 0171 499 6029, telex 269155, e-mail 100750.3717@compuserve.com)

VOAK, Jonathan Russell Saunders; s of Capt Allan Frederick Voak, of Bel-Air, St Brelade, Jersey, and Annette Mary, *née* Langlois; *b* 25 Oct 1960; *Educ* Victoria Coll Jersey, Leicester Poly (now De Montfort Univ) (BA); *m* 1 (m dis 1994); m 2, 1995, Colette Louise, *née* Townsend; *Career* curatorial asst to dir of V & A (Sir Roy Strong) 1984–87 (museum asst Metalwork Dept 1983–84), curator Aspley House Wellington Museum 1987–95 (also curator Ham House and Osterley Park House 1989–90), dir Hunt Museum 1996–; ed V&A Museum Report of the Bd of Tstees 1983–86 and 1986–89; co-ed: (with Sir Hugh Casson) V & A Album Gold Edition 1987, John Le Capelain exhbn catalogue Jersey 1988; contrib: Wellington in Spain exhbn catalogue Madrid 1988, Baixella da Victoria - Portugal's Gift of Silver to the Duke of Wellington 1992, London - World City exhbn catalogue Essen 1992; co-author and ed Apsley House, Wellington Museum 1995; memb: Museums Assoc, La Société Jersiase; tstee Chantry Tst, churchwarden Holy Trinity Rotherhithe; *Recreations* motor racing, painting; *Style*— Jonathan Voak, Esq; ✉ 217 The Circle, Queen Elizabeth Street, London SE1 2JN (☎ 0171 378 9651)

VOCKINS, Rev Michael David; OBE (1996); s of Arthur Donald Vockins, of Thatcham, Newbury, Berkshire, and Evelyn Margaret, *née* Mackay-Ellis; *b* 3 July 1944; *Educ* St Bartholomew's GS Newbury, Oxford Poly, Univ Coll of Wales (BSc), Gloucester Sch for Ministry; *m* 17 Dec 1966, Eileen Grace, da of Walter James Hayward; 2 da (Helen b 23 June 1970, Morag b 1 Jan 1973); *Career* sec Worcestershire County Cricket Club 1971–; mangr: Eng Counties XI Tour to Zimbabwe 1985, Eng Young Cricketers Tour to Aust 1990, Eng Under 19 XI Tour to NZ 1991, Eng A team tour Australia 1993, Eng A Team to Pakistan 1995; principally responsible for devising and promoting game of indoor cricket 1970–71; chm Test and County Cricket Bd Second XI Ctee, memb TCCB Ctee on Cricket, Registration; ordained Hereford Cathedral 1988, hon curate of Cradley, Mathon and Storridge Hereford 1988–; *Books* Indoor Cricket, Worcestershire County Cricket Club: An Illustrated History, Barclays World of Cricket (contrib); *Style*— The Rev Michael Vockins, OBE; ✉ Birchwood Lodge, Birchwood, Storridge, Malvern, Worcs WR13 5EZ (☎ 01886 884366); Worcestershire County Cricket Club, County Ground, New Road, Worcester WR2 4QQ (☎ 01905 748474, fax 01905 748005)

VOGT, (Susan) Harriet; da of Richard Vogt, of Washington DC, and Joan, *née* Davis; *b* 31 July 1952; *Educ* Sidwell Friends Sch Washington DC, Westonbirt Sch, Univ of Sussex (BAPsych); *common law husband*, Philip Gallagher, s of Patrick Gallagher, DFC; 2 s (Matthew Patrick Pierce Gallagher b 20 March 1991, James Conor Osmond Gallagher b 18 March 1993); *Career* dir of planning Ayer Advertising 1985–91 (dir 1984–91), corp cnsllr and strategist 1992–93, dir Portman Communications 1993–; *Recreations* consuming books, films, clothes, Italian food and culture, tennis, swimming; *Style*— Ms Harriet Vogt; ✉ 2 Dunollie Place, London NW5

VOLES, Prof Roger; s of Bertram Richard Edward Voles (d 1978), and Winifred Mabel, *née* Barnes (d 1988); *b* 20 July 1930; *Educ* Archbishop Tenison's Sch, London Univ (BSc, MTech, DTech); *m* 24 Sept 1966, Vida Margaret Murray, da of Alec Riley (d 1973); *Career* tech dir Thorn EMI Electronics 1989–91 (chief scientist 1974–89); ind conslt 1991–; visiting prof UCL 1993–; contributed 34 papers to jls of IEE and IEEE; granted 86 patents; organised 8 int confs; former chm: AGARD Avionics Panel, EEA Res Advsy Ctee, IEE Electronics Divnl Bd; Freeman Worshipful Co of Engrs 1984; FIEE 1971, FInstP 1971, FEng 1983, FIMA 1989; *Recreations* mountain walking, genealogy, travel; *Style*— Prof Roger Voles, FEng; ✉ 49 Park Rd, Chiswick, London W4 3EY

VOLK, Stephen Geoffrey; s of Dilwyn Mills Volk, of Pontypridd, S Wales, and Marion, *née* Hartnell; *b* 3 July 1954; *Educ* Coventry Sch of Art (BA), Univ of Bristol (postgrad cert in radio, film and TV studies); *m* Patricia; *Career* advtg copywriter 1977–85; writer; BBC/ASIFA/Icograda Prize for Animation 1976, London Advtg Award (for COI film 'Mark') 1979, D&AD Awards 1984 and 1985 *Screenplays* incl: Gothic (directed by Ken Russell), The Kiss (jtly), The Guardian (jtly, directed by William Friedkin), Ghostwatch (BBC), Massage (BBC), I'll Be Watching You (BBC); *Plays* incl: Answering Spirits, Smiling Like Lazarus; *Novel* Gothic; *Style*— Stephen Volk, Esq; ✉ 9 Coppice Hill, Bradford-on-Avon, Wilts BA15 1JT; c/o Seifert Dench Associates, 24 D'Arblay Street, London W1V 3FH (☎ 0171 437 4551, fax 0171 439 1355); c/o Frank Wuliger, Innovative Artists Talent and Literary Agency Inc, 1999 Avenue of the Stars, Suite No 2850, Los Angeles 90067, USA (☎ 00 1 213 553 5200, fax 00 1 213 557 2211)

VON ETZDORF, Georgina Louise; da of Roderick Rudiger von Etzdorf (d 1996), of Devizes, Wilts, and Audrey, *née* Catterns; *Educ* Downe House, St Martin's Sch of Art, Camberwell Sch of Art (BA); *Career* freelance textile designer 1978–79, freelance designer developing designs from paper work and silk screens on to fabric 1979–80, fndr Georgina von Etzdorf Partnership designing printing and selling wool and silk designs 1981, artistic dir in team producing biannual collections of clothing and accessories for men and women 1991–; lectures and teaching appointments: Cooper Hewitt Museum NYC, Nova Scotia Sch of Art and Design, Glasgow Coll of Art, St Martin's Sch of Art, Royal Coll of Art, The Crafts Cncl; Hon Dr in design Winchester Sch of Art Univ of Southampton 1996; *Exhibitions* Smithsonian Institution's Nat Museum of Design Washington, Cooper Hewitt Museum NY, V&A London; *Awards* BBC 4 Radio Enterprise Award for Small Businesses 1984, British Apparel Export Award 1986, British Gas Award Manchester Prize for Art and Indust 1988, highly commended Int Textile and Fashion Competition (Design Centre Stuttgart) 1988, finalist Export Awards (British Knitting and Clothing Export Cncl in conjunction with The Clothes Show) 1989; *Recreations* singing, dancing, playing the ukelele; *Clubs* Chelsea Arts; *Style*— Dr Georgina von Etzdorf; ✉ The Avenue, Odstock, Salisbury, Wiltshire SP5 4JA (☎ 01722 326625, fax 01722 338541)

VON MALLINCKRODT, George Wilhelm; Hon KBE (1997); s of Arnold Wilhelm von Mallinckrodt, of Riegsee, Germany, and Valentine, *née* von Joest; *b* 19 Aug 1930; *Educ* Schule Schloss Salem, Sch of Economics Hamburg; *m* 31 July 1958, Charmaine Brenda, da of Helmut Schroder; 2 s (Philip b 26 Dec 1962, Edward b 29 June 1965), 2 da (Claire b 11 Aug 1960, Sophie b 8 Aug 1967); *Career* merchant banker; Agfa AG (Munich) 1948–51, Münchmeyer & Co (Hamburg) 1951–53, Kleinwort Sons & Co (London) 1953–54, J Henry Schroder Banking Corporation (New York) 1954–55, Union Bank of Switzerland (Geneva) 1956–57; Schroders plc: rejoined J Henry Schroder Banking Corp NY 1957, joined J Henry Schroder & Co Limited 1960, dir Schroders plc 1977–, chm 1984–95, pres 1995–, chm J Henry Schroder Bank AG Zurich 1984–, chm Schroder Inc NY 1984–, dir Schroders Australia Holdings Ltd Sydney 1984–, dir Schroder Wertheim & Co Inc NY 1986–, dir Schroder International Merchant Bankers Ltd Singapore 1988–; also dir: Allianz of America Inc (NY) 1978–84, Banque Privée de Gestion Financière (Paris) 1980–83, Euris SA (Paris) 1987–, Siemens plc 1989–, Foreign & Colonial German Investment Trust 1992–; chm Cncl World Economic Forum Geneva; memb: Euro Advsy Ctee McGraw-Hill Inc 1986–89, City Advsy Gp CBI 1990–, Br N American Ctee; pres: German Chamber of Indust & Commerce UK 1992–95 (vice pres 1995–), German YMCA London; Hon Doctorate of Civil Law Bishop's Univ Quebec 1994; Cross of the Order of Merit FRG 1986, Offr's Cross of the Order of Merit FRG 1990; FRSA, CIMgt; *Recreations* theatre, shooting, skiing; *Style*— George W Mallinckrodt, Esq, KBE; ✉ Schroders plc, 120 Cheapside, London EC2V 6DS (☎ 0171 382 6345, fax 0171 288 2211, telex 885029)

von OTTER, Anne Sofie; *Educ* in Stockholm, Guildhall Sch of Music and Drama London; *Career* mezzo-soprano; studies with Vera Rozsa; appeared at venues incl: Royal Opera House Covent Garden, Wigmore Hall, Met Opera NY, La Scala Milan, Opera Houses of Berlin, Munich, Geneva, Lyon and Stockholm, BBC Proms; given recitals under conductors incl: Colin Davis, John Eliot Gardiner, Carlo Maria Giulini, James Levine, Riccardo Muti, Giuseppe Sinopoli, Sir Georg Solti, Andrew Davis; *Performances* incl: Oktavian in Der Rosenkavalier (with Met Opera under Carlos Kleiber and with Chicago Lyric Opera), Tancredi (Geneva), Cherubino in Le Nozze di Figaro (concert performances under Sir Georg Solti in London, Paris, Frankfurt and Cologne), title role in La Cenerentola (Covent Garden), Idamantes in Idomeneo (Met Opera), Romeo in I Capuleti (Covent Garden), Beatrice in Much Ado About Nothing (Glyndebourne); *Recordings* incl: Cosi fan Tutte (with Sir Neville Marriner), Orfeo (with John Eliot Gardiner), Hansel and Gretel (with Jeffrey Tate), Der Rosenkavalier (with Bernard Haitink), Le Nozze di Figaro (with James Levine), Schubert's Rosamunde (with Claudio Abbado), Bach B Minor Mass (with Sir Georg Solti), Lieder recitals of Wolf, Mahler and Brahms; *Style*— Ms Anne Sofie von Otter; ✉ IMG Artists Europe, Media House, 3 Burlington Lane, London W4 2TH (☎ 0181 747 9977, fax 0181 747 9131)

von PREUSSEN, Princess Nicholas; Hon Victoria; *née* Mancroft; da of 2 Baron Mancroft, KBE, TD; *b* 1952; *m* 1980, HRH Prince (Frederick) Nicholas von Preussen; 1 s (Frederick Nicholas Stormont b 11 June 1990), 3 da (Beatrice Victoria b 10 Feb 1981, Florence Jessica b 28 July 1983, Augusta Lily b 15 Dec 1986); *Style*— Princess Nicholas von Preussen; ✉ Maperton House, Wincanton, Somerset BA9 8EJ

von SCHRAMEK, Sir Eric Emil; kt (1982); s of Emil von Schramek (d 1947), and Annie von Schramek (d 1981); *b* 4 April 1921; *Educ* Stefans Gymnasium Prague, Tech Univ Prague (Dipl Ing Arch); *m* 1948, Edith, da of Dipl Ing W Popper; 1 s (Charles), 2 da (Annette, Therese); *Career* town planner Bavaria 1946–48; sr supervising architect Dept of Works and Housing Darwin NT 1948–51, chm von Schramek and Dawes Pty Ltd (formerly Evans, Bruer & Ptnrs) 1953–91; conslt to Hames Sharley International architects and planners 1989–; work includes: Nat Mutual Centre, State Govt Insur Building, Wales Ho, TAA Building; numerous churches throughout Australia and New Guinea; nat pres Building Sci Forum of Australia 1970–72; pres SA Chapter RAIA 1974–76; former nat dep chm Austcare; former cncllr Cncl of Professions; former chm various ctees Lutheran Church of Australia; KStJ 1995; life fellow RAIA, hon assoc (arch) SAIT; FRIBA, FIArbA; *Publications* contributions and articles in architectural pubns; *Recreations* music, reading, golf; *Style*— Sir Eric von Schramek; ✉ The Olives, PO Box 457, Yankalilla 5203, South Australia (☎ 00 61 85 583341)

von SIMSON, David; s of Prof Dr Werner von Simson (d 1996), of Freiburg, W Germany, and Kathleen, *née* Turner (d 1996); bro of Piers von Simson, *qv*; *b* 19 Sept 1950; *Educ* Lancing, New Coll Oxford (BA); *Children* 2 da (Alice b 5 June 1982, Rachel b 15 May 1984); *Career* mangr Samuel Montagu & Co Ltd 1976–79; dir: Hill Samuel Securities Ltd 1982–84, Hill Samuel & Co Ltd 1984–85 (mangr 1979–82); memb Supervisory Bd Bank von Ernst & Cie 1984–85, exec dir Swiss Bank Corporation International Ltd 1985–95, md SBC Warburg 1995–; non-exec dir Gardner Merchant Ltd; *Clubs* RAC; *Style*— David von Simson, Esq; ✉ SBC Warburg Group plc, 2 Finsbury Avenue, London EC2M 2PA (☎ 0171 395 2637, fax 0171 860 0901)

von SIMSON, Piers; s of Prof Werner von Simson (d 1996), of Freiburg, Germany, and Kathleen Aimee, *née* Turner (d 1996); bro of David von Simson, *qv*; *b* 23 Sept 1946; *Educ* Lancing, New Coll Oxford (BA), Univ of Calif Berkeley (LLM); *m* 1, 6 Aug 1977, Lindsay, da of Prof E J H Corner, formerly of Univ of Cambridge; 1 s (James Francis Louis b 16 April 1983), 2 da (Cara Isabel Camilla b 15 June 1978, Isabel Victoria b 17 April 1982); m 2, 17 April 1996, Sarah, da of David Phillips, of Prisk, Cowbridge, S Glamorgan; 1 s (Thomas Maximilian b 25 July 1996); *Career* called to the Bar Middle Temple 1969, dir S G Warburg & Co Ltd 1979–95 (joined 1972), dir S G Warburg Group plc 1989–95, md SBC Warburg 1995–96, dir Soditic Finance Company Ltd 1996–; *Recreations* opera, books, sailing, winter sports; *Clubs* Turf; *Style*— Piers von Simson, Esq; ✉ Soditic Finance Company Ltd, Brettenham House, Lancaster Place, London WC2E 7EQ (☎ 0171 872 7000, fax 0171 872 7100)

von WESTENHOLZ, Piers Patrick Frederick; Baron; s of Baron Henry Frederick Everard von Westenholz (d 1984), of Crackney, Widford, Herts; *b* 10 Dec 1943; *Educ* Downside; *m* 1, 1964 (m dis 1969), Sarah, da of Raimund von Hofmannstahl (s of the poet Hugo von Hofmannstahl) by his 2 w, Lady Elizabeth Paget (da of 6 Marquess of Anglesey, GCVO); m 2, 1979, Jane, da of Arthur Leveson, of Hall Place, Ropley, Hants; 1 s, 2 da; *Career* antique dealer and decorator; *Recreations* shooting, fishing, skiing; *Style*— Baron von Westenholz; ✉ Barrow Farm, Much Hadham, Herts

VOOS, John; s of Kurt Alias Voos, and Amy Jean, *née* Webb; *b* 6 May 1956; *Educ* Netteswell Comp Sch Harlow Essex, Harrow Coll of Technol and Art London; *m* 1 (m dis), Carmen Sik Heng, *née* Lim; m 2, Belinda Alison; 1 s (James Reith b 26 March 1988), 2 da (Jasmine Emma b 19 Nov 1983, Katy Jean Isobel b 15 May 1995); *Career* photographer Fleet St News Agency 1980–82, freelance photographer The Times 1982–86, staff photographer The Independent 1986–; included in World Press Photo Competition Book 1989 and 1991; *Recreations* sub-aqua diving, backgammon, swimming, walking, jogging; *Style*— John Voos, Esq; ✉ The Independent, 1 Canada Square, Canary Wharf, London E14 5DL (☎ 0171 293 2000, fax 0171 293 2435)

VORDERMAN, Carol Jean; *b* 24 Dec 1960; *Educ* Ysgol Mair Rhyl, Blessed Edward Jones HS Rhyl, Sidney Sussex Coll Cambridge (MA); *m* Patrick King; 1 da (Katie); *Career* civil engr Sir Alfred McAlpine 1981; broadcaster and TV personality; resident statistician Countdown (Channel 4) 1982– (first woman to appear on Channel 4), co-presenter Take Nobody's Word For It (BBC 1) 1986–90, devised, wrote and presented So We Bought a Computer (Channel 4) 1987, science expert Wide Awake Club (ITV) 1988–91, presenter Postcards from Down Under (BBC and Channel 7 Australia) 1989, co-presenter How 2! (ITV) 1990–, presenter Sum Chance (BBC 1) 1990, presenter A Way with Numbers (BBC1) 1991, The Parts (Radio 4) 1991–93, This Morning (ITV) 1992–, World Chess Championship Kasparov v Short (Channel 4) 1993, co-host Notes and Queries (BBC 2) 1993–94, educn corr GMTV 1993–94, anchor Tomorrow's World (BBC1) 1994–95, anchor Out of This World (BBC 1) 1996, anchor Entertainment Today (ITV) 1996–, columnist Daily Telegraph 1996–, presenter Millennium Science (Anglia Television) 1996–; guest/presenter numerous other TV and radio progs and corporate video prodns; guest appearances incl: Mrs Merton (BBC 2) 1995, You Bet (LWT) 1995, Teleganticmegavision (ITV) 1996; host various confs and awards ceremonies; md Rockhopper Ltd; dir Mensa 1989–92, memb DTI Task Force Action into Engrg 1995–; Assoc MICE; *Style*— Ms Carol Vorderman; ✉ c/o John Miles Organisation, Cadbury Camp Lane, Clapton-in-Gordano, Bristol BS20 9SB (☎ 01275 854675, fax 01275 810186)

VOS, Geoffrey Charles; QC (1993); s of Bernard Vos (d 1974), of London, and Pamela Celeste Rose, *née* Heilbuth; *b* 22 April 1955; *Educ* UCS, Gonville and Caius Coll Cambridge (MA); *m* 31 March 1984, Vivien Mary, da of Albert Edward Dowdeswell (d 1982), of Birmingham; 1 da (Charlotte b 1985), 1 step s (Carl b 1973), 2 step da (Maria b 1965, Louise b 1965); *Career* called to the Bar Inner Temple 1977, in practice Chambers of DR Stanford 1979–; hon sec Chancery Bar Assoc 1994–, subscriber Senate of the Inns of Ct; memb: Inner Temple, Lincoln's Inn; *Recreations* farming, wine, photography; *Clubs* United Oxford and Cambridge Univ, Worcs Golf; *Style*— Geoffrey Vos, Esq, QC; ✉ 3 Stone Buildings, Lincoln's Inn, London WC2A 3XL (☎ 0171 242 4937, fax 0171 405 3896)

VOSS, Prof Christopher Arnold; s of Dr H J Voss, of Cottingham, Northants, and Matthew, *née* Arnold (d 1989); *b* 23 Dec 1942; *Educ* Bedford Sch, Imperial Coll London (BSc), London Business Sch (MSc, PhD); *m* 14 Dec 1977, Carolyn Jill, da of Sir Richard Kingsland, DFC, of Canberra, Aust; 1 s (Barnaby b 1981), 1 da (Georgina b 1978); *Career* mangr Stuarts & Lloyds Ltd 1960–67, conslt Harbridge House Europe 1970–75, visiting prof Univ of Western Ontario 1975–77, lectr London Business Sch 1977–84, Alan Edward Higgs prof of mfrg strategy and policy Univ of Warwick 1984–90, BT prof of total quality mgmnt and dir Centre for Operations Mgmnt London Business Sch 1990–; chm European Ops Mgmnt Assoc; MBICS 1971, FRSA 1989, fell Br Acad of Mgmnt 1995 (memb Ctee); *Books* Operation Management in Service Industries and the Public Sector (1985), Just-In-Time Management (1988), Performance Measurement in Service Industries (1992), Manufacturing Strategy - Process and Content (1992), Made in Europe (1994); *Recreations* skiing, violin, book collecting; *Style*— Prof Christopher Voss; ✉ London Business School, Sussex Place, Regents Park, London NW1 4SA (☎ 0171 262 5050, fax 0171 724 7875)

VOSS, Dr Robert George Perceval; OBE (1984); s of Prof Vivian Voss, MBE (d 1988), of Cape Town, SA, and Florence Mary, *née* Perceval (d 1950); *b* 23 April 1928; *Educ* St Charles Coll Pietermaritzburg SA, Univ of Natal SA (BSc Eng), Univ of Oxford (Rhodes scholar, MA, DPhil); *m* 1960, Daisy Marie-Louise, da of John William Caisley; *Career* lectr Univ of Liverpool 1955–59, sr physicist Euro Orgn for Nuclear Res Geneva 1959–63; Daresbury Laboratory nr Warrington: construction of Nina Magnet 1963–66, head of experimental physics 1966–69, acting dir 1969–70, dep dir and head of design and construction of nuclear structure facility 1970–83; head of Engrg Div SERC Central Office Swindon 1983–90, assoc dir of sci and head of Sci Dept SERC Rutherford Appleton Laboratory 1990–93 (ret, hon scientist); Dr E G Malherbe Award for outstanding contrib to educn, sci and indust 1984; memb: American Physical Soc, Euro Physical Soc; CEng, CPhys; FInstP 1972, FIEE 1974, FRSA 1984, FEng 1987; *Recreations* walking, music, foreign travel, reading, France; *Style*— Dr Robert Voss, OBE, FEng; ✉ 11 Bannister Close, Oxford OX4 1SH (☎ 01865 251404)

VOWLES, Paul Foster; s of Ernest Foster Vowles (d 1929), of Bristol, and Georgina May, *née* Lawrence (d 1983), of Bristol; *b* 12 June 1919; *Educ* Bristol GS, CCC Oxford (MA); *m* 8 Jan 1948, Valerie Eleanor, da of Ralph Theodore Hickman (d 1967); 1 s (John b 1949), 2 da (Penelope b 1952, Deborah b 1955); *Career* Army 1939–46; cmmnd Gloucs Regt 1940, KAR 1942 (despatches), Maj; asst sec: Univ of Birmingham Appts Bd 1947, Inter-Univ Cncl for Higher Educn Overseas 1948–51, registrar Makerere Univ Coll East Africa 1951–63; Univ of London: sr asst to princ 1964–68, external registrar 1968–73, academic registrar 1973–82; vice-chm Cncl Westfield Coll Univ of London 1986–89; hon fell Queen Mary and Westfield College 1991; *Clubs* Athenaeum; *Style*— Paul Vowles, Esq; ✉ 13 Dale Close, Oxford OX1 1TU (☎ 01865 244042)

VRANCH, Richard Leslie; s of Leslie William Frank Vranch (d 1991), of Somerset, and Rea Helen, *née* Turner; *b* 29 June 1959; *Educ* Bristol GS, Trinity Hall Cambridge (MA, PhD); *Career* actor and musician; TV appearances incl: Whose Line Is It Anyway? (C4) 1988–, The Secret Policeman's Biggest Ball 1990, Jackanory (BBC) 1993 and 1994, The Music Game (C4) 1993, Cue the Music 1994–96, Beat That Einstein (C4) 1994, Just A Minute (Carlton) 1994, Paul Merton at the Palladium (BBC) 1994; theatre work incl: Aftertaste (with Tony Slattery, *qv*) 1981–, The Comedy Store Players 1986–, English Teaching Theatre (tour to Europe, ME and Mexico) 1988–94, Secret Policeman's Biggest Ball (Cambridge Theatre) 1990, Hysteria 2 and Hysteria 3 1991, Clive in The Dead Set 1992, Paul Merton Show (London Palladium) 1994; The Hot Club (BBC Radio 4) 1989; Plessey res fell St John's Coll Oxford 1984–85; *Publications* Defects in Irradiated MOS Structures (PhD thesis); *Recreations* cricket, travel in Europe and Latin America; *Clubs* Players, Arts; *Style*— Richard Vranch; ✉ c/o Talk Back, 36 Percy Street, London W1P 0LN

VYVYAN, Sir (Ralph) Ferrers Alexander; 13 Bt (E 1645), of Trelowarren, Cornwall; s of Sir John Stanley Vyvyan, 12 Bt (d 1995), and his 3 w, Jonet Noel, *née* Barclay; *b* 21 Aug 1960; *Educ* Charterhouse, Sandhurst, Architectural Assoc; *m* 1986, Victoria Arabella, yst da of M B Ogle, of Skerraton, Buckfastleigh, Devon; 4 s (Joshua Drummond b 10 Oct 1986, Frederick George b 21 Dec 1987, Rowan Arthur b 23 Oct 1989, Inigo Valentine b 14 Feb 1994); *Heir* s, Joshua Drummond Vyvyan b 10 Oct 1986; *Career* restoration of Trelowarren and its 18th century gardens and ancient woodlands; *Recreations* gardening and landscape, conservation; *Style*— Sir Ferrers Vyvyan, Bt; ✉ Trelowarren, Mawgan, Helston, Cornwall TR12 6AF (☎ 01326 221224)

W

WAAGE, Dr Jeffrey King; s of Prof Karl Mensch Waage, of Connecticut, USA, and Elizabeth, *née* King; *b* 15 March 1953; *Educ* Hopkins GS, Princeton Univ (AB, Phi Beta Kappa), Imperial Coll London (Marshall fell, PhD, DIC); *m* 18 March 1983, Cynthia, da of Dr Charles Day Masters; 1 da (Hannah b 23 Nov 1984), 3 s (Alexander b 26 Sept 1986, Nicholas b 29 March 1989, Theodore b 27 Feb 1994); *Career* postdoctoral work in entomology Univ of Texas Austin 1978, lectr in insect ecology Imperial Coll London 1978–86, dir Int Inst of Biological Control 1992– (joined as chief res offr 1986, subsequently dep dir); has worked extensively in tropical America, Africa and Asia on aspects of ecology and pest mgmnt since 1975; memb: Br Ecological Soc 1978, Royal Entomological Soc of London 1978; *Recreations* walking; *Style—* Dr Jeffrey Waage; ✉ International Institute of Biological Control, Silwood Park, Buckhurst Road, Ascot, Berks SL5 7TA (☎ 01344 872999)

WADDELL, Sir Alexander Nicol Anton; KCMG (1959, CMG (1955), DSC (1944); s of Rev Alexander Waddell; *b* 8 Nov 1913; *Educ* Fettes, Univ of Edinburgh, Gonville and Caius Coll Cambridge; *m* 1949, Jean Margot Lesbia, da of W Masters; *Career* WWII Serv; Lt RANVR 1942–44 (coastwatcher), Lt-Col (gen list) Br Mil Admin 1945–47; dist offr Br Solomon Islands 1938, DC 1945, princ asst sec N Borneo 1947–52, colonial sec Gambia 1952–56, dep gov Sierra Leone 1958–60 (colonial sec 1956–58), govr and C-in-C Sarawak 1960–63, UK cmmr Br Phosphate Commn 1965–78, memb Panel Ind Insprs Dept Environment 1979–85; *Recreations* golf, hill walking; *Clubs* East India and Sports; *Style—* Sir Alexander Waddell, KCMG, DSC; ✉ Pilgrim Cottage, Ashton Keynes, Wilts

WADDELL, Heather; yr da of Robert (Roy) Waddell (d 1980), of Hughenden, Glasgow, and Maureen, *née* Buchanan, MBE; *b* 11 July 1950; *Educ* Westbourne Sch Glasgow, St Leonard's Sch St Andrews, Univ of St Andrews (MA), Byam Shaw Sch of Art London (Dip in Fine Art, Leverhulme bursary), Univ of London (CertEd); *Career* publisher, art critic, author and photographer; lectr in English and gen studies Paddington Coll London 1978, researcher the Int Artists Exchange Prog in Aust and NZ under Gulbenkian scholarship (awarded 1979), int admin IVAEP ACME Gallery Covent Garden London 1980, Central Bureau for Educational Visits and Exchanges grant to set up art sch exchange links in Belgium and Holland 1980, fndr and md Art Guide Publications 1980–87 (art guides to London, NY, Paris, Berlin, Amsterdam, Madrid, Glasgow, Aust and UK), publisher Art Guide Publications imprint A & C Black 1987–90, arts events ed élan arts magazine The European 1990–91, visual arts ed Time Out Publications 1989–93, visual arts ed Chic magazine 1994–, lectr in art history American Univ Summer Sch Paris 1995–; freelance journalist: The Evening Standard 1974, The Artist 1974–75, TES 1977, The Glasgow Herald (London art critic 1980–84 and 1994–), Artnews USA 1986, New Art International Paris 1986, Artline UK 1985–92, Vie des Arts (London corr) 1979–89, The Independent 1988–89, Independent on Sunday 1993, The Times 1996; organiser New Scottish Prints Exhbn as part of Britain Salutes NY (toured USA) 1983, conslt Int Contemporary Art Fair London 1984–90, organiser Henri Goetz Exhibition London 1986, chm of judges The Art Show 1994; photographer: 5 + 1 Aust photos exhibition NSW House Art Gallery London 1979, Battersea Arts Centre 1980, Art Guides (London and Glasgow), Blue Guides (London and Paris), The Independent, The European, Time Out Publications, National Portrait Gallery London (20th Century Collection), Photo Agency Camera Press London; Int Assoc of Art Critics (AICA): memb 1980–, memb Exec Ctee 1982–, treas 1985–86, PRO 1990–; memb: Exec Ctee Int Assoc of Artists 1978–84, Soc of Young Publishers 1980–86, Ind Publishers' Guild 1980–89, Map and Guide Book Ctee and Art Book Publishers' Ctee Publishers' Assoc 1983–87; *Books* author of: London Art and Artists Guide (1979, 7 edn 1997), The Artists' Directory (1981, 3 edn 1989), Henri Goetz: 50 Years of Painting (1986); contrib: Encyclopaedia of London (Macmillan, 1986), L'Ecosse; lumière, granit et vent (1988), Blue Guide to Spain (1988), Londres (1997), Editions Autrement Paris, Time Out London Guide, Time Out New York Guide, Time Out Visitor's Guide, Time Out Shopping Guide, British Figurative Art 1980–92: Paintings of Hope and Despair (1992); *Recreations* travel, swimming, friends and their children, contemporary literature and films, enjoying life; *Style—* Heather Waddell; ✉ 27 Holland Park Avenue, London W11 3RW

WADDELL, Sir James Henderson; Kt (1974), CB (1960); s of Donald M Waddell and J C Fleming; *b* 5 Oct 1914; *Educ* George Heriot's Sch, Univ of Edinburgh (MA); *m* 1940, Dorothy Abbie, da of Horace Wright; 1 s, 1 da; *Career* Civil Serv 1936–75: under sec Cabinet Office 1961–63, dep sec Miny of Housing and Local Govt 1963–66, dep under sec Home Office 1966–75; dep chm Police Complaints Bd 1977–81, pres Open Air Museum Singleton 1990–94; *Style—* Sir James Waddell, CB; ✉ Long Meadow, East Lavant, Chichester, W Sussex (☎ 01243 527129)

WADDELL, Martin; s of Martin Mayne Waddell, and Alice, *née* Duffell; *b* 10 April 1941, Belfast; *Educ* Eaton House Sch London, St Clemence Danes Sch London, Down HS Downpatrick; *m* Dec 1969, Rosaleen Margaret, da of Thomas Arthur Carragher; 3 s (Thomas Mayne (Tom) b 1970, David Martin b 1972, Peter Matthew b 1975); *Career* writer (also writes as Catherine Sefton) 1966–; former work experience incls bookselling and junk-stalling; NI Arts Cncl sch speaker in children's literature; memb: Soc of Authors, Irish Writers' Union, Children's Literature Assoc of Ireland; *Books include* Starry Night (The Other Award, runner-up Guardian Young Fiction Award), Can't You Sleep Little Bear (Smarties Prize, Sheffield Book Award, Prix de Critiques de Livres pour Enfants de la Communauté Française de Belgique, Prix Verselle), The Park in the Dark (Emil/Kurt Maschler Award), The Hidden House (Emil/Kurt Maschler Award short list), Rosie's Babies (Best Book for Babies Award), Squeak-a-Lot, Grandma's Bill (runner-up Bisto Book of the Year Award, Acorn Award short list), Farmer Duck (Smarties Prize, Emil/Kurt Maschler Award short list); *Style—* Martin Waddell, Esq; ✉ c/o David Higham Associates, 5–8 Lower John Street, Golden Square, London W1R 4HA (☎ 0171 437 7888, fax 0171 437 1072)

WADDELL, Robert Steele (Robin); s of Col Herbert Waddell, CBE, HLI (d 1988), and Jean Cameron, *née* Wallace (d 1994); *b* 3 Aug 1931; *Educ* Glasgow Acad, St Mary's Melrose, Fettes, Univ of Cambridge; *m* 8 July 1960, Margaret Eileen Monro, da of Dr John Sturrock (d 1994); 4 da (Elizabeth-Anne (Mrs Wilson) b 1961, Nicola (Dr Markland) b 1963, Alexandra (Mrs Hardie) b 1966, Victoria (Mrs Vestey) b 1967); *Career* Nat Serv 41 Field Regt RA, Egypt; with Thomson McLintock Glasgow 1955–59, Speirs and Jeffrey Ltd 1960– (sr ptnr 1979, chm 1986–95, constl 1995–); *Recreations* golf; *Clubs* Elie Golf, Prestwick Golf, Glasgow Golf, Muirfield, R and A; *Style—* Robin Waddell, Esq; ✉ 34 Ann Street, Edinburgh EH4 1PJ (☎ 0131 332 3496); Speirs & Jeffrey Ltd, 36 Renfield Street, Glasgow G2 1NA (☎ 0141 248 4311, fax 0141 221 4764)

WADDELL, Rear Adm William Angus; CB (1981), OBE (1966); s of late James Whitefield Waddell, and late Christina, *née* Maclean; *b* 5 Nov 1924; *Educ* Univ of Glasgow (BSc, Cleland Gold Medal); *m* 1950, Thelma Evelyn Tomlins; 1 s, 1 da; *Career* Sub Lt RNVR (Special Branch) 1945, Offr i/c RN Polaris Sch 1966–68, Instr Capt Staff of SACLANT (Dir Info Systems Gp) 1969–72, Dean RN Coll Greenwich 1973–75, assoc teacher The City Univ 1973–75, Dir Naval Offr Appts (Instr) 1975–78, ADC to HM The Queen 1976–79, Chief Naval Instr Offr 1978–81, Rear Adm 1979, Flag Offr Admty Interview Bd 1979–81; Sec and Chief Exec Royal Inst of Public Health and Hygiene 1982–90; Hon FRIPHH; FIEE, CEng; *Style—* Rear Adm W A Waddell, CB, OBE; ✉ c/o National Westminster Bank, 80 Lewisham High Street, London SE13 5JJ

WADDINGTON, Bill; *Career* actor; writer and prodr numerous shows Army 1939–45, then stage comic, currently plays Percy Sugden in Coronation Street (Granada); *Style—* Bill Waddington; ✉ c/o Coronation Street, Granada TV Centre, Quay Street, Manchester M60 9EA (☎ 0161 832 7211, fax 0161 953 0298)

WADDINGTON, Baron (Life Peer UK 1990), of Read in the County of Lancashire; David Charles Waddington; GCVO (1994), PC (1987), QC (1971), DL (Lancashire 1991); s of late Charles Waddington, JP, of Read, Lancs, and Minnie Hughan Waddington; *b* 2 Aug 1929; *Educ* Sedbergh, Hertford Coll Oxford; *m* 1958, Gillian Rosemary, da of Alan Green, CBE, of Sabden, Lancs; 3 s (Hon James Charles b 1960, Hon Matthew David b 1962, Hon Alistair Paul b 1965), 2 da (Hon Jennifer Rosemary b 1965, Hon Victoria Jane b 1971); *Career* 2 Lt 12 Royal Lancers 1951–53; called to the Bar Gray's Inn 1951, recorder Crown Court 1972; former dir: J J Broadley Ltd, J and J Roberts Ltd, Wolstenholme Rink Ltd; Parly candidate (Cons): Farnworth 1955, Nelson and Colne 1964, Heywood and Royton 1966; MP (C): Nelson and Colne 1968–74, Clitheroe March 1979–83, Ribble Valley 1983–90; Lord Cmmr of the Treasy 1979–81, Parly under sec employment 1981–83, min of state Home Office 1983–87, govt chief whip 1987–89, home sec 1989–90; Lord Privy Seal and Leader of the House of Lords 1990–April 1992, govr and C-in-C Bermuda April 1992–June 1997; *Style—* The Rt Hon Lord Waddington, GCVO, PC, QC, DL; ✉ c/o Government House, Bermuda

WADDINGTON, Prof David James; s of Eric James Waddington (d 1958), of London, and Marjorie Edith, *née* Harding (d 1995); *b* 27 May 1932; *Educ* Marlborough, Imperial Coll (BSc, ARCS, DIC, PhD); *m* 17 Aug 1957, Isobel, da of Ernest Hesketh (d 1994), of Tibshelf, Derbyshire; 2 s (Matthew b 1963, Rupert b 1964), 1 da (Jessica b 1970); *Career* head Sci Dept Wellington Coll 1961–64 (teacher 1956–64); York Univ 1965–: prof of chemical educn 1978–, head dept 1983–92, pro-vice-chllr 1985–91; pres Educn Div Royal Soc Chem 1981–83, chm Ctee Teaching Chemistry, Int Union Pure and Applied Chem 1981–85, sec Ctee Teaching Sci Int Cncl Sci Unions 1985–89 (chm 1989–94), Nyholm medal Royal Soc Chem 1985, Brasted Award American Chem Soc 1988; *Books* Modern Organic Chemistry (1985), Kinetics and Mechanism: Case Studies (1977), Chemistry, The Salters' Approach (1989), Salters' Advanced Chemistry (1994); ed: Teaching School Chemistry (1984), Chemistry in Action (1987), Education Industry and Technology (1987), Bringing Chemistry to Life (1992), Science for Understanding Tomorrow's World: Global Change (1994), Global Environmental Change: Science Education and Training (1995), Partners in Chemical Education (1996); *Recreations* golf; *Style—* Prof David Waddington; ✉ Department of Chemistry, Univ of York, Heslington, York YO1 5DD (☎ 01904 432600/1, fax 01904 432605)

WADDINGTON, Leslie; s of Victor Waddington, and Zelda, *née* Levine; *b* 9 Feb 1934; *Educ* Portora Royal Sch NI, Sorbonne, Ecole du Louvre Paris (dip); *m* 1, 1967 (m dis 1983), Ferriel, *née* Lyle; 2 da; m 2, 1985, Clodagh Frances, *née* Fanshawe; *Career* chm and jt fndr Waddington Galleries 1957– (md 1966–); *Recreations* reading, walking, chess; *Style—* Leslie Waddington, Esq; ✉ Waddington Galleries, 11 Cork St, London W1X 1PD (☎ 0171 437 8611)

WADDINGTON, Prof Peter Anthony James; s of James William Harker Waddington (d 1980), and Patricia Ann, *née* Nil; *b* 6 March 1947; *Educ* Moseley Road Sch of Art, Matthew Boulton Tech Coll, Univ of London (external BSc), Univ of Leeds (MA, PhD); *m* 1968, Diane Anita, da of George Atherley; 1 s (Daniel Bevan b 15 Nov 1978), 1 da (Claire Shelley b 9 April 1980); *Career* Univ of Leeds: SSRC studentship 1969–70, res offr/fell Dept of Adult Educn 1970–74, lectr in sociology 1974–76; Univ of Reading: lectr in sociology 1976–92, reader in police studies Univ of Reading 1992–95, prof of sociology 1995–; *Books* The Training of Prison Governors (1983), Arming an Unarmed Police (1988), The Strong Arm of the Law (1991), Calling the Police (1993), Liberty and Order (1995); *Recreations* squash; *Style—* Prof Peter Waddington; ✉ Department of Sociology, University of Reading, PO Box 218, Reading, Berks RG6 2AA (☎ 0118 931 6763, fax 0118 931 8922)

WADDINGTON, Robert; s of George Waddington (d 1967), of Lytham, Lancs, and Mary Gwendoline, *née* Briggs; *b* 20 Jan 1942; *Educ* Uppingham; *m* 24 Jan 1976, Jennifer Ann, da of late Sir Anthony Banks Jenkinson, 13 Bt (d 1989); 2 s (Thomas Anthony b 10 May 1977, Guy George b 6 Sept 1979); *Career* Peat Marwick Mitchell 1960–64; Hambros Bank Ltd 1971– (dir 1984); FCA; *Recreations* shooting, golf, gardening; *Clubs* Turf Club; *Style—* Robert Waddington, Esq; ✉ 41 Tower Hill, London EC3 (☎ 0171 480 5000, fax 0171 488 9994)

WADDINGTON, Sue; MEP (Lab) Leicestershire and S Lincolnshire (majority 20,284); *Educ* Blyth GS Norwich, Univ of Leicester (BA, MEd); *Career* former community project leader and lectr in social policy, dir Community Educn Serv Birmingham until 1994, MEP (Lab) Leicestershire and S Lincolnshire 1994–; memb Euro Parliament: Social Affrs and Employment Ctee, Environment, Public Health and Consumer Affrs Ctee, Women's Rights Ctee, Delegation for relations with Slovenia; EPLP spokesperson on Women; former leader Leicester CC (elected cncllr 1973); contested gen election Leicestershire NW 1987; memb UNISON; *Style—* Ms Susan Waddington, MEP; ✉ Euro Office, Room 210, The Town Hall, Town Hall Square, Leicester, Leicestershire LE1 9BG (☎ 0116 247 1221, fax 0116 247 1331)

WADDLE, Christopher Roland (Chris); s of Joseph Waddle (d 1991), and Elizabeth, *née* Ashton; *b* 14 Dec 1960; *Educ* Heworth Grange Comp Sch; *m* 25 June 1983, Lorna, da of Douglas Bruce; 1 s (Jack b 2 Dec 1993), 1 da (Brooke b 31 May 1988); *Career* professional footballer; Newcastle Utd 1979–85, Tottenham Hotspur 1985–89, Marseille

1989–92, Sheffield Wednesday 1992–96, Bradford City 1997; with Sheffield Wednesday: runners-up Coca-Cola Cup 1993, runners-up FA Cup 1993; England caps: 1 under 21, 62 full; set then Br transfer record of £4.25m from Tottenham Hotspur to Marseille; Football Writers' Player of the Year 1993, Carling Player of the Month Jan 1995; occasional TV and radio commentator and pundit; *Recreations* music, family, TV, watching football; *Style*— Chris Waddle, Esq

WADE, Christopher Edward Huddart; s of Dr Edward Geoffrey Wade, and Dr Mary Wade, *née* Huddart, of Manchester; *b* 6 Feb 1944; *Educ* Cheadle Hulme Sch Cheshire (head boy), Gonville & Caius Cambridge (MA), Dept of Educn Univ of Nottingham (post grad CertEd); *m* 1 Nov 1968, Susan Marchant, da of Roland Batte; 2 da (Susannah Helen b 19 Sept 1970, Philippa Jane b 22 March 1972); *Career* chemistry teacher Dulwich Coll 1967–72, head of science Bassaleg Sch Newport Gwent 1972–77, dep head Fulston Manor Sch Kent 1977–80, dep head Moulsham HS Essex 1980–83, headmaster Bramston Sch Witham Essex 1984–90, headmaster Hewett Sch Norwich 1990–; memb: SHA 1984–, Assoc for Science Educn 1967–; *Books* Understanding Chemistry (1972); *Recreations* hill walking, island visiting (ambition/intention to visit every inhabited British island), cycling (gently), reading, cooking; *Clubs* Witham Rotary, Norwich Rotary; *Style*— Christopher Wade, Esq; ✉ Hewett School, Cecil Road, Norwich NR1 2PL (☎ 01603 628181, fax 01603 764129)

WADE, David Anthony; s of Col Harold Wade (d 1945), and Olive, *née* Baldwin (d 1961); *b* 22 Dec 1925; *Educ* Stonyhurst; *m* 1, 1 Dec 1949, Nancy (d 1965), da of Col R Stalker; 4 da (Linda b 9 Oct 1950, Louise b 2 June 1952 d 1953, Judith b 6 Jan 1955, Annabel b 6 June 1957); m 2, 29 March 1968, Amy Kathrine, da of Thomas Culley (d 1982), of Nova Friburgo, Brazil; 2 s (Mark b 13 March 1969, Sebastian b 2 Feb 1970), 1 da (Alexandra b 21 May 1971); *Career* served WWII Queens Regt 1943, cmmnd 2 KEO Gurkha Rifles, served Assam and Burma 1944–47; FO Singapore Burma and Germany 1947–50; called to the Bar Inner Temple 1959 (practised 1983–95); gen mangr: Synthetic Fibres Div Courtaulds Group 1961–65 (joined 1951), Wm Brandts Sons & Co Ltd 1965–66; gp md Alfred Dunhill Ltd 1967–69, md Australasian Assets Ltd 1969–72, chm Camel Investments Ltd 1975–92, dir Intrum Justitia International Ltd 1990–93; memb London Court of Int Arbitrators 1991–93; FCIArb 1984; *Books* Disaster (1987); *Recreations* fly fishing, sailing; *Clubs* Reform; *Style*— David Wade, Esq; ✉ Roman Way, Benenden, Kent TN17 4ES (☎ 01580 240873)

WADE, Dr John Philip Huddart; s of Dr Edward Geoffrey Wade, of Cheadle Hulme, Cheshire, and Mary Ward Pickering, *née* Huddart; *b* 19 April 1950; *Educ* Cheadle Hulme Sch, Univ of Cambridge (BA), Manchester Med Sch (MB BChir), Univ of Cambridge (MD); *m* 26 April 1976, Charlotte, da of Dr Elozor Leslie Feinmann (d 1985) and Sylvia Feinmann (d 1989); 1 da (Jessica Alice Feinmann), 1 s (Charles Louis Feinmann); *Career* registrar St Thomas's Hosp 1978, sr registrar Nat Hosp for Nervous Disease London and St Bartholomew's Hosp 1984–86, res fell Cerebrovascular Disease Univ of Western Ontario 1985–86, currently conslt neurologist Charing Cross Hosp and conslt neurologist Wexham Park Hosp Slough; present research interests incl: role of functional neuroimaging in neurology, early diagnosis of dementia, evaluation of individual patients with severe extracranial occlusive vascular disease; memb Assoc Br Neurologists 1986, fell Stroke Cncl American Heart Assoc 1988, FRCP 1992; *Publications* papers incl: Reactivity of the cerebral circulation in patients with occlusive carotid disease (with M M Brown, R W Ross Russell and C Bishop, 1986), CBF and vasoreactivity in patients with arteriovenous malformations (with J K Farrar and V C Hachinski, 1987); various invited chapters in books; abstract papers incl: Cerebral blood flow in subjects with high oxygen affinity haemoglobin at Euro Conf of Haemorheology London (with T C Pearson), Impact of contra lateral ICA stenosis on outcome of symptomatic ICA occlusion at Associates of Br Neurologists Glasgow (with V Hachinski and H J M Barnett, 1989); *Recreations* sailing; *Style*— Dr John Wade; ✉ 11 Gardnor Rd, Hampstead, London NW3 (☎ 0171 431 2900); Department of Neurosciences, Charing Cross Hospital, Fulham Palace Road, London W6 (☎ 0181 846 1303, fax 0181 846 1187)

WADE, Keith Martin; s of Alec Raymond Wade, of Leicester, and Maureen Briggs; *b* 5 Oct 1961; *Educ* Bosworth Coll Desford Leicester, LSE (BSc, MSc); *m* 20 Jan 1990; 1 s, 1 da; *Career* res offr Centre for Economic Forecasting London Business Sch 1984–88; Schroders: joined 1988, UK economist 1988–91, chief economist 1992–; placed third FT Poll of UK Economists 1992; memb Soc of Business Economists; *Books* Macroeconomics (co-author, 1995); *Recreations* cricket, soccer; *Style*— Keith Wade, Esq; ✉ Schroders plc, 120 Cheapside, London EC2V 6DS (☎ 0171 382 6000)

WADE, Prof Kenneth; s of Harry Kennington Wade (d 1983), of Sleaford, Lincs, and Anna Elizabeth, *née* Cartwright (d 1992); *b* 13 Oct 1932; *Educ* Carre's GS Sleaford Lincs, Univ of Nottingham (BSc, PhD, DSc); *m* 14 July 1962, Gertrud Rosmarie (Trudy), da of Willy Hetzel (d 1965), of Grenchen, Solothurn, Switzerland; 1 s (Alan b 1963), 2 da (Marianne b 1965, Julia b 1968); *Career* postdoctoral res fell: Univ of Cambridge 1957–59, Cornell Univ 1959–60; lectr in chemistry Derby Coll of Technol 1960–61; Univ of Durham: lectr in chemistry 1961–71, sr lectr 1971–77, reader 1977–83, prof 1983–, chm Dept of Chemistry 1986–89; pres Dalton Div RSC 1995–97; FRSC, FRS 1989; *Books* Organometallic Compounds: The Main Group Elements (with G E Coates, 1967), Principles of Organometallic Chemistry (with G E Coates, M L H Green and P Powell 1968), Electron Deficient Compounds (1971), Chemistry of Aluminium, Gallium, Indium and Thallium (with A J Banister 1976), Hypercarbon Chemistry (with G A Olah, G K S Prakash, R E Williams, and L D Field 1987), Electron Deficient Boron and Carbon Clusters (with G A Olah and R E Williams, 1990); *Recreations* walking; *Style*— Prof Kenneth Wade, FRS; ✉ Chemistry Department, University of Durham Science Laboratories, South Rd, Durham DH1 3LE (☎ 0191 374 3122, fax 0191 386 1127, e-mail kenneth.wade@durham.ac.uk)

WADE, Michael John; s of Peter Wade, and Lorna A M Harris; *b* 22 May 1954; *Educ* Royal Russell, N Staffs Coll; *Career* fndr and chm Holman Wade Ltd 1980–93, memb Lloyd's 1980–; dir Horace Clarkson plc 1986–93; memb: Cncl and Ctee Lloyd's 1987–92, Lloyd's Taskforce 1991; chm Lloyd's Community Prog 1988–94; fndr Corporate Lloyd's Membership Ltd 1993, chief exec CLM Insurance Fund plc; chm Opera Interludes Ltd 1990–; *Recreations* music, shooting, flying, architectural restoration; *Clubs* Turf; *Style*— Michael J Wade, Esq; ✉ Trafalgar Park, Near Salisbury, Wiltshire SP5 3QR (☎ 01722 710261, fax 01722 711307); CLM Insurance Fund plc, Fountain House, 130 Fenchurch Street, London EC3M 5EE (☎ 0171 283 7474, fax 0171 283 7478)

WADE, Neville Edward Henry; JP (Hertfordshire); *b* 5 Feb 1945; *Educ* Caludon Castle Sch Coventry, Coventry Tech Coll, Coventry Coll of Art, CAM (Dip in PR); *m*; 2 c; *Career* PR conslt; clerical offr Coventry Corporation 1961–64, PR offr Coventry Climax Engines Ltd 1965–1969, PR mangr Lansing Limited 1970–79, dir/ptnr Zaxhurst Limited Winchester 1979–85, dir Welbeck Golin/Harris Communications Ltd 1985–91, ind conslt 1991–; dir: Fluentplan Ltd 1980–, Ilex Court Management Ltd 1992–, Intersel Partnership Ltd 1994–, Strategic Partnership (London) 1994–; PRCA: past chm Educn & Trg Ctee, past bd memb; past appts incl: pres Inst of PR 1983, chief examiner CAM Dip in PR, fndr chm Basingstoke Publicity Club, jt fndr Alresford Pigs Assoc, memb New Alresford PC, pres Winchester Jr Chamber, dep pres Winchester C of C, Chm of Govrs Sun Hill Schs, chm Electric Vehicle Assoc of GB; winner first Inst of PR CAM Dip award, awarded Sir Stephen Tallent's Medal (for servs to IPR and practice of PR) 1994; moderator: CAM PR Dip, Watford Int PR Dip; chm IPR Disciplinary Ctee; FIPR, fell CAM Fndn; *Style*— Neville Wade, Esq, JP; ✉ 6 Ilex Court, Montague Rd, Berkhamsted, Herts HP4 3DY (☎ 01442 866656, fax 01442 870839, e-mail 100647.336@compuserve.com)

WADE, Prof Owen Lyndon; CBE (1983); s of James Owen David Wade, OBE (d 1962), of Cardiff, and Kate, *née* Jones (d 1974); *b* 17 May 1921; *Educ* Repton, Emmanuel Coll Cambridge, UCH (MA, MB BCh, MD, MRCP); *m* 6 March 1948, Margaret, da of Reginald John Burton (d 1972), of Ilfracombe and New Milton; 3 da (Robin Elizabeth b 1949, Josephine Margaret b 1951, Mary Sian b 1953); *Career* RMO UCH 1946, clinical asst Pneumokoniosis Res Unit MRC 1948–51, lectr Dept of Med Univ of Birmingham 1951–56, sr lectr and conslt physician Utd Birmingham Hosps 1956–57, Whitla prof of therapeutics Queen's Univ Belfast and conslt physician NI Hosps Authy 1957–71, dep dean Faculty of Med Queen's Univ Belfast 1968–71, prof of therapeutics and clinical pharmacology Univ of Birmingham and conslt physician Queen Elizabeth Hosp Birmingham 1971–85, vice princ and pro vice chllr Univ of Birmingham 1984–85 (dean Faculty of Med and Dentistry 1978–84); memb: NI Gen Health Servs Bd 1957–71, Standing Med Advsy Ctee Min of Health and Social Security NI 1968–71 (Chm Sub Ctees on Community Med and Psychogeriatric Care 1969), Jt Formulary Ctee for the Br Nat Formulary 1963–85 (chm 1978–85), Dunlop Ctee on Safety of Drugs Miny of Health London 1963–70 (chm Sub of Adverse Reactions to Drugs 1967–70), Medicines Cmmn DHSS London 1969–77; chm: Ctee of Review of Medicines 1977–83, Clinical Res Bd MRC 1970–74; conslt advsr WHO: med educn 1960, 1963 and 1965, drug monitoring 1964, intensive hosp drug monitoring 1968, drug monitoring 1968, drug consumption in Europe 1969, Drug Utilisation Res Gp 1968–86; vice pres Res Def Soc 1990–, tstee Arthur Thomson Charitable Tst 1974– (chm 1984–94); Hon MD Queen's Univ of Belfast 1989; memb: Physiological Soc, Br Pharmacological Soc, Assoc of Physicians of GB and Ireland, Med Res Soc; FRCP 1962, Hon FRCPI 1969; *Books* Adverse Reactions to Drugs (2 edn, 1976), Cardiac Output and Regional Blood Flow (with J M Bishop, 1962), The Romance of Remedies (1996); contrib: Jl of Physiology, Clinical Science, Jl of Clinical Investigation; *Recreations* sailing, woodturning, reading, grandchildren; *Clubs* Athenaeum; *Style*— Prof Owen Wade, CBE; ✉ The Medical School, University of Birmingham, Birmingham B15 2TJ (☎ 0121 414 4049)

WADE, Robert Edward; s of late Edward William Wade, and Rosina Alice, *née* Gill; *b* 29 Dec 1949; *m* 26 April 1975, Monica Jane, da of late Alex Rennie; 1 da (Joanne Lisa b 7 May 1980); *Career* dir: Bisgood Bishop 1984–86, County Bisgood 1986, Citicorp Scrimgeour Vickers 1986–88, Robert Fleming Securities 1988–90; chm: Bexley Developments Ltd, Media Sales and Publishing Ltd, The Essential Guides Ltd; dir: Homescene Ltd, Media Design Consultants Ltd, The New Concept Group Ltd; MSI (memb Stock Exchange 1975); *Recreations* golf; *Clubs* Royal Blackheath Golf; *Style*— Robert Wade; ✉ Glebe House, Chislehurst Rd, Bickley, Bromley, Kent BR1 2NJ (☎ 0181 467 8964, fax 0181 295 0498)

WADE, Air Chief Marshal Sir Ruthven Lowry; KCB (1974, CB 1970), DFC (1944); *b* 1920; *Educ* Cheltenham, RAF Cranwell; *Career* RAF 1939–78: Staff Offr Air HQ Malta, Cdr RAF Gaydon 1962–65, Air Exec to Dep for Nuclear Affrs SHAPE 1967–68, AOC 1 Gp Strike Command 1968–71, Dep Cdr RAF Germany 1971–72, vice chief Air Staff 1973–76, Air Marshal 1974, Air Chief Marshal 1976, Chief Personnel & Logistics MOD 1976–78; *Style*— Air Chief Marshal Sir Ruthven Wade, KCB, DFC; ✉ White Gables, Westlington, Dinton, Aylesbury, Bucks HP17 8UR (☎ 01296 748884)

WADE, (Sarah) Virginia; OBE (1986, MBE 1969); da of Canon Eustace Holland Wade (d 1988), and Joan Barbara, *née* Gowie (d 1989); *b* 10 July 1945; *Educ* Durban Girls' HS, Tunbridge Wells GS, Univ of Sussex (BSc); *Career* tennis player; winner: US Open Tennis Championships 1968, Aust Open 1972, Italian Open 1972, Wimbledon 1977, Seven Grand Slam titles (three singles, four doubles); played in Wightman Cup for GB twenty times, elected to the Int Tennis Hall of Fame 1989; commentator for BBC and American TV; memb Wimbledon Ctee 1982–92, vice pres Greater London Fund for the Blind; Hon LLD Univ of Sussex 1985; *Books* Courting Triumph (1978), Ladies of the Court (1986); *Clubs* All England Lawn Tennis, Queen's; *Style*— Miss Virginia Wade, OBE; ✉ International Management Group, Pier House, Strand on the Green, Chiswick, London W4 3NN (☎ 0181 994 1444, fax 0181 994 9606)

WADE, Sir (Henry) William Rawson; kt (1985), QC (1968); s of Col Henry Oswald Wade, DSO, TD (d 1941), and Eileen Lucy *née* Rawson-Ackroyd (d 1973); *b* 16 Jan 1918; *Educ* Shrewsbury, Gonville and Caius Coll Cambridge (BA, MA, LLD), Harvard; *m* 1, 1943, Marie (d 1980), da of G E Osland-Hill (d 1958), of Bucks; 2 s (Michael, Edward); m 2, 1982, Marjorie Grace Hope, wid of B C Browne, da of Surgn-Capt H Hope Gill RN (d 1956), of Devon; *Career* called to the Bar Lincoln's Inn, hon bencher 1964; prof of law: Univ of Oxford 1961–76, Univ of Cambridge 1978–82; master Gonville and Caius Coll Cambridge 1976–88; hon fell: St John's Coll Oxford 1976, Trinity Coll Cambridge 1991; FBA 1969 (vice pres 1981–83); *Books* numerous books and articles on administrative, constitutional and real property law; *Recreations* climbing, gardening, music; *Clubs* Alpine; *Style*— Sir William Wade, QC, FBA; ✉ Gonville and Caius College, Cambridge CB2 1TA (☎ 01223 332400, fax 01223 332456); 1A Ludlow Lane, Fulbourn, Cambridge CB1 5BL (☎ 01223 881745)

WADE-GERY, Sir Robert Lucian; KCMG (1982), KCVO (1983); o s of late Prof Henry Theodore Wade-Gery, MC, FBA, and Vivian, *née* Whitfield; *b* 22 April 1929; *Educ* Winchester, New Coll Oxford; *m* 16 June 1962, Sarah, da of Adam Denzil Marris, CMG (d 1983); 1 s (William Richard b 1967), 1 da (Laura Katharine (Mrs Jack Hanbury-Tenison b 1965); *Career* entered Foreign Serv 1951; served: London, Bonn, Tel Aviv, Saigon; under sec Central Policy Review Staff 1971–73; min: Madrid 1973–77, Moscow 1977–79; dep sec of the Cabinet 1979–82, high cmmr New Delhi 1982–87; vice chm Barclays de Zoete Wedd Ltd 1994– (exec dir 1987–93); fell All Souls' Oxford 1951–73 and 1987–89; chm Govrs London School of Oriental and African Studies 1990–, chm Anglo-Spanish Soc 1995– (dep chm 1993–95), hon treas Int Inst for Strategic Studies 1993–; *Recreations* walking, sailing, history, travel; *Clubs* Boodle's; *Style*— Sir Robert Wade-Gery, KCMG, KCVO; ✉ 7 Rothwell St, London NW1A 8YH (☎ 0171 722 4754); c/o BZW, Ebbgate House, 2 Swan Lane, London EC4R 3TS (☎ 0171 956 4849, fax 0171 956 3006); Church Cottage, Cold Aston, Cheltenham, Glos GL54 3BN (☎ 01451 821115)

WADE OF CHORLTON, Baron (Life Peer UK 1990), of Chester in the County of Cheshire; Sir (William) Oulton Wade; kt (1982), JP; s of Samuel Norman Wade, of Chester, and Joan Ferris, *née* Wild; *b* 24 Dec 1932; *Educ* Birkenhead Sch, Queen's Univ Belfast; *m* 1959, Gillian Margaret, da of Desmond Leete, of Buxton, Derbyshire; 1 s (Hon Christopher James Oulton b 1961), 1 da (Hon Alexandra Jane b 1964); *Career* farmer and cheesemaker; chm Marlow Wade mktg conslts; pres CHPA, chm NIMTECH; dir: Murray Vernon Ltd, Murray Vernon (Holdings) Ltd, John Wilman Ltd, Campus Venture Ltd; former Cheshire Cncllr, former chm City of Chester Cons Assoc 1973–76, jt hon treas Cons Pty 1982–90; pres Energy From Waste Assoc; chm Rural Economy Gp, chm Chester Heritage Tst; chm English Cheese Export Cncl 1982–84; Liveryman Worshipful Co of Farmers, Freeman City of London; *Clubs* Carlton, Farmers', Chester City, St James's (Manchester); *Style*— The Rt Hon Lord Wade of Chorlton; ✉ Chorlton Lodge, Chorlton by Backford, Chester CH2 4DB

WADHAMS, Dr Peter; s of Frank Cecil Wadhams (d 1971), and Winifred Grace, *née* Smith; *b* 14 May 1948; *Educ* Palmer's Sch Grays Essex, Churchill Coll Cambridge (Coll scholar, BA, MA), Scott Polar Res Inst Univ of Cambridge (PhD), Univ of Cambridge (ScD 1994); *m* 11 Oct 1980, Maria Pia, da of Renato Casarini, of Milan; *Career* res scientist Bedford Inst of Oceanography Dartmouth Canada (participant in Hudson-70, first expedition to circumnavigate Americas) 1969–70, postdoctoral fell Inst of Ocean Sciences Victoria BC Canada 1974–75; Scott Polar Research Inst Univ of Cambridge: res assoc 1976–81, asst dir of res 1981–88, dir 1988–92, reader in Polar studies 1992–; sr res fell Churchill Coll Cambridge 1983–93; visiting prof of arctic marine science US Naval Postgrad Sch Monterey Calif 1980–81, Green scholar Scripps Inst of Oceanography La Jolla Calif 1987–88, Walker-Ames prof Univ of Washington Seattle 1987–88, visiting prof Nat Inst of Polar Research Tokyo Japan 1995; UK del Arctic Ocean Sciences Bd, memb Cmmn for Sea Ice IAPSO, memb SCAR Gp of Specialists on Climate Change, memb Working Gp on Global Change Int Artic Sci Ctee; awarded: W S Bruce Prize (Royal Soc of Edinburgh) 1977, Polar Medal 1987, Italgas Prize for Environmental Sciences (Italy) 1990; memb: Int Glaciological Soc 1970, American Geophysical Union 1976, Challenger Soc 1983, Remote Sensing Soc 1984; fell Arctic Inst of N America 1983, FRGS 1989; *Books* Ice Technology for Polar Operations (co-ed, 1990), Advances in Ice Technology (co-ed, 1992), Marine, Offshore and Ice Technology (co-ed, 1994), The Arctic and Environmental Change (co-ed, 1996); *Recreations* painting, sailing; *Style*— Dr Peter Wadhams; ✉ Scott Polar Research Institute, University of Cambridge, Lensfield Rd, Cambridge CB2 1ER (☎ 01223 336542, fax 01223 336549, telex 81240 CAMSPLG, e-mail pw11@cus.cam.ac.uk)

WADLEY, Veronica; da of Neville John Wadley, and Anne Hawise Colleton, *née* Bowring; *b* 28 Feb 1952; *Educ* Francis Holland Sch London, Benenden; *m* 1 June 1985, Tom Bower, s of George Bower; 1 s (Alexander b 4 Oct 1990), 1 da (Sophie b 18 April 1986); *Career* journalist; Conde Nast Publications 1971–74, Sunday Telegraph Magazine 1978–81, Mail on Sunday 1982–86; Daily Telegraph: features ed 1986–89, asst ed 1989–94, dep ed 1994–95; assoc ed Daily Mail 1995–; *Style*— Miss Veronica Wadley; ✉ Daily Mail, Northcliffe House, 2 Derry Street, Kensington, London W8 5TT (☎ 0171 938 6000, fax 0171 937 4463)

WADSWORTH, David Grant; s of Fred Wadsworth (d 1960), and Lona, *née* Booth (d 1970); *b* 30 Dec 1944; *Educ* Hipperholme GS Yorks, Oriel Coll Oxford (MA), Univ of Newcastle-upon-Tyne (MPhil); *Career* teacher Gloucestershire and Blackpool 1966–73, admin posts Educn Dept Leeds City Cncl 1973–85, dep dir of educn Northumberland 1985–89, chief educn offr Bedfordshire 1989–96, chief exec Serice Children's Educn 1997–; memb: Yorkshire CCC and RFU, Cambridge Univ RUFC, Harlequins RFC, Luddites RFC; memb Soc of Educn Offrs; Hon DEd De Montfort Univ 1996; Chev l'Ordre des Palmes Académiques 1992, Cavaliere dell'Ordine Al Merito della Repubblica Italiana 1994; FRSA 1989; *Recreations* rugby and cricket (passively), epicurean delights; *Clubs* Royal Over-Seas League; *Style*— David G Wadsworth, Esq; ✉ HQ SCE, BFPO 140

WADSWORTH, James Patrick; QC (1981); s of Francis Thomas Bernard Wadsworth (d 1940), of Newcastle, and Geraldine Rosa, *née* Brannan (d 1953); *b* 7 Sept 1940; *Educ* Stonyhurst, Univ Coll Oxford (MA); *m* 1963, Judith, da of Morrison Scott, of Newport on Tay; 1 s (Francis b 1967), 1 da (Katharine (Mrs Ousterman) b 1964); *Career* called to the Bar Inner Temple 1963, bencher 1988, recorder of the Crown Ct 1980–; *Style*— James Wadsworth, Esq, QC; ✉ 4 Paper Buildings, Temple, London EC4Y 7EX (☎ 0171 353 3366, fax 0171 353 5778)

WADSWORTH, Roger Leonard; s of Leonard Wadsworth (d 1985), and Irene Nellie, *née* Hughes; *b* 2 May 1950; *Educ* Hurstpierpoint, Kingston Poly (BA); *m* 1988, Sandra Anne, da of RA Carney, of Barry County, Missouri; *Career* chm and md: Wadsworth Holdings Ltd, Leonard Wadsworth Group Ltd; chm: Wadsworth Electronics Ltd, Wadsworth Belgium BV; fndr Knoydart Deer Mgmnt Gp, sec Wealden Deer Mgmnt Gp; *Recreations* wildlife management, African game and habitat conservation, stalking, big game hunting, shooting; *Clubs* RAC, Outrigger (Honolulu), NRA, British Sporting Rifle; *Style*— Roger Wadsworth, Esq; ✉ Wadsworth Holdings Ltd, Central Avenue, West Molesey, Surrey KT8 0QB; Colony Surf, Honolulu, Hawaii, USA

WADSWORTH, Thomas Gordon; s of Samuel Bertram Wadsworth (d 1955), and Elizabeth Jane, *née* Brown (d 1987); *b* 13 Jan 1930; *Educ* Liverpool Coll, Univs of Liverpool and Wales (MChOrth, LLM (Legal Aspects of Med Practice)); *Career* formerly sr lectr in hand surgery and dir Arthritis Hand Unit Med Coll of St Bartholomew's Hosp Univ of London, currently consulting orthopaedic and hand surgn The Royal Hosps Tst (Royal Hosp of St Bartholomew, Royal London Hosp and London Chest Hosp), emeritus conslt orthopaedic and hand surgn Homerton Hosp; former examiner in pathology and section chm Primary FRCS England, examiner in surgery with special interest in pathology FRCSEd, examiner United Examining Bd; corresponding memb: American Acad of Orthopaedic Surgns, American Soc for Surgery of the Hand; memb American Shoulder and Elbow Surgns; former memb Cncl: Professions Supplementary to Med, Br Soc for Surgery of the Hand; fndr memb and former memb Ctee Br Elbow and Shoulder Soc, memb Euro Elbow and Shoulder Soc; Freeman City of London, Liveryman Worshipful Soc of Apothecaries; FBOA, FRCS, FRCSE, FACS, FICS, FAE 1996; *Recreations* walking in country, classical music, travel; *Clubs* Reform, City Livery, Savile; *Style*— Thomas Wadsworth, Esq; ✉ 32 Shepherd St, Mayfair, London W1Y 7LJ (☎ 0171 723 5785)

WADWELL, David Martin; s of George Wadwell, of Callow Hill, Virginia Water, Surrey, and Marie, *née* Pickering; *b* 12 March 1946; *Educ* Ipswich Sch, Univ of Southampton (BSc), LSE (MSc); *m* 5 June 1971 (m dis 1978), Valerie, da of Peter Arthur Wilks; *Career* CA; Ernst & Whinney 1968–72, ptnr de Zoete & Bevan Stockbrokers 1972–86, dir Barclays de Zoete Wedd 1986–; FCA, MSI; *Recreations* sailing, travel; *Style*— David Wadwell, Esq; ✉ 7 Hippodrome Mews, Clarendon Cross, Kensington, London W11 4NN (☎ 0171 229 0493); Barclays de Zoete Wedd Securities Ltd, Ebbgate House, 2 Swan Lane London EC4R 3TS (☎ 0171 623 2323, fax 0171 626 1879, telex 888 221)

WADWELL, (George) Richard; s of George Wadwell, of Virginia Water, Surrey, and Marie, *née* Pickering; *b* 25 Oct 1942; *Educ* Ipswich Sch Suffolk; *m* 28 Nov 1970, Gladys Yolanda, da of Señor Bricenio Amable Ramirez (d 1972), of Guayaquil, Ecuador; 2 da (Ingrid b 1974, Deborah b 1976); *Career* articled clerk rising to audit sr Touche Ross and Co London and Cape Town 1960–68, gp accountant Surinvest London 1968–69, asst to Fin Dir NORAM Ltd London and Nassau 1969–70, accountant central mktg BOAC Heathrow 1974–76 (various head office fin posts 1970–74), mangr asset and gp accounting British Airways Bd Heathrow 1981–86 (fin analyst 1976–81), mangr fin reporting British Airways plc 1996– (gp fin accountant 1986–); FCA 1977; *Recreations* radio ham, marathon running, travel; *Style*— Richard Wadwell, Esq; ✉ 7 Barkhart Drive, Wokingham, Berks RG40 1TW (☎ 0118 979 1398); Manager Financial Reporting, British Airways plc, PO Box 10, Hounslow, Middlesex TW6 2JA (☎ 0181 562 0579, fax 0181 562 8764)

WAGNER, Lady; Dame Gillian Mary Millicent; *née* Graham; DBE (1994, OBE 1977); eldest da of Maj Henry Archibald Roger Graham (d 1970), of Micheldever, Hants, and Hon Margaret Beatrice Lopes (d 1984), 3 da of 1 Baron Roborough; *b* 25 Oct 1927; *Educ* Cheltenham Ladies' Coll, Geneva Univ (Licencès Sciences Morales), LSE (Dip Social Admin), PhD London (1977); *m* 26 Feb 1953, Sir Anthony Richard Wagner, KCB, KCVO (d 1995); 2 s (Roger Henry Melchior Wagner, *qv* b 28 Feb 1957, Mark Anthony b 18 Dec 1958), 1 da (Lucy Elizabeth Millicent (Mrs Richard McCarraher) b 22 Oct 1954); *Career* chm: Review into Residential Care 1985–88, Barnardos 1978–84 (memb Cncl 1984–), Thomas Coram Fndn 1990–95; pres: SKILL Nat Bureau for Students with Disabilities 1978–91, IAPS 1984–90, Volunteer Centre 1993– (chm 1984–89), Abbeyfield 1996–; chm: Felixstowe Coll 1978–87, Carnegie UK Tst 1995–, Leche Tst; govr: Nat Inst for Social Work 1988–96, LSE 1991–96; tstee Princess Royal Tst for Carers 1992–; Freeman City of London; Hon Dr of Social Sciences Univ of Bristol 1989, Hon LLD Univ of Liverpool 1990; FRSA 1996; *Books* Barnardo (1979), Children of the Empire (1982), The Chocolate Conscience (1987); *Recreations* sailing, gardening, travelling; *Clubs* Aldeburgh Yacht; *Style*— Dame Gillian Wagner, DBE; ✉ 10 Physic Place, Royal Hospital Road, London SW3 4HQ (☎ 0171 352 0934); Wyndham Cottage, Crespigny Rd, Aldeburgh, Suffolk (☎ 01728 45 2596)

WAGNER, Michael (Mike); *b* 26 April 1956; *Educ* John Abbott Coll St Anne de Bellevue Quebec Canada, Concordia Univ Montreal Quebec (BComm, MBA, fin medal, Fin Execs Inst silver medal, graduate teaching fellowship), Canadian Securities Course; *m*; 1 da; *Career* mktg mangr Bell Canada 1979–85, strategic mktg conslt Bell Canada International NZ 1986; Bell Canada: section mangr Serv Devpt 1987–88, dir Business Planning 1989–90, dir Int Mktg 1991–92; md Corp Devpt then Long Distance Mktg Strategy Stentor Resource Center Inc 1993–95, vice pres Alliances Bell Canada Jun-Nov 1995; dir of mktg and sales Personal Communications Div British Telecommunications plc April 1996– (head of network mktg Nov 1995–April 1996); *Style*— Mike Wagner, Esq; ✉ BT Personal Communications, BT Westside, PPC1001, London Road, Hemel Hempstead, Herts HP3 9YF (☎ 01442 295131/2, fax 01442 241481)

WAGNER, Dr Nicholas Alan Giles; s of Thomas Donald Wagner, of Croydon, Surrey (d 1980), and Valerie Jacqueline Cameron Peers, *née* Kemp, of Marlow, Bucks; *b* 17 Jan 1945; *Educ* Whitgift Sch, The Med Coll of St Bartholomew's Hosp Univ of London (MB BS, DPM, MRCPsych); *m* 2, Linda Iris, da of James Halstead, of Brentford, Middx; 1 s (Alexander Jonathan Halstead); *Career* conslt: psychiatrist W Middx Univ Hosp 1978–88, mental health for the elderly Herefordshire Community Health NHS Tst 1988–; hon sr lectr Charing Cross and Westminster Med Sch 1984–88; fndn chm Herefordshire Alzheimer's Disease Soc; *Style*— Dr Nicholas Wagner; ✉ Department of Mental Health for the Elderly, Stonebow Unit, The County Hospital, Hereford HR1 2ER (☎ 01432 355444, fax 01432 364058)

WAGNER, Roger Henry Melchior; s of Sir Anthony Richard Wagner, KCB, KCVO (d 1995), and Dame Gillian Wagner, DBE, *qv*; *b* 28 Feb 1957; *Educ* Eton, Lincoln Coll Oxford (open scholar, BA), Royal Acad Schs; *Career* artist; *Exhibitions* incl: solo exhbns Anthony Mould Ltd 1985, 1988 and 1995, solo exhbn 42nd Aldeburgh Festival 1989, touring gp exhbn New Icons (Mead Gallery Univ of Warwick, The Royal Albert Museum Exeter and The Usher Gallery Lincoln) 1989–90, gp exhbn Images of Christ (Albermarle Gallery) 1991, gp exhbn Images of Christ (Northampton Museum and Art Gallery and St Paul's Cathedral) 1993, solo retrospective Ashmolean Museum Oxford 1994, solo exhbn Out of the Whirlwind: illustrations to the Book of Job (Bartlemas Chapel Oxford) 1995; *Publications* Fire Sonnets (1984), In a Strange Land (1988), The Book of Praises (1994), A Silent Voice (1996); *Clubs* Reynolds; *Style*— Roger Wagner, Esq; ✉ 5 Northmoor Road, Oxford OX2 6UW (☎ 01865 558007); c/o Anthony Mould Ltd, 173 New Bond Street, London W1Y 9PB (☎ 0171 491 4627, fax 0171 355 3865)

WAGSTAFF, Ven Christopher John Harold; s of Harold Maurice Wagstaff (d 1982), of London, and Kathleen Mary, *née* Bean (d 1979); *b* 25 June 1936; *Educ* Bishop's Stortford Coll, Essex Inst of Agric, St David's Coll Lampeter (BA); *m* 1964, Margaret Louise, da of John Park Alan Macdonald, of Scotland; 2 s (Alasdair b 1966, Robert b 1968), 1 da (Marianne b 1972); *Career* curate All Saints' Queensbury London 1963–68; vicar: St Michael Wembley 1968–72, Coleford with Staunton Gloucester 1972–82; rural dean South Forest 1975–82; archdeacon of Gloucester 1982–; Freeman City of London, memb Ct of Assts Worshipful Co of Armourers and Brasiers; *Recreations* gardening, travel; *Style*— The Ven the Archdeacon of Gloucester; ✉ Glebe House, Church Road, Maisemore, Gloucester GL2 8EY (☎ 01452 528500, fax 01452 381528)

WAIN, Prof (Ralph) Louis; CBE (1968); s of George Wain (d 1941), of Hyde, Cheshire, and Eliza, *née* Hardy (d 1948); *b* 29 May 1911; *Educ* Hyde Co GS Cheshire, Univ of Sheffield (BSc, MSc, PhD), Univ of London (DSc); *m* Joan, da of Thomas Bowker (d 1941), of Denton, Lancs; 1 s (Michael Louis b 1948), 1 da (Rosemary Joan b 1944); *Career* dir Agric Res Cncl Res Unit Wye Coll Univ of London 1953–78 (prof of chemistry 1950–78), hon prof of chemistry Univ of Kent 1978–; Hon DAgSci Ghent 1963, Hon DSc: Kent 1976, Lausanne 1977, Sheffield 1977; FRS 1960; *Recreations* painting, travel; *Style*— Prof Louis Wain, CBE, FRS; ✉ Crown Point, Scotton St, Wye, Kent TN25 5BZ (☎ 01233 812157); University of Kent, Canterbury, Kent (☎ 01227 764000, telex 965 449)

WAINE, David Michael; s of Capt Leslie Arthur Waine (d 1984), and Linda, *née* Pridmore; *b* 12 June 1944; *Educ* Reading Collegiate Sch; *m* 23 April 1966, Elizabeth Ann, da of John Halls (d 1967); 1 da (Nicola Frances b 1969); *Career* sports ed Newbury Weekly News 1960–64; BBC TV and radio reporter: Radio 4 Today prog, World at One, World Serv, TV news and current affrs, South Today, Points West 1964–67; BBC mgmnt: prog organiser Radio Brighton 1967–70, mangr Radio Bristol 1970–78, regnl TV mangr South West (Plymouth) 1978–83, head Network Prodn Centre Pebble Mill 1983–86, head of bdcasting Midlands 1986–92, head of bdcasting Midlands and East 1992–94; dir Production Devpt Non-Metropolitan Radio 1994–, ptnr David Waine Associates 1994–; pres Birmingham Press Club 1988–94; chm Birmingham Repertory Theatre Co 1996– (dir 1993–96), chm Birmingham Media Devpt Agency/Screen Cmmn; FRTS; *Recreations* sport, arts, gardening; *Style*— David Waine, Esq; ✉ NMR, Coach House, North Road, Nottingham

WAINE, Rt Rev John; KCVO (1996); s of late William Waine; *b* 20 June 1930; *Educ* Prescot GS, Univ of Manchester (BA), Ridley Hall Cambridge; *m* 1957, Patricia Zena, da of late Bertram Stevenson Haikney; 3 s; *Career* Pilot Offr RAF; ordained: deacon 1955, priest 1956; vicar: Ditton 1960–64, Holy Trinity Southport 1964–69; rector Kirkby 1969–75, bishop suffragan of Stafford 1975–78, bishop of St Edmundsbury and Ipswich 1978–86, entered House of Lords 1985, bishop of Chelmsford 1986–96, ret; chm: Churches Main Ctee 1991–96, Cncl Univ of Essex 1995; Clerk of the Closet to HM The Queen 1989–96; Hon Chaplain Worshipful Co of Glass Sellers (memb Ct of Assts); ChStJ (sub-prelate 1991); *Clubs* RAF; *Style*— The Rt Rev John Waine, KCVO; ✉ Broadmere, Ipswich Road, Grundisburgh, Woodbridge, Suffolk IP13 6TJ (☎ 01473 738296)

WAINE, Peter Edward; s of Dr Theodore Edward Waine, of Bilton, Rugby, Warwickshire, and Mary Florence, *née* Goodson; *b* 27 June 1949; *Educ* Bilton Grange, Worksop Coll, Univ of Bradford (BSc); *m* 21 June 1973, Stefanie Dale (niece of C P Snow, novelist), da of Philip Albert Snow, OBE, JP, *qv*, of Angmering, Sussex; 1 da (Philippa Wigmore b 21 May 1981); *Career* personnel mangr: GEC 1970–74, Cape Industries 1974–79, Coopers & Lybrand 1979–83; dir: CBI 1983–88, Blue Arrow 1988–90, W R Royle & Sons (non-exec) 1988–, SSK Ltd 1994–; co-fndr and chief exec Hanson Green 1990–; non-exec chm: Corecare Ltd 1990–92, Arkley House Finance Ltd 1990–92, The Sales Training Co 1994–; formerly: chm Welwyn Garden City Soc, memb Cncl Euro Business Sch; memb Current Affairs Ctee ESU; Parly candidate (Cons) Nottingham North 1979, nat vice chm The Bow Group 1972 (chm Birmingham Gp 1971); cncllr Rugby DC 1973–77; non-exec dir: East Herts Dist Health Authy 1990–92, East Herts Tst 1994–; visiting fell Bradford Business Sch 1994–; memb Int Cricket Cncl 1994–; chm The Tree Cncl; Freeman: City of London 1978, Worshipful Co of Carmen; FIMgt (former memb Cncl); *Publications* Spring Cleaning Britain (1974), Withering Heights (1976), The Independent Board Director (with Dr David Clutterbuck, *qv*, 1993); weekly columnist under pseudonym for London newspaper (1984–87); *Recreations* gardening, walking, tennis; *Clubs* MCC; *Style*— Peter Waine, Esq; ✉ West House, Digswell Place, Welwyn,

Herts (☎ 01707 330714); Hanson Green, 43 North Audley St, London W1 (☎ 0171 493 0837, fax 0171 355 1436)

WAINSCOAT, Dr James Stephen; s of Arnold John Wainscoat, and Mary Hilda, *née* Bateman (d 1989); *b* 7 May 1949; *Educ* Holme Valley GS, Univ of Liverpool (MB ChB), Univ of Birmingham (MSc); *m* 14 Aug 1971, Beverly Susan, da of Walter Hannah (d 1987); 1 s (Luke), 2 da (Emma, Nancy); *Career* conslt haematologist Oxford Radcliffe Hosp 1985–, sr lectr Univ of Oxford 1986–, hon dir Molecular Haematology Unit Leukaemia Res Fund Univ of Oxford 1988–; FRCP 1991 (MRCP 1976), FRCPath 1992 (MRCPath 1980); *Recreations* music, sport; *Style*— Dr James Wainscoat; ✉ Department of Haematology, Oxford Radcliffe Hosp, Headington, Oxford (☎ 01865 220330)

WAINWRIGHT, Dr (Anthony) Christopher; yr s of Robert Everard Wainwright, CMG (d 1990), of Shaftesbury, Dorset, and Bridget Doris, *née* Alan-Williams; *b* 25 Oct 1943; *Educ* Marlborough, St Thomas's Hosp Univ of London (MB BS); *m* 6 Sept 1968, Ursula, da of Ernest Herbert Jeans (d 1977), 1 s (James b 1972), 1 da (Sophie b 1975); *Career* sr registrar Univ Hosp Wales 1971–72, lectr anaesthesia Univ of Bristol 1972–75, conslt anaesthetist Univ of Southampton Hosps 1975–, hon clinical teacher Univ of Southampton 1975–; memb: New Forest Advsy Ctee of Nat Tst, Assoc of Anaesthetists, BMA; co fndr Wig and Scalpel Soc, former chm Copythorne Parish Cncl; FRCA 1971; *Books* chapters in Anaesthesia Review 4 and Co2 Lasers in Otolaryngology; author of papers on ophthalmic anaesthesia; *Recreations* horses, music, medieval architecture; *Style*— Dr Christopher Wainwright; ✉ Ashton Cottage, Kewlake Lane, Cadnam, Southampton SO40 2NS (☎ and fax 01703 812642); Shackleton Department of Anaesthetics, The General Hospital, Tremona Rd, Southampton SO16 6YD (☎ 01703 796135)

WAINWRIGHT, Geoffrey John; MBE; s of Frederick Wainwright, and Dorothy, *née* Worton; *b* 19 Sept 1937; *Educ* Pembroke Docks Sch, Univ of Wales, Univ of London; *m* 23 Dec 1977, Judith; 1 s (Nicholas b 1966), 2 da (Rhiannon b 1961, Sarah b 1963); *Career* prof of environmental archaeology Univ of Baroda India 1961–63, princ inspector of ancient monuments DOE 1980–89 (inspector 1963–80), chief archaeologist English Heritage 1989–; visiting prof: Univ of Southampton 1991, Inst of Archaeology UCL 1995–; fell Univ of Wales Coll of Cardiff 1985, hon fell Univ of Wales Lampeter 1996; memb Royal Cmmn on Ancient Monuments (Wales), pres Prehistoric Soc 1981–85, dir Soc of Antiquaries 1984–90; MIFA, FSA, FRSA; *Books* Coygan Camp (1967), Stone Age in India (1967), Durrington Walls (1971), Mount Pleasant (1979), Gussage All Saints (1979), The Henge Monuments (1989), Balksbury Camp Hampshire (1995); *Recreations* rugby, racing, food and drink, walking; *Style*— Geoffrey Wainwright, Esq, MBE, FSA; ✉ English Heritage, Fortress House, 23 Savile Row, London W1X 1AB (☎ 0171 973 3013)

WAINWRIGHT, Robert Ian (Rob); s of James Frederick Wainwright, of Glenalmond, and Jean, *née* Palmer-Lewis; *b* 22 March 1965; *Educ* Lathallan Sch, Glenalmond Coll Perth, Magdalene Coll Cambridge (BA, MBBChir); *m* 29 Aug 1992, Romayne Christina Garrioch, da of John Craig, of Bridge of Weir, Renfrewshire; *Career* rugby union flanker; 3 blues for Cambridge 1986–88, Edinburgh Academicals 1990–94 (winners Alloa Cup), West Hartlepool 1994, currently with Watsonians; rep: Scotland B (3 caps) 1988, 1990 and 1992 (capt), Scotland A (1 cap), Scotland (24 caps) 1992– (capt 1995–, following World Cup); memb World Cup squad 1995; Barbarians: 2 Hong Kong 7s 1989 and 1992, v NZ 1993, v French Barbarians 1994 (capt), v South Africa 1994; doctor with NHS 1990–91, Army doctor 1991– (current rank of Major); *Recreations* fishing, natural history, Scotland, hill walking, falconry; *Style*— Rob Wainwright, Esq

WAINWRIGHT, Sam; CBE (1982); *b* 2 Oct 1924; *Educ* LSE; *m* Ruth Strom; 3 s, 1 da; *Career* dep City ed Glasgow Herald 1952, md Rea Bros (merchant bankers) until 1977, md Nat Girobank 1977–85, dep chm Bd PO 1981–85, dir BICC plc 1985–90, chm Manders (Holdings) plc 1986–87, dir Amdahl (UK) Ltd 1988–93, chm Jigsaw Day Nurseries plc 1991–95; memb MMC 1985–91; *Style*— Sam Wainwright, Esq, CBE; ✉ Flat 5, 29 Warrington Crescent, London W9 1EJ (☎ 0171 286 8050)

WAITE, David Nicholas; s of George Frederick Waite (d 1989), of Leeds, and Constance, *née* Bouskill; *b* 28 March 1943; *Educ* Leeds GS, Magdalen Coll Oxford (exhibitioner, BA); *m* 1, 1967 (m dis 1979), Valerie May Fortune; 1 s (John b 1968); m 2, 1979, Frances Ann, da of Dominic Sarro; 1 s (Nicholas Sarro-Waite b 1981), 1 da (Mary Sarro-Waite b 1982); *Career* sales asst (later asst mangr Ore Purchases) Noranda Sales Corporation London and Toronto 1964–72, dir of trading (later pres NY brokerage subsid) Rudolf Wolff & Co Ltd London and NY 1972–78, vice pres i/c Metals Energy and Trade Finance Units Drexel Burnham Lambert Inc NY 1978–90, md i/c Commercial Futures and Foreign Exchange Div (and dir UK subsid) Paine Webber Inc NY and London 1990–93, dir of mktg Rudolf Wolff & Co Ltd London and NY 1993–; *Books* Commodities and the Third World (contrib 1974), Rudolf Wolff's Guide to the London Metal Exchange (contrib 1976); *Recreations* family, travel, tennis, squash, reading, gardening, movies; *Clubs* Copper (New York); *Style*— Mr David Waite; ✉ Rudolf Wolff & Co Ltd, Plantation House, 31–35 Fenchurch Street, London EC3M 3DX (☎ 0171 626 8765, fax 0171 626 3939)

WAITE, (Winston Anthony) John; s of John Clifford Waite (d 1969), of Gawsworth, Cheshire, and Margaret Ada, *née* Van Schuyk-Smith; *b* 26 Feb 1951; *Educ* Wilmslow GS, Univ of Manchester (BA); *m* 13 July 1984, Cate Anne Valerie, da of Stuart-Campbell, of Islington, London; *Career* BBC: graduate trainee 1973–76, radio presenter 1976–; progs incl: Face the Facts (Radio 4), You and Yours (Radio 4); *Recreations* music, reading, wine; *Style*— John Waite, Esq; ✉ BBC, Broadcasting House, London W1A 1AA (☎ 0171 580 4468)

WAITE, Rt Hon Lord Justice; Rt Hon Sir John Douglas Waite; kt (1982), PC (1993); s of Archibald Waite; *b* 3 July 1932; *Educ* Sherborne, CCC Cambridge; *m* 1966, Julia Mary, da of Joseph Tangye; 3 s and 2 step s; *Career* 2 Lt RA 1951–52; called to the Bar Gray's Inn 1956, bencher 1981; QC 1975, judge of the High Ct of Justice (Family Div) 1982–92, Lord Justice of Appeal 1993–; pres Employment Appeal Tribunal 1983–85, presiding judge North Eastern Circuit 1990–92; *Style*— The Rt Hon Lord Justice Waite; ✉ Royal Courts of Justice, Strand, London WC2A 2LL (☎ 0171 936 6255)

WAITE, Jonathan Gilbert Stokes; s of Capt Henry David Stokes Waite, of Cranleigh, Surrey, and Joan Winifred, *née* Paull; *b* 15 Feb 1956; *Educ* Sherborne, Trinity Coll Cambridge (MA); *Career* called to the Bar Inner Temple 1978, practised in common law SE Circuit 1979–; hon sec Bar Golfing Soc 1987–93; *Recreations* golf, bridge, skiing; *Clubs* Woking Golf, Aldeburgh Golf; *Style*— Jonathan Waite, Esq; ✉ 76 Forthbridge Rd, Battersea, London SW11 5NY (☎ 0171 228 4488); One Paper Buildings, Temple, London EC4Y 7EP (☎ 0171 583 7355, fax 0171 353 2144)

WAITES, Prof William Michael; s of Lt-Col William Harland Waites (d 1986), and Kathleen, *née* Inglett (d 1985); *b* 18 July 1939; *Educ* Harwich GS, Univ of Durham (BSc), Univ of Sheffield (PhD); *m* 13 Aug 1966 (m dis 1991), Janet Ashworth; 2 s (Michael b 24 Feb 1968, Richard b 15 Oct 1969); *Career* postdoctorates: Nat Inst For Med Res London 1965–66, Univ of Oxford 1966–69; AFRC Inst of Food Res: PSO 1969–85, dep head of microbiology 1981–85; Univ of Nottingham: prof of food microbiology 1985–, vice dean of faculty and head of dept 1987–90; convenor Microbiology Sub-Gp on Food Safety Applied Nutrition Res Consultative Ctee 1988–89, chm Food Safety Advsy Centre 1989–; vice-pres Soc for Applied Bacteriology 1992–93, pres Soc for Applied Bacteriology 1993–94; memb Technology Foresight Food and Drink Panel 1994–95; FIFST 1985; *Recreations* walking, gardening; *Style*— Prof William Waites; ✉ Dept of Applied Biochemistry and Food Science, Faculty of Agricultural and Food Sciences, Nottingham University, Sutton Bonington Campus, Loughborough, Leics LE12 5RD (☎ 0115 951 6160, fax 0115 951 6162)

WAKE, Sir Hereward; 14 Bt (E 1621), of Clevedon, Somerset, MC (1942), DL (Northants 1955); s of Maj-Gen Sir Hereward Wake, 13 Bt, CB, CMG, DSO, JP, DL (d 1963, himself tenth in descent from the 1 Bt; the latter was in turn fifteenth in descent from Hugh Wac or Wake, feudal Baron by tenure of Bourne and Deeping *temp* King Stephen; this family's descent from Hereward the Wake, albeit in the female line, seems probable although not proven); *b* 7 Oct 1916; *Educ* Eton, RMC; *m* 1952, Julia Rosemary, JP, da of Capt Geoffrey W M Lees, of Falcutt House, nr Brackley, Northants; 1 s, 3 da; *Heir* s, Hereward Charles, b 22 Nov 1952; *Career* served 1937–46 with 1, 2, 7 and 9 Bns 60 Rifles (Burma, Egypt, N Africa, NW Europe and Greece), Maj, ret 1947; High Sheriff Northants 1955, Vice Lord-Lt Northamptonshire 1984–91; Liveryman Worshipful Co of Merchant Taylors; *Style*— Sir Hereward Wake, Bt, MC, DL; ✉ Courteenhall, Northampton (☎ 01604 862204)

WAKE-WALKER, David Christopher; s of Capt Christopher Baldwin Hughes Wake-Walker, RN, and Lady Anne, da of 7 Earl Spencer; 1 cous to Diana, Princess of Wales; *b* 11 March 1947; *Educ* Winchester, Univ of St Andrews; *m* 1979, Jennifer Rosemary, only da of late Capt Patrick Vaulkhard; 2 s (Frederic b 1981, Nicholas b 1985); *Career* dir Kleinwort Benson Limited 1981 (joined 1969), md Kleinwort Benson (Hong Kong) Limited 1983–86, dir Kleinwort Benson Group plc 1990–95; *Clubs* Wanderers, Aldeburgh Yacht, Hong Kong, Shek O Country, Hurlingham; *Style*— David Wake-Walker Esq; ✉ 82 Royal Hill, London SE10 8RT (☎ 0181 691 4666)

WAKEFIELD, Derek John; CB (1982); s of Archibald John Thomas Wakefield (d 1971), and Evelyn Bessie, *née* Goddard (d 1971); *b* 21 Jan 1922; *Educ* The Cwlth Sch; *m* 1951, Audrey Ellen, da of Johnathan Smith (d 1961); 1 da (Isobel); *Career* Lt Royal Pioneer Corps 1942–47, served in N Africa, Italy and ME; Air Miny 1939–42 and 1947–52, GCHQ 1952–82 (under sec 1978–82); govr Barnwood House Tst Gloucester 1973–89, memb Airship Assoc; *Recreations* airships; *Clubs* Naval and Military; *Style*— Derek Wakefield, Esq, CB; ✉ Dunhurst, Bay Lane, Gillingham, Dorset SP8 4ER (☎ 01747 822932)

WAKEFIELD, Gerald Hugo Cropper (Hady); yr s of Sir Edward Birkbeck Wakefield, 1 Bt, CIE (d 1969), and (Constance) Lalage, *née* Thompson; *b* 15 Sept 1938; *Educ* Eton, Trinity Coll Cambridge (MA); *m* 4 Dec 1971, Victoria Rose, da of Maj Cecil Henry Feilden; 1 s (Edward Cecil b 7 March 1973); *Career* Nat Serv Lt 12 Royal Lancers 1957; memb Lloyd's; joined Joseph W Hobbs & Co 1961, Anderson Finch Villiers (Insurance) Ltd 1963; dir CTB (Insurance) Ltd 1972; chm: CTB Reinsurance Ltd 1988–92, Carpenter Bowring Ltd 1992–93, C T Bowring & Co 1996– (joined 1968, dir 1983–), Guy Carpenter & Co Inc NY 1996– (dep chm 1990–93, pres 1993–96); *Recreations* skiing, shooting, fishing; *Clubs* White's, The Brook (NY); *Style*— Hady Wakefield, Esq; ✉ Bramdean House, Alresford, Hants; The Bowring Group Ltd, Bowring Building, Tower Place, London EC3 (☎ 0171 357 2400, fax 0171 283 9629, telex 882191); Guy Carpenter & Co Ltd, 2 World Trade Center, NYC, New York 10038, USA (☎ 00 1 212 323 1323, fax 00 1 212 313 4928)

WAKEFIELD, Sir (Edward) Humphry Tyrrell; 2 Bt (UK 1962), of Kendal, Co Westmorland; s of Sir Edward Birkbeck Wakefield, 1 Bt, CIE (d 1969, himself yr bro of 1 Baron Wakefield of Kendal); *b* 11 July 1936; *Educ* Gordonstoun, Trinity Coll Cambridge (MA); *m* 1, 1960 (m dis 1964), Priscilla, da of (Oliver) Robin Bagot; m 2, 1966 (m dis 1971), Hon Elizabeth Sophia Sidney, da of 1 Viscount De L'Isle, VC, KG, GCMG, GCVO, PC; 1 s; m 3, 1974, Hon Katherine Mary Alice Baring, da of 1 Baron Howick of Glendale, KG, GCMG, KCVO (d 1973); 1 s (and 1 s decd), 1 da; *Heir* s, Lieut Maximilian Edward Vereker Wakefield, Royal Hussars (PWO), b 1967; *Career* Capt 10 Royal Hussars; fndr Stately Homes Collection, exec vice pres Mallett America Ltd 1970–75, former dir Mallett & Son (Antiques) Ltd; chm: Tyrrell & Moore Ltd 1975–91, Sir Humphry Wakefield & Ptnrs Ltd; former dir Spoleto Festival, dir Tree of Life Fndn (UK charity); memb Standing Cncl Baronetage; pres: Northumberland Mountain Rescue Services, Avison Tst; patron Actors Centre (North); memb Ctee Northumberland Branch Historic Houses Assoc; fell Pierrepont Morgan Library USA; awarded Freedom of Kansas City; hon citizen Cities of Houston and New Orleans; Hon Col Louisiana; joined membs of NZ Everest Expedition on their first ascent of Mt Wakefield NZ 1992; *Publications* author of numerous articles on antique furniture and architecture; *Clubs* Harlequins, Cavalry and Guards', Turf, Scott Polar; *Style*— Sir Humphry Wakefield, Bt; ✉ Chillingham Castle, Alnwick, Northumberland; c/o Barclays Bank, St James's St, Derby

WAKEFIELD, 11 Bishop of 1992–; Rt Rev Nigel Simeon McCulloch; patron of 74 livings and the archdeaconries and canonries in his cathedral; s of Pilot Offr Kenneth McCulloch, RAFVR (ka 1943), and Audrey Muriel, *née* Ball; *b* 17 Jan 1942; *Educ* Liverpool Coll, Selwyn Coll Cambridge (MA), Cuddesdon Theol Coll Oxford; *m* 15 April 1974, Celia Hume, da of Rev Canon Horace Lyle Hume Townshend, of Norwich, Norfolk (*see* Burke's Irish Family Records, 1976); 2 da (Kathleen b 1975, Elizabeth b 1977); *Career* ordained 1966, curate of Ellesmere Port Merseyside 1966–70, chaplain Christ's Coll Cambridge 1970–73, dir of theol studies Christ's Coll Cambridge 1970–75 (permission to officiate Dio of Liverpool 1970–73); diocesan missioner Norwich Diocese 1973–78, chaplain Young Friends of Norwich Cathedral 1974–78, rector St Thomas's and St Edmund's Salisbury 1978–86, archdeacon of Sarum 1979–86, hon canon Salisbury Cathedral and prebendary of Ogbourne 1979–86, prebendary of Wanstrow in Wells Cathedral 1986–91; bishop of Taunton 1986–91; chm Cambridge War on Want 1971–73, chm C of E Decade of Evangelism Steering Gp 1989–96; memb: Br Cncl of Churches USA Exchange (Church Growth) 1972–75, Archbishops Cncl for Evangelism Res and Trg Gp 1974–79; govr: Westwood St Thomas, St Edmund & St Mark's Salisbury 1979–86, Salisbury-Wells Theol Coll 1981–82, Royal Sch of Church Music 1984–, Marlborough Coll 1985–91, Kings Bruton 1987–92, Somerset Coll of Art and Technol 1987–89, Huddersfield Univ 1996–; pres Somerset Rural Music Sch 1986–92; chaplain Royal Bath and West Show 1991–92, chm Somerset County Scout Assoc 1987–92; memb: Gen Synod Working Gp Organists & Choirmasters 1984–85, Bath and Wells Zambia Link Programme 1987–92; chm Fin Ctee ABM 1987–92, pres Central Yorkshire Scout Assoc 1992–; chm: C of E Communication Unit 1993–, BOM Mission Renewal & Evangelism Ctee 1996–; memb: C of E Gen Synod 1990–, House of Bishops 1990–; *Books* A Gospel to Proclaim (1992), Barriers to Belief (1994); *Recreations* music, walking in the Lake District, broadcasting, gardening, brass bands; *Style*— The Rt Rev the Bishop of Wakefield; ✉ Bishop's Lodge, Woodthorpe Lane, Wakefield, W Yorks WF2 6JL (☎ 01924 255349, fax 01924 250202)

WAKEFIELD, Paul; s of James Wakefield, of Poole, Dorset, and Emily, *née* Hurst; *b* 13 Aug 1949; *Educ* King George V Sch Hong Kong, Seaford Coll E Sussex, Bournemouth Coll of Art, Birmingham Coll of Art; *m* May 1988, Helen, da of Gordon Cowcher; *Career* freelance photographer (for publishers and record cos 1973–80, advtg agencies 1980–); clients incl: Volvo, Volkswagen, Mercedes, BMW, British Gas, Jamiesons Whiskey, Kronenberg 1664, National Trust; *exhibitions* Photographers Gallery London 1984, Theatr Clwyd Mold 1986, Gallery of Photography Dublin 1991, Zelda Cheatle Gallery London 1991 and 1994, Association of Photographers Gallery London 1994, Saatchi Gallery London 1994; memb Assoc of Photographers; *Books* Wales: The First Place (with Jan Morris, 1982), Britain: A World by Itself (1984), Scotland: A Place of Visions (with Jan Morris, 1986), Ireland: Your Only Place (with Jan Morris, 1990); *Recreations* fly fishing; *Style*— Paul Wakefield, Esq; ✉ 41 Charterhouse Square, London EC1M 6EA (☎ 0171 606 6505, fax 0171 726 2968)

WAKEFIELD, Sir Peter George Arthur; KBE (1977), CMG (1973); s of John Bunting Wakefield; *b* 13 May 1922; *Educ* Cranleigh Sch, CCC Oxford; *m* 1951, Felicity Maurice-Jones; 4 s, 1 da; *Career* art consultant and diplomat; RA 1942–47, Mil Govt Eritrea 1946–47; Hulton Press 1947–49; joined Dip Serv 1949, ME Staff Coll for Arab Studies 1950, second sec Amman 1950–52, FO 1953–55; first sec: Nicosia 1955–56, Cairo 1956; Admin Staff Coll Henley 1957; first sec: Vienna 1957–60, Tokyo 1960–63; FO 1964–66, consul gen and cnsllr Benghazi 1966–69, econ and commercial cnsllr Tokyo 1970–72, econ and commercial min Tokyo 1973, seconded BOTB as Japanese market special advsr 1973–75; ambass: Lebanon 1975–78, Belgium 1979–82, ret; dir Nat Art Collections Fund 1982–92 (fndr Wakefield fund 1992); chm: Richmond Theatre Tst, Heritage Coordination Gp 1992–, Asia House London 1993–; dir Tst for Museum Exhibitions 1992–; *Recreations* looking at pictures, collecting pots; *Clubs* Travellers', Arts; *Style*— Sir Peter Wakefield, KBE, CMG; ✉ Lincoln House, 28 Montpelier Row, Twickenham, Middx TW1 2NQ (☎ 0181 892 6390, fax 0181 744 0961); La Molineta, Frigiliana, Provincia de Malaga, Spain (☎ 52 53 3175)

WAKEFIELD, His Hon Judge; Robert; *b* 14 Feb 1946; *Educ* Univ of Birmingham (LLB), Brasenose Coll Oxford (BCL); *Career* called to the Bar Middle Temple 1969, recorder 1993–96, circuit judge (SE Circuit) 1996–; *Style*— His Hon Judge Wakefield; ✉ 17 Old Buildings, Lincoln's Inn, London WC2A 3UP (☎ 0171 405 9653, fax 0171 404 8089)

WAKEFORD, Air Marshal Sir Richard Gordon; KCB (1976), LVO (1961), OBE (1958), AFC (1952); s of Charles Edward Augustus Wakeford; *b* 20 April 1922; *Educ* Kelly Coll; *m* 1948, Anne Butler; 2 s, 1 da (and 1 da decd); *Career* served RAF 1941–78, Cdr The Queen's Flight 1958–61, Air Offr Scotland and NI 1970–72, dir Service Intelligence MOD 1972–73, ANZUK Force Cdr Singapore 1974–75, dep chief Def Staff MOD (Intelligence) 1975–78; dir RAF Benevolent Fund Scotland 1978–89, vice chm (air) Lowland TA & VRA 1980–87; tstee McRoberts Tsts (chm 1982–94); dir: Thistle Fndn, Cromar Nominees; cmmr Queen Victoria Sch Dunblane 1980–90; CStJ 1986 (OStJ 1981); *Style*— Air Marshal Sir Richard Wakeford, KCB LVO, OBE, AFC; ✉ Sweethome Cottage, Inchberry Road, Fochabers, Moray (☎ 01343 820436)

WAKEHAM, Baron (Life Peer UK 1992), of Maldon in the County of Essex; John Wakeham; PC (1983), JP (Inner London 1972); s of Maj Walter John Wakeham (d 1965), of Godalming, Surrey; *b* 22 June 1932; *Educ* Charterhouse; *m* 1, 1965, Anne Roberta (k 1984), da of late Harold Edwin Bailey; 2 adopted s (Jonathan Martin b 1972, Benedict Ian b 1975); m 2, 1985, Alison Bridget, MBE, da of Ven Edwin James Greenfield Ward, LVO, *qv*; 1 s (Hon David Robert b 1987); *Career* CA; contested (C): Coventry East 1966, Putney Wandsworth 1970; MP (C): Maldon 1974–83, Colchester S and Maldon 1983–92; former sec Cons Small Businesses Ctee, asst Govt whip 1979–81, a Lord Cmmr to the Treasy (Govt whip) 1981, under sec of state for Indust 1981–82, min of state Treasy 1982–83, Parly sec to the Treasy and chief whip 1983–87, Lord Privy Seal 1987–88, Lord Pres of the Cncl 1988–89, ldr of the House of Commons 1987–89, sec of state for Energy July 1989–92, responsible for devpt of presentation of Govt policies 1990–92, Lord Privy Seal and ldr of the House of Lords 1992–94, chm Press Complaints Cmmn 1995–; non-exec dir Bristol & West Building Society 1994–; chm: Michael Page Gp plc 1995–, Kalon Gp plc 1995–, Vosper Thornycroft Holdings plc 1995–; non-exec dir: N M Rothschild & Sons Ltd 1995–, Enron Corporation 1994–; chm British Horseracing Bd 1995–; tstee and memb Ctee of Management RNLI 1995–; *Recreations* sailing, farming, racing, reading; *Clubs* Buck's, Carlton (chm 1992–), Garrick, Royal Yacht Squadron, St Stephen's Constitutional; *Style*— The Rt Hon Lord Wakeham, PC, JP; ✉ c/o House of Lords, London SW1A 0PW (☎ 0171 353 1248)

WAKEHAM, Prof William Arnot; s of Stanley William Wakeham (d 1969), of Bristol, and Winifred Gladys, *née* Crocker (d 1946); *b* 25 Sept 1944; *Educ* Bristol Cathedral Sch, Univ of Exeter (BSc, PhD, DSc); *m* 1, 1969 (m dis 1978), Christina Marjorie, da of Kenneth Stone, of Weymouth, Dorset; 1 s (Leigh b 1974); m 2, 23 Dec 1978, Sylvia Frances Tolley; 2 s (Russell Jon b 1983, Nicholas Ashley b 1986); *Career* res assoc Brown Univ Providence USA 1969–71; Imperial Coll London: lectr dept of chemical engrg 1971–79, reader in chemical physics of fluids 1979–85, prof of chemical physics 1985–, head of dept of chemical engrg 1988–96, pro-rector (research) 1996–; CEng, CPhys; FIChemE, FInstP, FIEE; *Books* Intermolecular Forces: Their Origin and Determination (1981), The Forces Between Molecules (1986), The Transport Properties of Fluids (1989), International Thermodynamic Tables of the Fluid State: Vol 10 - Ethylene (1989), Measurement of the Transport Properties of FLuids (1991), Status and Future Developments in the Study of Transport Properties (1992); *Recreations* waterskiing; *Style*— Prof William Wakeham; ✉ Department of Chemical Engineering & Chemical Technology, Imperial College of Science, Technology & Medicine, London SW7 2BY (☎ 0171 594 5005, fax 0171 594 5558, telex 929484 IMPCOL G)

WAKEHURST, 3 Baron (UK 1934); (John) Christopher Loder; s of 2 Baron Wakehurst, KG, KCMG (d 1970), and Margaret, Lady Wakehurst, DBE, *née* Tennant (d 1994); *b* 23 Sept 1925; *Educ* Eton, King's Sch Sydney, Trinity Coll Cambridge (MA, LLB); *m* 1, 27 Oct 1956, Ingeborg (d 1977), da of Walther Krumbholz; 1 s (Timothy Walter b 28 March 1958), 1 da (Christina Anne b 13 Dec 1959); m 2, 10 Sept 1983, (Francine) Brigid, da of William Noble, of Cirencester, Glos; *Heir* s, Hon Timothy Loder; *Career* serv WWII RANVR and RNVR; called to the Bar 1950; former chm: Anglo & Overseas Trust plc until 1996, The Overseas Investmt Trust plc until 1995, Morgan Grenfell Equity Income Trust plc until 1995; dep chm London and Manchester Group plc until 1995; dir Morgan Grenfell Latin American Companies Trust plc until 1996; CStJ; *Clubs* City of London, Chelsea Arts; *Style*— The Rt Hon the Lord Wakehurst; ✉ 26 Wakehurst Road, London SW11 6BY (☎ 0171 223 9410)

WAKELEY, Amanda Jane (Mrs Neil Gillon); da of Sir John Cecil Nicholson Wakeley, 2 Bt, *qv*; *b* 15 Sept 1962; *Educ* Cheltenham Ladies' Coll; *m* 25 July 1992, Neil David Gillon, yst s of Norman Keith Gillon, of Perth, W Australia; *Career* fashion designer; early career experience working in fashion indust NY 1983–85, in business working for private cmmns 1987–90, fndr Amanda Wakeley label 1990; collections sold in England, Europe and USA, opened flagship shop Chelsea Sept 1993; winner Glamour category British Fashion Awards 1992, 1993 and 1996; *Recreations* boating, water-skiing, snow-skiing, driving, horseback riding; *Style*— Ms Amanda Wakeley; ✉ 80 Fulham Road, London SW3 6HR (☎ 0171 584 4009, fax 0171 584 3186)

WAKELEY, Sir John Cecil Nicholson; 2 Bt (UK 1952), of Liss, Co Southampton; s of Sir Cecil Pembrey Grey Wakeley, 1 Bt, KBE, CB, FRCS (d 1979), and Dr Elizabeth Muriel Wakeley, *née* Nicholson-Smith (d 1985); *b* 27 Aug 1926; *Educ* Canford, Univ of London (MB BS); *m* 10 April 1954, June, o da of Donald Frank Leney; 2 s, 1 da (Amanda Jane Wakeley, *qv*); *Heir* s, Nicholas Jeremy Wakeley b 17 Oct 1957; *Career* former: chief inspr City of London Special Constabulary, sr consulting surgn W Cheshire Gp of Hosps; formerly memb: Liverpool Regional Hosp Bd, Mersey Regnl Health Authy, Cncl Royal Coll of Surgns of Eng; hon conslt advsr (civilian) to RAF; Liveryman: Worshipful Co of Barbers, Worshipful Soc of Apothecaries; FRCS, FACS; CStJ 1957; *Recreations* photography, music, model railway; *Style*— Sir John Wakeley, Bt; ✉ Mickle Lodge, Mickle Trafford, Chester CH2 4EB (☎ 01244 300316)

WAKELEY, Dr Richard Michael; s of Sir Cecil Wakeley, 1 Bt, KBE, CB, FRCS (d 1979), and Dr Elizabeth Muriel Wakeley, *née* Nicholson-Smith (d 1985); *b* 31 Jan 1933; *Educ* Winchester, King's Coll London (MB BS); *Career* house surgn King's Coll Hosp 1958; actor 1960–66; literary agent 1968–95; Freeman City of London 1956; memb: City Co of Barber Surgns, Worshipful Soc of Apothecaries; *Recreations* music, tennis; *Style*— Dr Richard Wakeley; ✉ 1 Wordsworth Mansions, Queens Club Gardens, London W14 9TE (☎ 0171 385 0908); Coves Cottage, St Peters, Broadstairs, Kent CT10 2TH

WAKELEY, Robin Anthony Wade; GSM (1955); s of Leslie Stuart Pembrey Wakeley (d 1961), of Welwyn Garden City, Herts, and Mary Louise Lloyd, *née* Wade; *b* 1 March 1937; *Educ* Hitchin GS for Boys, King's Coll London, King's Coll Hosp (BDS, Prosthetics prize); *m* 1, 1964 (m dis 1980), Pamela Margaret, da of Trevor James; 1 s (Roderick Stuart James b 15 Oct 1965), 2 da (Annabel Jane b 29 June 1967, Sophie Louise Wade b 1 Nov 1971); m 2, 1987, Carolyn, da of Frank Dakin; *Career* Nat Serv; res house surgn King's Coll Hosp 1964, pt/t lectr Guy's Hosp 1967–71 (pt/t registrar 1965–67), in private practice Harley Street 1971– (pt/t private practice 1965–71); Freeman City of London, Liveryman Worshipful Soc of Apothecaries 1976; *Recreations* golf, walking, collecting antiques; *Clubs* Reform; *Style*— Robin Wakeley, Esq; ✉ 106 Harley St, London W1N 1AF (☎ 0171 935 1196, fax 0171 486 9240)

WAKELEY, Timothy Grey (Tim); s of late William Grey Pembury Wakeley, Fitzalan Court, Rustington, Sussex, and Daisy Lillian, *née* Poole; *b* 13 Dec 1943; *Educ* Carshalton Coll; *m* 29 April 1967, Anne Caroline Duyland, da of Adm Sir John Fitzroy Duyland Bush, GCB; 2 s (Oliver Grey b 20 Aug 1969, Adam Grey b 2 Oct 1978), 2 da (Fenella Duyland b 8 April 1971, Melissa Emily (twin) b 2 Oct 1978); *Career* ptnr W Greenwell & Co 1972–86 (trainee 1961), md Greenwell Montagu Stockbrokers 1986–92, investmt mgmnt dir James Capel & Co 1993–; assoc memb Soc of Investmt Analysts, MSI; *Recreations* tennis, fly fishing, skiing, vintage cars; *Clubs* City of London; *Style*— Tim Wakeley, Esq; ✉ Little Green, Thursley, nr Godalming, Surrey GU8 6QE (☎ 01252 702320); 14 Arnold Mansions, Queen's Club Gardens, London W14 9RD (☎ 0171 381 4948); James Capel & Co, 6 Bevis Marks, London EC3A 7JQ

WAKELING, Rt Rev (John) Denis; MC (1945); s of Rev John Lucas Wakeling (d 1939), and Mary Louisa, *née* Glover (d 1923); *b* 12 Dec 1918; *Educ* Dean Close Sch Cheltenham, St Catharine's Coll Cambridge (MA), Ridley Hall Cambridge; *m* 4 April 1941, Josephine Margaret, da of Benjamin Charles Broomhall (d 1961); 3 s (Antony James b 1943, (John) Gerald b and d 1949, (John) Jeremy b 1954); *Career* Actg Maj Royal Marines 1939–45; clerk in Holy Orders; ordained: deacon 1947, priest 1948; asst curate Barwell Leics 1947–50; chaplain Clare Coll Cambridge and Cambridge Pastorate 1950–52, vicar Emmanuel Plymouth 1952–59, preb Exeter Cathedral 1957 and preb emeritus 1959, vicar Barking Essex 1959–65, archdeacon of West Ham 1965–70, bishop of Southwell 1970–85, entered House of Lords 1974; Hon DD Univ of Nottingham 1985; *Recreations* watching any sport live and on television, hearing classical music live and recorded; *Clubs* Hawks (Cambridge); *Style*— The Rt Rev Denis Wakeling, MC; ✉ 50 St Ann Place, Salisbury, Wilts SP1 2SU (☎ 01722 322016)

WAKELING, Richard Keith Arthur; s of late Eric George Wakeling, and Dorothy Ethel Wakeling; *b* 19 Nov 1946; *Educ* Enfield GS, Churchill Coll Cambridge (prize scholar, MA); *m* 9 Oct 1971, Carmen; 3 s (Simon, David, Nicholas); *Career* called to the Bar Inner Temple 1971; gp treas BOC Group plc 1977–83, fin dir John Brown plc 1983–86; Charter Consolidated plc: fin dir 1986–88, acting chief exec 1988–89; Johnson Matthey plc: dep chief exec 1990, chief exec 1991–94; non-exec dir: Costain Group PLC 1992–, Laura Ashley Holdings PLC 1994–95, Logica plc, Staveley Industries plc, HTR Income & Growth Split Trust plc, Oxford Instruments plc, Bain Hogg Group PLC; dep chm Celtic Group Holdings Ltd; FCT; *Recreations* medieval history and architecture, golf, gardening; *Style*— Richard Wakeling, Esq; ✉ 46 The Bourne, Southgate, London N14 6QS (☎ and fax 0181 886 8143); Costain Group plc, 111 Westminster Bridge Road, London SE1 7UE (☎ 0171 705 8444, fax 0171 705 8599)

WAKELY, Dr Peter George; s of George James Louis Wakely (d 1963), and Winifred Grace Florence, *née* Osborne (d 1961); *b* 15 Feb 1925; *m* 3 April 1954, Constance Mary (Babs), da of Samuel Jeffcote (d 1969); 2 s (Timothy b 1958, Nicholas b 1960); *Career* mathematician and engr previously at: GEC, English Electric Co, Queen's Univ Belfast, Univ of Southampton; hon prof of engrg sci Univ of Warwick 1968–77, chm and md Assoc Engrg Devpts Ltd 1971–80, engrg conslt 1980–; churchwarden St Michael and All Angels Cosby 1965–89, pres Inst of Mathematics and its Applications 1969, chm CSTI 1969, chm Jt Affrs Ctee CEI and CSTI 1970–71, govr Coventry Poly 1970–73, assessor on Cncl SERC 1977–88, memb Ctee of Inquiry into the Teaching of Mathematics in Schools (The Cockcroft Ctee) 1978–81; former chm: Jt SERC and Dept of Indust Advsy Panel on Computer Aided Engrg, SERC Cooperative Res Grants Panel, Steering Gp for the Nat Physical Laboratory Numerical Analysis and Computing Div; former memb numerous engrg, scientific and industl ctees; FIMA 1964; *Recreations* social history, sailing; *Style*— Dr Peter Wakely

WAKEMAN, Sir Edward Offley Bertram; 6 Bt (UK 1828), of Perdiswell Hall, Worcestershire; s of Capt Sir Offley Wakeman, 4 Bt, CBE (d 1975), and his 2 w, Josceline Etheldreda, *née* Mitford (d 1996, in her 103rd year); suc his half-bro Sir (Offley) David Wakeman, 5 Bt 1991; *b* 31 July 1934; *Heir* none; *Style*— Sir Edward Wakeman, Bt

WAKEMAN, Prof Richard John; s of Ronald Wakeman, of Exmouth, Devon, and Kathleen, *née* Smith; *b* 15 April 1948; *Educ* King Edward VI GS Bury St Edmunds, UMIST (BSc, MSc, PhD); *m* 24 July 1971, Patricia Joan, da of Jack Morris; 2 s (Simon Richard b 24 June 1976, Mark Andrew b 4 April 1979); *Career* chemical engr Lennig Chemicals Ltd 1970, research asst UMIST 1972–73; Univ of Exeter: lectr 1973–86, reader in particle technol 1986–90, prof of process engrg 1990–95; prof of chemical engrg Loughborough Univ 1995–; visiting engr Univ of California at Berkeley 1980; Filtration Soc: memb Cncl 1982–89, chm 1987–89, tstee 1989–; chm Working Party Euro Fedn of Chemical Engrs 1996– (memb 1984–); non-exec dir: The Filtration Society Ltd 1983–89, Exeter Enterprises Ltd 1987–90; author of over 200 research articles, patents and books/book contribs 1971–; FIChemE 1989 (MIChemE 1977), FRSA 1989, FEng 1996; *Awards* Moulton Medal Instn of Chemical Engrs 1991 and 1995 (Jr Moulton Medal 1978), Gold Medal Filtration Soc 1993 (Suttle Award 1971); *Recreations* philately, antiquities, industrial archaeology; *Style*— Prof Richard Wakeman, FEng; ✉ 19 Clyst Valley Road, Clyst St Mary, Exeter EX5 1DD (☎ and fax 01392 874398); Department of Chemical Engineering, Loughborough University, Loughborough, Leics LE11 3TU (☎ 01509 222506, fax 01509 223923, mobile 0850 570197, e-mail R.J.Wakeman@lboro.ac.uk)

WAKERLEY, (John) Charles; OBE (1974); s of Charles William Wakerley (d 1978), of Welton, nr Lincoln, and Gladys MacLennon, *née* Skelton (d 1986); bro of Richard Wakerley, QC, *qv*; *b* 18 Jan 1936; *Educ* Lincoln Sch, Univ of Nottingham (LLB); *m* 1, 1958 (m dis 1987), Peggy, da of late George Hayward, of Lincoln; m 2, 1987, Diana Louise Seton Adams, da of Fenmore Roger Seton, of North Haven, Conn, USA (former pres Rehabilitation Int); 2 step s (Christopher Adams b 1969, James Adams b 1971); *Career* cmmd Army Legal Serv 1960, ret as Lt-Col 1974; called to the Bar Gray's Inn 1960, admitted NY Bar 1982; currently sr vice pres and dir General Counsel US SmithKline Beecham plc (joined 1974); *Recreations* old clocks, American Civil War; *Style*— Charles Wakerley, Esq, OBE; ✉ Legal Operations Group, SmithKline Beecham plc, 1 New Horizons Court, Brentford, Middlesex TW8 9EP (☎ 0181 975 2000, fax 0181 975 2072)

WAKERLEY, Richard MacLennon; QC (1982); s of Charles William Wakerley (d 1978), and Gladys MacLennon, *née* Skelton (d 1986), of Lincoln; bro of Charles Wakerley, OBE, *qv*; *b* 7 June 1942; *Educ* De Aston Sch Market Rasen, Emmanuel Coll Cambridge

(MA); *m* 1966, Marian Heather, da of Stanley William Dawson, of Lincoln; 2 s (Paul b 1968, Simon b 1971), 2 da (Helen b 1966, Emma b 1973); *Career* called to the Bar Gray's Inn 1965, bencher 1991, head of chambers; recorder of the Crown Court 1982–, ldr Midland and Oxford Circuit 1992–; *Recreations* bridge, gardening, theatre; *Style—* Richard Wakerley, Esq, QC; ✉ Croft House, Grendon, Atherstone, Warwickshire (☎ 01827 712 329); 4 Fountain Court, Steelhouse Lane, Birmingham (☎ 0121 236 3476)

WALCOT, Prof Peter; s of Cedric Ernest William Walcot (d 1956), of London, and Harriet, *née* Reed (d 1988); *b* 10 May 1931; *Educ* Wilson's GS London, UCL (BA, PhD), Yale Univ (MA); *m* 28 Jan 1956, Jean Margaret Ellen; 2 s (Timothy, Christopher), 1 da (Alison); *Career* Nat Serv Flying Offr RAF 1955–57; visiting prof UCLA 1982, visiting lectr Univ of Florida 1983, visiting lectr New York Univ 1994; prof: Univ Coll Cardiff 1974–88 (asst lectr 1951–59, lectr 1959–66, sr lectr 1966–74), Univ of Wales Coll of Cardiff 1988–96; Webster Meml lectr Stanford Univ 1991; ed Greece and Rome 1970–; moderator in classics Univ of London Schools Examination Bd 1974–96; memb: Soc For Promotion of Hellenic Studies 1948, Classical Assoc 1957; *Books* Hesiod and the Near East (1966), Greek Peasants Ancient and Modern (1970), Greek Drama in its Theatrical and Social Context (1976), Envy and the Greeks (1978); *Recreations* walking; *Style—* Prof Peter Walcot; ✉ 28 Rowan Way, Lisvane, Cardiff CF4 5TD (☎ 01222 756653)

WALD, Prof Nicholas John; s of Adolf Max Wald, of London, and Frieda Shatsow (d 1986); *b* 31 May 1944; *Educ* Owen's Sch, UCH (MB BS), Univ of London (DSc); *m* 2 Jan 1966, Nancy Evelyn, *née* Miller; 3 s (David b 1968, Richard b 1971, Jonathan b 1977), 1 da (Karen b 1966); *Career* MRC Epidemiology and Med Care Unit 1971– (memb sci staff), ICRF Cancer Epidemiology and Clinical Trials Unit Oxford 1972–83, prof and head of Dept of Environmental and Preventive Med Bart's 1983– (founding chm Wolfson Inst of Preventive Medicine 1992–95); ed in chief Jl of Medical Screening (inaugural ed) 1994–; hon dir Cancer Research Campaign Screening Gp, hon conslt East London & City and Oxford RHA's; Advsy Cncl on Sci and Technol: memb Med Res and Health Ctee 1991–92; MRC: memb Steering Ctee of the MRC Study on Multivitamins and Neural-Tube Defects 1982–, chm Smoking Review Working Gp 1986–90, chm Study Monitoring Ctee of the MRC Randomised Clinical Trial of Colo-Rectal Cancer Screening 1986–; Dept of Health: memb Advsy Ctee on Breast Cancer Screening 1986–, memb Ind Sci Ctee on Smoking and Health 1983–91, Central Research and Devpt Ctee 1991–, memb Chief Medical Offr's Health of the Nation Working Gp 1991–, memb Chief Medical Offr's Advsy Gp on Folate Supplementation in the Prevention of Neural Tube Defects 1991–92, memb Central Res and Devpt Ctee 1991–, memb Scientific Ctee on Tobacco and Health 1993–; Royal Coll of Physicians: memb Ctee on Ethical Issues in Medicine 1988–, memb Sub-Ctee on Ethical Issues in Clinical Genetics 1988–91, memb Special Advsy Gp to Med Info Technol Ctee 1984; memb Action on Smoking and Health Res Ctee 1982–; memb Wellcome Trust Physiology and Pharmacology Panel 1995–; NE Thames RHA: memb Clinical Genetics Advsy Sub-Ctee 1984–, chm Breast Cancer Screening Evaluation Ctee 1988–, memb Dist Res Ethics Ctee 1990–95, cncl memb Coronary Prevention Gp 1993–94; memb Editorial Bds: Prenatal Diagnosis, Br Jl of Cancer, Cancer Epidemiology Biomarkers and Prevention; FFPHM 1982, FRCP 1986, FRCOG 1992; *Books* Alpha-Fetoprotein Screening - The Current Issues (ed with J E Haddow, 1981), Antenatal and Neonatal Screening (ed, 1984), Interpretation of Negative Epidemiological Evidence for Carcinogenicity (ed with R Doll, 1985), The Epidemiological Approach (1985), UK Smoking Statistics (jt ed, 1988 and 1991), Nicotine Smoking and the Low Tar Programme (ed with P Froggatt, 1989), Smoking and Hormone Related Disorders (ed with J Baron, 1990), Passive Smoking: A Health Hazard (jt ed, 1991), International Smoking Statistics (co-author, 1994); *Recreations* skiing, boating, economics; *Clubs* Athenaeum; *Style—* Prof Nicholas Wald; ✉ Department of Environmental and Preventive Medicine, Wolfson Institute of Preventive Medicine, The Medical College of St Bartholomew's Hospital, Charterhouse Square, London EC1M 6BQ (☎ 0171 982 6269, fax 0171 982 6270)

WALDEGRAVE, (Linda Margaret) Caroline; da of Maj Richard Burrows, of Royal Chase, Tunbridge Wells, Kent, and Molly, *née* Hollins; *b* 14 Aug 1952; *Educ* Convent of the Sacred Heart Woldingham Surrey, Cordon Bleu Sch of Cookery; *m* 1977, Rt Hon William Waldegrave, MP, *qv*, s of Earl Waldegrave, KG, GCVO, TD (d 1995); 1 s (James Victor b 12 Dec 1984), 3 da (Katharine Mary b 15 Sept 1980, Elizabeth Laura b 27 Oct 1983, Harriet Horatia b 28 Jan 1988); *Career* joined Leith's Catering as jr cook 1972; proprietor: Leith's Sch of Food and Wine 1994– (estab with Prue Leith 1975), Leith's Restaurant 1995–; dir Waldegrave Farms Ltd 1994–; *Books* Leith's Cookery School (with Prue Leith, 1985), The Healthy Gourmet (1986), Sainsbury's Low Fat Gourmet (1987), Leith's Cookery Bible (with Prue Leith, 1991), Leith's Complete Christmas (jtly, 1992), Leith's Fish Bible (jtly, 1995), Leith's Easy Dinner Parties (jtly, 1995); *Recreations* tennis, bridge; *Style—* Mrs Caroline Waldegrave; ✉ Leith's School of Food and Wine Ltd, 21 St Albans Grove, Kensington, London W8 5BP (☎ 0171 229 0177, fax 0171 937 5257); Leith's Restaurant Ltd, 92 Kensington Park Road, London W11 2PN (☎ 0171 229 4481)

WALDEGRAVE, 13 Earl (GB 1729); Sir James Sherbrooke Waldegrave; 17 Bt (E 1643), of Hever Castle, Co Kent; also Baron Waldegrave (E 1686) and Viscount Chewton (GB 1729); s of 12 Earl Waldegrave, KG, GCVO, TD (d May 1995), and Mary Hermione, *née* Grenfell (d Nov 1995); *b* 8 Dec 1940; *Educ* Eton, Trinity Coll Cambridge (MA, pres Boat Club, stroke Univ Crew 1962 and 1963); *m* 12 April 1986 (m dis 1996), Mary Alison Anthea, da of Sir Robert Allason Furness, KBE, CMG (d 1954); 2 s (Viscount Chewton b 1986, Hon Arthur Riversdale b 1989); *Heir* s, Edward Robert, Viscount Chewton b 10 Oct 1986; *Clubs* Beefsteak, Leander, HLYC; *Style—* The Rt Hon Earl Waldegrave; ✉ Chewton House, Chewton Mendip, Bath (☎ 01761 241264, fax 01762 241527)

WALDEGRAVE, Rt Hon William Arthur; PC (1990), MP (C) Bristol West (majority 6,071); 2 s of 12 Earl Waldegrave, KG, GCVO, TD (d May 1995), and Mary Hermione, *née* Grenfell (d Nov 1995); *b* 15 Aug 1946; *Educ* Eton, CCC Oxford, Harvard Univ; *m* 1977, Caroline Waldegrave, *qv*, da of Maj Richard Burrows, of Royal Chase, Tunbridge Wells, Kent; 1 s (James Victor b 12 Dec 1984), 3 da (Katharine Mary b 15 Sept 1980, Elizabeth Laura b 27 Oct 1983, Harriet Horatia b 28 Jan 1988); *Career* fell All Souls Oxford 1971–78 and 1979–86; CPRS 1971–73, on political staff 10 Downing St 1973–74, head of Political Office of Rt Hon Edward Heath (as ldr of the oppn) 1974–75; with GEC Ltd 1975–81, memb IBA Advsy Cncl 1980–; MP (C) Bristol W 1979–, jt vice chm Fin Ctee to Sept 1981, under sec of state DES (for Higher Educn) 1981–83, chm Ctee for Local Authy Higher Educn 1982–83, under sec of state DOE 1983–85; min of state DOE 1985, min of state FCO 1988, sec of state for Health 1990–92, Chancellor of the Duchy of Lancaster (with responsibility for the Citizen's Charter and Sci) 1992–94, min for agriculture fisheries and food 1994–95, chief sec to the Treasy 1995–; *Books* The Binding of Leviathan - Conservatism and the Future (1977), Changing Gear - What the Government Should Do Next (pamphlet, co-author, 1981); *Clubs* Beefsteak, Pratt's; *Style—* The Rt Hon William Waldegrave, MP; ✉ House of Commons, London SW1A 0AA

WALDEN, George Gordon Harvey; CMG (1981), MP (C) Buckingham (majority 19,791); s of G G Walden; *b* 15 Sept 1939; *Educ* Latymer Upper Sch, Jesus Coll Cambridge, Univ of Moscow, Univ of Hong Kong; *m* 1970, Sarah Nicolette Hunt; 2 s, 1 da; *Career* FO 1962–65, second sec Peking 1967–70, first sec Soviet Desk FCO 1970–73, École Nationale d'Administration Paris 1973–74, first sec Paris 1974–78, head of planning staff FCO 1982–83; MP (C) Buckingham 1983–97 (standing down at 1997 Gen Election); PPS to Rt Hon David Owen 1978–79, Rt Hon Lord Carrington 1979–81, PPS to Sec of State for Educn and Sci 1984–85; Parly under sec of state DES 1985–87; columnist Daily Telegraph 1988–94, contrib Evening Standard 1994–; chm Booker Prize 1995; fell Harvard Univ 1981–82; *Books* Ethics and Foreign Policy, We Should Know Better: Solving the Education Crisis; *Style—* George Walden, Esq, CMG, MP; ✉ House of Commons, London SW1A 0AA (☎ 0171 219 6346)

WALDEN, Herbert Richard Charles; CBE (1986); s of Reginald George Walden (d 1954), and late Matilda Ethel, *née* Baker; *b* 6 Oct 1926; *Educ* Westgate Sch Warwick; *m* 1950, Margaret (d 1995), da of Percy Harold Walker (d 1957); 2 da (Ann, Judith); *Career* serv WWII 1944–47, Royal Warwicks Regt, Capt Royal Leicestershire, serv UK and Gold Coast; dir and gen mangr: Warwick Building Society 1962–67, Rugby and Warwick Building Soc 1967–74; dir and gen mangr then chief exec Heart of England Building Soc 1974–86; chm The Bldg Socs Assoc 1983–85 (memb Cncl 1974–86), pt/t cmmr Bldg Socs Cmmn 1986–95; memb Bd Housing Corp 1985–88; chm S Warwickshire HMC 1964–72, fndr pres Warwick Rotary Club 1965, govr Warwicks Schs Fndn 1962–90 (chm 1986–90), vice pres Warwicks Scout Cncl (former co treas), tstee various Warwick charities; FCIS, FCIB; *Recreations* watching cricket and soccer; *Clubs* Naval and Military; *Style—* Herbert Walden, Esq, CBE; ✉ Fieldgate House, 24 Hill Wootton Rd, Leek Wootton, Warwick CV35 7QL (☎ 01926 854291)

WALDIE, Ian Michael; s of George Alistair (Ted) Waldie, of Queensland, Aust, and Dulcie Michel, *née* Clark; *b* 21 Jan 1970; *Educ* Burnside HS Nambour Aust, Queensland Coll of Art Brisbane Aust (Assoc Dip of Arts in Applied Photography); *Career* news photographer; cadet photographer The Sunshine Coast Daily (Maroochydore Queensland) 1988–89, photographer The Brisbane Courier Mail (Brisbane Queensland) 1989–92, freelance photographer Scotland 1992–93 (working for The Herald, The Scotsman, The Daily Record, The Sunday Mail, Take-A-Break and Rex Features), stringer photographer (covering Scotland for the Reuters UK and int serv) Reuters Ltd 1993–96, staff photographer Reuter UK Pictures (based London) 1996–; notable assignments since 1993 incl: numerous royal visits and functions, state visits by John Major, Mikhail Gorbochev, Nelson Mandela, Paul Keating, The Dalai Lama, Mother Theresa, the PM of Finland and The King and Queen of Norway, Scottish Cup Finals 1993 and 1994, Rugby Five Nations Tournament 1992, 1993, 1994 and 1995, Scottish Open Golf Championships 1993, 1994 and 1995, Alfred Dunhill Cup Golf Championships 1993, 1994 and 1995, Cons Pty Conf 1994 and 1995, Lab Pty Conf 1995, Rugby World Cup SA 1995, World Championships in Athletics Gothenburg 1995, conflict in NI over Protestant marching season in Portadown, Belfast, Londonderry, Inneskillen and Bellaghy; memb: Australian Journalists Assoc (AJA) 1988–93, NUJ 1992; *Awards* Best Sports Picture (Scottish Sports Photography Awards) 1994, Best News Picture (Scottish Airports Press Photography Awards) 1994, Photographer of the Yr, Young Photographer of the Yr and Best News Photographer of the Yr (Br Picture Eds Guild) 1994; *Recreations* surfing (in Australia), music (ex-drummer), squash, rally driving, various other sports; *Style—* Ian Waldie, Esq; ✉ c/o Reuters UK Pictures, 85 Fleet Street, London EC4P 4AJ (☎ and fax 0141 946 3373, mobile 0850 608097)

WALDMANN, Dr Carl; s of Leon Waldmann (d 1970), and Rene, *née* Schafer; bro of Prof Herman Waldmann, *qv*; *b* 25 March 1951; *Educ* Forest Sch Snaresbrook, Sidney Sussex Coll Cambridge (BA), London Hosp (MA, MB BChir, DA); *m* 27 July 1980, Judith; 1 da (Anna b 1981); *Career* Flt-Lt Unit MO RAF Brize Norton 1977–78, Sqdn Ldr 1981–82, sr specialist anaesthetics RAF Ely 1980–82 (specialist 1978–80); sr registrar in intensive care Whipps Cross Hosp 1982–83; sr registrar in anaesthetics: London Hosp 1984–85 (houseman 1975–76, sr house offr in anaesthetics 1976–77, lectr in anaesthetics 1983–84), Great Ormond St Hosp 1985–86; conslt in anaesthetics and dir of intensive care Royal Berks and Battle Hosps Reading 1986–; European dip in Intensive Care Med 1993; memb Ed Bd Care of the Critically Ill; FFARCS 1980; *Books* Pocket Consultant Intensive Care (1985), Respiration: The Breath of Life (1985), Hazards and Complications of Anaesthesia (1987), Kaufman, Anaesthesia Reviews; *Recreations* fencing, squash, skiing, water-skiing; *Clubs* Kirtons Farm Country (Reading); *Style—* Dr Carl Waldmann; ✉ The Tennyson, Sussex Lane, Spencers Wood, Reading RG7 1AT (☎ 0118 988 4460); Intensive Therapy Unit, Royal Berks Hosp, Reading, Berks (☎ 0118 987 7256, fax 0118 987 7250)

WALDMANN, Prof Herman; s of Leon Waldmann (d 1970), and Rene, *née* Schafer; bro of Dr Carl Waldmann, *qv*, and David Waldmann; *b* 27 Feb 1945; *Educ* Sir George Monoux GS Walthamstow, Sidney Sussex Coll Cambridge (exhibitioner, hon scholar, BA, MA, PhD), London Hosp Med Sch (open scholar, MB BChir, MRCPath, MRCP, Hutchinson prize for clinical res); *m* 1971, Judith Ruth; *Career* house physician and surgeon London Hosp 1969–70, MRC jr res fell 1970–73; Dept of Pathology Univ of Cambridge: demonstrator 1973–76, lectr 1975–76, reader in therapeutic immunology 1985, Kay Kendall prof of therapeutic immunology 1989–94; King's Coll Cambridge: res fell 1973–78, side tutor 1975–76, fell 1985–94; Univ of Oxford: prof of pathology Sir William Dunn Sch 1994–, fell Lincoln Coll 1994–; visiting scientist with Dr C Milstein Laboratory of Molecular Biology Cambridge 1978–79, sr house offr Dept of Med Royal Postgrad Med Sch London 1982, Eleanor Roosevelt fell Stanford USA 1987; memb Advsy Ctee MRC Cell Bd 1986–91; invited speaker at numerous symposia in the areas of immunology, haematology and transplantation; Graham Bull prize RCP 1989–90; FRS 1990; *Publications* author of numerous articles in learned jls; *Recreations* family, friends, food, travel, music; *Style—* Prof Herman Waldmann, FRS; ✉ 11 Gurney Way, Cambridge CB4 2ED; Sir William Dunn School of Pathology, South Parks Road, Oxford OX1 3RE (☎ 01865 275500)

WALDRON, Lady Olivia Elsie June; *née* Taylour; da of 5 Marquess of Headfort, TD (d 1960), and Elsie Florence, *née* Tucker (d 1972); *b* 20 June 1929; *Educ* St Catherine's Melbourne Australia, St Mary's Convent Ascot; *m* 1955, Victor Echevarri Waldron, *qv*, s of Ernest Victor Echevarri; 2 da (Sarah b 1956, Gina b 1957); *Career* started first health food shop in Windsor, Berks 1971; memb: Soil Assoc, Henry Doubleday Research Assoc, Royal Commonwealth Soc; dir The Hunger Project Ltd (UK) 1980–84, tstee The Hunger Project Tst 1984–89, memb SID 1983–, memb SID Exec UK 1984–94, chm Waldron Properties Ltd, memb Exec Cncl UK Chapter Soc for Int Devpt 1989–92, chm Advsy Cncl The Hunger Project Tst 1989–92, patron The Hunger Project 1994–; *Recreations* gardening, reading, friends and family; *Style—* The Lady Olivia Waldron; ✉ Idleigh Cottage, Meopham, Kent DA13 0JR (☎ 01474 872363, fax 01474 879232); P O Box 1626, Holmes Beach, Florida 34218–1626, USA (☎ 1 941 778 0354, fax 1 941 778 1248)

WALDRON, Victor Echevarri; s of Ernest Echevarri, ggs of Don Juan Ignacio Echevarri, of Bilbao, a Basque grandee and prominent activist in the Carlist uprising, who was naturalized 1821; adopted by deed poll surname of Waldron 1947; *Educ* West Ham Tech Coll, King's Coll London, King Alfred Naval Offr Trg Coll; *m* 1, 1947, Gladys Leila (d 1953), o da of Col Sir William Waldron; 1 s (William b 1948), 1 da (Carola b 1953); m 2, 1955, Lady Olivia Elsie June Waldron, *qv*, o da of 5 Marquess of Headfort (d 1960); 2 da (Sarah b 1956, Gina b 1957); *Career* serv RN 1940–45, Lt RNVR; memb Cons Central Office 1946–53, Parly candidate 1951, fin advsr to constituencies 1954; chm: Waldron Group of Cos, Roundwood Development Ltd; fndr dir Waldron Charity (private fndn); formerly: exec memb Nat Fedn of Property Owners, hon treas Property Cncl, dir The Hunger Project Tst; UK correspondent the Hunger Project Newspaper, ed Aware Digest 1988; author, journalist, news analyst and campaigner to end world hunger 1958–; contrib: Daily Telegraph, Cape Town Argus, Herald Tribune, etc; Lionel Fifield Writers' Award 1983; pres: World Runners UK 1980–, Peterborough Benevolent Soc 1991–; memb: Foreign Press Assoc, Overseas Press Club of NY, Journalists Devpt Gp of World Aware, Sports Aid Fndn; Liveryman and Freeman City of London; FRGS; *Publications* incl: Ageing for Beginners, The Man with Cloth Ears, The Wind at my Back (Minerva Press, 1995); *Clubs* Naval and Military, United and Cecil, Royal Corinthian Yacht; *Style*— Victor E Waldron, Esq; ✉ Idleigh Cottage, Meopham, Kent DA13 0JR (☎ 01474 872363); 516 74 Street, Holmes Beach, Florida USA

WALDUCK, (Hugh) Richard; JP (Middx 1974); s of Hugh Stanley Walduck (d 1975), of Long Meadow, Hatfield, Herts, and Enid Rosalind (Wendy) Walduck; *b* 21 Nov 1941; *Educ* Harrow, Univ of Cambridge (MA); *m* 1, 1969 (m dis 1980), Meintje Marianne, *née* Stibbe; 2 s (Alexander b 1971, Nicholas b 1972), 2 step s (Richard b 1966, Simon b 1968), 1 step da (Nicola b 1971); m 2, 27 Aug 1981, Susan Marion, da of Frank Sherwood; *Career* dir and sec Imperial London Hotels Ltd 1964–; Liveryman Worshipful Co of Basketmakers 1968; county pres St John Ambulance Hertfordshire 1990; *Recreations* history, skiing, beekeeping; *Style*— Richard Walduck, Esq, JP; ✉ Lower Woodside, Hatfield, Herts AL9 6DJ; c/o Director's Office, Imperial Hotel, Russell Sq, London WC1B 5BB (☎ 0171 837 3655, fax 0171 837 4653, telex 263951 RUSIMP LDN)

WALES, Archbishop of 1991–; Most Rev Alwyn Rice Jones; s of John Griffith Jones (d 1948), of Capel Curig, Gwynedd, and Annie, *née* Roberts (d 1945); *b* 25 March 1934; *Educ* Llanrwst GS Denbighshire, St David's UC Lampeter (BA), Fitzwilliam Coll Cambridge (Welsh Church scholar, BA, MA); *m* 15 April 1968, Meriel Ann, da of Roland William Thomas (d 1982), of 3 Bryn Haul, Llanfairfechan, Gwynedd; 1 da (Nia Rice b 8 March 1969); *Career* ordained Dio of Bangor: deacon 1958, priest 1959; asst curate Llanfairisgaer Bangor 1958–62, sec and chaplain Student Christian Movement Colls Wales 1962–65, chaplain St Winifred's Sch Llanfairfechan 1965–67, diocesan dir of educn Dio of Bangor 1965–75, diocesan youth chaplain 1967–72, diocesan warden of ordinands 1970–75, hon canon Bangor Cathedral 1975, vicar of Porthmadog 1975–79, preb Llanfair Bangor Cathedral 1978–79, dean of Brecon and vicar St Mary's with Battle 1979–82, bishop of St Asaph 1982–; pres CCBI 1997–; asst tutor in religious educn UCNW Bangor 1973–76, memb Religious Advsy Panel IBA 1973–75, chm Religious Panel S4C TV 1987; *Recreations* music, walking; *Style*— The Most Rev the Archbishop of Wales; ✉ Esgobty, St Asaph, Clwyd LL17 0TW (☎ 01745 583503, fax 01745 584301)

WALES, Anthony Edward; s of Albert Edward Wales, of Collingham, Nottinghamshire, and Kathleen May, *née* Rosenthal; *b* 20 Dec 1955; *Educ* Stamford Sch Lincs, Worcester Coll Oxford (MA); *m* 1 Sept 1984, Lynda, da of Leonard Page (d 1987), of Swansea, W Glamorgan; 2 s (Edward b 1987, Thomas b 1989), 1 da (Victoria b 1993); *Career* slr; ptnr Turner Kenneth Brown 1986–94 (joined 1979), company sec The Economist Newspaper Ltd 1994–; memb: Law Soc 1981, Law Soc Hong Kong 1986; *Style*— Anthony Wales, Esq; ✉ The Economist, 25 St James's Street, London SW1A 1HG (☎ 0171 830 7000, fax 0171 839 2968)

WALES, Gregory John; s of A J Wales, of Guildford, Surrey, and B Wales, *née* Read; *b* 17 May 1949; *Educ* Guildford RGS; *m* 29 July 1972, Jennifer Hilary, da of E Brown, of St Albans; 2 s (Nicholas b 1978, Andrew b 1981); *Career* CA 1974; sr lectr City 1976–79, mgmnt conslt 1976–80, mangr Arthur Andersen & Co 1980–82, ptnr Coombes Wales Quinnell 1982–90; dir: Meyer Communications Ltd, Sherbourne Foundation, MacLaurin Communications Ltd; Freeman City of London; FCA; *Recreations* cricket, squash, real tennis; *Clubs* MCC; *Style*— Gregory Wales, Esq; ✉ 9 The Avenue, Richmond, Surrey TW9 2AL (☎ 0181 940 9909); Sherbourne Foundation, 22 Berghem Mews, London W14 0HN

WALEY-COHEN, Hon Mrs (Felicity Ann); *née* Samuel; da of 3 Viscount Bearsted, TD, DL, and his 1 w, (Elizabeth) Heather (later Lady Grierson, d 1993), da of G Firmston-Williams; *b* 3 April 1948; *m* 1975, Robert Waley-Cohen, *qv*, 2 s of Sir Bernard Waley-Cohen, 1 Bt (d 1991); 3 s (Marcus b 1977, Sam b 1982, Thomas b 1984), 1 da (Jessica 1979); *Career* Felicity Samuel Gallery 1972–81; chm Patrons of New Art Tate Gallery 1982–87; tstee: Tate Fndn 1986–, Serpentine Gallery 1987– (vice chm 1993–); memb Exec Ctee NACF 1988–; govr English Nat Ballet 1994–; *Style*— The Hon Mrs R Waley-Cohen; ✉ Upton Viva, Banbury, Oxon

WALEY-COHEN, Hon Lady (Joyce Constance Ina); *née* Nathan; only da of 1 Baron Nathan, TD, PC (d 1963); *b* 20 Jan 1920; *Educ* St Felix Sch, Girton Coll Cambridge (MA); *m* 1943, Sir Bernard Nathaniel Waley-Cohen, 1 Bt (d 1991); 2 s (Sir Stephen Harry Waley-Cohen, 2 Bt, *qv*, Robert Bernard Waley-Cohen, *qv*), 2 da (Rosalind Alice (Mrs Philip Burdon) b 1945, (Eleanor) Joanna (Dr Joanna Waley-Cohen) b 1952); *Career* JP: Middx 1949–59, Somerset 1959–87; memb Bd of Govrs Westminster Hosp Gp 1952–68; chm: Westminster Children's Hosp 1952–68, Gordon Hosp 1961–68, Governing Body St Felix Sch 1970–83 (memb 1945–83), Governing Bodies of Girls Schs Assoc 1974–79 (memb 1963–), Independent Schs Jt Ctee 1977–80; govr: Taunton Sch 1978–90, Wellington Coll 1979–90; pres Ind Schs Info Serv Cncl 1981–86 (memb 1972–86) and memb Mgmnt Ctee; *Style*— The Hon Lady Waley-Cohen, JP; ✉ Honeymead, Simonsbath, Minehead, Somerset TA24 7JX (☎ 01643 831 242)

WALEY-COHEN, Robert Bernard; 2 s of Sir Bernard Waley-Cohen, 1 Bt (d 1991), and Hon Joyce, *qv*, da of 1 Baron Nathan; *b* 10 Nov 1948; *Educ* Eton; *m* 1975, Hon Felicity Ann, *qv*, da of 3 Viscount Bearsted, TD; 3 s (Marcus Richard b 1977, Sam Bernard b 1982, Thomas Andrew b 1984), 1 da (Jessica Suzanna b 1979); *Career* exec Christie's 1969–81 (gen mangr USA 1970–73); chm and chief exec offr Alliance Imaging Inc 1983–88, chief exec Alliance Medical Ltd 1989–; Liveryman Worshipful Co of Clothworkers; *Recreations* the arts, conservation, racing (racehorses include: Sun Lion, Rustle, The Dragon Master, Bibendum, Won't Be Gone Long); *Clubs* Jockey; *Style*— Robert Waley-Cohen, Esq; ✉ 18 Gilston Rd, London SW10 9SR (☎ 0171 244 6022)

WALEY-COHEN, Sir Stephen Harry; 2 Bt (UK 1961), of Honeymead, Co Somerset; s of Sir Bernard Nathaniel Waley-Cohen, 1 Bt (d 1991), and Hon Lady Waley-Cohen, *qv*; *b* 22 June 1946; *Educ* Eton, Magdalene Coll Cambridge (MA); *m* 1, 1972 (m dis 1986), Pamela Elizabeth, yr da of J E Doniger, of Knutsford, Cheshire; 2 s (Lionel Robert b 7 Aug 1974, Jack David b 7 Sept 1979), 1 da (Harriet Ann b 20 June 1976); m 2, 1986, Josephine Burnett, yr da of Duncan M Spencer, of Bedford, New York; 2 da (Tamsin Alice b 4 April 1986, Freya Charlotte b 20 Feb 1989); *Heir* s, Lionel Robert Waley-Cohen b 7 Aug 1974; *Career* fin journalist Daily Mail 1968–73, ed Money Mail Handbook 1972–74, dir and publisher Euromoney Publications Ltd 1969–83, chief exec Maybox Group plc (theatre and cinema owners and managers) 1984–89; dir Publishing Holdings plc 1986–88, chm Willis Faber & Dumas (Agencies) Ltd 1992– (dir 1988), dir St Martin's Theatre Ltd 1989–, md Victoria Palace 1989–; chm: Thorndike Holdings plc 1989–, Policy Portfolio plc 1993–, First Call Group plc 1996–; dir: Stewart Wrightson Members Agency Ltd 1987–, Exeter Preferred Capital Investment Trust plc 1992–, Portsmouth & Sunderland Newspaper plc 1994–, Savoy Theatre Ltd 1996–; md Mousetrap Productions Ltd 1994–, advsy dir Theatres Mutual Insurance Co 1995–; memb Fin Ctee Univ Coll London 1984–89, chm JCA Charitable Fndn (formerly Jewish Colonisation Assoc) 1992– (memb Cncl 1984–), memb Soc of London Theatres 1984– (memb Bd 1993–), chm Exec Ctee Br American Project for the Successor Generation 1989–92; govr Wellesley House Sch; Liveryman Worshipful Co of Clothworkers; *Clubs* Garrick; *Style*— Sir Stephen Waley-Cohen, Bt; ✉ 1 Wallingford Ave, London W10 6QA

WALFORD, Sir Christopher Rupert; kt (1995); s of John Rupert Charles Walford, MBE, and Gladys Irene Walford, *née* Sperrin; *b* 15 Oct 1935; *Educ* Charterhouse, Oriel Coll Oxford (MA); *m* 1967, Anne Elizabeth, *née* Viggars; 2 s (Rupert, Lawrence) and 1 s decd; *Career* Nat Serv cmmnd RA 1954–56, HAC 1957–72, ret as Warrant Offr; ptnr Allen & Overy 1970–96 (joined 1959); cncllr Royal Borough of Kensington 1962–65; Royal Borough of Kensington and Chelsea: cncllr 1964–82, dep Mayor 1974–75, Mayor 1979–80; alderman Ward of Farringdon Within 1982–, memb Cncl CGLI 1984–; govr Bridewell Royal Hosp 1984– (vice pres 1996–); tstee: St Paul's Cathedral Choir Sch Fndn 1985–, Guildhall Sch Music and Drama Fndn 1989–, Morden Coll Blackheath 1991–; IOD: memb Cncl, memb Policy and Exec Ctee 1986–94; memb Ct of Assts and Fin Ctee Corp of the Sons of the Clergy 1989–, Sheriff City of London 1990–91, Lord Mayor of London 1994–95; Freeman City of London 1964; Liveryman: Worshipful Co of Makers of Playing Cards 1978 (Master 1987–88), Worshipful Co of Slrs of City of London 1983 (Master 1993–94); Hon Liveryman and memb Ct of Assts Worshipful Co of Builders' Merchants 1992–; memb Guild of Freemen; hon fell Oriel Coll Oxford 1995; Hon DCL City Univ 1994; FRSA; *Recreations* listening to music, opera, kitchen bridge, horse racing, watching rugby and cricket, hill walking; *Clubs* MCC, City Livery, United Wards, Farringdon Ward (patron), Berkhamsted Golf, Braemar Golf; *Style*— Sir Christopher Walford; ✉ 213 Cromwell Tower, Barbican, London EC2Y 8DD (☎ and fax 0171 256 8578)

WALFORD, Dr Diana Marion; da of Lt-Col Joseph Norton, of Birmingham, and Thelma, *née* Norton; *b* 26 Feb 1944; *Educ* Calder HS for Girls Liverpool, Univ of Liverpool (George Holt scholarship, BSc, MB ChB, MD, George Holt medal, J Hill Abram prize), Univ of London (MSc, N and S Devi prize); *m* 9 Dec 1970, Arthur David Walford, s of Wing Cdr Adolph A Walford, of Bushey Heath, Herts; 1 s (Alexander b 5 May 1982), 1 da (Sally b 8 Aug 1972); *Career* house surgn Liverpool Royal Infirmary March-Aug 1969 (house physician 1968–69); sr house offr: St Mary's Hosp 1969–70, Northwick Park Hosp 1970–71; sr registrar rotation 1972–75, N London Blood Transfusion Centre MRC res fell and hon sr registrar Clinical Res Centre Northwick Park Hosp 1975–76, hon consIt haematologist Central Middx Hosp 1977–87; Dept of Health: sr med offr Medicines Div 1976–79, princ med offr Sci Servs Equipment Building Div 1979–83, sr princ med offr and under sec Med Manpower and Educn Div 1983–86, sabbatical London Sch of Hygiene and Tropical Med 1986–87, sr princ med offr and under sec Int Health Microbiology of Food and Water and Communicable Disease Div 1987–89, dep chief med offr and med dir NHS Mgmnt Exec 1989–92, dir Public Health Laboratory Service 1993–; contrib to various medical books and jls; FRCPath 1986 (MRCPath 1974), FRCP 1990 (MRCP 1972), FFPHM 1994 (MFPHM 1989); *Style*— Dr Diana Walford; ✉ Public Health Laboratory Service Board, 61 Colindale Avenue, London NW9 5DF (☎ 0181 200 1295)

WALFORD, His Hon Judge; John de Guise; s of Edward Wynn Walford (d 1989), of Norton-on-Tees, Cleveland, and Dorothy Ann, *née* Bouchier; *b* 23 Feb 1948; *Educ* Sedbergh Sch, Queens' Coll Cambridge (MA); *m* 30 July 1977, Pamela Elizabeth, da of Dr Peter Russell; 1 da (Caroline Louise b 6 May 1978), 1 s (Charles de Guise b 17 Sept 1979); *Career* called to the Bar Middle Temple 1971, in practice NE Circuit 1974–93, recorder of the Crown Court 1989–93 (asst recorder 1985–89), standing counsel (Criminal) DSS NE Circuit 1991–93, circuit judge (NE Circuit) 1993–; *Recreations* cricket, tennis, opera, watching Middlesbrough FC; *Clubs* Hawks' (Cambridge), Free Foresters CC; *Style*— His Hon Judge Walford; ✉ c/o North Eastern Circuit Office, 17th Floor, West Riding House, Albion Street, Leeds LS1 5AA (☎ 0113 244 1841)

WALFORD, John Howard; s of Henry Howard Walford (d 1928), and Marjorie Josephine, *née* Solomon (d 1983); *b* 16 May 1927; *Educ* Cheltenham, Gonville and Caius Coll Cambridge (MA); *m* 6 Aug 1953, Peggy Ann, da of Cdr Richard Frederick Jessel, DSO, OBE, DSC, RN (ret) (d 1988); 2 s (Charles b 1955, Richard b 1960), 2 da (Veronica b 1957, Rosemary b 1964); *Career* admitted slr 1950; Bischoff & Co: ptnr 1953–88, sr ptnr 1979–88, consIt 1988–91; sr legal offr to Banking Ombudsman 1991–96; memb Cncl Law Soc 1961–69; govr: Coll of Law 1967–88, St John's Hosp for Diseases of the Skin 1967–82; pres Slrs Disciplinary Tbnl 1979–88; chm Skin Disease Res Fund Appeal Ctee 1974–94, memb Bd of Mgmnt Petworth Cottage Nursing and Convalescent Home 1988– (chm 1988–93); memb Arbitration Panel of The Securities and Futures Authy Consumer Arbitration Scheme 1988–94; hon memb British Assoc of Dermatologists 1993; Master City of London Solicitors Co 1981; Cdr Order of Bernardo O'Higgins (Chile) 1972; *Recreations* being in the country, fly-fishing, travelling abroad; *Clubs* Garrick, City Law, Leconfield Fly-fishing; *Style*— John Walford, Esq; ✉ Pheasant Court, Northchapel, Petworth, West Sussex GU28 9LJ (☎ 01428 707550)

WALFORD, John Thomas; OBE (1985); s of Frederick Thomas Walford (d 1973), of London, and Rose Elizabeth, *née* Froud (d 1964); *b* 6 Feb 1933; *Educ* Richmond and East Sheen County GS; *m* 1, 1955 (m dis 1970), June Muriel Harding; 2 s (Martin b 1958, David b 1961), 1 da (Susan Ann b 1964); m 2, 1996, Nancy Yvonne Long; *Career* Nat Serv RAF 1951–53; CC Wakefield & Co Ltd 1949–51 and 1953–55, Stanley Eades & Co 1955–60, MooCow Milk Bars Ltd 1960–64, gen sec of the Multiple Sclerosis Soc 1977–95 (vol 1954–64, dep gen sec 1965–77, vice-pres 1995–); DL 1988–95; memb RSM; *Recreations* collecting Victorian fairings; *Style*— John Walford, Esq, OBE; ✉ Rhoslyn, Talley, Llandeilo, Carmarthenshire SA19 7AX (☎ 01558 685744)

WALKER, *see:* Forestier-Walker

WALKER, Alexander; s of Alfred Walker (d 1979), of Portadown, NI, and Ethel, *née* Andrews (d 1974); *b* 22 March 1930; *Educ* Portadown Coll, Queen's Univ Belfast (BA), Salzburg Seminar in American Studies, Collège d'Europe Bruges (Diplomé), Univ of Michigan Ann Arbor USA; *Career* lectr in political philosophy Univ of Michigan Ann Arbor 1952–54, features ed Birmingham Gazette 1954–56, leader writer and film critic The Birmingham Post 1956–59, film critic London Evening Standard 1960–, columnist Vogue magazine 1974–86; memb Br Screen Advsy Cncl (formerly Wilson Interim Action Ctee on the Film Indust) 1977–92, govr Br Film Inst 1988–94; Critic of the Year Br Press Awards 1970 and 1974 (commended 1985), Chevalier de L'Ordre des Arts et des Lettres 1981, Golden Eagle of the Philippines for servs to int cinema 1982; *Books* incl: The Celluloid Sacrifice: Aspects of Sex in the Movies (1966), Stardom: The Hollywood Phenomenon (1970), Stanley Kubrick Directs (1971), Hollywood England: The British Film Industry in the Sixties (1974), Rudolph Valentino (1976), Double Takes: Notes and Afterthoughts on the Movies 1956–76 (1977), Superstars (1978), The Shattered Silents: How the Talkies Came to Stay (1978), Garbo (1980), Peter Sellers: The Authorized Biography (1981), Joan Crawford (1983), Dietrich (1984), No Bells on Sunday: Journals of Rachel Roberts (ed, 1984), National Heroes: British Cinema in the Seventies and Eighties (1986), Vivien: The Life of Vivien Leigh (1987), 'It's Only a Movie, Ingrid': Encounters On and Off Screen (1988), Elizabeth: The Life of Elizabeth Taylor (1990), Bette Davis; A Celebration (1992), Fatal Charm: The Life of Rex Harrison (1992), Audrey: Her Real Story (1994); *Recreations* skiing, persecuting smokers; *Style*— Alexander Walker, Esq; ✉ 1 Marlborough, 38–40 Maida Vale, London W9 1RW (☎ 0171 289 0985)

WALKER, Prof Andrew Charles; s of Maurice Frederick Walker, of Saffron Walden, Essex, and Margaret Florence, *née* Rust; *b* 24 June 1948; *Educ* Kingsbury County GS, Univ of Essex (BA, MSc, PhD); *m* 2 April 1972, Margaret Elizabeth, da of Arthur Mortimer, of Heckmondwike, Yorks; 1 s (Edmund b 1978), 1 da (Abigail (twin) b 1978); *Career* Nat Res Cncl of Canada postdoctoral fell Ottawa Canada, Sci Res Cncl fell Dept of Physics Univ of Essex 1974–75 (sr res studentship 1969–72), sr scientific offr UK AEA Culham Laboratory 1975–83; Heriot-Watt Univ: lectr in physics 1983–85, reader then prof of physics, chair of modern optics 1988–; memb Ctee: Quantum Electronics

Gp Inst of Physics 1979–82 (hon sec 1982–85), Scottish Branch Inst of Physics 1985–88; memb: SERC/DTI Advance Devices and Materials Ctee 1992–94, EPSRC Electronics and Photonics Coll 1994–; chm Scottish Branch Inst of Physics 1993–95 (vice-chm 1991–93); FInstP 1987, FRSE 1994; *Recreations* music (piano, guitar), skiing, sailing; *Style*— Prof Andrew Walker, FRSE; ✉ Department of Physics, Heriot-Watt University, Riccarton, Edinburgh EH14 4AS (☎ 0131 451 3036, fax 0131 449 5542)

WALKER, Andrew Douglas; s of Malcolm Douglas Walker, and Jean Catherine Arnold, *née* Ross-Scott; *b* 6 May 1945; *Educ* Giggleswick Sch, Exeter Coll Oxford (MA), Northwestern Univ Sch of Law Chicago; *m* 10 March 1973, Hilary Georgina, yr da of Robert George Smith; *Career* articled Wilkinson, Kimbers & Staddon 1968–70, admitted slr 1970; Lovell, White & King (now Lovell White Durrant): joined 1971, ptnr 1975, opened Hong Kong office 1982, admitted slr Hong Kong 1982, sr ptnr Hong Kong office 1982–87, managing ptnr Lovell, White & King 1987–88, managing ptnr Lovell White Durrant 1988–93, sr ptnr May 1996–; licensed advocate (High Ct (Civil)) 1995; Liveryman City of London Slrs' Co; memb Law Soc 1970; FCIArb 1994; *Recreations* opera, classical music, ornithology; *Clubs* Hong Kong; *Style*— Andrew Walker, Esq; ✉ 11 St Ann's Terrace, St John's Wood, London NW8 6PH (☎ 0171 586 9697); Lovell White Durrant, 65 Holborn Viaduct, London EC1A 2DY (☎ 0171 236 0066, fax 0171 248 4212)

WALKER, (Hon) Anna; er da of Baron Butterworth, CBE, *qv*; *b* 5 May 1951; *Educ* Oxford HS, Beneden Sch Kent, Bryn Mawr Coll USA (ESU scholarship), Lady Margaret Hall Oxford (MA); *m* 1983, Timothy Edward Hanson Walker, s of Harris Walker; 3 da (Sophie (adopted) b 1975, Beth b 1984, Polly b 1986); *Career* Br Cncl 1972–73, CBI 1973–74; HM Civil Serv: ME Div DTI 1975–76, Post and Telecommunications Div DTI 1976–77, private sec to Sec of State for Indust 1977–78, princ Shipping Policy Div DTI 1979–83, princ Fin Div DTI 1983–84, interdepartmental review of budgetary control 1985–86, Cabinet Office 1986–87, Personnel Div 1987–88, asst sec Competition Policy Div DTI 1988–91, dir of competition Office of Telecommunications (Oftel) 1991–94, dep DG Oftel 1994–; *Recreations* theatre, travel, cycling; *Style*— Mrs Anna Walker; ✉ Office of Telecommunications, 50 Ludgate Hill, London EC4M 7JJ (☎ 0171 634 8804, fax 0171 634 8940)

WALKER, Gen Sir Antony Kenneth Frederick; KCB (1987); s of Kenneth Frederick Andrews Walker (d 1966), and Iris Mary Walker (d 1983); *b* 16 May 1934; *Educ* Merchant Taylors', RMA Sandhurst; *m* 1, 1961 (m dis 1983), Diana Merran Steward; 1 s, 1 da; m 2, (m dis); m 3, 1991, Hannah Dorothy (Sqn Ldr WRAF), da of Edward and Olga Watts, of Cowes, Isle of Wight; *Career* cmmnd RTR 1954; served: BAOR, Libya, Ghana, NI (despatches), Hong Kong, UN Force in Cyprus; CO 1 RTR 1974–76, Cdr Task Force Gulf (11 Armd Bde) 1978–80, GOC 3 Armd Div 1982–84, Col Cmdt RTR 1983–94; COS HQ UKLF 1985–87, Dep CDS (Commitments) 1987–89, Cmdt RCDS 1990–91, ret Army 1992; sr mil advsr EDS 1993–; chm Salisbury Festival 1993–, chm Br Bobsleigh Assoc 1992–; conslt Porton International plc 1992–93, sec gen Opsis (Nat Assoc for Educn, Trg and Support of Blind and Partially Sighted People) 1992–; *Recreations* bird-watching, music, especially opera, fly-fishing, practical study of wine; *Clubs* RAF (associate memb); *Style*— Gen Sir Antony Walker, KCB; ✉ c/o National Westminster Bank, PO Box 237, 72/74 High Street, Watford, Herts WD1 2BQ

WALKER, Archibald George Orr; s of George Edward Orr Walker, MBE, TD, QC (d 1973), of Newark Castle, Ayr, and Margaret Sybil, *née* Orr; *b* 14 Feb 1937; *Educ* Eton; *m* 11 Feb 1967, Fiona Mary Elizabeth, da of Alison Lyle Barr, MC (d 1970), of Brannochlie, Bridge of Weir; 1 s (James b 1968), 1 da (Rosamund b 1970); *Career* Nat Serv 2 Lt Coldstream Gds 1955–57; apprentice CA McClelland Moores Glasgow 1957–62, qualified CA 1962, dep chm Singer and Friedlander Ltd 1983–90 (joined 1968, dir 1973); chm: Ashbourne PLC 1993–, Premium Underwriting plc 1993–; non-exec dir: Clyde Petroleum plc 1973–88, Scot Nat Tst plc 1984; exec dir Singer and Friedlander Gp plc 1987–90, non-exec dir Singer and Friedlander Gp plc 1991–, memb Irvine Devpt Corp 1987; memb Queen's Body Gd for Scotland (The Royal Co of Archers) 1968; *Recreations* golf, tennis, stalking, shooting, skiing; *Clubs* Western (Glasgow), Prestwick Golf, The Hon Co of Edinburgh Golfers, Machrihanish Golf, Royal & Ancient Golf (St Andrews); *Style*— Archibald Walker, Esq; ✉ Newark Castle, Ayr KA7 4ED (☎ 01292 441587, fax 01292 445578)

WALKER, Brian Wilson; s of Arthur Harrison Walker (d 1960), and Eleanor Charlotte Mary, *née* Wilson; *b* 31 Oct 1930; *Educ* Heversham Sch Westmorland 1940–50, Leicester Coll of Technol, Manchester Univ, Oxford Univ (MA); *m* 5 April 1954, Nancy Margaret, da of Samuel Henry Gawith (d 1967); 1 s (Peter b 1955), 5 da (Clare b 1957, Dorcas b 1958, Grainne b 1964, Siobhan b 1967, Sarah b 1968); *Career* gen mangr Bridge Port Brass Ltd 1961–74, dir gen Oxfam 1974–83, dir Independent Cmmn on Int Humanitarian Issues 1983–85, pres Int Inst for Environment and Devpt 1985–89, dir Earthwatch Europe 1990–95; fndr chm New Ulster Movement 1969; chm: Band Aid/Live Aid 1985–91, SOS Sahel 1989–93, Governing Bd Dallan Sch 1996–; tstee: Cambodia Tst 1989–95, IIED 1989–95, Artisan Tst 1992–; *Recreations* gardening, walking, reading; *Clubs* Athenaeum; *Style*— Brian W Walker, Esq; ✉ Biskets, Church Hill, Arnside, Cumbria LA5 0DW

WALKER, Catherine Marguerite Marie-Therese; da of Remy Baheux and Agnes Lefèbvre; *Educ* Univs of Lille and Aix-en-Provence (Maitre-es-Lettres Philosophy); *m* 1969, John David Walker (decd); 2 da (Naomi Carolyn b 1971, Marianne Emily b 1972); *Career* fashion designer; dir Film Dept French Inst London 1970, memb Lecture Dept French Embassy 1971, dir and proprietor The Chelsea Design Co Ltd 1977–; winner: Br Fashion Awards Designer of the Year for Couture 1990–91, Br Fashion Awards Designer of the Year for Glamour 1991–92; *Style*— Mrs Catherine Walker; ✉ The Chelsea Design Co Ltd, 65 Sydney St, Chelsea, London SW3 6PX (☎ 0171 352 4626)

WALKER, (Alfred) Cecil; JP (1966), MP (UU) Belfast North (majority 9,625); s of Alfred George Walker, and Margaret Lucinda Walker (d 1983); *b* 17 Dec 1924; *Educ* Methodist Coll Belfast; *m* 1953, Ann May Joan; 2 s; *Career* contested (UU) NI Assembly 1973, MP (UU) Belfast N 1983– (also contested 1979); former sales mangr; *Recreations* cruising (motor yacht 'Talisman'); *Clubs* Down Cruising; *Style*— A Cecil Walker, Esq, JP, MP; ✉ 1 Wynnland Rd, Newtownabbey, Belfast BT36 6RZ, NI (☎ 01232 833463, fax 01232 844697)

WALKER, Chris Ian; s of Peter Earnest Walker, of Hatfield Peveral, Essex, and Kathleen Mary, *née* Partridge; *b* 11 June 1967; *Educ* Manningtree Sch, Colchester Tech Coll; *Career* professional squash player 1986–, capt England 1994– (capt current World Team Champions); currently ranked world no 5 and England no 1; rep England at under 12, 14, 16 and 19 level, finalist Br under 23 Closed 1988, semi-finalist Austrian Open 1989, rep England Euro Team Championships 1989, 1990, 1991, 1993, 1994, 1995 and 1996 (as capt), Euro champion 1992 and 1993, rep England World Team Championships 1992 (runners-up); winner: Jamaican Open 1989, Tenerife Open 1990, Euro Closed 1990, 1991/92 and 1992/93, Bundesliga Team Champions for Kiel Squash Club 1991, 1992 and 1993, Cairns Open 1991, Austrian Bundesliga Team Champions for S C Reuter 1991 and 1994, Northern Transvaal and Western Province Open 1992, SPA Belgium Classic 1993, Leekes Welsh Wizards Br Premier League champions 1993/94, NY Apawamis Open 1996, Irish Invitation 1996; finalist: PSA Super Series 1993, World Super series 1996; semi finalist: Spanish Open and Br Closed 1992, World Open 1994, Leekes Classic 1994, Tours French Open 1994, British Open 1994, Hong Kong Open 1995, Al Ahram Egypt Open 1996; quarter finalist: Austrian Open, Malaysian Open, Hong Kong Open (all 1991), Brazilian Classic 1993; runner-up: Br Profesionals' Championship 1993, Mahindra Indian Classic 1995–96 season; memb and vice pres Professional Squash Assoc (PSA) 1994–95, co-fndr Br Squash Professionals' Assoc (BSPA) 1993; *Recreations* golf, all sports, music; *Clubs* Dolphin Square, Cannons, Lexden Squash; *Style*— Chris Walker, Esq; ✉ 1 Nelson House, Dolphin Square, London SW1V 3NY (☎ and fax 0171 798 8155)

WALKER, Christine; *b* 1953; *Educ* Rhodesia, Ireland, Univ of Exeter; *Career* initial career in publishing, subsequently with Media Unit Benton & Bowles advtg agency 1976–85, fndr memb Ray Morgan & Partners ind media co 1985 (sold to Saatchi & Saatchi plc 1988); Zenith Media (Saatchi & Saatchi media arm): fndr head of bdcast rising to md, chief exec until 1997; dir: Meridian Outdoor Advertising Ltd 1993–, The National Film and Television School Ltd 1993–, Equinox Communications Ltd 1994–; Adwoman of the Year 1990, voted amongst UK's top business women (Options and Cosmopolitan magazines) 1992; memb: Cncl IPA, Women's Advtg Club of London, Mktg Gp of GB; *Style*— Ms Christine Walker

WALKER, Sir Colin John Shedlock; kt (1991), OBE (1981); s of Arthur John Walker (d 1982), of The Rookery, Hacheston, Woodbridge, Suffolk, and Olave Gertrude, *née* Mann (d 1982); *b* 7 Oct 1934; *Educ* St Edwards Sch Oxford, Royal Agric Coll Cirencester; *m* 26 Sept 1963, Wendy Elizabeth, da of John Hicks Ellis, of Long Stratton, Norfolk; 2 s; *Career* landowner, farmer, businessman; memb: Suffolk CC 1976–80, Central Blood Laboratories Authy 1985–93; chm: Nat Blood Authy 1993–, East Suffolk Health Authy 1986–87, East Anglian RHA 1987–94 (memb 1983–86), Harwich Harbour Bd 1987–, Bd of Govrs Orwell Park Sch 1991–; FRSA; *Recreations* shooting; *Clubs* Royal Over-Seas League; *Style*— Sir Colin Walker, OBE; ✉ Blomvyle Hall, Hacheston, Woodbridge, Suffolk IP13 ODY (☎ 01728 746756, fax 01728 747737); National Blood Authority, Oak House, Reeds Crescent, Watford, Herts WD1 1QH

WALKER, (Louis) David; MBE, TD; s of Louis Charles Walker, MBE (d 1981), and Margaret Ann, *née* Phillips (d 1988); *b* 4 July 1932; *Educ* Chipping Sodbury GS, Merchant Venturers' Coll, Univ of Bristol; *m* 1, 29 Feb 1964 (m dis 1995); 1 da (Sarah b 3 Jan 1965); m 2, 10 Aug 1996, Jane; *Career* Nat Serv 2 Lt RA 1953, Lt (later Capt) Royal Aust Artillery (CMF) 1956, Lt RA (TA) 1959, Capt 4 Bn Wiltshire Regt 1963–67; Union International Group Aust 1955–58 (London 1958–62), Marsh Harris Group Calne 1962–65, G Brazil & Co Ltd 1965–68, Unilever Group London 1968–71, dir Robert Wilson & Sons (1849) Ltd Scot 1971–78; McKey Food Service Ltd: md 1978–90, chm 1990–; chm: McKey Holdings (Europe) Ltd 1990–, McKey Wholesale Ltd 1991–92, Key Meats Ltd 1991–, Key Country Foods Ltd 1991–95, Key Country Bacon Ltd 1992–, Key Country Provisions Ltd 1992–; watch offr Sail Trg Assoc; BMMA: memb Cncl 1981–, pres 1994–; chm McDonald's Euro Meat Prods Quality Control Ctee, cmmr for Meat and Livestock Cmmn 1994–, memb Cncl, Exec and Food Policy & Resources Ctee Food and Drink Fedn 1995–; underwriter Lloyd's 1990–; Freeman and Liveryman: Worshipful Co of Tallow Chandlers 1963–, Worshipful Co of Butchers 1985; memb Royal Inst of Meat 1959; FRSH 1985 (MRSH 1959); *Recreations* sailing, game shooting, military history; *Clubs* RTYC, RSYC, RAYC; *Style*— L David Walker, Esq, MBE, TD; ✉ The Grange, Mollington, Banbury, Oxfordshire (☎ 01295 758657, fax 01295 758887); McKey Holdings (Europe) Ltd, Northfield Drive, Northfield, Milton Keynes MK15 ODF (☎ 01908 665431, fax 01908 665606, car 0850 217985/0850 936929, mobile 0385 736673)

WALKER, David; s of Francis Allen Walker (d 1994), of Tibshelf, Derbyshire, and Dorothy, *née* Buck; *b* 23 Oct 1947; *Educ* Tupton Hall GS Derbyshire, Hertford Coll Oxford (BA, 4 times soccer blue, capt Univ XI); *m* 1972, Elizabeth Grace, *née* Creswell; 2 s (Simon David, Mark Jonathan (twins) b 17 Aug 1975), 1 da (Kathryn Elizabeth b 25 Feb 1978); *Career* graduate trainee Marley Buildings Ltd 1970–72; E J Arnold & Son Ltd: area mangr 1972–74, product mangr 1974–77, merchandise mangr 1977–79, divnl dir 1979–84; Lex Volvo (subsid of Lex Service plc): gen mangr 1984–86, ops dir 1987–89, divnl dir 1990–94; md Hyundai Car (UK) Ltd (also subsid of Lex Service plc) 1994–; MCIM; *Recreations* walking, cycling, family; *Style*— David Walker, Esq; ✉ Hyundai Car (UK) Ltd, St Johns Place, Easton Street, High Wycombe, Bucks HP11 1NL (☎ 01494 428600, fax 01494 428 699)

WALKER, David; s of John Walker, and Irene, *née* Connor; *b* 8 Nov 1950; *Educ* Corby GS, St Catharine's Coll Cambridge (scholarship, Figgis Prize, sr scholarship, MA), Univ of Sussex/Ecole Pratique des Hautes Etudes (MA); *m* 9 Feb 1974, Karen; 1 s (Michael b 7 Dec 1982); *Career* sub ed, reporter then sr reporter Times Higher Education Supplement 1973–77, Harkness fell, congressional fell and visiting scholar Graduate Sch of Public Policy Univ of California Berkeley 1977–79, journalist Britain section The Economist 1979–81, local govt corr and leader writer The Times 1981–86, educn corr Daily Telegraph 1986–87, chief leader writer London Daily News 1987, public admin corr The Times 1987–90; BBC Radio News and Current Affairs: presenter Analysis 1988–, urban affrs corr 1993–95; currently leader writer The Independent; Industrial Soc Industrial Journalist of the Year (Radio) 1992, RICS Radio Journalist of the Year 1993; *Books* Media Made in California (1981), Municipal Empire (1983), Sources Close to the Prime Minister (1984), The Times Guide to the State (1995); *Recreations* piano, clarinet, running; *Clubs* United Oxford and Cambridge; *Style*— David Walker, Esq; ✉ 19 Lynton Grange, Fortis Green, London N2 9EU (☎ 0181 883 7880); The Independent, 1 Canada Square, Canary Wharf, London E14 (☎ 0171 293 2032)

WALKER, Prof David Alan; s of Cyril Walker (d 1990), and Dorothy, *née* Dobson; *b* 18 Aug 1928; *Educ* South Shields HS, Univ of Durham (BSc, PhD, DSc); *m* 7 July 1956, Shirley Wynne, da of William Chambers Mason (d 1980); 1 s (Rick b 1960), 1 da (Marney b 1957); *Career* RNAS 1946–48; ICI post-doctoral res fell 1956–58, reader in botany QMC London 1963–65 (lectr 1958–63, Charles F Kettering Res Fellowship 1962), reader in enzymology Imperial Coll London 1965–70; Univ of Sheffield: prof of biology 1970–84, dir of Res Inst for Photosynthesis 1984–88, prof of photosynthesis Robert Hill Inst 1988–93 (emeritus prof 1993–); corresponding memb American Soc of Plant Physiologists 1979; von Humboldt Prize Award 1991, Leverhulme Emeritus Award 1991; FIBiol 1971, FRS 1979, memb Academia Europaea 1994; *Books* Energy, Plants and Man (1979, rewritten edn 1992), C3 C4 Mechanisms and Cellular and Enviromental Regulation of Photosynthesis (1983), The Use of the Oxygen Electrode and Fluorescence Probes in Simple Measurements of Photosynthesis (1987); *Recreations* singing the Sheffield carols, walking, eating and drinking in good company, remoulding "this sorry scheme of things entire" in 'The Cross Keys', Thropton; *Style*— Prof David Walker, FRS; ✉ Animal and Plant Sciences, PO Box 601, The University of Sheffield, Sheffield S10 2UQ (☎ and fax 0114 230 5904, e-mail david@alegba.demon.co.uk)

WALKER, Sir David Alan; kt (1991); *b* 31 Dec 1939; *Educ* Chesterfield Sch, Queens' Coll Cambridge (MA); *m* 20 April 1963, Isobel, *née* Cooper; 1 s (Jonathan b 29 Jan 1968), 2 da (Elspeth b 4 June 1966, Penelope b 12 April 1970); *Career* HM Treasy: joined 1961, private sec to Jt Perm Sec 1964–66, seconded Staff IMF Washington 1970–73, asst sec 1973–77; Bank of England: chief advsr then chief Econ Intelligence Dept, asst dir 1980, exec dir fin and indust 1982–88; chm: Johnson Matthey Bankers Ltd (later Minories Finance Ltd) 1985–88, Securities and Investmts Bd 1988–May 1992; chm The Agricultural Mortgage Corp plc 1993–94, dep chm Lloyds Bank plc 1992–94, exec chm Morgan Stanley Group (Europe) plc Dec 1994–; non-exec dir: Bank of England until 1993, National Power Plc 1993–94, British Invisibles 1993–, Reuters Holdings plc 1994–; chm Financial Markets Gp LSE 1987–94, pt/t memb Bd CEGB 1987–89, nominated memb Cncl Lloyd's 1988–92; chm Exec Ctee Int Orgn of Securities Cmmns 1990–92;

govr: Henley Mgmnt Coll 1993–, LSE 1993–; memb Gp of Thirty 1993–; hon fell Queens' Coll Cambridge; *Recreations* music, long-distance walking; *Clubs* Reform; *Style*— Sir David Walker; ✉ Morgan Stanley Group (Europe) plc, 25 Cabot Square, Canary Wharf, London E14 4QA (☎ 0171 513 8000)

WALKER, HE David Critchlow; CMG (1993), CVO (1989); s of John Critchlow Walker, and Mary, *née* Cross (d 1988); *b* 9 Jan 1940; *Educ* Manchester GS, Univ of Cambridge (MA, DipEd); *m* 1965, Tineke, da of Harmen ven der Leek; 3 s (Daniel b 1966, Alexander 1967, Julian b 1970); *Career* temp asst lectr Univ of Manchester 1962–63, Cwlth Relations Office 1963–65, Embassy Mexico City 1965–68, Embassy Brussels 1968–70, FCO 1970–73, Embassy Washington 1973–78, FCO 1978–83, consul-gen Sao Paulo 1983–86, Embassy Madrid 1986–89, FCO 1989–92, high cmmr to Ghana and concurrently ambass to Togo 1992–96, high cmmr to Bangladesh 1996–; *Recreations* hill walking, gardening, music; *Style*— HE Mr David Walker, CMG, CVO; ✉ c/o FCO (Dhaka), King Charles Street, London SW1A 2AH

WALKER, David Marshall; s of Edward Alexander Walker, of Shaftesbury, Dorset, and Joyce Walker; *b* 31 July 1953; *Educ* Alleynes GS Stevenage, Univ of Nottingham (BSc), Thames Valley Coll (DMS); *m* June 1984, Diane Elizabeth, da of Norman Curbishley, of Gosforth, Cumbria; 1 s (Robin b 12 June 1990), 1 da (Chloe b 3 July 1987); *Career* British Airways 1976–88: joined as grad trainee, various appts Paris, Brussels and Bombay, subsequently UK based mktg planner, product mangr Far East, resource and mktg mangr N Atlantic, sr strategy mangr Far and Middle East, commercial mangr Gatwick (following merger with British Caledonian) until 1988; commercial dir Novair International 1988–89, gen mangr GB Airways 1989–90, mktg dir Network SouthEast 1990–93, dir Branded Products and Servs Post Office Counters Ltd 1993–; various mktg awards incl ISP Gold Award and BTA Corporate Campaign Award; *Recreations* flying (PPL), tennis, golf, reading; *Clubs* Royal Berkshire; *Style*— David Walker, Esq; ✉ Post Office Counters Ltd, Drury House, 1–16 Blackfriars Road, London SE1 9UA (☎ 0171 922 1166)

WALKER, Prof David Maxwell; CBE (1986), QC (Scot 1958); s of James Mitchell Walker (d 1934), of Bishopbriggs, Glasgow, and Mary Paton Colquhoun, *née* Irvine (d 1971); *b* 9 April 1920; *Educ* Glasgow HS, Univ of Glasgow (MA, LLB, LLD), Univ of Edinburgh (PhD, LLD), Univ of London (LLB, LLD); *m* 1 Sept 1954, Margaret Walker, OBE, da of Robert Knox (d 1970), of Brookfield, Renfrewshire; *Career* WWII: NCO Cameronians (Scottish Rifles) 1939, 2 Lt HLI 1940, transferred to RIASC 1941, served India 1941–42 and N Africa 1942–43, 8 Indian Div Italy 1943–46 (Bde Supply and Tport Offr HQ 21 Indian Inf Brig); advocate Scottish Bar 1948, in practice Scottish Bar 1948–53, called to the Bar Middle Temple 1957; Univ of Glasgow: prof of jurisprudence 1954–58, dean Faculty of Law 1956–59, regius prof of law 1958–90, convenor Sch of Law 1984–88, sr res fell 1990–; dir Scottish Univs' Law Inst 1974–80; chm: HS of Glasgow Educn Tst, Hamlyn Tst 1988–93; hon pres Friends of Glasgow Univ Library; Hon LLD Univ of Edinburgh 1974; FBA 1976, FRSE 1980, FSA (Scot) 1966, FRSA 1991; *Books* Law of Damages in Scotland (1955), The Scottish Legal System (1959, 7 edn 1997), Law of Delict in Scotland (1966, 2 edn 1981), Principles of Scottish Private Law (2 vols 1970, 4 edn 4 vols 1988–89), Law of Prescription and Limitation in Scotland (1973, 5 edn 1996), Law of Civil Remedies in Scotland (1974), Law of Contracts and Related Obligations in Scotland (1979, 3 edn 1994), The Oxford Companion to Law (1980), Stair's Institutions of the Law of Scotland (ed 1981), Stair Tercentenary Studies (ed 1981), The Scottish Jurists (1985), A Legal History of Scotland (vol 1, 1988, vol 2 1990, vol 3 1995, vol 4 1996); author of numerous papers in legal journals; *Recreations* book-collecting, Scottish history; *Clubs* Royal Scottish Automobile; *Style*— Prof David M Walker, CBE, QC, FRSE, FBA; ✉ 1 Beaumont Gate, Glasgow G12 9EE (☎ 0141 339 2802); Department of Private Law, University of Glasgow, Glasgow, Scotland G12 8QQ (☎ 0141 339 8855 ext 4556, telex 777070 UNIGLA)

WALKER, Prof David Morrison; OBE (1993); s of David Walker, of Dundee (d 1992), and Ada Margaret, *née* Morrison; *b* 31 Jan 1933; *Educ* Morgan Acad Dundee, Dundee Coll of Art (Dip in Art, post dip scholarship, post dip endorsement); *m* 12 June 1971, Averil Mary Stewart, da of William McIlwraith, of Coalhall, Ayr; 1 s (David William b 7 June 1973); *Career* asst Nat Buildings Record Edinburgh 1952–56, Nat Serv Movement Control Sch Royal Engrs 1956–58; Educn Dept: City of Glasgow 1958–59, City of Dundee 1959–61; SO: sr investigator Historic Buildings Dundee 1961–71 and Edinburgh 1971–75, allowance holder i/c Historic Buildings Inspectorate 1975–76, princ investigator Historic Buildings 1976–78, princ inspr Historic Buildings and assessor Historic Buildings Cncl for Scotland 1978–88, chief inspr 1988–93; assoc prof of art history Univ of St Andrews 1994–; occasional lectr: Univ of Glasgow 1965–, The Architectural Assoc 1978–81, Univ of Edinburgh 1988–, Heriot-Watt Univ 1991–; visiting prof Univ of Victoria Canada 1971; Arts Cncl Award 1969, Alice Davis Hitchcock Medallion 1970; Hon LLD Univ of Dundee 1988; Hon FRIAS 1982, FSA 1991, FRSE 1992; *Books* Architects and Architecture in Dundee (1955), 19th Century Mansions in the Dundee Area (1958), The Architecture of Glasgow (with Prof A H Gomme, 1968), The Buildings of Scotland, Edinburgh (with J Gifford and C McWilliam, 1984), Dundee: An Illustrated Introduction (with C McKean, 1984), Central Glasgow (with C McKean and F Walker, 1989), St Andrew's House: An Edinburgh Controversy, 1912–39 (1989), author of numerous articles; *Clubs* NEW, Edinburgh; *Style*— Prof David Walker, OBE, FRSE; ✉ 22 Inverleith Row, Edinburgh EH3 5QH

WALKER, Douglas Macdonald; s of James Walker (d 1963), of Edinburgh, and Mary Alice, *née* Barton (d 1974); *b* 4 Feb 1928; *Educ* George Heriot's Sch Edinburgh, Edinburgh & East of Scotland Coll of Agric (NDA); *m* 18 Aug 1951, Helen Grant, da of Andrew Bell (d 1979), of Edinburgh; 2 s (Ian b 1956, Duncan b 1958), 1 da (Morag b 1953); *Career* lectr in farm machinery Lancashire Farm Inst 1948–50, lectr in agric engrg Shuttleworth Coll 1950–53, asst export sales mangr David Brown Tractors Ltd 1953–64, md John Deere Ltd 1965–93; hon fell Shuttleworth Coll; visiting fell Cranfield Univ 1993–; past pres: Agric Engrs Assoc, Inst of Agric Engrs, Motor Industries Benevolent Fund; vice pres Inst of the Motor Indust 1989–92; tstee Douglas Bomford Meml Tst 1986; Freeman City of London 1974, Liveryman Worshipful Co of Farmers 1975; FIMgt, FIMI, MCIM, FIAgrE, FRAgrS; *Recreations* walking, travel, photography, collecting wine labels; *Style*— Douglas M Walker, Esq; ✉ Pentland House, 25 Hallfields, Edwalton, Nottingham NG12 4AA (☎ and fax 0115 923 3239)

WALKER, Duncan Roy; s of John Hamilton Walker (d 1978), of Uddingston, Lanarkshire, Scotland, and Sarah Carmichael, *née* Leitch; *b* 1 May 1942; *Educ* Bellshill Acad, Univ of Glasgow; *m* 12 June 1969, Mary Frances, da of Ambrose McNulty (d 1986), of Glasgow; 3 s (Jonathan Johar b 1972, Evan Alexander b 1974, Duncan Robert b 1982), 1 da (Katherine Anne b 1975); *Career* cardiothoracic surgn: Killingbeck Hosp, Gen Infirmary Leeds, St James Univ Hosp 1978–; tstee Children's Heart Surgery Fund; fell RCS; *Recreations* reading, bee keeping, gardening; *Style*— Duncan Walker, Esq; ✉ 15 North Grange Mount, Headingley, Leeds LS6 2BY (☎ 0113 278 3130); Lilypond Cottage, Quinish Estate, Dervaig, Mull; The Killingbeck Hospital, York Rd, Leeds LS14 6UQ (☎ 0113 264 8164)

WALKER, Ernest John Munro (Ernie); CBE (1995, OBE 1989); s of Ernest Walker (d 1944), and Anne, *née* Munro; *b* 20 July 1928; *Educ* Queen's Park Sch Glasgow; *m* 9 July 1955, Anne, da of Thomas Smith; 1 s (Alan b 9 Nov 1956), 2 da (Lesley b 17 Nov 1963, Allison b 17 Jan 1965); *Career* Scottish Football Assoc 1958–90 (sec 1977–90); chm: UEFA Stadia Ctee 1990–, Scottish Stadia Ctee 1990–, Scottish Football's Independent Review Cmmn 1995–; dir: Euro-Sporting 1985–, Nat Stadium Hampden Park; exec dir UEFA Eastern Euro Asst Bureau 1993–; chm Health Educn Bd for Scotland 1991–95, currently: vice pres Newspaper Press Fund, independent advsr to Sec of State for Scotland on appointments to public bodies; memb: Saltire Soc, Nat Tst for Scotland; *Recreations* watching football and international rugby, golf, fishing, walking, music; *Clubs* Royal Over-Seas League, Haggs Castle Golf (capt 1977), Glasgow Gailes Golf, Boat of Garten Golf, Poloc Cricket; *Style*— Ernie Walker, Esq, CBE; ✉ 11/12 Burrell Court, 120 St Andrew's Drive, Glasgow G41 4RB (☎ 0141 427 5294, fax 0141 427 5722)

WALKER, Geoffrey Hurst; s of Raymond Bennet Walker, of Perth, Scotland, and Joan Edith Agnes, *née* Michie; *b* 7 Feb 1956; *Educ* Bell Baxter HS Cupar Fife, Univ of Edinburgh (BCom); *m* 1995, Rosaleen, da of John Fay (d 1992); *Career* audit mangr Arthur Young 1978–87; fin dir: Serif Cowells plc 1987–89, DPS Typecraft Ltd 1990–; Liveryman Worshipful Co of Gold & Silver Wyre Drawers; CA 1981; *Recreations* sailing, badminton, philately; *Style*— Geoffrey Walker, Esq; ✉ 15 Colburn Avenue, Caterham, Surrey CR3 6HW (☎ 01883 343576, fax 01883 341081); Acorn House, Great Oaks, Basildon, Essex SS14 1AH (☎ 01268 523471, fax 01268 281090)

WALKER, George Alfred; s of William James Walker, and Ellen, *née* Page; *b* 14 April 1929; *m* 1957, Jean Maureen, *née* Hatton; 1 s (Jason), 2 da (Sarah (Marchioness of Milford Haven), Romla); *Career* chief exec The Brent Walker Group PLC (leisure gp) 1981–92, chief exec Walkers International 1992–; *Recreations* skiing, climbing, sailing; *Clubs* RAC; *Style*— George Walker, Esq; ✉ Pell House, High Road, Fobbing, Essex SS17 9JJ

WALKER, Sir Gervas George; kt (1979), JP (Bristol 1969), DL (Avon 1982); s of Harry Walker; *b* 12 Sept 1920; *Educ* Monmouth Sch; *m* 1944, Eileen, *née* Maxwell; 2 s; *Career* formerly: chm Bristol Avon River Authy, memb SW Regnl Planning Cncl, ldr and oppn ldr Bristol City Cncl, chm and ldr Avon CC 1973–81, chm Bristol Cons Assoc 1975–79 and Assoc of CCs 1979–81 (vice chm 1978–79); *Style*— Sir Gervas Walker, JP, DL; ✉ Bulverton Well Farm, Sidmouth, Devon EX10 9DW (☎ 01395 516902)

WALKER, Graham Edwards; s of Eric Walker, of North Wales, and Mary, *née* Edwards; *b* 6 July 1939; *Educ* Wallasey GS; *m* Annabel; 2 s (Max b 1 Aug 1966, Jago b 20 Aug 1972), 1 da (Abbey b 15 Feb 1964); *Career* yachtsman; memb Br Admiral's Cup team 1983, 1985, 1987, 1989 and 1993 (capt 1983, 1987 and 1993), capt Br Southern Cross team 1983, world 3/4 ton champion 1986, chm Br Americas Cup challenge 1986–87; dir: Argyll Group 1983–89, Broad Street Group 1989–90; currently chm: Software City PLC, Europa Aviation, Raleigh Int Tst; *Recreations* yachting, shooting, vintage cars; *Clubs* Crusade Yacht, Royal Thames, Royal Lymington, NBFC (RU), RAC, BDC; *Style*— Graham Walker, Esq; ✉ 14 Lincoln Street, London SW3 2TP (☎ 0171 823 7455, fax 0171 823 7454)

WALKER, Graham Peter; s of John Henry Walker, of Gidea Park, Essex, and Edna May, *née* Best; *b* 17 June 1948; *Educ* Royal Liberty Sch Gidea Park Essex, The London Film Sch (Dip); *m* 23 April 1977, Josephine Mary, da of Hywel Williams (d 1988), of Birmingham; 1 step s (Simon b 22 May 1968), 1 s (Timothy b 7 May 1992); *Career* film editor; BBC film ed 1976–84 (progs incl: Play for Today, Target, Shoestring, Great River Journeys), BBC supervising film ed 1984–86 (progs incl: Bergerac, Miss Marple, Hard Travelling), freelance feature film ed 1986– (work incl: The Fourth Protocol, The Josephine Baker Story, The Last of the Finest (aka Blue Heat), Freefall, The Infiltrator, Deadly Voyage); steward Assoc of Cinematograph and TV Technicians 1982–86; memb Guild of Br Film Eds 1987; CEBA Award 1992; *Recreations* cinema and travel; *Style*— Graham Walker, Esq; ✉ 64 Chiltern View Rd, Uxbridge, Middx UB8 2PF (☎ 01895 230589)

WALKER, Rt Hon Sir Harold; kt (1992), PC (1979), MP (Lab) Doncaster Central (majority 10,682); s of Harold Walker, and Phyllis Walker; *b* 12 July 1927; *Educ* Manchester Coll of Technol; *m* 1, 1956, Barbara (decd), da of Cecil Hague; 1 da; *m* 2, 1984, Mary Griffin; *Career* Fleet Air Arm 1946–48; MP (Lab): Doncaster 1964–83, Doncaster Central 1983–; asst govt whip 1967, Parly under sec of state for employment and productivity 1968–70, oppn front bench spokesman on industl rels 1970–74, Parly under sec of state for employment 1974–76, min of state 1976–79, oppn spokesman 1979–83; chm Ways and Means Ctee and dep speaker 1983–92; former chm: Speaker's Panel of Chairmen, Standing Orders Ctee, Ct of Referees; *Style*— The Rt Hon Sir Harold Walker, MP; ✉ House of Commons, London SW1A 0AA

WALKER, Sir Harold Berners; KCMG (1991); s of Adm Sir Harold Walker, KCB, RN (d 1975), and Olive Marjory, *née* Berners (d 1991); *b* 19 Oct 1932; *Educ* Winchester, Univ of Oxford (MA); *m* 15 Oct 1960, Jane, da of late Capt C J L Bittleston, CBE, DSC, RN; 2 da (Caroline Jane b 7 Sept 1961, Katherine Baker b 26 Jan 1965), 1 s (Christopher Harold b 3 Sept 1963); *Career* HM Dip Serv 1955–92; served FO, ME Centre for Arab Studies, Dubai, Cairo, Damascus, Washington, Jedda, FCO; ambassador: to Bahrain 1979–81, UAE 1981–86, Ethiopia 1986–89, Iraq 1990–91; memb Cwlth War Graves Cmmn 1992–, pres Friends of the Imperial War Museum 1992–, chm Bahrain Soc 1993–, vice chm Jerusalem and the East Mission Tst 1994–; chm CARE International UK 1994–; memb Corp Woking Sixth Form Coll 1996–; assoc fell RUSI 1992–; *Clubs* United Oxford and Cambridge University; *Style*— Sir Harold Walker, KCMG; ✉ Turaco House, Hook Heath Avenue, Woking, Surrey GU22 0HX; CARE International UK, 36–38 Southampton Street, London WC2E 7AF (☎ 0171 379 5247, fax 0171 379 0543)

WALKER, Maj Sir Hugh Ronald; 4 Bt (UK 1906), of Pembroke House, City of Dublin; s of Maj Sir Cecil Edward Walker, 3 Bt, DSO, MC (d 1964), and Violet, *née* McMaster; *b* 13 Dec 1925; *Educ* Wellington; *m* 1971, Norna, da of Lt Cdr R D Baird; 2 s (Robert Cecil, Roy Edward b 10 Aug 1977); *Heir* s, Robert Cecil Walker, b 26 Sept 1974; *Career* Maj RA, ret; memb Assoc of Supervisory and Exec Engrs; *Style*— Maj Sir Hugh Walker, Bt; ✉ Ballinamona Stud, Hospital, Killmallock, Co Limerick, Republic of Ireland (☎ 00 353 61 385106); c/o Lloyds Bank Ltd, Somerton, Somerset

WALKER, Dr Isobel Deda; da of Dr Thomas Alfred Christie, of Auchterarder, Perthshire, Scotland, and Edith Anderson, *née* Young; *b* 4 Oct 1944; *Educ* Jordanhill Coll Sch Glasgow, Univ of Glasgow (MB, ChB, MD); *m* 13 April 1966, Dr Colin Alexander Walker; 2 s (Jason b 1969, Lewis b 1975), 3 da (Nicola b 1972, Emily b 1979, Abigail b 1982); *Career* conslt haematologist Gtr Glasgow Health Bd 1978–, hon clinical sr lectr Univ of Glasgow 1978–; sec Br Soc for Haematology; chm: Steering Ctee Nat External Quality Assur Scheme for Blood Coagulation Testing, Haemostasis and Thrombosis Task Force Br Soc for Haematology; FRCPath 1984, FRCPEd 1985; *Recreations* French language, needlework; *Style*— Dr Isobel Walker; ✉ Department of Haematology, Glasgow Royal Infirmary, Castle St, Glasgow G4 0SF (☎ 0141 552 5692, fax 0141 211 4919)

WALKER, Rev Dr James Bernard; s of Rev Dr Robert Bernard William Walker, of Edinburgh, and Grace Brownlee, *née* Torrance; *b* 7 May 1946; *Educ* Hamilton Acad Lanarkshire, Univ of Edinburgh (MA, BD), Merton Coll Oxford (DPhil); *m* 18 Aug 1972, Sheila Mary, da of Alexander Ballantyne Easton (d 1948), of Ilford, London; 3 s (Colin Alexander b 1975, Alastair Robert b 1975, Peter Donald b 1978); *Career* ordained Church of Scotland 1975, assoc min Mid Craigie Parish Church (with Wallacetown) Dundee 1975–78, min Old and St Paul's Parish Church Galashiels 1978–87, princ Queen's Theol Coll Birmingham 1987–93, chaplain St Andrew's Univ 1993–; *Books* Israel - Covenant and Land (1986); *Recreations* hill walking, golf, swimming; *Style*— The Rev Dr James B Walker; ✉ The Chaplaincy Centre, 3A St Mary's Place, St Andrews, Fife KY16 9UY (☎ 01334 462865, fax 01334 462697)

WALKER, Janet Sheila; da of David Walker, of Chew Magna, Bristol, and Sheila, *née* Rapps; *b* 21 April 1953; *Educ* Keynsham GS, Somerville Coll Oxford (MA PPE), L'Institut des Hautes Études Internationales Univ of Nice (graduated in Politics and Economics); *Career* Price Waterhouse 1976–80 (qualified ACA), chief accountant Handmade Films 1980–81, cost controller Channel 4 1981–82, head of prog fin Thames TV 1982–84, treas IPPA (predecessor of PACT) 1984–87, fin dir British Screen Finance 1987–88, dep dir of fin Channel 4 1988–94 (concurrently UK rep EURIMAGES film funding orgn), fin controller for regnl broadcasting BBC 1994–96, fin dir Granada Media Group 1996–; hon lectr Sch of Media Studies Univ of Stirling; fndr dir Women in Film and TV; ACA 1979, MInstD 1996; *Style*— Miss Janet Walker; ✉ Granada Media Group, The London Television Centre, Upper Ground, London SE1 9LT (☎ 0171 261 3549, fax 0171 261 3721)

WALKER, Jeremy; s of Raymond St John (Henry) Walker (d 1980), and Mary, *née* Dudley; *b* 12 July 1949; *Educ* Brentwood Sch, Univ of Birmingham (BA, Barber Prize for local history); *m* 1968, June, da of Robert Lockhart; 2 s (Patrick b 1968, Toby b 1974), 1 da (Tamsin b 1969); *Career* civil servant; admin trainee Dept of Employment 1971–73, private sec to chm MSC 1974–76, princ Health & Safety Executive 1976–77, Economic Secretariat Cabinet Office 1977–79, princ Employment Service MSC 1979–82, asst sec Australian Dept of Employment & Indust Rels Canberra 1982–84, regnl employment mangr for Yorks & Humberside MSC 1984–86, head of community progs and new job trg scheme MSC 1986–88, regnl dir Yorks & Humberside Dept of Employment 1988–94 (ldr Leeds/Bradford City Action Team 1990–94), regnl dir Govt Office for Yorkshire and the Humber 1994–; *Recreations* gardening, hobby farming; *Style*— Jeremy Walker, Esq; ✉ Government Office for Yorkshire and the Humber, City House, New Station Street, Leeds LS1 4US (☎ 0113 283 5200, fax 0113 244 9313)

WALKER, His Hon John David; DL (East Yorkshire); s of late Lawrence Cecil Walker, and late Jessie Walker; *b* 13 March 1924; *Educ* Oundle, Univ of Cambridge (MA); *m* 1954, Elizabeth Mary Emma, da of late Victor William Owbridge, of Yorks; 1 s (Nicholas b 1958), 2 da (Belinda b 1955, Emma b 1962); *Career* served WWII Capt Frontier Force Rifles IA 1942–47; called to the Bar Middle Temple 1951, recorder 1972; circuit judge 1972–89 (currently sits as dep circuit judge); pres Mental Health Review Tbnls 1986–96; judicial memb Parole Bd 1992–95; *Recreations* shooting, fishing; *Clubs* Lansdowne; *Style*— His Hon John Walker, DL; ✉ Arden House, North Bar Without, Beverley, East Yorkshire HU17 7AG

WALKER, Brig (Edward) John Worley; OBE (1987); s of Air Cdre SG Walker, CB, OBE (d 1975) of Bradford-on-Avon, Wilts, and Laura Mabel Mary, *née* Gorton (d 1992); *b* 5 Dec 1941; *Educ* Dulwich, RMA Sandhurst; *m* 12 June 1965, Susan Vera Anthea, da of Air Vice-Marshal Sir Thomas Shirley, KBE, CB (d 1983), and Lady Vera Shirley, *née* Overton, of Wellingore, Lincolnshire; 3 da (Joanna b 1 April 1967, Tamsin b 28 Oct 1968, Rebecca b 10 March 1972); *Career* cmmnd The Duke of Wellington's Regt 1962; regtl duty 1962–67, ADC to Dep Supreme Allied Cdr Europe 1967–69, Staff Coll Toronto 1975–76, staff appointments in HQ NI, HQ UKLF and MOD, CO Duke of Wellington's Regt 1984–87, Cdr 49 Inf Bde 1990–92; dir Lincolnshire Homes Orders St John Tst 1992–; dir Br Nordic Ski Team: Sarajevo 1984, Calagary 1988; memb Br Ski Fedn Nordic Biathlon Ctee, vice pres Lincolnshire and S Humberside Royal Br Legion 1992, memb Army Benevolent Fund Ctee E Midlands Region 1992, pres Normandy Veterans' Assoc Lincoln Branch 1994; Offr of Merit Br Assoc Sovereign Mil Order of Malta 1994; FIMgt 1988, memb Br Olympic Assoc; *Recreations* golf, rugby football, game shooting; *Clubs* Army & Navy, St James's, Blankney Golf; *Style*— Brig John Walker, OBE; ✉ c/o Royal Bank of Scotland, Lincoln Branch, PO Box 50, Stonebow Centre, Lincoln LN2 1DQ (☎ 01522 536355, fax 01522 510794)

WALKER, Julian Fortay; CMG (1982), MBE (1960); s of Kenneth MacFarlane Walker (d 1963), of W Sussex, and Eileen Marjorie Walker, later Mrs Dahlberg (d 1983); *b* 7 May 1929; *Educ* Harvey Sch NY, Stowe, Bryanston, Univ of Cambridge (MA); *m* 1983 (m dis 1995) Virginia Anne (Mrs Austin), da of Michael Stevens, of Lechdlade, Glos; 3 step da (Rachel b 17 Feb 1969, Kathryn b 6 Oct 1970, Elizabeth b 21 Oct 1972); *Career* Nat Serv RN 1947–49; undergraduate Univ of Cambridge 1949–52, Univ of London Sch of African and Oriental Studies 1952; Foreign Serv: MECAS 1953, asst political agent Trucial States 1953–55, 3 then 2 sec Bahrain 1955–57, FCO and frontier settlement Oman 1957–60, 2 then 1 sec Oslo 1960–63, News Dept spokesman FCO 1963–67, 1 sec Baghdad 1967, 1 sec Rabat Morocco 1967–69, FCO 1969–71, political agent Dubai Trucial States 1971, consul gen and cnsllr HM Embassy Dubai United Arab Emirates 1971–72, sabbatical leave Univ of Cambridge 1972–73, political advsr and head of chancery Br Mil Govt Berlin 1973–76, NI Office Stormont Castle 1976–77, dir MECAS 1977–78, ambass to Arab Repub Yemen and Repub of Jibuti 1979–84, ambass to Qatar 1984–87, Res Dept FCO 1987–93, special advsr (Syria and Iraq), ret 1993; Order of Isthqaq 1 Class (Qatar) 1985; *Publications* Boundaries of the UAE (Archive Editions, ed, 1994); *Recreations* sailing and sailboarding, music, gardening, tennis; *Style*— Julian Walker, Esq, CMG, MBE; ✉ 32 Corney Road, Chiswick, London W4 2RA (☎ 0181 995 3811)

WALKER, Malcolm Conrad; CBE (1995); s of Willie Walker (d 1960), and Ethel Mary, *née* Ellam (d 1987); *b* 11 Feb 1946; *Educ* Mirfield GS; *m* 4 Oct 1969, (Nest) Rhianydd, da of Benjamin Jones (d 1976); 3 c; *Career* trainee mangr F W Woolworth & Co 1964–71, jt fndr Iceland Frozen Foods plc 1970– (currently chm and chief exec); *Recreations* stalking, skiing, family, home; *Style*— Malcolm Walker, Esq, CBE; ✉ Iceland Frozen Foods Plc, Second Ave, Deeside Industrial Park, Deeside, Clwyd CH5 2NW (☎ 01244 830100, fax 01244 814531, telex 61321)

WALKER, Marjorie G; da of Girsh L Myers, of Miami Beach, Florida, and Miriam, *née* Goldstien, of Philadelphia; *b* 22 Dec 1938; *Educ* Temple Univ (BS), Univ of Miami (MSc, PhD); *m* (m dis); 1 s (Michael b 9 Aug 1967); *Career* writer; lectr Open Univ 1982–87; ed Newsletter New Art at Tate Gallery 1989– (patron 1985–); bd memb: Patrons of New Art Tate Gallery, Br-American Arts Assoc, Coral Atkins Children's Home; *Books* A Parent's Guide to Child Development - Birth to Adolescence (with Dr Richard Lansdown, 1991); *Clubs* Contemporary Art Soc, Nat Art Collectors Funds, Goucho's; *Style*— Ms Marjorie Walker; ✉ 7 Conway Street, London W1P 5HD (☎ 0171 637 8804)

WALKER, Martin Alan; s of Thomas Martin Walker, of Beaconsfield, Bucks, and Dorothy, *née* McNeil; *b* 23 Jan 1947; *Educ* Queen Elizabeth GS Darlington, Harrow Co GS, Balliol Coll Oxford (Brackenbury scholar, BA), Harvard Univ (Harkness fell), American Political Science Assoc (Congressional fell); *m* 1978, Julia, da of Graham Arthur Watson; 2 da (Kate Emily b 1981, Fanny Sophia b 1985); *Career* flying scholarship RAF 1965 (private pilots licence); journalist and author; reporter: The Star Johannesburg 1966, News/Check Johannesburg 1966–67; The Guardian: reporter Manchester 1971–72, reporter London 1972–, Moscow corr 1983–88, US Bureau chief 1988–; regular bdcaster for BBC Radio and TV, commentator on CNN, CBC, C-SPAN and CBS; book reviewer: Literary Review, Washington Post Book World, Philadelphia Inquirer, London Review of Books; guest lectr (1989–90): Univ of Moscow, Univ of Pittsburgh, Univ of Toronto, Columbia Univ NY, Canadian Inst of Int Affrs; assoc ed Demokratizatsiya Jl of Soviet Democratisation Moscow Univ; Reporter of the Year British Press Awards 1987, Foreign Corr of the Year Krokodil Press Awards Moscow 1988; memb NUJ 1971–, White House Correspondent's Assoc; *Books* non-fiction: The National Front (1977), Daily Sketches (1978), Powers of the Press (1981), The Waking Giant - Gorbachev's Soviet Union (1986), Martin Walker's Russia (1989), Independent Traveller's Guide to the Soviet Union (1989), The Cold War (1993); fiction: The Infiltrator (1978), A Mercenary Calling (1981), The Eastern Question (1983); *Recreations* downhill and cross country skiing, travel, opera, wine; *Style*— Martin Walker, Esq; ✉ US Bureau Chief, c/o The Guardian, 119 Farringdon Road, London EC1R 3ER

WALKER, Sir (Charles) Michael; GCMG (1976, KCMG 1963, CMG 1960); s of Col Charles William Garne Walker, CMG, DSO (d 1974), and Dorothy Frances (d 1965), da of F Hughes-Gibb, JP, of Tarrant Gunville, Dorset; *b* 22 Nov 1916; *Educ* Charterhouse, New Coll Oxford; *m* 1945, Enid Dorothy, da of William Alexander McAdam, CMG (d 1961); 1 s, 1 da (Lady Couper); *Career* served WWII RA (attained rank of Lt-Col); clerk House of Lords 1939, served Dominions Office 1947, 1 sec UK Embassy Washington DC 1949–51, High Cmmn New Delhi and Calcutta 1952–55, CRO 1955–58, IDC 1958, asst under sec CRO 1959–62, high cmmr Ceylon 1962–65 and concurrently ambass Maldives 1965, high cmmr Malaysia 1966–71, perm sec Overseas Devpt Admin 1971–73, high cmmr India 1974–76; chm: Cwlth Scholarship Cmmn UK 1977–87, Festival of India Tst 1980–83; *Style*— Sir Michael Walker, GCMG; ✉ Herongate House, West Chiltington Common, Pulborough, W Sussex (☎ 0179 881 3473)

WALKER, Michael; s of Wilfred Arthur Walker, of Sudbury, Suffolk, and Molly, *née* Castle; *b* 1 Nov 1948; *Educ* Thomas Lethaby Sch London; *m* 6 June 1970, Jacqueline Margaret, da of John Alexander Bowen, of Witham, Essex; 1 s (Christopher Andrew James b 1984), 2 da (Sarah Jane b 1973, Lucy Anne b 1975); *Career* banker; Clive Discount Company Ltd: md 1985–92, chief exec 1992–; dir: PIC Holdings Ltd 1992–, PRIcoa Realty Group Ltd; chm Clive Agency Bond Broking Ltd; FCIB, FRSA; *Recreations* fishing, clay shooting, photography; *Style*— Michael Walker, Esq; ✉ Clive Discount Co Ltd, Cannon Bridge, 25 Dowgate Hill, London EC4R 2AT (☎ 0171 283 9111, fax 0171 626 1213)

WALKER, Michael Giles Neish; CBE (1985); s of Sir William Giles Newsom Walker (d 1989), of Pitlair, Cupar, Fife, and Mildred Brenda, *née* Nairn (d 1983); *b* 28 Aug 1933; *Educ* Shrewsbury, St John's Coll Cambridge (MA); *m* 27 Jan 1960, Margaret Ruby, da of Lt-Col John D Hills, MC (d 1975), of Chirk, North Wales; 2 s (Simon Giles David b 1961, Geordie Michael b 1966), 1 da (Nicola Margaret (Mrs Jeremy Sturgess) b 1965); *Career* chm Sidlaw Group plc 1988– (joined 1957, chief exec 1976–88); non-exec dir: Scottish Hydro-Electric plc 1982–, Dunedin Smaller Companies Investment Trust PLC 1982–, Ivory + Sime Smaller Companies Trust plc 1990– (chm 1992); *Clubs* Cavalry & Guards, Royal & Ancient, Hon Co of Edinburgh Golfers; *Style*— Michael Walker, Esq, CBE; ✉ Sidlaw Group plc, Keith House, South Gyle, Edinburgh EH12 9DQ (☎ 0131 317 2600, fax 0131 317 2620)

WALKER, Michael Stewart Gordon (Mike); s of Archibald Gordon Walker (d 1987), and Irene Beatrice Walker (d 1983); *b* 28 Nov 1945; *Educ* Caversham Secdy Modern Sch Reading; *m* 1 Oct 1966, Jacqueline Mary, da of Frederick Francis Watkins; 1 da (Ursula Fiona b 20 Feb 1970), 2 s (Ian Michael b 31 Oct 1971, David b 16 March 1978); *Career* professional football manager; former goalkeeper: Reading 1961–64, 6 appearances Shrewsbury Town 1964–66, 60 appearances York City 1966–68, 137 appearances Watford 1968–72 (Div 3 champions), 1 appearance on loan Charlton Athletic 1972, 451 appearances Colchester Utd 1973–82 (promotion to Div 3); 4 Wales under 23 caps, memb full squad 8 times; manager: Colchester Utd 1986–87 (coach 1982–85), Norwich City 1992–94 (reserve team manager 1987–92), Everton Jan-Nov 1994, rejoined Norwich City 1996; Colchester Bells Manager of the Month Oct 1987, Barclays Manager of the Month Aug and Sept 1992, Carling Manager of the Month 1993/94; other sporting achievements: cricket rep Reading Schs and Berks, Berks & Oxon co teams, winner co triple jump medal for Berks; *Recreations* travel, some music, some reading, dining out; *Style*— Mike Walker, Esq; ✉ The Tithe Barn, Framingham Earl Road, Yelverton, Norwich, Norfolk NR14 7PD (☎ and fax 01508 492531)

WALKER, Hon Sir Miles Rawstron; kt (1997), CBE (1991), MHK (1976–); s of George Denis Walker (d 1970), and Alice, *née* Whittaker; *b* 13 Nov 1940; *Educ* Castle Rushen HS, Shropshire Coll of Agric; *m* 11 Oct 1966, Mary Lilian, da of Thomas Edward Cowell (d 1988); 1 s (Mark), 1 da (Claire); *Career* co dir gen farming and retail dairy trade; memb: House of Keys Rushen Isle of Man 1976– (memb Treasy Dept 1996–), Bd of Agric 1976–81, Bd of Local Govt 1976–81; chm Broadcasting Cmmn 1979–81; Local Govt Bd: chm 1981–86, memb Exec Cncl (now Cncl of Ministers) 1981–, memb Assessment Bd 1983–86; vice chm IOM PO 1984–86, chief min IOM Govt 1986–96; LLD (hc) Univ of Liverpool 1994; *Style*— The Hon Sir Miles Walker, CBE, MHK; ✉ Magher Feailley, Main Road, Colby, Isle of Man (☎ 01624 833728); Government Office, Douglas, Isle of Man

WALKER, Prof Nigel David; CBE; s of David Boughton Walker (d 1968), and Violet, *née* Johnson (d 1977); *b* 6 Aug 1917; *Educ* Tientsin GS, Edinburgh Acad, ChCh Oxford (hon scholar); *m* 1939, Sheila Margaret, da of J G Johnston (d 1938); 1 da (Valerie Joan (Dr O'Farrell) b 1942); *Career* Scottish Office 1939, Cameron Highlanders and Lovat's Scouts Br Army 1940–46 (wounded Appenines), demobbed as Staff Capt Allied Force HQ Italy; princ then asst sec Scottish Office (private sec to Earl of Home when Minister of State) 1946–61, reader in criminology Oxford 1961–73, professorial fell Nuffield Coll Oxford 1961–73; visiting prof: Berkeley California 1965, Yale 1973; dir Cambridge Inst of Criminology 1973–84, professorial fell King's Coll Cambridge 1973–84; prof of criminology Cambridge 1973–84, visiting prof: Stockholm 1975, Cape Town 1984; chm Home Secs Advsy Cncl on Probation and Aftercare 1970–73; pres: Nat Assoc of Probation Offrs 1980–83, Br Soc of Criminology 1984–87; DLitt Oxford 1970; Hon LLD: Leicester 1973, Edinburgh 1983; Hon FRCPsych 1987; *Books* Short History of Psychotherapy (1957), Morale in the Civil Service (1961), Crime and Punishment in Britain (1965), Sentencing in a Rational Society (1969), Crime and Insanity in England (2 vols, 1968, 1973), Crimes, Courts and Figures (1971), Behaviour and Misbehaviour (1975), Punishment, Danger and Stigma (1980), Sentencing Theory Law and Practice (1986, 2 edn 1996), Public Attitudes to Sentencing (jtly, 1987), Crime and Criminology (1988), Why Punish? (1991), Dangerous People (1996); *Recreations* chess, walking; *Clubs* RSM; *Style*— Prof Nigel Walker, CBE; ✉ 14A Chaucer Rd, Cambridge CB2 2EB

WALKER, Nigel Keith; s of Frank George Walker, and Joyce Merle, *née* Foster; *b* 15 June 1963; *Educ* Rumney HS; *m* Mary; 2 da (Rebecca b Aug 1993, Eleanor b March 1995); *Career* athlete; memb Cardiff Athletics Club; honours at 110m hurdles: UK champion 1983, AAA champion 1984, semi-finalist Olympic Games LA 1984, Bronze medal Euro Indoor Championships France and World Indoor Championships USA 1987; 26 UK int appearances 1983–92 (jr int 1980–82); ret from athletics July 1992; debut for Cardiff RFC Sept 1992, debut for Wales Feb 1993 v Ireland; civil servant 1982–93, devpt offr Sports Cncl for Wales 1993– (pt/t 1996–), fitness conslt Cardiff RFC 1996–, presenter HTV 1996–; *Recreations* DIY, broadcasting, journalism; *Style*— Nigel Walker, Esq; ✉ c/o Walker & Walker Management Services, Cardiff Athletic Club, Westgate Street, Cardiff

WALKER, Sir (Baldwin) Patrick; 4 Bt (UK 1856), of Oakley House, Suffolk; also hereditary Pasha of the Ottoman Empire; s of late Cdr Baldwin Charles Walker (d 1927; himself s of Sir Francis Elliot Walker, 3 Bt (d 1928), in his turn 2 surviving s of Adm Sir Baldwin Wake Walker, 1 Bt, KCB, who was Comptroller of the (Royal) Navy and sometime Adm in the Turkish service, whereby he was cr a Pasha), and Mary, *née* Barnett (d 1991); *b* 10 Sept 1924; *Educ* Gordonstoun; *m* 1, 1948 (m dis 1954), Joy Yvonne, da of Sir Arrol Moir, 2 Bt (d 1957); m 2, 1954, Sandra Stewart; m 3, 1966, Rosemary

Ann, da of late Henry Hollingdrake; 1 s, 1 da; m 4, 1980, Vanessa Joyce, da of Dr Alan Clay; *Heir* s, Christopher Robert Baldwin, b 25 Oct 1969; *Career* served RN 1942–58; Planned Music Ltd 1958–62, emigrated to S Africa 1962, with Findlays 1962–64, Uniswa Insurance 1964–68, farmer 1969–74, various solar energy cos 1975–83, Pennypinchers 1983–87, propr PW Marketing (mktg energy, space and money saving) 1988–; *Style*— Sir Patrick Walker, Bt; ✉ 5 Voortrekker Road, Blanco 6531, South Africa

WALKER, Dr Paul Crawford; JP; s of Dr Joseph Viccars Walker (d 1986), of Northants, and Mary Tilley, *née* Crawford (d 1984); *b* 9 Dec 1940; *Educ* Queen Elizabeth GS Darlington, Downing Coll Cambridge (MA, MB BChir); *m* 1962, Barbara Georgina, da of Albert Edward Bliss, of Cambridgeshire; 3 da (Kate, Victoria, Caroline); *Career* Capt RAMC(V) 1975–78; area med offr Wakefield Area Health Authority 1976–77, regnl med offr NE Thames RHA 1977–85, gen mangr Frenchay Health Authority 1985–88, hon conslt in community med Bristol and Weston Health Authy 1988–89, dir public health Norwich Health Authy 1989–93, dir Centre for Health Policy Res Univ of E Anglia 1990–93, sr lectr Univ of Wales Coll of Med 1993–; dir Independent Public Health 1993–; chm CAER Consortium 1985–89; memb: NHS Computer Policy Ctee 1984–85, Advsy Ctee on Misuse of Drugs 1984–87, Exec Ctee Gtr London Alcohol Advsy Service 1978–85, Mgmnt Ctee Kings Fund Centre 1980–84; Essex Cmmn for the Peace 1980–85, Avon Cmmn for the Peace 1985–89 and 1995–; vice chm Professional Advsy Gp NHSTA, 1987–88; hon sr lectr London Sch of Hygiene and Tropical Medicine 1983–85, visiting prof QMC London 1985, hon sr lectr Univ of E Anglia 1990–93, med assessor Independent Tbnl Serv 1996–; cncllr City and County of Bristol 1995–; *Recreations* railway history, anthropology; *Clubs* Athenaeum; *Style*— Dr Paul Walker, JP; ✉ Chagford, 8 Church Avenue, Stoke Bishop, Bristol BS9 1LD (☎ and fax 0117 968 2205); The Council House, College Green, Bristol BS1 5TR (☎ 0117 922 2000)

WALKER, Peter Frank; s of Wilfrid Herbert Hornsey Walker (d 1965), and Mildred Sheila, *née* Caddell (d 1984); *b* 27 June 1937; *Educ* Oundle, King's Coll London (BSc); *m* 27 March 1965, Susan Margaret, da of Geoffrey Hugh Sharp, of Leicester; 1 s (Richard b 1972), 2 da (Fiona b 1967, Julia b 1969); *Career* Nat Serv 2 Lt RE 1955–57; CChem; chm Usher-Walker plc 1985– (md 1974–92); pres Soc of Br Printing Ink Mfrs 1985–86 (memb Cncl 1973–76, 1979–82, 1983–87 and 1989–); MRIC, MIOP; *Recreations* racing, antiques, bridge; *Clubs* RAC; *Style*— Peter Walker, Esq; ✉ Usher-Walker plc, Usher-Walker House, 1 Datapoint Business Centre, 6 South Crescent, London E16 4TL (☎ 0171 712 7121, fax 0171 712 7122)

WALKER, Peter Michael; s of Oliver Walker (d 1965), of S Africa, and Freda Miller; *b* 17 Feb 1936; *Educ* Highlands North HS, Johannesburg S Africa; *m* 2, 1979, Susan, da of Harold Davies (d 1969); 1 s (Daniel), 2 other c (Justin and Sarah by previous marriage); *Career* former Glamorgan and England cricketer (3 caps v S Africa 1960), former chm Cricketers' Assoc, sports columnist for variety of papers and periodicals including The Times, Sunday Telegraph and Mail on Sunday; cricket commentator Refuge Assurance Sunday League (for BBC), presenter numerous TV and radio programmes on news, current affairs, sport; currently dir of cricket devpt Cricket Bd of Wales (fndr and former md), md Merlin Television Ltd; *Books* Winning Cricket, Cricket Conversations, The All Rounder; *Recreations* golf, music; *Style*— Peter Walker, Esq; ✉ 14 Chargot Rd, Llandaff, Cardiff (☎ 01222 212893); Cricket Board of Wales, Sophia Gardens, Cardiff CF1 9XR (☎ 01222 231735, fax 01222 377044)

WALKER, Philip Andrew Geoffrey (Phil); *Educ* Howardian HS Cardiff; *Career* South Wales Echo 1962–64, Daily Sketch 1964–65, Evening Post Reading 1966–68, Daily Mail 1968–69, night ed Daily Mirror 1969–80, assoc ed Daily Express 1980–83, dep ed Daily Mirror 1983–88, freelance journalist 1988–90, ed Daily Star 1994– (dep ed 1990–94); *Recreations* natural history; *Style*— Phil Walker, Esq; ✉ Daily Star, Ludgate House, 245 Blackfriars Road, London SE1 9UX (☎ 0171 928 8000, fax 0171 620 1641)

WALKER, Raymond Augustus; QC (1988); s of Air Chief Marshal Sir Augustus Walker, GCB, CBE, DSO, DFC, AFC, (d 1986), and Dorothy Brenda, *née* Brewis; *b* 26 Aug 1943; *Educ* Radley, Univ of Cambridge (BA); *m* 2 Sept 1976, June Rose, da of Thomas Wisby; 1 s (James b 19 June 1979); *Career* called to the Bar Middle Temple 1966, recorder 1993–, head of chambers; *Recreations* golf, tennis, skiing, sailing, opera; *Clubs* Garrick, Royal West Norfolk Golf, Huntercombe Golf; *Style*— Raymond Walker, Esq, QC; ✉ 1 Harcourt Buildings, Temple EC4 (☎ 0171 353 0375)

WALKER, Raymond James (Ray); OBE (1990); s of Cyril James Walker (d 1984), and Louie, *née* Hopes (d 1964); *b* 13 April 1943; *Educ* Univ of Lancaster (BA); *m* 29 March 1968, Mary Eastwood, da of George Whittaker (d 1956); 1 da (Claire Louise b 1969); *Career* formerly md of specialised int servs co in textile indust and export dir of key div with leading branded product; currently chief exec Simpler Trade Procedures Bd for HM Govt; chm (co-chm 1987) UN/EDIFACT (UN Economic Cmmn for Europe's New Int Standard for Electronic Data Interchange), Western Euro rapporteur, vice-chm Western Euro Bd; special award American Standards Community (ANSI X.12) for outstanding contrib to int data exchange 1986, Man of the Year award International Data Exchange Assoc 1988; *Recreations* collecting wine labels, maps, jazz (at Ronnie Scott's); *Clubs* RAC, Royal Over-Seas League; *Style*— Ray Walker, Esq, OBE; ✉ 29 Glasshouse Street, London W1R 5RG (☎ 0171 287 3525, fax 0171 287 5751)

WALKER, Prof Raymond William (Ray); s of William Frederick Walker (d 1991), and Gwendoline Elizabeth, *née* Liddle; *b* 25 Jan 1936; *Educ* Ilkeston GS, Archbishop Holgate GS Barnsley, Univ of Hull; *m* 29 July 1961, Jennifer Mary, da of William Henry Morris; 3 s (Nicholas b 7 Dec 1962, Timothy b 21 Aug 1964, d 1980, Matthew b 21 Aug 1966), 1 da (Natalie b 21 April 1969); *Career* Univ of Hull: demonstrator in physical and inorganic chemistry 1958–61, asst lectr 1961–64, lectr 1964–71, sr lectr 1971–80, reader in combustion chemistry 1980–89, prof of combustion chemistry 1989–, dean School of Chemistry 1992–95, pro-vice-chllr 1995–; memb Combustion Inst; Royal Soc of Chemistry Medal 1987; FRSC 1985; *Publications* author of 15 major reviews and book chapters, and also over 100 papers in learned jls; *Recreations* sport (cricket, rugby league and union), travelling abroad, historical biography, theatre; *Style*— Prof Ray Walker; ✉ 14 The Croft, Beverley, East Yorkshire HU17 7HT; School of Chemistry, University of Hull, Hull, East Yorkshire HU6 7RX (☎ 01482 465449, fax 01482 466880)

WALKER, His Hon Judge Richard; s of Edwin Roland Walker (d 1980), of Epsom, and Barbara Joan, *née* Swann (d 1985); *b* 9 March 1942; *Educ* Epsom Coll, Worcester Coll Oxford (MA); *m* 29 March 1969, Angela Joan, da of John Robert Hodgkinson, of Minehead; 2 da (Rosemary b 1972, Sarah b 1974); *Career* called to the Bar Inner Temple 1966; asst cmmr: Parly Boundary Cmmn 1978–89, Local Govt Boundary Cmmn 1982–89; recorder 1989, circuit judge 1989–; commissary gen City and Diocese of Canterbury 1995–; chm Pathfinders (Anglican Youth Movement) 1978–84, vice chm Church Pastoral-Aid Soc 1978–85; *Books* Carter-Ruck on Libel and Slander (jt ed 3 edn, 1985 and 4 edn, 1992); *Style*— His Hon Judge Richard Walker; ✉ Knightsbridge Crown Court, 1 Pocock Street, London SE1 0BT

WALKER, Richard John Boileau; s of Kenneth Ralph Walker, and Caroline Jean, *née* Livingstone-Learmonth; *b* 4 June 1916; *Educ* Harrow, Univ of Cambridge, Courtauld Inst; *m* 26 Oct 1946, Margaret Ann Firebrace, da of Brig Roy Firebrace, CBE; 1 s (Nicholas b 3 Oct 1947), 2 da (Susan (Mrs McAlpine) b 8 Oct 1949, Frances (Mrs Goudge) b 23 July 1954); *Career* Lt RNVR 1939–45; asst keeper Tate Gallery 1946–49, govt picture advsr 1949–76, curator Palace of Westminster 1950–76; cataloguer: Nat Portrait Gallery 1976–85, Royal Collection 1985–90, Nat Tst 1990–; tstee: Nat Maritime Museum 1977–84, Army Museums Ogilby Tst 1979–90, Pennington-Mellor Tst 1988–; FSA 1967; *Books* Old Westminster Bridge (1979), Regency Portraits (1985), Royal Collection: Eighteenth Century Miniatures (1992); *Clubs* Athenaeum, United Oxford and Cambridge Univ; *Style*— Richard Walker, Esq, FSA; ✉ 31 Cadogan Place, London SW1X 9RX

WALKER, Hon Mr Justice; Hon Sir Robert; kt (1994); s of Ronald Robert Antony Walker, of Thaxted, Essex, and Mary Helen, *née* Welsh; *b* 17 March 1938; *Educ* Downside, Trinity Coll Cambridge (BA); *m* 3 Sept 1962, Suzanne Diana, *née* Leggi; 1 s (Robert Thomas b 1963), 3 da (Penelope Mary b 1966, Julian Diana b 1968, Henrietta Solveig b 1972); *Career* 2 Lt Nat Serv RA 1959–61; barr in practice at Chancery Bar 1961–94, QC 1982–94, judge of the High Court of Justice (Chancery Div) 1994–; bencher Lincoln's Inn 1990; *Style*— The Hon Mr Justice Walker; ✉ Royal Courts of Justice, Strand, London WC2A 2LL

WALKER, Robin Charles; s of Charles Walker (d 1961), of London, and Annie, *née* Vine; *b* 11 July 1932; *Educ* Cardinal Vaughan, Shoreditch Coll, Cardiff Coll of Physical Educn; *m* 16 Aug 1958, Margaret Elizabeth, 2 s (Jeffrey Charles b 1960, Andrew Robin b 1970), (1 da Suzanne Elisabeth b 1972); *Career* Nat Serv RAF 1950–52; teacher Hillbrooke Sch Tooting 1955–56, head of Dept Tylers Croft Sch 1956–61, sr lectr Physical Educn Dept Regent St Poly (now Poly of Central London) 1961–88 (head of Dept 1972–88); sport conslt 1988–; trampolinist 1958–, organiser and mangr first Br team to compete abroad (v W Germany) 1961; Br Trampoline Fedn: fndr and sec 1964, sr coach 1970–, tech dir 1980–, chief exec 1990–; judge World and Euro Championships 1965–82, fndr memb FIT (pres Safety Ctee); rep Middx Basketball 1964, nat grade coach Amateur Basketball Assoc 1964; *Books* Trampolining: Beginner to Competition (1983), Trampolining for Coaches and Performers (1988); *Recreations* music, ornithology, sports psychology, performing arts; *Style*— Robin Walker, Esq; ✉ British Trampoline Federation Ltd, 146 College Road, Harrow, Middlesex HA1 1BH (☎ 0181 863 7278)

WALKER, Sir Rodney Myerscough; kt (1996); s of Norman Walker (d 1943), of Wakefield, and Lucy, *née* Kitchen (d 1987); *b* 10 April 1943; *Educ* Thornes House GS Wakefield; *m* 16 March 1974, Anne Margaret, da of Walter Aspinall (d 1972), of Leeds; 2 s (Alexander b 1976, Timothy b 1977); *Career* currently: maj and controlling shareholder Myerscough Holdings Ltd, chm W Yorks Broadcasting Plc (Radio Aire), non-exec dir Bain Hogg Ltd, non-exec dir EMAP Radio, pres NHS Tst Fedn, chm Yorkshire Cable Gp, chm The Rugby Football League 1993, chm the Sports Cncl 1994–; former chm and pres Wakefield Round Table; chm: Wakefield Met Festival, Wakefield Theatre Tst; memb Senate Univ of Leeds 1993; tstee: St Oswald Charitable Tst, The Rowland St Oswald (1984) Charitable Tst, The Clarke Hall Farm Tst Ltd, London Marathon Tst, Sports Aid Fndn; FRSA; *Recreations* golf, charity work; *Clubs* Landsdowne; *Style*— Sir Rodney Walker; ✉ Walker House, Bond St, Wakefield, West Yorkshire WF1 2QP (☎ 01924 379443, fax 01924 290289, car 0836 222814, mobile 0802 252281)

WALKER, Prof Roger Michael; s of Jack Walker (d 1986), of Huddersfield, and Lily, *née* Pennock; *b* 25 July 1938; *Educ* Huddersfield Coll Sch, Univ of Manchester (BA), Birkbeck Coll London (PhD); *m* 10 Sept 1960 (m dis 1980), Patricia Mary, da of Maximilian Edmund Eccles (d 1960), of Huddersfield; 1 s (Julian b 1961), 1 da (Sara b 1962); *Career* asst lectr in Spanish Univ of Bristol 1961–63, prof of Spanish Medieval Studies Birkbeck Coll London 1980– (lectr 1963–72, reader 1972–80, vice-master 1988–93), ed Modern Language Review 1985–93; memb Ctee Modern Humanities Res Assoc, pres London Medieval Soc 1990–92, chm Br branch Société Rencesvals 1990–92; FSA 1983, FRHistS 1994; *Books* Estoria de Santa Maria Egiçiaca (1972), Tradition and Technique in 'El Libro del Cavallero Zifar' (1974), Camões e o Pensamento Filosófico do Seu Tempo (1979), El Cavallero Plaçidas (1982), MHRA Style Book (1991); *Recreations* heraldry, cricket, beer; *Clubs* Wig and Pen; *Style*— Prof Roger Walker, FSA; ✉ Dept of Spanish, Birkbeck College, University of London, Malet Street, London WC1E 7HX (☎ 0171 580 6622 ext 6143, fax 0171 383 3729)

WALKER, (Christopher) Roy; CB (1992); s of Christopher Harry Walker, of Eastwood, Essex, and Dorothy Jessica (d 1972); *b* 5 Dec 1934; *Educ* Sir George Monoux GS, Sidney Sussex Cambridge (BA), Free Univ Brussels; *m* 1961, Hilary Mary, da of Thomas William Biddiscombe; 2 s (Michael b 1967, Thomas b 1968); *Career* Bd of Trade 1958–68, private sec to Ldr House of Lords 1968–71, asst sec Civil Serv Dept 1971–73, Coal Div Dept of Energy 1973–74, seconded to Euro Secretariat Cabinet Office 1973–74, Indust Div Dept of Energy 1975–77, under sec DES 1977–86, Dept of Employment 1986–89, seconded to Business in the Cities 1989, dep head Science and Technol Secretariat Cabinet Office 1989–92, seconded as assoc dir Royal Inst of Public Admin 1992, chief offr Jt Nature Conservation Ctee 1993–96; *Recreations* dinghy sailing, hill walking, photography, archaeology, architecture; *Clubs* Chipstead Sailing; *Style*— Roy Walker, Esq, CB; ✉ 54 The Drive, Sevenoaks, Kent TN13 3AF (☎ 01732 455168)

WALKER, Sarah Elizabeth Royle (Mrs R G Allum); CBE (1991); da of Alan Royle Walker, and Elizabeth Brownrigg; *Educ* Pate's GS for Girls Cheltenham, RCM; *m* 1972, Graham Allum; *Career* mezzo-soprano; maj appearances in Br, America, Aust, NZ, Europe; operatic débuts incl: Coronation of Poppea (Kent Opera 1969, San Francisco Opera 1981), La Calisto (Glyndebourne 1970), Les Troyens (Scottish Opera 1972, Wienstaatsoper 1980), princ mezzo-soprano ENO 1972–77, Die Meistersinger (Chicago Lyric Opera 1977), Werther (Covent Gdn 1979), Giulio Caesare (Le Grand Theâtre Genève 1983), Capriccio (Brussels 1983), Teseo (Siena 1985), Samson (NY Metro Opera 1986); Marcellina in Le Nozze di Figaro (Covent Garden) 1995; Numerous Records and video recordings incl title role in Britten's Gloriana; Prince Consort prof of singing RCM 1993–; pres Cheltenham Bach Choir 1986–; FRCM 1987, LRAM; Hon GSM 1988; *Recreations* interior design, encouraging husband with gardening; *Style*— Miss Sarah Walker, CBE; ✉ c/o Lies Askonas, 6 Henrietta Street, London WC2E 8LA (☎ 0171 379 7700, fax 0171 242 1831)

WALKER, Simon Edward John; s of Louis Charles Vivian Walker, of London, and Joan Wallace, *née* Keith (d 1979); *b* 28 May 1953, South Africa; *Educ* S African Coll Sch Cape Town, Balliol Coll Oxford (pres of union); *m* Mary Virginia, *née* Strang; 1 s (Jeremy b 26 Oct 1985), 1 da (Gini b 3 June 1992); *Career* TV journalist NZ 1975–79, professional journalism fell Stanford Univ 1979–80, dir of communications/dir Parly Oppn Research Unit NZ 1980–84, concurrently presenter Fair Go (TVNZ); dir: Communicor Public Relations Wellington NZ 1984–89, NZ Centre for Independent Studies 1987–89; Hill & Knowlton: dep head of public affrs London 1989–90, dir of Euro public affrs and md Brussels 1990–94; ptnr Brunswick Public Relations 1994–; special advsr to the PM No 10 Policy Unit 1996–97; memb NZ Bdcasting Tbnl 1987–88; *Books* Rogernomics: Economic Reform in New Zealand 1984–1989 (ed, 1989); *Recreations* reading, politics; *Clubs* Travellers'; *Style*— Simon Walker, Esq; ✉ 86 Brook Green, London W6 7BD (☎ 0171 602 3883, fax 0171 602 0771); Brunswick Public Relations Ltd, 17 Lincoln's Inn Fields, London WC2A 3ED (☎ 0171 404 5959, fax 0171 831 2823)

WALKER, Simon Jeremy; s of Alan William Walker, of Oxfordshire, and Shirley Ann Lillian, *née* Fremel; *b* 2 April 1967; *Educ* Abingdon Sch, Trent Poly (BA); *m* 11 Aug 1990, Frances Mary, da of William Godfrey Townsend; 1 da (Daisy Megan b 28 Dec 1996); *Career* photographer; freelanced for various Br newspapers and magazines 1988–89, The Independent 1989, Sunday Telegraph 1990 (joined 1989), Sunday Express 1990–91, Sunday Times 1991, The Times 1993– (joined Staff 1995); contrib Gamma Press Agency 1991–; David Hodge/Observer Young Photojournalist of the Year 1987, Nikon Press Photographer of the Month July 1989, runner-up Most Promising Newcomer Category Br Press Photographer of the Year awards 1990 (commended 1989); *Books*

Para - Inside the Parachute Regiment (1993); *Recreations* preparing for baby and a dalmation, travel; *Style*— Simon Walker, Esq; ✉ 6 Queen Margarets Grove, Islington, London N1 4QD (☎ and fax 0171 275 7328, mobile 0831 451212)

WALKER, (Brian) Stuart; s of William Walker (d 1975), and Annie, *née* Jackson (d 1990); *b* 5 March 1932; *Educ* Blackpool Sch of Art (NDD), Royal Acad Schs London (David Murray scholar, Dip, Bronze Medal for painting, Silver Medal for drawing); *m* 1961 (sep), Adrienne Elizabeth Atkinson; 2 da (Anna b 5 April 1963, Lucy b 27 July 1965); *partner* since 1988, Francesca Elizabeth Boyd; 1 s (Jack b 13 Sept 1995); *Career* sr designer BBC Television 1968–84 (designer 1961–68), prodn designer Handmade Films 1984, sr designer BBC Television 1984–90, freelance prodn designer working on TV film prodns and feature films 1990–; maj prodns since 1974 incl: The Love School, The Chester Mystery Cycle, Divoroce - a Trilogy, Bet Your Life, Private Lives, Exiles, Danton's Death, Romeo and Juliet, Measure for Measure, School Play, St Joan, Arabian Nights, Hot House, The Combination, Life After Death, Last Love, Minor Complications, Winnie, James Joyce, An Englishman Abroad (BAFTA Award for TV Design 1984), Desert of Lies, The Dog it Was, The Big H, In the Secret State, Private Function (feature film), Shoot for the Sun, Inappropriate Behaviour, Border, Road (RTS Prodn Design Award 1988), Deadline, Mountain Language, Mountain and the Molehill, Portrait of a Marriage (BAFTA Award for TV Design 1991), London Kills Me (feature film), The Camomile Lawn, The Clothes in the Wardrobe, Captives (feature film), Absence of War, Hollow Reed; RDI 1989; *Style*— Stuart Walker, Esq; ✉ c/o Casarotto Marsh Ltd, National House, 60–66 Wardour Street, London W1V 3HP (☎ 0171 287 4450, fax 0171 287 9128)

WALKER, Ted; s of Edward Joseph Walker (d 1991), of Lancing, Sussex, and Winifred Edith, *née* Schofield; *b* 28 Nov 1934; *Educ* Steyning GS, St John's Coll Cambridge (BA, MA); *m* 1, 1956, Lorna Ruth (d 1987), da of William Caleb Benfell; 2 s (Edward Joseph b 1958, William John b 1964), 2 da (Susan Mary b 1958, Margaret Ruth b 1959); m 2, 1988, Audrey Joan Hicks; *Career* writer, poet, short-story writer and dramatist; head of modern languages Bognor Regis Sch 1963–65, prof of creative writing and Eng lit New England Coll 1971–92 (prof emeritus 1992–); Hon DLitt Univ of Southampton 1995; FRSL 1975 *Awards* The Eric Gregory Award 1964, The Cholmondeley Award 1966, The Alice Hunt Bartlett Award 1968, Major Arts Cncl of GB bursary 1970, The Soc of Authors travel bursary 1978, The Campion Award for poetry, The Critical Quarterly Award, The Ackerley Award for literary autobiography 1982, The Southern Arts Assoc Lit Prize, BAFTA nomination for best screenplay for children's films 1996; *Publications* poetry: Fox on a Barn Door (1965), The Solitaries (1967), The Night Bathers (1970), Gloves to the Hangman (1973), Burning the Ivy (1978), The Lion's Cavalcade (1980), Hands at a Live Fire (1987), Grandad's Seagulls (children's verse, 1994); other books: The High Path (autobiography, 1982), You've Never Heard Me Sing (short stories, 1985), In Spain (travel, 1987), The Last of England (autobiography, 1992); television scripts: Big Jim and the Figaro Club (comedy series, BBC 1981), A Family Man (BBC 1984), The Wind in the Willows (ITV 1995), The Wind in the Willows (ITV 1996); *Recreations* walking, cookery, travel, Times crossword; *Style*— Ted Walker, Esq, FRSL; ✉ Argyll House, The Square, Eastergate, Chichester, West Sussex PO20 6UP (☎ and fax 01243 542260); c/o Sheil Land Associates Ltd, 48 Doughty Street, London WC1N 2LF (☎ 0171 405 9351, fax 0171 831 2127)

WALKER, Ven Thomas Overington; s of Ernest Thomas Walker (d 1980), and Ethel, *née* Fogden; *b* 7 Dec 1933; *Educ* Dorking County GS, Keble Coll Oxford (MA), Oak Hill Coll (Homiletics prize); *m* 6 July 1957, Molly Anne, da of late Capt Robert Gilmour; 1 s (Timothy Mark b 1969), 2 da (Charis Louise (Mrs Wilson) b 1960, Rachel Joy (Mrs Hopkinson) b 1962); *Career* archdeacon of Nottingham until 1996, ret; *Books* Renew us by Your Spirit (1982), From Here to Heavan (1987), Small Streams, Big Rivers (1991); *Recreations* reading, music, sport, dry stone walling; *Style*— The Ven Thomas Walker

WALKER, Tim Philip Buchanan; s of W L B Walker, and Claudine Ella, *née* Mawby; *b* 23 June 1963; *Educ* Millfield; *Career* journalist; regnl newspapers 1983–87, The Observer 1987–90, The European 1990–93, The Tatler 1993–94, The Daily Mail 1994–; freelance presenter LBC London 1989–94; Young Journalist of the Year Br Press Awards 1987; *Books* Norma - A Biography (1993); *Recreations* yachting; *Clubs* Royal Motor Yacht (Poole); *Style*— Tim Walker, Esq; ✉ The Daily Mail, Northcliffe House, 2 Derry Street, London W8 5TT (☎ 0171 938 7190)

WALKER, Timothy Edward Hanson; s of Harris, and Elizabeth Walker; *b* 27 July 1945; *Educ* Tonbridge Sch, Brasenose Coll Oxford (MA, DPhil); *m* 1, 1969, Judith, *née* Mann (d 1976); 1 da; m 2, 1983, Anna, *née* Butterworth; 2 da; *Career* res fell Univ Coll Oxford and exhibitioner of Royal Cmmn of 1851 Oxford and Paris 1969–71; Harkness fell: Commonwealth Fund of New York 1971, Univ of Virginia 1971, Northwestern Univ 1972; strategic planner GLC 1974–77, princ DTI 1977–83, Sloan fell London Business Sch 1983, DTI: asst sec 1983–85, head of Policy Planning Unit 1985–86, princ private sec to Secs of State for Trade and Indust 1986–87, under sec, dir Inf Engrg Directorate/dir Alvey Prog 1987–89, head of Atomic Energy Div 1989–95; dep sec and head of Immigration and Nationality Dept Home Office 1995–; non-exec dir: ICI Chemicals and Polymers Ltd 1988–89, Govt Div UKAEA 1994–95; govr IAEA (UK) 1989–94, chm Assembly of Donors EBRD Nuclear Safety Account 1993–95; contrib to scientific jls; *Recreations* collecting modern prints, gardening, cookery; *Style*— Timothy Walker, Esq; ✉ Home Office, Queen Anne's Gate, London SW1H 9AT

WALKER, Hon Mr Justice; Hon Sir Timothy Edward (Tim); kt (1996); s of George Edward Walker (d 1977), and Muriel Edith, *née* Brown (d 1981); *b* 13 May 1946; *Educ* Harrow, Univ Coll Oxford (Plumptre scholar, MA, Eldon law scholar); *m* 1968, Mary Jane, *née* Tyndall; 2 da (Charlotte Elizabeth b 25 May 1972, Annabel Sarah b 16 Nov 1975); *Career* called to the Bar Inner Temple 1968 (bencher 1996), QC 1985, recorder of the Crown Court 1986–96, judge of the High Court of Justice (Queen's Bench Div) 1996–; *Style*— The Hon Mr Justice Timothy Walker; ✉ Royal Courts of Justice, Strand, London WC2A 2LL

WALKER, Victor Stewart Heron; s and h of Sir James Heron Walker, 5 Bt, by his 1 w, Angela Margaret, *née* Beaufort (d 1993); *b* 8 Oct 1942; *Educ* Eton; *m* 1, 1969 (m dis 1982), Caroline Louisa, yst da of late Lt-Col Frederick Edwin Barton Wignall; 2 s, 1 da; m 2, 1982, Svea, only da of late Capt (Ernst) Hugo Gothard Knutson Borg and Mary Hilary Borg; *Career* late 2 Lt Gren Gds & Lt Royal Wilts Yeo & Royal Yeo; *Clubs* Royal Yacht Sqdn; *Style*— Victor Walker, Esq; ✉ Res Castellans, St Antonin du Var, 83510 France; Old Cadet House, Mont Mallet, St Martin, Jersey, Channel Islands JE3 6DZ

WALKER, Gen Sir Walter Colyear; KCB (1968, CB 1964), CBE (1959, OBE 1949), DSO (1946) and Bars (1953, 1965); s of Arthur Colyear Walker; *b* 11 Nov 1912; *Educ* Blundell's, RMC Sandhurst; *m* 1938, Beryl Catherine (d 1990), da of E N W Johnston; 2 s (Anthony, Nigel), 1 da (Venetia); *Career* served Bde of Gurkhas: Waziristan 1939–41 (despatches twice), Burma 1942 and 1944–46 (despatches), Malaya 1949–59 (Brevet Lt-Col, despatches twice), Atomic Trials Maralinga S Australia 1956, Maj-Gen 1961, dir of ops Borneo 1962–65, Col 7 Duke of Edinburgh's Own Gurkha Rifles 1964–75, dep chief of staff Allied Forces Central Europe 1965–67, Lt-Gen 1967, GOC-in-C Northern Cmd 1967–69, Gen 1969, C-in-C Allied Forces Northern Europe 1969–72; Paduka Stia Negara Brunei 1 class 1964, hon Panglima Mangku Negara Malaysia 1965; *Books* The Bear at the Back Door (1978), The Next Domino (1980); *Recreations* normal; *Style*— General Sir Walter Walker, KCB, CBE, DSO; ✉ Haydon Farmhouse, Sherborne, Dorset DT9 5JB

WALKER, William Connoll (Bill); MP (C) Tayside North (majority 3,995); s of Charles and Willamina Walker; *b* 20 Feb 1929; *Educ* Dundee: Logie and Blackness Schs, Trades Coll, Coll of Arts; Coll of Distributive Trades London; *m* 1956, Mavis Lambert, 3 da; *Career* Sqdn-Ldr RAFVR; md Retail Stores Group; Parly candidate (C) Dundee East Oct 1974; MP (C) Perth and E Perthshire 1979–83, Tayside N 1983–; memb: Select Ctee on Scottish Affrs 1979–, Select Ctee on Parly Cmmn for Admin 1979–; jt sec Aviation Ctee, jt vice chm Cons Backbench Euro Affrs Ctee 1982–; sec: Scottish Cons Ctee 1991–, RAF Parly Gp, Cons Defence Ctee 1993–; chm: Scottish Cons Back-Bench Ctee, Cons Aviation Ctee 1993–, Cons Pty Orgn Ctee 1993–, All Pty Scout Gp; vice-chm: All Pty Scotch Whisky Gp, All Pty Scottish Sports Gp, World Parly Scout Union; pres: Cons for Euro Reform, Walker Associates; treas Br-Zimbabwe Parly Gp; *Clubs* RAF; *Style*— Bill Walker, Esq, MP; ✉ Candletrees, Longacres, Burrelton, Perthshire PH13 9NY (☎ 01828 670407)

WALKER-ARNOTT, Edward Ian; s of Charles Douglas Walker-Arnott (d 1980), of Woodford, Essex, and Kathleen Margaret, *née* Brittain; *b* 18 Sept 1939; *Educ* Haileybury, Univ of London (LLB), UCL (LLM); *m* 11 Sept 1971, (Phyllis) Jane, da of Lt-Col J M Ricketts, MC (d 1987), of Weston, Honiton, Devon; 1 s (William b 9 Nov 1981), 2 da (Emily b 7 April 1974, Hannah b 9 July 1979); *Career* admitted slr 1963, ptnr Herbert Smith 1968– (sr ptnr 1993–); non-exec dir Sturge Holdings plc 1989–95; memb: Cork Ctee on Review of Insolvency Law 1977–82, Insolvency Practitioners Tbnl; memb Cncl: Lloyd's 1983–88 (hon memb 1988), Haileybury Coll (treas 1977–88), Benenden Sch 1988–93; Freeman Worshipful Co of Slrs, memb Ct of Assts Worshipful Co of Loriners; memb Law Soc; *Recreations* cricket, tennis, gardening; *Clubs* City of London; *Style*— Edward Walker-Arnott, Esq; ✉ Manuden Hall, Manuden, nr Bishops Stortford, Herts CM23 1DY; Herbert Smith, Exchange House, Primrose St, London EC2A 2HS (☎ 0171 374 8000)

WALKER-ARNOTT, (Brian) Richard; s of (Charles) Douglas Walker-Arnott (d 1980), and Kathleen Margaret, *née* Brittain; *b* 8 Sept 1937; *Educ* Haileybury (scholar), Trinity Hall Cambridge (exhibitioner, MA); *m* 23 Jan 1988, Deborah Clare, da of John Ounsted; 1 s (Charles Laurence b 12 Oct 1989), 1 da (Harriet Rose b 8 July 1992); *Career* PR Dept Procter & Gamble Limited (Newcastle upon Tyne) 1960–68, Charles Barker 1968–73, FJ Lyons 1974–76; dir Charles Barker 1976–91; chief exec Assoc of Recognised English Language Servs 1992–; cncllr Royal Borough of Kensington and Chelsea 1974– (former chm various ctees and chief whip Majority Pty, dep ldr Majority Pty 1991), chm Kensington Cons Assoc 1980–83; Master Worshipful Co of Loriners 1990 (memb Ct of Assts); MIPR 1968, DipCam 1978; *Recreations* mountain walking; *Clubs* City Livery, Tyne Rowing; *Style*— Richard Walker-Arnott, Esq; ✉ 27 Finstock Rd, London W10 6LU (☎ 0181 968 4448)

WALKER OF WORCESTER, Baron (Life Peer UK 1992), of Abbots Morton in the County of Hereford and Worcester Peter Edward Walker; MBE (1960), PC (1970); s of Sydney Walker, and Rose, *née* Dean; *b* 25 March 1932; *Educ* Latymer Upper Sch, Univ of NY (LLD); *m* 22 Feb 1969, Tessa Joan, da of Geoffrey Ivan Pout; 3 s (Hon Jonathan Peter b 1970, Hon Timothy Rupert b 1975, Hon Robin Caspar b 1978), 2 da (Hon Shara Jane b 1971, Hon Marianna Clare b 1985); *Career* memb Cons Party National Exec Ctee 1956, nat chm Young Cons 1958–60, Parly candidate (Cons) Dartford 1955 and 1959, MP (Cons) Worcester 1961–92; PPS to Leader of the House of Commons 1963–64; oppn spokesman: on fin and economics 1964–66, on tport 1966–68, on local govt, housing and land 1968–70; min for housing and local govt June-Oct 1970; sec of state: for the environment 1970–72, for trade and indust 1972–74; oppn spokesman: on trade and indust and consumer affrs Feb-June 1974, on def 1974–75; minister for agric, fisheries and food 1979–83, sec of state for energy June 1983–87, sec of state for Wales 1987–90; currently non-exec dir: Worcester Group plc, Tate & Lyle plc, Liffe (Holdings) plc; chm: Thornton & Co Ltd, Cornhill Insurance Co; chm English Partnerships; Cdr's Cross of Order of Merit of Federal Republic of Germany 1994, Chilean Order of Bernardo O'Higgins Degree Gran Official 1995; *Books* The Ascent of Britain (1976), Trust the People (1987), Staying Power (autobiog, 1991); *Recreations* tennis, reading, music; *Style*— The Rt Hon Lord Walker of Worcester, MBE, PC; ✉ Abbots Morton Manor, Gooms Hill, Abbots Morton, Worcestershire

WALKER-OKEOVER, Sir Peter Ralph Leopold; 4 Bt (UK 1886), of Gateacre Grange, Co Lancaster, and Osmaston Manor, Co Derby; DL (Staffs 1992); s of Sir Ian Peter Andrew Monro Walker-Okeover, 3 Bt, DSO, TD (d 1982), and (Dorothy) Elizabeth, *née* Heber Percy; *b* 22 July 1947, (King Leopold III of the Belgians stood sponsor); *Educ* Eton, RMA Sandhurst; *m* 1, 1972 (m dis 1991), Catherine Mary Maule, eldest da of Col George Patrick Maule Ramsay; 2 s (Andrew Peter Monro b 1978, (Patrick) Ralph b 1982), 1 da (Georgina Elizabeth b 1976); m 2, 1993, Patricia Margaret, eld da of Laurence Berry Sanderson; *Heir* s, Andrew Peter Monro Walker-Okeover, b 22 May 1978; *Career* Capt Blues and Royals; *Style*— Captain Sir Peter Walker-Okeover, Bt, DL; ✉ Okeover Hall, Ashbourne, Derbyshire; House of Glenmuick, Ballater, Aberdeenshire, Scotland

WALKER-SMITH, Prof John Angus; s of Dr Angus Buchanan Walker-Smith (d 1975), of Sydney, Australia, and Alexandra Buckingham, *née* Trindall (d 1970); *b* 1 Dec 1936; *Educ* Sydney C of E GS, Univ of Sydney (MB BS, MD); *m* 29 Aug 1969, Elizabeth Cantley, da of late George Blaikie, of Edinburgh; 1 s (James b 15 July 1978), 2 da (Louise b 13 Aug 1970, Laura b 17 March 1975); *Career* house physician: Hammersmith Hosp 1963, Brompton Hosp 1963; res fell: (gastroenterology) Royal Prince Alfred Hosp Sydney 1964–66 (res med offr 1960–61), Kinderklinik Zurich Switzerland 1968; student supervisor and hon assoc physician Royal Alexandra Hosp for Children 1969–72 (res med offr 1962–67, professorial registrar 1967–69), conslt paediatrician St Bartholomew's Hosp 1973–95 (prof of paediatric gastroenterology 1985–95), prof Univ Dept of Paediatric Gastroenterology Royal Free Sch of Med 1995–; memb Christ Church Wanstead; Freeman City of London, Liveryman Worshipful Soc of Apothecaries; FRACP, FRCP (London and Edinburgh); memb: BMA, Br Paediatric Assoc, Br Soc of Gastroenterology; *Books* Diseases of Small Intestine in Childhood (3 edns 1975, 1979, 1988), Practical Paediatric Gastroenterology (with J R Hamilton and W A Walker 1983, 2 edn 1995); *Recreations* swimming, photography, painting, philately; *Style*— Prof John Walker-Smith; ✉ 16 Monkham's Drive, Woodford Green, Essex IG8 0LQ (☎ 0181 505 7756); The University Department of Paediatric Gastroenterology, The Royal Free School of Medicine, Hampstead, London NW3 2QG (☎ 0171 794 0500 ext 6234)

WALKER-SMITH, (Hon) Sir (John) Jonah; 2 Bt (UK 1960), of Broxbourne, Co Herts; o s of Baron Broxbourne, TD, QC, PC (Life Peer and 1 Bt, d 1992), and Dorothy, *née* Etherton; *b* 6 Sept 1939; *Educ* Westminster, Ch Ch Oxford; *m* 1974, Aileen Marie, o da of late Joseph Smith; 1 s (Daniel Derek b 26 March 1980), 1 da (Charmian Lucinda b 23 Aug 1977); *Heir* s, Daniel Derek Walker-Smith b 26 March 1980; *Career* called to the Bar Middle Temple 1963; *Style*— Hon Sir Jonah Walker-Smith, Bt; ✉ Doughty Street Chambers, 11 Doughty St, London WC1N 2PG (☎ 0171 404 1313)

WALKINGTON, Alexander Stuart Burnett (Sandy); s of Capt Ian Alexander Greet Walkington, of Cheltenham, and Shelagh Winnifred Mary Mackenzie, *née* Munro (d 1994); *b* 5 Dec 1953; *Educ* Cheltenham Coll (scholar), Trinity Hall Cambridge (Dr Eden law student, MA Economics and Law), Coll of Law London, Tulane Univ New Orleans; *m* 1988, Francesca Mary, da of Francis Weal; 2 s (Edward Alexander Alban b 1 Nov 1988, Thomas Francis Pageant b 12 Oct 1990), 1 da (Dora Clementine Bianca b 25 Dec 1995); *Career* called to the Bar Gray's Inn 1976 (Gerald Moody scholar), Tulane Univ 1977–78, Parly asst to Emlyn Hooson, QC, MP (*see* Baron Hooson) 1978–79, head of research Parly Lib Pty 1979–81, various positions rising to mangr of external affrs Texaco Ltd 1981–91, mangr of int PR Texaco Inc NY 1991–92, head of corp affrs British Telecommunications plc 1995– (head of public affrs 1992–95); Parly candidate (Lib/SDP Alliance) St Albans 1983 and 1987, memb St Albans City Cncl 1984–91; memb St Mary's PCC Welwyn; MIPR, FRSA; *Recreations* family, walking, studying architecture; *Style*— Sandy Walkington, Esq; ✉ British Telecommunications plc, 81 Newgate Street, London EC1A 7AJ (☎ 0171 356 5000)

WALKLEY, Geoffrey; s of Alexander Joseph Charles Walkley, of Winwick, Cambs, and Vera Cecilia Walkley; *b* 25 July 1944; *Educ* East Ham GS for Boys, Univs of Durham and Newcastle (LLB); *m* 18 Jan 1969, Barbara Eunice, da of Ernest Dunstan; 1 s (Richard Andrew b 21 Dec 1970), 1 da (Sarah Elizabeth b 29 April 1973); *Career* admitted slr 1968; Bartlett & Gluckstein: articled 1966–68, asst slr 1968–71, ptnr 1971–78; ptnr Bartlett & Gluckstein Crawley & De Reya (later Bartletts, De Reya) 1978–88, ptnr Nabarro Nathanson 1988–93, ptnr Penningtons 1993– (currently head of Commercial Dept); memb: Law Soc, Slrs' Benevolent Assoc, Licensing Executives' Soc, Soc for Computers and Law, Royal Yachting Assoc (memb Sailboat Organising Ctee), Royal Horticultural Soc; *Recreations* sailing, skiing, books, gardening, carpentry; *Clubs* Maylandsea Bay Yacht Club (hon auditor), Kestrel Owners' Assoc (chm), International 505 Assoc of GB; *Style*— Geoffrey Walkley, Esq; ✉ Penningtons, Bucklersbury House, 83 Cannon Street, London EC4N 8PE (☎ 0171 457 3000, fax 0171 457 3240)

WALKLING, (Anthony) Kim; s of William Charles Walkling (d 1989), and Vida Karina, *née* Beare; *b* 27 Sept 1957; *Educ* Sutton HS Plymouth, UCL (LLB); *m* 20 Sept 1986, (Margaret Caroline) Deirdre, *née* Moore, da of Samuel James Moore, of Purley, Surrey; *Career* articled clerk Slaughter and May 1980–82, asst slr Watson, Farley & Williams 1982–87, ptnr S J Berwin & Co 1987–92, ptnr Theodore Goddard 1992–; memb: Law Soc 1982, Holborn Law Soc 1988, European Air Law Assoc 1989; *Recreations* photography, music, good food and wine; *Style*— Kim Walkling, Esq; ✉ 150 Aldersgate Street, London EC1A 4EJ (☎ 0171 606 8855, fax 0171 606 4390, telex 884678)

WALL, (Dame) (Alice) Anne; DCVO (1981, CVO 1972, MVO 1964); da of Adm Sir Geoffrey Alan Brooke Hawkins, KBE, CB, MVO, DSC (d 1980), by his w Lady Margaret Ida, *née* Montagu-Douglas-Scott (d 1976), eldest da of 7 Duke of Buccleuch; *b* 31 March 1928; *Educ* Miss Faunce's PNEU Sch, Portsmouth Tech Coll; *m* 1975, Cdr Michael Edward St Quintin Wall, RN, s of Capt Bernard St Quintin Wall, Grenadier Gds (d 1976); *Career* asst press sec to HM The Queen 1958–81, extra woman of the bedchamber to HM The Queen 1981–; *Style*— Mrs Michael Wall, DCVO; ✉ Ivy House, Lambourn, Hungerford, Berks RG17 8PB (☎ 01488 72348); 6 Chester Way, Kennington, London SE11 4UT (☎ 0171 582 0692)

WALL, David Richard; CBE (1985); s of Charles Wall, and Dorothy Irene, *née* Barden; *b* 15 March 1946; *Educ* Haliford House Shepperton, Royal Ballet Sch White Lodge Richmond, Royal Ballet Sch Upper Sch; *m* 1 Aug 1967, Alfreda Thorogood, *qv*, da of Edward Thorogood (d 1966); 1 s (Daniel b 12 Dec 1974), 1 da (Annaliese b 15 Oct 1971); *Career* Royal Ballet 1963–: soloist 1964, princ dancer 1966–84; danced all major classical roles incl: Rakes Progress 1965, Swan Lake (with Margot Fonteyn) 1966, Giselle (Peter Wright prodn) 1968, Walk to the Paradise Garden 1972, Manon 1974, Dancers at a Gathering 1974, Romeo and Juliet 1975, La Bayadère 1975, Rituals 1975, Mayerling 1977; dir and gen sec Royal Acad of Dancing 1985–91, lectr and teacher Rambert Sch 1991–, dance conslt Remedial Dance Clinic 1991–, dir Boys' Classical Graduates Course London Studio Centre 1992; *Style*— David Wall, Esq, CBE

WALL, Malcolm Robert; s of Maj Gen Robert P W Wall, of Essex, and Patricia, *née* O'Brien, of York; *b* 24 July 1956; *Educ* Allhallows Sch Dorset, Univ of Kent (BA); *m* Elizabeth; 3 da (Emma b 4 Aug 1985, Josephine b 10 March 1987, Rebecca b 28 June 1991); *Career* sales exec Southern Television 1978–80, sales exec rising to sales dir Anglia Television Ltd 1980–87, sales and mktg dir Granada Television 1988–92, dep chief exec offr Meridian Broadcasting 1992–94, md Anglia Television Ltd 1994–96; currently dep dir United Broadcasting & Entertainment Ltd; non-exec dir The Television Corporation plc; *Clubs* Harlequin FC, MCC, RAC; *Style*— Malcolm Wall, Esq; ✉ United Broadcasting & Entertainment Ltd, Ludgate House, 245 Blackfriars Road, London SE1 (☎ 0171 579 440, fax 0171 579 4435)

WALL, Hon Mr Justice; Hon Sir Nicholas Peter Rathbone; kt (1993); s of Frederick Stanley Wall (d 1978), of London, and Margaret Helen, *née* Woods; *b* 14 March 1945; *Educ* Dulwich, Trinity Coll Cambridge (scholar, MA); *m* 31 August 1973, Margaret Diana Wall, JP, da of Norman Sydee (d 1992), of London; 4 c (Imogen b 1975, Emma b 1977, Rosalind b 1980, Simon b 1983); *Career* called to the Bar Gray's Inn July 1969, QC 1988, recorder of the Crown Court 1990–93, judge of the High Court of Justice (Family Div) 1993–; *Books* Rayden and Jackson on Divorce (jt ed 16 edn, 1991); *Recreations* collecting and binding books, opera, walking, composing clerihews; *Style*— The Hon Mr Justice Wall; ✉ Royal Courts of Justice, Strand, London WC2A 2LL

WALL, Prof Patrick David; s of Capt Thomas Wall, MC (d 1976), and Ruth, *née* Cresswell (d 1978); *b* 5 April 1925; *Educ* St Pauls, ChCh Oxford (BM, BCH, DM); *Career* instr in physiology Yale 1948–50, asst prof of anatomy Univ of Chicago 1950–53, instr in physiology Harvard 1953–55, assoc prof and prof of biology MIT 1955–67, prof of anatomy UCL 1967–90 (emeritus prof 1990); visiting prof Hebrew Univ Jerusalem 1972–; Hon MD Siena 1987, Hon MD Debrecen 1993; FRCP 1984, FRS 1989; *Books* Challenge of Pain (with R Melzack, 3 edn 1994), Textbook of Pain (3 edn 1994), Defeating Pain (with M Jones, 1991); *Style*— Prof Patrick Wall, FRS; ✉ 141 Gray's Inn Rd, London WC1X 8UB (☎ and fax 0171 833 0451)

WALL, Maj Sir Patrick Henry Bligh; kt (1981), MC (1945), VRD (1957); s of Henry Benedict Wall; *b* 14 Oct 1916; *Educ* Downside; *m* 1953, Sheila Elizabeth Putnam (d 1983); 1 da; *Career* served with RM 1935–50, Maj 1944; RN Staff Coll 1946, Jt Services Staff Coll 1947; memb Westminster City Cncl 1953–63; MP (C): Haltemprice 1954–55, E Yorkshire 1955–83, Beverley 1983–87; PPS to: Min AFF 1955–57, Chllr of the Exchequer 1958–59; delegate to UN Gen Assembly 1962, vice chm Cons Pty Def Ctee 1965–77, Select Ctee Def 1979–84; chm: Br SA Parly Gp 1970–87, Monday Club 1977–79, Br Taiwan Parly Gp 1979–87, Br Portuguese Parly Gp 1979–87; pres North Atlantic Assembly 1983–85 (chm Mil Ctee 1977–79, vice pres 1980–82); Freeman of Beverley 1988, Liveryman Worshipful Co of Fishmongers; fell Inst of Journalists 1988; US Legion of Merit 1944, Kt SMO Malta, Brilliant Star of Taiwan 1987; *Books* Soviet Maritime Thrust, Indian Ocean and the Threat to the West, Southern Ocean and the Security of the Free World; *Recreations* model ships & aircraft; *Clubs* RN Sailing Assoc; *Style*— Maj Sir Patrick Wall, MC, VRD, RM (ret); ✉ Lordington Park, Nr Chichester, West Sussex PO18 9DX (☎ 01293 370989); 8 Westminster Gdns, Marsham St, London SW1P 4JA (☎ 0171 828 1803)

WALL, Peter Mason; s of Kenneth Mason Wall, of Edgbaston, Birmingham, and Margaret, *née* Marsh; *b* 13 Jan 1947; *Educ* Uppingham, Univ of Bristol (BA); *m* 29 March 1975, Jennifer Mary, da of Frank James Evans (d 1983), of Harborne, Birmingham; 1 s (Nicholas James Mason b 14 Feb 1979), 1 da (Sarah Elizabeth b 29 Sept 1976); *Career* admitted slr 1972: managing ptnr Wragge & Co 1976–91, fin ptnr 1991–, dep sr ptnr 1993–; cmmr of Taxes 1980–89, memb Cncl Edgaston C of E Coll for Girls; memb Law Soc 1969; *Recreations* golf; *Clubs* Edgbaston Golf (ctee memb, capt 1995–97); *Style*— P M Wall, Esq; ✉ Wragge & Co, 55 Colmore Row, Birmingham B3 2AS (☎ 0121 233 1000, fax 0121 214 1099, telex 338728 WRAGGE G)

WALL, Maj-Gen Robert Percival Walter; CB (1978); s of Frank Ernest Wall, of Goodmayes, Essex (d 1981), and Ethel Elizabeth, *née* Collins (d 1980); *b* 23 Aug 1927; *Educ* Army & Jt Servs Staff Coll and Royal Coll of Defence Studies; *m* 1, 1953 (m dis 1985), Patricia Kathleen O'Brien; 2 s (Malcolm b 1956, Patrick b 1958), 1 da (Clare b 1961); m 2, 7 Feb 1986, Jennifer Hilary Anning; *Career* RM 1945; served Middle East, Far East, dir staff Jt Servs Staff Coll 1969–71, various MOD appointments, Maj-Gen RM Chief of Staff 1976–79; dir (Land) Decade Educn Cncl 1980–91; mgmnt conslt 1983–; former chm: Essex Family Practitioner Ctee 1985–90, Essex Family Health Servs Authy 1990; memb North East Thames Regional Health Authy 1990–94; pres Blackheath FC (RFU) 1983–85; Freeman City of London 1978, Craft Owning Freeman Co of Watermen and Lightermen 1979; FIMgt 1980; FRSA, JP City of London 1982; *Recreations* reading, walking, cricket, rugby; *Clubs* Army and Navy, MCC; *Style*— Maj-Gen Robert Wall; ✉ c/o Army & Navy Club, 36 Pall Mall, London SW1

WALL, Sir Robert William; kt (1987), OBE (1980); s of William George Wall, of Sellack (d 1980), and Gladys Perina, *née* Powell (d 1958); *b* 27 Sept 1929; *Educ* Monmouth, Bristol Coll of Technol; *m* 24 Feb 1968, Jean, da of Harry Clifford Ashworth; 1 s (Matthew b 1970, d 1986), 1 da (Gabrielle b 1971); *Career* cmmnd RAF 1955–58, OC Mountain Rescue Team RAF Valley 1956–58; engr 1958–88: Bristol Aeroplane Co, Br Aerospace plc; memb The Audit Cmmn 1986–94; pres Dolphin Soc 1994–95, pro chllr Univ of Bristol, memb Bristol Devpt Corp, cncl memb SS Great Britain Project; govr Bristol Old Vic Theatre Tst, pres Bristol Soc of Model and Experimental Engrs, ldr Cons Gp Bristol City Cncl; chm: Rail Users' Consultative Ctee for W Eng, memb Gen Purposes Ctee Nat Union of Conservative Assocs; Freeman: City of London 1986, Worshipful Co of Watermen and Lightermen; Hon MA Univ of Bristol 1982; MIMgt 1980, AMRAeS 1985, FCIT 1991, FRSA 1993; *Books* Bristol Channel Paddle Steamers (1973), Ocean Liners (1979), Airliners (1981), Bristol-Maritime City (1981), The Story of HMS Bristol (1986), Quayside Bristol (1992); *Recreations* hill walking, collecting postcards; *Clubs* Royal Over-Seas League, Clifton, Bristol Savages; *Style*— Sir Robert Wall, OBE; ✉ 1 Ormerod Rd, Stoke Bishop, Bristol BS9 1BA; The Glebe, Winsford, Somerset; The Council House, College Green, Bristol BS1 5TR (☎ 0117 926 6031, fax 0117 929 4512, telex 449819 CITBRI)

WALL, Sir (John) Stephen; KCMG, LVO; s of John Derwent Wall (d 1984), of Pulborough, W Sussex, and Maria Letitia, *née* Whitmarsh (d 1978); *b* 10 Jan 1947; *Educ* Douai Sch, Selwyn Coll Cambridge (BA); *m* 11 Oct 1975, Catharine Jane, da of Norman Reddaway, CBE, *qv*, of London; 1 s (Matthew b 1979); *Career* joined Her Majesty's Diplomatic Serv 1968; third sec Addis Ababa 1969–72, private sec to Ambass Paris 1972–74, press offr FCO and 10 Downing St 1974–77, asst private sec to Foreign Sec 1977–79, first sec Embassy Washington 1979–83, asst (later head) FCO Euro Community Dept 1983–88, private sec to Foreign Sec 1988–90, private sec to the Prime Minister 1991–93, ambass Portugal 1993–95, ambass and UK perm rep to EC 1995–; *Recreations* reading, walking, photography; *Style*— Sir Stephen Wall, KCMG, LVO; ✉ c/o Foreign and Commonwealth Office (UK Rep Brussels), King Charles St, London SW1 2AH

WALL, Prof (Charles) Terence Clegg; s of Charles Wall (d 1976), of Woodfield, Dursley, and Ruth, *née* Clegg; *b* 14 Dec 1936; *Educ* Marlborough, Trinity Coll Cambridge (BA, PhD); *m* 22 Aug 1959, Alexandra Joy, da of Prof Leslie Spencer Hearnshaw (d 1991), of West Kirby; 2 s (Nicholas b 1962, Alexander b 1967), 2 da (Catherine b 1963, Lucy b 1965); *Career* fell Trinity Coll Cambridge 1959–64, Harkness fell 1960–61, univ reader and fell St Catherine's Coll Oxford 1964–65, prof of pure mathematics Univ of Liverpool 1965–, Royal Soc Leverhulme visiting prof Mexico 1967, sr fell SERC 1983–88; treas: Wirral area SDP 1985–88, West Wirral SLD 1988–; fell Cambridge Philosophical Soc 1958–, memb American Mathematical Soc 1961–, pres London Mathematical Soc 1978–80 (memb 1961–, memb Cncl 1973–80 and 1992–); foreign memb Royal Danish Acad 1990–; FRS (memb Cncl 1974–76); *Books* Surgery on Compact Manifolds (1970), A Geometric Introduction to Topology (1970), The Geometry of Topological Stability (with Andrew du Plessis, 1995); *Recreations* gardening, home winemaking; *Style*— Prof C T C Wall, FRS; ✉ 5 Kirby Park, West Kirby, Wirral, Merseyside L48 2HA (☎ 0151 625 5063); Department of Pure Mathematics, Univ of Liverpool, PO Box 147, Liverpool L69 3BX (☎ 0151 794 4060, fax 0151 794 4061, telex 627095)

WALLACE, Prof (William) Angus; s of Dr William Bethune Wallace (d 1981), of Dundee, Scotland, and Dr Frances Barret, *née* Early (d 1992); *b* 31 Oct 1948; *Educ* Dundee HS, Univ of St Andrews (MB ChB); *m* 2 Jan 1971, Jacqueline Vera Studley, da of Dr George William Eglinton (d 1995), of East Finchley, London; 2 s (Malcolm b 1975, Andrew b 1979), 1 da (Suzanne b 1973); *Career* jr house offr Dundee Royal Infirmary and Maryfield Hosp 1972–73, demonstrator in anatomy Univ of Nottingham 1973–74; sr house offr: Nottingham 1974–75, Derby 1975; basic surgical trg registrar Newcastle and Gateshead Hosps 1975–77, orthopaedic registrar Nottingham Hosps 1978–81, res fell MRC 1979, lectr in orthopaedic surgery Univ of Nottingham 1981–84, visiting res fell Toronto W Hosp Canada 1983, sr lectr in orthopaedic surgery Univ of Manchester 1984–85, med dir North Western Orthotic Unit and med advsr Dept of Orthopaedic Mechanics Univ of Salford 1984–85, prof of orthopaedic and accident surgery Univ of Nottingham 1985–, med dir Sports Injury Clinic Univ of Nottingham; memb Cncl Royal Coll of Surgns of Edinburgh 1990–, Br rep on the Euro Soc for Shoulder and Elbow Surgery; chm: Clinical Curriculum Ctee Nottingham Med Sch 1992–95, Nat Osteoporosis Soc 1996–98; awarded Sir Walter Mercer Gold Medal by RCSEd 1985, Weigelt-Wallace Award for Med Care 1995; FRCSEd 1977, FRCSEd (orthopaedic) 1985, FRCS (Eng) 1997; memb RSM; *Recreations* narrowboat cruising, jogging, woodwork; *Style*— Prof Angus Wallace; ✉ University Hospital, Queen's Medical Centre, Nottingham NG7 2UH (☎ 0115 970 9407, fax 0115 942 3656)

WALLACE, Brian Godman; s of James Alexander Gaul Wallace, and Phyllis May, *née* Godman; *b* 1 March 1954; *Educ* Royal High Sch Edinburgh, Univ of St Andrews (MA); *m* Brenda Cameron; 1 da (Fiona b 11 March 1984), 1 s (Callum James b 27 April 1986); *Career* mangr Price Waterhouse CAs Dubai 1980–82 (asst mangr London 1976–80); Schlumberger: chief accountant Dubai 1982–84, Euro financial controller London 1984–85, Middle E financial controller Dubai 1985–87, Eastern Hemisphere fin dir Paris 1987–89; gp financial controller APV plc London 1989–90, fin dir Geest plc 1990–95, gp fin dir Ladbroke Group plc 1995–; ACA; *Recreations* golf, tennis, theatre; *Style*— Brian Wallace, Esq; ✉ Ladbroke Group plc, Maple Court, Central Park, Reeds Crescent, Watford, Herts WD1 1HZ (☎ 0171 856 8000, fax 0171 856 8001)

WALLACE, Prof David Alexander Ross; *b* 24 Nov 1933; *Educ* Univ of St Andrews (BSc), Univ of Manchester (PhD); *m* 12 July 1958, Elizabeth Anne, *née* Law (d 1963), 1 da (Elizabeth (Mrs Morrison) b 3 July 1961); *Career* instr Princeton Univ 1958–59, Benjamin Peirce Instr Harvard 1959–60, lectr Univ of Glasgow 1961–65, sr lectr Univ of Aberdeen 1965–73; prof of mathematics: Univ of Stirling 1973–86, Univ of Strathclyde 1986–96, ret; FRSE 1978, FRSA 1984; *Books* Groups (1974); *Recreations* tennis, badminton, swimming, cultural interests; *Style*— Prof D A R Wallace, FRSE; ✉ 27 Colquhoun Drive, Bearsden, Glasgow G61 4WQ (☎ 0141 942 4766); Department of Mathematics, University of Strathclyde, Livingstone Tower, 26 Richmond Street, Glasgow G1 1XH (☎ 0141 552 4400, fax 0141 552 8657, telex 77472)

WALLACE, Prof David James; CBE (1996); s of Robert Elder Wallace, and Jane McConnell, *née* Elliott; *b* 7 Oct 1945; *Educ* Hawick HS, Univ of Edinburgh (BSc, PhD); *m* 1970, Elizabeth Anne Yeats; 1 da; *Career* Harkness fell Dept of Physics Princeton Univ 1970–72, reader Dept of Physics Univ of Southampton 1978–79 (lectr 1972–78),

Tait prof of mathematical physics Univ of Edinburgh 1979–93 (head of physics 1984–87), vice-chllr Loughborough Univ 1994–; assoc dir Research Initiative on Pattern Recognition RSRE Malvern 1986–90; dir: Edinburgh Concurrent Supercomputer 1987–89, Edinburgh Parallel Computing Centre 1990–93; memb Cncl and chm Tech Opportunities Panel Engrg and Physical Scis Research Cncl 1994–, memb Scientific and Industl Award Ctees Royal Soc 1990–95; Euro Cmmn: memb High Performance Computing and Networking Advsy Ctee 1991–92, memb Physics Panel Human Capital and Mobility Prog 1991–94, memb Large Scale Facilities Evaluation Panel 1995–; memb Scottish Higher Educn Funding Cncl 1993–; pres Physics Section Br Assoc for the Advancement of Sci 1994; Maxwell Medal Inst of Physics 1980; author of pubns in research and review jls in various areas of theoretical physics and computing; FRS 1986, FRSE 1982, FInstP; *Recreations* running, eating at La Potiniėe, mycophagy; *Style*— Prof David Wallace, CBE, FRS, FRSE; ✉ Loughborough University, Loughborough, Leics LE11 3TU (☎ 01509 222001, fax 01509 223900, e-mail D.J.Wallace@lboro.ac.uk)

WALLACE, (James) Fleming; QC (Scot 1985); s of James Fleming Baird Wallace (d 1957), and Margaret Braidwood, *née* Gray; *b* 19 March 1931; *Educ* The Edinburgh Acad, Univ of Edinburgh (MA, LLB); *m* 1, 15 Sept 1964, Valerie Mary (d 1986), da of Leslie Lawrence (d 1957), of Wilts; 2 da (Jennifer b 1966, Gillian b 1969); m 2, 16 Aug 1990, Linda Ann, da of Robert Grant (d 1982); *Career* Nat Serv RA 2 Lt 1954–56, TA RA Lt 1956–60; advocate Scots Bar 1957–60, Scottish Parly draftsman and legal sec to the Lord Advocate London 1960–79, counsel Scottish Law Cmmn Edinburgh 1979–93, pt/t chm Industrial Tbnls (Scotland) 1993–; memb Faculty of Advocates 1957; *Books* Stair Memorial Encyclopaedia of the Laws of Scotland (contrib, 1988); *Recreations* choral singing, hill walking, golf, badminton; *Style*— Fleming Wallace, Esq, QC

WALLACE, Prof Frank Julius; s of Max Wallach, and Melly, *née* Hollaender; *Educ* Dean Close Sch Cheltenham, Univ of Birmingham (BSc, MSc, PhD, DSc); *m* 8 June 1946, Ruth Betty Ida, da of George Emil Aronstein (d 1942); 2 s (Paul George b 1952, Mark Jonathan b 1967), 1 da (Catherine Melly b 1948); *Career* lectr Univ of Birmingham 1951–56, chief res engr ABE Ltd 1956–60, prof of thermodynamics of fluid mechanics (former reader) Queen's Univ Belfast 1960–66, prof of mechanical engrg Univ of Bath 1966–89, conslt 1989–; sr dir F J Wallace & Associates Ltd; author of 75 published papers; memb Power Div Inst Mechanical Engrs 1985–89; FIMechE 1972; elected fell American Soc of Automotive Engrs 1980, FEng 1983; *Books* Engineering Thermodynamics (1964); *Recreations* tennis, languages; *Style*— Prof Frank Wallace, FEng; ✉ Cedarwood Cottage, 22 Sion Rd, Bath BA1 5SG (☎ 01225 314033); School of Mechanical Engineering, University of Bath, Bath BA2 7AY (☎ 01225 826399)

WALLACE, Prof Ian; s of Francis Jardine Wallace, and Edith, *née* Reay; *b* 8 Dec 1942; *Educ* Carlisle GS, Univ of Oxford (Cutlers Scholar, DAAD Scholar, MA, BLitt); *m* 8 July 1967, Trudy, da of Paul Johann Breitenmoser; 1 s (Daniel Frederick b 16 Nov 1976); *Career* asst prof in German Univ of Maine USA 1969–72 (instr 1967–69), lectr in German Univ of Dundee 1972–84; Univ of Loughborough: prof of modern languages 1984–91, head Dept of European Studies 1987–90; Univ of Bath: prof of German 1991–, head Sch of Modern Languages and Int Studies 1992–95; *Books* The Writer and Society in the GDR (ed, 1984), Volker Braun (1986), East Germany (1987), The German Revolution of 1989 (co-ed, 1992), Berlin (1993), Aliens (ed, 1994); *Recreations* sport, music; *Style*— Prof Ian Wallace; ✉ MLIS, University of Bath, Claverton Down, Bath BA2 7AY (☎ 01225 826244, fax 01225 826099)

WALLACE, Ian Bryce; OBE (1983); s of Sir John Wallace (d 1949), of London, and Mary McAdam Bryce Temple (d 1985); *b* 10 July 1919; *Educ* Charterhouse, Trinity Hall Cambridge (MA); *m* 1948, Patricia Gordon, da of Michael Gordon Black, OBE (d 1946), of Scotland; 1 s (John), 1 da (Rosemary); *Career* singer, actor, writer and broadcaster; pres Cncl for Music in Hosps 1988–; Hon DMus Univ of St Andrews 1991; *Books* Promise Me You'll Sing Mud (1975), Nothing Quite Like It (1982), Reflections on Scotland (1988); *Recreations* walking, reading, photography and watching sport; *Clubs* Garrick, MCC; *Style*— Ian Wallace, Esq, OBE; ✉ c/o Fraser & Dunlop Ltd, 5th Floor, The Chambers, Chelsea Harbour, Lots Road, London SW10 0XF (☎ 0171 344 1010)

WALLACE, Sir Ian James; kt (1982), CBE (1971, OBE (Mil) 1942); s of John Madder Wallace, CBE; *b* 25 Feb 1916; *Educ* Uppingham, Jesus Coll Cambridge; *m* 1942, Catherine Frost Mitchell; 1 s, 1 da; *Career* WWII Cdr (A) RNVR Fleet Air Arm; dir: Massey Ferguson Holdings 1952–72, Coventry Motor and Sundries Ltd 1986–91; chm SNR (Bearings) UK Ltd 1978–85, commercial conslt TRW Valves; Lloyd's underwriter; chm CBI Midland Regnl Cncl 1967–69; vice pres West Midlands Cons Cncl (chm 1967–70, pres 1972–74); pres: Coventry C of C 1972–74, West Worcestershire Cons Assoc 1995– (vice chm 1990–95), Fedn of Coventry Cons Assoc 1987–92 (chm 1968–87); life pres Mid Worcestershire Cons Assoc; former memb West Midlands Econ Planning Cncl and Severn-Trent Water Authy; pres: Birmingham and Midlands Inst 1991, Hereford and Worcestershire Rifle Assoc; FIMgt, FRSA, FInstD; *Recreations* rifle shooting, antiquarian horology; *Clubs* Carlton, Naval and Military, North London Rifle, Drapers (Coventry); *Style*— Sir Ian Wallace, CBE; ✉ Little House, 156 High St, Broadway, Worcs WR12 7AJ (☎ 01386 852414)

WALLACE, Ian Norman Duncan; QC (1973); s of Duncan Gardner Wallace (d 1939, HBM Crown Advocate in Egypt), of Alexandria, Egypt, and Eileen Agnes, *née* Wilkin (d 1991), of Bournabat, Smyrna, Turkey; *b* 21 April 1922; *Educ* Loretto, Oriel Coll Oxford (MA); *m* 25 March 1961 (m dis 1965), Valerie Mary, da of Rudolf Karl Walter Hollmann of Beckenham, Kent; *Career* Ordinary Seaman RN 1940–41, Lt RNVR 1941–46; called to the Bar Middle Temple 1948, practising barr and arbitrator specialising in construction law; visiting scholar Univ of California at Berkeley 1977–, visiting prof King's Coll London 1987–; FSA; *Publications* Hudson on Building and Civil Engineering Contracts (1959, 1965, 1970, 1979 and 1995 edns), Building and Civil Engineering Standard Forms (1969), Further Building Standard Forms (1973), ICE Conditions (1978), The International Civil Engineering Contract (1980), Construction Contracts: Principles and Policies (Vol 1 1986, Vol 2 1996); contrib: Law Quarterly Review, Construction Law Journal, International Construction Law Review; memb Editorial Bd Construction Law Journal; *Recreations* tennis, shooting; *Clubs* Lansdowne, Hurlingham; *Style*— Ian N D Wallace, Esq, QC, FSA; ✉ 53 Holland Park, London W11 3RS (☎ 0171 727 7640, fax 0171 727 8569); 1 Atkin Building, Gray's Inn, London WC1R 5BQ (☎ 0171 404 0102, fax 0171 405 7456, telex 298 623 HUDSON G)

WALLACE, James Robert; MP (Lib Dem) Orkney and Shetland (majority 5,033); s of John Fergus Thomson Wallace, of Annan, Dumfriesshire, and Grace Hannah, *née* Maxwell; *b* 25 Aug 1954; *Educ* Annan Acad, Downing Coll Cambridge (MA), Edinburgh Univ (LLB); *m* 9 July 1983, Rosemary Janet, da of William Grant Paton Fraser, OBE, TD, of Milngavie, Glasgow; 2 da (Helen b 1985, Clare b 1987); *Career* admitted Faculty of Advocates 1979; memb Scottish Lib Pty Nat Exec 1976–85 (vice chm 1982–85), Parly candidate (Lib) Dumfries 1979, Euro Parly candidate (Lib) S Scotland 1979; MP (Lib until 1988, now Lib Dem) Orkney and Shetland 1983–, Lib Parly spokesman on defence and dep whip 1985–87, Alliance election spokesman on tport 1987, Lib chief whip and defence spokesman 1987, Lib Dem chief whip 1988–92, Lib Dem spokesman on employment and fisheries 1988–92, Lib Dem spokesman on Scotland, maritime affairs and fishing 1992–, ldr Scottish Lib Dems 1992–; Elder of Church of Scotland; *Recreations* music, golf, travel; *Clubs* Caledonian, Scottish Liberal; *Style*— James Wallace, Esq, MP; ✉ Northwood House, Tankerness, Orkney KW17 2QS (☎ 01856 861383); House of Commons, London SW1A OAA (☎ 0171 219 6254, fax 0171 219 6437, e-mail jim.wallace@zetnet.co.uk)

WALLACE, John Williamson; OBE (1995); s of Christopher Kidd Wallace, of Glenrothes, Fife, and Ann Drummond, *née* Allan; *b* 14 April 1949; *Educ* Buckhaven HS, King's Coll Cambridge (MA); *m* 3 July 1971, Elizabeth Jane, da of Prof Ronald Max Hartwell, of Oxford; 2 s (Cosmo b 1979, Esme b 1982); *Career* asst princ trumpet LSO 1974–76, princ trumpet Philharmonia 1976–, performed obligato trumpet at Royal Wedding 1981, performed first performance Malcolm Arnold Concerto 1982, Sir Peter Maxwell Davies trumpet concerto Hiroshima 1988, Tim Souster Trumpet Concerto 1988, Robert Saxton, Dominic Muldowney, James Macmillan Trumpet Concerto 1993; trumpet duets: Prime Number (1990), Odd Number (1991), Even Number (1991); soloist Last Night of the Proms 1996; formed Wallace Collection Brass Ensemble 1986 (19 solo and gp recordings); hon memb RCM 1982, FRAM, FRSAMD, memb Royal; *Books* First Book of Trumpet Solos (1985), Second Book of Trumpet Solos (1985); *Style*— John Wallace, Esq, OBE; ✉ c/o (☎ 0171 609 7839, fax 0171 700 3310)

WALLACE, Julie T; da of Andrew Keir, and Julia, *née* Wallace; *Educ* Ysgol Y Drenywydd, Twickenham Sixth Form Coll, LAMDA; *Career* actress; *Theatre* incl: Billy the Kid and Barrel of Laughs (Upstream Theatre Club), The House of Usher (Theatre West), Beauty and the Beast (Bristol), The Worlds (Royal Court), The Cherry Orchard (Dundee), Misery (Criterion) 1993; *Television* incl: The Life and Loves of a She Devil (BBC TV, best actress nomination BAFTA), Stolen (LWT), Selling Hitler (ITV), Lovejoy (BBC), Comic Strip (BBC); *Films* incl: The Living Daylights, The Threepenny Opera, Hawks, The Lunatic, The Anchoress; *Recreations* going to the cinema, watching TV (esp Barry Norman!); *Style*— Ms Julie T Wallace; ✉ c/o Annette Stone Associates, 9 Newburgh Street, London W1V 1LH (☎ 0171 734 0626, fax 0171 434 2014)

WALLACE, Keith; s of William Wallace, CMG (d 1990), and Sheila Agnes, *née* Hopper; *b* 5 June 1945; *Educ* Mill Hill Sch; *m* 17 March 1973, Christine, da of Alan Beautement (d 1970); 3 s (Jasper b 1975, William b 1977, Dougal b 1983); *Career* admitted slr 1971; ptnr Bird & Bird 1972–84, clerk Richard Cloudesley's Charity 1976–, ed Pension Lawyer 1984–, ptnr Richards Butler 1985–; memb Takeover Panel 1994; chm: Legal Educn Ctee Soc for Computers and Law 1982–83, Maldon Unit Trust Managers Ltd 1987–, Independent Pension Trustee Ltd 1990–; dir Beaufort Trust Corporation Ltd 1985–; ed/commentator (Pensions) Television Educn Network 1992–; vice pres Holborn Law Soc 1983–84; The Assoc of Corporate Tstees (TACT): memb Cncl, dep chm Pensions Ctee; memb: Ctee Assoc Pension Lawyers 1984–89, Euro Ctee Int Fndn of Employee Benefit Plans 1989–93, NAPF Investmt Ctee 1991–96, Cncl Occupational Pensions Advsy Service 1992–; *Style*— Keith Wallace, Esq; ✉ Richards Butler, Beaufort House, 15 St Botolph Street, London EC3A 7EE (☎ 0171 247 6555, fax 0171 247 5091)

WALLACE, Maj Malcolm Charles Robarts; s of Lionel John Wallace, MBE, of Farnham, Surrey, and Maureen Winefride, *née* Robarts; *b* 12 June 1947; *Educ* Blackrock Coll County Dublin; *m* 1, 15 March 1974, Caroline Anne, da of Maj Philip Edward Churton Vigors Doyne Ditmas (d 1980); 1 s (Harry b 8 April 1980), 1 da (Philippa b 7 Oct 1981); m 2, 13 July 1991, Mrs Jane Barbara Thelwall; 2 s (Thomas b 24 Sept 1993, Charlie b 22 July 1995); *Career* Cmmnd RA 1967, served Far East and with RHA in BAOR, mounted duty with King's Troop RHA 1970–74, post CO King's Troop RHA 1982–85, ret 1985; chef d'equipe int and Olympic three day event team 1979–84, team mangr equestrian teams Seoul Olympics 1988 and Barcelona Olympics 1992, steward Sandown Park and Warwick 1987–94; dir gen Br Equestrian Fedn 1985, ret 1994, dir of regulation Jockey Club 1994–; Freeman: City of London 1984, Worshipful Co of Saddlers; *Books* The King's Troop, Royal Horse Artillery (1984); *Recreations* racing, equestrian sports, field sports; *Clubs* Cavalry and Guards'; *Style*— Maj Malcolm Wallace; ✉ Fishponds Farm, Stoke Albany, Market Harborough, Leics LE16 8PZ (☎ 01858 85250, fax 01858 85499); The Jockey Club, 42 Portman Square, London W1H 0EN (☎ 0171 486 4921, fax 0171 935 8703, car 0385 390325)

WALLACE, Richard Alexander; s of Lawrence Mervyn Wallace, and Norah Wallace; *b* 24 Nov 1946; *Educ* Clifton, King's Coll Cambridge (MA); *m* 1970, Teresa Caroline Harington Smith; 4 c (1 decd); *Career* asst master Woking Co GS for Boys 1967, Miny of Social Security 1968, princ DHSS 1972, asst sec 1981, under sec and head Tport Planning Water and Environment Gp Welsh Office 1988–90 (joined 1986), princ fin offr Welsh Office 1990–; *Style*— R A Wallace, Esq; ✉ Welsh Office, Cathays Park, Cardiff CF1 3NQ

WALLACE, Robin John; s of Patrick John Wallace, of Chandler's Ford, Hants, and (Lauretta Elizabeth) Anne, *née* Peters; bro of Shaun Wallace, *qv*; *b* 28 March 1964; *Educ* Thornden Sch Chandlers Ford, Barton Peveril Coll Eastleigh, Open Univ (BSc); *m* 1990, Jilly Mary Curry, *qv*, da of (Thomas) Peter Ellison Curry, QC, *qv*; 1 s (Lloyd Ellison b 13 Feb 1995); *Career* skier; second place Euro Freestyle Skiing Championships 1987, ninth place in freestyle Calgary Winter Olympics 1988, Br Freestyle Skiing Champion 1989, winner eight nat titles; nat coach to British Freestyle Skiing Team 1993; pres Br Acrobatic Sports Club; currently computer professional with Radio Computing Services UK Ltd; *Recreations* trampolining, computers, chess; *Style*— Robin Wallace, Esq; ✉ 3 Forest Road, Chandler's Ford, Hampshire SO5 1NA (☎ 01703 265214)

WALLACE, (George) Roger; *b* 20 April 1946; *m* 28 June 1969, Susan (Sue); 1 s (Mark b 25 July 1975), 1 da (Helen (twin) b 25 July 1975); *Career* Coalite Group Ltd (formerly Coalite Group plc): gp accountant 1976–80, gp fin controller 1980–82, fin dir 1982–89; dir CTC Fisheries Ltd 1986–, fin dir Anglo United plc 1990– (chief fin offr 1989–90); MCIMA; *Style*— Roger Wallace, Esq; ✉ Anglo United plc, Newgate House, Broombank Rd, Chesterfield, Derbys S41 9QJ (☎ 01246 454583, fax 01246 453787)

WALLACE, Shaun Patrick; s of Patrick John Wallace, of Chandler's Ford, Hants, and (Lauretta Elizabeth) Anne, *née* Peters; bro of Robin Wallace, *qv*; *b* 20 Nov 1961; *Educ* Thornden Sch Chandler's Ford, Barton Peveril Coll Eastleigh, Univ of Nottingham (BSc); *m* 10 Oct 1995, Tina, *née* Crownover; *Career* professional racing cyclist; memb: Crabwood Cycling Club Southampton 1977–80, VC Nottingham 1981–85, Harlow Cycling Club 1996–; achievements incl: nat jr km champion 1979, English schs 10 mile champion and record holder 1981, nat 4000m pursuit champion 1982, Silver medal 4000m pursuit Cwlth Games Brisbane 1982 and Victoria 1994, nat 20km, pursuit and 1km champion 1983, nat 20km and 1km champion 1984, GB rep Olympic Games 1984 and 1996, Silver medal professional 5000m pursuit World Championships Stuttgart 1991 and Valencia 1992, first Br rider invited to Japanese Keirin Sch and Int Series 1992, nat 1km champion 1995 and 1996, nat 20km champion 1996; records: world amateur flying km 1985, world professional flying km 1986; *Recreations* chess, bicycle development, car design, skiing, network marketing; *Style*— Shaun Wallace, Esq; ✉ 3 Forest Road, Chandler's Ford, Eastleigh, Hants SO53 1NA (☎ 01703 265214)

WALLACE, (Wellesley) Theodore Octavius; s of Dr Caleb Paul Wallace (d 1981), of Whitecroft, West Clandon, Surrey, and Dr Lucy Elizabeth Rainsford, *née* Pigott (d 1968); *b* 10 April 1938; *Educ* Charterhouse, Christ Church Oxford (MA); *m* 23 Jan 1988, Maria Amelia, o da of Sir Ian George Abercromby, 10 Bt; 1 s (James Abercromby Octavius b 18 Jan 1989), 1 da (Lucy Mary Diana b 4 Nov 1991); *Career* 2 Lt RA 1958, Lt Surrey Yeomanry TA 1959; called to the Bar Inner Temple 1963; memb Lloyd's; govr Inner London Sch 1966–86, chm Chelsea Cons Assoc 1981–84, chm VAT and Duties Tribunal 1992– (pt/t chm 1989–92), special cmmr 1992–; hon sec Taxation Sub-Ctee Soc of Cons Lawyers 1975–92; Cons candidate: Pontypool Feb 1974, South Battersea Oct 1974 and May 1979; *Books* The Case Against Wealth Tax (with Rt Hon

John Wakeham, MP, 1968), A History of Hans Town Chelsea (1986); *Recreations* tennis, racing, skiing; *Style*— Theodore Wallace, Esq; ✉ Whitecroft, West Clandon, Surrey GU4 7TD (☎ 01483 222574); 46 Belleville Rd, London SW11 4QT (☎ 0171 228 7740); Combined Tax Tribunals, 15–19 Bedford Avenue, London WC1B 3AS

WALLACE, Vivien Rosemary Lumsdaine; da of late Capt James Edward Lumsdaine Wallace, and late Gwynne Wallace, *née* Jones; *b* 11 Feb 1944; *Educ* St Martin's Sch Solihull, Emma Willard Troy New York (on English speaking Union Scholarship), Arts Cncl of GB bursary to study theatre admin; *m* 1, 2 Sept 1964, Anthony Thomas Etridge; m 2, 27 June 1981, Terence Francis Frank Coleman, *qv*; 1 s (Jack b 1984), 1 da (Eliza b 1983); *Career* press offr London Festival Ballet 1969–71, first ever press offr Royal Ballet Covent Garden 1972–74, chief press offr National Theatre 1975–77; Granada Television International: NY mangr 1979, head of sales 1981, dir of sales 1983, chief exec 1987–92; md Lippin-Wallace (television mktg co based London and LA) 1993–96, head of public affairs National Theatre 1996–; dir: Granada Television Ltd 1987–92, Nat Assoc of TV Production Executives USA 1988–92; chm TBA Films and Television Hamburg 1989–92; FRSA; *Style*— Miss Vivien Wallace; ✉ Royal National Theatre, Upper Ground, South Bank, London SE1 9PX (☎ 0171 928 2033)

WALLACE, Walter Wilkinson; CVO (1977), CBE (1974, OBE 1964), DSC (1944); s of Walter Wilkinson Wallace (d 1960), and Helen Morgan, *née* Douglas (d 1992); *b* 23 Sept 1923; *Educ* George Heriot's Sch Edinburgh; *m* 11 June 1955, Susan Blanche, da of Brig F W B Parry, CBE (d 1989); 1 s (Andrew Douglas b 1960), 1 da (Susan Emma b 1956); *Career* Capt RM 1942–46; Colonial Serv: successively dist cmmr, provincial cmmr then devpt sec Sierra Leone 1948–64, estab sec Bahamas 1964–67, sec to the Cabinet Bermuda 1968–73; Dip Serv: govr Br Virgin Is 1974–78, FCO 1980–; constitutional cmmr: St Helena 1987, Cayman Is 1991, Turks and Caicos Is 1992, British Virgin Is 1993, Falkland Is 1995; *Clubs* Army and Navy; *Style*— Walter Wallace, Esq, CVO, CBE, DSC; ✉ Becketts, Itchenor, West Sussex PO20 7DE (☎ 01243 512438); Foreign & Commonwealth Office, King Charles St, London SW1 (☎ 0171 270 2693)

WALLACE-HADRILL, Prof Andrew Frederic; s of John Michael Wallace-Hadrill (d 1985), of Oxford, and Anne, *née* Wakefield; *b* 29 July 1951; *Educ* Rugby (scholar), CCC Oxford (Charles Oldham scholar, Hertford and da Paravicini scholar, Craven and Ireland scholar, BA, DPhil); *m* 31 July 1975, Josephine Claire, da of John Temple Forbes Braddock; 1 da (Sophie Margaret Anne b 22 Sept 1980), 1 s (Michael Sutherland b 9 June 1984); *Career* fell and dir of studies in classics Magdalene Coll Cambridge 1976–83, jt lectr in classics Jesus Coll Cambridge 1979–83, lectr in ancient history Univ of Leicester 1983–87, prof of classics and head of dept Univ of Reading 1987–95, dir British Sch at Rome 1995–; ed Jl of Roman Studies 1990–95; memb Soc for the Promotion of Roman Studies 1973–; *Books* Suetonius: the scholar and his Caesars (1983), Ammianus Marcellinus - The Later Roman Empire AD 354–378 (1986), Patronage in Ancient Society (ed, 1989), City and Country in the Ancient World (jt ed, 1991), Augustan Rome (1993), Houses and Society in Pompeii and Herculaneum (1994); *Style*— Prof Andrew Wallace-Hadrill; ✉ The British School at Rome, via Gramsci 61, 00197 Rome, Italy (☎ 00 39 6 3230743)

WALLACE OF CAMPSIE, Baron (Life Peer UK 1974), of Newlands, Co of City of Glasgow; George Wallace; JP (1968), DL (Glasgow 1971); s of John Wallace and Mary Pollock; *b* 13 Feb 1915; *Educ* Queen's Park Secondary Sch, Univ of Glasgow; *m* 1977, Irene Alice Langdon, er da of Ernest Phipps, of Glasgow; *Career* admitted slr of the Supreme Ct 1950–, Hon Sheriff Hamilton 1971–; dir South of Scotland Electricity Bd 1966–69, chm East Kilbride Devpt Corp 1969–75, dir Smith and Nephew plc 1972–77, fndr memb Scottish Devpt Agency 1976–78, pres Wallace Cameron Hldgs 1977–; vice pres Scottish Assoc of Youth Clubs, memb Advsy Bd Salvation Army Strathclyde; active with many other gps and assocs; memb: Law Soc of Scotland, Royal Faculty of Procurators, Int Bar Assoc; Hon LLD Univ of Strathclyde 1993; FRSA, FCIM, FIMgt, FSA (Scot); KStJ; *Style*— The Lord Wallace of Campsie, JP, DL; ✉ 14 Fernleigh Rd, Newlands, Glasgow (☎ 0141 637 3337)

WALLACE OF COSLANY, Baron (Life Peer UK 1974), of Coslany, City of Norwich; George Douglas Wallace; s of George Wallace, of Cheltenham, Glos; *b* 18 April 1906; *Educ* Central Sch Cheltenham; *m* 1932, Vera, da of William Joseph Randall, of Guildford, Surrey; 1 s (Hon Michael George b 1944), 1 da (Hon Elizabeth Anne b 1933); *Career* sits as Lab Peer in House of Lords; MP (Lab): Chislehurst 1945–50, Norwich N 1964–74; Govt whip 1947–50, Lord in Waiting 1977–79, oppn whip 1979–84, oppn spokesman (Lords) on Health 1983–84; memb: Chislehurst and Sidcup UDC 1937–46, Kent CC 1948–53; pres: Radio Soc of GB 1977, League of Friends Queen Mary's Hosp Sidcup; *Recreations* gardening, amateur radio; *Style*— The Rt Hon the Lord Wallace of Coslany; ✉ 44 Shuttle Close, Sidcup, Kent (☎ 0181 300 3634)

WALLACE OF SALTAIRE, Baron (Life Peer UK 1995), of Shipley in the County of West Yorkshire; William John Lawrence Wallace; s of William Edward Wallace, and Mary Agnes, *née* Tricks; *b* 12 March 1941; *Educ* Westminster Abbey Sch, St Edwards Sch Oxford, King's Coll Cambridge (BA), Cornell Univ USA (PhD); *m* 25 Aug 1968, Helen Sarah, da of Edward Rushworth (d 1975); 1 s (Hon Edward b 1981), 1 da (Hon Harriet b 1977); *Career* lectr in govt Univ of Manchester 1966–67, dir of Studies Royal Inst of Int Affrs 1978–90, Hallstein fell St Antony's Coll Oxford 1990–95, reader in int relations LSE 1995–; visiting prof of int studies Central European Univ 1994–; memb various Liberal Pty and SDP Liberal Alliance Nat Ctees 1973–88; Parly candidate Liberal Pty: Huddersfield West 1970, Manchester Moss Side 1974, Shipley 1983 and 1987; *Books* The Transformation of Western Europe (1990), The Foreign Policy Process of Britain (1976), Policy Making in the European Community (1983), Regional Integration: the West European Experience (1994); *Style*— The Rt Hon Lord Wallace of Saltaire; ✉ Department of International Relations, London School of Economics, London WC2A 2AE (☎ 0171 405 7686, fax 0171 955 7446)

WALLDEN, Richard James; s of Frederick Edward Wallden, of Frinton on Sea, Essex, and Olive Maud, *née* Jones; *b* 7 Oct 1946; *Educ* Bancroft's Sch Woodford Green Essex; *m* 9 Oct 1971, Sally Barbara, da of Herbert James Ford, of Woodford Green, Essex; 4 s (James b 1975, Toby b 1977, Luke b 1980, Benjamin b 1981); *Career* Barclays Bank plc: mangr 1977–85, dir London NW Region 1985–89, dir Personnel Dept 1989–90; risk management dir UK Domestic Bank 1990–94, dir Barclays Life Assurance 1994–; memb Fyfield PCC 1974–; ACIB; *Recreations* rugby football; *Clubs* Bancroft RFC; *Style*— Richard Wallden, Esq; ✉ Business, Design and Development Director, Barclays Life Assurance Co Ltd, Fleetway House, 25 Farringdon Street, London EC4A 4JA (☎ 0171 832 3277)

WALLER, Gary Peter Anthony; MP (C) Keighley (majority 3,596); s of John Waller (d 1965), and Elizabeth Waller; *b* 24 June 1945; *Educ* Rugby, Univ of Lancaster; *Career* contested (C) Rother Valley Feb and Oct 1974; MP (C): Brighouse and Spenborough 1979–83, Keighley 1983–; memb House of Commons Select Ctee on Tport 1979–82, PPS to Rt Hon David Howell as Sec of State for Tport 1982–83; chm: All Party Wool Textile Gp 1984–89, House of Commons Information Select Ctee 1992– (memb 1991–); vice chm Cons Parly Tport Ctee 1992–; memb Cncl Consumers' Assoc 1995–; *Style*— Gary Waller, Esq, MP; ✉ House of Commons, London SW1A OAA (☎ 0171 219 4010, fax 0171 219 4935)

WALLER, Rt Hon Sir George Stanley; kt (1965), OBE (1945), PC (1976); s of James Stanley Waller; *b* 3 Aug 1911; *Educ* Oundle, Queens' Coll Cambridge; *m* 1936, Hon Elizabeth Margery, da of 1 Baron Hacking; 2 s (1 of whom The Rt Hon Sir Mark Waller, *qv*), 1 da; *Career* RAFO 1931–36; served WWII: RAFVR, 502 Sqdn 1940–41, Wing Cdr 1943 (despatches); called to the Bar Gray's Inn 1934, QC 1954; recorder: Doncaster 1953–54, Sunderland 1954–55, Bradford 1955–57, Sheffield 1957–61, Leeds 1961–65; slr gen Durham 1957–61, attorney gen Co Palatine of Durham 1961–65, justice of the High Court (Queen's Bench Div) 1965–76, presiding judge NE Circuit 1973–76, Lord Justice of Appeal 1976–84, ret; former memb: Gen Cncl of the Bar, Parole Bd, Criminal Law Revision Ctee 1977–85; chm Policy Advsy Ctee on Sexual Offences 1977–85; *Style*— The Rt Hon Sir George Waller, OBE; ✉ Hatchway, Hatch Lane, Kingsley Green, Haslemere, Surrey GU27 3LJ (☎ 01428 644629)

WALLER, Jane Ashton; da of Charles Ashton Waller, of Bucks, and Barbara Mary *née* Batt; *b* 19 May 1944; *Educ* Ladymede Sch Little Kimble, Croham Hurst Sch Croydon, Hornsey Art Sch (BA), Royal Coll of Art (MA); *m* 11 June 1983, Michael Hugh Vaughan-Rees, s of Lyle Vaughan-Rees (d 1962); *Career* since 1982: exhibited in London and many other parts of the country also in Kuwait, collections in LA, Chicago and Miami; work is sold at Bonhams and Sothebys; author of articles in Ceramic Review; started successful one woman campaign to save the Oxo Tower on the South bank; involved in Coin St Orgn; *Books* A Stitch in Time (1972), Some Things for the Children (1974), A Man's Book (1977), The Thirties Family Knitting Book (1981), Below the Green Pond (1982), The Man's Knitting Book (1984), Women in Wartime (jt 1987), Women in Uniform (jt 1989), Handbuilt Ceramics (1990), Blitz (jtly 1990), Saving the Dinosaurs (1994), The Sludge-Gulpers (1997); *Recreations* reading, gardening, knitting, writing, conservation, cooking, ceramics, walking in the country, collection of fashion magazines and knitting leaflets 1920–60; *Style*— Ms Jane Waller

WALLER, Jonathan Neil; s of Douglas Victor Waller, of Fareham, Hampshire, and Kristine Daphne Desmond Rieley (d 1982); *b* 16 April 1956; *Educ* Cherry Orchard HS Northampton, Northampton GS, Nene Coll Northampton, Coventry (Lanchester) Poly, Chelsea Sch of Art (BA, MA); *Career* artist; painting fellowship S Glamorgan Inst of Higher Educn Cardiff 1985–86, full time artist London 1987–; *Solo Exhibitions* Paton Gallery London 1986 and 1988, Flowers East London 1990, 1992, 1993 and 1994, Doncaster Museum and Art Gallery 1994; *Gp Exhibitions* New Contemporaries (ICA) 1984, Midland View 3 (Nottingham and tour) 1984, Four New Painters (Paton Gallery) 1986, Royal Over-Seas League London 1986, London Glasgow New York (Metropolitan Museum New York) 1988, The New British Painting (Cincinnatti USA and tour) 1988, Pacesetters (City Art Gallery Peterborough) 1988, The Thatcher Years: An Artistic Retrospective (Flowers East) 1989, Confrontation: Three British Artists (Joy Emery Gallery Detroit USA) 1989, Angela Flowers Gallery 1990 Barbican 1989, Flowers at Moos (Gallery Moos NY) 1990, This Sporting Life (Flowers East) 1990, Kunst Europa (Badischer Kunstverein Karlsruhe Germany) 1991, Nudes (Watermans Arts Centre Brentford) 1991, Artists Choice (Flowers East) 1992, Human Form (Parnham House Dorset) 1992, Heads (Royal Museum and Art Gallery Canterbury) 1993, But Big is Better... (Flowers East) 1993, New Figurative Painting (Salander-O'Reilly Galleries/Fred Hoffman Beverly Hills Calif) 1993, By Underground to Kew (London Transport Museum and Kew Gardens Gallery) 1994, Six Gallery Artists (Angela Flowers Gallery) 1994, After Redoute (Flowers East) 1994, Twenty-fifth Anniversary (Flowers East) 1995, The Discerning Eye (Mall Galleries London) 1995; cmmns: poster for London Underground on subject of Kew Gardens 1994, two paintings for Terminal 3 Heathrow Airport on subject of London parks 1995; work in the collections of: Metropolitan Museum NY, Contemporary Art Soc, Unilever plc, Dept of the Environment, Bankers Trust, Readers Digest London and NY, London Underground, Br Airports Authy; grants incl: Welsh Arts Cncl 1986, British Cncl 1990; awards: first prize Midland View 3 1984, Mark Rothko Meml Tst travelling scholarship to USA 1988; *Style*— Jonathan Waller, Esq; ✉ Studio 51, Acme Studios, 105–107 Carpenters Rd, Stratford, London E15 (☎ 0181 519 5240); c/o Matthew Flowers, Flowers East, 199–205 Richmond Road, Hackney, London E8 3NJ (☎ 0181 985 3333, fax 0181 985 0067)

WALLER, Rt Hon Lord Justice; Rt Hon Sir (George) Mark; kt (1989), PC (1996); s of The Rt Hon Sir George Stanley Waller, OBE, *qv* (a former Lord Justice of Appeal), and Hon Lady Elizabeth Margery Waller; *b* 13 Oct 1940; *Educ* Oundle, Univ of Durham (LLB); *m* 1967, Rachel Elizabeth, da of His Hon Christopher Beaumont, MBE, *qv*, of Boroughbridge, N Yorks; 3 s (Charles b 1968, Richard b 1969, Philip b 1973); *Career* called to the Bar Gray's Inn 1964, QC 1979, recorder of the Crown Court 1986–89, judge of the High Court of Justice (Queen's Bench Div) 1989–96, presiding judge (NE Circuit) 1992–95, judge i/c Commercial List 1995–96, a Lord Justice of Appeal 1996–; *Recreations* tennis, golf; *Clubs* Garrick, MCC, Huntercombe; *Style*— The Rt Hon Sir Mark Waller; ✉ c/o Royal Courts of Justice, Strand, London WC2A 2LL

WALLER, Michael Garnet; s of Richard Garnet Waller (d 1984), and Joan May Kendrew; *b* 22 Aug 1939; *Educ* Uppingham; *m* 1967, Susan, da of Charles Ernest Mercer (d 1979); 2 da; *Career* CA; ptnr Price Waterhouse 1972– (joined 1958); FCA (ACA 1964); *Recreations* shooting, golf, tennis; *Clubs* MCC, Oriental, Royal Ashdown Forest Golf; *Style*— Michael Waller, Esq; ✉ Highbrook House, Ardingly, W Sussex RH17 6SS; Price Waterhouse, Southwark Towers, 32 London Bridge St, London SE1 9SY (☎ 0171 939 2151)

WALLER, Rev Dr Ralph; *b* 11 Dec 1945; *Educ* John Leggot GS Scunthorpe, Univ of Oxford (MA), Richmond Coll Divinity Sch Univ of London (BD, Westcott New Testament Greek prize, Hodson Smith Church History prize), Univ of Nottingham (MTh), Univ of London (PhD); *m* 28 Dec 1968, Carol, *née* Roberts; 1 da (Elizabeth b 24 June 1983); *Career* VSO teacher and house master Shri Shivajh Mil Sch Poona India 1967–68; teacher Riddings Comp Sch Scunthorpe Sept 1968; student Richmond Coll Divinity Sch Univ of London 1969–72; Methodist min Melton Mowbray Circuit 1972–75 (ordained 1975); min of Elvet Methodist Church Durham City and Methodist chaplain Univ of Durham 1975–79; chaplain St Mary's Coll and St Aidan's Coll Univ of Durham 1979–81; chaplain Westminster Coll Oxford (also tutor in theology and res tutor) 1981–88; princ Harris Manchester Coll and tutor in theology 1988–; dir Fndn for the Study of Christianity and Soc 1990–; Alfred North Whitehead distinguished visiting lectr Univ of Redlands USA 1992; select preacher Univ of Oxford 1992; individual winner Templeton UK Award 1994; govr: St Mary's Coll Univ of Durham 1978–81, Kingswood Sch 1994–; memb: Dr Barnardo's Adoption Ctee 1979–81, Ecclesiastical History Soc, chm Univ of Oxford Faculty of Theology; tstee: Farmington Tst, Idreos Tst, Joan Crewdson Tst; *Publications* Faith and Freedom (contrib to vol 39 1985, and vol 47 1994), Truth, Liberty and Religion (contrib, 1986), Grace and Freedom (contrib, 1988), Studies in Church History (contrib to vol 25, 1988), A Response to the Challenge of Continuing Education (1992); *Recreations* walking, swimming, browsing round second-hand bookshops; *Style*— The Rev Dr Ralph Waller; ✉ Harris Manchester College, Oxford OX1 3TD (☎ 01865 271006)

WALLER, Sir Robert William; 9 Bt (I 1780), of Newport, Tipperary; s of 8 Bt (d 1958); *b* 16 June 1934; *Educ* Newark Coll of Engineering, Farleigh Dickinson Univ; *m* 1960 (m dis 1975), Carol Anne, da of John Edward Hines, of Hampton, New Hampshire, and Lynn, Mass, USA; 3 s (1 decd), 2 da; *Heir* s, John Michael Waller b 14 May 1962; *Career* engineer General Electric Co, ret; *Style*— Sir Robert Waller, Bt; ✉ 5 Lookout Terrace, Lynnfield, Mass 01940, USA

WALLER, His Hon Judge; Stephen Philip; s of Ronald and Susannah Waller; *b* 2 Jan 1950; *Educ* Mill Hill Sch, UCL (LLB); *m* 1, 1972 (m dis), Anne Brooksbank; 1 s, 1 da; m 2, 1986, Jenny Welch; 1 da; *Career* called to the Bar Inner Temple 1972, circuit judge (SE Circuit) 1996–; *Recreations* music; *Style*— His Hon Judge Waller; ✉ c/o Snaresbrook Crown Court, Hollybush Hill, Snaresbrook, London E11 1QW

WALLEY, Joan Lorraine; MP (Lab) Stoke-on-Trent North (majority 14,777); da of Arthur Simeon Walley (d 1968), and Mary Emma, *née* Pass (d 1991); *b* 23 Jan 1949; *Educ* Biddulph GS, Univ of Hull (BA), Univ Coll of Swansea (Dip); *m* 2 Aug 1980, Jan Ostrowski, s of Adam Ostrowski; 2 s (Daniel b 1981, Tom b 1983); *Career* local govt offr NACRO, memb Lambeth Cncl 1982–86, MP (Lab) Stoke-on-Trent N 1987–; oppn front bench spokesman on: environment 1988–90, transport 1990–95; memb: All Pty Parly Football Ctee, All Party Parly Street Lighting Gp; vice pres: Instn of Environmental Health Offrs, SERA; pres: West Midlands Home and Water Safety Cncl, Stoke on Trent Primary Sch Sports Assoc; *Style*— Joan Walley, MP; ✉ House of Commons, London SW1A 0AA

WALLEY, Sir John; KBE (1965), CB (1950); s of R M Walley; *b* 3 April 1906; *Educ* Hereford HS, Hereford Cathedral Sch, Merton Coll Oxford; *m* 1934, Elisabeth Mary Pinhorn; 2 s, 2 da; *Career* Postmaster Merton Coll Oxford 1924–28; asst princ Miny of Labour 1929, sec Cabinet Ctee on Unemployment 1932, princ Miny of Labour 1934, asst sec Miny of Nat Serv 1941, promoted under-sec to take charge of legislation and other preparations for Beveridge Nat Insur Scheme in New Miny of Nat Insur 1945, dep sec 1958–66; chm Dental Benefit Cncl 1945–48; chm Hampstead Centre Nat Tst 1969–79 (pres 1980–90); *Books* Social Security - Another British Failure? (1972), and contribs to others; *Style*— Sir John Walley, KBE, CB; ✉ Brookland House, 24 High Street, Cottenham, Cambs CB4 4SA (☎ 01954 250931)

WALLING, Tony Roy; s of Ray Frederic George Walling, and Olive May, *née* Hill; *b* 29 March 1948; *Educ* Walderslade Boys Sch Chatham Kent, Medway Coll of Art (DipAD); *m* 18 Sept 1971, Judith, da of John Williams Powell; 3 da (Aimée Lois b 30 Jan 1973, Adrienne Alice b 16 Feb 1975, Elizabeth Olivia b 2 Sept 1979); 1 s (Lewis Alexander b 31 July 1977); *Career* graphic designer Butterworth Group Publishers London 1969 (studio mangr 1971), pt/t consultancy work 1972–73, formed own consultancy London 1973; clients incl: STC Components, Japan Air Lines, Union Carbide Corporation, Imperial Cancer Res Fund, ICI Ltd, Newsweek International, Trident Television; joined Borodin Management & Communications Group 1987 (creative dir of subsid co Borodin Design Associates Ltd York 1987–92); design consultancy work abroad incl: Rhône-Poulenc France, Finlux Television, AMEC Properties, Imperial Cancer Res Fund; dir Phoenix Multimedia Solutions Ltd Harrogate 1992–; operating own design consultancy in Harrogate 1993–; memb Industl Liaison Ctee York Coll of Art & Technol, nat jt winner in competition for designing product guide for Reed Group; *Recreations* computer animation, multimedia, classical guitar playing, weight training; *Style*— Tony Walling, Esq; ✉ 2 Sundew Heath, Hillcrest View, Killinghall Moor, Harrogate, N Yorks HG3 2XZ (☎ 01423 526179)

WALLINGER, John David Arnold; s of Sir Geoffrey Arnold Wallinger, GBE, KCMG (d 1979), and Diana, *née* Peel Nelson (d 1986); *b* 1 May 1940; *Educ* Winchester, Clare Coll Cambridge (BA); *m* 16 Feb 1966, Rosamund Elizabeth, da of Jack Philip Albert Gavin Clifford-Wolff, MBE; *Career* ptnr: Panmure Gordon & Co 1972–75, Rowe & Pitman 1975–86; dir S G Warburg Securities 1986–, vice chm S G Warburg International 1994–95; exec dir SBC Warburg 1995–; SIA; *Recreations* golf, fishing, shooting, racing; *Style*— John Wallinger, Esq; ✉ SBC Warburg, 1 Finsbury Ave, London, EC2M 2PA (☎ 0171 606 1066, fax 0171 382 4800)

WALLINGER, Karl; *b* 19 Oct 1957; *Career* musician; formerly with: Quasimodo, Zero Zero, Invisible Body Club, Out, The Waterboys; fndr memb World Party 1986–; albums with The Waterboys: A Pagan Place (1984), This is the Sea (1985, UK no 37); albums with World Party: Private Revolution (1987, UK no 56), Goodbye Jumbo (1990, UK no 36), Bang! (1993, UK no 2); musical dir The Rocky Horror Show 1983; *Style*— Karl Wallinger, Esq; ✉ c/o Chrysalis Records Ltd, The Chrysalis Building, Bramley Road, London N10 6SP (☎ 0171 221 2231, fax 0171 221 6455)

WALLINGTON, Jeremy Francis; s of Ernest Francis Wallington (d 1962), and Nellie, *née* Howe (d 1953); *b* 7 July 1935; *Educ* Royal GS High Wycombe; *m* 22 Oct 1955, Margaret Ivy, da of Clifford Samuel Willment (d 1988); 3 s (Rupert Francis b 1958, Jake Samuel b 1962, Benjamin Geoffrey b 1965), 1 da (Abigail Margaret b 1959); *Career* asst ed: Sunday Times 1964–65 (co-fndr Insight 1963), Daily Mail 1965–66; ed World in Action 1968–70 (fndr Investigation Unit 1967), head of documentaries Granada TV 1970–77, prodr Philby, Burgess and Maclean 1977, dir of programmes Southern TV 1977–81, fndr Southern Pictures 1978, fndr and chief exec Limehouse Studios 1982–86, chief exec Headwater Cross-Media Ltd 1990–; *Recreations* France, cycling, singing; *Clubs* Boot and Flogger; *Style*— Jeremy Wallington, Esq; ✉ 28 Merrick Square, London SE1 4JB (☎ 0171 403 0570)

WALLIS, Bill; s of Albert Levi Wallis (d 1967), of Farnham, Surrey, and Edith Annie Robinson (d 1985); *b* 20 Nov 1936; *Educ* Farnham GS, St John's Coll Cambridge; *m* 1, 3 Feb 1960 (m dis 1979), Jean, da of Cdr R L Spalding, RN (decd), of Farnham, Surrey; 2 c (Kathryn b 1960, Dickon b 1970); m 2, 21 Aug 1979, Jane Karen, da of A S H Mills, of Steep, Hants; 2 c (Rose b 1982, Albert b 1984); *Career* comic and dramatic actor; professional debut Stratford on Avon Royal Shakespeare Theatre for two seasons (with Sir Peter Hall); W End appearances incl: Beyond the Fringe, Mrs Wilson's Diary (as Harold Wilson); numerous TV appearances; in repertory nationwide incl at: Newcastle, Leicester, Young Vic, Old Vic, Nat Theatre, RSC; established radio actor incl twenty three years of BBC Radio 4 Week Ending; *Recreations* heavy reading and light drinking; *Style*— Bill Wallis, Esq; ✉ c/o 108 Leonard Street, London EC2A 4RH (☎ 0171 739 6200, fax 0171 739 4101)

WALLIS, Prof David Ian; s of Leonard Stephen Wallis (d 1974), Stevenage, Herts, and Kathleen Muriel, *née* Culpin (d 1991); *b* 12 March 1934; *Educ* Alleynes GS Stevenage, Downing Coll Cambridge (MA, PhD); *m* 30 April 1960, Mary Elizabeth, da of John Cecil Ford (d 1985), of Soham, Cambs; 2 s ((David) Stephen b 1965, Dominic John b 1966), 1 da (Naomi Natasha b 1963); *Career* NATO Res Fell Univ of Pennsylvania 1959–61, sr res fell in physiology Aberdeen 1961–67; Univ of Wales Coll Cardiff: lectr in physiology 1967–71, sr lectr 1971–76, reader 1976–83, personal chair and prof 1983, head of dept 1987–94, established chair and prof of physiology 1989; memb Editorial Bd British Journal of Pharmacology 1981–88; chm Ctee of Br Pharmacological Soc 1993–95; memb: Physiological Soc, Br Pharmacological Soc, Brain Res Assoc; *Books* Cardiovascular Pharmacology of 5HT: Prospective Therapeutic Applications, Electrophysiology: A Practical Approach; *Recreations* painting, music; *Style*— Prof David Wallis; ✉ Unit of Physiology, School of Molecular and Medical Biosciences, University of Wales, College of Cardiff, PO Box 911, Cardiff CF1 3US (☎ 01222 874036, fax 01222 874094)

WALLIS, Prof Kenneth Frank; s of Leslie Wallis (d 1982), of Wath-on-Dearne, Yorks, and Vera Daisy, *née* Stone (d 1993); *b* 26 March 1938; *Educ* Wath-on-Dearne GS, Univ of Manchester (BSc, MScTech), Stanford Univ (PhD); *m* 26 July 1963, Margaret Sheila, da of William Harold Campbell, of Churchill, Somerset; *Career* lectr and reader LSE 1966–77, professor of econometrics Univ of Warwick 1977–, dir ESRC Macroeconomic Modelling Bureau 1983–; exec memb NUS 1961–63; cncl memb: RSS 1972–76, Royal Econ Soc 1989–94, Econometric Soc 1995–97; chm HM Treasy Acad Panel 1987–91 (memb 1980–); fell Econometric Soc 1975, FBA 1994; *Books* Introductory Econometrics (1972, 1981), Topics in Applied Econometrics (1973, 1979), Models of the UK Economy 1-4 (1984–87), Macroeconometric Modelling (1994), Time Series Analysis and Macroeconometric Modelling (1995); *Recreations* travel, music, gardening, swimming; *Style*— Prof Kenneth F Wallis, FBA; ✉ Department of Economics, University of Warwick, Coventry CV4 7AL (☎ 01203 523468, fax 01203 523032)

WALLIS-KING, Maj-Gen Colin Sainthill; CBE (1975, OBE 1971); s of Lt-Col Frank King, DSO, OBE (d 1934), of Hill House, Northrepps, nr Cromer, Norfolk, and Colline Ammabel, *née* St Hill (d 1985); *b* 13 Sept 1926; *Educ* Stowe; *m* 10 Nov 1962, Lisabeth, da of Swan P Swanstrøm (d 1970), of Oslo, Norway; 2 da (Kathrine, Marianne); *Career* HG 1942–44, enlisted Coldstream Gds 1944 (cmmnd 1945), liaison offr Fleet Air Arm 1954–56, Army Staff Coll 1960–61, Regtl Adj Coldstream Gds 1961–63, seconded to Parachute Regt 1963, ACOS G4 Comland Norway 1965–68, 2 i/c 1 Bn Coldstream Gds 1968–69, Cdr 2 Bn Coldstream Gds 1969–72, Dep Cdr 8 Inf Bde 1972, Col GS Combat Devpt MOD 1972–73, Cdr 3 Inf Bde 1973–75, Brig Intelligence MOD 1975–77, Dir Serv Intelligence 1977–80, ret 1980; dir Kongsberg Ltd 1982–87, UK rep Norsk Forsvarsteknologi 1987–93; *Recreations* equitation, fishing, sailing, music, cross-country skiing; *Clubs* Cavalry & Guards'; *Style*— Maj-Gen C S Wallis-King, CBE; ✉ c/o Royal Bank of Scotland, Holts Branch, Lawrie House, Victoria Road, Farnborough, Hants GU14 7NR

WALLOP, Hon Nicholas Valoynes Bermingham; s of 9 Earl of Portsmouth (d 1984); *b* 1946; *Educ* Stowe; *m* 1969, Lavinia, da of David Karmel, CBE, QC; 1 s (Henry b 1974), 1 da (Victoria b 1972); *Career* art dealer; *Clubs* Boodle's; *Style*— The Hon Nicholas Wallop; ✉ 15 Tregunter Road, London SW10 9LS (☎ 0171 930 4221, fax 0171 370 0959)

WALLS, (William) Alan; s of Harold Walls, of Sedgefield, Cleveland, and Marjorie, *née* Orton; *b* 18 Sept 1956; *Educ* Trinity Hall Cambridge (MA); *m* 29 July 1978, Julie, da of John Brown; 2 s (Thomas William b 4 Sept 1985, Adam Edward b 11 Feb 1991), 1 da (Rachel Hannah Louise b 8 June 1987); *Career* slr; Linklaters & Paines: articled 1979–81, slr 1981–87, ptnr 1987–, licensed insolvency practitioner 1990–; memb: Int Bar Assoc, London Slrs Litigation Assoc, Assoc Européenne des Practiceans de Procedures Collectives, City of London Slrs Co 1987, Law Soc; *Recreations* walking, sailing; *Style*— Alan Walls, Esq; ✉ Linklaters & Paines, Barrington House, 59–67 Gresham St, London EC2V 7DA (☎ 0171 606 7080, fax 0171 606 5113, telex 884349/888167)

WALLS, Geoffrey Nowell; s of Andrew Nowell Walls (d 1990), of Canberra, Aust, and Hilda Margaret, *née* Thompson; *b* 17 Feb 1945; *Educ* Trinity GS Melbourne Aust, Univ of Melbourne Aust (BComm); *m* 8 Aug 1975, Vanessa, da of Capt Alan John Bodger, DFC (d 1995), of London; 1 s (Robert Walls b 20 Jan 1968), 3 da (Tanya b 12 Nov 1969, Jennie b 18 Jan 1977, Sacha b 21 March 1978); *Career* 2 Lt RAAOC 1966–69, active serv S Vietnam 1967–68; Aust Dip Serv: asst trade cmmr (Bahrain, Cairo, Singapore, Jakarta, Mecas) 1970–75, trade cmmr Manila 1975–76, asst dir ME Section Dept of Trade and Resources Canberra 1976–78, trade cmmr Baghdad 1978–79, regnl dir Adelaide Cwlth Depts of Trade and Indust and Commerce 1980–83; gen mangr central region ATCO Industs Aust 1983–86, agent gen State of S Aust London 1986–; *Recreations* gardening, golf, reading, tennis; *Clubs* RAC, East India; *Style*— Geoffrey Walls, Esq; ✉ State of South Australia, Australia Centre, Melbourne Place, Strand, London WC2B 4LG (☎ 0171 240 8585, fax 0171 240 8686, car 0589 132937)

WALLS, Stephen Roderick; s of Ronald William Walls (d 1982); *b* 8 Aug 1947; *Educ* Morecambe GS; *m* 1, 1971 (m dis 1991), Lynette Janice; 1 s (Roderick William b 28 Jan 1976); m 2, 10 May 1996, Mrs Ruth Barry, o da of J Nadler, of Westville, Natal, S Africa; *Career* articled clerk Tyson Westall & Co 1963–69, audit sr Deloitte & Co 1969–71, fin planning exec Lindustries Ltd 1971–74, gp fin exec Vernons Ltd 1974–75; Chesebrough Ponds Inc: area fin dir Africa 1975–77, fin dir UK 1977–80, fin dir Europe 1980–81, vice pres fin US and Worldwide 1981–87; fin dir, md and chief exec designate Plessey Co plc 1987–89, chief exec Arjo Wiggins Appleton plc (formerly Wiggins Teape Appleton plc) 1989–92; The Albert Fisher Group PLC: chm 1992–, chief exec 1993–; non-exec dir: Lonrho plc 1993, Servisair plc 1994; FCA; *Recreations* running, flying, music; *Clubs* RAC; *Style*— Stephen Walls, Esq; ✉ The Albert Fisher Group PLC, 'C' Sefton Park, Bells Hill, Stoke Poges, Bucks SL2 4HS

WALLWORK, Geoffrey James; s of James Albert Wallwork (d 1986), and Winifred Mary, *née* Dyke; *b* 14 March 1941; *Educ* Boteler GS Warrington, Manchester GS; *m* 5 Aug 1967, Sheila Margaret, da of late Frank Oakley; 1 s (Andrew James b 30 July 1969), 2 da (Rachel Anne b 27 Nov 1971, Susan Catherine b 5 Jan 1978); *Career* CA; articled clerk Walton Watts and Co Manchester 1959, ptnr Thornton Baker & Co (became Grant Thornton) 1976–93; currently business conslt and co dir; Manchester Soc of Chartered Accountants: treas 1986–89, dep pres 1989–90, pres 1990–91; memb Cncl Central Fin Bd of the Methodist Church; FCA (ACA 1965); *Recreations* DIY, gardening, travel; *Style*— Geoffrey J Wallwork, Esq; ✉ Higher Town Farmhouse, 4 Warwick Close, Knutsford, Cheshire WA16 8NA (☎ 01565 634603)

WALLWORK, John; s of Thomas Wallwork, and Vera, *née* Reid; *b* 8 July 1946; *Educ* Accrington GS, Univ of Edinburgh (BSc, MB CHB), Univ of Cambridge (MA); *m* 1973, Elizabeth (Ann), da of John Selwyn Medley (d 1988), of New Plymouth, NZ; 1 s (Nicolas b 25 March 1982), 2 da (Sarah b 18 April 1977, Alice b 9 May 1989); *Career* surgical registrar Royal Infirmary Edinburgh 1975–76; sr registrar: Royal Infirmary Glasgow 1978–79, Bart's 1979–81, Adelaide Hosp S Aust 1977–78; chief res in cardiovascular and cardiac transplant surgery Stanford Univ 1980–81, currently conslt cardiothoracic surgn and dir of transplant serv Papworth Hosp Cambs; memb: Br Transplant Soc, Cardiac Soc, Int Soc for Heart & Lung Transplantation, Scot Thoracic Soc, Soc of Thoracic and Cardiovascular Surgns of GB and Ireland, Euro Assoc for Cardio-Thoracic Surgery, Transplant Soc, Euro Soc for Organ Transplantation; past pres Int Soc for Heart & Lung Transplants; Lister Professorship (RCSEd) 1985–86; FRCSEd; *Books* Heart Disease: What it is and How it is Treated (1987), Heart and Heart-Lung Transplantation (1989); *Clubs* Caledonian; *Style*— John Wallwork, Esq; ✉ Papworth Hospital, Papworth Everards, Cambs CB3 8RE (☎ 01480 830541, fax 01480 831281)

WALMSLEY, Claire; da of John Patrick Slavin (d 1971), of Blackpool, and (Margaret) Mabel, *née* Reader; *b* 6 May 1944; *Educ* Convent of the Holy Child Jesus Blackpool, Royal Coll of Music; *m* 1, 1964 (m dis 1982), Christopher Roberts Walmsley (d 1995); 2 da (Frances b 18 Nov 1964, Jennie b 13 April 1968), 1 s (Alexis b 14 April 1971); m 2, 1988, Stephen Charles Whittle, *qv*; *Career* BBC: joined 1976, radio reporter The Today Programme, Woman's Hour, You & Yours, World Service, TV prodr and documentary film maker Red Dynasty (Chinese trilogy), Horizon, Everyman, 40 Minutes, Newsnight, The Money Programme, left BBC 1990; md Boxclever Productions Ltd (ind TV prodn co) and Boxclever Communication Training 1990–; OFFER memb London Electricity Consumers' Ctee 1992–95; memb: BAFTA, RTS, IOD, Forum, Fawcett Soc, Network; FRSA; *Books* Assertiveness - The Right to be You (1991), Letting Go (1993); *Recreations* family, theatre, creative cooking, gardening, travel, reading; *Style*— Ms Claire Walmsley; ✉ Boxclever Communication Training, The Maples, 144 Liverpool Road, London N1 1LA (☎ 0171 619 0606, fax 0171 700 2248, e-mail CLAIRE@BOXCLEVER.CO.UK)

WALMSLEY, Rt Rev Francis Joseph; CBE (1979); *b* 9 Nov 1926, Woolwich, London; *Educ* St Joseph's Coll Mark Cross Tunbridge Wells, St John's Seminary Wonersh Guildford; *Career* served MN 1944–46 (N Atlantic convoys, Med and Indian Ocean); ordained RC priest (Dio of Southwark) 1953; asst priest: Woolwich 1953–58, Shoreham-by-Sea and Steyning Sussex 1958–60; chaplain RN 1960: Aircraft Carrier Sqdn (HM Ships Ark Royal, Victorious, Centaur and Hermes Far East and Med) 1961–63, Naval Base Devonport then RNEC Manadon 1961–63, Chatham 1965–67, served HM Ships Bulwark and Fearless 1967, base chaplain HMS Terror Singapore

1967–69, Rosyth 1969–72, RN Hosp Haslar 1972–74, princ RC chaplain and vicar gen to Bishop Gerard Tickle 1975–79; prelate of honour to His Holiness Pope Paul VI 1975; RC bishop to HM Forces and titular bishop of Tamalluma 1979–; *Style*— The Rt Rev Francis J Walmsley, CBE; ✉ 26 The Crescent, Farnborough, Hants GU14 7AS (☎ 01252 373699)

WALMSLEY, Dr Katharine Mary (Kate); da of David Robert Walmsley, of Ickleford, Hitchin, Herts, and Muriel Jean, *née* McKelvie (d 1990); *b* 5 May 1948; *Educ* Hitchin Girls' GS, Univ of Bristol (MB ChB); *m* 23 Sept 1972 (m dis 1991), Dr (John) Roy Davies; 2 da (Claire Louise b 18 July 1980, Angharad Caroline Mary b 6 Nov 1984); *Career* registrar and sr registrar in radiology Middx Hosp London 1974–79; conslt radiologist: UCLH 1979–, Royal Free Hosp 1979–92, King Edward VII's Hosp 1986–; FRCR 1977; *Recreations* my family; *Style*— Dr Kate Walmsley; ✉ Flat 6, Harmont House, 20 Harley St, London W1N 1AL (☎ 0171 580 1442)

WALMSLEY, Kevin James Thomas; s of James Walmsley, and Evelyn Grace, *née* Bunnett; *b* 20 Aug 1959; *Educ* Southlands Lancs, Runshaw Coll Lancs, Univ of Liverpool (BA); *m* 30 June 1990, Dr Sara Rosalind, da of Raymond Percy Luck, JP (d 1982); *Career* with King & Co CAs; memb Cons Pty 1974–; Dartford Borough Cncl (Gundulf Ward): cncllr 1983–95 (ret), served various ctees incl Policy, Strategy, Planning, Contracts, Resources, Dartforce, Housing, Performance Mgmnt (chm), Fin (chm), Personnel (chm), Fin and Corp Business (sr chm); Dartford Cons Assoc: treas 1986–87, dep chm 1987–89 and 1995–96, chm 1989–91, vice chm 1991–92; Parly candidate (C) Woolwich 1992 (prospective Parly candidate 1989–92); memb Nat Tst; ACCA; *Recreations* travel, walking, current affairs, reading, photography, gardening; *Style*— Kevin Walmsley, Esq; ✉ Dartford Conservative Association, 17 Highfield Road, Dartford, Kent DA1 2JS (☎ 01322 220704); King & Co Chartered Accountants, 12 Fife Road, Kingston upon Thames, Surrey KT1 1SZ (☎ 0181 546 7562, fax 0181 541 1387); King & Co Chartered Accountants, King & Co Suite, London House, Thames Road, Crayford, Kent DA1 4SB (☎ 01322 559152)

WALMSLEY, Dr Thomas (Tom); s of Prof Robert Walmsley, of St Andrews; *b* 15 Aug 1946; *Educ* Fettes, Univ of Dundee (MB ChB), Univ of Edinburgh (DPM); *m* 1, 1973 (m dis 1981), Jane Walsh, of Edinburgh; 1 da (Anna); m 2, 1981, Linda Hardwick, of Arbroath, Scotland; 2 s (William George, Christopher Robert (Kit)); *Career* lectr in psychiatry Univ of Edinburgh 1975–77, conslt psychiatrist Royal Edinburgh Hosp 1977–81, conslt psychiatrist Wessex RHA 1981–, psychiatric tutor Knowle Hosp 1983–92; visiting prof Univ of Kuwait 1994; MRCPsych 1974 (memb Central Approval Panel 1993–); *Recreations* reading, walking, maps; *Style*— Dr Tom Walmsley; ✉ Longcroft, Botley Road, Shedfield, Southampton SO32 2HN; Osborn Clinic, Fareham, Hants PO16 7ES (☎ 01329 288331)

WALPOLE, 10 Baron (GB 1723); Robert Horatio Walpole; JP (Norfolk); also 8 Baron Walpole of Wolterton (GB 1756); patron of 6 livings; s of 9 Baron Walpole, TD (d 1989); *b* 8 Dec 1938; *Educ* Eton, King's Coll Cambridge (MA, Dip Agric); *m* 1, 30 June 1962 (m dis 1979), (Sybil) Judith (d 1993), yr da of late Theodore Thomas Schofield, of Harpenden, Herts; 2 s (Hon Jonathan Robert Hugh b Nov 16 1967, Hon Benedict Thomas Orford b 1 June 1969), 2 da (Hon Alice Louise b 1 Sept 1963, Hon Emma Judith b 10 Oct 1964); m 2, 1980, Laurel Celia, o da of Sidney Tom Ball, of Swindon, Wilts; 2 s (Hon Roger Horatio Calibut b 1980, Hon Henry William b 1982), 1 da (Hon Grace Mary b 1986); *Heir* s, Hon Jonathan Robert Hugh Walpole; *Career* sits as crossbencher in House of Lords; memb: Agric Sub-Ctee of Select Ctee on European Communities 1991–94, Environment Sub-Ctee of Select Ctee on European Communities 1995–; *Style*— The Rt Hon the Lord Walpole, JP; ✉ Mannington Hall, Norwich, Norfolk NR11 7BB

WALSH, Amanda (Mrs Brian Stewart); da of David Joseph Walsh, of Thurlestone, S Devon, and Eileen Julia Frances Walsh; *b* 27 Nov 1955; *Educ* St Mary's Convent Worcester, Univ of Kingston (BA); *m* 28 Sept 1989, Brian Stewart; 1 step s (James b 1 Jan 1984), 1 step da (Sophie b 25 Sept 1982); *Career* sales and mktg exec Tek Translation Ltd 1978–80, account exec Wasey Campbell Ewald Advertising 1980–83; WCRS: joined 1984, bd dir 1987–89, client servs and new business dir 1990–93, md 1993–95; ptnr and md Walsh Trott Chick Smith 1995–; memb Mktg Soc 1991, MIPA; *Style*— Ms Amanda Walsh; ✉ Walsh Trott Chick Smith, 9–11 Broadwick Street, London W1V 1FN (☎ 0171 734 0050)

WALSH, Andrew Geoffrey; s of Dr Geoffrey Parkin Walsh, of Blackburn, Lancs, and Dorothy, *née* Baldwin; *b* 26 July 1954; *Educ* Westholme Sch Blackburn, Queen Elizabeth GS Blackburn, Magdalen Coll Oxford (MA), Trinity Hall Cambridge (LLB); *m* 2, Sept 1989, Emma Belmonte; *Career* admitted slr 1979; ptnr Pinsent Curtis (London office) 1993–; memb City of London Slrs' Co; *Books* Bus Company Privatisation (1992), Privatisation of London Buses (1993), Privatisation of Next Step Agencies (1994), Rail Privatisation (1994–95), PFI Projects in the Health Sector (1995), Trust Ports Privatisation (1995); *Recreations* soccer, gym, cycling, historic buildings, theatre; *Clubs* Broadgate; *Style*— Mr Andrew Walsh; ✉ Pinsent Curtis, Dashwood House, 69 Old Broad Street, London EC2M 1NR (☎ 0171 418 7000, fax 0171 418 7050)

WALSH, Arthur Stephen; CBE; s of Wilfrid Walsh (d 1977), and Doris, *née* Gregory; *b* 16 Aug 1926; *Educ* Midsomer Norton GS Somerset, Selwyn Coll Cambridge (MA); *m* 1 (m dis 1983), Gwendoline Mary; 1 s (Gordon Thomas b 1962), 1 da (Catherine Mary b 1964); m 2, Feb 1984, Judith Marth, da of Paul Balmer (d 1983), of Johannesburg, SA; *Career* ed: Marconi Space and Defence Systems 1969–82, The Marconi Group 1982–85; dir GEC 1983 (various sr posts 1952–69); STC plc (later Northern Telecom Europe): chief exec 1985–91, chm 1989–91; chm: Telemetrix, National Transcommunications Ltd 1991–; dep chm FKI plc 1993–; Hon DSc: Univ of Ulster 1988, Univ of Southampton 1993; FEng 1980, FIEE; *Recreations* sailing and skiing; *Style*— Arthur Walsh, Esq, CBE, FEng; ✉ NTL Ltd, Crawley Court, Winchester, Hampshire SO21 2QA (☎ 01962 822280, fax 01962 822555)

WALSH, Barbara Ann; da of James Walsh, of Chelford, Cheshire, and Audrey, *née* Dean; *b* 1 March 1955; *Educ* Manchester HS, Univ of Birmingham (BSc); *m* 1; 1 da (Emma Jane b 29 Oct 1981), 1 s (James Nicholas b 26 Aug 1984); m 2, Peter Charles Wozencroft; *Career* gen mangr Hillingdon Health Authy 1985–88, chief exec Riverside Mental Health NHS Tst 1988–93, chief exec Community Health Sheffield NHS Tst 1993–; MHSM 1981; *Recreations* family, walking, cooking, reading; *Style*— Ms Barbara Walsh; ✉ Community Health Sheffield NHS Trust, Fulwood House, Old Fulwood Road, Sheffield S10 3TH (☎ 0114 271 6374)

WALSH, His Hon Judge; Brian; QC (1977); s of Lt-Col Percy Walsh (d 1978), of Leeds, and Sheila, *née* Frais (d 1988); *b* 17 June 1935; *Educ* Leeds GS, Gonville and Caius Coll Cambridge (MA, LLB, Pres of the Union); *m* 19 August 1964, Susan Margaret, da of Eli Kay Frieze (d 1985), of Leeds; 2 da (Belinda Dayane b 8 June 1967, Alyson Gay b 28 May 1969); *Career* served as Pilot Offr RAF 1954–56; called to the Bar Middle Temple 1961, Blackstone entrance scholar, Harmsworth law scholar, bencher 1988; joined N Eastern Circuit 1961, recorder of the Crown Court 1972–96, ldr N Eastern Circuit 1990–94, sr circuit judge (NE Circuit) 1996–; govr: Leeds GS 1977–, Leeds Girls' HS 1978–; Yorkshire CCC: memb Ctee 1984–93, chm 1986–91, vice pres 1993–; *Recreations* golf, cricket, music; *Clubs* National Liberal; *Style*— His Hon Judge Walsh, QC; ✉ Park Court Chambers, 40 Park Cross St, Leeds LS1 2QH (☎ 0113 243 3277, fax 0113 242 1285, telex 666135)

WALSH, Colin Stephen; *b* 26 Jan 1955; *Educ* Portsmouth GS, Ch Ch Oxford (MA); *Career* asst organist Salisbury Cathedral 1978–85, organist and master of the music St Albans Cathedral 1985–88, organist and master of the Choristers Lincoln Cathedral 1988–; conductor Lincoln Choral Soc; has given many organ recitals in UK and overseas: French organ music from Salisbury 1985, French organ music from St Albans 1987, Great European Organ Series Lincoln Cathedral 1989, Vierne 24 Pieces en Style Libre 1991, English organ music 1992; ARCM 1972, FRCO 1977; *Recreations* walking, dining out, travel, theatre; *Style*— Colin Walsh, Esq; ✉ Lincoln Cathedral, 12 Minster Yard, Lincoln LN2 1PJ (☎ 01522 544544)

WALSH, (Bernard) David James; TD (1956); s of Maj Bernard John Merlin Walsh (d 1928), of Stourbank, Nayland, Suffolk, and Violet Jennie, *née* Pearson (d 1973); *b* 12 July 1923; *Educ* Eton, Trinity Hall Cambridge; *m* 28 Aug 1954, (Gladys) Angela Margot, da of Maj Henry Berry Lees, MC (d 1967), of Stour House, Nayland, Suffolk; 3 da (Sarah (Mrs Blake) b 1955, Jenny (Mrs Pickford) b 1957, Charlotte (Mrs Johnston) b 1960); *Career* WWII RA 1943, cmmnd 1944, serv Field and Medium Regts in UK 1944–45, instr Army Signal Sch India 1945 (cmd Artillery & Engrg Wing 1946–47), 304 Essex Yeo RHA Field Regt RA (UK) 1948–57, ret Maj 1957; called to the Bar Inner Temple 1952; private practice and SE Circuit 1954–62 and 1974–81, Govt Legal Serv (MPNI) 1962–63, asst registrar Criminal Appeals 1969–74 (dep asst registrar 1963–69), standing counsel for DHSS 1979–81, chm Social Security Appeal Tbnls 1983–95; author of various articles in Railway Magazine and other periodicals; pres: Gt Eastern Railway Soc 1973–, Stour Valley Railway Preservation Soc 1990–91, E Anglian Railway Museum 1991–; chm Consultative Panel for the Preservation of Br Tport Relics 1977–82 (hon sec and treas 1958–61), hon sec Essex Yeo Assoc 1981–91, pres Railway Club 1982–94 (hon sec 1951–68, vice pres 1968–82); *Books* The Stour Valley Railway (edns 1971–87); *Recreations* study of railway operating and history, photography; *Clubs* Carlton, Railway; *Style*— B D J Walsh, Esq, TD; ✉ The Old Rectory, Burgate, Diss, Norfolk IP22 1QD

WALSH, Henry George (Harry); *b* 28 Sept 1939; *Educ* West Hill Sch, McGill Univ, Univ of Cambridge; 3 da (Catherine b 1973, Rebecca b 1978, Harriet b 1994); *Career* HM Treasy: joined 1966, various posts Prices and Incomes and Monetary Policy Divs 1971–73, private sec to Chllr of the Duchy of Lancaster (Mr Harold Lever) 1974–76, asst sec European Secretariat Cabinet Office 1976–80, econ cnsllr British Embassy Washington 1980–85, asst sec and head of Monetary Policy Div 1985–86, head of IMF and Debt Div 1986–89, under sec Fin Insts and Markets Gp 1989–91; dep chm Building Societies Cmmn 1991–95 (conslt to Cmmn 1995–); *Style*— Harry Walsh, Esq; ✉ Building Societies Commission, 15 Great Marlborough Street, London W1V 2LL (☎ 0171 437 9992, fax 0171 437 1612)

WALSH, Rt Rev (Geoffrey David) Jeremy; s of Howard Wilton Walsh, OBE (d 1969), and Helen Maud Walsh, *née* Lovell (d 1985); *b* 7 Dec 1929; *Educ* Felsted, Pembroke Coll Cambridge (MA), Lincoln Theol Coll; *m* 1961, Cynthia Helen, da of Francis Philip Knight (d 1985); 2 s (David b 1962, Andrew b 1967), 1 da (Helen b 1964); *Career* vicar St Matthew's Bristol 1961–66; rector: Marlborough 1966–76, Elmsett with Aldham Suffolk 1976–80; archdeacon of Ipswich 1976–86, bishop of Tewkesbury 1986–95, ret; *Recreations* golf, gardening, bird-watching; *Style*— The Rt Rev Jeremy Walsh; ✉ 6 Warren Lane, Martlesham Heath, Ipswich IP5 7SH (☎ 01473 620797)

WALSH, Dr John; *b* 9 Dec 1937; *Educ* Phillip Exeter Acad New Hampshire, Yale (Ranking scholar, BA), Columbia Univ (Faculty scholar, MA, PhD, President's fell, Frederick J E Woodbridge hon fell, Fulbright graduate fell), Univ of Leyden The Netherlands; *m* 1962, Virginia Alys, *née* Galston; 3 c; *Career* US Naval Reserve 1957–63 (active duty Petty Offr 3 Class on USS Fiske 1957–59); lectr and res asst The Frick Collection 1966–68; Met Museum of Art: assoc for higher educn 1968–71, vice chm Dept of Euro Paintings 1974–75 (assoc curator 1970–72, curator 1972–74); Columbia Univ: lectr in art history 1969–70, adjunct assoc prof of art history 1970–72, adjunct prof 1972–75; prof of art history Barnard Coll and Columbia Univ 1975–77, Mrs Russell W Baker curator of paintings Museum of Fine Arts Boston 1977–83, visiting prof of fine arts Harvard Univ 1979, dir J Paul Getty Museum 1983–; memb Editorial Bd: Metropolitan Museum Journal 1970–75, Art Bulletin 1987–; memb: Museum Panel New York State Cncl on Fine Arts 1974–77, Governing Bd Yale Univ Art Gallery 1975–, Tstee Ctee on Educn Museum of Modern Art 1976–, Cmmr's Panel on Art Internal Revenue Service 1979–81, Indemnity Panel Nat Endowment for the Arts 1981–84; memb Advsy Bd: Int Fndn for Art Res 1975–, Gazette des Beaux-Arts 1980–; dir: The Museums Collaborative NY 1976–77, Arts International Inc 1979–87; dir and memb Exec Ctee Coll Art Assoc of America 1979–81; memb Visiting Ctee: Sherman Fairchild Paintings Conservation Center Met Museum of Art 1980–, Harvard Univ Art Museums 1981–90; pres Assoc of Art Museum Dirs 1989–90 (memb 1983–); memb: American Antiquarian Soc 1984–, Bd of Fellows Claremont Graduate School 1989–, Smithsonian Cncl 1990–; author of numerous catalogues and articles in art jls; *Style*— Dr John Walsh; ✉ J Paul Getty Museum, PO Box 2112, Santa Monica, Calif 90406, USA

WALSH, John Henry Martin; s of Martin Walsh (d 1986), of Galway, Eire, and Anne, *née* Durkin; *b* 24 Oct 1953; *Educ* Wimbledon Coll, Exeter Coll Oxford (BA), Univ Coll Dublin (MA); *partner* Carolyn Hart; 2 da (Sophie Matilda Hart-Walsh b 11 Aug 1987, Clementine Hart-Walsh b 5 July 1995), 1 s (Max Henry Thomas Hart-Walsh b 30 Aug 1991); *Career* journalist 1978–; Advtg Dept The Tablet, Gollancz publishers 1977–78, assoc ed The Director Magazine 1978–82; freelance feature writer and reviewer for various newspapers and magazines incl: The Times, The Independent, Time Out, Tatler, London Portrait, Executive Travel, Books and Bookmen; lit ed then features and lit ed Evening Standard 1986–88, lit ed and feature writer The Sunday Times 1988–93, ed Independent Magazine 1993–95, diarist and feature writer The Independent 1996– (lit ed 1995–96); broadcaster Books and Company (Radio 4), TV ed Book Choice (Channel 4) 1995–; dir Cheltenham Literary Festival 1997; *Books* Growing Up Catholic (1989); *Recreations* drinking, talking, music; *Clubs* Groucho's; *Style*— John Walsh, Esq; ✉ The Independent, 1 Canada Square, Canary Wharf, London E14 5DL (☎ 0171 293 2000)

WALSH, Jonathan George Michael; s of Charles Arthur Walsh (d 1978), of India, and Surrey, and Joan Violet Braidwood, *née* Allen (d 1969); *b* 21 April 1944; *Educ* Eton, Sorbonne Univ; *m* 24 Feb 1968, Angela Mary, da of Rear-Adm Sir Anthony Cecil Capel Miers, VC, KBE, CB, DSO (d 1985); 4 s (David b 1969, William b 1971, James b 1974, Harry b 1981); *Career* admitted slr 1969; ptnr: Joynson-Hicks London 1972, Taylor Joynson Garrett 1989, Stephenson Harwood 1991–; Freeman City of London 1982, Liveryman Worshipful Co of Tin Plate Workers 1982; memb Law Soc 1969; *Recreations* real tennis, lawn tennis, shooting; *Clubs* Boodle's, Queen's, MCC; *Style*— Jonathan Walsh, Esq; ✉ Quarley Down House, Cholderton, nr Salisbury, Wilts SP4 ODZ; 2 Wymond Street, London SW15 1DY (☎ 0181 788 9907); Stephenson Harwood, One St Pauls Churchyard, London EC4M 8SH (☎ 0171 329 4422, fax 0171 606 0822)

WALSH, Michael Anthony; s of Martin Walsh, of Chapel Rd, Ballinrobe, Co Mayo, Eire, and Bridget Walsh (d 1991); *b* 13 Oct 1946; *Educ* Ballinrobe Christian Brothers Sch, London Poly; *m* 16 July 1977, Bridget Teresa, da of John Heneghan; 2 da (Katharine Anne b 31 May 1978, Helen Bridget b 4 March 1981); *Career* PR gp fin dir; cost clerk Decca Radio & Television 1965, sr cost clerk Redifon Telecommunications 1966–67, mgmnt accountant Hobson Bates & Ptnrs 1967–73; Dewe Rogerson Ltd: fin controller 1973–78, assoc dir 1978, fin dir 1980; Dewe Rogerson Group Ltd; gp fin dir 1987–, co sec of all gp cos 1987–; MIPA 1989; *Recreations* golf, sailing; *Clubs* St Monicas (Southgate), Old Fold Manor Golf; *Style*— Michael Walsh, Esq; ✉ Dewe Rogerson

Group Limited, 3 1/2 London Wall Buildings, London Wall, London EC2M 5SY (☎ 0171 638 9571, fax 0171 638 7091)

WALSH, Michael Jeffrey; s of Kenneth Francis Walsh, of Alford, Lincs, and Edith, *née* Hudson; *b* 1 Oct 1949; *Educ* Hulme GS Oldham, Univ of Durham; *m* Sally, da of Rev Ronald Forbes Shaw; 1 s, 1 da; *Career* advertising exec; Young & Rubicam: graduate trainee 1972, account exec 1972–74, account mangr 1974–78, account dir 1978–80, bd dir 1980, new business dir 1981–82, memb UK Exec Ctee; Ogilvy & Mather: dir Bd and mgmnt supervisor 1983–84, head of account mgmnt 1984–85, dir of client service 1985–86, md 1986–89, elected to Worldwide Bd 1989, chm 1989–90, UK Gp chm 1990–, chief exec offr Europe, M East and Africa 1994–; chm Alkrington Young Conservatives 1966–67, vice chm British Red Cross 1994–; worldwide tstee WWF 1996–; *Recreations* collecting Victorian & Edwardian children's books, antiques, tennis, sailing, golf; *Clubs* RAC, Hunstanton Golf, Highgate Golf, Marks, Annabel's, Royal West Norfolk Golf; *Style*— Michael Walsh, Esq; ✉ Ogilvy & Mather, 10 Cabot Square, Canary Wharf, London E14 4QB (☎ 0171 345 3000)

WALSH, (Mary) Noelle (Mrs Heslam); da of late Thomas Walsh, and Mary Kate, *née* Ferguson; *b* 26 Dec 1954; *Educ* Univ of East Anglia (BA); *m* 15 Oct 1988, David Howard Heslam, s of Capt James William Heslam; 1 da (Ciara b 15 Aug 1989), 1 s (Calum b 17 May 1991); *Career* news ed Cosmopolitan Magazine 1979–85, ed Good Housekeeping Magazine 1987–91 (dep ed 1985–87), journalist Daily Telegraph 1991–92, dir The Value for Money Co Ltd 1992–; memb 300 Gp; FRSA; *Books* Hot Lips - The Ultimate Kiss and Tell Guide (1985), Ragtime to Wartime - The Best of Good Housekeeping 1922–1939 (1986), The Home Front - The Best of Good Housekeeping 1939–1945 (1987), Good Housekeeping - The Christmas Book (1988), Food Glorious Food - Eating and Drinking with Good Housekeeping 1922–42 (1990), Things My Mother Should Have Told Me - The Best of Good Housekeeping 1922–40 (1991), Childhood Memories - Growing Up with Good Housekeeping 1922–1942 (1991), The Good Deal Directory 1994 (1993), The Home Shopping Handbook (1994), The Good Deal Directory 1995 (1994), Baby on a Budget (1995), The Good Deal Directory 1996 (1995), Wonderful Weddings (1996), Factory Shopping and Sightseeing Guide (1996), The Good Mail Order Guide (1996), The Good Deal Directory 1997 (1996); *Recreations* gardening, bargain hunting, antiques, sailing; *Clubs* Network, Forum UK, Groucho; *Style*— Miss Noelle Walsh; ✉ Pip Cottage, Filkins, Lechlade, Glos GL7 3JJ (☎ 01367 860017, fax 01367 860013)

WALSH, Most Rev Patrick Joseph; *see:* Down and Connor, Bishop of (RC)

WALSH, Prof (Patrick Gerard) Peter; s of Peter Walsh (d 1985), and Joanna, *née* Fitzpatrick (d 1975); *b* 16 Aug 1923; *Educ* Preston Catholic Coll, Univ of Liverpool (BA, MA); *m* 18 July 1953, Eileen Benson, da of William Friel Quin (d 1979); 4 s (Anthony b 1954, Stephen b 1960, John b 1964, David b 1967), 1 da (Patricia b 1957); *Career* Intelligence Corps 1944–46; lectr in ancient classics Univ Coll Dublin 1952–59, lectr, reader and prof Dept of Humanity Univ of Edinburgh 1959–72, prof of humanity Univ of Glasgow 1972–93 (dean Faculty of Arts 1985–88); visiting prof: Toronto 1966, Yale 1970, Univ of N Carolina 1978, Georgetown 1989; Hon DLitt Edinburgh 1992; KCSG 1993; FRSE 1982; *Books* Livy, His Historical Aims and Methods (1961), Letters, Poems of Paulinus of Nola (1966–75), The Roman Novel (1970), Thirty Poems from the Carmina Burana (1974), Andreas Capellanus On Love (1982), Tragedies of George Buchanan (1982); edns of Livy: XXI (1973), XXVI to XXVII (1982), XXVIII to XXX (1986), XXXVI, XXXVII, XXXVIII, XXXIX, XL (1990–96); edn of William of Newburgh 1 (with M J Kennedy, 1988), Cassiodorus Explanation of the Psalms 3 vols (1990–91), Love-Lyrics from the Carmina Burana (1993), Apuleius, The Golden Ass (1994), Petronius, The Satyricon (1996); *Recreations* tennis, travel; *Style*— Prof Peter Walsh; ✉ 17 Broom Rd, Glasgow G43 2TP (☎ 0141 637 4977); c/o Department of Classics, Univ of Glasgow, Glasgow G12 8QQ

WALSH, Stephen John; s of C A Walsh, LLM, of Winchester and E B Walsh, *née* Boardman; *b* 14 Sept 1945; *Educ* Lancing, Coll of Law Guildford, Royal Coll of Art (MA); *m* 22 Feb 1975, Georgina Elizabeth, da of George William Stott; 3 da (Jessica Anne Elizabeth b 18 Oct 1980, Antonia Sarah Georgina b 29 May 1982, Clarissa Rachel Emily b 20 Jan 1989); *Career* articled clerk to Messrs Arnold Cooper and Tompkins Slrs 1965–67, designer Apple Ltd (The Beatles record co) 1967–68, postgrad student RCA 1968–73, pt/t creative dir Scenses Art Gallery London 1972–73, design conslt DI Design and Development Consultants Inc 1974–78, regnl dir (Middle East) Fitch & Co 1978–82, md Fitch (International) Ltd 1982–84, fndr and chief exec Crighton Ltd 1984–90, md Crighton McColl 1990–92, dir Business Design Group McColl 1992–95, md Hanseatica Projekt Design 1995–, dir ARCH 1995–; memb: Br Cncl of Shopping Centres 1985, Int Cncl of Shopping Centres 1985, Airports Cncl Int 1991; FCSD; *Recreations* tennis, sailing, skiing, swimming, riding, drawing; *Clubs* Durban Country (Natal); *Style*— Stephen Walsh, Esq; ✉ Hewshotts, Hewshott Lane, nr Liphook, Hampshire GU30 7SS (☎ 01428 723229); Hanseatica Projekt Design, Dusternstrasse 1, 20355 Hamburg (☎ 00 49 40 37640271, fax 00 49 40 37640279)

WALSH, Tom John; *b* 22 Oct 1950; *Educ* Univ of Leeds (BA), Central London Poly (Postgrad Dip in Town Planning); *m* Bee Yan, *née* Ong; 2 da (Patricia Clara, Victoria Siobhan); *Career* graduate trainee Planning Dept London Borough of Lewisham 1973–74, planning asst Architecture and Planning Dept City of London Corporation 1974–75, sr planner Docklands Team London Borough of Newham 1975–76, princ planning offr Planning Dept Grampian Regnl Cncl 1976–80, asst prof of urban and regnl planning King Abdul Aziz Univ Saudi Arabia 1980–85, dep co-ordinator Planning Aid for Londoners RTPI 1985–86; British Council: educn cnsllr Singapore 1986–90, projects mangr Pakistan 1990–93, dir Rio de Janeiro 1994–; MRTPI 1977, FRGS 1992; *Publications* Planning and Urban Change in Saudi Arabia (1985), A Householder's Guide to Planning Permission (1986), A Selection of Interesting Cases (1986); *Recreations* travel, photography, international and current affairs; *Style*— Tom Walsh; ✉ c/o FCO (Rio de Janeiro), King Charles Street, London SW1A 2AH

WALSHAM, Sir Timothy John; 5 Bt (UK 1831), of Knill Court, Herefordshire; o s of Rear Adm Sir John Scarlett Warren Walsham, 4 Bt, CB, OBE (d 1992), and Sheila Christina, *née* Bannerman; *b* 26 April 1939; *Educ* Sherborne; *Heir* kinsman, Percy Robert Stewart Walsham b 1904; *Style*— Sir Timothy Walsham, Bt; ✉ 19 Beckford Close, Tisbury, Wiltshire

WALSINGHAM, 9 Baron (GB 1780); John de Grey; MC (1951); patron of 2 livings; s of 8 Baron Walsingham, DSO, OBE, JP, DL (d 1965, half-n of 6 Baron, FRS); *b* 21 Feb 1925; *Educ* Wellington, Aberdeen Univ, Magdalen Coll Oxford (MA), Royal Mil Coll of Sci; *m* 30 July 1963, Wendy, er da of Edward Sidney Hoare; 1 s, 2 da (Hon Sarah b 1964, Hon Elizabeth b 1966); *Heir* s, Hon Robert de Grey, b 21 June 1969; *Career* Lt-Col RA; co dir; hon life memb Mark Twain Soc (for contributions to world peace); FInstD; *Recreations* etymology; *Clubs* Army and Navy, Special Forces, Norfolk; *Style*— The Rt Hon the Lord Walsingham, MC; ✉ The Hassocks, Merton, Thetford, Norfolk IP25 6QP (☎ 01953 885385, office 01953 883370, fax 01953 885385)

WALTER, Harriet Mary; da of Roderick Walter (d 1996), of London, and Xandra Carandini, *née* Lee (now Lady de Trafford); *b* 24 Sept 1950; *Educ* Cranborne Chase Sch, LAMDA; *Career* actress; debut Duke's Playhouse Lancaster 1974; nat tours 1975–78 with: 7:84, Joint Stock, Paines Plough; assoc artist RSC 1987, artistic assoc Royal Exchange Theatre Manchester; memb: Amnesty Int, Friends of the Earth, Arts for Labour *Theatre* Royal Court Theatre 1980–81 incl: Cloud Nine, The Seagull, Ophelia in Hamlet (with Jonathan Pryce); RSC incl: Nicholas Nickleby, Helena in All's Well That Ends Well (with Dame Peggy Ashcroft, dir Trevor Nunn, toured Broadway 1983), The Castle by Howard Barker 1985, Twelfth Night, A Question of Geography, The Three Sisters, title role in The Duchess of Malfi; RNT incl: A Fair Quarrel, Lady Croom in Tom Stoppard's Arcadia, Karen in The Children's Hour; other work incl: The Possessed (Almeida, also Paris, Milan and Bologna), The Merchant of Venice (Royal Exchange Manchester) 1987, Biddy in Three Birds Alighting in a Field (Royal Court and Manhattan Theatre Club NY), Anna in Old Times (Wyndhams), Clare in Sweet Panic (Hampstead), title role in Hedda Gabler (Chichester); *Television* incl: The Imitation Game (by Ian McEwan), Harriet Vane in Dorothy L Sayers Mysteries, The Price, Benefactors (by Michael Frayn), The Men's Room, Ashenden, Inspector Morse; *Films* incl: Turtle Diary, Reflections, The Good Father, Louis Malle's Milou en Mai, The Hour of the Pig, Sense and Sensibility; *Awards* Olivier Award nomination for Best Actress (for The Castle) 1985; winner: Olivier Award for Best Actress (The Three Sisters) 1988, Sony Radio Best Actress 1988 and 1992; *Books* contrib: Women and Theatre (1984), Clamorous Voices - Shakespeare's Women Today (1988), Players of Shakespeare Vol 3 (1993), Mother's Reflections by Daughters (1995); *Style*— Ms Harriet Walter; ✉ c/o Conway van Gelder Robinson Ltd, 18–21 Jermyn Street, London SW1Y 6HP (☎ 0171 287 0077, fax 0171 287 1940)

WALTER, Jeremy Canning; s of Maj Richard Walter, OBE, and Beryl, *née* Pugh; *b* 22 Aug 1948; *Educ* King's Sch Canterbury, Sidney Sussex Coll Cambridge (MA, LLB); *m* 1, 24 Aug 1973 (m dis 1985), Judith Jane, da of Dr Denton Rowlands, of Tamworth, Staffs (d 1987); 2 da (Emma b 1976, Alison b 1979); m 2, 17 Oct 1992, Dawna Beth, da of Sidney Rosenberg (d 1965), of Lawrence, Mass, USA; *Career* Ellis Piers & Young Jackson 1971–73, admitted slr 1973; currently head Corp Insurance Gp Simmons & Simmons (ptnr 1976–, also responsible for activities in Middle East and Central and Eastern Europe); memb: Law Soc, Exec Ctee Br Polish Legal Assoc, Br Privatisation Export Cncl, Int Bar Assoc (East-West Forum (Business Law Section)), American Bar Assoc (Int Law and Practice Section), Int C of C Fin Servs Cmmn, Insurance Law Sub-Ctee of Law Soc, The Securities Assoc; *Clubs* MCC; *Style*— Jeremy Walter, Esq; ✉ Simmons & Simmons, 21 Wilson Street, London EC2M 2RJ (☎ 0171 628 2020, fax 0171 628 2070)

WALTER, Michael; s of late Leonard Walter (d 1990), of 4 Griffin Close, Saxon Park, Blacon, Chester, and Anne, *née* Rue; *b* 6 May 1956; *Educ* The King's Sch, Christ's Coll Cambridge (BA, MA); *m* 27 Nov 1982, Joan Margaret, da of Arthur Colin Hubbard (d 1978), of Paeroa, nr Auckland, NZ; 1 s (Matthew b 1987), 1 da (Helen b 1984); *Career* admitted slr 1981 (England, Wales and Hong Kong); Stephenson Harwood: articled clerk 1979–81, asst slr 1981–86, ptnr 1986–; Freeman: City of London 1987, Worshipful Co of Slrs 1987; memb: Law Soc, Law Soc of Hong Kong; *Books* Moores & Rowlands Orange Tax Guides; *Recreations* sailing, scuba diving, running, reading, music; *Clubs* Royal Hong Kong Yacht, Royal Hong Kong Jockey, Hong Kong FC; *Style*— Michael Walter, Esq; ✉ Stephenson Harwood, One St Paul's Churchyard, London EC4M 8SH (☎ 0171 329 4422, fax 0171 606 0822)

WALTER, Robert John; s of Richard Walter, of Warminster, Wilts, and Irene; *b* 30 May 1948; *Educ* Warminster, Univ of Aston (BSc); *m* 28 Aug 1970, Sally (d 1995), da of Donald Middleton (d 1976); 2 s (Charles b 1976, Alexander b 1977), 1 da (Elizabeth b 1974); *Career* investmt banker and farmer; dir: FW Holst (Europe) Ltd 1984–86, TV-UK Ltd 1988; vice pres Aubrey G Lanston & Co Inc 1986–; visiting lectr Central London Poly; farmer in West Country; Parly candidate (C) Bedwellty 1979, prospective Parly candidate (C) N Dorset 1996–; chm: Aston Univ Cons Assoc 1967–69, W Wilts Young Cons 1972–75, Euro Democrat Forum 1979–84, Foreign Affrs Forum 1985–87, Cons Gp for Europe 1992–95 (vice chm 1984–86, dep chm 1989–92); memb Sir Francis Chichester Meml Appeal Ctee, chm Bd of Govrs Tachbrook Sch 1980–; Freeman City of London 1983, Liveryman Worshipful Co of Needlemakers 1983; AMIIMR, MSI; *Recreations* sailing, shooting; *Clubs* Carlton; *Style*— Robert Walter, Esq; ✉ Bracken House, 1 Friday St, London EC4M 9JA (☎ 0171 248 3955, fax 0171 236 2781, telex 945771)

WALTER, Thomas James (Tom); s of Ernest Thomas Walter (d 1975), and Mary, *née* Jacks (d 1972); *Educ* High Pavement GS Nottingham (head boy), Christ Church Oxford (MA, Fell Exhbn), Univ of Manchester (dip); *m* 2 Aug 1964, Dorothy, da of Ronald Clarke; 1 s (David Ronald James b 17 July 1965); *Career* asst master Shrewsbury Sch 1956–58, housemaster and head of classics St Bees Sch 1958–61, housemaster and head of English Lawrence Coll (British Cncl appt) Ghora Gali W Pakistan 1962–64, asst master Davy Hall Billingham Co Durham 1965, asst master Magdalen Coll Sch Oxford 1965–67, head of classics and dir of sixth form studies Balderstone Sr HS Rochdale 1967–72, headmaster Brinkburn Comp Sch Hartlepool, schoolmaster fell commoner St John's Coll Cambridge 1980, princ Hartlepool Sixth Form Coll 1983–95; memb: Sr Common Room Van Mildert Coll Durham, Sr Common Room St Chad's Coll Durham (govr 1986–89), SHA, Assoc of Sixth Form Coll Principals; sec Durham & Cleveland Ctee of the Prince's Trust 1979–; *Recreations* reading, theatre, watching rugby and cricket, swimming; *Clubs* West Hartlepool Rugby Football, Durham Co Cricket; *Style*— Tom Walter, Esq; ✉ 14 College Close, Dalton Piercy, Hartlepool TS27 3JA (☎ 01429 264248)

WALTERS, Sir Alan Arthur; kt (1983); s of James Arthur Walters, and Claribel, *née* Heywood; *b* 17 June 1926; *Educ* Alderman Newtons Sch Leicester, Univ Coll Leicester (BScEcon London), Nuffield Coll Oxford (MA); *m* 1975, Margaret Patricia, da of Leonard Wilson, of Leeds, Yorks; 1 da by previous m (Louise); *Career* Cassel prof of econs LSE 1968–76, prof of political economy Johns Hopkins Univ Maryland USA 1976–91; econ advsr to World Bank 1976–80 and 1984–88, personal econ advsr to PM (on secondment) 1981–84 and 1989; vice chm and dir AIG Trading Group Inc Washington DC 1991–; Hon DLitt Univ of Leicester 1981; Hon DSocSc: Univ of Birmingham 1984, Univ Francisco Marroquin Guatemala City 1994; *Recreations* music, tennis, Thai porcelain; *Clubs* Political Economy; *Style*— Sir Alan Walters; ✉ 2820 P Street NW, Washington, DC 20007, USA; AIG Trading Group Inc, 1200 19th St NW, Suite 605, Washington DC 20036, USA (☎ 00 1 202 861 8671, fax 00 1 202 775 2436)

WALTERS, Sir Dennis Murray; kt (1988), MBE (1960); s of Douglas L Walters (d 1964), and Clara, *née* Pomello (d 1992); *b* 28 Nov 1928; *Educ* Downside, St Catharine's Coll Cambridge (MA); *m* 1, 1955 (m dis 1969), Vanora, da of Sir Archibald McIndoe, CBE (d 1960); 1 s (Nicholas McIndoe Walters, *qv*, b 1957), 1 da (Lorian b 1960); m 2, 1970 (m dis 1979), Hon Celia Mary, da of Baron Duncan Sandys, CH (d 1987); 1 s (Dominic b 1971); m 3, 22 Jan 1981, Bridgett Louise, da of J F Shearer, CBE, of Wimbledon; 1 s (Oliver Charles b 1985), 1 da (Camilla Clare b 1982); *Career* interned in Italy during early part of WWII, joined Resistance Movement for 11 months; fndr memb Bow Group, chm Fedn of Univ Cons and Unionist Assocs 1949–50, PA to Viscount Hailsham, QC (now Lord Hailsham of Saint Marylebone) as Chm of Cons Pty 1957–69; Parly candidate (C) Blyth 1959 and 1960 by-election, MP (C) Westbury 1964–92; jt chm Cncl of Advancement of Arab-Br Understanding 1970–82, jt vice chm Cons Parly Foreign Affairs Ctee 1974–78 (jt sec 1965–71), chm Cons Middle East Cncl 1980–92 (pres 1992–); writer and broadcaster; tstee ANAF Foundation, memb Kuwait Investmt Advsy Ctee; chm Asthma Res Cncl 1968–88; Order of the Cedar of Lebanon 1969; *Books* Not Always With The Pack (autobiographical memoirs, 1989); *Recreations* reading, tennis; *Clubs* Boodle's; *Style*— Sir Dennis Walters, MBE; ✉ Orchardleigh, Corton, Warminster,

Wiltshire (☎ 01985 850369); 43 Royal Avenue, London SW3 4QE (☎ 0171 730 9431, fax 0171 823 5938)

WALTERS, Very Rev (Rhys) Derrick Chamberlain; OBE (1994); s of Ivor Chamberlain Walters, and Rosamund Grace, *née* Jackson; *b* 10 March 1932; *Educ* Gowerton Boys' GS, LSE, Ripon Hall Oxford (BSc); *m* 28 Dec 1959, Joan, da of William George Fisher, 2 s (David b 1962, Michael b 1964); *Career* curate of Manselton Swansea 1957–58, anglican chaplain of Univ Coll Swansea and curate of St Mary's 1958–62; vicar of: All Saints Totley 1962–67, St Mary's Boulton by Derby 1967–74; diocesan missioner Diocese of Salisbury 1974–82, vicar of Burcombe 1974–79, non residentiary canon of Salisbury Cathedral 1978 (canon and treas 1979–82), dean Liverpool 1983–; hon fell John Moores Univ (formerly Liverpool Poly) 1988; *Recreations* escapist literature, croquet, classical music; *Style—* The Very Rev the Dean of Liverpool, OBE; ✉ Liverpool Cathedral, St James Mount, Liverpool L1 7AZ (☎ 0151 709 6271, fax 0151 709 1112)

WALTERS, Sir (Frederick) Donald; s of Percival Donald Walters, and Irene Walters; *b* 5 Oct 1925; *Educ* Howardian HS Cardiff, LSE (LLB); *m* 1950, Adelaide Jean, *née* McQuistin; 1 s; *Career* called to the Bar Inner Temple 1946; practised Wales and Chester circuit 1948–59; memb: Bd Welsh Devpt Agency 1980–93 (dep chm 1984–92), Devpt Bd for Rural Wales 1984–; dir Chartered Trust plc 1959–85; cncl chm Univ of Wales Coll of Cardiff 1988–, vice chm Welsh Nat Opera 1990–, chm Wales Cncl for Vol Action 1987–93; chm Llandough Hosp NHS Tst 1993–; High Sheriff S Glamorgan 1987–88; *Style—* Sir Donald Walters; ✉ 120 Cyncoed Rd, Cardiff CF2 6BL

WALTERS, Eric; *b* 3 Aug 1944; *Educ* Bablake Sch Coventry, Selwyn Coll Cambridge (MA); *m* 12 Aug 1967, Katharina; 1 s (Eric Andrew b 28 Sept 1976), 1 da (Katya b 25 May 1973); *Career* res offr British Petroleum Co plc 1965–67, conslt Cape Industries plc 1967–69, sr conslt International Systems Research Ltd 1969–72, divnl mangr Lex Service Group plc 1976–80 (planner 1972–76); Grand Metropolitan plc: md CC Soft Drinks Ltd 1980–82, chm Soft Drinks and Overseas Brewing 1982, chief exec Retailing Div 1984; gp md Dominion International Group plc 1986–87, ptnr Schroder Ventures 1987–; currently dir: Goldsmith Group plc, Century Inns plc, The Old English Pub Co plc, Beck & Pollitzer Engineering Ltd, Paramount Hotels plc, Enfield Community Care Tst, Schroder Partenaires SA France, Kundert International Ltd, Tetley Group Ltd, Sytner Group Ltd; non-exec dir Silvermines Group plc 1994–; *Recreations* skiing, hiking, swimming; *Clubs* RAC; *Style—* Eric Walters, Esq; ✉ 136 Wades Hill, London N21 1EH; Schroder Ventures, 20 Southampton St, London WC2E 7QG (☎ 0171 632 1020, fax 0171 240 5072)

WALTERS, John Owen; s of Harry Thomas Walters, of Ipswich, and Mable Rose, *née* Oakley (d 1989); *b* 28 June 1966; *Educ* Northgate GS for Boys Ipswich, Univ of Birmingham (BA); *Career* magazine editor and croquet player; first tournament Hunstanton Norfolk 1980 (won all 3 events), winner World Croquet Championship 1991 (runner-up 1992); rep: Colchester Club 1984–85, Eastern Counties 1985– (winners 1985, 1986, 1988 and 1991), Ipswich Club 1986–, England 1991–, GB in Solomon Trophy v USA 1992 and Macrobertson Shield 1993; design and pubns conslt 1989–91, proprietor Eastern Rose Publishing 1990–92; ed: Townsend's Croquet Almanack 1988–92, Croquet (Croquet Assoc magazine) 1992–94, Radio Control Model Mart 1994, Telecard Collector International 1994; cncllr Croquet Assoc 1988–92 (chm Tournament Ctee 1991–92); *Recreations* bridge, badminton, tennis, politics, philosophy, films; *Style—* John Walters, Esq; ✉ c/o Croquet Association, Hurlingham Club, Ranelagh Gardens, London SW6 3PR (☎ and fax 0171 736 3148)

WALTERS, Rear Adm John William Townshend; CB (1984); s of William Bernard Walters, and Lilian Martha, *née* Hartridge; *b* 23 April 1926; *Educ* John Fisher Sch Purley; *m* 1949, Margaret Sarah Patricia Jeffkins; 2 s, 1 da; *Career* joined RN 1944, Supply Offr HMS Albion 1967–69, sec to Chief of Fleet Support 1969–72, Chief Naval Judge Advocate 1972–75, Capt Naval Drafting 1975–78, dir Naval Admin Planning 1978–80, Asst Chief of Def Staff (Personnel and Logistics) 1981–84, ret RN 1984; called to the Bar Middle Temple 1956; chm Industl Tbnls 1984– (Central London 1984–87, Southampton 1987–), dep chm Data Protection Tbnl 1985–; memb Royal Naval Sailing Assoc; *Clubs* Army and Navy; *Style—* Rear Adm John Walters, CB; ✉ Good Holding, 5 Hollycombe Close, Liphook, Hants GU30 7HR

WALTERS, Joyce Dora; da of Wilfred John Davies (d 1961), and Florence May, *née* Fisher; *b* 10 Dec 1932; *Educ* St Anne's Coll Oxford (MA); *m* 29 July 1979, Lt-Col Howard Corey Walters IV (d 1983), s of Col Howard Corey Walters III (d 1982), of California; 1 s by prev m (Nicholas John Warwick Bailey b 18 Sept 1962); *Career* headmistress: St Mary's Calne 1972–85, Clifton HS 1985–95; *Recreations* reading, cooking, travel; *Style—* Mrs Joyce Walters; ✉ 4 Longwood House, Failand, Bristol (☎ 0127 539 2092)

WALTERS, Julie; *b* 22 Feb 1950; *Career* actress; *Theatre* incl: seasons at Everyman Theatre Liverpool and Bristol Old Vic, Educating Rita (RSC Warehouse and Piccadilly Theatre), Having a Ball (Lyric), Jumpers (Royal Exchange), Fool for Love (NT and Lyric), When I was a Girl I Used to Scream and Shout (Whitehall), Frankie and Johnnie, Serafina in The Rose Tattoo (dir Sir Peter Hall), Sister My Sister 1995; *Television* incl: The Birthday Party, Secret Diary of Adrian Mole, Victoria Wood - As Seen on TV (BAFTA nomination), Boys From the Blackstuff (BAFTA nomination), She'll Be Wearing Pink Pyjamas, Say Something Happened (by Alan Bennett, BAFTA nomination), Intensive Care (by Alan Bennett), Talking Heads (by Alan Bennett), GBH (by Alan Bleasdale), Julie Walters & Friends (TV special Christmas 1991, 2 BAFTA nominations), Wide Eyed and Legless (Screen One, BBC (BAFTA nomination)), Bambino Mio (Screen One) 1994, Pat and Margaret (Screen One) 1994, Jakes Progress (Channel 4, by Alan Bleasdale) 1995, Little Red Riding Hood and the Wolfe (BBC, by Roald Dahl) 1995, Bathtime (short film, BBC) 1995, Brazen Hussies (BBC Screen Two film) 1996; *Films* incl: Rita in Educating Rita (Oscar nomination, BAFTA Award, Golden Globe Award), Buster, Personal Services (BAFTA nominee), Joe Orton's mother in Prick Up Your Ears, Killing Dad, Steppin' Out (Variety Club Award, BAFTA nomination) Just Like a Woman 1992, Clothes in the Wardrobe 1993; *Style—* Ms Julie Walters; ✉ c/o ICM Ltd, Oxford House, 76 Oxford Street, London W1N 0AX (☎ 0171 636 6565, fax 0171 323 0101)

WALTERS, Prof Kenneth; *b* 14 Sept 1934; *Educ* Dynevor GS Swansea, Univ Coll Swansea (state scholar, BSc, MSc, PhD), Univ of Wales (DSc); *m*; 3 c; *Career* res assoc Brown Univ USA and asst prof San Diego State Coll USA 1959–60; Univ of Wales Aberystwyth: lectr in applied mathematics 1960–65, sr lectr 1965–70, reader 1970–73, prof 1973–; pres Br Soc of Rheology 1974–76; memb Editorial Bd: Rheologica Acta 1972–, Jl of Rheology 1988–; exec ed Jl of Non-Newtonian Fluid Mechanics 1975–; Gold Medal Br Soc of Rheology 1984; hon fell Univ Coll Swansea 1992, foreign assoc Nat Acad of Engrg USA; FRS 1991; *Books* Rheometry (1975), Rheometry: Industrial Applications (ed, 1980), Numerical Simulation of non-Newtonian Flow (with M J Crochet and A R Davies, 1984), An Introduction to Rheology (with H A Barnes and J F Hutton, 1989), Rheological Phenomena in Focus (with D V Boger, 1993); *Style—* Prof Kenneth Walters, FRS; ✉ Department of Mathematics, University of Wales, Aberystwyth, Dyfed SY23 3BZ (☎ 01970 622750, fax 01970 622777)

WALTERS, Minette Caroline Mary; da of Samuel Henry Doddington Jebb (d 1960), and Minette Colleen Helen, *née* Paul; *b* 26 Sept 1949; *Educ* Godolphin Sch Salisbury, Univ of Durham (BA); *m* 1978, Alexander Hamilton Walters, s of Dr F J H Walters; 2 s (Roland Francis Samuel b 13 Dec 1979, Philip Gladwyn Hamilton b 12 Jan 1982); *Career* sub-ed then ed IPC Magazines 1972–76, freelance writer 1976–; prison visitor HM Prison Winchester; *Books* The Ice House (1992, Crime Writers' Assoc John Creasey Award), The Sculptress (1993, Edgar Allen Poe Award, Macavity Award), The Scold's Bridle (1994, Crime Writers' Assoc Gold Dagger Award), The Dark Room (1995); *Recreations* DIY, sailing, books, Radio 4, films, tv, theatre, crossword puzzles; *Style—* Mrs Minette Walters; ✉ c/o Gregory & Radice, 3 Barb Mews, London W6 7PA (☎ 0171 610 4676, fax 0171 610 4686)

WALTERS, Nicholas McIndoe; s of Sir Dennis Walters, MBE, *qv*, of London, and Vanora, *née* McIndoe; *b* 16 May 1957; *Educ* Downside, Univ of Exeter; *m* 1 Aug 1987, Emma Mary, yr da of David Blamey; 2 s (Benedict McIndoe b 15 Jan 1992, Alexander Bowman b 2 April 1994); *Career* legislative asst to Howard Baker, majority ldr The Senate, Washington DC 1980–81; exec: The Marconi Company 1981–82, Paul Winner Marketing Ltd 1982–83; dir Good Relations Ltd 1983–88, dep md GCI Group (formerly McAvoy Bayley Ltd) 1988–; Parly candidate (Cons) Merthyr Tydfil 1987; MIPR; *Recreations* skiing, tennis; *Clubs* Annabel's, Raffles, Hurlingham; *Style—* Nicholas Walters, Esq; ✉ 124 Bennerley Road, London SW11 6DY (☎ 0171 223 5277); GCI Group, 1 Chelsea Manor Gardens, London SW3 5PN (☎ 0171 351 2400)

WALTERS, Sir Peter Ingram; kt (1984); *b* 11 March 1931; *Career* exec chm BP plc 1981–90 (an md 1973–80), chm Midland Bank plc 1991–94; non-exec chm: Blue Circle Industries plc 1990–96 (dir 1989–96), SmithKline Beecham plc 1994– (dir 1989–); non-exec dep chm: EMI Group plc (formerly THORN EMI plc) 1990– (dir 1989–), HSBC Holdings plc 1993– (dir following takeover of Midland Bank 1992–); non-exec dir Cordiant plc (formerly Saatchi & Saatchi Co plc) 1994–; formerly chllr IOD; currently: memb Advsy Bd The LEK Partnership, dir Inst of Economic Affrs, memb Cncl Inst of Business Ethics, chm of Tstees Police Fndn, memb Ctee of Mgmnt RNLI; Liveryman Worshipful Co of Shipwrights; *Style—* Sir Peter Walters; ✉ SmithKline Beecham plc, New Horizons Court, Brentford TW8 9EP (☎ 0181 975 2000, fax 0181 975 2040)

WALTERS, Sir Roger Talbot; KBE (1971, CBE 1965); s of Alfred Walters, of Sudbury, Suffolk; *b* 31 March 1917; *Educ* Oundle, AA Sch of Architecture, Univ of Liverpool; *m* 1976, Claire Chappell; *Career* served RE WWII; chief architect (devpt) Directorate of Works WO 1959–62, dep dir gen res and devpt Miny Public Bldgs and Works 1962–67, dir gen prodn 1967–69; architect and controller construction servs GLC 1971–78; Hon FAIA, FRIBA, FIStructE; *Clubs* Reform; *Style—* Sir Roger Walters, KBE; ✉ 46 Princess Rd, London NW1 8JL (☎ 0171 722 3740)

WALTERSON, Inga Ruth; da of Francis Sinclair Walterson, of W Burrafirth, Shetland, and Mary Olive, *née* Bowie; *b* 27 May 1964; *Educ* Univ of Aberdeen (MA); *m* Ian James Douglas Anderson, s of John Robertson Anderson (d 1987), of Lerwick, Shetland, and Ella, *née* Morrison (d 1986); *Career* md Shetland Islands Broadcasting Company Ltd; *Style—* Ms Inga Walterson; ✉ Shetland Islands Broadcasting Company Ltd, Market St, Lerwick, Shetland ZE1 0JN (☎ 01595 695299, fax 01595 695696)

WALTHER, Robert Philippe; s of Prof David Philippe Walther (d 1973), and Barbara, *née* Brook; *b* 31 July 1943; *Educ* Charterhouse, Christ Church Oxford (MA); *m* 21 June 1969, Anne, da of Lionel Wigglesworth, of Woldingham, Surrey; 1 s (Luke b 1978), 1 da (Julie Clare b 1973); *Career* Clerical Medical Investment Group: joined 1965, dep investmt mangr 1972, investmt mangr 1976, asst gen mangr (investments) 1980, dir 1985–, gp chief exec 1994–; chm Investmt Ctee Assoc of Br Insurers; FIA 1970, AIIMR 1969; *Recreations* hockey, golf, bridge, squash, sailing; *Clubs* United Oxford and Cambridge; *Style—* Robert Walther, Esq; ✉ Ashwell's Barn, Chesham Lane, Chalfont St Giles, Bucks HP8 4AS (☎ 01240 75575); Clerical Medical Investment Group, 15 St James's Square, London SW1Y 4LQ (☎ 0171 930 5474, fax 0171 321 1846, telex 27432 CMG LDN)

WALTON, Alastair Henry; s of Sir Raymond Henry Walton (d 1988), of Wimbledon, London, and Helen Alexandra, *née* Dingwall; *b* 26 Aug 1954; *Educ* Winchester, Balliol Coll Oxford (BA); *m* 28 July 1984, Hon Mary Synolda, *née* Butler, da of 28 Baron Dunboyne, *qv*, of Chelsea, London; 4 da (Alexandra Mary b 1985, Christina Frances b 1986, Stephanie Katherine b 1988, Florence Lucy b 1992); *Career* called to the Bar Lincoln's Inn 1977, in practice 1978–; *Recreations* lawn tennis; *Style—* Alastair Walton, Esq; ✉ 26 Paradise Walk, Chelsea, London SW3 4JL (☎ 0171 376 5304); 7 Stone Bldgs, Lincoln's Inn, London WC2A 3SZ (☎ 0171 405 3886, fax 0171 242 8502)

WALTON, Anthony Michael; QC (1970); s of Henry Herbert Walton (d 1975), of Dulwich, and Clara Martha, *née* Dobrantz (d 1974); *b* 4 May 1925; *Educ* Dulwich, Hertford Coll Oxford (MA, BCL, pres Oxford Union Trinity 1945); *m* 1955, Jean Frederica, da of William Montague Hey (d 1936), of London; 1 s (Martin b 1969); *Career* called to the Bar Middle Temple 1950, bencher 1978, master reader autumn 1996; Liveryman Worshipful Co of Gunmakers; *Publications* Patent Law of Europe and the UK (1978), Russell on Arbitration (1982); *Style—* Anthony Walton, Esq, QC; ✉ 62 Kingsmead Rd, Tulse Hill, London SW2 3JG (☎ 0181 674 9159); 8 New Square, Lincoln's Inn, London (☎ 0171 405 4321)

WALTON, Dr Bryan; s of Henry Walton (d 1985), and Helen, *née* Pincus (d 1989); *b* 29 Aug 1943; *Educ* City of London Sch, London Hosp Med Coll Univ of London (MB BS, FRCA); *m* 7 July 1968, (Sarah) Ruth, da of Philip Levitan (d 1989); 1 s (Jonathan b 1976), 1 da (Ann b 1973); *Career* conslt anaesthetist London Hosp 1974–95, advsr on anaesthesia and intensive care Princess Grace Hosp London 1984–, dir of intensive care London Ind Hosp 1989–; memb: Med Def Union 1966, Assoc of Anaesthetists 1972, Anaesthetic Res Soc 1980, Hunterian Soc 1985, Chelsea Clinical Soc 1989; *Books* chapters: Adverse Reactions to Anaesthetic Drugs (1981), Scientific Foundations of Anaesthesia (3 edn 1982, 4 edn 1990), Hazards and Complications of Anaesthesia (1987, 2 edn 1993), Medicine in the Practice of Anaesthesia (1989); many pubns on anaesthesia and the liver, and anaesthesia and immunology; *Recreations* classical music; *Style—* Dr Bryan Walton; ✉ 28 Makepeace Avenue, Highgate, London N6 6EJ (☎ 0181 341 3139, fax 0181 342 8832)

WALTON, Christopher Henry; s of Frank Pearson Walton (d 1966), of Eastbourne, and Marion Ada Beasley (d 1989); *b* 20 June 1930; *Educ* Stockport GS, Gonville and Caius Coll Cambridge (MA); *m* 25 April 1959, Judith Vivien, da of Ernest Leslie Philp (d 1950), of Alexandria, Egypt; *Career* 2 Lt Lancs Fus 1949–51, Capt Royal Fus TA 1951–59; Cwlth Devpt Corp 1954–65, initiator and dir Kenya Tea Devpt Authy 1959–65; exec and dir: Kyle Products Ltd Gp 1965–67, Eastern Produce Ltd Gp 1967–69; div chief Projects Dept Eastern and Western Africa World Bank Washington 1969–87; Wolfson Coll Oxford: bursar 1987–95, emeritus fell 1995–; fin advsr Oxford Union Soc 1995–; pres UN Student Assoc 1954–55, on Cons Party Candidates List 1966–69, dep chm Cons Party Overseas Devpt Ctee 1967–68; govr: Pusey House Oxford, Stowe Sch; tstee Oxfordshire Historic Churches Tst; *Recreations* ecclesiastical architecture, Conservative politics, rowing; *Clubs* Oriental, Leander; *Style—* Christopher Walton, Esq; ✉ The Corner House, Foxcombe Lane, Boars Hill, Oxford OX1 5DH (☎ 01865 735179, fax 01865 736604)

WALTON, David; JP (Glasgow 1981); s of Isidore Aaron Walton, CBE, JP (d 1979), of Glasgow, and Lena, *née* Franklin (d 1984); *b* 4 Aug 1943; *Educ* Glasgow HS, Lycée Jaccard Lausanne Switzerland; *m* 12 Oct 1964, Carole, da of Michael Schuster-Davis (d 1953), of Glasgow; 2 s (Michael b 18 Oct 1965, John Richard b 1 Dec 1967); *Career* stockbroker; chm: The Scottish Metropolitan Property plc 1979–, Stirling Hendry & Co stockbrokers 1987–; chm and fndr tstee The Isidore and David Walton Fndn 1979; Hon LLD Glasgow 1980, Hon FRCPS Glasgow 1980; CStJ 1981; memb Int Stock Exchange 1964; *Recreations* bridge, travel; *Clubs* Western (Glasgow); *Style—* David Walton, Esq,

JP; ✉ The Scottish Metropolitan Property plc, 100 Queen Street, Glasgow G1 3DL (☎ 0141 248 7333); Stirling Henry & Co, 100 Queen Street, Glasgow G1 3DL (☎ 0141 248 6033)

WALTON, Col Dennis; CBE (1967, OBE 1962), MC, TD; s of Harry Walton (d 1966), of Bury, Lancs, and Eva Kathleen Walton (d 1969); *b* 7 Feb 1920; *Educ* Bury GS, Emmanuel Coll Cambridge (MA, Soccer blue); *m* 1949, Barbara Shirley, da of Leonard Bertram Jones, JP (d 1948), a former Mayor of Bury; 2 da; *Career* served WWII N Africa and Europe; Col RA (TA), Dep Cdr RA 42 Div 1962–67; md Dalkeith Knitwear Ltd 1963–78, bd memb Coats Patons Knitwear Div 1976–78; memb Cncl Nat Artillery Assoc 1962–; pres Nottingham and Dist Hosiery Mfrs Assoc 1967–69; chm: E Midland Further Educn Cncl Textiles Panel 1973–77, Technician Educn Cncl Ctee 1975–80; sr advsr Small Firms Serv (DE) 1978–89, business advsr Nottingham Business Venture 1989–; pres: E Midland Further Educ Cncl 1985–93, RA Offrs' Assoc of the North-West 1985–; Bolton Volunteer Artillery Assoc 1985–; capt Riber Cricket Club 1980–94; FIMgt, FInstD, FIBC; *Clubs* Royal Over-Seas League; *Style*— Col Dennis Walton, CBE, MC, TD; ✉ Riber Manor, Matlock, Derbyshire DE4 5JU (☎ 01629 583864)

WALTON, Ernest Ward; TD (1968); s of Herbert Walton, JP (d 1968), of Newcastle upon Tyne, and Eleanor, *née* Ward (d 1986); *b* 10 July 1926; *Educ* Univ of Durham (MB BS, MD); *m* 11 Oct 1952, Greta Elizabeth, da of Leonard Wray (d 1978), of Newcastle upon Tyne; 3 s (David b 1954, Paul b 1955, Hugh b 1961), 1 da (Caroline b 1959); *Career* Nat Serv 1950–52; TA 1952–72, Maj RAMC 1958; lectr in pathology Univ of St Andrews 1957–60, conslt pathologist N Tees Health Dist 1960–91, clinical lectr in pathology Univ of Newcastle upon Tyne 1978–91; chm Cleveland Med Laboratories 1981–; JP 1978, med advsr Nat Assoc of Funeral Dirs 1986–93, pres Stockton Rotary Club 1990–91; FRCPath 1972 (memb 1963); *Recreations* fell walking, travel, cross country skiing; *Clubs* Nat Lib; *Style*— Ernest Walton, Esq, TD; ✉ 32 The Green, Norton, Stockton on Tees, Cleveland TS20 1DX (☎ 01642 554653); Cleveland Medical Laboratories Ltd, Letch Lane, Carlton, Stockton on Tees, Cleveland TS21 1EE (☎ 01642 673737, fax 01642 602609)

WALTON, Field Laurence Joseph; s of Joseph Field Horace Walton (d 1982), and Marie Joan, *née* Lennard (d 1984); *b* 17 April 1940; *Educ* Loughborough Univ (BTech, MSc, played rugby for Eng Univs 1st XV); *m* 26 May 1965, Susan Thompstone, da of Basil Rowe; 1 da (Virginia Mary Spencer b 15 Dec 1966), 1 s (Francis Joseph Field b 1 Feb 1968); *Career* electrical apprentice then project engr Hawker Siddeley 1964–67, project mangr John Laing plc 1968–70, planning mangr Plessey plc 1970–71, engrg analyst Cazenove & Co 1971–74, engrg analyst Quilter Hilton Goodison 1974–77, investmt mangr Electra Funds and md Temple Bar Fund Managers 1977–85, md Guinness Mahon Fund Managers 1985–89, chm Guinness Mahon Asset Managers 1989–92; chm: Eleco Holdings plc 1983–, Henry Cooke Group plc 1993–95; independent dir: Temple Bar Properties 1982–, Temple Bar Investment Trust 1983–, Martin International Holdings plc 1994–, Romney, Hythe & Dymchurch Railway Plc 1995–; assoc MacArthur & Co Ltd 1995–; Freeman: City of London, Worshipful Co of Glass Sellers; CEng, FIEE, FIMgt, MSI; *Recreations* golf; *Clubs* Leicester FC, Harewood Downs Golf, Beaconsfield Golf; *Style*— Field Walton, Esq; ✉ Christow Cottage, Seer Green Lane, Jordans, Bucks HP9 2ST (☎ and fax 01494 874971)

WALTON, The Ven Geoffrey Elmer; s of Maj Harold Walton (d 1978), and Edith Margaret, *née* Dawson (d 1983); *b* 19 Feb 1934; *Educ* West Bridgford GS, Univ of Durham (BA), Queen's Coll Birmingham (Dip Theol); *m* 9 Sept 1961, Edith Mollie, da of John Patrick O'Connor (d 1970); 1 s (Jeremy Mark b 1968); *Career* vicar of Norwell Notts and Dio Youth chaplain 1965–69, recruitment and selection sec Advsy Cncl for the Church's Min London 1969–75, hon canon of Salisbury Cathedral 1981, rural dean of Weymouth 1980–82, archdeacon of Dorset 1982–, incumbent of Witchampton with Long Crichel and Moor Crichel 1982–, chm Dorset Co Scouts, chm E Dorset Housing Assoc, chm Dio Bd of Miny; *Recreations* religious drama, conjuring, walking; *Style*— The Ven the Archdeacon of Dorset; ✉ The Vicarage, Witchampton, Wimborne, Dorset BH21 5AP (☎ 01258 840422)

WALTON, John Cannell; *b* 26 Jan 1946; *Educ* King Edward VI Sch Norwich, UCL (BSc Econ); *Career* investmt analyst then head of investmt res Hill Samuel & Co 1968–72, acquisitions analyst Sterling Land 1972–74, investmt mangr then dir of investmts Imperial Life Assurance 1975–85, md Clan Asset Management Ltd 1985–95, dir Ivory & Sime Asset Management Ltd 1995–; investmt dir British Empire Securities & General Trust plc 1985–, dir French Property Trust plc 1990–; AIIMR; *Style*— John Walton, Esq; ✉ Ivory & Sime Asset Management Ltd, 14th Floor, One Angel Court, London EC2R 7HJ (☎ 0171 600 6655, fax 0171 600 4371)

WALTON, Lt-Col John Cusack; DL (1987); s of Col Granville Walton, CMG, OBE, DL, JP (d 1974), and Joan, *née* McCraken (d 1975); *b* 16 April 1928; *Educ* Marlborough; *m* 29 Jan 1971, Elsabe, da of Brig James Whetstone, OBE (d 1956); 1 s (David b 29 Feb 1972), 1 da (Joanna b 7 Nov 1973); *Career* cmmnd Royal Scots Greys 1947, Capt 1949–58, Adj 1955–58, Maj 1960–71, Lt-Col 1971–77, served Aden, Bahrain, Libya, Germany, UK, ret 1977; chm: Regtl Assoc 1984–92 (vice pres 1992–), Old Berks Hunt 1984–96, Oxon Scout Cncl 1984–94 (vice pres 1994–), Thames Valley Police Authy 1985–91 (memb 1995–); cncllr Oxon CC 1981–, memb E Wessex TAVR Assoc 1981–, memb Oxon CLA Ctee 1982–93, tstee Police Convalescent Home Flint House 1991–, vice chm Wantage Constituency Conservative Assoc 1994–; *Recreations* field sports; *Clubs* Cavalry and Guards'; *Style*— Lt-Col John Walton, DL; ✉ Longworth Manor, Abingdon, Oxfordshire OX13 5DY (☎ 01865 820223, fax 01865 820071)

WALTON, John Victor; s of Eric Roscoe Walton (d 1961), of 18 Beech Ave, Radlett, Herts, and Ethel Marjorie, *née* Addinsell (d 1983); *b* 5 Dec 1925; *Educ* Aldenham, Ruskin Sch of Drawing Oxford, Slade Sch of Fine Art London, Univ of London (Dip Fine Art); *m* 1950 (m dis 1970), Annette Rolande Francoise D'Exea; 2 s (James Andre b 1950, Roland Dominic b 1966), 1 da (Victoria Ann b 1953); m 2, 1989, Alice Ellsworth, *née* Low; *Career* portrait painter; princ Heatherley Sch of Fine Art 1974–; exhibitions incl: RA, Royal Soc of Portrait Painters, Paris Salon (hon mention), Institut de France, Academie des Beaux Arts; paintings in national instns and private collections in GB & abroad; co sec Thomas Heatherley Educnl Tst 1976–, chm Fedn of Br Artists 1990– (govr 1982–); RP 1976 (memb Cncl 1979–81 and 1983–90); *Recreations* painting, cycling, history; *Clubs* Chelsea Arts; *Style*— John Walton, Esq; ✉ 30 Park Road, Radlett, Herts; The Heatherley School of Fine Art, Upcerne Road, Chelsea SW10 0SH (☎ 0171 351 4190)

WALTON, Julian Frederick John; *b* 24 Oct 1946; *Educ* Downside; *m* 3 c; *Career* articled clerk Walton & Ryan Kings Lynn and Witham Weld & Co (admitted 1970); Frere Cholmeley Bischoff (formerly Bischoff & Co): joined 1970, ptnr 1975–, head Company Commercial Dept Bischoff & Co 1991–93, ptnr merged firm 1993–, head Company Commercial Dept Frere Cholmeley Bischoff 1994–; non-exec dir: Millicom (UK) Ltd, Liberty Communications Ltd; treas Marriage Care Wimbledon Centre 1980–95; memb: Law Soc, Slrs' Benevolent Fund, IBA, American C of C, CBI; *Recreations* all sports, theatre, cinema and reading; *Clubs* Royal Wimbledon Golf (capt 1995–96); *Style*— Julian Walton, Esq; ✉ Frere Cholmeley Bischoff, 4 John Carpenter Street, London EC4Y 0NH (☎ 0171 615 8000, fax 0171 615 8080)

WALTON, Miles Henry; s of Rae Walton, MC, AFC, TD, of Tynemouth, and Anne Elizabeth, *née* Flisher; *b* 15 July 1955; *Educ* Ratcliffe Coll, Brasenose Coll Oxford (MA); *m* 11 May 1985, Lorraine, da of Jack Nunn (d 1966); 1 s (Jack b 14 Nov 1987), 1 da (Rachel b 25 June 1989); *Career* admitted slr 1980; ptnr Wilde Sapte (currently head Corporate Tax); memb Law Soc, ATII; *Recreations* wine, sailing, saxophone, scuba diving, skiing; *Style*— Miles Walton, Esq; ✉ Wilde Sapte, 1 Fleet Place, London EC4M 7WS (☎ 0171 246 7000, fax 0171 246 7777)

WALTON, Peter; s of Michael Walton, of Alnwick, and Anne Walton; *b* 3 June 1969; *Educ* Merchiston Castle Sch, Royal Agric Coll Cirencester; *m* Diana; *Career* Rugby Union flanker; clubs: Alnwick 1988–91, Newcastle Gosforth 1991–92, Northampton 1992–95, Newcastle 1995–; Scotland: 3 A caps, 6 full caps, memb World Cup squad 1995; winner of several Player of the Year Awards; currently professional rugby player and pt/t livestock fieldsman; *Recreations* all sports; *Style*— Peter Walton, Esq; ✉ c/o Newcastle Rugby Club, New Ground, Great North Road, Gosforth, Newcastle upon Tyne NE3 2DT (☎ 0191 214 0422)

WALTON, Col Peter Sinclair; s of late Col William Patrick Everard Walton, CBE, and Ruby Marcella Bloomfield, *née* Maffett, of Tenterden, Kent; *b* 3 Jan 1939; *Educ* St John's Sch Leatherhead; *m* 3 July 1971, Michelle Frances, da of Philip Edward Aldous, OBE, of Cape Province, SA; 1 s (David Sinclair b 1972), 1 da (Victoria Louise b 1978); *Career* HAC 1957, Int Corps 1958, cmmnd RAOC 1961, Lt-Col HQ BAOR 1979, COS Br Mil Advsy and Trg Team Zimbabwe 1983, CO 2 Ordnance Bn 1983, Materials Mgmnt Strategy Review Team MOD 1987–89 (Col 1985), Hon Col RLC TA 1993; tstee and designer RAOC Museum 1976–; memb Cncl: Assoc of Independent Museums 1990–95, Friends of Nat Army Museum 1991–95, Br Assoc of Friends of Museums 1996–; memb Standing Conf on Archives and Museums 1993–95, sec Army Museums Ogilby Tst 1989–95, vice pres Victorian Mil Soc; chm Corps of Drums Soc; memb: RUSI, SAHR; Sultan of Oman's DSM 1975; *Books* Simkin's Soldiers - The British Army in 1890 (vol I 1982, vol II 1986); *Recreations* kicking myself for not doing today what I shall think of tomorrow; *Clubs* HAC; *Style*— Col Peter Walton; ✉ 127 High Street, Tenterden, Kent TN30 6JS

WALTON, Stuart Michael; s of James Walton, of 11 Evistones Rd, Gateshead, Tyne and Wear, and Blanche May, *née* Crawley; *b* 22 Jan 1945; *Educ* Gateshead GS, Univ of Newcastle (MB BS); *m* 6 Dec 1969, Jennifer Lois, da of James Mathewson (d 1942); 2 s (Jonathan James b 29 Oct 1970, Nicholas Paul b 30 Jan 1972), 1 da (Abigail Naomi b 28 Jan 1976); *Career* obstetrician and gynaecologist: registrar Newcastle 1969–74, lectr Univ of Nairobi Kenya 1974–76, sr lectr Wellington Clinical Sch of Med Univ of Otago NZ 1977–80, conslt North Tees Health Dist 1980– (clinical dir of Obstetrics & Gynaecology 1989–93); rep: Nat Family Planning Bodies, regnl trg ctees; FRCOG 1985, MFFP 1993; *Recreations* pastel painting, modern art history, wine; *Style*— Stuart Walton, Esq; ✉ The Downs, The Spital, Yarm, Cleveland TS15 9EU (☎ 01642 783898); Department of Obstetrics and Gynaecology, North Tees General Hospital, Stockton-on-Tees, Cleveland TS19 8PE (☎ 01642 672122)

WALTON JONES, Howard; s of Alfred (Freddie) Hayter Walton Jones (d 1996), of Majorca, and Carmen Mary, *née* Rowlands; ggf A Jones founded A Jones & Sons 1857 London; Co now has 100 shops in Britain with int reputation for high quality; *b* 18 Feb 1945; *Educ* Monkton Combe Sch Bath; *m* 20 July 1968, Susan Dorothy Ann, da of John Brian Edwards Penn (d 1980); 2 da (Emma b 1972, Katy b 1975); *Career* md A Jones & Sons plc (shoe retailers) 1976–; dir: Church & Co plc (shoe mfrs) 1976–, Babers of Oxford St (shoe retailers) 1976–; *Recreations* tennis; *Style*— Howard Walton Jones, Esq; ✉ A Jones & Sons plc, 18 Maple Road, Eastbourne, E Sussex BN23 6NZ (☎ 01323 730532, fax 01323 738272)

WALTON OF DETCHANT, Baron (Life Peer UK 1989); John Nicholas Walton; kt (1979), TD (1962); s of Herbert Walton; *b* 16 Sept 1922; *Educ* Alderman Wraith GS, King's Coll Med Sch Univ of Durham (MD), Univ of Newcastle (DSc); *m* 1946, Elizabeth (Betty) Harrison; 1 s, 2 da; *Career* Col (late RAMC) CO I (N) Gen Hosp (TA) 1963–66, Hon Col 201 (N) Gen Hosp (T & AVR) 1968–73; conslt neurologist Univ of Newcastle Hosps 1958–83, prof of neurology Univ of Newcastle 1968–83; chm: Muscular Dystrophy Gp GB 1970–95, Hamlyn Nat Cmmn on Educn 1991–93; memb Gen Med Cncl 1971–90 (chm Educn Ctee 1975–82, pres 1982–89), pres BMA 1980–82, ASME 1982–94, ABN 1987–88; first vice pres World Fedn of Neurology 1981–89 (pres 1989–97); warden Green Coll Oxford 1983–89; pres RSM 1984–86; Hon DUniv Aix Marseille, Laurea (hc) Genoa, Hon MD Sheffield; Hon DSc: Leeds, Leicester, Hull, Oxford Brookes; Hon DCL Newcastle; FRCP; *Clubs* Athenaeum, United Oxford and Cambridge Univ; *Style*— The Rt Hon Lord Walton of Detchant, TD; ✉ 13 Norham Gardens, Oxford OX2 6PS (☎ 01865 512492, fax 01865 512495)

WALWYN, Peter Tyndall; s of Lt-Col C T Walwyn, DSO, OBE, MC (d 1959), and Alexandra Adelaide Walwyn (d 1959); *b* 1 July 1933; *Educ* Charterhouse; *m* 5 Jan 1960, Virginia Clementina, da of Auriol S Gaselee (d 1987); 1 s (Edward b 1969), 1 da (Kate b 1972); *Career* racehorse trainer; leading trainer on the flat 1974–75, leading trainer Ireland 1974–75; over 1,800 races won worldwide; major races won incl: One Thousand Guineas 1970, Irish Derby 1971, Oaks Stakes 1974, Epsom Derby, King George and Queen Elizabeth Stakes and Irish 2000 Guineas 1975; chm Lambourn Trainers' Assoc; *Recreations* foxhunting, shooting; *Clubs* Turf, Jockey Club Rooms; *Style*— Peter Walwyn, Esq; ✉ Windsor House, Lambourn, Berks RG13

WAMBOLD, Ali Edward; s of William Henry Wambold, of Mandelieu, France, and Southampton, NY, and Princess Guity Afrouz Qajar; *b* 10 April 1954; *Educ* Harvard Univ (BA, Magna Cum Laude), Columbia Univ NY (MBA, Beta Gamma Sigma); *m* 21 Nov 1981, Monica Fleur, da of John Gerard-Sharp; 3 da (Marina b 9 July 1988, Daniela b 2 March 1990, Dominica b 8 Dec 1992); *Career* vice pres Lehman Brothers NY 1981–84; Lazard Frères & Co NY: vice pres 1985, gen ptnr 1987–95, md (following incorporation) 1995–; fndr and md Lazard Frères Corporate Partners 1988, chief exec Lazard Frères & Co Ltd London 1990–94, md Lazard Brothers & Co Ltd London 1993–; non-exec dir: Tomkins plc 1995–, Albert Fisher Group plc; Chartered Financial Analyst 1979, MSI 1994; *Style*— Ali Wambold, Esq; ✉ Lazard Brothers & Co Ltd, 21 Moorfields, London EC2P 2HT (☎ 0171 528 9966); Lazard Frères & Co LLC, 30 Rockefeller Plaza, New York, NY 10020, USA (☎ 00 1 212 632 6000)

WAN, Dr Horatio Ho-Hee; s of Cheuk-ming Wan (d 1988), of Hong Kong, and Shun-Hing, *née* Au (d 1979); *b* 24 June 1935; *Educ* Ling-nan Middle Sch Hong Kong, Univ of Hong Kong (MB BS), Univ of Manchester (MSc); *m* 24 Feb 1960, Octavia Huang long-long, da of Chen-Ying Huang, of Hong Kong; 1 s (Dennis Jit-Yin b 1971), 1 da (Valeria Jit-Wing Wan Ricci b 1961); *Career* MO Nethersole Hosp Hong Kong, sr house offr Aberdeen Teaching Hosps 1972–74, med registrar SE Kent 1974–75, res fell and med registrar Christie Hosp Manchester 1975–77, lectr and sr med registrar Univ Hosp of S Manchester 1977–78, clinical dir Tameside Gen Hosp 1996– (conslt physician in geriatric med 1979–); author of articles in various med jls incl: British Jl of Cancer, Postgraduate Medical Jl, Int Jl of Immunopharmacology; pres Manchester Chinatown Lions Club Int 1987–88; FRCP 1992 (MRCP 1975); *Recreations* travel, reading, investment, walking; *Style*— Dr Horatio Wan; ✉ Tameside General Hospital, Ashton-under-Lyne, Lancashire OL6 9RW (☎ 0161 331 5151); 2nd Floor, 16 Nicholas Street, Manchester M1 2TR (☎ 0161 228 2548)

WAN, Joseph Sai Cheong; *b* 27 Feb 1954; *Educ* in Hong Kong; *m* Flora Mei Yee; 2 da (Samantha Anne b 1987, Stephanie Eve b 1989); *Career* Peat Marwick (now KPMG Peat Marwick): joined as CA Hong Kong 1978, in London 1985–86, associate Hong Kong 1986–87; gp fin dir Dickson Concepts Ltd Hong Kong 1987–92 (responsible for acquisition of S T Dupont France 1987 and Harvey Nichols 1991), md Harvey Nichols & Co Ltd 1992–; FCA (ACA 1978); *Clubs* Royal Hong Kong Jockey; *Style*— Joseph Wan,

Esq; ✉ Harvey Nichols & Co Ltd, 67 Brompton Road, London SW3 1EF (☎ 0171 584 0011, fax 0171 823 1571)

WANAMAKER, Zoë; da of Sam Wanamaker, CBE (d 1993), and Charlotte Holland (d 1997); *Educ* King Alfred Sch, Sidcot Sch Somerset, Hornsey Coll of Art, Central Sch of Speech and Drama; *m* 7 Nov 1994, Gawn Grainger; *Career* actress; Hon DLitt Southbank Univ 1995; *Theatre* Manchester 69 Co incl: A Midsummer Night's Dream 1970, Guys and Dolls 1972; Edinburgh Lyceum Theatre incl: The Cherry Orchard 1971 (also at the Stables Theatre Club 1970), Dick Whittington 1971–72; Young Vic 1974 incl: Tom Thumb, Much Ado About Nothing; Nottingham Playhouse 1975–76 incl: A Streetcar Named Desire, Pygmalion, The Beggar's Opera, Trumpets and Drums; Piccadilly Theatre incl: Wild Oats 1977, Once in a Lifetime 1979–80 (RSC 1978–79, SWET Award 1979); RSC Stratford and London 1976– incl: The Devil's Disciple, Wild Oats (also West End), Ivanov, The Taming of the Shrew, Captain Swing, Piaf (also West End and Broadway, Tony nomination 1981), A Comedy of Errors, Twelfth Night and The Time of Your Life 1983–85 (all Olivier Award nominations), Mother Courage (Drama Award 1985), Othello (Olivier Award nomination 1989); NT incl: The Importance of Being Earnest 1982–83, The Bay at Nice and Wrecked Eggs 1986–87, Mrs Klein (also West End, Olivier Award nomination) 1988–89, The Crucible 1990–91 (Olivier Award nomination); other credits incl: Twelfth Night (Leeds Playhouse 1971, Cambridge Theatre Co 1973–74), Cabaret (Farnham) 1974, Kiss Me Kate (Oxford Playhouse) 1974, The Taming of the Shrew (New Shakespeare Co Round House) 1975, Loot (Manhattan Theatre Club, Music Box Theatre Broadway, Tony nomination 1986), Made in Bangkok (Mark Taper Forum LA) 1988, The Last Yankee (Young Vic) 1993, Dead Funny (Hampstead and West End) 1994, The Glass Menagerie (Donmar and Comedy (Olivier Award nomination for Best Actress 1996)) 1995, Sylvia (Apollo) 1996; *Television* Sally For Keeps 1970, The Eagle Has Landed 1972, Between the Wars 1973, The Silver Mask 1973, Lorna and Ted 1973, The Confederacy of Wives 1974, The Village Hall 1975, Danton's Death 1977, Beaux Strategem 1977, The Devil's Crown 1978–79, Strike 1981, Baal 1981, All the World's A Stage 1982, Richard III 1982, Enemies of the State 1982, Edge of Darkness 1985, Paradise Postponed 1985, Poor Little Rich Girl 1987, Once in a Lifetime 1987, The Dog it was that Died 1988, Ball Trap on the Côte Sauvage 1989, Othello 1989, Prime Suspect 1990, Love Hurts (BAFTA nomination) 1991, 1992 and 1993; *Radio* incl: The Golden Bowl, Plenty 1979, Bay at Nice 1987, A February Morning 1990, Carol (book reading) 1990, Such Rotten Luck 1991 (series I & II 1989); *Films* incl: Inside the Third Reich 1982, The Raggedy Rawney 1987; TV films: The Blackheath Poisonings (Central) 1991, Memento Mori (BBC) 1991, Countess Alice (BBC) 1991, The English Wife 1994, The Widowing of Mrs Holroyd (BBC) 1995; *Recreations* music, art galleries, films, TV, listening to the radio, dancing, seeing friends, reading, junkshops, shopping, the countryside, the garden; *Style—* Ms Zoë Wanamaker; ✉ c/o Conway van Gelder Robinson Ltd, 18–21 Jermyn Street, London SW1Y 6HP (☎ 0171 287 0077, fax 0171 287 1940)

WANLESS, Derek; s of Norman Hall Wanless (d 1980), and Edna Mary, *née* Charlton; *b* 29 Sept 1947; *Educ* Royal Grammar Sch Newcastle upon Tyne, King's Coll Cambridge (MA), Harvard Univ; *m* 25 Sept 1971, Vera, da of William West; 4 da (Marie Clare b 26 Aug 1974, Helen Kathryn b 24 Feb 1976, Rachael Louise and Christine Ruth (twins) b 20 Feb 1979), 1 s (Steven William b 7 Jan 1985); *Career* National Westminster Bank Plc: with Statistics Section Market Intelligence 1970–73, PA to Gen Mangr Financial Control 1973–75, planning mangr Domestic Banking Div 1975–78, asst mangr 15 Bishopsgate Branch 1978–79, sr project mangr Domestic Banking Div 1979–80, area dir North East Area 1982–85, area dir W Yorks Area 1985–86, dir of personal banking servs 1986–88, gen mangr UK Branch Business 1989–90, chief exec UK Financial Servs 1990–92, gp main bd dir 1991–, dep gp chief exec and gp head NatWest Markets Feb-March 1992, gp chief exec March 1992–, dir NatWest Markets 1992–; former dir: NatWest Life, Ulster Bank, Isle of Man Bank, National Westminster Home Loans, National Westminster Insurance Services, Lombard North Central; dir MasterCard International and vice chm Eurocard International 1989–90, chm MasterCard and Eurocard Members (UK and Republic of Ireland) Forum Ltd 1989; memb Advsy Ctee on Business and the Environment I 1991–93 (chm Financial Sector Working Gp 1992–93); chm: Advsy Ctee on Business and the Environment II 1993–95, Nat Forum for Mgmnt Educn and Devpt 1996– (memb Cncl 1993–); memb: Nat Advsy Cncl for Educn and Targets, Int Advsy Bd of the British-American C of C 1993–, Institut Int d'Etudes Bancaires 1992–, Bd World Business Cncl for Sustainable Devpt 1993–, Consultative Forum on the Environment Euro Cmmn 1994–; Freeman City of London 1992; Hon DSc City Univ 1995; MIS 1973, AIB 1978, FCIB 1990, FRSA 1991, CIMgt 1992; *Recreations* all sports, chess, music, walking, gardening; *Clubs* Reform; *Style—* Derek Wanless, Esq; ✉ National Westminster Bank Plc, 41 Lothbury, London EC2P 2BP (☎ 0171 726 1000, fax 0171 726 1174)

WAPSHOTT, Nicholas Henry; s of Raymond Gibson Wapshott (d 1995), of Hereford, and Olivia Beryl, *née* Darch (d 1970); *b* 13 Jan 1952; *Educ* Rendcomb Coll Cirencester, Univ of York; *m* Louise Nicholson, da of (Royden) Joseph Nicholson; 2 s (William Henry Joseph Nicholson b 5 Aug 1988, Oliver Evelyn Samuel Nicholson b 4 July 1990); *Career* journalist and author; The Scotsman 1973–76, The Times 1976–83, political ed The Observer 1988–92 (features ed 1983–88), ed Times Magazine (formerly The Saturday Review) 1992–; Liveryman Worshipful Co of Leathersellers; *Books* Peter O'Toole (1982), Thatcher (with George Brock, 1983), The Man Between: A Biography of Carol Reed (1990), Rex Harrison (1991); *Recreations* watching films, travelling, elephants, flirting; *Clubs* Reform, Morton's; *Style—* Nicholas Wapshott, Esq; ✉ 35 Cross St, Islington, London N1 2BH (☎ 0171 226 5278)

WARBURG, (Christina) Clare Barham; da of Dr (Alan) Barham Carter (d 1995), of Weybridge, Surrey, and Mollie Christina, *née* Sanders (d 1995); *Educ* St Michael's Sch, Université de Poitiers; *m* 1, 8 June 1968 (m dis 1975), Andrew Oscar Warburg, s of late Brig Thomas Raphael Warburg, CBE, of Maidstone, Kent; 2 s (Mark b 9 Jan 1971, Daniel b 2 Dec 1972); m 2, 28 Feb 1983 (m dis 1987) Peter Brian Adie; m 3, 13 May 1995, Dr Stuart St Pierre Slatter; *Career* paper conservator and watercolour restorer; fine art dealer 1975–: Kensington Park Galleries 1975–78, freelance 1978–; memb Kensington Ctee Save The Children Fund; *Recreations* gardening, antiques, photography; *Style—* Mrs Clare Warburg; ✉ 18 Park Place Villas, London W2 1SP

WARBURTON, Dame Anne Marion; DCVO (1979, CVO 1965), CMG (1977); da of Capt Eliot Warburton, MC; *b* 8 June 1927; *Educ* Barnard Coll Columbia Univ (BA), Somerville Coll Oxford (BA, MA); *Career* Marshall Plan Administration London 1949–52, NATO Paris 1952–54, Lazard Bros 1955–57; joined FO 1957, served FO/FCO 1957–59 and 1965–70; UK perm mission: UN NY 1959–62, Bonn 1962–65; head Guidance and Info Policy Dept FCO 1975–76, ambass Denmark 1976–83, ambass and perm UK rep to UN and other int orgns Geneva 1983–85 (former cnsllr UK Mission to UN Geneva 1970–75), pres Lucy Cavendish Coll Cambridge 1985–94; cmmr Equal Opportunities Cmmn 1986–87; memb: Bd Br Library 1989–95, Cncl UEA 1991–, Nolan Ctee (ctee on standards in public life) 1994–97; head EC mission into treatment of Bosnian Muslim women 1992–93; Grand Cross of Dannebrog (Denmark), Verdienstkreuz I Klasse (Germany), Lazo de Dama Order of Isabel la Catlina (Spain),; hon LLD Univ of Arkansas; hon fell: Somerville Coll 1977, Lucy Cavendish Coll 1994; FRSA 1986–93; *Style—* Dame Anne Warburton, DCVO, CMG; ✉ Ansted, Thornham Magna, Eye, Suffolk

WARBURTON, David; s of Harold Warburton, (d 1988), of Shipley Yorks, and Ada, *née* Sinfield (d 1960); *b* 10 Jan 1942; *Educ* St Walburgas Sch Shipley, Cottingley Manor Sch Bingley, Coleg Harlech N Wales; *m* 15 Oct 1966, Carole Anne Susan, da of Frank Tomney (d 1984), of Rickmansworth, and former MP for Hammersmith; 2 da (Sara Anne b 25 Sept 1968, Caroline Susan b 28 July 1970); *Career* GMWU educn offr 1965–67 (regnl offr 1967–73), nat industl offr GMBATU 1973–90, nat offr APEX 1990–95; vice pres Int Fedn Chemical and Energy Workers 1986–92, sec UK Chemical Unions Cncl 1978–85, chm TUC Gen Purpose Ctee 1984–95; memb: NEDC 1973–86, Cwlth Devpt Corp 1979–87, MOD Industl Cncl 1988–91, Civil Air Tport Nat Jt Cncl 1992–95, Industl Tbnl 1995–; dir ULS Leisure 1995–; sec Friends of Palestine 1983–; memb: Upper Wharfedale Museum Soc 1978–, Yorkshire Soc 1983–; co-ordinator Friends of the Speaker 1996–; *Books* Pharmaceuticals for the People (1973), Drug Industry (1975), UK Chemicals: The Way Forward (1977), Economic Detente (1980), The Case for Voters Tax Credits (1983), Forward Labour (1985), Facts Figures and Damned Statistics (1987); contrib numerous articles to leading jls; *Recreations* hill climbing, music, 1930–50 film memorabilia; *Clubs* Harlequins RFC, Victoria (Westminster); *Style—* David Warburton, Esq; ✉ 47 Hill Rise, Chorleywood, Rickmansworth, Herts WD3 2NY (☎ 01923 778726)

WARBURTON, Ernest; s of Arthur Warburton (d 1946), of Irlam, Lancs, and Jane Warburton (d 1942); *b* 10 June 1937; *Educ* Royal Masonic Sch, Wadham Coll Oxford (MA, DPhil); *m* 31 Dec 1960, (Anne) Jennifer, da of Harry Carding (d 1971), of Cadishead, Lancs; 2 s (Matthew b 1964, Jonathan b 1966); *Career* BBC: head of music North of Eng 1970–77, head of music progs Radio 1977–81, ed of music Radio Three 1982–85, external servs music organiser 1986–88, managing ed World Serv 1988–90, ed World Serv English 1990–95; freelance writer and music ed 1995–; ed: The Collected Works of Johann Christian Bach 1984–, The Librettos of Mozart's Operas; author of numerous articles on music incl for: The New Grove, The Grove Dictionary of Opera, The Musical Times, The Listener, Musik in Geschichte und Gegenwart, The Bach Yearbook; recordings: Deutsche Gramophon, CPO; Leverhulme fell 1972 and 1989; FRCO 1968; *Recreations* music, travel, architecture, reading, things Italian; *Style—* Ernest Warburton, Esq; ✉ 10a Park Ave, St Albans, Herts AL1 4PB (☎ and fax 01727 852589)

WARBURTON, Ivor William; s of Dennis Warburton (d 1990), and Edna Margaret, *née* Ridgway; *b* 13 Aug 1946; *Educ* Dulwich, Queens' Coll Cambridge (BA, MA), Univ of Warwick (MSc); *m* 16 Aug 1969 (m dis 1982), Carole-Ann, *née* Ashton; 3 da (Penny b 1970, Hazel b 1970, Catherine b 1975); *Career* British Railways: local prodn mgmnt posts 1968–74, divnl passenger mangr Bristol 1974–78, overseas tourist mangr Bd HQ 1978–82, chief passenger mangr Eastern Region York 1982–84, dir passenger mktg servs Bd HQ 1984–85, asst gen mangr London Midland Region Birmingham 1985–87, employee rels mangr Bd HQ 1987–88, dir of ops Bd HQ 1988–90, gen mangr London Midland Region Birmingham 1990–92, md InterCity W Coast 1992–; dir Transecon 1984–85; memb: ESRC Indust Econ and Environment Res Devpt Gp 1989–92, Res Centres Bd 1992–93, West Midlands Regnl Cncl CBI 1990–; pres Railway Study Assoc 1993–94; Liveryman Worshipful Co of Marketors 1987; FCIT 1989, FCIM 1993 (MCIM 1987); *Recreations* cooking Chinese style, music, opera, handicapped scouting; *Style—* Ivor Warburton, Esq; ✉ 34 St Clair's Road, Croydon CR0 5NE (☎ 0181 688 2742); British Rail InterCity West Coast, Stanier House, 10 Holliday St, PO Box 4505, Birmingham B1 1SN (☎ 0121 654 4200, fax 0121 654 4557)

WARBURTON, John Kenneth; CBE (1983); s of Frederick Hammond Warburton (d 1989), of Wolstanton, Newcastle-under-Lyme, and Winifred Eva, *née* Abbotts (d 1990); *b* 7 May 1932; *Educ* Newcastle-under-Lyme HS, Keble Coll Oxford (MA); *m* 25 June 1960, Patricia Naomi Margaret, da of Stewart Frank Glennie Gordon, ISM (d 1962), of Shrewsbury; 1 da (Moira b 1961); *Career* RAOC 1950–52; called to the Bar Gray's Inn 1977, CEDR accredited mediator; with London C of C 1956–59, DG and chief exec Birmingham Chamber of Indust and Commerce 1978–94 (joined 1959); memb: Steering Ctee Int Bureau of Cs of C 1976–94, Nat Cncl Assoc of Br Cs of C 1978–94, Review Body on Doctors and Dentists Remuneration 1982–92, BOTB Euro Trade Ctee and Business Link 1979–87, BOTB E Euro Trade Cncl 1984–93, MSC Task Gp on Employment Trg 1987–88; regnl sec W Midlands Regnl Gp of Cs of C 1978–94, pres Br C of C Execs 1979–81; dir: Business in the Community 1981–91, Nat Garden Festival 1986 Ltd 1983–87, National Exhibition Centre Ltd 1989–95; memb Cncl Univ of Birmingham 1982–; chm: Advsy Cncl W Midlands Industl Devpt Assoc 1983–86, Birmingham Chamber Trg Ltd 1987–94, Birmingham Macmillan Nurse Appeal 1994–; tstee Holy Child Sch Edgbaston Birmingham 1992–96; memb: Lord Chllr's Birmingham Advsy Ctee 1993–, Newman Coll Fin and Gen Purposes Ctee 1993–, Disciplinary Panels FIMBRA 1989–94; visiting BESO advsr in Slovakia and Mongolia 1994 and 1995; FRSA; *Style—* John Warburton, Esq, CBE; ✉ 35 Hampshire Drive, Edgbaston, Birmingham B15 3NY (☎ 0121 454 6764)

WARCHUS, Matthew; *b* 24 Oct 1966; *Educ* Univ of Bristol (BA special commendation for practical work in drama); *Career* director; dir Nat Youth Theatre of GB 1989 and 1990, Bristol Old Vic 1991, asst dir RSC 1991–92, assoc dir W Yorkshire Playhouse 1993; also freelance dir; *Theatre* for RSC (as dir) incl: Henry V 1995, The Devil is an Ass (The Swan & Pit) 1995; for West Yorkshire Playhouse: Life is A Dream (nominated TMA Best Dir), Who's Afraid of Virginia Woolf, Fiddler on the Roof, The Plough and the Stars, Death of a Salesman, Betrayal, True West; other prodns incl: The Life of Stuff (Donmar), True West (Donmar) 1994, Volpone (RNT) 1995, Art (Wyndhams) 1997; *Awards* Shakespeare's Globe Award for Most Promising Newcomer 1994, The Sydney Edward's Award for Best Director (for Volpone and Henry V) 1995; Olivier Award nomination for Best Director (for Volpone, Henry V) 1996; *Style—* Matthew Warchus, Esq; ✉ c/o The Royal Shakespeare Company, Barbican Theatre, Silk Street, London EC2Y 8BQ

WARD, Dr Adam Anthony; s of Dennis Harold Ward, of Crowborough, East Sussex, and Margaret Maud, *née* Record; *b* 15 June 1947; *Educ* Tonbridge, Springhill Sch, King's Coll London, Westminster Med Sch Univ of London (MB BS), LSHTM (MSc), Hotel Dieu Univ of Paris (DipOrthMed); *Career* clinician, lectr and broadcaster; ed Broadway Magazine 1970, lectr and hon sr registrar (epidemiology) Westminster Med Sch 1978–79; physician: Dept of Orthopaedic Med Hotel Dieu Paris 1982–83, Royal London Homoeopathic Hosp 1983–; conslt musculoskeletal physician and specialist in complementary med; memb: Cncl The British Inst of Musculoskeletal Med, Cncl The Faculty of Homoeopathy London, Ctee The British Medical Acupuncture Soc, Editorial Bd Acupuncture in Medicine jl; *Recreations* walking, skiing and relaxing; *Style—* Dr Adam A Ward; ✉ 41 Frankfield Rise, Tunbridge Wells, Kent TN2 5LF (☎ 01892 525799)

WARD, Rt Hon Lord Justice; Rt Hon Sir Alan Hylton; kt (1988), PC (1995); s of Stanley Victor Ward (d 1974), and Mary, *née* Whittingham; *b* 15 Feb 1938; *Educ* Christian Bros Coll Pretoria, Univ of Pretoria (BA, LLB), Pembroke Coll Cambridge (MA, LLB); *m* 1, 1963 (m dis 1982); 1 s (Mark b 1968), 2 da (Wendy b 1965, Emma b 1966); m 2, 1983 Helen Madeleine, da of Keith Gilbert, of Marbella, Spain; 2 da (Amelia b 1984, Katharine (twin) b 1984); *Career* attorney Supreme Ct SA 1959–61, called to the Bar Gray's Inn 1964, QC 1984, judge of the High Court of Justice (Family Div) 1988–95, Lord Justice of Appeal 1995–; former liaison judge for Midland and Oxford Circuit; *Recreations* mowing the lawn, but dreaming of my cover drive; *Clubs* MCC; *Style—* The Rt Hon Lord Justice Ward; ✉ Royal Courts of Justice, Strand, London WC2A 2LL (☎ 0171 936 6761)

WARD, Anthony John (Tony); s of William Cyril Ward (d 1960), and Gladys Mary, *née* Colling (d 1980); *b* 3 Nov 1940; *Educ* Devonport HS; *m* 13 March 1965 (m dis 1984), 1 s (Ian James b 30 Sept 1972), 1 da (Lucy Anne b 5 Aug 1975); *Career* on staff National Assistance 1959–89, chief exec Resettlement Agency 1989–94, dir of ops and dep chief exec Child Support Agency 1994–96; *Recreations* travel, cricket; *Style*— Tony Ward, Esq

WARD, Anthony Robert; s of Stanley Roy Ward, of Worcestershire, and Jeanette, *née* Mantle; *b* 6 Jan 1957; *Educ* Wrekin Coll, Wimbledon Sch of Art (BA); *partner* Mark Thompson, *qv*, theatre designer; *Career* costume and set designer; worked extensively in rep incl: Royal Exchange Manchester, Bristol Old Vic, Derby Playhouse, Haymarket Theatre Leicester, Nottingham Playhouse, Theatre Royal Plymouth, Theatre Royal York; *Theatre* for RSC incl: A Midsummer Night's Dream, King Lear, The Tempest, Artists & Admirers, The Winter's Tale, The Alchemist, The Virtuoso, Troilus & Cressida; for RNT incl: Sweet Bird of Youth, Napoli Milionaria, The Way of the World, La Grande Magia, John Gabriel Borkman; other credits incl: Oliver! (London Palladium), The Rehearsal, A Hard Heart (both Almeida), Assassins (Donmar Warehouse), Nine (Donmar Warehouse); *Opera* for Opera North incl: La Bohème, Yolande, The Nutcracker, L'Etoile, Gloriana (also ROH); other credits incl: The Makropulos Case (Metropolitan Opera, NY), Tosca (De Vlaamse Opera, Antwerp), Manon Lescaut (Opera de Paris, Bastille & De Vlaamse Opera); *Ballet* The Nutcracker (Adventures in Motion Pictures, Sadlers Wells); *Film* A Midsummer Night's Dream (RSC prodn, dir Adrian Noble, *qv*); *Awards* Olivier Award nominations incl: Best Costume & Set Design (for A Winter's Tale) 1994, Best Set Design (for Sweet Bird of Youth and The Tempest) 1995; Tony Award nomination for Scenic Design (for A Midsummer Night's Dream) 1995–96; winner Olivier Award Best Costume Design (for A Midsummer Night's Dream, La Grande Magia and The Way of the World) 1996; *Style*— Anthony Ward, Esq; ✉ c/o Agent, Harriet Cruickshank, 97 Old South Lambeth Road, London SW8 1XU (☎ 0171 735 2933, fax 0171 820 1081)

WARD, Antony John (Tony); s of Edgar Frank Ward (d 1979), of Northampton, and Kathleen Muriel Ward, MBE, *née* Hobbs (d 1995); *b* 23 June 1947; *Educ* Northampton Trinity HS, Lanchester Poly Coventry (LLB); *Career* local govt legal serv 1969–78, slr of Supreme Ct 1971, ptnr Coward Chance 1985–87 (joined 1978), ptnr Clifford Chance 1987–; memb Law Soc Planning Law Ctee 1985–95; memb and past chm: Bar Cncl, RICS, Law Soc Jt Planning Law Conf Ctee 1985–; numerous lectures and articles for professional orgns and pubns; Freeman City of London 1980, Liveryman Worshipful Co of Slrs 1983; memb Law Soc 1980; *Recreations* tennis, squash; *Style*— Tony Ward, Esq; ✉ Clifford Chance, 200 Aldersgate Street, London EC1A 4JJ (☎ 0171 600 1000, fax 0171 600 5555, telex 887 847 LEGIS G)

WARD, Bernard Leonard; s of Leonard Ward (d 1968), of W Midlands, and Louisa Elizabeth, *née* Knock; *b* 18 July 1934; *Educ* Holyhead Rd Secdy Modern Wednesbury W Midlands; *m* 26 July 1958, Shiela Mary, da of Thomas Maguire (d 1948); 2 da (Karen Lesley b 1958, Stephanie Ann b 1966); *Career* served with N Staffs Regt Korea; photographer; began career Far East, apprenticed to world's leading photographers, in sole practice (specialising in portraits of people and animals) 1979–; recipient of numerous awards from BIPP, Master Photographic Assoc, Kodak and London Portrait Gp; memb MPS; FBIPP, FRPS, FMPA, FRSA; *Recreations* tennis, sailing, skating, golf, fly fishing, horse riding; *Clubs* Telford Racquet; *Style*— Bernard Ward, Esq; ✉ Bernard's Gallery, 70 Lucknow Road, Willenhall, West Midlands WV12 4QG (☎ 01902 602985)

WARD, Cecil; CBE (1989); s of William Ward (d 1975), of Belfast, and Mary Caroline, *née* Gray (d 1969); *b* 26 Oct 1929; *Educ* Belfast Tech HS, Belfast Coll of Technol, Queen's Univ Belfast (MA); *Career* Belfast Corp: clerk 1947–60, ctee clerk 1960–73; Belfast City Cncl: chief clerk 1973–77, asst town clerk 1977–79, town clerk and chief exec 1979–89, ret 1989; chm Greater Shankill Partnership Bd 1994–; memb: Bd Ulster Orch 1980–94 (chm 1990–94), Exec Cncl Soc of Local Authy Chief Execs 1980–89, Arts Cncl NI 1980–85 and 1987–89, NI Ctee of IBA 1983–88, NI Local Govt Staff Cmmn 1983–89, Bd Grand Opera House 1987–, Bd Tstees Ulster Museum 1989–95, Senate Queen's Univ Belfast 1990–, Bd Mater Hosp Tst 1994–; *Recreations* music, walking; *Clubs* Malone Golf, Reform (NI); *Style*— Cecil Ward, Esq, CBE, JP; ✉ 24 Thornhill, Malone, Belfast BT9 6SS Northern Ireland (☎ 01232 668960); Hatter's Field, Drumaweir, Greencastle, Co Donegal, Republic of Ireland

WARD, Christopher John; s of late John Stanley Ward, and Jacqueline Law Hume, *née* Costin (d 1996); *b* 25 Aug 1942; *Educ* King's Coll Sch Wimbledon; *m* (m dis 1987); 1 s (William b 15 April 1979), 2 da (Sadie b 13 Aug 1973, Martha b 6 April 1976); m 2, 1991, Nonie Niesewand; *Career* reporter: Driffield Times 1959, Newcastle Evening Chronicle 1960–63; asst ed Daily and Sunday Mirror 1976–81 (joined 1963); ed Daily Express 1981–83, jt fndr and dir Redwood Publishing Ltd 1983–, non-exec dir Acorn Computer Group plc 1983–; tstee World Wide Fund for Nature 1994–; winner Mark Boxer Award Br Soc of Magazine Editors 1995; *Books* How to Complain (1974), Our Cheque is in the Post (1980); *Recreations* shooting, fell walking; *Clubs* Savile; *Style*— Christopher Ward, Esq; ✉ 7 Rochester Road, London NW1 9JH (☎ 0171 267 9070); Redwood Publishing Ltd, 12–26 Lexington Street, London W1R 4HQ (☎ 0171 312 2757, fax 0171 312 2609)

WARD, Christopher John Ferguson; s of Maj Harry Leeming Ferguson Ward, and Barbara Dorothy, *née* Gurney; *b* 26 Dec 1942; *m* 1 (m dis), Elizabeth (now Lady Loader); 2 s (Julian b 1963, Alexander b 1969), 1 da (Samantha (Mrs Lawrie Lewis) b 1967); m 2, Janet Theresa, da of Ronald Kelly; 1 s (Rupert b 1986), 1 da (Sarah b 1984); *Career* admitted slr 1965; managing ptnr Clarks Solicitors 1990–; MP for Swindon 1969–70, former memb Berks CC (ldr 1979–81); chm: Chiltern Nursery Trg Coll (1989–91), Assoc of Nursery Trg Colls 1990; *Clubs* United and Cecil (hon sec 1982–87, hon treas 1992–); *Style*— Christopher Ward, Esq; ✉ Ramblings, Maidenhead Thicket, Berks SL6 3QE; Clarks, Great Western House, Station Road, Reading RG1 1SX (☎ 0118 958 5321)

WARD, Christopher Margrave; s of Dr Gerald Margrave Ward (d 1979), and Pamela Gwyneth, *née* Owen-Williams; *b* 17 June 1941; *Educ* Felsted, London Hosp Medical Sch, Univ of London (BSc, MB BS); *m* 7 July 1971, Wendy Ann, da of Capt Leslie Edward Campion, of 14 Charlwood, Courtwood Lane, Croydon; 1 s (Matthew b 1972), 1 da (Naomi b 1974); *Career* clinical res fell plastic surgery Hosp for Sick Children Toronto Canada 1976–77, sr registrar plastic surgery Postgrad Med Sch Hammersmith Hosp 1977–78, memb Monospecialist Ctee for Plastic Surgery within EEC 1986–1990; conslt plastic surgn: W Middx Hammersmith and Central Middx Hosps 1978–88, Charing Cross and W Middx Univ Hosps 1988–95 (hon conslt 1995–); currently dean of admissions Charing Cross and Westminster Med Sch; advsr: Nat Breast Care and Mastectomy Assoc, Nat Disfigurement Guidance Centre; examiner plastic surgery specialists FRCS intercollegiate exam; pres: Plastic Surgn Section RSM 1986–87, W London Cleft Lip and Palate Assoc; Eng int hockey player 1965; FRCS; *Books* Cosmetic Surgery - Facing The Facts (1986); *Recreations* real tennis; *Clubs* Queen's and Hampton Court Real Tennis; *Style*— Christopher Ward, Esq; ✉ 44 Wensleydale Rd, Hampton, Middlesex TW12 2LT (☎ 0181 979 2897); 15 Cumberland Road, Kew Gdns, Richmond, Surrey TW9 3DU (☎ 0181 948 4990)

WARD, Clive Richard; s of William Herbert Ward (d 1982), and Muriel, *née* Wright; *b* 30 July 1945; *Educ* Sevenoaks Sch, Univ of Cambridge (MA); *m* 9 Sept 1972, Catherine Angela, da of Lt Cdr Godfrey Joseph Hines, of Hildenborough, Kent; 3 da (Joanna b 1975, Diana b 1977, Emily b 1979); *Career* CA 1971, asst sec Take Over Panel 1975–77, ptnr Ernst and Young 1979–90 (head corp fin London 1987), corp devpt dir Shandwick plc 1990–91, dir The Capita Group plc 1992–94, ptnr and head of corp fin S Regn Ernst & Young 1994–; Freeman: Worshipful Co of Barbers 1985, Worshipful Co of Tobacco Pipe Makers and Tobacco Blenders 1975; FCA 1979; *Books* Guide to Company Flotation (1989); *Recreations* fishing, music, gardening; *Style*— Clive Ward, Esq; ✉ Market Heath House, Brenchley, Tonbridge, Kent TN12 7PA (☎ 01892 722172); Ernst & Young, Apex Plaza, Reading RG1 1YE (☎ 0118 950 0611, fax 0118 950 7744)

WARD, Constance Cluett; da of George Bywater Cluett, II (d 1957), of NY, and Marion, *née* Ticknor (d 1980); *b* 25 Oct 1928; *Educ* Knox Sch NY, Finch Coll NY; *m* 1, 1949 (m dis 1963), Louis D Sage; 3 da (Deborah Sage Rockefeller b 1951, Marion (Viscountess Thurso) b 1954, Martha (Mrs Simon E Berry) b 1959); m 2, 1975, Alexander Reginald (Reggie) Ward (d 1987); *Career* hotelier; proprietor Kinnaird Dunkeld Perthshire 1987–; 4 red roofs Michelin Guide, 3 rosettes AA Guide, AA Country House Hotel of Yr 1992, RAC Blue Ribbon 1995; memb Relais et Chateaux; *Recreations* music, books, grandchildren; *Clubs* The Colony (NYC); *Style*— Mrs Constance Cluett Ward; ✉ Balmacneil House, Kinnaird Estate, Dunkeld, Perthshire PH8 0LB; Kinnaird, Kinnaird Estate, Dunkeld, Perthshire PH8 0LB (☎ 01796 482440, fax 01796 482289); 116 Swan Court, Chelsea Manor Street, London SW3 (☎ 0171 352 3743)

WARD, David; s of Frank Ward, of Darfield, and Elizabeth, *née* Pattinson (d 1989), of Westmorland; *b* 23 Feb 1937; *Educ* Dame Allan's School Newcastle-upon-Tyne, Queen Elizabeth GS Penrith, St Edmund Hall Oxford (BA); *m* 22 July 1978, Antoinette, da of Maj-Gen Desmond Alexander Bruce Clarke; 2 s (Andrew b 1981, Robin b 1982), 1 da (Rachel b 1979); *Career* admitted slr 1962; with Atkinson Ritson and Lightfoot (formerly Atkinson and North) since articles, now sr ptnr; pres The Law Soc 1989–90 (cncl memb 1972–91), memb Lord Chllr's Advsy Ctee on Legal Educn and Conduct 1991–; *Recreations* mountaineering, choral singing; *Clubs* Carlisle Mountaineering; *Style*— David Ward, Esq; ✉ The Green, Caldbeck, Wigton, Cumbria CA7 8ER (☎ 01697 478220); 15 Fisher St, Carlisle, Cumbria CA3 8RW (☎ 01228 25221, fax 01228 515409)

WARD, David James; s of Lesley Edward Ward, of Egham, Surrey, and Margaret, *née* Cook; *b* 1 May 1946; *Educ* Manor Croft Sch Egham, Brookland Tech Coll, Richmond Coll of Technol; *m* 10 April 1971, Glenora Ann, da of late Robert Gordon Tott; 2 da (Joanna Louise b 1 March 1980, Sarah Michele b 30 July 1982); *Career* freelance photographer 1978–; press photographer, work published in various magazines papers and books, photographer of Royalty, show business people and actors, specialist in portraiture; winner of many merits and awards incl: Press Photographer of the Year, Kodak Photographer of the Year, Panorama Photographer of the Year, Kodak Gold Award for Portrait Photography 1993, UK Portrait Photographer of the Year 1996; Master Photographic Assoc 1986, Br Photographers' Assoc 1990; FBIPP 1994; *Books* Wonderful World Series (1985); *Recreations* jogging, squash, cycling; *Clubs* Roundtable (Egham); *Style*— David Ward, Esq; ✉ Latchets, Harpesford Ave, Virginia Water, Surrey GU25 4RE (☎ 01344 843421); The Studio, Latchets, Harpesford Ave, Virginia Water, Surrey GU25 4RE (☎ 01344 843421)

WARD, Dr Dermot Joseph; s of Richard Ward (d 1985), of Dublin, and Margaret, *née* Whitty (d 1962); *b* 7 June 1933; *Educ* St James Secdy Sch Dublin; *m* 3 Aug 1961, Ruth Eva, da of George Nathaniel Stedmond (d 1978), of Dublin; 2 s (Jonathan Dermot b 1965, Simon Richard b 1969); *Career* sr registrar in psychiatry Bath Clinical Area 1965–68, med dir St Lomans Hosp Dublin 1979–86 (conslt psychiatrist 1969–86); conslt psychiatrist: Graylingwell Hosp Chichester 1986–88, St Davids Hosp Carmarthen 1988–; pubns in: Br Med Jl, Irish Med Jl, Br Jl of Psychiatry; memb Inst of Economic Affrs 1983; LRCPI, LRCSI, LM, FRCPI, FRCPsych, DPM, memb BMA 1961, FRSM 1983; *Recreations* writing, literature, theatre, films and travel; *Clubs* Royal Soc of Med; *Style*— Dr Dermot Ward; ✉ 4 Jubilee Terrace, Chichester, West Sussex; Llysneddyg, Jobswell Rd, Carmarathen, Dyfed; St Davids Hosp, Camarthen, Dyfed SA31 3HB (☎ 01269 237481)

WARD, Ven Edwin James Greenfield; LVO (1963); s of Canon Frederick Greenfield Ward, MC (d 1963); *b* 26 Oct 1919; *Educ* St John's Leatherhead, Christ's Coll Cambridge; *m* 1946, Grizell Evelyn (d 1985), da of Capt Harry Gurney Buxton (d 1936); 1 s, 2 da (Alison Bridget (*see* Lord Wakeham), Joanna Grizelda (*see* C J E Spicer); *Career* Lt King's Dragoon Guards 1940–46; ordained 1948, vicar of North Elmham 1950–55; chaplain to: HM The Queen 1955–89 (extra chaplain 1989–), Windsor Great Park 1955–67; archdeacon of Sherborne and rector of W Stafford 1967–84, archdeacon emeritus 1985–; *Recreations* fishing; *Style*— The Ven Edwin Ward, LVO; ✉ 14 Arle Close, Alresford, Hampshire SO24 9BG (☎ 01962 735501)

WARD, Elizabeth Despard; OBE (1992, MBE 1978); da of Denys Ashley Ferion Rynd (d 1965), of Brookhurst Brook, nr Godalming, Surrey, and Joyce, *née* Fleming (d 1987); *b* 11 Oct 1926; *Educ* Cheltenham Ladies Coll; *m* 1, 21 June 1946 (m dis 1952), Capt Michael Aston; 1 da (Susan b 19 May 1947); m 2, 3 May 1952, Nigel Yeoward Peirce Ward, s of Robert Geoffrey Ward (d 1971); 1 s (Timothy Nigel Peirce b 3 Jan 1953, d 1987), 1 da (Rebecca Elizabeth b 8 Feb 1954); *Career* sales dir NYP Ward and Co 1957–66, PRO Bonhams Fine Art Auctioneers 1959–61, JP 1974–83; local rep SAAFA, vol After Prison Care Serv, founder pres Br Kidney Patient Assoc; Hon LLD Univ of Dundee 1990; memb RSM, FInstD; *Books* Timbo, A Struggle for Survival (1986); *Recreations* walking, bicycling, opera; *Clubs* Arts, Royal Society of Medicine; *Style*— Mrs Elizabeth Ward, OBE; ✉ Oakhanger Place Cottage, nr Bordon, Hampshire GU35 9JP (☎ 01420 487757); British Kidney Patient Association, Bordon, Hants (☎ 01420 472021, fax 01420 475831)

WARD, Gerald John; CBE; s of Col Edward John Sutton Ward, LVO, MC (d 1990); *b* 31 May 1938; *Educ* Eton, Sandhurst, RAC Cirencester; *m* 1967 (m dis 1983), Rosalind Elizabeth, da of Hon Richard Lygon (d 1972), 2 da; m 2, 1984, Amanda, da of Sir Lacey Vincent, 2 Bt (d 1963); *Career* Capt RHG; industrialist and farmer; chm: UK Solenoid Ltd, Chilton Farms Ltd; Extra Equerry to HRH The Prince of Wales 1987; *Clubs* White's; *Style*— Gerald Ward, Esq, CBE; ✉ Chilton Park Farm, Hungerford, Berks (☎ 01488 682329); 179 Cranmer Court, Whiteheads Grove, London SW3 (☎ 0171 589 6955)

WARD, Graham Norman Charles; s of Ronald Charles Edward Ward, and Hazel Winnifred, *née* Ellis; *b* 9 May 1952; *Educ* Dulwich, Jesus Coll Oxford (MA, Boxing blue); *m* 1, 1975 (m dis 1981), Ingrid Imogen Sylvia, da of Hubert Edward Philip Peter Baden-Powell (d 1994); 2 s (Peter Ronald Norman b 15 June 1978, Andrew Charles Richard b 16 Sept 1980); m 2, 1993, Ann, da of Joseph Mistri; 1 s (Alexander Christopher Edward b 14 Feb 1996); *Career* Price Waterhouse: articled clerk 1974–77, personal tech asst to chm Account Standards Ctee 1978–79, seconded to HM Treasy 1985, ptnr 1986–, dir Electricity Services Europe 1990–94, dir Business Development 1993–94, chm World Utilities Gp 1994–, dep chm World Energy Gp 1996–; chm: Young Chartered Accountants Group 1980–81, London Soc of Chartered Accountants 1989–90 (memb Ctee 1983–91); memb Cncl ICAEW 1991–, membership sec Pensions Res Accountants Gp 1985–90, memb Cncl Soc of Pension Conslts 1988–90; vice pres: Univ of Oxford Amateur Boxing Club 1990–, Soc of Cons Accountants 1992–; pres: Jesus Coll Assoc 1990–91, Chartered Accountants Students' Soc of London 1992–96 (vice pres 1987–92); Freeman: Worshipful Co of CAs 1994, City of London 1994; FCA 1983 (ACA 1977); *Books* The Work of a Pension Scheme Actuary (1987), Pensions: Your Way Through The Maze (1988); *Recreations* boxing, rugby, opera, ballet; *Clubs* Carlton, Vincent's (Oxford); *Style*— Graham Ward, Esq; ✉ Price Waterhouse, Southwark Towers, 32

London Bridge Street, London SE1 9SY (☎ 0171 939 3101, fax 0171 939 3134, car 0860 609211)

WARD, Dr (Richard) Humphry Thomas; s of Brig Dr William Roy Ward, TD, QHS (d 1985), and Alice Anita Marjorie Ward (d 1983); *b* 29 April 1938; *Educ* Shrewsbury, St John's Coll Cambridge (MA, MB BChir); *m* 31 July 1965, Hilary Patricia, da of Cedric Ivor Tuckett, OBE (d 1975); 2 s ((William) Harvey Charles b 1967, Jeremy Edward Humphry b 1971), 1 da (Charlotte Rosemary Lucy b 1968); *Career* conslt obstetrician and gynaecologist UCH London 1972–; FRCOG, memb RSM; *Recreations* gardening, skiing; *Style*— Humphry Ward, Esq; ✉ University College Hospital Private Consulting Rooms, Grafton Way, London WC1 (☎ 0171 387 8323)

WARD, Prof Ian Macmillan; *b* 9 April 1928; *Educ* Royal GS Newcastle upon Tyne, Magdalen Coll Oxford (BA, DPhil); *m*; 3 c; *Career* tech offr Fibres Div ICI Ltd Harrogate 1954–61, res assoc Div of Applied Mathematics Brown Univ USA 1961–62, head Basic Physics Section ICI Fibres 1962–66 (ICI res assoc 1965–66), sr lectr in physics of materials H H Wills Physics Laboratory Univ of Bristol 1966–70; Univ of Leeds: prof of physics 1970–94, chm of dept 1975–78 and 1987–89, Cavendish prof 1987–94, dir Interdisciplinary Res Centre in Polymer Sci and Technol 1989–94, research prof 1994–; chm: Br Polymer Physics Gp Inst of Physics 1971–75 (sec 1967–71), Macromolecular Physics Section Euro Physical Soc 1976–81; pres Br Soc of Rheology 1984–86; assoc ed Jl of Macromolecular Science (Physics) 1966–, jt ed Solid State Science Series Cambridge Univ Press 1966–, ed Polymer 1974–; memb Editorial Bd: Jl of Materials Science 1974–, Plastics and Rubber Processing and Applications 1981–, Jl of Polymer Science 1989–, Jl of Applied Science 1989–; A A Griffiths Silver Medal Inst of Materials 1982, S G Smith Meml Medal Textile Inst 1984, Swinburne Medal Plastics and Rubber Inst 1988, Charles Vernon Boys Medal and Prize Inst of Physics 1993; hon degree Univ of Bradford 1993; FRS 1983, FInstP, FPRI; *Publications* Mechanical Properties of Solid Polymers (1971, 2 edn 1983), Structure and Properties of Oriented Polymers (ed, 1975), Ultra High Modulus Polymers (ed jtly, 1979), Advances in Oriented Polymers - 1 (ed, 1982), Advances in Oriented Polymers - 2 (1987), An Introduction to the Mechanical Properties of Solid Polymers (with D W Hadley, 1993); around 500 papers in polymer science; *Style*— Prof Ian M Ward, FRS; ✉ IRC in Polymer Science and Technology, University of Leeds, Leeds LS2 9JT (☎ 0113 233 3808, fax 0113 233 3846)

WARD, (William) Ian Roy; s of William Gerald Roy Ward (d 1977), of St Leonards-on-Sea, and Ellinor Ward, *née* Ostergaard (d 1964); *b* 17 Sept 1936; *Educ* Bembridge Sch, Thames Nautical Trg Coll HMS Worcester; *m* 21 Nov 1964, Vivienne, da of George Edward Garton Watson (d 1971), of Capetown; 1 s (Duncan b 30 Sept 1969), 2 da (Michele b 4 Sept 1967, Alison b 31 Aug 1975); *Career* Lt RNR until 1965; Merchant Navy 1954–58 and 1962–64, called to the Bar Admiralty Chambers 1962, ptnr (specialising in shipping) Lovell White Durrant 1976–95, conslt Holman Fenwick & Willam 1996–; dir British & International Sailors' Soc; Freeman Worshipful Co of Solicitors; memb Law Soc 1976; FCIArb 1972; *Recreations* sailing, walking; *Clubs* East India; *Style*— Ian Ward, Esq; ✉ 67 The Avenue, Kew, Richmond, Surrey TW9 2AH (☎ 0181 940 0260); Castle Hill, Newport, Dyfed SA42 OQD (☎ 01239 820263)

WARD, Ivor William (Bill); OBE (1969); s of Stanley James (d 1943), of Plymouth, and Emily, *née* Smith (d 1944); *b* 19 Jan 1916; *Educ* Hoe GS; *m* 1, 1939, Patricia Aston, *née* Gold (m dis 1967); m 2, 1970, Betty, *née* Wager (m dis 1981); m 3, 22 Dec 1987, Sandra Calkins Hastie, da of Cdr William Calkins, USN, of Pacific Grove, California, USA; 2 s (David Terence, Martin Sean), 1 da (Mary Kathleen); *Career* gunner RA TA 1939, WO1 REME TA 1942–46 (seconded to SAS 1946); BBC: engr's asst 1932, tech asst Alexandra Palace 1936, maintenance engr 1937, returned to Alexandra Palace as studio mangr 1946, light entertainment to prodr 1947 (responsible for How do you View, This is Show Business, and others), sr light entertainment producer 1951; ITV: head of light entertainment ATV 1955, prodn controller ATV 1956, exec controller TV 1963, bd memb ATV (Network) Ltd 1955, dir of progs and exec dir ATV Ltd 1968, memb ITV Network Prog Ctee 1970, chm Network Sports Ctee 1971, memb EBU Sports Working Party 1973, chm EBU Football Ctee 1974, dep md ATV Ltd 1974, head EBU Ops Gp for all euro broadcasters for coverage of FIFA World Football Cup in Argentina 1978 (Summer Olympic Games in Moscow 1980), assisted Thomson Fndn in improving Thailand's TV prodn techniques 1981, memb UNESCO team assisting Ethiopian Govt in media devpt planning 1982, exec prodr Highway 1983; dir various episodes of Press Gang 1991–94; responsible for shows such as Sunday Night at The Palladium and the Royal Variety Shows working with performers such as: Bob Hope, Nat King Cole, Bing Crosby, Sir Harry Secombe, Shirley Bassey, and many others; chm Richmond Films and Television 1985; Awards: Guild of TV Producers-Light Entertainment Producer 1959, BAFTA Desmond Davies Award 1976, Royal TV Soc Cyril Bennett Award 1991; Liveryman Fletchers' Co; FRSA 1974, FRTS 1990; *Recreations* golf; *Clubs* Lord's Taverners; *Style*— Bill Ward, Esq, OBE; ✉ Nichols Nymet Cottage, North Tawton, Devon EX20 2BR (☎ 0171 734 9313, fax 0183 782 602)

WARD, Most Rev John Aloysius; *see:* Cardiff, Archbishop of (RC)

WARD, Prof John Dale; s of John Ward, and Lily, *née* Dale; *b* 25 Dec 1935; *Educ* Mount St Mary's Coll Derbyshire, The London Hosp Med Coll (BSc, MD); *m* 22 Sept 1962, Ann Deirdre, da of Gp Capt Francis Sumerling, OBE (d 1967); 1 s (Timothy Jerome b 1969), 3 da (Clare Caroline b 1963, Susannah Elizabeth b 1965, Helen Louise b 1967); *Career* med trg The London Hosp 1954–61, res study Guy's Hosp 1968–89, conslt physician in med and diabetes Royal Hallamshire Hosp Sheffield 1971–; Claude Bernard lectr Euro Assoc for the Study of Diabetes Vienna 1996; chm: Med and Scientific Section Br Diabetic Assoc 1993–95, Patient Servs Cmmn Br Diabetic Assoc; second vice-pres Royal Coll of Physicians (London) 1996–; hon treas Euro Assoc for the Study of Diabetes 1989–92; memb American Diabetes Assoc 1987, FRCP 1976; *Books* The Foot in Diabetes (co-ed 1987); *Recreations* golf, music; *Clubs* Sickleholme Golf (Derbyshire); *Style*— Prof John Ward; ✉ Department of Medicine, Royal Hallamshire Hospital, Glossop Road, Sheffield S10 2JF (☎ 0114 271 2938)

WARD, John Devereux; CBE (1973), MP (C) Poole (majority 12,831); s of Thomas Edward Ward (d 1981), and Evelyn Victoria Ward (d 1986); *b* 8 March 1925; *Educ* Romford County Tech Sch, Univ of St Andrews (BSc Eng); *m* 1955, Jean Miller, da of Andrew Aitken (d 1974); 1 s, 1 da; *Career* RAF 1943–47; chartered civil and structural engr; Taylor Woodrow Ltd 1958–92, md Taylor Woodrow Arcon 1976–78; Parly candidate (C) Portsmouth North Oct 1974, MP (C) Poole 1979–; PPS: to Fin Sec to Treasy 1984–86, to Sec of State for Social Security 1987–89, to PM 1994–; jt sec Cons Backbench Indust Ctee 1982–83, vice chm Cons Trade and Indust Ctee 1983–84, representative of UK Parliament at Cncl of Europe and Western Euro Union 1983–87 and 1989–94, chm Br Gp Inter-Parly Union 1993–94 (memb Exec Ctee 1982–94); fndr memb Cons Cwlth Cncl; memb: Nat Union Exec Cons Pty 1965–78, Cons Pty Central Bd of Fin 1969–78; *Style*— John Ward, Esq, CBE, MP; ✉ House of Commons, London SW1A 0AA

WARD, John Stanton; CBE (1985), RA (1965, ARA 1956), RP 1952; s of Russell Stanton Ward (d 1927), of Hereford, and Jessie, *née* Watson (d 1965); *b* 17 Oct 1917; *Educ* St Owen's Sch Hereford, Hereford Sch of Art and Crafts, RCA (Drawing prize); *m* Alison Christine, da of Richard Myrddin Williams; 4 s (William b 1952, George b 1954, Jack b 1959, Toby 1965), 2 da (Celia b 1957, Charlotte (twin) b 1957); *Career* served WWII RE 1939–46; with Vogue magazine 1948–52, illustrated Cider with Rosie (Laurie Lee) 1958, freelance portrait painter, book illustrator and architectural draughtsman 1958–; exhibitions incl: Wildenstein Gallery, Trafford Gallery, Arthur Jefferies Gallery, Maas Gallery; Retrospective exhibitions: Canterbury 1988, Agnews Gallery London 1990; painter to the Dilettante Soc 1980; Hon DLitt Univ of Kent at Canterbury; Freeman City of Hereford; memb Royal Soc of Watercolour Painters; *Clubs* Athenaeum, Buck's, Harry's Bar; *Style*— John Ward, Esq, CBE, RA, RP; ✉ Bilting Court, Ashford, Kent TN25 4HF (☎ 01233 812478)

WARD, John Streeton; OBE (1989); s of Charles Eric Ward, of Stamford, Lincs, and Agnes Anne, *née* Streeton; *b* 28 Sept 1933; *Educ* Stamford Sch; *m* 28 Sept 1957, Dorothy Sheila; 2 s (Graham b 1960, Richard b 1966); *Career* Barclays Bank: joined 1950, local dir Preston 1974–79, sr local dir Newcastle upon Tyne 1983–88 (local dir 1979–83), regnl dir Barclays Bank plc 1988–93 (chm Barclays Northern Regnl Bd); dir and dep chm North England Building Society 1993–94, dir and jt dep chm Northern Rock Building Society (following merger) 1994–; non-exec dir: Tyne & Wear Enterprise Trust Ltd (ENTRUST) 1981–90, Northern Investors Company PLC 1984–, Tyne & Wear Development Corp (dep chm) 1987–, The Newcastle Initiative 1988– (chm 1990–93), Theatre Royal Trust Ltd 1988–, Northumbrian Water Group plc 1989– (dep chm 1993–96), Grainger Trust PLC 1994–, T Cowie plc 1994–; non-exec chm Waters & Robson Ltd 1996–; memb: Bd Business in the Community Tyne & Wear & Northumberland (chm 1985–90), Bd of Govrs Newcastle upon Tyne Poly until 1992, Cncl Univ of Durham 1993–, N of England Industl Devpt Bd 1995–, Newcastle upon Tyne West End Ptnrship City Challenge Bd 1992–, Appeal Ctee Marie Curie Cancer Care; vice chm Tyneside Stables Project Ltd St Thomas St Workshops; chm: Cruddas Park Community Tst Newcastle upon Tyne, British Olympic Appeal NE Region 1984 and 1988; ACIB; *Recreations* golf, theatre going, Newcastle United FC supporter; *Clubs* Royal and Ancient (St Andrews), Northumberland Golf; *Style*— John S Ward, Esq, OBE; ✉ office ☎ 0191 415 0092, fax 0191 529 5741, home ☎ 0191 529 3036)

WARD, (Christopher) John William; s of Gp Capt Thomas Maxfield Ward, CBE, DFC (d 1969), and Peggy, *née* Field; *b* 21 June 1942; *Educ* CCC Oxford (BA Lit Hum), Univ of E Anglia (DipEcon); *m* 1971 (m dis 1988), Diane, *née* Lelliott; *Career* Bank of England 1965–74; gen sec: Bank of England Staff Organisation 1974–80, Assoc First Div of Civil Servants 1980–88; head of devpt Opera North 1988–94, dir of corp affairs West Yorkshire Playhouse 1994–; chm Swindon Supporters in London 1987–88; *Style*— John Ward, Esq; ✉ West Yorkshire Playhouse, Playhouse Square, Leeds LS2 7UP (☎ 0113 244 2141)

WARD, Sir Joseph James Laffey; 4 Bt (UK 1911), of Wellington, New Zealand; s of Sir Joseph George Davidson Ward, 3 Bt (d 1970), and Joan Mary Haden, *née* Laffey (d 1993); *b* 11 Nov 1946; *m* 1968, Robyn Allison, da of William Maitland Martin, of Rotorua, NZ; 1 s (Joseph James Martin b 1971), 1 da (Theresa Jane b 1972); *Heir* s, Joseph James Martin Ward b 20 Feb 1971; *Style*— Sir Joseph Ward, Bt; ✉ 3 Regal Place, Milford, Auckland, New Zealand

WARD, Prof (John Stephen) Keith; s of John Ward (d 1983), of Hexham, Northumberland, and Evelyn, *née* Simpson; *b* 22 Aug 1938; *Educ* Hexham GS, Univ of Wales (BA), Linacre Coll Oxford (BLitt), Trinity Hall Cambridge (MA); *m* 21 June 1963, Marian, da of Albert Trotman (d 1942), of Ystrad Rhondda, S Wales; 1 s (Alun James b 1968), 1 da (Fiona Caroline b 1966); *Career* lectr in logic Univ of Glasgow 1964–69, lectr in philosophy Univ of St Andrews 1969–71, lectr in philosophy of religion King's Coll London 1971–76, fell and dean Trinity Hall Cambridge 1976–83, F D Maurice prof of moral and social theology Univ of London 1983–86, prof of history and philosophy of religion King's Coll London 1986–91, regius prof of divinity Univ of Oxford and Canon of Christ Church 1991–; ordained priest C of E 1972; pres World Congress of Faiths, memb Cncl Royal Inst of Philosophy; *Books* Kant's View of Ethics (1972), The Concept of God (1974), Rational Theology and the Creativity of God (1982), The Living God (1984), Images of Eternity (1987), Divine Action (1990), A Vision to Pursue (1991), Religion and Revelation (1994), Religion and Creation (1996), God Chance and Necessity (1996); *Recreations* music, walking; *Style*— Prof Keith Ward; ✉ Christ Church, Oxford OX1 1DP (☎ 01865 276246)

WARD, His Hon Judge Malcolm Beverley; s of Edgar Ward (d 1966), and Dora Mary, *née* Dutton (d 1974); *b* 3 May 1931; *Educ* Wolverhampton GS, St John's Coll Cambridge (MA, LLM); *m* 12 July 1958, Muriel Winifred, da of Dr Edwin Daniel Mackay Wallace (d 1973); 2 s (Simon b 1963, Nicholas b 1967), 2 da (Louise b 1965, Amanda b 1970); *Career* called to the Bar 1956, recorder 1974–79, circuit judge (Midland and Oxford Circuit) 1979–; chm Wolverhampton GS 1981– (govr 1972–); *Recreations* golf, music, (in theory) horticulture; *Style*— His Hon Judge Malcolm Ward; ✉ Midland and Oxford Circuit Office, The Priory Courts, 33 Bull Street, Birmingham B4 6DW (☎ 0121 627 1700)

WARD, Malcolm Stanley; s of Hugh Ward (d 1979), and Rebecca, *née* Rogerson; *b* 24 Sept 1951; *Educ* Gilberd Sch Colchester; *Career* dep ed Gulf News Dubai 1978–79, ed Woodham and Wickford Chronicle Essex 1979–81, dep ed Gulf Times Qatar 1981–84, dir Daily News Birmingham 1986–91 (ed 1986–91), ed Metronews Birmingham 1991–92, ed Evening News Worcester 1992–95, md Dar Al Sharq (Qatar) 1995–; *Recreations* writing, travel, soccer, driving, tennis; *Style*— Malcolm Ward, Esq; ✉ c/o Dar Al Sharq, PO Box 3488, Doha, Qatar, Arabian Gulf (☎ 00 974 663945)

WARD, Maxwell Colin Bernard; s of Maj Bernard Maxwell Ward, LVO (d 1991), and Margaret Sunniva, *née* Neven-Spence (d 1962); *b* 22 Aug 1949; *Educ* Harrow, St Catharine's Coll Cambridge (MA); *m* 17 April 1982, Sarah, da of Lt-Col Peter William Marsham, MBE (d 1970); 2 s (Charles Bernard Maxwell b 27 Feb 1986, Frederick Peter Neven b 15 Feb 1989), 2 da (Laura Sunniva b 2 April 1984, Antonia Hersey b 27 Sept 1993); *Career* ptnr Baillie Gifford & Co 1975– (investment trainee 1971–74); dir: Scottish Equitable Life Assurance Society 1988–94, Scottish Equitable plc 1995–; main bd memb Capability Scotland 1981–; *Recreations* tennis, squash, bridge, country pursuits, golf; *Clubs* New (Edinburgh), Cavalry and Guards; *Style*— Maxwell Ward, Esq; ✉ Stobshiel House, Humbie, East Lothian EH36 5PD (☎ 01875 833646); Baillie Gifford & Co, 1 Rutland Court, Edinburgh EH3 8EY (☎ 0131 222 4000, fax 0131 222 4488)

WARD, Michael Jackson; CBE (1980); s of Harry Ward, CBE (d 1988), and Dorothy Julia, *née* Clutterbuck (d 1974); *b* 16 Sept 1931; *Educ* Drayton Manor GS, UCL (BA), Univ of Freiburg Germany, CCC Oxford; *m* 1, Oct 1955, Eileen Patricia, da of John Foster (d 1985); 1 s (Michael b 1962), 1 da (Victoria b 1959); *Career* Nat Serv 2 Lt Royal Signals 1953–55; dist cmmr and asst sec to Govt Gilbert and Ellice Islands HMCOS 1956–61; Br Cncl: Schs Recruitment Dept 1961–64, regnl rep Sarawak 1964–68, dep rep Pakistan 1968–70, dir Appts Servs Dept 1970–72, dir Personnel Dept 1972–75, controller Personnel and Appts Div 1975–77, rep Italy 1977–81, controller Home Div 1981–85, asst dir gen 1985–90, dir Germany 1990–91, ret, hon memb 1991; *Recreations* music, golf; *Clubs* Gog Magog Golf; *Style*— Michael Ward, Esq, CBE; ✉ 1 Knapp Rise, Haslingfield, Cambridge, CB3 7LQ (☎ 01223 871557)

WARD, Michael John; s of Stanley Ward (d 1985), of Romford, and Margaret, *née* Gill (d 1987); *b* 7 April 1931; *Educ* Royal Liberty GS Gidea Park Essex, Univ of Manchester (BA); *m* 1953, Lilian, da of Frederick Lomas (d 1994), of Hadleigh, Essex; 2 da (Alison, Susan); *Career* Flt Lt RAF 1952–57; MP (Lab) Peterborough 1974–79, ldr London Borough of Havering Cncl 1971–74 (memb 1958–78), sponsored Unfair Contract Terms Act 1977, PPS to Sec of State for Educn and Science, min for overseas devpt, min of state FCO 1976–79, dir of info Inner London Educn Authy 1984–86, public affairs offr Gas Consumers Cncl 1986–88; exec offr to Rt Hon Paddy Ashdown MP 1988–89, asst gen sec Assoc of Chief Offrs of Probation 1989–95, co sec Blackheath Cator Estate

Residents Ltd 1995–; Parly candidate SDP/Lib All Tonbridge & Malling 1987; memb Cncl and chm Professional Practices Ctee Inst of PR 1992–94; FIPR, FRSA 1992; *Recreations* music, gardens; *Style—* Michael Ward, Esq; ✉ 5 The Lane, Blackheath Park, London SE3 9SL (☎ 0181 852 5836 and 0181 297 8691)

WARD, Hon (Edward) Nicholas; s of 7 Viscount Bangor (d 1993), and his 4 w, Marjorie Alice, *née* Banks (d 1991); hp of half-bro, 8 Viscount; *b* 16 Jan 1953; *Educ* Westminster, Univ of Edinburgh (MA); *m* 1985, Rachel Mary, 2 da of Hon Hugh Waldorf Astor, *qv*; 2 da (Anna Roxelana b 1987, Zoë Rachel b 1990); *Career* investment analyst with Smith New Court; independent tv producer; *Style—* The Hon Nicholas Ward; ✉ 9 Kildare Terrace, London W2

WARD, (Charles John) Nicholas; *b* 1 Aug 1941; *Educ* Charterhouse, INSEAD (MBA); *m* 1967, Deirdre Veronica; 2 da; *Career* early career spanned several cos engaged in retailing, distribution, healthcare, leisure and property sectors; currently: chm Ryan Group Ltd 1995–, chm NHS Supplies Authy 1995–, non-exec dir Albert E Sharp Holdings plc 1996–, non-exec dir and chm of Audit Ctee Central Transport Rental Group plc 1996–, chm The Volunteering Partnership 1995–, chm Make a Difference Team 1994–, chm Nat Assoc for Lay Visiting 1992–; Liveryman Worshipful Co of Tylers and Bricklayers (Master 1991–92); FCA 1964; *Clubs* Carlton, Royal Society of Medicine; *Style—* C J Nicholas Ward, Esq; ✉ Bacon House, Greatworth, nr Banbury, Oxon OX17 2DX (☎ and fax 01295 712732); Flat 2, 77 Warwick Square, London SW1V 2AR (☎ and fax 0171 834 9175)

WARD, Hon Peter Alistair; 3 s of 3 Earl of Dudley, MC, TD (d 1969), and his 1 w, Rosemary Millicent Ednam, *née* Leveson-Gower, RRC (who d 1930 prior to 2 Earl's death in 1932), da of 4 Duke of Sutherland, KG; *b* 8 Feb 1926; *Educ* Eton, Univ of British Columbia, ChCh Oxford; *m* 1, 1956 (m dis 1974), Claire Leonora, only da of A E G Baring; 1 s (Alexander b 1961), 2 da (Rachel b 1957, Tracy b 1958); m 2, 1974, Elizabeth Rose, da of Richard V C Westmacott, of Ascona, Switzerland; 2 s (Jeremy b 1975, Benjamin b 1978); *Career* Royal Canadian Air Force 1943–45 and Fleet Air Arm; chm Baggeridge Brick plc; *Clubs* White's, Pratt's, Royal Yacht Squadron; *Style—* The Hon Peter Ward; ✉ 7 Elm Park Lane, London SW3 (☎ 0171 351 2890); Cornwell Manor, Chipping Norton, Oxon (☎ 01608 658555, fax 01608 659040)

WARD, Dr Peter Roger; s of late Edmund Ward, AMIEE, of Moelfre, Anglesey, and Mona MacPhail; *b* 26 Aug 1927; *Educ* Univ of Manchester (MB ChB, DMRD); *m* 7 Dec 1954, Helen Ruth, da of late William Ballantyne, of Douglas, Lanarkshire; 1 s (Alistair b 1961), 3 da (Fiona (Mrs Cruickshank) b 1958, Frances (Mrs Trainer) b 1959, Kathleen b 1962); *Career* Nat Serv Med Branch RAF 1953–55; conslt radiologist Aberdeen Hosps and clinical sr lectr Univ of Aberdeen 1963–92, conslt radiologist Grampian Healthcare Tst 1993–; FRCR 1962; *Recreations* mountains; *Clubs* Cairngorm; *Style—* Dr Peter Ward; ✉ X-ray Department, Woodend Hospital, Aberdeen AB15 6XS (☎ 01224 404160)

WARD, Peter Terry; *b* 8 Oct 1945; *m*; 1 da, 1 s; *Career* Standard-Triumph Motor Co: service liaison offr 1967–69, area mangr field service engrg and parts 1969–71, parts sales supervisor 1971–72, seconded to British Leyland France 1972, parts sales mangr Jaguar Rover Triumph Ltd (following gp reorganisation) 1973–75; Unipart Ltd: commercial mangr 1975–76, mangr distributor devpt 1976–77, sales dir 1977–79; dir parts ops Talbot Motor Co (and md subsid Motaquip Ltd) 1979–83; Rolls-Royce Motor Cars Ltd: dir sales and mktg 1983–84, md Sales and Mktg Div 1984–86, md 1986, md and chief exec 1987, chief exec Rolls-Royce Motors Holdings Ltd 1990, exec dir Vickers PLC (parent co of Rolls-Royce) 1991–May 1995, chm and chief exec Rolls-Royce Motor Cars Ltd 1991–94 (chm only 1995, resigned Feb), md ops Vickers PLC 1993–94; former chm and chief exec Cunard Line and exec dir Trafalgar House plc (taken over by Kvaerner ASA 1996); non-exec dir Bridon plc 1994–; pres Soc of Motor Manufacturers and Traders 1994–95 (also chm SMMT Int Trade Ctee), bd memb Association des Constructeurs European d'Automobiles, chm Crewe Economic Devpt Exec, vice pres Motor and Allied Trades Benevolent Fund (BEN); Liveryman Worshipful Co of Coachmakers & Coach Harness Makers; *Style—* Peter Ward, Esq; ✉ Cunard Line Ltd, 555 Fifth Avenue, New York, NY 10017, USA (☎ 00 1 212 880 7500)

WARD, Philip; s of Albert Edwin Ward, of Doncaster, and Mildred, *née* Elsey; *Educ* Haberdashers' Aske's Sch Hampstead, Perugia, Coimbra, MECAS (Lebanon); *m* 4 April 1964, Audrey Joan, da of Lawrence Monk, of Newport, Essex; 2 da (Carolyn b 1966, Angela b 1968); *Career* coordinator Library Servs Libya 1963–71, Unesco expert Library Servs and Documentation Egypt 1973, Unesco dir of Nat Library Serv Indonesia 1973–74, professional writer 1974–; fndr Private Libraries Assoc 1956–, FRGS, FRSA, ALA; *Books* The Oxford Companion to Spanish Literature 1978, A Dictionary of Common Fallacies (2 vols, 1978–80), A Lifetime's Reading (1982); novels: Forgotten Games (1984); poetry: Lost Songs (1981); plays: Garrity (1970); travel books incl: Japanese Capitals (1985), Travels in Oman (1986), Finnish Cities (1987), Polish Cities (1988), Bulgaria (1989), Wight Magic (1990), South India (1991), Western India (1991), Bulgarian Voices: Letting the People Speak (1992), Sofia (1993), Bahrain: a Travel Guide (1993), Gujarat, Daman, Diu: a Travel Guide (1994); *Recreations* meditative basketball (following the teachings of Hirohide Ogawa) and reading; *Style—* Philip Ward, Esq

WARD, Maj-Gen Sir Philip John Newling; KCVO (1976), CBE (1971, OBE 1967); s of George William Newling Ward (d 1953), of Clapham, nr Worthing, and Mary Florence Ward; *b* 10 July 1924; *Educ* Monkton Combe Sch; *m* 1948, Pamela Ann, da of William Horace Edmund Glennie; 2 s, 2 da; *Career* cmd 1 Bn Welsh Gds 1965–67, Cdr LF Gulf 1969–71, GOC London Dist and Maj-Gen Cmd Household Div 1973–76, Cmdt RMA Sandhurst 1976–79 (Adj 1960–62); dir corp affrs (IDV) International Distillers & Vintners (UK) 1980–89; chm: Hamilton Ingram Ltd 1985–89; memb Southern Regnl Bd Lloyds Bank 1983–90; cmmr Chichester Cathedral 1980–83; chm: Royal Soldiers' Daughters' Sch until 1983, Queen Alexandra's Hosp Home; govr cmdt Church Lads and Church Girls Bde until 1986; High Sheriff of W Sussex 1985–86, Lord Lt W Sussex 1994– (DL 1981, Vice Lord Lt 1990); Freeman City of London; KStJ 1994; *Recreations* gardening; *Clubs* Cavalry and Guards' (chm 1987–90), Buck's; *Style—* Maj-Gen Sir Philip Ward, KCVO, CBE; ✉ 15 Tarrant Wharf, Arundel, W Sussex BN18 9NY (☎ 01903 884122)

WARD, Phillip David; s of Frederick William Ward, of E Retford, Notts, and Phyllis Mavis, *née* Hawker; *b* 1 Sept 1950; *Educ* Sir John Talbot's GS Salop, Univ of Sheffield (BJur); *m* 1974, Barbara Patricia, da of Wilfred Taylor; 2 da (Joanna Claire b 21 April 1980, Justine Nichola b 15 Nov 1982); *Career* DOE: joined 1973, seconded to Hackney/Islington Inner City Partnership 1978–80, head Local Govt Fin Taxation Div 1985–88, Nuffield/Leverhulme scholar 1988–89, head Global Atmosphere Div 1989–90, princ private sec to Sec of State 1990–92, dir Construction Sponsorship 1992–; *Recreations* cinema, theatre, travel; *Style—* Phillip Ward, Esq; ✉ Department of the Environment, 2 Marsham Street, London SW1P 3EB (☎ 0171 276 4139, fax 0171 276 3369)

WARD, Reginald George (Reg); s of Thomas George Ward, of Blandford Forum (d 1988), and Ada May, *née* Lane (d 1989); *b* 6 July 1942; *Educ* Univ of Leicester (BSc), Univ of Aberdeen, Univ of Oxford (dip in statistics), London Business Sch (MBA); *m* 19 Dec 1964, Chandan, da of Ranchhod Mistry; 1 da (Karen b 26 May 1966), 2 s (Stephen b 4 Aug 1978, Nicholas b 26 Jan 1984); *Career* lectr Univ of St Andrews 1965–69, analyst NCR 1969–70, economist ICL 1970–71, statistician DTI 1971–78; chief statistician: HM Treasy 1978–82, Cabinet Office 1982–86; under sec DTI 1986–89, asst dir Central Statistical Office 1989–94, dir Statistics and Economics Office Inland Revenue 1994–; *Books* Keeping Score (1991); *Recreations* sailing, photography; *Style—* Reg Ward, Esq; ✉ Inland Revenue, Room F3, Somerset House, Strand, London WC2R 1LB (☎ 0171 438 6609, fax 0171 438 7106)

WARD, Maj-Gen Robert William; CB (1989), MBE (1972); s of Lt-Col William Denby Ward (d 1973), of Fleet, Hants, and Monica Thérèse, *née* Collett-White (d 1985); *b* 17 Oct 1935; *Educ* Rugby, RMA Sandhurst; *m* 16 April 1966, Lavinia Dorothy, da of Col (Alexander James) Henry Cramsie, OBE, DL, JP (d 1982), of O'Harabrook, Ballymoney, Co Antrim, N Ireland; 2 s (Thomas b 1968, James b 1973), 1 da (Gemma b 1970); *Career* cmmnd The Queen's Bays (later Queen's Dragoon Gds) 1955; served: Jordan, Libya, Germany, NI, Borneo, 1955–64; student RN Staff Coll 1967, GSO2 Intelligence Bahrain 1968–69, cdr A Squadron, QDG Berlin 1970–72, Nat Def Coll 1972–73, MA to C in C BAOR 1973–75, CO 1 Queen's Dragoon Gds 1975–77, Col GS Army Staff Coll 1977–78, cmd 22 Armoured Bde 1979–82, student Nat Def Coll Canada 1982–83, asst COS Northern Army Gp 1983–86, GOC Western District 1986–89; Col 1 Queen's Dragoon Gds 1991–, Hon Col Royal Mercian & Lancastrian Yeo 1995–; landscape and garden design conslt; sec Game Conservancy (Shropshire) 1993–, pres SSAFA Shropshire 1994–, chm Shropshire Historic Parks and Gardens Tst 1996–; *Recreations* gardening, outdoor sports, country pursuits, food, wine, travel; *Clubs* Cavalry and Guards', MCC, I Zingari; *Style—* Maj-Gen Robert Ward, CB, MBE

WARD, Prof Roy Charles; s of Charles Henry Ward (d 1996), of Oxford, and Hilda May, *née* Norris (d 1987); *b* 8 July 1937; *Educ* Reading Sch, Univ of Reading (BA, PhD); *m* 2 April 1966, (Georgina) Kay, da of Percy Frederick Kirby (d 1962); 2 da (Katie b 1970, Sally Ann b 1973); *Career* prof Univ of Maryland USA 1968–69; Univ of Hull: lectr 1960, sr lectr 1972–77, reader 1977–1981, prof 1981–92 (emeritus prof 1992), dean of Sci Faculty 1986–87, pro vice chllr 1987–91; chm GEOWISE (environmental consultancy); chm Minister's NE Regnl Advsy Panel MAFF; memb: Rural Devpt Cmmn, Humberside Business Ctee 1987–95; chm of Govrs Scarborough Coll 1992–95; memb Inst of Br Geographers, FRGS; *Books* Floods (1978), Principles of Hydrology (3 edn, 1989); *Recreations* walking, wine; *Style—* Prof Roy Ward; ✉ GEOWISE, 64 Newbiggin, Malton, N Yorks YO17 0JF (☎ 01653 698408, fax 01653 698408)

WARD, Simon; *b* 16 Oct 1941; *Educ* Alleyns Sch Dulwich; *m*; 3 da; *Career* actor; joined Nat Youth Theatre aged 13 (roles incl Hamlet and Richard II), with Birmingham Rep Co 1964–65 and Oxford Playhouse Co 1965–66; *Theatre* West End debut The Fourth of June (St Martin's), Loot (Criterion), Wise Child (Wyndham's), The Unknown Soldier, The Tempest and The Skin of our Teeth (all Chichester Theatre Co) 1968, Spoiled (Haymarket) 1970, Hamlet and Troilus and Cressida (NT), A Meeting By The River (USA), Rear Column (Globe), Whose Life Is It Anyway, House Guest (Savoy), Dial M For Murder (Vaudeville), Heartbreak House (Theatre Royal Haymarket), Treats (USA) 1983, York Mystery Plays 1984, The Devil and the Good Lord 1984, How the Other Half Loves 1985, Perchance to Dream 1985, Ross 1986, The Cocktail Party (Phoenix) 1986, Portraits (Savoy) 1987, Paris Match (Theatre Clwyd) 1988, Dangerous Obsession 1989, Henceforward 1990, Rumours (Chichester Festival Theatre) 1990, Revenge (Redgrave Theatre Farnham) 1991, Don't Dress For Dinner (Apollo) 1992 (Duchess) 1994, Cell Mates (Albery) 1995; *Television* BBC: Carried By Storm, Bloomsday, French Cricket, Flowering Cricket, The World of Wooster, The Flying Swan, Smith as Killer, Calf Love, The Son, The Dark Number, Jackanory, Spoiled, Chips With Everything, The Black Tulip, Roads to Freedom, The Breakthrough, The Rear Column, An Inspector Calls, Lovejoy; other: Accolade (Rediffusion), The Misfit (ATV), The Leather Funnel (Anglia), Diamonds (ATV), Allo Beatrice (Fildebroc), A Taste for Death (Anglia); *Films* Frankenstein Must Be Destroyed, I Start Counting, The Three Musketeers, All Creatures Great and Small, Young Winston, Aces High, Holocaust 2000, Dominique, The Four Feathers, Zulu Dawn, Raising Daisy Rothschild, La Sabina, The Monster Club, Hitler - The Last Ten Days, Tug of Love, The Corsican Brothers, Supergirl, Double X, Ghost Writers; *Style—* Simon Ward, Esq; ✉ c/o ICM Ltd, Oxford House, 76 Oxford Street, London W1N 0AX (☎ 0171 636 6565, fax 0171 323 0101)

WARD, Simon Charles Vivian; s of Maj Vivian Horrocks Ward, of Sudbury, Suffolk, and Leila Penelope, *née* Every; *b* 23 March 1942; *Educ* Shrewsbury, Trinity Coll Cambridge (MA); *m* 18 Sept 1965, Jillian Eileen, da of Thomas Roycroft East (d 1980), of Dublin; 3 da (Victoria Penelope Jane (Mrs Matthew Doull) b 1969, Antonia Lisa b 1971, Lucinda Fiona b (twin) 1971); *Career* trainee stockbroker Govett Sons & Co 1963–65; ptnrs' asst: Hedderwick Hunt Cox and Co 1965–67, Hedderwick Borthwick and Co 1967–70; ptnr Montagu Loebl Stanley and Co 1972–86; dir: Fleming Montagu Stanley Ltd 1986–89, Fleming Private Asset Management Ltd 1989–; chm Fleming Private Fund Management Ltd 1989 (dir 1975–); MSI (memb Int Stock Exchange 1968); *Recreations* skiing, tennis, shooting, gardening, opera, ballet; *Clubs* Boodle's; *Style—* Simon Ward, Esq; ✉ The Dower House, Bulmer, Sudbury, Suffolk CO10 7EN (☎ 01787 373257); Fleming Private Asset Mgmnt Ltd, 20 Finsbury Street, London EC2Y 2AQ (☎ 0171 814 2827, fax 0171 814 2800, telex 885941)

WARD, Tony; *b* 18 July 1931; *Educ* Loughborough Univ; *m* Gwenda Mary; 1 s (Timothy Matthew); *Career* Southern Amateur Athletic Assoc Admin 1965–68, Recreation Div 3M 1968–79, md Setars (UK) 1979–82, PR conslt offr Amateur Athletic Assoc/BAAB/BAF 1986–; *Books* Modern Distance Running (1968), Athletics For the Seventies (1969), Linford Christie (with Linford Christie, 1989), Athletics - The Golden Decade (1991); *Recreations* theatre, literature; *Style—* Tony Ward, Esq; ✉ 7 Garlands Close, Burghfield Common, Berkshire RG7 3JX (☎ 0118 983 3739, fax 0118 983 4865); British Athletic Federation, 225A Bristol Road, Edgbaston, Birmingham B5 7UB (☎ 0121 440 5000)

WARD, Tony; *Educ* Univ of Leeds (BSc); *Career* various personnel positions Grand Metropolitan plc until 1992, dir of human resources Kingfisher plc 1992–; dep chair Cmmn for Racial Equality 1993–95 (cmmr 1990–95); memb CBI Employment Ctee 1995–FIPD; *Style—* Tony Ward, Esq; ✉ Kingfisher plc, North West House, 119 Marylebone Road, London NW1 5PX (☎ 0171 724 7749)

WARD-BOOTH, Maj-Gen John Antony (Tony); OBE (1969), DL (1987); s of Rev John Vernon Ward Ward-Booth (d 1973); *b* 18 July 1927; *Educ* Worksop Coll; *m* 1952, Margaret Joan, da of Rev Aubrey Hooper, MC; 2 s, 2 da; *Career* joined Army 1945, CO 3 Bn Parachute Regt 1967–69, Cdr 16 Parachute Bde 1970–73, Nat Defence Coll Canada 1973–74, DAG HQ BAOR 1974–75, Maj-Gen 1976, Dir Army Air Corps 1976–79, GOC Western Dist 1979–82, ret; sec Eastern Wessex TAVRA 1982–89; chm Southampton Div SSAFA 1982–93, Dep Col R Anglian Regt 1982–86; memb Paracute Regt Cncl 1982–93; chm Cncl: Clayesmore Sch 1985, govr Enham Village Centre 1982; *Recreations* sports; *Clubs* Army and Navy, MCC; *Style—* Maj-Gen Tony Ward-Booth, OBE, DL; ✉ 22 Winchester Gardens, Andover, Hants SP10 2EH (☎ 01264 354317)

WARD-HOWLETT, Ronald Peter Henry; s of Ronald Desmond Ward-Howlett (d 1972), of Gerrards Cross, Bucks, and Hilda May, *née* Stopforth-Rimmer (d 1970); *b* 5 May 1932; *Educ* Ealing Coll; *Career* served RAF 1950–52; fin investmt controller Ernst & Young (formerly Arthur Young) 1984–93, currently conslt Armstrong Tomkins (taxation and accountancy servs); govr Ainsdale HS 1989–93; life memb Br Herpetological Soc, fndr memb Jersey Wildlife Preservation Soc; fndr tstee Howlett Mabrouk Shanekoe Fndn; FIMgt, FInstAA, FZS, FLS; *Recreations* herpetology, numismatics; *Clubs* Royal Over-Seas League, The Victory Services; *Style—* Ronald Ward-Howlett, Esq; ✉ 13 Brandon Park Court, Argyle Road, Southport, Lancashire PR9 9LG (☎ 01704 545366); Armstrong Tomkins, Egerton House, Tower Road, Birkenhead, Wirral L41 1FN (☎ 0151 650 6981)

WARD-JACKSON, (Audrey) Muriel; *née* Jenkins; da of William James Jenkins (d 1974), of Roehampton, and Alice, *née* Glyde (d 1967); *b* 30 Oct 1914; *Educ* Queenswood Sch Hatfield Herts, Lady Margaret Hall Oxford (BA, MA); *m* 14 March 1946, George Ralph Norman Ward-Jackson (d 1982), s of late Ralph Stapleton Ward-Jackson; *Career* Civil Serv: asst princ 1937, princ 1942, asst sec 1946–55 (served in Miny of Works, Town and Country Planning, HM Treasy, Housing and Local Govt); John Lewis Partnership 1955–74: gen inspr and fin dir, dir 1957–74, dir John Lewis Properties Ltd 1969–74, chm Pensions Trust 1964–74; served on Civil Serv Arbitration Tbnl 1959–64, chm Consumer Ctees (Agric Mktg) 1971–75; govr Br Film Inst 1962–65; memb: Cncl Bedford Coll Univ of London 1967–72, Nat Savings Review Ctee 1971–73, Royal Cmmn on Standards of Conduct in Public Life 1974–76; *Recreations* swimming; *Clubs* Lansdowne; *Style—* Mrs Muriel Ward-Jackson; ✉ The Grange, Grange Close, Goring-on-Thames, Oxon RG8 9DY (☎ 01491 872843)

WARD-JONES, Norman Arthur; CBE (1990), VRD (1959); s of Alfred Thomas Ward-Jones, and Claire Mayall, *née* Lees; *b* 19 Sept 1922; *Educ* Oundle, Brasenose Coll Oxford; *m* Pamela Catherine Ainslie, *née* Glessing; *Career* Capt RM 1941–46; RM Reserve 1948–64, Lt-Col and CO RMR (City of London) 1961–64 (Hon Col 1968–74); admitted slr 1950; sr ptnr Lawrence Messer Co 1981–85, hon slr Magistrates' Assoc 1960–85; JP N Westminster 1966–92; chm East Anglian Real Property Co Ltd 1970–80 (non exec dir 1980–89), memb Gaming Bd for GB 1984– (chm 1986–92); pres The Brasenose Soc 1991–92; *Recreations* wine drinking; *Clubs* East India; *Style—* Norman Ward-Jones, Esq, CBE, VRD; ✉ The Cottage, Barnhorne Manor, 75 Barnhorn Road, Little Common, Bexhill-on-Sea, E Sussex TN39 4QB

WARD-THOMAS, Evelyn; *see:* Anthony, Evelyn Bridgett Patricia

WARD THOMPSON, Catharine Joan; da of Peter Michaeljohn Ward, of Waterdell House, Croxley Green, Herts, and Janet Mary, *née* Bruce (*see* Debrett's Peerage, Bruce, Bt cr 1628); *b* 5 Dec 1952; *Educ* Holy Cross Convent Chalfont St Peter Bucks, Rickmansworth GS, Univ of Southampton (BSc), Univ of Edinburgh (DipLA); *m* 30 Dec 1983, Henry Swift Thompson, s of Henry Swift Thompson, of Grass Valley, California, and Hancock Point, Maine, USA; 1 s (James b 21 Nov 1987), 2 da (Emma b 27 Sept 1985, Joanna b 19 Sept 1991); *Career* landscape asst Justice and Webb Landscape Architects Vancouver BC Canada 1974–75, landscape architect and sr landscape architect W J Cairns & Ptnrs 1976–81, princ LDS Assocs Landscape Architects and Landscape Scientists 1986–90, head Dept of Landscape Architecture Edinburgh Coll of Art Heriot-Watt Univ 1989– (lectr 1981–88); visiting research scholar: Univ of Pennsylvania, Harvard 1994–95; memb: Amnesty International, World Devpt Movement; ALI; *Recreations* dance, choreography, theatre; *Clubs* University of Edinburgh Staff; *Style—* Mrs Catharine Ward Thompson; ✉ 11 Douglas Crescent, Edinburgh EH12 5BB (☎ 0131 337 6818); Hancock Point, Maine 04640, USA; Department of Landscape Architecture, Edinburgh College of Art, Heriot-Watt University, Lauriston Place, Edinburgh EH3 9DF (☎ 0131 221 6091, fax 0131 221 6005)

WARDALE, Sir Geoffrey Charles; KCB (1979, CB 1974); *b* 29 Nov 1919; *Educ* Altrincham GS, Queens' Coll Cambridge; *m* 1944, Rosemary Octavia Dyer; 1 s, 1 da; *Career* Civil Serv Miny Tport: joined 1942, asst sec 1957–66, under sec 1966–70; DOE: joined 1970, dep sec 1972–78, 2 perm sec 1978–80; vice patron Brighton College 1992– (govr 1981–92, chm 1985–90), memb Cncl Univ of Sussex 1986–92, pres Lewes Area CAB 1987–, pres Friends of Lewes Soc 1993–; *Style—* Sir Geoffrey Wardale, KCB; ✉ 89 Paddock Lane, Lewes, E Sussex (☎ 01273 473468)

WARDE, His Hon John Robins; *b* 25 April 1920; *Educ* Radley, Corpus Christi Coll Oxford (MA); *m* 16 Aug 1941, Edna Holliday (Holly), *née* Gipson; 3 s (Robin b 1944, Simon b 1946, Nicholas b 1952); *Career* served WWII 1940–45 Lt RA, liaison offr with HQRA 53 (W) Div, awarded C-in-C's Certificate for outstanding good service in the Campaign in NW Europe; admitted slr 1950, ptnr Waugh & Co Haywards Heath and E Grinstead E Sussex 1960–70, registrar Clerkenwell County Ct 1970–77, recorder Crown Ct 1972–77, circuit judge SE Circuit 1977–90; cncllr Devon CC 1946–49; memb: Devon Agric Exec Ctee 1948–53, W Regnl Advsy Cncl of BBC 1950–53, Cncl and Ct of Govrs The Univ Coll of the SW 1948–53, Soc of Sussex Downsmen, Assoc of Br Members of the Swiss Alpine, Br Schs Exploring Soc, Law Soc; Freeman City of London 1983, Liveryman Worshipful Co of Gardeners 1983; *Recreations* mountaineering, watching cricket, listening to music; *Clubs* MCC, Sussex CC, Forty; *Style—* His Hon John Warde; ✉ 20 Clifton Terrace, Brighton, E Sussex BN1 3HA

WARDE-ALDAM, Maj William; JP (S Yorks 1972), DL (S Yorks 1979); s of Lt-Col John Ralph Patientius Warde-Aldam, TD (d 1973); *b* 14 June 1925; *Educ* Eton; *m* 1960, Gillian Margaret, da of Malcolm Scott, of Lyons Hall, Great Leighs, Essex; 2 s, 1 da; *Career* served with Coldstream Guards: Germany, Italy, Norway, Malaya, Kenya 1943–64; High Sheriff Hallamshire 1971; pres Yorks Agric Soc 1990; chm: Badsworth Hunt 1971–, Yorks Residential Sch for the Deaf and Doncaster Coll for the Deaf 1966–91; *Clubs* Cavalry and Guards', MCC, Pratt's; *Style—* Maj William Warde-Aldam, JP, DL; ✉ Frickley Hall, Doncaster DN5 7BU (☎ 01977 642854); Ederline, Ford, Lochgilphead, Argyll PA31 8RJ (☎ 01546 810284)

WARDE-NORBURY, (William George) Antony; DL (S Yorks, 1989); s of Harold George Warde-Norbury, of Hooton Pagnell Hall, nr Doncaster, Yorks, and Mary Betty Warde-Aldam; *b* 13 March 1936; *Educ* Eton, Sandhurst; *m* 15 April 1961, Philippa Marjorie, da of Col Philip Ralph Davies-Cooke, CB, of Gwysaney Hall, Mold, N Wales; 2 s (Mark b 1962, Alistair b 1966); *Career* Capt Coldstream Gds 1957–64; Allied-Lyons plc: joined 1964, jt md Allied Breweries 1986–88 (dir 1979–88), gp main bd dir 1986–88, also dir subsids incl European Cellars and Britvic Corona 1986–88; non-exec chm: Provident Financial plc, NED Gallup Orgn, various other cos; High Sheriff of South Yorkshire 1996–97; *Recreations* field sports, agriculture, golf, music; *Clubs* Cavalry and Guards', Boodle's, RAC; *Style—* Antony Warde-Norbury, Esq; ✉ Hooton Pagnell Hall, Doncaster DN5 7BW (☎ 01977 642850, fax 01977 644213, car tel 0374 833616)

WARDELL, Gareth Lodwig; MP (Lab) Gower (majority 7,018); s of John Thomas Wardell and Jenny Ceridwen Wardell; *b* 29 Nov 1944; *Educ* Gwendraeth GS, LSE (BSc, MSc); *m* 1967, Jennifer Dawn Evans; 1 s (Alistair); *Career* former teacher, sr lectr in geography Trinity Coll Carmarthen 1973–82; election agent then res asst to Dr Roger Thomas as MP for Carmarthen 1979–82, MP (Lab) Gower 1982–, chm Select Ctee on Welsh Affrs 1984–; lay memb GMC 1995 (memb 1994); FRGS; *Recreations* swimming, cross-country running; *Style—* Gareth Wardell, Esq, MP; ✉ 67 Elder Grove, Carmarthen, Dyfed SA31 2LH

WARDEN-OWEN, Edward (Eddie); s of Norman Warden-Owen, of Trearddur Bay, Holyhead, Gwynedd, and Gwladys Elinor, *née* Jones; *b* 25 June 1949; *Educ* Holyhead Co Secdy Sch, Cardiff Coll of Educn; *m* 18 Aug 1989, Susan Virginia, da of Thomas Henry Alexander Gill, of Havant, Hants; 2 s (Myles Elliot b 1991, Marcus Lloyd b 1994); *Career* teacher of physical educn 1972–74, began career in sailmaking 1974, currently co dir of Bruce Banks Sails Ltd; sporting highlights in yachting: 470 class rep Olympic Games 1980, helmsman of Phoenix, memb Br Admirals Cup Team 1985 (top scoring boat overall), Skipper of Indulgence V, winner 3/4 Ton Cup 1986, navigator of White Crusader in Br challenge for America's Cup 1986–87, Silk Cut Helmsman of the Year 1987, winner Congressional Cup 1987, Nippon Cup 1988 and Omega Gold Cup 1991, skipper of Crusader in 12 Metre World Championships 1988 (winner Midnight Sun Cup Race), skipper of Indulgence VII, memb British Admirals Cup winning team 1989, runner up One Ton Cup 1989, coach to NZ Team America's Cup Challenge 1991–92, coach to Spanish Americas Cup Challenge 1995, skipper Indulgence winner of Fastnet Race 1993, skipper Mumm a Mia winner of Mumm 36 Euro Championships 1994 and Fastnet Race (Mumm 36 class) 1995, memb winning Italian team Admirals Cup 1995, skipper Babbalaas winner of Southern Ocean Racing Circuit 1996; *Recreations* squash, tennis, skiing, golf, horse riding; *Clubs* Royal Ocean Racing, Royal Thames Yacht, Holyhead Sailing; *Style—* Eddie Warden-Owen, Esq; ✉ Bruce Banks Sails Ltd, 372 Brook Lane, Sarisbury, nr Southampton, Hampshire (☎ 01489 582444, fax 01489 589789)

WARDINGTON, 2 Baron (UK 1936); Christopher Henry Beaumont Pease; s of 1 Baron Wardington (d 1950), and Dorothy Charlotte, *née* Forster (d 1983); *b* 22 Jan 1924; *Educ* Eton; *m* 9 Sept 1964, (Margaret) Audrey, da of John White (d 1962), and former w of Jack Dunfee; 1 adopted s (Christopher William Beaumont b 18 April 1970), 2 adopted da (Lucy Anne (Mrs John Vallance Petrie) b 23 Sept 1966, Helen Elizabeth b 24 Dec 1967); *Heir* bro, Hon William Simon Pease; *Career* served Scots Gds Italy, Capt 1942–47; ptnr Hoare Govett Ltd 1950–86; cmmr Public Works Loan Bd 1964–69; memb: Cncl of Stock Exchange 1963–81, Corp for Bond Holders 1967–80; Alderman Broad St Ward London 1960–63, tstee Royal Jubilee Tsts 1965–95; chm: Athlone Tst, Friends of British Library 1986–95; Liveryman Worshipful Co of Goldsmiths; *Recreations* books, gardening, golf; *Clubs* RAC, Garrick, Roxburghe, All England Lawn Tennis (Wimbledon); *Style—* The Lord Wardington; ✉ 29 Moore St, London SW3 (☎ 0171 584 5245); Manor House, Wardington, Banbury, Oxon (☎ 01295 750202, fax 01295 750805)

WARDLAW, Prof Alastair Connell; s of Prof Claude Wilson Wardlaw (d 1985), of Bramhall, Cheshire, and Jessie, *née* Connell (d 1971); *b* 20 Jan 1930; *Educ* Manchester GS, Univ of Manchester (BSc, MSc, PhD, DSc); *m* 1 July 1954, Jacqueline Shirley, da of Reginald Ormsby Jones, of Durrus, Ireland; 1 s (Malcolm b 1963), 2 da (Joanna b 1958, Valerie b 1961); *Career* res fell: Western Reserve Univ Cleveland Ohio USA 1953–55, St Mary's Hosp Med Sch London 1955–58; res memb Connaught Med Res Laboratories Toronto 1958–66; prof of microbiology: Univ of Toronto 1966–70, Univ of Glasgow 1970–96; memb: Marshall Aid Scholarship Cmmn, American Soc for Microbiology 1978; FRSE 1972, FIBiol 1988, FRSA 1989; *Books* Sourcebook of Experiments for the Teaching of Microbiology, Practical Statistics for Experimental Biologists, Pathogenesis and Immunity in Pertussis; *Recreations* cultivation of ferns, ceramics, bicycle-camping; *Style—* Prof Alastair Wardlaw, FRSE; ✉ 92 Drymen Rd, Bearsden, Glasgow G61 2SY (☎ 0141 942 2461); Division of Infection and Immunity, University of Glasgow, Glasgow G12 8QQ (☎ 0141 339 8855 ext 4001, fax 0141 330 4600)

WARDLAW, Sir Henry John; 21 Bt (NS 1631), of Pitreavie, Fifeshire; s of Sir Henry Wardlaw, 20 Bt (d 1983), and Ellen, *née* Brady (d 1977); *b* 30 Nov 1930; *Educ* Melbourne Univ (MB, BS); *m* 1962, Julie-Ann, da of late Edward Patrick Kirwan; 5 s ((Henry) Justin b 10 Aug 1963, Edward Patrick b 1 July 1964, Simon John b 19 June 1965, Anthony James b 1 Oct 1968, Adrian Stewart b 2 April 1971), 2 da (Janet Montgomerie b 7 Sept 1967, Marie Ellen b 29 Sept 1977); *Heir* s, (Henry) Justin Wardlaw b 10 Aug 1963; *Style—* Sir Henry Wardlaw, Bt; ✉ Mandalay, 75–77 Two Bays Road, Mt Eliza 3930, Victoria, Australia

WARDLE, Anthony Peter; s of Peter John Wardle, of Minehead, Somerset, and Caroline Mina Gertrude, *née* Salter; *b* 9 Aug 1948; *Educ* Hertford GS, Thames Nautical Training Coll, Univ of Southampton Sch of Navigation; *m* 24 June 1972, Susan Margaret, *née* Lewis; 2 da (Jessica Ann b 3 June 1979, Eleanor Katherine b 18 June 1981); *Career* navigating apprenticeship Peninsular & Oriental Steam Navigation Co 1966–69, sales and mktg mgmnt Ross Foods 1972–73, BBDO Advertising 1973–74, dir Promotional Campaigns Ltd 1977–79 (joined 1975), dir and shareholder Merchandising Strategy Ltd 1979–81, co bought out to form Mann Wardle Ltd (jt chm 1981–87); co later became Mann Wardle Group Ltd (acquired by Saatchi & Saatchi plc 1987); chm 1987–91: Saatchi & Saatchi/Spa, Saatchi & Saatchi Business Communications, Saatchi & Saatchi Integrated; chm Saatchi & Saatchi/Equator UK Ltd 1989–; fndr Genius Publishing Ltd 1991, chm Wardle & Associates (Mktg and Communications Conslts); memb: BFSS, The Game Conservancy; *Recreations* shooting, fishing, tennis, food, wine; *Style—* Anthony Wardle, Esq; ✉ Norton House, Norton St Philip, Bath, Somerset BA3 6LW (☎ 01373 834239, car 0410 095779)

WARDLE, Charles Frederick; MP (C) Bexhill and Battle (majority 16,307); s of Frederick Maclean Wardle (d 1975), and Constance, *née* Roach; *b* 23 Aug 1939; *Educ* Tonbridge, Lincoln Coll Oxford, Harvard Business Sch; *m* 1964, Lesley Ann, da of Sidney Wells (d 1967), and Dorothy, *née* Martin; 1 da (Sarah b 1969); *Career* chm Benjamin Priest Group 1977–84; MP (C) Bexhill and Battle 1983–, PPS to Sec of State for Social Servs 1984–87, chm One Nation Forum 1989–90, PPS to Sec of State for Scotland 1990–92, under sec of state Home Office 1992–94, under sec of state DTI 1994–95; memb: CBI Cncl 1980–84, Trade and Indust Ctee 1983–84, Treasy and Civil Ctee 1990–91; *Style—* Charles Wardle, Esq, MP; ✉ House of Commons, Westminster, London SW1A 0AA

WARDLE, (John) Irving; s of John Wardle (d 1975), of Bolton, and Nellie, *née* Partington (d 1930); *b* 20 July 1929; *Educ* Bolton Sch, Wadham Coll Oxford (BA), RCM (ARCM); *m* 1, Joan (decd); m 2 (m dis), Fay; 2 s (Benjamin b 1964, Thomas b 1967); m 3, Elizabeth Rosalind; 1 s (Alexander b 1972), 1 da (Judith b 1974); *Career* sub ed Times Educational Supplement 1957–60, dep theatre critic The Observer 1960–63, theatre critic The Times 1963–89, ed Gambit Int Theatre Magazine 1970–72, theatre critic The Independent on Sunday 1990–; *Plays* The Houseboy (Open Space Theatre 1973), Dolls (Soho Poly Theatre 1987), Faust at Elsinore (Theatr Clwyd 1995); *Books* The Theatres of George Devine (1978), Theatre Criticism (1992); *Recreations* piano playing; *Style—* Irving Wardle, Esq; ✉ 51 Richmond Rd, New Barnet, Herts EN5 1SF; The Independent on Sunday, 1 Canada Square, Canary Wharf, London E14 5AP (☎ 0171 293 2000, fax 0171 293 2435)

WARDLE, Piers; s of late Dr Christopher John Wardle, of Devon, and Mary, *née* Haworth; *b* 20 April 1960; *Educ* Exeter Art Coll, Ruskin Sch of Drawing Oxford; *Career* artist; *Solo Exhibitions* incl: Northcott Theatre Exeter 1979, The Acme Gallery London 1981, Pomeroy Purdy Gallery London 1989, 1990 and 1992, Eastbourne Clark Gallery Florida 1990, Bernard Baron Gallery London 1990; *Group Exhibitions* incl: The Museum of Modern Art Oxford 1982, The London Group (Royal College of Art) 1985, The Crypt London 1987 and 1988, The Summer Show (Richard Pomeroy Gallery) 1988, New Work By Gallery Artists (Pomeroy Purdy Gallery) 1990, John Moores 17 1991, The Poetry Show (Rebecca Hossack Gallery) 1992, Gallery Artists (Purdy Hicks Gallery) 1993, Lemon 1993, Es la Manera (Factual Nonsense) 1993, Ssexcess (Factual Nonsense) 1993, Fête Worse than Death 1993 and 1994, Candyman II (Tower Bridge Business Complex) 1994, Hardcore (Factual Nonsense) 1994, ArtFocus (Tel Aviv) 1994, Hanging Picnic 1995, Make Believe (Royal College of Art) 1995; work in the collection of The Courtauld Institute; contrib to The Late Show (on Chaos Theory and Art) BBC TV 1990; *Books* Longinus and Stephaton (with Tim Long, 1990); *Style—* Piers Wardle; ✉ c/o Workfortheeyetodo, 51 Hanbury Street, London E1 (☎ and fax 0171 426 0579)

WARDROPE, James (Jim); s of James Wardrope, of Bathgate, W Lothian, and Elizabeth Wilson, *née* Young (d 1989); *b* 14 March 1954; *Educ* Bathgate Acad, Univ of Edinburgh (BSc, MB ChB); *m* 31 March 1978, Diana Jane, da of Bruce Stuart Fothergill, of Sheffield; 1 s (Alistair b 1988), 1 da (Katie b 1986); *Career* registrar and res registrar Leeds Gen Infirmary 1982–85, sr registrar Royal Hallamshire Hosp Sheffield 1985–87, conslt in accident and emergency med Northern Gen Hosp Sheffield 1987–; memb: BAEM Academic Sub Ctee and Disaster Sub Ctee, Nat Hosp Jr Staff Ctee 1982–85, Exec

Ctee Sheffield Div BMA 1985–; FRCS (Edin) 1982, FRCS 1982; *Books* The Management of Wounds and Burns (with J A R Smith, OUP, 1992); *Recreations* cycling, running, gardening; *Style*— Jim Wardrope, Esq; ✉ Accident and Emergency Department, Northern General Hospital, Herries Rd, Sheffield S5 7AU (☎ 0114 243 4343)

WARE, Jeremy John; OBE (1993); s of Col Robert Remington Ware (d 1952), of Collingham, Newark, Notts, and Barbara, *née* Lewellyn (d 1995); *b* 29 Oct 1932; *Educ* Winchester, Lincoln Coll Oxford (MA); *m* 23 April 1960, Patricia Jane, da of Maj Horace Maylin Vipan Wright; 3 s (Julian b 1963, Henry b 1965, Maylin b 1968); *Career* admitted slr 1958; ptnr Tallents Godfrey & Co; pres: Notts Law Soc 1986–87, Grantham Div Cons Assoc 1986–94 (chm 1978–86); chm Lincs & E Notts Euro Parly Constituency 1988–91; memb Law Soc; *Recreations* shooting, fishing, gardening; *Style*— J J Ware, Esq, OBE; ✉ Lister Place, Brant Broughton, Lincoln; 3 Middlegate, Newark, Notts (☎ 01636 71881)

WARE, Michael John; CB (1985), QC (1988); s of Kenneth George Ware (d 1967), and Phyllis Matilda, *née* Joynes (d 1984); *b* 7 May 1932; *Educ* Cheltenham GS, Trinity Hall Cambridge (BA, LLB); *m* 4 June 1966, Susan Ann, da of late Gp Capt C E Maitland, DFC, AFC; 3 da (Victoria b 1967, Johanna b 1970, Katherine b 1974); *Career* called to the Bar Middle Temple 1955; Legal Dept Bd of Trade (later DTI) 1957–73, legal advsr Office of Fair Trading 1973–77; under-sec (legal) DTI (co inspections and prosecutions) 1977–80; slr Dept of Environment 1980–92, chm Meat Hygiene Appeals Tbnl for England and Wales and for Scotland 1993–; *Style*— Michael Ware, Esq, CB, QC; ✉ 12 Hill Road, Haslemere, Surrey GU27 2JN

WARE, Robert; s of Dr M Ware, and W E Ware, *née* Boyce; *b* 1951; *Educ* Bryanston; *Career* mgmnt trainee Dunlop (asst advtg mangr Dunlop Sports Co Ltd) 1969–72, transferred as account mangr to Sharps (now part of Saatchi & Saatchi) 1971–74, account dir then assoc dir Winship Webber & Co (advtg agency, later merged with Vernon Stratton Ltd) 1974–78, account dir DPP (creative consultancy) 1978–79, UK md JPP International 1979, md (Hitchin) then gp bd dir Bartlett Ray & Jarvis Ltd (advtg agency) 1979–85, chm and chief exec Ware Anthony Rust Ltd (initially advtg agency, now full mktg and PR consultancy) 1985–; winner ISP awards for New Berry Fruits and Toblerone (with Bartlett Ray & Jarvis Ltd); chm Mktg Ctee: Children's Haven Appeal, Cambridge Arts Theatre appeal; memb Worshipful Soc of Apothecaries; MIPA; *Recreations* golf, cricket, wining and dining; *Clubs* Gog Magog Golf; *Style*— Robert Ware, Esq; ✉ Ware Anthony Rust Ltd, Newnham Mill, Newnham Road, Cambridge CB3 9EX (☎ 01223 566212)

WAREING, Robert Nelson; MP (Lab) Liverpool West Derby (majority 20,425); s of Robert Wareing (d 1960), and Florence Patricia, *née* Mallon (d 1964); *b* 20 Aug 1930; *Educ* Ranworth Square Sch, Alsop HS Liverpool, Bolton Coll of Educn, Univ of London (BSc, external degree); *m* 1962, Betty (d 1989), da of Thomas Coward (d 1964); *Career* local govt offr 1946–48, LAC RAF 1948–50, local govt offr 1950–56, coll lectr 1957–83, chm Merseyside Econ Devpt Co Ltd 1981–86; Parly candidate (Lab): Berwick-upon-Tweed 1970, Liverpool Edge Hill March 1979 (by-election) and May 1979; MP (Lab) Liverpool West Derby 1983–, asst opposition whip 1987–92, chm Br-Yugoslav Parly Gp 1994–, memb Select Ctee on Foreign Affrs 1992–, vice chm Br-Russian Parly Gp 1992–, vice-pres Br-Southern Slav Soc; Merseyside CC: cncllr 1981–86, chief whip Lab Gp 1981–83; memb: Hansard Soc, Br-Russia Centre, Br-East West Centre; *Recreations* concert-going, soccer, travel; *Clubs* Dovecot Labour (Liverpool), Victoria Dining (London); *Style*— Robert Wareing, Esq, MP; ✉ House of Commons, London SW1A 0AA (☎ 0171 219 3482)

WARENIUS, Prof Hilmar Meek; s of Tor Adolph Warenius (d 1971), and Ruby Gwendoline, *née* Meek; *b* 12 Jan 1942; *Educ* Penzance GS, Downing Coll Cambridge (MA, PhD), Middlesex Hosp Med Sch London (MB BChir (Cantab), DMRT); *m* 19 Aug 1972, Rosamund Jean Talbot, da of Leopold Edward Hill (d 1957); 1 s (Christopher b 1976), 2 da (Eleanor b 1979, Fleur b 1985); *Career* sr house offr Royal Marsden Hosp 1970–71, registrar in radiotherapy Middlesex Hosp 1972–74; first asst to Prof Mitchell at Addenbrooke's Hosp Cambridge 1974–75, MRC clinical res fell Univ of Cambridge 1975–79, first asst to Mr William Ross Univ of Newcastle and Newcastle Gen Hosp 1979–80, conslt in radiotherapy and oncology in Newcastle 1980–82, CRC prof of radiation oncology Univ of Liverpool 1982–90, MRC hon clinical coordinator Fast Neutron Studies 1982–89, currently prof and dir Cancer Res Campaign Oncology Res Unit Dept of Med Univ of Liverpool; visiting prof and hon conslt Dept of Clinical Oncology Hammersmith Hosp London; FRCR, FRCP; *Recreations* swimming, guitar, choral society, cooking; *Style*— Prof Hilmar Warenius; ✉ 14 Delavor Rd, Heswall, Wirral, Merseyside (☎ 0151 342 3034); Cancer Research Campaign, Oncology Research Unit, Department of Medicine, The University of Liverpool, PO Box 147, Liverpool L69 3BX (☎ 0151 706 4530, fax 0151 706 5802)

WARHURST, Alan; CBE (1990); s of William Warhurst (d 1965), and Margaret, *née* Holden (d 1953); *b* 6 Feb 1927; *Educ* Canon Slade GS Bolton, Univ of Manchester (BA); *m* 5 Sept 1953, Sheila Lilian, da of John Bradbury (d 1957), of Atherton; 1 s (Nicholas b 1964), 2 da (Alyson b 1958, Frances b 1960); *Career* Nat Serv cmmnd Lancs Fus 1946–48; dir: City Museum Bristol 1960–70, Ulster Museum Belfast 1970–77, Manchester Museum 1977–93; pres: South Western Fedn of Museums and Galleries 1966–68, North Western Fedn of Museums and Galleries 1979–80, The Museums Assoc 1975–76; chm: Irish Nat Ctee ICOM 1973–75, North West Museums Serv 1992– (dep chm 1987–92), Gtr Manchester Archaeological Fedn 1983–93, Hulme Hall Ctee Univ of Manchester 1986–93; hon sec The Univ Museums Gp 1987–93, tstee Canon Slade GS 1987–93, memb Museums and Galleries Cmmn 1994–; Hon MA Queen's Univ Belfast 1983; FSA 1953, FMA 1958; *Recreations* English ceramics, hillwalking; *Style*— Alan Warhurst, Esq, CBE, FSA; ✉ Calabar Cottage, Woodville Road, Altrincham, Cheshire WA14 2AL (☎ 0161 928 0730)

WARHURST, Paul; *b* 26 Sept 1969; *Career* professional footballer; Manchester City 1987–88, 67 appearances Oldham Athletic 1988–91, with Sheffield Wednesday 1991–93, joined Blackburn Rovers 1993–; honours: Oldham Athletic runners up League Cup 1990, Sheffield Wednesday runners up FA Cup 1993; *Style*— Paul Warhurst, Esq; ✉ Blackburn Rovers FC, Ewood Park, Blackburn BB2 4JF (☎ 01254 55432)

WARIN, Dr Andrew Peter; s of Dr John Fairbairn Warin, OBE (d 1990), of Iffley, Oxford, and Dr Kathleen Warin; *b* 16 Jan 1945; *Educ* Radley, Guy's Hosp Med Sch London (MB BS); *m* 1, 3 Sept 1966 (m dis 1987), Dr Judith M Warin, da of V D H Rutland, of Farnborough, Hants; 1 s (Benjamin b 2 Jan 1974), 2 da (Fiona b 11 Nov 1969, Joanna b 10 Nov 1970); m 2, 21 April 1993, Stella, *née* Purcell; *Career* conslt dermatologist and sr lectr St John's Hosp for Diseases of Skin 1976–80, conslt dermatologist Exeter 1980–; author of articles on psoriasis, mycosis, fungoides and glucagonoma syndrome; FRSM, FRCP, memb Br Assoc of Dermatologists; *Recreations* swimming, running, tennis, skiing, clarinet; *Style*— Dr Andrew Warin; ✉ 14 Barnfield Hill, Exeter, Devon EX1 1SR; Royal Devon and Exeter Hospital, Barrack Rd, Exeter, Devon (☎ 01392 402613)

WARING, Sir (Alfred) Holburt; 3 Bt (UK 1935); s of Sir Alfred Waring, 2 Bt (d 1981), and Winifred, Lady Waring; *b* 2 Aug 1933; *Educ* Rossall; *m* 1958, Ana, da of Valentine Medinilla; 1 s, 2 da; *Heir* s, Michael Holburt Waring, b 3 Jan 1964; *Career* dir: SRM Plastics, Waring Investments, Property Realisation Co Ltd; *Recreations* tennis, golf, squash, swimming; *Clubs* Moor Park Golf; *Style*— Sir Holburt Waring, Bt; ✉ 30 Russell Rd, Moor Park, Northwood, Middx

WARKE, Rt Rev Robert Alexander; *see:* Cork, Cloyne and Ross, Bishop of

WARKENTIN, Juliet; da of John and Germaine Warkentin, of Toronto, Canada; *b* 10 May 1961; *Educ* Univ of Toronto (BA); *m* Andrew Lamb; *Career* former ed: Toronto Life Fashion, Drapers Record; currently ed marie claire; Canadian Nat Magazine Award 1989, Business and Professional Magazine Editor of the Year PPA Awards 1995; *Style*— Ms Juliet Warkentin; ✉ marie claire, 2 Hatfields, London SE1 9PG (☎ 0171 261 5177, fax 0171 261 5277)

WARLAND, Philip John; s of Ernest Alfred Henry Warland, of Christchurch, and Winifred Mary, *née* Poyntz-Owen (d 1991); *b* 25 Dec 1945; *Educ* KCS; *m* 19 Sept 1970, Sandra, da of Jack Cross (d 1987); 3 s (David b 1972, Richard b 1973, John b 1978); *Career* head Info Div Bank of England 1985–89, gp personnel resources mangr Standard Chartered Bank 1989–90, dir gen Assoc of Unit Tsts and Investment Funds 1991–; chm Oasis Charitable Tst 1986–; *Recreations* squash, golf, cricket, walking; *Style*— Philip Warland, Esq; ✉ Association of Unit Trusts and Investment Funds, 65 Kingsway, London WC2B 6TD (☎ 0171 831 0898)

WARLOW, Prof Charles Picton; s of Charles Edward Picton Warlow (d 1988), and Nancy Mary McLellan, *née* Hine (d 1987); *b* 9 Sept 1943; *Educ* Univ of Cambridge (BA, MB BChir, MD), St George's Hosp Med Sch London; *m* 4 Sept 1976, Ilona Patricia, da of Max McDowell, of Auckland, NZ; 2 s (Benjamin b 1 Aug 1980, Oliver b 27 Oct 1984), 1 da (Margaret b 25 March 1982); *Career* clinical reader in neurology Univ of Oxford 1977–86, fell Green Coll Oxford 1979–86, prof of med neurology Univ of Edinburgh 1987–; memb: Assoc of Br Neurologists, Br Stroke Res Gp, Euro Neurological Soc, Atherosclerosis Discussion Gp, American Neurological Assoc; FRCP, FRCPEd, FRCPGlas; *Books* Transient Ischaemic Attacks (1982), Dilemmas in the Management of the Neurological Patient (1984), More Dilemmas in the Management of the Neurological Patient (1987), Stroke and Living with Stroke (with Barbara Woodhouse, 1987), Handbook of Neurology (1991), Transient Ischaemic Attacks of the Brain and Eye (1994), Stroke - a practical guide to management (jtly); *Recreations* sailing, photography, mountains; *Style*— Prof Charles Warlow; ✉ Department of Clinical Neurosciences, Western General Hospital, Crewe Road South, Edinburgh EH4 2XU (☎ 0131 537 2082)

WARMAN, Alister Seager; *Educ* Harrow, Courtauld Inst of Art Univ of London; *Career* lectr Poly of Newcastle upon Tyne 1970–74, Art Dept Arts Cncl of GB 1975–85, dir Serpentine Gallery London 1985–91, princ Byam Shaw Sch of Art 1991–; *Style*— Alister Warman, Esq; ✉ Byam Shaw School of Art, 2 Elthorne Road, London N19 4AG (☎ 0171 281 4111, fax 0171 281 1632)

WARMAN, Oliver Byrne; *b* 10 June 1932; *Educ* Stowe, Univ of Exeter, Balliol Coll Oxford; *Career* cmmnd Welsh Guards 1953, GSO III Cabinet Office, instr Staff Coll RMCS, ret 1970; artist; first exhibited RA 1980; exhibited: RBA, RWA, RSMA, ROI, NEAC; work in collections incl: Royal Family, Sultan of Oman, Emir of Kuwait, US Embassy, Nat West Bank and all clearing banks, S G Warburg, Co-op Bank Crown Cmmn; dir: Ship & Boat Builders Fedn 1972, Falmarine 1973, Ashlyns' Wine Shippers 1978, Tulsemead Wine Shippers 1983; chief exec Fedn of Br Artists 1984–93; memb Cncl: CBI, Army Ski Assoc; RBA 1984, ROI 1989; *Books* Arnhem 1944 (1970), Royal Society of Portrait Painters (1986); contrib to anthologies on wine, painting, military history; *Recreations* painting, France, food, military history, sailing, wine; *Clubs* Cavalry & Guards', Chelsea Arts, Royal Cornwall Yacht; *Style*— Oliver Warman, Esq; ✉ 1 and 2 The Row, Mollington, Banbury, Oxon OX17 1BH (☎ 01295 750300, fax 01295 750951); Le Moulin de la Roque, Montpinchon, 50210 Cerisy-La-Salle, Manche, France

WARMINGTON, Anthony Marshall; s of Sir Marshall Warmington, 3 Bt, of Swallowfield Park, Reading, Berkshire (d 1995), and Eileen Mary, *née* Howes (d 1969); *b* 1 July 1946; *Educ* Charterhouse, Univ of Grenoble; *m* 1973 (m dis 1987), Carolyn Patricia (d 1993), da of late Micky Simonds; 1 s (Oliver Marshall Simonds b 30 Sept 1974), 1 da (Katherine Louise b 22 Feb 1977); *Career* Lt Queen's Dragoon Gds, served NI Aden Germany 1965–68; Kitcat and Aitken 1968–71, Bisgood Bishop & Co 1971–72, investmt mangr Ionian Bank 1972–74, investmt mangr Kitcat and Aitken 1974–77; dir: Streets Financial PR 1980–87 (joined 1977), PR Manning Selvage & Lee 1987–89; dir: Burson-Marsteller 1989–91, Burson-Marsteller Financial 1989–91 (head int investor rels); dir Financial Public Relations Ltd 1991–; advsr to Republic of Lithuania under EU PHARE Prog Feb-Jul 1994, advsr to Republic of Macedonia on privatisation 1995–96; memb MENSA 1990; *Recreations* golf, shooting, theatre, tennis; *Clubs* MCC; *Style*— Anthony Warmington, Esq; ✉ Financial Public Relations Ltd, International Press Centre, 76 Shoe Lane, London EC4A 3JB (☎ 0171 353 8906, fax 0171 353 7550, e-mail Warmington@antwarm.demon.co.uk)

WARMINGTON, Sir (Marshall Denham) Malcolm; 4 Bt (UK 1908), of Pembridge Square, Royal Borough of Kensington; s of Sir Marshall George Clitheroe Warmington, 3 Bt (d 1995), and his 1 w, Mollie, *née* Kennard; *b* 5 Jan 1934; *Educ* privately; *Heir* half-bro, David Marshall Warmington b 14 Feb 1944; *Style*— Sir Malcolm Warmington, Bt; ✉ c/o David Warmington, Esq, 139 Highlands Heath, London SW15 3TZ

WARNE, (Ernest) John David; CB (1982); s of John Warne (d 1954), and Amelia, *née* Hawking (d 1928); *b* 4 Dec 1926; *Educ* Univ of London (BA); *m* 1953, Rena (d 1995), da of Col Vladimir Vasilievich Alexandrov (d 1937), of Leningrad (now St Petersburg), Russia; 3 s (Anthony, Steven, Richard); *Career* univ lectr 1951–53; Civil Service: princ 1953–64, asst sec 1964–72, under sec 1972–79, dep sec 1979–82; sec ICAEW 1982–90; conslt 1990–; *Recreations* reading, collecting prints, theatre, walking; *Style*— John Warne, Esq, CB; ✉ 16 Carlton Mews, Wells, Somerset BA5 1SG (☎ and fax 01749 671286)

WARNER, Deborah; da of Roger Harold Metford Warner, of Oxfordshire, and Ruth Ernestine, *née* Hurcombe; *b* 12 May 1959; *Educ* Sidcot Sch Somerset, St Clare's Coll Oxford, Central Sch of Speech and Drama London; *Career* artistic dir Kick Theatre Co 1980–86, res dir RSC 1987–89, assoc dir RNT 1990–; Chevalier de l'Ordre des Arts et des Lettres (France) 1992; *Productions* Kick Theatre Co: The Good Person of Sichuan 1980, Woyzeck 1981 and 1982, The Tempest 1983, Measure for Measure 1984, King Lear 1985, Coriolanus 1986; RSC: Titus Andronicus (Best Dir Olivier Awards, Best Dir Evening Standard Awards 1989) 1987, King John 1988, Electra 1988 and 1990; RNT: The Good Person of Sichuan 1989, King Lear 1990, Richard II 1995–96; other credits incl: Hedda Gabler 1991 (Abbey Theatre Dublin and Playhouse Theatre London, Best Director and Best Prodn Olivier Awards 1992 (TV version 1992)), Wozzeck (Opera North) 1993 and 1996, Coriolan (Salzburg Festival) 1993–94, Footfalls (The Garrick) 1994, Don Giovanni (Glyndebourne Festival Opera and Channel 4) 1994 and 1995, The Waste Land (Fitzroy Prodns) 1995–96, The St Pancras Project (LIFT Festival) 1995; *Recreations* travelling; *Style*— Ms Deborah Warner; ✉ c/o Conway van Gelder Robinson Ltd, 18–21 Jermyn Street, London SW1Y 6HP (☎ 0171 287 0077, fax 0171 287 1940)

WARNER, Sir Edward Redston; KCMG (1965, CMG 1955), OBE (1948); s of Sir George Redston Warner, KCVO, CMG (d 1978), and Margery Catherine, *née* Nicol (d 1963); *b* 23 March 1911; *Educ* Oundle, King's Coll Cambridge; *m* 1943, Grizel Margaret, da of Col Paul Robert Clerk Rattray, CBE, JP, DL, RE (d 1937); 3 s (Paul (now Ramsay of Bamff), Nigel, Alan), 1 da (Elizabeth (Mrs Berry)); *Career* FO 1935–70: served Athens, dep UK delegate OEEC Paris 1956–59, min Tokyo 1959–62, ambass Cameroon 1963–66, UK rep Econ and Social Cncl UN 1966–67, ambass Tunisia 1968–70, memb Staff Appeals Bd OECD Paris 1971–83; pt/t ed Historical Manuscripts Cmmn 1971–74; Liveryman Worshipful Co of Grocers; *Clubs* Utd Oxford and Cambridge; *Style*— Sir Edward Warner, KCMG, OBE; ✉ Old Royal Oak, Blockley, Glos GL56 9EX

WARNER, Francis Robert Le Plastrier; s of Rev Hugh Compton Warner (d 1955), of Epsom, Surrey, and Nancy Le Plastrier, *née* Owen (d 1992); *b* 21 Oct 1937; *Educ* Christ's Hosp, London Coll of Music, St Catharine's Coll Cambridge (BA, MA), Univ of Oxford (MA); *m* 1, 1958 (m dis 1972), Mary, *née* Hall; 2 da (Georgina b 1962, Lucy b 1967); m 2, 2 July 1983, Penelope Anne, da of John Hugh Davis, of Blagdon, nr Bristol; 1 s (Benedict b 1988), 1 da (Miranda b 1985); *Career* poet and dramatist; Univ of Cambridge: supervisor St Catharine's Coll 1959–63, staff tutor in Eng, memb Bd of Extramural Studies 1963–65; Univ of Oxford: Lord White fell in Eng lit and sr Eng tutor St Peter's Coll 1965–, fell librarian 1966–76, univ lectr 1967–, dean of degrees 1984–, vice-master 1987–89, pro-proctor Univ of Oxford 1989–90 and 1996–97; Messing Int Award (USA) for Distinguished Contribs to Lit 1972, awarded Silver medal Benemerenti of the Constantinian Order of St George (Italy) 1990, elected academico correspondente estrangeiro Portuguese Academia de Letras e Artes 1993; memb Southern Arts Drama Panel Arts Cncl of GB 1976–78 (chm 1978–79 and 1979–80); *Poetry* Perennia (1962), Early Poems (1964), Experimental Sonnets (1965), Madrigals (1967), The Poetry of Francis Warner (USA, 1970), Lucca Quartet (1975), Morning Vespers (1980), Spring Harvest (1981), Epithalamium (1983), Collected Poems 1960–84 (1985), Nightingales: Poems 1985–96 (1996); *Plays* Maquettes, a trilogy of one-act plays (1972); Requiem: Pt 1 Lying Figures (1972), Pt 2 Killing Time (1976), Pt 3 Meeting Ends (1974); A Conception of Love (1978), Light Shadows (1980), Moving Reflections (1983), Living Creation (1985), Healing Nature: The Athens of Pericles (1988), Byzantium (1990), Virgil and Caesar (1993), Agora: an Epic (1994), King Francis 1st (1995), Goethe's Weimar (1997); *Editor* Eleven Poems by Edmund Blunden (1965), Garland (1968), Studies in the Arts (1968); *Recreations* children, cathedral music, travel; *Clubs* Athenaeum; *Style*— Francis Warner, Esq; ✉ St Peter's College, Oxford OX1 2DL (☎ 01865 278 900)

WARNER, Eur Ing Prof Sir Frederick Edward; kt (1968); s of Frederick Warner; *b* 31 March 1910; *Educ* Bancroft's Sch, UCL; *m* 1, Margaret Anderson McCrea; 2 s, 2 da; m 2, Barbara Reynolds; *Career* chemical engr; Cremer & Warner: joined 1956, sr ptnr 1963–80; visiting prof: Bartlett Sch of Architecture UCL 1970–83, Imperial Coll London 1970–78 and 1993–, Essex Univ 1983–; chm London Univ Sch of Pharmacy 1971–78, pro chllr Open Univ 1974–79, pres Br Standards Inst 1980–83 (formerly chm Exec Bd and dep pres); memb Ct Essex Univ; fell UCL 1967; Hon DUniv: Open Univ 1980, Essex 1992; Hon DSc: Aston 1970, Cranfield 1978, Heriot-Watt 1978, Newcastle 1979; Hon DTech Bradford 1969; hon fell UMIST; medal Insinöö-riliitto Finland 1969, Leverhulme medal Royal Soc 1978, Buchanan medal 1982, environment medal Tech Inspectorate of the Rheinland 1984, Gerard Piel award 1991, World Fedn of Engrg Orgns medal 1993; Hon FRSC, Hon FICE, Hon FIChemE; FRS 1976, FEng 1977, FIMechE; *Books* Problems in Chemical Engineering Design (with J M Coulson, 1949), Technology Today (ed de Bono, 1971), Standards in the Engineering Industries (NEDO, 1977), Risk Assessment (Royal Soc, 1983 and 1992), Radioecology after Chernobyl (ed with R M Harrison, 1992); papers on quality assurance, Kuwait oil fires, nuclear winter, underground gasification of coal, air and water pollution, contracts, planning, risks and safety, professional and continuous education; *Clubs* Athenaeum; *Style*— Eur Ing Prof Sir Frederick Warner, FEng, FRS; ✉ Univ of Essex, Wivenhoe Park, Colchester CO4 3SQ (☎ 01206 873370, fax 01206 873370)

WARNER, Sir Gerald Chierici; KCMG (1995, CMG 1984); s of Howard Warner and Elizabeth, *née* Chierici-Kendall; *b* 27 Sept 1931; *Educ* Univ of Oxford (BA); *m* 1956, Mary Wynne Davies; 2 da, 1 s (decd); *Career* HM Dip Serv: 3 sec Peking 1956–58, 2 sec Rangoon 1960–61, 1 sec Warsaw 1964–66 and Geneva 1966–68, cnsllr Kuala Lumpur 1974–76, cnsllr FCO 1976–90; memb Police Complaints Authy 1990–91, intelligence co-ordinator Cabinet Office 1991–96; *Style*— Sir Gerald Warner, KCMG; ✉ c/o Cabinet Office, 70 Whitehall, London SW1 2AS

WARNER, James Royston; s of Peter John Warner, of Broadway, Worcs, and Joan Emily May, *née* Hodge; *b* 27 Aug 1948; *Educ* Prince Henry's GS Evesham, Gonville and Caius Coll Cambridge (MA); *m* 23 May 1992, Melissa, da of Ronald Brooks, of Tollerton; 1 da (Chloe Jane Brooks b 15 July 1985); *Career* industl engr British Leyland 1970–73; Mars Ltd: mgmnt servs mangr 1973–75, distribution mangr 1975–78, materials and purchasing mangr 1978–80, factory mangr 1980–82; Coopers & Lybrand: conslt 1982–85, ptnr 1985–, practice ldr Manufacturing and Logistics (Europe) 1990 (head (UK) 1988), worldwide co-ldr Supply Chain Management Practice 1993; fell: Inst of Logistics, Br Inst of Prodn and Inventory Control; *Recreations* music, walking on Dartmoor, cooking, spending time with my family; *Style*— James Warner, Esq; ✉ Coopers & Lybrand, 1 Embankment Place, London WC2N 6NN (☎ 0171 213 4637, fax 0171 213 2407, mobile 0850 988212)

WARNER, Sir Jean-Pierre Frank Eugene; kt (1981); s of Frank Cloudesley ffolliott Warner, and Louise Marie Blanche, *née* Gouet; *b* 24 Sept 1924; *Educ* Sainte Croix de Neuilly, Ecole des Roches, Harrow, Trinity Coll Cambridge; *m* 1950, Sylvia Frances, da of Sir Ernest Goodale, CBE, MC; 2 da; *Career* serv WWII Rifle Bde; called to the Bar Lincoln's Inn 1950; jr counsel: Restrictive Trading Agreements Registrar 1961–64, Treasury (Chancery) 1964–72; QC 1972, advocate gen European Communities Ct of Justice 1973–81, vice pres UK Assoc European Law 1975–83 (pres 1983–89), High Ct judge (Chancery) 1981–94, judge of Restrictive Practices Ct 1982–94; master of the walks Lincoln's Inn 1982, keeper of the Black Book 1983, dean of the Chapel 1984, treas 1985; former cncllr Kensington and Chelsea; former dir Warner & Sons; Liveryman Worshipful Co of Weavers; Hon LLD: Univ of Exeter 1983, Univ of Leicester 1984, Univ of Edinburgh 1987; *Style*— Sir Jean-Pierre Warner; ✉ 32 Abingdon Villas, London W8 6BX (☎ 0171 937 7023)

WARNER, Prof John Oliver; s of Henry Paul Warner (d 1992), and Ursula, *née* Troplowitz, of London; *b* 19 July 1945; *Educ* The Lawrence Sherrif Sch Rugby, Univ of Sheffield Med Sch (MB ChB, MD, DCH, Pleasance prize in paediatrics, FRCP 1986); *m* 1990, Dr Jill Amanda Warner, da of Maurice Halliday; 2 da (Olivia b 26 May 1991, Abigail b 21 Aug 1994); *Career* jr hosp posts Sheffield 1968–72; Hosp for Sick Children Great Ormond St: registrar 1972–74, res fell 1974–77, sr registrar 1977–80; conslt paediatric chest physician Royal Brompton Nat Heart & Lung Hosp (jt hosp and acad appt with Nat Heart & Lung Inst) 1980, subsequently sr lectr then reader in paediatrics Univ of London until 1990, prof of child health Univ of Southampton 1990–; assoc ed Thorax; memb Editorial Bd: Clinical and Experimental Allergy, Paediatric Allergy and Immunology, Paediatric Pulmonology; fndr chm Cystic Fibrosis Holiday Fund Charity 1986–90, memb Exec Ctee Br Allergy Fndn, hon conslt Pilgrims Sch (Invalid Children's Aid nationwide nat sch for children with asthma and eczema); memb: Br Paediatric Assoc 1976, RSM 1976, Br Soc for Allergy and Clinical Immunology 1979 (former sec), Br Thoracic Soc 1983, American Thoracic Soc 1992, Euro Respiratory Soc 1991 (head of Paediatric Assembly 1993–); *Publications* Childhood Asthma: a guide for parents and children (with S J Goldsworthy, 1981, 1982 and 1983), Scoliosis: Prevention (proceedings of Phillips Zorab symposium, 1983), Help for the New Cystic Fibrosis Family (1988), Eczema in the Home (1988), British Medical Bulletin (scientific ed, 1992), A Colour Atlas of Paediatric Allergy (with W F Jackson, 1994); also author of over 200 published papers; *Recreations* cricket, horse riding; *Clubs* MCC; *Style*— Prof John Warner; ✉ Cannizaro, 40 Wilderness Heights, West End, Southampton SO18 3PS (☎ 01703 470600); Department of Child Health, University of Southampton Clinical Medical School, Southampton General Hospital, Level G, Centre Block, Southampton SO16 6YD (☎ 01703 796160, fax 01703 796378)

WARNER, Marina Sarah (Mrs John Dewe Mathews); da of Col Esmond Pelham Warner, TD (d 1982), of Cambridge, and Emilia, *née* Terzulli; *b* 9 Nov 1946; *Educ* Lady Margaret Hall Oxford (MA); *m* 1, 31 Jan 1972 (m dis 1980), Hon William Hartley Hume Shawcross, *qv*, s of Baron Shawcross, *qv*; 1 s (Conrad Hartley Pelham b 1977); m 2, 16 Dec 1981, John Piers Dewe Mathews, s of Denys Cosmo Dewe Mathews (d 1986), of London; *Career* writer; Getty Scholar Getty Center for the History of Art and the Humanities 1987–88, Tinbergen prof Erasmus Univ Rotterdam 1991, Reith lectr 1994; visiting prof: Queen Mary and Westfield Coll London 1994–, Univ of Ulster 1994–95, Univ of York 1996, Mellon prof of history of art Univ of Pittsburgh 1997; Whitney J Oates fell Princeton 1996; memb: Advsy Bd Royal Mint to 1993, Mgmnt Ctee Nat Cncl for One Parent Families, Advsy Cncl Br Library, Arts Cncl Literature Panel, Exec Ctee Charter 88 1993; Hon DLitt: Univ of Exeter 1995, Sheffield Hallam Univ 1995, Univ of York 1997; FRSL 1985; *Books* The Dragon Empress (1972), Alone of All Her Sex: The Myth and the Cult of the Virgin Mary (1976), Queen Victoria's Sketchbook (1980), Joan of Arc: The Image of Female Heroism (1981), Monuments and Maidens: The Allegory of the Female Form (1985), Into the Dangerous World: Childhood and its Costs (1991), L'Atalante (1993), Managing Monsters: Six Myths of Our Time (Reith lectures, 1994), Wonder Tales (ed, 1994), From the Beast to the Blonde: On Fairy Tales and Their Tellers (1995); fiction: In A Dark Wood (1977), The Skating Party (1983), The Lost Father (1988), Indigo (1992), The Mermaids in the Basement (short stories, 1993); children's books: The Impossible Day (1981), The Impossible Night (1981), The Impossible Bath (1982), The Impossible Rocket (1982), The Wobbly Tooth (1984); juvenile: The Crack in the Teacup (1979); libretti: The Queen of Sheba's Legs (1994), In the House of Crossed Desires (1996); contrib: Times Literary Supplement, Washington Post, London Review of Books, Independent, Independent on Sunday, New York Times Book Review, Times Higher Ed; *Recreations* travel, looking at pictures; *Style*— Miss Marina Warner; ✉ c/o Rogers, Coleridge and White, 20 Powis Mews, London W11 1JN (☎ 0171 221 3717)

WARNER, Norman Reginald; s of Albert Henry Edwin Warner, and Laura Edith, *née* Bennett; *b* 8 Sept 1940; *Educ* Dulwich, Univ of Calif Berkley (MA, Harkness fell), Nuffield Coll Oxford (Gwilym Gibbon fell); *m* 1 (m dis 1981), Anne Lesley; 2 s (Andrew Simon b 1967, Joel James Stephen b 1981), 1 da (Justine Emma b 1969); m 2, Suzanne Elizabeth; *Career* DHSS: various posts concerned with NHS 1960–74, principal private sec to Sec of State for Social Services 1974–76, asst sec Supplementary Benefit 1976–79, asst sec Operational Planning 1979–81, regnl controller Wales and SW Region 1981–83, under sec Supplementary Benefit and Housing Benefit 1984–85; dir Social Services Kent County Cncl 1985–91, chm City and East London Family Services Authy 1991–94, md Warner Consultancy and Training Services, chm National Inquiry into Children's Homes 1992, memb Local Govt Cmmn 1995–96, sr policy advsr to Shadow Home Sec 1996–; sr res fell in Euro social welfare and chm Euro Inst of Social Servs Univ of Kent; chm: The Residential Forum, Royal Philanthropic Soc 1993–; tstee Leonard Cheshire Fndn and MacIntyre Care 1994–, memb Assoc of Dirs of Social Services 1985–; FRSA; *Recreations* walking, reading, cinema, theatre; *Style*— Norman Warner, Esq; ✉ 8 College Gardens, Dulwich, London SE21 7BE (☎ 0181 693 8083); The Residential Forum, National Institute for Social Work, 5 Tavistock Place, London WC1H 9SN (☎ 0171 387 9681)

WARNER, Peter Mark; s of Dr Marcel Mark Warner, of Weybridge, Surrey, and late Birthe Johanna Warner; *b* 21 June 1959; *Educ* Woking County GS, Kingston Poly Business Sch (BA Hons); *m* Carolyn Frances, *née* Rice; *Career* account exec Tim Arnold and Associates (sales promotion agency) 1981–83, client services dir IMP Ltd 1989–93 (joined as account exec 1983), ptnr Howell Henry Chaldecott Lury and Partners 1993–; *Recreations* gardening, fell walking, motorcycling, canal restoration; *Clubs* The Little House; *Style*— Peter Warner, Esq; ✉ Howell Henry Chaldecott Lury and Partners, Kent House, 14–17 Market Place, Great Titchfield Street, London W1N 7AJ (☎ 0171 436 3333, fax 0171 436 2677)

WARNER, Philip Courtenay Thomas; s and h of Sir (Edward Courtenay) Henry Warner, 3 Bt, and Jocelyn Mary Beevor; *b* 3 April 1951; *Educ* Eton; *m* 1982, Penelope Anne, yr da of John Lack Elmer (d 1973); 1 s, 4 da; *Career* dir: Lewin & Warner Ltd, Warner Estate Hldgs plc; *Recreations* power-boating, sailing; *Style*— Philip Warner, Esq; ✉ 6 Holland Park Mews, London W11 3TG

WARNER, Simon Metford; s of Roger Harold Metford Warner, of Burford, Oxford, and Ruth Ernestine, *née* Hurcombe; *b* 12 Jan 1951; *Educ* Downs Sch Colwall Herefordshire, Leighton Park Sch Reading, Churchill Coll Cambridge (MA), Univ of Bristol; *m* 1974, Judith, da of Capt W Adams; 1 s (Leo b 1980); *Career* staff photographer Sotheby's 1973–75, freelance photographer 1975–; contrib to many books incl: Best Views of Britain (Geoffrey Young), Wild Britain (Douglas Botting), Brontë Country (ed by Glenda Leeming), Pennine Landscapes (with Judith Warner, 1984), South Pennines and Brontë Country (with Judith Warner, 1984); illustrator of: Pennine Way North (1989), Pennine Way South (1990), These Lonely Mountains (1987), Peddar's Way and Norfolk Coast Path (1991), Wolds Way (1982), Made in Yorkshire (1992), The Lake District (1995); exhibitions incl: Leeds Playhouse Gallery, Cliffe Castle Art Gallery, Keighley (Bradford Museums) 1988, Grassington Festival; *Recreations* cycling, theatre; *Style*— Simon Warner, Esq; ✉ Whitestone Farm, Stanbury, Keighley, W Yorks BD22 0JW (☎ 01535 644644)

WARNFORD-DAVIS, (Karelyn) Mandy; da of John David Warnford-Davis, and Ruth Grace, *née* Clift; *b* 19 June 1954; *Educ* Heathfield Sch Ascot Berks, St Hugh's Coll Oxford (BA); *m* 1993, Richard Russell; 1 s, 1 da; *Career* admitted slr 1979; slr Titmuss Sainer and Webb 1979–82, ptnr Rowe and Maw 1985– (joined 1982); non-exec dir Hodder Headline plc 1995–; memb Law Soc; *Recreations* opera, cinema, music, travel; *Style*— Miss Mandy Warnford-Davis; ✉ Rowe & Maw, 20 Black Friars Lane, London EC4V 6HD (☎ 0171 248 4282, fax 0171 248 2009, telex 262787 MAWLAW G)

WARNOCK, Hon Felix Geoffrey; er s of Sir Geoffrey Warnock (d 1995), and Baroness Warnock (Life Peer), *qv*; *b* 18 Jan 1952; *Educ* Winchester, Royal Coll of Music (ARCM); *m* 27 Aug 1975, Juliet, da of Arthur Robert Lehwalder, of Seattle, Washington, USA; 1 s (Daniel Arthur Richard b 1985), 2 da (Eleanor Denise b 1982, Polly Patricia b 1986); *Career* bassoonist: Acad of St Martin-in-the-Fields 1975–89, Albion Ensemble 1980–92, Acad of Ancient Music 1981–89; prof of bassoon Trinity Coll of Music 1985–90; gen mangr Orchestra of the Age of Enlightenment 1989–94, dir of early music RAM 1993–95, gen mangr The English Concert 1995–; memb Musicians' Union; *Recreations* cricket, golf; *Style*— The Hon Felix Warnock; ✉ 5 Kingsbridge Road, London W10 6PU (☎ 0181 969 5738); The English Concert, 8 St George's Terrace, London NW1 8XJ (☎ 0171 911 0905, fax 0171 911 0904)

WARNOCK, Baroness (Life Peer UK 1985), of Weeke in the City of Winchester; Dame (Helen) Mary Warnock; DBE (1984); da of Archibald Edward Wilson (d 1924), of Winchester, and Ethel Mary (d 1952), eldest da of Sir Felix Otto Schuster, 1 Bt; *b* 14 April 1924; *Educ* St Swithun's Winchester, Lady Margaret Hall Oxford (MA, BPhil); *m* 1949, Sir Geoffrey Warnock (d 1995), s of James Warnock, OBE, MD (d 1953), of Leeds; 2 s (Hon Felix Geoffrey b 1952, *qv*, Hon James Marcus Alexander b 1953), 3 da (Hon Kathleen (Kitty) b 1950, Hon Stephana (Fanny) (Hon Mrs Branson) b 1956, Hon (Grizel) Maria (Hon Mrs Jenkins) b 1961); *Career* fell and tutor in philosophy

St Hugh's Coll Oxford 1949–66, former headmistress Oxford HS; former memb SSRC, chm Ctee of Enquiry into Human Fertilisation, former memb IBA; chm: Advsy Ctee on Animal Experiments, Ctee of Enquiry into Education of Handicapped; memb Royal Cmmn on Environmental Pollution 1979–85; Talbot Res fell LMH until 1976, FCP; mistress Girton Coll Cambridge 1985–91 (life fell); hon degrees: Open Univ, Essex, Melbourne, Bath, Exeter, Manchester, Glasgow, York, Warwick, Liverpool, London, St Andrews; *Books* Ethics Since 1900, Existentialism, Imagination, Schools of Thought, What Must We Teach? (with T Devlin), Education: A Way Forward, Memory, A Common Policy for Education, The Uses of Philosophy, Imagination and Time, Women Philosophers; *Recreations* gardening, music; *Style*— The Rt Hon the Lady Warnock, DBE; ✉ 3 Church Street, Great Bedwyn, nr Marlborough, Wilts SN8 3PE

WARRELL, Prof David Alan; s of Alan Theophilus Warrell, ISO, of Abingdon, and late Mildred Emma, *née* Hunt; *b* 6 Oct 1939; *Educ* Portsmouth GS, ChCh Oxford (MA, DM, BCh, DSc), St Thomas's Hosp Med Sch; *m* 11 Oct 1975, Mary Jean, da of George Prentice, of London; 2 da (Helen b 1981, Clare b 1985); *Career* lectr and conslt physician Royal Postgrad Med Sch London 1974–75, conslt physician Radcliffe Infirmary Oxford 1975–79, fell St Cross Coll Oxford 1977–, hon conslt physician Oxfordshire Health Authy 1979–, fndr dir Wellcome-Mahidol Univ of Oxford Tropical Med Prog Bangkok 1979–86, hon clinical dir Alistair Reid Venom Res Unit Liverpool Sch of Tropical Med 1983–, prof of tropical med and infectious diseases and dir Centre for Tropical Med Univ of Oxford 1987–; hon conslt in malariology to the Army 1989–, hon med advsr RGS 1994–; chm AIDS Therapeutic Trials Ctees MRC 1987–93; pres Br Venom Gp 1992–, pres elect Int Fedn for Tropical Med 1996 (vice pres 1992–96), vice pres Royal Soc of Tropical Med and Hygiene 1996–; WHO: conslt on malaria, rabies and snake bites, memb Steering Ctee for Chemotherapy of Malaria 1986–91, memb Expert Advsy Panel on Malaria 1989–; tstee Tropical Health and Educn Tst 1988–, patron Cambodia Tst 1991–; hon fell: Ceylon Coll of Physicians, Australasian Coll of Tropical Med, Australasian Soc for Infectious Diseases; FRCP, MRCS, FZS 1967; FRGS 1989; *Books* Rabies - The Facts (1986), Oxford Textbook of Medicine (1987, 3 edn 1996), Bruce-Chwatt's Essential Malariology (1993); *Recreations* music, hill walking, natural history, book collecting; *Style*— Prof David Warrell; ✉ Centre for Tropical Medicine, University of Oxford; John Radcliffe Hospital, Headington, Oxford OX3 9DU (☎ 01865 220968, fax 01865 220984, e-mail david.warrell@ndm.ox.ac.uk)

WARREN, Very Rev Alan Christopher; s of Arthur Henry Warren (d 1987), of Durdham Court, Bristol, and Gwendoline Catherine, *née* Hallett; *b* 27 June 1932; *Educ* Dulwich Coll, Corpus Christi Coll Cambridge (MA), Ridley Hall Theol Coll; *m* 24 Aug 1957, Sylvia Mary, da of Charles Edwin Matthews (d 1988), of West Wickham, Kent; 3 da (Susan Rachel b 1958, Catherine Linda b 1960, Helen Judith b 1963); *Career* curate: St Paul's Margate 1957–59, St Andrew's Plymouth 1959–62; chaplain Kelly Coll Tavistock 1962–64, vicar Holy Apostles' Leicester 1964–72, diocesan missioner Coventry 1972–78, hon canon Coventry Cathedral 1972–78, proctor in convocation 1977–78 and 1980–85, provost Leicester Cathedral 1978–92; memb Cathedral's Statutes Cmmns 1981–89, chm Leicester Cncl of Christians and Jews 1982–92; pres: Leicester Civic Soc 1984–92, Leicester Cncl of Churches 1982–92, Alleyn Club 1991–92; vice pres Leicester Bach Choir; tutor Norfolk Adult Educn 1993–, musical dir West Norfolk Singers; formerly MCC and minor counties cricketer; *Books* Putting it Across (1975), Dulwich Memories (1990); *organ prelude* Et Incarnatus Est (1979); *Recreations* music, golf, steam trains, cricket umpiring; *Clubs* Free Foresters, Hunstanton Golf; *Style*— The Very Rev the Emeritus Provost of Leicester; ✉ 9 Queen's Drive, Hunstanton, Norfolk PE36 6EY (☎ 01485 534533)

WARREN, Andrew David; s of Walter Warren, of Oxford, and Monica Joyce Warren; *b* 9 May 1944; *Educ* Royal GS High Wycombe, Wadham Coll Oxford (MA); *m* 27 Oct 1973, Joan Mary, da of Arthur Webb; 2 s (Paul b 1978, Ian b 1980), 1 da (Clare b 1976); *Career* Centrefile 1966–69; Deloitte Haskins & Sells: joined 1969, ptnr mgmnt consultancy 1975–79, ptnr i/c Computer Servs Div 1979–85, ptnr i/c Mgmnt Consultancy Div 1985–90; exec ptnr i/c Mgmnt Consultancy Coopers & Lybrand Deloitte (following merger) 1990–91, exec ptnr i/c Eastern Europe Coopers & Lybrand Europe 1991–; MBCS 1968, FIMC 1987; *Recreations* flying, sailing, theatre, photography; *Clubs* Le Micro; *Style*— Andrew Warren, Esq; ✉ 7 Arran Mews, Ealing, London W5 3QA (☎ 0181 992 0673); Coopers & Lybrand, 1 Embankment Place, London WC2N 6NN (☎ 0171 583 5000, fax 0171 213 2459, telex 887470)

WARREN, Sir (Brian) Charles Pennefather; 9 Bt (I 1784), of Warren's Court, Co Cork; s of Col Sir Thomas Warren, 8 Bt, CBE, DL (d 1961); *b* 4 June 1923; *Educ* Wellington; *m* 1976 (m dis 1983), Nicola Louise, da of Capt Edward de Lérisson Cazenove, of Great Dalby, Leics, and his w Grania (ggda of Sir John Kennedy, 1 Bt); *Heir* kinsman, Michael Blackley Warren b 1918; *Career* serv with 2 (Armoured) Bn Irish Gds 1941–45; *Style*— Sir Charles Warren, Bt; ✉ The Wilderness, Castle Oliver, Kilmallock, Co Limerick, Ireland

WARREN, Dr Graham Barry; s of Charles Graham Thomas Warren, and Joyce Thelma, *née* Roberts; *b* 25 Feb 1948; *Educ* Willesden Co GS, Pembroke Coll Cambridge (BA, MA, PhD); *m* 18 June 1966, Philippa Mary Adeline, da of Alexander Edward Temple-Cole (d 1981), of Shoreham, Kent; 4 da (Joanna b 5 Nov 1966, Eleanor b 20 Aug 1969, Katya b 13 Nov 1979, Alexandra b 7 Dec 1980); *Career* MRC jr res fell Nat Inst for Med Res London 1972–74, res fell Gonville and Caius Coll Cambridge and Stothert res fell of the Royal Soc Biochemistry Dept Univ of Cambridge 1975–77, sr scientist Euro Molecular Biology Lab Heidelberg W Germany (formerly gp ldr) 1977–85, prof and head of Dept of Biochemistry Univ of Dundee 1985–88, princ scientist Imperial Cancer Res Fund 1988–; memb Euro Molecular Biology Orgn; *Style*— Dr Graham Warren; ✉ 17 Grosvenor Rd, London N10 2DR (☎ 0181 444 5808); Imperial Cancer Research Fund, P O Box 123, Lincoln's Inn Fields, London WC2A 3PX (☎ 0171 269 3561)

WARREN, John; QC (1994); s of Frank Warren (d 1973), of Oldham, Lancs, and Dora, *née* Thomas (d 1985); *b* 25 Aug 1945; *Educ* Chadderton GS, Univ of Nottingham (LLB); *m* 17 Aug 1968, Anne, da of late James Henry Marlor; 1 s (James Quentin b 29 Sept 1974), 1 da (Laura Jane (twin)); *Career* called to the Bar Gray's Inn 1968, recorder Midland and Oxford Circuit 1993–; *Recreations* supporting Nottingham Forest FC, classical music (particularly opera); *Clubs* Nottingham and Notts United Services, Keyworth and Ruddington Rotary; *Style*— John Warren, Esq, QC; ✉ 1 High Pavement, Nottingham NG1 1HF (☎ 0115 941 8218, fax 0115 941 8240)

WARREN, John Anthony; *b* 11 June 1953; *Educ* Tiffin Sch, Univ of Bristol (BSc); *m* 1975, Anna; 2 s; *Career* Ernst & Young 1974–81; United Biscuits (Holdings) plc: chief accountant rising to fin dir UK, Int Sr Mgmnt Programme Harvard Busines Sch 1990, gp fin dir (main bd) 1990–, chief exec Asia Pacific 1995–; non-exec dir Rexam plc 1994–; ACA 1977; *Style*— John Warren, Esq; ✉ United Biscuits (Holdings) plc, Church Road, West Drayton UB7 7PR (☎ 01895 432100, fax 01895 448848)

WARREN, John Cecil Turnbull; s of Cecil George Warren (d 1971), and Jessie Eileen, *née* Parker; *b* 25 April 1931; *Educ* Collyer's Sch Horsham, Univ of Durham (BArch), Univ of Newcastle (MLitt); *m* 11 Sept 1957, Judith Boulton, da of Ernest Kershaw (d 1985); 1 s (Philip Heath b 1963), 1 da (Rebecca Jane b 1966); *Career* Pilot Offr RAF 1957; architect and town planner, fndr and sr ptnr Architectural and Planning Partnership (ret 1991), currently conslt to The Conservation Practice; hon fell Univ of York, exhibitor RA Summer Exhibitions; fndr tstee and hon architect Weald and Downland Open Air Museum Singleton Chichester (ret 1991), vice pres Chalkpits Museum Amberley; ARIBA 1959, FRTPI 1961, FSA 1981; *Books* Wealden Buildings (ed), Greek Mathematics and the Architects to Justinian I, Traditional Houses in Baghdad, Conservation in Baghdad, The History of Architecture by Sir Banister Fletcher (contrib, 18, 19 and 20 edns), The World's Great Architecture (ed Nuttgens), Architecture of the Islamic World (ed Michell), Edwardian Architecture (ed Service), Conservation and Rehabilitation of Buildings (ed Markus); contrib to: Architectural Review, Art and Archaeology Res Papers, Architectural Design, Industrial Archaeology; *Recreations* painting, writing, travelling, forestry; *Style*— John Warren, Esq, FSA; ✉ Parsons Farm, Coltstaple Lane, Horsham, W Sussex RH13 7BB (☎ 01403 730022); Consultant, The Conservation Practice, 19–23 Blackfriars Bridge Road, London SE1 8NY (☎ 0171 902 2210, fax 0171 902 2211)

WARREN, Eur Ing Sir Kenneth Robin; kt (1994); s of Edward Charles Warren (d 1987); *b* 15 Aug 1926; *Educ* Midsomer Norton, Aldenham, De Havilland Aeronautical Tech Sch, Univ of London (Fulbright scholar USA); *m* 1962, Elizabeth Anne, da of Russell Chamberlain; 1 s, 2 da; *Career* aero and electronics engr; De Havilland Aircraft 1947–51, BOAC 1951–57, Smiths Industries Ltd 1957–60, Elliott Automation Ltd 1960–69; currently chm Warren Woodfield Assocs; dir: Lockheed-Martin Defence Systems Ltd, Luther Pendragon Ltd; chm: Merchants Ltd, Electronic Share Information Ltd, Computer Security Advsy Bd LSE; cncllr Paddington BC 1953–65, Parly candidate (C) St Pancras N 1964; MP (C): Hastings 1970–83, Hastings and Rye 1983–92; chm: Parly Ctee on Offshore Technol 1974–75, Cons Parly Aviation Ctee 1974–76, Western European Union Science, Technol and Aerospace Ctee 1977–80; memb Select Ctee on Science and Technol, PPS to Rt Hon Sir Keith Joseph as Sec of State for Industry 1979–81 and for Educn and Sci 1981–83; chm: Select Ctee on Trade and Indust 1983–92, Br-Soviet Parly Gp 1986–92; Freeman City of London; Liveryman: Worshipful Co of Coachmakers and Harness Makers, Worshipful Co of Air Pilots and Navigators; fell Univ of Exeter 1994–; Eur Ing, CEng, FRAeS, FCIT, FRSA; *Clubs* Athenaeum, Garrick, Special Forces; *Style*— Eur Ing Sir Kenneth Warren; ✉ Woodfield House, Goudhurst, Kent TN17 2NN (☎ 01580 211590)

WARREN, Maurice Eric; s of Frederick Leonard Warren, and Winifred Warren (d 1936); *b* 21 June 1933; *Educ* St Brendan's Coll Bristol; *m* 21 Aug 1954, Molly, da of Herbert Slater, of Bristol; 1 s (Stephen), 1 da (Sally (Mrs Wilkinson)); *Career* RAF 1951–53; md: Dalgety Agriculture Ltd 1976–81, Dalgety UK Ltd 1981–87; Dalgety plc: md 1987–89, chief exec 1989–93, chm 1993–96; chm: South Western Electricity plc 1993–95, CAMAS plc 1994–, Great Western Hotels Ltd 1996–; FCCA; *Recreations* golf; *Style*— Maurice Warren, Esq; ✉ Dalgety plc, 100 George St, London W1H 5RH (☎ 0171 486 0200, fax 0171 493 0892, telex 23874); Great Western Holdings Ltd, Milford House, 1 Milford Street, Swindon SN1 1HL (☎ 01793 499400, fax 01793 499451)

WARREN, Michael Christopher; s of Joseph Henry Warren (d 1971), and Helen, *née* Ashworth (d 1946); *b* 30 Dec 1944; *Educ* Palmers Sch for Boys Thurrock, Central Sch of Speech and Drama; *m* 1, 1969 (m dis 1978), Kathleen Mary, *née* Reindorp; m 2, 1992 Lindsay Kathlyn, da of William Heathcote Roberts; 1 da (Rebecca Roberts-Warren b 19 Aug 1983); *Career* journalist Essex and Thurrock Gazette 1963–65, various theatre work (incl 69 Theatre Co Manchester) 1969–71, res exec and assoc dir Research Services Ltd 1971–81, head of Survey Unit Consumers' Assoc 1981–86, dir of res COI 1986–93, DG Market Research Soc 1993– (memb 1975–, memb Professional Standards Ctee 1988–91, memb Educn Ctee 1992–93); memb Research Resources and Trg Bds ESRC 1994–; fndr memb Social Research Assoc; author of various articles on research techniques and mgmnt; FRSA 1995; *Recreations* jazz, cricket, competitive model aviation; *Clubs* Ronnie Scott's, Harlequins; *Style*— Michael Warren, Esq; ✉ Market Research Society, 15 Northburgh Street, London EC1V 0AH (☎ 0171 490 4911)

WARREN, Nicholas Roger; QC (1993); s of Roger Warren (d 1991), and Muriel Reeves; *b* 20 May 1945; *Educ* Bryanston, Univ Coll Oxford (scholar, BA); *m* 1, 1979 (m dis 1989); 2 s, 1 da; m 2, 1995; *Career* called to the Bar Middle Temple 1972 (Astbury scholar); asst recorder 1995–; *Recreations* music, sailing; *Style*— Nicholas Warren, Esq, QC; ✉ Wilberforce Chambers, 8 New Square, Lincoln's Inn, London WC2A 3QP (☎ 0171 306 0102, fax 0171 306 0096)

WARREN, Ven Norman Leonard; s of Arthur Henry Warren (d 1987), and Gwendoline Catharine, *née* Hallett; *b* 19 July 1934; *Educ* Dulwich, CCC Cambridge (MA), Ridley Hall Cambridge; *m* 15 April 1961, Yvonne Sheather; 3 s (Andrew Mark b 1962, Philip James b 1966, David John Chi Hanh b 1970), 2 da (Ruth Elizabeth b 1963, Sarah Rachel b 1968); *Career* RN 1953–55; vicar St Paul's Leamington Spa 1963–77, rector Morden Surrey 1977–89, rural dean Merton 1986–89, archdeacon Rochester 1989–; memb: Gen Synod of the C of E 1989–95, Cncl Royal Sch of Church Music; pres Music in Worship Tst; *Books* Journey into Life (1963), The Way Ahead (1965), Directions (1968), Signposts (1974), What's The Point? (1986), A Certain Faith (1988), The Path of Peace (1988), Is God There? (1990), Why Believe (1993), Responsorial Psalms; *Recreations* music, walking; *Style*— The Ven the Archdeacon of Rochester; ✉ The Archdeaconry, Rochester, Kent ME1 1SX (☎ 01634 842527)

WARREN, Prof Peter Michael; s of Arthur George Warren (d 1947), and Alison Joan, *née* White (d 1942); *b* 23 June 1938; *Educ* Sandbach Sch, Llandovery Coll, UCNW Bangor (BA), Corpus Christi Coll Cambridge (BA, MA, PhD); *m* 18 June 1966, Elizabeth Margaret, da of Percy Halliday, of Beaconsfield, Bucks; 1 s (Damian b 1984), 1 da (Diktynna b 1979); *Career* reader in Aegean archaeology Univ of Birmingham 1976 (lectr 1972–74, sr lectr 1974–76); Univ of Bristol: prof of ancient history and classical archaeology 1977–, dean Faculty of Arts 1988–90, pro-vice-chllr 1991–95, fell 1995–96; visiting prof Univ of Minnesota 1981, Geddes-Harrower prof of Greek art and archaeology Univ of Aberdeen 1986–87, Félix Neubergh lectr Univ of Göteborg 1986; vice pres Cncl Bristol and Glos Archaeological Soc 1989–93 (vice chm 1980–81, chm 1981–83); pres: Wotton-under-Edge Historical Soc 1986–90, Bristol Anglo-Hellenic Cultural Soc 1987–, Birmingham and Midlands Branch Classical Assoc 1996–97; chm Managing Ctee Br Sch Athens 1979–83 (memb 1973–77, 1978–79, 1986–90, 1994–), memb Cncl Soc for the Promotion of Hellenic Studies 1978–81; hon fell Archaeological Soc of Athens 1987, corresponding fell Soc for Cretan Historical Studies 1992; FSA 1973; *Books* Minoan Stone Vases (1969), Myrtos An Early Bronze Age Settlement in Crete (1972), The Aegean Civilizations (1975 and 1989), Minoan Religion as Ritual Action (1988), Aegean Bronze Age Chronology (with V Hankey, 1989); *Recreations* contemporary Br politics, Manchester Utd, history of Mediterranean botany; *Style*— Prof Peter Warren, FSA; ✉ Claremont House, 5 Merlin Haven, Wotton-under-Edge, Glos GL12 7BA (☎ 01453 842 290); Department of Archaeology, University of Bristol, 11 Woodland Rd, Bristol BS8 1TB (☎ 0117 928 8255/ 928 8877)

WARREN, Dr Peter Tolman; s of late Hugh Alan Warren, OBE, of Sanderstead, Surrey, and late Florence Christine, *née* Tolman; *b* 20 Dec 1937; *Educ* Whitgift Sch S Croydon, Queens' Coll Cambridge (BA, MA, PhD); *m* 9 Sept 1961, Angela Mary, da of late Thomas Henry Curtis, of Sanderstead, Surrey; 2 s (Simon b 1965, Timothy b 1970), 1 da (Katherine b 1967); *Career* princ scientific offr Br Geological Survey (previously Inst Geological Sci/Geological Survey & Museum) 1962–72 (formerly scientific offr), princ scientific offr Cabinet Office Whitehall 1972–76, safety advsr NERC 1976–77, exec sec Royal Soc of London 1985– (dep exec sec 1977–85); vice-pres: Geological Soc 1992–96, Parly and Scientific Ctee 1995–; memb Cncl GPDST 1989–, govr Croydon HS for Girls; FGS, ChGeol; *Books* Geology of the Country around Rhyl and Denbigh (jtly,

1984); *Recreations* gardening, geology; *Clubs* Athenaeum; *Style*— Dr Peter Warren; ✉ Flat One, 6 Carlton House Terrace, London SW1Y 5AG (☎ 0171 839 5260); The Royal Society, 6 Carlton House Terrace, London SW1Y 5AG (☎ 0171 839 5561, fax 0171 930 2170, telex 917876)

WARREN, Prof Raymond Henry Charles; s of Arthur Henry Warren (d 1987), and Gwendoline, *née* Hallett; *b* 7 Nov 1928; *Educ* Bancroft's Sch, Corpus Christi Coll Cambridge (MA, DMus); *m* 9 April 1953, Roberta, da of Frederick Smith (d 1985); 3 s (Timothy b 1954, Christopher b 1956, Benedict b 1960), 1 da (Clare b 1965); *Career* prof of music: Queen's Univ Belfast 1967–72 (lectr 1955–67), Univ of Bristol 1972–94; princ compositions: The Passion (1962), Symphony No 1 (1965), Symphony No 2 (1969), Symphony No 3 (1996), In the Beginning (Opera 1982), Oratorio Continuing Cities (1989); chm Bristol Chamber Choir; memb and former chm: Incorporated Soc Musicians (Bristol Centre); emeritus prof Univ of Bristol 1994–; memb: Composers' Guild, ISM, Assoc of Professional Composers; FRSA; *Recreations* walking; *Style*— Prof Raymond Warren; ✉ 9 Cabot Rise, Portishead, Bristol BS20 9NX (☎ 01275 844289)

WARREN, Robert John; s of Dr John Nettleton Warren, of Arundel, Sussex, and Mary, *née* Clayton; *b* 29 Dec 1935; *Educ* Lancing, Brighton Coll of Tech and Arts; *m* 1962, Madeline Lee, da of Fred Redfearn; 1 da (b 4 July 1965), 1 s (b 4 Jan 1968); *Career* schoolmaster 1955, Nat Serv RNVR Sub Lt 1955–57, reporter Hampshire Chronicle 1957–58, reporter Coventry Evening Telegraph 1958–60, reporter/sub ed Chronicle Herald Halifax Canada 1960–61, sub ed Montreal Star 1961–63; News of the World: reporter 1963–71, dep news ed 1971–74, news ed 1974–93, asst ed 1985–93, assoc ed 1993–95, exec ed 1995–; *Recreations* golf, tennis, squash, gardening; *Clubs* National Liberal, Wig and Pen; *Style*— Robert Warren, Esq; ✉ The News of the World, 1 Virginia Street, London E1 9XR (☎ 0171782 4000)

WARREN, Dr Roderic Ellis; s of Ronald Thomas Warren (d 1970), of Tadworth, Surrey, and Mabel Elsie Warren; *b* 24 Oct 1948; *Educ* Whitgift Sch Croydon, Gonville and Caius Coll Cambridge (MA, MB BChir), Westminster Hosp Med Sch; *m* 6 Sept 1976, Pamela Rose, da of Frederick John Taft (d 1976), of Canterbury; 1 s (Charles), 2 da (Elizabeth, Eleanor); *Career* conslt microbiologist Addenbrooke's Hosp 1976–93, assoc lectr Univ of Cambridge 1977–93, dir Public Health Laboratory Royal Shrewsbury Hosp 1993–95, gp dir Public Health Laboratory Service Midlands 1995–; treas Br Soc for Antimicrobial Chemotherapy; FRCPath 1989; *Recreations* occasional; *Style*— Dr Roderic Warren; ✉ Public Health Laboratory, Royal Shrewsbury Hospital, Mytton Oak Road, Shrewsbury SY3 8XQ (☎ 01743 261161)

WARREN, Stanley Anthony Treleaven (Tony); CB (1984); s of Stanley Howard Warren, and Mable Harriet, *née* Ham; *b* 26 Sept 1925; *Educ* King's Coll London (BSc); *m* 1950, Sheila Gloria May, *née* Rowe; 2 s, 1 da; *Career* Sub Lt RN 1945–47, Constructor Lt RCNC 1947–51, designer Royal Yacht Britannia 1951–54, frigate modernisations 1954–57, constructor HM Dockyard Malta 1957–60, Admty constructor overseer John Brown and Yarrow 1960–64, Polaris submarine design 1964–67, PNO Cammell Laird 1967–72, project mangr HMS Invincible 1972–76, dep dir of Submarines (Polaris) MOD (PE) 1976–79, dir gen Submarines MOD (PE) 1979–85; CEng, FRINA, FIMechE, RCNC; *Style*— Tony Warren, Esq, CB

WARRENDER, Hon Robin Hugh; 3 s of 1 Baron Bruntisfield, MC (d 1993), and his 1 w, Dorothy Etta, *née* Rawson (d 1975); *b* 24 Dec 1927; *Educ* Eton, Trinity Coll Oxford; *m* 1951, Gillian Elizabeth, da of Leonard Lewis Rossiter and his w Elsie Rose, da of late Sir Bernard Oppenheimer, 1 Bt; 1 s, 2 da; *Career* former chm London Wall Holdings plc 1986; underwriting memb of Lloyd's 1953, Tudor & Co (Insur) Ltd 1958–62, md Fenchurch Insurance Holdings Ltd 1963–69, dep chm A W Bain & Sons Ltd 1970, chm Bain Dawes plc and other gp cos 1973–86; dir: Comindus SA (France) 1980–, Worms & Co 1981–; Varity Corp (Canada) 1982; Varity Holdings Ltd 1982–, Heritable Group Holdings Ltd 1983–, Société Centrale Preservatrice Foncière Assurances 1986–89, Group Athena 1989–; memb: Cncl of Bath Univ 1979–82, Cncl and Ctee Lloyd's 1983–86; Royal Choral Soc 1979–; Liveryman Worshipful Co of Fishmongers; *Clubs* White's; *Style*— The Hon Robin Warrender; ✉ Capps Lodge House, Fulbrook, Burford, Oxon OX18 4DB (☎ 01993 822262)

WARRINGTON, Bishop of 1996–; Rt Rev John Richard Packer; s of Rev Canon John William Packer, of Bridge, Canterbury, and Hilda Muriel, *née* Hatch; *b* 10 Oct 1946; *Educ* Manchester GS, Keble Coll Oxford (BA Modern History, BA Theol, MA), Univ of York (Dip); *m* 30 Dec 1971, Barbara Priscilla Deborah, da of Donald Fingland Jack, of Scarborough; 2 s (Richard James b 1978, Timothy Stephen b 1980), 1 da (Catherine Ruth b 1976); *Career* curate St Peter's St Helier Morden Surrey 1970–73, dir of pastoral studies Ripon Hall 1973–75, Ripon Coll Cuddesdon Oxon 1975–77, chaplain St Nicolas' Abingdon Oxon 1973–77, vicar Wath upon Dearne with Adwick upon Dearne 1977–86, rural dean Wath 1983–86, rector Sheffield Manor 1986–91, rural dean Attercliffe 1990–91, archdeacon of W Cumberland 1991–96, priest i/c Bridekirk 1995–96; memb Gen Synod Church of England 1985–91 and 1992–96; *Recreations* history, cricket, walking; *Style*— The Rt Rev the Bishop of Warrington; ✉ 34 Central Avenue, Eccleston Park, Prescot, Merseyside L34 2QP (☎ 0151 426 1897, fax 0151 493 2479)

WARWICK, Bishop of 1996–; Rt Rev Anthony Martin Priddis; s of John Edward Priddis (d 1982), and Joan, *née* Humphries; *b* 15 March 1948; *Educ* Watford Boys' GS, CCC Cambridge (MA Biochemistry), Cuddesdon Theol Coll, New Coll Oxford (DipTheol, MA (by incorporation)); *m* 28 July 1973, Kathy, da of Ted and Mia Armstrong; 2 s (Michael b 7 July 1975, James b 16 Aug 1977), 1 da (Sarah b 25 March 1981); *Career* ordained deacon 1972, priest 1973; asst curate St Edward's New Addington Surrey 1972–75, coll chaplain Christ Church Oxford 1975–80, team vicar St John's High Wycombe Bucks 1980–86, rector of Amersham 1986–96, rural dean of Amersham 1992–96, hon canon of Christ Church 1995; tstee and chm Amersham United Charities 1986–96, chm governing bodies of 2 schs 1986–96, fndr memb Bd Chilterns Hundred Housing Assoc 1988–92; *Books* The Study of Spirituality (contrib, 1986); *Recreations* walking, gardening, sport (including golf), music, reading; *Style*— The Rt Rev the Bishop of Warwick; ✉ Warwick House, 139 Kenilworth Road, Coventry CV4 7AF (☎ 01203 416200, fax 01203 415254)

WARWICK, Archdeacon of; *see:* Paget-Wilkes, Ven Michael Jocelyn James

WARWICK, Diana; *b* 16 July 1945; *Educ* Univ of London (BA); *m* 1969, Sean Terence Bowes Young; *Career* tech asst NUT 1969–72, asst sec Civil and Public Servs Assoc 1972–83, gen sec Assoc of Univ Teachers 1983–92, first chief exec Westminster Fndn for Democracy (all-pty advsy gp for newly democratised countries) 1992–95, chief exec Ctee of Vice-Chllrs and Principals (CVCP) 1995–; chm Tstees Ctee VSO 1994–; memb: Bd Br Cncl 1985–95, Employment Appeals Tbnl 1987–, Exec Bd Industl Soc 1987–93, Gen Cncl TUC 1989–92, Nolan Ctee 1995–; govr Cwlth Inst 1988–95; *Style*— Ms Diana Warwick; ✉ The Committee of Vice-Chancellors and Principals, 29 Tavistock Square, London WC1H 9EZ (☎ 0171 387 9231, fax 0171 388 8649)

WARWICK, 9 Earl Brooke (GB 1746) and of (GB 1759); Guy David Greville; also Baron Brooke (E 1621); s of 8 Earl of Warwick (d 1996), and Sarah Anne Chester, *née* Beatty; *b* 30 Jan 1957; *Educ* Eton, Ecole des Roches; *m* 1981 (m dis 1992), Susan (Susie) McKinley, da of George William McKinley Wilson, of Melbourne, Australia, and formerly w of Nicholas Sydney Cobbold; 1 s (Lord Brooke), 2 step c; *Heir* s, Charles Fulke Chester Greville, Lord Brooke b 27 July 1982; *Recreations* golf, surfing; *Clubs* White's; *Style*— The Rt Hon the Earl of Warwick; ✉ 4 Walter Street, Claremont, Perth, W Australia 6010

WARWICK, Richard Carey; s of Dennis Bliss Winter, of Redmarley, Glos, and Margaret Joan, *née* Simpson; *b* 29 April 1945; *Educ* Dean Close Sch Cheltenham, RADA; *Career* actor; appeared with: Nat Theatre at Old Vic, Young Vic Co, Cambridge Theatre Co; *Theatre* incl: While the Sun Shines, In Praise of Love, The Real Thing; *Television* icl: The Vortex, The Last of the Mohicans, A Fine Romance; *Film* appearances incl: Romeo and Juliet, If..., The Bedsitting Room, Nicholas and Alexandra, Sebastiane, The Tempest, The Breaking of Bumbo, White Hunter White Heart, Hamlet; *Recreations* running, cycling, swimming, music, reading, dancing; *Clubs* YMCA, CND, Troll, Heaven; *Style*— Richard Warwick, Esq; ✉ Peter Charlesworth Ltd, 68 Old Brompton Road, London SW7 3LQ (☎ 0171 581 2478)

WARWICK THOMPSON, Dr Paul; s of Prof Sir Michael Warwick THOMPSON, *qv*, and Sybil, *née* Spooner; *b* 9 Aug 1959; *Educ* Bryanston Sch, Univ of Bristol (BA), UEA (MA, PhD); *m* 1985, Adline, da of Max Finlay; 1 da (Roberta Beatrice b 1987), 1 s (Oscar Leo b 1990); *Career* English teacher St Bede's Sch Eastbourne, scriptwriter/researcher The Design Cncl 1987–88; Design Museum London: curator Contemporary Design 1988–90, curator 1990–92, curatorial dir 1992–94, dir 1994–; memb: Design Forum, Int Advsy Ctee Nagoya Int Design Centre Japan 1992–; FRSA; *Books* Review 1 New Design (1989), Review 2 New Design (1990); *Style*— Dr Paul Warwick Thompson; ✉ 18 Clifton Avenue, London W12 9DR (☎ 0181 740 6536); The Design Museum, Butlers Wharf, London SE1 2YD (☎ 0171 403 6933, fax 0171 378 6540)

WASHINGTON, Joan; *Educ* Central Sch of Speech and Drama (distinction), Univ London (Dip); *m* 1 Nov 1986, Richard E Grant (the actor), *qv*; 1 da (Olivia b 4 Jan 1989); *Career* accent/dialogue coach; began career teaching in remand homes, comprehensive schs, RCN; taught over 320 accents, has taught regularly at RADA and Central; *Theatre* West End prodns incl: Anything Goes, Orpheus Descending (Broadway), Crazy for You, City of Angels, She Loves Me, Sunset Boulevard; RNT: Guys and Dolls, Beggar's Opera, Brighton Beach Memoirs, A View from the Bridge, Cat on a Hot Tin Roof, The Shaughraun, The Crucible, After the Fall, Pygmalion, Carousel, Sweeney Todd, Angels in America, The Children's Hour, Sweet Bird of Youth, Broken Glass, The Ends of the Earth; RSC: The Merchant of Venice, The Jew of Malta, Across Oka; Royal Court: Rat in the Skull, The Edward Bond Season, Serious Money, The Queen and I, Simpatico; *Television* incl: The Singing Detective, Lorna Doone, Old Times, Top Girls, Roots, Suddenly Last Summer, Middlemarch, Scarlett, Our Friends from the North, Cold Lazarus; *Films* incl: Yentl, The Bounty, Greystoke, Plenty, Prick up your Ears, A World Apart, The Trial, Damage, Second Best, Carrington, Jane Eyre, Jude, French Kiss, Fierce Creatures; *Style*— Ms Joan Washington

WASON, (Robert) Graham; s of Cathcart Roland Wason, and Margaret Ogilvie, *née* Lamb; gs of Rear Adm Cathcart Romer Wason, CMG, CIE (d 1941), ggs of Rt Hon Eugene Wason, MP (Liberal MP and Chm Scottish Liberal Party), gggs of P R Wason, MP for Ipswich, Promoter of Reform Bill 1832 and co-fndr of Reform Club; *b* 6 Jan 1951; *Educ* Alleyne's GS Stevenage, Univ of Surrey (BSc); *Career* ptnr Deloitte & Touche Consulting Group (Greene Belfield-Smith Div) 1983–; formerly in tourism and hotels ops in Europe and Africa and 'Holiday Which?'; chm Tourism Leisure Sports and Recreation Ctee Br Consultants Bureau until 1995; fell Hotel and Catering Int Mgmnt Assoc, fell Br Assoc of Hotel Accountants, fell Tourism Soc; affiliate memb World Tourism Orgn; *Recreations* golf, tennis, travel; *Style*— Graham Wason, Esq; ✉ Deloitte and Touche Consulting Group, Greene Belfield-Smith Division, Stonecutter Court, 1 Stonecutter Street, London EC4A 4TR (☎ 0171 936 3000, telex 884739 TRLNDN G)

WASS, Sir Douglas William Gretton; GCB (1980, KCB 1975, CB 1971); s of Arthur William Wass (d 1978), of Hampton, Middx, and Winifred Elsie, *née* Gretton (d 1955); *b* 15 April 1923; *Educ* Nottingham HS, St John's Coll Cambridge (BA, MA); *m* 14 July 1954, Dr Milica, da of Tomislav Pavicic (d 1932), of Belgrade, Yugoslavia; 1 s (Andrew b 1960), 1 da (Alexandra b 1958); *Career* entered HM Treasy 1946; private sec to: Chllr of Exchequer 1959–61, Chief Sec Treasy 1961–62; asst sec Treasy 1962, alternate exec dir IMF and fin cnsllr Br Embassy Washington 1965–67; Treasy: under-sec 1968, dep sec 1970–73, second perm sec 1973–74, perm sec 1974–83; jt head Home Civil Serv 1981–83; chm: Equity & Law plc (now AXA Equity & Law) 1986–95, Nomura International Ltd 1986–, NCM (UK) Ltd 1991–95; dir: Barclays Bank 1984–87, De La Rue Company plc 1984–93, Compagnie du Midi SA (now AXA SA) 1987–95, The Equitable Companies Inc 1992–; Reith lectr 1983, Shell Int lectr St Andrews 1985, Harry Street Memorial lectr Univ of Manchester 1987; dep chm Centre for Policy Studies Inst 1980–84; chm: Br Selection Ctee of Harkness Fellowships 1981–84, UN Advsy Gp on Fin Flows to Africa 1987–88; dep chm African Capacity Building Fndn 1990–; memb Cncl: Overseas Development Inst 1990–, Br Heart Fndn 1990–; govr Centre for Econ Policy Res 1983–90, pres Mkt Res Soc 1987–91; memb Cncl Univ of Bath 1985–91, govr Ditchley Fndn; hon fell St John's Coll Cambridge; Hon DLitt Univ of Bath 1985; *Books* Government and the Governed (1984); *Recreations* swimming; *Clubs* Reform; *Style*— Sir Douglas Wass, GCB; ✉ 6 Dora Rd, London SW19 7HH (☎ 0181 946 5556, fax 0181 241 4626); Nomura International Ltd, 1 St Martin's-le-Grand, London EC1A 4NP (☎ 0171 236 8811, fax 0171 248 5958, telex 883119)

WASS, Prof John Andrew Hall; s of Samuel Hall Wass (d 1970), and June Mary Vaudine, *née* Blaikie (d 1992); *b* 14 Aug 1947; *Educ* Rugby, Guy's Hosp Med Sch London (MB BS, MD); *m* 4 April 1970, Valerie Jean, *née* Vincent; 1 s (Samuel b 1979), 1 da (Katherine b 1974); *Career* registrar: KCH London 1973–74, Guy's Hosp London 1974–75; sub-dean of Med Coll and prof of clinical endocrinology St Bartholomew's Hosp London 1989–95 (univ lectr 1976–81, sr lectr 1982–85, reader 1985–89), conslt in endocrinology Radcliffe Infirmary Oxford 1995–; Linacre fell RCP 1994–; advsr to BACUP 1985–, med dir Bart's City Life Saver 1993–; sec: Endocrine Section RSM 1988–92, Assoc of Clinical Profs Univ of London 1993–; vice chm Ctee of Mgmnt Royal Med Benevolent Fund 1990–94 and 1996– (memb 1982–94), memb Exec Ctee Euro Fedn of Endocrine Socs 1994–, memb Exec Ctee Int Soc of Endocrinology 1996–, sec Clinical Endocrinology Tst 1996–; co-fndr The Pituitary Fndn 1994; chm Bart's Choral Soc 1992–95; Freeman City of London 1983, Liveryman Worshipful Co of Barbers; memb: American Endocrine Soc, Assoc of Physicians; fell Green Coll Oxford (MA) 1995; FRCP 1986 (MRCP 1973), FRSM; *Publications* Neuroendocrine Perspectives (1987), Acromegaly, 100 years of treatment (1994), Clinical Endocrine Oncology (ed, 1996), Oxford Textbook of Endocrinology (ed, 1997); also author of articles and chapters on: acromegaly, pituitary tumours, growth hormone, growth factors, osteoporosis; ed Clinical Endocrinology jl 1991–94; *Recreations* music, opera, theatre, wine, Scotland; *Clubs* Garrick; *Style*— Prof John Wass; ✉ West Wing, Kirtlington Park, Kirtlington, Oxon OX5 3JN (☎ 01869 350375); Department of Endocrinology, Radcliffe Infirmary, Woodstock Road, Oxford OX2 6HE (☎ 01865 224765, fax 01865 224617)

WASTELL, Prof Christopher; s of Edgar Barker Wastell (d 1963), and Doris Emmeline, *née* Pett (d 1965); *b* 13 Oct 1932; *Educ* Drax GS, Guy's Hosp Med Sch (MB BS), Univ of London (MS, FRCS); *m* 2 April 1958, Margaret Anne, da of Joseph Fletcher (d 1976); 1 s (Giles Richard b 1965), 2 da (Jacqueline Anne b 1961, Vivien Clare b 1963); *Career* house physician Joyce Green, house surgn Farnborough Kent, sr house offr Bristol Royal Infirmary, house surgn Great Ormond St, registrar Westminster Hosp, lectr Westminster Med Sch 1964–67, C and H J Gaisman res fell Mount Sinai Hosp NY USA 1965–66, sr lectr and hon conslt surgn Westminster Med Sch and Hosp 1968–73 (reader 1973–82); conslt to accident and emergency Westminster Hosp 1971–85; prof and hon conslt surgn: Charing Cross and Westminster Med Sch London Univ at

Westminster Hosp 1983–92, Chelsea and Westminster Hosp 1992–96; hon conslt surgn: Royal Hosp Chelsea 1993–, Royal Brompton Hosp 1996–; FRCS; *Books* Chronic Duodenal Ulcer (1972), Westminster Hospital Symposium on Chronic Duodenal Ulcer (1974), Surgery for Nurses (with Ellis, 1976), Surgery of the Stomach and Duodenum (with Nyhus, 1977 and 1986), Cimetidine, The Westminster Hospital Symposium (1978), Surgery of the Esophagus, Stomach and Small Intestine (with Nylus and Donahue, 1995); *Recreations* sailing, gardening, walking; *Clubs* Chipstead Sailing, RSM; *Style*— Prof Christopher Wastell; ✉ 7 Manor Way, Beckenham, Kent BR3 3LH; 3 North Rd, Kingsdown, Deal, Kent CT14 8AG; Surgical Unit, Chelsea and Westminster Hospital, 369 Fulham Road, London SW10 9NH (☎ 0181 746 8000/8463, fax 0181 746 8282)

WASTELL, David John; s of Ian Wastell, of London, and Audrey, *née* Overton; *b* 3 Jan 1957; *Educ* Latymer Sch Edmonton, New Coll Oxford (MA); *Career* Tavistock Times and Sunday Independent (Mirror Group Newspapers Grad Trainee Scheme) 1979–81, feature writer Scottish Daily Record 1981–86; Sunday Telegraph: reporter/feature writer 1986–88, political corr 1988–92, political ed 1992–; *Recreations* mountaineering, walking, sailing, skiing; *Style*— David Wastell, Esq; ✉ The Sunday Telegraph, 1 Canada Square, Canary Wharf, London E14 5DT (☎ 0171 538 7353, House of Commons ☎ 0171 219 6116)

WASTELL, William; s of Capt Charles Henry Wastell, MN (d 1939), and Elsie Alice Perham; *b* 13 Dec 1939; *Educ* Brentwood Sch, Regent St Poly Sch of Architecture; *m* 26 Nov 1966, Rosamund, da of Harold Geoffrey Haden; 3 da (Kerry b 1969, Miranda b 1970, Cindy b 1972); *Career* md Wastell and Porter Architects Ltd; ARIBA; *Recreations* photography, bridge, travel; *Style*— William Wastell, Esq; ✉ Oak House, Mardley Heights, Welwyn, Herts (☎ 01438 716808); Wastell and Porter, Troopers Yard, 23 Bancroft, Hitchin, Herts SG5 1JW (☎ 01462 422440, fax 01462 420403)

WATCHMAN, David; *b* 18 Jan 1937; *Educ* Bishop Gore Sch; *m* Dorothy; 1 s (Hugh), 1 da (Helen); *Career* account exec Park Advertising Ltd London 1958–63, dir ATA Advertising Group London 1963–73, md Intext Inc Australia 1976–79, chief exec West Sydney Radio Pty Ltd 1979–84; dir: Atkins Bros plc (and subsid cos) 1985–90, Mors Technology SA 1988–, Mors SA 1991–, Mors Technology UK Ltd 1991–; chief exec Royal Acad of Dancing 1991–; JP (Aust); FInstD, FInstM, FRSA; *Recreations* opera, ballet, reading, golf, gardening; *Style*— David Watchman, Esq; ✉ Royal Academy of Dancing, 36 Battersea Square, London SW11 (☎ 0171 223 0091)

WATERFORD, 8 Marquess of (I 1789); Sir John Hubert de la Poer Beresford; 12 Bt (I 1665); also Baron of Le Poer (I 1375), Viscount Tyrone, Baron Beresford (both I 1720), Earl of Tyrone (I 1746), and Baron Tyrone (GB 1786, in which title he sits in House of Lords); s of 7 Marquess of Waterford (d 1934); *b* 14 July 1933; *Educ* Eton; *m* 23 July 1957, Lady Caroline Olein Geraldine Wyndham-Quin, da of 6 Earl of Dunraven and Mount-Earl (d 1965); 3 s (Earl of Tyrone, Lord Charles Richard de la Poer b 1958, Lord James Patrick de la Poer b 1965), 1 da (Lady Alice Rose de la Poer b 31 July 1970); *Heir* s, Earl of Tyrone; *Career* Lt RHG Supp Reserve; *Clubs* White's; *Style*— The Most Hon the Marquess of Waterford; ✉ Curraghmore, Portlaw, Co Waterford (☎ 00 353 51 387102, fax 00 353 51 387481)

WATERHOUSE, Keith Spencer; CBE (1991); s of Ernest Waterhouse, and Elsie Edith Waterhouse; *b* 6 Feb 1929; *Educ* Osmondthorpe Cncl Sch Leeds, Leeds Coll of Commerce; *m* 1 (m dis); 1 s, 2 da; m 2, 1984 (m dis); *Career* writer and journalist 1950–; columnist: Daily Mirror 1970–86, Daily Mail 1986–; contrib to various pubns; *Plays* Mr & Mrs Nobody 1986, Jeffrey Bernard is Unwell 1989 (Evening Standard Comedy of the Year award 1990), Bookends 1990, Our Song 1992; plays (with Willis Hall) incl: Billy Liar 1960, Celebration 1961, England Our England (revue, music by Dudley Moore), Squat Betty & the Sponge Room, All Things Bright and Beautiful 1963, Say Who You Are 1965, Children's Day 1969, Who's Who 1972, Saturday Sunday Monday and Filumena (adaptions from plays by Eduardo de Filippo) 1973, The Card (musical adaption from novel by Arnold Bennett, music and lyrics Tony Hatch and Jackie Trent) 1973, Worzel Gummidge (music Dennis King), Budgie (musical, lyrics Don Black, music Mort Schuman); *Screenplays* (with Willis Hall) incl: Whistle Down the Wind, Billy Liar, A Kind of Loving, Man in the Middle, Pretty Polly, Lock up your Daughters; *TV Films* incl: There is a Happy Land, The Warmonger, Charlie Muffin (from Brian Freemantle's novel) 1983, This Office Life (from own novel) 1985, The Great Paper Chase (from the book Slip Up by Anthony Delano) 1986; *TV Series* incl: The Upchat Line, West End Tales, The Happy Apple, Charters and Caldicott, Andy Capp; TV series with Willis Hall: Queenie's Castle, Budgie, The Upper Crusts, Billy Liar, Worzel Gummidge (character created by Barbara Euphan Todd); *Awards* Granada Columnist of the Year 1970, IPC Descriptive Writer of the Year 1970, IPC Columnist of the Year 1973, British Press Awards Columnist of the Year 1978, Granada Special Quarter Century award 1982, British Press Awards Columnist of the Year 1990; hon fell Leeds Metropolitan Univ; *Novels* incl: There is a Happy Land (1957), Billy Liar (1959), Jubb (1963), The Bucket Shop (1968), Billy Liar on the Moon (1975), Office Life (1978), Maggie Muggins (1981), In the Mood (1983), Thinks (1984), Our Song (1988), Bimbo (1990), Unsweet Charity (1992); *General* The Passing of the Third Floor Buck (anthology of Punch pieces, 1974), Mondays, Thursdays (Daily Mirror columns 1976), Rhubarb, Rhubarb (1979), Fanny Peculiar (1983), Mrs Pooter's Diary (1983), Waterhouse at Large (1985), The Collected Letters of a Nobody (1986), The Theory and Practice of Lunch (1986), The Theory and Practice of Travel (1988), Waterhouse on Newspaper Style (1989, revised and expanded from Daily Mirror Style 1980), English Our English (1991), City Lights (memoirs, 1994), Streets Ahead (memoirs, 1995); *Clubs* Garrick, Pen, Chelsea Arts; *Style*— Keith Waterhouse, Esq, CBE; ✉ 29 Kenway Road, London SW5 0RP; agent: Alexandra Cann Representatives, 200 Fulham Road, London SW10 9PN (☎ 0171 352 6266); Literary Agent: David Higham Associates, 5–8 Lower John Street, London W1R 3PE (☎ 0171 437 7888)

WATERHOUSE, Norman; s of Norman Waterhouse, and Jean Gardner Hamilton Reid; *b* 13 Oct 1954; *Educ* Salesian Coll Farnborough, Univ of Birmingham Med Sch (MB ChB); *Career* plastic surgn trg: Frenchay Hosp Bristol, Hospital Tondu Bordeaux, South Australian Craniofacial Unit Adelaide, Mount Vernon Hosp Northwood, Tokyo Metropolitan Hosp; former conslt in plastic and reconstructive surgery: St Bart's Hosp and The London Hosp Whitechapel 1989–91, Charing Cross Hosp, St Mary's Hosp Paddington, Westminster Hosp; currently conslt in plastic and reconstructive surgery Chelsea & Westminster Hosp; memb European Craniofacial Soc; FRCS 1982, FRCSEd 1982, FRCS (plastic surgery) 1988; *Recreations* rock climbing, mountaineering, Wado-ryu karate (1st Dan); *Style*— Norman Waterhouse, Esq; ✉ 55 Harley St, London W1N 1DD (☎ 0171 636 4073, fax 0171 436 1645)

WATERHOUSE, Dame Rachel Elizabeth; *née* Franklin; DBE (1990, CBE 1980); da of Percival John Franklin (d 1955), and Ruby Susanna, *née* Knight; *b* 2 Jan 1923; *Educ* King Edward's HS for Girls Birmingham, St Hugh's Coll Oxford (MA), Univ of Birmingham (PhD); *m* 16 Aug 1947, John Alfred Humphrey Waterhouse, s of (Thomas Alfred) Foster Waterhouse, of Edgbaston, Birmingham; 2 s (Matthew b 21 Sept 1950, Edmund b 4 Feb 1952), 2 da (Deborah (Mrs De Haes) b 11 March 1956, Rebecca (Mrs Morgan) b 20 Oct 1958); *Career* WEA/extra-mural tutor 1944–47; res fell Univ of Birmingham 1948–52; memb: Potato Mktg Bd 1969–81, Price Cmmn 1977–79, Nat Consumer Cncl 1975–86, Duke of Edinburgh's Enquiry into Br Housing 1984–85 and 1990–91; chm Consumers' Assoc 1982–90 (memb Cncl 1966–96); memb: Nat Economic Devpt Cncl 1981–91, Securities & Investmts Bd 1983–92, Cncl of Banking Ombudsman 1986–95, Advsy Bd Inst of Food Res 1988–93; chm Cncl for Licensed Conveyancers 1986–89, memb Health and Safety Cmmn 1990–95, tstee Joseph Rowntree Fndn 1990–; memb Advsy Ctee Microbiological Safety of Food 1991–95; chm: Res Inst for Consumer Affairs 1991–94 (memb 1994–), Lunar Soc Birmingham 1991–96 (vice chm 1996–); dir Birmingham Foundation 1995–96; memb Ct of Govrs Univ of Birmingham 1991–, tstee Affirming Catholicism 1992–; Hon DLitt Loughborough Univ 1980, Hon DSocSci Univ of Birmingham 1990; Hon CGIA 1988; CIMgt 1988; *Books* History of the Birmingham and Midland Institute 1854–1954 (1954), A Hundred Years of Engineering Craftsmanship (1957), Children in Hospital, 100 Years of Child Care in Birmingham (1962); *Style*— Dame Rachel Waterhouse, DBE; ✉ 252 Bristol Rd, Birmingham B5 7SL (☎ 0121 472 0427)

WATERHOUSE, Prof Roger William; s of Ronald and Dorothy May Waterhouse; *b* 29 April 1940; *Educ* King Edward VII Sch Sheffield, Corpus Christi Coll Oxford (MA); *m* 1, 1962 (m dis), Mania, *née* Jevinsky; 2 da, 1 s; m 2, 1979, Jaqueline Mary, *née* Dymond; 1 da, 1 s; *Career* lectr Shoreditch Coll of FE 1961–62, teacher Kibbutz Ma'abarot 1962–64, head of economics Myers Grove Comp Sch 1964–66, subsequently asst lectr, lectr, sr lectr and princ lectr Hendon Coll of Technol 1966–73, head Dept of Humanities and dean of humanities Middx Poly 1973–86, dep dir academic planning Wolverhampton Poly 1986–89, dir Derbys Coll of HE 1989–92, fndr vice-chllr Univ of Derby 1992–; chm: Interfaculty Studies Bd CNAA, Derbyshire Careers Service Ltd; memb: Philosophy Panel CNAA, Working Pty on Credit Accumulation and Transfer Scheme (CATS), Ctee for Arts and Social Sciences CNNA, Derby Educn Ctee; fndr and first chair SE England Consortium for CATS (SEEC), fndr and first pres Trans-European Exchange and Transfer Consortium (TEXT); FRSA; *Recreations* wood-turning; *Style*— Prof Roger Waterhouse; ✉ University of Derby, Kedleston Rd, Derby DE22 1GB (☎ 01332 622200, e-mail RWWaterhouse@derby.ac.uk)

WATERHOUSE, Hon Sir Ronald Gough Waterhouse; kt (1978); s of Thomas Waterhouse, CBE (d 1961), and Doris Helena Gough (d 1993); *b* 8 May 1926; *Educ* Holywell GS, St John's Coll Cambridge (MA, LLM); *m* 1960, Sarah Selina, da of Capt Ernest Augustus Ingram (d 1954), of Bletchley Park Stud; 1 s, 2 da; *Career* RAFVR 1944–48; called to the Bar Middle Temple 1952, bencher 1977, treas Middle Temple 1995, QC 1969; dep chm: Cheshire QS 1964–71, Flintshire QS 1966–71; recorder of the Crown Court 1972–77, judge of the High Court of Justice (Queen's Bench Div) 1988–96 (Family Div 1978–88), ret; judge of Employment Appeal Tbnl 1979–88, presiding judge Wales and Chester Circuit 1980–84; chm Tbnl of Inquiry into Child Abuse in N Wales 1996–; chm Local Govt Boundary Cmmn for Wales 1974–78, vice pres Zoological Soc of London 1981–84 and 1991–92 (sometime cncl memb 1972–92); pres: Llangollen Int Musical Eisteddfod 1994–, St John's Wood Soc 1994–97; Hon LLD Univ of Wales 1986; *Recreations* golf, watching cricket, music; *Clubs* Garrick, MCC, Cardiff and County, Pilgrims; *Style*— The Hon Sir Ronald Waterhouse; ✉ Greystone House, Walford, Ross-on-Wye, Herefordshire HR9 5RJ

WATERLOW, Sir Christopher Rupert; 5 Bt (UK 1873), of London; s of (Peter) Rupert Waterlow (d 1969), of Knightsbridge, London, and Jill Elizabeth, *née* Gourlay (d 1961); gs of Sir Philip Alexander Waterlow, 4 Bt (d 1973), and 3 cous twice removed of Sir Thomas Waterlow, 3 Bt, CBE, of Harrow Weald; *b* 12 Aug 1959; *Educ* Stonyhurst Coll; *m* 6 Sept 1986, Sally-Ann, o da of Maurice Bitten, of Abbey Wood, London; *Heir* kinsman, Nicholas Anthony Ronald Waterlow b 30 Aug 1941; *Career* musician; distributor for Amway (UK) Ltd; memb: Stonyhurst Assoc, Berchman Soc; *Recreations* music, shooting, squash; *Clubs* Wasps RUFC; *Style*— Sir Christopher Waterlow, Bt; ✉ 26 Barfield Road, Bromley, Kent BR1 2HS

WATERLOW, Lady; Diana Suzanne; *née* Skyrme; da of Sir Thomas Skyrme, KCVO, CB, CBE, TD, JP, *qv*, of Blockley, Gloucs, and Hon Barbara Suzanne, *née* Lyle, da of 1 Baron Lyle of Westbourne; *b* 21 March 1943; *m* 10 July 1965, Sir (James) Gerard Waterlow, 4 Bt, *qv*; 1 s, 1 da; *Career* actress 1963–68; dir The Securities and Futures Authy (formerly The Securities Assoc); appointed JP S Westminster 1972, transferred to W Berkshire 1982; memb Bd of Holloway Prison; ptnrship in interior design business W Squared Interiors; *Recreations* tennis, bridge; *Style*— Lady Waterlow; ✉ Rushall Lodge, Pewsey, Wilts SN9 6EN

WATERLOW, Sir (James) Gerard; 4 Bt (UK 1930), of Harrow Weald, Middlesex; s of Sir Thomas Waterlow, 3 Bt, CBE (d 1982); *b* 3 Sept 1939; *Educ* Marlborough, Trinity Coll Cambridge; *m* 1965, Diana Suzanne, *qv*, yr da of Sir Thomas Skyrme, KCVO, CB, CBE, TD, JP, *qv*; 1 s, 1 da (Amanda Jane (Mrs Jason Howard) b 1968); *Heir* s, Thomas James Waterlow b 20 March 1970; *Style*— Sir Gerard Waterlow, Bt; ✉ Rushall Lodge, Pewsey, Wilts SN9 6EN

WATERMAN, Clive Adrian; s of Harvey Waterman (d 1967), of Hendon, London, and Hannah, *née* Spector (d 1995); *b* 13 Aug 1949; *Educ* Haberdashers' Aske's Sch Elstree, London Hosp Med Coll (BDS), Royal Dental Hosp of London (MSc); *Career* clinical asst London Hosp 1973–75 (house surgn 1973), registrar Eastman Dental Hosp 1976–77, pt/t clinical asst Guy's Hosp 1977–84, gen and specialist practice 1977–, pt/t lectr King's Coll 1985–; chm GP Section Br Soc of Periodontology 1990–94, asst sec BSP 1994–95; memb: Kingston and Richmond Local Dental Ctee 1988–, Cncl BSP 1990–95, memb BDA Scientific Programme Sub-Ctee 1990–; *Recreations* cricket, skiing, squash, wine, dining; *Clubs* Riverside, Reform; *Style*— Clive Waterman, Esq; ✉ 4 Elm Grove Rd, Barnes, London SW13 0BT (☎ 0181 392 2288, office 0181 878 8986, fax 0181 878 9755)

WATERMAN, Dennis; *b* 24 Feb 1948; *Educ* Corona Theatre Sch; *m* 1, Patricia Maynard; 2 da (Hannah, Julia); m 2, Rula Lenska, *qv*; *Career* actor; began career with Children's Film Fndn, joined RSC Stratford aged 12; singer; has reached number 1 in Aust/NZ and number 3 in UK, toured UK with Friends on Tour, hosted own TV special With A Little Help From My Friends; *Theatre* Winthrop Parroo in The Music Man (West End), Carving a Statue (West End), began three-year engagement at Royal Court when aged 16 (credits incl Saved, Twelfth Night and Sergeant Musgrave's Dance), Alfie (tour), Saratoga (RSC), Windy City (West End musical), Same Time Next Year (tour Aust/NZ) 1984, Buttons in Cinderella (Beck Theatre Millingdon) 1984, Same Time Next Year (UK tour and Old Vic) 1985, The Real Thing (Yvonne Arnaud Theatre Guildford then Perth Aust) 1986, Double Double (tour) 1987, Jeffrey Bernard Is Unwell (Aust tour 1991–92, UK tour) 1993, A Slice of Saturday Night (Strand Theatre), Fools Rush Inn (Richmond) 1996; *Television* Just William (series), Fair Exchange (USA), Member of the Wedding (USA), The Sweeney 1974–78, Minder (5 series), Minder On The Orient Express (Christmas film special) 1985, The Lives and Loves of a She Devil (BBC) 1986, Who's Our Little Jenny Lind (Yorkshire) 1986, Northern Lights (Yorkshire) 1988, Stay Lucky (4 series, Yorkshire), On The Up (3 series, BBC), Circles of Deceit (series, Yorkshire) 1994; *Films* Up the Junction, Man in the Wilderness, The Eyes Have It, The Belstone Fox, Smashing Bird I Used To Know, Scars of Dracula, The Sweeney 1976, The Sweeney II 1977, The First World Cup - A Captain's Tale (also co-prodr, Emmy nomination), The First Kangaroos, Cold Justice (also prodr); *Recreations* watching all sports, playing golf; *Style*— Dennis Waterman, Esq; ✉ c/o M M & M, Pinewood Studios, Pinewood Road, Iver, Bucks SL0 0NH (☎ 01753 650808, fax 01753 650705)

WATERMAN, Dr Fanny; OBE (1971); da of Myer Waterman (d 1984), of Leeds, and Mary, *née* Behrmann (d 1978); *b* 22 March 1920; *Educ* Chapel Allerton HS Leeds, RCM; *m* Dr Geoffrey de Keyser; *Career* concert pianist and teacher of int repute; chm Harvey Leeds Int Pianoforte Competition, jury memb of prestigious piano competitions incl the Tchaikovsky, Rubinstein (vice pres), First Chinese Int Piano Competition, and Leeds Int (pres); vice pres World Fedn of Int Music Competition 1992–; regular broadcaster tv and radio, author of over thirty books on piano-playing and teaching; FRCM; Hon DMus Leeds 1992, Dr Univ of York 1995; *Books* incl: Me and My Piano Repertoire, Duets Books 1 & 2, The Young Pianist's Dictionary; *Recreations* travel, reading, voluntary work, cooking; *Style—* Dr Fanny Waterman, OBE; ✉ Woodgarth, Oakwood Grove, Leeds, W Yorks LS8 2PA (☎ 0113 265 5771, fax 0113 265 0754)

WATERMAN, Howard John; *b* 23 May 1953; *Educ* Univ of Southampton (LLB), Coll of Law; *m* 1 Nov 1981, Sharon; 1 s (Craig b 31 Dec 1992), 1 da (Lauren b 1 Sept 1988); *Career* admitted slr 1977; ptnr Cameron Markby Hewitt 1984–94, ptnr Sidley & Austin 1994–; memb City of London Slrs Co; memb Law Soc 1977; *Recreations* chess, bridge, sports; *Style—* Howard Waterman, Esq; ✉ The Folly, 2 Newgate Street Village, nr Hertford, Herts SG13 8RA (☎ 01707 875338); Sidley & Austin (☎ 0171 360 3600)

WATERMAN, Ivan David; s of Harry Waterman (d 1990), of London, and Lilian Maud, *née* Shapiro; *b* 26 Feb 1949; *Educ* Dame Alice Owen's GS Islington; *m* Jill, da of Douglas Palmer; 1 da (Alice b 16 June 1988); *Career* journalist; East London Advertiser 1968–71 (chief reporter, ed Film and Diary Pages), reporter North London News Agency and Fleet Street News Agency 1971–72, news ed and exec dir Thames Valley News Agency 1972–73, News of the World (showbusiness reporter, film and theatre critic, showbusiness ed) 1973–89, Today (theatre critic, dep showbusiness ed, then showbusiness ed) 1989–95 (following paper's closure), currently theatre critic OK! Magazine; also freelance contrib to: Independent on Sunday, Mail on Sunday, The Times; memb: Critics' Circle, Broadcasting Press Guild; *Books* Keith Moon - The Life and Death of a Rock Legend (biography, 1979); *Recreations* golf, tennis, cricket, backgammon, rugby, football, staying in five star hotels; *Clubs* Sheen Lawn, Scribes, Old Owen's Assoc; *Style—* Ivan Waterman, Esq; ✉ 99 Queen's Road, Richmond, Surrey TW10 6HF (☎ 0181 940 6063, fax 0181 948 5468); 17 Defoe House, Barbican, London EC2

WATERMAN, Peter Alan (Pete); s of John Edward Waterman, of 94 Burlington Rd, Coventry, and Stella, *née* Lord (d 1978); *b* 15 Jan 1947; *Educ* Frederick Bird Secdy Modern Coventry; *m* 1, 1970, Elizabeth Reynolds; 1 s (Paul Andrew b 1972); m 2, 1980, Julie Reeves; 1 s (Peter Alan b 1982); m 3, 1991, Denise Gyngell; 2 da (Toni Tuesday b 1990, Charlie Ella b 1991); *Career* record producer; former disc jockey at local pubs and Mecca dancehall, former Arts and Repertoire man for various record cos; formed Loose Ends Productions with Peter Collins working with artists incl Musical Youth and Nick Kershaw until 1983, fndr ptnr Stock Aitken Waterman (with Mike Stock and Matt Aitken) 1984; has won numerous Silver, Gold and Platinum Discs since 1985 for writing and/or producing artists incl: Princess, Hazell Dean, Dead or Alive, Bananarama, Mel and Kim, Sinitta, Rick Astley, Kylie Minogue, Brother Beyond, Jason Donovan, Donna Summer, Sonia, Big Fun, Cliff Richard; involved with charity work incl SAW Goes to the Albert (Royal Marsden Hosp) and records: Let it Be (Ferry Aid), The Harder I Try (Young Variety Club of GB), Help (Comic Relief), Lets All Chant, I Haven't Stopped Dancing Yet and Use It Up and Wear It Out (Help a London Child), Ferry 'Cross the Mersey (Mersey Aid), Do They Know It's Christmas? (Ethiopia Famine Appeal), You've Got a Friend (Childline); *Awards* BPI Best British Producers 1988; Music Week Top Producers for: Singles (1st) and Albums (3rd) 1987, Singles (1st) and Albums (1st) 1988 and 1989; Ivor Novello awards (UK): Songwriters of the Year 1987, 1988 and 1989, Writers of Most Performed Works 1987, 1988 and 1989; BMI awards (USA) Writers of Most Performed Works 1987, 1988 and 1989, Jasrac awards (Japan) and Cash awards (Hong Kong) Writers of Most Performed Foreign Works 1989; *Recreations* steam railways, model railways, car collection, Koi Carp farming; *Style—* Pete Waterman, Esq; ✉ PWL Records, 4–7 The Vineyard, Sanctuary St, London SE1 1QL (☎ 0171 403 0007, fax 0171 403 8202)

WATERMAN, Prof Peter George; s of George Leonard Waterman (d 1992), and Queenie Rose Waterman (d 1988); *b* 28 April 1946; *Educ* Judd GS Tonbridge, Univ of London (BPharm, DSc), Univ of Strathclyde (PhD); *m* 1968, Margaret, da of Carl Humble; *Career* Univ of Strathclyde: asst lectr 1969–72, lectr 1972–83, sr lectr 1983, reader 1983–87, personal prof 1987, currently prof of phytochemistry Dept of Pharmaceutical Sciences; currently dir of natural projects prog Strathclyde Inst for Drug Research; sr res Nat Museums of Kenya 1983–85; conslt: Forestry Res Inst of Malaysia, Western Australian Herbarium, Australian Nat Herbarium, ODA; Tate and Lyle award Phytochemical Soc of Europe 1983; Hon Dr Université de Franche-Comte 1994; memb: Phytochemical Soc of Europe, American Soc for Pharmacognosy, Linnean Soc, Int Soc for Chemical Ecology; FRSE 1991; author of 6 books and numerous papers in scientific jls; exec ed Biochemical Systematics and Ecology; *Recreations* ornithology; *Style—* Prof Peter G Waterman, FRSE; ✉ Phytochemistry Research Laboratories, University of Strathclyde, Glasgow G1 1XW (☎ 0141 552 4400, fax 0141 552 6443)

WATERPARK, 7 Baron (I 1729); Sir Frederick Caryll Philip Cavendish; 8 Bt (GB 1755); s of Brig-Gen Frederick Cavendish, bro of 6 Baron and 6 in descent from William Cavendish, natural s of 3 Duke of Devonshire; suc unc 1948; *b* 6 Oct 1926; *Educ* Eton, RMC Medal of Honour; *m* 17 April 1951, Danièle, da of Roger Guirche, of Paris; 1 s, 2 da; *Heir* s, Hon Roderick Cavendish; *Career* served: Gren Gds, Kenya Police Reserve; md Spartan Air Services 1955–60; dir: Handley Page Ltd 1968–70, Airborne Group plc 1990–93; CSE Aviation Ltd: sales dir 1962, dep chm 1984, chief exec 1989–90; dep chm and md CSE Int 1984–90; dir D T Dobie (East Africa) Ltd 1995–; tstee RAF Museum 1994–; *Clubs* Cavalry and Guards'; *Style—* The Rt Hon Lord Waterpark; ✉ 2/74 Elm Park Rd, London SW3 (☎ 0171 351 3663)

WATERS, Brian Richard Anthony; s of Montague Waters, QC, of London, and late Jessica Freedman; *b* 27 March 1944; *Educ* City of London Sch, St John's Coll Cambridge (MA), (Dip Arch, PCL DipTP); *m* 1 Nov 1974, Myriam Leiva, da of José Ramon Leiva Alvarez, of Bogota, Colombia; *Career* chartered architect & town planner; memb RIBA, RTPI; pres Cities of London and Westminster Soc of Architects 1980–82, vice pres RIBA 1988–89 and 1991–92 (memb Cncl 1987–92); chm Nat Architecture Conf London 1991, London Planning Devpt Forum 1990–; princ The Boisot Waters Cohen Partnership (design), ptnr Studio Crown Reach; dir: Gray Lucas Management Ltd, Land Research Unit Ltd; jt publishing ed Planning in London; ed Architectural Journalist of the Year commendation 1979, 1982, 1984 and 1986; Freeman: City of London, Co of Chartered Architects (memb Ct 1991–); *Books* author of books, articles and reviews for various architectural pubns, Inst Economic Affairs and CPC; *Recreations* tennis, dressage, pots, Siberian huskies; *Clubs* RAC, Hurlingham; *Style—* Brian R A Waters, Esq; ✉ Studio Crown Reach, 149a Grosvenor Road, London SW1V 3JY (☎ 0171 828 6555, fax 0171 834 9470)

WATERS, Brian Wallace; s of Stanley Wallace Waters (d 1993), of Harpenden, Herts, and Kathleen, *née* Thake; *b* 24 Nov 1936; *Educ* City of London Sch, Harvard Business Sch; *m* 1 April 1961, Gillian, da of Herbert William Harris (d 1976); 4 s (Andrew b 1963, James b 1965, Richard b 1967, Mark b 1975); *Career* Ernst & Young: ptnr 1968, exec vice chm (Europe) 1979–82, chm (Europe) 1982–85, managing ptnr Ernst & Young Birmingham 1993–96, managing ptnr Midlands Region 1995–; chm London Soc of Chartered Accountants 1976–77, memb Cncl ICAEW 1983–87, memb Exec Ctee Union Européennes des Experts Comptables 1983–87; memb Horserace Betting Levy Appeal Tbnl 1986–; Liveryman: Worshipful Co of Chartered Accountants, Worshipful Co of Drapers; FCA 1960, FCMA 1962; *Recreations* cricket, field sports, racing, real tennis; *Clubs* MCC, Institute of Directors, Lord's Taverners, Wig and Pen; *Style—* Brian Waters, Esq; ✉ Ernst & Young, One Colmore Row, Birmingham B3 2DB (☎ 0121 232 4000)

WATERS, David Frobisher; *b* 20 Sept 1949; *Educ* The King's Sch Canterbury, Univ of Cape Town (BComm, MIndAd); *m* 1, 12 June 1971 (m dis); 2 s (Marcus Damian Napier b 2 Dec 1973, Fraser Henry Hamilton b 31 March 1976); m 2, 8 Dec 1990, Brigid Mary Dowling; 1 s (Caspar Rudyard Van Der Byl b 14 July 1992), 1 da (Sacha Lucinda b 21 March 1995); *Career* ptnr Ernst & Young Jersey 1986–; ATII 1969, FCA 1970, CA (SA) 1972; *Recreations* sport, games and puzzles; *Clubs* Hon Artillery Co, Royal Cape Yacht, Western Province Sports, Victoria (Jersey), Mensa; *Style—* David Waters, Esq; ✉ Green Lanes, Pont Au Bre, St Peter, Jersey, Channel Islands (☎ 01534 485718); Ernst & Young, Le Gallais Chambers, 54 Bath St, St Helier, Jersey, Channel Islands (☎ 01534 501000)

WATERS, Mrs Frank; Denise Jeanne Marie Lebreton; *see:* Brown, Denise Jeanne Marie Lebreton

WATERS, Donald Henry; OBE (1994); s of Henry Lethbridge Waters (d 1978), of Edinburgh, and Jean Manson, *née* Baxter (d 1987); *b* 17 Dec 1937; *Educ* George Watson's Coll Edinburgh, Inverness Royal Acad; *m* 5 May 1962, June Leslie, da of Andrew Hutchison (d 1984), of Forres, Moray; 1 s (Andrew Henry Lethbridge b 1969), 2 da (Jennifer Dawn b 1963, Gillian Claire b 1966); *Career* Grampian Television plc: dir 1979–, chief exec 1987–, dep chm 1993–; dir: John M Henderson Ltd 1972–76, Glenburnie Properties Ltd 1976– (chm 1993–), Scottish Television and Grampian Sales Ltd (STAGS) 1980–, Blenheim Travel Ltd 1981–90, Moray Firth Radio Ltd 1982–, Independent Television Publications Ltd 1987–90, Cablevision Scotland plc 1987–91, Central Scotland Radio Ltd 1994–96 (chm 1995–96), GRT Bus Group plc 1994–95, British Linen Bank Group Ltd 1994–; visiting prof of film and media studies Univ of Stirling 1991; memb: Independent Television Association Ltd 1994–, Ct British Linen Bank Ltd 1994–; dir: Aberdeen Royal Hosps NHS Tst 1996–, Scottish Post Office Bd 1996–; vice chm BAFTA Scotland 1992–, chm Celtic Film and TV Assoc 1994–96 (tstee Scotland 1990–); memb: Royal Television Soc 1988, BAFTA UK 1988–; chm Police Dependent Tst Grampian Region 1992–95; memb: Cncl SATRO, CBI Scotland Cncl 1994–; memb: Grampian Initiative, Grampian and Islands Family Tst (GIFT) 1988–; a Burgess of Guild Aberdeen 1979; past chm Royal Northern and Univ Club; MICAS 1961, FRSA 1990; *Recreations* gardening, travel, hillwalking; *Clubs* Royal Northern and Univ Aberdeen; *Style—* Donald Waters, Esq, OBE; ✉ Balquhidder, 141 North Deeside Road, Milltimber, Aberdeen AB13 0JS (☎ 01224 867131); Grampian Television plc, Queens Cross, Aberdeen AB15 4XJ (☎ 01224 846846)

WATERS, Prof (William) Estlin; s of Dr Edward Thomas Waters (d 1977), and Dr Cicely Waters, *née* Weatherall (d 1985); *b* 6 Nov 1934; *Educ* Cardiff HS, Univ of London (MB BS), Univ of St Andrews (DIH); *m* 14 March 1964, Judith Isabel, da of David Harold Lloyd (d 1963); 2 s (Robert b 26 April 1966, David b 8 Aug 1967); *Career* Nat Serv Capt RAMC; Univ of Southampton: sr lectr and reader in clinical epidemiology and community med 1970–75, prof of community medicine 1976–90, emeritus prof 1990–, professorial fell 1990–94; sec Exec Ctee Int Epidemiological Assoc 1974–77 (memb Cncl 1971–77 and 1981–84), ed Int Jl of Epidemiology 1990; MFCM 1974, FFCM 1976 FFPHM 1989; *Books* Community Medicine (1983 and 1987), Headache, Clinical Epidemiology Series (1986), author of over 130 medical papers; *Recreations* ornithology, collecting books, visiting and reading about remote islands; *Clubs* British Trust for Ornithology, British Ornithologists'; *Style—* Prof Estlin Waters; ✉ Orchards, Broxmore Park, Sherfield English, Romsey, Hants SO51 6FT (☎ 01794 884254)

WATERS, (Suzanne) Fiona; s of Capt Michael Theodore Waters, of Ambleside, Cumbria, and Sylvia, *née* Tingle; *b* 10 April 1956; *Educ* Felixstowe Ladies' Coll; *children* 1 da (Poppy), 1 s (Liam); *Career* production co-ordinator Knightsbridge Theatrical Productions 1976, press offr Royal Court Theatre 1980, head of press and network co-ordinator Satellite TV plc 1982, head of press Sky Channel 1984, dir of press and publicity Sky TV (later British Sky Broadcasting) 1988–91, fndr Fiona Waters Associates PR consultancy 1991; MIPR; *Recreations* gardening, writing; *Style—* Ms Fiona Waters; ✉ 57 Temple Fortune Hill, London NW11 7XR

WATERS, Gen Sir (Charles) John; GCB (1995, KCB 1988), CBE (1981, OBE 1977); s of Patrick George Waters (d 1952), and Margaret Ronaldson, *née* Clark (d 1991); *b* 2 Sept 1935; *Educ* Oundle, RMA Sandhurst; *m* 1962, Hilary Doyle, da of Harry Sylvester Nettleton (d 1983); 3 s (Patrick, Harry, George); *Career* instr Army Staff Coll Camberley 1973–75, CO 1 Bn The Gloucestershire Regt 1975–77, Col Gen Staff 1 Armd Div 1977–79, Cmd 3 Inf Bde 1979–81, RCDS 1982, Dep Cmd Land Forces Falklands 1982, Cmd 4 Armd Div 1983–85, Cmdt Staff Coll Camberley 1986–88, GOC and dir of ops NI 1988–90 (despatches 1990), Col The Gloucestershire Regt 1985–91; Col Comdt POW Div 1988–92, C-in-C UKLF 1990–93, Dep Supreme Allied Cdr Europe April 1993–94, ADC Gen to HM The Queen 1992–94, Hon Col Wessex Yeo 1991; Kermit Roosevelt lectr 1992; memb: Advsy Cncl Victory Meml Museum Arlon Belgium, Cncl Cheltenham Coll, Admiral Army Sailing Assoc 1990–93; Hon Col Royal Devon Yeo 1991, Admiral Infantry Sailing Assoc 1990–93; FRSA; *Recreations* sailing, skiing, painting, reading, walking; *Clubs* Army and Navy, British Kiel Yacht; *Style—* Gen Sir John Waters, GCB, CBE; ✉ c/o Lloyds Bank, Colyton, Devon EX13 6DY

WATERS, John Stephen; s of Ronald Neil Waters (d 1976), of Ufford Place, Woodbridge, Suffolk, and Eva Louise, *née* Porter (d 1989); *b* 22 Oct 1934; *Educ* Queen Elizabeth's Sch Barnet, Charing Cross Hosp Med Sch (MB BS), FRCS, MS; *m* 10 July 1960, Faith, da of Edward Hindle; 3 da (Lynn b 28 May 1963, Jill b 10 July 1966, Susan b 26 Dec 1967); *Career* med trg Charing Cross Hosp: house surgn, house physician, casualty offr; surgical registrar 1960–64: Royal Surrey Co Hosp, Prince of Wales Hosp London, St George's Hosp; sr surgical registrar 1965–71: Norfolk and Norwich Hosp, St George's Hosp, Royal Marsden Hosp; conslt surgn Morriston and Singleton Hosps Swansea 1971–; hon tutor Univ of Wales Coll of Med; elected to Welsh Bd RCS; memb: BMA, RSM, Assoc of Surgeons; *Recreations* sailing, walking; *Style—* John Waters; ✉ 12 Grange Rd, West Cross, Swansea, West Glamorgan SA3 5ES

WATERS, Rev Robert; MBE (1996); s of Robert Waters (d 1962), and Frances, *née* Galloway; *b* 8 July 1930; *Educ* Boroughmuir Sch Edinburgh, Univ of Edinburgh (MA), Scottish Congregational Coll (exit cert), Univ of Chicago (Fulbright scholar), Chicago Theol Seminary (World Church fell); *m* 1956, Magdalene Moyes Forrest; 1 s (Derek Graham b 1962), 1 da (Nicola Fay b 1965); *Career* trainee seedsman 1945–48, Nat Serv RAF 1948–50, miner 1950–54, Univ of Edinburgh 1956–60, Univ of Chicago 1960–61, Scottish Congregational Coll 1954–56 and 1961–62, ordained 1962; min: E Kilbride Congregational Church 1962–69, Augustine Bristo Church Edinburgh 1969–71; gen sec: Congregational Union of Scotland 1971–95, (chm 1970–71), Scottish Congregational Church 1993–96; chm: SCAWD Investment Assoc Ltd 1979–89, Church Leaders' Forum 1983–, Scottish Churches Housing Liaison 1984–93, Livingston Sponsors Cncl 1984–86 and 1992–, Multilateral Church Conversation 1988–; chm of Corporations Cncl for World Mission 1989–91, convenor Cncl of Shared Interest 1989–93; *Recreations* trout fishing (memb various fishing clubs), carpentry, gardening, landscape painting, reading, computer studies, radio-control aircraft building; *Style—* The Rev Robert Waters, MBE; ✉ 10 Gartcows Drive, Falkirk FK1 5QQ (☎ 01324 624898)

WATERS, Prof Ronald Thomas; s of David John Waters (d 1978), of Caerphilly, and Mary Evelyn Rees (d 1982)); *b* 20 June 1930; *Educ* Caerphilly GS, Univ Coll Of Swansea (BSc, PhD); *m* 2 April 1956, Catherine Margaret, da of Richard Cullen (d 1978), of Swansea; 2 da (Janet b 1957, Deborah b 1961); *Career* res engr: AEI Ltd 1954–63; Univ of Wales 1963–95 (head Electrical Engrg Div Cardiff Sch of Engrg, prof emeritus 1995); FInstP, FIEE, CEng; *Books* Gas Discharges and the Electricity Supply Industry (1962), Electrical Breakdown of Gases (1978); *Recreations* golf, gardening, travel; *Clubs* Cardiff Golf; *Style*— Prof Ronald Waters; ✉ 7 South Rise, Llanishen, Cardiff, South Glamorgan CF4 5RF (☎ 01222 754602); University of Wales Cardiff, PO Box 917, Cardiff CF2 1XH (☎ 01222 874000, fax 01222 874420)

WATERSON, Nigel Christopher; MP (C) Eastbourne (majority 5,481); s of late James Waterson, and Katherine Mahon; *b* 12 Oct 1950; *Educ* Leeds GS, The Queen's Coll Oxford; *m* 1 (m dis); m 2, Bernadette Anne, da of late Denis O'Halloran; *Career* slr and barr, fndr and sr ptnr Waterson Hicks slrs; pres Oxford Univ Cons Assoc 1970, res asst to Sally Oppenheim MP 1972–73, chm Bow Gp 1986–87, Parly candidate (C) Islington S and Finsbury 1979, MP (C) Eastbourne 1992–, PPS to Gerald Malone as Min for Health 1995–; former vice chm: Cons Backbench Tport and Tourism Ctees, All Pty Head Injuries Gp; currently vice chm: All Pty Br-Greek Gp, All Pty Daylight Extra Gp; former sec Cons Backbench Shipping and Shipbuilding Ctee; currently sec: Br-Cyprus Cwlth Parly Assoc Gp, All Pty Cyprus Gp; memb: All Pty Parly Gp for Pensioners, Parly Gp for Engrg Devpt, All Pty Disablement Gp, Br-American Parly Gp, Parly Maritime Gp, All Pty Parly Arts and Heritage Gp, Lords and Commons Solicitors Gp, All Pty Br-Caribbean Gp, All Pty Czech and Slovak Gp, Inter-Parly Union, Parly Advsy Cncl for Tport Safety, All Pty Cricket Gp; hon patron Bow Group 1993–95; memb IPU; pres SE Area Cons Educn Advsy Ctee; cncllr London Borough of Hammersmith and Fulham 1974–78; chm: Hammersmith Cons Assoc 1987–90, Hammersmith and Fulham Jt Mgmnt Ctee 1988–90; memb Mgmnt Ctee Stonham Housing Assoc Hostel for Ex-Offenders 1988–90, vice pres Eastbourne Branch BLESMA; *Recreations* sailing, polo, reading, music; *Clubs* Carlton, Eastbourne Constitutional, Guards Polo, Coningsby, Sussex CCC; *Style*— Nigel Waterson, Esq, MP; ✉ House of Commons, London SW1A 0AA

WATERSTONE, David George Stuart; CBE (1991); s of Malcolm Stuart Waterstone, MBE (d 1977), and Sylvia Catherine, *née* Sawday (d 1967); *b* 9 Aug 1935; *Educ* Tonbridge, St Catharine's Coll Cambridge (MA); *m* 1 (m dis), Dominique, *née* Viriot; 1 s (Mark), 2 da (Caroline, Isabelle); m 2, 10 April 1988, Sandra Kaye, da of George Edward Willey, of Aust; *Career* PO 601 County of London Sqdn RAF 1953–56, Lt 21 SAS 1956–59; HM Dip Serv 1959–70, sr exec IRC 1970–71, md Commercial BSC 1972–77; exec chm: BSC Chemicals 1977–81, Redpath Dorman Long 1977–81; chief exec: Welsh Devpt Agency 1983–90, Energy and Technical Services Group PLC 1990–95; chm Ansaldo International 1995–; non-exec dir: Portsmouth and Sunderland Newspapers plc 1984–, Hunting plc 1995–, Precoat International plc 1995–; memb Bd BSC 1976–81, chm Combined Heat and Power Assoc 1993–95; CIMgt 1975; *Recreations* sailing, walking, furniture making, painting; *Clubs* Reform; *Style*— David Waterstone, Esq, CBE; ✉ 1 Prior Park Buildings, Prior Park Rd, Bath BA2 4NP; Ansaldo International, 14 Headfort Place, London SW1X 7DH (☎ 0171 838 8910, fax 0171 259 5197)

WATERSTONE, Timothy John Stuart; s of Malcolm Stuart Waterstone, MBE (d 1977), of Maresfield, Sussex, and Sylvia Catherine, *née* Sawday (d 1967); *b* 30 May 1939; *Educ* Tonbridge, St Catharine's Coll Cambridge (MA); *m* 1, Oct 1962 (m dis 1971), Patricia Harcourt-Poole; 2 s (Richard b 1963, Martin b 1965), 1 da (Sylvia b 1969); m 2, Oct 1972 (m dis 1990), Clare Perkins; 2 da (Amanda b 1975, Maya b 1977), 1 s (Oliver b 1980); m 3, Feb 1991, Mary Rose Alison; 2 da (Lucy Rose b 1992, Daisy Alison b 1994); *Career* Carritt Moran & Co Calcutta 1962–64, Allied Breweries plc 1965–73, W H Smith Group plc 1973–81, fndr and exec chm Waterstone & Co 1982–93, chm Priory Investments Ltd 1990–95, dep chm Sinclair-Stevenson Publishers Ltd 1990–92; memb Bd: Futurestart (BT Venture Capital Fund) 1991–, Yale Univ Press 1992–, Troika BVI 1992–93, Virago Publishers 1995–96; tstee International House 1986–92, memb Ctee Booker Prize 1986–93; chm: Princes Youth Business Tst Awards 1990, Shelter 25th Anniversary Appeal 1991–92, London Int Festival of Theatre 1990–92, The Elgar Fndn 1992–; co-fndr Bookaid 1992; dir: The Academy of Ancient Music 1990–95, The London Philharmonic Orchestra 1990–; *Fiction* Lilley & Chase (1994), An Imperfect Marriage (1995), A Passage of Lives (1996); *Recreations* books, music; *Clubs* Garrick; *Style*— Timothy Waterstone, Esq; ✉ 1/11 Hay Hill, London W1X 7LF (☎ 0171 409 7339, fax 0171 409 7089)

WATERTON, John Brian; s of Laurence Maude Waterton (d 1976); *b* 10 March 1934; *Educ* Giggleswick Sch Yorks; *m* 1959, Jane Pollack, da of Harry Anthony Pitt Wilkinson (d 1966); 2 s, 2 da; *Career* co dir and gp mktg dir: Dawson International plc 1978–89, House of Hardy Ltd 1989–91; mktg dir Int Business Scottish Equitable plc 1991–; *Recreations* golf; *Clubs* Caledonian; *Style*— John Waterton, Esq; ✉ Scottish Equitable plc, International Business, Edinburgh Park, Edinburgh EH12 9SE (☎ 0131 339 9191, fax 0131 459 1107)

WATES, Michael Edward; s of Sir Ronald Wates (d 1986), and Phyllis Mary, *née* Trace; *b* 19 June 1935; *Educ* Oundle, Emmanuel Coll Cambridge (MA), Harvard Business Sch (PMD); *m* 24 June 1959, Caroline Josephine, *née* Connolly; *Career* Nat Serv RM 1953–55; Wates Ltd: joined 1959, dir Wates Construction 1963–, dir Wates Built Homes 1966–, chm Wates Group 1974; chm Br Bloodstock Agency plc 1986–92; past master Worshipful Co of Innholders (Liveryman 1958), Liveryman Worshipful Co of Coachmakers & Coach Harness Makers; Hon FRIBA; *Style*— Michael Wates, Esq; ✉ Manor House, Langton Long, Blandford Forum, Dorset DT11 9HS (☎ 01258 455241); Wates Ltd, 1260 London Rd, Norbury, London SW16 4EG (☎ 0181 764 5000)

WATHEN, Julian Philip Gerard; s of Gerard Anstruther Wathen, CIE (d 1958), and Melicent Louis, *née* Buxton (d 1984); bro of Rev Mark W G Wathen, TD, *qv*; *b* 21 May 1923; *Educ* Harrow; *m* 1948, Priscilla Florence, da of Maj-Gen Bevil Thomson Wilson, CB, DSO (d 1975); 1 s (Simon), 2 da (Lucy (Mrs Floyer-Acland), Henrietta (Mrs Goodall)); *Career* joined Barclays Bank DCO 1948, served Kenya, Tanganyika, Cyprus, New York, Sudan, Ghana; vice chm Barclays Bank 1979–84 (gen mangr 1966); dir Mercantile & Gen Reinsurance 1977–91; pres Royal African Soc 1984–88 (now hon vice pres), vice chm London Goodenough Tst for Overseas Graduates 1983–89 (now govr), chm City of London Endowment Tst for St Paul's Cathedral 1983–; chm Hall Sch Charitable Tst 1972–, chm St Paul's Sch, dep chm Thomas Telford Sch, govr Dauntsey's Sch; memb Cncl Book Aid International; Master Worshipful Co of Mercers 1984–85; *Clubs* Travellers'; *Style*— Julian Wathen, Esq; ✉ Woodcock House, Owlpen, Dursley GL11 5BY (☎ and fax 01453 860214); 1 Montagu Place, Marylebone, London W1H 1RG (☎ 0171 935 8569)

WATHEN, Rev Mark William Gerard; TD (1946); s of Gerard Anstruther Wathen, CIE (d 1958), and Melicent Louis, *née* Buxton (d 1984); bro of Julian P G Wathen, *qv*; *b* 18 Sept 1912; *Educ* Gresham's Sch Holt; *m* 1940, Rosemary, da of Charles Hartridge, of Findon Place, W Sussex, and his w Kathleen, er da of Sir Fortescue Flannery, 1 Bt; 2 s (Roderick b 1940, Jonathan b 1951), 2 da (Primula b 1946 d 1991, Erica (Mrs Jonathan Strange) b 1949); *Career* dir Barclays Bank (City, Ipswich, Norwich) 1948–72; High Sheriff Norfolk 1968; memb Gen Synod C of E 1970–80, church cmmr 1973–78, ordained deacon and priest 1982, priest i/c St Columba's Church Isle of Skye 1982–92; Master Mercers' Co 1963; *Recreations* the church, reading and writing; *Clubs* Brooks's, MCC; *Style*— The Rev Mark Wathen, TD; ✉ Tollgate Cottage, Marsham, Norwich NR10 5PX (☎ 01263 732673)

WATKIN, Dr Bernard Curtis; s of Harold Victor Watkin (d 1989), and Mary Curtis (d 1965); *b* 29 Aug 1931; *Educ* Hymer's Coll, Tiffin Sch, Univ of London (MB BS), St Bartholomew's Hosp (DPhysMed); *m* 21 Oct 1967, Jennifer Ann, da of Dr Edward Street; 2 da (Eleanor Curtis b 5 April 1971, Jessica Kate b 5 Feb 1973); *Career* hon clinical asst in rheumatology St Stephen's Hosp London; registrar Arthur Stanley Inst of Rheumatology Middx Hosp London, registrar in physical med St Thomas's Hosp London, scientific advsr in orthopaedics ICI Ltd, sports injury conslt to IMG (International Management Group); med offr to BCU at 1972 Olympics; memb: Br Assoc of Manipulative Med, Soc of Orthopaedic Med; *Books* contrib to various books on lumbar disorders; paper on Tempero-Mandibula R Joint in Rheumatoid Arthritis (1969); *Style*— Dr Bernard Watkin; ✉ 62 Wimpole Street, London W1M 7DE (☎ 0171 486 8684, fax 0171 935 8269)

WATKIN, (Francis) David; s of John Wilfrid Watkin, and Beatrice Lynda Dadswell; *b* 23 March 1925; *Career* director of photography; served Army 1944–47; American Academy Award 1985, Br Academy Award 1986; *Films* incl: The Knack, Help, Marat Sade, The Charge of the Light Brigade, Catch 22, The Devils, The Boyfriend, Jesus of Nazareth, Chariots of Fire, White Nights, Out of Africa, Moonstruck, Memphis Belle, Hamlet, This Boy's Life, Jane Eyre, Bogus; *Documentary* films incl The England of Elizabeth; *Recreations* music, reading; *Style*— David Watkin; ✉ 6 Sussex Mews, Brighton BN12 1GZ

WATKIN, Dr David John; s of Thomas Charles Watkin, and Vera Mary, *née* Saunders (d 1996); *b* 7 April 1941; *Educ* Farnham GS, Trinity Hall Cambridge (MA, PhD, LittD); *Career* Univ of Cambridge: fell Peterhouse 1970–, lectr in history of art 1972–, head Dept of History of Art Univ of Cambridge 1989–92, reader in history of architecture 1993–; memb: Historic Bldgs Advsy Ctee, Historic Bldgs and Monuments Cmmn 1980–95, Exec Ctee Georgian Gp; Hon Dr of Arts De Montfort Univ 1996; FSA 1979; *Books* Thomas Hope 1769–1831 and The Neo-Classical Idea (1968), The Life and Work of CR Cockerell RA (1974), Morality and Architecture (1977), English Architecture: A Concise History (1979), The Rise of Architectural History (1980), Neo-Classical and Nineteenth Century Architecture (with Robin Middleton, 1980), Athenian Stuart: Pioneer of the Greek Revival (1982), The English Vision: The Picturesque in Architecture, Landscape and Garden Design (1982), A History of Western Architecture (1986, 2 edn 1996), German Architecture and the Classical Ideal: 1740–1840 (with Tilman Mellinghoff, 1987), Sir John Soane: Enlightenment Thought and the Royal Academy Lectures (1996); *Clubs* Beefsteak, Travellers'; *Style*— Dr David Watkin, FSA; ✉ Peterhouse, Cambridge CB2 1RD (☎ 01223 338200)

WATKIN, Steven Llewellyn; s of John Watkin, of Port Talbot, West Glamorgan, and Sandra, *née* Davies; *b* 15 Sept 1964; *Educ* Cymer Afan Comp Sch, Glan Afan Comp Sch, Swansea Coll of Further Educn, S Glamorgan Inst of Higher Educn (BA); *Career* professional cricketer; Glamorgan CCC: debut v Worcs 1986, awarded county cap 1989; 11 caps Welsh Secdy Schs 1981–84; tours: England A to Kenya/Zimbabwe 1990, Pakistan/Sri Lanka 1991 and WI/Bermuda 1992, Br Colls to W Indies 1987, Glamorgan to W Indies 1989, memb team touring W Indies 1993/94; 3 test matches Eng v W Indies (Headingley and Lords) 1991, memb squad Ashes series 1993, played last test match Eng v Aust (Oval) 1993; jt leading wicket taker with 94 wickets 1989, leading wicket taker with 92 wickets 1993; Players Player of the Year 1993; soccer cap Welsh Boys under 16; *Recreations* carpentry, gardening, watching TV, listening to music, a quiet pint, motor mechanics, all sports; *Style*— Steven Watkin, Esq; ✉ c/o Glamorgan CCC, Sophia Gardens, Cardiff CF1 9XR (☎ 01222 343478)

WATKINS, Alan (Rhun); s of David John Watkins (d 1980), of Tycroes, Dyfed, and Violet, *née* Harris (d 1986); *b* 3 April 1933; *Educ* Amman Valley GS Ammanford, Queens' Coll Cambridge (MA, LLM); *m* 1955, Ruth Howard (d 1982); 1 s, 1 da (and 1 da decd); *Career* Flying Offr Educn Branch RAF 1955–57; called to the Bar Lincoln's Inn 1957, res asst Dept of Govt LSE 1958–59, editorial staff Sunday Express 1959–69 (NY corr 1961, crossbencher columnist 1963–64); political corr: Spectator 1964–67, New Statesman 1967–76; political columnist Sunday Mirror 1968–69, dir The Statesman and Nation Publishing Co 1973–76, columnist Evening Standard 1974–75, political columnist Observer 1976–93, columnist Independent on Sunday 1993–; rugby columnist: Field 1984–86, Independent 1986–; chm Political Advsy Gp Br Youth Cncl 1979–81, memb (Lab) Fulham Borough Cncl; *Books* The Liberal Dilemma (1966), The Making of the Prime Minister (with A Alexander, 1970), Brief Lives (1982), Sportswriter's Eye (1989), A Slight Case of Libel (1990), A Conservative Coup (1991, 2 edn 1992); *Recreations* reading, walking; *Clubs* Beefsteak, Garrick; *Style*— Alan Watkins, Esq; ✉ 54 Barnsbury St, London N1 1ER (☎ 0171 607 0812)

WATKINS, Brian; CMG (1993); s of James Edward Watkins (d 1981), of Newport, Gwent, and Gladys Ann, *née* Fletcher (d 1942); *b* 26 July 1933; *Educ* Newport HS, LSE (BSc(Econ)), Worcester Coll Oxford; *m* 1, 26 Oct 1957 (m dis 1979), Thelma, da of Thomas Horace Waite (d 1963), of Newport, Gwent; 1 s (Mark b 1958); m 2, 31 Dec 1982, Elisabeth, da of Arfon Jones; 1 da (Caroline b 1985); *Career* RAF 1954–58; HMOCS Sierra Leone 1959–63, local govt 1963–66, admin Tristan da Cunha 1966–69; admitted slr 1970; lectr Univ of Manchester 1969–71; HM Dip Serv: FCO 1971–73, NY 1973–76, NI Office 1976–78, FCO 1978–81, cnsllr and dep govr Bermuda 1981–83, cnsllr (econ) and consul gen Islamabad 1983–86, consul gen Vancouver 1986–90, high cmmr to Swaziland 1990–93 (ret); pt/t immigration adjudicator 1993–; memb: Law Soc, Cncl BCEL; OStJ 1994 (memb Gwent Cncl); *Recreations* reading, dancing, theatre; *Clubs* St James's; *Style*— Brian Watkins, Esq, CMG

WATKINS, David John; s of Thomas George Watkins (d 1986), and Alice Elizabeth, *née* Allen (d 1955); *b* 27 Aug 1925; *Educ* S Bristol Central Sch, Merrywood GS, Bristol Tech Coll; *Career* Nat Serv RAF 1945–48; engr in indust 1941–45 and 1948–66; MP (Lab) Consett 1966–83 (memb Lab Pty 1950–); chm Courtlands Estate (Richmond) Ltd 1990– (dir 1987–); hon treas Cncl for Advancement of Arab-Br Understanding 1990– (memb 1968–, dir 1983–90); memb Amalgamated Engrg and Electrical Union (AEEU, formerly Amalgamated Engrg Union) 1941–; hon treas Med Aid for Palestinians 1995– (tstee 1984–); *Books* Labour and Palestine (1975), Industrial Common Ownership (1978), The World and Palestine (1980), The Exceptional Conflict (1984), Palestine - An Inescapable Duty (1992), Seventeen Years In Obscurity (1996); *Recreations* reading, music, swimming; *Clubs* Royal Cwlth Soc; *Style*— David Watkins, Esq; ✉ The Arab-British Centre, 21 Collingham Rd, London SW5 0NU (☎ 0171 373 8414, fax 0171 835 2088)

WATKINS, Rev Gordon Derek; s of Clifford Henry Watkins (d 1967), of Bristol, and Margaret Caroline, *née* Grimley (d 1974); *b* 16 July 1929; *Educ* St Brendan's Coll Clifton; *m* 3 Jan 1957, Beryl Evelyn Watkins, da of Thomas Henry Whitaker (d 1959), of Sydney, NSW; *Career* Nat Serv RAOC 1947–49; minor canon of Grafton Cathedral NSW 1953–56, vicar of Texas Queensland 1956–61, curate of St Wilfrid's Harrogate 1961–63, vicar of Upton Park 1963–67; rector of: Great and Little Bentley 1967–73, Great Canfield 1973–78; asst sec Chelmsford Diocesan Synod 1973–78, sec Chelmsford Redundant Churches Uses Ctee 1973–78, pastoral sec Diocese of London 1978–84, vicar St Martin-within-Ludgate City of London 1984–89, sec London Diocesan Advsy Ctee 1984–94, priest vicar of Westminster Abbey 1984–89, Priest-in-Ordinary to HM The Queen 1984–96; chaplain: Ward of Farringdon within City of London 1984–89, Knights of the Round Table 1984–89; Freeman City of London 1984; Chaplain Co of Makers of Playing Cards 1987–88, Hon Freeman Co of Pipe Makers and Tobacco Blenders 1994– (Chaplain 1985–94); *Recreations* reading, television, the country; *Clubs* Athenaeum; *Style*— The Rev Gordon Watkins; ✉ 21 Crammond Place, Dalgety Bay, Dunfermline, Fife KY11 5LS (☎ 01383 822634)

WATKINS, Maj-Gen Guy Hansard; CB (1986), OBE (1974); s of Col Alfred Norman Mitchell Watkins (d 1970), of Milford-on-Sea, Hants, and Sylvia Christine, *née* Downing (d 1988); *b* 30 Nov 1933; *Educ* The King's Sch Canterbury; *m* 15 Feb 1958, Sylvia Margaret, da of William Lawrence Grant, of Walton-on-the-Hill, Surrey; 2 s (Michael b 1959, Peter b 1971), 2 da (Anne-Marie b 1961, Carol b 1965); *Career* cmmnd RA 1953, Instr Staff Coll 1971, CO 39 Regt RA (BAOR) 1973, Task Force Cdr (BAOR) 1977, Dir Public Relations (Army) 1980, Cmd Artillery Div (BAOR) 1982, Dir Gen Army Manning and Recruiting 1985, ret 1986; chief exec The Royal Hong Kong Jockey Club 1986–96; dir: British Bloodstock Agency plc 1996–, Racecourse Holdings Trust 1996–; hon chm Metro Manila Turf Club 1996–; Liveryman Worshipful Co of Farriers; *Recreations* riding, golf, fishing; *Clubs* Royal Hong Kong Jockey, Army and Navy, West Sussex Golf, Littlehampton Golf, Oriental; *Style*— Maj-Gen Guy Watkins, CB, OBE; ✉ British Bloodstock Agency plc, Queensberry House, High Street, Newmarket, Suffolk CB8 9BD (☎ 01638 665021, fax 01638 660283)

WATKINS, James Arthur; s of William Arthur Watkins, of York, England, and Mary Lilian Chapman; *b* 26 Sept 1945; *Educ* Archbishop Holgate's Sch York, Univ of Leeds (LLB); *m* 1, 4 March 1967 (m dis), Ursula Barbara; 2 da (Philippa Jane Langford b 1975, Victoria Joanne Langford b 1977); m 2, 7 Jan 1993, Lisa, *née* Cattermole; 1 s (Oscar George James b 6 Sept 1995), 1 da (Cosima Amelia Clementine b 6 Nov 1996); *Career* Linklaters & Paines: articled clerk 1967, asst slr 1969, ptnr 1975–94; legal dir Trafalgar House plc 1994–96, legal dir Schroders plc 1996–; dir Bankers' Trustee Co; memb Worshipful Co of Solicitors 1976, Freeman City of London 1976; memb: Law Soc 1969, Int Bar Assoc 1978, Union Internationale des Avocats 1980; *Recreations* golf, tennis, reading, music, food and wine; *Clubs* Hurlingham, Annabel's, Hanbury Manor Golf and Country, Hong Kong, Shek-O Country; *Style*— James Watkins, Esq; ✉ 2 Montpelier Square, London SW7 1JT (☎ 0171 589 9819)

WATKINS, Prof Jeffrey Clifton; s of Colin Hereward Watkins (d 1983), and Amelia Miriam Watkins (d 1981); *b* 20 Dec 1929; *Educ* Perth Modern Sch Western Aust, Univ of Western Aust (BSc, Hackett travelling studentship award), Univ of Cambridge (PhD); *m* 1973, Beatrice Joan, da of Morton Thacher; 1 s (Timothy Douglas b 10 Sept 1973), 1 da (Katherine Helen b 9 Oct 1975); *Career* post-doctoral research fell: Univ of Cambridge (Rockefeller fell) 1954–55, Yale Univ 1955–57, Aust Nat Univ Canberra 1958–65 (fell 1961–65); scientific offr ARC Inst of Animal Physiology Babraham Cambridge 1965–67, memb Scientific Staff MRC Neuropsychiatry Unit Carshalton Surrey 1968–73; Univ of Bristol Sch of Med: sr research fell Depts of Physiology and Pharmacology 1973–83, hon sr research fell Dept of Pharmacology 1983–89, hon prof of pharmacology 1989–; Wakeman Award (USA) for outstanding achievement in neuroscience 1992, Dana Award (USA) for pioneering achievement in health 1994, Bristol-Myers Squibb Award (USA) for distinguished achievement in neuroscience research 1995; memb: Int Brain Research Orgn 1969, Br Pharmacological Soc 1974, Br Physiological Soc 1975, (American) Soc for Neuroscience 1988; FRS 1988, memb Academia Europaea 1989; *Books* The NMDA Receptor (ed with G L Collingridge, 1989, 2 edn 1995); *Recreations* the countryside; *Style*— Prof Jeffrey Watkins, FRS; ✉ 8 Lower Court Road, Lower Almondsbury, Bristol BS12 4DX (☎ 01454 613829); Department of Pharmacology, School of Medical Sciences, University Walk, Bristol BS8 1TD (☎ 0117 928 7639, fax 0117 927 9839)

WATKINS, John; s of Charles Watkins, and Kathleen Myrtle, *née* Cullis (d 1969); *b* 16 Dec 1943; *Educ* Yeovil Sch Somerset; *m* 2 Sept 1967, Diane Mary, da of Cyril Charles Hooper; 2 s (James Charles Cullis b 24 Oct 1969, Alastair John Cullis b 2 Aug 1972), 2 da (Philippa Louise b 11 Sept 1974, Gemma Kate b 7 Sept 1978); *Career* articled clerk Howard Howes & Co 1962–68; ptnr: Neville Russell 1972–89, Ernst & Young 1989–; FCA (ACA 1968), assoc memb Lloyd's of London 1986; *Clubs* RAC; *Style*— John Watkins, Esq; ✉ Ernst & Young, Private Client Services, Rolls House, 7 Rolls Buildings, Fetter Lane, London EC4A 1NH (☎ 0171 931 2808)

WATKINS, Karen; *see:* John, Katherine

WATKINS, Nowell St John; s of Josceline Charles Shaw Watkins (d 1974), and Anne Agnes St John Beddow, *née* Hickman (d 1989); *b* 20 Aug 1930; *Educ* Haileybury; *m* 27 April 1957, Penelope Mary, da of James Herbert Harris, MC (d 1981), of Mayfield; 1 s (Timothy James b 16 May 1961), 1 da (Amanda Mary St John b 14 Jun 1959); *Career* admitted slr 1954, NP and ptnr in firm variously known as Steward Vulliamy and Watkins & Stewards 1960–86, sr ptnr Watkins Stewart & Ross 1986–; HM Coroner for Ipswich Dist of Suffolk, chm Social Security Appeal Tbnl and Disability Appeal Tbnls; *Recreations* cricket, racing, gardening; *Clubs* MCC, Ipswich Rotary; *Style*— Nowell Watkins, Esq; ✉ Watkins Stewart & Ross, 8 Lower Brook St, Ipswich IP4 1AL (☎ 01473 226 266, fax 01473 230 052)

WATKINS, Dr Peter John; s of Kenneth Harold Watkins (d 1938), and Irmgard Madeleine, *née* Herrmann (d 1989); *b* 6 Feb 1936; *Educ* Ampleforth, Gonville and Caius Coll Cambridge/St Bartholomew's Hosp London (MA, MB BChir, MD, FRCP); *m* 1, 1970, Gillian Barbara (d 1985), da of Eric Fowler; 2 da (Julia Rachel b 7 Feb 1971, Sara Helen b 12 Dec 1972), 1 s (Benedict Kenneth b 27 Nov 1974); m 2, 1993, Valerie Joan Brown; 2 step s (Thomas Dominic Brown b 31 Oct 1974, Adam Robert Brown b 29 Sept 1976); *Career* jr resident appts Bart's London 1961–65; Gen Hosp Birmingham: sr house offr 1965–66, research fell 1966–68, sr registrar 1968–71; KCH London: consIt physician 1971–, dir of postgrad educn 1989–; hon sr lectr King's Coll Sch of Med and Dentistry 1987–; visiting prof Amsterdam Med Centre 1985; Br Diabetic Assoc: chm Med Advsy Ctee 1980–83, chm Med and Scientific Section 1990–93; chm: Clinical Autonomic Research Soc 1986–87, Specialist Advsy Ctee on Endocrinology and Diabetes 1987–90; hon sec and treas Assoc of Physicians of GB and I 1983–93, hon sec Choosing Priorities in the NHS RCP 1994–95; pres Euro Diabetic Nephropathy Study Gp 1996–; Castelli-Pedroli Prize and Golgi Lecture Euro Assoc for the Study of Diabetes 1990, Charles Best Lecture Toronto Diabetes Assoc 1996; memb: Assoc of Physicians of GB and I, Med and Scientific Section Br Diabetic Assoc, RSM; *Books* Long-term Complications of Diabetes (ed, 1986), ABC of Diabetes (3 edn, 1993), Diabetes and its Management (5 edn, 1996); *Recreations* hill walking, music; *Style*— Dr Peter J Watkins; ✉ 31 Lancaster Avenue, London SE27 9EL (☎ 0181 761 8086); King's Diabetes Centre, King's College Hospital, Denmark Hill, London SE5 9RS (☎ 0171 346 3241, fax 0171 346 3407)

WATKINS, Peter Rodney; s of Frank Arthur Watkins (d 1990), of Seaton, Devon, and Mary Gwyneth, *née* Price, of Brentwood, Essex; *b* 8 Oct 1931; *Educ* Solihull Sch, Emmanuel Coll Cambridge (MA); *m* 23 Aug 1971, Jillian Ann, da of Henry John Burge (d 1973); 2 da (Anna Mary b 1972, Katharine Ruth b 1975); *Career* Nat Serv FO RAF 1954–56; history master E Ham GS 1956–59, sixth form history master and house tutor Brentwood Sch Essex 1959–64, sr history master Bristol GS 1964–69; headmaster: King Edward's Five Ways Sch Birmingham 1969–74, Chichester HS for Boys 1974–79; princ Price's Sixth Form Coll Fareham Hants 1980–84, chief exec Sch Curriculum Devpt Ctee 1988 (dep chief exec 1984–88), dep chief exec Nat Curriculum Cncl 1988–91, educnl conslt 1991–, OFSTED inspector 1993–; exec Secondary Heads Assoc 1980–84, chm Christian Educn Movement 1980–87, govr: Bedales Sch Hants 1986–88, St Luke's Sch Portsmouth 1992–; reader St Peter's Bishops Waltham 1989–; *Books* The Sixth Form College in Practice (1982), Modular Approaches to the Secondary Curriculum (1986), St Barnabas' Swanmore 1845–1995 (1995); *Recreations* fell walking, local history, theology; *Style*— Peter R Watkins, Esq; ✉ 7 Crofton Way, Swanmore, Southampton, Hampshire SO32 2RF (☎ 01489 894789); office: The Old Chapel House, Pound Hill, Alresford SO24 9BU (☎ 01962 732307, fax 01962 735597)

WATKINS, Richard Valentine; *b* 23 Sept 1950; *Educ* Wellington, Loughborough Univ of Technol (BSc); *m* 1978, Charlotte, *née* de Laszlo; 2 s, 1 da; *Career* Phillips & Drew Inc 1972–77, mangr and overseas rep Kleinwort Benson 1977–83, md Phillips & Drew Inc (NY) 1983–86, pres Hoare Govett Inc (NY) 1986–88, chm Burns Fry Hoare Govett Inc (NY) 1988, exec dir J Henry Schroder Wagg & Co Ltd 1988–92, former chief exec Schroder Securities Ltd and dir of related cos in SE Asia, Japan, Korea, Switzerland; fndr dir and chief exec LatInvest Holdings and dir related cos 1992–, dir Morgan Grenfell Latin American Companies Trust plc; *Recreations* skiing; *Style*— Richard Watkins, Esq; ✉ LatInvest Holdings (UK) Ltd, 1 Angel Court, London EC2 (☎ 0171 600 3999, fax 0171 600 4144)

WATKINS, Roger Malcolm; s of Ronald Alan Watkins, of London, and Molly Elsie, *née* Bullen; *b* 15 Jan 1952; *Educ* Latymer Upper Sch, Emmanuel Coll Cambridge (MA), Westminster Med Sch Univ of London (MB MChir); *m* 4 April 1981, Mary Jane, da of Maj John Strelley, MBE, of Hereford; *Career* sr registrar in surgery Westminster Hosp London 1984–87, sr registrar and lectr in surgery Royal Marsden Hosp London 1987–88, conslt surgn Derriford Hosp Plymouth 1988–; memb: RSM, BMA, Br Assoc of Surgical Oncology, Assoc of Surgns of GB; FRCS; *Books* Aids to Postgraduate Surgery (1989); *Style*— Roger Watkins, Esq; ✉ Bay Tree House, The Crescent, Crapstone Yelverton, Devon PL20 7PS (☎ 01822 852504); Derriford Hospital, Plymouth PL6 8DH (☎ 01752 792108)

WATKINS, Rt Hon Sir Tasker Watkins; VC (1944), GBE (1990), kt (1971), DL (Glamorgan 1956), PC (1980); s of Bertram Watkins and Jane Watkins; *b* 18 Nov 1918; *Educ* Pontypridd GS; *m* 1941, Eirwen Evans; 1 s (decd), 1 da (Mair, *see* John Griffith Williams, Esq, QC); *Career* WWII Maj Welch Regt; called to the Bar Middle Temple 1948, QC 1965, dep chm Carmarthenshire QS 1966–71, dep chm Radnor QS 1962–71; recorder: Merthyr Tydfil 1968–70, Swansea 1970–71; High Ct judge: Family Div 1971–74, Queen's Bench 1974–80; presiding judge Wales and Chester Circuit 1975–80 (ldr 1970–71), Lord Justice of Appeal 1980–93, sr presiding judge England and Wales 1983–91, dep chief justice 1988–93; chm Judicial Studies Bd 1979–80; chm Wales Region Mental Health Review Tribunal 1960–71; Hon LLD: Wales 1979, Glamorgan Univ 1996; Hon FRCS England 1992; *Style*— The Rt Hon Sir Tasker Watkins, VC, GBE, DL; ✉ 5 Pump Court, Middle Temple, London EC4; Fairwater Lodge, Fairwater Rd, Llandaff, Cardiff, S Glamorgan

WATKINS, Thomas Frederick; s of Frederick (Ginger) Watkins, and Patricia Daphne (Lilly Loop); *b* 21 Sept 1949; *Educ* London Coll of Furniture (Dip, Lon Cert Art and Design); *partner* Darren Sven Coppin; *Career* design asst Conran Design Gp, designer Tom Law Assoc, sr designer Richard Ellis & Co, mgmnt design conslt to music indust; currently dir Massive Management (chm Massive Gp of Cos); sometime mangr Bros, Pet Shop Boys, East 17; memb: 3 T's Soc, Mickey Mouse Collectors Club, Pelham Puppets Assoc, Steif (teddy bear club); *Recreations* collecting Mickey Mouse memorabelia; *Style*— Thomas Watkins, Esq; ✉ Massive Management, 26 Drysdale Street, London N1 8LS (☎ 0171 613 2457, fax 0171 613 4395)

WATKINS, William George; s of W H E Watkins, and A M Brown; *b* 29 Aug 1933; *Educ* King's Sch Canterbury, Univ Coll Oxford (MA); *m* Anne, *née* Roper; 3 s (David b 1966, James b 1971, John b 1971), 1 da (Emma b 1968); *Career* Nat Serv 2 Lt 40 Field Regt RA 1952–54; asst slr Slaughter and May 1960–69 (articled clerk 1957–60); Lovell White Durrant (formerly Durrant Piesse, previously Durrant Cooper and Hambling): joined 1969, ptnr 1970–95, conslt 1995–; Liveryman City of London, memb City of London Solicitors' Co; memb: Law Soc, Int Bar Assoc; *Recreations* walking, industrial archaeology; *Style*— William Watkins, Esq; ✉ Bramshott Manor, Church Rd, Bramshott, Liphook, Hants GU30 7SQ; Lovell White Durrant, 65 Holborn Viaduct, London EC1A 2DY (☎ 0171 236 0066, fax 0171 248 4212)

WATKINSON, David Robert; s of late Robert Douglas Watkinson, of St Johns, Woking, Surrey, and Muriel Winifred, *née* Reeves; *b* 6 Oct 1947; *Educ* Woking GS for Boys, Clare Coll Cambridge (MA, LLB); *partner* Suzanne Eve Tarlin; 1 da (Eva Rose b 1 July 1980); *Career* called to the Bar Middle Temple 1972; fndr memb chambers Wellington St London 1974–88 (committed to working in social welfare areas of law), specialist in housing law; memb: Exec Ctee Family Squatting Advsy Ctee 1972–75, N Islington Law Centre 1974–78; memb and legal advsr to campaign against criminal trespass laws 1974–78, occasional legal advsr Advsy Serv to Squatters 1975–, concerned with publicity for campaign of limitation of rights of defence in W Germany late 1970s, campaigned to extend grant of Legal Aid in particular to Magistrates' Cts 1979–80, memb Stop the Criminal Trespass Law Campaign 1983–84, teacher of housing law Univ of Warwick 1984, observer on behalf of Haldane Soc for Socialist Lawyers and on behalf of Agric Allied Workers Branch Tport and Gen Workers Union at trial of agric day labourers in Spain 1986, lectures on legal aspects of housing S Bank Poly and other instns 1988, assoc dir Nat Housing Law Serv 1991–93, memb Legal and Parly Ctee SQUASH (Squatters Action for Secure Homes) 1993–94; vice-chm Housing Law Practitioners Assoc 1994–; author of reviews and articles on housing 1974– (Legal Action Gp Bulletin, Roof, Law Soc's Gazette, Haldane Soc Bulletin); memb: Haldane Soc Socialist Lawyers Legal Action Gp, Admin Law Bar Assoc, Housing Law Practitioners' Assoc, Nicaragua Solidarity Campaign; *Books* contrib: Law in a Housing Crisis (1975), NCCL Civil Rights Guide (1978), Squatting - The Real Story (1980), Critical Lawyers Handbook (1992); Squatting Trespass and Civil Liberties (jtly, 1976); *Recreations* travel, theatre, cinema, ethnic music, history, archaeology, fiction, swimming; *Style*— David Watkinson, Esq; ✉ 2 Garden Court, Temple, London EC4 9BL (☎ 0171 353 1633, fax 0171 353 4621)

WATKINSON, Douglas Arthur; s of Raymond Arthur Watkinson (d 1947), and Joan Lilian, *née* Crawley (d 1972); *b* 5 July 1945; *Educ* Haberdashers' Aske's, East Fifteen Acting Sch; *m* 20 June 1972, Lesley Moira, da of Stanley Thompson; 2 s (Callum Neil b 21 Aug 1979, Duncan Clyde b 23 Feb 1981), 2 da (Fenella Laurie b 31 May 1978, Ailsa Morag b 2 Nov 1983); *Career* freelance writer; began as actor, script ed BBC 1972–75, freelance writer 1975–; contrib to TV series/serials incl: Z Cars, The Brothers, Owen MD, Duchess of Duke Street, Spy Trap, Onedin Line, Juliet Bravo, The Bill, Boon, Maybury, Lovejoy, Poirot, Anna Lee; sole writer of series: For Maddie With Love, Strange True Stories, The New Statesman, Forever Green, Land of Promise; stage plays: Let's Do It My Way, The Dragon's Tail, Caesar and Me; memb Writers' Guild; *Recreations* travel, photography, bonsai, reading; *Clubs* National Liberal; *Style*— Douglas Watkinson, Esq; ✉ Dinton Cottage, Dinton, Bucks HP17 8UH (☎ 01296 748270, fax 01296 747439); c/o MBA Literary Agents, 45 Fitzroy St, London W1P 5HR (☎ 0171 387 2076)

WATKINSON, Ernest Cooper; s of John Ernest Watkinson (d 1960), and Margaret Hannah, *née* Cooper (d 1971); *b* 4 Sept 1937; *Educ* Skerry's Coll, Sch of Architecture King's Coll Durham (H B Saint Meml Prize, Br Paints Prize, Dip Arch); *m* 1961, Sheila Joan (d 1994), da of Victor Ernest Strong (d 1974); 2 s (Neil b 1964, Simon b 1966); *Career* Williamson Faulkner Brown & Partners (amalgamation of W H Williamson and H F Brown 1962): joined 1960, assoc 1963, ptnr 1965; practice became Faulkner-Brown Hendy Watkinson Stonor 1972 then FaulknerBrowns 1986; external examiner Sch of Architecture Univ of Newcastle upon Tyne 1986–88, hon architect Newcastle upon Tyne Cncl for Vol Serv; *Awards* practice won over 50 incl RIBA Architecture Awards, Civic

Tst Awards, Structural Steel Awards, Concrete Soc Awards; Freeman City of London 1985, memb Guild of Freemen City of London 1986, Liveryman Worshipful Co of Chartered Architects 1989; FRIBA 1962, memb Assoc of Conslt Architects 1988; *Recreations* travel, theatre, gardening, Rotary; *Clubs* East India; *Style*— Ernest Watkinson, Esq; ✉ FaulknerBrowns, Dobson House, Northumbrian Way, Killingworth, Newcastle upon Tyne NE12 0QW (☎ 0191 268 3007, fax 0191 268 5227)

WATLING, His Hon Judge; (David) Brian Watling; QC (1979); s of Russell Watling and Stella, *née* Ridley; *b* 18 June 1935; *Educ* Charterhouse, King's Coll London; *m* 1964, Noelle Bugden, WRNS; *Career* called to the Bar 1957, Crown Ct recorder 1979–81, circuit judge (SE Circuit) 1981–; memb Prosecuting Cncl to the Crown Central Criminal Court 1972–79; Univ of Buckingham: visiting lectr 1977–80, prof in law 1980–84; *Style*— His Hon Judge Watling, QC; ✉ Chelmsford Crown Court, PO Box 9, New Street, Chelmsford CM1 1EL

WATNEY, (John) Adrian; s of Maj John Douglas Watney, RA (d 1983), of Dorking, Surrey, and Barbara Ann, *née* Smith; *b* 3 Oct 1943; *Educ* Sherborne; *m* 9 Sept 1967, Angela Winifred, da of Dudley Partridge (d 1982), of Horsley, Surrey; 1 s (Christopher b 1981), 3 da (Katherine b 1970, Sarah b 1972, Victoria b 1976); *Career* admitted slr 1968; currently ptnr Masons Solicitors; Freeman: City of London 1964, Worshipful Co Mercers (Master 1990–91); memb Law Soc; chm Classical Road Show; tstee: Stiftelsen Carpe Vitum, Marrown Environmental Fund, The Kingwood Tst; special tstee St Bartholomew's Hosp; govr: Sherborne Sch, St Paul's Boys' Sch (chm), St Paul's Girls Sch (chm), Glenesk Sch; *Recreations* golf, cricket, rugby, opera; *Clubs* Royal and Ancient Golf (St Andrews), MCC, Rye Golf, Walton Heath Golf, Lucifers GS, Hon Co of Edinburgh Golfers; *Style*— Adrian Watney, Esq; ✉ Masons, 30 Aylesbury Street, London EC1R 0ER (☎ 0171 490 4000, fax 0171 490 2545)

WATSON, *see also:* Inglefield-Watson, Milne-Watson

WATSON, Dr Adam; s of Adam Watson, of Banchory, Kincardineshire, and Margaret Isabella Spence, *née* Rae; *b* 14 April 1930; *Educ* Turriff Acad, Univ of Aberdeen (BSc, PhD, DSc); *m* 19 March 1955, Jenny Mortimer, *née* Sutherland; 1 s (Adam Christopher b 7 Oct 1963), 1 da (Jenny b 13 July 1958); *Career* demonstrator in biological sciences McGill Univ Montreal 1952–53, teacher of sci Aberdeen Acad 1956–57, sr res fell Univ of Aberdeen 1957–60 (asst lectr Dept of Natural History 1953–56), princ scientific offr Nature Conservancy and offr in charge Mountain and Moorland Res Station 1966–71, sr princ scientific offr Inst of Terrestrial Ecology Banchory 1971–90; memb Cairngorms Partnership Bd 1995–; Neill prize of RSE 1983–85; CBiol, fell Arctic Inst of N America, FRSE 1971, FIBiol; *Books* Animal Populations in Relation to their Food Resources (ed, 1970), The Cairngorms (1975 and 1992), The Cairngorms (with D Nethersole-Thompson, 1981), The Place Names of Upper Deeside (1984); *Recreations* hill walking, mountaineering, cross-country skiing; *Clubs* Scot Mountaineering, Scot Ornithologists; *Style*— Dr Adam Watson, FRSE; ✉ Clachnaben, Crathes, Banchory, Kincardineshire AB31 3JE (☎ 01330 844609); c/o Institute of Terrestrial Ecology, Hill of Brathens, Glassel, Banchory, Kincardineshire AB31 4BY (☎ 01330 823434)

WATSON, Alan Carlos; s of William Carlos Watson (d 1990), and Doris May, *née* Putwain; *b* 26 Oct 1940; *Educ* Willesden Tech Coll (HNC); *m* 12 Sept 1964, Sandra Mary, da of John Bruce Garner; 1 s (Ashley b 8 April 1966), 1 da (Martine b 11 Dec 1968); *Career* student apprentice Matthew Hall Mechanical Services Ltd, ptnr Building Design Partnership 1988– (joined 1972); expert witness for House of Commons Select Ctee Channel Tunnel Hybrid Bill; FCIWEM; *Recreations* golf; *Style*— Alan Watson, Esq; ✉ 17 Silver Close, Harrow, Middlesex HA3 6JT; Building Design Partnership, 16 Gresse St, London W1A 4WD (☎ 0171 631 4733, fax 0171 631 0393)

WATSON, Prof Alan John; CBE (1985); s of Rev John William Watson (d 1980), of Bognor Regis, and Edna Mary, *née* Peters (d 1985); *b* 3 Feb 1941; *Educ* Kingswood Sch Bath, Jesus Coll Cambridge (MA); *m* 1965, Karen, da of Hartwig Lederer (d 1966), of Frankfurt-on-Main; 2 s (Stephen b 1966, Martin b 1968); *Career* history scholar and res asst to Regius Prof of Modern History Cambridge 1962–64; broadcaster; presenter The Money Programme (BBC 2) and Panorama (BBC 1) 1964–76, head of radio & TV EEC Cmmn 1976–80; presenter: You and 92 (BBC 1) 1990, The Germans (C4) 1992, Key Witness (BBC Radio 4) 1996; chief exec Charles Barker City Ltd 1980–83, dep chm Sterling PR Ltd 1985–86; chm: City and Corporate Counsel Ltd 1987–93, Corporate Vision Ltd 1989–, Threadneedle Publishing Group plc 1989–94, Corporate Television Networks Ltd 1992–, Burson-Marsteller UK 1994–96, Burson-Marsteller Europe 1996–; visiting fell Louvainium Business Sch Brussels 1990–94, Erasmus visiting prof Catholic Univ of Louvain 1990–; pres Lib Pty 1984–85, vice chm Euro Movement 1995–; memb: Exec Bd UNICEF 1985–92, Exec Jesus Coll Cambridge Soc 1987–94, Bd Prince of Wales Business Leaders' Forum 1996–, BT Bd Community and Charities Ctee 1996–; chm: Royal Television Soc 1992–94, British-German Assoc 1992–; chm: Bd of Govrs Westminster Coll Oxford 1988–94, Richmond Theatre Appeal 1990–91; pres Heathrow Assoc for the Control of Aircraft Noise 1991–95; govr: Kingswood Sch 1984–90, English Speaking Union 1993– (dep chm 1995–); Hon Doctorate St Lawrence Univ 1992; German Order of Merit 1995; FRTS 1992; *Books* Europe at Risk (1974), The Germans (1992, 1994 and 1995); *Recreations* travel, wines, boating; *Clubs* Brooks's, RAC, Kennel; *Style*— Prof Alan Watson, CBE; ✉ Cholmondeley House, 3 Cholmondeley Walk, Richmond, Surrey; Somerset Lodge, Nunney, Somerset; Burson-Marsteller, 24–28 Bloomsbury Way, London WC1A 2PX (☎ 0171 831 6262, fax 0171 404 1146)

WATSON, Prof (George) Alistair; s of George Arthur Watson (d 1972), and Grace Ann, *née* MacDonald; *b* 30 Sept 1942; *Educ* Breadalbane Acad, Univ of Edinburgh (BSc, MSc), Australian Nat Univ (PhD); *m* 6 April 1971, (Margaret) Hilary, da of Robert Whitton Mackay (d 1971); 1 da (Kirsty b 1989); *Career* Univ of Dundee: lectr 1970–82, sr lectr 1982–84, reader 1984–88, prof 1988–, head Dept of Mathematics and Computer Sci 1992–; FIMA 1972; FRSE 1996; *Books* Computational Methods for Matrix Eigenproblems (with A R Gourlay, 1973), Approximation Theory and Numerical Methods (1980); *Recreations* opera, photography, gardening; *Style*— Prof Alistair Watson, FRSE; ✉ 7 Albany Rd, Broughty Ferry, Dundee DD5 1NS, (☎ 01382 779473); Department of Mathematics and Computer Science, University of Dundee, Dundee DD1 4HN (☎ 01382 344472)

WATSON, Sir (James) Andrew; 5 Bt (UK 1866), of Henrietta Street, Cavendish Sq, St Marylebone, Co Middx; s of Sir Thomas Watson, 4 Bt (d 1941), and Ella, Lady Watson; *b* 30 Dec 1937; *Educ* Eton; *m* 1965, Christabel Mary, eldest da of Maj Kenneth Ralph Malcolm (Peter) Carlisle (d 1983), and sister of Sir Kenneth Melville Carlisle, MP, *qv*; 2 s, 1 da; *Heir* s, Roland Victor Watson; *Career* Lt Life Gds; called to the Bar Inner Temple 1966; recorder of the Crown Court; *Style*— Sir Andrew Watson, Bt; ✉ Talton House, Newbold-on-Stour, Stratford-on-Avon, Warwicks CV37 8UB

WATSON, Dr (Nicholas) Andrew; s of Phillip Charles Watson, of 2 Station New Rd, Brundall, Norwich, and Venetia Madeline Le Poer, *née* Wyon; *b* 25 Aug 1952; *Educ* Boston GS, Univ of Nottingham Med Sch (BMedSci, MB BS, Dip Child Health); *m* 18 Nov 1977, Elaine Alma, da of late Jack Attack; 1 s (Edward Phillip b 29 Oct 1984), 1 da (Helen Ruth b 5 Jan 1983); *Career* jr house offr Derby Royal Infirmary and Nottingham City Hosp 1975–76; sr house offr in Depts of: Geriatric Med City Hosp 1976–77, Med City Hosp Feb 1977 - July 1977, Traumatology Queens Med Centre Feb 1978 - July 1978, Paediatrics Queen's Med Centre 1978–79; postgrad traineeship in gen practice Nottingham 1977–78 and Feb 1979 - July 1979; princ in gen practice Keyworth 1979–82, specialist in orthopaedic med 1982–; lectr in USA and UK with Soc of Orthopaedic Med 1982–; author of numerous published papers letters and articles on orthopaedic med; pres Soc of Orthopaedic Med 1992– (elected to Cncl 1982, chm 1988–92); MRCGP 1979, fell Soc of Orthopaedic Med 1982 (memb 1981); *Recreations* music (has played piano, viola, mandolin and crumhorn), plays jazz guitar in a jazz band; *Style*— Dr Andrew Watson; ✉ 10 Golf Course Rd, Stanton on the Wolds, Notts NG12 5BH (☎ 0115 937 3603); 32 Wimpole St, London W1M 7AE (☎ 0171 486 2160)

WATSON, Maj-Gen Andrew Linton; CB (1981); s of Col William Linton Watson, OBE (d 1961), of Bridge of Allan, and Dorothy Ellen, *née* Lea (d 1950); *b* 9 April 1927; *Educ* Wellington; *m* 23 Feb 1952, Mary Elizabeth (Ginty), da of Albert S Rigby (d 1965), of Co Down; 2 s (Alastair Alexander Linton b 15 Feb 1953, Patrick Adrian Richard John b 4 April 1955), 1 da (Shane Elizabeth Annabel b 2 Aug 1960); *Career* cmmnd Black Watch 1946; 1 and 2 Bns served: UK, Germany, Cyprus, Br Guyana, UN Force Cyprus; Staff Coll 1958, Jt Servs Staff Coll 1964, GSO1 HQ 17 Div Malaya Dist 1966–68; cmd 1 Bn Black Watch 1969–71: Malaya, UK, Gibraltar, NI; Cdr 19 Airportable Bde 1971–73, Royal Coll Def Studies 1974, Cdr Br Army Staff and mil attaché Washington DC 1975–77, GOC Eastern Dist 1977–80, chief of staff Allied Forces Northern Europe 1980–82, Col The Black Watch 1981–92; chm Inner London Branch Army Benevolent Fund 1983–, Lt govr Royal Hosp Chelsea 1984–92; *Recreations* golf, walking; *Clubs* Army and Navy, Highland Brigade; *Style*— Maj-Gen Andrew Watson, CB; ✉ c/o Royal Bank of Scotland, 12 Dunkeld Road, Perth, Scotland PH1 5RB

WATSON, Andrew Stewart; s of Leslie Donald Watson, of Malvern, Worcestershire, and Joan Beatrice, *née* Everton; *b* 29 March 1950; *Educ* King's Sch Worcester, St John's Coll Oxford; *m* 11 Dec 1976, Lea Karin, da of Eino Arvid Nordberg (d 1963); *Career* admitted slr 1975; Thomson Snell and Passmore: articled clerk 1973, ptnr 1981, head Litigation Dept 1986; pres Mental Health Review Tbnl 1995; memb: Legal Aid Area Ctee 1986, Local Advsy Ctee Headway Gp, Law Soc (memb specialist personal injury and medical negligence panels); *Recreations* running, reading, music, cooking; *Style*— Andrew Watson, Esq; ✉ 3 Lonsdale Gardens, Tunbridge Wells, Kent TN1 1NX (☎ 01892 510000)

WATSON, Anthony; s of Lt Cdr Andrew Patrick Watson, RNR, and Harriet, *née* Hewardine (d 1981); *b* 2 April 1945; *Educ* Campbell Coll Belfast, Queen's Univ Belfast (BSc); *m* 29 July 1972, Heather Jane, da of Lt Cdr Wilfred Norman Dye, RNR (d 1988); 2 s (Edward b 1975, Tom b 1976), 1 da (Tilly b 1980); *Career* barr Lincoln's Inn; dir: Touche Remnant & Co 1978–85, Touche Remnant Hldgs 1978–85; chief investmt offr Citibank NA 1985–90; chm: Citifunds Ltd 1985–90, Citicare Ltd 1985–90; md AMP Asset Management PLC 1996– (dir int investment 1991–96); dir: Cathay Holdings Ltd 1992–96, Asian Infrastructure Fund Ltd 1994–, Virgin Direct Finanacial Services Ltd 1996–; played for London Irish RFC first XV 1967–68; AIIMR 1971; *Clubs* RAC; *Style*— Anthony Watson, Esq

WATSON, Anthony Gerard (Tony); s of George Maurice Watson, JP, of Market Deeping, Lincs, and Anne, *née* McDonnell; *b* 28 May 1955; *Educ* St John Fisher Peterborough, North Staffs Poly (BA); *m* 1, 17 Sept 1982, Susan Ann, da of Malcolm Gutteridge, of Stockton on Tees; 2 s (Samuel John b 3 Sept 1983, Tom b 10 Jan 1985), 1 da (Emily Anne b 7 Feb 1987); m 2, 1994, Sylvie Helen, *née* Pask; 1 s (Daniel James b 6 Sept 1993); *Career* reporter Stamford Mercury 1978–79, news ed Evening Despatch Darlington 1983–84 (reporter 1979–81); Yorkshire Post: reporter 1984–86, dep ed 1988–89, ed 1989–; res World in Action Granada TV 1986–88; awarded Br Press Awards 1986 and 1987, YTV Journalist of the Year 1986; memb Guild of Editors; *Style*— Tony Watson, Esq; ✉ The Yorkshire Post, Wellington St, Leeds LS1 1RF (☎ 0113 243 2701, fax 0113 244 3430, telex 55245)

WATSON, Antony Edward Douglas; QC (1986); s of William Edward Watson, of Hanchurch, Staffs, and Margaret Douglas; *b* 6 March 1945; *Educ* Sedbergh, Sidney Sussex Coll Cambridge (MA); *m* 15 Sept 1972, Gillian Mary, da of Alfred John Bevan-Arthur, of Bramishall, Staffs; 2 da (Edwina b 1978, Willa b 1981); *Career* 2 Lt Staffs Yeomanry (TA) 1964–67; called to the Bar Inner Temple 1968; specialising in Intellectual Property Law; dep chm The Copy Right Tribunal 1994; *Recreations* country pursuits, wine, opera; *Style*— Antony Watson, Esq, QC; ✉ 3 New Square, Lincoln's Inn, London WC2A 3RS (☎ 0171 405 1111)

WATSON, Sir Bruce Dunstan; kt (1985); s of James Harvey Watson, and Edith Mary, *née* Crawford; *b* 1 Aug 1928; *Educ* Toowoomba GS, Univ of Queensland (BEng, BComm); *m* 30 Dec 1952, June, da of Harry Woolston Kilgour; 1 s (Timothy), 2 da (Sally, Jenny); *Career* engr Tasmanian Hydroelectricity Cmmn and Townsville Electricity Bd 1950–56, design engr and dep chief engr Copper Refineries Pty Ltd 1956–70; MIM Holdings Ltd: gp industl rels mangr 1973–75, exec dir coal ops and jt ventures 1977–80, md 1980–81, chief exec offr 1981–90, chm 1983–91; gen mangr Agnew Nickel Mine 1975–77; pres Australasian Inst of Mining and Metallurgy 1992; dir: National Australian Bank Ltd 1992, Boral Ltd 1990; pres Australian Inst of Company Directors 1992–95; Hon DEng Univ of Queensland, Hon DUniv Griffith Univ 1992; Cdrs Cross of Order of Merit Fed Rep of Germany 1991; FIE, FAIM; *Recreations* golf; *Clubs* Brisbane, Queensland, Lions; *Style*— Sir Bruce Watson; ✉ MIM Holdings Limited, 410 Ann St, Brisbane, Queensland 4000, Australia (☎ 00 61 7 833 8000, fax 00 61 7 832 2426, telex AA40160)

WATSON, Christopher John; s of Allan John Watson (d 1965), of Uxbridge, and Dorothy C, *née* Perry; *b* 21 June 1940; *Educ* Leighton Park Sch, Univ of Bristol (BA); *m* 20 July 1963, Mary, da of Andrew Warden Vincent (d 1986), of Hereford; 2 s (Angus b 1969, Peter b 1972), 1 da (Clare b 1967); *Career* King's Coll Univ of London 1962–63, Northumberland CC 1963–65, Univ of Sussex 1966–68, res offr Scottish Devpt Dept 1968–72; Univ of Birmingham Centre for Urban and Regional Studies: res fell 1972–79, lectr 1979–83, sr lectr 1983–, head of dept 1988–93, dir of int affrs 1984–94, dir The Japan Centre 1994–; memb Board of Management and chair Housing Services Ctee Mercian Housing Assoc Ltd; *Books* Housing in Clydeside 1970 (with J B Cullingworth, 1971), Housing Policy and the Housing System (with Alan Murie and Pat Niner, 1975), contrib to various books and jls; *Recreations* music, travel; *Style*— Christopher Watson, Esq; ✉ The Japan Centre, The University of Birmingham, Edgbaston, Birmingham B15 2TT (☎ 0121 414 3303, fax 0121 414 3270, telex 333762 UOBHAM G)

WATSON, David Alan; s of John Watson, of Ledsham, N Yorks, and Elizabeth, *née* Bentley; *b* 29 April 1950; *Educ* Nottingham HS, St John's Coll Cambridge (exhibitioner, MA); *m* 21 July 1984, Christine Elizabeth, da of Victor Hutchinson; *Career* asst account exec Pressmark 1972; Infopress: joined as account exec 1972, successively account dir, assoc dir, dir then md, chief exec 1992–; MIPR 1981; *Recreations* fly fishing; *Style*— David Watson, Esq; ✉ Chief Executive, Infopress, 2–3 Salisbury Court, Fleet Street, London EC4Y 8AA (☎ 0171 353 2320, fax 0171 583 9437)

WATSON, David Robert; s of Herbert Lawrence Watson (d 1991), and Elizabeth May Grant, *née* Hill; *b* 9 April 1952; *Educ* St Anselm's Sch Bakewell, Oundle, Worcester Coll Oxford (BA(Eng)); *m* 1978, Elizabeth Anne, da of Francis Stewart Orwin (d 1995); 1 da (Emma b 1979), 1 s (George b 1981); *Career* Peat Marwick Mitchell 1973–76; British Petroleum: project accountant 1977–79, New Zealand 1979–81, business analyst 1981–83, USA 1983–85, mangr Acquisitions and Disposals 1985–89, mangr Business Support 1989–91, vice pres Corporate Development BP Canada 1991–92, mangr Wytch Farm Oil Field 1992–94; seconded as chief exec Oil and Gas Projects and Supplies Office DTI 1994–96, gp treas British Petroleum Co plc 1996–; FCA; *Recreations* cricket, music, gardening; *Style*— David Watson, Esq; ✉ British Petroleum Company plc, 1 Finsbury Circus, London EC2M 7BA (☎ 0171 496 5039, fax 0171 496 5048)

WATSON, David Saxton; s of Alfred Ralph Cecil Watson, of Windlesham, and Marion Joy, *née* Saxton (d 1967); *b* 16 April 1942; *Educ* Stowe, Univ of St Andrews; *m* 1, 29 Sept 1965 (m dis), Victoria Jane, da of Rodney Sykes; 1 s (James Daniel b 29 May 1971), 1 da (Juliet Natasha b 4 March 1968); m 2, 22 Dec 1990, Helen, da of Harry Fogarty; *Career* articled clerk then CA Safferys 1962–70, Safferys Champness 1970–; vice chm City Dist Training Bd ICA; FCA; *Recreations* flying (private pilots licence), golf, skiing; *Clubs* West London Aero, Richmond Golf; *Style—* David Watson, Esq; ✉ Saffery Champness, Fairfax House, Fulwood Place, Gray's Inn, London WC1V 6UB (☎ 0171 405 2828, fax 0171 405 7887, telex 889108 RYSAF G)

WATSON, Prof Douglas Hugh; s of John Douglas Drummond Watson (d 1975), of Drymen, and Marion Allison, *née* Smellie (d 1991); *b* 20 Nov 1931; *Educ* King Edward VII Sheffield, Stirling HS, Univ of Glasgow (BSc, PhD); *m* 1, 2 Sept 1959 (m dis 1984), Dolina Munro; 1 s (Donald John b 20 June 1960), 1 da (Shirley Anne b 9 March 1965); m 2, 20 Nov 1993, Hilary Bower; *Career* Univ of Glasgow: asst lectr in chemistry 1953–57, ICI fell Chemistry Dept 1957–60, MRC Experimental Virus Unit 1960–64; Univ of Birmingham: sr res fell Dept of Virology 1964–67, sr lectr 1967–69, reader 1967–69; Univ of Leeds: prof of microbiology 1972–93, dean of staff 1989–91, pro vice chllr 1991–93, prof emeritus 1993; ed in chief Jl of Gen Virology 1971–75; treas Soc for Gen Microbiology 1980–87; FIBiol 1972; *Style—* Prof Douglas Watson; ✉ 11 Rosewood, Woodley, Reading RG5 3QU (☎ 0118 966 6910)

WATSON, Sir (Noel) Duncan; KCMG (1967, CMG 1960); s of Harry Watson, of Bradford, Yorks; *b* 16 Dec 1915; *Educ* Bradford GS, New Coll Oxford; *m* 1951, Aileen (d 1980), da of Charles Bell, of Dublin; *Career* Colonial Admin Serv: admin offr Cyprus 1938–43, asst colonial sec Trinidad 1943–45, seconded to Colonial Office 1946, princ private sec to Sec of State for Colonies 1947–50, asst sec Colonial Office 1950–62, under sec Central Africa Office 1963, asst under sec Colonial Office and CRO 1964–67; transferred to HM Dip Serv 1965; political advsr to C-in-C Far East 1967–70, high cmmr Malta 1970–72, dep under sec FCO 1972–75; ret HM Dip Serv 1975; dep chm Central Cncl of Royal Cwlth Soc 1983–87 (vice pres 1987); *Style—* Sir Duncan Watson, KCMG; ✉ Sconce, Steels Lane, Oxshott, Leatherhead, Surrey KT22 0QH

WATSON, Sir Duncan Amos; kt (1993), CBE (1986); s of Duncan Watson (d 1980), of Sheffield, and Sybil Watson (d 1984); *b* 10 May 1926; *Educ* Worcester Coll for the Blind, St Edmund Hall Oxford (BA); *m* 2 June 1954, Mercia Margaret, da of Gilbert S Casey (d 1963), of Auckland, NZ; *Career* Treasy Slrs Dept 1957–86, ret as princ asst treasy slr; chm Exec Cncl Royal Nat Inst for the Blind 1975–90, pres World Blind Union 1988–92, chm Access Ctee for England 1989–93; *Recreations* reading, listening to music; *Clubs* MCC; *Style—* Sir Duncan Watson, CBE; ✉ 19 Great Russell Mansions, 60 Great Russell St, London WC1B 3BE (☎ 0171 242 7284)

WATSON, (Angus) Gavin; s of late Herbert Edward Watson, of Carlisle, and late Marjorie, *née* Reid; *b* 14 April 1944; *Educ* Carlisle GS, Merton Coll Oxford, Peterhouse Cambridge; *m* 29 April 1967 (m dis 1991), Susan Naomi, da of late Eric Beal, of Manchester; 2 s (Matthew b 1974, Nicholas b 1980); *Career* DOE: joined 1971, princ 1974, Sec of State's Private Office 1975–78, asst sec 1979, under sec 1986–95, head Govt Offices Central Unit 1995–; chm Environment and Tport Branch Assoc of First Div Civil Servants 1983–85; hon fell Inst of Bldg Control 1987; FRSA 1994; *Recreations* fell walking, looking at buildings, industrial archaeology; *Style—* Gavin Watson, Esq; ✉ Department of the Environment, 2 Marsham Street, London SW1P 3EB (☎ 0171 276 4209, fax 0171 276 4402)

WATSON, Gerald Walter; s of Reginald Harold Watson (d 1970), and Gertrude Hilda, *née* Ruffell (d 1979); *b* 13 Dec 1934; *Educ* King Edward VI Norwich Sch, CCC Cambridge (MA); *m* 30 Dec 1961, Janet Rosemary, da of Benjamin Henry Hovey (d 1954); 1 s (Rupert b 1968), 2 da (Candida b 1966, Meriel b 1971); *Career* Pilot Offr RAF 1953–55; W O 1958–64, MOD 1964–69; Civil Serv Dept 1969–73 (and 1975–81), NI office 1973–75, HM Treasy 1981–86; dir: Central Computer and Telecommunications Agency 1978–82, Bank of England 1983, dep chm Bldg Socs Cmmn 1986–88; ptnr Arthur Young 1989, ptnr Ernst & Young 1989–; FBCS 1980; *Recreations* opera, theatre, equestrian sports; *Style—* Gerald Watson, Esq; ✉ Ernst & Young, Rolls House, 7 Rolls Buildings, Fetter Lane, London EC4A 1NH

WATSON, Graham Forgie; s of George William Forgie Watson (d 1982), and Margaret Kinlay, *née* Hogg (d 1983); *b* 14 Jan 1958; *Educ* George Heriot's Sch Edinburgh, Univ of Edinburgh (LLB); *m* 3 May 1983, (Elspeth) Margaret, da of Alexander Brewster (d 1983); 2 da (Rebecca b 1989, Sally b 1991); *Career* CA 1982; KPMG 1979–83, dir Noble Grossart Ltd 1984–91, md The Carnegie Partnership Ltd 1991–93, ptnr Deloitte & Touche 1994–; *Recreations* golf, squash, skiing; *Clubs* New (Edinburgh), Bruntsfield Links Golf, Golf House Club Elie; *Style—* Graham F Watson, Esq; ✉ Deloitte & Touche, 39 George Street, Edinburgh EH2 2HZ (☎ 0131 225 6834, fax 0131 226 6764)

WATSON, Graham Robert; MEP (Lib Dem) Somerset and N Devon (majority 22,540); s of Gordon Graham Watson (d 1991), and Stephanie, *née* Revill-Johnson; *b* 23 March 1956; *Educ* City of Bath Boys' Sch, Heriot-Watt Univ (BA); *m* 5 Sept 1987, Dr Rita Giannini, da of Dr Mario Giannini; 1 da (Frederica b 26 Jan 1992), 1 s (Gregory b 27 April 1995); *Career* freelance interpreter and translator 1979–80, administrator Paisley Coll of Technology (now Paisley Univ) 1980–83, head private office ldr Lib Pty (Rt Hon (now Sir) David Steel MP) 1983–87, sr press offr TSB Gp PLC 1987–88; HSBC Holdings PLC: sr public affairs mangr 1993–94 (public affairs mangr 1988–93, seconded to EBRD 1991); MEP (LD) Somerset and N Devon 1994–; fndr memb Euro Community's Youth Forum 1980; gen sec Int Fedn of Liberal and Radical Youth 1979–81 (vice-pres 1977–79); memb Governing Bd Euro Youth Centre 1980–82; MIL, MIPR; *Books* The Liberals in the North-South Dialogue (ed, 1980); *Recreations* walking the dog, choir singing, writing; *Clubs* National Liberal; *Style—* Graham Watson, Esq, MEP; ✉ The European Parliament, Rue Belliard, B-1040 Brussels, Belgium; Somerset and North Devon Liberal Democrats, 10 Belvedere Rd, Taunton, Somerset TA1 1BW

WATSON, Maj-Gen Henry Stuart Ramsay; CBE (1973, MBE 1954); s of Maj Henry Angus Watson, CBE, MVO (d 1952), and Dorothy Bannerman Watson, OBE, *née* Ramsay (d 1968); *b* 9 July 1922; *Educ* Winchester; *m* 1965, Susan, o da of Col William Hall Jackson, CBE, DL, of Barford, nr Warwick; 2 s (Angus b 1967, William b 1969), 1 da (Edwina b 1971); *Career* cmmnd 2 Lt 13/18 Royal Hussars 1942, Lt 1943, Capt 1945, Adj 13/18 H 1945–46 and 1948–50; psc 1951, GSO2 HQ 1 Corps, 1952–53, instr RMA Sandhurst 1955–57, instr Staff Coll Camberley 1960–62, CO 13/18 Royal Hussars 1962–64 Col GS, SHAPE 1965–68, Col Def Policy Staff MOD 1968, IDC 1969, BGS HQ BAOR 1970–73, dir Def Policy Staff MOD 1973–74, sr Army Directing Staff RCDS 1974–76, Col 13/18 Royal Hussars 1979–90; dep dir gen IOD 1985–88 (exec dir 1977–85), dir Treasurer's Dept Cons Central Office 1992–94 (dep dir 1989–92); *Recreations* golf, gardening; *Clubs* Cavalry and Guards', Huntercombe Golf; *Style—* Maj-Gen H S R Watson, CBE; ✉ The White Cross, Askett, Princes Risborough, Bucks HP27 9LR (☎ and fax 01844 347601)

WATSON, Ian; *b* 20 April 1943, St Albans; *Educ* Tynemouth Sch, Balliol Coll Oxford (scholar, BA); *m* 1 Sept 1961, Judith, *née* Jackson; 1 da (Jessica b 1973); *Career* author; Eng and French lit res Oxford 1963–65 (res degree 1965), lectr in lit UC Dar es Salaam Tanzania 1965–67, lectr in Eng lit Tokyo Univ of Educn 1967–70 (pt/t Keio Univ Tokyo and Japan Women's Univ), lectr then sr lectr in complementary studies Sch of History of Art Birmingham Poly and course teacher in sci fiction and futures studies 1970–76; memb Cncl Sci Fiction Fndn London 1974–91; features ed Foundation - The Review of Science Fiction 1974–91 (reg contrib sci fiction criticism), Euro ed SFWA Bulletin 1983–; memb Towcester and Dist Lab Pty 1980–, CND 1980–; CC candidate (Lab): Helmdon Div Northamptonshire 1981, Towcester Div Northamptonshire 1984, Middleton Cheney Div Northamptonshire 1989; *Books* incl: Japan - A Cat's Eye View (1969), The Embedding (1973, Prix Apollo 1975, Premios Zikkurath for best foreign novel in Spanish trans 1978), The Jonah Kit (1975, Br Sci Fiction Orbit award 1976, Br Sci Fiction Assoc award 1977), Orgasmachine (1976), The Martian Inca (1977), Japan Tomorrow (1977), Alien Embassy (1977), Miracle Visitors (1978), The Very Slow Time Machine - Science Fiction Stories (1979, finalist World Sci Fiction Achievement (Hugo) award), God's World (1979), The Gardens of Delight (1980), Under Heaven's Bridge (with Michael Bishop, 1981), Deathhunter - Pictures at an Exhibition (ed, 1981), Sunstroke and Other Stories (1982), Chekhov's Journey (1983), Changes (ed, 1983), The Book of the River (1984), Converts (1984), The Book of the Stars (1984), The Book of Being (1985), The Book of Ian Watson (1985), Slow Birds and Other Stories (1985), Afterlives (ed, 1986), Queenmagic Kingmagic (1986), Evil Water and Other Stories (1987), The Power (1987), The Fire Worm (1988), Whores of Babylon (1988), Meat (1988), Salvage Rites and Other Stories (1989), The Flies of Memory (1990), Inquisitor (1990), Stalin's Teardrops (1991), Space Marine (1993), Lucky's Harvest: the first book of Mana (1993), The Coming of Vertumnus and other stories (1994), The Fallen Moon: the second book of Mana (1994), Harlequin (1994), Chaos Child (1995), Hard Questions (1996); *Style—* Ian Watson, Esq; ✉ c/o Victor Gollancz Ltd, Wellington House, 125 Strand, London WC2R 0BB (☎ 0171 420 5555)

WATSON, James Kenneth; s of late James Edward Watson, and Helen Grace, *née* Kilby (d 1960); *b* 16 Jan 1935; *Educ* Watford GS, Stanford Univ California; *children* 2 s (Jamie Nicholas b 6 April 1970, Mark Robin (twin) b 6 April 1970), 1 da (Sara Ann b 11 Dec 1965); *Career* fin dir Br Road Servs 1968–77; chm: NFC plc (formerly Nat Freight Corp) 1991–Dec 1994 (fin dir 1977–85, dep chm 1985–90), Watson & Philip plc 1993–; non-exec dir: Gartmore plc 1993–96, Henlys Group plc 1993–, National Express Group plc 1993–; chm Inst of Mgmnt 1993–96; Freeman City of London, Liveryman Worshipful Co of Carmen 1980; FCA; *Recreations* cricket, theatre, history; *Clubs* RAC, MCC, Mark's; *Style—* James Watson, Esq; ✉ Watson & Philip plc, 17 Welbeck Street, London W1M 7PF (direct ☎ 0171 935 4669, fax 0171 935 1284)

WATSON, Prof James Patrick; s of Hubert Timothy Watson (d 1964), of London, and Grace Emily, *née* Mizen (d 1957); *b* 14 May 1936; *Educ* Roan Sch Greenwich, Trinity Coll Cambridge (BA, MB, MD); *m* 4 April 1962, Christine Mary, da of Rev Norman Tasker Colley (d 1987), of Midsomer Norton; 4 s (Peter b 1963, Andrew b 1964, John b 1970, Robert b 1972); *Career* jr hosp appts 1960–64, trainee psychiatrist Inst of Psychiatry 1964–70, sr lectr and hon conslt psychiatrist St George's Hosp and Med Sch 1970–74; prof of psychiatry: Guy's Hosp Med Sch 1974–, The United Med and Dental Schs of Guy's and St Thomas's Hosp 1984–; FRCPsych 1977, FRCP 1978; *Recreations* music (especially Mozart), sport in general; *Clubs* Nat Lib; *Style—* Prof James Watson; ✉ Guy's Hosp, London SE1 9RT (☎ 0171 955 4247)

WATSON, Ven Jeffrey John Seagrief; s of John Cole Watson (d 1987), and Marguerite Freda Rose, *née* Seagrief, of Histon, Cambs; *b* 29 April 1939; *Educ* Univ Coll Sch Hampstead, Emmanuel Coll Cambridge (minor scholar, MA), Clifton Theol Coll Bristol; *m* 20 Sept 1969, Rosemary Grace, da of Harold Arnold John Lea; 1 da (Rachel Helen b 16 Jan 1971), 1 s (David John Seagrief b 18 April 1973); *Career* curate: Christ Church Beckenham (Dio of Rochester) 1965–69, St Jude Southsea (Dio of Portsmouth) 1969–71; vicar Christ Church Winchester (Dio of Winchester) 1971–81, examining chaplain to the Bishop of Winchester 1976–93, vicar of Bitterne (Dio of Winchester) 1981–93, rural dean of Southampton 1983–93, proctor in convocation 1985–95, hon canon of Winchester Cathedral 1991–93, archdeacon of Ely 1993–, hon canon of Ely Cathedral 1993–; chm Church of England Vocations Advsy Sub-Ctee 1991–; *Recreations* photography, travel, walking, friends, singing barbershop; *Style—* The Ven the Archdeacon of Ely; ✉ St Botolph's Rectory, 1a Summerfield, Cambridge CB3 9HE (☎ and fax 01223 515725)

WATSON, Dr John David; *b* 7 Feb 1946; *Educ* The Academy Omagh, Trinity Coll Dublin (BA, MB BCh, BAO), LM (Rotunda Hosp), DObstRCOG (London), Univ of Edinburgh (DipSocMed), FFCM London 1986 (MFCM 1977); *m*; 3 c; *Career* house offr Adelaide Hosp Dublin 1971–72, clinical clerk (SHO) Rotunda Hosp Dublin July-Dec 1972, SHO Royal Maternity Hosp Belfast Feb-July 1973, registrar in community med Eastern Health and Social Servs Bd (later seconded to Univ of Edinburgh for DipSocMed) 1973–74, sr tutor/sr registrar in community med Queen's Univ Belfast/Eastern Health and Social Servs Bd 1975–77 (tutor/registrar in community med 1974–75), asst chief admin med offr Eastern Health and Social Servs Bd 1977–81, dir of public health Northern Health and Social Servs Bd 1989– (chief admin med offr 1981–89); author of published papers in learned jls; former memb: NI Faculty Affrs Ctee Faculty of Public Health Med, NI Health and Social Servs Trg Cncl, NI Ctee on Aids; memb: Soc for Social Med, Faculty of Med Queen's Univ of Belfast, Clinical Res Awards Advsy Ctee NI, NHS Health Economics Gp, Med Ctee Central Servs Agency; fell Ulster Med Soc; *Clubs* Tyrone County, Lough Erne Yacht; *Style—* Dr John Watson; ✉ Dervaghroy House, Beragh, Omagh, Co Tyrone BT79 0UR

WATSON, John Grenville Bernard; s of Norman Victor Watson (d 1969), of Leeds, and Rugby Ernestine, *née* Hawker (d 1962); *b* 21 Feb 1943; *Educ* Bootham Sch York, Coll of Law; *m* 12 June 1965, da of Jack Wood (d 1970), of Sheffield; 1 s (Alexander b 1973), 2 da (Melinda b 1975, Sophie b 1975); *Career* asst slr Hepworth & Chadwick 1967–69, mgmnt trainee John Waddingtons Ltd 1969–73, md Waddingtons Games Ltd 1976–79 (mktg dir 1973–76), dir Main Bd John Waddingtons plc 1979–89; MP (C): Skipton 1979–83, Skipton and Ripon 1983–87; PPS 1981–86; dir Goddard Kay Rogers (Northern) Ltd 1989–93; memb Leeds Devpt Corp 1988–93, chief exec Bradford City Challenge Ltd 1992–, non-exec dir Yorkshire Building Society 1995–; nat chm Young Cons 1970–72, chm Cons Candidates Assoc 1975–79, pres Br Youth Cncl 1979–83, Freeman City of London, memb Ct Worshipful Co of the Makers of Playing Cards; memb Law Soc; *Books* Home from Home (1973), Changing Gear (contrib, 1982), View From The Terrace (contrib, 1986); *Recreations* walking, bungee jumping, travel; *Style—* John Watson, Esq; ✉ Bay Horse Corner, Ling Lane, Scarcroft, Leeds LS14 3HY (☎ 0113 289 2209); Bradford City Challenge Ltd, Mitre Court, Cutler Heights Lane, Bradford BD4 9JY (☎ 01274 653030, fax 01274 653252)

WATSON, John Henry; s of Henry William Watson (d 1963), and Rose Hannah, *née* Abley (d 1982); *b* 25 Jan 1944; *Educ* Wolverhampton GS; *m* 1966, Marigold Anne, da of Rev William Young Milne, Rector of Malvern Wells; 1 s (decd), 3 da; *Career* articled with Worcester Country Practice 1960–66, mgmnt conslt Touche Ross & Co 1968–71, fin dir Pillsbury UK Ltd 1975–85, sr vice-pres Pillsbury Canada Ltd 1985; vice-pres int fin The Pillsbury Co USA; chief fin offr and exec vice pres Rank America 1989–; FCA; *Recreations* music; *Style—* John Watson, Esq; ✉ 110 Spalding Mill, Dunwoody, Georgia 30350, USA

WATSON, Malcolm Charles; s of George Edward Watson (d 1994), of Sutton Coldfield, and Florence Margaret, *née* Hickson (d 1989); *b* 27 Jan 1946; *Educ* Liverpool Coll, St Paul's Coll (CertEd), Open Univ (BA), Univ of Birmingham (MEd); *m* 23 Aug 1969, Sheila Christine, da of Raymond Quick Paton; 2 da (Sarah Louise b 24 Nov 1972, Katherine Anna b 11 Jan 1976); *Career* asst teacher Hutton GS Lancs 1968–71; Brockworth Sch Glos: head of dept 1971–74, head of house 1974–76; head of Lower Sch

Hodge Hill Sch Birmingham 1976–84, headteacher John Willmott Sch 1989– (dep head 1984–89); memb British Educnl Mgmnt and Admin Soc 1982–; FIMgt 1996; *Recreations* literature, theatre and golf; *Clubs* Sutton Coldfield Rotary; *Style*— Malcolm Watson, Esq; ✉ John Willmott School, Reddicap Heath Road, Sutton Coldfield, West Midlands B75 7DY (☎ 0121 378 1946, fax 0121 311 1437)

WATSON, Marilyn Jane; da of Edwin John Watson, DFC, of Norfolk, and Mary Irene Love, *née* Willmott; *b* 17 Sept 1952; *Educ* St Mary's Convent Bishop's Stortford, Cambridge Coll of Arts and Technol; *children* 1 s (Luke b 1988); *Career* dir MPR Leedex Group Ltd 1986–89, md Watsons 1989–; MIPR, MCB; *Recreations* gardening, riding, swimming; *Style*— Ms Marilyn Watson; ✉ Watsons, Terrace Gardens, Barnes, London SW13 OHD (☎ 0181 392 2332, fax 0181 392 2347)

WATSON, Mervyn Edward Robert; s of Robert George Watson, of Darlington, Co Durham, and Beryl May, *née* Lord; *b* 23 Aug 1945; *Educ* Queen Elizabeth GS Darlington, Univ of Nottingham (BSc), Univ of Sask Canada (BA); *Career* trainee mangr BSC 1963–68, res metallurgist Hudson Bay Mining and Smelting Co Manitoba Canada 1968–70, actor Coventry Theatre in Educn Co 1972–75, actor and assoc dir Humberside Theatre Hull 1975–77, assoc dir Alan Ayckbourn's Theatre in the Round Scarborough, playwright and freelance theatre dir 1979–80, sr prodr Granada TV 1980–91, dep head of drama series BBC TV Drama Group 1991–94 (actg head June 1993), dep controller of drama Yorkshire Television 1994–; *Television* prodr/exec prodr progs for Granada TV incl: Coronation Street 1982–84 and 1989–91 (prodr over 700 episodes), First Among Equals (by Jeffrey Archer) 1985–86, Floodtide (by Roger Marshall) 1987, Wipe Out (by Martin Stone and Ric Maher) 1988; for BBC TV incl: Harry, Pie in the Sky; for Yorkshire TV incl Emmerdale; *Plays* incl: Big Deal (stage play for 9 to 11 year olds) 1975, Reversed Charges (stage and radio) 1978, Hands (with Rosemary Leach, TV play) 1980, Family Man (with Julie Walters and John Duttine, TV play) 1983; *Recreations* DIY, hill walking, skiing; *Style*— Mervyn Watson, Esq; ✉ Yorkshire Television Ltd, Leeds LS3 1JS (☎ 0113 243 8283)

WATSON, Col Michael Colvin; OBE (1966), MC (1944), TD, DL (Wilts 1979–86, Glos 1986); s of Lt-Col Forrester Colvin Watson, OBE, MC (d 1951), and Cecilia, *née* Grimston (descended from 1 Earl of Verulam, d 1960); *b* 30 Sept 1918; *Educ* Stowe, Sandhurst; *m* 18 April 1942, Hon (Joan) Sybil, *née* Berry (d 1988), da of 1 Baron Buckland (d 1928); 1 s (Rupert b 1949), 2 da (Mrs Longsdon b 1946, Mrs Hurrell b 1951); *Career* cmmnd 17/21 Lancers 1938, ret 1947; cmd Royal Wilts Yeo 1961–65 (joined 1954), Col TAVR 1967–73, ADC (TAVR) to HM The Queen 1969–73, Col 17/21 Lancers 1975–83; High Sheriff Gloucestershire 1981, Vice Lord Lt Gloucestershire 1987–89; *Recreations* field sports; *Clubs* Cavalry and Guards'; *Style*— Col M C Watson, OBE, MC, TD, DL; ✉ The Dower House, Barnsley, Cirencester, Gloucestershire GL7 5EF (☎ 01285 740508)

WATSON, Michael Goodall (Mike); MP (Lab) Glasgow Central (majority 11,019); s of Clarke Carter Watson (d 1995), and Agnes Hope, *née* Goodall (d 1991); *b* 1 May 1949; *Educ* Dundee HS, Heriot-Watt Univ (BA); *m* 31 Oct 1986, Lorraine Therese, da of William McManus (d 1985); *Career* devpt offr and tutor Mid-Derbyshire Workers Educnl Assoc 1974–77, trade union official ASTMS (now MSF) 1977–89 (divnl offr 1977–87, regnl offr 1987–89); MP (Lab) Glasgow Central 1989– (by-election); memb: Select Ctee on Parly Cmmr for Admin 1990–95, Public Accounts Ctee 1995–, Leadership Campaign Team (with responsibility for foreign affairs) 1995–; chm PLP Ctee on Overseas Devpt Aid 1991–, sec PLP Trade Union Gp 1990–; memb Exec Ctee Lab Pty Scot Cncl 1987–90; *Books* Rags to Riches - The Official History of Dundee United Football Club (1985); *Recreations* running, watching Dundee Utd FC, reading; *Style*— Mike Watson, Esq, MP; ✉ House of Commons, London SW1A 0AA (☎ 0171 219 5804, fax 0171 219 2457)

WATSON, Dr Michael Leonard; s of Col Edgar Stewart Watson, OBE, of Bridlington and Dorothy, *née* Mansfield; *b* 29 March 1949; *Educ* Merchiston Castle Sch, Univ of Edinburgh (BSc Hons, MB ChB, MD); *m* 1, 27 March 1971, Penelope Ann, da of William H A Bartlett, of Elvanfoot; 1 s (James Stuart Michael b 31 Jan 1979), 1 da (Fiona Jane b 15 Oct 1976); m 2, 6 Sept 1992, Marion, da of R T Emond, of London; *Career* travelling fell MRC 1981–82, conslt physician Royal Infirmary Edinburgh 1984–, head of Med Services Royal Infirmary Edinburgh 1996–; chair Symposium Ctee RCP Edinburgh; FRCP 1986–90; *Recreations* mountaineering; *Style*— Dr Michael L Watson; ✉ 44 Ann Street, Edinburgh EH4 1PJ (☎ 0131 332 2205); Medical Renal Unit, Lauriston Place, Royal Infirmary, Edinburgh EH3 9YW (☎ 0131 229 2477)

WATSON, Hon Miles Ronald Marcus; s and h of 3 Baron Manton; (triplet with Hon Thomas and Hon Victoria); *b* 7 May 1958; *Educ* Eton; *m* 17 Oct 1984, Elizabeth A, eldest da of J R Story, of Westcott, Surrey; 2 s (Thomas b 19 April 1985, Ludovic Waldo Rupert b 31 March 1989); *Style*— The Hon Miles Watson

WATSON, Moray Robin Philip Adrian; s of Capt Gerard Arthur Watson (ka 1940), and Jean, *née* MacFarlane (d 1969); *b* 25 June 1928; *Educ* Eton, Webber-Douglas Acad for Singing and Dramatic Art; *m* 28 June 1955, Pamela Phyllis, da of Percy Garfield Marmont (d 1977); 1 s (Robin Guy Stewart b 1959), 1 da (Emma Kate b 1957); *Career* actor; cmmnd 5 Bn Northamptonshire Regt 1948, served Austria; London debut Small Hotel (St Martin's) 1955; *Theatre* incl: A River Breeze, Plaintiff in a Pretty Hour, The Grass is Greener, The Bad Soldier, Smith (title role), The Doctor's Dilemma (with Wilfred Hyde White and Anna Massey) 1963, The Public Eye (Broadway) 1963–64, You Never Can Tell (with Ralph Richardson and Harry Andrews) 1965, The Rivals (with Ralph Richardson and Margaret Rutherford) 1966, Hay Fever (with Penelope Keith), Lettice and Lovage (with Geraldine McEwan), Under Their Hats (Flanders and Swann Revue); one person show The Incomparable Max (based on the writings of Sir Max Beerbohm); *Television* incl: Compact 1962–63, Pride and Prejudice, The Pallisers, Nobody's Perfect, Rumpole of the Bailey, Seal Morning, The Body in the Library, The Darling Buds of May; *Films* incl: The Grass is Greener, The Valiant, Operation Crossbow, The Sea Wolves; *Clubs* The Garrick; *Style*— Moray Watson, Esq; ✉ 81 Elm Grove Road, Barnes, London SW13 0BX; c/o Michael Whitehall Ltd, 125 Gloucester Road, London SW7 4TE (☎ 0171 244 8466, fax 0171 244 9060)

WATSON, Prof Peter Anthony; s of Henry Watson (d 1974), and Elsie Watson (d 1988); *b* 28 June 1941; *Educ* Queen Elizabeth GS Darlington, Univ of Durham (BSc, PhD); *m* 19 Feb 1966, Joy Carolyn, da of James William Gartside, of Grimsby, Lincs; 3 da (Vivienne b 1967, Jennifer b 1969, Alison b 1970); *Career* sr scientific offr PO Res Dept London 1962–70 (formerly scientific offr); Univ of Bradford: lectr 1970–75, sr lectr 1975–78, reader 1978–80, prof of communications engrg 1980–94, head of dept 1991–94; seconded as devpt dir BIT Ltd 1984–86 (Euro Space Agency Netherlands 1977–79); prof and head of dept Univ of York 1994–96; chm York Electromagnetic Services Ltd 1995–; dir York Electronics Centre 1996–; delivered IEE Appleton lecture 1980, awarded Marconi Premium Prize IEE 1978 and 1987, J J Thomson Premium 1989, IERE Benefactors Premium 1991; memb and chm various nat ctees IEE, memb Br Nat Ctee for Radio Sci, memb various ctees Int Union of Radio Sci; FIEE; *Recreations* classical music, walking; *Style*— Prof Peter Watson; ✉ Department of Electronics, University of York, Heslington, York YO1 5DD (☎ 01904 432338, fax 01904 432335)

WATSON, Peter Frank Patrick; s of Frank Patrick Watson (d 1963), of Birmingham, and Lilian Ethel, *née* Hopwood (d 1993); *b* 23 April 1943; *Educ* Cheltenham, Univ of Durham (Psychology prize), Univ of London, Univ of Rome; *m* 1 (m dis), Nichola Theodas; m 2 (m dis), Lesley Rowlatt; *Career* intern Tavistock Clinic 1966–68; dep ed New Society 1968–71, Sunday Times 1971–81, The Times 1981–83, The Observer 1985–; regular contrib New York Times; Italian Govt music scholarship 1964, US Govt bursary 1970, Crime Writers of Britain Gold Dagger 1982; memb: PEN 1988, Br Psychological Soc; *Books* War on the Mind: the Military Uses and Abuses of Psychology (1973), Twins (1980), The Caravaggio Conspiracy (1982), Wisdom & Strength: the Biography of a Renaissance Masterpiece (1990), From Manet to Manhattan: the Rise of the Modern Art Market (1992), Nureyev: a Biography (1994), The Death of Hitler (with Ada Petrova, 1995); author of 5 novels set in the art world; books translated into 14 languages; *Recreations* opera, cricket, fishing; *Clubs* Garrick; *Style*— Peter Watson, Esq; ✉ Business Desk, The Observer, 119 Farringdon Road, London EC1 3ER (☎ 0171 278 2332)

WATSON, Peter Gordon; s of Ralph Watson, and Renee, *née* Smith; *b* 30 April 1930; *Educ* The Leys Sch, UCH London, Queens' Coll Cambridge (MA, MB BChir); *m* 6 Aug 1955, Ann Wollaston, da of John Macintosh; 3 s (Andrew Brailsford b 1957, James Bartholomew Wollaston b 1959, Hamish Charles John b 1963), 2 da (Louisa Harriet b 1961, Elizabeth Emma Hutton b 1965); *Career* Nat Serv 2 Lt RHA 1948–50; sr lectr Inst of Ophthalmology London 1962–63; posts held 1965–95: sr conslt ophthalmic surgn Addenbrooke's Hosp Cambridge, conslt Moorfields Eye Hosp London, assoc lectr Faculty of Clinical Med Univ of Cambridge, sr lectr Inst of Ophthalmology Univ of London, ed Eye journal; vice pres Coll of Ophthalmologists 1965–95; acad organiser Cambridge Ophthalmological Symposium 1970–95; memb Cncl and chm Educn Ctee Int Cncl of Ophthalmology 1994–; former dep hospitaller Order of St John of Jerusalem; Freeman City of London, memb Worshipful Soc of Apothecaries; fell commoner Queens' Coll Cambridge 1985; FRCS 1963, FCOphth 1988; *Books* Metabolic Integrations (1954), The Sclera and Systemic Disorders (1976); *Recreations* tennis, sailing, shooting; *Clubs* RSM; *Style*— Peter Watson, Esq; ✉ 17 Adams Rd, Cambridge CB3 9AD (☎ 01223 353789, 01223 362900, fax 01223 460910)

WATSON, Peter James; s of Thomas Joseph Watson (d 1975), and Dorothy Marion, *née* Smith; *b* 12 March 1944; *Educ* John Ruskin GS Croydon; *m* 2 July 1979, Sheila Jane, *née* Byars; *Career* trainee reporter Croydon Times 1960–63, sports sub ed Daily Sketch 1963–65; London Evening News: sports sub ed 1965–69, chief sports sub ed 1969–73, sports ed 1973–79; sports sub ed Daily Express 1979–81, account dir Sports Bureau Int 1981–87, md PSW Sports Consultants 1981–87, sports ed Sunday Express 1989–June 1994 (dep sports ed 1987–89), assoc sports ed Daily Star July-Aug 1994, asst ed (sport) Sunday Express Aug 1994–95; memb: Sports Writers Assoc, Football Writers Assoc; *Books* My Greatest Training Triumph (1982), Long Live The National (1983); *Recreations* gardening, theatre, golf; *Clubs* MCC, Eastbourne Golf; *Style*— Peter Watson, Esq; ✉ Petshe, 9 Hyde Tynings Close, Meads, Eastbourne, East Sussex BN20 7TQ (☎ 01323 725818)

WATSON, Vice Adm Sir Philip Alexander; KBE (1976), LVO (1960); s of Alexander Henry St Croix Watson (d 1963); *b* 7 Oct 1919; *Educ* St Alban's Sch; *m* 1948, Jennifer Beatrice, *née* Tanner; 1 s, 2 da; *Career* joined RNVR 1940, transferred to RN 1945, Rear Adm 1970, Dir-Gen Weapons (Navy) MOD 1970–77, Vice Adm 1974, Chief Naval Engr Offr 1974–77, ret 1977; adm pres Midland Naval Offrs Assoc 1979–85; dir: Marconi International Marine Co Ltd, Marconi Radar Systems Ltd (chm 1977–85); naval conslt GEC Marconi Electronics Ltd 1977–85, conslt to Marconi Gp of Companies 1985–87; memb Cncl IEE 1975–78, 1982–87 and 1988–91; CEng, FIEE 1963, CIMgt 1973; *Clubs* Army and Navy; *Style*— Vice Adm Sir Philip Watson, KBE, LVO; ✉ The Hermitage, Bodicote, Banbury, Oxon OX15 4BZ

WATSON, Prof (John) Richard; s of Reginald Joseph Watson, and Alice Mabel, *née* Tennant; *b* 15 June 1934; *Educ* Magdalen Coll Oxford (BA, MA), Univ of Glasgow (PhD); *m* 21 July 1962, Pauline Elizabeth, *née* Roberts; 1 s (David James b 1966), 2 da (Elizabeth Emma b 1968, Rachel Clare b 1971); *Career* 2 Lt RA 1953–55; lectr: Univ of Glasgow 1962–66, Univ of Leicester 1966–78; prof of English Univ of Durham 1978– (public orator 1989–); memb Archbishops' Cmmn on Church Music 1988–92, chm Modern Humanities Res Assoc 1990–, vice-pres Charles Wesley Soc 1994–, pres Int Assoc of Univ Profs of English 1995–; *Books* Wordsworth's Vital Soul (1982), Everyman's Book of Victorian Verse (ed, 1982), English Poetry of the Romantic Period 1789–1830 (1985), The Poetry of Gerard Manley Hopkins (1987), Companion to Hymns and Psalms (with K Trickett, 1988), A Handbook to English Romanticism (with J Raimond, 1992); *Recreations* playing the cello, cycling, hill-walking; *Style*— Prof Richard Watson; ✉ Stoneyhurst, 27 Albert Street, Western Hill, Durham DH1 4RL (☎ 0191 384 5716); University of Durham, English Department, Elvet Riverside, New Elvet, Durham (☎ 0191 374 2731)

WATSON, Robert John; s of Donald George James Watson, and Nabiha, *née* Bulis; *b* 29 June 1955; *Educ* Sir Walter St John Sch, Oxford Sch of Architecture (BA, Dip Arch); *m* 11 Aug 1984, Au, da of Dr Hing Tsung Lam; 1 s (Oliver Kai b 7 Nov 1992); *Career* ptnr Lam and Watson and Woods Partnership, dir and ptnr First Design Gp, dir Mitrech Ltd; hon consulting architect to London Chinatown Assoc and specialist in traditional Chinese architecture and oriental design; fndr memb Progress Architectural Gp; RIBA; *Recreations* private aviation, vintage transport, speed, futurism; *Style*— Robert Watson, Esq; ✉ 370 Upper Richmond Road, London SW15 6TS (☎ 0181 780 9606); Lam, Watson & Woods Architects, 25 Abbeville Mews, 88 Clapham Park Rd, London SW4 7BX (☎ 0171 720 9609)

WATSON, Ronald Norman Stewart; s of Kenneth Watson, of Yeovil, Somerset, and Dorothy Fraser, *née* Peat; *b* 12 Feb 1942; *Educ* Tauntons' GS Southampton; *m* 2 Dec 1972, Sally Virginia, da of Arthur John Wilson; 2 s (Ben b 1974, Ross b 1979); *Career* mangr computer servs Conoco Europe 1969–74, mgmnt conslt Booz Allen & Hamilton 1974–76, fin mangr BNOC 1977–83, fin mangr Britoil 1983–86, gp fin dir Howden Group plc 1987–93, chief exec Precision Technology Group 1993–; FCA 1964; *Recreations* sailing, golf; *Clubs* Helensburgh GC, RNC Yacht; *Style*— Ronald Watson, Esq; ✉ Precision Technology Group Ltd, RNCYC House, Rhu, Dunbartonshire G84 8NG (☎ 01436 820110 and fax 01436 820383)

WATSON, (James) Roy; CBE (1990), QFSM (1985); s of Edwin Watson (d 1981), of Leigh, Lancs, and Sarah, *née* Isaacs (d 1989); *b* 25 Aug 1936; *Educ* Westleigh Sch Leigh Lancs, Leigh Mining and Tech Coll; *m* 8 Feb 1958, Josephine Mary, da of Vincent Foster, of Leigh, Lancs; 1 s (Ian Mark b 1959, d 1983), 2 da (Tessa Marie b 1962, Janet Elizabeth b 1970); *Career* Lancs Co Fire Brigade: joined 1962, divnl cdr 1976, dep chief offr 1981, chief fire offr 1983–92, ret; chm Fire Servs Sports and Athletics Assoc Angling Soc, vice pres Fire Servs Nat Benevolent Fund (chm 1989–90); German Fire Servs Assoc Medal for int co-operation 1989; hon fell Univ of Central Lancashire 1992; FIFireE 1983; *Recreations* golf, music, caravanning; *Style*— Roy Watson, Esq, CBE, QFSM; ✉ 2a Ambleside Drive, Darwen, Lancashire BB3 3BG (☎ 01254 725317)

WATSON, Sheila Mary; da of Joseph Herbert Watson, OBE, MC (d 1990), and Evelyn Ada, *née* Patching (d 1993); *b* 8 March 1931; *Educ* The Warren Worthing, King's Coll London, Univ of Bordeaux (BA); *m* 1, 2 Sept 1961 (m dis), Neil Francis Elliot Blackmore, s of late William Blackmore, MD; 2 da (Karen Anne b 30 May 1964, Laura b 10 Sept 1967); m 2, 15 April 1972, David Hugh Arthur Christie-Murray; *Career* dir David Higham Associates (authors' agents) 1955–71, dir and sec Bolt & Watson Ltd 1971–83, md Watson Little Ltd 1983–; *Recreations* reading, walking; *Style*— Ms Sheila Watson; ✉ Capo Di Monte, Windmill Hill, London NW3 6RJ (☎ 0171 431 6819); Watson Little Ltd, (☎ 0171 483 0770)

WATSON, Shirley; da of Andrew Johnson, of Hexham, Northumberland, and Adella, *née* Cowen; *b* 24 May 1955; *Educ* Queen Elizabeth GS, Univ of Bradford (BSc); *m* 22

Sept 1979, David Alan Watson, s of Harold Roy Watson (d 1971); *Career* articled clerk rising to asst mangr Ernst & Young CAs 1984–88, mgmnt accountant rising to fin dir Marketing Solutions Ltd 1988–89, UK fin controller Boase Massimi Pollitt advtg agency 1988–89, fin dir BMP DDB Needham Worldwide 1989–; ACA 1981, MIPA 1990; *Style*— Mrs Shirley Watson; ✉ 37 Oakhurst Avenue, East Barnet, Herts EN4 8DL (☎ 0181 368 8300); BMP DDB Needham Worldwide Ltd, 12 Bishop's Bridge Road, London W2 6AA (☎ 0171 258 3979, fax 0171 723 9846)

WATSON, Simon John; s of John Charles Watson, of Reigate, Surrey, and Lorna Kathleen, *née* Whitehouse; *b* 13 May 1958; *Educ* Maidstone GS, St Catherine's Coll Oxford (MA); *Career* admitted slr 1983; ptnr Simmons & Simmons 1988– (articled clerk 1981–83, asst slr 1983–88); memb Law Soc; *Recreations* opera, bridge; *Style*— Simon Watson, Esq; ✉ 21 Wilson Street, London EC2M 2TX (☎ 0171 628 2020, fax 0171 588 4129, telex 888562)

WATSON, Prof Stephen Roger; s of John Cole Watson, MBE (d 1987), of Steyning, Sussex, and Marguerite Freda Rose, *née* Seagrief; *b* 29 Aug 1943; *Educ* Univ Coll Sch Hampstead, Emmanuel Coll Cambridge (BA, MA, PhD); *m* 26 July 1969, Rosemary Victoria, da of Rt Rev Cyril James Tucker, CBE (d 1992), of Cambridge; 1 s (Oliver b 5 Feb 1972), 1 da (Emily b 18 Feb 1975); *Career* planning asst Shell International Petroleum Co 1970–71, fell Emmanuel Coll Cambridge 1971– (res fell 1968–70); Cambridge Univ: lectr Engrg Dept 1971–86, Peat Marwick prof of mgmnt studies 1986–94, dir Judge Inst of Mgmnt Studies 1990–94; dean Management Sch Univ of Lancaster 1994–; dir: Cambridge Decision Analysts 1984–94, Environmental Resources Management 1989–95; FSS; *Books* Decision Synthesis (with D M Buede, 1988); *Recreations* overseas development, singing; *Style*— Prof Stephen Watson; ✉ 8 Castle Park, Lancaster LA1 1YQ (☎ 01524 64755); Management School, Univ of Lancaster, Lancaster LA1 4YX (☎ 01524 593998, fax 01524 381454, e-mail s.watson@lancaster.ac.uk)

WATSON, Steve; *b* 1 April 1974; *Career* professional footballer (defender); joined Newcastle Utd FC 1990; memb England under 21 team; *Style*— Steve Watson, Esq; ✉ c/o Newcastle United FC, St James Park, Newcastle upon Tyne NE1 4ST (☎ 0191 232 8361)

WATSON-GANDY, Dr Carl Donald Tyndale; s of Lt-Col Campbell Vere Watson-Gandy, OBE (d 1996), and Edith Laura, *née* Falck; *b* 2 March 1939; *Educ* Eton, Univ of Edinburgh (BSc), Univ of London (MSc, PhD, DIC); *m* 22 July 1976, Patricia Marion, da of Alexander Hugh Ramsay (d 1962), of Auckland, NZ; 1 s (Hugh b 1981), 1 da (Vere b 1979); *Career* mining engr N Rhodesia 1961–64, lectr Imperial Coll 1967–88, visiting prof Univ of Copenhagen 1984; dir: IPDM Ltd 1981–85, Burman Association Ltd 1984–; sr lectr in logistics RMCS Cranfield 1988–91, ind academic and conslt 1991–; sec Swindon Chapter FGBMFI 1989–94; Liveryman Worshipful Co of Gardeners 1981; FIMgt 1980, FILog 1981; *Books* Distribution Management: Mathematic Modelling and Practical Analysis (co author 1971); *Recreations* gardening; *Style*— Dr Carl Watson-Gandy

WATT, *see:* Harvie-Watt

WATT, Alison; da of James Watt, and Annie (Nancy), *née* Sinclair; *b* 11 Dec 1965; *Educ* Glasgow Sch of Art (BA, postgrad studies, first prize Glasgow Competition, Armour prize for still life painting); *Career* artist; *Solo Exhibitions* One Woman Show (The Scottish Gallery, London) 1990, One Woman Show - Contemporary Art Season (Glasgow Art Gallery and Museum, Kelvingrove) 1990, Flowers East Gallery 1993 and 1995; *Group Exhibitions* incl: Student Competition (Royal Scottish Acad) 1986, British Inst Fund (Royal Acad) 1986, Student Competition (Royal Scottish Acad Edinburgh) 1987, Nat Portrait Competition (Nat Portrait Gallery London) 1987, Recent Graduates (Compass Gallery Glasgow) 1988, Six Women Artists (Scottish Gallery Edinburgh) 1988, London Opening (Scottish Gallery London) 1989, Royal Scottish Portrait Award (Royal Scottish Acad Edinburgh) 1989, The Compass Contribution (Tramway Glasgow) 1990, Scottish Art in the 20th Century (Royal West of England Acad Bristol) 1991, The Portrait Award (Nat Portrait Gallery London) 1992, Cabinet Paintings (Gillian Jason Gallery London) 1992, Plymouth City Museum & Art Gallery 1992, LA Art Fair 1992, Art '93 London 1993, Decouvertes (Paris Art Fair) 1993, Fred Hoffman Gallery LA 1993, Inner Visions Flowers East 1994, After Redoute: Recent flower paintings, drawings and photographs Flowers East 1994, The Twenty Fifth Anniversary Exhibition flowers East at London Fields 1995; *Commissions* HRH Queen Elizabeth The Queen Mother (Nat Portrait Gallery London), Glasgow Art Gallery and Museum, Kelvingrove, The Observer, EMI Records, News Scotland Ltd, Mirror Group Newspapers, Collins Publishers, numerous private cmmns; *Works in Collections* Nat Portrait Gallery, Glasgow Art Gallery and Museum, BBC, Robert Fleming Holdings Ltd London, Robert and Susan Kasen - Summer NY, Aberdeen Art Gallery, National Westminster Bank plc, McMaster Univ Art Gallery; *Awards* first prize for painting Br Inst Fund (Royal Acad) 1986, winner John Player Portrait award (Nat Portrait Gallery) 1987, Elizabeth Greenshields Fndn award Montreal Canada 1989, special commendation Morrison Scottish Portrait award (Royal Scottish Acad, Edinburgh) 1989; *Style*— Ms Alison Watt; ✉ c/o Flowers East, 199–205 Richmond Road, London E8 3NJ (☎ 0181 985 3333)

WATT, Arthur Alexander; Baron of Wester Fernie; Barony re-established and confirmed by the Lord Lyon 20 Feb 1990 from a petition dated 24 Oct 1988; *b* 22 May 1940; *Educ* George Heriot's Sch Edinburgh, Falkirk HS; *m* 1, 1965 (m dis 1977); 2 s, 1 da; m 2, 1979, Judith Mary, *née* Mangles; 2 s, 1 da; *Career* CA; conslt PA Management Consultants Ltd 1968–71, fin dir Cooper & Turner Ltd 1971–73, gp fin dir/md Aurora Holdings Ltd 1973–83; chm Arden Ltd 1983–, chm and chief exec James Wilkes PLC 1988–94, chm CSC Group Ltd 1995–; *Recreations* running, climbing, skiing; *Clubs* Oriental; *Style*— Arthur Watt, Baron of Wester Fernie; ✉ Greenhall, Madderty, Crieff PH7 3NY (☎ 01764 683350, fax 01738 630360)

WATT, Prof Graham Charles Murray; s of Alan Crombie Robertson Watt (d 1989), of Skene, Aberdeenshire, and Helen, *née* Hughes; *b* 3 Jan 1952; *Educ* Aberdeen GS, Univ of Aberdeen (BMedBiol, MB ChB, MD, Cardno prize in anatomy, McWillie prize in biochemistry and physiology, Durno prize and Lizard medal in anatomy, Munday and Venn prize, Watt prize in social med); *m* 29 Dec 1983, Elizabeth Anne, da of John Munro; 2 da (Nuala Catherine Morley b 12 Dec 1984, Vari Helen Munro b 29 May 1986); *Career* med HO City Hosp Aberdeen 1976–77, surgical HO Gilbert Bain Hosp Lerwick 1977, registrar in histopathology and morbid anatomy Leicester General Hosp 1977–78, SHO in general med Aberdeen Hosps 1978–80, registrar in geriatric med Dept of Health Care of the Elderly Sherwood Hosp Nottingham 1980, res registrar MRC Epidemiology and Med Care unit Northwick Park Hosp 1980–82, paediatric vocational trainee in general practice Ladywell Med Centre and Sch of Community Paediatrics Univ of Edinburgh 1982–83, head MONICA Project Centre and res fell Dept of General Practice Univ of Glasgow 1983–86, hon lectr Cardiovascular Epidemiology Unit Univ of Dundee 1983–86, trainee GP Townhead Health Centre Glasgow 1986, trainee in community med Greater Glasgow Health Bd 1986–87, sr med offr Chief Scientist Office Scottish Home and Health Dept 1987–89, prof of general practice Univ of Glasgow 1994– (sr lectr in public health 1990–94); currently hon conslt in public health med Greater Glasgow Health Bd; memb: BMA, British Hypertension Soc, Soc of Social Med, Assoc of Univ Depts of General Practice; MRCP 1979, MRCGP 1986, FRCPGlas 1991, FFPHM 1994 (MFPHM 1987); *Publications* author of numerous research pubns and invited scientific presentations on epidemiology of cardiorespiratory disease, inequalities in health, environmental health and health servs research; *Clubs* Kettle; *Style*— Prof Graham Watt; ✉ University Department of General Practice, Woodside Health Centre, Barr Street, Glasgow G20 7LR (☎ 0141 332 8118, fax 0141 353 3402)

WATT, Hew Matthew Brown; OBE (1973), JP (Essex 1951); s of William Orr Watt (d 1949), of Orsett, Grays, Essex, and Jeanie, *née* Dunlop (d 1951); *b* 16 Sept 1915; *Educ* Palmers GS Grays Essex, Essex Inst of Agric; *m* 9 Oct 1937, Molly Annie, da of William John Payne (d 1972), of Grays, Essex; 1 da (Dr Trudy Watt b Jan 1953); *Career* Lt Army Cadet Corp 1941–45; agric broadcaster and writer 1951–, chm Thurrock Licensing Ctee 1961–85, memb Agric Advsy Ctee BBC 1964–76, agric visits to 22 countries incl China and Soviet Union 1967–86, dep chm Thurrock Bench 1970–85, memb Guild Agric Journalists 1970–, chm Apple & Pear Devpt Cncl 1972–77, memb Nature Conservancy Cncl 1972–82; memb and pres Thurrock Rotary Club 1947–, organiser Orsett Agric Show 1950–71, treas and deacon Orsett Congregational Church 1964–95; memb and pres Farmers' Club London 1964–; fndr chm: Thurrock Christian Social Cncl 1965–75, chm Thurrock Marriage Guidance Cncl 1968–75, vice pres Royal Agric Benevolent Inst; Paul Harris fell Rotary Int 1993, hon fell Writtle Coll Anglian Poly Univ 1993; Freeman City of London, Liveryman Worshipful Co of Fruiterers 1977; FRAgS 1985; *Recreations* talking, live theatre; *Style*— Hew Watt, Esq, OBE, JP; ✉ Wingfield Cottage, Prince Charles Ave, Orsett, Grays, Essex RM16 3HS

WATT, Iain Alasdair; s of Dr Andrew Watt, of Edinburgh, and Margaret Fawns, *née* Brown (d 1967); *b* 30 March 1945; *Educ* Edinburgh Acad, Univ of Hull (BSc); *m* 30 Jun 1971, Lynne Neilson, da of Harold Livingston (d 1984), of Kirkcaldy; 3 s (Nicholas b 15 Feb 1973, Christopher Nial b 25 April 1975, Oliver Noel b 10 July 1980), 1 da (Gemma Stephanie Margaret b 12 April 1985); *Career* joined Bank of Scotland Group 1964, dir British Linen Bank Ltd (subsid) 1986–, currently chief exec Edinburgh Fund Managers Group plc; dir other cos incl: Edinburgh Dragon Trust, Edinburgh New Tiger Trust; memb Cncl Queens Nursing Inst in Scotland; AIB; *Recreations* tennis, golf; *Clubs* Golf House Elie, Bruntsfield Golf, N Berwick Golf, Aberdour Tennis, Dean Tennis; *Style*— I A Watt, Esq; ✉ Sycamore Bank, North Queensferry, Fife (☎ 01383 413645); Edinburgh Fund Managers Group plc, Donaldson House, 97 Haymarket Terrace, Edinburgh EH12 5HD (☎ 0131 313 1000, fax 0131 313 6311)

WATT, Ian Glendinning; CBE (1992); s of Edward Glendinning Watt (d 1974), of Eastbourne, and Violet Isabel, *née* Eeley; *b* 6 Dec 1932; *Educ* Eastbourne Coll; *m* 27 Sept 1958, Pauline Ann, da of Bertram Roy Shaw (d 1972), of Fareham; 1 s (Jonathan b 1962), 1 da (Louise b 1963); *Career* chartered accountant 1957–; ptnr: KMG Thomson McLintock 1963–87 (chm 1987), KPMG Peat Marwick 1987–92; advsr to Govrs and head Special Investigations Unit Bank of England 1992–; jt liquidator Rolls-Royce Ltd 1971, DTI inspr into Alexander Howden Group plc 1982 and Guinness plc 1986, assessor to BCCI Inquiry 1991; dep chm Caffyns plc 1993–; govr: Eastbourne Coll 1965–, Roedean 1976–88, Brambletye Sch E Grinstead (chm) 1969–94; FCA; *Recreations* fishing, cricket, golf; *Clubs* MCC, Caledonian, Royal Ashdown Forest Golf; *Style*— Ian Watt, Esq, CBE; ✉ Rough Acre, Furners Green, Uckfield, East Sussex TN22 3RP (☎ 01825 740 392); Bank of England, Threadneedle Street, London EC2R 8AH (☎ 0171 601 3801, fax 0171 601 5032)

WATT, Surgn Vice Adm Sir James; KBE (1975); s of Thomas Watt (d 1944), and Sarah Alice, *née* Clarkson; *b* 19 Aug 1914; *Educ* King Edward VI Sch Morpeth, Univ of Durham (MB BS, MS), Univ of Newcastle (MD); *Career* joined RN as Surgn Lt RNVR 1941; served: HMS Emerald Far E, HMS Roxborough N Atlantic 1943, HMS Asbury USA 1944, HMS Arbiter Pacific 1945 (despatches), Surgn Lt Cdr, demobbed 1946; rejoined RN as surgical registrar RN Hosp Haslar 1948; surgical specialist: NI 1949, HM Hosp Ship Maine (Korean War) 1951, RN Hosp Hong Kong 1954; conslt in surgery: RN Hosp Plymouth 1956 (Surgn Cdr), RN Hosp Haslar 1959, RN Hosp Malta 1961, RN Hosp Haslar 1963, Surgn Capt and 1 jt prof of naval surgery RCS and RN Hosp Haslar 1965, Surgn Rear Adm 1 dean of naval med and med offr i/c Inst of Naval Med 1969, Surgn Vice Adm and med dir gen of the Navy 1972, ret 1977; visiting fell Univ House Aust Nat Univ Canberra 1986; author of numerous papers on: surgery, burns injury, hyperbaric oxygen therapy, Christian ethics, med aspects of the history of sea warfare, voyages of discovery, the slave trade and the founding of Australia; pres: Med Soc of London 1980–81 (tstee 1983–), RSM 1982–84, ECHO International Health Services Ltd 1989–; vice pres: Soc for Nautical Res, Churches Cncl for Health and Healing 1988–; pres Inst of Religion and Med 1989–91; chm Bd of Tstees Naval Christian Fellowship 1968–75, tstee Royal Sailors Rests 1972–81, pres RN Lay Readers Soc 1974–83; Erroll Eldridge Prize 1968, Gilbert Blane Gold Medal 1971; Hon Freeman Worshipful Co of Barbers 1978, hon memb Smeatonian Soc of Civil Engrs 1978 (pres 1996); Hon FRCS Edinburgh 1976, Hon DCh Newcastle 1978; FRCS, FRCP, FRSM, FICS, FRGS, FSA, fell Assoc of Surgns of GB & Ireland; Cdr OStJ of Jerusalem 1968; *Books* various on medical and historical subjects; *Recreations* mountain walking; *Clubs* Royal Over-Seas League; *Style*— Surgeon Vice Adm Sir James Watt, KBE, FSA

WATT, Dr Jean Barbara; da of Capt Douglas Maxwell Watt, MM (d 1967), of Kingsheath, Birmingham, and Barbara Gwenllian Havard, *née* Jones; *b* 15 Dec 1948; *Educ* Howells Sch Llandaff Cardiff, King Edward VI Sch for Girls Kings Heath Birmingham, Univ of Birmingham (MB ChB); *m* 15 July 1978, Gavin Neil McKenzie, s of Roderick Charles McKenzie (d 1969), of Warlingham, Surrey; 2 da (Molly b 1980, Charlotte b 1985); *Career* sr house offr Univ Hosp of Wales Cardiff 1973–76, registrar The Hosp for Sick Children Great Ormond Street 1976–79, sr registrar in paediatrics St Mary's Hosp Paddington London 1982–87, conslt paediatrician Royal Shrewsbury Hosp 1987–; FRCP 1994 (MRCP 1975); *Recreations* gardening; *Style*— Dr Jean Watt; ✉ Cross Houses Hospital, Cross Houses, nr Shrewsbury, Shropshire SY5 (☎ 01743 761242)

WATT, John Gillies McArthur; QC (Scot 1992); s of Peter Julius Watt (d 1978), and Nancy, *née* McArthur; *b* 14 Oct 1949; *Educ* Clydebank HS, Univ of Glasgow, Univ of Edinburgh (LLB); *m* 1 (m dis 1988), Catherine, yr da of Robert Russell, of Toronto; 2 da (Rowan b 5 Nov 1976, Harriet b 27 Dec 1979); m 2, Nov 1988, Susan, o da of Dr Tom C Sparks Jnr, of Ardmore, Oklahoma and Breckenridge, Colorado; *Career* law apprentice Messrs Mackenzie Roberton Glasgow, admitted slr 1974, ptnr Stewart & Bennett Argyll 1975–78, admitted Faculty of Advocates 1979, advocate depute 1989, temp sheriff 1991, called to the English Bar Middle Temple 1992; memb Incorporation of Coopers of Glasgow 1976–; *Recreations* shooting, sailing, skiing, opera; *Clubs* Lansdowne, Royal Western Yacht (Glasgow); *Style*— John Watt, Esq, QC; ✉ 6511 Devinney Court, Arvada, CO 80004, USA (☎ 00 1 303 456 1548); c/o Advocates' Library, Parliament House, Edinburgh EH1 1RF (☎ 0131 226 5071, fax 0131 225 3642, clerk ☎ 0131 226 2881)

WATT, Capt Kenneth Rupert; s of Gerald Allingham Watt, of Thornhill, Co Londonderry, NI, and Gladys Kathleen, *née* Macky; *b* 12 Sept 1914; *Educ* Malvern, RMC Sandhurst, Trinity Coll Cambridge, (MA); *m* 1946, Elisabeth, da of Capt Edward Hodgson, of Barnfield, Cowfold, Sussex; *Career* regular soldier 15/19 The King's Royal Hussars, active serv France, invalided 1945; sr ptnr Tattersalls 1951–83 (chief shareholder); landowner, salmon fishery mangr, shoot and bird reserve owner; Lord of the Manor of Boulge (Suffolk); *Recreations* hunting, polo, shooting, fishing, music, opera, wildlife sanctuary (private); *Clubs* White's, Cavalry and Guards', Jockey Club Rooms (Newmarket); *Style*— Capt Kenneth Watt; ✉ Dingle Estate, Dunwich, Suffolk; Barclays, Cambridge; Tattersalls, Terrace House, Newmarket, Suffolk CB8 9BT

WATT, Dr Robert Mackay; s of Robert Mackay Watt, of Southfield Cottage, Summerfield Rd, Dunbar, Scotland, and Helen Good, *née* Pollock (d 1975); *b* 5 Feb 1941; *Educ* Aberdeen GS, Manchester GS, Univ of Edinburgh (BSc, MB ChB, PhD, Dip Comm Med); *m* 28 June 1969, Christine Wendy, da of James Clifford Gregory (d 1990), of Innisfree, 10 Outgaits Close, Hunmanby, Filey, Yorks; 2 s (Andrew b 1970, Mark b 1972); *Career* fell in community med Univ of Edinburgh Med Sch 1975–77 (lectr in physiology 1970–75), superintending inspr Cruelty to Animals Act 1876 1984–87 (inspr 1977–84), chief inspr Animals (Scientific Procedures) Act 1987–; CBiol, FIBiol 1989; *Recreations* painting, model making, wood carving, aviation; *Style*— Dr Robert Watt; ✉ Home Office, Animals (Scientific Procedures) Inspectorate, 50 Queen Anne's Gate, London SW1H 9AT (☎ 0171 273 2347)

WATT, Robert Strachan; CBE (1990); s of William Watt, of Stonehaven (d 1986); *b* 13 Oct 1932; *Educ* Robert Gordon's Coll Aberdeen, Univ of Aberdeen (MA); *m* 1958, Lorna Jean, *née* Beattie; 1 s (Martin b 1959), 2 da (Gillian b 1961, Alison b 1965); *Career* IBM 1957–65; dir: Systems Consultants Ltd 1965–75, Telex Ltd 1976–77, Lothian and Edinburgh Enterprise Ltd 1990–; chm: Scotbyte Computers Ltd 1979–95, Livingston Devpt Corp 1982–, W Lothian NHS Trust 1993–; memb Court Heriot-Watt Univ 1985–91; FBCS 1969, FRSA 1992; *Recreations* golf, tennis; *Clubs* Royal Burgess Golfing Society (Edinburgh); *Style*— Robert Watt, Esq, CBE; ✉ Livingston Development Corporation, 1 Bell Square, Brucefield, Livingston, West Lothian EH54 6QA

WATT, Prof William Smith; s of John Watt, and Agnes, *née* Smith; *b* 20 June 1913; *Educ* Univ of Glasgow (MA), Balliol Coll Oxford; *m* 7 July 1944, Dorothea, da of Robert James Codrington Smith; 1 s (Robert b 1951); *Career* lectr in Greek Univ of Glasgow 1937–38, fell and tutor in classics Balliol Coll Oxford 1938–52, civilian offr Admty Naval Intelligence Div 1941–45; Univ of Aberdeen: regius prof of humanity 1952–79, curator of library 1954–59, dean of Faculty of Arts 1963–66, Univ Ct 1966–77, vice princ 1969–72; memb: Scot Cncl for Trg of Teachers 1964–67, Gen Teaching Cncl 1967–71 and 1975–78; chm Governing Body Aberdeen Coll of Educn 1971–75 (vice chm 1964–67, govr 1959–75); convener Scot Univs Cncl on Entrance 1973–77 (memb 1968–77), pres Scot Classical Assoc 1983–88, sr fell Br Acad 1989; *Books* Ciceronis Epistulae (vol 3 1958, vol 2.1 1965, vol 1 1982), George Buchanan's Miscellaneorum Liber (jtly, 1982), Vellei Paterculi Historiae (1988); *Clubs* Aberdeen Business and Professional; *Style*— Prof W S Watt, FBA; ✉ 38 Woodburn Gardens, Aberdeen AB15 8JA (☎ 01224 314369)

WATTERS, James Andrew Donaldson; s of Andrew James Watters, of Dumfriesshire, and Elsa Donaldson, *née* Broatch; *b* 16 March 1948; *Educ* King's Coll Sch Wimbledon, Pembroke Coll Oxford (BA); *m* 21 July 1973, Lesley Jane Aves, da of Cyril Joseph Churchman (d 1963); 2 s (Alexander b 4 March 1978, Rupert b 11 June 1980), 1 da (Flora b 16 May 1985); *Career* admitted slr 1972, articled clerk and slr Stephenson Harwood 1970–75, slr Norton Rose Botterell & Roche 1976–79, sr legal advsr Investors in Industry plc 1980–82; ptnr: Goodwille & Co 1982–85, Stephenson Harwood 1985–92, Watson Farley & Williams 1992–; Freeman: City of London, Worshipful Co of Slrs; memb Law Soc 1972; *Style*— James Watters, Esq; ✉ 59 De Beauvoir Rd, London N1 5AU (☎ 0171 503 9080); Watson Farley & Williams, 15 Appold Street, London EC2A 2HB (☎ 0171 814 8000, fax 0171 814 8141/2)

WATTIS, Dr John Philip; s of Philip William Wattis, of Leeds, and (Elizabeth) Joan, *née* Nickson; *b* 4 Feb 1949; *Educ* St Joseph's Coll Blackpool, Univ of Liverpool Med Sch (MB ChB); *m* 12 July 1969, Florence Elizabeth (Libby), da of David John Roberts (d 1980); 2 s (Mark b 1980, Peter b 1985), 2 da (Sharon b 1982, Ruth b 1988); *Career* house offr The Royal Infirmary Liverpool 1972–73, med supt Amudat Mission Hosp Uganda 1973–75, registrar in psychiatry John Conolly Hosp Birmingham 1975–78, lectr in health care of the elderly Univ of Nottingham 1978–81, sr lectr and conslt in old age psychiatry St James's Univ Hosp Leeds 1986–95 (conslt 1981–86), medical dir Leeds Community and Mental Health NHS Trust 1995–; chm Section for Psychiatry of Old Age RCPsych (past hon sec and public educn offr); memb Dementia Working Gp Christian Cncl on Ageing (past chm); former chm and fndr Leeds Branch Alzheimer's Disease Soc; FRCPsych 1991 (MRCPsych 1981); *Books* Practical Psychiatry of Old Age (2 edn with C Martin, 1993), Psychological Assessment of Old People (ed with I Hindmarsh, 1988), Confusion in Old Age (1989); *Recreations* mountain biking, photography; *Style*— Dr John Wattis; ✉ Leeds C&MHT, The Mansion, Meanwood Park Hospital, Tongue Lane, Leeds LS6 4QB (☎ 0113 275 8721, fax 0113 274 5172)

WATTS, Sir Arthur Desmond; KCMG (1989, CMG 1977), QC (1988); s of Col Arthur Edward Watts (d 1958), and Eileen May, *née* Challons (d 1981); *b* 14 Nov 1931; *Educ* Haileybury, RMA Sandhurst, Downing Coll Cambridge (MA, LLB, Whewell scholar in Int Law); *m* 1957, Iris Ann Collier; 1 s (Christopher), 1 da (Catherine); *Career* called to the Bar Gray's Inn 1957, bencher 1996; HM Dip Serv: legal asst FO 1957–59, legal advsr Br Property Cmmn (later Br Embassy) Cairo 1959–62, asst legal advsr FO 1962–67, legal advsr Br Embassy Bonn 1967–69, asst slr Law Offrs Dept 1969–70, legal cnsllr FCO 1970–73, cnsllr (legal advsr) Office of UK Permanent Rep to EEC 1973–77, legal cnsllr FCO 1977–82, dep legal advsr FCO 1982–87 and legal advsr 1987–91, ret; in practice at the Bar 1991–; special negotiator for succession issues in former Yugoslavia 1996–; memb: Bd of Mgmnt Br Inst of Int and Comparative Law 1987–, Bd Inst of Advanced Legal Studies 1988–91, Advsy Bd Institut für Internationales Recht Kiel 1989–, Editorial Ctee Br Year Book of Int Law 1991–; assoc memb Institut de Droit International 1991–; pres Br Branch Int Law Assoc 1992–; *Books* Legal Effects of War (4 edn with Lord McNair, 1966), Encyclopaedic Dictionary of International Law (jt ed, 1986), Oppenheim's International Law (vol 1, 9 edn with Sir Robert Jennings, 1992), International Law and the Antarctic Treaty System (1992); contribs to int legal pubns incl British Year Book of International Law and International and Comparative Law Quarterly; *Style*— Sir Arthur Watts, KCMG, QC; ✉ 20 Essex Street, London WC2R 3AL

WATTS, Prof Cedric Thomas; s of Thomas Henry Watts (d 1964), of Cheltenham, and Mary Adelaide, *née* Cheshire (d 1965); *b* 19 Feb 1937; *Educ* Cheltenham GS, Pembroke Coll Cambridge (BA, MA, PhD); *m* 3 Jan 1963, Judith Edna Mary, da of Charles Edward Hill (d 1974), of Bath; 1 s (William b 1967), 2 da (Linda b 1964 d 1985), (Sarah b 1972); *Career* Nat Serv RN 1956–58; asst lectr Cambs Coll of Arts and Technol 1964–65, prof English and American Sch Univ of Sussex 1983– (lectr 1965–79, reader 1979–83); *Books* Conrad's Heart of Darkness: A Critical and Contextual Discussion (1977), Cunninghame Graham: A Critical Biography (jtly, 1979), A Preface to Conrad (1982), R B Cunninghame Graham (1983), The Deceptive Text (1984), A Preface to Keats (1985), William Shakespeare: Measure for Measure (1986), Hamlet (1988), Joseph Conrad: A Literary Life (1989), Literature and Money (1990), Joseph Conrad: Nostromo (1990), Romeo and Juliet (1991), Thomas Hardy: Jude the Obscure (1992), Joseph Conrad (1994), A Preface to Greene (1997); *Style*— Prof Cedric Watts; ✉ University of Sussex, Brighton, East Sussex BN1 9QN (☎ 01273 606755)

WATTS, Charles Robert (Charlie); *b* 2 June 1941; *m* 14 Sept 1964, Shirley Anne, *née* Shepherd; 1 da; *Career* drummer; joined Rolling Stones 1963; signed recording contracts with: Impact Records/Decca 1963, London Records/Decca 1965, Rolling Stones Records, CBS 1983, Virgin 1992; albums with Rolling Stones: The Rolling Stones (1964, reached UK no 1), The Rolling Stones No 2 (1965, no 1), Out of Our Heads (1965, UK no 2), Aftermath (1966, UK no 1), Big Hits (High Tide and Green Grass) (compilation, 1966, UK no 4), got LIVE if you want it! (live, 1967), Between The Buttons (1967, UK no 3), Flowers (US compilation, 1967, US no 3), Their Satanic Majesties Request (1967, UK no 3), Beggars Banquet (1968, UK no 3), Through The Past Darkly (Big Hits Volume 2) (compilation, 1969, UK no 2), Let It Bleed (1969, UK no 1), Get Yer Ya-Ya's Out! (live, 1970, UK no 1), Stone Age (compilation, 1971, UK no 4), Sticky Fingers (1971, UK no 1), Hot Rocks 1964–71 (US compilation, 1972, US no 9), Goats Head Soup (1973, UK no 1), It's Only Rock'N'Roll (1874, UK no 2), Made In The Shade (compilation, 1975, UK no 14), Rolled Gold - The Very Best of The Rolling Stones (compilation, 1975, UK no 7), Black and Blue (1976, UK no 2), Love You Live (live, 1977, UK no 3), Some Girls (1978, UK no 2), Emotional Rescue (1980, UK no 1), Tattoo You (1981, UK no 2), Still Life (American Concert 1981) (live, 1981, UK no 4), Undercover (1983, UK no 3), Rewind 1971–84 (compilation, 1984, UK no 23), Dirty Work (1986, UK, no 4), Steel Wheels (1989, UK no 2), Flashpoint (live, 1991, UK no 6); has toured with The Charlie Watts Orchestra 1985–86; solo albums: Charlie Watts Orchestra - Live at Fulham Town Hall 1986, From One Charlie (with book Ode to a High Flying Bird) 1992, Warm & Tender 1993, From One Charlie 1995, Long Ago & Far Away 1996; concert films: Sympathy For The Devil (dir Jean Luc Godard) 1969, Gimme Shelter 1970, Ladies and Gentleman, The Rolling Stones 1977, Let's Spend The Night Together (dir Hal Ashby) 1983, Flashpoint (film of 1990 Steel Wheels Tour) 1991; *Books* Ode To A High Flying Bird (1965); *Recreations* jazz; *Style*— Charlie Watts, Esq; ✉ c/o Munro Sounds, 5 Church Row, Wandsworth Plain, London SW18 1ES

WATTS, Christopher Charles Philip; s of Rev Bertram Philip Knight Watts (d 1978), and Ethel Mary, *née* Palmer; unc Sir Henry Lumby of Ormskirk, Lord Lieut of Lancs (d 1989); *b* 21 Jan 1943; *Educ* Liverpool Coll, St John's Leatherhead, Northern Poly London (Dip Arch); *m* 5 Sept 1964, Ann Elizabeth, da of George Richard Harding; 1 da (Melanie-Ann b 1969); *Career* architect to the media, television and sound recording industs; conslt to the Virgin Cos; designer patentee of the Frolic fun boat and others; Liveryman: Worshipful Co of Needlemakers, Guild of Air Pilots and Air Navigators; *Recreations* mountain pursuits, flying, the Arts; *Style*— Christopher Watts, Esq; ✉ Christopher Watts Associates, Tressan House, Chapmans Lane, Deddington, Oxon OX15 0SU (☎ 01869 338883, fax 01869 338868)

WATTS, Christopher Nigel Stuart; s of Maj Ronald Henry Watts (d 1982), of Carlisle, and Eva Maria-Louise, *née* Gliese; *b* 6 March 1954; *Educ* Univ of Aberdeen (MA); *m* 24 Dec 1986, Nicola Clare, da of Wilfred Albert Mason, of Ashby de la Zouche; 3 s (Billy b 1990, Joscelyn b 1991, Rollo b 1992), 1 da (Poppy Mason-Watts b 1988); *Career* admitted slr 1980; ptnr Whitehead Watts; dir Mason-Watts Fine Art; former legal memb Mental Health Act Cmmn, pres Mental Health Review Tbnl; chm Mental Health Strategy and Review Ctee Warwicks Health Authy 1993–96, memb Ceredigion Community Health Cncl, chm of Govrs Sch Gp; *Recreations* music, opera, theatre; *Clubs* Lansdowne; *Style*— Christopher Watts, Esq; ✉ Plas Aberceri, Newcastle Emlyn, West Wales (☎ 01239 710250)

WATTS, Dr David; s of John Mark Watts (d 1956), of Chapel-en-le-Frith, Derbyshire, and Eva Jane, *née* Waterhouse (d 1973); *b* 14 June 1935; *Educ* New Mills GS, UCL (BSc), Univ of California Berkeley (MSc), McGill Univ Montreal (PhD); *m* 1, 7 Aug 1961 (m dis 1966), Judith Harriet, da of Jack Koota (d 1968), of NY; 1 s (Christopher b 1963); m 2, 18 April 1981, Pamela Anne, da of Charles Lee (d 1983), of Montreal; m 3, 7 June 1996, Nancy Priscilla, da of Sanford Clark Smith (d 1962); *Career* reader Sch of Geography and Earth Resources Univ of Hull 1989– (lectr 1963–73, sr lectr 1973–89, dean 1988–91); visiting appts incl: McGill Univ Montreal 1966 and 1968, Flinders Univ of S Australia 1980, Univ of Adelaide 1980, Inst of Geography Kunming China 1993, Univ of Habana Cuba 1995; fndr ed Jl of Biogeography 1974–80; vice chair Soc for Caribbean Studies 1991–92; memb: Inst of British Geographers 1973 (memb Cncl 1977–79), Caribbean Studies Assoc 1973 (memb Cncl 1988–90), Biogeography Res Gp 1976 (chm UK 1979–82), Consumers' Assoc 1987, RSPB 1987, RGS 1994; *Books* incl: Principles of Biogeography (1971), The West Indies: Patterns of Development, Culture and Environmental Change since 1942 (1987 and 1990), Las Antillas Occidentales (1992), The Plant Geography of Korea (1993), Vegetation and Environment of the Sand Seas of Saudi Arabia (1995), Population Density, Land Degradation and the Water Resource in Tropical Islands (1996); *Recreations* theatre, opera, mountain walking, travel, wine; *Style*— Dr David Watts; ✉ 21 Hall Walk, Walkington, Beverley, N Humberside HU17 8TF (☎ 01482 861137); School of Geography and Earth Resources, University of Hull, Hull HU6 7RX (☎ 01482 465421, fax 01482 466340)

WATTS, Edward (Ted); s of Edward Samuel Window-Watts (d 1975), of Hornchurch, and Louise, *née* Coffee; *b* 19 March 1940; *Educ* East Ham GS for Boys, South West Essex Tech Coll; *m* 18 June 1960, Iris Josephine, da of Edward John Frost, MBE; 2 s (Mark Edward b 3 March 1963, Paul Jonathan b 27 June 1968), and 1 da decd; *Career* Cotton Ballard & Blow Architects 1959–62, E Wookey & Co General Practice Surveyors 1962–64, chief surveyor Ian Fraser & Assoc (Architects & Town Planners) 1964–66, team leader Housing Devpt Br GLC 1966–67, fndr Edward Watts & Co 1967 (now Watts & Partners, currently chm); dir: RICS Journals Ltd 1982–88 (chm 1986–88), Surveyors Holdings 1983–88, People Need Homes Plc 1991–96, WASP PLC 1994–, Buildingcare Ltd 1994–; non-exec dir: WSP Group 1993–, Thamesmead Town 1994–; fndr chm Hyde Housing Assoc 1967–70 (memb until 1985), chm Tech Ctee Building Conservation Tst 1984–86; memb: Gen Cncl RICS 1982– (pres 1991–92), ARCUK 1991–, Urban Villages Group 1992–, Bd Coll of Estate Mgmnt 1994–, Ministerial Advsy Bd PACE 1995–, Home Office Steering Gp on strategy for Central London accommodation 1995–; Hon DSc Southbank Univ 1992; Freeman City of London, Liveryman Worshipful Co of Chartered Surveyors; MInstD; FRICS 1971 (ARICS 1962), ACIArb 1964, FIMgt 1982; *Recreations* sailing, cruising, racing offshore; *Clubs* Royal Ocean Racing, Island Sailing, Royal Lymington Yacht, RAC; *Style*— Ted Watts, Esq; ✉ Watts & Partners, 11 Haymarket, London SW1Y 4BP (☎ 0171 930 6652, fax 0171 839 4740)

WATTS, John Arthur; MP (C) Slough (majority 514); *b* 19 April 1947; *Educ* Bishopshalt GS, Hillingdon, Gonville and Caius Coll Cambridge (MA); *m* 1974, Susan Jennifer, *née* Swan; 1 s, 3 da; *Career* CA 1972, sec Parly and Law Affairs Ctee ICAEW 1981–83; former chm Cambridge Univ Cons Assoc, chm Uxbridge Cons Assoc 1973–76, memb Hillingdon BC 1973–86 (former dep ldr and leader of oppn, ldr 1978–84); MP (C) Slough 1983–; PPS to: Min of Housing and Construction 1984–85, Min of State Treasy 1985; min of state Dept of Tport 1994–; chm Treasy and CS Select Ctee 1992–94 (memb 1986–); FCA; *Style*— John Watts, Esq, MP; ✉ House of Commons, London SW1A 0AA

WATTS, John Clifford; s of Clifford Watts (d 1987), and Edith, *née* Fenby (d 1972); *b* 13 June 1933; *Educ* Hull GS, Hull Coll of Technol; *m* 1954, Marion Edith, da of John Holroyd (d 1983), of Hull; 2 s (Christopher, Nicholas); *Career* gp chief exec Witshier plc 1986–; *Recreations* flying (holder of private pilot's licence); *Clubs* IOD; *Style*— John Watts, Esq; ✉ 11 West Drive, Sonning, nr Reading, Berks (☎ 0118 969 3349); Manor Court, Harmondsworth, Middx (☎ 0181 759 3331, fax 0181 564 7545)

WATTS, Mark Francis; MEP (Lab) Kent E (majority 635); s of Albert Charles Watts, of Maidstone, Kent, and Carol Emmah, *née* Fleishman; *b* 11 June 1964; *Educ* Maidstone GS, LSE (MSc(Econ)); *m* 27 Aug 1988, Kim, da of Emmanuel Burton McEachan, and Elizabeth, *née* Hird; 2 s (Alastair Thomas b 28 Dec 1988, James Matthew McEachan b 6 Sept 1993); *Career* employed Royal Borough of Kingston Upon Thames 1988–94, cncllr Maidstone BC 1986–95 (ldr Lab Gp 1990–94), MEP Kent E 1994–, Euro Parly spokesman for transport and tourism 1994–; *Recreations* walking, swimming, enjoying the countryside, spending time with my family; *Style*— Mark Watts, Esq, MEP;

✉ Transport House, Apsley Street, Ashford, Kent TN 23 1LF (☎ 01233 663668, fax 01233 663510)

WATTS, Michael George; s of late George Watts, OBE, and Barbara Grace, *née* Young; *b* 3 Dec 1934; *Educ* St Edward's Sch, Oxford Sch of Architecture, SW Essex Sch of Art; *m* 1, 13 April 1957 (m dis 1979), (Edith) Sylvia, da of Albert Edward Matthews, MBE (d 1975); 3 s (Simon Michael b 1959, Martin Andrew b 1964, Julian b 1967), 1 da (Alison Barbara b 1962); m 2, 15 Dec 1979, Margaret Jennifer (Meg), da of Alfred Cooper (d 1973); *Career* RE 1956–58; formerly architect public authy housing, with EPR Architects Ltd 1985–91 (bldgs incl offices in central London and Glaxo Gp Res Bldgs); paintings exhibited in various galleries incl RIBA and Llewellyn Alexander, cartoons and caricatures syndicated nationally under pseudonym Septimus Pike, articles illustrations and cartoons in local and nat pubns; memb various art socs countrywide; memb Cons Pty: N Shropshire, London, W Sussex; ARIBA 1965, MFPS 1989; *Recreations* travelling, painting, DIY; *Clubs* Thames Art; *Style*— Michael Watts, Esq; ✉ Trinity Cottage, Edgmond, Shropshire TF10 8LB (☎ 01952 813864); Cavalaire, West Drive, Bracklesham Bay, Chichester, W Sussex PO20 8PH (☎ 01243 670614); Michael Watts Chartered Architect, 27–31 Sutherland Street, London SW1V 4JU (☎ 0171 630 6004)

WATTS, Michael John Colin; s of Colin Ernest Watts, of Northwood, Middx, and Jenny Brearly, *née* Eatough; *b* 17 July 1947; *Educ* Rugby, Univ of Cambridge (MA); *m* 23 Sept 1983, Katherine Elizabeth, da of Jim Spivey; *Career* CA 1973; articled clerk Cooper Brothers 1969–73, Morgan Grenfell & Co Limited: joined 1973, seconded Br Trade Devpt Office NY 1976–78, dir Morgan Grenfell Finance Limited 1985–87; dir Brown Shipley & Co Limited 1987–91, dir Robert Fleming & Co Ltd 1991–; Freeman City of London 1989, memb Worshipful Co of Pattenmakers 1990; FCA 1978; *Clubs* MCC; *Style*— Michael Watts, Esq; ✉ Robert Fleming & Co Ltd, 25 Copthall Avenue, London EC2R 7DR (☎ 0171 638 5858, fax 0171 256 5036)

WATTS, Nigel John; s of John Charles, of Bishops Waltham, and Joane Louise Margaret, *née* Martin; *b* 24 June 1957; *Educ* Crewkerne GS, Bristol Poly (BA), Trent Poly (PGCE), Univ of East Anglia (PhD 1995); *m* 1991, Sahera, da of Kewal Chohan; *Career* writer; teacher Date Gaigo Gakuin Japan 1982–84, pt/t temp teacher London 1984–87, pt/t temp creative writing teacher Richmond Adult Coll 1989–95, fndr The Writing Room creative writing courses London 1990–95; memb Soc of Authors 1989–; Betty Trask Award 1989, Arts Cncl Award 1990, Oppenheimer/John Downes Award 1991, K Blundell Trust Award 1992, Br Library Penguin Books fell 1995; practitioner's cert in Shiatsu Brit Sch of Shiatsu; *Books* The Life Game (1989), Billy Bayswater (1990), We All Live in a House Called Innocence (1992), Twenty Twenty (1994), The Penknife (1995), Writing a Novel (1996); *Style*— Nigel Watts, Esq; ✉ c/o Hodder & Stoughton Ltd, 338 Euston Road, London NW1 3BH

WATTS, Reginald John; s of Wilfred John Lionel Watts (d 1963), and Julia Doris Watts; *b* 28 Jan 1931; *Educ* Bishop's Stortford Coll; *m* 13 July 1960, (Susan) Roscoe Watts, *qv*, da of Charles Roscoe Cushman; 1 s (Marcus Redmayne b 1962), 1 da (Charlotte Amelia Roscoe b 1964); *Career* chm Burson-Marsteller 1968–85, fndr chm Reginald Watts Assoc 1985–91, dep chm Citigate Corporate Ltd 1991–95; memb Metropolitan Police Ctee 1995–; non-exec dir of various cos; cncllr: Southend BC 1954–63, Westminster City Cncl 1974–82 (dep Lord Mayor 1981–82); memb CBI London Regnl Cncl, chm BIM Public Affrs Ctee 1989, pres Inst of PR 1989; hon sr visiting fell City Univ Business Sch; visiting fell Univ of Wolverhampton 1992–; hon steward Westminster Abbey; FIPR; *Books* Public Relations for Top Management, Reaching the Consumer, The Businessman's Guide to Marketing, The Corporate Revolution; *Recreations* art, ballet, polo, squash; *Clubs* Carlton (memb Mgmnt Ctee 1992–95), Hurlingham, RAC, Guards' Polo, MCC; *Style*— Reginald Watts, Esq; ✉ 29 West Hill, London SW18 1RB

WATTS, (Susan) Roscoe; da of Charles Roscoe Cushman, of Lamberhurst Quarter, Kent, and Marjorie Cushman; *b* 13 Feb 1937; *Educ* Blackheath HS, Rachel McMillan Teacher Trg Coll (teaching Cert), Inst of Educn Univ of London (MA); *m* 13 July 1960, Reginald John Watts, *qv*; 1 s (Marcus Redmayne b 1962), 1 da (Charlotte Amelia Roscoe b 1964); *Career* lectr in child devpt N London Coll, past princ Montessori St Nicholas Centre; formerly vice-chair: Teaching Cncl Br Assoc of Early Childhood, NNEB Tutors Assoc, govr Dartford Teachers Trg Coll; *Recreations* collecting builders with few skills, creating gardens; *Clubs* Hurlingham; *Style*— Mrs Roscoe Watts; ✉ Montessori St Nicholas Centre, 23–24 Prince's Gate, London SW7 1PT (☎ 0171 225 1277, fax 0171 823 7557)

WATTS, His Hon Judge Victor Brian; s of Percy William King Watts (d 1981), and Doris Milicent *née* Peat (d 1971); *b* 7 Jan 1927; *Educ* Cofe's GS, Univ Coll Oxford (MA, BCL); *m* 31 July 1965, Patricia Eileen, da of Richard Cuthbert Steer, of Ferndown, Dorset (d 1982); 1 s (Martin b 1969), 1 da (Julia b 1967); *Career* Flying Offr Educn Branch RAF 1950–52; called to the Bar Middle Temple 1950; memb Western Circuit; recorder Crown Ct 1972–80; circuit judge (SE Circuit) 1980–; *Recreations* the arts, tennis, riding; *Clubs* Hurlingham; *Style*— His Hon Judge Victor Watts; ✉ 28 Abinger Rd, Bedford Park, London W4 1EL (☎ 0181 994 4435); Southwark Crown Court, 1 English Grounds, off Battlebridge Lane, London SE1 2HU

WATTS, Vincent Challacombe; s of Geoffrey Hilton Watts (d 1987), and Lillian Florence, *née* Pye (d 1955); *b* 11 Aug 1940; *Educ* Sidcot Sch, Peterhouse Cambridge (MA), Univ of Birmingham (MSc); *m* 17 June 1967, Rachel Mary, da of John Arthur Rosser (d 1986); 1 s (Ben b 1977), 1 da (Hannah b 1981); *Career* CA; ptnr Andersen Consulting 1976– (joined 1963); projects incl: performance indicators for NHS and govt agencies, memb HM Treasy Fin Mgmnt Unit 1982–85, info technol strategies for NHS, BR and MOD; memb Cncl: ICAEW 1987–89, Operational Res Soc 1974–76; FCA, FIMC; *Recreations* squash; *Clubs* Utd Oxford and Cambridge Univ, Jesters; *Style*— Vincent Watts, Esq; ✉ Andersen Consulting, 2 Arundel St, London WC2R 2PS (☎ 0171 438 3560)

WATTS-RUSSELL, David O'Reilly; s of Cdr Nevill David Watts-Russell (d 1962), and Jean, *née* McNair (d 1974); *see* Burke's Landed Gentry 18 edn vol II, 1969; *b* 21 Jan 1944; *Educ* Gordonstoun; *m* 5 April 1974, Susan; 1 s (Edward David b 1976), 3 da (Miranda Jane b 1980, Emily Susan b 1983, Tabitha Rose b 1986); *Career* dir: Greig Middleton & Co Ltd 1986–92, Caledonian European Securities Ltd 1992–; memb Ayrshire and Arran Health Bd 1987–91; *Recreations* music, reading, shooting, fishing, travel; *Clubs* New (Edinburgh), Glasgow Arts; *Style*— David Watts-Russell, Esq; ✉ Glenlogan, Sorn, Mauchline, Ayshire KA5 6JE

WAUGH, Auberon Alexander; s of Evelyn Waugh (d 1966), the novelist, by his 2 w Laura (d 1973), yst da of Hon Aubrey Herbert, 2 s of 4 Earl of Carnarvon; *b* 17 Nov 1939; *Educ* Downside, Christ Church Oxford; *m* 1 July 1961, Lady Teresa Onslow, da of 6 Earl of Onslow, KBE, MC, TD (d 1971); 2 s (Alexander b 1963, Nathaniel b 1968), 2 da (Sophia b 1962, Daisy b 1967); *Career* served Royal Horse Guards 1957–58; journalist and novelist; formerly with: Catholic Herald, Mirror Group, Times; former chief fiction reviewer Evening Standard 1973–80; columnist: Private Eye 1970–86, The Spectator 1976–96 (political corr 1967–70, chief fiction reviewer 1970–73), The Sunday Telegraph 1981–90; chief book reviewer: Daily Mail 1981–86, Independent 1986–90; book reviewer Sunday Telegraph 1990–, Way of the World columnist Daily Telegraph 1990–; former contributor Books and Bookmen; editor Literary Review 1986–; contested (Dog Lovers Party) N Devon Gen Election 1979; Nat Press Critic of the Year commendations 1976 and 1978; Granada TV What the Papers Say Columnist of the Year 1978 and 1988; *Books* Foxglove Saga (1960), Path of Dalliance (1963), Who are the Violets Now? (1966), Consider the Lilies (1968), A Bed of Flowers (1971), The Last Word - The Trial of Jeremy Thorpe (1980), Four Crowded Years - The Diaries of Auberon Waugh 1972–1976, A Turbulent Decade - 1976–85 (1985), Waugh on Wine (1986), Will This Do? (autobiography, 1991), Way of the World (collected journalism, 1995); *Recreations* gossip, wine; *Style*— Auberon Waugh, Esq; ✉ Combe Florey House, Combe Florey, Taunton, Somerset (☎ 01823 432297)

WAUGH, Dr Michael Anthony; s of Anthony Lawrence Waugh, of Richmond, Surrey, and Nancy Genevieve, *née* Vernon; *b* 19 Sept 1943; *Educ* St George's Coll Weybridge Surrey, Charing Cross Hosp Med Sch Univ of London (MB BS); *Career* conslt physician genito-urinary medicine Gen Infirmary Leeds 1975–, pt/t secondment Aids Unit Dept of Health 1992–93; pres Med Soc for Study of Venereal Diseases 1989–91 (hon sec 1981–89); Int Union Against Venereal Diseases and Treponematoses: sec gen 1984–95, pres 1995–; dep ed Int Jl of STD and Aids 1993, observer Venereology and Dermatovenereology Specialists Ctee Union of Euro Med Specialists 1984–92; hon sr lectr Univ of Leeds 1985– (Soc of Apothecaries lectr in history of medicine 1984–); hon librarian, offr and memb Cncl RSM 1995–; corresponding memb Austrian Soc for Dermatology and Venereology 1990, memb Bd Euro Acad of Dermatology and Venereology 1994–, fell The Netherlands Soc for Dermatology and Venereology 1996; Liveryman Worshipful Co Apothecaries 1970; DHMSA 1970, Dip Venereology 1974; fell Assoc Australasian Coll of Venereologists (FACSHP) 1996, FRCPI 1994 (MRCPI 1993), FRCP 1995; *Books* venereology section of Oxford Companion to Medicine (1986), contrib Sexually Transmitted Diseases (2 edn, 1990), History of Sexually Transmitted Diseases (1990); *Recreations* gardening, travelling; *Style*— Dr Michael Waugh; ✉ Wellfield House, 151 Roker Lane, Pudsey, Leeds LS28 9ND (☎ and fax 0113 256 5255); Dept of Genito-Urinary Medicine, General Infirmary Leeds LS1 3EX (☎ 0113 292 6762, fax 0113 292 6387)

WAUGH, Lady Teresa Lorraine; *née* Onslow; da of 6 Earl of Onslow, KBE, MC, TD (d 1971); sister of 7 Earl of Onslow; *b* 1940; *m* 1961, Auberon Waugh, *qv*; 2 s, 2 da; *Career* translator and novelist; *Books* Painting Water (1984), Waterloo Waterloo (1986), An Intolerable Burden (1988), Song at Twilight (1989), Sylvia's Lot (1994); *Style*— The Lady Teresa Waugh; ✉ Combe Florey House, Combe Florey, Taunton, Somerset (☎ 01823 432297)

WAVERLEY, 3 Viscount (UK 1952); John Desmond Forbes Anderson; o s of 2 Viscount Waverley (d 1990), and Lorna Myrtle Ann, *née* Ledgerwood; *b* 31 Oct 1949; *Educ* Malvern; *m* 4 Jan 1994, HE Dr Ursula Helen Barrow, MA, LLM, PhD, High Cmmr for Belize, da of Raymond Hugh Barrow, Barrister-at-law, SC, of Belize City, Belize; 1 s (Hon Forbes Alastair Rupert b 15 Feb 1996); *Heir* s, Hon Forbes Alastair Rupert; *Career* landscape contractor (Europe and ME) 1975–85, publishers' agent (Latin America/Africa) 1985–93, emerging mkts support 1993–; chm: Lomé Parly Gp, Internal Political Parly Gp, All-Party Nigeria Gp; vice chm Royal Yacht Parly Gp, memb Exec Ctee Cwlth Parly Assoc 1994–95, sec All-Party Export Gp; observer San José X Ministerial Conf 1994, Cwlth observer Bangladesh Gen Election 1996; memb: Inter-Parly Union, Def Study Gp, Br Latin American All-Party Gp, All-Party Belize Gp; active interests in foreign affrs, overseas devpt, conflict resolution and UK export performance; memb RIIA, companion Inst of Export; *Recreations* golf, scuba diving, walking, travel; *Clubs* Rye Golf; *Style*— The Rt Hon the Viscount Waverley; ✉ c/o House of Lords, London SW1A 0PW (☎ 01426 846747)

WAX, Ruby; da of Edward Wax, and Berta, *née* Goldmann; *b* 19 April 1953; *Educ* Evanston Township HS, Univ of Denver, Univ of Berkeley, RSAMD (Gold Medal in acting); *m* 16 May 1988, Edward Richard Morison Bye; 1 s (Maximillian b 11 Nov 1988), 2 da (Madeline b 10 Dec 1990, Marina b 5 Nov 1993); *Career* actor and comedienne; *Theatre* Crucible Theatre 1976, RSC 1978–82, Wax Acts 1992 (one woman show, UK tour and West End); *Television* Not The Nine O'Clock News (writer) 1983, Girls On Top 1984–85, Don't Miss Wax 1985–87, Hit and Run 1988–89, Full Wax 1989–94, Ruby Meets.... 1996; documentaries incl: Miami Memoirs 1987, East Meets Wax 1988, Ruby Takes a Trip 1992; *Awards* performer of the year British Comedy Awards 1993; *Style*— Miss Ruby Wax; ✉ Peters Fraser & Dunlop Ltd, 503 The Chambers, Chelsea Harbour, Lots Road, London SW10 0XF (☎ 0171 344 1010, fax 0171 352 8135)

WAXMAN, Dr Jonathan; s of David Waxman, and Shirley, *née* Friedman; *b* 31 Oct 1951; *Educ* Haberdashers' Aske's, UCL (BSc, MB BS, MD); *m* Clare Petronella Florence, da of Basil Taylor; 1 da (Thea Millie b 22 Dec 1993), 1 s (Frederick Merlin b 24 April 1996); *Career* trained in med UCH London, registrar in med St Mary's Hosp London 1979–81, sr registrar in oncology Bart's 1981–86, conslt oncologist Royal Postgrad Med Sch Hammersmith 1986–; memb: Assoc of Physicians, Assoc of Cancer Physicians, American Soc of Clinical Oncology, American Assoc of Cancer Research; FRCP; *Books* The New Endocrinology of Cancer (jtly, 1988), The Molecular Biology of Cancer (jtly, 1989), Urological Oncology (jtly, 1992), Interleukin II (jtly, 1992), Molecular Endocrinology of Cancer (1995); *Style*— Dr Jonathan Waxman; ✉ Department of Oncology, Royal Postgraduate Medical School, Du Cane Road, London W12 0NN (☎ 0181 743 2030 ext 4660, fax 0181 743 8766)

WAY, Adam Gerald Richmond (Bertie); s of Col A G Way, MC; *b* 29 Feb 1952; *Educ* Eton; *Career* short serv cmmn Gren Gds 1972–75; dir i/c gp business devpt Lowe Bell Communications Ltd 1991– (joined 1986); non-exec chm The Blomfield Group (exec search and recruitment consits); memb Cncl WellBeing (health research charity for women and babies), memb Bd Starlight Fndn; *Recreations* country pursuits; *Clubs* Boodle's; *Style*— A G R Way, Esq; ✉ Lowe Bell Communications Ltd, 7 Hertford Street, London W1Y 8LP (☎ 0171 495 4044, fax 0171 493 3212)

WAY, John Stanley; s of Stanley George Godwin Way (d 1985), of Weybridge, Surrey, and Margaret Jean, *née* Edwards; *b* 18 Dec 1946; *Educ* St John's Sch Leatherhead; *m* 1 Feb 1975, (Diana) Jayne, da of Maj Thomas Herbert Sills, MBE, TD, DL (d 1988), of Sandy, Beds; 2 s (Robert b 1979, Duncan b 1986); *Career* Coopers & Lybrand 1969–73; Continental Illinois Nat Bank & Tst Chicago: Far East regnl auditor 1974–79, Euro/Latin America regnl auditor London 1979–83, int auditor 1983–87; int auditor worldwide Prudential Insur Co of America 1987–90, sr conslt The Bank Relationship Consultancy 1991–92, gp audit dir Inchcape plc 1992–; FCA 1969, FHKSA 1977, MIMgt 1978, IIA 1978; *Recreations* golf, tennis, cricket; *Clubs* RSAC, Surrey CCC, IOD; *Style*— John Way, Esq; ✉ Passworth, School Lane, Ockham, Surrey GU23 6PA

WAY, Patrick Edward; s of John Francis Way (d 1996), of Solihull, and Margaret Helen Laura, *née* Ewins; *b* 6 Feb 1954; *Educ* Solihull Sch, Univ of Leeds (BA); *m* 10 June 1978, Judith Anne, da of Dr Peter Orchard Williams, CBE, of Bletchingdon; 3 s (Oliver Christopher Patrick b 16 Dec 1983, Frederick William Patrick b 6 Feb 1987, Dominic Hugo Patrick b 29 Nov 1988); *Career* admitted slr 1979, asst slr Lawrence Graham 1979–82, tax ptnr Nabarro Nathanson 1985–87 (asst 1982–85), ptnr and head of Corp Tax Dept Gouldens 1987–94, called to the Bar Lincoln's Inn 1994, tax barr Gray's Inn 1994–; founding ed Trusts and Estates 1985, tax ed The BES Magazine 1986; ctee memb BES Assoc, memb Revenue Bar Assoc; *Books* Death and Taxes (1985), Maximising Opportunities under the BES (1986), The BES and Assured Tenancies - The New Rules (1988), Tax Advice for Company Transactions (ed and contrib, 1992), Tolley's Tax Planning (contib, 1996–97), The Enterprise Investment Scheme (1994), Joint Ventures (ed and contrib, 1994); *Recreations* theatre-going, mini rugby coaching; *Style*— Patrick Way, Esq; ✉ 8 Gray's Inn Square, Gray's Inn, London WC1R 5AZ (☎ 0171 242 3529)

WAY, Penny; da of David Reginald Way, of Cargreen, Cornwall, and Sheila, *née* Cornell; *b* 3 April 1962; *Educ* Callington Comp Sch Cornwall, Devonport HS for Girls Plymouth; *Career* windsurfer; took up windsurfing and began racing 1980, memb Sibleyback and Christchurch Windsurfing Club; achievements incl: nat champion 1981–85, Aust champion 1981 and 1982, Euro champion 1984 and 1988, world champion 1986, 1990 and 1991, Gold medal Pre-Olympics 1990, winner Palma Olympic Regatta 1992, sixth place Olympic Games 1992, UK nat champion (Olympic class) 1993 and 1994, winner 1995 Olympic Selection trials for 1996 Olympics; awards: Windsurfing Personality of the Year 1989–91, Silk Cut Helmsman of the Year 1990, Yachtsperson of the Year 1991, Sports Aid Fndn Sir John Cohen Meml Award 1991, Outstanding Young Person of the Year Br Jr C of C 1992; *Books* Competitive Windsurfing, Windsurfing Sports Guide, The Usborne Book of Windsurfing; *Recreations* mountain biking in stunning scenery; *Style*— Ms Penny Way; ✉ Cavendish Cottage, 25c The Park, Nottingham NG7 1BB

WAY, Philip John Robert; s of Philip William Frederick Way (d 1969), of Enfield, Middx, and Ellen Gladys, *née* Wallace (d 1981); *b* 16 March 1940; *Educ* Higher Grade Sch, Ealing Tech Coll; *m* 29 May 1965, Joan Dawn, da of Alfred Richard Maclannan; 1 s (Duncan Edward b 6 Dec 1971), 1 da (Alison Ruth b 15 Dec 1975); *Career* actively engaged in industl photography for the electricity supply indust 1962–92 (latterly mangr), ptnr in visual resource mgmnt consultancy 1992–95, proprietor Philip Way Photography 1995–; hon photographer: St Paul's Cathedral 1982–95, 'Not Forgotten' Assoc; winner Black and White Photography category Financial Times Photographic Awards, twice winner Martini Royal Photographic Annual Awards; pres BIPP 1995–96 (variously memb Regional Ctee/regional treas and regional chm, memb Nat Cncl/nat treas); currently chm BIPP Benevolent Soc; ARPS, Hon FBIPP; *Style*— Philip Way, Esq; ✉ 2 Green Moor Link, Winchmore Hill, London N21 2ND (☎ 0181 360 5876); Philip Way Photography, 426–432 Essex Road, London N1 3PJ (☎ 0171 704 0494, fax 0171 226 0435)

WAY, Sir Richard George Kitchener; KCB (1961, CB 1957), CBE (1952); s of Frederick Way; *b* 15 Sept 1914; *Educ* Poly Secdy Sch London; *m* 1947, Ursula Starr; 1 s, 2 da; *Career* dep under sec WO 1955–57, dep sec MOD 1957–58, dep sec Miny Supply 1958–59, perm under sec WO 1960–63, perm sec Miny Aviation 1963–66; chm: Lansing Bagnall 1967–69, London Transport 1970–74, Royal Cmmn for Exhibition of 1851 1978–87; princ King's Coll London 1975–80; dir: BOAC 1967–73, Dobson Pk Industs Ltd 1975–85; treas Cncl London Zoological Soc 1983–84 (memb 1977, vice-pres 1979–82 and 1984–87); Hon DSC Univ of Loughborough; CStJ; *Clubs* Brooks's; *Style*— Sir Richard Way, KCB, CBE; ✉ The Old Forge, Shalden, Alton, Hants (☎ 01420 82383)

WEALE, Prof Albert Peter; s of Albert Cecil Weale (d 1978), of Brighton, and Elizabeth Margaret, *née* Granger (d 1975); *b* 30 May 1950; *Educ* Varndean GS for Boys Brighton, Clare Coll Cambridge (MA, PhD); *m* 1, 17 Sept 1976 (m dis 1985), Jane, *née* Leresche; m 2, 28 Jan 1994, Jan, *née* Harris; *Career* Sir James Knott res fell Dept of Politics Univ of Newcastle upon Tyne 1974–76, lectr in politics 1976–85, asst dir Inst for Res in the Social Sciences Univ of York 1982–85, prof of politics UEA 1985–92, prof of govt Univ of Essex 1992–; chm Nuffield Cncl of Bioethics Working Party on Ethics of Xenotransplantation; memb: Grants Ctee The King's Fund, Advsy Ctee Centre for the Study of Regulated Industries; co-ed Br Jl of Political Science 1995–96; FRSA; *Books* Equality and Social Policy (1978), Political Theory and Social Policy (1983), Lone Mothers, Paid Work and Social Security (1984), Cost and Choice in Health Care (ed, 1989), Controlling Pollution in the Round (1991), Innovation and Environmental Risk (ed, 1991), The New Politics of Pollution (1992), Environmental Standards in the European Union in an Interdisciplinary Framework (co-ed, 1995); *Recreations* walking, piano, company of friends, swimming; *Style*— Prof Albert Weale; ✉ Department of Government, University of Essex, Wivenhoe Park, Colchester, Essex CO4 3SQ (☎ 01206 872127, fax 01206 873598)

WEALE, Martin Robert; *b* 4 Dec 1955; *Educ* Highgate Sch, Clare Coll Cambridge (BA); *Career* ODI fell Nat Statistical Office Malawi 1977–79, research offr Dept of Applied Economics Cambridge 1979–87, lectr Faculty of Economics and Politics Univ of Cambridge 1987–95, dir NIESR 1995–; memb HM Treasy Ind Panel of Economic Forecasting Advsrs 1996–; treas Alzheimer's Research Tst; *Books* British Banking (1986), Macroeconomic Policy - Inflation, Wealth and the Exchange Rate (1989), Reconciliation of National Income and Expenditure (1995); *Clubs* Athenaeum; *Style*— Martin Weale, Esq; ✉ National Institute of Economic and Social Research, 2 Dean Trench Street, London SW1P 3HE (☎ 0171 222 7665, e-mail mweale@niesr.ac.uk)

WEALE, Robert Arthur; s of William Noel Morris Weale, of Presteigne, Powys, and Elizabeth May, *née* Rogers; *b* 3 April 1963; *Educ* John Beddoes Comp Sch Presteigne, Poly of Wales Pontypridd (HND); *partner* Shirley Badham; 1 da (Rhiannon Nancy May b 1 Dec 1993); *Career* flat green bowls player; memb: Presteigne Bowling Club (outdoor) 1974–, Park Hall Hereford (indoor) 1989–92, Radnorshire (indoor) 1992–; outdoor rep Wales 1982– (capt 1991), indoor rep Wales 1993–; honours incl: Welsh under 25's singles champion 1984 and 1986, winner Welsh nat fours (with father and two brothers) 1984, Br Isles under 25's singles champion 1985, winner Welsh nat pairs 1986, Gold medal fours Cwlth Games Edinburgh 1986, Bristol & West singles (Eng v Wales) champion 1988, Bronze medal pairs World Championships Auckland 1988 (fifth place singles), Gold medal pairs Aust Bicentennial Games Tweed Heads 1988, fourth place pairs Cwlth Games Auckland 1990, winner Welsh nat mixed pairs 1991 and 1994, winner Welsh fours (with three brothers) 1992, winner Br Isles fours 1992 (runners-up 1985), winner Welsh pairs 1992, winner Jersey Classic pairs 1993, Bronze Hong Kong Pairs Classic 1993, Silver medal pairs Cwlth Games Victoria 1994; youngest Welsh outdoor int capt 1991; highways admin: Hereford & Worcester CC 1985–89, Powys CC 1989–90; highways technician Hereford & Worcester Contracting 1990–95; *Recreations* keen interest in most sports (especially cricket, soccer and rugby), fishing, music; *Style*— Robert Weale, Esq; ✉ 28 Gosmore Road, Clehonger, Hereford HR2 9SN (☎ 01981 251082); Presteigne Bowling Club, 24 Hereford St, Presteigne, Powys (☎ 01544 267151)

WEALE, Timothy Donald; s of Donald Jones Weale (d 1971), of Basingstoke, Hants, and Freda Jessy, *née* Gardiner (d 1991); *b* 10 April 1951; *Educ* Magdalen Coll Oxford, Coll of Estate Mgmnt Reading; *m* 12 Oct 1974, Pamela Anne, da of Gerard Gordon Moore (d 1972), of Tadley, Hants; 1 s (Edward b 15 April 1981), 1 da (Alice b 21 April 1983); *Career* TA Maj; Wessex Regt (Rifle Vols) 1979–86, Inns of Ct and City Yeo 1986; vice pres Royal Yeomanry Band; ptnr Pearsons (auctioneers, estate agents surveyors) 1984–86, dir Prudential Property Services 1986–89, ptnr Healey and Baker 1989–; pres Farnborough Div St John Ambulance 1996; Freeman City of London 1996; FSVA 1978, ARVA 1979; *Recreations* sailing, skiing, vintage cars, gardening, field sports, music, antiques; *Clubs* VSCC, Cavalry and Guards', Greywell Flyfishers, Leander; *Style*— Timothy Weale, Esq; ✉ Thackham Court, Hartley Wintney, nr Basingstoke, Hants RG27 8JG (☎ 01252 843900); Healey and Baker, 29 St George St, Hanover Square, London W1 3BG (☎ 0171 629 9292)

WEARE, Dr (Trevor) John; OBE (1990); s of Trevor Leslie Weare, and Edna Margaret, *née* Roberts; *b* 31 Dec 1943; *Educ* Aston Tech Coll, Imperial Coll London (Granville studentship prize in physics); *m* 20 June 1964, Margaret Ann, da of Harry Wright; 2 s (Michael John b 1969, Stuart Martin b 1972); *Career* post-doctoral res fell Dept of Theoretical Physics: McGill Univ Montreal Canada 1968–70, Univ of Oxford 1970–72; Hydraulics Res Station: sr scientific offr 1972–75, princ scientific offr 1975–78, sr princ scientific offr 1978–81, chief scientific offr 1981–82; chief exec HR Wallingford Group Ltd (formerly Hydraulics Research Ltd) 1982–; FRSA 1987, FIWEM 1989; *Style*— Dr John Weare, OBE; ✉ HR Wallingford Group Ltd, Howbery Park, Wallingford, Oxon OX10 8BA (☎ 01491 835381, fax 01491 825430)

WEARNE, Prof Stephen Hugh; s of Hugh Wearne (d 1941), and Phyllis Marion, *née* Stevens (d 1966); *b* 29 June 1928; *Educ* Woolwich Poly (BSc), Imperial Coll London (DIC), Univ of Manchester (PhD); *m* 3 Oct 1959, (Elizabeth) Jean, da of Prof W E Morton (d 1984), of Hale, Cheshire; 1 s (Christopher b 1960), 1 da (Susan b 1963); *Career* apprentice 1945–50, design, planning and co-ordination of water power projects in Spain, Scotland and S America 1952–57, construction design and mgmnt of nuclear power projects 1957–64, sr lectr UMIST 1964–73, prof of technol mgmnt Univ of Bradford 1973–84, emeritus prof; chm UK Engrg Project Mgmnt Forum 1983–86; CEng, FICE, FIMechE, FAPM; *Books* Principles of Engineering Organization (1973, 2nd edn 1993), Control of Engineering Projects (ed, 1989), Civil Engineering Contracts (1989); *Recreations* work, family, music; *Style*— Prof Stephen Wearne; ✉ Project Management Group, UMIST, PO Box 88, Manchester M60 1QD (☎ 0161 200 4615, fax 01625 585536)

WEATHERALL, Prof Sir David John; s of Harry Weatherall (d 1973), and Gwendoline Charlotte Miriam, *née* Tharme (d 1985); *b* 9 March 1933; *Educ* Calday Grange GS, Univ of Liverpool (MB ChB, MD); *m* 20 June 1962, Stella Mayorga Isobel, da of Rev Campo Mayorga, of Bogota, Colombia; 1 s (Mark b 1968); *Career* Regius prof of med Univ of Oxford 1992– (Nuffield prof of clinical med 1974–92); hon dir: MRC Molecular Haematology Unit 1980, Inst of Molecular Med Univ of Oxford (1984); Hon MD: Univ of Leeds, Univ of Sheffield, Univ of Nottingham, Oxford Brookes Univ, South Bank Univ; Hon DSc: Univ of Manchester, Univ of Edinburgh, Univ of Leicester, Univ of Aberdeen, Univ of London, Univ of Keele; Hon LLD: Univ of Liverpool, Univ of Bristol; overseas memb Nat Acad of Sciences USA 1990, vice pres Royal Soc 1990–91 (Royal medal 1990, Buchanan medal 1994), hon fell Imperial Coll, Hon FRCOG, Hon FRACP, Hon FACP, FRCP, FRCPath, FRCPE, FRS; *Books* The Thalassaemia Syndromes (with J B Clegg, 3 edn 1982), Blood and Its Disorders (with R M Hardisty, 2 edn 1982), The Oxford Textbook of Medicine (with J G G Ledingham and D A Warrell, 3 edn 1995), The New Genetics and Clinical Practice (3 edn, 1991), Science and the Quiet Art (1995); *Recreations* music, oriental food; *Style*— Prof Sir David Weatherall, FRS; ✉ 8 Cumnor Rise Rd, Cumnor Hill, Oxford OX2 9HD (☎ 01865 862467); Institute of Molecular Medicine, John Radcliffe Hosp, Oxford (☎ 01865 222359, fax 01865 222501)

WEATHERALL, Vice Adm Sir James Lamb (Jim); KBE (1989); s of Lt Cdr Alwyne Thomas Hirst Weatherall, RNR (d 1939), and Olive Catherine Joan, *née* Cuthbert (d 1977); *b* 28 Feb 1936; *Educ* Gordonstoun; *m* 12 May 1962, Jean Stewart, *née* Macpherson, da of 1 Baron Drumalbyn, KBE, PC; 2 s (Niall b 1967, Ian b 1976), 3 da (Sarah b 1968, Annie b 1974, Elizabeth b 1976); *Career* cadet BRNC Dartmouth, HMS Triumph 1954, midshipman HMS Albion 1955–56; Sub Lt: HMS Scotsman 1956, HM Yacht Britannia 1958; Lt: HMS Lagos 1959–60, HMS Wizard 1960–61, Long Navigation Course 1961–62, HMS Houghton 1962–64, HMS Tartar 1964, HMS Eastbourne 1965–66; Lt Cdr Advanced Navigation Course 1966, HMS Soberton 1966–67 (i/c), HMS London 1968–70; Lt Cdr/Cdr HMS Ulster 1970–72 (i/c); Cdr: MOD 1972–74, HMS Tartar 1975–76 (i/c), Cdr Sea Trg 1976–77, HMS Ark Royal 1978; Capt: Nato Def Coll 1979, MOD-Naval Plans 1979–81, HMS Andromeda (i/c), and 8 Frigate Sqdn 1982–84 (incl Falklands), RN Presentation Team 1984–85, HMS Ark Royal (i/c) 1985–87; ADC HM The Queen 1986–87; Rear Adm Staff of Supreme Allied Cdr Europe 1987–89; Vice Adm Dep Supreme Allied Cdr Atlantic 1989–91, HM Marshal of the Diplomatic Corps 1992–; chm Sea Cadet Assoc 1992–, chm Sea Cadet Cncl 1992–; tstee Marnell Preservation Tst 1992–; pres Int Social Service 1996–; govr: Box Hill Sch 1992– (chm 1993–), Gordonstoun Sch 1993– (chm 1996–); Liveryman Worshipful Co of Shipwrights 1985 (asst Ct 1989), Freeman City of London 1985, Younger Brother Trinity House 1986; *Recreations* fishing, stamp collecting; *Clubs* RN of 1765 and 1785; *Style*— Vice Adm Sir James Weatherall, KBE; ✉ Ambassadors Court, St James's Palace, London SW1A 1BL

WEATHERHEAD, Alexander Stewart (Sandy); OBE (1985), TD (1964 and clasp 1973); s of Kenneth Kilpatrick Weatherhead (d 1979), and Katharine, *née* Stewart (d 1994), of Glasgow; *b* 3 Aug 1931; *Educ* George Watson's Edinburgh, Larchfield Sch Helensburgh, Glasgow Acad, Univ of Glasgow (MA, LLB); *m* 22 Dec 1972, (Harriett) Foye, da of Rev Arthur Organ, DD, of Toronto, Canada; 2 da (Foye b 1974, Alison b 1975); *Career* Nat Serv 1950–52 2 Lt RA 1950; TA 1952–76; Lt-Col cmdg 277 (A & SH) Field Regt RA (TA) 1965–67, Lowland Regt RA (T) 1967, Univs of Glasgow and Strathclyde OTC 1971–73; Col TAVR (Lowlands West) 1974–76, ADC to HM The Queen 1977–81, Hon Col Univs of Glasgow and Strathclyde OTC 1982–, chm Lowland TAVRA 1990–93 (memb 1967–); admitted slr 1958; ptnr Tindal Oatts Slrs Glasgow 1960–97 (conslt 1997–); hon vice pres Law Soc of Scotland 1983–84 (Cncl memb 1971–84), Temp Sheriff 1985–92; chm Soc for Computers and Law 1982–84 (hon memb 1986); memb: Royal Faculty of Procurators in Glasgow 1960– (dean 1992–95), Royal Artillery Cncl of Scotland 1972–, Royal Cmmn on Legal Servs in Scotland 1976–80; memb Law Soc of Scotland 1958; *Recreations* reading, sailing, music, tennis; *Clubs* New (Edinburgh), Royal Western Yacht (cdre 1995–), Clyde Cruising, Royal Highland Yacht; *Style*— A S Weatherhead, Esq, OBE, TD; ✉ 52 Partickhill Rd, Glasgow G11 5AB (☎ 0141 334 6277); 48 St Vincent St, Glasgow G2 5HS (☎ 0141 221 8012, fax 0141 221 7803)

WEATHERHEAD, Very Rev Dr James Leslie; CBE (1997); *b* 29 March 1931; *Educ* Dundee HS, Univ of Edinburgh (MA, LLB, sr pres Students' Rep Cncl), New Coll Univ of Edinburgh (pres Univ Union); *m* 3 March 1962, Dr Anne Shepherd; 2 s; *Career* Nat Serv Temp Actg Sub-Lt RNVR 1955–56 (HMS Eagle Suez War); licensed by Presbytery of Dundee 1960, ordained by Presbytery of Ayr 1960; asst min Auld Kirk of Ayr 1960–62; min: Trinity Church Rothesay 1962–69, Old Church Montrose 1969–85; princ clerk Gen Assembly of Church of Scotland 1985–93 and 1994–Sept 1996 (moderator 1993–94), chaplain to HM The Queen in Scotland 1991–; memb Church of Scotland Tst, former memb Bdcasting Cncl for Scotland (BBC); Hon DD Univ of Edinburgh 1993; *Publications* author of numerous published articles (religious and non-religious) in The Scotsman and Yachting Monthly; *Recreations* sailing (20–ft yacht), music (especially playing baroque music on recorder); *Style*— The Very Rev Dr James L Weatherhead, CBE; ✉ Newton Park, 59 Brechin Road, Kirrie Muir DD8 4DE (☎ 01575 572237)

WEATHERILL, (Hon) Bernard Richard; QC (1996); s of The Rt Hon the Lord Weatherill, DL, *qv*, and Lyn, *née* Eatwell; *b* 20 May 1951; *Educ* Malvern, Principia Coll Illinois (int scholar), Univ of Kent (BA); *m* 1977, Sally Maxwell, da of late John Ronald Fisher; 1 da (Julia Rosemary b 12 April 1982), 1 s (Thomas Bernard b 3 March 1984); *Career* called to the Bar Middle Temple 1974, memb Gen Cncl of the Bar 1990–92 and 1993–95; memb: Chancery Bar Assoc, Professional Negligence Bar Assoc; *Recreations* wine, lawn tennis, real tennis, squash, golf, avoiding gardening; *Clubs* All England Lawn Tennis and Crocquet, Hurlingham, Royal Tennis Court, Jesters; *Style*— Bernard Weatherill, QC; ✉ 3 New Square, Lincoln's Inn, London WC2A 3RS (☎ 0171 405 5577, fax 0171 404 5032)

WEATHERILL, Baron (Life Peer UK 1992), of North East Croydon in the London Borough of Croydon; (Bruce) Bernard Weatherill; PC (1980), DL (Kent 1992); s of late Bernard Weatherill, of Spring Hill, Guildford, and Annie Gertrude, *née* Creak; *b* 25 Nov 1920; *Educ* Malvern; *m* 1949, Lyn, da of late Henry Thomas Eatwell, of Whitehall, Sandwich Bay, Kent; 2 s ((Hon) Bernard Richard Weatherill, QC, *qv* b 1951, Hon Henry Bruce b 1953), 1 da (Hon Virginia (Hon Mrs Lovell) b 1955); *Career* serv WWII 4/7 Royal Dragoon Gds & Indian Army in 19th KGVO Lancers; pres (former md) Bernard Weatherill Ltd (Savile Row tailors); MP (C) Croydon NE 1964–92, oppn whip 1967, a Lord Cmmr of the Treasy (Govt whip) 1970–71, vice chamberlain HM Household 1971–72, comptroller 1972–73, treas HM Household and Govt dep chief whip 1973–74, oppn dep chief whip 1974–79, chm Ways and Means Ctee 1979–83, Speaker of the House of Commons 1983–92; chm Cwlth Speakers and Presiding Offrs 1986–88; chm Industry & Parly Tst 1993–; formerly: chm Guildford Cons Assoc, memb Nat Union Cons Party; High Bailiff Westminster Abbey 1989–; convenor of Cross Bench Peers House of Lords 1995–; Hon Bencher Lincoln's Inn 1989; Hon DCL Univ of Kent at Canterbury, Hon DCL William & Mary Univ of Virginia 1988, Hon DUniv Open Univ 1993; Hon Freeman Worshipful Co of Merchant Taylors, Hon Asst Worshipful Co of Blacksmiths, Liveryman Worshipful Co of Gold & Silver Wyre Drawers; vice-chllr Order of St John of Jerusalem 1992; *Clubs* Cavalry and Guards', Reform; *Style—* The Rt Hon the Lord Weatherill, PC, DL; ✉ c/o House of Lords, London SW1A OPW

WEAVER, Barrie Keith; s of James Richard Weaver (d 1977), of Corton, Norfolk, and Theresa, *née* Cooper; *b* 10 Dec 1946; *Educ* Wallington Sch Surrey, Central Sch of Art (BA); *m* 15 Nov 1996, Angela Wendy, da of Stephen Douglas Hawksley, of Davenham, Cheshire; *Career* designer: Conran Assocs 1971–73, Pentagram Design 1973–76; fndr Roberts Weaver Design 1977, personally retained by Hitachi Japan and Zebra Japan as design dir 1989, fndr chm Weaver Associates 1990; cmmns incl: TI Group 1978–80, British Telecom 1982–84, STC 1984–85, Applied Materials USA 1985–87, Nixdorf 1986–88, Plessey 1985–87, Matsushita Japan 1988–89, Nissan Japan 1990–91, Samsung Korea 1991–92, Airbus 1992, BICC 1991–92, Stiga 1992, Whirlpool 1993, Mizuno Japan 1994, British Telecom 1995, Braun Germany 1996, Medison Korea 1996, Ransomes UK 1996; recipient: four Br Design Awards, Industrie Form Germany 1988 and 1996, Prince Philip Award, Designer of the Year 1990, Good Design Award Norway 1993, Design Innovations Award Germany 1994 and 1995; memb Design Cncl 1989–95; FRSA 1984, FCSD 1982; *Recreations* antiques, painting, travel, looking at buildings; *Style—* Barrie Weaver, Esq; ✉ 53 Brookville Rd, London SW6 7BH (☎ 0171 385 7112); Weaver Associates, 2a Westbourne Grove Mews, London W11 2RU (☎ 0171 221 4420, fax 0171 727 1880)

WEAVER, (Christopher) Giles Herron; s of Lt-Col John Frederick Herron Weaver (d 1993), of Greywalls, Gullane, Lothian, and Ursula Priscilla Marie Gabrielle, *née* Horlick; *b* 4 April 1946; *Educ* Eton, London Business Sch (MSc); *m* 30 July 1974, Rosamund Betty, da of Lionel Mayhew (d 1992), of Alton, Hants; 2 s (Freddy b 1977, Jack b 1986), 2 da (Flora b 1975, Johanna b 1983); *Career* CA; articles with Arthur Young 1966–71; asst to chm: Jessel Securities 1973–75, Berry Wiggins 1975–76; i/c pension funds Ivory and Sime plc 1976–86, md pensions mgmnt Prudential Portfolio Mangrs 1986–90; Murray Johnstone Ltd: investmt dir 1990–93, md 1993–; proprietor Greywalls Hotel Gullane Lothian 1976–; ACA 1970, FCA 1977; *Recreations* skiing, golf, tennis, stalking, bridge; *Clubs* New (Edinburgh), HCEG (Muirfield), Hurlingham, Denham; *Style—* Giles Weaver, Esq; ✉ Greywalls, Gullane, Lothian (☎ 01620 843205); 48 Thurloe Sq, London SW7; Murray Johnstone Ltd, 7 West Nile St, Glasgow G1 2PX (☎ 0141 226 3131, fax 0141 248 5420, car 0374 896471)

WEAVER, Leonard John; CBE (1990); s of Alfred Wallace Weaver (d 1994), and Anne, *née* Geleyns; *b* 10 June 1936; *Educ* St Mary's Sch, Univ of Surrey; *m* 1963, Penelope Ann, *née* Sturge-Young; 5 s (Richard b 1963, Adrian b 1965, Nicholas b 1968, Simon b 1975, David b 1977), 1 da (Sophie b 1966); *Career* served Kenya Regt 1955–57; AEI Ltd 1962–64, works mangr PYE-TMC 1964–66; P E Consulting Group: joined 1966, dir 1975, md 1979–82; chm: Polymark International plc 1982–92, Pearson Engineering Ltd 1985–88, The Engineering Link Ltd 1986, Jones & Shipman plc 1988–, Manifold Industries Ltd 1982–95, Eutech Engineering Solutions Ltd 1995–; memb Steering Bd Nat Physical Laboratory 1993–95; memb Cncl: BIM 1978–83 and 1991– (vice chm 1993–), Inst of Mfrg Engrs 1980–91 (pres 1990–91), IEE 1991–96; pres Inst of Mgmnt Conslts 1983–84; Hon DUniv Surrey; Freeman City of London, memb Ct of Assts Worshipful Co of Engrs; CEng, FIEE, FIM, CIMgt, FIMC, FRSA, fell Soc of Mfrg Engrs (USA); *Recreations* cricket, book-collecting, shooting; *Clubs* Reform, MCC; *Style—* Leonard Weaver, Esq, CBE; ✉ Crab Apple Court, Oxshott Rd, Leatherhead, Surrey KT22 0DQ (☎ 01372 843647, fax 01372 843318)

WEAVER, Oliver; QC (1985); s of Denis Weaver, and Kathleen Nesville, *née* Lynch; *b* 27 March 1942; *Educ* Friends' Sch Saffron Walden, Trinity Coll Cambridge (MA, LLM); *m* 3 Oct 1964, Julia Mary, *née* MacClymont; 1 s (James b 1969), 2 da (Lucy (Mrs Piers Moreau) b 1967, Mary-Ann b 1970); *Career* pres Cambridge Union Soc 1963; called to the Bar: Middle Temple 1965, Lincoln's Inn 1969; memb: Bar Cncl 1981–84, Panel of Chairmen of Authorisation and Disciplinary Tribunals of the Securities and Futures Assoc 1988–93, Cncl of Law Reporting 1986–93; *Recreations* fishing, racing, gun dogs; *Style—* Oliver Weaver, Esq, QC; ✉ Kennel Farm, Albury End, Ware, Herts SG11 2HS; Erskine Chambers, 30 Lincoln's Inn Fields, London WC2A 3PF (☎ 0171 242 5532)

WEAVER, (Richard) Paul; s of Richard Franklyn Henderson Weaver (the author and poet, d 1979), of Brighton, and Ellen, *née* O'Sullivan; *b* 10 Jan 1952; *Educ* Anstey Comp, Belvoir HS, Felixstowe Comp; *Career* news reporter Sussex Express Lewes 1970–71, Hayters Sports Agency 1971–72, sports freelance Brighton 1972–75, chief sportswriter Southend Evening Echo 1975–78, sports ed Westminster Press 1978–79; cricket corr: News of the World 1979–86, Daily Mirror 1986–89; sr sportswriter Today 1989–91, freelance sportswriter (Guardian and Sunday Telegraph) 1991–; winner: BBC Short Story Award 1969, Sportswriter of the Year (provincial newspapers) 1976, Best Sports Journalist 1977 (local award); memb The Cricket Writers' Club; *Recreations* reading, theatre, classical music, pubs; *Clubs* The Cricketers, Coolhurst Tennis; *Style—* Paul Weaver, Esq; ✉ 14 South Grove House, Highgate Village, London N6 6LP (☎ 0181 348 6768, fax 0181 348 4293)

WEAVER, Sir Tobias Rushton (Toby); kt (1973), CB (1962); s of Sir Lawrence Weaver, KBE (d 1930), of London, and Kathleen Purcell (d 1927); *b* 19 July 1911; *Educ* Clifton, Corpus Christi Coll Cambridge (MA); *m* 1941, Marjorie, da of Rt Hon Sir Charles Trevelyan, 3 Bt, of Wallington Hall, Northumberland; 1 s (Lawrence b 1948), 3 da (Kathleen (Mrs Nicholas Abbott), Caroline (Mrs Michael Baker), Rachel (Mrs Charles Munn)); *Career* former master Eton and Barking, Admty 1941, civil servant DES 1946–73 (dep sec 1962–73); prof of educn: Univ of Southampton 1973, Univ of London Inst of Educn 1974, Open Univ 1976–78; fell Imperial Coll London 1986; *Recreations* calligraphy; *Style—* Sir Toby Weaver, CB; ✉ 14 Marston Close, London NW6 4EU (☎ 0171 624 4263)

WEBB, Prof Adrian Leonard; s of Leonard Webb, of Melksham, Wilts, and Rosina, *née* Staines; *b* 19 July 1943; *Educ* St Julian's HS Newport Gwent, Birmingham Univ (B Soc Sci), LSE (MSC), Loughborough Univ (DLitt); *m* 1, (m dis); 2 s (Rhicert b 20 April 1967, Geraint b 17 July 1971); m 2, 1996, Monjulee, da of Dass, of Kuala Lumpur, Malaysia; *Career* lectr LSE 1966–74, res dir Personal Social Servs Cncl 1974–76; Loughborough Univ: prof of social policy 1976–93, dir Centre for Res in Social Policy 1982, pro-vice-chllr 1988–93; vice-chllr Univ of Glamorgan 1993–; memb: DHSS Res Liaison Gps 1975–90, Sociology and Social Admin Ctee SSRC 1976–80, Cncl on Tbnls 1985–91, Eng Nat Bd on Nursing Midwifery and Health Visiting 1988–93, Dearing Ctee of Enquiry on Higher Educn 1996–; chm Social Admin Assoc 1977–80, nat chm Bd of Govrs Volunteer Centre 1978–84, chm Ctee on Workforce Planning and Trg in Social Servs 1987–88, chm Dept of Health Task Force on Nursing Research 1992–93; sci advsr Chief Scientist's Departmental Res Ctee DHSS 1987–90, vice-pres Leics Regnl Cncl Guideposts Tst Ltd 1988–93, advsr on social policy and social work Univ Funding Cncl 1989–92, Leics DHA 1992–93, NHS Wales R&D Forum 1993–, CBI Wales 1993–; memb: Social Policy Assoc, Br Sociological Assoc, Political Studies Assoc; FRSA 1987; *Books* numerous articles and books on social policy incl (jtly): Change Choice and Conflict in Social Policy (1975), Planning Need and Scarcity - Essays on the Personal Social Services (1986), The Economic Approach to Social Policy (1986), Social Work Social Care and Social Planning (1987), Joint Approaches to Social Policy - Rationality and Practice (1988); *Recreations* walking, painting (water colour), ornithology; *Clubs* Nat Liberal; *Style—* Prof Adrian Webb; ✉ University of Glamorgan, Pontypridd, Mid Glamorgan CF37 1DL (☎ 01443 482001, fax 01443 482390, e-mail ALWEBB@GLAMORGAN.AC.UK)

WEBB, Anthony Michael Francis; CMG (1963), QC (1961), JP (1966); s of Sir Ambrose Henry Webb, QC (d 1964), and Agnes Ellen, *née* Gunn (d 1969); *b* 27 Dec 1914; *Educ* Ampleforth, Magdalen Coll Oxford (MA); *m* 1948, Diana Mary, da of Capt Graham Farley (d 1942); 1 s (Simon), 1 da (Amanda); *Career* 2 Lt Queen's Bays 1940, SOE ME and Europe 1941–46, Maj; called to the Bar Gray's Inn 1939; Colonial Legal Serv: Malaya 1947–55, Kenya 1955–64 (AG and min for legal affrs); dep sec of cmmns and head of court business Lord Chllr's Office 1964–78, chm Indust Tbnls 1978–87; *Clubs* Special Forces; *Style—* Anthony Webb, Esq, CMG, QC, JP; ✉ 19 Crittle's Court, Wadhurst, E Sussex TN5 6BY

WEBB, Anthony Ronald; s of late Ronald Alfred Webb, of Tenterden, Kent, and Muriel Dorothy, *née* Empleton; *b* 17 July 1947; *Educ* Chislehurst and Sidcup GS, Univ of Bristol (LLB); *m* 29 Sept 1979, Sarah Lynette, da of Denzil Edward Kieft, of Lagos, Portugal; 1 da (Camilla b 1986), 2 s (Guy b 1989, Piers b 1994); *Career* called to Bar Inner Temple 1970, recorder of the Crown Court 1993– (asst recorder 1989–93); *Recreations* equestrian, travel, gardening; *Clubs* Kent CCC; *Style—* Anthony Webb, Esq; ✉ Capel Cross, Grovehurst Lane, Horsmonden, Tonbridge, Kent TN12 8BB (☎ 01892 723973); Farrar's Building, Temple, London EC4Y 7BD (☎ 0171 583 9241, fax 0171 583 0090)

WEBB, Brian James; s of Frederick William Webb (d 1972), of Liverpool, and Esther, *née* Foxall; *b* 15 Jan 1945; *Educ* Brookfield Sch Liverpool, Liverpool Coll of Art, Canterbury Coll of Art (DipAD); *m* 1969, Gail Elizabeth, da of George Henderson Barker (d 1986); 1 s (James William Robin b 4 Jan 1980), 1 da (Holly Katharine b 4 Feb 1976); *Career* asst graphic designer Michael Tucker Assocs 1967–69, graphic designer Derek Forsyth Partnership 1969–71, designer and dir Trickett & Webb Ltd 1971–; work has been exhibited and published throughout the world; contrib Penrose Annual, Best of British Packaging, Best of British Corporate Identity and other jls; winner of numerous awards D & AD, Donside and Nat Calendar Awards for work on clients incl: Thames TV, Midland Bank, Royal Mail; memb: Cncl CSD 1980–87 and 1989– (chm Graphics Gp 1980–85), Exec Ctee D & AD 1987–89; memb juries: D & AD 1975–, Design Bursary RSA 1980–; visiting lectr numerous colls in UK, USA and ASIA, external assessor CNAA UK; memb D & AD 1972, fell CSD 1972, FRSA 1980; *Recreations* walking, sailing, working; *Style—* Brian Webb, Esq; ✉ Trickett and Webb Ltd, The Factory, 84 Marchmont Street, London WC1N 1HE (☎ 0171 388 5832, fax 0171 387 4287)

WEBB, Bryan Wyndham; s of Bernard Webb (d 1979), of Crumlin, Wales, and Elsie May Skillen, *née* Smith; *b* 6 Aug 1960; *Educ* Greenfield Secdy Sch Newbridge Gwent; *m* 2, Susan; 1 s (Christopher b 23 Jan 1985); *Career* chef; The Crown Whitebrook Gwent 1976–78, The Drangway Swansea 1978–83, Kirroughtree Hotel Newton Stewart Scotland 1983–85, Café Rouge (not chain) London 1985–87, Hilaire Restaurant London 1987–; William Heptinstall Award 1980; Hilaire Restaurant: Good Food Guide 3*, AA Guide 3 stars, Egon Ronay 1 star, Michelin red M; *Recreations* eating in restaurant, working out at local health club; *Clubs* Holmes Place Chelsea; *Style—* Bryan Webb, Esq; ✉ Hilaire, 68 Old Brompton Road, London SW7 3LQ (☎ 0171 584 7601, fax 0171 581 2949)

WEBB, Christine; da of Horace John Webb, of Hythe, Kent, and Marjorie Alice, *née* Spurgeon; *b* 28 March 1945; *Educ* Waterloo Park Co GS Liverpool, Univ of Manchester (BA), Univ of London (MSc, PhD); *Career* staff nurse Middx Hosp 1968, night sister Northwick Park Hosp 1971–72, ward sister Royal Free Hosp 1972–73, pupil midwife Whittington Hosp 1973; nurse tutor: Middx Hosp Aug-Oct 1975 (unqualified nurse tutor 1973–74), Miny of Health Mozambique Oct 1975–78; sr nurse tutor UCH 1978–80, research asst Chelsea Coll Univ of London 1980–82, pt/t clinical teacher Royal Free Hosp 1981–82, lectr Dept of Nursing Univ of Manchester 1982–84, princ lectr in nursing Bristol Poly 1984–89; Univ of Manchester: prof of nursing 1989–96, head Sch of Nursing Studies 1990–95; prof of health studies Univ of Plymouth 1996–; hon dir of nursing research S Manchester HA 1989–96, memb Nursing Research Ctee N Manchester HA 1994–96; advsr: Southport Nursing Devpt Unit 1991–93, ESRC project on the regulation of legal and med professions 1991–93; memb RCN; *Books* Sexuality, Nursing and Health (1985), Feminist Practice in Women's Health Care (ed, 1986), Women's Health - Midwifery and Gynaecological Nursing (ed, 1986), Textbook of Adult Nursing (jt ed, 1992), Working Together? Interprofessional Relations in Health Care (jtly, 1994); book reviews for various learned jls; memb Editorial Bd Midwifery, ed Clinical Nursing 1997–; *Recreations* walking, dogs, reading; *Style—* Prof Christine Webb; ✉ Institute of Health Studies, University of Plymouth PL4 8AA (☎ 01752 233247)

WEBB, Prof Colin Edward; s of Alfred Edward Webb (d 1985), and Doris, *née* Collins (d 1966); *b* 9 Dec 1937; *Educ* Erith GS, Univ of Nottingham (Ford (Dagenham) Trust scholar, BSc), Univ of Oxford (DPhil, Prize in Waverley Gold Medal Competition for Scientific Essay); *m* 1, 6 June 1964, Pamela Mabel Cooper (d 1992), da of Maj Wilfred Alan Cooper White (d 1984); 2 da (Susan Patricia b 17 March 1967, Julie Diane (Mrs T Pottle) b 28 August 1970); m 2, 25 July 1995, Margaret Helen Marshall, da of Gordon Dewar (d 1968); *Career* memb tech staff Bell Telephone Labs Murray Hill NJ USA 1964–68; Clarendon Lab Univ of Oxford: AEI res fell in physics 1968–71, lectr 1971–90, reader in physics 1990–92, prof of laser physics 1992–; sr res fell in physics Jesus Coll Oxford 1988– (official tutorial fell 1973–88); visiting prof Dept of Physics Univ of Salford 1988–; chm and fndr Oxford Lasers Ltd 1977– (Achievement Award of Worshipful Company of Scientific Instrument Makers 1986, Queen's Award for Export 1987, Queen's Award for Technol 1989 and 1991); Optical Soc of America: memb 1960–88, fell 1988–, dir-at-large 1991–94; FInstP 1985 (memb 1968–85, Duddell Medal and Prize 1985), FRS 1992; *Publications* over 80 papers in scientific jls and numerous chapters in books; *Recreations* music, photography, travel, reading; *Clubs* Royal Society; *Style—* Prof Colin Webb, FRS; ✉ Department of Atomic and Laser Physics, University of Oxford, The Clarendon Laboratory, Parks Road, Oxford OX1 3PU (☎ 01865 272210, fax 01865 272400); Oxford Lasers Ltd, Abingdon Science Park, Barton Lane, Abingdon, Oxfordshire OX14 3YR (☎ 01235 554211, fax 01235 554311)

WEBB, Prof David John; s of Alfred William Owen Webb, of London, and Edna May, *née* Parrish; *b* 1 Sept 1953; *Educ* Dulwich Coll London (Kent scholar), The Royal London Hosp (MB BS, MD), FRCPEd, FFPM (UK), FRCP (London); *m* 23 June 1984, Dr Margaret Jane Cullen, da of Dr Archibald Skinnider Cullen; 2 s (David Matthew b 29 July 1992, Matthew Owen Cullen b 28 Aug 1995); *Career* MRC clinical research fell MRC Blood Pressure Unit Glasgow 1982–85, lectr in clinical pharmacology Dept of Pharmacology and Clinical Pharmacology St George's Hosp Med Sch Univ of London 1985–89; Univ of Edinburgh: sr lectr Dept of Med and dir Clinical Research Centre 1990–95, Christison prof of therapeutics and clinical pharmacology Clinical Pharmacology Unit and Research Centre 1995–; hon conslt physician Western Gen Hosps NHS Tst Edinburgh 1990–; hon tstee and jt research dir High Blood Pressure Fndn 1991–; memb: MRS 1982, Scottish

Soc for Experimental Med 1982 (memb Cncl 1994–), Br Hypertension Soc 1985 (memb Exec Ctee 1991–94), Euro Soc of Hypertension 1987, Int Soc of Hypertension 1988, Br Pharmacological Soc 1988 (memb Exec 1994–, hon sec, dir and tstee 1996–), Scottish Cardiac Soc 1992, Faculty of Pharmaceutical Med RCP UK 1992, Research Defence Soc 1992, American Heart Assoc 1994, Euro Network of Therapeutics Teachers (assoc) 1994, Assoc of Physicians of GB and I 1994, Scottish Soc of Physicians 1995, Assoc of Clinical Profs of Med 1996, Soc for Meds Research 1996; Biennial SmithKline Beecham Fndn Prize for Research Br Pharmacological Soc 1994; memb: British Mountaineering Council, Scottish Malt Whisky Society; *Books* The Molecular Biology and Pharmacology of the Endothelins (Molecular Biology Intelligence Unit Monograph Series, with G A Gray, 1995), The Endothelium in Hypertension (ed with P J T Vallance, 1996); *Recreations* summer and winter mountaineering, opera, bridge, chess; *Style—* Prof David Webb; ✉ Clinical Pharmacology Unit and Research Centre, University Department of Medicine, Western General Hospital, Edinburgh EH4 2XU (☎ 0131 332 1205, fax 0131 343 6017, e-mail d.j.webb@ed.ac.uk)

WEBB, George Hannam; CMG (1984), OBE (1974); s of George Ernest Webb, and Mary Hannam, *née* Stephens; *b* 24 Dec 1929; *Educ* Malvern Coll, King's Coll Cambridge (MA); *m* 1956, Josephine Chatterton (now a JP); 2 s, 2 da; *Career* serv 14/20 King's Hussars 1948–49, Parachute Regt (TA) 1950–53; Colonial Serv Kenya 1953–63 (dist offr Central and North Nyanza, dist cmmr Moyale, secretariat Nairobi); Diplomatic Serv 1963–85 (first sec Bangkok and Accra, cnsllr Tehran and Washington), ret 1985; sr fell City Univ London 1989–93 (dir of mgmnt devpt 1985–89); memb Cncl: Royal Soc for Asian Affairs 1984–91, Gresham Coll 1988– (clerk to cncl 1992–94); tstee Hakluyt Soc 1986–; dep chm Cncl of Friends of Nat Army Museum 1988–95; tstee Encounter 1989–91; Liveryman Worshipful Co of Scriveners 1989; FRSA; *Publications* Kipling Journal (ed, 1980–), The Bigger Bang: Growth of a Financial Revolution (1987), Kipling's Japan (ed with Sir Hugh Cortazzi, 1988); *Recreations* books and travel; *Clubs* Travellers', Beefsteak, Royal Commonwealth Society; *Style—* G H Webb, Esq, CMG, OBE; ✉ Weavers, Danes Hill, Woking, Surrey GU22 7HQ

WEBB, Iain Andrew; s of Eric Webb, of York, and Oris, *née* Dyson; *b* 30 March 1959; *Educ* Scalby Secdy Sch Scarborough, Joseph Rowntree Secdy Sch York, Rambert Sch of Ballet London, The Royal Ballet Sch London; *m* 30 July 1982, Margaret, da of Ettore Barbieri; 1 s (Jason Alexander b 29 July 1987); *Career* Sadlers Well's Royal Ballet (now The Birmingham Royal Ballet) 1979–89; princ roles: Oberon in Ashton's The Dream, The Young Man in Ashton's The Two Pigeons, Franz in Wright's Coppelia, Colas and Alain in Ashton's La Fille mal Gardée, Prince Siegfried and Benno in Wright's Swan Lake, Pas de Quatre in Nureyev's Raymonda Act III, Blue Bird and Pas de Quatre in Wright's Sleeping Beauty, The Poet in Les Sylphides; Balanchine's The Prodigal Son, Van Manen's 5 Tango's, Kay in Bintley's The Snow Queen; created roles in: Bintley's Polonia, Night Moves, Choros The Swan of Tuonela, Flowers of the Forest; performed Petrushka 1988/89 season; joined The Royal Ballet at Covent Garden 1989; debut as the King of the South in MacMillan's The Prince of the Pagodes, Mercury in Bintley's The Plants, danced in first performances of Balanchine's Violin Concerts and Page's Bloodline, Alain in Ashton's La Fille mal Gardée, guest appearances in Spain and SA 1989 and 1992, received sponsorship to study with Royal Danish Ballet March 1992, prog organiser and conslt for the Celebration of Classical Dance evening Harrogate Festival 1992; 1992–93 season: Bottom in The Dream, Mrs Tiggywinkle and Alexander Bland Pig in The Tales of Beatrix Potter, the small ugly sister (Ashton's Role) in Ashton's Cinderella, Sancho Panza in Mikhail Barysnikov's Don Quixote and the Pas de Quatra in MacMillian's Gloria; 1993–94 season: The Doctor in MacMillan's Different Drummer, Gallison in Anthony Dowell's Sleeping Beauty; prod and dir Patrick Armand and Friends Gala for 1993 Harrogate Int Festival, co-prodr an evening with principals and soloists of the Stuttgart Ballet 1994, prodr gala performance for the 150th anniversary of the Shaftesbury Homes at the Banqueting House 1994; co-dir The Dance Agency 1993–, fndr Dance Cares 1994, memb Bd of Dirs Adventures in Motion Pictures 1994; *Recreations* history of ballet, collecting ballet memorabilia, music, photography; *Style—* Iain Webb, Esq; ✉ The Royal Ballet, Royal Opera House, Covent Garden, London WC2E 9DD

WEBB, Jeremy Richard; s of C R Webb, OBE, MC (d 1976); *b* 25 March 1931; *Educ* Radley, Hertford Coll Oxford; *m* 1956, Clover Margaret, da of Maj J Suckling (d 1981); 3 s; *Career* 2 Lt Royal Sussex Regt; advertising (creative dir): Foote Cone & Beldins 1956–61, Lintas Ltd 1961–65, Wasey Campbell Ewald 1966–71, Ferrero & Co Spa Turin 1971–74, Wasey Campbell Ewald 1974–75, Everetts Ltd 1975–85; dir and creative dept mangr Allen Brady and Marsh 1985–87; dir The Word Process 1987–; *Recreations* bridge, swimming, painting, writing; *Style—* Jeremy Webb, Esq; ✉ 79 Cowleigh Rd, Malvern, Worcs WR14 1QL (☎ 01684 574748)

WEBB, (Anthony) John; s of Charles Reginald Webb (d 1972), of Bristol, and Gwendoline, *née* Moon; *b* 29 Dec 1929; *Educ* Cotham GS Bristol, Univ of Bristol (MB ChM); *m* 5 March 1955, Audrie Ruth; 2 s (Mark Idris, Dr Jason Crispin Webb), 2 da (Dominique Louise, Charlotte Anne); *Career* Nat Serv RAMC 1955–57 Lt/Capt 5 Field Ambulance; conslt surgn Bristol Royal Infirmary and Royal Hosp for Sick Children Bristol 1967, conslt surgn Bristol Royal Infirmary 1985–94, currently sr res fell in surgery Univ of Bristol; memb: Br Soc of Clinical Cytology, Br Assoc of Endocrine Surgns (pres), IAC; FRCS 1957, fell Int Acad of Cytology; *Books* Operative Surgery and Management (contrib, 1984–94), Practical Aspiration Cytology (contrib, 1985), General Surgical Operations (contrib, 1987–94); *Recreations* choral singing, gardening; *Clubs* Jenner, Bristol Royal Infirmary; *Style—* John Webb, Esq; ✉ 7 Percival Rd, Clifton, Bristol BS8 8EL (☎ 0117 973 8349)

WEBB, Justin Oliver; s of Charles Webb (d 1983), and Gloria, *née* Crocombe; *b* 3 Jan 1961; *Educ* Friends' Sch Sidcot, LSE (BSc(Econ)); *Career* BBC: news trainee 1984–86, reporter BBC Radio Ulster 1986–87, reporter Today prog Radio 4 1987–88, news reporter and foreign affrs corr BBC Radio and Television 1988–93 (assignments incl Gulf War, Russia, USA, Middle E, India, Western and Eastern Europe and S Africa, Bosnia), full-time presenter Breakfast News 1994– (occasional presenter 1993–94); memb RIIA; *Style—* Justin Webb, Esq; ✉ BBC Breakfast News, Television Centre, Wood Lane, London W12 7RJ (☎ 0181 576 7501)

WEBB, Keith Stewart; s of Arthur Saunders Webb, of Walsall, and Doris Martha, *née* Cheadle; *b* 19 March 1947; *Educ* Joseph Leckie Sch Walsall, Matthew Boulton Coll Birmingham, Sch of Art and Design Walsall; *m* 13 Aug 1972, Gillian, da of Anthony Anson; 2 da (Nicola Lucy b 5 Aug 1978, Amy Francesca b 27 Dec 1984); *Career* Lucas Industries: in trg Group Advertising Facility 1964–67, prodn controller 1967–68, press offr Lucas Electrical 1968–69, chief press offr 1969–70, dep gp PR mangr 1970–72; Edson Evers and Associates: joined 1973, assoc ptnr 1974–85, ptnr 1985–; MIPR 1974, Dip in Communication and Mktg 1976; *Recreations* swimming, yachting; *Style—* Keith Webb, Esq; ✉ Yew Tree House, 366 Birmingham Rd, Walsall, West Midlands WS5 3NX (☎ 01922 21032); Edson Evers & Associates, Priory House, Friars Terrace, Stafford ST17 4QG (☎ 01785 249237/255146, fax 01785 211518)

WEBB, Lizbeth; *see:* Campbell, Elizabeth

WEBB, Patrick John Ryall; s of Kenneth Edmund Ryall Webb, of Tadworth, Surrey, and Marjorie Eveline Ryall, *née* Nuthall; *b* 31 March 1944; *Educ* St Edward's Sch Oxford, Trinity Hall Cambridge; *m* 22 March 1969, Dr Joanna Webb, da of Thomas Gilbert Burton (d 1976), of Hull; 1 s (Edward b 1970), 2 da (Georgina b 1971, Elly b 1975); *Career* articled clerk Ernst and Young 1965–69, mangr Peat Marwick McLintock 1969–81; co sec: Touche Remnant and Co 1981–85, James Capel and Co 1986–91; dir James Capel Unit Trust Management Ltd 1989–91; md G W Hutton & Co (Underwriting Agency) Ltd 1991–95, fin dir J H Chappell (Underwriting Agencies) Ltd 1994–; dir Walton Heath Golf Club 1985–93, chm and govr Bramley Sch 1975–95; FCA 1970, FRSA; *Recreations* golf, music, tennis; *Style—* Patrick Webb, Esq; ✉ 17 Tower Road, Tadworth, Surrey KT20 5QY (☎ 01737 814606); J H Chappell (Underwriting Agencies) Ltd, 78 Leadenhall St, London EC3 (☎ 0171 626 4617, fax 0171 220 7185)

WEBB, Richard; s of Lt-Col Richard Webb (d 1988), and Iris Webb (d 1996); *b* 26 July 1943; *Educ* Marlborough; *m* 25 Feb 1992, Gillian Blane, *née* Jenkins; *Career* Condé Nast Publications Ltd 1966–70, dir Michael Joseph Ltd publishers London 1970–74, co-fndr and md Webb & Bower (Publishers) Ltd/Richard Webb Ltd 1975–; *Clubs* Dartmouth Yacht; *Style—* Richard Webb, Esq; ✉ Hope Cottage, Lower Ferry Slip, Dartmouth, Devon TQ6 9AW; Richard Webb Ltd, 9 Duke Street, Dartmouth, Devon TQ6 9PY (☎ 01803 835525, fax 01803 835552)

WEBB, Richard Murton Lumley; s of Richard Henry Lumley Webb, and Elizabeth Martin Munro, *née* Kerr; *b* 7 March 1939; *Educ* Winchester, New Coll Oxford; *m* 1966, Juliet Wendy English, *née* Devenish; 1 s (b 1973), 1 da (b 1974); *Career* articled clerk then CA Brown Fleming & Murray 1961–68; Morgan Grenfell & Co Ltd: joined 1968, dir 1973–, dep chm 1988–89, chm 1989–96; dir Morgan Grenfell Group plc 1988–; MICAS 1965; *Recreations* music, reading; *Clubs* Hurlingham; *Style—* Richard Webb, Esq

WEBB, Robert Stopford; QC (1988); s of R V B Webb, MC, of Styal, Cheshire, and Isabella Raine, *née* Hinks; *b* 4 Oct 1948; *Educ* Wycliffe Coll, Univ of Exeter (LLB); *m* 1 April 1975, Angela Mary, da of Bernard Bruce Freshwater (d 1978), of Darlington, Co Durham; 2 s (Alfred b 1978, William b 1980); *Career* called to the Bar Inner Temple 1971, recorder 1993–, head of chambers 5 Bell Yard; chm Air Law Ctee Royal Aeronautical Soc 1988–92, vice chm Air Law Ctee Int Bar Assoc 1990–92, rep of Bar Int Bar Assoc 1994–; memb: Bd Int Acad of Trial Lawyers, Chllr's Advsy Cncl Univ of Exeter; membre de la Commission d'Arbitrage Aerien et Spatial (Paris) 1994; FRAeS; *Recreations* golf, fly fishing; *Clubs* Royal Wimbledon Golf, Royal Lytham St Anne's Golf, Prestbury Golf; *Style—* Robert Webb, Esq, QC; ✉ 5 Bell Yard, London WC2A 2JR (☎ 0171 333 8811, fax 0171 333 8831)

WEBB, Rodney Anson John; JP; s of Ernest Herbert Webb (d 1983), of Norwich, and Irene Maud, *née* Gotts; *b* 24 April 1944; *Educ* Bracondale Sch Norwich; *m* 8 Nov 1969 (m dis), Angela Delys, da of Frederick Lukies (d 1981), of Salhouse, Norfolk; 3 da (Alison b 1971, Victoria b 1977, Hannah b 1986); *Career* md: Bowater Flexible Packaging 1978, Bowater Cartons 1980, Crest Packaging 1985–; memb Ctee Br Carton Assoc 1980–81, pres Flexible Packaging Assoc 1983–84; vice pres: Euro Flexible Packaging Assoc 1984–86, UK spokesman Euro Aluminium Foil Assoc 1988–91, pres Euro Aluminium Foil Assoc Converters 1992; FCA; *Recreations* golf, tennis, skiing, water skiing; *Clubs* Bearsted Golf; *Style—* Rodney Webb, Esq, JP; ✉ Angley House, Angley Park, Cranbrook, Kent TN17 2PN (☎ 01580 714773); Crest Packaging Limited, Courteney Rd, Gillingham, Kent ME8 0RX (☎ 01634 234444, fax 01634 387035, telex 96153)

WEBB CARTER, Brig David Brian Wynn; OBE (1982), MC (1967)2; s of Brig Brian Wolseley Webb Carter, DSO, OBE (d 1982), and (Evelyn) Rosemary, *née* Hood (d 1978); *b* 5 Nov 1940; *Educ* Eton, RMA Sandhurst, Nat Defence Univ USA; *m* 15 Oct 1973, Felicity Elizabeth, da of William Lytton de Burgh Young, DL (d 1980), of Drewsteignton, Devon; 1 s (Oliver b 1975), 2 da (Margot b 1977, Camilla b 1983); *Career* cmmnd Irish Gds 1961; served BAOR, Libya, Cyprus, Middle East, Singapore, Hong Kong, Belize and USA; CO 1 Bn Irish Gds 1979–81, CBF Belize 1984–87, ACOS Int HQ BAOR 1988–91, Dir Personnel Army MOD 1992–95, Hon ADC to HM The Queen 1994–95; sec The Corviglia Ski Club St Moritz 1995–; *Books* The Illicit Drug Trade in Britain and Latin America: A Changing Relationship (1989); *Recreations* skiing, cricket, travel; *Clubs* White's, MCC; *Style—* Brig David Webb Carter, OBE, MC; ✉ c/o Guards & Cavalry Section, Lloyds Bank, 6 Pall Mall, London SW1

WEBBER, John Anthony; s of Walter James Webber (d 1972), of Birmingham, and Edith, *née* Lloyd (d 1964); *b* 15 Feb 1951; *Educ* Birmingham Secdy Sch, Birmingham Coll of Food and Domestic Arts (City & Guilds), Westminster Coll of Food London (City & Guilds); *m* 5 Aug 1987, Caroline Isobel, da of Ian Jackson, of Appin, Argyll; 1 s (Nigel John b 10 Feb 1989), 2 da (Chloe Caroline b 4 Jan 1992, Abigail Louise b 14 Feb 1995); *Career* chef; first commis chef rising to chef de partie Park Lane Hotel Piccadilly 1969–73; Dorchester Hotel Park Lane: second commis chef 1973–75, first commis chef 1975–76, chef de partie 1976–79, sous chef 1979–80; head chef: Gidleigh Park Hotel Chagford Devon 1980–85 (Michelin rosette 1982), Clivedon Taplow Bucks 1985–88; exec chef 'Kinnaird' Kinnaird Estate nr Dunkeld 1988– (Michelin rosette 1992, 4/5 Good Food Guide 1996); Cert of Merit (Salon Culinaire de Londres) 1976, Silver Medal (City of Truro Festival of Culinary Arts) 1980, Gold Medal (Torquay Gastranomic Festival) 1981; Master Craftsman Craft Guild of Chefs, Master Chef Master Chefs Inst; *Recreations* fishing, eating out, music; *Style—* John Webber, Esq; ✉ Kinnaird, Kinnaird Estate, By Dunkeld, Tayside PH8 0LB (☎ 01796 482440, fax 01796 482289)

WEBBER, Lesley Anne; da of Capt Dennis John Webber, of Felpham, West Sussex, and Constance Acie, *née* Greenaway; *b* 10 April 1956; *Educ* Sydenham HS, Univ of Birmingham (LLB); *m* 17 Sept 1983, Nigel Cleevely Wagland, s of James Leslie William Wagland, DFC, of New Milton, Hants; 2 s (Christopher b 1989, James b 1991); *Career* admitted slr 1980; Freshfields 1980–84; Masons: joined 1984–93; ptnr Property Litigation and Planning Dept Dibb Lupton Broomhead 1993–; FCIArb, memb Law Soc, hon memb Arbrix; *Recreations* skiing, theatre; *Style—* Miss Lesley Webber; ✉ Dibb Lupton Broomhead, 125 London Wall, London EC2Y 5AE (☎ 0171 600 0202, fax 0171 600 1650)

WEBBER, Suzanne Laura; da of Edwin Howard Webber, of Bristol, and Thelma, *née* Parkinson; *b* 27 Feb 1958; *Educ* Clifton HS, Univ of Oxford (BA); *m* 25 June 1988, Richard Henry Struan Birkett; 2 s (James Howard Struan b 10 Dec 1990, Robert Alexander b 25 May 1993), 1 da (Imogen Claire b 30 Oct 1995); *Career* publisher; Thomas Nelson and Son Ltd Publishers: Thomson publishing trainee 1981–82, desk ed English Language Teaching Books 1982–84; commissioning ed W Foulsham Publishers 1984–85, commissioning ed Ebury Press 1985–87; BBC Books: sr commissioning ed 1987–91, jt editorial dir 1991–; *Recreations* mountain walking, reading, tennis, swimming; *Style—* Ms Suzanne Webber; ✉ BBC Books, 80 Wood Lane, London W12 0TT (☎ 0181 576 2274)

WEBBER, Terence Frank Lees (Terry); s of late Leslie Clifford Ebb Webber, and late Harriet Marjorie, *née* Lees; *b* 28 July 1934; *Educ* Mill Hill Sch; *m* 1970, Susan Yvonne, *née* Knightley; 2 da (Penelope Jane b 12 April 1972, Elizabeth b 19 Aug 1974); *Career* Nat Serv Royal Army Educn Corps 1957–59; articled Percy Mason & Co 1951–56; Peat Marwick Mitchell & Co: sr asst 1959, sr mangr 1968, ptnr ME 1970, ptnr London 1974; transfd to KPMG Bristol 1985–93, conslt 1993–95; *Style—* Terry Webber, Esq; ✉ Frampton Court, Frampton Cotterell, Bristol BS17 2DW (☎ 0145 477 7417)

WEBER, David Henry; s of Humphrey Norden Weber, of London, and Queenie, *née* Temple; *b* 11 Aug 1953; *Educ* Haberdashers' Aske's, Clare Coll Cambridge (MA), Coll of Law London; *m* 2 da (Clare Louise b 10 July 1981, Helen Victoria b 29 Aug 1984); *Career* articled clerk Linklaters & Paines London 1976, slr 1978, seconded Fulbright & Jaworski (attorneys) Houston Texas 1980–81, ptnr Linklaters & Paines 1984–; memb: Law Soc, Major Projects Assoc, Int Bar Assoc; memb City of London Solicitors' Co; *Recreations* music, sailing, travel; *Style—* David H Weber; ✉ Linklaters & Paines, 59–67

Gresham Street, London EC2V 7JA (☎ 0171 606 7080, fax 0171 606 5113, telex 884349/888167)

WEBER, Prof Richard Robert; s of Richard Robert Weber (d 1988), and Elizabeth, *née* Bray; *b* 25 Feb 1953; *Educ* Walnut Hills HS, Solihull Sch, Downing Coll Cambridge (MA, Mayhew Prize, PhD); *Career* Univ of Cambridge: research fell Queens' Coll 1977–78, tutor and dir of studies in mathematics, manufacturing engrg and management studies Queens' Coll 1978–92, lectr Dept of Engrg 1984–92 (asst lectr 1978–84), reader in management sci 1992–94, Churchill prof of mathematics for operational research Dept of Pure Mathematics and Mathematical Statistics 1994–, vice pres Queens' Coll 1996–; memb: Operational Research Soc, Operations Research Soc of America; FRSS; *Recreations* hiking, fitness training, travel; *Style*— Prof Richard Weber; ✉ Queens' College, Cambridge CB3 9ET (☎ 01223 335570); Department of Pure Mathematics and Mathematical Statistics, Statistical Laboratory, University of Cambridge, 16 Mill Lane, Cambridge, Cambridgeshire CB2 1SB (☎ 01223 337953, fax 01223 337956)

WEBSTER, Rev Dr Alan Brunskill; KCVO (1988); *b* 1 July 1918; *Educ* Oxford (MA, BD), City Univ (DD Hon); *m* 1951, Margaret; 2 s, 2 da; *Career* curate in Sheffield 1942–46, staff of Westcott House 1946–52, vicar of Barnard Castle 1952–59, warden of Lincoln 1959–70, dean of Norwich 1970–78, dean of St Paul's 1978–87; pres Cathedral Camps 1982; *Books* Joshua Watson, Broken Bones May Joy, Julian of Norwich; contrib to: Historic Episcopate, Strategist of the Spirit, The Reality of God; *Recreations* writing, gardening, travel; *Style*— The Rev Dr Alan Webster, KCVO; ✉ 20 Beechbank, Norwich NR2 2AL (☎ 01603 455833)

WEBSTER, Alistair Stevenson; QC (1995); s of His Hon Ian Webster, *qv*, of Rochdale, and Margaret, *née* Sharples; *b* 28 April 1953; *Educ* Hulme GS Oldham, BNC Oxford (BA); *m* 4 June 1977, Barbara Anne, da of Dr Donald Longbottom (d 1961); 2 da (Elizabeth b 1982, Alexandra b 1985); *Career* called to the Bar Middle Temple 1976, hon sec Northern Circuit of the Bar 1988–93, recorder 1996– (asst recorder 1992); memb Gen Cncl of the Bar 1994–95; *Recreations* skiing, cricket, tennis; *Clubs* Manchester Racquets, Rochdale Racquets, I Volenti CC; *Style*— Alistair Webster, Esq, QC; ✉ Ashworth Hall, Ashworth Rd, Rochdale, Lancs OL11 5UP (☎ 01706 30779); Lincoln House, Deansgate, Manchester (☎ 0161 832 5701, fax 0161 832 0839)

WEBSTER, Maj-Gen Bryan Courtney; CB (1986), CBE (1981); s of Capt Herbert John Webster (ka 1940), and Mabel, *née* Harrison (d 1970); *b* 2 Feb 1931; *Educ* Haileybury, RMA Sandhurst; *m* 1957, Elizabeth Rowland Waldron, da of Prof Sir David Waldron Smithers; 2 s (Julian, Justin), 1 da (Lucinda); *Career* cmmnd Royal Fusiliers 1951, Airborne Forces 1953–56; served: Germany, Korea, Egypt, Gibraltar, Hong Kong, Malta; directing staff Staff Coll 1969–71; cmd: 1 RRF 1971–73, 8 Inf Bde 1975–77; MID 1977, Chief of Staff SE Dist 1977–78, Indian Nat Def Coll 1979, dir of admin Planning (Army) 1980–82, dir Army Quartering 1982–86; Dep Col (City of London) RRF 1976–89, chm Army Benevolent Fund Surrey; cncllr Wine Guild of the UK; Freeman City of London 1984; FIMgt; *Recreations* field sports, ornithology, wine; *Style*— Maj-Gen Bryan Webster, CB, CBE; ✉ c/o Midland Bank, 69 High Street, Sevenoaks, Kent

WEBSTER, (James) Colin Eden; OBE; s of George Webster (d 1975), and Daphne Milman, *née* Bisset (d 1995); *b* 5 March 1936; *Educ* Wellington Coll, Trinity Coll Oxford; *m* 1965, Susan Scarff; 1 da, 2 s; *Career* joined British Petroleum plc 1959, exec vice pres BP America Inc 1987–89, joined National Power Div CEGB (before privatisation) 1989, exec dir National Power plc 1990–96, md National Power UK until 1996; non-exec dir: Seafield Resources plc, Unitech plc until 1996; *Recreations* sailing, opera, travel; *Style*— Colin Webster, Esq, OBE

WEBSTER, David Gordon Comyn; s of Alfred Edward Comyn Webster, of St John's Town of Dalry, Castle Douglas, Scotland, and Meryl Mary, *née* Clutterbuck (d 1970); *b* 11 Feb 1945; *Educ* Glasgow Acad, Univ of Glasgow (LLB); *m* 12 Feb 1972, (Pamela) Gail, da of Dr Dennis Frank Runnicles, of Sevenoaks, Kent; 3 s (Michael Gordon Comyn b 20 Sept 1974, Nicholas Gordon Comyn b 9 Jan 1978, Jonathan Hugo Comyn b 9 Feb 1983); *Career* Lt RNR, ret 1970; admitted slr 1968, corp fin Samuel Montagu & Co 1968–72, Wm Brandts 1972–73, fin dir Oriel Foods Ltd 1973–76; Safeway plc (formerly Argyll Group plc): dir 1977– (from formation of Argyll Group), fin dir 1977–89, exec dep chm 1989–96, chief exec 1996–; non-exec dir: Reed International plc 1992–, Reed Elsevier plc 1993–; memb Nat Employers' Liaison Ctee; govr Lockers Park Sch Tst Ltd; *Recreations* military history, gardening, skiing, shooting; *Style*— David Webster, Esq; ✉ Rodinghead, Ashridge Park, Berkhamsted, Hertfordshire; Safeway plc, Safeway House, Millington Road, Hayes UB3 4AY (☎ 0181 848 8744)

WEBSTER, Derek Adrian; CBE (1979); s of James Tulloch and Isobel Webster; *b* 24 March 1927; *Educ* St Peter's Bournemouth; *m* 1966, Dorothy Frances Johnson; 2 s, 1 da; *Career* RN 1944–48; reporter Western Morning News 1943, staff journalist Daily Mail 1949–51, joined Mirror Group 1952, Northern ed Daily Mirror 1964–67, ed Daily Record 1967–72, chm and editorial dir Scottish Daily Record and Sunday Mail Ltd 1974–87, dir Mirror Group Newspapers 1974–87; memb Press Cncl 1981–83 (jt vice chm 1982–83), vice chm Age Concern Scotland 1977–83, hon vice pres Newspaper Press Fund; *Recreations* travel, reading; *Style*— Derek Webster, Esq, CBE; ✉ 32 Athole Gardens, Dowanhill, Glasgow G12 9BD (☎ 0141 339 6239)

WEBSTER, Gary Ian; s of Reginald John Webster (d 1991), of Brentwood, Essex, and Kathleen Elenor, *née* Short; *b* 3 Feb 1964; *Educ* Brentwood Co HS, London Acad of Music and Dramatic Art (pres Union); *Career* actor; *Theatre* Skylight in Class Enemy (Manchester Library Theatre) 1986, Above All Courage (New End Theatre Hampstead) 1987, Kevin in Groping For Words (Manchester Library Theatre) 1990; *Television* Graham in EastEnders 1987, various roles in Boon, Taggart and The Bill, Ray Daley in Minder 1990–95; *Films* Empire State (Channel 4) 1986, Out of Order (Channel 4/BFVW) 1987; *Recreations* nightclubbing, football, cricket, golf, sailing, former Essex county badminton player; *Style*— Gary Webster, Esq; ✉ c/o Sally Hope Associates, 108 Leonard Street, London EC2A 4RH (☎ 0171 613 5353)

WEBSTER, His Hon Ian Stevenson; s of Harvey Webster by his w Annabella, *née* McBain; *b* 20 March 1925; *Educ* Rochdale GS, Univ of Manchester; *m* 1951, Margaret, *née* Sharples; 2 s (one of whom Alistair Stevenson Webster, *qv*); *Career* serv Sub-Lt RNVR in WWII, Fleet Air Arm pilot; barr Middle Temple 1948, recorder Crown Ct 1972–76 (asst recorder Oldham 1970, Salford 1971); chm Manchester Industl Tribunals 1976–81; circuit judge (Northern Circuit) 1981–95, ret; hon recorder Burnley 1991–95; *Style*— His Hon Ian Webster; ✉ 1 Higher Lodge, Norden, Rochdale OL11 5TZ

WEBSTER, Jan; da of William Stuart McCallum (d 1940), of Blantyre, Lanarkshire, and Margaret Henderson (d 1977); *b* 10 Aug 1924; *Educ* Hamilton Acad; *m* 1946, Andrew Webster, OBE, s of William Webster; 1 s (Stephen William b 1951), 1 da (Lyn Margaret b 1950); *Career* journalist: Glasgow Evening News and Scottish Sunday Mail 1942–46, Kemsley Newspapers London 1946–48; freelance journalist and writer of short stories 1948–; *Books* incl: Colliers Row (1977), Saturday City (1978), Beggarman's Country (1979), Due South (1982), Muckle Annie (1985), One Little Room (1987), The Rags of Time (1987), A Different Woman (1989), Abercrombie's Aunt and Other Stories (1990), I Only Can Dance With You (1990), Bluebell Blue (1991), Lowland Reels (1992), Tallie's War (1993), Makalienski's Bones (1995), Pinkmount Drive (1996); *Recreations* teaching creative writing, studying Shakespeare; *Style*— Mrs Jan Webster; ✉ c/o Robert Hale Ltd, Clerkenwell House, 45–47 Clerkenwell Green, London EC1R OHT

WEBSTER, Prof John; s of Albert Ashcroft Webster (d 1955), of Kirkby-in-Ashfield, Notts, and Alice, *née* Street (d 1957); *b* 25 May 1925; *Educ* Univ Coll Nottingham (external London BSc), Univ of London (external PhD, DSc); *m* 1 Aug 1950, Mary Elizabeth (Brom), da of Thomas Jireh Bromhead (d 1981), of Clenchwarton, Norfolk; 1 s (Christopher b 1956), 1 da (Sarah b 1959); *Career* lectr in botany Univ of Hull 1946–49, lectr, sr lectr then reader in botany Univ of Sheffield 1950–69; Univ of Exeter: prof of biological scis 1969–90 (emeritus prof 1990), head of Dept 1969–86; author of numerous pubns on taxonomy and ecology of fungi; Int Mycological Assoc: vice pres 1977–83, pres 1983–90, hon life pres 1990; Br Mycological Soc: memb 1946, sec 1953–57, pres 1969 and 1996, hon memb 1987; hon memb Mycological Soc of America 1987; FIBiol 1970; *Books* Introduction to Fungi (1980), Fungal Ecology (with N J Dix, 1995); *Recreations* gardening, walking; *Style*— Prof John Webster; ✉ University of Exeter, Hatherly Laboratories, Prince of Wales Road, Exeter EX4 4PS (☎ 01392 263784, fax 01392 263700)

WEBSTER, John Dudley; *b* 13 Nov 1939; *Educ* Merchant Taylors', Univ Coll London (BSc); *m* 1967, Barbara Joan; 1 da (Katherine b 1969); *Career* dir and sec Sun Life Corporation plc until 1992; dir: Sapphire Petroleum plc 1981–88, Group Investors plc 1984–86, The Fleming Geared Income & Assets Investment Trust plc 1984–, Hoare Govett Smaller Companies Index Investment Trust plc 1992–, FIM Services Ltd 1992–, The Housing Finance Corporation Ltd 1993–, HCG Lloyd's Investment Trust PLC 1993–, Leeds Life Assurance Ltd 1994–96, USDC Investment Trust plc 1994–96, Save & Prosper Linked Investment Trust plc 1994–, Venturi Investment Trust plc 1994–; chm: Second Consolidated Trust plc 1992–, SEC Group PLC 1993–, Equitas Holdings Ltd 1995–; chm GT Income Growth Trust plc 1996–; chm Br Insur Assoc Investmt Protection Ctee 1982–84, lay memb Cncl of Stock Exchange 1985–86 and 1988–91 (dir Stock Exchange 1991–92), ind dir Securities Assoc 1986–90, tstee COIF Charity Funds 1988–; FIA; *Clubs* City of London; *Style*— John Webster, Esq; ✉ 10 Merrydown Way, Chislehurst, Kent BR7 5RS (☎ and fax 0181 467 9148)

WEBSTER, Prof (Anthony) John Francis; s of Flt Lt John Terence Webster, DFC (ka 1940), and Lilian Hypatia, *née* Mogg; *b* 24 Aug 1938; *Educ* Wellingborough Sch, St John's Coll Cambridge (MA, Vet MB), Univ of Glasgow (PhD); *m* 31 Aug 1964, Maureen Anne Sanderson, da of Joseph Blair (d 1959); 1 s (Mark b 1965), 1 da (Joanne b 1967); *Career* assoc prof Univ of Alberta Canada 1966–70, princ vet res offr Rowett Res Inst Aberdeen 1970–77, prof of animal husbandry Univ of Bristol 1977– (head Sch of Vet Sci 1993–); pres: Br Soc of Animal Prodn 1991, Nutrition Soc 1992–95; MRCVS 1963 (memb Cncl 1993–97); *Books* Calf Husbandry Health and Welfare (1981), Understanding the Dairy Cow (1987), Animal Welfare: A Cool Eye Towards Eden (1995); *Recreations* sailing, music; *Style*— Prof John Webster; ✉ Department of Clinical Veterinary Science, University of Bristol, School of Veterinary Science, Langford, Bristol BS18 7DU

WEBSTER, Vice Adm Sir John Morrison; KCB (1986); s of Frank Martin Webster (d 1986), of Lymington, and Kathleen Mary, *née* Morrison (d 1986); *b* 3 Nov 1932; *Educ* Pangbourne Coll; *m* 15 Dec 1962, Valerie Anne, da of Vice Adm Sir Michael Villiers KCB, OBE (d 1990), of Melton, Woodbridge; 1 s (Thomas b 1970 d 1994), 2 da (Lucilla (Mrs Harry Sinanian) b 1964, Rozelle b 1966); *Career* joined RN 1951, specialised in navigation 1959; served: UK, Far East, Australia; staff appts at Dartmouth and MOD; cmd: HMS Argonaut 1970–71, HMS Cleopatra 1977–79; Naval Advsr and RNLO Ottawa 1974–76, dir Naval Warfare (MOD) 1980–81, Rear Adm 1982, Flag Offr Sea Trg 1982–84, chief of staff to C-in-C Fleet 1984–86, Vice Adm 1985, Flag Offr Plymouth and Naval Base Cdr Devonport 1987–90; landscape and marine painter, exhibitions in Canada and London (King St Gallery 1981 and 1984, Oliver Swann Gallery 1986, 1988, 1991 and 1993, Tryon Swann 1996); pres Royal Naval Benevolent Tst 1991–; govr Canford Sch, chm Pangbourne Coll; Yr Bro Trinity House 1970; *Recreations* painting, sailing; *Clubs* Royal Cruising, Royal Naval Sailing Assoc; *Style*— Vice Adm Sir John Webster, KCB; ✉ Old School House, Soberton, Hampshire SO32 3PF

WEBSTER, John Walter; s of Norman Alan Webster (d 1982), and Francis Kate, *née* Simons; *b* 21 Jan 1936; *Educ* De Aston Sch Market Rasen Lincs, LSE (BSc); *m* 12 Aug 1961, Constance Anne, da of Arthur Cartwright (d 1944), of Sch House, Admaston, Rugeley, Staffs; 1 da (Elizabeth b 1966), 1 s (Graham b 1968); *Career* mangr Price Waterhouse & Co 1961–71; gp dir gen The Penguin Group 1992–Jan 1996, ret; FCA; *Recreations* skiing, travel, reading; *Style*— John Webster, Esq; ✉ Woodmans Cottage, Bramley Rd, Silchester, Hants (☎ 0118 970 0670); School House, Admaston, nr Rugeley, Staffs (☎ 01889 21285)

WEBSTER, Maj (Richard) Michael Otley; s of Brig Frederick Richard Webster, of Mere, Wilts, and Beryl Helena Sellars, *née* Otley; *b* 11 Aug 1942; *Educ* Charterhouse, RMA Sandhurst, Army Staff Coll Camberley; *m* 12 June 1971, Joanna Gay Enid, da of Lt Col Richard Henry Oothout Simpson, DSO; 2 s (Jonathan Richard b 4 July 1972, Rupert James b 21 June 1974); *Career* cmmnd RA, served Germany, Aden and UK, cmd The King's Troop RHA 1962–79; jockey in amateur steeplechases 1967–77; joined United Racecourses Ltd 1979–96; clerk of the course: Kempton Park 1980–96 (gen mangr 1981–94), Lingfield Park 1986–87, Epsom Downs 1988–95; clerk of the course and mangr Bangor-on-Dee 1996–; memb Horseracing Advsy Cncl 1987–90, dist cmmr Garth South Pony Club 1987–90; memb Hon Corps of Gentlemen at Arms (HM Body Guard) 1993–; *Recreations* shooting, cricket and walking; *Clubs* Cavalry and Guards; *Style*— Maj Michael Webster; ✉ Coopers Farm, Hartley Wespall, Hook, Hants RG27 0BQ (☎ 01256 882413); Bangor-on-Dee Races Ltd, The Racecourse, Bangor-on-Dee, Wrexham LL13 0DA (☎ 01978 780323)

WEBSTER, Prof Nigel Robert; s of Derek Stanley Webster, of Walsall, and Sheila Margaret Flora, *née* Squire; *b* 14 June 1953; *Educ* Univ of Leeds (BSc, MB ChB, PhD); *m* 2 July 1977, Diana Christina Shirley, da of Brian Robert Galt Hutchinson, of York, 1 s (Oliver James b 1986), 2 da (Lorna Elizabeth b 1984, Lucy Anne b 1987); *Career* memb Scientific Staff Div of Anaesthesia MRC Clinical Res Centre 1986–88, conslt in anaesthesia, dir of transplant anaesthesia and co-dir of intensive care St James' Univ Hosp Leeds 1988–94, prof Dept of Anaesthesia and Intensive Care Univ of Aberdeen and hon conslt Aberdeen Royal Infirmary 1994–; memb: Intensive Care Soc, Euro Soc of Intensive Care Med, Soc for Free Radical Res, Elgar Soc; FFARCS, FRCP; *Books* Research Techniques in Anaesthesia (1988), Intensive Care: Developments and controversies (1992); *Recreations* flying, music, gardening; *Style*— Prof Nigel Webster; ✉ Wickerinn Farmhouse, Banchory AB31 5QX; Aberdeen Royal Infirmary, Forester Hill, Aberdeen AB9 2ZB (☎ 01224 681818)

WEBSTER, Norman; s of George Wyndham Webster (d 1974), of Dover, and Naomi, *née* Wardill (d 1969); *b* 6 May 1924; *Educ* Dover GS, Tunbridge Wells Sch of Art, Royal Coll of Art (royal exhibitioner ARCA); *m* 1947, Joan Winifred, da of James Tristram Augustus Simpson; 3 s (Matthew Norman b 14 Aug 1955, Simon Julian b 10 July 1956, Mark Wardill b 23 Aug 1960); *Career* lectr in drawing and engraving College of Art Leeds 1949 then sr lectr in printmaking Fine Art Dept Leeds Poly (following amalgamation) until 1985; solo exhbns: Northern Artists Gallery Leeds 1969, Goosewell Gallery Menston 1977, Northern Artists Gallery Harrogate 1978, The Hart Holes Studios Holmfirth 1978, Manor House Gallery Ilkley 1980; exhbns incl: Bankside Gallery Blackfriars, Royal Academy, New English Art Club, Yorkshire Printmakers America, Canada, Israel and Germany; collections: Arts Council of GB, Ashmolean Museum, FA, Univ of Salford, DOE, Leeds City Art Gallery, Wakefield City Art Gallery, Harrogate Art Gallery; sr fell RE 1994 (fell 1973, ARE 1951), sr fell RWS 1994 (fell 1975, ARWS 1966); *Recreations* reading, classical music, walking the dog; *Style*— Norman Webster, Esq

WEBSTER, Sir Peter Edlin; kt (1980); s of Herbert Edlin Webster, of Cookham, by his w Florence Helen; *b* 16 Feb 1924; *Educ* Haileybury, Merton Coll Oxford; *m* 1, 1955 (m dis), Susan Elizabeth, da of the late Benjamin William Richards; 1 s, 2 da; m 2, 1968, Avril Carolyn Simpson, da of the late Dr John Ernest McCrae Harrisson; *Career* Nat Serv RNVR 1943–46 and 1950; lectr in law Lincoln Coll Oxford 1950–52, called to the Bar Middle Temple 1952; standing jr counsel to Labour Miny 1964–67; QC 1967; chm: London Common Law Bar Assoc 1975–79, Senate of the Inns of Court and the Bar 1976–77; dir Booker McConnell 1978–79; High Ct judge (Queen's Bench) 1980–92; chm: Judicial Studies Bd 1981–83, Review Bd for Govt Contracts 1993–; memb City Disputes Panel 1994–; *Style*— Sir Peter Webster

WEBSTER, Richard Edward; s of William Graham Webster, of Port Tennant, Swansea, and June Elizabeth, *née* Richards; *b* 9 July 1967; *Educ* Cefn Hengoed Secdy; *m* 1 da (Kelly Joanne Webster b 11 July 1987); *Career* rugby union flanker; clubs: Bonymaen RFC (capt youth team 1984–85 and 1985–86), Swansea RFC, Barbarians RFC; rep: Wales Youth 1985–86, Wales U21 1987; Wales: debut v Aust 1987, memb World Cup Squad 1987, 13 caps; memb British Lions' team touring NZ 1993; bricklayer, sales rep Manor Bricks; *Recreations* DIY, horse riding, keep fit; *Style*— Richard Webster, Esq

WEBSTER, Richard Joseph; s of Peter Joseph Webster, of Dulwich, London; *b* 7 July 1953; *Educ* William Penn Sch Dulwich; *m* 1980, Patricia Catherine, da of Gerald Stanley Edwards, of East Grinstead, Sussex; 1 s (James Joseph b April 1985), 1 da (Victoria Catherine b Sept 1983); *Career* Lloyd's insur broker; various sr exec posts 1977– (incl chm R J Webster Insurance Services Ltd 1987–90), currently md Non-Marine Div Alexander Howden Group Ltd; *Recreations* family, golf, tennis, watching rugby; *Clubs* various incl Capital, East Sussex National, Lloyd's of London; *Style*— Richard J Webster, Esq; ✉ 23a The Glen, Farnborough Park, Locksbotton, Kent BR6 8LP; 8 Devonshire Square, London EC2M 4PL (☎ 0171 216 3329, fax 0171 972 9855, telex 882171 HOWDEN G)

WEBSTER, Sinclair Aubrey; s of Rae Walter Webster, of Felpham, W Sussex, and Alphonsine Maria Brulez; *b* 19 Nov 1948; *Educ* Worth Sch, Trinity Hall Cambridge (MA, DipArch); *m* 3 July 1971, Stephanie Jane, da of E D John Walter Pollard; 1 s (Hugh Sinclair b 23 May 1980), 1 da (Isabel Mary b 29 Sept 1982); *Career* architect; ptnr Sheppard Robson 1988–95, chm Sinclair Webster Ltd 1995–; cncllr (Cons) Woking Borough Cncl 1990– (chm Housing and Community Servs Ctee 1993); govr St Dunstan's RC Primary Sch; RIBA 1975; *Recreations* painting, reading, politics, walking, shooting, stalking; *Style*— Sinclair Webster, Esq; ✉ Sinclair Webster Ltd, The Studio, Wych-Elm House, Ashwood Road, Woking, Surrey GU22 7JW (fax 01483 740915, mobile 0973 225639)

WEBSTER, Dr Stephen George Philip; s of George Stephen Webster (d 1982), and Winifred Ella, *née* Tice (d 1971); *b* 30 Sept 1940; *Educ* County HS for Boys Ilford Essex, The London Hosp Med Coll (MB BS, MD); *m* 23 July 1960, Susan Jane, da of Maurice Hills, of 2 Fulbourn, Cambs; 3 s (Matthew John b 15 June 1968, Thomas Edward b 9 Jan 1970, Richard George b 14 April 1971); *Career* conslt physician in gen and geriatric med 1973, assoc lectr Faculty of Clinical Med Univ of Cambridge 1975; hon sec and public info offr Br Geriatrics Soc 1984–90, memb Geriatrics Ctee RCP 1989, chm CAMTAD Cambridge, med advsr Counsel and Care of the Elderly, pre Age Concern Cambs; Hon MA Univ of Cambridge 1975; FRCP 1988; *Books* Ageing: The Facts (1984), Geriatric Medicine (contrib, 1988); *Recreations* reading, skiing; *Style*— Dr Stephen Webster; ✉ 1 Water Street, Cambridge CB4 1NZ (☎ 01223 359037); Department of Geriatric Medicine, Addenbrooke's Hospital, Cambridge CB2 2UF (☎ 01223 245151)

WEBSTER, Trevor; s of Samuel Webster (d 1982), and Winifred, *née* Chapman (d 1977); *b* 1 Nov 1937; *Educ* Leeds GS, Univ of Leeds (LLB); *m* (m dis); *Career* customs offr Rhodesia and Nyasaland 1956–57, reporter 1960–64 (Financial World, Investors Review, Stock Exchange Gazette), reporter Daily Express 1966; The Scotsman city ed 1970–86 (dep city ed 1964–70), dep city ed Daily News 1987, Questor ed Daily Telegraph 1987–88, city ed Daily Express 1989–91 (dep city ed 1988–89), business travel ed Evening Standard 1992–; *Books* Corfu and the Ionian Isles (1986), Athens and Greek Mainland (1987), Rhodes and the Dodecanese (1988), Crete and the Cyclades (1989), Greek Island Delights (1990), Where To Go In Greece (1995); *Recreations* tennis, skiing, travel, wine, theatre, cinema; *Clubs* National Liberal, Hunters, City Golf; *Style*— Trevor Webster, Esq

WEDDERBURN, Prof Dorothy; da of Frederick C Barnard (d 1953), and Ethel C, *née* Lawrence (d 1969); *b* 18 Sept 1925; *Educ* Walthamstow HS For Girls, Girton Coll Cambridge (MA); *m* 1 (m dis), William A Cole; m 2, 1962 (m dis 1969), as his 2 w, Prof Kenneth William Wedderburn (now Baron Wedderburn of Charlton, *qv*); *Career* res offr Dept of Applied Economics Univ of Cambridge 1950–65; Imperial Coll of Sci and Technol: lectr in industl sociology 1965–70, reader 1970–77, prof 1977–81, dir Industl Sociology Unit 1973–81, head Dept of Social and Econ Studies 1978–81; princ: Bedford Coll 1981–85, Royal Holloway and Bedford New Coll 1985–90; sr res fell Imperial Coll of Sci and Technol 1990–, emeritus prof of industl sociology Univ of London 1990–; hon pres Fawcett Soc 1986–, pt/t memb Royal Cmmn on the Distribution of Income and Wealth 1974–78; non-exec dir Kensington, Chelsea and Westminster Dist Health Authy 1992–; memb: Cncl Advsy Conciliation and Arbitration Serv 1976–82, ESRC 1976–82, Bd Anglo-German Fndn 1987–, Cncl Loughborough Univ 1990–93, Medical Manpower Standing Advsy Ctee Dept of Health 1991–96, Ct City Univ 1992–, Cncl Goldsmiths' Coll Univ of London 1994–; govr London Guildhall Univ 1989–; Hon DLitt: Univ of Warwick 1984, Loughborough Univ 1989; Hon DUniv Brunel 1990, Hon LLD Cantab 1991, Hon DSci City Univ 1991; fell Ealing Coll of Higher Educn 1985; hon fell: Imperial Coll Univ of London 1986, Royal Holloway and Bedford New Coll London 1991; *Books* White Collar Redundancy (1964), Redundancy and the Railwaymen (1964), The Aged in the Welfare State (with P Townsend, 1965), Workers' Attitudes and Technology (1972); *Recreations* politics, walking, cooking; *Style*— Prof Dorothy Wedderburn; ✉ Management School, Imperial College, 52/53 Prince's Gate, Exhibition Road, London SW7 2PG (☎ 0171 594 9119)

WEDDERBURN OF CHARLTON, Baron (Life Peer UK 1977), of Highgate, Greater London; Kenneth William Wedderburn; QC (1990); s of Herbert John Wedderburn; *b* 13 April 1927; *Educ* Aske's (Hatcham) GS, Whitgift Sch, Queens' Coll Cambridge (MA, LLB); *m* 1, 1951 (m dis 1962), Nina, da of Dr Myer Salaman; 1 s (Hon David Roland b 1956), 2 da (Hon Sarah Louise b 1954, Hon Lucy Rachel b 1960); m 2, 1962 (m dis 1969), Dorothy Enid, da of Frederick C Barnard and formerly w of William A Cole; m 3, 1969, Frances Ann, da of Basil F Knight; 1 s (Hon Jonathan Michael b 1972); *Career* served RAF 1949–51; sits as Lab peer in House of Lords (Lab employment spokesman 1980–1993); barr Middle Temple 1953, fell at Clare Coll and lectr in Faculty of Law Univ of Cambridge 1952–64, Cassel prof of commercial law LSE 1964–92 (prof emeritus 1992–); visiting prof: UCLA Law Sch 1967, Harvard Law Sch 1969–70; chm: London and Provincial Theatre Cncls 1973–92, Ind Review Ctee 1976–; ed Modern Law Review 1970–88, memb ed Bd Int Labour Law Review 1975–; fell Br Acad 1981–; Hon Dott Giur Univ of Pavia 1987, Hon Dott Econ Univ of Siena 1991, Hon Dott Law Univ of Stockholm; *Publications include* The Worker and the Law (1986), Cases and Materials on Labour Law (1967), Employment Grievances and Disputes Procedures (with P L Davies, 1969), Labour Law and Industrial Relations (with R Lewis and J Clark, 1982), Diritto del Lavoro in Europa (with B Veneziani and S Ghimpu, 1987), Clerk and Lindsell on Torts (jt ed, 1995), Employment Rights in Britain and Europe (1991), Labour Law and Freedom (1995); *Recreations* Charlton Athletic FC; *Style*— Prof the Rt Hon the Lord Wedderburn of Charlton, QC, FBA; ✉ 29 Woodside Ave, Highgate, London N6 4SP (☎ and fax 0181 444 8472); LSE, Aldwych, London WC2A 2AE (☎ 0171 405 7686, fax 955 7366, telex 24655 BLPES G)

WEDDERSPOON, Very Rev Alexander Gillan; s of Rev Robert John Wedderspoon (d 1956), and Amy Beatrice, *née* Woolley (d 1972); *b* 3 April 1931; *Educ* Westminster, Jesus Coll Oxford (MA, BD); *m* 2 Aug 1968, Judith Joyce Wynne, da of Arthur Fitzwalter Wynne Plumptre, CBE (d 1977); 1 s (Alexander Michael Wynne b 1975), 1 da (Caroline Joyce b 1972); *Career* Nat Serv 1949–51, cmmnd RA; curate Kingston Parish Church 1961–63, lectr in religious educn Univ of London 1963–66, educn advsr C of E Schools Cncl 1966–69, priest i/c St Margaret's Westminster 1969–70, canon residentiary Winchester Cathedral 1970–87 (vice dean 1980–87), dean of Guildford 1987–; *Books* Religious Education 1944–84 (1964), The Durham Report on Religious Education (1970), Grow or Die (1981); *Recreations* walking, travel; *Style*— The Very Rev the Dean of Guildford; ✉ Cathedral Office, Stag Hill, Guildford GU2 5UP (☎ 01483 65287)

WEDDLE, Stephen Norman; s of Norman Harold Weddle, Sutton Coldfield, W Midlands, and Irene, *née* Furniss; *b* 1 Jan 1950; *Educ* Fairfax High Sch Sutton Coldfield, NE London Poly (BSc), Bedford Coll London; *m* July 1977 (m dis 1980), Brigid, da of late Edward Couch; *Career* graduate trainee journalist Birmingham Post and Mail 1972–75, reporter BBC Radio Stoke-on-Trent 1975–76; BBC TV: prodr Cool It 1985–90, ed Daytime Live 1987–90, ed Daytime UK 1990–91, ed Pebble Mill 1991–94 (researcher, dir and prodr 1976), ed Special Projects 1994–; *Awards* winner RTS Best Original TV Achievement award 1987, Variety Clubs International Media award 1993, Royal Television Soc Midland Centre award; *Recreations* supporting Tottenham Hotspur FC, cinema, travel, reading novels, comedy and politics, eccentric dancing; *Style*— Stephen Weddle, Esq; ✉ BBC TV, Pebble Mill, Special Projects, Birmingham B5 7QQ (☎ 0121 414 8888, telex 265781, fax 0121 414 2552)

WEDEL, Claus Viggo; *b* 1 April 1940; *Educ* Denmark; *m* Judi; 1 s (Anders), 3 da (Susse, Anna, and Harriett); *Career* fndr chm and md Anglo-Norden Ltd 1966–, chm JMC Timber Ltd 1980–; *Recreations* shooting, sailing; *Style*— Claus Wedel, Esq; ✉ Anglo-Norden Ltd, Orwell Terminal, Duke Street, Ipswich, Suffolk IP3 0AJ (☎ 01473 233266, fax 01473 230805)

WEDELL, Prof (Eberhard Arthur Otto) George; s of Rev Dr H Wedell (d 1964), of Haslemere and Dusseldorf, and Gertrude, *née* Bonhoeffer (d 1982); *b* 4 April 1927; *Educ* Cranbrook Sch, LSE (BScEcon); *m* 5 April 1948, Rosemarie, da of Rev Dr Paul Winckler; 3 s (Martin b 1950, Crispin b 1954, Philip b 1956), 1 da (Rebecca b 1957); *Career* princ Miny of Educn 1955–60 (asst princ 1950–55), fndr sec gen Bd for Social Responsibility Gen Assembly of the C of E 1958–60 (secondment from Civil Serv), sec ITA 1961–64 (dep sec 1960–61), prof of adult educn and dir extra-mural studies Univ of Manchester 1964–75, head Community Employment Div Cmmn of the Euro Communities 1973–82, visiting prof of employment policy Manchester Business Sch 1975–83, prof of communications policy Univ of Manchester 1983–92 (prof emeritus 1992), dir-gen Euro Inst for the Media 1983–93 (vice chm Govrs 1993–), visiting prof Int Acad of Bdcasting 1993–, emeritus fell Leverhulme Tst 1994–96; chm: Wyndham Place Tst 1983–, Beatrice Hankey Fndn 1984–; candidate (Lib) Greater Manchester West Euro elections 1979, Greater Manchester Central (Alliance) Euro elections 1984; Chevalier de L'Ordre des Arts et des Lettres (France) 1989, Officer of the Order of Merit (FRG) 1991, Cdr of the Order of Merit (Portugal) 1993; hon memb Royal Exchange Theatre Company 1989 (dir 1968–89); Hon MEd Univ of Manchester 1968, Dr (hc) Int Journalistics Inst of Kazakstan 1995; memb Int Inst of Communications 1969, FRTS 1982, FRSA 1972; Lord of the Manor of Clotton Hoofield; *Books* The Use of Television in Education (1963), Broadcasting and Public Policy (1968), Teaching at a Distance (with HD Perraton, 1968), Structures of Broadcasting (ed, 1970), Study by Correspondence (with R Glatter, 1971), Correspondence Education in Europe (1971), Teachers and Educational Development in Cyprus (1971), Education and the Development of Malawi (ed, 1973), Broadcasting in the Third World (with E Katz, 1977, Book of the Year NAEB USA 1978), Mass Communications in Western Europe (with G M Luyken and R Leonard, 1985), Making Broadcasting Useful (ed, 1986), Media in Competition (with G M Luyken, 1986), Radio 2000 (with P C Crookes, 1991), Der Segen des Glaubens (with R Rocholl, 1995), The Media and Democracy in Africa (with A J Tudesq, 1997); *Recreations* gardening, music, theatre; *Clubs* Athenaeum, St James (Manchester), Fondation Univ (Brussels); *Style*— Prof George Wedell; ✉ 18 Cranmer Rd, Manchester M20 6AW (☎ 0161 445 5106, fax 0161 448 2884); 94 Eton Place, London NW3 2DT (☎ 0171 722 0299); Vigneau, Lachapelle 47350 Seyches, France (☎ 00 33 53 83 88 71)

WEDGE, Prof Peter Joseph; s of John Wedge (d 1983), and Nellie, *née* Clemson (d 1978); *b* 13 June 1935; *Educ* Queen Mary's Sch Walsall, Univ of Oxford (MA), LSE (certificates in social and public admin and applied social studies); *m* 26 Aug 1961, Dorothy Charlton, da of John Charlton Grieves; 2 s (John, David), 2 da (Sarah, Catherine); *Career* Nat Serv RAF 1953–55; probation offr Hertfordshire 1961–64, res offr Preston 1964–65, tutor caseworker Univ of Manchester and Family Welfare Assoc 1965–68; Nat Children's Bureau 1968–81: sr res offr, princ res offr, asst dir, dep dir (res); UEA: sr lectr then prof of social work 1981–, dean Sch of Econ and Social Studies 1990–93, dean Sch of Health and Social Work 1993–96, professorial fell 1996–; vice chm Norwich Community Partnership NHS Tst 1993–95; dir Ormiston Tst, memb Child Tst; memb: SPA 1966, ACPP 1969; *Books* Preston Family Welfare Survey (1966), Growing Up Adopted (1972), Born to Fail? (1973), Continuities in Childhood Disadvantage (1982), Children in Adversity (1982), Finding Families for Hard-to-Place Children (1986), Sibling Groups and Social Work (1991); *Recreations* singing, walking; *Style*— Prof Peter Wedge; ✉ Schools of Health & Social Work, University of East Anglia, Norwich, Norfolk NR4 7TJ (☎ 01603 593632, fax 01603 593552)

WEDGWOOD, Antony John; s of Dr John Wedgwood, CBE, *qv*, and Margaret Webb Mason (d 1995); *b* 31 Jan 1944; *Educ* Marlborough, Trinity Coll Cambridge (MA); *m* 18 July 1970, Angela Margaret Mary, da of Dr E D Page; 1 s (Tom b 20 April 1978), 2 da (Elizabeth b 15 July 1975, Caroline b 7 July 1991); *Career* Peat Marwick Mitchell & Co (now KPMG): articled 1966 (qualified 1969), ptnr 1981–, banking and fin tech ptnr for UK 1986–; memb various professional ctees and working parties Auditing Practices Bd, ICAEW and Br Bankers' Assoc; FCA (ACA 1969); *Publications* A Guide to the Financial Services Act 1986 (jtly 1986), author of various articles on banking and finance; *Recreations* reading, vintage cars, travel; *Clubs* Athenaeum; *Style*— Antony Wedgwood, Esq; ✉ KPMG, 1–2 Dorset Rise, Blackfriars, London EC4Y 8AE (☎ 0171 311 1000)

WEDGWOOD, Dennis Leveson; s of Stanley Leveson Wedgwood, of Pawlett, Somerset, and Hilda, *née* Millington (d 1977), of Biddulph, Staffs; *b* 14 Sept 1936; *Educ* Bury GS, Univ of London (BDS, MB BS); *m* 18 June 1966, Jean, da of Arthur Oliver (d 1989), of Minsterley, Shrops; 2 da (Elizabeth b 20 May 1968, Rosalind b 5 April 1970); *Career* Col, serv Falkland Islands and S Georgia 1960–62, dental practice 1962–64, house surgn and registrar Westminster Hosp 1964–66, sr registrar Univ Coll and Mt Vernon Hosps 1972–75, prof and chm Oral and Maxillo-Facial Surgery Univ of Manitoba Winnipeg Canada 1975–80, conslt Oral and Maxillo-Facial Surgn Shrops HA 1980–; dental post grad tutor Shrops Health Dist; memb: BMA, BAOMFS, HCSA; FDSRCS, FRCSEd, FRCD(C); *Books* approx 20 scientific pubns on oral and maxillo-facial surgery; *Recreations* walking, sailing, restoration of steam vehicles; *Style*— Dennis Wedgwood;

✉ Royal Shrewsbury Hospital, Mytton Oak Rd, Copthorne, Shrewsbury SY3 8XF (☎ 01743 261151)

WEDGWOOD, Dr John; CBE (1987); s of Hon Josiah Wedgwood (d 1968, yr s of 1 Baron Wedgwood and sometime chm of Josiah Wedgwood and Sons and dir of Bank of England 1942–46), of Damson Hill, Stone, Staffs, and Dorothy Mary Wedgwood, OBE, *née* Winser; hp to 1 cous once removed, 4 Baron Wedgwood; *b* 28 Sept 1919; *Educ* Abbotsholme, Trinity Coll Cambridge (MA, MD); *m* 1, 17 July 1943 (m dis 1971), Margaret, da of Alfred Sidell Mason, of Bury St Edmunds; 3 s (Antony John, *qv*, b 31 Jan 1944, Simon James Josiah b 3 Oct 1949, Nicholas Ralph b 30 June 1951), 2 da (Judith Margaret (Mrs Dominic Brennan) b 24 Aug 1946, Katherine Sarah (Mrs Ian Stanbury) b 24 Nov 1955); m 2, 1972, Jo Alice, da of Harold Swann Ripsher (d 1958); *Career* Surgn-Lt RNVR, Europe and Far East 1943–46; conslt Middx Hosp 1968–80, med dir Royal Hosp Putney 1980–86, conslt emeritus Middx Hosp 1980–; chm Royal Surgical Aid Soc 1987–; dir Wedgwood plc 1967–87, tstee Wedgwood Museum 1967–93; Liveryman Worshipful Soc of Apothecaries; FRCP; *Recreations* ceramics, history, sailing; *Clubs* Athenaeum, Liveryman Soc of Apothecaries; *Style—* Dr John Wedgwood, CBE; ✉ 156 Ashley Gardens, Thirleby Rd, London SW1P 1HW (☎ 0171 828 8319)

WEDGWOOD, Pamela, Lady; *see:* Tudor-Craig, Dr Pamela

WEDGWOOD, 4 Baron (UK 1942); Piers Anthony Weymouth Wedgwood; s of 3 Baron Wedgwood (d 1970, 5 in descent from Josiah Wedgwood, first MP for the newly enfranchised Stoke-on-Trent 1832–34 and s of Josiah Wedgwood, FRS, who founded the pottery), by his 2 w, Jane Weymouth, *née* Poulton; *b* 20 Sept 1954; *Educ* Marlborough, RMA Sandhurst; *m* 30 May 1985, Mary Regina Margaret Kavanagh, da of late Edward Quinn, of Philadelphia, USA; 1 da (Hon Alexandra Mary Kavanagh b 3 Oct 1987); *Heir* first cous once removed, Dr John Wedgwood, CBE, *qv*; *Career* late Capt Royal Scots (The Royal Regt); *Style—* The Rt Hon the Lord Wedgwood; ✉ House of Lords, London SW1

WEDGWOOD, Dame (Cicely) Veronica; OM (1969), DBE (1968, CBE 1956); da of Sir Ralph Wedgwood, 1 Bt, sis of late Sir John Wedgwood, 2 Bt, aunt of Sir Martin Wedgwood, 3 Bt, and 1 cous twice removed of 4 Baron Wedgwood; *b* 20 July 1910; *Educ* Norland Place Sch, Lady Margaret Hall Oxford; *Career* historian, particularly of sixteenth and seventeenth centuries; memb Royal Cmmn on Historical MSS 1953–78; pres: English Assoc 1955–56, English Centre of Int PEN Club 1951–57, Soc of Authors 1972–77; memb: Arts Cncl 1958–61, Arts Cncl Literature Panel 1965–67, Inst for Advanced Study Princeton USA 1953–68, Advsy Cncl V & A Museum 1960–69; tstee Nat Gallery 1962–68 and 1969–76; hon memb: American Acad of Arts and Letters 1966, American Acad of Arts and Scis 1973, American Philosophical Soc 1973; special lectr UCL 1962–90; hon fell: Lady Margaret Hall Oxford 1962, UCL 1965, LSE 1975; hon bencher Middle Temple 1978; Hon LLD Glasgow, Hon LittD Sheffield; Hon DLitt: Smith Coll, Harvard, Oxford, Keele, Sussex, Liverpool; Offr Order of Orange-Nassau 1946, Goethe Medal 1958; FRHistS 1952, FBA 1975; *Books* Strafford (1935, revised edn Thomas Wentworth, 1961), The Thirty Years' War (1938), Oliver Cromwell (1939, revised edn 1973), Charles V by Carl Brandi (trans, 1939), William the Silent (1944, James Tait Black Prize), Auto da Fé by Elias Canetti (trans, 1946), Velvet Studies (1946), Richelieu and the French Monarchy (1949), Seventeenth Century English Literature (1950), Montrose (1952), The King's Peace (1955), The King's War (1958), Truth and Opinion (1960), Poetry and Politics (1960), The Trial of Charles 1 (1964), Milton and His World (1969), The Political Career of Rubens (1975), The Spoils of Time vol 1 (1984), History and Hope: collected essays (1987); *Style—* Dame Veronica Wedgwood, OM, DBE, FBA; ✉ 17 Ashley Court, Morpeth Terrace, London SW1P 1EN

WEDLAKE, William John; s of William John Wedlake, of South Zeal, Devon, and Patricia Mary, *née* Hunt; *b* 24 April 1956; *Educ* Okehampton GS, Exeter Coll of Educn, Univ of Warwick (BSc); *m* 4 July 1987, Elizabeth Kessick, da of late Brian Kessick Bowes; 2 s (Joshua William b 2 May 1989, James Henry b 29 Aug 1990), 1 da (Sophie Elizabeth b 16 April 1992); *Career* formerly with: Arthur Andersen Bristol, Price Waterhouse USA and London, Continental Bank London; fin dir Schroders 1987–93, fin dir Guardian Insurance (Guardian Royal Exchange) 1993–96, chief fin offr Terra Nova Group 1996–; FCA; *Recreations* horse riding, walking, golf; *Style—* William J Wedlake, Esq; ✉ Terra Nova Group, 41–43 Mincing Lane, London EC3R 7SP (☎ 0171 283 3000, fax 0171 396 5150)

WEDLEY, Dr John Raymond; s of Raymond Wedley (d 1988), of Wallasey, Cheshire, and Marjorie Elizabeth, *née* Howell (d 1993); *b* 24 April 1945; *Educ* Oldershaw GS, Univ of Liverpool (MB ChB); *m* 27 July 1968, Susan, da of Thomas Reginald Wakefield, of Fovant, nr Salisbury, Wilts; *Career* sr lectr Guy's Hosp Med Sch and hon conslt on anaesthetics Guy's Hosp 1976–81, conslt on anaesthetics and pain relief Guy's Hosp 1981–, hon conslt on anaesthetics and pain relief St Luke's Hosp for the Clergy 1990–, hon conslt in pain relief to the Army 1991–; memb Anaesthetics Specialist Sub Ctee SE Thames RHA 1978–79, clinical rep for Guy's Med Academic Staff Ctee BMA 1978–81, Guy's linkman to Assoc of Anaesthetics GB and Ireland 1978–81; pres Ctee SE Thames Soc of Anaesthetists 1996–97 (memb 1982–85, hon sec 1991–94), memb Cncl Section of Anaesthetics RSM 1987–90; FFARCS 1974; *Books* A Handbook of Clinical Techniques in the Management of Chronic Pain (jtly, 1994); chapters in: Emergency Anaesthesia (1986), Surgery for Anaesthetists (1988), Symptom Control (1989), Bone Metastases Diagnosis and Treament (1991); *Recreations* walking, theatre, music, gardening; *Clubs* Royal Society of Medicine; *Style—* Dr John Wedley; ✉ 16 Glamorgan Rd, Hampton Wick, Kingston upon Thames, Surrey KT1 4HP (☎ 0181 241 7405); Suite 304, Emblem House, London Bridge Hospital, 27 Tooley St, London SE1 2NP (☎ 0171 403 3876)

WEEDON, Prof Basil Charles Leicester; CBE (1974); s of Charles William Weedon (d 1954), and Florence May Weedon (d 1963); *b* 18 July 1923; *Educ* Wandsworth Sch, Imperial Coll of Sci and Technol (PhD, DSc); *m* 21 March 1959, Barbara Mary, da of Leonard Sydney Dawe (d 1963); 1 s (Matthew b 1967), 1 da (Sarah b 1962); *Career* hon prof Univ of Nottingham 1988– (vice chllr 1975–88), fell Queen Mary and Westfield Coll London 1984 (prof of organic chemistry 1960–76); scientific ed Pure and Applied Chemistry 1960–75; chm: Food Additives and Contaminants Ctee 1968–83, Cncl Nat Stone Centre 1985–91 (memb 1985–93), Electricity Consumers' Ctee E Midlands Region 1990–95; memb: Sci Bd Sci Res Cncl (chm Enzyme Chemistry and Technol Ctee) 1972–75, Univ Grants Ctee (chm Physical Sciences Sub Ctee) 1974–76, EEC Scientific Ctee for Food 1974–81; FRS 1971; Hon DTech Univ of Brunel 1975, Hon LLD Univ of Nottingham 1988; *Recreations* reading, music, walking; *Style—* Prof Basil Weedon, CBE, FRS; ✉ Sheepwash Grange, Heighington Rd, Canwick, Lincoln LN4 2RJ (☎ 01522 522488)

WEEKES, Rt Rev Ambrose Walter Marcus; CB (1970); s of Lt Cdr William Charles Tinnoth Weekes, DSO (d 1958), and Ethel Sarah Weekes, JP (d 1964); *b* 25 April 1919; *Educ* Rochester Cathedral Choir Sch, Sir Joseph Williamson's Rochester, King's Coll London, AKC 1941, FKC 1970, Scholae Cancellarii Lincoln; *Career* ordained: deacon 1942, priest 1943; Chaplain RN 1944–72, The Chaplain of the Fleet 1969–72; QHC 1969, dean of Gibraltar 1973–78; asst bishop of Gibraltar 1978; suffragan bishop of Gibraltar in Europe 1980–86; dean Pro-Cathedral of the Holy Trinity Brussels 1980–86; hon asst bishop of Rochester 1986–88, chaplain of St John's Montreux Switzerland 1988–92, asst bishop Diocese in Europe 1988–; *Recreations* music, yachting; *Clubs* MCC, Army and Navy; *Style—* The Rt Rev Ambrose Weekes, CB

WEEKS, Clive Anthony; s of Donald Alfred Frederick Weeks, of Ewell, and Beryl Mary, *née* Moreton; *b* 5 Sept 1947; *Educ* Wimbledon Coll; *m* 1970, Teresa Mary, da of Rupert Alan Forrester; 1 s (Nicholas Edward Clive b 1986), 2 da (Clare Elizabeth b 1971, Katherine Frances b 1973); *Career* articled clerk then C A F Rowland & Co 1964–70, fin accountant W S Atkins & Partners 1970–71; ptnr: Rowland & Co 1975–76 (staff and training mangr 1971–75), Rowland Nevill & Co 1976–85, Moores Rowland 1985– (London managing ptnr 1992–95, managing ptnr 1995–); ACA 1969; *Recreations* family, music, books, cricket; *Style—* Clive Weeks, Esq; ✉ Moores Rowland, Clifford's Inn, Fetter Lane, London EC4A 1AS (☎ 0171 831 2345, fax 0171 831 6123)

WEEKS, John; CBE (1986); s of Victor John Weeks (d 1983), and Beatrice Anne, *née* Beasley (d 1975); *b* 5 March 1921; *Educ* Dulwich, Architectural Assoc Sch (Dip); *m* 7 Sept 1955, Barbara Lilian, da of Thomas Harry Nunn (d 1937); 1 s (Timothy b 1959), 1 da (Julia b 1957); *Career* dep dir Nuffield Fndn Div of Architectural Studies 1956–60, architect in partnership with Richard Llewelyn-Davies (cr Baron 1963, d 1981) 1960–81, chm Llewelyn-Davies Weeks 1981–86 (conslt 1986–91); sr lectr Univ Coll London 1961–72; works include: Student Housing Imperial Coll of Tropical Agric Trinidad (1960), Rushbrooke Village Suffolk (West Suffolk Award 1957, listed 1996), Northwick Park Hospital Harrow (1961), Univ Children's Hosps Leuven Belgium (1970), Flinders Medical Centre Adelaide S Aust (1972), redevelopment of St Mary's Hosp Paddington London (1978–88); exhibitions: This is Tomorrow (London 1956), Cybernetic Serendipity (London 1968); cncl memb Architectural Assoc London 1975–83 (vice pres 1976–78), chm Br Health-Care Export Cncl 1982–84; chm St Mary's Hosp Arts Ctee 1985–95; hon memb China Soc of Architects Beijing 1985; FRIBA 1964, FRSA 1980; *Books* Investigation into the Functions and Design of Hospitals (jtly, 1955); many articles and lectures internationally on hosp architecture incl: Indeterminate Architecture (1964), Multi-Strategy Buildings (1969), Design for Research-Principles of Laboratory Architecture (1986); *Clubs* Architectural Assoc; *Style—* John Weeks, Esq, CBE; ✉ 39 Jackson's Lane, London N6 5SR

WEEKS, Wilfred John Thomas (Wilf); s of William Weeks, of Launceston, Cornwall, and Kathleen, *née* Penhale; *b* 8 Feb 1948; *Educ* Shebbear Coll, KCL (BD); *m* 10 June 1981, Anne Veronica, da of late Arnold Harrison; 3 s (Orlando b 8 Aug 1983, Matthew b 20 May 1985, Caspar b 10 Jan 1988); *Career* youth and community offr/educn offr and sec Fedn of Cons Students 1974–76, head of the private office of Rt Hon Sir Edward Heath, MP 1976–80, fndr chm GJW Government Relations 1980–; chm Friends of the Tate Gallery 1990–, tstee Dulwich Picture Gallery and chm Dulwich Picture Gallery Tst 1994–; *Recreations* gardening, collecting; *Style—* Wilf Weeks, Esq; ✉ GJW Government Relations, 2 Little Smith Street, SW1

WEEPLE, Edward John (Ed); s of Edward Weeple, of Glasgow, and Mary Catherine, *née* McGrath; *b* 15 May 1945; *Educ* St Aloysius' Coll Glasgow, Univ of Glasgow (MA); *m* 27 June 1970, Joan Anne, *née* Shaw; 3 s (Stephen b 9 Feb 1972, Michael b 8 Aug 1974, Timothy b 14 June 1982), 1 da (Paula b 11 Oct 1975); *Career* teacher Uganda 1967–68, Miny of Health DHSS 1968–78 (private sec to Min of Health 1972–74); Scottish Office: Economic Planning Dept 1978–80, Home and Health Dept 1980–85, Agric and Fisheries Dept 1985–90, Industry Dept (grade 3) 1990–95, Educn and Indust Dept (under sec) 1995–; *Style—* Ed Weeple, Esq; ✉ 19 Lauder Road, Edinburgh EH9 2JG (☎ 0131 668 1150); The Scottish Office, Education and Industry Department, Victoria Quay, Leith, Edinburgh (☎ 0131 244 0623, fax 0131 244 7122)

WEETMAN, Prof Anthony Peter; s of Kenneth Weetman (d 1991), and Evelyn, *née* Healer; *b* 29 April 1953; *Educ* Univ of Newcastle Med Sch (MB BS, MD, DSc); *m* 20 Feb 1982, Sheila Lois, da of John Seymour Thompson, OBE, (d 1985); 1 s (James b 1986), 1 da (Chloe b 1989); *Career* MRC trg fell 1981–83, MRC travelling fell 1984–85, Wellcome sr res fell 1985–89, lectr in med Univ of Cambridge and hon conslt physician Addenbrooke's Hosp 1989–91, prof of med Univ of Sheffield 1991–; MRCP 1979, FRCP 1990, Goulstonian lectr RCP 1991; *Recreations* fell walking; *Style—* Prof Anthony Weetman; ✉ Department of Medicine, University of Sheffield Clinical Sciences Centre, Northern General Hosp, Sheffield S7 5AU (☎ 0114 243 4343, fax 0114 256 0458)

WEIDENFELD, Baron (Life Peer UK 1976), of Chelsea in Greater London; (Arthur) George Weidenfeld; kt (1969); s of Max and Rosa Weidenfeld; *b* 13 Sept 1919; *Educ* Piaristen Gymnasium Vienna, Vienna Univ, Konsular Akademie; *m* 1, 1952, Jane, da of J Edward Sieff; 1 da (Hon Laura Miriam Elizabeth (Hon Mrs Barnett) b 1953); m 2, 1956 (m dis 1961), Barbara (d 1996), da of Maj George Skelton and former wife of Cyril Connolly; m 3, 1966 (m dis 1973), Sandra, da of Charles Shipman Payson; m 4, 14 July 1992, Annabelle, da of late Cdr Nicholas Whitestone; *Career* served WWII BBC Monitoring Serv 1939–42, news commentator with BBC 1942–45; fndr Contact Magazine and Books 1945, columnist News Chronicle 1945–46, fndr chm Weidenfeld & Nicolson Ltd 1948–; spent 1 year as political advsr and chief of cabinet to Chaim Weizmann (Pres of Israel 1948–52); dir Great Universal Stores Europe AG 1990–, chm Bd of Govrs Ben Gurion Univ of Negev Beer-Sheva; govr: Univ of Tel Aviv, Weizmann Inst of Sci, Bezalel Acad of Arts Jerusalem, Jerusalem Fndn; chm Mitchell Prize for History of Art; memb Bd: South Bank 1986–, English Nat Opera 1988–; tstee Nat Portrait Gallery 1988–95; hon fell: St Peter's Coll Oxford, St Anne's Coll Oxford 1994; vice chm: Oxford Univ Campaign 1992–95, Oxford Univ Devpt Campaign 1995–; Hon Senator of Bonn Univ 1996; conslt: Bertelsmann Fndn (Germany) 1995–, Burda Medien (Munich) 1995–; memb bd of govrs Landau Forte Coll Derby 1994–; Chevalier de l'Ordre National de la Legion d'Honneur 1990; Knight Cdrs Cross (Badge and Star) of the Order of Merit of the Fed Republic of Germany, holder Golden Knight's Cross with Star of the Austrian Order of Merit; *Recreations* opera, travel; *Clubs* Garrick, Athenaeum; *Style—* The Rt Hon Lord Weidenfeld; ✉ 9 Chelsea Embankment, London SW3 (☎ 0171 351 0042)

WEIGH, Brian; CBE (1982), QPM (1976); s of Edwin Walter Weigh (d 1958), and Ellen, *née* Wignall (d 1969); *b* 22 Sept 1926; *Educ* St Joseph's Coll Blackpool, Queen's Univ Belfast; *m* 1952, Audrey, da of Arthur Leonard Barker (d 1968); 1 da (Amanda); *Career* Metropolitan Police 1948–67, dep chief constable Somerset and Bath Constabulary 1969–74 (asst chief constable 1967–69), dep chief constable Avon and Somerset Constabulary 1974–75; chief constable: Gloucestershire Constabulary 1975–79, Avon and Somerset 1979–83; HM inspr of constabulary for SW England and pt of E Anglia 1983–88; memb Royal Life Saving Soc (vice pres UK Branch and Cwlth); *Recreations* golf, fell walking, gardening; *Style—* Brian Weigh, Esq, CBE, QPM; ✉ c/o Home Office, HM Chief Inspector of Constabulary, Queen Anne's Gate London SW1H 9AT

WEIGHILL, Francis James; s of Francis Weighill (d 1943), and Ellen, *née* Parkinson (d 1989); *b* 12 Feb 1939; *Educ* Wrekin Coll, Univ of Liverpool (MB ChB, MChOrth); *m* 12 July 1969, Christine Ann Elizabeth, da of Leslie Daniel Houghton (d 1987); 3 s (Michael Francis b 13 May 1970, Peter James b 3 April 1972, Robert Edward Leslie b 8 Nov 1976); *Career* house offr Liverpool Royal Infirmary 1964–65, surgical registrar Leith Edinburgh 1967–68, sr orthopaedic registrar Liverpool 1973, clinical res fell Hosp for Sick Children Toronto 1974–75; Univ Hosp of Manchester: conslt orthopaedic surgn 1977, hon clinical lectr, clinical examiner in surgery; tutor RCS 1982–88; fell Br Orthopaedic Assoc, FRCSE 1969, FRCS 1969; *Recreations* sailing, painting; *Style—* Francis Weighill, Esq; ✉ Lane End, 90 Cherry Lane, Lymm, Cheshire WA13 0PD (☎ 01925 752726); 15 St John Street, Manchester M3 4DG (☎ 0161 834 7373)

WEIL, Prof Daniel; s of late Dr Alfredo Leopoldo Weil, and Mina, *née* Rosenbaum; *b* 7 Sept 1953; *Educ* Universidad Nacional de Buenos Aires (Arquitecto FAU UMBA), RCA

(MA); *Career* industrial designer and lectr; unit master Dip Sch Architectural Assoc 1983–86, external examiner MA design Glasgow Sch of Art 1987–90; visiting lectr: RCA, Middx Poly, Kingston Poly, Sch of Architecture Univ of Milan, Bezadel Sch of Art Jerusalem; md Parenthesis Ltd 1982–90, fndr and ptnr Weil and Taylor (design consultancy for maj clients) 1985–91, ptnr Pentagram design conslts 1992–, prof of industl design RCA; exhibitions incl: Memphis Milan 1982, 100 Designers Trienala of Milan 1983, Design Since 1945 (Philadelphia Museum of Art) 1983, Heavy Box (Architectural Assoc) 1985, Contemporary Landscape (Museum of Modern Art Kyoto) 1985, British Design (Kunstmuseum Vienna) 1986, Inspiration (Tokyo, Paris, Milan) 1988, Metropolis (ICA London) 1988, The Plastic Age (Victoria & Albert Museum) 1990; work in public collections incl The Bag Radio (Museum of Modern Art NY); memb Design Sub-Ctee D&AD, juror BBC Design Awards 1990; FCSD 1989; *Style*— Prof Daniel Weil; ✉ Pentagram Design Ltd, 11 Needham Road, London W11 2RP (☎ 0171 229 3477)

WEIL, Peter Leo John; s of Robert Weil of Berlin, Germany, and Renate Scheyer; *b* 7 Sept 1951; *Educ* Methodist Coll Belfast, Queens' Coll Cambridge (BA); *Career* researcher Granada TV 1973–77 (Granada Reports, World in Action); BBC: prodr BBC TV Current Affairs 1977–84 (Nationwide, Newsnight, Panorama), head of Youth Progs BBC NI 1984–86 (actg dep head of progs 1986), ed Open Air BBC NW 1986–88, exec prodr Wogan 1988–89, head of topical features 1989–90, head of network TV BBC North 1990–92; head of progs Barraclough Carey North Productions 1992–; exec prodr: People's Parliament, The Other Side of Midnight, First Edition; *Recreations* cinema, walking, good food; *Style*— Peter Weil, Esq; ✉ 19 Waterlane House, 5 Waterlane, Richmond, Surrey TW9 1TJ (☎ 0181 940 0651)

WEINBERG, Prof Felix Jiri; s of Victor Weinberg (d 1988), and late Nelly, *née* Altschul; *Educ* Univ of London (BSc, DIC, PhD, DSc); *m* 24 July 1954, Jill Nesta, da of Jack Alfred Piggott (d 1970); 3 s (John Felix b 27 April 1958, Peter David (twin) b 27 April 1958, Michael Jonathan b 8 Jan 1969); *Career* Dept of Chemical Engrg and Chemical Technol Imperial Coll London: res asst 1951–54, asst lectr 1954–56, lectr 1956–60, sr lectr in combustion 1960–64, reader in combustion 1964–67, prof of combustion physics 1967–93, emeritus prof of combustion physics and sr research fell 1993–; visiting prof at various univs and insts across the world; fndr and first chm Combustion Physics Gp Inst of Physics 1974–, chm Br Section Combustion Inst 1975–80, cncl memb Inst of Energy (formerly Inst of Fuel) 1976–79; conslt to numerous bodies incl: Geo Centers, OSCA, BP, US Army, Univ of California; prolific contrib to scientific literature and memb editorial bds of various specialist jls; Silver Combustion medal The Combustion Inst Pittsburgh 1972, Bernard Lewis Gold medal Univ of Waterloo Canada 1980, Rumford medal Royal Soc 1988, Italgas prize for research and innovation in energy science Turin Acad 1991; Hon DSc Technion Israel 1990; fell Inst of Energy 1960, CEng 1960, FInstP 1960, FRS 1983; *Style*— Prof Felix Weinberg, FRS; ✉ Department of Chemical Engineering and Chemical Technology, Imperial College, Prince Consort Rd, London SW7 2BY (☎ 0171 594 5580, fax 0171 594 5604)

WEINBERG, Sir Mark Aubrey; kt (1987); s of Philip Weinberg (d 1933); *b* 9 Aug 1931; *Educ* King Edward's Johannesburg, Witwatersrand Univ, LSE; *m* 1980, Anouska (Anouska Hempel, the fashion designer), da of Albert Geissler (d 1980); *Career* md Abbey Life Assurance 1961-70, chm Allied Dunbar Assurance 1971–90, dir BAT Industs 1985–89, dep chm Securities and Investmts Bd 1986–90; chm: St James's Place Capital 1991–, J Rothschild Assurance plc 1991–, Life Assurance Holding Corp 1995–; tstee Tate Gallery 1985–92, jt chm The Per Cent Club 1985–, chm Stock Exchange Ctee on Private Share Ownership 1995–; *Books* Take-overs and Mergers (5 edn, 1989); *Recreations* skiing, bridge; *Clubs* Portland; *Style*— Sir Mark Weinberg; ✉ St James's Place Capital, Spencer House, 27 St James's Place, London SW1A 1NR (☎ 0171 493 8111)

WEINSTOCK, Baron (Life Peer UK 1980), of Bowden, Co Wilts; Arnold Weinstock; kt (1970); s of Simon and Golda Weinstock; *b* 29 July 1924; *Educ* Albion Road Central Sch N London, LSE (BScEcon); *m* 1949, Netta, da of Sir Michael Sobell (d 1993); 1 s (Hon Simon Andrew Weinstock b 1952, d 1996), 1 da (Dr The Hon Susan Gina Lacroix b 1955); *Career* jr admin offr Admiralty 1944–47; Radio & Allied (Holdings) Ltd: joined 1954, md 1955, merged with GEC plc 1961, dir GEC 1961, md GEC 1963–96, ret; dir Rolls-Royce Ltd 1971–73; sits as independent in House of Lords 1980–; hon master of the bench Gray's Inn 1982–; tstee: Br Museum 1985–96, Royal Philharmonic Soc Fndn Fund; Hon FRCR; Hon DSc: Univ of Salford 1975, Aston Univ 1976, Univ of Bath 1978, Univ of Reading 1978, Univ of Ulster 1987; Hon LLD: Univ of Leeds 1978, Univ of Wales 1985; Hon DTech Loughborough Univ 1981; Hon DUniv Anglia Polytechnic Univ 1994; hon fell: LSE, Peterhouse Cambridge; Officier Legion d'Honneur France 1991, Commendatore Order of Merit Italy 1991; FRSS; *Recreations* racing, breeding horses, classical music; *Clubs* Jockey, Pratt's; *Style*— The Rt Hon Lord Weinstock; ✉ c/o General Electric Company plc, 1 Stanhope Gate, London W1A 1EH (☎ 0171 493 8484, fax 0171 493 1974)

WEIR, Rear Adm Alexander Fortune Rose; CB (1981), JP (Bodmin 1985), DL (Cornwall 1993); s of Cdr Patrick Wylie Rose Weir, RN (d 1971), and Minna Ranken Forrester, *née* Fortune (d 1983); *b* 17 June 1928; *Educ* RNC Dartmouth, RNC Greenwich; *m* 5 Sept 1953, Ann Ross Hamilton, da of Col John Atchison Crawford, RAMC (d 1982), and Norah Katherine, *née* Smyth (d 1968); 4 da (Phillipa b 1954, Joanna b 1956, Margaret b 1958, Nicola b 1959); *Career* Cadet 1945–46, Midshipman HMS Glasgow 1946–47, Actg Sub Lt HMS Zephyr, Portland 1947, Sub Lt professional courses 1947–48, Sub Lt and Lt, HMS Loch Arkaig 1949–51, ADC to Govr of Victoria Aust 1951–53; HMS Mariner 1953–54, Navigating Offr 1954, HMS St Austell Bay WI, Navigating Offr 1955–56, HMS Wave, Fishery Protection Sqdn Home Arctic and Iceland 1956–58, Lt Cdr Advanced Navigation Course 1958; Staff ND Offr, Flag Offr Sea Trg at Portland Dorset 1958–61, HMS Plymouth, Staff Offr Ops, 4 Frigate Sqdn, Far East Station 1961–62, Cdr 1962, Trg Cdr, BRNC Dartmouth 1962–64, CO HMS Rothesay WI Station 1965–66, Staff of C-in-C Portsmouth, Staff Offr Ops 1966–68, 2 in Cmd and Exec Offr HMS Eagle 1968–69, Capt 1969; jssc 1969–70; pres Far East Cmd Midshipman's Bd 1970, Asst Dir Naval Operational Requirments MOD(N) 1970–72, Capt (F) 6 Frigate Sqdn (8 ships) and HMS Andromeda Far East, Mediterranean & Home Waters 1972–74, NATO Def Coll Rome 1974–75, ACOS Strategic Policy Requirements and Long Range Objectives SACLANT 1975–77, Capt HMS Bristol 1977–78; Rear Adm 1978; Dep Asst Chief of Staff (Ops) to SACEUR 1978–81; ret RN 1981; joined Capt Colin McMullen and Associates (Marine Consultants) 1981 and took over 1983– (co renamed McMullen Associates in 1990); memb: Nautical Inst, Royal Inst of Navigation; pres: Delabole Branch RNA 1984–, Padstow Unit Sea Cadets 1985–; memb Ctee League of Friends St Lawrence's Hosp Bodmin 1985–; licensed RN lay reader 1981, licensed lay reader Parish of Westbourne Diocese of Chichester 1981, licensed reader St Kew Parish Diocese of Truro 1984–, warden of readers Diocese of Truro 1995, lay canon Truro Cathedral 1996; JP: Chichester 1982–84, Bodmin 1985; assoc Victoria Coll of Music, FIMgt; *Recreations* sailing, shooting, golf; *Clubs* Naval, IOD, RYS, RYA, RNSA; *Style*— Rear Adm Alexander Weir, CB, JP, DL; ✉ McMullen Associates (Marine Consultants), Tipton Farm, St Kew, Bodmin, Cornwall PL30 3ET (☎ 01208 841289, fax 01208 841675); Yeoman House, Croydon Rd, Penge SE20 7TP (☎ 0181 663 6565, fax 0181 659 5568, telex 946171)

WEIR, David; s of James Weir (d 1981), and Margaret, *née* Barclay; *b* 18 Nov 1944; *Educ* Cumnock Acad, Univ of Glasgow; *m* 4 March 1969, Patricia Irene; 2 da (Katharine Anne, Jennifer Bronwen); *Career* articled clerk William Duncan & Co Ayr, qualified CA 1968, ptnr Ernst & Young (formerly Arthur Young) 1978– (joined 1968); dir: Merseyside Enterprise Bd 1985–89, Business Opportunities on Merseyside 1989–93; memb: NW Industrial Devpt Bd 1988–, Merseyside Objection One Tech Panel for Industl Devpt 1996–; ATII 1968; *Recreations* golf; *Style*— David Weir, Esq; ✉ Ernst & Young Chartered Accountants, Silkhouse Court, Tithebarn Street, Liverpool L2 2LE (☎ 0151 236 8214)

WEIR, The Hon Lord; David Bruce; s of James Douglas Weir (d 1981), of Argyll, and Kathleen Maxwell, *née* Auld (d 1975); *b* 19 Dec 1931; *Educ* The Leys Sch Cambridge, Univ of Glasgow (MA, LLB); *m* 1964, Katharine Lindsay, da of The Hon Lord Cameron (decd); 3 s (Donald b 1965, Robert b 1967, John b 1971); *Career* admitted to Faculty of Advocates 1959, QC (Scot) 1971, advocate depute 1979–82, senator of the Coll of Justice in Scotland 1985–; chm: Med Appeal Tbnl 1972–77, Pension Appeals Tbnl for Scotland 1978–84 (pres 1984–85), NHS Tbnl Scotland 1983–85; memb: Criminal Injuries Compensation Bd 1974–79 and 1984–85, The Parole Bd for Scotland 1988–91; govr Fettes Coll 1986–95 (chm 1989–95); *Recreations* sailing (Tryad), music; *Clubs* New (Edinburgh), Royal Highland Yacht; *Style*— The Hon Lord Weir; ✉ Parliament House, High St, Edinburgh EH1 1RQ (☎ 0131 225 2595)

WEIR, David Ian; s of Dr Harold Ross Weir, of Scotland, and Masterton, NZ, and Helen Bain Dougal Weir (d 1995); *b* 2 July 1935; *Educ* Dundee High GS Scotland, Strathallan Sch, Wairarapa Coll Masterton NZ, Univ of NZ (BDS), MGDS RCS (Eng); *m* 29 Dec 1959, Joan Anne, da of late Capt William Patrick Sinclair, of Sliva, Fiji; 2 s (Ian Kenneth Sinclair b 7 July 1960, John Fraser b 16 Sept 1961), 2 da (Temo Fiona (Mrs Donovan) b 27 Aug 1962, Linley Ann b 30 Nov 1964); *Career* gen dental practice Masterton NZ 1959–60, assoc Hammersmith dental practice 1960–61, princ practitioner Associate Dentists in Practice 1961–84, private practice Harley St 1975–; pt/t dental surgn: Marks & Spencers stores Hammersmith & Chiswick 1979–93, Bush Boake & Allen Ltd 1986–92; course tutor MGDS Group 1988–92, dir and hon conslt Maurice Wohl Centre King's Coll Sch of Med and Dentistry 1993– (pt/t clin lectr 1989–90); fndr memb: Harley St Occlusion Gp, Br Endosseous Pin Implant Soc; memb: Br Periodontal Soc, Br Dental Assoc, Soc for Advancement of Anaesthesia in Dentistry, Asian Odontological Soc (former memb Ctee), Assoc of Industl Dental Surgns (memb Ctee), Med Protection Soc, Dental Practitioner Assoc; former positions: sec London Branch Br Dental Health Fndn, memb London Chapter Alpha-Omega Soc, treas Acad of Gnathology (superceded by Pankey UK); contrib to numerous learned dental jls; *Recreations* sailing, golf, classical music, Highland bagpipe (tutor Highland bagpipe Sherborne Sch Dorset 1993), Gaelic language, reading, writing; *Style*— David Weir, Esq; ✉ White Gates, 5 Prospect Road, Long Ditton, Surrey KT6 5PY (☎ 0181 339 0249, e-mail 101477.344@compuserve.com); 46 Harley Street, London W1N 1AD (☎ 0171 636 5213, fax 0171 631 5213); Maurice Wohl GDP Centre, King's Coll Sch of Medicine and Dentistry, 45–47 Caldecot Road, London SE5 9RW (☎ 0171 346 3088/9)

WEIR, Prof Donald MacKay; s of Dr Henry James Weir, of Dumbartonshire, and Gwendoline, *née* MacKay (d 1981); *b* 16 Oct 1928; *Educ* Edinburgh Acad, Univ of Edinburgh (MB ChB, MD); *m* 1, 1956, Dr Sylvia Eva Leiman (m dis 1976); 3 s (Michael b 1957, David b 1959, Philip b 1961); m 2, 6 June 1976, Dr (Cecelia) Caroline Blackwell, da of Cecil Blackwell (d 1987), of Texas; *Career* res fell Rheumatism Res Unit MRC Taplow 1957–61, personal chair in microbiology and immunology Univ of Edinburgh 1983– (lectr Bacteriology Dept 1961–67, sr lectr and hon conslt 1967–78, reader 1978–83), prof emeritus and hon fell Univ of Edinburgh 1994–; hon visiting prof Inst Pasteur Athens Greece 1989–92; memb: Br Soc of Immunology, Br Soc of Cell Biology; FRCPE; *Books* Handbook of Experimental Immunology (1967, 1973, 1983 and 1986), Immunology (1970, 1971, 1973, 1977, 1983, 1988 and 1993), Principles of Infection and Immunity in Patient Care (1981), Aids To Immunology (1986); *Recreations* sailing; *Clubs* Royal Forth Yacht; *Style*— Prof Donald Weir; ✉ 36 Drummond Place, Edinburgh EH3 6PW (☎ 0131 556 7646); University of Edinburgh Medical School, Department of Medical Microbiology, Teviot Place, Edinburgh EH8 9AG (☎ 0131 650 3170, fax 0131 650 6531, telex 727442)

WEIR, George Wilson (Doddie); s of John Wilson Weir, and Margaret Anne, *née* Houston; *b* 4 July 1970; *Educ* Daniel Stewart's and Melville Coll, E of Scot Coll of Agric; *Career* rugby union No 8 and lock forward; toured NZ with Scottish Schs 1988; clubs: Melrose RFC 1988–95 (over 180 appearances), Newcastle RFC 1996–; rep: South of Scot (20 appearances), Scottish Students, Scotland under 19, Scot under 21, Scot B; Scotland: toured NZ 1990 and 1996, debut v Argentina 1990, memb World Cup squad 1991 and 1995, Aust 1992, South Seas 1993, 39 caps; former farmer, currently professional rugby player and pt/t sales rep Carlsberg-Tetley Alloa; *Recreations* horse riding (one day eventing), clay pigeon shooting, swimming, golf; *Style*— Doddie Weir, Esq; ✉ Cortleferry Farm, Stow, Galashiels, Scotland (☎ 01578 760760)

WEIR, Dame Gillian Constance; DBE (1996, CBE 1989); da of Cecil Alexander Weir (d 1941), of Martinborough, NZ, and Clarice Mildred Foy, *née* Bignell (d 1965); *b* 17 Jan 1941; *Educ* Wanganui Girls Coll Wanganui NZ, RCM London; *m* 1, 1967 (m dis 1971), Clive Rowland Webster; m 2, 1972, Lawrence Irving Phelps, s of Herbert Spencer Phelps (d 1979), of Somerville, Mass, USA; *Career* int concert organist 1965–; concerto appearances incl: all leading Br orchs, Boston Symphony Orch, Seattle Symphony Orch, Aust ABC Orchs, Euro orchs; regular performer at int festivals incl: Edinburgh, Bath, Flanders, Proms, Europhalia, Aldeburgh; performed in major int concert halls and cathedrals incl: Royal Albert Hall, Royal Festival Hall, Sydney Opera House, Palais des Beaux Arts, Lincoln Center, Kennedy Center; frequent nat and int radio and TV appearances (incl own 6 part series The King of Instruments (BBC), and 60 Minutes documentary on life/career), adjudicator int competitions, artist in residence at major univs, organ conslt (incl Symphony Hall Birmingham), lectures and master classes held internationally; recordings for: Virgin Classics, Argo, Chandos, Koss Classics, Decca, Collins Classics (Complete Works of Olivier Messiaen released 1994); prizes incl: St Albans Int Organ Competition 1964, Countess Munster Award 1965, Int Performer of the Year American Guild of Organists NY USA 1981, Musician of the Year Int Music Guide 1982, Turnovsky Fndn Award 1985; first woman pres: Incorporated Assoc of Organists 1981–83, Royal Coll of Organists 1994–96; pres Incorporated Soc of Musicians 1992–93; co-opted to Cncl Royal Philharmonic Soc 1995; tstee Eric Thompson Tst; Hon DMus Univ of Victoria Wellington NZ 1983; hon memb RAM, Hon FRCO 1975, hon fell Royal Canadian Coll of Organists 1983; *Recreations* theatre; *Style*— Dame Gillian Weir, DBE; ✉ 78 Robin Way, Tilehurst, Berks RG31 4SW (☎ 0118 941 4078)

WEIR, Dr Hugh William Lindsay; s of Maj Terence John Collison Weir (d 1958), and Rosamund Suzanne, *née* Gibson; *b* 29 Aug 1934; *Educ* Ireland and abroad, DLitt; *m* 1973, Hon Grania Rachel O'Brien, da of 16 Baron Inchiquin (d 1968); *Career* teacher, illustrator, journalist, author and publisher; md: Weir Machinery Ltd 1965–75, Ballinakella Press, Bell'Acards; memb Church of Ireland Representative Body 1980–89; Irish Heritage historian 1980–; environment corr The Clare Champion and regular contrib Church of Ireland Gazette; pres: Young Environmentalist Fedn, Clare Young Environmentalists; vice pres Clare Archeological and Historical Soc; Nat Monuments advsr Clare Co Cncl, diocesan lay preacher Limerick and Killaloe; memb: Killaloe Diocesan Synod, General Synod; FRGS; *Books* O'Brien - People and Places (1984), Houses of Clare (1986), Ireland - A Thousand Kings (1988), Trapa - An Adventure in Spanish and English (1990), O'Connor - People and Places (1994); Oidhreacht Award 1990 for journalism and environmental promotion; *Recreations* writing, art, boating and angling, travel; *Style—* Dr Hugh Weir; ✉ Ballinakella Lodge, Whitegate, Co Clare, Ireland (☎ and fax 01619 27030)

WEIR, Hon James William Hartland; s and h of 3 Viscount Weir, *qv*; *b* 6 June 1965; *Career* accountant; *Style—* The Hon James Weir; ✉ 27 Albany St, Edinburgh EH1 3QN

WEIR, Judith; CBE (1995); *b* 1954; *Educ* King's Coll Cambridge, Tanglewood Summer Sch (Koussevitsky fellowship); *Career* composer; studied under John Tavener, Robin Holloway and Gunther Schuller; sometime memb Nat Youth Orch; composer in residence Southern Arts Assoc 1976–79, lectr Music Dept Univ of Glasgow 1979–82, creative arts fell Trinity Coll Cambridge 1983–85, Guinness composer in residence RSAMD 1988–91, Fairbairn composer-in-assoc City of Birmingham Symphony Orch 1995–97; winner Critics' Circle Music Section Award for most outstanding contribution to Br musical life 1994, hon doctorate Univ of Aberdeen 1995; *Operas* A Night at the Chinese Opera (cmmnd BBC for Kent Opera) 1987, Heaven Ablaze in His Breast (opera and dance collaboration with Ian Spink and Second Stride, screened BBC, winner Int Opera Screen Festival Helsinki 1991) 1989, Blond Eckbert (cmmnd ENO) 1994; *Orchestral works* Scipio's Dream (BBC 2) 1991, Music Untangled, Heroic Strokes of the Bow, Combattimento II 1993, music for Sir Peter Hall's The Gift of the Gorgon (RSC), music for Caryl Churchill's The Skriker (RNT) 1994, Musicians Wrestle Everywhere 1995, Moon and Star (premiere BBC Proms) 1995; *Style—* Ms Judith Weir, CBE; ✉ c/o Chester Music Ltd, 8–9 Frith Street, London W1V 5TZ (☎ 0171 434 0066, fax 0171 287 6329)

WEIR, Sir Michael Scott; KCMG (1980, CMG 1974); s of Archibald Weir; *b* 28 Jan 1925; *Educ* Dunfermline HS, Balliol Coll Oxford; *m* 1, 1953, Alison Walker; 2 s, 2 da; m 2, 1976, Hilary Reid; 2 s; *Career* WWII RAF; joined FO 1950; served: Trucial States, San Francisco, Washington, Cairo; cllr and head Arabian Dept FO 1966–68, dep political resident Bahrain 1968–71, head of chancery, UK Mission to UN (NYC) 1971–73, asst under sec FCO 1974–79, ambassador Cairo 1979–85, ret 1985; princ dir 21 Century Tst 1990–; pres Egypt Exploration Soc 1988–, chm British Egyptian Soc 1990–; *Style—* Sir Michael Weir, KCMG; ✉ 37 Lansdowne Gardens, London SW8 2EL

WEIR, (John) Paul; s of John Weir, and Elizabeth, *née* Melville; *b* 16 Sept 1967; *Educ* Greenwood Acad Irvine; *Career* professional boxer (flyweight); amateur career: Gold medal Belfast Diamond Jubilee 1989, Silver medal Norway Box Cup 1989, Bronze medal Euro Championships 1990, Bronze medal Canada Cup 1990 and 1991, 160 contests (won 140); turned professional 1992; professional career: WBO strawweight champion 1993–, defended vs Lindi Memani 1993, undefeated in 5 contests; Scottish int; *Recreations* running, horse riding and fast cars; *Style—* Paul Weir, Esq; ✉ c/o St Andrew's Sporting Club, Forte Crest Hotel, Bothwell Street, Glasgow G2 7EN (☎ 0141 248 5461, fax 0141 221 8986)

WEIR, Richard Stanton; s of Brig Richard Ambrose Weir, OBE (d 1972), and Dr Margaret Lucretia, *née* Cowan (d 1988); *b* 5 Jan 1933; *Educ* Repton, Christ Church Oxford (MA); *m* 17 June 1962, Helen Eugenie, da of Andrew Guthrie (d 1979); 1 da (Nicola Helen (Mrs Wilkinson) b 1964); *Career* cmmnd 3 Carabiniers (Prince of Wales's Dragoon Guards) 1951; called to the Bar Inner Temple 1957; head of Legal Dept Soc of Motor Manufacturers and Traders Ltd 1958–61, exec British Motor Corporation Ltd 1961–64, dep co sec Rank Organisation Ltd 1964–67, head of admin Rank Leisure Services 1967–69, sec CWS Ltd 1969–74; dir The Retail Consortium 1975–81; memb Consumer Protection Advsy Ctee 1973–76, sec gen & chief exec Bldg Socs Assoc 1981–86; dir-gen: The Retail Consortium 1986–89, Br Retailer Assoc 1986–89, Institutional Fund Managers' Assoc 1989–95; *Clubs* United Oxford and Cambridge University; *Style—* Richard Weir, Esq; ✉ PO Box 427, Umhlali 4390, KwaZulu Natal, Rep of South Africa (☎ 00 27 322 5773); 10 Fort Gate Newhaven, East Sussex BN9 9DR (☎ 01273 516851)

WEIR, Sir Roderick Bignell; kt (1984), JP (NZ 1972); s of Cecil Alexander Weir (d 1940), of Palmerston, NZ, and Clarice Mildred Foy (d 1965); *b* 14 July 1927; *Educ* Wanganui Boys Coll; *m* 1, 1952, Loys Agnes Wilson (d 1984); 1 da (Lesley Alex (Mrs Donaldson) b 28 March 1953); m 2, 22 March 1986, Anna Jane, da of Richard T Peacock, of Barton Rd, Heretaunga, Wellington; *Career* chm: McKechnie Pacific Ltd, Amuri Corporation Ltd, Rod Weir and Co Ltd, New Zealand Casing Company Ltd, Crown Meats Ltd, Rangatira Ltd; dir: Sun Alliance Insurance Ltd, Sun Life Assurance Co Ltd, Bain Clarkson; former dir: McKenzies NZ Ltd, Development Finance Corporation Ltd, James Smith Ltd, Allied Farmers Ltd, Crown Corporation Ltd, Dalgety NZ Ltd, Newton King Ltd, de Pelichet McLeod Ltd, Gisborne Sheepfarmers Mercantile Co Ltd, Canterbury Farmers Cooperative Assoc Ltd; conslt NZ Apple & Pear Mktg Bd; memb: Advsy Bd Salvation Army, Cncl Wellington Medical Res Fndn Inc; patron and memb Bd Massey Coll Univ Agric Res Fndn; chm and patron: Massey Coll Business & Property Tst, NZ National Party Business House Ctee, ASEAN/NZ Business Cncl, Electoral Holdings Inc; memb Fin & Property Ctee NZ Nat Party; tstee: NZ Inst of Economic Res (Inc), Medic Alert, Wanganui Boys Coll; memb: Cncl Wellington Sch of Med, Justice of Peace Assoc; tstee Winston Churchill Meml Tst; Hon DSc Massey Univ 1993; *Recreations* shooting, boxing, fishing; *Clubs* Wellington Men's (Wellington), Wellington Golf (Heretaunga), Levin (Levin); *Style—* Sir Roderick Weir, JP; ✉ Jellicoe Towers, 5/189 The Terrace, Wellington, New Zealand (☎ 00 64 4 472433 fax 00 64 4 4732685); The Grove, Main Road North, Waikanae, New Zealand (☎ 00 64 4 2936373, fax 00 64 4 2936373)

WEIR, Dr Ronald John; s of John Bishop Weir (d 1974), and Susan Davies, *née* McCleverty (d 1977); *b* 6 April 1935; *Educ* Jordanhill Coll Sch Glasgow, Univ of Glasgow (MB ChB, MD); *m* 2 June 1961, Janette MacKay, da of Thomas Wilson (d 1971); 3 s (Cameron John b 1966, Clifford Ronald b 1967, Gavin MacKay b 1972), 1 da (Kendra-Lynne Isobel b 1969); *Career* conslt physician and hon sr clinical lectr Gartnavel Gen Hosp and Western Infirmary Glasgow 1974–; chm Glasgow Area Med Audit Ctee; memb: Int Soc of Hypertension, Euro Soc of Hypertension, Br Hypertension Soc, Br Diabetic Assoc, Scot Soc of Physicians, Assoc of Physicians of GB and Ireland, Bd of Examiners Royal Coll of Physicians and Surgns of Glasgow, Med Panel Church of Scotland; FRCPG 1976; *Recreations* hill walking, gardening, reading; *Style—* Dr Ronald Weir; ✉ 10 Moorfoot Way, Bearsden, Glasgow G61 4RL (☎ 0141 943 1367); Gartnavel General Hospital/Western Infirmary, 1053 Great Western Rd, Glasgow G12 0YN (☎ 0141 211 3000)

WEIR, 3 Viscount (UK 1938); William Kenneth James Weir; also Baron Weir (UK 1918); s of 2 Viscount Weir, CBE (d 1975), of Montgreenan, Kilwinning, Ayrshire, and his 1 w, Lucette Isabel, *née* Crowdy (d 1972); *b* 9 Nov 1933; *Educ* Eton, Trinity Coll Cambridge (BA); *m* 1, 1964 (m dis 1972), Diana Lucy, da of late Peter Lewis MacDougall of Ottawa, Canada; 1 s (Hon James William Hartland), 1 da (Hon Lorna Elizabeth b 17 May 1967); m 2, 6 Nov 1976 (m dis), Mrs Jacqueline Mary Marr, da of late Baron Louis de Chollet, of Fribourg, Switzerland; m 3, 24 Nov 1989, Marina, da of late Marc Sevastopoulo; 1 s (Hon Andrew Alexander Marc b 1989); *Heir* s, Hon James William Hartland Weir b 6 June 1965; *Career* Nat Serv with RN 1955–57; chm: Great Northern Investment Trust Ltd 1975–82, Weir Group PLC 1983– (vice chm 1981–83, chm and chief exec 1972–81); co-chm RIT and Northern plc 1982–83, vice chm St James's Place Capital plc; dir: British Steel Corporation 1972–76, BICC plc 1977– (chm 1996–), Br Bank of the Middle East 1977–79 Canadian Pacific Ltd 1989–, L F Rothschild Unterberg Towbin 1983–85; memb: Ct of Bank of England 1972–84, Scottish Econ Cncl 1972–84, Engrg Industries Cncl 1975–80, London Advsy Ctee of Hongkong and Shanghai Banking Corp 1980–92; chm: Engrg Design Res Centre 1988–91, Patrons of Nat Galleries of Scotland 1984–; pres BEAMA 1988–89 and 1993–95; Hon DEng Univ of Glasgow 1993; FIBF 1984, MIES 1985, FRSA 1987, Hon FEng 1993; *Recreations* golf, shooting; *Clubs* White's; *Style—* The Rt Hon the Viscount Weir; ✉ Rodinghead, Mauchline, Ayrshire KA5 5TR (☎ 0156 388 4233); The Weir Group PLC, Cathcart, Glasgow G44 4EX (☎ 0141 637 7111, fax 0141 637 2221, telex 77161 WPLCRT G)

WEISKRANTZ, Prof Lawrence; s of Benjamin Weiskrantz (d 1935), of Russia and the USA, and Rose, *née* Rifkin; *b* 28 March 1926; *Educ* Swarthmore Coll (BA), Oxford Univ (MSc), Harvard (PhD); *m* 11 Feb 1954, Barbara Edna, da of William Collins (d 1979); 1 s (Conrad b 1963), 1 da (Julia b 1966); *Career* cryptographer USAF 1944–46, served Europe, Africa and Middle East; assoc Inst of Living 1952–55, teaching asst Harvard Univ 1952–53, pt/t lectr Tufts Univ 1952, sr post-doctoral fell US Nat Acad of Sci Univ of Oxford 1955–56; Univ of Cambridge: res assoc 1956–61, asst dir of res 1961–66, reader in physiological psychology 1966–67; prof of psychology Univ of Oxford 1967–93; FRS 1980, memb US Nat Acad of Sci 1987; *Recreations* music, walking; *Style—* Prof Lawrence Weiskrantz, FRS; ✉ c/o Magdalen Coll, Oxford; Department of Experimental Psychology, South Parks Rd, Oxford OX1 3UD (☎ 01865 271444, fax 01865 310447)

WEISMAN, Malcolm; s of David Weisman (d 1969), and Jeanie Pearl Weisman (d 1980); *Educ* Parmiter's Sch, Harrogate GS, LSE, St Catherine's Coll Oxford (MA); *m* 1958, Rosalie, da of Dr A A Spiro (d 1963), of St John's Wood; 2 s (Brian b 1959, Daniel b 1963); *Career* Jewish chaplain RAF 1956, hon chaplain Univ of Oxford 1971–, sr chaplain HM Forces 1972–, sec gen Allied Air Forces Chiefs of Chaplains Ctee 1980–92 (hon pres 1993), sec Former Chiefs of Air Forces Chaplains Assoc 1994; called to the Bar Middle Temple 1961, asst cmmr Parly Boundaries 1976, recorder Crown Ct 1980, head of chambers 1982–90; memb Cts of Univs of East Anglia, Sussex, Kent, Lancaster, Essex and Warwick; memb Sr Common Room Univs of Kent and East Anglia; fell Univ of Essex Centre for Study of Theol; ed Menorah magazine; memb: MOD Advsy Ctee on Mil Chaplaincy, Cabinet of Chief Rabbi of Cwlth; Man of the Year Award 1980, Chief Rabbi's award for Excellence 1993; religious advsr to small Jewish communities and Hillel cnsllr to New Univs; hon chaplain to: Lord Mayor of Westminster 1992–93, Mayor of Barnet 1994–95; *Recreations* reading, walking, doing nothing; *Style—* Malcolm Weisman, Esq; ✉ 1 Gray's Inn Square, London WC1R 5AA (☎ 0171 405 8946, fax 0171 405 1617)

WEISS, John Roger; s of Ernst Weiss (d 1983), and Betsy, *née* Hallam (d 1989); *b* 27 Dec 1944; *Educ* St Helen's Coll Thames Ditton Surrey, Carshalton Coll of FE; *m* 16 Sept 1967, Hazel Kay, da of Alfred Lang; *Career* tax offr Inland Revenue 1961–64; ECGD: exec offr 1964–70, higher exec offr 1970–76, sr exec offr 1976–78, princ 1978–82, asst sec 1982–90, group dir 1990–; *Recreations* music, walking; *Style—* John Weiss, Esq; ✉ Export Credits Guarantee Department, PO Box 2200, 2 Exchange Tower, Harbour Exchange Square, London E14 9GS (☎ 0171 512 7376, fax 0171 512 7400)

WEISS, Prof Nigel Oscar; s of Oscar Weiss (d 1994), of Cape Town, and Ursula Mary, *née* Kisch; *b* 16 Dec 1936; *Educ* Hilton Coll South Africa, Rugby, Clare Coll Cambridge (MA, PhD, ScD); *m* 29 June 1968, Judith Elizabeth, da of Brig Ronald Martin, OBE, MC; 2 da (Catherine Anne b 4 Oct 1970, Naomi Alison b 1 Nov 1982), 1 s (Timothy Francis b 5 March 1973); *Career* res assoc UKAEA Culham Lab 1962–65; Univ of Cambridge: lectr Dept of Applied Mathematics and Theoretical Physics 1965–79, fell Clare Coll 1965, dir of studies in mathematics Clare Coll 1966–79, tutor for graduate students Clare Coll 1970–73, reader in astrophysics 1979–87, prof of mathematical astrophysics 1987–, chm Cncl Sch of Physical Sciences 1993–; visiting prof Sch of Mathematical Sciences Queen Mary and Westfield Coll London 1986–; temporary appointments: Res Lab of Electronics MIT 1960–61, Max Planck Inst für Astrophysik Munich 1966, 1971, 1972, 1975, 1977, 1984, 1990 and 1991, Nat Solar Observatory Sacramento Peak New Mexico 1968, 1979, 1983, 1987, 1989 and 1992, Courant Inst of Mathematical Sciences NY Univ and Inst for Space Studies NY 1968, Dept of Astronomy Columbia Univ 1976, Woods Hole Oceanographic Inst 1978, 1981, 1985, 1987 and 1990, Harvard-Smithsonian Center for Astrophysics Cambridge Mass 1978–79, 1983, 1991 and 1993, Jt Inst for Lab Astrophysics Univ of Colorado Boulder 1982 and 1986; RAS: memb Cncl 1987–90, memb Fin Ctee 1988–, vice pres 1989–90; memb: Astronomy and Planetary Physics Bd and RAS assessor SERC 1987–90, Solar Physics Section Bd Euro Physical Soc 1982 (chm 1984–88); sr fell SERC 1987–92; FRS 1992; *Publications* papers on astrophysics, fluid mechanics and nonlinear dynamics; *Recreations* travel; *Style—* Prof Nigel Weiss, FRS; ✉ 10 Lansdowne Road, Cambridge CB3 0EU (☎ 01223 355032); Department of Applied Mathematics and Theoretical Physics, University of Cambridge, Silver Street, Cambridge CB3 9EW (☎ 01223 337910, fax 01223 337918)

WEISS, Prof Robert Anthony (Robin); s of Hans Weiss, and Stefanie, *née* Löwensohn; *b* 20 Feb 1940; *Educ* UCL (BSc, PhD); *m* 1 Aug 1964, Margaret Rose D'Costa; 2 da (Rachel Mary b 1966, Helen Anne b 1968); *Career* lectr in embryology UCL 1963–70, Eleanor Roosevelt Int Cancer Res fell Univ of Washington Seattle 1970–71, visiting assoc prof of microbiology Univ of Southern Calif 1971–72, staff scientist Imperial Cancer Res Fund Laboratories 1972–80, dir of res Inst of Cancer Res 1990– (dir 1980–89); FRCPath 1985, Hon MRCP 1989; Gustav Stern Award in Virology 1973; *Books* RNA Tumor Viruses (1982, 2 edn 1985), Aids and The New Viruses (1990), HIV, Aids and Cancer (1991); author of various articles on cell biology, virology and genetics; *Recreations* music, natural history; *Style—* Prof Robin Weiss; ✉ Chester Beatty Laboratories, Institute of Cancer Research, Fulham Road, London SW3 6JB (☎ 0171 352 8133, fax 0171 352 3299)

WELANDER, Rev Canon David Charles St Vincent; s of Charles Ernest Sven Welander, of Uppsala, Sweden, and Lousia Georgina Downes, *née* Panter; *b* 22 Jan 1925; *Educ* Unthank Coll Norwich, Univ of London (BD), Univ of Toronto; *m* 12 July 1952, Nancy O'Rourke, da of Dr George Weldale Stanley, MC (d 1960); 2 s (Richard David Edward b 1955, Christopher Peter Graham b 1959), 3 da (Rosemary Aileen Nancy b 1953, Sarah Jane Mary b 1957, Claire Elizabeth Georgina b 1960); *Career* ordained: deacon 1948, priest 1949; chaplain and lectr in New Testament studies London Coll of Divinity Univ of London 1950–56; vicar: Iver Bucks 1956–61, Christ Church Cheltenham 1962–74; rural dean Cheltenham 1972–75, canon residentiary Gloucester Cathedral 1975–91, canon-librarian Gloucester; memb Gen Synod of C of E 1970–85, sr inspr Theol Colls 1975–82; tstee Stained Glass Museum Ely Cambs 1984–; memb Cncl: Malvern Girls Coll 1982–91, King's Sch Gloucester; FSA 1979; *Books* Gloucester Cathedral (with David Verey, 1979), The Stained Glass of Gloucester Cathedral (1985), Gloucester Cathedral: Its History, Art and Architecture (1991); *Recreations* walking, golf, music, European travel; *Style—* The Rev Canon David Welander, FSA; ✉ 1 Sandpits Lane, Sherston Magna, nr Malmesbury, Wilts SN16 0NN (☎ 01666 840180)

WELBANK, (John) Michael; s of William Stephenson Welbank (d 1970), of London, and Alice Mary, *née* Robson (d 1973); *b* 2 Aug 1930; *Educ* Highgate Sch, UCL (BA, Dip TP); *m* 25 Aug 1956, Alison Mary, da of Cecil William Hopkins (d 1973), of London; 2 s (Julian b 1 Feb 1959, William David b 22 Oct 1961), 1 da (Katherine Elizabeth Rose b 29 July 1963); *Career* Nat Serv 2 Lt RA 1948–50; planning offr LCC 1951–59, architect Miny of Educn 1959–62, sr architect Miny of Housing and Local Govt 1962–64, dir Shankland Cox 1964–94, conslt ENTEC 1995–; chm Cncl Br Conslt Bureau 1985, memb Exec Ctee ICOMOS 1986–91, pres Royal Town Planning Inst 1992 (vice pres 1991), govr Chartered Surveyors Trg Tst 1994–, chm of tstees RTPI Tst 1995–; Churchill Fellowship 1990, visiting prof Oxford Brookes Univ 1993–; Freeman City of London 1952, Liveryman Worshipful Co of Chartered Architects 1988 (Master 1994); ARIBA 1958,

MRTPI 1962, MAE, FRSA; *Recreations* sailing, antiquities; *Clubs* Reform, City Livery; *Style*— Michael Welbank, Esq; ✉ 24 South Hill Park, London NW3 2SB (☎ and fax 0171 794 6766); ENTEC, 17 Angel Gate, City Road, London EC1V 2PT (☎ 0171 278 8338, fax 0171 833 9090)

WELBY, Sir (Richard) Bruno Gregory Welby; 7 Bt (UK 1801), of Denton Manor, Lincolnshire; s of Sir Oliver Welby, 6 Bt, TD (d 1977, s of Lady Maria Hervey, sis of 4 Marquess of Bristol), by his w, Barbara Angela, da of John Gregory, CB, CMG, and gda of Sir Philip Gregory; n of Dowager Lady Saltoun, and Viscountess Portal of Hungerford; *b* 11 March 1928; *Educ* Eton, Ch Ch Oxford; *m* 1952, Jane Biddulph, da of the late Ralph Hodder-Williams, MC; 3 s, 1 da; *Heir* s, Charles William Hodder Welby; *Style*— Sir Bruno Welby, Bt; ✉ 20 St Mary Abbot's Terrace, London W14

WELBY, Charles William Hodder; s and h of Sir (Richard) Bruno Welby, 7 Bt, of Denton Manor, by Jane Biddulph; *b* 6 May 1953; *Educ* Eton, RAC; *m* 1978, Suzanna, da of Maj Ian Stuart-Routledge (d 1981), of Harston Hall, Grantham; 3 da (Venetia b 1981, Zinnia b 1985, Isadora b 1993); *Career* 2 Lt 1974 Worcestershire and Sherwood Foresters TAVR; chartered surveyor, ptnr Humberts Grantham, dep dir Cons Bd of Fin 1987, dir Constituency Fin to 1992; dir H E W Fund-raising Ltd 1993; contested (C) Caerphilly 1983; FRICS; *Style*— Charles Welby, Esq; ✉ Stroxton House, Grantham, Lincs (☎ 0147 683 232)

WELCH, Ann Courtenay; OBE (1966, MBE 1953); da of Maj Courtenay Harold Wish Edmonds, OBE (d 1953), and Edith Maud, *née* Austin (d 1945); *b* 20 May 1917; *m* 1, 1939 (m dis 1948), Alfred Graham Douglas, DFC; 2 da (Vivien Redman b 1943, Elizabeth Douglas b 1945); m 2, 21 June 1953, Patrick Palles Lorne Elphinstone Welch, s of Brig Gen Malcolm Hammond Edward Welch, CB, CMG (d 1947); 1 da (Jan b 1955); *Career* pilot A licence 1934, Air Tport Aux ferry pilot 1940–42; gliding instr for 40 years, 20 as nat examiner of instrs, fndr Surrey Gliding Club 1938, mangr Br Gliding Team 1948–68; pres Int Jury for championships in gliding, hang gliding, paragliding and microlight flying 1970–; worldwide ed and prodr annual bulletin Féderation Aéronautique Internationale 1978–90, ed Royal Aero Club Gazette, holder Womens Nat Goal Distance Gliding Record 1961–; pres: Br Hang Gliding and Paragliding Assoc, Br Microlight Assoc; chm Light Aviation Group RAes, hon pres 2 cmmns Féderation Aéronautique Internationale, hon vice chm Royal Aero Club; FRAeS, FRMetS, MRIN; Gold Air Medal, Lilienthal Medal, Silver Medal Royal Aero Club, Bronze Medal, Pelagia Mejewska medal of Féderation Aéronautique Int; *Books* Silent Flight (1939), Cloud Reading for Pilots (1944), Gliding and Advanced Soaring (1947), Woolacombe Bird (1964), Story of Gliding (1965), Pilots Weather (1973), Accidents Happen (1978), Happy to Fly (1983), Complete Microlight and Soaring Guides (1983, 1986); *Recreations* sailing, painting; *Clubs* Royal Aero, Surrey & Hants Gliding, Bosham Sailing; *Style*— Mrs Ann Welch, OBE; ✉ 14 Upper Old Park Lane, Farnham, Surrey GU9 0AS (☎ and fax 01252 715991)

WELCH, Clifford William; CBE (1994); s of William Henry Welch, and Ethel, *née* Games; *b* 1925; *Educ* Christ's Coll Finchley, Plastics Research Inst, Delft Tech HS Holland; *m* 1954, Jill Price Simpson; *Career* former visiting lectr Nat Coll of Rubber & Plastics Technol Univ of London; Temple Press Ltd: asst ed Plastics 1953, ed Plastics 1957, editorial dir 1958–60; md Heywood-Temple Industrial Publications Ltd and Tothill Press Ltd 1960–66, dep chm Business Publishing Div and chief exec IPC Business Press Overseas Ltd/International Publishing Corporation Ltd 1966–73; Lloyd's of London Press Ltd: fndr chief exec and subsequent dep chm 1973–91; chm Lloyd's Maritime Information Services Ltd 1989–92; dep chm Design Council 1991–93 (chm Publications Ctee 1988–93); memb Royal Free Hosp Sch of Med, chm Katharine Dormandy Tst Royal Free Hosp London; tstee Newsvendors Ben Inst; memb: Bd Mercury Theatre Colchester, Ct City Univ; Freeman City of London 1957, Liveryman and memb Ct of Assts Worshipful Co of Horners (Master 1982) FIM; *Publications* contrib: The Penguin Science Survey, History of the British Plastics Federation; various papers to IUPAC and other socs; *Clubs* City of London, Oriental, MCC, Flyfishers'; *Style*— Clifford Welch, Esq, CBE; ✉ Orchard House, Coles Oak Lane, Dedham, Colchester, Essex CO7 6DR (☎ 01206 322277)

WELCH, (James) Colin Ross; s of James William Welch, of Ickleton Abbey, Cambridgeshire, and Irene Margherita, *née* Paton; *b* 23 April 1924; *Educ* Stowe, Peterhouse Cambridge (maj scholar, BA); *m* 1950, Sybil Russell; 1 s, 1 da; *Career* serv WWII cmmnd Royal Warwickshire Regt 1942, served NW Europe, twice wounded; journalist Glasgow Herald 1948, Colonial Office 1949; Daily Telegraph: leader writer, columnist (Peter Simple, with Michael Wharton), Parly sketch writer 1950–64, dep ed 1964–80, reg columnist 1981–83; ed Chief Executive magazine 1980–82; columnist and book critic The Spectator 1982–91, Parly sketch writer Daily Mail 1984–92, columnist The Independent 1993, currently freelance reviewer and columnist; awards: Granada Journalist of the Year 1974, Specialist Writer Br Press Awards 1986; Knight's Cross Order of Polonia Restituta 1972; *Publications* Sir Frederick Ponsonby - Recollections of Three Reigns (ed, 1951), Nestroy - Liberty Comes to Krähwinkel (trans with Sybil Welch, 1954); author of numerous articles in: Encounter, Spectator, New Statesmen, American Spectator; contribs to symposia incl The Future That Doesn't Work (1977); *Style*— Colin Welch, Esq; ✉ 4 Goddard's Lane, Aldbourne, Wilts SN8 2DL (☎ 01672 540010)

WELCH, Dr Janet Mary (Jan); da of Patrick Palles Lorne Elphinstone Welch, of Farnham, and Ann Courtenay, *née* Edmunds; *b* 11 June 1955; *Educ* Farnham Girls' GS, Farnborough Tech Coll, St Thomas's Hosp Med Sch (Tite scholar, entrance scholar, BSc, MB BS, FRCP); *m* 1989, Gary Richards, s of Jack Richards; 1 da (Fabia Rosamund Welch-Richards b 2 Oct 1990), 1 s (Toby Lorne Welch-Richards b 8 June 1993); *Career* house surgn St Mary's Hosp Portsmouth 1980, house physician then SHO in microbiology St Thomas's Hosp London 1981, SHO in haematology Exeter then in med Reading 1982, registrar in infectious diseases London 1983, sr registrar in genitourinary med St Thomas's Hosp London 1987–90 (in virology 1984–87), conslt in genitourinary med King's Coll Hosp 1990–; SE Thames regnl audit co-ordinator in genitourinary med and HIV, memb Med Advsy Ctee Brook Advsy Centres 1994–; *Books* Looking After People with Late HIV Disease (1990); *Recreations* gardening, skiing; *Style*— Dr Jan Welch; ✉ Department of Genitourinary Medicine, King's Healthcare NHS Trust, Denmark Hill, London SE5 9RS (☎ 0171 346 3470, fax 0171 346 3486)

WELCH, Sir John Reader; 2 Bt (UK 1957), of Chard, Co Somerset; s of Sir Cullum Welch, 1 Bt, OBE, MC (d 1980); *b* 26 July 1933; *Educ* Marlborough Coll, Hertford Coll Oxford (MA); *m* 25 Sept 1962, Margaret Kerry, o da of Kenneth Victor Douglass; 1 s, 2 da; *Heir* s, James Douglass Cullum, b 10 Nov 1973; *Career* slr; ptnr: Bell Brodrick & Gray 1961–71, Wedlake Bell 1972–96; chm: John Fairfax (UK) Ltd 1977–90, London Homes for the Elderly 1981–90; registrar Archdeaconry of London, memb Court of Common Cncl (City of London) 1975–86 and chm Planning and Communications Ctee 1981–1982; Liveryman and memb of Ct of Assts Haberdashers' Co (Master 1990–91), Freeman and past Master Parish Clerks' Co, pres The Grand Charity of Freemasons 1985–95; memb City Livery Club (hon slr 1983–90, pres 1986–87), chm Walbrook Ward Club 1978–79; CStJ 1981; FRSA 1991; *Clubs* Surrey CCC, Hurlingham; *Style*— Sir John Welch, Bt; ✉ 28 Rivermead Court, Ranelagh Gardens, London SW6 3RU; office: 16 Bedford St, Covent Gdn, London WC2E 9HF (☎ 0171 379 7266, fax 0171 836 6117)

WELCH, Melvin Dennis (Mel); s of Robert Charles Welch (d 1991), of Watford, and Rose Elizabeth, *née* Oakley (d 1993); *b* 21 Nov 1946; *Educ* Bushey GS, Univ of Sussex (BSc, MSc); *m* 18 Sep 1971, Susan Jane, da of Arthur Jeffcoatt (d 1976), of Coventry; 1 s (Timothy b 1972), 1 da (Josephine b 1974); *Career* sec: English Basketball Assoc 1970–91, Br and Irish Basketball Fedn 1970–, Cwlth Basketball Fedn 1978–91; co-ordinator Carnegie Nat Sports Devpt Centre 1991–, sec Yorks and Humberside Fedn of Sport & Recreation 1991–; memb: Eligibility Ctee Int Basketball Fedn 1984–, Olympic Review Ctee Sports Cncl 1985–86; chm Br Inst of Sports Admin 1994– (fndr memb 1979, memb Exec Ctee 1985–, vice-chm 1992–94, fell 1995–); Sports Aid Fndn: memb UK Grants Ctee 1986–, chm Eng Grants Ctee 1996–, govr and memb Exec Ctee Sports Aid Fndn 1996–; coaching review panel Sports Cncl 1989–91; dir: Basketball Publishing Ltd 1986–91, Basketball Marketing Ltd 1986–87; tournament referee N Leeds tennis league; life vice-pres English Basketball Assoc 1991–; *Books* EBBA Yearbook (1971–91), Intersport Basketball (1981), Encyclopaedia Britannica Book of Year (contrib, 1985–90), Getting Things Done (1992), Raising Money (1992), Running Meetings (1992), Running a Club (1992), Looking after the Money (1992), Getting It Right (1994), Making Your Point (1994), Making A Match (1994); *Recreations* tennis, basketball; *Style*— Mel Welch, Esq; ✉ 5 Thorn Lane, Roundhay, Leeds LS8 1NF (☎ 0113 266 8751); Carnegie National Sports Development Centre, Beckett Park, Leeds LS6 3QS

WELCH, Peter John; s of Cyril Vincent Welch (d 1961), of Sutton Coldfield, and Elsie Lilian Ramsden; *b* 4 Jan 1940; *Educ* St Philip's Sch Edgbaston; *m* 12 June 1962, Margaret Mary, da of John Lavelle Bates, of Birmingham; 4 s (Peter b 1963, Andrew b 1964, Julian b 1966, Ian b 1975), 1 da (Elspeth b 1968); *Career* dir: Unicorn Industries plc 1972–78 and 1980–87 (chm 1980–84), Foseco MINSEP plc 1978–87, Thermal Scientific plc 1987–88, Jeyes Group plc 1987–, Holliday Chemical Holdings plc 1988– (dep chm 1992–), Dunham Bush Ltd 1989–95, Associated British Consultants plc 1989–93 (chm 1990–93), Meconic Ltd 1990–, WSP Group 1993– (chm 1993–); chm Unitary Tax Campaign (Ltd) 1978–; FCA 1961; *Recreations* bridge, music, reading; *Style*— Peter Welch, Esq; ✉ Frankfield, Spinfield Lane, Marlow, Buckinghamshire SL7 2LB (☎ 01628 485975)

WELCH, Prof Robert; s of Patrick Welch (d 1995), and Kathleen, *née* Kearney (d 1989); *b* 25 Nov 1947; *Educ* Coláiste Chriost Ri Cork (nat scholar, Univ Coll Cork (Univ scholar, BA, MA), Univ of Leeds (PhD); *m* 1970, Angela, da of Pearse O'Riordan; 4 c (Rachel b 16 Jan 1971, Killian b 23 July 1975, Egan 31 Jan 1980, Tiernan b 1 March 1981); *Career* temp lectr Univ of Leeds 1971–73, lectr in English Univ of Ife Nigeria 1973–74, lectr in English Univ of Leeds 1974–84; Univ of Ulster: prof of English 1984–, sometime head of Dept, dir Centre for Irish Literature & Bibliography 1994–; Arts Cncl for Northern Ireland: memb Bd 1990–96, chm Creative Arts Ctee 1991–96, vice-chm 1992–93; chm Int Assoc for the Study of Irish Literature 1988–91; assessor HEFC 1994–95; *Books* Irish Poetry from Moore to Yeats (1980), Changing States: Transformations in Modern Irish Literature (1993), The Kilcolman Notebook (novel) 1994, The Oxford Companion to Irish Literature (1996); *Recreations* walking, fishing, gardening, wine; *Clubs* Kildare Street & University, Carlton; *Style*— Prof Robert Welch; ✉ 34 Station Road, Portstewart, N Ireland BT55 7DA; Leamagowra Lodge, Leamagowra, Glencolumcille, Co Donegal, Ireland; Coleraine Centre for Irish Literature and Bibliography, University of Ulster, Coleraine, N Ireland BT52 1SA (☎ 01265 832823, fax 01265 324914)

WELDON, Anthony Henry David; s of Max Weldon (d 1979), and Regina Charlotte, *née* Gideon; *b* 23 Dec 1945; *Educ* Uppingham; *m* 1, 1970 (m dis 1984), Claire Ellen, *née* Gessler; 2 s (Julian b 1972, Oliver b 1975), 1 da (Alexandra b 1974); m 2, 1984 (m dis 1994), Manina Anne, *née* Mitchell; *Career* dir: Durrington Holdings Ltd 1991, N P Record plc 1993; chm Advsy Bd Royal Acad of Arts, memb Exec Ctee RCM; memb Worshipful Co of Masons; hon fell St Peter's Coll Oxford; FRCM; *Recreations* sport, opera; *Clubs* MCC, RAC, Royal Hampton Court Tennis, Annabel's, Mark's, Brooks's, Hurlingham, Chelsea Arts, Queens, Cumberland Lawn Tennis, Highgate Golf; *Style*— Anthony Weldon, Esq; ✉ 808 St James Court, Flatts Village, Hamilton Parish FL04, Bermuda

WELDON, Sir Anthony William; 9 Bt (I 1723), of Dunmore, Co Carlow; s of Sir Thomas Weldon, 8 Bt (d 1979), by his w Marie, Lady Weldon, who subseq m 6 Earl Cathcart, *qv*; *b* 11 May 1947; *Educ* Sherborne; *m* 1980, Amanda, formerly w of Anthony Wigan, and da of Maj Geoffrey North, MC, by his w, Hon Margaret de Grey (2 da of 8 Baron Walsingham, DSO, OBE, JP, DL); 2 da (Alice Louise b 13 Nov 1981, Oonagh Leone b 6 Oct 1983); *Heir* 2 cous, Kevin Weldon; *Career* late Lt Irish Gds, awarded S Arabian GSM; md BFP Design and Communications and Bene Factum Publishing Ltd; *Recreations* stalking, champagne, cricket; *Clubs* White's, The Stranded Whales; *Style*— Sir Anthony Weldon, Bt

WELDON, Duncan Clark; s of Clarence Weldon (d 1980), of Southport, and Margaret Mary Andrew; *b* 19 March 1941; *Educ* King George V GS Southport; *m* 1 (m dis 1971), Helen Shapiro; m 2, 9 July 1974, Janet, da of Walter Mahoney (d 1982); 1 da (Lucy Jane b Oct 1977); *Career* theatrical producer, formerly photographer; co-fndr Triumph Theatre Productions Ltd 1970; dir: Duncan C Weldon Productions Ltd, Triumph Proscenium Productions Ltd, Triumph Film & Television Ltd, Richmond Theatre, The Chichester Festival Theatre 1994–; first stage prodn A Funny Kind of Evening (with David Kossoff, Theatre Royal Bath) 1965, first London prodn Tons of Money (Mayfair) 1968, presentations also in Europe, Aust, Russia, Canada and Hong Kong; *Productions* presented over 175 in London incl; 1970: When We Are Married; 1971: The Chalk Garden, Big Bad Mouse, The Wizard of Oz; 1972: Lord Arthur Savile's Crime, Bunny, The Wizard of Oz; 1973: Mother Adam, Grease, The King and I; 1974: Dead Easy; 1975: The Case in Question, Hedda Gabler (RSC), Dad's Army, Betzi, On Approval; 1976: 13 Rue de l'Amour, A Bedful of Foreigners, Three Sisters, Fringe Benefits, The Seagull, The Circle; 1977: Separate Tables, Stevie, Hedda Gabler, On Approval, The Good Woman of Setzuan, Rosmersholm, Laburnum Grove, The Apple Cart; 1978: Waters of the Moon, Kings and Clowns, The Travelling Music Show, A Family, Look After Lulu, The Millionairess; 1979: The Crucifer of Blood; 1980: Reflections, Rattle of a Simple Man, The Last of Mrs Cheyney, Early Days (RNT); 1981: Virginia, Overheard, Dave Allen, Worzel Gummidge; 1982: Murder in Mind, Hobson's Choice, A Coat of Varnish, Captain Brassbound's Conversion, Design For Living, Uncle Vanya, Key for Two, The Rules of the Game, Man and Superman; 1983: The School for Scandal, Dash, Heartbreak House, Call Me Madam, Romantic Comedy, Liza Minnelli, Beethoven's Tenth (also Broadway), Edmund Kean (also Broadway), Fiddler on the Roof, A Patriot for Me, Cowardice, Great and Small, The Cherry Orchard, Dial M for Murder, Dear Anyone, The Sleeping Prince, The School for Scandal, Hi-De-Hi!; 1984: Hello Dolly!, The Aspern Papers, Strange Interlude (also Broadway), Serjeant Musgrave's Dance, Aren't We All? (also Broadway), American Buffalo, The Way of the World, Extremities; 1985: The Wind in the Willows, The Lonely Road, The Caine Mutiny Court-Martial, Other Places, Old Times (also in LA), The Corn is Green, Waste (RSC), Strippers, Guys and Dolls (RNT), Sweet Bird of Youth, Interpreters, Fatal Attraction, The Scarlet Pimpernel; 1986: The Applecart, Across from the Garden of Allah, Antony and Cleopatra, The Taming of the Shrew, Circe & Bravo, Annie Get Your Gun, Long Day's Journey into Night, Rookery Nook, Breaking the Code (also Broadway), Mr and Mrs Nobody; 1987: A Piece of My Mind, Court in the Act!, Canaries Sometimes Sing, Kiss Me Kate (RSC), Melon, Portraits, Groucho - A Life in Review, A Man for all Seasons, You Never Can Tell, Babes in the Wood; 1988: A Touch of the Poet, The Deep Blue Sea, The Admirable Crichton, The Secret of Sherlock Holmes, A Walk in the Woods, Orpheus Descending (also Broadway), Richard II; 1989: Richard III, The Royal Baccarat Scandal, Ivanov, Much Ado About Nothing, The Merchant of Venice (also Broadway), Frankie & Johnny, Veterans Day, Another Time, The Baker's Wife, London Assurance; 1990: Salome (RNT), Bent (RNT),

An Evening with Peter Ustinov, The Wild Duck, Henry IV, Kean, Love Letters, Time and the Conways; 1991: The Homecoming, The Philanthropist, The Caretaker, Becket, Tovarich, The Cabinet Minister; 1992: Talking Heads, Heartbreak House, A Woman of No Importance (RSC), Lost in Yonkers, Trelawny of the Wells, Cyrano de Bergerac; 1993: Macbeth (RSC), Relative Values, Two Gentlemen of Verona (RSC); 1994: Travesties (RSC), A Month in the Country, Rope, An Evening with Peter Ustinov, Arcadia (RNT), Home, Saint Joan, Lady Windermere's Fan, The Rivals; 1995: Dangerous Corner, Cell Mates, The Duchess of Malfi, Taking Sides, Old Times, Communicating Doors, Hobson's Choice, The Hothouse; 1996: Uncle Vanya, When We Are Married, Talking Heads, The Cherry Orchard; other Broadway prodns incl: Brief Lives 1974, Wild Honey (NT) 1986, Blithe Spirit and Pygmalion 1987, Taking Sides 1996; *Style*— Duncan C Weldon, Esq; ✉ Duncan C Weldon Productions Ltd, Suite 4, Wardorf Chambers, 11 Aldwych, London, WC2B 4DA (☎ 0171 836 0186, fax 0171 240 7511)

WELDON, Fay; *née* Franklin Birkinshaw; da of Dr Frank Birkinshaw (d 1947), of N Zealand, and Margaret, *née* Jepson; *b* 22 Sept 1931; *Educ* Christ Church Girls HS (NZ), South Hampstead HS, Univ of St Andrews (MA); *m* 1; 1 s (Nicholas b 1954); m 2, June 1961 (m dis 1994), Ron Weldon; 3 s (Daniel b 1963, Thomas b 1970, Samuel b 1977); m 3, 1995, Nicolas Fox; *Career* screen writer, novelist, critic, essayist; chm of judges Booker McConnell Prize 1983; Hon DLitt Univ of St Andrews 1992; *Books* The Fat Woman's Joke (1967), Down Among the Women (1971), Female Friends (1975), Remember Me (1976), Little Sisters (1978), Praxis (1978, Booker Prize nomination), Puffball (1980), Watching Me Watching You (1981), The President's Child (1982), Life and Loves of a She Devil (1984, televised 1986), Letters to Alice-on First Reading Jane Austen (1984), Polaris and Other Stories (1985), Rebecca West (1985), The Shrapnel Academy (1986), Heart of the Country (1987, televised 1987), The Hearts and Lives of Men (1987), The Rules of Life (1987), Leader of the Band (1988), The Cloning of Joanna May (1989), Darcy's Utopia (1990), Growing Rich (1990, televised 1990), Moon Over Minneapolis or Why She Couldn't Stay (1991), Life Force (1992), Affliction (1994), Splitting (1995), Worst Fears (1996); children's books: Wolf the Mechanical Dog (1988), Party Puddle (1989); *Style*— Mrs Fay Weldon; ✉ c/o Curtis Brown, Haymarket House, 28/29 Haymarket, London SW1Y 4SP; c/o Casarotto Co Ltd, National House, 60–66 Wardour St, London W1V 3HP

WELEMINSKY, Judy Ruth; da of Dr Anton Weleminsky, of Leeds, and Gerda, *née* Loewenstamm; *b* 25 Oct 1950; *Educ* Pontefract & Dist Girls' HS, Roundhay HS, Univ of Birmingham (BSc), Univ of Lancaster (MA); *partner* Robert J A Smith; 2 da (Emma Jane Weleminsky Smith b 6 Feb 1991, Alice Rose Weleminsky Smith b 13 Feb 1993); *Career* personnel and training offr Lowfield (S & D) Ltd 1973–75, community rels offr Lambeth Cncl for Community Rels 1975–78, equal opportunities offr Wandsworth BC 1978–80, employment devpt offr Nat Assoc for Care and Resettlement of Offenders (NACRO) 1980–82; dir: Nat Fed of Community Orgns 1982–85, Nat Schizophrenia Fellowship 1985–90, NCVO 1991–94; mgmnt conslt 1994–, ptnr Managing Directors 1995–; assoc: Volprof 1994, Compass Partnership 1994; FRSA 1992; *Recreations* family, friends and food; *Style*— Ms Judy Weleminsky; ✉ 3 Chelwood Gardens, Kew, London TW9 4JG (☎ 0181 876 5087)

WELFARE, Jonathan William; s of Kenneth William Welfare (d 1966), of Stradbroke, Suffolk, and (Dorothy) Patience Athole, *née* Ross; *b* 21 Oct 1944; *Educ* Bradfield Coll Berkshire, Emmanuel Coll Cambridge (MA); *m* 6 Sept 1969, Deborah Louise, da of James D'Arcy Nesbitt, of Neston, Cheshire; 1 s (Oliver b 1987), 3 da (Harriet b 1973, Laura b 1975, Amy b 1979); *Career* corp planning mangr Milton Keynes Devpt Corp 1970–74, chief economist and dep chief exec S Yorkshire Met CC 1974–84, dir The Landmark Tst 1984–86; co-fndr The Oxford Ventures Gp 1986; dir: Granite TV Ltd 1988–, Oxford Innovation Ltd 1988–; md Venture Link Investors Ltd 1990–95, chief exec Bristol 2000 1995–; tstee: The Oxford Tst (chm 1985–95), The Northmoor Tst (chm 1986–95); Freeman Co of Info Technologists, Freeman City of London; FRSA; *Books* Sources of EEC Funding for Local Authorities (1977); *Recreations* tennis (real and lawn), cricket, sailing; *Clubs* Hawks' (Cambridge); *Style*— Jonathan Welfare, Esq; ✉ Rooks Orchard, Little Wittenham, Abingdon, Oxfordshire (☎ 01865 407765)

WELFARE, Simon Piers; s of Kenneth William Welfare (d 1966), of Stadbroke, Suffolk, and Dorothy Patience, *née* Ross; *b* 21 Nov 1946; *Educ* Harrow, Magdalen Coll Oxford; *m* 3 Aug 1968, Mary Katharine Welfare, da of Marquess of Aberdeen and Temair, CBE (d 1974), of Haddo House, Aberdeenshire; 1 s (Toby b 29 March 1973), 2 da (Hannah b 30 Sept 1969, Alice b 6 Sept 1971); *Career* broadcaster and writer Yorkshire TV Ltd 1968–81, freelance prodr 1982–, md Granite Film and TV Prodns 1989–; *Books* Arthur C Clarke's Mysterious World (with A C Clarke and John Fairley, 1980), Arthur C Clarke's World of Strange Powers (with A C Clarke and J Fairley, 1984), Great Honeymoon Disasters (1986), Arthur C Clarke's Chronicles of the Strange & Mysterious (with A C Clarke and J Fairley, 1987), Red Empire (with Gwyneth Hughes, 1990), The Cabinet of Curiosities (with J Fairley, 1991), Days of Majesty (with Alastair Bruce, 1993), Arthur C Clarke's A-Z of Mysteries (with J Fairley, 1993); *Recreations* collecting arcane knowledge, flying; *Style*— Simon Welfare, Esq; ✉ The Den of Keithfield, Tarves, Ellon, Aberdeenshire AB41 0NU (☎ 01651 851510/851760)

WELHAM, George; s of George Leslie Welham (d 1986), of London, and Dorothy Emily, *née* Peckham; *b* 9 July 1938; *Educ* Dulwich; *m* 1, Yvonne, *née* Adams; 3 s; m 2, Penelope, *née* Connell; 2 step da; *Career* fin journalist 1960–69; co fndr and first chm Welham-McAdam Public Relations 1969–76, dir Extel PR & Advertising 1976–79, dir and dep md Hill & Knowlton London 1979–84, md Gavin Anderson & Co London 1984–88, chief exec then chm Burson-Marsteller Financial Ltd 1988–92, dir Burson-Marsteller Ltd (memb Exec Ctee) 1988–92, dep chm Financial Dynamics Ltd 1993–; *Style*— George Welham, Esq; ✉ Financial Dynamics Ltd, 30 Furnival Street, London EC4A 1JE (☎ 0171 831 3113)

WELLDON, Dr Estela Valentina; da of Gildo D'Accurzio (d 1983), and Julia, *née* Barbadillo (d 1957); *b* 3 Nov 1936; *Educ* Universidad de Cuyo Argentina (MD), Menninger Sch of Psychiatry USA, Univ of London; *m* Ronald Michael Charles Welldon (d 1970); 1 s (Daniel Alexis b 2 Feb 1970); *Career* psychiatrist Henderson Hosp 1964; Portman Clinic London: conslt psychiatrist 1975–, clinic tutor 1987–92; private practice 121 Harley Street; specialist in the application of group analysis to social and sexual deviancy, pioneer in teaching of forensic psychotherapy, fndr in forensic psychotherapy Univ of London; pres Int Assoc for Forensic Psychotherapy 1991–95 (hon pres 1995–); assessor British Journal of Psychiatry, expert on female crime and sexual deviation Panel of Specialists RCPsych, Br corr and memb Editorial Bd Argentinian Journal of Group Psychotherapy; currently sr lectr: BPMF Univ Coll London, Dept of Psychiatry Sassari Univ Sardinia Italy, Dept of Psychology Univ of Bologna Italy; Visitante Distinguido Univ & City of Cuzco Peru 1989; memb: Gp Analytic Soc 1968, Br Assoc of Psychotherapists 1972, Inst for Study and Prevention of Delinquency, American Gp Psychotherapy Assoc, Int Assoc of Gp Psychotherapy, Inst of Group Analysis; fndr memb Bd of Dirs Int Acad of Law and Mental Health, memb Bd of Dirs Int Assoc of Group Psychotherapy; memb Soc of Authors; FRCPsych 1987 (MRCPysch 1973); *Books* Mother, Madonna, Whore (1988), A Practical Guide to Forensic Psychotherapy (1996); *Recreations* opera, theatre, swimming; *Clubs* Groucho; *Style*— Dr Estela Welldon; ✉ 121 Harley St, London W1N 1DH (☎ 0171 935 9076, fax 0171 586 0713)

WELLER, (William) Leslie; DL (West Sussex, 1992); s of Frederick Leslie Weller (d 1977), of Horsham, W Sussex, and Blanch Mary, *née* Kemp (d 1994); *b* 23 April 1935; *Educ* Collyers GS, Cranleigh; *m* 1, 6 June 1959 (m dis), Joyce Elizabeth; 1 s (Adrian Leslie b 21 June 1963); m 2, Brenda Olive Wilson; *Career* Nat Serv RAF 1957–59; chartered surveyor: Newland Tompkins and Taylor 1951–55, King and Chasemore 1959–78 (ptnr 1961–78); dir Sotheby's London 1978–94 (md Sotheby's Sussex 1978–91), Weller King 1994–; chm Olumpia Fine Art and Antiques Fairs 1980–, chm Cncl Sussex Archaeological Soc, chm Chichester Cathedral Fabric Advsy Cncl, tstee Chichester Cathedral Tst 1979– (chm 1979–86); Freeman: Worshipful Co of Ironmongers 1984 (memb Ct 1992), City of London 1986; FRICS 1961, FSVA 1976; *Recreations* reading, gardening, the arts, book-collecting; *Clubs* Naval & Military (vice chm) and Sussex; *Style*— Leslie Weller, Esq, DL; ✉ Hobshorts House, Rook Cross Lane, West Grinstead, Horsham, West Sussex RH13 8LL (☎ 01403 711821); Weller King, 36 High Street, Steyning, West Sussex BN44 3YE (☎ 01903 816633, fax 01903 816644, car 0850 914357)

WELLER, Prof Malcolm Philip Isadore; s of Solomon George Weller (d 1958), and Esther, *née* Black; *b* 29 May 1935; *Educ* Perse Sch, Univ of Cambridge (MA, prize winner, capt coll athletics team), Univ of Newcastle (MB BS, prize winner), Br Cncl travel award; *m* 8 May 1966, (Celia) Davina, da of Solomon Reisler (d 1973), of Manchester; 2 s (Ben b 19 Aug 1969, Adrian b 17 Dec 1970); *Career* psychiatrist; conslt St Ann's Hosp, hon prof Middlesex Univ; formerly lectr and first asst Charing Cross Hosp Sch of Med; visiting fell Fitzwilliam Coll Cambridge 1994–95; pubns incl over 100 chapters, papers and editorials on psychiatric and medico-legal subjects; co-opted memb London Univ Bd of Studies in Psychology & Higher Degrees Sub Ctee; external examiner Univs of Manchester and Singapore; RCPsych: former memb Gen Psychiatry, Social Community and Rehabilitation Exec Ctees, former memb Working Gps, currently co-opted memb Psychopharmacology Ctee; chm: CONCERN, N Thames Regnl Psychiatric Ctee, Haringey Div of Psychiatry 1992–94; former vice chm NE Thames Regnl Ctee for Hosp Med Servs; former organiser Newcastle Music Festival, former co-opted memb Mgmnt Ctee Laing Art Gallery; former local cncllr, former chm of govrs Gosforth Middle Sch; memb Central Ctee BMA; FBPsS 1986, FCINP 1987, FRCPsych 1987; *Books* Scientific Basis of Psychiatry (1983 and 1992), International Perspectives in Schizophrenia (1990), MCQs on the Basic Sciences (1992), Dimensions of Community Care (1993), Progress in Clinical Psychiatry (1996); Bailliere's Clinical Psychiatry Series (ed in chief, 7 vols); *Recreations* history of art, music; *Clubs* New York Acad of Sciences, RSM; *Style*— Prof Malcolm Weller; ✉ 30 Arkwright Rd, Hampstead, London NW3 6BH (☎ 0171 794 5804, fax 0171 431 1589)

WELLER, Prof Roy Oliver; s of Leonard Albert Ernest Weller (d 1969), and Myrtle Passie, *née* Vivash (d 1979); *b* 27 May 1938; *Educ* St Olave's and St Saviour's GS London, Guy's Med Sch Univ of London (MD, PhD); *m* 22 Dec 1960, Francine Michelle, da of Robert Arthur Cranley; 1 s (Timothy b 1965), 1 da (Adrienne b 1964); *Career* US Public Health Serv post doctoral fell Albert Einstein Coll of Med 1967–68, sr lectr in pathology Guy's Med Sch 1969–72 (lectr 1964–67 and 1968–69), conslt neuropathologist Guy's and Maudsley Hosps 1972, clinical serv dir of pathology Southampton Univ Hosp's Tst 1989–93 (sr lectr and reader in neuropathology 1973–78, prof of neuropathology 1978, dep dean of med 1980–84); ed Neuropathology and Applied Neuropathology; memb Br Neuropathological Soc, FRCPath 1982; *Books* Pathology of Peripheral Nerves (1977), Clinical Neuropathology (1983), Atlas of Neuropathology (1984), Systemic Pathology: Nervous System Muscle and Eyes (ed 1990); also author of over 150 research papers, current work mainly on neuroimmunology related to multiple sclerosis; *Recreations* pottery, music, walking; *Style*— Prof Roy O Weller; ✉ 22 Abbey Hill Rd, Winchester, Hants SO23 7AT (☎ 01962 867465); Department of Pathology, Level E, South Pathology Block, Southampton General Hospital, Tremona Rd, Southampton SO9 6YD (☎ 01703 796669, fax 01703 796869, e-mail row@soton.ac.uk)

WELLER, Walter; s of Walter Weller (d 1982), and Anna Katharina Weller (d 1990); *b* 30 Nov 1939; *Educ* Gymnasium HS of Music Vienna; *m* 8 June 1966, Elisabeth Maria, da of Prof Franz Samohyl, of Vienna; 1 s (Andreas b 18 June 1978); *Career* musician and conductor; Vienna Philharmonic Orch 1956–57, fndr Weller Quartet 1957–67, first Konzertmeister Vienna Philharmonic 1961, debut as conductor 1966, princ conductor RPO 1980–85, conductor laureate Royal Liverpool Philharmonic Orch (princ conductor and artistic advsr), princ guest conductor Nat Orch of Spain 1990– (princ guest conductor 1987–90), chief conductor and music dir Royal Scottish Orchestra 1991–, chief conductor Basel Symphony Orchestra and gen music dir Allgemeine Basler Musikgesellshaft 1994; recordings incl: complete Prokofiev and Rachmaninov symphonies, complete Beethoven symphonies and piano concertos, Mendelssohn, Smetana, Shostakovitch, Grieg, Bartok, Dukas; operas incl: Fidelio and Der Rosenkavalier (Scottish Opera), Der Fliegende Hollander and Ariadne auf Naxos (ENO), Der Frieischutz (Teatro Comunale Bologna), Der Fliegende Hollander (La Scala); conductor of leading orchestras: Britain, Europe, Scandinavia, America; Honoured Cross for Art and Sci (Austria), Mozart Interpretation prize, Beethoven Gold medal; *Style*— Walter Weller, Esq; ✉ c/o Harrison-Parrott Ltd, 12 Penzance Place, London W11 4PA (☎ 0171 229 9166, fax 0171 221 5042, telex 892791 BIRDS G)

WELLING, Mark Ronald; s of Kenneth Ronald Welling, of Derby, and Margaret Dorothy, *née* Hunter; *b* 22 March 1956; *Educ* Derby Sch, Emmanuel Coll Cambridge (MA); *m* 28 March 1987, Vanessa Jane, da of W Richard Barker, of Farnley Tyas, W Yorks; *Career* admitted slr 1981; ptnr Allen & Overy 1987–; cncllr (Lib Dem) Royal Borough of Kingston upon Thames 1986–90; chm Mgmnt Ctee Kingston CAB 1995–96; memb City of London Slrs' Co 1987–; memb Law Soc 1981; *Recreations* bassoon, clarinet and piano playing; *Style*— Mark Welling, Esq; ✉ Allen & Overy, One New Exchange, London EC4M 9QQ (☎ 0171 330 3000, fax 0171 300 9999, telex 8812801)

WELLINGHAM, Air Cdre (John) Bernard; s of Claude Bernard Wellingham (d 1963), and Annetta, *née* Jagoe (d 1980); *b* 21 June 1925; *Educ* Trinity Sch Croydon, Christ's Coll Cambridge (MA), Royal Coll of Military Sci Shrivenham, RAF Staff Coll Bracknell, Jt Servs Staff Coll Latimer; *m* 24 July 1948, Patricia Margaret, da of Wing Cdr Patrick John Murphy (d 1965); 2 s (John b 1949, Charles b 1953); *Career* RAF 1945, cmmnd 1946, communications devpt Royal Aircraft Establishment Farnborough 1946–50, served RAF Shaluffa and Abu Sueir 1951–53, HQ RAF Fighter Cmd 1953–54, sr tech offr RAF Patrington 1954–56, Guided Weapons Devpt Royal Radar Estab Malvern 1957–60, Operational Requirements Staff Air Miny 1961–63, Cmd Telecomms Offr NEAF 1964–67, chief instr RAF Coll Cranwell 1967–68, memb Air Force Bd Ctee on RAF Career Structure 1968–69, asst dir signals MOD 1969–72, controller Def Communications Network 1972–74, Air Offr Wales and Station Cdr RAF St Athan 1974–76, Air Cdre Signals RAF Support Cmd 1976–78; Mid Suffolk DC: cncllr 1983–95, chm Policy and Resources Ctee 1990–92, chm of Cncl 1992–94, ldr 1990–95; chm Wingfield Parish Cncl, churchwarden; CEng, FRAes 1976, FIMgt 1976; *Recreations* tennis, shooting, horticulture; *Clubs* RAF; *Style*— Air Cdre Bernard Wellingham; ✉ The White House, Wingfield, Diss, Norfolk IP21 5QT (☎ 01379 384 639)

WELLINGS, David Gordon; s of Gordon Henry Wellings (d 1970), of Middleton, Manchester, and Muriel, *née* Giddings; *b* 13 Dec 1940; *Educ* Alkrington County Sch, Manchester Grammar, Oriel Coll Oxford (Heath Harrison Travel Scholarship, MA); *m* 1962, Jennifer Christine, da of John Eric Simpson; 1 da (Karen Julie b 22 Sept 1963), 1 s (Antony David b 16 March 1968); *Career* mangr Biscuits Product Gp Cadbury Bros Ltd 1962–68, mktg mangr then mktg dir Associated Fisheries Foods Ltd 1968–73, md Northray Foods Ltd 1973–78; Imperial Group plc 1978–86: variously ops dir Ross Foods Ltd, chm and md Golden Wonder Ltd, HP Foods Ltd and Lea & Perrins Ltd, business devpt dir Imperial Foods Ltd; Cadbury Schweppes plc: md Cadbury Ltd 1986–89, md Confectionery Stream 1986–93, gp chief exec 1993–96; non-exec dir Signet Group plc 1992–; *Recreations* golf, ornithology; *Style*— David Wellings, Esq; ✉ Signet Group plc, Zenith House, The Hyde, London NW9 6EW (☎ 0181 905 9000, fax 0181 200 9466)

WELLINGS, Sir Jack Alfred; kt (1975), CBE (1970); s of late Edward Josiah Wellings, of Surrey; *b* 16 Aug 1917; *Educ* Selhurst GS, London Poly; *m* 1946, Greta, da of late George Tidey, of Sunderland; 1 s, 2 da; *Career* vice pres Hawker Siddeley (Canada) Ltd 1952–62; chm: The 600 Group Ltd 1968–87 (md 1963–84), On Line Business and Scientific Systems Ltd 1984–, Craigmore House Ltd 1985–; memb Nat Enterprise Bd 1977–79; pt/t memb: NCB 1971–77, Br Aerospace 1980–87; Liveryman Worshipful Co of Founders; *Style*— Sir Jack Wellings, CBE; ✉ Boundary Meadow, Collum Green Rd, Stoke Poges, Bucks SL2 4BB (☎ 01753 662978)

WELLINGS, Victor Gordon; QC (1973); s of late Gordon Arthur Wellings, and Alice Adelaide Wellings (who later m Charles Arthur Poole, decd); *b* 19 July 1919; *Educ* Reading Sch, Exeter Coll Oxford (MA); *m* 1948, Helen Margaret Jill, da of late Henry Lovell; 3 s; *Career* Capt IA 17 Dogra Regt and Int Corps India 1940–46; called to the Bar Gray's Inn 1949, in practice 1949–73; dep High Court judge 1975–92, pres Lands Tbnl 1989–92 (memb 1973–88); Hon ARICS 1993; *Recreations* golf, fishing; *Clubs* United Oxford and Cambridge University; *Style*— Victor Wellings, Esq, QC; ✉ Cherry Tree Cottage, Whitchurch Hill, Nr Reading, Berks RG8 7PT

WELLINGTON, 8 Duke of (UK 1814); Arthur Valerian Wellesley; KG (1990), LVO (1952), OBE (1957), MC (1941), DL (Hants 1975); also Baron of Mornington (I 1746), Earl of Mornington, Viscount Wellesley (both I 1760), Viscount Wellington of Talavera and of Wellington, Baron Douro (both UK 1809), Conde do Vimeiro (Portugal 1811), Earl of Wellington (UK 1812), Marquess of Wellington (UK 1812), Duque de Ciudad Rodrigo and a Grandee of the 1 Class (Spain 1812), Duque da Victoria, Marques de Torres Vedras (both Portugal 1812), Marquess of Douro (UK 1814), and Prince of Waterloo (Netherlands 1815); s of 7 Duke of Wellington, KG (d 1972); *b* 2 July 1915; *Educ* Eton, New Coll Oxford; *m* 1944, Diana, da of Maj-Gen Douglas McConnel, CB, CBE, DSO, of Knockdolian, Ayrshire; 4 s, 1 da; *Heir* s, Marquess of Douro; *Career* patron of 4 livings; Brig (ret) RHG, CO 1955–58; Silver Stick in Waiting and Lt-Col cmdg Household Cav 1959–60 & OC 22 Armd Bde 1960–61; cdr RAC BAOR 1962–64; defence attaché Madrid 1964–67; Col-in-Chief The Duke of Wellington's Regt 1974–; Hon Col 2 Bn Wessex Regt TA & VRA; nat vice-pres Royal Br Legion; dir Massey Ferguson Holdings 1967 and Massey Ferguson Ltd 1973–89; vice pres and cncl memb Zoological Soc of London 1973–89; pres and dep pres the Game Conservancy 1976–87; pres: Rare Breeds Survival Tst 1982–86, Cncl for Environmental Conservation 1983–86, Atlantic Salmon Trust 1983–, Hampshire Association of Parish Councils 1994–, National Canine Defence League 1996–; Queen's Tstee Bd of Royal Armouries 1983–95; chm Pitt Club, govr Wellington Coll; tstee: Lawes Agric Tst 1989–, Centre for Agric Strategy Univ of Reading 1988–95, World Wildlife Fund (UK) 1985–90; tstee and dep chm Thames Salmon Tst 1986–; vice pres The Kennel Club 1987–; dep pres RASE 1993 (hon vice pres and memb Cncl); Gd Cross Order of Isabel the Catholic (Spain) 1986, Légion d'Honneur (France); *Clubs* Buck's, Cavalry and Guards'; *Style*— His Grace the Duke of Wellington, KG, LVO, OBE, MC; ✉ Stratfield Saye House, Basingstoke, Hants RG27 0AS; Apsley House, Piccadilly, London W1V 9FA

WELLINGTON, John Treloar; s of Basil Wellington (d 1986), of Melbourne, Aust, and Eunice, *née* Lowe; *b* 18 March 1945; *Educ* Thornbury Sch Melbourne, Northcote Sch Melbourne; *Career* 3MA Mildura Vict Aust 1961, Victorian Bdcasting Network 1962–64, Tasmanian Bdcasting Network 1964–66, Aust Bdcasting Cmmn (now Corp) and overseas serv Radio Aust Melbourne 1966–73, fndr memb Capital Radio London 1973–74, fndr memb Metro Radio Newcastle upon Tyne 1974–75, fndr memb Radio Orwell Suffolk 1975–77, London Bdcasting Co and Ind Radio News London 1977–79, fndr memb Nat Bdcasting Sch London 1979–81, fndr memb Essex Radio Chelmsford and Southend 1981–84, fndr memb Radio Mercury Reigate and Crawley 1984– (merged with County Sound Radio Guildford to become Allied Radio plc, 1992); Allied Radio plc: gp prog dir 1992–93, non-exec dir 1993–; fndr London Country Radio (Country 1035) 1993; non-exec dir: KFM (Kent and Sussex Radio Ltd) 1995–, Alice Soundtech plc 1995–, Spartan Media Holdings Ltd 1995–, Spartan Communications Ltd 1995–; pres Reigate Opera 1992–96; *Recreations* music, films, television, travel, food and wine; *Style*— John Wellington, Esq; ✉ c/o PO Box 1, Crawley, West Sussex RH11 9TT (☎ 01293 519161)

WELLMAN, Glenn; s of Edward John Wellman, of Castleshaw, Delph, Yorkshire, and Isabella Jean, *née* Fordyce; *b* 5 Jan 1948; *Educ* Audenshaw GS Lancs, Imperial Coll London (BSc), Manchester Business Sch (MBA); *m* 1973, Barbara Ann Howe; 1 s (Benjamin Alexander b 1977), 1 da (Rachel Lucy b 1978); *Career* asst investmt mangr Esso Petroleum Company 1976 (investmnt analyst 1970), sr vice pres and md Alliance Capital Management 1985 (vice pres 1979), md CSFB Investment Management 1993; memb Inst of Personnel Management 1970, assoc Soc of Investment Analysts 1973; *Publications* author of various papers and articles in learned journals; *Recreations* gardening, history, theatre; *Style*— Glenn Wellman, Esq; ✉ CS Investment Management Ltd, Beaufort House, 15 St Botolph Street, London EC3A 7JJ

WELLS, Alan Peter; s of Ernest William Charles Wells, of Newhaven, and Eunice Mae, *née* Dyke; bro of Colin Wells, *qv*; *b* 2 Oct 1961; *Educ* Tideway Comp Sch Newhaven; *m* 26 Sept 1987, Melanie Elizabeth, da of Barry William Last; 1 s (Luke William Peter b 29 Dec 1990); *Career* professional cricketer; Sussex CCC: debut 1981, awarded county cap 1986, 270 first class appearances, capt v Leics 1990 (won game and scored undefeated century), capt 1992–; NCA under 19 tour Canada 1979; England: Young England v India 1981, unofficial tour SA 1989–90 (1 test match, 2 one day ints), vice capt A team to SA 1993–94, capt A team to India and Bangladesh 1994–95; record partnership for brothers in first class cricket with Colin Wells scoring 303 undefeated v Kent 1987; Sussex Player of the Year 1989 and 1993, Sussex leading batsman 1989–94; off-seasons: laboratory asst Artex 1981, insurance salesman 1984–87, proprietor corporate outwork business Newhaven 1988–94 (brother and father co-directors); *Recreations* country pubs, Indian cuisine, music of Sting, other sports; *Style*— Alan Wells, Esq; ✉ Sussex CCC, County Ground, Eaton Road, Hove BN3 3AN (☎ 01273 732161)

WELLS, Allan; MBE (1982); s of George Jackson Wells (d 1991), of Edinburgh, and Catherine, *née* Ramsey (d 1990); *b* 3 May 1952; *Educ* Liberton HS; *m* 29 June 1974, Margot Cumming, da of John Wilkie; 1 da (Zoe Allana b 1 Feb 1985), 1 s (Simon Allan b 24 June 1987); *Career* former int athlete; competed at 100m, 200m and 4 x 100m relay, memb Edinburgh Southern Harriers, Scot and GB int; honours incl: Gold medal 200m, Silver medal 100m and Gold medal 4 x 100m Cwlth Games 1978, runner-up Golden Sprint 1979, Gold medal 100m and Silver medal 200m Europa Cup, Gold medal 100m and Silver medal 200m Olympic Games 1980, winner Golden Sprint 1981, Gold medal 100m and Silver medal 200m World Cup 1981, Gold medal 200m and Silver medal 100m Europa Cup 1981, Gold medal 100m/200m and Bronze medal 4 x 100m Cwlth Games 1982; Br records: 60m indoor 1978, 100m 1978–86, 200m 1978–87; Scot Sportsman of the Year 1978–82; marine engr 1967–80, public relations 1980–82, currently fitness conslt; Hon Doctorate Univ of Surrey; *Recreations* formula 1 motor racing, training; *Style*— Allan Wells, Esq, MBE; ✉ 14 Oakley Dell, Merrow Park, Guildford, Surrey GU4 7HJ (☎ 01483 37683)

WELLS, (William Arthur) Andrew; TD (1984); s of Sir John Wells, DL, *qv*; *b* 14 June 1949; *Educ* Eton, Birmingham and N London Univs (BA); *m* 19 Oct 1974, Tessa Margaret, da of Lt-Col Jocelyn Eustace Gurney, DSO, MC, DL (d 1973), of Tacolneston Hall, and Sprowston, Norfolk, n of John Gurney, *qv*; 2 s (William b 1980, Frederick b 1982), 1 da (Augusta b 1984); *Career* TA: cmmnd Wessex Yeo (Royal Glos Hussars) 1971, visiting lectr Jr Div Staff Coll 1978–79, Maj Royal Green Jackets 1981–90; publishing 1969–81, property management Minories Holdings Ltd and Watermen's Co 1981–91, agent and curator Leeds Castle Kent 1992–, dir Leeds Castle Enterprises Ltd 1996–; tstee Chevening Estate 1992–; memb: Kent TA Ctee, Exec Ctee Friends of Kent Churches, Exec Ctee CPRE (Kent); Hon Freeman Watermen's Co 1991; *Recreations* architectural and art history, country interests; *Style*— Andrew Wells, Esq, TD; ✉ Mere House, Mereworth, Maidstone, Kent ME18 5NB; Leeds Castle, Maidstone, Kent ME17 1PL (☎ 01622 765400, ☎ and fax 01622 880249)

WELLS, Archdeacon of; *see:* Acworth, Ven Richard Foote

WELLS, (Petrie) Bowen; MP (C) Hertford and Stortford (majority 20,210); s of late Reginald Laird Wells by his w Agnes, *née* Hunter; *b* 4 Aug 1935; *Educ* St Paul's, Univ of Exeter, Regent St Poly Mgmnt Sch; *m* 1975, Rennie Heyde; 2 s; *Career* Nat Serv RN 1954–56; schoolmaster Colet Court 1956–57, sales trainee British Aluminium 1957–58, Commonwealth Developments Corpn 1961–73 (various positions incl co sec and industl rels mangr Guyana Timbers 1965–67), owner mangr Substation Group Services Ltd 1973–79; MP (C): Hertford and Stevenage 1979–83, Hertford and Stortford 1983–; PPS to: Michael Alison as Min of State for Employment 1982–83, Roger Freeman as Public Tport Min and the Earl of Caithness as Min for Aviation and Shipping 1992–94; asst Govt whip 1994–95, Lord Cmmr of HM Treasy (Govt whip) 1995–; memb: Foreign Affrs Select Ctee 1981–92, Euro Legislation Select Ctee 1983–92; chm: UN Parly Gp 1983–92, Br-Caribbean Gp; jt sec All Pty Gp on Overseas Devpt, memb Gen Cncl of Conservative Gp for Europe; memb Exec Cwlth Parly Assoc (CPA) 1984–, regnl rep Int CPA; govr: Inst of Devpt Studies Univ of Sussex 1980–94, Centre for Caribbean Studies Univ of Warwick; tstee Indust and Parly Tst 1985–; *Books* Managing Third World Debt, Growing Out of Debt; *Recreations* music, walking, gardening, cooking, sailing; *Style*— Bowen Wells, Esq, MP; ✉ House of Commons, London, SW1A 0AA

WELLS, Boyan Stewart; s of Gordon Tebbutt Wells, of Bristol, and Vera, *née* Stanisic; *b* 3 June 1956; *Educ* Colston's Sch Bristol, Wadham Coll Oxford (MA, Hockey blue); *m* 11 Aug 1984, Alison Jayne, da of Michael Albert Good, of Bristol; 3 da (Holly Catharine b 8 May 1987, Elena Rose b 2 Dec 1988, Laura Elizabeth b 9 Dec 1994); *Career* ptnr Allen & Overy 1987– (joined 1979); Freeman: City of London, Worshipful Co of Slrs 1987; memb: Friends of Dulwich Soc, Law Soc; *Recreations* golf, cinema; *Clubs* Richmond Hockey, Dulwich Golf; *Style*— Boyan Wells, Esq; ✉ Allen & Overy, One New Change, London EC4M 9QQ (☎ 0171 330 3000, fax 0171 330 9999)

WELLS, (Jennifer) Brigid Ellen; JP (Brighton 1980); da of Dr Leonard John Haydon, TD (late Col RAMC, d 1976), of Speldhurst, nr Tunbridge Wells, Kent, and Susan Eleanor, *née* Richmond (d 1958); *b* 18 Feb 1928; *Educ* Francis Holland Sch London, Malvern Girls' Coll (fndn scholar), Beaver Co Day Sch Boston Mass, Branksome Hall Toronto (Govr-Gen's medal), Masters' Sch Dobbs Ferry NY, Univ of Edinburgh, Lady Margaret Hall Oxford (scholar, MA), Univ of Brighton (PG Dip in counselling 1995); *m* 10 Feb 1962, Ian Vane Wells, s of Edgar George Wells (d 1944), of IOW; 3 da (Susanna Ellen Vane (Mrs Evans) b 1963), Elena Mary (Mrs Munro) b 1964, Jessica Isabel b 1968); *Career* Cwlth Relations Office: asst princ 1949–56, 2nd sec UK High Cmmn Wellington NZ 1952–54, private sec to Parly Under Sec of State for Cwlth Relations 1954–56; princ MAFF 1956–62; teacher ILEA 1962–63 and 1969–75; head of dept: Camden Sch for Girls 1973–75, St David & St Katharine's Sch Hornsey 1975–77; headmistress Brighton & Hove HS GPDST 1978–88; JP (Inner London) 1972–78; memb Broadcasting Complaints Cmmn 1986–93 (chm Jan-June 1992), assessor Civil Serv Selection Bd 1989–95, chm Friends of the GPDST 1991–; project mangr USA GAP Activity Projects Ltd 1988–91; chm designate W Sussex Ambulance Serv NHS Tst 1993–94; govr Woldingham Sch 1989–, cmmr Duke of York's Royal Military Sch 1993–, ARCS sch inspr 1995–; *Recreations* travel, gardening, choral singing; *Style*— Mrs Brigid Wells, JP; ✉ Cherry Trees, Bradford Road, Lewes, East Sussex BN7 1RD

WELLS, Sir Christopher Charles; 3 Bt (UK 1944), of Felmersham, Co Bedford; s Sir Charles Maltby Wells, 2 Bt, TD (d 1996), and Katharine Boulton, *née* Kenrick; *b* 12 Aug 1936; *Educ* McGill Univ, Toronto Univ (MD); *m* 1, 1960 (m dis 1984), Elizabeth, da of I Griffiths, of Outrement, Quebec; 2 s (Michael b 1966, Geoffrey b 1970), 2 da (Felicity b 1964, Megan b 1969); m 2, 1985, Lynda Ann Cormack, of Toronto, Ontario; 1 s (Andrew b 1983); *Heir* s, Michael Christopher Gruffydd Wells b 1966; *Career* MD in family practice; *Style*— Sir Christopher Wells, Bt; ✉ 1268 Seaforth Crescent, R R Number 3, Lakefield, Ontario, KOL 2HO, Canada

WELLS, Dr (John) Christopher Durant; s of late Colin Durant Wells, of Cae Coch, Bryn Siencyn, Anglesey, and Barbara Gwynneth, *née* Williams; *b* 5 Oct 1947; *Educ* Manchester GS, Univ of Liverpool (MB, ChB); *m* 14 Aug 1971, Sheila Frances, da of Patrick Joseph Murphy, of Wallasey, Merseyside; 2 da (Amanda b 1973, Sally b 1977); *Career* various hosp appts 1970–82, conslt anaesthetist Mersey RHA 1982–95; dir: Centre For Pain Relief and Regnl Neuroscience Unit Walton Hosp Liverpool 1983–94, Pain Relief Res Inst Liverpool 1983–; hon conslt: in pain relief Marie Curie Homes 1984–, Clatterbridge Centre for Oncology 1992–, Neurosciences Unit Walton Hosp 1996–; hon sr lectr Depts of Anaesthesia and Neurological Sciences Univ of Liverpool 1985–; recently completed res projects incl: acupuncture analgesia, effects of percutaneous cordotomy, mechanism of action of pituitary ablation in pain relief, treatment and prevention of post-herpetic neuralgia, the use of opiods and other drugs via the spinal route, causes and treatment of trigeminal neuralgia, new treatments in migraine; current res incl: the use of implanted drug delivery systems, the management of back pain, the rehabilitation of chronic pain sufferers; pioneered rehabilitation progs in the UK for chronic pain sufferers, starting with first continuously running prog in 1982; numerous presentations at maj nat and int meetings incl: morphine in cancer pain Toronto 1984, mgmnt of chronic back pain Aust 1991, pain relief in the 90's Jordan 1996, update on relief of cancer pain Istanbul 1996; pres: Self Help In Pain, People In Pain; memb Ctee Pain Soc of GB and NI (chm Educ and Sci Sub-Ctee); memb: BMA, Int Assoc for Study of Pain, Royal Soc of Pain Clinicians; fndr memb and past pres Pain Interest Gp; LRCP 1970, MRCS 1970, LMCC 1973, FFARCS 1978; *Books* numerous pubns on pain incl: The Clinical Neurology of Old Age (contrib, 1989), Ballieres Clinical Rheumatology (contrib, 1987), Pain Mechanisms and Management (1991), In Pain? (1993); *Recreations* curling (for Wales), skiing, horse-riding, samba music, chess; *Style*— Dr Christopher Wells; ✉ 45a Rodney Street, Liverpool L1 9EW (☎ 0151 708 9344, fax 0151 707 0609)

WELLS, Colin Mark; s of Ernest William Charles Wells, of Newhaven, East Sussex, and Eunice Mae, *née* Dyke; bro of Alan Wells, *qv*; *b* 3 March 1960; *Educ* Tideway Sch Newhaven; *m* 25 Sept 1982 (m dis), Celia Lilian, da of George James Corbett; 1 da (Jessica Louise b 2 Oct 1987); *Career* professional cricketer; Sussex CCC: first class debut 1979, awarded county cap 1982, over 300 appearances, vice capt 1988–90; joined Derbyshire CCC 1994–97 (cap 1995), 2nd XI coach/capt Somerset CC 1997–; Border South Africa 1980–81, Western Province South Africa 1984–85; represented MCC v Championship winners 3 times, 2 one day ints England (v Aust and Pakistan) 1985; amateur player Newhaven and Brighton & Hove; *Recreations* all sports, keep fit, cooking, wines; *Style*—

Colin Wells, Esq; ✉ c/o Derbyshire CCC, County Cricket Ground, Nottingham Road, Derby DE2 6DA

WELLS, Prof David Arthur; s of Arthur William Wells (d 1993), of Lancing, West Sussex, and Rosina Elizabeth, *née* Jones (d 1986); *b* 26 April 1941; *Educ* Christ's Hosp Horsham, Gonville and Caius Coll Cambridge (MA, PhD); *Career* lectr in German: Univ of Southampton 1966–69, Bedford Coll London 1969–74; prof of German: The Queen's Univ of Belfast 1974–87, Birkbeck Coll London 1987–; hon sec Modern Humanities Res Assoc 1969–, sec-gen Int Fedn for Modern Languages and Literatures 1981–; FRSA 1985; *Books* The Vorau Moses and Balaam (1970), The Wild Man from the Epic of Gilgamesh to Hartmann von Ave's Iwein (1975), A Complete Concordance to the Vorauer Bücher Moses (1976), The Years Work in Modern Language Studies (jt ed, 1976–); *Recreations* travel; *Style*— Prof David Wells; ✉ 128 Belgrave Rd, London SW1V 2BL (☎ 0171 834 6558); Department of German, Birkbeck College, Malet St, London WC1E 7HX (☎ 0171 631 6103, fax 0171 383 3729)

WELLS, David George; s of George Henry Wells, of Welford, Northants, and Marian, *née* Trolley (d 1988); *b* 6 Aug 1941; *Educ* Market Harborough GS, Univ of Reading (BA); *m* 27 Oct 1967, Patricia Ann, da of George Fenwick (d 1983), of Southampton; 2 s (Jonathan b 1968, Colin b 1971); *Career* Hancock Gilbert & Morris 1962–67, Esso Chemical Ltd 1967–69, Gas Cncl 1969–72; British Gas: chief acct admin 1973–76, chief investmt acct (HQ) 1976, dir fin (SE Region) 1976–83, dep chm (W Midlands regn) 1983–88, SE regnl chm (plc) 1988–93, md Regnl Servs 1993, md Service 1993–; dep chm Metrogas Bldg Soc 1979–83 (dir 1978–86); chm South London Trg and Enterprise Cncl 1989–93; dir Port Greenwich Ltd 1989–94; FCA 1966, CIMgt 1990, Companion IGasE 1988; FRSA 1991; *Recreations* walking, reading, photography, gardening; *Style*— David Wells, Esq; ✉ British Gas, Service, Lakeside House, 30 The Causeway, Staines, Middlesex TW18 3BY (☎ 01784 874001)

WELLS, David Patrick Casey; s of late Frank Wells, and Bridget Theresa, *née* Casey; *b* 24 Nov 1950; *Educ* St Joseph's Coll Blackpool Lancs, QMC London (LLB); *m* 28 Dec 1991, Michele Jane; 2 da (Holly, Hannah); *Career* admitted slr 1976, slr Herbert Smith 1976–81; ptnr: Reynolds Porter Chamberlain 1981–88, Titmuss Sainer & Webb (now Titmuss Sainer Dechert) 1988–96; memb Law Soc; *Recreations* rugby (Blackheath), swimming, reading and family; *Style*— David Wells, Esq

WELLS, Dean of; *see:* Lewis, Very Rev Richard

WELLS, Prof George Albert; s of George J Wells (d 1960), and Lilian Maud, *née* Bird (d 1986); *b* 22 May 1926; *Educ* Stationers' Company's Sch, UCL (BA, MA, PhD, BSc); *m* 29 May 1969, Elisabeth, da of Franz Delhey, of Aachen; *Career* Nat Serv in coal mines 1944–45; lectr in German UCL 1949–64 (reader 1964–68), prof of German Birkbeck Coll London 1968–88; emeritus prof Univ of London 1988–, hon assoc Rationalist Press Assoc; *Books* Herder and After (1959), The Plays of Grillparzer (1969), The Jesus of the Early Christians (1971), Goethe and the Development of Science (1978), The Historical Evidence for Jesus (1982), Did Jesus Exist? (1986), The Origin of Language (1987), J M Robertson - Liberal, Rationalist and Scholar (ed, 1987), Religious Postures (1988), Who Was Jesus? - A Critique of the New Testament Record (1989), Belief and Make-Believe (1991), What's in a Name? Reflections on Language, Magic and Religion (1993), The Jesus Legend (1996); jt ed of three books by F R H Englefield: Language, Its Origin and Relation to Thought (1977), The Mind at Work and Play (1985), Critique of Pure Verbiage - Essays on Abuses of Language in Literary, Religious and Philosophical Writing (1990); *Recreations* walking; *Style*— Prof George Wells; ✉ 35 St Stephens Ave, St Albans, Herts AL3 4AA (☎ 01727 851347)

WELLS, Graham Holland; s of Edmund Holland Wells, RD (d 1974), and Pamela Doris, *née* Siddall; *b* 28 May 1959; *Educ* Shrewsbury, Brasenose Coll Oxford (MA); *m* 21 Jan 1984, Dr Susan Margaret Wells, da of James Edgar Riley Tompkin, of Desford, Leicestershire; *Career* called to the Bar Middle Temple 1982; *Recreations* rowing, skiing, hill walking, water colour and oil painting; *Style*— Graham Wells, Esq; ✉ Derby Square Chambers, Refuge Assurance House, Derby Square, Liverpool, Merseyside L2 1TS (☎ 0151 709 4222, fax 0151 708 6311)

WELLS, John Campbell; s of Rev Eric George Wells (d 1984), and Dorothy Mary, *née* Thompson (d 1960); *b* 17 Nov 1936; *Educ* Eastbourne Coll, St Edmund Hall Oxford (MA); *m* Teresa, da of Sir Christopher Chancellor, of The Old Priory, Ditcheat, Somerset; *Career* author, playwright and actor; 2 Lt Royal Sussex Regt 1955; writer: Mrs Wilson's Diary (with Richard Ingrams), The Dear Bill Letters (with Richard Ingrams), play Anyone for Denis? (in which he played the lead, Whitehall Theatre) 1982, Rude Words: a discursive history of the London Library (1990), screenplay Princess Caraboo (jtly, also acted) 1994, Princess Caraboo: Her True Story (1994), A Brand from the Burning (1995); various translations include: Danton's Death, The Marriage of Figaro (NT), La Vie Parisienne (Scottish Opera), The Magic Flute (City of Birmingham Touring Opera), Cyrano de Bergerac (Haymarket) 1992; dir: La Vie Parisienne, Mikado (D'Oyly Carte), The Bold Fisherman (TVS), A Brand from the Burning (RSC) 1995; memb: The Literary Soc, The Dramatists' Club; *Recreations* walking, talking; *Style*— John Wells, Esq; ✉ 1a Scarsdale Villas, London W8 6PT (☎ 0171 937 0534)

WELLS, Prof John Christopher; s of Rev Philip Cuthbert Wells (d 1974), of Walton-on-Trent, and Winifred May, *née* Peaker; *b* 11 March 1939; *Educ* St John's Sch Leatherhead, Trinity Coll Cambridge (BA), Univ Coll London (MA, PhD); *Career* UCL: asst lectr in phonetics 1962–65, lectr 1965–82, reader 1982–88, prof 1988–; former pres World Esperanto Assoc, former chm London Esperanto Club; FBA 1996; *Books* Teach Yourself Concise Esperanto Dictionary (1969), Practical Phonetics (1971), Jamaican Pronunciation in London (1973), Accents of English (1982), Longman Pronunciation Dictionary (1990); *Style*— Prof J C Wells, FBA; ✉ Department of Phonetics & Linguistics, University College, Gower St, London WC1E 6BT (☎ 0171 380 7175, fax 0171 383 4108)

WELLS, Capt John Gerard; CBE (1964), DSC (1940); s of Vice Adm Sir Gerard Aylmer Wells, KBE (d 1943); *b* 22 Sept 1915; *Educ* Summer Fields Oxford, RNC Darmouth; *m* 1947, Diana, da of Lt-Gen Sir Edmond Schreiber, KCB, DSO; 2 s; *Career* served RN 1929–64; WWII served Atlantic, Med and Pacific; cmd: HMS Dainty 1959, HMS Excellent 1961, HMS Kent 1963; ret Capt; gen mangr Aviemore Centre 1964–70, dir Clarkson Holidays 1970–74, conslt Wakeman Trower & Ptnrs 1975–76, gen mangr Gulfspan 1977–78, Mgmnt Business Servs (London) 1980–81, res historian HMS Warrior (1860) 1981–87, chm Warrior Assoc 1985; *Books* Whaley - The Story of HMS Excellent 1830–1980, The Immortal Warrior, Britain's First and Last Battleship, The Royal Navy - an Illustrated Social History 1870–1982; *Recreations* sailing, skiing, shooting, stalking, golf, naval historical research; *Clubs* Army and Navy, Royal Cruising; *Style*— Capt John Wells, CBE, DSC, RN; ✉ High Firs House, Hatch Lane, Liss, Hants (☎ 01730 893343)

WELLS, Sir John Julius; kt (1984), DL (Kent 1992); o s of Rev (Arthur) Reginald Kemble Wells (d 1964), and Margaret Evelyn, *née* Hodgson; ggg nephew of John Wells, JP, DL, MP for Maidstone 1820–30; *b* 30 March 1925; *Educ* Eton, CCC Oxford (MA); *m* 31 July 1948, Lucinda Mary Helen Francis, eld da of Francis Ralph Meath Baker, JP, of Hasfield Court, Glos; 2 s ((William Arthur) Andrew *qv*, Oliver Reginald b 5 Nov 1955), 2 da (Julia Jane (Mrs James Luard) b 1 Feb 1951, Henrietta Frances b 27 Feb 1952); *Career* served WWII in HM Submarines; contested (C) Smethwick 1955, MP (C) Maidstone 1959–87; chm: Cons Pty Horticultural Ctee 1965–71 and 1973–87, Horticulture Sub Ctee of Agric Select Ctee 1968, Parly Waterways Gp 1974–80; vice chm Cons Agric Ctee 1970; memb Mr Speaker's Panel of Chairmen 1974–87; pres Nat Inst of Fresh Produce 1984–90; Master Worshipful Co of Fruiterers 1977, Hon Freeman of Maidstone 1979; Knight Cdr Order of Civil Merit (Spain) 1972, Cdr Order of Lion (Finland) 1984; *Style*— Sir John Wells, DL; ✉ Mere House Barn, Mereworth, Kent ME18 5NB; Acheillie Lodge, Rogart, Sutherland

WELLS, Malcolm Henry Weston; s of Lt Cdr Geoffrey Weston Wells (d 1988), and Inez Brenda, *née* Williams (d 1967); *b* 26 July 1927; *Educ* Eton; *m* 20 Dec 1952, (Helen) Elizabeth Agnes, da of Rt Rev Bishop Maurice Henry Harland (d 1986); 1 s (Nicholas Weston b 1954), 1 da (Caroline Felicity b 1956); *Career* RNVR 1945–48; Peat Marwick Mitchell 1948–58 (articled clerk, latterly asst mangr), SIEBE plc 1958–63 (sec, latterly md); dir: Charterhouse Japhet plc 1963–73 (chm 1973–80), Charterhouse Group 1964–80 (joined 1963), Civil Aviation Authy 1974–77; chm: Charterhouse Petroleum plc 1977–82, BWD Securities plc 1987–95, German Securities Investment Trust plc 1985–89; dir: Carclo Engineering Group plc 1982–, Nat Home Loans Holdings plc 1989–93, Bank in Liechtenstein Ltd 1981–90 (London rep, latterly md); memb Solicitors Disciplinary Tbnl 1975–81; *Recreations* sailing; *Clubs* City of London; *Style*— M H W Wells, Esq; ✉ 100 Palace Gardens Terrace, London W8 4RS (☎ 0171 727 5228)

WELLS, Prof Michael; s of John Thomas Wells (d 1975), of Cannock, Staffs, and Lily, *née* Ellis; *b* 7 Aug 1952; *Educ* Pool Hayes Sch Willenhall, Univ of Manchester (BSc, MB ChB, MD); *m* 1, 21 Dec 1974 (m dis 1992), Jane Cecila, da of John Parker Gill, of Gosforth Cumbria; 1 s (James b 1980), 1 da (Rosemary b 1982); m 2, 27 May 1994, Lynne Margaret Austerberry, da of Raymond George Walker, of Blythe Bridge, Staffs; *Career* lectr in pathology Univ of Bristol 1978–79, sr lectr in pathology Univ of Leeds 1988–93 (lectr 1980–88); hon conslt Utd Leeds Teaching Hosps NHS Trust 1983–93; clinical sub dean: Leeds West Univ of Leeds Sch of Med 1988–91, St James's Univ Hosp 1994–96; hon conslt pathologist St James's Univ Hosp Leeds 1993–96, ptnr Roundhay Pathologists (BUPA Hosp) Leeds 1993–96; prof of gynaecological pathology: Univ of Leeds 1993–96, Univ of Sheffield Med Sch 1997–; hon conslt histopathologist Central Sheffield Univ Hosps 1997–; memb: Assoc of Clinical Pathologists Speciality Ctee on Histopathology 1989–93, Exec Ctee Int Soc of Gynaecological Pathologists 1991–94, Cncl Br Gynaecological Cancer Soc 1990–92 (pres 1994–97), Part 1 MCQ Sub-ctee RCOG 1989–95, Sub-ctee for the Co-ordination of Research into Gynaecological Cancer of the UK Co-ordinating Ctee on Cancer Research 1991–, Jt RCOG/Wellbeing Research Advsy Ctee 1996–, Panel of Examiners in Histopathology RCPath, Editorial Advsy Bd Placenta 1990–95; memb Editorial Bd: Epithelial Cell Biology, Histopathology, Int Jl of Gynaecological Pathology; assoc ed Papillomavirus Report 1990–93; hon sec Br Div of the Int Acad of Pathology 1988–93, meetings sec Pathological Soc of GB and I 1996–; FRCPath 1995 (MRCPath 1983); *Books* Haines and Taylor Obstetrical and Gynaecological Pathology (asst ed, 4 edn, 1995); author/co-author of 125 chapters, review articles and original papers; *Recreations* reading, choral singing, cycling, gardening; *Style*— Prof Michael Wells; ✉ 8 Rosebank, Burley-in-Wharfedale, Ilkley, W Yorkshire LS29 7PQ (☎ 01943 862719, e-mail mike@mikewell.demon.co.uk, mobile 0973 426554); Department of Pathology, The University of Sheffield Medical School, Beech Hill Road, Sheffield S10 2RX (☎ 0114 271 2733, fax 0114 278 0059)

WELLS, Prof Peter Bernard; s of Kenneth Edward Bainton Wells (d 1974), and Kathleen Mary Newman Wells (d 1988); *b* 9 Aug 1936; *Educ* Marling Sch Stroud Glos, Univ of Hull (BSc, PhD); *m* 28 Dec 1963, Maureen, da of Alfred Stephenson (d 1983); 1 s (Richard Peter Kerwin b 1970), 2 da (Catherine Mary b 1964, Sarah Judith b 1967); *Career* Univ of Hull: asst lectr in chemistry 1961, subsequently lectr, sr lectr, reader in physical chemistry, prof of physical chemistry 1981–89, G F Grant prof of chemistry 1989–, assoc dir Res Centre for Surface Engrg 1991–; author of several papers on heterogeneous catalysis, surface engrg and corrosion sci; chm Prog Mgmnt Ctee SERC/DTI LINK Prog on New Catalysts and Catalytic Processes; FRSC; *Publications* author of over 100 scientific papers on heterogeneous catalysis; *Recreations* music; *Style*— Prof Peter Wells; ✉ University of Hull, School of Chemistry, Hull HU6 7RX (☎ 01482 465660, fax 01482 466410)

WELLS, Dr Peter George; s of Joseph Frederick Wells (d 1973), and Daisy Irene, *née* Sissons (d 1963); *b* 27 April 1925; *Educ* Giggleswick Sch, Univ of Sheffield (MB ChB, Dip Child Health, Dip Obstetrics, Dip Psychological Med); *m* 28 Nov 1970, (Finola) Fidelma; 1 s ((John) Oliver Lancaster b 1972), 1 da (Mary Jane b 1973); *Career* RN 1943–46, Sub Lt RNVR 1945 (midshipman 1944); conslt for adolescent psychiatric servs Mersey and NW RHAs 1970–92, assoc lectr Univ of Manchester, hon clinical teacher Univ of Liverpool; memb: Nat Exec Assoc for Psychiatric Study of Adolescence 1978–83, Exec Ctee NW Div RCPsych 1982–86, BMA; founder and developer of Richmond Fellowship Mental After-Care Home Chester and Mental After Care Social Clubs Cheshire 1964–70; Silver medal (for film) BMA 1969, survey and report on the mental health needs of adolescents in the Hunter Valley (Health Cmmn NSW Aust) 1980–81; Cheadle prize (for res paper Inpatient treatment of 165 adolescents with emotional and conduct disorders - a study of outcome) 1992; MRCPsych 1971, FRCPsych 1979, MRANZCP 1981, FRANZCP 1983; *Recreations* sailing, skiing, ornithology, family history, surveying the lie of the land; *Style*— Dr Peter Wells; ✉ High Trees, Dark Lane, Henbury, Macclesfield, Cheshire SK11 9PE

WELLS, Prof Peter Neil Temple; s of Sydney Parker Temple Wells (d 1976), and Elizabeth Beryl Wells (d 1987); *b* 19 May 1936; *Educ* Clifton Coll Bristol, Univ of Aston (BSc), Univ of Bristol (MSc, PhD, DSc); *m* 15 Oct 1960, Valerie Elizabeth, da of Charles Edward Johnson (d 1982), of Burnham-on-Sea, Somerset; 3 s (Andrew b 1963, Alexander b 1965, Thomas b 1970), 1 da (Lucy b 1966); *Career* res asst United Bristol Hosps 1960–71, prof of med physics Univ of Wales Coll of Med (formerly Welsh Nat Sch of Med) 1972–74, area physicist Avon AHA (teaching) 1975–82; chief physicist: Bristol and Weston Health Authy 1982–91, United Bristol Healthcare NHS Tst 1991–; hon prof in clinical radiology Univ of Bristol 1986–; over 250 pubns mainly on med applications of ultrasonics; former pres Br Inst of Radiology, vice pres World Fedn for Ultrasound in Med and Biology, pres Instn of Physics and Engrg in Medicine and Biology (FIPEMB 1995); FInstP 1970, FIEE 1978, FEng 1983, Hon FRCR 1987; *Books* Physical Principles of Ultrasonic Diagnosis (1969), Biomedical Ultrasonics (1977); *Style*— Prof Peter Wells, FEng; ✉ Department of Medical Physics and Bioengineering, Bristol General Hospital, Bristol BS1 6SY (☎ 0117 928 6274)

WELLS, Chief Constable Richard Burton; QPM (1987); s of Walter Percival (Bill) Wells (d 1969), of Ramsgate, and Daphne Joan, *née* Harris (d 1982); *b* 10 Aug 1940; *Educ* Sir Roger Manwood's GS Sandwich, Priory Sch Shrewsbury, St Peter's Coll Oxford (open exhibition, MA); *m* Patricia Ann, da of Lewis Edward James Smith (d 1942), of Kent; 1 s (James b 1973), 1 da (Caroline b 1975); *Career* Met Police: joined 1962, uniform and CID Constable Bow St 1962–66, Special Course Police Staff Coll 1966–67, uniformed duties Sergeant and station Sergeant 1967–68, uniformed duties Inspr Commercial St and Leman St 1968–70, uniformed duties Inspr Hendon Trg Sch 1970–73, operational cmd Chief Inspr Whetstone 1973, community liaison offr as Chief Inspr then Supt Notting Hill, Kensington and Chelsea 1973–76, operational cmd as Supt Hampstead 1976–79, operational cmd as Chief Supt Hammersmith 1979–80, Chief Supt Community Relations Branch New Scotland Yard 1980–81, Sr Cmd Course Police Staff Coll 1981, operational cmd as dist Chief Supt Paddington, Marylebone and Harrow Rd 1981–82, Chief Supt then Cdr Hendon Trg Sch 1982–83, Dep Asst Cmmr 1983–90, dir of public affrs 1983–86, operational cmd (7 area) NW London 1986–90; Chief Constable S Yorks 1990–; chm ACPO Personnel and Trg Ctee; memb Fulbright Cmmn; pres: Young

Enterprise for S Yorks, Deepcar Brass Band 1992; Freeman City of London 1992, Offr Brother Order of St John 1994; CIMgt; *Recreations* Tai Chi, hockey (capt Shropshire county schoolboys XI 1959), walking, gardening, music, painting, reading, genealogy and historical research; *Style*— Chief Constable Richard Wells, QPM; ✉ South Yorkshire Police HQ, Snig Hill, Sheffield S3 8LY (☎ 0114 252 3400, fax 0114 252 3481, telex 547996)

WELLS, Richard Michael; s of Peter Michael Wells, of S Yorks, and Mary, *née* Target; *b* 30 April 1947; *Educ* Wombwell Secdy Modern Sch S Yorks, Univ of Sheffield (BA); *m* July 1988, Jacqueline Elizabeth, da of late Stanley Everett, of Teesside; 1 step s (Kevin), 1 step da (Jessica); *Career* indentureship South Yorkshire Times 1964–68, gen reporter Sheffield Morning Telegraph 1968–71, mature student Univ of Sheffield 1971–74; BBC Radio: reporter then prodr BBC Radio Sheffield 1974–78, reporter London 1978–80, freelance 1980–85, rejoined BBC Radio as N of England corr 1985–, also assignments in India and Saudi Arabia; memb Nat Cncl RSPB 1978–83 and 1984–89 (chm Info and Educn Ctee 1985–88); *Recreations* hunting, birdwatching; *Clubs* National Hunting, RSPB; *Style*— Richard Wells, Esq; ✉ BBC Broadcasting Centre, Woodhouse Lane, Leeds LS2 1PN (☎ 0113 243 6076, fax 0113 242 0652, mobile 0860 373624)

WELLS, Prof Stanley William; s of Stanley Cecil Wells, MBE (d 1952), of Hull, and Doris, *née* Atkinson (d 1986); *b* 21 May 1930; *Educ* Kingston HS Hull, UCL (BA), The Shakespeare Inst Univ of Birmingham (PhD); *m* 23 April 1975, Susan Hill, the novelist, *qv*; 3 da (Jessica b 1977, Imogen b and d 1984, Clemency b 1985); *Career* Nat Serv RAF 1951 (invalided out); Shakespeare Inst: fell 1962–77, lectr 1962, sr lectr 1971, reader 1973–77, hon fell 1979–88; prof of Shakespeare studies and dir Shakespeare Inst Univ of Birmingham 1988–; conslt in Eng Wroxton Coll 1964–80, head of Shakespeare Dept OUP 1978–88, sr res fell Balliol Coll Oxford 1980–88, fell UCL 1994; dir Royal Shakespeare Theatre Summer Sch 1971–, pres Shakespeare Club of Stratford-upon-Avon 1972–73; memb: Exec Ctee Shakespeare's Birthplace 1976–78 and 1988– (tstee 1975–81 and 1984–, dep chm 1990, chm 1991–); Royal Shakespeare Co: govr 1974–, memb Exec Ctee 1976–, chm Membership Ctee 1991–, chm Collections Ctee 1991–, vice chm Bd of Govrs 1991–; guest lectr at Br and overseas univs, Br Acad Annual Shakespeare lectr 1987, Br Cncl Melchiori lecture Rome 1991; govr King Edward VI GS for Boys 1973–77; assoc ed New Penguin Shakespeare 1967–, gen ed Oxford Shakespeare 1978–, ed Shakespeare Survey 1980–; author of contribs to: Shakespeare Survey, Shakespeare Quarterly, Shakespeare Jahrbuch, Theatre Notebook, Stratford-upon-Avon Studies, TLS, and others; Hon DLitt Furman Univ 1976; memb: Soc for Theatre Res 1963–, Cncl Malone Soc 1967–90, tstee Rose Theatre 1991–, dir Globe Theatre Tst 1990–; Walford Prize (for sustained contribs to bibliographies) Library Assoc 1994; *Books* Thomas Nashe, Selected Writings (ed, 1964), A Midsummer Night's Dream (ed, 1967), Richard II (ed, 1969), Shakespeare, A Reading Guide (1969 and 1970), Literature and Drama (1970), The Comedy of Errors (ed, 1972), Shakespeare (ed 1973, 2 edn 1990), English Drama Excluding Shakespeare (ed, 1975), Royal Shakespeare (1977 and 1978), Nineteenth Century Burlesques (compiled in 5 vols, 1977), Shakespeare: An Illustrated Dictionary (1978 and 1985), Shakespeare: The Writer and his Work (1978), Thomas Dekker, The Shoemaker's Holiday (ed with RL Smallwood, 1979), Modernizing Shakespeare's Spelling, with Three Studies in the Text of Henry V (with Gary Taylor, 1979), Re-editing Shakespeare for the Modern Reader (1984), Shakespeare's Sonnets (ed, 1985), The Complete Oxford Shakespeare (ed with Gary Taylor *et al*, 1986), The Cambridge Companion to Shakespeare Studies (ed, 1986), William Shakespeare: A Textual Companion (with Gary Taylor *et al*, 1987), An Oxford Anthology of Shakespeare (1987), Shakespeare: A Dramatic Life (1994), Shakespeare and the Morning Image (ed, with E A Davies, 1994), Twelfth Night (ed, with Roger Warren, 1994); *Recreations* music, travel; *Style*— Prof Stanley Wells; ✉ Longmoor, Ebrington, Chipping Campden, Glos GL55 6NW (☎ 01386 593352, fax 01386 593443); The Shakespeare Institute, Stratford upon Avon, Warwicks (☎ 01789 293138)

WELLS, Sir William Henry Weston; kt (1997); s of Sir Henry Wells, CBE (d 1970), and Rosemary Halliday, *née* Whitchurch (d 1977); *b* 3 May 1940; *Educ* Radley, Magdalene Coll Cambridge (BA); *m* 1 Jan 1966, Penelope Jean, da of Col R B Broadbent (d 1979); 3 s (Rupert d 1969, George b 1971, Henry b 1972); *Career* chm: Land and House Property Group 1977, Frincon Holdings Ltd 1977–87, Chesterton 1983–; dir: London Life Association 1984–89, London Life Ltd 1990–, Pearl Group plc 1994–, Norwich & Peterborough Building Society 1994–; memb Bd of Govrs: Royal Free Hosp 1968–74, Camden and Islington AHA 1972–82; chm Special Tstees of the Royal Free Hosps 1979–, memb Cncl Royal Free Hosp Sch of Med 1977–91, pres Royal Free Hosp Retirement Fellowship 1994–; chm: Hampstead Health Authy 1982–90, Royal Free Hampstead NHS Tst 1991–94, S Thames RHA 1994–96, South Thames Regional Office 1996–; memb Cncl NHS Tst Fedn 1991–93 (vice chm 1992–93), memb NHS Policy Bd 1994–; hon treas: Royal Coll of Nursing 1988–, Nat Assoc of Leagues of Hosp Friends 1992–; dir AMP UK Bd 1989–; FRICS; *Recreations* family, philately, gardening; *Clubs* Boodle's; *Style*— Sir William Wells; ✉ 54 Brook St, London W1A 2BU (☎ 0171 499 0404)

WELLWOOD, James McKinney; s of James Wellwood (d 1967), of Belfast, and Violet Armstrong McKinney (d 1978); *b* 18 Dec 1940; *Educ* Fettes, Univ of Cambridge, St Thomas' Hosp Medical Sch London; *m* 1, 8 March 1975, Frances Alexandria Ruth, da of Stephen Howard, of Hertfordshire, England; m 2, 24 July 1982, Anne Margaret, da of Sydney Jones Samuel, of Llanelli, Wales; 1 s (James b 1984), 1 da (Laura b 1988); *Career* conslt surgn Whipps Cross Hosp Leytonstone London 1979, hon sr lectr Med Coll of St Bartholomew Smithfield London 1979, clinical tutor Waltham Forest District 1983–91, clinical dir of surgery Whipps Cross Hosp 1991–; hon overseas sec The Br Assoc of Surgical Oncology 1986–91 (hon sec 1982–86), Br del The European Soc of Surgical Oncology 1986–90; memb: Educn Advsy Ctee Assoc of Surgns of GB and Ireland 1987–90, Waltham Forest DHA 1983–90, UK Cncl Assoc of Endoscopic Surgns of GB and I 1994–; Queen's Commendation for Brave Conduct 1971; Liveryman Worshipful Soc of Apothecaries; *Recreations* skiing, shooting, travel; *Clubs* Athenaeum, Royal Soc of Medicine; *Style*— James Wellwood, Esq; ✉ 50 Clifton Hill, St John's Wood, London NW8 0DG (☎ 0171 625 5697); Whipps Cross Hospital, Leytonstone, London E17 (☎ 0181 539 5522); 134 Harley St, London W1N 1AH (☎ 0171 487 4212)

WELSBY, John Kay; CBE (1990); *b* 26 May 1938; *Educ* Univ of Exeter (BA), Univ of London (MSc); *m* 1964, Jill Carole Richards; 1 s, 1 da; *Career* Govt Economic Serv 1966–81; British Railways Bd: dir Provincial Services 1981–83, dir Mfrg and Maintenance Policy 1984–86, md Procurement and Special Projects 1986–87, bd memb 1987–, chief exec 1990–95, chm 1995–; memb Cncl Industrial Soc 1995, tstee Industry in Educn; Liveryman Worshipful Co of Carmen's 1992, Freeman City of London 1992; CIMgt 1991, FCIT; *Recreations* walking, music, swimming; *Style*— John Welsby, Esq, CBE; ✉ British Railways Board, Euston House, 24 Eversholt St, London NW1 1DZ (☎ 0171 922 6300, fax 0171 922 4003)

WELSER-MÖST, Franz; *b* 16 Aug 1960; *Career* conductor; music dir: London Philharmonic Orch 1990–96 (music dir emeritus 1996–), Zurich Opernhaus 1995–; previously held positions in Lausanne and Winterthur Switzerland and Norrköping Sweden, int debut Salzburg Festival 1985; has worked with orchs incl: NY Philharmonic, St Louis, Boston and Chicago Symphony Orchs, Philadelphia Orch, Cleveland Orch, Oslo Philharmonic, Bayerischer Rundfunk; *Performances* operatic engagements incl: Rossini's L'Italiana in Algeri (Vienna State Opera) 1987, The Marriage of Figaro (Vienna State Opera) 1988, La Clemenza di Tito (Deutsche Oper Berlin) 1991, Der Rosenkavalier (Zurich Opernhaus) 1992, Rusalka (Zurich Opernhaus) 1994, Peter Grimes (Glyndebourne Festival) 1994, Werther (Zurich Opernhaus) 1996, Parsifal (Zurkch Opernhaus) 1996; *Recordings* for EMI incl: Mendelssohn Symphonies No 3 and 4, Bruckner Symphony No 7, Strauss Waltzes, Orff Carmina Burana, Stravinsky Oedipus Rex, Bartok Miraculous Mandarin with Kodaly Peacock Variations, Lehar Die Lustige Witwe, Bruckner Symphony No 5 (live with LPO), Beethoven Symphony No 5 (live with LPO), Schmidt Symphony No 4; *Style*— Franz Welser-Möst, Esq; ✉ c/o Kathryn Enticott, IMG Artists Europe, Media House, 3 Burlington Lane, London W4 2TH (☎ 0181 233 5800, fax 0181 233 5801)

WELSH, Andrew Paton; MP (SNP) Angus East (majority 954); s of William Welsh (d 1979), and Agnes Paton, *née* Reid (d 1977); *b* 19 April 1944; *Educ* Univ of Glasgow (MA, Dip Ed); *m* 1971, Sheena Margaret, da of Douglas Henry Cannon (d 1972); 1 da (Jane b 1980); *Career* Parly candiate (SNP): Dumbarton Central Feb 1974, Angus E 1983; MP (SNP): Angus S Oct 1974–1979, Angus E 1987–; SNP chief Parly whip 1978–79 and 1987–; SNP spokesman on: housing and agric 1974–79 and 1987–, small businesses and self employment 1975–79 and 1987–; chief SNP whip 1987–; Parly Select Ctee on Members Interests 1990–, Parly Select Ctee on Scottish Affairs 1992–; SNP exec vice chm: admin 1979–82, local govt 1983–86; SNP vice pres 1987–, lectr in public admin and economics Dundee Coll of Commerce 1979–83, sr lectr in business and admin studies Angus Coll of Further Educn 1983–87; memb Stirling DC 1974, memb and provost Angus DC 1984–87; *Recreations* music, horse riding, languages; *Style*— Andrew Welsh, Esq, MP; ✉ office: SNP, Community Centre, Marketgate, Arbroath DD11 1HR (☎ 01241 874522, fax 01241 871561); House of Commons, London SW1A OAA

WELSH, Prof (James Anthony) Dominic; s of James Welsh (d 1967), of Port Talbot, and Teresa, *née* O'Callaghan; *b* 29 Aug 1938; *Educ* Bishop Gore Sch Swansea, Merton Coll Oxford (exhibitioner, MA, DPhil), Carnegie Mellon Univ USA (Fulbright Scholar); *m* 1965, Bridget Elizabeth, da of Very Rev John Francis Pratt; 3 s (James Justin Siderfin b 16 June 1967, Simon David Patrick b 19 Nov 1969, John Francis b 3 Oct 1971 d 1990); *Career* research Bell Telephone Labs Murray Hill NJ USA 1961; Univ of Oxford: lectr Mathematical Inst 1966–90 (jr lectr 1963–66), fell Merton Coll 1966, tutor in mathematics Merton Coll 1966–90, ad hominem reader in mathematical scis 1990–92, ad hominem prof of mathematics 1992–; research visitor Univ of Michigan 1968; visiting prof: Univ of Waterloo 1969, Univ of Calgary 1974; John von Neumann prof Univ of Bonn 1990–91; chm Univ of Oxford: Dean's Ctee 1972–73, Faculty of Mathematics 1976–78, Faculty Bd of Mathematics 1984–86; Merton Coll Oxford: princ of postmasters 1970–73, sub-warden 1982–84; chm Br Combinatorial Soc 1983–87, memb London Mathematical Soc 1964 (memb Cncl 1972–76); *Books* Matroid Theory (1976), Probability; an Introduction (with G R Grimmett, 1986), Codes and Cryptography (1988), Complexity: Knots Colourings and Counting (1993); *Recreations* mosts sports (particularly rugby and real tennis), art, walking; *Style*— Prof Dominic J A Welsh; ✉ South Lodge, Rose Lane, Oxford OX1 4DT (☎ 01865 247449); Mathematical Institute, 24–26 St Giles, Oxford, OX1 3LB (☎ 01865 276325, fax 01865 276383)

WELSH, Frank Reeson; s of Francis Cox Welsh (d 1974), of Westmorland, and Doris (Reeson) Ibbet; *b* 16 Aug 1931; *Educ* Blaydon GS, Magdalene Coll Cambridge (MA); *m* 1954, Agnes, da of John Embleton Cowley, OBE, of Co Durham; 2 s (Benjamin, John), 2 da (Jane, Sophie); *Career* dir: William Brandts Sons 1965–72, Grindlays Bank 1972–85, The Trireme Trust 1983–; chm: Cox & Kings 1972–77, Jensen Motors Ltd 1968–72, Hadfields Ltd 1967–79, Robey of Lincoln 1967–78, The London Industl Assoc 1984–88; memb: Royal Cmmn on the NHS 1976–79, Br Waterways Bd 1975–81, Gen Advsy Cncl IBA 1976–80, Health Educn Cncl 1978–80; CIMgt; *Books* The Profit of the State (1982), The Afflicted State (1983), First Blood (1985), Bend'or (with George Ridley, 1985), Uneasy City (1987), Building the Trireme (1988), Companion Guide to the Lake District (1989, 2 edn 1997), A History of Hong Kong (US edn, A Borrowed Place) (1993, revised 1997); *Recreations* sailing (barge 'Remercie'), building triremes; *Clubs* Utd Oxford and Cambridge; *Style*— Frank Welsh, Esq; ✉ Bonnezac 86250, France

WELSH, John Christopher; s of Thomas A Welsh, and Mary, *née* Croker, of Cumbria; *b* 29 March 1962; *Educ* William Ellis Sch, Ulverston Victoria HS, Sedbergh Coll, Univ of Durham; *Career* draughtsman Brian Clouston & Ptnrs 1984–87, asst ed Designers' Journal 1987–89, buildings ed Building Design 1990–93 (features writer 1989–90), ed RIBA Journal 1993–; *Books* Rick Mather's Zen Restaurants (1992), Massimiliano Fuksas (1994), Modern house (1995); *Style*— John Welsh, Esq; ✉ RIBA Journal, 40 Marsh Wall, London E14 9TP (☎ 0171 560 4000)

WELSH, Michael John; s of Cdr David Welsh, RN; *b* 22 May 1942; *Educ* Dover Coll, Lincoln Coll Oxford; *m* 1963, Jennifer Pollitt; 1 s, 1 da; *Career* formerly with Levi Strauss & Co Europe (dir of market devpt 1976); MEP (EDG) Lancs Central 1979–94; chm Chorley and Dist NHS Tst 1994–, res assoc Univ of Central Lancs 1994–, chief exec Action Centre for Europe Ltd 1995–; *Books* Labour Market Policy In The European Community - The British Presidency (1987), Collective Security - The European Community and the Preservation of Peace (1988), German Unification - The Challenge of Assimilation (1990), Accountability - The Role of Westminster and the European Institutions (1990), Europe United? The European Community and the retreat from Federalism (1995); *Clubs* Carlton; *Style*— Michael Welsh, Esq; ✉ Watercrook, 181 Town Lane, Whittle le Woods, Chorley, Lancs PR6 8AG (☎ 01257 276992, fax 01257 231254)

WELSH, Maj-Gen Peter Miles; OBE (1973), MC (1966); s of Brig (William) Miles Moss O'Donnell Welsh, DSO, MC (d 1965), of Lismore, Sonning, Berks, and Mary Margaret Edith Gertrude Louise, *née* Hearn (d 1991); *b* 23 Dec 1930; *Educ* Winchester, RMA Sandhurst; *m* 1974, June Patricia, da of Francis MacAdam, of Buenos Aires, Argentina, widow of M E McCausland; 2 step s, 1 step da; *Career* army offr; directing staff Staff Coll 1968–71, CO 2 Royal Green Jackets 1971–74, cmd 5 Inf Bde 1974–76, RCDS 1977, BGS HQ BAOR 1978–80, Brig Lt Div 1980–83, pres Regular Cmmns Bd 1983–85; *Recreations* golf, shooting; *Clubs* MCC, I-Zingari, Free Foresters, Berks Golf; *Style*— Maj-Gen Peter Welsh, OBE, MC; ✉ Streeve Hill, Limavady, Co Londonderry BT49 0HP

WEMYSS, Rear Adm Martin La Touche; CB (1981); s of Cdr David Edward Gillespie Wemyss, DSO, DSC, RN (d 1989), of Luthrie, Fife, and Edith Mary Wemyss (d 1930); *b* 5 Dec 1927; *Educ* Shrewsbury; *m* 1 (m dis), Ann Hall; 1 s, 1 da; m 2, 1973, Elizabeth Loveday, da of Col Robert Harper Alexander, RAMC (d 1969), of Kingston Gorse, Sussex; 1 s, 1 da; *Career* Cmdg Offr: HMS Sentinel, HMS Alliance, Submarine COs Qualifying Course, HMS Norfolk, 3 Submarine Sqdn; Dir Naval Warfare 1974–76, Flag Offr Second Flotilla 1977–78, Rear Adm 1977, asst chief of Naval Staff (Ops) 1979–81; Clerk Worshipful Co of Brewers 1981–91; *Recreations* sailing, gardening; *Clubs* White's, Army & Navy; *Style*— Rear-Adm Martin Wemyss, CB; ✉ The Old Post House, Emberton, nr Olney, Bucks MK46 5BX (☎ 01234 713838)

WEMYSS AND MARCH, 12 (and 8) Earl of (S 1633 & 1697); Francis David Charteris; KT (1966), JP (E Lothian); also Lord Wemyss of Elcho (S 1628), Lord Elcho and Methil (S 1633), Viscount Peebles, Lord Douglas of Neidpath, Lyne, and Munard (S 1697), and Baron Wemyss of Wemyss (UK 1821); s of Lord Elcho (ka 1916, s and h of 11 Earl, but predeceased him) and Lady Violet Manners (d 1971), 2 da of 8 Duke of Rutland; suc gf 1937; *b* 19 Jan 1912; *Educ* Eton, Balliol Coll Oxford, Trinity Coll Cambridge; *m* 1, 24 Feb 1940, Mavis Lynette Gordon (d 1988), er da of Edwin Edward Murray, of Hermanus, Cape Province, SA; 1 s, 1 da (and 1 s, 1 da decd); m 2, 29 April 1995, Mrs Shelagh Kathleen Kennedy, da of George Ernest Thrift, of Vancouver, BC,

Canada; *Heir* s, Lord Neidpath; *Career* Basutoland Admin Serv 1937–44 (war serv with Basuto troops ME 1941–44); landowner; former dir: Standard Life Assurance, Scottish Television; conslt Wemyss and March Estate Mgmnt Co Ltd; chm: Nat Trust for Scotland 1946–67 pres 1967–91, pres emeritus 1991–; chm Royal Cmmn on Ancient and Hist Monuments and Constructions of Scotland 1949–84, Lord High Cmmr to Gen Assembly of Church of Scotland 1959, 1960 and 1977, pres Nat Bible Soc of Scotland 1962–83, Lord Lt E Lothian 1976–87, Lord Clerk Register of Scotland and Keeper of the Signet 1974–, Lt Royal Co of Archers (Queen's Body Guard for Scotland), hon pres The Thistle Fndn; Hon LLD St Andrews 1953, Hon DUniv Edinburgh 1983; *Clubs* New (Edinburgh); *Style*— The Rt Hon the Earl of Wemyss and March, KT, JP; ✉ Gosford House, Longniddry, East Lothian EH32 0PX (☎ 01875 87200)

WEN, Eric Lewis; s of Adam Kung Wen, of California, and Mimi, *née* Seetoo; *b* 18 May 1953; *Educ* Dalton Sch, Columbia Univ (BA), Yale Univ (MPhil), Churchill Coll Cambridge (res award); *m* 3 June 1989, Louise Anne, da of Sir Brian Barder, KCMG, *qv*; 2 da (Lily Havala b 5 Nov 1990, Florence Lydia b 26 May 1993); *Career* lectr in music: Yale Univ 1977–78, Guildhall Sch of Music and Drama 1978–84, Goldsmiths' Coll London 1980–84, Mannes Coll of Music 1984–86; ed: The Strad 1986–89, The Musical Times 1988–90; md Biddulph Recordings and Publishing 1990–; *Books* Schenker Studies (contrib, 1990), Trends in Schenkerian Research (contrib, 1990), The Cambridge Companion to the Violin (contrib, 1992); *Publications* The Heifetz Collection (ed, 1995); *Recreations* chess, cookery, film, card magic; *Style*— Eric Wen, Esq; ✉ 34 St George St, Hanover Square, London W1R 0ND (☎ 0171 491 8621, fax 0171 495 1428)

WENBAN-SMITH, Hugh Boyd; s of William Wenban-Smith, CBE, CMG, of Lymington, Hants, and Ruth Orme, *née* McElderry; *b* 6 Nov 1941; *Educ* Bradfield Coll, King's Coll Cambridge (open minor scholar, MA), UCL (MSc); *Career* Miny of Fin then Bank of Zambia (ODI/Nuffield Fellowship Scheme) Zambia 1964–67, NIESR 1967–68, econ advsr on progs in E Africa Miny of Overseas Devpt 1968–70, seconded to FCO as first sec to British High Cmmn New Delhi India 1970–74, econ advsr on steel, shipbuilding and rescue cases DTI 1975–77, sr econ advsr Price Cmmn 1977–79, seconded to Coopers and Lybrands Assocs 1979–80, head Water Fin and Econs Div DOE 1980–84; Dept of Tport: dir fin mgmnt 1984–89, under sec and head Marine Directorate 1989–93, head Civil Aviation Directorate 1993–95, dir Nat Roads Policy 1996–; *Style*— Hugh Wenban-Smith, Esq; ✉ Department of Transport, Great Minster House, 76 Marsham Street, London SW1P 4DP (☎ 0171 271 4969)

WENDT, Robin Glover; CBE (1996), DL (Cheshire 1990); s of William Romilly Wendt (d 1995), of Keswick, Cumbria, and Doris May, *née* Glover (d 1958); *b* 7 Jan 1941; *Educ* Hutton GS, Wadham Coll Oxford (MA); *m* 1965, Prudence Ann, da of Arthur Dalby; 2 da (Julia Margaret b 1967, Catherine Susan b 1970); *Career* asst princ Miny of Pensions and Nat Insurance 1962–65, princ Miny of Social Security/DHSS 1965–72 (princ private sec 1970–72), asst sec DHSS 1972–75, chief exec Cheshire CC 1979–89 (dep sec 1975–79), sec Assoc of County Councils 1989–; clerk Cheshire Lieutenancy 1979–90; vice pres Cheshire Magistrates Assoc 1990–, tstee Independent Living Funds 1993–; memb: Soc of Local Authy Chief Execs 1979–, Advsy Ctee Social Security 1982–, Poly and Colls Funding Cncl 1988–93; *Recreations* swimming, travel, music, following sport, gardening; *Style*— Robin Wendt, Esq, CBE, DL; ✉ Association of County Councils, Eaton House, 66A Eaton Square, London SW1W 9BH (☎ 0171 201 1517, fax 0171 235 5674)

WENNIKE, Helge; *b* 10 Nov 1944; *Educ* Commercial Coll Copenhagen; *m* 17 Feb 1973, Grete Else-Marie; 1 s (Nicolai b 1973), 1 da (Anne-Marie b 1976); *Career* mangr Privatbanken until 1978; md: RB-Banken 1978–80, Finansbank 1980–81, Jyske Bank 1981–84; dep md: Scandinavian Bank Group plc 1984–90, SVP Skandinaviska Enskilda Banken 1990–94; dir Pridecorp 1994–; chm Steff's Ltd; *Recreations* golf, tennis; *Clubs* RAC; *Style*— Helge Wennike, Esq; ✉ 6 Vincent House, Regency Street, London SW1P 4BX (☎ 0171 834 7258); 2 Grosvenor Gardens, London SW1W 0DH (☎ 0171 823 4034, fax 0171 823 4022)

WENSLEY, Dr Richard Thomas; s of Thomas Henry Wensley (d 1984), of Liverpool, and Florence Caroline, *née* Palmer; *b* 15 Oct 1939; *Educ* Merchant Taylors' Sch Crosby, Univ of Liverpool (MB ChB); *m* 24 Aug 1963, (Juliet) Patricia, da of James Ahearn (d 1972), of Cork, Ireland; 1 s (Richard James b 1966), 3 da (Carolyn Anne b 1964, Susan Kathrine (Mrs Martin Pickton) b 1965, Gillian Elizabeth b 1969); *Career* sr registrar in haematology Bristol Royal Infirmary 1969–74, dir Regnl Haemophilia Centre Manchester Royal Infirmary 1979–92 (conslt haematologist 1974–); numerous papers published and presented at Int Congress on Haemophilia; memb Br Soc of Haematology; MRCP 1973, FRCPath 1982 (MRCPath 1970); *Recreations* playing classical piano music, cooking exotic cuisine; *Style*— Dr Richard Wensley; ✉ The Manchester Clinic, A Floor, Manchester Royal Infirmary, Oxford Rd, Manchester M13 9WL (☎ 0161 276 4812)

WENSLEY, Prof (John) Robin Clifton; s of Maj George Leonard Wensley, and Jeanette Marion, *née* Robbins, of Cambridge; *b* 26 Oct 1944; *Educ* Perse Sch Cambridge, Univ of Cambridge (BA), London Business Sch (MSc, PhD); *m* 19 Dec 1970, Susan Patricia, da of Kenneth Royden Horner (d 1975), and Irene Lucy Horner; 2 da (Helen Rebecca b 1973, Ruth Elizabeth b 1975), 1 s (Benjamin Royden b 1978); *Career* brand mangr Rank Hovis McDougall 1966–69 (former PA), conslt Tube Investments Ltd 1971–73, asst dir of Studies Ashridge Coll 1973–74, sr lectr London Business Sch 1974–85 (former lectr), chm Warwick Business Sch 1989– (prof 1985–), dir BRL Ltd 1987–; memb ESRC Res Grants Bd 1993–, jt chair Assoc of Business Schs 1993–, memb Cncl Tavistock Res Inst 1992–; *Books* Marketing Strategy: Planning, Implementation and Control (1986), Readings in Marketing Strategy (1989), Interface of Marketing and Strategy (1990); *Recreations* badminton, gardening, DIY; *Style*— Prof Robin Wensley; ✉ Warwick Business School, University of Warwick, Coventry CV4 7AL (☎ 01203 523923, fax 01203 523719, telex 317472)

WENT, David; s of Arthur Edward James Went (d 1980), of Dublin, and Phyllis, *née* Howell (d 1980); *b* 25 March 1947; *Educ* High Sch Dublin, Trinity Coll Dublin (BA, LLB); *m* 4 Nov 1972, Mary, da of Jack Milligan (d 1972), of Belfast; 1 s (James b 1976), 1 da (Kate b 1978); *Career* barr King's Inn Dublin; gen mangr Citibank Dublin 1974 (Jeddah 1975), banking dir Ulster Investment Bank Dublin 1976 (chief exec 1982); chief exec: Ulster Bank 1988–94, Coutts & Co Group 1994–; FIBI 1978; *Recreations* tennis, reading; *Clubs* Royal Belfast Golf, Royal North of Ireland Yacht, University (Dublin), Fitzwilliam Lawn Tennis; *Style*— David Went, Esq; ✉ Coutts & Co Group, 27 Bush Lane, Cannon Street, London EC4R 0AA (☎ 0171 203 4770)

WENT, Rt Rev John Stewart; *see:* Tewkesbury, Bishop of

WENTWORTH, Stephen; s of Ronald Wentworth, OBE (d 1983), of London, and Elizabeth Mary, *née* Collins (d 1967); *b* 23 Aug 1943; *Educ* King's Coll Sch Wimbledon, Merton Coll Oxford (MA, MSc); *m* 9 May 1970, Katharine Laura, da of Rev Arthur John Hopkinson, CIE (d 1953), of, Aislaby, N Yorks; 3 da; *Career* Civil Serv: princ MAFF 1970–78 (asst princ 1967–70), on loan to Civil Serv Selection Bd 1974–75, Personnel Div MAFF 1975–76, on loan to HM Dip Serv as first sec (agric) Office of the UK Perm Rep to the Euro Communities Brussels 1976–78, asst sec head of Beef Div MAFF 1978–80, seconded Cabinet Office 1980–82, head of Milk Div MAFF 1982–85, head of Euro Communities Div 1985–86, promoted to grade 3 head of Meat Gp 1986–89, head of Livestock Products Gp 1989–91, head of Euro Community and External Trade Policy Gp 1991–93, Fisheries sec 1993–; *Style*— Stephen Wentworth, Esq; ✉ Ministry of Agriculture Fisheries & Food, Nobel House, Smith Square, London SW1P 3JR

WENTWORTH-STANLEY, (David) Michael; s of Geoffrey David Wentworth-Stanley, and Bridget, *née* Pease; *b* 29 Feb 1952; *Educ* Eton; *m* 7 Oct 1975, Jane, da of Col Tom Hall, OBE; 3 da (Laura b 12 Dec 1978, Emma b 28 May 1981, Harriet b 7 Aug 1985); *Career* CA 1974; Cazenove Inc NY 1981–83, ptnr Cazenove & Co 1982– (joined 1975); memb Bd Securities and Futures Authy 1995–; ACA 1974, FCA 1979; *Recreations* countryside, gardening, skiing; *Clubs* White's, MCC; *Style*— Michael Wentworth-Stanley, Esq; ✉ 41 Old Church St, London SW3 5BS (☎ 0171 352 3419); Cazenove & Co, 12 Tokenhouse Yard, London EC2R 7AN (☎ 0171 588 2828, fax 0171 606 9205)

WENTZELL, Pamela; *née* Moran; da of Herbert Thomas Moran, of London, and Teresa McDaid, *née* Conway; *b* 3 Feb 1950; *Educ* Pitman's Sch Ealing, Marlborough Coll London; *m* 18 Oct 1969, Christopher John, s of Charles John Wentzell, of Gurnard, IOW; *Career* md JP Communicators Ltd (PR consultancy) 1980–; former chm Southampton Publicity Assoc 1985–86, chm elect Wessex Branch IPR 1996–97; MIPR 1980, FInstD 1989; *Recreations* theatre going, classical music, gardening; *Style*— Mrs Pamela Wentzell; ✉ Roke Hollow, Woodington Lane, East Wellow, Hampshire (☎ 01794 517583); JP Communicators Ltd, Bedford House, 81 Bedford Place, Southampton SO1 2DF (☎ 01703 632738, fax 01703 230516)

WEST HAM, Archdeacon of; *see:* Fox, Ven Michael John

WESCHKE, Karl Martin; *b* 7 June 1925; *m* 1, 1948 (m dis 1957), Alison de Vere; 2 s (Benjamin, Lucas), 2 da (Lore, Rachel); m 2, 1963 (m dis 1968), Liese Dennis; *Career* artist and art lectr, came to Britain as POW 1948, designed sets for Berto Pasuka's Les Ballets Negres 1951–54, collaborated with Alison de Vere on Psyche and Eros (animated film cmmnd by Channel 4) 1989–94; *Work in Public Collections* incl: Arts Cncl of GB, City Art Gallery Bristol, Central Selling Orgn, Contemporary Art Soc London, Cornwall Educn Ctee, Ferens Art Gallery Hull, Govt Art Collection, City Art Gallery Plymouth, Tate Gallery London, Nat Museum of Wales Cardiff, Baltimore Museum of Art Maryland (Print Collection), Museum of Modern Art NY (Print Collection), Nat Gallery of Victoria Melbourne, Art Gallery of NSW Sydney; *Solo Exhibitions* incl: New Vision Centre Gallery London 1958, Woodstock Gallery London 1959, Matthiesen Gallery London 1960, Arnolfini Gallery Bristol 1964 and 1968, Grosvenor Gallery London 1964, Dartington Hall 1968, Bear Lane Gallery Oxford 1971, travelling exhibition 1971–72, Kettle's Yard Cambridge 1980, Moira Kelly Fine Arts London 1981, Redfern Gallery 1984, 1987, 1989, 1992 and 1994; *Retrospective Exhibitions* Whitechapel Art Gallery 1974, Newlyn Art Gallery Penzance 1974, travelling exhibition 1980–81; contrib to numerous major mixed exhibitions of Br art since 1959 in UK, USA, Asia, Germany and Austria; *Extended Display Exhibitions* Tate Gallery London Oct 1996 (transferring to Tate Gallery St Ives Nov 1996–April 1997); *Awards* incl: Arts Cncl of GB Major Award 1976, S W Arts Major Award 1978, prizewinner John Moores Exhibition 1978, Arts Cncl of GB Purchase Award 1980, shortlisted Jerwood Painting Prize 1995 (exhibited Royal Scottish Acad Edinburgh and Royal Acad of Arts London 1995); Hon DA Univ of Plymouth 1994; *Style*— Karl Weschke, Esq; ✉ Ruston, Cape Cornwall, St Just, Penzance, Cornwall TR19 7NL (☎ and fax 01736 788389)

WESKER, Arnold; s of Joseph Wesker (d 1959), and Leah, *née* Perlmutter (d 1976); *b* 24 May 1932; *Educ* Upton House Central Sch Hackney; *m* 1958, Doreen Cecile, da of Edwin Bicker, of Norfolk; 2 s (Daniel, Lindsay Joe), 2 da (Tanya Jo, Elsa Sarah); *Career* playwright and director; Nat Serv RAF 1950–52 (material gathered for later play Chips with Everything); various positions Norfolk 1952–54 (incl seed sorter, farm labourer and kitchen porter), trained pastry cook London and Paris 1954–56; awarded Arts Cncl grant 1958 and Writers' Bursary 1996; artistic dir Centre Fortytwo 1961–70, chm Br Centre of Int Theatre Inst 1978–82, pres Int Playwrights' Ctee 1979–83; *Stage Plays*: The Kitchen (1957), Chicken Soup with Barley (1958), Roots (1959), I'm Talking About Jerusalem (1960), Chips with Everything (1962), The Four Seasons (1965), Their Very Own and Golden City (1966), The Old Ones (1970), The Friends (1970), The Journalists (1972), The Wedding Feast (1974), Shylock (1976), Love Letters on Blue Paper (stories 1974, play 1976), One More Ride on the Merry-Go-Round (1978), Fatlips (book 1978, play 1980, renamed His Own Wings), Caritas (1980), Sullied Hand (1981), Anne Wobbler (1982), Four Portraits - of Mothers (1982), Yarsdale (1983), Cinders (1983), Whatever Happened to Betty Lemon (1986), When God Wanted a Son (1986), Badenheim 1939 (1987), Shoeshine & Little Old Lady (1987), Lady Othello (1987), Beorhtel's Hill (1988), The Mistress (1988), Three Women Talking (1990), Letter To A Daughter (1990), Blood Libel (1991), Wild Spring (1992), Circles of Perception (1996); *Film Scripts* The Wesker Trilogy (1979), Lady Othello (1980), Homage to Catalonia (1991), Maudie (1995); *Radio and TV Plays* Menace (1971), Breakfast (1981), Bluey (radio play 1984, stage play 1993), Thieves in the Night (4 part adaptation of Arthur Koestler's novel, 1984–85), Diary of a Good Neighbour (4 part adaptation of Doris Lessing's novel 1989); stories, essays and other writings incl: Six Sundays in January (1971), Say Goodbye You May Never See Them Again (1974), Love Letters on Blue Paper (1974), Words - as definition of experience (1976), Journey into Journalism (1977), Said The Old Man to The Young Man (1978), Fatlips (1978), Distinctions (1985), A Mini-Biography (1988), As Much As I Dare (autobiography, 1994); stage dir: The Four Seasons (Havana) 1968, The Friends (Stockholm and London) 1970, The Old Ones (Munich) 1973, Their Very Own and Golden City (Aahus) 1974, Love Letters on Blue Paper (Nat Theatre 1978 and Oslo 1980), The Entertainer (Theatre Clwyd) 1983, Annie Wobbler (Birmingham and London) 1984, Yarsdale (RSC Actor's Festival Stratford) 1985, Yarsdale and Whatever Happened to Betty Lemon (London) 1987, Shylock (workshop prodn, London) 1989, The Merry Wives of Windsor (Oslo) 1989–90, The Kitchen (Univ of Wisconsin USA) 1990, The Mistress (Rome) 1991, The Wedding Feast (Denison Univ of Ohio USA); Hon DLitt UEA 1989, Hon Dr of Humane Letters Denison Univ of Ohio 1997; Hon Fell Queen Mary and Westfield Coll 1995; FRSL; *Style*— Arnold Wesker, Esq; ✉ 37 Ashley Road, London N19 3AG (☎ 0171 272 0034, fax 0171 272 5370); c/o National Westminster Bank plc, 298 Seven Sisters Road, London N4 2AF

WESLEY, Mary Aline (Mary Siepmann); CBE (1995); da of Col Harold Mynors Farmar, CMG, DSO (d 1958), of Yarmouth, IOW, and Violet Dalby (d 1972); *b* 24 June 1912; *Educ* at home by foreign governesses, finishing sch Paris, LSE; *m* 1, 1937 (m dis 1945), 2 Baron Swinfen (d 1977); 2 s (Roger (3 Baron Swinfen), Hon Toby Eady); m 2, 1952, late Eric Siepmann, s of Otto Siepmann, of Clifton, Bristol; 1 s (William b 1953); *Career* writer; hon fell LSE; hon degree: Open Univ, Univ of Exeter; *Books* incl: Speaking Terms (for children, 1968), The Sixth Seal (for children, 1968), Haphazard House (for children, 1983), Jumping the Queue (1983), The Camomile Lawn (1984), Harnessing Peacocks (1985), The Vacillations of Poppy Carew (1986), Not That Sort of Girl (1987), Second Fiddle (1988), A Sensible Life (1990), A Dubious Legacy (1992), An Imaginative Experience (1994), Part of the Furniture (1997); *Recreations* reading; *Style*— Ms Mary Wesley, CBE; ✉ c/o Tessa Sayle Agency, 11 Jubilee Place, London SH3 3TE (☎ 0171 823 3883)

WESSON, Jane Louise; da of George Graham, resident France, and Joyce Mary, *née* Benson; *b* 26 Feb 1953; *Educ* Wolverhampton Girls' HS, Univ of Kent at Canterbury (BA, Anthony London prize); *m* 8 Oct 1977, William Jonathan Rhodes Wesson, s of William Herbert Beech Wesson; 1 da (Anna Clare b 22 Feb 1981), 1 s (William Alexander Henry b 28 Jan 1983); *Career* Lancaster Coll of Law 1975–76, articled clerk Pothecary & Barratt London 1976–78, slr Hepworth & Chadwick Leeds 1978–89; non-exec dir: Pontefract Health Authy 1990–93, Wakefield Health Authy 1993; a chm Child Support

Appeal Tbnls 1992–, chm Harrogate Healthcare NHS Tst 1993–; memb Bd Northern Counties Housing Assoc 1994–; *Recreations* sailing, singing, gardening; *Style*— Mrs Jane L Wesson; ✉ Harrogate Healthcare NHS Trust, Ebor Rise, Cornwall Road, Harrogate, N Yorks HG1 2PU (☎ 01423 885959, fax 01423 501391)

WEST, Rear Adm Alan William John; DSC (1982); *b* 1948; *Educ* BRNC Dartmouth; *m* Rosemary; 3 c; *Career* CO HMS Yarnton 1973, princ warfare offr 1977 (whereafter specialist appts on HMSS Juno, Ambuscade and Norfolk), Cdr 1980, CO HMS Ardent 1980–82 (served Indian Ocean, Arabian Gulf, Med, Atlantic and Falklands Campaign where sunk), in Directorate of Naval Plans MOD 1982–84, Capt 1984, Asst Dir of Naval Staff Duties 1985–86, Navy memb Interim Working Gp MOD 1986–87, CO HMS Bristol and Capt Dartmouth Trg Sqdn 1987–88, led study on future employment of women in RN 1988, head Maritime Intelligence Directorate 1989–92, RCDS 1992, HCSC 1993, Dir of Naval Staff Duties 1993–94, Rear Adm 1994, Naval Sec and DG Naval Manning 1994–96, COMUKTG/CASWSF (Commander United Kingdom Task Gp/Commander Anti-Submarine Warfare Striking Force) 1996–; *Style*— Rear Adm A W J West, DSC; ✉ COMUKTG/CASWSF, 7–8 The Parade, HM Naval Base, Portsmouth PO1 3NA (☎ 01705 726620, fax 01705 726647)

WEST, Brian John; s of Herbert Frank West, and Nellie, *née* Painter; *b* 4 Aug 1935; *Educ* Tiffin Sch Kingston-upon-Thames; *m* 2 April 1960 (m dis 1986), Patricia Ivy, da of Reginald White (d 1985), of Old Windsor, Berks; 2 s (Nicholas Guy b 7 July 1962, Jason Philip b 12 July 1966); m 2, 11 April 1987, Gillian, da of Anthony Bond (d 1984), of Flint, Clwyd; *Career* Sub Lt (O) Fleet Air Arm RN 1956–58; journalist 1952–60 (Richmond Herald, Surrey Comet, Western Morning News); ed: Surrey Comet 1964–70 (asst ed 1960–64), Leicester Mercury 1970–74; head of advtg and PR Littlewoods Organisation plc 1974–83, dir AIRC 1983–88, dir and chief exec AIRC 1988–95, ret; dir Radio Joint Audience Research Ltd (RAJAR) 1991–94, dir West Media 1995–; govr Communications Advtg and Mktg Fndn 1983–89; memb: Cncl Radio Acad 1985–91, Cncl and Exec Ctee Advtg Assoc 1987–95; chm Organising Ctee UK Radio Festival 1989–95, fndr pres Assoc of Euro Radios 1992; Winston Churchill fell 1995, fell Beaverbrook Fndn 1995, fell Radio Acad 1995; *Books* Radio Training in the United States (1996); *Recreations* riding, walking, gardening, photography, music, computers; *Style*— Brian West, Esq

WEST, Christopher John Rodney; s of Norman (Peter) Hartley West (d 1963), of Rio de Janeiro, Brasil, and Epsom, and Lucy Catherine West, *née* Skey (d 1962); *b* 6 April 1932; *Educ* St George's Coll Buenos Aires Argentina, Haileybury, UCL (BSc); *m* 31 March 1956, Patricia Anne, da of Kenneth Arthur Alexander Neilson (d 1972); 1 da (Helen b 1958), 2 s (Martin b 1960, Ian b 1964); *Career* Nat Serv Sub Lt RNVR; indust career plant mangr in ICI Plastics Div and Br Visqueen Ltd 1955–68, gen mgmnt BOC Gases Div 1968–71, dir Courtenay Mgmnt Selection Consultants 1971–; chm Assoc of Search and Selection Conslts; MIPM; *Recreations* sailing, walking; *Clubs* Naval, Devonshire House Dining; *Style*— Christopher West, Esq; ✉ Courtenay, 3 Hanover Sq, London W1R OAT (☎ 0171 491 4014, fax 0171 493 3183)

WEST, Prof David Richard Frederick; s of Sydney West (d 1990), and Frederica May, *née* Horsman (d 1986); *b* 7 March 1926; *Educ* Bromley County Sch, Univ Coll Cardiff (BSc), Imperial Coll London (PhD, DIC, DSc); *m* 23 June 1951, Phyllis Edith, da of Robert Wade (d 1956), of Bromley, Kent; 2 s (Peter Robert b 1954, Michael John b 1964), 1 da (Elisabeth Susan b 1957); *Career* scientific offr MOS 1949–50; Imperial Coll London: lectr 1950–63, sr lectr 1963–70, reader 1970–86, sr tutor in metallurgy and materials 1966–91, memb Governing Body 1981–89, prof of physical metallurgy 1986–91, emeritus prof and sr res fell 1991–; vice pres Inst of Materials 1990–91 (memb Cncl, chm Materials Sci and Technol Div); memb Rochester Diocesan Synod, lay chm Bromley Deanery Synod; FIM 1978, CEng 1978; *Books* Ternary Equilibrium Diagrams (1982); *Recreations* music, reading; *Style*— Prof David West; ✉ 39 St Mary's Avenue, Bromley, Kent BR2 0PU (☎ 0181 460 1567)

WEST, James Glynn; *b* 21 April 1947; *Educ* Eton; *Career* md Globe Investment Trust PLC 1987–90 (joined 1973), an md Lazard Bros & Co Ltd and chief exec Lazard Investors Ltd 1990–94; currently chm: Gartmore Micro Index Trust PLC, Principal Health Care Finance Ltd; currently non-exec dir: Abtrust New Dawn Investment Trust PLC, Abtrust Convertible Trust PLC, British Assets Trust PLC, Bensons Crisps PLC, Middlesex Holdings PLC, First Equity Ltd, LEPCO Ltd, Candover Investments PLC; FCA; *Clubs* City; *Style*— James West, Esq; ✉ Orchard House, Eastling, Nr Faversham, Kent ME13 0AZ (☎ 01795 890432, fax 01795 890353)

WEST, Prof John Clifford; CBE (1977); s of John Herbert West (d 1958), of Hindley, Lancs, and Ada, *née* Ascroft (d 1984); *b* 4 June 1922; *Educ* Hindley and Abram GS, Univ of Manchester (BSc, PhD, DSc); *m* 7 Jan 1946, Winefride Mary, da of Francis Herbert Turner, of Blackpool, Lancs (d 1973); 3 da (Angela b 1946, Julia b 1951, Clare b 1960); *Career* Nat Serv, Electrical Lt Anti-Submarine Warfare Branch RNVR 1943–46; lectr Univ of Manchester 1946–57, prof of electrical engrg Queen's Univ Belfast 1958–65, dean of applied sciences Univ of Sussex 1965–78, vice chancellor Univ of Bradford 1979–89, pres IEE 1984–85; chm: Civil Serv Cmmn Special Merit Promotions Panel 1966–72, Crawford Cmmn on Broadcasting Coverage 1973–74, Cncl for Educnl Technol 1980–85, Asian Inst of Business Bradford 1987–89, Int Review Cmmn Univ of Botswana 1990; consultat de l'Enseignement Supérieur Madagascar 1992; memb UGC 1973–78, tstee Br Philatelic Tst 1989–, treas Yorkshire Cancer Res Camp 1989–; Hon DSc Univ of Sussex 1988, Hon DUniv Bradford 1990; FIEE 1962, FRPSL 1970, FEng 1983, Hon FInstMC 1984, FRGS 1988, Hon FIEE 1992; *Books* Servomechanisms (1953), Analytical Techniques for Non-Linear Control Systems (1960), The Postmarks of Valparaiso (1994); *Recreations* philately; *Clubs* Athenaeum; *Style*— Prof John C West, CBE, FEng; ✉ 6 Park Crescent, Guiseley, Leeds LS20 8EL (☎ 01943 872605, fax 01943 879910); 11 Windlesham Hall, Windlesham Ave, Brighton BN1 3AH (☎ 01273 726913)

WEST, Martin Graham; s of Edward Graham West, of Bury, and Dorothy West (d 1987); *b* 7 Nov 1938; *Educ* Bury GS; *m* 1962, Jacqueline, da of Alfred Eric Allen (d 1959); 1 s (Jeremy b 1970), 2 da (Angela b 1965, Janine b 1967); *Career* dir British Mail Order Corporation Ltd 1973–76; London Scottish Bank plc: dir 1976–, chief exec 1988–, chm 1995–; FCA; *Recreations* classic car restoration, bridge, philately; *Clubs* St James's (Manchester); *Style*— Martin Graham West, Esq; ✉ The Chaplain's House, West Lane, High Legh, Knutsford, Cheshire WA16 6LR (☎ 01925 754448); London Scottish Bank plc, London Scottish House, 24 Mount Street, Manchester M2 3LS (☎ 0161 834 2861, fax 0161 834 2536)

WEST, Dr Martin Litchfield; s of late Maurice Charles West, and Catherine Baker, *née* Stainthorpe; *b* 23 Sept 1937; *Educ* St Paul's, Balliol Coll Oxford (Craven scholar, Hertford scholar, de Paravicini scholar, Dean Ireland's scholar, MA, DPhil, DLitt, Chancellor's prizes, Conington prize); *m* 31 Dec 1960, Stephanie Roberta, da of late Robert Enoch Pickard; 1 da (Rachel Ann b 17 July 1963), 1 s (Robert Charles b 17 May 1965); *Career* Univ of Oxford: Woodhouse jr res fell in classics St John's Coll 1960–63, fell and praelector in classics Univ Coll 1963–74; prof of Greek Univ of London 1974–91, sr res fell All Souls Coll Univ of Oxford 1991–; visiting lectr Harvard Univ 1967–68, res fell Japan Soc for the Promotion of Science 1980, visiting prof UCLA 1986; memb: Hellenic Soc, Classical Assoc, Jt Assoc of Classical Teachers, Oxford Philological Soc, London Classical Soc, Ancient Monuments Soc; hon memb Hungarian Classical Soc 1984, corresponding memb Akademie der Wissenschaften zu Göttingen 1991; FBA 1973; *Books* Hesiod, Theogony (ed, 1966), Fragmenta Hesiodea (ed with R Merkelbach, 1967), Early Greek Philosophy and the Orient (1971), Sing Me, Goddess (1971), Iambi et Elegi Graeci (ed, 1971–72), Textual Criticism and Editorial Technique (1973), Studies in Greek Elegy and Iambus (1974), Hesiod, Works and Days (ed, 1978), Theognidis et Phocylidis Fragmenta (1978), Delectus ex Iambis et Elegis Graecis (1980), Greek Metre (1982), The Orphic Poems (1983), Carmina Anacreontea (1984), The Hesiodic Catalogue of Women (1985), Euripides, Orestes (ed, 1987), Introduction to Greek Metre (1987), Hesiod (trans, 1988), Aeschyli Tragoediae (1990), Studies in Aeschylus (1990), Ancient Greek Music (1992), Greek Lyric Poetry (trans, 1993); author of over 300 articles in learned jls; *Recreations* music; *Style*— Dr Martin West, FBA; ✉ All Souls College, Oxford OX1 4AL

WEST, Morris Langlo; AM (1985); s of Charles Langlo West, and Florence Guilfoyle, *née* Hanlon; *b* 26 April 1916; *m* Joyce, *née* Lawford; *Career* writer; Lt Australian Imp Forces 1939–43; recipient Dag Hammarskjold Prize (Grand Collar of Merit) 1978; memb World Acad of Arts and Sciences; Hon DLitt: Santa Clara Univ 1968, Mercy Coll NY 1982, Univ of Western Sydney 1993, Australian Nat Univ Canberra 1995; FRSL; *Books* Gallows on the Sand (1955), Kundu (1956), Children of the Sun (1957), The Crooked Road (in England The Big Story, 1957), The Concubine (1958), Backlash (in England The Second Victory, 1958), The Devil's Advocate (Nat Brotherhood award Nat Cncl of Christians and Jews, James Tait Black Meml award, 1960), 1959 (William Heinemann award Royal Soc, filmed 1977, 1960), The Naked Country (1960), Daughter of Silence (1961, play 1961), The Shoes of the Fisherman (1963), The Ambassador (1965), Tower of Babel (1968), Scandal in the Assembly (with R Francis, 1970), The Heretic: A Play in Three Acts (1970), Summer of the Red Wolf (1971), The Salamander (1973), Harlequin (1974), The Navigator (1976), Proteus (1979), The Clowns of God (1981), The World is Made of Glass (1983), Cassidy (1986), Masterclass (1988), Lazarus (1990), The Ringmaster (1991), The Lovers (1993), Vanishing Point (1996), A View From The Ridge (1996); *Style*— Morris West, Esq, AM, FRSL; ✉ PO Box 102, Avalon, NSW 2107, Australia

WEST, Peter; s of Harold William West (d 1975), and Dorcas Ann West (d 1972); *b* 12 Aug 1920; *Educ* Cranbrook Sch; *m* 1946, Pauline Mary, da of Lt Cdr Evan Cuthbert Pike, RNVR (d 1929); 2 s (Simon, Stephen), 1 da (Jacqueline); *Career* radio and TV sports commentator/presenter 1947–; sports journalist, rugby corr The Times 1971–82; *Books* Fight for the Ashes (1953), Fight for the Ashes (1956), Flannelled Fool and Muddied Oaf (autobiography 1986), Clean Sweep (1987), Denis Compton-Cricketing Genius (1989); *Recreations* gardening, rubber bridge; *Style*— Peter West; ✉ The Paddock, Duntisbourne Abbotts, Cirencester, Glos (☎ 01285 821380)

WEST, Prof Richard Gilbert; s of Arthur Gilbert Dixon West (d 1949), and Daisy Elizabeth Lovesay, MBE (d 1992); *b* 31 May 1926; *Educ* King's Sch Canterbury, Clare Coll Cambridge (MA, PhD, ScD); *m* 30 June 1973, Hazel Violet; *Career* Univ of Cambridge: dir Sub Dept Quaternary Res 1966–87, prof of botany 1977–91, emeritus prof 1991–; FRS 1968, FGS, FSA, Hon MRIA; *Books* Pleistocene Geology and Biology (second edn 1977), Preglacial Pleistocene of the Norfolk and Suffolk Coasts (1980), Pleistocene Palaeoecology of Central Norfolk (1991); *Style*— Prof Richard West, FRS, FSA; ✉ 3A Woollards Lane, Gt Shelford, Cambridge CB2 5LZ; Department of Plant Sciences, University of Cambridge

WEST, Dr Richard James; s of Edward West (d 1982), of Edinburgh, and Doreen, *née* Rutherford; *b* 5 Feb 1944; *Educ* Edinburgh Acad, Univ of Edinburgh (MB ChB); *m* 12 April 1969, Christine, da of Reginald Paul (d 1975); 2 s (Timothy b 1970, Gregory b 1981), 2 da (Sophie b 1971, Madeleine b 1977); *Career* conslt radiologist Queen Elizabeth Hosp Birmingham, hon sr clinical lectr Univ of Birmingham, examiner in surgical neurology RCSE(d) 1986–; author of pubns on biliary and interventional radiology 1978–; memb BMA, FRCR 1973; *Books* Advanced Medicine 23 (contrib, 1987), Philosophical Ethics in Reproductive Medicine (contrib, 1990); *Recreations* singing badly in a choir; *Style*— Dr Richard West

WEST, Prof Richard John; s of Cecil John West (d 1987), and Alice, *née* Court; *b* 8 May 1939; *Educ* Tiffin Boys' Sch, Middx Hosp Med Sch (MB BS, MD); *m* 15 Dec 1962, Dr Jenny Winn, da of Leslie Gaius Hawkins (d 1976); 1 s (Simon b 1964), 2 da (Sarah b 1967, Sophie b 1972); *Career* lectr Inst of Child Health 1974–75, dean St George's Hosp and Med Sch 1982–87 (sr lectr and conslt paediatrician 1975–91), postgrad med dean S Western Region and prof of postgrad med educn Univ of Bristol 1991–; hon conslt paediatrician Royal Hosp for Sick Children Bristol; memb: Cncl Br Paediatric Assoc 1974–76, Wandsworth Health Authy 1981–82 and 1990, SW Thames RHA 1982–88, Clinical Outcomes Gp Dept of Health 1992–, Nursing Forum Dept of Health 1993–, Performance Review Dept of Health 1993–95; chm Dist Med Ctee Wandsworth and E Merton 1978–80; sch govr: Tiffin Boys' Sch 1983–86, Wimbledon HS 1987–91; gen sec Inst of Med Ethics 1989– (memb Cncl 1986–); MRCP 1967, FRCP 1979; *Books* The Family Guide to Children's Ailments (1983), Royal Society of Medicine Child Health Guide (1992); *Recreations* reading, travel, medical history; *Style*— Prof Richard West; ✉ 4 Old Vicarage Place, Apsley Road, Bristol BS8 2TD; Medical Postgraduate Department, Academic Centre, Frenchay Hospital, Bristol BS16 1LE (☎ 0117 975 7050)

WEST, Robert John; s of Clifford Lennard West (d 1996), of Maidenhead, Berks, and Joan, *née* Naylor (d 1983); *b* 1 Jan 1952; *Educ* Maidenhead GS, Clare Coll Cambridge (MA); *m* 13 June 1987, Elisabeth, da of Sydney and Joyce Hynd; 2 s (David Robert b 29 May 1988, Andrew James b 5 Jan 1990); 1 da (Annabel b 22 Nov 1991); *Career* asst slr Freshfields 1977–82 (articled clerk 1975–77), ptnr Baker & McKenzie 1985– (asst slr 1982–85); memb: Law Soc, Assoc of Pension Lawyers; *Books* Butterworths Law for Accountants (1993); *Recreations* football, tennis, golf; *Style*— Robert West, Esq; ✉ Baker & McKenzie, 100 New Bridge Street, London EC4V 6JA (☎ 0171 919 1000, fax 0171 919 1999)

WEST, Dr Stephanie Roberta; da of Robert Enoch Pickard (d 1993), of Adderbury, Oxon, and Ruth, *née* Batters; *b* 1 Dec 1937; *Educ* Nottingham HS for Girls GPDST, Somerville Coll Oxford (Ireland scholar, Derby scholar, BA, DPhil, Gaisford prize); *m* 1960, Martin Litchfield West, s of late Maurice Charles West; 1 da (Rachel Ann b 17 July 1963), 1 s (Robert Charles b 17 May 1965); *Career* Univ of Oxford: Mary Ewart research fell Somerville Coll 1965–67, lectr in classics Hertford Coll 1966–90, lectr in Greek Keble Coll 1981–, sr research fell in classics and fell librarian Hertford Coll 1990–; memb Cncl GPDST 1974–87; FBA 1990; *Books* The Ptolemaic Papyri of Homer (1967), Omero Odissea i (libri i-iv, 1981), A Commentary on Homer's Odyssey i (with A Heubeck and J B Hainsworth, 1988); *Style*— Dr Stephanie West, FBA; ✉ 42 Portland Road, Oxford OX2 7EY (☎ 01865 556060); Hertford College, Oxford OX1 3BW (☎ 01865 279452)

WEST, Timothy Lancaster; CBE (1984); s of (Harry) Lockwood West (d 1989), actor, and Olive Carleton-Crowe; *b* 20 Oct 1934; *Educ* John Lyon Sch Harrow, Regent St Poly; *m* 1, 1956 (m dis), Jacqueline Boyer; 1 da; m 2, 1963, Prunella Scales, *qv*; 2 s; *Career* actor; chm: LAMDA, All Change Arts Ltd; Hon DUniv Bradford; Hon DLitt: Univ of West of England, Univ of East Anglia; FRSA; *Theatre* West End debut in Caught Napping (Piccadilly Theatre) 1959; other performances incl: Gentle Jack, The Trigon, The Italian Girl, Abelard and Heloise, Exiles, The Constant Couple, Laughter, The Homecoming, Beecham, Master Class, The War at Home, When We Are Married, The Sneeze, Long Day's Journey into Night, It's Ralph, King Lear (Dublin), Willy Loman in Death of a Salesman (Theatr Clwyd), Iago in Othello (Nottingham), Sir Anthony Absolute in The Rivals (Chichester), Mail Order Bride and Getting On (West Yorkshire

Playhouse); with RSC 1962–66 (London and Stratford season 1964–66) incl: debut in Nil Carborundum and Afore Night Come (Arts Theatre) 1962, Hedda Gabler (tour Aust, Canada and USA); with Prospect Theatre Co 1966–82: King Lear, Prospero in The Tempest, Claudius in Hamlet, Enobarbus in Antony and Cleopatra, Shylock in The Merchant of Venice, Bolingbroke in Richard II, Mortimer in Edward II, Shpigelsky in A Month in the Country, Emerson in A Room with a View; with Bristol Old Vic Co incl: Trelawny, Falstaff in Henry IV (both parts), Sartorius in Widowers' Houses, Solness in The Master Builder, Lord Ogleby in The Clandestine Marriage, Vanya in Uncle Vanya; most recently Twelve Angry Men (Comedy) 1996; *Television* incl: Edward VII, Horatio Bottomley, Hard Times, Crime and Punishment, Churchill and the Generals, Brass, The Last Bastion, The Monocled Mutineer, A Very Peculiar Practice, The Good Doctor Bodkin Adams, What the Butler Saw, Harry's Kingdom, The Sealed Train, When We Are Married, Breakthrough at Reykjavik, Strife, A Shadow on the Sun, The Contractor, Blore, MP, Beecham, Survival of the Fittest, Why Lockerbie?, Framed, Smokescreen, Eleven Men Against Eleven, Cuts, Rebecca; *Film* incl: Twisted Nerve, Nicholas and Alexandra, The Day of the Jackal, Oliver Twist, Hedda, Joseph Andrews, The Devil's Advocate, Agatha, Masada, The Thirty Nine Steps, Rough Cut, Cry Freedom; *Recreations* listening to music, travelling; *Style*— Timothy West, Esq, CBE; ✉ c/o James Sharkey Associates, 21 Golden Square, London W1R 3PA (☎ 0171 434 3801, fax 0171 494 1547)

WEST, William Todd; s of Alfred William West (d 1963), of Humberside, and Annie Beatrice, *née* Todd (d 1969); *b* 7 Aug 1924; *Educ* Sedbergh, Univ of London (LLB); *m* 7 July 1956, Beryl Josephine, da of William Fletcher Taylor (d 1966), of Scarborough, N Yorks; 1 s (Nicholas William b 1958); *Career* slr, ret; called to the Bar Gray's Inn 1989; elected legal memb of Royal Town Planning Inst 1975–86 (legal assoc memb 1969–75); memb Humberside Valuation Tbnl; *Books* Drugs Law (1982), The County Court (1983), A Shop Hours Casebook (1984), The Trial of Lord de Clifford (1985, 2 edn 1990), Fifty Years of Irish Cricket 1940 to 1990 (1991), Bridlington in The Time of Edward II (1991), Irish Women International Cricketers 1982 to 1992 (1993), An Anthology of the Cricket Writings of E H D Sewell (1993), Gentlemen and Players - The First Seventy Years (1995); *Recreations* bird watching, watching county cricket, exercising a rabbiting terrier, fishing, golf; *Style*— William West, Esq; ✉ Lindis, Roundhay Road, Bridlington, North Humberside YO15 3JZ (☎ 01262 673116)

WEST-KNIGHTS, Laurence James; s of Maj Jan James West West-Knights (d 1990), and Amy Winifred, *née* Gott; *b* 30 July 1954; *Educ* Perse Sch, Hampton Sch, Emmanuel Coll Cambridge (MA); *m* Joanne Anita Florence, *née* Ecob; 1 s (Frederick Hugh Merriman b 11 March 1994), 1 da (Imogen Amy b 26 Aug 1992); *Career* seaman offr London Div RNR 1981–94 (Lt Cdr); called to the Bar Gray's Inn 1977, practising barr 1978–, asst recorder 1994–; cncl memb Soc for Computers and Law 1995–, chm Bar Cncl Working Party on e-mail and IT 1995–, memb Ed Bd Judicial Studies Bd Bulletin 1996–; FCIArb; *Recreations* sailing, cricket, amateur radio; *Clubs* Royal Solent Yacht, Bar Yacht, Radio Soc of GB, Surrey CCC; *Style*— L J West-Knights, Esq; ✉ 27 Marlborough Road, Chiswick, London W4 4EU; 4 Paper Buildings, Temple, London EC4Y 7EX (☎ 0171 353 3366, fax 0171 353 5778, e-mail ljwk@lix.compulink.co.uk)

WEST-RUSSELL, His Hon Sir David Sturrock; kt (1986); s of Sir Alexander West-Russell (d 1962), and Agnes, *née* Sturrock (d 1930); *b* 17 July 1921; *Educ* Rugby, Pembroke Coll Cambridge (MA), Harmsworth Law Sch (1952); *m* 30 April 1949, Christine, *née* Tyler; 1 s (Christopher), 2 da (Fiona, Sarah); *Career* War Serv 1940–46: Buffs, cmmnd Queen's Own Cameron Highlanders 1941, Parachute Regt 1942–46, N Africa, Italy, France, Greece, Norway, Palestine (despatches), ret Maj; managment trainee Guest Keen & Nettlefold 1948–50; called to the Bar Middle Temple 1953, bencher 1986, practising SE Circuit, dep chm Inner London QS 1966–72, circuit judge 1972, senior circuit judge Inner London Crown Ct 1979–82 and Southwark Crown Ct 1983–84; pres Industl Tribunals for England and Wales 1984–91, memb Departmental Ctee on Legal Aid in Criminal Proceedings 1964–65, cmmr NI Emergency Provisions Act 1974–; chm: Lord Chancellor's Advsy Ctee on Appointments of Magistrates for Inner London 1976–87, Home Sec's Advsy Bd on Restricted Patients 1985–91; pres Inner London Magistrates Assoc 1979–85; memb: Inner London Probation Ctee 1979 (chm 1988–90), Lord Chancellor's Advsy Ctee on Training of Magistrates 1980–85, Judicial Studies Bd 1980–84 and 1987–90, Parole Bd 1980–82, Parole Review Ctee 1987–88, Criminal Injuries Compensation Bd 1991–; *Clubs* Garrick; *Style*— His Hon Sir David West-Russell; ✉ Old Sarum Cottage, Teffont Magna, Salisbury, Wilts SP3 5QX (☎ 01722 716261)

WESTABY, Mark; s of Donald Westaby, of Winterton, S Humberside, and Patricia, *née* Morwood; *b* 26 June 1955; *Educ* Frederic Gough, Brunel Univ (BSc); *m* Sarah Frances Elizabeth, *née* Cox; 1 da (Sofia Elizabeth Olga); *Career* Ove Arup & partners and Res Dept British Gas 1979–81; former PRO: John Drewry Associates, HPS Ltd 1983–84, Countrywide Communications (London) 1984–90 (latterly dir, work on Tandem Computers responsible for PR Indust Best Consultancy award 1987); Kinnear Ltd management conslts in communication 1990–93; dir rising to jt md Portfolio Communications Ltd 1993–; chm Business & Technol Gp PR Consultants Assoc (chm elect 1989–91); *Recreations* all sports, music, reading, travel; *Style*— Mark Westaby, Esq; ✉ Portfolio Communications Ltd, 26 West Street, London WC2H 9NA (☎ 0171 240 6959, fax 0171 240 4849)

WESTBROOK, Michael John David (Mike); OBE (1988); s of Philip Beckford Westbrook (d 1981), of Devon, and Vera Agnes, *née* Butler; *b* 21 March 1936; *Educ* Kelly Coll Tavistock Plymouth Coll of Art (NDD), Hornsey Coll of Art (ATD); *m* 1; 1 s (Anthony Guy b 9 April 1964), 1 da (Joanna Maria b 14 June 1966); m 2, 23 Sept 1976, Katherine Jane (Kate), da of Prof Alec Naraway Duckham, CBE (d 1988); *Career* composer, pianist and bandleader; formed first band at Plymouth Art Sch 1958; moved to London 1962 and has since led a succession of gps incl: The Mike Westbrook Brass Band (with Phil Minton) 1973–, The Mike Westbrook Orchestra 1974–, The Westbrook Trio (with Kate Westbrook and Chris Biscoe) 1982–; has toured in Britain, Europe, Australia, Canada, NY, Singapore and Hong Kong, has written cmmnd works for festivals in GB and Europe; has composed music for theatre, opera, dance, radio, TV and films and has made numerous LPs and recordings incl: Marching Song (1967), Metropolis (1969), Tyger (1971), Citadel/Room 315 (1974), On Dukes Birthday (1984), Big Band Rossini (1987), Off Abbey Road (1988), Bean Rows and Blues Shots (saxophone concerto, 1991); TV scores incl Caught on a Train (1980), cinema score Moulin Rouge (1990); concert works with Kate Westbrook incorporating Euro poetry and folk song: The Cortege (1979), London Bridge is Broken Down (1987), music theatre pieces incl: Mama Chicago (1978), Westbrook Rossini (1984), The Ass (1985), Pier Rides (1986), Quichotte (1989); recent works incl: Goodbye Peter Lorre (with Kate Westbrook and John Alley), Good Friday 1663 (an opera for TV, with Kate Westbrook), Coming Through Slaughter (with Michael Morris, based on novel by Michael Ondaatje), Measure for Measure (1992), Blue Terenzi (1995); current projects incl: Bar Utopia (big band cabaret, lyrics by Helen Simpson), Stage Set (duo with Kate Westbrook); *Recreations* walking by the Erme Estuary; *Clubs* John Clare Soc, The Blake Soc (St James), Ronnie Scotts; *Style*— Mike Westbrook, Esq, OBE; ✉ Flat 17, Tamar House, 12 Tavistock Place, London WC1H 9RA

WESTBROOK, Sir Neil Gowanloch; kt (1988), CBE (1981); s of Frank Westbrook, and Dorothy; *b* 21 Jan 1917; *Educ* Oundle, Clare Coll Cambridge (MA); *m* 1945, Hon Mary Joan Fraser, da of 1 Baron Strathalmond, CBE; 1 s, 1 da; *Career* WWII Actg Lt Col RE and Gen Staff Offr (despatches); chm and mangr: Trafford Park Estates PLC, Port of Manchester Warehouses Ltd; farmer; memb CBI NW Regnl Cncl 1982–88, chm CBI NW Inner Cities Study Gp 1985–88, memb IOD Manchester and Area Branch Ctee 1967–86, chm North West Industl Cncl 1982–87, dep chm Trafford Ctee Manchester C of C and Indust 1983–86; memb: Trafford Indust Cncl 1975–86, Assoc of Br C of C Ctee on Rates and Local Govt Fin 1975–77, Bd of Fin Cons Pty 1984–87, Nat Union Industl and Trade Forum 1982–87, Nat Union Exec Ctee 1975–81, NW Area Fin and Gen Purposes Ctee 1974–87; chm of Manchester Cons Assoc 1974–83 (vice chm 1973–74, hon treas 1964–73), chm Greater Manchester Co-ordinating Ctee 1978–86, memb Manchester City Cncl 1949–72 (dep ldr 1968–69), Lord Mayor City of Manchester 1969–70, chm Greater Manchester South Euro Div 1978–84; chm NW Museum and Art Gallery Serv 1965–68, memb Nat Cncl Museums Assoc 1965–69; *Recreations* shooting, fishing; *Clubs* Carlton, Manchester Tennis and Racquets; *Style*— Sir Neil Westbrook, CBE; ✉ Neil House, Twining Road, Ashburton Road, Trafford Park, Manchester M17 1AT (☎ 0161 872 5426)

WESTBROOK, HE Roger; CMG (1990); s of Edward George Westbrook, of Bearsted, Kent, and Beatrice Minnie, *née* Marshall; *b* 26 May 1941; *Educ* Dulwich, Hertford Coll Oxford (MA); *Career* HM Dip Serv: FO 1964, asst private sec to the Chllr of the Duchy of Lancaster and Min of State FCO 1965, Yaoundé 1967, Rio de Janeiro 1971, Brasilia 1972, private sec to Min of State FCO 1975, head of chancery Lisbon 1977, dep head News Dept FCO 1980, dep head Falkland Islands Dept FCO 1982, Overseas Inspectorate FCO 1984, high cmmr Negara Brunei Darussalam 1986, ambass Republic of Zaire 1991–92, high cmmr Tanzania 1992–95, ambass Portugal 1995–; *Clubs* Travellers'; *Style*— HE Mr Roger Westbrook, CMG; ✉ Foreign and Commonwealth Office (Lisbon), King Charles Street, London SW1A 2AH

WESTBURY, 5 Baron (UK 1861); David Alan Bethell; CBE (1994), MC (1942), DL (N Yorks 1973); s of Capt Hon Richard Bethell (d 1929, s of 3 Baron, whom he predeceased), and Lady Agatha Tollemache, sis of 9 Earl of Dysart; suc bro, 4 Baron, 1961; *b* 16 July 1922; *Educ* Harrow, RMC; *m* 21 Oct 1947, Ursula Mary Rose, CBE (1990), er da of Hon Robert James (3 s of 2 Baron Northbourne), and his 2 w, Lady Serena Lumley, da of 10 Earl of Scarbrough; 2 s, 1 da; *Heir* s, Maj Hon Richard Bethell, MBE; *Career* served WWII with Scots Guards in N Africa & Italy (despatches); sits as Conservative peer in House of Lords; equerry to HRH Duke of Gloucester 1947–49; chm Cwlth Health Fndn; vice pres: Forces Help Soc, Lord Roberts Workshops; pres Northern Police Convalescent Home, memb Exec Ctee of Int Fedn of Multiple Sclerosis Socs; patron: Action Around Bethlehem Children with Disability, Yorks Assoc of Boys' Clubs; KStJ 1977, Bailiff of Egle 1988–93, Bailiff Grand Cross 1988, GCStJ 1988; *Clubs* White's, Jockey, Pratt's, Buck's; *Style*— The Rt Hon the Lord Westbury, CBE, MC, DL; ✉ Barton Cottage, Malton, N Yorks YO17 0AT (☎ 01653 692293); 8 Ropers Orchard, Danvers St, London SW3 5AX (☎ 0171 352 7911)

WESTBURY, Prof David Rex; s of Harold Joseph Westbury (d 1966), of Rubery, Worcs, and Kathleen, *née* Hedderley (d 1996); *b* 24 June 1942; *Educ* Bromsgrove Co HS Worcestershire, ChCh Oxford (MA, BSc, BM BCh, DM); *m* 19 Feb 1966, Pauline, da of James Robinson (d 1988), of Darlington, Co Durham; 1 s (Paul b 1969), 1 da (Claire b 1971); *Career* Univ of Birmingham: lectr 1968–74, sr lectr 1974–82, reader 1982–86, exec dean Med Faculty 1984–92, prof 1987–, vice princ 1992–; dir: Birmingham Research and Development Ltd 1993–, S Birmingham Mental Health NHS Tst 1994–; memb Physiological Soc 1968; *Recreations* eating, walking, amateur radio communications; *Clubs* Athenaeum; *Style*— Prof David Westbury; ✉ 120 Bunbury Rd, Northfield, Birmingham B31 2DN (☎ 0121 4757404), University of Birmingham, Edgbaston, Birmingham B15 2TT (☎ 0121 414 5939, fax 0121 414 4534)

WESTCOTT, John Miles; s of Leonard George Westcott (d 1977), of Chipping Campden, Glos, and Marion Blanche, *née* Field; *b* 22 Feb 1929; *Educ* Taunton Sch; *m* 1 Sept 1956, Anne Milne, da of Capt Robert Porter, OBE (d 1956), of Blundellsands, Liverpool; 2 s (Andrew John b 1959 d 1969, Timothy Edmund James b 1963), 1 da (Catherine May b 1961); *Career* Nat Serv 2 Lt 13/18 Royal Hussars 1949, Lt North Somerset Yeomanry 1950–52; admitted slr 1956; managing ptnr Veale Wasbrough 1988, currently exec dir Kingswood Foundation Ltd; legal chm (pt/t) Pensions Appeals Tbnl 1989–; former pres Bristol Law Soc; vice pres Avon Youth Assoc; contrib Family Law; memb Law Soc; *Recreations* village cricket, dry stone wall building; *Clubs* Royal Commonwealth Soc; *Style*— John Westcott, Esq; ✉ Old Farm, Southwood, Baltonsborough, Glastonbury, Somerset (☎ 01458 850416); Kingswood Foundation Ltd, Kingswood, Bristol BS15 2DB (☎ 0117 947 7948)

WESTCOTT, Dr Nicholas James; s of John Hugh Westcott, of Oxshott, Surrey, and Helen Fay, *née* Morgan; *b* 20 July 1956; *Educ* Epsom Coll, Sidney Sussex Coll Cambridge (Walter Frewin Lord prize, Smuts studentship, MA, PhD); *m* 2 Jan 1989, Miriam, da of Francis Pearson; *Career* res assoc Univ of Dar Es Salaam 1979–80; HM Diplomatic Service 1982–: Cultural Relations Dept FCO 1982–84, seconded to EC Brussels 1984–85, first sec UK Permanent Representation Brussels 1985–89, on planning staff FCO 1989–90, EC Dept 1990–92, head CFSP Unit and European corr 1992–93, dep high cmmr British High Cmmn Dar Es Salaam 1993–96, head Economic Rels Dept 1996–; memb RIIA 1982, memb Royal African Soc 1979; FRGS 1991; *Books* Managed Economies In World War II (with P Kingston and R G Tiedemann, 1991); author of various articles in jls; *Recreations* reading, travelling, gardening, tennis; *Style*— Dr Nicholas Westcott; ✉ Foreign and Commonwealth Office, King Charles Street, London SW1A 2AH (☎ 0171 270 3000)

WESTCOTT, Richard Henry; s of Charles Westcott (d 1984), of S Molton, Devon, and Ruby Alice, *née* Addicott (d 1979); *b* 5 Nov 1947; *Educ* Barnstaple Boys' GS; *m* 26 Nov 1983, Susan, da of George Frederick Read (d 1991), of Middlesbrough, Cleveland; 1 s (Charles George Frederick b 20 April 1987), 1 da (Emily Margaret Alice b 29 Aug 1985); *Career* called to the Bar Lincoln's Inn 1978; articled then sr clerk Moore Bedworth & Co CA's Barnstaple 1964–73, tax mangr Arthur Andersen CA's London 1973–75; dir: Morgan Grenfell & Co Ltd 1983–86 (exec mangr 1975–83), Warburg, Akroyd, Rowe & Pitman, Mullens Securites Ltd 1986–89; md Merrill Lynch International Ltd 1989–91; business conslt 1991–95; non-exec dir: TBI plc 1992–, Fairview New Homes PLC 1992– (dep chm), Herring Baker Harris Group plc 1994–95; FCA 1970, FTII 1974, ACIB 1979; *Recreations* walking, reading, carpentry, music, golf; *Style*— Richard Westcott, Esq

WESTERBY, (Stuart) Marcus; s of Ernest (Tim) Westerby (d 1976), and Pollie Westerby (d 1992); *b* 1 April 1934; *Educ* Leys Sch Cambridge; *m* 30 July 1959, Josephine (Jo), da of Stanley Clegg (d 1982); 3 da (Sally Anne, Penny Jane, Emma Gail); *Career* Nat Serv RN 1952–53 (Royal Gd at HM Queen Elizabeth's Coronation 1953); dir Moët & Chandon (London) Ltd 1956–94, ret; hon vice pres Golf Club Stewards Assoc UK; fell Zoological Soc of London; *Recreations* golf, shooting; *Clubs* Br Racing Drivers' (hon life memb), Veteran Car Club of GB (hon life memb), British Automobile Racing, Moor Park Golf; *Style*— Marcus Westerby, Esq; ✉ Woodcroft, Trout Rise, Loudwater, Rickmansworth, Herts WD3 4JS (☎ and fax 01923 772773)

WESTHEAD, (John) Simon; s of Stanley Westhead (d 1986), of Clitheroe, and Ellen Fanny, *née* Hargraves (d 1977); *b* 17 June 1938; *Educ* Giggleswick Sch; *m* 21 Sept 1962, Gillian Mary, da of Maurice Collinge; 2 s (Edward Paul b 10 Dec 1963, Nicholas Charles b 28 June 1965); *Career* accountant; Waterworth Rudd & Hare: articled clerk 1956–62, ptnr 1968–, sr ptnr 1987–; memb NW Dist Soc of Chartered Accountants 1965–93, NW rep on Cncl Inst of Chartered Accountants 1977–87; non-exec dir Blackburn Hyndburn and Ribble Valley Health Care NHS Tst 1993–; ACA 1962, AInstT 1962, memb Soc of Practitioners of Insolvency 1990; *Recreations* cricket, squash, walking, Rugby Union (spectator), golf, collecting; *Clubs* Dist & Union (Blackburn), Clitheroe Cricket, Cryptics Cricket, Blackburn RUFC (pres 1995–); *Style*— Simon Westhead, Esq; ✉ Waterworth Rudd & Hare, Central Buildings, Richmond Terrace, Blackburn, Lancashire BB1 7AP (☎ 01254 51123)

WESTLAKE, Rev Peter Alan Grant; CMG (1972), MC (1943); s of Alan Robert Cecil Westlake, CSI, CIE (d 1978), and Dorothy Louise, *née* Turner (d 1966); *b* 2 Feb 1919; *Educ* Sherborne, CCC Oxford (MA), Univ of Wales (MSc, BD); *m* 1943, Katherine Gertrude (d 1990), da of Rev Harold Charles Spackman; 2 s; *Career* FRAS; RA in Libya and Tobruk (adj 1 RHA) and Italy (despatches), Capt 1939–46; entered Foreign Serv 1946, head of Chancery Tel Aviv 1955–57; cnsllr: Washington 1965, Canberra 1967–71; min Br Embassy Toyko 1971–76, UK cmmr gen Int Ocean Expo Okinawa 1975; ordained deacon 1981, priest Church in Wales 1982–; Order of Rising Sun (Japan) 1975; *Books* The Lord of Snow (1992), The Katogle (1994); *Recreations* oceanography; *Style*— The Rev Peter Westlake, CMG, MC; ✉ 53 Church St, Beaumaris, Gwynedd LL58 8AB (☎ 01248 810114)

WESTMEATH, 13 Earl of (I 1621); William Anthony Nugent; also Baron Delvin (I before 1489, evolved from a feudal Barony, of which the date of origin is uncertain); s of 12 Earl of Westmeath (d 1971); *b* 21 Nov 1928; *Educ* Marlborough, RMA Sandhurst; *m* 31 July 1963, Susanna Margaret, o da of His Hon Judge James Charles Beresford Whyte Leonard, of Sutton Courtenay, Berks; 2 s; *Heir* s, Lord Delvin; *Career* RA 1947–61, ret as Capt; sr master St Andrew's Sch Pangbourne, ret 1988; *Style*— The Rt Hon the Earl of Westmeath; ✉ Farthings, Bradfield, Reading, Berks RG7 6LL (☎ 0118 974 4426)

WESTMINSTER, Anne, Duchess of; Anne Winifred; da of Brig-Gen Edward Sullivan, CB, CMG, of Glanmire House, Co Cork; *m* 1947, as his 4 w, 2 Duke of Westminster, GCVO, DSO (d 1953); *Style*— Her Grace Anne, Duchess of Westminster; ✉ Lochmore, Lairg, Sutherland (☎ 01971 500 222); Eaton Lodge, Eccleston, Chester (01244 674 797)

WESTMINSTER, Archbishop (RC) of 1976–; His Eminence the Cardinal (George) Basil Hume; s of late Sir William Errington Hume, CMG, and late Marie Elisabeth, *née* Tisseyre; *b* 2 March 1923; *Educ* Ampleforth, St Benet's Hall Oxford, Fribourg Univ Switzerland; *Career* ordained priest 1950; Ampleforth Coll: sr modern language master 1952–63, housemaster 1955–63, prof of Dogmatic Theology 1955–63, magister scholarum of the English Benedictine Congregation 1957–63, abbot 1963–76; Cardinal Archbishop of Westminster 1976; pres: Cncl of Euro Bishops' Conferences 1978–87, Bishops' Conference England and Wales 1979–, Cncl of Christians and Jews; jt pres Churches Together in England 1990–; memb: Congregation for Eastern Churches 1994–, Congregation for Religious and Secular Insts, Pontifical Cncl for Promotion of Christian Unity, Pontifical Cncl for Pastoral Assistance to Health Care Workers; appointed relator for the Synod on Consecrated Life 1994; Hon Bencher Inner Temple; Hon DD: Cambridge 1979, Newcastle 1979, London 1980, Oxford 1981, York 1982, Kent 1983, Durham 1987, Collegio S Anselmo Rome 1987, Hull 1989, Univ of Keele 1990; Hon DHL: Manhattan Coll NY USA 1980, Catholic Univ of America 1980; Hon LLD Univ of Northumbria at Newcastle 1992, Hon DUniv Surrey 1992; Hon Freeman: Newcastle-upon-Tyne 1980, City of London 1980, Worshipful Co of Skinners 1994; *Books* Searching for God (1977), In Praise of Benedict (1981), To Be a Pilgrim (1984), Towards a Civilisation of Love (1988), Light in the Lord (1991), Remaking Europe (1994), Footprints of the Northern Saints (1996); *Style*— His Eminence the Cardinal Archbishop of Westminster; ✉ Archbishop's House, Westminster, London SW1P 1QJ (☎ 0171 798 9033)

WESTMINSTER, Dean of; *see:* Carr, Very Rev Dr (Arthur) Wesley

WESTMINSTER, 6 Duke of (UK 1874); Sir Gerald Cavendish Grosvenor; 15 Bt (E 1622), OBE (Mil 1995), TD (1994), DL (Cheshire 1982); also Baron Grosvenor (GB 1761), Earl Grosvenor, Viscount Belgrave (both GB 1784), and Marquess of Westminster (UK 1831); s of 5 Duke of Westminster, TD (d 1979), and Hon Viola Lyttelton (d 1987), da of 9 Viscount Cobham; *b* 22 Dec 1951; *Educ* Harrow; *m* 1978, Natalia Ayesha, yst da of Lt-Col Harold Pedro Joseph Phillips, and Georgina (da of Sir Harold Wernher, 3 Bt, GCVO, TD, and Lady Zia, CBE, *née* Countess Anastasia Mikhailovna, da of HIH Grand Duke Michael of Russia); sis of Duchess of Abercorn; 1 s (Earl Grosvenor b 29 Jan 1991), 3 da (Lady Tamara Katherine b 20 Dec 1979, Lady Edwina Louise b 4 Nov 1981, Lady Viola Georgina b 12 Oct 1992); *Heir* s, Hugh Richard Louis, Earl Grosvenor b 29 Jan 1991; *Career* joined Queen's Own Yeo 1970, cmmnd 1973, Capt 1979, Maj 1985, Lt-Col 1992, Commanding Regt 1992, Col 1995; sat as Cons Peer in House of Lords until 1993; landowner; dir: Grosvenor Estate Holdings, Marcher Sound Ltd, North West Business Leadership Team, Royal & Sun Alliance Insurance Group plc 1995–, Sutton Ridge Pty Ltd, Claridges 1981–92, Harland & Woolfe 1984–87, Coutts & Co Jan-Dec 1985, Business in the Community 1988–92, Countryside Movement 1996–; chm of tstees: Thomas Cubbitt Meml Tst, Falcon Tst, Royal Agric Soc of the Cwlth, TSB Fndn of England and Wales, Wesminster Fndn, Nuffield Tst for the Forces of the Crown; tstee Westminster Abbey Tst; chllr: Manchester Metropolitan Univ, Keele Univ 1986–93; pres of various orgns incl: Arthritis Care, Br Limbless Ex-Servicemen's Assoc, Br Assoc for Shooting and Conservation, Drug and Alcohol Fndn, The Game Conservancy Tst, Holstein Freisan Soc (patron), London Fedn of Clubs for Young People, RNIB, SCOPE (formerly The Spastics Soc); vice pres of various orgns incl: CLA, NSPCC, Royal Engrs Museum Fndn; patron of various orgns incl: Br Kidney Patients' Assoc, Dyslexia Inst, Royal Fine Art Cmmn, Worcestershire CCC; govr Royal Agric Soc of England; memb Cncl Nat Army Museum; Freeman: City of London, City of Chester; Liveryman Worshipful Cos of: Marketors, Goldsmiths, Fishmongers, Armourers and Braziers, Gunmakers, Weavers; Liveryman Guild of Air Pilots and Air Navigators; Hon LLD: Keele Univ, Westminster Coll Foulton Missouri; Hon DLitt Manchester Metropolitan Univ; hon memb RICS; fell: Inst of Clerk of Works of GB, Liverpool John Moores Univ, Royal Agric Socs; FCIB, FRSA; KStJ 1991; *Recreations* shooting, fishing, scuba diving; *Clubs* Royal Yacht Squadron (Cowes), Brooks's, Cavalry & Guards', MCC, St James's, Australian, British Deer Society, Chester Business, Chester City, Chester Lions, Downhurst, Hon Officers' Association of British Columbia, Nairobi Safari, Pitt, Rotary Club of Chester, Royal Green Jackets, Tarporley Hunt, Vancouver (Canada); *Style*— His Grace the Duke of Westminster, OBE, TD, DL; ✉ Eaton Hall, Chester, Cheshire CH4 9ET; Eaton Estate Office, Eccleston, Chester (☎ 01244 684400)

WESTMORE, Geoffrey David (Geoff); s of Alan Herbert Westmore, of Guildford, Surrey, and Mary Elspeth, *née* Brooking; *b* 28 Aug 1950; *Educ* Royal GS Guildford; *m* 21 July 1979, Paula, *née* Clemett; 1 s (Jonathan Henry Clemett b 1987), 1 da (Kathryn May Clemett b 1983); *Career* Deloitte Haskins & Sells (now Coopers & Lybrand): mangr 1975–83, ptnr 1983–; FCA 1972; *Recreations* sport, music, theatre, films; *Style*— Geoff Westmore, Esq; ✉ Coopers & Lybrand, Plumtree Court, London EC4A 4HT (☎ 0171 583 5000)

WESTMORELAND, Graham James; s of Ronald Westmoreland, of Castleford, and Audrey, *née* Beaumont; *b* 31 July 1959; *Educ* Castleford HS, Wakefield Coll of Technol and Arts; *m* 8 May 1982, Janet Ann, da of Dennis Arnold Davies; 1 da (Alexandra Brooke b 3 March 1989), 1 s (James Anthony b 27 Dec 1991); *Career* Vernons Advertising London 1976–80, Advertising Bureau Leeds 1980–84, Brahm Leeds 1984–86, creative dir Advertising Principles Leeds 1988–89 (recipient 4 Roses and included in D&AD), freelance photographer 1989– (Association of Photographers Merit and Silver award); *Style*— Graham Westmoreland, Esq; ✉ 18 Carr Lane, Middlestown, nr Wakefield, W Yorkshire WF4 4QJ (☎ 01924 276493, fax 01924 276389)

WESTMORELAND, (George) Michael; s of George Sawden Westmoreland (d 1955), of Leeds, and Gladys, *née* Fowler (d 1954); *b* 16 Nov 1931; *Educ* Leeds Moden Sch, Leeds Coll of Art (NDD), Univ of Leeds (Art Teachers' Cert); *m* 1966, Joanne Jennifer, da of Jack Camm; 2 s (Thomas Patrick b 1967, Daniel Joseph b 1976); *Career* freelance artist; full and pt/t teacher and lectr 1953–67 (Leeds Coll of Art, Wakefield Sch of Art, Margaret McMillan Coll Bradford, Northumberland Coll of Educn), freelance photographer and film-maker 1967– (ran various courses in film and photography Leicester Coll of Educn 1967–76), sr lectr Educnl Technol Centre Leicester Poly 1976–85; *Exhibitions* one-man show Photographers Gallery London 1979, 12 Images Nat Museum of Photography Bradford 1985, A Panoramic View (travelling one-man show) 1986–95, invited contributor to Tomorrow Exhibition (Royal Festival Hall) 1986 and Panoramania Exhibition (Barbican Centre) 1988, various gp shows UK and abroad, various works in public and private collections and numerous Cmmns for panoramic projects; winner: Kodak Bursary 1980, Richard Farrand Award 1984 (jt RPS/BIPP presentation for tech distinction in applied photography); write-up of works: British Journal of Photography (May 1979), Design Magazine (Dec 1980), Camera Magazine (Jan 1985), SLR Magazine (May 1987); FRPS 1982, FBIPP 1983; *Recreations* badminton, snooker; *Style*— Michael Westmoreland, Esq; ✉ 358 Victoria Park Rd, Leicester LE2 1XF (☎ and fax 0116 270 5828)

WESTMORLAND, 16 Earl of (E 1624); Anthony David Francis Henry Fane; also Baron Burghersh (E 1624); s of 15 Earl of Westmorland, GCVO, DL (d 1993), and Barbara Jane, da of Lt-Col Sir Roland Lewis Findlay, 3 and last Bt (d 1979); *b* 1 Aug 1951; *Educ* Eton, Spain; *m* 1985, Mrs Caroline E Fairey, da of Keon Hughes, and former w of Charles Fairey; 1 da (Lady Daisy Caroline b 18 Jan 1989); *Heir* bro, Hon Harry St Clair Fane b 19 March 1953; *Career* dir Phillips Internat Auctioneers 1994–; mktg conslt; memb Orbitex Arctic Ocean Research Project Expedition to North Pole 1990; life pres St Moritz Sporting Club, govr Guild of Veteran Pilots and Racing Drivers; FRGS; *Style*— The Rt Hon the Earl of Westmorland; ✉ 31 Langton Street, London SW10 0JL

WESTOLL, James; DL (Cumbria 1963); s of James Westoll (d 1969); *b* 26 July 1918; *Educ* Eton, Trinity Coll Cambridge (MA); *m* 1946, Sylvia Jane, MBE, da of Lord Justice Luxmoore (d 1944); 2 s, 2 da; *Career* served 1939–46 NW Europe (despatches), Maj Border Regt; farmer; called to the Bar 1952; chm Cumberland CC 1958–74, memb NW Electricity Bd 1959–66, dep chm Cumberland QS 1960–71, High Sheriff 1964, chm Cumbria CC 1973–76; memb Ct of Assts Worshipful Co of Clothworkers (Master 1983–84); Hon LLD Univ of Leeds 1984; CStJ 1977, KStJ 1984; *Recreations* gardening, shooting; *Clubs* Boodle's, Farmers'; *Style*— James Westoll, Esq, DL; ✉ Dykeside, Longtown, Cumbria (☎ 01228 791235)

WESTON, Adrian Robert; s of Harold Gibbons Weston (d 1987), of Leicester, and Alwyne Gabrielle, *née* Applebee; *b* 7 June 1935; *Educ* Ratcliffe Coll, Queen's Coll Oxford (MA); *m* 29 Sept 1963, Bridget Ann, da of William Henry Smith (d 1964), of Leicester; 1 s (Thomas b 1968), 1 da (Alexandra b 1967); *Career* admitted slr 1961; dir: Atkinson Design Associates Ltd 1982–, Everards Brewery Ltd 1984–, Pal International Ltd 1985–, LET Ltd 1989–; sr ptnr Harvey Ingram Owston Slrs; capt Leics Co Hockey Assoc 1965–66; vice pres: The Hockey Assoc 1979– (chm 1972–78), Leics CCC; chm of govrs Ratcliffe Coll Leicester 1990–; *Recreations* golf, reading, music; *Clubs* Leicestershire Golf, RAF; *Style*— Adrian R Weston, Esq; ✉ Home Farm, Smeeton Westerby, Leicester LE8 0QJ (☎ 0116 279 2514); Harvey Ingram Owston Solicitors, 20 New Walk, Leicester LE1 6TX (☎ 0116 254 5454)

WESTON, Anthony Paul Cartade (Tony); s of Robert Jean Marcel Cartade Weston, of Bristol, and Edna Lavinia Jago-Burton (d 1949); *b* 14 May 1936; *Educ* King Edwards Southampton, Fairfield Bristol, The West of England Coll of Art (NDD, ATD, MAH); *m* 28 Dec 1961, Jennifer Anne Blaise, da of Arthur Frederick Gore Bird (d 1971); 1 s (Nicholas b 1964), 1 da (Rebecca b 1965); *Career* painter, sculptor, antiquarian, paintings in many private collections, author; exhibitor at The Royal West of England Acad; *Books* The Late Drawings of Mantegna, Paduan Sculpture, West of England Horology et al; *Recreations* riding to hounds, literary research; *Clubs* The Clifton Yacht; *Style*— Tony Weston, Esq; ✉ The Old Garden, Old Bristol Road, Lower Langford, nr Bristol BS18 7BW

WESTON, Bryan Henry; s of Henry James Weston (d 1973), and Rose Kate Weston (d 1989); *b* 9 April 1930; *Educ* St George GS Bristol, Bristol Tech Coll, Rutherford Tech Coll, Oxford Tech Coll; *m* 21 July 1956, Heather Grace (d 1995), da of Henry Gordon West, of Redhill, Avon; 2 s (Richard b 21 Jan 1958, Robert b 21 Dec 1960), 2 da (Rebecca b 13 Sept 1962, Rachel b 21 Sept 1967); *Career* 2 Lt RE 1954–56; apprentice engr SW Electricity Bd 1949, various engrg and commercial posts with SW Electricity Bd 1956–73 (latterly commerical mangr 1973); dep chm Yorks Electricity Bd 1977, chm and chief exec Manweb plc (formerly MANWEB (Merseyside and N Wales Electricity Bd)) 1985–90 (chm 1990–94), ret 1994; CEng, FIEE, CIMgt; *Recreations* gardening, walking, caravanning, DIY; *Style*— Bryan Weston, Esq; ✉ Fountainhead Cottage, Brassey Green, nr Tarporley, Cheshire CW6 9UG

WESTON, Celia Anne; da of Geoffrey Weston, of London, and Elizabeth, *née* Denny; *b* 13 Feb 1956; *Educ* Clifton HS for Girls, City of Bath Girls' Sch, Poly of North London (BSc); *Career* journalist; reporter The Morning Star 1979–82, asst ed The Teacher 1982–87, SDP Policy and Press Office 1987, freelance journalist (specialising in educn) 1987–88; The Guardian: Educn corr 1988–91, Labour corr 1991–93, Industrial corr 1993–, Enterprise ed 1995–, Careers ed 1995–; fndr memb North Kensington Women's Refuge 1974; memb: North Kensington Law Centre Mgmnt Ctee 1973–75, NUS Women's Ctee 1975–78, London Student Orgn Exec 1974–77, Br Youth Cncl 1977–78; memb Mgmnt Ctee and vice chairwoman Nat Cncl for One Parent Families 1985–, conslt on devpt of training policy 1987–; memb NUJ 1979, fell British American Project; commended Industl Journalist of the Year Awards 1991; *Recreations* gardening, scrabble, bridge; *Style*— Ms Celia Weston; ✉ Industrial Correspondent, The Guardian, 119 Farringdon Rd, London EC1R 3ER (☎ 0171 278 2332)

WESTON, Rear Adm Charles Arthur Winfield; CB (1978); s of Charles Winfield Weston (d 1958), of Barton-on-Sea, Hants; *b* 12 July 1922; *Educ* Merchant Taylors'; *m* 1946, Jeanie Findlay, da of William Dick Brown Miller; 1 s, 1 da; *Career* joined RN as cadet 1940, served WWII home waters, Med, Indian Ocean, Atlantic, sec to 2 Sea Lord 1965–67, Capt 1967, CSO to C-in-C Naval Home Cmd 1969–71, dir Naval Physical Trg and Sport 1972; dir: Def Admin Planning Staff 1973–75, Quartering (RN) 1975–76; ADC to HM The Queen 1976, adm pres RNC Greenwich 1976–78, appeals sec King Edward VII's Hosp for Offrs 1979–87; Freeman Worshipful Co of Shipwrights; *Recreations* golf, gardening; *Clubs* MCC, Norfolk; *Style*— Rear Adm C A W Weston, CB; ✉ Flinten Barn, Little Thornage, Holt, Norfolk NR25 7JD (☎ 01263 713523)

WESTON, Christopher John; s of Eric Tudor Weston, of Plaxtol, Kent, and Evelyn, *née* Snell; *b* 3 March 1937; *Educ* Lancing; *m* 12 July 1969, Josephine Annabel, da of Dr Moir; 1 da (Annabel b 1973); *Career* RAF 1955–57; chm and chief exec Phillips Son & Neale and assoc cos 1972–; dir: Foreign & Colonial Pacific Investment plc 1984–, Hodder Headline plc 1986– (non-exec chm 1997–), Foreign & Colonial Enterprise Trust plc 1987–, Oxford Molecular Group plc 1994–; chm Bradford Peters (Holdings) Ltd 1987–;

pres Soc of Fine Art Auctioneers; chm QUIT (Nat Soc of Non Smokers) 1993–; Freeman City of London, Liveryman Worshipful Co of Painter-Stainers; FIA (Scot), FRSA; *Recreations* theatre, music; *Clubs* Oriental; *Style*— Christopher Weston, Esq; ✉ Phillips, 101 New Bond St, London W1Y 0AS (☎ 0171 629 6602, fax 0171 629 8876)

WESTON, Rev Canon David Wilfrid Valentine; s of The Rev William Valentine Weston (d 1937), and Gertrude Hamilton, *née* Erby (d 1979); *b* 8 Dec 1937; *Educ* St Edmund's Sch Canterbury, Univ of Lancaster (PhD); *m* 9 June 1984, Helen Strachan, da of James R Macdonald; 2 s (Luke b 1986, Alexander b 1990); *Career* monk of Nashdom Abbey 1960–84; ordained: deacon 1967, priest 1968; novice master 1969–74, prior of Nashdom 1971–74, abbot 1974–84; vicar of Pilling 1985–89, chaplain to the Bishop of Carlisle 1989–94; canon residentiary of Carlisle Cathedral 1994–, canon librarian 1995–; Freedom City of London 1959, memb Worshipful Co of Salters 1959; *Recreations* history; *Style*— The Rev Canon David Weston, PhD; ✉ 3 The Abbey, Carlisle, Cumbria CA3 8TZ (☎ 01228 21834)

WESTON, Ven Frank Valentine; s of Rev William Valentine Weston, VD (d 1937), and Gertrude Hamilton, *née* Erby (d 1979); *b* 16 Sept 1935; *Educ* Christ's Hosp, Queen's Coll Oxford (BA, MA); *m* 20 April 1963, Penelope Brighid, da of Marmaduke Carver Middleton Athorpe (d 1973), formerly of Dinnington Hall, Yorkshire; 1 s (Simon b 1964), 2 da (Victoria b 1966, Lucy b 1968); *Career* 2 Lt RA 1954–56 (Nat Serv); curate St John the Baptist Atherton Lancs 1961–65, chaplain Coll of the Ascension Selly Oak Birmingham 1965–69, princ 1969–76, princ and Pantonian prof of theology Edinburgh Theological Coll 1976–82, archdeacon of Oxford and canon of Christ Church Oxford 1982–; govr: Tudor Hall Sch Banbury 1988–, Christ's Hosp 1988– (almoner 1996–), St Augustine's Upper Sch Oxford 1984–; Master Worshipful Co of Salters 1992–93 (Liveryman 1957, memb Ct of Assts 1984–); *Recreations* walking, listening to music; *Style*— The Ven the Archdeacon of Oxford; ✉ Archdeacon's Lodging, Christ Church, Oxford OX1 1DP (☎ 01865 276185)

WESTON, (Willard Gordon) Galen; OC (1990); s of W Garfield Weston (d 1978, sometime Cons MP), of Toronto, Canada and London, by his 1 w, Reta Lila Howard (d 1967); yr bro of Garry, *see* Garfield Howard Weston; *for further details see* Debrett's Illustrated Guide to The Canadian Establishment; *b* 29 Oct 1940; *m* 1966, Hilary Mary Frayne; 2 children; *Career* chm George Weston Limited; chm: Wittington Investments Limited, Holt, Renfrew & Co Limited, Loblaw Companies Limited, Weston Foods Limited, Weston Resources Limited; vice chm Fortnum & Mason plc (UK); dir: Associated British Foods plc (UK), Brown Thomas Group Limited (Ireland), Canadian Imperial Bank of Commerce, Wittington Investments Ltd (UK); dir: The Lester B Pearson Coll of the Pacific, Utd World Colls (UK), Canadian Meml Fndn (Canada) Tst; pres The W Garfield Weston Fndn; hon tstee Upper Canada Coll Fndn; life memb: Art Gallery of Ontario, Royal Ontario Museum; Hon LLD Univ of Western Ontario; Officer of the Order of Canada (OC); *Recreations* golf, tennis; *Clubs* Badminton & Racquet (Toronto), Guards Polo (UK), Lyford Cay (Bahamas), Toronto Club, York (Toronto), Windsor (Florida), Brooks (NY), White's (UK); *Style*— W Galen Weston, OC; ✉ George Weston Limited, 22 St Clair Avenue East, Toronto M4T 2S7, Canada (☎ 00 1 416 922 2500, fax 00 1 416 922 4394, telex 06 22781 WESTLOB)

WESTON, Garfield Howard (Garry); DL; s of Willard Garfield Weston (d 1978, sometime Cons MP), of Toronto, Canada and London, by his 1 w, Reta Lila, *née* Howard (d 1967); er bro of Galen Weston, *qv*; *b* 28 April 1927; *Educ* Sir William Borlase Sch, New Coll Oxford (BA), Harvard; *m* 8 Aug 1959, Mary Ruth, da of Maj-Gen Sir Howard Karl Kippenberger (d 1957); 3 s (Guy, George, Garth), 3 da (Jana (Mrs Antoine Khayat), Kate (Mrs William Hobhouse), Sophia (Mrs Charles Mason)); *Career* md: Ryvita Co Ltd UK 1951–54, Weston Biscuit Co Aust 1954–67; chm: Associated British Foods plc 1967– (vice chm 1960), Fortnum & Mason PLC 1979–, Wittington Investments Ltd UK 1979–, British Sugar PLC 1991–; *Style*— Garry Weston, Esq, DL; ✉ Associated British Foods plc, Weston Centre, Bowater House, 68 Knightsbridge, London SW1X 7LQ (☎ 0171 589 6363, fax 0171 584 8560)

WESTON, HE Sir (Philip) John; KCMG (1992, CMG 1985); s of Philip George Weston, of London (d 1969), and Edith Alice Bray, *née* Ansell (d 1976); *b* 13 April 1938; *Educ* Sherborne, Worcester Coll Oxford; *m* 28 Jan 1967, Margaret Sally, da of Robert Hermann Ehlers, of Bridgwater; 2 s (Ben b 1969, Rufus b 1973), 1 da (Gabriel b 1970); *Career* served as 2 Lt with 42 Commando RM 1956–58; entered Dip Serv 1962, FO 1962–63, Treasy Centre for Admin Studies 1964, Chinese languages student Hong Kong 1964–66, Peking 1967–68, FO 1969–71, office of Perm Rep to EEC 1972–74, asst private sec to Sec of State for Foreign and Cwlth Affrs (Rt Hon James Callaghan, Rt Hon Anthony Crosland) 1974–76, head of EEC Presidency Secretariat FCO 1976–77, visiting fell All Souls Coll Oxford 1977–78, cncllr Washington 1978–81, head Def Dept FCO 1981–84, asst under sec of State FCO 1984–85, min Paris 1985–88, dep sec to the Cabinet 1988–89, dep under sec of state FCO 1989–90, political dir FCO 1990–91; UK perm rep: at NATO Brussels 1992–July 1995, to Western European Union 1993–July 1995; UK perm rep and ambass to UN and on Security Cncl NY July 1995–; *Recreations* fly-fishing, running, birds, poetry; *Clubs* Flyfishers', Garrick, Utd Oxford and Cambridge Univ; *Style*— HE Sir John Weston, KCMG; ✉ c/o Foreign and Commonwealth Office (UKMIS New York), King Charles St, London SW1

WESTON, John Pix; s of Lt John Pix Weston (d 1968), of Harborne, Birmingham, and Margaret Elizabeth, *née* Cox (d 1946); *b* 3 Jan 1920; *Educ* King Edward's Birmingham, Aston Univ Birmingham (BSc), LSE (BSc), Univ of Georgia USA (Dip); *m* 5 Aug 1948, Ivy, da of Walter Glover, of Northallerton, Yorks; 3 s (John b 1951, David b 1958, Ian Christopher b 1963); *Career* Nat Serv Sgt RAMC 1939, 203 Mil Liaison Mission SA 1940–44, Allied Mil Liaison HQ (Albania) and GHQ (Southern) Cairo 1944–45, HQ NI Dist 1945–46; City of Birmingham Police Dept 1936–39, various posts in electricity supply industry 1946–58, ops mangr Jamaica Public Service Co 1958–61, princ asst engr and acting asst chief commercial offr MEB 1961–64, asst chief commercial offr SSEB 1964–66, sr econ advsr to Min of Transport 1966–69, sr economist and engr Int Bank for Reconstruction and Devpt Washington 1968–70, sr mangr Michelin Tyre Co 1970–72, dir Post Experience Courses Open Univ 1972–75, dir-gen Royal Soc for the Prevention of Accidents 1974–78, industl devpt offr Argyll and Bute DC 1977–79, health and safety advsr Newcastle Poly and Northants CC 1979, chief admin offr W Bromwich Coll of Commerce and Technol 1979–85, conslt engr and economist 1985–; Birmingham Photographic Soc 1979–85: prog sec, competition sec, outings sec, memb Cncl; memb Cncl Midland Counties Photographic Fedn 1982–85, chm Upper Marlbrook Residents' Assoc 1982–87; lectr: Allen Tech Inst Kendal 1951–58, Ipswich Civic Coll 1958–60, Halesowen Coll of Further Educn 1961–64, Bromsgrove Coll of Further Educn 1961–64, Aston Univ Birmingham 1961–64; SBStJ 1965; author of numerous papers on educn, engrg, tport and safety; CEng 1953, AMIEE 1958, FSS 1957, FREconS 1957, MAPLE 1958, MIEE 1964, FIEE 1966, FIMgt 1973; *Recreations* fell walking, swimming, gardening, cine and still photography; *Clubs* Farmers', St John House; *Style*— John Weston, Esq; ✉ Brook Mill and Woodside, Brook, Pendine, Dyfed SA33 4NX (☎ 01994 427477)

WESTON, Keith Andrew; s of Walter Henry Ernest Weston, of Beaconsfield, and Sheila Mary, *née* Anderson; *b* 19 Dec 1953; *Educ* Royal GS High Wycombe, Portsmouth Poly; *m* 28 Aug 1984, Jane Elizabeth; 2 s (Luke David b 18 May 1988, James Henry b 7 Feb 1991); *Career* chartered accountant; R M Blaikie & Co 1974–76; Saffery Champness: joined 1976, ptnr 1983–, head Harrogate office 1992–; ACA 1979; *Recreations* participating in golf and squash, spectator of most sports including rugby, football, golf and cricket; *Clubs* RAC; *Style*— Keith Weston, Esq; ✉ Saffery Champness, 6 Windsor Court, Clarence Drive, Harrogate, N Yorks HG1 2PE (☎ 01423 568012, fax 01423 501798, mobile 0831 692124)

WESTON, Dame Margaret Kate; DBE (1979); da of Charles Edward and Margaret Weston; *b* 7 March 1926; *Educ* Stroud HS, Coll of Technology Birmingham (now Univ of Aston); *Career* engrg apprenticeship and devpt work General Electric Company Ltd; asst keeper Dept of Electrical Engrg and Communications Sci Museum 1955 (dep keeper 1962, keeper of Dept of Museum Servs 1967); dir Sci Museum 1973–86; govr: Imperial Coll of Sci and Technol 1974–89, Ditchley Fndn 1985– (memb Cncl of Mgmnt); pres Assoc of Ind Railway and Preservation Socs; vice pres Tport Tst; chm Horniman Museum 1988–97; tstee: Brooklands Museum, Hunterian Collection, Fleet Air Arm Museum; memb: Museum and Galleries Cmmn 1988–96, 1851 Cmmn 1988–95, Ct RCA, SE Electricty Bd 1981–90, Cncl RSA 1985–90; Hon DSc: Univ of Aston 1974, Univ of Salford 1984, Univ of Leeds 1987; Hon DEng: Univ of Bradford 1984, Univ of Loughborough 1987; Hon DUniv Open Univ 1987; fell: Imperial Coll London 1975, Newnham Coll Cambridge 1986; sr fell RCA 1986, FMA, FINucE, FRSA; Medal Inst of Engrs and Shipbuilders in Scotland; *Recreations* music, travel, gardening, getting involved in a few things; *Style*— Dame Margaret Weston, DBE; (☎ 01737 355885)

WESTON, Sir Michael Charles Swift; KCMG (1992), CVO (1979); s of Edward Charles Swift Weston (d 1982), Kathleen Mary, *née* Mockett (d 1996); *b* 4 Aug 1937; *Educ* Rose Hill Sch Tunbridge Wells, Dover Coll Dover, St Catharine's Coll Cambridge (exhibitioner, MA); *m* 1 (m dis); 2 s (Simon b 1963, Justin b 1965), 1 da (Antonia-Jane b 1970); m 2, 1990, Christine Julia Ferguson; 1 s (Tobias b 1993), 1 da (Catharine b 1996); *Career* HM Dip Serv: joined 1961, third sec Kuwait 1962–65, second sec FCO 1965–68, first sec Tehran 1968–70, UK Mission NY 1970–74, FCO 1974–77, cnsllr Jedda 1977–80, RCDS 1980–81, cnsllr (info) Paris 1981–84, cnsllr Cairo 1984–87, head of Southern Euro Dept FCO 1987–90, ambass Kuwait 1990–92, UK perm rep to Conf on Disarmament Geneva (with personal rank of ambass) 1992–; *Recreations* squash, tennis, walking, bridge; *Clubs* United Oxford and Cambridge Univ; *Style*— Sir Michael Weston, KCMG, CVO; ✉ c/o FCO (Geneva), King Charles Street, London SW1A 2AH (Geneva ☎ 00 41 22 918 2300)

WESTON, Prof Richard Henry; s of Raymond Charles Weston (d 1982), and Winifred May, *née* Hook (1985); *b* 20 March 1944; *Educ* Univ of London (BSc), Univ of Southampton (PhD); *m* 1, 14 Feb 1962 (m dis 1976), Sylvia June, *née* Gregg; 2 s (Keith Richard b 1962, Ian Michael b 1964); m 2, 25 May 1985, Betty, da of Leonard Whitear, of Loughborough; 1 da (Nicola Michelle b 1980); *Career* pro-vice chllr res and prof of engrg Loughborough Univ of Technol, head MSI Res Inst; supervisor of over 50 postgrad students, various overseas educnl appts, princ investigator for over 20 major UK and Euro res studies in mfrg, retained conslt by numerous UK companies, tech advsr to Sci and Engrg Res Cncl, DTI and ICL; author of in excess of 200 res pubns on mfrg engrg topics with special interest in manufacturing systems integration, information systems and robotics; memb: Bd of Int Jls, Br and Euro Standards Bodies; FIEE 1984, FRSA; *Books* incl: Software for Modular Robots (contrib, 1984), Integrating Robots Within Production Systems Encyclopaedia of Systems and Control (contrib, 1988), The Automated Manufacturing Directory (ed 4 edns, 1985), Fluid Power 8 (contrib, 1988), Modular Robots Encyclopaedia of Systems and Control (contrib, 1988), Contouring with Pneumatic Servo-Driven Robots (contrib, 1988); *Recreations* golf, bridge, squash, football (Univ colours); *Style*— Prof Richard Weston; ✉ Department of Manufacturing Engineering, Loughborough University, Loughborough, Leics LE11 3TU (☎ 01509 222907, fax 01509 267725)

WESTON SMITH, John Harry; s of Cdr Weston Smith, OBE, RN (1986); *b* 3 Feb 1932; *Educ* Fettes, St John's Coll Cambridge (MA); *m* 1955, Margaret Fraser, da of Prof E A Milne, FRS (d 1954); 1 s (Hugh b 1961), 2 da (Miranda b 1956, Lucinda b 1964); *Career* jt gen mangr Abbey National 1968–69 (sec 1961–68), with N M Rothschild 1969–71; British Land Co PLC: joined as co sec 1971, dir 1973–, fin dir 1989–, md British Land Corporation 1991–; dir various other cos; chm Govrs of St Christopher's Sch Hampstead; FCIS, ACII, ACIB; *Style*— John Weston Smith, Esq; ✉ 10 Eldon Grove, London NW3 (☎ 0171 435 5069); Sydenhams Farm House, Bisley, Glos (☎ 01452 770047)

WESTROPP, Anthony Henry (Harry); s of Col Lionel Henry Mountefort Westropp (d 1991), and Muriel Constance Lilian, *née* Jorgensen; *b* 22 Dec 1944; *Educ* Sherborne, King's Coll London; *m* 1, 7 Dec 1977 (m dis 1991), Zoë Rosaleen, da of (Charles) Douglas Neville Walker, of Paris; m 2, 6 May 1993, Hon Victoria Monica Watson, da of 3 Baron Manton; 1 da (Marina b 1993); *Career* with Lazard Bros & Co Ltd 1967–72, dir of subsidiaries Trafalgar House Gp 1972–75, md private gp of cos 1975–81; gp md: Bardsey plc 1981–90, The Beckenham Group plc 1990–91; non-exec dir: Portman Building Society 1982–, Nickerson Group Rothwell Ltd 1991– (chm), MCD UK Ltd 1994–, Marling Industries plc 1994–; chm: Britton Group PLC 1992–95, Abacus Polar Group plc 1994–, Norbain plc 1996–; Freeman Co of Cutlers (Sheffield) 1982; *Recreations* hunting, fishing, skiing; *Clubs* Boodle's; *Style*— Harry Westropp, Esq; ✉ Wootton Downs Farmhouse, Woodstock, Oxon OX20 1AF (☎ 01869 83222)

WESTROPP, Eric Mountefort; CBE (1982); s of Col Lionel Henry Mountefort Westropp, and Muriel Constance Lilian, *née* Jorgensen; *see* Burkes Irish Family Records; *b* 30 March 1939; *Educ* Wellington, Camberley Staff Coll; *m* 18 Oct 1963, Jill Mary, da of Rear Adm I G Aylen, of Honiton, Devon; 2 s (Richard b 1965, Patrick b 1966), 1 da (Victoria b 1969); *Career* cmmnd 11 Hussars (PAO) 1958, served NI, ME, BAOR, Bde Maj 51 Inf Bde Hong Kong 1972–74, exec offr to Dep SACEUR at SHAPE in Belgium 1976–78, cmd Royal Hussars (PWO) 1978–80, Brig 33 Armd Bde BAOR 1983–85, ret; joined Control Risks Ltd 1985 (dir 1986), md Control Risks Response Services Ltd 1987–; *Recreations* riding, skiing, photography, reading; *Clubs* Special Forces; *Style*— Eric Westropp, Esq, CBE; ✉ The White House, Bloxworth, Wareham, Dorset (☎ 01929 459356); Control Risks Ltd, 83 Victoria St, London SW1 (☎ 0171 222 1552)

WESTROPP, George Victor; s of Edward L Westropp (d 1962), of Epsom, Surrey, and Mary Breward, *née* Hughes (d 1973); *b* 2 Nov 1943; *Educ* Bedford Sch; *m* 12 Jan 1972 (m dis 1973), Alexander Jeanne, da of Joseph Steinberg; m 2, 9 May 1977 (m dis 1988), Christine June, da of Alan Ashley, of London; 2 s (Edward b 1980, Kit b 1982); *Career* reporter City Press 1961–63, city reporter Sunday Express 1963, fin journalist Evening Standard 1963–68, Extel (asst city ed 1968–69); dir Shareholder Relations Ltd 1969–73, fin PR exec PPR International Ltd 1974–76, md Hemingway Public Relations Ltd 1977–79, nat dir of communications Touche Ross (now Deloitte & Touche) 1979– (ptnr 1985–); MIPR, FRSA; *Books* The Lake Vyrnwy Fishing Book (1979), Lake Vyrnwy - The Story of a Sporting Hotel (1992); *Recreations* salmon and trout fishing, gardening; *Clubs* London Press (chm 1990–), Room 74; *Style*— George Westropp, Esq; ✉ 36 Holley Rd, London W3 7TS (☎ 0181 743 1752); Deloitte & Touche, Stonecutter Court, 1 Stonecutter Street, London EC4A 4TR (☎ 0171 936 3000, car tel 0374 412480)

WESTWELL, Dr Alan Reynolds; OBE (1996); s of Stanley Westwell (d 1980), of Liverpool, and Margaret, *née* Reynolds (d 1962); *b* 11 April 1940; *Educ* Old Swan Coll, Liverpool Poly (ACT Hons), Univ of Salford (MSc), Univ of Keele (PhD); *m* 30 Oct 1967, (Elizabeth) Aileen, da of John Birrell (d 1975), of Fife, Scotland; 2 s (Stephen b 1972, Colin (twin) b 1972), 1 da (Julie b 1970); *Career* asst works mangr (previously engrg apprentice and tech asst) Liverpool City Tport Dept 1956–67; chief engr: Southport Corp Tport Dept 1967–69, Coventry Corp Tport Dept 1969–72, Glasgow Corp Tport Dept

1972–74; dir of public tport Tayside Regnl Cncl 1974–79, dir gen Strathclyde Passenger Tport Exec 1979–86, chm and md Strathclyde Buses Ltd 1986–90; chief exec and md: Greater Manchester Buses Ltd 1991–93, Greater Manchester Buses (North) Ltd 1993–; public tport professional advsr Convention of Scottish Local Authorities (COSLA) 1975–85; Int Public Tport Union (UITP, based Brussels): chm Br Membership 1993–, memb Exec Mgmnt Ctee 1992–, memb Euro Action Ctee, memb Public Tport and Urban Planning Cmmn; elder Hale Utd Reformed Church; CEng, FCIT, MIMechE, MIEE; *Recreations* golf, swimming, tennis, music, reading; *Style—* Dr Alan Westwell, OBE; ✉ 6 Amberley Drive, Hale Barns, Cheshire WA15 0DT (☎ 0161 980 3551); Greater Manchester Buses (North) Ltd, Wallshaw Street, Oldham OL1 3TR (☎ 0161 627 2929, fax 0161 627 5845)

WESTWICK, Christopher Alan; s of Edward Westwick (d 1977), of Whitley Bay, and Winifred, *née* Shrimpton (d 1981); *b* 30 Oct 1933; *Educ* St Paul's Sch, LSE (BSc); *m* 1966, Dr Wendy Josephine Griffin; 1 s (Robert David b 21 Dec 1974), 1 da (Rachel Jane b 14 May 1973); *Career* CA; sr project exec Centre for Interfirm Comparison 1960–69, mgmnt conslt Associated Industrial Consultants 1969–71, tech under sec ICAEW 1971–75, sec Inflation Accounting Steering Gp 1976–77, tech dir ICAEW 1977–78, res fell LSE 1978–79, sr memb Arthur Andersen UK Tech Gp 1979–93, conslt 1993–; sec Cathedral Accounts Working Pty 1993–; lectures widely and is author of numerous articles in professional jls; FCA; *Publications* A study of profitability in the hosiery and knitwear industry (1971), Accuracy of profit forecasts in bid situations (1972), Investment appraisal for the clothing industry (1973), Accounting for Inflation: a working guide to the accounting procedures (1973), How to use management ratios (1973, 2 edn 1987), Investment Appraisal and Inflation (with P S D Shohet, 1976), Property Valuation and Accounts (1980), Sources of British Business Comparitive Performance Data (1980, 2 edn with W Westwick 1986), Current Cost Accounting (with P R Hinton, 1980), Do the Figures Make Sense? A practical guide to analytical review (1981), Inflation Accounting Around the World (with Ian Hay Davison, 1981), Profit forecasts: how they are made, reviewed and used (1983), Accounting for overseas operations (1986); *Recreations* walking, skating, skiing, sailing, model engineering, reading, music, good food and wine, country dancing; *Style—* C A Westwick, Esq; ✉ 20 Brookway, London SE3 9BJ

WESTWOOD, 3 Baron (UK 1944); (William) Gavin Westwood; s of 2 Baron Westwood, JP (d 1991), and Marjorie, *née* Bonwick; *b* 30 Jan 1944; *Educ* Fettes; *m* 1969, Penelope, FCA, da of Charles Edgar Shafto, VRD, MB (d 1994); 2 s (Hon William Fergus b 1972, Hon Alistair Cameron b 1974); *Heir* s, Hon William Fergus Westwood b 24 Nov 1972; *Career* co dir; *Style—* The Rt Hon Lord Westwood; ✉ Ferndale, Clayton Road, Newcastle upon Tyne, NE2 1TL

WESTWOOD, Hon Nigel Alistair; yr s of 2 Baron Westwood, JP (d 1991), and Marjorie, *née* Bonwick; *b* 1950; *Educ* Fettes; *m* 1977, Joan Elizabeth, yr da of Reginald Ibison, CBE; 2 s (David Alistair b 1983, Peter Robert b 1986); *Career* chartered surveyor; hon Norwegian consul, chllr Consular Corps Newcastle upon Tyne; Knight First Class Royal Norwegian Order of Merit 1995; FRICS, FRSA; *Clubs* Northern Counties, Den Norske; *Style—* The Hon Nigel Westwood; ✉ 7 Fernville Rd, Gosforth, Newcastle-upon-Tyne NE3 4HT

WESTWOOD, Vivienne; OBE (1992); *b* 8 April 1941; *Career* fashion designer; a series of influential avant garde collections showcased at World's End 430 King's Road (formerly named Let it Rock, Too Fast to Live Too Young to Die, Sex, Seditionaries) 1971–82; collections: Pirate (Olympia) 1981, Savage (Olympia) 1981, Buffalo (Olympia) 1982, Punkature (Court de Louvre Paris) 1982, Witches (Court de Louvre Paris) 1983, Hypnos (Court de Louvre Paris, Best of Five Tokyo) 1983, Clint Eastwood (Paris) 1985, Mini Crini (Paris, Limelight NY) 1985, Harris Tweed (Olympia) 1987, Pagan I (Olympia) 1988, Time Machine (Olympia) 1988, Civilizade (Olympia) 1989, Voyage to Cythera (Olympia) 1989, Pagan V (Olympia) 1989, Portrait (IOD) 1990, Cut & Slash (Villa de Gamberaia) 1990, Cut Slash & Pull (IOD) 1990, Dressing Up (Azzedine Alaia, Paris) 1991, Salon (Azzedine Alaia, Paris) 1991, Always on Camera (Le Monde de l'Art, Paris) 1992, Grand Hotel (Grand Hotel, Paris) 1992, Anglomania (Cercle Republicain, Paris) 1993, Cafe Society (Grand Hotel, Paris) 1993, On Liberty (Le Carrousel du Louvre, Paris) 1994, Erotic Zones 1994, Vive la Cocotte 1995, Les Femmes 1995, Storm in a Teacup 1995, first showed menswear collection in Milan 1996; opened shop in: Davies St Mayfair 1990, Tokyo 1996; prof of fashion: Vienna Acad of Applied Arts 1989–91, Berlin Hochschule 1993–; profiled South Bank Show (LWT) 1990; British Designer of the Year 1990 and 1991; *Style—* Ms Vivienne Westwood, OBE; ✉ Vivienne Westwood Ltd, Westwood Studios, 9–15 Elcho Street, Battersea, London SW11 4AU (☎ 0171 924 4747)

WESTWOOD, Rt Rev William John; s of Ernest, and Charlotte Westwood; *b* 28 Dec 1925; *Educ* Grove Park GS Wrexham, Emmanuel Coll Cambridge (MA), Westcott House Cambridge; *m* 1954, Shirley Ann, yr da of Dr Norman Jennings; 1 s, 1 da; *Career* served Army 1944–47; rector of Lowestoft 1957–65, vicar of St Peter Mancroft Norwich 1965–75, rural dean of Norwich 1966–70, hon canon Norwich Cathedral 1969–75, city dean of Norwich 1970–73, area bishop of Edmonton 1975–84, bishop of Peterborough 1984–95, ret; memb Archbishops' Cmmn on Church and State 1966–70, church cmmr 1973–78 and 1985–92; memb Press Cncl 1975–81, chm of govrs Coll of All Saints Tottenham 1976–78; memb Ct: Nene Coll Northampton, Univ of Leicester, Univ of Nottingham 1985–95; tstee: Uppingham Sch 1985–95 (chm 1993–95), Oakham Sch 1985–95; chm C of E Ctee for Communications 1979–86; memb IBA Panel of Religious Advrs 1983–87; memb: BBFC Video Consultative Cncl 1985–89, Bdcasting Standards Cncl 1988–92, Health Educn Authy 1992–, Volunteering Partnership 1995–; pres: English Churches Housing Tst 1985–95 (formerly chm 3 housing assocs), Nat Deaf-Blind League 1991–95, E of England Agricultural Soc 1994–95; hon fell Emmanuel Coll Cambridge, Hon LLD Univ of Leicester; Freeman City of London 1988; *Recreations* the countryside, wine bars, art galleries; *Style—* The Rt Rev William Westwood; ✉ 102 Thwaite Street, Cottingham, East Riding, Yorkshire HU16 4RQ

WETHERED, (James) Adam Lawrence; *b* 2 April 1953; *Educ* Eton, Christ's Coll Cambridge (BA, LLB); *m* Dr Diana Wethered; 5 c; *Career* called to the Bar Inner Temple 1975; J P Morgan: joined 1976, corp fin banker Shipping and Scandinavian Depts 1977–83, Energy and Minerals Dept 1983–84, head Shipping Fin Dept London 1984–86, head Specialised Fin Dept London 1986–88, Strategic Planning and Mgmnt Reporting, Securities Servs, Ops Products and Global Support NY 1988–89, memb London Mgmnt Ctee i/c Ops, Technol, Audit, Financial, Legal & Compliance, Personnel, Facilities and Servs 1990–91, i/c Cost Restructuring Prog NY 1991, fixed income underwriting mangr Europe 1991–93, chief exec J P Morgan Securities Ltd and chm London Mgmnt Ctee 1993–, also head of credit Europe, Middle E and Africa and memb Global Corp Fin Mgmnt Ctee, dir J P Morgan et Cie and Morgan Guaranty International Finance Corporation; bd dir SFA 1993–; *Style—* Adam Wethered, Esq; ✉ J P Morgan Securities Ltd, 60 Victoria Embankment, London EC4Y 0DX (☎ 0171 600 2300)

WETHERED, Simon Richard; s of Dr Rodney Richard Wethered (d 1995), of Nupend House, Stonehouse, Glos, and Sarah Meriel, *née* Long-Price; *b* 1 March 1945; *Educ* Clifton, Worcester Coll Oxford (BA); *m* 9 Sept 1978, Victoria, da of Adm of the Fleet Sir Michael Le Fanu, GCB, DSC (d 1970); 2 s (Edward b 1983, Charles b 1988), 1 da (Anna b 1981); *Career* admitted slr 1970; ptnr: Simmons & Simmons 1974–78, Alsop Wilkinson (formerly Wilkinson Kimbers) 1978–; licensed insolvency practitioner 1987–; memb Soc of Practitioners of Insolvency and Insolvency Practitioners Assoc, dir Academy Concerts Soc 1984–; dir FIMBRA 1987–, memb: PIA Appeals Tbnl, Law Soc 1970–; visitor HMP Wormwood Scrubs 1984–; Liveryman Worshipful Co of Distillers; *Recreations* wine, music, sailing, walking; *Clubs* City Law, Bosham Sailing, Hogarth; *Style—* Simon Wethered, Esq; ✉ 29 Burlington Road, London W4 4BQ (☎ 0181 994 6392); 6 Dowgate Hill, London EC4R 2SS (☎ 0171 248 4141, fax 0171 623 8286, telex 885543, car tel 0860 828 664)

WETHERELL, Gordon Geoffrey; s of Geoffrey Wetherell, of Addis Ababa, Ethiopia, and Georgette Maria, *née* Matkovitch; *b* 11 Nov 1948; *Educ* Bradfield, New Coll Oxford (BA, MA), Univ of Chicago (MA); *m* 11 July 1981, Rosemary Anne, da of Cdr Terence Macrae Myles, RN, ret, of Crieff, Perthshire; 4 da (Christine b 1982, Stephanie b 1985, Emily b 1987, Alexandra b 1989); *Career* FCO (concurrently third sec/vice consul to Br Embassy Chad) 1973–74, third then second sec E Berlin 1974–77; first sec: UK delegation to comprehensive test ban negotiations Geneva 1977–80, New Delhi 1980–83, NATO Desk Defence Dept FCO 1983–85; secondment to HM Treasy 1986–87, asst head Euro Communities Dept (External) FCO 1987–88, cnsllr and dep head of mission Warsaw 1988–92, cnsllr Bonn 1992–94, head Personnel Servs Dept FCO 1994–; *Recreations* tennis, travel, reading, Manchester Utd FC; *Clubs* Oxford and Cambridge; *Style—* Gordon Wetherell, Esq; ✉ FCO, King Charles Street, London SW1A 2AH (☎ 0171 270 2533)

WETHERELL, John Michael Hugh Paxton; s of Paxton Wetherell, MBE (d 1978), of Whitstable, Kent, and Catherine Wilson, *née* Collins (d 1992); *b* 24 Oct 1942; *Educ* Ampleforth; *m* 2 May 1964, Elizabeth Ann, da of Harold Thompson (d 1988), of Broadstairs, Kent; 1 s (Joseph b 1979), 5 da (Laura b 1966, Kate b 1968, Beatrice b 1972, Gabrielle b 1974, Jessica b 1978); *Career* Lloyd's underwriter Janson Green/Bolton Ingham Non-Marine Syndicate 1983; dir: Bolton Ingham Agency Ltd 1983–88, Janson Green Management Ltd 1986–91, Cater Allen Syndicate Management Ltd 1992–94, Liberty Syndicate Management Ltd 1994–; memb Lloyd's 1973; *Recreations* reading, music, racing; *Clubs* City University; *Style—* John Wetherell, Esq; ✉ c/o Liberty Syndicate Management Ltd, 1 Minster Court, Mincing Lane, London EC3R 7AA

WEYLAND, HE Joseph; s of Adolph Weyland (d 1981), and Marie, *née* Kox (d 1985); *b* 24 April 1943; *Educ* Luxembourg, Univ of Paris (LLD), Institut d'Etudes Politiques Paris (dipl); *m* Bénédicte, *née* Boucquéau; 2 s (Serge b 16 Nov 1973, Philippe b 23 June 1977); *Career* Luxembourg diplomat; attaché Foreign Miny Luxembourg 1968–69, sec Luxembourg Embassy Bonn 1969–72, dep dir of protocol 1972–76, dep perm rep to the EEC 1976–79, dir for foreign trade Foreign Miny Luxembourg 1979–83, perm rep to the UN NYC 1983–84, perm rep to the EEC Brussels 1984–91, sec gen Foreign Miny Luxembourg 1991–92, ambass to the Ct of St James's 1993–; chm Intergovernmental Conf on Political Union leading to Maastricht Treaty 1991, rep of Luxembourg to Intergovernmental Conf leading to Single European Market 1985; *Books* Le Traité de Maastricht (co-author, 1993); *Clubs* Rotary, RAC; *Style—* HE Mr Joseph Weyland; ✉ Embassy of Luxembourg, 27 Wilton Crescent, London SW1X 8SD (☎ 0171 235 6961)

WHADDON, Baron (Life Peer UK 1978), of Whaddon, Co Cambridge; (John) Derek Page; s of John Page and Clare, *née* Maher; *b* 14 Aug 1927; *Educ* St Bede's Coll Manchester, Univ of London (BSc); *m* 1, 1948, Catherine Audrey (d 1979), da of John William Halls; 1 s (Hon John Keir b 1955), 1 da (Hon Eve-Ann (Hon Mrs Prentice) b 1952); m 2, 1981, Angela Rixson, da of Luigi della Bella, of Treviso, Italy; *Career* dir: Cambridge Chemicals 1962–89, Rindalbourne 1983–90; chm: Microautomatics Ltd 1981–87, Daltrade 1983–, Skorimpex-Rind 1985–; MP (Lab) King's Lynn 1964–70, joined SDP 1981 (Lib Democrats since 1989); memb Mgmnt Cncl COSIRA 1976–83; *Recreations* flying; *Clubs* Reform; *Style—* The Rt Hon Lord Whaddon; ✉ c/o House of Lords, London SW1A 0PW; The Old Vicarage, Whaddon, Royston, Herts

WHALE, James; s of David L Whale (d 1979), of London, and Anne Elizabeth, *née* Price; *b* 13 May 1951; *Educ* various schs Surrey (Surrey Jr Archery Champion 1965), Marion Ross Sch of Drama; *m* 10 March 1970, Melinda Jane Maxted; 2 s (James, Peter); *Career* radio and TV presenter; worked in repertory theatre 1970–71; *Radio*: fndr DJ Radio Top Shop Oxford Circus 1971–73; presenter: Metro Radio Newcastle 1973–80, Line Up (BBC Radio Derby) 1980–81, Whale Up The Tees (Radio Tees) 1981–82, Friday File (Radio Aire Leeds) 1982–90; other appearances: Midweek (BBC R4) 1985, Atlantic 252 1990, Radio York 1993, GLR 1993, LBC 1994, Century Radio (Newcastle upon Tyne) 1994, Talk Radio UK 1995–; *Television* Three's Company (Tyne Tees TV) 1981–82, Eleanor Live (HTV) 1986, Open Exchange (Channel Four) 1987, The James Whale Radio Show (YTV) 1988–92, It's Your Round (BSB) 1991, Pick of the Week (Yorkshire TV) 1991–93, Central Weekend (Central TV) 1991–95, James Whale Paper Round (Tyne Tees TV) 1991, Parents (YTV) 1992, People Today (BBC TV) 1992, Dial Midnight (LWT) 1992, The James Whale Debate (YTV) 1993, Whale On..... (LWT) 1993 and 1994, You're Booked (LWT) 1994, The James Whale Show (LWT) 1995; *Awards* three Sony Awards, Smash Hits Local Personality of the Year 1984; nominations incl: Best Phone In Show 1976, Radio Personality of the Yeard 1994 (TRIC Awards); *Recreations* eating, archery and enjoying life; *Style—* James Whale, Esq; ✉ Stuart Hobday Associates, 30 Winchester Avenue, Ashton-under-Lyne, Lancashire OL6 8BU (☎ and fax 0161 308 4044)

WHALEN, Sir Geoffrey Henry; kt (1995), CBE (1989); s of Henry Charles Whalen (d 1981), and Mabel Elizabeth Whalen (d 1965); *b* 8 Jan 1936; *Educ* East Ham GS, Magdalen Coll Oxford (MA); *m* 1961, Elizabeth Charlotte, da of Dr Eric Waud, of Helperby, Yorks; 2 s (Thomas b 1967, Henry b 1977), 3 da (Catherine b 1963, Anna b 1965, Georgina b 1975); *Career* personnel dir Leyland Cars British Leyland 1975–78; Peugeot Talbot Motor Co PLC: asst md 1981–84, md 1984–90, dep chm and md 1990–95, non-exec dir 1995–; former dir: Robins and Day Ltd, Talbot Ireland Ltd, Proptal UK Ltd, Motaquip Ltd, Sunbeam-Talbot Ltd; pres Soc of Motor Manufacturers & Traders 1988–90 and 1993–94; govr Coventry Univ (formerly Poly) 1989–95; non-exec dir: Coventry Building Society, T & N Plc, Lombard North Central plc, Caradon Plc, Hall Engineering (Holdings) Plc; chm Hills Precision Components Ltd; Liveryman Worshipful Co of Coachmakers & Coach Harness Makers; Hon DBA; CIMgt, FIMI; Chevalier de la Legion d'Honneur 1990; *Recreations* cricket, tennis, golf; *Clubs* United Oxford and Cambridge Univ; *Style—* Sir Geoffrey Whalen, CBE; ✉ 8 Park Crescent, Abingdon, Oxfordshire; c/o Peugeot Talbot Motor Co PLC, Aldermoor House, PO Box 227, Aldermoor Lane, Coventry CV3 1LT (☎ 01203 884000, fax 01203 884001)

WHALLEY, Guy Ainsworth; s of Philip Guy Rothay Whalley, CBE (d 1950), and Norah Helen, *née* Mawdsley (d 1981), direct descendant of Col Edward Whalley, cousin of Oliver Cromwell and Signatory of The Death Warrant of King Charles I; *b* 26 May 1933; *Educ* Rugby, Gonville and Caius Coll Cambridge (BA, MA); *m* 22 Aug 1959, Sarah, da of Walter William Knight (d 1966); 1 s (Philip Mark b 1961), 1 da (Katherine Jane b 1962); *Career* Nat Serv 2 Lt Royal Fus 1951–53, active serv Korean War 1952–53; slr Supreme Ct 1959, ptnr Freshfields Slrs 1964–93, non-exec dir Higgs and Hill plc 1972–94; chm Ctee of Mgmnt RAM 1990– (dir and memb 1982–); govr Beechwood Park Sch 1974–88 (chm 1975–84), co-opted memb Oxford Univ Appointments Ctee 1982–92; tstee: Rugby Sch War Meml Fund 1980–, Rugby Sch Gen Charitable Tst 1986–; vice chm Jt Servs Ctee Herts Family Health Servs Authy 1994–; *Recreations* gardening, music, cricket, golf, painting; *Clubs* MCC; *Style—* Guy Whalley, Esq; ✉ Woodmans Farm, Chipperfield, Hertfordshire (☎ and fax 01923 263794); 8B Wyndham Place, London W1 (☎ 0171 258 0469)

WHALLEY, Jeffrey; *b* 20 Nov 1942; *Career* FKI plc: joined 1980, gp md 1980–89, non-exec chm 1989–; md: Gartland & Whalley Securities Ltd 1989–, Gartland & Whalley Holdings Ltd 1989–, Crossley House Developments Capital Ltd; non-exec dep chm Babcock International Group PLC, non-exec dir Quadramatic plc; *Style—* Jeffrey Whalley, Esq; ✉ Gartland & Whalley Securities Ltd, Crossley House, Hopwood Lane Halifax, West Yorkshire HX1 5EB (☎ 01422 349401, fax 01422 349395); FKI plc, West House, King Cross Road, Halifax, W Yorkshire HX1 1EB (☎ 01422 330267, fax 01422 330084)

WHALLEY, John Mayson; s of George Mayson Whalley (d 1968), and Ada Florence, *née* Cairns (d 1989); *b* 14 Sept 1932; *Educ* The Grammar Sch Preston, Univ of Liverpool (BArch (1st Class Hons), MCD, Sir Charles Reilly medal), Univ of Pennsylvania (MLA); *m* 21 May 1966, (Elizabeth) Gillian, da of Walter Hide; 1 s (James b 1972), 2 da (Emma b 1968, Tamsin b 1970); *Career* landscape architecture Oskar Stonorov Philadelphia 1958–60, architect and landscape architect Grenfell Baines & Hargreaves and Building Design Partnership Preston 1960–62, assoc Derek Lovejoy & Associates 1963–68, ptnr Derek Lovejoy & Partners 1968–93; fndr and sr ptnr: DLP Manchester 1963–93, J M W International Preston 1993–; Leverhulme and Italian govt fellowships for study in Scandinavia and Univ of Rome 1957–58, Fulbright scholar 1958, Manchester Soc of Architects Winstanley fellowship 1965; Civic Tst awards: W Burton Power Station 1968, Cheshire Constabulary HQ 1969, Rochdale Canal 1973, Royal Life Offices Peterborough 1992; first prize int competition: Cergy-Pontoise Urban Park France 1970, regnl park at La Courneuve Paris 1972; first prizes design competition: Liverpool Int Garden Festival 1984, Stoke-on-Trent Garden Festival 1986, Glasgow Garden Festival 1988, Urban Park Vitoria-Gasteiz Spain 1990, Nanatsudo Park Mito City Japan 1991; Civic Tst Awards assessor 1970–92; chm RIBA NW Region 1984–85, pres Manchester Soc of Architects 1980–81, nat pres Landscape Inst 1985–87; contrib radio and TV programmes, author tech press articles and papers; memb French Order of Architects 1977, FRIBA 1968, FRTPI 1971, FLI 1970, FRSA 1986; *Recreations* jazz, salmon fishing, cricket, photography, travel, good food and wine; *Clubs* Ronnie Scott's, St James' (Manchester); *Style—* John M Whalley, Esq; ✉ J M W International, Dilworth House, Longridge, nr Preston PR3 3ST (☎ 01772 783262, fax 01772 783262)

WHALLEY, Prof Lawrence Jeffrey; s of James Anthony Whalley (d 1980), of St Annes-on-Sea, Lancs, and Florence Evelyn Whalley (d 1964); *b* 12 March 1946; *Educ* St Joseph's Coll, Univ of Newcastle (MB BS, MD), DPM; *m* 1969, Patricia Mary, da of Denis McCarthy; 3 da (Charlotte Louise b 1970, Amanda Sophie b 1971, Elizabeth Natalia b 1972); *Career* trainee psychiatrist, memb Clinical Scientific Staff MRC 1977–86, sr lectr in psychiatry Univ of Edinburgh 1986–91, Crombie Ross prof of mental health and head Dept of Mental Health Univ of Aberdeen 1992–; FRCPsych 1990; *Books* Ace Inhibitors: Central Actions (with Dr John Starr, 1994); author of over 100 scientific reports and articles; *Style—* Prof Lawrence Whalley; ✉ Department of Mental Health, Medical School, Foresterhill, Aberdeen AB9 2ZD (☎ 01224 681818, fax 01224 663145)

WHALLEY, Capt Richard Carlton; s of Frederick Seymour Whalley, MC (d 1958), of The Lawn, Marlow, Bucks, and Gwendolen, *née* Collingwood (d 1984); *b* 4 July 1922; *Educ* Shrewsbury, 151 OCTU; *m* 1 Aug 1945, Mary Christian, da of George Bradley (d 1954), of Hilltop Farm, Croxton Kerrial, Grantham, Lincs; 2 s (Jonathon b 1946, Peter b 1948), 2 da (Mary b 1951, Margaret (twin) b 1951); *Career* Regular Army 1940, cmmnd Royal Signals 1942, Indian Assam Burma Adj 2 Div Signals 1942–45 (despatches 1945), Staff Capt War Office 1945–48, GHQ Singapore 1948–51; Vulcan Foundry Ltd locomotive builders 1952–68 (asst sec, commercial mangr, gen mangr), mangr Diesel Engine Div English Electric, dir and gen mangr Glacier Metals 1968–70, dep chm and md Millspaugh Group 1971–77, divnl md Sulzer Bros UK, memb Bd Br Shipbuilders 1978–81, chm and md Ewden Associates Ltd 1982–; chm Working Pty NEDO, memb Industl Tbnls 1972–91; Freeman Worshipful Co of Cutlers; FInstD; *Recreations* rowing, walking; *Clubs* National Liberal, London Rowing, Sheffield; *Style—* Capt Richard Whalley; ✉ Sunnybank Farm, Bolsterstone, Sheffield S30 5ZL (☎ 0114 288 3116); Ewden Associates Ltd, Ewden House, Bolsterstone, Sheffield S30 5ZL (☎ and fax 0114 288 3116)

WHALLEY, Maj-Gen William Leonard; CB (1985); s of William Whalley (d 1952), and Doris Patricia, *née* Hallimond (d 1992); *b* 19 March 1930; *Educ* Sir William Turner's Sch Coatham, Royal Mil Coll of Sci; *m* 30 July 1955, (Honor) Mary, da of Maj Cyril Golden (d 1985); 1 da (Elisabeth Anne Mary b 7 July 1956); *Career* DG Ordnance Services 1983–85; Col cmdt: RAOC 1986–93, RLC 1993–94; life vice pres Army Boxing Assoc; pres: Little Aston Cons Branch, RAOC Charitable Tst; tstee Corby CTC Tst, chm of govrs Brooke Weston City Technol Coll 1991–96; *Recreations* cabinet making, bridge, information technology; *Style—* Maj-Gen William Whalley, CB; ✉ c/o Midland Bank plc, 8 High Street, Sutton Coldfield B72 1XB

WHARNCLIFFE, 5 Earl of (UK 1876) Richard Alan Montagu Stuart Wortley; also Baron Wharncliffe (UK 1826) and Viscount Carlton (UK 1876); er s of Alan Ralph Montagu Stuart Wortley (d 1986), and Virginia Ann, *née* Claybaugh; suc his kinsman 4 Earl of Wharncliffe (d 1987); *b* 26 May 1953; *Educ* Wesleyan Univ; *m* 1979, Mary Elizabeth, da of Rev William Wellington Reed, of Keene, NH, USA; 3 s (Viscount Carlton, Hon Christopher James b 1983, Hon Otis Alexander b 14 Feb 1991); *Heir* s, Reed Montagu Stuart Wortley, Viscount Carlton, b 5 Feb 1980; *Career* construction foreman; *Style—* The Rt Hon the Earl of Wharncliffe; ✉ 15 Sweetser Road, N Yarmouth, Maine 04097, USA

WHARTON, Dr Christopher Frederick Percy; s of John Christopher Wharton, of Banbury, Oxon, and Gertrude Margaret, *née* Dingwall; *b* 19 Feb 1937; *Educ* Shrewsbury Sch, Worcester Coll Oxford (BM BCh, MA, DM), MRCS, FRCP; *m* 10 Aug 1963 (m dis 1980), Andrea Mary Puckle, da of Andrew Gordon Leslie Puckle (d 1988), of Loxwood, W Sussex; 2 da (Antonia Helen Jane b 30 May 1969, (Virginia Phillippa Gertrude) Rose b 29 Oct 1972); m 2, 23 May 1980, Pamela Mary, da of Sqdn Ldr William Henry Deane, of Pretoria, SA; *Career* house offr and registrar in cardiology and gen med Guy's 1963–73, conslt physician in med and cardiology Bromley Acute Tst 1963–, hon tutor Guy's Med Sch 1979–, teacher Univ of London 1986– (clinical tutor 1974–84), dist tutor RCP 1989–94, cons rep Acute Tst Bd; chm: Bromly Acute Med Advsy Ctee, Mgmnt Ctee Chipstead Lake Cheshire Home; Freeman City of London 1982, Liveryman Worshipful Co of Gunmakers; FRCP 1980; memb: British Cardiac Soc 1982, BMA; *Books* Cardiological Problems in Practice (1981), Management of Common Disease in Practice Cardiology (with A R Archer, 1986); *Publications* various pubns on echocardiography (1967–72), Myocardial Infarct - Management and Rehabilitation article in Cardiac Update (1987), A Case of Angina - Dual Pathology (1989), Silent Ischaemia - What Implications (1989); *Recreations* shooting, golf, tennis, skiing, Chelsea FC, travel, wine and food; *Clubs* Athenaeum; *Style—* Dr Christopher Wharton; ✉ 24–26 High St, Chipstead, nr Sevenoaks, Kent TN13 2RP (☎ 01732 452906); The Medical Unit, Farnborough Hospital, Farnborough Common, Orpington, Kent (☎ 01689 814098)

WHARTON, Rt Rev (John) Martin; *see:* Kingston, Bishop of

WHARTON, Baroness (E 1544/5); Myrtle Olive Felix (Ziki) Robertson; *née* Arbuthnot; er da of David Arbuthnot (s of Maj John Arbuthnot, MVO, gn of Sir Robert Arbuthnot, 2 Bt), and Baroness Wharton, tenth holder of the title (d 1974); suc as eleventh holder of the title on termination of the abeyance in her favour 1990; *b* 20 Feb 1934; *m* 1958, Henry Macleod Robertson (d 1996), s of Henry Robertson, of Elgin; 3 s (Hon Myles Christopher David b 1964, Hon Christopher James b 1969, Hon Nicholas Charles (twin) b 1969), 1 da (Hon Patricia Lesley b 1966); *Heir* s, Hon Myles Christopher David Robertson b 1 Oct 1964; *Career* sits as cross bencher in House of Lords; memb: All Pty Media Gp, All Pty Gp for Animal Welfare; Hon Assoc Br Veterinary Assoc; licentiate of Royal Photographic Soc; *Style—* The Rt Hon Lady Wharton

WHATELY, Julian Richard; s of Gerald Arthur Whately, OBE (d 1985), and Nina Abigail Whately, *née* Finlayson; *b* 10 Aug 1949; *Educ* Eton, Univ of Bristol (BA); *m* 1973, Clare Magdalen Hallett; 3 s (Richard Marcus b 11 March 1977, Hugo Thomas b 4 May 1979, Benjamin William b 26 Sept 1980); *Career* admitted slr 1974; ptnr Lee and Pembertons; tstee Herbert and Peter Blagrave Charitable Tst, govr Research into Ageing, memb Main Ctee RUKBA; *Recreations* golf, hill walking, fishing, skiing; *Clubs* Boodle's, The Kandahar; *Style—* Julian Whately, Esq; ✉ The Manor House, Holybourne, Alton, Hampshire

WHATELY, Kevin; s of Richard Whately (d 1968), of Humshaugh, Northumberland, and Mary, *née* Pickering; *b* 6 Feb 1951; *Educ* Humshaugh Sch, Barnard Castle Sch, Central Sch of Speech and Drama; *m* 30 April 1984, Madelaine, da of Jack Newton (d 1983); 1 da (Catherine Mary b 13 April 1983), 1 s (Kieran John Richard b 12 Oct 1984); *Career* actor; memb Northumberland and Durham County Cross Country Running Team 1968; Ambassador: The Prince's Trust, Newcastle-upon-Tyne; HonD Univ of Northumberland; *Theatre* incl: Sep in Whistling at Milestones (Half Moon) 1977, Terry Ellis in Sir is Winning (Roundhouse) 1978, The Rivals and King Lear (Old Vic Co) 1979, Lamb in Raffles (Far East tour) 1979, Eric in A Nightingale Sang (Br tour) 1980, Prince Hal in Henry IV Part 1 (Newcastle) 1981, Andy in Accounts (Edinburgh and London) 1982, title role in Billy Liar (nat tour) 1983, John Proctor in The Crucible (Leicester) 1989, Daines in Our Own Kind (Bush) 1991, Twelve Angry Men (Comedy) 1996; *Television* incl: Norman in Angels (BBC) 1981, Kevin in Coronation St (Granada) 1981, Bob in The Dig (BBC) 1981, Adams in Shackleton (BBC) 1982, Neville in Auf Wiedersehen Pet (Central) 1982–84, Sgt Lewis in Inspector Morse (Central) 1985–92, Steve in B & B (Thames) 1992, Jack Kerruish in Peak Practice (Central) 1993–95, Hardy in The English Patient (Miramax) 1995, Trip Trap (BBC) 1995; *Awards* incl: Pye Comedy Performance of the Year Award 1983, Variety Club Northern Personality of the Year 1990; *Recreations* looking over the next horizon, charity golf events; *Style—* Kevin Whately, Esq; ✉ c/o Caroline Dawson Associates, Apartment 9, 47 Courtfield Road, London SW7 4DB (☎ 0171 370 0708, fax 0171 835 1403)

WHATLEY, Prof Frederick Robert; *b* 26 Jan 1924; *Educ* Univ of Cambridge (ARC scholar, BA, PhD); *Career* res assoc Dept of Plant Nutrition Univ of California Berkeley 1948–50, sr lectr Univ of Sydney 1951–53, Guggenheim fell Univ of Oxford and Nobel Inst Stockholm 1959–60; Univ of California Berkeley: asst plant physiologist Dept of Soils and Plant Nutrition 1953–59 and 1960–62, assoc biochemist Dept of Cell Physiology 1962–64; prof of botany King's Coll London 1964–71, Sherardian prof of botany Univ of Oxford 1971–91 (emeritus prof 1991–), visiting res fell Res Sch of Biology ANU 1979, head of Dept of Plant Scis Univ of Oxford 1985–91; author of 160 res pubns; FRS 1975; *Books* Light and Plant Life (with J M Whatley); *Style—* Prof F R Whatley, FRS; ✉ Department of Plant Sciences, University of Oxford, Oxford OX1 3RB (☎ 01865 275000, fax 01865 275144)

WHATMORE, Andrew; s of late Charles Sydney Whatmore, and Monica Mabel, *née* Tucker, of Boxworth, Cambs; *b* 18 June 1946; *Educ* The Skinners' Sch Tunbridge Wells, Woolwich Poly, Univ of London (BSc(Eng)); *m* 17 Dec 1983, Elizabeth, da of late James Stewart Morrison Sim, and Isobel McLuckie, *née* Russell, of Dollar, Clacks; 1 s (Charles Stewart b 1984), 1 da (Kathryn Elizabeth b 1985); *Career* resident engr: (EAEC) Kenya 1980, Roughton and Ptnrs Al Ain UAE 1981; chief engr Taylor Woodrow Int Ghana 1983, agent Christiani & Nielsen S Wales 1987, dep chief engr Geoffrey Osborne Chichester 1988, sr planning engr Edmund Nuttall Kilsyth Glasgow 1989, chief engr Skye Crossing Miller-Dywidag 1992, regnl chief engr Birse Construction Northampton 1994, chief engr Mid Orient Technical Services 1995, planner Balfour Beatty Kingston Bridge Glasgow 1996; CEng, MICE; *Recreations* riding, walking, beach-combing; *Style—* Mr Andrew Whatmore; ✉ West Netherton Farm, Milnathort, Tayside KY13 7SB (☎ 01577 865018)

WHEARE, Thomas David; s of Sir Kenneth Clinton Wheare, CMG (d 1979), of Oxford, and Joan, *née* Randell; *b* 11 Oct 1944; *Educ* Dragon Sch Oxford, Magdalen Coll Sch Oxford, King's Coll Cambridge (MA), Ch Ch Oxford (DipEd); *m* 29 Oct 1977, Rosalind Clare, da of J E Spice, of Winchester; 2 da (Clare b 1980, Frances b 1981); *Career* asst master Eton 1967–76, housemaster Shrewsbury Sch 1976–83, headmaster Bryanston Sch 1983–; hon treas Headmasters' Conf 1993–; *Recreations* music; *Style—* Thomas Wheare, Esq; ✉ The Headmaster's House, Bryanston School, Blandford, Dorset DT11 0DA (☎ 01258 452728)

WHEAT, Kenneth James (Ken); s of Arthur James Wheat, of Kenilworth, Warwickshire, and Freda, *née* Glasson; *b* 16 April 1948; *Educ* Castle HS Kenilworth, Royal Agricultural Coll Cirencester (MRAC); *m* 2 Oct 1981, Trudi Elizabeth, da of Percival McDonald, of Stratford upon Avon, Warwick; *Career* sr writer: KMP Manchester 1975–77, Cogent Elliot 1977–82, Ayer Barker 1982–83, Crawford Halls 1984–86; creative dir: Brookes and Vernons 1986–93, Alliance (Midlands) Ltd 1993–94; freelance writer 1994–96; memb D&AD; *Recreations* Alpine walking, skiing, gardening, rare breeds; *Style—* Ken Wheat, Esq; ✉ 21 Lindisfarne Drive, Kenilworth, Warwickshire CV8 2PQ

WHEATCROFT, Christopher John Wildin; s of Harold Wheatcroft (d 1952), and Doris, *née* Wildin; *b* 7 May 1938; *Educ* Winchester Coll; *m* 30 June 1966, (Thelma Clare) Greer, da of Joseph Allison Corkey; 2 s (James b 14 Aug 1970, Jonathan b 10 July 1980), 1 da (Jessica b 28 Feb 1973); *Career* Nat Serv cmmnd Somerset Light Infantry 1956–58; ptnr Spicer and Pegler 1971 (articled clerk 1958–63), ptnr Touche Ross (after merger with Spicer and Pegler 1990, now Deloitte & Touche); FCA; *Style—* Christopher Wheatcroft, Esq; ✉ Deloitte & Touche, Hill House, 1 Little New Street, London EC4A 3TR (☎ 0171 936 3000, fax 0171 583 8517)

WHEATER, Prof Roger John; OBE (1991); s of Alfred Wheater, MBE (d 1993), and Rosa Ida, *née* Brown; *b* 24 Nov 1933; *Educ* Brighton, Hove and Sussex GS, Brighton Tech Coll; *m* 29 Nov 1963, Jean Ord, *née* Troup; 2 c (David and Jennifer (twins) b 22 March 1973); *Career* cmmnd Royal Sussex Regt 1953, 3 Bn Gold Coast Regt 1953–54, intelligence offr 4/5 Bn Royal Sussex Regt (TA) 1954–56; Colonial Police Uganda: asst supt 1956, first i/c Crime Div Masaka Dist 1956–57, OC Crime Div Karamoja Dist 1957, Office of the Dir of Public Prosecutions 1959, OC Special Force W Province 1960–61; Uganda National Parks: chief warden Murchison Falls National Park 1961–70, dir 1970–72 (acting dir 1965–69), dir National Park Lodges Uganda Ltd 1970–72; dir Royal Zoological Society of Scotland 1972–; conslt: Sultanate of Oman 1990 and 1991, International Bank for Redevelopment (World Bank) 1974–, World Tourist Orgn (UN) 1980–; Sec of State's inspr Zoo Licensing Act 1984–; memb: Co-ordinating Ctee Nuffield Unit of Tropical Animal Ecology 1970–72, Scientific and Tech Ctee E African Wildlife Soc 1970–72, Bd of Govrs Mweke Coll of Wildlife Management 1970–72, Int Union of Directors of Zoological Gardens 1974–93 (pres 1988–91), Ctee on Educn and Information Scottish Wildlife Tst 1982–, Ad Hoc Ctee on Zoo Licensing Act DOE 1986–, UK Ctee Int Union for the Conservation of Nature and Natural Resources (IUCN) 1988–, IUCN Conservation Breeding Specialist Gp 1988–, Cncl Flora and Fauna Preservation Soc 1990–94; chm: Advsy Ctee Cammo Estate 1980–95, Fedn of Zoological Gardens of Great Britain and Ireland 1993–96 (vice chm 1980–93), Euro Assoc of Zoos and Aquaria 1994–

(memb Cncl 1992–, chm Membership Ctee 1992–94, vice chm 1994); memb Editorial Bd International Zoo Year Book 1987–; pres Assoc of British Wild Animal Keepers 1984–, vice pres World Pheasant Assoc Int 1994–, UK tstee Dian Fossey Gorilla Fund 1993–, fndr patron Dynamic Earth Appeal Fund 1993–; memb Bd: Costorphine Primary Sch 1989–95, Scottish Natural Heritage 1995–; memb SNH Scientific Advsy Ctee 1995–, chm Access Forum 1996–, memb Cncl Zoological Soc of London 1995–, chm Edinburgh Centre for Rural Research 1993–; Hon Prof Faculty of Veterinary Med Univ of Edinburgh 1993; hon FRSGS 1995–; CBiol, FIBiol 1988, FRSE 1985, FRSA 1991; *Recreations* country pursuits, painting, photography and gardening; *Style*— Prof Roger Wheater, OBE, FRSE; ✉ Royal Zoological Society of Scotland, Edinburgh Zoological Park, Murrayfield, Edinburgh EH12 6TS (☎ 0131 334 9171/2/3, fax 0131 316 4050)

WHEATLEY, Alan Edward; s of Edward Wheatley (d 1991), and Margaret Rosina Turner; *b* 23 May 1938; *Educ* Ilford GS; *m* 30 June 1962, Marion Frances, da of John Douglas Wilson (d 1968); 1 da (Susan b 1966), 2 s (Michael b 1968, Jonathan b 1974); *Career* Price Waterhouse 1960–92 (sr ptnr London Office 1985–92), chm 3i Group plc 1992–93; non-exec dir: EBS Investments Ltd (Bank of England subsid) 1977–90, British Steel plc 1984–94, Babcock International Group Plc 1993–, Legal & General Group Plc 1993–, Forte Plc 1993–96, NM Rothschild & Sons Ltd 1993–; non-exec dep chm: Cable & Wireless plc 1984–85 (govt dir 1981–84), Ashtead Group Plc 1994–; non-exec chm: Foreign & Colonial Special Utilities Investment Trust PLC 1993–, New Court Financial Services Ltd 1996–; dir Industl Devpt Advsy Bd 1985–92; tstee V&A Museum 1996–, tstee dir V&A Enterprises Ltd 1996–; govr Solefield Sch; FCA; *Recreations* golf, tennis, music, bridge; *Clubs* Wildernesse Golf; *Style*— Alan E Wheatley, Esq; ✉ New Court, St Swithin's Lane, London EC4P 4DU (☎ 0171 280 5406, fax 0171 280 5431)

WHEATLEY, Rear Adm Anthony; CB (1988); s of Edgar Christian Wheatley, and Audrey Grace Barton Hall, *née* Phillips (d 1982); *b* 3 Oct 1933; *Educ* Berkhamsted Sch, RNC Dartmouth, RN Engrg Coll Manadon; *m* 17 Nov 1962, Iona Sheila, da of Major Oliver Peter Haig (d 1987); 1 da (Charlotte Emma (Mrs Charles Edmund Mayris Sylvester) b 1 Oct 1963); *Career* RN joined 1950, HMS Ceylon 1958–60, HMS Ganges 1960–61, HMS Cambrian 1962–64, Staff of RNEC Manadon 1964–67, Staff of Cdr Br Navy Staff Washington 1967–69, HMS Diomede 1970–72, Staff of C-in-C Fleet 1972–74, Exec Offr RNEC Manadon 1975–76, MOD Procurement Exec 1977–79, Br naval attaché Brasilia 1979–81, RCDS 1982, HMS Collingwood (in cmd) 1982–85; Flag Offr Portsmouth, Naval Base Cdr and Head of Estab of Fleet Maintenance and Repair Orgn Portsmouth 1985–87, ret 1988; gen mangr Nat Hosp for Neurology and Neurosurgery 1988–96; *Recreations* cricket, golf, music; *Clubs* Army and Navy, Free Foresters; *Style*— Rear Adm Anthony Wheatley, CB; ✉ 172 Rivermead Court, Ranelagh Gardens, London SW6 3SF

WHEATLEY, Rev Canon Arthur; s of George Wilson Wheatley (d 1971), of Edinburgh, and Elizabeth, *née* Mackenzie (d 1987); *b* 4 March 1931; *Educ* Alloa Acad, The Episcopal Theol Coll Edinburgh; *m* 1 Aug 1959, (Sheena) Morag, *née* Wilde; 2 s (Christopher b 2 Oct 1961, Kenneth b 3 Nov 1969), 2 da (Paula b 1 Sept 1960, Virginia b 14 June 1964); *Career* ordained: deacon 1970, priest 1970; curate St Salvador's Dundee Brechin and St Ninian's Dundee 1970–71, priest i/c St Ninian's Dundee 1971–76, rector Holy Trinity Elgin with St Margaret's Lossiemouth Dio of Moray Ross and Caithness 1976–80, canon St Andrews Cathedral 1978–80 and 1983–95 (provost 1980–83, hon canon 1995–), priest i/c St Columba's Grantown-on-Spey with St John's Rothiemurchus 1983–95; chaplain: HM Prison Porterfield Inverness 1978–, RAF Grantown-on-Spey 1983–96; *Recreations* shooting, fishing, bee-keeping; *Style*— The Rev Canon Arthur Wheatley; ✉ Wester Curr Cottage, Dulnain Bridge, Grantown-on-Spey PH26 3LX (☎ 01479 851273)

WHEATLEY, Derek Peter Francis; QC (1981); s of Edward Pearse Wheatley (d 1967), of Exeter, and Gladys Eugenie, *née* Williams; *b* 18 Dec 1925; *Educ* Leys Sch Cambridge, Univ Coll Oxford (MA); *m* 1955, Elizabeth Pamela, da of John Morgan Reynolds (d 1983), of Penarth; 2 s (Simon, Jonathan), 1 da (Claire); *Career* 8 King's Royal Hussars, Lt 1946–48, served BAOR; called to the Bar 1951, practised until 1974 and 1990–, memb Hon Soc of the Middle Temple and (ad eundem) Gray's Inn, recorder Crown Ct 1971–74, memb Bar Cncl 1975–78, 1980–83, 1986–90 and 1995–, memb Bar Cncl/Law Soc Ctee on Banking Law 1976–, chm Legal Ctee Ctee of London and Scottish Bankers 1984–86, chief legal advsr Lloyds Bank plc 1974–90, banking conslt in private practice and to Watson Farley and Williams; vice-pres Bar Assoc for Commerce Fin and Indust; FRSA 1993; *Recreations* yachting; *Clubs* Roehampton, Bar Yacht; *Style*— Derek Wheatley, Esq, QC; ✉ 3 The Wardrobe, Old Palace Yard, Richmond, Surrey (☎ 0181 940 6242); Verulam Chambers, Gray's Inn, London WC1X 8LZ (☎ 0171 813 2400, fax 0171 405 3870, DX 436 CHANCERY LANE)

WHEATLEY, Sheriff John Francis; QC (Scot 1992); s of Baron Wheatley, PC (Life Peer, d 1988), and Agnes Mary, da of Samuel Nichol; *b* 9 May 1941; *Educ* Mount St Mary's Coll Derbyshire, Univ of Edinburgh (BL); *m* 1970, Bronwen Catherine, da of Alastair Fraser, of Dollar; 2 s; *Career* called to the Bar Scot 1966, advocate depute 1974–78; Sheriff of Perthshire and Kinross-shire 1980–; *Recreations* gardening, music; *Style*— Sheriff John Wheatley, QC; ✉ Braefoot Farmhouse, Fossoway, Kinross-shire (☎ 0157 74 212); Sheriff Court House, Tay St, Perth (☎ 01738 20546)

WHEATLEY, John Robert Glamis; s of Arthur William Robert Wheatley (d 1971), of Westcliff-on-Sea, Essex, and Marjorie, *née* Leeds; *b* 21 Aug 1930; *Educ* Brentwood Sch, Regent Street Poly (Frederick James French travelling scholarship in architecture); *m* 1964, Pamela Christine, da of Maj Victor George Guest; 2 c (Torquil William Glamis b 10 June 1969, Camilla Victoria Jill b 25 May 1971); *Career* asst: Housing Div GLC 1955–58, Campbell-Jones & Sons Architects 1958–59; Covell Matthews & Partners: gp ldr 1959–63, assoc ptnr 1963–66, ptnr 1966; Covell Matthews Wheatley: fndr dir 1976, chm 1977–84, dir 1984–92; dir: CMW Group plc 1990–92, Thames Estuary Airport Ltd 1991–94; chm Covell Matthews Partnership Ltd 1982–88; Worshipful Co of Chartered Architects: fndr memb 1984, Master 1990–91; Freeman City of London 1983; RIBA 1959, FRSA 1990; *Recreations* music, cricket; *Style*— John R G Wheatley, Esq; ✉ Cato Cottage, 24 Esher Green, Esher, Surrey KT10 8AD (☎ and fax 01372 464224)

WHEATLEY, Ven Paul Charles; s of Charles Lewis Wheatley (d 1984), and Doris Amy, *née* Kerslake; *b* 27 May 1938; *Educ* Wycliffe Coll, St John's Coll Durham, Lincoln Theol Coll; *m* 1 Aug 1963, Iris Mary, da of Horace Lacey; 2 s (Andrew Charles b 26 July 1964, Timothy John b 6 July 1966), 1 da (Fenella Ruth b 11 April 1969 d 1994); *Career* curate St Michael and All Angels Bishopston Bristol 1963–68, Bishop of Bristol's youth chaplain 1968–73, vicar of Covingham and team rector Dorcan Swindon 1973–79, team rector Ross on Wye with Brampton Abbotts, Bridstow and Peterstow 1979–91, rural dean Ross and Archenfield Deanery 1979–91, Hereford diocesan ecumenical offr and preb Hereford Cathedral 1987–91, archdeacon of Sherborne 1991–, priest i/c West Stafford with Frome Billett and canon Salisbury Cathedral 1991–; memb: HM Govt's Pop Festivals Cmmn 1972–74, Warborough PC 1976, Ross Town Cncl 1986–79; *Recreations* travel, gardening, model railways, opera; *Style*— The Ven the Archdeacon of Sherborne; ✉ West Stafford Rectory, Dorchester, Dorset DT2 8AB (☎ 01305 264637, fax 01305 260640)

WHEATLEY, Ven Peter William; er s of late William Nobes Wheatley, and late Muriel, *née* Ounsted; *b* 7 Sept 1947; *Educ* Ipswich Sch, Queen's Coll Oxford (MA), Pembroke Coll Cambridge (MA), Coll of the Resurrection Mirfield, Ripon Hall Oxford; *Career* ordained deacon 1973, priest 1974; asst curate All Saints Fulham 1973–78; vicar: Holy Cross with St Jude and St Peter St Pancras 1978–82, St James W Hampstead 1982–95; priest i/c: All Souls Hampstead and St Mary Kilburn 1982–90, St Mary with All Souls Kilburn 1990–95; dir of post ordination trg (Edmonton Episcopal Area) 1985–94, area dean of N Camden (Hampstead) 1988–93; archdeacon of Hampstead 1995–; *Style*— The Ven the Archdeacon of Hampstead; ✉ 27 Thurlow Road, Hampstead, London NW3 5PP (☎ 0171 435 5890, fax 0171 435 6049)

WHEATLY, Richard John Norwood; s of Patrick Wheatly (d 1986), of Watford, and Doris Mary, *née* Norwood; *b* 9 Feb 1946; *Educ* Watford GS, St John's Coll Cambridge (MA); *m* 1, 8 July 1968 (m dis 1974), Jane Margaret Phillips, da of Frank Thomas, of Rickmansworth, Herts; 1 da (Sophie Catherine Jane b 26 June 1970); m 2, 9 Feb 1980 (m dis 1993), Susan Angela Seider, da of Stuart Masson, of Watford, Herts; *Career* mktg mangr Unilever 1968–72; gp exec: Garland Compton Advertising 1972–73, McCann Erickson Advertising 1973–74; divnl mangr Johnson & Johnson 1974–78, chm Leo Burnett Advertising 1978–94, chief exec Rainbow consortium competing for National Lottery licence 1994, Golden Rose Communications plc: chief exec 1995–, md subsid Jazz FM 1995–; non-exec dir Hamilton Wright (direct mktg agency) 1996–; FIPA 1988; *Recreations* riding, shooting; *Clubs* United Oxford and Cambridge Univ; *Style*— Richard Wheatly, Esq; ✉ Golden Rose Communications, 26–27 Castlereagh Street, London W1H 6DJ (☎ 0171 706 4100)

WHEATON, Rev Canon David Harry; s of Harry Wheaton, MBE (d 1982), and Kathleen Mary, *née* Hyde-Frost (d 1957); *b* 2 June 1930; *Educ* Abingdon, St John's Coll Oxford (MA), London Bible Coll (BD); *m* 23 March 1956, Helen Joy, da of Leonard Forrer (d 1953); 1 s (Mark b 1965), 2 da (Mary b 1964, Joanna b 1967); *Career* tutor Oak Hill Coll 1954–62; rector Ludgershall Bucks 1962–66, vicar of St Paul's Onslow Sq London 1966–71, chaplain Brompton Hosp 1969–71; princ Oak Hill Coll 1971–86, vicar of Christ Church Ware 1986–96, ret 1996; Hon Canon of St Albans 1976–96 (canon emeritus 1996), rural dean of Hertford 1988–91, hon chaplain to HM The Queen 1990–; dir: Church Soc Tst (chm 1981–88), Church Pastoral-Aid Society Tst; *Books* New Bible Dictionary (contrib, 1962), New Bible Commentary (contrib, revised edn 1970, 21st century edn 1994), Evangelical Dictionary of Theology (contrib, 1984), Here We Stand (contrib, 1986), Restoring the Vision (contrib, 1990); *Recreations* walking, DIY; *Style*— The Rev Canon David Wheaton; ✉ 43 Rose Drive, Chesham, Bucks HP5 1RR (☎ 01494 783862)

WHEELER, Adrian Christopher de Vaux Cathcart; s of Paul Murray Wheeler, and Lucinda Mary de Vaux Cathcart Mure, *née* McKerrell, of St Germans, Cornwall; *b* 5 Nov 1949; *Educ* Dulwich Coll, Clare Coll Cambridge (open exhibitioner, MA); *m* Dawn Harverson; *Career* dir Brian Dowling Ltd 1974–76 (exec 1971–74), md Sterling Public Relations 1976–87, md GCI Group London 1994–; memb Mktg Soc, MIPR 1972; *Recreations* skiing, sailing, tennis; *Clubs* Savile, Royal Ocean Racing, Egypt Exploration Soc; *Style*— Adrian Wheeler, Esq; ✉ GCI Group, 1 Chelsea Manor Gardens, London SW3 5PN (☎ 0171 351 2400, fax 0171 352 6244)

WHEELER, Sir (Harry) Anthony; kt (1988), OBE (1973); s of Herbert George Wheeler (d 1976), of Stranraer, and Laura Emma, *née* Groom; *b* 7 Nov 1919; *Educ* Stranraer HS, Glasgow Sch of Architecture, Univ of Strathclyde (BArch); *m* 6 Oct 1944, Dorothy Jean, da of David Campbell; 1 da (Pamela Jane b 24 Sept 1953); *Career* served RA 1939–46, demobbed as Capt; asst to: city architect Oxford 1948, Sir Herbert Baker & Scott 1949; sr architect Glenrothes New Town 1949–51, sr lectr Dundee Sch of Architecture 1952–58, commenced private practice Fife 1952, formed partnership Wheeler & Sproson 1954; princ works incl: Woodside Shopping Centre and St Columba's Parish Church Glenrothes, St Peter's Episcopal Church Kirkcaldy, Hunter Bldg Edinburgh Coll of Art, Students' Union Univ of St Andrews, Leonard Horner Hall and Students' Union Heriot-Watt Univ, reconstruction The Giles Pittenweem, redevpt Dysart and Old Buckhaven, town centre renewal Grangemouth; memb: Royal Fine Art Cmmn Scotland 1967–86, Scottish Housing Advsy Ctee 1971–75; tstee Scottish Civic Tst 1970–83; MRTPI 1953, ARSA 1963, RSA 1975 (treas 1978–80, sec 1980–83, pres 1983–90), FRSA 1988, FRIBA (vice-pres 1973–75), pres Royal Incorpn of Architects Scotland 1973–75, hon pres Sattire Soc 1995; Hon RA 1983, Hon RHA 1983, Hon RBS 1984, Hon RGI 1986, Hon DDes 1991; *Recreations* watercolour painting, sketching, fishing, gardens, music, drama; *Clubs* Scottish Arts, New (Edinburgh); *Style*— Sir Anthony Wheeler, OBE; ✉ Hawthornbank House, Dean Village, Edinburgh EH4 3BH (☎ 0131 225 2334); The Steading, Logierait, Ballinluig, Perthshire PH9 0LH (☎ 01796 482282); 118 Hanover St, Edinburgh EH2 1DR (☎ 0131 226 3338, fax 0131 220 4136)

WHEELER, Arthur William Edge; CBE (1979, OBE 1967); eldest s of Arthur William Wheeler (d 1969), of Dublin, and Rowena; *b* 1 Aug 1930; *Educ* Mountjoy Sch, Trinity Coll Dublin; *m* 1956, Gay; 2 s, 1 da; *Career* called to the Bar Gray's Inn 1960; crown counsel Nigeria 1955, acting legal sec Southern Cameroons and memb Exec Cncl and House of Assembly 1958, princ crown counsel Fedn of Nigeria 1961, dir Public Prosecutions N Nigeria 1966, high ct judge N Nigeria 1967, chief judge Kaduna State of Nigeria 1975, cmmr for Revision of the Laws of Northern States of Nigeria 1980; chm Foreign Compensation Cmmn 1983–; Social Security cmmr 1992–; *Recreations* watching sport, music; *Clubs* Royal Cwlth Soc, MCC, Kildare Street and University (Dublin); *Style*— Arthur Wheeler, Esq, CBE; ✉ c/o Office of the Social Security Commissioners, Harp House, 83 Farringdon Street, London EC4A 4DH

WHEELER, (Selwyn) Charles (Cornelius-); s of Wing Cdr Charles Cornelius-Wheeler, RFC and RAFVR (d 1972), and Winifred Agnes, *née* Rees (d 1973); *b* 26 March 1923; *Educ* Cranbrook Sch; *m* 29 March 1962, Dip Singh; 2 da (Shirin Caroline b 1963, Marina Claire b 1964); *Career* journalist and bdcaster; with Daily Sketch 1940; BBC: joined as sub-ed 1946, Euro serv corr Berlin 1950–53, prodr Panorama 1956–58, corr S Asia 1959–62, corr Berlin 1962–65, corr Washington and chief corr USA 1965–73, chief corr Europe 1973–76, subsequently presenter and corr Panorama and Newsnight; freelance 1979–; RTS Journalist of the Year 1988, RTS Int Documentary Award 1989, James Cameron Meml Prize 1989, RTS Special Commendation 1992, RTS Cyril Bennett Award 1993, Broadcasting Press Guild Harvey Lee Award 1995; Hon DUniv Open Univ 1992, Hon DLitt Univ of Sussex 1995; *Recreations* gardening; *Style*— Charles Wheeler, Esq; ✉ 10a Portland Rd, London W11 (☎ 0171 221 4300)

WHEELER, Colin; s of Stanley Arthur Thomas Wheeler (d 1978), of Hindhead, Surrey, and Lilian Mary, *née* Covey (d 1985); *b* 23 Feb 1938; *Educ* Farnham GS, Farnham Sch of Art, Royal Academy Schs London; *m* 1962, Jacqueline Anne Garelli Buchanan, da of Neville R Buchanan; 3 da (Andrée b 1963, Jacqueline b 1966, Vivien b 1968); *Career* cartoonist; asst lectr Bolton Coll of Art then High Wycombe Coll of Art 1961–63 then various pt/t teaching appts London, first published cartoon Times Educnl Supplement c 1963; freelance contrib of cartoons, illustrations and occasional writing to Daily Telegraph and other national broadsheet press, Private Eye, New Statesman, TES and The Teacher until 1986, front page cartoonist, illustrator and writer The Independent 1986–; *Books* A Thousand Lines (1979), Off the Record (1980); *Recreations* painting and drawing, the protection of old buildings and the encouragement of good modern architecture; *Style*— Colin Wheeler, Esq; ✉ 76 West Street, Farnham, Surrey; The Independent, 1 Canada Square, Canary Wharf, London E14 5DL (☎ 0171 293 2000, fax 0171 293 2435)

WHEELER, David Michael; s of Antony Wheeler, of London, and Edith Wheeler, LVO, *née* Dawkins; *b* 20 March 1940; *Educ* Eton; *m* 21 Oct 1961, Margita, da of The Hon Andrew Vanneck, MC (d 1965), of Heveningham Hall, Suffolk; 2 s (Andrew b 20 July 1963, James b 28 Oct 1966); *Career* ptnr Strauss Turnbull & Co London until 1974, fndr chm and chief exec Ermitage Group Ltd 1974–88; chm: Ermitage International Ltd 1988–, Michael Simpson Ltd 1993–, Harris & Dixon Holdings 1994– (dep chm 1984–94); non-exec dir: Le Masurier, James & Chinn 1986–, Western Quebec Mines 1988–, Sotheby's London 1989–92; MSI (memb Stock Exchange 1963); *Recreations* walking, reading, museum visiting; *Clubs* White's, Travellers' (Paris); *Style*— David Wheeler, Esq; ✉ Broadlands, La Hougue Bie, Grouville, Jersey, CI (☎ 01534 854216); Ermitage International Ltd, PO Box 79, St Helier, Jersey, CI (☎ 01534 876007, fax 01534 879151, telex 4192135)

WHEELER, HE Frank Basil; CMG (1990); s of Harold Gifford Wheeler (d 1975), and Lucy, *née* Childs (d 1970); *b* 24 April 1937; *Educ* Mill Hill Sch; *m* 1, 1959, Catherine Saunders Campbell (d 1979); 1 s (Paul b 1962); m 2, 1984 (m dis 1988), Alyson Ruth Lund, *née* Powell; m 3, Susana Plaza Larrea; *Career* HM Forces 1956–58; HM Dip Serv: joined FO 1958, asst private sec to Min of State FO 1963–65, second sec (commercial) Berne 1965–68, first sec FCO 1968–72, first sec and head of Chancery Wellington 1972–75, FCO 1975–77, cnsllr and head of Chancery Prague 1977–79, home inspr 1979–80, head of Home Inspectorate 1980–82, head of Personnel Policy Dept FCO 1982–84, cnsllr and head of Chancery UK Delgn to NATO Brussels 1984–86, cnsllr FCO 1986, on loan to DTI 1986–89, ambass to Ecuador 1989–93, ambass to Chile 1993–; *Style*— HE Mr Frank Wheeler, CMG; ✉ c/o Foreign and Commonwealth Office (Santiago), King Charles Street, London SW1A 2HA

WHEELER, Rt Hon Sir John Daniel; kt (1990), PC (1993), JP (Inner London 1978), DL (Greater London 1989), MP (C) Westminster North (majority 3,733); s of late Frederick Harry Wheeler, and Constance Elsie, *née* Foreman; *b* 1 May 1940; *Educ* County Sch Suffolk, Staff Coll Wakefield; *m* 1967, Laura Margaret Langley; 1 s, 1 da; *Career* former asst prison governor; MP (C): Paddington 1979–83, Westminster N 1983–; min of state for N Ireland 1993–; memb: Home Office Standing Ctee on Crime Prevention 1977–85 (chm Sub-Ctee on Mobile Crime 1983–84), Home Office Steering Ctee on Crime Prevention 1985–93; chm: Residential Burglary Working Gp 1986–87, All-Party Penal Affairs Gp 1986–93 (vice-chm 1979–86), Home Affairs Select Ctee Sub-ctee on Race Relations and Immigration 1980–87, Home Affairs Select Ctee 1987–92 (memb 1980–92), Conservative Greater London Area Members' Ctee 1983–90 (jt sec 1979–83), Policy Gp for London 1988–93, British-Pakistan Parly Gp 1988–93; vice-chm: Conservative Urban Affairs and New Towns Ctee 1980–83, Conservative Home Affairs Ctee 1987–93 (jt sec 1980–87); CStJ 1992 (Officer Brother 1991), Hilal-i-Quaid-i-Azam (knight) of Pakistan 1991; *Style*— The Rt Hon Sir John Wheeler, JP, DL, MP; ✉ House of Commons, London SW1A 0AA (☎ secretary 0171 219 6427, fax 0171 219 2546)

WHEELER, John Frederick; s and h of Sir John Wheeler, 3 Bt, and Gwendolen Alice, da of late Alfred Ernest Oram; *b* 3 May 1933; *Educ* Bedales, London Sch of Printing, The Life Guards; *m* 1963, Barbara Mary, da of Raymond Flint, of Stoneygate, Leicester; 2 s (John Radford b 1965, Andrew Charles b 1969), 1 da (Jane Louise b 1964); *Career* company dir and farmer; *Recreations* sailing, field sports; *Style*— John F Wheeler, Esq; ✉ Round Hill, Aldeburgh, Suffolk IP15 5PG (☎ 01728 452748)

WHEELER, Sir John Hieron; 3 Bt (UK 1920), of Woodhouse Eaves, Co Leicester; s of Sir Arthur Wheeler, 1 Bt, DL, JP (d 1943), and Mary, *née* Pullman (d 1938); bro of 2 Bt (d 1964); *b* 22 July 1905; *Educ* Charterhouse; *m* 24 July 1929, Gwendolen Alice, da of late Alfred Ernest Oram, of Walberton, Kirby Muxloe, nr Leicester; 2 s (John Frederick, Benjamin b 1935); *Heir* s, John Frederick Wheeler, *qv*; *Style*— Sir John Wheeler, Bt; ✉ 39 Morland Ave, Stoneygate, Leicester

WHEELER, John Michael; s of Sir Charles Wheeler, KBE (d 1976), and Frieda, *née* Close (d 1972); *b* 8 Nov 1931; *Educ* Shrewsbury Sch, Queens' Coll Cambridge (BA), Harvard Business Sch (PMD); *m* 1956, Jean Ruth Kirsty, da of Capt John McMyn Gilmour, MC (d 1950); 1 s (Richard John Gilmour b 1960), 2 da (Fiona Elizabeth Gilmour b 1962, Tanya Kirsty b 1963); *Career* Grenadier Guards 1950–52; H Clarkson & Co Ltd: trainee (Norway and USA) 1956–59, dir 1967–90; dir: Building Trades Exhibitions Ltd 1990–93, Andry Montgomery Ltd 1993–; conslt Mitsubishi Corporation (UK) plc 1990–96; chm Help the Aged (Bucks) 1990–94, vice chm International Social Service UK 1992–, memb Cncl Univ of Buckingham 1994–; High Sheriff for Co of Buckinghamshire 1994–95; master of hounds 1970–92, master Worshipful Co of Broderers 1995–96; *Recreations* golf, country sports, wine tasting; *Clubs* MCC, City University, Tasting; *Style*— John Wheeler, Esq; ✉ Sly Corner, Lee Common, Great Missenden, Bucks HP16 9LD (☎ 01494 837232, fax 01494 837941)

WHEELER, John Vashon Tyrwhitt; s of Wing Cdr Vashon James Wheeler, MC, DFC (ka 1944), and Josephine Hermione, *née* Spencer-Phillips (d 1977); *b* 24 Oct 1931; *Educ* Eton, Trinity Coll Cambridge (BA, MA); *m* 1, 7 Sept 1957, Geraldine (d 1970), da of William Noel Jones (d 1982), of Little Gables, Glasllwch Lane, Newport; 3 s (James Vashon b 1960, Nicholas Charles Tyrwhitt b 1965, Justin Alexander Noel b 1970), 1 da (Susan Verity (Mrs Cummings) b 1958); m 2, 1978, Mrs Caroline Susan Chance, da of Patrick Edward Michael Holmes, MBE; 2 step s (Timothy William Holmes b 1966, Henry Charles Hugh b 1969), 1 step da (Lucy Emma b 1971); *Career* Nat Serv Flying Offr; dir Wolseley-Hughes plc 1970–82 (chief exec agric div); chm and md: Benson Heating Ltd 1982–84, Benson Group plc 1984–90; chm Richardson (Bitterley) Ltd 1970–; memb: Shropshire CC, Bitterley Parish Cncl; MIMechE 1965, FIAgrE 1978; *Recreations* land management; *Clubs* RAF; *Style*— John Wheeler, Esq; ✉ Bitterley Court, Ludlow, Shropshire (☎ 01584 890265, fax 01584 891098)

WHEELER, Air Vice-Marshal Leslie William Frederick; s of George Douglas Wheeler (d 1982), and Susan Wheeler (d 1993); *b* 4 July 1930; *Educ* Creighton Sch Carlisle; *m* 1961, Joan Elizabeth, da of Harry Newton Carpenter (d 1969); 2 da; *Career* RAF cmmnd 1952, OC 360 Sqdn 1970–72, Station Cdr RAF Finningley 1977–79, Dir Gen RAF Personal Serv 1983–84; independent inspr Public Inquiries 1984–93; chm Appt Bd MOD 1984–93; *Recreations* walking, golf, philately; *Clubs* RAF; *Style*— Air Vice-Marshal Leslie Wheeler; ✉ c/o Midland Bank plc, Brampton, Cumbria

WHEELER, Prof Michael David; s of David Mortimer Wheeler, and Hilda Lois Stansfield, *née* Eke; *b* 1 Sept 1947; *Educ* St Albans Sch, Magdalene Coll Cambridge (scholar, MA), UCL (PhD); *m* 1970, Vivienne Rees; 1 s (Joshua b 1973), 2 da (Charlotte b 1975, Emily (twin) b 1975); *Career* Quain student (lectr) Univ of London 1972–73; Univ of Lancaster: lectr in English 1973–85, sr lectr 1985–90, head of dept 1984–86, assoc dean of humanities 1989–91, prof of English literature 1990–; dir: Ruskin Prog (interdisciplinary res gp) 1990–, Ruskin Collection Project 1990–; visiting lectr USA, Canada, Denmark, India, Iraq, Japan, Poland, Yugoslavia, Switzerland, Italy, Turkey and Norway 1975–; Gladstone Fndr's Day lectr 1991; tstee: St Deiniol's Library Hawarden 1994, Armiitt Library 1996; Companion Guild of St George 1992; *Publications* The Art of Allusion in Victorian Fiction (1979), English Fiction of the Victorian Period 1830–1890 (1985, 2 edn 1994), Death and the Future Life in Victorian Literature and Theology (1990, winner US Conf on Christianity and Literature award, 1991–92, abridged as Heaven, Hell and the Victorians 1994), The Lamp of Memory: Ruskin, Tradition and Architecture (co-ed, 1992), Ruskin and Environment: The Storm-Cloud of the Nineteenth Century (ed, 1995); Longman Literature in English Series 47 vols (jt gen ed, 1980–), Whitehouse Edition of John Ruskin (jt gen ed, 1994–), Time and Tide: Ruskin Studies 1996 (ed, 1996), Works of John Ruskin (introduction to CD-Rom, 1996); *Recreations* choral singing; *Clubs* United Oxford and Cambridge; *Style*— Prof Michael Wheeler; ✉ 15 Meadowside, Lancaster LA1 3AQ (☎ 01524 60097)

WHEELER, Air Chief Marshal Sir (Henry) Neil George; GCB (1975, KCB 1969, CB 1967), CBE (1957, OBE 1949), DSO (1943), DFC 1941 (and Bar 1943), AFC 1954; s of Thomas Henry Wheeler (d 1933), of Pretoria, S Africa; *b* 8 July 1917; *Educ* St Helen's Coll Southsea, RAF Coll Cranwell; *m* 1942, Alice Elizabeth, da of William Henry Weightman, CMG (d 1970); 2 s, 1 da; *Career* joined RAF 1935, served in Bomber, Fighter and Coastal Cmds WWII, Gp Capt 1954, ADC to HM The Queen 1957–61, Air Cdre 1961, Air memb Research Policy Staff MOD 1962–63, Air Vice-Marshal 1963, SASO RAF Germany 1963–66, Dep Chief of Defence Staff (Operational Requirements) MOD 1967 (asst chief 1966–67), Air Marshal 1967, Cdr Far East Air Force 1969–70, Air memb Supply and Organisation MOD 1970, Air Chief Marshal 1972, controller of Aircraft MOD Procurement Exec 1973–75, ret 1976; dir: Rolls-Royce Ltd 1977–82, Flight Refuelling Ltd 1977–85; vice pres Cncl of the Air League; chm Anglo-Ecuadorian Soc 1986–89; Liveryman Guild of Air Pilots and Air Navigators (Master 1986–87); CIMgt, FRAeS; *Recreations* fly-fishing, painting, gardening; *Clubs* Flyfishers', RAF; *Style*— Air Chief Marshal Sir Neil Wheeler, GCB, CBE, DSO, DFC, AFC; ✉ Boundary Hall, Cooksbridge, Lewes, Sussex (☎ 01273 400201)

WHEELER, Nicholas Hugh; s of David Hugh Wheeler (d 1979), and Rosemary Margaret Jean, *née* Leaney; *b* 3 Oct 1953; *Educ* St Lawrence Coll Ramsgate Kent (first team tennis capt), Harlow Tech Coll; *m* 6 Sept 1975, Sylvia Mabel, *née* Wiffil; 2 da (Victoria Kate b 28 Sept 1978, Alexandra Rosemary b 12 July 1982); *Career* journalist; South London Press 1972, reporter Western Morning News and Western Evening Herald Plymouth 1972–77, reporter Coventry Evening Telegraph 1977–79, reporter/prodr BBC Radio Solent 1979–84, BBC Newsbeat 1984; Capital Radio: ed of news and showbusiness prog The Way It Is 1985–87, head of News and Talks Dept 1987–94, prog controller Capital FM and Capital Gold 1994–95, ed Independent Radio News 1995–; *Recreations* squash, cycling, surfing, motorbikes; *Style*— Nicholas Wheeler, Esq; ✉ IRN, Independent Television News, 200 Grays Inn Road, London WC1X 8XZ (☎ 0171 833 3000)

WHEELER, Dr Patrick Clive Gage; s of Cdr Leonard Gage Wheeler, of Alresford, Hants, and Nancy Dorathea, *née* Cross; *b* 6 Oct 1943; *Educ* St Edward's Sch Oxford, Christ Church Oxford (MA, DM, BM BCh), St Thomas' Hosp London (MRCP); *m* 7 June 1975, Diana Lilian, da of Cdr Edward Stanley, of Waldringfield, Suffolk; 3 da (Anna b 1976, Kate b 1978, Gemma b 1981); *Career* med registrar St Thomas' Hosp 1971–75, sr med registrar King's Coll Hosp 1975–80, conslt physician and gastroenterologist S Kent Hosp's Tst 1980–; author of various articles on gastrointestinal and liver disease in scientific pubns; memb Br Soc of Gastroenterology; FRCP 1987; *Recreations* fly-fishing, opera, Francophilia; *Clubs* Army & Navy; *Style*— Dr Patrick Wheeler; ✉ Elham Manor, Elham, Canterbury, Kent CT4 6UL; William Harvey Hospital, Ashford, Kent

WHEELER, Paul; s of Dennis Wheeler, and Joan Margaret, *née* Crawte; *b* 8 Nov 1952; *Educ* Wallingford GS, Coll of Law Guildford; *m* 17 Dec 1977, Sally Anne, da of Arthur (Bob) Robert; 2 s (Lewis b 1983, Nicholas b 1986); *Career* slr 1977; lectr Coll of Law 1977–78, prosecuting slr Thames Valley Police 1978–82, ptnr Hedges Wallingford and Didcot 1985; memb: Law Soc 1985 (Berks, Bucks and Oxon), Oxford Dist Slrs Assoc 1987; *Recreations* hockey, clarinet; *Clubs* Wallingford Sports and Social, Wallingford Dist Lions, Goring and Streatley Band; *Style*— Paul Wheeler, Esq; ✉ Hedges, Market Place, Didcot, Oxon OX11 7LJ (☎ 01235 811888, fax 01235 816322)

WHEELER, Raymond Leslie; s of Edmund Francis Wheeler (d 1969), and Ivy Geraldine, *née* Fryer (d 1979); *b* 25 Oct 1927; *Educ* Newport Co Secdy GS, Univ Coll Southampton (BSc), Imperial Coll London (MSc); *m* 22 March 1950, Jean, da of Colin McInnes (d 1942); 1 s (Douglas b 1956), 2 da (Lesley (Mrs Rathmann) b 1952, Jennifer (Mrs Harrison) b 1954); *Career* chief structural designer Saunders-Roe Div Westland Aircraft Ltd 1965–66 (chief stress 1962–65), tech dir Br Hovercraft Corp Ltd 1972–85 (chief designer 1966–85), business devpt dir Westland Aerospace Ltd 1985–89, dir systems support Westland Aerospace Ltd 1989–91 (ret), conslt 1992–; pres IOW Area Bd Young Enterprise, chm of govrs Whippingham Co Primary Sch, chm of govrs IOW Coll; FRAeS, FRINA, RDI 1995; *Books* From Sea to Air - The Heritage of Sam Saunders (with A E Tagg, 1989), From River to Sea - The Marine Heritage of Sam Saunders; *Recreations* hockey, photography, archaeology; *Style*— Raymond Wheeler, Esq, RDI; ✉ Brovacum, 106 Old Road, East Cowes, IOW PO32 6AX (☎ 01983 292994)

WHEELER, Gen Sir Roger Neil; GCB (1997, KCB 1993), CBE (1984); s of Maj-Gen Norman Wheeler (d 1990), of Sudbury, Suffolk, and Helen Wheeler; *b* 16 Dec 1941; *Educ* All Hallows Sch Devon, Hertford Coll Oxford (MA); *Career* cmmnd into RUR 1961, CO 2 Royal Irish 1979–82, Bde Cdr 11 Armoured Bde 1984–86, GOC 1 Armoured Div 1989–90, ACGS 1990–93, GOC Northern Ireland 1993–96, C-in-C UK Land Command 1996–97, Chief of the Gen Staff 1997–; *Recreations* fly fishing, rugby, hill walking; *Clubs* Army and Navy; *Style*— Gen Sir Roger Wheeler, GCB, CBE; ✉ MOD, Main Building, Horseguards Avenue, London SW1A 2HB

WHEELER, Timothy Carpenter; s of Andrew Wheeler (d 1950), of Philadelphia, USA, and Molly Wheeler (d 1991); *b* 20 Sept 1933; *Educ* Beaumont Coll, Law Soc Sch of Law; *m* Nov 1967, Diana Katherine, *née* Hillson; 1 da (Katherine Margaret Elizabeth); *Career* Nat Serv RAC 1957–58; articled to Lewis and Lewis and Gisborne 1951–56, admitted slr 1957; ptnr Clifford-Turner 1964–87 (joined as asst slr 1958), ptnr Clifford Chance 1987–93; chm Sub-Ctee on Land Law City of London Law Soc 1985–90; memb: City of London Slrs' Co (incorporating City of London Law Soc), Law Soc, Int Bar Assoc, Br Property Fedn; *Recreations* walking, gardening, travelling; *Style*— Timothy Wheeler, Esq; ✉ Clifford Chance, 200 Aldersgate St, London EC1A 4JJ (☎ 0171 600 1000, fax 0171 600 5555)

WHEELER-BENNETT, Richard Clement; s of Dr Clement Wheeler Wheeler-Bennett (d 1957), and Enid Lucy, *née* Boosey (d 1975); *b* 14 June 1927; *Educ* Radley, ChCh Oxford (MA), Harvard Business Sch; *m* 8 May 1954, Joan Ellen (DL Greater London 1991), da of late Prof Eric Alfred Havelock, of Connecticut, USA; 1 s (Clement b 1965 d 1986), 2 da (Joanna b 1957, Emily b 1960); *Career* RM Lt Commando 1944–48; banker; mangr First National City Bank of New York 1960–66, gen mangr (Europe) Australia and New Zealand Banking Group 1978–80 (exec dir 1967–78), chm Thomas Borthwick & Sons Ltd 1980–85; dir: Fleming Int High Income Investmt Tst 1983–92, ANZ Grindlays Bank 1993–96; chm ANZ Pensions (UK) Ltd; chm Roehampton Club Ltd 1988–92; *Recreations* fishing, golf, shooting, viticulture; *Clubs* Brooks's, Pratt's, MCC; *Style*— Richard Wheeler-Bennett, Esq; ✉ The Mill House, Calstone Wellington, nr Calne, Wilts SN11 8QF (☎ 01249 813241); 50E Cornwall Gardens, London SW7 4BG (☎ 0171 937 6276)

WHEELER-BOOTH, Sir Michael Addison John; KCB (1994); s of Addison James Wheeler, and Mary Angela, *née* Blakeney-Booth; *b* 25 Feb 1934; *Educ* Leighton Park Sch, Magdalen Coll Oxford (MA); *m* 1982, Emily Frances Smith; 1 s (Alfred James b 1990), 2 da (Kate 1985, Charlotte b 1987); *Career* Nat Serv Midshipman RNVR 1952–54; clerk House of Lords 1960, private sec to Ldr of House of Lords and Govt Chief Whip 1965, seconded as jt sec Inter Party Conf on House of Lords Reform 1967, clerk of the Journals 1970, chief clerk Overseas and Euro Office 1972, princ clerk 1978, reading clerk House of Lords 1983–88, clerk asst of the Parliaments 1988–90, Clerk of the Parliaments 1991–; *Publications* Griffith & Ryle on Parliament (contrib, 1989), Halsbury's Laws of England on Parliament (ed), contrib to parly jls; *Recreations* reading, entertaining, swimming, opera, the countryside; *Clubs* Brooks's, Garrick; *Style*— Sir Michael Wheeler-Booth, KCB; ✉ Northfields, Sandford St Martin, Chipping Norton, Oxon OX7 7AG (☎ 01608 683632); 11 Dewhurst Road, London W14 0ET (☎ 0171 602 0838)

WHEELHOUSE, Alan; s of George William Wheelhouse (d 1990), of Nottingham, and Dorothy Marion, *née* Hickling (d 1974); *b* 4 March 1934; *Educ* Nottingham HS, Emmanuel Coll Cambridge (MA, LLM); *m* 1963, Jennifer Mary, da of Donald Stewart Robinson (d 1974), of Nottingham; 3 da (Heather Jane b 1964, Julie Ann b 1966, Emma Louise b 1969); *Career* slr, sr ptnr Freeth Cartwright 1974–94, pres Nottinghamshire Law Soc 1985–86; chm Nottingham First 1994–; govr Nottingham HS 1988–; *Sporting Career* Cambridge Cricket blue 1959, Nottinghamshire Co Cricket 1961 (ctee memb 1987–, chm Cricket Ctee 1991–95, chm 1994–), capt Notts 50+ Cricket XI 1985–88, dist chm XL Club 1985–; chm Registration Ctee TCCB 1994–; chm Gunn & Moore Club Cricket Alliance 1983–85; pres: Old Nottinghamians Soc 1982, Old Nottinghamians Cricket Club 1988–89 (former capt), Notts Cricket Assoc 1989–; *Recreations* cricket, watching sport, concert and theatre going, eating-out; *Clubs* Hawks, Forest Nottinghamians CC (life memb), XL Club, Notts CCC, Caythorpe CC (vice pres), Nottinghamshire Football (vice-pres); *Style—* Alan Wheelhouse, Esq; ✉ Bracken House, Bracken Hill, Caythorpe, Nottingham NG14 7EF (☎ 0115 966 3047); Willoughby House, 20 Low Pavement, Nottingham (☎ 0115 936 9369, fax 0115 936 9370)

WHEEN, Francis James Baird; s of James Francis Thorneycroft Wheen, and Patricia Winifred, *née* Ward; *b* 22 Jan 1957; *Educ* Copthorne Sch Sussex, Harrow, Royal Holloway Coll London (BA); *m* Julia Thorogood; 4 s (Jack, Frank, Bertie, Archie), 1 da (GeorgeAnna); *Career* journalist; editorial asst The Guardian 1974–75, staff writer New Statesman 1978–84, news ed New Socialist 1983–84, contributing ed Tatler 1985, diarist The Independent 1986–87, contributing ed Sunday Correspondent Magazine 1989–90, diarist Independent on Sunday 1990–91, reg contrib to Private Eye 1987–, contributing ed Vanity Fair 1992–93; columnist: Observer 1993–, Esquire 1993–, Guardian 1994–; freelance work for numerous pubns GB and overseas incl: The Times, Daily Mirror, London Evening Standard, Sunday Telegraph, Los Angeles Times, The Nation (NY), The New Yorker, Literary Review; was for several years reg presenter of News-Stand (BBC Radio) and What The Papers Say (Granada TV); *Books* The Sixties (1982), World View 1982 (1982), Television: A History (1985), The Battle For London (1985), Tom Driberg: His Life And Indiscretions (1990), The Chatto Book of Cats (1993), Lord Gnome's Literary Companion (1994), The Vintage Book of Cats (ed, 1996); *Clubs* Academy (Soho); *Style—* Francis Wheen; ✉ Sokens, Green Street, Pleshey, Near Chelmsford, Essex CM3 1HT (☎ 01245 231566)

WHEEN, Richard Francis; s of Rear Adm Charles Kerr Thorneycroft Wheen, CB (d 1989), and Veryan Rosamond, *née* Acworth; *b* 27 May 1941; *Educ* Harrow, Peterhouse Cambridge (MA); *m* 14 Jan 1983, Anne, da of Patrick Joseph Keegan, of Ireland (d 1980); 5 s (Timothy b 1983, Patrick (twin) b 1983, Jonathan b 1985 (d 1987), Christopher b 1986, Peter b 1988), 1 da (Elizabeth b 1991); *Career* slr; ptnr Linklaters & Paines, ret 1996; Lt Cdr RNR, ret 1978; author Bridge Player series of programs for home computers 1983–; *Recreations* family, bridge, shooting, piano, golf, skiing, editing parish magazine, writing bridge articles for publication, writing doggerel; *Clubs* Army and Navy, Worplesdon Golf, Reigate Heath Golf, St Enedoc Golf; *Style—* Richard F Wheen, Esq; ✉ The Grange, Rectory Lane, Buckland, Betchworth, Surrey RH3 7BH (☎ 01737 842193)

WHELAN, Prof Michael John; s of William Whelan, ISM (d 1978), of Aldershot, Hants, and Ellen, *née* Pound (d 1972); *b* 2 Nov 1931; *Educ* Farnborough GS, Gonville and Caius Coll Cambridge (MA, PhD); *Career* Univ of Cambridge: demonstrator in physics 1961–65, asst dir of res in physics 1965–66, fell Gonville and Caius Coll 1958–66; reader in physical examination of materials Univ of Oxford 1966–92; prof of microscopy of materials Univ of Oxford 1992– (fell Linacre Coll 1968–); hon professor Univ of Sci & Technol Beijing 1995; FRS 1976, FInstP 1976; *Books* Electron Microscopy of Thin Crystals (co-author), Worked Examples in Dislocations; *Recreations* gardening, tinkering, Japanese language; *Style—* Prof M J Whelan, FRS; ✉ 18 Salford Rd, Old Marston, Oxford OX3 0RX (☎ 01865 244556); Department of Materials, Oxford University, Parks Rd, Oxford OX1 3PH (☎ 01865 273700, fax 01865 273789, telex 83295 NUCLOX G)

WHELAN, Michael Joseph; s of Michael Whelan (d 1972), and Mary, *née* Hynes (d 1991); *b* 1 May 1932; *Educ* Castleknock Coll Dublin, Univ Coll Dublin (BA), Columbia Univ NY (MSc); *m* 3 June 1955, Maureen Therese, da of John Ryan (d 1972); 3 s (Gerard b 1959, Brian b 1962, Roger b 1966), 1 da (Ann-Maeve b 1956); *Career* called to the Bar King's Inn Dublin 1953; corporate lawyer Shell Oil: Toronto 1955–59, NY 1959–60; devpt and commercial mangr Aer Lingus NY and Dublin 1960–63, mktg dir Irish Tourist Bd Dublin 1963–71, fndr and chief exec Aran Energy plc Dublin and London; FInstPet, FInstD; *Recreations* sailing; *Clubs* Royal Irish Yacht, Fitzwilliam, St Stephens Green, Milltown Golf, Royal Irish Automobile (all Dublin); *Style—* Michael J Whelan, Esq; ✉ 51 Mount St, Mayfair, London W1; The Cove, Baltimore, Co Cork; Ardoyne House, Ballsbridge, Dublin 4; Clanwilliam Court, Dublin 2

WHELAN, Paul David; s of Don Whelan, of NZ, and Beris, *née* Pashby; *b* 29 Sept 1966; *Educ* Wellington Conservatoire NZ, RNCM (Marianne Mathy scholar); *Career* baritone; studied with Flora Edwards, Patrick McGuigan, Robert Alderson and David Harper; *Concerts* conducted by: Sir Simon Rattle, Gary Bertini, Kent Nagano, Richard Hickox, Sir Yehudi Menuhin, Paolo Olmi, Sir David Willcocks, Sir Charles Farncombe; performed with: LSO, City of Birmingham Symphony Orch, Hallé Orch, BBC Philharmonic Orch, BBC Symphony Orch, City of London Sinfonia, London Sinfonietta, English Chamber Orch, RIAS Berlin Chamber Choir, Budapest Symphony Orch; venues incl: Wigmore Hall, St David's Hall Cardiff, Blackheath Concert Halls, Cheltenham Festival; *Opera roles* incl: title role in The Doctor of Myddfai (debut for Welsh Nat Opera), Figaro in The Marriage of Figaro (Scottish Opera), Shaklovity in Khovanshchina (ENO), Marcello in La Bohème (Glyndebourne Touring Opera), Flint in Billy Budd (Geneva Opera), Schaunard in La Bohème (Netherlands Opera, Stuggart Opera, Royal Opera House, Metropolitan Opera NY), Guglielmo in Cosi fan Tutte (Dublin Grand Opera), Masetto in Don Giovanni (Bordeaux), Demetrius in A Midsummer Night's Dream (Australian Opera), title role in Don Giovanni (Australian Opera) 1997, title role in Eugene Onegin (Australian Opera) 1997, Ned Keene in Peter Grimes (Metropolitan Opera) 1997; *Recordings* A Midsummer Night's Dream (with LSO under Sir Colin Davis), Kurt Weill's Silbersee (under Markus Stenz); *Awards* winner Webster Booth-Esso Award, Brigitte Fassbaender Award for Lieder, winner Lieder Prize Cardiff Singer of the World 1993; scholarships incl: Wolfson Fndn, Countess of Munster Musical Tst, Peter Moores Fndn; *Recreations* tennis, hiking; *Style—* Paul Whelan, Esq; ✉ c/o IMG Artists Europe, Media House, 3 Burlington Lane, London W4 2TH (☎ 0181 747 9977, fax 0181 747 9131)

WHELAN, Paul William; s of William James Whelan (d 1966), and Carol, *née* O'Leary (d 1990); *b* 24 Sept 1935; *Educ* Southgate County GS, LSE, Borough Road Training Coll; *m* (m dis); 2 s (Patrick John Paul b 7 July 1971, Alexander James b 15 March 1978), 2 da (Holly Anne b 9 June 1969, Rosalind Elizabeth b 31 Dec 1981); *Career* teacher training 1958–59, teacher and lectr 1959–62; joined: Brunning Advertising & Marketing 1963, Thomson Group Marketing 1968, Doyle Dane Bernbach 1970; estab: first co Byfield Mead & Partners (later Byfield Whelan Osborn & Cruttenden) 1971, second co Noble Whelan O'Connell (later AAP-Ketchum) 1978, third co Clifford Whelan Oldrey (formerly Paul Whelan & Partners, then Whelan Oldrey) 1990; dir Shandwick 1987; various Creative Circle, D & AD and Clio awards for press and TV advtg; MIPA, memb Mktg Soc; *Style—* Paul Whelan, Esq; ✉ Clifford Whelan Oldrey, Congress House, 23–28 Great Russell Street, London WC1B 3PX (☎ 0171 753 0005)

WHELAN, Peter; s of Thomas Whelan (d 1959), lithographic artist, of Stoke-on-Trent, and Bertha, *née* Brookes; *b* 3 Oct 1931; *Educ* Hanley GS, Univ of Keele (BA); *m* 1958, Frangcon Hood, da of John Frederick Price, pottery designer; 2 s (Timothy John b 1958, Lawrence Peter b 1961), 1 da (Megan Nell b 1976); *Career* writer and playwright; worked in advtg 1957–78, dir Garland Compton advtg agency 1975–78; memb Theatre Writers' Union *Television* In Suspicious Circumstances, The Trial of Lord Lucan; *Plays* Lakota (with Don Kincaid, Cockpit Theatre London, 1970), Double Edge (with Les Darbon, Vaudeville London, 1975), Captain Swing (RSC Stratford & London, 1978), The Accrington Pals (RSC London, 1981), Clay (RSC London, 1983), Worlds Apart (by Jose Triana, adaption, RSC London, 1987), The Bright and Bold Design (RSC London, 1991, Best Play nomination Writers' Guild 1992), The School of Night (RSC Stratford & London, 1992–93, Best Play nomination Writers' Guild 1993), The Herbal Bed (The Other Place Stratford, 1996); *Style—* Peter Whelan, Esq; ✉ c/o The Agency, 24 Pottery Lane, London W11 4LZ (☎ 0171 727 1346, fax 0171 727 9037)

WHELAN, Terence Leonard; s of Thomas James Whelan (d 1939), and Gertrude Beatrice, *née* Chick (d 1968); *b* 5 Dec 1936; *Educ* Oakfield Secdy Sch Anerley London, Beckenham Coll of Art (NDD); *m* 1, 1961 (m dis 1971); 2 s; m 2, 15 Dec 1972, Margaret Elizabeth, da of Brinley John Bowen, of Middx; 1 da; *Career* Nat Serv 14 Field Ambulance RAMC Germany 1956–58; art ed Condé Nast Publishers 1959–68 (worked on Vogue Pattern Book, Vogue South Africa, Br Vogue); Ideal Home magazine: art ed 1968–74, asst ed and art dir 1974–77, ed 1977–95; md Satellite Editorial Publications Ltd 1996–, editorial dir Lifestyle magazine 1996–; freelance editorial conslt, writer and broadcaster on home interest; voted Ed of the Year (Special Interest Section) British Soc Magazine Editors 1988; memb Soc Typographic Designers 1972; FRSA 1993; *Style—* Terence Whelan, Esq

WHELDON, David Robert; s of Derek Wheldon (d 1962), of Silsoe, and Joan Mary, *née* Neville; *b* 15 Aug 1956; *Educ* Royal Masonic Schs Bushey Hertfordshire, Univ of Kent Canterbury (BA); *m* 10 Sept 1982, Macarena, da of Jaime Ruiz-Larrea Cangas (d 1981); 2 s (Daniel b 8 Feb 1986, Alexander b 25 March 1989); *Career* teacher of English 1978–82; Saatchi & Saatchi: account exec 1983, account supervisor 1984, account dir 1985, Bd dir 1986, gp account dir 1987; gp account dir then jt managing ptnr WCRS Mathews MarCantonio 1989, md Lowe Howard-Spink 1989–93; The Coca-Cola Company (Atlanta): vice pres and worldwide dir of advtg 1993–96, appointed dir of mktg Gtr Europe 1996; pres BBDO Europe 1996–; *Recreations* cinema, music, reading, tennis, travel, cooking, playing with the children; *Clubs* Savile, Riverside; *Style—* David R Wheldon, Esq; ✉ BBDO Europe, 239 Old Marylebone Road, London NW1 5QT (☎ 0171 298 7070, fax 0171 724 5995)

WHELDON, Juliet Louise; CB (1994); da of John Wheldon, and Ursula Mabel, *née* Caillard; *b* 26 March 1950; *Educ* Sherborne Sch for Girls, Lady Margaret Hall Oxford (Tullis exhibitioner, Thackeray prize, BA); *Career* called to the Bar Gray's Inn 1975, advsy Div Treasury Solicitor's Dept 1976–83, Law Offices' Dept 1983–84, Treasury Solicitor's Dept 1984–86, asst legal sec Law Offices' Dept 1986–87, head Central Advsy Div Treasury Solicitor's Dept 1987–89, legal sec to Law Offices 1989–; *Style—* Miss Juliet Wheldon, CB; ✉ 9 Buckingham Gate, London SW1E 6JP (☎ 0171 828 1968)

WHELER, Sir Edward Woodford; 14 Bt (E 1660, of City of Westminster, Co London); s and h of Sir Trevor Wood Wheler, 13 Bt (d 1986), and Margaret Idris, *née* Birch (d 1987); *b* 13 June 1920; *Educ* Radley; *m* 2 July 1945, Molly Ashworth, da of late Thomas Lever; 1 s (Trevor), 1 da (Dinah); *Heir* s, Trevor Woodford b 11 April 1946; *Career* joined army (RA) 1940, cmmnd Royal Sussex Regt 1941, attached 15 Punjab Regt IA 1941–45 Colonial Audit Service Uganda and Ghana 1948–58; Automobile Association of E Africa 1958–70; Benson & Hedges Ltd 1971–81 (dir 1978–81); company sec Robert Lewis (St James's) Ltd 1981–90; Freeman of City of London 1980; *Style—* Sir Edward Wheler, Bt; ✉ 34 St Carantoc Way, Crantock, Newquay, Cornwall (☎ 01637 830965)

WHELON, (Charles) Patrick Clavell; s of Charles Eric Whelon (d 1975), and Margaret Ethel Salter (d 1960); *b* 18 Jan 1930; *Educ* Wellington, Pembroke Coll Cambridge (MA); *m* 6 Jan 1968, Prudence Mary, da of Samuel Lesley Potter (d 1966); 1 s (Charles b 1969), 1 da (Emily b 1971); *Career* called to the Bar Middle Temple 1954, recorder of the Crown Court 1978–; Liveryman Worshipful Co of Vintners; *Recreations* gardening, travel, drawing; *Style—* Patrick Whelon, Esq; ✉ Russetts, Pyott's Hill, Old Basing, Hants RG24 8AP; 2 Harcourt Buildings, Temple, London EC4Y 9DB (☎ 0171 353 2112)

WHETNALL, Andrew Donard; CB; s of Donard Whetnall (d 1950), and Joan, *née* Mummery; *b* 18 May 1948; *Educ* King's Norton GS, Univ of Sussex (MA), Univ Coll Cambridge (CertEd); *m* 1972, Jane Lepel, da of Lt Col H P L Glass; 2 da (Francesca b 1975, Elizabeth b 1977), 2 s (George b 1979, Thomas b 1983); *Career* teacher 1972–75, DOE 1975–80, princ Dept of Tport 1980–83; DOE: princ 1983–87, asst sec water legislation 1988–89 (inner cities 1987–88); under sec Cabinet Office 1993–96 (asst sec 1989–93), dir Local Govt Machinery of Govt and Standards Gp DOE 1996–; *Recreations* reading, music; *Style—* Andrew Whetnall, Esq, CB; ✉ Department of the Environment, Zone 5/C2, eland House, Bressenden Place, London SW1E 50U (☎ 0171 890 4198, fax 0171 890 4189)

WHETSTONE, Rear Adm Anthony John (Tony); CB (1982); s of Albert Whetstone (d 1949), and Hannah Elizabeth (Anne), *née* Hubbard (d 1963); *b* 12 June 1927; *Educ* King Henry VIII Sch Coventry; *m* 7 April 1951, Elizabeth Stewart (Betty), da of Robert Bruce Georgeson; 3 c (Elizabeth Anne b 1952, Alison Mary b 1954, Robert Anthony Stewart b 1963); *Career* RN: joined 1945, cmmnd Sub-Lt 1947, cmd HMS Sea Scout (submarine) 1955–56, cmd HMS Artful (submarine) 1959–61, Cdr 1963, Ops Offr to Flag Offr Submarines 1963–65, cmd HMS Repulse (Polaris submarine) 1967–69, Capt 1969, asst dir Naval Warfare 1970–72, cmd HMS Juno 1972–73, COS to Flag Offr Submarines 1974–75, RCDS 1976, cmd HMS Norfolk 1977–78, Flag Offr Sea Trg 1978–80, Rear Adm 1979, Asst Chief of Naval Staff (ops) 1981–83, ret 1983; dir gen: Cable TV Assoc 1983–86, Nat TV Rental Assoc 1983–87; dir DESC Ltd 1991–96; asst sec Def Press and Bdcasting Ctee 1987–92, sec Special Tstees St George's Hosp 1988–93, memb Cncl Offrs Pension Soc 1984–96, area pres Royal Naval Assoc Kent and Surrey 1985–95, nat pres Submarine Old Comrades Assoc; chm: Tstees RN Submarine Museum, Civil Serv Drama Fedn 1985–92; FIMgt 1976; *Recreations* fly fishing, hill walking, amateur theatre; *Clubs* Army and Navy, Naval, Civil Service; *Style—* Rear Adm Tony Whetstone, CB; ✉ 17 Anglesey Road, Alverstoke, Hants PO12 2EG (☎ 01702 680632)

WHEWELL, Roger William; s of Alfred Thomas Whewell (d 1969), and Dorothy Annie Whewell (d 1988); *b* 24 Jan 1940; *Educ* Harrison Coll Barbados, Clifton; *m* 9 May 1964, (Edith) Elaine, da of George Turcan Chiene, DSO, TD, MC (d 1992), of Edinburgh; 2 s (Andrew b 1966, Rupert b 1969), 1 da (Lisa b 1968); *Career* CA; articled clerk Jackson Taylor Abernethy & Co 1958–64; KPMG: joined 1964, ptnr 1974, gen ptnr 1985–96; memb Policyholders' Protection Bd; Liveryman Worshipful Co of Chartered Accountants; FCA 1964; *Recreations* equestrian and country pursuits; *Style—* Roger Whewell, Esq; ✉ Innerwick House, Glenlyon, By Aberfeldy, Perthshire PH15 2PP

WHICHER, Prof John Templeman; s of Leonard Sydney Whicher, of Piddinghoe, Sussex, and Ethel Adelaid, *née* Orton; *b* 30 July 1945; *Educ* Sherborne, Univ of Cambridge (MA, MB BChir), Westminster Hosp Med Sch, Univ of London (MSc); *m* 1 (m dis 1982), Alba Heather Phyllida Leighton Crawford; 1 s (Hugo b 1975), 1 da (Emma b 1973); m 2, 17 Sept 1982, Jennefer Whitney, da of Dr Arthur Benson Unwin, of London; 2 da (Alexandra b 1986, Charlotte b 1989); *Career* dep dir Protein Reference Unit Westminster Hosp 1975–78, conslt chem pathologist Bristol Royal Infirmary 1978–87; Univ of Leeds: prof of chem pathology 1987–91, prof of molecular pathology 1991–96; former chm Scientific Ctee Assoc of Clinical Biochemists, former conslt advsr to Chief MD DHSS, memb Geologists' Assoc; FRCPath; *Books* Immunochemistry in Clinical Laboratory Medicine (jointly, 1978), A Short Textbook of Chemical Pathology (jointly, 1989), The Biochemistry of Inflammation (jointly, 1990); *Recreations* hot air ballooning, speleology, geology; *Clubs* British Balloon and Airship; *Style*— Prof John Whicher; ✉ Rush House, Deighton, York YO4 6HG (☎ 01904 87237); Research School of Medicine, University of Leeds, 24 Hyde Terrace, Leeds LS2 9LN (☎ 0113 233 6871)

WHICKER, Alan Donald; o s of late Charles Henry Whicker, and Anne Jane, *née* Cross; *b* 2 Aug 1925; *Educ* Haberdashers' Aske's; *Career* Capt Devonshire Regt, dir Army Film and Photo Section with 8 Army and US 5 Army, war corr in Korea; foreign corr, novelist, writer, television and radio broadcaster; joined BBC TV Tonight programme 1957; writer and presenter of documentary series for: BBC TV 1959–68 and 1982–92, Yorkshire TV 1968–82 and 1992–; author of articles for various publications, Sunday newspaper columns; various awards incl: Screenwriters' Guild Best Documentary Script 1963, Guild of Television Producers and Directors Personality of the Year 1964, Silver Medal RTS 1968, Dumont Award Univ of California 1970; Best Interview Programme Award, Hollywood Festival of TV 1973, Dimbleby Award BAFTA 1978, TV Times Special Award 1978, Royal TV Soc's first Hall of Fame 1993; FRSA; *TV Series* for BBC 1: Whicker's World 1959–60 and 1965–66, Whicker Down Under 1961, Whicker on Top of the World! 1962, Whicker in Sweden, Whicker in the Heart of Texas, Whicker down Mexico Way 1963, The Alan Whicker Report series including The Solitary Billionaire (J Paul Getty), Whicker's World - the First Million Miles (six retrospectives) 1982, Whicker's World - a Fast Boat to China 1984, Whicker's World - Living with Uncle Sam 1985, Whicker's World - Living with Waltzing Matilda 1988, Whicker's World - Hong Kong 1990, Whicker's World - A Taste of Spain 1992; for BBC 2: Whicker! (talk show) 1984; for Yorkshire TV: Whicker's World Specials on Gen Stroessner of Paraguay, Count von Rosen and Pres Duvalier of Haiti, Whicker in Europe, Whicker's Walkabout, Broken Hill-Walled City, Gairy's Grenada, World of Whicker, Whicker's Orient, Whicker within a Woman's World 1972, Whicker's South Seas, Whicker Way Out West 1973, Whicker's World series on Cities 1974, Whicker's World Down Under 1976, Whicker's New World 1977, Whicker's World - India 1978, Whicker's World - Indonesia 1979, Whicker's World - California 1980, Peter Sellers Meml programme 1980, Whicker's World Aboard the Orient Express 1982, Around Whicker's World in 25 years (three retrospective progs) 1982, Around Whicker's World - The Ultimate Package! (four progs) 1992, Whicker's World - The Absolute Monarch (The Sultan of Brunei) 1992, Whickers' World South Africa (two progs) 1993, Whicker's Miss World 1993, Whicker's World - The Sun King 1993, In South-East Asia: Whicker's World - The Real Oriental Express 1994, Whicker - The Mahathir Interview (Dr Mahathir Mohammed, PM of Malaysia) 1994, Whicker's World - Pavarotti in Paradise 1994; *Radio* for BBC: writer/presenter various programmes, chaired Start the Week 1982, Whicker's Wireless World 1983; *Cinema* various films incl The Angry Silence 1964; *Books* Some Rise By Sin (1949), Away - with Alan Whicker (1963), Within Whicker's World (1982), Whicker's New World (1985), Whicker's World Down Under (1988); *Style*— Alan Whicker, Esq; ✉ Le Gallais Chambers, St Helier, Jersey

WHILE, Prof Alison Elizabeth; da of Harold Arthur Armstrong While, MBE, TD (d 1983), and Janet Bell Symington Clark; *b* 24 July 1953; *Educ* Wycombe Abbey, Univ of Southampton (BSc), Poly of the South Bank (MSc), Univ of London (PhD), St Thomas' Hosp (RGN), Univ of Southampton (RHV); *m* Philip Allan Gore-Randall, *qv*; 2 s (William b 1986, Edward b 1987); *Career* health visitor N Kensington 1977–80, lectr Chelsea Coll Univ of London 1980–89, prof of community nursing King's Coll London 1992– (sr lectr 1989–92); memb: Royal Coll of Nursing 1977, Health Visitors' Assoc 1977; Freeman City of London 1979, Liveryman Worshipful Co of Farriers 1979; *Books* Research in Preventive Community Nursing Care (1986), Health in the Inner City (1989), Caring for Children (1991); *Recreations* riding, tennis, good food, travel, The Cotswolds; *Style*— Prof Alison While; ✉ 21 Rylett Road, London W12 9SS (☎ 0181 743 7054); Department of Nursing Studies, King's College London, Cornwall House, Waterloo Road, London SE1 8WA (☎ 0171 872 3022, fax 0171 872 3219)

WHIMSTER, Prof William Frederick; s of Dr William Swanson Whimster (d 1969), of Nottingham, and Dr Madge Elizabeth Whimster, *née* Edwards (d 1975); *Educ* Sedbergh, Queens' Coll Cambridge (MA, MB BChir, MD), Guy's Hosp London, DObstRCOG; *m* 1958, Sybil Harrison, da of George Wallace; 2 da (Claire Elizabeth b 4 June 1961, Suzanne Jane b 18 Dec 1966), 2 s (Peter William b 21 Feb 1963, James Richard b 13 Aug 1968); *Career* house surgn Lewisham Hosp London 1958–59, house physician Lewisham Hosp Nottingham 1959; Nat Serv S Pacific Health Serv (Colonial Office) 1960–63: MO i/c med beds Lautoka Hosp Fiji 1960–61, chief MO Niue Island (NZ Island Territories) 1961–63; SHO (pathology) Lewisham Hosp London 1963–64; Royal Free Hosp: registrar (haematology) 1964–65, lectr in morbid anatomy 1967–68; lectr/conslt in morbid anatomy (on secondment) Univ of WI Jamaica 1968–70, sr lectr (MRC) in experimental pathology Inst of Diseases of the Chest London 1971–72, memb Scientific Staff MRC Air Pollution Unit Bart's Med Coll 1972–74; King's Coll Sch of Med and Dentistry: lectr/hon conslt in morbid anatomy 1974–83, actg head of dept 1983–85, head Dept of Morbid Anatomy (now Dept of Histopathology) 1985–91, contract prof of pathology Univ of Ancona Italy 1989–91, prof and head Dept of Histopathology 1991–, Soc of Apothecaries lectr on the history of med 1994–; visiting lectr Universidad Nacional de Colombia Bogota 1978; memb: Cncl RSM 1979–84, Advsy Ctee on Undergraduate Trg in Pathology Euro Soc of Pathology 1983–; UK memb for Anatomic Pathology Euro Union of Med Specialists 1990–; ed RCPath Bulletin 1988–, assoc ed E Euro Med Jl 1992–; memb Editorial Bd: Bahrain Med Bulletin 1977–, Electronic Jl of Pathology 1994–; Freeman City of London 1982, Liveryman Worshipful Soc of Apothecaries 1982; memb: Assoc of Clinical Pathologists, BMA, Br Thoracic Soc, Euro Soc of Analytical Cellular Pathology, Euro Soc of Pathology, Fellowship of Postgraduate Med, Int Acad of Pathology, Pathological Soc of GB and I, RSM, W Kent Medico-Chirurgical Soc; FRCPath, FRCP(London); *Books* Tumours of the Trachea, Bronchus, Lung and Pleura - Diagnostic Tumour Bibliographies 1 (1983); *Recreations* windsurfing, teaching medical writing for publication, quantitative pathology, roadside workman signs, skiing, reading history; *Clubs* Athenaeum; *Style*— Prof William Whimster; ✉ Department of Histopathology, King's College School of Medicine and Dentistry, Denmark Hill, London SE5 8RX (☎ 0171 346 3004, fax 0171 346 3670, mobile 0385 243099)

WHINES, Nicholas Rudwick; s of Rudwick Albert Whines, of Salisbury, and Patricia May, *née* Smith; *Educ* Bishop Wordsworth Sch Salisbury, Fitzwilliam Coll Cambridge (BA); *m* 4 April 1975, Jennifer Elizabeth Susan, da of Archibald Frederick Aldhous; 1 s (Thomas Edward Rudwick b 1979), 1 da (Harriet Frances Dora b 1981); *Career* prodr: BBC Schs Radio 1972–86, BBC Schs TV 1986–88, Schs Bdcasting TV 1991; head of Schs Bdcasting BBC Radio 1988–90, sr prodr BBC Schools TV 1991–; BAFTA award for children's documentary and educn 1989; *Recreations* gardening, swimming; *Style*— Nicholas Whines, Esq; ✉ BBC, 201 Wood Lane, White City, London W12 7TS (☎ 0181 752 5252)

WHINNEY, Rt Rev Michael Humphrey Dickens; s of Humphrey Charles Dickens Whinney (d 1982), and Evelyn Lawrence Revell, *née* Low (d 1979); gggs of Charles Dickens; *b* 8 July 1930; *Educ* Charterhouse, Pembroke Coll Cambridge (MA), Ridley Hall Cambridge, General Theol Seminary NY (pt/t, STM); *m* 1958, Veronica, da of late Lt-Col Derek Webster; 2 s (Timothy b 1959, David b 1966), 1 da (Kathryn b 1961); *Career* Nat Serv 5 Regt RHA 1949–50, TA Serv Surrey Yeo (Queen Mary's) Regt 1950–52; articled clerk Whinney Smith & Whinney CAs (now Ernst & Young) 1950–52; curate St Helen's Rainham with S Hornchurch and Wennington Essex 1957–60, head Univ of Cambridge Mission Settlement Bermondsey London 1960–67, vicar St James with Christ Church Bermondsey 1967–73, archdeacon and borough dean of Southwark London 1973–82, suffragan bishop of Aston Birmingham 1982–85, bishop of Southwell Nottingham 1985–88, asst bishop Dio of Birmingham 1988–95, hon asst bishop Dio of Birmingham 1996–, canon residentiary Birmingham Cathedral 1992–95, diocesan dir for mission 1993–95; chm: dirs Whitchester Christian Centre, tstees Enterprise Sailing; memb Lee Abbey Cncl; conslt Caret Consulting Ltd; registered practitioner Br Assoc of Psychological Type, gen memb W Midlands Inst of Psychotherapy; a vice pres Dickens Fellowship; *Books* Episcopacy Today and Tomorrow (1990); *Style*— The Rt Rev Michael Whinney; ✉ Moorcroft, 3 Moor Green Lane, Moseley, Birmingham B13 8NE (☎ and fax 0121 449 2856)

WHIPHAM, Thomas Henry Martin; CBE (1990); s of Harry Rowland Whipham (d 1942), and Anne Hilda Muriel Martin (d 1975); *b* 18 May 1923; *Educ* Malvern; *m* 6 May 1972, Bridget Elizabeth, da of Hugh Roger Greville Montgomery (d 1952); 1 da (Sandra Claire b 24 June 1975); *Career* WWII Army 1941–46, cmmnd Lt RAC Duke of Wellington's Regt 1943, served N Africa, Italy, Middle East; called to the Bar Lincoln's Inn 1949 (ad eundem Middle Temple); pres London Rent Assessment Panel 1986–94 (a vice pres 1978–86), pres Central London Valuation Tbnl 1987–94, nat vice pres Valuation Tbnls 1991–94; hon steward Westminster Abbey 1985–; Parly candidate (Cons) Shoreditch and Finsbury by-election 1958 (also gen election 1959); memb: London Electricity Consultative Cncl 1961–70, Friern Hosp Mgmnt Ctee 1960–73, Marylebone Borough Cncl 1962–65, Westminster City Cncl 1968–86 (chm Ctees on: Road Safety, Highways and Works, Town Planning), Lord Mayor of Westminster 1982–83; Freeman: City of London, Worshipful Co of Goldsmiths; Cdr of Order of Orange Nassau 1982; *Recreations* swimming, walking, opera, theatre, reading, travel, enjoying life; *Clubs* MCC, Carlton, Hurlingham; *Style*— Thomas Whipham, Esq, CBE; ✉ 28 Ashworth Road, London W9 1JY (☎ 0171 289 5609)

WHIPP, Dr Elisabeth Clare; da of Dr Brian Whipp (d 1985), and Margery Eileen Whipp (d 1977); *b* 9 Sept 1947; *Educ* St Helen's Sch Northwood, Lady Margaret Hall Oxford; *Career* conslt oncologist Bristol Royal Infirmary 1981–; *Style*— Dr Elisabeth Whipp; ✉ Bristol Oncology Centre, Horfield Rd, Bristol BS8 2BZ (☎ 0117 928 2417, fax 0117 973 4211)

WHIPPMAN, Michael; s of Matthew Whippman (d 1973), and Adelina Miriam, *née* Abrahams (d 1994); *b* 20 Sept 1938; *Educ* King Edward VII Sch Johannesburg, Univ of Witwatersrand (Univ scholar, UNICO medal, BSc), Clare Coll Cambridge (PhD); *m* 1967, Constance Lorae, da of Robert and Martha Baskett; 2 da (Sarah Caroline b 8 June 1970, Ruth Katherine b 3 March 1974); *Career* Univ of Pennsylvania: res fell 1963–65, asst prof 1965–71; sr res fell Univ of Helsinki 1971–73; DHSS (now DSS): princ 1973–80, asst sec 1980–88, under sec 1988–90 and 1994–; under sec HM Treasy 1990–93; fell American Physical Soc 1972; *Recreations* opera, walking; *Style*— Michael Whippman, Esq; ✉ Policy Director, DSS, The Adelphi, 1–11 John Adam Street, London WC2N 6HT (☎ 0171 962 8361, fax 0171 712 2235)

WHISHAW, Anthony Popham Law; s of Robert Whishaw, and Joyce Evelyn Mary, *née* Wheeler (d 1996); *b* 22 May 1930; *Educ* Tonbridge (Higher Cert), Chelsea Sch of Art, RCA (travelling scholarship, drawing prize); *m* 1957, Jean Gibson; 2 da (Phoebe, Zoe); *Career* artist; *Collections* incl: Arts Cncl GB, Coventry Art Gallery, Euro Parl Strasbourg, Leicester City Art Gallery, Museo de Bahia Brazil, Nat Gallery Victoria Melbourne, Museum of Contemporary Art Helsinki, Royal Acad, Power Art Gallery Sydney Aust, Ferens Art Gallery Hull, City Art Galleries Sheffield, Chantry Bequest, The Tate Gallery, Christchurch Kensington, The Long Term Credit Bank of Japan, Andersen Consulting, Ashikaga Bank of Tokyo, Zeneca, Bolton Art Gallery, The Financial Times, M A M Ladbrokes; *One-Man Exhibitions* incl: Liberia Abril Madrid 1957, Roland Browse & Delbanco 1960, 1961, 1963, 1965 and 1968, Hoya Gallery London 1974, Acme Gallery 1978, from Landscape (Kettle's Yard Cambridge, Ferens Art Gallery Hull, Bede Gallery Jarrow) 1982–84, Work on Paper (Nicola Jacobs Gallery London) 1983, Reflections After Las Meninas (tour) 1987, Royal Acad of Arts Diploma Galleries London 1987, Hatton Gallery Newcastle 1988, Mead Gallery Warwick Univ 1988, Hansard Gallery Southampton 1988, Spacex Gallery Exeter 1988, Infaust Gallery Hamburg 1989, Infaust Gallery Shanghai 1989, Blasón Gallery London 1991, Artspace London 1992, 1994 and 1995, RWA Bristol 1993, On Memory and Reflection (nat touring exhbn ending at Barbican) 1994–95; *Gp Exhibitions* incl: Ashmolean Museum Oxford 1957–72, Br Painting 1952–77 (Royal Acad of Arts London) 1977, Walker Art Gallery Liverpool 1980, Hayward Annual (Hayward Gallery London) 1980 and 1982, Nine Artists (Helsinki, touring) 1983, Three Decades 1953–83 (Royal Acad of Arts London) 1983, 30 London Painters (Royal Acad of Arts London) 1985, Whitechapel Open (Whitechapel Art Gallery London) 1981–83, 1987 and 1994, The Romantic Tradition in Contemporary British Painting (Madrid, Murcia, touring) 1988, 8 Contemporary Br Artsists (Galerie Sapet Valeree France) 1988, Le Paysage Contemporaine 1991/92 (touring Belgium, France); *Prizes* Perth International Biennale 1973, Bayer Int Painting 1973, South East Arts Assoc Painting 1975, GLC Painting 1981, John Moores Minor Painting 1982; scholarships: Spanish Govt 1956, Abbey Minor 1956, Abbey Premier 1982, Lorne 1982–83; Greater London Arts Assoc Grant 1977, Arts Cncl GB Award 1978, RA Picture of the Year 1996 (for Korn Ferry); RA 1989 (ARA 1980), ARCA, RWA 1992; *Style*— Anthony Whishaw, Esq, RA; ✉ c/o The Royal Academy, Burlington House, London W1V 0DJ

WHISHAW, Sir Charles Percival Law; kt (1969); 2 s of Montague Law Whishaw (d 1946), of London, and Erna Louise, *née* Spies; *b* 29 Oct 1909; *Educ* Charterhouse, Worcester Coll Oxford; *m* 1936, (Margaret) Joan (d 1989), da of Col Thomas Henry Hawkins, CMG (d 1944), of Formby, Lancs; 1 s, 2 da; *Career* called to the Bar 1932, admitted slr 1938, ptnr Freshfields 1943–74; tstee Calouste Gulbenkian Fndn 1956–81; Liveryman City of London Solicitors' Co; Comendador of Order of Infante D Henrique Portugal 1982; *Style*— Sir Charles Whishaw; ✉ Clare Park, nr Farnham, Surrey GU10 5DT (☎ 01252 851333, 01252 850681)

WHISTLER, Laurence; CBE (1973, OBE 1955); s of Henry Whistler (d 1940), of Salisbury, and Helen, *née* Ward; *b* 21 Jan 1912; *Educ* Stowe, Balliol Coll Oxford (MA); *m* 1, 12 Sep 1939, Jill (d 1944), da of Sir Ralph Furse, KCMG, DSO (d 1963); 1 s (Simon b 1940), 1 da (Caroline b 1944); m 2, 15 Aug 1950 (m dis 1986), Theresa, yr sis of Jill Furse; 1 s (Daniel b 1954), 1 da (Frances b 1957); m 3, 24 March 1987 (m dis 1991), Carol, da of John Groves, CB; *Career* WWII RCS 1940–41, 2 Lt RB 1941, Capt RB 1942–45; glass engraver and author; work on glass incl: engraved church windows and panels Moreton Dorset, Sherborne Abbey Dorset, Guards' Chapel London, Salisbury Cathedral, Curry Rivel Somerset, Dacre Cumbria, Abbots Ripon Hunts, St Hilda's Coll Oxford; exhibitions: Agnews Bond St 1969, Marble Hill Twickenham 1972, Corning Museum USA 1974, Ashmolean 1976 and 1985, Sotheby's 1992, Salisbury Museum 1993;

hon fell Balliol Coll Oxford 1974, first pres Guild of Glass Engravers 1975–80; Hon DLit Oxford 1992; *Books* on glass incl: The Engraved Glass of Laurence Whistler (1952), Engraved Glass 1952–58 (1959), Pictures on Glass (1972), The Image on The Glass (1975), Scenes And Signs On Glass (1985), Point Engraving on Glass (1992); poetry incl: The World's Room - Collected Poems (1949), To Celebrate Her Living (1967), Enter (1987); prose incl: The English Festivals (1947), The Initials In The Heart, The Story of a Marriage (1975); on his brother: Rex Whistler, His Life and Drawings (1948), The Work of Rex Whistler (with Ronald Fuller, 1969), The Laughter And The Urn (biography, 1985); on architecture incl: Sir John Vanbrugh (biography, 1938), The Imagination of Vanbrugh (1954); *Style*— Laurence Whistler, Esq, CBE; ✉ Scriber's Cottage, Watlington, Oxford

WHISTON, John; *Educ* Edinburgh Acad, Balliol Coll Oxford (BA); *Career* BBC: joined as gen trainee 1983, asst prodr BBC Music & Arts 1985–87 (worked on progs incl Timewatch, Bookmark and Omnibus), prodr BBC Music & Arts 1987–94 (a sr prodr The Late Show, prodr Edinburgh Nights), head of Youth and Entertainment Features 1994–; prodr progs for BBC Music & Arts incl: Naked Hollywood (BAFTA Best Documentary, ACE Award, Emmy Nomination), Absurdistan (BFI Grierson Best Documentary Award), Archive Productions progs (incl The Lime Grove Story, A Night with Alan Bennett, TV Hell, Granadaland, Cops on the Box, A Night in with David Attenborough); progs 1994– incl: The Mrs Merton Show (BAFTA Award), Rough Guides, The Travel Show, The Big Trip, The Sunday Show, Kicking & Screaming, Great Railway Journeys, The Sunday Show, Dennis Pennis, themed nights incl Weird Night and George Best Night; *Style*— John Whiston, Esq; ✉ BBC Television, New Broadcasting House, Oxford Road, Manchester M60 1SJ (☎ 0161 244 3602)

WHITAKER, Barry Carnaby; s of Maj Kenneth Henry Whitaker (d 1987), of Tilford, Surrey, and Millicent, *née* Carnaby (d 1984); *b* 5 Nov 1940; *Educ* Marlborough; *m* 21 Nov 1968, Jacqueline, da of Sqdn Ldr Harold Rothwell; 2 s (Jason b 7 Feb 1970, Max b 11 Dec 1975); *Career* qualified CA; Peat Marwick Mitchell & Co 1959–64; ptnr: Joseph Sebag & Co 1970–79 (joined 1965), Carr Sebag & Co 1979–84, Grieveson Grant & Co 1984–86, Kleinwort Benson Ltd 1986–88, C L Alexanders Laing & Cruickshank Gilts Ltd 1988–89, Brown Shipley Stockbroking Limited 1990–96, Shaw & Co Ltd 1996–; chm Tilford Parish Cncl 1980–92 (memb 1977–92), pres Tilford Cons Assoc 1988–92 (chm 1983–88); FCA 1974 (ACA 1964), MSI 1961; *Recreations* country sports, bridge, reading; *Clubs* Boodle's, Royal London YC; *Style*— Barry Whitaker, Esq; ✉ The Old House, Lodsworth, Petworth, West Sussex GU28 9DA (☎ 01798 861418); Shaw & Co Ltd, Camomile Court, 23 Camomile Street, London EC3A 7PP (☎ 0171 444 816, fax 0171 444 8625, car 0836 266763)

WHITAKER, Benjamin Charles George (Ben); 3 s of Maj-Gen Sir John Albert Charles Whitaker, 2 Bt, CB, CBE (d 1957), and Pamela Lucy Mary, *née* Snowden (d 1945); bro of Sir James Whitaker, 3 Bt, *qv*; *b* 15 Sept 1934; *Educ* Eton, New Coll Oxford (BA); *m* 18 Dec 1964, Janet Alison, da of Alan Harrison Stewart, of Beeston, Notts; 2 s (Daniel b 1966, Rasaq b 1972), 1 da (Quincy b 1968); *Career* Lt Coldstream Guards; called to the Bar Inner Temple 1959; MP (Lab) Hampstead 1966–70, Parly sec to Min for Overseas Devpt 1969–70; exec dir The Minority Rights Gp 1971–88, UK memb The UN Human Rights Sub Cmmn 1975–88, dir The Gulbenkian Fndn (UK) 1988–; Lt Order of Merit (Portugal); *Books* Parks for People (1971), The Foundations (1974), The Police in Society (1979), A Bridge of People (1983), The Global Connection (1987); *Recreations* writing, water-colour painting; *Style*— Ben Whitaker, Esq; ✉ c/o The Gulbenkian Foundation, 98 Portland Place, London W1N 4ET (☎ 0171 636 5313)

WHITAKER, Catherine (Kati); da of Dennis Whitaker, of Totteridge, London, and Florence, *née* Gregory; *b* 11 Dec 1957; *Educ* Queen Elizabeth Girls Sch Barnet, Somerville Coll Oxford (read PPE), Coll of Law Lancaster Gate; *m* 29 May 1989, Andrew Jackson Hughes, s of Brian Jackson Hughes, of Aldershot, Hants; 2 da (Alice Chloe b 27 Aug 1991, Georgia Bryony b 21 July 1993); *Career* freelance radio and TV journalist 1973–; presenter Radio 4 documentaries and magazine progs: Does He Take Sugar 1987–95, Sunday 1988–90; presenter: Visions (Thames TV) 1992, audio magazine for doctors; reporter Breakfast News BBC Television; *Recreations* music, dance, cinema, travel; *Style*— Ms Kati Whitaker; ✉ 5 Wilkinson Street, London SW8 1DD (fax 0171 787 2061)

WHITAKER, David Brian; OBE (1989); s of Denis Whitaker (d 1996), of Hexton, Hitchin, Herts, and Phyllis, *née* Clark; *b* 16 Aug 1948; *Educ* Hitchin Boys' GS, Loughborough Univ (BEd); *m* 18 July 1970, Christine (Chris), da of George Clements (d 1987); 2 s (Kester Mark Clement b 19 Dec 1974, Alexander John Clement b 16 May 1977); *Career* teacher: Hitchin Boys' Sch 1972–76, Sherrardswood Sch 1976–78, Marlborough 1978–85; int hockey player and coach; player: Blueharts 1973–74, Southgate 1974–80, 104 caps England and GB 1973–80; coach England and GB 1980–88 and 1993–, dir of coaching Hockey Assoc 1986–89 (professional coach 1985–86); honours as player: Southgate Euro Club champions 1976, 1977, 1978, played in World Cup 1975 and 1978, Euro Cup 1974 and 1977; honours as coach: Bronze Medal Olympic Games 1984, Silver Medal World Cup 1986, Silver Medal Euro Cup 1987, Gold Medal Olympic Games 1988, Champions Trophy 1981–88; UK coach of the year 1985 and 1988; ptnr Performance Consultants; *Books* Coaching Hockey (1986), Coaching Workshop (1992); *Recreations* DIY, golf, history; *Style*— David Whitaker, Esq, OBE; ✉ The Cedars, Stockton-on-Teme, Worcester WR6 6UT

WHITAKER, David Haddon; OBE (1991); s of Edgar Haddon Whitaker, MA, OBE (d 1985), and Molly Marion, *née* Seely; *b* 6 March 1931; *Educ* Marlborough, St John's Coll Cambridge (MA); *m* 1, 1959, late Veronica, *née* Leach; m 2, 1976 (m dis), Audrey, *née* Curl; m 3, 1994, Marguerite, *née* Van Reenen; *children* 2 s (Martin, Rupert), 2 da (Lee, Jane); *Career* Nat Serv Coldstream Gds 1949, 2 Lt Queen's Own Royal West Surrey Regt 1950; chm: Soc of Bookmen 1984–86 (sec 1969–78), Br Standards Inst's Working Pty for Standard Book Numbering 1966–67, ISBN 1968–69, J Whitaker & Sons Ltd 1980– (dir 1966–); dir Teleordering Ltd 1984–90; ed The Bookseller 1976–80; memb Library and Info Servs Cncl of the Office of Arts and Libraries 1984–89 (chm Working Pty on Financing the Public Library Service 1988–89); chm: Book Trade Electronic Data Interchange Standards Ctee 1986–90, Advsy Panel of Int Standard Book Numbering Agency Berlin 1989 (dep chm 1986), Sec of State for Nat Heritage Advsy Panel for Public Lending Right 1988–93, Working Pty on Library and Book Trade Rels 1988–91 (memb 1965), Br Nat Bibliography Res Fund 1991, Information and Library Services Lead Body for National Vocational Qualifications 1991 (resigned 1995); hon vice pres The Library Assoc 1990; *Recreations* walking, reading, tennis; *Clubs* Garrick, Leander, Thames Rowing; *Style*— David Whitaker, Esq, OBE; ✉ The Ship, Boscastle, Cornwall PL35 0HD (☎ 01840 250555); J Whitaker & Sons Ltd, 12 Dyott St, London WC1A 1DF (☎ 0171 420 6000)

WHITAKER, Prof Dorothy Stock; da of Charles William Stock (d 1958), of Chicago, Illinois, and Martha Emily, *née* Utesch (d 1985); *b* 30 March 1925; *Educ* Univ of Chicago (PhB, MA, PhD); *m* 21 Dec 1963, Frederic Philip Galvin, s of Capt Charles Frederick Whitaker (d 1988), of Baildon, W Yorks; 1 s (Weem b 1965); *Career* res assoc Dept of Educn Univ of Chicago 1952–55, res psychologist VA Res Hosp Chicago 1955–57, assoc prof of psychology Univ of Chicago 1957–64 (former asst prof), lectr Dept of Psychology Univ of Leeds 1964–73, prof of social work Dept of Social Policy and Social Work Univ of York 1973–; memb: American Psychological Assoc 1952, American Gp Psychotherapy Assoc 1956, Gp Analytic Soc 1964, Inst for Group Analysis 1980; *Books* Psychotherapy Through The Group Process (with Morton Lieberman, 1964), Using Groups to Help People (1985), Research by Social Workers (with J Lesley Archer, 1989); *Recreations* sailing, walking; *Style*— Prof Dorothy Whitaker; ✉ Iriss - Block 4, University of York, Heslington, York YO1 5DD (☎ 01904 433488, fax 01765 620253, telex 57933 YORKUL)

WHITAKER, James Edward Anthony; s of George Edward Dudley Whitaker, OBE (d 1983), and Mary Evelyn Austin, *née* Haslett (d 1989); *b* 4 Oct 1940; *Educ* Cheltenham Coll; *m* 1965, Iwona, da of late Andrzej Karol Milde, of Poland; 2 s (Edward b 1965, Thomas b 1966), 1 da (Victoria b 1973); *Career* journalist: Daily Mail, Daily Express, The Sun, Daily Star; currently Royal corr Daily Mirror; *Books* Prince Charles, Prince of Wales, Settling Down, Diana v Charles; *Recreations* racing, shooting, skiing; *Clubs* City Golf; *Style*— James Whitaker, Esq; ✉ c/o Mirror Group Newspapers, One Canada Square, Canary Wharf, London E14 5AP (☎ 0171 510 3000)

WHITAKER, Sir James Herbert Ingham; 3 Bt (UK 1936), of Babworth, Nottinghamshire; OBE (1996); s of Maj-Gen Sir John Albert Charles Whitaker, 2 Bt, CB, CBE (d 1957), and Pamela Lucy Mary, *née* Snowden (d 1945); bro of Benjamin Charles George Whitaker, *qv*; *b* 27 July 1925; *Educ* Eton; *m* 26 July 1948, Mary Elisabeth Lander, JP (who m 1940, Capt David Urling Clark, MC, d 1942), da of Ernest Johnston (d 1965), of Cockshut, Reigate, Surrey, and sis of Sir Charles Hepburn Johnston, GCMG (d 1986); 1 s, 1 da (Shervie, m David W J Price, *qv*); *Heir* s, John James Ingham Whitaker b 23 Oct 1952, *qv*; *Career* Capt Coldstream Gds 1944, served in N W Europe, Egypt and Palestine 1945, ret 1947; dep chm Halifax Building Society 1973–94, ret; govr Atlantic Coll; High Sheriff Notts 1969; *Recreations* shooting; *Style*— Sir James Whitaker, Bt, OBE; ✉ Auchnafree, Dunkeld, Perthshire (☎ 01350 725233); Babworth Garden House, Babworth, Retford, Notts (☎ 01777 703454)

WHITAKER, John James Ingham (Jack); s and h of Sir James Herbert Ingham Whitaker, 3 Bt; *b* 23 Oct 1952; *Educ* Eton, Univ of Bristol, (BSc); *m* 31 Jan 1981, Elizabeth Jane Ravenscroft, da of L J R Starke, of NZ; 1 s (Harry James Ingham b 1984), 3 da (Lucy Harriet Ravenscroft b 1982, Alix Catherine Hepburn b 1987, Eleanor Mary Harvie b 1989); *Career* FCA, AMIEE; *Style*— Jack Whitaker, Esq; ✉ The Cottage, Babworth, Retford, Notts DN22 8EW

WHITAKER, Martin; s of Maj Robert Edmund Whitaker, TD (d 1993), of Shropshire, and Priscilla Kynaston, *née* Mainwaring; *b* 24 Sept 1938; *Educ* Sherborne, RAC Cirencester; *m* 16 July 1966, Susan Mary Sheila, da of Francis Spenceleigh Walker, of Standlake, Oxon; 1 s (Alexander b 1972), 1 da (Anabel b 1969); *Career* chartered surveyor; dir Lane Fox (Residential) Ltd 1987–; FRICS; *Recreations* shooting, hunting; *Style*— Martin Whitaker, Esq; ✉ Dovecote House, Driffield, Cirencester, Glos GL7 5PY (☎ 01285 851465); 15 Dyer Street, Cirencester, Glos

WHITAKER, Michael; s of Donald Whitaker, and Enid, *née* Lockwood; *b* 17 March 1960; *Educ* Salendine Nook Secdy Modern Sch; *m* 13 Dec 1980, Veronique Dalems, da of Dino Vastapane; *Career* professional show jumper; Jr Euro Team 1976, winner Jr Championships under 16 and under 21, winner Jr Euro Team Championship 1978; Grand Prix wins: Hickstead 1986, Dortmund 1986 and 1995, Wembley 1987, Birmingham 1989, Calgary 1989; other wins incl: Hickstead Derby 1980, King George V Gold Cup 1982 and 1989, Euro Team Championships 1985, 1987, 1989, Euro Team Championships 1985, 1987, 1989, nat champion 1984 and 1989; runner-up Euro Championships 1989, Silver medal World Team Championships 1986 (Bronze medal 1990), Silver medal team event Olympics LA 1984; 45 int appearances; world bareback high jump record Dublin 1980; Martini Equestrian Personality Award 1993; *Recreations* sport, spending time at home; *Style*— Michael Whitaker, Esq

WHITAKER, Patrick James; s of John Henry Foord Whitaker, of The Garden House, Dunorlan Farm, Tunbridge Wells, Kent, and Anne Jennifer, *née* Cheveley; *b* 9 April 1965; *Educ* Garth Hill Comp, Berkshire Coll of Art & Design (RSA art bursary, BTEC), St Martin's Sch of Art (BA); *Career* fndr designer Whitaker Malem (with Keir Malem, *qv*) 1988– (annual collections of hand crafted leatherwear for specialist int retail); launched new line of male and female leather torsos (with Adel Roostein) 1995; special assignments incl: body sculptures for re-opening of Bauhaus Dessau, outfit for Naomi Campbell in Vauxhall advertising campaign 1993; cmmns for: Mick Jagger, Cher, Pamela Anderson, Gloria Estefan, Janet Jackson, Jerry Hall, Bono; film cmmns incl: Mortal Kombat 1995, The Changeling 1995; Unlaced Grace (Banbury Museum and nat touring exhbn) 1994–95; finalist Smirnoff Fashion Awards 1985, nominated British Fashion Awards 1992; appearances on TV and subject of press profiles in quality fashion magazines, fashion lectr at various colleges of art and design; *Recreations* film collection; *Style*— Patrick Whitaker, Esq; ✉ Whitaker Malem, Top Floor, Candid Studios, 3 Torrens Street, Angel, Islington, London EC1V 1NQ (☎ 0171 278 6332, fax 0171 278 6332)

WHITAKER, Sheila Hazel; da of Charles Whitaker (d 1975), and Hilda Dixon (d 1987); *b* 1 April 1936; *Educ* Cathays HS for Girls Cardiff, King's Norton GS Birmingham, Univ of Warwick (BA); *Career* chief stills offr Nat Film Archive BFI 1968–74, dir Tyneside Cinema, Tyneside Film Festival Newcastle Upon Tyne 1979–84, head of programming Nat Film Theatre BFI 1984–90, dir London Film Festival 1987–; memb Int Jury Venice Film Festival 1992; Chevalier de l'Ordre des Arts et des Lettres (France) 1996; *Clubs* Groucho; *Style*— Ms Sheila Whitaker; ✉ London Film Festival, South Bank, Waterloo, London SE1 8XT (☎ 0171 815 1320, fax 0171 633 0786)

WHITAKER, Steven Dixon; s of George Dixon Whitaker, of Exeter, and Elsie Whitaker; *b* 28 Jan 1950; *Educ* Burnley GS, Churchill Coll Cambridge (MA); *m* 4 Sept 1976, Jacqueline, da of William Ernest Branter (d 1985); 1 da (Emma Louise); *Career* called to the Bar Middle Temple 1973; *Recreations* horses, music, the arts, foreign travel; *Style*— Steven Whitaker, Esq; ✉ Via Marconi 7, Brucciano Mollazana, 55020 Lucca, Italy; 199 Strand, London WC2R 1DR (☎ 0171 379 9779, fax 0171 379 9481); All Saints Chambers, 9/11 Broad Street, Bristol BS1 2HP (☎ 0117 921 1966, fax 0117 927 6493)

WHITBOURN, Dr Philip Robin; OBE (1993); s of Edwin Arthur Whitbourn (d 1953), of Badgers Mount, Sevenoaks, Kent, and Kathleen, *née* Sykes; *b* 10 March 1932; *Educ* Sevenoaks Sch Kent, UCL (PhD); *m* 10 Jan 1959, Anne Pearce, da of Peter Melrose Marks (d 1938), of Glasgow; 1 s (James b 1963), 1 da (Katherine b 1960); *Career* architect; Sir Edwin Cooper RA and Partners 1955–58, Stewart Hendry and Smith 1958–60, Fitzroy Robinson Partnership 1960–66, Historic Bldgs Div GLC 1966–86; English Heritage: joined 1986, divnl architect London Region 1988–92, dir South Region 1992–94, chief architect Conservation Gp 1992–95; sec ICOMOS UK (Int Cncl on Monuments and Sites) 1995–; sec to Tstees INTACH (UK) Tst (Indian Nat Tst for Art and Cultural Heritage) 1995–; pres Royal Tunbridge Wells Civic Soc 1995– (chm 1969–70, 1972–73, 1978–80 and 1990–91), memb Southwark Diocesan Advsy Ctee for the Care of Churches 1973–; FRIBA 1968, FRTPI 1983, FSA 1984; *Style*— Dr Philip Whitbourn, OBE, FSA; ✉ Rosaville Lodge, 40 Beulah Road, Tunbridge Wells, Kent TN1 2NR (☎ 01892 523026, fax 01892 537873); ICOMOS UK, 10 Barley Mow Passage, London W4 4PH (☎ 0181 994 6477, fax 0181 747 8464)

WHITBREAD, David Anthony Llewellyn; s of Sqdn Ldr Jack Leonard Whitbread, of Hertford, and late Eunice, *née* Llewellyn; *b* 20 July 1936; *Educ* Latymer Upper Sch, Selwyn Coll Cambridge (MA); *m* 3 April 1965, Margaret Lilias, da of Geoffrey Luffingham, of Pietermaritzburg, S Africa; 3 da (Emily Jane b 1966, Harriet Ann b 1969, Rosemary b 1973); *Career* MOD 1960–67, sr asst educn offr Norfolk CC 1967–73, princ asst educn offr Hertfordshire CC 1973–84; Assoc of CCs: under sec for educn 1984–96, educn offr 1996–; FRSA; *Style*— David Whitbread, Esq; ✉ Association of County

Councils, Eaton House, 66A Eaton Square, London SW1W 9BH (☎ 0171 201 1535, fax 0171 235 8458)

WHITBREAD, Fatima; MBE (1987); *b* 3 March 1961; *Career* mktg conslt; javelin thrower, now ret; WAAA champion 1981–84 and 1986–87, UK champion 1981–85 and 1987–88; Gold medal Euro Jr Championships Poland 1979; Cwlth Games: Bronze medal Brisbane 1982, Silver medal Edinburgh 1986; Gold medal Euro Championships Stuttgart 1986; World Championships: Silver medal Helsinki 1983, Gold medal Rome 1987; Olympic Games: Bronze medal LA 1984, Silver medal Seoul 1988; holder of world, Euro, Cwlth and UK record (77.44m at Stuttgart) 1986–; former women's rep Br Olympic Assoc; former memb: Euro Athletics Assoc, Athletics Cmmn; govt non-exec dir Thameside Community Healthcare Bd; pres Chafford Hundred Athletic Club; *Books* Fatima (autobiography, 1988); *Recreations* theatre; *Style—* Miss Fatima Whitbread, MBE; ✉ c/o Chafford Hundred Information Centre, Elizabeth Road, Chafford Hundred, Grays, Essex RM16 6QZ (☎ 01375 391099)

WHITBREAD, Robin Peter; s of Peter Whitbread (d 1995), of Devon, and Joyce, *née* Cripps (d 1968); *b* 8 Jan 1951; *Educ* Ardingly Coll Sussex; *m* 21 May 1988, Sarah Louise, da of Michael Swallow; *Career* J Sainsbury plc: joined as mgmnt trainee 1969, PA to Chm 1974–77, sr mangr Produce Div 1980–83, departmental dir of mktg 1983–87, dir Shaw's Bd (wholly owned subsid based New England USA) 1987–90, main bd dir 1990–, mktg dir 1990–94, trading dir 1994–; Mktg Soc Marketer of the Yr 1993; memb Rabobank UK Food and Agribusiness Advsy Bd 1996–; chm Shere and Gomshall Branch Cons Assoc; memb Mktg Soc; *Recreations* cricket, squash, gardening; *Clubs* Old Ardinians Cricket (pres); *Style—* Robin Whitbread, Esq; ✉ J Sainsbury plc, Stamford House, Stamford Street, London SE1 9LL (☎ 0171 921 6000, fax 0171 921 7610)

WHITBREAD, Samuel Charles (Sam); JP; s of Maj Simon Whitbread (d 1985), of Southill, Bedfordshire, and Helen Beatrice Margaret, *née* Trefusis; family settled in Bedfordshire at time of Conquest, founded Brewery 1742, 1 Tory and 5 Whig/Liberal MPs; *b* 22 Feb 1937; *Educ* Eton, Trinity Coll Cambridge; *m* 1961, Jane Mary, da of Charles William John Hugh Hayter (d 1985), of Oxfordshire; 3 s (Charles, Henry, William), 1 da (Victoria (Mrs Sebastian Morley)); *Career* non-exec dir Whitbread plc 1972– (chm 1984–92); dir: Whitbread Investment Co plc 1977–94, Brewers' Soc Cncl 1984–92, Whitbread Share Ownership Tstees Ltd 1984–92, Whitbread Pension Tstees Ltd 1984–92, S C Whitbread Farms 1985, Sun Alliance Group 1989–92; pres: E of England Agric Soc 1991–92, Shire Horse Soc 1990–92; landowner (10,800 acres); Lord-Lt for Bedfordshire 1991– (DL 1974); Liveryman Worshipful Co of Brewers; Bledisloe Gold Medal RASE 1989; KStJ; *Recreations* shooting, painting, music, travel; *Clubs* Brooks's; *Style—* Sam Whitbread, Esq, JP; ✉ Southill Park, Biggleswade, Beds SG18 9LL (☎ 01462 813272)

WHITBREAD, (Hugh) William; s of Col William Henry Whitbread, TD (d 1994), and his 2 w, Betty Parr, *née* Russell; *b* 11 Feb 1942; *Educ* Eton, Cambridge Univ, Harvard Univ; *m* 1972, Katherine Elizabeth, *née* Hall; 4 c; *Career* HM Diplomatic Serv 1966–71, second sec Vientiane 1968–70 (third sec 1966–68); md Thomas Wethereds of Marlow 1976–80, specialist dir Whitbread & Co 1981–89, investmt mangr Whitbread Investment Co PLC 1989–94, dir Whitbread Investment Co PLC 1992–94; Liveryman: Worshipful Co of Skinners, Worshipful Co of Brewers; *Recreations* fishing, shooting; *Clubs* Brook's, RAC; *Style—* William Whitbread Esq; ✉ The Old Rectory, Dennington, Woodbridge, Suffolk

WHITBURN, Vanessa Victoria; *Educ* Mount St Mary's Convent Sch Exeter, Exeter Coll of FE, Univ of Hull (BA); *Career* BBC: studio mangr Broadcasting House and Bush House London 1974–76, asst floor mangr TV Drama Television Centre 1976–77 (work incl The Onedin Line), prodr Radio Drama Pebble Mill 1977–83 (work incl The Archers) sr prodr Radio Drama Pebble Mill 1983–88 (prodr/dir numerous plays and classic serials for Radio 3 and 4); prodr Brookside (Mersey Television for Channel Four) 1988–90, rejoined BBC as prodr/dir BBC TV Pebble Mill 1990–91, ed The Archers (BBC Radio 4) 1991–94, ed The Archers and radio drama BBC Midlands and East 1995–; fndr memb Mgmnt Bd Theatre Foundry 1985, chm Education on Screen (independent video prodn co), memb Bd The Birmingham Repertory Theatre; has also directed stage, radio and TV drama prodns for various groups incl Derby Playhouse and WGBH Boston 1985; conslt for ODA on Ndiga Nacio (Kenyan radio soap opera) 1993; *Style—* Ms Vanessa Whitburn; ✉ BBC Midlands and East, Broadcasting Centre, Pebble Mill Road, Birmingham B5 7QQ

WHITBY, Charles Harley; QC (1970); s of Arthur William Whitby (d 1983), of Acton, Middx, and Florence, *née* Edwards (d 1982); *b* 2 April 1926; *Educ* St John's Leatherhead, Peterhouse Cambridge (MA); *m* 11 Sept 1981, Eileen May, da of Albert George Scott (d 1978), of Palmers Green, London; *Career* RAFVR 1944–48; called to the Bar Middle Temple 1952, bencher 1977, memb Bar Cncl 1969–71 and 1972–78, recorder of the Crown Court 1972–; Criminal Injuries Compensation Bd 1975–; memb Governing Cncl St John's Leatherhead 1977– (chm 1985–); contrib: Halsbury's Laws of England, Atkins Encyclopedia of Court Forms; *Recreations* reading, golf, watching soccer, fishing, swimming; *Clubs* Utd Oxford and Cambridge Univ, RAC (steward 1985–), Garrick, Woking Golf; *Style—* Charles Whitby, Esq, QC; ✉ 12 King's Bench Walk, Temple, London EC4Y 7EL (☎ 0171 583 0811)

WHITBY, Prof (Lionel) Gordon; s of Sir Lionel Ernest Howard Whitby, CVO, MC, MD (d 1956), of The Master's Lodge, Downing Coll, Cambridge, and Ethel, *née* Murgatroyd (d 1994); *b* 18 July 1926; *Educ* Eton, King's Coll Cambridge (BA, MA, PhD, MB BChir, MD), Middx Hosp Med Sch London; *m* 29 July 1949, Joan Hunter, da of William Sanderson (d 1969), of Edinburgh; 1 s ((Lionel) Michael b 1952), 2 da (Anne Rosemary (Mrs Priestley) b 1950, Pamela Jean (Mrs Molyneaux) b 1954); *Career* fell King's Coll Cambridge 1951–55, jr med appts in London 1956–59, Rockefeller travelling fellowship in med Nat Inst of Health USA 1959–60, univ biochemist Addenbrooke's Hosp Cambridge 1960–63, fell Peterhouse Cambridge 1961–62, prof of clinical chemistry Edinburgh Univ 1963–91 (dean Faculty of Med 1969–72 and 1983–86, vice-princ 1979–83); tstee Nat Library of Scotland 1982–91, vice-pres Royal Soc of Edinburgh 1983–86, memb Br Library Advsy Cncl 1986–91, chm Advsy Ctee on Distinction Awards Scottish Sub-Ctee 1991 and 1993–95 (memb 1989–91); memb: Dept of Health, Scottish Office Home and Health Dept, professional advsy ctees 1965–81, Med Laboratory Technicians Bd, Cncl for Professions Supplementary to Med 1978–94; memb Worshipful Co of Glovers of London; MRCS, LRCP 1956, FRCPE 1968, FRSE 1968, FRCP 1972, FRCPath 1972, FIBiol 1988; *Books* Lecture Notes on Clinical Chemistry (with A F Smith, G J Beckett and S W Walker, 5 edn 1993), Principles and Practice of Medical Computing (with W Lutz, 1971); *Recreations* gardening, photography; *Style—* Prof Gordon Whitby, FRSE; ✉ 51 Dick Place, Edinburgh EH9 2JA (☎ and fax 0131 667 4358)

WHITBY, Mark; s of George Whitby, MBE, FRIBA (d 1972), of London, and Rhona Carmian, *née* Butler; *b* 29 Jan 1950; *Educ* Ealing GS for Boys, King's Coll London (BSc Civil Engrg); 1 s by prev partnership (Alex b 25 Sept 1982); m 19 Jan 1991, Janet, *née* Taylor; 1 s (Ralph b 24 May 1993), 2 da (Harriet b 29 Feb 1992, Katherine b 28 Oct 1996); *Career* ptnr Whitby & Bird Engineers; engrg projects throughout Europe incl: Igus Factory Cologne, Olivetti Research Centre Bari, Stock Exchange Berlin, British Embassies Berlin and Dublin, Merchants Bridge Manchester, Mappa Mundi Museum Hereford, King's Fund HQ London, Anvil Theatre Basingstoke, David Mellor Factory Hathersage; FICE 1992, FIStructE 1996, FEng 1996; *Media* Secrets of Lost Empires (1996); *Recreations* walking, gardening, engineering history, being taken to Glyndebourne; *Style—* Mark Whitby, Esq, FEng; ✉ Whitby & Bird, 54 Newman Street, London W1P 4DA (☎ 0171 631 5291, fax 0171 323 4645 and 0171 631 3032)

WHITE, Adrian Harold Michael; s of Brig Gilbert William White, MBE (d 1977), and Clodagh Marie, *née* Austin (d 1977); *b* 20 Nov 1945; *Educ* Ampleforth; *m* 25 June 1970, Helen Frances McKay, da of Sir Herbert (Charles Fahie) Cox, QC (d 1973); 1 s (Hugh b 5 March 1978); *Career* CA; audit sr Peat Marwick Mitchell & Co 1964–70; exec: Brown Shipley & Co Ltd 1970–72, Old Broad St Securities Ltd 1972–75, Hill Samuel & Co Ltd 1975–78; sr asst dir Morgan Grenfell & Co Ltd 1978–87, dep md Midland Montagu Asset Management 1987–92, currently dep chief exec and chief operating offr Hermes Pensions Management Ltd; FCA; *Recreations* rifle shooting, racing; *Clubs* MCC, North London Rifle; *Style—* Adrian White, Esq; ✉ c/o Hermes Pensions Management, Standon House, 21 Mansell Street, London E1 8AA

WHITE, Alan Geoffrey; s of John White, and Rose, *née* Dallin; *b* 8 July 1934; *Educ* Mitcham GS; *m* Melanie (decd); *Career* RAF Photographic 1952–57; freelance photographer 1958–67, Colour Processing Laboratories 1967–85, own company Stilled Movie Ltd 1986– (producing specialised plate photography and translights for film sets and visual effects in feature film and TV indust), photographer Alan White Photography (undertaking makeover portrait photography); has presented papers at various confs; FBIPP, FRPS, memb RTS, MBKS, MMPA, hon memb Br Film Designers Guild; *Recreations* golf, theatre, travel; *Clubs* Hurlingham Luncheon, Tenterden Golf; *Style—* Alan White, Esq; ✉ Bramble Cottage, Church St, Hartfield, East Sussex TN7 4AG; Stilled Movie Ltd, Shepperton Studios, Studios Rd, Shepperton, Middx TW17 OQD (☎ 01932 562611 ext 2010, fax 01932 568989, mobile 0860 399888)

WHITE, Angela Mary; da of Henry William Orman (d 1973), of London, and Irene Isobel, *née* Searle (d 1995); *Educ* Bromley HS, City of London Coll (Louis H Keik travelling scholarship); *m* 1962, Roger Lowrey White, JP; *Career* advertising agencies 1960–68, dep advtg mangr Br Tourist Authy 1968–71, advtg and mktg mangr English Tourist Bd 1971–90, dir external relations Royal Mail Streamline 1992–96 (joined Royal Mail 1990); cncllr (Cons) London Borough of Bromley 1967–71; chm Status of Women Ctee 1976–83, memb Ct of Assts Worshipful Co of Marketors 1990, Freeman City of London 1990; FCIM 1989 (memb 1974, nat vice chm 1990–91); *Clubs* United and Cecil, Women in Direct Marketing; *Style—* Mrs Angela M White; ✉ The White House, 9 Dartmoor Drive, Huntingdon, Cambs PE18 8XT

WHITE, Prof Christopher John; CVO (1995); s of Gabriel Edward Ernest Francis White, CBE (d 1988), of London, and Elizabeth Grace, *née* Ardizzone (d 1958); *b* 19 Sept 1930; *Educ* Downside, Courtauld Inst of Art, Univ of London (BA, PhD), Univ of Oxford (MA); *m* 14 Dec 1957, Rosemary Katharine Alice, da of Gordon Paul Desages (d 1960), of London; 1 s (Sebastian Gabriel b 1965), 2 da (Arabella Elizabeth b 1959, Clarisa Grace b 1961); *Career* asst keeper Dept of Prints and Drawings British Museum 1954–65, dir Messrs P and D Colnaghi London 1965–71, curator of graphic arts Nat Gallery of Art Washington DC 1971–73, dir of studies Paul Mellon Centre for Studies in British Art London 1973–85, assoc dir Yale Centre for British Art New Haven Connecticut 1973–85, dir Ashmolean Museum 1985–, fell Worcester Coll Oxford 1985–, prof of the arts of the Netherlands Univ of Oxford 1992–; dir Burlington Magazine 1981–; FBA 1989; *Books* Rembrandt and His World (1964), The Flower Drawings of Jan van Huysum (1965), Rubens and His World (1968), Rembrandt as an Etcher (1969), Rembrandt's Etchings: A Catalogue Raisonné (jtly, 1970), Dürer: The Artist and his Drawings (1972), English Landscape 1630–1850 (1977), Dutch Paintings in the Collection of HM The Queen (1982), Rembrandt in Eighteenth-century England (ed, 1983), Rembrandt (1984), Peter Paul Rubens: Man and Artist (1987), Drawing in England from Hilliard to Hogarth (jtly, 1987), Old Master Drawings from the Ashmolean Museum (jtly, 1992), The Dutch and Flemish Drawings at Windsor Castle (jtly, 1994), Anthony van Dyck: Thomas Howard, The Earl of Arundel (1995); *Recreations* music, travel; *Style—* Prof Christopher White, CVO, FBA; ✉ 14 South Villas, London NW1 9BS (☎ 0171 485 9148); 39 St Giles, Oxford OX1 3LW (☎ 01865 512289); Shingle House, St Cross, Nr Harleston, Norfolk IP20 0NT (☎ 01986 782264); Ashmolean Museum, Oxford OX1 2PH (☎ 01865 278005, fax 01865 278018)

WHITE, Sir Christopher Robert Meadows White; 3 Bt (UK 1937), of Boulge Hall, Co Suffolk; s of Sir (Eric) Richard Meadows White, 2 Bt (d 1972); *b* 26 Aug 1940; *Educ* Bradfield; *m* 1962 (m dis 1968), Anne Marie Ghislaine, da of late Maj Tom Brown, OBE, MC; m 2, 1968 (m dis 1972), Dinah Mary Sutton; m 3, 1976, Ingrid Carolyn, da of Eric Jowett, of Gt Baddow, Essex; *Heir* none; *Career* schoolmaster 1961–72, professore Istituto Shenker Rome and Scuala Specialisti Aeronauta Macerata 1962–63, housemaster St Michael's Sch Ingoldisthorpe Norfolk 1963–69, hon pres Warnborough House Oxford 1973–; *Style—* Sir Christopher White, Bt; ✉ c/o Hangersley House, Hangersley, Ringwood, Hants BH24 3JH

WHITE, Craig; *b* 16 Dec 1969; *Career* professional cricketer; debut Yorkshire CCC 1990; England: first cap 1994, memb squad 7 match one day series v S Africa 1996, memb team touring Zimbabwe and New Zealand 1996/97; *Style—* Craig White, Esq; ✉ c/o Yorkshire CCC, Headingley Cricket Ground, Leeds, W Yorks LS6 3BU (☎ 0113 278 7394)

WHITE, Sir David Harry; kt (1992), DL (Notts 1989); s of Harry White, OBE (d 1975), of Nottingham, and Kathleen, *née* Sadler; *b* 12 Oct 1929; *Educ* Nottingham HS, HMS Conway; *m* 5 April 1971, Valerie Jeanne; *Career* apprentice rising to Master Mariner 1946–56; National Freight Consortium plc: dep chm and dir 1981–89, gp md Property Gp 1984–87, non-exec chm NFC Trustees Ltd 1986–; chm: Nottingham Development Enterprise Ltd 1987–93, Mansfield Brewery plc 1993–; chm: Nottingham Health Authority 1986–, Bd of Govrs Nottingham Trent Univ 1987–, The Coal Authy 1994–; tstee Djanogly City Technol Coll 1989, hon pres Notts Co Branch RSPCA 1987–, govr Nottingham HS 1987–; *Clubs* RAC; *Style—* Sir David White, DL; ✉ Mansfield Brewery plc, Littleworth, Mansfield, Notts NG18 1AB (☎ 01623 425355, fax 01623 25725)

WHITE, David Julian; s of Arthur John Stanley White, CMG, OBE, of Mere, Wilts, and Joan, *née* Davies; *b* 17 July 1942; *Educ* Marlborough; *m* 24 June 1967, Claire Rosemary, da of Rowland Emett, OBE, of Ditchling, Sussex; 3 da (Juliet b 1969, Sarah b 1972, Victoria b 1974); *Career* Union Discount Co of London Ltd plc 1965–79; Cater Allen Holdings plc 1979– (dep chm 1985–); *Recreations* tennis; *Style—* David White, Esq; ✉ 20 Birchin Lane, London EC3V 9DJ (☎ 0171 623 2070, fax 0171 929 1641)

WHITE, David Thomas (Tom); CBE (1990); s of Walter Henry White (d 1985), of Ystradgynlais, Swansea, and Anne, *née* Williams (d 1988); *b* 10 Oct 1931; *Educ* Maesydderwyn GS, UC Swansea, LSE; *m* 1956, Eileen May Moore; 1 s (David (decd)), 2 da (Vivienne Gwyneth, Ceri Ann); *Career* Devon CC 1957–61 (child care offr, sr child care offr, area children's offr), dep children's offr Monmouthshire CC 1961–65, dep co children's offr Lancs CC 1965–70, dir of social servs Coventry City Cncl 1970–85, princ and chief exec NCH Action for Children (formerly National Children's Home) 1990–96 (dir of social work 1985–90), ret; formerly pres: Assoc of Child Care Offrs, Assoc of Dirs of Social Servs; memb Br Assoc of Social Workers; fell: Inst of Social Welfare, Social Care Assoc; *Books* Across Three Decades (contrib), On Second Thoughts (contrib, 1987), Social Work - The Media and Public (contrib, 1991); *Recreations* golf, gardening; *Style—* Tom White, Esq, CBE; ✉ 102 Kenilworth Rd, Coventry, W Midlands CV4 7AH (☎ 01203 419949); NCH Action for Children, 85 Highbury Park, London N5 1VD (☎ 0171 226 2033, fax 0171 226 2537)

WHITE, Prof Douglas John; s of Douglas John White, of Sutton Coldfield, W Midlands, and Gladys May, *née* Robins; *b* 31 Oct 1933; *Educ* Handsworth GS Birmingham, Magdalen Coll Oxford (MA, Jr Math Prize), Univ of Birmingham (MSc, PhD, DSc); *m* 29 March 1958, Hazel Margaret, da of Albert Edward Roberts (d 1967); 1 s (David John b 29 March 1963), 1 da (Alison Vanessa b 16 Aug 1967); *Career* Nat Serv RAF air radar fitter 1951–53; Kenward res fell Univ of Birmingham 1960–62, prof and head of Dept of Operational Res Univ of Strathclyde 1968–71 (reader in operational res 1965–68), prof and head of Dept of Decision Theory Univ of Manchester 1971– (sr res fell 1962–64); Univ of Virginia: MacWade prof of systems engrg 1987–90, chm Dept of Systems Engrg 1988, Neal and Nancy Wade prof of systems engrg 1994–96; memb Center for Advanced Studies; author of many pubns in maths of operational res and decision theory; former: chm Educn and Res Ctee for Operational Res Soc (former chm of Ctee of Profs in Operational Res, memb USA Soc, memb UK Soc); res assessor for SERC and Nat Sci Fndns of Hong Kong, USA and Canada; Beale Medal Operational Research Soc UK 1993; fell Inst of Mathematics and its Applications; hon MA Univ of Manchester 1974; CMath; *Books* Dynamic Programming (1969), Decision Theory (1969), The Role and Effectiveness of Theories of Decision in Practice (with K C Bowen, 1973), Operational Research Techniques (with Donaldson and Lawrie, 1969), Operational Research Techniques (vol 2, with Donaldson, Lawrie, Jardine, McKenzie, McFarlane, 1974), Decision Methodology (1975), Fundamentals of Decision Theory (1976), Finite Dynamic Programming (1978), Recent Developements in Markov Decision Processes (with Thomas and Hartley, 1980), Optimality and Efficiency (1982), Multi Objective Decision Making (with French, Thomas and Hartley, 1983), Operational Research (1985), Introduction to Operational Research (with French, Thomas and Hartley, 1986), Mavkov Decisions Processes (1993); Heldermann Sigma Series in Applied Mathematics (series ed); *Recreations* walking, gardening, reading, listening to music; *Style*— Prof Douglas White; ✉ Bollicello, 24 Springbank, Bollington, Macclesfield, Cheshire SK10 5LQ (☎ 01625 572768)

WHITE, Baroness (Life Peeress UK 1970), of Rhymney, Co Monmouth; Eirene Lloyd White; da of Thomas Jones, CH, LLD (d 1955), of Aberystwyth, and Eirene Theodora, *née* Lloyd (d 1935); *b* 7 Nov 1909; *Educ* St Paul's Girls' Sch, Somerville Coll Oxford; *m* 1948, John Cameron White (d 1968); *Career* former journalist and civil servant; MP (Lab) Flint E 1950–70; min of state: Foreign Affrs 1966–67, Welsh Office 1967–70; chm Labour NEC 1968–69, takes Lab whip in Lords, chm Select Ctee EEC and princ dep chm Ctees House of Lords 1979–82, a dep Speaker House of Lords 1979–89; memb Royal Commission on Environmental Pollution 1974–80, pres Montgomeryshire Soc 1981–82; chm Cncl UWIST 1984–88, vice pres UCW Cardiff 1989–93; hon fell Somerville Coll Oxford; Hon LLD: Univ of Wales 1979, Queen's Univ Belfast 1982, Univ of Bath 1983; *Style*— The Rt Hon Lady White; ✉ 64 Vandon Court, Petty France, SW1H 9HF (☎ 0171 222 5107); House of Lords, London SW1A 0PW (☎ 0171 219 5435)

WHITE, His Hon Judge Frank John; s of Frank Byron White (d 1954), of Reading, and Renée Marie Thérèse, *née* Cachou (d 1972); *b* 12 April 1927; *Educ* Reading Sch, King's Coll London (LLB, LLM); *m* 11 April 1953, Anne Rowlandson, da of Sir Harold Gibson Howitt, GBE, DSO, MC; 2 s (Stephen b 29 Sept 1955, Simon b 27 Aug 1963), 2 da (Teresa b 31 Aug 1958, Louise b 8 Sept 1961); *Career* Sub Lt RNVR 1945–47; called to the Bar Gray's Inn 1951, memb Gen Cncl of the Bar 1969–73, dep chm Berks QS 1970–72, recorder of the Crown Ct 1972–74, circuit judge (SE Circuit) 1974, sr circuit judge 1994–, pres Cncl HM Circuit Judges 1990–91; chm County Ct Rule Ctee 1993– (memb 1991–); memb: Lord Chllr's Legal Aid Advsy Ctee 1977–83, Judicial Studies Bd 1985–89; *Books* Bench Notes for Assistant Recorders (1988); *Recreations* walking, gardening; *Clubs* Athenaeum, Roehampton; *Style*— His Hon Judge Frank White; ✉ 8 Queens Ride, London SW13 0JB; Central London County Court, 13–14 Park Crescent, London W1N 3PD

WHITE, Frank Richard; JP (1968); s of Arthur Leslie White (d 1944), and Edna Phylis Jackson, *née* Meade (d 1976); *b* 11 Nov 1939; *Educ* Bolton Tech Coll; *m* 28 Jan 1967, Eileen, da of Frank Crook of Bolton; 2 s (John Richard Alexander b 1 Sept 1968, Christopher Niel b 10 July 1973), 1 da (Elizabeth Caroline b 30 July 1970); *Career* MP (Lab) Bury and Radcliffe 1974–83, parly sec Dept of Indust 1975–76, govt whip 1976–79, oppn spokesman church affrs 1979–83; chm: NW Lab MPs 1979–83, All Party Paper Indust Gp 1979–83; memb Select Ctee Employment 1979–83 (presented Home Workers Bill), oppn whip 1980–82, dir trg GMB Trade Union 1988–; memb: Bolton Town Cncl 1963–74, 1986–90 and 1994–, Gtr Manchester CC 1973–75; chm Bolton Magistrates' Bench 1992–95; vice pres East Lancs Railway Preservation Soc 1983; pres: Bolton Utd Servs Veterans' Assoc 1988, Bolton Male Voice Choir 1992; memb: IMS 1966, IPM 1971; hon fell Bolton Inst 1993; *Recreations* history, walking, caravanning, Richard III supporter; *Clubs* Tonge Cricket, Tonge Lab; *Style*— Frank White, Esq, JP; ✉ 4 Ashdown Drive, Firwood Fold, Bolton, Lancs BL2 3AX (☎ 01204 308547); National College, College Rd, Whalley Range, Manchester M16 8BP (☎ 0161 861 8788)

WHITE, Air Vice-Marshal George Alan; CB (1984), AFC (1973); s of James Magee White, and Evangeline, *née* Henderson; *b* 11 March 1932; *Educ* Queen's Univ Belfast, Univ of London (LLB); *m* 1955, Mary Esmé, *née* Magowan; 2 da; *Career* pilot 1956, RAF Staff Coll 1964, HQ Middle East Command 1966–67, cmd 5 Sqdn 1970–72, Nat Defence Coll 1972–73, cmd RAF Leuchars 1973–75, RCDS 1976, Dir of Ops (Air Defence and Overseas) 1977–78, Sr Air Staff Offr HQ No 11 Gp 1979–80, Air Cdre Plans HQ Strike Cmd 1981–82, Dep Cdr RAF Germany 1982–84, Cmdt RAF Staff Coll 1984–87, ret; FRAeS; *Style*— Air Vice-Marshal G A White, CB, AFC; ✉ PO Box 2048, Paphos, Cyprus

WHITE, Sir George Stanley James; 4 Bt (UK 1904), of Cotham House, Bristol; s of Sir George Stanley Midelton White, 3 Bt (d 1983, md Bristol Aeroplane Co, and ggs of Sir George White, 1 Bt, pioneer of Electric Street Traction, fndr first Eng aeroplane factory and responsible for introduction of Bristol Biplanes and Monoplanes), and Diane, Lady White; *b* 4 Nov 1948; *Educ* Harrow; *m* 1974 (m dis 1979); 1 da (Caroline Morwenna); m 2, Elizabeth, da of Sir William Reginald Verdon-Smith; 1 s (George Philip James), 1 da (Kate Elizabeth); *Heir* s, George Philip James b 1987; *Career* conslt horologist; pres: Bristol Branch Br Horological Inst 1993–, Gloucestershire Soc 1993; chm Bristol and Glos Archaeological Soc 1992–95; memb Glos Diocesan Advsy Ctee for Faculties and the Care of Churches 1985– (clocks advsr to the Dio 1986–); High Sheriff Avon 1989, JP 1991–95; Worshipful Co of Clockmakers: Liveryman 1986, Keeper of the Collection 1988, memb Ct of Assts 1994; FSA; *Books* English Lantern Clocks (1989), Tramlines to the Stars (1995); *Style*— Sir George White, Bt, FSA

WHITE, Prof Gillian Mary; da of Albert George White (d 1990), of Ilford, Essex, and Mabel Bathurst (d 1988); *b* 13 Jan 1936; *Educ* Ilford Co HS, King's Coll London (LLB, PhD); *m* 1 April 1978, Colin Arthur Fraser, s of Arthur David Fraser (d 1962); *Career* asst examiner estate duty office Inland Revenue 1954–57; called to the Bar Gray's Inn 1960; editorial asst Sweet and Maxwell publishers London 1960–61, res and editorial asst to Mr Elihu Lauterpacht Trinity Coll Cambridge 1961–67, res fell in law and dir of studies in law New Hall Cambridge 1964–67; Faculty of Law Univ of Manchester: lectr 1967–71, sr lectr 1971–73, reader 1973–75, prof of int law 1975–91, dean 1979–81 and 1988–90, prof emeritus 1991–; contrib to jls on int law and EC law; chm exec Manchester Univ Settlement 1974–80, memb Jt Cncl St Peter's House University of Manchester 1972–89; hon life fell New Hall Cambridge 1977; memb: Soc of Public Teachers of Law, Br Inst of Int and Comparative Law, American Soc of Int Law, Int Law Assoc, UK Assoc for Euro Law, Univs Assoc for Contemporary Euro Studies, Bar Euro Gp; *Books* Nationalization of Foreign Property (1961), The Use of Experts by International Tribunals (1965), Melland Schill Monographs on International Law (gen ed); *Recreations* travel, classical music, cooking, history of architecture; *Style*— Prof Gillian White

WHITE, Graham Stewart; s of Cecil Thomas White, and Kathleen May, *née* Banwell; *b* 24 March 1947; *Educ* Sir John Lawes Sch Harpenden; *m* 29 April 1972, Sylvia Mary, da of John Morris Done; 2 s (Oliver Lewis b 15 Dec 1974, Anthony Joe b 25 Feb 1977); *Career* Scholl: mktg dir 1977–80, md 1980–84; business devpt dir Schering-Plough Consumer Products 1984–87; chief exec Londis (Holdings) Ltd 1987–, non-exec dir Nisa-Todays Ltd 1987–; memb Mktg Soc; *Recreations* rugby football; *Style*— Graham S White, Esq; ✉ Eurogroup House, 67–71 High St, Hampton Hill, Middlesex TW12 1LZ (☎ 0181 941 0344, fax 0181 941 6499)

WHITE, Hugh Collins; s of William Mitchell White (d 1991), of Maybole, Ayrshire, and Mary Ann Luke, *née* Collins; *b* 21 Oct 1944; *Educ* Kilmarnock Acad, MacIntosh Sch of Architecture (Cert in Architecture); *m* 23 Aug 1968, Betsy, da of Bernard Lizar Zive (d 1977), of Ayr; 2 da (Kirstine b 1971, Sheona b 1974); *Career* chartered architect in private practice; corp memb RIBA, ARIAS; *Recreations* equestrian driving, photography, restoring horse drawn vehicles, the Brass Band Movement; *Style*— Hugh White, Esq; ✉ 17 Cargill Road, Maybole, South Ayrshire KA19 8AF; (☎ and fax 01655 882260)

WHITE, Adm Sir Hugo Moresby; GCB (1995, KCB 1991), CBE (1985); s of Hugh Fortescue Moresby White, CMG (d 1979), and Betty Sophia Pennington, *née* Brandt (d 1993); *b* 22 Oct 1939; *Educ* Dragon Sch, NC Pangbourne, RNC Dartmouth; *m* 16 April 1966, Josephine Mary Lorimer, da of Dr John Meavious Pedler, of Adelaide, S Aust; 2 s (Jonathan b 26 Feb 1968, Thomas b 8 Jan 1971); *Career* RN; Lt HMS Blackpool 1960–61 Kuwait; in diesel submarines: HMS Tabard 1962–64, HMS Tiptoe 1964, HMS Odin 1964–65; navigation course HMS Dryad 1966, navigator HMS Warspite 1966–68, 1 Lt HMS Osiris 1968–69, CO HMS Oracle 1970–71, staff BRNC Dartmouth 1971–73 Cdr Submarine Sea Trg Faslane 1973–75, CO HMS Salisbury 1975–77 (Cod War), with Naval Secs Dept MOD 1977–78, Capt Naval Plans MOD 1978–80, CO HMS Avenger and Capt 4 Frigate Sqdn (Falklands) 1981–82, Cdre PSO to CDS MOD 1982–85, CO HMS Bristol and Flag Capt to FOF2 1985–87, Rear Adm Flag Offr Flotilla 3 and Cdr ASW Strike Force 1987–88, Asst Chief of Naval Staff MOD 1988–91, Vice Adm 1991, Flag Offr Scotland and NI 1991–92, Adm 1992, C-in-C Fleet, C-in-C EASTLANT 1992–94, C-in-C COMNAVNORTHWEST 1994–95; govr of Gibraltar 1995–96; *Recreations* sailing, travelling, reading, gardening; *Clubs* Army and Navy; *Style*— Adm Sir Hugo White, GCB, CBE

WHITE, Ian Shaw; s of Frank White, of May Hill, Glos, and Joan, *née* Shaw; 1 s (Howard b 1994); *b* 30 July 1952; *Educ* Bromsgrove, Churchill Coll Cambridge (MA); *m* 18 Oct 1980, Susan Elizabeth (d 1989), da of Capt Alan Francis Bacon, of Purley, Surrey; 2 s (Duncan b 1985, Gordon b 1988); m 2, 28 March 1992, Barbara Jolanda, da of Maj Wladyslaw Arzymanow (d 1968); 1 s (Howard); *Career* ptnr W Greenwell and Co 1984–86; dir: Greenwell Montagu 1986–88 (head of res 1987–88), Kleinwort Benson Securities 1988–93, Robert Fleming Securities 1993–; AMIIMR; *Recreations* travel, philosophy, family; *Style*— Ian White, Esq; ✉ 22 Blomfield Road, Little Venice, London W9 1AD (☎ 0171 286 4360); Robert Fleming Securities, 25 Copthall Avenue, London EC2R 7DR (☎ 0171 638 5858, fax 0171 374 8042, telex 297451)

WHITE, Rev Canon John Austin; s of Charles White (d 1976), and Alice Emily, *née* Precious (d 1967); *b* 27 June 1942; *Educ* Batley GS Yorks, Univ of Hull (BA), Coll of the Resurrection Mirfield; *Career* asst curate St Aidan's Church Leeds 1966–69, asst chaplain Leeds Univ 1969–73, chaplain Northern Ordination Course 1973–82, canon St George's Chapel Windsor Castle 1982– (canon precentor 1984–); memb directing staff St George's House Windsor Castle 1982–, tstee and treas Full Employment UK; *Publications* A Necessary End (with Julia Neuberger, 1991); *Recreations* medieval iconography, cooking, poetry; *Style*— The Rev Canon John White; ✉ 8 The Cloisters, Windsor Castle, Windsor SL4 1NJ (☎ 01753 860409, fax 01753 860414); 2 Queen's Staithe Mews, York

WHITE, Prof John Edward Clement Twarowski; CBE (1983); s of Brig A E White, and Suzanne, *née* Twarowska; *b* 4 Oct 1924; *Educ* Ampleforth, Trinity Coll Oxford, Courtauld Inst of Art, Univ of London (BA, PhD); *m* 19 Oct 1950, Xenia, *née* Joannides (decd); *Career* WWII Pilot RAF 1943–47, demobbed as Flt Lt; reader in history of art Courtauld Inst 1958–59 (lectr 1952–58), Alexander White visiting prof Univ of Chicago 1958, Pilkington prof of history of art Univ of Manchester and dir of Whitworth Art Gallery 1959–66, Ferens visiting prof of fine art University of Hull 1961–62, chm Art Advsy Panel NW Museum and Art Gallery Servs 1962–66, prof of history of art and chm Dept of History of Art Johns Hopkins Univ Baltimore 1966–71; UCL: Durning-Lawrence prof of history of art UCL 1971–90, vice provost 1984–88, pro-provost for external affairs 1990–95; vice pres Comité International d'Histoire de l'Art 1986–92, chm Assoc of Art Historians 1976–80; memb: Bd of Dirs Coll Art Assoc 1970, Advsy Cncl V & A 1973–76, Exec Ctee Assoc of Art Historians 1974–81, Art Panel Arts Cncl 1974–78, Reviewing Ctee on Export of Works of Art 1975–82, Visiting Ctee RCA 1976–86, Armed Forces Pay Review Body 1986–92; tstee Whitechapel Art Gallery 1976–92; Hon MA Manchester 1963; FSA, AAH, CIHA; *Books* Perspective in Ancient Drawing and Painting (1956), The Birth and Rebirth of Pictorial Space (1957, 3 edn 1987), Art and Architecture in Italy 1250–1400 (1966, 2 edn 1987), Duccio: Tuscan Art and the Medieval Workshop (1979), Studies in Renaissance Art (1983), Studies in Late Medieval Italian Art (1984); articles in: Art History, Art Bulletin, Burlington Magazine, Jl of Warburg and Courtauld Insts; *Clubs* Athenaeum; *Style*— Prof John White, CBE, FSA; ✉ 25 Cadogan Place, London SW1X 9SA (☎ and fax 0171 235 4034)

WHITE, John Jameson; s of Jameson Richard White (d 1989), of Chalkwell, Essex, and Betty Annette, *née* Payne (d 1993); *b* 6 July 1938; *Educ* Wrekin Coll; *m* 1, 18 April 1964, Carolyn Helen (d 1991), da of Thomas Lyle Morgan (d 1988); 1 s (Matthew Jameson b 22 March 1968), 2 da (Sarah Michele b 19 Sept 1966, Amanda Clare b 23 May 1970); m 2, 23 May 1992, Carolyn Margery, da of Prof Gilbert Walton (1990), and Edna Walton; *Career* Cameron Markby Hewitt (formerly Cameron Kemm & Co): articled clerk 1957–62, admitted slr 1963, ptnr 1964– (currently head of Banking Dept); lectr on banking circuit, memb Editorial Bd Journal of Int Fin Law; memb Law Soc 1964; FCIB 1992; *Books* Legal Issues of Cross-Border Banking (contrib, 1989); *Recreations* hockey, student of port; *Clubs* Athenaeum, W Herts; *Style*— John White, Esq; ✉ Cameron Markby Hewitt, Sceptre Court, 40 Tower Hill, London EC3N 4BB (☎ 0171 702 2345, fax 0171 702 2303, mobile 0831 384396)

WHITE, Prof John William; CMG (1981); s of George Alexander John White (d 1977), of New Lambton HTS, Newcastle, and Jean, *née* Mackay; *b* 25 April 1937; *Educ* Newcastle Boys HS NSW Aust, Sydney Univ (BSc, MSc), Univ of Oxford (MA, DPhil); *m* 23 July 1966, Ailsa Barbara, da of Arthur Ambrose Vise, of Southport, Queensland; 1 s (David George Blithe b 1973), 3 da (Sarah Kirsten Jean b 1968, Catherine Naomi b 1970, Rachel Mary b 1974); *Career* Univ of Oxford: ICI fell Lincoln Coll 1961–63, official fell St John's Coll 1963–85, assessor 1981–82; neutron beam co-ordinator AERE Harwell 1973–75, Tilden lectr RSC 1976, dir Institut von Laue Langevin Grenoble 1977–80 (dep dir 1975–77); Aust Nat Univ (ANU) Canberra: prof of physical and theoretical chem 1985–, pro vice chllr 1992, chm of bd Inst of Advances Studies 1992, dean Research Sch of Chemistry 1995–; Marlowe medal Faraday Soc 1968, Tilden lectr Royal Soc of

Chemistry 1976, Argonne fell Univ of Chicago and Argonne Nat Laboratory USA 1985–90, Hinshelwood lectr Univ of Oxford 1991, Christenson fell St Catherine's Coll Oxford 1991, fndn lectr Assoc of Asian Chemical Studies 1991, hon fell St John's Coll Oxford 1996; church warden Rhone Alps Parish 1976–80; memb Cncl: Epsom Coll 1980–85, Wycliffe Hall Oxford 1981–85; pres: Royal Aust Chem Inst Canberra 1987, Aust Soc of Crystallographers 1987 (pres Nat Ctee for Crystallographers 1992–); chm: Neutron Scattering Cmmn Int Union of Crystallography 1994–, Oxford-Aust Scholarships Ctee 1996–; FRSC 1981, FRACI 1985, FAIP 1986, FAA 1991, FRS 1993; *Recreations* skiing, squash, family; *Style*— Prof John White, CMG, FRS; ✉ 2 Spencer St, Turner ACT 2601, Australia (☎ 00 61 6 2486836); Research School of Chemistry, Australian National University, PO Box 414, Canberra 2601 ACT, Australia (☎ 00 61 6 2493578, fax 00 61 6 2494903)

WHITE, Sir John Woolmer; 4 Bt (UK 1922), of Salle Park, Norfolk; s of Sir Headley Dymoke White, 3 Bt (d 1971), and Elizabeth Victoria Mary, *née* Wrightson (d 1996); *b* 4 Feb 1947; *Educ* Cheltenham Coll, Royal Agric Coll Cirencester; *m* 1987, Joan, da of late T D Borland, of Flemington, W Linton, Peeblesshire; 1 s; *Heir* s, Kyle Dymoke Wilfrid White b 16 March 1988; *Career* md Salle Farms Co; *Clubs* Athenæum; *Style*— Sir John White, Bt; ✉ Salle Park, Reepham, Norfolk NR10 4SG

WHITE, Keith Christopher; s of Frank White (d 1963), and Gladys Louise, *née* Moore (d 1960); *b* 14 July 1933; *Educ* Glyn GS Epsom, Univ of London (BSc); *m* 10 Sept 1960, Jennifer Mary (Jenny), da of Thomas Mayhew Lewin (d 1985); 1 s (Paul b 1961), 2 da (Gillian b 1963, Judith b 1968); *Career* Lt Col Engr and Tport Staff Corps RE (TA) 1991 (Maj 1986); consltg engr; ptnr R Travers Morgan & Ptnrs Consltg Engrs 1971, chm and chief exec Travers Morgan Consltg Gp 1991–93 (dir 1988); memb Bd Welsh Health Common Servs Authy 1982–, vice chm Construction Industry Cncl 1991–93; Freeman City of London 1966, Liveryman Worshipful Co of Paviors 1966 (memb Ct of Assts); FIStructE 1969 (pres 1987–88), FIHT 1974, FICE 1987, FEng 1989; *Recreations* golf, reading, watching cricket, travel; *Clubs* RAC; *Style*— Keith White, Esq, FEng; ✉ Longmead, 8 Hillcroft Avenue, Purley, Surrey CR8 3DG (☎ and fax 0181 660 9883)

WHITE, Keith George; *b* 12 Oct 1948; *Educ* MA; *Career* Crown Agents: joined in 1973, corp sec 1980–, dir Professional Servs 1992–; chm various Crown Agents Gp Cos; pres H F Holidays Ltd; FRSA; occasional lectr and contrib articles to orgns and pubns; *Recreations* family, fencing, walking; *Clubs* Royal Over-Seas League; *Style*— Keith G White, Esq; ✉ The Crown Agents, St Nicholas House, St Nicholas Road, Sutton, Surrey SM1 1EL (☎ 0181 643 3311, fax 0181 643 6518)

WHITE, Sir Lynton Stuart; kt (1985), MBE (Mil 1943), TD; s of Sir Dymoke White, 2 Bt, JP, DL (d 1968), and Isabelle Stuart, *née* MacGowan (d 1982); *b* 11 Aug 1916; *Educ* Harrow, Trinity Coll Cambridge (MA); *m* 1945, Phyllis, da of Sir Newnham Worley, KBE (d 1976); 4 s (Anthony, Richard, Robert, Philip), 1 da; *Career* TA; 2 Lt RA 1939, served WWII UK 1939–40, Far East 1940–45 (despatches), Hon Lt-Col RA (TA) 1946, TARO 1948–71; memb Hampshire CC 1970 (vice chm 1976, chm 1977–85); DL Hants (ret); *Style*— Sir Lynton White, MBE

WHITE, (Edward) Martin Everatt; s of Frank White (d 1983), of Shrewsbury, and Norah Kathleen, *née* Everatt (d 1959); *b* 22 Feb 1938; *Educ* Priory Boys GS Shrewsbury, King's Coll Cambridge (MA); *m* 10 May 1969, Jean Catherine, da of James Orr Armour (d 1987), of Manchester; 1 s (Robert b 1978), 1 da (Susannah b 1975); *Career* admitted slr 1962; chief exec: Winchester City Cncl 1974–80, Bucks CC 1980–88, Nat Assoc of Citizens Advice Bureau 1988–90; chm Curlew Partnership Ltd 1990–92; pt/t lectr Sch of Business Oxford Brookes Univ 1990–; pt/t immigration adjudicator 1993–; CIMgt 1987; *Books* The Role of the Chief Executive in Information Technology (1987); *Recreations* gardening, walking, other outdoor pursuits; *Style*— Martin White, Esq; ✉ 1 School Lane, Itchen Abbas, Winchester, Hants SO21 1BE (☎ 01962 779617)

WHITE, Michael; s of Albert Ernest White (d 1979), and Doris Mary, *née* Harvey; *b* 4 April 1955; *Educ* Langdon Sch, Univ of Oxford (MA), Inns of Court Sch of Law; *Career* called to the Bar Middle Temple (Harmsworth scholar); chief music critic of The Independent on Sunday, broadcaster and librettist; *Opera Librettos* The Adjudicator, Touristen Dachau; *Publications* Wagner for Beginners, Collins Guide to Opera and Operetta (gen ed); *Recreations* travel, composition, the Church of England (occasionally); *Style*— Michael White, Esq; ✉ The Independent on Sunday, 1 Canada Square, Canary Wharf, London E14 5AP (☎ 0171 293 2000, fax 0171 293 2435)

WHITE, Michael Charles; s of Henry Wallis White (d 1967), of St Just, Penwith, Cornwall, and Kay, *née* Wood (d 1957); *b* 21 Oct 1945; *Educ* Bodmin GS Cornwall, UCL (BA); *m* 2 Feb 1973, Patricia Vivienne, da of (Harold) Lawrence Gaudin; 3 s (Samuel Wallis b 21 Sept 1974, Joseph Lawrence b 11 Aug 1976, Henry John b 7 Dec 1978); *Career* reporter: Reading Evening Post 1966–70, London Evening Standard 1970–71; The Guardian: sub ed, feature writer and diarist 1971–76, parly sketchwriter 1977–84, Washington corr 1984–88, assoc ed 1989–, political ed 1990–; columnist: Health Service Journal 1977–84 and 1992–, The Listener 1989–91; co-presenter Week in Westminster Radio 4 1989–; lectr Woodrow Wilson Fellowship Fndn Princeton USA 1990–; chm Parly Press Gallery 1995; Granada TV sketchwriter of the year 1982; memb: NUJ 1966–, Notting Hill Housing Tst 1977–; *Clubs* Beefsteak; *Style*— Michael White, Esq; ✉ The Guardian, 119 Farringdon Road, London EC1R 3ER (☎ 0171 278 2332)

WHITE, Michael Simon; s of Victor R White, and Doris G White; *b* 16 Jan 1936; *Educ* Lyceum Alpinum Zuoz Switzerland, Pisa Univ, Sorbonne Paris; *m* 1, 1965 (m dis 1973), Sarah Hillsdon; 2 s, 1 da; m 2, 1985, Louise, da of Nigel Moores (d 1977); 1 s (b 1985); *Career* theatre and film producer; asst to Sir Peter Daubeny 1956–61; *Theatre* London prodns incl: Rocky Horror Show, Sleuth, America Hurrah, Oh Calcutta!, The Connection, Joseph and the Amazing Technicolor Dreamcoat, Loot, The Blood Knot, A Chorus Line, Deathtrap, Annie, Pirates of Penzance, On Your Toes, Metropolis, Bus Stop; recent prodns incl: Crazy for You 1993, Me and Mamie O'Rourke 1994, She Loves Me 1994, Fame The Musical 1995; *Films* incl: Monty Python and the Holy Grail, Rocky Horror Picture Show, My Dinner with André, Ploughman's Lunch, Moonlighting, Stranger's Kiss, The Comic Strip Presents, The Supergrass, High Season, Eat The Rich, White Mischief, Nuns on the Run, The Pope Must Die, The Turn of the Screw, Widows Peak; *Books* Empty Seats (1984); *Recreations* art, skiing, racing; *Clubs* RAC; *Style*— Michael White, Esq; ✉ 13 Duke Street, St James's, London SW1Y 6DB (☎ 0171 839 3971)

WHITE, Michael William; s of Joseph White, and Mary, *née* Ruth; *b* 11 April 1945; *Educ* North Staffs Poly Beaconside, Stafford (BSc); *m* Mary Doris White, 2 da (Elizabeth Ann b 16 Aug 1973, Catherine Frances b 20 Sept 1976); *Career* sr electrical engr GEC Electrical Projects Ltd 1971–74 (began as student apprentice); IDC Consultants Ltd: sr electrical engr, princ mechanical and electrical engr 1974–78, tech mangr electrical and control engrg 1980–82; ptnr Building Design Partnership 1985–93 (assoc engr 1983–85), assoc dir Amec Design and Management 1993–; CEng, FIEE, FCIBSE; *Recreations* hill-walking; *Clubs* Long Distance Walkers Assoc; *Style*— Michael White, Esq; ✉ Amec Design and Management, Timothy's Bridge Road, Stratford-upon-Avon, Warwickshire CV37 9NJ (☎ 01789 204288)

WHITE, (Eur Ing) Dr Norman Arthur; s of Charles Brewster White (d 1969), of Co Durham, and Lilian Sarah, *née* Finch (d 1975); *b* 11 April 1922; *Educ* Univ of London (BSc(Eng)), UMIST (AMCT), Harvard Business Sch (AMP), Univ of Westminster (DMS), Univ of Philippines (MSc), LSE (PhD); *m* 1, 1944, Joyce Marjorie (d 1982), *née* Rogers; 1 s (Howard Russell b 1945), 1 da (Lorraine Avril b 1949); m 2, 1983, Marjorie Iris, da of William Colenso Rushton (d 1947), of London; *Career* Royal Dutch Shell Group: petroleum res engr Thornton Res Centre 1945–51, progressed through various assignments in technological devpt and commercial mgmnt rising to dep Gp Mktg Co-ordinator 1966–68, chm and dir Shell Oil and mining cos in UK and Europe 1963–72, chief exec New Enterprises Div 1968–72, plural assignments 1972–; dir: Norman White Assocs 1972–94 (princ exec 1972–93), Environmental Resources Ltd 1973–87, Tanks Oil & Gas Ltd 1974–85, Henley Centre for Forecasting 1974–92 (dep chm 1974–87), Com-Tek Resources Inc Colorado 1988–93, Proscyon Partners Ltd 1992–; dep chm Strategy International Ltd 1976–82; chm: KBC Advanced Technologies Ltd 1979–90, Ocean Thermal Energy Conversion Systems Ltd 1982–, Gearhart Tesel plc 1983–85 (dir 1980–85), Process Automation & Computer Systems Ltd 1984–94, Andaman Resources plc 1986–90, Technology Transfer Centre Surrey Ltd 1990–, Delta Media Solutions Ltd 1990–92, Millennium Satellite Centre Ltd 1995–; memb int energy and petroleum delgns 1979–97: Russia, China, Rumania, East Germany, Hungary, Japan, Korea, Indonesia, India, Mexico, Argentina, Venezuela, Brazil, South Africa; memb Parly and Scientific Ctee House of Commons 1977–83 and 1987–92; WPC: chm Br Nat Ctee 1987–94 (vice chm 1977–87), treas 1983–91 and 1994–97, vice pres World Petroleum Congresses 1991–94; memb: UK CAA Ctee of Enquiry on Flight Time Limitations (Bader Ctee) 1972–73, Cncl IMechE 1980–85 and 1987–91, Cncl Inst of Petroleum 1975–81 (vice pres), Royal Soc Mission to People's Republic of China 1985; visiting prof: Henley Mgmnt Coll 1979–90, Univ of Manchester 1981–90 (visiting ind dir 1971–81), The City Univ 1989–96; memb Senate Univ of London 1974–87; chm: Jt Bd for Engrg Mgmnt (IMechE, ICE, IEE, IChemE) 1990–93, Transnational Satellite Educn Centre Univ of Surrey 1991–94; govr: King Edward VI Royal GS Guildford 1976–, Reigate GS 1976–93; Presidential Award IMechE 1994, Cncl Award Inst of Petroleum 1996; Freeman City of London; Liveryman: Worshipful Co of Engineers, Worshipful Co of Spectacle Makers, Co of World Traders; Hon Calgarian (Alberta Canada); memb Royal Inst of Int Affrs and Royal Inst; Eur Ing, CEng, FInstD, FIMgt, FRSA, FIMechE; *Books* Financing the International Petroleum Industry (1979), Handbook of Engineering Management (1989); *Recreations* family, country and coastal walking, wild life, browsing, international affairs, comparative religions, domestic odd-jobbing; *Clubs* Athenaeum, City Livery, Harvard (London), IOD, LSE, County (Guildford); *Style*— Dr Norman A White; ✉ Green Ridges, Downside Road, Guildford, Surrey GU4 8PH (☎ 01483 567523, fax 01483 504314); 9 Park House, 123–125 Harley Street, London W1N 1HE (☎ 0171 935 7387, fax 0171 704 6060)

WHITE, Adm Sir Peter; GBE (1977, KBE 1976, CBE 1960, MBE 1944); s of William White (d 1936), and Gertrude Frances, *née* Turner (d 1972), of Amersham, Bucks; *b* 25 Jan 1919; *Educ* Dover Coll; *m* 1947, Audrey Eileen (d 1991), da of Ernest Wallin, of Kingsthorpe, Northampton; 2 s (John, Andrew); *Career* served RN 1937–1977, Adm (princ staff offr to CDS 1967–69, dir-gen Fleet Services 1969–71, Port Adm Rosyth 1972–74, chief of fleet support 1974–77); conslt Wilkinson Match Ltd 1978–79; assoc dir: Educn for Industl Soc 1979–88, Business in the Community 1988–; chm cncl Offrs' Pension Soc 1982–90, memb Fndn Ctee Gordon Boys' Sch 1980–90; *Recreations* riding, gardening; *Clubs* Army and Navy; *Style*— Admiral Sir Peter White, GBE

WHITE, Peter Richard; MBE (1991); s of Ernest George White, of Stratford-on-Avon, and Eileen Agnes, *née* Hayter; *b* 20 March 1942; *Educ* King Edward VI Sch Stratford-on-Avon, Birmingham Sch of Architecture (DipArch); *m* 25 Sept 1965, Paula, da of Thomas Howard Jeffries Gilman; 1 s (Oliver Richard Gilman b 13 May 1981), 2 da (Emma b 7 Oct 1968, Kate b 4 Sept 1971); *Career* architect: James Roberts Architects 1964–66, Ralph Calder Assocs Detroit Michigan USA 1965; gp ldr City Architects Dept Birmingham 1967–70; Waterway Environment Servs British Waterways: architect/planner 1970–87, chief architect/design and planning mangr 1987–92, conslt 1992–; waterside planning aspects of maj schemes incl: Limehouse Basin, Paddington, Kings Cross; master plans incl: Maryport and Hayle Harbour, Canal du Midi Corridor (Service Navigation France); *Awards* Civic Tst award 1969 and 1973, 6 Euro Architectural Heritage Year awards 1975, Business Panel for the Environment award 1983 and 1987, special medal for a continuing contrib to conservation (awarded by HRH The Duke of Edinburgh); ARCUK 1964, RIBA 1970; *Books* Waterway Environment Handbook (1972), Canals - A New Look (1985); *Recreations* industrial archaeology, oil painting, sketching, restoring historic boats; *Style*— Peter White, Esq, MBE; ✉ Waterway Environnment Services, British Waterways Board, The Locks, Hillmorton, nr Rugby, Warwicks CV21 4PP (☎ 01788 570625, fax 01788 541076)

WHITE, Peter Richard; *b* 11 Feb 1942; *m* Mary; 1 s, 1 da; *Career* chartered accountant Price Waterhouse 1965–69, mgmnt accountant, chief internal auditor then financial controller and treas Abbey National Building Society 1970–82; Alliance & Leicester Building Society: gen mangr (fin and mgmnt servs) Alliance Building Society 1982–85, gen mangr (admin and treasy) Alliance & Leicester (following merger) 1985–87, dir and gen mangr (devpt and treasy) 1987–89, dep gp chief exec and md 1989–91, gp chief exec 1991–; dir: Alliance & Leicester Pensions Investments Ltd, Electonic Funds Transfer (Clearing) Ltd, Electronic Funds Transfer (POS) Ltd; chm Girobank plc 1996–; formerly: dep chm Building Socs Assoc, chm Met Assoc of Building Socs; currently: chm Cncl of Mortgage Lenders, memb Cncl Br Bankers Assoc; Freeman City of London; memb IOD; FCA 1985, fell ACT 1993, CIMgt 1993, FCIB 1993; *Recreations* watching sport, playing golf, opera; *Style*— Peter White, Esq; ✉ Alliance & Leicester Building Society, 49 Park Lane, London W1Y 4EQ (☎ 0171 629 6661, fax 0171 408 1399)

WHITE, Peter Roland; s of Norman Leonard White, and Gene Elwin, *née* McGrah; *b* 9 July 1945; *Educ* Bournville Boys' Tech Sch, Univ of Birminghm (BDS); *m* 1, 23 March 1968 (m dis 1980), Elizabeth Susan, da of Thomas Colin Graty, of Leigh Sinton Worcs; 2 s (Gordon Michael White b 6 Aug 1970, Adam Edward White b 12 Jan 1973), 1 da (Frances Elizabeth Graty b 8 Nov 1968); m 2, 20 Dec 1980, Elisabeth Anne, da of Fred Haworth; *Career* conslt oral surgn; Dudley Rd Hosp Birmingham 1968, Birmingham Dental Hosp 1969–70, Wordsley Hosp Stourbridge 1970–71, Univ of Manchester Dental Sch 1971–73, St Luke's Hosp Bradford 1973–74, Liverpool Dental Hosp and Broad Green Hosp 1974–77; conslt oral surgn NW Regnl Health Authy 1977–, clinical dir Rochdale Healthcare Tst 1992–93, dep med dir Rochdale Healthcare Tst 1994–; postgrad tutor Rochdale and Oldham 1989–94 (Rochdale 1980–87); memb numerous NHS local ctees; publications in learned jls; memb BDA (pres E Lancs E Cheshire Branch 1995), FBAOMS 1977 (memb 1971–77), FDSRCS (Eng), memb Manchester Med Soc 1979 (pres Odontological Section 1990); *Recreations* music, genealogy, sailing; *Clubs* Elton Sailing; *Style*— Peter R White, Esq; ✉ 65 Highcroft Way, Syke, Rochdale, Lancs (☎ 01706 353577); 14 St John Street, Manchester (☎ 0161 832 7904)

WHITE, Phil John; s of Herbert Henry White, of Ashford, Kent, and Rosena Agnes May, *née* Clay; *b* 30 Aug 1960; *Educ* Norton Knatchbull Sch Ashford, Trent Poly (BA); *m* 2 July 1988 (sep 1994), Pauline Catriona, da of Terence Armstrong; *Career* prodr BBC Radio Cleveland 1985–88; TFM Radio: presenter 1988–91, features prodr 1991–93; prog dir Viking FM 1995–96 (prog controller 1993–95), freelance broadcaster, writer and illustrator 1996–; *Recreations* watching TV, listening to radio, art, travel, music, food, tennis, golf, football, life; *Style*— Phil White, Esq; ✉ Craig Cottage, 19 Main Street, Elloughton, N Humberside HU15 1JS

WHITE, Richard Hamilton Hayden; s of Charles Henry Hayden White (d 1995), and Helen Margherita, *née* Hamilton (d 1996); *b* 9 Aug 1939; *Educ* Sutton Valence Sch, Trinity Coll Oxford (MA); *Career* admitted slr 1963, asst slr Freshfields 1963–67, lectr then sr lectr in law Univ of Birmingham 1967–74; Lord Chancellor's Dept: temp legal advsr then sr legal advsr 1974–81, asst slr 1981–92, under sec and head Legal Gp 1992–95, the legal advsr 1995–; *Publications* contrib: Social Needs and Legal Action (1973), Legal Services in Birmingham (1975), Lawyers in their Social Setting (1976), Rechtsbedürfuis and Rechtschilfe (1978), EEC Conventions on Jurisdiction and Enforcement of Judgements (1992); *Recreations* Sicily, rural pursuits; *Style*— Richard White, Esq; ✉ Legal Group, Lord Chancellor's Department, Selborne House, 54–60 Victoria Street, London SW1E 6QW (☎ 0171 210 3530)

WHITE, Prof Robert Stephen; s of James Henry White, of Uley, Glos, and Ethel Gladys, *née* Cornick; *b* 12 Dec 1952; *Educ* Market Harborough Comp, West Bridgford Comp, Emmanuel Coll Cambridge (Senior Scholar, MA, Bachelor Scholar, PhD); *m* Helen Elizabeth, da of Dennis J Pearce; 1 s (Mark James b 1979), 1 da (Sarah Rosemary b 1981); *Career* guest investigator Woods Hole Oceanographic Instn USA 1977 (also 1988 and 1990), research asst Dept of Geodesy and Geophysics Univ of Cambridge 1978, postdoctoral scholar Woods Hole Oceanographic Instn USA 1978–79; Univ of Cambridge: research fell Emmanuel Coll 1979–82, NERC research fell Dept of Earth Scis 1979–81, sr asst in research 1981–85, asst dir of research 1985–89, fell St Edmund's Coll 1988–, prof of geophysics 1989–, acting head Dept of Earth Scis 1991 and 1993; Cecil & Ida H Green Scholar Scripps Instn of Oceanography Univ of California San Diego summer 1987; awarded Stichting Fund for Sci Tech and Research Schlumberger Ltd 1994; fell American Geophysical Union; FGS (Bigsby Medal 1991), FRS 1994; *Publications* author of numerous articles in international journals; *Style*— Prof Robert White, FRS; ✉ Bullard Laboratories, Madingley Road, Cambridge CB3 0EZ (☎ 01223 337187)

WHITE, Robin Graham; s of Alan White, of Salisbury, and late Celia White; *b* 21 July 1955; *Educ* Oundle; *m* 8 June 1985, Ann, da of Patrick Ingram, of Clare, Suffolk; 2 da (Sarah Celia b 23 March 1988, Madeline Jane b 25 Jan 1990); *Career* reporter; Northants Evening Telegraph 1973–76, Piccadilly Radio Station Manchester 1977, IRN 1978, ITN 1978–96 (crime corr 1990–92), media advsr Shell International 1996–; *Recreations* golf, shooting, reading, music; *Style*— Robin White, Esq; ✉ Shell International, Shell Centre, London SE1 7NA (☎ 0171 934 1234)

WHITE, Roderick Douglas Thirkell; s of Noel Thirkell White (d 1974), and Margaret Douglas, *née* Robertson; *b* 27 March 1939; *Educ* Marlborough, Trinity Coll Oxford (MA); *m* 1964, Stephanie Francis, da of C S Powell; 2 s (Jestyn Noel b 17 Sept 1968, Tristram Benedict b 23 Feb 1971); *Career* advertising exec; J Walter Thompson: graduate trainee Marketing Dept 1962–65, marketing gp head 1965, asst dir 1967; head of unit J Walter Thompson Consultancy Unit 1972–75 (memb staff 1968–75), J Walter Thompson Development Group 1975–77; planning dir: Lansdowne Marketing 1979 (head of planning 1977), Landsdown Conquest (formerly LansdownEuro) 1981–; President's Gold medal IPA 1967; MIPA 1967, assoc memb MRS 1980; *Books* Consumer Product Development (1973), Advertising: What It Is and How To Do It (1980); *Recreations* walking, windsurfing, cinema, music; *Style*— Roderick White, Esq; ✉ Lansdown Conquest Ltd, 4 Flitcroft Street, London WC2H 8DJ (☎ 0171 240 4949, fax 0171 240 9094)

WHITE, Roger; s of Geoffrey White, of The Old Post Office, Westonbirt, Glos, and Zoe, *née* Bowler; *b* 1 Sept 1950; *Educ* Ifield GS, Christ's Coll Cambridge (BA), Wadham Coll Oxford; *Career* Hist Building Div GLC 1979–83, sec Georgian Gp 1984–91, exec sec Garden History Soc 1992–96; visiting res fell Yale Center for British Art 1990; pres Oxford Univ Architectural Soc 1975–76; memb: Ctee Painswick Rococo Garden 1985–94, Chiswick House Advsy Panel 1991–, Pell Wall Preservation Tst 1993–; FSA 1986; *Books* John Vardy (in The Architectural Outsiders, 1985), Georgian Arcadia: Architecture for the Park and Garden (exhibition catalogue, 1987), The Architectural Evolution of Magdalen College (1993); *Recreations* looking at old buildings; *Style*— Roger White, Esq, FSA; ✉ 76 Clapham Common North Side, London SW4 9SD (☎ and fax 0171 350 0085)

WHITE, Roger John Graham; s of Alfred James White (d 1976), of Kingston Hill, Kingston, and Doris Elizabeth, *née* Robinson (d 1973); *b* 30 April 1940; *Educ* Tiffin Sch; *m* 18 Jun 1966, Elizabeth, da of Tom Lionel Greenwood, of Esher, Surrey; 2 s (Graham b 1968, Andrew b 1970), 1 da (Katherine b 1977); *Career* articled clerk Knox Cropper CAs; KPMG: joined 1962, sr mangr 1970, tax ptnr 1974, sr tax ptnr UK 1981–, chm KPMG Int Tax Ctee 1990–94; memb: professional and industry tax ctees, Bd and Ops Ctee 1988; lectr and writer on tax matters; Income and Corporation Taxes Act 1988: appointed by Lord Chllr to membership of Tbnl under section 706 Income and Corporation Taxes Act (ICTA) 1988, appointed by Chllr of the Exchequer to the Advsy Panel under section 765 ICTA 1988; FCA 1962, FTII 1970; *Books* The Trading Company (1978), Purchase of Own Shares (1983); *Recreations* bridge, gardening, books; *Clubs* Addington Soc (chm 1991–93), Reform; *Style*— Roger White, Esq; ✉ KPMG, 8 Salisbury Square, London EC4Y 8BB (☎ 0171 311 1000, fax 0171 311 8885 (Group 3), telex 8811541 PMM LON G)

WHITE, (Wilfred) St John; s of Richard St John White (d 1932), of Wellington Lodge, Bristol, and (Gladys) Lucy, *née* Jones; *b* 28 Nov 1922; *Educ* Merchant Venturers' Coll, Univ of Bristol; *m* 22 Aug 1974, Kyoko (d 1978), da of Dr Ray Igarashi (d 1938), of Tokyo, Japan; *Career* res engr Telecommunications Res Estab 1942–46 (devpt of RADAR for RAF); Decca Ltd (later Racal Decca Ltd) 1946–92: devpt engr later dir of up to forty cos within the gp, invented Hi-Fix Electronic Position Fixing System (won Queen's Award for Technological Innovation 1969), dir responsible for mktg of Decca Navigational System (international standard), dir Decca Avionics Mktg, as dir of four oil cos was involved in devpt of North Sea Resources 1963–92, advsr to chief exec Offr Dowty Group 1989–92, advsr to Chm TI Group plc 1992–95, advsr to chm and chief exec Messier-Dowty and Dowty Aerospace 1995–; memb: Sales and Export Ctee SBAC 1982–89, Cncl Electronic Engrg Assoc 1976–88; MIEE 1947, FInstD 1954, MRIN 1955; memb: Air League 1982, Royal Aeronautical Soc 1986; *Books* Christmas Island Cracker (1987); *Recreations* swimming and squash; *Clubs* The Naval & Military; *Style*— St John White, Esq; ✉ Dolphin Square, London SW1V 3NR (☎ 0171 828 3600); Mukoyama, Nerimaku, Tokyo (☎ 00 81 3 3990 2546)

WHITE, Stephen Frank; s of Judge Frank John White, of Queens Ride, London, and Anne Rowlandson, *née* Howitt, MBE; *b* 29 Sept 1955; *Educ* Eton, Univ of Bristol (BA); *Career* accountant Price Waterhouse and Co 1977–81, with Phillips and Drew 1981–83, Hill Samuel Investment Management Ltd 1983–85; dir: Foreign & Colonial Management Ltd 1985–, Foreign & Colonial Eurotrust plc and Foreign & Colonial German Investment Trust plc; Liveryman of the Merchant Taylors' Co; ACA; *Recreations* opera, gardening, walking; *Clubs* Brooks'; *Style*— Stephen F White, Esq; ✉ c/o Foreign & Colonial Management Ltd, Exchange House, Primrose St, London EC2A 2NY (☎ 0171 628 8000)

WHITE, Stephen John; s of George Edward White, and Doreen Ivy White; *b* 23 July 1948; *Educ* St Olaves GS; *m* 1, 1971; 2 da (Claire Louise b 1975, Victoria Emily b 1978); m 2, 28 September 1991; 1 s (Charles Edward John b 1996); *Career* dir: Aegis Group plc (formerly WCRS Group plc), TMDH plc; dep chief exec Carat International until 1993; fndr: European Media Management 1993–, Fairbrother White 1994–, Sponsorship Science 1996–; MAA, MIPA, MCAM; *Recreations* tennis, power boating, vintage cars; *Clubs* RAC, Vanderbilt; *Style*— Stephen White, Esq; ✉ European Media Management, Douglas House, 3 Richmond Buildings, London W1V 5AE (☎ 0171 437 3956, fax 0171 437 3960)

WHITE, Stewart Dale; s of Theo Jeffrey White (d 1979), of Sydney, Aust, and Mary Jean, *née* Stewart; *b* 23 July 1951; *Educ* Newington Coll, St Andrew's Coll Univ of Sydney (BA, LLB), Downing Coll Cambridge (LLM); *m* 20 Sept 1980, Elisabeth Mary Hargreaves, da of Geoffrey John Bolton (d 1968), of Eton Coll; 1 s (Andrew b 1 Aug 1983), 1 da (Victoria b 1 July 1982); *Career* admitted slr: NSW 1976, England and Wales 1979; sr assoc Allen Allen and Hemsley Sydney 1979–83; ptnr: Blake Dawson Waldron Sydney 1983–88, Denton Hall Burgin and Warrens London 1988–94, Ashurst Morris Crisp 1994–; councillor Section on Business Law of Int Bar Assoc and fndr chm Communications Law Ctee of Int Bar Assoc; chm: Standing Ctee Media and Communications Lawasia 1986–92, Legal Symposium ITU-COM 1989, Regulatory and Economic Symposium ASIA TELECOM '93; appointed expert to Econ and Social Ctee of EC to advise on Green Papers on Satellite Policy and Mobile Communications and Cmmn's proposed Directives on Digital Short Range Radio and High Definition TV, founding conslt ed EC Telecommunications Law 1993; memb: Legal Symposium TELECOM 87 and TELECOM 91 and Strategy Summit TELECOM 95, NSW Ctee Cambridge Cwlth Tst, Ctee on Computers, Telecommunications and IT Int C of C; memb: Law Soc, Int Bar; *Publications* Vol 39 Butterworth's Encylopedia of Forms and Precedents on Telecommunication (ed), EC Telecommunications Law (European Practice Library Chancery, fndr conslt ed), Satellite Communications in Europe: Law and Regulation (jt author, 1993); *Recreations* swimming, sailing, walking, bridge, opera; *Clubs* Australian, Royal Sydney Yacht Squadron, Bembridge Sailing, Sea View Yacht, Little Ship, Henley Royal Regatta, Australian Jockey, Royal Sydney Golf, Sydney Cricket Ground; *Style*— Stewart White, Esq; ✉ Ashurst Morris Crisp, Broadwalk House, 5 Appold Street, London EC2A 2HA (☎ 0171 638 1111, fax 0171 972 7990, telex 887067)

WHITE, Tom; *see:* White, David Thomas

WHITE, Tony; s of Richard Charles White (d 1989), and Dorothy Maud Dempster White; *b* 27 Aug 1947; *Educ* Eastbrook Secdy Modern Sch (represented Essex in athletics), East Ham Tech Coll (finalist Letraset Student awards); *m* 3 April 1971, Patricia Margaret, da of Charles Felton; 2 da (Sarah Jane b 8 June 1972, Anna Louise b 23 Sept 1973); *Career* dir and animator; head of design Halas & Batchelor: writer and dir Quartet (first prize Chicago Film Festival), A Short Tall Story (represented GB in int animation festivals, used by UN to promote peace), Jackson Five TV series; dir the Ink Thief children's mixed-media TV drama series (Animus Entertainments/Yorkshire-Tyne Tees TV); films with Richard Williams incl: A Christmas Carol (Academy award), The Pink Panther Strikes Again (D&AD award); prodr, dir and animator Hokusai - An Animated Sketchbook (Br Academy award); fndr Animus Productions (films incl TV specials Cathedral and Pyramid), fndr Animus Entertainments (films for TV and multi-media projects); lectured extensively in the US, Europe and UK; FSIA; *Books* The Animator's Workbook (Phaidon Press, 1988); *Style*— Tony White, Esq; ✉ Animus Productions, Prominent Studios, 68A Delancy Street, London NW1 7RY (☎ 0171 284 4812, fax 0171 284 4813)

WHITE, Victor Oscar; s of Arthur Albert White (d 1976), and Gisela Lydia, *née* Wilde; *b* 30 Aug 1936; *Educ* Michael Hall Sch Forest Row, London Univ (LLB); *m* 28 March 1967, Susan Raynor, da of Raynor Leslie Jones (d 1991); 2 s (Christopher b 1968, Jonathan b 1974), 1 da (Katherine b 1971); *Career* slr; ICI: joined Legal Dept 1965, gp slr 1980–96, gp sec 1992–96; conslt Beachcroft Stanleys slrs 1996–; memb Law Soc; *Style*— Victor White, Esq; ✉ Beachcroft Stanleys, 20 Furnival Street, London EC4 (☎ 0171 242 1011, fax 0171 831 6630)

WHITE-JONES, John Dale; s of George David White-Jones (d 1979), of Llangollen, N Wales, and Vera, *née* Dale (d 1979); *b* 3 Oct 1934; *Educ* Llandovery Coll; *m* 13 May 1972, Hilary Anne, da of Thomas Richard William Porter; 2 da (Gemma b 23 Sept 1975, Kate b 24 March 1977); *Career* Nat Serv RA 1953–55; prodn dir Thames TV plc 1986–91, mktg dir Teddington Studios Ltd 1991–93, ret; dir Kingston Training and Educn Cncl 1988–89; chm Runnymede Alzheimer's Soc, chm Spelthorne Housing Assoc; govr Halliford Sch; *Style*— John White-Jones, Esq; ✉ 6 St Nicholas Drive, Shepperton, Middlesex TW17 9LD

WHITE-THOMSON, Christopher Trefusis; yr s of Maj Walter Norman White-Thomson (3 s of Rt Rev Leonard White-Thomson, sometime Bishop of Ely, by his w Hon Margaret Trefusis, 3 da of 20 Baron Clinton); *b* 22 Feb 1940; *Educ* Harrow, RMA Sandhurst; *m* 1967, Juanita Maria, da of Frederick Arthur Rowlands, of Catania, Sicily; 1 s (Charles b 1969), 1 da (Kate b 1971); *Career* formerly Capt Royal Fusiliers; joined Cater Ryder & Co 1969, chief exec Oppenheimer Fund Management 1982–87; dir Mercantile House Hldgs 1980–87, Parrish plc 1988–90; *Clubs* Army and Navy; *Style*— Christopher White-Thomson, Esq; ✉ Baggaretts, White Colne, Colchester, Essex CO6 2QH

WHITEHALL, Barry John; JP (1987); s of Jack Baxter Whitehall (d 1969), and Norah Louise, *née* Kellond (d 1989); *b* 28 Aug 1936; *Educ* Ampleforth; *m* 1, (m dis 1979), Lavinia Antonia, da of Col R P Baily; 1 s (Richard Andrew b 26 April 1969), 1 da (Sarah Christina b 16 Sept 1972); m 2, 1979, Christine Barbara, da of Ralph Coates; *Career* RAF 1953–57; BBC: joined 1957, head of bdcasting Br Solomon Islands Protectorate 1968–70, head of overseas admin World Serv 1980–88, gen mangr monitoring World Serv 1988–91, controller of resources World Serv 1991–96; *Recreations* tennis, bridge; *Clubs* East India; *Style*— Barry Whitehall, Esq, JP; ✉ Anchor House, St Leonards Lane, Wallingford, Oxon OX10 0HA (☎ 01491 35937, fax 01491 832850)

WHITEHEAD, Hon Mrs (Annabel Alice Hoyer); *née* Millar; LVO (1986); yr da of 1 Baron Inchyra, GCMG, CVO (d 1989); *b* 25 Jan 1943; *m* 1973, Christopher James Bovill Whitehead; 1 s (Robert William Bovill b 1977), 1 da (Christina Daisy Elizabeth b 1975); *Career* lady-in-waiting to HRH The Princess Margaret, Countess of Snowdon 1971–75 and 1992– (extra lady-in-waiting 1975–92); *Style*— The Hon Mrs Whitehead, LVO; ✉ 5 Vicarage Gdns, London W8

WHITEHEAD, David; s of Prof Thomas Paterson Whitehead, of Leamington Spa, Warwicks, and Doreen Grace, *née* Whitton; *b* 31 May 1952; *Educ* Warwick Sch, Univ of Birmingham, Birmingham Poly (BA), Avery Hill Coll of FE (PGCE); *m* Mary Teresa, da of Denis McGeeney; 1 s (Thomas David b 18 June 1981), 1 da (Rachel Brigid b 27 March 1984); *Career* section head Oyez Stationery Ltd 1975–78, mgmnt trainee rising to asst sales mangr Fyffes Group Ltd 1978–82, sec Br Poultry Fedn 1985–90 (asst sec 1982–85), dir Br Ports Assoc 1992– (dir of policy 1990–92); chm Environment Ctee Euro Sea Ports Orgn 1993–, advsr on ports to EC Economic and Social Ctee 1994; *Books* European Sea Ports Organisation's Environmental Code of Practice (jtly, 1994); *Recreations* reading, gardening, music, walking; *Clubs* Athenaeum; *Style*— David Whitehead, Esq; ✉ British Ports Association, Africa House, Kingsway, London WC2B 6AH (☎ 0171 242 1200, fax 0171 405 1069)

WHITEHEAD, Dr Denis Sword; s of Henry Whitehead (d 1979), and Alice, *née* Sword (d 1942); *b* 8 May 1927; *Educ* Uppingham, Univ of Cambridge (MA, PhD); *m* 9 June 1951, Frances Cabot Paine (Frankie), da of Frank Cabot Paine (d 1952), yacht designer and builder, of Wayland, Mass; 3 s (Henry, Frank, Ian), 1 da (Anne (Mrs Prebensen)); *Career* with Rolls-Royce 1948–54, lectr and reader Univ of Cambridge 1957–85; engrg conslt 1985–; fell Jesus Coll Cambridge 1962–; contrib chapter on Aerolasticity in Turbomachines to AGARD Manual; MIMechE, MRAeS, CEng; *Recreations* sailing, golf, fishing; *Clubs* RAC; *Style*— Dr Denis Whitehead; ✉ Inwoods, Farleigh Wick, Bradford-on-Avon, Wilts BA15 2PU (☎ 01225 863207)

WHITEHEAD, Frances; da of Frank Whitehead (d 1968), and Alice Archibald, *née* Pemberton (d 1972); *Educ* Queen Mary Sch Lytham, St Hilda's Coll Oxford (BA, MA), Univ of Sheffield (MA); *Career* librarian Lancs Co libraries 1970–71, freelance writer 1973–85, editorial dir Mills & Boon 1987–94 (ed 1973, dep editorial dir 1985–87), independent editorial conslt 1994–; author, speaker and bdcaster on aspects of writing and mass market fiction; *Books* And Then He Kissed Her ..., A Guide to Writing Fiction (jtly); *Recreations* Times crossword, sumo wrestling, theatre, travel off the beaten track; *Clubs* Soc of Genealogists; *Style—* Ms Frances Whitehead; ✉ 12 Grimwood Road, Twickenham, Middlesex TW1 1BX (☎ 0181 892 6185)

WHITEHEAD, John Michael Stannage; CBE (1990), JP (1968), DL (1988); s of (Arthur) Stannage Whitehead, JP (d 1946), of Stechford, Elms Rd, Leicester, and Isaline, *née* Baker, JP (d 1974); *b* 19 Dec 1927; *Educ* Uppingham, Leicester Tech Coll; *m* 28 April 1962, Alanda Joy, da of Geoffrey Taylor Bentley (d 1987), of Acorns, Esher Park Ave, Esher, Surrey; 1 s (Michael John Stannage b 1968), 2 da (Penelope Josephine b 1963, Belinda Louise b 1964); *Career* 2 Lt Army Cadet Corps 1945–48, Special Constabulary 1950–68; dir: G Stibbe & Co Ltd 1948–74, J & H Hadden Ltd 1954–63; md Stibbe-Hadden Ltd 1963–74 (chm 1963–72), chm John Whitehead Textiles Ltd 1974–91, chm H Harrison & Co Finishers Ltd 1987–91, tax cmmr 1966; chm govrs Leicester Poly 1974–90 (vice chm 1971–74), chm govrs Leicester Poly Higher Educn Corp 1988–92 (pro chllr 1990–92), vice chm and pro-chllr De Montfort Univ (formerly Leicester Poly) 1992–, hon fell De Montfort Univ 1993; memb various charities; memb Lloyd's 1979–; High Sheriff of Leicestershire 1994; Freeman: City of London, City of Leicester; Worshipful Co Merchant Taylors: Liveryman 1951, Second Upper Warden and memb Ct 1992, Master 1995; Worshipful Co of Framework Knitters: Liveryman 1952, Master 1978, currently memb Ct of Assts; FRSA 1978; *Recreations* watching rugby football, sailing, gardening, reading; *Clubs* Leicestershire; *Style—* John Whitehead, Esq, CBE, JP, DL; ✉ The Poplars, Main St, Houghton on the Hill, Leicestershire LE7 9GD (☎ and fax 0116 241 2244)

WHITEHEAD, Sir John Stainton; GCMG (1992, KCMG 1986, CMG 1976), CVO (1978); s of John William Whitehead (d 1946), and Kathleen Mary Whitehead (d 1981); *b* 20 Sept 1932; *Educ* Christ's Hosp Horsham, Hertford Coll Oxford (MA); *m* 1 Feb 1964, (Mary) Carolyn, da of Henry Whitworth Hilton (d 1970); 2 s (Simon b 1966, James b 1973), 2 da (Sarah b 1968, Jessica b 1971); *Career* HM Forces 1950–52; HM Dip Serv: FO 1955–56, 3 sec then 2 sec Tokyo 1956–61, FO 1961–64, 1 sec Washington 1964–67, 1 sec (econ) Tokyo 1968–71, FCO 1971–76, head Personnel Servs Dept 1973–76, cnsllr Bonn 1976–80, min Tokyo 1980–84, dep under-sec of state (chief clerk) FCO 1984–86, ambass to Japan 1986–92; non-exec dir: Cadbury Schweppes plc 1993–, Serco Group plc 1994–96, BPB Industries plc 1995–; advsr on Japanese affrs to the Pres of the Bd of Trade 1992–95, sr advsr Morgan Grenfell Group 1992–, advsr/conslt various cos and orgns; memb Cncl Buckingham Univ 1992–95, tstee Monteverdi Choir and Orchestra 1991–, memb Royal Opera House Tst 1992–93, memb UK-Japan 2000 Gp 1992–, memb Cncl The Japan Soc 1992–, memb Mgmnt Cncl Great Britain Sasakawa Fndn 1992–96; hon fell Hertford Coll Oxford 1991; *Recreations* new challenges, post-retirement work, music, travel, golf, tree-felling; *Clubs* Beefsteak, United Oxford and Cambridge Univ, Liphook Golf, MCC (assoc memb); *Style—* Sir John Whitehead, GCMG, CVO; ✉ Bracken Edge, High Pitfold, Hindhead, Surrey GU26 6BN

WHITEHEAD, Dr (John Ernest) Michael; s of Dr Charles Ernest Whitehead (d 1939), of London, and Bertha Ivy, *née* Harding (d 1945); *b* 7 Aug 1920; *Educ* Merchant Taylors', Gonville and Caius Coll Cambridge (MA, MB BChir), St Thomas's Hosp Med Sch (Dip Bact); *m* 3 Aug 1946, Elizabeth Bacchus (d 1996), da of Col George Walker Cochran, DSO, IA (d 1970), of Parkstone, Dorset; 1 s (Stephen Michael b 1947), 1 da (Anne Elizabeth b 1951); *Career* Co Cdr 7 Bn Cambridgeshire HG 1940–42; lectr in bacteriology St Thomas's Hosp Med Sch London 1948–52, dep dir Public Health Laboratory Sheffield 1953–58, hon lectr in bacteriology Univ of Sheffield 1954–58, dir Public Health Laboratory Coventry 1958–75, hon lectr in bacteriology Univ of Birmingham 1962–75, dir Public Health Laboratory Serv 1981–85 (dep dir 1975–81), conslt advsr in med microbiology DHSS 1981–85, temp advsr WHO 1976–80; specialist advsr to House of Commons Select Ctees on Agric 1988–93 and Social Servs 1989–90; FRCPath (1974, vice pres 1983–86), chm Assoc of Med Microbiologists 1983–85; *Recreations* modern languages, house and garden maintenance; *Clubs* Athenaeum; *Style—* Dr Michael Whitehead; ✉ Martins, Churchend, Slimbridge, Gloucester GL2 7BL (☎ 01453 890726)

WHITEHEAD, Neil Anthony; s of H Whitehead and P J Whitehead, *née* Gripe; *b* 7 Feb 1956; *Educ* King's Sch Gloucester, Kingston Poly (BA 3–D Design); *m* Fiona, da of J B Mackie; *Career* designer; formerly with Murdoch Design and Jeremy Farmer; Fitch plc 1984–: successively assoc dir, dir Retail Div, creative dir then head of retail design, currently sr dir in jt charge of London Gp; clients incl: Kingfisher, BT, BSkyB; various appearances on design progs for BBC TV incl Colour in Design and History of Retail Design (both BBC2), conf presentations at various indust events; Design Week Award (Exhbn Environment) 1995; memb Mktg Soc, MCSD, fell Int Real Estate Fedn (FIABCI); *Sporting Achievements* played 1st team Richmond RFC 1980–86, winner Middx Sevens 1983, also played for Middx 1981–85; *Recreations* all sports including tennis and rugby; *Clubs* Richmond RFC, Raffles; *Style—* Neil Whitehead, Esq; ✉ Fitch plc, Commonwealth House, 1 New Oxford Street, London WC1A 1WW (☎ 0171 208 8000, fax 0171 208 0200)

WHITEHEAD, Dr Philip John; s of Lionel Gilbert Whitehead (d 1974), and Leslie Broadbridge, *née* Phillips (d 1985); *b* 13 April 1938; *Educ* Wennington Sch Wetherby, Univ of Bristol (MB ChB); *m* 4 April 1964, Mary Elizabeth, da of Harry Fisher (d 1983); 3 da (Sarah b 1964, Naomi b 1966, Rebecca b 1973); *Career* conslt pathologist W Cumberland Hosp Whitehaven Cumbria 1970–79, conslt haematologist Frenchay Hosp Bristol 1979–; MRCPath 1970, FRCPath 1982; *Recreations* reading, music, walking; *Style—* Dr Philip Whitehead; ✉ Department of Haematology, Frenchay Hospital, Bristol BS16 1LE (☎ 0117 970 1212)

WHITEHEAD, Phillip; MEP (Lab) Staffs E and Derby (majority 52,196); s of Harold Whitehead (d 1961), and Frances May, *née* Kingman (d 1966); *b* 30 May 1937; *Educ* Lady Manners Sch Bakewell, Exeter Coll Oxford (MA); *m* 1967, Christine Hilary, da of Thomas George Usborne, of Surrey; 2 s (Joshua b 1969, Robert b 1971), 1 da (Lucy b 1974); *Career* writer and TV prodr; cmmnd Sherwood Foresters 1956; producer 1961–67, ed This Week (Thames TV) 1967–70; MP (Lab) Derby N 1970–83, front bench spokesman Higher Educn 1981–83; MEP (Lab) Staffs E and Derby 1994–, chm Euro Parly Intergroup on Consumer Policy 1994–, memb Environment and Culture Ctees 1994–, memb Special Ctee of Enquiry into BSE 1996–97; chm Fabian Soc 1978–79; presenter Credo LWT 1983–85; columnist The Times 1983–85; dir: Goldcrest Film & TV Holdings 1984–87, Consumers Assoc 1982– (chm 1990–94); chm: New Society Ltd 1985, Statesman & Nation Publications 1984–90 (chm 1985–90); dir Brook Productions (1986) Ltd 1986–; visiting fell in communications Goldsmiths' Coll London 1985–; FRSA; *Style—* Phillip Whitehead, Esq, MEP; ✉ Mill House, Rowsley, Matlock, Derbys DE4 2EB (☎ 01629 732659); 206 Rue du Trône, Brussels 1040, Belgium; Brook Productions, 21–24 Bruges Place, Randolph St, London NW1 0TF (☎ 0171 482 6111); European Constituency Office, 53 High Street, Burton-on-Trent DE14 1JS

WHITEHEAD, Prof Rex Raymond; s of Athol George Whitehead, of Melbourne, Aust, and Mavis Caroline, *née* Cumming; *b* 30 May 1941; *Educ* Essendon HS Melbourne, Univ of Melbourne (MSc, PhD), Univ of Glasgow (DSc, Kelvin Gold medal and prize); *m* 27 Aug 1971, Hilary Joan, da of John Rutherford; 1 da (Joanne Caroline Brenda b 10 Sept 1973), 1 s (Christopher George John b 18 Feb 1977); *Career* Univ of Glasgow: res fell 1967–69, lectr 1969–78, reader 1978–86, titular prof 1986–, memb Univ Ct 1992–96, dean Faculty of Science 1993–96, clerk of Senate 1996–2001; visiting fell Aust Nat Univ 1975; visiting prof: Michigan State Univ 1974, Florida State Univ 1986–87; memb various ctees SERC since 1980, hon asst keeper Hunterian Museum 1980–; FInstP 1975, FRSE 1985; *Recreations* archery, tea tasting, nicotinage; *Clubs* College (Glasgow); *Style—* Prof Rex Whitehead, FRSE; ✉ 2 Durness Avenue, Bearsden, Glasgow G61 2AQ (☎ 0141 942 7391); Department of Physics and Astronomy, University of Glasgow, Glasgow G12 8QQ (☎ 0141 339 8855)

WHITEHEAD, Roland James; s of (Edwin Francis) Romilly Whitehead, of Burghclere, nr Newbury, Berks, and Diana Elizabeth Whitehead; *b* 30 May 1964; *Educ* Eton, Univ of Southampton (BSc), RCA, MDes (RCA), Imperial Coll of Sci and Technol and Med (DIC Industl Design Engrg); *m* Katie Annette Walker; *Career* industl designer; Julian Everitt Yacht Designs 1982, Kelsall Yacht Design 1983, PA Design 1986, Mortimer Technology 1987–88, Prowess Creative 1988–94, Continuum 1994–; winner: PA Design and PA Technol bursary 1985–87, Guardian PC Rewards south and south east regions; designer Br challenge for Little America's Cup 1987; MCSD (chm Product Gp 1990–94), assoc memb RINA; *Recreations* yacht racing, music; *Clubs* British Canoe Union, Utopia Yacht, UK International C Class Catamaran Assoc; *Style—* Roland Whitehead, Esq; ✉ Myrtle Cottage, Broadford Bridge Road, West Chiltington, West Sussex RH20 2LA; Continuum, Warnham, West Sussex RH12 3RZ (☎ 01403 271888, fax 01403 272127)

WHITEHEAD, Sir Rowland John Rathbone; 5 Bt (UK 1889), of Highfield House, Catford Bridge, Kent; ggs of 1 Bt, sometime Lord Mayor of London; s of Maj Sir Philip Henry Rathbone Whitehead, 4 Bt (d 1953); *b* 24 June 1930; *Educ* Radley, Trinity Hall Cambridge (BA); *m* 3 April 1954, Marie-Louise, da of late Arnold Christian Gausel, of Stavanger, Norway; 1 s, 1 da; *Heir* s, Philip Henry Rathbone Whitehead; *Career* pres Inst of Translation & Interpreting 1996–; chm: tstees Rowland Hill Benevolent Fund (PO) 1982–, govrs Appleby Sch Cumbria, The Baronets' Tst 1985–88 (also fndr), Exec Ctee Standing Cncl of the Baronetage 1984–; tstee: Kelmscot House Tst 1970–, Brogdale Horticultural Tst 1994–; memb Ct of Assts Worshipful Co of Fruiterers (Master 1995), Freeman City of London; *Books* Cybernetics: Communication and Control (Handbook of Management Technology); *Recreations* poetry, rural indolence; *Clubs* Arts; *Style—* Sir Rowland Whitehead, Bt; ✉ Sutton House, Chiswick Mall, London W4 2PR (☎ 0181 994 2710); Walnut Tree Cottage, Fyfield, Lechlade, Glos GL7 2TT (☎ 0136 7850 267)

WHITEHEAD, Prof Thomas Patterson (Tom); CBE (1985); *b* 7 May 1923; *Educ* Salford Royal Tech Coll, Univ of Birmingham (PhD); *m* 20 Sept 1947, Doreen Grace, *née* Whitton; 2 s (Paul b 1948, David b 1952), 1 da (Jill b 1955); *Career* biochemist S Warwicks Hosp Gp 1950–60, conslt biochemist Queen Elizabeth Hosp Birmingham 1960–86, dir Wolfson Res Laboratories 1972–84, dean Faculty of Medicine Univ of Birmingham 1984–87; scientific advsr BUPA Health Care 1969–95; MRCP (Hon), FRCPath, FRSC; *Books* Quality Control in Clinical Chemistry (1976), Clinical Chemistry and Haematology Adult Reference Values (1994); *Recreations* growing and exhibiting sweet peas; *Clubs* Athenaeum; *Style—* Prof Tom Whitehead, CBE; ✉ 70 Northumberland Rd, Leamington Spa, Warwickshire CV32 6HB (☎ 01926 421974)

WHITEHORN, Katharine Elizabeth; da of Alan Drummond Whitehorn (d 1980), of Marlborough and London, and Edith Marcia, *née* Gray (d 1982); *Educ* Blunt House, Roedean, Glasgow HS for Girls, Newnham Coll Cambridge (MA); *m* 4 Jan 1958, Gavin Tudor Lyall, *qv*, s of Joseph Tudor Lyall; 2 s (Bernard b 1964, Jake b 1967); *Career* publisher's reader 1950–53, teacher Finland 1953–54, graduate asst Cornell Univ USA 1954–55, Picture Post 1956–57, Woman's Own 1958, Spectator 1959–61; columnist The Observer 1960– (assoc ed 1980–88); dir: Nationwide Building Society 1983–91, Nationwide Anglia Estate Agents 1987–90; memb: Latey Ctee on Age of Majority 1965–67, BBC Advsy Gp on Social Effects of Television 1971–72, Bd Br Airports Authy 1972–77, Cncl RSM 1982–85; rector Univ of St Andrews 1982–85; vice-pres The Patients Assoc 1983–; Hon LLD Univ of St Andrews 1985; memb NUJ; *Books* Cooking in a Bedsitter (1960), Roundabout (1961), Only on Sundays (1966), Whitehorn's Social Survival (1968), Observations (1970), How to Survive in Hospital (1972), How to Survive Children (1975), Sunday Best (1976), How to Survive in the Kitchen (1979), View from a Column (1981), How to Survive your Money Problems (1983); *Recreations* river boat; *Clubs* Royal Soc of Med, Royal Soc of Arts; *Style—* Ms Katharine Whitehorn; ✉ c/o The Observer, 119 Farringdon Road, London EC1R 3ER

WHITEHOUSE, Prof David John; s of Joseph Whitehouse (d 1989), of Wolverhampton, and Alice Gertrude, *née* Roberts (d 1985); *b* 15 Oct 1937; *Educ* Univ of Bristol (BSc), Univ of Leicester (PhD), Univ of Warwick (DSc); *m* 17 July 1965, Ruth Lily Epsley, da of William Pannell; 1 s (Steven Charles b 6 April 1971), 1 da (Anne Frances b 14 Jan 1969); *Career* devpt engr Switchgear Wolverhampton 1958–61, res engr Rank Taylor Hobson Leicester 1961–68, chief engr Rank Precision Industries 1968–78, sr fell SERC Univ of Warwick 1985 (prof of mech engrg 1978, prof of engrg sci, chief scientist 1990, dir of Centre for Micro Engrg and Metrology 1981), sr fell SERC 1986–90; author of 140 tech and scientific papers; memb: BSI, CIRP 1976, JSPE, MASPE; fell: Inst of Prodn and Control, Inst of Control of Instrumentation, Inst of Mgmnt Engrs; FInstP, FIEE; *Books* Mean Line of Surface Texture (1965), Nano Technology (Inst of Physics, 1991), Handbook of Surface Metrology (Inst of Physics, 1994), Optical Methods in Surface Metrology (SPIE, 1996); *Recreations* swimming, weight lifting, music; *Style—* Prof David Whitehouse; ✉ 171 Cromwell Lane, Burton Green, Coventry CV4 8AN (☎ 01203 473558); Department of Engineering, University of Warwick, Coventry CV4 7AL (☎ 01203 523154, fax 01203 418922, telex 311904)

WHITEHOUSE, David Rae Beckwith; QC (1990); s of (David) Barry Beckwith Whitehouse, FRCS, FRCOG, and late Mary Whitehouse, JP, *née* Boffey; *b* 5 Sept 1945; *Educ* Ellesmere Coll Shropshire, The Choate Sch Connecticut USA (ESU scholar), Trinity Coll Cambridge (MA); *m* 1 Jan 1971, Linda Jane, da of Eric Vickers, CB, of Oakham, Rutland, Leics; 1 s (Benedict Harry Beckwith b 1978); *Career* called to the Bar Gray's Inn 1969; asst recorder 1983, recorder 1987–; memb: Criminal Bar Assoc 1969–, International Bar Assoc 1990–; *Recreations* architecture, music, wild gardening; *Style—* David Whitehouse, Esq, QC; ✉ 3 Raymond Buildings, Gray's Inn, London WC1R 5BH (☎ 0171 831 3833, fax 0171 242 4221)

WHITEHOUSE, Dr David Robert; s of Derick William Whitehouse, of Birmingham, and Anne Valmai, *née* Mallet; *b* 7 Jan 1957; *Educ* Duddeston Manor Sch, Univ of Manchester (BSc, PhD); *m* 3 April 1982, Jillian Dorothy, da of Bernard Carey, of Preston; 1 s (Christopher David b 2 May 1985), 2 da (Lucy Claire b 8 June 1987, Emily Kate b 3 June 1991); *Career* Nuffield Radio Astronomy Laboratories Jodrell Bank 1978–82, Space Science Laboratory UCL 1982–85, conslt ed Space magazine 1987–91, freelance space technol conslt, writer, broadcaster 1985–88, science corr BBC 1988–; pres Soc for Popular Astronomy 1995–; FRAS 1979; *Books* New Scientist Special Publication; Man in Space (ed), numerous articles in int press and academic jls; *Recreations* mountaineering, music; *Style—* Dr David Whitehouse; ✉ BBC, BBC Broadcasting House, London W1A 1AA (☎ 0171 927 4474, fax 0171 636 4295, e-mail david.whitehouse@bbc.co.uk)

WHITEHOUSE, Prof Graham Hugh; s of Raymond Hugh Whitehouse (d 1955), of Hatch End, Middx, and Joyce Miriam Moreton, *née* Powell; *b* 24 Nov 1939; *Educ* Harrow

Co GS, Kings Coll London, Westminster Med Sch (MB BS); *m* 22 March 1969, Jacqueline Meadows, da of Benjamin Alfred Charles (d 1987), of Worcester Park, Surrey; 1 s (Richard b 1973), 1 da (Victoria b 1975); *Career* asst prof of radiology Univ of Rochester NY USA 1975–76, prof of diagnostic radiology Univ of Liverpool 1976– (sr lectr 1972–75); examiner RCR, ed British Journal of Radiology; FRCR 1971, FRCP 1983; *Books* Gynaecological Radiology (1981), Techniques in Diagnostic Radiology (co ed, 1 edn 1983, 3 edn 1995), Self Assessment in Diagnostic Radiology (jtly, 1986), Exercises in Diagnostic Imaging (jtly, 1989), Radiology for Anaesthetists (jtly, 1995); *Recreations* oil painting, choir singing, cricket, reading widely; *Style*— Prof Graham Whitehouse; ✉ 9 Belmont Rd, West Kirby, Merseyside L48 5EY (☎ 0151 625 6933); Department of Radiodiagnosis, University of Liverpool, PO Box 147, Liverpool L69 3BX (☎ 0151 794 5775, fax 0151 794 5766, telex 627095)

WHITEHOUSE, Mary; CBE (1980); da of James Hutcheson, and Beatrice Ethel, *née* Searanckle; *b* 13 June 1910; *Educ* Chester City GS For Girls, Cheshire Co Training Coll Crewe; *m* 23 March 1940, Ernest Raymond Whitehouse; 3 s (Paul b 4 Jan 1941, Richard b 8 June 1944, Christopher b 30 Dec 1945); *Career* art specialist at Wednesfield Sch Wolverhampton 1932–40, Brewood GS 1943, sr mistress and sr art mistress Madeley Sch Shrops 1960–64; co-fndr Clean Up TV Campaign 1964, hon gen sec Nat Viewer's and Listener's Assoc 1965–80 (pres 1980–94, pres emeritus 1994); freelance journalist/broadcaster; *Books* Cleaning Up TV (1966), Who Does She Think She Is? (1971), Whatever Happened to Sex? (1977), A Most Dangerous Woman (1982), Mightier than the Sword (1985), Mary Whitehouse, Quite Contrary (autobiog, 1993); *Recreations* reading, walking, tennis, gardening; *Style*— Mrs Mary Whitehouse, CBE; ✉ Ardleigh, Colchester, Essex C07 7RH (☎ 01206 230123)

WHITEHOUSE, Prof (Julian) Michael Arthur; s of Arthur Arnold Keer Whitehouse, of Olney, Bucks, and Kathleen Ida Elizabeth, *née* Elliston (d 1989); *b* 2 June 1940; *Educ* Queens' Coll Cambridge (MA, MB BChir), St Bartholomew's Hosp of London (MD); *m* 10 April 1965, Diane France, da of Dr Raymond Maximillien Theodore de Saussure (d 1972), of Geneva, Switzerland; 1 s (Michael Alexander de Saussure b 1966) 2 da (Fiona Geraldine b 1968, Vanessa Caroline b 1972); *Career* hon conslt physician, sr lectr and acting dir Dept of Med Oncology Bart's 1976; currently prof of med oncology and hon conslt physician Southampton Univ Hosps, dir CRC Wessex Med Oncology Unit Southampton; visiting prof: Univ of Boston 1981, Christchurch Clinical Sch of Med NZ 1986; former vice pres Euro Soc of Med Oncology; chm: UICC Clinical Oncology Ctee, Jt Cncl for Clinical Oncology RCP and RCR; vice chm Scientific Ctee CRC; ed Haematological Oncology; govr Canford Sch Dorset; Freeman City of London, Liveryman Worshipful Soc of Apothecaries; FRCP 1979, FRCR 1992, FRCPEd 1994; *Books* CNS Complications of Malignant Disease (1979), A Pocket Consultant in Clinical Oncology (1989), Investigation and Management (with Christopher J Williams, 1984–85), Recent Advances in Clinical Oncology (1982 and 1986), Cancer - the Facts (with Maurice Slevin, 1996); *Recreations* skiing, sailing, travelling; *Clubs* Athenaeum; *Style*— Prof Michael Whitehouse; ✉ CRC Wessex Medical Oncology Unit, CF99 Southampton General Hospital, Tremona Rd, Southampton SO16 6YD (☎ 01703 796185, fax 01703 783839)

WHITEHOUSE, Michael G; *b* 28 Sept 1946; *Educ* Harvard Business Sch; *Career* Halifax Building Society: joined 1964, computer dept 1965, mangr Computer Systems 1973, controller Computer Systems Services 1975, exec 1982, asst gen mangr 1983, gen mangr Business Info Systems 1986, main bd and ops dir 1989–92; former dir: Halifax Loans Ltd (chm), Halifax Credit Card Ltd (chm), Halifax Premises Ltd; non-exec dir Skipton Building Soc 1993; dir of ops National Westminster UK Branch Bank 1993–94, dir NatWest Home Loans 1995–, chief operating offr NatWest Retail Bank 1995–; CIMgt 1990, FBCS 1991; *Style*— Michael G Whitehouse, Esq; ✉ National Westminster Bank, Drapers Gardens, 12 Throgmorton Avenue, London EC2N 2DL

WHITEHOUSE, Prof Norman Harold; s of late Norman Lester Whitehouse and late Maud Whitehouse; *b* 22 April 1938; *Educ* Queen Mary's GS Walsall, Univ of Leeds (LDS, BChD), Univ of Birmingham (DDH, DDPH RCS); *m* 1963, Barbara, da of late Jack Palmer; 1 da (Emma Louise b 1966), 1 s (Matthew John b 1967); *Career* dental offr Salop CC 1962–64, dental offr and area dental offr Norfolk CC 1964–69, chief dental offr City of Nottingham 1969–74, chief administrative dental offr and specialist in community dental health S Glamorgan and E Dyfed HAs 1974–86, chief exec and sec BDA 1986–93, chief administrative dental offr and dir of dental public health Mid Glamorgan HA 1993–95, hon conslt S and Mid Glamorgan HAs 1993–, prof of dental public health and dean Dental Sch Univ of Wales Coll of Med 1993–; chief exec: Dental Hosp of the S Glamorgan HA 1993–95, Univ Dental Hosp NHS Tst 1995–; memb GDC 1993–; memb: BDA 1962, Int Coll of Dentists 1988, Pierre Fauchard Acad 1988, Acad of Dentistry Int 1987; hon memb American Dental Assoc 1993; FRCSEd (ad hominem) 1995, FDSRCSEng (by election) 1995; *Recreations* hill-walking; *Style*— Prof Norman Whitehouse; ✉ Dental School, University of Wales College of Medicine, Heath Park, Cardiff CF4 4XY (☎ 01222 742470, fax 01222 766343)

WHITEHOUSE, Chief Constable Paul Chapple; QPM (1993); s of John Cecil Whitehouse, of Little Shelford, Cambs, and Beatrice May, *née* Chapple; *b* 26 Sept 1944; *Educ* Emmanuel Coll Cambridge (MA Economics); *m* 1970, Elizabeth Frances Carolyn, da of Eric Dinsmore (d 1970), of Surrey; 1 s, 1 da; *Career* joined Durham Constabulary 1967, supt Northumbria Police 1977–83 (joined 1974), asst chief constable (personnel and trg) Greater Manchester 1983–87, dep chief constable W Yorkshire Police 1987–93, chief constable Sussex Police 1993–; *Recreations* collecting people, IT, steam, disputation, keeping the peace; *Clubs* Royal Over-Seas League; *Style*— Mr Paul Whitehouse, QPM; ✉ Sussex Police HQ, Malling House, Lewes, East Sussex BN7 2DZ (☎ 01273 404001, fax 01273 404263)

WHITEHOUSE, Sarah Alice; da of Rev William Beadon Norman, and Beryl, *née* Welch; *b* 13 Jan 1961; *Educ* Felixstowe Coll Suffolk, Univ of St Andrews (MA, pres Univ Debating Union, pres Univ Cons Assoc), Univ of Westminster (pro exam in law), Inns of Ct Sch of Law (1992–93); *m* 15 Oct 1988, Andrew Timothy Brian, s of late Brian Paul Whitehouse; 1 da (Elizabeth Julia b 30 Dec 1992); *Career* National Westminster Bank plc 1983–85, sr mangr Fuji International Finance Ltd 1985–90, asst dir Barclays De Zoete Wedd Ltd 1990–91; Parly candidate (C) Warley West 1992; memb Lincoln's Inn 1991–, barr 1993–; *Recreations* riding, walking, music; *Clubs* Carlton (assoc memb); *Style*— Ms Sarah Whitehouse; ✉ 56 Drakefield Road, London SW17 8RP (☎ 0181 672 8366, fax 0181 675 6890, car 0831 613358); 6 King's Bench Walk, Temple, London EC4Y 7DR (☎ 0171 583 0410)

WHITELAW, Prof Andrew George Lindsay; s of Dr Robert George Whitelaw, DL, of 64 Garvock Hill, Dunfermline, Scotland, and Cicily Mary, *née* Ballard; *b* 31 Aug 1946; *Educ* George Watson's Coll Edinburgh, King's Coll Cambridge (MA, MB BChir, MD); *m* 1, 7 Sept 1968 (m dis 1990), Sara Jane, da of Capt Jack Sparks (d 1979), of Peaslake, Surrey; 1 s (Benjamin Cameron b 12 May 1972), 2 da (Nicola Jane b 26 Dec 1970, Rebecca Catrin b 18 April 1974); *m* 2, 4 Aug 1990, Marianne, da of Dr Otto Thoresen, of Horten, Norway; 1 s (Thomas Thoresen b 31 Oct 1990); *Career* specialist paediatric training at Gt Ormond St and in Toronto 1972–79, conslt neonatologist and hon sr lectr Royal Postgrad Med Sch Hammersmith Hosp 1981–90, prof paediatrics Univ of Oslo 1995– (assoc prof 1990–95); chm perinatal servs ctee NW Thames, dep chm res ethics ctee Hammersmith Hosp, memb res ctee Birthright; FRCP 1988; *Books* The Very Immature Infant Under 28 Weeks Gestation (with Cooke, 1988); *Recreations* music, mountains, theatre; *Style*— Prof Andrew Whitelaw; ✉ Aker University Hospital, 0514 Oslo, Norway (☎ 00 47 22 894599, fax 00 47 22 468467)

WHITELAW, Billie Honor; CBE (1991); da of Percival Whitelaw (d 1942), of Bradford, Yorks, and Frances Mary, *née* Williams (d 1980); *b* 6 June 1932; *Educ* Thornton GS; *m* 1, 1952 (m dis 1965), Peter Vaughan; m 2, Robert Muller; 1 s (Matthew Norreys b 1967); *Career* actress; first appearance aged 11 BBC Northern Region 1943, first West End appearance Hotel Paradiso 1954; Annenberg fell Univ of Reading, John Hopkins Award Dartmouth Coll NH USA, Award of Distinction Washington Coll USA; guest lectr at many US Univs, incl Smith, Wellesley, Barnard NYC, UCLA, Univ of Calif Santa Barbara, Madison Wisconsin, De Kalb Chicago, Boston Library and others; Hon DLitt Bradford Univ 1981; *Theatre* NT at Old Vic 1963–66 incl: Desdemona to Olivier's Othello, Hobson's Choice, Beckett's Play; seasons at Chichester, Moscow and Berlin; RSC incl: After Haggerty 1971, The Greeks 1979, Passion Play 1981; Royal Court with Samuel Beckett 1971–89 incl: Not I, Happy Days, Footfalls (written especially for her); opened Samuel Beckett Theatre New York with: Rockaby, Footfalls, Enough (also performed in LA 1984); other West End plays incl: Alphabetical Order 1975, Molly 1976, Tales of Hollywood (NT) 1984, Who's Afraid of Virginia Woolf (Young Vic) 1987; *Television* over 100 TV appearances incl: No Trams to Lime St, The Fifty Pound Note, Beyond the Horizon, Anna Christie, Wessex Tales, Jamaica Inn, The Picnic, The Entertainer, Firm Friends, Born to Run; *Radio* Rough, The Female Messiah, Alpha Beta, The Cherry Orchard, All That Fall and Embers, Vassa Zheleznova, The Wireless Lady; *Films* incl: Charlie Bubbles (1968, American Film Critics Award and Br Film Acad Best Supporting Actress), Start The Revolution Without Me, Leo the Last, Gumshoe, Frenzy, The Omen, The Dressmaker, Maurice, Joyriders, The Krays, Jane Eyre; *Awards* incl: TV Actress of the Year 1960, Best TV Actress 1972, Evening Standard Best Actress 1977, Variety Club Best Actress 1977, Best Radio Actress 1987, Br Film Award Evening Standard Best Actress 1988; *Books* Billie Whitelaw - Who He! (autobiography, 1995); *Style*— Ms Billie Whitelaw, CBE; ✉ c/o Michael Foster, ICM Ltd, Oxford House, 76 Oxford Street, London W1N 0AX (☎ 0171 636 6565, fax 0171 323 0101)

WHITELAW, Dr Douglas Dixon; s of George Whitelaw (d 1983), of Glasgow, and Jean, *née* Forrester (d 1986); *b* 4 March 1952; *Educ* HS of Glasgow, Univ of Glasgow (BSc(Hons), MSc, PhD); *m* 31 Dec 1974, Elspeth Martin, da of John Campbell; 2 s (Fraser Martin b 9 Nov 1981, Lindsay Elder b 21 Sept 1987); *Career* Wellcome Trust research fell Univ of Glasgow 1975–80, sr scientist Int Lab for Research on Animal Diseases (ILRAD) Nairobi Kenya 1980–88, EC sr research fell Univ of Glasgow 1989–90; Br Cncl: dep dir/sci offr Australia and NZ 1990–93, asst dir rising to dir Enugu Nigeria 1993–94, dir Kano Nigeria 1994–95, dep dir (sci) Korea 1996–; author of over seventy pubns in int scientific jls; *Recreations* music, golf, cricket; *Clubs* Nairobi, Royal Over-Seas League; *Style*— Dr Douglas Whitelaw; ✉ 13 St Dunstan's Park, Melrose, Roxburghshire TD6 (☎ 01896 822125); c/o The British Council, 10 Spring Gardens, London SW1A 2BN (☎ 0171 930 8466, fax 0171 389 4589)

WHITELAW, Prof James Hunter (Jim); s of James Whitelaw, and Jean Ross, *née* Scott; *b* 28 Jan 1936; *Educ* Glasgow HS, Univ of Glasgow (BSc, PhD), Univ of London (DSc); *m* 10 July 1959, Elizabeth, da of David Dewar Williamson Shields; 3 s (Alan Scott b 1962, David Stuart b 1964, James Douglas b 1968); *Career* res assoc Brown Univ 1961–63, prof Imperial Coll London 1974– (lectr 1963–69, reader 1969–74); ed Experiments in Fluids 1982–; Hon DSc Univ of Lisbon 1980, Hon DSc Univ of Valencia 1996; FIMechE, FEng 1991, FRS 1996; *Books* Principles and Practice of Laser-Doppler Anemometry (with F Durst and A Melling, 1981), Calculation Methods for Engineering Flows (with P Bradshaw and T Cebeci, 1981); series ed Combustion Treatise; jt ed over 20 books, author of over 300 technical papers; *Recreations* music, garden, travel; *Style*— Prof Jim Whitelaw, FRS, FEng; ✉ 149A Coombe Lane West, Kingston Upon Thames, Surrey KT2 7DH (☎ 0181 942 1836); Department of Mechanical Engineering, Imperial College, London SW7 (☎ 0171 594 7028)

WHITELAW, 1 Viscount (UK 1983), of Penrith, Co Cumbria; William Stephen Ian Whitelaw; KT (1990), CH (1974), MC (1944), PC (1967), DL (Cumbria 1974, Cumberland 1967); s of William Alexander Whitelaw (s of William Whitelaw, MP Perth and chm LNER, whose unc, Alexander *m* Dorothy, da of Ralph Disraeli and niece of Benjamin, 1 and last Earl of Beaconsfield) and Helen (da of Maj-Gen Francis Russell, CMG, JP, DL, of a family long domiciled in Scotland, one of whom served under Edward III at the siege of Berwick and saw action at Hallydon Hill in 1333; her mother was Philippa, maternal gda of 6 Viscount Strangford, diplomat and author; 7 Viscount Strangford was George Smythe, supposed model for Disraeli's Coningsby); *b* 28 June 1918; *Educ* Winchester, Trinity Coll Cambridge; *m* 1943, Cecilia Doriel, yr da of Maj Mark Sprot, Royal Scots Greys, of Roxburghshire, and Meliora, herself er da of Sir John Hay, 9 Bt; 4 da; *Career* served Scots Gds WW II; landowner; DL Dunbartonshire 1952–66; MP (C) Penrith and Cumberland Borders 1955–83; PPS to pres BOT 1956 and to chllr of Exchequer 1957–58, asst govt whip 1959–61, lord cmmr of Treasury 1961–62, Parly sec Miny of Labour 1962–64, chief oppn whip 1964–70, lord pres of Cncl and leader of House of Commons 1970–72; sec state: Northern Ireland 1972–73, Employment 1973–74; chm Cons Party 1974–75, dep leader of Oppn and Home Affairs spokesman 1975–79, home secretary 1979–83, lord pres of Cncl and leader of House of Lords 1983–88, ret; Hon Freeman Worshipful Co of Merchant Taylors; *Clubs* White's, Carlton, Royal and Ancient Golf of St Andrew's; *Style*— The Rt Hon the Viscount Whitelaw, KT, CH, MC, PC, DL; ✉ House of Lords, London SW1A 0PW

WHITELEY, *see:* Huntington-Whiteley

WHITELEY, Lady Angela Mary; *née* North; yr da of Francis George, Lord North (d 1940), er s of 8 Earl of Guilford; sister of 9 Earl; raised to the rank of an Earl's da 1950; *b* 28 May 1931; *m* 18 July 1955, Peter John Henry Whiteley, eldest s of late Brig John Percival Whiteley, OBE, TD, MP, of The Grange, Bletchley, Bucks; 2 s, 1 da; *Style*— The Lady Angela Whiteley; ✉ 10 Henning St, London SW11 3DR (☎ 0171 223 3601)

WHITELEY, Gen Sir Peter John Frederick; GCB (1979, KCB 1976), OBE (1960), DL (Devon 1987); s of John George Whiteley (d 1958), by his w Irene, *née* Izzard (d 1964); *b* 13 Dec 1920; *Educ* Bishop's Stortford Coll, Bembridge Sch, Ecole des Roches; *m* 1948, Nancy Vivian, da of William Carter Clayden (d 1943); 2 s, 2 da; *Career* joined RM 1940, Fleet Air Arm 1946–51, Staff Offr Staff Coll Camberley 1960–63, CO 42 Commando Malaysia 1965–66 (despatches), NATO Def Coll 1968, Cdr 3 Commando Bde 1968–70, Maj-Gen Commando Forces 1970–72, COS Allied Forces Northern Europe 1972–75, Cmdt Gen RM 1975–77, C-in-C Allied Forces Northern Europe 1977–79, Lt-Govr and C-in-C Jersey 1979–85; pres Devon St John's Ambulance 1987–96, dep chm Bd of Theatre Royal Plymouth, tstee Jersey Wildlife Preservation Tst; past master Guild of Freeman of the City of London; Hon Asst Worshipful Co of Fletchers; KStJ 1980; CIMgt; *Recreations* sailing, skiing, music, dogs; *Clubs* Royal Commonwealth Society; *Style*— Gen Sir Peter Whiteley, GCB, OBE, DL; ✉ Stoneycross, Yealmpton, Devon PL8 2JZ (☎ 01752 880462)

WHITELEY, (John) Richard; s of Thomas Kenneth Whiteley, and Margaret Sarah Whiteley; *b* 28 Dec 1943; *Educ* Giggleswick Sch N Yorks, Christ's Coll Cambridge (MA); *m* (m dis); 1 s (James); *Career* TV reporter and presenter; ed Varsity Cambridge Univ 1965, trainee ITN 1965–68, reporter and presenter various programmes Yorkshire TV 1968–, presenter Countdown (C4) 1982–; chm Minster Sound Radio (York) Ltd; first face on Channel 4 (2 Nov 1982), Personality of the Year Yorkshire TV 1987 and 1991; govr Giggleswick Sch, tstee Royal Armouries 1995–; *Recreations* watching Coronation Street, all news programmes, reading newspapers, window shopping in antique shops, talking about Yorkshire, racing; *Style*— Richard Whiteley, Esq; ✉ Yorkshire Television, Leeds LS3 1JS (☎ 0113 243 8283)

WHITELOCKE, Rodger Alexander Frederick; s of Leslie W S Whitelocke (d 1955), of Bulstrode Park, Jamaica, and Ruth, *née* Hopwood; descendant of Sir James Whitelocke b 1570 (and Family Tree in Plantagenet Roll Exeter Vol) and Bulstrode Whitelocke, Keeper of the Great Seal b 1605 (s Sir James); *b* 28 Feb 1943; *Educ* Taunton Sch, Univ of London, Bart's (MB BS); *m* 28 July 1973, Eleonora Valerie, da of Professor W F Maunder, of Tiverton, Devon; 2 s (Nicholas b 1979, James b 1984), 1 da (Katherine b 1978); *Career* house surgn St Bartholomew's Hosp 1969–70, research on prostaglandins in ocular inflammation Inst of Ophthalmology 1971–73 (PhD London), sr resident surgical offr Moorfields Eye Hosp 1976, sr registrar St Bartholomew's 1977–80; conslt ophthalmic surgn: St Bartholomew's Hosp, Royal Marsden Hosp London; hon conslt St Luke's Hosp for Clergy, visiting prof of visual scis City Univ London 1988–91; Freeman City of London; FRCS; *Recreations* music, antiques, travel, gardening; *Clubs* The Fountain, Athenaeum; *Style*— Rodger Whitelocke, Esq; ✉ Westwood, Heather Drive, Sunningdale, Berks; 152 Harley Street, London W1N 1HH (☎ 0171 935 3834)

WHITEMAN, Prof John Robert; s of Robert Whiteman, and Rita, *née* Neale; *b* 7 Dec 1938; *Educ* Bromsgrove Sch, Univ of St Andrews (BSc), Worcester Coll Oxford (DipEd), Univ of London (PhD); *m* 8 Aug 1964, Caroline Mary, da of Oswald B Leigh (d 1941); 2 s (Angus b 1967, Hamish b 1969); *Career* sr lectr RMCS Shrivenham 1963–67; asst prof: Univ of Wisconsin USA 1967–68, Univ of Texas at Austin USA 1968–70; Brunel Univ 1970–: reader numerical analysis 1970–76 (on leave Richard Merton Gäst prof Univ of Münster FRG 1975–76), prof of numerical analysis and dir Brunel Inst of Computational Mathematics 1976– (head Dept of Mathematics and Statistics 1982–90), vice princ 1991–; visiting prof: Univ of Pisa 1985, Univ of Kuwait 1986, Texas A and M Univ USA 1986–, Univ of Stuttgart 1990; memb: SERC Mathematics Ctee 1981–86, SERC Sci Bd 1989–92, Amersham Deanery Synod C of E; chm SERC Sci Bd Educn and Trg Panel 1991–92; Freeman City of London 1979, Liveryman Worshipful Co of Glass Sellers 1979; hon doctorate Univ of West Bohemia 1995; FIMA 1970, CMath 1991; *Books* numerous pubns on numerical solution of differential equations (particularly finite element methods) incl: The Mathematics of Finite Elements and Applications vols 1–8 (ed 1973–94), Numerical Methods for Partial Differential Equations (ed journal); *Recreations* walking, swimming, golf, tennis, orchestral music; *Style*— Prof John Whiteman; ✉ Institute of Computational Mathematics, Brunel University, Uxbridge, Middlesex UB8 3PH (☎ 01895 203270, fax 01895 203303)

WHITEMAN, Prof Peter George; QC (1977); s of David Whiteman (d 1988), and Betsy Bessie, *née* Coster; *b* 8 Aug 1942; *Educ* Warwick Secdy Mod Sch, Leyton Co HS, LSE (LLB, LLM); *m* 24 Oct 1971, Katherine Ruth, da of Gershon Ellenbogen; 2 da (Victoria Elizabeth b 1975, Caroline Venetia b 1977); *Career* lectr Univ of London 1966–70, called to the Bar Lincoln's Inn 1967; bencher Lincoln's Inn 1985, recorder of the Crown Ct 1986–, dep High Court Judge 1994–, jt head of chambers; memb Bar Cncl; memb Faculty of Laws Univ of Florida 1977–, prof of Law Univ of Virginia 1980–; attorney and cnsllr NY State 1982; visiting prof: Univ of Virginia 1978, Univ of California at Berkeley 1980; memb: Ctee Unitary Tax Campaign (UK) 1982–, Ed Bd Virginia Jl of Int Law 1982–; author numerous articles in learned jls; pres and chm Dulwich Village Preservation Soc 1987–, memb Advsy Ctee The Dulwich Estate Scheme of Mgmnt 1988–, chm Dulwich Jt Residents Ctee 1991–; memb: Consultative Ctee Dulwich Picture Gallery 1990–; FRSA 1976; *Books* Whiteman on Income Tax (1988), Whiteman on Capital Gains Tax (1988), British Tax Encyclopedia (1988); *Recreations* tennis, jogging, hill-walking, croquet, opera and theatre; *Style*— Prof Peter G Whiteman, QC; ✉ Hollis Whiteman Chambers, Queen Elizabeth Building, The Temple, London EC4Y 9BS (☎ 0171 936 3131, 0171 353 0551, 0171 583 5766, fax 0171 353 1937)

WHITEMAN, The Ven Rodney David Carter; s of Leonard Archibald Whiteman (d 1955), and Sybil Mary, *née* Morshead (d 1990); *b* 6 Oct 1940; *Educ* St Austell GS Cornwall, Ely Theological Coll; *m* 28 Oct 1969, Christine Anne, da of Edward Thomas James Chelton, of Cheltenham, Glos; 1 s (James Rodney Charles b 1975), 1 da (Rebecca Mary De Mornay b 1972); *Career* ordained Birmingham Cathedral: deacon 1964, priest 1965; curate All Saints Kings Heath 1964–70, vicar: St Stephen Rednal 1970–79, St Barnabas Erdington 1979–89; rural dean of Aston 1981–89, hon canon Birmingham Cathedral 1985–89, Archdeacon of Bodmin 1989–, hon canon of Truro Cathedral 1989–, priest in charge Cardynham with Helland 1989–94; *Style*— The Ven the Archdeacon of Bodmin; ✉ The Rectory, Cardynham, Bodmin, Cornwall PL30 4BL (☎ 01208 821614)

WHITEMORE, Hugh John; s of Samuel George Whitemore (d 1987), and Kathleen, *née* Fletcher; *b* 16 June 1936; *Educ* Judd Sch Tonbridge, King Edward VI Sch Southampton, RADA; *m* 1, July 1961 (m dis 1976), Jill, *née* Brooke; m 2, May 1976 (m dis 1994), Sheila, *née* Lemon; 1 s (Tom b 1976); *Career* playwright; stage plays: Stevie 1977, Pack of Lies 1983, Breaking the Code 1986, The Best of Friends 1988, It's Ralph 1991; films incl 84 Charing Cross Road (Royal Film Performance 1987), Jane Eyre (1995); many TV plays and dramatisations incl contribs to: The Wednesday Play, Armchair Theatre, Play for Today; *Recreations* music, movies, reading; *Style*— Hugh Whitemore, Esq; ✉ 67 Peel Street, London W8 7PB

WHITEOAK, John Edward Harrison; *b* 5 July 1947; *Educ* Keighley Secdy Tech, Univ of Sheffield (MA, CIPFA); *m* 1, Margaret Elizabeth, *née* Blakey (d 1980); 1 s (Roger b 1969), 2 da (Juliet b 1971, Olivia b 1973); m 2, 23 Sept 1983, Dr Karen Lynne Wallace, *née* Stevenson; 2 da (Georgia b 1988, Francesca b 1990); *Career* positions in local govt 1966–79 (Skipton, Solihull, Cleveland), gp dir Resources Cheshire CC 1994– (dep co treas 1979–81, co treas 1981–94); fin advsr ACC 1984–; princ negotiator on Local Govt Fin for England 1994–; chm Corp Governance Panel CIPFA; vice pres Soc of Co Treasurers 1996– (memb 1981–); memb: Accounting Standards Ctee 1984–87, Tech Ctee CIPFA 1984–, Exec Ctee SCT 1987–; *Books* Public Sector Accounting and Financial Control (co-author, 1992); *Recreations* golf, tennis; *Clubs* RAC, Chester City Club and Eaton Golf; *Style*— John Whiteoak, Esq; ✉ Huntington Hall, Chester CH3 6EA; County Hall, Chester, Cheshire CH1 1SG

WHITER, John Lindsay Pearce; s of Nugent Whiter (d 1966), and Jean Dorothy, *née* Pearce; *b* 10 May 1950; *Educ* Eastbourne GS; *m* 5 July 1975, Janet Dulcie Sarah, da of Dr Kenneth Oswald Albert Vickery, of Eastbourne; 2 s (Timothy b 1976, William b 1989), 1 da (Nancy b 1979); *Career* articled clerk and audit sr Honey Barrett & Co Eastbourne 1968–72, mangr Brebner Allen & Trapp 1973–74, sr ptnr (London) Neville Russell 1992–93 (ptnr 1977–88, managing partner (London) 1988–92), fin dir The Benfield Group Ltd 1994–; Freeman City of London, Bishopsgate Ward, Langbourn Ward; memb: Guild of Freeman of the City of London, Worshipful Co of Chartered Accountants in England and Wales; FCA 1973, FInstD, FRSA; *Recreations* golf, tennis, the arts; *Clubs* The Nat, City of London; *Style*— John Whiter, Esq; ✉ 29 Dry Hill Rd, Tonbridge, Kent TN9 1LU (☎ 01732 355088); The Benfield Group Ltd, 55 Bishopsgate, London EC2N 3AS (☎ 0171 578 7000, fax 0171 578 7001)

WHITEREAD, Rachel; da of Thomas Whiteread (d 1988), of London, and Pat, *née* Lancaster; *b* 20 April 1963; *Educ* Brighton Poly (BA), Slade Sch of Art UCL (DipHe in sculpture); *Career* artist and sculptor; involved in teaching on various postgrad and undergrad courses; *Solo Exhibitions* incl: Carlile Gallery London 1988, Ghost (Chisenhale Gallery London) 1990, Arnolfini Gallery Bristol 1991, Karsten Schubert Ltd London 1991, Rachel Whiteread Recent Sculpture (Luhring Augustine Gallery NY) 1992, House (E London) 1993, Basel Kunsterein (Switzerland) 1995, ICA Philadelphia (USA) 1995, ICA Boston (USA) 1995, Rachel Whiteread: Shedding Life (Tate Gallery Liverpool) 1996–97; *Selected Gp Exhibitions* incl: Whitworth Young Contemporaires Manchester 1987, Riverside Open London 1988, Whitechapel Open London 1989, Deichtorhallen Hamburg 1989–90, British Art Show (touring) 1990, Karsten Schubert Ltd London 1990, Metropolis (Martin-Gropius Bau Berlin) 1991, Broken English (Serpentine Gallery) 1991, Gp Show (Luhring Augustine NY) 1991, Turner Prize Exhibition (Tate) 1991 and 1993, Double Take (Hayward and Kunstalle Vienna) 1992, Documenta IX (Kassel Germany) 1992, Carnegie International (USA) 1995; *Awards* The Elephant Trust 1989, GLA Prodn Grant 1989, nominated Turner Prize 1991, DAAD Stipendum Berlin 1992, winner Turner Prize 1993; *Style*— Ms Rachel Whiteread; ✉ Anthony d'Offay Gallery, 9 Dering Street, London W1R 9AA (☎ 0171 499 4100)

WHITFIELD, Adrian; QC (1983); s of Peter Henry Whitfield (d 1967), and Margaret Mary Whitfield; *b* 10 July 1937; *Educ* Ampleforth, Magdalen Coll Oxford (MA); *m* 1, 1962 (m dis), Lucy Caroline, *née* Beckett; 2 da (Teresa, Emily); m 2, 1971, Niamh, da of Prof Cormac O'Ceallaigh, of Dublin; 1 s (Adam), 1 da (Katharine Anna); *Career* called to the Bar Middle Temple 1964, memb Western Circuit, recorder 1981–, head of chambers, chm NHS Tbnl 1993–; *Style*— Adrian Whitfield, Esq, QC; ✉ 47 Faroe Rd, London W14 0EL (☎ 0171 603 8982); 3 Serjeants' Inn, London EC4Y 1BQ (☎ 0171 353 5537)

WHITFIELD, Alan; s of Jonathon Whitfield (d 1982), and Annie, *née* Fothergill Rawe (d 1969); *b* 19 April 1939; *Educ* Consett GS, Sunderland and Newcastle Colls of Advanced Technol; *m* 24 Oct 1964, Sheila, da of John Thomas Carr (d 1976); 2 s (Simon Mark b 12 Jan 1968, Andrew Jonathon b 16 March 1972); *Career* asst engr then surveyor NCB 1956–62, various posts rising from engrg asst to team leader Northumberland Co Cncl 1962–70; Civil Serv: maingrade 1970–73, princ prof 1973–76, supt engr 1976–78, on secondment to establishments as personnel mangr 1978–80, dep dir Midlands Road Construction Unit 1980–83, dir of tport E and W Midlands 1983–89, regional dir DOE and Dept of Tport Eastern Region 1989, road programme dir Dept of Tport (now Highways Agency) 1989–95; chief highways engr Ove Arup and Partners 1995–; memb Nat Cncl Inst of Highway Engrs (memb Ctee Midland Branch, dep chm Construction Bd); CEng, MICE, FIHT; *Recreations* golf, music; *Clubs* RAC; *Style*— Alan Whitfield, Esq; ✉ Ove Arup and Partners, The Oaks, Westwood Way, Coventry CV4 8JB (☎ 01203 474347, fax 01203 466690)

WHITFIELD, Dr Ann; da of Dr Gerald A W Whitfield (d 1971), of Lindfield, Sussex, and Dr Nancy L Jones; *b* 28 July 1935; *Educ* Sherborne, Kings Coll Hosp Univ of London (MB BS, DA); *m* 2 Dec 1961, Robert Evan Kendell, s of Owen Kendell (d 1955), of Enfield, Middx; 2 s (Patrick b 1968, Harry b 1970), 2 da (Katherine b 1965, Judith b 1966); *Career* clinical fell Univ of Vermont Med Sch USA 1969–70; conslt anaesthetist: Lewisham Hosp London 1972–74, Royal Infirmary Edinburgh 1976–; FFARCS 1965, MRCS, LRCP; *Recreations* hill walking, cooking, music; *Style*— Dr Ann Whitfield; ✉ 3 West Castle Rd, Edinburgh EH10 5AT (☎ 0131 229 4966); Department of Anaesthetics, Royal Infirmary of Edinburgh, Edinburgh (☎ 0131 229 2477)

WHITFIELD, Hugh Newbold; s of Rev George Joshua Newbold Whitfield, of Exmouth, Devon, and Audrey Priscilla, *née* Dence; *b* 15 June 1944; *Educ* Canford, Gonville and Caius Coll Cambridge and St Bartholomew's Hosp London (MA, MChir); *m* Penelope Joy, da of William Craig; 2 s (Angus Hugh Newbold b 18 April 1976, Alastair James Newbold b 14 Jan 1981); *Career* cmmnd RAMC 1967–74; various house jobs Bart's, res fell Inst of Urology 1974–76; Bart's: chief asst Dept of Urology 1976–79, conslt urologist 1979–93, clinical dir Dept of Urology and dir Lithotripter Unit 1991–; ed Br Jl of Urology 1993–; former memb Nat Youth Orch of GB; memb: BMA 1968, Br Assoc of Urological Surgns 1974; FRSM 1975, FRCS 1972; *Books* Textbooks of Genito-Urinary Vols I and II (ed with W F Hendry, 1985), Urology: Pocket Consultant (1985), Genitourinary Surgey (ed 5 edn vols I-III, 1992); *Recreations* music, country pursuits, golf; *Clubs* Athenaeum; *Style*— Hugh Whitfield, Esq; ✉ Institute of Urology and Nephrology, The Middlesex Hospital, 48 Riding House Street, London W1F 7PN; Central Middlesex Hospital, Department of Urology, Acton Lane, Park Royal, London NW10 7NS (☎ 0181 965 5733); 43 Wimpole Street, London W1M 7AF (☎ 0171 935 3095, fax 0171 935 3147)

WHITFIELD, June; OBE (1985); da of John Herbert Whitfield (d 1955), and Bertha Georgina, *née* Flett (d 1982); *b* 11 Nov 1925; *Educ* Streatham Hill HS, RADA; *m* 1955, Timothy John Aitchison, s of Cdr J G Aitchison, OBE; 1 da (Suzy b 4 June 1960); *Career* actress; stage debut ASM Pinkstring & Sealing Wax (Duke of York's) 1944; *Theatre* incl: Ace of Clubs (Cambridge Theatre and tour) 1950, Love from Judy (Saville) 1952, From Here and There (Royal Court) 1955, Jack and the Beanstalk (Chichester 1982, Bath 1985, Guildford 1986), An Ideal Husband (Chichester) 1987, Over My Dead Body (Savoy) 1988, Babes in the Wood (Croydon) 1990 (Plymouth 1991, Cardiff 1992), Cinderella (Wimbledon) 1995; *TV and radio* incl: Take It From Here 1953–60, Hancock 1956, Benny Hill 1961, Dick Emery 1973, subject of This is Your Life 1976 and 1995, Happy Ever After (5 series) 1974–78, Terry and June (9 series) 1979–87, The News Huddlines 1984–96, French and Saunders 1988, Cluedo 1990, Absolutely Fabulous! 1992–94 (two specials 1996), Huddlines, Variety Special, Miss Marple in Murder at the Vicarage 1993, A Pocket Full of Rye 1994, At Bertram's Hotel 1995, Whats My Line 1994 and 1995, At Bartram's Hotel 1995, Common as Muck 1996, Family Money 1996, The 4.50 from Paddington 1996; *Films* Carry on Nurse 1958, Spy with the Cold Nose 1966, The Magnificent Seven Deadly Sins 1971, Carry on Abroad 1972, Bless This House 1972, Carry on Girls 1973, Romance with a Double Base 1974, Not Now Comrade 1975, Carry On Columbus 1992, Jude the Obscure 1995; *recordings* Up Je T'aime, Wonderful Children's Songs 1972; *Style*— Miss June Whitfield, OBE; ✉ c/o April Young Limited, 11 Woodlands Road, Barnes, London SW13 0JZ (☎ 0181 876 7030, fax 0181 878 7017)

WHITFIELD, Prof Michael; s of Arthur Whitfield (d 1990), of Wirral, Merseyside, and Ethel, *née* Woodward (d 1986); *b* 15 June 1940; *Educ* King's Sch Chester, Univ of Leeds (BSc, PhD); *m* 31 July 1961, Jean Ann (d 1984), da of Stanley Beige Rowe (d 1964); 1 s (Benjamin b 1968), 3 da (Katherine b 1962, Clare b 1964, Juliet b 1965); *Career* res scientist CSIRO Fisheries and Oceanography Sydney Australia 1964–69, dir Marine Biological Assoc Plymouth 1987– (sr princ res scientist 1970–87), dir Plymouth Marine Laboratory 1994–95 (dep dir 1988–94); hon prof Univ of Plymouth 1995–; vice pres Sir Alister Hardy Fndn for Ocean Sci, pres Challenger Soc for Marine Sci 1996–; memb Royal Soc: Scientific Ctee on Oceanic Research, Scientific Ctee on Problems in the Environment, Int Geosphere Biosphere Programme; tstee: National Marine Aquarium Ltd, Gaia Tst, Estuarine and Coastal Sciences Assoc; memb: Freshwater Biological Assoc, Scottish Assoc for Marine Science; Hon DSc Univ of Göteborg 1991; FRSC, FRSA, FIBiol; *Books* Ion-selective Electrodes for the Analysis of Natural Waters (1970), Marine Electro Chemistry (1981), Tracers in the Ocean (1988), Light & Life in the Sea (1990); *Recreations* hill walking, photography, watching wildlife, running; *Style*— Prof Michael Whitfield; ✉ The Marine Biological Association of the UK, The Laboratory, Citadel Hill, Plymouth PL1 2PB (☎ 01752 633331, fax 01752 669762, e-mail miw@mba.ac.uk)

WHITFIELD, Patrick John; s of Albert Victor Whitfield (d 1978), and Rose Anna, *née* Maye (d 1971); *b* 7 Nov 1931; *Educ* Wandsworth Sch, King's Coll London, St George's Hosp Med Sch (MB BS, LRCP); *m* 23 July 1955, Doris Eileen, da of Herbert Nelson Humphries (d 1962); 2 da (Roseanne Louise (Mrs Paul Roblin) b 8 Sept 1968, Natalie Anne b 17 Nov 1975); *Career* jr hosp appts 1958–64, trained at Regnl Plastic Surgery

Centre Queen Mary's Univ Hosp; sr registrar: seconded Plastic Surgery Centre Oxford 1966, Queen Mary's Univ Hosp 1967–72 (seconded to Paris, Rome, NY); conslt plastic surgn: Westminster Hosp and SW Thames Regnl Health Authy 1972, Royal London Hosp Tst 1996–; recognised teacher in plastic surgery Univ of London (Westminster and Charing Cross Hosps), Plastic Surgery Section RSM 1973–81 (hon sec, memb Cncl, vice pres, pres), memb Res Ctee Br Assoc of Plastic Surgns 1974–77, hon sec Br Assoc of Aesthetic Plastic Surgns 1977–83; FRSM 1968, FRCS; memb: Br Assoc of Plastic Surgns 1972, Br Assoc of Aesthetic Plastic Surgns 1978 (fndr); *Books* Operative Surgery (contrib); *Recreations* golf, scuba-diving, tennis, art appreciation; *Clubs* Athenaeum, Royal Wimbledon Golf; *Style—* Patrick Whitfield, Esq; ✉ 17 Harley St, London W1N 1DA (☎ 0171 580 6283)

WHITFIELD, Paul Martin; s of Christopher Gilbert Whitfield, FSA (d 1968), of Chipping Campden, Glos, and Frances Audrey, *née* Chandler (d 1993); *b* 9 Dec 1942; *Educ* Stowe, Middle Temple; *m* 1, 3 July 1965, Rowan, da of late Norman Fleming, of Broadway, Worcs; 1 s (Benjamin b 1971), 1 da (Lucy b 1968); m 2, 22 Sept 1982, Alison, da of late Dr I A B Cathie, of Barton House, Warwick; 1 s (Orlando b 1987), 1 da (Lily b 1988); *Career* dir Christie's International and Group of Companies (resigned 1987), dep chm W & FC Bonham Ltd (auctioneers) 1987–94, sr dir Sotheby's 1994–; govr Stowe Sch 1980–92; *Recreations* music, literature; *Clubs* Brooks's; *Style—* Paul Whitfield, Esq; ✉ Sotheby's, 34–35 New Bond Street, London W1A 2AA (☎ 0171 408 5481, fax 0171 408 5941)

WHITFIELD, Prof Roderick; s of late Prof John Humphreys Whitfield, and Joan, *née* Herrin; *b* 20 July 1937; *Educ* King Edward's Sch Birmingham, Sch of Oriental and African Studies, St John's Coll Cambridge (BA, MA), Princeton Univ (MFA, PhD); *m* 1, 11 July 1963 (m dis 1983), Dr Frances Elizabeth, da of Prof Richard Charles Oldfield; 1 s (Aldus b 1970), 2 da (Martha-Ming b 1965, Tanya b 1967); m 2, 25 Aug 1983, Dr Youngsook Pak; *Career* Offr Cadet Jt Serv Sch for Linguists, RAF 1955–57, PO RAFVR 1957, Flying Offr RAFVR; res assoc and lectr Princeton Univ 1964–66, res fell St John's Coll Cambridge 1966–68, asst keeper 1st class Dept of Oriental Antiquities The Br Museum 1968–84, prof of Chinese and East Asian Art Univ of London and head of Percival David Fndn of Chinese Art 1984–93, Percival David chair of Chinese and East Asian art SOAS 1993–; memb Cncl Oriental Ceramic Soc 1984–93, tstee Inst of Buddhist Studies; memb Int Inst of Conservation; *Books* In Pursuit of Antiquity (1969), The Art of Central Asia, The Stein Collection at the British Museum (3 vols, 1982–85), Treasures From Korea (ed 1984), Korean Art Treasures (ed 1986), Caves of the Thousand Buddhas (1990), Fascination of Nature: Plants and Insects in Chinese Painting and Ceramics of the Yuan Dynasty 1279–1368 (1993), The Problem of Meaning in Early Chinese Ritual Bronzes (ed, 1993), Dunhuang, Caves of the Singing Sands: Buddhist Art from the Silk Road (2 vols, 1995), The Arts of Central Asia: the Pelliot Collection in the Musée Guimet (collaborative translator, 1996); *Style—* Prof Roderick Whitfield; ✉ Department of Art and Archaeology, School of Oriental and African Studies, Thornhaugh Street, Russell Square, London WC1H 0XG (☎ 0171 323 6376, fax 0171 436 3844, e-mail rw5@soas.ac.uk)

WHITFORD, Dr Frank Peter; s of Percy Whitford, and Katherine Ellen, *née* Rowe (d 1996); *b* 11 Aug 1941; *Educ* Peter Symonds' Sch Winchester, Wadham Coll Oxford (BA), Courtauld Inst (MA), Freie Universität Berlin, RCA (higher doctorate); *m* 1972, Cecilia Josephine, da of Stanley Dresser; *Career* contrib ed Studio International 1964–74, tutor Slade Sch of Art 1969–72, lectr in history of art Homerton Coll Cambridge 1972–86, tutor in cultural history RCA 1986–91, art critic Sunday Times 1991–93, writer and broadcaster; *Books* Expressionism (1970), Japanese Prints and Western Painters (1977), Bauhaus (1983), Kokoschka - A Life (1986), Klimt (1991), and numerous others on 19/20th century art; *Recreations* cooking; *Clubs* Savile; *Style—* Frank Whitford, Esq

WHITFORD, Sir John Norman Keates Whitford; kt (1970); s of Harry Whitford; *b* 24 June 1913; *Educ* Univ Coll Sch, Munich Univ, Peterhouse Cambridge; *m* 1946, Rosemary, da of John Barcham Green by his w Emily Paillard; 4 da; *Career* served WW II RAFVR; QC 1965; High Court judge (Chancery) 1970–80; barr: Inner Temple 1935, Middle Temple 1946; chm Departmental Ctee Copyright & Design Law 1974–76; *Style—* Sir John Whitford; ✉ 140 High Street, West Malling, Kent ME19 6NE

WHITHEAR, (Edward) Roy; s of William Albert Henry Whithear, of Englefield Green, Surrey; *b* 10 July 1940; *Educ* Isleworth GS, Sherwood Union HS, Univ of Westminster (BA); *m* Ann Whithear, da of William John Mager; 3 c (Samantha Jane b 8 Feb 1970, Peter James b 20 July 1971, Jonathan Paul b 22 June 1976); *Career* British Airways 1958–65, The Observer Ltd 1965–67, IBM (UK) 1967–77, dir of fin & admin Kingston RBC 1977–78, fin & admin dir Computer Tech Ltd 1978–80, Gestetner Group 1980–85 (fin dir Operating subsids, gp fin controller, gen mangr Mfrg); Midland Bank Group 1985–92, fin dir Greenwell Montagu Stockbrokers and Smith Keen Cutler; sec-gen Assoc for Child Psychology and Psychiatry 1993–94, dir fin and sec Cancer Research Campaign 1994–; FCCA, FIMgt, FRSA, MCIT, MBCS; *Recreations* association football (Watford FC supporter), theatre; *Style—* Roy Whithear, Esq; ✉ Cancer Research Campaign, 10 Cambridge Terrace, London NW1 4JL (☎ 0171 935 1655, fax 0171 487 4310)

WHITING, Alan; s of Albert Edward Whiting, and Marjorie Irene, *née* Rodgers; *b* 14 Jan 1946; *Educ* Acklam Hall Secdy GS Middlesbrough, UEA (BA), UCL (MSc); *m* 17 Aug 1968, Annette Frances, da of James Kitchener Pocknee; 2 s (Matthew Peter b 27 June 1977, Paul Michael b 11 Nov 1982), 2 da (Alison Jane b 8 March 1976, Claire Louise b 17 Dec 1979); *Career* res assoc and asst lectr UEA 1967–68, cadet economist HM Treasy 1968–69, economic asst Dept of Econ Affairs and Miny of Technol 1969–70; economist: Euro Free Trade Assoc Geneva 1970–72, CBI 1972–73; DTI: econ advsr 1974–78, sr econ advsr 1979–83, Industl and Commercial Policy Div 1983–85, under sec Economics Div 1985–88, Econ Mgmnt and Educn Div 1989, Fin and Resource Mgmnt Div 1989–92, Financial Services Div 1992; HM Treasy: under sec Securities and Investmt Services Gp 1992–95, dep dir Financial Regulation 1995–; *Books* The Trade Effects of EFTA and the EEC (jtly, 1972), The Economics of Industrial Subsidies (ed, 1975); *Recreations* building, gardening, sport, music; *Clubs* Littleton Sailing; *Style—* Alan Whiting, Esq; ✉ HM Treasury, Parliament Street, London SW1P 3AG (☎ 0171 270 4448, fax 0171 270 5563, telex 9413704)

WHITING, Prof Brian; s of Leslie George Whiting (d 1971), and Evelyn Irene Edith, *née* Goss; *b* 6 Jan 1939; *Educ* Stockport GS, Univ of Glasgow (MB ChB, MD); *m* Marlene Shields, *née* Watson; 2 da (Gillian b 1969, Lanie b 1971); *Career* RNR 1965–73, ret as Surgn Lt Cdr; visiting prof of clinical pharmacology Univ of California San Francisco 1978–79, dir Clinical Pharmacokinetics Laboratory Dept of Materia Medica Stobhill Gen Hosp 1980–91 (former res and hosp posts), visiting prof of clinical pharmacology Univ of Auckland NZ 1987, currently dean Faculty of Med and prof of clinical pharmacology Dept of Med and Therapeutics Univ of Glasgow; non-exec memb Greater Glasgow Health Bd; author of pubns on: clinical pharmacology, pharmacokinetics, population pharmacokinetics; clinical sec treas Br Pharmacological Soc 1987–91; memb: Assoc of Physicians of GB and I, Ctee on Dental and Surgical Materials 1989–92, Gen Medical Cncl; FRCP (Glasgow), FFPM; *Books* Lecture Notes on Clinical Pharmacology (4 edn, 1992); *Recreations* music, painting, photography, mountaineering; *Style—* Prof Brian Whiting; ✉ 2 Milner Rd, Jordanhill, Glasgow G13 1QL (☎ and fax 0141 959 2324); Faculty of Medicine, University of Glasgow, Glasgow G12 8QQ (☎ 0141 330 4249, fax 0141 330 5440, e-mail B.Whiting@clinmed.gla.ac.uk)

WHITING, Derek Alan; OBE (1991); s of William Thomas Whiting (d 1981), of Beckenham, Kent, and Gladys Dudfield Whiting (d 1970); *b* 2 Aug 1931; *Educ* Tonbridge Sch; *m* 1, 5 June 1962, Lady Frances Esmee, *née* Curzon, da of 5 Earl Howe, PC (d 1964); 2 s (Francis b 1965, Alexander b 1967); m 2, 14 Dec 1972, Angela Clare Forbes, da of Sir Archibald Forbes, GBE, (d 1989); *Career* Nat Serv cmmnd The Buffs 1950, ADC to Govr and C-in-C Br Somaliland 1951, Actg Capt; commodity trading & broking 1952–90; underwriting memb Lloyds 1972–80; chm: Int Petroleum Exchange 1986–90, London Sugar Futures Mkt 1984–87, AFBD 1984–87, Comfin Trading Ltd 1980–89, Sucden (UK) Ltd 1980–90, Buckingham Asset Management 1992–95, Tonbridge Sch Appeal 1992–94; played rugby for: Harlequins (former chm and hon sec), Kent; Liveryman Worshipful Co of Skinners; *Recreations* shooting, golf, reading; *Clubs* Swinley Forest, Hurlingham, Harlequins; *Style—* Derek Whiting, Esq, OBE; ✉ 4 Gertrude Street, London SW10 0JN (☎ 0171 352 6220, fax 0171 351 1804, car 0860 763502)

WHITING, Rev Peter Graham; CBE (1984); s of Rev Arthur Whiting (d 1993), of Wimborne, Dorset, and Olive, *née* Stebbings (d 1986); *b* 7 Nov 1930; *Educ* Yeovil GS, Irish Baptist Coll, Dublin (Dip Theol); *m* 9 Jan 1960, Lorena, da of Albert Inns (d 1982), of Northampton; 2 s (Julian b 1962, Toby b 1964), 3 da (Clare b 1960, Sophie b 1967, Anna b 1973); *Career* cmmnd RAChD 1962, Regtl Chaplain 1962–69, Chaplain 1 Bn Parachute Regt 1964–66, Sr Chaplain 20 Armd Bde BAOR and Lippe Garrison BAOR 1969–72, Staff Chaplain HQ BAOR 1972–74, Sr Chaplain 20 Airportable Bde 1974–75, Dep Asst Chaplain Gen W Midland Dist Shrewsbury 1975–78, Sr Chaplain Young Entry Units 1976–78, Asst Chaplain Gen 1 Br Corps BAOR 1978–81, Dep Chaplain Gen to the Forces (Army) 1981–84; ordained Baptist Minister 1956; minister: Kings Heath Northampton 1956–62, Beechen Grove Baptist Church Watford 1985–95, ret; Queen's Hon Chaplain 1981–84; memb Cncl of Churches; *Style—* The Rev P G Whiting, CBE; ✉ 16 Hermitage Close, North Mundham, Chichester, West Sussex PO20 6JZ

WHITLAM, Michael Richard; s of Richard William Whitlam (d 1971), and Mary Elizabeth, *née* Land (d 1983); *b* 25 March 1947; *Educ* Morley GS, Tadcaster GS, Coventry Coll of Educn, Univ of Warwick (CertEd), Cranfield Inst of Technol (MPhil); *m* 24 Aug 1968, Anne Jane, da of William McCurley (d 1987); 2 da (Rowena b 1971, Kirsty b 1973); *Career* former teacher Ripon Co GS; asst govr 1969–74: HM Borstal Hollesley Bay, HM Prison Brixton; dir: Hammersmith Teenager Project Nat Assoc of Care and Resettlement of Offenders, UK Ops Save The Children Fund 1978–86 (former dep dir); chief exec Royal Nat Inst for the Deaf 1986–90, dir City Literature Inst 1990–91, DG British Red Cross Society 1991–; dir: BritCross Ltd, British Red Cross Events Ltd, Charity Appointments 1994–; chm: London Intermediate Treatment Assoc 1979–82, Nat Intermediate Treatment Assoc 1980–83, Sound Advantage plc 1989–90, ACENVO 1988–91 (chm Policy Ctee 1994–); memb: Exec Cncl Howard League 1974–84, Community Alternative Young Offenders Ctee NACRO 1979–82, Exec Cncl Nat Children's Bureau 1980–86, Bd REACH 1996–; FRSA; *Recreations* painting, walking, keeping fit, family activities, opera, management of the voluntary sector, recently joined United Reform Church; *Style—* Michael Whitlam, Esq; ✉ Director General, British Red Cross Society, 9 Grosvenor Crescent, London SW1X 7EJ (☎ 0171 201 5272, fax 0171 235 5194, mobile 0802 927236)

WHITLEY, His Hon John Reginald; s of Reginald Joseph Ashley Whitley (d 1979), and Marjorie Rose, *née* Orton (d 1994); *b* 22 March 1926; *Educ* Sherborne, Corpus Christi Coll Cambridge; *m* 1966, Susan Helen, *née* Kennaway; 1 da (Elizabeth Rose b 1967); *Career* served KRRC 1944–48; called to the Bar Gray's Inn 1953, practiced Western Circuit 1953–86, recorder 1978–86, circuit judge (Western Circuit) 1986–96; *Recreations* golf; *Style—* His Hon J R Whitley; ✉ Kingsrod, Fridays Hill, Kingsley Green, Haslemere, Surrey GU27 3LL

WHITLEY, Air Marshal Sir John René; KBE (1956, CBE 1945), CB (1946), DSO (1943), AFC and bar (1937, 1956); s of Arthur Noel Joseph Whitley (d 1940); *b* 7 Sept 1905; *Educ* Haileybury; *m* 1, 1932, Barbara Alice Patricia (d 1965), da of F R Liscombe; 3 s (Christopher, David, Piers) and 1 s (Guy d 1978); m 2, 1967, Alison (d 1986), widow of John Howard Russell, and da of Sir Nigel Campbell (d 1948, s of Adela Harriet, 2 da of Lord Charles Pelham Clinton, 2 s of 4 Duke of Newcastle); *Career* served RAF 1926–62: India 1932–37, Bomber Cmd 1937–45, Singapore 1946, India 1947, Dir Organisation (Estabs) Air Miny 1948–49, IDC 1950, AO Admin 2 TAF Germany 1951–52, AOC 1 Gp Bomber Cmd 1953–56, Air Memb Personnel 1957–59, Inspr-Gen RAF 1959–62, ret; controller RAF Benevolent Fund 1962–68; *Style—* Air Marshal Sir John Whitley, KBE, CB, DSO, AFC; ✉ The Grange, Steep, Petersfield, Hampshire GU32 2DB (☎ 01730 267232)

WHITMORE, Sir Clive Anthony; GCB (1988, KCB 1983), CVO 1983; s of Charles Arthur and Louisa Lilian Whitmore; *b* 18 Jan 1935; *Educ* Sutton GS, Christ's Coll Cambridge; *m* 1961, Jennifer Mary Thorpe; 1 s, 2 da; *Career* private sec to Perm Under Sec of State War Office 1961, asst private sec to Sec of State for War 1962, princ 1964, private sec to Perm Under Sec of State MOD 1969, asst sec 1971, asst under sec of state (Def Staff) MOD 1975, under sec Cabinet Office 1977, princ private sec to PM 1979–82, dep sec 1981, perm under sec of state MOD 1983–88, perm under sec of state Home Office 1988–94, ret; non-exec dir: Boots Co plc 1994–, Morgan Crucible Co plc 1994–, Racal Electronics plc, NM Rothschild & Sons Ltd; *Recreations* music, gardening; *Style—* Sir Clive Whitmore, GCB, CVO; ✉ c/o Morgan Crucible Co plc, Morgan House, Madeira Walk, Windsor, Berks SL4 1EP (☎ 01753 837000)

WHITMORE, Sir John Henry Douglas; 2 Bt (UK 1954), of Orsett, Co Essex; s of Col Sir Francis Henry Douglas Charlton Whitmore, 1 Bt, KCB, CMG, DSO, TD (d 1962, maternal gs of Sir William Cradock-Hartopp, 3 Bt, while his paternal grandmother was Lady Louisa Douglas, eldest da of 5 Marquess of Queensberry); *b* 16 Oct 1937; *Educ* Eton; *m* 1, 1962 (m dis 1969), Ella Gunilla, da of Sven A Hansson, of Danderyd, Sweden; 1 da; m 2, 1977, Diana Elaine, da of Fred A Becchetti, of Calif; 1 s; *Heir* s, Jason Whitmore b 26 Jan 1983; *Career* sports psychologist, also concerned with psychology of int relations; dep dir Centre for Int Peacebuilding, author of books on the mental aspects of sport, life and work; *Recreations* squash, skiing, motor racing; *Clubs* British Racing Drivers; *Style—* Sir John Whitmore, Bt; ✉ Southfield, Leigh, nr Tonbridge, Kent TN11 8PJ (☎ 01732 454490)

WHITNEY, John Norton Braithwaite; s of Dr Willis Bevan Whitney, and Dorothy Anne, *née* Robertson; *b* 20 Dec 1930; *Educ* Leighton Park Friends' Sch Reading; *m* 9 June 1956, Roma Elizabeth Duncan (former dancer with London Festival Ballet), da of George Hodgson; 1 s (Alexander b 31 Jan 1961), 1 da (Fiona b 17 Nov 1958); *Career* radio prodr 1951–64; fndr: Ross Radio Productions Ltd 1951, Autocue Ltd 1955, Radio Antilles 1963; fndr dir Sagitta Productions 1968–82; dir: Consolidated Productions (UK) Ltd 1980–82, Satellite TV plc 1982; md: Capital Radio 1973–82, Really Useful Group Ltd 1989–90 (chm 1990–95); dir gen IBA 1982–89, non-exec chm Trans World Communications plc 1991–94, dir Friends Provident Life Office 1982–, chm Friends Provident Stewardship Ctee 1985–; non-exec chm: Friends Provident Ethical Investment Trust plc 1994–, Friends Provident NYC; chm: Radio Joint Audience Research Ltd 1992–, Sony Radio Awards 1992–, Nat Bowl Milton Keynes for Sony 1991–95; chm: Advsy Panel Guinness Mahon Global Rights Div Fund 1993–, Caspian Publishing 1996–, The Radio Partnership 1996–; non-exec dir VCI plc 1995–; fndr Recidivists Anonymous Fellowship Tst 1962, co fndr and chm Local Radio Assoc 1964, chm Assoc Ind Radio Contractors 1973–75 and 1980, dir Duke of York's Theatre 1979–82, memb Bd Royal Nat Theatre 1982–94; RCM: memb Centenary Devpt Fund (formerly Appeal Ctee)

1982–94, chm Media and Events Ctee 1982–94; memb: Cncl Royal London Aid Soc 1966–90, Cncl Fairbridge Drake Soc (formerly Drake Fellowship) 1981, Films TV and Video Advsy Ctee Br Cncl 1983–89, Indust and Commerce Liaison Ctee Royal Jubilee Tsts 1986– (memb Admin Cncl of Tsts 1981–85), Intermediate Technol Gp 1982–85, Cncl for Charitable Support 1989–93, Bd Open Coll 1987–89, Bd City of London Sinfonia 1994–; chm tstees: Soundaround (nat sound mag for the blind) 1981–, Artsline 1983–; tstee Venture Tst 1982–86, vice chm Japan Festival 1991 (chm Japan Festival Media Ctee 1991–92), dir Japan Festival Educn Tst 1992–, tstee Nat Assoc of Hospital Bdcasting Assocs 1993–; chm Br American Arts Assoc 1992–95; vice pres: Cwlth Youth Exchange Cncl 1982–85, RNID 1988–; pres London Marriage Guidance Cncl 1983–90; pres TV and Radio Industs Club 1985–86 (memb Cncl 1979–); govr: English Nat Ballet (formerly London Festival Ballet) 1989–91, Performing Arts & Technol Sch 1992–; chm Theatre Investmt Fund 1990–, patron MusicSpace Tst 1990, FRTS (vice pres 1986–89), hon memb BAFTA, hon fell RCM, memb SWET; FRSA; *Recreations* chess, photography, sculpture; *Clubs* Garrick, Whitefriars, Pilgrims; *Style—* John N B Whitney, Esq; ✉ 4 Clifford Street, London W1X 1RB (☎ 0171 734 5121)

WHITNEY, Dr Paul Michael; s of John Henry Whitney (d 1980), of Bexhill, and Irene, *née* Tither; *b* 4 May 1948; *Educ* Judd Sch Tonbridge, Aston Univ (BSc, PhD (Physical Chemistry)), Cranfield Sch of Mgmnt (MBA); *m* 1971, Melanie Jane, da of Gordon E A Hounslow; 1 da (Natasha Louise b 12 March 1973), 2 s (Benjamin Paul b 10 Nov 1974, Jonathan Mark b 20 Sept 1977); *Career* paper mill tech mangr Courtaulds/CDC Swaziland 1974–79 (research chemist/mgmnt trainee 1972–74), with Industrial and Commercial Finance Corp (now 3i plc) 1980–83; CIN Management Ltd: venture capital dir 1984, venture capital md 1985, chief exec 1988–93; md NatWest Asset Managers and chief exec NatWest Investment Management Ltd 1993–96, chief exec Sun Life Asset Management Ltd 1996–; non-exec dir: MFI Furniture Group plc, Phytopharm plc, Malvern plc; *Recreations* windsurfing, sleeping; *Clubs* RAC; *Style—* Dr Paul Whitney; ✉ Sun Life Asset Management Ltd, 107 Cheapside, London EC2V 6DU (☎ 0171 606 7788, fax 0171 600 6097)

WHITNEY, Sir Raymond William (Ray); kt (1997), OBE (1968), MP (C) Wycombe (majority 17,076); o s of late George Whitney, of Northampton; *b* 28 Nov 1930; *Educ* Wellingborough Sch, RMA Sandhurst, Univ of London (BA), Hong Kong and Australia Nat Univs; *m* 1956, Sheila Margot Beswick Prince; 2 s; *Career* RA Northants Regt 1951–64, seconded to Aust Army HQ 1960–63, served Trieste, Korea, Hong Kong, Germany; FO 1964–78: served Peking, head of Chancery Buenos Aires 1969–72, dep high cmmr Dacca 1973–76, head Overseas Info Dept FCO 1977–78; MP (C) Wycombe April 1978– (by-election), PPS to Treasy Mins 1979–80, vice chm Cons Backbench Employment Ctee 1980–83, chm Cons Foreign Affrs Ctee 1981–83, Parly under sec of state FCO 1983–84; Parly under sec of state for: social security 1984–85, health 1985–86; chm: All Party Br Latin American Gp, Mountbatten Community Tst, Cncl for Def Info, The Cable Corporation, The Positive European Gp; *Style—* Sir Ray Whitney, OBE, MP; ✉ The Dial House, Kings Road, Sunninghill, Berks SL5 0AG (☎ 01344 23164); House of Commons, London SW1A 0AA (☎ 0171 219 5099)

WHITROW, Benjamin John; s of Philip Benjamin Whitrow, TD (d 1966), and Mary Isabella, *née* Flounders (d 1984); *b* 17 Feb 1937; *Educ* Dragon Sch Oxford, Tonbridge, RADA; *m* 13 Jan 1972, Catherine Elizabeth, da of Jack Kenneth Cook (d 1986); 1 s (Thomas George b 1976), 1 da (Hannah Mary b 1973); *Career* actor; Nat Serv King's Dragoon Gds 1956–58; debut Liverpool Playhouse 1959; rep work Birmingham, Bristol, Harrogate; joined NT under Sir Laurence Olivier 1967–74; *Theatre* West End incl: Otherwise Engaged 1975, Dirty Linen 1976, Ten Times Table 1978, What the Butler Saw 1979, Passion Play 1982, Noises Off 1983, A Little Hotel on the Side (NT) 1984, Uncle Vanya 1988, Racing Demon (RNT) 1991, Falstaff in Merry Wives of Windsor (RSC) 1992, Camillo in The Winters Tale (RSC) 1992, Fiodor in Mischa's Party (RSC) 1993, Ephraim Smooth in Wild Oats (RNT) 1995; *Television* for BBC incl: Ulysses in Troilus and Cressida, By George, The Devil's Disciple, Bergerac, Hay Fever, Mr Bennet in Pride and Prejudice; other credits incl: Ffizz, J R Ackerley in We Think the World of You, A Little Bit of Singing and Dancing (Granada), Natural Causes (YTV), Harry's Game (YTV), Chancer (Central), *Radio* incl: comedy series After Henry, own adaptation Mary Russell Mitford's Letters, own adaptation My Grandfather and Father Dear Father by Dennis Constanduras; *Films* incl: Clockwise, Personal Services, Quadrophenia, On the Black Hill, A Shocking Accident (Oscar for Best Short Film 1982); *Recreations* golf, reading, bridge; *Clubs* Richmond Golf; *Style—* Benjamin Whitrow, Esq; ✉ c/o Lou Coulson, 37 Berwick Street, London W1V 3RF (☎ 0171 734 9633, fax 0171 439 7569)

WHITSEY, Fred; *b* 18 July 1919; *m* 1947, Patricia Searle; *Career* ed Popular Gardening 1967–82 (asst ed 1948–64, assoc ed 1964–67); gardening corr: Sunday Telegraph 1961–71, Daily Telegraph 1971–; contrib Country Life and The Garden; Gold Veitch Meml Medal 1979, Victoria Medal of Honour 1986, Garden Writers' Guild Lifetime Achievement Award 1994; vice pres Royal Horticultural Soc 1996–; *Books* Sunday Telegraph Gardening Book (1966), Fred Whitsey's Garden Calendar (1985), Garden for all Seasons (1986); *Recreations* music, gardening; *Style—* Fred Whitsey; ✉ Avens Mead, 20 Oast Rd, Oxted, Surrey RH8 9DU

WHITSON, Keith Roderick; s of William Cleghorn Whitson, and Ellen, *née* Wade; *b* 25 March 1943; *Educ* Alleyn's Sch Dulwich; *m* 26 July 1968, Sabine Marita, da of Ulrich Wiechert; 1 s (Mark James b 26 July 1980), 2 da (Claudia Sharon b 31 Aug 1971, Julia Caroline b 2 May 1973); *Career* HSBC Holdings plc group: joined Hongkong and Shanghai Banking Corporation 1961, mangr Frankfurt 1978–80, mangr Indonesia 1981–84, asst gen mangr fin Hong Kong 1985–87, chief exec offr Hongkong and Shanghai Banking Corporation UK 1987–89, exec dir Marine Midland Banks Inc 1989–93, chief exec offr Midland Bank plc London 1994–; dir HSBC Holdings plc (parent co of Midland) 1994–; chm: Midland Life, Forward Trust Group Ltd London 1993–; non-exec dir BET plc; former chm: Carroll McEntee and McGinley Inc, Concord Leasing USA; *Style—* Keith Whitson, Esq; ✉ Midland Bank plc, 27 Poultry, London EC2P 2BX (☎ 0171 260 8000, fax 0171 260 7065)

WHITTAKER, (George) Anthony; s of George Whittaker (d 1980), by his w Muriel (d 1975); *b* 10 May 1930; *Educ* McGill Univ Montreal (BEng), Inst of Technol Charlottesville Virginia USA (MS); *m* 1964, Elizabeth Anne, da of R E Smyth; 1 s, 2 da; *Career* 2 Lt REME; dir: Smith and Nephew Overseas Ltd 1956–63, Deering Milliken Ltd 1963–68 (and int vice pres), Guinness Peat Group Ltd 1968–82; md Grosvenor Place Amalgamations Ltd 1982–; non-exec dir: Spillers Ltd 1979–80, Albert Fisher Group plc 1982– (dep chm 1992–), Robin Marlar Ltd 1983–84, Norman Reeves plc 1983–86, Edeco Holdings Ltd 1985–89, UK Paper plc 1988–90; chm Bright Walton Homes plc 1986–93; *Recreations* cricket, walking, fishing; *Clubs* MCC, IOD, Lansdowne; *Style—* G Anthony Whittaker, Esq; ✉ Craigie Lea, Church Lane, Stoke Poges, Bucks SL2 4NZ

WHITTAKER, (Thomas) Geoffrey; s of Maj William Whittaker (d 1983), and Nellie May, *née* Crabtree (d 1989); *b* 2 March 1937; *Educ* Ermysted's Sch Skipton, Lincoln Coll Oxford (MA), London Coll of Violinists; *m* 8 Nov 1960, Florence McKay, da of John Glasgow (d 1943); 2 s (William Robert b 1961, Edward Norman b 1963 d 1995), 1 da (Katherine Margaret (Mrs Saner) b 1966); *Career* Nat Serv radar tech Cyprus 1955–57; dir and gen mangr Harlander Coats AG Austria 1969, md Laidlaw & Fairgrieve Scotland 1983, dir Invergordon Distillers plc Scotland 1983–94; chm GMI Ltd 1995–; dir Grampian Country Foods Ltd 1994–; playing memb Edinburgh Symphony Orch; memb: Galashiels Mfrs' Corp 1975, Soc of Coopers of Glasgow 1984, Keepers of the Quaich 1988, Br Wool Textiles Export Cncl; former deacon Galashiels Mfrs' Assoc, former chm Scottish Wool Spinners Fedn; Liveryman: Worshipful Co of Grocers of Paisley 1962, Glasgow Co of Coopers 1984; Freeman Citizen of Glasgow at Far Hand 1984; *Recreations* music, bridge; *Clubs* Caledonian (Edinburgh); *Style—* Geoffrey Whittaker, Esq; ✉ Beechlaw Langside Drive, Peebles, Tweeddale EH45 8RF (☎ 01721 721452); CMI Ltd, Inchinnan Industrial Estate, Renfrew

WHITTAKER, (Rosemary) Jane; da of Robert Charnock Whittaker, of Blackpool, Lancs, and Betty, *née* Howard; *b* 27 Feb 1955; *Educ* Queen Mary's Sch Lytham, Univ of Manchester (LLB); *m* 6 Aug 1987, Colin Michael Brown; *Career* articled clerk Manchester (admitted slr 1978), slr International Computers Ltd (ICL) 1982–88, ptnr Macfarlanes slrs 1988–; chair Cons Lawyers' Assoc; memb: Law Soc (memb Cncl 1995–), Assoc of Women Slrs (chair 1994–95), London C of C; *Books* The Role of Directors in the European Community (1992); *Recreations* swimming, theatre, entertaining and cooking; *Clubs* Richmond Riverside; *Style—* Ms Jane Whittaker; ✉ Macfarlanes, 10 Norwich Street, London EC4A 1BD (☎ 0171 831 9222, fax 0171 831 9607)

WHITTAKER, Malcolm George; s of Rev George Henry Whittaker (d 1995), of Ilkley, Yorks, and Katherine Clarissa, *née* Salter (d 1995); *b* 24 Dec 1937; *Educ* Ermysteds GS Skipton Yorks, Univ of Leeds (MB ChB), Univ of Glasgow, Univ of London; *m* 22 March 1969, Susan Jane, *née* Allan; 1 s (James Benjamin b 17 Aug 1976), 1 da (Helen Rachel b 1 Feb 1971); *Career* lectr in surgery UCH London, currently sr conslt surgn Darlington and Northallerton Health Dists and lectr in clinical surgery Univ of Newcastle upon Tyne; hon clinical teacher the Middlesex and Univ Coll Hosps London; pres North of England Surgical Soc 1996–97; former vice pres Section of Surgery RSM, memb Société Internationale de Chirurgie; FRCS, FRCSEd; *Recreations* walking, reading, skiing; *Clubs* Royal Automobile, Kandahar, Swiss Alpine; *Style—* Malcolm Whittaker, Esq; ✉ 12 Southend Ave, Darlington (☎ 01325 484293)

WHITTAKER, (Alan) Mark; s of Alan Whittaker, of Darwen, Lancs, and Jean, *née* Almond; *b* 17 April 1957; *Educ* John Ruskin HS Croydon, Univ of Durham (BA); *Career* grad trainee Thomson Regnl Newspapers Newcastle-upon-Tyne 1979, reporter Lancashire Evening Telegraph 1980–82, BBC Radio Lancashire 1983–86, BBC Radio West Midlands 1986–88; presenter: Newsbeat BBC Radio 1 1988–96, Costing the Earth Radio 4 1994–, Kershaw and Whittaker Radio 5 Live 1994–, You & Yours Radio 4 1996–; *Recreations* hiking, football, public houses; *Clubs* Blackburn Rovers FC, Kidderminster Harriers; *Style—* Mark Whittaker, Esq; ✉ 12 St George's Terrace, Kidderminster, Worcs; BBC Broadcasting House, Portland Place, London W1A 1AA (☎ 0171 765 4649)

WHITTAKER, Michael William Joseph; s of Harry Whittaker, of Dorchester, and Hylda, *née* Roach; *b* 28 Jan 1941; *Educ* Normain Coll Chester, Miller Acad Thurso, Weymouth and Brunel Tech Coll Bristol; *m* 8 Aug 1972, Brenda Pauline, da of Thomas Marsh (d 1987), of Thurnscoe, Yorks; 2 da (Helena Amanda b 7 March 1963, Lindsay Jane b 30 Dec 1974); *Career* self employed design conslt; private light aircraft projects, 6 aircraft designed and developed 1973–93, 90 flying MW5 and MW6 microlights manufactured under licence; winner numerous design awards; CEng, MIMechE, FRAeS; *Recreations* restoration of vintage motorcycles, design and development of light aircraft; *Style—* Michael Whittaker, Esq; ✉ Appletree Cottage, Churchfield Road, Clayton, Doncaster, S Yorks DN5 7BZ

WHITTAKER, Nigel; *b* 1948; *Educ* Clare Coll Cambridge, Yale Law Sch; *Career* barr; head of Legal Dept Roche Products Ltd 1974–77, Gen Cncl Br Sugar 1977–82, exec dir Kingfisher plc 1983–95 (joined 1982), chm Cardcast plc 1996–; proprietor NW Corporate Affairs Consultancy 1995–; non-exec dir: European Smaller Companies plc 1993–, Wickes plc 1996–; chm CBI's Distributive Trades Survey Panel 1987–94, memb UK Ecolabelling Bd 1992–, chm Br Retail Consortium 1995; *Style—* Nigel Whittaker, Esq

WHITTAKER, Roger Henry Brough; s of Edward Whittaker (d 1989), and Valda Viola, *née* Showan; *b* 22 March 1936; *Educ* Prince of Wales Sch Nairobi Kenya, Univ of Cape Town SA, Univ of Wales Bangor (BSc); *m* 15 Aug 1964, Natalie Deirdre, da of Edward (Toby) O'Brien (d 1979); 2 s (Edward Guy b 1974, Alexander Michael b 1978), 3 da (Emily Clare (Mrs Kennedy) b 1968, Lauren Marie b 1970, Jessica Jane b 1973); *Career* Nat Serv Kenya Regt in Kenya, TA; singer/songwriter; first recorded hit Steelmen (1962), first continental hit If I were a Richman, Mexican Whistler (1967), first UK hit Durham Town (1969), I Don't Believe In If Anymore (1970), New World in the Morning (1970), What Love Is (1971), Why (1971), Mammy Blue (1971); first USA hit The Last Farewell (1976), over 11 million copies sold worldwide, earning major acclaim throughout Europe, Canada, Australia, N Zealand and the third world; Skye Boat Song (with Des O' Connor) 1986; TV series incl: Whittaker's World of Music (LWT 1971), Hallelujah It's Christmas (Thames 1975), Roger Whittaker Show (Westward 1977), Sing Out (Ulster 1987); TV specials in Denmark, Germany, Canada, USA, Australia; films incl Roger Whittaker in Kenya (a musical safari) SOS (Stars Orgn for Spastics), Birthright (fund raising aim of Royal Soc of Gynaecologists), Rescue the Rhino; memb: Lord's Taverners, Br Acad of Songwriters and Composers; L'Invite d'Honneur (Juan Les Pins, Antibes) 1971, key to the City of Atlanta 1975; hon citizen: Baltimore 1978, Winnipeg 1978, Houston 1983, Lowell Mass 1985; B'Nai B'Rith Humanitarian Award 1980, Ambassador of Goodwill (Chatanooga) 1983, Seal of the Cwlth of Mass 1985, Gold Badge of Merit Basca 1988; hon fell Univ Coll of N Wales Bangor 1994; MCPS (pres); *Books* So Far So Good; *Recreations* squash, golf, fishing, photography, backgammon, gardening; *Style—* Roger Whittaker, Esq; ✉ agent (☎ 00 1 904 471 3711)

WHITTALL, (Harold) Astley; CBE (1978); s of Harold Whittall, and Margaret Whittall; *b* 8 Sept 1925; *Educ* Handsworth GS, Tech Coll Birmingham; *m* 1952, Diana Margharita Berner; *Career* former chm Amalgamated Power Engrg; former pres Engrg Employers' Fedn; chm: Ransomes plc until 1993, BSG International plc until 1994; trg bd dir APV holdings plc until 1995; dir: Sykes Pickervant Holdings plc until 1994, Bain Hogg Ltd, R Platnauer Ltd; chm Engrg Trg Authy 1990–94; CEng, FIMechE, FIEE, FIMarE, CIMgt; *Recreations* shooting; *Clubs* RAC, IOD; *Style—* Astley Whittall, Esq, CBE

WHITTEMORE, Prof Colin Trengove; s of Hugh Ashcroft Whittemore (d 1983), of Mollington, Chester, and Dorothea, *née* Nance; *b* 16 July 1942; *Educ* Rydal Sch, Harper Adams Agric Coll, Univ of Newcastle upon Tyne (BSc, PhD, DSc, NDA, FIBiol); *m* 24 Sept 1966, Christine, da of John Leslie Featherstone Fenwick (d 1964), of Corbridge, Northumberland; 1 s (Jonathan b 1974), 3 da (Joanna b 1970, Emma b 1976, Rebecca b 1985); *Career* head of Animal Prodn Advsy and Devpt E of Scotland Coll of Agric 1978–84, head of Animal Sci Div Edinburgh Sch of Agric 1984–90, head of Dept of Agric Univ of Edinburgh 1989–90 (lectr in agric 1970–78, prof of animal prodn 1984–90); head Univ of Edinburgh Inst of Ecology and Resource Mgmnt 1990– (prof of agric and rural economy 1990–); Sir John Hammond Prize, RASE Gold medal, Mignini Oscar and David Black award for scientific contribs and res; memb: Community Cncl, BSAS; FRSE; *Books* Practical Pig Nutrition (with F W H Elsley, 1976), Lactation (1980), Pig Production (1980), Pig Science (1987), The Science and Practice of Pig Production (1993); *Recreations* skiing, horses; *Clubs* Farmers'; *Style—* Prof Colin Whittemore, FRSE; ✉ Agriculture Building, University of Edinburgh, West Mains Rd, Edinburgh EH9 3JG (☎ 0131 667 1041, fax 0131 667 2601, telex 727617)

WHITTINGDALE, John Flasby Lawrance; OBE (1990), MP (C) Colchester South and Maldon (majority 21,821); s of John Whittingdale (d 1974), and Margaret Esmé Scott, *née* Napier; *b* 16 Oct 1959; *Educ* Winchester, UCL (BSc); *m* 1990, Ancilla Campbell

Murfitt; 1 s (Henry John Flasby b 26 May 1993), 1 da (Alice Margaret Campbell b 20 Dec 1995); *Career* head of political section Cons Res Dept 1982–84, special advsr to Sec of State for Trade and Indust 1984–87, mangr NM Rothschild 1987, political sec to Rt Hon Margaret Thatcher as PM 1988–90 and mangr of her private office 1990–92, MP Colchester S and Maldon 1992–, sec Cons Parly Home Affairs Ctee 1992–94, memb Parly Health Select Ctee 1993–, former PPS to Eric Forth, MP (Min of State Dept for Educn and Employment) resigned 1996; memb: Selsdon Gp, British Mensa; *Clubs* Essex; *Style—* John Whittingdale, Esq, OBE, MP; ✉ c/o House of Commons, London SW1A 0AA (☎ 0171 219 3577, fax 0171 219 2522)

WHITTINGHAM, Michael (Mike); s of Francis Sadler Whittingham (d 1972), of London, and Jean Mary, *née* Tarlton (d 1989); *b* 11 June 1954; *Educ* Alleyn's Sch Dulwich, Univ of Leicester (BA, MA), Univ of Loughborough (PGCE); *m* Christine Paterson, da of Alexander McMeekin; *Career* athletics coach; memb Herne Hill Harriers; represented: London Schs, English Schs, Surrey Co, Southern Cos, Br Univs, 25 GB caps (400m hurdles, 800m, 4 x 400m); best performances: semi-final Euro Indoor Championships 1981, fourth Cwlth Games 1982; nat sr event coach 400m 1990– (jr event coach 400m hurdles 1987–88); coach and coached: Jon Rigeon, Roger Black, Kriss Akabusi, John Regis, Marcus Adam, Christine McMeekin, Jacqui Parker, Claire Bleasdale, Colin Anderson, Maria Akara; Post Office Counters Coach of the Year 1992; lectr Univ of Lyon France 1978–80, teacher 1980–85, dir of sport and physical educn 1985–88, head of leisure servs Waverley Borough Cncl 1988–92; Direction Sportive (sports mgmnt & devpt co) 1992–; Minister's nominee on Regnl Cncl Sports Cncl 1993–96; Winston Churchill fell 1990; memb: Inst of Leisure Amenity Mgmnt, Int Athletics Club, Nat Tst, UK/S Africa Initiative; *Recreations* languages, piano, reading, arts, natural history, recreational sport; *Style—* Mike Whittingham, Esq; ✉ Rhodens, The Green, Sands, Farnham, Surrey GU10 1LL (☎ 01252 781140, fax 01252 782223); British Athletics Federation, 225A Bristol Road, Edgbaston, Birmingham B16 8NM

WHITTINGTON, Prof Geoffrey; s of Bruce Whittington (d 1988), and Dorothy Gwendoline, *née* Gent; *b* 21 Sept 1938; *Educ* Sir Roger Manwood's GS, Dudley GS, LSE, Fitzwilliam Coll Cambridge; *m* 7 Sept 1963, Joyce Enid, da of George Smith (d 1963); 2 s (Alan Geoffrey b 1972, Richard John b 1976); *Career* res posts Dept of Applied Economics Cambridge 1962–72, fell Fitzwilliam Coll Cambridge 1966–72; prof of accountancy and finance: Univ of Edinburgh 1972–75, Univ of Bristol 1975–88; Univ of Bristol: head of Dept of Economics 1981–84, dean Faculty of Social Sciences 1985–87; Price Waterhouse prof of fin accounting Univ of Cambridge 1988–, fell Fitzwilliam Coll Cambridge 1988–; memb: MMC 1987–, Accounting Standards Bd 1994–; FCA 1973 (ACA 1963); *Books* Growth Profitability and Valuation (with A Singh, 1968), The Prediction of Profitability (1971), Inflation Accounting (1983), The Debate on Inflation Accounting (with D Tweedie, 1984), The Elements of Accounting (1992); *Recreations* music, squash, badminton, walking; *Style—* Prof Geoffrey Whittington; ✉ Faculty of Economics and Politics, Austin Robinson Building, Sidgwick Ave, Cambridge CB1 4RT (☎ 01223 335208, fax 01223 335475)

WHITTINGTON, Prof Graeme; s of Walter Whittington (d 1985), and Ethel Elizabeth Garrett (d 1985); *b* 25 July 1931; *Educ* King Edward VI Sch Guildford, Univ of Reading (BA, PhD); *Career* Ernest Ridley scholar Univ of Reading 1956–59, visiting lectr Univ of Natal 1971, chm Dept of Geography and Geology Univ of St Andrews 1987–92; Univ of St Andrews: lectr 1959–72, sr lectr 1972–80, reader 1980–95, chm Dept of Geography 1985–87 and 1993–96, chm Dept of Geography and Geology 1987–92, prof 1995–96; Leverhulme Emeritus fell 1996; memb Cncl Royal Scottish Geographical Soc 1992–95; FRGS 1963, memb Inst Br Geographers 1963; *Books* Environment and Land Use in Africa (jt ed with M F Thomas, 1969), An Historical Geography of Scotland (jt ed with I D Whyte, 1983), Fragile Environments (ed, 1996); *Recreations* gardening; *Style—* Prof Graeme Whittington; ✉ School of Geography and Geology, The University, St Andrews, Fife KY16 9ST (☎ 01334 463915, fax 01334 463949, e-mail gw@st-andrews.ac.uk)

WHITTINGTON, Dr Richard Michael; s of Dr Theodore Henry Whittington (d 1982), and Cecily Grace, *née* Woodman (d 1973); *b* 9 Sept 1929; *Educ* St Edwards Sch Oxford, Oriel Coll Oxford (MA); *m* 1954, Dorothy Margaret, da of William Fraser Darroch Gardner (d 1977); 1 s (Richard), 1 da (Alison); *Career* HM Coroner Birmingham and Solihull 1976; vice pres Coroner's Soc of England and Wales; former univ physician Aston Univ (Hon DSc); author of numerous papers in med jls on sudden death; Liveryman Worshipful Soc of Apothecaries; memb Br Acad of Forensic Sci, FRSM; *Recreations* contract bridge, country walking; *Style—* Dr Richard Whittington; ✉ Clanrickarde House, 11 Four Oaks Rd, Sutton Coldfield, W Midlands B74 2XP; Coroners Court, Newton St, Birmingham B4 6NE (☎ 0121 235 2930, fax 0121 235 3228)

WHITTLE, Prof Martin John; *b* 6 July 1944; *Educ* William Grimshaw Secdy Mod Sch London, Southgate Tech Coll London, Univ of Manchester Med Sch (MB ChB, MRCOG, MD); *m* 12 July 1969, Lindsay Hall, da of late Sydney Jones; 1 s (Nicolas John b 29 July 1972); *Career* house physician then house surgn Manchester Royal Infirmary 1972–73; SHO in obstetrics and gynaecology: Musgrove Park Hosp Taunton 1973–74, St Mary's Hosp Manchester 1974–75; clinical tutor Univ Hosp of S Manchester 1976–77 (SHO in obstetrics and gynaecology 1975–76), registrar in obstetrics and gynaecology Queen Mother's Hosp/Western Infirmary Glasgow 1977–78, research fell LAC-USC Med Center Women's Hosp Los Angeles Calif 1978–79, lectr in obstetrics and gynaecology and hon sr registrar Queen Mother's/Western Infirmary Glasgow 1979–82, conslt obstetrician Queen Mother's Hosp Glasgow and conslt gynaecologist Royal Samaritan Hosp for Women Glasgow 1982–, dir of fetal med Univ Dept of Midwifery Queen Mother's Hosp Glasgow 1986–91, prof of fetal med Birmingham Women's Hosp Univ of Birmingham 1991– (dir RCOG Fetal Med Prog 1992–); memb: Scientific Advsy and Pathology Ctee RCOG 1983–86, Working Gp on Infertility Servs in Scotland 1989–90, MRC Working Pty on Phenylketonuria 1991–92, Subspecialist Bd RCOG 1989–92 (chm Regnl Obstetric Ultrasound Gp W Midlands 1991), Birthright/RCOG Research Ctee 1991, RCOG Working Pty on Down's Screening 1992; chm Standing Jt Ctee RCOG and RCR 1993– (memb 1987–90, vice chm 1990–93); memb Editorial Bd: Prenatal Diagnosis 1990–, Current Obstetrics and Gynaecology 1990–, Archives of Disease in Childhood 1991–, Br Jl of Midwifery 1993–, Br Jl of Obstetrics and Gynaecology 1994–; regular reviewer: Br Jl of Obstetrics and Gynaecology, American Jl of Obstetrics and Gynaecology, Ultrasound in Obstetrics and Gynaecology, Lancet, BMJ; examiner RCOG, external examiner Med Sch Univs of Nottingham, Sheffield and Aberdeen and Royal Coll of Surgns Dublin; memb: Blair Bell Research Soc, Glasgow Obstetrical and Gynaecological Soc, Perinatal Club, Soc for Perinatal Obstetricians USA, Int Fetoscopy Working Gp, Gynaecological Visiting Soc; FRCPGlas 1987 (MRCPGlas 1985), FRCOG 1988; *Books* Prenatal Diagnosis in Obstetric Practice (with Prof J M Connor, 1989, 2 edn 1995); *Publications* author of various book chapters and numerous articles; *Recreations* flying (PPL), keen yachtsman, enjoying classical music and art; *Style—* Prof Martin Whittle; ✉ Department of Fetal Medicine, Birmingham Women's Hospital, Edgbaston B15 2TT (☎ 0121 627 2775, fax 0121 415 4837)

WHITTLE, Prof Peter; s of Percy Whittle (d 1970), and Elsie, *née* Tregurtha (d 1993); *b* 27 Feb 1927; *Educ* Wellington Boys' Coll NZ, Univ of NZ (BSc, MSc), Uppsala Univ Sweden (PhD); *m* 20 May 1951, Kathe Hildegard, da of Viktor Blomquist, of Raisio, Finland; 3 s (Martin b 1952, Miles b 1955, Gregory b 1961), 3 da (Lorna b 1954, Jennifer b 1962, Elsie b 1968); *Career* Docent Uppsala Univ 1951–53, NZ DSIR 1953–59 (rising to sr princ scientific offr), lectr Univ of Cambridge 1959–61, prof of mathematical statistics Univ of Manchester 1961–67, Churchill prof of mathematics of operational res Univ of Cambridge 1967–94, prof emeritus Univ of Cambridge 1994–; Hon DSc Victoria Univ NZ 1987; memb Royal Soc NZ, FRS 1978; *Books* Hypothesis Testing in Time Series Analysis (1951), Prediction and Regulation (1963), Probability (1970), Optimisation under Constraints (1971), Optimisation over Time (vol 1 1982, vol 2 1983) Systems in Stochastic Equilibrium (1986), Risk-Sensitive Optimal Control (1990), Probability via Expectation (1992), Optimal Control: basics and beyond (1995); *Style—* Prof Peter Whittle, FRS; ✉ 268 Queen Edith's Way, Cambridge CB1 4NL (☎ 01223 245422); Statistical Laboratory, 16 Mill Lane, Cambridge CB2 1SB (☎ 01223 337965, fax 01223 337956)

WHITTLE, Stephen Charles; s of Charles William Whittle, and Vera Lillian, *née* Moss; *b* 26 July 1945; *Educ* St Ignatius Coll Stamford Hill, UCL (LLB); *m* 1988, Claire Walmsley, *qv*, *née* Slavin; *Career* asst ed New Christian 1968–70; World Cncl of Churches Geneva: communications offr 1970–73, ed One World 1973–77, asst head Communications Dept 1975–77; BBC: sr prodr Religious Progs Manchester 1977–82, prodr Newsnight 1982, ed Songs of Praise and Worship 1983–89, head of religious programmes 1989–93, chief advsr on editorial policy 1993–96; dir Broadcasting Standards Cncl April 1996–; Freeman City of London 1990; *Books* Tickling Mrs Smith (1970); *Recreations* cinema, theatre, music, reading, exercise; *Style—* Stephen Whittle, Esq; ✉ The Broadcasting Standards Council, 5–8 The Sanctuary, London SW1P 3JS (☎ 0171 233 0544, fax 0171 233 0397)

WHITTLESEA, Michael Charles; s of Sydney Charles Whittlesea (d 1982), of London, and Rose, *née* Grimshaw; *b* 6 June 1938; *Educ* Harrow Sch of Art (Nat Dip Design); *m* 1 June 1963, Jill Diana, da of Leslie Gilbert Henry Morris; *Career* artist; exhibitions incl: World of Newspapers Exhibition (prize winner, Sothebys and Royal Acad), Royal Acad Summer Exhibition 1985–88, The Singer and Friedlander Sunday Times Watercolour Exhibition 1987–95 (prize winner 1991), Drawing Matters (Bankside Gallery) 1995; work in public collections incl Bury Art Gallery & Museum; RWS, NEAC; *Awards* Painter Stainers Award 1985, selected Hunting Gp Awards 1985; *Books* The Complete Water Colour Course, The Complete Step by Step Watercolour Course; *Clubs* Chelsea Arts; *Style—* Michael Whittlesea, Esq; ✉ Richmond Cottage, High Street, Hurley, Berks SL6 5LT (☎ 01628 824393)

WHITTY, Baron (Life Peer UK 1996), of Camberwell in the London Borough of Southwark; (John) Lawrence Whitty; s of Frederick James Whitty (d 1981), and Kathleen May Whitty (d 1967); *b* 15 June 1943; *m* 1, 11 Jan 1969 (m dis 1986), Tanya Margaret, da of Tom Gibson; 2 s (Hon Michael Sean b 1970, Hon Daniel James b 1972); m 2, 1 June 1993, Angela, da of James Forrester; *Career* Hawker Siddeley 1962; Civil Serv 1965–70, Miny of Aviation, UKAEA, Miny of Technol; Economics Dept TUC 1970–73, nat res and political offr GMBATU (formerly Gen and Municipal Workers Union) 1973–85, Euro sec Lab Pty 1994– (gen sec 1985–94); memb: Lab Pty (Islington, Greenwich, Dulwich, Battersea, Peckham, Westminster South), Fabian Soc; cr a life peer 1996; *Recreations* swimming, walking, theatre; *Style—* The Rt Hon Lord Whitty; ✉ 33 Gilbert House (☎ 0171 834 6890)

WHITWORTH, John Vincer; s of Hugh Hope Aston Whitworth, MBE (d 1996), of Strawberry Hill, Middlesex, and Elizabeth, *née* Boyes (d 1959); *b* 11 Dec 1945; *Educ* Royal HS Edinburgh, Merton Coll Oxford (MA, BPhil), Univ of Edinburgh; *m* 2 Aug 1975, Doreen Ann, da of Cecil Roberts; 2 da (Eleanor Ruth b 1 Jan 1984, Catherine Rebecca b 20 March 1987); *Career* poet; teacher of: English Colchester English Studies Centre 1970–71, business studies and economics Centre of Economic and Political Studies 1971–82 (exec dir until 1982); reviewer Poetry Review and The Spectator, poetry bdcast on BBC TV 1994 and 1995; *Awards* Alice Hunt Bartlett Award of the Poetry Society 1980, South East Arts Award 1980, Observer Book of the Year (for Poor Butterflies) 1982, Barbara Campion Memorial Prize 1983, prizewinner National Poetry Competition 1984, Cholmondeley Award for Poetry 1988; *Books* Unhistorical Fragments (1980), Poor Butterflies (1982), Lovely Day for a Wedding (1985), Tennis and Sex and Death (1989), The Faber Book of Blue Verse (ed, 1990), Landscape With Small Humans (1993), The Complete Poetical Works of Phoebe Flood (1996); *Recreations* cooking, playing with my daughters, suffering with the England cricket team, rearing guinea-pigs; *Style—* John Whitworth, Esq; ✉ 20 Lovell Road, Rough Common, Canterbury, Kent CT2 9DG (☎ 01227 462400)

WHITWORTH, Maj-Gen Reginald Henry (Rex); CB (1969), CBE (1963); s of Aymer William Whitworth (d 1976), and Alice Lucy Patience, *née* Hervey (d 1973, gda of Lord Arthur Hervey (d 1894), Bishop of Bath and Wells and s of 1 Marquess of Bristol); *b* 27 Aug 1916; *Educ* Eton, Balliol Coll and Queen's Coll Oxford; *m* 1946, June Rachel (d 1994), da of Col Sir Bartle Mordaunt Edwards, CVO, MC, JP, DL (d 1977), of Hardingham Hall, Norfolk; 2 s (and 1 decd), 1 da; *Career* Grenadier Gds 1940, Bde Maj 24 Gds Bde 1945–46; Cdr: 1 Grenadier Gds 1956–57, Berlin Inf Bde Gp 1961–63, GOC Yorks and Northumberland Dists 1966–68, COS Southern Cmd 1968–70; fell and bursar Exeter Coll Oxford 1970–81; former chm St Mary's Sch Wantage; Historic Churches Preservation Tst; USA Bronze Star 1946; *Books* Field Marshal Earl Ligonier, Famous Regiments: The Grenadier Guards, Gunner at Large, William Augustus - Duke of Cumberland (1992); *Recreations* fishing, military history; *Clubs* Army and Navy; *Style—* Maj-Gen Rex Whitworth, CB, CBE; ✉ Abbey House Farm, Goosey, nr Faringdon, Oxon SN7 8PA (☎ 01367 710252)

WHORWELL, Dr Peter James; s of Arthur Victor Whorwell, of Canterbury, and Beryl Elizabeth, *née* Walton; *b* 14 June 1946; *Educ* Dover Coll, Univ of London (BSc, MB BS, MRCS, FRCP, MD); *Career* conslt physician and sr lectr in med Univ of Manchester 1981–; dir S Manchester Functional Gastrointestinal Diseases Serv, med advsr Int Fndn for Functional Gastrointestinal Disorders, memb Euro Expert Panel for Functional Gastrointestinal Disorders, med conslt to many pharmaceutical cos; numerous pubns on gastrointestinal diseases; memb: Br Soc Gastroenterology, American Gastroenterology Assoc; *Style—* Dr Peter Whorwell; ✉ Department of Medicine, University Hospital of South Manchester, Manchester M20 8LR (☎ 0161 291 3826); home (☎ 0161 291 3826)

WHYBREW, Edward Graham (Ted); s of Ernest Whybrew (d 1968), and Winifred Maud, *née* Castle (d 1968); *b* 25 Sept 1938; *Educ* Hertford GS, Balliol Coll Oxford (BA, soccer and cricket first elevens), Nuffield Coll Oxford (studentship); *m* 9 Sept 1967, Julia Helen, da of Michael Baird (d 1969); 1 s (Adam b 1970), 2 da (Katherine b 1973, Anna b 1975); *Career* econ advsr: NEDO 1963–64, Dept of Econ Affrs 1964–69; Dept of Employment: econ advsr 1969–73, sr advsr 1973–77, asst sec youth and employment policy 1977–81, asst sec industl rels 1981–85, under sec industl rels, pay and equal opportunities 1985–89, under sec Dir of Personnel 1989–92; Certification Offr Trade Unions and Employers' Assocs 1992–; assoc ptnr Jamieson/Scott exec search 1993–, ptnr Museum Replicas 1996–; treas Triangle Adventure Playground Assoc 1973–; *Recreations* horseriding, gardening, cricket; *Style—* E G Whybrew, Esq; ✉ Certification Office, 180 Borough High Street, London SE1 1LW (☎ 0171 210 3730)

WHYBROW, Christopher John; QC (1992); s of Herbert William Whybrow, OBE (d 1973), of Colchester, Essex, and Ruby Kathleen, *née* Watson; *b* 7 Aug 1942; *Educ* Colchester Royal GS, King's Coll London (LLB); *m* 1, 11 Sep 1969 (m dis 1976), Marian, da of John Macaulay, of Ramsey, Essex; m 2, 4 April 1979 (m dis 1990), Susan, da of Edward Christie Younge, of Loddiswell, Devon; *Career* called to the Bar Inner Temple

1965; dep social security cmmr 1996–; *Recreations* cricket, tennis, gardening, country life; *Clubs* MCC, Lansdowne; *Style*— Christopher Whybrow, Esq, QC; ✉ 1 Serjeants Inn, London EC4Y 1NH

WHYTE, Donald; JP (City of Edinburgh); s of late John Whyte, of Almondhill, Kirkliston, and late Catherine Dunachie; *b* 26 March 1926; *Educ* Crookston Sch Musselburgh, Inst of Heraldic and Genealogical Studies Canterbury; *m* 1950, Mary, da of George Laird Burton; 3 da; *Career* conslt genealogist, author, lectr; contrib to numerous academic jls; pres Assoc of Scot Genealogists and Record Agents 1981–; vice pres: Scot Genealogy Soc 1983–, family history socs at Glasgow, Aberdeen and Dundee; granted armorial bearings Lyon Office 1986; Citation of Recognition, Ontario Genealogical Soc 1987; FSG, FHG; *Books* Kirkliston: A Parish History (latest edn, 1991), Dictionary of Scottish Emigrants to the USA pre-1855 (1972, reprinted 1981, vol 2 1986), Introducing Genealogical Research (5 edn 1985), Dictionary of Scottish Emigrants to Canada Before Confederation (1986, Vol 2 1995), Walter MacFarlane: Clan Chief and Antiquary (1988), The Scots Overseas: A Selected Bibliography (1995), Scottish Clock and Watch Makers, 1453–1900 (1996); *Recreations* motoring, heraldry, black and white photography; *Style*— Donald Whyte, Esq, JP; ✉ 4 Carmel Rd, Kirkliston, West Lothian EH29 9DD (☎ 0131 333 3245)

WHYTE, John Stuart; CBE (1976); s of William Walter Whyte (d 1951), and Ethel Kate, *née* Budd (d 1983); *b* 20 July 1923; *Educ* The John Lyon Sch Harrow, Northampton Engrg Coll, Univ of London (BSc Eng, MSc Eng); *m* 10 March 1953, (Edna) Joan Mary (d 1995), da of Frank Stark Budd (d 1942); 1 s (Peter b 1954), 1 da (Anne (Mrs McCulloch) b 1959); *Career* HM Treasy 1965–68, Post Office Telecommunications 1968–79, dep md British Telecom 1979–81, md and engr-in-chief British Telecom 1981–83, chm Plessey Telecommunications International 1983–88, pres Stromberg Carlson Corporation (USA) 1984–85; chm: Astronet Corporation 1984–86, GEC/Plessey Telecommunications International 1988–89; vice pres Royal Inst 1972–74, dep chm Nat Electronics Cncl 1976–, pres Inst of Br Telecommunications Engrs 1977–83 (hon memb 1983), govr Int Cncl for Computer Communications 1982–91, pres Assoc of Br Membs of Swiss Alpine Club 1988–90; Freeman City London 1979, Liveryman Worshipful Co of Scientific Instrument Makers 1979; CEng 1951, FIEE 1966 (vice pres 1981–84), FEng 1982, CIMgt 1982; *Recreations* mountaineering, opera, genealogy; *Clubs* Alpine, Cambridge Alpine; *Style*— John Whyte, Esq, CBE, FEng; ✉ Wild Hatch, Coleshill Lane, Amersham, Bucks HP7 0NT (☎ 01494 722663)

WIBLIN, Derek John; CB (1992); s of late Cyril G H Wiblin, and Winifred, *née* Sandford; *b* 18 March 1933; *Educ* Bishopshalt Sch Hillingdon, Univ of Birmingham (BSc); *m* 1960, Pamela Jeanne Hamshere; 1 s, 1 da; *Career* served RAF 1954–57; Courtaulds Ltd 1957–58, DSIR Building Res Station 1958–67, Civil Serv Cmmn 1967–71, DOE 1971–79, Ports Div Dept of Tport 1979–81, Estabs Div DOE 1981–83; under sec, princ estab and fin offr: Lord Chllr's Dept 1984–88, Crown Prosecution Serv 1988–93; *Recreations* making violins; *Clubs* Athenaeum, RAF; *Style*— Derek Wiblin, Esq, CB; ✉ 19 Woodwaye, Oxhey, Watford, Herts WD1 4NN (☎ 01923 228615)

WICKENS, Prof Alan Herbert; OBE (1980); s of Leslie Herbert Wickens (d 1986), of Birmingham, and Sylvia Amelia, *née* Hazelgrove (d 1968); *b* 29 March 1929; *Educ* Ashville Coll Harrogate, Loughborough Univ of Technol (DLC, DSc), Univ of London (BSc); *m* 1, 12 Dec 1953, Eleanor Joyce Waggott (d 1984); 1 da (Valerie Joanne b 1958); m 2, 2 July 1987, Patricia Anne McNeil, da of Willoughby Gervaise Cooper, of Dawlish; *Career* res engr: Sir W G Armstrong Whitworth Aircraft Ltd 1951–55, Canadair Ltd Montreal 1955–59, A V Roe & Co Ltd 1959–62; BR: Res Dept 1962–68, dir of advanced projects 1968–71, dir of res 1971–84, dir of engrg devpt and res 1984–89; Dept of Mechanical Engrg Loughborough Univ of Technol: industl prof 1972–76 and 1992–, prof of dynamics 1989–92; writer of various pubns on dynamics of railway vehicles, high speed trains and railway technol; jt winner Macrobert award 1975; pres Int Assoc of Vehicle System Dynamics 1981–86, hon fell Derbyshire Coll of Higher Educn 1984, chm Office of Research and Experiment Union Internationale de Chemin de Fer Utrecht 1988–90; Hon DTech CNAA 1978, Hon Doctorate Open Univ 1980; MAIAA 1958, MRAeS 1963, FIMechE 1971, FEng 1980; *Recreations* gardening, travel, music; *Clubs* RAF; *Style*— Prof Alan Wickens, OBE, FEng; ✉ Department of Mechanical Engineering, University of Technology, Loughborough LE11 3TU (☎ 01509 223201, fax 01509 232029)

WICKERSON, Sir John Michael; kt (1987); s of Walter Wickerson, of London, and Ruth Ivy Constance Field; *b* 22 Sept 1937; *Educ* Christ's Hosp, Univ of London (LLB); *m* 1963, Shirley Maud, da of Andrew Best (d 1980); 1 s (Andrew John b 1968); *Career* admitted slr 1960, managing ptnr Ormerod Wilkinson Marshall Slrs; pres: London Criminal Cts Slrs Assoc 1981–83, Law Soc of England and Wales 1986–87; chm: R Mansell Ltd, Investors Compensation Scheme Ltd, Croydon Community NHS Tst; memb Royal Cmmn on Criminal Justice 1991–93; hon memb: American Bar Assoc, Canadian Bar Assoc, NZ Law Soc; *Books* Motorist and the Law; *Recreations* sport, music; *Style*— Sir John Wickerson; ✉ 40 Homefield Road, Warlingham, Surrey (☎ 01883 622126)

WICKHAM, (William) Jeffry Alexander; RD (1974); s of Lt-Col Edward Thomas Ruscombe Wickham, MVO (d 1957), and Rachel Marguerite, *née* Alexander (d 1955); *b* 5 Aug 1933; *Educ* Eton, Balliol Coll Oxford (BA, MA), LAMDA; *m* April 1962, Clare Marion, da of A R M Stewart (d 1958), of Fearnan; 2 s (Caspar (Fred) b 1962, Rupert b 1964), 1 da (Saskia b 1967); *Career* actor; Nat Serv RN 1952–54, Russian interpreter 1954; cncllr Br Actors' Equity Assoc (vice pres 1986–92, pres 1992–94), memb Cncl Actors' Benevolent Fund; Liveryman Worshipful Co of Skinners 1956; *Theatre* West End appearances incl: Othello (Old Vic) 1963, Catch My Soul (The Rock Othello) (Prince of Wales) 1970, The Unknown Soldier and his Wife (New London) 1973, The Marrying of Ann Leete (Aldwych) 1975, Donkeys' Years (Globe) 1976, The Family Reunion (Vaudeville) 1979, Anyone for Denis? (Whitehall) 1981, Amadeus (Her Majesty's) 1982, Interpreters (Queen's) 1985, Beyond Reasonable Doubt (Queen's) 1987, Exclusive (Strand) 1989, The Revengers' Comedies (Strand) 1991, An Ideal Husband (Globe) 1993, The Woman in Black (Fortune) 1994; Nat Theatre 1983–85, 1986–87 and 1993–94 incl: Saint Joan, The Spanish Tragedy, A Little Hotel on the Side, The Magistrate, The Madness of George III; RSC 1996–97 incl: Much Ado About Nothing, Camino Real; *Television* incl: Trainer, Clarissa, Mother Love, The Old Boy Network, Yes Prime Minister, Hotel du Lac, Diana, Strangers and Brothers, Edward VII, An Age of Kings; *Films* incl: The Remains of the Day, Clockwise, Another Country, Ransom, Waterloo; *Recreations* walking, languages; *Style*— Jeffry Wickham, Esq; ✉ c/o Markham & Froggatt Ltd, 4 Windmill St, London W1 (☎ 0171 636 4412)

WICKHAM, John Ewart Alfred; s of Alfred James Wickham (d 1931), of Chichester, Sussex, and Hilda May, *née* Cummins (d 1977); *b* 10 Dec 1927; *Educ* Chichester GS, Univ of London St Bartholomew's Med Coll (BSc, MB BS, MS); *m* 28 July 1961, (Gwendoline) Ann, da of James Henry Loney (d 1975); 3 da (Susan Jane b 31 May 1962, Caroline Elizabeth b 28 July 1963, (Ann) Clare b 4 July 1966); *Career* Nat Serv RAF 1947–49; sr conslt urological surgn St Barts Hosp London 1966–85, surgn St Peters Hosp London 1967–93, sr lectr Inst of Urology London 1967–, surgn King Edward VIII Hosp for Offrs London 1973, surgn urologist RAF 1973–, sr res fell and conslt surgn Guy's and St Thomas's Hosp 1993–; dir: Academic Unit Inst of Urology Univ of London 1979–93, London Clinic Lithotripter Unit 1987–, N E Thames Regnl Lithotripter Unit 1987–93; pres RSM Urological Section 1984, first pres Int Soc of Endo-Urology 1983, first pres Int Soc of Minimal Invasive Surgery 1989; dir: Rencal Ltd, London Lithotripter Co Ltd, Atraumatic Ltd; Freeman City of London 1971, Liveryman Worshipful Co of Barber Surgns 1971; Hunterian prof and medal RCS 1970, James Berry prize and medal for contribs to renal surgery RCS 1982, Cutlers prize and medal Assoc Surgns GB for surgical instrument design 1985, St Peters Medal Br Assoc of Urological Surgns 1985, Cecil Joll prize RCS 1993, John Latymer medal American Urological Assoc, Rovsing medal Danish Surgical Soc; Hon MD Univ of Gothenburg 1994; FRCS 1959, FRSM, FRCP, FRCR; Fulbright scholar of USA 1964; *Books* Urinary Calculous Disease (1979), Percutaneous Renal Surgery (1983), Intra-Renal Surgery (1984), Lithotripsy II (1987), Renal Tract Stone Metabolic Basis and Clinical Practice (1989), Minimal Invasive Therapy (ed, 1991); *Recreations* mechanical engineering, tennis; *Clubs* Athenaeum, RAC; *Style*— John Wickham, Esq; ✉ Stowe Maries, Balchins Lane, Westcott, Surrey RH4 3LR (☎ 01306 885557); 29 Devonshire Place, London W1N 1PE (☎ 0171 935 2232, fax 0171 224 0684)

WICKHAM, John Francis; *b* 17 Sept 1934; *Educ* Bedales, S Berks Coll of Further Educn (ONC), LCC Central Sch of Arts and Crafts (Dip in Design, NDD); *Career* apprentice engr Chilton Electric Products 1952–55, asst designer Robert Welch Associates 1960–63, estab freelance consultancy 1963–, formed Bell Wickham Associates (with Peter Bell now ret) 1972, ptnr Webster Wickham 1992–; RSA bursary (used for travel throughout Europe) 1958; Design Cncl awards: Ilford photographic dryer 1975, LKB Biochrom Ultraspec spectrophotometer 1984, Oxford Medical EEG monitor 1985; Br design award: Nautech Autohelm Seatalk instrument range 1990, Nautech Autohelm Wheel Pilot 1990, NautechAutohelm Sea Talk Autopilot 1992, Oxford Sonicaid TEAM Foetal Monitor 1993; Minerva Award 1993; FCSD; *Style*— John Wickham, Esq; ✉ Pittams Farm, Wappenham, Towcester, Northamptonshire NN12 8SP (☎ 01307 860 236, fax 01327 860 990)

WICKHAM, His Hon Judge; William Rayley; s of Rayley Esmond Wickham (d 1970), and Mary Joyce, *née* Thom (d 1965); *b* 22 Sept 1926; *Educ* Sedbergh, Brasenose Coll Oxford (MA, BCL); *m* 11 May 1957, Elizabeth Mary, da of John Harrison Thompson (d 1957); 1 s (Christopher b 1961), 2 da (Katharine b 1958, Sarah b 1959); *Career* Army 1944–47 Lt; called to the Bar Inner Temple 1951; chief magistrate Aden 1957 (magistrate 1953), crown counsel Tanganyika 1959, asst to law offrs Tanganyika 1961–63, recorder 1972–75, circuit judge 1975–, sr circuit judge in Liverpool 1992, hon recorder of Liverpool 1992; *Style*— His Hon Judge Wickham; ✉ 115 Vyner Rd South, Bidston, Birkenhead, Merseyside (☎ 0151 652 2095); Queen Elizabeth II Law Courts, Liverpool

WICKRAMASINGHE, Prof (Nalin) Chandra; s of Percival Herbert Wickramasinghe, of Sri Lanka, and Theresa Elizabeth, *née* Soysa; *b* 20 Jan 1939; *Educ* Royal Coll Colombo, Univ of Ceylon, (BSc), Univ of Cambridge (MA, PhD, ScD); *m* 5 April 1966, (Nelum) Priyadarshini, da of Cecil Eustace Pereira; 1 s (Anil Nissanka b 1970), 2 da (Kamala Chandrika b 1972, Janaki Tara b 1981); *Career* fell Jesus Coll Cambridge 1963–73, prof and head Dept of Applied Mathematics and Astronomy Univ Coll Cardiff 1973–88, dir Inst of Fundamental Studies and advsr to Pres of Sri Lanka 1982–84; prof of applied maths and astronomy Univ of Wales 1988–; visiting prof of physics Univ of W Indies Mona Kingston 1994; co-author with Prof Sir Fred Hoyle of a series of books of cosmic theory of life 1978–88; Powell Prize for English Verse Trinity Coll Cambridge 1962, Int Dag Hammarskjöld Gold Medal for Science 1986, Scholarly Achievement Award Inst of Oriental Philosophy Japan 1988, conferred title of Vidya Jyothi (Sri Lankan Nat Honour) 1992, Soka Gakkai Int Peace and Culture Award 1993, Int Sahabdeen Award for Sci 1996; *Books* Interstellar Grains (1967), Light Scattering Functions (1973), Lifecloud (with F Hoyle, 1978), Diseases from Space (1979), Evolution from Space (1981), Space Travellers (1981), Living Comets (1985), From Grains to Bacteria (1984), Archaeopteryx (1986), Cosmic Life Force (1988), The Theory of Cosmic Grains (1991), Our Place in the Cosmos (1992), Mysteries of the Universe and Life (with D Ikeda, 1994), Glimpses of Life, Time and Space (1994); *Recreations* photography, poetry, history of science; *Clubs* Icosahedron Dining (Cardiff); *Style*— Prof Chandra Wickramasinghe; ✉ 24 Llwynypia Rd, Lisvane, Cardiff CF4 5SY (☎ 01222 752146, fax 01222 753173); School of Mathematics, University of Wales Cardiff, Senghennydd Rd, Cardiff CF2 4AG (☎ 01222 874811, fax 01222 371921, telex 498635, e-mail smancw@thor.cf.ac.uk)

WICKREMESINGHE, HE Sarath Kusum; s of Martin Wickremesinghe (d 1976), and Prema, *née* de Silva; *b* 26 Jan 1928; *Educ* St Thomas' Coll Colombo Sri Lanka, Univ of Ceylon (BSc); *m* 12 Oct 1953, Damayantha, da of Herbert Alexander Jayatillaka Hulugalle (former Sri Lankan ambass to Italy); *Career* Sri Lankan diplomat; exec ICI (Export) Ltd Colombo 1951; Chemical Industries (Colombo) Ltd (assoc co of ICI): dir 1964, chm and chief exec 1966; subsequently chm subsid/assoc cos in Sri Lanka of: British American Tobacco, Eagle Star Insurance, Standard Chartered Bank; concurrently chm/dir over 20 local cos; variously: memb Securities and Exchange Cmmn of Sri Lanka, memb Nat Educn Cmmn, memb Bd of Mgmnt Sri Lanka Inst of Devpt Admin, tstee and memb Cncl Employers' Fedn of Ceylon, memb Bd of Mgmnt Postgraduate Inst of Mgmnt Univ of Sri Jayawardenapura, memb Bd of Mgmnt Univ of Colombo Devpt Fund; Sri Lankan ambass to the Ct of St James's 1995–; *Clubs* Royal Over-Seas League, Royal Colombo Golf; *Style*— HE Mr S K Wickremesinghe; ✉ Sri Lanka High Commission, 13 Hyde Park Gardens, London W2 2LU (☎ 0171 262 1841, fax 0171 262 7970)

WICKS, Anne; da of Alfred George Miles, of Halstead, nr Sevenoaks, Kent, and Jessie Katherine, *née* Lidbury; *b* 23 Oct 1938; *Educ* Bromley GS, Bedford Coll London (BSc); *m* 29 Nov 1957, Anthony John Wicks (d 1965), s of Bernard John Wicks; 1 s (James b 1 July 1977), 2 da (Kate b 27 Aug 1969, Lucinda b 1981); *Career* graduate trainee Research Services Ltd 1961–62; The Thomson Organisation: res exec mangr 1962–71, dir of food and drink res 1971–72; res exec dir McCann Erickson Advertising Ltd 1972–82, planning dir Grandfield Rork Collins 1982–86, strategic planning dir DMB&B Ltd 1986–; memb: Market Res Soc 1965, Marketing Gp of GB, Women's Advtg Club of London (pres 1983–84); MIPA; *Recreations* family, gardening; *Style*— Mrs Anne Wicks; ✉ D'Arcy Masius Benton & Bowles, 123 Buckingham Palace Road, London SW1W 9DZ (☎ 0171 630 0000, fax 0171 630 0033)

WICKS, Brian Cairns; TD; s of Henry Gillies Wicks (d 1970), of Eastbourne, and Ethel (d 1968); *b* 26 March 1934; *Educ* Sedbergh, Univ of Cambridge (BA); *m* 31 March 1959, Judith Anne, da of Kennedy Harrison (d 1961); 1 s (Robert b 1965), 1 da (Pippa b 1962); *Career* Maj 4/5 Btn Green Howards (TA), A/G AVT 1 W African Field Battery Nigeria 1952–54; div sec ICI plc Paints Div 1975–86, dep dir gen Nat Farmers Union 1986–95; dir: Fatstock Marketing Co 1985–95, NFUM Finance Leasing Co Ltd 1988–95; pres S Bucks and E Berks C of C and Indust 1981–83, chm Berks Business Gp 1983–87, memb Deregulation Panel of the Enterprise & Deregulation Unit DTI 1989–91; Freeman City of London, Liveryman Worshipful Co of Glovers 1988; *Recreations* fishing, shooting, gardening; *Style*— Brian C Wicks, Esq; ✉ Gracefield Main Road, Lacey Green, Nr Princes Risborough, Bucks HP27 0QU

WICKS, Caroline Philippa (Pippa); da of Brian Cairns Wicks, of Bucks, and Judith Anne Wicks; *b* 18 Dec 1962; *Educ* Lady Verney HS High Wycombe, Haileybury Coll, St Hugh's Coll Oxford (open scholar, Irene Shringley Zoology scholar, MA, Univ Hockey First XI), London Business Sch (Dip Corp Fin); *m* 4 July 1987, Michael Charles Wright, s of Arthur Wright; *Career* Bain & Co mgmnt conslts: assoc conslt 1984–86, conslt in trg 1986–87, conslt 1987–90, mangr 1990–91; Courtaulds Textiles plc: business devpt mangr 1991–93, fin dir 1993–; *Recreations* hockey, squash, tennis, skiing, wine, theatre, travel, antiques; *Style*— Mrs Pippa Wicks; ✉ Courtaulds Textiles plc, 13–14 Margaret Street, London W1A 3DA (☎ 0171 331 4500)

WICKS, Malcolm; MP (Lab) Croydon North West (majority 1,527); s of Arthur Wicks, and Daisy Wicks; *b* 1 July 1947; *Educ* Elizabeth Coll Guernsey, NW London Poly, LSE (BSc); *m* 7 Sept 1968, Margaret, *née* Baron; 1 s, 2 da; *Career* fell Dept of Social Admin Univ of York 1968–70, res worker Centre for Environmental Studies 1970–72, lectr in social admin Dept of Govt Studies Brunel Univ 1970–74, social policy analyst Urban Deprivation Unit Home Office 1974–77, lectr in social policy Civil Service Coll 1977–78, res dir and sec Study Cmmn on the Family 1978–83, dir Family Policy Studies Centre 1983–92, co-dir Euro Family and Social Policy Unit 1992; MP (Lab) Croydon NW 1992–; shadow social security min 1995–; memb Select Ctee on Social Security 1994–95; chm Winter Action on Cold Homes 1986–92, sec PLP Social Security Ctee 1994–95, sponsor Carers (Recognition and Services) Act 1995; memb Euro Inst of Social Security; tstee Nat Energy Fndn 1988–94; *Publications* Old and Cold - Hypothermia and Social Policy (1978), Government and Urban Poverty (jtly, 1983), A Future for All - Do We Need a Welfare State? (1987), Family Change and Future Policy (jtly, 1990), A New Agenda (jtly, 1993), The Active Society: defending welfare (1994); *Recreations* music, walking, gardening, white water rafting; *Clubs* Ruskin House Labour (Croydon); *Style*— Malcolm Wicks, MP; ✉ House of Commons, London SW1A 0AA

WIDDECOMBE, Rt Hon Ann Noreen; PC (1997), MP (C) Maidstone (majority 16,286); da of James Murray Widdecombe, CB, OBE, and Rita Noreen Widdecombe; *b* 4 Oct 1947; *Educ* La Sainte Union Convent Bath, Univ of Birmingham, LMH Oxford (MA); *Career* sr admin Univ of London 1975–87; Runnymede dist cncllr 1976–78, fndr and vice chm Women and Families for Def 1983–85; Parly candidate (C): Burnley 1979, Plymouth Devonport 1983; MP (C) Maidstone 1987–; Parly under-sec: for social security 1990–93, for employment 1993–94; min of state Dept of Employment 1994–95, min of state Home Office 1995–; *Books* Layman's Guide to Defence (1984); *Recreations* reading; *Style*— The Rt Hon Ann Widdecombe, MP; ✉ 9 Tamar House, Kennington Lane, London SE11 4XA (☎ 0171 735 5192); House of Commons, London SW1A 0AA (☎ 0171 219 5091)

WIDDOWSON, Prof Henry George; s of George Percival Widdowson (d 1986), of East Runton, Norfolk, and Edna May, *née* Garrison (d 1980); *b* 28 May 1935; *Educ* Alderman Newton's Sch Leicester, King's Coll Cambridge (MA), Univ of Edinburgh (PhD); *m* 15 July 1966, Dominique Nicole Helene, da of Jean Dixmier, of Paris; 2 s (Marc Alain b 24 May 1968, Arnold b 18 Oct 1972); *Career* Nat Serv RN 1956; English language offr Br Cncl Sri Lanka and Bangladesh 1962–68, lectr Dept of Linguistics Univ of Edinburgh 1968–77, currently prof of educn Inst of Educn Univ of London and prof of applied linguistics Univ of Essex, chm Advsy Ctee Br Cncl English Teaching 1982–91, fndr ed Applied Linguistics, memb Kingman Ctee on the Teaching of English Language; Hon Doctorate Univ of Oulu; *Books* Stylistics and the Teaching of Literature (1975), Teaching Language as Communication (1978), Explorations in Applied Linguistics (vol I 1979, vol II 1984), Learning Purpose and Language Use (1983), Language Teaching: A Scheme for Teacher Education (ed, 1987), English in the World (with Randolph Quirk, 1985), Aspects of Language Teaching (1990), Practical Stylistics (1992); *Recreations* reading, walking, travel, poetry; *Style*— Prof H G Widdowson; ✉ Institute of Education, 20 Bedford Way, London WC1H 0AL (☎ 0171 580 1122)

WIDDUP, (Stanley) Jeffrey; s of Terence Widdup (d 1985), of Farnham Royal, Bucks, and Barbara Widdup (d 1995); *b* 10 July 1951; *Educ* Haileybury, Inns of Court Sch of Law; *m* Aug 1981, Janet, da of late Jack Clark; 1 s (Jack b 17 Jan 1983); *Career* called to the Bar Gray's Inn 1973, head of chambers 1981–, asst recorder of the Crown Court 1993–; memb Ctee Relate Guildford; *Recreations* golf, growing vegetables; *Clubs* Bramley Golf, Bigbury Golf, Guildford County; *Style*— Jeffrey Widdup, Esq; ✉ Stoke House, Leapale Lane, Guildford, Surrey GU1 4LY (☎ 01483 39131, fax 01483 300542)

WIDE, Charles Thomas; QC (1995); s of Nicholas Scott Wide, of Felpham, W Sussex, and Ruth Mildred Norton, *née* Bird; *b* 16 April 1951; *Educ* The Leys Sch Cambridge, Univ of Exeter (LLB); *m* 1979, Hon Ursula Margaret Bridget Buchan, da of 3 Baron Tweedsmuir, *qv*; 1 da (Emily Susan b 10 June 1982), 1 s (Thomas Nicholas Buchan b 20 March 1984); *Career* called to the Bar Inner Temple 1974, recorder of the Crown Court 1995– (asst recorder 1991–95), standing counsel HM Customs & Excise (Crime) Midland & Oxford Circuit 1989–95, standing counsel Inland Revenue (Crime) Midland & Oxford Circuit 1991–95; *Recreations* fell walking; *Style*— Charles Wide, Esq, QC; ✉ 9 Bedford Row, London WC1R 4DB (☎ 0171 242 3555, fax 0171 242 2511)

WIEGOLD, Prof James; s of Walter John Wiegold (d 1967), and Elizabeth, *née* Roberts (d 1960); *b* 15 April 1934; *Educ* Caerphilly Boys' GS, Univ of Manchester (BSc, MSc, PhD), Univ of Wales (DSc); *m* 7 April 1958, (Edna) Christine, da of Lewis Norman Dale (d 1989); 1 s (Richard), 2 da (Helen (Mrs Fish), Alison (Dr Sharrock)); *Career* asst lectr Univ Coll N Staffs 1957–60, lectr UMIST 1960–63, prof Univ Coll Cardiff (now Univ Wales Coll Cardiff following merger with UWIST) 1974– (lectr 1963–67, sr lectr 1967–70, reader 1970–74); memb Mathematical Sciences Sub Ctee UGC 1981–86; FIMA 1979; *Books* The Burnside Problems and Identities in Groups (translated from the Russian of S I Adian, with J C Lennox, 1979), Around Burnside (translated from the Russian of A I Kostrikin, 1990); *Recreations* music (choral singing), walking, language; *Style*— Prof James Wiegold; ✉ 131 Heol y Deri, Rhiwbina, Cardiff, Wales CF4 6UH (☎ 01222 620469); School of Mathematics, University of Wales, College of Cardiff, Senghenydd Rd, Cardiff CF2 4AG (☎ 01222 874194, fax 01222 874199, telex 498635)

WIELD, (William) Adrian Cunningham; s of Captain Ronald Cunningham Wield, CBE, RN (d 1981), of Coburg, Chudleigh, S Devon, and Mary, *née* MacDonald (d 1991); *b* 19 Feb 1937; *Educ* Downside; *m* 8 June 1979, Benedicte, da of Poul Preben Schoning (d 1984), of Copenhagen; 1 s (Alexander b 1983), 1 da (Isobel b 1980); *Career* 2 Lt Duke of Cornwall LI 1955–57; stockbroker; ptnr W Mortimer 1967–68, dir EB Savory Milln (later SBCI Savory Milln) 1985–88 (ptnr 1968–85), dir Albert Sharp & Co 1988–, non-exec dir Buzzacot Investment Management Co 1990–94; chm Reed Brook Ltd 1993–94, chm Boisdale Ltd 1995–; memb London Stock Exchange 1959–1988, MSI; *Books* The Special Steel Industry (published privately, 1973); *Recreations* golf, shooting, sailing; *Clubs* Reform; *Style*— Adrian Wield, Esq; ✉ Tysoe Manor, Tysoe, Warwicks (☎ 01295 680709, fax 01295 688018); Scott House Sekforde St, London EC1; c/o Albert Sharp & Co, Moor House, 119 London Wall, London EC2 (☎ 0171 638 7275, fax 0171 638 7270, telex 336550)

WIELER, Anthony Eric; s of Brig Leslie Frederic Ethelbert Wieler, CB, CBE, JP (d 1965), of Hambledon, Surrey, and Elisabeth Anne, *née* Parker (d 1984); *b* 12 June 1937; *Educ* Shrewsbury, Trinity Coll Oxford (MA); *Career* Nat Serv 1958–60, 2 Lt 7 Duke of Edinburgh's Own Gurkha Rifles (in 1967 organised the appeal which raised £1.5m for Gurkha Welfare Tsts); joined L Messel & Co, memb London Stock Exchange until 1967, sr investmt mangr Ionian Bank Ltd until 1972; fndr chm: Anthony Wieler & Co Ltd 1972–89, Anthony Wieler Unit Trust Management 1982–89; dir: Lorne House Trust IOM 1987, Arbuthnot Fund Managers Ltd 1988–89; assoc dir Albert E Sharp & Co 1989–92, English Trust Co Ltd (i/c Investmt Mgmnt Div) 1992–; Action Research: memb Cncl, memb Finance Ctee, chm Corporate Support Gp; fndr Oxford Univ Modern Pentathlon Assoc 1957 (organised first match against Cambridge), chm Hambledon PC 1965–76, initial subscriber Centre for Policy Studies 1972 (memb Wider Ownership Sub Ctee), fndr One Million Club for XVI Universiade, memb and tstee numerous other charities particularly concerning Nepal incl King Mahendra Tst for Nature Conservation in Nepal (UK) and Pestalozzi Childrens Village Tst, Surrey county vice pres Order of St John; hon sec AIIM 1974–88; MSI 1993–; OStJ; *Recreations* tennis; *Clubs* Boodle's; *Style*— Anthony Wieler, Esq; ✉ Feathercombe, Hambledon, nr Godalming, Surrey GU8 4DP (☎ 01483 860200); English Trust Co Ltd, 12a Charterhouse Square, London EC1M 6AX (☎ 0171 608 0888, fax 0171 608 2684)

WIENS, Edith; da of Rev David Wiens (d 1981), of Canada, and Gertrud Wiens-Janz (d 1979); *b* 9 June 1950; *Educ* Oberlin Coll USA (BMus, MMus), Hanover Germany (Master of Performance), masterclass with E Werba Munich; *m* Kai Moser, professional cellist, s of Prof Dr Hans Joachim Moser, of Berlin; 2 s (Johannes b 14 June 1979, Benjamin b 3 May 1981); *Career* soprano, specialising in concerts and recitals; sung with orchs incl: London, Berlin, Israel, Munich and New York Philharmonic Orchs, Boston, Chicago, Montreal, Amsterdam Concertgebouw, Leipzig Gewandhaus and Bavarian Radio Symphony Orchs; operatic roles incl: Donna Anna in Don Giovanni (Glyndebourne, with Bernard Haitink), the Countess in Le Nozze di Figaro (Buenos Aires), Ilia in Idomeneo (Japan, with Seiji Ozawa); worked with other conductors incl: Daniel Barenboim, Sir Colin Davis, Sir Neville Marriner, Sir Georg Solti, Kurt Masur; prizewinner at various int competitions incl Salzburg Mozart competition, ARD Munich and Zwickau Schumann competition (Gold medal); recitals in NY, Paris, Vienna Musikverein, Berlin, Moscow, Munich, Frankfurt, Cologne, Florence and Amsterdam; various festival appearances in Salzburg, Montreux, Tanglewood, Lockenhaus, Aix-en-Provence, Lucerne, Schleswig-Holstein, Dresden, Berlin, Vienna and the London Proms; *Recordings incl* Peer Gynt (as Solveig), Das Paradies und die Peri (as the Peri, Grammy award 1990), Parsifal (erstes Blumenmädchen), Dona Nobis Pacem, Mendelssohn's 2nd Symphony and A Midsummer Night's Dream, Haydn's Creation, Beethoven's 9th Symphony, Mozart's Mass in C Minor and Requiem, Mahler's 2nd, 4th and 8th Symphonies, Zemlinsky's Lyric Symphony, Schubert, Strauss, Schumann and Brahms Lieder; *Style*— Ms Edith Wiens; ✉ Georg-Schuster Strasse 10, 82152 Krailling, Germany (☎ 00 49 89 857 4281, fax 00 49 89 856 2218); c/o Matthew Sprizzo, 477 Durant Avenue, Staten Island, NY 10308, USA (☎ 00 1 718 948 5402, fax 00 1 718 984 8996)

WIGART, (Bengt) Sture; s of Bengt Eric Wigart (d 1979), and Elsa Margareta Westberg (d 1983); *b* 11 May 1934; *Educ* Univ of Stockholm, Univ of Munich; *m* 1, 1959, Anne Outram; 3 s; m 2, 1981 (m dis); m 3, 1985; m 4, 1994, Hon Julia Collbran Groves, *née* Cokayne; *Career* chm: Wigart Management Ltd, Sub Contract UK, Company Clothing Information Services Ltd, Byggfakta Scandinavia AB; *Recreations* sailing, art; *Clubs* Royal Lymington Yacht, Naval and Military; *Style*— Sture Wigart, Esq; ✉ Oxleys, Dock Lane, Beaulieu, Hants SO42 7YJ (☎ 01590 612216)

WIGG, Simon Antony; s of William Antony Wigg, of Aylesbury, and Rosemary Evelyn Wigg, *née* Smith-Wright; *b* 15 Oct 1960; *Educ* Woodbridge Sch Suffolk, John Hampden Sch High Wycombe; *Career* speedway racer; Br Grass Track champion 1981, 1982, 1983, 1985, 1989 and 1990, Br Open Pairs champion 1985 and 1986, runner-up World Pairs Championship 1987, Br Speedway champion 1988 and 1989, World Long Track champion Germany 1990 and 1993 (Czech Republic 1994, Czechoslovakia 1989, Denmark 1985, runner-up Germany 1987), Cwlth Speedway champion 1989, runner-up World Speedway Championship Munich 1989 and 1995; capt English team 1986, 1987 and 1988, memb English World Cup winning side 1989, winner several int events and four Br League gold medals 1983, 1985, 1986 and 1989; *Recreations* skiing, water sports (all, including jetskiing and windsurfing), squash, motorcross, keep-fit; *Style*— Simon Wigg, Esq; (fax 01296 730004)

WIGGIN, Sir Alfred William (Jerry); kt (1993), TD (1970), MP (C) Weston-super-Mare (majority 5,342); s of Col Sir William Wiggin, KCB, DSO and Bar, TD, DL, JP, sometime chm Worcs TA & AF Assoc (gs of Sir Henry Wiggin, 1 Bt, being s of Alfred Wiggin, Sir Henry's 4 s, and Margaret, da of Edward John Nettlefold, whose f was fndr of the firm of Nettlefold & Chamberlain and J S Nettlefold & Sons, the latter eventually becoming part of the Guest Keen & Nettlefold conglomerate); *b* 24 Feb 1937; *Educ* Eton, Trinity Coll Cambridge; *m* 1, 1964 (m dis 1981), Rosemary Janet, da of David Orr; 2 s, 1 da; m 2, 15 Dec 1991, Mrs Morella C M Bulmer; *Career* 2 Lt Queen's Own Warwicks & Worcs Yeo (TA) 1959, Maj Royal Yeo 1975–78, Hon Col 'A' (WWY) Sqdn The Royal Mercian and Lancastrian Yeomanry 1992–; Parly candidate (C) Montgomeryshire 1964 and 1966, MP (C) Weston-super-Mare 1969– (by-election); PPS to Lord Balniel at MOD then FCO 1970–74, PPS to Sir Ian Gilmour at MOD 1971–72, parly sec MAFF 1979–81, parly under sec of state MOD 1981–83; chm: Select Ctee on Agric 1987–, Econ Ctee N Atlantic Assembly 1991–; memb Ct of Assts Worshipful Co of Goldsmiths; *Clubs* Beefsteak, Pratt's, Royal Yacht Squadron; *Style*— Sir Jerry Wiggin, TD, MP; ✉ The Court, Axbridge, Somerset BS26 2BN (☎ 01934 732527); House of Commons, London SW1A 0AA (☎ 0171 219 4466)

WIGGIN, Maj Sir Charles Rupert John; 5 Bt (UK 1892), of Metchley Grange, Harborne, Staffs; s of Sir John Henry Wiggin, 4 Bt, MC (d 1991), and his 1 w, Lady Cecilia Evelyn, *née* Anson (d 1963), da of 4 Earl of Lichfield; *b* 2 July 1949; *Educ* Eton; *m* 1979, Mrs Mary Burnett-Hitchcock, o da of Brig S Craven-Chambers, CBE; 1 s (Richard Edward John b 1980), 1 da (Cecilia Charlotte b 1984); *Heir* s, Richard Edward John Wiggin b 1 July 1980; *Career* Maj Grenadier Guards; *Style*— Maj Sir Charles Wiggin, Bt; ✉ c/o Child & Co, 1 Fleet Street, London EC4Y 1BD

WIGGINS, Prof David; s of late Norman Wiggins, OBE, and Diana, *née* Priestley (d 1995); *b* 8 March 1933; *Educ* St Paul's, Brasenose Coll Oxford (MA); *m* 1980 (sep), Jennifer Hornsby; 1 s (Peter Joshua Wiggins b 1987); *Career* asst princ Colonial Office 1957–58, Jane Eliza Procter visiting fell Princeton Univ 1958–59, lectr then fell New Coll Oxford 1959–67, prof of philosophy Bedford Coll London 1967–80, fell and praelector in philosophy Univ Coll Oxford 1981–89, prof of philosophy Birkbeck Coll London 1989–93, Wykeham prof of logic Univ of Oxford 1994–; visiting appts: Stanford Univ 1964 and 1965, Harvard Univ 1968 and 1972, All Souls Coll Oxford 1973, Princeton Univ 1980; author of various articles in learned jls; memb: Ind Cmmn on Tport 1973–74, Central Tport Consultative Ctee 1977–79; chm Tport Users Consultative Ctee for SE 1977–79; memb: London Tport and Amenity Assoc, Aristotelian Soc; hon foreign memb American Acad of Arts and Sciences (1992); FBA 1978; *Books* Identity and Spatio Temporal Continuity (1967), Truth, Invention and the Meaning of Life (1978), Sameness and Substance (1980), Needs, Values, Truth (1987); *Style*— Prof David Wiggins, FBA; ✉ New College, Oxford OX1 3BN

WIGGINS, (Anthony) John; s of late Rev Sydney Arthur Wiggins, of Wilts, and Mavis Ellen, *née* Brown; *b* 8 July 1938; *Educ* Highgate, The Hotchkiss Sch USA, Oriel Coll Oxford (MA), Harvard Univ (MPA); *m* 1962, Jennifer Anne, da of late John Wilson Walkden, of Northampton; 1 s (Nicholas b 1963), 1 da (Victoria b 1967); *Career* asst princ HM Treasy 1961, princ Dept of Econ Affrs 1966, asst sec HM Treasy 1972, PPS to Chllr of the Exchequer 1980–81, under sec head of Oil Div Dept of Energy 1981–84, memb Bd BNOC 1982–84, under sec Cabinet Office 1985–86, under sec Dept of Educn and Sci 1987–88, dep sec 1988–92; memb Ct of Auditors of the EC 1993–; *Recreations* mountaineering, skiing, opera; *Clubs* Alpine; *Style*— John Wiggins, Esq; ✉ Court of Auditors of the European Communities, 12 rue Alcide de Gasperi, 1615 Luxembourg (☎ 00 352 439 845372)

WIGGINTON, Prof Michael John; s of Lt-Col Sydney Isaac Wigginton, OBE (d 1945), and Eunice Olive, *née* Piper; *b* 26 March 1941; *Educ* Nottingham HS, Gonville and Caius Coll Cambridge (MA, DipArch); *m* 1, 1969 (m dis), Margaret Steven; 1 s (Alexander Steven b 1974), 1 da (Julia Caroline b 1972); m 2, 1988, Jennifer, da of Lester Bennett; 1

s (Dominic James Michael b 19 July 1993), 1 da (Annabel Marie Olivia b (twin) 19 July 1993); *Career* architect and author; with YRM architects and planners 1966–85 (responsible for the design of a series of bldgs incl an innovatory office bldg in the Netherlands, a maj energy sensitive hosp in Singapore and co-designer The Sultan Qaboos Univ in Oman), ptnr Richard Horden Assoc 1987–94, fndr the Designers Collaborative 1994; organiser Glass in the Environment Conf Crafts Cncl 1986; architect memb UK/USA Govt sponsored res on energy responsive bldg envelopes; chm RIBA Professional Lit Ctee 1996–; teacher/lectr 1990–95: Scott Sutherland Sch of Arch Aberdeen, Univ of Wales, Harvard Univ, Pennsylvania State Univ, Westminster Univ, Trondheim Univ Norway, Royal Coll of Art, Plymouth Univ, Portsmouth Univ; prof of architecture Plymouth Univ 1996–; occasional contrib BBC Kaleidoscope; with Richard Horden: winner The Stag Place Competition London 1987, winner Epsom Club Stand Competition 1989, winner Shell UK HQ Competition 1990, Financial Times Award for Architecture 1993; with the Designers Collaborative: Commended Design Award Zephyr Low Energy Project Competition 1994; co-inventor SERRAGLAZE refactive glazing device 1993–94; RIBA, FRSA; *Publications* Window Design (1969), Office Buildings (1973), Practice in the Netherlands (1976), Design of Health Buildings in Hot Climates (1976), Glass To-day (1987), Silicon can Shine (1988), Towards the Chromogenic Century (1990), Can We Have a Theory, Please (1991), Building Intelligence (1992), Notes Towards a Theory of Architecture (1992), The Building Skin: Scientific Principle vs Conventional Wisdom (essay in Companion to Contemporary Architectural Thought, 1993), Better Buildings Means Better Business (ed, 1993), Glass in Architecture (1996); *Recreations* music, reading, tennis; *Style*— Prof Michael Wigginton; ✉ 41 Chiddingstone St, London SW6 3TQ (☎ 0171 371 5855, fax 0171 731 8785); Plymouth University School of Architecture, The Hoe Centre, Notte Street, Plymouth PL1 2AR (☎ 01752 233600, fax 01752 233634)

WIGGLESWORTH, David Cade; CBE (1993), DL; s of Air Cdre Cecil George Wigglesworth, CB, AFC (d 1961), and Margaret, *née* Cade Bemrose (d 1963); *b* 25 March 1930; *Educ* Tonbridge, London Coll of Printing; *m* 11 Feb 1956, Anne, da of John Cairns Hubbard, of Esher, Surrey; 2 s (George b 1957, Lloyd b 1959), 2 da (Sally b 1962, Joanna b 1963); *Career* Nat Serv as pilot, FO RAFVR 1948–50; Bemrose Corp plc: salesman London 1952–55, London sales mangr 1955–65, gen mangr Bemrose Flexible Packaging Spondon Derbyshire 1965–69, md Bemrose Derby Ops 1969–71, gp chief exec 1971–91, chm 1992–95; started acquisitions in USA 1984; chm: CBI Economic Situation Ctee 1984–92, Hobson plc 1994–95, East Midlands Devpt Co Ltd, Bd of Govrs Trent Coll Long Eaton Derbys; High Sheriff for Derbyshire 1992–93 (also started Crimebeat); capt Derbyshire Co Golf Team 1974–75; Freeman City of London, Liveryman Worshipful Co of Stationers & Newspaper Makers; memb Faculty Assoc of Mgmnt Centre Europe (of American Mgmnt Assoc); *Recreations* golf, gardening, skiing; *Clubs* Chevin Golf (Derby), Pine Valley Golf (USA), Trevose Golf (Cornwall); *Style*— David Wigglesworth, Esq, CBE, DL; ✉ Manor Quarry, Duffield, Derbyshire DE56 4BG (☎ and fax 01332 841200)

WIGGLESWORTH, Jack; s of Jack Wigglesworth (d 1989), of London, and Gladys Maud, *née* Haywood; *b* 9 Oct 1941; *Educ* Jesus Coll Oxford (MA PPE); *m* 25 July 1970, Carlota Josefine Páez; 1 s (Antony John b 8 March 1972), 1 da (Jacqueline Mary b 11 Aug 1974); *Career* gilts desk economist and institutional salesman Phillips & Drew 1963–71, govt bond desk W Greenwell & Co 1971–86, head of sales for govt bond co Lloyds Merchant Bank 1986–87, LIFFE and SFA (to implement Fin Servs Act (1986)) 1988, head Int Fixed Interest Investmt Henderson Administration Ltd 1989–91, business devpt dir J P Morgan Futures Inc 1992–93, dir of mktg Citifutures Ltd 1993–; LIFFE: memb Founding Working Party and Steering Ctee 1982, Bd dir 1982–, designed Long Gilt Contract, chm Membership & Rules Ctee 1988–92, dep chm 1992–95, chm LIFFE 1995–; memb Authorisation Ctee and Individuals' Registration Panel SFA (formerly The Securities Assoc) 1987–, founding dir of Bd Securities Inst 1992–, memb Fin Servs Strategy Gp City & Inner London North TEC (CILNTEC) 1992–, dir Futures and Options Assoc 1995–; *Recreations* boating, music, films, computers, Latin American concerns; *Style*— Jack Wigglesworth, Esq; ✉ 3 Deacons Heights, Elstree, Herts WD6 3QY (☎ and fax 0181 953 8524); LIFFE, Cannon Bridge, London EC4R 3XX (☎ 0171 623 0444, fax 0171 379 2546, mobile 0850 938252, e-mail jack@wigs.demon.co.uk)

WIGGLESWORTH, Prof Jonathan Semple; s of Sir Vincent Brian Wigglesworth, CBE (d 1994), of Lavenham, Suffolk, and Mabel Katherine, *née* Semple (d 1986); *b* 2 Dec 1932; *Educ* Gordonstoun, Gonville and Caius Coll Cambridge (BA), UCH (BChir, MD); *m* 21 July 1960, (Margaret) Joan, da of Christopher Every Rees (d 1974); 3 da (Sara b 1961, Sian b 1965, Kirsty b 1968); *Career* house physician UCH 1960, house surgn Nat Temperance Hosp 1960–61, Graham scholar in morbid anatomy 1961–62, Beit Memorial fell 1962–64, lectr in morbid anatomy 1964–65, reader in paediatric pathology Dept of Paediatrics Hammersmith Hosp 1980–85 (sr lectr 1965–79), hon conslt in neonatal histopathology NW Thames Region 1983–, prof of perinatal pathology Royal Postgrad Med Sch 1985–; memb: Br Paediatric Assoc, Paediatric Pathology Soc, Br Paediatric Pathology Assoc, Neonatal Soc; FRCPath 1977; *Books* Haemorrhage Ischaemia and the Perinatal Brain (with K Pape, 1979), Perinatal Pathology (1984, 2 edn 1996), Textbook of Fetal and Perinatal Pathology (with D Singer, 1990); *Recreations* fly-fishing, gardening; *Clubs* Athenaeum, RSM; *Style*— Prof Jonathan Wigglesworth; ✉ Wason House, Upper High St, Castle Cary, Somerset BA7 7AT (☎ 01963 350360); 55 Stamford Court, Goldhawk Rd, London W6 0XD (☎ 0181 748 6806); Department of Histopathology, Royal Postgraduate Medical School, Hammersmith Hospital, Du Cane Rd, London W12 0HS (☎ 0181 383 3280, fax 0181 740 7417)

WIGGLESWORTH, Mark; *Career* assoc conductor BBC Symphony Orch 1991–93; music dir: Opera Factory 1991–94, The Premiere Ensemble, BBC Nat Orch of Wales 1996–; guest conductor: BBC Symphony Orch, BBC Scottish Symphony Orch, LPO, Bournemouth Symphony Orch, English Chamber Orch, Scottish Chamber Orch, Royal Scottish Nat Orch, EU Youth Orch, Salzburg Festival, Berlin Philharmonic, Deutsches Symphonie-Orchester Berlin, Royal Concertgebouw, Rotterdam Philharmonic, Residentie Orch, Netherlands Radio Philharmonic, Netherlands Wind Ensemble, Oslo Philharmonic, Swedish Radio Orch, Deutsche Kammerphilharmonie, Chicago Symphony, Philadelphia Orch, Minnesota Orch, San Francisco Symphony, Los Angeles Philharmonic Orch; work with Opera Factory: Birtwistle Yan Tan Tethera, Mozart Da Ponte operas, first recording Schoenberg arrangement of Mahler's Das Lied von der Erde (winner Gramophone Magazine Award); Welsh Nat Opera: Elektra, The Rake's Progress; *Style*— Mark Wigglesworth, Esq; ✉ c/o Harold Holt Ltd, 31 Sinclair Road, London W14 0NS (☎ 0171 603 4600, fax 0171 603 0019, telex 22339 HUNTER)

WIGGLESWORTH, William Robert Brian; s of Sir Vincent Brian Wigglesworth, CBE (d 1994), of Suffolk, and Mabel Katherine, *née* Semple (d 1986); *b* 8 Aug 1937; *Educ* Marlborough, Magdalen Coll Oxford (BA); *m* 1969, Susan Mary, da of Arthur Baker, JP (d 1980), of Suffolk; 1 da (Elizabeth b 1979), 1 s (Benjamin b 1982); *Career* Nat Serv 2 Lt Royal Signals 1956–58; Ranks Hovis McDougall Ltd 1961–70 (gen mgmnt and PA to Chief Exec); princ Bd of Trade 1970; asst sec: Dept of Prices and Consumer Protection 1975, Dept of Indust 1978; dep DG of telecommunications 1984– (acting DG 1992–93); dir Reedheath Ltd (telecommunications regulatory advice) 1994–; jt dir Int Inst for Regulators in Telecommunications City Univ; sr advsr Telecommunications Forum Int Inst of Communications (IIC) London; memb Bd JNT Assoc (UKERNA); FRSA; *Recreations* fishing, gardening, history; *Style*— William Wigglesworth, Esq; ✉ Millfield House, Heath Road, Polstead, Colchester, Essex CO6 5AN (☎ 01787 210590, fax 01787 210592)

WIGGS, His Hon Judge; (John) Samuel; s of Kenneth Ingram Wiggs, and Marjorie Ruth, *née* Newton; *b* 23 Nov 1946; *Educ* Chigwell Sch, Univ of Southampton (LLB); *m* 1, Elizabeth, *née* Jones (decd); m 2, Kerry, da of Brian Martley; 4 da (Rebecca, Catherine, Nicola, Elizabeth); *Career* called to the Bar Middle Temple 1970, recorder of the Crown Court 1991–95, circuit judge (Western Circuit) 1995–; life govr Imperial Cancer Research Fund; memb Bar Law Reform Ctee 1990–94; *Recreations* playing the bassoon, gardening, hill walking; *Style*— His Hon Judge Wiggs; ✉ c/o The Law Courts, Winchester, Hants SO23 9EL (☎ 01962 841212)

WIGHT, Robin Alexander Fairbairn; s of William Fairbairn Wight (d 1972), of Alwoodley, Leeds, and Olivia Peterina, *née* Clouston (d 1988); *b* 5 June 1938; *Educ* Dollar Acad, Magdalene Coll Cambridge (MA); *m* 27 July 1963, Sheila Mary Lindsay, da of James Forbes (d 1963), of Edinburgh; 3 s (James William Fairbairn b 1966, Alasdair Robin Forbes b 1968, Douglas Clouston Fullerton b 1973), 1 da (Catriona Mary Susan b 1965); *Career* ptnr Coopers & Lybrand CAs 1971–96; Coopers & Lybrand Scotland: regnl ptnr 1977–95, exec chm 1990–96; chm Arville Holdings 1990–; FCA 1976; *Recreations* golf, watching rugby, skiing, business, bridge; *Clubs* Caledonian, RAC; *Style*— Robin Wight, Esq; ✉ 22 Regent Terrace, Edinburgh EH7 5BS (☎ 0131 556 2100, fax 0131 558 1104); Arville Holdings, Sandbeck, Wetherby, West Yorkshire LS22 7BQ (☎ 01931 582735, fax 01937 580196, car 0385 258098)

WIGHTMAN, Very Rev (William) David; s of William Osborne Wightman (d 1988), of Leicester, and Madge, *née* Hargreaves (d 1972); *b* 29 Jan 1939; *Educ* Alderman Newton's GS Leicester, George Dixon GS Birmingham, Univ of Birmingham (BA), Wells Theol Coll; *m* 1963, Karen Elizabeth, da of George Harker; 2 s (William Michael b 7 Oct 1964, Matthew John b 30 Sept 1968), 2 da (Bridget Caroline b 3 Dec 1965, Joanna Rachel b 15 Oct 1971); *Career* asst curate: St Mary and All Saints Rotherham 1963–67, St Mary Castlechurch 1967–70; vicar: of St Aidan Buttershaw Bradford 1970–76, of St John the Evangelist Cullingworth 1976–83; rector of St Peter Peterhead 1983–91, chaplain HM Prison Peterhead 1989–91, rector of St John Longside, St Drostan Old Deer and All Saints' Strichen 1990–91, Aberdeen and Orkney diocesan dir of trg 1989–92, provost of St Andrew's Cathedral Aberdeen 1991–, priest-in-charge St Ninian Aberdeen 1991–, hon canon of Christ Church Cathedral Hartford Connecticut 1991–; *Style*— The Very Rev David Wightman; ✉ 15 Morningfield Road, Aberdeen AB2 4AP (☎ 01224 314765); St Andrew's Cathedral, King Street, Aberdeen (☎ 01224 640119)

WIGHTMAN, David Richard; s of John William Wightman, of Leatherhead, Surrey, and Nora, *née* Martin; *b* 3 April 1940; *Educ* KCS Wimbledon; *m* Rosalind Jill, *née* Diaper; *Career* Turner Kenneth Brown (merged with Nabarro Nathanson May 1995): articled clerk 1957–62, asst slr 1962–65, ptnr 1965–87, sr ptnr 1987–; ed-in-chief Int Construction Law Review 1983–; Freeman City of London, memb Worshipful Co of Slrs 1983; memb: Law Soc 1962, Int Bar Assoc 1976, IOD 1982, Soc of Construction Law 1986, Cncl London C of C; FRSA 1990; *Recreations* tennis, farming; *Clubs* Travellers'; *Style*— David Wightman, Esq; ✉ Nabarro Nathanson, 50 Stratton Street, London W1X 6NX (☎ 0171 493 9933, fax 0171 629 7900)

WIGHTMAN, John Martin; s of John William Wightman, of Leatherhead, Surrey, and Nora, *née* Martin; *b* 27 Jan 1944; *Educ* The Oratory; *m* 17 Oct 1970, Anne Leigh, da of William Laurence Paynter, MBE, of Leatherhead, Surrey; 2 s (Dominic Martin b 20 Dec 1972, Patrick John b 22 March 1983), 5 da (Antonia Leigh b 7 Dec 1971, Georgina Mary b 13 July 1975, Francesca Katherine b 13 May 1978, Gemma Theresa b 25 June 1981, Christiana Bernadette b 11 March 1986); *Career* David A Bevan Simpson & Co (now Barclays de Zoete Wedd): joined 1968, ptnr 1978, dir de Zoete & Bevan Ltd 1986–, dir Barclays de Zoete Wedd Securities Ltd 1986–; memb: Euro Govt Business Rels Cncl, City Liaison Group, Cons Assoc Shamley Green; AIIMR, MSI, MInstD; *Recreations* sports; *Clubs* Little Ship, Guildford and Godalming RFC; *Style*— John Wightman, Esq; ✉ The Manor House, Shamley Green, Surrey GU5 0UD (☎ 01483 893269); de Zoete & Bevan Ltd, Ebbgate House, 2 Swan Lane, London EC4R 3TS (☎ 0171 623 2323)

WIGHTMAN, Nigel David; s of Gerald Wightman (d 1983), of Church Brampton, Northants, and Margaret Audrey, *née* Shorrock; *b* 19 July 1953; *Educ* Bolton Sch, Kent Coll, Dundee HS, Brasenose Coll Oxford (MA), Nuffield Coll Oxford (MPhil); *m* 21 Feb 1987, Christine Dorothy, da of Hubert Alexander Nesbitt, of Bangor, Co Down, NI; 3 s (Patrick Gerald Wisdom b 1987, Hugo William Joseph b 1989, Jack David Alexander b 1991); *Career* Samuel Montagu and Co 1976–80, Chemical Bank 1980–84, NM Rothschild and Sons 1984–95, chief exec Rothschild Asset Management Asia Pacific Ltd until 1995, chief exec Wheelock NatWest Investment Management Ltd 1995–; *Recreations* seasonal; *Clubs* Wildernesse Golf, Aberdeen Marina (Hong Kong), Royal Hong Kong Yacht; *Style*— Nigel Wightman, Esq; ✉ Wheelock NatWest, 43F NatWest Tower, Times Square, Causeway Bay, Hong Kong

WIGLEY, Dafydd; MP (Plaid Cymru) Caernarfon (majority 14,476); s of Elfyn Edward Wigley; *b* 1 April 1943; *Educ* Caernarfon GS, Rydal Sch Colwyn Bay, Univ of Manchester; *m* Elinor, da of Emrys Bennett Owen, of Dolgellau; 3 s (2 s decd), 1 da; *Career* industl economist; formerly with: Ford Motor Co, Mars Ltd, Hoover Ltd; MP (Plaid Cymru) Caernarfon Feb 1974–, pres Plaid Cymru 1981–84 and 1991–, vice chair All Party Disablement Gp 1992–; candidate Euro Parliament elections 1994; vice pres Fedn of Industl Devpt Authorities; hon fell Univ Coll of North Wales Bangor 1994; *Books* An Economic Plan for Wales (1970), O Ddifri (1992), Dal Ati (1993), A Democratic Wales in a United Europe (1995), A Real Choice for Wales (1996); *Style*— Dafydd Wigley, Esq, MP; ✉ House of Commons, London SW1A 0AA (☎ 0171 219 5021, constituency office ☎ 01286 672076)

WIGLEY, David Lanceley; s of Rev Alfred Lanceley Wigley (d 1985), of Knaresborough, and Constance, *née* Durham (d 1932); *b* 20 Aug 1932; *Educ* Harrogate GS, New Coll Oxford (Open scholar, MA, MSc); *m* 11 Aug 1956, Brenda Elizabeth, da of (George) Kenneth Moralee; 2 s (Stephen David b 1959, Andrew Michael Durham b 1961), 1 da ((Elizabeth) Janet (now Mrs Millward) b 1962); *Career* product devpt with Procter and Gamble: UK 1956–61, USA 1961–63, UK 1963–66, Scandinavia (mangr) 1966–69, Italy (dir) 1969–77, Latin America 1977–82; chief exec Methodist Homes for the Aged 1982–, dir and sec Methodist Homes Housing Assoc 1982–, chm VOICES (Vol Orgns Involved in Caring in the Elderly Sector) 1993–96; chm of Govrs Rydal Sch Colwyn Bay 1986–95, chm of Govrs Rydal Penrhos Colwyn Bay 1995–, sec Methodist Church Div of Social Responsibility 1982–96; FRSA 1991; *Recreations* sport, Italy; *Style*— David Wigley, Esq; ✉ The Boat House, 36 Broadway, Duffield, Derbyshire DE56 4BU (☎ 01332 842951); Chief Executive, Methodist Homes for the Aged, Epworth House, Stuart Street, Derby DE1 2EQ (☎ 01332 296200, fax 01332 296925)

WIGLEY, Peter; s of John Henry Wigley (d 1982), of Sheffield, and Mary Avis, *née* Bloodworth (d 1981); *b* 3 Nov 1931; *Educ* High Storrs GS Sheffield, Queens' Coll Cambridge (MA); *m* 27 Oct 1956, Barbara, da of late Colin McPherson Grant; 3 da (Deborah Susan (Mrs Hensby) b 9 Aug 1957, Heather Louise (Mrs Haslam) b 2 Dec 1964, Annette Rachel b 1 Sept 1970), 2 s (Michael David b 8 Nov 1959, Graham Mark b 8 Sept 1961); *Career* copywriter and trainee accounts exec Ripley Preston & Co Ltd (advtg agents) 1956–57, tech interfactory corr Dunlop Rubber Co Ltd (tyre mfrs) 1957–60, merchandising offr Courtaulds Ltd (textile mfrs) 1960–62, advtg and sales promotion mangr Wades Departmental Stores Ltd (retailer gp) 1962–65, PRO East Kilbride Development Corporation 1965–69, chief publicity offr Sheffield City Cncl

1969–86, PRO Sheffield Utd FC (following early retirement 1986) 1986–89, conslt 1989–; FIPR 1985 (MIPR 1969); *Recreations* bridge, natural history, music, reading, touring France; *Style—* Peter Wigley, Esq; ✉ 11 Twentywell View, Sheffield S17 4PX (☎ 0114 235 1228)

WIGLEY, (Francis) Spencer; s of Frank Wigley (d 1970), Dep Cmmr of Police of Fiji, and Lorna, *née* Wattley; gf Sir Wilfrid Wigley, Chief Justice Leeward Islands, WI; *b* 28 Oct 1942; *Educ* Dean Close Sch, Univ of Nottingham (BA); *m* 1969, Caroline, *née* Jarratt; 2 s (Francis b 1972, Edward b 1973); 1 da (Elizabeth b 1979); *Career* admitted slr 1967; sec and head of corp admin The RTZ Corporation plc 1983–92 (legal advsr 1976–83), sec and gen counsel Bass plc 1992– (memb Exec Ctee of Bd 1995–); govr: Amesbury Sch 1983–95 (chm 1987–93), Cranleigh Sch 1989–; *Recreations* sailing, sporting activities, photography; *Clubs* RAC; *Style—* Spencer Wigley, Esq; ✉ Bass plc, 20 North Audley Street, London W1Y 1WE (☎ 0171 409 1919)

WIGMORE, His Hon Judge; James Arthur Joseph; s of Arthur John Ormsey Wigmore (d 1948), and Kathleen May, *née* Jowett (d 1935); *b* 7 Aug 1928; *Educ* Downside, Royal Military Acad Sandhurst, English Coll Gregorian Univ Rome (PhL, STL); *m* 1966, Diana, da of Henry Holemans; 3 da (Rebecca b 1 Feb 1967, Philippa b 28 June 1969, Stephanie b 5 Dec 1970); *Career* RCS 1946–52; lectr in philosophy: Downside Abbey 1960–63, Oscott Coll 1963–66; called to the Bar Inner Temple 1971, dep coroner Bristol 1976–88, recorder 1989–90, circuit judge (Western Circuit) 1990–; *Clubs* Naval & Military; *Style—* His Hon Judge Wigmore; ✉ c/o Western Circuit Office, Bridge House, Sion Place, Clifton, Bristol BS8 4BN

WIGODER, Baron (Life Peer UK 1974), of Cheetham, in City of Manchester; Basil Thomas Wigoder; QC (1966); s of Philip I Wigoder, LRCPI, LRCSI, of Deansgate, Manchester; *b* 12 Feb 1921; *Educ* Manchester GS, Oriel Coll Oxford (MA); *m* 1948, Yoland, da of Ben Levinson; 3 s (Hon Justin b 1951, Hon Charles Francis b 1960, Hon Giles b 1963), 1 da (Hon Carolyn b (twin) 1963); *Career* serv WWII Lt RA N Africa, Italy, Greece; sits as Lib Democrat in House of Lords; contested (Lib): Bournemouth 1945, Westbury 1959 and 1964; pres Oxford Union 1946, barr 1946, vice pres Lib Pty 1966, memb Crown Ct Rules Ctee 1971–80, master of bench Gray's Inn 1972 (treas 1989), recorder Crown Ct 1972–87; Lib dep whip House of Lords 1976–77, chief whip 1977–86; chm Health Servs Bd 1977–80, memb Cncl on Tbnls 1980–86; chm BUPA and dir BUPA Hosps 1981–92, vice pres BUPA 1992–; Liveryman Worshipful Co of Coopers; *Recreations* cricket, music; *Clubs* Nat Lib, MCC; *Style—* The Rt Hon the Lord Wigoder, QC; ✉ House of Lords, London SW1 (☎ 0171 219 3114)

WIGRAM, Hon Andrew Francis Clive; MVO (1986); s and h of 2 Baron Wigram, MC, JP, DL; *b* 18 March 1949; *Educ* Winchester, RMA Sandhurst, RAC Cirencester; *m* 1974, Gabrielle, yst da of R Moore, of NZ; 3 s (Harry Richard Clive b 1977, Robert Christopher Clive b 1980, William Michael Clive b 1984), 1 da (Alice Poppy Louise b 1989); *Career* Maj Grenadier Guards 1969–86; Extra Equerry to HRH The Duke of Edinburgh 1982–86; Steward Henley Royal Regatta; Liveryman Worshipful Co of Cordwainers; *Clubs* Leander, Farmers'; *Style—* Maj the Hon Andrew Wigram, MVO; ✉ Poulton Fields Farms, Poulton, Cirencester, Glos GL7 5SS (☎ 01285 851388, fax 01285 850120)

WIGRAM, Rev Canon Sir Clifford Woolmore; 7 Bt (UK 1805), of Walthamstow, Essex; s of Robert Ainger Wigram (d 1915), and Evelyn Dorothy, *née* Henslowe (d 1960); suc unc, Sir Edgar Thomas Ainger Wigram, 6 Bt (d 1935); *b* 24 Jan 1911; *Educ* Winchester, Trinity Coll Cambridge (MA); *m* 24 Aug 1948, Christobel Joan (d 1983; who m 1, Eric Llewellyn Marriott, CIE d 1945), da of late William Winter Goode, of Curry Rivel, Somerset; 1 step s, 1 step da; *Heir* bro Edward Robert Woolmore Wigram, b 19 July 1913; *Career* ordained 1934, vicar Marston St Lawrence with Warkworth and Thenford, non residentiary canon Peterborough Cathedral 1973, ret 1983, canon emeritus Peterborough Cathedral; *Style—* The Rev Canon Sir Clifford Wigram, Bt; ✉ Flat 8, Emden House, Barton Lane, Headington, Oxford OX3 9JU (☎ 01865 750887)

WIGRAM, 2 Baron (UK 1935); (George) Neville Clive Wigram; MC (1945), JP (Glos 1959), DL (1969); s of 1 Baron Wigram, GCB, GCVO, CSI, PC, Equerry to George V both as Prince of Wales and King (d 1960, himself ggs of Sir Robert Wigram, 1 Bt), and his w Nora, da of Sir Neville Chamberlain; *b* 2 Aug 1915; *Educ* Winchester, Magdalen Coll Oxford; *m* 19 July 1941, Margaret Helen (d 1986), da of Gen Sir Andrew Thorne, KCB, CMG, DSO, and Hon Margaret Douglas-Pennant, 10 da of 2 Baron Penrhyn, JP, DL; 1 s, 2 da; *Heir* s, Hon Andrew Wigram; *Career* late Lt-Col Gren Gds; page of honour to HM 1925–32; mil sec and comptroller to Govr-Gen NZ 1946–49; govr Westminster Hosp 1967–74; *Clubs* Cavalry and Guards', MCC; *Style—* The Rt Hon Lord Wigram, MC, JP, DL; ✉ Poulton Fields, Cirencester, Glos GL7 5SS (☎ 01285 851250)

WIJETUNGE, Don B; s of Don Dines Wijetunge (d 1963), of Colombo, Sri Lanka, and Prem, *née* Jayatilake; *b* 24 Jan 1941; *Educ* Royal Coll Colombo Sri Lanka, Univ of Ceylon (MB BS); *m* 20 April 1971, Indra, da of Andrew Amerasinghe, of Kandy, Sri Lanka; 1 s (Aruna b 1973), 1 da (Sonalee b 1974); *Career* conslt surgn Univ Hosp Damman Saudi Arabia 1980–82, dir of emergency serv Abdulla Fouad Univ Hosp Saudi Arabia 1982–84, conslt surgn and head Dept of Emergency Serv St George's Hosp London 1984– (first asst Dept of Surgery 1976–80); memb: American Coll of Emergency Physicians, BMA; fell Faculty of Accident and Emergency Medicine (FFAEM), FRCSEd; *Recreations* computer applications in medicine; *Style—* Don Wijetunge, Esq; ✉ Accident & Emergency Service, St George's Hospital, Blackshaw Rd, London SW17 0QT (☎ 0181 715 3585)

WILBERFORCE, Baron (Life Peer UK 1964), of City and Co of Kingston-upon-Hull; Sir Richard Orme Wilberforce; kt (1961), CMG (1965), OBE (1944), PC (1964); s of Samuel Wilberforce, of Lavington House, Petworth, Sussex (d 1954, 4 s of Reginald Wilberforce, JP, DL, by Anna Maria, da of Hon Richard Denman, 3 s of 1 Baron Denman; Reginald was 2 s of the Bishop of Oxford who founded Cuddesdon Theological Coll and was himself 3 s of William Wilberforce, the philanthropist) and Katherine, *née* Sheepshanks (d 1963); the family name derives from a Yorkshire village, Wilberfoss (Wild-Boar-Foss); *b* 11 March 1907; *Educ* Winchester, New Coll Oxford (MA); *m* 10 July 1947, Yvette Marie, da of Roger Lenoan, Judge of the Cour de Cassation, Paris; 1 s (Hon Samuel Herbert b 1951), 1 da (Hon Anne Catherine (Hon Mrs Burn) b 1948); *Career* served WWII Norway, France and Germany as Brig, Chief Legal Div Control Cmmn Germany 1944–45, under sec Control Office Germany and Austria 1945–46; called to the Bar 1932; QC 1954, High Ct judge (Chancery) 1961–64, Lord of Appeal in Ordinary 1964–82, chm Exec Cncl Int Law Assoc 1967–90, memb Perm Ct of Arbitration; pres: Fédération Internationale du Droit Européen 1978, Anti-Slavery Int; fell All Souls Oxford 1932; hon fell: New Coll Oxford 1965, Wolfson Coll Oxford 1990; high steward Univ of Oxford 1967–90, chllr Univ of Hull 1978–94; Hon FRCM, Hon CRAeS; hon memb: Scottish Faculty of Advocates, Canadian Bar, American Soc of Int Law, American Law Inst; Hon DCL Oxford 1967; Hon LLD: London 1972, Hull 1973, Bristol 1983; Diplôme d'Honneur Corp des Vignerons de Champagne; Gd Cross St Raymond of Penafort (Spain) 1976, Bronze Star (US) 1944; *Clubs* Athenaeum, Oxford and Cambridge; *Style—* The Rt Hon the Lord Wilberforce, CMG, OBE, PC; ✉ c/o House of Lords, London SW1

WILBRAHAM, *see:* Baker Wilbraham

WILBRAHAM, Philip Neville; s of Anthony Basil Wilbraham, of N Humberside, and Sheila Eleanor, *née* Neville; *b* 25 Nov 1958; *Educ* Woodleigh Sch, Radley, Univ of Aston Birmingham (BSc); *m* 1981, Stephanie Jane, da of Ian William McClaren Witty; 2 s (Samuel b 1984, Dominic b 1987), 2 da (Rachel b 1982, Rosemary b 1986); *Career* chm: Northumbrian Fine Foods plc 1993–, Prospect Industries plc; Liveryman Worshipful Co of Shipwrights; *Recreations* shooting, politics; *Clubs* Carlton, City Livery; *Style—* Philip Wilbraham, Esq; ✉ Welton Hill, Kidd Lane, Welton, East Yorks HU15 1PH; Prospect Industries plc, Ferriby Hall, North Ferriby HU14 3JP (☎ 01482 633385, fax 01482 633520)

WILBY, Prof Charles Bryan; s of Charles Edward Wilby (d 1974), of Leeds, and Olive Eleanor, *née* Whitehead (d 1970); *b* 13 July 1926; *Educ* Leeds Mod Sch, Univ of Leeds (BSc, PhD); *m* 19 Aug 1950, Jean Mavis, da of John William Broughton (d 1987), of Leeds; 3 s (Charles b 1952, Christopher b 1955, Mark b 1962); *Career* engr Yorkshire Hennebique Contracting Co Ltd 1949–52, dep chief engr Twisteel Reinforcement Ltd Manchester 1952–54, devpt engr Stuart's Granolithic Co Ltd 1954–59, lectr and pt/t conslt Univ of Sheffield 1959–63, prof of civil and structural engrg Univ of Bradford (now emeritus); conslt Robinson Consulting Engineers Bradford 1984–93; concurrently pt/t lectr at colls of technol and further educn: Derby, Hull, Leeds, Stockport; currently private conslt and author; chm Civil Engrg Panel Yorkshire Cncl for Further Educn, memb Cncl London and chm Yorkshire Branch IStructE, dep chm Yorkshire Assoc, chm Students Section ICE, memb Panel Intermediate Technol, memb Ct Univ of Sheffield, memb Ct, Cncl and Senate Univ of Bradford; FICE, FIStructE, CEng; *Books* 18 books incl: Basic Building Science (1963), Concrete Shell Roofs (1977), Post-tensioned Prestressed Concrete (1981), Structural Concrete (1983), Concrete Materials and Structures (1992), Concrete Domes (1993); author of over 40 technol papers; *Recreations* various and varying, European and USA travel; *Style—* Prof C B Wilby; ✉ Flat 27, Esplanade Court, Harrogate HG2 0LW (☎ 01423 569061)

WILBY, David Christopher; s of Alan Wilby, of Baildon, Yorks, and June, *née* Uppard; *b* 14 June 1952; *Educ* Roundhay Sch Leeds, Downing Coll Cambridge (MA); *m* 23 July 1976, Susan Christine, da of Eric Arding (d 1977), of Bardsey, nr Wetherby, Yorks; 1 s (Edward b 1985), 3 da (Victoria b 1981, Christina b 1983, Charlotte b 1987); *Career* called to the Bar Inner Temple 1974; memb: NE circuit, Hon Soc of Inner Temple; *Recreations* golf, watching association and rugby football, being in Tenerife; *Clubs* Pannal Golf, Golf Del Sur (Tenerife), Taverners Headingley, 100, Leeds United AFC; *Style—* David Wilby, Esq; ✉ Stray Holt, Slingsby Walk, Harrogate, North Yorks (☎ 01423 888 019); Flat 3, 26 Cheniston Gardens, Kensington, London W8; San Andres, San Miguel, Tenerife, Canary Islands; 199 Strand, London WC2R 1DR (☎ 0171 379 9779); 5th Floor, St Paul's House, 23 Park Square, Leeds LS1 2NI (☎ 0113 245 5866)

WILBY, James Jonathon; s of Geoffrey Wilby, of Isle of Man, and Shirley, *née* Armitage; *b* 20 Feb 1958; *Educ* Sedbergh Sch, Univ of Durham, RADA; *m* 25 June 1988, Shana Louise, da of late Garth John Loxley Magraw; 1 s (Barnaby John Loxley b 9 Nov 1988), 1 da (Florence Hannah Mary b 18 Oct 1992); *Career* actor; *Theatre* incl: Another Country (Queen's Theatre) 1983, As You Like It (Manchester Royal Exchange), Jane Eyre (Chichester Festival Theatre), The Tempest (Chichester Festival Theatre), The Common Pursuit (Lyric) 1988, The Trial (Young Vic) 1993, A Patriot for Me (RSC) 1995; *Television* incl: Dutch Girls (LWT), A Tale Of Two Cities (Granada), Mother Love (BBC) 1992, Tell Me That You Love Me (BBC), Adam Bede (BBC), You Me And It (BBC) 1993, Lady Chatterley (BBC) 1993, Crocodile Shoes (BBC) 1994, Witness against Hitler (BBC) 1995; *Films* incl: Maurice, A Summer Story, A Handful of Dust, Immaculate Conception, Howards End, Une partie d'Échec 1994; *Awards* Venice Film Festival Best Actor Award (for Maurice) 1987; *Style—* James Wilby; ✉ c/o Paul Lyon-Maris, ICM Ltd, Oxford House, 76 Oxford Street, London W1N 0AX (☎ 0171 636 6565, fax 0171 323 0101)

WILBY, Peter John; s of Lawrence Edward Wilby (d 1981), and Emily Lavinia, *née* Harris (d 1995); *b* 7 Nov 1944; *Educ* Kibworth Beauchamp GS Leics, Univ of Sussex (BA); *m* 5 August 1967, Sandra, da of Alfred James; 2 s (David Paul b 29 Dec 1971, Michael John b 1 Oct 1973); *Career* reporter The Observer 1968–72; educn corr: The Observer 1972–75, New Statesman 1975–77, Sunday Times 1977–86; educn ed The Independent 1986–89; Independent on Sunday: home ed 1989–91, dep ed 1991–95, ed 1995–96; *Books* Parents' Rights (1983); *Recreations* reading, lunching, cooking; *Style—* Peter Wilby, Esq; ✉ 51 Queens Road, Loughton, Essex IG10 1RR (☎ 0181 508 9483)

WILCOCK, Christopher Camplin; CB (1997); s of Arthur Camplin Wilcock, of Ipswich, Suffolk, and Dorothy Wilcock, *née* Haigh; *b* 13 Sept 1939; *Educ* Berkhamsted Sch, Ipswich Sch, Trinity Hall Cambridge (maj scholar, BA, MA); *m* 5 June 1965, Evelyn Clare; da of late Geoffrey Joseph Gollin; 2 da (Alice Emily b 1967, Florence Mary b 1969); *Career* HM Dip Serv: Arabian Dept FO 1962–63, third sec HM Embassy Khartoum 1964–66, Econ Rels Dept FO 1966–67, UK del NATO 1968–70, W European Dept 1970–72; Hospital Building Div DHSS 1972–74; Dept of Energy: Petroleum Prodn (subsequently Continental Shelf Policy) Div 1974–78 (promoted to asst sec 1976), Electricity Div 1978–81, seconded to Shell UK 1982–83, Estab and Fin Div 1984–88 (promoted to Grade 4 1986), head of Electricity Div A 1988–91 (promoted to Grade 3 1988), head of Electricity Div 1991–94 (in DTI from 1992), head of Electricity and Nuclear Fuels Div 1994–95, head of Nuclear Power Privatisation Team 1995–96; dir Corp Fin Dept Price Waterhouse 1996–; Order of the Two Niles, Fifth Class (Republic of the Sudan) 1965; *Recreations* reading, history, cinema; *Style—* Christopher Wilcock, Esq, CB; ✉ 22 Luttrell Avenue, London SW15 6PF

WILCOX, His Hon Judge David John Reed; s of Leslie Leonard Kennedy Wilcox (d 1990), and Ada Margaret Reed, *née* Rapson (d 1958); *b* 8 March 1939; *Educ* Wednesbury Boys' HS, King's Coll London (LLB); *m* 22 June 1962, Wendy Feay Christine, da of Ernest Cyril Whiteley (d 1974), of Singapore; 1 s (Giles Frederick Reed b 16 Nov 1962), 1 da (Hester Margaret Reed b 2 Jan 1965); *Career* called to the Bar Gray's Inn 1962, Capt Directorate Army Legal Servs 1962–65 (Far East Land Forces Singapore 1963–65), crown counsel Hong Kong 1965–68, memb Hong Kong Bar 1968, practised Midland and Midland & Oxford Circuits 1968–85 (recorder 1979–85), circuit judge (Midland and Oxford Circuit) 1985–; liaison judge Lincs and S Humberside Magistrates 1988–94, assigned Co Ct judge Lincs and S Humberside 1988–94, resident judge Great Grimsby 1988–94, assigned Co Cts judge and designated care judge Birmingham 1994–96, judge Official Referees' Ct 1996– (official referee 1989); vice pres Lincs and S Humberside Magistrates' Assoc 1988–94, memb Humberside Probation Ctee 1988–94; chm Nottingham Friendship Housing Assoc 1969–75; *Recreations* gardening, travel; *Style—* His Hon Judge David Wilcox; ✉ Official Referees' Courts, St Dunstan's House, 133–137 Fetter Lane, London EC4A 1HD (☎ 0171 936 7429)

WILCOX, Rt Rev David Peter; s of John Wilcox (d 1961), and Stella May, *née* Bower (d 1977); *b* 29 June 1930; *Educ* Northampton GS, St John's Coll Oxford (MA), Lincoln Theological Coll; *m* 11 Aug 1956, Pamela Ann, da of Herbert Leslie Hedges; 2 da (Sara b 1957, Frances b 1959), 2 s (Peter b 1961, Christopher b 1968); *Career* asst curate St Helier Morden Southwark 1954–56, staff sec Student Christian Movement and asst curate Univ Church Oxford 1956–59; Theological Coll posts: Lincoln 1959–64, Bangalore S India 1964–70; vicar Gt Gransden and rector Lt Gransden Ely 1970–72, canon Derby Cathedral and warden E Midlands Jt Ordination Scheme 1972–77, princ Ripon Coll Cuddesdon and vicar Cuddesdon Oxford 1977–86, bishop of Dorking 1986–95; asst bishop diocese of Chichester 1995–; *Recreations* walking, music, painting; *Style—* The Rt Rev D P Wilcox; ✉ 4 The Court, Hoo Gardens, Willingdon, Eastbourne BN20 9AX

WILCOX, Desmond John; s of late John Wallace Wilcox, and Alice May, *née* Whittle (d 1992); *b* 21 May 1931; *Educ* Cheltenham GS, Christ's Coll London, Outward Bound Sea Sch (sail trg apprentice); *m* 1, 6 Jan 1954, Patsy, da of late Harry Price; 1 s (Adam b 1961), 2 da (Cassandra b 1959, Claire (twin) b 1961); m 2, 2 Dec 1977, Esther Rantzen, OBE, *qv*, da of Henry Barnato (Harry) Rantzen (d 1992); 1 s (Joshua b 1981), 2 da (Emily b 1978, Rebecca b 1980); *Career* deckhand Merchant Marine 1948, cmmnd Nat Serv Army 1949–51; reporter weekly papers 1949, news agency reporter 1951–52, reporter and foreign corr Daily Mirror (incl New York bureau and UN) 1952–60, reporter This Week ITV 1960–65; joined BBC 1965, co-ed and presenter Man Alive 1965, formed Man Alive Unit 1968, head of gen features BBC TV 1972–80, writer and presenter Americans (TV documentaries) 1979, presenter and chm Where it Matters (ITV discussion series) 1981; prodr and presenter BBC TV series: The Visit 1982 and 1984–91, The Marriage 1986, Black in Blue 1989–91; presenter 60 Minutes BBC TV 1983–84; prodr and presenter for Carlton TV: Day in the Life 1993, The Visit 1993–94; SFTA award for Best Factual Programme Series 1967, Richard Dimbleby award SFTA for Most Important Personal Contrib in Factual TV 1971; tstee: WALK Fund (Walk Again Limb Kinetics), Disfigurement Guidance Centre, Wessex HEARTBEAT; memb Conservation Fndn, patron: Harefield Hosp Fund, All Hear Cochlear Implant Charity, Children's Head Injury Tst, Br Deaf Assoc, Hearing Research Tst 1996; chief patron Mildmay Centenary Appeal; md Desmond Wilcox Productions Ltd, chm Man Alive Group (documentaries, series, independent prodns and corporate videos); *Publications* Explorers (jtly, 1975), Americans (1978), Return Visit (1991); with Esther Rantzen: Kill the Chocolate Biscuit: or Behind the Screen (1981), Baby Love (1985); *Recreations* riding; *Clubs* Arts, Groucho; *Style—* Desmond Wilcox, Esq; ✉ Desmond Wilcox Productions Ltd, Westpoint, 33–34 Warple Way, Acton, London W3 0RG (☎ 0181 743 7431, fax 0181 740 7454)

WILCOX, Baroness (Life Peer UK 1995), of Plymouth in the County of Devon; Judith Ann Wilcox; *née* Freeman; da of John and Elsie Freeman, of Plymouth, Devon; *b* 31 Dec 1939; *Educ* St Mary's Convent Wantage, Univ of Plymouth; *m* 1, 1961 (m dis 1986), Keith Davenport, s of Harold Cornelius Davenport, of Plymouth; 1 s (Hon Simon b 1963); m 2, 1986, as his 2 w, Sir Malcolm George Wilcox, CBE (d 1986), s of late George Harrison Wilcox; *Career* fndr Channel Foods Ltd Cornwall 1983; ptnr Morinie et Cie France 1990–; chm Nat Consumer Cncl 1990–96, currently pres Nat Fen of Consumer Gps; former chm: Local Govt Commission, Inland Revenue; chm: Citizen's Charter Advsy Panel, Port of London Authy, Ctee Automobile Assoc; FRSA; *Recreations* fishing, sailing; *Clubs* Reform, St Mawes Sailing; *Style—* The Rt Hon Lady Wilcox; ✉ 17 Great College Street, London SW1

WILD, (Charles) Barrie; s of Charles Wild (d 1960), of Skellow, Doncaster, and Dorothy Mary Wild (d 1982); *b* 6 Aug 1934; *Educ* Sir Percy Jackson GS; *m* 22 Aug 1959, Beryl Margaret, da of late Reginald Joseph Lowe, of York; 2 da (Karen Beverley b 1962, Katrina Lorraine b 1964); *Career* accountant: Brown Bayley Steels Ltd Sheffield 1960–65, Joseph Terry & Sons Ltd chocolate mfrs York 1965–67, Northern Ideal Homes Ltd Barnsley 1968; auditor: Thomson McLintock (now KPMG) 1969–79, Milk Marketing Bd 1979–95; ptnr Wild & Co CAs York 1981–; FCA 1964 (ACA 1959), registered auditor 1991; *Recreations* cricket, rugby league, horse racing, gardening; *Style—* Barrie Wild, Esq; ✉ 34 Dringthorpe Road, Dringhouses, York YO2 2LG (☎ 01904 707227)

WILD, John Vernon; CMG (1960), OBE (1955); s of James Wild (d 1964), and Ada Gertrude, *née* Clark (d 1947); *b* 26 April 1915; *Educ* Taunton Sch, King's Coll Cambridge (MA, Cricket blue); *m* 1, 17 Oct 1942, Margaret Patricia, *née* Rendell (d 1975); 1 s (Paul b 1949 d 1986), 1 da (Judith b 1944); m 2, 30 Dec 1976, Marjorie Mary Lovatt Robertson, da of Francis William Lovatt Smith (d 1975); *Career* Colonial Admin Serv Uganda: asst dist offr 1938, asst chief sec 1950, estab sec 1951, admin sec 1955–60, chm Constitutional Ctee 1959; mathematics teacher Hele's Sch Exeter 1960–71, lectr in maths Exeter Sixth Form and Tech Coll 1971–76; *Books* Early Travellers in Acholi (1950), The Uganda Mutiny (1953), The Story of the Uganda Agreement (1957); *Recreations* golf, gardening; *Clubs* Rye Golf; *Style—* J V Wild, Esq, CMG, OBE; ✉ Maplestone Farm, Brede, nr Rye, E Sussex TN31 6EP (☎ 01424 882261)

WILD, Kenneth (Ken); s of Ernest Wild, and Ethel Harriet, *née* Singleton; *b* 25 July 1949; *Educ* Chadderton GS, Univ of York (BA); *m* 6 April 1974, Johanna Regina Elizabeth, da of Karl Heinrich Christian Wolf, of Cheltenham; 1 s (Philip b 1981), 1 da (Victoria b 1978); *Career* CA; Peat Marwick Mitchell & Co 1974–78, under sec ICAEW 1978–80; Touche Ross (now Deloitte & Touche): mangr then sr mangr 1980–84, tech ptnr 1984–; ICAEW: memb Cncl 1989–90 and 1991–, chm Business Law Ctee 1996– (vice chm 1990–96), memb Accounting Standards Bd 1994–, memb Fin Reporting Advsy Bd to Treasy 1996–; FCA 1978; *Books* An Accountants Digest Guide to Accounting Standards - Accounting for Associated Companies (1982), Company Accounting Requirements, A Practical Guide (jtly, 1985), The Financial Reporting and Accounting Service (jtly, 1990), Cash Flow Statements: A Practical Guide (jtly, 1991), Accounting for Subsidiary Undertakings: A Practical Guide (jtly, 1992), Reporting Financial Performance: A Practical Guide to FRS 3 (jtly, 1993), Financial Reporting and Accounting Manual (jtly, 1994); *Recreations* reading, gardening; *Style—* Ken Wild, Esq; ✉ Deloitte & Touche, Hill House, 1 Little New Street, London EC4A 3TR (☎ 0171 303 4449, fax 0171 353 9820, telex 884739 TRLNDN G)

WILD, Prof Raymond (Ray); s of Frank Wild, of Chinley, Derbyshire, and Alice, *née* Large; *b* 24 Dec 1940; *Educ* Glossop GS, Stockport Tech Coll, Salford Coll of Tech, John Dalton Coll, Univ of Bradford (MSc (x 2), PhD) Brunel Univ (DSc); *m* 25 Sept 1965, Carol Ann, da of William Mellor, of Birchvale, Derbys; 1 s (Duncan Francis b 19 March 1970), 1 da (Virginia Kate b 10 June 1972); *Career* in industry 1957–67: apprentice and draughtsman 1957–62, design engr 1962–64, res engr 1964–66, prodn controller 1966–67; Univ of Bradford: res fell 1967–69, lectr 1969–73; prof Henley Mgmnt Coll 1973–77; Brunel Univ: head of Depts 1977–89, pro vice chllr 1988–89; princ Henley Mgmnt Coll 1990–; coll govr, Whitworth fell; FIMechE, FIEE, FIMgt, FRSA, CEng; *Books* Work Organization (1975), Concepts For Operations Management (1977), Mass Production Management (1972), Techniques of Production Management (1971), Management And Production (1972), Production and Operations Management (1978, 5 edn 1995), How To Manage (1982, 2 edn 1994), and 7 others; *Recreations* writing, travel, theatre, painting, sports, DIY; *Style—* Prof Ray Wild; ✉ Broomfield, New Rd, Shiplake, Henley-on-Thames, Oxfordshire RG9 3LA (☎ 0118 940 4102); Henley Management College, Greenlands, Henley on Thames, Oxon RG9 3AU (☎ 01491 571454, fax 01491 571635, e-mail RayW@Henleymc.ac.uk)

WILD, (John) Robin; JP (Ettrick and Lauderdale 1982); s of John Edward Brooke Wild (ka 1943), of Whin Brow, Cloughton, Scarborough, Yorks, and Teresa, *née* Ballance; *b* 12 Sept 1941; *Educ* Sedbergh, Univ of Edinburgh (BDS), Univ of Dundee (DPD); *m* 31 July 1965, (Eleanor) Daphne, da of Walter Gifford Kerr (d 1975), surgeon, of Edinburgh; 1 s (Richard b 1978), 2 da (Alison b 1967, Rosemary b 1977); *Career* princ in gen dental practice Scarborough Yorks 1965–71, dental offr E Lothian CC 1971–74, chief admin dental offr Borders Health Bd 1974–87, regnl dental postgrad advsr SE Regnl Ctee for Postgrad Med Educn 1982–87, dir of studies (dental) Edinburgh Postgrad Bd for Med 1986–87, chief dental offr Scottish Office Home and Health Dept 1993–97 (dep chief dental offr 1987–93), dir of Dental Services Scotland NHS 1993–97, chief dental offr Dept of Health 1997–; hon sr lectr Univ of Dundee 1993–; vice chm Tweeddale Ettrick & Lauderdale Cons & Unionist Assoc 1982–87, chm Scottish Cncl Br Dental Assoc 1985–87; hon fell Univ of Edinburgh 1984–; FDSRCS (Edinburgh); *Recreations* restoration and driving of vintage cars, music, gardening; *Clubs* Royal Cwlth Soc, RSAC; *Style—* Robin Wild, Esq, JP; ✉ Braehead House, St Boswells, Roxburghshire TD6 0AZ; Department of Health, Richmond House, 79 Whitehall, London SW1A 2NS

WILDASH, Richard James; s of Arthur Ernest Wildash, of London, and Sheila Howard, *née* Smith; *b* 24 Dec 1955; *Educ* St Paul's, Corpus Christi Coll Cambridge (MA); *m* 29 Aug 1981, (Elizabeth) Jane, da of Peter Edward Walmsley, of Dundee; 2 da (Joanna Helen b 1987, Bethany Jane b 1996); *Career* Dip Serv: FCO 1977, E Berlin 1979, Abidjan 1981, FCO 1984, Harare 1988, FCO 1992, first sec Br High Cmmn New Delhi 1994–; memb Inst of Linguists; FRGS; *Recreations* music, literature, the country; *Style—* Richard Wildash, Esq; ✉ Foreign and Commonwealth Office, King Charles St, London SW1A 2AH (☎ 0171 270 3000)

WILDBLOOD, (Christopher) Michael Garside; s of Richard Garside Wildblood, of Ouseburn, N Yorks, and Rita Muriel, *née* Jellings; *b* 9 Oct 1945; *Educ* Rugby, Corpus Christi Coll Cambridge (MA, Dip Arch); *m* 30 July 1971, Anne Somerville, da of Alun Roberts, of Radyr, Glamorgan; 1 s (Thomas Garside b 1976), 3 da (Shân Catherine Somerville b 1978, Jane Somerville b 1987, Rachel Somerville b 1989); *Career* chartered architect; ptnr and principal Wildblood Macdonald, Chartered Architects 1975–; chm: RIBA Leeds Soc of Architects 1985–87, RIBA Yorkshire Region 1985–86; pres W Yorkshire Soc of Architects 1993–95; ARIBA; *Recreations* golf, choral singing, watercolour painting; *Clubs* Alwoodley Golf, Old Rugbeian Golfing Soc (Northern Sec); *Style—* Michael Wildblood, Esq; ✉ Hammonds, Lower Dunsforth, Ouseburn, N Yorks YO5 9SA; Wildblood Macdonald, Chartered Architects, Audby Studio, Audby Lane, Wetherby LS22 4FD (☎ 01937 585225)

WILDE, Dr Colin Ernest; s of James Wright Wilde (d 1982), of Poynton, Cheshire, and Maria, *née* Booth; *b* 17 Oct 1937; *Educ* Ashton under Lyne GS, Univ of Birmingham (BSc, PhD); *m* 29 Dec 1962, (Marjorie) Julie, da of James Garth Garner, of Doncaster; 2 da (Colette Elizabeth b 16 Jan 1969, Debbie-Jane b 10 Aug 1970); *Career* conslt clinical chemist Doncaster Royal Infirmary 1974–, hon lectr Univ of Sheffield Med Sch 1976–; memb: Scientific Advsy Ctee 1975–84 (chm), Pathology Advsy Ctee RHA 1978–82, Dept of Health Nat External Quality Assessment Scheme Steering Ctee 1979–, Advsy Ctee for Dangerous Pathogens 1981–87, Health Servs Advsy Ctee HSC 1983–92, IFCC Educn Ctee Mexico project 1984–; advsr in clinical chemistry Br Cncl 1984–, hon nat treas Assoc of Clinical Biochemists 1987–94 (hon nat sec 1981–85), memb Panel of Examiners RCPath; FRSC 1964, FRCPath 1973; *Style—* Dr Colin Wilde; ✉ Department of Clinical Chemistry, Royal Infirmary, Doncaster, S Yorks DN2 5LT (☎ 01302 553106)

WILDE, Ernest; s of Leonard Wilde (d 1970), of Thornton-Cleveleys, Lancs, and Harriet, *née* Hulmes (d 1988); *b* 22 Jan 1936; *Educ* Ashton-under-Lyne GS, Univ of Leeds (BSc, PhD); *m* 21 Aug 1962, Mary Constance, da of William Ingham (d 1960), of Manchester; *Career* Royal Aircraft Estab Bedford 1960–62, lectr Royal Coll of Advanced Technol 1962–66; Univ of Salford: lectr 1966–68, sr lectr 1968–91, dir of overseas educnl devpt 1982–, pro vice chllr 1987–91; CEng, CMath, MRAeS, FIMA; *Recreations* travel, walking, gardening; *Style—* Ernest Wilde, Esq; ✉ 10 Stiles Ave, Marple, Stockport, Cheshire SK6 6LR (☎ 0161 427 4608); The University of Salford, Salford M5 4WT (☎ 0161 745 5476, fax 0161 745 5999)

WILDE, HE John; *b* 6 Oct 1941; *m* 1965, Jeanette Grace, *née* Reed; 1 s (Jason b 1969), 1 da (Joanna b 1974); *Career* HM Dip Serv: joined FO 1959, Conakry (Guinea) 1962–64, Pretoria 1964–65, Kuwait 1965–68, Tripoli 1968–69, FCO 1969–72, Zagreb 1972–76, Singapore 1976–79, FCO 1979–82, asst to Dep Govr Gibraltar 1982–85, JSDC 1985, FCO 1985–87, dep high cmmr Lilongwe 1987–91, asst head W Indian and Atlantic Dept FCO 1991–94, high cmmr The Gambia 1995–; *Recreations* golf, reading, music; *Style—* HE Mr John Wilde; ✉ c/o Foreign & Commonwealth Office (Banjul), King Charles Street, London SW1A 2AH

WILDE, Malcolm James; s of Malcolm John Wilde, and Irene Doris, *née* Rickwood; *b* 9 Oct 1950; *Educ* Bishopshalt Sch; *m* 1 Sept 1973, (Helen) Elaine, da of John Bartley, and Doris Bartley; 1 s (Alastair James Rory b 27 Feb 1987), 2 da (Joanne Caroline b 6 July 1976, Julia Felicity b 10 Feb 1981); *Career* mangr Western American Bank (Europe) Ltd 1970–75, vice pres Crocker National Bank 1975–77; dir: Guinness Mahon Holdings Ltd, Guinness Mahon & Co Ltd 1977–87; md: BCMB Group Ltd, British & Commonwealth Merchant Bank plc 1987–92; dir Standard Bank London Ltd 1992–; *Recreations* golf, sport generally, opera, antique furniture; *Clubs* Piltdown Golf; *Style—* Malcolm Wilde, Esq; ✉ Copyhold House, Copyhold Lane, Cuckfield, Sussex; Standard Bank London Ltd, Cannon Bridge House, 25 Dowgate Hill, London EC4R 2SB (☎ 0171 815 3000, fax 0171 815 3093)

WILDE, Martin Henry; s of Robert Christopher Wilde (d 1989), of Exeter, Devon, and Margaret Alexandra, *née* Forsyth; *b* 22 July 1961; *Educ* King George II Sch, Univ of Oxford (BA), Open Univ (MBA); *Career* trainee journalist Thomson Regional Newspapers 1983–85, freelance financial journalist London then Hong Kong 1985–89, a princ conslt Robertson Mayhew Chang insurance conslts Hong Kong 1989–93, independent insurance conslt Hong Kong and UK 1993–; tstee King George II Tst; *Recreations* golf, skiing, opera, reading; *Style—* Martin Wilde, Esq; ✉ 6 Olive Close, New Costessey, Norwich NR5 0AR

WILDER, Jess; da of David Wilder, of Henley-on-Thames, Oxon, and Mary Wilder; *b* 15 April 1953; *Educ* St Joseph's Convent Reading Berks, Henley GS, Univ of E Anglia (BA); *Career* with Galerie de Seine Paris 1977–78, co-owner Portal Gallery London 1988– (gallery asst 1975–77); artists exhibited incl: Beryl Cook, Jane Lewis, Guy Taplin; *Recreations* many and various; *Clubs* Groucho, Chelsea Arts; *Style—* Ms Jess Wilder; ✉ Portal Gallery, 16a Grafton Street, Bond Street, London W1X 3LF (☎ 0171 493 0706, fax 0171 629 3506)

WILDING, Richard William Longworth; CB (1979); s of Longworth Allen Wilding (d 1963), of Oxford, and Elizabeth Olga Fenwick, *née* Stokes (d 1968); *b* 22 April 1929; *Educ* Winchester, New Coll Oxford; *m* 1954, Mary Rosamund, da of Sir Nicolas de Villiers (d 1958), of London; 1 s (James), 2 da (Lucy, Clare); *Career* civil servant (ret); head Office of Arts and Libraries 1984–88; former dep sec: HM Treasy, Civil Serv Dept; *Style—* Richard Wilding Esq, CB; ✉ 14 The Lodge, Kensington Park Gardens, London W11 3HA

WILDMAN, David Aubrey; s of Ronald Aubrey Wildman, of Luton, Beds, and Bridget Teresa, *née* Cotter; *b* 4 July 1955; *Educ* Denbigh HS, Luton Coll; *m* 11 Oct 1975, Gillian, da of Edward Ambrose Close, of Richmond, N Yorks; 1 s (Philip b 1986), 1 da (Sophie b 1992); *Career* Chase Manhattan Bank 1973–75, Mobil Oil Co 1975–80, Herald Fin Servs 1980–88, md General and Medical Finance plc 1988–; *Recreations* theatre, good food, family; *Style—* David A Wildman, Esq; ✉ Forest Thatch, Pilton, Oundle, Peterborough PE8 5SN (☎ 01832 720692); General & Medical Finance plc, Forest House, Pilton, Peterborough PE8 5SN (☎ 01832 720795, fax 01832 720311)

WILDSMITH, Brian Lawrence; s of Paul Wildsmith, of Yorks, and Annie Elizabeth Oxley (d 1984); *b* 22 Jan 1930; *Educ* De La Salle Coll, Slade Sch of Fine Art UCL (DFA); *m* 1955, Aurélie Janet Craigie, da of Bernard Ithurbide (d 1957); 1 s (Simon), 3 da (Clare, Rebecca, Anna); *Career* freelance artist 1957–, prodn design, illustrations, titles and graphics for first USA-USSR Leningrad film co prodn of the Blue Bird, artist and maker of picture books for young children; Brian Wildsmith Museum opened in Izu, Japan 1994; winner: Kate Greenaway medal 1962, Soka Gakkai Educnl medal 1988, The Ushio Culture award 1991; *Books* ABC (1962), The Lion and the Rat (1963), The North Wind and the Sun (1964), Mother Goose (1964), 123 (1965), The Rich Man and the Shoemaker (1965), The Hare and the Tortoise (1966), Birds (1967), Animals (1967), Fish (1968), The Miller, the Boy, and the Donkey (1969), The Circus (1970), Puzzles (1970), The Owl and the Woodpecker (1971), The Twelve Days of Christmas (1972), The Little Wood Duck

(1972), Squirrels (1974), Pythons Party (1974), Blue Bird (1976), The True Cross (1977), What The Moon Saw (1978), Hunter and his Dog (1979), Animal Shapes (1980), Animal Homes (1980), Animal Games (1980), Animal Tricks (1980), Seasons (1980), Professor Noah's Spaceship (1980), Bears Adventure (1981), Cat on the Mat (1982), The Trunk (1982), Pelican (1982), Apple Bird (1983), The Island (1983), All Fall Down (1983), The Nest (1983), Whose Shoes (1984), Toot Toot (1984), Daisy (1984), Give a Dog a Bone (1985), What A Tale (1986), My Dream (1986), Goats Trail (1986), Giddy Up (1987), If I Were You (1987), Carousel (1988), The Christmas Story (1989), The Snow Country Prince (1990), The Cherry Tree (1991), The Princess and The Moon (1991), Over the Deep Blue Sea (1992), The Easter Story (1993), The Tunnel (1993), Noah's Ark (1994), Saint Francis (1995), The Creation (1995), Katie and the Dream-Eater (in collaboration with HIH Princess Takamado, 1996), Brian Wildsmith's Wonderful World of Words (1996); in collaboration with Rebecca Wildsmith: Look Closer, Wake Up, Wake Up, What Did I Find, Whose Hat Was That (1993); *Recreations* piano, tennis; *Clubs* Reform; *Style—* Brian L Wildsmith, Esq; ✉ 11 Castellaras, 06370 Mouans-Sartoux, Alpes-Maritimes, France (☎ 00 33 93 75 24 11)

WILDSMITH-TOWLE, Alan Geoffrey; s of Frederick William Towle (d 1973), of Broadmede, Derby, and Cissie Wildsmith, *née* Steeples; *b* 24 July 1939; *Educ* Joseph Wright Sch of Art, Derby and Dist Coll of Art; *Career* photographer and painter; served RAF photographer 1960–63; in family pharmaceutical business 1957–60, photographer Rolls-Royce Derby 1964–68, started own photographic business 1968, returned studio in St Neots Huntingdonshire 1972, moved back to Derbyshire 1976, opened studio in Belper 1977–; regular photographic exhibitions USA; winner of over 100 int awards in photography; FBIPP 1977, FRPS 1990, FRSA 1990; *Recreations* art, photography, the environment, painting and drawing, agriculture, horses; *Style—* Alan Wildsmith-Towle, Esq; ✉ Wildsmith-Towle, Photographic Artist, St George's House, Bridge St, Belper, Derbyshire DE56 1AZ (☎ 01773 825101)

WILES, Eric Allen; s of Arthur Wiles, of Brandesburton, E Yorks, and Doris May, *née* Grantham (d 1978); *b* 12 Dec 1956; *Educ* Hornsea Sch, Univ of Warwick (BA); *m* 9 June 1984, Carole Anne, da of Montague Carl Henry Docwra; 1 da (Olivia Alexandra b 5 Aug 1994); *Career* chartered accountant/tax conslt; trainee Binder Hamlyn 1978–82, Thornton Baker 1982–84, tax conslt Deloitte Haskins & Sells 1984–86; Forward Trust Group Ltd: tax mangr 1986–88, sr mangr Customer Serv 1988–91, fin controller 1991–93, sr mangr Business Devpt 1993–; currently memb Cncl ICAEW; vice chm Worcestershire Gp of CAs 1996, assoc FIMA 1979, assoc Chartered Inst of Taxation 1985, FCA 1992 (ACA 1982), FRSA 1995; *Recreations* golf, gardening, travel, historical studies; *Style—* Eric Wiles, Esq; ✉ The Chapel, Chapel Lane, Upton Snodsbury, Worcester WR7 4NH (☎ 01905 381270); Forward Trust Business Finance Ltd, Metropolitan House, 1 Hagley Road, Edgbaston, Birmingham B16 8TH (☎ 0121 455 4607, fax 0121 456 1431, car 0374 756874)

WILEY, (William) Struan Ferguson; s of John Nixon Wiley (d 1968), of Hartlepool, and Muriel Isobel, *née* Ferguson (d 1969); *b* 13 Feb 1938; *Educ* Fettes, Univ of New Hampshire USA; *m* 1, 25 Jan 1964 (m dis 1977), Margaret Louise, da of Ian Graham Forsyth, of Crinan, Scotland; 1 s (Fergus b 1966), 2 da (Sarah b 1964, Anna b 1969); m 2, 21 Dec 1977, Rosemary Anne, da of Sir John Cameron, OBE, of Cowesby, Yorks; *Career* Nat Serv 2 Lt 10 Royal Hussars 1956–58, TA 1958–68, Lt Queens Own Yorks Yeo 1958–68; dir: Chunky Chicks (Nichols) Ltd 1962, Sterling Poultry Prods Ltd 1965, Ross Poultry Ltd 1970, Allied Farm Foods Ltd 1970, Imperial Foods Ltd 1975; chm and md Ross Poultry and Ross Buxted Nitrovit Ltd 1977; chm: J B Eastwood Ltd 1978, J Lyons Catering Ltd 1981, Normand Ltd 1981, Embassy Hotels Ltd 1983, Almear Ltd 1995–; asst md J Lyons & Co Ltd 1981–90, dir Allied-Lyons plc 1986–90, Normand Motor Gp Ltd (and chief exec) 1990–94; non-exec dir: Golden Lay Eggs UK Ltd, Wembley Stadium Ltd, John Clark (Holdings) Ltd 1996–, Stadium Group plc 1996–; non-exec chm: Kingsbury Group plc 1995–, Mayfair Taverns Ltd 1996–; chm Br Poultry Breeders and Hatcheries Assoc 1976; memb: Governing Body Houghton Poultry Res Station 1974–82, Grand Cncl Hotel Catering Benevolent Assoc 1983, Leisure Industs Ctee NEDC 1987, Strategy Ctee Retail Motor Indust Fedn 1990–94; winner Poultry Indust Mktg Award 1977; Freeman: City of London 1980, Worshipful Co of Poulters 1981; *Recreations* golf, shooting, collecting old golf clubs; *Clubs* Cavalry and Guards, Woodhall Spa Golf, Sunningdale Golf; *Style—* Struan Wiley, Esq; ✉ Old Rectory, Withcall, Louth, Lincs LN11 9RL (☎ 01507 343 218)

WILEY, Dr Yvonne Victoria; da of Samuel Victor McGaffin (d 1980), of Portadown, NI, and Emily, *née* Ferris (d 1982); *b* 24 Dec 1934; *Educ* Banbridge Acad, Queen's Univ (MB BCh, BAO), DPM (London), FRCPsych; *m* 1959, David James Wiley, s of James Browne Wiley; 2 s (Mark b 1962, Gareth b 1963), 1 da (Louise b 1964); *Career* conslt psychiatrist: Bath Health Dist 1975–79, Stoke Park Hosp 1979–96; sr lectr Univ of Bristol 1984–92; currently med memb Mental Health Review Tbnls, second opinion appointed doctor Mental Health Act Cmmn; Royal Coll of Psychiatrists: chm Mental Handicap Section 1990–94, chm SW Div 1992–96; pres: Bristol Mencap 1984–94, Bristol BMA 1986–87; memb: Bd of Dirs Bristol Industl Therapy Orgn, Bristol Medico Chirurgical Soc, RSM; fell Int Assoc of the Scientific Study of Intellectual Disability (FIASSID); *Recreations* antiques, theatre; *Style—* Dr Yvonne Wiley

WILFORD, Sir (Kenneth) Michael; GCMG (1980, KCMG 1976, CMG 1967); s of George McLean Wilford (d 1965), and Dorothy Veronica, *née* Wilson, MBE (d 1945); gs of Sir Thomas Wilford, KCMG, KC, NZ High Cmmr in London 1929–33; *b* 31 Jan 1922, Wellington, NZ; *Educ* Wrekin Coll Shropshire, Pembroke Coll Cambridge (MA); *m* 1944, Joan Mary, da of Capt E F B Law, RN (d 1977); 3 da; *Career* RE WWII (despatches); entered Foreign Service 1947, Berlin 1947–49, asst private sec to Sec State Foreign Affrs 1949–52 and 1959–60, Paris 1952–55, Singapore 1955–59, private sec to Lord Privy Seal 1960–62, Rabat 1962–64, consul gen Peking 1964–66, cnsllr Washington 1967–69, asst under sec FCO 1969–73, dep under sec 1973–75, ambass Japan 1975–80; dir Lloyds Bank International 1982–87, advsr Baring Int Investment Mgmnt 1982–90; visiting fell All Souls Coll Oxford 1966–67; hon pres Japan Assoc 1981–, chm Royal Soc for Asian Affairs 1984–94; FInstD; *Recreations* golf, gardening; *Style—* Sir Michael Wilford, GCMG; ✉ Brook Cottage, Abbotts Ann, Andover, Hants SP11 7DS (☎ 01264 710509)

WILKES, Prof Maurice Vincent; s of Vincent J Wilkes, OBE (d 1971), of Hagley, Worcestershire, and Helen, *née* Malone (d 1968); *b* 26 June 1913; *Educ* King Edward's Sch Stourbridge, St John's Coll Cambridge (BA, MA, PhD); *m* 1947, Bertie Mary (Nina), da of Bertie Twyman (d 1914), British Consul Shanghai, China; 1 s (Anthony b 1950), 2 da (Helen b 1951, Margaret b 1953); *Career* WWII serv: sci offr ADRDE, Army Ops Res Gp, TRE 1939–42 (sr sci offr 1942–45); Univ of Cambridge: univ demonstrator 1937–45, head Computer Laboratory (formerly Mathematical Laboratory) 1945–80, prof of computer technol (now emeritus prof) 1965–80, fell St John's Coll 1950–; computer engr Digital Equipment Corp Maynard MA USA 1980–86, memb for res strategy Olivetti Res Bd 1986–90 (currently staff advsr); Hon ScD Univ of Cambridge 1993; Hon DSc: Univ of Newcastle 1972, Univ of Hull 1974, Univ of Kent 1975, City Univ 1975, Free Univ of Amsterdam 1978, Tech Univ of Munich 1978, Univ of Bath 1987, Univ of Pennsylvania 1996; Hon DTech Linköping Sweden 1975; FRS 1956, FEng 1976, FBCS, FIEE; foreign assoc: US Nat Acad of Sci, US Nat Acad of Engrg; foreign hon memb American Acad of Arts and Scis, Kyoto Prize 1992; *Books* Memoirs of a Computer Pioneer (1985), Computing Perspectives (1994); author of various technical books and papers in sci jls; *Clubs* Athenaeum; *Style—* Prof Maurice Wilkes, FRS, FEng; ✉ 130 Huntingdon Rd, Cambridge CB3 0HL; Olivetti Research Ltd, 24A Trumpington St, Cambridge CB2 1QA (☎ 01223 343 300, fax 01223 313542)

WILKES, HE Gen Sir Michael; KCB (1991), CBE (1988, OBE 1979); *Educ* King's Sch Rochester, RMA Sandhurst; *m* Anne; 2 s (Jonathan, Jeremy); *Career* cmmnd RA 1960, joined 7 Parachute Regt RHA, served Middle E and Cyprus, Adj 42 Medium Regt RA Devizes, psc, Bde Maj HQ 3 Div RA Bulford; cmd The Chestnut Troop 1 Regt RHA 1975–77, mil asst to Chief of Gen Staff MOD, COS HQ 3 Armd Div Soest Germany, Cdr 22 Armd Bde BAOR, GOC 3 Armd Div BAOR 1988–90, Cdr UK Field Army and Inspr Gen TA 1990, land dep to Jt Cdr HQ Strike Cmd High Wycombe under Operation Granby, memb Army Bd and Adj Gen 1993–95; Lt Govr Jersey 1995–; *Recreations* sailing, golf, hillwalking, skiing, reading; *Style—* HE Gen Sir Michael Wilkes, KCB, CBE; ✉ Government House, St Saviour, Jersey, CI JE2 7GH

WILKES, Prof (Francis) Michael; s of Francis Wilkes, of Dudley, Staffs, and Cecilia Josephine, *née* Grealey; *b* 9 Nov 1941; *Educ* St Philip's GS Birmingham, Univ of Birmingham (BSocSc, PhD); *m* Vivienne Mary, da of Alfred William Ernest Sawyer; 3 s (John Francis b 19 Oct 1972, David James (twin) b 19 Oct 1972, Stephen Mark b 9 March 1977); *Career* prof of business investment and mgmnt and dean Faculty of Commerce and Social Sci Univ of Birmingham 1991– (lectr then sr lectr with secondments to Univ of Aston Birmingham and Northwestern Univ USA 1962–91); memb (SDP and independent) Birmingham City Cncl 1984–92; memb Br Acad of Mgmnt; *Books* Management of Company Finance (with J M Samuels, 1971, 6 edn 1995), Capital Budgeting Techniques (2 edn, 1983), Mathematics for Business Finance and Economics (1994); *Recreations* walking, cricket; *Style—* Prof Michael Wilkes; ✉ The Business School, University of Birmingham, Edgbaston, Birmingham B15 2TT (☎ 0121 414 4948, fax 0121 414 6707)

WILKES, Richard Geoffrey; CBE (1990, OBE (mil) 1969), TD (1958), DL (Leics 1967); s of Geoffrey William Wilkes (d 1963), of Leicestershire, and Kathleen Mary, *née* Quinn (d 1932); *b* 12 June 1928; *Educ* Repton; *m* 1953, Wendy Elaine, da of Rev Clarence Oliver Ward (d 1982), of Hampshire; 1 s (Timothy), 3 da (Judi, Jane, Louise); *Career* cmmr RHA 1947, serv TA Leics 1948–72, Cdr Royal Leicestershire Regt (TA) 1965–69, TA Col E Midlands Dist 1969–72, ADC (TAVR) to HM The Queen 1972–77, Dep Hon Col (TA) Royal Anglian Regt (Leics) 1981–88; chm Leicester Co TAVRA 1981–89, vice chm E Midland TAVRA 1981–89; cmdt Leics Special Constabulary 1972–79; chartered accountant; ptnr Price Waterhouse London 1969–90, dir Cassidy Davis Insurance Group 1989–; pres: ICAEW 1980–81, Int Fedn of Accountants 1987–90; advsr to Lloyd's of London on self-regulation 1983–85; chm: SSAFA Leics 1991–, Care for Mentally Handicapped 1995– (govr 1972–); memb Ct of Assts Worshipful Co of Chartered Accountants (Master 1991–92); FCA 1952; *Recreations* shooting, sailing; *Clubs* Army and Navy; *Style—* Richard Wilkes, Esq, CBE, TD, DL; ✉ The Hermitage, Foxton, Leicestershire (☎ 01858 545213)

WILKES, Roderick Edward; s of Ernest Lawrence Wilkes (d 1987), of Staffordshire, and Sabra Whitehouse Johnson; *b* 26 Feb 1945; *Educ* Kingshill Sch Secdy Modern for Boys Wednesbury, Wednesbury Coll of Commerce (HND, DipM); *m* 28 March 1970, Marie, da of Harold Page; 1 s (James Edward b 6 June 1972), 1 da (Victoria Louise b 6 May 1974); *Career* Guest Keen & Nettlefolds Ltd 1960–70, commercial conslt GKN Sankey Ltd 1970–73, mktg dir Morlock Industries Ltd 1973–84, gp mktg dir Ellison Circlips Group 1984–86, md sr RFS 1987–94 (gen mangr 1986–87), md Phoenix Metal Products Ltd 1994–; past nat chm Chartered Inst of Mktg (Pres Award), nat chm Specialist Ceilings and Interiors Assoc; MCAM, FInstD, FCIM, FIMgt; *Recreations* theatre, swimming, travel, DIY; *Style—* Roderick E Wilkes, Esq; ✉ Monmoor Farm, Eardington, nr Bridgnorth, Shropshire WV16 5LA (☎ and fax 01746 763076)

WILKIE, David Andrew; MBE (1974); s of Henry George White Wilkie, of Aberdeen, Scotland, and Jean Angus, *née* McDonald; *b* 8 March 1954; *Educ* Royal Overseas Childrens' Sch Sri Lanka, Daniel Stewarts Coll Edinburgh, Univ of Miami Florida (BA); *ptnr* Helenè Margareta, da of Olof Isacson; 1 da (Natasha Louisa b 25 June 1989), 1 s (Adam Henry); *Career* international swimmer; first represented GB 1969, currently competes in masters swimming events worldwide; Cwlth Games: Bronze medal 200m breaststroke 1970, Gold medal 200m breaststroke 1974, Gold medal 200m individual medley 1974, Silver medal 100m breaststroke 1976; Olympic Games: Silver medal 200m breaststroke 1972, Gold medal 200m breaststroke 1976, Silver medal 100m breaststroke 1976; World Championships: Gold medal 200m breaststroke 1973, Bronze medal 200m individual medley 1973, Gold medal 200m breaststroke 1975, Gold medal 100m breaststroke 1975; Euro Championships: Gold medal 200m breaststroke 1974, Gold medal 200m individual medley 1974, Silver medal 400m medley relay 1974; records broken: 5 world, 23 Cwlth, 16 Euro, 30 Br; records held: Euro and Br 200m breaststroke, Scot nat 100m and 200m breaststroke 1976–, 3 world in masters events; former ptnr Sports Perception; former TV presenter: Splash (Channel 4), Wings Wheels and Water (Channel 4), Winning With Wilkie (STV), Wilkie on Water (STV), Wilkie in Winter (STV); currently swimming analyst Eurosport, Sky Sports and Prime Sports; md Health Perception; memb Worldwide Fund for Nature; *Books* Wilkie (autobiography), Winning with Wilkie, Splash, The Handbook of Swimming; *Recreations* scuba diving, travelling; *Style—* David Wilkie, Esq, MBE; ✉ Health Perception Ltd, Woodbine Stores Cottage, Chavey Down Road, Winkfield Row, Berks RG12 8NY (☎ 01344 890115, fax 01344 890116)

WILKIE, (Alex) Ian; s of Frederick James Wilkie (d 1976), and Florence Gladys Bell (d 1989); direct descendant of Sir David Wilkie, RA (1785–1841); *b* 1 Sept 1935; *Educ* Lancing, Poole Coll of Tech, Brighton Tech Coll (HNC Metallurgy); *m* 4 May 1963, Pamela May, da of William Frank Ross, of Hove, Sussex; 1 s (Andrew b 19 Jan 1964), 2 da (Jill and Philippa (twins) b 14 Jan 1966); *Career* Military Serv The Gordon Highlanders; dir: The Association of British Pewter Craftsmen Ltd, md British Pewter Designs Ltd, Anzon Ltd (subsid of Cookson Group plc) 1980–84; head of corporate relations worldwide Cookson Group plc 1985–92; sec to the Adjudicators of The Cookson Conservation and Restoration Award 1992–, tstee Historic Churches Preservation Tst; memb: Country Landowners' Assoc, Game Conservancy, Br Assoc for Shooting and Conservation, Br Field Sport Soc; regular contributor of articles on marketing, advertising and corporate affrs; Liveryman Worshipful Co of Pewterers, Freeman City of London; *Recreations* shooting (shoot mangr Stow Longa Shoot), stalking, fishing, golf, gardening, property restoration; *Clubs* East India, Wig and Pen, Lime Street Ward, London Metal Exchange Golf Assoc (life-vice pres); *Style—* A Ian Wilkie, Esq; ✉ The Old Post Office, Hail Weston, Cambs PE19 4JW; 38 High Street, Hail Weston, Cambs (☎ 01480 472965, fax 01480 477300, car 0831 247553)

WILKINS, Sir Graham John (Bob); kt (1980); s of George Wilkins; *b* 22 Jan 1924; *Educ* Yeovil Sch, Univ Coll SW of England Exeter (BSc); *m* 1, 1945, late Daphne Haynes; m 2, 1990, Helen Catherine MacGregor; *Career* chm and chief exec: Thorn EMI 1985–88 (dir 1978, chm 1988–89), Beecham Group 1974–86 (exec vice chm 1974); dir: Beecham Inc 1967–86, Beecham AG 1973–74, Courtaulds 1975–85, Hill Samuel 1977–88, Rowntree Mackintosh 1984–88, Courage Pensions 1984–, Eastern Group plc (formerly Eastern Electricity plc) 1989–95; memb Doctors and Dentists Remuneration Review Body 1980–87 (chm 1987–90); pres Advertising Assoc 1983–89, chm ICC UK 1985–89; pres: Assoc of Br Pharmaceutical Indust 1969–71, European Fedn of Pharmaceutical Industs Assoc 1978–82; memb BOTB 1977–80, chm Cncl Sch of Pharmacy Univ of London 1988– (memb 1984–); Hon FRCP 1985; *Style—* Sir Graham Wilkins

WILKINS, John Anthony Francis; s of Edward Manwaring Wilkins (d 1988), and Ena Gwendolen Francis Wilkins (d 1988); *b* 20 Dec 1936; *Educ* Clifton, Clare Coll Cambridge (major scholar and fndn scholar, BA); *Career* 2 Lt 1 Bn Glos Regt 1955–57; asst ed Frontier, asst ed The Tablet 1967–72, scriptwriter BBC External Servs 1972–81 (Ondas radio prize 1973), ed The Tablet 1982–; *Recreations* ornithology; *Style*— John Wilkins, Esq; ✉ The Tablet, 1 King Street Cloisters, Clifton Walk, London W6 0QZ (☎ 0181 748 8484, fax 0181 748 1550)

WILKINS, Prof Malcolm Barrett; s of Barrett Charles Wilkins (d 1962), of Cardiff, and Eleanor Mary, *née* Jenkins; *b* 27 Feb 1933; *Educ* Monkton House Sch Cardiff, King's Coll London (BSc, PhD, DSc); *m* 10 July 1959, (Mary) Patricia, da of Lt-Cdr James Edward Maltby, RNR, RD; 1 s (Nigel Edward Barrett b 7 Aug 1961), 1 da (Fiona Louise Emma Barrett b 14 Jan 1965 d 1980); *Career* lectr in botany King's Coll London 1959–64 (asst lectr 1958–59), prof of biol Univ of E Anglia 1965–67 (lectr 1964–65), prof of plant physiology Univ of Nottingham 1967–70, Regius prof of botany Univ of Glasgow 1970–; chm: Life Sciences Advsy Ctee Euro Space Agency 1987–89, Laurel Bank Sch Co Ltd Glasgow 1980–87; memb Incorporation of Gardeners City of Glasgow, memb Ct Univ of Glasgow, tstee Royal Botanic Gdns Edinburgh 1990– (dep chm 1993–94, chm 1994–); memb Advsy Ctee Scottish Agric Coll; hon memb American Soc for Plant Physiology; FRSE 1972 (vice pres 1994–); *Books* Plantwatching (1988), Advanced Plant Physiology (ed, 1984), The Physiology of Plant Growth and Development (ed, 1969); *Recreations* fishing, sailing, model engrg; *Clubs* Caledonian, New (Edinburgh); *Style*— Prof Malcolm Wilkins, FRSE; ✉ 5 Hughenden Drive, Glasgow G12 9XS (☎ 0141 334 8079); Botany Dept, Glasgow University, Glasgow G12 8QQ (☎ 0141 330 4450/0141 339 339 8855, ext 4450, fax 0141 330 4447, telex 777070 UNIGLA)

WILKINS, Roger Frederick Laurence; s of Laurence Rea Wilkins (d 1988), of Hall Green, Birmingham, and Joan Muriel, *née* Marklew (d 1991); *b* 28 Sept 1940; *Educ* King Edward's Sch Birmingham, Univ of Manchester (BSc), Univ of Nottingham (PGCE); *m* 1 (m dis 1993); 1 da (Catharine Marguerite b 1968), 1 s (Matthew Laurence b 1970); m 2, 1994, Francine Catherine, *née* Corris; *Career* successively educn offr, head of science, dep headmaster and headmaster Kigezi Coll Uganda 1963–70; British Council: asst rep Malawi 1971–75, asst dir Service Conditions Dept 1975–78, educn offr Nepal 1978–82, head of gp HE Div 1982–85, dir S Pacific 1985–88, regnl dir Manchester 1989–92, advsr to Asst DG 1992–93, dir Uganda 1993–; *Recreations* photography, cricket, wildlife conservation; *Clubs* Old Edwardians Assoc; *Style*— Roger Wilkins, Esq; ✉ The British Council, c/o FCO (Kampala), King Charles Street, London SW1A 2AH

WILKINSON, Rev Canon Alan Bassindale; s of Rev John Thomas Wilkinson (d 1980), of Knighton, Powys, and Marian, *née* Elliott (d 1980); *b* 26 Jan 1931; *Educ* William Hulme's GS Manchester, St Catharine's Coll Cambridge (BA, MA, PhD), Coll of the Resurrection Mirfield; *m* 1, 27 July 1961 (m dis 1975), Eva Leonore, da of Curt Michelson (d 1981), of Lausanne; 2 s (John b 1964, Conrad b 1968), 1 da (Sarah b 1962); m 2, 29 Dec 1975, Fenella Ruth, da of Col Rupert Thurstan Holland, CBE, DSO, MC (d 1959), of Salisbury; *Career* ordained: deacon 1959, priest 1960; asst curate St Augustine's Kilburn 1959–61, chaplain of St Catharine's Coll Cambridge 1961–67, vicar of Barrow Gurney 1967–70, chaplain and lectr of St Matthias' Coll Bristol 1967–70, princ Chichester Theol Coll 1970–74, warden Verulam House St Albans 1974–75, sr lectr Crewe and Alsager Coll 1975–78, dir of training Ripon Diocese 1978–84, priest i/c Darley Thornthwaite and Thruscross 1984–88, hon priest of Portsmouth Cathedral 1988–, diocesan theologian 1993–, cathedral chaplain 1994–; Open Univ tutor 1988–, visiting fell Chichester Inst of HE 1995–; select preacher: Cambridge 1967, Oxford 1982; memb: Gen Synod Bd of Educn 1982–86; memb: Governing Body Coll of Ripon and York St John 1984–88, Governing Body SPCK 1982–91; hon canon: of Chichester 1970, of Ripon 1984; *Books* The Church of England and the First World War (1978), Would You Believe It? (1983), Christian Choices (1983), More Ready to Hear (1983), Dissent or Conform? War, Peace and the English Churches 1900–1945 (1986), The Community of the Resurrection - A Centenary History (1992); *Style*— The Rev Canon Alan Wilkinson; ✉ Hope Cottage, 27 Great Southsea St, Portsmouth PO5 3BY (☎ 01705 825788)

WILKINSON, Sheriff Alexander Birrell; QC (Scot 1993); s of Capt Alexander Wilkinson, MBE (d 1938), of Perth, Scotland, and Isabella Bell, *née* Birrell (d 1977); *b* 2 Feb 1932; *Educ* Perth Acad, Univ of St Andrews (MA), Univ of Edinburgh (LLB); *m* 10 Sept 1965, Wendy Imogen, da of Capt Ernest Albert Barrett, RE (d 1949), of Belfast; 1 s (Alan b 1974), 1 da (Jennifer b 1970); *Career* Nat Serv RAEC 1954–56; faculty of advocates 1959, in practice Scottish Bar 1959–69, lectr in Scots law Univ of Edinburgh 1965–69, Sheriff of Stirling Dunbarton and Clackmannan at Stirling and Alloa 1969–72, prof of private law Univ of Dundee 1972–86 (dean of Faculty of Law Univ of Dundee 1974–76 and 1986); Sheriff: of Tayside Central and Fife at Falkirk 1986–91, of Glasgow and Strathkelvin 1991–96, of Lothian and Borders at Edinburgh 1996–; a temp judge of the Ct of Session 1993–; chm: Industl Tbnls (Scotland) 1972–86, Scottish Marriage Guidance Cncl 1974–77, Legal Servs Gp Scottish Assoc of CAB 1979–83; vice-pres The Sheriffs' Assoc 1995–; chllr Diocese of: Brechin 1981–, Argyll and The Isles 1985–; *Books* Gloag and Henderson's Introduction To The Law of Scotland (jt ed, 1980 and 1987), The Scottish Law of Evidence (1986), The Law of Parent and Child in Scotland (co-author, 1993); *Recreations* collecting books and pictures, reading, travel; *Clubs* New (Edinburgh); *Style*— Sheriff A B Wilkinson, QC; ✉ 25 Glencairn Crescent, Edinburgh EH12 5BT (☎ 0131 346 1797); Sheriffs' Chambers, Sheriff Court House, 27 Chambers Street, Edinburgh EH1 1LB (☎ 0131 225 2525)

WILKINSON, Charles Edmund; s of Dr Oliver Charles Wilkinson (d 1987), of Riverholme, Thames St, Wallingford, Oxon, and Sheila Muriel, *née* McMullan; *b* 6 June 1943; *Educ* Haileybury and ISC, Clare Coll Cambridge; *m* 3 June 1967, Gillian Margaret, da of Thomas Patrick Madden Alexander, of East Grinstead, Sussex; 2 da (Claire b 10 March 1972, Juliet b 13 June 1973); *Career* slr; sr ptnr Blyth Dutton 1980–91 (ptnr 1974), ptnr Lawrence Graham (following merger) 1991–; memb Worshipful Co of Coachmakers and Coach Harness Makers, Freeman City of London; memb Law Soc; *Clubs* Brooks's, Hurlingham, Roehampton; *Style*— Charles Wilkinson, Esq; ✉ Lawrence Graham, 190 The Strand, London WC2R 1JN (☎ 0171 379 0000, fax 0171 379 6854)

WILKINSON, Prof Christopher David Wicks (Chris); s of Charles Norman Wilkinson (d 1942), and late Doris Margaret, *née* Wicks; *b* 1 Jan 1940; *Educ* Queen Elizabeth's GS Blackburn, Balliol Coll Oxford (MA), Stanford Univ (PhD); *m* 25 June 1962, Dr Judith (Judy) Anne Hughes, da of late Ronald Sydney Hughes; 2 da (Rona Elizabeth b 4 Oct 1969, Maggie Alison b 19 July 1974), 1 s (Kit Alexander b 27 May 1971); *Career* engr English Electric Valve Co Chelmsford 1967–69; Dept of Electronics and Electrical Engrg Univ of Glasgow: lectr 1969–75, sr lectr 1975–79, reader 1979–82, titular prof 1982–92, James Watt prof 1992–; memb APS; FRSE 1987; *Recreations* hill walking, allotment holder; *Style*— Prof Chris Wilkinson, FRSE; ✉ Department of Electronics and Electrical Engineering, The University, Glasgow G12 8QQ (☎ 0141 330 5219, fax 0141 330 6010, e-mail chrisw@elec.gla.ac.uk)

WILKINSON, Christopher John (Chris); s of Maj Edward Anthony Wilkinson, of Welwyn Garden City, Herts, and Norma Doreen, *née* Trevelyan-Beer; *b* 1 July 1945; *Educ* St Albans Sch, Regent Street Poly Sch of Architecture (DipArch, RIBA); *m* 3 April 1976, Diana Mary, da of Alan Oakley Edmunds, of Limpsfield Chart, Surrey; 1 s (Dominic b 1980), 1 da (Zoe b 1978); *Career* princ ptnr Chris Wilkinson Architects 1983–; formerly with Richard Rogers and Ptnrs, Michael Hopkins Architects and Foster Assocs; assessor on BSC Colorcoat Award 1986 and 1987, British Steel Student Architectural Award 1994 and 1995; chm RIBA SE Region Awards 1996; works exhibited: RA Summer Exhbn 1986, 1987, 1988, 1991 and 1995, The Architecture Fndn 1992 and 1995, Tokyo Design Centre 1995; projects incl: Stratford Market Depot and Stratford Station for Jubilee Line Extension, Liverpool St Station Devpt and Arcade Ticket Hall for CrossRail Link, Winsor Park Housing, Refurbishment of Ten Trinity Sq for Willis Corroon Gp, 18/19 Clerkenwell Green; *Awards* Eric Lyons Award 1993, Canary Wharf Bridge Competition 1994, Hulme Bridge Competition 1995, Bedford Bridge Competition 1995, CSD Designer of the Yr 1996; *Books* Supersheds (1991), Supersheds II (1995); *Recreations* golf, painting, travel; *Style*— Chris Wilkinson, Esq; ✉ 52 Park Hall Rd, West Dulwich, London SE21 8BW (☎ 0181 761 7021); Studio 2, 10 Bowling Green Lane, London EC1R 0BD (☎ 0171 251 8622, fax 0171 251 8419)

WILKINSON, Christopher Richard; s of Rev Thomas R Wilkinson (d 1978), and Frances, *née* Steel; *b* 3 July 1941; *Educ* Heath GS Halifax, Selwyn Coll Cambridge (BA, MA); *Career* Cwlth Secretariat 1963–65, OECD Paris and Madrid 1965–66, World Bank Washington DC and Lagos 1966–73; European Commission Brussels: head of div Directorate Gen for Regnl Policy 1973–78, head of div Directorate Gen for Internal Market and Industl Affrs 1978–82, head of div Directorate Gen for Telecommunications, Info Industs and Innovation 1983–93, advsr Telecommunications and Postal Affairs 1993–; visiting fell Center for Int Affrs Harvard Univ 1982–83; *Recreations* mountain walking, gardening, cooking; *Style*— Mr Christopher Wilkinson; ✉ European Commission, 200 rue de la Loi, B-1049 Brussels, Belgium (☎ 00 322 296 9538)

WILKINSON, Brig Clive Anthony; CBE (1987); s of George Wilkinson (d 1974), of Cheltenham, and Elsie Annie Wilkinson, *née* Reid; *b* 14 Feb 1935; *Educ* Bishop Cotton Sch Simla India, Wrekin Coll Wellington Shropshire; *m* 4 July 1959, Nadine Elizabeth Wilkinson, da of William Humphreys (d 1979), of Southport; 2 da (Juliette b 1960, Caroline b 1962); *Career* cmmnd RA 1955, Staff Coll Camberley 1967, military asst to C in C AFCENT 1974–77, instr German Armed Forces Staff Coll 1977–79, CO 7 Bn UDR 1979–81, Col Strategic Planning Team NATO HQ 1982–84, asst COS logistics HQ BAOR 1985–86, Cdr 107 (Ulster) Bde 1987–89; dir The Gin and Vodka Assoc of GB 1990–, vice pres Confédération Européenne des Producteurs de Spiritueux 1993–96; FIMgt 1989; *Recreations* sailing, golf, walking; *Clubs* Army and Navy; *Style*— Brig Clive Wilkinson, CBE; ✉ c/o Army and Navy Club, 36–39 Pall Mall, London SW1Y 5JN

WILKINSON, David; CB (1994); *b* 1947; *Educ* Boteler GS Warrington Lancs, Wigan and District Mining and Tech Coll, Bedford Coll London (BA), LSE, Moscow State Univ (postgrad study); *m* 3 da; *Career* Dept of Educn and Science: served as trainee 1974–79, incl period on Secretariat of Inquiry into Sch Govt (Taylor Ctee), and as private sec to Perm Sec (Sir James Hamilton), Higher Educn Policy 1979–81, schs territorial offr NW Eng 1981–84, negotiator Sch Teacher's Pay and Conditions 1984–86, head of Information Branch and chief press offr to Rt Hon Kenneth Baker MP 1986–88, dep princ and establishment offr 1988–89, head of Science Branch 1989–92, head of Science and Engrg Base Gp Office of Science and Technol Cabinet Office 1992–94, study leave RCDS 1995; *Style*— David Wilkinson, Esq, CB; ✉ Cabinet Office, Office of Science, Government Offices, Great George Street, London SW1P 3AL

WILKINSON, Sir Denys Haigh; kt (1974); s of Charles Wilkinson, and Hilda Wilkinson; *b* 5 Sept 1922; *Educ* Loughborough GS, Jesus Coll Cambridge; *m* 1, 1947 (m dis 1967), Christiane, *née* Clavier; 3 da; m 2, 1967, Helen, *née* Sommers; 2 step da; *Career* dir Int Sch of Nuclear Physics Erice Sicily 1974–83, vice chllr Univ of Sussex 1976–87; chm: Br Cncl Scientific Advsy Panel and Ctee 1977–86, Radioactive Waste Mgmnt Advsy Ctee 1978–83; memb: Wilton Park Acad Cncl 1979–83, Cncl Assoc Cwlth Univs 1980–87; pres Inst of Physics 1980–82, foreign memb Royal Swedish Acad of Scis 1980–, Hon FilDr Uppsala; Hon DSc: Saskatchewan, Utah State, Guelph, Queen's (Kingston), Coll of William and Mary Williamsburg; Hon LLD Univ of Sussex; FRS 1956; *Style*— Sir Denys Wilkinson, FRS; ✉ Gayles Orchard, Friston, Eastbourne, E Sussex BN20 0BA (☎ 01323 423333)

WILKINSON, Donald John; s of Frederick Wilkinson, of Wigan Lancs, and Tina, *née* Cameron; *b* 14 Feb 1955; *Educ* Lancaster Royal GS, Keble Coll Oxford (MA, MLitt); *m* 1 Aug 1979, Janet Margaret, da of Stanley Wilkinson; 1 s (Ian b 1984), 1 da (Rachael b 1983); *Career* teacher Manchester GS 1979–84, head of history Oakham Sch 1984–86, head of Sixth Form Newcastle-under-Lyme Sch 1987–89, headmaster Cheadle Hulme Sch 1990–; FRSA; *Publications* The Normans in Britain (jtly, 1988), various articles on seventeenth century English history; *Recreations* sport (especially cricket and running), walking, theatre, reading modern novels; *Style*— Donald Wilkinson, Esq; ✉ Cheadle Hulme School, Claremont Rd, Cheadle Hulme, Cheshire SK8 6EF (☎ 0161 488 3330)

WILKINSON, Brig (Charles) Edward; CBE (1982, OBE 1977), TD (1964, and Clasps 1970, 1976 and 1982), DL (Derbyshire 1985); s of Charles Dean Wilkinson, of Ashford in the Water, Derbyshire, and Florence, *née* Wakefield; *b* 5 May 1932; *Educ* Repton, Manchester Business Sch; *m* 15 Sep 1956, Joy Maureen, da of Arthur Locke, of Colchester, Essex (d 1946); 1 s (Timothy), 1 da (Sarah); *Career* Nat Serv cmmnd Sherwood Foresters 1951, TA, Mercian Volunteers, Worcester-Foresters Staff 1952–85; Brig TA 1982–85; dir numerous cos including Leigh Interests plc 1990–94; Hon Col 3 Worcester Foresters 1983–94; chm E Midlands TAVRA 1985–94; vice chm Cncl of TAVRAs 1990–94; govr Repton Sch 1993–; High Sheriff of Derbyshire 1996–97; Liveryman and memb Ct of Assts Worshipful Co of Fuellers (Master 1996–97), Freeman City of London; *Recreations* Territorial Army, photography, spectator sports; *Clubs* Army and Navy, Royal Fowey Yacht; *Style*— Brig Edward Wilkinson, CBE, TD, DL; ✉ Thornbury, Ashford in the Water, Bakewell, Derbyshire DE45 1QH (☎ and fax 01629 812535)

WILKINSON, Geoffrey Crichton; CBE (1986), AFC (1957); s of Col William Edward Duncan Wilkinson (d 1980), and Evelyn Katherine Wilkinson (d 1996); *b* 7 Nov 1926; *Educ* Bedford Sch, Royal Indian Mil Coll; *m* 6 Dec 1958, Virginia Mary, da of Russell Broom (d 1963), of Rodinghead, Mauchline, Ayrshire; 2 da (Susannah (Mrs Wright) b 1961, Samantha (Mrs Barber) b 1963); *Career* RN 1944–47; aeronautical engrg trg 1948–49, pilot RAF 1949–59, seconded USAF Korea 1952–53, Empire Test Pilot Sch 1956, engrg test pilot 1957–59, ret 1959; Turner and Newall 1959–61, dir Mercury Airlines 1961–65, dep chief inspr air accidents Dept of Trade 1981 (inspr 1965, ret as chief inspr accidents 1986); Air medal USA 1953; FRAeS 1970; *Recreations* sailing; *Clubs* RAF; *Style*— Geoffrey Wilkinson, Esq, CBE, AFC; ✉ Buckingham House, 50 Hyde St, Winchester, Hants SO23 7DY (☎ 01962 865823)

WILKINSON, Glen Alexander Low; s of Cdr James Henry Wilkinson, of Gosport, Hants, and Alexia Menny, *née* Low; *b* 2 Sept 1950; *Educ* Churchers Coll Petersfield Hants, Birmingham Univ Med Sch (MB ChB); *m* 26 March 1976, Diana Joy, da of George Norman Purdy, of Halesowen; 1 s (Matthew James b 11 Feb 1988), 3 da (Rebecca b 9 Feb 1978, Angela b 9 March 1979, Laura b 19 May 1986); *Career* sr registrar in cardiothoracic surgery W Midlands RHA 1985–88, sr fell (actg instr) in cardiothoracic surgery Univ Hosp Washington Seattle USA 1986–87, currently conslt cardiothoracic surgn Sheffield Health Authy and Northern Gen Hosp; FRCS 1978, memb Soc of Cardiothoracic Surgns of GB and I 1986; *Recreations* model railway running and collecting, model boat building, photography; *Style*— Glen Wilkinson, Esq; ✉ 31 Meadow Bank Ave, Cherry Tree Hill, Nether Edge, Sheffield S7 1PB (☎ 0114 258 3197); Northern General Hospital, Herries Rd, Sheffield S5 7AU (☎ 0114 243 4343, fax 0114 256 0472)

WILKINSON, Sir (David) Graham Brook; 3 Bt (UK 1941), of Brook, Witley, Co Surrey; s of Sir David Wilkinson, 2 Bt, DSC (d 1972); *b* 18 May 1947; *Educ* Millfield, ChCh Oxford; *m* 1977, Sandra Caroline, da of Dr Richard Rossdale; 2 da (Louise Caroline Sylvia b 1979, Tara Katherine Juliet b 1982); *Heir* none; *Career* dir Orion Royal Bank Ltd 1971–85, md SEIC Services (UK) 1985–89; non-exec dir: Galveston-Houston Co USA 1986–89, Lamport Gilbert Ltd 1992–; memb Ct of Assts Worshipful Co of Farmers, Liveryman Worshipful Co of Goldsmiths; CStJ 1994; *Clubs* Royal Yacht Sqdn, White's; *Style*— Sir Graham Wilkinson, Bt

WILKINSON, Howard; s of Jack Wilkinson, of Sheffield, and Doris, *née* Winfield; *b* 13 Nov 1943; *Educ* Nether Edge GS, Abbeydale Boys' GS, Sheffield Coll of Educn, Univ of Sheffield (BEd); *m* twice; 2 s (Damian James, Alistair Benjamin), 1 da (Anna Marie); *Career* former professional football manager and player; playing career: Hallam 1960–62, Sheffield Wednesday 1962–66, Brighton & Hove Albion 1966–71, Boston Utd 1971–77 (player-mangr 1972–77), Mossley 1977–78 (player/mangr), represented England youth; mangr: Notts County 1981–83 (formerly coach), Sheffield Wednesday 1983–88, Leeds Utd 1988–96; technical dir Football Association 1997–; sometime mangr England semi-professional, B and under 21 levels; sometime coach England A, B and under 21 levels; honours as mangr: promotion to Div 1 Notts County 1981, runners-up Div 2 Sheffield Wednesday 1984, Div 2 Championship Leeds Utd 1990, League Championship Leeds Utd 1992; Div 2 Mangr of the Season Barclays Bank 1990, Mangr of the Year Barclays Bank 1991–92 season; first chm League Managers' Assoc; sch teacher 1976–78, FA Regnl Coach 1978–81; Hon MBA Leeds Metropolitan Univ 1993; *Books* Managing to Succeed (autobiography, 1992); *Recreations* wine, reading, music, sport; *Style*— Howard Wilkinson, Esq; ✉ c/o The Football Association, 16 Lancaster Gate, London W2 3LW

WILKINSON, James Hugh; s of Hugh Davy Wilkinson (d 1972), and Marjorie, *née* Prout (d 1965); *b* 19 Sept 1941; *Educ* Westminster Abbey Choir Sch, Sutton GS, King's Coll London (BSc), Churchill Coll Cambridge (CertEd); *m* 11 Nov 1978, Elisabeth Ann, da of John Morse, of Cheltenham; 2 s (Christopher b 1979, Matthew b 1982); *Career* science and health corr Daily Express 1964–74, science and aviation corr BBC Radio 1974–83, science corr BBC TV News 1983–; visiting fell Agric and Food Res Cncl's Inst of Food Res Reading Berks; sec Brotherhood of St Edward the Confessor Westminster Abbey 1982–; *Books* Conquest of Cancer (1973), Tobacco (1986), Green or Bust (1990); *Recreations* music, fishing; *Style*— James Wilkinson, Esq; ✉ BBC TV Centre, Wood Lane, London W12 7RJ (☎ 0181 576 4671, fax 0181 749 9016)

WILKINSON, Jeffrey Vernon; s of Arthur Wilkinson (d 1965), and Winifred May Allison (d 1989); *b* 21 Aug 1930; *Educ* Matthew Humberstone Sch, King's Coll Cambridge (MA), Sorbonne; *m* 1955, Jean Vera, da of George Farrow Nurse (d 1959); 2 da (Julie Katherine b 1962, Elizabeth Jane b 1964); *Career* Joseph Lucas Ltd: joined as graduate apprentice 1954, dir CAV 1963, dir and gen mangr Diesel Equipment CAV 1967, dir 1974, divnl md 1978; dir Simon Engineering 1968, dir and gen mangr Lucas Electrical 1974, jt gp md Lucas Industries plc 1979–84, dir APAX Partners & Co 1986– (and chm or dir various assoc cos); chm and chief exec offr Spear and Jackson plc 1992–; chm: Automotive Components Manufacturers 1979–84, Plastics Processing Economic Devpt Ctee 1985–88; memb Cncl and Exec SMMT 1979–84; Liveryman Worshipful Co of Wheelwrights 1971; FBCS, CIMgt; *Recreations* tennis, swimming, water skiing, reading, theatre; *Style*— Jeffrey Wilkinson, Esq; ✉ Hillcroft, 15 Mearse Lane, Barnt Green, Birmingham B45 8HG (☎ 0121 447 7750)

WILKINSON, John Arbuthnot DuCane; MP (C) Ruislip Northwood (majority 19,791); s of Denys Wilkinson; *b* 23 Sept 1940; *Educ* Eton, RAF Coll Cranwell, Churchill Coll Cambridge; *m* 1, 1969 (m dis 1987), 1 da; *m* 2, 1987, Cecilia, da of Raul Cienfuegos Lyon; 1 s; *Career* RAF Flying Instructor, Civil Aviation; MP (C): Bradford W 1970–74 (also contested Feb and Oct 1974), Ruislip - Northwood 1979–; PPS to: Min of State Indust 1979–80, John Nott as Sec of State Defence 1981–82; chm Anglo-Asian Cons Soc 1979–82, head Univs Dept Cons Central Office 1967–68, chm Cons Aviation Ctee 1983–85 and 1992–93, chm Space Sub-Ctee Cons Indust Ctee 1986–90, chm Cons Defence Ctee 1993–94 and 1996– (vice chm 1983–85 and 1990–93); formerly PA to Chm BAC, formerly sales mangr Klingair Ltd; sometime tutor Open Univ, delegate to Cncl of Europe and WEU 1979–90; *Books* The Uncertain Ally - British Defence Policy 1960–90 (with Michael Chichester), British Defence - a Blueprint for Reform; *Recreations* cross country skiing, fell running; *Style*— John Wilkinson Esq, MP; ✉ House of Commons, London SW1A 0AA

WILKINSON, John Francis; s of Col W T Wilkinson, DSO (d 1950), and Evelyn Sybil (d 1975); *b* 2 Oct 1926; *Educ* Wellington, Univ of Edinburgh, Cambridge and London Univ Colonial Course; *m* 11 Aug 1951, Alison Jessie, da of Hugh Wilmott Malcolm (d 1961); 2 (Anthony Hugh b 5 April 1953, Roderick William b 26 Oct 1954), 1 da (Julian Margaret Marion b 24 Sept 1960); *Career* trainee pilot Fleet Air ARM 1945, RN 1945–47; HM Colonial Serv Nigeria: asst dist offr Bida 1949, asst sec Land & Mines Kanduna 1950, private sec to Chief Cmmr N Nigeria 1951; Nigerian Bdcasting Serv: controller N Region 1952, controller Nat Progs Lagos 1956–58; BBC African Service: orgn African Prog 1958, E and Central Africa Prog 1961, asst head 1964, head 1969–76; head of prodn and planning BBC World Service 1976; sec BBC 1977, dir Public Affrs BBC 1980–85; vice pres The Centre for Int Briefing Farnham Castle 1987– (chm 1977–87), tstee One World Bdcasting Tst 1990– (dir 1986–90), dir One World Week Ltd 1989–, vice pres Royal African Soc 1978–80 (chm Speakers and Publications Ctee 1970–78); memb Cncl Mgmnt Worldaware 1988–94; Hon Master Open Univ 1989; *Recreations* sailing, occasional golf; *Clubs* Commonwealth Trust; *Style*— John Wilkinson, Esq; ✉ Compass Cottage, Minchinhampton, nr Stroud, Gloucester GL6 9HD (☎ 01453 833072, fax 01453 833617)

WILKINSON, John Parker; JP (Cambridgeshire, 1975); s of Lt-Col William Currington Wilkinson (d 1993), MC, TD, of Peterborough, and Brenda Mary, *née* Parker (d 1989); *b* 3 July 1939; *Educ* Kings Sch Peterborough, Architecture Assoc (AADipl), Nottingham Coll of Art and Design (DipTP); *m* 29 June 1963, Barbara Ann, da of John George Metcalf (d 1984), of Peterborough; 1 s (James b 1968), 1 da (Anna b 1966); *Career* asst architect Barlett and Gray Nottingham 1962–65, architect Co Planning Dept Huntingdon 1965–68, ptnr Ruddle Wilkinson Ptnrship Peterborough 1972–91, princ John Wilkinson Architects & Planners Peterborough 1991–; dir: Abbeyfields (Peterborough) Soc Ltd 1993–, Cresset Leisure Services Ltd 1994–, Abbey Planning Supervisers Ltd 1995–; pres Peterborough Rotary Club 1981–82, memb Peterborough Civic Soc; ARIBA 1964, MRTPI 1968, FInstD 1986; *Recreations* swimming, photography, walking, geology; *Style*— John Wilkinson, Esq, JP; ✉ 100 Park Road, Peterborough, Cambridgeshire PE1 2TJ (☎ 01733 66731, fax 01733 892437)

WILKINSON, Rev Canon Keith Howard; s of Kenneth John Wilkinson, of Leicester, and Grace Winifred, *née* Bowler; *b* 25 June 1948; *Educ* Beaumont Leys Coll Leicester, The Gateway GS Leicester, Univ of Hull (BA), Emmanuel Coll Cambridge (MA), Westcott House Cambridge; *m* 27 Aug 1972, Carolyn, da of Lewis John Gilbert (d 1985), of Wokingham; 2 da (Rachel b 1979, Claire b 1979); *Career* head of religious studies Bricknell HS 1970–72, head of faculty (humanities) Kelvin Hall Comprehensive Sch Kingston upon Hull 1972–74; ordained: deacon 1976, priest 1977; asst priest St Jude Westwood Peterborough 1976–79, educn offr to the church Peterborough 1977–79, asst master and chaplain Eton Coll 1979–84, sr chaplain and head of religious studies Malvern Coll 1984–89 (sr tutor 1988–89), headmaster Berkhamsted Sch 1989–96, headmaster The King's Sch Canterbury 1996–; hon canon Cathedral Church of Christ Canterbury; FRSA 1994; *Recreations* films, music, drama, ecology, walking, buildings, the Archers; *Clubs* East India; *Style*— The Rev Canon Keith Wilkinson; ✉ The King's School, Canterbury, Kent, CT1 2ES (☎ 01227 595501, fax 01227 595595)

WILKINSON, Dr Laura Margaret; da of William Low Wilkinson, of Ayr, and Dorothy, *née* Smith; *Educ* Ayr GS, Wellington Sch Ayr, Univ of Glasgow (MB ChB); *Career* house offr in med then surgery Gartnavel Gen/Western Infirmary Glasgow 1984–85, SHO in gen med Monklands Dist Gen Hosp Airdrie 1985–87; Gartnavel Gen/Western Infirmary Glasgow: registrar then sr registrar in radiology 1987–93, conslt radiologist W of Scotland Breast Screening Serv Gartnavel Gen Hosp and Western Infirmary Glasgow 1993–; Royal Coll of Radiologists: W of Scotland Jr Forum rep 1991–95, memb Scottish Standing Ctee 1991–95, chm Exec Jr Radiologists Forum 1993–95; sec Jr Forum Euro Assoc of Radiology 1995–; FRCR 1992; *Recreations* golf, skiing, aerobics; *Clubs* Royal Scottish Automobile; *Style*— Dr Laura Wilkinson; ✉ 1/L 54 Polwarth Street, Hyndland, Glasgow G12 9TL (☎ 0141 334 5540); West of Scotland Breast Screening Centre, Gartnavel General Hospital, Glasgow G12 0YN (☎ 0141 211 3118/3114, fax 0141 211 8000, mobile 0831 420492)

WILKINSON, Dr Mark Lawrence; s of Rev Canon Raymond Stewart Wilkinson, QHC, of Warwick, and Dorothy Elinor, *née* Church; *b* 19 May 1950; *Educ* Birkenhead Sch, The Middx Hosp Med Sch, Univ of London (BSc, MB BS, MD); *m* 4 Jan 1975, Anna Maria, da of Nicola Ugo Dante Cassoni, of Kenton, Harrow; 1 s (Nicholas b 1979), 1 da (Elinor b 1985); *Career* registrar Middx Hosp 1979–81; Liver Unit King's Coll Sch of Med: res fell 1981–84, lectr 1984–86; sr lectr and conslt physician Guy's Hosp and UMDS of Guy's and St Thomas' Hosps 1986–, clinical dir of specialist med Guy's and St Thomas' Hosps' Tst 1995–; memb Jt Advsy Gp on Endoscopy 1995–, trg offr Endoscopy Ctee of Br Soc of Gastroenterology 1995–, sec Br Assoc for Study of the Liver 1993–96; FRCP 1992 (MRCP 1977); *Recreations* books, walking, Italy; *Style*— Dr Mark Wilkinson; ✉ Gastroenterology Unit, United Medical and Dental Schools of Guy's and St Thomas' Hospitals, 18th Floor, Guy's Tower, St Thomas' St, London SE1 9RT (☎ 0171 955 4564, fax 0171 955 4230)

WILKINSON, Rear Adm Nicholas John; CB (1994); s of Lt Col M D Wilkinson, of Manningtree, and J M Cosens; *b* 14 April 1941; *Educ* English Sch Cairo, Cheltenham Coll, Britannia RNC Dartmouth; *m* 1969 (m dis 1996), Penelope Ann Stephenson; 3 s (Sacheverell b 1969, Isambard b 1971, Augustus b 1976), 1 da (Gezina b 1977); *Career* with RN; served HM Ships: Venus, Vidal, Hardy, Hermes, Fife, Endurance, London 1960–78; 1964–82: RN Air Station Arbroath, RNC Greenwich (Lieutenants' Course Prize) 1967, Office of Vice Chief of Naval Staff, Army Staff Course (Mitchell Essay Prize) 1973, Clyde Submarine Base, sec to ACNS (Policy), Trg Cdr HMS Pembroke; NATO Def Coll Rome 1982–83, mil asst to Dir Int Mil Staff NATO HQ 1983–85, RCDS 1986, dir Def Logistics MOD 1986–89, sec to First Sea Lord 1989–90, sr mil memb Prospect Team MOD 1991–92, DG Naval Manpower and Trg 1992–94, Chief Naval Supply and Secretariat Offr 1993–, Commandant Joint Service Def Coll 1994–; govr Princess Helena Coll; FIMgt 1991; *Publications* articles in Naval Review 1985–; *Recreations* swimming, cricket, opera, jazz, cuisine Perigourdine; *Clubs* MCC; *Style*— Rear Adm Nicholas Wilkinson, CB; ✉ Joint Service Defence College, RNC Greenwich, London SE10 9NN (☎ 0181 858 2154 ext 4006, fax 0181 853 5739, e-mail comdt@jsdc.demon.co.uk)

WILKINSON, Nigel Vivian Marshall; QC (1990); s of John Marshall Wilkinson (d 1993), of E Horsley, Surrey, and Vivien, *née* Gwynne-James; *b* 18 Nov 1949; *Educ* Charterhouse, Christ Church Oxford (MA, Holford Exhibitioner); *m* 20 April 1974, Heather Carol Hallett, QC, *qv*, da of late Hugh Victor Dudley Hallett; 2 s (James b 4 June 1980, Nicholas b 20 April 1982); *Career* called to the Bar Middle Temple 1972, Astbury scholar 1972, memb Midland and Oxford circuit 1972–, recorder of the Crown Ct 1992–; dep chm Cricket Cncl Appeals Ctee 1992–; *Recreations* sport and entertainment; *Clubs* MCC, I Zingari, Invalids CC, Armadillos CC, Vincent's (Oxford), Butterflies CC, Rye, Royal Wimbledon, Roehampton Golf; *Style*— Nigel Wilkinson, Esq, QC; ✉ 2 Crown Office Row, Temple, London EC4Y 7HJ (☎ 0171 797 8100)

WILKINSON, Prof Paul; s of Walter Ross Wilkinson (d 1985), of Bristol, and Joan Rosemary, *née* Paul; *b* 9 May 1937; *Educ* Lower Sch of John Lyon Harrow, Univ Coll Swansea (MA); *m* 19 March 1960, Susan Sherwyn, da of Charles William John Flook (d 1968), of Newport, Gwent; 2 s (John Paul b 1964, Charles Ross b 1969), 1 da (Rachel Margaret b 1962); *Career* served RAF 1959–65, ret as Flt Lt; Univ Coll Cardiff: asst lectr in politics 1966–68, lectr 1968–75, sr lectr 1975–78; visiting prof Simon Fraser Univ Canada 1973, reader in politics Univ of Wales 1978–79; prof of int relations: Univ of Aberdeen 1979–89 (head Dept Politics and Int Relations 1985–89), Univ of St Andrews 1990– (head Sch of History and Int Relations 1994–); chm Res Fndn for the Study of Terrorism 1986–89, dir Res Inst for the Study of Conflict and Terrorism 1989–94; jt ed Terrorism And Political Violence (scholarly jl) 1988–; hon fell Univ Coll Swansea; FRSA 1995; memb: RIIA, British Int Studies Assoc, Political Studies Assoc; *Books* Social Movement (1971), Political Terrorism (1974), Terrorism versus Liberal Democracy (1976), Terrorism and the Liberal State (1977, revised edn 1986, 3rd edn 1994), Terrorism: Theory and Practice (jtly, 1978), British Perspectives on Terrorism (1981), The New Fascists (revised edn, 1983), Contemporary Research on Terrorism (1987), Lessons of Lockerbie (1989), Terrorist Targets and Tactics (1990), Northern Ireland: Reappraising Republican Violence (1991), Technology and Terrorism (1993), Terrorism: British Perspectives (1993), The Victims of Terrorism (1994); *Recreations* walking, modern painting, poetry; *Clubs* Savile; *Style*— Prof Paul Wilkinson; ✉ Department of International Relations, University of St Andrews, St Andrews, Fife KY16 9AJ (☎ 01334 462900, fax 01334 462914, telex 9312110846 SAG)

WILKINSON, Lt-Col Sir Peter Allix; KCMG (1970, CMG 1960), DSO (1944), OBE (1944); s of Capt Osborn Cecil Wilkinson (ka 1915) (3 s of late Maj-Gen George Allix Wilkinson), by his w Esmé Barbara, da of Sir Alexander Wilson; *b* 15 April 1914; *Educ* Rugby, Corpus Christi Coll Cambridge; *m* 1945, Mary Theresa (d 1984), da of Algernon Hyde Villiers (ka 1917, 3 s of Rt Hon Sir Francis Hyde Villiers, GCMG, GCVO, CB, sometime ambass Brussels, 4 s of 4 Earl of Clarendon) by his w Beatrix (who subsequently m (1919) 4 Baron Aldenham & (2 Baron) Hunsdon, by whom she was mother of 5 Baron Aldenham); 2 da (Virginia b 1947, m 1971, Daniel Worsley; 1 s, 1 da; Alexandra b 1953; 1 s, 2 da); *Career* cmmnd 2 Bn Royal Fusiliers 1935, served WWII (Poland, Fr, Balkans, Central Euro, Italy), cmmnd 6 SOE 1943–45, Lt-Col, ret 1947; joined Dip Serv 1947; 1 sec: Vienna 1947, Washington 1952; cnsllr Bonn 1955–60, under sec Cabinet Office 1963–64, sr civilian instr IDC 1964–66, ambass Vietnam 1966–67, asst under sec FO 1967–68, dep under sec and chief admin Dip Serv 1968–70, ambass Vienna 1970–71, ret 1972; re-employed as co-ordinator of intelligence Cabinet Office 1972–73; Polish Cross of Valour 1940, Czech Order of White Lion 1945, Order of Yugoslav Banner (hon) 1984; *Publications* Gubbins & SOE (with Joan Bright Astley); *Recreations* reading, trout-fishing; *Clubs* White's, Army and Navy; *Style*— Lt-Col Sir Peter Wilkinson, KCMG, DSO, OBE; ✉ 28 High St, Charing, Kent (☎ 01233 712306)

WILKINSON, Prof Peter Charles; s of Michael Charles Wilkinson (d 1980), and Helen Craig, *née* Wilcox (d 1975); *b* 10 July 1932; *Educ* London Hosp Med Coll (MB BS, MD); *m* 29 Nov 1958, Eileen Mary, da of Joseph Baron (d 1983); 2 s (Anthony b 1960, James b 1964), 1 da (Catherine b 1962); *Career* lectr London Hosp Med Coll 1960–63; Immunology Dept Univ of Glasgow: lectr 1964–69, sr lectr 1969–77, reader 1977–82, prof 1982–; visiting prof Rockefeller Univ New York 1979, hon conslt immunology

Western Infirmary Glasgow 1970–; FRSE 1983, FIBiol 1987; *Books* Dictionary of Immunology (4 edn, 1995), Chemotaxis and Inflammation (2 edn, 1982), approximately 200 sci papers; *Recreations* books; *Style*— Prof Peter Wilkinson, FRSE; ✉ Immunology Department, University of Glasgow, Western Infirmary, Glasgow G11 6NT (☎ 0141 211 2728, fax 0141 337 3217)

WILKINSON, Sir Philip William; kt (1988); *b* 8 May 1927; *Educ* Leyton County HS; *m* 1951, Eileen Patricia, *née* Malkin (d 1991); 1 s (Peter), 2 da (Anne, Susan); *Career* National Westminster Bank plc: dir 1979–90, dep gp chief exec 1980, gp chief exec 1983–87, dep chm 1987–90; dir: International Westminster Bank 1982–90, Handels Bank Nat West Zürich (dep chm) 1983–90, British Aerospace plc 1987–91, National Power plc 1990–92; memb Cncl: CBI 1983–89, Indust Soc 1982–89, Imperial Cancer Res Fund; dir Eng Nat Opera 1987–93, tstee Baptist Building Fund; a vice pres: The Leprosy Mission, The Boys' Bde, The Chartered Inst of Bankers; chm The Wishbone Tst; FCIB; *Recreations* golf, watching sport; *Clubs* RAC; *Style*— Sir Philip Wilkinson

WILKINSON, HE Richard Denys; CVO (1992); s of Denys Cooper Wilkinson (d 1961), of Pill House, Llanmadoc, and Gillian Avice, *née* Nairn (d 1973); *b* 11 May 1946; *Educ* Eton, Trinity Coll Cambridge (MA, MLitt), Ecole Nationale des Langues Orientales Vivantes, Paris, Ecole des Langues Orientales Anciennes Institut Catholique de Paris; *m* 8 Dec 1982, (Maria) Angela, da of Frederick Edward Morris; 2 s (Wilfred b 17 Dec 1983, Samuel b 4 Feb 1986), 1 da (Eleanor b 19 March 1991); *Career* Hayter post-doctor in Soviet Studies Sch Slavonic and East Euro Studies Univ of London 1971–72; HM Dip Serv: entered 1972, Madrid 1973–77, FCO 1977–79, visiting prof faculty of history Univ of Michigan Ann Arbor 1980, FCO 1980–83, Ankara 1983–85, cnsllr and head of chancery Mexico City 1985–88, info cnsllr Paris 1988–92, head Policy Planning Staff FCO 1993–94, head Eastern Dept FCO 1994–97, HM ambass Venezuela 1997–; *Recreations* sightseeing, oriental studies; *Clubs* United Oxford and Cambridge; *Style*— HE Mr Richard Wilkinson, CVO; ✉ c/o FCO (Caracas), King Charles St, London SW1A 2AH

WILKINSON, Robert Purdy; OBE (1990); s of Robert Purdy Wilkinson (d 1958), and Lily Ingham, *née* Robson (d 1987); *b* 23 Aug 1933; *Educ* Robert Richardson GS, Univ of Durham (BA, sec Durham Union Soc, rugby 1 XV); *m* 21 Dec 1957, June, da of late Godfrey Palmer; 2 da (Katharine Jane (Dr Warner), Susanna Jean (Mrs Edge-Partington)); *Career* Kleinwort Sons & Co 1958–62, Estabrook & Co 1962–64, W I Carr Sons & Co 1964–81; Stock Exchange: ptnr and memb 1966, memb Cncl 1978, chm Firms Accounts Ctee 1980–81, first SE inspr 1981, dir Surveillance Div 1984–90, dep chief exec and dir Enforcement The Securities Assoc 1987–90, ret 1991; DTI inspr 1987, 1989 and 1991; special advsr Johannesburg Stock Exchange and SA Fin Services Bd 1991, govr World Economic Forum 1991; conslt Morgan Grenfell & Co, advsr Assoc of Swiss Stock Exchanges 1991, advsr Czech Miny of Fin 1995; dir: Invesco Group Ltd 1994–, Tradepoint plc 1994–; chm of Govrs Sevenoaks Sch; *Recreations* walking, skiing, gardening, schools sport; *Style*— Robert Wilkinson, Esq, OBE; ✉ Bessels House, Bessels Green, Sevenoaks, Kent TN13 2PS (☎ and fax 01732 457782)

WILKINSON, Sally Ann; da of Derek George Wilkinson (d 1978), of London, and Kathleen Mary Patricia, *née* O'Callaghan (d 1989); *b* 1 Nov 1953; *Educ* Westonbirt Sch Gloucestershire, Watford Coll of Technol (HND); *Career* trainee exec Image Makers Ltd 1973, account exec Crawford Heard Ltd 1974, divnl press offr Thorn Domestic Appliances 1975–78, account exec rising to creative dir Kingsway Rowland 1978–89, divnl md The Rowland Co 1990–92, md SAW Associates 1993–94, dep gen mangr Edelman Worldwide London 1994–95, md SAW Associates 1995–, md Brook Wilkinson 1996–; memb: Inst of Mktg 1978, Assoc of Women in PR 1990; *Recreations* theatre, music, writing, art and painting; *Style*— Miss Sally Ann Wilkinson; ✉ Brook Wilkinson, 89 Notting Hill Gate, London W11 3JZ (☎ 0171 229 9907, fax 0171 229 8809)

WILKINSON, (George) William; s of Thomas Nutter Wilkinson (d 1985), and Elizabeth, *née* Hurst; *b* 21 Oct 1948; *Educ* Chorlton GS Manchester, Univ of Nottingham (BSc); *m* 27 Dec 1969, Carol Susan, da of Albert James Henry Petre; 3 s (Matthew Jon b 13 Nov 1978, Daniel James b 23 June 1982, Samuel Luke b 26 Aug 1989); *Career* actuarial trainee Sun Alliance 1969, overseas posting as chief actuary Protea Assurance Cape Town 1977–80; Sun Alliance: asst mangr 1980–83, business mangr 1983–88, pensions admin mangr 1988–90, pensions mangr 1990–93, mangr Re-Engineering 1993–95, mangr Pensions Review Project 1995–96, mangr Ops Devpt 1996–; sch govr 1988; FIA 1975; *Recreations* family, squash, golf, keeping fit; *Clubs* Christ's Hosp; *Style*— William Wilkinson, Esq; ✉ Sun Alliance Group plc, Stane Court, Chart Way, Horsham, West Sussex RH12 1XA (☎ 01403 230403, fax 01403 233249)

WILKINSON, Dr William Lionel; CBE (1986); s of Lionel Wilkinson (d 1978), and Dorothy, *née* Steels; *b* 16 Feb 1931; *Educ* Holgate GS Barnsley, Christ's Coll Cambridge (MA, PhD, ScD); *m* 3 Sept 1955, (Josephine) Anne, da of Charles Dennis Pilgrim (d 1954), of Bedford; 5 s (David William b 6 March 1957, Andrew Charles b 15 Nov 1958, Iain Francis b 5 March 1962, Richard John b 24 March 1965, Stephen James b 6 Feb 1970); *Career* lectr Univ Coll Swansea 1956–59, UKAEA 1959–67, prof of chem engrg Univ of Bradford 1967–79, BNF plc 1979–92 (dep chief exec and chm of fuel and engr gp 1986–92), dep chm dir Allied Colloids plc; chm Br Nuclear Industry Forum 1992–, pres European Atomic Forum 1994–; Hon DEng Bradford 1989; Freeman Worshipful Co of Salters 1985; FIChemE 1957, FEng 1980; FRS 1990; *Books* Non-Newtonian Fluids (1960); *Recreations* fell walking; *Clubs* Athenaeum; *Style*— Dr William Wilkinson, CBE, FRS, FEng; ✉ Tree Tops, Legh Rd, Knutsford WA16 8LP (☎ 01565 653 344); British Nuclear Industry Forum, 22 Buckingham Gate, London SW1E 6LB (☎ 0171 828 0116)

WILKS, Capt Antony Hugh Francis; MBE; s of Walter Hugh Wilks (d 1964), of Bushey, Herts, and Frances Mary Bradford, *née* Pratt; *b* 29 Dec 1936; *Educ* Oundle; *m* 4 Sept 1971, Susan Chaloner, *née* Reed; 1 s (Rupert b 1973), 1 da (Lalage b 1976); *Career* serv HM Submarines 1958–67, i/c HMS Belton 1967–69, Staff Coll India 1970, HMS Jupiter 1971–72, BRNC Dartmouth 1973–75, ADC to HE Govr Hong Kong 1976, Naval Staff 1977–78; i/c: Royal Brunei Navy 1979–80, HMS Aurora 1981–82, RNC Greenwich 1983–85; Dep Cdr Naval Base Rosyth Scotland and Queen's Harbourmaster Rosyth and Cromarty 1986–90; chief harbourmaster Firth and Forth 1990–96; chm Forth Estuary Forum; memb: East Bd Scottish Environment Protection Agency, South East Scotland Bd Scottish Natural Heritage 1995; Yr Brother Trinity House London 1976; Liveryman Worshipful Co of Wheelwrights 1965; Perwira Agong Negara Brunei (first class) 1979, Dato Seri Laila Jasa (Brunei Knighthood) 1980; MNI; *Recreations* music, squash; *Clubs* St Moritz Tobogganing, Jesters; *Style*— Capt Antony Wilks, MBE; ✉ Easter Fossoway, Kinrosshire (☎ 01577 840255)

WILKS, Stanley David (Jim); CB (1979); *b* 1 Aug 1920; *Educ* Polytechnic Sch London; *m* 1947, Dorothy Irene, *née* Adamthwaite; 1 s (Howard John b 1955), 1 da (Penelope Jane b 1958); *Career* RAC 1939–46, served with 48 Bn RTR, 3 Carabiniers (Imphal 1944); Home Office 1946–50; BOT (later DTI) 1950–80: 1 sec Br Embassy Washington 1950–53, later involved with GATT, non-ferrous metals, ECGD and airports policy, chief exec BOTB 1975–80; dep chm: Technology Transfer Group 1986–89 (formerly DG 1981–86), Strategy International Ltd 1990–92 (conslt dir 1981–90), The Business Development Group 1994–; dir: Matthew Hall Business Development Ltd 1981–89, Hadson Petroleum International plc 1981–91, Hadson Corporation (USA) 1985–93, Associated Gas Supplies Ltd 1987–90; regnl dir James Hallam Ltd 1984–, chm Export Network Ltd 1985–89; MIEx 1980; *Recreations* sailing; *Clubs* Medway Yacht; *Style*— Jim Wilks, Esq, CB; ✉ 6 Foxgrove Avenue, Beckenham, Kent BR3 5BA

WILLACY, Michael James Ormerod; CBE (1989); s of James Willacy (d 1977), of Plymouth, Devon, and Majorie Winifred, *née* Sanders; *b* 7 June 1933; *Educ* Taunton Sch Somerset; *m* 1, 25 Nov 1961, Merle Louise, da of Johannes Schrier, of Denia, Spain; 2 s (Richard b 1962, Peter b 1969), 1 da (Jennifer b 1963); m 2, Victoria Stuart, da of Cecil Stuart John, of Mobberley, Cheshire; 3 s (James b 1985, Michael b 1986, David b 1990), 1 da (Elizabeth b 1988); *Career* gen mangr Shell UK Materials Services 1983–85, dir HM Govt Central Unit on Purchasing 1985–90, purchasing advsr HM Treasy 1991–92; md Michael Willacy Associates Ltd 1991–; chm Macclesfield C of C 1981–83, fndr chm Macclesfield Business Ventures 1982–83; Old Tauntonian Assoc: gen sec 1978–91, pres 1988–89, vice pres 1989–; FCIPS; *Recreations* golf, travel, gardening; *Clubs* Royal Cwlth Soc; *Style*— Michael Willacy, Esq, CBE; ✉ PO Box 20, Ivybridge, Devon PL21 9XS (☎ 01548 830591, fax 01752 894985)

WILLATS, Stephan; *b* 17 Aug 1943; *Educ* Ealing Sch of Art; *m* Stephanie Willats; *Career* artist; ed and publisher Control magazine 1965–, pt/t lectr 1965–72, dir The Centre for Behavioural Art 1972–73, DAAD fell W Germany 1979–80, convenor Art Creating Society Symposium Museum of Modern Art Oxford 1990; *Solo Exhibitions* incl: Visual Automatics and Visual Transmitters (Museum of Modern Art Oxford) 1968, The Artist as an Instigator of Changes in Social Cognition and Behaviour (Gallery House London) 1973, Coding Structure and Behaviour Parameters (Gallery Banco Bresco Italy) 1975, Allitudes within Four Relationships (Lisson Gallery London) 1976, Questions About Ourselves (Lisson Gallery) 1978, Concerning our Present Way of Living (Whitechapel Art Gallery) 1979, Berlin Wall Drawings (Galerie Rudiger Schottle Munich) 1980, Mens en Omgeving De Beyard Centram voor beeldende Kanst (Breda Holland) 1981, Meta Filler and Related Works (Tate Gallery) 1982, Inside the Night (Lisson Gallery) 1983, Dopelganger (Lisson Gallery) 1985, City of Concrete (Ikon Gallery Birmingham) 1986, Concepts and Projects Bookworks (Nigel Greenwood Books, London) 1987, Between Objects and People (Leeds City Art Gallery) 1987, Secret Language (Cornerhouse Gallery Manchester) 1989, Mosaics (Galerie Kaj Forsblom Helsinki) 1990, Multiple Clothing (ICA) 1993, Museum Mosaic (Tate Gallery London) 1994, Random Life (Victoria Miro Gallery London) 1994, Living Together (Tramway Glasgow) 1995, Writing On The Wall (Galerie Kaj Forsblom Helsinki) 1995; *Group Exhibitions* incl: Kinetic Art (Hayward Gallery) 1970, Art as Thought Process (Serpentine Gallery London) 1974, Social Criticism and Art Practice (San Francisco Art Inst) 1977, La Parola e le Imagine (Commune di Milano) 1979, Sculpture in the Twentieth Century (Whitechapel Art Gallery London) 1981, New Art at the Tate Gallery (Tate Gallery) 1983, Eye Level (Van Abbemuseum Eindhoven) 1986, 100 years of British Art (Leeds City Art Gallery) 1988, The New Urban Landscape (World Fin Centre NYC) 1990, Excavating the Present (Kettle Yard Gallery Cambridge) 1991, Instruction and Diagrams (Victoria Miro Gallery London) 1992, Visione Britannica (Valentina Moncada Rome Italy) 1994, Temples (Victoria Miro Gallery London) 1995, Ideal Standard Summertime (Lisson Gallery London) 1995; works in public collections incl: Art Museum Zurich, The Scottish Nat Gallery of Modern Art Edinburgh, The Tate Gallery London, The Arts Cncl of GB, The V & A Museum, The British Museum, Museum of Contemporary Art Utrecht Holland, Stichting Volkshuisvesting in de Kunst Den Hag Holland, Van Abbe Museum Eindhoven Holland, Stadtische Galerie Stuttgart; *Style*— Stephan Willats, Esq; ✉ Lisson Gallery (London) Ltd, 67 Lisson Street, London NW1 5DA (☎ 0171 724 2739)

WILLATTS, Dr Sheila Margaret; da of Charles William Chapman (d 1978), and Joyce Margaret Chapman; *b* 6 June 1943; *Educ* UCL, UCH Med Sch London (MB BS, MD), FRCP, FRCA; *m* 1, 16 July 1966, David George Willatts, s of Bertram George Willatts; 2 da (Nicola b 14 April 1971, Ellen Laura b 1 Nov 1975), 1 s (Stephen Chapman b 5 Jan 1973); m 2, 25 Feb 1989, Michael Crabtree; *Career* registrar trg in anaesthetics Brook Hosp and KCH, sr registrar King's Coll Hosp until 1978, conslt anaesthetist Frenchay Hosp Bristol 1978–85, conslt i/c Intensive Therapy Unit Bristol Royal Infirmary 1985–, conslt advsr in anaesthetics to the Chief Med Offr 1991–; sec and subsequently chm Intensive Care Soc 1980–84, memb Cncl Royal Coll of Anaesthetists 1986– (chm Examinations Ctee, Quality of Practice Ctee, Hosp Recognition Ctee, Equivalence Ctee and Intercollegiate Bd for Trg in Intensive Care Med); memb: Assoc of Anaesthetists 1976, RSM 1978, Br Medico Legal Soc 1985, BMA 1989; *Books* Lecture Notes in Fluid and Electrolyte Balance (2 edn, 1982), Anaesthesia and Intensive Care for Neurosurgery (1984), Principles and Protocols in Intensive Therapy (1991), Confidential Enquiries into Maternal Deaths Triennial Report 1991–93 (1996); *Recreations* travel, keep fit, gardening; *Style*— Dr Sheila Willatts; ✉ 6 Westbury Park, Durdham Down, Bristol BS6 7JB (☎ 0117 974 3447, fax 0117 946 6429); Directorate of Anaesthesia, Bristol Royal Infirmary, Bristol BS2 8HW (☎ 0117 928 2163, fax 0117 928 2098, mobile 0374 135721)

WILLCOCKS, Alison Ann; da of Patrick MacNamara, and Sibyl MacNamara; *b* 22 July 1952; *Educ* St Francis' Coll Letchworth, New Hall Cambridge (MA), Univ of Birmingham (BMus); *m* 1976 (sep), Jonathan Willcocks; 1 s, 1 da; *Career* asst mistress Portsmouth HS 1976–79; Bedales Sch: history teacher 1980–83, housemistress 1983–88, dep head 1988–94, head 1995–; *Recreations* writing, music, reading; *Style*— Mrs Alison Willcocks; ✉ Bedales School, Church Road, Steep, Petersfield, Hants GU32 2DG (☎ 01730 300100)

WILLCOCKS, Sir David Valentine; kt (1977), CBE (1971), MC (1944); s of late Theophilus Herbert Willcocks, and Dorothy, *née* Harding; *b* 30 Dec 1919; *Educ* Clifton, King's Coll Cambridge (MA, MusB); *m* 1947, Rachel Gordon Blyth, da of late Rev Arthur Cecil Blyth, fell of Selwyn Coll Cambridge; 2 s (1 decd), 2 da; *Career* serv WWII DCLI, Capt NW Europe; organist Salisbury Cathedral 1947–50, master of choristers and organist Worcester Cathedral 1950–57, music lectr Cambridge 1957–74, fell and organist King's Coll Cambridge 1957–73 (hon fell 1979), univ organist 1958–74, musical dir Bach Choir 1960–, gen ed OUP Church Music 1961–; pres Assoc of British Choral Directors 1993–; past pres: RCO, ISM, Nat Fedn of Music Socs, Birmingham and Midland Inst; former chm Assoc Bd Royal Schs of Music; former conductor: Cambridge Philharmonic, Salisbury Music Soc, Worcester Festival Choral Soc, City of Birmingham Choir, Bradford Festival Choral Soc, Cambridge Univ Music Soc; dir RCM 1974–84; Freeman City of London 1981; Hon RAM, Hon GSM, Hon FTCL, Hon MA Bradford; Hon DMus: Exeter, Leicester, Bristol, Westminster Choir Coll, Princeton, St Olaf Coll; Hon DLit Sussex; Hon DSLitt Trinity Coll Toronto; FRCM, FRCO, FRNCM, FRSAMD, FRSCM; hon fell Royal Canadian Coll of Organists; *Clubs* Athenaeum, Arts; *Style*— Sir David Willcocks, CBE, MC; ✉ 13 Grange Road, Cambridge CB3 9AS (☎ 01223 359559, fax 01223 355947)

WILLCOCKS, Maj-Gen Michael Alan; CB (1997); s of Henry Willcocks, and Georgina Bernadette, *née* Lawton (d 1990); *b* 27 July 1944; *Educ* St John's, RMA Sandhurst, Univ of London (BSc); *m* 10 Dec 1966, Jean Paton, da of James Burnside Paton Weir (d 1967); 1 s (Julian b 20 June 1968), 2 da (Jessica b 28 April 1971, Hannah b 26 Feb 1976); *Career* cmmnd RA 1964, serv Malaya, Borneo, UK, Germany 1965–72, MOD 1977–79, Comd M Battery RHA 1979–80, Staff Coll Directing Staff 1981–82, CO 1 Regt RHA 1983–85, DACOS HQ UKLF 1985–87, Asst COS Intelligence/Ops HQ UKLF 1988, Cmd RA 4 Armd Div 1989–90, RCDS 1991, ACOS Land Operations Joint War HQ Gulf War (and aftermath), Dir Army Plans and Programme 1991–93, DG Land Warfare 1993–94, COS Allied Command Europe Rapid Reaction Corps 1994–96, COS Land Component of Peace Implementation Force (IFOR) Bosnia-Herzogovina 1995–96, Asst CGS 1996–; *Books* Airmobility and the Armoured Experience (1989); *Recreations* books, music, tennis, fishing, sailing; *Clubs* National Liberal, European-Atlantic Group; *Style*— Maj-Gen Michael Willcocks, CB; ✉ Assistant Chief of the General Staff, Ministry of Defence, Whitehall, London SW1A 2HB

WILLCOX, Toyah Ann; da of Beric Arnold Willcox, of Birmingham, and Barbara Joy, *née* Rollinson; *b* 18 May 1958; *Educ* Edgbaston C of E Coll, Birmingham Old Rep Theatre Sch; *m* 16 May 1986, Robert Fripp, s of Arthur Fripp (d 1985), of Wimbourne; *Career* actress and singer songwriter; vice pres Nat Assoc of Youth Clubs; patron: Bournemouth Hosp, Salisbury Festival, Inspire Salisbury Spinal Injury Unit, Sch for the Performing Arts, hon asst Womens Cncl of GB; *Theatre* incl: Tales from the Vienna Woods (NT) 1977, American Days (ICA) 1978, Sugar and Spice (Royal Court) 1979, Trafford Tanzi (Mermaid) 1983, Cabaret (Strand) 1987, Three Men on a Horse (NT) 1987, A Midsummer Nights Dream (Birmingham Rep) 1988, Whale (RNT) 1989–90, Therese Raquin (Nottingham Playhouse) 1990, Taming of the Shrew (Cambridge Theatre Co) 1990, Amadeus (Compass Theatre) 1991, The Choice 1992, Memoirs of a Survivor (both Salisbury Playhouse) 1992, Carrington 1993, Peter Pan (both Chichester Festival Theatre) 1994, A Midsummer Night's Dream (Regent's Park) 1995; *Television* incl: Little Girls Don't 1980, Ebony Tower 1983, Ink Thief 1993, Tomorrow Calling 1993, Kavanagh QC 1994, The Good Sex Guide Late 1996, Watchdog 1996, Holidays Out 1996; *Films* incl: Jubilee 1978, The Corn is Green 1978, Quadrophenia 1978, The Tempest 1979, URG The Music War 1979, Battle Ship Redwing 1985, Murder 1985, Midnight Breaks 1987, Little Pig Robertson 1990, The Anchoress 1992, Julie and the Cadillacs 1996; *Albums* Sheep Farming in Barnet 1978, Blue Meaning 1979, Toyah Toyah 1980, Anthem 1981, Changeling 1982, Warrior Rock 1982, Love is the Law 1983, Minx 1985, Lady or the Tiger 1985, Desire 1987, Pro 1988, Ophelia's Shadow 1991, Kneeling At The Shrine 1991, Dreamchild 1993, Kiss of Reality 1993, LEAP 1994; *singles* incl: It's a Mystery, I Wanna be Free, Thunder in the Mountains, Good Morning Universe, Brave New World, World in Action, Echo Beach, Out of the Blue, Now and Then; *Style—* Ms Toyah Willcox; ✉ c/o Jon Roseman Agencies Ltd, 46 Sutton Court Road, London W4 4NL (☎ 0181 742 0552, fax 0181 742 0554)

WILLESDEN, Bishop of 1992–; Rt Rev (Geoffrey) Graham Dow; s of Ronald Graham Dow (d 1983), of Harpenden, Herts, and Dorothy May, *née* Christie; *b* 4 July 1942; *Educ* St Albans Sch, Queen's Coll Oxford (BA, BSc, MA), Univ of Birmingham (Dip in Pastoral Studies), Univ of Nottingham (MPhil); *m* 23 July 1966, Molly Patricia, da of Roland Eric Sturges; 3 s (Alastair Graham b 8 Dec 1968, James Peter Graham (Jamie) b 12 Dec 1970, Michael Graham b 10 Jan 1975), 1 da (Lindsay Patricia b 26 April 1972); *Career* ordained (Rochester): deacon 1967, priest 1968; asst curate Tonbridge Parish Church 1967–72, chaplain student St John's Coll Oxford 1972–75 (acting chaplain 1974–75), lectr in Christian doctrine St John's Coll Nottingham 1975–81, supr Univ of Nottingham 1975–81, vicar Holy Trinity Coventry 1981–92, canon theologian Coventry Cathedral 1988; Coventry Dio: memb Bishop's Cncl for Miny 1981–87, memb Bishop's Cncl 1982–85, memb Deanery and Diocesan Synods 1982–, chm Coventry Christian Trg Project 1982–88 (dir Christian Trg Prog 1988–92), tstee Church Patronage Tst 1985; chm Bd of Social Responsibility London Dio 1992–; chaplain Coventry Branch Owen Owen PLC 1981–92, govr Blue Coat Sch Coventry 1981–92 (tstee 1981–87); *Publications* incl: The Local Church's Political Responsibility (1980), Whose Hand on the Tiller? (1983), Those Tiresome Intruders (1990), Christian Renewal in Europe (1992), Explaining Deliverance (1991), A Christian Understanding of Daily Work (1994); *Recreations* steam and model railways, travel, music; *Style—* The Rt Rev the Bishop of Willesden; ✉ 173 Willesden Lane, London NW6 7YN (☎ 0181 451 0189, fax 0181 451 4606, mobile 03744 21678)

WILLETT, Allan Robert; s of Robert Willett, and Irene Grace Priscilla, *née* Weigall; *b* 24 Aug 1936; *Educ* Eastbourne Coll; *m* 1, 13 April 1960 (m dis 1993), Mary, da of Joseph Hillman; 2 da (Joanna, Katherine), 1 s (Robert); m 2, 5 Oct 1993, Anne, da of Hubert Steed; *Career* cmmnd The Buffs Royal East Kent Regt and seconded to 23 King's African Rifles 1955–57, Kenya Campaign Medal 1956; gp md G D Peters Ltd 1969–71, chm Northampton Machinery Co 1970–74, dep chm Rowen and Boden 1973–74, formed Willett Cos 1974, chm Willett International Ltd GB (mfr of coding, labelling and inspection systems with subsid ops in 25 countries) 1983–; chm: E Kent Initiative, Industl Devpt Bd London and South East, Centre for Tomorrow's Company (set up by RSA 1995); Queen's Award for Export Achievement 1989 and 1994, Businessman of Northamptonshire 1994, UK Export Excellence Award (Nat West Bank and FT Exporter) 1995; *Recreations* walking, military history, golf, skiing; *Style—* Allan Willett, Esq; ✉ Willett International Limited, Cumberland Cottage, The Street, Chilham, Canterbury, Kent CT4 8BX (☎ 01227 738800, fax 01227 738855)

WILLETT, Prof Frank; CBE (1985); s of Thomas Willett (d 1965), of Bolton, Lancs, and Frances, *née* Latham (d 1978); *b* 18 Aug 1925; *Educ* Bolton Municipal Secdy Sch, Univ Coll Oxford (MA); *m* 24 July 1950, (Mary) Constance, da of Charles Hewitt (d 1952), of Bolton Lancs; 1 s (Steven b 1955), 3 da (Margaret Mary b 1952, Pauline b 1958, Jean b 1962); *Career* linguist RAF 1943–44; keeper of ethnology and gen archaeology Manchester Museum 1950–58, govt archaeologist i/c Ife Museum Nigeria 1958–63, Leverhulme res fell 1964, res fell Nuffield Coll Oxford 1964–66, prof of African art and archaeology Northwestern Univ USA 1966–76, visiting fell Clare Hall Cambridge 1970–71, dir Hunterian Museum and Art Gallery Univ of Glasgow 1976–90, hon sr res fell Hunterian Museum 1990–, research collaborator Smithsonian Inst Washington DC 1993–; fndr Univ Museums in Scot, memb Scot Catholic Heritage Cmmn 1981–93, also memb various other ctees; curator RSE 1992–; Arts Cncl of the African Studies Assoc USA Leadership Award 1995; fell Royal Anthropological Inst 1949, hon fell Bolton Inst of Higher Educn 1990; FRSE 1979; *Books* Ife In The History of West African Sculpture (1967), African Art: An Introduction (1971, revised edn 1993), Treasures of Ancient Nigeria (with Ekpo Eyo, 1980); *Recreations* baiting architects, relaxing, walking; *Clubs* Royal Cwlth Soc; *Style—* Prof Frank Willett, CBE, FRSE; ✉ The Hunterian Museum, The University of Glasgow, Glasgow G12 8QQ (☎ 0141 339 8855 ext 4384, fax 0141 954 7028, telex 777070 UNIGLA)

WILLETT, Michael John; *b* 2 Oct 1944; *Educ* Tottenham GS, Open Univ (BA), Open Business Sch (MBA); *m* 1967, Gillian Margaret, *née* Pope (m dis 1993); 2 s, 1 da; *Career* pilot RAF 1963–71; pilot Laker Airways Ltd 1972–82; CAA: joined 1982, subsequently chief flight ops inspr, memb Bd, gp dir Safety Regulation 1992–; chm Exec Bd and Ctee Jt Aviation Authorities 1996–; Freedom City London, Liveryman and Asst to Court Guild of Air Pilots and Air Navigators; FRAeS 1992; *Recreations* horse-riding; *Style—* Michael Willett, Esq; ✉ Group Director Safety Regulation, Civil Aviation Authority, Aviation House, Gatwick Airport South, West Sussex RH6 0YR (☎ 01293 573078, fax 01293 573997)

WILLETT, Peter Stirling; s of Maj Kingsley Willett, MC (d 1946), of South Cadbury House, Yeovil, Somerset, and Agnes Mary, *née* Stirling (d 1972); *b* 19 July 1919; *Educ* Wellington, Univ of Cambridge (MA); *m* 1, 1954 Anne Marjorie, *née* Watkins (d 1965); 2 s (David Henry Stirling b 1955, Stephen Murray b 1958); m 2, 1971, Chloë Lister Beamish; *Career* The Queen's Bays 1941–46 (Middle East, Italy); author, journalist, thoroughbred breeding conslt; dir: Goodwood Racecourse 1977–, National Stud 1986–93; pres Thoroughbred Breeders Assoc 1980–85, chm tstee Br Euro Breeders Fund 1983–95; FRSA; *Books* An Introduction to the Thoroughbred (1960), The Thoroughbred (1970), The Classic Racehorse (1981), Makers of the Modern Thoroughbred (1986), Tattersalls (1987), A History of the General Stud Book (1991); *Recreations* tennis, following cricket, reading, bridge; *Clubs* Army and Navy, Jockey; *Style—* Peter Willett, Esq; ✉ Paddock House, Rotherwick, Hook, Hants RG27 9BG (☎ 01256 76 2488)

WILLETTS, David Lindsay; MP (C) Havant (majority 17,584); s of John Roland Willetts, and Hilary Sheila Willetts; *b* 9 March 1956; *Educ* King Edward's Sch Birmingham, ChCh Oxford (BA); *m* 1986, Hon Sarah Harriet Ann, da of Baron Butterfield (Life Peer), *qv*; 1 da, 1 s; *Career* res asst to Nigel Lawson MP 1978; HM Treasury 1978–84: energy policy 1978–79, public expenditure control 1980–81, private sec to Fin Sec 1981–82, monetary policy 1982–84; memb PM's Downing St Policy Unit 1984–86, dir of studies Centre for Policy Studies 1987–92, conslt dir Cons Res Dept 1987–92, MP (C) Havant 1992–, Parly private sec to Chm of the Cons Pty Sir Norman Fowler 1993–94, asst whip 1994–95, Lord Cmmr of HM Treasy 1995, Parly under sec Office of Public Serv 1995–96, Paymaster Gen 1996–Dec 1996 (resigned); memb: Lambeth Southwark and Lewisham FPC 1987–90, Parkside Health Authy 1988–90, Social Security Advsy Ctee 1989–92; non-exec dir: Retirement Security Ltd 1988–94 (chm 1991–94), Electra Corporate Ventures Ltd 1989–94; writer and broadcaster; lectr Deutsch-Englische Gesellschaft; *Books* Modern Conservatism (1992), Civic Conservatism (1994), Blair's Gurus (1996); *Style—* David Willetts, Esq, MP; ✉ House of Commons, London SW1A 0AA (☎ 0171 219 4570)

WILLIAMS, *see also:* Ffowcs Williams

WILLIAMS, Prof Adrian Charles; s of Geoffrey Francis Williams, OBE, of Aberystwyth, and Maureen, *née* Wade; *b* 15 June 1949; *Educ* Epsom Coll, Univ of Birmingham (MB ChB, MD); *m* 19 April 1980, Linnea Marie, da of Gerald Olsen, of Colorado, USA; 2 s (Alec b 1984, Henry b 1986), 1 da (Sarah b 1981); *Career* visiting fell Nat Inst Health USA 1976–79, registrar Nat Hosp London 1979–81, conslt neurologist Queen Elizabeth Hosp Birmingham 1981–, Bloomer prof clinical neurology Univ of Birmingham 1988–; memb Assoc Br Neurologists; FRCP 1986; *Recreations* sailing, skiing, gardening; *Style—* Prof Adrian Williams; ✉ 53 Weoley Hill, Selly Oak, Birmingham B29 4AB (☎ 0121 472 0218); Department of Neurology, Queen Elizabeth Hospital, Edgbaston, Birmingham B15 2TT (☎ 0121 472 1311)

WILLIAMS, Prof Alan; CBE (1995); s of Ralph James Williams (d 1942), and Muriel, *née* Williams; *b* 26 June 1935; *Educ* Cyfarthfa GS Merthyr Tydfil, Univ of Leeds (BSc, PhD); *m* 30 July 1960, Maureen Mary, da of Sydney Bagnall, of Leeds; 3 s (Christopher b 1964, Nicholas b 1967, Simon b 1971); *Career* Livesey prof in fuel and combustion sci and head of Dept of Fuel and Energy Univ of Leeds 1973– (dean of engrg 1991–94); memb: DTI Advsy Ctee on Coal Research 1991–96, DTI Energy Advsy Panel 1993–96; memb OST Technol Foresight Energy Panel 1994–; author Combustion of Liquid Fuel Sprays; former pres and hon sec Inst of Energy; FRIC, FInstE, FInstPet, FInstGasE; *Style—* Prof Alan Williams, CBE; ✉ Department of Fuel and Energy, Leeds University, Leeds LS2 9JT (☎ 0113 233 2508, fax 0113 244 0572)

WILLIAMS, Alan Harding; s of Edward Todd Williams (d 1964), of Tredegar, and Anne, *née* Harding (d 1972); *b* 24 July 1925; *Educ* Thomas Richards Tech Coll, Cross Keys Coll, Crumlin Tech Coll, Britannia Sch of Mines; *m* 27 Nov 1946, Marie, da of David Halliday; 1 da (Sandra b 14 May 1947); *Career* lawn bowls administrator; Int Bowling Bd: memb 1981–, memb Exec 1987–, pres World Bowls Bd 1992–94; Br Isles Bowling Cncl: Welsh Bowling Assoc del 1982–84, pres 1983, del 1987–; Welsh Bowling Assoc: memb Exec 1974–85, pres 1981, hon asst sec 1985–87, hon sec 1987–; Welsh Bowls Umpires Assoc: memb Mgmnt Ctee 1976–, chm 1979–81, memb Umpires Panel 1987–89, officiated at various int events; Bedwellty Park Bowls Club Tredegar: memb 1961–, sec Mgmnt Ctee 1969–, pres 1978–, sec 1987–90, life memb 1990; fndr memb Merthyr Tydfil Indoor Bowls Club 1975–; Rhymney & Sirhowy Valley Bowling Assoc: offr and memb Mgmnt Ctee 1969–, chm 1971, life memb 1990, pres 1994; Monmouthshire Bowling Assoc: memb Mgmnt Ctee 1969–, hon sec 1974–87, memb Exec 1974–, pres 1977; Barbarians Bowls Assoc: memb Mgmnt Ctee 1981–87, hon sec and treas 1984–88, pres 1990; memb: Welsh Bowls Coaching Panel 1987–89, Exec Cwlth Games Cncl for Wales 1987– (Welsh Bowling Assoc rep 1985–86); formerly: coal mining engr, memb Work Study Practitioners Assoc; *Recreations* bowls; *Style—* Alan Williams, Esq; ✉ 48 Pochin Crescent, Tredegar, Gwent NP2 4JS (☎ 01495 723836)

WILLIAMS, Prof Alan Harold; s of Sgt Harold George Williams (d 1968), and Gladys May Clark (d 1962); *b* 9 June 1927; *Educ* King Edward's Sch Birmingham, King Edward's High Sch Birmingham, Univ of Birmingham (BCom); *m* 7 Nov 1953, June Frances, da of Sgt Edward Alexander Porter; 2 s (Mark Alan b 1956, Paul Robert b 1961), 1 da (Susan Heather b 1959); *Career* RAF 1945–48 Corpl; lectr Univ of Exeter 1954–63, visiting lectr MIT 1957–58, visiting fell Princeton 1963–64, sr lectr, reader then prof Univ of York 1964–, dir of economic studies HM Treasury Centre for Admin Studies; former memb: Yorkshire Water Authy, Nat Water Cncl, Royal Cmmn on NHS; Hon DPhil Lund Sweden 1977; memb Royal Economic Soc, ISTANC; *Books* Public Finance and Budgetary Policy (1961), Efficency in the Social Services (with Robert Anderson, 1977), Principles of Practical Cost Benefit Analysis (with Robert Sugden, 1978); *Recreations* music, walking, teasing; *Style—* Prof Alan Williams; ✉ Centre for Health Economics, University of York, York YO1 5DD (☎ 01904 433651, fax 01904 433764)

WILLIAMS, Rt Hon Alan John; PC (1977), MP (Lab) Swansea West (majority 9,478); s of Emlyn Williams (d 1951); *b* 14 Oct 1930; *Educ* Cardiff HS, Cardiff Coll Technol, Univ Coll Oxford; *m* 1957, (Mary) Patricia Rees; 2 s, 1 da; *Career* serv RAF 1956–58; former econ lectr and journalist; memb: Lab Pty 1950–, Fabian Soc and Co-op Pty; Parly candidate (Lab) Poole 1959, MP (Lab) Swansea West 1964–; chm Welsh PLP and PPS to PMG 1966–67, Parly under-sec Dept of Econ Affrs 1967–69, Parly sec Miny of Technol 1969–70, oppn spokesman on consumer protection, small businesses and minerals 1970–74; min of state: for prices and consumer protection 1974–76, for indust 1976–79; oppn spokesman: on Wales 1979–81, on Civil Service 1981–83, on indust 1983–87; dep shadow leader of the House 1983–89, shadow sec of state for Wales 1987–88; memb Select Ctee on Public Accts 1990–, memb Lord Chancellor's Advsy Ctee (pubn of official records); *Style—* The Rt Hon Alan Williams, MP; ✉ House of Commons, London SW1A 0AA

WILLIAMS, Alan Lee; OBE (1973); *b* 29 Nov 1930; *Educ* Roan Sch Greenwich, Ruskin Coll Oxford; *Career* RAF Signals 1949–51; pt/t messenger Nat Fire Serv 1944–45, cncllr Greenwich Borough Cncl 1951–53, nat youth offr Lab Pty 1955–62, head of UNA Youth Dept 1962–66, memb Cncl of Europe and Parly Assembly W Euro Union 1966–70, ldr UK Delgn to Fourth Ctee UN Gen Assembly 1969; MP (Lab): Hornchurch 1966–70, Hornchurch and Havering 1974–79; PPS to Sec of State for: Def 1969–70 and 1974–76, NI 1976–79; chm BNC World Assembly of Youth 1960–66, dep dir Euro Movement 1972–79, chm CSIS Euro Working Gp Washington DC 1974–, ldr Parly Delgn to N Atlantic Assembly 1974–79, memb Cncl RUSI 1974–78, memb Tri-Lateral Cmmn 1976–, chm Parly Lab Pty Def Ctee 1976–79, industl fell Plessey 1978–79, dir gen ESU 1979–86, memb FO Advsy Ctee on Disarmament and Arms Control and Advsy Ctee PRO 1977–81, chm Peace Through NATO 1983–92; chm Tport on Water 1974–; chm NATO Fellowships Ctee (Brussels) 1980–87, bd memb Attlee Fndn 1987–89, warden and chief exec Toynbee Hall 1987–92, dir City Coll 1987–, chm Ceder Centre 1988–, dir Br-Atlantic Ctee 1992–, dir Atlantic Cncl 1993–; Freeman: City of London 1969, Co of Watermen and Lightermen 1952; fell Queen Mary and Westfield Coll London 1994; DLitt (hc) Schiller Int Univ; FRSA; *Publications* Radical Essays (1966), Europe or the Open Sea (1971), Crisis in European Defence (1973), The European Defence Initiative: Europe's Bid for Equality (1985), The Decline of the Labour Party and the Fall of the SDP (1989), Islamic Resurgence (1991), Prospects for a Common European Foreign and Security Policy (1995), NATO's Future in the Balance: Time for a Rethink? (1995), International

Terrorism: Failure of International Response (1995), NATO and European Defence: A New Era of Partnership (1996); *Clubs* Reform, Pilgrims; *Style*— Alan Lee Williams, Esq, OBE

WILLIAMS, Alan Peter; s of Ronald Benjamin Williams, of Lindfield, Sussex, and Marcia Elizabeth, *née* Lister; *b* 27 Oct 1944; *Educ* Merchant Taylors', Univ of Exeter (LLB, capt cricket XI, editor Univ Newspaper); *m* 21 Sept 1968, Lyn Rosemary, da Reginald Ewart Campling; 1 da (Laura Kate Elisabeth b 3 April 1974); *Career* articled clerk Burton Yeates & Hart 1966–67; Denton Hall (and predecessor firms): articled clerk 1967–68, admitted slr 1969, ptnr 1972–, opened Hong Kong office 1976, currently head of Media and Technol Dept; memb: Publishing Law Gp Publishers' Assoc 1983–, Int Media Law Editorial Bd 1986–; Liveryman Worshipful Co of Pewterers; memb: Law Soc 1969, RSA 1990; assoc memb Inner Magic Circle; memb: Richard III Soc, Friends of Shakespeare's Globe; *Books* Publishing Agreements (by Charles Clark, contrib), Intellectual Property The New Law (jtly), Multimedia: Contracts, Rights and Licensing (jtly); *Recreations* cricket, music, walking, photography, theatre; *Clubs* MCC, Groucho, Whitefriars, Wig & Pen, City Law, Omar Khayyam; *Style*— A P Williams, Esq; ✉ Denton Hall, Five Chancery Lane, Clifford's Inn, London EC4A 1BU (☎ 0171 242 1212, fax 0171 404 0087, e-mail apw@dentonhall.com)

WILLIAMS, Dr Alan Wynne; MP (Lab) Carmarthen (majority 2,922); s of Tom Williams (d 1980), and Mary Hannah Williams, *née* Thomas; *b* 21 Dec 1945; *Educ* Carmarthen GS, Jesus Coll Oxford (BA, DPhil); *m* 1973, Marian, da of Tom Williams, of Gwynedd; *Career* lectr in environmental science Trinity Coll Carmarthen 1971–87; MP (Lab) Carmarthen 1987–; memb: Select Ctee on Welsh Affrs 1987–91, Select Ctee on Sci and Technol 1992–; *Recreations* reading, watching sport; *Style*— Dr Alan Williams, MP; ✉ Gwendraeth, 79 Parklands Road, Penybanc, Ammanford, Dyfed (☎ 01269 594710); House of Commons, London SW1A 0AA (☎ 0171 219 4533)

WILLIAMS, Prof Allan Peter Owen; s of Thomas Williams (d 1995), of Cardiff, and Hilda Marie Williams (d 1983); *b* 14 Oct 1935; *Educ* Eastbourne GS, Univ of Manchester (BA), Birkbeck Coll London (MA, PhD); *m* 25 July 1959, Rosella, da of Maj Honorio Jose Muschamp d'Assis Fonseca (d 1984); 1 s (Edmond b 1965), 2 da (Hélène b 1963, Roselyne b 1967); *Career* res exec (later res gp head) Marplan Ltd 1960–63; City Univ Business Sch: lectr 1963–74, sr lectr 1974–83, reader 1983–88, prof 1988–, dep dean 1996–; City Univ: dir Centre for Personnel Res and Enterprise Devpt 1978–, pro-vice-chllr 1987–93, head Dept of Business Studies 1993–; dir Organisation Surveys Ltd 1966–69, conslt psychologist Civil Serv Selection Bd 1966–80; hon treas Br Psychological Soc 1971–74 (chm occupational psychology section 1979–80), memb Army Personnel Res Ctee MRC 1983–94, chm Personnel Psychology Panel APRC 1987–94; memb Exec Ctee: Int Assoc of Applied Psychology, Br Acad of Mgmnt; memb Ct of Assts Guild of Mgmnt Consultants; FBPsS 1979, CPsychol 1988, FBAM 1995; *Books* The Role and Educational needs of Occupational Health Nurses (1982), Using Personnel Research (1983), Changing Culture: New Organisational Approaches (1989 and 1993), The Competitive Consultant (1994); *Recreations* lawn tennis, photography, philately, bibliophile; *Clubs* Barnet Lawn Tennis; *Style*— Prof Allan Williams; ✉ City University Business Sch, Frobisher Crescent, Barbican Centre, London EC2Y 8HB (☎ 0171 477 8000, fax 0171 477 8880)

WILLIAMS, Sir Alwyn; kt (1983); s of D D Williams; *b* 8 June 1921; *Educ* Aberdare Boys' GS, Univ Coll of Wales Aberystwyth; *m* 1949, Joan Bevan; 1 s, 1 da; *Career* Univ of Wales fell 1947–48 (Harkness fell 1948–50), lectr in geology Univ of Glasgow 1950–54, prof of geology Queen's Univ Belfast 1954–74 (pro vice chllr 1965–74); Lapworth prof of geology and head of dept Univ of Birmingham 1974–76; Univ of Glasgow: princ and vice chllr 1976–88, hon palaeobiology res fell 1988–; chm Bd of Tstees BM (NH) 1974–79; pres RSE 1985–88, chm Scot Hosps Endowments Res Tst 1988–96; FRS, FRSE 1958, MRIA; *Books* Treatises and Monographs in Geology and Palaeontology; *Recreations* music, art; *Style*— Sir Alwyn Williams, FRS, FRSE; ✉ Palaeobiology Unit, Department of Geology and Applied Geology, Univ of Glasgow, Glasgow G12 8QQ

WILLIAMS, Andrew Edward; s of Graham Edward Williams, of Baschurch House, Shrewsbury, and Rosaline Joan Amphlett; *b* 16 Sept 1952; *Educ* Wakeman Sch Shrewsbury, Univ of Warwick (LLB), Univ of Sheffield (MA); *Career* called to the Bar Lincoln's Inn 1975; memb Legal Aid Area Ctee (London); acting metropolitan stipendiary magistrate; memb Criminal Bar Assoc; *Style*— Andrew E Williams, Esq; ✉ 3 Hare Court, Temple, London EC4Y 7BJ (☎ 0171 353 7561, fax 0171 353 7741)

WILLIAMS, Dr Anthony Ffoulkes; s of Edward Gordon Williams, of Birkenhead, and Sarah Elizabeth, *née* Wearing (d 1972); *b* 7 May 1951; *Educ* Birkenhead Sch, UCL (BSc), Westminister Med Sch (MB BS), St Catherine's Coll Oxford (DPhil); *Career* res fell Dept of Paediatrics Univ of Oxford 1981–85, lectr in child health Univ of Bristol 1985–87, sr lectr in child health and conslt paediatrician St George's Hosp Med Sch 1987–; memb: Nutrition Soc, British Paediatric Assoc, British Assoc for Perinatal Med; FRCP 1993 (MRCP 1978); *Style*— Dr Anthony Williams; ✉ Department of Child Health, St George's Hospital Medical School, Cranmer Terrace, London SW17 0RE (☎ 0181 725 2986, fax 0181 725 2858)

WILLIAMS, Anthony Frederick Davies (Tony); s of Evan Glyndwr Morgan Davies Williams (d 1963), of Caerphilly, Wales, and Gwendolen Delilah, *née* Naish, latterly Mrs Calder (d 1994); *b* 12 Aug 1940; *Educ* Christ Coll Brecon, City of London Business Sch; *m* 21 June 1969, Lorna Elizabeth, da of Geoffrey Thomas Southern Harborne; 2 s (Nicholas Geoffrey Calder b 26 April 1973, Andrew Christian Calder b 15 Jan 1976); *Career* chartering clerk Cayzer Irvine Group 1958–62, chartering mangr Tate & Lyle 1963–74, dir London shipping div Louis Dreyfus Corp 1974–86, chartering broker Denholm Coates & Co Ltd 1986–88, divnl dir Tate & Lyle International 1988–96, md Kentships (div of Tate & Lyle International) 1988–96; memb Baltic Exchange 1961–; Freeman City of London 1988; Hon Artillery Co: cmmnd 2 Lt 1968, Co of Pikemen & Musketeers 1988–; MICS 1961; *Recreations* rugby football, military ceremonial activities, golf, classical music, sailing; *Clubs* Harlequins RFC, Richmond RFC, Marine Engrs; *Style*— Tony Williams, Esq; ✉ 29 Clive Road, Strawberry Hill, Twickenham, Middlesex TW1 4SQ (☎ 0181 892 7534)

WILLIAMS, Anthony Touzeau; s of Frank Chauncy Williams (d 1971), of Keymer, Sussex, and Yvonne Romaine, *née* Touzeau (d 1967); *b* 14 March 1927; *Educ* Cranleigh Sch, A A Sch of Architecture (Dip Arch); *m* 16 May 1953, Eleanor Brigitte, da of Dr Ernst Jellinek (d 1977), of Harpenden; 3 s (Simon b 1956, Michael b 1959, Peter b 1962); *Career* asst architect: Herts CC 1949–56, Br Standards Inst 1956–58, head Tech Dept RIBA 1958–63; ptnr: Alex Gordon & Ptnrs 1963–66, Anthony Williams & Burles 1966–76; series ed Building Dossiers 1973–, Anthony Williams & Ptnrs 1976–94; chm SGS Yarsley: International Certification Services Ltd 1985–94, Certification Cncl 1994–97; dir Sign Design Soc 1993–94; memb Cncl Bldg Standards Gp of Br Standards Soc, past chm Modular Soc; FRIBA, FCSD, FRSA; *Books* Signs (1984), Energy Design Guide (1985); *Recreations* semiotics, historic gardens; *Style*— Anthony Williams, Esq; ✉ 43A West Common, Harpenden, Herts AL5 2JW (☎ and fax 01582 460994)

WILLIAMS, Bernard Arthur Owen; s of Owen Pasley Denny Williams (d 1975), of Swaffham Bulbeck, Cambs, and Hilda Amy, *née* Day (d 1991); *b* 21 Sept 1929; *Educ* Chigwell Sch Essex, Balliol Coll Oxford (MA); *m* 1, 1955 (m dis 1974), Shirley Vivienne Brittain, da of Sir George Catlin; 1 da (Rebecca b 1961); m 2, 1974, Patricia Law Skinner, da of Frederick Dwyer; 2 s (Jacob b 1975, Jonathan b 1980); *Career* Nat Serv pilot RAF 1951–53; Univ of Oxford: fell All Souls Coll 1951–54, tutor in philosophy New Coll 1954–59, fell New Coll 1954–59; lectr in philosophy UCL 1959–64, prof of philosophy Bedford Coll London 1964–67, Knightbridge prof of philosophy Univ of Cambridge and fell King's Coll 1967–79, provost King's Coll Cambridge 1979–87, White's prof of moral philosophy Univ of Oxford and fell of CCC Oxford 1990–96; visiting appts: Univ of Ghana 1958–59, Princeton 1963 (sr fell in Humanities 1978), Harvard 1973; Univ of California Berkeley: visiting appt 1986, Monroe Deutsch prof of philosophy 1988–, Sather prof of classics 1989; memb: Public Schs Cmmn 1965–70, Royal Cmmn on Gambling 1976–78; chm Ctee on Obscenity and Film Censorship 1977–79; Cmmn on Social Justice 1992–94; Hon Litt D Dublin 1981, Hon Fell Balliol Coll Oxford 1984, Hon D Litt: Univ of Aberdeen 1985, Univ of Keele 1995; foreign hon memb American Acad of Arts and Sciences 1983; FBA 1971; *Books* British Analytical Philosophy (co-ed with A C Montefiore, 1966), Morality (1972), A Critique of Utilitarianism in Utilitarianism: For and Against (J J C Smart and Bernard Williams, 1973), Problems of the Self (1973), Descartes: The Project of Pure Enquiry (1978), Moral Luck (1981), Utilitarianism and Beyond (co-ed with A K Sen, 1982), Ethics and the Limits of Philosophy (1985), Shame and Necessity (1993), Making Sense of Humanity (1995), Festschrift: World, Mind and Ethics (1995); *Style*— Prof Bernard Williams, FBA; ✉ 18 Farndon Road, Oxford OX2 6RT (☎ 01865 558500); Corpus Christi College, Oxford OX1 4JF

WILLIAMS, Dr Brian Owen; s of William Wood Williams (d 1988), of Kilbarchan, Scotland, and Joan Scott, *née* Adam; *b* 27 Feb 1947; *Educ* Kings Park Sch Glasgow, Univ of Glasgow (MD, MB, ChB); *m* 3 Dec 1970, Martha MacDonald, da of James Carmichael (d 1974), of Glasgow; 2 da (Jennifer b 1976, Linzie b 1978); *Career* maj RAMC 32 Scot Signal Regt TA 1976–83; conslt geriatrician Victoria Infirmary Glasgow 1976–79, sr lectr Univ of Glasgow 1979–82, conslt in admin charge W Glasgow Geriatric Med Serv 1982–, hon sr clinical lectr Univ of Glasgow 1982–; author of over 100 pubns on health care of the elderly; past hon sec: Royal Coll of Physicians & Surgns of Glasgow, Scottish Royal Colls; memb: BMA, BGS, Scot Soc Physicians; FRCP; *Books* Practical Management of the Elderly (with Sir Ferguson Anderson, 4 edn, 1983, 5 edn, 1988); *Recreations* swimming, writing, hill walking; *Style*— Dr Brian Williams; ✉ 15 Thorn Drive, High Burnside, Glasgow G73 4RH (☎ 0141 634 4480); Gartnavel General Hospital, 1053 Great Western Rd, Glasgow G12 0YN (☎ 0141 211 3167)

WILLIAMS, Bryn Owen; BEM (1990); s of Hugh James Owen Williams (d 1983), and Ivy, *née* Heffer; *b* 20 Aug 1933; *Educ* Southgate County GS, Pitman's Coll, Italia Conti Stage Sch; *m* 6 July 1957, Ann Elizabeth Rheidol, da of David Rheidol Powell (d 1932), adopted da of Stephen Llewellyn Jones (d 1963), of Dulwich; 1 s (Timothy Dorian b 7 April 1959), 1 da (Tracy-Jane b 11 June 1961); *Career* professional toastmaster 1950; co fndr (with father) Nat Assoc of Toastmasters 1956 (pres 1962 and 1990, life vice pres 1984), chm Toastmaster Training Ltd 1988, officiated at over fourteen thousand events in over twenty countries; memb Grand Order Water Rats 1965, pres of the Soc of Past Chm of the Licensed Victuallers Nat Homes 1993; Freeman City of London 1980, Liveryman Worshipful Co of Butchers 1985; intronized into the Jurade of the Vineyards of St Emilion 1989; MIOD 1990; *Recreations* golf, classical music; *Clubs* Wig & Pen, Muswell Hill Golf, Concert Artists Assoc, City Livery, Variety Club of GB Golf Soc (life memb), Jaguar Drivers (life memb); *Style*— Bryn Williams, Esq, BEM; ✉ Tanglewood, 50 The Ridgeway, Enfield, Middx EN2 8QS (☎ 0181 366 0012 and 0181 336 1398); Bryn Williams Enterprise (fax 0181 367 8248)

WILLIAMS, Caroline Ann; da of Maurice Henry Jackson, of Almeria, Spain, and Dorothy, *née* Ludlow; *b* 2 March 1954; *Educ* Convent of the Cross Sch Waterlooville Hants, St Hugh's Coll Oxford, Univ of Southampton (LLB); *m* 17 March 1973, Richard David Brooke Williams, s of Gp Capt Richard David Williams, CBE, of Hampshire; 1 s (Richard David b 6 Aug 1987), 1 da (Rowena b 27 June 1982); *Career* admitted slr 1978; ptnr Blake Lapthorn; chm Portsmouth Area Ctee Hampshire Incorporated Law Soc 1993–95; govr and chm Univ of Portsmouth 1993–, govr Portsmouth HS 1995–; govr and vice chm Portsmouth Coll of Art Design and Further Educn 1989–94, memb industl advsy bd Portsmouth Univ Business Sch; memb Law Soc 1978; FRSA 1995; *Publications* A Practical Legal Guide to Occupational Pension Schemes (with Philip Harwood-Smart, 1993); *Recreations* sailing; *Style*— Mrs Caroline Williams; ✉ 4 Grand Parade, Old Portsmouth, Hants; Blake Lapthorn, New Court, 1 Barnes Wallis Rd, Segensworth, Fareham PO15 5UA (☎ 01489 579990, fax 01489 579126)

WILLIAMS, Christopher; s of Henry Edward Williams (d 1957), of Bristol, and Beatrice May, *née* Somers (d 1990); *Educ* Colstons Sch Stapleton Bristol, St Cuthbert's Society Univ of Durham (BA); *Career* W & T Avery Ltd Soho Foundry Birmingham 1964–69, md Frenchay Transport Group 1969–; chm Frenchay Community Health Cncl 1980–81 (memb 1976–81, vice chm 1978–80), chm Frenchay Health Authy 1990–91 (memb 1981–91), chm Frenchay Healthcare NHS Tst 1992– (chm designate 1991–92); memb: NHS Nat Fire Policy Advsy Gp 1993–, Standing Fin and Capital Ctee NHS Tst Fedn 1993–, Cncl NHS Tst Fedn 1994–; Northavon DC: cncllr (C) 1976–96, chm Fin and Gen Purposes Ctee 1980–90, chm of Cncl 1986–88, ldr Cons Gp 1991–96; chm Bd of Govrs Frenchay Park Hosp Sch 1978–94, dir Bristol/Avon Groundwork Tst 1990–96; *Recreations* music, reading, travel; *Style*— Christopher Williams, Esq; ✉ Frenchay Healthcare NHS Trust, Trust Headquarters, Beckspool Road, Frenchay, Bristol BS16 1ND (☎ 0117 975 3801, fax 0117 975 3806)

WILLIAMS, Dr Christopher Beverley; s of Dr Denis John Williams, CBE (d 1990), and Dr Joyce Beverley Williams, MBE, *née* Jewson (d 1996); *b* 8 June 1938; *Educ* Dragon Sch, Winchester, Trinity Coll Oxford (MA, BM BCh), Univ Coll Hosp London (LRCS, MRCS, FRCP); *m* 25 April 1970, Dr Christina Janet Seymour Williams, da of Rex Seymour Lawrie; 1 da (Caroline Frances Aitken b 7 July 1972), 1 s (Duncan Nicholas Grant b 21 Nov 1973); *Career* house appts: UCH 1965, Brompton Hosp 1966, Hammersmith Hosp 1967, Nat Hosp for Neurology Whittington 1966; subsquently registrar UCH; currently: conslt physician St Mark's Hosp for Diseases of the Colon and Rectum (formerly sr registrar) and King Edward VII Hosp for Officers, hon conslt physician Royal Free Hosp, Hosp for Sick Children Great Ormond St, Queen Elizabeth Hosp Hackney and St Luke's Hosp for the Clergy; worldwide lectr on colonoscopy and colonoscopic polypectomy incl Quadrennial Review Lecture in Polypectomy (World Congress of Gastroenterology 1990), author of numerous articles on colonoscopy, colonic neoplasia and related topics; Gold medal BMA internal film competition, BLAT trophy for teaching films; Liveryman Worshipful Soc of Apothecaries 1958; memb: Br Soc of Gastroenterology 1973 (endoscopy fndn lectr 1976 and 1995, endoscopy vice pres 1987), Societé Belge de l'Endoscopie Digestive (hon memb) 1973, Societé Medicale Internationale d'Endoscopie et de Radio-Cinema (hon memb and int ed) 1973; fell Med Soc of London 1981 (Lettsomian lectr 1983), FRSM 1970 (memb Proctology Section), FRCP 1983; *Books* Colorectal Disease - an introduction for physicians and surgeons (jt ed), Practical Gastrointestinal Endoscopy (1983, 4 edn 1995), Gastrointestinal Endoscopy (annually, 1989–); *Recreations* travel, fine wine and food, skiing, scuba; *Clubs* St Albans Medical Dining; *Style*— Dr Christopher Williams; ✉ 11 Frognal Way, London NW3 (☎ 0171 435 4030, fax 0171 435 5636, e-mail 100732.2460@compuserve.com); St Mark's Hospital Endoscopy Unit, Northwick Park, Harrow, London HA1 3UJ (☎ 0181 235 4130, personal sec ☎ 0181 440 1063); London Clinic Endoscopy Unit, 20 Devonshire Place, London W1 (bookings sec ☎ 0171 244 3681, fax 0171 486 1755)

WILLIAMS, Clifford; s of George Frederick Williams (d 1932), and Florence Maud Gapper Williams Maycock; *b* 30 Dec 1926; *Educ* Highbury County GS London; *m* 1962, Josiane Eugenie, da of Auguste Camille Joseph Peset (d 1972), of Paris; 2 da (Anouk, Tara); *Career* director and writer; Lt RAOC 1946–48; fndr and dir Mime Theatre Co

1950–53, dir of prodns Marlow Theatre Canterbury 1956 and Queen's Theatre Hornchurch 1957, assoc dir Royal Shakespeare Co 1963–; has dir for Nat Theatres of UK, Finland, Yugoslavia, Bulgaria, Mexico, Spain, France, Denmark, Sweden, Germany, Japan, Canada, Aust, New Zealand and USA; prodns in London and NY incl premieres of plays by: Friedrich Dürrenmatt, Eugene Ionesco, David Rudkin, Anthony Shaffer, Alan Bennett, Peter Ustinov, Rolf Hochhuth, Alexander Solzhenitsyn, Peter Nichols and Hugh Whitemore; recently dir Harvey by Mary Chase (Savoy) 1995, Private Lives (NZ) 1996, The Father (NY) 1996; dir Man and Superman (film, 1988); author of plays incl: The Sleeping Princess, The Goose Girl, The Secret Kingdom (with Donald Jonson), Stephen Hero (adaptation of James Joyce with Donald Jonson), Rebecca (adaptation of Daphne du Maurier), Bellman's Opera (with Martin Best), Matters Matrimonial, Keys of the Kingdom; fell Trinity Coll of Music 1956, govr Welsh Coll of Music and Drama 1980–89 (fell 1994); chm: British Theatre Assoc 1978–90, UK Centre of Int Amateur Theatre Assoc 1980–; *Recreations* motor sport; *Style*— Clifford Williams, Esq; ✉ 62 Maltings Place, London SW6 2BY (☎ 0171 736 4673)

WILLIAMS, Adm Sir David; GCB (1977, KCB 1975), DL (Devon 1981); s of A Williams; *b* 22 Oct 1921; *Educ* Yardley Ct Sch Tonbridge, RNC Dartmouth; *m* 1947, Philippa Stevens; 2 s; *Career* joined RN as Cadet 1935, Flag Offr and 2 i/c Far East Fleet 1970–72, dir-gen Naval Manpower and Trg 1972–74, Vice-Adm 1973, Adm 1974, Chief Naval Personnel and Second Sea Lord 1974–77, C-in-C Naval Home Cmd and ADC to HM The Queen 1977–79, Gentleman Usher to HM The Queen 1979–82, Extra Gentleman Usher 1982–, govr and C-in-C Gibraltar 1982–85; memb Cwlth War Graves Cmmn 1980–89 (vice-chm 1986–89); pres (Navy) Not Forgotten Assoc; Hon Liveryman Worshipful Co of Fruiterers; KStJ 1983; *Clubs* Royal Yacht Sqdn, Army and Navy; *Style*— Admiral Sir David Williams, GCB, DL; ✉ Barnhill, Stoke Gabriel, Totnes, Devon TQ9 6SJ

WILLIAMS, David; s of Trevor Kenneth Stuart Williams (d 1961), and Peri Rene Mavis, *née* Morgan (d 1987); *b* 8 June 1926; *Educ* Cathedral Sch Hereford, St John's Coll Oxford (MA); *m* 18 Aug 1951, Brenda Yvonne, da of Dan Campbell Holmes, OBE (d 1964); 1 s (Jonathan b 1955), 1 da (Linda b 1957); *Career* Sub Lt RNVR 1944–47; dir Gordon and Gotch Advertising 1950–58, chm David Williams and Ketchum 1958–78, dir Ketchum Communications Inc USA 1968–86; govr Pusey House Oxford 1963–; vice chm Royal Cwlth Soc for the Blind 1969–85; memb Cncl: Inst Practice in Advtg 1959–78, Advtg Assoc 1963–78, Advtg Standards Authy 1976–80, Impact Fndn 1985–91, Chest Heart and Stroke Assoc 1987–92; memb: Detection Club 1988–, The Welsh Acad 1996–; Freeman City of London 1959, Liveryman Worshipful Co of Stationers and Newspaper Makers 1960; MCAM 1959, FIPA 1962; *Novels* Unholy Writ (1976), Treasure by Degrees (1977), Treasure up in Smoke (1978), Murder for Treasure (1980), Copper, Gold & Treasure (1982), Treasure Preserved (1983), Advertise for Treasure (1984), Wedding Treasure (1985), Murder in Advent (1985), Treasure in Roubles (1986), Divided Treasure (1987), Treasure in Oxford (1988), Holy Treasure! (1989), Prescription for Murder (1990), Treasure by Post (1991), Planning on Murder (1992), Banking on Murder (1993), Last Seen Breathing (1994), Death of a Prodigal (1995), Dead in the Market (1996), A Terminal Case (1997); numerous short stories; archive at The Mugar Meml Library Boston Univ USA; *Recreations* golf, music, looking at churches; *Clubs* Carlton, Wentworth Golf; *Style*— David Williams, Esq; ✉ Blandings, Pinewood Rd, Wentworth, Virginia Water, Surrey GU25 4PA (☎ 01344 842055, fax 01344 843045)

WILLIAMS, David; s of Frederick Williams, and Janet, *née* North; *b* 7 Aug 1966; *Educ* St John HS Sittingbourne; *Career* yachtsman; began sailing catamarans 1984, winner Olympic trg qualifier 1989, nat champion 1990 and 1991, tenth place Olympic Games Barcelona 1992, winner Olympic qualifier 1995 (sailing a Tornado Catamaran), thirteenth place Olympic Games Savannah 1996; *Recreations* sailing, swimming, skiing; *Style*— David Williams, Esq; ✉ 56 London Rd, Teynham, Kent ME9 9QN (☎ 01795 521650)

WILLIAMS, Prof Sir David Glyndwr Tudor; kt (1991), Hon QC (1994), DL (1995); s of Tudor Williams, OBE (d 1955), and Anne, *née* Rees (d 1980); *b* 22 Oct 1930; *Educ* Queen Elizabeth GS Carmarthen, Emmanuel Coll Cambridge (MA, LLB), Harvard Law Sch, Univ of California at Berkeley (LLM); *m* 1959, Sally, *née* Cole; 2 da (Rhiannon b 1963, Siân b 1968), 1 s (Rhys b 1965); *Career* called to the Bar Lincoln's Inn 1956; lectr: Univ of Nottingham 1958–63, Keble Coll Oxford 1963–67; Univ of Cambridge: lectr Emmanuel Coll 1967–76, sr tutor Emmanuel Coll 1970–76, reader in public law 1976–83, pres Wolfson Coll 1980–92, Rouse Ball prof of English law 1983–92, vice-chllr 1989–96 (vice-chllr emeritus 1996–), prof of law 1996–; distinguished anniversary fell ANU Canberra Oct-Dec 1996; pres Nat Soc for Clean Air 1983–85; memb: Cncl on Tbnls 1972–82, Royal Cmmn on Environmental Pollution 1976–83, Cmmn on Energy and the Environment 1979–82, Animal Procedures Ctee 1987–89; hon degrees: Univ of Loughborough, Univ of Hull, Anglia Poly, Univ of Nottingham, Univ of Liverpool, Davidson Coll (N Carolina), Wm Jewell Coll (Missouri), McGill Univ, Sydney Univ, Duke Univ; *Books* Not in the Public Interest (1965), Keeping the Peace (1967); *Recreations* reading, sport; *Clubs* Athenaeum; *Style*— Prof Sir David Williams, QC, DL; ✉ Emmanuel College, Cambridge CB2 3AP (☎ 01223 334200, fax 01223 334426)

WILLIAMS, Sir David Innes; kt (1985); s of Gwynne Evan Owen Williams (d 1957), and Cecily Mary, *née* Innes; *b* 12 June 1919; *Educ* Sherborne, Trinity Hall Cambridge, Univ Coll Hosp Med Sch (MB BCh, MA, MD, MCh); *m* 19 Sept 1944, Margaret Eileen, da of Victor Harding (d 1956); 2 s (Martin Gwynne b 13 March 1948, Michael Innes b 14 Nov 1949); *Career* Maj RAMC 1945–48 (surgical specialist); surgn St Peter's Hosp London 1950–78, urological surgn The Hosp for Sick Children Gt Ormond St 1952–78; urologist: King Edward VII Hosp for Offrs 1961–72, Royal Masonic Hosp 1962–72; civil conslt urologist to RN 1971–78, dir Br Post Grad Med Fedn Univ of London 1978–86, pro vice chllr Univ of London 1985–87; pres: Br Assoc of Urological Surgns 1976–78, BMA 1988–89, RSM 1990–92; vice pres: Int Soc of Urology 1973–74, RCS 1983–85; chm: Cncl for Post Grad Med Educn Eng and Wales 1985–88, Cncl Imperial Cancer Res Fund 1982–91; hon fell UCL 1986; FRCS Eng 1944, Hon FACS 1983, Hon FRCSI 1984, Hon FDSRCS Eng 1986; *Books* Urology of Childhood (1952), Urology of Childhood (1958), Paediatric Urology (1968, 1982), The London Lock (1995); *Recreations* gardening; *Clubs* RSM; *Style*— Sir David Innes Williams; ✉ 66 Murray Rd, Wimbledon Common, London SW19 4PE (☎ 0181 879 1042); The Old Rectory, East Knoyle, Salisbury, Wilts SP3 6AQ

WILLIAMS, Chief Constable David John; QPM (1992); s of John Isaac Williams (d 1957), of Clydach, and Edith, *née* Stoneham; *b* 7 April 1941; *Educ* Ystalyfera GS, UCL (LLB), National Executive Inst USA; *m* 1962, Johanna, da of Samuel Murphy; 2 s (Steven John b 12 Sept 1965, Ian David b 16 Jan 1969); *Career* cadet rising to chief supt Metropolitan Police Service 1958–84, asst chief constable Hertfordshire Constabulary 1984–89, chief constable Surrey Police 1991– (dep chief constable 1989–91); chm Traffic Ctee ACPO 1995; awarded Queen's Commendation for Bravery 1976; OStJ 1995; *Recreations* opera, music, rugby football, countryside walking, keeping fit; *Style*— Chief Constable David J Williams, QPM; ✉ Surrey Police HQ, Mount Browne, Sandy Lane, Guildford, Surrey GU3 1HG (☎ 01483 571212, fax 01483 300279)

WILLIAMS, Dr David John; s of Frank Williams, CBE (d 1979), and Kathleen, *née* Davies (d 1989); *b* 23 April 1938; *Educ* Highgate Sch, Hotchkiss Sch USA, Trinity Coll Cambridge (MA), St Thomas' Hosp Med Sch (MB BChir), FRCP, FFAEM, MRCGP; *m* 1977, Ann Andrews, da of William Walker-Watson; 1 s (Jonathan b 4 Sept 1979), 1 da (Antonia b 31 March 1981); *Career* jr med posts St Thomas' Hosp, Kingston Hosp, Guy's/Maudsley Neurosurgical Unit 1964–65; resident MO: Nat Heart Hosp 1966, Middx Hosp 1967–70; registrar Maudsley Hosp 1970–71, GP 1971–72; conslt in A&E med: Middx Hosp 1973–84, St Thomas' Hosp 1984–93; clinical dir for A&E servs Guy's and St Thomas' Hosps Tst 1993–; sec Casualty Surgns Assoc 1978–84; pres: Br Assoc for A&E Med 1987–90, Intercollegiate Faculty of A&E Med 1993–; invited memb Cncl Royal Coll of Physicians, Royal Coll of Surgns and Royal Coll of Anaesthetists 1994–; faculty rep: Senate of Surgery of GB and I 1994–, Acad of Med Royal Colls and Faculties in Scot 1996–; hon memb American Coll of Emergency Physicians 1990; *Recreations* reading, collecting books, theatre, travel; *Style*— Dr David Williams; ✉ 13 Spencer Hill, Wimbledon, London SW19 4PA (☎ 0181 946 3785); Accident and Emergency Department, St Thomas' Hospital, Guy's and St Thomas' Hospitals Trust, Lambeth Palace Road, London SE1 7EH (☎ 0171 928 9292, fax 0171 922 8260)

WILLIAMS, David Lincoln; s of Lewis Bernard Williams (d 1976), of Cardiff, and Eileen Elizabeth, *née* Cadogan (d 1989); *b* 10 Feb 1937; *Educ* Cheltenham; *m* 1959, Gillian Elisabeth, da of Dr William Phillips (d 1977); 1 s (Jonathan), 1 da (Sophie); *Career* chm: Allied Profiles Ltd 1981–, John Williams of Cardiff plc 1983–88 (dir 1969–88), Cox (Penarth) Ltd 1984–, Costa Rica Coffee Co 1988–; pres Vale of Glamorgan Festival 1994– (chm 1978–94); chm: Cardiff Broadcasting plc 1979–84, Friends of Welsh Nat Opera 1980–; memb Welsh Arts Cncl 1987–94 (chm Music Ctee 1988–94); Liveryman Worshipful Co of Founders; *Recreations* opera, sailing; *Clubs* Cardiff & County; *Style*— David Williams, Esq; ✉ Rose Revived, Llantrithyd, Cowbridge, S Glam (☎ 01446 781357)

WILLIAMS, Prof David Raymond; OBE (1993); s of late Eric Thomas Williams, and Amy Gwendoline Williams; *b* 20 March 1941; *Educ* UCNW Bangor (BSc, PhD), Univ of St Andrews (DSc); *m* 22 Aug 1964, Gillian Kirkpatrick, da of late Adam Murray; 2 da (Caroline Susan b 1 Nov 1970, Kerstin Jane b 20 July 1973); *Career* lectr Univ of St Andrews 1966–77, prof of speciation and analytical chemistry Univ of Wales Cardiff 1977–; chm Br Cncl Sci Advsy Ctee 1986–94; EurChem, CChem, FRSC, FRSA; *Books* The Principles of Bioinorganic Chemistry, The Metals of Life, Analysis Using Glass Electrodes, Trace Element Medicine and Chelation Therapy; *Recreations* swimming, cycling, travel, photography; *Style*— Prof David R Williams, OBE; ✉ Department of Chemistry, University of Wales Cardiff, PO Box 912, Cardiff CF1 3TB (☎ 01222 874778, fax 01222 874778, telex 497368 G)

WILLIAMS, Deryk Meredith; s of Edward Meredith Williams (d 1987), of Criccieth, and Enid Meredith Williams, *née* Jones; *b* 11 Feb 1942; *Educ* Ysgol Eifionydd Porthmadog, Univ Coll Oxford (BA); *m* 1978, Mair Elizabeth Catlin; 1 s (Huw Meredith b 14 Sept 1979), 2 da (Nia Meredydd b 1 April 1982, Sara Meredydd b 13 April 1985); *Career* sub-ed TWW (then Wales regnl ITV co) Cardiff 1964–67 (joined as researcher 1963); BBC Wales: dir 1967–74, prodr 1974–78, ed Heddiw (Today) daily magazine prog 1978–82, ed Newyddion Saith (News at Seven) for S4C 1982–87; dir of progs Sianel Pedwar Cymru (S4C) 1991– (dep dir of progs 1987–91); *Recreations* cricket, other sports, reading novels, music; *Style*— Deryk Williams, Esq; ✉ Sianel Pedwar Cymru, Parc Ty Glas, Llanishen, Cardiff CF4 5GG (☎ 01222 747444, fax 01222 754444)

WILLIAMS, Desmond James; OBE (1988); s of Sydney Williams (d 1982), and Eleanor Williams; *b* 7 July 1932; *Educ* Douai Sch, Xaverian Coll, Univ of Manchester (Dip Arch); *m* 1 (m dis 1982); 3 s (Dominic Blair b 1965, Andrew Francis b 1970, Jeremy (twin) b 1970), 1 da (Sarah Frances b 1967); m 2, 30 Dec 1988, Susan Alexandra, da of John Richardson, of Shaldon, Devon; *Career* architect; in private practice 1964–, specialising in educnl and leisure buildings, security design, residential devpts and hotels; consultancy clients incl World Bank and Asian Devpt Bank, given lectures at Univs of London and Manchester and in Canada, London and Manchester; author of articles in: Education (1980), Building (1988 and 1989), Architects Journal (1989), Security Magazine (1990); past pres Manchester Soc of Architects 1988, examiner Sch of Architecture Univ of Manchester, chm NW regn RIBA 1990–92; memb Nat Mktg Ctee RIBA 1993–94; RIBA 1967; *Recreations* music, opera, walking, painting, travel; *Style*— Desmond Williams, Esq, OBE; ✉ Ellis Williams Partnership, Pennine House, Carrs Rd, Cheadle, Cheshire SK8 1BW (☎ 0161 428 0808, fax 0161 428 0812)

WILLIAMS, Sir Donald Mark; 10 Bt (UK 1866), of Tregullow, Cornwall; s of Sir Robert Ernest Williams, 9 Bt (d 1976); *b* 7 Nov 1954; *Educ* W Buckland Sch; *m* 1982, Denise, o da of Royston H Cory, of Kashmir, Raleigh Hill, Bideford, Devon; 1 s (Matthew b and d 1985), 1 da (Hannah Louise b 1987); *Heir* bro, Barton Matthew Williams, b 21 Nov 1956; *Style*— Sir Donald Williams, Bt; ✉ Kamsack, Saskatchewan, Canada; Upcott House, Barnstaple, N Devon

WILLIAMS, Douglas; CB (1977), CVO (1966); s of James Eli Williams (d 1977), and Elizabeth, *née* Thomas (d 1943); *b* 14 May 1917; *Educ* Wolverhampton GS, Exeter Coll Oxford (MA); *m* 4 Dec 1947, Marie Agathe, da of Charles Leon Jacquot (d 1959); *Career* WWII Maj RA (despatches 1945); princ Colonial Office 1947, colonial attaché Br Embassy Washington 1956–60, memb and Br Co chm Caribbean Cmmn 1956–60, asst sec Colonial Office (Head of West Indian Div) 1960–67, Miny of Overseas Devpt 1967, under sec i/c multilateral aid 1968, govr Asian Development Bank and African Development Bank 1968–73 (dep sec 1973–77), ret 1977; memb: Bd of Crown Agents 1978–84, Econ and Social Ctee Euro Community 1978–82, Overseas Devpt Inst Governing Cncl 1979–85; tstee Help the Aged 1984–92 (chm various ctees); vice chm: Help the Aged Int 1984–92, Nonsuch Park and Dist Res Assoc Epsom 1984–93; *Books* The Specialised Agencies of the United Nations (1987), contrib to The United Kingdom - The United Nations; *Clubs* United Oxford and Cambridge Univ, Cwlth Tst; *Style*— Douglas Williams, Esq, CB, CVO; ✉ 14 Gomshall Rd, Cheam, Sutton, Surrey SM2 7JZ (☎ 0181 393 7306)

WILLIAMS, Prof Dudley Howard; s of Lawrence Williams (d 1990), and Evelyn Williams (d 1982); *b* 25 May 1937; *Educ* Pudsey GS Yorks, Univ of Leeds (BSc, PhD), Univ of Cambridge (MA, ScD); *m* 9 March 1963, Lorna Patricia Phyllis, da of Phillip Anthony Herbert Bedford; 2 s (Mark Howard b 1966, Simon Bedford b 1968); *Career* post doctoral fell and res assoc Stanford Univ USA 1961–64; Univ of Cambridge: asst dir of res 1966–74, reader in organic chemistry 1974–96, prof of biological chemistry 1996–; Churchill Coll Cambridge: fell 1964–89, extraordinary fell 1989–96, professorial fell 1996–; chm Scientific Bd Xenova plc 1993–; author of numerous scientific articles and books; memb Academia Europaea 1990–; FRS 1983; *Books* Spectroscopic Methods in Organic Chemistry (with I Fleming, 5 edn); *Recreations* squash, piano playing; *Style*— Prof Dudley Williams, FRS; ✉ 7 Balsham Rd, Fulbourn, Cambridge CB1 5BZ (☎ 01223 502341); University Chemical Laboratory, Lensfield Rd, Cambridge CB2 1EW (☎ 01223 336368, fax 01223 336913)

WILLIAMS, Air Cdre Edward Stanley; CBE (1975, OBE 1968); s of William Stanley Williams (d 1957), of Wallasey, Cheshire, and Ethel, *née* Jones (d 1953); *b* 27 Sept 1924; *Educ* Wallasey Central Sch, Sch of Slavonic and Eastern European Studies London Univ, Univ Coll London, St John's Coll Cambridge (MPhil); *m* 12 July 1947, Maureen, da of William Joseph Donovan (d 1974), of Oxton, Merseyside; 2 da ((Susan) Jane b 3 Feb 1950, Sally (Ann) b 23 June 1955); *Career* joined RAF 1942, WWII training in Canada, served in flying boats 1944, seconded BOAC 1944–48, 18 Sqdn RAF Waterbeach 1949, instr Central Navigation Sch RAF Shawbury 1950–52, Russian language study 1952–54; flying appts 1954–61: MEAF, A & AEE Boscombe Down, 216 Sqdn Tpt Cmd; OC RAF Element Army Intelligence Centre 1961–64, asst air attaché Moscow 1964–67, first RAF def fell 1967–68, Sch of Serv Intelligence 1968–71, chief Target Plans HQ Second ATAF 1971–73, chief intelligence offr Br Forces Near East 1973–75, cmd Jt Air Reconnaissance

Intelligence Centre (UK) 1976–77, def and air attaché Moscow 1978–81, ret RAF 1981; conslt Soviet mil affrs MOD 1982–85, Soviet res assoc RUSI 1985–; vice-chm (air) TAVR and RAFVR Assoc (NW Area) 1988–93; *Books* The Soviet Military (1987), Soviet Air Power: Prospects for the Future (1990), An Attaché's Report (1997); *Recreations* walking; *Clubs* RAF; *Style*— Air Cdre E S Williams, CBE; ✉ c/o Midland Bank, 2 Liscard Way, Wallasey, Merseyside L44 5TR

WILLIAMS, Prof (William) Elwyn; s of Owen Williams (d 1972), of Anglesey, and Maggie, *née* Jones (d 1977); *b* 6 July 1931; *Educ* Holyhead Co Secdy Sch, Univ of Manchester (BSc, MSc, PhD, DSc); *m* 1, Judith (d 1976), da of Evan Davies (d 1932), of Llandovery; 1 s (Richard Aled b 26 Jan 1960); m 2, 6 Sept 1984, Janet Hazel, da of Leonard Knight Adams (d 1989), of Guildford; *Career* lectr then sr lectr in applied mathematics Univ of Liverpool 1957–65, prof of mathematics Univ of Surrey 1965–96 (emeritus prof 1996–); FIMA 1966; *Books* Fourier Series and Boundary Vale Problems (1973), Dynamics (1975), Partial Differential Equations (1982), Applied Mathematics for A-Level (with A R Waltham, 1985); *Style*— Prof Elwyn Williams; ✉ Department of Mathematics, University of Surrey, Guildford, Surrey GU2 5XH (☎ 01483 259640, fax 01483 300803)

WILLIAMS, Emrys; *b* 18 Jan 1958; *Educ* Slade Sch of Art (Boise Travelling scholar, Robert Ross scholar, BA), Stewart Powell Bowen fellowship 1983; *Career* artist in residence: Mostyn Art Gallery Llandudno 1983, South Hill Park Arts Centre and Wilde Theatre Bracknell 1985; *Solo Exhibitions* Andrew Knight Gallery Cardiff 1984, Pastimes Past (Wrexham Arts Centre) 1984, The Welsh Mountain Zoo (South Hill Park Arts Centre, Bracknell) 1985, Off Season - Winter Paintings (Oldham Art Gallery) 1985, Lanchester Poly Gallery Coventry 1986, Benjamin Rhodes Gallery London 1986, 1989 and 1991, Wrexham Arts Centre 1990; *Gp Exhibitions* incl: Clwyd Ten (Wrexham Arts Centre) 1981, Thorugh Artists Eyes (Mostyn Art Gallery, Llandudno) 1982, John Moores Liverpool Exhibiiton XIII 1982–83, Serpentine Summer Show II (Serpentine London) 1983, Pauline Carter & Emrys Williams (Chapter Gallery) Cardiff 1984, John Moores Liverpool Exhibition XIV 1985, Group 56 (Bratislava Czechoslavakia) 1986, David Hepher and Emrys Williams (Castlefield Gallery) Manchester 1987, Big Paintings (Benjamin Rhodes Gallery) 1988, Ways of Telling (Mostyn Art Gallery, Llandudno) 1989, Group 56 (Glynn Vivian Museum, Swansea), 1990; *Work in Public Collections* Contemporary Art Soc of Wales, Arthur Andersen & Co, Glynn Vivian Art Gallery and Museum Swansea, Govt Art Fund, Clwyd County Cncl, Clwyd Fine Art Trust, Metropolitan Museum of Art NY; numerous works in private collections in Britian and USA; *Awards* minor prize John Moores Liverpool Exhibition 1983, third prize Royal Nat Eisteddfod of Wales 1985, third prize Royal Over-Seas League London (Wardair Travel prize to Canada) 1988, Welsh Arts Cncl award for travel to Normandy 1988, Welsh Arts Cncl award for travel to Germany 1991; *Style*— Emrys Williams, Esq; ✉ Benjamin Rhodes Gallery, 4 New Burlington Place, London W1X 1SB (☎ 0171 534 1768/9, fax 0171 287 8841)

WILLIAMS, Euryn Ogwen; s of Alun Ogwen Williams (d 1970), and Lil Evans (d 1968); *b* 22 Dec 1942; *Educ* Mold Alun GS, UCNW (BA Dip Educ); *m* 1 Jan 1966, Jenny Lewis, da of John Edward Jones, of The Knap, Barry; 1 s (Rhodri Ogwen b 10 May 1968), 1 da (Sara Lisa Ogwen b 17 March 1971); *Career* media conslt and prodr; prog dir TWW, prodr HTV, dir EOS Independent Production Co, dir BBC Radio, dep chief exec and prog controller S4C, hon lectr Univ of Wales; *Books* Pelydrau Pell (1973), Images of Europe (1995); *Recreations* reading, television viewing, spectator sports; *Style*— Euryn Williams, Esq; ✉ 12 Maes-y-Coed, The Knap, Barry, South Glamorgan CF6 8SZ (☎ 01446 734864)

WILLIAMS, Faynia Roberta; da of Michael Manuel Jeffery (d 1968), of Brighton, Sussex, and Sally Caroline, *née* Stone (d 1968); *b* 10 Nov 1938; *Educ* Brighton and Hove HS, RADA (Dip), Univ of London (BA), Univ of Oxford, Nat Film Sch (short course); *m* 1, 1961, Michael Brandis Williams (d 1968), s of Walter Williams; 2 da (Sabra Mildred b 1964, Teohna Eloise b 1966); m 2, 1975, Richard Arthur Crane, s of Rev Robert Bartlett Crane; 2 s (Leo Michael b 1977, Samuel Richard b 1979); *Career* producer, director of theatre, television, radio and film; formerly actress; fell in theatre: Univ of Bradford 1974–78, Univ of Lancaster 1978; Granada TV artist in residence and visiting prof Univ of Calif 1984; Freedom of the City of London 1959; memb: Equity 1959, Eastern Arts Assoc Drama Panel 1986 (vice chm 1989), Cncl Int Theatre Inst and Dramatic Arts Ctee 1989–; Fedn of Audiovisual Dirs 1990; vice chm Dir Guild of GB 1990–92 and 1995– (vice pres 1988–89); *Theatre* first professional appearance Bridlington Repertory Theatre 1958, Stephen Joseph's Theatre in the Round (with Harold Pinter and Alan Ayckbourn) 1958–60; contract artist MGM USA 1960–61; first directed The Oz Trial (Oxford Playhouse) 1971; artistic dir: Oxford Free Theatre 1972–74, Oxford Arts Festival 1973, Bradford Theatre in the Mill 1974–78, Brighton Theatre 1980–85, Tron Theatre Glasgow 1983–84, Univ of Essex Theatre 1985–89; freelance dir: Royal Court, Fortune, Bush, Young Vic; theatres abroad incl USSR, Poland, Aust, Sweden, USA, Budapest 1993 and NT Romania 1991; prodns incl: Brothers Karamazov (with Alan Rickman, Edinburgh Int Festival 1981, Fortune Theatre London and USSR), King Lear (RSC, RNT and Acter Co USA); *Television* incl: Signals, Channel 4 arts documentaries 1990; *Films* 2 shorts: Sleepy, Prelude; *Radio* prodr BBC Radio Drama 1992– incl: Moscow Stations (starring Tom Courtenay, nominated Radio Times Award) and Vlad the Impaler (starring John Hurt, nominated Sony Award); prodr BBC Radio Features 1993– interviews incl: Joan Littlewood, Pina Bausch, Peter Stein, Patrice Chèreau, Peter Sellars, Dame Iris Murdoch and Ariel Dorfman; also Movers and Shakers (feature series, Radio 3), Bausch of Wuppertal (Radio 3 and World Service) and Starboy (with Ian Drury and Shirley Anne Field, drama Radio 3) 1995–96; *Awards* incl: Edinburgh Festival Fringe First Award 1974, 1975, 1977, 1979, 1980, 1986, 1987, 1988 and 1989; nominated: Best Dir/Designer for Satan's Ball London Critics' Award 1977, Best Dir for Brothers Karamazov 1981; *Recreations* bellringing, the sea, travel to lesser-known places; *Style*— Ms Faynia Williams; ✉ c/o Nathan Joseph, N J Media Enterprises Ltd, 10 Clorane Gardens, London NW3 7PR (☎ 0171 794 0414, fax 0171 437 0238)

WILLIAMS, Francis Owen (Frank); CBE (1987); s of Owen Garbett Williams, of Liverpool; *b* 16 April 1942; *Educ* St Joseph's Coll Dumfries; *m* 1974, Virginia Jane, da of Raymond Berry, of Marlow, Bucks; 3 c; *Career* md Williams Grand Prix Engineering Ltd; *Clubs* BRDC; *Style*— Frank Williams, Esq, CBE; ✉ Stargroves, nr Newbury, Berkshire; Williams Grand Prix Engineering Ltd, Grove, Wantage, Oxon (☎ 01235 777700)

WILLIAMS, Prof Frederic Ward (Fred); s of Prof Sir Frederic Calland Williams (d 1977), of Cheshire, and Gladys, *née* Ward; *b* 4 March 1940; *Educ* St John's Coll Cambridge (MA, ScD), Univ of Bristol (PhD); *m* 11 April 1964, Jessie Anne Hope, da of Rev William Wyper Wilson (d 1988), of Weston-Super-Mare, Avon; 2 s (Frederic b 21 Aug 1968, David b 11 Feb 1970); *Career* asst engr Freeman Fox and Ptnrs 1964; lectr in civil engrg: Ahmadu Bello Univ Nigeria 1964–67, Univ of Birmingham 1967–75; prof in civil engrg Univ of Wales Inst of Sci and Technol 1975–88, head of Div of Structural Engrg Univ of Wales Cardiff 1988–, fndr and chm Cardiff Advanced Chinese Engrg Centre 1993–; conslt to NASA, Br Aerospace; author of numerous papers in jls; sec Llanishen and Lisvane Cncl of Churches; FICE 1984, FIStructE 1985, FRAeS 1990; *Recreations* hill walking, jogging; *Style*— Prof Fred Williams; ✉ Brandelhow, 12 Ridgeway, Lisvane, Cardiff CF4 5RS (☎ 01222 761772); Head of Structural Engineering, Cardiff School of Engineering, University of Wales, Cardiff, PO Box 917, Cardiff CF2 1XH (☎ 01222 874826, fax 01222 874209, telex 498635)

WILLIAMS, (John) Gage; OBE (1987); s of Col George Torquil Gage Williams, DL, of Menkee, St Mabyn, Cornwall, and Yvonne Marguerite, *née* Ogilvy; *b* 12 March 1946; *Educ* Eton, RMA Sandhurst, Magdalene Coll Cambridge (MA); *m* 4 Jul 1970, Elizabeth Anne Kyffin, da of Stephen Marriott Fox (d 1971), of Burlorne, Weybridge, Surrey; 1 s (James b 1973), 2 da (Rebecca b 1971, Meg b 1978); *Career* cmmnd Somerset and Cornwall Light Inf 1966 (The Light Inf 1967); Platoon Cdr: Ethiopia, Aden, Canada, Norway, Kenya, Germany; GSO 3 ops 19 Airportable Bde England and Cyprus 1974–75, instr tactics Sch of Inf Fort Benning USA 1975–77, Royal Mil Coll Sci 1977, Royal Staff Course Greenwich 1978; Co Cdr: Ireland, Canada, Cyprus (UN) 1978–80; GSO2 Jt Warfare MO1 1980–82, Special Ops Liaison Offr Washington DC 1982–83, Mil Asst GOC NI 1983–84; cmmnd 1 Bn Light Inf: Lancs, Falklands, Canada, NI 1985–87; Liaison Col to Sch of Advanced Mil Studies Fort Leavenworth Kansas 1987–88, Col Higher Cmd and Staff Course Camberley 1988–90, Col Def Studies, cmmnd UKMF/1 Inf Bde 1991–92, dir of resettlement 1992–95, ret as Brig; Dep Col Light Inf (Somerset and Cornwall); dir CASE Global plc; non-exec dir The Ecodome; memb Ed Bd The Officer Magazine; *Recreations* shooting, fishing, skating, golf, skiing, squash, tennis; *Clubs* Cavalry and Guards', Light Infantry, Hawks, Cornish, Beefsteak, St Enodoc GC, IOD, Hockley Golf; *Style*— J G Williams, Esq, OBE; ✉ c/o Menkel, St Mabyn, Bodmin, Cornwall PL30 3DD (☎ 01962 884188, office ☎ 0171 496 0551)

WILLIAMS, Gareth James; s of Rev Daniel James Williams, (d 1967), of Cardiff, and Elizabeth Beatrice May, *née* Walters (d 1974); *b* 22 Dec 1944; *Educ* Cardiff HS, Univ of Exeter; *m* 2 Aug 1969, Ruth Elizabeth, da of Sub Lt Albert Gordon Laugharne (d 1944); 1 s (Geraint b 1975), 2 da (Rhian b 1971, Catherine b 1974); *Career* Marks and Spencer plc: joined 1967, exec responsibilities for buying and distribution systems 1974–86, sr exec 1986–87, Business Devpt Gp NY USA 1987–88, divnl dir for Physical Distribution, Retail Systems Logisitics and Info Tech 1988–92; princ mgmnt conslt in logistics and retail in UK and Europe with BMS/Bossard 1992–96, chief exec Al-Futtaim Sons Dubai 1996–; memb: Directors' Prog 3i 1992–, Euro Retail Advsy Bd Templeton Coll Oxford 1994–; chm London Welsh RFC 1996– (memb Exec Ctee 1995–96); memb: Cons Pty, Chalfont St Giles Parish Church, Friend of Covent Garden; hon vice pres Cardiff HSOB RFC; sport: Cardiff and Cardiff HSOB Rugby Clubs 1964–67, capt Univ of Exeter RFC 1967, played for Br Univs Athletic Union 1967, advsr Br Acad 1985–87; Fell Inst of Logistics 1989; *Recreations* sport (esp rugby), music (esp opera), education; *Clubs* Rugby (London), Cardiff HSOBRFC; *Style*— Gareth Williams, Esq; ✉ Dolphin Cottage, Deep Acres, Cheschen Bois, Bucks HP6 5NX (☎ 01494 432168); Al-Futtaim Sons, PO Box 7976, Dubai (☎ 00 971 4 277553)

WILLIAMS, Geoffrey Copeland Meirion; s of William Meirion Williams (d 1939), of Hastings, and Winifred Marjorie, *née* Brice (d 1987); *b* 31 Aug 1937; *Educ* Eastbourne Coll; *m* 29 May 1965, (Carin) Marianne, da of Col Arne Persson (d 1971), of Stockholm; 1 s (Anthony b 1977), 2 da (Ingela b 1968, Katherine b 1968); *Career* md Ansvar Insurance Co Ltd 1977– (gen mangr 1969–77); dir UK Temperance Alliance Ltd; vice pres Friends of the Towner Gallery Eastbourne, chm Eastbourne and Co Health Tst; FCII 1970; *Recreations* reading, jazz; *Style*— Geoffrey Williams, Esq; ✉ Ansvar House, St Leonards Rd, Eastbourne, E Sussex BN21 3UR (☎ 01323 737541, fax 01323 430977)

WILLIAMS, Geoffrey Guy; s of Capt Alfred Guy Williams, OBE (d 1956), and Margaret, *née* Thomas (d 1995); *b* 12 July 1930; *Educ* Blundell's, Christ's Coll Cambridge (MA, LLM); *Career* solicitor; ptnr Slaughter & May 1961–66 (joined 1952); J Henry Schroder Wagg & Co Ltd: dir 1966–90, vice chm 1974, dep chm 1977–90; chm Nat Film Fin Corpn 1976–85 (dir 1970); dir: Bass plc 1971–91, Schroders plc 1976–90, John Brown plc 1977–85, Standard Chartered plc 1990–94; chm Issuing Houses Assoc 1979–81, loan cmmr Public Works 1990–; Freeman City of London; *Clubs* Brooks's; *Style*— Geoffrey Williams, Esq; ✉ 18G Eaton Square, London SW1W 9DD (☎ 0171 235 5212)

WILLIAMS, Dr Geoffrey James; s of Idris Williams (d 1985), of Risca, Gwent, and Emily Edith, *née* James (d 1971); *b* 6 July 1936; *Educ* Pontywaun GS Risca, Univ Coll Swansea (BA, PhD); *m* 25 July 1959, Lorna, da of Ernest John McKay (d 1972); 2 s (Jonathan Rhodri b 24 May 1962, David Huw b 30 May 1967), 2 da (Cerys Sîan b 26 April 1961, Lucy Lenora b 6 Jan 1980); *Career* Nat Park asst Brecknock Co Planning Office 1961–62; lectr in geography: Fourah Bay Coll Univ of Sierra Leone 1963–69, Univ Coll Swansea 1969–70; sr lectr in geography Ahmadu Bello Univ Northern Nigeria 1970–74, prof of geography Univ of Zambia 1974–87, hon res fell Univ Coll Swansea 1987–90, dir of studies King George VI & Queen Elizabeth Fndn of St Catharine's Cumberland Lodge 1988–; FRGS 1957, memb Inst of Br Geographers 1957; *Books* A Bibliography of Sierra Leone (1971), Development and Ecology in the Lower Kafue Basin in the Nineteen Seventies (co-ed, 1977), Independent Zambia, A Bibliography of the Social Sciences 1964–79 (1984), The Peugeot Guide to Lusaka (1984), Lusaka and its Environs: A Geographical Study of a Planned City in Tropical Africa (1987), Geographical Perspectives on Development in Southern Africa (co-ed, 1987); *Recreations* books, travel, photography; *Style*— Dr Geoffrey Williams; ✉ Penyrheolrhyn, Ffawyddog, Llangattock, Crickhowell, Powys NP8 1PY (☎ 01873 811300); Mews Cottage, Cumberland Lodge, The Great Park, Windsor, Berkshire SL4 2HP (☎ 01784 433566); King George VI and Queen Elizabeth Foundation of St Catharine's, Cumberland Lodge, The Great Park, Windsor, Berkshire SL4 2HP (☎ 01784 432316 and 01784 434893, fax 01784 438507)

WILLIAMS, George Mervyn; CBE (1977), MC (1944), TD; yr s of Owain Lloyd Joseph Williams (d 1930), and Maude Elizabeth, *née* Morgan (d 1941); *b* 30 Oct 1918; *Educ* Radley; *m* 1, 8 March 1941 (m dis 1946), Penelope, da of late Sir Frank Herbert Mitchell, KCVO, CBE; m 2, 19 Aug 1950, Grizel Margaretta Cochrane, DStJ, da of Maj Walter Peter Stewart, DSO, late Highland LI, of Davo House, Kincardineshire; 1 s (Owain Anthony Mervyn b 8 Jan 1955); *Career* Maj Royal Fusiliers N Africa, Italy, Greece; chm: Christie-Tyler plc 1950–86, S Wales Regnl Bd Lloyds Bank Ltd 1975–87, Williams & Morgan Ltd 1986–; High Sheriff Glamorgan 1966, Vice Lord Lt Mid Glamorgan 1986–93 (JP 1965–70, DL 1967–86); Liveryman Worshipful Co of Furniture Makers; CStJ; *Clubs* Brooks's, Cardiff and County; *Style*— George Williams, Esq, CBE, MC, TD; ✉ Llanharan House, Llanharan, Mid Glamorgan CF7 9NR; office: 27 Broad Street, Ludlow, Shropshire SY8 1NJ (☎ 01584 872877, fax 01584 872833)

WILLIAMS, Gerard; s of Frank Williams, of Manchester, and Margaret Rose, *née* Lockwood; *b* 9 July 1959; *Educ* Manchester HS of Art, Manchester Poly, Brighton Poly; *Career* artist; *Solo Exhibitions* Interim Art 1986 and 1990, Anthony d'Offay Gallery 1989, Galleria Franz Paludetto Turin 1990, Patrick de Brock Gallery Antwerp 1991, Todd Gallery London 1993, Galerie 102 Düsseldorf 1993, Aldebaran, Baillargues France 1993, Galerie du Tableau Marseille 1994, The Showroom (London) 1994, Galerie 102 (Düsseldorf) 1996; *Group Exhibitions* incl: Whitechapel Open 1985, 1986, 1987 and 1988, Summer Show (Anthony d'Offay Gallery) 1988, That Which Appears is Good, That Which is Good Appears (Tanja Grunert Gallery Cologne) 1988, Home Truths (Castello di Rivara) 1989, Richard Wentworth Grenville Davey Gerard Williams (Sala Uno Rome) 1989, Its a Still Life (Arts Cncl of GB, touring) 1989–91, Leche Vitrines (Le Festival ARS Musica Brussels) 1990, TAC 90 (Sala Parpallo/Diputacion de Valencia, touring) 1990, Realismi (Galleria Giorgio Persano Turin, Ileana Toynta Contemporary Art Centre Athens) 1990, What is a Gallery? (Kettles Yard, Univ of Cambridge), Maureen Paley Interim Art 1990–91, Anni Novanta (Bologna, Cattolica and Rimini) 1991, Lithuanian

Artists Assoc Symposium 1991, Koji Tatsuno: 03.91 (Palais Galliera Paris) 1991, Made for Arolsen (Museumverein Arolsen Germany) 1992, Rencontres No 1 (Assoc La Vigie Nimes France) 1992, In House, Out House (Unit Seven London) 1993, Five British Artists (Patrick de Brock Gallery Antwerp) 1993, The East Wing Collection (Courtauld Inst London) 1993–96, Escale a Marseille (Tour du Roy Rene Marseille) 1994, Sous Reserve de Modification (Montpellier France) 1994, Seeing the Unseen (Fliesig Coll London) 1994, Arte Inglese d' Oggi (Turin, Galleria Civica di Modena Italy) 1994, Taking Form (The Fruitmarket Gallery Edinburgh) 1995, A Matter of Facts (Städtische Ausstellungshalle Münster) 1996, Good News (102 Galerie Düsseldorf) 1996, Open Exhbn (Whitechapel Art Gallery) 1996; *Style—* Gerard Williams, Esq; ✉ 175 Swaton Road, London E3 4EP (☎ and fax 0171 515 2739, mobile 0937 530533)

WILLIAMS, Prof Sir Glanmor; kt (1995), CBE (1981); s of Daniel Williams (d 1957), of Dowlais, Glamorganshire, and Ceinwen, *née* Evans (d 1970); *b* 5 May 1920; *Educ* Cyfarthfa Sch Merthyr Tydfil, Univ Coll of Wales Aberystwyth (BA, MA, DLitt); *m* 6 April 1946, (Margaret) Fay, da of late William Harold Davies, of Cardiff; 1 s (Huw b 1 Dec 1953), 1 da (Margaret b 31 March 1952); *Career* Univ Coll of Swansea: asst lectr 1945, sr lectr 1952–57, prof of history 1957–82, vice princ 1975–78; vice pres Univ Coll of Wales 1986–; chm Royal Cmmn on Ancient Monuments (Wales) 1986–90 (memb 1962–); memb: Historic Bldg Cncl (Wales) 1962–89, Bd of Celtic Studies Univ of Wales 1969–90, Ancient Monuments Bd (Wales) 1983–95, Ctee Welsh Nat Folk Museum 1986–90; chm: Nat Broadcasting Cncl of Wales 1965–71, Br Library Bd 1973–80, Br Library Advsy Cncl 1980–85; govr BBC 1965–71, pres Assoc of Teachers of History of Wales 1983–94; Cymmrodorion medal 1991; FRHistS 1954, FSA 1979, FBA 1986; *Books* The Welsh Church From Conquest to Reformation (1962), Welsh Reformation Essays (1967), Religion Language and Literature in Wales (1979), Wales 1415–1642 (1987), Glamorgan County History Vols I-VI (ed 1971–88), Swansea: an Illustrated History (1990), The Welsh and their Religion (1991); *Recreations* music, walking; *Style—* Prof Sir Glanmor Williams, CBE, FBA, FSA; ✉ 11 Grosvenor Rd, Sketty, Swansea SA2 0SP (☎ 01792 204113)

WILLIAMS, Prof Glanville Llewelyn; QC (1968); s of Benjamin Elwey Williams (d 1971), of Bridgend, Glamorgan, and Gwladys Llewelyn (d 1959); *b* 15 Feb 1911; *Educ* Cowbridge GS, UCW Aberyswyth, St John's Coll Cambridge (MA, PhD, LLD); *m* 19 Oct 1939, Lorna Margaret, da of Francis Wilfrid Lawfield (d 1950); 1 s (Rendel b 1941); *Career* called to the Bar Middle Temple 1935; fell St John's Coll Cambridge 1936–42; Univ of London 1945–55: reader in English law, prof of public law, Quain prof of jurisprudence; fell Jesus Coll Cambridge 1955 (hon fell 1978); Univ of Cambridge: reader in English law 1957–66, prof 1966, Rouse Ball prof of English law 1968–78; Carpentier lectr Columbia Univ 1956, Cohen lectr Univ of Jerusalem 1957, first Walter E Meyer visiting res prof NY Univ 1959–60, Charles Inglis Thompson guest prof Univ of Colorado 1965; special conslt for American Law Inst Model Penal Code 1956–58; memb: Standing Ctee on Criminal Law Revision (Home Office) 1959–80, Law Cmmn working party on codification of criminal law 1967, Ctee on Mentally Abnormal Offenders (Home Office and DHSS) 1972; pres Abortion Law Reform Assoc 1962–; Hon LLD: Nottingham 1963, Wales 1974, Glasgow 1980, Sussex 1987; Hon DCL Durham 1984, Hon LittD Cambridge 1995; Hon Bencher Middle Temple 1966, FBA 1957, fell Galton Inst, foreign hon memb American Acad of Arts and Scis 1985; *Books* Liability for Animals (1939), Chapters in McElroy's Impossibility of Performance (1941), The Law Reform (Frustrated Contracts) Act (1944), Learning The Law (1 edn 1945, 11 edn 1982), Crown Proceedings (1948), Joint Obligations (1949), Joint Torts and Contributory Negligence (1950), Speedhand Shorthand (1952, 8 edn 1980), Criminal Law: The General Part (1955, 2 edn 1964), The Proof of Guilt (1955, 3 edn 1963), The Sanctity of Life and the Criminal Law (US edn 1956, UK edn 1958), The Mental Element in Crime (1965), Foundations of the Law of Tort (with B A Hepple, 1976, 2 edn 1984), Textbook of Criminal Law (1978, 2 edn 1983); *Style—* Prof Glanville Williams, QC; ✉ Merrion Gate, Gazeley Lane, Cambridge CB2 2HB (☎ 01223 841175)

WILLIAMS, Prof Glynn Anthony; s of Idris Merrion Williams, of Bayston Hill, nr Shrewsbury, and Muriel Elizabeth, *née* Purslow (d 1953); *b* 30 March 1939; *Educ* Wolverhampton GS, Wolverhampton Coll of Art (NDD); *m* 6 July 1963, Heather, da of Cyril Woodhall (d 1952); 2 da (Victoria b 2 Jan 1964, Sophie b 7 Aug 1967); *Career* regular exhibitor of sculpture 1967– (represented by Bernard Jacobson Gallery London), currently prof of sculpture and head Sch of Fine Art Royal Coll of Art; has exhibited internationally, represented GB in the third Kotara Takamura Exhibition in Japan; work in nat and int public collections incl Tate Gallery, Nat Portrait Gallery and V&A; cmmns incl: Henry Purcell Meml for City of Westminster, Gateway of Hands sited by P & O at Chelsea Harbour; author of articles on sculpture published in various art magazines and reviewer for the Times Literary Supplement; subject panel memb CNAA; Prix de Rome 1961, hon fell Wolverhampton Poly 1989; FRCA, FRBS 1992, FRSA 1996; *Recreations* music, walking, crossword puzzles, cooking; *Clubs* Chelsea Arts; *Style—* Prof Glynn Williams; ✉ Royal College of Art, Kensington Gore, London SW7 2EU (☎ 0171 584 5020)

WILLIAMS, Prof (James) Gordon; *b* 13 June 1938; *Educ* Toxteth Tech Inst, Farnborough Tech Coll, Imperial Coll London (BSc, PhD, DSc); *Career* Imperial Coll London: res student 1961–62, asst lectr 1962–64, lectr 1964–70, reader 1970–75, prof of polymer engrg 1975–91, head Mechanical Engrg Dept 1990–, prof of mech engrg 1991–; consultancies: BP Chemicals UK 1967–, Quantum Chemicals USA 1977–, Du Pont USA 1982–, ICI; memb Editorial Advsy Bd Polymer, hon ed Plastics and Rubber - Processing and Applications, regnl ed International Journal of Fracture 1983–; FPRI 1979, FIMechE 1979, FEng 1982, FCGI 1986, FRS 1994 *Awards* Unwin scholarship 1961, Swinburne Medal Plastics & Rubber Inst 1986; *Books* Stress Analysis of Polymers (2 edn, 1980), Fracture Mechanics of Polymers (1985); *Style—* Prof J G Williams, FRS, FEng; ✉ Breda, 16 Bois Lane, Chesham Bois, Amersham, Buckinghamshire HP6 6BP (☎ 01494 726248); Mechanical Engineering Department, Imperial College, Exhibition Road, South Kensington, London SW7 2BX

WILLIAMS, Gordon; s of Charles Williams, of Anfield, Liverpool, and Marjorie Gerard, *née* Bradborn (d 1984); *b* 27 June 1945; *Educ* Bishop Vesey's GS Sutton Coldfield, UCH Med Sch (MB BS); *m* 1 (m dis 1989), Susan Mary Gubbins; 2 da (Katherine Louise b 1970, Victoria Mary b 1972); m 2, 20 Sept 1989, Clare, da of (Montgomery) Derek Sanderson (d 1976); *Career* conslt urologist and transplant surgn Hammersmith Hosp and hon sr lectr RPMS 1978–, external examiner Univ of Addis Ababa; visiting surgn: Syria, Burma, Poland; numerous pubns on urology, urological cancer, impotence and diseases of the prostate; chm NW Thames Urologists; memb Cncl: Br Assoc of Urological Surgns, Int Soc of Urology, Euro Soc of Urology, Euro Transplant Soc; memb Worshipful Soc of Apothecaries 1984, Freeman City of London 1985; MS Univ of London 1988, FRCS; *Recreations* travel, Indian food; *Style—* Gordon Williams, Esq; ✉ Department of Surgery, Hammersmith Hospital and Royal Post Graduate Medical School, Ducane Road, London W12 0HS (☎ 0181 740 3218, fax 0181 740 3443)

WILLIAMS, Air Vice-Marshal Graham Charles; AFC (1971, and bar 1975); s of Charles Francis Williams (d 1968), and Molly, *née* Chapman (d 1988); *b* 4 June 1937; *Educ* Marlborough, RAF Coll Cranwell; *m* 3 March 1962, Judy Teresa Ann, da of Reginald Walker (d 1972); 1 s (Mark b 1963), 1 da (Kim b 1966); *Career* Pilot 54 Sqdn Odiham 1958–60, instr 229 OCU Chivenor 1961–63, Flt-Cdr 8 Sqdn Khormaksar 1964–65, Empire Test Pilots' Sch 1966, 'A' Sqdn (fighter test) A and AEE Boscombe Down 1967–70, RAF Staff Coll Bracknell 1971, OC 3 (F) Sqdn Wildenrath 1972–74, jr directing staff RCDS 1975–77, Stn Cdr RAF Bruggen 1978–79, Gp Capt Ops HQ RAF Germany 1980–82, CO Experimental Flying RAE Farnborough 1983, Cmdt A and AEE Boscombe Down 1984–85, DOR (Air) MOD 1986, Asst Chief of Def Staff Operational Requirements (Air) 1987–90, Cmdt Gen RAF Regt and Dir Gen Security (RAF) 1990–91; aerospace/defence conslt GW Associates 1991–93, mil mktg advsr Loral International Inc 1993–96, dir UK Lockhead Martin Int SA 1996–; FRAeS 1984, FInstMgt 1992; Harmon Trophy USA 1970; *Recreations* squash, golf; *Clubs* RAF; *Style—* Air Vice-Marshal Graham Williams, AFC; ✉ Gate Cottage, Horsenden, Princess Risborough, Bucks HP27 9NF

WILLIAMS, Graham John; s of Hubert John Williams (d 1976), and Marguerite Madeleine Williams; *b* 24 April 1943; *Educ* Cranleigh, Univ of Edinburgh, INSEAD Fontainebleau (MBA); *m* Valerie Jane, *née* Dobson; 2 s (Alex b 18 Sept 1973, Nicholas b 21 March 1989), 1 da (Sara b 13 April 1992); *Career* articled clerk C F Middleton & Co CAs 1962–67, CA Coopers & Lybrand 1967–68, INSEAD 1968–69; Charterhouse Group: product mangr 1969, exec UK Venture Capital 1970–74, dir Charterhouse SA Paris 1975–79; dep md (and jt fndr) Barclays Development Capital Ltd 1979–84; Hays plc: fin dir 1984–, involved in MBO 1987 and subsequent listing 1989, gp corporate devpt dir 1992–; MICAS 1967; *Recreations* golf, tennis, sailing, skiing, swimming, squash; *Clubs* Old Cranleighans, Walton Heath Golf, RAC; *Style—* Graham Williams, Esq; ✉ Hays plc, Hays House, Millmead, Guildford, Surrey GU2 5HJ (☎ 01483 302203, fax 01483 300388)

WILLIAMS, Prof (Daniel) Gwyn; s of Rev Daniel James Williams (d 1967), of Cardiff, and Elizabeth Beatrice Mary Walters (d 1974); *b* 7 March 1940; *Educ* Cardiff HS, Univ Coll Cardiff (MB BCh), Welsh Nat Sch of Med (MD); *m* 21 Jan 1967, Angela Mary, da of John Edwin Davies (d 1974), of Petts Wood, Kent; 4 da (Rachel b 1968, Sian b 1970, Hannah b 1972, Leah b 1976); *Career* jr hosp appts at Cardiff Royal Infirmary and The Radcliffe Infirmary Oxford, sr registrar in med Radcliffe Infirmary, res fell and asst lectr Royal Postgrad Medical Sch London, consIt physician and prof of med United Medical and Dental Schs of Guy's and St Thomas's Hosp Univ of London; MRS, The Renal Assoc; FRCP 1978; *Books* The Oxford Textbook of Medicine (contrib, 1987), The Oxford Textbook of Clinical Nephrology (contrib, 1990); *Style—* Prof Gwyn Williams; ✉ The Renal Unit, Guy's Hospital, St Thomas's St, London SE1 9RT (☎ 0171 955 4481)

WILLIAMS, Prof (John) Gwynn; CBE (1997); s of Rev John Ellis Williams (d 1969), of Rhyl, Clwyd, and Annie Maude, *née* Rowlands; *b* 19 June 1924; *Educ* Holywell GS Clwyd, Univ Coll of N Wales Bangor (BA, DipEd, MA); *m* 24 July 1954, Beryl, da of Rev Stafford Henry Morgan Thomas (d 1968); 3 s (William Gwynn b 1965, Gruffudd Rowland b 1969, Thomas Ellis b 1972); *Career* RN 1943–46; staff tutor Dept of Extra Mural Studies Univ of Liverpool 1951–54; Univ of N Wales: asst lectr 1955, prof of Welsh history 1963–83, dean Faculty of Arts 1972–74, vice princ 1974–79, vice pres 1993–; chm Press Bd Univ of Wales 1979–91 (memb Cncl 1973–85), dir Gregynog Press 1979–; pres: Nat Library of Wales 1986– (vice pres 1984–86), Cambrian Archaeological Assoc 1987–88; vice pres Hon Soc of Cymmrodorion 1988–, hon memb Gorsedd of Bards (White Robe); memb Royal Cmmn on Ancient and Historical Monuments in Wales 1967–91; *Publications* The Founding of the University College of North Wales, Bangor (1985), The University College of North Wales: Foundations (1985), University and Nation: 1893–1939, The Thomas Jones Pierce Memorial Lecture (1992), The Report on the Proposed University of Wales (ed, 1993), The University Movement in Wales (1993); contrib works on seventeenth century Wales to learned jls; *Recreations* travelling, walking; *Style—* Prof J Gwynn Williams, CBE; ✉ Llywenan, Siliwen, Bangor, Gwynedd LL57 2BS (☎ 01248 353065)

WILLIAMS, (Richard) Hall; s of late Edward Hall Williams, and late Kitty Williams; *b* 21 Oct 1926; *Educ* Barry Sch S Glamorgan, UC of Wales Aberystwyth (BSc); *m* 1949, Nia Wynn, *née* Jones; 2 da (Beti Wyn, Carys), 2 s (Huw, Gareth); *Career* various appts in local govt, indust and mgmnt educn until 1967; Welsh Office: entered 1967, subsequent appts in Health and Economic Planning and Agriculture Gps, under sec Agricultural Dept 1981–86; treas Ministerial Bd Presbyterian Church in Wales 1986–95, dep chm Local Govt Boundary Cmmn for Wales 1989–96, vice chm Age Concern Wales 1990–93; *Recreations* enjoying all things Welsh; *Style—* Hall Williams, Esq; ✉ Argoed, 17 West Orchard Crescent, Llandaff, Cardiff CF5 1AR (☎ 01222 562472)

WILLIAMS, Helen Elizabeth Webber; da of Maj Alwyn Thomas, JP, of Llwydcoed, Glamorgan, and Eleanor, *née* Evans; *b* 28 April 1938; *Educ* Redland HS Bristol, Girton Coll Cambridge (scholar, MA, DipEd); *m* 1963 (m dis 1974), Prof Peter Williams; 1 s (Daniel b 1969), 1 da (Lucy b 1968); *Career* asst English mistress: St Paul's Girls' Sch 1962–63, St George's Sch Edinburgh 1963–64; lectr in English and dir of studies Faculty of Arts Univ of Edinburgh 1967–78 (asst lectr Dept of English 1964–67), headmistress Blackheath HS 1978–89, high mistress St Paul's Girls' Sch 1989–92 (resigned), English teacher The Brearley Sch New York 1993–94, princ RNIB New College Worcester 1995–; govr: SOAS, Stowe Sch; *Books* T S Eliot: The Wasteland (1968); *Recreations* music, drama, cookery, gardening; *Style—* Mrs Helen Williams; ✉ The Principal's House, RNIB New College, Whittington Road, Worcester

WILLIAMS, Helen Mary; da of Percy Graham Myatt, of Leeds, and Mary Dodgson, *née* Harrison; *b* 30 June 1950; *Educ* Allerton HS Leeds, St Hilda's Coll Oxford (BA); *m* 1, 1975 (m dis 1982), Ian Vaughan Williams; m 2, 1993, David Michael Forrester, s of Reginald Forrester; 1 s (James b 31 March 1983), 1 da (Natasha b 9 Jan 1986); *Career* civil servant; DES 1972–93: joined as admin trainee 1972, private sec to Joan Lestor then Margaret Jackson (both Parly Secs DES) 1975–76, princ 1976–84, asst sec DES 1984–93; under sec Office of Science and Technology (OST), Office of Public Serv and Science and Cabinet Office 1993– (OST transferred to DTI 1995); *Recreations* family life, walking, bellringing; *Style—* Mrs Helen Williams; ✉ Office of Science and Technology, Albany House, 94–98 Petty France, London SW1H 9ST (☎ 0171 271 2020, fax 0171 271 2018)

WILLIAMS, Dr Helen Mary Sefton (Mrs Maynard); *b* 17 Nov 1955; *Educ* Sleaford HS for Girls, Stamford HS for Girls, Univ of Wales (MB BCh, MRCPath); *Career* house offr in gen med Singleton Hosp Swansea 1979–80; Univ Hosp of Wales Cardiff: house offr in surgery 1980, SHO in clinical haematology 1980–81, SHO in clinical pathology (rotation) 1981–82, registrar in med microbiology 1982–84; sr registrar in med microbiology Mayday Hosp Croydon 1984–86, lectr/hon sr registrar in med microbiology St Thomas' Hosp London 1986–88, locum consIt med microbiologist Mayday Hosp Croydon 1988–89, consIt med microbiologist Norwich Public Health Lab 1989–; hon consIt microbiologist: Norfolk and Norwich Health Care Tst, Mental Health Care Tst, Community Servs Tst; hon lectr UEA; Royal Coll of Pathologists: memb Cncl 1993–96, memb Specialty Advsy Ctee on Med Microbiology 1993–96, memb Academic Activities Ctee 1994–, chm Clinical Audit Ctee and dir of Clinical Audit 1995–, memb Pubns Ctee 1995–; memb PHLS Audit Ctee 1994–, chm Anglia Med Microbiology Devpt Gp 1996–; hon sec Norwich Med Chirurgical Soc 1993–95; memb: Assoc of Clinical Pathologists, Assoc of Med Microbiologists, Med Women's Fedn, BMA; *Style—* Dr Helen M S Williams; ✉ Public Health Laboratory, Bowthorpe Road, Norwich NR2 3TX (☎ 01603 611816, fax 01603 620190)

WILLIAMS, Hilary Elizabeth Rita; da of Stanley John Williams (d 1991), of Bath, and Kathleen Doris, *née* Orchard; *b* 21 Feb 1944; *Educ* Bath HS GDPST, St Mary's Coll Univ of Durham (BA), Cranfield Sch of Mgmnt (MBA); *Career* trainee mangr and co dir Geo V Williams & Sons Ltd 1967–68, asst govr various estabs HM Prison Serv 1968–72, sr devpt offr Social Servs Dept Wilts CC 1972–77, career devpt advsr Mobil Oil Co Ltd 1978–81, mgmnt conslt Hay Management Consultants Ltd 1981–83, South Western Region British Gas plc 1983–92 (consecutively business studies mangr, customer serv mktg mangr, dist serv mangr (Torquay), regnl mktg servs mangr), chief exec The Guide Association (formerly The Girl Guides' Assoc) 1992–; non-exec dir Royal Utd Hosp Bath NHS Tst 1991–96; external examiner postgrad DMS courses Middx Univ Business Sch 1993–96; memb Fundraising Ctee Minerva Fund (GPDST); memb ACENVO; MIMgt 1982; *Recreations* theatre and classical music, networking, hot air ballooning, gentle horse riding, sedate skiing, having a go at virtually anything new and personally challenging - especially if out of the ordinary; *Clubs* Royal Over-Seas League; *Style*— Ms Hilary Williams; ✉ Chief Executive, The Guide Association, 17–19 Buckingham Palace Road, London SW1W 0PT (☎ 0171 834 6242, fax 0171 828 8317, mobile 0585 330716)

WILLIAMS, Prof (Morgan) Howard; s of Morgan Williams, of Port Elizabeth, and Ellen Frances, *née* Reid; *b* 15 Dec 1944; *Educ* Grey HS, Rhodes Univ (BSc, BSc (Hons), PhD, DSc); *m* 13 Dec 1969 (sep), Jean, da of Rev Reginald Charles Doe; 2 s (Christopher b 6 May 1975, Michael 5 May 1977); *Career* physicist in Antarctic expedition 1967–69, Rhodes Univ 1970–80 (lectr, sr lectr, prof of computer sci), prof of computer sci Heriot-Watt Univ 1980–; FBCS, FRSA, CEng; *Books* Proceedings of BNCOD 7 (1989), Proceedings of RIDS (1993), Database Programming Languages (1995); various contribs to other publications; *Recreations* swimming, rambling, gardening; *Style*— Prof Howard Williams; ✉ 3 House O'Hill Brae, Edinburgh EH4 5DQ (☎ 0131 336 1215); Department of Computing and Electrical Engineering, Heriot-Watt University, Riccarton, Edinburgh EH14 4AS (☎ 0131 451 3430, fax 0131 451 3431)

WILLIAMS, Howard Glyn; *b* 3 Sept 1941; *Educ* King's Coll Sch Wimbledon; *m* 1970, Angela Margaret, *née* Fitzgerald; 1 s, 1 da; *Career* ptnr i/c Investgations Gp dealing with mergers and acquisitions, flotations, fundraising and financial investigations Clark Whitehill CAs (chm of ptnrship 1990–94); *Recreations* family, theatre, tennis, skiing; *Style*— Howard Williams, Esq; ✉ Clark Whitehill, 25 New Street Square, London EC4A 3LN (☎ 0171 353 1577, fax 0171 583 1720, telex 887422)

WILLIAMS, Hugh; *see:* Bonneville, Hugh Richard

WILLIAMS, Huw Rhys Charles; s of David Charles Williams (d 1984), of Llanelli, Carmarthenshire, and Glenys Margaret, *née* Williams; *b* 4 Jan 1954; *Educ* Llanelli GS, Jesus Coll Oxford (MA); *m* 22 Jan 1994, Kathleen Mary, da of Capt Melville Desmond John Hooper (d 1990), of Penarth, Vale of Glamorgan; *Career* admitted slr 1978; princ asst slr Mid Glamorgan CC 1984, ptnr i/c public, planning and environmental law Edwards Geldard (Cardiff, Deeside, Derby and Nottingham) 1988– (joined 1987); chm Cardiff and SE Wales branch The Oxford Soc; memb Law Soc 1978; *Recreations* skiing, swimming, architecture and art history; *Clubs* United Oxford and Cambridge Univ, Cardiff and County; *Style*— Huw Williams, Esq; ✉ Edwards Geldard, Dumfries House, Dumfries Place, Cardiff CF1 4YF (☎ 01222 238239, fax 01222 237268)

WILLIAMS, Huw Tregelles; *b* 13 March 1949; *Educ* Llanelli Boys' GS, Univ Coll of Wales Cardiff (BMus, MA); *Career* BBC Wales: music prodr 1973–78, sr prodr 1978–86, head of music 1986–92, currently dir BBC Nat Orch of Wales; organ performer on Radio 3 and TV, prodr of several major series for BBC TV, recitalist at inaugural recital St David's Hall Organ Cardiff; hon fell Welsh Coll of Music and Drama 1995; memb: Welsh Arts Cncl, Music Panel Llangollen Int Music Festival; FRCO (Turpin prize 1971); *Clubs* Cardiff and County; *Style*— Huw Tregelles Williams, Esq; ✉ BBC National Orchestra of Wales, BBC Broadcasting House, Llandaff, Cardiff CF5 2YQ (☎ 01222 572888, fax 012227 572575)

WILLIAMS, Prof (Edward) Idris; OBE (1995); *b* 14 Aug 1930; *Educ* Univ of Manchester (MB ChB, MD); *m* Kathleen; 3 da (Mary (Mrs Campbell), Diana (Mrs Tivey), Sarah (Mrs Hossak)); *Career* Capt RAMC 1955–58; principal GP Bolton 1960–79, sr lectr GP Univ of Manchester 1979–85, prof GP Univ of Nottingham 1985–95, emeritus prof Univ of Nottingham 1995–; advsr in primary health care NHS Exec 1994–96; FRCGP, memb BMA; *Books* Caring for Older People in the Community (3 edn, 1995); *Recreations* gardening, fell walking, music; *Style*— Prof Idris Williams, OBE; ✉ Barn Howe, Lyth, nr Kendal, Cumbria LA8 8DF (☎ 01539 568666)

WILLIAMS, James Gareth Branston; s of Dr Ronald Branston Williams, of Glos, and Dorothy Elizabeth, *née* Lindop (d 1971); *b* 13 April 1946; *Educ* Kingswood Sch Bath, CCC Oxford (scholar, MA); *m* 1980, Julia May, da of Sidney Thomas White (d 1982); 1 da (Charlotte Louise Dorothy b 25 March 1983), 1 s (Oliver Thomas Branston b 17 May 1988); *Career* advtg exec; account planner Boase Massimi Pollitt 1972–75 (trainee account planner 1971–72), planning dir/ptnr SJIP 1975–80, account dir/planner SJIP/BBDO 1980–82; Young & Rubicam: dep planning dir 1982, planning dir 1983–84, sr vice pres/dir of strategy and research Europe 1984–94, exec vice pres/dir of strategy and research Europe 1994–; memb: Market Research Soc 1973 (full memb 1990), Mktg Soc 1980, ESOMAR 1984; *Recreations* jigsaws, computing, food and wine; *Clubs* RAC, Hurlingham; *Style*— James Williams, Esq; ✉ Young & Rubicam Europe, Greater London House, Hampstead Road, London NW1 7QP (☎ 0171 611 6461, fax 0171 611 6942, mobile 0468 464347)

WILLIAMS, Jennifer Mary (Jenny); da of The Rt Hon the Lord Donaldson of Lymington, PC, *qv*, and Dame (Dorothy) Mary Donaldson, GBE, *qv*; sis of Hon Michael Donaldson, *qv*; *b* 26 Sept 1948; *m* 1970, Mike Williams, *qv*; 3 s; *Career* currently head of Railways Privatisation & Regulation Directorate Dept of Tport; non-exec dir Morley Coll 1993–; *Style*— Mrs Jenny Williams; ✉ Zone 3/29, Great Minster House, 76 Marsham Street, London SW1P 4DR (☎ 0171 271 5239, fax 0171 271 5249)

WILLIAMS, John; AO (1987), OBE (1980); *b* 24 April 1941, Australia; *Educ* Accademia Musicale di Siena Italy (scholarship), Royal Coll of Music; *Career* guitarist; taught by father from age 4, later studied with Andrés Segovia, USA and Japan debuts 1963; appeared with many Br orchs and at many Br festivals, toured extensively in Europe, N and S America, Soviet Union, Far E and Australia; one of the first classical musicians to appear at Ronnie Scott's jazz club, fndr memb of popular music gps SKY 1979–84 and John Williams and Friends 1983–, formed contemporary music ensemble ATTACCA 1991 (with whom toured UK and Australia 1992); artistic dir and music advsr South Bank Summer Music Festival 1984–85, artistic dir Melbourne Arts Festival Australia 1987; work written for him by composers incl: Leo Brouwer, Peter Sculthorpe, Stephen Dodgson, André Previn; performed with orchs incl: Royal Philharmonic, LSO, City of Birmingham Symphony, English Chamber, Australian Chamber, Bournemouth Sinfonietta, Acad of St Martin-in-the-Fields, all other major Br orchs; appeared at venues incl: Queen Elizabeth Hall, Royal Festival Hall, Barbican Hall, Symphony Hall Birmingham, Fairfield Hall, Salle Pleyel Paris, Hong Kong Cultural Centre (inaugural concerts 1989), NEC Birmingham (10th Anniversary concert, with CBSO); appeared at festivals incl: BBC Proms, Cheltenham, Chichester, Exeter, Cardiff, Perth and Adelaide Festivals Aust, Toronto Int Guitar Festival, South Bank Latin American Festival, Lichfield, St Albans, Melbourne Arts Festival; performed European première of Nigel Westlake's Antarctica (for guitar and orch) with LSO under Kent Nagano Barbican Hall 1992; numerous TV appearances incl LWT South Bank Show documentary on life and work, regularly performs with Julian Bream, Paco Pena, Itzhak Perlman, André Previn; *Recordings* major guitar works, numerous concertos, most recently Iberia, The Seville Concert and The Great Paraguayan; six albums with Sky, The Guitar is the Song (with John Williams and Friends) 1983; *Style*— John Williams, Esq, AO, OBE; ✉ c/o Harold Holt Ltd, 31 Sinclair Road, London W14 0NS (☎ 0171 603 4600, fax 0171 603 0019)

WILLIAMS, Prof (Lawrence) John; s of Arthur John Williams, of Cardiff, and Elizabeth Jeanetta, *née* Charlton; *b* 12 June 1927; *Educ* Univ of Wales (BA, MA); *m* 18 Aug 1951, Mair Eluned; 2 s (Stephen Richard b 1955, Roger b 1959), 1 da (Katherine b 1958); *Career* Nat Serv RAF 1948–51; res offr Cabinet Office 1951–52; UCW (now Univ of Wales Aberystwyth): lectr then sr lectr until 1987, prof of economics 1987–94, prof emeritus 1994–; *Books* incl: The South Wales Coal Industry, 1841–75 (with J H Morris, 1958), Britain and the World Economy (1971), Why Are the British Bad at Manufacturing? (with K Williams and D Thomas, 1983), Welsh Historical Statistics (2 Vols, 1985), The Aberystwyth Report on Coal (with K Williams and A Cutler, 1985), Modern South Wales: essays in economic history (ed with C Baber, 1986), 1992: The Struggle for Europe (1989), Cars: Analysis and History, Cases (1994), Was Wales Industrialised and other essays (1995); *Recreations* hill-walking; *Style*— Prof John Williams; ✉ 22 Danycoed, Aberystwyth, Dyfed; Department of Economics, University of Wales, Aberystwyth (☎ 01970 622502)

WILLIAMS, John; s of Roy Albert John Williams, of Ramsgate, Kent, and Barbara, *née* Love; *b* 20 Feb 1954; *Educ* Sir Roger Manwood's GS Sandwich Kent, Highbury Tech Coll Portsmouth (James Arlott Meml prize); *m* Pamela Blackburn; 2 s (Tom b 16 Jan 1980, Jack b 12 August 1984), 1 da (Rosie b 10 May 1982); *Career* Chatham News and Standard 1974–77, industl corr Birmingham Evening Mail 1978–80 (district reporter 1977–78); London Evening Standard: industl corr 1980–85, political corr 1985–93; political ed The Mirror 1993–; *Recreations* family; *Style*— John Williams, Esq; ✉ Mirror Group Newspapers, 1 Canada Square, Canary Wharf, London E14 5AP (☎ 0171 219 4377, fax 0171 293 3975)

WILLIAMS, John Albert Norman; s of Albert George Williams, of Harbour View, Ilston Way, Mumbles, Swansea, and Norma May Williams; *b* 14 Jan 1948; *Educ* Oystermouth Secdy Sch Swansea; *m* 14 June 1971, Susan Mary, da of Ronald Francis Davies; 3 da (Emma Jayne b 23 June 1972, Claire Louise b 10 April 1974, Katie Victoria b 23 July 1975); *Career* racehorse jockey; apprentice to Fulke Walwyn 1963–65 then Dr A Jones, first ride Worcester 1965, first winner on flat Kempton 1967, first winner nat hunt Newton Abbott 1969, flat racing only 1984– (mainly nat hunt 1965–84); nat hunt achievements: twice winner Norwegian Grand Nat, winner Grosser Preis der Speilbank Germany 1982, ridden in Grand Nat 4 times, ridden in numerous int races Europe and USA, leading jockey West Country courses; flat racing achievements: winner Stewards Cup Goodwood, winner Ayr Gold Cup, Leslie & Godwin Spitfire Stakes Goodwood 1992, Gammage Stakes 1993, John O Gaunt, Cezarawitch 1993, ridden various maj races Scandinavia, rode five winners in a day 1990, best season 64 winners 1990 and 1993, winner Prix Gladiator Longchamp 1993, Flying Childers Doncaster 1993; *Recreations* golf; *Style*— John Williams, Esq; ✉ Paddock View, Tolldown Way, Burton, nr Chippenham, Wilts SN14 7PD (☎ 01454 218622)

WILLIAMS, John Arthur; s of Arthur Williams (d 1984), and May Lilian, *née* Read (d 1991); *b* 2 June 1933; *Educ* Guildford GS, Perth W Australia, Charterhouse, Jesus Coll Cambridge; *Career* HM Overseas Civil Serv Kenya 1957–62, asst sec rising to under sec responsible for pubns, dist socs, PR, HQ rebuilding ICAEW 1962–71, Australian Def Dept Canberra 1971–72, under sec responsible for gen policy and fin, EC and int ICAEW 1972–95, dir int affairs ICAEW 1990–95; int consit to accounting profession 1995–; *Recreations* sailing, skiing, tennis, walking, music, stamp collecting; *Clubs* Hurlingham, Royal Philatelic Soc; *Style*— John Williams, Esq; ✉ 71 Winchendon Rd, London SW6 5DH (☎ 0171 736 3545); c/o The Institute of Chartered Accountants in England & Wales (ICAEW), Moorgate Place, London EC2P 2BJ (☎ 0171 920 8457, fax 0171 374 2060)

WILLIAMS, Dr John Charles; OBE (1997); s of Frank Williams (d 1968), of Princes Risboro, Bucks, and Miriam, *née* Keene (d 1988); *b* 17 July 1938; *Educ* High Wycombe Royal GS, Queen Mary Coll London (BSc, PhD, Univ Year prize); *m* 1968, Susan Winifred, *née* Ellis; 1 s (Matthew Richard b 1976), 1 da (Rachel Joanna b 1972); *Career* engr; researcher, conslt and project leader Philips Res Laboratories 1964–77, mangr MSDS Res Laboratory Marconi Space & Defence Systems Ltd 1980–82 (mangr Advanced Shipborne Terminals 1978–80), dir GEC Marconi Res Centre 1987–88 (dir Marconi Res Centre Gt Baddow 1982–85, md GEC Research Ltd 1985–87), md Cranfield Industrial Development Ltd 1988–89, sec and chief exec Inst of Electrical Engrs 1989–; fell Queen Mary and Westfield Coll 1995; FIEE, SMIEEE (USA), FIE (Aust), FEng 1990, MRI; *Recreations* bridge, jazz; *Style*— Dr John C Williams, OBE, FEng; ✉ Institution of Electrical Engineers, Savoy Place, London WC2R 0BL (☎ 0171 240 1871, fax 0171 497 8863, car 0836 340495)

WILLIAMS, John Charles Wallis; s of Peter Alfred Williams, of Menston, West Yorks, and Mary, *née* Bower (d 1990); *b* 12 Dec 1953; *Educ* St Peter's York, Queen's Coll Oxford (MA); *m* 28 June 1980, Wendy Irene, da of Harold Doe, of Whitton, Middx; 2 da (Sarah b 1984, Clare b 1988); *Career* advertising exec J Walter Thompson Co 1975–86, PR exec Valin Pollen Ltd 1986–90 (head res and planning 1988–90, asst md 1989–90), md Fishburn Hedges 1995– (fndr dir 1991); FRSA; *Recreations* cinema, music, good food and wine; *Style*— John Williams, Esq; ✉ 23 Blenheim Road, London W4 1UB (☎ 0181 995 8747); Fishburn Hedges, 1 Northumberland Ave, Trafalgar Square, London WC2N 5BW (☎ 0171 839 4321, fax 0171 839 2858)

WILLIAMS, Dr John Edmund; s of John Edgar Williams (d 1971), of Penarth, Glamorgan, and Catherine Letitia, *née* Edmunds (d 1958); *b* 27 Aug 1930; *Educ* Penarth GS, Univ Coll Cardiff (BSc), Welsh Nat Sch of Med (MB BCh, DMRD); *m* Gwen Elizabeth, da of Ewart Price (d 1952), of Bethesda, Caenarvonshire; 1 s (Paul Martyn), 2 da (Ann Catherine (Mrs Loeppky), Elizabeth Siân (Mrs West)); *Career* conslt radiologist United Cardiff Hosp 1963–72, asst prof of radiology Univ of Washington Seattle USA 1968–69; St George's Hosp London: dir of radiology and conslt radiologist 1972–95, hon sr lectr, chm of radiology; currently med advsr Nuffield Hosps; warden RCR 1986–90; Hon FFR RCSI 1988, FRCPE, FRCP, FRCR; *Recreations* theatre, music, golf, woodcarving; *Clubs* Wimbledon Park Golf, London Welsh RFC; *Style*— Dr John Williams; ✉ 29 Margin Drive, Wimbledon, London SW19 5HA (☎ 0181 946 6640)

WILLIAMS, John Fagan; s of Frank Thomas Williams, and Margaret, *née* Fagan; *b* 7 Jan 1948; *Educ* Rishworth Sch; *m* 1, Lynne, *née* Boothby; 1 da (Kate); *m* 2, Rita, *née* Rowe; *Career* local, regional and nat newspaper journalist 1967–76; fndr Staniforth Williams PR consultancy 1976–86, fndr jt md Mason Williams PR consultancy 1986– (over 28 awards for business excellence 1988–); memb: Bd PRCA 1994, Arthouse (non-exec), Red Snapper; MIPR 1979, FInstD 1990; *Sporting Achievements* int sports car racing driver (Europe and USA) 1981–90, 8th place World Sports Car Championship 1989; *Recreations* race driving, sailing, music; *Clubs* British Racing Drivers', RAC; *Style*— John Williams, Esq; ✉ Mason Williams Ltd, Tanzaro House, Ardwick Green, Manchester M12 6FZ (☎ 0161 273 5923, fax 0161 273 7127)

WILLIAMS, John Griffith; QC (1985); s of Maj Griffith John Williams, TD, of Hedd-yr-Ynys, Common Lane, Beer, Seaton, Devon, and Alison Rundle, *née* Bennett; *b* 20 Dec 1944; *Educ* Kings Sch Bruton, The Queen's Coll Oxford (BA); *m* 3 April 1971, Mair, o da of Major The Right Hon Sir Tasker Watkins VC, GBE, PC, DL; 2 da (Joanna b 1972, Sarah b 1976); *Career* Lt 4 Bn Royal Welch Fus (TA) Welsh Volunteers (TAVR); barr Grays Inn 1968, bencher 1994, in practice Wales and Chester Circuit (treas 1993–95, leader 1996–), recorder Crown Ct 1984–; asst cmmr Parly Boundary Commission for Wales 1994; memb Bar Cncl 1990–92; fell Woodard Corp (Western Div) 1994–; dep chllr

Diocese of Llandaff 1996; *Recreations* golf; *Clubs* Army and Navy, Cardiff and County, Cardiff, Royal Porthcawl Golf; *Style*— John Griffith Williams, Esq, QC; ✉ 144 Pencisely Rd, Llandaff, Cardiff CF5 1DR (☎ 01222 562981); Goldsmith Building, Temple, London EC4Y 7BL (☎ 0171 353 7881, fax 0171 353 5319)

WILLIAMS, Rev John Herbert; LVO (1989); s of Thomas Williams (d 1932), of Gwent, and Mary Williams, *née* Davies (d 1956); *b* 15 Aug 1919; *Educ* Lewis Sch Pengam, St David's Coll Lampeter (BA), Salisbury Theological Coll; *m* 1948, Joan Elizabeth, da of Archibald Morgan, of Gwent; 1 s (Michael); *Career* clerk in Holy Orders; chaplain (Prison Dept): Manchester 1951, Holloway 1952, Birmingham 1957, Wormwood Scrubs 1964; regional chaplain SE 1971, dep chaplain gen (Home Office) 1974–83, priest-in-ordinary to HM The Queen 1979–83; chaplain of the Queen's Chapel of the Savoy 1983–89, chaplain of the Royal Victorian Order 1983–89; chaplain to HM The Queen 1988–89; *Recreations* music (classical, opera, church), rugby, stamp collecting; *Clubs* City Livery; *Style*— The Rev John Williams, LVO; ✉ 75 Monks Drive, London W3 0ED (☎ 0181 992 5206)

WILLIAMS, J(ohn) Leighton; QC (1986); s of Reginald John Williams, of Skewen, Neath, Glamorgan, and Beatrice Beynon; *b* 15 Aug 1941; *Educ* Neath Boys GS, King's Coll London (LLB), Trinity Hall Cambridge (MA); *m* 9 Oct 1969, Sally Elizabeth, da of Howard Jones Williams, of Abergavenny, Gwent; 2 s (Nicholas b 1970, Thomas b 1972); *Career* called to the Bar Gray's Inn 1964, recorder of the Crown Court 1985–, Queens Cncl 1986, Master of the Bench Gray's Inn 1994; memb Criminal Injuries Compensation Bd 1987–; *Style*— J Leighton Williams, Esq, QC; ✉ Farrar's Building, Temple, London EC4Y 7BD (☎ 0171 583 9241)

WILLIAMS, John Llewellyn; s of David John Williams (d 1948), of Dronfield, nr Sheffield, and Anne Rosamund, *née* White; *b* 24 Jan 1938; *Educ* Christ's Hosp Horsham, Guy's Hosp Dental Sch London (BDS, LDS RCS, Evelyn Sprawson prize), Guy's Hosp Med Sch London (MB BS), FDSRCS; *m* 1960, Gillian Joy, *née* Morgan; 3 da (Amanda Jill (Mrs Henderson) b 1962, Jacqueline Mary (Mrs Lytton) b 1963, Anne-Marie b 1970); *Career* formerly sr registrar Westminster Hosp, Queen Mary's Roehampton and UCH; conslt oral and maxillofacial surgn: St Richard's Hosp Chichester, Southlands and Worthing Hosps, St Luke's Hosp Guildford; hon conslt: Queen Mary's Hosp Roehampton, King Edward VII Hosp Midhurst; formerly hon civilian conslt Cambridge Mil Hosp Aldershot, hon clinical tutor United Med and Dental Schs of Guy's and St Thomas' Hosps; memb: Cncl Royal Coll of Surgns of England 1993– (dean Faculty of Dental Surgery 1995–), GDC 1995–; sec gen Euro Assoc of Cranio-Maxillofacial Surgery (pres-elect); memb: Jt Conslts Ctee 1989–, Clinical Outcomes Gp Dept of Health 1993–, Clinical Standards Advsy Gp 1994–; Downs Surgical Prize (Br Assoc of Oral and Maxillofacial Surgns) 1995; memb: BDA, BMA, Br Assoc of Maxillofacial Surgns, Euro Assoc of Cranio-Maxillofacial Surgery; FRCSEd (by election) 1991; *Books* Maxillofacial Injuries (2 Vols, ed, 2 edn 1995); *Recreations* horticulture (contrib National Gardens Scheme), skiing, sailing (RYA race training instructor), chasing good wine!; *Clubs* Royal Yachting Association, Hayling Island Sailing, Royal Horticultural Society, Oral Surgery Club of GB; *Style*— John Llewellyn Williams, Esq; ✉ Dean, Faculty of Dental Surgery, Royal College of Surgeons of England, Lincoln's Inn Fields, London WC2A 3PN (☎ 0171 405 3474)

WILLIAMS, Hon John Melville; QC (1977); s of Baron Francis-Williams (Life Peer, d 1970); *b* 20 June 1931; *Educ* St Christopher Sch Letchworth, St John's Coll Cambridge (BA); *m* 1955, Jean Margaret, da of Harold Lucas (d 1995); 3 s, 1 da; *Career* called to the Bar Inner Temple 1955, bencher 1985, recorder 1986–94, head of chambers; pres Assoc of Personal Injury Lawyers 1990–94, co-chm Int Section Assoc of Trial Lawyers of America 1991–93; *Style*— The Hon John Melville Williams, QC; ✉ Old Square Chambers, 1 Verulam Buildings, Gray's Inn, London WC1R 5LQ (☎ 0171 831 0801, fax 0171 405 1387, e-mail 100605.1147@compuserve.com); Deers Hill, Abinger Hammer, Dorking, Surrey RH5 6PS

WILLIAMS, Dr John Peter Rhys; MBE (1977); s of Peter Rhys Jervis Williams, of Bridgend, and Margaret, *née* Rhodes; *b* 2 March 1949; *Educ* Bridgend GS, Millfield and St Marys Hosp Med Sch (MB BS, MRCS, LRCP); *m* 10 May 1973, Priscilla, da of Michael Parkin, of Buxton, Derbys; 1 s (Peter b 1987), 3 da (Lauren b 1977, Anneliese b 1979, Francine b 1981); *Career* conslt orthopaedic surgn Princess of Wales Hosp Bridgend 1986–; Br jr tennis champion 1966, 55 Welsh International rugby caps 1969–81, memb Br Lions tour NZ 1971 and South Africa 1974; memb Br Orthopaedic Assoc, FRCSE; *Books* JPR Autobiography (1977); *Recreations* all sports especially squash, tennis, rugby; *Clubs* Wig & Pen, Lord's Taverners; *Style*— Dr John Williams, MBE; ✉ Llansannor Lodge, Llansannor, Cowbridge, South Glamorgan CF7 7RX (☎ 01446 772590); Princess of Wales Hospital, Coity Road, Bridgend, Mid Glamorgan CF31 1RQ (☎ 01656 752752)

WILLIAMS, Sir John Robert; KCMG (1982, CMG 1973); s of Sydney James Williams, of Salisbury; *b* 15 Sept 1922; *Educ* Sheen Co Sch, Fitzwilliam Coll Cambridge; *m* 1958, Helga Elizabeth, da of Frederick Konow Lund, of Bergen; 2 s, 2 da; *Career* CRO New Delhi and N Malaya; high cmmr Suva 1970–74, min Lagos and non-resident ambass Benin 1974–79, asst under-sec FCO 1979, high cmmr Nairobi and perm Br rep UN Environment Programme and HABITAT (UN Centre for Human Settlements) 1979–82, ret; chm: Cwlth Inst London 1984–87, Salisbury & S Wilts Museum 1988–95; hon fell Fitzwilliam Coll Cambridge 1983; *Style*— Sir John Williams, KCMG; ✉ Eton House, Hanging Langford, Salisbury

WILLIAMS, John Robert; s of Edward S Williams (d 1986), of London, and Frances Madge, *née* Porter; *b* 7 April 1931; *Educ* Enfield GS, Queens' Coll Cambridge (MA); *m* 12 Sept 1959, Teresa, da of Joseph Wareing (d 1956), of Preston, Lancs; 3 da (Catherine b 1960, Joanna b 1962, Helen b 1967); *Career* Ogilvy & Mather: res exec, mktg mangr, res dir, account dir, client servs dir, int mgmnt supervisor 1956–68, appointed to Bd 1968, vice chm 1981; chm Wimbledon CC 1974–89, pres The Wimbledon Club (cricket, lawn tennis, hockey clubs, Lakeside squash club) 1995– (chm 1985–90); FIPA 1968; *Recreations* cricket, tennis, squash, theatre; *Clubs* MCC, RAC; *Style*— John Williams, Esq; ✉ 61 Murray Rd, London SW19 4PF (☎ 0181 946 9363)

WILLIAMS, John Thomas; s of John T Williams, of South Shields, and Margaret Williams; *b* 20 Aug 1958; *Educ* Mortimer Road Sch South Shields, S Shields Marine & Tech Coll, Westminster Catering Coll (City and Guilds); *m* 12 Nov 1984, Patricia, da of George Judith; 1 da (Sabrina b 27 Nov 1985), 1 s (Jeremy b 21 Dec 1989); *Career* commis chef Percy Arms Hotel Northumberland 1974–75, chef de cuisine Royal Roof Restaurant The Royal Garden Hotel London 1975–84, pt/t commis chef Ma Cuisine Restaurant March-Sept 1982, chef dir Restaurant le Crocodile London 1984–86, head chef Claridge's 1986–93, maitre chef de cuisine The Berkeley Hotel London 1994–95, maitre chef de cuisines Claridge's 1995–; memb Academie Culinaire de France; *Awards* incl finalist Commis Chef of the Year 1977, various medals Hotelolympia 1977–84, finalist Pierre Tattinger Int Culinary Prize 1987 and 1992, regnl finalist Egon Ronay Br Meat Competition 1990, finalist MOGB '91; *Recreations* golf, cooking; *Style*— John Williams, Esq; ✉ Claridge's Hotel, Brook Street, London W1A 2JQ (☎ 0171 629 8860, fax 0171 499 8011)

WILLIAMS, Juliet Susan Durrant; da of Robert Noel Williams (d 1972), of Gower, W Glamorgan, and Frances Alice, *née* Durrant (d 1995); *Educ* Leeds Girls HS, Cheltenham Ladies' Coll, Bedford Coll London (BSc), Hughes Hall Cambridge (PGCE); *Career* ed Macmillan & Co (publishers) 1966–68, asst ed The Geographical Magazine 1968–73, md Readers Union Gp of Book Clubs 1973–79, chief exec Marshall Cavendish Mail Order 1979–82, md Brann Direct Marketing 1982–88, dir The BIS Gp Ltd 1985–91, chief exec Bd Mktg Communications Div BIS 1988–91, chief exec Strategic Management Resources 1991–; full blue lacrosse Univ of Cambridge; FRGS 1970, MInstM 1975; *Recreations* labrador retrievers, the countryside, motor sport; *Style*— Ms Juliet Williams; ✉ Treeton Cottage, Abbotskerswell, Newton Abbot, Devon TQ12 5PW (☎ 0831 097946); Strategic Management Resources, PO Box 800, Swindon, Wilts SN2 5QF (☎ 01793 410039, fax 01793 410029)

WILLIAMS, Chief Constable Kenneth Robert; QPM (1992); s of Sidney Williams (d 1980), of Urmston, and Margaret Elizabeth, *née* Howell (d 1995); *b* 28 April 1944; *Educ* Wellacre Secdy Modern Sch Flixton, Univ of Manchester (Cert in Police, Penal and Social Studies), Open Univ (BA Social Scis); *m* 27 June 1969, Jean Margaret, da of Jack Reginald Ballantyne; 2 da (Alison Jane b 16 March 1972, Jennifer Anne b 23 Oct 1974); *Career* Gtr Manchester Police: constable Salford City Police 1963 (Salford South Div 1963–68), sergeant North Manchester Div 1968–72, patrol inspr Salford Div 1973–74, inspr then chief inspr HQ 1974–76, sub-divnl cmd Bolton Div 1976–78 (North Manchester Div 1978–79); directing staff Police Staff Coll Bramshill 1979–81; returned to Gtr Manchester Police: sub-divnl cmd Manchester Central Div 1981, sub-divnl cmd Manchester Int Airport 1981–84, departmental cmd Computer Project Branch HQ 1984–85, departmental cmd Ops Support Branch HQ 1985–86, divnl cmd North Manchester 1986–87, Sr Cmd Course Police Staff Coll Bramshill 1987, asst chief constable Gtr Manchester Police 1987–90; dep chief constable Durham Constabulary 1990–93, chief constable Norfolk Constabulary 1993–; memb ACPO 1987; *Recreations* swimming, walking, reading, music; *Style*— Chief Constable Kenneth Williams, QPM; ✉ Norfolk Constabulary HQ, Martineau Lane, Norwich, Norfolk NR1 2DJ (☎ 01603 768769, fax 01603 276161)

WILLIAMS, Kit; *b* 28 April 1946; *Career* artist; began painting in Navy, first exibited at Portal Gallery 1973, exhibitions in Japan, Germany and New York; *Books* Masquerade (1979), The Bee on the Comb (1984), Out of One Eye - The Art of Kit Williams (1986); *Style*— Kit Williams, Esq

WILLIAMS, (John) Kyffin; OBE (1982), DL (Gwynedd 1985); s of Henry Inglis Wynne Williams (d 1942), and Essyllt Mary, *née* Williams (d 1964); *b* 9 May 1918; *Educ* Shrewsbury, Slade Sch of Fine Art UCL; *Career* 1 Lt 6 Bn RWF (TA) 1937, invalided 1941; artist; sr art master Highgate Sch London 1944–73; works in the collections of: Arts Cncl, Nat Museum of Wales, Nat Library of Wales, Walker Art Gallery Liverpool, Nat Portrait Gallery, Contemporary Art Soc, Glyn Vivian Art Gallery Swansea, Chantrey Bequest, Univ of Wales, Imperial Coll London; memb Art Ctee Nat Museum of Wales, pres Royal Cambrian Acad 1992; Winston Churchill fellowship 1968; hon fell: Univ Coll of Swansea 1989, Univ Coll of N Wales Bangor 1991, Univ Coll of Wales Aberystwyth; Hon MA Univ of Wales 1973, Hon DLitt Univ of Wales 1993; medal of the Hon Soc of Cymmrodorion 1991; RA 1974 (ARA 1970); *Books* Across the Straits (autobiography, 1973), A Wider Sky (autobiography, 1991), Portraits (1996), Boyo Ballads (1995), Portraits (1996); *Recreations* countryside sports; *Style*— Kyffin Williams, Esq, OBE, DL, RA; ✉ Pwllfanogl, Llanfairpwllgwyngyll, Gwynedd LL61 6PD (☎ 01248 714693)

WILLIAMS, Sir Lawrence Hugh; 9 Bt (GB 1798), of Bodelwyddan, Flintshire; s of Col Lawrence Williams, OBE, JP, DL (d 1958), by his 2 w and 1 cous once removed, Elinor, da of Sir William Williams, 4 Bt, JP, DL; suc half-bro Sir Francis John Watkin Williams, 8 Bt, QC, JP (d 1995); *b* 25 Aug 1929; *Educ* RNC Dartmouth; *m* 1952, Sara Margaret Helen, 3 da of Prof Sir Harry Platt, 1 Bt, MD, MS, FRCS; 2 da (Emma Louise (Mrs Radcliffe Percy Royds) b 1961, Antonia Margaret b 1963); *Heir* none; *Career* cmmnd RM 1947; served in: Korea 1951, Cyprus 1955, Near East 1956; Capt 1959, ret 1964; Lt Cdr RNXS 1965–87; farmer; chm Parciau Caravans Ltd 1964–, underwriting memb Lloyd's; High Sheriff Anglesey 1970; *Clubs* Army and Navy, RNSA; *Style*— Sir Lawrence Williams, Bt; ✉ Parciau, Marianglas, Anglesey LL73 8PH

WILLIAMS, Sir Leonard; KBE (1981), CB (1975); *b* 19 Sept 1919; *Educ* St Olave's GS, King's Coll London; *m* Anne Taylor Witherley; 3 da; *Career* Inland Revenue 1938, War Serv RA 1940–47, MOD 1948, NATO 1951–54, Miny of Supply (later Aviation) 1954, Miny of Technol (later DTI) 1964, IDC 1966, Dept of Energy 1974–76, DG for Energy Commission of the European Communities 1976–81; *Style*— Sir Leonard Williams, KBE, CB; ✉ Blue Vines, Bramshott Vale, Liphook, Hants GU30 7PZ

WILLIAMS, Leonard Edmund Henry; CBE (1981), DFC (1944); s of William Edmund Williams (d 1965), and Elizabeth, *née* Restall (d 1969); *b* 6 Dec 1919; *Educ* Acton Co Sch; *m* 23 March 1946, Marie Eirina, da of John Harries-Jones (d 1939); 4 s (Graham b 1949, Martin b 1957, Simon b 1961, Andrew b 1965), 1 da (Jennifer b 1947); *Career* served RAF WWII; Acton Borough Cncl 1939–49, Gas Cncl 1949–53; Nationwide Building Society: fin offr 1954–61, dep gen mangr 1961–67, chief exec 1967–81, dir 1975, chm 1982–87; dir: Peachey Property Corporation plc 1982–88, Y J Lovell (Holdings) plc 1982–89; chm Nationwide Anglia Building Society 1987–88 (pres 1989–91), dep chm British United Provident Association Ltd 1988–90 (govr 1982–90); chm: Bldg Socs Assoc 1979–81, Met Assoc of Bldg Socs 1972–73 (pres 1989–92), Third Age Challenge Trust 1993–; Freeman City of London 1974, Liveryman Worshipful Co of Basketmakers 1979 (memb Ct of Assts 1992–); FCA, FCIB, IPFA, CIMgt, FRSA; *Books* Building Society Accounts (1966); *Recreations* golf, reading; *Clubs* RAF, City Livery; *Style*— Leonard Williams Esq, CBE, DFC; ✉ The Romanys, 11 Albury Rd, Burwood Park, Walton-on-Thames, Surrey KT12 5DY (☎ 01932 242758)

WILLIAMS, Lia Jane; da of Bernard Hather Williams (d 1993), and Brenda, *née* Whitehead; *b* 26 Nov 1963; *Educ* Arts Educational Schs Tring Park, The London Studio Centre; *m* 1 s (Joshua James b 9 Sept 1989); *Career* actress; *Theatre* Sybil in Daisy Pulls It Off (West End), Outside Broadcast (Birmingham Rep), When Did You Last See Your...Trousers? (Garrick), Spotted Dick (Watford Palace), She Stoops To Conquer (Leeds Playhouse), Doris and Doreen, Angie in Body Language (both Stephen Joseph theatre Scarborough), Goneril in King Lear (Royal Court), Oleanna (Royal Court and Duke of York's), The Revengers' Comedies (Strand), Skylight (RNT, Wyndhams and Broadway) 1995–96; *Television* BBC: Happy Families, Bread, Casualty, Mr Wroe's Virgins, Paula in Seaforth, Flowers of the Forest (screen 2); other credits incl: Annika (series, Central), Shrinks (Euston Films), Lucy in The Yob (Comic Strip film); *Films* Bella in Dirty Weekend, Firelight, The Fith Province; *Awards* Most Promising Newcomer The Critics' Circle London Drama Awards 1991; Olivier Award nominations incl: Best Comedy Performance (for The Revengers' Comedies) 1992, Best Actress (for Skylight) 1996; *Recreations* gardening, being with Joshua; *Style*— Ms Lia Williams; ✉ c/o Hamilton Asper Management, Ground Floor, 24 Hanway Street, London W1P 9DD (☎ 0171 636 1221, fax 0171 636 1226)

WILLIAMS, HE Martin John; CVO (1983), OBE (1979); s of John Henry Stroud Williams, of Cricklade, Wilts, and Barbara, *née* Benington; *b* 3 Nov 1941; *Educ* Manchester GS, Corpus Christi Coll Oxford (BA); *m* 6 April 1964, Susan, da of Albert Mervyn (Peter) Dent (d 1984); 2 s (Nicholas b 1966, Peter b 1967); *Career* CRO 1963; Dip Serv: joined 1968, Manila 1966–69, Milan 1970–72, Civil Service Coll 1972–73, FCO 1973–77, Tehran 1977–80, Overseas Devpt Admin 1980–82, New Delhi 1982–86, Rome 1986–90, FCO 1990–92, NI Office 1993–95, high cmmr Zimbabwe 1996–; *Style*— HE Mr Martin Williams, CVO, OBE; ✉ c/o Foreign and Commonwealth Office (Harare), King Charles Street, London SW1A 2AH

WILLIAMS, (John) Michael; s of George Keith Williams (d 1980), and Joan Doreen, *née* Selby (d 1969); *b* 15 Oct 1942; *Educ* Cheltenham, Worcester Coll Oxford (MA); *Career*

admitted slr 1967, ptnr Cooper Sons Hartley & Williams; sec Buxton & High Peak Law Soc 1984–, pres E Midlands Assoc of Law Socs 1996–97; conductor Buxton Musical Soc 1968–, organist St John's Buxton 1985–, vice chm Buxton Opera House 1978–, dir Buxton Arts Festival Ltd 1993–, memb Panel of Music Advsrs to North West Arts 1995–; *Recreations* music, cricket; *Style*— Michael Williams, Esq; ✉ 143 Lightwood Rd, Buxton, Derbyshire (☎ 01298 24185); Cooper Sons Hartley & Williams, 25 Market St, Chapel-en-le-Frith, High Peak, Derbyshire SK12 6HP (☎ 01298 812138)

WILLIAMS, Dr Michael; s of late Benjamin Williams, and Ethel Mary, *née* Marshell (d 1954); *b* 24 June 1935; *Educ* Univ Coll Swansea (BA), Univ of Wales (PhD, DLitt), St Catharine's Coll Cambridge (DipEd), Univ of Oxford (MA); *m* 25 June 1955, Eleanore, da of Leopold Lorenz Lerch (d 1940); 2 da (Catherine Dilys b 1962, Tess Jane b 1965); *Career* demonstrator Dept of Geography Swansea Univ Coll 1957–60, lectr rising to reader Univ of Adelaide SA 1960–78, pt/t lectr in planning SA Inst Technol Aust 1963–70; Univ of Oxford: lectr in geography 1978–89, fell Oriel Coll 1978–, lectr in charge St Anne's Coll 1978–, reader in geography 1990–, dir Environmental Change and Mgmnts Environmental Change Unit 1994–, prof in geography 1996–; temp academic appointments: visitor UCL 1973 (visitor and lectr 1966–67); visiting fell: Dept of Geography Univ of Wisconsin-Madison USA 1973–74 (distinguished visitor 1994), Dept of Geography Flinders Univ SA 1984; visiting prof: Ctee on Geographical Studies Univ of Chicago 1989, UCLA 1994; contrib to many academic jls; Inst of Br Geographers: hon ed Transactions of the Institute 1983–88, chm Pubns Ctee 1983–88, memb Special Pubns Ctee 1983–88 (memb Cncl 1983–88); memb: Editorial Advsy Bd RGS 1984–92, Editorial Ctee Progress in Human Geography 1990–, Int Relations Sub Ctee Cncl Br Geography 1990–93; ed Global Environmental Change 1993–96; John Lewis Gold medal RGS (SA) 1979, Hidy medal and award Forest and Conservation History Soc USA 1988 (hon fell 1989), Charles A Weyerhaeuser award 1991; travel and res grants: Australian Res Grant Cmmn, Br Acad, Royal Soc; FBA 1989 (memb Cncl 1993–96, chm Section N until 1996); *Books* The Making of the Australian Landscape (1974, Biennial literary prize Adelaide Festival of Arts, 1976), Australian Space, Australian Time: Geographical Perspectives 1788–1914 (jt ed, 1975), The Americans and their Forests: A Historical Geography (1989), Wetlands: A Theatened Landscape (ed, 1991), Planet Management (ed, 1992); *Style*— Prof Michael Williams, FBA; ✉ Westgates, Vernon Avenue, Harcourt Hill, Oxford OX2 9AU (☎ 01865 243725); School of Geography, Mansfield Rd, Oxford OX1 3TB (☎ 01865 271924, fax 01865 271929)

WILLIAMS, Michael Duncan; s of Harry Duncan Williams, of Oxford, and Irene Pamela, *née* Mackenzie; *b* 31 March 1951; *Educ* Oundle, Trinity Hall Cambridge (MA); *Career* vice pres and UK sr credit offr Bank of America NT and SA 1973–89, dir: SFE Bank Ltd, Banque SFE 1988–89; dep gen mangr credit Nomura Bank Int plc 1989–93, dir Credit Risk Mgmnt Swiss Bank Corporation 1993–94, head Portfolio Mgmnt European Bank for Reconstruction and Development 1994–; hon treas: FISA, The International Rowing Fedn, Amateur Rowing Assoc; vice pres London Rowing Club, steward Henley Royal Regatta; memb Chartered Inst of Bankers; *Recreations* rowing, golf; *Clubs* Leander; *Style*— Michael Williams, Esq; ✉ 113 Deodar Rd, London SW15 2NU; European Bank for Reconstruction and Development, One Exchange Square, London EC2A 2EH

WILLIAMS, Michael John; s of Stanley Williams, and Phyllis Mary, *née* Wenn; *b* 23 July 1948; *Educ* William Ellis Sch London, Univ of Liverpool (Oliver Elton prize for English literature, BA); *m* 1971, Carol; 2 da (Stella b 1983, Amy b 1988); *Career* indentured graduate trainee Liverpool Daily Post & Echo 1970–73, features sub ed and news sub ed Birmingham Evening Mail 1973–75, home news sub ed The Times 1975–78, asst to editorial dir Thames & Hudson Book Publishers 1978–79; New Society Magazine: diary ed and feature writer 1979–84, dep ed 1984–86; features ed Today 1986; The Sunday Times: dep news ed 1986–87, news ed 1987–89, asst ed (news) 1989–90, managing ed (news) 1990–92, managing ed (features) 1993–94; exec ed The Independent 1996– (exec news ed 1994–); *Books* British Society (1984), Britain Now Quiz (1985), Society Today (1986); *Recreations* walking in the Himalayas; *Style*— Michael Williams, Esq; ✉ 33 Kelly Street, Camden Town, London NW1 8PG (☎ 0171 482 5318); The Independent, 1 Canada Square, Canary Wharf, London E14 5DL

WILLIAMS, Rev Canon Michael Joseph; s of James Williams (d 1972), of West Bromwich, Staffs, and Edith, *née* Unsworth (d 1988); *b* 26 Feb 1942; *Educ* West Bromwich Secondary Tech Sch, West Bromwich Tech Coll (HNC) St John's Coll Durham (BA); *m* 31 July 1971, (Mary) Miranda, da of Lawrence Gordon Bayley, MBE, of Stockport; 1 s (James Matthew b 3 Nov 1978), 1 da (Victoria Louise b 5 March 1976); *Career* team vicar St Philemon Toxteth Liverpool 1975–78 (curate 1970–75), dir of pastoral studies St John's Coll Durham 1978–88, princ The Northern Ordination Course 1989–; visiting lectr Chester Coll and Univ Coll of Ripon York St John 1993–; hon lectr Univ of Manchester, pres The Northern Fedn for Training in Miny 1991–93, hon canon Liverpool Cathedral 1993; *Books* The Power and the Kingdom (1989); *Recreations* woodwork; *Style*— The Rev Canon Michael Williams; ✉ 75 Framingham Rd, Brooklands, Sale, Cheshire M33 3RH (☎ 0161 962 7513, e-mail mike@noc2.u-net.com); Northern Ordination Course, Luther King House, Brighton Grove, Manchester M14 5JP (☎ 0161 225 6668)

WILLIAMS, Michael Leonard; s of Michael Leonard Williams (d 1987), of Stratford-upon-Avon, and Elizabeth, *née* Mulligan (d 1982); *b* 9 July 1935; *Educ* St Edward's Coll Liverpool, RADA; *m* 5 Feb 1971, Dame Judi Dench, DBE, *qv*, da of Dr Reginald Arthur Dench (d 1964), of York; 1 da (Finty b 24 Sept 1972); *Career* actor; Nat Serv RAF 1953–55; Coronation scholar RADA 1957, Nottingham Playhouse 1959–61, West End debut 1961, assoc memb RSC 1963–77; chm Catholic Stage Guild 1977–88, fndr memb The Surrey Soc of Cncl for the Protection of Rural England; patron: Cumbria Theatre Tst, Chicken Shed; life govr Imperial Cancer Fund; *Theatre* RSC roles incl: Puck in A Midsummer Night's Dream, the herald in Marat/Sade (London and NY), Arthur in Tango, Petruchio in Taming of the Shrew, Troilus in Troilus and Cressida, Orlando in As You Like It, the Fool in King Lear, Charles Courtly in London Assurance, title role in Henry V, Private Meek in Too True to be Good, Autolycus in A Winter's Tale; West End roles incl: George Pigden in Out of Order, Charles Pooter in Mr and Mrs Nobody, George Pigden in Two into One, Bob in Pack of Lies (Lyric) 1983, George in Two Into One (Shaftesbury) 1984, Charles in Mr and Mrs Nobody (Garrick) 1986; *Television* incl: Elizabeth R 1971, A Raging Calm 1974, My Son My Son 1978, Love In A Cold Climate 1980, A Fine Romance 1980–82, Bukovsky 1984, Blunt 1986, Double First 1988, Angel Voices 1989, Can You Hear Me Thinking? 1990, September Song 1992, Conjugal Rites 1993; *Films* incl: Dead Cert 1974, Enigma 1981, Educating Rita 1982, Henry V 1989; *Recreations* cricket, gardening, painting; *Clubs* Garrick; *Style*— Michael Williams, Esq; ✉ c/o Julian Belfrage Associates, 46 Albemarle Street, London W1X 4PP (☎ 0171 491 4400, fax 0171 493 5460)

WILLIAMS, Michael Lodwig (Mike); s of John Leslie Williams, of Cardiff, and Eileen Mary, *née* Sanders; *b* 22 Jan 1948; *Educ* Wycliffe Coll Glos, Trinity Hall Cambridge (MA), Nuffield Coll Oxford; *m* 1970, Jenny Mary Williams, *qv*, *née* Donaldson; 3 s; *Career* Miny of Fin Lusaka 1969–71; HM Treasy: joined in 1973, seconded to Price Waterhouse 1980–81, head industl policy issues 1992–; *Style*— Mike Williams, Esq; ✉ Deputy Director, Industry, HM Treasury, Parliament Street, London SW1P 3AG (☎ 0171 270 4449, fax 0171 270 4332)

WILLIAMS, Michael Roy; s of Edgar Harold Williams, and Joyce, *née* Smith; *b* 29 March 1947; *Educ* Selhurst GS, Univ of Exeter (BA); *Career* UCMDS trainee Unilever plc/prod mangr Bird's Eye Foods 1969–72, account dir Leo Burnett advtg 1972–78, dir Geers Gross plc 1978–86, md Geers Gross UK 1978–86, dir Charles Barker plc 1986–89, chief exec Ayer Ltd 1986–90, dir Ayer Europe 1986–90, managing ptnr Serendipity Brand Makers Ltd 1990–; *Recreations* films, music, windsurfing, travel, France, SE Asia; *Style*— Michael R Williams, Esq; ✉ Serendipity Brand Makers Ltd, 30 Gray's Inn Road, London WC1X 8HR

WILLIAMS, (Garnet) Montague Eveleigh; s of Garnet Montague Williams (d 1939), of Coulsdon, Surrey, and Ellen, *née* Eveleigh (d 1968); *b* 19 Dec 1917; *Educ* Reigate GS, London Polys (BSc); *m* 8 May 1948, Phyllis Olive, da of Capt Thomas Mann (d 1950), of Margate, Kent; 1 s (Oliver b 19 March 1961 d 26 Dec 1973), 1 da (Sara b 5 Nov 1957); *Career* sr sci offr Armament Res & Devpt Estab Miny of Supply 1941–55, sr engr Tech Div PE Consulting Group 1955–59, head of dept City Univ London and Northampton CAT 1959–67 (memb Univ Cncl 1989–), tech dir Ferraris Med Ltd & Associates 1967–86, pt/t conslt chartered engr 1986–; life memb Old Reigatian Assoc (chm 1960–61), chm Governing Body City Literary Inst 1988–; memb: Parly and Sci Ctee 1971–74, Barbican Assoc London 1977–, Governing Body Birkbeck Coll 1991–93, Standing Ctee City Univ Convocation 1988–, Central London Regnl Ctee Engrg Cncl 1993–, Ctee City Univ Soc 1993–; chm UK Automation Cncl 1971–74; common cncllr Aldersgate Ward Corp of London 1985–93; memb: City and Hackney Community Health Cncl 1986–93, City and Hackney Dist Health Authy Jt Consultative Ctee 1987–93 (vice chm 1991), London Fire and Civil Defence Authy 1988–93, City of London Archeological Tst 1993–; Freeman City of London 1966; Liveryman: Worshipful Co of Scientific Instrument Makers 1966, Worshipful Co of Engrs 1988, Worshipful Co of Blacksmiths 1990; CEng, FIEE 1991 (MIEE 1954), FIMfgE 1990, FInstMC 1976, FRSA 1969,; *Recreations* reading, theatre, cinema, photography, good living, France; *Clubs* Guildhall, City Livery, Players Theatre; *Style*— Montague Williams, Esq; ✉ Orland, Church Avenue, Clent, Stourbridge, West Midlands DY9 9QS; Milton House, 24 Richmond Rd, Horsham, Sussex

WILLIAMS, Nicholas Michael Heathcote; s of late Sir Edgar Trevor Williams, CB, CBE, DSO, DL, of Oxford, and Gillian, *née* Gambier-Parry; *b* 5 Nov 1954; *Educ* Marlborough, St Catharine's Coll Cambridge (Briggs scholar, MA); *m* 19 Dec 1987, Corinna Mary, da of David and Barbara Mitchell, of Oxford; 2 s (Benjamin b 1988, Joshua b 1990), 1 da (Rebecca b 1993); *Career* RMA Sandhurst 1977, 2 Lt Royal Green Jackets 1977, Lt 1977; called to the Bar Inner Temple 1976; *Recreations* reading, looking at pictures, walking, cricket; *Clubs* Royal Green Jackets; *Style*— Nicholas Heathcote Williams, Esq; ✉ 12 King's Bench Walk, Inner Temple, London EC4 (☎ 0171 583 0811, fax 0171 583 7228)

WILLIAMS, Nigel Phillip; s of Stanley Phillip Williams, of Rainham, Kent, and Freda Frances, *née* Stone; *b* 9 May 1956; *Educ* Gillingham GS, LSE (BSc); *Career* W Greenwell & Co 1977–78, assoc memb Grieveson Grant & Co 1978–84, md William Cooke Lott & Kissack Ltd 1984–90, advsr Czechoslovenska Obchodni Banka 1990–91, chm Mgmnt Bd Creditanstalt Investment Co 1991–96, chm Emerging Europe Asset Management; non-exec dir: Marienbad Waters, Guinness Flight Global Strategy Fund, Guinness Flight International Accumulation Fund, Czech Value Fund; memb: SBE 1978, SE 1983; *Recreations* sailing, skiing, shooting; *Clubs* Royal London Yacht, Carlton; *Style*— Nigel Williams, Esq; ✉ Creditanstalt Investment Company, Voršilská 5, 11000 Prague, Czech Republic (☎ 00 42 2 249 93 200, fax 00 42 2 249 93 201)

WILLIAMS, Prof Norman Stanley; s of Julius Williams, of Harewood, nr Leeds, and Mable, *née* Sundle (d 1978); *b* 15 March 1947; *Educ* Roundhay Sch Leeds, Univ of London (MB BS, MS); *m* Linda, da of Reuben Feldman, of London; 1 s (Benjamin b 1983), 1 da (Charlotte b 1979); *Career* res fell UCLA 1980–82, sr lectr in surgery Leeds Gen Infirmary 1982–86 (res fell 1977–78, lectr 1978–80), winner Patey Prize 1978, Fulbright scholar 1980, Moynihan fellowship 1985, prof of surgery The Royal London Hosp 1986– (house surgn and physician 1970–71, surgical registrar 1971–76); author of numerous chapters and papers on gastroenterological disease; chm UKCCCR Sub-ctee on colorectal cancer, pres Ileostomy Assoc of GB, vice chm Editorial Ctee British Journal of Surgery, pres Euro Digestive Surgery 1997; memb Editorial Bd: Int Jl of Colorectal Disease, Jl of Surgical Oncology; jt winner Bupa Prize for Medically Illustrated Textbook 1995, Nessim Habif Prize for Surgery 1995; memb: Br Soc of Gastroenterology, Surgical Res Soc, Assoc of Surgeons, Int Surgical Gp; FRCS 1975; *Books* Surgery of the Anus Rectum and Colon (jt author), Colorectal Cancer (ed); *Recreations* long distance swimming, theatre, cinema; *Style*— Prof Norman Williams; ✉ Academic Dept of Surgery, The Royal London Hospital, Whitechapel, London E1 1BB (☎ 0171 377 7079, fax 0171 377 7283)

WILLIAMS, Sir (Michael) Osmond; 2 Bt (UK 1909), of Castell Deudraeth, and Borthwen, Co Merioneth; MC (1944), JP (Gwynedd 1960); s of Capt Osmond Trahairn Deudraeth Williams, DSO (d 1915), by his w Lady Gladys Finch Hatton (da of 13 Earl of Winchilsea); suc gf, Sir Arthur Osmond Williams, 1 Bt, JP, sometime Lord-Lt and MP Merionethshire, 1927; *b* 22 April 1914; *Educ* Eton, Freiburg Univ; *m* 1947, Benita Mary, da of G Henry Booker (d 1953); 2 da; *Heir* none; *Career* 2 Lt Royal Scots Greys 1933–37 and 1939; Mid East, Italy and NW Europe WW II 1939–45, Capt 1940, Maj 1945; memb Merioneth Pk Planning Ctee 1971–74, govr Rainer Fndn Outdoor Pursuits Centre 1963–75, chm Quarry Tours Ltd 1973–77; Chev Order of Leopold II with Palm, Croix de Guerre with Palm (Belgium) 1940; *Recreations* music, travelling; *Clubs* Travellers'; *Style*— Sir Osmond Williams, Bt, MC; ✉ Borthwen, Penrhyndeudraeth, Gwynedd LL48 6EN (☎ 01766 770215)

WILLIAMS, Owen John; s of Owen John Williams (d 1975), of St Clears, and Dilys, *née* Evans; *b* 17 May 1950; *Educ* Ysgol Abermâd Aberystwyth, Harrow, Univ Coll Oxford (MA); *m* 2 March 1984; 1 da (Olivia b 23 Dec 1986); *Career* called to the Bar Middle Temple 1974, memb Wales and Chester Circuit 1975; chm O J Williams Ltd Group of Cos 1975–; dir St Clears Market Co; Parly candidate (Cons) Ceredigion & Pembroke N 1987 and 1992, Euro candidate Mid & West Wales 1989, prospective Parly candidate (Cons) Carmarthen West and S Pembrokeshire 1996; memb Hon Soc Cymmrordorion, govr United Counties Agric Soc, pres St Clears Sr Citizens' Assoc, non-exec memb E Dyfed Health Authy 1990–95, govr Marlborough Primary Sch 1993; Lloyd's underwriter 1978; MInstD; *Recreations* racing, rugby, country & western music; *Clubs* Carlton; *Style*— O J Williams, Esq; ✉ 4 Brick Court, Temple, London EC4Y 9AD (☎ 0171 583 8455, fax 0171 353 1699); O J Williams Ltd, St Clears, Dyfed SA33 4BN (☎ 01994 230355, fax 01994 230732)

WILLIAMS, Prof (Hilary) Paul; s of John Kenneth Williams, and Margaret Rosalind Williams; *b* 22 June 1943; *Educ* Redruth GS, Univ of Cambridge (MA), Univ of Leicester (PhD); *m* 27 Aug 1971, Eileen, da of Ernest Hewart; 1 s (Alexander Paul b 18 Feb 1975), 2 da (Anna Morwenna b 17 Nov 1972, Eleanor Mary b 20 April 1982); *Career* devpt analyst for IBM 1968–71, lectr Univ of Sussex 1971–76, prof of mgmnt sci Univ of Edinburgh 1976–84; Univ of Southampton: prof of operational res 1984–, dean Faculty of Mathematical Studies 1987–90 and 1992–93; memb: Operational Res Soc, Mathematical Programming Soc, Royal Instn of Cornwall; *Books* Model Building In Mathematical Programming (1978, 3rd edn 1990), Model Solving in Mathematical Programming (1993); *Recreations* running, walking; *Style*— Prof Paul Williams; ✉ 72 Olivers Battery Rd, Winchester, Hants SO22 4JB (☎ 01962 52575); Faculty of

Mathematical Studies, The University, Southampton SO9 5NH (☎ 01703 593794, fax 01703 593939, telex 47661)

WILLIAMS, Paul Adrian; s of Ronald Harry Williams (d 1993), of Abingdon, Oxon, and Phyllis Mabel, *née* Silvester (d 1994); *b* 3 May 1947; *Educ* Abingdon Sch; *m* 1975, Katy Ebtehaj, *née* Kohanim; 2 da (Sarah Anoosha b 1978, Lisa Susan b 1982); *Career* chartered accountant; trainee Wenn Townsend & Co Oxford 1966–72, audit mangr Whinney Murray & Co London 1972–78, currently ptnr responsible for computer audit and security servs Binder Hamlyn London (joined 1978); memb Ctee of Enquiry into Failure of London Ambulance Serv Computer-Aided Despatch System 1992; ICAEW: memb Cncl, chm Faculty of IT 1994–96; Freeman City of London 1995, Freeman Worshipful Co of Info Technologists 1994; FCA 1972, MBCS 1984; *Books* Expert Systems in Auditing (1990); *Recreations* golf, 8-track recording, music; *Style—* Paul Williams, Esq; ✉ Binder Hamlyn, 180 The Strand, London WC2R 1EA

WILLIAMS, Paul Michael; *b* 25 June 1948, Wales; *Educ* DipHSM, Postgrad Dip in Mgmnt Studies (CNAA Poly of Wales); *m*; *Career* Welsh admin trainee Welsh Hosp Bd 1966–69, nat admin trainee S Western Regnl Hosp Bd and Univ of Manchester 1969–71, sr admin asst Welsh Hosp Bd 1971–72, hosp sec Whitchurch Hosp Cardiff 1972–73, asst gen mangr S Glamorgan HA 1973–74, project admin Welsh Health Tech Servs Orgn (WHTSO) 1974–76, dist planning offr Mid Glamorgan HA 1980–82 (asst dist planning offr 1976–80), unit admin Morgannwg Health Unit 1982–86, asst dist gen mangr Mid Glamorgan HA 1986–90, unit gen mangr Ogwr Health Unit 1990–92, chief exec Bridgend and Dist NHS Tst 1992–; former chm: Tst Chief Execs in Wales (currently memb Advsy Gp), Welsh Ctee on Drug Misuse; currently chm Mgmnt Gp NHS Staff Coll Wales; former memb: Welsh Health Planning Forum, Welsh Office Organisational Devpt Gp and Community Resource Mgmnt Gp; currently memb: Standing Ctee for Postgrad Med Educn (Wales), Welsh Divnl Cncl IHSM (chm 1984–85 and 1985–86); govr Bridgend Coll of FE and HE, dir Wales Quality Centre, vice chm Princess of Wales Hosp Macmillan Cancer Centre Appeal; FIMgt 1988 (MIMgt 1974), FHSM 1995 (MHSM 1972); *Recreations* flyfishing, travel, art, music, gardening, running; *Style—* Paul Williams, Esq; ✉ Bridgend and District NHS Trust, Trust Headquarters, 71 Quarella Road, Bridgend, Mid Glamorgan CF31 1YE (☎ 01656 752752)

WILLIAMS, Dr Paul Randall; CBE (1996); s of Fred Williams (d 1986), and Eileen Westbrook, *née* Stafford (d 1964); *b* 21 March 1934; *Educ* Baines' GS, Loughborough Coll (DLC, BSc), Univ of Liverpool (PhD); *m* 7 Sept 1957, Marion Frances, da of Frederick Gee Lewis (d 1981); 1 s (John Lewis b 1959), 1 da (Judith Sarah b 1962); *Career* ICI res fell Univ of Liverpool 1957, res physicist Br Nat Bubble Chamber 1958–62, Rutherford Laboratory SRC 1962–79, head Engrg Div SERC 1981–83 (head of Astronomy Radio and Space Div 1979–81); dir: Rutherford Appleton Laboratory 1987–94 (dep dir 1983–87), Daresbury and Rutherford Appleton Laboratories 1994–95; chm and chief exec Cncl for the Central Laboratory of the Res Cncls (CCLRC) 1995–; govr: Westminster Coll Oxford, Abingdon Coll, Abingdon Sch; lay preacher Methodist Church; Glazebrook Medal and Prize Inst of Physics 1994; Hon DSc Univ of Keele 1996; FInstP; *Recreations* sailing, walking, skiing, choral singing; *Style—* Dr Paul Williams, CBE; ✉ 5 Tatham Rd, Abingdon, Oxon OX14 1QB (☎ 01235 524654); Council for the Central Laboratory of the Research Councils, Rutherford Appleton Laboratory, Chilton, Didcot, Oxon OX11 0QX (☎ 01235 445533, fax 01235 445147, telex 83159 RUTHLB G)

WILLIAMS, Dr Penry Herbert; s of Douglas Herbert Williams (d 1939), of Cheshunt, Herts, and Dorothea Adelaide Blanche, *née* Murray (d 1982); *b* 25 Feb 1925; *Educ* Marlborough, New Coll Oxford, St Antony's Coll Oxford (MA, DPhil); *m* 10 Sept 1952, June Carey (d 1991), da of George Carey Hobson (d 1945), of Cape Town; 1 s (Jonathan b 1960), 1 da (Sarah b 1957); *Career* RA 1943–45 (cmmnd 1945), Royal Indian Artillery 1945–47 (Lt 1946); Univ of Manchester: asst lectr 1951–54, lectr 1954–63, sr lectr 1963–64; fell lectr and tutor New Coll Oxford 1964–92 (fell emeritus 1992), chm New Coll Devpt Ctee 1992–; ed English Historical Review 1982–90; FRHistS; *Books* The Council in the Marches of Wales (1958), Life in Tudor England (1964), The Tudor Regime (1979), New College 1379–1979 (ed, with John Buxton, 1979), The Later Tudors. England 1547–1603 (1995); *Recreations* hill walking, opera; *Style—* Dr Penry Williams; ✉ Green Corner, Wood Green, Witney, Oxon OX8 6DQ (☎ 01993 702545); New College, Oxford OX1 3BN (☎ 01865 279509)

WILLIAMS, Peter; CBE (1984); s of late Humphrey Richard Williams; *b* 4 Oct 1916; *Educ* St Paul's; *m* 1940, Nona (d 1995), da of late William Cook-Davies; 1 da (Lowri); *Career* dep chm Wedgwood plc 1975–84, chm Staffs Devpt Assoc 1984–92; FCA; *Recreations* golf, reading, music; *Style—* Peter Williams, Esq, CBE; ✉ Una, Barlaston, Staffs ST12 9AA (☎ 01782 373907)

WILLIAMS, (John) Peter; s of John Ronald Williams, of Malvern, Worcs; *b* 29 June 1953; *Educ* Kingston GS, St John's Coll Cambridge (MA); *m* 1980, Geraldine Mary, *née* Whelan; 1 s (Dominic b 1982), 2 da (Frances b 1984, Caroline b 1987); *Career* articled clerk Thomson McLintock CAs 1975–79, finance accountant Grindlays Bank 1979–82; Associated Newspapers Holdings Ltd: gp accountant 1982–90, fin dir Associated Newspaper Holdings 1990, fin dir Daily Mail and General Trust plc (parent co of Associated Newspapers) 1991–; non-exec dir The Bristol Evening Post plc 1991–; FCA 1989 (ACA 1979); *Recreations* opera, golf, swimming, philately; *Style—* Peter Williams, Esq; ✉ Daily Mail and General Trust plc, Northcliffe House, 2 Derry Street, London W8 5TT (☎ 0171 938 6000, fax 0171 938 4626)

WILLIAMS, (William) Peter; s of William Edgar Williams (d 1983), of Canterbury, and Gladys Mary, *née* Thomas (d 1985); *b* 21 Sept 1933; *Educ* King Edward GS Totnes, Cotham GS Bristol; *m* 1, 1960 (m dis 1986), Ann Veronica; 2 s, 4 da; m 2, 1986, Jo Taylor Williams, da of Alexander Thomas Taylor, of Timaru, NZ; 1 da; *Career* journalist with Bristol Evening Post and BBC Radio in South West 1954–64, reporter Day by Day Southern Television 1964–65, reporter and prodr This Week (later TV Eye) Thames Television 1965–79, reporter Panorama and presenter/exec prodr Open Secret BBC 1979–82, controller of factual progs TVS 1982–92; md: Peter Williams TV International Ltd 1992–, Studio Z 1992–; prodr Just Williams series of documentaries, originated The Human Factor series; awards incl: Test Tube Explosion 1983 (runner up Prix Italia), Just Williams - The Mercenaries 1984 (San Francisco Golden Gate award), The Human Factor - Boy on a Skateboard 1985 (Asia Bdcasting Union Premier Documentary award), Unit 731 - Did the Emperor Know? 1985 (San Francisco Golden Gate award, Gold Medal NY Int Film and TV Festival 1986), The Human Factor - Vicar of Bangkok 1989 (Sanford St Martin Merit Award for Religious Bdcasting), Charlie Wing 1990 (RTS Best UK Regnl Prog, Rheims Euro TV Festival Best Documentary 1991), Ambulance! (Indies Best Regnl Prog 1995); chm Canterbury Festival 1987–, pres Optimists Club 1988–; dir: E Kent Enterprise Agency 1987, CT FM Radio 1996; Hon MA Univ of Kent at Canterbury 1992; *Books* Winner Stakes All, McIndoe's Army, Unit 731 - The Secret of Secrets; *Recreations* theatre, music, tennis, cricket; *Clubs* Kent CCC (life memb); *Style—* Peter Williams, Esq; ✉ Boughton-under-Blean, Faversham, Kent

WILLIAMS, HE Peter Keegan; CMG (1992); s of William Edward Williams, and Lilian, *née* Spright; *b* 3 April 1938; *Educ* F Calday Grange GS, Univ de Lille, Pembroke Coll Oxford (MA); *m* 1969, Rosamund Mary de Worms; 2 da; *Career* joined Dip Serv 1962, first sec FCO 1973, first sec, head of Chancery and Consul Rabat 1976 (chargé d'Affaires 1978 and 1979), cnsllr GATT UK Mission Geneva 1979–83 (chm GATT Panel on US-Canada Tuna Dispute 1981–82, chm GATT Ctee on Finance and Personnel 1981–83), ambass S Yemen 1983–85, head UN Dept FCO 1986–89, ambass to Socialist Republic of Vietnam 1990–; FRGS; *Recreations* wine, walking; *Clubs* Travellers', United Oxford and Cambridge Univ; *Style—* HE Mr Peter Williams, CMG; ✉ British Embassy, 16 Pho Ly Thuong Kiet, Hanoi, Vietnam

WILLIAMS, Dr Peter Orchard; CBE (1991); s of Robert Orchard Williams, CBE (d 1967), and Agnes Annie, *née* Birkinshaw (d 1972); *b* 23 Sept 1925; *Educ* Caterham Sch, Queen's Royal Coll Trinidad, St John's Coll Cambridge (MA), St Mary's Hosp Med Sch (MB BChir); *m* 19 Dec 1949, Billie Innes, da of William Williams Brown (d 1985); 2 da (Judith Anne Way b 1953, Sheridan Petrea Ford b 1955); *Career* med appts: St Mary's Hosp, Royal Free Hosp 1950–53, med specialist RAMC 1953–55; MO MRC 1956–60, dir Wellcome Tst 1965–91 (memb staff 1960–65, conslt 1992–93), hon dir Wellcome Inst for History of Med; chm: Hague Club (Euro Fndns), Assoc Med Res Charities, Fndns Forum, various med ctees; currently chm Health Research Ethics Ctee HM Prisons; pres Royal Soc of Tropical Med and Hygiene 1991–93; Liveryman Worshipful Soc of Apothecaries 1988; Hon DSc: Univ of Birmingham 1989, Univ of the West Indies 1991, Univ of Glasgow 1992; Hon DM: Univ of Nottingham 1990, Univ of Oxford 1993; Mary Kingsley medal Liverpool Sch Tropical Med 1983, hon fellowship London Sch of Hygiene and Tropical Med; FRCP 1970 (MRCP 1952); *Books* Careers in Medicine (1952), Personal Recollections (1993); *Recreations* gardening, travel, golf; *Clubs* RSM; *Style—* Dr Peter Williams, CBE; ✉ Courtyard House, Bletchingdon, Kidlington, Oxon OX5 3DL (☎ 01869 350171, fax 01869 350789)

WILLIAMS, Dr Peter Richard; s of Calvert Percy Halliday Williams, of Christchurch, Dorset, and Joan Lillian, *née* Cook; *b* 13 July 1946; *Educ* Bedford Mod Sch, Univ of Oxford, Univ of Saskatchewan, Univ of Reading (BA, MSc, PhD); *m* 2 Dec 1972, Esther May, da of Louis Van Der Veen, of Saskatoon, Saskatchewan, Canada; *Career* res fell: Univ of Birmingham 1975–80, Australian Nat Univ 1980–83; dep dir Inst of Housing 1986–88 (asst dir 1980–86), prof of housing mgmnt and dir Centre for Housing Mgmnt and Devpt Univ of Wales Cardiff 1989–94 (visiting fell 1994–95), currently dep sec and head of research and external affairs BSA and Cncl of Mortgage Lenders; visiting prof Sch of Public Policy Univ of Bristol; memb Bd Housing Corp; memb Editorial Bd: Housing Studies, Roof Magazine; gen ed Housing Practise book series; formerly: memb Bd Tai Cymru (Housing for Wales), chm Housing Mgmnt Advsy Panel for Wales, chm Housing Studies Assoc; memb: RGS, Inst Br Geographers, Chartered Inst of Housing; *Books* Urban Political Economy (author and ed, 1982), Social Process and The City (ed, 1983), Conflict and Development (ed, 1984), Gentrification and The City (author/ed, 1986), Class and Space (author/ed, 1987), Home Ownership (co-author, 1990), Safe as Houses (co-author, 1991); *Recreations* walking, sailing; *Style—* Dr Peter Williams; ✉ BSA/Council of Mortgage Lenders, 3 Savile Row, London W1X 1AF (☎ 0171 437 0655, fax 0171 434 3791)

WILLIAMS, Brig Peter Richard Godber; DL (Cambridgeshire 1989); s of Maj William Washington Williams, TD, FRGS (d 1995), of Appin, Argyll, and Katharine Beatrice, *née* Godber; *b* 2 Jan 1936; *Educ* The Leys Sch Cambridge, RMA Sandhurst; *m* 30 Oct 1964, Margaret Ellen Nina, da of Maj-Gen John MacKenzie, Matheson, OBE, TD, of Edinburgh; 1 s (Richard b 12 March 1968), 1 da (Charlotte b 18 Dec 1965); *Career* Nat Serv 1954, cmmnd Welsh Gds 1957, 1 Bn Welsh Gds UK/BAOR 1957–61, Gds Parachute Co 1962–63, Staff Captain Cyprus 1964, Co Cdr Welsh Gds 1964–66, Staff Coll 1967, Bde-Maj 16 Para Bde 1967–70, 2 i/c 1 Bn Welsh Gds BAOR N Ireland 1970–72, Lt-Col 1972, Staff Cdr 1 Bn Welsh Gds UK Cyprus Berlin 1975–77, Col MOD and HQ UKLF 1977– 85, Brig Cdr 54 Inf Bde E Midlands Area 1985–88, ret 1989; bursar St Mary's Sch Cambridge 1989; rugby Army XV 1958, churchwarden St James's Croxton, cmdt Cambs ACF 1989–94, chm Cambs TAVRA 1995 (vice chm 1993); author of various articles in mil pubns; *Recreations* tennis, shooting, fishing, music; *Clubs* Army and Navy; *Style—* Brig Peter Williams, DL; ✉ Croxton Old Rectory, Eltisley, Huntingdon, Cambs PE19 4SU (☎ 01480 880344)

WILLIAMS, Sir (Robert) Philip Nathaniel; 4 Bt (UK 1915), of Bridehead, Co Dorset; JP (1992), DL (Dorset 1995); s of Sir David Philip Williams, 3 Bt, DL (d 1970), by his 2 w, Elizabeth, Lady Williams, DL; *b* 3 May 1950; *Educ* Marlborough, Univ of St Andrews (MA); *m* 1979, Catherine Margaret Godwin, da of Canon Cosmo Gabriel Rivers Pouncey, of Church Walk, Littlebredy, Dorchester, Dorset; 1 s (David b 1980), 3 da (Sarah b 1982, Margaret b 1984, Clare b 1987); *Heir* s David Robert Mark Williams b 31 Oct 1980; *Career* landowner (2500 acres); *Clubs* MCC; *Style—* Sir Philip Williams, Bt, JP, DL; ✉ Bridehead, Littlebredy, Dorchester, Dorset DT2 9JA (☎ 01308 482232)

WILLIAMS, Raymond Lloyd; CBE (1987); s of late Walter Raymond Williams, and Vera Mary Williams; *b* 27 Feb 1927; *Educ* Bournemouth Sch, St John's Coll Oxford (Gibbs scholar, BA, MA, DPhil, DSc); *m* 1956, Sylvia Mary Lawson, *née* Whitaker; 1 s, 1 da; *Career* Pressed Steel Co res fell 1951–53, Harkness res fell Univ of California Berkeley 1953–54; Explosives R & D Estab: sr res fell 1955–56, sr scientific offr 1956–58, princ scientific offr 1958–60; princ scientific offr Admiralty Materials Laboratory 1960–62; Explosives R & D Estab: sr princ scientific offr 1962, supt Analytical Servs Gp 1962–65, supt Non-metallic Materials Gp 1965–68; dir Met Police Laboratory 1968–87; visiting prof Sch of Chemical Scis Univ of E Anglia 1968–, ed Forensic Science International 1978–, jt ed Forensic Science Progress 1985–91; Forensic Sci Soc: pres 1983–85, chm Professional Awards Ctee 1985–96; Home Office conslt on fingerprints 1988–90; Royal Soc of Chemistry: Theophilus Redwood lectr 1984, schs lectr Analytical Div 1988–89, public lectr 1990, Dalton lectr 1995; Adelaide Medal Int Assoc of Forensic Sciences 1993; CChem 1980, FRSC; *Publications* author of over 60 papers in scientific jls; *Recreations* tennis (played for Civil Serv and Oxfordshire); *Style—* Raymond Williams, Esq, CBE; ✉ 9 Meon Road, Bournemouth, Dorset BH7 6PN (☎ 01202 423446)

WILLIAMS, Prof Rhys Watcyn; s of Rev Morgan John Williams, and Barbara, *née* John; *b* 24 May 1946; *Educ* The Bishop Gore Sch Swansea, Jesus Coll Oxford (MA, DPhil); *m* Kathleen, da of William Henry Gould, of Bournemouth; 2 s (Daniel b 1978, Thomas b 1982); *Career* tutorial res fell Bedford Coll Univ of London 1972–74, lectr in German Univ of Manchester 1974–84; Univ of Wales Swansea (formerly Univ Coll Swansea): prof of German 1984–, dean Faculty of Arts 1988–91; pres Int Carl Einstein Soc 1988–92; *Books* Carl Sternheim, A Critical Study (1982); *Style—* Prof Rhys Williams; ✉ 48 Derwen Fawr Rd, Sketty, Swansea SA2 8AQ (☎ 01792 280921); Department of German, University of Wales Swansea, Singleton Park, Swansea SA2 8PP (☎ 01792 295173)

WILLIAMS, Richard Charles John; s of Herbert Charles Lionel Williams (d 1957), and Barbara Dorothy, *née* Moenich; *b* 19 Oct 1949; *Educ* Highgate Sch, London Coll of Printing (DipAD); *m* Agnieszka Wanda, da of Zygmunt Jan Skrobanski; 1 da (Mary Barbara Daisy b 31 July 1981), 1 s (Peter Crispin John b 4 April 1986); *Career* asst designer Industrial Design Unit Ltd 1973–74, sr designer J Sainsbury Ltd 1974–77, dir of packaging Allied International Designers 1977–86, co-fndr/md Design Bridge 1986–96; exec memb DBA 1989–90; *Recreations* motor sports; *Style—* Richard Williams, Esq

WILLIAMS, Dr Richard James Willson; s of Ernest James Williams, of Downend, Bristol, and Eleanor Mary Willson, *née* Rickard; *b* 5 Feb 1949; *Educ* Bristol GS, Univ of Birmingham (MB ChB, Marjorie Hutchings prize in psychiatry); *m* 21 May 1971, Janet May, da of Ronald Phillip Simons (d 1990); 2 da (Anna May b 12 July 1975, Katharine Alice Jane b 21 Nov 1977), 1 s (James Christopher Willson b 13 Aug 1981); *Career* house physician Selly Oak Hosp Birmingham 1972–73, house surgn Worcester Royal Infirmary 1973, registrar in psychiatry S Glamorgan AHA 1974–77 (sr house offr in psychiatry

1973–74), sr registrar in child and adolescent psychiatry S Glamorgan AHA and Welsh Nat Sch of Med 1977–80, conslt child and adolescent psychiatrist 1980– (Avon AHA 1980–82, Bristol and Weston Health Authy 1982–91, Utd Bristol Healthcare NHS Tst 1991–); dir NHS Health Advsy Serv 1992–; Univ of Bristol: clinical teacher in mental health 1980–89, clinical lectr in mental health 1989–94, hon sr lectr in mental health 1994–, govr Inst of Child Health 1988–94, memb Ct 1990–93; sr fell Health Servs Mgmnt Centre Univ of Birmingham 1996–; asst ed Jl of Adolescence 1990–, co-ed Child and Adolescent Psychiatry Section Current Opinion in Psychiatry 1993–; RCPsych: memb Cncl 1986–90 and 1993–, chm S Western Div 1996–; chm Assoc for the Psychiatric Study of Adolescents 1987–93; memb: Assoc for Child Psychology and Psychiatry 1978–, Assoc for Professionals in Servs for Adolescents 1979–, Assoc of Univ Teachers of Psychiatry 1989–, Br Paediatric Assoc 1987–96; DPM 1976, FRCPsych 1990 (MRCPsych 1976), FRSM 1992, MHSM 1994, MInstD 1994, MCPCH 1996; *Publications* The APSA Register of Adolescent Units (5 edn 1990), A Concise Guide to the Children Act 1989 (1992), A Unique Window on Change (1993), Comprehensive Mental Health Services (1994 and 1995), Clinicians in Management (1994 and 1995), Suicide Prevention (1994), Comprehensive Health Services for Elderly People (1994), Drugs and Alcohol (1994), Guiding Through Change (1994), Together We Stand (1995), A Place in Mind (1995), The Substance of Young Needs (1996), Making a Mark (1996), Safeguards for Young Minds (1996); *Recreations* licensed radio amateur, dinghy sailing, motorsport (med offr at racing circuit); *Clubs* Athenaeum, IOD; *Style*— Dr Richard Williams; ✉ NHS Health Advisory Service, Sutherland House, 29–37 Brighton Road, Sutton, Surrey SM2 5AN (☎ 0181 642 6421, fax 0181 770 7327)

WILLIAMS, Richard Wayne; s of David Victor Williams (d 1964), and Sarah Irene, *née* Jones; *b* 13 June 1948; *Educ* Ystalyfera GS Swansea, Univ Coll of Wales Aberystwyth (LLB), Univ of London (LLM); *m* 7 Sept 1974, Linda Pauline, da of Cecil Ernest Elvins; 2 s (Rhodri Christopher Wyn b 18 Jan 1982, Robin Owen Wyn b 12 Sept 1985); *Career* admitted slr 1973; ptnr Ince & Co 1978–; speaker at conferences on shipping matters UK and abroad; conslt on shipping matters to UN agencies and other int bodies; memb: Baltic Exchange, London Maritime Arbitrators Assoc; memb Law Soc; *Books* Limitation of Liability for Maritime Claims (1986, 2 edn 1991); *Recreations* archaeology, reading, guitar, travel; *Style*— Richard Williams, Esq; ✉ Ince & Co, Knollys House, 11 Byward St, London EC3R 5EN (☎ 0171 623 2011, fax 0171 623 3225, telex 8955043 INCES G)

WILLIAMS, Robbie; *b* 13 Feb 1974; *Career* singer; memb Take That 1990–95, solo 1995–; credits with Take That: 11 top ten singles incl 6 no 1's (Pray 1993, Relight My Fire 1993, Babe 1993, Everything Changes 1994, Sure 1994, Back For Good 1995); albums with Take That: Take That and Party (1992, UK no 2), Everything Changes (1993, UK no 1), Nobody Else (1995); awards incl: Best British Single (for Could It Be Magic) BRIT Awards 1993, Nordoff Robbins Silver Clef Levi's Original Talent Award 1993, Best British Single and Best British Video (for Pray) BRIT Awards 1994, Best Group MTV Euro Pop Awards 1994; videos: Take That and Party (1992, UK no 1), Take That - The Party Live At Wembley (1993, UK no 1), Everything Changes (1994, UK no 1), Take That - Berlin (1994, UK no 1); released first solo single Freedom (Chrysalis Records, 1996, UK no 2); host MTV Europe Awards 1996; *Recreations* rollerblading, Port Vale FC; *Style*— Robbie Williams, Esq; ✉ c/o PR Department, Chrysalis Records, EMI House, 43 Brook Green, London W6 7EF

WILLIAMS, Robert Charles; s of (Charles) Bertram Williams, of Sutton Coldfield, and Marjorie Iris, *née* Jones; *b* 29 Sept 1949; *Educ* Bromsgrove Sch, Worcester Coll Oxford (MA); *m* 4 Aug 1976, Caroline Ursula Eanswythe, da of Rev David Allan Pope; 3 s (Henry b 1979, George b 1981, Alfred b 1982); *Career* called to the Bar Inner Temple 1973; ed The Law Reports and The Weekly Law Reports 1996– (managing ed The Weekly Law Reports 1990–96); hon sec PCC All Saints' Blackheath London; *Recreations* music; *Style*— Robert Williams, Esq; ✉ 65 Micheldever Rd, London SE12 8LU (☎ 0181 318 0410); 1 Crown Office Row, Temple, London EC4Y 7HH

WILLIAMS, Prof Robert Charles Gooding; OBE (1969); s of Robert Williams (d 1941), of Westminster, London, and Alice Grace, *née* Gooding (d 1935); *b* 28 Dec 1907; *Educ* Westminster City, Imperial Coll of Sci, Technol and Med (BSc, DIC, PhD); *m* 16 Dec 1937, Edith Emma (Molly) (d 1974), da of Albert James Morrow (d 1948), of Highgate, London; 1 da (Fiona Molly (Mrs Hunt) b 1940); *Career* chief engr Murphy Radio Ltd 1935–45, exec engr N American Philips Inc NY 1946–47, chief engr Philips Electronics and Associated Industries 1948–69, dir Guildford and Counties Broadcasting Co Ltd 1970–93, princ Professional and Scientific Services 1974–; visiting prof of electronics Univ of Surrey 1969–74; originated and disseminated basic concept of integrated multimedia teaching prog based on TV adopted by the Open Univ and of nat electronic grid for telecommunications and cable TV, played a leading role in estab of Univ of Surrey in Guildford, founded the gp awarded the franchise for the Guildford area commercial radio station; memb Cncl IEE 1962–65 (chm Radio and Telecommunications Section 1956–57, chm Electronics Div 1963–64); chm IEE int confs on: Ferrites 1958, Transistors 1959, Med Electronics 1960, TV 1962, Educn 1974; dir IEEE USA 1967–68 (fndr chm UK and Repub of Ireland Section 1961–66), memb Br Electrotechnical Approvals Bd 1967–86; pres: IEEIE 1969–75 (chm Cncl 1966–69), Industl Cncl Educnl and Trg Technol 1982–86 (fndr chm 1966–82); memb Ctee: Cncl Royal TV Soc 1958–60 and 1963–65, Res Degrees of CNAA 1964–68, Nat Cncl for Educnl Technol 1967–72; chm Ctee Int Electrotechnical Cmmn on: Safety of Household Appliances 1967–74, Data Processing Equipment and Office Machines 1974–84; memb: Bd of Govrs Guildford Coll of Technol 1962–89, W Surrey Coll of Art & Design 1970–85, Bd of Tstees Yvonne Arnaud Theatre Guildford; Freeman City of London, Liveryman Worshipful Co of Clothworkers 1946; MRI, FCGI, Hon FIEIE, FIEEE (USA), FInstP, CEng, FIMechE, FIEE, FRSA; *Publications* author of numerous professional papers and feature articles; *Recreations* arboriculture, theatre, antique maps; *Clubs* Athenaeum, Pilgrims of GB; *Style*— Prof Robert C G Williams, OBE; ✉ Field Plot, The Flower Walk, Guildford, Surrey GU2 5EP (☎ 01483 577777)

WILLIAMS, Sir Robert Evan Owen; kt (1976); s of Gwynne Williams; *b* 30 June 1916; *Educ* Sherborne, UCL, Univ Coll Hosp (MD); *m* 1944, Margaret Lumsden; 1 s, 2 da; *Career* former memb MRC and pres RCPath; prof bacteriology London Univ 1960–73, dean St Mary's Hosp Medical Sch 1967–73, dir Public Health Laboratory Service 1973–81, chm Genetic Manipulation Advsy Gp and Ctee on Genetic Manipulation (HSE) 1981–86; Liveryman Worshipful Soc of Apothecaries; fell UCL 1968; Hon FRCPA, Hon MD Uppsala, Hon DSc Bath, Dr Hon Causa Lisbon 1992; FRCP, FRCPath, FFCM; *Recreations* horticulture; *Clubs* Athenaeum; *Style*— Sir Robert Williams; ✉ Little Platt, Plush, Dorchester, Dorset (☎ and fax 01300 348320)

WILLIAMS, Prof Robert Hughes; s of Emrys Williams (d 1972), of Rhydsarn, Llanuwchllyn, Bala, Gwynedd, N Wales, and Catherine, *née* Hughes; *b* 22 Dec 1941; *Educ* Bala Boys' GS, Univ Coll of N Wales Bangor (BSc, PhD, DSc); *m* 18 March 1967, Gillian Mary, da of Basil Harrison, of Bournemouth, Dorset; 1 s (Alun Hughes b 14 Aug 1972), 1 da (Sian Hughes b 17 Dec 1970); *Career* lectr, reader then prof New Univ of Ulster NI 1968–83, prof of physics and head of Dept Univ of Wales Cardiff 1984–94, dep princ Univ of Wales Cardiff 1993–94, vice chllr and princ Univ of Wales Swansea 1994–; author of several chapters, articles and papers; chm S Wales Branch and Semiconductor Gp of Inst of Physics; Br Vacuum Cncl medal 1988, Max Born medal German Physics Soc 1989; CPhys, FInstP 1976, FRS 1990; *Books* Metal Semiconductor Contacts (1988); *Recreations* walking and fishing; *Style*— Prof Robert Williams, FRS; ✉ Dolwerdd, Trerhyngyll, Cowbridge, S Glamorgan (☎ 01446 773402); University of Wales Swansea, Singleton Park, Swansea SA2 8PP (☎ 01792 29514, fax 01792 295655)

WILLIAMS, Robert James; s of Capt Thomas Edwin Williams, MBE, of Lutterworth, Leicestershire, and Joan Winifred, *née* Nelson; *b* 20 Sept 1948; *Educ* King Edward VII Sch Sheffield, Univ Coll Oxford (BA); *m* 29 July 1972, Margaret, da of late Charles Neville Hillier, of Guernsey; 2 da (Katherine b 6 Aug 1979, Caroline b 24 Aug 1983); *Career* Linklaters & Paines: articled clerk 1971–73, asst slr 1973–81, Hong Kong Office 1978–80, ptnr 1981–93; exec dir The Law Debenture Corporation plc 1993–; non-exec dir: 'Nationwide Premier' BES Companies 1993–, The Hoare Govett Smaller Companies Index Investment Tst PLC 1994–, The Hoare Govett 1000 Index Investment Tst PLC 1994–; memb City of London Slrs Co 1980; memb Law Soc 1973; *Recreations* swimming, walking, eating, sleeping; *Style*— Robert Williams, Esq; ✉ 84 Alleyn Rd, London SE21 8AH (☎ 0181 244 9104, fax 0181 761 1536); Princes House, 95 Gresham St, London EC2V 7LY (☎ 0171 606 5451, fax 0171 606 0643, telex 888347)

WILLIAMS, Prof Robert Joseph Paton; s of Ernest Ivor Williams (d 1968), and Alice, *née* Roberts (d 1988); *b* 25 Feb 1926; *Educ* Wallasey GS, Merton Coll Oxford (BA, MA, DPhil); *m* 19 July 1952, Jelly Klara, da of Mattheüs Jacobus Christiaan Buchli, of The Netherlands; 2 s (Timothy Ivor b 1955, John Matthew b 1957); *Career* Univ of Oxford: jr res fell Merton Coll 1951–55, lectr in chemistry 1955–72, fell 1956–, tutor in biochemistry Wadham Coll 1956–72, reader in chemistry 1972–74, Royal Soc Napier res prof Univ of Oxford 1974–91, sr res fell Wadham Coll 1991–93, emeritus fell Wadham Coll 1993–, hon fell Merton Coll 1991–; Buchman Memorial lectr California Inst of Technol 1972; visiting lectr: Princeton Univ 1976, Univ of Toronto 1980, Univ of Newfoundland 1983; Walter J Chute lectr Univ of Dalhousie 1984, Katritsky lectr UEA 1986, Garland lectr Univ of Dundee 1990, A D Little lectr Massachusetts Inst of Technol 1990, UK/Canada Rutherford lectr Royal Soc 1996, numerous other named lectures; foreign memb: Lisbon Acad of Sci 1981, Royal Soc of Sci Liège 1981, Royal Swedish Acad of Sci 1984, Nat Acad of Sci Czechoslovakia 1989; memb: Lindemann Tst, Oxford Preservation Tst; delegate Oxford Univ Press; Hon DSc: Univ of Liège Belgium 1980, Univ of Leicester 1985, Univ of E Anglia 1992, Univ of Keele 1994, Univ of Lisbon Portugal 1996; memb Academia Europaea 1994; FRS 1972; *Awards* incl: Tilden lectr and medallist Chem Soc 1970, Keilen medal Biochem Soc 1972, Hughes medal The Royal Soc 1979, Claire Brylants medal Univ of Louvain 1980, Sir Hans Krebs medal Euro Biochem Societies 1985, Linderstrom-Lang medal Carlsberg Fndn Copenhagen, Sigillum Magnum Univ of Bologna 1987, Heyrovsky medal Int Union of Biochemistry 1988, Sir Frederick Gowland Hopkins medal Biochem Soc 1989, Royal medal The Royal Soc 1995; *Books* Inorganic Chemistry (with C G S Phillips 1966), Biomineralization (with S Mann and J Webb, 1989), The Biological Chemistry of the Elements (with J R R Frausto da Silva, 1991), The Natural Selection of the Chemical Elements (with J R R Frausto da Silva, 1996); *Recreations* walking in the country; *Style*— Prof Robert Williams, FRS; ✉ 115 Victoria Rd, Oxford OX2 7QG (☎ 01865 558926); Wadham College, Oxford OX1 3QR (☎ 01865 272600, fax 01865 272690)

WILLIAMS, Sir Robin Philip; 2 Bt (UK 1953), of Cilgeraint, Co Caernarvon; s of Sir Herbert Geraint Williams, 1 Bt, sometime MP (Reading and also Croydon S) and Parly sec BOT 1928–29 (d 1954), and Dorothy Frances, *née* Jones (d 1957); *b* 27 May 1928; *Educ* Eton, St John's Coll Cambridge; *m* 19 Feb 1955, Wendy Adele Marguerite, da of late Felix Joseph Alexander, of Hong Kong; 2 s; *Heir* s, Anthony Geraint Williams, b 22 Dec 1958; *Career* Lt RA 1947; called to the Bar Middle Temple 1954; insurance broker 1952–91, memb Lloyd's 1961–; chm: Bow Group 1954, Anti Common Market League 1969–84; councillor Borough of Haringay 1968–74; hon sec: Safeguard Britain Campaign 1975–90, Campaign for an Independent Britain 1990–; Liveryman Worshipful Co of Merchant Taylors; *Style*— Sir Robin Williams, Bt; ✉ 1 Broadlands Close, Broadlands Rd, Highgate, London N6 4AF

WILLIAMS, Rev Canon (John) Roger; s of Sir Gwilym Tecwyn Williams, CBE (d 1989), and Kathleen Isobel Rishworth, *née* Edwards (d 1989); *b* 6 Oct 1937; *Educ* Denstone Coll, Lichfield Theol Coll, Westminster Coll Oxford (DipTh 1995); *Career* ordained Lichfield Cathedral; deacon 1963, priest 1964; asst curate: Wem Shropshire 1963–66, St Peter's Collegiate Church Wolverhampton 1966–69; rector Pudleston-cum-Whyle with Hatfield and priest i/c Stoke Prior Humber and Docklow Hereford 1969–74, vicar Christ Church Fenton Stoke-on-Trent 1974–81, rector Shipston-on-Stour with Honington and Idlicote 1981–92, rural dean Shipston 1983–90, hon canon Coventry Cathedral 1990–; rector of Lighthorne, vicar of Chesterton, vicar of Newbold Pacey with Moreton Morrell (all 1992–); chaplain to High Sheriff of Warwicks 1987–88 and 1991–93; *Recreations* art, architecture, walking, travel; *Style*— The Rev Canon Roger Williams; ✉ The Rectory, Church Lane, Lighthorne, Warwick CV35 0AR (☎ 01926 651279)

WILLIAMS, Prof Roger Stanley; CBE (1993); s of Stanley George Williams, and Doris, *née* Dagmar; *b* 28 Aug 1931; *Educ* St Mary's Coll Southampton, London Hosp Med Coll (MB, MD, LRCP, MRCP); *m* 1, 8 Aug 1954 (m dis 1977), Lindsay Mary, *née* Elliott; 2 s (Robert b 8 March 1956, Andrew b 3 Jan 1964), 3 da (Anne b 5 March 1958, Fiona b 24 April 1959, Deborah b 12 July 1961); m 2, 15 Sept 1978, Stephanie Gay, da of Gp Capt Patrick de Laszlo (d 1980); 1 s (Aiden b 16 May 1981), 2 da (Clemency b 28 June 1979, Octavia b 4 Sept 1983); *Career* Capt RAMC 1956–58; jr med specialist Queen Alexandra Hosp Millbank 1956–58, med registrar and tutor Royal Postgraduate Med Sch 1958–59, lectr in med Royal Free Hosp 1959–65, conslt physician Royal S Hants and Southampton Gen Hosp 1965–66, dir Inst of Liver Studies and conslt physician King's Coll Hosp and Med Sch 1966–96, prof of hepatology King's Coll London 1994–96, dir Inst of Hepatology UCL 1996–; memb scientific gp on viral hepatitis WHO Geneva 1972, conslt Liver Res Unit Tst 1974–, memb Advsy Gp on Hepatitis DHSS 1980– (memb Transplant Advsy Panel 1974–83), memb Clinical Standards Advsy Ctee Dept of Health 1994–; attended Melrose meml lecture Glasgow 1970, Goulstonian lecture RCP 1970, Searle lecture American Assoc for Study of Liver Disease 1972, Fleming lecture Glasgow Coll of Physicians and Surgns 1975, Sir Arthur Hurst meml lecture Br Soc of Gastroenterology 1975, Skinner lecture Royal Coll of Radiologists 1978; Sir Ernest Finch visiting prof Sheffield 1974, hon conslt in med to Army 1988–; memb: RSM (sec of section 1962–71), Euro Assoc for Study of the Liver (sec and treas 1968–71, pres 1984); pres Br Soc of Gastroenterology 1989–90, UK rep Select Ctee of Experts Organ Transplantation 1989–, second vice pres RCP 1991–, chm Cons Med Soc; Freeman City of London, Liveryman Worshipful Soc of Apothecaries; FRCP, FRCS, FRCPEd, FRACP, Hon FACP; fell King's Coll London 1992; *Books* ed: Fifth Symposium on Advanced Medicine (1969), Immunology of the Liver (1971), Artificial Liver Support (1975), Immune Reactions in Liver Diseases (1978), Drug Reactions and the Liver (1981), Variceal Bleeding (1982), The Practice of Liver Transplantation (1995), International Developments in Health Care: A Review of Health Systems in the 1990s (1995); author of over 1,500 scientific papers, review articles and book chapters; *Recreations* tennis, sailing, opera; *Clubs* Carlton, Saints and Sinners, Royal Yacht Sqdn, Royal Ocean Racing; *Style*— Prof Roger Williams, CBE; ✉ 8 Eldon Rd, London W8 (☎ 0171 937 5301); Reed House, Satchell Lane, Hamble, Hants; Institute of Hepatology, University College London Medical School, 69–75 Chenies Mews, London WC1E 6HX (☎ 0171 380 0401, fax 0171 380 0405)

WILLIAMS, Ronald Millward; CBE, DL; s of George Williams (d 1982), of Benfleet, Essex, and Gladys, *née* Millward (d 1989); *b* 9 Dec 1922; *Educ* Leeds Coll of Technol;

m 1943, Joyce, da of late Ernest Stead; 1 s (Michael b 13 May 1945), 2 da (Janet b 3 March 1947, Susan b 31 Oct 1949); *Career* apprentice draughtsman rising to commissioning engr Yorkshire Switchgear and Engineering Co Ltd 1942–54, refinery electrical maintenance engr rising to industl engrg supt Mobil Oil Co Ltd 1954–82; chm: Southend Health Authy 1981–91, Southend Health Care NHS Trust 1991–96; memb Harwich Harbour Bd 1986–89, chm St George's Abbeyfield Soc 1986–89, vice-pres Southend Battalion Boy's Brigade 1975–; dist cncllr 1960–86 (former cncl chm and chm Policy Ctee), county cncllr 1970–93 (former cncl chm, chm Highways Ctee, chm Planning Ctee, leader Cons Gp); *Recreations* photography, reading, travel, work; *Style*— Ron Williams, Esq, CBE, DL; ✉ 41 Poors Lane, Hadleigh, Benfleet, Essex SS7 2LA (☎ and fax 01702 559565)

WILLIAMS, Ronald William; s of Albert Williams (d 1942), and Katherine Teresa, *née* Chilver (d 1962); *b* 19 Dec 1926; *Educ* City of London Sch, Downing Coll Cambridge (BA, LLB); *Career* RN 1945–48; Iraq Petroleum Co and Philips Electrical Industries 1952–64, conslt then sr conslt PA Management Consultants 1964–69; asst sec Nat Bd for Prices and Incomes 1969–71; Civil Serv Dept: asst sec 1973–80, UK Govt rep ILO Convention 1975, under sec 1980; dir of The Office of Manpower Econs 1980–86 (asst sec 1971–73); sr advsr Coopers and Lybrand 1986–93, currently independent mgmnt conslt; *Recreations* books, music; *Style*— Ronald Williams, Esq; ✉ 126 Defoe House, Barbican, London EC2Y 8ND (☎ 0171 638 5456)

WILLIAMS, Roy; CB (1989); s of Eric and Ellen Williams; *b* 31 Dec 1934; *Educ* Univ of Liverpool (BA), Univs of Chicago and Berkeley USA; *m* 1959, Shirley, da of Capt O Warwick; 1 s (Justin b 1966), 1 da (Adela b 1961); *Career* asst princ Miny of Power 1956 (princ 1961), princ private sec Miny of Power 1969, paymaster gen 1969, asst sec DTI 1971, princ private sec to Sec of State for Indust 1974, under sec 1976; dep perm sec DTI responsible for: int trade policy 1984–87, sponsorship of manufacturing indust 1987–91, regnl policy, inward investment and small firms 1991–94; *Style*— Roy Williams, Esq, CB

WILLIAMS, Sally Ann; *b* 31 Oct 1962; *Educ* Cardiff Poly, NCTJ qualified journalist; *Career* journalist Essex County Newspapers 1983–85, head of newsroom The Post Office Nat HQ 1990–94 (joined The Post Office 1985), dir Countrywide Porter Novelli Ltd (formerly Countrywide Communications Ltd) 1994–; *Style*— Ms Sally Williams; ✉ Countrywide Porter Novelli Ltd, Bowater House East, 68 Knightsbridge, London SW1X 7LH (☎ 0171 584 0122, fax 0171 584 6655)

WILLIAMS, Simon; s of Hugh Williams (d 1969), and Margaret, *née* Vyner (d 1993); *b* 16 June 1946; *Educ* Harrow; *m* Eve Lucinda (actress as Lucy Fleming), da of Col (Robert) Peter Fleming, OBE, and Dame Celia Johnson; *Career* actor and writer; co-chm (with Angela Thorne) The Actors' Charitable Trust; *Theatre* trained in repertory at Worthing, Birmingham and Bath; early work incl: Hay Fever, The Collector, No Sex Please..., Gigi, The Last of Mrs Cheney, An Ideal Husband (nat tour), They're Playing Our Song (nat tour), Death Trap (nat tour); recent credits incl: The Common Pursuit (Lyric Hammersmith), The Lover (Young Vic), A Marriage Has Been Arranged (NT Studio), The Black Prince (Aldwych), The Winslow Boy (The Globe), Switchback (Theatre Royal Windsor); *Television* incl: Upstairs Downstairs (BBC), First Among Equals, Don't Wait Up (BBC), The Mixer 1992, Law and Disorder (Thames), Agony Again; US TV incl: The Return of the Man From UNCLE (Viacom), Sam McCloud In London (Universal), lead role in Alfred Hitchcock Presents...; *Film* incl: The Prisoner of Zenda (Universal Pictures), The Fiendish Plot of Dr Fu Manchu (Orion), The Breaking Of Bumbo, Joanna, The Incredible Sarah, The Odd Job, No Longer Alone; *Plays* Switchback, Kiss My Aunt; *Novels* Talking Oscars, Kill The Lights; *Style*— Simon Williams, Esq; ✉ Peters Fraser & Dunlop Ltd, 503 The Chambers, Chelsea Harbour, Lots Road, London SW10 0XF (☎ 0171 352 4446, fax 0171 352 7356)

WILLIAMS, Stanley Killa; s of Jack Killa Williams (d 1972), and Gwyneth Mary, *née* Jenkins; *b* 2 July 1945; *Educ* Bromsgrove Sch, Merton Coll Oxford (MA Jur), Coll of Law (Herbert Ruse Prize); *m* 15 July 1972, Dheidre Rhona, *née* Westerman; 1 da (Esther Catrin b 22 Dec 1975), 1 s (Justin Gareth Killa b 22 July 1977); *Career* slr Devon CC 1969–74 (trainee slr 1966–68), asst county sec Oxon CC 1974–80, dep co sec and slr Rowntree Mackintosh plc 1980–89; BTR plc: co sec and slr 1989–93, gp commercial attorney 1993–96; chm York Ebor Round Table 1985–86; memb Law Soc 1969; *Recreations* theatre, tennis, squash; *Clubs* RAC; *Style*— Stanley Williams, Esq

WILLIAMS, Prof Stanley Thomas; s of Thomas Raymond Williams (d 1959), and Martha Alice Rowlands (d 1973); *b* 8 March 1937; *Educ* Birkenhead Sch, Univ of Liverpool (BSc, PhD, DSc); *m* 26 April 1962, Grace Katharine, da of Capt Cyril Twentyman (d 1973); 1 s (decd), 1 da (Anne Margaret b 12 Jan 1966); *Career* post doctoral fell Univ Coll Dublin 1962–64; Univ of Liverpool: lectr 1964–73, sr lectr 1973–78, reader 1978–87, prof 1987–; Workers Educnl Assoc; chm Bergey Tst 1994–; memb: Br Mycological Soc 1961–, Soc Gen Microbiology 1962–, American Soc Microbiology 1965–; *Books* Soil Organisms (1971), Methods in Soil Microbiology (1972), Biology of Actinomycetes (1983); *Recreations* opera, swimming, gardening, politics; *Style*— Prof Stanley Williams; ✉ 10 Brimstage Ave, Bebington, Merseyside L63 5QH (☎ 0151 608 5385); Dept Genetics and Microbiology, Liverpool University, PO Box 147, Liverpool L69 3BX (☎ 0151 794 5125, fax 0151 794 4401, telex 627095 UNILPL G)

WILLIAMS, Susan Elizabeth; da of Ernest George Fost, of Congresbury, Avon, and late of Royal Horse Artillery, and Kathleen Beatrice Maud, *née* Hewlett; *b* 30 Oct 1942; *Educ* Weston-super-Mare GS for Girls, Bristol Royal Hosp for Sick Children (Registered Sick Children's Nurse), Bristol Royal Hosp (Registered Gen Nurse), Univ of London (Extramural Dip in Nursing), Wolverhampton Poly (CertEd, BEd, Post Grad Dip in Psychology); *m* 1, 1964, Dennis Norman Carnevale (d 1975); 1 s (Marcus b 1968), 1 da (Maria b 1964); m 2, 7 May 1976 (sep), Keith Edward Williams, s of Philip Edward Williams, of Shrewsbury; *Career* ward sister Bristol Children's Hosp 1972–75, nurse tutor Shrewsbury Sch of Nursing 1976–80, sr nurse tutor Dudley Health Authy 1980–84, regnl nurse (educn and res) W Midlands RHA 1984–87, chief nurse advsr and dir of nurse educn Bromsgrove and Redditch Health Authy 1987–88, regnl dir of nursing and quality assurance W Midlands RHA 1988–93, dep dir of nursing NHS Management Executive 1993–94, dir of Nursing Greater Glasgow Community and Mental Health Tst 1994–; memb Nat Tst; memb RCN 1960–; *Recreations* mountain walking, classical music; *Style*— Ms Susan Williams; ✉ Trust Headquarters, Gartnavel Royal Hospital, 1055 Great Western Road, Glasgow G12 0XH (☎ 0141 211 3647)

WILLIAMS, Susan Eva; MBE (1958); da of Robert Henry Williams (d 1963), of Bonvilston House, S Glamorgan, by his w, Dorothy Marie (d 1976); *b* 17 Aug 1915; *Educ* St James's Sch W Malvern; *m* 1950, Charles Crofts Llewellyn Williams (d 1952), s of Charles Williams, of The Heath, Cardiff (d 1912); *Career* Wing Offr WAAF WWII; JP Glamorgan 1961, High Sheriff 1968; DL Glamorgan 1973, HM Lt for S Glamorgan 1981–85; Lord Lt S Glamorgan 1985–90; *Recreations* nat hunt racing; *Clubs* RAF; *Style*— Mrs Susan Williams, MBE; ✉ Caercady, Welsh St Donat's, Cowbridge, S Glamorgan CF71 7ST (☎ 0144 677 2346)

WILLIAMS, Prof Thomas Eifion Hopkins; CBE (1980); s of David Garfield Williams (d 1974), of Cwmtwrch, Breconshire, and Annie Mary, *née* Hopkins (d 1949); *b* 14 June 1923; *Educ* Ystradgynlais GS, Univ of Wales (BSc, MSc), Univ of Durham (PhD), Univ of California Berkeley (Post Doctoral); *m* 28 June 1947, (Elizabeth) Lois, da of Evan Rees Davies (d 1979), of Cwmtwrch, Breconshire; 1 s (Huw b 2 Feb 1960), 2 da (Maelor b 5 April 1948, Amanda b 19 May 1955); *Career* res Stressman Sir W G Armstrong Whitworth Aircraft 1945, asst engr Trunk Rds Div Glamorgan CC 1946, asst lectr Univ Coll of Swansea 1947, lectr and reader King's Coll Univ of Durham 1948–63, resident conslt engr RT James & Ptnrs 1952, visiting prof Northwestern Univ Illinois 1957, reader and prof Univ of Newcastle upon Tyne 1963–67, res prof Dept of Civil Engrg and Transportation Univ of Southampton 1983–93 (prof 1967–83, emeritus prof 1993–); memb and chm NEDO EDC Civil Engrg 1969–78, chm Dept of Tport Trunk Rd Assessment Standing Advsy Ctee 1980–87, pres Inst of Highway Engrs 1979–80, memb Public Policy Ctee RAC 1981–, memb Cncl Church Schs Co 1982–90, visitor Traffic Engr Div Tport & Rd Res Laboratory 1982–88; specialist advsr: H of C Tport Select Ctee 1989, House of Lords Euro Communities Ctee 1990; CEng, FICE, FIHT, FCIT; *Books* ed: Urban Survival & Traffic (1961), Inter-City VTOL: Traffic & Sites (1969), Transportation & Environment (1973), Urban Road Appraisal Report (chm, 1986); *Recreations* music; *Clubs* RAC; *Style*— Prof Thomas Williams, CBE; ✉ Willowdale, Woodlea Way, Ampfield, Romsey, Hants SO51 9DA (☎ 01703 253 342)

WILLIAMS, Walter Gordon Mason; CB (1983); s of Rees John Williams DSO (d 1960), of Cardiff, and Gladys Maud Williams, *née* Hull (d 1967); *b* 10 June 1923; *Educ* Cardiff HS, Coll of Estate Mgmnt; *m* 1950, Gwyneth Joyce, da of Thomas Gwyn Lawrence (d 1941), of Caerphilly; 2 da (Lois, Ann); *Career* chartered surveyor; district valuer: Tower Hamlets 1967–68, Westminster 1968–69; superintending valuer North Midlands 1969–73, asst chief valuer 1973–79, dep chief valuer (under sec) 1979–83, vice pres London Rent Assessment Panel 1984–94; *Recreations* reading, music, theatre, rugby union football; *Style*— Walter Williams, Esq, CB; ✉ 33A Sydenham Hill, London SE26 6SH (☎ 0181 670 8580)

WILLIAMS, Sir William Maxwell Harries (Max); kt (1983); s of Llwyd and Hilary Williams; *b* 18 Feb 1926; *Educ* Nautical Coll Pangbourne; *m* 1951, Jenifer, da of Rt Hon Edward Leslie Burgin (d 1945); 2 da; *Career* served 178 Assault Fd Regt RA Far East (Capt) 1943–47; admitted slr 1950; sr ptnr: Clifford-Turner 1984–87, Clifford Chance 1987–90; non-exec dep chm: Royal Insurance Holdings plc 1992–95 (dir 1985–), 3i Group plc 1993–96 (dir 1988–); memb Cncl Law Soc 1962–85 (pres 1982–83), Royal Cmmn on Legal Servs 1976–79, memb Ctee of Mgmnt of Inst of Advanced Legal Studies 1980–86, Crown Agents for Overseas Govts and Admin 1982–86, lay memb Stock Exchange Cncl 1984–91, chm Review Bd for Govt Contracts 1986–93, memb Stock Exchange Disciplinary Appeals Ctee 1989–; chm Police Appeals Tbnl 1993–; hon memb: Canadian Bar Assoc, American Bar Assoc; memb Cncl Wildfowl Trust (hon treas 1974–80, currently vice pres); pres City of London Law Soc 1986–87; Master Worshipful Co of Slrs' 1986–87; Hon LLD Univ of Birmingham 1983; *Recreations* fishing, golf, ornithology; *Clubs* Garrick; *Style*— Sir Max Williams; ✉ 200 Aldersgate Street, London EC1A 4JJ (☎ 0171 600 1000, fax 0171 600 5555)

WILLIAMS, William Trevor (Bill); s of Percy Trevor Williams (d 1987), of Liverpool, and Edith, *née* Hible; *b* 3 June 1935; *Educ* Liverpool Coll Sch; *m* 1, 23 June 1956, Jane Williams; 2 s (Bruce b 1956, Shaun b 1959), 1 da (Heidi b 1961); m 2, 25 March 1967, Pamela Hilda, da of Albert Victor Saunders (d 1988), of Westminster; 1 da (Justine b 1970); *Career* Nat Serv RAF 1953–55; mangr RMC Ltd: Wales 1963–73, E Midlands 1973–76, London 1976–78; divnl dir North of England RMC (UK) Ltd 1978–84, md Hall & Co Ltd 1984–93; tstee Surrey Vol Serv Cncl 1996–; Freeman City of London, Liveryman Worshipful Co of Builders Merchants; *Recreations* fly-fishing, gardening; *Clubs* Flyfishers', Bishopstoke Fishing; *Style*— Bill Williams, Esq; ✉ Quarry House, Springbottom Lane, White Hill, Bletchingley, Surrey RH1 4QZ (☎ 01737 643876)

WILLIAMS, Col William Trevor (Bill); s of Francis Harold Williams (d 1951), and Ethel Mabel, *née* Gwyther (d 1964); *b* 16 Oct 1925; *Educ* Whitchurch GS, Univ of Kent (MA); *m* 6 Feb 1951, Elizabeth, da of Brig A H Goldie (d 1967); 2 s (Stephen b 15 May 1952, Richard b 16 Nov 1961), 2 da (Mandy b 11 June 1958, Mary b 13 April 1967 d 1994); *Career* enlisted Grenadier Gds 1943, cmmnd Black Watch, served with Royal Scots RCT, GS until 1977, served Malaysia, South America, Ethiopia, Libya, Germany and Singapore, ret as full Col; dir SATRA (GB) 1978–79, dir gen Engineering Industries Association 1980–; memb SATRO; FIMgt 1965, FCIS 1979, MCIT 1980; *Recreations* golf, photography; *Clubs* IOD; *Style*— Col Bill Williams; ✉ 15 Mill Lane, Lower Harbledown, Canterbury, Kent CT2 8NE (☎ 01227 768170)

WILLIAMS-BULKELEY, Michael; yr s of Lt-Col Sir Richard Harry David Williams-Bulkeley, 13 Bt (d 1992), and Renée Arundell, *née* Neave (d 1994); *b* 2 April 1943; *Educ* Eton; *m* 4 May 1968, Ellen-Marie, eldest da of L Falkum-Hansen (d 1972), of Oslo, Norway; 2 s (James b 1970, David Haakon b 1973); *Career* Lt Welsh Gds, served Aden 1965–66; dir: CT Bowring Reinsurance Ltd 1981–89, Bowring Int Insur Brokers Ltd 1988–91; md: Marsh & McLennan Worldwide 1988–91, Adams Johnson Green Ltd 1991; *Recreations* golf, gardening, shooting; *Clubs* Boodle's, New Zealand GC; *Style*— Michael Williams-Bulkeley, Esq; ✉ Pigeon Hill, Lilley Bottom, nr Luton LU2 8NH (☎ 01582 31971)

WILLIAMS-BULKELEY, Sir Richard Thomas; 14 Bt (E 1661), of Penrhyn, Caernarvonshire; er s of Sir Richard Harry David Williams-Bulkeley, 13 Bt, TD, JP (d 1992), and Renée Arundell, *née* Neave (d 1994); *b* 25 May 1939; *Educ* Eton; *m* 1964, Sarah Susan, eldest da of Rt Hon Lord Justice (Sir Henry Josceline) Phillimore, OBE (d 1974); 2 s (Richard Hugh b 1968, Harry David b (twin) 1968), 1 da (Victoria Mary b 1973); *Heir* s, Richard Hugh Williams-Bulkeley b 8 July 1968; *Career* Capt Welsh Gds 1963; High Sheriff Gwynedd 1993–94; FRICS; *Recreations* astronomy; *Clubs* Army and Navy; *Style*— Sir Richard Williams-Bulkeley, Bt; ✉ Red Hill, Beaumaris, Anglesey, Gwynedd LL58 8YS

WILLIAMS OF CROSBY, Baroness (Life Peer UK 1993), of Stevenage in the County of Hertfordshire; Prof Shirley Vivian Teresa Brittain Williams; PC (1974); da of Prof Sir George Catlin and the writer, Vera Brittain (Mrs Catlin); *b* 27 July 1930; *Educ* Somerville Coll Oxford, Columbia Univ New York; *m* 1, 1955 (m dis 1974), Prof Bernard Williams; 1 da (Hon Rebecca Clare); m 2, 19 Dec 1987, Prof Richard E Neustadt; *Career* contested (Lab): Harwich 1954 and 1955, Southampton Test 1959; MP (Lab) Hitchin 1964–74, Hertford and Stevenage 1974–79; MP (SDP) Crosby 1981–83 (by-election, converted Cons majority of 19,272 to SDP one of 5,289); PPS to Min of Health 1964–66, Parly sec Miny of Lab 1966–67; Min of State: Educn and Sci 1967–69, Home Office 1969–70; oppn spokesman on: Social Serv 1970–71, Home Affrs 1971–73, Prices and Consumer Protection 1973–74 (Sec of State Prices and Consumer Protection 1974–76); Sec of State Educn and Sci and Paymaster Gen 1976–79; chm Fabian Soc 1980 (gen sec 1960–64), memb Lab NEC 1970–81, pres SDP 1982–88 (co-fndr 1981); prof of elective politics Kennedy Sch of Govt Harvard Univ 1988–; memb: Advsy Cncl to Sec-Gen UN Fourth World Women's Conference 1995, Comité des Sages Euro Cmmn 1995, Bd International Crisis Gp NY, Educn Devpt Center Newton MA; tstee Twentieth Century Fund (New York), dir Project Liberty 1990–; visiting fell Nuffield Coll Oxford 1966–74; Godkin lectr Harvard 1979, Janeway lectr Princeton 1990, Regents lectr Calif at Berkeley 1991, Darwin lectr Cambridge 1995, Strathclyde lectr 1995, Dainton lectr Br Library 1995; assoc fell Center for Euro Studies; hon fell: Somerville Coll Oxford, Newnham Coll Cambridge; *Books* Politics is for People (1981), A Job to Live (1985); *Television* Shirley Williams in Conversation (series, 1980), Snakes and Ladders (BBC Diary, 1996); *Recreations* hillwalking, swimming, music; *Style*— The Rt Hon Lady Williams of Crosby, PC; ✉ Kennedy School of Government, 79 John F Kennedy Street, Cambridge, Mass 02138, USA (☎ 00 1 617 495 8866, fax 00 1 617 496 4474)

WILLIAMS OF ELVEL, Baron (Life Peer UK 1985), of Llansantffraed in Elvel, Co Powys; Charles Cuthbert Powell Williams; CBE (1980); s of Dr Norman Powell Williams, DD (d 1943), and Muriel de Lerisson (d 1979), da of Arthur Philip Cazenove; *b* 9 Feb 1933; *Educ* Westminster, Christ Church Oxford (MA), LSE; *m* 1 March 1975, Jane Gillian, da of Maj Gervase Edward Portal (d 1960); *Career* British Petroleum Co Ltd 1958–64, Bank of London and Montreal 1964–66, Eurofinance SA Paris 1966–70, Baring Brothers & Co Ltd 1970–77 (md 1971–77), chm Price Cmmn 1977–79, md Henry Ansbacher & Co Ltd 1980–82, chief exec Henry Ansbacher Holdings plc, chm Henry Ansbacher & Co Ltd 1982–85, dir Mirror Group Newspapers plc 1985–92; *Clubs* Reform, MCC; *Style*— The Rt Hon the Lord Williams of Elvel, CBE; ✉ 48 Thurloe Square, London SW7 2SX

WILLIAMS OF MOSTYN, Baron (Life Peer UK 1992), of Great Tew in the County of Oxfordshire; Gareth Wyn Williams; QC (1978, NI 1993); s of Albert Thomas Williams (d 1964), and Selina Williams (d 1985); *b* 5 Feb 1941; *Educ* Rhyl GS, Queens' Coll Cambridge (MA, LLM); *m* 1, Aug 1962 (m dis), Pauline, da of Ernest Clarke (d 1962); 1 s (Hon Daniel b 1969), 2 da (Hon Martha b 1963, Hon Emma b 1966); m 2, 1994, V M Russell; 1 da (Hon Imogen); *Career* called to the Bar Gray's Inn 1965 (bencher 1991), recorder of the Crown Court 1978, ldr Wales and Chester circuit 1987–89, head of chambers; chm Bar Cncl 1992; pres: Prisoners' Rights 1993, Cwlth and Ethnic Bar Assoc 1993, Welsh Coll of Music and Drama 1993; memb Cncl of Justice 1993, memb Eire Bar (King's Inns) 1993; pro-chllr Univ of Wales 1994, fell Univ Coll of Wales Aberystwyth 1993; *Style*— The Rt Hon Lord Williams of Mostyn, QC; ✉ Poplars Farmhouse, Evenlode, Glos GL5 0NN; Farrar's Building, Temple, London EC4Y 7BD (☎ 0171 583 9241, fax 0171 583 0090)

WILLIAMS-WYNN, Sir (David) Watkin; 11 Bt (E 1688), of Gray's Inn, Co Middx; DL (Clwyd 1969); s of Sir (Owen) Watkin Williams-Wynn, 10 Bt, CBE, JP (d 1988), and his 1 w, Margaret Jean, *née* McBean; *b* 18 Feb 1940; *Educ* Eton; *m* 1, 1968 (m dis 1981), (Harriet) Veryan Elspeth, da of late Gen Sir Norman Hastings Tailyour, KCB, DSO; 2 s (Charles Watkin b 1970, Robert Watkin b 1977), 2 da (Alexandra 1972, Lucinda b (twin) 1972); m 2, 1983, Victoria Jane, da of Lt-Col Ian Dudley De Ath, DSO, MBE (d 1960), and formerly w of Lt-Col R E Dillon, RM; 2 s (Nicholas Watkin b 1988, Harry Watkin b (twin) 1988); *Heir* s, Charles Watkin Williams-Wynn b 1970; *Career* Lt Royal Dragoons 1959, Maj Queen's Own Yeo 1970; memb Agric Lands Tbnl (Wales) 1978; High Sheriff Clwyd 1990; *Style*— Sir Watkin Williams-Wynn, Bt, DL; ✉ Plas-yn-Cefn, St Asaph, Clwyd LL17 0EY (☎ 01745 582200)

WILLIAMS-WYNNE, Col John Francis; CBE (1972), DSO (1945), JP (Gwynedd 1974); s of Maj Frederick Williams-Wynn, CB (s of Lady Annora Williams-Wynne, yr da of 2 Earl Manvers (Earldom extinct 1955), and ggs of Sir Watkin Williams-Wynn, 4 Bt, by his 2 w Charlotte, *née* Grenville, aunt of Richard Grenville, 1 Duke of Buckingham); Col Williams-Wynne took the name Williams-Wynne instead of Williams-Wynn in 1940; *b* 9 June 1908; *Educ* Oundle, Magdalene Coll Cambridge; *m* 1938, Margaret Gwendolen Hayward (d 1991), da of Rev George Eliot Roper; 1 s (William Robert Charles Williams-Wynne, *qv* b 7 Feb 1947), 2 da (Merion; m 1, Maj Peter Abbot-Davies; 2 s; m 2, HH Sayyid Faher bin Taimour Al-Said; Jane Margaret; m 15 Earl of Home, *qv*; 1 s, 2 da); *Career* RA 2 Lt 1929, served WWII India and Burma, Col 1954, Hon Col 7 Cadet Bn Royal Welsh Fus 1964–74; Parly candidate (C) Merioneth 1950; pres: Wales and Monmouth Cons and Unionist Assoc 1948–49, Royal Welsh Agric Soc 1967–68 (chm Cncl 1972–76), Timber Growers' Orgn 1974–76; former chm BBC Wales Agric Advsy Ctee, chm and md Cross Foxes Ltd; chm Advsy Ctee Miny of Agric Experimental Farm Trawscoed 1955–76, fndr and chm Flying-Farmers Assoc 1974–82 (pres 1982); memb: Gwynedd River Bd 1957–63, Nat Parks Cmmn 1961–66, Forestry Cmmn 1963–65, Forestry Ctee of GB 1967–76, Prince of Wales's Ctee 1971–76, Airline Users' Ctee CAA 1973–80; pt/t memb Merseyside and N Wales Electricity Bd 1953–65; constable of Harlech Castle 1964–; Merioneth: JP 1950, DL 1953, Vice-Lt 1954, Lt 1957–74; Gwynedd: JP 1974, Lt 1974–80, Vice Lord-Lt 1980–85; CStJ, FRAgS; *Clubs* Pratt's, Army and Navy; *Style*— Col John Williams-Wynne, CBE, DSO, JP; ✉ Peniarth, Tywyn, Merioneth, Gwynedd LL36 9UD (☎ 01654 710178)

WILLIAMS-WYNNE, William Robert Charles; s of Col John Francis Williams-Wynne, CBE, DSO, JP, *qv*, and late Margaret Gwendolin, *née* Roper (d 1991); *b* 7 Feb 1947; *Educ* Packwood Haugh, Eton; *m* 18 Oct 1975, Hon Veronica Frances, da of Baron Buxton of Alsa, MC, of Oldhall Farm, Stiffkey, Norfolk; 3 da (Chloë b 14 Oct 1978, Leonora b 20 Oct 1980, Rose b 17 Feb 1983); *Career* Williams Wynne Farms 1969, Mount Pleasant Bakery 1983; JP 1974; contested Gen Election as Cons candidate for Montgomery 1974, F and GP RWAgS, memb Cncl RASE, chm WASEC, cmmr Nat Parks 1983, memb Prince of Wales Ctee 1983; FRICS 1972; *Style*— William Williams-Wynne, Esq; ✉ Williams Wynne Farms, Tywyn, Gwynedd LL36 9LG (☎ 01654 710101/2, fax 01654 710103)

WILLIAMSON, Anthony Evelyn (Tony); CBE (1990); s of Arthur Evelyn Williamson (d 1944), and Lucy; *b* 2 Jan 1932; *Educ* East Lane Secondary Modern, Willesden Tech Coll; *m* 17 Sept 1955, Sylvia Elizabeth, da of James Lawler (d 1969); 2 da (Sandra b 1960, Joanne b 1962); *Career* md Hoover plc UK 1986–92; vice-chm Queen's Park Rangers FC until 1987 (resigned); Freeman City of London; Liveryman Worshipful Co of the Makers of Playing Cards; *Recreations* sport, golf; *Style*— Tony Williamson, Esq, CBE; ✉ 7 Crofta, Lisvane, Cardiff CF4 5EW

WILLIAMSON, Anthony William (Tony); OBE; s of Rev Joseph Williamson (d 1988), of St Paul's, Dock St, London, and Audrey Hollist, *née* Barnes (d 1974); *b* 2 Sept 1933; *Educ* Marlborough, Trinity Coll Oxford, Cuddesdon Theological Coll Oxford; *m* 10 Oct 1959, Barbara Jane, da of Louis Freeman (d 1970), of Gullet Lane, Kirby Muxloe, Leicester; 3 s (Paul Joseph b 19 March 1962, Hugh Anthony b 3 May 1964, Ian Thomas b 17 Jan 1967), 1 da (Ruth Elizabeth b 16 Sept 1960); *Career* Nat Serv 1951–53; fork-lift driver Pressed Steel Co Cowley Oxford (now Rover Cowley) 1958–87; ordained: deacon 1960, priest 1961; chm: BBC Radio Oxford Local Radio Cncl 1970–73, TGWU Cowley Body Plant 1971–87; currently diocesan dir of educn (schools) Oxford; Oxfordshire CC: memb 1973–88, jt ldr 1985–87, jt chm of educn 1987–88; Oxford City Cncl: memb 1961–67 and 1970–88, former chm of housing, ldr 1980–83, Lord Mayor 1982–83; *Recreations* tennis, hill walking; *Style*— The Rev Canon Tony Williamson, OBE; ✉ 9 The Goggs, Watlington, Oxford OX9 5JX (☎ 01491 612143); Education Dept (Schools), Oxford Diocesan Church House, North Hinksey, Oxford OX2 0NB (☎ 01865 244566)

WILLIAMSON, (Robert) Brian; CBE; *b* 16 Feb 1945; *Educ* Trinity Coll Dublin (MA); *m* June 1986, Diane Marie Christine de Jacquier de Rosée; *Career* PA to Rt Hon Maurice Macmillan MP (later Viscount Macmillan) 1967–71, ed Int Currency Review 1971; GNI Group: md Gerrard & National Holdings plc 1978–89, chm GNI Ltd 1985–89, chm Gerrard & National Holdings plc 1989–; chm LIFFE 1985–88 (dir 1980–88), memb Cncl British Invisible Exports Cncl 1985–88 (memb European Ctee 1988–90), bd memb Securities and Investments Board 1986–, memb Ct Bank of Ireland 1990– (dir Bank of Ireland British Holdings 1986–90), dir Fleming International High Income Investment Trust plc 1990–, dir Electra Investment Trust 1994–; dir NASDAQ Int Bd 1993–; govr at large Nat Assoc of Securities Dealers (USA) 1995; dir The River and Rowing Museum Henley 1992–94; Parly candidate (C): Sheffield Hillsborough 1974, Truro 1976–77; cmmnd HAC 1975; FRSA 1991; *Clubs* Pratt's, Kildare Univ (Dublin); *Style*— Brian Williamson, Esq, CBE; ✉ Gerrard & National Holdings plc, Cannon Bridge, 25 Dowgate Hill, London EC4R 2GN (☎ 0171 337 3500)

WILLIAMSON, David Francis; CB (1984); s of late Samuel Charles Wathen Williamson, of Bath, and late Marie Eileen Williamson; *b* 8 May 1934; *Educ* Tonbridge, Exeter Coll Oxford (MA); *m* 1961, Patricia Margaret, da of Eric Cade Smith, of Broadclyst, Exeter; 2 s; *Career* civil servant; MAFF 1958–65 and 1967–77, seconded to HM Dip Serv for Kennedy Round Trade Negotiations 1965–67, dep dir Gen Agric European Cmmn Brussels 1977–83, dep sec Cabinet Office 1983–87, sec gen Euro Cmmn Brussels 1987–; *Style*— David Williamson, Esq, CB; ✉ European Commission, 200 Rue de la Loi, 1049 Brussels, Belgium

WILLIAMSON, David Geoffrey; o s of Geoffrey Williamson (d 1976), of Folkestone, Kent, and Margaret Lloyd, *née* Roberts (d 1988); *b* 25 Feb 1927; *Educ* Merchant Taylors'; *Career* publishing asst Geoffrey Bles Ltd 1945–50, editorial asst Burke's Peerage Ltd 1950–53, re-joined Geoffrey Bles Ltd 1953–58, co-fndr and mangr antique dealing co 1958–71, freelance contributor to all Burke's Peerage publications (rising to sr contributing ed) until 1982; princ contrib: Burke's Guide to the Royal Family (1973), Burke's Presidential Families of the United States of America (1975, 2 edn 1981), Burke's Royal Families of the World (vol I, 1977, vol II, 1980); Debrett's Peerage Ltd: joined as co-ed Debrett's Peerage and Baronetage 1983, ed Debrett's Distinguished People of Today (now People of Today) 1988 (sr ed subsequent edns until 1995), consltg ed Debrett's Peerage Ltd 1995–; freelance contrib to magazines, newspapers and television on genealogical and royal subjects; life memb Soc of the Friends of St George's and Descendants of the Knights of the Garter; memb: Association of Genealogists and Record Agents (AGRA) (chm Cncl 1985–89, memb Cncl 1994–), Exec Ctee English Genealogical Congress 1991– (pres 7th Congress 1997), The Bookplate Soc 1995–; FSA 1991, FSA Scot 1982, FSG 1983; *Books* The Counts Bobrinskoy - A Genealogy (1962), Debrett's Book of the Royal Engagement (with Jean Goodman, 1986), Debrett's Kings and Queens of Britain (1986), Debrett's Kings and Queens of Europe (1988), Debrett's Presidents of the United States of America (1989), Kind Heart and Coronet: A selection of genealogical work by Patrick Montague-Smith (ed with Charles Kidd, 1989), Debrett's Guide to Heraldry and Regalia (1992), The Imperial House of Mexico (contrib, 1994), Brewer's British Royalty (1996); *Recreations* genealogy, reading, television, numismatics, visual arts, archaeology, travel; *Clubs* Royal Over-Seas League; *Style*— David Williamson, Esq, FSA; ✉ 7 Bonchurch Road, London W10 5SD (☎ 0181 968 5420); Debrett's Peerage Ltd, 73–77 Britannia Road, London SW6 2JY (☎ 0171 736 6524, fax 0171 731 7768)

WILLIAMSON, David Stewart Whittaker; JP (1972); s of John Watt Williamson (d 1951), and Annie Simpson, *née* Stewart (d 1989); *b* 18 Jan 1943; *Educ* Hamilton Acad, Univ of Glasgow; *m* 1 March 1969, Joy Delia Francis, da of Walter Elliot Francis Wilson (d 1959); 2 s (Robin b 1970, John b 1979), 2 da (Jill b 1972, Nicola b 1975); *Career* CA in private practice, ptnr David Williamson 1967–; pt/t lectr in accountancy Univ of Glasgow 1966–76; memb Local Authy Accounts in Scotland 1986–93; cncllr (Cons): Burgh of Hamilton 1966–75, Hamilton Dist 1975–84; magistrate 1973–75; *Recreations* tennis, hillwalking, swimming, politics; *Style*— David Williamson, Esq, JP; ✉ 3 Alder Ave, Hamilton, Lanarkshire ML3 7LL (☎ 01698 422882); David Williamson, Chartered Accountant, 47 Cadzow St, Hamilton ML3 6ED (☎ 01698 284888)

WILLIAMSON, Hazel Eleanor (Mrs Harvey Marshall); QC (1988); da of Geoffrey Briddon, of Barton on Sea, Hants, and the late Nancy Briddon, *née* Nicholson; *b* 14 Jan 1947; *Educ* Wimbledon HS for Girls GPDST, St Hilda's Coll Oxford (BA, MA); *m* 1, 24 June 1969, R Williamson; m 2, 16 Sept 1983, H Marshall, FRICS; *Career* called to the Bar Gray's Inn 1972 (Atkin Scholar), bencher 1996; recorder 1996–; chm Chancery Bar Assoc 1994; memb Property Advsy Gp DOE 1994; FCIArb 1992; *Recreations* gardening, opera, occasional offshore sailing; *Style*— Miss Hazel Williamson, QC; ✉ 13 Old Square, Lincoln's Inn, London WC2 (☎ 0171 404 4800, fax 0171 405 4267)

WILLIAMSON, Prof Hugh Godfrey Maturin; s of Thomas Broadwood Williamson (d 1962), and Margaret Frances, *née* Davy; *b* 15 July 1947; *Educ* Rugby, Trinity Coll Cambridge (MA), St John's Coll Cambridge (PhD, DD); *m* 1971, Julia Eiluned, *née* Morris; 2 da (Laura Ruth Eiluned b 13 April 1973, Halcyon Clare b 13 Sept 1975), 1 s (Nathan Paul Maturin b 17 Sept 1978); *Career* Univ of Cambridge: asst lectr in Hebrew and Aramaic 1975–79, lectr 1979–89, reader 1989–92, fell Clare Hall 1985–92; Regius prof of Hebrew Univ of Oxford and Student of Christ Church 1992–; Tyndale fell for biblical res 1970; memb: Soc for Old Testament Study 1975, Soc of Biblical Literature 1985, Cncl Br Sch of Archaeology in Jerusalem, Cncl Palestine Exploration Fund; chm Anglo-Israel Archaeological Soc; Biblical Archaeology Soc Award 1985; FBA 1993; *Books* Israel in the Books of Chronicles (1977), 1 and 2 Chronicles (1982), Ezra, Nehemiah (1985), The Future of Biblical Studies (jt ed, 1986), Annotated key to Lambdin's Introduction to Biblical Hebrew (1987), Ezra and Nehemiah (1987), It Is Written: Essays in Honour of Barnabas Lindars (jt ed, 1988), Jesus Is Lord (1993), The Book called Isaiah: Deutero-Isaiah's Role in Composition and Redaction (1994), Wisdom in Ancient Israel: Essays in Honour of J A Emerton (jt ed, 1995); *Style*— Prof H G M Williamson, FBA; ✉ Christ Church, Oxford OX1 1DP (☎ 01865 278200, fax 01865 278190)

WILLIAMSON, John Peter; s of John William Stephen Williamson (d 1979), of Camberwell, and Ellen Gladys, *née* Naulls; *b* 19 Jan 1943, Amersham, Bucks; *Educ* Addey and Stanhope GS, Hackney Tech Coll, Thames Poly; *m* 17 Oct 1964, Dorothy Shirley Esther, da of Leonard Frederick Farmer, of Blackheath; 2 s (Earl John Grant b 1975, Craig Stephen b 1980); *Career* engr mangr Production Dept Rolex Watch Co 1960–63 (fndr Rolex Sports Club, fndr Rolex Rocketry Soc); jt md and financial controller Dynamic Reading Inst 1968–69, international instr in speed reading, memory and mind training techniques, fndr chm BIM Younger Mangr Assoc 1969–70, gp financial controller, co sec and asst md Hunter-Print Group plc 1971–74, asst to Company Controller ITT/STC 1975 (responsibility for 26 Divs); corp planner; UK chm: Investigations, Operational Reviews and Computer Audits (mangr 1976–80), ITT Bd (USA); conslt: C E Heath & Co insurance brokers, Liberty Life, Trident Life, Sun Life Unit Services, Coll of Taxation; princ J P Williamson & Co 1981–86; md: Prestige Micro-Systems Ltd 1979–, Guardian Independent PLC 1983–, Guardian Independent Executors Ltd 1994–, Guardian Independent Wills & Trusts Ltd 1994–, Guardian Independent Group International Ltd 1995–, Guardian Independent Finance Corporation Ltd 1995–, Guardian Independent General Insurance Services Ltd 1995–, Guardian Independent Publishing Corporation Ltd 1995–; licensed credit broker; fndr chm and conslt to several local and nat computer clubs 1975–80, co fndr Assoc of London Hobby Computer Clubs 1980; chm SE London Area Soc of Chartered Accountants 1992–93; memb: Inst of Chartered Accountants SIB Vetting Panel, Main Ctee, Ethics and Regulation Review Panel and London Business Bd London Soc of Chartered Accountants, Regional Ctee Life Insur Assoc, Million Dollar Round Table Inner Circle (top 6 per cent of fin advsrs in world), LIA Achievement Forum Inner Circle (top 39 fin advsrs in UK); fndr memb I Fin Planning 1987; Freeman City of London 1986; memb: PIA, FIMBRA, Life Insurance Assoc; FCA, CInstSMM, MCIM, FInstD, MIMgt, MIIM, MLIA (Dip), ALIMA (Dip), ACFB; *Books* author ITT/STC EDP Audit Manual; *Recreations* computers, reading, shooting, martial arts; *Style*— J P Williamson, Esq; ✉ c/o Guardian Independent PLC, PO Box 56, Eltham, London SE9 1PA (☎ 0181 850 4195, fax 0181 294 1597)

WILLIAMSON, John Robin; s of Samuel Charles Wathen Williamson (d 1991), and Marie Eileen, *née* Denney (d 1962); *b* 11 May 1931; *Educ* Tonbridge, St John's Coll Cambridge (MA); *m* 28 June 1958, Rosemarie Dorothea, da of Rev Carl Hugo Stelzner (d 1967), of St Jacobus, Pesterwitz, Germany; 2 da (Catherine Anne b 1959, (Susan) Jane b 1962); *Career* Iraq Petroleum Co 1956–68, Qatar and Abu Dhabi Petroleum Cos 1968–77, BP plc 1977–82 (mangr Forties Oilfield, gen mangr Exploration and Prodn, dir BP Petrol Devpt Ltd), dir and md oil and gas subsid cos Trafalgar House plc 1984–89; FIMechE, FInstPet; *Style*— John Williamson, Esq; ✉ 56 Palace Court, London W2 4JB

WILLIAMSON, Marshal of the RAF Sir Keith Alec; GCB (1982, KCB 1979), AFC (1968); s of Percy and Gertrude Williamson; *b* 25 Feb 1928; *Educ* Bancroft's Sch, Market Harborough GS, RAF Coll Cranwell; *m* 1953, Patricia Anne, da of Wing Cdr F M N Watts; 2 s, 2 da; *Career* cmmnd 1950, served RAAF Korea, cmd RAF Gütersloh W Germany 1968–70, RCDS 1971, Dir of Air Staff Plans 1972–75, Cmdt RAF Staff Coll 1975–77, ACOS SHAPE Plans and Policy 1977–78; AOC-in-C: RAF Support Cmd 1978–80, RAF Strike Cmd and C-in-C UK Air Forces 1980–82; Chief of Air Staff 1982–85, Air ADC to HM The Queen 1982–85, Marshal of the RAF 1985; *Style*— Marshal of the RAF Sir Keith Williamson, GCB, AFC; ✉ c/o NatWest Bank, Fakenham, Norfolk

WILLIAMSON, (George) Malcolm; s of George Williamson (d 1969), and Margery Williamson; *b* 27 Feb 1939; *Educ* Bolton Sch; *Career* regnl gen mangr (London) Barclays Bank plc 1983–85, memb PO Bd 1985–89, md Girobank plc 1985–89, gp exec dir Standard Chartered Plc 1989–91, md Standard Chartered Bank 1991–92, gp chief exec Standard Chartered plc 1993–; non-exec dir National Grid Group plc 1995–; FCIB, CIMgt; *Recreations* mountaineering, running, chess; *Clubs* Rucksack, Manchester Pedestrian; *Style*— Malcolm Williamson, Esq; ✉ Standard Chartered Plc, 1 Aldermanbury Square, London EC2V 7SB (☎ 0171 280 7500, fax 0171 280 7791)

WILLIAMSON, Sir Malcolm Benjamin Graham Christopher; kt (1996), Hon AO (1987), CBE (1976); s of Rev George Williamson, of Sydney, and Bessie, *née* Wrigley; *b* 1931; *Educ* Barker Coll Hornsby NSW, Sydney Conservatorium of Music; *m* 9 Jan 1960, Dolores Irene Daniel; 1 s, 2 da; *Career* composer, pianist and organist; Master of The Queen's Music 1975–; performed in numerous countries incl: Africa, Australia, Asia, Canada, Denmark, Finland, France, Scandinavia, UK, USA, USSR, Yugoslavia; asst organist Farm St London, organist St Peter's Limehouse London 1958–60, lectr in music Central Sch of Speech and Drama London 1961–62, composer in residence Westminster Choir Coll Princeton NJ 1970–71 (hon fell 1971), composer in residence Florida State Univ 1975, visiting prof of music Univ of Strathclyde 1983–86; creative arts fell Australian Nat Univ 1974–81, Ramasciotti Medical Research Fellowship Univ of NSW 1981; pres: Beauchamp Sinfonietta 1972–, Birmingham Chamber Music Soc 1975–, Univ of London Choir 1976–, Purbeck Festival of Music 1976–, Royal Philharmonic Orchestra (London) 1977–82, Sing for Pleasure 1977–, Br Soc for Music Therapy 1977–, Stevenage Music Soc 1987–, Ditchling Choral Soc 1989–, Finchley Children's Music Group 1991–; vice pres: The Elgar Fndn, St Michael's Singers, Nat Music Cncl of GB, Nat Youth Orch of GB; also involved with: London Adventist Chorale, Primavera Chamber Orch and Ensemble, Michael James Music Tst, Friends of Gaudeamus, Richmond upon Thames Arts Cncl, Cncl of the Friends of The Musicians' Chapel, London Charity Concert Orch, Temple Music Tst, Australian Sinfonia, Macclesfield Arts Festival, Saffron Walden Choral Soc, N Herts Hospice Care Assoc, Westminster Catholic Choristers Tst, Harlow Chorus, Hatfield Philharmonic Chorus, NE London Poly Chorus; Hon DMus: Westminster Choir Coll Princeton 1970, Univ of Melbourne 1982, Univ of Sydney 1982; Hon DUniv Open Univ 1983; *Operatic works* grand operas: Our Man in Havana (also orchestral suite and concert suite for chorus and orch), The Violins of Saint-Jacques, Lucky Peter's Journey; chamber operas: English Eccentrics, The Happy Prince, Julius Caesar Jones, Dunstan and the Devil, The Growing Castle, The Red Sea, The Death of Cuchulain, The Musicians of Bremen; operatic sequence: The Brilliant and the Dark; choral operas and cassations: The Moonrakers, Knights in Shining Armour, The Snow Wolf, Genesis, The Stone Wall, The Winter Star, The Glitter Gang, The Terrain of the Kings, The Valley and the Hill, The Devil's Bridge; ballets: Sinfonia Concertante, The Display, Sun into Darkness, Spectrum, BigfellaTootsquoodgeandNora (sic) (to Pas de Quatre), Perisynthion, Heritage, Have Steps Will Travel (to Piano Concerto no 3); *Orchestral works* incl: Santiago de Espada, Sinfonia Concertante, Sinfonietta, Concerto Grosso, Symphonic Variations, Serenade and Aubade, Epitaphs for Edith Sitwell, The Bridge that Van Gogh Painted, The House of Windsor Orchestral Suite, Fiesta, Ochre, Fanfarade, Ode for Queen Elizabeth, In Thanksgiving - Sir Bernard Heinze, Cortège for a Warrior, Lento for Stings, Bicentennial Anthem, seven symphonies; concertos: three piano concertos, Concerto for Two Pianos and Strings, Organ Concerto, Violin Concerto, Lament in Memory of Lord Mountbatten of Burma, Au Tombeau du Martyr Juif Inconnu; *Chamber music* incl: Variations for Violoncello and Piano, Concerto for Wind Quartet and Two Pianos, Serenade for Flute, Piano and String Trio, Pas de Quatre for Piano and Woodwind Quartet, Pietà, The Feast of Eurydice, Champion Family Album, Channukkah Sketches for Flute and Guitar; *Scores and title music* film scores incl: The Brides of Dracula, Thunder in Heaven, Crescendo, The Horror of Frankenstein, Nothing but the Night, Watership Down (title music and prologue), The Masks of Death, various documentaries; for TV and radio: The Golden Salamander, Bald Twit Lion, Strange Excellency, Choice, Gallery, Chi Ming, Churchill's People, The House of Windsor; musicals: No Bed for Bacon, Trilby; *Choral and vocal works* various works for solo voice and piano and solo voice and orchestra, numerous hymns and psalms, numerous choral works; *Solo piano works* incl: two piano sonatas, seven books of travel diaries, five preludes, Ritual of Admiration, Himna Titu, Springtime on the River Moskva for Piano Duet; *Recreations* literature; *Style*— Sir Malcolm Williamson, AO, CBE; ✉ c/o Campion Press, Sandon, Buntingford, Herts SG9 0QW (☎ 01763 247287, fax 01763 249984)

WILLIAMSON, Dame (Elsie) Marjorie; DBE (1973); da of Leonard Williamson; *b* 30 July 1913; *Educ* Royal Holloway Coll London; *Career* dep vice chllr Univ of London 1970–71 and 1971–72; princ: St Mary's Coll Univ of Durham 1955–62, Royal Holloway Coll 1962–73; lectr in physics Bedford Coll 1945–55; memb Cwlth Scholarship Cmmn 1975–84, fell Bedford Coll London; *Style*— Dame Marjorie Williamson, DBE; ✉ Priory Barn, Lower Raydon, Ipswich, Suffolk (☎ 01473 824033)

WILLIAMSON, Prof Mark Herbert; OBE (1994); s of Herbert Stansfield Williamson (d 1955), and Winifred Lilian, *née* Kenyon (d 1990); *b* 8 June 1928; *Educ* Groton Sch Mass USA, Rugby, ChCh Oxford (DPhil); *m* 5 April 1958, Charlotte Clara Dallas, da of Hugh Macdonald (d 1958); 1 s (Hugh b 1961), 2 da (Emma b 1963, Sophia b 1965); *Career* demonstrator in zoology Univ of Oxford 1952–58, with Scottish Marine Biological Assoc Edinburgh 1958–62, lectr in zoology Univ of Edinburgh 1962–65, prof (fndr and head of Dept) Dept of Biology Univ of York 1965–; FIBiol 1966; *Books* Analysis of Biological Populations (1972), Ecological Stability (1974), Island Populations (1981), Quantitative Aspects of Biological Invasions (1987), Biological Invasions (1996); *Recreations* natural history, walking; *Style*— Prof Mark Williamson; ✉ Dalby Old Rectory, Terrington, York YO6 4PF (☎ 01347 888244); Department of Biology, University of York, York YO1 5DD (☎ 01904 432806, fax 01904 432860)

WILLIAMSON, Martin; s of Albert Williamson (d 1986), and Jocelyn Marjorie, *née* Roe (d 1968); *b* 30 July 1944; *Educ* Wyggeston GS Leicester, Birmingham Catering Coll, Portsmouth Catering Coll, Cornel Univ NY; *m* 29 Jan 1972, Susan Anne Williamson, JP; 1 s (James Andrew b 8 Jan 1982), 1 da (Victoria b 16 Sept 1974); *Career* trainee mangr Strand Hotels Ltd 1964–65, asst mangr Ireland Caterers Fountain Hotel Cowes 1966, Belmont Hotel & Golf Club Bermuda 1966–67; resident mangr: Queen's Hotel Southsea Hants 1968–70, Bay Roc Hotel Montego Bay Jamaica 1970–72; relief mangr Gooderson Group of Hotels Durban SA 1972–73, gen mangr Bear Hotel Havant Hants 1973–84, hotel proprietor (The Miller of Mansfield Goring-on-Thames) 1984–; fndr memb The Master Innholders 1978, Freeman City of London 1978; FHCIMA; *Recreations* rugby, cricket, golf; *Clubs* MCC; *Style*— Martin Williamson, Esq; ✉ Pond House, High Street, South Stoke, Oxon RG8 0JS; The Miller of Mansfield, High St, Goring on Thames, Reading RG8 9AW (☎ 01491 872829, fax 01491 874200)

WILLIAMSON, Neil Morton; s of John Glynn Williamson (d 1987), and Vera May, *née* Morton; *b* 14 May 1943; *Educ* Tonbridge, Worcester Coll Oxford (MA); *Career* Henry Ansbacher & Co Ltd 1965–78 (dir 1972–78), 3i Corporate Finance Ltd 1978– (md 1979–); memb Ct of Assts Worshipful Co of Skinners (Liveryman 1972), Freeman City of London 1970; *Recreations* golf, opera, ballet; *Clubs* East India, Royal and Ancient Golf (St Andrews), Royal St George's Golf, Rye Golf, Walton Health Golf; *Style*— Neil Williamson, Esq; ✉ 3i Corporate Finance Ltd, 91 Waterloo Rd, London SE1 8XP (☎ 0171 928 3131, fax 0171 975 3399)

WILLIAMSON, Sir Nicholas Frederick Hedworth; 11 Bt (E 1642), of East Markham, Notts; s of Maj William Hedworth Williamson (ka 1942), and Diana (who m 2, 1 and last Baron Hailes, and d 1980), o da of Brig-Gen Hon Charles Lambton, DSO, 4 s of 2 Earl of Durham; suc unc, Sir Charles Williamson, 10 Bt (d 1946); *b* 26 Oct 1937; *Educ* Eton; *Heir* none; *Career* Nat Serv cmmnd 4/7 Royal Dragoon Gds 1957; farmer; *Style*— Sir Nicholas Williamson, Bt; ✉ Abbey Croft, Mortimer, Reading, Berks (☎ 0118 933 2324)

WILLIAMSON, Nigel; s of Neville Albert Williamson, now of Arizona, and Ann Maureen Kitson; *b* 4 July 1954; *Educ* Chislehurst and Sidcup GS, UCL; *m* 1976, Dr Magali Patricia; 2 s (Adam b 1977, Piers b 1978); *Career* ed: Tribune 1984–87, Labour Party News 1987–89, New Socialist 1987–89; The Times: political corr and columnist 1989–90, diary ed 1990–92, home news ed 1992–95, Whitehall corr 1995–96; freelance writer for among others The Times, Harpers and Queen, and Mojo 1996–; *Books* The SDP (1982), The New Right (1984); *Recreations* cricket, music, modern fiction; *Clubs* St James's, Skyliners Cricket; *Style*— Nigel Williamson, Esq; ✉ High Beeches, 60 Sutherland Ave, Biggin Hill, Westerham, Kent TN16 3HG (☎ 01959 571127)

WILLIAMSON, Dr Paul Eric Dominic; s of Peter Williamson, of London, and Mary Teresa, *née* Meagher; *b* 4 Aug 1954; *Educ* Wimbledon Coll, Univ of East Anglia (BA, MPhil, LittD); *m* 11 Aug 1984, Emmeline Mary Clare, da of James Mandley (d 1983), of London; *Career* V & A Museum: asst keeper Dept of Sculpture 1979–89, acting keeper Dept of Sculpture 1989, curator Sculpture Collection 1989–96, chief curator 1996–; memb: Wells Cathedral West Front Specialist Ctee 1981–83 (memb Exhibitions Organising Ctee for English Romanesque Art 1984 and Age of Chivalry 1987), wall paintings sub ctee Cncl for the Care of Churches 1987–90, Ctee Br Acad Corpus of Romanesque Sculpture in Br and Ireland, Lincoln Cathedral Fabric Cncl 1990–; expert advsr on sculpture Reviewing Ctee on the Export of Works of Art 1989–, foreign advsr to Int Center of Medieval Art 1991–94; Guild Freeman of Preston 1972; FSA 1983; *Books* An Introduction to Medieval Ivory Carvings (1982), Catalogue of Romanesque Sculpture in the Victoria and Albert Museum (1983), The Medieval Treasury: The Art of the Middle Ages in the Victoria and Albert Museum (ed, 1986, 2 edn 1996), The Thyssen-Bornemisza Collection: Medieval sculpture and works of art (1987), Northern Gothic Sculpture 1200–1450 (1988), Early Medieval Wall Painting and Painted Sculpture in England (ed with S Cather and D Park, 1990), Gothic Sculpture 1140–1300 (1995), European Sculpture at the Victoria and Albert Museum (ed, 1996); author of numerous articles and book reviews in The Burlington Magazine and others; *Recreations* wine, tennis, second-hand bookshops; *Style*— Dr Paul Williamson, FSA; ✉ 53 St Maur Rd, London SW6 4DR (☎ 0171 384 1446); Sculpture Department, Victoria and Albert Museum, South Kensington, London SW7 2RL (☎ 0171 938 8399, fax 0171 938 8404)

WILLIAMSON, Philip Nigel; s of Leonard James Williamson, and Doris, *née* Chapell; *b* 23 Sept 1948; *Educ* Mill Hill, Newcastle Univ (BA, BArch); *m* 27 May 1983, Victoria Lois, da of Joseph Samuel Brown, of Clwyd, N Wales; 2 s (Nicholas James b 1984, Christopher Patrick b 1988); *Career* architect; chm and md: PNW Associates Ltd (architects and interior designers) 1985–, PNW Properties Ltd 1985–; memb RIBA; *Recreations* sailing, tennis, winter sports; *Clubs* The Queen's; *Style*— Philip Williamson, Esq; ✉ Lower Pennington Farmhouse, Lower Pennington Lane, Lymington, Hampshire SO41 8AL (☎ 01590 672699); 6 North Road, Richmond, Surrey (☎ 0181 878 8427)

WILLIAMSON, Robert Algie (Robin); s of Thomas Algie Williamson (d 1955), of Glasgow, and Laura Evelyn, *née* Littler; *b* 11 Aug 1931; *Educ* Merchiston Castle Edinburgh, Harvard Business Sch (Advanced Mgmnt Prog); *m* 1, 25 Aug 1956, (Sheila) Patricia Langdon (d 1985), da of Air-Cdre Richard Grice, OBE, DFC (d 1952); 2 s (Eric Duncan b 26 June 1958, d 1958, Roy Eric b 26 Oct 1963), 2 da (Susan Kay b 18 Feb 1960, Lois Ann b 31 Aug 1961); m 2, 17 Dec 1994, (Helen) Anne Lacy, da of Capt Clive Cyril Anthony Bayley, GC, CIH (d 1949); *Career* RAF Pilot Offr Flying Trg 1954–56; sec and fin dir John Brown & Co (Clydebank) Ltd 1958–68, fin dir Upper Clyde Shipbuilders Ltd Glasgow 1968–69, gp fin dir Samuel Osborn & Co Ltd Sheffield 1969–78, fin dir Surface Electronics Ltd Poole Dorset 1984–93, md Seatic Marine Ltd Dorset 1984–95; dir: Forelle Ltd 1987–92, Forelle Construction Holdings Ltd 1992–, Bourne Steel Ltd 1988–95; chm: Cristie Electronics Ltd 1995–96, Squadron Marine Ltd 1994–96; Freeman Worshipful Co of Cutlers of Hallamshire 1972; MICAS 1954, FIMgt; *Recreations* fishing, sailing; *Clubs* RAF; *Style*— Robin A Williamson, Esq; ✉ Dullar Farm House, Sturminster Marshall, nr Wimborne, Dorset BH21 4AB (home ☎ 01258 857344, office ☎ 01258 858233, fax 01258 858244)

WILLIAMSON, Rt Rev Robert (Roy) Kerr; *see:* Southwark, Bishop of

WILLIAMSON, Prof Robin Charles Noel; s of James Charles Frederick Lloyd Williamson (d 1970), of Hove, Sussex, and Helena Frances, *née* Madden (d 1984); *b* 19 Dec 1942; *Educ* Rugby, Univ of Cambridge and Bart's Med Sch (BA, BChir, MA, MB MChir, MD); *m* 21 Oct 1967, Judith Marjorie, da of Douglas John Bull (d 1982), of London; 3 s (Richard b 1968, Edward b 1970, James b 1977); *Career* house surgn Bart's 1968, surgical registrar Royal Berks Hosp Reading 1971–73, sr surgical registrar Bristol Royal Infirmary 1973–75, clinical and res fell surgery Mass Gen Hosp and Harvard Med Sch 1975–76; Univ of Bristol: lectr in surgery 1977, conslt sr lectr in surgery 1977–79, prof of surgery 1979–87; prof and dir of surgery Royal Postgraduate Med Sch and Hammersmith Hosp 1987–, sr ed British Journal of Surgery 1991–96; Arris and Gale lectr RCS 1977–78, Moynihan fell Assoc of Surgns of GB and I 1979, Hunterian Prof RCS 1981–82, Res Med Br Soc of Gastroenterology 1982, co sec Br Jl of Surgery Soc 1983–91, pres Pancreatic Soc of GB and I 1984–85; sec gen World Assoc of Hepatopancreatobiliary Surgery 1990–94 (treas 1986–90); pres: Int Hepatopancreatobiliary Assoc 1996– (sec-gen 1994–96), Assoc of Upper Gastrointestinal Surgns 1996–; vice pres and chm Scientific Ctee Assoc of Surgns of GB and I 1996–; Finlayson lectr RCS Glasgow 1985, Sir Gordon Bell lectr RACS (NZ) 1988; hon fell Royal Coll of Surgns of Thailand 1992; Hallett prize RCS 1970; Hon PhD Mahidol Univ Thailand 1994; FRCS 1972; *Books* Colonic Carcinogenesis (jtly, 1982), General Surgical Operations (jtly, 1987), Emergency Abdominal Surgery (jtly, 1990), Surgical Management (jtly, 1991), Gastrointestinal Emergencies (jtly, 1991), Scott: An Aid to Clinical Surgery (jtly, 1994); *Recreations* travel, military uniforms and history; *Clubs* United Oxford and Cambridge; *Style*— Prof Robin Williamson; ✉ The Barn, 88 Lower Rd, Gerrards Cross, Bucks SL9 8LB (☎ 01753 889816); Department of Surgery RPMS,

Hammersmith Hospital, Ducane Rd, London W12 0NN (☎ 0181 383 3210, fax 0181 383 3023)

WILLIAMSON, Rosemary; da of Frank Chance, of Bury St Edmunds, and Nancy, *née* Bramley; *b* 28 Dec 1947; *Educ* Ilford Co HS, Worcester Coll of Educn (cert ed), Cambridge Inst (Advanced DipEd); *m* 14 Oct 1972, Albert Michael Williamson, s of Albert Edward Williamson; *Career* maths and PE teacher: Dane Secdy Sch Ilford 1969–70, Eastbrook Comp Barking 1970; peripatetic teacher of dance Newham Educn Authy 1970–72, teacher in charge of PE Elmgreen First Sch Thetford 1972–75, headmistress South Lee Sch 1981– (teacher and dep head 1976–81); inspection team memb for independent schs ISIS East Ctee 1984–, memb IAPS 1981–; *Recreations* fund raising for Cancer Research Campaign, reading, crosswords, jigsaws, travel; *Clubs* Bury St Edmunds Farmers; *Style—* Mrs Rosemary Williamson; ✉ South Lee School, Nowton Road, Bury St Edmunds, Suffolk IP33 2BT (☎ 01284 754654, fax 01284 706178)

WILLIAMSON, Prof Stephen; s of Donald Williamson (d 1986), and Patricia Kathleen Mary, *née* Leyland; *b* 15 Dec 1948; *Educ* Burnage GS Manchester, Imperial Coll of Sci & Technol London (scholar, BSc, PhD, DSc, Sylvanus P Thompson prize); *m* 19 Dec 1970, Zita, da of Philip Mellor (d 1975); 1 s (Samuel Thurston b 1975), 2 da (Rebecca Anne b 1977, Lucy Frances b 1981); *Career* lectr in engrg Univ of Aberdeen 1973–81, reader in engrg Imperial Coll London 1985–89 (sr lectr 1981–85), prof of engrg Univ of Cambridge 1989–, fell St John's Coll Cambridge 1990–; FIEE 1988, fell City and Guilds of London Inst 1990, FIEEE 1995, FEng 1995; *Recreations* gardening, reading; *Style—* Prof Stephen Williamson, FEng; ✉ Cambridge University Engineering Department, Trumpington Street, Cambridge CB2 1PZ (☎ 01223 332664, fax 01223 332662)

WILLINGHAM, Derrick; *b* 29 Dec 1932; *Educ* Brunts GS Mansfield Notts, Nottingham Univ (BA); *m* 1956, Nancy Patricia, *née* Webb; 1 s, 1 da; *Career* dep fin dir and gp controller Dunlop Holdings Ltd 1970–74, fin dir Stone-Platt Industries Ltd 1974–77, chm and chief exec Hayward Tyler Pump Gp 1977–85, pres Sterling Pump Cos 1984–85, sr vice pres Vulcan Industrial Services 1985–87, dep chm TWIL Limited 1991–94 (chief exec 1987–91); chm Br Pump Mfrs Assoc 1984–85; pres Chartered Inst of Mgmnt Accountants 1982–83, pres Br Iron and Steel Prodrs Assoc 1992; non-exec: Ellison Circlips Group Ltd 1992–, Kings Mill Centre for Health Care Servs 1993–; memb House Ctee St Luke's Hospice 1995– (chm 1996–), memb Yorkshire regnl ctee RSA 1996–; pres Rother Valley Cons Assoc 1996–; Master Cutler The Co of Cutlers in Hallamshire 1993–94, Liveryman Worshipful Co of Tin Plate Workers (aka Wire-Workers); FCMA; *Recreations* golf, tennis, theatre, travel; *Clubs* RAC, Lindrick Golf, Harvard Business School Club of London; *Style—* Derrick Willingham, Esq; ✉ Lindrick Lodge, Lindrick Road, Woodsetts, Nr Worksop, Notts S81 8AY (☎ 01909 568276, fax 01909 561758)

WILLINK, Sir Charles William; 2 Bt (UK 1957), of Dingle Bank, City of Liverpool; s of Rt Hon Sir Henry Urmston Willink, 1 Bt, MC, QC (d 1973, ggs of Daniel Willink, sometime Dutch Consul in Liverpool), and his 1 w, Cynthia Frances (d 1959), da of Herbert Morley Fletcher, MD, FRCP, of Harley Street; *b* 10 Sept 1929; *Educ* Eton, Trinity Coll Cambridge (MA, PhD); *m* 7 Aug 1954, Elizabeth, er da of Humfrey Andrewes, of North Grove, Highgate; 1 s, 1 da; *Heir* s, Edward Daniel Willink b 18 Feb 1957; *Career* asst master: Marlborough 1952–54, Eton 1954–85 (housemaster 1964–77); FRSA; *Books* Euripides' Orestes (ed with commentary, 1986); *Recreations* bridge, field botany, music (bassoon); *Style—* Sir Charles Willink, Bt; ✉ 22 North Grove, Highgate, London N6 4SL (☎ 0181 340 3996)

WILLIS, Alan James; CBE (1992); s of William Ross Willis (d 1995), of Dunblane, Scotland, and Georgina Agnes, *née* Cheape (d 1976); *b* 19 Nov 1936; *Educ* Daniel Stewart's Coll Edinburgh, Sch of Architecture Edinburgh Coll of Art (Andrew Grant scholarship, DipArch); *m* 25 March 1967, June, da of George Victor Cook Creasey; 3 s (James Richard b 4 Aug 1970, Andrew Charles b 3 April 1972, Peter Robert b 2 Aug 1973), 1 da (Emma Sophie b 20 July 1977); *Career* architect; with Sir Frank Mears & Partners 1953–56, Architect Res Unit Univ of Edinburgh 1960–63, directing architect Notts Co Architects' Dept 1963–73; county architect: Durham CC 1973–76, Essex CC 1976–90; dir of property servs Essex CC 1990–96; hon treas RIBA 1993–95; winner various Civic Tst and RIBA design awards and commendations 1968–93; RIBA 1960, FRSA 1975; *Recreations* watercolour painting, sailing, model railway construction, art director Chelmsford Cathedral Festival; *Clubs* MCC, Waldringfield Sailing; *Style—* Alan Willis, Esq, CBE; ✉ Waterside, East Street, Coggeshall, Colchester, Essex CO6 1SJ (☎ 01376 561677)

WILLIS, Antony Martin Derek; s of late Thomas Martin Willis, of Marton, NZ, and Dawn Marie, *née* Christensen; *b* 29 Nov 1941; *Educ* Wanganui Collegiate Sch Wanganui NZ, Victoria Univ Wellington NZ (LLB); *m* 1, 10 Feb 1962 (m dis), Diane Elizabeth, da of late Frederick Willis Gorton (d 1987), of Feilding, NZ; 3 da (Kirsty Elizabeth b 13 April 1963, Sara Jane b 7 June 1966, Nicola Mary b 6 Nov 1968); m 2, 12 April 1975, Diana Alice Cockburn, da of Robert Dermot McMahon Williams, of Redhill, Surrey; 1 s (Matthew William Dermot b 22 Aug 1988), 2 da (Charlotte Emily Christensen b 5 Jan 1978, Joanna Catherine Dalrymple b 7 Dec 1981); *Career* slr; ptnr: Perry Wylie Pope & Page NZ 1967–70, Coward Chance London 1970–87 (managing ptnr 1987); Clifford Chance (merged firm of Coward Chance with Clifford Turner): jt managing ptnr 1987–88, sr litigation and arbitration ptnr 1989–; Freeman City of London 1975, Liveryman Worshipful Co of Slrs; memb: Law Soc, City of London Slrs' Co, American Arbitration Assoc, Int Bar Assoc, Wellington Dist Law Soc (NZ); accredited mediator Centre for Dispute Resolution; memb: CPR Inst for Dispute Resolution NY, Int Panel of Distinguished Mediators; FCIArb; *Recreations* music; *Clubs* Reform, Wellington, Hurlingham; *Style—* Antony Willis, Esq; ✉ Clifford Chance, 200 Aldersgate Street, London EC1A 4JJ (☎ 0171 600 1000, direct ☎ 0171 959 0137, fax 0171 600 5555)

WILLIS, David; s of William Willis (d 1986), of Consett, Co Durham, and Rachael Elizabeth, *née* Cant; *b* 13 Jan 1949; *Educ* Consett GS, Univ of Edinburgh (BArch); *m* 12 July 1970, Patricia Ann, da of Charles Cedric Endley, DSO, of Cape Town, S Africa; 2 s (Robert b 1984, Steven b 1988), 1 da (Jennifer b 1978); *Career* architect; ptnr Crichton Lang Willis & Galloway; projects incl: New Lanark Restoration 1974– (RICS/The Times Conservation Award, Europa Nostra Medal of Honour 1988), Old Coll Univ of Edinburgh 1974–87; architect Thirlestane Castle Tst 1987–; dir: The Caledonian Racing Club, Countlocal; RIBA, FRIAS; *Recreations* racehorse owner; *Clubs* Caledonian Racing; *Style—* David Willis, Esq; ✉ 3 Maryfield Place, Bonnyrigg, Midlothian (☎ 0131 663 5487); Crichton Lang Willis & Galloway, 38 Dean Park Mews, Edinburgh EH4 1ED (☎ 0131 315 2940, fax 0131 332 0224)

WILLIS, Frank William; s of Prof Frank McIlveen Willis (d 1991), of South Littleton, Worcs, and Jonette Constance, *née* Van Praag; *b* 6 April 1947; *Educ* Bradford GS, Magdalen Coll Oxford (BA, BPhil); *m* 15 July 1972, Jennifer Carol, da of Cecil Stanley Arnold (d 1964); 2 da (Laura b 1973, Harriet b 1976); *Career* diplomat; third sec FCO 1971, third then second sec HM Embassy Moscow 1972–74, Ecole Nationale D'Administration Paris 1974–75, first sec FCO 1975–79, principal then asst sec DTI 1980–87; controller of advertising IBA 1987–90, dir of advtg and sponsorship ITC 1991–; memb Solus Club; *Recreations* reading, cinema, hill walking; *Style—* Frank Willis, Esq; ✉ ITC, 33 Foley St, London W1P 7LB (☎ 0171 306 7713, fax 0171 306 7717)

WILLIS, Maj-Gen John Brooker; CB (1981); William Noel Willis (d 1976), and Elaine (d 1978); *b* 28 July 1926; *Educ* Redhill Tech Coll; *m* 1959, Yda Belinda Jane, da of Lt-Col G C Firbank, MC (d 1947); 2 s (Christopher Guy b 1960, Hugo b 1968), 2 da (Richenda b 1961, Abigail b 1967); *Career* cmmnd 10 Hussars 1947, cmd 1964–67, Brig 1974, Maj-Gen 1977, DG Fighting Vehicles and Engrg Equipment 1977–81; ret; *Recreations* golf, aviation, amateur dramatics; *Clubs* Army and Navy; *Style—* Maj-Gen John Willis, CB

WILLIS, John Edward; s of Baron Willis (Life Peer; d 1992), and Audrey Mary, *née* Hale; does not use courtesy style of Hon; *Educ* Eltham Coll, Fitzwilliam Coll Cambridge (MA), Univ of Bristol (Postgrad Cert in Radio, Film and TV); *m* 1972, Janet, da of Kenneth Sperrin; 1 s (Thomas b 1975), 1 da (Beth b 1978); *Career* researcher ATV Network Ltd 1969–70; Yorkshire Television: researcher 1970–74, prodr/dir 1975–82, controller of documentaries and current affrs and ed First Tuesday 1983–88; Channel Four Television: controller of factual progs 1988–89, dep dir of progs 1990–92, dir of progs 1993–; memb BAFTA, FRTS 1993; *Awards* incl: BAFTA Best Documentary, Prix Jeunesse and RTS Outstanding Achievement as a Dir awards for Johnny Go Home 1976, Int Emmy, RTS Best Investigative Journalism and Matthew Trust Award for The Secret Hospital 1979, Prix Futura and Bdcasting Critics' Prize for Alice: A Fight for Life 1983, Special Jury Award San Francisco for The Chinese Geordie 1983, 12 int environmental awards for Windscale: The Nuclear Laundry (co-dir) 1983, John Grierson Best Documentary Award for From the Cradle to the Grave 1987, RTS Silver Medal 1988; *Books* Johnny Go Home (1975), Churchill's Few (1983); *Style—* John Willis, Esq; ✉ Channel Four Television, 124 Horseferry Road, London SW1P 2TX (☎ 0171 306 8400, fax 0171 306 8356)

WILLIS, Air Chief Marshal Sir John Frederick; KCB (1993, CB 1991), CBE (1988); s of Frederick Arthur Willis (d 1994), and Kathleen Enid, *née* Grindle (d 1993); *b* 27 Oct 1937; *Educ* Dulwich Coll, RAF Coll Cranwell; *m* 1959, Merrill, *née* Thewliss; 5 c; *Career* RAF Coll Cranwell 1955–58, cmmnd pilot 1958, various appts rising to OC No 27 Sqn (Vulcans) until 1977, staff duties Directorate of RAF Forward Policy then Air Plans Directorate MOD 1977–82, OC RAF Akrotiri Cyprus 1982–84, Dir of Air Staff Briefing MOD 1984, promoted Air Cdre 1985, Chief of Special Weapons Branch SHAPE 1985–89, promoted Air Vice-Marshal 1989, ACDS (Policy and Nuclear) 1989–91, DG Trg (RAF) 1991–92, promoted Air Marshal 1992, AOC-in-C RAF Support Cmd 1992–94, COS RAF Logistics Cmd 1994–95, promoted Air Chief Marshal 1995, Vice Chief of the Defence Staff MOD 1995–; *Clubs* RAF; *Style—* Air Chief Marshal Sir John Willis, KCB, CBE, RAF; ✉ Vice Chief of the Defence Staff, MOD, Room 6177, Main Building, Whitehall, London SW1A 2HB

WILLIS, Prof John Raymond; s of John Vindon George Willis, of Bicester, Oxon, and Loveday Gwendoline, *née* Parkin; *b* 27 March 1940; *Educ* Southall GS, Imperial Coll London (BSc, ARCS, PhD, DIC), Univ of Cambridge (MA); *m* 3 Oct 1964, Juliette Louise, da of Horace Albert Edward Ireland (d 1979); 3 da (Estelle b 1966, Lucy b 1967, Charlotte b 1969); *Career* asst lectr Imperial Coll London 1962–64, res assoc Courant Inst NY 1964–65, asst dir of res Univ of Cambridge 1968–72 (sr asst 1965–67), prof of applied mathematics Univ of Bath 1972–94, prof of theoretical solid mechanics Univ of Cambridge 1994–; ed in chief Jl of the Mechanics and Physics of Solids 1982–92 (jt ed 1992–); memb: SRC Mathematics Ctee 1975–78, SERC Mathematics Ctee 1984–87, Int Congress Ctee, Int Union for Theoretical and Applied Mechanics 1982–90); FIMA 1966, FRS 1992; *Recreations* music, swimming; *Style—* Prof John Willis, FRS; ✉ Department of Applied Mathematics and Theoretical Physics, University of Cambridge, Silver Street, Cambridge CB3 9EW (☎ 01223 339251, fax 01223 337918)

WILLIS, Rear Adm Kenneth Henry George; CB (1981); s of Henry (d 1976), and Elsie Nellie Willis (d 1993); *Educ* St Olave's GS, Jesus Coll Cambridge (BA); *m* Sheila Catherine; 3 da (Lois, Laura, Sharon); *Career* Chief of Staff to C-in-C Naval Home Cmmnd to Sept 1981; dir gen Home Farm Trust Ltd Bristol 1982–88; tstee Fndn Tst for the Mentally Handicapped, tstee Home Farm Tst Retirement Benefits Scheme; MInstD, FRSA; *Recreations* rowing, life-saving, amateur theatricals; *Style—* Rear Adm Kenneth H G Willis, CB; ✉ c/o Barclays Bank, 1 Manvers St, Bath; Bath and County Club, Queen's Parade, Bath

WILLIS, Very Rev Robert Andrew; s of Thomas Willis, of Kingswood, Bristol, and Vera Rosina, *née* Britton (d 1985); *b* 17 May 1947; *Educ* Kingswood GS, Warwick Univ, Worcester Coll Oxford (BA), Cuddesdon Coll Oxford (DipTheol); *Career* ordained: deacon 1972, priest 1973; curate: St Chad's Shrewsbury 1972–75, vicar choral Salisbury Cathedral and chaplain to Cathedral Sch 1975–78, team rector Tisbury Wilts 1978–87, chaplain Cranborne Chase Sch and RAF Chilmark 1978–87, rural dean of Chalke 1982–87, vicar of Sherborne with Castleton and Lillington Dorset 1987–92, chaplain Sherborne Sch for Girls 1987–92, rural dean of Sherborne 1991–92, canon and prebendary of Salisbury Cathedral 1988–92, proctor in convocation 1985–92 and 1994–, dean of Hereford 1992–; memb: Cncl Partnership for World Mission 1990–, Cathedral Fabric Cmmn for England 1994–, C of E Liturgical Cmmn 1994–; govr: Cranborne Chase Sch 1985–87, Sherborne Sch 1987–92; chm of govrs Hereford Cathedral Sch 1993–; sub chaplain OStJ 1991; FRSA 1993; *Books* Hymns Ancient and Modern (contrib, 1983), The Choristers' Companion (jtly, 1989); *Recreations* music, literature, travel; *Clubs* United Oxford and Cambridge Univ; *Style—* The Very Rev Robert Willis; ✉ The Deanery, The Cloisters, Hereford HR1 2NG (☎ 01432 359880, fax 01432 355929)

WILLIS, Robert George Dylan (Bob); MBE (1982); s of Edward Woodcock Willis (d 1982), and Anne Margaret, *née* Huntington; *b* 30 May 1949; *Educ* King Edward VI Royal GS Guildford; *m* 1980, Juliet, da of William and Barbara Smail, of Wilts; 1 da (Katie-Anne b 1984); *Career* former professional cricketer, currently broadcaster and chm Nat Sporting Club; capt: Warwickshire 1980–84, England 1982–84; 90 tests for England, record number of wickets for England on retirement (325); chm In Style Promotions Ltd, cricket commentator Sky Sports; *Books* co-author of nine cricket books; *Recreations* opera, classical music, wine, real ale; *Clubs* MCC, IOD, Nat Sporting, RAC, Surrey CCC, Friends of Covent Garden, Warwickshire CCC; *Style—* Bob Willis, Esq, MBE; ✉ 10 West Place, London SW19 4UH; Café Royal, 68 Regent St, London W1R 6EL (☎ 0171 437 0144, fax 0171 437 5441)

WILLIS, His Hon Judge Stephen Murrell; s of John Henry Willis (d 1936), of Hadleigh, Suffolk, and Eileen Marian, *née* Heard (d 1984); *b* 21 June 1929; *Educ* Christ Church Cathedral Choir Sch Oxford (chorister), Bloxham Sch (scholar); *m* 1, 1953 (m dis 1974), Jean Irene, *née* Eve; 1 s (Rev Geoffrey Willis), 3 da (Susanna (Mrs Ravestein-Willis), Barbara (Mrs Tregear), Jill (Mrs Warner)); m 2, 1975, Doris Florence Davies, *née* Redding; 2 step da (Mrs Jill Lockhart, Mrs Janette Davies); *Career* Nat Serv RS 16 Ind Para Bde Gp 1948–50; articles Gotelee and Goldsmith 1950–55, admitted slr 1955; ptnr: Chamberlin Talbot and Bracey 1955–63, Pearless de Rougemont & Co 1964–85; dep circuit judge 1975–80, rec 1980–85, circuit judge (SE Circuit) 1986–94, chm Lord Chllr's Advsy Ctee for SE London Area 1987–; fndr The Suffolk Singers 1962, fndr and dir The Prodigal Singers 1964–; *Recreations* performing early music, sailing, walking, travel; *Clubs* The Noblemen and Gentlemen's Catch; *Style—* His Hon Judge Stephen Willis; ✉ Croydon Combined Court Centre, Altyre Rd, Croydon CR9 5AB (☎ 0181 681 2533); Villa Callisto, PO Box 1040, Paphos, Cyprus

WILLISON, Lt-Gen Sir David John; KCB (1973), OBE (1958), MC (1945); s of Brig Arthur Cecil Willison, DSO, MC, of Parracombe, N Devon, and Hyacinth D'Arcy, er da of Maj Philip Urban Walter Vigors, DSO, of Basingstoke; *b* 25 Dec 1919; *Educ* Wellington, RMA Woolwich; *m* 1, 1941, Betty Vernon (d 1989), da of Air Vice-Marshal Sir Leslie Bates, KBE; 1 s (Robin), 2 da (Celia, Janet); m 2, 15 Oct 1994, Trisha, *née* Tennent, widow of Cdr Kim Clitherow, RN; *Career* 2 Lt RE 1939, served NW Europe, Java, Malaya, Egypt, Middle East, Berlin and Aden, CO 38 Engr Regt 1960–63; BGS:

Intelligence MOD 1967–70, HQ BAOR Northag 1970–71; dir of Serv Intelligence MOD 1971–72, dep chief of Def Staff Intelligence MOD 1972–75, dir gen Intelligence MOD 1975–78, Col Cmdt RE 1973–82, Chief RE 1977–82; int affrs conslt: Nat Westminster Bank Gp 1980–84, County NatWest Investment Management 1984–91, Pareto Ptnrs 1991–95; pres SJA Western Area Hants 1987–93, chm RE Widows' Soc 1987–91; Freeman City of London; *Clubs* Naval and Military, Royal Lymington Yacht; *Style*— Lt-Gen Sir David Willison, KCB, OBE, MC; ✉ The Old Coach House, Fairfield Close, Lymington, Hants SO41 3NP (☎ 01590 673325)

WILLISON, Sir John Alexander; kt (1970), OBE (1964), QPM (1970), DL (Worcs 1968); s of John Willison Gow Willison (d 1942), and Mabel Willison (d 1964); *b* 3 Jan 1914; *Educ* Sedbergh; *m* 1947, Jess Morris (d 1996), da of late John Bruce; *Career* chief constable: Berwick Roxburgh and Selkirk Police 1952–58, Worcs Constabulary 1958–67, W Mercia Constabulary 1967–74; KStJ 1970; *Recreations* country pursuits; *Style*— Sir John Willison, OBE, QPM, DL; ✉ Ravenhills Green, Lulsley, Worcs (☎ 01886 821688)

WILLMAN, John Romain; s of John Sydney Willman (d 1993), and Millicent Charlotte, *née* Thornton; *b* 27 May 1949; *Educ* Bolton Sch Lancs, Jesus Coll Cambridge (MA), Westminster Coll Oxford (CertEd); *m* 1 April 1978, Margaret, da of Dr John Shanahan (d 1981), of Maida Vale; 1 s (Michael b 1982), 2 da (Kate b 1984, Claire b 1987); *Career* asst teacher Brentford Sch for Girls Middx 1972–76, fin researcher Consumers' Assoc 1976–79, ed of Taxes and Assessment (jls of Inland Revenue Staff Fedn) 1979–83, pubns mangr Peat Marwick Mitchell & Co 1983–85, gen sec Fabian Soc 1985–89, freelance writer and journalist, ed Consumer Policy Review 1990–91; Financial Times: public policy ed 1991–94, features ed 1994–; assoc Inst for Public Policy Res 1990–91; *Books* Make Your Will (1989), Labour's Electoral Challenge (1989), Sorting out Someone's Will (1990), Lloyds Bank Tax Guide (10 edn, 1996), Which? Guide to Planning and Conservation (1990), Work for Yourself (1991), Labour and the Public Services (1994); *Recreations* skiing; *Clubs* Wessex Cave, Inst of Contemporary Art; *Style*— John Willman, Esq; ✉ 143 Jerningham Road, London SE14 5NJ (☎ 0171 639 3826); Financial Times, 1 Southwark Bridge, London SE1 9HL (☎ 0171 873 3854, fax 0171 873 3196, e-mail willman@willman.demon.co.uk)

WILLMER, John Franklin; QC (1967); s of Rt Hon Sir Henry Gordon Willmer (d 1983), of London, and Mary Barbara, *née* Hurd; according to the privately printed History of the Wilmer Family (1888), the name in various spellings is found in public records from the 12th century and existed prior to the Norman Conquest; *b* 30 May 1930; *Educ* Winchester, CCC Oxford (MA); *m* 1, 1958 (m dis 1979), Nicola Ann Dickinson; 1 s (Stephen), 3 da (Susan, Jennifer, Katherine); m 2, 1979, Margaret Lilian, da of Chester B Berryman (d 1995), of Marlborough, Wilts; *Career* Nat Serv 1949–50, 2 Lt TA 1950–57, Capt; called to the Bar Inner Temple 1955, bencher 1975, ldr of the Admiralty Bar 1992–95; ret 1995; memb: Panel of Lloyd's Arbitrators in Salvage Cases 1967–91, Panel from which wreck cmmrs apptd 1967–79, Admiralty Ct Ctee 1980–95; Lloyd's appeal arbitrator in salvage cases 1991–; gen cmmr Income Tax for Inner Temple 1982–, re-appointed a wreck cmmr 1987–; Freeman Worshipful Co of Arbitrators 1992; *Recreations* walking, visiting ancient buildings and archaeological sites; *Clubs* United Oxford and Cambridge Univ; *Style*— J F Willmer, Esq, QC; ✉ Flat 4, 23 Lymington Rd, London NW6 1HZ (☎ 0171 435 9245); 7 King's Bench Walk, Temple, London EC4Y 7DS (☎ 0171 583 0404, fax 0171 583 0950, telex 887491 KBLAW)

WILLMORE, Prof (Albert) Peter; s of Albert Mervyn Willmore (d 1957), and Kathleen Helen, *née* O'Rourke (d 1987); *b* 28 April 1930; *Educ* Holloway Sch London, UCL (BSc, PhD); *m* 1, 1962 (m dis 1972), Geraldine Anne; 2 s (Nicholas b 1963, Andrew b 1964); m 2, 6 Aug 1972, Stephanie Ruth, da of Leonard Alden, of Surrey; 1 s (Ben b 1976), 1 da (Lucy b 1973); *Career* res fell, lectr, reader then prof of physics UCL 1957–72, prof of space res Univ of Birmingham 1972–; Tsiolkowsky Medal USSR 1987; FRAS 1960, memb Int Acad of Astronautics 1996; *Recreations* ancient history, music, sailing; *Style*— Prof Peter Willmore; ✉ School of Physics and Space Research, University of Birmingham, Edgbaston, Birmingham B15 2TT (☎ 0121 414 6452, fax 0121 414 3722, telex 338938)

WILLMOT, Derrick Robert; s of Jack Willmot (d 1982), and Olive, *née* Yarnall (d 1986); *b* 29 April 1947; *Educ* Chesterfield Boys' GS, UCL and UCH London (BDS, LDS); *m* 9 Jan 1971, Patricia Marie, da of Robert Creighton, of San Luis, Menorca, Spain; 2 s (Mark b 1973, Andrew b 1974); *Career* dental house surgn Royal Portsmouth Hosp 1970, gen dental practitioner Ashbourne Derbyshire 1971, sr registrar UCH 1979 (registrar 1977); conslt orthodontist: Chesterfield Royal Hosp 1984–92, Charles Clifford Dental Hosp Univ of Sheffield 1992–; sec Conslt Orthodontists Gp 1989–94, dental advsr Med Protection Soc 1992–, memb Bd Faculty of Dental Surgery RCS England 1994–; memb Round Table 1972–87: Ashbourne, St Albans, Chesterfield; memb Chesterfield Scarsdale Rotary Club 1988–; vice chm Bd of Govrs Chesterfield Sch 1988–92, pres S Yorks BDA 1992–93; FDS 1978, DDO 1980, MOrthRCS 1987; *Style*— Derrick Willmot, Esq; ✉ Ashcroft, Matlock Rd, Walton, Chesterfield, Derbyshire S42 7LD (☎ 01246 239847); Charles Clifford Dental Hospital, University of Sheffield, Sheffield S10 2SZ (☎ 0114 271 7809)

WILLMOTT, Dennis James; CBE (1988), QFSM (1981); s of James Arthur Willmott (d 1970), and Esther Winifred Maude, *née* Styles (d 1989); *b* 10 July 1932; *Educ* St Albans County GS; *m* 1958, Mary Patricia, da of Walter Ball-Currey (d 1975), of Liverpool; 3 s (Stephen, Christopher, Andrew); *Career* served Korea 1951–52, Royal Norfolk Regt 1950–57, Sgt; joined Fire Serv 1957; dep chief fire offr: Isle of Wight Fire Bde 1972–74, Wiltshire 1976; chief staff offr London Fire Bde 1976–81, dep chief fire offr London 1981–83; chief fire offr Merseyside Fire Bde 1983–88; gp contingency mangr Avon Rubber plc 1988–93 (emergency planning conslt 1993–); cncllr: Avon & Cannings Dist Wilts CC 1993–, Kennet District Cncl W Lavington 1991 and 1995–; memb Inst Fire Engrs 1970; *Recreations* walking; *Clubs* Royal Br Legion; *Style*— Dennis Willmott, Esq, CBE, QFSM; ✉ 27 Highlands, Potterne, Devizes (☎ 01380 725672)

WILLMOTT, Edward George; CB (1990), OBE (1980); s of Thomas Edward Willmott (d 1983), of Alvechurch, Worcs, and Eileen Ruth, *née* Murphy; *b* 18 Feb 1936; *Educ* Redditch Co HS, Gonville and Caius Coll Cambridge (MA); *m* 18 June 1960, Sally Penelope, da of George Philip Banyard (d 1946); 2 s (Philip b 1961, Christopher b 1964), 1 da (Georgina b 1962); *Career* RMCS Shrivenham and Camberley 1967–68, DAA and QMG 8 Inf Bde 1969–70, OC 8 Field Sqdn RE 1971–73, memb Directing Staff RMCS Shrivenham 1973–75; CO: 23 Engr Regt 1976, 2 Armd Div Engr Regt 1976–78; Col MGO Secretariat MOD (PE) 1979–80, Cdr 30 Engr Bde, RCDS 1983, dep Cmdt RMCS Shrivenham 1984–85, pres (Army) Ordnance Bd MOD 1986–88 (vice pres 1985–86), dir gen Weapons (Army) MOD 1988–90, ret as Maj-Gen 1991; pres Inst of Royal Engrs 1987–90, Col Cmdt Royal Engrs 1988–; chief exec Construction Indust Trg Bd 1991–; govr Roedean Sch 1994–; Liveryman and Asst Worshipful Co of Engrs 1991; FICE 1989, CEng 1989; *Recreations* walking, gardening; *Clubs* IOD; *Style*— E G Willmott, Esq, CB, OBE

WILLMOTT, Prof John Charles; CBE (1983); s of Arthur George Willmott (d 1960), of Goodmayes, Essex, and Annie Elizabeth, *née* Darby (d 1964); *b* 1 April 1922; *Educ* Bancroft's Sch Woodford, Imperial Coll London (ARCS, BSc, PhD); *m* 10 May 1952, Sheila Madeleine, da of Stanley Dumbell, OBE (d 1966), of Birkenhead; 2 s (Nigel b 24 Sept 1956, Philip b 13 March 1963), 1 da (Stella b 19 April 1954); *Career* serv WWII Lt REME 1942–46; Univ of Liverpool: asst lectr 1948–49, lectr 1949–58, sr lectr 1958–63, reader 1963–64; Univ of Manchester: prof of nuclear physics 1964–67, dir physical labs 1967–89, pro vice chllr 1982–85; memb: Nuclear Physics Bd SERC 1968–73 and 1976–82 (memb Cncl 1978–82), Physical Scis Sub Ctee UGC 1970–80, NATO Sci for Stability Steering Gp 1981–; FInstP 1968; *Books* Tables of Coefficients for the Analysis of Triple Angular Correlations of Gamma-Rays from Aligned Nuclei (1968), Atomic Physics (1975); *Recreations* walking; *Style*— Prof John Willmott, CBE; ✉ 37 Hall Moss Lane, Bramhall, Cheshire SK7 1RB (☎ 0161 439 4169)

WILLMOTT, Peter; s of Benjamin Merriman Willmott (d 1959), and Dorothy Nellie, *née* Waymouth (d 1926); *b* 18 Sept 1923; *Educ* Tollington Sch London, Ruskin Coll Oxford, Univ of London (BSc); *m* 31 July 1948, Phyllis Mary, da of Alec George Noble (d 1966); 2 s (Lewis b 1949, Michael b 1952); *Career* res offr Inst of Community Studies 1960–64, co dir 1964–78, dir Centre for Environmental Studies 1978–80, head central policy unit GLC 1981–83, sr fell Policy Studies Inst 1983–, ed Policy Studies 1988–95; Hon DUniv Orleans 1990; memb Br Sociological Assoc; *Books* Family and Kinship in East London (with Michael Young, 1957), Family and Class in a London Suburb (with Michael Young, 1957), The Evolution of a Community (1963), Adolescent Boys of East London (1966), The Symmetrical Family (with Michael Young, 1973), Inner London: policies for dispersal and balance (with Graeme Shankland and David Jordan, 1977), Inner City Poverty in Paris and London (with Charles Madge, 1981), Unemployment, Poverty and Social Policy: a comparative study in Britain, France and Germany (with Roger Mitton and Phyllis Willmott, 1983), Social Networks, Informal Care and Public Policy (1986), Friendship Networks and Social Support (1987), Social Polarisation and Social Housing: the British and French Experience (with Alan Murie, 1988), Community Initiatives: Patterns and Prospects (1989), Urban Trends 1 (with Robert Hutchison, 1992), Urban Trends 2 (1994); *Style*— Peter Willmott, Esq; ✉ Policy Studies Institute, 100 Park Village East, London NW1 3SR (☎ 0171 468 0468, fax 0171 388 0914)

WILLOCKS, Dr Timothy; s of Joseph Roy Willocks, of Stalybridge, Cheshire, and Ann Willocks; *b* 27 Oct 1957; *Educ* Xaverian Coll Manchester, UCL (BSc), UCH (MB BS); *Career* psychiatrist 1983–; co-fndr Kurtz Theatre Co; *Novels* Bad City Blues (1990), Green River Rising (1994), Bloodstained Kings (1995); *Screenplays* A Martial Kind of Men (1994), Love's Executioner, Usher's Blood, Green River Rising; *Recreations* karate (first dan black belt); *Style*— Dr Timothy Willocks; ✉ c/o Michelle Kass Associates, 36–38 Glasshouse Street, London W1R 5RH (☎ 0171 439 1624, fax 0171 734 3394)

WILLOTT, Robert Graham; s of William Arthur Willott (d 1968), and Vera Joanna, *née* Ashton; *b* 9 March 1942; *Educ* Hitchin GS; *m* 1968, Patricia Ann (d 1981); 2 da (Sian Elizabeth b 1971, Carys Ann b 1973); *Career* Pawley & Malyon CAs: articled clerk 1959–65, mangr 1965–68, ptnr 1968–69; Haymarket Publishing Ltd: ed Accountancy Age 1969–72, publisher 1972–75, dir 1975–76; ICAEW: sec Parly and Law Ctee 1976–78, tech dir 1978–81; Touche Ross (formerly Spicer and Pegler, Spicer & Oppenheim): ptnr 1981–91, i/c Client Devpt Unit 1981–86, fndr and ptnr i/c West End Practice 1987–91, memb Nat Exec 1985–86 and 1988; ptnr Willott Kingston Smith & Assocs 1991–, special prof Sch of Mgmnt and Finance Univ of Nottingham 1992–; ICAEW: past memb Parly and Law Ctee, past memb Company Law Sub-Ctee, Sub-Ctee Auditing Practice Ctee; special advsr DTI; chm Initial Working Pty and advsr to Design Business Assoc 1985–; dir and hon treas The Direct Marketing Association (UK) Ltd 1996–; dir Cheviot Capital Ltd 1985–; memb Mktg Soc, FCA (1976, ACA 1965), MInstD; *Books* Going Public (ed 1971–73), Current Accounting Law and Practice (1976–85 and 1992–), Guide to Price Controls 1977–78 (1977), The Purchase or Redemption by a Company of its Own Shares (Tolley's, jtly 1982), How Advertising Agencies Made Their Profits (1984–90), Financial Performance of Marketing Services Companies (annual, 1991–); *Style*— Robert Willott, Esq; ✉ Willott Kingston Smith & Associates, 10 Bruton Street, London W1X 7AG (☎ 0171 304 4646, fax 0171 304 4647)

WILLOUGHBY, Anthony James Tweedale; s of John Lucas Willoughby, OBE (d 1985), of Mere, Wilts, and Hilary Winifred Tweedale Tait; *b* 29 Sept 1944; *Educ* Westminster; *m* 8 Feb 1975, Joanna, da of Capt David Clayhills-Henderson, of Stoneygroves Farm, by Liff, Dundee; 2 s (James b 23 July 1978, Nicholas b 21 Jan 1982), 1 da (Rachel b 9 June 1976); *Career* admitted slr 1970; The Distillers Co Ltd 1970; ptnr: Herbert Smith 1977–94, Willoughby & Partners (formerly Rouse & Co) 1994–; govr Westminster Sch 1990–; MITMA 1975; *Recreations* cricket, golf, tennis; *Clubs* The Hurlingham, Royal Wimbledon Golf, Blairgowrie Golf, The Royal Tennis Court, Royal & Ancient; *Style*— Anthony Willoughby, Esq; ✉ Willoughby & Partners, The Isis Building, Thames Quay, 193 Marsh Wall, London E14 9SG (☎ 0171 345 8888, fax 0171 345 4555)

WILLOUGHBY, Ven David Albert; s of John Robert Willoughby (d 1982), and Jane May, *née* Lilley; *b* 8 Feb 1931; *Educ* Bradford GS, St John's Coll Univ of Durham (BA, Dip Theol); *m* 1959, Brenda Mary, da of Dennis Watson (d 1953); 2 s (Simon, Andrew); *Career* asst curate: St Peter's Shipley 1957–60, Barnoldswick with Bracewell 1960–62; rector St Chad's New Moston Manchester 1962–72; vicar: Marown IOM 1972–80, St George's with All Saints' Douglas IOM 1980–96; rural dean Douglas 1980–82, archdeacon IOM 1982–96; memb Gen Synod 1982–96; *Recreations* singing and involvement in light entertainment; *Style*— The Ven David Willoughby; ✉ Vista Montana, 19 Glen Vine Park, Glen Vine, Isle of Man, IM4 4EZ (☎ 01624 852493)

WILLOUGHBY, Hon Michael Charles James; s and h of 12 Baron Middleton, MC; *b* 14 July 1948; *Educ* Eton; *m* 1974, Hon Lucy Corinna Agneta Sidney, da of 1 Viscount De L'Isle, VC, KG, GCMG, GCVO, PC; 2 s (James William Michael b 1976, Charles Edward Henry b 1986), 3 da (Charlotte Jacqueline Louise b 1978, Emma Coralie Sarah b 1981, Rose Arabella Julia b 1984); *Career* Lt Coldstream Gds and Queen's Own Yeomanry; farmer; *Style*— The Hon Michael Willoughby; ✉ North Grimston House, Malton, N Yorks YO17 8AX

WILLOUGHBY, Rt Rev Noel Vincent; *see:* Cashel and Ossory, Bishop of

WILLOUGHBY, Prof Peter Geoffrey; OBE (1995), JP (Hong Kong 1982); s of George James Willoughby, LRAM (d 1976), and Enid Alberta Willoughby, LRAM, *née* Nye (d 1995); *b* 17 Feb 1937; *Educ* Merchant Taylors', LSE (LLB, LLM); *m* 20 Jan 1962, Ruth Marylyn, da of Frederick William Brunwin (d 1981); 1 s (Richard Stephen William b 1967), 1 da (Sara Jane Bandele b 1964); *Career* RNVR 1954–59; admitted slr (Hons) 1962, lectr Gibson & Weldon Law Tutors 1962, barr and slr Nigeria 1962, sr lectr The Nigerian Law Sch 1962–66, princ lectr (formerly lectr and sr lectr) The Coll of Law 1966–73, slr Hong Kong 1973, dir of professional legal educn Univ of Hong Kong 1973 (prof of law 1975–86), ptnr Turner Kenneth Brown (London and Hong Kong) 1986–92, conslt to Deacons, Graham & James (Hong Kong) 1992–, dir Guinness Flight and Calder Sarl 1992–; visiting prof City Univ of Hong Kong 1992–, visiting professorial fell Queen Mary and Westfield Coll Univ of London 1996–; Hong Kong: memb Advsy Ctee on Legal Educn 1973–86, chm Ctee of Inquiry into Public Works Dept 1977, chm Ctee on Insur Law Reform 1981–85, chm Hong Kong Law Soc Revenue Law Ctee 1974–87; memb: Hong Kong Law Soc Disciplinary Panel 1983–92, Hong Kong Free Legal Advice Panel 1974–87, Hong Kong Inland Revenue Bd of Review 1977–, Hong Kong Law Reform Cmmn 1980–87, Hong Kong Standing Ctee on Company Law Reform 1983–91, Hong Kong Securities Cmmn 1984–89, Hong Kong Air Traffic Licensing Authy 1987–92, Jt Liaison Ctee on Hong Kong Taxation 1992– (chm 1986–92); memb: English Law Soc 1962 (VAT Ctee 1972–73 and 1988–92, Revenue Law Ctee 1990–92), City of London Slrs' Co 1987–92, Law Soc and Bar Cncl Ctee on China 1988–92; *Publications* Encyclopedia Hong Kong Revenue Law (4 vols, loose-leaf), Registration of Titles in Hong Kong, Guide to Hong Kong Stamp Duty, Guide to Hong Kong Estate Duty;

numerous articles and published public lectures; *Recreations* sailing, sport generally, music, gardening, Asian cats, classic cars; *Clubs* Royal Ocean Racing, Royal Hong Kong Yacht, Royal Fowey Yacht, Lagos Yacht, Alderney Sailing, Royal Channel Islands Yacht, Middlesex CCC; *Style*— Prof Peter Willoughby, OBE, JP; ✉ Old Mill House, La Hêche, St Anne, Alderney, Channel Islands (☎ 01481 823925, fax 01481 823228); Deacons, Graham & James, Alexandra House, 3rd-6th Floors, Hong Kong (☎ 00 8522 825 9211, fax 00 8522 810 0431)

WILLOUGHBY, Philip John; JP (City of London 1990); s of George James Willoughby (d 1976), of Cawsand, Cornwall, and Enid Alberta, *née* Nye (d 1995); *b* 6 Oct 1939; *Educ* Merchant Taylors'; *m* 16 May 1964, Susan Elizabeth, da of John Humphriss (d 1971), of Northwood, Middlesex; 1 s (Andrew James b 17 Sept 1965), 1 da (Caroline Louise b 3 March 1969); *Career* RNVR Seaman's Branch 1957–60; articled to predecessor of Clark Whitehill 1957, ptnr 1968; CA 1964; dir Moor Park Golf Club Ltd 1992–95; hon treas (formerly chm) Pottery and Glass Trades Benevolent Inst, govr Northwood Coll Sch; memb Old Merchant Taylors' Soc, pres Bishopgate Ward Club 1989–90; memb Ct of Common Cncl for Bishopsgate 1985–, chief commoner and chm City Lands and Bridge House Estates 1996–, chm Libraries, Art Galleries and Records Ctee 1991–93, chm of Govrs City of London Freemen's Sch 1994–95; Freeman City of London 1971, Master Worshipful Co of Glass Sellers 1986–87 (Liveryman 1971, hon clerk 1976–89), Liveryman Worshipful Co of Chartered Accountants, Liveryman Worshipful Co of Clockmakers, pres City Livery Club 1993–94; FCA 1968; Offr Order of the Niger 1989; *Recreations* the family, sailing, cricket, rugby, music, golf; *Clubs* MCC, City Livery, Moor Park Golf; *Style*— Philip Willoughby, Esq, JP; ✉ Penlee, 28 Valley Road, Rickmansworth, Herts WD3 4DS (☎ 01923 447602); Clark Whitehill, 25 New Street Square, London EC4A 3LN (☎ 0171 353 1577, fax 0171 583 1720)

WILLOUGHBY, Roger James; s of Hugh Lloyd Willoughby (d 1965), and Gerd, *née* Pers-Pleym (d 1989); *b* 30 Sept 1939; *Educ* Shrewsbury, Balliol Coll Oxford (BA); *m* 21 March 1970, (Jane Helen) Veronica, da of Francis Alfred Lepper, of St Wenn, Cornwall; *Career* House of Commons: clerk 1962, dep princ clerk 1975, sec to UK Delgn to Euro Parl 1976, clerk of Home Affrs Ctee 1979, clerk of supply Public Bill Office 1984, clerk of private bills 1988–, registrar of members' interests 1994–; *Recreations* literature, cricket, walking, bonfires; *Style*— Roger Willoughby, Esq; ✉ House of Commons, London SW1 (☎ 0171 219 3277)

WILLOUGHBY DE BROKE, 21 Baron (E 1491); (Leopold) David Verney; s of 20 Baron Willoughby de Broke (d 1986, descended from the 1 Baron, who was so cr by Henry VII after being on the winning side at Battle of Bosworth Field (1485), and was 4 in descent from 4 Baron Willoughby de Eresby), and Rachel, *née* Wrey (d 1991); *b* 14 Sept 1938; *Educ* Le Rosey, New Coll Oxford; *m* 1965 (m dis 1989), his kinswoman Petra, 2 da of Col Sir John Aird, 3 Bt, MVO, MC, and Lady Priscilla Heathcote-Drummond-Willoughby (yr da of 2 Earl of Ancaster); 3 s (Rupert Greville b 1966, John Mark b 1967, Edmund Peyto b 1973); *Heir* s, Rupert Greville b 1966; *Career* chm: S M Theatre Ltd 1991–, St Martin's Magazines plc 1992–, Compton Verney Opera and Ballet Project 1992–; pres Heart of England Tourist Bd 1996–; patron Warwicks Assoc of Boys' Clubs 1991–; FRGS 1993; *Clubs* White's; *Style*— The Rt Hon Lord Willoughby de Broke; ✉ Ditchford Farm, Moreton-in-Marsh, Glos GL56 9RD

WILLOUGHBY DE ERESBY, Baroness (E 1313) (Nancy) Jane Marie Heathcote-Drummond-Willoughby; DL (Lincolnshire 1993); da of 3 Earl of Ancaster (d 1983, when Earldom of Ancaster and Barony of Aveland became extinct, and the Baronetcy of Heathcote passed to his kinsman) and Hon (Nancy) Phyllis Louise Astor (d 1975), da of 2 Viscount Astor; succeeded father in Barony of Willoughby de Eresby; *b* 1 Dec 1934; *Educ* m; *Heir* co-heiresses; *Career* a train bearer to HM The Queen at the Coronation 1953; *Style*— The Rt Hon the Lady Willoughby de Eresby, DL; ✉ Grimsthorpe, Bourne, Lincs PE10 0LZ

WILLS, Dr Arthur William; OBE (1990); s of Archibald Wills (d 1950), of Market St, Warwick, and Violet Elizabeth, *née* Davies (d 1971); *b* 19 Sept 1926; *Educ* St John's Sch Coventry, St Nicholas Coll Canterbury, Univ of Durham (BMus, DMus); *m* 14 Nov 1953, Mary Elizabeth, da of John Titterton (d 1955), of Downham Rd, Ely; 1 s (Colin b 1956), 1 da (Rachel b 1958); *Career* dir of music King's Sch Ely 1953–65, composer and organist Ely Cathedral 1958–90, prof and academic tutor RAM 1964–1992, examiner Royal Schools of Music 1966–96; recitals in: Europe, USA, Canada, Australia, Hong Kong; Hon RAM, Hon FLCM, ARSCM; FRCO 1948 (cncl memb 1966); *Books* Organ (Menuhin Music Guide Series 1984, 2 edn, 1993); *Compositions* Symphonic Suite The Fenlands (for brass band and organ), Symphony in A Minor, Piano Sonata "1984", Opera "1984", Sonata (for guitar), Concerto (for guitar and organ), A Muse of Fire (overture for brass band and organ), Concerto Lirico (for guitar quartet), Choral Concerto: The Gods of Music (for organ, choir and orchestra); song cycles: Love's Torment (for counter tenor and guitar or piano/harpsichord), The Dark Lady (for baritone and piano), When the Spirit Comes (for mezzo and piano), A Woman in Love (for Mezzo and guitar), Three Poems of EE Cummings (for tenor, oboe and piano); Sacrae Symphoniae: Veni Creator Spirit (for double wind quintet), Benedicite, Missa Eliensis, Missa Sanctae Etheldredae, Resurrection (for organ); *Recreations* travel, antiques, reading; *Clubs* RAM; *Style*— Dr Arthur Wills, OBE; ✉ 26 New Barns Rd, Ely, Cambs CB7 4PN (☎ and fax 01353 662084)

WILLS, Colin Spencer; s of late Sir John Spencer Wills, of E Sussex and London, and Elizabeth Drusilla Alice Clare, *née* Garcke (d 1995); *b* 25 June 1937; *Educ* Eton, Queens' Coll Cambridge (MA); *Career* dir: Thames Television plc 1970–91, Euston Films Co 1971–91, ENO 1975–87, BAFTA 1980–94, Wembley Stadium 1975–84, govr Eng Nat Ballet 1988–94, govr English Nat Ballet Sch 1989–; chm Visiting Arts Office of GB and NI 1990–; FCA 1962; *Recreations* music, theatre, walking; *Clubs* White's; *Style*— Colin S Wills, Esq; ✉ 12 Campden Hill Square, London W8 7LB (☎ 0171 727 0534); Old Brick Farm, Burwash, E Sussex (☎ 01435 882 234)

WILLS, Sir (Hugh) David Hamilton; kt (1980), CBE (1971, MBE 1946) TD (1964), DL (1967); yr s of Frederick Noel Hamilton Wills (d 1927, himself yr bro of 1 Baron Dulverton) by his w Margery Hamilton, da of Hon Sir Hugh Fraser, sometime High Court Judge; Mrs Wills m 1942, as her 2 husb, Wing Cdr Huntly Sinclair, RCAF; *b* 19 June 1917; *Educ* Eton, Magdalen Coll Oxford; *m* 1949, Eva Helen Wills, JP, yst da of late Maj Arthur Thomas McMorrough Kavanagh, MC; 1 s (decd), 1 da; *Career* served WWII Queen's Own Cameron Highlanders (TA); France 1940, Aruba 1940–41, GSO 111 (Ops) GHQ Home Forces 1941–42, GSO 11 (Ops) HQ Southern Command 1943–44; chm of Tstees Rendcomb Coll 1955–84, High Sheriff Oxfordshire 1961, memb Governing Body Atlantic Coll 1963–73 and 1980–; dir Farmington Tst; fndr and pres Ditchley Fndn; *Recreations* fishing, sailing; *Clubs* Boodle's, Grillions; *Style*— Sir David Wills, CBE, TD, DL; ✉ Sandford Park, Sandford St Martin, Chipping Norton, Oxford OX7 7AJ (☎ 01608 683238)

WILLS, David James Vernon; s and h of Sir John Vernon Wills, 4 Bt, *qv*; *b* 2 Jan 1955; *Career* memb cncl Royal Bath & West and Southern Counties Soc; *Recreations* shooting; *Style*— David Wills, Esq

WILLS, Frederick Hugh Philip Hamilton; yr twin s of Capt Michael Desmond Hamilton Wills, MC (ka 1943), and Mary Margaret Gibbs, *née* Mitford; *b* 31 May 1940; *Educ* Eton, RAC Cirencester; *m* 1969, Priscilla Annabelle, da of Capt Alec David Charles Francis (d 1993), of Malmesbury, Wilts; 2 s (Michael b 1972, Edward b 1974), 1 da (Clare (twin) b 1974); *Career* II Hussars (PAO) 1959–66; TA Royal Wilts Yeomanry 1967–75; hon treas Cirencester and Tewkesbury Cons Assoc 1976–86; High Sheriff for Co of Gloucestershire 1995; *Recreations* country pursuits; *Style*— Frederick H P H Wills, Esq; ✉ The Old House, Rendcomb, Cirencester, Glos GL7 7EY (☎ 01285 831671, fax 01285 831494)

WILLS, Hon Mrs (Jean Constance); *née* Elphinstone; LVO (1983); da of 16 Lord Elphinstone, KT, (d 1955), and Lady Mary Bowes-Lyon, DCVO (d 1961), 2 da of 14 Earl of Strathmore and sis of HM Queen Elizabeth The Queen Mother; *m* 1936, Maj John Lycett Wills, Life Gds (ret), s of Capt Arnold Wills and gs of Sir Edward Wills, 1 Bt, KCB; 1 s (Andrew *see* Hon Mrs Elizabeth Wills), 1 da (Susan (Mrs Charles Bertie)), and 2 da decd; *Career* extra Lady-in-Waiting to HRH The Princess Margaret 1970–; *Style*— The Hon Mrs Wills, LVO; ✉ Allanbay Park, Binfield, Berks (☎ 01734 343215); 11 Rutland Mews East, London SW7 (☎ 0171 584 5876)

WILLS, Sir John Vernon; 4 Bt (UK 1923), of Blagdon, Co Somerset, TD, JP (Somerset 1962); s of Sir George Vernon Proctor Wills, 2 Bt (d 1931) and bro of 3 Bt (ka 1945); Sir George, 1 Bt, was pres of Imperial Tobacco Co of GB and Ireland of which 2 Bt was a dir; *b* 3 July 1928; *Educ* Eton; *m* 1953, Diana Veronica Cecil (Jane), da of late Douglas Ryan Midelton Baker, of Winsford, Minehead, Somerset; 4 s (David, Anthony, Rupert, Julian); *Heir* s, David James Vernon Wills, *qv*; *Career* Lt-Col (TA) 1965–67, Bt-Col 1967; Somerset Co: alderman 1970, High Sheriff 1968, DL 1968; Lord-Lt and Keeper of the Rolls of Avon 1974–96, Lord-Lt of Somerset 1994–; chm Wessex Water Authority to 1982; dep chm: Bristol Evening Post 1978– (dir 1973–), Bristol Waterworks Co 1983– (chm 1986); chm Bristol & West Building Society 1988–93 (dir 1969–93); memb: Nat Water Cncl 1973–82, Bristol Local Bd Barclays Bank to 1987; pro chllr Univ of Bath 1979–; KStJ 1978; Hon LLD Univ of Bristol 1986, Hon DLitt Univ of Bath 1993; hon Capt RNR 1988, FRICS; *Clubs* Cavalry and Guards'; *Style*— Sir John Wills, Bt, TD, JP; ✉ Langford Court, Langford, Bristol BS18 7DA (☎ 01934 862338)

WILLS, Gp Captain (Alan) Marcus; CVO (1988), OBE (1982); s of Alan Oliver Wills, OBE, of Brent Knoll, Somerset, and Rosamond Margaret, *née* Batty; *b* 21 Sept 1943; *Educ* Sherborne, RAF Coll Cranwell; *m* 23 Sept 1967, Victoria Katrina, da of Dr Derek Harold Johnson (d 1995), of Dartmouth, Devon; 3 s (Matthew b 1971, Adam b 1973, Edward b 1976); *Career* RAF 1966–94: 111 Sqdn 1966–68, ADC to AO C in C Air Support Cmd 1968–70, 10 Sqdn 1970–76, RAF Staff Coll 1976–78, CO 10 Sqdn 1978–82, COS Secretariat MOD 1982–83, Personal SO to CAS 1983–85, Station Cdr RAF Benson, Dep Capt Queen's Flight, ADC to HM The Queen 1985–87, Int Military Staff HQ NATO Brussels 1987–90, MOD Central Staff 1991–94; Air Equerry to HM The Queen 1995–; memb Ct of Assts Worshipful Co of Coachmakers & Coach Harness Makers (Liveryman 1982); *Recreations* computers, photography; *Clubs* RAF; *Style*— Gp Capt Marcus Wills, CVO, OBE; ✉ Office of HM Senior Air Equerry, Royal Air Force Northolt, Middlesex HA4 6NG

WILLS, Nicholas Kenneth Spencer; s of late Sir John Spencer Wills, of Beech Farm, Battle, Sussex, and Elizabeth Drusilla Alice Clare Garcke (d 1995); *b* 18 May 1941; *Educ* Rugby, Queens' Coll Cambridge (MA); *m* 1, 1973 (m dis 1983), Hilary Ann Flood; 2 s, 2 da; m 2, 1985, Philippa Trench Casson; 1 da; *Career* chm: Argus Press Holdings plc 1974–83, Electrical Press plc 1974–83, Initial plc 1979–87, The Eclectic American Catalogue Co (UK & USA) 1992; md: Birmingham & District Investment Trust plc 1970–91, Electrical & Industrial Investment plc 1970–91, Nat Electric Construction plc 1971–91; BET plc: dir 1975–92, md 1982–91, chief exec 1985–91, chm 1991–92; dir: American C of C (UK) 1985– (vice pres 1988–), St George Assurance Co Ltd 1974–81, National Mutual Life Assurance Society 1974–85, Colonial Securities Trust Co Ltd 1976–82, Cable Trust Ltd 1976–77, Globe Investment Trust plc 1977–90, Boulton and Paul plc 1979–84, Drayton Consolidated Trust plc 1982–92, National Westminster Bank plc (City & West End Advsy Bds) 1982–91, Bradbury Agnew and Co Ltd 1974–83, United World Colleges (International) Ltd 1987–95 (fin dir 1987–93), National Mutual Life Assurance Society 1991– (dep chm 1992–), Hitchin Priory Ltd 1992– (dep chm 1994–), Baring Tribune Investment Tst plc 1992–, Manchester Trading & Commercial LLC 1995–, Toye & Co PLC 1996–; chm: BET Building Services Ltd 1984–87, Onslow Commercial and Trading 1994–; dep chm National Mutual Home Loans 1994–96; memb: Cncl CBI 1987–92 (memb Overseas Ctee 1987–91, Public Expenditure Task Force 1988, memb Economic Affairs Ctee 1991–), Cncl Business in the Community 1987–92, Advsy Bd Fishman-Davidson Center for the Study of the Service Sector Univ of PA 1988–92, Advsy Bd Charterhouse Buy-Out Funds 1990–, Cncl Industl Soc 1991–; Prince's Youth Business Tst 1988–: memb Advsy Cncl 1988–, hon treas 1989–92, memb Investment Ctee 1992–; chm Involvement & Participation Assoc 1991–; tstee Int Fedn Keystone Youth Orgns 1988–, chm IFKYO Int Tstees 1990–; treas and churchwarden Church of St Bride Fleet St 1978–, govr Haberdashers' Aske's Schs Elstree 1989– (chm Girls' Sch Ctee 1994–); memb Ct of Assts Worshipful Co of Haberdashers 1981 (Jr Warden 1987–89); hon fell Queens' Coll Cambridge 1990; FCA; CIMgt, FCT, FRSA; *Recreations* shooting, sailing, trying to farm in the Highlands; *Clubs* White's, RAC, City Livery, Clyde Cruising; *Style*— Nicholas Wills, Esq; ✉ International Consultant, 75 Brook Street, London W1Y 2EB (☎ 0171 495 8919, fax 0171 499 4351)

WILLS, Peter Gordon Bethune; TD (1967); s of Lionel Wills (d 1967), and Sita, *née* Stapleton (d 1982); *b* 25 Oct 1931; *Educ* Malvern, Corpus Christi Coll Cambridge; *m* 1, 1957, Linda Hutton; 2 s, 1 da; m 2, 1967 (m dis 1981) Gloria Rayner; m 3, 1982, Faith Hines; *Career* served Royal Inniskilling Fusiliers in NI and Korea 1950–52, London Irish Rifles (TA) 1952–67; ptnr Sheppards and Chase (Stockbrokers) 1960–85 (joined 1955); memb Cncl of Stock Exchange 1973–86 (dep chm 1979–82); chm: Security Settlements Options Ltd 1979–92, Sheppards Moneybrokers Ltd 1985–89; dir: Wills Group plc 1969–87, The Securities Assoc 1986–89, London Clear Ltd 1987–89, BAII Holding Ltd 1986–89, LIFFE 1982, Hambro Clearing Ltd 1992–93, Securities Institute 1992–93; specialist advsr Social Security Ctee House of Commons 1993; FSI 1993 (memb Stock Exchange 1960); *Style*— Peter Wills, Esq; ✉ 2 Wellswood Park, Torquay TQ1 2QB (☎ 01803 291219)

WILLS, Sir (David) Seton; 5 Bt (UK 1904), of Hazelwood, Stoke Bishop, Westbury-on-Trym, Glos, and Clapton-in-Gordano, Somerset; s of Maj George Wills by his first w, Lilah, da of Capt Percy Hare, gs of 2 Earl of Listowel; suc unc, Sir Edward Wills, 4 Bt (d 1983); *b* 29 Dec 1939; *Educ* Eton; *m* 1968, Gillian, twin da of Albert Eastoe; 1 s, 3 da; *Heir* s, James Seton Wills, b 1970; *Career* FRICS; *Style*— Sir Seton Wills, Bt; ✉ Eastridge House, Ramsbury, Marlborough, Wilts SN8 2HJ (☎ 01672 520015); Estate office (☎ 01672 520042, fax 01672 520556)

WILLS, Maj (Michael) Thomas Noel Hamilton; DL (1991); s of Capt Michael Desmond Hamilton Wills, MC (ka 1943), and Mary Margaret, *née* Mitford; *b* 31 May 1940; *Educ* Eton, Royal Agric Coll Cirencester; *m* 23 Oct 1982, Penelope Ann, da of Ben Howard-Baker, of Glascoed Hall, Llansilin, Oswestry, Shropshire; 1 s (Nicholas James Noel Hamilton b 9 Sept 1983), 1 da (Camilla Jane Hamilton b 27 June 1985); *Career* Coldstream Gds 1959–73; memb: CLA, Timber Growers' Assoc, Royal Forestry Soc; pres League of Friends Stroud Hosp, vice pres Glos Scout Assoc, chm of tstees Rendcomb Coll; High Sheriff Glos 1985; Exon Queen's Body Guard of the Yeoman of the Guard 1993; *Recreations* country pursuits; *Clubs* Boodle's; *Style*— Maj Thomas Wills, DL; ✉ Misarden Park, Stroud, Glos (☎ 01285 821309); Coulags, Achnashellach, Ross-shire

WILLSON, Prof (Francis Michael) Glenn; s of Christopher Glenn Willson (d 1940), and Elsie Katrine, *née* Mattick (d 1924); *b* 29 Sept 1924; *Educ* Carlisle GS, Univ of

Manchester (BA), Balliol Coll and Nuffield Coll Oxford (MA, DPhil); *m* 23 June 1945, Jean, da of Malcolm Nicol Carlyle (d 1957); 2 da (Judith b 1946, Rosanne b 1953); *Career* MN 1941–42, RAF 1943–47, PO 1944, Flying Offr 1945, Flt Lt 1946; res offr RIPA 1953–60; Univ of Oxford: res fell Nuffield Coll 1955–60, lectr in politics St Edmund Hall 1958–60; Univ Coll of Rhodesia & Nyasaland: prof of govt 1960–64, dean Faculty of Social Studies 1962–64; Univ of California Santa Cruz: prof of govt and politics 1965–74, provost Adlai Stevenson Coll 1967–74, vice chllr coll and student affairs 1973–74, visiting prof 1985–92; princ Univ of London 1975–78 (warden Goldsmiths' Coll 1974–75); Murdoch Univ W Aust: vice chllr 1978–84, emeritus prof 1985; memb: Political Studies Assoc of UK; *Books* Administrators in Action (1961), The Organization of British Central Government (with D N Chester, 2 edn 1964), A Strong Supporting Cast: The Shaw Lefevres 1789–1936 (1993), Our Minerva. The Men and Politics of the Univ of London 1836–1858 (1995); *Recreations* reading, listening to music; *Style*— Prof Glenn Willson; ✉ 32 Digby Mansions, Hammersmith Bridge Rd, London W6 9DF (☎ 0181 741 1247)

WILLSON, John Michael; CMG (1988); s of Richard Willson (d 1972), of New Malden, Surrey, and Kathleen, *née* Aldridge (d 1983); *b* 15 July 1931; *Educ* Wimbledon Coll, University Coll Oxford (MA), Trinity Hall Cambridge; *m* 25 Sept 1954, (Phyllis Marian) Dawn, da of William John Richards (d 1974), of Barcombe, Sussex, and Phyllis, *née* Holman, OBE (d 1971); 2 s (Simon b 8 July 1955, Richard b 17 May 1957), 2 da (Melanie b 2 April 1960, Amanda b 5 March 1962); *Career* Nat Serv Army 1949–51; HM Overseas Civil Serv Northern Rhodesia 1955–64, Min Overseas Devpt London 1965–70; FCO 1970–90: HM ambassador 1983–87 (Ivory Coast, Niger, Burkina), Br High Cmmr Zambia 1988–90; conslt Africa Business and Investment Ltd 1990–; *Recreations* photography, music, gardening; *Clubs* Royal Cwlth Soc; *Style*— John Willson, Esq, CMG; ✉ c/o C Hoare & Co, 37 Fleet Street, London EC4P 4DQ

WILLSON, Quentin; s of Prof Harold Bernard Willson, of Leicester, and Agnes Grieve, *née* Gullon; *b* 23 July 1957; *Educ* Wyggeston Boys' GS Leicester, Univ of Leicester; *m* 25 June 1988, Helen Margaret; *Career* motoring journalist; dep ed Buying Cars magazine 1989–92, dep ed Car Choice magazine 1992–93, presenter Top Gear (BBC2) 1992–, assoc ed BBC Top Gear magazine 1993–; *Books* The Good Car Guide (1993–96), The Ultimate Classic Car Book (1995), The Classic American Car Book (1997); *Recreations* reading T S Eliot; *Style*— Quentin Willson, Esq; ✉ Willson Fane, PO Box 325, Leicester LE7 9LD (☎ 0116 259 5367, fax 0116 259 5425); Top Gear, BBC Broadcasting Centre, Pebble Mill Road, Birmingham B5 7QQ

WILLSON, Stephen Phillips; s of Douglas Stephen Willson, and Sheila, *née* Phillips; *b* 27 July 1948; *Educ* Battisborough Sch Plymouth Devon, Coll of Law; *m* 20 Dec 1975, Susan Mary, da of Gavin Miller Hunter (d 1978); 1 s (Guy Edward Phillips b 23 Nov 1983), 2 da (Sophie Anna b 1 Nov 1977, Sabine Lara b 22 Jan 1979); *Career* Burton & Ramsden: articled clerk 1966–71, asst slr 1971–73, ptnr 1973–82; ptnr S J Berwin & Co 1982– (currently head Property); memb Law Soc; *Recreations* squash, tennis; *Clubs* RAC; *Style*— Stephen Willson, Esq; ✉ S J Berwin & Co, 222 Grays Inn Road, London WC1X 8HB (☎ 0171 533 2222, fax 0171 533 2000)

WILMOT, Chief Constable David; QPM (1989), DL (Greater Manchester 1996); *b* 12 March 1943; *Educ* Baines GS Poulton-Le-Fylde Lancs, Univ of Southampton (BSc); *m* Ann Marilyn, *née* Doyle; *Career* Lancs Constabulary: constable 1962–67, sgt 1967–69, inspr 1969–74; Merseyside Police: chief inspr 1974–77, supt 1977–81, chief supt 1981–83; dep chief constable W Yorks Police 1985–87 (asst chief constable 1983–85); chief constable Gtr Manchester Police 1991– (dep chief constable 1987–91); memb ACPO; *Recreations* reading, gardening; *Style*— Chief Constable David Wilmot, QPM, DL; ✉ Greater Manchester Police HQ, PO Box 22 (SW PDO), Chester House, Boyer Street, Manchester M16 0RE (☎ 0161 872 5050, fax 0161 856 2666/1506)

WILMOT, Gary; s of Harold Wilmot (d 1960), of London; *b* 8 May 1954; *Career* actor and entertainer; showbusiness debut 1976, formed double act Gary Wilmot and Judy touring theatres and clubs; numerous TV and pantomime appearances, toured in over 300 theatres, writer of children's books, singer/songwriter; awarded Silver Heart for Most Promising Artiste Variety Club of GB 1987, patron of several charities; *Theatre* credits incl: Bill Snibson in Me & My Girl (Adelphi 1989–91, nat tour 1992–93), Teething Troubles (tour), Joe in Carmen Jones (Old Vic) 1991–92, Copacabana (Prince of Wales 1994–95, nat concert tour 1996); *Television* debut on New Faces 1977–78, appeared in Royal Variety Performance 1985 and 1988, subject of This Is Your Life 1986, own TV series and Christmas specials 1986–88, Showstoppers (series) 1995; *Films* Trigger Pullers 1992; *Recordings* The Album (with LSO), Copacabana (cast album); *Recreations* DIY, sports enthusiast; *Style*— Gary Wilmot, Esq; ✉ c/o Dee O'Reilly Management Ltd, 112 Gunnersbury Ave, London W5 4HB (☎ 0181 993 7441, fax 0181 992 9993)

WILMOT, Sir Henry Robert; 9 Bt (GB 1759), of Chaddesden, Derbyshire; s of Capt Sir Robert Arthur Wilmot, 8 Bt (d 1974, sometime equerry to HRH The Duke of Gloucester), of Pitcarlie, Auchtermuchty, Fife, and Juliet Elvira, *née* Tufnell; *b* 10 April 1967; *Educ* Eton; *m* 29 April 1995, Susan C, elder da of John Malvern, of Roehampton, London; *Heir* kinsman, Maj Martyn Sacheverel Wilmot b 2 Sept 1914; *Recreations* six-axis motion; *Clubs* Buck's, Boodle's, London; *Style*— Sir Henry Wilmot, Bt

WILMOT-SITWELL, Peter Sacheverell; s of Capt Robert Bradshaw Wilmot-Sitwell, RN (d 1946), and Barbara Elizabeth Fisher (d 1991); *b* 28 March 1935; *Educ* Eton, Univ of Oxford (BA); *m* 1960, Clare Veronica, LVO (1991), da of Ralph H Cobbold; 2 s, 1 da; *Career* memb Stock Exchange 1960, chm Rowe & Pitman stockbrokers 1986 (sr ptnr 1982–86); chm: (following merger) S G Warburg Securities 1986–94 (jtly 1986–90), Mercury World Mining Trust 1993–; vice chm S G Warburg Group plc until 1994; non-exec dir: Minorco plc, Foreign Colonial Income Growth Investment Trust, Close Brothers PLC, Southern Africa Investors Ltd; *Recreations* shooting, golf; *Clubs* White's, Swinley Forest Golf; *Style*— Peter Wilmot-Sitwell, Esq; ✉ Portman House, Dummer, nr Basingstoke, Hants RG25 2AD; Minorco plc, 40 Holborn Viaduct, London EC1N 2PQ (☎ 0171 404 2060)

WILMOT-SMITH, Richard James Crosbie; QC (1994); s of John Patrick Wilmot-Smith (d 1993), and Rosalys Vida, *née* Massy; *b* 12 May 1952; *Educ* Charterhouse, Univ of N Carolina (John Motley Morehead scholar, AB); *m* 1978, Jenny, da of Richard William Castle; 2 da (Antonia b 12 Nov 1981, Claudia b 23 July 1984), 1 s (Freddie b 12 April 1986); *Career* called to the Bar Middle Temple 1978 (Benefactors Law scholar), asst recorder of the Crown Court 1994–; *Recreations* cricket; *Clubs* Kent CCC; *Style*— Richard Wilmot-Smith, Esq, QC; ✉ 39 Essex Street, London WC2A 3AT (☎ 0171 583 1111)

WILMSHURST, John; s of Alfred William Wilmshurst, and Frances May, *née* Handy; *b* 30 Jan 1926; *Educ* Maidstone GS, Univ Coll Oxford (MA); *m* 31 March 1951, Patricia Edith, da of R John W Hollis, MBE; 1 s (Jonathon b 1968), 3 da (Letitia b 1953, Felicity b 1955, Priscilla b 1960); *Career* Lt RASC 1945–48; patents offr Glaxo Laboratories Ltd 1950–52, gp advertising mangr Reed International Ltd 1952–59, dir Roles & Parker Ltd 1959–67, md Stuart Advertising Ltd 1967–71, chm and chief exec John Wilmshurst Marketing Consultants Ltd 1971–94, princ conslt Duncan Alexander and Wilmshurst 1994–; memb: Gen Cncl Church Missionary Soc 1970–78, Kent Playing Fields Assoc; chm Kent Branch Chartered Inst of Mktg 1972, church warden Farleigh Parish Church 1979–82; Freeman City of London, memb Ct of Assts Worshipful Co of Carmen; FCIM 1986, FCAM 1982; *Books* The Fundamentals and Practice of Marketing (1978), The Fundamentals of Advertising (1985), Below the Line Publicity (1994); *Recreations* birdwatching, horse racing, theatre, music, collecting first editions; *Style*— John Wilmshurst, Esq; ✉ The Stable Cottage, East Farleigh, Kent (☎ 01622 728241)

WILSEY, Gen Sir John Finlay Willasey; GCB (1996, KCB 1991), CBE (1985, OBE 1983), DL (Wilts 1996); s of Maj Gen John Harold Owen Wilsey (d 1961), of Jersey, and Beatrice Sarah Finlay, *née* Best; *b* 18 Feb 1939; *Educ* Sherborne, RMA Sandhurst; *m* 1975, Elizabeth Patricia, da of C R E Nottingham; 1 da (Alexandra Claire Willasey b 18 Aug 1977), 1 s (James Nicholas Charles b 1 May 1979); *Career* cmmnd Devonshire and Dorset Regt 1959, despatches 1976 and 1981, cmd 1 Inf Bde 1984–86, RCDS 1987, COS HQ UK Land Forces 1988–90, GOC Northern Ireland 1990–93, C-in-C UK Land Command 1993–96, ADC (Gen) to HM The Queen 1994–96; Col Devonshire and Dorset Regt 1990–, Col Cmdt RLC 1993–96, Hon Col Jersey Field Sqdn RE; chm Western Provident Association 1996–; govr: Sherborne Sch 1995–, Prince's Mead Winchester 1995–, Sherborne Sch for Girls 1996–, Royal Hosp Chelsea 1996–, Sutton's Hosp in Charterhouse 1996–; *Recreations* skiing, sailing, fishing, collecting old English watercolours; *Clubs* Army and Navy, St Moritz Tobogganing, Scientific Exploration Society; *Style*— Gen Sir John Wilsey, GCB, CBE, DL; ✉ Western Provident Association, Rivergate House, Blackburn Park, Taunton, Somerset TA1 2PE (☎ 01823 623502)

WILSHIN, Richard Douglas; s of Douglas William Wilshin, MBE (d 1994), of Hastings, and Joan Winifred, *née* Bishop; *b* 28 Nov 1939; *Educ* Hastings GS, Law Soc Sch of Law, Coll of Law Guildford; *m* 1966, Gwendoline Margaret, da of late Robert Smith; 2 s (David Richard b 11 Oct 1968, Ian Douglas b 18 Feb 1971); *Career* general clerk then articled clerk 1956–63, asst slr Hart Reade & Co 1963–64, dep chief exec and slr Battle Rural DC 1967–73 (asst slr 1964–67), dir of admin E Hants DC 1973–85, registrar General Optical Council 1985–; Freeman City of London 1989, Liveryman Worshipful Co of Spectacle Makers 1992; memb Law Soc; FIMgt 1984, FRSA 1992; *Publications* Word Processing for Councils (1983), The General Optical Council and Opticians in the UK (1986); author of various articles and papers on mgmnt and admin; *Recreations* computing, theatre, music; *Style*— Richard Wilshin, Esq; ✉ General Optical Council, 41 Harley Street, London W1N 2DJ (☎ 0171 580 3898, fax 0171 436 3525, car 0486 586286)

WILSHIRE, Prof Brian; s of Edmund Wilshire, of Swansea, and Eileen, *née* Nicholls; *b* 16 May 1937; *Educ* Rhondda County GS for Boys, Univ Coll Swansea (BSc, PhD, DSc, basketball rep Wales and Univ of Wales); *m* 1956, Marian, da of Sidney Rees Teague; 3 s (Keith b 1957, Neville b 1959, Ralph b 1962); *Career* Univ of Wales Swansea (formerly Univ Coll Swansea): lectr 1960–72, sr lectr 1972–78, reader 1978–82, personal professorship 1982–, head Dept of Material Engrg 1985–; dir Eidawn Materials Research Ltd 1984–; ACTA Metallurgica lectr 1991–93; Platinum Medal Inst of Materials 1995; FIM 1976, FEng 1993; *Books* Technological and economic trends in the steel industries (1983), Creep of Metals and Alloys (1985), Introduction to Creep (1993); *Style*— Prof Brian Wilshire, FEng; ✉ Cwrt-y-Berllan, Reynoldston, Gower, Swansea SA3 1AE (☎ 01792 390870); Department of Materials Engineering, University of Wales Swansea, Singleton Park, Swansea SA2 8PP (☎ 01792 295243, fax 01792 295244); Eidawn Materials Research Ltd, Singleton Abbey, Singleton Park, Swansea SA2 8PP (☎ 01792 295243)

WILSHIRE, David; MP (C) Spelthorne (majority 19,843); *b* 16 Sept 1943; *Educ* Kingswood Sch Bath, Fitzwilliam Coll Cambridge; *m* 1967, Margaret; 1 s (Simon b 1971), 1 da (Sarah b 1969, d 1981); *Career* MP (C) Spelthorne 1987–; PPS: to Min of State for Def Procurement MOD 1991–92, to Min of State Home Office 1992–94; Cons Backbench Environment Ctee: vice chm 1990–91, sec 1995–; Cons Backbench NI Ctee: sec 1990–91, vice chm 1995–; memb: NI Select Ctee, British-Irish Parly Body; ptnr Western Political Res Servs; former: co-dir Political Mgmnt Prog Brunel Univ, ldr Wansdyke DC (Avon), memb Avon CC; *Style*— David Wilshire, Esq, MP; ✉ 55 Cherry Orchard, Staines, Middx (☎ 01784 450822); House of Commons, London SW1A 0AA (☎ 0171 219 3534)

WILSKI, Andrew; s of Ingénieur Boguslaw Jaloszynski, of Piotrowek, Warsaw, and Janina Zofia Zalewska; *b* 2 April 1947; *Educ* Reytan GS, Med Acad Warsaw (DM), Univ of London (DPM, MRCPsych); *m* 2 April 1982, Phillippa, da of Patrick Green, of Freshfields, Harpenden, Herts; 3 s (Alexis b 1983, Nicholas b 1984, Piers b 1986), 1 da (Francesca b 1989); *Career* conslt psychiatrist Royal Tunbridge Wells Health Authy, former conslt psychotherapist Univ of Essex, lectr Herts Coll of Art, community psychiatrist Mental Health Centre London, sr registrar Westminster Hosp, memb Assoc of Christian Psychiatrists, tstee Mordechai Vanunu Tst, memb Movement for Christian Democracy; *Books* Cultural Resources and Psychiatric Rehabilitation (1985); *Recreations* travel, reading, arts, photography; *Style*— Andrew Wilski, Esq; ✉ 4 Berkeley Rd, Mount Sion, Royal Tunbridge Wells, Kent (☎ 01892 27304)

WILSON, Prof Alan Geoffrey; s of Harry Wilson (d 1987), of Darlington, County Durham, and Gladys, *née* Naylor (d 1990); *b* 8 Jan 1939; *Educ* Queen Elizabeth GS Darlington, Corpus Christi Coll Cambridge (BA, MA); *m* 17 April 1987, Sarah Caroline Fildes; *Career* scientific offr Rutherford Laboratory 1961–64, res offr Inst of Econs and Statistics Univ of Oxford 1964–66, mathematical advsr Miny of Tport 1966–68, asst dir Centre for Environmental Studies 1968–70; Univ of Leeds: prof of urban and regnl geography 1970–, chm bd of arts econs and social studies and law 1984–86, pro vice chllr 1989–91, vice chllr 1991–; memb Oxford City Cncl 1964–67, memb and vice chm Kirklees AHA 1979–81, vice chm Dewsbury DHA 1982–86; chm NHS Complaints Review Ctee 1993, memb Northern and Yorkshire Regnl Health Authy 1994–96; Fndr's Medal Royal Geographical Soc 1992; FBA 1994; *Books* Entropy in Urban and Regional Modelling (1970), Catastrophe Theory and Bifuration (1981), Geography and the Environment (1981), Modelling the City: Performance, Policy and Planning (jtly, 1994), Intelligent GIS, Location Decisions and Strategic Planning (jtly, 1996); *Recreations* fell running; *Clubs* Athenaeum; *Style*— Prof Alan Wilson, FBA; ✉ Vice Chancellor's Lodge, Grosvenor Rd, Leeds LS6 2DZ; Vice Chancellor's Office, University of Leeds, Leeds LS2 9JT (☎ 0113 233 3000, fax 0113 233 4122)

WILSON, Alan James; s of Dr John Stanley Wilson, and Ellen Wilson; *b* 23 March 1948; *Educ* Univ of Brimingham (MB, ChB, MD), Univ of Glasgow (MSc); *m* 30 March 1976, Pauline Logan, da of Paul Weatherley, FRS, of Torphins, Aberdeenshire; 2 da (Margaret b 1978, Grace b 1982); *Career* lectr in surgery King's Coll Hosp 1984–87, conslt surgn Whittington Hosp 1987–; FRCSGlas; *Recreations* mountaineering; *Style*— Alan Wilson, Esq; ✉ 54 Grasmere Rd, Muswell Hill, London N10 (☎ 0181 883 1880); Whittington Hospital, Highgate, London N19 (☎ 0171 272 3070)

WILSON, Alastair James Drysdale; QC (1987); s of Alastair Robin Wilson, ERD, of Sudbury, Suffolk, and Mary Damaris, *née* Dawson; *b* 26 May 1946; *Educ* Wellington Coll, Pembroke Coll Cambridge; *Career* called to the Bar Middle Temple 1968, recorder 1996–; *Recreations* gardening, restoring old buildings; *Style*— Alastair Wilson, Esq, QC; ✉ Rainthorpe Hall, Tasburgh, Norfolk NR15 1RQ (☎ 01508 470 618, fax 01508 470 793); 19 Old Buildings, Lincoln's Inn, London WC2A 3UP (☎ 0171 405 2001, fax 0171 405 0001)

WILSON, Alexander William (Alex); s of William Wilson (d 1965), and Jemima Helen, *née* Jeffrey, of Cathcart, Glasgow; *b* 9 July 1927; *Educ* Queen's Park Glasgow; *m* 2 March 1955, Elizabeth Margaret (Betty), da of George Gilmour Wilson; 2 s (Alasdair Jeffrey b 1 Sept 1956, Colin George b 18 Aug 1961); *Career* served RE BAOR 1945–48; various positions in indust, selling/mktg accountancy/computer systems then in mgmnt consultancy (self-employed, Coopers & Lybrand, AIC/Inbucon) 1949–72; Wilson Hughes plc (formerly computer serv bureau, now microcomputer dealership): jt fndr and md 1973–90, hon pres (after MBO) 1990–92; UK Business Computer Dealer of the Year

1985; memb Cncl CIMA 1968–69 (pres Glasgow Branch 1966–68); memb: Caledonian Soc of London (pres 1991–92), Burns Club of London (pres 1988–90); life govr Royal Scottish Corp, life dir Royal Caledonian Schs (vice chm 1995); FCMA 1965 (ACMA 1952); *Recreations* golf, collecting Mauchlineware (antique Scottish souvenir woodware), studying the works of Robert Burns; *Clubs* Caledonian (chm 1991–94), Porters Park Golf; *Style*— Alex Wilson, Esq; ✉ 9 Lodge Avenue, Elstree, Herts WD6 3LX (☎ 0181 953 3032)

WILSON, Air Chief Marshal Sir (Ronald) Andrew Fellowes; KCB (1991), CB (1990), AFC (1978); s of Ronald Denis Wilson (d 1982), of Great Bookham, Surrey, and Gladys Vera Wilson; *b* 27 Feb 1941; *Educ* Tonbridge, RAF Coll Cranwell; *m* 1, 4 Aug 1962 (m dis 1979), Patricia Lesley, da of B D Cauthery (d 1986), of Effingham, Surrey; 1 da (Hayley Ann Fellowes b 7 Oct 1972); m 2, 21 May 1979, Mary Christine, da of Stanley Anderson (d 1978), of Darfield, Yorks; *Career* Flying Instr RAF Leeming 1963–65, Pilot 2 Sqdn RAF Gutersloh 1966–67, ADC to C-in-C RAF Germany 1967–68, Flt Cdr 2 Sqdn RAF Gutersloh 1968–70, Sqdn Ldr 1970, Flt Cdr 2 Sqdn RAF Laarbruch 1970–72, RAF Staff Coll Bracknell 1973, SO HQ Strike Cmd 1974–75, Wing Cdr 1975, OC 2 Sqdn 1975–77, SO Air Plans MOD 1977–79, Gp Capt 1980, OC RAF Lossiemouth 1980–82, Air Cdr Falkland Is and OC RAF Stanley 1982, SO Commitments Staff MOD 1983–85, Air Cdre 1985, Dir of Ops (Strike) MOD 1985, Dir Air Offensive MOD 1986–87, Air Vice-Marshal 1987, SASO Strike Cmd and DCSO HQUKAIR 1987–88, AOC 1 Gp 1989–91, Cdr Br Forces ME Aug-Nov 1990; Air Marshal 1991; C-in-C RAF Germany and Cdr 2 Allied Tactical Air Force 1991–93, Air Chief Marshal 1993, Air ADC to HM The Queen 1993, Air Memb for Personnel and AOC-in-C Personnel and Trg Command 1993–95, ret 1995; awarded: QCVSA 1973, Arthur Barratt Meml Prize 1973; govr: Tonbridge Sch 1984–, Skinners' Sch 1996–; memb Cncl Br Ski Fedn 1986–90; Freeman City of London 1966, Liveryman Worshipful Co of Skinners 1970 (Extra Memb of Ct 1984–87, Third Warden 1996–); FRAeS; CIMgt; *Recreations* skiing, golf, painting, furniture restoration, photography; *Clubs* Royal Air Force; *Style*— Air Chief Marshal Sir Andrew Wilson, KCB, AFC; ✉ c/o Royal Air Force Club, 128 Piccadilly, London SW1

WILSON, Andrew Norman; s of Lt-Col Norman Wilson (d 1985), and Jean Dorothy, *née* Crowder; *b* 27 Oct 1950; *Educ* Rugby, New Coll Oxford (BA, MA, Chllr's essay prize, Ellerton theol prize); *m* 1, 1971 (m dis 1990), Katherine Dorothea, da of late Prof Austin Ernest Duncan-Jones; 2 da; m 2, 1991, Ruth Guilding; *Career* author; asst master Merchant Taylors' Sch 1975–76, lectr St Hugh's Coll and New Coll Oxford 1976–81; literary ed: Spectator 1981–84, Evening Standard 1990–; FRSL 1981; *Books* The Sweets of Pimlico (1977, John Llewellyn Rhys Meml prize 1978), Unguarded Hours (1978), Kindly Light (1979), The Laird of Abbotsford (1980, John Llewellyn Rhys Meml prize 1981), The Healing Art (1980, Somerset Maugham award 1981), Who Was Oswald Fish? (1981), Wise Virgin (1982, W H Smith Literary award 1983), The Life of John Milton (1983), Scandal (1983), Hilaire Belloc (1984), How Can We Know? (1985), Gentlemen in England (1985), Love Unknown (1986), Stray (1987), The Lion and the Honeycomb (1987), Penfriends from Porlock (1988), Tolstoy (1988, Whitbread Biography award), Incline Our Hearts (1988), The Tabitha Stories (1988), Eminent Victorians (1989), C S Lewis (1990), A Bottle in The Smoke (1990), Daughters of Albion (Sinclair-Stevenson, 1991), Jesus (1992), The Rise and Fall of the House of Windsor (1993), The Vicar of Sorrows (1993), Hearing Voices (1995), A Watch in the Night (1996); *Clubs* Travellers; *Style*— Andrew Wilson, Esq, FRSL

WILSON, Sir Anthony; kt (1988); s of Charles Ernest Wilson (d 1930), of Kirkstall, Leeds, and Martha Clarice, *née* Mee (d 1943); *b* 17 Feb 1928; *Educ* Giggleswick Sch; *m* 18 June 1955, (Margaret) Josephine, da of Maj Joseph Henry Hudson, CBE, MC, DL (d 1977), of Wetherby, Yorkshire; 2 s (Duncan Henry b 1957, Oliver Charles b 1964), 1 da (Victoria Margaret (Mrs Mathews) b 1960); *Career* CA; ptnr Price Waterhouse 1961–84, head Govt Accountancy Serv and chief accountancy advsr to HM Treasy 1984–88, non-exec dir The Capita Group plc 1989–92; memb: UK Review Body on Top Salaries 1989–, Mgmnt Bd of SW Arts 1983–91 (chm 1988–91), Cncl ICAEW 1985–88, Accounting Standards Ctee 1984–88, Auditing Practices Ctee 1987–88; chm: Jt Disciplinary Scheme of the UK accountancy profession 1990–93, Dorset Musical Instruments Tst 1994–; vice chm Sherborne House Tst 1995–, pres Chandos Chamber Choir 1986–88, chm Dorset Opera 1988–93, dir Opera - 80 1989–91; Freeman City of London, memb Ct Worshipful Co of Needlemakers 1988, Liveryman Worshipful Co of CAs; FCA; *Recreations* fishing, golf, gardening, opera, music; *Clubs* Reform, Royal Over-Seas League; *Style*— Sir Anthony Wilson; ✉ The Barn House, 89 Newland, Sherborne, Dorset DT9 3AG (☎ 01935 815674)

WILSON, Anthony Joseph (Joe); MEP (Lab) Wales North (majority 15,242); s of Joseph Samuel Wilson (d 1987), of Birkenhead, and Eleanor Annie, *née* Jones (d 1990); *b* 6 July 1937; *Educ* Birkenhead Sch, Loughborough Coll (DLC), Univ of Wales (BEd); *m* 1 Aug 1959 (m dis 1987), June Mary, da of Charlie Sockett (d 1985), of Wolverhampton; 1 s (Joseph Glen b 1964), 2 da (Carla Jane b 1965, Jessica Lee b 1967); *Career* Nat Serv RAPC 1955–57; teacher in Guernsey 1960–66, gen mangr St Mary's Bay Kent 1966–69, lectr NE Wales Inst 1969–89; MEP (Lab): N Wales 1989–94, Wales N 1994–; *Recreations* basketball, camping; *Style*— Joe Wilson, Esq, MEP; ✉ 79 Ruabon Rd, Wrexham, North Wales LL3 7PU (☎ 01978 352808); Labour Euro Office, 67 Regent Street, Wrexham LL11 1PG (☎ 01978 362363, fax 01978 366163); Swydfa Ewropeadd, 58 Stryd Lyyn, Caernarfon LL65 2AF (☎ 01286 78950, fax 01286 78950)

WILSON, Dr Ashley John; s of late John Wilson, of Harton, South Shields, Tyne & Wear, and Gladys Wilson; *b* 2 Nov 1950; *Educ* South Shields GS, Bedford Coll, Univ of London (BSc), Univ of York (DPhil); *m* 2 Jan 1976, Sheila, da of James Mather, of South Shields, Tyne & Wear; *Career* mangr Centre for Cell and Tissue Res Univ of York 1980–; ed Procedures in Electron Microscopy 1993–; memb: Br Humanist Assoc, Nat Secular Soc; active memb and sec York Humanist Gp, fell Royal Microsopical Soc; MIBiol 1975, CBiol 1979; *Books* An Atlas of Low Temperature Scanning Electron Microscopy (1984), Foams: Chemistry, Physics and Structure (1989), Resins for Light and Electron Microscopy (1992); *Recreations* singing, wine tasting, architectural history, badminton; *Style*— Dr Ashley J Wilson; ✉ 8 Manor Drive South, Acomb, York YO2 5SA (☎ 01904 330943); Centre for Cell and Tissue Research, University of York, York YO1 5SA (☎ 01904 432935, fax 01904 432936)

WILSON, Vice Adm Sir Barry Nigel; KCB (1990); s of Rear Adm Guy Austin Moore Wilson, CB (d 1986), and Dorothy Wilson, BEM, *née* Watson (d 1993); *b* 5 June 1936; *Educ* St Edward's Sch Oxford, Britannia RN Coll (Queen's Sword, Queen's Gold Medal); *m* 26 Dec 1961, Elizabeth Ann, da of William Hardy (d 1986); 1 s (Robert Guy b 1967), 1 da (Harriet Jane b 1965); *Career* CO HMS Mohawk 1973–74, CO HMS Cardiff 1978–80; RCDS 1982, Dir Navy Plans 1983–85, Flag Offr Sea Training 1986–87, ACDS (Programmes) 1987–89, Dep Chief of Defence Staff (Programmes and Personnel) 1989–92, ret 1992; chm: Soldiers' Sailors' and Airmens' Family Assoc (SSAFA), Cncl Bede House Assoc Bermondsey, Cncl RN Museum, Bd of Visitors HM Prison Guys Marsh; *Recreations* campanology, gardening; *Style*— Vice Adm Sir Barry Wilson, KCB

WILSON, Brian David Henderson; MP (Lab) Cunninghame North (majority 2,939); s of late John Forrest Wilson, and Marion, *née* McIntyre; *b* 13 Dec 1948; *Educ* Dunoon GS, Univ of Dundee (MA), Univ Coll (Dip Journalism Studies); *m* 1981, Joni, *née* Buchanan; 1 da, 2 s; *Career* publisher and founding ed West Highland Free Press 1972–; MP (Lab) Cunninghame N 1987–; oppn front bench spokesman: on Scot Affrs 1988–92, on citizen's rights and open govt 1992, tport 1992–94 and 1995–96, on trade and indust 1994–95, election planning 1996–; first winner Nicholas Tomalin Meml award 1975; contrib to: The Guardian, Glasgow Herald; Spectator Parliamentarian of Year Awards 1990; FSA(Scot); *Books* Celtic: a century with honour (1988); *Clubs* Kilbirnie Place Golf, Garnock Labour; *Style*— Brian Wilson, Esq, MP; ✉ 219 Queen Victoria Drive, Glasgow (☎ 0141 959 1758); Miavaig House, Isle of Lewis (☎ 01851 672357); office: 37 Main St, Kilbirnie, Ayrshire (☎ 01505 682847); House of Commons, London SW1A 0AA (☎ 0171 219 4033)

WILSON, Brian John; s of Andrew Wilson (d 1983), and Alice Margaret, *née* Dickel; *b* 17 May 1944; *Educ* Enfield GS; *m* 26 March 1966, Pamela Florence, da of Joseph Thomas Wansell; 2 da (Jane b 1967, Susan b 1971); *Career* CA 1966; articled clerk Charles Comins & Co 1960–66; Ernst & Young 1966–: joined 1966, ptnr 1973–, i/c public sector servs 1983–88, i/c specialist industs 1988–91, i/c multinationals gp 1992–94; FCA; *Recreations* golf, sailing; *Style*— B J Wilson, Esq; ✉ Ernst & Young, Becket House, 1 Lambeth Palace Rd, London SE1 7EU (☎ 0171 931 3635, fax 0171 928 1345)

WILSON, Brian Vincent; s of Reginald Wilson (d 1976), of Dublin, and Josephine, *née* Murphy (d 1980); *b* 10 July 1945; *Educ* Clongowes Wood Coll Co Kildare Ireland, Univ Coll Dublin (BA), Trinity Coll Dublin (MBA); *m* 16 Oct 1968, Frances Mary Carroll, da of Thomas Carroll (d 1978), of Dublin; 1 s (Stephen b 11 Dec 1973), 2 da (Samantha b 24 July 1969, Eugenie b 25 May 1971); *Career* private indust 1968–71, sr exec Industl Credit Co 1971–73, mangr banking (later dir and gen mangr GB) Allied Investment Bank 1974–83, gp gen mangr GB Allied Irish Banks 1983–89, dir and gp gen mangr Ireland AIB Group 1989–95; ret; *Recreations* cricket, golf, rugby, tennis, opera; *Clubs* Reform, Wentworth Golf, MCC, Fitzwilliam Lawn Tennis; *Style*— Brian V Wilson, Esq

WILSON, Dr Bryan Ronald; *b* 25 June 1926; *Educ* Univ Coll Leicester, LSE (Hutchinson medal for res), Univ of London (BSc, PhD), Univ of Oxford (MA, DLitt); *Career* lectr in sociology Univ of Leeds 1955–62 (warden Sadler Hall 1959–62); Cwlth Fund fell Univ of Calif Berkeley 1957–58; Univ of Oxford: reader in sociology 1962–93, fell All Souls Coll 1963–93, emeritus fell 1993, sub warden All Souls Coll 1988–90; Hon DLitt: Soka Univ Japan, Univ of Louvain Belgium; hon pres Int Soc for the Sociology of Religion 1991–; FBA 1994; *Books* Sects and Society (1961), Religion in Secular Society (1966), Patterns of Sectarianism (ed, 1967), Religions Sects (1970), The Youth Culture and the Universities (1970), Rationality (ed, 1970), Magic and the Millennium (1973), Education, Equality and Society (ed, 1975), The Noble Savages (1975), Contemporary Transformations of Religion (1976), The Social Impact of New Religious Movements (ed, 1981), Religion in Sociological Perspective (1982), Human Values in a Changing World (co-author, 1984), Values (ed, 1988), The Social Dimensions of Sectarianism (1990), Religion - Contemporary Issues (ed, 1992), A Time to Chant: Soka Gakkai Buddhists in Britain (co-author, 1994); *Style*— Dr Bryan Wilson, FBA; ✉ 12 Victoria Court, London Road, Oxford OX3 7SP (☎ 01865 744818)

WILSON, Catherine Mary; OBE (1996); da of Arthur Thomas Bowyer, of Nettleham, Lincoln, and Kathleen Edith May, *née* Hawes (d 1993); *b* 10 April 1945; *Educ* Windsor County GS; *m* 1968, Peter John Wilson, s of Henry Wilson; *Career* museum and gallery asst City and County Museum Lincoln 1964–72, curator Museum of Lincolnshire Life 1972–83, asst dir recreational servs Lincs Co Cncl 1983–91, dir Norfolk Museums Service 1991–; memb Bd: Museums & Galleries Cmmn 1996–, Museums Trg Inst 1994–; FMA, FSA 1989; *Recreations* steam engines, industrial archaeology, local history; *Clubs* Norfolk; *Style*— Mrs Catherine Wilson, OBE, FSA; ✉ Norfolk Museums Service, Castle Museum, Norwich NR1 3JU (☎ 01603 223620)

WILSON, Charles Martin; s of Adam Wilson (d 1964), and Ruth Ann Wilson (d 1974); *b* 18 Aug 1935; *Educ* Eastbank Acad Glasgow; *m* 1, 18 Jan 1968 (m dis 1973), Anne Robinson, *qv*; 1 da (Emma Alexandra b 1970); m 2, 2 Oct 1980, Sally Angela O'Sullivan, da of L J Connell; 1 s (Luke Adam b 1981), 1 da (Lily Joan b 1985); *Career* dep night news ed Daily Mail 1963, followed by exec jobs at The Daily Mail including sports ed and dep Northern ed, asst ed London Evening News; ed: Glasgow Evening Times 1976, Glasgow Herald 1981, The Sunday Standard from its launch 1982; exec ed The Times 1982, ed Chicago Sun Times 1984, ed The Times Nov 1985–90 (jt dep ed 1984), dir News International March-Dec 1990, md and ed in chief The Sporting Life 1991–, editorial dir Mirror Group Newspapers plc 1991–92, md MGN plc 1992–, acting ed The Independent 1995–96; *Recreations* writing, reading, watching steeplechasing; *Clubs* Reform; *Style*— Charles M Wilson, Esq; ✉ Mirror Group plc, One Canada Square, Canary Wharf, London E14 5AP

WILSON, Hon Charles Thomas; s of 3 Baron Nunburnholme (d 1974) by his 1 w, late Lady Mary Alexander Thynne, youngest da of 5 Marquess of Bath; hp of bro, 4 Baron; *b* 27 May 1935; *Educ* Ludgrove, Eton; *m* 1969 (m dis), Linda Kay, only da of Cyril James Stephens, of Woodlands, Challock Lees, Ashford, Kent; 1 s (Stephen), 1 da (Nathalia); *Career* page of honour to HM King George VI 1950–52; memb Stock Exchange 1956–66; co dir; *Clubs* White's; *Style*— The Hon Charles Wilson; ✉ c/o Banco Fonseca Y Burnay, Portimao, Portugal

WILSON, Prof Colin Alexander St John; *b* 14 March 1922; *Educ* Felsted Sch, Corpus Christi Coll Cambridge (BA), Univ of London (Dip); *m* 1, 1955 (m dis 1971), Muriel Lavender; m 2, 1972, Mary Jane, *née* Long; 1 s, 1 da; *Career* Nat Serv RNVR 1942–46; asst Housing Div London Co Cncl 1950–55, architect to Devpt Co 1955–56, in private practice with Sir Leslie Martin 1956–64, own private practice Colin St John Wilson & Partners 1965–; *Buildings* Univ of Cambridge: Harvey Court, Stone Building, extension to Sch of Architecture; 3 libraries Oxford Univ, Biochemistry Laboratory Babraham ARC, extension to Br Museum, Br Library, Queen Mary Coll Library (SCONUL award for design excellence), Bishop Wilson Meml Library, Chicago Public Library; *Projects* Liverpool Civic and Social Centre, HQ and res campus Lucas Industries Ltd, Hong Kong Poly; memb: Bd Arts Cncl 1990–94, Cncl RA 1991; chm: Architecture Ctee RA 1991–, Architecture Unit Arts Cncl 1992–94, Nat Lottery Architecture Working Gp 1993–; tstee Nat Gall 1977–80, Tate Gall 1973–80; prof and head Dept of Architecture Univ of Cambridge 1975–89 (now emeritus prof); fell: Churchill Coll Cambridge 1962–71, Pembroke Coll Cambridge 1975–89; visiting critic Sch of Architecture Yale Univ 1960, 1964 and 1983; Cdr Order of the Lion (Finland); FRSA, RA, FRIBA; *Publications* Architectural Reflections (1992), The Other Tradition (1995); author of numerous articles in various pubns; *Style*— Prof Colin St John Wilson, RA; ✉ Colin St John Wilson & Partners, Highbury Crescent Rooms, 27 Horsell Road, London N5 1XJ (☎ 0171 354 2030, fax 0171 704 9925)

WILSON, Colin Christopher; s of late Ninian Jameson Reid-Wilson, of Bournemouth, England, and Margaret Elizabeth, *née* Briscoe (d 1958); *b* 6 Sept 1941; *Educ* St Peter's Sch Bournemouth, Coll of Law; *m* 11 Sept 1965, Priscilla Joan, da of Bruce Osborne (d 1960), of Calcutta, India; 2 s (Simon Christopher b 1971, Daniel James b 1977); *Career* admitted slr 1966, sr ptnr Turners Bournemouth 1985–; hon slr and tstee St Thomas Garnet Sch; memb Law Soc; *Recreations* sailing, tennis, skiing; *Style*— Colin Wilson, Esq; ✉ Chalbury Grange, Chalbury, Wimborne, Dorset (☎ 01258 840465); Turners, 1 Poole Rd, Bournemouth, Dorset (☎ 01202 291291, fax 01202 553606)

WILSON, Colin Henry; s of Arthur Wilson, and Annetta Wilson; *b* 26 June 1931; *Educ* Leicester Gateway Sch; *m* 1; 1 s (Roderick); m 2, 1973, Pamela Joy, da of John Arthur Stewart (d 1972); 2 s (Damon, Rowan), 1 da (Sally); *Career* author; writer in residence Hollins Coll Va 1966–67; visiting prof: Univ of Washington Seattle 1967, Rutgers Univ New Brunswick NJ 1974; *Books* incl: The Outsider (1956), Ritual in the Dark (1960), The

Mind Parasites (1966), The Black Room (1970), The Occult (1971), Criminal History of Mankind (1983), The Essential Colin Wilson (1984), The Personality Surgeon (1986), Spiderworld (1987), Encyclopaedia of Unsolved Mysteries (with Damon Wilson, 1987), Aleister Crowley - The Nature of the Beast (1987), The Misfits - A Study of Sexual Outsiders (1988), Beyond the Occult (1988), Written in Blood (1989), Serial Killers (with Donald Seaman, 1990), Mozart's Journey to Prague (play, 1991), Spiderworld - The Magician (1992), The Strange Life of P D Ouspensky (1993), A Plague of Murder (with Damon Wilson, 1995), From Atlantis to the Sphinx (1996), Atlas of Sacred Sites and Holy Places (1996); *Recreations* walking, swimming; *Clubs* Savage; *Style—* Colin Wilson, Esq; ✉ Gorran Haven, Cornwall PL26 6NT

WILSON, Sir David; 3 Bt (UK 1920), of Carbeth, Killearn, Co Stirling; s of Sir John Mitchell Harvey Wilson, 2 Bt, KCVO (d 1975), by his w, Mary Elizabeth (d 1979); *b* 30 Oct 1928; *Educ* Deerfield Acad Mass USA, Harrow, Oriel Coll Oxford; *m* 1955, Eva Margareta, da of Tore Lindell, of Malmö, Sweden; 2 s, 1 da; *Heir* s, Thomas David Wilson; *Career* called to the Bar Lincoln's Inn 1953, admitted solicitor 1962; conslt Simmons & Simmons 1992–93 (ptnr 1963–92); *Recreations* sailing; *Clubs* Arts, Royal Southern Yacht; *Style—* Sir David Wilson, Bt; ✉ Tandem House, Queen's Drive, Oxshott, Surrey KT22 0PH

WILSON, David; *b* 6 July 1960; *Educ* Anglia Poly (BA), LSE (LLM); *Career* admitted slr 1986; slr Holman Fenwick & Willan 1987–88, slr Gouldens 1988–90; BAT Industries plc: slr 1990–93, gp co sec 1993–; memb Law Ctee Law Soc; author of various articles in legal jls and business publications; *Books* The Guide to Best Practice at the AGMs of Companies (1996); *Recreations* music, theatre, swimming; *Style—* David Wilson, Esq; ✉ BAT Industries plc, Windsor House, 50 Victoria St, London SW1H 0NL (☎ 0171 222 7979, fax 0171 222 4269)

WILSON, David Geoffrey; OBE (1986), DL (Greater Manchester, 1985); s of Cyril Wilson (d 1950), and Winifred, *née* Sutton (d 1944); *b* 30 April 1933; *Educ* Leeds GS, Oldham Hulme GS; *m* 10 Aug 1980, Dianne Elizabeth, da of Rupert George Morgan (d 1980); *Career* Nat Serv RAOC 1951–53, TA Manchester Regt 9 Battalion 1958–68, ret Maj; sec Williams Deacon's Bank 1965–70, area mangr Williams & Glyn's Bank 1977–81 (sec 1970–72, mangr 1973–76), regnl dir Enterprise Bd NW 1981–85, dir of banking The British Linen Bank Ltd 1986–91, non-exec dir Lancastrian Building Society 1991–92; chm: North Manchester Health Authority 1991–94, North Manchester Healthcare NHS Tst 1994–; memb Advsy Bd (NW) Northern Rock Building Soc 1992–95, chm Manchester Business Link 1993–, chm E Manchester Partnership 1996–; dir NW Arts Bd 1991–; pres: Manchester C of C & Indust 1978–80 (currently a dir), Manchester Literary and Philosophical Soc 1981–83; High Sheriff of Greater Manchester 1991–92; dep chm: Hallé Concerts Soc, Bd of Fin Manchester Diocese 1994–; hon consul for Iceland, memb Ct Univ of Manchester; chm: Manchester PO Advsy Ctee, Manchester Telecommunications Advsy Ctee; govr Salford Coll of Technol 1988–96, memb Cncl Univ of Salford 1996–; Hon MA Univ of Manchester 1983, Hon MA Univ of Salford 1995; FIMgt, FCIB; *Recreations* gardening, music; *Clubs* St James's (Manchester), Army and Navy, MCC, Lancashire CCC; *Style—* David Wilson, Esq, OBE, DL; ✉ Winton, 28 Macclesfield Rd, Wilmslow, Cheshire SK9 2AF (☎ 01625 524133, fax 01625 520605); North Manchester Healthcare NHS Trust, Central Drive, Crumpsall, Manchester M8 5RL (☎ 0161 740 9942, fax 0161 720 2834)

WILSON, David John; s of Samuel Charles Wilson (d 1974), of Chingford, Essex, and Elizabeth Marie, *née* Coleman (d 1980); *b* 13 Sept 1938; *Educ* Sir George Monoux GS Walthamstow London, Univ of St Andrews (MA), Univ of Leicester (post grad cert in educn), Univ of Newcastle upon Tyne (MEd); *m* 1971, Brenda Mary, da of Charles Edward Caley, of Harlow, Essex; 2 s (Jeremy Daniel b 14 May 1975, Adam Giles David b 4 June 1977); *Career* teacher of English and drama Ambrose Fleming Tech GS Enfield 1963–67, head English Dept Passmores Comp Sch Harlow 1967–71, dep headteacher Mandeville Sch Aylesbury Bucks 1971–73, headteacher Warsett Comp Sch Brotton Cleveland 1973–78, headteacher Tong Upper Sch Bradford 1978–86, headteacher Oulder Hill Community Sch Rochdale 1986–; pt/t tutor in educn Open Univ 1982–93, schoolteacher fell Corpus Christi Coll Cambridge 1997; guest lectr in educn: Univ of York, Univ of Manchester, Univ of Huddersfield; examiner in educn Univ of Lancaster; contrib to several BBC educn programmes inc The Way Ahead (BBC North); convener SHA Rochdale 1989–; FIMgt 1987; *Books* The Technical and Vocational Education Initiative - The Agony and the Ecstasy (1988); *Recreations* travel, photography, reading, cricket; *Style—* David Wilson, Esq; ✉ The Oaklands, Savile Road, Hebden Bridge, West Yorkshire HX7 6BY (☎ 01422 842392); Oulder Hill Community School, Hudsons Walk, Rochdale OL11 5EF (☎ 01706 45522, fax 01706 48404)

WILSON, Sir David Mackenzie; kt (1984); s of Rev Joseph Wilson (d 1988), of Castletown, Isle of Man; *b* 30 Oct 1931; *Educ* Kingswood Sch, St John's Coll Cambridge (MA, LittD), Lund Univ Sweden; *m* 1955, Eva, da of late Dr G Sjögren, of Stockholm; 1 s, 1 da; *Career* asst keeper Br Museum 1954–66 (dir 1977–92); reader in archaeology of Anglo-Saxon period Univ of London 1966–71 (prof of medieval archaeology 1971–76), jt head Dept of Scandinavian Studies UCL 1973–76 (dean of Faculty of Arts 1973–76); govr Museum of London 1976–81, tstee Nat Museums of Scotland 1985–87, memb Ancient Monuments Bd for England 1976–84, former pres Br Archaeological Assoc, cmmr English Heritage 1990–; hon fell: St John's Coll Cambridge, UCL; FSA, FBA; Order of Polar Star (Sweden, first class) 1977; *Books incl*: The Anglo Saxons, Viking Art, Catalogue of Anglo-Saxon Metalwork 700–1100 in the British Museum; pubns on the Vikings, St Ninian's Isle Treasure and the Bayeux Tapestry; *Clubs* Athenaeum, Brooks's; *Style—* Sir David Wilson, FSA, FBA; ✉ The Lifeboat House, Castletown, Isle of Man IM9 1LD

WILSON, David Steel; s of John Mill Wilson (d 1954), and Elizabeth Garth, *née* Steel (d 1987); *b* 21 Jan 1936; *Educ* Bishopbriggs HS, Glasgow Coll of Technol (Dip in Mktg); *m* 24 Aug 1965, Patricia Ann, da of James MacDowall Docherty; 1 s (Byron David Kingsley b 10 Dec 1970), 1 da (Saskia Claire Kingsley b 2 Jan 1973); *Career* Nat Serv RAF 1957–59; Fyfe & McGrouther Ltd: apprentice 1953–57, sales rep 1959–66, sales mangr 1966–67; area sales mangr James Neill & Co Ltd Sheffield 1967–69, mktg mangr Pneumatic Components (RTZ Group) 1969–70, commis chef and trainee mangr Pheasant Inn Keyston 1970–72, proprietor The Peat Inn Fife 1972–, dir Taste of Scotland Ltd 1996–; Cellar of the Year UK Wine award Egon Ronay Guide 1985, chef laureate Br Gastronomic Acad 1986, Michelin star 1986, Restaurateur of the Year Catey award 1989, 4/5 Good Food Guide 1996; memb: Master Chefs of GB 1983– (chm Exec Ctee 1987–), Academie Culinaire de France; FRSA 1992; *Recreations* music, sport, travel; *Style—* David Wilson, Esq; ✉ The Peat Inn, Peat Inn, by Cupar, Fife KY15 5LH (☎ 01334 84206, fax 01334 84530)

WILSON, Derek; s of William Lawson Wilson (d 1980), of Blaydon, Co Durham, and Bertha, *née* Heppell (d 1982); *b* 21 Sept 1932; *Educ* Blaydon GS, Univ of Durham (BDS), Univ of London (MB BS); *m* 25 Oct 1958, da of Walter Parkinson (d 1978), of Blaydon, Co Durham; 1 s (David John Sinclair b 1966), 1 da (Kathryn Jane b 1963); *Career* surgn Lt RN 1958–61; conslt oral and maxillo facial surgn Charing Cross Hosp 1972–; hon conslt: St Thomas' Hosp 1972–, Cambridge Mil Hosp Aldershot 1976–; former dean of admissions and chm Selection Ctee Charing Cross and Westminster Med Sch; memb: BMA, Euro Acad of Facial Surgery; FDS RCS 1970, fell BAOMS; *Recreations* golf, tennis, bridge; *Clubs* Walton Heath Golf; *Style—* Derek Wilson, Esq; ✉ Sumners, 28 The Street, West Horsley, Leatherhead, Surrey KT24 6AX (☎ 014865 3791); Department of Oral & Maxillo-Facial Surgery, Charing Cross Hospital, Fulham Palace Rd, London W6 8RF (☎ 0181 846 1471)

WILSON, Des; s of Albert H Wilson (d 1989), of Oamaru, NZ, and Ellen, *née* Hoskins; *b* 5 March 1941; *Educ* Waitaki Boys' HS NZ; *m* 1 (m dis 1984); 1 s (Timothy), 1 da (Jacqueline); *m* 2, 24 May 1985, Jane, *née* Dunmore, of Brighton; *Career* journalist; columnist: The Guardian 1968–71, The Observer 1971–75; ed Social Work Today 1976–79, dep ed The Illustrated London News 1979–81; dir Shelter 1967–71, memb Nat Exec Nat Cncl for Civil Liberties 1971–73, head public affrs RSC 1974–76; chm: CLEAR 1982–90, Friends of the Earth 1983–86, Citizens Action 1984–90, Campaign for Freedom of Info 1984–90; Lib Pty: pres 1986–87, memb Fed Exec 1988–89, dir Gen Election Campaign Lib Democrats 1990–92; vice chm public affrs worldwide Burson Marsteller 1993–94, dir of corp and public affairs BAA 1994–; *Books* I Know it Was the Place's Fault (1970), Des Wilson's Minority Report - A Diary of Protest (1973), So You Want to Be a Prime Minister - A Personal View of British Politics (1979), The Lend Scandal (1982), Pressure - The A to Z of Campaigning in Britain (1984), The Environmental Crisis (ed, 1984), The Secrets File (ed, 1984), The Citizen Action Handbook (1986), Battle for Power - Inside the Alliance General Election Campaign (1987); novels: Costa del Sol (1990), Campaign (1992); *Clubs* Groucho; *Style—* Des Wilson, Esq; ✉ 48 Stapleton Hall Road, London N4 3OG

WILSON, Sir (Robert) Donald; KBE (1995), kt (1987), DL (Cheshire 1987); s of John Wilson, and Kate Wilson; *b* 6 June 1922; *Educ* Grove Park Sch Wrexham Clwyd; *m* 1946, Edna Elizabeth; *Career* RAF; landowner; tyre industry 1946–60, dir of various farming and property cos 1954–; chm: Cheshire CLA 1979–81, Electricity Consultative Cncl (NW) 1981–85, Mersey RHA 1982–94, Midlands RHA 1993; North West RHA 1994–; bd memb NW Electricity Bd (NORWEB) 1981–85; memb: NHS Bd 1986–88, Sch Teachers' Review Body 1991–92; pres Ayrshire Cattle Soc 1966–67; High Sheriff Cheshire 1985–86; Hon LLD Univ of Liverpool; fell John Moores Univ Liverpool; *Recreations* fishing, countryside generally; *Clubs* Chester City, Farmers; *Style—* Sir Donald Wilson, KBE, DL; ✉ The Oldfields, Pulford, Chester

WILSON, Edward; s of Edward William Wilson, of Wingrove House, South Shields, and Thomasina, *née* Moore; *b* 13 July 1947; *Educ* South Shields GS for Boys, Univ of Manchester (BA); *Career* actor Nat Youth Theatre 1965–70, played leading repertory theatres incl a season with the Traverse Theatre Edinburgh; dir Newbury Community Theatre 1984, artistic dir Fiftieth Anniversary of the Royal Jubilee Tst (staged The Way of Light St Paul's Cathedral) 1984; dir for Nat Youth Theatre 1981– (artistic dir 1987–): Murder in the Cathedral (London, Edinburgh Festival Moscow Arts Theatre), A Man For All Seasons, The Royal Hunt of the Sun (Jeanetta Cochrane Theatre London), The Taming of the Shrew, Othello, Night Shriek (Shaw), Caucasian Chalk Circle (His Majesty's Aberdeen, Tyne Opera House Newcastle, Bloomsbury Theatre), Marat Sade and Blitz (Playhouse Theatre), Blood Wedding (Bloomsbury Theatre, Teatro Principal Valencia), The Rivals (Greenwich, Theatre Royal Brighton, His Majesty's Aberdeen), Maggie May (Royalty Theatre), Amphibious Spangulatos (Greenwich), Godspell (nat tour for Vance Productions), Pippin (Bloomsbury), Othello (Bloomsbury); dir Brit Cncl tours 1986, 1989 and 1990; TV appearances in When the Boat Comes In and Rockliffe's Babies; memb: Actors' Equity, Directors' Guild of GB; chm Northern Arts Awards; *Recreations* music; *Clubs* Royal Over-Seas League; *Style—* Edward Wilson, Esq; ✉ National Youth Theatre of Great Britain, 443–445 Holloway Rd, London N7 6LW (☎ 0171 281 3863, fax 0171 281 8246, car 0860 386894)

WILSON, Elizabeth Anne (Mitzie); da of Kenneth Gordon Wilson, of Sidmouth, Devon, and Eileen Ray Wilson; *b* 30 April 1957; *Educ* Sidmouth Community Coll, Exeter Tech Coll, Birmingham Coll of Food and Domestic Arts (Dip in Home Economics); *m* 18 April 1992, David Nigel Johnson, s of Thomas Johnson; 1 da (Angelica Lois b 4 Oct 1994); *Career* Woman's Own 1978–82, dep cookery ed Family Circle 1982–84, cookery ed Woman's Own 1984–87, Best Magazine 1987–89 (initially established Cookery Dept, subsequently dep ed i/c fashion, beauty, home and cookery), currently ed-in-chief BBC Good Food Magazine (launch ed 1989); launched BBC: Vegetarian Magazine 1992, Gourmet Magazine 1992; memb Guild of Food Writers 1989–; *Books* Can't Fail Cakes (1995); *Style—* Mitzie Wilson; ✉ BBC Worldwide Publishing, Woodlands, 80 Wood Lane, London W12 0TT (☎ 0181 576 2000)

WILSON, Eric; *b* 8 July 1935; *Educ* Houghton-le-Spring GS; *m* 26 Dec 1963, Irene; 1 s (Mark); *Career* Nat Serv RAF 1953–55; Lloyds Bank 1956–57; various mgmnt appts with: Bank of W Africa 1958–65, Martins Bank 1965–67, Barclays Bank 1968–80; corp fin dir Barclays Bank 1980–84, chief exec and regnl dir TSB Scotland plc 1989–90 (gen mangr of banking 1984–86, sr gen mangr 1986–87, chief gen mangr 1987, md 1987–89), fin conslt 1990–; memb CBI Scot Cncl 1987–90; chm Customer Services Ctee for Yorks OFWAT; assoc Univ of York, lectr in mgmnt subjects and former MBA advsr Univ of Wales (for Chartered Inst of Bankers); FIB (Scotland), FCIB; *Recreations* running, music, reading and travelling; *Style—* Eric Wilson, Esq; ✉ Calabar, 5 Manor Farm Close, Copmanthorpe, York YO2 3GE (☎ 01904 702995, fax 01904 706188)

WILSON, Geoffrey Alan; s of late Lewis Wilson, and Doris, *née* Shrier; *b* 19 Feb 1934; *Educ* Haberdashers' Aske's, Coll of Estate Mgmnt; *m* 1963, Marilyn Helen Freedman; 1 s (James Lewis b 12 Aug 1965), 2 da (Sophie Louise b 20 Dec 1968, Annabel Jane b 23 Dec 1971); *Career* 2 Lt RA 1955–56; private practice 1957–60, dir Amalgamated Investment Property Co 1961–70, co-fndr and dir Sterling Land Co 1971–73, chm Greycoat PLC 1985–94 (dir 1976–94), chm Equity Land Ltd 1994–; memb W Met Conciliation Ctee Race Rels Bd 1969–71, memb Governing Cncl Univ Coll Sch 1991–, memb Cncl CBF World Jewish Releif 1993–, cmmr English Heritage 1992–; tstee: ORT Tst 1980–, Public Art Devpt Tst 1990–; FRICS 1958; *Recreations* reading, architecture, art, film; *Clubs* Reform, RAC; *Style—* Geoffrey Wilson, Esq; ✉ Equity Land Ltd, 7 Cavendish Square, London W1M 9HA (fax 0171 636 7078)

WILSON, Hon Geoffrey Hazlitt; CVO (1989); yr s of 1 Baron Moran, MC (d 1977), and Dorothy, *née* Dufton, MBE (d 1983); *b* 28 Dec 1929; *Educ* Eton, King's Coll Cambridge (BA); *m* 19 May 1955, (Barbara) Jane, o da of William Edward Hilary Hebblethwaite, of Itchen Stoke, Alresford, Hants; 2 s (Nicholas b 1957, Hugo b 1963), 2 da (Laura b 1966, Jessica b 1967); *Career* 2 Lt RHG 1948–49; joined English Electric 1956, dep comptroller 1965, fin controller (overseas) GEC 1968; Delta plc: fin dir Cables Div 1969, elected to Main Bd as gp fin dir 1972, jt md 1977, dep chief exec 1980, chief exec 1981–88, chm 1982–94; chm: W Midlands and Wales Bd Nat Westminster Bank plc 1990–92 (dir 1985–92), Southern Electric plc 1993–96; dep chm Johnson Mathey plc 1994–; dir: Blue Circle Industries plc (non-exec) 1981–, Drayton English & International Trust plc 1978–95; dep pres Engrg Employers' Fedn 1986–90 (vice pres 1990–), pres British Electro-Technical and Allied Manufacturers' Assocs 1987–88 (counsellor 1988–94); hon memb Hundred Gp 1985 (chm 1979–81); memb: Fin Reporting Cncl 1990–93, Cncl Inst of Cost and Management Accountants 1972–78, Accounting Standards Ctee 1978–79, Admin Cncl The Royal Jubilee Tsts 1979–88 (hon treas 1980–88), Cncl Winchester Cathedral Tst, Cncl St Mary's Hosp Med Sch 1985–88; memb Mgmnt Bd and hon treas Prince's Royal Jubilee Tsts 1988–89; Worshipful Co of CAs: memb Ct of Assts, Jr Warden 1986–87, Sr Warden 1987–88, Master 1988–89, currently Hon Memb of Ct; CIMgt, FCA 1955, FCMA 1959; *Recreations* family, reading, walking, skiing, vintage cars; *Clubs* Boodle's, RAC; *Style—* The Hon Geoffrey Wilson, CVO; ✉ Johnson Matthey plc, 2–4 Cockspur Street, Trafalgar Square, London SW1Y 5BQ (☎ 0171 269 8400, fax 0171 269 8433)

WILSON, Sir Geoffrey Masterman; KCB (1969, CB 1968), CMG (1962); s of Alexander Wilson; *b* 7 April 1910; *Educ* Manchester GS, Oriel Coll Oxford; *m* 1, 1946 (m dis 1979), Julie Strafford Trowbridge; 2 s, 2 da; m 2, 1989, Stephanie Adrienne, widow of Charles Stainsby, of Chadlington, Oxfordshire; *Career* vice pres Int Bank Washington DC 1961, perm sec Miny Overseas Dept 1968–70 (dep sec 1966–68), dep sec gen Cwlth Secretariat 1971, chm Race Rels Bd 1971–77, chm Oxfam 1977–83; hon fell: Wolfson Coll Cambridge 1971, Oriel Coll Oxford 1994; *Style—* Sir Geoffrey Wilson, KCB, CMG; ✉ 4 Polstead Rd, Oxford

WILSON, Gerald Robertson; CB (1991); s of Charles Robertson Wilson, of Edinburgh, and Margaret, *née* Early (d 1995); *b* 7 Sept 1939; *Educ* Univ of Edinburgh (MA); *m* 11 May 1963, Margaret Anne, da of John Wight, of Edinburgh (d 1970); 1 s (Christopher b 1968), 1 da (Catherine b 1964); *Career* private sec Civil Serv to: Min of State for Scot 1965–66, Lord Privy Seal 1972–74; cnsllr UK Representation Brussels 1977–82, asst sec Scottish Office 1974–77 (and 1982–84), under sec Indust Dept for Scotland 1984–88, sec Scot Educn Dept 1988–95, sec and head Scottish Office Educn and Indust Dept 1995–; *Recreations* music; *Clubs* Royal Cwlth Soc, New (Edinburgh); *Style—* Gerald Wilson, Esq, CB; ✉ The Scottish Office Education and Industry Department, Victoria Quay, Edinburgh EH6 6QQ

WILSON, (Robert) Gordon; s of Robert George Wilson, of Glasgow; *b* 16 April 1938; *Educ* Douglas HS, Univ of Edinburgh (BL), Univ of Dundee (LLD); *m* 1965, Edith Margaret Hassall; 2 da; *Career* MP (SNP) Dundee East Feb 1974–87; SNP: nat sec 1964–71, vice chm 1972–73, sr vice chm 1973–74, dep ldr Parly Gp 1974–79, chm 1979–90, vice pres, former treas spokesman; slr; memb Ct Univ of Abertay Dundee, chm Marriage Counselling (Tayside) 1989–92, rector Univ of Dundee 1983–86; *Style—* Gordon Wilson, Esq; ✉ 48 Monifieth Rd, Broughty Ferry, Dundee DD5 2RX (☎ 01382 79009)

WILSON, Guy Edward Nairne Sandilands; s of John Sandilands Wilson (d 1963), of 36 Egerton Crescent, London, and Penelope Ann, *née* Fisher-Rowe; *b* 10 April 1948; *Educ* Heatherdown Sch, Eton, Univ of Aix-en-Provence; *m* 20 Oct 1979, (Marianne) Susan, da of James Drummond D'Arcy Clark, of Oxwold House, Barnsley, Glos; 2 s (John b 5 Feb 1984, Hugh b 27 Aug 1986); *Career* CA; Ernst & Young: joined 1967, ptnr 1979–, seconded to HM Treasy 1989–92; FCA; *Recreations* cricket, golf, tennis, squash, football, gardening; *Clubs* Brooks's, MCC, IZ, Arabs, Royal St George's Golf, Berkshire Golf; *Style—* Guy Wilson, Esq; ✉ Ernst & Young, Becket House, 1 Lambeth Palace Rd, London SE1 7EU (☎ 0171 931 3860, fax 0171 928 0467)

WILSON, Guy Murray; s of Capt Rowland George Wilson (d 1950), of Tolleshunt D'Arcy, Essex, and Mollie, *née* Munson (d 1987); *b* 18 Feb 1950; *Educ* New Coll Oxford (MA), Univ of Manchester (Dip Art Gallery and Museum Studies); *m* 28 Oct 1972, Pamela Ruth, da of Alan Robert McCredie, OBE, of Yorkshire; 2 s (John b 1976, David b 1986), 2 da (Rebecca b 1978, Elizabeth b 1983); *Career* Royal Armouries HM Tower of London: keeper of edged weapons 1978–81, dep master 1981–88, master of the armouries 1988–; memb: Br Cmmn for Mil History, Arms and Armour Socs of GB and Denmark, Advsy Ctee on Hist Wreck Sites; Liveryman Worshipful Co of Gunmakers; FSA 1984, FRSA 1992; *Books* Treasures from The Tower of London (jtly, 1982), The Royal Armouries in Leeds: The Making of a Museum (jtly, 1996); *Recreations* walking, reading; *Style—* Guy Wilson, Esq, FSA; ✉ Tang Croft, Tang Road, High Birstwith, Harrogate, North Yorkshire HG3 2JU (☎ 01423 770648); The Royal Armouries, HM Tower of London, London EC3N 4AB (☎ 0171 480 6358, fax 0171 481 2922); The Royal Armouries Museum, Armouries Drive, Leeds, W Yorks LS10 1LT (☎ 0113 220 1999, fax 0113 220 1954)

WILSON, His Hon Judge Harold; s of late Edward Simpson Wilson, of Harpenden, Herts, and late Catherine, *née* Donovan; *b* 19 Sept 1931; *Educ* St Albans Sch, Sidney Sussex Coll Cambridge (state scholar, MA); *m* 1, 1958, Diana Marion, da of late Guy Philip Dudley Sixsmith; 3 s 1 da; m 2, 1973, Jill, da of late Charles Edward Walter Barlow; 1 step s, 1 step da; *Career* Nat Serv pilot offr RAF 1950–51, Flg offr RAFVR 1951–54, Flt Lt RAuxAF 1954–disbandment; admin trainee King's Coll Hosp then med records offr 1954–57; sch master St Julian's Secdy Mod Sch St Albans 1957–59; called to the Bar Gray's Inn 1958 (Holker exhibitioner), pupillage with Roger Gray QC Queen Elizabeth Bldgs Temple 1959–60, practice on Oxford Circuit 1960–71 (jr 1964–65, dep chm Monmouthshire QS 1970), practice on Midland & Oxford Circuit 1971–75, recorder 1971–75, chm Industrial Tbnls Birmingham 1976–81, circuit Judge (Midland and Oxford Circuit) 1981–, res judge Coventry Crown Ct 1983–92, liaison judge Coventry City Magistrates 1986–92, care judge Coventry Care Centre 1991–92, resident judge Oxford Crown Ct 1993–, liaison judge Oxfordshire Magistrates 1993–96, care judge Oxford Care Centre 1993–, liaison judge Oxfordshire Family Proceedings Panel 1996–; pres Tport Tbnl 1991–96, chm Reparations Advsy Ctee Coventry 1991–92, chm Thames Valley Area Criminal Justice Liaison Ctee 1996–; memb: Matrimonial Rules Ctee 1984–88, W Midlands Probation Ctee 1985–92, Oxfordshire Probation Ctee 1993–; hon recorder of Coventry 1986–93; *Recreations* watching rugby football, being with my wife, reading, listening to music; *Clubs* RAF; *Style—* His Honour Judge Harold Wilson; ✉ Oxford Combined Court Centre, St Aldates, Oxford OX1 1TX (☎ 01865 246200); 2 Harcourt Buildings, Temple, London EC4Y 9DB (☎ 0171 353 6961)

WILSON, Harold James Arthur (Jim); OBE (1995); s of James Wilson (d 1965), of Houghton Park, Ampthill, Bedfordshire, and Winifred Wilson (d 1956); *b* 16 April 1935; *Educ* Gresham's; *m* Judith Anne Linda, da of George Badman; 2 s (Jonathan Paul b 1959, Christopher James b 1965); *Career* Nat Serv RAF 1953–55; Eastern Counties Newspapers 1956–64; Anglia TV 1964–94: head of news 1967–74, controller of news 1988, dir news and regnl devpt Anglia Broadcasting 1989–94, ret; chm Int PR Ctee Rotary Int 1989–90, currently dir All-Anglia Radio Ltd; vice-chm Anglia Crimestoppers Bd, memb RTS, ind memb Norfolk Police Authy, memb Broadland Housing Assoc; *Recreations* restoring and maintaining Elizabethan farmhouse; *Style—* Jim Wilson, Esq, OBE; ✉ Ash Farm, Carleton Rode, Norfolk NR16 1RU

WILSON, Harry; s of Henry Wilson (d 1960), of Welwyn Garden City, and Elsie, *née* Day (d 1987); *b* 18 Aug 1926; *Educ* Handside Sch Welwyn Garden City, Hatfield Poly; *Career* athletics coach; as athlete represented: Herts at every distance from 100m-Marathon, Wales at 10000m and Cross-Country; started coaching sprinters 1959 (success with Ann Jenner Olympics 1960, Janet Simpson Olympics 1968 and 1972), moved to coaching endurance events 1960 (first success with Richard Jones Euro jr record holder for The Mile 4m 2.8s), has since coached 65 GB internationals incl 10 Olympians; best known incl: Steve Ovett (Euro 1500m champion 1978, Olympic 800m champion 1980, Cwlth 5000m champion 1986, world record holder for Mile, 1500m, 2 miles), Kirsty Wade (Cwlth 800m champion 1982, Cwlth 800m and 1500m champion 1986, former British record holder 800m), Tony Simmons (Euro Silver medallist 10000m 1974, fourth place Olympics 10000m 1976), Jill Hunter (Cwlth Silver medallist 10000m 1989), Angela Tooby (Silver medallist World Cross Country Championships 1988), Julian Goater (Cwlth 5000m Bronze medallist 1982), Jo White (Euro Jr 800m Bronze medallist 1977), Nicky Morris (Euro Indoor 3000m Silver medallist 1988), Simon Mugglestone (4 consecutive wins in Varsity Cross Country Match); coach to: GB Team for Olympics World and Euro Championships 1978–91, Indian Nat Endurance squad 1988–89, Sri Lanka Endurance Squad 1990–91; lectr and organiser of training courses in numerous countries worldwide; Master Coach award BAAB 1989, awards for services to athletics from Assocs of Spain Zambia and Finland; mktg mangr Engrg Indust Trg Bd 1968–87; *Books* Complete Middle Distance Runner, Running Dialogue, Running My Way; previously industl magazine ed Rank Organisation; *Style—* Harry Wilson, Esq; ✉ 90 Windmill Drive, Croxley Green, Rickmansworth, Hertfordshire WD3 3FE (☎ 01923 897486)

WILSON, Prof Herbert Rees; s of Thomas Rees Wilson (d 1971), of Nefyn, N Wales, and Jane, *née* Humphreys (d 1982); *b* 28 Jan 1929; *Educ* Pwllheli GS, Univ Coll of North Wales Bangor (BSc, PhD); *m* 30 Dec 1952, Elizabeth, da of John Thomas Turner (d 1966), of Nefyn, N Wales; 1 s (Neil b 28 June 1957 d 1996), 2 da (Iola b 14 June 1955, Helen b 5 Sept 1961); *Career* post doctoral res scientist Wheatstone Physics Laboratory King's Coll London 1952–57, lectr in physics Univ of St Andrews and Queen's Coll Dundee 1957–64, res assoc Harvard Med Sch Boston 1962, sr lectr and reader in physics Univ of Dundee 1964–83, prof of physics Univ of Stirling 1983–90 (prof emeritus 1990); memb Br Fulbright Scholars Assoc; FInstP 1975, FRSE 1975, FRSA 1989; *Books* Diffraction of X-Rays by Proteins Nucleic Acids and Viruses (1966); *Recreations* literature, the theatre, travel; *Style—* Prof Herbert Wilson, FRSE; ✉ Lower Bryanston, St Margaret's Drive, Dunblane FK15 0DP (☎ 01786 823105); School of Natural Sciences, University of Stirling, Stirling FK9 4LA (☎ 01786 73171 ext 7761)

WILSON, Ven (John) Hewitt; CB (1977); s of John Joseph Wilson (d 1959), of Ireland, and Marion Wilson, *née* Green (d 1980); *b* 14 Feb 1924; *Educ* Kilkenny Coll, Mountjoy Sch Dublin, Trinity Coll Dublin (BA, MA); *m* 1951, Gertrude Elsie Joan, da of Rev Robert Edward Weir (d 1957), of Dublin; 3 s (John, Peter, Timothy), 2 da (Kathryn, Sarah); *Career* clergyman; ordained 1947 for St George's Church Dublin; joined RAF 1950, Staff Chaplain Air Miny 1961–63, Asst Chaplain in Chief Far E Air Force 1966–69, Strike Cmd 1969–73, Chaplain in Chief RAF 1973–80; archdeacon 1973, canon and preb Lincoln Cathedral 1974–80, canon emeritus 1980–; incumbent Heyfords with Rousham and Somerton 1981–93; hon chaplain to HM The Queen 1972–80; Freeman and Hon Chaplain Worshipful Co of Coachmakers and Coach Harness Makers; *Recreations* tennis, gardening, golf, travel; *Clubs* RAF; *Style—* The Ven Hewitt Wilson, CB; ✉ Glencree, Philcote St, Deddington, Banbury, Oxford OX15 0TB (☎ 01869 338903)

WILSON, Ian; s of Burns Lumsdon Wilson, of Sunderland, and Valerie, *née* Guy; *b* 19 Dec 1970; *Educ* Southmoor Comp Sch, Univ of Sunderland; *Career* swimmer; memb: City of Sunderland Amateur Swimming Club, City of Leeds Swimming Club; competes in 1500m freestyle; jr England and GB int 1985 and 1986, nat youth team boys capt 1986, finalist Euro Jr Championships 1985 and 1986, rep England nat intermediate squad (under 19) 1987 and 1988, sr England debut 1988, sr GB debut 1989; achievements incl: winner 5 Gold, 9 Silver and 2 Bronze medals at nat age gp championships 1983–88, winner 21 Gold, 10 Silver and 2 Bronze nat sr medals 1987–, fifth Cwlth Games Auckland 1990, winner int meeting Rome 1990, fourth World Championships Perth 1991, Gold medal World Student Games Sheffield 1991 (only Br swimming medallist), second Euro Championships Athens 1991, fifth Olympic Games Barcelona 1992, fourth Cwlth Games Victoria 1994 (men's team capt), seventh World Championships Rome 1994, second World Short Course Championships Rio de Janeiro 1995; records: English sr long course record 1500m freestyle (15:03:72) Athens 1991, Br sr short course record 1500m freestyle (14:40:69) Sheffield 1995, Br and English sr long course record 800m freestyle (8:00:63) Athens 1991; Amateur Swimming Assoc: swimmers' rep Tech Swimming Ctee 1993–, inaugural chm Athletes Cncl 1995–; *Recreations* listening to music, watching TV; *Style—* Ian Wilson, Esq; ✉ c/o Amateur Swimming Association, Harold Fern House, Derby Square, Loughborough, Leics LE11 5AL (☎ 01509 230431, fax 01509 610720)

WILSON, Lt-Gen Sir (Alexander) James; KBE (1974, CBE 1966, MBE 1948), MC (1945), DL (Notts, 1993); s of late Maj-Gen Bevil Thomson Wilson, CB, DSO, of Chelsea, and Florence Erica, da of Sir John Starkey, 1 Bt, JP, DL; *b* 13 April 1921; *Educ* Winchester, New Coll Oxford (MA); *m* 3 Oct 1958, Hon Jean Margaret, da of 2 Baron Rankeillour (d 1958); 2 s, 1 step s, 2 step da (1 decd); *Career* WWII served Rifle Bde N Africa and Italy (despatches), Adj Indian Mil Acad Dehra Dun 1945–47, priv sec to C-in-C Pakistan 1947–49, psc 1950, Co Cdr 1 Bn Rifle Bde BAOR 1951–52, Bde Maj 11 Armd Div BAOR 1952–54, Kenya (despatches) 1954–55, Lt-Col 1955, Instr Staff Coll Camberley 1955–58, 2 cmd 3 Green Jackets BAOR 1959–60, GSO1 Sandhurst 1960–62, CO 1 Bn XX Lancs Fus 1962–64, COS UN Force Cyprus 1964–66 (Actg Force Cdr 1965–66), Cdr 147 Inf Bde (TA) 1966–67, dir Army Recruiting MOD 1967–70, GOC NW Dist 1970–72, Vice Adj-Gen 1972–74, GOC SE Dist 1974–77, Dep Col (Lancs) RRF 1973–77, Col Royal Regt Fus 1977–82; Col Cmdt: Queen's Div 1974–77, RAEC 1975–79, Royal Green Jackets 1977–81; Hon Col Oxford Univ OTC 1978–82; Sunday Times football corr 1957–90; chm Tobacco Advsy Cncl 1977–83 (chief exec 1983–85); dir: Standard Commercial Corpn 1983–92, Standard Wool 1986–92; advsr in politics and econs 1992–; memb: Sports Cncl 1973–82, Cncl CBI 1977–85; hon vice pres FA 1976–82, vice chm NABC (CYP) 1977–90 (vice pres 1990–), chm RUSI 1973–76; pres: Notts Assoc of Boys' and Keystone Clubs 1986– (now Notts Clubs for Young People), Broadway Lodge 1989–, Crown and Manor Boys' Club Hoxton 1995– (chm 1977–95); review ed Army Quarterly 1985–; *Recreations* cricket, association football; *Clubs* Travellers, MCC, Nottinghamshire CCC; *Style—* Lt-Gen Sir James Wilson, KBE, MC, DL; ✉ 151 Rivermead Court, London SW6 3SF (☎ 0171 736 7228)

WILSON, Hon James McMoran; s and heir of 2 Baron Moran; *b* 6 Aug 1952; *Educ* Eton, Trinity Coll Cambridge; *m* 7 June 1980, Hon (Mary) Jane Hepburne-Scott, yst da of 10 Lord Polwarth; 2 s (David Andrew McMoran b 6 Nov 1990, Alistair Thomas Hay b 17 March 1993); *Career* dir Boston Ventures Management; *Clubs* Somerset, Flyfishers; *Style—* The Hon James Wilson; ✉ 65 Upland Rd, Brookline, Mass 02146, USA

WILSON, James Noel Chalmers Barclay; OBE (1996); s of Alexander Wilson (d 1957), and Isobel Barbara, *née* Fairweather (d 1961); *b* 25 Dec 1919; *Educ* King Henry VIII Sch Coventry, Univ of Birmingham (MB ChB, ChM); *m* 3 Sept 1945, Patricia Norah, da of Harold Norman McCullough (d 1927); 2 s (Michael b 3 Dec 1956, Richard b 24 March 1960), 2 da (Sheila (Mrs Edwards) b 20 Aug 1947, Jane (Mrs Wentworth) b 30 April 1950); *Career* regtl MO RAMC 1943–46, discharged W/S Capt, qualified as parachutist and served 1 Airborne Div; res surgical posts: Birmingham Gen Hosp 1943 and 1947, Coventry and Warwicks Hosp 1948, Robert Jones and Agnes Hunt Orthopaedic Hosp 1949–52; conslt orthopaedic surgn: Cardiff United Hosps and Welsh Regnl Bd 1952–55, Royal Nat Orthopaedic Hosp London and Stanmore 1955–84, Nat Hosp Queen Square 1962–84; surgn i/c accident serv Stanmore 1955–84, hon conslt orthopaedic surgn Garston Med Rehabilitation Centre Watford 1955–84, teacher in orthopaedics Univ of London 1955–84, BOA travelling fell USA 1954; emeritus orthopaedic surgn and conslt: Royal Nat Orthopaedic Hosp, Nat Hosp for Nervous Diseases Queen Square; prof of orthopaedics Addis Ababa Univ 1989; UK vice chm World Orthopaedic Concern (pres 1979–84), vice chm IMPACT (Initiative Against Avoidable Disablement), RCS Watson-Jones lectr 1988, Duraiswami Meml Oration New Delhi 1989, Jackson Burrows Medal lectr 1991; MRCS 1943, LRCP 1943, FRCS 1948, sr fell Br Orthopaedic Assoc (editorial sec 1972–76), FRSM (pres orthopaedic section 1982 and hon memb 1989); memb: Egyptian Orthopaedic Assoc, Bangladesh Orthopaedic Soc (patron 1994); *Books* Watson-Jones Fractures and Joint Injuries (ed, 5 and 6 edns); *Recreations* golf, gardening, photography, old cars; *Clubs* RSM; *Style—* J N Wilson, Esq, OBE; ✉ The Chequers, Waterdell, nr Watford, Herts WD2 7LP (☎ 01923 672364)

WILSON, Sir James William Douglas; 5 Bt (UK 1906), of Airdrie, New Monkland, Co Lanark; s of Sir Thomas Douglas Wilson, 4 Bt, MC (d 1984), and Pamela Aileen, da of Sir Griffin Wyndham Edward Hanmer, 7 Bt; *b* 8 Oct 1960; *Educ* Marlborough, Univ of London; *m* 1985, Julia Margaret Louise, da of Joseph Charles Francis Mutty, of Mulberry Hall, Melbourn, nr Royston, Herts: 2 s (Thomas Edward Douglas b 1990, Harry William Patrick b 1995), 2 da (Jessica Sarah b 1988, Katrina Elizabeth b 1992); *Heir* s, Thomas Edward Douglas Wilson b 1990; *Career* farmer; *Style*— Sir James Wilson, Bt; ✉ Lillingstone Lovell Manor, Buckingham MK18 5BQ (☎ 01280 860643)

WILSON, Prof Janet Ann; da of Henry Donald Wilson (d 1991), of Edinburgh, and Margaret Penuel MacGregor, *née* Robertson; *b* 10 Nov 1955; *Educ* George Watson's Ladies' Coll Edinburgh, Univ of Edinburgh Med Sch (BSc, MB ChB, MD, Ellis Prize in Paediatrics), FRCS, FRCSEd; *m* 1987 (m dis 1996), Mark Nicholas Gaze, s of John Owen Gaze; 1 s (Donald John b 1991); *Career* house offr: in gen med Eastern Gen Hosp Edinburgh 1979–80, in gen surgery The Royal Infirmary Edinburgh 1980; demonstrator in anatomy Univ of Edinburgh 1980–81; SHO: in gen surgery Dept of Clinical Surgery Univ of Edinburgh 1981–82, in otolaryngology City Hosp Edinburgh 1982–83; registrar in otolaryngology City Hosp, Royal Hosp for Sick Children Edinburgh and Bangour Hosp 1983–85, lectr in otolaryngology Univ of Edinburgh 1985–87, sr registrar in otolaryngology City and Associated Hosps Edinburgh 1987–92, conslt otolaryngologist and hon sr lectr Royal Infirmary Glasgow 1992–95, prof of otolaryngology, head and neck surgery Univ of Newcastle upon Tyne 1995–; memb Cncl: Otorhinolaryngological Research Soc 1988–90 (hon sec 1990–94), Royal Soc of Med 1994–95, Royal Coll of Surgns of Edinburgh 1995–; chm Educn and Trg Subctee Br Assoc of Otorhinolaryngologists - Head and Neck Surgns 1996–; Euro Rhinologic Soc Prize 1986, Br Academic Conf ORL Research Prize 1987, Angell James Prize 1988, Royal Soc of Med Downs Prize 1989, Lionel Coll Meml Fellowship 1990, Ernest Finch visiting prof Sheffield 1996; travel awards: EEC Concerted Action 1987, Ethicon Fndn Fund 1988, Head and Neck Fndn 1990; memb: Otorhinolaryngological Research Soc 1985, Euro Rhinologic Soc 1986, Scottish Otolaryngological Soc 1987, Br Soc of Otolaryngologists 1987, Caledonian Soc of Gastroenterology 1989, BMA 1989, Br Soc of Gastroenterology 1992, Br Soc of Audiology 1992; *Books* Stell and Maran's Head and Neck Surgery (jt ed, 3 edn); also 10 book chapters; *Recreations* performing arts, the company of friends; *Style*— Prof Janet A Wilson; ✉ Oak House, 1 Jesmond Dene Road, Newcastle upon Tyne NE2 3QJ (☎ 0191 284 0251); Department of Otolaryngology, Head and Neck Surgery, University of Newcastle, Freeman Hospital, Newcastle upon Tyne NE7 7DN (☎ 0191 284 3111, fax 0191 213 1968)

WILSON, Dr Jean Lesley; da of Alan Herbert Wilson (d 1957), and Beryl, *née* Wagstaff; *b* 2 Aug 1945; *Educ* King Edward VI HS for Girls Edgbaston (fndn scholar), Newnham Coll Cambridge (MA, PhD, Clothworkers' exhibitioner, Charles Oldham Shakespeare scholar); *m* 1972, Prof Norman Hammond, *qv*, s of William Hammond; 1 s (Gawain Jonathon Curle b 2 Dec 1975), 1 da (Deborah Julian Curle b 13 Sept 1982); *Career* lectr in English Univ of Edinburgh 1970–72, fell King's Coll Cambridge 1972–75 (memb High Table 1975–), adjunct assoc prof of English Boston Univ 1990–; FSA 1980; *Books* Entertainments for Elizabeth I (1980), The Archaeology of Shakespeare (1995); author of numerous articles in jls and newspapers; *Recreations* riding, needlework; *Style*— Dr Jean Wilson, FSA; ✉ Wholeway, Harlton, Cambridge CB3 7ET (☎ 01223 262376); 83 Ivy Street, No 32, Brookline, MA 02146–4073, USA (☎ 00 1 617 739 9077)

WILSON, John; s of George Wilson (d 1987), and Winefred May, *née* Ball (d 1979); *b* 15 Feb 1941; *Educ* Lordsfield Boarding Sch, Ealing Coll; *m* Malgorzata Janina, da of Jerzy Wojciechowski; 1 da (Amy Janina b 18 Aug 1988); *Career* Colour Processing Labs Ltd 1960–61, prodn dir Golderstat Ltd 1961–; chm: John Wilson Ltd 1979–, Colour Centre Ltd 1985– (dir 1973–); FBIPP; *Recreations* golf; *Style*— John Wilson, Esq; ✉ John Wilson Ltd, 16A D'Arblay St, London W1V 3FP (☎ 0171 437 1057)

WILSON, Sir John Foster; kt (1975), CBE (1965, OBE 1955); s of Rev George Henry Wilson (d 1959); *b* 20 Jan 1919; *Educ* Worcester Coll for the Blind, St Catherine's Coll Oxford; *m* 1944, Chloe Jean, *née* McDermid, OBE; 2 da; *Career* int health administrator; dir Royal Cwlth Soc for the Blind 1950–83, pres Int Agency for the Prevention of Blindness 1975–83 (now hon life pres); sr conslt UN Devpt Programme (IMPACT) 1983–, pres Brighton Soc for the Blind 1988–; *Books* various publications on disability and travel; *Clubs* Royal Over-Seas League (vice-pres 1993–); *Style*— Sir John Wilson, CBE; ✉ 22 The Cliff, Roedean, Brighton, E Sussex BN2 5RE (☎ 01273 607667, fax 01273 679624)

WILSON, John Robert; *b* 13 June 1949; *Educ* Univ of Southampton (BA), LSE (MSc); *m* Dec 1971, Lesley; 1 s (James b June 1983), 1 da (Alice b Aug 1989); *Career* sec: Clothing Manufacturers' Federation, Shirt Manufacturers' Federation, Tie Manufacturers' Assoc and the Corsetry Manufacturers' Assoc 1977–81 (joined secretariat 1972); British Clothing Industry Assoc: gen sec 1981–84, dep dir 1984, dir 1985–; dir and sec Mens' and Boys' Wear Exhibitions Ltd 1985–93 (sec 1984–91); dir: British Knitting and Clothing Export Cncl 1987–91, British Fashion Cncl, Apparel Marketing Services (Export) Ltd, European Designer Collections, Clothing Technology Centre; DG Br Knitting and Clothing Confederation 1991–, chief exec British Apparel Centre 1987–, DG British Apparel & Textile Confederation 1992–; *Publications* The UK Fashion Designer Scene (report for DTI, 1986); *Style*— John Wilson, Esq; ✉ British Clothing Industry Association Ltd, British Apparel and Textile Centre, 5 Portland Place, London W1N 3AA (☎ 0171 636 7788)

WILSON, His Hon Judge John Warley; s of late John Pearson Wilson, of Kenilworth, and late Nancy Wade, *née* Harston; *b* 13 April 1936; *Educ* Warwick Sch, St Catharine's Coll Cambridge (MA); *m* 2 June 1962, Rosalind Mary, da of Raymond Harry Pulford; *Career* called to the Bar Lincoln's Inn 1960, practised Midland and Oxford Circuit until 1982, recorder 1979–82, circuit judge (Midland and Oxford Circuit) 1982–; *Recreations* gardening, national hunt racing; *Style*— His Hon Judge John Wilson; ✉ Victoria House, Farm Street, Harbury, Leamington Spa, Warwickshire CV33 9LR (☎ 01926 612572)

WILSON, Julian David Bonhôte; s of Peter Jardine Bonhôte Wilson, OBE (d 1981), and Helen Angela Mann (d 1961); *b* 21 June 1940; *Educ* Harrow; *m* 1, 29 Dec 1970 (m dis 1980), Carolyn Anne, da of Vivian Michael, of Geneva; 1 s (Thomas b 1973); m 2, 22 June 1981, Alison Christian Findlay, da of late Hugh Ramsay, of W Chiltington, Sussex; *Career* racing corr BBC TV 1966–; *Books* Lester Piggott - The Pictorial Biography (1985), 100 Greatest Racehorses (1987), The Racing World (1991); *Recreations* cricket, Cresta run; *Clubs* St Moritz Tobogganing; *Style*— Julian Wilson, Esq; ✉ 45 Old Church Street, London SW3 (☎ 0171 352 4449); Home Farm Cottage, Burrough Green, Newmarket, Suffolk CB8 9LY (☎ 01638 507395, fax 01638 508333); BBC Television Centre, Wood Lane, London W12 7RJ (☎ 0181 225 6491, fax 0181 749 3560)

WILSON, Keith Drummond; s of Gordon Drummond Wilson, of Maldon, Victoria, Aust, and Heather, *née* Lindsay (d 1994); *b* 18 July 1960; *Educ* The King's Sch Parramatta Aust, Royal Melbourne Inst of Technol; *m* 12 July 1990, Pamela Elizabeth, da of John Angus Mackay; 2 da (Elizabeth Rose b 1993, Olivia Catherine b 1996); *Career* news reporter The Herald Melbourne 1979–83, features ed The News and Travel International (TNT) London 1983; Amateur Photographer: news ed 1984–85, dep tech ed 1985–87, features ed 1987–88; launch ed What Camera? 1988–89; ed: Amateur Photographer 1989–, Photo Technique 1993–95; gp ed IPC Photographic titles 1994–; mangr Photo Panel Euro Imaging & Sound Assoc 1995–; MRPS 1992; *Books* Focus On Photography (1994); *Recreations* photography, hill walking, cricket, cooking, cinema; *Style*— Keith Wilson, Esq; ✉ Group Editor, Amateur Photographer, IPC Magazines, King's Reach Tower, Stamford Street, London SE1 9LS (☎ 0171 261 5100, fax 0171 261 5404)

WILSON, Lynn Anthony; s of Connolly Thomas Wilson (d 1970), of Northampton, and Frances, *née* Chapman (d 1975); *b* 8 Dec 1939; *Educ* Oakham Sch Rutland; *m* 4 April 1964, Judith Helen, da of late Jack Ronald Mann; 2 s (Nicholas b 30 May 1967, Giles b 27 May 1969); *Career* chm Wilson (Connolly) Holdings plc 1982– (md 1966); nat pres The House Builders Fedn 1981, chm Northants CCC; FCIOB, CIMgt; *Recreations* cricket, golf, horseracing, shooting; *Style*— Lynn Wilson, Esq; ✉ Wilson (Connolly) Holdings plc, Thomas Wilson House, Tenter Rd, Moulton Park, Northampton NN3 6QJ (☎ 01604 790909, fax 01604 492387)

WILSON, (William) Mark Dunlop; s of Maj Thomas Dunlop Wilson, of Glasgow, and Paule Juliette, *née* Durand; *b* 23 Jan 1949; *Educ* Univ of Glasgow (BSc), Univ of Illinois (MSc, PhD); *m* 11 Aug 1973, Nancy, da of Donald Lyle Anderson, of PO Box 127, Hoffman, Illinois 62250, USA; 1 s (Clark Andrew Dunlop b 18 March 1979), 1 da (Megan Christine b 3 Dec 1982); *Career* World Bank: agric professional offr in Europe and Middle E 1975–76, S Asia 1976–80, and Latin America 1988–90, currently div chief Latin America Agriculture IV; memb: Lions Club, Presbyterian Church, American Soc of Animal Sciences, Cncl for Agricultural Sciences and Technol USA, Br Soc of Animal Sciences; *Recreations* hiking, soccer coach, riding, chm Boy Scout Troop; *Style*— Mark D Wilson; ✉ World Bank, 1818 H St NW, Washington DC, 20433 USA (☎ 00 1 202 473 9200, fax 00 1 202 552 3132, telex RCA 248423 WORLD BANK)

WILSON, Ven Mark John Crichton; s of Rev William Hubert Wilson, of St Andrews, Fife, and Gladys Margaret, *née* Goode; *b* 14 Jan 1946; *Educ* St John's Sch Leatherhead, Clare Coll Cambridge (choral exhibitioner, MA Natural Scis, CertTheol), Ridley Hall Cambridge; *m* 4 April 1970, Rev Canon Mavis Kirby Wilson; 3 da (Naomi b 6 Nov 1971, Susannah b 13 Aug 1976, Rachel b 31 May 1979), 1 s (Edward b 24 Oct 1973); *Career* ordained deacon 1969, priest 1970; curate: Luton with E Hyde (Dio of St Albans) 1969–72, Ashtead (Dio of Guildford 1972–77); chaplain Epsom Coll Surrey 1977–81, vicar Christ Church Epsom Common (Dio of Guildford) 1981–96, rural dean 1987–91, archdeacon of Dorking (Dio of Guildford) 1996–; *Recreations* cricket, gardening; *Style*— The Ven the Archdeacon of Dorking; ✉ Littlecroft, Heathside Road, Woking, Surrey GU22 7EZ (☎ 01483 772713, fax 01483 757353)

WILSON, (Alan) Martin; QC (1982); s of Joseph Norris Wilson (d 1986), of London, and Kate, *née* Clusky (d 1982); *b* 12 Feb 1940; *Educ* Kilburn GS, Univ of Nottingham (LLB); *m* 1, 1966 (m dis 1975), Pauline Frances Kibart; 2 da (Rebecca b 1968, Anna b 1971); m 2, 20 March 1976, Julia Mary, da of Patrick Maurice George Carter, OBE, of Malvern, Worcs; 1 da (Alexandra b 1980); *Career* called to the Bar Gray's Inn 1963; recorder of the Crown Ct (Midland and Oxford Circuit) 1979–; occasional memb Hong Kong Bar 1988–, Malaysian Bar 1995; *Recreations* sailing, shooting, literature, travel; *Clubs* Bar Yacht, Sloane; *Style*— Martin Wilson, Esq, QC; ✉ 1 Serjeants' Inn, Fleet Street, London EC4Y 1LL (☎ 0171 353 9901, fax 0171 583 2033)

WILSON, Brig Sir Mathew John Anthony; 6 Bt (UK 1874), of Eshton Hall, Co York, OBE (Mil 1979, MBE Mil 1971), MC (1972); s of Anthony Thomas Wilson (d 1979), by his 1 w Margaret (d 1980), formerly w of Vernon Motion and da of late Alfred Holden; suc unc, Sir (Mathew) Martin Wilson, 5 Bt 1991; *b* 2 Oct 1935; *Educ* Trinity Coll Sch Port Hope Ontario; *m* 1962, Janet Mary, er da of late Edward Worsfold Mowll, JP, of Walmer; 1 s (Mathew Edward Amcotts b 1966), 1 da (Victoria Mary b 1968); *Heir* s, Mathew Edward Amcotts Wilson b 13 Oct 1966; *Career* Brig King's Own Yorks LI, ret 1983; exec dir Wilderness Fndn (UK) 1983–85; pres and chief exec offr Dolphin Voyaging Inc 1995; *Books* Taking Terrapin Home: A Love Affair with a Small Catamaran (1994); *Clubs* Explorers; *Style*— Brig Sir Mathew Wilson, Bt, OBE, MC; ✉ Vermont, USA

WILSON, Dr Michael Anthony; s of Charles Kenneth Wilson (d 1995), and Bertha, *née* Poppleton (d 1987); *b* 2 June 1936; *Educ* Roundhay Sch, Univ of Leeds (MB ChB, FRCGP, DObstRCOG); *m* 24 Jan 1959, Marlene; 2 s (Mark Edward b 3 May 1960, Ian Gregory b 2 May 1962); *Career* princ in GP Strensall N Yorks 1961–; pres Yorks Regnl Cncl BMA 1975–79, chm Gen Med Servs Ctee 1984–90 (dep chm 1979–84); memb: Cncl BMA 1977–90 and 1992–, Standing Med Ctee to DHSS 1967–69 and 1978–90 (dep chm 1986–90), Gen Med Cncl 1989–, Code of Practice Authy Assoc of Br Pharmaceutical Indust 1990–, Advsy Bd Med Protection Soc 1990–, Jt Conslts Ctee 1991–, NHS Clinical Standards Advsy Gp 1991–93; fell BMA 1979, FRSM 1985; *Recreations* travel, Rotary, golf; *Clubs* East India, Rotary Club of York, York Golf, Ampleforth Coll Golf; *Style*— Dr Michael Wilson; ✉ Longueville, Mill Hill, Huntington, N Yorks YO3 9PY (☎ 01904 768861, fax 01904 762012); Dr M A Wilson & Partners, Southfields Rd, Strensall, N Yorks YO3 5UA (☎ 01904 490532, fax 01904 491927)

WILSON, Michael Gerald; s of John Charles Wilson (d 1992), of Hove, Sussex, and Dorothy Beatrice, *née* Harmer (d 1985); *b* 6 Dec 1942; *m* 22 Aug 1964, Maureen Brenda, da of Arthur Charles Hiron (d 1982); 1 s (James Michael b 27 Oct 1981), 1 da (Sarah Michelle b 28 March 1973); *Career* admitted slr 1975 with Slaughter & May; ptnr Berwin Leighton 1979– (currently head Fin Instns Dept); Freeman: City of London, Worshipful Co of Slrs; memb: Law Soc 1975, Int Bar Assoc 1975, S Western Legal Fndn 1982, Asia Pacific Lawyers Assoc 1985, Inter Pacific Bar Assoc 1990; assoc memb Lloyd's of London 1987; FRSA; *Recreations* tennis, squash, swimming, travel, reading, music; *Clubs* RAC; *Style*— Michael Wilson, Esq; ✉ Berwin Leighton, Adelaide House, London Bridge, London EC4R 9HA (☎ 0171 623 3144, fax 0171 623 4416, telex 886420)

WILSON, Michael John Francis Thomond; s of Sir Michael Thomond Wilson, MBE (d 1983), of Clytha, South Ascot, Berks, and Lady Jessie Babette, *née* Winnington (d 1984); *b* 9 Sept 1934; *Educ* Rugby, Oriel Coll Oxford (MA); *m* 4 May 1968, (Katharine) Mary Rose, da of Lt-Col Robert Macauley Fanshawe (d 1974), and Mary Marjoribanks Fanshawe, of Barrasford, Hexham, Northumberland; 3 s (James b 1970, Andrew b 1972, Richard b 1976); *Career* Nat Serv Lt RA 1953–55; admitted slr 1961; Stephenson Harwood (formerly Stephenson Harwood and Tatham): ptnr 1966–96, head of Litigation Dept 1969–92, conslt 1996–; *Recreations* horse racing, tennis; *Style*— Michael Wilson, Esq; ✉ Andridge House, Radnage, High Wycombe, Bucks HP14 4DZ (☎ 01494 482215); Stephenson Harwood, 1 St Paul's Churchyard, London EC4M 8SH (☎ 0171 329 4422, fax 0171 410 9217)

WILSON, Michael Sumner; s of Cdr Peter Sumner Wilson, AFC (d 1993), and Margaret Kathleen, *née* Letchworth (d 1996); *b* 5 Dec 1943; *Educ* St Edward's Sch Oxford; *m* 5 June 1975, Mary Dorothy Wordsworth, da of John Alexander Drysdale (d 1986); 1 da (Amanda Wordsworth Sumner b 12 March 1976); *Career* Equity & Law 1963–68, Abbey Life 1968–71; Hambro Life/Allied Dunbar: broker mangr 1971–73, exec dir 1973–76, main bd dir 1976–82, jt dep md 1982–84, jt md 1984–88, gp chief exec 1988–90; dir BAT Industs 1989–90, chief exec J Rothschild Assurance plc 1991–; non-exec dir Vendôme Luxury Group plc 1993–; tstee Mental Health Fndn; *Recreations* tennis, racing; *Style*— Michael Wilson, Esq; ✉ 42 Eaton Place, London SW1X 8AL; J Rothschild Assurance plc, J Rothschild House, Dollar St, Cirencester, Glos G27 2AQ (☎ 01285 640302, fax 01285 642772)

WILSON, Michael Thomas; s of Thomas Wilson (d 1967), and Blanche, *née* Dunne; *b* 27 April 1938; *Educ* Rothwell GS, Univ of Manchester (BA); *m* 1 Sept 1962, Diana Frances, da of Harold Frank Pettit (d 1968); 1 s (Simon b 1964), 2 da (Victoria b 1966, Emmeline b 1977); *Career* supervisor truck mktg Ford Motor Co 1959–62, dir residential studies Inst of Mktg 1962–64, md Marketing Improvements Ltd 1964–88, chm

Marketing Improvements Group plc 1988–, visiting prof Cranfield Sch of Mgmnt 1989; FInstM 1985, FInstD 1966; *Books* Managing a Sales Force (1970), The Management of Marketing (1980); *Recreations* sport, theatre, cinema, reading; *Style*— Michael Wilson, Esq; ✉ Ulster House, 17 Ulster Terrace, Regents Park Outer Circle, London NW1 (☎ 0171 487 5811, fax 0171 935 4839)

WILSON, Miles Robert; s of Maurice James Wilson (d 1969), of Colchester, Essex, and Kathleen Isobel Wilson; *b* 28 Sept 1946; *Educ* Chinthurst Sch Tadworth Surrey, Carshalton Coll Surrey; *m* 1985 (m dis); *Career* professional broadcaster and radio presenter 1964–78; involved in the tourist indust; fndr PR-advtg agency 1983, chm and md The Wasp Group of Companies (advtg, PR and mktg agency) Worthing Sussex 1986–92, freelance PR and mktg conslt 1995–, alumni rels offr De Montfort Univ 1996–; fndr Bedroom Browser publication (for hotels) 1985; pres Sussex Coast Business Club 1990–92; chm Worthing Post Office Advsy Cncl 1991–92, exec memb Worthing Coll Tourism Liaison Ctee 1987–92; memb: Tourism Soc 1983, PATAC Leicestershire 1992–, Ctee Burton Business Club 1992–93; community advsr: Leicestershire County Cncl 1983–, West Sussex County Cncl 1989–90; memb: Worthing Soc (life memb) 1988–, Trevithick Soc 1992–; MIPR 1985, MIMgt 1989; *Books* Fort Newhaven History (co-author 1984), The Hewes of Leicestershire (1996/97); *Recreations* sailing, country pursuits, music, antiques, enjoying good food, wine and classical music; *Style*— Miles R Wilson, Esq; ✉ Glenholm, Ravenstone, Leicestershire LE67 2AR (☎ 01530 832345); De Montfort University, The Gateway, Leicester LE1 9BH (☎ 0116 257 7348, fax 0116 257 7023, e-mail mrjw@dmu.ac.uk)

WILSON, Prof Nairn Hutchison Fulton; s of William Fulton Wilson, of Kilmarnock, Ayrshire, and Anne Hutchison, *née* Stratton; *b* 26 April 1950; *Educ* Strathallan Sch, Univ of Edinburgh (BDS), Univ of Manchester (MSc, PhD); *m* 1; 2 da (Kirsty b 1972, Shona b 1976); m 2, 12 April 1982, Margaret Alexandra, *née* Jones; 1 s (Iain b 1984), 1 da (Hannah b 1983); *Career* lectr in restorative dentistry Univ of Edinburgh 1974–75; Univ of Manchester: lectr 1975–82, sr lectr 1982–86, prof of restorative dentistry Univ of Manchester 1986–, dean and clinical dir Univ Dental Hosp of Manchester 1992–95; non-exec dir North Manchester NHS Healthcare Tst 1994–; pres: Br Assoc of Teachers of Conservative Dentistry 1992, Section of Odontology Manchester Medical Soc 1993–94, Br Soc for Restorative Dentistry 1994–95; ed Jl of Dentistry 1986–; dean Faculty of Dental Surgery Royal Coll of Surgns of Edinburgh 1995–; fndr tstee Manchester Dental Educn Tst 1993–, tstee Oral and Dental Research 1995–, chm Manchester Dental Educn Centre 1995–; fell: American Coll of Dentists, Acad of Dental Materials; memb: Pierre Fauchard Acad, Acad of Operative Dentistry; FDS(Ed), DRD(Ed), FDS(Eng); *Recreations* various; *Style*— Prof Nairn Wilson; ✉ Unit of Conservative Dentistry, University Dental Hospital of Manchester, Higher Cambridge St, Manchester M15 6FH (☎ 0161 275 6660, fax 0161 275 6710)

WILSON, Hon Mr Justice; Hon Sir Nicholas Allan Roy; kt (1993); s of late (Roderick) Peter Garratt Wilson, of Fittleworth, Pulborough, W Sussex, and (Dorothy) Anne, *née* Chenevix-Trench; *b* 9 May 1945; *Educ* Bryanston Sch, Worcester Coll Oxford (BA); *m* 14 Dec 1974, Margaret, da of Reginald Frank Higgins (d 1986); 1 s (Matthew b 1977), 1 da (Camilla b 1981); *Career* called to the Bar Inner Temple 1967, practised Western Circuit, recorder of the Crown Court 1987–93, QC 1987, judge of the High Court of Justice (Family Div) 1993–; *Style*— The Hon Mr Justice Wilson; ✉ Royal Courts of Justice, Strand, London WC2A 2LL

WILSON, Nicholas Samuel; s of Dr John Alexander George Wilson, of Sheffield (d 1985), and Grace, *née* Twiselton (d 1974); *b* 27 Sept 1935; *Educ* Repton, Univ of Sheffield (LLB), Harvard Univ (LLM), Univ of California at Berkeley (postgrad res); *m* 1, 1961 (m dis 1980), Rosemary Ann Wilson; 2 s (Simon John b 1964, Justin Nicholas b 1966), 1 da (Sophie Rachael b 1973); m 2, 11 Oct 1982, Penelope Mary Elizabeth Moore; *Career* Nat Serv 2 Lt RA 1954–56, Capt TA 1956–61; articled with Keeble Hawson Steele Carr & Co Sheffield 1956–61, ptnr Slaughter and May 1968–90 (asst slr 1961–67), advsr National Westminster Bank Plc 1990–95; memb: DTI Advsy Ctee on Company Law 1970–74, Ctee of Inquiry on Indust Democracy 1975–76, City Capital Markets Ctee 1980–94 (chm 1990–94), Legal Risk Review Ctee 1991–92, Financial Law Panel 1993–95, Nat Art Collections Fund Devpt Bd 1991–95; chm Governing Body Repton Sch 1992– (memb 1982–); tstee COIF Charity Funds 1995–; Freeman Worshipful Co of Slrs; *Recreations* music, gardening, wine; *Clubs* City of London; *Style*— Nicholas Wilson, Esq; ✉ Overponds, Puttenham, Surrey GU3 1BG (☎ 01252 703261, fax 01252 703815)

WILSON, Nick; s of Stanley Wilson (d 1981), and Dorothy Wilson, of Winchester; *b* 21 April 1949; *Educ* Buxton Coll, Univ of Manchester (BA Drama); *m* Sept 1984, Annie; 3 da (Sadie b 7 March 1986, Abigail and Zoe (twins) b 26 March 1989), 1 s (Bradley b 29 May 1995), 1 step s (Robin b 31 Oct 1974); *Career* dir and prodr children's progs BBC 1975–84, ed children's progs TV-am 1984–87 (devised Wide Awake Club, Wacaday and Are You Awake Yet?), ed children's and youth progs Granada TV 1988–89, dir of progs The Children's Channel 1993–94, ptnr Clear Idea Television 1989– (prodr numerous progs incl Top Banana, Hitman & Her and Coast to Coast), controller of children's progs and sport Channel 5 Broadcasting 1996–; memb: BAFTA, RTS; *Awards* BAFTA nomination for Best Children's Factual Prog 1986, TRIC Award for Best Children's Prog 1987; *Recreations* tennis, horse racing, family; *Clubs* Royal County of Berkshire Health and Racquets; *Style*— Nick Wilson, Esq; ✉ Channel 5 Broadcasting Ltd, 22 Long Acre, London WC2E 9LY (☎ 0171 550 5555, fax 0171 497 5222)

WILSON, Nigel Guy; s of Noel Wilson, and Joan Louise, *née* Lovibond; *b* 23 July 1935; *Educ* Univ Coll Sch, CCC Oxford (BA, MA); *m* 1996, Hanneke Marion Wirtjes; *Career* lectr Merton Coll Oxford 1957–62, fell and tutor in classics Lincoln Coll 1962–; visiting prof: Univ of Padua 1985, École Normale Supérieure Paris 1986; FBA 1980; *Books* Menander Rhetor (with D A Russell, 1981), Scribes and Scholars (with L D Reynolds, 3 edn 1991), Scholars of Byzantium (1983, 2 edn 1996), Oxford Classical Text of Sophocles (with Sir Hugh Lloyd-Jones, 1990), From Byzantium to Italy (1992), Photius: The Bibliotheca (1994), Aelian: Varia Historia (1997); *Recreations* tennis (not lawn), oenology, travel, bridge; *Style*— Nigel Wilson, Esq, FBA; ✉ Lincoln College, Oxford, Oxfordshire OX1 3DR (☎ 01865 279794, fax 01865 279802)

WILSON, Nigel Richard; s of Lt-Col Richard Wilson (d 1992), of Stamford, Lincolnshire, and Jean Dorothy, *née* Jamieson (d 1992); *b* 18 Feb 1946; *Educ* Radley; *m* 8 July 1971, Ann (d 1990), da of John Rowlands, of Canada; 1 s (William Pennington b 1974), 1 da (Rebecca Pennington b 1977); m 2, 19 July 1991, Jennifer, da of Dudley Clark, of Thornborough, Bucks; *Career* ptnr McAnally Montgomery 1975–83 (memb Mgmnt Ctee 1982–83), ptnr Laing and Cruickshank 1983, dir Alexander Laing & Cruickshank 1983–88, md Laing & Cruickshank Investment Management Services Ltd 1987–88, dep md Cantrade Investment Management Ltd (formerly CS Investment Ltd) 1988–; chm: Ski Club of GB 1979–82, Royal Tokaji Wine Company 1993–, Chateau de Landiras Investments 1994–; dir: Nat Ski Fedn 1979–82, Tonbridge Services 1993–; hon steward All England Lawn Tennis & Croquet Club 1969–90, memb Multiple Sclerosis Fin Ctee 1983–; hon treasurer: Tonbridge Sch 1993–96, Sir Andrew Judd Fndn 1993–96; Freeman City of London 1972, Liveryman Worshipful Co of Skinners 1982 (memb Ct 1993); *Books* Silk Cut Ski Guide (1974); *Recreations* skiing, golf, tennis, cricket, shooting, fishing; *Clubs* City of London, Fly Fishers', Ski Club of GB; *Style*— Nigel Wilson, Esq; ✉ Old Manor Farm, Cublington, Leighton Buzzard, Bedfordshire LU7 0LE (☎ 01296 681279, fax 01296 688510); Cantrade Investment Management Ltd, No 4 Chiswell Street, Finsbury Square, London EC1Y 4UP (☎ 0171 614 8000, fax 0171 454 0888)

WILSON, Paul; s of Thomas William Wilson (d 1947), of Newcastle upon Tyne, and Gladys Rawden, *née* Scaife (d 1989); *b* 2 Aug 1947; *Educ* Univ of Northumbria and Univ of London (Dip in Nursing), Univ of Northumbria and CNAA (DMS), Henley Management Coll and Brunel Univ (MBA); *Career* registered mental nurse St Nicholas Hosp Newcastle 1965–68, head of nursing in intensive therapy (formerly staff nurse) Royal Victoria Infirmary Newcastle 1970–74 (registered gen nurse 1968–70), mangr of night nursing services West Sector Hosps Northumberland Health Authy 1974–76, staff offr to area nursing offr Merton Sutton and Wandsworth Area Health Authy 1976–77, divnl nursing offr Roehampton Health Dist 1977–82, dir policy and planning Maidstone Health Authy 1985–87 (chief nursing offr 1982–85), gen mangr Mental Health Services Greater Glasgow Health Bd 1987–91, dir of health care contracting Lothian Health Bd 1994–95 (dir of operations 1991–94), dir NHS Tsts NHS in Scotland Management Executive 1995–; *Recreations* cats, children, Moi, food, travel, music; *Style*— Paul Wilson; ✉ The Scottish Office, St Andrews House, Edinburgh EH1 3DG (☎ 0131 244 2179)

WILSON, Peter George Kirke; s of Col H W Wilson, OBE, TD (d 1965), of Enton, Surrey, and Lilian Rosemary, *née* Kirke; *b* 22 Oct 1942; *Educ* Winchester; *m* 18 Sept 1965, Susan Mary, da of Capt David Baynes, MC, DSO (d 1958); 2 s (Nigel b 1968, David b 1971), 1 da (Fiona b 1967); *Career* formerly with Deloitte Haskins & Sells, currently chm Stanton Chase International; FCA 1966; *Recreations* golf, tennis, study of WWII, old Morris cars; *Style*— Peter Wilson, Esq; ✉ Dormers, Kiln Way, Grayshott, Hindhead, Surrey GU26 6JF; 84 Ashbury Rd, London SW11; Stanton Chase International, Finland House, 56 Haymarket, London SW1Y 4RN (☎ 0171 930 6314)

WILSON, Peter Michael; s of Michael de Lancey Wilson, of Salisbury, and Mary Elizabeth, *née* Craufurd (d 1972); *b* 9 June 1941; *Educ* Downside, Oriel Coll Oxford (MA); *m* 5 Sept 1964, Lissa, da of Olaf Trab (d 1993); 1 s (Mark b 1974), 1 da (Juliet b 1972); *Career* chm Gallaher Ltd 1994–; *Style*— Peter Wilson, Esq; ✉ Gallaher Ltd, Members' Hill, Brooklands Rd, Weybridge, Surrey (☎ 01932 859777)

WILSON, Prof Peter Northcote; CBE (1987); s of L William Charles Montgomery Wilson (d 1980), and Fanny Louise, *née* White (d 1975); *b* 4 April 1928; *Educ* Whitgift Sch, Wye Coll London (BSc, MSc), Univ of Edinburgh, Univ of London (PhD); *m* 9 Sept 1950, (Maud Ethel) Bunny, da of William Ernest Bunn (d 1962); 2 s (David Richard b 1953, John Peter b 1959), 1 da (Rosemary Margaret b 1951); *Career* lectr in agric Makerere Coll Uganda 1951–57, sr lectr in animal prodn Imp Coll of Tropical Agric 1957–61, prof of agric Univ of W Indies 1961–64, dir Trinidad & Tobago Agric Credit Bank 1962–64, sr scientist and head of biometrics Unilever Research 1964–68, agric devpt dir SLF 1968–71, chief agric advsr BOCM Silcock 1971–83, prof of agric and rural economy Univ of Edinburgh 1984–90, princ E of Scotland Coll of Agric 1984–90, head Edinburgh Sch of Agric 1984–90, sci dir Edinburgh Centre for Rural Res 1990–, emeritus prof Univ of Edinburgh 1991–; visiting prof Univ of Reading 1975–83; govr Eastern Caribbean Farm Inst 1961–64, chm Frank Parkinson Agric Tst 1972–, pres Br Soc of Animal Prodn 1977–78 (hon memb 1990), memb Medicines Cmmn 1976–79, sec Inst of Biology 1992–96 (vice pres 1977–79 and 1991–92), sec-gen Scottish Agric Colls 1986–87, chm Agric Vet and Food Sci Sub Ctee Higher Educn Fundin Cncl 1992 and 1996, gen sec Royal Soc of Edinburgh 1996–; pres: Scotia Club 1991–94, Edinburgh Agric Soc 1992–94; life fell Wye Coll 1992; CBiol 1963, FIBiol 1963, FRSE 1987, FRSA 1989; *Books* Agriculture in The Tropics, Improved Feeding of Cattle and Sheep; *Recreations* photography, philately, ornithology, hill walking; *Clubs* Farmers', New (Edinburgh); *Style*— Prof Peter Wilson, CBE, FRSE; ✉ 8 St Thomas Rd, Edinburgh EH9 2LQ (☎ 0131 667 3182); Waddington Building, Kings Buildings, West Mains Rd, Edinburgh EH9 3JG (☎ 0131 650 5542)

WILSON, Peter Stafford; s of Sir Geoffrey Wilson, and Judy Chamberlain, *née* Trowbridge; *b* 12 Jan 1951; *Educ* St Albans Sch Washington DC, Westminster, Exeter Coll Oxford; *m* 1, (m dis); m 2, 1980, Patricia Clare, da of R Q Macarthur Stanham, of Camden Park, NSW, Aust; 3 s, 1 da; *Career* asst dir Welsh Nat Drama Co 1974–75, co dir Bush Theatre London 1975–76; assoc dir: Horsehoe Theatre Co Basingstoke 1976–79, Lyric Theatre Hammersmith 1980–83; ind prodr 1983–; credits incl: Edmund Kean with Ben Kingsley, Showpeople with David Kernan, A Betrothal with Ben Kingsley and Geraldine James, The Woman in Black, An Inspector Calls (UK, USA and Aust), Victor Spinetti Diaries, Julian Glover's Beowolf, Wind in the Willows, An Evening with Gary Lineker, Broken Glass, Michael Feinstein/Miriam Margolyes' Dickens Women, The Wind in the Willows, Old Wicked Songs, Birdy; chief exec: PWP Ltd 1983–, HM Tennent Ltd 1988–90, Norwich Theatre Royal 1992–; dir/prodr Mobil Touring Theatre 1985–; *Books* Forty Games for Frivolous People, The After Dinner Olympics; *Recreations* tennis, swimming; *Style*— Peter Wilson, Esq; ✉ PWP Ltd, The Penthouse, 7 Leicester Place, London WC2H 7BP (☎ 0171 734 7184, fax 0171 734 7185)

WILSON, (Edward) Philip; s of Peter Wilson, and Grace Helen Wilson; *b* 2 Nov 1940; *Educ* Bryanston, Conservatoire de Musique Paris; *m* 1970, Lady Alexandra Jellicoe, er da of 2 Earl Jellicoe, PC, DSO, MC; *Career* chm Philip Wilson Publishers Ltd (art book publishing and retail); *Style*— Philip Wilson, Esq; ✉ Philip Wilson Publishers Ltd, 143/149 Great Portland Street, London W1N 5FB (☎ 0171 436 4426)

WILSON, Sir Reginald Holmes; kt (1951); s of Alexander Wilson; *b* 1905; *Educ* St Lawrence Ramsgate, Univ of London (BCom); *m* 1, 1930, Rose Marie von Arnim; 1 s, 1 da; m 2, 1938, Sonia Havell; *Career* CA (Scot) 1927; ptnr Whinney Murray & Co 1937–72, princ asst sec Miny Shipping 1941, dir fin Miny War Tport 1941, under sec Miny Tport 1945, memb Royal Cmmn on the Press 1946, vice chm Hemel Hempstead Devpt Corp 1946–56, comptroller Br Tport Cmmn (BTC) 1947, govr LSE 1954–58; chm BTC: Eastern Area Bd 1955–60, London Midland Area Bd 1960–62; memb Ctee of Enquiry into Civil Air Tport 1967–69; chm: Thomas Cook & Son Ltd 1966–75, Transport Holding Co 1967–70 (dep chm 1962–67), Nat Freight Corp 1969–70, Transport Development Group Ltd 1971–75, Bd for Simplification of Int Trade Procedures 1976–79; chm Brompton Hosp Cardiographic Inst 1960–80; chm Bd Govrs: Hosp for Diseases of the Chest 1960–71, Nat Heart Hosp 1969–71, Nat Heart and Chest Hosps 1971–80; hon treas Int Hosp Fedn; Liveryman Worshipful Co of Carmen; FCIT, FBIM; *Style*— Sir Reginald Wilson; ✉ 49 Gloucester Square, London W2 2TQ

WILSON, Richard; OBE (1994); s of John Boyd Wilson (d 1975), and Euphemia, *née* Colquhoun (d 1960); *b* 9 July 1936; *Educ* Greenock HS, RADA; *Career* actor/director; *Theatre Actor* lead roles in Operation Bad Apple, An Honourable Trade, May Days, Normal Service (Hampstead Theatre); Edinburgh Traverse: title role in Uncle Vanya, Vladamir in Waiting for Godot; Stephen Feeble in The Weekend (tour and West End), Kabak in Occupations (Stables Theatre Manchester); Dr Rance in What the Butler Saw (RNT) 1995; *Plays Directed* Royal Court: Women Laughing, God's Second In Command, Other Worlds, Heaven and Hell, A Wholly Healthy Glasgow; Royal Exchange Manchester: The Lodger, Women Laughing (Best New Play Manchester Evening News, Writers' Guild of GB Award for regnl theatre), An Inspector Calls, A Wholly Healthy Glasgow; Hampstead Theatre: Imagine Drowning (John Whiting Award), President Wilson in Paris, Lenz; Bush Theatre: View of Kabul, Commitments; also Prin (Lyric Hammersmith and Lyric Shaftesbury), Simply Disconnected (Chichester) 1996; *TV Actor*, BBC: One Foot in the Grave (5 series), One Foot in the Algarve, The Vision Thing, Unnatural Pursuits, Fatherland, Normal Service, Tutti Frutti, The Holy City, Poppyland; Granada/Actor: Cluedo, Sherlock Holmes; YTV/Actor: High and Dry, Room at the Bottom, Emmerdale Farm; Under the Hammer, The Other Side of Paradise

(Central/Grundy), Inspector Morse (Zenith), Mr Bean (Thames), Selling Hitler (Euston), The Woman I Love (HTV), Murder by the Book (TVS), Walking the Plank (Yorkshire), Sweeney, Only When I Laugh (4 series), Victorian Scandals, Sharp Intake of Breath (2 series), My Good Woman (3 series), Crown Court, Gulliver's Travels (Channel 4) 1996; *TV Directed* BBC: Changing Step (winner Best Feature BANFF TV), A Wholly Unhealthy Glasgow, Under the Hammer, Remainder Man, Commitments; *Films Actor* Soft Top Hard Shoulder, Carry on Columbus, A Dry White Season, How to get ahead in Advertising, Fellow Travellers, Prick up your Ears, Whoops Apocalypse, Passage to India; British Comedy Award for Top TV Comedy Actor 1991, BAFTA Award for Light Entertainment 1991 and 1993, Scottish BAFTA for Best TV Actor 1993; *Recreations* squash, swimming and eating; *Clubs* RAC, Groucho's; *Style—* Richard Wilson, Esq, OBE; ✉ Conway van Gelder Ltd, 18–21 Jermyn Street, London SW1 6HP (☎ 0171 287 0077)

WILSON, Richard Henry; *b* 1953; *Educ* London Coll of Printing, Hornsey Coll of Art (Dip AD), Univ of Reading (MFA); *Career* artist; DAAD artist in residence Berlin 1992–93; contrib to numerous art pubns, work in various public and private collections; also musician (co-fndr and performer Bow Gamelan Ensemble 1983–); *Solo exhibitions* incl: 20:50 (Matt's Gallery London) 1987, One Piece at a Time (installation inside Tyne Bridge Newcastle) 1987, Art of Our Time (Saatchi Collection and Royal Scot Acad Edinburgh) 1987, Leading Lights (Brandts Kunsthallen Odense Denmark) 1989, Sea Level (Arnolfini Gallery Bristol) 1989, She Came in Through the Bathroom Window (Matt's Gallery London) 1989, High-Tec (MOMA Oxford) 1989, Take Away (Centre of Contemporary Art Warsaw 1990, Saatchi Gallery 1991), Lodger (Galerie Valeria Belvedere Milan) 1991, Swift Half and Return to Sender (Galerie de l'Ancienne Poste Calais) 1992, Drawings (Kunstlerhaus Bethanien Berlin) 1993, Matt's Gallery London 1994, Butler Gallery Kilkenny Castle Ireland 1994, LA/UK Festival Museum of Contemporary Art Los Angeles 1994, Galerie Klaus Fischer Berlin 1995, Galerie Valeria Belvedere Milan 1996, Room 6 Channel View Hotel Towner Art Gallery Eastbourne 1996, Formative Processes Gimpel Fils London 1996, Jamming Gears Serpentine Gallery 1995; *Group Exhibitions* incl: Up a Blind Alley (Trigon Biennale Graz Austria) 1987, Hot Live Still (Plymouth Art Centre) 1987, High Rise (São Paulo Bienal Brazil 1989, UK and USSR 1990), All Mod Cons (Edge Biennale Newcastle) 1990, Heatwave (Serpentine Gallery London) 1992, Galleria Mazzocchi Parma Italy 1992, Sydney Biennale 1992, Museet for Samtidskunst Oslo 1993, Private Kunstwerk Berlin 1993, The Boatshow (Cafe Gallery London) 1993, Time Out Billboard Project London 1993, Sendezeit: A Space without Art (Alexanderplatz Berlin) 1993, Tachikawa Public Art Project Tokyo 1994, Art Unlimited: Artists' Multiples (South Bank touring) 1994, Negev Desert Symposium Israel 1995, Contemporary Art Soc Drawing Show 1995, Nomad: Six European Sculptors (Stadtische Ausstellunshalle Munster) 1996, Art-itecture: Ten Artists (Museum of Contemporary Art Barcelona) 1996, Islands (Nat Museum of Contemporary Art Canberra Australia); *Awards* Boise travel scholarship 1977, Arts Cncl minor award 1977, Gtr London Arts Project award 1978, 1981 and 1989, RSA award 1996; *Style—* Richard Wilson, Esq; ✉ Matt's Gallery, 42–44 Copperfield Rd, London E3 4RR (☎ 0181 983 1771, fax 0181 983 1435)

WILSON, Sir Richard Thomas James; KCB (1997, CB 1991); s of Richard Ridley Wilson (d 1982), and Frieda Bell, *née* Finlay (d 1980); *b* 11 Oct 1942; *Educ* Radley, Clare Coll Cambridge (BA, LLB); *m* 25 March 1972, Caroline Margaret, da of Rt Hon Sir Frank Lee, GCMG, KCB (d 1971); 1 s (Tom b 10 March 1979), 1 da (Amy b 16 Feb 1981); *Career* called to the Bar Middle Temple 1965, private sec Bd of Trade 1969–71 (asst princ 1966–), princ Cabinet Office, asst sec Dept of Energy 1977 (joined Dept 1974), team leader privatisation of Britoil 1982, promoted to princ estab and fin offr (under sec) 1982, mgmnt and personnel office Cabinet 1986, economic secretariat (dep sec) Cabinet Office 1987–90, dep sec HM Treasy 1990–92, permanent sec DOE 1992–94, permanent under sec of state Home Office 1994–; *Style—* Sir Richard Wilson, KCB; ✉ Home Office, 50 Queen Anne's Gate, London SW1H 9AT

WILSON, Prof Sir Robert; kt (1989), CBE (1978); s of Robert Graham Wilson (d 1966), and Anne, *née* Riddle (d 1985); *b* 16 April 1927; *Educ* South Shields HS, Univ of Durham (BSc), Univ of Edinburgh (PhD); *m* 4 June 1986, Fiona, da of Lt-Col Kenneth Wheeler Nicholson; *Career* sr scientific offr Royal Observatory Edinburgh 1952–57, res fell Dominion Astrophysical Observatory Canada 1957–58, leader Plasma Spectroscopy Gp Harwell 1959–61, head Spectroscopy Divn Culham Lab 1962–68, dir Astrophysics Res Unit (SRC) 1968–72, head Dept of Physics and Astronomy UCL 1987–93 (Perren prof of astronomy 1972–94, dean of sci 1982–85); Herschel Medal RAS 1986, US Presidential Award 1988, Massey Award Royal Soc/COSPAR 1994; foreign memb American Philosophical Soc 1996; Hon DSc Queen's Univ Belfast 1995; FInstP 1966, FRS 1975; *Style—* Prof Sir Robert Wilson, CBE, FRS; ✉ Department of Physics & Astronomy, University College London, Gower St, London WC1E 6BT (☎ 0171 380 7154, fax 0171 380 7145, telex 28722 UCPHYS G)

WILSON, Robert (Bob); s of late William Smith Wilson, of Stubton, Notts, and Catherine Wingate, *née* Primrose (d 1991); *b* 30 Oct 1941; *Educ* Tapton House GS, Chesterfield GS, Loughborough Coll (Dip Physical Ed); *m* 25 July 1964, Margaret Vera, da of Stanley Miles; 2 s (John Richard b 2 Aug 1965, Robert James b 24 April 1969), 1 da (Anna Louise b 7 Dec 1966); *Career* PE teacher 1963–64; professional footballer (goalkeeper) Arsenal FC 1964–74: winner Euro Fairs Cup 1970, League and Cup double 1971; rep: Eng Schoolboys, Eng Grammar School, Br Univs, Derbyshire Schools Football, Eng Amateur Squad, full int Scot 1971–72; FA Coaching Award Full Badge 1967–; chm London Football Coaches' Assoc; pres: Arsenal Supporters' Club, Loughborough Colls FC; with BBC 1974–94 (presenter Football Focus and other sports progs), joined ITV (presenter Network Football) 1994–; dir Bob Wilson's Goalkeeping Sch 1981–; Hon DLitt Univ of Loughborough 1989; *Books* Goalkeeping, The Art of Goalkeeping (1973), You've Got To Be Crazy (1989); *Style—* Bob Wilson, Esq; ✉ Threepwood Leisure Services Ltd, 27 Great North Road, Brookmans Park, Nr Hatfield, Herts AL9 6LB (☎ 01707 654698, fax 01707 664276)

WILSON, Robert Julian (Robin); s of Prof Frank Percy Wilson (d 1963), and Joanna, *née* Perry-Keene (d 1985); *b* 6 July 1933; *Educ* St Edward's Sch Oxford, Trinity Coll Cambridge (Exhibition); *m* 6 April 1957, Caroline Anne, da of John Edward Maher; 2 da (Dr Katharine Joanna b 1959, Dr Olivia Jane b 1964); *Career* lectr Univ of Münster Westphalia 1955–58, asst master St Peter's Sch York 1958–62, head of English Nottingham HS 1962–72, headmaster Trinity Sch of John Whitgift Croydon 1972–94; chm HMC 1993, memb Cncl GPDST 1994–; govr: Brentwood Sch 1994–, St Peter's Sch York 1995–; FRSA 1982; *Books* Bertelsmann Sprachkursus Englisch (jt ed, 1959), Shakespeare: The Merchant of Venice (ed, 1971); *Recreations* drama, travel, skiing, golf; *Clubs* E India, Devonshire, Addington Golf; *Style—* Robin Wilson, Esq; ✉ 22 Beech House Rd, Croydon, Surrey CR0 1JP (☎ 0181 686 1915)

WILSON, Robert Peter; s of Alfred Wilson (d 1951), and Dorothy Eileen Wilson, MBE, *née* Mathews (d 1991); *b* 2 Sept 1943; *Educ* Epsom Coll, Univ of Sussex (BA), Harvard Business Sch (AMP); *m* 7 Feb 1975, Shirley Elisabeth, da of George Robson, of Hunmanby, Yorks; 1 s (Andrew), 1 da (Nicola); *Career* asst economist Dunlop Ltd 1966–67, economist Mobil Oil Co Ltd 1968–70; Rio Tinto Zinc Group: joined 1970, md A M and S Europe Ltd 1979–82, head of planning and devpt RTZ plc 1982–87, chief exec RTZ Corporation plc 1991–97 (dir 1987–), chm RTZ Corporation plc 1997–; non-exec dir: CRA Ltd (Australia) 1990– (unified with RTZ Dec 1995), Boots Company plc 1991–; Hon DSc Univ of Exeter 1993; *Recreations* theatre, opera, tennis; *Style—* Robert Wilson, Esq; ✉ The RTZ Corporation plc, 6 St James's Square, London SW1Y 4LD (☎ 0171 930 2399/071 895 9077, fax 0171 930 3249, telex 24639)

WILSON, Robert William; s of Alfred Wilson (d 1968), of Retford, Notts, and Winifred, *née* Scarborough (d 1964); *b* 18 Sept 1926; *Educ* Retford GS; *m* 24 March 1951, Pamela Marjorie, da of Horace Utley Dixon (d 1962), of Retford; 2 da (Jillian b 1954, Carol b 1956); *Career* Intelligence Corps 1945–48 (latterly in India); admitted slr 1951; cmmr for oaths 1957, HM Coroner for E Berks 1971–, conslt slrs Maidenhead 1989–; memb Coroners' Soc for England and Wales 1970, Lloyd's underwriter 1978, sec Lloyd's of Windsor; memb Law Soc 1960; *Recreations* yachting (yacht 'Nirvana Star'); *Style—* Robert Wilson, Esq; ✉ Oak Trees, West End, Waltham St Lawrence, Berks RG10 0NN (☎ 0118 934 3406, fax 0118 932 0599)

WILSON, Dr the Hon Robin James; elder s of Baron Wilson of Rievaulx, KG, OBE, PC, FRS (Life Peer, d 1995); *b* 5 Dec 1943; *Educ* University Coll Sch Hampstead, Balliol Coll Oxford (BA, MA), Univ of Pennsylvania (MA, PhD), MIT; *m* 1968, (Margaret Elizabeth) Joy, da of Brian and Sallie Crispin, of Dawlish; 2 da (Jennifer b 1975, Catherine (twin) b 1975); *Career* sr lectr in mathematics Jesus Coll Oxford 1969–72; Open Univ: sr lectr in mathematics 1972–, actg head Dept of Pure Mathematics 1990–92, dean and dir of studies Mathematics and Computing Faculty 1995–; pt/t sr lectr in mathematics: Keble Coll Oxford 1980–, Lady Margaret Hall Oxford 1988–94; several times visiting prof of mathematics Colorado Coll USA; *Books* Introduction to Graph Theory (1972), Let Newton Be! (jtly, 1988), fourteen other mathematics books, Gilbert and Sullivan: The D'Oyly Carte Years (jtly, 1984), three other music books; *Recreations* music (performing and listening), travel, philately; *Style—* Dr the Hon Robin Wilson; ✉ 15 Chalfont Rd, Oxford OX2 6TL

WILSON, Robin Lee; CBE (1992); s of Henry Eric Wilson, OBE (d 1958), of Jos, Nigeria, and Catherine Margaret, *née* Lee (d 1935); *b* 4 March 1933; *Educ* Glenalmond Coll Perthshire, Univ of Glasgow (BSc); *m* 1956, Gillian Margaret, da of L J N Kirkby; 1 s (James David b 1962), 2 da (Jacqueline Margaret b 1957, Ginnette Mary b 1960); *Career* trainee then asst engr Sir William Halcrow & Partners consulting engrs 1952–56; R Travers Morgan & Partners: sr engr Nigeria 1956–60, ptnr Belfast practice 1965, ptnr London 1966, sr ptnr 1985, gp chm 1988–91; dir Travers Morgan Ltd conslts 1988–91 (conslt 1991–94), chm Thomas Telford Ltd publishers 1990–94, dir Mid Kent Holdings plc 1994–; chm: Construction Industry Cncl 1994–96, Bd of Engrs' Regulation 1994–; Coopers Hill Meml prize ICE 1989, Inst of Highways & Transportation award 1990; memb Cncl: ICE 1977–80, 1983–86 and 1987–93, ACE 1985–88, Construction Indust Cncl 1990–; senator Engrg Cncl 1992–; pres ICE 1991–92; Min's nominee SE Cncl for Sport and Recreation 1987–90; memb Cncl Glenalmond Coll 1985–; Liveryman: Worshipful Co of Paviors 1972 (memb Ct of Assts), Worshipful Co of Engrs 1989; Hon DSc City Univ 1991; FICE 1966, FIHT 1966, MConsE 1966, FCIT 1992, FEng 1986; *Publications* author of papers in learned jls on highway engrg and related subjects; *Recreations* sailing, golf; *Clubs* Royal Thames Yacht, Itchenor Sailing, W Sussex Golf; *Style—* Robin Wilson, Esq, CBE, FEng; ✉ The Grove House, Little Bognor, Pulborough, Sussex RH20 1JT (☎ 01798 865569, fax 01798 865672)

WILSON, Rodney Herbert William; *b* 21 June 1942; *Educ* Windsor GS for Boys, Berkshire Coll of Art, Camberwell Sch of Art (NDD), Hornsey Coll of Arts (ATD); *Career* asst lectr Loughborough Coll of Art 1965–69; Arts Council: film offr 1970–85, dir Film, Video and Broadcasting Dept 1986–; memb: PACT, RTS, IMZ; *Style—* Rodney Wilson, Esq; ✉ Arts Council of England, 14 Great Peter Street, London SW1P 3NQ (☎ 0171 973 6443, fax 0171 973 6581)

WILSON, Ronald George; s of Robert Paterson Wilson (d 1951), of Aberdeen, and Ena Watson Cowie Wilson (d 1965); *b* 20 April 1937; *Educ* Aberdeen GS, Univ of Aberdeen (MB ChB, MD); *m* 1, 6 April 1963 (m dis 1992), Muriel, da of James Hutcheon (d 1968), of Aberdeen; 1 s (James Robert b 13 Oct 1967), 1 da (Fiona Alys b 18 Nov 1970); m 2, 29 March 1996, Susan, da of Steven Blackett, of Newcastle; *Career* surgn Lt RN with 40 Commando RM 1963–65, with Med Branch Royal Marine Reserves until 1982; sr house offr in surgery (Aberdeen 1966–68), Bristol Trg Scheme 1968–70, registrar in gen surgery Bristol 1970–71, res in breast cancer Edinburgh Royal Infirmary 1971–73, lectr in surgery Univ of Nottingham 1973–77; conslt surgn Gen Hosp Newcastle upon Tyne; Breast Screening Prog mangr until 1996, ret; currently regnl QA mangr for screening: Regnl and Nat Organisational Ctees, Nat Ctee for Evaluation; FRCSEd; *Clubs* Moyniham Chirurgical; *Style—* Ronald Wilson, Esq; ✉ 14 Hudshaw Gardens, Hexham, Northumberland NE46 1HY (☎ and fax 01434 606180); Quality Assurance Reference Centre for Screening, Newcastle upon Tyne (☎ 0191 273 8811 ext 22602, fax 0191 272 5620); Leeds office (☎ 0113 292 4490, fax 0113 292 4492)

WILSON, Simon; *Career* jewellery designer/retailer; co-fndr (with Nicky Butler) Butler and Wilson Antiquarius Market King's Road Chelsea 1968, opened flagship shop Fulham Rd 1974, cmmnd to design Christmas light display for Regent Street 1979–80 and 1980–81, Export Dept opened 1983, cmmnd to design exclusive range for Giorgio Armani 1984, second shop opened South Molton St 1985, joined London Designer Collections (first show Olympia) and opened concession at Harrods 1986, opened second concession at Jaeger Regent St 1987, shops opened West Hollywood Calif, Glasgow and at Selfridges 1988, major restrospective exhbn celebrating 21st anniversary 1989, subject of book Rough Diamonds (author Vivienne Becker) 1990, launched extended accessory line (belts and handbags) 1991, retail ops extended to Heathrow Airport 1992, joined QVC home shopping channel 1993, cmmnd to design exclusive range for tourists visiting Tower of London 1994; *Style—* Simon Wilson, Esq; ✉ Butler and Wilson, 189 Fulham Road, London SW3 (☎ 0171 352 3045, 0171 352 8255) and 20 South Molton Street, London W1 (☎ 0171 409 2955)

WILSON, Stephen Richard Mallett (Sam); s of Dr Peter Remington Wilson, of Taunton, and Kathleen Rosemary Hough, *née* Mallett (d 1988); *b* 12 Oct 1941; *Educ* Uppingham, Clare Coll Cambridge (MA), Coll of Law Guildford; *m* 1969, Marycita Jane, da of Gwynn Craven Hargrove; 2 da (Gemma Harriet b 11 April 1972, Alexandra Jane b 17 Jan 1974), 1 s (Thomas William Gwynn b 1 Sept 1979); *Career* articled clerk Simmons & Simmons (admitted 1966); ptnr: Westhorp Ward & Catchpole 1968–89, Birkett Westhorp & Long 1989–95, Birketts 1995–; non-exec dir Boydell & Brewer Ltd (publishers); memb Cncl Law Soc 1990– (chm Standards & Guidance Ctee 1996–), pres Suffolk & North Essex Law Soc 1988 (sec 1980–88), clerk to Gen Cmmrs of Income Tax (Stowmarket Div); memb: Law Soc 1964, Soc of Tst and Estate Practitioners; *Recreations* tennis, golf, hunting, sailing, skiing, bridge, crosswords, classical music (particularly opera); *Style—* Sam Wilson, Esq; ✉ Birketts, 24/26 Museum Street, Ipswich, Suffolk IP1 1HZ (☎ 01473 232300)

WILSON, (Catherine) Thelma; da of John Matters (d 1964), of Ashington, Northumberland, and Eleanor Irene, *née* Hudson (d 1979); *b* 9 June 1929; *Educ* St Margaret's HS Gosforth, Central Newcastle HS, King's Coll Durham Univ (BA); *m* 26 Sept 1953, Noel, s of the late Andrew Wilson, of Ashington, Northumberland; 2 s ((Peter) Lawrence b 16 Jan 1956, Michael David b 5 Aug 1959); *Career* geriatric social worker Wimbledon Guild of Social Welfare 1952–56, lectr several Colls in London 1958–65, princ lectr in social policy E London Univ (formerly Poly) 1965–94; conslt on preparation for retirement Tate & Lyle Refineries London 1968–93, UK rep on the Int Ctee Euro Regnl Clearing House for Community Work 1971–78, cncl memb for the educn and trg of health visitors 1973–83, short term expert Social Devpt Fund UN 1973, hon sec Social

Admin & Social Work Ctees of the Jt Univ Cncl for Social & Public Admin 1972–79, memb Exam Ctee Local Govt Trg Bd and several related activities 1979–96, expert assignment Regnl Office for Euro World Health Orgn 1981, advsr Nursing and Social Work Serv Soldiers' Sailors & Airmen's Families Assoc 1983–, mangr (Mental Health Act) Goodmayes Hosp 1990–93, conslt with Bray Leino Trg for Change 1994–, asst sec The Friends of St Thomas' Hosp 1995–96; winner: CEC Erasmus and Tempus awards 1990, 1991, 1992, 1993 and 1994, British Cncl awards 1990 and 1991; Medal of Honour Med Acad Poznan Poland; Freeman City of London 1984, Liveryman Worshipful Co of Chartered Secs and Admins 1984; MISW 1964, FCIS 1974 (ACIS 1964), FRSA 1990; *Books* over 40 pubns including Penal Services for Offenders; comparative studies of England and Poland 1984–85 (1987); *Recreations* reading, travel; *Clubs* Royal Over-Seas League; *Style*— Mrs Thelma Wilson; ✉ 163 Clarence Gate Gardens, Glentworth Street, London NW1 6AP (☎ and fax 0171 262 9712)

WILSON, Prof Thomas; OBE (1945); s of John B Wilson (d 1945), and Margaret, *née* Ellison (d 1977); *b* 23 June 1916; *Educ* Methodist Coll Belfast, Queen's Univ Belfast (BA), Univ of London (PhD), Univ of Oxford (MA); *m* 6 July 1943, Dorothy Joan, da of Arthur Parry; 1 s (John), 2 da (Moya, Margaret); *Career* WWII Miny of Econ Warfare 1940–41, Miny of Aircraft Prodn 1941–42, War Cabinet Offices 1942–45; Econ Section Cabinet 1945–46; fell Univ Coll Oxford 1946–58, Adam Smith prof of political economy Univ of Glasgow 1958–82; visiting fell All Souls Coll Oxford 1974–75; numerous govt consultancies; hon fell LSE 1979; Hon DUniv Stirling 1981; FBA 1976, FRSE 1980; *Books* Fluctuations in Income and Employment (1942), Oxford Studies in the Price Mechanism (ed, 1951), Inflation (1961), Planning and Growth (1964), Essays on Adam Smith (jt ed with A S Skinner, 1975), The Market and the State (jt ed with A S Skinner, 1976), Welfare State (with D J Wilson, 1982), Inflation, Unemployment and the Market (1984), Ulster - Conflict and Consent (1989), The State and Social Welfare (jt ed with D J Wilson, 1991), Churchill and the Prof (1995); *Recreations* hill walking, photography; *Clubs* Athenaeum; *Style*— Prof Thomas Wilson, OBE, FRSE, FBA; ✉ 1 Chatford House, The Promenade, Clifton Down, Bristol BS8 3NG (☎ 0117 973 0741)

WILSON, Thomas Brendan; CBE (1990); s of Thomas Joseph Wilson (d 1971), of Glasgow, and Maureen, *née* O'Doherty (d 1975); *b* 10 Oct 1927; *Educ* Blairs Coll Aberdeen, Univ of Glasgow, Royal Coll of Music; *m* 20 Sept 1952, Margaret, *née* Rayner; 3 s (Brendan b 20 March 1954, Martin b 21 Jan 1957, Stephen b 28 June 1958); *Career* composer and lectr; Nat Serv RAF 1945–48; Music Dept Univ of Glasgow: lectr 1957–71, reader 1971–77, personal chair 1977 (now emeritus); advsy positions: Arts Council, New Music Group of Scotland, SPNM, Composers' Guild of Great Britain (chm 1985–88), Scottish Society of Composers (hon pres); compositions incl: Variations for Orchestra, Second Symphony 1964, Concerto for Orchestra 1967, Touchstone (portrait for orchestra) 1967, Third Symphony 1979, Introit 1982, Piano Concerto 1985, St Kentigern Suite 1985, Viola Concerto 1987, Violin Concerto 1993, Sunset Song (BBC), Trumpet Concerto (for John Wallace), Concerto for Trombone, Concerto for Guitar, Carillon; cmmns for: BBC Proms, Scottish Opera, Scottish Ballet, Edinburgh Festival, Cheltenham Festival, City of London Festival, Musica Nova, BBC, Glasgow Cathedral (850th anniversary), Paisley (500th anniversary as Royal Burgh) and New International Concert Hall Glasgow inaugural concert; recordings incl: complete Piano Music, Piano Concerto and Introit, Piano Sonata, St Kentigern Suite, Chamber Symphony, Violin Concerto; Hon DMus Univ of Glasgow 1991; FRSAMD 1991, FRSE 1994; *Recreations* golf, talking shop; *Style*— Thomas Wilson, Esq, CBE; ✉ 120 Dowanhill Street, Glasgow G12 9DN (☎ and fax 0141 339 1699)

WILSON, Thomas Charles; s of Jeremy Charles Wilson, DFC, of Fulmer, Bucks, and June Patricia, *née* Bucknill; *b* 2 June 1946; *Educ* Eton, Aix-en-Provence Univ; *m* 5 Dec 1980, (Elizabeth) Jane, da of Lt-Gen Sir Napier Crookenden, KCB, DSO, OBE; 1 s (James b 1984), 1 da (Tobina b 1981), 1 step s (Geoffrey b 1977); *Career* sr ptnr corp fin Price Waterhouse 1987– (articled clerk 1965–77, ptnr 1977–); FCA 1974; *Recreations* golf, tennis, fishing, bridge; *Clubs* Hurlingham Denham Golf; *Style*— Thomas Wilson, Esq; ✉ Price Waterhouse, No 1 London Bridge, London SE1 9QL (☎ 0171 939 3000, fax 0171 403 2283)

WILSON, Thomas David; s and h of Sir David Wilson, 3 Bt, *qv*; *b* 6 Jan 1959; *Educ* Harrow; *m* 21 July 1984, Valerie, er da of Vivian David Davies Stogdale, of Monks Farm, Shotover, Oxon; 2 s (Fergus b 24 April 1987, Oscar b 10 June 1989); *Recreations* skiing, shooting, fishing, tennis, sailing; *Clubs* Royal Southern Yacht, Mill Reef (Antigua); *Style*— Thomas D Wilson, Esq; ✉ Argyll House, 120 Balham Park Road, London SW12 8EA (☎ 0181 767 7599); R Mears & Co Ltd, Latham House, 16 Minories, London EC3N 1AX (☎ 0171 702 3571, fax 0171 702 0154)

WILSON, Timothy Hugh; s of Hugh Walker Wilson (d 1965), and Lilian Rosemary, *née* Kirke; *b* 8 April 1950; *Educ* Winchester Coll, Mercersburg Acad USA, Corpus Christi Coll Oxford (MA), Warburg Inst Univ of London (MPhil), Univ of Leicester; *m* 12 May 1984, Jane, da of Francis George Lott and Anne Josephine Lott; 2 s (Alastair James Johnnie b 11 June 1983, David George Lorenzo b 15 March 1992), 1 da (Julia Annie Jane b 17 Sept 1986); *Career* res asst National Maritime Museum 1977–79, asst keeper Dept of Medieval and Later Antiquities British Museum 1979–90, keeper of Western Art Ashmolean Museum 1990–; tstee Ruskin Fndn 1994; fell: Villa I Tatti Florence 1984, Balliol Coll Oxford 1990, Royal Soc of Painter Printmakers 1990; FSA 1989; *Books* Flags At Sea (1986), Ceramic Art of the Italian Renaissance (1987), Maiolica: Italian Renaissance Ceramics in the Ashmolean Museum (1989), Itlian Maiolica of the Renaissance (1996); contrib to books and exhbn catalogues, various articles in specialist jls on Renaissance ceramics and related subjects; *Style*— Timothy Wilson, Esq, FSA; ✉ Balliol College, Oxford OX1 3BJ; Department of Western Art, Ashmolean Museum, Oxford OX1 2PH (☎ 01865 278041, fax 01865 278056)

WILSON, Col Timothy John Michael; s of Lt-Col A C Wilson (d 1975), of Kent and Devon, and Margaret Beverley, *née* Iliffe; *b* 23 March 1932; *Educ* Cranbrook Sch Kent, Canadian Army Staff Coll, Nat Defence Coll, Indian Nat Defence Coll; *m* 23 Sept 1961, Kitty Maxine, da of Maj Seymour Norton-Taylor, of Poole, Dorset; 2 da (Vanessa b 1963, Jennifer b 1965); *Career* 2 Lt and Lt 1950–53, Lt 2 i/c RM Detachment HMS Gambia 1953–55 (memb earthquake relief team Zante Ionian Islands 1953), Troop Subaltern 40 Commando RM 1955–57, served Cyprus, Near East (severely wounded at Port Said Landings 1956, despatches); housemaster RM Sch of Music 1957–59, motor tport course 1959–60, local Capt ADC to C-in-C Near East HQ Near East Cyprus 1960–61, Capt Motor Tport Offr RM Poole 1961–63, staff course Canadian Army Staff Coll 1963–65, Adj and Co Cdr 40 Commando RM (subsequently Maj) 1965–68 (served Malaysia 1965–67), Maj GSO 2 (instr) Jr Div Army Staff Coll Warminster 1968–70, Bde Maj UK Commandos GSO 2 Ops and Planning HQ Commando Forces RM 1970–72, staff course Nat Def Coll 1972–73, Lt-Col Royal Marines Rep USMC Devpt and Educn Cmd 1973–75, CO 42 Commando RM 1975–78 (served N Ireland 1976), Col Dir drafting and records RM HMS Centurion 1978–79, staff course Indian Nat Def Coll New Delhi 1979–80, Asst Adj Gen to Cmdt Gen RM MOD London 1980–83, ADC to HM The Queen 1982–83, memb HM Bodyguard of the Hon Corps of Gentlemen of Arms 1984–; working volunteer memb Kent and E Sussex Steam Railway, Hon MSc (def studies) Allahabad 1980; *Recreations* beagling, golf, tennis, travel; *Clubs* Army and Navy; *Style*— Col Timothy Wilson

WILSON, Warren; s of Robert Wilson, of Ashton-under-Lyne, Lancs, and Flora Wilson; *b* 8 Aug 1945; *Educ* Hathershan Sch; *m* 1, Linda; 1 s (Luke Russell b 8 Dec 1970), 1 da (Miranda Jane b 28 Aug 1968); m 2, Wendy Monica; 1 da (Nathalie May b 19 Nov 1990), 1 s (Harry John b 21 May 1993); *Career* reporter Oldham Evening Chronicle 1964–68, sub ed Express and Star Wolverhampton 1968–70; Shropshire Star: Shropshire liaison 1970–72, dep news ed 1972–77, news ed 1977–91, ed 1991–94; ed Express and Star Wolverhampton 1995–; memb Guild of Br Newspaper Eds; *Recreations* gardening, wine, golf, music; *Clubs* Telford Hotel Golf and Country; *Style*— Warren Wilson, Esq; ✉ 27 Exeter Drive, Old College Fields, Wellington, Shropshire (☎ 01952 245579); Express and Star Ltd, Queen Street, Wolverhampton, West Midlands WV1 3BU (☎ 01902 313131, car 0802 218731)

WILSON, Dr William; *b* 29 Oct 1928; *Educ* Glasgow HS, Univ of Glasgow (MB ChB); *m* 14 June 1958, Isabel, da of Col David Mackie, MC (d 1966), of Stamford House, Dundonald, Ayrshire; 1 s (David b 1965), 1 da (Anne b 1961); *Career* sr conslt ophthalmologist Glasgow Royal Infirmary 1962–, hon clinical lectr Univ of Glasgow 1962–; conslt: St Vincent Sch for the Blind Glasgow, Kelvin Sch for Partially Sighted Children; examiner: RCSEd and Glasgow 1964–, Coll Ophthalmologists 1988–; pres Scottish Ophthalmological Soc 1982–84; FRCSEd 1958, FCOphth; *Recreations* gardening, DIY; *Clubs* Royal Scottish Automobile; *Style*— Dr William Wilson; ✉ 34 Calderwood Rd, Newlands, Glasgow G43 2RU; Crossways, Muthill, Perthshire (☎ 0141 637 4898)

WILSON-JOHNSON, David Robert; s of Harry Kenneth Johnson, of Irthlingborough, Northants, and Sylvia Constance, *née* Wilson; *b* 16 Nov 1950; *Educ* Wellingborough Sch, Br Inst of Florence, St Catharine's Coll Cambridge (BA), RAM; *Career* baritone; Royal Opera House Covent Garden debut We Come to the River 1976, Paris Opera debut Die Meistersinger 1989, US debut with Cleveland Orch 1990, NY debut with NY Philharmonic 1992; ARAM 1984, FRAM 1988; *Performances* at Covent Garden incl: Billy Budd 1982, L'Enfant et les Sortilèges 1983 and 1987, Boris Godunov 1984, Die Zauberflöte 1985, 1986 and 1987, Turandot 1987, Madam Butterfly 1988, St François d'Assise (title role) 1988 (winner Evening Standard Award for Opera); others incl: Eight Songs for a Mad King (Paris) 1979, Last Night of the Proms 1981 and 1986; Paris Opera incl: Die Meistersinger, Die Zavberflötè, Billy Budd; Netherlands Opera incl: Punch and Judy (Birtwistle) 1992, Von Heute Auf Morgen (Schoenberg) 1995, The Nose (Schostakovich) 1996, Oedipe (Enescu's) 1996; festival appearances at: Glyndebourne, Edinburgh, Bath, Bergen, Berlin, Geneva, Graz, Holland, Hong Kong, Jerusalem, Orange, Paris, Vienna; *Recordings* incl: Schubert Winterreise, Schoenberg Ode to Napoleon, La Traviata, Lucrezia Borgia, Mozart Masses from King's College, Haydn Nelson Mass, Belshazzar's Feast, Elgar The Kingdom, Berlioz L'Enfance du Christ, Tippett The Ice Break, Bach Cantatas and B Minor Mass; *Films* The Midsummer Marriage (Sir Michael Tippett), The Lighthouse (Sir Peter Maxwell Davies); *Recreations* swimming, slimming, gardening, growing walnuts at house in the Lot; *Style*— David Wilson-Johnson, Esq; ✉ 28 Englefield Road, London N1 4ET (☎ 0171 254 0941); c/o Lies Askonas Ltd, 6 Henrietta Street, Covent Garden, London WC2E 8LA (☎ 0171 379 7700, fax 0171 242 1831, telex 921104 ASKONA G)

WILSON OF LANGSIDE, Baron (Life Peer UK 1969), of Broughton, in Co Edinburgh; Henry Stephen Wilson; PC (1967), QC (Scot 1965); s of James Wilson, of Glasgow, solicitor; *b* 21 March 1916; *Educ* Glasgow HS, Univ of Glasgow (MA, LLB); *m* 1942, Jessie Forrester (d 1996), da of late William Nisbet Waters, of Paisley; *Career* serv WWII HLI and RAC; barr 1946, slr-gen Scotland 1965–67, lord-advocate 1967–70, Sheriff Princ Glasgow and Strathkelvin 1975–77; contested (Lab): Dumfriesshire 1950 and 1955, Edinburgh W 1951; joined SDP 1981, sits as cross bench Peer in House of Lords; *Style*— The Rt Hon the Lord Wilson of Langside, PC, QC

WILSON OF RADCLIFFE, Baroness; Freda; *née* Mather; *b* 23 Jan 1930; *m* 1976, as his 2 w, Baron Wilson of Radcliffe (d 1983, former Lab Peer and chief exec offr Co-operative Wholesale Soc); 1 step da; *Style*— The Rt Hon the Lady Wilson of Radcliffe; ✉ 10 Gisburn Drive, Walshaw, Bury BL8 3DH

WILSON OF TILLYORN, Baron (Life Peer UK 1992), of Finzean in the District of Kincardine and Deeside and of Fanling in Hong Kong; Sir David Clive Wilson; GCMG (1991, KCMG 1987, CMG 1985); s of Rev William Skinner Wilson (d 1942), and Enid, *née* Sanders; *b* 14 Feb 1935; *Educ* Trinity Coll, Glenalmond, Keble Coll Oxford (scholar, MA), Univ of Hong Kong, Columbia Univ NY (visiting scholar), Univ of London (PhD); *m* 1 April 1967, Natasha Helen Mary, da of late Bernard Gustav Alexander; 2 s (Hon Peter Michael Alexander b 31 March 1968, Hon Andrew Marcus William b 21 June 1969); *Career* HM Dip Serv: joined SE Asia Dept FO 1958, third sec Vientiane 1959–60, language student Hong Kong 1960–62, third then second sec Peking 1963–65, first sec Far Eastern Dept 1965–68, resigned 1968; ed The China Quarterly (Contemporary China Inst SOAS Univ of London) 1968–74; rejoined HM Dip Serv 1974, Cabinet Office 1974–77, political advsr to Govr of Hong Kong 1977–81, head S Euro Dept FCO 1981–84, asst under sec of state responsible for Asia and the Pacific FCO 1984–87, Govr and C-in-C of Hong Kong 1987–92; chm Scottish Hydro-Electric plc 1993–, dir Martin Currie Pacific Trust plc; chllr Univ of Aberdeen 1997–; chm Scottish Ctee British Cncl 1993–, pres Bhutan Soc of the UK 1993–, vice pres Royal Scottish Geographical Soc 1996–; memb: Governing Body SOAS, Cncl Glenalmond Coll, N Cncl CBI Scotland; Hon LLD: Univ of Aberdeen 1990, Univ of Abertay Dundee 1995, Chinese Univ of Hong Kong 1996; Hon DLitt Univ of Sydney 1991; *Recreations* mountaineering, skiing, reading; *Clubs* Alpine, New (Edinburgh); *Style*— The Rt Hon Lord Wilson of Tillyorn, GCMG; ✉ Tillyorn, Finzean, Aberdeenshire AB31 6PN; Scottish Hydro-Electric plc, 10 Dunkeld Road, Perth PA1 5WA (☎ 01738 455200)

WILTON, (James) Andrew Rutley; *Career* asst keeper: British Art Walker Art Gallery Liverpool 1965–67, Dept of Prints and Drawings British Museum 1967–76; curator Prints and Drawings Yale Center for British Art New Haven 1976–80, asst keeper Dept of Prints and Drawings British Museum 1980–84, keeper of The British Collection Tate Gallery 1989– (curator Turner Collection The Clore Gallery 1985–89); *Books* Constable's English Landscape Scenery (1976), The Wood Engravings of William Blake (1976), British Watercolours 1750–1850 (1977), Turner in Switzerland (with John Russell, 1977), William Pars: Journey through the Alps (1979), The Life and Work of J M W Turner (1979), Turner Abroad (1982), Turner in his Time (1987); author of numerous exhibition catalogues; FRSA, Hon OWCS; *Recreations* music, walking, architecture; *Clubs* The Athenaeum; *Style*— Andrew Wilton, Esq; ✉ Tate Gallery, Millbank, London SW1P 4RG (☎ 0171 887 8046, fax 0171 887 8047)

WILTON, Sir (Arthur) John; KCMG (1979, CMG 1967), KCVO (1979), MC (1945); s of Walter Wilton (d 1944); *b* 21 Oct 1921; *Educ* Wanstead HS, St John's Coll Oxford; *m* 1950, Maureen Elizabeth Alison, *née* Meaker; 4 s, 1 da; *Career* Royal Ulster Rifles 1942 (despatches), Maj; HM Dip Serv 1947–79: dir MECAS Shemlan 1960–65, dep high cmmr Aden 1966–67, ambass Kuwait 1970–74, under sec FCO 1974–75, ambass Jedda 1976–79; dir London House for Overseas Graduates 1979–86, chm Arab-Br Centre 1981–86, govr Hele's sch 1989–92, pres Plymouth Branch English Speaking Union 1991–; FRSA 1982–92; *Recreations* reading and current affairs, gardening; *Style*— Sir John Wilton, KCMG, KCVO, MC

WILTON, Penelope; *m* 1990, Ian Holm, *qv*; *Career* actress; *Theatre* incl: NT: The Philanderer, Betrayal, Sisterly Feelings, Man and Superman, Much Ado About Nothing, Major Barbara, The Secret Rapture, Piano, Landscape; Greenwich Theatre: Measure for Measure, All's Well that Ends Well, The Norman Conquests; Royal Court: The Philanthropist, West of Suez; Nottingham Playhouse: King Lear, Widowers House; other credits incl: The Cherry Orchard (Lyceum Theatre Edinburgh), The Seagull (Chichester), Bloomsbury (Phoenix), The Deep Blue Sea (Almeida and Apollo), Andromache (The

Old Vic), Vita and Virginia (Ambassadors), Moon Light (Pinter Festival), Landscape (Gate Theatre Dublin), Cherry Orchard (RSC); *Television* BBC: Mrs Warren's Profession, The Song of Songs, The Pearcross Girls, Othello, King Lear, The Widowing of Mrs Holroyd, Pasmore, Country, The Norman Conquests, The Monocled Mutineer, The Tale of Beatrix Potter, Ever Decreasing Circles, Screaming, The Borrowers (2 series), The Deep Blue, Madly in Love, Landscape; *Films* incl: Joseph Andrews, French Lieutenant's Woman, Slaughter House, Clockwise, Cry Freedom, Blame it on the Bellboy, The Secret Rapture, Carrington; *Style*— Ms Penelope Wilton; ✉ c/o Julian Belfrage Associates, 46 Albemarle Street, London W1X 4PP (☎ 0171 491 4400, fax 0171 493 5460)

WILTON, Rosalyn Susan; *née* Trup; da of Samuel Trup, and Celia, *née* Aronson; *b* 25 Jan 1952; *Educ* Univ of London (BSc); *m* 11 April 1978, Gerald Parselle Wilton, s of Orville Wilton; 2 da (Georgina b 1979, Emily b 1981); *Career* sterling money broker Butler Till Ltd 1973–79; dir: GNI Ltd 1982–84, Drexel Burnham Lambert Ltd (md Institutional Financial Futures and Options and md Int Fixed Income) 1984–90, md Transaction Products Reuters Ltd 1992- (sr vice pres 1990–92); dir The London Int Financial Futures Exchange 1985–90; *Style*— Mrs Rosalyn Wilton; ✉ Reuters Limited, 85 Fleet St, London EC4P 4AJ (☎ 0171 250 1122)

WILTON, 7 Earl of (UK 1801); Seymour William Arthur John Egerton; also Viscount Grey de Wilton (UK 1801); s of 6 Earl of Wilton (d 1927, gs of 2 Earl, himself yr bro of 2 Marquess of Westminster and er bro of 1 Baron Ebury); *b* 29 May 1921; *Educ* Eton; *m* 1962, Diana, da of Roy Galway and formerly w of David Naylor-Leyland, MVO, 3 s of Sir Edward Naylor-Leyland, 2 Bt; *Heir* 4 cous, 6 Baron Ebury; *Clubs* White's; *Style*— The Rt Hon the Earl of Wilton; ✉ The Old Vicarage, Castle Hedingham, Halstead, Essex CD9 3EZ

WILTSHIRE, Earl of; Christopher John Hilton Paulet; s and h of 18 Marquess of Winchester, *qv*; *b* 30 July 1969; *Style*— Earl of Wiltshire; ✉ c/o Marquess of Winchester, 6a Main Rd, Irene 1675, Transvaal, South Africa

WILTSHIRE, James Gordon; s of Arthur Thomas Wiltshire (d 1984), of Oxshott, and Barbara Gordon, *née* Donald (d 1990); *b* 17 Jan 1928; *Educ* Dean Close Sch Cheltenham, Queens' Coll Cambridge (BA); *m* 19 May 1961, Philippa Katharine, da of Philip Milholland (d 1976), of Wimbledon; 1 s (Philip Gordon b 1965), 2 da (Nicola Viva b 1962, Penelope Ara b 1967); *Career* Lt RE Ghana 1947–48; Kennedy & Donkin (now Rust, Kennedy & Donkin) consulting engrs: asst engr 1951–57, ptnr 1958–86, jt sr ptnr 1975–86, chief exec 1984–86; conslt Rust, Kennedy & Donkin Ltd 1987–95; memb Smeatonian Soc of Civil Engrs 1977- (hon treas 1981–94, pres 1995); Freeman City of London 1989, Liveryman Worshipful Co of Engrs 1990; FEng 1987, FICE, FIEE; *Recreations* tennis, golf, sailing, philately, DIY; *Clubs* Royal Wimbledon Golf, Burhill Golf, Dynamicables, Blythe Sappers; *Style*— James Wiltshire, Esq, FEng; ✉ Willow Bend, Moles Hill, Oxshott, Surrey KT22 0QB; Rust, Kennedy & Donkin Ltd, Westbrook Mills, Godalming, Surrey GU7 2AZ (☎ 01483 425900, telex 859373 KDHO G, fax 01483 425136)

WILTSHIRE, Kenneth Frank; s of Theo Wiltshire (d 1977), and Constance Maud, *née* Baker (d 1985); *b* 26 March 1929; *Educ* Bournemouth GS, Royal W of England Acad Bristol; *m* 1, Anne Elizabeth Muschamp (d 1991), da of Arthur William Pickard (d 1946); 2 s (Andrew b 28 Nov 1952, Tim b 22 June 1965); m 2, Susan Gay, da of Kenneth Grahame Cotman; *Career* Lethaby scholar SPAB 1955; restoration of: Longford Castle 1958–91, Wilton House 1963–75, Binghams Melcombe 1963–85, Milton Abbey 1966–, Dodington House 1972–77, Romsey Abbey 1974–, Wimborne Minster 1975–94, Sherborne Abbey 1976–95, Farnham Castle 1976–95, Wilbury Park 1977–95, Wadham and All Souls Coll Oxford 1978–, Worcester Cathedral 1986–96, Pershore Abbey 1990–; chm: Design Awards Ctee Nat Stone Fedn, Jt Nat Ctee for Natural Stone 1991–; vice pres Salisbury Civic Soc, chm Cathedral Architects Assoc 1993–96; Freeman City of London, memb Worshipful Co of Masons 1985; FRIBA, FRSA; *Recreations* walking, photography; *Clubs* Nat Liberal; *Style*— Kenneth Wiltshire, Esq; ✉ De Vaux House, Salisbury, Wilts (☎ 01722 335306)

WILTSHIRE, Timothy John; s of Raymond Wiltshire (d 1983), of Farmborough, Bath, Avon, and Kathleen Grace Wiltshire; *b* 18 April 1953; *Educ* S Bristol Poly (Dip Engrg), Lackham Coll of Agric; *m* 14 June 1975, Bridget Eileen, da of Rodney Holbrook Acheson-Crow, of Bristol, Avon; 3 s (Benjamin b 1978, Robert b 1980, Jonathon b 1986), 1 da (Eleanor b 1983); *Career* branch mangr Lloyds Abbey Life plc 1973–82, mgmnt fin serv Property Growth Assurance Ltd 1982–83, formed financial servs brokerage 1983, dir Hamiltons Southern Ltd (business and property investmt servs) 1987; memb C of C, govr Royal Bath & West Soc, clerk and cncllr to Driffield and Harnhill Parish Cncl, chm Ampneys Cons Assoc; *Recreations* shooting, water sports, historic building conservation; *Style*— Timothy Wiltshire, Esq

WIMBORNE, 4 Viscount (UK 1918); Sir Ivor Mervyn Vigors Guest; 6 Bt (UK 1838); also Baron Wimborne (UK 1880) and Baron Ashby St Ledgers (UK 1910); s of 3 Viscount Wimborne (d 1993), and his 1 w, Victoria, *née* Vigors; *b* 19 Sept 1968; *Educ* Eton; *Heir* uncle, Hon Julian John Guest b 12 Oct 1945; *Style*— The Rt Hon the Viscount Wimborne; ✉ c/o House of Lords, Westminster, London SW1A OPW

WINCH, Prof Donald Norman; s of Sidney Winch, and Iris May, *née* Button; *b* 15 April 1935; *Educ* Sutton GS, LSE (BSc Econ), Princeton Univ (PhD); *m* 5 Aug 1983, Doreen Alice, *née* Lidster; *Career* visiting lectr Univ of Calif Berkeley 1959–60, lectr in economics Univ of Edinburgh 1960–63; Univ of Sussex: lectr 1963–66, reader 1966–69, prof of the history of economics 1969–, dean Sch of Social Scis 1968–74, pro vice chllr arts and social studies 1986–89; pubns sec Royal Econ Soc 1971–; FBA 1986, FRHistS 1987; *Books* Classical Political Economy and Colonies (1965), James Mill: Selected Economic Writings (1966), Economics and Policy (1969), The Economic Advisory Council (with S K Howson, 1976), Adam Smith's Politics (1978), That Noble Science of Politics (with S Collini and J Burrow, 1983), Malthus (1987), Riches and Poverty (1996); *Recreations* gardening; *Style*— Prof Donald Winch; ✉ University of Sussex, Falmer, Brighton, E Sussex BN1 9QN (☎ 01273 606755, fax 01273 678466)

WINCHESTER, Archdeacon of; *see:* Clarkson, Ven Alan Geoffrey

WINCHESTER, Dean of; *see:* Till, Very Rev Michael Stanley

WINCHESTER, Bishop of 1995–; Rt Rev Michael Charles Scott-Joynt; s of Rev Albert George Scott-Joynt (d 1979), and Bettine, *née* Young (d 1991); *b* 15 March 1943; *Educ* Bradfield Coll Berks, King's Coll Cambridge (hon scholar, MA); *m* 24 July 1965, (Mary) Louise, da of Colin White (d 1964), and Margot, *née* Rumens (d 1964); 2 s (Jeremy Charles b 1970, Matthew James b 1970), 1 da (Hannah Margaret b 1968); *Career* curate Cuddesdon Oxon 1967–70, tutor Cuddesdon Coll 1967–72, team vicar Newbury Berks 1972–75, rector Bicester area team miny Oxon 1975–81, dir of ordinands and in-service trg and canon residentiary St Albans Cathedral 1982–87, bishop of Stafford 1987–95; *Recreations* walking, opera; *Style*— The Rt Rev the Bishop of Winchester; ✉ Wolvesey, Winchester, Hants SO23 9ND (☎ 01962 854050, fax 01962 842376)

WINCHESTER, 18 Marquess of (Premier Marquess of England, cr 1551); Nigel George Paulet; also Baron St John of Basing (E 1539) and Earl of Wiltshire (E 1550); s of George Paulet (1 cous of 17 Marquess, who d 1968; also eighth in descent from 5 Marquess); *b* 22 Dec 1941; *m* 1967, Rosemary Anne, da of Maj Aubrey John Hilton, of Harare, Zimbabwe; 2 s (Earl of Wiltshire, *qv*, Lord Richard George b 1971), 1 da (Lady Susan b 1976); *Heir* s, Earl of Wiltshire; *Career* dir Rhodesia Mineral Ventures Ltd, Sani-Dan Servs Ltd, Rhodesia Prospectors Ltd; *Style*— The Most Hon the Marquess of Winchester; ✉ 6a Main Rd, Irene 1675, Transvaal, South Africa

WINCHILSEA AND NOTTINGHAM, 16 and 11 Earl of (E 1628 and 1681); Sir Christopher Denys Stormont Finch Hatton; 17 and 11 Bt (E 1611 and 1660), of Eastwell and Raunston respectively; also Baron Finch (E 1675), Viscount Maidstone (E 1623) and Hereditary Lord of Royal Manor of Wye; s of 15 and 10 Earl of Winchilsea and Nottingham (d 1950), by his 1 w, Countess Gladys Széchényi (d 1978), 3 da of Count Lászlo Széchényi (sometime Hungarian min in London); *b* 17 Nov 1936; *Educ* Eton, Gordonstoun; *m* 1962, Shirley, da of late Bernard Hatfield, of Wylde Green, Sutton Coldfield; 1 s (Viscount Maidstone), 1 da (Lady Alice b 2 May 1970); *Heir* s, Viscount Maidstone, *qv*; *Style*— The Rt Hon the Earl of Winchilsea and Nottingham; ✉ South Cadbury House, nr Yeovil, Somerset

WINDEBANK, Dr (William) John; s of William Hori Windebank (d 1989), of Keinton Mandeville, Somerton, Somerset, and Kathleen, *née* Saunders; *b* 1 Nov 1939; *Educ* Purbrook Park Co HS Purbrook Hants, Univ of Glasgow Med Sch (BSc, MB ChB); *m* 25 March 1961, Peggy Julia, da of Norman Miles, of 24 Ilex Walk, Hayling Island, Hants; 1 s (Michael b 17 June 1968), 1 da (Jillian b 6 Oct 1966); *Career* sr registrar in gen and thoracic med Glasgow Hosps 1971–73, conslt physician in gen med and thoracic med Derby Hosps 1973–, conslt in charge Respiratory Div Cardiothoracic Measurement Dept Derbyshire Royal Infirmary 1973–, sr lectr anatomy and physiology Derby Sch of Occupational Therapy 1974–, hon clinical teacher Univ of Nottingham Med Sch 1978–, hon lectr in physiological measurement People's Coll Nottingham 1980–, resuscitation trg offr Derby Hosp 1987–; surgn St John Ambulance Bde Derbyshire S area; med offr: Derby Marathon, Darley Moor motorcycle racing club, Locko Park horse trials; SBOStJ 1981 (Serv medal 1981, Vol Med Serv medal 1970); memb: BMA 1966, Scot Thoracic Soc 1968, BTS 1976; MRCP 1970, ARTP 1975, FRCP Glasgow 1980, FRCP London 1994; *Recreations* first aid, wine and bread making; *Style*— Dr John Windebank; ✉ Derbyshire Royal Infirmary, London Road, Derby DE1 2QY

WINDELER, John Robert; s of Alfred Stewart, and Ethela Marie, *née* Boremuth; *b* 21 March 1943; *Educ* Ohio State Univ USA (BA, MBA); *m* 15 June 1965, Judith Lynn, da of Robert Francis Taylor; 2 s (Stewart, James); *Career* Irving Tst Co NY: vice pres Liability Mgmnt 1973–75, sr vice pres Money Market Div 1975–80, mangr Loan Syndication Devpt 1981, gen mangr London 1981–83, exec vice pres Investmt Banking Gp 1984; md Irving Trust International Ltd London 1984–, pres Irving Securities Inc NY 1987–91; chief fin offr National Australia Bank Melbourne 1991–93, chief exec Insurance Div National Australia Group UK Ltd 1993–94; dir Alliance & Leicester Building Society 1994–, dir BMS Associates; *Recreations* skiing, tennis, running, history; *Clubs* Hurlingham; *Style*— John Windeler, Esq; ✉ Alliance & Leicester Building Society, 49 Park Lane, London W1Y 4EQ (☎ 0171 629 6661, fax 0171 408 1399)

WINDER, Anne; *Educ* Ursuline Convent HS Brentwood Essex; *Career* BBC Radio: prodr Current Affrs then Talks and Documentaries Depts, ed Kaleidoscope until 1988, head of Arts, Science and Features Radio 1988–; chair BBC Radio Equal Opportunities Implementation Gp; *Recreations* sailing; *Style*— Ms Anne Winder; ✉ BBC Radio, Broadcasting House, London W1A 1AA (☎ 0171 765 4809, fax 0171 765 5454)

WINDER, Prof Anthony Frederick (Tony); s of Fred Winder (d 1996), and Ida Winifred, *née* Ellis (d 1982); *b* 7 March 1938; *Educ* Manchester GS, BNC Oxford (open scholar, MRC trg scholar, MA, MSc, BM BCh, DM), St Mary's Hosp Med Sch London (Harmsworth scholar), Guy's Hosp Med Sch London (PhD); *m* 3 Aug 1993, Sylvia Margaret, da of late Rev Charles Thomas Campbell, of Boston, Lincs; *children* 2 s (Christopher Philip b 14 Aug 1964, Charles David b 20 Nov 1971), 1 da (Clare Elizabeth Jane (Mrs Hitchcock) b 21 Jan 1966); *Career* house physician to Professorial Paediatric and Metabolic Units St Mary's Hosp London 1963–64, house surgn Mayday Hosp Croydon 1964; Univ of London 1964–: lectr in biochemistry Guy's Hosp Med Sch 1965–69 (jr lectr 1964–65), recognised teacher Faculty of Med (attached Bds of Studies in Biochemistry, Pharmacology and Pathology) 1969–82 and (attached Bd of Pathology) 1988–, univ sr lectr in pharmacology with responsibility for biochemical pharmacology 1971–73 (lectr 1969–71), sr lectr in chemical pathology and head Div of Chemical Pathology Dept of Pathology Inst of Ophthalmology 1973–82, hon conslt in chemical pathology Moorfields Eye Hosp 1974–82, hon clinical asst Dept of Lipids and Diabetes and hon lectr in chemical pathology Bart's Med Coll 1978–82, conslt in chemical pathology Leics HA(T) and clinical teacher and hon reader in med Univ of Leciester Med Sch 1982–88, prof of chemical pathology and head Dept of Chemical Pathology and Human Metabolism Royal Free Hosp Sch of Med and hon conslt in chemical pathology Royal Free Hampstead NHS Tst 1988–, hon conslt in chemical pathology Moorfields Eye Hosp and Inst of Ophthalmology 1992–93; hon conslt SE Thames RHA 1991–; memb: Trent Region Research Ctee 1985–89, Enfield HA 1989–91; med dir Family Heart Assoc 1992–95; contrib chapters to academic books; memb: Biochemical Soc 1971, Assoc of Clinical Biochemists 1973, RSM 1975 (hon treas Lipid Forum), Br Hyperlipidaemia Assoc 1985 (memb Ctee 1990–93), Assoc of Clinical Pathologists (scientific meetings sec 1992–96, pres 1996), Euro Atherosclerosis Soc 1995; FRCPath 1985, MRCP 1988; *Recreations* playing clarinet, tenor and baritone saxophones, enjoying jazz and most forms of music, swimming; *Style*— Prof Tony Winder; ✉ Department of Chemical Pathology and Human Metabolism, Royal Free Hospital School of Medicine and NHS Hospital Trust, Rowland Hill Street, London NW3 2PF (☎ 0171 830 2258, fax 0171 794 9537, e-mail tony_w@rfhsm.ac.uk)

WINDER, John Lindsay; JP (Furness and District 1969); s of Harold Vickers Winder (d 1969), of Barrow in Furness, and Mary Dick, *née* Card; *b* 8 Nov 1935; *Educ* Barrow GS; *Career* CA 1959; sr ptnr J L Winder & Co; chm Furness Building Soc 1993- (dir 1973–, vice chm 1988–93); pres Barrow Scout Mgmnt Ctee; FCA; *Recreations* fell-walking, gardening, golf; *Style*— John L Winder, Esq, JP; ✉ 32 Dane Avenue, Barrow in Furness LA14 4JS (☎ 01229 821726); 125 Ramsden Square, Barrow in Furness, Cumbria LA14 1XA (☎ 01229 820390)

WINDER, Robert James; s of Herbert James Winder (d 1984), of London, and Mary, *née* Dalby; *b* 26 Sept 1959; *Educ* Bradfield Coll, St Catherine's Coll Oxford (BA); *m* 1989, Hermione, *née* Davies; 1 s (Luke b 1993); *Career* on staff Euromoney 1982–86, literary ed The Independent until 1995 (joined 1986), currently occasional contrib The Independent; *Books* No Admission (1988), The Marriage of Time and Convenience (1994); *Recreations* eating, drinking, being merry, etc; *Style*— Robert Winder, Esq; ✉ The Independent, 1 Canada Square, Canary Wharf, London E14 5DL (☎ 0171 293 2000, fax 0171 293 2435)

WINDHAM, John Jeremy; er s of Sir Ralph Windham (d 1980), formerly of Waghen Hall, Yorks and later of Kingscote, and Lady Kathleen Mary Windham; descended from the ancient family of Wyndham of Felbrigg and Crownthorpe (NW of Wymondham) Norfolk and direct descendant of the family of Smith of Hill Hall, Essex; kinsman and hp of Sir Thomas Bowyer-Smyth, 15 Bt, *qv*; *b* 22 Nov 1948; *Educ* Wellington Coll; *m* 1976, (Rachel) Mary, da of Lt-Col (Walter) George Finney, TD (d 1973); 1 s ((Thomas) Ralph b 1985), 2 da (Katharine Anne b 1981, Emma Georgina b 1983); *Career* Capt Irish Gds and 22 SAS, ret; Br Trans-Americas Expdn (Darien Gap) 1972, Kleinwort Benson Ltd 1978–84, fndr and dir Defence Systems Ltd 1980–85, Enterprise Oil plc 1984–88, fndr md Integrated Defence Ltd 1988–; *Recreations* shooting, navigation, farming; *Style*— John Windham, Esq; ✉ The Hyde, Woolhope, Herefordshire HR1 4RE; Integrated Defence Ltd (☎ 01989 740689, fax 01989 740685)

WINDLE, Prof Alan Hardwick; s of Stuart George Windle (d 1979), of Croydon, Surrey, and Myrtle Lilian, *née* Povey (d 1960); *b* 20 June 1942; *Educ* Whitgift Sch,

Imperial Coll London (BSc (Eng), ARSM, Bessemer medal, RSA Silver medal), Trinity Coll Cambridge (PhD); *m* 14 Sept 1968, Janet Susan, da of Dr Claude Morris Carr; 3 da (Emma Rachel b 16 Oct 1969, Lucy-Clare b 17 June 1971, Rosemary Joy b 9 July 1976), 1 s (Roy Dudley Andrew b 22 Feb 1973); *Career* ICI 1966–67, lectr in metallurgy Imperial Coll London 1967–75; Univ of Cambridge: lectr in materials sci 1975–92, fell Trinity Coll 1978– (tutor 1983–91), prof of materials sci 1992–, acting dir Melville Lab for Polymer Synthesis 1993–94, head Dept of Materials Sci and Metallurgy 1996–; Rosenhain medal Inst of Metals 1987, Swinburne medal and prize Plastics and Rubber Inst 1992; MInstP 1971, FIM 1992; *Books* A First Course in Crystallography (1978), Liquid Crystalline Polymers (with Dr A M Donald, 1992); *Recreations* flying light aircraft; *Style*— Prof Alan Windle; ✉ Department of Materials Science and Metallurgy, University of Cambridge, Pembroke Street, Cambridge CB2 3QZ (☎ 01223 334321, fax 01223 335637)

WINDLE-TAYLOR, Paul Carey; s of Dr Edwin Windle-Taylor, CBE (d 1990), and Diana, *née* Grove (d 1987); *b* 25 Nov 1948; *Educ* Mill Hill, Emmanuel Coll Cambridge (MA, MB BChir), St Thomas Hosp London, MBA, FRCS, FRSM; *m* 1973 (m dis); *Career* conslt otolaryngologist; corresponding fell American Acad of Otolaryngology; *Recreations* fly fishing, fine wines; *Clubs* Flyfishers', MCC; *Style*— Paul Windle-Taylor, Esq; ✉ 151 Durnford Street, Plymouth, Devon PL1 3QR; Nuffield Hospital, Derriford Rd, Plymouth PL6 8BG (☎ 01752 775861)

WINDLESHAM, 3 Baron (UK 1937); Sir David James George Hennessy; 3 Bt (UK 1927), CVO, PC (1973); s of 2 Baron Windlesham (d 1962), by his 1 w Angela (d 1956), da of Julian Duggan; *b* 28 Jan 1932; *Educ* Ampleforth, Trinity Coll Oxford; *m* 22 May 1965, Prudence Loveday (d 1986), yr da of Lt-Col Rupert Trevor Wallace Glynn, MC; 1 s (Hon James b 1968), 1 da (Hon Victoria b 1966); *Heir* s, Hon James Rupert Hennessy b 9 Nov 1968; *Career* served Grenadier Gds, Lt; sits as Cons peer in House of Lords; min of state: Home Office 1970–72, NI 1972–73; Lord Privy Seal and ldr House of Lords 1973–74; chm: ATV Network 1981 (md 1975–81), Parole Bd 1982–88; dir: The Observer 1981–89, W H Smith Group 1986–95; chm: Oxford Preservation Tst 1979–89, Oxford Soc 1985–88; tstee: British Museum 1981–96 (chm 1986–96), Community Service Volunteers 1981–, Royal Collection Tst 1993–; govr and memb cncl (1983–) and vice-chm (1987–) Ditchley Fndn; memb Museums and Galleries Cmmn 1984–86; pres Victim Support 1992–; hon fell Trinity Coll Oxford 1982, visiting fell All Souls' Coll 1986, princ Brasenose Coll Oxford 1989–; Hon DLitt Univ of Oxford 1995; *Books* Communication and Political Power (1966), Politics in Practice (1975), Broadcasting in a Free Society (1980), Responses to Crime (vol 1 1987, vol 2 1993, vol 3 1996), The Windlesham/Rampton Report on Death on the Rock (with Richard Rampton, QC, 1989); *Style*— The Rt Hon the Lord Windlesham, CVO, PC; ✉ Brasenose College, Oxford OX1 4AJ

WINDRAM, Dr Michael David (Mike); s of Gordon Howard Windram (d 1990), of Halesowen, W Midlands, and Ethel May, *née* Hudson (d 1977); *b* 21 Sept 1945; *Educ* King Edward's Sch Birmingham, Queens' Coll Cambridge (MA, PhD); *m* 28 March 1970, Joycelyn Mary, da of Leslie Albert Marsh (d 1972); 2 s (Christopher b 20 Dec 1973, Richard b 7 April 1977); *Career* radio astronomer Univ of Cambridge 1966–69, physicist and sr engr Marconi Avionic Systems Ltd 1969–71; Radio Frequency Section IBA: engr 1971–73, sr engr 1973–77, head of section 1978–82; head of Video and Colour section Experimental and Devpt IBA 1982–87, head of Experimental and Devpt Dept IBA 1987–90; NTL (National Transcommunications Ltd): exec mangr R&D 1991–93, dir of advanced products 1993–95; md DMV (Digi-Media Vision Ltd) 1995–; FIEE 1991, FRTS 1992, graduate memb Inst of Physics 1993, FEng 1993; *Recreations* music, DIY, caravaning; *Style*— Dr Mike Windram, FEng; ✉ 1 Hickory Drive, Harestock, Winchester, Hants SO22 6NJ (☎ 01962 880226); DMV, Stoneham Rectory, Stoneham Lane, Eastleigh, Hants SO50 9NW (☎ 01703 573002, fax 01703 573015)

WINDSOR, *see also:* Royal Family section

WINDSOR, Barbara; da of John Deeks, and Rose, *née* Ellis; *b* 6 Aug 1937; *Educ* Our Lady's Convent London, Aida Foster's Stage Sch; *Career* actress; began career aged 13 in pantomime, subsquently toured singing in cabaret (incl Ronnie Scott Band); numerous appearances on chat and quiz shows; *Theatre* incl: Love from Judy (West End debut), Fings Ain't Wot They Used to Be (Garrick), Oh' What a Lovely War (Broadway), Come Spy with Me (Whitehall, with Danny La Rue), Marie Lloyd in Sing A Rude Song (Garrick), The Threepenny Opera (with Vanessa Redgrave), The Owl and the Pussycat, Carry on London (Victoria Palace), A Merry Whiff of Windsor (one woman show, UK and world tour), Maria in Twelfth Night (Chichester Festival Co), Calamity Jane (nat tour), Kath in Kenneth William's prodn of Entertaining Mr Sloane (Lyric Hammersmith), The Mating Game, Miss Adelaide in Guys and Dolls (tour), Kath in first nat tour of Entertaining Mr Sloane (nominated Martini Regional Theatre Award for Best Actress); *Pantomime* numerous appearances incl: Babes in the Wood (Palladium), Fairy Godmother in Cinderella (Orchard Dartford) 1995–96; *Television* incl: Dreamers Highway, The Jack Jackson TV Show, Six Five Special, The Rag Trade (BBC), subject of This Is Your Life (Thames), Obituary Show (Channel Four), One Foot in the Grave (BBC), currently Peggy Mitchell in EastEnders, host Funny World (BBC) 1996; *Films* incl: Sparrers Can't Sing, Carry on films (first Carry on Spying 1964), Lost, Too Hot to Handle, Flame in the Street, On the Fiddle, Hair of the Dog, Chitty Chitty Bang Bang, A Study in Terror, Comrades, The Boyfriend, Double Vision; *Radio* numerous incl Fancy A Bit; *Albums* numerous incl single Sparrers Can't Sing (top 30 hit); *Books* Laughter and Tears of a Cockney Sparrow; *Style*— Miss Barbara Windsor; ✉ c/o Barry Burnett Organisation Ltd, Suite 42–43, Grafton House, 2–3 Golden Square, London W1R 3AD (☎ 0171 437 7048/9, fax 0171 437 1098)

WINDSOR, Dean of; *see:* Mitchell, Very Rev Patrick Reynolds

WINDSOR, Viscount; Ivor Edward Other Windsor-Clive; s and h of 3 Earl of Plymouth, DL, *qv*, and Caroline, *née* Rice; *b* 19 Nov 1951; *Educ* Harrow, RAC Cirencester; *m* 1979, Caroline, da of Frederick Nettlefold and Hon Mrs Juliana Roberts (da of 2 Viscount Scarsdale); 3 s (Hon Robert, Hon Frederick b 1983, Hon Edward b 1994); 1 da (Hon India Harriet b 1988); *Heir* s, Hon Robert Other Ivor Windsor-Clive b 25 March 1981; *Career* co-fndr and dir Centre for Study of Modern Art 1973, dir Plymouth Estates; *Recreations* cricket, football; *Style*— Viscount Windsor; ✉ Oakly Park, Ludlow, Shropshire (☎ Bromfield 393); 6 Oakley Street, London, SW3

WINDSOR, Col Rodney Francis Maurice; CBE (1972), DL (Co Antrim 1967, Aberdeenshire 1989); s of Maurice Windsor, MBE (d 1945), and Elsie, *née* Meredith (d 1959); *b* 22 Feb 1925; *Educ* Tonbridge; *m* 1, 26 April 1951, Deirdre Willa (d 1991), da of Col Arthur O'Neill Cubitt Chichester, OBE, MC, DL (d 1972), of Co Antrim; 2 s (Anthony b 1955, Nicholas b 1961), 1 da (Patricia b 1953); m 2, 6 April 1994, Mrs Angela H Stainton; *Career* served Royal Armoured Corps 1943, The Queen's Bays 1944–52, Capt 1949, ADC to High Cmmr and C-in-C Austria 1949–50; N Irish Horse TA 1959–67, Lt-Col cmdg 1964–67, Col TA N Ireland 1967–71, ADC TA to HM The Queen 1970–75; farmer; chm Banff and Buchan Dist Valuation Appeal Ctee 1989–96 (memb 1982–96); memb: Co of Aberdeen Red Cross, District Ctee Scottish Veterans Garden City Assoc 1993–; *Recreations* field sports, golf; *Style*— Col Rodney F M Windsor, CBE, DL; ✉ Mains of Warthill, Meikle Wartle, Aberdeenshire AB51 5AJ (☎ 01651 821273)

WINDSOR, Stuart James; s of E J Windsor (d 1965), and Gwendoline Knott (d 1979); *b* 26 May 1946; *Educ* Chace Sch; *m* Oct 1971, Janet Elizabeth Davidson-Lungley; 3 s (Alexander b 3 Nov 1976, Miles b 4 Jan 1985, Freddie b 26 Dec 1988); *Career* photographer; journalist until 1970, Fleet St photographer 1970–73 (Times, Observer, Daily Mail); photographic projects incl: coast to coast trip of America documenting lifestyles, living with Kabre Tribe in N Togo (as part of Nat Geographic anthropological educnl field trip), project in Galapagos Islands, coverage of Mount Kinabulu Borneo climb 1988; solo exhibition of retrospective work Embankment Gallery 1979; contrib to magazines and books on numerous travel and architectural topics, picture library contains 100,000 worldwide images, produces masterclasses on photographic and visual arts subjects, estab photo library Capital City Pictures devoted to London; *Books* Images of Egypt (1993), France and French Lifestyles (1994), Australia - This Beautiful Land, Dream Machines - BMW; French Experience (CD-ROM); *Recreations* travel, writing, classic cars, photography, design, architecture; *Clubs* Richmond RFC; *Style*— Stuart Windsor, Esq; ✉ 1 Salisbury Rd, Wimbledon, London SW19 4EZ (☎ 0181 946 9878)

WINDSOR-LEWIS, Geoffrey; s of Dr H Windsor Lewis (d 1982), of Cambridge, and Phyllis Mary, *née* Harris (d 1989); *b* 7 April 1936; *Educ* Leys Sch Cambridge, Trinity Hall Cambridge (MA); *m* Jacqueline, *née* Harty; 3 s (Steve b 12 Nov 1962, Guy b 2 April 1964, Tom b 5 Sept 1982); *Career* Nat Serv cmmnd 2 Regt RHA 1954–56; former rugby union player: Wales 1960, Barbarians, Univ of Cambridge 1956–58 (capt 1958); hon sec Barbarian Football Club 1966–; chartered surveyor; jt sr ptnr Buckell & Ballard 1978–84; dir: Arundell House plc 1985–90, Harcourt Properties Ltd 1990–; chm Rugby Park Properties 1994–; conslt Chancellors Group of Estate Agents; govr: Dragon Sch Oxford, Leys Sch; Liveryman Worshipful Co of Chartered Surveyors; FRICS; *Recreations* vegetable gardening, golf; *Clubs* East India, Frewen (Oxford), Hawks (Cambridge); *Style*— Geoffrey Windsor-Lewis, Esq; ✉ Wilcote Place, Ramsden, Oxfordshire OX7 3BA (☎ 01993 868370)

WINDUST, Jeremy Paul; s of Norman Albert Windust (d 1963), of Glos, and Pamela Rosie, *née* Frampton (d 1969); *b* 6 Jan 1952; *Educ* Marling Sch Stroud, Middx Poly (BA), Brunel Univ (MA); *m* 8 Jan 1972, Elaine Rosemary, da of Lionel Hubert Jordan; 2 s (Alexander b 1973, Benjamin b 1976), 1 da (Kathryn b 1978); *Career* exec offr GCHQ Cheltenham 1975–87; memb ctee to re-establish trade union rights at GCHQ, co-applicant against Govt's union ban at GCHQ in High Ct, Ct of Appeal and House of Lords 1984 and before European Ct of Human Rights Strasbourg 1987; ed Warning Signal 1985–87; proprietor Willow Press (letterpress printing shop); gen sec (chief negotiator) Retail Book Assoc 1988–93, memb Retail Wages Cncl of GB 1988–93, negotiator Inst of Professionals, Managers and Specialists 1993–, leader Lab Gp Cotswold DC 1995–; *Recreations* music; *Style*— Jeremy Windust, Esq; ✉ 29 Morestall Drive, Cranhams Lane, Cirencester, Glos (☎ 01285 641047)

WINEARLS, Dr Christopher Good; s of late Capt James Robert Winearls, and Sheila, *née* Boardman; *b* 25 Sept 1949; *Educ* Diocesan Coll Rondebosch Capt Town, Univ of Cape Town (MB ChB), Univ of Oxford (DPhil); *m* 6 Dec 1975, Beryl Claire, da of Dr Wilmer Edward George Butler, of Cairns, Queensland, Aust; 4 s (James b 1979, Alastair b 1982, Stuart b 1985, Robert Frederick Good b 1991); *Career* sr lectr in med Royal Postgrad Med Sch London 1986–88, conslt nephrologist Churchill Hosp Oxford 1988–; hon sec Renal Assoc of GB; Rhodes scholar 1972; FRCP; *Recreations* sailing; *Style*— Dr Christopher Winearls; ✉ Renal Unit, Churchill Hosp, Oxford OX3 7LJ (☎ 01865 225804, fax 01865 225773)

WINFIELD, Peter Stevens; s of Harold Stevens Winfield (d 1945), of Chelsea, and Susan, *née* Cooper (d 1973); *b* 24 March 1927; *Educ* Sloane Sch Chelsea, West London Coll of Commerce; *m* 29 June 1955, Mary Gabrielle, da of Patrick John Kenrick (d 1955), of Chelsea; 4 s (John b 28 May 1961, Michael b 18 Jan 1965, Peter Anthony b 18 May 1966, Edward b 4 April 1968), 2 da (Susan (Mrs Wood) b 10 March 1958, Katherine (Mrs Cardona) b 18 Nov 1959); *Career* RA 1944–48, BQMS, India, Egypt and Palestine; joined Healey & Baker 1951 (sr ptnr 1975–88); dir: London Auction Mart Ltd 1970–92 (chm 1980–92), Osprey Management Company Ltd 1989–91, Golden Square Properties Ltd 1990–96; memb: Lloyd's of London 1978–, Property Investmt Ctee Save and Prosper Group Ltd 1980–, Horserace Totalisator Bd 1981–92, Cncl of The Racehorse Owners Assoc 1995–; non-exec dir Manders plc 1987–, chm Letinvest plc 1987–94, dir Kingston Theatre Tst 1990–; special tstee: Guy's Hosp 1974–96 (govr 1973–74), Guy's and St Thomas's Hosp 1996–; Liveryman: Worshipful Co of Farriers 1967, Worshipful Co of Feltmakers 1972 (Master 1990–91); FRICS 1953; *Recreations* horseracing, cricket, swimming, reading; *Clubs* Buck's, United and Cecil, Mark's, MCC, RAC; *Style*— Peter S Winfield, Esq; ✉ 29 St George St, Hanover Square, London W1A 3BG (☎ 0171 629 9292, fax 0171 514 2365)

WING, Dr Antony John; s of (Harry) John Tayler Wing (d 1962), of Oxford, and Helen, *née* Foster; *b* 2 May 1933; *Educ* Rugby, Univ of Oxford (MA, BM BCh, DM), St Thomas' Hosp Med Sch; *m* 23 Jan 1960, Rachel Nora, da of Norman Gray, of Eastbourne, Sussex; 3 s (Mark b 1962, Charles b 1964, Michael b 1970), 1 da (Nicola b 1961); *Career* Sqdn Ldr RAF Med Branch 1960–64; registrar St Thomas' Hosp 1964–66, sr registrar Charing Cross Hosp 1967–68, Nuffield res fell Makerere Univ Uganda 1968–69, conslt physician St Thomas' Hosp 1969–94, conslt nephrologist St George's Hosp 1994–; examiner Soc of Apothecaries 1970–, chm of registry Euro Dialysis and Transplant Assoc 1976–85; memb Grants Ctee: Nat Kidney Res Fund 1979–86, Br Kidney Patients Assoc 1985–; chief med offr: Colonial Mutual Assur Soc 1980, United Friendly Assur Soc 1988; memb Governing Body Stowe Sch 1988–, lay reader St Stephen's Church Twickenham, chm Cicely Northcote Tst 1977–83; Liveryman Worshipful Soc of Apothecaries 1973, Freeman City of London 1974; FRSM 1966, FRCP 1976, fell Assurance Med Soc; *Books* The Renal Unit (with M Magowan, 1972), Decision Making in Medicine (with G Scorer, 1979); *Recreations* golf, tennis, skiing; *Clubs* Vincent's, MCC, Roehampton; *Style*— Dr Antony Wing; ✉ St George's Hospital, London SW17 0QT (☎ 0181 725 2145, fax 0181 725 1673)

WING, Prof John Kenneth; CBE (1990); *Educ* Strand Sch, UCL (MB BS, MD, PhD); *Career* RNVR 1942–46, Lt (A); med and specialist trg 1947–56, scientific staff MRC 1957–64, dir MRC Social Psychiatry Res Unit 1965–89, prof of social psychiatry Inst of Psychiatry and London Sch of Hygiene 1970–89 (emeritus prof Univ of London 1989–); memb MRC 1985–89; conslt College Research Unit RCPsych 1995– (dir 1989–94); Hon MD Univ of Heidelberg 1976; FRCPsych; *Books* Institutionalism and Schizophrenia (1970), Measurement and Classification of Psychiatric Symptoms (1974), Reasoning about Madness (1978), Measurement for Mental Health (1995); *Style*— Prof J K Wing, CBE; ✉ Royal College of Psychiatrists, 11 Grosvenor Crescent, London SW1X 7EE (☎ 0171 235 2351 ext 125, fax 0171 235 2954)

WING, Dr Lorna Gladys; OBE; da of Bernard Newbury Tolchard (d 1969), and Gladys Ethel, *née* Whittell (d 1962); *b* 7 Oct 1928; *Educ* Chatham GS, UCH London (MD, MB BS); *m* 15 May 1950, Prof John Kenneth Wing, CBE, *qv*, s of William Sidney Wing (d 1928); 1 da (Susan b 1956); *Career* scientific staff MRC Social and Community Psychiatry Unit 1964–90, hon conslt psychiatrist Maudsley Hosp London 1972–90, hon sr lectr Inst of Psychiatry London 1974–90; conslt psychiatrist Nat Autistic Soc 1990– (fndr memb and vice pres); FRCPsych 1980; *Books* Early Childhood Autism (ed, 1976), Hospital Closure and the Resettlement of Residents (1989), The Autistic Spectrum - A Guide for Parents and Professionals (1996); *Recreations* walking, reading, gardening; *Style*— Dr Lorna Wing, OBE; ✉ Centre for Social and Communication Disorders (Diagnosis and Assessment), Elliot House, 113 Masons Hill, Bromley, Kent BR2 9HT (☎ 0181 466 0098, fax 0181 466 0118)

WINGATE, Capt Sir Miles Buckley; KCVO (1982); s of Terrence Wingate; *b* 17 May 1923; *Educ* Taunton GS, Prior Park Coll; *m* 1947, Alicia Forbes Philip; 3 da; *Career* with Royal Mail Lines 1939; master mariner; memb Bd Trinity House 1968–88 (dep master 1976–88); Liveryman Worshipful Co of Master Mariners; FNI; *Style*— Captain Sir Miles Wingate, KCVO; ✉ Trinity House, Tower Hill, London EC3N 4DH (☎ 0171 480 6601)

WINGATE-SAUL, Michael Anthony; s of Anthony Sylvester Wingate-Saul, and Brenda Maxwell, *née* Stoddart (d 1987); *b* 8 Feb 1938; *Educ* Rugby, King's Coll Cambridge (MA); *m* 23 Sept 1967, Eleanor Jane, da of Alan Lawrence Brodie (d 1972); 2 da (Polly b 1969, Rebecca b 1971); *Career* Nat Serv 1956–58, 2 Lt 4 Regt RHA Germany; slr, sr ptnr Letcher & Son, NP; memb Ctee Hants Branch CLA 1993–, govr Bryanston Sch 1982–; *Recreations* music, theatre, photography, walking, tennis, skiing; *Style*— Michael A Wingate-Saul, Esq; ✉ Sandle Lodge, Sandleheath, Hampshire SP6 1PF (☎ 01425 652261); 24 Market Place, Ringwood, Hampshire BH24 1BS (☎ 01425 471424, fax 01425 470917)

WINGFIELD DIGBY, (Kenelm) Simon Digby; TD (1946), DL (1953); s of Col Frederick James Bosworth Wingfield Digby, DSO (d 1952), and Gwendolen, *née* Hamilton Fletcher (d 1975); Sir Simon Digby and his brothers fought beside Henry Tudor at Bosworth Field, granted Manor of Coleshill which is still in the family; *b* 13 Feb 1910; *Educ* Harrow, Trinity Coll Cambridge (MA); *m* 1936, Kathleen Elizabeth, da of Hon Mr Justice Courtney Kingstone, of Canada; 1 s (John), 1 da (Venetia); *Career* barr; MP (C) West Dorset 1941–74, Cons whip 1948–51, Civil Lord of Admty 1951–57, ldr Br Delgn Cncl Europe Assembly 1972–74; Order of Leopold, Order of the White Lion; landowner (estates at Sherborne, Dorset and Coleshill, Warwickshire); *Recreations* shooting, fishing; *Clubs* Carlton; *Style*— Simon Wingfield Digby, Esq, TD, DL; ✉ Sherborne Castle, Sherborne, Dorset (☎ 01748 22650); Coleshill House, Warwickshire; Digby Estate Office, Sherborne, Dorset (☎ 01935 813182)

WINGFIELD DIGBY, Stephen Hatton; s of Archdeacon Basil Wingfield Digby, MBE (d 1996), of Salisbury, and Barbara Hatton Budge (d 1987); *b* 17 Nov 1944; *Educ* Sherborne, Univ of Bristol (BSc), Queen's Univ Belfast (MBA); *m* 1968, Sarah Jane, da of Osborne Lovell, of Dorset; 2 s (William b 1974, Alexander b 1983), 1 da (Claire b 1972); *Career* dir: Bass Sales Ltd 1978–81, Bass Wales & West Ltd 1981–83, The Harp Lager Co 1983–, Buckleys Brewery plc 1988–93, Crown Brewery plc 1989–93; account dir Guinness Brewing GB 1994–; chm Assoc of London Brewers and Licensed Retailers (formerly London Brewers' Cncl) 1990–94; warden The Brewers' Company 1994–; *Recreations* fishing, shooting; *Clubs* MCC; *Style*— Stephen Wingfield Digby, Esq; ✉ The Coach House, Gregories Farm Lane, Beaconsfield Bucks HP9 1HJ; Guinness Brewing GB, Park Royal Brewery, London NW10 7RR (☎ 0181 965 7700)

WINKELMAN, Joseph William; s of George William Winkelman (d 1956), of Keokuk, Iowa, USA, and Cleo Lucretia, *née* Harness (d 1978); *b* 20 Sept 1941; *Educ* Keokuk HS, Univ of the South Sewanee Tennessee (BA, pres of graduating class), Wharton Sch of Fin Univ of Pennsylvania, Ruskin Sch of Drawing, Univ of Oxford (Cert in Fine Art); *m* 8 Feb 1969, Harriet Lowell, da of Gaspard D'Andelot Belin, of Cambridge, Mass; 2 da (Alice Mary b 21 March 1973, Harriet Lowell b 28 May 1974); *Career* secondary sch master for US Peace Corps Tabora Sch Tanzania 1965–66; memb Cncl of Mgmnt Bankside Gallery London 1986–95, chm Nat Assoc of Blood Donors 1994–95, govr Windmill First Sch Oxford 1994–; artist; working mainly in relief and intaglio printmaking 1974–96, handmaking own autographic prints; hon fellowship: Printmakers' Cncl 1988, RWS 1996; prizes: Int Miniature Print Exhibitions Cadaques Spain 1982 and Seoul Korea 1982, Royal W of Eng Acad Bristol for painting 1985; vice pres Oxford Art Soc, pres Royal Soc of Painter-Printmakers (RE) 1989–95; memb Arts Club; fell Royal Soc of Painter-Printmakers 1982 (assoc 1979), academician Royal W of Eng Acad (RWA) 1989 (assoc 1983); *Recreations* gardening, hill walking, theatre; *Style*— Joseph Winkelman, Esq; ✉ The Hermitage, 69 Old High St, Headington, Oxford OX3 9HT (☎ 01865 62839)

WINKLE, Anthony Webbe; OBE (1997); s of Harry Downing Winkle (d 1974), of Edinburgh, and Gladys, *née* Hughes (d 1977); *b* 28 Dec 1931; *Educ* Newcastle HS, George Watson's Coll, Heriot-Watt Univ; *m* 1959, Patricia Emily Mary, da of George Alfred Parker (d 1984), of Edinburgh; 2 s (Philip b 1964 d 1990, Paul b 1966); *Career* Nat Serv RAF pilot, Flying Offr 1956–58; project mangr; conslt E C Harris; farmer; *Clubs* New (Edinburgh); *Style*— Anthony W Winkle, OBE; ✉ Whitmuir Lamancha, West Linton, Peeblesshire EH46 7BB (☎ 01968 660431); E C Harris, Hailes House, Hailes Ave, Lanark Rd, Edinburgh EH13 OLZ (☎ 0131 441 5363, fax 0131 441 5348)

WINKLEMAN, Barry Lester David; s of Leonard Winkleman (D 1978), of London, and Fay, *née* Goldstein (d 1989); *b* 21 May 1939; *Educ* Hall Sch Hampstead, Carmel Coll Wallingford, Sorbonne Paris (dip), Balliol Coll Oxford (MA); *m* 1, 8 Dec 1968 (m dis), Eve Pollard, *qv*; 1 da (Claudia b 15 Jan 1972); m 2, Cindy Black, *née* Macdonald; 1 da (Sophie b 5 Aug 1980); *Career* creative asst Clifford Bloxham Partners 1962–64, guide Club Mediterranée 1964–65; The Times: Promotions Dept 1966, mangr Special Pubns 1967, asst publishing mangr 1967–73, publishing mangr 1973–75; md Times Books 1975–94, md City Magazines 1981–87, md Angus & Robertson UK 1982–91, publisher The Times Supplements 1988–89, md Gen Div William Collins & Sons 1989–91, md Bartholomew/Times (Royal warrant holder Supplier of Maps to HM The Queen, a div of HarperCollins) 1992–94, md Prion Books 1994–, publishing columnist Tatler magazine 1995–96; *Publications* The Times Atlas of World History (editorial dir, 1978); *Recreations* reading, family, painting; *Clubs* Groucho; *Style*— Barry Winkleman, Esq; ✉ c/o Prion Books, Unit L, 32–34 Gordon House Road, London NW5 1LP

WINKLEY, Dr Linda Mary; da of Reginald Bertram Holland (d 1984), and Vera Mary, *née* Mills; *b* 1 June 1942; *Educ* King Edward's HS for Girls Edgbaston Birmingham, Univ of Birmingham (MB ChB, DPM, DCH, DRCOG); *m* 22 July 1967, David Ross Winkley, s of Donald Winkley, of Sutton Coldfield, Birmingham; 1 s (Joseph b 15 June 1973), 1 da (Katherine b 23 June 1971); *Career* in gen practice 1967–70, trained in adult psychiatry Warnford Hosp Oxford 1970–72, sr registrar Midland Trg Scheme in Child Psychiatry 1973–75, conslt child psychiatrist Selly Oak Hosp Birmingham 1976–, regnl speciality clinical tutor in child psychiatry 1989– (developed child psychotherapy servs in Midlands and set up course for psychotherapeutic work with children 1980), clinical dir Children's Hosp Birmingham 1993–94; memb Client Gp Planning Team, chm Children's Mental Health Promotion Sub-Ctee W Midlands, chm Div of Child Health and Paediatrics Selly Oak Hosp 1988–93; fndr memb and treas W Midlands Inst of Psychotherapy; memb: ACP 1973, APP 1985; MACP 1986, FRCPsych 1989; *Recreations* theatre, music, squash; *Style*— Dr Linda Winkley; ✉ Oaklands, Selly Oak Hospital, Raddlebarn Rd, Selly Oak, Birmingham B29 6JD (☎ 0121 627 8231)

WINKLEY, Dr Stephen Charles; s of George William Dinsdale Winkley (d 1987), and Eunice Kate, *née* Golding (d 1992); *b* 9 July 1944; *Educ* St Edward's Sch Oxford, Brasenose Coll Oxford (MA, DPhil); *m* 1, 1968 (m dis 1978), Georgina Mary, *née* Smart; 2 s (Nicholas Leo b 1971, Howard Mungo Alaric b 1972); m 2, 1983, Jennifer Mary, *née* Burt; 2 da (Imogen Daisy Arabella b 1987, Isabella Alice Rose b 1994); *Career* asst master Cranleigh Sch 1969–85, second master Winchester Coll 1985–91, headmaster Uppingham Sch 1991–; *Recreations* water colour painting; *Style*— Dr Stephen Winkley; ✉ Spring Back Way, Uppingham, Rutland LE15 9TT (☎ 01572 822688); Uppingham School, Rutland LE15 9QE (☎ 01572 822216)

WINKWORTH, Peter Leslie; s of Francis William Henry Winkworth (d 1975), and Ruth Margaret Llewllin, *née* Notley; *b* 9 Aug 1948; *Educ* Tonbridge; *m* 16 June 1973, Tessa Anne, da of Sir Alexander Warren Page (d 1993); 1 s (Piers b 1976), 2 da (Victoria b 1975, Jessica b 1978); *Career* merchant banker and CA; dir: Close Brothers Group plc 1984–, Close Brothers Ltd 1977–, Close Consumer Finance Ltd 1991–, Close Investment Management Ltd, Safeguard Investments Ltd 1984–, Winterflood Securities Ltd 1993–, Arkstar Ltd 1984–88, Clifford Brown Group plc 1987–93, Jackson-Stops & Staff Ltd 1990–92; *Recreations* tennis, horse breeding and racing, national hunt trainer; *Clubs* St George's Hill Lawn Tennis; *Style*— Peter Winkworth, Esq; ✉ Merton Place, Dunsfold, Surrey GU8 4NP; Close Brothers Group plc, 12 Appold Street, London EC2A 2AA (☎ 0171 426 4000, fax 0171 247 1203)

WINN, Hon Charles Rowland Andrew; s and h of 5 Baron St Oswald, *qv*; *b* 22 July 1959; *m* 1985, Louise Alexandra, da of Stewart Mackenzie Scott; 1 s (Rowland Charles Sebastian Henry b 1986), 1 da (Henrietta Sophia Alexandra b 1993); *Career* landowner; *Style*— The Hon Charles Winn

WINN, Geoffrey Frank; s of Capt Frank Winn (d 1987), of Scarborough, and Hettie, *née* Croft (d 1983); *b* 13 Dec 1938; *Educ* Scarborough HS, Univ of Leeds (BCom); *m* 9 July 1966, Jennifer Lynne Winn, JP, da of Jack Winter, DFC, of Scarborough; 2 da (Deborah b 1967, Susie b 1970); *Career* CA; in practice Winn & Co (Scarborough and branch offices) 1962–; chm Scarborough Bldg Soc 1994– (dir 1984–); chm Scarborough Flower Fund Homes 1986– (memb 1970–); pres: Humberside & Dist Soc of CAs 1991–92; memb Cncl ICAEW 1995–; tstee Scarborough CC; FCA 1962; *Recreations* golf, skiing, badminton; *Clubs* CLA; *Style*— Geoffrey Winn, Esq; ✉ Barmoor House, Scalby, Scarborough, N Yorks YO13 OPG (☎ 01723 362 414); Winn & Co, 62/63 Westborough, Scarborough, N Yorks YO11 1TS (☎ 01723 364341, car 0831 344940)

WINNER, Michael Robert; s of George Joseph Winner (d 1972), and Helen, *née* Zlota (d 1984); *b* 30 Oct 1935; *Educ* St Christopher Sch Letchworth Herts, Downing Coll Cambridge (MA); *Career* chm: Scimitar Films Ltd, Michael Winner Ltd, Motion Picture & Theatrical Investments Ltd 1957–; memb Cncl and chief censorship offr and tstee Dirs Guild of GB 1983–, fndr and chm Police Meml Tst 1984–; dir: Play It Cool 1962, The Cool Mikado (also writer) 1962, West Eleven 1963, The Mechanic 1972; prodr and dir: The System 1963, I'll Never Forget What's 'is name 1967, The Games 1969, Lawman 1970, The Nightcomers 1971, Chato's Land 1971, Scorpio 1972, The Stone Killer 1973, Death Wish 1974, Won Ton Ton The Dog That Saved Hollywood 1975, Firepower 1978, Scream for Help 1984, Death Wish III 1985; prodr dir and writer: You Must be Joking 1965, The Jokers 1966, Hannibal Brooks 1968, The Sentinel 1976, The Big Sleep 1977, Death Wish II 1981, The Wicked Lady 1982, Appointment with Death 1987, A Chorus of Disapproval 1988, Bullseye! 1989, Dirty Weekend 1992; theatre prodns: The Tempest 1974, A Day in Hollywood A Night in the Ukraine 1978; *Recreations* being wonderful and difficult; *Style*— Michael Winner, Esq; ✉ 6–8 Sackville St, London W1X 1DD (☎ 0171 734 8385)

WINNER, Paul; JP (North Westminster Bench 1972); s of Emmanuel Winner (d 1967), of Oakwood Ct, London, and Bessie, *née* Taylor (d 1983); *Educ* St Lawrence Coll Ramsgate, Westminster City Sch, La Sorbonne Paris, St John's Coll Oxford; *m* Mary, da of Frank Oppenheimer; 1 s (Daniel b 3 May 1968), 1 da (Sonya b 21 March 1966); *Career* sec Oxford Univ Ctee World Univ Serv 1953–56, exec Gilbert McAllister & Partners 1959–62, asst dir World Parliament Assoc 1959–63, exec dir Lonsdale Information Ltd 1963–67, fndr Paul Winner Marketing Communications Ltd 1967–84, dir Good Relations plc 1984–85, fndr chm Paul Winner Consultants Ltd 1986–, fndr md Strategic Partnerships International Ltd 1995–; mktg advsr CBI 1985–; Parly candidate: (Lib) Spelthorne May & Oct 1974 and 1979, (Lib/SDP Alliance) Windsor and Maidenhead 1983; co-ordinator Alliance gen election fund raising campaign 1987; memb Magistrates' Domestic Panel 1980–92; memb Exec Cncl of Christians and Jews 1980–; fndr Real Age Initiative 1994; Freeman City of London 1981, Liveryman Worshipful Co of Marketors; MCIM, FInstD, FRSA; *Books* Effective PR Management - A Guide to Corporate Survival (Kogan Page, 1987), Da Cuneo Tutto, Da Torino Tutto Interno; *Recreations* art, tennis, travel; *Clubs* Reform, Savile, Hurlingham, Hon Society of the Knights of the Round Table, Rotary Club of London; *Style*— Paul Winner, Esq, JP; ✉ Paul Winner Consultants Limited, 141 Sloane St, London SW1X 9AY (☎ 0171 730 8525, fax 0171 730 7133)

WINNICK, David Julian; MP (Lab) Walsall North (majority 3,824); *b* 26 June 1933; *Educ* LSE; *Career* memb Willesden Cncl 1959–64, Brent Cncl 1964–66; contested (Lab) Harwich 1964, MP (Lab) Croydon South 1966–70, contested Croydon Central Oct 1974 and Walsall Nov 1976, MP (Lab) Walsall North 1979–; memb Select Ctees on: Race Relations and Immigration 1969–70, Environment 1980–83, Procedure 1989–; vice-pres APEX 1983–88; chm UK Immigrants Advsy Service 1984–; *Style*— David Winnick, Esq, MP; ✉ House of Commons, London SW1A 0AA

WINNIFRITH, Charles Boniface; s of Sir (Alfred) John Digby Winnifrith, KCB (d 1993), and Lesbia Margaret, *née* Cochrane (d 1981); *b* 12 May 1936; *Educ* Tonbridge, ChCh Oxford (MA); *m* 1, 21 April 1962, Josephine Joy, MBE (d 1991), da of Roger Spencer Poile (d 1974), of Kingston, Kent; 1 s (John b 1964), 2 da (Charlotte b 1966, Laura b 1968); m 2, 29 May 1993, Sandra Ann, da of William Mitchell Stewart (d 1970), of Hexham, Northumberland; *Career* Nat Serv 2 Lt RAEC 1958–68; Dept of the Clerk of House of Commons 1960–: second clerk of Select Ctees 1983–87, clerk of Select Ctees 1987–89, princ clerk of Table Office 1989–95, clerk of Ctees 1995–; memb Gen Synod of the C of E 1970–90, chm House of Laity Canterbury Diocesan Synod 1979–91; govr Ashford Sch Kent 1973–93; *Recreations* cricket, American soap opera; *Clubs* MCC; *Style*— Charles Winnifrith, Esq; ✉ Gale Lodge Farm, Long Buckby, Northants NN6 7PH (☎ 01604 770396); Cliffe Cottage, St Margaret's at Cliffe, Kent CT15 6BJ (☎ 01304 853280); House of Commons, London SW1 (☎ 0171 219 3313)

WINNIFRITH, Thomas John; s of Sir (Alfred) John Digby Winnifrith, KCB (d 1993), of Hall House Farm, Appledore, Kent, and Lesbia Margaret, *née* Cochrane (d 1981); *b* 5 April 1938; *Educ* Tonbridge, ChCh Oxford (MA), CCC Oxford (MPhil), Univ of Liverpool (PhD); *m* 1, 3 July 1967, Joanna Victoria Lee (d 1976); da of John Booker (d 1986); 1 s (Thomas John Zacchaeus b 1968), 2 da (Tabitha Jessie Ann b 1969, Naomi Miranda Alice b 1971); m 2, 19 March 1988, Helen Mary, da of Sir George Peregrine Young, CMG (d 1960); *Career* asst master Eton Coll 1961–66, E K Chambers student Corpus Christi Oxford 1966–68, William Noble fell Univ of Liverpool 1968–70, sr lectr Univ of Warwick 1977–95 (lectr 1970–77); *Books* The Brontës and their Background (1973), The Brontës (1977), Brontë Facts and Problems (jtly, 1983), Nineteen Eighty-Four and All's Well (jtly, 1984), The Vlachs (1987), A New Life of Charlotte Brontë (1988), Charlotte and Emily Brontë (jtly, 1989), Fallen Women in the Nineteenth Century Novel (1994), Balkan Fragments (1995); *Style*— Thomas Winnifrith, Esq; ✉ 40 Newbold Terrace East, Leamington Spa, Warwickshire CV32 4EY (☎ 01926 883543); Department of English, University of Warwick, Coventry CV4 7AL (☎ 01203 523523)

WINNING, Most Rev Thomas Joseph; *see:* Glasgow, Archbishop of (RC)

WINNINGTON, Anthony Edward; s of Col Thomas Foley Churchill Winnington, MBE, *qv*, of Hurlingham, London, and Lady Betty, *née* Anson, da of late 4 Earl of Lichfield; *b* 13 May 1948; *Educ* Eton, Univ of Grenoble; *m* 5 Dec 1978, Karyn Kathryn Kettles, da of Joanne Dayton, of Palm Beach, Florida, USA; 1 s (Edward b 1987), 2 da (Victoria b 1981, Sophia b 1985); *Career* dir of equity sales Hoare Govett Securities Ltd 1984–92 (joined 1969), dir Robert Fleming Securities 1992–; MSI (memb Stock Exchange 1984); *Recreations* music, fishing; *Clubs* Boodle's, City of London, Pratt's, Annabel's; *Style*— Anthony Winnington, Esq; ✉ 20 Baskerville Rd, London SW18 3RW (☎ 0181

870 8466); Robert Fleming Securities, 25 Copthall Ave, London EC2R 7DR (☎ 0171 638 5858)

WINNINGTON, Sir Francis Salwey William; 6 Bt (GB 1755); s of Francis Salwey Winnington (d 1913), and gs of Sir Francis Winnington, 5 Bt, JP, DL (d 1931); *b* 24 June 1907; *Educ* Eton; *m* 1944, Anne Beryl Jane, da of late Capt Lawrence Drury-Lowe, Scots Gds; 1 da; *Heir* bro, Col Thomas Foley Churchill Winnington, MBE, *qv* b 16 Aug 1910; *Career* Lt Welsh Gds 1928–32; re-employed 1939 (despatches); patron of three livings; landed proprietor (4,700 acres); *Clubs* Lansdowne House; *Style—* Sir Francis Winnington, Bt; ✉ Brockhill Court, Shelsley Beauchamp, Worcs

WINNINGTON, Col Thomas Foley Churchill; MBE (1948); s of Francis Winnington (d 1913), and Blanche Emma, *née* Casberd-Boteler, (d 1968); hp to bro, Sir Francis Winnington, 6 Bt, *qv*; *b* 16 Aug 1910; *Educ* Eton, Balliol Coll Oxford (BA); *m* 20 May 1944, Lady Betty Winnington, *née* Anson, da of 4 Earl of Lichfield (d 1960); 2 s (Anthony Edward, *qv*, b 1948, Henry b 1961), 2 da (Sarah (Viscountess Campden, LVO) b 1951, Emma (Mrs Christopher Milne) b 1956); *Career* joined Grenadier Gds 1933: served WWII Dunkirk and NW Europe (despatches) cmd 3 Bn Malaya (despatches) 1948, Col cmdg 1952–55; pres WO Selection Bd 1955, ret 1957; Reed Int 1958–75; appeals advsr Help The Aged 1976–96; *Clubs* Pratt's, Hurlingham, MCC; *Style—* Col Thomas Winnington, MBE; ✉ 182 Rivermead Ct, Ranelagh Gdns, London SW6 3SG (☎ 0171 731 0697)

WINRAM, Steven George; s of Alistair George Ian Winram, of Leicester, and Irene Josephine, *née* Harvey; *b* 30 Jan 1960; *Educ* Dulwich, Pembroke Coll Cambridge (MA); *Career* Saatchi & Saatchi Co plc: Investor Rels and Corporate Communications Div 1982–85, Acquisitions and Corporate Fin Div 1985–88, worldwide media res and info dir Zenith Media 1988–93; media analyst and dir Barclays de Zoete Wedd Ltd 1994–; *Recreations* tennis, squash, choral music, politics, flying (PPL); *Style—* Steve Winram, Esq; ✉ Barclays de Zoete Wedd Ltd, Ebbgate House, 2 Swan Lane, London EC4R 3TS (☎ 0171 623 2323, fax 0171 956 4615)

WINSER, Nigel de Northop; s of Robert Stephen Winser, of Kintbury, Berks, and Anne, *née* Carrick; *b* 4 July 1952, Kisumu, Kenya; *Educ* Bradfield Coll, Poly of Central London; *m* 17 July 1982, Shane, da of Arthur James Wesley-Smith, of Sheffield; 1 s (Philip b 1984), 1 da (Kate b 1987); *Career* Royal Geographical Soc/Inst of Br Geographers: field dir Mulu Sarawak expedition 1976, expedition offr 1978 (expeditions carried out in Karakoram Pakistan, Kora Kenya, Wahiba Oman, Kimberley Aust, Temburong Brunei, Mkomazi Tanzania, Badia Jordan), estab Expedition Advsy Centre 1980, asst dir and head of exploration 1988, dep dir 1991–; exploration fell commoner Corpus Christi Coll Cambridge 1990; Patrons Gold Medal for leadership of Wahiba Sands project 1988, Mrs Patrick Ness Award for expdn leadership 1977, Mungo Park Medal Royal Geographical Soc Scotland 1995; fndr: Exploration Univ 1991, Sponsor Our Species 1992, Geographical Observatories Prog 1994; dep chm Friends of Conservation (UK) 1996; *Books* Sea of Sands and Mists (1989), contributing ed History of World Exploration (1991); *Recreations* fly fishing on the Kennet, photography, travel; *Clubs* Geographical, Rainforest; *Style—* Nigel Winser, Esq; ✉ Royal Geographical Society (with the Institute of British Geographers), 1 Kensington Gore, London SW7 2AR (☎ 0171 589 5466, fax 0171 584 6150, e-mail n.winser@rgs.org)

WINSKELL, Cyril; MBE (1982); s of Robert Winskell (d 1963), of South Shields, and Margaret Wiley (d 1970); *b* 29 Aug 1932; *Educ* South Shields HS, Rutherford GS, King's Coll Newcastle upon Tyne, Univ of Durham (certificate in architecture); *m* 24 Sept 1960, Patricia, da of Leonard George Dolby (d 1967), of North Shields; 4 s (Cy b 1961, Scott b 1962, Dane b 1968, Mark b 1968), 1 da (Patricia b 1965); *Career* Nat Serv Sapper Christmas Island 1956–57; architect; fndr Winskell Chartered Architects Urban Consultants 1982–96, conslt Greenall Design Group & Winskell 1996–; visiting critic and occasional lectr at various schs of architecture 1972–, one man show Gallery Colbert Durham City 1977, chm Northern Region RIBA 1980–82, chm Northumbria Branch RIBA 1984–86, convenor Newcastle Cityscape 1984–; external examiner Sch of Architecture Queen's Univ Belfast 1987–92; architect for the restoration of: St Thomas's Neighbourhood Newcastle upon Tyne 1978–81, Canning Area Liverpool 1984–87, Lowther Village Cumbria 1993–, Mitford Estate Northumerland 1995–; memb Historic Areas Advsy Ctee English Heritage 1987–88, pres Northern Architectural Assoc 1990–94; FRIBA 1971 (ARIBA 1956); *Recreations* painting, travel; *Style—* Cyril Winskell, Esq, MBE; ✉ 7 Collingwood St, Newcastle upon Tyne NE1 1JE (☎ 0191 261 4436)

WINSKILL, Air Cdre Sir Archibald Lyttle (Archie); KCVO (1980, CVO 1973), CBE (1960), DFC (and Bar), AE; s of James Winskill, of Penrith; *b* 24 Jan 1917; *Educ* Penrith and Carlisle GS; *m* 1947, Christiane Amélie Pauline, da of M Bailleux, of Calais; 1 s (decd), 1 da (Francoise Elizabeth, who m Christopher Meyer, CMG, *qv*); *Career* served WWII: Fighter Pilot Battle of Britain 1940, French Resistance 1941, N Africa 1942–43; Station Cdr Turnhouse and Duxford, Gp Capt ops RAF Germany 1957–60, Air Cdre 1963, air attaché Paris 1964–67, dir PR (Air) MOD 1967–68, Capt of HM The Queen's Flight 1968–82, extra equerry to HM The Queen 1968–; ret RAF 1982; *Clubs* RAF, Ham Manor Golf; *Style—* Air Cdre Sir Archie Winskill, KCVO, CBE, DFC, AE; ✉ Anchors, 58 Coastal Rd, East Preston, W Sussex BN16 1SN (☎ 01903 775439)

WINSLET, Christopher James; s of Frank Winslet, and Margaret, *née* Martin; *b* 27 May 1955; *Educ* Strodes GS, Univ of Wales (BSc(Econ)); *m* 1976, Jane Margaret, da of John Albert King; 1 da (Eleanor Jane b 4 Aug 1980), 1 s (Edward Simon b 14 Aug 1982); *Career* Deloitte & Co 1976–87: joined as trainee accountant, qualified CA 1979, taxation specialist 1980; ptnr Deloitte Haskins & Sells 1987 (merged with Coopers & Lybrand 1989), ptnr i/c Fin Servs Tax Div Coopers & Lybrand 1993–; frequent writer and speaker on taxation of insurance cos; FCA 1979, ATII 1980; *Books* Noah (1992), George and the Dragon (1993); *Recreations* writing musicals, tennis, reading, dieting; *Clubs* Coopers Hill Tennis; *Style—* Christopher Winslet, Esq; ✉ Coopers & Lybrand, 1 Embankment Place, London WC2N 6NN (☎ 0171 583 5000, fax 0171 213 4409)

WINSTANLEY, Alan Kenneth; s of (Albert) Kenneth Winstanley (d 1973), and Doreen, *née* Dunscombe, of Mansfield, Notts; *b* 2 Nov 1952; *Educ* St Clement Danes GS for Boys London; *m* 5 Oct 1975, Christine Susan Ann, da of Raymond Henry Osborne; 1 s (James Alan Kenneth b 7 Jan 1983), 1 da (Eve Alexis b 24 Oct 1978); *Career* record prodr; recording engr (work incl Amii Stewart's Knock on Wood, early Stranglers' records) 1970–79, freelance prodr Stranglers LP The Raven 1979, prodr (in partnership with Clive Langer) 1979–; jt fndr: West Side Studios London 1984, residential studio Henley 1987; artists produced incl: Madness 1981–85, Teardrop Explodes 1981, Dexy's Midnight Runners 1982, Elvis Costello 1983–84, Marilyn 1983, Lloyd Cole and the Commotions 1985, David Bowie, Sade, Style Council, Ray Davies, Gil Evans (for Absolute Beginners) 1985, Bowie and Jagger (Dancing in the Street) 1985, China Crisis 1986, Hothouse Flowers 1987–90, The Adventures 1989, Morrissey 1989–91, They Might Be Giants 1989, Bush 1995, Aztec Camera 1995; Platinum albums: One Step Beyond (Madness) 1980, Absolutely (Madness) 1981, Complete Madness 1982, Too-Rye Ay (Dexy's Midnight Runners) 1982, Sixteen Stone (Bush) 1995; Gold albums: The Raven (The Stranglers) 1980, Dance Craze 1981, 7 (Madness) 1981, Kilimanjaro (Teardrop Explodes) 1982, The Rise and Fall (Madness) 1983, Punch the Clock (Elvis Costello) 1983, Easy Pieces (Lloyd Cole) 1985, People (Hothouse Flowers) 1988, Home (Hothouse Flowers) 1990, Flood (They Might Be Giants) 1994; Silver albums: Goodbye Cruel World (Elvis Costello) 1984, Mad Not Mad (Madness) 1985; Platinum single: Come On Eileen (Dexy's Midnight Runners) 1982; Gold singles: Baggy Trousers 1980, Embarrassment 1981, It Must Be Love 1981, Our House 1982 (all by Madness), Dancing in the Street (Bowie & Jagger) 1985; Silver singles: One Step Beyond 1980, My Girl 1980, Work Rest and Play EP 1981, Return of the Los Palmas 7 1981, Shut Up 1981, Grey Day 1981, Driving in my Car 1982, Wings of a Dove 1983 (all by Madness), Reward (Teardrop Explodes) 1981, Swords of a Thousand Men (Tenpole Tudor) 1981, Calling Your Name (Marilyn) 1983; *Awards* Top Producer (singles) Music Week award 1982, nominee Best British Producer BPI awards 1982 and 1983; *Recreations* tennis, golf, skiing, cycling, travelling; *Style—* Alan Winstanley, Esq; ✉ West Side Studios, Olaf Centre, 10 Olaf St, London W11 4BE (☎ 0171 221 9494, fax 0171 727 0008)

WINSTANLEY, His Hon Judge; Robert James; s of Morgan James Winstanley (d 1980), and Joan Martha, *née* Cuthbert, of Epsom; *b* 4 Nov 1948; *Educ* Glyn GS Epsom, St Catharine's Coll Cambridge (MA), Coll of Law London; *m* 19 Aug 1972, Josephine, *née* Langhorne; 2 s (Jonathan Robert b 18 Aug 1978, Richard Frances b 24 June 1980); *Career* asst slr Dawson & Co 1973–75 (articled clerk 1971–73), ptnr Winstanley - Burgess 1975–96, circuit judge (SE Circuit) 1996–; memb Cncl Law Soc 1985–96; memb Law Soc 1973; *Recreations* cricket, motorcycling, bridge; *Clubs* United Oxford and Cambridge University; *Style—* His Hon Judge Winstanley; ✉ c/o South Eastern Circuit Office, New Cavendish House, 18 Maltravers Street, London WC2R 3EU

WINSTON, Prof Brian Norman; s of Reuben Winston (d 1989), of Wembley, and Anita, *née* Salamons (d 1983); *b* 7 Nov 1941; *Educ* Kilburn GS, Merton Coll Oxford (MA); *m* 1978, Adèle, da of Aleck Jackson; 1 da (Jessica b 1979), 1 s (Matthew b 1983); *Career* freelance journalist 1974–; researcher/prodr Granada TV 1963–66, prodr/dir BBC TV 1966–69, prodr/dir Granada TV 1969–72, lectr Bradford Coll of Art 1972–74, res dir Dept of Sociology Univ of Glasgow 1974–76, head of gen studies Nat Film & TV Sch Beaconsfield 1974–79, prof and head of film studies Tisch Sch of the Arts New York Univ 1979–86 (visiting prof of film 1976–77), dean Sch of Communications Pennsylvania State Univ 1986–92, prof and dir Centre for Journalism Studies Univ of Wales Coll of Cardiff 1992–; produced The Third Walker (starring William Shatner and Colleen Dewhurst) Canada 1976; winner Emmy for documentary script writing for Heritage: Civilization and the Jews part 8 (WNET-TV, NY); chair Welsh Film Cncl 1995– (memb 1993–), govr BFI; *Books* Dangling Conversations - The Image of the Media (1973), Dangling Conversations - Hardware Software (1974), Bad News (1976), More Bad News (1980), Misunderstanding Media (1986), Working with Video (with Julia Keydel, 1986), Claiming the Real (1995), Technologies of Seeing (1996); *Recreations* cooking; *Style—* Prof Brian Winston; ✉ Centre for Journalism Studies, University of Wales College of Cardiff, 69 Park Place, Cardiff, Wales CF1 3AS (☎ 01222 874786, fax 01222 238832)

WINSTON, Malcolm John; s of John Winston (d 1982), of Bexhill, and Sarah, *née* Bates; *b* 8 Nov 1930; *Educ* Stationers' Co Sch; *m* 16 June 1962, Cynthia Mary Boorne, da of Hugh Napier Goodchild (d 1981), of Norwich; 1 s (Mark Jonathan Napier b 1964), 1 da (Sarah Catherine Louise (Mrs Bray) b 1967); *Career* Bank of England 1950–75, seconded Central TSB 1973, sr asst gen mangr Central TSB 1981 (asst gen mangr 1975), joined TSB England & Wales upon merger with Central TSB 1986; pres Assoc of Int Savings Banks in London 1985– (fndr 1980, chm 1983–84), chm Lombard Assoc 1989–90, dir Tyndall Bank plc 1991–94, dir Bankgesellschaft Berlin (UK) PLC 1995– (sr advsr Bankgesellschaft Berlin 1994–); sr advsr Landesbank Berlin 1993–; chm Alkenmind Ltd 1994–; Freeman City of London 1952, Liveryman Worshipful Co of Makers of Playing Cards 1979; fell Assoc of Corp Treasurers 1979; ISBI medal of Honour ISBI World Congress (Rome) 1990; *Recreations* beagling, tennis; *Clubs* Overseas Bankers'; *Style—* Malcolm Winston, Esq; ✉ Maze Pond, Wadhurst, East Sussex (☎ 01892 782074, fax 01892 783698); Bankgesellschaft Berlin, 1 Crown Court, Cheapside, London EC2V 6JP (☎ 0171 572 6700, fax 0171 572 6799)

WINSTON, Baron (Life Peer 1995), of Hammersmith in the London Borough of Hammersmith and Fulham; Robert Maurice Lipson Winston; s of Lawrence Winston (d 1949), of London, and Ruth, *née* Lipson; *b* 15 July 1940; *Educ* St Paul's, Univ of London (MB BS); *m* 8 March 1973, Lira Helen, da of Simon Joseph Feigenbaum (d 1971), of London; 2 s (Hon Joel, Hon Benjamin), 1 da (Hon Tanya); *Career* sr res accoucheur The London Hosp 1965, sr lectr Inst of Obstetrics and Gynaecology 1975–81, visiting res prof Catholic Univ of Leuven Belgium 1976–77, conslt obstetrician and gynaecologist Hammersmith Hosp 1978– (sr res fell 1975–78), presenter of Your Life in Their Hands BBC TV 1979–87, prof of gynaecology Univ of Texas San Antonio 1980–81, reader in fertility studies Royal Postgrad Med Sch 1981–86, prof of fertility studies Univ of London 1986–, dean Inst of Obstetrics and Gynaecology Royal Postgraduate Med Sch 1995–; author of over 200 scientific papers on reproduction; chm Br Fertility Soc 1990–93 (fndr memb); pres: Int Fallopius Soc 1987–88, Progress All Party Parliamentary Gp for Res In Reproduction 1991; Cedric Carter Medal Clinical Genetics Soc 1992, Victor Bonney Prize Royal Coll of Surgns of Eng 1993, Chief Rabbinate Open Award for Contributions to Society 1993; hon fell Queen Mary and Westfield Coll 1996; FRCOG, FRSA; *Books* Reversibility of Sterilization (1978), Tubal Infertility (1981), Infertility - A Sympathetic Approach (1986), What We Know About Infertility (1987), Getting Pregnant (1989), Infertility, a postgraduate handbook (1993), Making Babies (1996); *Recreations* theatre, music, skiing, wine, broadcasting; *Clubs* RSM, Athenaeum; *Style—* The Rt Hon Lord Winston; ✉ 11 Denman Drive, London NW11 6RE (☎ 0181 455 7475); Royal Postgraduate Medical School, Hammersmith Hospital, Ducane Rd, London W12 0HS (☎ 0181 749 5579, fax 0181 749 6973, car 0836 639339)

WINTER, David; OBE; s of Cecil Winter, and Cissie Winter; *b* 24 Oct 1931; *Educ* Clifton, UCL (LLB); *children* 4 s (Harry, Adam, Mateusz, Bartusz), 1 da (Lucy); *Career* slr; conslt Baker & McKenzie on East West trade; rep and chm for the UK of the UN Economic Cmmn for Europe Working Party on Int Contract Practices in Industry, memb Cncl Sch of Slavonic & E Euro Studies and GB-Russia Centre, dep chm Exec Cncl Russo British Chamber of Commerce, chm British-Russian Law Assoc; author of numerous publications in the field of East West trade; Freeman City of London, asst and hon legal advsr Guild of Air Pilots and Air Navigators; listed arbitrator on various int panels; *Recreations* flying light aircraft; *Style—* David Winter, Esq, OBE; ✉ Baker & McKenzie, 100 New Bridge Street, London EC4 (☎ 0171 919 1000)

WINTER, Rev Canon David Brian; s of Walter George Winter (d 1952), of London, and Winifred Ella, *née* Oughton (d 1972); *b* 19 Nov 1929; *Educ* Machynlleth Co Powys, Trinity GS London, King's Coll London (BA), Inst of Educn London (PGCE), Oak Hill Theological Coll; *m* 15 April 1961, Christine Ellen, da of Bernard Martin, of Hitcham, Suffolk; 2 s (Philip b 1963, Adrian b 1969), 1 da (Rebecca b 1964); *Career* Nat Serv RAF 1948–50; sch teacher 1955–59, ed Crusade 1959–70, freelance writer and broadcaster 1970–71, prodr BBC Radio 1971–, head of religious progs BBC Radio 1982–87, head of religious bdcasting BBC 1987–89; priest i/c Ducklington Oxfordshire 1989–95, hon curate Hermitage and Cold Ash Berks 1995–; hon canon Christ Church Oxford 1995–; memb Radio Acad 1985–; *Books* incl: Truth in the Son (1985), Battered Bride? (1988), What's in a Word (1994), Where Do We Go From Here? (1996); *Recreations* watching cricket; *Style—* Rev Canon David Winter; ✉ The Vicarage, Cold Ash, Thatcham, Berks RG18 9PT (☎ 01635 864395)

WINTER, Donovan; *b* 29 Sept 1930; *Educ* Surrey Boy's GS, Central Sch of Speech and Drama; *Career* writer, producer and director; Sub Lt RNVR(A) Fleet Air Arm; actor then scriptwriter for radio and low budget feature films (also playing leading parts); writer/prodr/dir/ed: The Awakening Hour and The Great Expedition (documentaries); fndr Donwin Productions Ltd 1960; prodns for Donwin incl: The Trunk, World Without

Shame, Sunday in the Park, A Penny For Your Thoughts, Promenade, Come Back Peter, All Lovers are Strangers, The Deadly Females, Give Us Tomorrow, Roller Force (documentary) 1980; also dir TV commercials; fndr memb: BAFTA (blacklisted 1982), BAFTA LA (resigned 1988), Writers' Guild of GB (transferred to Writers' Guild of America 1980), Directors' Guild of GB; *Publications* The Winters of My Discontent (autobiography); numerous film scripts and articles on the errant ways of admin of the film industry; *Recreations* truly Don Quixote - inveterate litigant and persistant campaigner denouncing the corruption and hypocrisy of govt bureaucracy, exposing injustice and decrying the pomposity and duplicity of the courts and legal profession (the battle continues relentlessly - often in ct); black humour, travel and entertaining beautiful young women in season; *Style*— Donovan Winter, Esq; ✉ 7 St James' House, Kensington Square, London W8 5HD (☎ 0171 937 4491)

WINTER, Frederick Thomas (Fred); CBE (1963); s of Frederick Neville Winter (d 1965), of Newmarket, and Anne Flanagan (d 1987); *b* 20 Sept 1926; *Educ* Ewell Castle; *m* 1956, Diana Ruth, da of Col T R Pearson (d 1945), of Derby; 3 da (Joanna b 1957, Denise (twin) b 1957, Philippa b 1958); *Career* former racehorse jockey and trainer; Lt 6 Bn Para Regt 1944–47; flat jockey 1939–42, national hunt jockey 1947–64, champion jockey 4 times; won: Grand National (twice), Gold Cup (twice), Champion Hurdle (3 times); trainer 1964–88, champion trainer 8 times; won: Grand Nat (twice), Cheltenham Gold Cup, Champion Hurdle (3 times); ret 1988; *Recreations* golf, gardening; *Style*— Fred Winter, Esq, CBE; ✉ Montague House, Eastbury, Newbury, Berks RG17 7JN (☎ 01488 71438)

WINTER, Prof Gerald Bernard; s of Morris Winter (d 1974), and Edith Winter (d 1984); *b* 24 Nov 1928; *Educ* Coopers' Co Sch, London Hosp Med Coll Univ of London (BDS, MB BS, DCH); *m* 24 April 1960, (Brigitte) Eva, da of Dr Hans Heinemann Fleischhacker (d 1965), of London; 1 s (Simon Michael b 1961), 1 da (Caroline Rosalind b 1965); *Career* Nat Serv RADC 1948–49; dental house surgn 1955, house surgn and house physician 1958, lectr Royal Dental Hosp 1959–62; Inst of Dental Surgery Eastman Dental Hosp London: conslt dental surgn 1962–66, prof of children's dentistry 1966–94, dean and dir of studies 1983–93; pres Br Soc of Paediatric Dentistry (formerly Br Paedodontic Soc) 1970–71 and 1993–94 (hon sec 1961–64), hon sec Int Assoc of Dentistry for Children 1971–79, pres Br Soc of Dentistry for the Handicapped 1976–77; FDSRCS, FFDRCSI; *Style*— Prof Gerald Winter; ✉ c/o Eastman Dental Institute, Eastman Dental Hospital, 256 Gray's Inn Road, London WC1X 8LD (☎ 0171 915 1000, fax 0171 915 1012)

WINTER, John Anthony; MBE (1984); s of Frank Oliver Winter (d 1989), of Norwich, and Sybil Mary, *née* Rudd (d 1976); *b* 16 May 1930; *Educ* Bishops Stortford Coll, Architectural Assoc Sch of Architecture (AA Dip), Yale Univ (MArch); *m* May 1956, Valerie Ursula, *née* Denison; 2 s (Timothy b 1960, Henry b 1963), 1 da (Martha b 1966); *Career* architect; princ John Winter & Assocs; works incl: Morley Coll Lambeth, housing devpt at Lucas Place Milton Keynes, office devpt at 83 Mansell St London E1; frequent contrib to architectural jls and videos; memb: Royal Fine Art Cmmn 1986–96, Cncl of Architectural Assoc 1989–95 (tstee 1995–); FRSA 1988; *Books* Modern Buildings (1969), Industrial Buildings (1971); *Style*— John Winter, Esq, MBE; ✉ 81 Swains Lane, London N6 (☎ 0181 340 9864); 80 Lamble St, London NW5 4AB (☎ 0171 267 7567)

WINTER, Brig John Quentin; LVO 1985 (MVO 1982); s of Lt Cdr The Rev Henry Winter, RN (d 1977), and Lawrell, *née* Quentin (d 1992); *b* 28 Jan 1943; *Educ* The Judd Sch Tonbridge, RMA Sandhurst; *m* 7 Jan 1967, Susan Elizabeth Jane, da of Arthur John Mortimer (d 1982), of London; 2 s (Guy b 1972, James b 1975); *Career* cmmnd Parachute Regt 1963, served worldwide, CO 10th Battalion Parachute Regt 1982–84; Cdr Cwlth Military Advsy Team Ghana 1987–89, Military Sec HQ UK Land Forces 1989–91, Military Attaché British Embassy Moscow 1993–96; Equerry to HRH The Prince of Wales 1980–82, Extra Equerry to HRH The Prince of Wales 1989–; Freeman City of London 1985; *Recreations* fishing, hill walking; *Clubs* Army and Navy; *Style*— Brig John Winter, LVO; ✉ c/o The Royal Bank of Scotland, Holts Farnborough Branch, Victoria Rd, Farnborough, Hants GU14 7NR

WINTER, Richard Thomas; s of Thomas Alfred Baldwin Winter, of Warwickshire, and Ruth Ethel, *née* Newbury; *b* 6 March 1949; *Educ* Warwick Sch, Univ of Birmingham (LLB); *m* Dorothy Sally, da of Peter Hancock Filer; 2 da (Hannah Louise b 2 Sept 1990, Fiona Ruth b 5 Aug 1992); *Career* articled clerk and asst slr Evershed & Tomkinson 1971–75, slr Fisons plc 1975–78, ptnr Evershed Wells & Hind 1981–94 (joined 1978), ptnr Eversheds Slrs 1989–94, managing ptnr London office Eversheds 1991 (joined 1987); head Group Legal Dept Bass PLC 1994–; memb: Law Soc, Slrs Euro Gp; *Recreations* tennis, sailing, skiing; *Clubs* Royal Corinthian Yacht, Solway Yacht, Roehampton; *Style*— Richard Winter, Esq; ✉ Bass PLC, 20 North Audley Street, London W1Y 1WE (☎ 0171 409 1919, fax 0171 409 8526)

WINTERBONE, Prof Desmond Edward; s of Edward Frederick Winterbone (d 1986), of Tenby, Dyfed, and Phoebe Hilda, *née* Lane (d 1986); *b* 15 Jan 1943; *Educ* Tenby GS, Rugby Coll of Engrg Technol (CNAA BSc, English Electric Student Apprentice prize), Univ of Bath (PhD), Univ of Manchester (DSc); *m* 24 Sept 1966, Veronica Mary, da of Thomas Frank Cope; 1 s (Edward Joseph b 24 April 1974), 1 da (Anne Caroline b 28 Oct 1971); *Career* student apprentice English Electric Co Ltd Rugby 1960–65 (design engr Diesel Engine Div 1965–67), res fell Univ of Bath 1967–70; UMIST: lectr Dept of Mechanical Engrg 1970–78, sr lectr 1978–80, prof of mechanical engrg 1980–, head Dept of Mechanical Engrg 1981–83, vice princ for external affairs 1986–88, dep princ 1987–88, head Thermodynamics and Fluid Mechanics Div 1990–, head Dept of Mechanical Engrg 1991–94, pro-vice-chllr 1995–; chair professorship Nanjing Aeronautical Inst 1985, Mombusho fellowship Univ of Tokyo 1989, Erskine fell Canterbury Univ NZ 1994; doctorate hc Univ of Ghent 1991; FIMechE, MSAE (US), FEng 1989; *Books* The Thermodynamics and Gas Dynamics of Internal Combustion Engines Vols I and II (jt ed, 1982 and 1986), Internal Combustion Engineering: Science and Technology (contrib, 1990), Advanced Thermodynamics for Engineers (1997); *Recreations* running, cycling (time trials), mountaineering, travel; *Style*— Prof Desmond Winterbone, FEng; ✉ UMIST, Department of Mechanical Engineering, PO Box 88, Manchester M60 1QD (☎ 0161 200 3710, fax 0161 200 3723)

WINTERBOTTOM, David Stuart; s of Samuel Winterbottom (d 1986), and Gladys Winterbottom; *b* 25 Nov 1936; *Educ* Roundhay Sch Leeds; *m* 24 June 1961, Gillian Margaret; 1 s (Richard David Charles b 19 June 1966), 1 da (Fiona Louise b 14 Feb 1964); *Career* articled clerk Alexander Sagar & Co Leeds Chartered Accountants, sr auditor Price Waterhouse & Co Leeds, fin dir Chester Barrie Ltd, md Arbuthnot Latham & Co Ltd Industl Div, gp chief exec Evode Group plc until March 1993, ret; chm: Emblem Technology plc, Tricom Group Holdings Ltd, Barr & Wallace Arnold Trust PLC, Coal Products Holdings Ltd, Lightlink Group Ltd, Crompton Lighting Holdings Ltd; dep chm T J Hughes PLC; non-exec dir: Biotrace International PLC, Electrocomponents PLC, Remploy Ltd; FCA, FCT; *Recreations* golf, travel, gardening; *Clubs* E India, Devonshire, Sports and Public Schs, Lilleshall Hall Golf, Stone Golf, British Pottery Manufacturers' Association; *Style*— David S Winterbottom, Esq; ✉ Walnut Tree Farm, Cowley, Gnosall, Stafford ST20 0BE (☎ 01785 822438, fax 01785 823119)

WINTERBOTTOM, Prof Michael; s of Allan Winterbottom (d 1982), of East Budleigh, Devon, and Kathleen Mary Winterbottom (d 1990); *b* 22 Sept 1934; *Educ* Dulwich, Pembroke Coll Oxford (MA, D Phil); *m* 1, 31 Aug 1963 (m dis 1983), Helen, da of Harry Spencer (d 1977), of Willenhall, Staffs; m 2, Nicolette Janet Streatfeild Bergel, da of Henry Shorland Gervis (d 1968), of Sherborne; 2 s (Peter, Jonathan); *Career* lectr in Latin and Greek UCL 1962–67, fell and tutor in classics Worcester Coll Oxford 1967–92 (reader in classical languages 1990–92), Corpus Christi prof of Latin 1993– (fell Corpus Christi Coll 1993–); Dr hc Besançon 1985; FBA 1978; *Books* Quintilian (ed 1970), Ancient Literary Criticism (with D A Russell, 1972), Three Lives of English Saints (1972), The Elder Seneca (ed and translated, 1974), Tacitus, Opera Minora (ed with R M Ogilvie, 1975), Gildas (ed and translated 1978), Roman Declamation (1980), The Minor Declamations Ascribed to Quintilian (ed with commentary, 1984), Sopatros the Rhetor (with D C Innes 1988), Cicero De Officiis (ed, 1994); *Recreations* hill walking, travel; *Style*— Prof Michael Winterbottom, FBA; ✉ 53 Thorncliffe Road, Oxford OX2 7BA

WINTERBOTTOM, Sir Walter; kt (1978), CBE (1972, OBE 1963); s of James Winterbottom; *b* 31 March 1913; *Educ* Chester Coll of Educn, Carnegie Coll of Physical Educn; *m* 1942, Ann Richards; 1 s (decd), 2 da; *Career* dir of coaching and mangr England Team FA 1946–62; gen sec Central Cncl Physical Educn 1963–72, dir Sports Cncl 1965–78; *Style*— Sir Walter Winterbottom, CBE; ✉ 15 Orchard Gdns, Cranleigh, Surrey (☎ 01483 271593)

WINTERFLOOD, Brian Martin; s of Thomas George Winterflood (d 1978), of Slough, and Doris Maud, *née* Waddington; *Educ* Frays Coll Uxbridge Middx; *m* 10 Oct 1966, Doreen Stella, da of Albert Frederick McCartney, of London; 2 s (Guy b 2 April 1970, Mark b 8 March 1973), 1 da (Sarah b 9 July 1974); *Career* Nat Serv 1955–57; Greener Dreyfus & Co 1953–55; Bisgood Bishop & Co: joined 1957, ptnr 1967, dir 1971 (Co inc), md 1981 (co taken over by County NatWest Investment Bank 1986), md market making 1986; exec dir County NatWest Securities 1986–88, md Winterflood Securities Equities 1988–, exec dir Union Discount Co of London plc 1991–93, dir Close Brothers Group plc 1993–, md Winterflood Securities Limited Gilts 1994; MSI 1966; vice-pres REMEDI (Rehabilitation and Med Res Tst), jt chm USM initiative for The Prince's Youth Business Tst; *Recreations* family, work, travel; *Style*— Brian Winterflood; ✉ 5 Church Hill, Wimbledon, London SW19 7BN (☎ 0181 946 4052); Winterflood Securities Ltd, 23–29 Walbrook, London EC4N 8LA (☎ 0171 621 0004, fax 0171 623 9482)

WINTERS, (Leonard) Alan; s of Geoffrey Walter Horace Winters, of Ipswich, and Christine Agnes, *née* Ive; *b* 8 April 1950; *Educ* Chingford Co HS, Univ of Bristol (BSc), Univ of Cambridge (MA, PhD); *m* (sep); 2 da (Victoria b 1972, Catherine b 1973); *Career* jr res offr and res offr Dept of Applied Economics Univ of Cambridge 1971–80, lectr in economics Univ of Bristol 1980–86, economist The World Bank 1983–85, prof of economics Univ Coll of N Wales Bangor 1986–90, prof of economics Univ of Birmingham 1990–94, div chief of int trade World Bank 1994–; res fell Centre for Econ Policy Res, assoc ed: Economic Jl, Jl of Common Market Studies; former chm English Folk Dance and Song Soc; *Books* An Econometric Model of The Export Sector: The Determinants of British Exports and Their Prices (1981), International Economics (1985, new edn 1991), Europe's Domestic Market (1988), Eastern Europe's International Trade (1994); *Recreations* music, cricket, walking; *Style*— Mr L Alan Winters; ✉ International Trade Division (IECIT), The World Bank, Room N-5043, 1818 H-Street NW, Washington DC 20433, USA (☎ 00 1 202 473 3845)

WINTERSGILL, Matthew William; s of Harold Heap Wintersgill (d 1973), of Bedford, and Patricia, *née* Gregory; *b* 12 July 1949; *Educ* Stratton Sch Beds, Canterbury Sch of Architecture; *m* 16 Sept 1978, Sara Neill, da of Gerald Bradley (d 1970), and Sheila Neill (d 1985), of London; *Career* architect; Powell and Moya 1973–78 (incl: Cripps Bldg project for Queen's Coll Cambridge, Sch for Advanced Architectural Studies Bristol, Nat West Bank Devpt Shaftesbury Ave London), Thompstone Harris Design Assocs 1978–80, ptnr Wintersgill & Faulkner 1980– (formerly Thompstone Wintersgill Faulkner); work projects for: BAA, Bowater Corp, BP Oil Int, The Sci Museum, Reuters, Prudential Assurance Co, IVECO Ford Truck Ltd, The PO, Nat West Bank, Rank Leisure, FCO; memb W End Soc of Architects; registered memb ARCUK 1974, RIBA 1975; *Recreations* drawing, swimming, travel, walking; *Style*— Matthew Wintersgill, Esq; ✉ Wintersgill & Faulkner, 7–11 Lexington St, London W1R 4BU (☎ 0171 734 8671, fax 0171 434 1808)

WINTERSON, Jeanette; *b* 27 Aug 1959; *Educ* Accrington Girls' HS, St Catherine's Coll Oxford (BA); *Career* author; *Books* Oranges Are Not the Only Fruit (1985, BBC TV adaptation 1990), The Passion (1987), Sexing The Cherry (1989), Written on the Body (1992), Art and Lies (1994), Art Objects (critical essays, 1995), Gut Symmetries (1997); *Film* Great Moments in Aviation (1992); *Awards* Whitbread First Novel award 1985, John Llewelyn Rhys prize 1987, Commonwealth Writers' award 1988, E M Forster award (American Acad of Arts and Letters) 1989, Golden Gate San Francisco Int Film Festival 1990, Best Drama Euro TV Festival 1990, FIPA D'Argent Cannes 1991, BAFTA Best Drama 1991, Prix Italia 1991; *Recreations* I try to live my life in one piece, so work is recreation and recreations are also work; *Style*— Ms Jeanette Winterson; ✉ c/o Jonathan Cape Ltd, 20 Vauxhall Bridge Road, London SW1V 2SA

WINTERTON, (Jane) Ann; MP (C) Congleton (majority 11,120); da of late Joseph Robert and Ellen Jane Hodgson, of Sutton Coldfield; *b* 6 March 1941; *Educ* Erdington GS for Girls; *m* 1960, Nicholas Raymond Winterton MP, *qv*; 2 s, 1 da; *Career* MP (C) Congleton 1983–, memb Agric Select Ctee 1987–, chm All Party Pro-Life Gp 1991–, hon treas Parly and Scientific Ctee 1994–; jt master S Staffs Hunt 1959–64; memb W Midlands Cons Women's Advsy Ctee 1969–71, memb The Chms' Panel 1992–; *Style*— Mrs Ann Winterton, MP; ✉ House of Commons, London SW1A 0AA

WINTERTON, Nicholas Raymond; MP (C) Macclesfield (majority 22,767); s of Norman H Winterton (d 1971), of Lysways House, Longdon Green, Staffs; *b* 31 March 1938; *Educ* Rugby; *m* 1960, Jane Ann Winterton MP, *qv*, da of J R Hodgson, of Sutton Coldfield; 2 s, 1 da; *Career* Nat Serv 2 Lt 14/20 King's Hussars 1957–59; sales exec trainee Shell-Mex and BP Ltd 1959–60, sales and gen mangr Stevens and Hodgson Ltd 1960–80; cncllr Warwickshire CC 1967–1972 (dep chm County Educn Ctee 1970–72, chm Co Youth Serv Sub-Ctee 1969–72); Parly candidate (C) Newcastle-under-Lyme 1969 (by-election) and 1970, MP (C) Macclesfield 1971– (by-election); Parly advsr to Construction Plant Hire Assoc; non-exec dir: Bridgewater Paper Co Ltd, Emerson International Inc, MSB Ltd; chm: Br-Namibian Parly Gp 1983–90, Anglo-Danish Parly Gp, All Pty Parly Media Gp, All Pty Parly Cotton and Allied Textile Gp 1979–, All Pty Parly Paper and Bd Indust Gp 1983–; vice chm Anglo Swedish Parly Gp; jt vice chm Br Indonesian Parly Gp; treas: Br Bahamas Parly Gp, Br-Taiwan Parly Gp; vice chm: Br-SA Parly Gp 1979–90, UK Falkland Islands Gp; memb Select Ctees: Social Servs 1979–90, Standing Orders 1981–; chm Health Ctee 1991–92, memb House of Commons Chairmen's Panel 1986–; memb Exec Ctee Anglo-Austrian Soc; Freeman City of London, Liveryman and Memb Ct of Assts Worshipful Co of Weavers; *Clubs* Cavalry and Guards'; *Style*— Nicholas Winterton, Esq, MP; ✉ House of Commons, Westminster, London SW1A 0AA

WINTOUR, Charles Vere; CBE (1980, MBE (Mil) 1945); s of Maj-Gen F G Wintour, CB, CBE (d 1948), of Broadstone, and Alice Jane Blanche, *née* Foster (d 1977); *b* 18 May 1917; *Educ* Oundle, Peterhouse Cambridge (BA, MA); *m* 1, 1940 (m dis 1979), Eleanor Trego, er da of Prof R J Baker; 3 s (Gerald Jackson b 1940 (decd), James Charles b 1948, Patrick Walter b 1956), 2 da (Anna, Hilary Nora); m 2, 9 Nov 1979, Audrey Cecilia, da of Frederick George Smith, former w of W A Slaughter; *Career* Royal Norfolk Regt 1940, GSO 2 COSSAC 1944, GSO 2 SHAEF 1945 (despatches); Evening Standard: joined 1946, political ed 1952, dep ed 1959–76 and 1978–80; asst ed Sunday Express 1952–54, managing ed Daily Express 1957–59; ed: Sunday Express Magazine 1981–82, UK Press Gazette 1985–86; dir: Evening Standard Co Ltd 1959–82, Express (formerly Beaverbrook) Newspapers Ltd 1964–82, TV-am (News) Ltd 1982–84, Wintour Publications 1984–85; ombudsman Sunday Times 1990–96; memb Press Cncl 1978–79; Croix de Guerre: France 1945, Belgium 1945; Bronze Star (US) 1945; *Books* Pressures on the Press (1972), Rise and Fall of Fleet Street (1989); *Recreations* theatre going; *Clubs* Garrick; *Style—* Charles Wintour, Esq, CBE; ✉ 60 East Hatch, Tisbury, Wilts SP3 6PH (☎ 01747 870880)

WINWOOD, Dr Robert Sidney; s of Robert Winwood, of Poole, Dorset, and Mary Theodore, *née* Watson; *b* 31 Dec 1932; *Educ* Univ of London (MB BS); *m* 28 Aug 1954, June Margaret, da of Leslie Frank Sansom, of Broadstone, Dorset; 3 s (Robert Julian b 3 June 1958, Paul John b 9 Aug 1961, Andrew Leslie b 15 June 1969); *Career* Capt and jr med specialist RAMC 1958–62; conslt physician and cardiologist; FRCP; memb: BMA 1957, Hunterian Soc 1964, Ramblers' Assoc, Nat Tst, CPRE; *Books* Essentials of Clinical Diagnosis in Cardiology (1981), current textbooks of Anatomy and Physiology, Materia Medica and Medicine for Nurses, chapters in other med textbooks; *Recreations* music, photography, running, hill walking; *Clubs* Holmes Place, Barbican Health; *Style—* Dr Robert S Winwood; ✉ Holly House Hospital, Buckhurst Hill, Essex (☎ 0181 505 3311, fax 0181 502 9735); Roding Hospital, Ilford, Essex (☎ 0181 551 1100); St Bartholomew's Hospital, London EC1A 7BE

WINWOOD, Steve; *b* 12 May 1948; *m* 2, 1987, Eugenia, *née* Crafton; 4 c; *Career* musician; memb gps: Spencer Davis Group 1963–67, Traffic 1967–69, 1970–74 and 1994–, Blind Faith 1969, Ginger Baker's Airforce 1970; has worked with: Eric Clapton, *qv*, Jimi Hendrix, Sandy Denny, Howling Wolf, Muddy Waters, George Harrison and others; albums with Traffic: Mr Fantasy (1968, UK no 8), Traffic (1968, UK no 9), Last Exit (1969), Best of Traffic (compilation, 1970), John Barleycorn Must Die (1970, UK no 11), Welcome To The Canteen (1971, US no 26), Low Spark Of High Heeled Boys (1972, US no 7), Shoot-Out At The Fantasy Factory (1973, US no 6), Traffic - On The Road (1973, UK no 40), When The Eagle Flies (1974, UK no 31), Heavy Traffic (compilation, 1975), More Heavy Traffic (compilation, 1975), Far From Home (1994); album Blind Faith (1969, UK no 1); solo albums: Steve Winwood (1977, US no 22), Arc Of A Diver (1981, UK no 13), Talking Back To The Night (1982, UK no 6), Back In The High Life (1986, UK no 8), Chronicles (compilation, 1987, UK no 12), Roll With It (1988, UK no 4), Refugees Of The Heart (1990); *Style—* Steve Winwood, Esq; ✉ c/o Virgin Records, Kensal House, 553–579 Harrow Road, London W10 4RH

WISBECH, Archdeacon of; *see:* Rone, Ven Jim

WISCARSON, Christopher; s of John Xavier Wiscarson, and Jean Eileen, *née* Eckhoff; *b* 25 March 1951; *Educ* Welbeck Coll, King's Coll London (BSc), Harvard Business Sch (PMD 1985); *m* 25 Nov 1972, Gillian Elizabeth, *née* Deeks; 2 da (Annabel Julia b 4 Sept 1978, Verity Michelle b 5 April 1980); *Career* gen mangr Southern Life Cape Town South Africa until 1986, chief exec Save and Prosper Insurances 1986–90; fin dir Lloyds Abbey Life plc 1990–93, md Black Horse Financial Services 1993–; chm Johannesburg Centenary Arts Ctee 1984–86; FIA; *Publications* paper Mergers - Strategy Beyond Finance presented to Henley Mgmnt Coll 1988; *Recreations* painting, interpretation of art; *Clubs* Phyllis Court (Henley-on-Thames); *Style—* Christopher Wiscarson, Esq; ✉ Black Horse Financial Services, Mountbatten House, Military Road, Chatham, Kent ME4 4JF (☎ 01634 836011, fax 01634 836009, mobile 0589 163084)

WISDOM, Dr Anthony Rodwell; s of Col George E C Wisdom, CMG (d 1958), of Edenbridge, Kent, and Dorothea, *née* Rodwell (d 1978); *b* 30 Sept 1930; *Educ* Epsom Coll, London Hosp Med Coll, Univ of London; *m* 1, 25 Feb 1956 (m dis 1966), Charlotte Hartstein; 3 s (Oliver b 1958, Michael b 1960, Julian b1961), 1 da (Lucy b 1956); m 2, 14 Aug 1974, Vaneska, da of Col R Fleury of Rio de Janeiro, Brazil; *Career* Nat Serv RN med branch 1955–57; jr dr 1954–64, conslt physician 1964–; MSSVD, fell Hunterian Soc; *Books* Atlas of Sexually Transmitted Diseases (1 edn 1973, 2 edn 1989); *Recreations* rowing, travelling, food especially foreign; *Clubs* Leander, Tideway Scullers, London Rowing; *Style—* Dr Anthony Wisdom; ✉ GU Clinic, Oldchurch Hospital, Romford, Essex RM7 0BE (☎ 01708 746090)

WISDOM, Julia Mary; da of Dennis Wisdom (d 1985), and Rosemary Jean, *née* Cutler; *b* 24 Sept 1958; *Educ* Cranborne Chase, Bryanston, King's Coll London (BA); *Career* commissioning ed of crime fiction Victor Gollancz Ltd until 1993, editorial dir HarperCollins Publishers Ltd 1994–; memb: Crime Writers' Assoc 1987, Dorothy L Sayers Soc 1992; *Recreations* music, travel, reading; *Clubs* Academy; *Style—* Ms Julia Wisdom; ✉ HarperCollins Publishers Ltd, 77–85 Fulham Palace Road, London W6 8JB (☎ 0181 741 7070, fax 0181 307 4440)

WISE, Gp Capt Adam Nugent; LVO (1983), MBE (1976); s of Lt-Col (Alfred) Roy Wise, MBE, TD (d 1974), and Cassandra Noel Wise (d 1982); *b* 1 Aug 1943; *Educ* Repton, RAF Coll Cranwell, Univ of London (BA); *m* 1983, Jill Amabel, da of (Cyril) Geoffrey Marmaduke Alington, of Lincs (d 1987); 1 s, 1 da; *Career* cmmnd RAF 1965; served Middle East, Far East, Germany; ADC to Cdr FEAF 1970–71, exchange pilot Federal German Air Force 1972–75, OC Univ of Wales Air Sqdn 1979–80, Equerry to HM The Queen 1980–83, OC Univ of London Air Sqdn 1983–86, private sec to TRH The Duke of York and The Prince Edward 1983–87, RAF Coll Cranwell 1988–91, OC RAF Benson, Dep Capt The Queen's Flight and ADC to HM The Queen 1991–93, Military and Air Attaché British Embassy Madrid 1994–, Liveryman Worshipful Co of Golsmiths; *Recreations* sailing, riding; *Clubs* RAF, Royal Ocean Racing; *Style—* Gp Capt Adam Wise, LVO, MBE; ✉ FCO (Madrid), King Charles Street, London SW1A 2AH

WISE, Audrey; MP (Lab) Preston (majority 12,175); *Career* MP (Lab) Preston 1987–; *Style—* Mrs Audrey Wise, MP; ✉ House of Commons, London SW1A 0AA (☎ 0171 219 3000)

WISE, Hon Christopher John Clayton; s and h of 2 Baron Wise, *qv*; *b* 19 March 1949; *Educ* Norwich Sch, Southampton Univ; *Career* MIBiol; *Clubs* Farmers; *Style—* Dr the Hon Christopher Wise; ✉ Demeter, Woodmancote, Cirencester, Glos GL7 7EF

WISE, Dennis Frank; s of Frank Dennis Wise, and Pamela June Wise; *b* 16 Dec 1966; *Educ* Christopher Wren Sch London (now Hammersmith Sch); *Career* professional footballer; Wimbledon FC: joined 1985, debut v Cardiff City, 135 league appearances (31 goals), 23 cup appearances (3 goals), winners FA Cup 1988; Chelsea FC: joined 1990–, debut v Derby County, over 60 appearances (18 goals), runners-up FA Cup 1994; England caps: 1 under 21, 3 B, 6 full; *Recreations* golf, snooker, tennis; *Style—* Dennis Wise, Esq; ✉ Chelsea FC, Stamford Bridge, Fulham Rd, London SW6 1HS (☎ 0171 385 5545)

WISE, Ernie; *see:* Wiseman, Ernest

WISE, Herbert; s of Zsiga Weisz (d 1963), and Juliska, *née* Stern (d 1951); *b* 31 Aug 1924; *Educ* Austria Vienna, Oxted Co Secdy Sch Surrey, New Era Acad of Drama; *m* 1, 1963 (m dis 1972), Moira Redmond; m 2, 1988, Fiona Walker; 1 s (Charlie Walker-Wise b 15 May 1978), 1 da (Susannah Walker-Wise b 25 Jan 1973); *Career* TV, film and theatre dir of over 300 prodns in UK incl I Claudius; actor and/or dir in rep 1950–56, artistic dir Dundee Rep Theatre 1952–55, dir Granada TV 1956–60, freelance dir BBC and ITV 1960–; work in Germany, Austria and USA incl: Skokie 1981, Pope Paul II 1984, Strange Interlude 1987; BAFTA Desmond Davis Award for outstanding creative contrib to TV 1978, Emmy Award (for I Claudius) 1979, Dirs' Guild of America Award for best film prodn (for Skokie) 1982; memb: Dirs' Guild of America, Dirs' Guild of GB, BAFTA; *Recreations* astronomy, chess, music, films, theatre; *Style—* Herbert Wise, Esq; ✉ c/o Nigel Britten, NG Management, Garden Studios, 11–15 Betterton Street, London WC2H 9BP (☎ 0171 379 0344, fax 0171 379 0801)

WISE, 2 Baron (UK 1951); John Clayton Wise; s of 1 Baron Wise, DL (d 1968); *b* 11 June 1923; *m* 1, 1946 (m dis 1986), Margaret Annie, da of Frederick Victor Snead, of Banbury; 2 s; m 2, 19 Dec 1993, Mrs Janice Harman Thompson, da of late Albert John Harman, of NSW, Australia; *Heir* s, Hon Christopher Wise; *Career* farmer; *Style—* The Rt Hon Lord Wise; ✉ Lynn Cottage, Castle Hill, Hemyock, Devon EX15 3RU

WISE, Prof Michael John; CBE (1979), MC (1945); s of Harry Cuthbert Wise (d 1954), of Birmingham, and Sarah Evelyn, *née* Lawton (d 1962); *b* 17 Aug 1918, Stafford; *Educ* Saltley GS Birmingham, Univ of Birmingham (BA, DipEd, PhD); *m* 4 May 1942, Barbara Mary, da of C L Hodgetts (d 1951), of Wolverhampton; 1 da ((Barbara) Janet (Mrs Meyer) b 1 June 1946), 1 s (John Charles Michael b 6 Sept 1949); *Career* cmmnd RA 1941, serv Middle E 1942–44, Maj 1944, The Northamptonshire Regt 1944–46, serv Italy 1944–46; lectr in geography Univ of Birmingham 1946–51; LSE: lectr in geography 1951–54, Sir Ernest Cassel reader in econ geography 1954–58, prof of geography 1958–83, pro dir 1983–85; Erskine fell Univ of Canterbury NZ 1970; chm: Departmental Ctee of Inquiry into Statutory Smallholdings Miny of Agric 1964–68, Landscape Advsy Ctee Dept of Tport 1981–90 (memb 1971–90), Sir Dudley Stamp Meml Tst 1988–; pres: Inst of Br Geographers 1974, Geographical Assoc 1976–77, Int Geographical Union 1976–80, Royal Geographical Soc 1980–82; memb Social Sci Res Cncl 1976–82, chm of govrs Birkbeck Coll London 1983–89; hon fell LSE 1988, fell Birkbeck Coll London 1990; Fndrs Medal Royal Geographical Soc 1977; Hon DUniv Open 1978, Hon DSc Univ of Birmingham 1982, Lauréat d'Honneur Int Geographical Union (1984); FRGS, FRSA, fell Inst of Environmental Sci; Alexander Körösi Csoma Medal Hungarian Geographical Soc 1980, Tokyo Geographical Soc Medal 1981, hon memb Geographical Socs of Paris, Poland, USSR and Mexico, hon fell Landscape Inst 1991; *Books* Birmingham and its Regional Setting (hon ed, 1950); consultant: An Atlas of World Resources (1979), The Great Geographical Atlas (1982), Ordnance Survey Atlas of Gr Britain (1982); *Recreations* gardening, music, watching cricket; *Clubs* Athenaeum, Geographical; *Style—* Prof Michael Wise, CBE, MC; ✉ 45 Oakleigh Ave, Whetstone, London N20 9JE (☎ 0181 445 6057); London School of Economics, Houghton St, Aldwych, London WC2A 2AE (☎ 0171 405 7686)

WISE, Dr Peter Hermann; s of James Wise, of Adelaide, Aust, and Matilda, *née* Benedikt; *b* 20 April 1937; *Educ* St Peter's Coll Adelaide, Univ of Adelaide (MB BS), Univ of London (PhD); *m* 19 Nov 1964 (m dis 1992), Carole Margaret, da of Otto Kornitzer (d 1983); 2 s (Nicholas Simon, Daniel Jeremy); *Career* dir of endocrinology Royal Adelaide Hosp Aust 1969–75, assoc prof of med Flinders Univ of S Aust 1976–79, conslt physician Charing Cross Hosp London 1979–; ctee memb: Br Diabetic Assoc, Ethical Res Ctee, RCGP; FRACP 1971, FRCP 1978; *Books* Knowing About Diabetes (1994), Atlas of Endocrinology (1994), Essential Endocrinology (1995); *Recreations* tennis, music; *Style—* Dr Peter Wise; ✉ 67 Chartfield Avenue, London SW15 6HN (☎ 0181 789 1859)

WISE, Prof Richard; s of A R James Wise (d 1993), of Eastbourne, and Joan, *née* Richards; *b* 7 July 1942; *Educ* Burnage HS, Univ of Manchester (MB ChB, MD); *m* 16 Feb 1979, Dr Jane Marion Symonds, da of R C Symonds, of Sedbergh; 1 s (Peter Richard b 1970 d 1989), 1 da (Katherin b July 1972); *Career* conslt and dir W Midlands Antibiotic Res Laboratory Dudley Rd Hosp Birmingham 1974–, hon prof Univ of Birmingham 1995– (reader in clinical microbiology 1985–95); author of papers and books on antibiotic therapy; FRCPath; *Recreations* viticulture; *Style—* Prof Richard Wise; ✉ Department of Medical Microbiology, City Hospital, Dudley Road, Birmingham B18 7QH (☎ 0121 554 3801)

WISEMAN, Carol Mary; *b* 20 Nov 1942; *Educ* Southport HS, Lady Margaret Hall Oxford (MA); *Career* director; BBC TV 1965–79: res dir Schools TV, asst dir Drama; Freelance Film TV drama dir 1979–; prodns incl: Coming Out (play, BBC) 1979, A Question of Guilt (serial, BBC) 1980, Bognor-Deadline (serial, Thames) 1981, Pictures (serial, Central) 1982, Big Deal (series, BBC) 1983–84, Dog Ends (play) 1985, Dear Box Number (play) 1985, A Matter of Will (play) 1985, Cats Eyes (series, TVS) 1986, A Little Princess (BAFTA Award for Best Childrens Drama) 1987, Somewhere to Run (Prix Europa) 1988, May Wine (film, Canal Plus), 1989, Finding Sarah (play, Channel 4) 1990, Does This Mean We're Married (film, Canal Plus) 1990, Love Hurts (series, BBC) 1991, Face the Music (film, Movie Group), Goggle-Eyes (serial, BBC) 1992, Blue Heaven (serial, Channel 4), Ghosts - The Shadowy Third (film, BBC) 1993, The Queen's Nose (serial, BBC) 1995–96; *Style—* Ms Carol Wiseman

WISEMAN, David John; s of James Wiseman (d 1982), and Marjorie, *née* Ward; *b* 25 March 1944; *Educ* St John's Sch Leatherhead, Britannia RNC Dartmouth, RNEC Manadon Plymouth (BSc), Univ of Surrey (MSc); *Career* RN 1962–74, Lt 1967–74; asst sec DTI 1980–87 (princ 1974–80), co dir Kingsway Rowland 1987–89, md Rowland Public Affairs 1988–91, md The Rowland Co Brussels 1989–91, md Counsellors in Public Policy Ltd 1991–; FIEE 1974, CEng 1974, MIMgt 1986, MIPR 1989; *Recreations* travel, gardening, music; *Clubs* Athenaeum; *Style—* David Wiseman, Esq; ✉ 35 Blandford Street, London W1H 3AE (☎ 0171 935 0348); Counsellors in Public Policy Ltd, 52 Broadwick St, London W1V 1FF (☎ 0171 734 0313, fax 0171 494 1667)

WISEMAN, Ernest (Ernie Wise); OBE (1976); s of Harry Wiseman, and Connie, *née* Wright; *b* 27 Nov 1925; *Educ* Cncl Sch; *m* 1953, Doreen, da of Henry James William Blyth; *Career* radio, variety, TV and film actor, long running comedy partnership with the late Eric Morecambe; *Theatre* Royal Command Performances: 1955, 1964, 1966, 1968 and 1984; The Mystery of Edwin Drood (Savoy) 1987, Run for your Wife (Criterion) 1988, the King in Sleeping Beauty (Theatre Royal Windsor) 1992–93; *Television* incl: Too Close for Comfort (TV Los Angeles) 1986, NZ Telethon 1989 and 1990, This is Your Life 1990, The Importance of Being Ernie (40 Minutes, BBC) 1993; *Awards* SFTA Awards: 1963, 1971, 1972, 1973; BAFTA Award Light Entertainment TV 1973, Silver Heart Variety Club 1964 and 1976, Water Rats 1970, Radio Indust 1971 and 1972, Sun Newspaper 1973; *Books* with Eric Morecambe: Eric and Ernie - an autobiography of Morecambe and Wise (1973), Scripts of Morecambe and Wise (1974), Morecambe and Wise Special (1977), There's No Answer to That (1981); Still On My Way To Hollywood (autobiography, 1990); *Recreations* boating, swimming; *Style—* Ernie Wise, Esq, OBE; ✉ Gable End, 22 Dorney Reach Rd, Dorney Reach, Maidenhead, Berks SL6 01DX

WISEMAN, Sir John William; 11 Bt (E 1628), of Canfield Hall, Essex; s of Sir William Wiseman, 10 Bt, CB, CMG (d 1962), and his 3 w, Joan, Lady Wiseman; *b* 16 March 1957; *Educ* Millfield, Hartford Univ Conn USA; *m* 1980, Nancy, da of Casimer Zyla, of New Britain, Conn, USA; 2 da (Elizabeth b 1983, Patricia Alison b 1986); *Heir* fifth cous, Thomas Alan Wiseman b 8 July 1921; *Style—* Sir John Wiseman, Bt

WISEMAN, Dr Martin Jeremy; s of Leslie Wiseman, of Faversham, Kent, and Sonia Wiseman, *née* Linder; *b* 18 April 1953; *Educ* King's Sch Canterbury, Guy's Hosp Med Sch (MRCP); *m* 5 May 1979, Jane Carol, da of Dennis Bannister, of Bournemouth, Dorset; 1 s (Daniel b 1987), 2 da (Jessica b 1982, Anna b 1985); *Career* res fell Metabolic Unit Guys Hosp 1981–86, head of Nutrition Unit Dept of Health 1986–; author of publications on diabetes nutrition and kidney disease; memb: Br Diabetic Assoc, Nutrition Soc; *Recreations* gastronomy, travel, family, Times crossword; *Style—* Dr Martin Wiseman; ✉ Department of Health, London SE1 (☎ 0171 972 5325)

WISEMAN, Prof (Timothy) Peter; s of Stephen Wiseman (d 1971), of Manchester, and Winifred Agnes Wiseman; *b* 3 Feb 1940; *Educ* Manchester GS, Balliol Coll Oxford

(MA, DPhil); *m* 15 Sept 1962, (Doreen) Anne, da of Harold Williams, of Atherton, Lancs; *Career* reader in Roman history Univ of Leicester 1973–76 (lectr in classics 1963–73), visiting prof of classics Univ of Toronto 1970–71, prof of classics Univ of Exeter 1977–; vice pres British Academy 1992–94, pres Roman Soc 1992–95; Hon DLitt Durham 1988; FSA 1977, FBA 1986; *Books* Catullan Questions (1969), New Men in the Roman Senate (1971), Cinna the Poet (1974), Clio's Cosmetics (1979), Catullus and His World (1985), Roman Studies (1987), Death of an Emperor (1991), Talking to Virgil (1992), Historiography and Imagination (1994), Remus: A Roman Myth (1995); *Style*— Prof Peter Wiseman; ✉ Department of Classics, The Queen's Building, University of Exeter, Exeter EX4 4QH (☎ 01392 264201, fax 01392 264377, telex 42894 EXUNIV G)

WISEMAN, Thomas Alan; s of Thomas Edward Wiseman (d 1959, 5 in descent from Sir Thomas Wiseman, 6 Bt), and Anna Louisa, *née* Allen; hp to fifth cous, Sir John Wiseman, 11 Bt; *b* 8 July 1921; *Educ* Gravesend Co Sch for Boys; *m* 11 Dec 1946, Hildemarie (d 1991), da of Gustav Domnik, of Allenstein, formerly E Prussia; 1 s (Thomas b and d 1947), 1 da (Susan b and d 1949); *Career* Army 1941–46; ships' agent Hamburg 1937–38, temp civil servant Gravesend 1939–41, English corr and interpreter Brussels 1946–52, ships agent 1952–75 admin offr Forest Prods Terminal 1975–86, ret 1986; *Style*— Thomas Wiseman, Esq; ✉ 14 Havisham Rd, Chalk, Gravesend, Kent DA12 4UN (☎ 01474 361575)

WISHART, John MacKeand (Jock); s of Thomas Wishart, of Dumfries, and Marion Jane MacKeand Hood, BEM; *b* 6 Feb 1953; *Educ* Dumfries Acad, Univ of Durham (BA, pres Union and Univ Boat Club); *m* 28 July 1984, Deborah Jane, da of Wilfred Preston; 1 s (Gregory John MacKeand b 16 Sept 1986), 1 da (Laurie Isla b 3 May 1991); *Career* PA to gp sales and promotions dir Lillywhites 1974–78, sales dir Ravelle Wrightweights 1978–80, conslt 1980–84; Hill and Knowlton: assoc dir 1984–89, sponsorship dir 1989–91, conslt 1991–; dir JGI 1991–; head of public rels Rugby World Cup 1991, memb Organising Ctee World Corporate Games London 1992; memb London Int Sport 1994–, fndr memb Top 100 Club; sporting achievements: GB rowing rep World Jr Championships, winner Br Univ Championship medals for rowing, canoeing and weightlifting, rowing rep Scotland, finalist Wyfolds Cup Henley Royal Regatta 1978 and 1979, America's Cup challenger Newport RI 1980, past holder Round Britain Powerboat Record 1989, winner all major trophies Cowes Week IOW during period 1983–91, Br Dragon Boat champion 1989, 1990 and 1992, fourth place Dragon Boat World Championships 1990, European champion 1993 and 1995, winner Br Skiffing Championships 1991 and 1993; memb Br Polar Team (first men to walk unsupported to N Geomagnetic pole) 1992, organiser Ultimate Challenge (largest ever party and first televised trek to N Magnetic Pole) 1996; vice pres Palatinate Assoc (Univ of Durham Old Boys); *Recreations* sailing, dragon boat paddling, rowing, skiing, rugby; *Clubs* Leander, Mosimanns, Molesey Boat (capt 1978), Royal Canoe, Kingston Rowing, Royal Hong Kong Yacht, Tamesis, Skiff, London Corinthian Sailing, Kingston Royals Dragon Boat (chm 1987–95); *Style*— Jock Wishart, Esq; ✉ c/o J G I, 5 Albert Drive, London SW19 6LP (☎ 0181 780 5270, fax 0181 780 5273)

WISHART, (Margaret) Ruth (Mrs R McLeod); da of John Wishart (d 1960), and Margaret Smith, *née* Mitchell (d 1989); *b* 27 Aug 1945; *Educ* Eastwood Senior Secdy Sch; *m* 16 Sept 1971, Roderick McLeod, s of Roderick McLeod; *Career* women's ed Scottish Daily Record 1973–78; asst ed: Sunday Mail 1978–82, Sunday Standard 1982–83; freelance journalist and broadcaster 1983–86, sr asst ed The Scotsman 1986–88; columnist and broadcaster 1988–; memb: Scottish Ctee Assoc Business Sponsorship of Arts, Scottish Advsy Ctee to Br Cncl; dir Assembly Theatre; hon vice pres Scottish Action on Dementia; memb: Scottish Cncl Royal Glasgow Inst; Hon Dr Univ of Stirling 1994; *Recreations* theatre, concerts, gardening, galleries, curling; *Style*— Ms R Wishart; ✉ Wilson Court, Wilson St, Glasgow; Eyry House, Kilcreggan, Argyll (☎ and fax 0141 552 0367); BBC Scotland (☎ 0141 338 2376)

WISHEART, James Dunwoody; s of Rev James Wisheart (d 1986), of Belfast, and Ena Mary, *née* Dunwoody (d 1986); *b* 2 March 1938; *Educ* Methodist Coll Belfast, Queen's Univ Belfast (BSc, MB, MCh), Univ of Alabama; *m* 11 Sept 1965, Janet Mary, da of Cecil Walter Gibson (d 1973), of Dublin; 2 s (Michael b 1969, Andrew b 1973), 1 da (Linda b 1968); *Career* conslt cardiothoracic surgn Bristol Royal Infirmary and Royal Children's Hosp 1975–, med dir United Bristol Healthcare Tst 1992–; assoc ed Thorax 1984–90; memb Methodist Church; memb: BMA, Br Cardiac Soc, Soc Cardiothoracic Surgns, Euro Assoc Cardiothoracic Surgns; FRCS, FRCSEd (memb bd cardiothoracic surgery 1982–); *Recreations* music, walking, sailing; *Style*— James Wisheart, Esq; ✉ Department of Cardiac Surgery, Bristol Royal Infirmary, Bristol BS2 8HW (☎ 0117 9 28 2821)

WISNER, George John; s of George Phillip Wisner, and Lillian Florence, *née* Butler; *b* 1 June 1949; *Educ* Haverstock Hill Sch, Chelsea Sch of Art; *m* 26 March 1977, Romayne Siobhan, da of Derek Dobson Wood; 2 da (Alice Willow b 29 Dec 1977, Shelley Rose b 11 Feb 1980); *Career* set designer; BBC: apprentice carpenter 1965–70, design asst 1971–74, designer 1974–80, sr TV designer 1980–91, head of design Open Univ Prodn Centre 1991–; host visitor Liaison Dept BBC TV Centre London 1990–91, ptnr: Blakesley Gallery Northants 1991–, Pebbles Two 1994–; freelance designer; BBC prodns designed incl: Day in the Death of Joe Egg, The Gambler by Dostoyevsky, The Prime of Miss Jean Brodie, The Grand Inquisitor, End Game, Macbeth, Miss Julie, numerous childrens progs; FRSA 1987; memb: BAFTA, RSA; *Recreations* cycling, swimming; *Style*— George Wisner, Esq; ✉ Barton House, Blakesley, nr Towcester, Northamptonshire NN12 8RE (☎ 01327 860282)

WISZNIEWSKI, Adrian Ryszard; s of Witold Eugene Wiszniewski, of Renfrew, Glasgow, and Elspeth Mary, *née* Hyland; *b* 31 March 1958; *Educ* Mackintosh Sch of Architecture, Glasgow Sch of Art (BA, postgrad Dip); *m* 11 May 1985, Diane Lennox, da of Ronald Alexander Foley, of Nairn; 2 s (Max Tristan Charles b 26 June 1987, Louis Lennox Highland b 26 Nov 1993), 1 da (Holly b 21 April 1990); *Career* artist; work in painting, printmaking, ceramics, tapestry, neon, sculpture, writing, film; solo exhibitions in London, Belgium, Australia and Japan; also exhibited in several important int gp exhibitions and surveys throughout the world; Mark Rothko Scholarship 1984; *Books* For Max (1988), A Man Tied-Up in His Own Composition (1996); *Style*— Adrian Wiszniewski, Esq; ✉ 2 Shields, Castle Semple, Lochwinnoch, Renfrewshire PA12 4HL

WITCHELL, Nicholas N H; s of William Joseph Henshall Witchell, and Barbara Sybil Mary, *née* MacDonald; *b* 23 Sept 1953; *Educ* Epsom Coll, Univ of Leeds (LLB); *Career* joined BBC News 1976, reporter NI 1979–81, reporter London 1981–83, Ireland corr 1984; presenter: 6 O'Clock News 1984–89, BBC Breakfast News 1989–94; corr Panorama 1994, diplomatic corr BBC 1995–; assoc prodr: News 39 1989, News 44 1994, News 45 1995; chm Project Urquhart, govr Queen Elizabeth's Fndn for Disabled People; OStJ; FRGS; *Books* The Loch Ness Story (1974, 1975, 1982 and 1989); *Style*— Nicholas Witchell; ✉ BBC TV News, BBC TV Centre, London W12 7RJ (☎ 0181 743 8000)

WITHERIDGE, Rev John Stephen; s of Francis Edward Witheridge (d 1988), and Joan Elizabeth, *née* Exell; *b* 14 Nov 1953; *Educ* St Albans Sch, Univ of Kent at Canterbury (BA), Christ's Coll Cambridge (MA); *m* 1975, Sarah Caroline, da of The Rev Peter Phillips; 2 s (George b 1983, Henry b 1986), 2 da (Charlotte b 1978, Harriet b 1981); *Career* curate Luton Parish Church 1979–82, head of religious studies and asst chaplain Marlborough Coll 1982–84, chaplain to the Archbishop of Canterbury 1984–87, conduct (sr chaplain) Eton Coll 1987–96, headmaster Charterhouse 1996–; author various articles and reviews; *Recreations* family, theatre, travel, history, gardening, running; *Clubs* East India; *Style*— The Rev John Witheridge; ✉ Charterhouse, Godalming, Surrey GU7 2DJ (☎ 01483 291600, fax 01483 291647)

WITHEROW, John Moore; s of Cecil John Rhodes Witherow, of Menton, France, and Millicent Frances, *née* Wilson; *b* 20 Jan 1952; *Educ* Bedford Sch, Univ of York (BA), Univ of Cardiff (Dip in Journalism); *m* 1985, Sarah Jane Linton; 2 s (Sam b 1985, Roly b 1988), 1 da (Anna b 1996); *Career* trainee Reuters London and Madrid 1977–80, home and foreign corr The Times 1980–83; The Sunday Times: defence corr 1984–85, diplomatic corr 1985–87, focus ed 1987–89, foreign ed 1989–92, managing ed (news) 1992–94, acting ed 1994, ed 1995–; memb PCC; *Books* The Winter War: The Falklands (with Patrick Bishop, 1982), The Gulf War (1993); *Recreations* skiing, sailing; *Clubs* RAC; *Style*— John Witherow, Esq; ✉ The Sunday Times, 1 Pennington Street, London E1 9XW (☎ 0171 782 5640, fax 0171 782 5420)

WITHEROW, Air Cdre Marcus Spence; s of Lt-Col T M Witherow (d 1970), of Dumfries, and Florence Eileen, *née* Spence (d 1971); *b* 17 Aug 1936; *Educ* Holt Sch Dumfriesshire; *m* 15 March 1969, Mary Craigie, da of George Henry Paulin, ARSA (d 1962), of Glasgow and Hampstead; 2 s (Rupert b 1971, Dominic b 1973); *Career* RAF 1955–90; cmmnd RAF Regt 1956 (served Aden, Bahrain, Trucial Oman, Libya and Germany), ADC to C-in-C RAF Tport/Air Support Cmd 1966–68, Sqdn Ldr 1968, cmd 26 Sqdn RAF Regt 1968–70, graduated RAF Staff Coll 1971, Wing Cdr 1974, HQ AAFCE 1974–76, graduated Air Warfare Course 1976, cmd 3 Wing RAF Regt 1976–78, Gp Capt 1978, ADC to HM The Queen 1980–82, cmd RAF Regt Depot Catterick 1980–82, graduated Royal Coll of Def Studies 1983, HQ RAF Germany 1984–85, Air Cdre 1985, Dir of Ground Personnel RAF 1985–87, Dir RAF Regt 1987–90, ret as Air Cdre 1990; business admin 1991–95, head of indust and public sector rels Coutts Consulting Group plc 1996–; memb Cncl Offrs' Pensions Soc 1996–; Freeman City of London 1992; FIMgt 1981; *Recreations* shooting, fishing, photography, natural history, gardening, conservation of nature, reading, current affairs; *Clubs* RAF; *Style*— Air Cdre Marcus Witherow; ✉ c/o Drummonds, The Royal Bank of Scotland, Admiralty Arch, 49 Charing Cross, London SW1A 2DX

WITHEROW, Ross O'Neill; s of Cecil John Witherow, of Monte Carlo, and Millicent Frances, *née* Wilson; *b* 2 Jan 1945; *Educ* Bedford Sch, UCH Med Sch London (Grenfell student scholar, MB BS, MS, Eschmann prize); *m* 1, 1977 (m dis 1982), Michelle, *née* Heimsoth; 1 s (Alexander Guy O'Neill b 2 March 1981); m 2, 14 Sept 1990, Bridget Margaret Rossiter, da of Michael Christopher Alfred Codrington; 1 s (Thomas Edward b 12 Oct 1991), 1 step s (Peter Goodman Rossiter b 27 Aug 1983); *Career* house offr: UCH London 1968, Addenbrooke's Hosp Cambridge 1968–69; ship's surgn Union Castle Line 1969–70, SHO UCH 1971, registrar in surgery Edgware Gen Hosp 1972, sr registrar in gen surgery UCH 1974–75 (registrar 1973), postgrad res fell in urology Univ of Calif San Francisco 1976–77 (lectr 1978), lectr and hon sr registrar in urology London Hosp 1978–79, resident asst surgn St Paul's Hosp 1979–80, conslt urologist St Mary's Hosp London and clinical sr lectr (recognised teacher) Univ of London 1981–; memb: Br Assoc of Urological Surgns 1981, Société Internationale d'Urologie 1982; FRCS 1973, FRSM 1979, FEBU 1992; *Books* Surgical Infection (1977), Genito-Urinary Surgery (contrib, 1985), Radiounclide Evaluation of the Impotent Male in the Diagnosis and Management of Male Erectile Dysfunction (1992); *Recreations* skiing, golf, opera, cooking; *Clubs* Carlton, RAC, Bowood Golf and Country; *Style*— Ross Witherow, Esq; ✉ 26 Harmont House, 20 Harley Street, London W1N 1AN (☎ 0171 935 1252, fax 0171 637 5373)

WITHERS, Georgette Lizette (Googie); AO (1980); da of Capt Edgar Clements Withers, CIE, CBE, RN (d 1951), and Lizette Catharina Wilhelmina, *née* Van Wageningen (d 1976); *b* 12 March 1917; *Educ* Fredville Park Nonnington Kent, Sch of the Holy Family London; *m* 1948, John Neil McCallum, AO, CBE (chm & chief exec Fauna Films, Australia, also actor & prodr, as well as sometime pres Australian Film Cncl and theatre manager), s of John Neil McCallum (d 1957), of Brisbane; 1 s (Nicholas), 2 da (Joanna, Amanda); *Career* actress (as Googie Withers) 1933–; over 50 films incl: One of Our Aircraft is Missing, On Approval, It Always Rains on Sunday; plays incl: Deep Blue Sea, Winter Journey, Hamlet, Much Ado About Nothing, The Cherry Orchard, The Skin Game, Private Lives, The Kingfisher, The Circle, The Importance of Being Earnest, School for Scandal, Time and the Conways, The Chalk Garden, An Ideal Husband (Old Vic); numerous TV plays incl: Within These Walls, Time After Time (Best Actress award), Hotel du Lac, Northanger Abbey; Chichester Festival Theatre: Hay Fever, Ring Round The Moon; The Cocktail Hour (UK and Aust tour), High Spirits (Aust tour), On Golden Pond (UK tour); USA Ace award Best Actress, BAFTA Best Actress award 1954, Sun Best Actress award 1974; *Recreations* travelling, reading, interior decorating; *Clubs* Queen's (Sydney); *Style*— Miss Googie Withers, AO; ✉ 1740 Pittwater Rd, Bayview, NSW 2104, Australia

WITHERS, Michael John; s of Harold Leslie Withers (d 1985), of Dawlish, Devon, and Kathleen Veronica, *née* Chudleigh (d 1988); *b* 15 Jan 1938; *Educ* South West Essex Tech Sch, City Univ (dip in tech engrg, BSc), Univ of Birmingham (MSc); *m* 1962, Marguerite, *née* Beckett; 1 s (Richard John b 1965), 1 da (Justine Marguerite b 1966); *Career* Radio Indust Cncl apprenticeship Cossor Ltd 1955–60, radar engr Cossor Radar 1960–63, lectr Dept of Electronic and Electrical Engrg Univ of Birmingham 1963–72, visiting prof of telecommunications Tech Inst of Aeronautics Sao Jose dos Campos Brazil 1969–70, hon princ sci offr Royal Signals and Radar Establishment Malvern 1970–72, sr systems engr Br Aerospace Stevenage 1972–77, engrg mangr Andrew Corporation Inc Fife 1977–83, mangr RF Technology Division 1983–87, md and chief exec ERA Technology Ltd 1987–, Fellowship of Engrg visiting prof in principles of design Loughborough Univ 1991–; published over 50 tech papers and patents; FIEE 1983 (MIEE 1966), FEng 1990; *Recreations* photography, video and film production, cabinet-making, gardening; *Style*— Michael Withers, Esq, FEng; ✉ The Hollies, Arford Rd, Headley, Bordon, Hants GU35 8LJ (☎ 01428 712175); ERA Technology Ltd, Cleeve Rd, Leatherhead, Surrey KT22 7SA (☎ 01372 367000)

WITHERS, Roy Joseph; CBE (1983); s of Joseph Withers (d 1973), and Irene Ada, *née* Jones; *b* 18 June 1924; *Educ* Tiffin Sch Kingston-upon-Thames, Trinity Coll Cambridge; *m* 20 Dec 1947, Pauline Mary Gillian, *née* Johnston; 4 s (Christopher, Stephen, Paul, Robert); *Career* sr engr ICI 1948–55, tech dir Humphreys & Glasgow 1955–63, engrg dir Davy Power Gas Corporation 1963–70 (md 1970–71), chm exec Davy Powergas 1972–73; Davy Corporation: md 1973–83, dep chm 1983–86, vice chm 1986–91; non-exec dir Vosper Thornycroft (UK) Ltd 1990– (chm 1985–90), chm Transmark Worldwide 1987–93 (dep chm 1985–87); memb BOTB 1983–86, chm Overseas Projects Bd 1983–86; FEng 1983, FIMechE, FIChemE; *Recreations* golf, painting; *Clubs* Carlton, Hampstead Golf, Bramshaw Golf; *Style*— Roy Withers, Esq, CBE, FEng; ✉ Wheelwrights Cottage, Bramshaw, Lyndhurst, Hants SO43 7JB

WITHERSPOON, Dr (Edward) William; s of Edward William Witherspoon (d 1982), of Liverpool, and Maude Miranda, *née* Goff (d 1987); *b* 19 Dec 1925; *Educ* King Edward's Sch Birmingham, Univ of Birmingham (MB ChB), Univ of London DTM & H, RCP (Lond), RCS (Eng); *m* 10 June 1954, Jean (d 1988), da of John McKellar (d 1956); *Career* Maj RAMC 2 i/c 3 Field Ambulance, 4 RTR Suez Canal Zone and Cyprus 1951–53; physician (tropical diseases and clinical pharmacology); asst govt med offr Medico-Legal Dept Sydney 1958–60; med dir: Burroughs Wellcome 1960–71, ABPI Trade Mission Japan 1968, Abbott Labs 1971–77, Warner Lambert/Parke Davis 1977–82; Roussel Labs 1983–91, conslt Regulatory Agencies 1992–, chm Pharmaceutical Physicians Gp Ctee BMA 1986–92; Freeman City of London 1993, Yeoman Worshipful Soc of Apothecaries;

FRSH 1971, FFPM 1990; *Publications* The Hunter Years 1728–93 (annals RACS, 1994), The Pharmaceutical Physician (BMA monograph 1989), Thalidomide - The Aftermath (Pharmaceutical Med 1988); *Recreations* travel, National Trust for Scotland; *Clubs* City Livery, Royal Soc of Medicine; *Style*— Dr William Witherspoon; ✉ Brook Cottage, 4 Manor Rd, Oakley, nr Aylesbury, Bucks HP18 9QD (☎ 01844 237722)

WITT, Margaret June; da of Henry Witt (d 1976), of 2 Clarendon Rd, Walthamstow, London; *b* 14 June 1930; *Educ* Walthamstow Co HS for Girls, Bart's Med Coll (BSc, MB BS, Treasurer's Prize in Anatomy, Harvey Prize in Physiology, Matthew Duncan Prize and Gold Medal), FRCS 1961, FRCOG 1979; *Career* successively: house surgn Gynaecology and Obstetrics Unit then house surgn Gen Surgery and Medicine Unit Bart's, sr house offr Casualty Dept Mayday Hosp, registrar then sr registrar in obstetrics and gynaecology Bart's, lectr in anatomy Anatomy Dept Bart's Med Coll, surgical registrar Elizabeth Garrett Anderson Hosp and Peace Meml Hosp, sr house offr Queen Charlotte's Hosp, two locum appts St Stephen's Hosp Watford, sr house offr Hosp for Women Soho Square, registrar Dulwich Hosp (branch of King's Coll Hosp), conslt obstetrician and gynaecologist N Middx Hosp; hon lectr in obstetrics and gynaecology Bart's and Royal Free Hosp Med Sch, hon conslt St Luke's Hosp for the Clergy, hon conslt in gynaecological endocrinology Bart's; Freeman City of London 1990; memb: Farringdon Ward Club, Royal Soc of St George (Parent Body and City Branch), Hunterian Soc 1972, Med Soc of London 1973; *Recreations* photography, travel; *Style*— Miss Margaret Witt; ✉ 95 Harley St, London W1 (☎ 0171 935 0588)

WITTICH, John Charles Bird; s of Charles Cyril Wittich (d 1976), and Minnie Amelia Victoria, *née* Daborn (d 1991); *b* 18 Feb 1929; *Educ* privately (BA); *m* 10 July 1954, June Rose, da of Thomas Frederick Taylor (d 1972); 1 s (Andrew Paul b 1961), 1 da (Margaret Judith b 1957); *Career* professional librarian 1946–86; freelance writer and lectr 1986–, lectr in adult educn circles, memb Minor Order of Readers of the C of E 1980–; Freeman City of London 1971, Master Parish Clerks Co 1995–96, Liveryman Worshipful Co of Woolmen 1977; FRSA 1980; *Books* Off-Beat Walks in London (1969, new edn 1995), London Curiosities (1973, new edn 1996), London Villages (1976, revised 1992), London Street Names (1977, new edn 1995), London's Inns & Taverns (1978, new edn 1996), London's Parks & Squares (1981, new edn 1997), Catholic London (1988), Churches, Cathedrals & Chapels (1988), Guide to Bayswater (1989), Exploring Cathedrals (1992, new edn 1996), Regent's Park (1992), Curiosities of Surrey (1994), History and Guide Church of St Magnus the Martyr (1994), Explorers' London (1995), Spot it London (1995), Walks Around Haunted London (1996), London Bus Top Tourist (1997); *Clubs* City Livery; *Style*— John Wittich, Esq; ✉ 88 Woodlawn Street, Whistable, Kent (☎ 01227 772619)

WITTS, Diana Katharine; da of Maj Gen Frederick Vavasour Broome Witts (d 1969), and Alice Mary, *née* Wrigley (d 1990); *b* 14 May 1936; *Educ* Brondesbury-at-Stocks, Univ of Bristol (BSc Physics); *Career* hosp physicist Charing Cross Hosp 1958–59, research asst Royal Victoria Hosp Montreal 1959–61; maths and physics teacher: Parliament Hill Sch London 1961–63, Highlands Sch Eldoret (Kenya) 1963–65; community memb Lee Abbey Lynton Devon 1966, maths and physics teacher and running a house Alliance Girls HS Kikuyu (Kenya) 1966–70, maths and physics teacher Headington Sch Oxford 1971, sr mistress Gordonstoun Sch 1971–75; with Church Mission Society 1975–: vocational trg for Maasai girls in Kenya 1976–79, tutor Crowther Hall 1979, viability study for rural devpt in Anglican Church of Zaire 1980, actg asst regnl sec Kenya, Uganda and Zaire (based Nairobi) 1981–83, estab basic level course on Theological Educn by Extension (in Swahili) NE Zaire 1983–85, regnl sec W Africa, Sudan and Zaire 1985–95, gen sec Church Mission Soc 1995–; tstee Africa Educnl Tst, reader C of E 1991– (memb Bd of Mission); awarded Cross of St Augustine (by Archbishop of Canterbury) 1994; *Recreations* climbing, sailing, swimming; *Style*— Diana K Witts; ✉ General Secretary, Church Mission Society, Partnership House, 157 Waterloo Road, London SE1 8UU (☎ 0171 928 8681, fax 0171 401 3215)

WITTY, (John) David; CBE (1985); s of Harold Witty (d 1948), of Molescroft, E Yorks, and Olive, *née* Scaife (d 1977); *b* 1 Oct 1924; *Educ* Beverley GS, Balliol Coll Oxford (MA); *m* 1955, Doreen, da of John William Hanlan (d 1952), of Hull; 1 s (Simon); *Career* served RN 1943–46; slr; chief exec Westminster City Cncl 1977–84; hon sec London Boroughs Assoc 1978–84; chm London Enterprise Property Co 1984–85; lawyer memb London Rent Assessment Panel 1984–92; dir Great Portland Estates plc 1987–; Order of Infante D Henrique (Portugal) 1978, Order of Right Hand (Nepal) 1980, Order of King Abdul Aziz (Saudi Arabia) 1981, Order of Oman 1982, Order of Orange Nassau 1982; *Recreations* golf, motoring; *Clubs* Royal Mid Surrey Golf; *Style*— David Witty, Esq, CBE; ✉ 14 River House, 23/24 The Terrace, Barnes, London SW13 0NR (☎ 0181 876 0038)

WIX, Jonathan; s of Harold Wix, of London, and Bernice Beare, of Durban, S Africa; *b* 3 Nov 1951; *Educ* Carmel Coll Wallingford Berks; *m* 1977, Carolyn; 1 s (James b 1983), 1 da (Amelia b 1986); *Career* wine rep Grierson Blumenthal 1976–77, Vanston Estates 1978–79, owner Inebriated Newt Clapham 1979–85, set up restaurants in Wimbledon (sold 1983), Fulham 1982, Shepherds Bush 1985 (both sold to Kennedy Brookes 1985); md Br and Foreign Tobacco Co 1984–85; bought and developed: Stamford Brook Power Station 1984, Wood Hall 1986 (hotel opened 1988), Nidd Hall Knaresborough 1988, 42 The Calls Leeds 1989 (hotel opened 1991), Victoria Hotel Bradford 1995; *Awards* for 42 The Calls: Co Hotel of the Year 1992, Leeds Award for architecture 1992, Intercity Hotel of the Year 1994, Caterer and Hotelkeeper Hotel of the Year 1995, Good Hotel Guide César Award, Johansens City Hotel of the Year 1996; *Recreations* skiing, shooting, building hotels; *Style*— Jonathan Wix, Esq; ✉ 42 The Calls, Leeds LS2 7EW (☎ 0113 244 0099, fax 0113 234 4100)

WIXLEY, Gordon Robert Alexander; CBE (1979, OBE Mil 1955), TD (1959), DL (1976); s of Walter Henry James (d 1959), and Maud Mary, *née* Neave (d 1971); *b* 22 Nov 1914; *Educ* Lindisfarne Coll; *Career* HAC 1939, RA 1939–46; 290 Field Regt RA (City of London) TA 1947–54, CO 1951–54; Col TA 1955–58; CA; memb Ct of Common Cncl (City of London) 1964– (chief commoner 1985), vice chm Greater London TAVRA 1967–73; chm bd of govrs: Bethlem Royal and Maudsley Hosp 1980–82, City of London Freemen's Sch 1977–78; chm ctee of mgmnt Inst of Psychiatry 1984–87; vice chm Nat Biological Standards Bd 1976–89; ADC (TA) to HM The Queen 1967–73; Liveryman: Worshipful Co of Fletchers, Worshipful Co of Chartered Accountants; *Recreations* travel, walking, reading; *Clubs* Bucks, Athenaeum, Army and Navy, City Livery; *Style*— Gordon Wixley, Esq, CBE, TD, DL; ✉ 947 Chelsea Cloisters, Sloane Ave London SW3 3EU (☎ 0171 589 3109)

WIXON, Capt David George; s of John Charles Wixon (d 1957), and Eneta Mary Saunders, *née* Watts (now Mrs Rushmer); *b* 16 May 1937; *Educ* Aylesbury GS, Britannia RNC, RNEC Manadon Devon (BScEng), RNC Greenwich (AME(N)); *m* 3 April 1961, Rosamond Mary, da of Geoffrey Howard Stevens (d 1991); 1 s (Rufus b 1965), 2 da (Miranda b 1962, Theresa b 1963); *Career* RN served aboard: HMS Newcastle 1957–58, HMS Aurochs 1963–64, HMS Valiant 1966–69, HMS Courageous 1968–72; sr lectr Dept Nuclear Sci and Technol RNC Greenwich 1972–75 (promoted Cdr 1974), CSST (sub sea trg) 1975–77, Cdr RNEC 1980–83 (promoted Capt 1983), CSSE (Strategic Systems Exec MOD) 1983–86, Job Evaluation judge RN 1987–90, CO HMS Drake 1990–92; mangr White Ensign Assoc 1992–; Liveryman Worshipful Co of Blacksmiths 1992; MIMechE 1974; *Recreations* rugby football, classic cars, collecting hollow stemmed wine glasses; *Clubs* Allard Owners, Devonport Servs RFU; *Style*— Capt David Wixon, RN; ✉ Stroll, Yelverton, Devon PL20 6BX

WNEK, Marek Stanislaw; s of Andrew Wnek (d 1989), and Andrée Gabrielle, *née* Zaliwska; *b* 19 Feb 1958; *Educ* Dulwich, Gonville and Caius Coll Cambridge (MA); *m* 1, 1985 (m dis 1988), Clare Ann Birch; m 2, 14 Sept 1991, Samantha Mary Constance, da of Martin Donovan Boyce, of Beaulieu, Hants; *Career* freelance journalist/English teacher Spain 1980–82; sr writer/bd dir: Ogilvy & Mather advtg 1985–90 (copywriter 1982–85), Lowe Howard-Spink advtg 1990–94; exec creative dir and managing ptnr Euro RSCG Wnek Gosper advtg 1994–, memb Bd Euro RSCG Worldwide 1996–; creator of Guinness - Pure Genius campaign; winner various awards and commendations from D&AD, British TV Advtg, Cannes, Campaign Press, Eurobest, Epica, Creative Circle and Clio Awards; memb: D&AD, Creative Circle; *Recreations* running, tennis, shooting; *Clubs* The Union; *Style*— Marek Wnek, Esq; ✉ Euro RSCG Wnek Gosper, 10 Great Newport Street, London WC2H 7JA (☎ 0171 240 4111, fax 0171 465 0552)

WODEHOUSE, Lord; John Armine Wodehouse; s and h of 4 Earl of Kimberley, *qv*; *b* 15 Jan 1951; *Educ* Eton, Univ of E Anglia (BSc, MSc); *m* 1973, Hon Carol Lylie, 2 da of 3 Baron Palmer (d 1990); 1 s, 1 da (Hon Katherine b 1976); *Heir* s, Hon David Simon John Wodehouse b 10 Oct 1978; *Career* systems programmer with Glaxo 1979–96 (joined as res chemist 1974), advanced technol and informatics specialist Glaxo Wellcome 1996–; chm: UK Info Users Gp 1981–83, UIS Users Gp 1991–93; fell Br Interplanetary Soc 1984– (assoc fell 1981–83); FRSA, MBCS 1988, CEng 1993; *Recreations* photography, computing, running; *Style*— Lord Wodehouse; ✉ Kingswood, Henley Road, Medmenham, Marlow, Bucks SL7 2EU; Advanced Technology & Informatics, Glaxo Wellcome Research & Development, Medicines Research Centre, Gunnels Wood Road, Stevenage, Herts SG1 2NY (☎ 01438 745745)

WOFFENDEN, Kenneth John; s of James Harold Woffenden (d 1991), of Wilmslow, Cheshire, and Agnes, *née* Grisenthwaite (d 1976); *b* 22 Oct 1954; *Educ* Manchester GS, Pembroke Coll Cambridge (Fndn scholar, MA, Ziegler Law Prize), Coll of Law Guildford; *m* 2 July 1982, Glesni Myfanwy, da of Gwynfor Thomas Davies; 2 da (Catherine b 28 Oct 1987, Emily b 18 Oct 1989), 1 s (Thomas b 8 April 1993); *Career* Simmons & Simmons: articled clerk 1977–79, admitted slr 1979, asst slr Corp Dept 1979–84, ptnr Corp Dept 1984–, admitted slr Hong Kong 1986, head Corp and Banking Gp Hong Kong 1987–90, ptnr Corp Dept 1990–95 (head of Gp 1994–95), managing ptnr Hong Kong office 1995–; memb: Law Soc of England and Wales, Law Soc of Hong Kong, Int Bar Assoc, Inter-Pacific Bar Assoc; *Recreations* music, cricket, family life; *Clubs* Carlton, Hong Kong, Hong Kong Country; *Style*— Kenneth Woffenden, Esq; ✉ Simmons & Simmons, 24th Floor, Jardine House, One Connaught Place, Central Hong Kong (☎ 00 852 2868 1131, fax 00 852 2810 5040)

WOGAN, Michael Terence (Terry); s of late Michael Thomas Wogan, and Rose Wogan; *b* 3 Aug 1938; *Educ* Crescent Coll Limerick, Belvedere Coll Dublin; *m* 24 April 1965, Helen, da of Timothy J Joyce; 2 s (Alan Terence b 1 Oct 1967, Mark Paul b 13 April 1970), 1 da (Katherine Helen b 31 Sept 1972); *Career* with Royal Bank of Ireland 1956–60, announcer/newsreader Radio Telefis Eireann 1961–66, presenter various TV and radio progs 1966–69; BBC: own show Radio 1 1969–72, morning show Radio 2 1972–84 and 1993–, presenter numerous BBC TV progs incl Blankety Blank, Wogan, Do The Right Thing, Auntie's Sporting Bloomers, Children in Need Appeal, BAFTA and Variety Club Awards Ceremonies, Come Dancing, A Song for Europe and the Eurovision Song Contest, Miss World, Wogan's Island, various documentaries; *Awards* numerous from: Variety Club of GB, Radio Industries Club, Sony Radio Awards, Pye Radio Awards, TV Times, Daily Mail, Sunday Express, Carl-Alan Awards; *Books* Banjaxed (1979), The Day Job (1981), To Horse To Horse (1982), Wogan on Wogan (1987), Wogan's Ireland (1988), Terry Wogan's Bumper Book of Togs (1995); *Recreations* tennis, golf, reading; *Clubs* Garrick, Stephens Green (Dublin), Temple Golf, Stoke Poges Golf, Lahinch Golf, London Irish RFC; *Style*— Terry Wogan, Esq; ✉ c/o Jo Gurnett Personal Management, 2 New Kings Road, London SW6 4SA

WOLF, Martin Harry; s of Edmund Wolf, of London, and Rebecca, *née* Wijnschenk (d 1993); *b* 16 Aug 1946; *Educ* Univ Coll Sch, Corpus Christi Coll Oxford (open scholar, MA), Nuffield Coll Oxford (MPhil); *m* Aug 1970, Alison Margaret, da of late Herbert Kingsley Potter, of Newbury, Berks; 2 s (Jonathan Thomas b 24 Jan 1975, Benjamin Jacob b 11 Jan 1977), 1 da (Rachel Janet b 11 June 1985); *Career* World Bank: joined Young Professional programme 1971, Office of Vice Pres for East Africa 1972–74, sr economist India Div 1974–77, involved with World Devpt Report 1977–78, sr economist Int Trade and Capital Flows Div 1979–81; dir of studies Trade Policy Res Centre 1981–87; Financial Times: joined 1987, chief economics leader writer and assoc ed 1990–96, economics commentator and assoc ed 1996–; conslt to various orgns, advsr and rapporteur to Eminent Persons Gp on World Trade 1990 (winner New Zealand 1990 Commemoration Medal), jt winner Wincott Fndn Sr Prize for excellence in financial journalism 1990, winner RTZ David Watt Memorial Prize 1995; visiting fell: UCL 1978, Nuffield Coll Oxford 1978–79; memb: Nat Consumer Cncl 1987–93, Awards Ctee American Express Bank Review Essay Competition 1994, cncl Royal Economic Soc 1991–96; special prof Univ of Nottingham 1993–; *Publications* incl: Textile Quotas against Developing Countries (with Donald B Keesing, 1980), India's Exports (1982), Costs of Protecting Jobs in Textiles and Clothing (1984), Global Implications of the European Community's Programme for Completing the Internal Market (1989), Meeting the World Trade Deadline: Path to a Successful Uruguay Round (1990), The Resistible Appeal of Fortress Europe (1994); *Recreations* theatre, reading, skiing; *Clubs* Reform; *Style*— Martin Wolf, Esq; ✉ Financial Times, 1 Southwark Bridge, London SE1 9HL (☎ 0171 873 3673/3421)

WOLF, (Colin) Piers; s of Peter Wolf, of Claverdon, nr Stratford upon Avon, and Gladys Mary, *née* Williams; *b* 26 Jan 1943; *Educ* Bedford Sch; *m* 8 April 1972, Jennifer Elisabeth, da of Kingsley Richard Fox, of Surbiton, Surrey; 1 s (Guy Daniel b 1976), 1 da (Jocelyn Ruth b 1975); *Career* admitted slr 1966; ptnr Evershed & Tomkinson 1973– (now Eversheds); memb Law Soc 1972 (memb Standing Ctee on Co Law 1989); *Recreations* music, reading, walking, cycling; *Style*— Piers Wolf, Esq; ✉ Eversheds, Churchgates House, Cutler Street, Ipswich IP1 1UR (☎ 01473 284428, fax 01473 233666)

WOLFE, Anthony James Garnham; s of Herbert Robert Inglewood Wolfe, VRD (d 1970), and Lesley Winifred, *née* Fox; *b* 30 Aug 1952; *Educ* Haileybury ISC, Univ of Bristol (BSc); *m* 4 Sept 1982, Ommar Aung, da of Lionel Aung Kwa Takwali (d 1956); *Career* chartered accountant; London and Hong Kong Offices Peat Marwick Mitchell 1974–81, GT Mgmnt London and Hong Kong Offices 1981–91, Signature Financial Group 1992–94, Henderson Administration Group PLC 1994–; FCA; *Recreations* rugger, golf, travel, canoeing, walking; *Clubs* Royal Wimbledon Golf, Royal Canoe; *Style*— Anthony Wolfe, Esq; ✉ c/o Henderson Administration Group PLC, 3 Finsbury Avenue, London, EC2M 2PA

WOLFE, John Henry Nicholas; s of Herbert Robert Inglewood Wolfe (1970), and Lesley Winifred, *née* Fox; *b* 4 June 1947; *Educ* Eastbourne Coll, St Thomas's Hosp Univ of London (MB BS, MS); *m* 1, 23 June 1973 (m dis 1990), Jennifer, da of Geoffrey Sutcliffe; 3 s (Robert, Owen, Matthew), 2 da (Tara, Roshean); m 2, 1 Oct 1994, Dorothy Carey; *Career* res fell Harvard Med Sch Brigham Hosp 1981–82, sr registrar St Thomas's Hosp 1982–84, Hunterian prof RCS 1983; conslt surgn: St Mary's Hosp Med Sch 1984, Royal Postgrad Med Sch Hammersmith Hosp, Edward VII Hosp for Offrs; memb: Surgical Res Soc, Assoc of Surgns (memb Speciality Bd), Cncl Vascular Soc of GB and I, Euro

Soc of Vascular Surgery (chm Vascular Advsy Ctee), Int Soc of Cardiovascular Surgery; FRCS; memb Editorial Bd Euro Jl of Vascular Surgery; *Books* Vascular Surgery (ed 1985, 1989), ABC of Vascular Diseases (1992); *Recreations* sailing, cooking for children, walking; *Clubs* RSM; *Style*— John Wolfe, Esq; ✉ 66 Harley St, London W1N 1AE (☎ 0171 580 5030, fax 0171 631 5341)

WOLFE, Richard John Russell; s of late Maj John Claude Frank Wolfe, of Surrey, and Betty Doris, *née* Hopwood; *b* 15 July 1947; *Educ* Ackworth Sch Ackworth Yorks; *m* 1, 28 Nov 1970 (m dis 1977), Lorraine Louise Hart; 1 da (Pandora b 12 July 1976); m 2, 23 July 1994, Irene Mehmet; *Career* mgmnt trainee NM Rothschild and Son Ltd 1964–68, investmt dealer British and Continental Bank 1968–72, fund mangr Hill Samuel and Co Ltd 1972–75, corporate fin offr NM Rothschild and Sons Ltd 1976–80, first vice pres and head of real estate fin UK Security Pacific Nat Bank 1980–90, md and head of Euro real estate Bankers Trust Co 1990–92, fin conslt 1992–; tstee: Inlight Tst, Truemark Tst 1994–; AIB 1978; *Books* Real Estate Finance (contrib 1988); *Recreations* choir singing, swimming, training, study of ancient civilisations; *Style*— Richard Wolfe, Esq; ✉ 52 Claylands Road, London SW8 1NZ; 45–47 Queen Victoria Street, London EC4N 4SA

WOLFE MURRAY, James Archibald; s of Lt-Col Malcolm Victor Alexander Wolfe Murray, DL (d 1985; ggs of James Murray, who as a Lord of Session took the title Lord Cringletie; he was gggs of Alexander Murray, 2 Bt, of Blackbarony), and his 1 w, Lady Grizel Mary Boyle (d 1942), eldest da of 8 Earl of Glasgow; *b* 25 April 1936; *Educ* Eton, Worcester Coll Oxford; *m* 1, 8 June 1963 (m dis 1976), Hon (Lady until 1963 and again from 1995) Diana Lucy Douglas-Home, da of Baron Home of the Hirsel, KT (14 Earl of Home until 1963); 1 s (Rory James b 1965), 2 da (Fiona Grizel (Mrs Andrew Shufflebotham) b 1964, Clare Elizabeth (Mrs John Flett) b 1969); m 2, 17 July 1978, Amanda Felicity, da of Anthony Frank Street (d 1974); 1 s (Andrew Alexander b 1978); *Career* 2 Lt Black Watch 1954–56; export dir James Buchanan & Co 1969–75; vice chm and md: Macdonald Greenlees Ltd 1975–82, John Haig & Co 1982–87; md White Horse Distillers 1987–95, strategic affairs dir United Distillers 1994–95 (regnl dir 1988–94), ret; *Recreations* golf, fishing, shooting, cricket; *Clubs* White's, Royal St George's Golf, MCC, Hon Co Edinburgh Golfers; *Style*— James Wolfe Murray, Esq; ✉ Chesterhall, Eildon, Melrose TD6 9HE (☎ 01835 823064)

WOLFENDALE, Prof Sir Arnold Whittaker; kt (1995); s of Arnold Wolfendale (d 1963), and Doris, *née* Hoyle (d 1983); *b* 25 June 1927; *Educ* Stretford GS, Univ of Manchester (BSc, PhD, DSc); *m* 1952, Audrey, da of Arnold Darby (d 1968); 2 s (twins, Colin and David); *Career* prof of physics Univ of Durham 1965–92, SIO, RTSO, RSA Civil Defence 1958–81, chm N Region Manpower Service Cmmn's Job Creation Programme 1975–78; pres: Royal Astronomical Soc 1981–83, Antiquarian Horological Soc 1993–; chm: Cosmic Ray Cmmn of IUPAP 1982–84, Astronomy & Planetary Science Bd SERC 1988–94 (memb SERC 1988–94); pres Durham Univ Soc of Fells 1988–94; Astronomer Royal 1991–95; Freeman Worshipful Co of Clockmakers 1991, Hon Freeman Worshipful Co of Scientific Instrument Makers 1993; Hon DSc: Potchefstroom, Lodz, Central Lancs, Teeside, Newcastle upon Tyne, Open Univ and Lancaster; awarded Univ of Turku medal 1987, Observatory medal Armagh 1992, Marian Smoluchowski medal Poland 1992; foreign fell: Nat Acad of Sciences of India 1990, Indian Nat Sci Acad 1991, Tata Inst of Fund Research Bombay; foreign assoc Royal Soc of S Africa; FRS, FInstP (pres 1994–96), FRAS; *Recreations* gardening, travel; *Style*— Prof Sir Arnold Wolfendale, FRS; ✉ Ansford, Potters Bank, Durham DH1 3RR

WOLFF, Prof Heinz Siegfried; s of Oswald Wolff (d 1968), of W Germany, and Margot, *née* Saalfeld; *b* 29 April 1928; *Educ* City of Oxford Sch, UCL (BSc); *m* 21 March 1953, Joan Eleanor Mary, da of Charles Heddon Stephenson, MBE (d 1968); 2 s (Anthony b 1956, Laurence b 1961); *Career* head Div of Biomedical Engrg Nat Inst for Med Res 1962–70 (joined 1954), head Div of Bioengineering Clinical Res Centre 1970–83, dir Brunel Inst for Bioengineering Brunel Univ 1983–95 (emeritus prof 1995–); chm: Life Sci Working Gp ESA 1976–82, Microgravity Advsy Ctee ESA 1982–91, Microgravity Panel Br Nat Space Centre 1986–87; vice pres REMAP 1995–; presenter TV series incl: BBC TV Young Scientist of the Year 1968–81, Royal Inst Christmas Lectures 1975, The Great Egg Race 1978–86, Great Experiments which Changed the World 1985–86; Harding Award Action Research 1989, Edinburgh Medal for Servs to Science and Society 1992, Donald Julius Goen Prize IMechE 1994; Hon Doctorate: Open Univ 1993, De Montfort Univ 1995; fell UCL 1987; memb: Physiological Soc, Biological Engrg Soc, Ergonomics Res Soc; FIBiol, FIEE, FBES; *Books* Biological Engineering (1969); *Recreations* working, dignified practical joking; *Style*— Prof Heinz Wolff; ✉ Brunel Institute for Bioengineering, Brunel University, Uxbridge, Middlesex UB8 3PH (☎ 01895 271206, fax 01895 274608, telex 261173)

WOLFF, Michael Gordon; s of Sergei Mikhailovich Wolff (d 1979), of St Petersburg, and Mary, *née* Gordon; *b* 12 Nov 1933; *Educ* Greshams, Architectural Assoc Sch of Architecture; *m* 1, 14 Aug 1976 (m dis 1987), Susan, da of Brig Sydney Kent; 1 da (Rebecca Rose b 27 Oct 1981); m 2, July 1989, Martha Anne *née* Newhouse; *Career* fndr and creative dir Wolff Olins 1965–83, fndr and creative dir The Consortium 1983–87, worldwide creative dir Addison Design Consultants Ltd 1987–92; currently: gp design conslt W H Smith, non-exec dir Newell and Sorrell Ltd; pres D&AD Assoc 1971, pres CSD 1985–87; dir The Hunger Project (UK) 1978–83 (memb bd of tstees 1983–); FRSA, PPCSD; *Recreations* family life, seeing and walking; *Style*— Michael Wolff, Esq; ✉ c/o Newell and Sorrell, 7 Chalcot Road, London NW1 8LH (☎ 0171 722 1113)

WOLFFE, Andrew John Antony; s of Antony Curtis Wolffe, MBE, of Gatehouse-of-Fleet, and Alexandra Lorna, *née* Graham; *b* 6 July 1964; *Educ* Kirkcudbright Acad, Edinburgh Coll of Art (BA); *Career* graphic designer; creative dir Tayburn Design (joined 1986); projects incl: Grampian Holdings annual reports 1987, 1988 and 1989 (each won Stock Exchange Best Annual Report prizes), Scottish Enterprise corp identity 1990, Scottish Electricity Cos privatisation identity 1991, Balmoral International Hotels identity, Scottish & Newcastle Breweries plc annual report 1991, Bank of Scotland annual report 1992, 1993, 1994 and 1995, Royal Mail (Burns commemorative stamps 1995); tstee Edinburgh Photography Workshop Tst 1991–; MSTD; *Recreations* tennis, fly-fishing; *Clubs* Scottish Arts, Drummond Tennis; *Style*— Andrew Wolffe, Esq; ✉ Tayburn, 15 Kittle Yards, Causewayside, Edinburgh EH9 1PJ (☎ 0131 662 0662, fax 0131 662 0606)

WOLFSON, Sir Brian Gordon; s of Gabriel Wolfson (d 1950), of Liverpool, and Charlotte Eve, *née* Carr (d 1967); *b* 2 Aug 1935; *Educ* Liverpool Coll, Univ of Liverpool; *m* 10 March 1957, Helen, da of Lewis Grodner, of Liverpool; 1 s (David b 28 March 1964), 1 da (Gaye b 5 July 1961); *Career* gp jt md Granada Group 1967–70 (joined 1962); chm: Anglo Nordic Holdings 1976–87, Wembley Stadium Ltd 1986–95, Wembley plc 1988–95; dir: Fruit of the Loom Inc Chicago, Kepner-Tregoe Inc Princeton USA, Autotote Inc Delaware; chm: EDC Ctee on Leisure & Tourism 1986–92, Nat Training Task Force 1989–93, Nat Leadership Body for Investors in People UK 1993–; memb: Nat Economic Devpt Cncl 1989–92, Advsy Bd William H Wurster Centre for Int Mgmnt Studies Univ of Pennsylvania, Bd Joseph H Lauder Inst Univ of Pennsylvania; govr: Nat Inst of Economic & Social Res 1992–95, Ashridge Mgmnt Coll 1992– (chm MBA Prog); first non-North American pres Young Presidents' Orgn 1979–80; Hon DBA The Liverpool John Moores Univ (formerly Liverpool Poly) 1989; CIMgt (chm 1986–88, vice pres 1988–93, Verulam Gold Medal 1994), fell Br Inst of Engrs; *Recreations* archaeology, wildlife films; *Style*— Sir Brian Wolfson; ✉ 44 Welbeck Street, London W1M 7HF (☎ 0171 486 6216, fax 0171 496 6217)

WOLFSON, Baron (Life Peer UK 1985), of Marylebone in the City of Westminster; Sir Leonard Gordon Wolfson; 2, kt (1977), Bt (UK 1962), of St Marylebone, Co London; o s of Sir Isaac Wolfson, 1 Bt, FRS (d 1991), and Edith, *née* Specterman (d 1981); *b* 11 Nov 1927; *Educ* King's Sch Worcester; *m* 1, 1949 (m dis 1991), Ruth, da of Ernest A Sterling; 4 da (Hon Janet Frances b 1952, Hon Laura b 1954, Hon Deborah b 1959, Hon Elizabeth b 1966); m 2, 1 Sept 1991, Estelle, widow of Michael Jackson; *Career* chm Wolfson Fndn 1972– (fndr tstee 1955–); chm: Great Universal Stores plc 1981– (dir 1952, md 1962), Burberrys Ltd 1978–; hon fell: St Catherine's Coll Oxford, Wolfson Coll Cambridge, Wolfson Coll Oxford, Worcester Coll Oxford, UCL, LSHTM 1985, Queen Mary Coll 1985, Univ of Westminster 1991, Imperial Coll London 1991; tstee Imperial War Museum 1988, patron Royal Coll of Surgns 1976; Hon FRCP 1977, Hon FRCS 1988, Hon FBA 1986; Hon DCL: Oxon 1972, E Anglia 1986; Hon LLD: Strathclyde 1972, Dundee 1979, Cantab 1982, London 1982; Hon DSc: Hull 1977, Wales 1984; Hon DUniv Surrey 1990, Hon DM Birmingham 1992; Hon PhD: Tel Aviv 1971, Hebrew Univ 1978, Weitzmann Inst 1988; Hon DHL Bar Ilan Univ 1983; Winston Churchill Award British Technion Soc 1989; pres Jewish Welfare Bd 1972–82, tstee Imperial War Museum 1988–94; Liveryman Worshipful Co of Pattenmakers; *Style*— The Rt Hon the Lord Wolfson; ✉ 18–22 Haymarket Road, London SW1Y 4DQ

WOLFSON, (Geoffrey) Mark; MP (C) Sevenoaks (majority 19,154); s of Capt Vladimir Wolfson, RNVR (d 1954); *b* 7 April 1934; *Educ* Eton, Pembroke Coll Cambridge; *m* 1965, Edna Webb, *née* Hardman; 2 s; *Career* warden Brathay Hall Centre Cumbria 1962–66, head of youth servs Industl Soc 1966–70, dir and head of personnel Hambros Bank 1970–88; MP (C) Sevenoaks 1979–; PPS: to Min of State for NI 1983–84, to Min of State for Def Procurement 1984–85, to Min for the Armed Servs 1987–88; memb NI Select Ctee 1994–; *Style*— Mark Wolfson, Esq, MP; ✉ House of Commons, London SW1A 0AA

WOLFSON, Ruth, Baroness; Ruth; *née* Sterling; da of Ernest A Sterling (d 1986), of London, and Fay, *née* Ogus; *Educ* St Albans HS; *m* 14 Nov 1949 (m dis 1991), as his 1 w, Baron Wolfson (Life Peer), *qv*; 5 da (1 decd); *Career* tstee: Wolfson Fndn 1982–91, Wolfson Family Charitable Tst, Edith and Isaac Wolfson (Scotland) Tst; memb Prince of Wales' Ctee Queen's Silver Jubilee Appeal 1976; hon fell St Catherine's Coll Oxford 1988; *Recreations* gardening, photography; *Style*— Ruth, Lady Wolfson; ✉ 1 Mount Row, London W1Y 5DD

WOLFSON OF SUNNINGDALE, Baron (Life Peer UK 1991), of Trevose in the County of Cornwall; Sir David Wolfson; kt (1984); s of Charles and Hylda Wolfson; *b* 9 Nov 1935; *Educ* Clifton, Trinity Coll Cambridge (MA), Stanford Univ California (MBA); *m* 1, 1962 (m dis 1967), Patricia Elizabeth (now Baroness Rawlings, *qv*), da of Louis Rawlings; m 2, 1967, Susan E, da of Hugh Davis; 2 s (Hon Simon Adam b 1967, Hon Andrew Daniel b 1969), 1 da (Hon Deborah Sarah b 1973); *Career* Great Universal Stores 1960–78 and 1993– (dir 1973–78 and 1993–); sec to shadow cabinet 1978–79, chief of staff Political Office 10 Downing St 1979–85; chm: Alexon Group plc (formerly Steinberg Group plc) 1982–86, Next plc 1990–; non-exec dir: Stewart Wrightson Holdings plc 1985–87, Next 1989–; Hon Fell Hughes Hall Cambridge 1989, Hon FRCR 1978, Hon FRCOG 1989; *Recreations* golf, bridge; *Clubs* Portland, Sunningdale, Woburn Golf; *Style*— The Rt Hon Lord Wolfson of Sunningdale; ✉ c/o House of Lords, London SW1A 0PW

WOLKIND, Dr Stephen Nathaniel; s of Leonard Wolkind (d 1978), and Nettie, *née* Barbitsky; *b* 5 Aug 1939; *Educ* Christ Coll Finchley, Middlesex Hosp Med Sch, Univ of London (MB BS, MD); *m* 29 Jan 1963, Lilliane Camille Juliette Marcelle, da of Edmond Stanislavs Marie Vin (d 1966); 2 s (Ivan b 14 Oct 1967, Philip b 18 Nov 1969), 1 da (Helen b 14 July 1965); *Career* sr lectr and hon conslt in Child Psychiatry London Hosp 1972–85, conslt in child psychiatry Maudsley Hosp 1985; advsr on child and adolescent psychiatry Dept of Health, psychiatric advsr parents for children adoption agency and the bridge; FRCPsych 1981 (MRCPsych 1971, memb Ct of Electors); *Books* Pregnancy, A Psychological and Social Study (1978), Medical Aspects of Adoption and Foster Care (1979), Child Psychiatry and the Law (1989); *Recreations* walking, wine tasting, cinema; *Style*— Dr Stephen Wolkind; ✉ Children's Department, Maudsley Hospital, Denmark Hill, London SE5 8AZ (☎ 0171 703 6333)

WOLMAN, Clive Richard; s of Lionel Wolman (d 1969), of Sheffield, and Estelle, *née* Davidson; *b* 5 April 1956; *Educ* King Edward VII Sheffield, Carmel Coll Wallingford, St Catherine's Coll Oxford (MA), Poly of Central London (Dip Law), London Business Sch (MBA); *m* Anna, *née* Roden; *Career* Reading Evening Post reporter 1978–80, Jerusalem Post Israel energy housing and telecoms corr 1980–81; Financial Times: co comments writer 1982–83, personal fin ed 1983–85, securities industry corr (covered Big Bang and City Regulation) 1986–89; city ed (i/c financial, business, personal fin sections) The Mail on Sunday 1989–95, ed-in-chief London Financial News 1996–; *Recreations* archaeology, cycling; *Style*— Clive Wolman, Esq; ✉ London Financial News, 18–20 Scrutton Street, London EC2A 4EN (☎ 0171 426 3333)

WOLMER, Viscount; William Lewis Palmer; s and h of 4 Earl of Selborne, *qv*; *b* 1 Sept 1971; *Educ* Eton, Christ Church Oxford; *Style*— Viscount Wolmer

WOLPERT, Prof Lewis; CBE (1990); *b* 19 Oct 1929; *Educ* Univ of Witwatersrand SA (BSc), Imperial Coll London (DIC), King's Coll London (PhD); *m* (m dis); 2 s, 2 da; *Career* civil engr 1951–54: SA Cncl for Scientific and Industl Res, Israel Water Planning Dept; career changed to cell biology 1954, reader in zoology Dept of Zoology at King's Coll London 1964, prof of Biology as Applied to Medicine Univ Coll London Medical Sch 1966–; Scientific Medal of the Zoological Soc 1968; visiting lectr: Univ of Warwick, Collège de France; TV presenter for Antenna (BBC 2) 1988–89, various interviews and documentaries for Radio 3; Christmas lectures Royal Instn 1986; Hon MRCP London 1986, Hon DSc CNAA 1992; FRS 1980; *Books* A Passion for Science (1988), The Triumph of the Embryo (1991), The Unnatural Nature of Science (1992); *Recreations* cycling, tennis; *Style*— Prof Lewis Wolpert, CBE, FRS; ✉ Department of Anatomy & Developmental Biology, University College and Middlesex School of Medicine, Windeyer Building, Cleveland Street, London W1P 6DB (☎ 0171 380 9345, fax 0171 380 9346)

WOLSELEY, Sir Charles Garnet Richard Mark; 11 Bt (E 1628), of Wolseley, Staffs; s of Capt Stephen Wolseley (ka 1944, s of Sir Edric Wolseley, 10 Bt, JP (d 1954); the Wolseleys of Mt Wolseley, Co Carlow, who produced Sir Garnet, the Victorian general cr Visc Wolseley are a cadet branch) and Pamela, Lady Wolseley; *b* 16 June 1944; *Educ* Ampleforth, RAC Cirencester; *m* 1, 1968 (m dis 1984), Anita, da of Hugo Fried, of Epsom; 1 s, 3 da; m 2, 1984, Mrs Imogene E Brown; *Heir* s, Stephen Garnet Hugo Charles b 1980; *Career* ptnr Smiths Gore Chartered Surveyors 1979–87 (conslt 1987–); FRICS; *Recreations* shooting, fishing, water-colour painting; *Clubs* Farmers', Shikar; *Style*— Sir Charles Wolseley, Bt; ✉ Wolseley Park, Rugeley, Staffs WS15 2TU (☎ 01889 582346)

WOLSELEY, Sir James Douglas; 13 Bt (I 1745), of Mount Wolseley, Co Carlow; s of James Douglas Wolseley (d 1960), and Olive, *née* Wofford; *b* 17 Sept 1937; *m* 1, 1965 (m dis 1971), Patricia Lynn, da of William R Hunter, of Mount Shasta, California, USA; m 2, 1984, Mary Anne, da of Thomas G Brown, of Hilo, USA; *Heir* kinsman, John Walter Wolseley b 1938; *Style*— Sir James Wolseley, Bt

WOLSTENHOLME, Sir Gordon Ethelbert Ward; kt (1976), OBE (1944); s of Ethelbert Wolstenholme (d 1940), of Sheffield; *b* 28 May 1913; *Educ* Repton, Corpus Christi Coll Cambridge, Middx Hosp Med Sch (MB BChir); *m* 1, Mary Elizabeth (d 1985), da of Rev Herbert Spackman; 1 s, 2 da; m 2, Dushanka, only da of Arthur Messinger; 2 da; *Career* WWII RAMC 1940–47, serv France, Med, Middle E; dir Ciba Fndn 1949–78; memb: Exec Bd UK Ctee WHO 1961–70 (fndr memb 1954), Cncl Westfield Coll Univ of London 1965–73, Planning Bd Univ Coll Buckingham 1969; chm Nuffield Inst for Comparative Med 1969–70, memb Gen Med Cncl 1973–83, tstee and chm Academic Bd St George's Univ Sch of Med 1978–90, Harveian librarian RCP 1979–89, dir and chief scientific advsr Info Retrieval 1980–88, vice pres Assoc of Special Libraries and Info Bureaux 1979–82, pres Br Soc of History of Med 1983–85, patron Fund for the Replacement of Animals in Med Experiments (FRAME), fndr and first chm Action in Int Med 1988–, tstee and chm Oral and Dental Research Tst 1989–; hon life govr Middx Hosp 1938, hon fell Hunterian Soc (orator 1976), hon FACP, hon FRSM 1982 (hon sec 1964–70, pres library res 1968–70, chm working pty on Soc's future 1972–73, pres 1975–77 and 1978); asst emeritus Worshipful Soc of Apothecaries; fell UCL 1991; Hon LLD Univ of Cambridge 1968, Hon DTech Univ of Brunel 1981, Hon MD Grenada 1983; Hon FDSRCS 1991, MRCS, FRCP, FIBiol; *Style*— Sir Gordon Wolstenholme, OBE; ✉ 10 Wimpole Mews, London W1M 7TF (☎ 0171 486 3884)

WOLSTENHOLME, His Hon Judge; (John) Scott; s of Donald Arthur Wolstenholme, of Rainton, N Yorks, and Kathleen Maye, *née* Humphrys (d 1987); *b* 28 Nov 1947; *Educ* Roundhay Sch Leeds, Univ Coll Oxford (MA); *m* (Margaret) Lynne, da of Wilfred Harrison (d 1989); 3 s (Ian b 22 June 1974, Adam b 3 April 1976, Max b 11 Nov 1979), 1 da (Helen (twin) b 11 Nov 1979); *Career* called to the Bar Middle Temple 1971, in practice NE Circuit 1971–92, recorder of the Crown Court 1992–95, chm Industl Tbnls 1992–95, circuit judge (NE Circuit) 1995–; *Recreations* playing the drums, walking, photography; *Style*— His Hon Judge Wolstenholme; ✉ Leeds Combined Court Centre, Oxford Row, Leeds LS1 3BE

WOLSTENHOLME, Susan Elizabeth (Sue); da of Sir Gordon Wolstenholme, OBE, *qv*, of London, and Mary Elizabeth, *née* Spackman (d 1985); *b* 5 Nov 1940; *Educ* Berkhamsted Sch for Girls, St Godric's Secretarial Coll; *Career* J Walter Thompson Co Ltd: joined 1963, mangr Entertaining/Social Functions 1965, assoc dir 1976–83; ran own catering business 1983–85; dir British Tennis Foundation (formerly LTA Trust) 1988–; chm Devpt, Coaching & Schs' Ctee LTA 1985; hon sec Herts LTA 1978–88, govr Berkhamsted Schs 1980–, hon sec Berkhamsted Old Girls' Guild 1971–95; *Recreations* tennis (former county player), sport, reading, cooking; *Clubs* Berkhamsted Squash Rackets & Tennis, Sloane; *Style*— Ms Sue Wolstenholme; ✉ The British Tennis Foundation, Queen's Club, West Kensington, London W14 9EG (☎ 0171 381 7140, fax 0171 381 6507, mobile 0831 218531)

WOLTON, Harry; QC (1982); s of Harry William (d 1943), and Dorothy Beatrice, *née* Meaking (d 1982); *b* 1 Jan 1938; *Educ* King Edward's Sch Birmingham, Univ of Birmingham; *m* 3 April 1971, Julie Rosina Josephine, da of George Edward Mason (d 1985); 3 s (Matthew Harry b 1972, Andrew b 1974, Edward b 1977); *Career* called to the Bar 1969; recorder Crown Ct 1985, dep High Ct judge 1990–; *Style*— Harry Wolton, QC; ✉ The Black Venn, Edwyn Ralph, Bromyard, Herefordshire HR7 4LU (☎ 01885 483302); 3 Redcliffe Mews, London SW10 9JT (☎ 0171 370 3940); 5 Fountain Ct, Steelhouse Lane, Birmingham B4 6DR (☎ 0121 606 0500); Devereux Chambers, Temple WC2R 3JJ (☎ 0171 353 7534)

WOLVERSON, Brig (Robert) Christopher; OBE (1982); s of Robert Archibald Wolverson (d 1963), of Cambridge, and Mary Isabel, *née* Barnes; *b* 9 June 1940; *Educ* Bedford Sch, Downing Coll Cambridge (MA); *m* 8 Sept 1973, Deborah Elizabeth, da of Dr James Charles Shee (d 1995), of Rhodesia and SA, and Catherine Mary, *née* Hartnett; 2 da (Joscelin b 1978, Thomasina b 1980); *Career* cmmnd Irish Guards 1962, served Germany, UK, Aden, Belize, NI, Zimbabwe, Cyprus, Falkland Is, Bangladesh, Adj Cambridge Univ OTC 1968–70, Staff Coll 1970–72, Bde Maj 4 Guards Armoured Bde 1974–76, DS Staff Coll 1978–80, Mil Asst C-in-C BAOR 1980–81, DS Zimbabwe Staff Coll 1981–82, cmd 1 Bn The Kings Own Royal Border Regt 1983–85, MOD 1985–89, cmd Br Mil Advsy Team Bangladesh 1990–92, cmd 43 (Wessex) Bde and Exeter Area 1992–95, ADC to HM The Queen 1995–96, ret; Regtl Lt Col Irish Guards 1995–; *Clubs* Army and Navy, MCC; *Style*— Brig Christopher Wolverson, OBE, ADC

WOLVERSON, Maurice Frank; s of Frank Wolverson (d 1990), of Wednesbury, W Mids, and (Edith Anne) Nancy, *née* Phillips (d 1973); *b* 7 June 1927; *Educ* Wednesbury Boys' HS; *m* 4 June 1949, (Kathleen) Merle, da of Philip Patrick Forrester (d 1986); *Career* conscripted 1946, RAOC 1947–49 (demobbed Sgt); ptnr Whitehouse Wolverson Armston Cox CAs (formerly Barnfield & Co) 1961–92, chm Parklands Housing Soc Ltd (now Accord Housing Group Ltd) 1989–93 and 1996– (pt/t treas 1966–82, memb Ctee 1982–, vice chm 1988–89 and 1993–96); tstee Crumps Almshouses and others, chm Walsall Family Practitioner Ctee 1983–89 (memb 1973–89, vice chm 1975–83), chm Walsall Health Authy 1992–95 (memb 1985–95, vice chm 1990–92); ACA 1959, FCA 1970; Maitre-Confrere de Confrerie St Etienne D'Alsace; *Recreations* wines, music, reading, keeping fit; *Style*— Maurice Wolverson, Esq; ✉ 6 Greenslade Rd, Park Hall, Walsall, W Mids WS5 3QH (☎ 01922 26133)

WOLVERTON, 7 Baron (UK 1869); Christopher Richard Glyn; er s of 6 Baron Wolverton, CBE (d 1988), and Dowager Baroness Wolverton; *b* 5 Oct 1938; *Educ* Eton; *m* 1, 1961 (m dis 1967), Carolyn Jane, yr da of late Antony Noel Hunter, of London SW3; 2 da (Hon Sara-Jane b 1963, Hon Amanda Camilla b 1966); m 2, 1975 (m dis 1989), Mrs Frances Sarah Elisabeth Stuart Black, eldest da of Robert Worboys Skene, of London W8; m 3, 1990, Gillian Konig; *Heir* bro, Hon Andrew John Glyn, *qv*; *Career* FRICS; *Style*— The Rt Hon the Lord Wolverton

WOMBWELL, Sir George Philip Frederick; 7 Bt (GB 1778), of Wombwell, Yorkshire; s of Maj Sir Philip Wombwell, 6 Bt, MBE (d 1977); *b* 21 May 1949; *Educ* Repton; *m* 1974, (Hermione) Jane, eldest da of Thomas S Wrightson, of Ulshaw Grange, Leyburn, N Yorks; 1 s (Stephen Philip Henry b 1977), 1 da (Sarah Georgina b 1980); *Heir* s, Stephen Philip Henry Wombwell b 12 May 1977; *Career* farmer; *Style*— Sir George Wombwell, Bt; ✉ Newburgh Priory, Coxwold, York YO6 4AS (☎ 0134 76 435)

WOMERSLEY, (John) Michael; s of John Basil Womersley (d 1979), of Yorkshire, and Ann Patricia, *née* Allured; *b* 18 Feb 1960; *Educ* King Edward's Sch Bath, Oxford Poly (HND); *m* 4 May 1991, Susanne Jayne, da of John Maurice George Garrard, and Sue, *née* Mullins; 1 s (Oliver Peter b 25 Oct 1995); *Career* asst mangr (Reading) British Tranport Hotels 1981, commis chef Gidleigh Park 1982–84, chef de partie Le Manoir aux Quat'Saisons 1984–86, successively legumier, commis patissier then baker L'Esperance Marc Meneau 1986–87, fish chef de partie Les Pres D'Eugenie Michel Guerard 1987, sr sous chef Cliveden Hotel 1988–89, head chef Lucknam Park Hotel 1989–95, chef proprietor Three Lions Restaurant Stuckton 1995–; memb Academie Culinaire de Grand Bretagne; *Awards* winner: first prize Yorkshire Fine Wine Competition 1990, third prize Mouton Cadet Competition, Prix des Deux Cartes 1994; finalist Pierre Tatinger Competition 1993; Lucknam Park Hotel awards: County Restaurant of the Yr Good Food Guide 1990, 4 AA red stars and 3 red rosettes 1991–, Ackerman clover 1991–95, Hotel of the Yr Exec Travel and Utell 1991, Michelin star 1992–95; Three Lions awards: Michelin Red M 1996, 3* and Hampshire Achiever Rosette Good Food Guide 1996; *Recreations* advanced diver, skiing, golf, Tai Chi; *Style*— Michael Womersley, Esq; ✉ Three Lions Restaurant, Stuckton, nr Fordingbridge, Hants SP6 2HF (☎ 01425 652489, fax 01425 652144)

WOMERSLEY, Sir Peter John Walter; 2 Bt (UK 1945), of Grimsby, Co Lincoln; JP (1991); s of late Capt John Walter Womersley (ka 1944), and gs of Rt Hon Sir Walter Womersley, 1 Bt, PC (d 1961); *b* 10 Nov 1941; *Educ* Charterhouse, RMA Sandhurst; *m* 1968, Janet Margaret, da of Alastair Grant; 2 s, 2 da; *Heir* s, John Gavin Grant Womersley b 7 Dec 1971; *Career* serv Regular Army, Offr Cadet at Sandhurst until 1962, 2 Lt King's Own Royal Border Regt 1962, Lt 1964, ret 1968; human resources serv mangr SmithKline Beecham 1993– (personnel offr 1968–72, personnel mangr 1972–93); MIPM; *Books* Collecting Stamps (with Neil Grant, 1980); *Recreations* breeding rare poultry, motor racing photography; *Style*— Sir Peter Womersley, Bt, JP; ✉ Broomfields, 23 Goring Rd, Steyning, W Sussex BN44 3GF

WONFOR, Andrea Jean; da of George Duncan (d 1995), of Matfen, Northumberland, and Audrey Joan, *née* Player (d 1991); *b* 31 July 1944; *Educ* Simon Langton Girls' Sch Canterbury, New Hall Cambridge (exhibitioner, BA); *m* 1, 1967 (m dis 1974), Patrick Masefield; 1 da (Abigail Jane b 1968); m 2, 1974, Geoffrey Wonfor; 1 da (Samantha Mia b 1975); *Career* broadcasting exec; trainee Granada TV 1966–67; Tyne Tees TV: researcher 1968–73, dir 1973–76, head of youth and children's progs 1976–82, dir of progs 1982–87; md Zenith North Ltd (TV prodn co) 1987–90; Channel Four Television: controller of arts and entertainment progs 1990–93, dep dir of progs 1993; Granada Television: dir of progs 1993–94, jt md 1994–; jt md Granada International Productions 1996–; govr British Film Inst 1989–94, chair Edinburgh Int Television Festival 1994; fell RTS; *Style*— Ms Andrea Wonfor; ✉ Granada Television Ltd, Granada Television Centre, Quay Street, Manchester M60 9EA

WONNACOTT, John Henry; s of Jack Alfred Wonnacott (d 1974), and Ethel Gwendoline Wonnacott; *b* 15 April 1940; *Educ* Univ Coll Sch, Slade Sch; *m* 10 Aug 1974, Anne Rozaha, da of Tadeusz Wesolowski (d 1980); 2 da (Elizabeth Anne b 1978, Emma Zofja b 1982), 1 s (Jack Henry Tadeus b 1994); *Career* artist; *Gp Exhibitions* incl: Painting and Perception (Univ of Sterling) 1971, British Painting '74 1974, British Painting' 52–77 (Royal Acad) 1977, Hard Won Image (Tate Gallery) 1984, Pursuit of the Real (Barbican) 1990; *Solo Exhibitions* incl: The Minories of Colchester 1977, Rochdale Art Gallery and tour 1978, Marlborough Fine Art 1980, 1985 and 1988, Scottish Nat Portrait Gallery 1986, Agnew's 1992 and 1996; work in public collections incl: Tate Gallery, Arts Cncl, Edinburgh Scottish Nat Portrait Gallery, Norwich Castle, Rochdale Gallery, British Cncl, Metropolitan NY, Imperial War Museum, Nat Maritime Museum Greenwich; *Style*— John Wonnacott, Esq; ✉ Thomas Agnew & Sons Ltd, 43 Old Bond Street, London W1X 4BA (☎ 0171 629 6176, fax 0171 629 4359)

WOOD, Andrew Marley; KCMG (1995, CMG 1986); s of Robert George Wood (d 1988), and Muriel, *née* du Feu; *b* 2 Jan 1940; *Educ* Ardingly, King's Coll Cambridge (MA); *m* 1, 15 Sept 1972, Melanie Leroy, *née* Masset (d 1977); 1 s (Matthew Thomas b 22 Aug 1975); m 2, 15 Sept 1978, Stephanie Lee, *née* Masset; 1 da (Laura Lee b 10 May 1981), 1 s (Patrick Andrew Robert b 5 Feb 1985); *Career* FO (now FCO): joined 1961, third sec Moscow 1964–67, second then first sec Washington 1967–70, seconded to Cabinet Office 1971–73, FCO 1973–76, first sec and head Chancery then cnsllr Belgrade 1976–79, head Chancery Moscow 1979–82, head West European Dept 1982–83, head Personnel Ops Dept 1983–85, ambass Belgrade 1985–89, min Washington 1989–92, dep under sec and chief clerk 1992–95, ambass Russian Fedn and Republic of Moldova 1995–; *Style*— Sir Andrew Wood, KCMG; ✉ c/o Foreign and Commonwealth Office (Moscow), King Charles Street, London SW1A 2AH

WOOD, Andrew Stephen; s of Robert Wood, of York, and Elizabeth Anne Wood; *b* 5 March 1966; *Educ* Ashfield Secdy Modern Sch, York Coll of Arts and Technol, Scarborough Tech Coll; *m* Joanne Mary, da of John Ramsey; *Career* 3 chef Hotel Dorink Franfurt, Ritz Hotel London, Royal Crescent Hotel Bath, currently head chef Middlethorpe Hotel York; winner cooking competition Amsterdam 1988; *Recreations* scuba diving (memb Br Sub Aqua Club); *Clubs* Excalibar Dive, York Squash and Racquets; *Style*— Andrew Wood, Esq; ✉ Middlethorpe Hall, Bishopthorpe Road, York YO1 1QB (☎ 01904 641241, fax 01904 620176)

WOOD, Anthony Hugh Boynton-; Lord of the Manor of Copmanthorpe, nr York (acquired 1568); o s of Frederick Anthony Boynton-Wood (d 1939; s of Capt Albert Charles Wood, JP, 8 QRI Hussars, of Hollin Hall, Ripon), and Gladys Gertrude (d 1986), yr da of Charles Frederick Wray, of Hobberley House, Shadwell (gs of William Wray, of Castle Wray, Co Donegal) (*see* Burke's LG 18 edn, vol III, 1972, Boynton-Wood); ninth in descent from Dame Frances Boynton, da and co-heir of John Barnard, Mayor of Hull, who refused Charles I entry to the city, and was great-uncle of Anne Boldero-Barnard, Lady Carrington; ggg nephew of Rev Prof Thomas Robert Malthus, of Haileybury Coll, author of the celebrated 'Essay on Principle of Population'; collateral descendant of Bl Edmund Sykes (martyred 23 March 1587, beatified 22 Nov 1987), through his niece Dame Frances Boynton; *b* 1 May 1917; *Educ* privately, Leeds Univ, Hull Univ; *Career* slr 1947; landowner (manages 1,000 acre ancestral estate (in family since 1719) and Hollin Arab Stud); received into Church of Rome at Ampleforth 1987; life memb: The Arab Horse Soc, The British Horse Society, Law Soc, Selden Soc (8 New Sq, Lincoln's Inn), Historic Houses Assoc, Cromwell Assoc, Nat Art-Collections Fund; vice pres Friends of York City Art Gallery; *Recreations* horse trials, riding, gardening, genealogy, heraldry, arts, music, theatre; *Style*— Anthony Boynton-Wood, Esq; ✉ Hollin Hall, Ripon, N Yorks HG4 3AB (☎ 01765 692466)

WOOD, Dr Anthony James (Tony); s of Harry Wood (d 1961), of Lowestoft, Suffolk, and Elizabeth Ann, *née* Calvert (d 1975); *b* 20 Nov 1938; *Educ* Lowestoft GS, Univ of Nottingham (BSc), Univ of London (PGCE), Univ of Southampton (PhD); *m* 1960, Marion Christine, da of Basil Archie Paine; 1 s (David Anthony b 10 July 1964), 2 da (Susan Nicola b 7 Oct 1965, Wendy Michelle b 23 March 1976); *Career* physics teacher Fairham Comp Nottingham 1961–62; Instr Lt RN 1962–67; sr lectr Weymouth Coll of Educn 1969–73 (lectr 1967–69); princ lectr and head of Mathematics Div Northampton Coll of Educn 1973–75; dean Faculty of Mathematics and Business Nene Coll Northampton 1975–84 (dean Blackwood Hodge Mgmnt Centre 1981–84); chief exec Luton Coll of HE 1989–93 (dir 1985–93, Leverhulme research fell 1985–86); vice chllr and chief exec Univ of Luton 1993–; chm Bedfordshire Family Practitioners' Ctee 1989–90; chm and non-exec dir: Bedfordshire FHSA 1990–94, Bedfordshire Health Authy 1994–; external examiner Univ of Southampton 1978–83; dir: Putteridge Bury Ltd 1989–, HE Business Enterprises 1991–93, HE Quality Cncl 1992–93; memb: Euro Fndn for Mgmnt Devpt 1981–, Access Courses Recognition Gp CNAA 1987–92, Instns Ctee CNAA 1989–92, Ctee for Degree Awarding Powers HE Quality Cncl 1992–93, R & D Ctee NW Thames RHA 1993–94, CVCP 1993–, Univs Liaison Ctee Anglia and Oxford RHA 1994–96; chm Standing Conference of Princs and Dirs of Colls and Insts of HE 1990–93; FIMA 1975, CMath 1992; *Books* Involving Parents in the Curriculum (1976), Curriculum Enrichment for Gifted Children (1979), Quicksilver Maths series (1982), Hedgehoppers series (1986); *Recreations* home and family; *Style*— Dr Tony Wood; ✉ Vice-Chancellor, University of Luton, Park Square, Luton, Bedfordshire LU1 3JU (☎ 01582 489226, fax 01582 489362); Chairman, Bedfordshire Health Authority, Charter House, Alma Street, Luton, Bedfordshire LU1 1PL (☎ 01582 744800, fax 01582 451718)

WOOD, Prof Bernard Anthony; s of Anthony Frederick Wood, of Burnham-on-Sea, Somerset, and late Joan Faith, *née* Slocombe; *b* 17 April 1945; *Educ* King's Sch Gloucester, Middx Hosp Med Sch Univ of London (BSc, MB BS, PhD); *m* 29 March 1982, Alison Margretta, da of Robert Richards, of Studham, Beds; 1 s (Nicholas b 1970), 2 da (Penny b 1972, Hannah b 1986); *Career* Univ of London: lectr 1973–75, sr lectr 1975–78, reader 1978–82, SA Courtauld prof 1982–85; Derby prof of anatomy Univ of Liverpool 1985–, dean Faculty of Med Univ of Liverpool 1996–; past pres Primate Soc of GB, vice pres Royal Anthropological Inst, past sec Br Assoc of Clinical Anatomists, pres Anatomical Soc of GB and Ireland 1996–; *Books* Human Evolution (1978), Major Topics in Primate and Human Evolution (1986), Hominid Cranial Remains (1991); *Recreations* research, walking; *Style—* Prof Bernard Wood; ✉ Dyer's Farm, Edge, Malpas, Cheshire SY14 7DN (☎ and fax 01829 250205); Faculty of Medicine, University of Liverpool, Liverpool L69 3BX (☎ 0151 706 4261, fax 0151 709 2601)

WOOD, Charles Anthony; OBE (1996); s of Anthony Mewburn Wood (d 1994), of Chiddingstone, Kent, and Margaret Kathleen, *née* Stordy; *b* 20 Nov 1938; *Educ* Downside, Pembroke Coll Oxford (MA); *m* 10 Oct 1964, Susan Mary, da of Henry Anderson, MBE (d 1975), of Wallingford; 3 s (Robert b 1969, Francis b 1979, Jonathan b 1982), 1 da (Juliette b 1971); *Career* Phillips & Drew 1962–71, L Messel & Co 1971–86; dir: Lehman Brothers Securities 1986–96, Greig Middleton & Co Ltd 1996–; chm Lehman Brothers Pension Scheme 1988–; chm New Islington and Hackney Housing Assoc 1984–95; AIIMR, MSI; *Recreations* houses, gardening, climbing; *Clubs* City of London, Alpine; *Style—* Charles Wood, Esq, OBE; ✉ 14 Compton Terrace, London N1 2UN (☎ 0171 226 4056); Greig Middleton & Co Ltd, 66 Wilson Street, London EC2A 2BL (☎ 0171 392 4000)

WOOD, Charles Gerald; s of John Edward Wood; *b* 6 Aug 1932; *Educ* Chesterfield GS, King Charles I Sch Kidderminster, Birmingham Coll of Art; *m* 1954, Valerie Elizabeth Newman; 1 s (John Charles b 1954), 1 da (Katrina b 1959); *Career* dramatist, screenwriter and writer for television and radio 1963–; 1949–63: soldier (17–21st Lancers), scenic artist, layout artist and stage mangr, cartoonist (The Stage, The Globe and Mail Toronto), Bristol Evening Post; memb Drama Panel SW Arts 1970–72, conslt Nat Film Devpt Fund 1980–82, memb Cncl BAFTA 1990–93; FRSL 1984; *Theatre* plays incl: Cockade, Dingo, Don't Make Me Laugh, Meals on Wheels, Fill the Stage with Happy Hours, H or Monologues at Front of Burning Cities, Tie Up the Ballcock, Welfare, The Garden, Veterans, The Script, Jingo, Red Star, Has Washington Legs, Across From the Garden of Allah, The Plantagenets, Man Beast and Virtue (Pirandello), Arabia, The Mountain Giants (Pirandello) 1993, The Tower (Dumas) 1995; *Television* plays: Not At All, Traitor in a Steel Helmet, Drill Pig, Prisoner and Escort, Drums Along the Avon, Mutzen Ab!, A Bit of a Holiday, A Bit of a Family Feeling, A Bit of Vision, A Bit of an Adventure, Death or Glory Boy, The Emergence of Antony Purdy Esq, Love Lies Bleeding, Do As I Say!; series: Don't Forget to Write, My Family and Other Animals (adaption), The Settling of the Sun, Sharpe's Company, Sharpe's Regiment, Sharpe's Waterloo, Mute of Malice; documentaries: Last Summer By the Sea; *Films* incl: The Knack, Help, How I Won the War, The Long Day's Dying, The Charge of the Light Brigade, The Bed Sitting Room, Cuba, Wagner, Red Monarch, Puccini, Wagner, Tumbledown (Prix Italia RAI Prize, Best Single Play BAFTA, Best Single Play RTS, Best Single Play BPG), An Awfully Big Adventure (Beryl Bainbridge), A Breed of Heroes (Alan Judd), England My England (John Osborne); *Radio 1962–72* Prisoner and Escort, Cowheel Jelly, Next to Being a Knight; *Publications* incl: Cockade, New English Dramatists 8, Dingo, H, Veterans, Man Beast and Virtue (Pirandello), The Mountain Giants (Pirandello), The Tower (Dumas); *Style—* Charles Wood, Esq; ✉ c/o William Morris Agency (UK) Ltd, 31/32 Soho Square, London W1V 6DG (☎ 0171 434 2191, fax 0171 437 0238)

WOOD, David Bernard; s of Richard Edwin Wood (d 1987), and Audrey Adele Whittle, *née* Fincham; *b* 21 Feb 1944; *Educ* Chichester HS for Boys, Worcester Coll Oxford (BA); *m* 1, 1966 (m dis 1970), Sheila, *née* Dawson; m 2, Jan 1975, Jacqueline, da of Prof Sydney William Stanbury; 2 da (Katherine b 1976, Rebecca b 1979); *Career* actor, writer, composer, playwright, theatre director and producer; West End acting credits incl: Hang Down Your Head and Die 1964, Four Degrees Over 1966, After Haggerty 1970, Jeeves 1975; film acting credits incl: If.... 1968, Aces High 1976, North Sea Hijack 1980; dir: WSG Productions Ltd/Whirligig Theatre 1966–, Verronmead Ltd 1982–, Westwood Theatrical Productions Ltd 1986–1994, W2 Productions 1995–; *Publications* many plays published by Samuel French incl: The Owl and the Pussycat Went to See (1968), The Plotters of Cabbage Patch Corner (1970), The Gingerbread Man (1977), The Selfish Shellfish (1983), The See-Saw Tree (1987), Save the Human (1990); children's books incl: The Operats of Rodent Garden (1984), The Discorats (1985), Playtheatres (1987), Sidney the Monster (1988), Happy Birthday Mouse (1990), Save the Human (1990), Baby Bear's Buggy Ride (1993); for Pop-up Theatre: Cinderella (1994), Bedtime Story (1995), The Magic Show (1995); stage adaptations of: Helen Nicoll and Jan Pieńkowski's Meg and Mog (1980), HRH The Prince of Wales' The Old Man of Lochnagar (1986), Roald Dahl's THE BFG (1991), The Witches (1992), Enid Blyton's Noddy (1993), More Adventures of Noddy (1995); film screenplays Swallows and Amazons (1974), Back Home (1989); *Recreations* conjuring (memb Magic Circle), collecting old books; *Clubs* Green Room; *Style—* David Wood, Esq; ✉ c/o Casarotto Ramsay Ltd, National House, 4th Floor, 60–66 Wardour Street, London W1V 4ND (☎ 0171 287 4450, fax 0171 287 9128)

WOOD, Rear Adm David John; s of John Herbert Wood (d 1982), and Nesta, *née* Jones; *b* 12 June 1942; *Educ* St Paul's Sch, Britannia RNC Dartmouth, RNEC Manadon (BSc(Eng)); *m* 1966, Hilary Jolly; 2 s (Thomas b 1971, Charles b 1972), 1 da (Anna b 1974); *Career* with RN; various Fleet Air Arm appts incl HMS Ark Royal and Sea Vixen and Wessex Sqdns 1965–73, Aircraft Support MOD 1973–76, Air Engr Offr Lynx Intensive Flying Trials Unit 1976–77, Army Staff Course 1978, Aircraft Procurement MOD (PE) 1979–81, Naval Sec's Dept MOD 1981–84, on staff FO Naval Air Command 1984–86, NATO Def Coll Rome 1986–87, asst dir for EH101 Project MOD (PE) 1987–89, dir Aircraft Support Policy (Navy) MOD 1989–91, dir Maritime Projects MOD (PE) 1991–95, DG Aircraft (Navy) 1995–; FRAeS 1993 (memb Cncl 1996), FIMgt 1995; *Recreations* cross country walking and running, choral singing, supporting local church; *Clubs* Army and Navy; *Style—* Rear Adm David Wood; ✉ Ministry of Defence, Whitehall, London SW1A 2HB

WOOD, David John Dargue; s of John Nöel Wood, MC (d 1976), of Sheffield, and Ruth Mary Dargue, *née* Moffitt (d 1987); *b* 17 April 1930; *Educ* King Edward VII Sch Sheffield, Wadham Coll Oxford (MA); *m* 23 March 1957, (Rosemary) Sepha, da of Lt-Col Philip Neill, TD (d 1986), of Whitby; 1 s (Justin b 1959), 1 da (Annabel b 1963); *Career* RAF Airfield Construction Branch Egypt and Libya 1953–54; ptnr Husband and Co consltg engrs 1967–88 (jt md 1988–90); pres Br Section Société des Ingenieurs et Scientifiques de France 1984–85; treas Assoc of Consulting Engrs 1980–81; FEng 1987, FICE 1964, FIWEM 1965, MConsE 1967; *Recreations* sailing; *Clubs* Royal Cruising, Royal Ocean Racing; *Style—* David Wood, Esq, FEng; ✉ Little Crofton Cottage, Titchfield, Hants PO14 3ER (☎ and fax 01329 847844)

WOOD, His Hon Judge; David Russell; s of Christopher Russell Wood (d 1987), of Riding Lea, Northumberland, and Muriel Wynne Wood; *b* 13 Dec 1948; *Educ* Sedbergh Sch Yorks, UEA (BA); *m* 24 Feb 1979, Georgina Susan, da of Maj Dudley Buckle; 2 s (John Dudley Russell b 4 June 1980, Robert James Russell b 12 May 1985), 1 da (Rose-Ann Florence b 19 May 1982); *Career* called to the Bar Gray's Inn 1973, recorder of the Crown Court 1990–95 (asst recorder 1984–90), circuit judge (NE Circuit) 1995–; memb: Bar Cncl, NE Circuit Criminal Bar Assoc; *Recreations* farming, shooting, fishing, golf, tennis, piano; *Clubs* Northern Counties (Newcastle-upon-Tyne); *Style—* His Hon Judge Wood; ✉ Newcastle upon Tyne Crown Court, Quayside, Newcastle upon Tyne (☎ 0191 201 2000, fax 0191 201 2001)

WOOD, Maj-Gen Denys Broomfield; CB (1978); s of Maj Percy Neville Wood (d 1952), of Hartfield, Sussex, and Meryl, *née* Broomfield (d 1964); *b* 2 Nov 1923; *Educ* Radley, Pembroke Coll Cambridge (BA, MA, Capt of Coll Boat Club and memb Goldie Crew); *m* 12 June 1948, Jennifer Nora, da of Air Cdre William Morton Page, CBE (d 1957), of Wimbledon; 1 s (Andrew Richard b 1950), 2 da (Joanna Margaret b 1954, Bridget Susan b 1956); *Career* War Serv UK and Far East 1944–47, cmmnd REME 1944, staff capt WO 1948; instr RMA Sandhurst 1949, staff coll 1953, DAA & QMG II Inf Bde Gp 1955, OC IO Inf Workshop Malaya 1958, Jt Servs Staff Coll 1960, directing staff Staff Coll 1961, Cmdg REME 3 Div 1963, operational observer Vietnam 1966–67, Col GS Staff Coll 1967, Imperial Def Coll 1970, dir admin planning (Army) 1971, dep mil sec 1973, dir Army Quartering 1975–78, Col Cmdt REME 1978–84; exec sec then sec CEI 1978–84; memb Lord Chllr's Panel of Ind Inquiry Inspectors 1984–93, gen cmmr of taxes 1985–, lay memb Adjudication Ctee Law Soc 1986–92; CEng, FIMechE, FRSA; *Clubs* Army and Navy; *Style—* Maj-Gen Denys Wood, CB; ✉ Elmtree House, Hurtmore Road, Godalming, Surrey GU7 2RA

WOOD, Derek Alexander; CBE (1995), QC (1978); s of Alexander Cecil Wood, and Rosetta, *née* Lelyveld; *b* 14 Oct 1937; *Educ* Tiffin Sch Kingston-upon-Thames, Univ Coll Oxford (BCL, MA); *m* 9 Aug 1961, Sally Teresa Scott Wood, step da of Sir Norman Randall Elliott, CBE; 2 da (Jessica Susan b 27 Oct 1965, Rebecca Lucy b 7 Sept 1968); *Career* called to the Bar Middle Temple 1964, recorder of the Crown Court 1985, bencher Middle Temple 1986, princ St Hugh's Coll Oxford 1991–; DoE: memb Advsy Gp on Commercial Property Devpt 1975–78, memb Working Gp on New Forms of Social Ownership in Housing 1976, memb Property Advsy Gp 1978–, chm Review of Rating of Plant and Machinery 1992; chm Standing Advsy Ctee on Trunk Rd Assessment Dept of Tport 1986–94; memb Cncl London Borough of Bromley 1975–78; dep chm Soc of Labour Lawyers 1978–91; hon fell Central Assoc of Agric Valuers 1988, hon ARICS 1991; FCIArb 1993; *Books* Leasehold Enfranchisement and Extension (ed, part of Halsbury's Laws of England series), Handbook of Arbitration Practice (jt ed with Ronald Bernstein, 1987, 2nd edn 1993); various works on agricultural law; *Recreations* music; *Clubs* Athenaeum, RAC; *Style—* Derek Wood, Esq, CBE, QC; ✉ St Hugh's College, Oxford OX2 6LE; Falcon Chambers, Falcon Court, London EC4Y 1AA (☎ 0171 353 2484, fax 0171 353 1261)

WOOD, Dudley Ernest; CBE (1995); s of Ernest Edward Wood, and Ethel Louise Wood; *b* 18 May 1930; *Educ* Luton GS, St Edmund Hall Oxford (BA); *m* 1955, Mary Christina, *née* Blake; 2 s; *Career* sr mangr ICI 1954–86, sec RFU 1986–95, ret; played rugby football for: Oxford Univ, Bedford and East Midlands, Rosslyn Park, Waterloo, Streatham Croydon, E Mids; hon life memb Squash Racquets Assoc 1984; *Recreations* squash, travel, dog-breeding, ME affrs; *Clubs* E India, Royal Over-Seas League; *Style—* Dudley Wood, Esq, CBE

WOOD, Edmund Michael; s of George Lockhart Wood (d 1959), and Joan, *née* Halsey; *b* 7 Sept 1943; *Educ* Maidwell Hall, Eton; *m* 6 Nov 1971, Elizabeth Anne, da of Sqdn Ldr Robert Roland Patrick Fisher (d 1991); 2 da (Sarah Georgina b 10 July 1974, Anne Louise b 15 Sept 1977); *Career* chartered accountant 1967; articled to Singleton Fabian & Co 1963, ptnr Singleton Fabian Derbyshire & Co 1969 (firm merged with Binder Hamlyn & Co 1974); currently: sr ptnr specialising in personal finance planning Binder Hamlyn, dir BH Matheson Investment Management; dir Lee Valley Water Co 1982–90; chm Hitchin Deanery Synod 1991–; FCA 1974 (ACA 1968); *Recreations* fishing, shooting, golf, gardening; *Clubs* Boodle's; *Style—* Edmund M Wood, Esq; ✉ The Old Rectory, Holwell, Hitchin, Hertfordshire SG5 3SP (☎ 01462 712228); Binder Hamlyn, Victoria Square, Victoria Street, St Albans, Hertfordshire AL1 3TF (☎ 01727 836363, fax 01727 840993)

WOOD, Sir Frederick Ambrose Stuart; kt (1977); s of Alfred Phillip Wood, of Goole, Yorks, and Patras, Greece, and Charlotte, *née* Barnes; *b* 30 May 1926; *Educ* Felsted Sch, Clare Coll Cambridge; *m* 1947, J R (Su) King; 2 s, 1 da; *Career* serv WWII Sub Lt Fleet Air Arm 1944–47; formerly chm Nat Bus Co 1972–78; chm Croda Int 1960–86 (md 1953, hon life pres 1986–), chm NEB 1981, NRDC 1979–81 (memb 1973) and first chm of the Br Tech Gp (after NEB and NRDC merged) 1981–83; Hon LLD Univ of Hull; *Style—* Sir Frederick Wood; ✉ Hearn Wood, The Mount, Headley, Hants GU35 8AG (☎ 01428 712134)

WOOD, Gareth Haydn; s of Haydn William George Wood, and Joyce, *née* Jenkins; *b* 7 June 1950; *Educ* Pontypridd Boys' GS, RAM; *Career* memb RPO 1972– (chm until 1994), composer of many pieces for brass bands incl Butlins Youth 1977 and Nat 4 Section 1980; cmmns incl: Overture Suffolk Punch (RPO), Festivities Overture (Philharmonia Orch), fanfares (100 years of the Financial Times), fanfare (150 years of Cunard), Sinfoniettas 2, 3 and 4 (Nat Youth Orch of Wales), Fantasy of Welsh Song (Welsh Prom Concerts), test-piece (European Brass Band Championships) 1992, The Land of Magic and Enchantment (40th anniversary of Pembs Nat Park), Fanfare for a New Beginning (opening of Kravis Centre W Palm Beach), Cardiff Bay Overture (Cardiff Bay Devpt Corp) 1993, Toduri (600th anniversary of City of Seoul Korea), Halifax Diptych (Halifax Building Society), Poems within a Prayer (Robert Tear (tenor)); ARAM; *Style—* Gareth Wood, Esq; ✉ 57 Marischal Road, Lewisham, London SE13 5LE (☎ and fax 0181 318 3312)

WOOD, Prof Graham Allan; s of William Wales Wood, of Glasgow, and Ann Fleming, *née* Blackwood; *b* 15 Aug 1946; *Educ* Hillhead HS, Univ of Glasgow (BDS), Univ of Dundee (MB ChB); *m* 23 Nov 1970, Lindsay, da of Alfred Balfour; 1 s (Alexander b 1985), 1 da (Nicola b 1975); *Career* gen dental practice 1968–70, house offr and sr house offr Glasgow Dental Hosp 1970–71, registrar in oral and maxillofacial surgery Canniesburn and Victoria Infirmary Hosps 1971–72, dental surgeon Int Grenfell Assoc 1972–73, registrar in oral and maxillofacial surgery Queen Elizabeth Hosp Birmingham 1973–74, sr registrar in oral and maxillofacial surgery N Wales 1979–83 (conslt 1983–95), conslt in oral and maxillofacial surgery Canniesburn Hosp Glasgow 1995–, hon clinical sr lectr Univ of Glasgow 1995–; clinical dir Glasgow: oral surgery, oral med, oral pathology, oral microbiology; clinical prof in oral and maxillofacial surgery Univ of Texas; postgrad tutor in Dentistry; dip in cleft lip and palate surgery Univ of Mexico; memb: BMA, BDA, BAOMS, BSI, Br Soc for Head and Neck Oncology, Craniofacial Soc of GB, Working Pty on Oro-facial Cancer in Wales, Specialty Accreditation Ctee for Oral and Maxillofacial Surgery; FDSRCPS Glasgow 1973, FRCSEd 1985; *Books* Cryosurgery of the Maxillofacial Region Vol II (contrib, 1986); *Recreations* golf, squash, sailing, hill walking, skiing (formerly Canadian ski patroller); *Clubs* Bowfield Country, Kilmacolm Golf; *Style—* Prof Graham A Wood; ✉ Abbotsford, Broomknowe Road, Kilmacolm, Renfrewshire PA13 4HX; Department of Oral and Maxillofacial Surgery, Canniesburn Hospital, Bearsden, Glasgow G61 1QL (☎ 0141 211 5787)

WOOD, Graham Barry; s of Anthony Philip Wood, of Dacre, Cumbria, and Jean Wissett, *née* Snelgrove; *b* 21 June 1959; *Educ* Merchant Taylors' Crosby, Univ of Salford (BSc); *m* 1, 6 Aug 1983 (m dis 1985), Hilene Susan, da of Wilson McCloud Henry, of Thornton, Merseyside; m 2, 2 Sept 1989, Yvonne Alison Owen Ditchfield, da of James Edward Owen, of Heaton Moor, Stockport; 2 s (Benjamin James b 7 April 1990, George Edward b 11 June 1992); *Career* CA; ptnr Bennett Brooks Cheshire 1985–; currently fin dir Armstrong Laing plc; FCCA 1990, MInstD 1992, FCA 1993 (ACA 1983); *Recreations* cooking, wine, gardening, skiing, travel; *Style—* Graham Wood, Esq; ✉ c/o Armstrong Laing Group, Chester House, 79 Dane Road, Sale, Manchester M33 7BP WA16 6BU (☎ 0161 972 4022, fax 0161 962 4000)

WOOD, Prof Graham Charles; s of Cyril Wood (d 1964), of Farnborough, Kent, and Doris Hilda, *née* Strange (d 1986); *b* 6 Feb 1934; *Educ* Bromley GS Kent, Christ's Coll Cambridge (MA, PhD, ScD); *m* 19 Dec 1959, Freda Nancy, da of Arthur Waithman (d 1973), of Bolton, Lancashire; 1 s (David b 1964), 1 da (Louise b 1963); *Career* Univ of Manchester Inst of Sci and Technol: lectr, sr lectr then reader in corrosion sci 1961–72, prof of corrosion sci and engrg 1972–, head of Corrosion Protection Centre 1972–82, vice princ Academic Devpt 1982–84, dep princ 1983, dean Faculty of Technol 1987–89, vice princ 1992–94, pro-vice chllr 1994–; pres Inst of Corrosion Sci Technol 1978–80, chm of Nat Cncl of Corrosion Soc 1986; chm Int Corrosion Cncl 1993–96 (vice chm 1988–93); FIM 1969, CEng, FEng 1990, FRSC 1969, CChem, FIMF 1972, FICorr 1968; *Awards* Sir George Beilby Medal 1973, U R Evans Award 1983, Carl Wagner Award 1983, Cavallaro Medal 1987, Hothersall Medal 1989; *Recreations* travel, cricket, walking; *Style—* Prof Graham Wood, FEng; ✉ 8 Amberley Close, Deane, Bolton, Lancashire BL3 4NJ (☎ 01204 63659); Corrosion and Protection Centre, University of Manchester Institute of Science and Technology (UMIST), PO Box 88, Sackville St, Manchester M60 1QD (☎ 0161 200 4851, fax 0161 200 4865, telex 666094)

WOOD, Prof Hamish Christopher Swan; CBE (1993); s of Joseph Wood (d 1958), of Hawick, Roxburghshire, and Robina Leggat, *née* Baptie (d 1959); *b* 8 May 1926; *Educ* Hawick HS, Univ of St Andrews (BSc, PhD); *m* 18 Dec 1951, Jean Dumbreck, da of George Mitchell (d 1995), of Hawick, Roxburghshire; 1 s (Colin Dumbreck b 16 Dec 1957), 1 da (Sheena Margaret (Mrs Walker) b 22 Feb 1953); *Career* lectr in chemistry Univ of St Andrews 1950–51, res fell Dept of Med Chemistry Aust Nat Univ 1951–53, reader in organic chemistry (also lectr and sr lectr) 1953–69; Univ of Strathclyde: prof of organic chemistry 1969–91, dep princ 1982–84, vice princ 1984–86, prof emeritus 1991–; chm Governing Body Glasgow Polytechnic 1987–93, chm Univ Ct Glasgow Caledonian Univ 1993–94; memb Universities Funding Cncl 1989–93; Hon DUniv Strathclyde 1992, Hon LLD Glasgow Caledonian Univ 1994; hon fell Scotvec 1993; FRSE 1968 (memb Cncl 1992–95), FRSC 1973, CChem 1973; *Style—* Prof Hamish Wood, CBE, FRSE; ✉ 26 Albert Drive, Bearsden, Glasgow G61 2PG (☎ 0141 942 4552); Department of Pure and Applied Chemistry, University of Strathclyde, Thomas Graham Building, 295 Cathedral St, Glasgow G1 1XL (☎ 0141 552 4400, fax 0141 552 5664, telex UNSLIB G)

WOOD, (John) Humphrey (Askey-); s of Lt-Col Edward Askey Wood, Leics Regt, and Irene Jeanne, *née* Parry; *b* 26 Nov 1932; *Educ* Winchester, CCC Cambridge (MA); *m* 1981, Katherine Ruth Stewart Reardon, da of Capt Horace Alan Peverley (d 1952), Canadian Grenadier Gds, of Wildwood, St Andrews East, Quebec Canada; 1 s from previous m (Jason b 1966), 1 step s (Alexander b 1965), 1 step da (Kate b 1968); *Career* De Havilland Aircraft Co Ltd 1956, Hawker Siddeley Aviation Ltd 1964 (dir and gen mangr Manchester 1969–76), md Industl and Marine Div Rolls-Royce Ltd 1976–79, chm Amey Roadstone Corp 1979–86, an md Consolidated Gold Fields plc 1979–89; non-exec chm: Vinten Group plc 1991–, Albrighton plc 1993–; dir: Gold Fields of South Africa Ltd 1986–89, Blue Tee Corp 1986–89; non-exec dir: Birse Group plc 1989–95, Albrighton plc 1990–93; Butten tstee PA Consulting Group 1991–; memb Cncl CBI 1983–89, vice pres Nat Cncl of Building Material Prodrs 1985–89; *Recreations* fly-fishing, sailing, painting; *Style—* Humphrey Wood, Esq; ✉ Albyn House, 239 New King's Rd, London SW6 4XG (☎ 0171 371 0042, fax 0171 736 2158)

WOOD, Sir Ian Clark; kt (1994), CBE (1982); s of John Wood (d 1986) and Margaret, *née* Clark (d 1981); *b* 21 July 1942; *Educ* Robert Gordon's Coll Aberdeen, Aberdeen Univ (BSc); *m* 1970, Helen, *née* Macrae; 3 s; *Career* chm and md John Wood Group plc, chm J W Holdings Ltd; awards: Grampian Industrialist of the Year, Young Scottish Businessman of the Year 1979, Scottish Free Enterprise 1985, Scottish Business Achievement Award Tst (jtly) 1992, Corporate Elite Leadership Award (Services) 1992, The Alick Buchanan-Smith Meml Award for Personal Achievement 1995; memb: Scottish Enterprise Bd, Bd Royal Bank of Scotland plc, Oil & Gas Projects & Supplies Office, Scottish Economic Cncl, Scottish HE Funding Cncl; jt chm Quincentenary Ctee Univ of Aberdeen; Hon LLD Aberdeen 1984; FRSA, CIMgt; *Recreations* squash, art, family; *Style—* Sir Ian Wood, CBE; ✉ Marchmont, 42 Rubislaw Den South, Aberdeen AB15 4BB (☎ 01224 313625); John Wood Group plc, John Wood House, Greenwell Rd, East Tullos, Aberdeen AB12 3AX (☎ 01224 851000, fax 01224 871997, telex 739977)

WOOD, James; *Educ* Univ of Cambridge (organ scholar), RAM; *Career* composer and conductor; prof of percussion Darmstadt Int Summer Courses 1982–94; fndr and dir: New London Chamber Choir, Centre for Microtonal Music London, Critical Band; conductor: BBC Symphony Orch, London Sinfonietta, Ensemble InterContemporain, l'Itinéraire, Netherlands Wind Ensemble, Percussion Group The Hague, Belgian Radio Philharmonic, Krakow Radio Orch, Tokyo Philharmonic Choir 1995–96, Netherlands Chamber Choir 1995–96; cmmns for: Arditti Quartet, the King's Singers, Electric Phoenix, Amadinda Percussion Group Budapest, Duo Contemporain, Robert Van Sice and BBC; cmmns BBC Proms: Oreion 1989 (conducted BBC Symphony Orch), Two men meet, each presuming the other to be from a distant planet (for Steven Schick and Critical Band) 1995; recordings incl: Stoicheia, Ho Shang Yao, Choroi Kai Thaliai, Rogosanti, Incantamenta, Two men meet, each presuming the other to be from a distant planet, Venancio Mbande talking with the trees, Phainomena; Gemini fellowship 1993, Arts Foundation Fellowship 1995/6, Holst Foundation Award; *Style—* James Wood, Esq; ✉ Bancroft, Rectory Lane, Fringford, Bicester, Oxon OX6 9DX

WOOD, James Alexander Douglas; s of Lt-Col Alexander Blythe Wood, TD, and Cynthia Mary, *née* Boot; *b* 25 June 1952; *Educ* Haileybury, Univ of Warwick (LLB); *m*; 2 s (Nathan b 1988, Tommy b 1990); *Career* called to the Bar Middle Temple 1975; memb: int mission of lawyers to Malaysia 1982, panel of inquiry into visit of Leon Brittan to Univ of Manchester Students Union in March 1985; involved for the defence in many civil rights cases incl: The Newham Seven, The Broad Water Farm Trials, The Miners Strike Trials, Birmingham Six Appeal; *Books* The Right of Silence, the Case for Retention (1989); *Recreations* parenting, gardening, the enhancement of civil liberties and the enforcement of civil rights; *Style—* James Wood, Esq; ✉ Doughty Street Chambers, 11 Doughty Street, London WC1N 2PG (☎ 0171 404 1313, fax 0171 404 2283)

WOOD, Jane Caroline; da of Duncan Patrick (d 1983), and Kathleen, *née* Smith (d 1959); *b* 17 Aug 1943; *Educ* Putney HS for Girls, Lucy Cavendish Coll Cambridge (MA); *m* 1, 1962 (m dis 1987), Christopher Wood; 1 da (Caroline b 1963), 2 s (Adam b 1965, Benjamin b 1966); m 2, 1996, Edward Russell-Walling; *Career* Secker & Warburg: asst to Barley Anderson 1982–83, ed 1983–85, exec ed 1985–87; ed dir Arrow Books 1987–90, ed dir MacMillan Ltd 1990–94, publishing dir Orion Books 1994–; *Recreations* reading, theatre, cinema, concerts, walking, skiing; *Clubs* Peg's; *Style—* Ms Jane Wood; ✉ Orion Books, Orion House, 5 Upper St Martin's Lane, London WC2H 9EA (☎ 0171 240 3444, fax 0171 379 6158)

WOOD, Dr Jane Diana Dudley; *b* 31 Aug 1937; *Career* conslt physician (care of the elderly) Glan Clywd Dist Gen Hosp; memb GMC 1994–; *Style—* Dr Jane Wood; ✉ Glan Clwyd District General Hospital, Rhyl, Clwyd LL18 5UJ (☎ 01745 583910)

WOOD, John; CB (1989); s of Maj Thomas John Wood, IA (d 1962), and Rebecca, *née* Grand (d 1990); *b* 11 Jan 1931; *Educ* King's Coll Sch Wimbledon, Law Soc Sch of Law; *m* 3 April 1958, Jean Iris, da of George Collier (d 1945), of London; 2 s (Simon b 1959, Nicholas b 1961); *Career* slr; dep dir Public Prosecutions 1985–87, dir Serious Fraud Office 1987–90, DPP Hong Kong 1990–94; conslt slr Denton Hall 1995; *Recreations* most sports, theatre, music; *Style—* John Wood, Esq, CB

WOOD, John Edward; OBE (1977); s of John Wood (d 1965), of Newcastle, Staffs, and Elsie, *née* Rose (d 1985); *b* 23 March 1924; *Educ* Wolstanton Co GS N Staffs, N Staffs Tech Coll (Dip in Mining Engrg), King's Coll Durham (BSc); *m* 9 Sept 1949, Valerie Joy, da of Frederick Heath Grindey; 2 s (Stephen John b 4 Oct 1954, Robert Geoffrey b 13 Dec 1959), 1 da (Helena Judith b 14 Sept 1952); *Career* underground coal miner and trainee mining engr 1940–50, various mgmnt posts rising to colliery mangr N Staffs 1951, mangr several collieries (incl E Midlands 1954) 1951–60; NCB: sr mgmnt posts at gp and area level 1960–71, area dir S Notts, Doncaster N Notts 1972–85; self-employed conslt mining engr 1985–96; awards: Futers Medal (IMinE) 1975, Lord Edward Cavendish Medal (Notts & N Derby Br Inst Mining Engrs) 1985; Freeman City of London 1979, former fndr memb Worshipful Co of Engrs; fell Inst of Mining Engrs 1940 (nat pres 1977), CEng 1970, FEng 1980, CIMgt, former pres Notts and N Derbyshire Branch Inst Mining Engrs; *Clubs* Freemason, St John; *Style—* John E Wood, Esq, OBE, FEng; ✉ 6 The Avenue, Mansfield, Nottinghamshire NG18 4PN (☎ 01623 23083)

WOOD, The Hon Sir John Kember; kt (1977), MC (1944); s of John Roskruge Wood; *b* 8 Aug 1922; *Educ* Shrewsbury, Magdalene Coll Cambridge; *m* 1952, Ann Lowe; 1 s, 1 da; *Career* WWII serv Rifle Bde 1941–46, ME and Italy (POW 1944); called to the Bar Lincoln's Inn 1949, bencher 1977; QC 1969, recorder Crown Ct 1975–77, judge Family Div High Ct 1977–93, pres Employment Appeals Tbnl 1988–93 (judge 1985–88); vice chm Parole Bd 1987–89 (memb 1986–89); *Style—* The Hon Sir John Wood, MC; ✉ 2 Lansdowne Road, Holland Park, London W11 3LW

WOOD, John Lockhart; JP, DL; s of George Lockhart Wood (d 1959), and Joan Wood, *née* Halsey; *b* 22 Aug 1935; *Educ* Eton, Trinity Coll Cambridge (MA); *m* 26 Oct 1963, (Rosemary) Sonia Despard, da of Richard Graham Hemsley Hopkins (d 1974); 1 s (Edmund b 1966), 1 da (Kirsty b 1968); *Career* Nat Serv 2 Lt 8 King's Royal Irish Hussars; McCorquodale plc: joined 1958, dir 1964–86, chief exec 1972–86, chm 1986; non-exec dir: Halifax Building Soc 1986– (vice chm 1991), Bibby Line Group Ltd 1987–, Domino Printing Sciences plc 1988–96; High Sheriff Hertfordshire 1988–89; *Recreations* gardening, fishing, travel; *Clubs* Cavalry and Guards'; *Style—* John Wood, Esq, JP, DL; ✉ The Hoo, Great Gaddesden, Hemel Hempstead, Herts HP2 6HD (☎ 01442 252689, fax 01442 233863)

WOOD, John Norris; s of Wilfrid Burton Wood, (d 1943) and Lucy Heald Sutcliffe Boston (d 1977); *b* 29 Nov 1930; *Educ* Bryanston Sch, Goldsmiths' Coll Sch of Art, E Anglian Sch of Painting & Design, RCA (Degree with Hons); *m* 12 June 1962, Julie Corsellis Guyatt, da of John Nicholls (d 1968); 1 s (Wilfrid Spencer Conal b 1968), 1 da (Dinah Elizabeth Georgia b 1971); *Career* artist and author; lectr in illustration Goldsmiths' Coll Sch of Art 1956–68, tutor Cambridge Coll of Art 1959–70; fndr scientific, tech, med illustration course at Hornsey Coll of Art 1965; fndr and i/c Natural History Illustration Unit and Ecological Studies Dept RCA 1971 (sr lectr to present day); regular Exhibits at RA Summer Exhibition; conslt to BBC Life on Earth; provided illustrations for: Time and Life, Knopf, Mathew Price Ltd, Longmans, BBC Publications, Post Office, Methuen, Penguins, Sunday Times and others; author and illustrator Hide and Seek (children's natural history book series, translated into 10 languages); memb Soc of Authors 1995, FRCA 1980; *Recreations* conservation, natural history, art, music; *Style—* John Norris Wood, Esq; ✉ The Brook, Dewhurst Lane, Wadhurst, E Sussex TN5 6QE; Royal Coll of Art, Dept Natural History and Ecological Studies, Stevens Building, Kensington Gore, London SW7

WOOD, John R; s of Maj-Gen and Mrs Harry S Wood; *b* 23 April 1945; *Educ* Cranbrook Sch Kent, RMA Sandhurst, Gonville and Caius Coll Cambridge (MA), RMCS Shrivenham (Div 1 Army Staff Course), RAF Advanced Staff Course Bracknell; *m* 23 Aug 1969, Gillian; 3 s (Nicholas b 23 Jan 1972, James b 15 May 1974, Edward b 12 April 1981); *Career* served gunner offr RA UK and Germany 1969–71, transferred REME 1972, various field appts REME UK and BAOR 1972–77, Army Staff Course 1978–79, various staff appts UK 1979–83, engrg support planning offr Challenger main battle tank 1983–86 (promoted Lt Col), staff offr grade 1 (Weapons) Automotive Trials cmdg Automotive Trials Wing Royal Armament R & D Estab Chertsey 1986–87, ret Army; tech dir and chief engr RAC Motoring Servs 1987–91, md Motor Industry Research Association (MIRA) 1991–; chm Sub Ctee on the Environment FIA 1989–91, chm Int Conf on Automotive Diagnostics 1990, chm IMechE Seminar on Impact of Regulations on Diesel Emissions 1990, memb Automotive Electronics Conf Planning Panels 1987, 1989 and 1991, memb Tech Ctee FISITA 1992, chm Third Autosports Int Tech Congress 1993, chm Automobile Div Bd IMechE 1993 (memb 1985, vice chm 1992), memb Cncl and Communications Bd IMechE 1993, chm Tech Advsy Panel RAC Motor Sports Assoc 1995–, memb Motor Sports Cncl 1995–, memb Senate Engrg Cncl 1996–; memb Cncl: FISITA 1994–, SMMT 1995–; CEng 1975, FIMechE 1989 (MIMechE 1975) FIMI, MSAE; *Papers and Publications* The Development of Automotive Diagnostic Systems for Armoured Fighting Vehicles in the British Army (IMechE Conf, 1985), Engineering for the Customer - Development and the Future (IMechE Proceedings Vol 207, 1993), The Response of Development Engineers to Future Needs (1993), The Development of the Speed Hill-Climb Car (IMechE Proceedings Vol 208, 1994); *Recreations* motor racing, shooting; *Style—* John Wood, Esq; ✉ MIRA, Watling Street, Nuneaton, Warwickshire CV10 0TU (☎ 01203 355344, fax 01203 355345)

WOOD, Leonard George; CBE (1978); s of Leonard George Wood (d 1955), and Miriam *née* Barnes (d 1924); *Educ* Bishopshalt Sch Hillingdon Middx, Univ of London (BCom); *m* 12 Sept 1936, Christine Florence (d 1978), da of William Cooper Reason (d 1935); *Career* Sgt RAF 1943, Flying Offr RAF 1944–46; exec dir Parent Bd EMI Ltd (now EMI Music plc) 1965–80, gp dir records and music EMI Ltd 1966–77, asst md EMI Ltd 1973–77; chm: EMI Records UK Ltd 1966–78 (md 1959–66), EMI Music Publishing Ltd 1972–78; dep chm Phonographic Performance Ltd 1967–80; chm: Cncl of IFPI 1968–73, BPI 1972–80 (hon pres 1980–), Record Merchandisers Ltd 1975–80; vice pres and memb Bd of Int Fedn of Prodrs of Phonograms and Videograms (IFPI) 1967–82 (pres and chm of Bd 1973–76), tstee Br Record Industs Tst 1989–94; *Recreations* gardening, music; *Style—* Leonard Wood, Esq, CBE; ✉ Lark Rise, 39 Howards Thicket Gerrards Cross, Buckinghamshire SL9 7NT (☎ 01753 884233); BPI Ltd, 25 Savile Row, London W1X 1AA (☎ 0171 287 2252)

WOOD, Mark William; s of Joseph Hatton Drew Wood, of Rainham, Kent; *b* 28 March 1952; *Educ* Gillingham GS, Univ of Leeds (BA), Univ of Warwick (MA), Univ of Oxford (CertEd); *m* 29 Dec 1986, Helen, da of Peter Frederick Lanzer, of Brussels; 1 da (Phoebe Elizabeth b 1989), 1 s (Rupert William Caspar b 1991); *Career* Reuters: joined 1976, corr Vienna 1977–78, corr E Berlin 1978–81, corr Moscow 1981–85, chief corr W Germany 1985–87, Euro ed 1987–89, ed-in-chief 1989–, exec dir 1990–96; chm Visnews Reuters Television 1992–; non-exec dir ITN 1993–; *Recreations* German literature, skiing; *Style—* Mark Wood, Esq; ✉ Reuters, 85 Fleet St, London EC4P 4AJ (☎ 0171 542 7900, fax 0171 542 5311)

WOOD, Rt Rev Maurice Arthur Ponsonby; DSC (1944); s of Arthur Wood, and Jane Elspeth Dalzell, *née* Piper; *b* 26 Aug 1916; *Educ* Monkton Combe Sch, Queens' Coll Cambridge (MA), Ridley Hall Cambridge; *m* 1, 1947, Marjorie, *née* Pennell (d 1954); 2 s, 1 da; m 2, 1955, Margaret, da of Rev E J Sandford, MC; 2 s, 1 da; *Career* ordained St Paul's Cathedral: deacon 1940, priest 1941; chaplain RN and Royal Marine Commandos 1943–46; hon chaplain Commando Assoc 1950–; rector St Ebbe's Oxford 1947–52, vicar and rural dean Islington 1952–61, princ Oak Hill Coll Southgate 1961–71, prebendary St Paul's Cathedral 1969–71, 69th bishop of Norwich 1971–85 (memb House of Lords

1975–85); hon asst bishop: Diocese of London 1985–, Diocese of Oxford 1988–94; chm Order of Christian Unity 1986–95 (pres 1995–), sponsor Christians in Sport 1988–; visitor: Langley Sch 1975–85, Luckley Oakfield Sch 1990–; govr Monkton Combe Sch; hon Freeman Worshipful Co of Weavers 1993– (Chaplain 1986–93); *Books* Like a Mighty Army (1954), Your Suffering (1956), Comfort in Sorrow (1957), Christian Stability (1972), Into the Way of Peace (1982), This is Our Faith (1985); *Clubs* Royal Cwlth Soc; *Style*— The Rt Rev Maurice A P Wood; ✉ Abbot's Cottage, Upper Street, Horning, Norwich, Norfolk NR12 8NE (☎ 01692 630908); 41 Fir Tree Walk, Enfield, London EN1 3TZ (☎ 0181 363 4491)

WOOD, Nicholas Andrew; s of Charles Stephen Wood, (d 1965), and Celia Patty Wood, *née* Underwood (d 1959); *b* 31 Jan 1943; *Educ* Lewes Co GS, Queen Elizabeth Sch Crediton; *m* 8 July 1972, Mary Kristina, da of Donald Bernard Naulin, of Williamsburg, Virginia; 2 da (Olivia Marian Vicary b 17 Oct 1984, Genevieve Anna Cordelia b 11 Oct 1987); *Career* called to the Bar Inner Temple 1970, bencher of the Inner Temple 1990; recorder 1993– (asst recorder 1987–93); Ordnance Survey 1960–61, Meridian Airmaps Ltd 1961–62, commercial artist, designer, copywriter 1962–67; *Recreations* people, places, art, music, transport; *Style*— Nicholas Wood, Esq; ✉ 5 Paper Buildings, Temple, London EC4Y 7HB (☎ 0171 583 9275, fax 0171 583 1926/2031)

WOOD, Nicholas Peter; s of Robin Wilfrid Jerrard Wood CBE, of Ilkley, W Yorks, and Anne, *née* Marlor; *b* 26 June 1956; *Educ* Sedbergh; *m* 1 Nov 1986, Adrienne Felicity, da of June Rosemary Tebbs; 1 s (Benjamin Thomas Scott b 11 June 1988), 1 da (Emma Louise Alice b 2 Feb 1990); *Career* regnl admin trainee Leeds Area Health Authy 1975–78, asst administrator Salisbury Gen Infirmary 1978–80, dep administrator Scunthorpe Gen Hosp 1980–83, administrator King George Hosp 1983–85, actg unit administrator Acute Servs Redbridge Health Authy 1985–86, dir of operational servs Bart's Hosp London 1986–88, unit gen mangr Hackney 1988–90 (dep gen mangr 1988), gen mangr clinical servs City and Hackney Provider Unit 1990–92, chief exec E Cheshire NHS Trust 1992–; IHSM: dist rep and preceptor for IHSM students 1986–91, chm NE Thames Regnl Cncl 1990–92; chm NW Region Mgmnt Trg Scheme Advsy Gp 1994–; AHSM 1985; *Recreations* sailing, golf, skiing, tennis, rugby, stamp collecting; *Clubs* Tytherington Golf, Ski Club of GB; *Style*— Nicholas Wood, Esq; ✉ East Cheshire NHS Trust, Trust Headquarters, Victoria Road, Macclesfield, Cheshire SK10 3BL (☎ 01625 661501, fax 01625 661644)

WOOD, (John) Peter; s of Walter Ralph Wood (d 1967), and Henrietta, *née* Martin (d 1944); *b* 27 March 1925; *Educ* Grove Park GS Wrexham, Seale Hayne Agric Coll Newton Abbott, Royal Horticultural Soc Wisley; *m* 1956, Susan Maye, da of Brig Lesley White (d 1971); 1 s (David), 1 da (Victoria); *Career* ed Amateur Gardening 1971–85, conslt ed 1985–89, freelance gardening journalist and broadcaster 1989–; ed The Rose 1986–; NDH, FIHort; *Recreations* choral singing, gardening; *Style*— Peter Wood, Esq; ✉ 1 Charlton House Court, Charlton Marshall, Blandford Forum, Dorset (☎ and fax 01258 454653)

WOOD, (John) Peter; s of late John Wood, and Louisa, *née* Herrington; *b* 18 June 1933; *Educ* Bradford GS, Univ of Durham (BSc); *m* 28 March 1958, Valerie, da of late William Spencer; 1 s (John b 1965), 1 da (Fiona b 1963); *Career* Nat Serv; J Bibby & Sons plc: md Palethorpes Ltd 1971–76, gen mangr Feeds and Seeds Div 1976–79, md Agricultural Gp 1979–84, chief exec 1984–89; chm Heart of England Building Society 1992–93 (dir 1990–93), dir Cheltenham & Gloucester Building Society 1993–; CIMgt; *Clubs* Oriental; *Style*— Peter Wood, Esq

WOOD, Prof Philip Henry Nicholls; s of Herbert Wood (d 1969), of Sheffield, and Frances Amelia, *née* Nicholls (d 1961); *b* 23 Oct 1928; *Educ* Churcher's Coll Petersfield, Bart's Med Coll, Univ of London (MB BS); *m* 30 July 1952, Cherry Norma, da of Norman Charlish (d 1928), of Brighton; 4 da (Julia b 1956, Vyvyan b 1958, Eleanor b 1959, Beatrix b 1965); *Career* Nat Serv chief clerk Mil Hosp York RAMC 1947–49; res asst prof of med State Univ of NY at Buffalo USA 1963–65; Univ of Manchester: sr res fell Rheumatism Res Centre 1965–67, dir Arthritis and Rheumatism Cncl Epidemiology Res Unit Med Sch 1968–88 (emeritus dir 1989), hon lectr Dept of Community Med 1968–77, hon reader 1977–83, hon prof 1983–89; conslt to WHO 1971–; memb Scientific Ctees Arthritis and Rheumatism Cncl 1971–89, hon memb Euro League Against Rheumatism (former ed), scientific advsr to chief scientist DHSS 1977–87, memb ctees various rheumatological and epidemiological learned socs; FFCM 1972, FRCP 1978 (memb 1971), FFPHM 1989; *Books* Salicylates, An International Symposium (ed 1963), Population Studies of the Rheumatic Diseases (ed, 1968), International Classification of Impairments, Disabilities and Handicaps (1980), Oxford Textbooks of Public Health (contrib, 1984), Geriatric Medicine (contrib, 1992); *Recreations* oil and water-colour painting, listening to music, English lit, local history studies; *Clubs* RSM; *Style*— Prof Philip Wood; ✉ Bephillick, Duloe, nr Liskeard, Cornwall PL14 4QA (☎ 01503 264635)

WOOD, Robert Wilson; s of Peter Wilson Wood, of Whitburn, Lothian, and Elizabeth Christie, *née* Campbell; *b* 18 Oct 1948; *Educ* Bathgate Acad, Univ of Strathclyde (BSc, Dip Mgmnt); *m* 6 Aug 1971, Mary Davidson, da of James Stewart Armadale (d 1962), of Lothian; 1 s (Alastair b 5 July 1982), 1 da (Lorna b 16 May 1979); *Career* gen mangr Volvo Trucks GB Ltd 1976–80, sales and serv dir Peugeot-Talbot Motor Co 1980–83, md Motor Div Godfrey Davis Holdings plc 1983–85, gp chief exec Henlys Ltd 1985–91, chief exec Henlys Group plc 1991–; vice chm Elstree and Borehamwood MENCAP, tstee The Devpt Tst for the Mentally Handicapped; FIMgt 1984, FInstD 1985, FIMI 1986; *Recreations* gardening, family; *Style*— Robert Wood, Esq; ✉ Henlys Group plc, 1 Imperial Place, Elstree Way, Borehamwood, Herts WD6 1JJ (☎ 0181 953 9953)

WOOD, Roderic Lionel James; QC (1993); s of Lionel James Wood (d 1969), and Marjorie, *née* Thompson; *b* 8 March 1951; *Educ* Nottingham HS, Lincoln Coll Oxford (MA jurisp); *Career* called to the Bar Middle Temple 1974; asst recorder 1994; memb: Family Law Bar Assoc 1988–, Supreme Ct Procedure Ctee 1990–, Bar Cncl 1993–, Professional Conduct Ctee of the Bar 1993–, Legal Aid and Fees Ctee 1995–, Supreme Court Users Group 1995–; jt chm Barristers Clerks Liaison Ctee 1994–95; memb Editorial Bd Longman Practitioner's Child Law Bulletin 1993–94; *Recreations* music, theatre, travel; *Style*— Roderic Wood, Esq, QC; ✉ 1 King's Bench Walk, Inner Temple, London EC4Y 7DB (☎ 0171 583 6266, fax 0171 583 2068)

WOOD, Roger Norman Alexander; s of Adrian Theodore Wood (d 1992), of Bristol, and Doreen Mary, *née* Gordon-Harris; *b* 13 Sept 1947; *Educ* The Leys Sch Cambridge, Univ of Bristol (BSc); *m* 1971, Mary Thomasine Howard, da of Howard Reginald Thomas; 1 s (Alexander b 1973), 2 da (Emily b 1975, Joanna b 1976); *Career* Guthrie Corp Ltd 1972–81, United City Merchants plc 1981–86, Burmah Castrol plc 1986–91, George Wimpey plc 1991–94, fin dir Automotive Products Group Ltd 1995–; FCA; *Clubs* Oriental, West Hill Golf, Tanglin, Sereban Int Golf; *Style*— Roger Wood, Esq; ✉ High Leybourne, Hascombe, Godalming, Surrey GU8 4AD (☎ 01483 208559)

WOOD, Prof Ronald Karslake Starr; s of Percival Thomas Evans Wood (d 1979), of Ferndale, and Florence Dix, *née* Starr (d 1989); *b* 8 April 1919; *Educ* Ferndale GS, Imperial Coll London (BSc, ARCSc, DIC, PhD); *m* 15 Dec 1947, Marjorie, da of Frank Schofield (d 1981), of Alnwick; 1 s (Richard Piers Karkslake b 1952), 1 da (Jessica Laura Anne b 1955); *Career* Imperial Coll London: lectr 1946, reader 1954, prof 1964; Cwlth Fund fell 1950, research fell Connecticut Exp Station 1957; hon fell: American Phytopathological Soc, Deutsche Phytomedizinische Gesellschaft; Otto Appel Denkmunze German Fed Repub, pres and first hon memb Int Soc for Plant Pathology, pres and second hon memb Br Soc for Plant Pathology, ed 6 books on plant pathology; memb governing bodies: Imperial Coll, East Malling Res Station, Inst of Horticultural Res; chm Biological Cncl, vice pres Inst of Biology; hon pres 7th Int Conference on Plant Pathology 1998; FRS 1976; *Books* Physiological Plant Pathology (1967); *Recreations* gardening; *Style*— Prof Ronald Wood, FRS; ✉ Pyrford Woods, Pyrford, Surrey GU22 8QL (☎ 01932 343827); Imperial College, London SW7 2BB (☎ 0171 589 5111, fax 0171 584 2056)

WOOD, Ronald (Ronnie); *b* 1 June 1947; *m* 1; 1 s (Jesse); *m* 2, 2 Jan 1985, Jo Howard; 1 s (Tyrone b 1983), 1 da (Leah b 1978); *Career* guitarist; played: bass guitar in The Jeff Beck Group 1968–69, guitar in The Faces 1969–75, The Rolling Stones 1975–; has played with: Bo Diddley (toured as The Gunslingers), Rod Stewart (with The Faces), Muddy Waters, Jerry Lee Lewis and others; albums with Jeff Beck Gp: Truth (1968), Beck-Ola (1969, reached UK no 39); albums with The Faces: First Step (1970, UK no 45), Long Player (1971, UK no 31), A Nod's As Good As A Wink...To A Blind Horse (1971, UK no 2), Ooh La La (1973, UK no 1), Coast To Coast Overtures And Beginners (live, 1974, UK no 3); signed solo record contract with CBS Records 1978; albums with The Rolling Stones: Black And Blue (1976, UK no 2), Love You Live (live, 1977, UK no 3), Some Girls (1978, UK no 2), Emotional Rescue (1980, UK no 1), Tattoo You (1981, UK no 2), Still Life (American Concert 1981) (1982, UK no 4), Undercover (1983, UK no 3), Rewind 1971–1984 (compilation, 1984, UK no 23), Dirty Work (1986, UK no 4), Steel Wheels (1989, UK no 2), Flashpoint (live, 1991, UK no 6), Voodoo Lounge (1994, UK no 1); solo albums inc: Slide On This (1992); concert films: Let's Spend the Night Together (dir Hal Ashby) 1983, Flashpoint (film of 1991 Steel Wheels Tour) 1991; *Style*— Ronnie Wood, Esq; ✉ c/o Marathon Music, 5 Church Row, Wandsworth Plain, London SW18 1ES

WOOD, Simon Richard Browne; s of Lt-Col Browne William Wood, of The Grange, Tadcaster, N Yorks, and Joan Radegunde, *née* Woollcombe; *b* 12 Dec 1947; *Educ* Eton; *m* 17 July 1970, Clare Launa, da of Lord Martin Fitzalan Howard, *qv* (bro 17 Duke of Norfolk), of Brockfield Hall, York; 1 s (Charles b 1973), 2 da (Alethea b 1975, Miranda b 1978); *Career* ptnr Sheppards and Chase 1975–80, dir Cater Allen Holdings plc 1981–, currently md Cater Allen Ltd; *Recreations* shooting, fishing; *Style*— Simon R B Wood, Esq; ✉ Brockfield Farmhouse, Warthill, York YO3 9XJ (☎ 01904 489362); Cater Allen Holdings plc, 20 Birchin Lane, London EC3V 9DJ (☎ 0171 623 2070, fax 0171 929 1641, telex 888553)

WOOD, Steve; s of Henry James Wood (d 1989), of Southampton, and Irene Rhoda, *née* Stare; *b* 8 March 1946; *Educ* St Nicholas' New Forest, Southampton Art Coll (NDD); *m* 12 May 1984, Sally Karen Jameson; 1 s (James David b 27 Feb 1991), 2 da (Laura Juliet b 12 March 1987, Natalie Lucy b 21 May 1988); *Career* photographer specializing in portraits of Royal Family since 1966 and fashion photographer; Photographer of the Year Br Press Awards 1992 (3 times runner-up); *Style*— Steve Wood, Esq

WOOD, Dr Susan Marion; da of Gerald Colomba Ryan (d 1986), of Guildford, Surrey, and Marion Audrey, *née* Webb (d 1984); *b* 20 July 1952; *Educ* Tormead Sch Guildford, King's Coll London (BSc), St Bartholomew's Hosp London (MB BS), Hammersmith Hosp (MD); *m* 30 Jan 1978, Dr John Roland Wood, s of Roland Wood; *Career* sr med offr Medicines Div DHSS 1983–87; princ med offr: Review of Medicines the Medicines Control Agency Dept of Health 1987, Drug Safety Unit Medicines Control Agency Dept of Health 1987–90; head Pharmacovigilance Unit Medicines Control Agency 1990–; author of pubns on endocrinology and adverse drug effects; UK rep of Safety and Pharmacovigilance Working Parties of Ctee on Proprietary Medicinal Products of EEC Brussels 1985–88 and 1988–, memb Advsy Gp of WHO Collaborate Centre for Adverse Drug Reaction Monitoring 1988–; FRSM, memb Br Pharmacological Soc; *Recreations* travel, oriental cuisine; *Style*— Dr Susan Wood; ✉ Medicines Control Agency, Dept of Health, Market Towers, 1 Nine Elms Lane, London SW8 (☎ 0171 273 0400, fax 0171 273 0675)

WOOD, Terence Courtney; CMG (1989); s of Courtney John Wood (d 1962), of Chelmsford, and Alice Lucretia, *née* Spall (d 1978); *b* 6 Sept 1936; *Educ* King Edward VI Sch Chelmsford, Trinity Coll Cambridge (BA); *m* 1, 1962, Kathleen Mary, *née* Jones; 1 s (Sebastian Courtney b 1965), 1 da (Claudia Harriet b 1969); *m* 2, 1982, Diana Humphreys-Roberts; *Career* Nat Serv RA 1955–57; joined HM Diplomatic Serv 1968, first sec FCO 1968–69, Embassy Rome 1969–73, FCO 1973–77, Sr Offrs' War Course Greenwich RNC 1977, cnsllr High Cmmn New Delhi 1977–81, political advsr Br Military Govt Berlin 1981–84, head S Asia Dept FCO 1984–86, visiting fell Center for Int Affairs Harvard Univ 1986–87, min Embassy Rome 1987–92, ambass to Vienna 1992–96, ret; *Recreations* painting, music; *Clubs* Travellers'; *Style*— Terence Wood, Esq, CMG; ✉ c/o Foreign & Commonwealth Office, King Charles Street, London SW1A 2AH

WOOD, Timothy John Rogerson; MP (C) Stevenage (majority 4,888); *b* 13 Aug 1940; *Educ* King James's GS Knaresborough Yorks, Univ of Manchester; *m* 1969, Elizabeth Mary Spencer; 1 s, 1 da; *Career* former project mangr ICL Ltd, MP (C) Stevenage 1983–; PPS to: Rt Hon John Stanley as Min for Armed Forces 1986–87, Min of State for NI 1987–88, Rt Hon Ian Stewart as Min of State for NI 1988–89, Rt Hon Peter Brooke as Sec of State for NI 1989–90; asst Govt whip 1990–92, Lord Cmmr of the Treasury (Govt whip) 1992–95; comptroller HM's Household 1995–; memb Bow Gp 1962–, chm Wokingham Cons Assoc 1980–83, vice chm Thames Valley Euro Constituency Cncl 1979–83; memb: Bracknell Dist Cncl 1975–83 (ldr 1976–78), Bracknell Devpt Corpn 1977–82; *Publications* Bow Gp pamphlets on educn, computers in Britain and the Post Office; *Style*— Timothy Wood, Esq, MP; ✉ House of Commons, London SW1A 0AA

WOOD, (René) Victor; s of Frederick Wood (d 1973); *b* 4 Oct 1925; *Educ* Jesus Coll Oxford; *m* 1950, Helen Morag, *née* Stewart; *Career* chief exec Hill Samuel Insurance and Shipping Holdings Ltd 1969–79 (and chm 1974–79), chm Lifeguard Assurance 1976–84; dir: Haslemere Estates plc 1976–86, Coalite Group plc 1977–89, Colbourne Insurance Co Ltd 1980–90, Wemyss Development Co Ltd 1982–, Criterion Insurance Co Ltd 1984–90, Scottinvest SA 1985–95, Wemyss Hotels France SA 1985–95, Domaine de Rimauresq SARL 1985–, Sun Life Corporation plc 1986–95, Worldwide and General Investment Company 1992–; vice pres Br Insur Brokers' Assoc 1981–84; *Books* (all jtly with Michael Pilch): Pension Schemes (1960 and 1979), New Trends in Pensions (1964), Pension Scheme Practice (1967), Company Pension Schemes (1971), Managing Pension Schemes (1974); *Style*— Victor Wood, Esq; ✉ Little Woodbury, Newchapel, nr Lingfield, Surrey RH7 6HR (☎ 01342 832054)

WOOD, Victoria; da of Stanley Wood, of Bury, Lancs, and Helen, *née* Mape; *b* 19 May 1953; *Educ* Bury GS, Univ of Birmingham (BA, Drama and Theatre Arts); *m* 1980, Geoffrey Durham; 1 da (Grace b 1988), 1 s (Henry b 1992); *Career* entertainer and writer; stage debut Talent at Crucible Theatre Sheffield 1978 (TV prodn of this won 3 Nat Drama Awards 1980), wrote stage musical Good Fun 1980; TV plays: Talent 1979, Nearly A Happy Ending 1980, Happy Since I Met You 1981, Pat and Margaret 1994; writer/performer TV series: Wood and Walters 1981–82, Victoria Wood As Seen on TV 1985 (Broadcasting Press Guilds Award, BAFTA Award), 2nd series 1986 (BAFTA Award), special 1987 (BAFTA Award), An Audience with Victoria Wood 1988 (BAFTA Award), Victoria Wood 1989, Victoria Wood's All Day Breakfast 1993 (Writer's Guild Award), Victoria Wood Live in Your Own Home 1994; stage revues: Funny Turns (Duchess) 1982, Lucky Bag (Ambassadors) 1985, Victoria Wood (Palladium) 1987, Victora Wood Up West 1990, Victoria Wood (Royal Albert Hall) 1996; Variety Club BBC Personality of the Year 1987, Br Comedy Award for Top Female Comedy Performer 1995; Hon DLitt: Lancaster 1989, Sunderland 1993, Bolton 1995, Birmingham

1996; *Books* Lucky Bag: The Victoria Wood Song Book (1985), Up To You Porky: The Victoria Wood Sketch Book (1986), Barmy: The 2nd Victoria Wood Sketch Book (1987), Mens Sana in Thingummy Doo-Dah (1990), Pat and Margaret (1994), Victoria Wood Live in Your Own Front Room (1994); *Recreations* walking, talking; *Style*— Miss Victoria Wood; ✉ c/o The Richard Stone Partnership, 25 Whitehall, London SW1A 2BS (☎ 0171 839 6421, fax 0171 839 5002)

WOOD, Rt Rev Dr Wilfred Deniston; *see:* Croydon, Bishop of

WOOD, William Jeremy (Jerry); s of Maj Peter Alexander Wood, RA, of Budleigh Salterton, Devon, and Gwendoline Marion, *née* Hebron; *b* 2 June 1947; *Educ* Liverpool Coll, Univ of Manchester (BSc); *m* 17 March 1973, Judienne, da of Anthony Bridgett, of London; 1 da (Alexis (Lekki) b 1981); *Career* Euro prod mktg mangr Avon Overseas Ltd 1973–79, conslt PE Consulting Group 1979–82, Euro strategic mktg dir Schering Plough Corporation 1983–85, bd dir Lowe Bell Financial Ltd 1986–, md First Financial 1996–; *Recreations* golf, skiing, travel; *Clubs* RAC; *Style*— Jerry Wood, Esq; ✉ Lowe Bell Financial Ltd, 1 Red Lion Court, London EC4A 3HE (☎ 0171 353 9203, fax 0171 353 6777)

WOOD, William Walker (Willie); MBE (1992); s of William Edward Wood (d 1981), of Gifford, and Jennie Aitken, *née* Bisset (d 1993); *b* 26 April 1938; *Educ* Knox Acad; *m* 12 Aug 1967, Morag Christie, da of John Turnbull (d 1976), of Garvald; 1 s (Colin b 1972), 1 da (Sylvia b 1968); *Career* Nat Serv craftsman REME 1956–59; bowler: Singles Gold medallist: SA Games 1973, Cwlth Games 1982; Singles winner Aust Mazda Tournament 1983; World Championships: Silver and Gold medal team winner 1984, Singles Silver and Triples Silver winner 1988; Singles runner-up Embassy World Indoor Championships 1989, Woolwich Scottish Masters champion 1990 and 1995, Gold medal fours Cwlth Games 1990, Midland Bank World Pairs runner-up 1991; World Championships: Gold medal fours, Gold medal team winner, Bronze medal triples; Scottish internationalist for 28 years, Gifford Club champion 18 times; memb E Lothian Team 1956–; memb Scottish Bowling Team: Outdoors 1966–, Indoors 1972–; *Recreations* bowls; *Clubs* Gifford Bowling, E Lothian Indoor Bowling; *Style*— Willie Wood, Esq, MBE; ✉ Willie Wood's Garage, 2 Tyne Close, Haddington, E Lothian (☎ 0162 0182 3579)

WOODALL, David; s of Walker Woodall (d 1960), of Knottingley, and Maud, *née* Robinson (d 1966); *b* 15 April 1950; *Educ* Batley HS, Wakefield Sch of Art, Dip in Advtg; *Career* formerly: illustrator Sharps Bradford, dir own co Scarborough, art dir Saatchi and Saatchi; currently a creative dir J Walter Thompson; winner: 2 Silvers Cannes Film Festival, 2 Silvers Br TV Awards, 3 Silvers D&AD Br Poster Awards, 2 Silvers Creative Circle Awards, 1 Silver and 1 Gold Euro Awards, Irish Film Festival Grand Prix Award, 1 Silver (and 1 nomination) D&AD; memb D&AD; *Recreations* windsurfing, running, painting; *Clubs* Barbican, Mortons; *Style*— David Woodall, Esq; ✉ J Walter Thompson, 40 Berkeley Square, London W1X 6AD (☎ 0171 499 4040, fax 0171 493 8432)

WOODALL, Pamela Diane; da of Ronald Albert Woodall, and Margaret, *née* Williams (d 1989); *b* 21 June 1954; *Educ* Solihull HS for Girls, Univ of Manchester (BA), LSE (MSc); *Career* Govt Econ Serv 1975–79, head of statistics The Economist 1979–83, economist Bank of America 1983–85, economics ed The Economist 1993– (economics corr 1985–93); *Recreations* skiing, squash, gardening; *Style*— Ms Pamela Woodall; ✉ The Economist, 25 St James's St, London SW1A 1HG (☎ 0171 830 7050)

WOODARD, Rear Adm Sir Robert Nathaniel; KCVO (1995); s of Francis Alwyne Woodard (d 1974), and Catherine Mary, *née* Hayes; *b* 13 Jan 1939; *Educ* Lancing; *m* 20 July 1963, Rosamund Lucia, da of Lt-Col Denis Lucius Alban Gibbs, DSO and Bar (d 1984), and Lady Hilaria Agnes, *née* Edgcumbe; 2 s (Rupert b 1964, Jolyon b 1969), 1 da (Melissa b 1967); *Career* aviator 1958–75; served carriers: Bulwark, Ark Royal, Eagle, Victorious; cmd: 771 and 848 Naval Air Sqdn (Lt-Cdr), HMS Amazon 1978–80 (Cdr), HMS Glasgow 1983–85 (Capt), HMS Osprey 1985–86; Cdre Clyde 1988–90, Flag Offr Royal Yachts 1990–95; Extra Equerry to HM The Queen 1992–; dir Woodard Schs (Western Div) 1985–; govr: King's Taunton Sch, King's Hall Sch, Bolitho Sch; vice pres RNA (Falmouth Branch), pres SSAF/FHS for Cornwall 1995–, chm Nat Tst (Devon and Cornwall) 1996–; Yr Bro Trinity House 1994–, memb Order of St John Ctee (Cornwall); FIMgt 1978, MInstD 1995; *Recreations* painting, shooting, fishing and village cricket; *Clubs* Royal Yacht Sqdn, Royal Cornwall Yacht, Naval and Military, Port Navas Yacht; *Style*— Rear Adm Sir Robert Woodard, KCVO; ✉ Restormel Manor, Lostwithiel, Cornwall PL22 0HN

WOODBERRY, (Graham) George John; adopted; *b* 21 Sept 1938; *Educ* secdy modern sch; *m* 1962, Sheilagh Moira Eblis; 1 s (David b 1969), 2 da (Lynn, Jane); *Career* RN Submarines 1952–65; dir Securicor International 1981–95 (conslt 1995–); *Style*— George Woodberry, Esq; ✉ 20 Sydenham Road, Croydon, Surrey; c/o Securicor International, Sutton Park House, Carlshalton Rd, Sutton, Surrey (☎ 0181 770 7000)

WOODBINE PARISH, Sir David Elmer; kt (1980), CBE (1964); s of Walter Woodbine Parish (d 1952), and Audrey, *née* Makins; *b* 29 June 1911; *Educ* Eton, Lausanne Switzerland; *m* 1939, Mona Blair McGarel (d 1991), da of Charles McGarel Johnston (d 1918), of Glynn, Co Antrim; 2 da (Vanessa b 1941, Miranda b 1944); *Career* industl conslt; dep chm Marine & General Mutual Life Assur Soc 1976–86; chm: St Thomas's Hosp Med Sch 1970–82, City and Guilds of London Inst 1967–78 (life vice pres 1979), Bovis Ltd 1959–66, Sussex Area Royal Sch Church Music, Florence Nightingale Museum Tst 1981–86; memb Bd of Govrs Clothworkers Fndn 1977–; memb Ct of Assts Worshipful Co of Clothworkers (Master 1974–75); memb Ct Russia Co 1937–85, fell Imperial Coll; Hon FCGI, Hon LLD Leeds 1975; CIMgt, FRSA; *Recreations* gardening, music; *Clubs* Boodle's; *Style*— Sir David Woodbine Parish, CBE; ✉ The Glebe Barn, Pulborough, W Sussex RH20 2AF (☎ 01798 872613)

WOODBRIDGE, Anthony Rivers; s of John Nicholas Woodbridge (d 1991), of Gerrards Cross, Bucks, and Patricia Madeleine, *née* Rebbeck (d 1996); *b* 10 Aug 1942; *Educ* Stowe, Trinity Hall Cambridge (MA); *m* 29 Sept 1976, Lynda Anne, da of Charles Henry Nolan (d 1992), of Stouffville, Ontario, Canada; 1 s (Christian b 30 March 1978); *Career* admitted slr 1967; ptnr Woodbridge & Sons Uxbridge 1969, sr ptnr Turberville Woodbridge Uxbridge 1983–; co sec: Abbeyfield Uxbridge Soc Ltd 1974–96, Burr Brown International Ltd 1992–; admin Uxbridge Duty Slr Scheme 1983–91, clerk Cmmrs Income Tax 1985–; chm of govrs Fulmer Sch Bucks 1988–96, memb Hillingdon Health Authy 1990–92; chm: Hillingdon Community Health NHS Tst 1992–94, Harrow and Hillingdon Healthcare NHS Tst 1994–; hon slr Age Concern Hillingdon 1989–, tstee Hillingdon Partnership Tst 1995–; memb Ct Brunel Univ 1995–; memb Law Soc 1967; *Recreations* walking, cycling, touring; *Clubs* Denham Golf; *Style*— Anthony Woodbridge, Esq; ✉ Cadogan House, 39 North Park, Gerrards Cross, Bucks SL9 8JL (☎ 01753 885442); 122 High St, Uxbridge, Middx UB8 1JT (☎ 01895 259871, fax 01895 258649)

WOODBRIDGE, Robert James; s of Bernard Woodbridge, of Norfolk, and Edith Ellen, *née* Holloway; *b* 2 Dec 1945; *Educ* Ealing GS, Univ of Liverpool (BA); *m* 31 July 1975, Gillian Margaret, da of Harold Morris; 1 s (Daniel b 19 Oct 1976), 1 da (Alice b 27 Oct 1978); *Career* merchant banker; Arthur Andersen & Co 1967–71, credit analyst Chase Manhattan Bank NA 1971–72, vice pres Merrill Lynch International Bank Ltd 1972–77, investor/fin advsr 1977–83, md Houston Financial Services 1983–85, exec vice pres Riggs National Bank of Washington DC 1985–91, md Riggs AP Bank 1989–91; chm: Riggs Valmet SA (Geneva) 1989–92, Riggs Bank Europe SA (France) 1990–92; conslt Policy Economics Gp E Europe SCS Holdings SA 1993–; FCA; *Recreations* skiing, golf, tennis, bridge; *Clubs* Ski Club of GB, RAC, Harbour, Highgate Golf; *Style*— Robert Woodbridge, Esq

WOODCOCK, Anthony Douglas Henry; s of Douglas Henry Woodcock (d 1982), and Doreen, *née* Wade; *b* 22 Nov 1951; *Educ* Brecon Boys GS, Univ Coll Cardiff (BMus); *m* 26 June 1971, Virginia, da of Ralph Harrison; 1 s (Thomas b 20 May 1983); *Career* music offr Welsh Arts Cncl 1974–77, asst dir South East Arts 1977–84, gen mangr City of London Sinfonia 1984–86, gen mangr St David's Hall Cardiff 1986–88, chief exec Royal Liverpool Philharmonic Soc 1988–91, md Bournemouth Orchestras 1991–; memb Music Ctee Welsh Arts Cncl, memb cmmnd team (for Welsh Arts Cncl) to review BBC Welsh Symphony Orch; former dir Assoc of Br Orchs, former chm and sec Music Offrs Gp Regnl Arts Assoc, former chm cmmnd team (for Scottish Arts Cncl) to review work of Royal Scottish Orch; *Recreations* tennis, squash, cycling; *Clubs* Royal Over-Seas League; *Style*— Anthony Woodcock, Esq; ✉ Bournemouth Orchestras, 2 Seldown Lane, Poole, Dorset BH15 1UF (☎ 01202 670611, fax 01202 687235)

WOODCOCK, Dr Ashley; s of Arthur Woodcock, of Stoke-on-Trent, and Vera, *née* Jones (d 1973); *b* 13 April 1951; *Educ* Univ of Manchester (BSc, MB ChB, MD); *m* 3 Aug 1974, Fiona Marilyn, da of Raymond Griffiths, of Gwaun-Cae Gurwen, Ammanford, Dyfed; 2 s (Daniel Ashley b 1984, (Benjamin) George b 1986), 1 da (Hannah Vera b 1982); *Career* specialist physician Gen Hosp Bandar-Seri-Begawan Brunei SE Asia 1977–79; jr dr 1979–86: Brompton Hosp, Nat Heart Hosp, Hammersmith Hosp, St James Hosp; conslt physician Manchester Royal Infirmary 1986–88, conslt physician and dir Regnl Lung Function Laboratory and dir Slumberland Sleep Laboratory 1988–; sec NW Thoracic Soc, public educn offr and memb Cncl and Exec Br Thoracic Soc, Clinical Section chm Euro Respiratory Soc; MRCP 1977, FRCP 1992; *Recreations* jogging, tennis; *Clubs* Hale Tennis; *Style*— Dr Ashley Woodcock; ✉ NW Regional Dept of Respiratory Physiology, Wythenshawe Hospital, Southmoore Road, Wythenshawe, Manchester M23 9LT (☎ 0161 291 2398)

WOODCOCK, (Evan) Clive; CBE (1996); s of Percy Woodcock (d 1985), and Lilian Mary, *née* Hanlon; *b* 11 Aug 1938; *Educ* King Edward VI Sch Stafford, Univ of Birmingham (LLB); *m* 7 Sept 1963, Hilary Anne, da of Christopher Allen Pither, (d 1970); 1 s (Andrew b 28 June 1967), 2 da (Susan (Mrs Rush) b 5 Nov 1964, Emma b 24 Aug 1973); *Career* admitted slr 1962; chief asst slr and co prosecuting slr Salop CC 1965–69, chief prosecuting slr Cheshire Police Authy 1969–86; chief crown prosecutor: Crown Prosecution Serv Merseyside 1986–93, Merseyside & Lancs 1993–96; pres Prosecuting Slrs Soc of England and Wales 1980–82 (cncl memb 1970–86); FIMgt 1986, FRSA 1996; *Recreations* fell-walking, photography, music; *Style*— Clive Woodcock, Esq, CBE; ✉ 8 Nield Court, Church Lane, Upton-by-Chester, Cheshire CH2 1DN (☎ 01244 381607)

WOODCOCK, Graham; CBE (1992, OBE 1980); s of Thomas Woodcock (d 1975), of Newfield, Haslingden, Rossendale, Lancs, and Beryl, *née* Duckworth (d 1951); *b* 25 July 1920; *Educ* Uppingham, St John's Coll Cambridge (BA, MA); *Career* Nat Serv WWII: enlisted RA 1939, active serv Gibraltar and India (seconded to Royal India Artillery) 1939–46, released with hon rank of Capt 1946; admitted slr 1949; ptnr Woodcock & Sons 1949–82 (conslt 1982–), hon legal advsr to RRF 1975–; pres: Bury and District Law Soc 1971–72, Haslingden Branch Royal Br Legion, Haslingden and Dist Civic Tst, Haslingden and Helmshore Band, Haslingden and Dist Fly-Fishing Assoc, Rossendale Search and Rescue Team; fndr chm Higher Mill Textile Museum Helmshore; cnclr Lancs CC 1969–81, chm N Western Area Cons Cncl 1989–92 (patron 1992–95, hon vice-pres 1995–), memb Fin Bd Nat Union of Cons and Union Assoc 1985–89 (memb Gen Purposes Ctee 1988–93, memb Exec Ctee 1975–); Guild Burgess of the Borough of Preston in the Co of Lancaster since the Guild Merchant of 1922; memb Law Soc; *Recreations* travel, walking, gardening; *Clubs* Royal Over-Seas League, Cambridge Union Soc; *Style*— Graham Woodcock, Esq, CBE; ✉ Heathfield, Haslingden, Rossendale, Lancs BB4 4BW (☎ 01706 214290)

WOODCOCK, Sir John; kt (1989), CBE (1983), QPM (1976); s of Joseph Woodcock (d 1967), and Elizabeth May, *née* Whiteside (d 1982); *b* 14 Jan 1932; *Educ* Preston Tech Coll; *m* 4 April 1953, Kathleen Margaret, da of John Abbott; 2 s (Clive John b 1954, Aidan Edward b 1956), 1 da (Karen Belinda b 1962); *Career* police cadet Lancs Constabulary 1947–50, Army Special Investigation Branch 1950–52, constable to chief inspr Lancs Constabulary 1952–65, supt and chief supt Beds and Luton Constabulary 1965–68, asst chief constable Gwent 1968–70; dep chief constable: Gwent 1970–74, Devon & Cornwall 1974–78; chief constable: N Yorks Police 1978–79, S Wales Constabulary 1979–83; HM Inspr of Constabulary 1983–90, HM Chief Inspr of Constabulary 1990–93; author Woodcock Report - Escapes from Whitemoor Prison 1994; Intermediate Cmd Course Police Coll 1965, Sr Cmd Course 1968, Study Bavarian Police 1977, Euro Discussion Centre 1977; lectr Int Police Course Sicily and Rome 1978; FBI Nat Exec: Washington 1981, Salt Lake City Utah 1986, Sun Valley Idaho 1988 and 1992, Arnhem Netherlands 1990; study of Royal Hong Kong Police 1989; vice pres Welsh Assoc of Youth Clubs 1981–87; chm Wales Ctee Royal Jubilee and Prince's Tst 1983–85; memb: Admin Cncl Royal Jubilee Tsts 1981–85, Prince's Tst Ctee for Wales 1981–84, Governing Bd World Coll of the Atlantic 1980–84; pres Police Mutual Assurance Soc 1990–94; non-exec dir Capital Corporation plc London 1994–; hon memb Swansea Lions; St John Cncl: N Yorks, S Glam, Mid Glam (chm), Hereford and Worcs 1978–90; CStJ 1993 (OStJ 1981); Papal knighthood 1984 (KSG); CIMgt 1980; *Recreations* table tennis, badminton, golf, walking, horticulture; *Style*— Sir John Woodcock, CBE, QPM

WOODCOCK, John Charles; OBE (1996); s of Rev Parry John Woodcock (d 1938), and Norah Mabel, *née* Hutchinson; *b* 7 Aug 1926; *Educ* Dragon Sch Oxford, St Edward's Sch Oxford, Trinity Coll Oxford (MA); *Career* Manchester Guardian 1952–54; cricket writer for: The Times 1954–, Country Life 1962–91; ed Wisden Cricketers' Almanack 1980–86; covered 40 Test Tours since 1950 incl: Aust (17 times), S Africa, West Indies, NZ, India, Pakistan; dir The Cricketer, memb Ctee MCC 1988–91 and 1993–95 (tstee 1996–), pres Cricket Writers' Club; patron of the living of Longparish Hants; Br Press Sportswriter of the Year 1987; *Books* The Ashes (1956), Barclays World of Cricket (with E W Swanton 1980, assoc ed 2 edn, conslt ed 3 edn 1986), Hockey for Oxford versus Cambridge (1946 and 1947); *Recreations* golf, country pursuits; *Clubs* Flyfishers', Vincent's (Oxford), St Enodoc Golf, MCC, Hampshire CCC (hon life memb), Surrey CCC (hon life memb), Arabs, Free Foresters, Cryptics, Oxford Harlequins, I Zingari; *Style*— John Woodcock, Esq, OBE; ✉ The Curacy, Longparish, nr Andover, Hants SP11 6PB (☎ 01264 720259)

WOODCOCK, Nigel; s of Barry Woodcock, of Chesterfield, Derbyshire, and Monica Ann, *née* Redfern; *b* 17 June 1958; *Educ* Chesterfield Sch, Leamington Coll, QMC London (BSc(Econ)), London Business Sch; *m* Anneliese, *née* Roughton-Skelton; 2 da (Jane b 11 Aug 1980, Catherine b 18 Sept 1993), 2 s (Thomas b 27 June 1985, Robert b 21 June 1988); *Career* national NHS admin trainee NE Thames RHA 1980–81, asst hosp administrator The London Hosp Mile End 1982, asst hosp administrator Whittington Hosp Islington 1983, dep hosp sec The London Hosp Whitechapel 1986 (asst hosp sec 1983–85), dir of facilities N Herts Health Authy 1986–88, unit gen mangr Lister Hosp Stevenage (N Herts HA) 1988–90, chief exec W Cumbria Health Care NHS Tst 1992– (unit gen mangr under W Cumbria HA 1990–92); *Recreations* cricket, soccer, current affairs; *Style*— Nigel Woodcock, Esq; ✉ West Cumbria Health Care NHS Trust, West Cumberland Hospital, Whitehaven, Cumbria CA28 8JG (☎ 01946 523700, fax 01946 523100)

WOODCOCK, Thomas; LVO (1996); s of Thomas Woodcock, of Hurst Green, Lancs, and Mary, *née* Woodcock; *b* 20 May 1951; *Educ* Eton, Univ of Durham (BA), Darwin Coll Cambridge (LLB); *Career* called to the Bar Inner Temple 1975; Rouge Croix Pursuivant 1978–82, Somerset Herald of Arms 1982–; FSA; *Books* Oxford Guide to Heraldry (with John Martin Robinson, 1988), Dictionary of British Arms Medieval Ordinary Vol One (Vol I, ed with D H B Chesshyre, 1992, Vol II, ed with Hon Janet Grant and Ian Graham, 1996); *Clubs* Travellers'; *Style—* Thomas Woodcock, Esq, LVO, FSA; ✉ College of Arms, Queen Victoria St, London EC4V 4BT (☎ 0171 236 3634)

WOODD, Hugh Basil; s of Rev Canon Frederick Hampden Basil Woodd (d 1986), and Emily Hornby, *née* Foss (d 1980); *b* 13 Nov 1940; *Educ* Canford, Univ of Bristol (BA); *m* 21 Oct 1967, Susan Mary (Sue), da of Norman Andrew Armitage, of Dorset; 1 s (Christopher b 24 Nov 1968), 2 da (Rachel b 29 June 1970, Anna b 8 June 1972); *Career* CA; Mann Judd & Co: London 1963–67 and 1969–88, Addis Ababa 1967–69, ptnr 1970; ptnr Touche Ross & Co (upon merger) 1979, ret 1988 to become sole practitioner in Winchester; hon treas: St Matthews PCC; St Matthews PCC; Freeman City of London 1964, Liveryman Worshipful Co of Salters 1964; ACA 1967; *Recreations* opera, mountain walking, DIY; *Style—* Hugh Woodd, Esq; ✉ Honeywick, 17 Bereweeke Ave, Winchester, Hants SO22 6BH (☎ 01962 852924)

WOODFIELD, Sir Philip John; KCB (1983, CB 1974), CBE (1963); s of late Ralph and Ruth Woodfield; *b* 30 Aug 1923; *Educ* Alleyn's Sch Dulwich, King's Coll London; *m* 1958, Diana, da of late Sydney, and Margaret, Herington; 3 da; *Career* served WWII RA; civil servant NI and Home Office; dep sec Home Office 1974–81, perm under sec NI Office 1981–84; chm: London and Metropolitan Govt Staff Cmmn 1984–91, Irish Soldiers and Sailors Land Tst 1986–, Scrutiny of Supervision of Charities 1987, Review of Br Tport Police 1987–88; memb Royal Cmmn on Criminal Justice 1991–93; staff cnsllr for the Security and Intelligence Servs 1987–95; *Recreations* music; *Clubs* Garrick, Beefsteak; *Style—* Sir Philip Woodfield, KCB, CBE; ✉ c/o Lloyds Bank, 7 Pall Mall, London SW1

WOODFORD, Anthony Arthur George; CB (1989); s of Arthur George Woodford (d 1989), and May, *née* McRea; *b* 6 Jan 1939; *Educ* Haberdashers' Aske's, Open Univ (BA), MA (Oxon) 1992; *m* 29 Aug 1965, Christine Barbara, da of John Tripp (d 1989); 1 s (Adrian b 1970), 2 da (Caroline b 1966, Sarah b 1969); *Career* cmmnd pilot 1959; served with Squadrons 12, 44, 53, 101, until 1978; directing staff RAF Staff Coll 1972–75, asst air attache Washington DC 1978–81, cmd RAF St Mawgan 1982–83, ADC to HM The Queen 1982–83; RCDS 1984, staff appts HQ RAF Strike Cmd 1985–89, asst chief of staff policy SHAPE 1989–92, ret Air Vice-Marshal; fell and home bursar Magdalen Coll Oxford 1992–; *Clubs* RAF; *Style—* Anthony Woodford, Esq, CB; ✉ Magdalen College Oxford, University of Oxford, Oxford OX1 4AU (☎ 01865 276000)

WOODFORD, Maj-Gen David Milner; CBE (1975); s of Maj Robert Milner Woodford, MC (d 1981), and Marion Rosa (Tessa), *née* Gregory (d 1955); *b* 26 May 1930; *Educ* Prince of Wales Sch Nairobi, Wadham Coll Oxford; *m* 1959 (m dis 1987), Mary, da of D E Jones, Esq (d 1963); *Career* served 1 Royal Fusiliers Korea, Egypt, Sudan and Middle East 1953–62, MA Vice Chief of Gen Staff 1964–66, CO 3 RRF 1970–72, Col Cyprus 1972–75, Cmd 3 Inf Bde 1976–77, dir Army Training 1981–82, SDS RCDS 1982–83, Cmdt Joint Serv Def Coll 1984–86, Col RRF 1982–86, ret 1986; memb Lord Chancellor's Panel of Independent Inspectors; *Recreations* literary, historical, golf; *Clubs* Army and Navy, New Zealand Golf; *Style—* Maj-Gen David Woodford, CBE; ✉ c/o Barclays Bank, Fleet, Hants;

WOODFORD, Dr F(rederick) Peter; s of Wilfrid Charles Woodford (d 1931), and Mabel Rose, *née* Scarff (d 1970); *b* 8 Nov 1930; *Educ* The Lewis Sch Pengam Glamorgan, Balliol Coll Oxford (BA, MA), Univ of Leeds (PhD); *m* 18 Dec 1964, Susan, da of E A Silberman (d 1969); 1 da (Julia Jacqueline b 21 Nov 1969); *Career* RAF 1956–57 (pilot offr, flying offr); res fell Leiden Univ 1958–62, visiting scientist and lectr Univ of Tennessee Medical Sch and NIH USA 1962–63, guest investigator Rockefeller Univ NY 1963–71, scientific historian Ciba Fndn and scientific assoc Wellcome Trust 1971–74, exec dir Inst for Res into Mental and Multiple Handicap 1974–77, PSO (Clinical Chemistry) DHSS 1977–84, chief scientific offr Dept of Health 1984–93, distinguished visitor Royal Free Sch of Medicine 1994–; managing exec ed: Jl of Atherosclerosis Res 1960–62, Jl of Lipid Res 1963–69, Proceedings of Nat Acad of Scis USA 1970–71; scientific ed Xth Int Symposium on Atherosclerosis (Montreal) 1994, ed Camden History Review 1995–; Hon DSc Univ of Salford 1993; FRCPath 1984, CChem, FRSC 1990, FBES 1993 (MBES 1991), fell Instn of Physics and Engrg in Med and Biology (FIPEMB) 1995; *Books* Scientific Writing for Graduate Students (1969), Medical Research Systems in Europe (1973), The Ciba Foundation: An Analytic History (1974), Writing Scientific Papers in English (1975), Training Manual for Technicians in Physiological Measurement (1988), Training Manual for Technicians in Medical Physics (1989), Training Manual for Medical Laboratory Assistants (1991), First-Level and Advanced Training Manuals for Rehabilitation Engineering Technicians (1993), Atherosclerosis Vol 109 (ed, 1994), Atherosclerosis X (1995), From Primrose Hill to Euston Road (1995), Oestrogen Replacement and the Menopause (1996); *Recreations* playing chamber music (pianist, chm Hampstead Music Club 1996–); *Style—* Dr F Peter Woodford; ✉ 1 Akenside Rd, London NW3 5BS (☎ 0171 435 2088, fax 0171 794 6695)

WOODFORD, Peggy Elizabeth Lainé (Mrs Aylen); da of Ronald Curtis Woodford, OBE (d 1970), of Assam, India, and Ruth Mahy, *née* Lainé (d 1987); *b* 19 Sept 1937; *Educ* Guernsey Ladies' Coll CI, St Anne's Coll Oxford (MA); *m* 1 April 1967, Walter Stafford Aylen, QC, *qv*, s of Rt Rev Charles Arthur William Aylen (d 1972); 3 da (Alison b 1968, Frances b 1970, Imogen b 1974); *Career* writer; Italian govt res scholar Rome 1960–61, script and res asst BBC TV 1962–63, sr tutor Sixth Form Coll Reading 1964–67; *Books* incl: Abraham's Legacy (1963), Please Don't Go (1972), Backwater War (1975), The Real Thing (1977), Rise of the Raj (1978), See You Tomorrow (1979), You Can't Keep Out the Darkness (1980), The Girl with a Voice (1981), Love Me Love Rome (1984), Misfits (1984), Monster in our Midst (1988), Schubert (2 edn, 1989), Out of the Sun (1990), Mozart (2 edn, 1990), Blood and Mortar (1994), Cupid's Tears (1995), On the Night (1996); *Style—* Miss Peggy Woodford; ✉ c/o David Higham Associates, 5–8 Lower John Street, Golden Square, London W1R 4HA (☎ 0171 437 7888, fax 0171 437 1072)

WOODFORD, Stephen William John; s of John Wilfred Stephen Woodford, of Longparish, Hampshire, and Barbara, *née* Wood; *b* 11 Feb 1959; *Educ* Tomlinscote Sch Frimley Surrey, City Univ London (BScEcon); *m* 30 April 1988, Amelia Wylton, da of Wylton Dickson; 2 s (William Nicholas b 3 Aug 1989, Miles Wylton John b 31 July 1992); *Career* graduate trainee Nestle Co Ltd 1980–82, account mangr Lintas Advertising 1982–85, account dir Waldron Allen Henry & Thompson 1985–89, account dir rising to gp account dir WCRS 1989–91, dep md Leo Burnett 1991–94, md WCRS 1995– (client servs dir 1994–95); *Recreations* young family and house in Cornall; *Style—* Stephen Woodford, Esq; ✉ WCRS, 161 Drury Lane, London WC2B 5PR (☎ 0171 242 2800)

WOODHEAD, Christopher Anthony (Chris); *b* 20 Oct 1946; *Educ* Univ of Bristol (BA, PGCE), Univ of Keele (MA); *Career* English teacher Priory Sch Shrewsbury 1969–72, dep head of English Newent Sch Glos 1972–74, head of English Gordano Sch Avon 1974–76, tutor in English Univ of Oxford 1976–82, advsr in English 1982–84, chief advsr Shropshire LEA 1984–88; dep chief educn offr: Devon LEA 1988–90, Cornwall LEA 1990–91; chief exec: Nat Curriculum Cncl 1991–93 (dep chief exec 1991), School Curriculum and Assessment Authy 1993–94; HM's chief inspr for schs OFSTED 1994–; special prof Univ of Nottingham 1993–95; *Recreations* fell running, rock climbing, second-hand bookshops; *Style—* Mr Chris Woodhead; ✉ OFSTED, Alexandra House, 33 Kingsway, London WC2B 6SE (☎ 0171 421 6762, fax 0171 421 6546)

WOODHEAD, David James; s of Frank Woodhead, of North Yorks, and Polly Woodhead; *b* 9 Nov 1943; *Educ* Queen Elizabeth GS Wakefield, Univ of Leicester (BA); *m* 21 July 1974, Carole, da of Arthur Vincent Underwood (d 1986); 2 s (Richard James b 1976, William Alexander b 1979); *Career* journalist: educn corr Cambridge Evening News 1965–68, The Sunday Telegraph 1968–75; chief press offr ILEA 1978–84 (press offr 1975–78), nat dir Ind Schools Info Serv (ISIS) 1985–; editorial dir The ISIS Magazine; tstee: Jt Educnl Tst, Nat Isis Strings Acad, the Oratory Gp; govr: Battle Abbey Sch 1988–91, St John's Sch Leatherhead 1994–; FRSA 1990; *Publications* Choosing Your Independent School (ed, annually 1985–), Good Communications Guide (1989); *Recreations* family, opera, classical music, travel; *Style—* David Woodhead, Esq; ✉ Independent Schools Information Service, 56 Buckingham Gate, London SW1E 6AG (☎ 0171 630 8793, fax 0171 630 5013)

WOODHEAD, Vice Adm Sir (Anthony) Peter; KCB (1992); s of Leslie Woodhead, and Nancy Woodhead; *b* 30 July 1939; *Educ* Leeds GS, Conway, BRNC Dartmouth; *m* 1964, Carol Woodhead; 1 s (Simon), 1 da (Emma (Mrs Jeremy Cave)); *Career* RN Seaman Offr, pilot 1962, aircraft carriers Borneo Campaign; CO HM Ships: Jupiter 1974, Rhyl 1975; NDC 1976, Naval Plans Div MOD 1977, CSO to Flag Offr Third Flotilla 1980, COS to FO cmdg Falklands Task Force 1982, Capt 4 Frigate Sqdn 1983, RCDS 1984, Dir Naval Ops 1985, CO HMS Illustrious 1986; Flag Offr: Flotilla Two 1988, Flotilla One 1989; Vice Adm 1991; Dep SACLANT 1991–93; Prisons Ombudsman 1994–; non-exec dir BMT 1996–; pres Marriage Resource 1994–, patron Homeless Fund 1996–, govr Aldro Sch 1996–; *Recreations* tennis, golf, lay reader; *Style—* Sir Peter Woodhead, KCB; ✉ 30 Orange Street, London WC2 7HH

WOODHEAD, Robin George; s of Walter Henry Woodhead (d 1976), of Zimbabwe, and Gladys Catherine Woodhead, of Johannesburg, SA; *b* 28 April 1951; *Educ* Mount Pleasant Sch Salisbury Rhodesia, Univ Coll of Rhodesia and Nyasaland (LLB); *m* 28 June 1980 (m dis 1992), Mary Fitzgerald, da of Fergus Hamilton Allen, CB, *qv*, of Berks; *Career* 1981–86: chm International Petroleum Exchange of London Ltd, md Premier Man Ltd, dir E D & F Man International Ltd; chm and chief exec National Investment Group plc and chief exec National Investment Holdings plc 1986–91, chief exec London Commodity Exchange 1992–; fndr tstee Whitechapel Gallery, chm Ballet Rambert; memb Law Soc 1978; *Recreations* skiing, tennis, riding, contemporary art, Zululand farmer; *Style—* Robin Woodhead, Esq; ✉ The London Commodity Exchange Ltd, 1 Commodity Quay, St Katharine Docks, London E1 9AX (☎ 0171 481 2080, fax 0171 702 9924)

WOODHEAD-KEITH-DIXON, Rev James Addison; s of James Keith-Dixon (d 1967), of Lorton Hall, Cockermouth, Cumbria, and Margaret Ann, da of James Wright, of Glossop, Derbys; *b* 20 July 1925; *Educ* St Aidan's Coll Birkenhead, Univ of Liverpool; *m* 1, 16 Oct 1951, Mary Constance (d 1977), da of Alfred Tindal Saul (d 1960), of Highcroft, Stanwix, Carlisle (d 1972); 1 s (Andrew James b 14 April 1953); m 2, 1 Aug 1981, Clodagh Anne, da of James Trevor Cather, of Icod, Tenerife; *Career* ordained: deacon 1948, priest 1949; curate: Upperby Carlisle 1948–50, Dalton-in-Furness 1950–52; vicar: Blawith-with-Lowick 1952–59, Lorton 1959–80; chaplain of Tenerife 1980–82, team vicar of Falstone, Thorneyburn and Greystead 1982, team rector 1983, lay rector Lorton; ret 1992; Lord of The Manors of Lorton Brigham and Whinfell; *Recreations* shooting, fishing, heraldry and genealogy; *Style—* The Rev James Woodhead-Keith-Dixon; ✉ Culpee House, Cree Bridge, Newton Stewart, Wigtownshire DG8 6NR

WOODHOUSE, Charles Frederick; s of Wilfrid Meynell Woodhouse (d 1967), of Chester Row, London, and Margaret (Peggy), *née* Kahl; *b* 6 June 1941; *Educ* Marlborough, McGill Univ, Peterhouse Cambridge (BA); *m* 25 Jan 1969, Margaret Joan, da of Thomas Wheatcroft Cooper (d 1991), of Hulland Ward, Derbyshire; 1 s (Timothy b 6 Dec 1973), 2 da (Rachel b 11 Nov 1969, Philippa b 1 Nov 1971); *Career* admitted slr; ptnr Farrer & Co 1969–; chm: The Cheviot Tst, Rank Pension Trustees Ltd; dir: Santos Europe Ltd, Santos USA Corp; legal advsr: Br Athletic Fedn, CCPR, Inst of Professional Sport; hon legal advsr Cwlth Games Cncl for Eng; memb Ctee Br Assoc for Sport and Law; tstee LSA Charitable Tst, pres Guildford CC, hon life vice pres Surrey Championship; memb Law Soc; *Recreations* cricket, golf; *Clubs* MCC, United Oxford and Cambridge, Worplesdon Golf, Surrey CCC, Free Foresters; *Style—* Charles Woodhouse, Esq; ✉ Selborne Lodge, 2 Austen Rd, Guildford, Surrey GU1 3NP (☎ 01483 573676); Farrer & Co, 66 Lincoln's Inn Fields, London WC2A 3LH (☎ 0171 242 2022, fax 0171 831 9748, telex 24318)

WOODHOUSE, Christopher Richard James; s of Col the Hon Christopher Montague Woodhouse, DSO, OBE, of Oxford, and Lady Davidema Katharine Cynthia Mary Millicent (Davina), *née* Bulwer-Lytton (d 1995), da of 2 Earl of Lytton, KG, GCSI, GCIE, PC; *b* 20 Sept 1946; *Educ* Winchester, Guy's Hosp Med Sch (MB BS); *m* 27 Feb 1975, Hon Anna Margaret, da of 3 Baron Milford; 1 s (Jack b 7 Dec 1978), 1 da (Constance b 1 Jan 1982); *Career* sr lectr Inst of Urology 1981; conslt urologist: Royal Marsden Hosp 1981, St George's Hosp 1985–95; hon conslt urologist: St Peter's Hosp 1981, Hosp for Sick Children Gt Ormond St 1981; numerous pubns in learned jls; corresponding memb American Urological Assoc 1985; Liveryman Worshipful Soc of Apothecaries; FRSM 1981, FRCS 1975, FEBU 1993; *Books* Physiological Basis of Medicine-Urology and Nephrology (1987), Long Term Paediatric Urology (1991); *Recreations* skiing, stalking; *Clubs* Leander; *Style—* Christopher Woodhouse, Esq; ✉ The Institute of Urology, 48 Riding House Street, London W1P 7PN (☎ 0171 380 9381, fax 0171 730 6204)

WOODHOUSE, James Stephen; s of Rt Rev John Walker Woodhouse (d 1956); *b* 21 May 1933; *Educ* St Edward's Sch Oxford, St Catharine's Coll Cambridge; *m* 1957, Sarah Maud, da of Col Hubert Blount, MC (d 1979); 3 s, 1 da; *Career* asst master Westminster Sch 1957–63, under-master and master of Queen's Scholars 1963–67; headmaster: Rugby Sch 1967–81, Lancing Coll 1981–93; dir ISIS East 1994; *Recreations* sailing, music, hill walking, natural history; *Clubs* East India, Sports and Public Sch; *Style—* James Woodhouse, Esq; ✉ Welcome Cottage, Wiveton, Holt, Norfolk NR25 7TH (☎ 01263 740 935)

WOODHOUSE, Prof John Robert; s of Horace Woodhouse (d 1983), and Iris Evelyn, *née* Pewton; *b* 17 June 1937; *Educ* King Edward VI GS Stourbridge, Hertford Coll Oxford (MA, DLitt), Univ of Pisa, Univ of Wales (PhD); *m* 5 Aug 1967, Gaynor, *née* Mathias; *Career* asst lectr in Italian Univ of Aberdeen 1961–62, Br Cncl scholar Scuola Normale Superiore Pisa 1962–63, asst lectr then lectr UCNW Bangor 1963–66, lectr then sr lectr Univ of Hull 1966–73; Univ of Oxford: lectr in Italian 1973–89, fell St Cross Coll 1973–84, lectr Jesus Coll 1973–89, lectr St Edmund Hall 1975–89, lectr Brasenose Coll 1976–89, fell Pembroke Coll 1984–89 (supernumerary fell 1991), fell Magdalen Coll 1990–, Fiat Serena prof of Italian studies 1990–; corresponding fell: Accademia Letteraria dell'Arcadia 1982–, Accademia della Crusca 1991, Commissione per i testi di lingua Bologna 1992; fell: Huntingdon Library Calif 1986, Newberry Library Chicago 1988; Old Dominion fndn fell Harvard Univ 1969–70, founding fell Centro Studi Dannunziani Pescara 1979, sr res fell Center for Medieval and Renaissance Studies UCLA 1985; memb: Exec Ctee Soc for Italian Studies 1979–85 and 1991–96, Exec Ctee Modern Humanities Res Assoc 1984–94 (hon life memb 1994), Editorial Bd Italian Studies jl 1987–91; ed (Italian) Modern Language Review 1984–94, fndr chm Oxford Italian Assoc 1990; Cavaliere Ufficiale al Merito della Repubblica Italiana 1991; FRSA 1983, FBA 1995; *Books* incl: Italo Calvino - a reappraisal and an appreciation of the trilogy (1968),

V Borghini 'Storia della nobiltà fiorentina' (ed, 1974), Baldesar Castiglione - a reassessment of the Cortegiano (1978), G d'Annunzio 'Alcyone' (ed, 1978), G Rossetti 'Lettere familiari' (jt ed, 1983), Idem 'Carteggi' (jt ed, Vol I 1984, Vol II 1988, Vol III 1992, Vol IV 1996) The Languages of Literature in Renaissance Italy (jt ed, 1988), From Castiglione to Chesterfield: The Decline in the Courtier's Manual (1991); *Recreations* hill walking, music, gardening; *Style*— Prof J R Woodhouse; ✉ Magdalen College, Oxford OX1 4AU (☎ 01865 276000, fax 01865 276094)

WOODHOUSE, (Ronald) Michael; s of Henry Alfred Woodhouse, of Woking, Surrey (d 1961), and Phyllis, *née* Gemmell (d 1983); *b* 19 Aug 1927; *Educ* Lancing, Queen's Coll Oxford; *m* 15 Oct 1955, Quenilda Mary, da of Rt Rev Neville Gorton, Bishop of Coventry (1942, d 1945); 1 s (Alexander b 1961), 3 da (Harriet b 1956, Isobel b 1958, Anna b 1964); *Career* Courtaulds PLC 1951–91; chm: The International Paint Co Ltd 1978–84, British Cellophane Ltd 1979–86, Courtaulds Fibres 1985–86; dep chm Courtaulds plc 1986–91 (dir 1976–91), chm Rexam PLC (formerly Bowater plc) 1993–96 (dir 1988–96); chm Princes Tst Volunteers 1991–, memb Volunteering Partnership 1995–; dir RSA Examination and Assessment Fndn 1991–; CIMgt 1988; *Clubs* Carlton; *Style*— Michael Woodhouse, Esq; ✉ Tankards, Wonersh, nr Guildford, Surrey (☎ 01483 892078); Dalehead, Hartsop, Patterdale, Cumbria CA11 0NZ (☎ 01768 482505)

WOODHOUSE, Hon (Christopher) Montague; DSO (1943), OBE (1944); s of 3 Baron Terrington, KBE (d 1961), and hp of bro, 4 Baron Terrington; *b* 11 May 1917; *Educ* Winchester, New Coll Oxford (MA); *m* 28 Aug 1945, Lady Davidema (Davina) Katharine Cynthia Mary Millicent Bulwer-Lytton (d 1995), da of 2 Earl of Lytton, and wid of 5 Earl of Erne; 2 s (Christopher Richard James b 1946, Nicholas Michael John b 1949), 1 da (Emma Davina Mary (Mrs Christopher Johnson-Gilbert) b 1954); *Career* serv WWII organising resistance in occupied Greece; dir-gen and dir of studies Royal Inst of Int Affrs 1955–59, visiting fell Nuffield Coll Oxford 1956–64; MP (C) Oxford 1959–66 and 1970–74, Parly sec Miny of Aviation 1961–62, jt under-sec of state Home Office 1962–64; dir of educn and trg CBI 1966–70, visiting prof King's Coll London 1978–89, fell Trinity Hall Cambridge 1949, corresponding memb Acad of Athens 1980, hon fellow New Coll Oxford 1982; chm Royal Soc of Literature 1977; FRSL 1951; *Books* Karamanlis, the Restorer of Greek Democracy (1982), Something Ventured (autobiography 1982), Gemistos Plethon (1986); *Style*— The Hon Montague Woodhouse, DSO, OBE, FRSL; ✉ 59 Pegasus Grange, Whitehouse Road, Oxford OX1 4QQ (☎ 01865 724642)

WOODHOUSE, The Rt Hon Sir (Arthur) Owen; KBE (1981), kt (1974), DSC (1944), PC (1974); s of Arthur James Woodhouse, and Wilhelmina Josephine, *née* Allen; *b* 18 July 1916; *Educ* Napier Boys' HS, Auckland Univ (LLB); *m* 1940, Margaret Leah Thorp; 4 s, 2 da; *Career* served 1939–45 War RNZNVR, Lt Cdr; asst to Naval Attaché HM Embassy Belgrade 1945; admitted barr and slr 1946; judge: Supreme Ct NZ 1961–86, Ct of Appeal 1974–86; pres Ct of Appeal 1981–86; first pres Law Cmmn 1985–91; chm Royal Cmmn on Personal Injury in NZ 1966–67, chm similiar inquiry in Australia 1973–74, pres NZ Section Int Cmmn of Jurists 1986–92; Hon LLD Victoria Univ of Wellington 1978, Hon LLD York Univ Canada 1981; *Style*— The Rt Hon Sir Owen Woodhouse, KBE, DSC, PC; ✉ 244 Remuera Road, Auckland 5, New Zealand (☎ 00 64 9 5244383)

WOODHOUSE, (Bernard) Raymond; s of (Thomas) Bernard Montague Woodhouse (d 1969), of Woodcote Park Ave, Purley, Surrey, and Betty, *née* Harvey (d 1956); *b* 24 Nov 1939; *Educ* Ardingly, St Dunstan's Catford, Nat Coll of Food Tech; *m* 6 Oct 1962, Judith, da of Robert Arnold Roach (d 1994), of Caterham; 2 s (Richard Thomas Raymond b 5 May 1965, Martyn Bernard Robert b 26 Jan 1970); *Career* chm TSJ Woodhouse Ltd 1973– (joined 1960); non-exec dir The Huge Cheese Company London Ltd 1994–; Freeman City of London 1979, Liveryman Worshipful Co of Butchers 1979; *Recreations* tennis, sailing, golf; *Clubs* Royal Smithfield (memb Cncl), Bletchingley Golf, Farmers'; *Style*— Raymond Woodhouse, Esq; ✉ T S J Woodhouse Ltd, 72–98 Blundell St, London N7 9TS (☎ 0171 609 2200, fax 0171 609 5513); The Backwater, Upper Ct Rd, Woldingham, Surrey CR3 7BF

WOODING, Sir Norman Samuel; kt (1992), CBE (1986); s of Samuel Wooding (d 1966), of Street Ashton, and Nellie, *née* White (d 1970); *b* 20 April 1927; *Educ* Lawrence Sheriff Sch Rugby, Univ of London (BSc), Univ of Leeds and Univ of Manchester (PhD); *m* 19 Sept 1949, Dorothy Elizabeth, da of Alfred Smith; 1 s (Richard b 1959), 2 da (Susan b 1956, Lucy b 1968); *Career* dep chm Courtaulds plc 1976–87 (dir 1973–87), non-exec chm Earlys of Witney plc 1978–83 (non-exec dir 1971–83), chm EIS Group PLC 1994–; non-exec dir: British Nuclear Fuels plc 1987–; non-exec dep chm Royal London Mutual Insurance Co Ltd 1987–96; non-exec chm: Agricultural Genetics Co Ltd 1988–93, British Textile Technology Group Ltd 1991–94 (non-exec dir 1988–91); chm E Euro Trade Cncl 1990–96, pres RBCC; memb: Cncl Britain-Russia Assoc, Governing Body Br Assoc for Central and Eastern Europe; chm Cncl Sch of Slavonik and E Euro Studies Univ of London; sr assoc memb St Antony's Coll Oxford; CIMgt 1983; *Recreations* gardening, mountain walking, cooking, fast cars; *Clubs* Reform; *Style*— Sir Norman Wooding, CBE; ✉ EIS Group PLC, 6 Sloane Square, London SW1W 8EE (☎ 0171 730 9187)

WOODING, Roy; s of Raymond Wooding (d 1957), and Elsie, *née* Lyons; *b* 11 Oct 1953; *Educ* Mexborough Co Secdy Sch; *m* 16 October 1976, Angela, da of George Jones; 1 da (Rachael Emma b 27 Sept 1978); *Career* photographer; M T Walters & Associates Ltd 1970–84 (apprentice then responsible for much of creative output), fndr ICS Photography 1984–, awarded BIPP Yorkshire Centre Indust/Photographer of the Year on seven occasions, BIPP bronze award for nat print exhibition 1990 and 1995; FBIPP 1982 (yst then in indust catagory, assoc BIPP 1976); *Books* contrib photographs to Photography Year Book (1983); *Recreations* Yorkshire league badminton, skiing, tennis, fishing; *Style*— Roy Wooding, Esq; ✉ 20 Farmoor Close, Harlington, Doncaster, South Yorkshire DN5 7JP (☎ 01709 896237); ICS Photography, The Studios, Dolcliffe Road, Mexborough, South Yorkshire S64 9AZ (☎ and fax 01709 570966)

WOODINGTON, Walter; s of Frederick William Woodington (d 1951), and Emily, *née* Shaw (d 1953); *b* 9 June 1916; *Educ* Woolwich Poly, City & Guilds Sch of Art; *m* Jacqueline, da of Richmond Shakespear Murray; *Career* portraitist; regular exhibitor in Royal Acad Summer Show since 1942; portraits in Royal Acad and Portrait Gall incl: Sir Mortimer Wheeler, Sir Kenneth Robson, Sir Eric Riches, Lord Banks, Sir Hugh Ferguson-Jones, Adm Sir Deric Holland-Martin, Brig H L B Salmon, Sir George Porter; pt/t teacher of drawing and painting St Martin's Sch of Art and Reigate Sch of Art, curator Royal Acad Schs 1961–85; RP, RBA, NEAC; *Recreations* music and walking; *Clubs* The Arts; *Style*— Walter Woodington, Esq; ✉ 5 Kenver Avenue, Finchley, London N12 0PG (☎ 0181 445 9334)

WOODLEY, Derek George; s of George Edward Woodley (d 1957), of Romford, Essex, and Dorothy Marjorie Gwendoline Roper; *b* 28 March 1931; *Educ* Royal Liberty Sch (Dip Arch); *m* 9 July 1955, Thelma Joan, da of Arthur Legg (d 1971); 2 s (David b 1962, Richard b 1968), 1 da (Jacqueline b 1963); *Career* Capt RE (survey), Cyprus survey and other classified work; chartered architect, sr ptnr Bell & Woodley 1980–; RIBA; *Recreations* cricket, golf; *Style*— Derek Woodley, Esq; ✉ Leap House, 45 Ferry Rd, Felixstowe, Suffolk (☎ 01394 284880); Bell & Woodley, 45 Ferry Rd, Old Felixstowe, Suffolk IP11 9LY (☎ 01394 284550)

WOODLEY, Keith Spencer; s of Charles Spencer Woodley, of Pleshey, Essex, and Hilda Mary, *née* Brown; *b* 23 Oct 1939; *Educ* Stationers Company's Sch; *m* 19 May 1962, Joyce Madeleine, *née* Toon; 1 s (Jonathan b 11 Jan 1972), 2 da (Rachel Jane b 8 March 1962, Helen Elizabeth b 17 July 1966); *Career* articled clerk Deloitte Plender Griffith and Co 1957–62, audit sr and mangr Deloitte & Co 1963–68; Deloitte Haskins & Sells: ptnr 1969–90, personnel ptnr 1978–82, memb Mgmnt Bd 1985–90; CA in private practice 1990–; non-exec dir: Royscot Trust PLC 1990–96, National & Provincial Building Society 1991–96, Abbey National PLC 1996–; complaints cmmr: Securities and Investment Bd 1990–94, Securities and Futures Authy and Int Stock Exchange 1990–, FIMBRA 1990–, Personal Investment Authy 1994–; hon treas Nat Assoc of CAB 1991–94; memb Cncl ICAEW 1989– (pres 1995–96); Liveryman: Worshipful Co of Stationers & Newspaper Makers, Worshipful Co of CAs; FCA 1963; *Recreations* hill-walking, theatre and listening to music; *Style*— Keith Woodley, Esq; ✉ 11 Sion Hill, Bath BA1 2UH (☎ 01225 484222, fax 01225 461683); 24 Gay Street, Bath BA1 2PL (☎ 01225 338733)

WOODLEY, Leonard Gaston; QC (1988); *Educ* Univ of London; *Career* called to the Bar Inner Temple 1963, head of chambers 8 King's Bench Walk, recorder of the Crown Court; memb Bar Trinidad; *Style*— Leonard Woodley, Esq, QC; ✉ 8 King's Bench Walk, Temple, London EC4Y 7DU

WOODLEY, Ven Ronald John; s of John Owen Woodley (d 1960), and Maggie Woodley, *née* Lord (d 1973); *b* 28 Dec 1925; *Educ* Montagu Rd Sch Edmonton London, Bishops' Coll Cheshunt Herts; *m* 1959, Patricia, da of Thomas Kneeshaw (d 1979); 1 s (John), 2 da (Rachel, Elizabeth); *Career* Sgt BAOR 1944–47; ordained: deacon 1953, priest 1954; curate: St Martin Middlesbrough 1953–58, Whitby 1958–61; curate i/c the Ascension Middlesbrough 1961–66, vicar 1966–71, rector of Stokesley 1971–85, rural dean 1977–84, canon and prebendary of York 1982–, archdeacon of Cleveland 1985–91 (archdeacon emeritus 1991–); *Recreations* walking, gardening, cinema, theatre, wine-making, cooking; *Style*— The Ven Ronald Woodley; ✉ Brierton House, 52 South Parade, Northallerton DL7 8SL (☎ 01609 778818)

WOODLEY, Sonia; QC (1996); da of Stanley Percival Woodley (d 1994), of Southampton, and Mabel Emily, *née* Hawkins; *b* 8 Oct 1946; *Educ* Convent HS Southampton, Inns of Court Sch of Law; *m* 8 Sept 1973 (m dis 1986), Peter Stuart McDonald; 2 s (James Alexander Heaton b 10 July 1977, William Edward Henry b 17 Aug 1981), 1 da (Laura Rose Jane b 5 July 1979); *Career* called to the Bar Gray's Inn 1968, recorder of the Crown Court 1987–; *Recreations* fishing, gardening, travelling; *Style*— Miss Sonia Woodley, QC; ✉ 9–12 Bell Yard, London WC2A 2LF (☎ 0171 400 1800, fax 0171 404 1405, mobile 0378 298496)

WOODMAN, Prof Anthony John; s of John Woodman (d 1988), of Newcastle upon Tyne, and Alma Clare, *née* Callender (d 1982); *b* 11 April 1945; *Educ* Ushaw Coll Durham, King's Coll Newcastle, Univ of Durham (BA), King's Coll Cambridge (PhD); *m* 21 July 1977, Dorothy Joyce, da of Gordon Charles Monk (d 1970), of N Shields; 2 s (David b 1981, John b 1983); *Career* reader in Latin lit Univ of Newcastle upon Tyne 1979–80 (lectr in classics 1968–79); prof of Latin: Univ of Leeds 1980–84, Univ of Durham 1984–; visiting prof Princeton Univ 1989–90, visiting fell Univ of Wisconsin/Madison 1995; *Books* Quality and Pleasure in Latin Poetry (jtly, 1974), Velleius Paterculus: the Tiberian Narrative (1977), Creative Imitation and Latin Literature (jtly, 1979), Velleius Paterculus: the Caesarian and Augustan Narrative (1983), Poetry and Politics in the Age of Augustus (jtly, 1984), Past Perspectives: Studies in Greek and Roman Historical Writing (jtly, 1986), Rhetoric in Classical Historiography (1988), Tacitus: Annals IV (jtly, 1989), Author and Audience in Latin Literature (jtly, 1992), Tacitus and the Tacitean Tradition (jtly, 1993), Tacitus: Annals III (jtly, 1996); *Style*— Prof A J Woodman; ✉ Department of Classics, 38 North Bailey, Durham DH1 3EU (☎ 0191 374 2072)

WOODROFFE, Peter Mackelcan; s of Kenneth Derry Woodroffe (d 1972), of London, and Raby Alfreda Mackelcan, *née* Ryan (d 1991); *b* 2 Aug 1927; *Educ* Mill Hill; *m* 15 June 1973, Amanda Aloysia Nicolette, da of Henry Forbes, of Berks; 2 s (Justin Mackelcan b 24 May 1977, Clifford Derry b 10 Dec 1979); *Career* joined Rifle Bde 1945, cmmnd 2 Lt Royal Northumberland Fus 1946 (Lt 1947), ret 1948; admitted slr 1953; sr ptnr Woodroffes 1963– (ptnr 1956–63); underwriting memb of Lloyd's; sec Ct of Govrs Mill Hill Sch, cncllr (C) Westminster City Cncl 1962–65; hon citizen State of Texas USA 1967, Freeman City of London 1984; memb Law Soc 1953; *Recreations* skiing, golf, tennis, palaeontology; *Clubs* Boodle's, Woodroffe's, Hurlingham, The Berkshire Golf, Rye Golf, Royal Cinque Ports Golf; *Style*— Peter Woodroffe, Esq; ✉ 13 Cadogan Street, London SW3 2PP (☎ 0171 589 9339); Stonewalls, Pett Level, nr Hastings, Sussex TN35 4EH (☎ 01424 813198); Woodroffes, 36 Ebury Street, London SW1W 0LU (☎ 0171 730 0001, fax 0171 730 0079)

WOODROOFE, Sir Ernest George; kt (1973); s of late Ernest Woodroofe; *b* 6 Jan 1912; *Educ* Cockburn HS, Univ of Leeds (PhD); *m* 1, 1938, Margaret Downes (d 1961); 1 da; m 2, 1962, Enid Arnold; *Career* chm: Unilever Ltd 1970–74, Leverhulme Tst 1974–82; memb British Gas Corporation 1973–82; dir: Schroders 1974–89, Burton Group 1974–83, Guthrie Corporation 1974–82; Hon DSc: Cranfield, Univ of Liverpool; Hon LLD Univ of Leeds, Hon DUniv Surrey, hon fell UMIST, Hon ACT Liverpool; memb Royal Cmmn for 1851 Exhibition 1968–84; FInstP, FIChemE; Cdr Order of Orange Nassau (Netherlands) 1972; *Style*— Sir Ernest Woodroofe; ✉ 44 The Street, Puttenham, Guildford, Surrey GU3 1AR (☎ 01483 810977)

WOODROW, (Donald) Alan; s of Donald Woodrow, of Toronto, Canada, and Barbara, *née* Brethour; *b* 22 Sept 1952; *Educ* George Vanier Secdy Sch Toronto, Royal Conservatory of Music Toronto; *m* 28 Nov 1995, Vivian Elizabeth Tierney (sop); 2 s from previous m (Jonathan b 9 Dec 1981, Alexander b 10 Jan 1984); *Career* tenor; princ artist ENO 1976–91; *Roles* incl: Pedrillo in Die Entführung aus dem Serail, Don Ottavio in Don Giovanni, Lindoro, Canio in Pagliacci, Herod in Salome, Herman in The Queen of Spades, Bacchus in Ariadne auf Naxos, Walter, Don Jose in Carmen, The Captain in Wozzeck; Sergei in Lady Macbeth of Mtsensk (Paris Opera and La Scala Milan) 1992, Kaiser in Die Frau ohne Schatten (Munich), Florestan in Fidelio (Bern); *Style*— Alan Woodrow, Esq; ✉ Athole Still International Management, 25–27 Westow Street, London SE19 3RY (☎ 0181 771 5271, fax 0181 771 8172)

WOODROW, Arabella Thomasine; da of Michael Henry Carlile Morris (d 1987), of Basingstoke, Hants, and Margaret Joyce, *née* Flannery (d 1984); *b* 31 March 1954; *Educ* Queen Anne's Sch Caversham Berks, Lady Margaret Hall Oxford (BA, DPhil); *m* 15 Dec 1979, Richard Erskine Woodrow, s of Cyril Erskine Woodrow (d 1960), of Scarborough; *Career* wine merchant; sales rep Harveys of Bristol 1979–84, Wine and Spirit Educn Tst dip 1981, Vintners scholarship from Vintners Co 1983, sales rep Christopher & Co Ltd 1984–85, wine buyer Cooperative Wholesale Soc 1986–; qualified Master of Wine 1986; memb: Inst of Masters of Wine 1986, Wine Devpt Bd 1986–92, Wine Standards Bd 1990; Freeman: Worshipful Co of Vintners 1995, City of London 1995; *Books* Wines Of The Rhone Valley; *Recreations* marathon running, triathlon, cookery, wine tasting; *Style*— Mrs Arabella Woodrow; ✉ CWS National Retail Buying, New Century House, PO Box 53, Manchester M60 4ES (☎ 0161 827 5353, fax 0161 827 5114)

WOODROW, Brian Guy; s of Guy Woodrow (d 1968), and Irene Adela, *née* Carr-Jackson (d 1976); *b* 12 June 1938; *Educ* Aldenham Sch, Magdalene Coll Cambridge (MA); *m* 12 Sept 1964, Sally Margaret, da of Herbert Jay Savours; 3 s (James Hugh b 9 May 1967, Nicholas Charles b 22 March 1969, Jeremy David b 21 March 1975); *Career* Nat Serv 2 Lt 1 RHA 1956–58; asst to Managing Dir Turton Brothers and Matthews (specialist steel mfrs) 1961–62, staff offr Coates Brothers Ltd (mfrs of printing inks, resins and paints) 1962–65, admin gen mangr of subsid then sr account mangr Masius Wynne-Williams Ltd (advtg agency) 1965–68, recruitment mangr Texas Instruments Ltd (mfrs of electronic components) 1968–71, ptnr Selection and Industrial Training

Administration Ltd (specialist trg consultancy) 1971–73; dir Harpur and Tunstall Ltd (mfrs of reprographic materials and equipment) 1977; MSL Group Ltd (human resource conslts) 1973–77 and 1978–: md of recruitment advtg agency 1981–82, md MSL UK 1982–87, non-exec dep chm 1987–; non-exec dir Bedford Hosp NHS Tst 1991–; High Sheriff of Beds 1995–96; chm: Bedford Sports Fndn, Bedford Hosps Charity; vice pres Beds Rural Communities Charity; fell Inst of Personnel and Devpt (FIPD); *Recreations* sport (currently golf and skiing, formerly hockey and squash); *Style*— Brian Woodrow, Esq; ✉ 55 Bushmead Avenue, Bedford MK40 3QW (☎ and fax 01234 359352); MSL Group Ltd, 32 Aybrook Street, London W1M 3JL (☎ 0171 487 5000, fax 0171 486 6939)

WOODROW, William Robert (Bill); s of Geoffrey William Woodrow, of Chichester, W Sussex, and Doreen Mary, *née* Fasken; *b* 1 Nov 1948; *Educ* Barton Peveril GS, Winchester Sch of Art, St Martin's Sch of Art, Chelsea Sch of Art (Higher Dip in Fine Art); *m* 12 Nov 1970, Pauline, da of John Neville Rowley; 1 s (Harry), 1 da (Ellen); *Career* sculptor; winner Anne Gerber award Seattle Museum of Art USA 1988, tstee Tate Gallery 1996–; *Exhibitions* numerous solo exhibitions in Europe, Australia, USA and Canada since 1972 incl Fool's Gold (Duveen Galleries Tate Gallery London, later Darmstadt Germany) 1996; group exhibitions incl: Br Sculpture in the 20th Century Whitechapel Art Gallery 1981, Biennale of Sydney 1982, Aperto 82 Venice 1982, XII Biennale of Paris 1982, New Art at the Tate Gallery 1983, Transformations Sao Paulo (also Rio de Janeiro, Mexico City, Lisbon) 1983, Int Survey of Recent Painting and Sculpture New York 1984, Skulptur im 20 Jahrhundert Basle 1984, ROSC '84 Dublin 1984, Space Invaders toured Canada 1985, The Br Show toured Australia 1985, Carnegie Int Pittsburgh 1985, Entre el objeto y la imagen toured Spain 1986, Painting and Sculpture Today Indianapolis 1986, Br Art of the 1980's Stockholm and Tampere 1987, Documenta 8 Kassel W Germany 1987, Starlit Waters Tate Liverpool 1988, British Now Montreal 1988, GB-USSR Kiev Moscow 1990, Metropolis Berlin 1991, XXI Sao Paulo Bienal 1991, Arte Amazonas (Rio de Janiero, Brasilia, Berlin, Dresden and Aachen) 1992–94, Collaborative Works (with Richard Deacon, Chisenhale Gallery London) 1993, Contemporary Br Art in Print Edinburgh and Yale 1995, Un Siecle de Sculpture Anglaise (Paris) 1996; *Museum Collections* incl: Arts Cncl GB, Br Cncl, Imperial War Museum, Kunsthaus Zurich, Malmö Konsthall, Muesum of Modern Art NY, Nat Gallery of Canada, Rijksmuseum Kröller-Müller, Tate Gallery; *Style*— W R Woodrow, Esq; ✉ c/o Lisson Gallery, 52–54 Bell Street, London NW1 5DA (☎ 0171 724 2739)

WOODRUFF, William Charles (Bill); CBE (1985); s of Thomas William Woodruff (d 1943), of Ramsgate, Kent, and Caroline Elizabeth, *née* Windsor (d 1966); *b* 14 Aug 1921; *Educ* St George's Sch Ramsgate; *m* 1, 9 May 1946, Ethel May (d 1981), da of late Frank Miles, of Rochester, Kent; 1 s (Gerald b 1948), 1 da (Pamela b 1951); m 2, 7 April 1987, Olivia Minerva, *née* Barnes; 3 step s (John b 1946, James b 1947, David b 1949); *Career* Flt-Lt navigator/observer 1409 Flight RAF 1941–46, POW 1943–45; Miny of Civil Aviation: joined 1945, air traffic controller at various airports and London HQ 1946–56, air traffic controller Heathrow 1956–62, sec PATCH long-term ATC Planning Gp 1960–61, dir civil air traffic ops 1967–69 (dep dir 1962–67), controller nat air traffic servs 1977–81 (jt field cdr 1969–74, dep controller 1974–77); aviation assessor airports public inquiries 1981–84, specialist advsr Parly Select Tport Ctee on air traffic control safety 1988–89; master Guild of Air Traffic Control Offrs 1956 (clerk of Guild 1952–56); FRAeS 1976; *Recreations* reading, gardening, crosswords; *Style*— Bill Woodruff, Esq, CBE; ✉ Great Oaks, 36 Court Rd, Ickenham, Uxbridge, Middx UB10 8TF (☎ 01895 639134)

WOODS, (Paul) Anthony John; s of Charles John Woods, of Streatham, London, and Joan Vera, *née* Margetts; *b* 14 June 1945; *m* 9 June 1979, Louise Head, da of Jason Richard Head Palmer, of Teddington, Middx; 1 s (Richard b 1982), 1 da (Eleanor b 1980); *Career* admitted slr: England and Wales 1969, NSW Australia 1973; ptnr Norton Rose 1980–94; Liveryman City of London Slrs Co 1981–; memb Law Soc 1969; *Recreations* theatre, reading, gardening, watching rugby union and cricket; *Clubs* MCC, Tanglin; *Style*— Anthony Woods, Esq; ✉ 44 Alleyn Road, London SE21 8AL

WOODS, His Hon Brian; DL (Derbyshire 1994); yr s of Edward Percival Woods, of Woodmancote, Cheltenham (d 1967), and Beulah Aileen Ruth, *née* Thomas (d 1977); *b* 5 Nov 1928; *Educ* City of Leicester Boys' Sch, Univ of Nottingham (LLB); *m* 23 April 1957, Anne Margaret, da of Frederic James Griffiths, of Parkgate, Wirral (d 1975); 3 da (Rachel b 1962, Helen b 1965, Diana b 1969); *Career* RAF 1947–49; called to the Bar Gray's Inn 1955; memb Midland Circuit, Circuit Judge 1975–94; dep chm Lincs (Lindsey) Quarter Sessions 1968; Anglican lay reader 1970–, chllr Diocese of Leicester 1977–79; memb Cncl of Abbots Bromley Sch of St Mary and St Anne 1977–92, fell Midland Div Woodard Corp 1978–92, legal memb Mental Heath Review Tbnls (Trent and Northern Regions) 1983–; *Recreations* musical music, taking photographs, avoiding complacency; *Style*— His Honour Brian Woods, DL

WOODS, Brian Edwin; s of Norman Eric Woods (d 1972), and Alice Louise, *née* Finch (d 1984); *b* 26 Feb 1940; *Educ* Leeds GS; *m* 10 July 1965 (m dis 1981), Judith Elizabeth, *née* Everitt; 1 da (Jane Louise b 7 Jan 1973); m 2, 2 Oct 1981, Josephine, da of Philip Bradley Canneaux, 1 da (Helen Josephine b 27 Aug 1983); *Career* articled clerk Whitfield & Co Leeds, qualified chartered accountant 1965; Thornton Baker: mangr Birmingham 1970–73, mangr Bedford 1973–75, ptnr 1975, managing ptnr 1983–95, sr ptnr 1995–; dir Bedfordshire Training and Enterprise Cncl 1990–95, memb Br Olympic Appeal Ctee for Bedfordshire 1995–96, dir (Eastern region) Children's Hospice, chm Bedford Branch Haven Children's Hosp Appeal; FCA 1975 (ACA 1965); *Recreations* photography, music, walking; *Clubs* Rotary (Bedford), Institute of Directors, Bedford Round Table; *Style*— Brian Woods, Esq; ✉ Grant Thornton, 49 Mill St, Bedford MK40 3LB (☎ 01234 211521)

WOODS, David Victor; *b* 7 May 1958; *Educ* Skegness GS, Selwyn Coll Cambridge (MA Law), Coll of Law Guildford; *Career* articled clerk Hill & Perks Slrs 1980–82, admitted slr 1982, ptnr Eversheds 1987– (chm Nat Commercial Practice Gp 1993–); *Clubs* Norwich Castle Round Table; *Style*— David Woods, Esq; ✉ Eversheds, Holland Court, The Close, Norwich NR1 4DX (☎ 01603 272727, fax 01603 610535)

WOODS, Elisabeth Ann; da of Norman Singleton, of London, and Cicely Margaret, *née* Lucas; *b* 27 Oct 1940; *Educ* S Hampstead HS, Girton Coll Cambridge (BA); *m* 1976, James Maurice Woods; *Career* asst princ Miny of Pensions and Nat Insurance 1963–69 (asst private sec to Min then private sec to Permanent Sec); DHSS (later DSS): princ 1969–76, asst sec 1976–88, (seconded to HM Treasy 1980–82), grade 3 Central Resource Mgmnt 1988, head of fin 1988–91; cmmr HM Customs and Excise 1992–: dir VAT Control 1992–95, dir Ops Compliance 1995–; *Recreations* cycling, reading, cooking; *Style*— Mrs Elisabeth Woods; ✉ HM Customs and Excise, New King's Beam House, 22 Upper Ground, London SE1 9PJ (☎ 0171 865 5978, fax 0171 865 5354)

WOODS, Prof (Hubert) Frank; s of Hubert George Woods (d 1959), of Leeds, and Julia Augusta, *née* Kamlinski (d 1963); *b* 18 Nov 1937; *Educ* St Bees Sch, Univ of Leeds (BSc), Univ of Oxford (BM BCh, DPhil); *m* 7 Jan 1966, Hilary Sheila, da of Ernest E Cox, of Sheffield; 1 s (Christopher b 21 Oct 1967), 2 da (Katharine b 23 Feb 1971, Rebecca b 5 June 1973); *Career* house offr posts NHS 1965–66, memb external med scientific staff MRC 1972–76, hon conslt physician Sheffield Health Authy 1976–, dean Faculty of Med and Dentistry Univ of Sheffield 1988– (prof of clinical pharmacology and therapeutics 1976–), sr external examiner in med Univ of Oxford 1988– (lectr in med 1967–72), examiner membership exam RCP 1989–, author 115 res papers and 3 books; memb GMC; regnl advsr RCP 1986–89; memb Hunterian Soc 1967, FRCP 1978 (MRCP 1968), FFPM 1989; *Books* Clinical and Biochemical Aspects of Lactic Acidosis (with R D Cohen, 1976); *Style*— Prof Frank Woods; ✉ Royal Hallamshire Hospital, Glossop Rd, Sheffield, S Yorks (☎ 0114 271 1900)

WOODS, Maj-Gen Henry Gabriel; CB (1979), MBE (1945), MC (1945), DL (N Yorks 1984); s of G S Woods (d 1961), of Bexhill-on-Sea, Sussex, and Flora, *née* MacNevin (d 1976); *b* 7 May 1924; *Educ* Highgate Sch, Trinity Coll Oxford (MA); *m* 29 April 1953, Imogen Elizabeth Birchenough, da of C E S Dodd (d 1975), of Bath; 2 da (Sarah b 1955, Arabella b 1958); *Career* cmmnd 5 Royal Inniskilling Dragoon Gds 1944, served NW Europe (Normandy to Baltic) 1944–45, 1945–51, 1960–62 and 1967–69, Adj Korea 1952, served Middle East 1954 and 1964–67, Mil Asst to Vice Chief of Def Staff 1962–64, cmd 5 Royal Inniskilling Dragoon Gds 1965–67, Asst Mil Sec to C-in-C BAOR 1967–69, Cdr RAC Centre 1969–72, Cdr Br Army Staff and Mil Attaché Br Embassy Washington USA 1972–75, GOC NE Dist 1976–80, Army Staff Coll 1956, Jt Servs Staff Coll 1960, RCDS 1972; head Centre for Industl and Educnl Liaison W and N Yorks 1980–87, dir St William's Fndn 1987–, dir Transpennine 1988–; chm: Bradford and W Yorks BIM 1982–84, Yorks Region RSA 1984–92, N Yorks Scout Cncl 1984–, 5 Royal Inniskilling Dragoon Gds Assoc 1979–92; pres: Royal Soc of St George (York and Humberside) 1986–88, Royal Dragoon Gds' Assoc 1992–; memb: York Area Mental Health Appeals Ctee 1984–90, TA&VR Assoc 1982–90, Yorks Agric Soc 1980–, Cncl RSA 1990–96; Vice Lord-Lt N Yorks 1986–; memb Merchants of the Staple of England 1982– (Mayor 1991–92), memb Merchant Adventurers of York 1989–; Hon DLitt Univ of Bradford 1988; FIMgt 1980, FRSA 1981; Order of Leopold Second Class (1966); *Books* Change and Challenge - History of the 5th Royal Inniskilling Dragoon Guards (with Gen Sir Cecil Blacker, 1976); *Recreations* gardening, walking, foot follower (hunting), military history; *Clubs* Cavalry and Guards', Ends of the Earth, 7 Armd Division Officers'; *Style*— Maj-Gen Henry Woods, CB, MBE, MC, DL; ✉ St William's Foundation, 5 College Street, York YO1 2JF (☎ 01904 642744)

WOODS, Humphrey Martin; s of Rev Howard Charles Woods, of Hindhead, Surrey, and Kathleen Ailsie Clutton, *née* Baker; descendant of the philosopher John Locke; *b* 23 Nov 1937; *Educ* Lancing, Trinity Coll Oxford (BA); *m* 1, 4 May 1963, Dona Leslie; m 2, 25 Jan 1977, Jennifer Mary, da of Brig Edward Hayden Tinker, of NZ; 2 da (Eleanor b 1977, Lucy b 1979), 3 s (Mark b 1981, Leo b 1984, Dominic b 1963); *Career* archaeologist with English Heritage (formerly Historic Bldgs & Monuments Cmmn for England) 1974–; tutor in archaeology Dept of Continuing Educn Univ of Oxford 1996–; FSA 1991; *Publications* Excavations on the Second Site of The Dominican Priory Oxford (in Oxoniensia Vol XLI, 1976), The Despoliation of the Abbey of SS Peter, Paul and Augustine Between the Years 1542 and 1793 (in Historical Essays in Memory of James Hobbs, 1980), The Completion of the Abbey Church of SS Peter, Paul and Augustine, Canterbury, by Abbots Wido and Hugh of Fleury (in British Archaeological Association Conference Transactions, 1982), Excavations at Eltham Palace 1975–79 (in Transactions of the London and Middx Archaeological Soc, 1982), Excavations on the Site of the Dominican Friary at Guildford in 1974 and 1978 (Research Vol No 9 of the Surrey Archaeological Soc, 1984), Excavations at Wenlock Priory 1981–86 (in Journal of the Br Archaeological Assoc, 1987), St Augustine's Abbey - report on excavations 1960–78 (Kent Archaeological Soc Monograph Series Vol IV, 1988), Romanesque West Front at The Church of the Holy Trinity Much Wenlock (in Transactions of the Shropshire Archaeological Soc, 1989), Excavations at Glastonbury Abbey 1987–1993 (in Proceedings of the Somerset Archaeological and Natural History Soc, Vol 138, 1994); *Recreations* walking in the Quantock hills, natural history; *Style*— Humphrey Woods, Esq, FSA; ✉ 20 Wembdon Hill, Bridgwater, Somerset TA6 7PX (☎ 01278 423 955)

WOODS, Prof John David; CBE (1991); s of Ronald Ernest Goff Woods (d 1968), and Ethel Marjorie Woods; *b* 26 Oct 1939; *Educ* Imperial Coll London (BSc, ARCS, PhD, DIC); *m* 7 April 1971 (m dis 1996), Irina Christine Alix, da of Bernd von Arnim; 1 s (Alexander Jan Roland b 1975), 1 da (Virginia Elizabeth Marina b 1980); *Career* res fell Meteorological Office 1966–72, prof of physical oceanography Univ of Southampton 1972–77, prof of oceanography and dir Institut Fuer Meereskunde Univ of Kiel 1977–86, dir of marine and atmospheric sciences NERC 1986–94; Imperial Coll Univ of London 1994–: dean Graduate Sch of Environment, head Dept of Earth Resources Engrg and prof of oceanography; hon prof of oceanography Univ of Southampton 1994–; contrib papers on oceanography and meteorology to various learned jls; fell Linacre Coll Oxford 1991–; memb: NERC 1979–82, Meteorological Res Ctee 1976–77 and 1987–96; Hon DSc: Univ of Liège 1980, Univ of Plymouth 1991; awarded RGS founder's medal 1996; FRGS 1966, FRMetSoc 1967, fndn memb Academia Europaea 1988; *Books* Underwater Science (1971), Underwater Research (1976); *Recreations* history; *Clubs* Athenaeum; *Style*— Prof John Woods, CBE; ✉ Department of Earth Resources Engineering, Imperial College, London SW7 2BP (☎ 0171 594 7400, fax 0171 594 7403)

WOODS, Dr Kevin J; *b* 9 Feb 1953; *Educ* Sale Co GS, QMC London (BSc, PhD); *m*; 3 da; *Career* lectr in health care Univ of London 1977–85, Australian studies visiting fell Flinders Univ S Australia 1984 (visiting lectr 1981), dir of planning and res and dep dist gen mangr N Derbyshire Health Authy 1985–89, dist gen mangr Chester Health Authy 1990, regnl gen mangr Trent Health 1993–94 (regnl dir of corp planning and exec memb Trent RHA 1991–93), sr fell Health Servs Mgmnt Unit Univ of Manchester until 1994, dir of purchasing NHS Mgmnt Exec The Scottish Office 1995–; special lectr in health care planning Faculty of Med Univ of Nottingham until 1995; author of published articles in academic jls; dir Chester and Wirral TEC until 1990, memb Nat Advsy Body of the Confidential Enquiry into Stillbirths and Deaths in Infancy; MHSM; *Books* The Social Geography of Medicine and Health (jtly with J Eyles); *Style*— Dr Kevin J Woods; ✉ NHS Management Executive, The Scottish Office, St Andrew's House, Edinburgh EH1 3DG (☎ 0131 244 1727)

WOODS, Prof Leslie Colin; s of Alexander Binny Woodhead (d 1983), of Auckland, NZ, and Gwendoline Isabel Annie, *née* Tew (d 1982); *b* 6 Dec 1922; *Educ* Auckland Univ (BSc, MSc, DSc, BE), Merton Coll Oxford (Rhodes scholar, MA, DPhil, DSc); *m* 1, 21 Aug 1943 (m dis 1977), (Gladys) Elizabeth; 5 da (Coral Anne (Mrs Schofield) b 1944, d 1993, Jillian Rebecca (Mrs Lloyd) b 1947, Diane Rose b 1949, Elizabeth Gladys b 1950, Patricia Beverley (Mrs Alvarez) b 1950); m 2, 11 Nov 1977 (m dis 1990), Helen Louise, *née* Troughton; m 3, 8 Feb 1990 (m dis 1996), Jacqueline Suzanne, *née* Griffiths; *Career* pilot 16/17 Fighter Sqdns RNZAF; served 1941–45: Pilot Offr 1942, Flying Offr 1943, Flt Lt 1944; prof of engrg Univ of NSW Sydney 1956–61; Univ of Oxford: fell and tutor in engrg sci Balliol Coll 1961–70 (emeritus fell 1990), prof of maths 1970–90 (emeritus prof 1990), chm Maths Inst 1984–89; Hon DSc Auckland Univ 1983; *Books* The Theory of Subsonic Plane Flow (1961), Introduction to Neutron Distribution Theory (1964), The Thermodynamics of Fluid Systems (1975), Principles of Magnetoplasma Dynamics (1987), Introduction to the Kinetic Theory of Gases and Magnetoplasmas (1993), Thermodynamic Inequalities in Gases and Magnetoplasmas (1996); *Recreations* gliding, clarinet playing; *Style*— Prof Leslie Woods; ✉ Balliol College, Oxford

WOODS, Maurice Eric; *b* 28 June 1933; *Educ* Moulsham Secdy Modern Sch Chelmsford, Univ of London (LLB, external); *m* 2 June 1956, Freda Pauline, *née* Schlosser; 2 s, 2 da; *Career* admitted slr 1965, in private practice 1965–84; pt/t chm: Supplementary Benefit Appeal Tribunals 1981–84, Social Security Appeal Tribunals June - Oct 1984; Industrial Tribunals: pt/t chm 1983–84, chm 1984–90, regnl chm 1990–; *Recreations* music, travel, reading, video photography; *Style*— Maurice Woods, Esq; ✉ Regional Office of Industrial Tribunals, 1st Floor, The Crescent Centre, Temple Back, Bristol BS1 6EZ (☎ 0117 929 8261)

WOODS, Michael Francis (Frank); s of late William Francis Woods, and Arana Cathryn, *née* Rowlands (d 1953); *b* 30 Oct 1933; *Educ* The Leys Sch Cambridge, Clare Coll Cambridge (DipArch, MA); *m* Judith Mary, da of James Marsh; 1 s (Simon Nicholas Michael b 4 Sept 1963); *Career* architect; Chamberlin, Powell & Bon (merged with Austin-Smith: Lord 1989): joined 1959, assoc 1963, ptnr 1978–86, sole practitioner and sr ptnr Chamberlin Powell Bon & Woods 1986–89, ptnr Austin-Smith: Lord; *Awards* RIBA Architecture Award (for work at Univ of Leeds), Structural Steel Award (for Wandsworth Refuse Transfer Station), RIBA Nat Award and Civic Trust Award (for Int Ecotechnology Res Centre, Cranfield Inst of Technol), Civic Trust Commendation (for Penarth Marina, nr Cardiff); ARIBA, FRSA; *Books* ACA Illustrated Directory of Architects (co-ed), Overlay Drafting (co-author); *Recreations* theatre, painting, silversmithing, photography; *Style*— Frank Woods, Esq; ✉ Austin-Smith: Lord, 17 Bowling Green Lane, London EC1R 0BD (☎ 0171 251 6161, fax 0171 608 3409)

WOODS, Michael John; s of Dr L H Woods, and Margery, *née* Pickard; *Educ* Bradfield; *m* 15 Jan 1966, Carolyn Rosemary, da of William Tadman, of Roborough, nr Winkleigh, N Devon; 1 s (Nicholas John b 13 Aug 1967), 1 da (Jennifer Sarah Rosemary b 29 May 1969); *Career* Nat Serv 1 Bn Royal Fus (serv Suez Crisis) 1955–77; trainee exec Mecca Ltd 1957–63; dir: Silver Blades Ice Rink Ltd 1963–70, Mecca Catering 1968–, Mecca Leisure Ltd 1973–; asst md: Mecca Bingo Social Clubs 1972–80, Mecca Leisure Ltd 1979–85; chm: Mecca Agency International 1983–85, Ison Bros (Newcastle) Ltd 1983–85, Pointer Motor Co 1983–85, Scot Automatic Printing 1983–85; md: Mecca Leisure Speciality Catering Div 1985–91, Speciality Catering Div Europe 1989–91; dir Saddle and Sirloin Restaurant Ltd 1991–; self employed catering conslt 1991–, gp catering exec Apollo Leisure (UK) Ltd 1993–; vice pres Variety Club of GB (co chm Sunshine Coaches); memb: Exec Ctee Actors' Charitable Tst, Confrérie de la Chaîne des Rôtisseurs, Hotel and Catering Benevolent Assoc; FInstD 1965, FHCIMA 1989; *Recreations* squash, swimming, shooting (clay and pheasant), fishing; *Style*— Michael Woods, Esq; ✉ Glendale, Farley Green, Albury, nr Guildford, Surrey (☎ 01483 202472)

WOODS, Rt Rev Robert Wilmer (Robin); KCMG (1980), KCVO (1971); s of Rt Rev Edward Sydney Woods (d 1953), Bishop of Lichfield, and Clemence Rachel, 2 da of Robert Barclay, JP; *b* 15 Feb 1914; *Educ* Gresham's, Trinity Coll Cambridge; *m* 1942, Henrietta Marion, JP (1966), da of late Kenneth H Wilson, OBE, JP; 2 s, 3 da; *Career* asst sec Student Christian Movement 1938–42; ordained priest 1939; army chaplain 1942–46, vicar of S Wigston 1946–51; Archdeacon: Singapore 1951–58, Sheffield 1958–62; Dean of Windsor, domestic chaplain to HM The Queen and Register Most Noble Order of the Garter 1962–71, Bishop of Worcester 1971–81, Prelate Order of St Michael and St George 1971–89, Asst Bishop Diocese of Gloucester 1982–; dir Christian Aid 1969–80, memb Prince of Wales Tst 1984; *Books* Robin Woods: an autobiography (1986); *Recreations* shooting, painting; *Clubs* Brooks's; *Style*— The Rt Rev Robin Woods, KCMG, KCVO; ✉ Torsend House, Tirley, Glos GL19 4EU (☎ 01452 780327)

WOODS, Prof William Alfred; *b* 26 May 1931; *Educ* Upholland GS Lancs, Univ of Liverpool (BEng, PhD, DEng, W H Wakinson prize, James Carlton Stitt Silver medal); *m*; 3 c; *Career* graduate apprentice English Electric Co Ltd Liverpool 1953–54, tech asst Aero Engine Div Rolls-Royce Ltd Derby 1956–59, pt/t conslt Res Laboratories General Motors Corporation Warren Michigan USA 1969–89; consulting experience incl: Br Ship Res Assoc 1959–68, Rocket Propulsion Estab Westcott 1960, Associated Octel Co 1960–, Nat Engrg Laboratory E Kilbride 1965–67, Ruston and Hornsby Ltd 1968, BR Bd 1968–88, CEGB 1971, UKAEA Harwell 1974, Aust Miny of Supply 1974, NZ Inventions Devpt Authy 1974, Rohm & Haas Co 1975–76, Kennedy and Donkin consulting engrs 1976, US Nat Bureau of Standards 1976–77; Dept of Mechanical Engrg Univ of Liverpool: lectr 1959–64, sr lectr 1964–67, reader 1967–79; academic sub-dean Univ of Liverpool 1972–75, visiting full prof Dept of Mechanical Engrg Mass Inst of Technol USA 1976–77 (visiting prof 1963); Univ of London: prof of mechanical engrg 1979–94 (prof emeritus 1994–), head Dept of Mechanical Engrg QMC 1979–87; visiting prof Sch of Mechanical and Prodn Engrg Nanyang Technological Inst Singapore 1988 and 1989; IMechE: former sec Merseyside and N Wales Sub-Branch and fndr memb Merseyside and N Wales Branch Ctee, former vice chm Headquarters Ctee Thermodynamics and Fluid Mechanics Gp, currently memb Energy and Fluid Transfer Ctee (chm 1984–87) and Univs' Internal Combustion Engine Gp, James Clayton Fund prize 1959, E Midlands Branch graduate prize 1960, N Western Branch graduate prize 1961, Viscount Weir prize 1962, James Clayton award 1963 and 1974, Sr Engr award 1989; Br Cncl award for tech exchange to visit Eidgenossishe Technische Hochschule Zurich Switzerland 1964; CEng, FEng 1989, FIMechE, FRSA; *Publications* ed Thermodynamics and Fluid Mechanics Div Commonwealth and International Library; fndr memb: Editorial Advsy Bd International Jl of Applied Engineering Education, Hon Editorial Advsy Bd International Jl of Heat and Fluid Flow; *Style*— Prof William Woods, FEng; ✉ c/o Department of Mechanical Engineering, Queen Mary and Westfield College, University of London, Mile End Road, London E1 4NS

WOODS-SCAWEN, Brian; s of Dennis Woods-Scawen, of Warwick, and Betty, *née* Runacres; *b* 2 Nov 1946; *Educ* Salesian Coll Farnborough, Univ of Sheffield (BA (Econ)), Univ of Warwick (MA); *m* 1988, Jane Woods-Scawen, JP, *qv*; 1 da (Suzannah b 28 April 1977), 1 s (Tristan b 2 Dec 1978); *Career* Coopers & Lybrand: articled clerk 1971–74, ptnr 1980, chm Corp Fin Midlands 1986, memb Partnership Bd 1994, chm Midlands Region 1995; FCA 1979, assoc memb Securities Inst 1994; *Books* Survey of Financial Management in Law Firms (1993, 1994, 1995); author of articles on strategic devpts in legal profession; *Style*— Brian Woods-Scawen, Esq; ✉ The Stables, Hunt Paddocks, Kenilworth, Warwickshire CV8 1NL (☎ 01926 58225); Coopers & Lybrand, Temple Court, 35 Bull Street, Birmingham B4 6JT (☎ 0121 265 5000, fax 0121 265 5959, car 0831 680025)

WOODS-SCAWEN, Jane; JP (1995); da of William Richard Grice (d 1985), of Wolverhampton, and Louisa May, *née* Gibbons; *b* 18 March 1950; *Educ* Wolverhampton HS for Girls, Univ of Birmingham (BCom, Theodore Mander prize, Doris Griffiths prize); *m* m 2, 27 May 1988, Brian Dennis Woods-Scawen, *qv*, s of Dennis Charles Woods-Scawen; 1 step da (Suzannah b 28 April 1977), 1 step s (Tristan b 2 Dec 1978); *Career* Coopers & Lybrand (formerly Cooper Brothers & Co): articled clerk 1971–74, seconded to Wolverhampton Met Borough Cncl 1982–83, ptnr 1983–92 (first female ptnr); counsellor RELATE 1992– (Cert CC 1996); dir Grand Theatre Wolverhampton 1982–87; Soroptimist International: memb Wolverhampton 1975–87 (pres 1983–84), memb Central Birmingham 1987–95, memb Kenilworth 1995–; memb Cncl Wolverhampton C of C 1982–87; FCA 1974, FRSA 1990; *Recreations* theatre, music, literature, food; *Style*— Jane Woods-Scawen, JP; ✉ The Stables, Hunt Paddocks, Rouncil Lane, Kenilworth, Warwickshire CV8 1NL (☎ 01926 858225)

WOODSTOCK, Viscount; Timothy Charles Robert Noel Bentinck; o s and h of 11 Earl of Portland, *qv*; *b* 1 June 1953; *Educ* Harrow, Univ of East Anglia (BA); *m* 1979, Judith Ann, da of John Robert Emerson, of Cheadle, Staffs; 2 s (Hon William Jack Henry b 1984, Hon Jasper James Mellowes b 1988); *Heir* s, Hon William Jack Henry Bentinck b 19 May 1984; *Career* actor as Timothy Bentinck; *Style*— Viscount Woodstock; ✉ 3 Stock Orchard Crescent, Islington, London N7 9SL

WOODVINE, John; *Career* actor; *Theatre* incl: Russian colonel in Every Good Boy Deserves Favour, Cutler Walpole in The Doctor's Dilemna, Mr Ormsby in Poor Horace, Jacky in Close the Coalhouse Door, Claudius in Hamlet, Mr Prince in Rocket to the Moon, Bustopher, Asparagus and Growltiger in Cats, The Chorus in Henry V, Falstaff in Henry IV parts I and II (Best Comedy Performance Olivier Awards 1987), Gregor in Between East and West (Hampstead), Chris Christopherson in Anna Christie (Young Vic), Father Jack in Dancing at Lughnasa (Garrick) 1991–92; English Shakespeare Co incl: title role in Volpone (also tour), Shylock in The Merchant of Venice, Prospero in The Tempest 1992, Duncan and The Porter 1992; RNT incl: Gens in Ghetto, George H Jones in Machinal; RSC incl: Banquo in Macbeth, Supple in The Alchemist, Dogberry in Much Ado About Nothing, Falstaff in The Merry Wives of Windsor, Malvolio in Twelfth Night, Uncle Ralph in Nicholas Nickelby (London, Broadway and Channel 4), Monsieur in The Hostage, Priuli in Venice Preserved; *Television* BBC incl: Detective Inspr Witty in Z-Cars, Chief Supt Kingdom in New Scotland Yard, All Creatures Great and Small, The Black and Blue Lamp, An Actor's Life For Me, Spender, The Browing Version, Swallows and Amazons, Edge of Darkness, Tell-Tale Heart, Henry IV (parts I & II); Yorkshire incl: Room at the Bottom, New Statesman, Runaway Bay (2 series), Heartbeat; Granada incl: The Dog It Was That Died, A Tale of Two Cities, Who Bombed Birmingham?, Medics; TVS incl: Knights of God, A Month in the Country; Thames incl: All in Good Faith, The Pirate Prince; other credits incl: Les Girls (Central), title role in Pontius Pilate (Brook Prodns), Dr Finlay (STV); *Films* incl: An American Werewolf in London, Murder With Mirrors, Deceptions, Squaring the Circle, Vote for Hitler, A Nightingale Sang, Danny Champion of the World, Count Down to War, Wuthering Heights, The Trial; *Style*— John Woodvine, Esq; ✉ c/o Scott Marshall Personal Management, 44 Perryn Rd, London W3 7NA (☎ 0181 749 7692, fax 0181 740 7342)

WOODWARD, His Hon Judge Barry; s of Wilfred Woodward, of Co Durham, and Mary Hannah, *née* Lax; *b* 13 June 1938; *Educ* Alderman Wraith GS Co Durham, Univ of Sheffield (LLB, LLM); *m* 21 Oct 1963, Patricia, da of Hamdon Holland; 2 da (Joanne Clair, LLB, b 24 Dec 1966, Alison Jane, LLB, b 23 Feb 1970 (both barristers)); *Career* various teaching posts and res 1961–70, called to the Bar Grays Inn 1970, in practice at Bar Northern Circuit 1970–84, chm of Industrial Tbnls 1984–90, recorder 1988–90, circuit judge (Northern Circuit) 1990–; *Style*— His Hon Judge Woodward; ✉ Manchester Crown Court, Crown Square, Manchester (☎ 0161 954 1800)

WOODWARD, (John) Charles; s of Eric Jackson Woodward (d 1978), of Belper, Derbyshire, and Maude Woodward, *née* Adams (d 1989); *b* 31 Oct 1935; *Educ* Herbert Strutt GS Belper Derbyshire, Univ of Manchester (BSc); *m* 11 Sept 1962, Kathy, da of Harry Ashton (d 1982), of Hazel Grove, Cheshire; 1 s (Giles b 15 Dec 1967), 2 da (Zoë b 14 Sept 1963, Sarah b 5 Jan 1965); *Career* memb London Stock Exchange 1971–75, ptnr Colegrave & Co 1972–75, investmt mangr Reed International 1975–83, chief exec BA Pensions 1984–91; Nat Assoc of Pension Funds: memb Cncl 1982–91, chm Investmt Ctee 1982–84, chm of Cncl 1987–89, vice pres 1989–91, chm Tstee Pension Scheme 1991–; investmt advsr Cleveland CC 1983–86; dir: Nat Freight Corporation Tstees Ltd 1986–, Legal and General Property Fund Managers Ltd 1991–, Kingfisher Pension Trustee Ltd 1992–, Marine and General Mutual Life Assurance Society 1994–; chm: BES Trustees plc 1992–, Albright & Wilson Pension Trustees Ltd 1993–, Trustees Porvait Pension Plan 1993–; tstee: Dunn & Co Pensions Scheme 1993–, Mansfield Brewery Group Pension Scheme 1994–; memb Ctee of Mgmnt Fleming General Exempt Fund 1994–; FIA 1965; *Style*— Charles Woodward, Esq; ✉ Foston House, 29 Brudenell Avenue, Canford Cliffs, Poole, Dorset BH13 7NW (☎ 01202 701171)

WOODWARD, Christopher Haldane; s of William Haldane Woodward, of Wirral, Cheshire, and Audrey Woodward; *b* 18 Nov 1946; *Educ* Calday Grange GS, Univ of Birmingham (BSocSc), Manchester Business Sch (MBA); *m* 9 Aug 1969, Frances Maria, da of Richard Alan Beatty, of Edinburgh; 1 s (Matthew b 1974), 2 da (Rosalind b 1976, Charlotte b 1980); *Career* graduate trainee and economist mktg asst GKN 1968–70, mktg mangr GKN Farr Filtration 1970–72, mktg exec Guthrie Corporation 1974–75, mktg and devpt exec Tay Textiles 1976–77 (gp mktg and planning controller 1978–79), Cape Insulation Ltd 1979–82 (mktg mangr, nat sales mangr, sales and mktg dir); mktg dir: Euro Uniroyal Ltd 1982–86, 3i plc 1986–94; md Total Communications 1994–; dir: Design for Learning Ltd, Anglo-Romanian Development Corporation Ltd; chief exec Molecular Solutions Ltd; memb MBA Soc; *Recreations* opera, theatre, music, art; *Clubs* RAC; *Style*— Christopher Woodward, Esq; ✉ Total Communications (☎ 01825 724030)

WOODWARD, Dagmar; *Career* hotelier; initial trg experience as chef Frankfurt Inter-Continental 1970, subsequently various positions within food and beverage depts London, Washington and Atlanta, resident mangr NY; gen mangr: Portman Inter-Continental until 1991, May Fair Inter-Continental 1991–; Hotelier of the Year 1992; memb: London Ctee BHA, RAGB, London West One Mangrs Assoc; chm Environment Ctee IHC; FHCIMA, Master Innholder; Dame de la Jurade de Saint Emilion; *Style*— Ms Dagmar Woodward; ✉ General Manager, The May Fair Inter-Continental London, Stratton Street, London W1A 2AN (☎ 0171 629 7777, fax 0171 629 1459)

WOODWARD, Edward; OBE (1980); *b* 1 June 1930; *Educ* RADA; *m* 1; 2 s (Timothy, Peter), 1 da (Sarah); m 2, Michele Dotrice; 1 da (Emily); *Career* actor; *Theatre* various rep work, West End debut Where There's a Will (Garrick) 1954, Owen Tudor in The Queen and the Welshman (Edinburgh Festival and Lyric Hammersmith), Salad Days, joined RSC 1958, Mercutio in Romeo and Juliet, Laertes in Hamlet, Thaliard in Pericles and Claudio in Much Ado About Nothing, Percy in Rattle of a Simple Man (West End and Broadway), lead in High Spirits (Broadway), lead roles in On Approval, The Wolf, The Dark Horse, The Male of the Species, Robin Hood in Babes in the Wood, Sydney Carton in Two Cities (Variety Award for Best Performance in a Musical), title role in Cyrano and Flamineo in The White Devil (NT), Macheath in The Beggar's Opera (also dir), lead in Richard III (Ludlow Festival) 1982; *Television* Callan (series, Best Actor Soc of Film and TV Arts (now BAFTA) 1969, Sun Awards 1970/71 and TV Times Awards 1972), Robert McCall in The Equalizer (series, Golden Globe Award and 5 Emmy nominations), Guy Crouchback in Sword of Honour, Cassius in Julius Caesar, Lopakin in The Cherry Orchard, Luigi in Saturday, Sunday, Monday, Mervyn Griffiths Jones, QC in The Trial of Lady Chatterley, F Scott Fitzgerald in A Dream Divided, Rod of Iron, A Bit of a Holiday, The Bass Player and the Blonde (mini-series), Sir Samuel Hoare in Churchill: The Wilderness Years, Royston in Codename Kyril, appearance in Common as Muck (BBC) 1994; host: World War II (Emmy Award 1990), In Suspicious Circumstances (Granada); in US: Simon Legree in Uncle Tom's Cabin (ACE Television Award nomination), The Man in the Brown Suit (Warner Bros), Hunted (Universal), Harrison (movie series, Paramount TV) 1994, The Woodward Files (Westcountry TV/HTV West) 1995; *Film* title in Breaker Morant, Saul in King David, Sargie in Mr Johnson, The Ghost of Christmas Present in A Christmas Carol, Josh Gifford in The Champions, Cdr Powell in Who Dares Wins, lead in The Wicker Man, Sgt Wellbeloved in Stand Up Virgin Soldiers, Sitting Target, The File on the Golden Goose, title role in Callan, Deadly Advice; *Music* 3 Edward Woodward Hour TV Specials, recorded 12 LP albums, Feelings (compilation), awarded 3 Gold discs; *Style*— Edward Woodward, Esq, OBE; ✉ c/o Peters Fraser & Dunlop Ltd, 503 The Chambers, Chelsea Harbour, Lots Road, London SW10 0XF (☎ 0171 352 4446, fax 0171 352 7356)

WOODWARD, Gerard Vaughan; s of Reginald Llewelwyn Woodward (d 1991), and Sylvia, *née* Walsh (d 1981); *b* 4 Dec 1961; *Educ* St Ignatius Coll London, Falmouth Sch of Art, LSE (BSc, Maurice Freedman Prize); *m* 1983, Suzanne Jane, da of Robin Anderson; *Career* freelance artist 1985–89, freelance writer 1989–; memb Soc Authors 1992–; *Poetry* The Unwriter and Other Poems (1989, Eric Gregory Award), Householder (1991, Poetry Book Soc choice 1991, Somerset Maugham Award 1992, shortlist J L Rhys Prize Mail on Sunday 1992), After the Deafening (1994, Poetry Book Soc Choice 1994);

Recreations chess, playing the piano, pathology; *Style*— Gerard Woodward, Esq; ✉ c/o Chatto & Windus Ltd, Random Century House, 20 Vauxhall Bridge Road, London SW1V 2SA (☎ 0171 973 9740, fax 0171 233 6123)

WOODWARD, Adm Sir John Forster (Sandy); GBE (1989), KCB (1982); *b* 1 May 1932; *Educ* RNC Dartmouth; *m* 1960, Charlotte Mary, *née* McMurtrie; 1 s, 1 da; *Career* RN 1946; served HMS: Maidstone, Sheffield, Zodiac; submarine specialist 1954; served HMS: Sanguine, Porpoise; CO HMS Tireless 1961–62; Lt Cdr 1962, CO HMS Grampus 1965, 1 Lt HMS Valiant to 1967; Cdr 1967; CO: qualifying course for COs 1967–69, CO HMS Warspite 1969–71; RCDS 1971–72, Capt 1972, Directorate of Naval Plans MOD 1972–74, Capt SM Sea Trg 1974–76, CO HMS Sheffield 1976–78, dir Naval Plans MOD 1978–81, Rear-Adm 1981, Flag Offr First Flotilla 1981–83, Sr Cdr (from HMS Hermes) S Atlantic Task Gps in Falklands War 1982, Flag Offr Submarines and NATO Cdr Submarines Eastern Atlantic 1983–85, Vice Adm 1984, Dep CDS (Commitments) MOD 1985–87, Adm 1987–89; C in C Naval Home Cmd 1987–89, ret 1989; conslt on defence matters, independent inspr Lord Chancellor's Panel; Hon Liveryman Worshipful Co of Glass Sellers; *Books* One Hundred Days (1992); *Recreations* sailing, golf, bridge, skiing, computers; *Style*— Adm Sir Sandy Woodward, GBE, KCB; ✉ c/o Naval Secretary, Room 161, Victory Building, HM Naval Base, Portsmouth PO1 3LS

WOODWARD, Dr Michael Trevor; s of Trevor Woodward, of Weare Giffard Hall, Weare Giffard, N Devon, and Beryl Gladys, *née* Barker; *b* 25 Nov 1957; *Educ* Dartmouth Comprehensive Sch Sandwell, Univ of Aberdeen (MA, PhD), Univ of Edinburgh (MBA); *m* Anne, *née* Russell; 2 da (Katherine Millar, Molly Jennifer); *Career* dir: Ivory and Sime plc 1990–95 (investmt mangr 1983), Ivory and Sime Investment Management plc 1995–; *Recreations* squash, racketball, golf; *Clubs* Sloane; *Style*— Dr Michael Woodward; ✉ 2 Corrennie Drive, Edinburgh EH10 6EQ (☎ 0131 447 2989); Ivory & Sime plc, 1 Charlotte Square, Edinburgh EH2 4DZ (☎ 0131 225 1357)

WOODWARD, Roger Robert; AC (1992), OBE (1980); s of Francis William Woodward, and Gladys, *née* Bracken, of Sydney, Australia; *b* 20 Dec 1942; *Educ* Sydney Conservatorium of Music (Dip SCM), Warsaw Acad of Music; *m* 16 April 1989, Patricia May, da of Edward Ludgate; 2 s (Benjamin, Elooy), 1 da (Asmira); *Career* concert pianist, conductor and composer; has worked with various major conductors incl Claudio Abbado, Pierre Boulez, Sir Charles Mackerras, Kurt Masur and Zubin Mehta; has appeared at over fifty international festivals (incl nine BBC Proms seasons) in forty countries, performed numerous world premieres; featured with Boulez, Stockhausen, Xenakis and John Cage in BBC documentary film, worked with numerous other major international composers, conductors and orchs; over forty recordings and videos on various major labels; artistic dir: Sydney Spring Int Festival of New Music, Kötschach-Mauthen Festival Austria, Saaremaa Summer Music Days Estonia; fell Frederic Chopin Int Soc 1976; Hon Dr of Creative Arts Woollong Univ 1992, Hon DMus Univ of Sydney 1995; Cdr Cross Order of Merit Poland 1992; *Style*— Roger Woodward, Esq, AC, OBE; ✉ c/o ECAM Ltd Concert Management, 130 Drayton Park, London N5 1LX (☎ 0171 354 3844, fax 0171 609 5644)

WOODWARD, Sarah Wendy Boston; da of Edward Albert Arthur Woodward (the actor), and Venetia Mary, *née* Battine; *b* 3 April 1963; *Educ* Moria House Sch Eastbourne, RADA (Bancroft Medal); *Career* actress; *Theatre* RSC: Henry V, Love's Labours Lost, Hamlet, Richard III, Camille and Red Noses 1984–85, Murder in the Cathedral 1993–94, Rosaura in The Venetian Twins, Miranda in The Tempest 1993–94, Rosaline in Love's Labours Lost 1995; Birmingham Repertory: Charley's Aunt, The Winter's Tale; other theatre incl: Artist Descending a Staircase (King's Head, Duke of York), The Rape of Lucrece (Almeida), Romeo and Juliet, Arms And The Man (Regent's Park Open Air Theatre), Angelus From Morning 'Til Midnight (Soho Poly), Build On Sand (Royal Court), Talk of the Devil (Bristol Old Vic), London Assurance (Chichester Theatre, Royal Haymarket), Schism in England (NT), Anne Danby in Kean (Old Vic, Toronto) 1990–91, Rose Jones in The Sea (RNT) 1991–92, Wild Oats (RNT) 1995, Connie Wicksteed in Habeas Corpus (Donmare Warehouse) 1996; *Television* incl: The Bill (LWT), Gems (Thames), The Two of Us (LWT), Sherlock Holmes (Granada), Poirot (Thames), Casualty (BBC); *Radio* incl: Scuttling Off (Radio 4) 1988, 84 Charing Cross Road (World Service) 1991; *Awards* Clarence Derwent Award for Artist Descending a Staircase 1989, nominated for Best Newcomer Shakespeare Globe Awards 1994; *Recreations* all sports, poker (winner Fulham Open Hold 'em Championship Trophy 1994), blackjack; *Style*— Miss Sarah Woodward; ✉ c/o ICM Ltd, Oxford House, 76 Oxford Street, London W1N 0AX (☎ 0171 636 6565, fax 0171 323 0101)

WOODWARD, Stephen James; s of Wesley James Woodward (d 1968), and Margery, *née* Gill (d 1978); *b* 25 May 1950; *Educ* King's Sch Rochester, W London Business Sch (BA); *m* 24 March 1973, Alison Linda, da of Robert Epps; 3 s (Paul James, David Robert, Michael Stephen); *Career* sponsored business undergraduate De La Rue Co 1968–72, product exec Nestle Co 1972–75, sr product mangr Carnation Co 1975–78, mktg dir Seagram UK 1978–86, gp dir Lowe Howard-Spink advtg 1987–89; chief exec: Brands Div Michael Peters Group plc 1989–90, Ayer Group UK 1990–93 (responsible for founding Ayer/DP&A Direct Marketing, Ayer Data Management), Leagas Shafron Davis Chick Ayer (after merger) 1993; chm DP&A Ltd 1993–; fndr dir: The Competitive Advantage Business Ltd 1994–, DWT Ventures; chm Inpost Ltd; chm external affrs The Marketing Soc; *Books* Understanding Brands - By Ten People Who Do (1991), Branding In Action (1993); *Style*— Stephen Woodward, Esq; ✉ The Competitive Advantage Business Ltd, River House, Restmor Way, Wallington, Surrey (☎ 0181 288 2000, fax 0181 288 2100)

WOODWARD, William Charles (Bill); QC (1985); s of Wilfred Charles Woodward, of Nottingham, and Annie Stewart, *née* Young; *b* 27 May 1940; *Educ* Nottingham HS, St John's Coll Oxford (BA); *m* 1965, Carolyn Edna, da of Francis Doughty Johns, of Kent; 2 s (William b 1968, Fergus b 1974), 1 da (Rebecca b 1966); *Career* called to the Bar Inner Temple 1964, memb Midland and Oxford Circuit, marshall to late Sir Donald Finnemore, head of Chambers 1987–95, recorder 1989–; memb Law Advsy Ctee Univ of Nottingham, fndr memb Nottingham Medico Legal Soc; *Recreations* sporadic cookery, swimming, gardening; *Clubs* Pre-War Austin Seven, Notts United Services; *Style*— W C Woodward, Esq, QC; ✉ 24 The Ropewalk, Nottingham NG1 5EF (☎ 0115 947 2581, fax 0115 947 6532, MDX 10,060)

WOOF, Richard Austin; s of Richard Woof (d 1983), of Launceston, Tasmania, and Avril Frances Chandler Hopkinson, *née* Clark (d 1984); *b* 14 June 1940; *Educ* King's Coll Taunton; *m* 17 June 1961, Christine Julia, da of Arthur Seymour Hodgkinson (d 1978), of Devon; 1 s (Julian b 1961), 1 da (Caroline b 1972); *Career* slr; sr ptnr Debenham & Co 1974–, commercial property ed The Law Society Gazette 1975–93; FRSA; *Recreations* carriage driving, quarter horse racing; *Style*— Richard A Woof, Esq; ✉ Gorebridge House, Loxhill, nr Godalming, Surrey GU8 4BH; Debenham & Co, 20 Hans Rd, Knightsbridge, London SW3 1RT (☎ 0171 581 2471, fax 0171 823 8977)

WOOL, Dr Rosemary Jane; CB (1995); *b* 19 July 1935; *Educ* Charing Cross Hosp Med Sch Univ of London (MB BS, DRCOG); *Career* princ in general practice 1963–70, psychiatric trg 1970–74; HM Prison Service: therapist HM Prison Grendon 1974–78, sr med offr HM Young Offenders' Inst Leicester 1979–82, princ med offr 1983–89, dir Prison Medical Services 1989–, dir Health Care 1991–96; head Educn and Trg Unit Dept of Addictive Behaviour St George's Hosp London 1996–, advsr to the Prisons Bd States of Jersey 1996–; sec gen Int Cncl Prison Medical Services; memb: Royal Soc Health, BMA, RSM; FRCPsych 1988 (MRCPsych 1974); *Style*— Dr Rosemary Wool, CB; ✉ Wicken House, 105 Weston Road, Aston Clinton, Aylesbury, Bucks HP22 5EP (☎ 01296 630448)

WOOLCOCK, Robin Arthur John; s of Arthur Woolcock (d 1977), of Hayes, Middx, and Minnie Elizabeth, *née* Dance, of Hitchin, Herts; *b* 6 Sept 1947; *Educ* Hayes Co GS, Queen Mary Coll London (BSc(Econ)); *m* April 1971, Ruth Monica, da of Fred Matthews, of Wirral; 2 da (Claire Elizabeth b 6 Aug 1975, Louise Jane b 17 Sept 1977); *Career* various sales and mktg positions Ford of Europe until 1978 (joined as graduate trainee 1969), product planning dir Leyland Truck and Bus 1978–82, UK ops dir Leyland (later Leyland DAF) 1982–88; Volkswagen AG Group/Lonrho: md MAN/VW Truck and Bus Ltd 1989–92, md Skoda UK Ltd 1993–94, head of Volkswagen at VAG (United Kingdom) Ltd 1994–; Freeman City of London, Liveryman Worshipful Co of Carmen; memb Inst of Road Transport Engrs, FCIT; *Recreations* Northampton RFC; *Style*— Robin Woolcock, Esq; ✉ VAG (United Kingdom) Ltd, Yeomans Drive, Blakelands, Milton Keynes, Bucks MK14 5AN (☎ 01908 601789, fax 01908 601607)

WOOLDRIDGE, Ian Edmund; OBE (1991); s of late Edmund James Wooldridge, and late Bertha Wooldridge; *b* 14 Jan 1932; *Educ* Brockenhurst GS; *m* 1, 1957 (m dis 1979), Veronica Ann, *née* Churcher; 3 s (Kevin, Simon, Max); m 2, 1 Dec 1980, Sarah Margaret, da of Leonard Chappell, of Great Easton, Essex; *Career* RN 1952–54; columnist and chief sportswriter Daily Mail 1972– (cricket corr 1963–71); Sports Cncl/Sports Writers' Assoc and British Press Awards: twice Columnist of the Year, five times Sportswriter of the Year, four times Sports Feature Writer of the Year; *Books* Cricket Lovely Cricket (1963), Mary P (with Mary Peters, 1974), MCC: The Autobiography of a Cricketer (with Colin Cowdrey, 1976), The Best of Wooldridge (1978), Travelling Reserve (1982), Sport in the 80's (1989); *Recreations* travel, golf, Beethoven, dry martinis; *Clubs* Reform; *Style*— Ian Wooldridge, Esq, OBE; ✉ 11 Collingham Gardens, London SW5; Daily Mail, Northcliffe House, London W8 (☎ 0171 938 6228)

WOOLDRIDGE, Michael James (Mike); s of James Wooldridge (d 1996), and Eveline Betty, *née* Carter; *b* 24 July 1947; *Educ* Bournemouth Sch for Boys, Harlow Tech Coll (later NCTJ Cert); *m* 1974, Ruth Kyre Holliday, da of Canon Keble Thomas (d 1992), and Gwyneth Thomas; 3 c (Beth b 1977, Simon b 1978, Sophie b 1981); *Career* reporter Eastern Counties Newspapers 1965–68, VSO Uganda 1968–69; with the BBC 1970–: World Service News 1970–78, reporter Radio News 1978–82, East Africa corr 1982–89, Southern Africa corr 1989–90, Religious Affrs and Community Rels corr 1990–96, S Asia corr 1997–; memb NUJ 1965; *Books* VSO in Action (1978), War Wounds (on Sudan, contrib 1988); *Recreations* family pursuits, walking, music, travel; *Clubs* Athenaeum; *Style*— Mike Wooldridge; ✉ c/o Foreign News, Room 3084, Broadcasting House, London W1A 1AA (☎ 0171 765 5284, fax 0171 636 9515)

WOOLDRIDGE, Susan Margot; da of John De Lacy Wooldridge, DSO, DFC, DFM (d 1958), and Margaretta, *née* Scott; *Educ* Convent of the Holy Child Jesus London, More House London, Central Sch of Speech and Drama London, Ecole Jacques Lecoq Paris; *Career* actress; *Theatre* incl: Map of the Heart, Night Mother, Look Back in Anger, Office Suite, Ubu Roi, Dusa Fish Stas and Vi, The Cherry Orchard, School for Scandal, The Merchant of Venice, Tartuffe, Hayfever; *Television* incl: The Jewel in the Crown (ALVA Award for Best Actress, BAFTA nomination for Best Actress), The Dark Room, The Devil's Disciple, Time and the Conways, Hay Fever, John MacNab, Ticket to Ride, The Small Assassin, Pastoral Care, The Last Place on Earth, Tickle on the Tum, The Naked Civil Servant, Rep (comedy series), The Racing Game, Changing Step, The Pied Piper, Crimestrike, Broke, An Unknown Woman, The Hummingbird Tree, Inspector Alleyn Mysteries, Bad Company, All Quiet on the Preston Front, Under the Hammer, Preston Front, The Writing Game; *Films* incl: How to Get Ahead in Advertising, Hope and Glory (BAFTA Award for Best Supporting Actress), Loyalties, Butley, The Shout, Dead Man's Folly, Frankenstein, Afraid of the Dark, Twenty-One, Just Like a Woman; *Style*— Ms Susan Wooldridge; ✉ London Management, 2–4 Noel Street, London W1V 3RB (☎ 0171 287 9000, fax 0171 287 3036)

WOOLF, Dr Anthony Derek; s of Douglas Langton Woolf, of Woodford, Essex, and Kathorn Beth Woolf, *née* Pearce (d 1980); *b* 12 June 1951; *Educ* Forest Sch, Snaresbrook, London Hosp Med Coll (BSc, MB BS); *m* 4 Dec 1975, Hilary Ann, da of Ronald Ruddock-West (d 1978); 1 s (Richard Thomas b 1981), 1 da (Sarah Louise b 1979); *Career* sr registrar Royal Nat Hosp for Rheumatic Diseases and Bristol Royal Infirmary 1983–87, conslt rheumatologist Royal Cornwall Hosp Truro Cornwall 1987; author of papers on rheumatology, med educn, viral arthritis and osteoporosis; ed Osteoporosis Review, ed Balliere's Clinical Rheumatology, memb Editorial Bd Annals of Rheumatic Diseases and Care of the Elderly, memb Cncl and treas Nat Osteoporosis Soc, chm EULAR Educn and Trg Ctee; Freeman Worshipful Soc of Apothecaries; FRCP 1979 (MRCP 1979); *Books* Osteoporosis - A Clinical Guide (1988 and 1990), How to Avoid Osteoporosis - A Positive Health Guide (1989), Osteoporosis - A Pocket Book (1994); *Style*— Dr Anthony Woolf; ✉ Royal Cornwall Hospital, Dept of Rheumatology, Infirmary Hill, Truro TR1 2HZ (☎ 01872 74242)

WOOLF, David; s of Raymond Woolf, of Newcastle-upon-Tyne and London, and Valerie Belle, *née* Robins (d 1954), of Plymouth; *b* 27 Jan 1945; *Educ* Clifton; *m* 19 June 1977, Vivienne Barbara, er da of Dr David Perk, of Johannesburg (d 1994); 2 s (James b 11 Jan 1979, John b 26 April 1982); *Career* trainee Keyser Ullman 1963–64, chartered accountant Chalmers Impey 1965–69, PA Corob Holdings 1969–71, fndr and chief exec Citygrove plc 1971–90, currently chm and chief exec Citygrove Leisure plc and Watford Leisure Corporation Ltd; memb Exec Ctee: British ORT 1989– (vice chm 1995–), British Technion Soc 1989–; memb Control Cmmn World ORT Union 1993–; govr ORT-Braude Int Inst of Technol 1989–; FCA 1969; *Recreations* sailing, tennis, opera; *Clubs* Royal Lymington Yacht; *Style*— David Woolf, Esq; ✉ Citygrove Leisure plc, 1–18 Chelsea Garden Market, Chelsea Harbour, London SW10 0XE (☎ 0171 352 8750, fax 0171 376 4918)

WOOLF, Dr Douglas Langton; s of Dr Abraham David Woolf (d 1961), and Celia, *née* Rutkowski (d 1976); *b* 20 Sept 1919; *Educ* St Aubyn's Sch, Grocers' Co Sch; *m* 1946, Kathorn Beth Pearce, da of Thomas Pearce (d 1948), of Melbourne; 1 s (Anthony b 1951), 1 da (Valerie b 1948); *Career* Mil Serv RAMC (capt) 1947–49; house surgn London Hosp 1945–46, registrar Br Red Cross Rheumatism Clinic 1946–47, sr registrar Dept of Rheumatology Middx Hosp 1949–53, conslt physician rheumatology Willesden Gen Hosp 1952–84, consulting rheumatologist Forest Healthcare 1984–, hon conslt Dept of Reumatology Guy's and St Thomas' Tst 1994–; med dir and conslt rheumatologist The Horder Centre for Arthritis 1982–89, memb Attendance Allowance Bd Dept of Health 1983–92; memb Exec Ctee Arthritis Care 1954– (chm Nat Servs Ctee, memb Cncl, hon chm 1982–88); vice pres: League of Friends Royal London Hosp 1986, Arthritis Care 1989, Horder Centre 1990; currently conducts arbitrations on behalf of Electricity Supply Pension Scheme; Liveryman Worshipful Soc of Apothecaries; hon memb Br Soc for Rheumatology, hon fell Hunterian Soc (pres 1979–80, Hunterian Orator 1986); fell Harveian Soc; FRSM, FMS London; *Publications* guest ed Clinics in Rheumatic Diseases, author of numerous articles on rheumatism and arthritis, past hon ed Hunterian Soc Transitions, past ed Rheumatology and Rehabilitation; *Recreations* gardening, antiques; *Style*— Dr Douglas Woolf; ✉ 2 The Green, Woodford, Essex IG8 0NF (☎ 0181 504 8877); 2 Harley St, London W1N 1AA (☎ 0171 580 1199)

WOOLF, Emile Harold; s of Samuel Woolf (d 1984), of London, and Ethel, *née* Smith (d 1967); *b* 17 Jan 1938; *Educ* Parktown Boys HS Johannesburg S Africa; *m* 1962, Anita, da of Kalman Weitzman; 5 c (Kelly b 1959, Carl b 1962, Alexander b 1964, Matthew b

1966, Gabrielle b 1974); *Career* former articled clerk Sinclairs; CA Deloittes 1962–65; dir: Foulks Lynch professional tutors 1965–72, London Sch of Accountancy 1972–75; fndr Emile Woolf & Assocs 1975, ptnr Kingston Smith 1984– (currently head of litigation servs); chm Practice Insur Requirements Ctee ICAEW; lectr on professional econ and business issues to govts, the profession and indust throughout the world; journalist; reg contrib to accountancy press; FCA 1962, FIMgt 1972, FCCA 1981, MAE 1991, FIIA 1994; *Awards* Int Author's Award Univ of Hartford Connecticut 1980 (only non-American to win); *Publications incl*: The Legal Liabilities of Practising Accountants (1985), Financial Services Act Compliance Workbook (1988), Understanding Accounting Standards (1988), Preserving your Right to Audit (1992), Accountants' Liability (1996), Auditing Today (1996); *Recreations* golf, opera; *Style—* Emile Woolf, Esq; ✉ Kingston Smith, Chartered Accountants, Devonshire House, 60 Goswell Road, London EC2M 7AD (☎ 0171 566 3754, fax 0171 566 4010)

WOOLF, Geoffrey Stephen; s of Edward Woolf, of London, and Ruth, *née* Rosenbaum; *b* 13 Oct 1946; *Educ* Harrow Co GS, King's Coll London (LLB); *m* 1, 19 March 1972 (m dis 1978), Marcia, da of late Joseph Levy; m 2, 14 Feb 1985, Dr Josephine Kay Likierman, da of Julian Likierman, of London; 3 s (Nicholas b 18 Nov 1986, Simon b 30 July 1988, Alexander b 20 June 1991); *Career* articled to Sir Anthony Lousada at Stephenson Harwood & Tatham 1968–70, admitted slr 1970, ptnr Stephenson Harwood 1975–; Freeman Worshipful Co of Solicitors 1975; memb Law Soc 1970; *Recreations* opera, theatre; *Style—* Geoffrey Woolf, Esq; ✉ Stephenson Harwood, 1 St Paul's Churchyard, London EC4M 8SH (☎ 0171 329 4422, fax 0171 606 0822)

WOOLF, Baron (Life Peer UK 1992), of Barnes in the London Borough of Richmond; Sir Harry Kenneth Woolf; kt (1979), PC (1986); s of late Alexander Woolf, and late Leah, *née* Cussins; *b* 2 May 1933; *Educ* Fettes, UCL (LLB); *m* 1961, Marguerite, da of late George Sassoon; 3 s (Hon Jeremy Richard George b 26 Aug 1962, Hon Andrew James David b 18 June 1965, Hon Eliot Charles Anthony b 29 July 1967); *Career* Nat Service cmmnd 15/19 Royal Hussars 1954, Capt Army Legal Service 1955; called to the Bar Inner Temple 1954 (Bencher 1976–), recorder Crown Ct 1972–79, jr counsel Inland Revenue 1973–74, first Treasy jr counsel in common law 1974–79, judge High Ct (Queen's Bench) 1979–86, presiding judge SE Circuit 1981–84, Lord Justice of Appeal 1986–92, Lord of Appeal in Ordinary 1992–96, Master of the Rolls 1996–; memb Senate of Bar and Bench 1981–85; chm: Lord Chllr's Advsy Ctee on Legal Educn 1987–90, Middx Justice's Advsy Ctee 1987–90, Bd of Mgmnt Inst of Advanced Legal Studies 1986–93, Butler Tst 1992–96 (pres 1996–), St Mary's Hosp Special Tstees 1993–, advsy cncl on Public Records 1996–; Hamlyn lectures 1989, Zamir & Woolf (2 edn) 1993, De Smith Woolf & Jowell: Judicial Review of Administrative Action (5 edn) 1995, Inquiry into Prison Disturbances 1990–91 and Access to Justice 1994–96; pres: Law Teachers Assoc 1985–90, Jt Ctee for Jewish Social Services 1988–, W London Magistrates' Assoc 1987–92; govr Oxford Centre for Hebrew Studies 1988–93 (emeritus 1993); pro-chllr Univ of London 1994–; hon memb: Public Soc of Teachers of Law 1988–, Ct Univ of London 1993–94, Nuffield Coll Oxford 1996–; Visitor UCL 1996–; Hon LLD: Buckingham, Bristol, London and Anglia, Manchester Metropolitan; hon fell Leeds Polytechnic (now univ); fell UCL 1981; *Clubs* Garrick; *Style—* The Rt Hon the Lord Woolf, PC; ✉ Royal Courts of Justice, Strand, London WC2A 2LL (☎ 0171 936 6002)

WOOLF, Dr Ian Lloyd; s of Dr Sidney Woolf (d 1967), of Newcastle upon Tyne, and Mildred, *née* Wiener (d 1986); *b* 25 Sept 1939; *Educ* Royal GS Newcastle upon Tyne, Univ of Oxford (MA), UCH Med Sch (BM BCh); *m* 7 Sept 1969, Gillian Louise, da of Jonas Bolchover (d 1989), of Manchester; 1 s (Sam b 17 Nov 1975), 1 da (Joanna b 7 Oct 1973); *Career* res fell Harvard Med Sch USA 1970–71, med registrar UCH 1969–70 and 1971–72; lectr in med: Univ of Manchester 1972–74, King's Coll Hosp Univ of London 1974–76; conslt physician North Middx Hosp London 1977–; hon lectr Dept of Med Royal Free Hosp Med Sch, med advsr Nat Assoc of Colitis and Crohns Disease; FRCP 1985; *Recreations* reading, tennis; *Style—* Dr Ian Woolf; ✉ 75 Cholmeley Crescent, Highgate, London N6 5EX (☎ 0181 340 8100); Department of Medicine, North Middlesex Hospital, Sterling Way, London N18 1QX (☎ 0181 887 2251)

WOOLF, Sir John; kt (1975); s of late Charles M Woolf, and Vera Woolf; *Educ* Institut Montana Switzerland; *m* 1955, Ann Saville; 2 s (1 decd); *Career* film and television producer; served WWII (Bronze Star USA 1945), asst dir Army Kinematography War Office (Lt Col) 1944–45; fndr and chm Romulus Films Ltd 1948–, co-fndr and exec dir Anglia TV Group plc 1958–83 (responsible for forming and directing Anglia TV's Drama Dept), chm British & American Investment Tst plc 1982– (formerly British & American Film Holdings plc), dir First Leisure Corporation plc 1982–; memb: Cinematograph Film Cncl 1969–79, Bd of Govrs Service Sound & Vision Corp (formerly Services Kinema Corp) 1974–83, tstee and memb Exec Ctee Cinema and TV Benevolent Fund; Freeman City of London 1982; FRSA 1978; *Television* prodns for Anglia TV incl: over 100 plays, 10 series of Tales of the Unexpected, Orson Welles Great Mysteries; *Films* prodns by Romulus Group incl: The African Queen, Pandora and the Flying Dutchman, Moulin Rouge, I am a Camera, Carrington VC, Beat the Devil, Story of Esther Costello, Room at the Top, Wrong Arm of the Law, The L-Shaped Room, Term of Trial, Life at the Top, Oliver!, Day of the Jackal, The Odessa File; *Awards* personal awards incl: British Film Acad Award for Best Film of 1958 (Room at the Top), Oscar and Golden Globe for Best Film of 1969 (Oliver!), special awards for contribution to British Film Industry from Cinematograph Exhibitors Assoc 1969, Variety Club of GB 1974; Romulus films awarded 14 Oscars in various categories; *Style—* Sir John Woolf; ✉ 214 The Chambers, Chelsea Harbour, London SW10 0XF (☎ 0171 376 3791)

WOOLF, Prof Neville; s of Barnett Woolf (d 1972), of Cape Town, SA, and Florence Charlotte, *née* Cohn (d 1973); *b* 17 May 1930; *Educ* Univ of Cape Town SA (MB ChB, MMed Path), Univ of London (PhD), FRCPath; *m* 31 March 1957, Lydia Paulette, da of Harry Joseph Mandelbrote (d 1971), of Cape Town, SA; 1 s (Adam b 1964), 1 da (Victoria (Mrs Coren) b 1960); *Career* reader and hon conslt St George's Hosp Med Sch 1968–74 (sr lectr and hon conslt 1965–68), Bland-Sutton prof of histopathology Univ Coll Sch of Medicine, currently vice dean and faculty tutor Faculty of Clinical Scis UCL Med Sch; former chm Bd of Studies in Pathology Univ of London, memb Pathological Soc; *Books* Cell, Tissue and Disease (1977 and 1986), Pathology of Atherosclerosis (1982); *Recreations* reading, music, cooking; *Style—* Prof Neville Woolf; ✉ University College School of Medicine, The Bland-Sutton Institute, 48 Riding House St, London W1P 7AA (☎ 0171 380 9401, fax 0171 380 9399)

WOOLFENDEN, (Kenneth) Alan; s of Frederick John Woolfenden (d 1971), and Mary, *née* Duff; *b* 25 July 1950; *Educ* N Manchester GS for Boys, Univ of Liverpool (MB ChB); *m* 1 April 1972, Susan Irene, da of Alan Eaton, of Manchester; 1 s (Jonathan Frederick b 12 Dec 1980); *Career* conslt urological surgn Royal Liverpool University Hospital Tst 1985–, clinical dir of urology Royal Liverpool and Broadgreen University Hospital Tst; hon lectr Dept of Surgery Faculty of Med Univ of Liverpool; dir Sr Registrar Trg Mersey Region; memb Cncl: Br Assoc of Urological Surgns, Liverpool Med Inst; memb Exec Cncl Mersey Region for Kidney Res; memb BMA 1973, FRCS 1978, FEBU 1992; *Style—* Alan Woolfenden, Esq; ✉ Riverside, Manorial Rd, Parkgate, South Wirral, Cheshire (☎ 0151 336 7229); 48 Rodney St, Liverpool L1 9AA (☎ 0151 709 2079)

WOOLFENDEN, Guy Anthony; s of Harold Arthur Woolfenden (d 1986), and Kathleen Norah Woolfenden (d 1978); *b* 12 July 1937; *Educ* Westminster Abbey Choir Sch, Whitgift Sch, Christ's Coll Cambridge (MA), Guildhall Sch of Music (LGSM), fell Birmingham Schs of Music (FBSM); *m* 29 Sept 1962, Jane, da of Leonard George Smerdon Aldrick, of Ewell, Surrey; 3 s (Richard b 1964, Stephen b 1966, James b 1969); *Career* head of music RSC 1963–, artistic dir Cambridge Festival 1986–91; compositions incl: scores for RSC, Comedie Française, Burgtheater and Norwegian Nat Theatre, four ballet scores, TV and film music, concert music; conducts concerts, opera and ballet in Britain and internationally; chm Denne Gilkes Meml Fund; vice pres: Beauchamp Sinfonietta, Katharine House Hospice Tst; memb: Nat Campaign for the Arts, MU, PRS, MCPS, Composers' Guild, Assoc of Professional Composers, SPNM; *Recreations* photography, table tennis, walking, cricket; *Style—* Guy Woolfenden, Esq; ✉ Malvern House, Sibford Ferris, Banbury, Oxfordshire OX15 5RG (☎ 01295 780679, fax 01295 788630); Royal Shakespeare Company, Royal Shakespeare Theatre, Stratford upon Avon, Warwickshire CV37 6BB (☎ 01789 296655)

WOOLFSON, Dr Gerald; s of late Joseph Samuel Woolfson, and late Lilian Woolfson; *b* 25 March 1932; *Educ* Milton Sch Bulawayo and Zimbabwe, Capetown Univ (MB); *m* 1, 1955, Sheila Charlaff; 2 s (David b 1955, Adrian b 1965), 1 da (Karen b 1959); m 2, 1980, Lynne Woolfson, *qv*; 1 s (Alexander b 1978); *Career* conslt psychiatrist Hammersmith and St Mary's Hosp Gp; hon sr lectr RPMS; FRSM, FRCP, FRCPsych; *Recreations* chess, doodling; *Style—* Dr Gerald Woolfson; ✉ 56 Redington Rd, London NW3 (☎ 0171 794 1974); 97 Harley St, London W1N 1DF (☎ 0171 935 3400)

WOOLFSON, Lynne; da of David Bernard Silver (d 1969), of London, and Fay Butchen (d 1977); *b* 4 July 1946; *Educ* Camden Sch for Girls, Univ of Manchester (BA, ed Manchester Independent newspaper), Courtauld Inst of Art (MA); *m* Dr Gerald Woolfson, *qv*; 1 s (Alexander b 1978); *Career* TV journalist 1968–78 (incl World in Action and David Frost and Russell Harty progs); art historian; film prodr; vice-pres Brian Gibson Films; *Recreations* white water rafting, gazing at paintings; *Style—* Lynne Silver

WOOLFSON, Prof Michael Mark; s of Maurice Woolfson (d 1956), of London, and Rose, *née* Solomons; *b* 9 Jan 1927; *Educ* Wellingborough GS, Jesus Coll Oxford (BA, MA), UMIST (PhD, DSc); *m* 19 July 1951, Margaret, da of Dr Mayer Frohlich; 2 s (Mark b 1954, Malcolm b 1957), 1 da (Susan b 1960); *Career* HG 7 Northants Bn 1942–44, Nat Serv cmmnd 2 Lt RE 1947–49; res asst Cavendish Laboratory Cambridge 1952–54, ICI res fell Cambridge 1954–55, reader in physics UMIST 1961–65 (lectr 1953–61), currently emeritus prof Univ of York (prof of theoretical physics 1965); pres: Yorks Philosophical Soc, York Astronomical Soc; FIP, FRAS, FRS; *Books* Direct Methods in Crystallography (1961), An Introduction to X-Ray Crystallography (1970), The Origin of the Solar System: The Capture Theory (1989), Physical and Non-Physical Methods of Solving Crystal Structures (1995); *Recreations* winemaking; *Style—* Prof Michael Woolfson, FRS; ✉ Sandmoor Green, Leeds, W Yorks LS17 7SB (☎ 0113 266 2166); Department of Physics, University of York, York, N Yorks YO1 5DD (☎ 01904 432230, fax 01904 432214)

WOOLFSON, Rosalind Anne; da of Myer Henry Woolfson (d 1962), of Glasgow, and Miriam, *née* Cohen; *b* 13 Feb 1945; *Educ* Glasgow HS for Girls, Principessa Colonna Sch Florence, Glasgow Sch of Art; *Career* Marks & Spencer; FJ Lyons PR, Shandwick Group 1975–91, bd dir Shandwick Communications 1985–91, estab own public relations co 1991; memb: IPR, AWPR; *Recreations* visual arts, travel, literature, music, opera; *Style—* Miss Rosalind Woolfson; ✉ Woolfson Communications, Number 2, Weavers Way, Camden Village, London NW1 0XE (☎ 0171 388 4381, fax 0171 388 4382)

WOOLHOUSE, Prof John George; CBE (1988); s of George Francis Woolhouse (d 1940), and Doris May, *née* Webber (d 1991); *b* 17 June 1931; *Educ* Ardingly Coll, BNC Oxford (MA); *m* 12 April 1958, Ruth Carolyn, da of Rev Thomas Edward Harrison; 2 s (Mark Edward John b 25 April 1959, Hugh Francis b 15 Nov 1961), 1 da (Elinor Clare (twin) b 15 Nov 1961); *Career* Nat Serv 2 Lt RCS 1950–51, Pilot Offr RAFVR 1951–54, RAuxAF Pilot Offr 1954–56; Rolls-Royce Ltd: various appts 1954–64, dir personnel and admin (Rolls-Royce and Assocs) 1965–68, co educn and training offr 1968–72; asst dir Kingston Poly 1972–78, dir Atkins Planning of WS Atkins Group Conslts 1978–82, under sec MSC and dir Tech and Vocational Educn Initiative 1983–87, prof of educn and dir Centre for Educn and Indust Univ of Warwick 1988–; FBIM, Hon FIIM; *Books* Organisation Development, Gower Handbook of Management (1983), The Reform of Post-16 Education and Training in England and Wales (1993); *Recreations* music, walking, boating, fishing; *Clubs* RAF; *Style—* Prof John Woolhouse, CBE; ✉ University of Warwick, Coventry CV4 7AL

WOOLLAMS, Christopher John (Chris); s of late George James Woollams, and Phyllis Joan, *née* Cox; *b* 4 July 1949; *Educ* Watford Boys' GS, St Peter's Coll Oxford (MA); *m* (m dis); 3 da (Catherine Louise b 1978, Georgina Clair b 1983, Stephanie Marie 1986); *Career* chm Spiral Cellars Ltd 1980–91, dir Ogilvy and Mather London 1980–83, md Publicis 1984, chm Ted Bates Group London 1985 (Euro and Worldwide Bd dir 1986), chm Fitness in Home Ltd 1986–91; chief exec: WMGO Group plc 1987–95, SRC (UK) Ltd 1996–; chm The Woollams Outsourcing (TWO) Company Ltd 1995–; MIPA 1983, FInstD 1986, memb Marketing Soc 1989; *Recreations* flying, golf, wine, writing, chess, skiing; *Clubs* RAC, IOD, Redhill Flying; *Style—* Chris Woollams; ✉ Hazelbirch, Woodland Way, Kingswood, Surrey KT20 6NN

WOOLLARD, Kenneth David; s of Harry Woollard (d 1950), of Clare, Suffolk, and Bush Hill Park, Middx, and Forence Jane, *née* Shore (d 1983); *b* 20 Nov 1930; *Educ* Tottenham Tech Coll; *m* 19 Feb 1955, Edna May, da of Frank Stallwood (d 1976), of London; 2 s (David Gordon b 1960, Peter Kenneth b 1963), 1 da (Karen Ann (twin) b 1963); *Career* Nat Serv RAOC N Africa 1948–50; commercial and mktg career in electrical engrg and telecommunications; regnl mangr major projects UK 1968–74, liaison mangr and conslt UK overseas offshore and onshore petro-chemical projects (Moss Moran, Morecambe Bay, Esso Fawley, Br Gas N Sea gas fields) 1974–78, project mangr (Delta Dunmurry) Br Coal and Steel Contracts 1978–87, Dept of Tport Motorway Communications M1, M4, M25 and M6 projects, British Rail telecommunications and cable TV projects 1987–91; dir Home Mkt Duratube Ltd 1991–94; MCIM 1974; *Recreations* sailing, golf; *Style—* Kenneth Woollard, Esq; ✉ Courtneys, 6 Langham Close, Marshalswick, St Albans, Herts AL4 9TH (☎ 01727 836861)

WOOLLCOMBE, James Humphrey George; s of Humphrey William Woollcombe (d 1968), of Hemerdon House, Plympton, Devon, and Dorothy Shepley, *née* Smith (d 1977); *b* 27 Aug 1925; *Educ* Charterhouse, Christ Church Oxford (MA, BCL); *m* 1, 13 Oct 1951, Félice George Ingle Finch (d 1981), da of Prof George Ingle Finch, FRS; 7 da (Catriona b 5 Feb 1954, Susannah b 15 July 1955, Sophia b 6 Feb 1958, Lucinda b 27 Dec 1959, Alexandra b 22 Nov 1962, Valentine b 23 Nov 1964, Magdalen b 17 March 1968); m 2, 21 April 1982, Jennifer Susan Platt, da of Lt-Cdr John Scott-Fox (d 1947); *Career* Life Gds 1943–47 (Capt 1947); called to the Bar Inner Temple 1955; Shell International 1953–82 (various legal and commercial posts, vice pres Shell International Trading Co 1975–82), ret; High Sheriff of Devon 1995–96; chm Political Ctee South Hams Cons Assoc 1987–89, cncllr Devon CC 1989–93; memb: Dartmoor Nat Park Ctee 1994–97, Dartmoor Nat Park Authy 1996–; chm: South Hams Amenity Fedn 1986–, Bd of Govrs Kelly Coll Tavistock 1988–, Cornwall and Devon Careers Ltd 1995–, New Palace Centre Plymouth 1996–; govr Ivybridge Community Coll 1984–94; Order of St John: chm Cncl Devon 1986–95, memb Chapter-Gen 1993–; CStJ 1993; *Recreations* music, books, family and general history, conservation of the countryside; *Clubs* Cavalry and Guards; *Style—* James Woollcombe, Esq; ✉ Hemerdon House, Plympton, Devon PL7 5BZ (☎ 01752 337350, fax 01752 331477)

WOOLLETT, Maj-Gen John Castle; CBE (1957, OBE 1955), MC (1945); o s of John Castle Woollett (d 1921), and Lily Bradley Woollett (d 1964); *b* 5 Nov 1915; *Educ* St Benedict's Sch, RMA Woolwich, St John's Coll Cambridge (MA); *m* 1, 1941 (m dis 1957), Joan Eileen, *née* Stranks; 2 s (and 1 s decd); m 2, 1959, Helen Wendy, *née* Braithwaite; 2 step s; *Career* cmmnd RE 1935, served 1939–45 and Korea, Maj-Gen, chief engr BAOR 1967–70 (ret), Col Cmdt RE 1973–78, planning inspr DOE 1975–81, memb Lord Chllr's Panel 1982–87; CEng, FICE; *Recreations* cruising, sailing (yacht 'Cymbeline'); *Clubs* Army & Navy, Royal Cruising, Royal Engineer Yacht, Royal Ocean Racing, Royal Lymington Yacht, Island Sailing (Cowes); *Style*— Maj-Gen John Woollett, CBE, MC; ✉ 42 Rhinefield Close, Brockenhurst, Hants SO42 7SU (☎ 01590 622417)

WOOLLEY, Brian Peter; s of Herbert Woolley, and Edna, *née* Hindley; *b* 28 April 1954; *Educ* Manchester GS, St John's Coll Oxford (MA); *m* 1978, Joy, da of Alan Harbottle; *Career* Citibank NA London 1975–79, Orion Bank Limited 1979–81, md and head of capital markets Citibank International plc 1984–96, md and regnl head Bank of China International (UK) Ltd 1996–; *Recreations* skiing, opera, golf; *Clubs* Wentworth; *Style*— Brian Woolley, Esq; ✉ 14 Argyll Road, London W8 7BG

WOOLLEY, David Rorie; QC (1980); s of Albert Walter Woolley, of Wallingford, Oxon, and Ethel Rorie, *née* Linn; *b* 9 June 1939; *Educ* Winchester, Trinity Hall Cambridge (MA); *Career* called to the Bar Middle Temple 1962, recorder Crown Ct 1982– inspr DOE Inquiry into Nat Gallery 1984, bencher Middle Temple 1988; Liveryman Worshipful Co of Coopers; *Publications* Town Hall and the Property Owner (1965); *Recreations* opera, real tennis, mountaineering; *Clubs* MCC, Oxford and Cambridge; *Style*— David Woolley, Esq, QC; ✉ 1 Serjeant's Inn, London EC4Y 1NH (☎ 0171 583 1355)

WOOLLEY, (William) Ian; JP (1963); s of William Edward Woolley (d 1989), of Blackburn, and Marion Elizabeth, *née* Aspinall (d 1982); *b* 22 June 1932; *Educ* Charterhouse, Univ of London (BPharm), Ohio State Univ (MSc); *m* 1957, Joyce Christine; 3 da (Bridget b 1958, Sonya b 1951, Gillian b 1964), 1 s (Stephen b 1959); *Career* md Cupal Pharmaceutical Laboratories until 1993 (joined ca 1953), ret; proprietor Ian Woolley Consultancies; memb N Western RHA 1982–84; chm: Blackburn Hyndburn & Ribble Valley DHA 1983–93, Blackburn Hyndburn & Ribble Valley Healthcare NHS Tst 1993–; variously: chm Blackburn YMCA, chm Blackburn Civic Soc, memb NW Indusl Devpt Bd; chm of govrs Westholme Ind Girls' Sch 1968–92; MRPharmS; *Recreations* golf, walking, reading, photography; *Clubs* Pleasington Golf, Senior Golfers' Society; *Style*— Ian Woolley Esq, JP; ✉ Blackburn, Hyndburn & Ribble Valley Healthcare NHS Trust, Trust HQ, Queens Park Hospital, Haslingden Road, Blackburn BB2 3HH (☎ 01254 293800, fax 01254 293803, mobile 0468 143507)

WOOLLEY, Dr Paul Kerrison; s of Robert Charles Woolley (d 1979), and Hilda Kerrison, *née* Barnsley; *b* 9 Nov 1939; *Educ* King Edward VI Sch Birmingham, Univ of York (BA, DPhil); *m* 31 July 1976, Penelope Ann, da of Albert Ewart Baines; 2 s (Nicholas Kerrison b 26 Oct 1977, Robert Ewart b 10 June 1980); *Career* ptnr Murray & Co Birmingham 1965–67 (joined 1959), Esmée Fairbairn lectr in fin Univ of York 1971–76, specialist advsr House of Lords Ctee on EEC 1975–76, advsr International Monetary Fund Washington DC 1980–83 (economist 1976–78, sr economist 1978–80); dir 1983–87: Baring Brothers & Co Ltd, Baring Investment Management, Baring International Investment Management, Baring Quantitative Management; fndr and md GMO Woolley Ltd London 1987–, ptnr Grantham Mayo Van Otterloo & Co Boston USA; author of various articles in academic and fin jls; memb Birmingham Stock Exchange 1964–67; *Recreations* walking, travel; *Clubs* Reform, City University; *Style*— Dr Paul Woolley; ✉ 17 Edwardes Square, London W8 6HE (☎ 0171 602 0476); GMO Woolley Ltd, 1 Angel Court, Throgmorton Street, London EC2R 7HJ (☎ 0171 814 9400, fax 0171 814 9405/6)

WOOLLEY, Prof Robert Peter; s of John S Woolley and Joan Grace Woolley; *b* 8 Jan 1954; *Educ* Eastbourne Coll, RCM, Inst of Educ Univ of London; *m* Sept 1982, Susan Jane, da of Michael Carrington; 1 da (Jessica Ruth Olivia b 1985); *Career* harpsichordist, fortepianist, organist and conductor; concerts in UK, USA, Japan and throughout Europe since 1973, regular BBC and World Serv bdcaster, taught in Austria and Portugal, early music advsr and prof of harpsichord and fortepiano RCM 1985–, memb Purcell Quartet; *Recordings* incl: Purcell - Complete Harpsichord Works and music by Handel, Frescobaldi, D Scarlatti, J S Bach, C P E Bach, Poglietti, Bohm; *Recreations* walking, reading, architecture, photography; *Style*— Prof Robert Woolley; ✉ 63 Mallinson Road, London SW11 1BW (☎ 0171 223 9184); Royal College of Music, Prince Consort Road, London SW7 2BS (☎ 0171 589 3643)

WOOLLEY, His Hon Judge Roy Gilbert; s of John Woolley (d 1974), and Edith Mary, *née* Holt (d 1958); *b* 28 Nov 1922; *Educ* Deeside, UCL (LLB); *m* 1953, Doreen, da of Humphrey Morris Farmer (d 1967); 2 s (Christopher, Peter), 2 da (Julie, Carolyn); *Career* served WWII Flying Offr RAF Coastal Cmd 1939–45; called to the Bar Lincoln's Inn 1951, recorder 1975–76, circuit judge (Wales and Chester Circuit) 1976–93; memb: Gen Synod of Church of England 1990–95, Legal Advsy Cmmn of the Church of England 1991–95; reader dioceses of: St Asoph Chester, Lichfield 1975–; *Recreations* reading, music, art, antiques; *Style*— His Hon Judge Woolley; ✉ Henlle Hall, Gobowen, Oswestry, Shropshire SY10 7AX (☎ 01691 661257)

WOOLLONS, Prof David John; s of Sydney Charles Woollons (d 1958), of Birmingham, and Eileen Annie, *née* Russell; *b* 10 June 1937; *Educ* Solihull Sch, Univ of Bristol (BSc, PhD); *m* 29 Sept 1961, Janice, da of William Hector Evans (d 1975), of Bridgend, Glamorgan; 2 s (Andrew b 1963, Martin b 1968), 1 da (Sian b 1966); *Career* res engr Philips Research Laboratories 1961–67, reader in engrg Univ of Sussex 1972–84 (lectr in engrg 1967–72), prof of engrg Univ of Exeter 1984–; memb Cncl Inst of Electrical Engrs (past chm Sci Educn and Technol Divnl Bd); FIEE; *Books* Introduction to Digital Computer Design (1972), Microelectronic Systems (1982); *Recreations* reading, walking, music, car renovation; *Style*— Prof David Woollons; ✉ Little Croft, 437 Topsham Road, Exeter, Devon EX2 7AB (☎ 01392 874270); School of Engineering, University of Exeter, North Park Road, Exeter EX4 4QF (☎ 01392 263628, fax 01392 217965)

WOOLMAN, (Joseph) Roger; CB (1997); s of Maurice Wollman (d 1971), and Hilda, *née* Boyers; *b* 13 Feb 1937; *Educ* Perse Sch, Trinity Hall Cambridge (exhibitioner, MA); *m* 19 May 1973, Elizabeth, da of late Eric Ingham; 1 da (Sarah b 1974), 1 s (Mark b 1975); *Career* admitted slr 1974; various positions Office of Fair Trading and DTI 1976–93 (under sec 1985–93); slr and legal advsr MAFF, Forestry Cmmn and Intervention Bd for Agricultural Produce 1993–; *Clubs* Reform, Hampstead Golf; *Style*— Roger Woolman, Esq, CB; ✉ Ministry of Agriculture, Fisheries and Food, 55 Whitehall, London SW1A 2EY (☎ 0171 270 8349)

WOOLMER, Robert Andrew (Bob); s of Clarence Shirley Woolmer, of Pinelands, SA, and Stella Kathleen, *née* Birks (d 1995); *b* 14 May 1948; *Educ* Skinners' Sch; *m* 9 Nov 1974, (Shirley) Gillian, da of Eddie Hall; 2 s (Dale Robert b 22 March 1979, Russell Christopher b 1 June 1982); *Career* cricket coach; former player: Tonbridge second XI 1961, Tunbridge Wells 1963, Kent schs 1965, England schs 1966, Kent CCC second XI 1966, Kent CCC 1968–84 (awarded county cap 1970), one day int debut 1972, 19 test matches 1975–81 (debut v Aust at Lords), DH Robins' XI to SA 1973, Natal 1974–76, MCC tour India 1976–77, Centenary Test Melbourne 1977, Avendale CC Capetown 1981–89 (first non-racial township side); coaching and devpt Avendale CC 1981– (11 jr teams, 5 sr teams); also coach: B Section Currie Cup team Boland SA, promoted to A Section 1993, SA National Team 1994–; dir of coaching Warwickshire CCC 1991–94; off-seasons: order clerk ICI 1966–68, teacher Holmewood House Prep Sch 1968–71, coach Transvaal Cricket Union 1970–71, Thwaites and Matthews Caterers 1975–77, proprietor Bob Woolmer Sports Tonbridge 1977–84, sports admin Herzlia HS SA 1985–87; memb Bd of Tstees John Passmore Tst SA; *Books* Pirate and Rebel (autobiog, 1984), Skilful Cricket (1993); The Bob Woolmer Way (cricket coach in video); *Recreations* hockey, photography, wine, food; *Style*— Bob Woolmer, Esq; ✉ 31 Peak Drive, Pinelands, Cape Town 7405, South Africa (☎ 00 27 21 5318512, fax 00 27 21 5310084)

WOOLNOUGH, Victor James (Vic); s of Lionel Victor Woolnough, of Basingstoke, Hampshire (d 1989), and Joyce Eileen, *née* Hodder; *b* 1 Nov 1943; *Educ* Queen Mary's GS (Hampshire schs jr 100 yards sprint champion 1957); *m* 21 March 1964, Carla Bettine, da of Albert Ernest Atherton; 1 da (Lisa b 19 Dec 1966); *Career* Lansing Bagnall Ltd (Basingstoke): trainee draughtsman and engrg apprentice 1961–66, detail draughtsman 1966–67, design draughtsman 1966–69; CA Blatchford & Sons Ltd: design draughtsman 1969–73, design engr 1973–87, chief designer 1988–92, research and devpt mangr 1992–; specialist in the design and devpt of artificial limbs (incl Blatchford Endolite System), sole or jt inventor of over a dozen patented mechanisms and devices; FIED 1981 (MIED 1976), IEng 1981; *Recreations* small boats, walking, personal computers and the Internet; *Style*— Vic Woolnough, Esq; ✉ Lawrenny, Mary Lane, North Waltham, Hampshire RG25 2BY; Chas A Blatchford & Sons Ltd, Lister Road, Basingstoke, Hampshire RG22 4LU (☎ 01256 465771, e-mail vic@vicw.demon.co.uk, internet http://www.vicw.demon.co.uk/)

WOOLRICH, John; *b* 3 Jan 1954; *Educ* Univ of Manchester (BA), Univ of Lancaster (MLitt); *Career* composer; Northern Arts fell Univ of Durham 1982–85, composer in res Nat Centre for Orchestral Studies London 1985–86, visiting lectr Goldsmith's Coll London 1986–87, composer in assoc Orch of St John's Smith Square 1994–95, lectr in music Royal Holloway Univ of London 1994–; dir The Composers Ensemble 1989–; hon FTCL; *Major works* Ulysses Awakes 1989, The Ghost in the Machine 1990, Viola Concerto 1993, Oboe Concerto 1996 (world première BBC Proms 1996), In The House of Crossed Desires 1996; *Style*— John Woolrich, Esq; ✉ c/o Faber Music, 3 Queens Square, London WC1N 3AU (☎ 0171 278 7436, fax 0171 278 3817)

WOOLTON, 3 Earl of (UK 1956); Simon Frederick Marquis; also Baron Woolton (UK 1939), Viscount Woolton (UK 1952), and Viscount Walberton (UK 1956); s of 2 Earl of Woolton (d 1969, s of 1 Earl of Woolton, CH, PC, JP, DL, chm Lewis's Investment Trust and associated cos, min of Food 1940–43, min of Reconstruction and memb War Cabinet 1943–45, lord pres Cncl 1945 and 1951–52, chllr of Duchy of Lancaster 1952–55, chm Cons Pty 1946–55) by his 2 w (Cecily) Josephine, er da of Sir Alastair Penrose Gordon-Cumming 5 Bt (now Countess Lloyd George of Dwyfor); *b* 24 May 1958; *Educ* Eton, Univ of St Andrews (MA); *m* 30 April 1987, Hon Sophie, o c of 3 Baron Birdwood, *qv*; 3 da (Lady Olivia Alice b 16 April 1990, Lady Constance Elizabeth b 14 Oct 1991, Lady Claudia Louise b 3 March 1995); *Heir* none; *Career* merchant banker; with S G Warburg & Co Ltd 1982–88; tstee Woolton Charitable Tst, co dir and landowner 1988–; *Clubs* Royal and Ancient (St Andrews), New (Edinburgh), White's, Pratt's, Brooks's, MCC; *Style*— The Rt Hon the Earl of Woolton; ✉ Glenogil, by Forfar, Angus DD8 3SX

WOOLWICH, Bishop of 1996–; Rt Rev Colin Ogilvie Buchanan; s of Prof Robert Ogilvie Buchanan (d 1980), and Kathleen Mary, *née* Parnell (d 1990); *b* 9 Aug 1934; *Educ* Lincoln Coll Oxford (MA), Tyndale Hall Bristol (Gen Ordination Examination); *m* 14 June 1963, Diana Stephenie, *née* Gregory; 2 da (Stephanie Joan b 24 Feb 1965, Judith Ruth b 8 April 1967); *Career* ordained deacon 1961, priest 1962; asst curate Cheadle PC 1961–64; memb staff: London Coll of Divinity Northwood 1964–70, St John's Coll Nottingham (formerly London Coll of Divinity) 1970–85 (princ 1979–85); hon canon Southwell Minster 1982–85, bishop of Aston 1985–89, asst bishop of Rochester 1989–96, vicar St Mark's Gillingham 1991–96; memb: Liturgical Cmmn 1964–86, Gen Synod 1970–85 and 1990–, Doctrine Cmmn 1986–91, Lambeth Conf 1988, Assembly CCBI 1990– (memb Steering Ctee 1990–92), Cncl for Christian Unity and Ctee of Minority Ethnic Anglican Concerns (nominated) 1991–96, Cncl for Christian Unity (elected) 1996–, Steering Gp Int Anglican Liturgical Consultations 1995–; Rochester diocesan ecumenical offr 1995–96; fndr proprietor Grove Books 1970–85 (co sec 1985–93); DD Lambeth 1993; pres Movement for Reform of Infant Baptism, vice pres Electoral Reform Soc; *Publications* Growing into Union (jtly, 1970), Open to Others (1992), Infant Baptism and the Gospel (1993), Cut the Connection (1994); ed News of Liturgy jl; *Recreations* armchair follower of sport, history, biography, electoral reform; *Style*— The Bishop of Woolwich; ✉ c/o Southwark Diocesan Office, Trinity House, 4 Chapel Court, Borough High Street, London SE1 1HW

WOOSNAM, Ian Harold; MBE (1992); s of Harold Woosnam, and Joan Woosnam; *b* 2 March 1958; *Educ* St Martins Modern Sch; *m* 12 Nov 1983, Glendryth, da of Terrance Mervyn Pugh; 1 s (Daniel Ian b 5 Feb 1985), 2 da (Rebecca Louise b 16 June 1988, Ami Victoria b 10 Sept 1991); *Career* professional golfer 1976–; tournament victories: News of the World under 23 match-play 1979, Cacharel under 25 Championship 1982, Swiss Open 1982, Silk Cut Masters 1983, Scandinavian Enterprise Open 1984, Zambian Open 1985, Lawrence Batley TPC 1986, 555 Kenya Open 1986, Hong Kong Open 1987, Jersey Open 1987, Cepsa Madrid Open 1987, Bell's Scottish Open 1987 and 1990, Lancome Trophy 1987 and 1993, Suntory World Match-Play Championship 1987 and 1990, Volvo PGA Championship 1988, Carrolls Irish Open 1988 and 1989, Panasonic Euro Open 1988, Mediterranean Open 1990 and 1991, Monte Carlo Open 1990, 1991 and 1992, Epson Grand Prix 1990, US F & G Classic 1991, US Masters 1991, PGA Grand Slam of Golf 1991, Murphy's English Open 1993, Air France Cannes Open 1994, British Masters 1994, Johnnie Walker Classic 1996, Heineken Classic 1996, Scottish Open 1996, German Open 1996; team events: Ryder Cup 1983, 1985 (winners), 1987 (winners), 1989 (winners), 1991, 1993 and 1995 (winners), Dunhill Cup 1985, 1986, 1988, 1989 and 1990, World Cup 1980, 1982, 1983, 1984, 1985, 1986, 1987 (team and individual winner), 1990, 1991 (individual winner), 1992, 1993 and 1994; finished top Order of Merit 1987 and 1990, ranked number 1 Sony world rankings 1991; *Recreations* snooker, water skiing, sports; *Style*— Ian Woosnam, Esq, MBE; ✉ c/o IMG, Pier House, Strand on The Green, London W4 3NN (☎ 0181 233 5000, fax 0181 233 5001)

WOOTTON, David Hugh; s of James Wootton, and Muriel Wootton; *b* 21 July 1950; *Educ* Bradford GS, Jesus Coll Cambridge (BA, MA); *m* 23 April 1977, Elizabeth Rosemary, da of Peter Knox; 2 s (James b 1979, Christopher b 1985), 2 da (Alexandra b 1978, Sophie b 1981); *Career* ptnr Allen & Overy 1979–; memb Law Soc 1975; Liveryman Worshipful Co of Fletchers; *Recreations* opera, rowing, skiing; *Clubs* Leander; *Style*— David Wootton, Esq; ✉ Allen & Overy, One New Change, London EC4M 9QQ (☎ 0171 330 3000, fax 0171 330 9999)

WOOTTON, Frank Albert Antony; OBE (1995); *b* 30 July 1914; *Educ* Eastbourne Coll of Art; *m* Virginia Ann; 1 s (Leigh Antony b March 1959), 1 da (Tracy Ann b Feb 1963); *Career* artist; official war artist RAF 1939–46; C P Robertson trophy Air Miny 1979, Royal Aero Club Silver medal 1985; companion Royal Aeronautical Soc 1985, Freeman Guild of Air Pilots and Air Navigators 1987, pres Guild of Aviation Artists 1970–88; *Exhibitions* Ackermanns Gallery London 1964, Stacy-Marks Gallery Eastbourne 1965, Incurable Collector Gallery NY 1969, Horse Artists of the World (Tryon Gallery London) 1969, Tryon Gallery London 1974, Nat Air and Space Museum Smithsonian Inst Washington DC 1983–84, EAA Museum Oshkosh Wisconsin, The Maestro (RAF Museum) 1992–93; *Books* How to Draw Aircraft (1940), How to Draw Cars (1949), The

Aviation Art of Frank Wootton (1976), At Home in the Sky (1984), The Landscape Paintings of Frank Wootton (1990), Frank Wootton - 50 Years of Aviation Art (1992); *Clubs* RAF; *Style*— Frank Wootton, Esq, OBE; ✉ Mayflower House, Alfriston, Sussex BN26 5QT (☎ 01323 870 343)

WOOTTON, (Harold) John; s of Harold Wootton (d 1980), of Bloxwich, Staffs, and Hilda Mary, *née* Somerfield (d 1989); *b* 17 Nov 1936; *Educ* Queen Mary's GS Walsall, Queen Mary's Coll Univ of London (BSc), Univ of California (MEng); *m* 1960, Patricia Ann, da of Cyril Ronald Riley; 2 s (David Ian b 1962, Neil Antony b 1964); *Career* lectr Dept of Civil Engrg Univ of Leeds 1959–62, tech dir Freeman Fox Wilbur Smith Associates 1963–67, jt md SIA Ltd 1967–71, chm Wootton Jeffreys Consultants Ltd 1971–91, chief exec Transport Research Laboratory 1991–; visiting prof: in computing King's Coll Univ of London 1987–89, in tport studies UCL 1989–92; jr vice pres Inst of Highways and Transportation; CEng, FCIT, FIHT, FBCS; *Recreations* cricket, golf, rotary, photography, travel; *Clubs* RAC; *Style*— John Wootton, Esq; ✉ Transport Research Laboratory, Old Wokingham Road, Crowthorne, Berks RG45 6AU (☎ 01344 770001, fax 01344 770761)

WOOTTON, Robert John (Bob); s of William Robert Wootton (d 1987), of Marlow, Bucks, and Linda Rosalie, *née* Gyton; *b* 30 June 1955; *Educ* Oundle, UCL; *Career* trainee media exec Lintas Ltd 1974–81, successively trainee media exec, head of TV then assoc media dir Wight Collins Rutherford Scott Ltd 1981–85, media dir HDM Horner Collis Kirvan Ltd then Griffin Bacal Ltd 1985–94, ptnr De Saulles Associates media consultancy 1994–96, dir of media servs ISBA 1996–; MIPA 1986; *Recreations* active and passive participation in music, cookery, food and wine, mycology; *Clubs* RAC, Fred's; *Style*— Bob Wootton, Esq; ✉ Incorporated Society of British Advertisers, 44 Hertford Street, London W1 (☎ 0171 499 7502)

WOOTTON, Dr (Leslie) Roger; s of Denis Stokes Wootton (d 1965), and Geraldine Amy, *née* Virgo; *b* 29 June 1944; *Educ* Kingston GS, City Univ (BSc, PhD); *m* 15 Sept 1979, Hilary Anne Robinson; 2 s (Marcus Desmond b 21 July 1981, Julian Michael b 12 Feb 1986); *Career* Nat Physical Laboratory 1962–71 (joined Aerodynamic Div; projects incl: wind effects on bldgs, vortex induced motion of towers and masts, deep water jetty Humber Estuary at Immingham), W S Atkins consltg engrs 1971–93; projects incl: BP Forties platform, Shell Tern devpt; dean Sch of Engrg City Univ London 1993–; NE Rowe medal Royal Aeronautical Soc, Telford Premium ICE; memb: Royal Aeronautical Soc, Wind Engrg Soc, Wind Energy Soc; FICE, FEng 1985; *Books* Dynamics of Marine Structures; *Recreations* being a husband and father, hot air ballooning (as means of escaping from former recreations!); *Clubs* Br Balloon and Airship Club; *Style*— Prof Roger Wootton, FEng; ✉ Hardwick Cottage, St Nicholas Hill, Leatherhead, Surrey KT22 8NE (☎ 01372 372654)

WORAM, Terence Annesley; s of Victor Henry Woram (d 1940), and Helena Mary, *née* Cox (d 1992); *b* 23 June 1933; *Educ* Christian Brothers Coll Kimberley SA, Univ of Capetown SA (BArch); *m* 14 Oct 1961, Patricia Eileen, da of Frederick Leslie Lawrence; 1 s (Michael Desmond b 27 Aug 1962, d 22 May 1980), 3 da (Catherine Ann b 17 Jan 1964, Frances Mary b 21 May 1965, Joanna Helen b 2 May 1967); *Career* Pallet and Price Salisbury Rhodesia 1953–56, Harrison and Abramovitz NY 1956–59, Trehearn Norman Preston and Ptnrs London 1960–64; ptnr: BL Adams Partnership London 1964–69, Green Lloyd and Adams London 1969–79; sr ptnr Terence Woram Associates 1979–; architectural awards: Richmond Soc 1983, Europa Nostra 1986, Aylesbury Soc 1988, Richmond Conservation-Design Awards 1993; rep cricket: combined SA Univs XI 1955, USA All Stars XI v W Indies 1958; chm York House Soc; RIBA; *Recreations* cricket, travel, old Hollywood films; *Clubs* Richmond Cricket (dep chm), Middx Cricket Union (chm); *Style*— Terence Woram, Esq; ✉ 48 Lebanon Park, Twickenham, Middx TW1 3DG

WORCESTER, Marquess of; Henry John Fitzroy Somerset; s and h of 11 Duke of Beaufort, *qv*; *b* 22 May 1952; *Educ* Eton; *m* 13 June 1987, Tracy Louise, the environmentalist, da of Hon Peter Ward, s of 3 Earl of Dudley; 2 s (Robert, Earl of Glamorgan b 20 Jan 1989, Lord Alexander b 3 Sept 1995), 1 da (Lady Isabella Elsa b 27 July 1991); *Heir* s, Earl of Glamorgan; *Career* conslt to Franc Warwick London W1; FRICS; *Recreations* hunting, shooting, golf, tennis, skiing, rock music; *Clubs* Turf; *Style*— Marquess of Worcester; ✉ Badminton House, Glos GL9 1DB

WORCESTER, Prof Robert Milton; s of late C M Worcester, of Kansas City, USA, and late Violet Ruth Worcester; *b* 21 Dec 1933; *Educ* Univ of Kansas (BSc); *m* 1, 1958 (m dis), Joann, *née* Ransdell; 2 s; m 2, 1982, Margaret Noel, *née* Smallbone; *Career* conslt McKinsey & Co 1962–65; controller Opinion Research Corporation 1965–68, chm Market & Opinion Research International (MORI) Ltd 1973–; visiting prof of: govt LSE, journalism City Univ London; conslt: The Times, Economist; past pres World Assoc for Public Opinion Research; tstee: Magna Carta Tst, World Wide Fund for Nature (UK) 1988–94; vice pres: European-Atlantic Group, Royal Soc for Nature Conservation; chm Pilgrims Soc; FRSA; *Books* Political Communications (co editor 1982), Political Opinion Polling: an International Review (ed 1983), Private Opinions Public Polls (co author 1986), We British (co author, 1990), British Public Opinion (1991), Typically British (co author, 1991); *Recreations* choral music (Bart's Hosp Choir), gardening, skiing; *Clubs* Reform; *Style*— Prof Robert Worcester; ✉ MORI (Market & Opinion Research International), 32 Old Queen Street, London SW1H 9HP (☎ 0171 222 0232, fax 0171 222 1653)

WORDIE, Sir John Stewart; kt (1981), CBE (1975), VRD (1963); s of Sir James Mann Wordie, CBE (d 1962), of Cambridge; bro of Peter J Wordie, CBE, TD, *qv*; *b* 15 Jan 1924; *Educ* Winchester, St John's Coll Cambridge (MA, LLM); *m* 1955, Patricia, da of Lt-Col Gordon Bryson Kynoch, CBE, TD, DL, of Keith, Banffshire; 4 s; *Career* served WWII RNVR, Cdr RNR 1967, Cdr London Div RNR 1969–71; called to the Bar Inner Temple 1950; chm: Burnham and Pelham Ctee 1966–87, Soulbury Ctee 1966–, Wages Cncls 1956–93, Nat Jt Cncl for Further Education 1980–93; memb: Agric Wages Bd for Eng and Wales 1974–95, Central Arbitration Ctee 1976–91, Cncl of ACAS 1986–90; Ct Asst Worshipful Co of Salters' 1971– (Master 1975); *Recreations* sailing, shooting, tennis; *Clubs* Travellers', RORC, Hawks, Army & Navy, Royal Tennis Ct, Clyde Corinthian Yacht; *Style*— Sir John Wordie, CBE, VRD; ✉ Dodington House, Breamore, Fordingbridge, Hants SP6 2EH

WORDIE, Peter Jeffrey; CBE, TD; s of Sir James Mann Wordie, CBE (d 1962), of Cambridge, and Gertrude Mary, *née* Henderson; bro of Sir John Wordie, *qv*; *b* 30 May 1932; *Educ* Winchester, Univ of Cambridge (BA); *m* 27 Feb 1959, Alice Elinor Michele, da of Nicolas de Haller, of St Legier, Vaud, Switzerland; 2 s (Roderick b 1960, Charles b 1969), 3 da (Chantal b 1961, Michaela b 1964, Philippa b 1966); *Career* Nat Serv 1 Argylls 1950–52, TA 8 Argylls 1952–69; dir and vice chm Harrisons (Clyde) Ltd 1959–93; chm Buildings of Scotland Trust 1990–; tstee Burrell Collection 1985–; memb Worshipful Co of Shipwrights 1988; Hon DUniv Stirling 1986; *Books* The Royal Game (1989); *Recreations* fishing, real tennis; *Clubs* Travellers'; *Style*— Peter Wordie, Esq, CBE, TD; ✉ The Row, Dunblane, Perthshire FK15 9NZ

WORDSWORTH, Antony Christopher Curwen; s of Lt-Col John Gordon Wordsworth, OBE (d 1995), of Hereford, and Doreen Blackwood, *née* Butler-Henderson; ggggs of William Wordsworth, maternal ggs of Lords Faringdon and Clarina; *b* 24 April 1940; *Educ* Repton; *m* 3 Nov 1962, Rosamond Anne, da of Maj John David Summers, of Old Romney, Kent; 1 s (Mark b 1965), 2 da (Lucy (Mrs Nicholas Brown) b 1968, Mary b 1972); *Career* Lt Irish Gds 1958–62; insurance loss adjuster; dir Tyler & Co (Adjusters) Ltd; fell Chartered Inst of Loss Adjusters; churchwarden Radwinter; *Recreations* country gardening, music, dogs, pony driving; *Style*— Antony Wordsworth, Esq; ✉ Little Brockholds Farm, Radwinter, Saffron Walden, Essex CB10 2TF (☎ 01799 599 458); Tyler & Co (Adjusters) Ltd, 1 Norton Folgate, Bishopsgate, London E1 (fax 0171 377 6355)

WORLEY, (Edward) Michael; JP (1972); *b* 29 March 1936; *Educ* Uppingham, Downing Coll Cambridge; *m* 1966, Ann; 2 s (Andrew, Thomas), 1 da (Rachel); *Career* Steel Co of Wales Ltd (Port Talbot) 1957–62; William King Ltd (West Bromwich): joined 1962, md 1963–, chm 1973–; chm Taxation Ctee Unquoted Companies Gp 1979–, dir Wesleyan Assurance Soc 1980– (vice chm 1987–93, dep chm 1993–), memb Birmingham Diocesan Bd of Fin 1980–91, chm Birmingham Botanical Gardens & Glasshouses 1981–, memb W Midlands Regnl Health Authy 1982–93 (vice chm 1990–93), memb Cncl Birmingham Chamber of Indust and Commerce 1984–90, memb Bd Black Country Development Corp 1987–, non-exec dir Birmingham Regnl Office Barclays Bank PLC 1987–92, pres Nat Assoc of Steel Stockholders 1988–90, govr Sandwell Coll of Further and Higher Educn 1988–, chm Sandwell Trg and Enterprise Cncl 1990–95, pres Fédération Internationale des Associations de Négociants en Aciers, Tubes et Métaux (FIANATM) 1995–; *Books* co-author: Regional Government (1968), Freedom to Spend (1971), Passing On (1973); *Recreations* gardening, sailing, reading; *Style*— Michael Worley, Esq, JP; ✉ William King Ltd, Atlas Centre, Union Rd, West Bromwich, West Midlands B70 9DR (☎ 0121 500 4100, fax 0121 553 2038)

WORLEY, Stephen Christopher; s of Norman George Worley, of Worcester, and Janette Rose, *née* Smith; *b* 14 July 1963; *Educ* Ewell Castle; *Career* jr in Prodn Dept Wight Collins Rutherford Scott advtg agency 1981–82, Creative Servs Dept J Walter Thompson Ltd 1982–85, commercials prodn mangr Edwards Baker Swannel Ltd prodn co 1985–88, fndr ptnr (with John Swannell) John Swannell Films Ltd 1988–90, md Swan Films (after assuming majority shareholding) 1990; numerous advtg awards from: D&AD, Creative Circle, British TV Awards, Cannes and NY Festivals; memb AFVPA 1988; *Recreations* motor racing, skiing, tennis; *Style*— Stephen Worley, Esq

WORLIDGE, (Edward) John; s of Robert Leonard Worlidge (d 1960), and Kathleen Frances, *née* Bonallack; bro of Capt Robert Worlidge, *qv*; *b* 31 May 1928; *Educ* Marlborough, St John's Coll Cambridge (MA); *m* 8 Jan 1955, Margaret Elizabeth (Margot), da of John Murray (d 1965); 3 s (David b 1956, Nigel b 1960, Mark b 1963); *Career* 2 Lt RE 1946–48; exec dir BAT Industries plc 1980–89, chm and chief exec Wiggins Teape Group 1984–89 (dir 1970–89); non-exec dir: Rugby Group plc 1987–94, Thames Water plc 1988–; pres Marlburian Club 1987, memb Cncl Marlborough Coll (chm Fin Ctee) 1988–, govr Woolmer Hill Sch Haslemere 1992–; rowed for: Cambridge v Oxford 1951, Cambridge v Harvard & Yale in USA 1951, Lady Margaret Boat Club winning Grand Challenge Cup Henley 1951, Leander Winners Grand Challenge Cup Henley 1952, GB VIII Olympics Helsinki 1952; Liveryman Worshipful Co of Ironmongers 1986; FRSA 1986; *Recreations* sailing, golf; *Clubs* Hawks, Leander, Royal Yacht Squadron, Royal and Ancient Golf, Army and Navy; *Style*— John Worlidge, Esq; ✉ East Dene, Midhurst Rd, Haslemere, Surrey, GU27 2PT (☎ and fax 01428 654633)

WORLIDGE, Capt Robert Alan; LVO (1977); s of Robert Leonard Worlidge (d 1960), and Kathleen Frances, *née* Bonallack; bro of John Worlidge, *qv*; *b* 26 Oct 1933; *Educ* Marlborough Coll, Dartmouth, Royal Naval Engrg Coll; *m* 1, 1961 Pauline Reynolds, da of Stewart Cathie Griffith, CBE, DFC, TD; 2 da (Claire b 1964, Sarah b 1967); m 2, 1979, Agnes Margaret (Molly), da of Maj-Gen Walter Rutherfoord Goodman, CB, DSO, MC (d 1976), of Woodbridge, Suffolk; *Career* joined RN 1952; HMS Renown 1965–70, HMRY Britannia 1975–77; Capt HMS Sultan 1983–85; John Brown Engineers & Constructors 1986–93, MD CJB Developments Ltd 1993–; MIMechE; *Recreations* golf, cricket, sailing, theatre; *Clubs* Royal Yacht Sqdn, Royal Cinque Ports Golf, MCC; *Style*— Capt Robert Worlidge, LVO, RN; ✉ Abbey Rectory, 17 Park Lane, Bath BA1 2XH; Airport Services Road, Portsmouth, Hants

WORLING, Dr Peter Metcalfe; s of Alexander Davidson Worling (d 1965), of Aberdeen, and Florence, *née* Metcalfe (d 1992); *b* 16 June 1928; *Educ* New Sch Darjeeling India, Robert Gordon's Coll Aberdeen, Univ of Bradford (PhD); *m* 20 March 1954, Iris Isabella, da of James Peacock McBeath (d 1962), of Dingwall; 1 s (Bruce b 26 Aug 1956 d 1984), 2 da (Helen (Mrs Hill) b 25 Aug 1958, Fiona b 13 Jan 1962); *Career* home sales mangr Carnegies of Welwyn 1954–56 (export exec 1950–54), sales mangr Bradley & Bliss Ltd 1961–66 (pharmacist 1956–61), md Vestric Ltd Cheshire 1979–88 (mangr Ruislip Branch 1965–66, regnl dir Edinburgh 1966–73, commercial dir Cheshire 1973–79, md Cheshire 1979–89), chm AAH Pharmaceuticals Ltd Cheshire 1989–91, conslt 1991–95; memb Ctee Edinburgh Branch Royal Pharmaceutical Soc 1968–73 and 1995– (chm Reading Branch 1963–64); chm: S Wholesale Druggists Assoc 1970 (memb 1966–73), Nat Assoc of Pharmaceutical Distributors 1983–85 (memb Ctee 1974–91, hon memb 1991–); pres Proprietary Articles Trade Assoc 1984–85 (hon memb Cncl 1991–); FRPharmS 1954; *Recreations* genealogy, gardening; *Style*— Dr Peter Worling; ✉ The Grange, 29 Fernielaw Avenue, Edinburgh EH13 0EF (☎ and fax 0131 441 5134)

WORMELL, Peter Roydon; s of Roydon Wormell (d 1959), of Mackay, Queensland, and Gladys Mary Barrow (d 1987); *b* 28 June 1928; *Educ* Colchester Royal GS, Univ of Essex (BA, 1995); *m* 1, 1951 (m dis 1976), Jean, *née* Holmes; 1 s (Stephen Peter b 1958), 1 da (Carol Elizabeth b 1956); m 2, 26 May 1979 (m dis 1992), M J Horkins (authoress Mary Lyons); *Career* landowner, author, broadcaster; presenter Radio Orwell Farming Prog 1976–87; ed in chief Farmers' Handbook 1976–90; chm: Eastern Area Cons Agric Ctee 1968–93, Cons Countryside Forum 1978–93; memb: Essex CC 1966–77 (chm and ldr 1973–77), Lexden and Winstree RDC 1961–67, Colchester Water Bd 1963–66, Eastern Sports Cncl 1968–71, Eastern Electric Consultative Cncl 1969–73, Ct Univ of Essex 1968–77; chm: N Essex VSO 1968–76, N Essex ESU 1971–75, Jt Ctee Farmers' Club 1975–78, Colchester Colne Round Table 1965 (pres 1970), chm Abberton Church Tst 1994; Liveryman Worshipful Co of Farmers 1975; memb: Guild of Agric Journalists 1967, Lloyd's 1977; *Books* Anatomy of Agriculture (1978), Abb and La'Hoe in Photographs (1995), Called to the Classroom (1995); *Recreations* farming, politics, writing; *Clubs* Farmers', Royal Over-Seas League; *Style*— Peter Wormell, Esq; ✉ The Estate Office, Langenhoe Hall, Abberton, Colchester CO5 7NA (☎ 01206 735265, fax 01206 735487)

WORONCOW, Barbara; da of Dr Aleksander Woroncow, of Haslemere, Surrey, and Aldona, *née* Kwapinska; *b* 2 Sept 1952; *Educ* Purbrook Park Co GS Hants, Univ of Cambridge (MA), Univ of Leicester (grad cert in mus studies), Leeds Poly (further educn teachers cert); *m* 25 June 1977, Adrian Norris; *Career* asst curator Kirklees Met Cncl 1975–76, asst keeper of ethnography Leeds City Museum 1976–83, dep dir Area Museum and Art Gallery Serv for Yorks and Humberside 1985–87 (asst dir 1983–85), dir Yorks and Humberside Museums Cncl 1987–; author of numerous articles for museum jls; chm Museum Ethnographers Gp 1982–84 (sec 1977–79); Museums Documentation Assoc: memb Exec Ctee 1983–87, memb Bd of Mgmnt 1989–91; Yorks and Humberside Fedn of Museums and Art Galleries: memb 1975–, exec ctee 1987–, vice pres 1992–94, pres 1994–96; Museums Assoc: vice pres 1994–96, pres 1996–; vice chair of govrs Jacob Kramer Coll (Art & Design) Leeds 1990–92; Silver Medal Soc of Dyers and Colourists 1989; FMA 1989 (AMA 1977, memb Cncl 1990–); *Recreations* travel, opera, good food; *Clubs* Naval and Military (assoc lady memb); *Style*— Ms Barbara Woroncow; ✉ Yorkshire and Humberside Museums Council, Farnley Hall, Hall Lane, Leeds LS12 5HA (☎ 0113 263 8909, fax 0113 279 1479)

WORRALL, Anna Maureen (Mrs G H G Williams); QC (1989); *Educ* Hillcrest Sch, Loreto Coll Llandudno, Univ of Manchester (LLB); *m* 1964, Graeme Williams; 2 da; *Career* called to the Bar Middle Temple 1959, in practice 1959–63, lectr in law Holborn Coll of Law, Language and Commerce 1964–69, dir ILEA Educnl Television Service 1969–71, in practice 1971–, recorder 1987–, pres Mental Health Review Tbnls (memb 1993–); *Style*— Miss Anna M Worrall, QC; ✉ Cloisters, 1 Pump Court, Temple, London EC4Y 7AA (☎ 0171 583 0303)

WORRALL-THOMPSON, Antony; s of Michael Worrall-Thompson, and Joanna Brenda, *née* Duncan; *b* 1 May 1952; *Educ* Kings Sch Canterbury, Westminster Coll (HND); *m* 1, 1975, Jill, *née* Thompson; m 2, 1983 (m dis), Molitza Jane Hamilton, da of Hugh Miller; 2 s (Blake Antony Cardew, Sam Michael Hamilton); m 3, 1996, Jacinta Shiel; 1 s (Toby Jack Duncan); *Career* chef; food and beverage mangr Coombe Lodge Hotel Essex 1972, head chef and mangr Golden Fleece Restaurant Brentwood 1972; head chef: Ye Olde Logge Brentwood 1974, Adriatico Restaurant Woodland Green 1976, Hedges Restaurant South Woodford 1977, Brinkley's Restaurant Fulham Rd 1978–79 (with 6 month sabbatical to France), Dan's Restaurant Chelsea 1980; Ménage à Trois: chef and patron Knightsbridge 1981, opened in Bombay 1983, opened New York 1985, opened in Melbourne 1986, sold 1988 (retains all consultancies); chef and patron Avoirdupois Kings Road 1984, opened Mise-en-Place Limited 1986, purchased KWT Foodshow 1988; chef and patron: One Ninety Queen's Gate 1989–, Bistrot 190 1990–, dell'Ugo 1992–, Zoë 1992–, Drones 1995–; md Simpsons of Cornhill plc 1993–97; columnist Sunday Times, capt quiz team on Question of Taste (Radio 4), appearances on various TV shows incl Ready Steady Cook; ctee memb: Restaurateurs' Assoc of GB (vice chm), Académie Culinaire of France; FHCIMA; *Awards* Meilleur Ouvrier de Grande Bretagne 1987 (life title), winner Mouton Rothschild menu competition 1988; *Books* The Small and Beautiful Cookbook (1984), Supernosh (1993), Modern Bistrot Cooking (1994), 30–Minute Menu (1995), Ready Steady Cook (with Brian Turner, 1996); *Recreations* wine, antiques, art, interior design, gardening, sport, classical music, travel; *Style*— Antony Worrall-Thompson, Esq; ✉ 2 Rivermead Cottages, Mill Lane, Lower Shiplake, Henley-on-Thames, Oxon RG9 3LZ

WORSLEY, Francis Edward (Jock); s of Francis Arthur Worsley, and Mary, *née* Diamond; *b* 15 Feb 1941; *Educ* Stonyhurst, Sorbonne; *m* 12 Sept 1962, Caroline Violet, da of James Hamilton Grey Hatherell (d 1968), of Manor House, Chacombe, Banbury, Oxon; 2 s (Richard, Edward), 2 da (Miranda, Joanna); *Career* CA 1964; chm: The Financial Training Co Ltd 1972–91, Lloyd's Members' Agency Services Ltd 1994–; dir Lautro 1990–94; non-exec dir: The Cleveland Trust Plc 1993–, Reece Plc 1994–; memb Building Societies Cmmn 1991–; pres ICAEW 1988–89 (memb Cncl until 1996); complaints cmmr Securities and Investments Bd 1994–; govr Ludgrove Sch; Freeman: City of London, Worshipful Co of Chartered Accountants (Master 1992–93); FCA 1964; *Recreations* tennis, wine, cooking; *Style*— F E Worsley, Esq; ✉ Building Societies Commission, 15 Great Marlborough Street, London W1V 2LL (☎ 0171 437 9992)

WORSLEY, Dr Giles Arthington; s of Sir Marcus Worsley, Bt, *qv*, and Hon Bridget Assheton, da of 1 Baron Clitheroe, PC; *b* 22 March 1961; *Educ* Eton, New Coll Oxford, Courtauld Inst Univ of London (PhD); *Career* architectural ed Country Life 1989–94 (architectural writer 1985–88), ed Perspectives on Architecture 1994–; Soc of Architectural Historians of GB: Essay Prize 1989, Reginald Taylor Essay Prize 1991; Alexander Prize Royal Historical Soc 1992; memb Ctee: Save Britain's Heritage 1985–, Georgian Gp 1990– (ed Jl 1991–94); memb: Royal Fine Art Cmmn 1994–, Historic Buildings and Areas Advsy Ctee English Heritage 1995–; FSA 1991; *Books* Architectural Drawings of the Regency Period (1991), Classical Architecture in Britain: The Heroic Age (1995); *Recreations* reading, walking, buildings; *Style*— Dr Giles Worsley, FSA; ✉ Perspectives on Architecture, 2 Hinde Street, London W1M 5RH (☎ 0171 224 1766, fax 0171 224 1768)

WORSLEY, Sir (William) Marcus John; 5 Bt (UK 1838), of Hovingham, Yorks, JP (N Yorks 1957), DL (1978); s of Col Sir William Arthington Worsley, 4 Bt (d 1973, descent from Oliver Cromwell; sis Katharine m HRH the Duke of Kent in 1961), and Joyce Morgan, *née* Brunner; *b* 6 April 1925; *Educ* Eton, New Coll Oxford; *m* 10 Dec 1955, Hon Bridget Assheton, da of 1 Baron Clitheroe, PC; 3 s (William b 1956, Dr Giles Worsley, FSA *qv* b 1961, Peter b 1963), 1 da (Sarah b 1958); *Heir* s, William Ralph Worsley; *Career* served Green Howards, India and W Africa, WWII; MP (C): Keighley 1959–64, Chelsea 1966–74; church cmmr 1970–84, chm Nat Tst Properties Ctee 1980–90, dep chm Nat Tst 1986–92, pres Royal Forestry Soc of England Wales and NI 1980–82; High Sheriff N Yorks 1982–83; Lord Lt N Yorks 1987; *Recreations* reading, walking, travel; *Clubs* Boodle's; *Style*— Sir Marcus Worsley, Bt; ✉ Hovingham Hall, York YO6 4LU (☎ 01653 628206)

WORSLEY, Michael Dominic; QC (1985); s of Paul Worsley, and Magdalen Teresa, *née* Pestel; *b* 9 Feb 1926; *Educ* Bedford Sch, Inns of Court Sch of Law; *m* 1, Oct 1962, Pamela, *née* Philpot (d 1980); 1 s (Benedict b 28 Sept 1967); m 2, 12 June 1986, Jane, da of late Percival Sharpe; *Career* RN 1944–45; called to the Bar Inner Temple 1955, head of chambers; prosecuting counsel: to the Inland Revenue in London 1968–69, London Sessions 1969–71; jr treas counsel Central Criminal Ct 1971–74 (sr treas counsel 1974–85); *Recreations* music, travelling; *Clubs* Garrick, Lansdowne; *Style*— Michael Worsley, Esq, QC; ✉ 6 King's Bench Walk, Temple, London EC4Y 7DR (☎ 0171 583 0410)

WORSLEY, Nicholas Jarvis; QC (1993); s of Edgar Taylor Worsley (d 1973), and Vida, *née* McCormick (d 1986); *b* 21 July 1943; *Educ* Clifton, Univ of Cambridge (MA, LLB); *m* 4 Nov 1967, Anna Maxine, da of Maxwell George Bekenn, of 55 West St, Stratford upon Avon; 2 da (Sophie Tamaris Worsley b 1970, Jessica Worsley b 1973); *Career* called to Bar Inner Temple 1966, chm Agricultural Tribunal 1980, recorder 1984–94; chm: Worcester Civic Soc 1974–77, City of Worcester Building Preservation Tst 1977–, Countess of Huntingdon Hall Ltd 1984–; *Recreations* everything foreign, contemporary British arts, architecture and crafts; *Style*— Nicholas Worsley, Esq, QC; ✉ 5 Fountain Court, Steelhouse Lane, Birmingham B4 6DR (☎ 0121 606 0500)

WORSLEY, Paul Frederick; QC (1990); s of Eric Worsley, MBE, GM, and Sheila Mary, *née* Hoskin; *b* 17 Dec 1947; *Educ* Hymers Coll Hull, Mansfield Coll Oxford (MA); *m* 14 Dec 1974, Jennifer Ann Avery, JP, da of late Ernest Avery; 1 s (Nicholas b 1975), 1 da (Charlotte b 1977); *Career* called to the Bar Middle Temple 1970 (Astbury Scholar), recorder Crown Ct 1987–; *Recreations* Spy prints, opera, sailing; *Clubs* Yorkshire (York); *Style*— Paul Worsley, Esq, QC; ✉ 40 Park Cross St, Leeds LS1 2QH (☎ 0113 243 3277); 1 Hare Court, Temple, London EC4Y 7BE (☎ 0171 353 5324)

WORSLEY, Gen Sir Richard Edward; GCB (1981, KCB 1976), OBE (1964); s of H Worsley, of Grey Abbey, Co Down; *b* 29 May 1923; *Educ* Radley; *m* 1, 1958, Sarah Mitchell; 1 s, 1 da; m 2, 1980, Caroline, Duchess of Fife (*see* Hon Lady Worsley); *Career* served WWII (Mid East & Italy) and Malayan Emergency in Rifle Bde, Instr RMA Sandhurst and Staff Coll Camberley 1948–51, CO Royal Dragoons 1962–64, Cdr 7 Armoured Bde 1965–67, COS Far East Land Force 1969–71; GOC 3 Div 1972–74, Cdr 1st (British) Corps 1976–78; QMG 1979–82 (Vice-QMG 1974–76), ret 1982; Pilkington Group 1982–86, chief exec Pilkington Electro-Optical Div 1982–86 (chm 1984–86), chm Barr and Stroud 1982–86; chm Western Provident Assoc 1989–; *Clubs* Cavalry & Guards; *Style*— Gen Sir Richard Worsley, GCB, OBE

WORSLEY, William Ralph; s and h of Sir (William) Marcus John Worsley, 5 Bt, of Hovingham, Yorkshire; *b* 12 Sept 1956; *Educ* Harrow, RAC; *m* 26 Sept 1987, Marie-Noëlle, yr da of Bernard H Dreesmann; 1 s (Marcus William Bernard b 2 Nov 1995), 2 da (Isabella Claire b 24 Oct 1988, Francesca Sylvia b 5 March 1992); *Career* former Lt Queen's Own Yeomanry TAVR; farmer; forester; chartered surveyor; dir: Guinness Flight Paterson Ltd, Scarborough Building Soc; conslt Humberts 1986–92; memb N York Moors Nat Park Authority; Liveryman Worshipful Company of Merchant Taylors; FRICS; *Recreations* shooting, skiing, reading; *Clubs* White's, Pratt's; *Style*— William Worsley, Esq; ✉ Wool Knoll, Hovingham, York (☎ 01653 628771, fax 01653 628668)

WORSLEY-TAYLOR, Annette Pamela; da of Sir John Godfrey Worsley-Taylor, 3 Bt (d 1952), and Anne, *née* Paget (now Anne, Lady Jaffray); *b* 2 July 1944; *Educ* Downham Sch Hatfield Heath Herts; *Career* fndr London Designer Collections 1975 (dir 1976–); conceived, launched and organised London Designer Show 1991–92, organised and marketed London Fashion Week, fndr memb British Fashion Cncl 1983 (memb exec 1987–); *Recreations* fashion, design, music, theatre; *Style*— Ms Annette Worsley-Taylor; ✉ 3/57 Drayton Gardens, London SW10 9RU (☎ 0171 835 0845, fax 0171 835 0846)

WORSTHORNE, Sir Peregrine Gerard; kt (1991); s of Col Alexander Koch de Gooreynd, OBE, formerly Irish Gds (d 1985), who assumed surname of Worsthorne by deed poll in 1923, but reverted to Koch de Gooreynd in 1937; *see also* er bro Simon Towneley from whose estate the Worsthorne name is derived (gd m Manuela, da of Alexandre de Laski by Joaquina, Marquesa de Souza Lisboa da of José Marques Lisboa, sometime Min Plenipotentiary of Emperor of Brazil to Ct of St James), and Priscilla, later Baroness Norman (d 1991); *b* 22 Dec 1923; *Educ* Stowe, Peterhouse Cambridge (BA), Magdalen Coll Oxford; *m* 1, 7 June 1950, Claudie Marie-Hélène (d 1990), da of Victor Edouard Bertrand de Colasse, of Paris, and former w of Geoffrey Baynham; 1 da (Dominique Elizabeth Priscilla b 18 Feb 1952), 1 step s (David); m 2, 11 May 1991, Lucinda Lambton, *qv*; *Career* cmmnd Oxford & Bucks LI 1942, Lt Phantom GHQ Liaison Regt 1944–45; journalist and writer; formerly on editorial staff of: The Glasgow Herald 1946–48, The Times 1948–55, Daily Telegraph 1955–61; ed Sunday Telegraph 1986–91 (assoc ed 1961–86), ret 1991; *Books* The Socialist Myth (1972), Peregrinations (1980), By The Right (1987), Tricks of Memory, an autobiography (1993); *Recreations* tennis, reading, walking; *Clubs* Garrick, Beefsteak, Pratt's; *Style*— Sir Peregrine Worsthorne; ✉ The Old Rectory, Hedgerley, Bucks SL2 3UY (☎ 01753 646167, fax 01753 646914)

WORSWICK, Dr Richard David; *b* 22 July 1946; *Educ* Magdalen Coll Sch Oxford, New Coll Oxford (MA, DPhil); *m* 1970, Jacqueline Brigit Isobel, *née* Adcock; 3 da (Helen b 1975, Catherine b 1978, Isobel b 1981); *Career* res asst Science Res Cncl Dept of Inorganic Chemistry Univ of Oxford 1972–73, res product mangr Boots Co plc 1973–76; Harwell Laboratory UK Atomic Energy Authy: on staff Mktg and Planning 1976–85, head Res Planning 1985–88, head Environmental and Med Sciences Div 1988–90; dir of Process Technol and Instrumentation AEA Industrial Technology 1990–91, govt chemist 1991–, chief exec Laboratory of the Govt Chemist (DTI Agency) 1991–96, chief exec LGC 1996–; FRSC 1991; *Recreations* listening to music, playing the violin, gardening; *Style*— Dr Richard Worswick; ✉ Laboratory of the Government Chemist, Queen's Road, Teddington, Middx TW11 0LY (☎ 0181 943 7300, fax 0181 977 0741)

WORTH, Brian Leslie; s of Leslie Worth (d 1988), of Brockenhurst, Hants, and Grace Alice, *née* Drake (d 1983); *b* 25 Jan 1938; *Educ* Haberdashers' Aske's; *m* (m dis); 1 s (Graham b 1966), 1 da (Susan b 1964); *Career* Nat Serv Sr Aircraftsman RAF 1960–62; CA; ptnr Whitehill Marsh Jackson & Co 1964, sr ptnr Fryer Whitehill & Co 1974–82, managing ptnr Clark Whitehill Chartered Accountants 1982–86; chm: Clark Whitehill Chartered Accountants 1984–90, Clark Kenneth Leventhal 1988–90, Bd of Res ICAEW 1990–, Folley Bros Holdings Ltd 1990–, Annual Survey of Published Accounts 1990–92; sr fell Centre for Empirical Res in Accounting and Finance 1993–; memb Main Ctee London Soc of CAs 1976–85 (chm 1983–84); hon treas Br Cncl of Churches 1973–79; FCA (memb Cncl 1985–), FCIArb; *Books* Planning Your Personal Finances (1973), Financing Local Government (1992); *Style*— Brian L Worth, Esq; ✉ 25 New Street Square, London EC4A 3LN (☎ 0171 353 1577)

WORTH, Irene; Hon CBE (1975); *b* 23 June 1916, Nebraska, USA; *Educ* UCLA (BE); *Career* actress; Hon Dr Arts Tufts Univ 1980, Hon DFA Queen's Coll NY 1986; Antoinette Perry award for distinguished achievement in the theatre 1965, NY Theatre Hall of Fame 1979, Obie award for outstanding achievement in the theatre 1989, NY Mayor's Award of Honor for Arts and Culture 1990; *Theatre* debut in Escape Me Never (NY) 1942, Broadway debut The Two Mrs Carrolls (Booth Theatre) 1943, studied for six months with Elsie Fogerty 1944–45, Love Goes To Press (Embassy then Duchess Theatre) 1946, Edward My Son (Lyric) 1948, Home is Tomorrow (Cambridge Theatre) 1948, Champagne for Deliah (New Theatre) 1949, The Cocktail Party (Edinburgh Festival then New Theatre and Henry Miller Theatre NY) 1949–50, Othello (Old Vic) 1951, Midsummer Night's Dream (Old Vic) 1952, Old Vic tour of S Africa (Macbeth, Othello, Midsummer Night's Dream, The Other Heart) 1952, The Merchant of Venice (Old Vic) 1953, All's Well That Ends Well and Richard III (Shakespeare Festival Theatre Ontario) 1953, A Day by the Sea (Haymarket) 1953–54, A Life in the Sun (Edinburgh Festival) 1955, The Queen and the Revels (Haymarket) 1955, Hotel Paradiso (Winter Garden) 1956, Mary Stuart (Phoenix Theatre NY and Old Vic) 1957–58, The Potting Shed (Globe) 1958, As You Like It (Shakespeare Festival Theatre Ontario) 1959, Toys in the Attic (Hudson Theatre) 1960 (NY Newspaper Guild Page One award 1960), season at Royal Shakespeare Theatre Stratford 1962, King Lear (Aldwych) 1962, The Physicists (Aldwych) 1963, The Ides of March (Haymarket) 1963, King Lear (RSC) 1964, Tiny Alice (Billy Rose Theatre NY) 1965 (Best Actress Tony Awards 1965), A Song at Twilight, Shadows of the Evening and Come into the Garden Maud (Noel Coward trilogy, Queen's Theatre) 1966 (Evening Standard award 1966), Heartbreak House (Chichester and Lyric) 1967 (Variety Club of GB award and Whitbread Anglo-American award for outstanding actress 1967), Seneca's Oedipus (NT) 1968, Tiny Alice (Aldwych) 1970, Hedda Gabler (Stratford Ontario) 1970, worked with Int Co for Theatre Resources Paris and Iran 1971, Notes on a Love Affair (Globe) 1972, The Seagull (Chichester and Greenwich) 1973–74, Sweet Bird of Youth (Lake Forest, Washington, NY) 1975 (Best Actress Tony Awards and Jefferson Awards 1975), Misalliance, Old Times and After the Season (Academy Festival Theatre) 1976–78, The Cherry Orchard (NY) 1977 (Best Actress Obie Awards, Drama Desk Awards and Critic's Choice Awards 1977), Happy Days (NY) 1979 (Best Actress Obie Awards 1979), The Lady from Dubuque (NY) 1980, L'Olimpiade (Edinburgh Festival) 1982, The Chalk Garden (NY) 1982, The Physicists (Washington) 1983, The Golden Age (NY) 1984, Coriolanus (NT) 1984, The Bay at Nice (NT) 1986, You Never Can Tell (Haymarket) 1987, Lost in Yonkers (NY) 1991 (Best Supporting Actress Tony Awards and Drama Desk Awards 1991); *Television* The Lady from the Sea 1953 (Daily Mail Nat TV award 1953), The Lake 1953 (Daily Mail Nat TV award 1954), Coriolanus 1984; *Films* Orders to Kill 1957 (Best Woman's Performance Br Film Acad Awards 1958), The Scapegoat 1958, King Lear 1970, Nicholas and Alexandra 1971, Eye Witness 1980, Deathtrap 1982, Fast Forward 1985; for television: Forbidden 1985, The Big Knife 1988, The Shell Seekers 1989; *Recreations* music; *Style*— Ms Irene Worth, CBE; ✉ c/o ICM Ltd, Oxford House, 76 Oxford Street, London W1N 0AX (☎ 0171 636 6565, fax 0171 323 0101)

WORTH, Prof Katharine Joyce; da of George Lorimer, and Elizabeth, *née* Jones; *b* 4 Aug 1922; *Educ* Univ of London (MA, PhD); *m* 30 Aug 1947, George, s of Ernest Worth; 2 s (Christopher George b 7 Nov 1952, Charles Robert Edmund b 4 July 1959), 1 da

(Elizabeth Lorimer b 5 Nov 1955); *Career* prof of drama and theatre studies Royal Holloway and Bedford New Coll Univ of London (formerly Royal Holloway Coll) 1978–87 (lectr Eng lit 1964–74, reader Eng lit 1974–78), visiting prof King's Coll London 1988–, hon res fell RHBNC 1990–; adaptor and prodr of Beckett's Company performed in Edinburgh 1987, London and New York 1988, Monaco and Dublin 1991, co-ed Theatre Notebook, memb Ed Bd of Yeats Annual and Modern Drama, frequent lectr abroad supported by the Br Cncl and foreign universities; memb: Soc for Theatre Res 1950, Soc of Authors 1988; Friend of the Royal Academy; *Books* Revolutions in Modern English Drama (1973), Beckett the Shape Changer (ed 1975), The Irish Drama of Europe from Yeats to Beckett (1978), Oscar Wilde (1983), Maeterlinck's Plays in Performance (1985), Where There is Nothing (ed 1987), Waiting for Godot and Happy Days (Text and Performance, 1990), Sheridan and Goldsmith (1992); *Recreations* theatre-going, walking, travel; *Style*— Prof Katharine Worth; ✉ 48 Elmfield Ave, Teddington, Middx TW11 8BT

WORTH, Peter Herman Louis; s of Dr L H Worth (d 1982), and Ruth, *née* Niemeyer (d 1967); *b* 17 Nov 1935; *Educ* Marlborough Coll, Trinity Hall Cambridge (MA, MB BChir), FRCS 1967, Middlesex Hosp Med Sch; *m* 8 Feb 1969, Judith Katherine Frances, da of Arthur Girling (d 1959), of Langham Essex; 1 s (Hugo b 1970), 1 da (Anna b 1972); *Career* conslt urological surgn: UCH 1976, St Peter's Hosps 1976, Middlesex Hosp 1984 (now UCL Hosps), Royal Masonic Hosp 1986, King Edward VII Hosp 1993; memb: Br Assoc of Urological Surgns, RSM; *Books* contrib chapters on urology in several medical text books; *Recreations* classical music, skiing, gardening; *Style*— Peter Worth, Esq; ✉ Broad Eaves, Mill Lane, Broxbourne, Herts EN10 7AZ (☎ 01992 462827); 31 Wimpole St, London W1M 7AE (☎ 0171 935 3593, fax 0171 224 1957)

WORTHEN, Prof John; s of Frederick Morley Worthen, and Dorothy Geach, *née* Barrett, of Bournemouth; *b* 27 June 1943; *Educ* Merchant Taylors' Sch, Downing Coll Cambridge (BA), Univ of Kent (MA. PhD); *m* 1983, Cornelia Linda Elfriede, da of Dr Helmut Rumpf; *Career* instructor Univ of Virginia 1968–69, jr res fell Univ of Edinburgh 1969–70; Univ Coll of Swansea: lectr in English 1970–85, sr lectr in English 1985–90, prof of English 1990–93; prof of D H Lawrence studies Univ of Nottingham 1994–; *Books* D H Lawrence - The Early Years 1885–1912 (1991), and numerous pubns on D H Lawrence; *Recreations* music; *Style*— Prof John Worthen; ✉ Department of English Studies, University of Nottingham, University Park, Nottingham NG7 2RD (☎ 0115 951 5151)

WORTHINGTON, His Hon George Noel; s of George Errol Worthington (d 1976), and Edith Margaret Boys, *née* Stones (d 1970); *b* 22 June 1923; *Educ* Rossall; *m* 10 July 1954, Jacqueline Kemble, da of George Lionel Spencer Lightfoot (d 1972), of Carlisle; 2 s (Nicholas b 1958, Jonathan decd), 1 da (Kate b 1962); *Career* serv RAC 1941–46; admitted slr 1949; recorder of the Crown Ct 1972–79, circuit judge 1979–94; memb Ct of Assts Worshipful Co of Wax Chandlers; *Recreations* gardening and theatre; *Clubs* Athenaeum, Hurlingham; *Style*— His Hon George N Worthington

WORTHINGTON, Prof John; s of Brig Roger Fraser Worthington (d 1984), and Mary, *née* Smith (d 1990); *b* 8 Aug 1938; *Educ* Gresham's, Architectural Assoc (Travelling scholar, Holloway Travelling scholar, AADipl), Univ of Philadelphia (MArch), Univ of California; *m* 1963, Susan Mary, da of late Air Marshal Sir John Davis; 1 s (Nicholas Fraser b 22 Dec 1969), 1 da (Samantha Jane b 27 June 1973); *Career* served Royal Enniskillen Fusiliers Berlin and Wuppertal 1957–59; architect: Alex Gordon & Partners 1964–65, Thompson, Berwick, Pratt & Partners Vancouver 1967–68, Ahrends, Burton & Koralek London 1969–70; res conslt Home Office 1970–71, fndr memb JFN Associates 1971–73, fndr ptnr Duffy Lange Giffone Worthington (now Duffy Eley Giffone Worthington) 1973–76, external dir URBED 1975–78; DEGW: ptnr 1976–90, fndr DEGW (Scotland) Ltd 1984, dir of main bd DEGW International Ltd 1990–, dep chm 1994–; dir Inst of Advanced Architectural Studies Univ of York 1992–; corp consultancy incl: NW Region HQ and SE Region Laboratories CEGB, Geneva HQ Digital Equipment Corporation Europe, corp HQ ESB Dublin, Engineering HQ BNFL, Conoco Oil, Midland Bank International, Kajima Corporation Tokyo, Scottish Equitable Assurance Soc Edinburgh, Carl Zeiss Jena, Irish Life Dublin, Basildon Development Corporation, Warrington Development Corporation, Welsh Development Agency, Hackney and Islington Inner City Project DOE, Scottish Development Agency, Scottish Education Department, Department of Education and Science, Department of Health, City of Birmingham, Greycoat, Stanhope Properties, Trafalgar House Developments, Imry Merchant Developers, Neinver Madrid, Chelsfield Europe, Intelligent Building in Europe; pt/t tutor: AA Sch of Architecture 1968, Canterbury Sch of Art 1969, Bartlett Sch of Architecture UCL 1969–74; visiting prof: Univ of Cincinnati 1978–79, Univ of Arizona 1986, Univ of Technol Sydney 1993 and 1994; external examiner: Bartlett Sch of Architecture UCL 1990–92 (Oxford Poly 1987–90), Univ of Manchester 1994–96, Univ of Kingston 1994–96; patron Urban Design Group, vice pres AA; memb: Ctee Br Cncl for Offices, Steering Ctee Vision for London; Harkness fell Commonwealth Fund 1965–67; *Books* Office Planner (conslt ed and contrib, 1976), Planning Office Space (with Duffy and Cave, 1976), Industrial Rehabilitation (with Eley, 1984), Fitting Out the Workplace (with Konya, 1988), Human Office (with Beucker and Murai, 1990); contrib to numerous pubns; *Recreations* sailing, travel; *Style*— Prof John Worthington; ✉ Institute of Advanced Architectural Studies, University of York, The King's Manor, York YO1 2EP (☎ 01904 433960, fax 01904 433949); DEGW International Ltd, Porters North, 8 Crinan Street, London N1 9SQ (☎ 0171 239 7777)

WORTHINGTON, Nick; s of David Worthington, of Stoke Abbott, Dorset, and Bridgit, *née* Petter; *b* 19 Oct 1962; *Educ* Fitzharry's Comp Abingdon Oxon, Banbury Sch of Art and Design, St Martin's Sch of Art (BA); *Career* advtg copywriter; trainee TBWA London 1984, Symington & Partners London 1984–86, Jenner Keating Becker London 1986–88, Bartle Bogle Hegarty London 1988–96, Abbott Mead Vickers BBDO 1996–; winner numerous advtg awards incl 2 Gold Lions Cannes (for Levi's 501); motor cycle racer, BMCRC & KRC 250cc champion 1991; *Recreations* motorcycle racing; *Clubs* Br Motorcycle Racing; *Style*— Nick Worthington, Esq; ✉ Abbott Mead Vickers BBDO Ltd, 191 Old Marylebone Road, London NW1 5DW (☎ 0171 402 4100)

WORTHINGTON, Philip Michael; s of Col Lancelot Jukes Worthington, TD, JP (d 1975), and 1 w Phyllis Mary, *née* Sadler (d 1981); *b* 24 April 1926; *Educ* Ashby-de-la-Zouch, Univ Coll Nottingham (BSc); *m* 1, 25 June 1955, Gillian Hazel, da of late Sir William Sidney Albert Atkins, CBE, of Chobham Place, Chobham, Surrey; 1 s (Nicholas b 1960), 1 da (Catherine b 1962); m 2, 29 July 1983, Judith Sonia May Worthington, JP, da of Henry Peter Robson Hamlin, of Ashby-de-la-Zouch, Leics; 1 da (Miranda b 1985); *Career* conslt engr and business and project conslt; md: WS Atkins and Partners 1971–78 (joined 1946, dir 1965–78), PM Worthington & Associates Ltd 1978–93; dir: Worthington Group plc 1972– (chm 1972–83, sec 1983–), Polycast Ltd 1984– (sec 1991–); exec dir Major Projects Assoc 1982–83, assoc fell Templeton Coll Oxford 1982–84; author of papers on engrg and economics; underwriting memb Lloyd's 1988–; CEng, FICE; *Books* The Worthington Families of Medieval England; *Style*— P M Worthington, Esq; ✉ The Knoll House, Knossington, Oakham, Leics LE15 8LT (☎ and fax 01664 454315)

WORTHINGTON, William Anthony (Tony); MP (Lab) Clydebank and Milngavie (majority 12,430); s of Malcolm Thomas Henry Worthington (d 1985), and Monica, *née* Wearden (d 1995); *b* 11 Oct 1941; *Educ* City Sch Lincoln, LSE (BA), Univ of Glasgow (MEd); *m* 26 March 1966, Angela May, da of Cyril Oliver, of The Moat House, Charing, Kent; 1 s (Robert b 1972), 1 da (Jennifer b 1970); *Career* lectr Jordanhill Coll Glasgow 1971–87, regnl cncllr Strathclyde 1974–87 (chm Fin Ctee 1986–87); MP (Lab) Clydebank and Milngavie 1987–; oppn front bench spokesman on: educn, employment, trg and social work in Scotland until 1992, overseas devpt 1992–93, foreign affrs 1993–94, NI 1995–; memb Scottish Community Educn Cncl 1980–87, chm Strathclyde Community Business 1984–87; *Recreations* running, gardening, reading, sailing; *Clubs* Radnor Park Bowling; *Style*— Tony Worthington, MP; ✉ 24 Cleddans Crescent, Hardgate, Clydebank, Dunbartonshire G81 5NW (☎ 01389 873195); House of Commons, London SW1 0AA (☎ 0171 219 3507)

WORTON, Prof Michael John; s of William Asquith Worton (d 1973), and Nan Scott Elliot, *née* Little; *b* 20 July 1951; *Educ* Dumfries Acad, Univ of Edinburgh (MA, Gold Medal, F C Green Prize, PhD); *Career* lectr in French Univ of Liverpool 1976–80; UCL: lectr in French language and literature 1980–91, sr lectr in French 1991–94, prof of French 1994–, currently dean Faculty of Arts, dir Centre for Interdisciplinary Research in the Arts and Humanities 1995–; assoc dir Inst of Romance Studies 1994–; hon research assoc Centre National de la Recherche Scientifique Paris; *Books* Intertextuality: Theories and practices (ed and introduced with Judith Still, 1990, reprinted 1993), Tournier: La Goutte d'or (1992, reprinted 1995), René Char: The Dawn Breakers/Les Matinaux (ed, introduced and translated, 1992), Textuality and Sexuality: Reading theories and practices (ed and introduced with Judith Still, 1993), Michel Tournier (ed, 1995); also author of numerous book chapters, and of articles and reviews in learned jls; *Recreations* hill walking, theatre, opera; *Style*— Prof Michael Worton; ✉ 146 Hornsey Lane, London N6 5NS (☎ 0171 272 4472); Faculty of Arts, University College London, Gower Street, London WC1E 6BT (☎ 0171 391 1347, fax 0171 813 2273, e-mail m.worton@ucl.ac.uk)

WOSNER, John Leslie; s of Eugen Wosner, of London, and Lucy, *née* Chajes; *b* 8 June 1947; *Educ* Hasmonean GS, Univ of Sheffield (BA); *m* 17 March 1974, Linda Jose, da of Abraham Freedman; 1 da (Dina b 1975), 2 s (Jeremy b 1979, Daniel b 1982); *Career* articled clerk and mangr Arthur Andersen 1969–73, Tax Consultancy Div Harmood Banner CA's 1973–74; Pannell Kerr Forster: tax mangr 1974–76, ptnr 1976–, head Home Counties Tax Dept 1986–90, ptnr i/c Luton 1990–92, managing ptnr 1992–; Freeman City of London; ATII, FCA; *Recreations* history, reading, football, country walks; *Clubs* Travellers; *Style*— John Wosner, Esq; ✉ Pannell Kerr Forster, New Garden House, 78 Hatton Garden, London EC1N 8JA (☎ 0171 831 7393, fax 0171 405 6736)

WOTHERSPOON, (William) Gordon; *b* 6 July 1947; *Career* Safeway plc (formerly Argyll Group plc): joined 1971, dir 1989–, currently md property and devpt; *Style*— Gordon Wotherspoon, Esq; ✉ Safeway plc, Safeway House, Millington Road, Hayes UB3 4AY (☎ 0181 848 8744)

WOTHERSPOON, (John Munro) Iain; TD, DL (Lochaber, Inverness, Badenoch and Strathspey 1982), WS (1950); s of Robert Wotherspoon (d 1968), of Inverness, and Jessie MacDonald, *née* Munro (d 1980); *b* 19 July 1924; *Educ* Inverness Royal Acad, Loretto, Trinity Coll Oxford (MA), Univ of Edinburgh (LLB); *m* 30 Aug 1952, Victoria Avril Jean, da of Sir Lawrie Edwards, KBE, DL (d 1968), of Newcastle upon Tyne; 2 s (James b 1955, Jonathan b 1957), 2 da (Ann b 1956, Victoria b 1960); *Career* slr and landowner; Lt Royal Signals Europe and Burma 1944–46, TA 1948–78, Lt-Col Cmdg 51 (Highland) Div Signals 1963–67, Col Dep Cdr 13 Signals Gp 1970–72, Hon Col 32 Scottish Signal Regt 1972–78, ADC to HM The Queen 1971–76; sr ptnr Macandrew & Jenkins WS Inverness; Dep Lt Inverness Lieutenancy Highland 1982–; clerk to the Lieutenancy 1985–; *Recreations* shooting, fishing, stalking; *Style*— Iain Wotherspoon, TD, DL; ✉ Maryfield, 62 Midmills Road, Inverness IV2 3QL (☎ 01463 233642); Macandrew & Jenkins, 5 Drummond Street, Inverness IV1 1QF (☎ 01463 233001, fax 01463 230743)

WRAGG, Prof Edward Conrad; s of George William Wragg, of Sheffield, and Maria, *née* Brandstetter; *b* 26 June 1938; *Educ* King Edward VII GS Sheffield, Hatfield Coll, Univ of Durham (BA, DipEd), Univ of Leicester (MEd), Univ of Exeter (PhD); *m* 29 Dec 1960, Judith, da of Beaumont King (d 1984), of Penistone, nr Sheffield; 1 s (Christopher Beaumont b 1975), 2 da (Josephine b 1966, Caroline Maria b 1967); *Career* master Queen Elizabeth GS Wakefield 1960–64, head of German Wyggeston Boys' Sch 1964–66, lectr in educn Univ of Exeter 1966–73, prof of educn Univ of Nottingham 1973–78, prof of educn Univ of Exeter 1978–; memb Devon Educn Ctee, chm Sch Broadcasting Cncl for UK (1981–86), chm Educnl Broadcasting Cncl for UK 1986–87, pres Br Educnl Res Assoc, chm BBC Regnl Advsy Cncl for SW 1989–92, chm BBC Regnl Cncl for South 1992–96; chartered fell Coll of Preceptors 1988; DUniv Open Univ 1989; radio/TV presenter: Chalkface (Granada), Crisis in Education (BBC), Education Roadshow (BBC); winner Jerwood award 1991; Hon DUniv Univ of Strathclyde 1993; *Books* Teaching Teaching (1974), Classroom Interaction (1976), Teaching Mixed Ability Groups (1976), A Handbook for School Governors (1980), Class Management and Control (1981), A Review of Research in Teacher Education (1982), Swineshead Revisited (1984), Classroom Teaching Skills (1984), The Domesday Project (1985), Education - An Action Guide for Parents (1986), Teacher Appraisal (1987), Education in the Market Place (1988), The Wragged Edge - Education in Thatcher's Britain (1988), Schools and Parents (1989), Riches from Wragg (1990), Mad Curriculum Disease (1991), Class Management (1993), Questioning (1993), Explaining (1993), Primary Teaching Skills (1993), Parents' File (1993), No, Minister! (1993), An Introduction to Classroom Observation (1994), The Flying Boot Reading Scheme (1994), Effective Teaching (1994), The Parent's Guide to the National Curriculum (1995), The Ted Wragg Guide to Education (1995), Teacher Appraisal Observed (1996), The Longman Parent's and Students' Guides (1996), The Last Quango (1996); *Recreations* football watching, playing and coaching, music, running, cooking; *Style*— Prof Edward Wragg; ✉ 14 Doriam Close, Exeter EX4 4RS (☎ 01392 491052); School of Education, University of Exeter EX1 2LU (☎ 01392 264877, fax 01392 264746)

WRAGG, John; s of Arthur Wragg, of York, and Ethel, *née* Ransom; *b* 20 Oct 1937; *Educ* York Sch of Art, Royal Coll of Art; *Career* artist; *Solo Exhibitions* Hanover Gallery 1963, 1966 and 1970, Gallerie Alexandre Iolas Paris 1968, York Festival 1969, Bridge Street Gallery Bath 1982, Katherine House Gallery Marlborough 1984, Quinton Green Fine Art 1985, Devizes Museum Gallery 1994 and 1996, England & Co London 1994, L'Art Abstract Gallerie 1995, Monumental' 96 Belgium 1996; *Group Exhibitions* incl: Lords Gallery 1959, L'Art Vivant 1965 and 1968, Arts Cncl Gallery Belfast 1966, Pittsburg Int 1967, Britische Kuns heute Hamburg 1968, Fndn Maeght 1968, Bath Festival Gallery 1977 and 1984, Artists Market 1978, Biennale di Scultura di Arese (Milan) 1980, King Street Gallery Bristol 1980, Gallerie Bollhagen Worpswede Germany 1981 and 1983, Quinton Green Fine Art 1984, 1985, 1986 and 1987, Abstraction 89 (Cleveland Bridge Gallery) 1989, Sculptors Drawings (Cleveland Bridge Gallery) 1990, Contemporary Br Drawing (Cleveland Bridge Gallery) 1989, The Hunting Art Prizes Exhibition 1991, Best of British (Simpsons and Connaught Brown) 1993; *Work in Collections* Sainsbury Centre UEA, Israel Museum Jerusalem, Tate Gallery, Arts Cncl of GB, Arts Cncl of NI, Contemporary Art Soc, Wellington Art Gallery NZ, Nat Gallery of Modern Art Edinburgh, Chancery Bequest 1981; ARCA 1960, RA 1991; *Recreations* walking; *Style*— John Wragg, Esq, RA; ✉ 6 Castle Lane, Devizes, Wilts SN10 1HJ (☎ 01380 727087)

WRAGG, Lawrence de Villamil; s of Arthur Donald Wragg (d 1966), of Buxton, Derbys, and Lilia Mary May, *née* Adcock (d 1990); *b* 26 Nov 1943; *Educ* Rendcomb Coll Glos, Univ of Bristol (BA), Sorbonne Paris (Dip), Manchester Business Sch (MBA); *m* 23

July 1971, Aureole Margaret Willoughby, da of Lt-Col Edward Cole Willoughby Fowler (d 1985), of Chislehurst, Kent; 1 s (David b 1979), 2 da (Isabel b 1977, Helen b 1988); *Career* systems analyst National Data Processing Service 1968–69, mgmnt conslt Price Waterhouse Assocs 1969–72, exec dir Chemical Bank International (formerly London Multinational Bank Ltd) 1974–82; dir: Charterhouse Japhet 1982–86, Standard Chartered Merchant Bank 1987–89; dep chm and chief exec Ketton Investments 1990–; chm: Lawrence Wragg Associates Ltd 1989–, Proscyon Partners Ltd 1990–; dir: The Bookshed Ltd 1993–, Bivar Ltd 1993–, Curzon Mortgages Ltd 1996–; chm: Govrs of Duxford Sch 1985–90, The Ickleton Soc 1982–; vice chm Ickleton PC 1988–90, chm London Banks Composite Currency Ctee 1980–84; memb: Assoc of MBAs 1974–, Cambridge City and S Cambridgeshire Ctee CPRE; MSI, FRSA; *Books* Composite Currencies (ed, 1984); *Recreations* music, mountaineering, skiing, gardening, aviation; *Clubs* London Mountaineering (treas); *Style*— Lawrence Wragg, Esq; ✉ 105 Brewery Road, Pampisford, Cambs CB2 4EW (☎ and fax 01223 830811)

WRAIGHT, Sir John Richard; KBE (1976), CMG (1962); s of Richard George Wraight (d 1964), and Kathleen Elizabeth Mary, *née* Robinson (d 1974); *b* 4 June 1916; *Educ* Selhurst GS, Sch of Slavonic Studies Univ of London (extension courses); *m* 1947, Marquita (Maggie), *née* Elliott; *Career* employed City of London 1932–39; 1939–45: Gunner to Maj HAC and RHA, Western Desert (Alamein), then ADC to Mil Cdr Cairo Area, Balkans Section, Min of Economic Warfare mission Cairo, economic warfare advsr HQ Med Allied Air Forces Caserta; joined FO 1945, special asst to chief of UNRRA ops in Europe 1946, Dip Serv 1947, first sec Athens 1948, Tel Aviv 1950, Washington 1953, asst head econ rels FO 1957, commercial cnsllr Cairo and Damascus 1959, Brussels and Luxembourg 1962, UK cmmr on Tripartite Cmmn for Restitution of Monetary Gold Brussels 1962–68, min and consul gen Milan 1968–73, ambass Switzerland 1973–76, ret; co dir and co conslt 1976–, int conslt to London stockbrokers Phillips & Drew 1976–88; pres Co Scout Cncl of Gtr London SW 1977–; Cdr of the Order of the Crown (Belgium) 1966; veteran memb Hon Artillery Co; memb RIIA; *Books* The Swiss and the British (1987), The Swiss in London: A History of the City Swiss Club 1856–1991 (1991); *Recreations* music, gardening, birdwatching; *Style*— Sir John Wraight, KBE, CMG; ✉ 35 Jameson Street, London W8 7SH

WRANGHAM, Peter John; *b* 30 April 1934; *m* 5 Jan 1963, Bridget Ann; 1 da (Fiona); *Career* currently dir: Johnson Electric Holdings, Hongkong and Cosmopolitan Textiles Ltd; former exec dir Hongkong & Shanghai Banking Corp; former non-exec dir: Cathay Pacific Airways, Hutchinson Whampoa, James Capel & Co, Midland Bank plc; *Style*— Peter Wrangham, Esq

WRATTEN, Donald Peter; s of Frederick George Wratten (d 1936), of Folkestone, Kent, and Majorie, *née* Liverton (d 1979); *b* 8 July 1925; *Educ* Harvey GS Folkestone, LSE (BScEcon), Open Univ (BA); *m* 6 Sept 1947, Margaret Kathleen, da of Frank Marsh (d 1938), of London; 1 s (Mark b 1955), 1 da (Isobel b 1958); *Career* RAF Meteorological Wing 1943–47; PO: asst princ 1950, private sec to Asst PMG 1955–56, princ POHQ 1956–65, private sec to PMG 1965–66, head of Mktg Div PO Telecom 1966–67, dir E Region PO Telecom 1967–69; chief exec: Nat Girobank 1969–74, Nat Data Processing Serv 1974–75; sr dir personnel Br Telecom 1975–81, mgmnt conslt 1981–85, non-exec dir National Counties Building Society 1985–96; chm Radlett Soc, pres Stereoscopic Soc, memb Cncl Int Stereoscopic Union, memb then chm Advsy Panel City Univ Business Sch 1974–80; memb: Business Educn Cncl 1975–82, Ct Cranfield Inst of Technol 1975–81; FIMgt 1960, LRPS 1984, FRSA 1985; *Books* The Book of Radlett and Aldenham; *Recreations* stereoscopic photography, social history; *Style*— Donald Wratten, Esq; ✉ 10 Homefield Rd, Radlett, Herts WD7 8PY (☎ 01923 854500, fax 01923 853011)

WRAXALL, Sir Charles Frederick Lascelles; 9 Bt (UK 1813), of Wraxall, Somerset; s of Sir Morville William Lascelles Wraxall, 8 Bt (d 1978), and Irmgard Wilhelmina Maria, *née* Schnidrig; *b* 17 Sept 1961; *Educ* Archbishop Tenison's GS Croydon; *m* 1983, Lesley Linda, da of William Albert Allan; 1 s (William b 3 April 1987), 1 da (Lucy Rosemary Lascelles b 8 Oct 1992); *Heir* s, William Nathaniel Lascelles Wraxall b 3 April 1987; *Career* civil servant DHSS 1978–80, trainee auditor Woolworths Pty Cape Town 1980–81, trainee accountant British Steel Corporation 1982–87, asst accountant Morgan Stanley Int 1987–; *Recreations* DIY, football, stamp collection; *Style*— Sir Charles Wraxall, Bt

WRAXALL, 2 Baron (UK 1928); George Richard Lawley Gibbs; DL (Somerset 1996); s of 1 Baron Wraxall, TD, PC (d 1931, s of Antony Gibbs, of the banking family and 2nd cousin of 4 Baron Aldenham), and his 2 w, Hon Ursula Mary Lawley, OBE, RRC (d 1979), er da of 6 and last Baron Wenlock, GCSI, GCIE, KCMG (for whom Queen Mary was Sponsor); *b* 16 May 1928; *Educ* Eton, RMA Sandhurst; *Heir* bro, Hon Sir Eustace Gibbs, KCVO, CMG, *qv*; *Career* Maj N Somerset and Bristol Yeo, Lt Coldstream Gds; chm: N Somerset Cons Assoc 1970–74, N Somerset Yeomanry Assoc 1987– (tstee 1980–); govr and chm St Katherine's Comprehensive Sch 1974–81, chm Avon County Scout Cncl 1976–95, pres Avon County Scouts 1995–, CLR memb Agricultural Land Tribunals (SW) 1960–, fell Woodard Corpn (Western Div) Ltd 1980–92 (memb Exec Woodard Corpn 1980–92); tstee Wells Cathedral Preservation Tst 1975–; pres: Assoc of Professional Foresters 1991–95, Woodspring Cons Assoc 1992–; patron and former pres N Somerset Agric Show 1985–; patron Benefice of: Flax Bourton Somerset, Exwick Devon, Clyst St George Devon; landowner; *Recreations* shooting, estate management; *Clubs* RAC, Cavalry and Guards, Clifton (Bristol); *Style*— The Rt Hon the Lord Wraxall, DL; ✉ Tyntesfield, Wraxall, Bristol, Somerset BS19 1NU (☎ 01275 462923); Estate Office (☎ 01275 462021, fax 01275 463771)

WRAY, Denis Gage; s of Capt Gerald Gage Wray (d 1956), and Mary Alice Elaine, *née* Todd (d 1976); *b* 21 May 1928; *Educ* Rossall Sch, Univ of Edinburgh (MB ChB), Univ of Liverpool (MCh Orth); *m* 23 March 1953, Jean, da of Thomas Henry Simpson (d 1967); 2 s (Peter b 1961, Brian b 1967), 2 da (Sheila b 1955, Carol b 1958); *Career* sr examiner in surgery Br Assoc of Occupational Therapists 1962–82, conslt orthopaedic surgn Stockport Health Authy 1965–89, pt/t conslt orthopaedic surgn in private practice 1968–; memb and sec Orthopaedic Engrg Sub Ctee Br Orthopaedic Assoc 1981–84, memb various ctees of BSI 1983–87; fell: Manchester Med Soc, Br Orthopaedic Assoc; FRCS (Ed); *Books* Journal of Trama (contrib, 1981), Journal of RCS Edinburgh (1982), Journal of Clinical Practice (1983); *Recreations* tennis, squash, bowls; *Style*— Denis Wray, Esq; ✉ 11 Clifford Rd, Poynton, Cheshire SK12 1HY (☎ and fax 01625 872537); 432 Buxton Rd, Stockport SK2 7JQ (☎ 0161 483 9333, fax 0161 419 9913)

WRAY, Prof Gordon Richard; s of Joseph Wray (d 1975), of Farnworth, Bolton, Lancs, and Letitia, *née* Jones (d 1978); *b* 30 Jan 1928; *Educ* pt/t Worsley and Bolton Tech Coll (ONC, HNC), Univ of Manchester (BSc, MSc, PhD), Loughborough Univ of Technol (DSc); *m* 20 Nov 1954, Dr Kathleen Wray, da of Harold Greenwood Senior (d 1984), of Rastrick, Brighouse, Yorks; 1 s (Vaughan Richard b 24 Oct 1959), 1 da (Amanda Diane b 19 July 1961); *Career* engrg apprentice Bolton Lancs 1943–49, Sir Walton Preston scholar Univ of Manchester 1949–52, devpt engr Platt Bros Ltd Manchester 1952–53, lectr in mechanichal engrg Bolton Tech Coll 1953–55, lectr in textile engrg UMIST 1955–66; Loughborough Univ of Technol: reader in mechanical engrg 1966–70, prof (later head) Dept of Mechanical Engrg 1970–88, dir Engrg Design Inst 1988–91, Royal Academy of Engrg prof in the principles of engrg design 1988–93, emeritus prof 1993–; visiting prof Univ of California (Berkeley) 1977; memb: Dept of Industs Chief Scientist's Requirement Bd 1974–75, Interdisciplinary Bd CEI/CSTI 1978–83 (Brunel lectr Br Assoc Annual Meeting 1980), Ctee on Innovation SEFI Brussels 1980–82, Royal Soc Working Gp on Agric Engrg 1981–82, Applied Mechanics Ctee SERC 1982–85, Fellowship of Engrg Working Pty on Dept of Indust Requirement Bds 1982, Working Pty on Engrg Design SERC 1983, Royal Soc Sectional Ctee 4(i) 1986–89, Ctee Engrg Profs Conf 1986–88, Mullard Award Ctee Royal Soc 1986–91, Royal Soc/SERC Industl Fellowships Panel 1986–89, Royal Soc Technol Activities Ctee 1989–93; chm Engrg Cncl/Design Cncl Working Pty on Attaining Competences in Engrg Design (ACED Report) 1989–91; memb Cncl IMechE 1964–67 (chm Manipulative and Mechanical Handling Machinery Gp 1969–71); IMechE: Viscount Weir Prize 1959, Water Arbitration Prize 1972, James Clayton Prize 1975, 76th Thomas Hawksley Meml lectr 1989; Warner Medal of the Textile Inst 1976, SG Brown Prize of the Royal Soc 1978; Hon MIED 1990; FRS 1986, FEng 1980, FIMechE 1973, FTI 1963, FRSA 1974; Euro Engr (Eur Ing) Paris 1987 (first recipient of title); *Books* Modern Yarn Production from Man-Made Fibres (1960), Modern Developments in Weaving Machinery (1961), An Introduction to the Study of Spinning (3 edn, 1962), Design or Decline: A National Emergency? (in Proceedings of IMechE, Vol 205, 1991); *Recreations* photography, fell walking, steam traction engines, theatre, music, gardening, DIY; *Style*— Eur Ing Prof Gordon Wray, FRS, FEng; ✉ c/o Engineering Design Institute, Department of Mechanical Engineering, Loughborough University, Loughborough, Leics LE11 3TU (☎ 01509 223201, fax 01509 232029, telex 34319)

WRAY, James; MP (Lab) Glasgow Provan (majority 10,703); *Career* MP (Lab) Glasgow Provan 1987–; *Style*— James Wray, Esq, MP; ✉ House of Commons, London SW1A 0AA (☎ 0171 219 3000)

WRAY, Nigel; *b* 9 April 1948; *Educ* Mill Hill Sch, Univ of Bristol (BSc); *Career* chm: Fleet Street Letter plc 1976–83, Burford Holdings plc 1988–, Trocadero plc, Carlisle Grop plc; non-exec dir: Carlton Communications plc 1983–, Singer and Friedlander plc 1987–, Saracens plc 1995–, Grantchester plc 1996–, SkyePharma plc; *Recreations* all sport (played rugby for Hampshire), cinema, musicals, reading a bit; *Style*— Nigel Wray, Esq; ✉ Burford Holdings plc, 20 Thayer Street, London W1 (☎ 0171 224 2240)

WREFORD-BROWN, Capt Christopher Louis; DSO (1982); s of Louis Carless Wreford-Brown (d 1995), of Devon, and Anne, *née* Ridgeway; *b* 10 Aug 1945; *Educ* Rugby, CDipAF; *m* 29 March 1969, Jenny, da of John Lawrence Pinsent, of Devon; 1 s (Paul b Sept 1972), 2 da (Julia b Feb 1970 (Mrs W Scott), Amanda b May 1976); *Career* joined RN 1963, joined submarine service 1969, qualified as navigating offr and princ warfare offr, Lt Cdr Co HMS Opossum 1976, 2 i/c HMS Courageous, staff 2 Submarine Sqdn, Cdr 1980, Nat Def Coll 1981; CO: HMS Dreadnought, HMS Conqueror, HMS Valiant; MOD, Capt 1986, CO HMS Cornwall 1987, Capt 8 Frigate Sqdn 1988, Royal Coll of Def Studies 1989, defence progs staff MOD 1990, Capt 2 Submarine Sqdn 1992–95; Freeman City of London 1988; MInstD 1994; FIMgt 1988; *Recreations* hunting, gardening; *Style*— Capt Christopher Wreford-Brown, DSO

WREN, Dr John Josiah; s of Leslie Josiah Wren, of Hertford Heath, and Agnes Eva, *née* Sims; *b* 10 April 1933; *Educ* Hertford GS, Christ's Coll Cambridge (MA, PhD); *m* 1, 13 April 1955, Beryl Wilson (d 1980), da of Geoffrey Alfred Victor Brampton (d 1955), of Sudbury, Suffolk; 2 s (Hugh Josiah b 1959, Colin John b 1962), 1 da (Catherine b 1961); *m* 2, 5 Aug 1991, Rachel, da of Stephen Denis Garrett, FRS (d 1989), of Cambridge; *Career* res fell Calif Inst of Technol 1956–58, J Lyons & Co 1959–69, Grand Metropolitan plc 1969–86 (sr exec and dir of subsid cos), in consultancy 1986–89, gen sec Soc of Chemical Indust 1989–96 (chm Cncl 1987–88); memb Parly and Scientific Ctee, tstee Catalyst Museum 1989–96; memb: MAFF Steering Gp on Food Surveillance 1981–90, Euro Fedn of Food Sci and Technol, Euro Fedn of Biotechnology; tstee Nat Centre for Initial Teacher Trg in Primary Sch Sci (SCIcentre) Univ of Leicester and Homerton Coll Cambridge 1996–; FRSC 1965, CChem, FIFST 1966, MFC 1984; *Books* Food Quality and Preference (co-ed, 1988), author of various pubns on sci and technol; *Recreations* listening to music, choral singing, walking; *Clubs* Glyndebourne Festival Soc; *Style*— Dr John Wren; ✉ Greensand, East Chiltington, East Sussex BN7 3QU (☎ and fax 01273 890177)

WRENBURY, 3 Baron (UK 1915); Rev John Burton Buckley; s of 2 Baron Wrenbury (d 1940), and Helen, *née* Graham (d 1981); *b* 18 June 1927; *Educ* Eton, King's Coll Cambridge (MA); *m* 1, 1956 (m dis 1961), Carolyn Joan Maule, da of Col Ian Burn-Murdoch, OBE; *m* 2, 1961, Penelope Sara Frances, da of Edward Dimond Fort; 1 s, 2 da (Hon Elizabeth Margaret (Hon Mrs Grey-Morgan) b 1964, Hon Katherine Lucy (Hon Mrs Schaale) b 1968); *Heir* s, Hon William Edward Buckley b 19 June 1966; *Career* slr 1952, dep legal advsr Nat Tst 1955–56, ptnr: Freshfields 1956–74, Thomson Snell & Passmore 1974–90; landowner (390 acres); ordained deacon 1990, ordained priest 1991; Liveryman: Worshipful Co of Merchant Taylors, City of London Solicitors' Co; *Clubs* Oriental; *Style*— The Rev the Rt Hon Lord Wrenbury; ✉ Oldcastle, Dallington, Heathfield, Sussex TN21 9JP (☎ 01435 830400, fax 01435 830968)

WRENCH, Charles Hector; s of Hector Wrench (d 1981), and Sheelagh Mary Veronica, *née* Lynch; *b* 19 Sept 1960; *Educ* Downside, Pembroke Coll Oxford (MA, Lacrosse half blue); *m* 24 June 1989, Amanda, da of Stuart Henry Hodgson; 2 s (Bertie Alexander Stockdale b 19 Nov 1990, Harry Hector b 24 Aug 1992); *Career* co-dir Freelance Ltd 1983–85 (joined 1981), Lowe Howard-Spink advtg 1985–89, bd dir/head of account mgmnt Young & Rubicam Ltd advtg 1990–; *Recreations* golf, cricket, skiing, water sports, squash, tennis, football; *Style*— Charles Wrench, Esq; ✉ Young & Rubicam Ltd, Greater London House, Hampstead Road, London NW1 7QP (☎ 0171 387 9366)

WREXHAM, Bishop of (RC) 1994–; Rt Rev Edwin Regan; s of James Regan (d 1974), of Port Talbot, W Glam, and Ellen Elizabeth, *née* Hoskins (d 1991); *b* 31 Dec 1935; *Educ* Port Talbot Co GS, St John's Coll Waterford Eire, Corpus Christi Coll London (Dip in RE); *Career* curate Neath 1959–66, Corpus Christi Coll London 1966–67, religious educn advsr Archdiocese of Cardiff 1967–85, chaplain St Clare's Convent Porthcawl 1967–71, admin St David's Cathedral Cardiff 1971–84; parish priest: St Helens Barry 1984–89, St Mary's Bridgend 1989–94; memb: Amnesty Int, World Devpt Movement; *Recreations* hill walking; *Style*— The Rt Rev the Bishop of Wrexham; ✉ Bishop's House, Sontley Road, Wrexham, Clwyd LL13 7EW (☎ 01978 262726, fax 01978 354257)

WREY, Benjamin Harold Bourchier; s of Maj Christopher Bourchier Wrey, TD (d 1976), and Ruth, *née* Bowden; *b* 6 May 1940; *Educ* Blundell's, Clare Coll Cambridge (MA); *m* 19 Feb 1970, (Anne) Christine Aubrey Cherry, da of Col Christopher B Stephenson (d 1970); 1 da (Tanya b 20 Jan 1971); *Career* Pensions Advsy Dept Legal & General Assurance Society Ltd 1963–66, investmt analyst Hambros Bank Ltd 1966–69; Henderson plc (formerly Henderson Administration Group plc): joined 1969, dir 1971–, jt md 1981–82, dep chm 1983–92, chm 1992–; dir Electric and General Investment Co plc; chm Institutional Fund Managers Assoc; memb: Institutional Investors Advsy Ctee London Stock Exchange, Fin Practitioners Panel City Disputes Panel; *Recreations* shooting (represented Univ of Cambridge, Co of London, England and GB teams in full-bore target rifle shooting in UK and overseas, winner Bisley Grand Aggregate 1966 and 1969), fishing, ballet and opera; *Clubs* Boodle's, City of London, Hurlingham; *Style*— Benjamin Wrey, Esq; ✉ Henderson plc, 3 Finsbury Ave, London EC2M 2PA (☎ 0171 638 5757, fax 0171 377 5742, telex 884616)

WREY, Sir (George Richard) Bourchier; 15 Bt (E 1628), of Trebitch, Cornwall; s of Sir (Castel Richard) Bourchier Wrey, 14 Bt (d 1991), and Sybil Mabel Alice, *née* Lubke; *b* 2 Oct 1948; *Educ* Eton; *m* 1 Aug 1981, Lady Caroline Janet Lindesay-Bethune, da of 15 Earl of Lindsay (d 1989); 2 s (Harry David Bourchier b 1984, Humphrey George

Bourchier b 1991), 1 da (Rachel Pearl b 1987); *Heir* s, Harry David Bourchier Wrey b 3 Oct 1984; *Career* property developer and farmer; *Recreations* all types of sport, shooting; *Clubs* Turf; *Style—* Sir Bourchier Wrey, Bt; ✉ 60 The Chase, London SW4 0NH (☎ 0171 622 6625); Hollamoor Farm, Tawstock, Barnstaple, N Devon (☎ 01271 73466)

WRIGGLESWORTH, Sir Ian William; kt (1991); s of Edward Wrigglesworth, of Stockton on Tees; *b* 8 Dec 1939; *Educ* Stockton GS, Stockton Billingham Tech Coll, Coll of St Mark and St John Chelsea; *m* 1968, Patricia Susan, da of Hugh L Truscott; 2 s, 1 da; *Career* PA to Sir Ronald Gould as gen sec NUT 1966–68, head Co-op Pty Res Dept 1968–70, press and public affrs mangr Nat Giro 1970–74; MP (Lab and Co-op 1974–81, SDP 1981–87) Thornaby, Teesside Feb 1974–83, Stockton South 1983–87; PPS: to Alec Lyon when Min of State Home Office 1974, to Roy Jenkins when Home Sec 1974–76; sec Manifesto Gp within Lab Party 1976–81, vice chm Lab Econ Fin and Taxation Assoc 1976–81, oppn spokesman Civil Service 1979–81, SDP home affrs spokesman Nov 1982–May 1983, SDP econ and industl affrs spokesman 1983–87, Alliance trade and indust spokesman 1987; chm: UK Land Estates Ltd, Prima Europe Ltd; dep chm John Livingston & Sons Ltd; dir: Fairfield Industries Ltd, CIT Holdings Ltd, Med Div Smiths Industries plc, UK Cabin Co Ltd, Northern Devpt Co; chm Northern Region CBI 1992–94; govr Univ of Teesside; Liveryman Worshipful Co of Founders; *Recreations* walking, water sports, music; *Clubs* Reform, National Liberal; *Style—* Sir Ian Wrigglesworth; ✉ Prima Europe Ltd, 14 Soho Square, London W1V 5FB (☎ 0171 287 6676, fax 0171 287 8139)

WRIGHT, Hon Mrs (Alison Elizabeth); *née* Franks; da of Baron Franks, PC, OM, GCMG, KCB, CBE (Life Peer, d 1992); *b* 1945; *m* 1973, Stanley Harris Wright, *qv*; *Career* currently director general British Invisibles; *Style—* The Hon Mrs Wright; ✉ 6 Holly Place, Holly Walk, Hampstead, London NW3 (☎ 0171 435 0237); British Invisibles, 6th Floor, Windsor House, 39 King Street, London EC2V 8DQ (☎ 0171 600 1198, fax 0171 606 4248)

WRIGHT, Allan Grant; s of John Johnstone Wright (d 1984), and Mary, *née* Armstrong; *b* 11 Aug 1944; *Educ* Wallace Hall Acad, West of Scot Coll of Agric (SDA); *m* 26 March 1965, Ann Campbell, da of Thomas Savage (d 1944); 1 s (Grant b 1970), 1 da (Shelley b 1967); *Career* reporter The Scottish Farmer 1964–67, dep agric ed The Glasgow Herald 1967–73, agric ed The Press and Journal 1973–79, with BBC 1979–89 (agric ed 1984–89), freelance journalist and PR consit 1989–92, communications mangr Semex UK 1992–94, Scottish corr Farmers Weekly 1994–; hon assoc BVA 1991, FGAJ 1987, ARAgS 1989; *Style—* Allan Wright, Esq; ✉ Halfacre, The Shotts, Thornhill, Dumfriesshire DG3 5JT (☎ and fax 01848 331640)

WRIGHT, Andrew Paul Kilding; s of Harold Maurice Wright (d 1983), and Eileen Mary, *née* Kilding; *b* 11 Feb 1947; *Educ* Queen Mary's GS Walsall, Univ of Liverpool (BArch); *m* 10 Oct 1970, Jean Patricia, da of Alfred John Cross; 1 s (Samuel b 1976), 2 da (Hannah b 1973, Sarah b 1985); *Career* architect; Sir Basil Spence Glover & Ferguson 1973–78, ptnr Law & Dunbar-Nasmith 1981– (assoc 1978–81); Inverness Architectural Assoc: memb Cncl 1981–90, pres 1986–88; memb: Rural Design and Building Assoc 1985–, Cncl RIBA 1988–94 and 1995–, Ecclesiastical Architects and Surveyors Assoc 1989–, Scottish Soc of Conservators and Restorers 1990–; Royal Incorporation of Architects in Scotland: memb Cncl 1985–94 and 1995–, pres 1995– (vice pres 1986–88), membership convener 1992–94, convenor Conservation Working Gp 1994–95; assessor Civic Tst Awards 1994–; one of four RIBA/UK delegates to Architects Cncl of Europe 1995–, memb Bd Glasgow 1999 UK City of Architecture and Design 1995–, Sec of State appointed Bd memb Ancient Monuments Bd for Scotland 1996–; diocesan architect Dio of Moray Ross and Caithness 1988–, conslt architect Mar Lodge Estate (for Nat Tst for Scotland) 1996–; hon architectural advsr Scottish redundant Churches Trust 1996–; RIBA, PRIAS; *Recreations* music, railway history, fishing; *Clubs* Highland; *Style—* Andrew P K Wright, Esq; ✉ Craiglen, Sanquhar Road, Forres, Moray IV36 0DG (☎ 01309 672749); Law & Dunbar-Nasmith, 29 St Leonards Rd, Forres, Moray IV36 0DN (☎ 01309 673221, fax 01309 676397)

WRIGHT, Dr Anne Margaret; CBE (1997); da of Herbert Holden (d 1973), of Kent, and Florence, *née* Kelly (d 1980); *b* 27 July 1946; *Educ* Holy Trinity Ind GS Bromley Kent, King's Coll London (Merchant Taylors' Co exhibition, William Henry Gladstone exhibition, BA, Lillian M Faithfull prize, Early Eng Text Soc prize, George Smith studentship, Inglis studentship, PhD); *m* 25 July 1970, Martin Wright, s of Robert Wright (d 1981), of London; 1 da (Amy Laura b 1982); *Career* lectr in English Univ of Lancaster 1969–71, lectr rising to reader in modern English studies Hatfield Poly 1971–84, registrar for Arts and Humanities CNAA 1984–86, dep rector (academic) Liverpool Poly 1986–90, vice chllr Univ of Sunderland (formerly Sunderland Poly) 1990–; chm: Sunderland Common Purpose 1990–, Cmmn on Univ Career Opportunity 1993–; dir: Everyman Theatre Liverpool 1988–90, Entrust Newcastle upon Tyne 1990–93, North Regnl Mgmnt Centre Washington 1990–93, The Wearside Opportunity 1991–93, Northern Sinfonia 1991–96, Northern Arts Bd 1991–95, Higher Educn Quality Cncl 1992–, Wearside TEC 1993–, Open Learning Fndn 1993–95; memb: Eng Studies Bd CNAA 1978–84, Arts and Humanities Res Sub-Ctee CNAA 1979–84, Ctee for Int Co-operation in HE Br Cncl 1990–, Further Educn Funding Cncl 1992–96, Hong Kong Univ and Poly Grants Ctee 1992–, Cncl for Indust and HE 1994–, North East C of C Cncl 1995–, CBI Regnl Cncl 1996–; FRSA 1991, CIMgt 1994; *Books* Literature of Crisis 1910–1922, Bernard Shaw's Saint Joan (1984), Harley Granville Barker (critical biography in Modern British Dramatists 1900–1945, 1982), Tom Stoppard (critical biography in Dictionary of Literary Biography, 1982); various publications on Shaw, Lawrence, T S Eliot and others; *Recreations* theatre, opera, the Arts; *Style—* Dr Anne Wright, CBE; ✉ University of Sunderland, Langham Tower, Ryhope Rd, Sunderland SR2 7EE (☎ 0191 515 2035 or 0191 515 2036, fax 0191 515 2044)

WRIGHT, Dr Anthony Wayland (Tony); MP (Lab) Cannock and Burntwood (majority 1,506); s of Frank Wright, and Maud Wright; *b* 11 March 1948; *Educ* Kettering GS, LSE (BSc(Econ)), Harvard Univ (Kennedy scholar), Balliol Coll Oxford (DPhil); *m* 21 July 1973, Moira Elynwy, da of Edmor Phillips; 3 s (and 1 s decd); *Career* lectr in politics UCNW Bangor 1973–75, lectr, sr lectr then reader in politics Sch of Continuing Studies Univ of Birmingham 1975–92; MP (Lab) Cannock and Burntwood 1992–; chm S Birmingham Community Health Cncl 1983–85, parent govr St Laurence Church Schs Northfield Birmingham 1989–92; *Books* Who Do I Complain To? (1997); *Recreations* tennis, football, secondhand bookshops, walking, gardening; *Style—* Dr Tony Wright, MP; ✉ House of Commons, London SW1A 0AA

WRIGHT, Brig Antony Peter (Tony); MBE (1974); s of Capt Dennis Gordon Wright (ka France 1944), and Vera Rose Jean, *née* Mills (d 1991); *b* 13 Jan 1939; *Educ* Blundell's RMA Sandhurst; *m* 20 June 1964, Ann Jennifer, da of Harry Thomas Lucas, of Trimley St Martin, nr Felixstowe, Suffolk; 1 s (Jeremy Gordon b 10 Sept 1968), 2 da (Nicola Louise b 14 May 1970, Sally Victoria b 4 Oct 1974); *Career* cmmnd Sherwood Foresters 1958, RMCS Div II 1970, Staff Coll 1971, cmd 1 WFR 1979–82, Col project mangr Inf Weapons 1986–88, vice pres (Army), Brig Ordnance Bd 1988–89, ret 1989; mktg dir SDE Ltd 1989–91, sec/mangr Ipswich Golf Club 1991–; *Recreations* golf, mountain walking, gardening; *Style—* Brig A P Wright, MBE; ✉ Ipswich Golf Club, Purdis Heath, Ipswich IP3 8UQ (☎ 01473 728941)

WRIGHT, Barbara Janet; da of Lt John Sutherland (d 1994), and Betty Dorothy Gladys, *née* Durrant, of Woodbridge, Suffolk; *b* 16 March 1955; *Educ* Romford County HS for Girls, Univ of Sheffield (LLB); *m* 23 Oct 1981, Lynton Wright, s of John (Jack) Wright of Stockport, Cheshire; *Career* asst slr Gill Turner and Tucker Maidstone 1979–80 (articled clerk 1977–79); asst slr Cripps Harries Hall and Co: Tunbridge Wells 1980–82, Crowborough 1982–84; Walkers 1984–87 (ptnr from 1986), ptnr Thomson Snell and Passmore Tunbridge Wells 1987–; chm Kent Slr's Family Law Assoc 1990–; memb: Family Mediator's Assoc 1993–, Soroptimist Int of Turnbridge Wells; hon arbitrator Tunbridge Wells Equitable Friendly Soc 1987–93, hon legal advsr W Kent Relate 1992–, hon treas Tunbridge Wells Tonbridge and Dist Law Soc 1993–; memb Kent Archaeological Soc; memb Law Soc 1979; *Style—* Mrs Barbara Wright; ✉ 3 Lonsdale Gardens, Tunbridge Wells, Kent TN1 1NX (☎ 01892 510000, fax 01892 549884)

WRIGHT, Bernard Bucknall; s of Clifford Joseph Wright (d 1963), and Catherine Mary, *née* Bucknall (d 1939); *b* 22 Dec 1933; *Educ* West Park GS St Helens, Univ of Liverpool (LLB); *m* 23 May 1964, Jennifer, da of George Richard Cockram; 5 s (Simon Andrew b 15 Feb 1965, Paul Nicholas b 31 May 1966, Christopher David b 8 Feb 1968, Michael Jonathan b 11 Jan 1970, Nicholas James b 15 June 1980); *Career* Nat Serv educn offr RAF 1957–59; ptnr Cuff Roberts & Co Liverpool 1960– (articled clerk 1954–57); memb Law Soc 1959–; Law Soc Liverpool: memb 1959, hon sec 1979–82, pres 1983; *Recreations* golf, skiing, interest in most sports especially rugby, food and wine; *Clubs* New Brighton Rugby Union (former pres), Heswall Squash, Heswall Golf (former capt), Liverpool Artists; *Style—* Bernard Wright, Esq; ✉ Cuff Roberts, 100 Old Hall St, Liverpool L3 9TD (☎ 0151 227 4181, fax 0151 227 2584)

WRIGHT, Bruce; *b* 8 May 1944; *Educ* Battersea GS, Univ of Leicester (BA, MA); *Career* financial controller Mars Confectionery 1978–81, fin dir Courage 1981–85, with Grand Metropolitan plc 1986–87, fin dir Meyer International plc 1987–; ACIS 1971; *Style—* Bruce Wright, Esq; ✉ Meyer International plc, Aldwych House, 81 Aldwych, London WC2B 4HQ (☎ 0171 400 8792)

WRIGHT, Christopher Norman; s of late Walter Reginald Wright, of 3 Butts Lane, Tattersall, Lincs, and Edna May, *née* Corden; *b* 7 Sept 1944; *Educ* King Edward VI GS Louth Lincs, Univ of Manchester (BA), Manchester Business Sch; *m* 15 March 1972, Carolyn Rochelle (Chelle), da of Lloyd B Nelson, of California, USA; 2 s (Timothy b 1973, Thomas b 1974), 1 da (Chloe b 1978); *Career* operator Univ and Coll Booking Agency Manchester 1965–67, formed Ellis Wright Agency (with Terry Ellis) 1967, changed name to Chrysalis 1968, chm 1985–, now international music publishing, television, film and radio gp Chrysalis plc (which also owns Sheffield Sharks Basketball team), owner (following £10m takeover) Queens Park Rangers FC and Wasps Rugby Club 1996–; *Recreations* tennis, breeding racehorses; *Clubs* Turf; *Style—* Christopher Wright, Esq; ✉ Chrysalis Group plc, The Chrysalis Building, Bramley Road, London W10 6SP (☎ 0171 221 2213)

WRIGHT, Claud William; CB (1969); s of Horace Vipan Wright (d 1945), of E Yorks, and Catherine Margaret, *née* Sales (d 1963); *b* 9 Jan 1917; *Educ* Charterhouse, ChCh Oxford (MA); *m* 1947, Alison Violet, da of John Jeffrey Readman, of Dumfries; 1 s (Crispin), 4 da (Dione, Daphne, Ianthe, Oenone); *Career* WO 1939, Private Essex Regt 1940, 2 Lt KRRC 1940, WO 1942–45, GSO 2; joined MOD 1947, asst under sec (Pol) 1961–66, asst under sec (P Air) 1966–68, dep under sec (Air) 1968–71, dep sec Arts and Libraries Dept of Educn and Sci 1971–76, res fell Wolfson Coll Oxford 1977–83; fil Dr hc Univ of Uppsala 1979, Hon DSc Univ of Hull 1987; Lyell Fund 1947, RH Worth prize 1958, Prestwich medal Geological Soc London 1987, Foulerton award Geologists Assoc 1955, Phillips medal Yorks Geological Soc 1976, Strimple award Paleontological Soc of America 1988; author of numerous papers on geological, palaeontological and archaeological subjects; *Books* Monographs on fossil crabs (with J S H Collins, 1972), ammonites of the middle chalk (with W J Kennedy, 1981), ammonites of the lower chalk (with W J Kennedy, 1984–91), Cretaceous Sea-Urchins (with A B Smith, 1990–); *Recreations* archaeology, botany, palaeontology; *Clubs* Athenaeum; *Style—* C W Wright, Esq, CB; ✉ Old Rectory, Seaborough, Beaminster, Dorset DT8 3QY (☎ 01308 868426)

WRIGHT, (Idonea) Daphne; da of Claud William Wright, of Dorset, and Alison Violet, *née* Readman; *b* 19 May 1951; *Educ* St Mary's Wantage; *Career* sec and editorial asst Chatto & Windus 1976–77, ed Hutchinson 1977–83, editorial dir Quartet 1983–84, Bellew Publishing 1984–86; winner Tony Godwin Meml Tst award 1980; memb: Crime Writers Assoc 1989, Soc of Authors 1990; *Books* The Distant Kingdom (1987), The Longest Winter (1989), The Parrot Cage (1990), Never Such Innocence (1991), Dreams of Another Day (1992), The Tightrope Walkers (1993); as Natasha Cooper: Festering Lilies (1990), Poison Flowers (1991), Bloody Roses (1992), Bitter Herbs (1993), Rotten Apples (1995), Fruiting Bodies (1996), Sour Grapes (1997); as Kate Hatfield: Drowning in Honey (1995), Angels Alone (1996), Marsh Light (1997); *Recreations* reading, entertaining, tennis; *Style—* Ms Daphne Wright; ✉ c/o Jennifer Kavanagh, 44 Langham Street, London W1N 5RG (☎ 0171 636 2477, fax 0171 636 2479)

WRIGHT, David Anthony; s of George Henry Wright, of Hornsea East Yorks, and Theresa, *née* Rooke; *b* 21 March 1949; *Educ* Marist Coll Hull, Sidney Sussex Coll Cambridge (MA, memb cast Oxford and Cambridge Shakespeare Co Tour of USA 1969–70 directed by Jonathan Miller); *m* 1979, Susan Iris, da of F W Benson, of Salford, Lancs; 1 s (Daniel), 1 da (Fernanda Maria); *Career* freelance documentary film-maker in TV 1979–; films incl: The Christians, This England, The Pennines: A Writer's Notebook, Years of Lightning, N Division, 617: Last Days of a Vulcan Squadron, Village Earth, In the Footsteps of The Incas, Learning How the Maasai See, The Tribe That's Fighting Back, Think Dream Laugh, The World: A Television History, Last Voyage of The Arctic Raider, Abbeystead - The Aftermath, Akong and The Big Shrine Room, Bellamy's Bugle; set up own co 54th Parallel 1988; films: The Heat is On - The Making of Miss Saigon, Under The Sacred Bo Tree; for First Tuesday (UK) and Arts & Entertainment Networks (USA): Bad Trip to Edgewood (1992), Follow the Flag (1993); for The Discovery Channel (Europe and USA) First Tuesday - Toxic Border (1994), First Tuesday - From Fury to Forgiveness (1994), Witness - From Fury to Forgiveness (Channel 4, 1995), Discovery Journal - Born to Run (USA and Europe, 1995), Discovery Journal - Supermax (USA and Europe, 1995); *Recreations* travel, walking, reading, swimming, chopping logs; *Style—* David Wright, Esq; ✉ Wood Hall, Old Ellerby, Hull HU11 5AJ (☎ 01482 811265); 54th Parallel Productions, Wood Hall, Old Ellerby, Hull HU11 5AJ (☎ 01482 811265)

WRIGHT, David Frederick; s of Harry George Durie Wright (d 1989), of St Annes on Sea, Lancs, and Dorothy Emily, *née* Forster (d 1986); *b* 2 Oct 1937; *Educ* Bec Sch London, Christ's Coll Cambridge (MA), Lincoln Coll Oxford; *m* Anne-Marie, da of George MacDonald (d 1992), OBE, of Edinburgh; 1 s (Andrew b 1968), 1 da (Jennifer b 1970); *Career* dean of Faculty of Divinity Univ of Edinburgh 1988–92 (lectr in ecclesiastical history 1964–73, sr lectr 1973–, memb Univ Ct 1984–87); former memb: Cncl of Mgmnt Keston Coll Kent, Cncl of Scot Church History Soc, Bd Nat Bible Soc of Scot; chm Tyndale Fellowship for Biblical and Theol Res; memb: Praesidium Int Congress on Calvin Res, Assoc Int d'études Patristiques, N American Patristics Soc, Ecclesiastical History Soc, Center of Theological Inquiry Princeton NJ; *Books* Common Places of Martin Bucer (1972), Essays in Evangelical Social Ethics (ed, 1978), New Dictionary of Theology (jt ed, 1988), Bible in Scottish Life and Literature (ed and contrib, 1988), Chosen by God: Mary in Evangelical Perspective (ed and contrib, 1989), Encyclopaedia of the Reformed Faith (conslt ed, 1992), Dictionary of Scottish Church History and Theology (chief gen ed, 1993), Calvin's Old Testament Commentaries (chief ed, 1993–), Martin Bucer: Reforming Church and Community (ed and contrib, 1994), Disruption to

Diversity: Edinburgh Divinity 1846–1996 (ed and contrib, 1996); *Recreations* walking, gardening; *Style—* David Wright, Esq; ✉ 3 Camus Road East, Edinburgh EH10 6RE (☎ 0131 445 1960); New College, Mound Place, Edinburgh EH1 2LX (☎ 0131 650 8976, fax 0131 650 6579, telex 727442 UNIVED G)

WRIGHT, HE Sir David John; KCMG (1996, CMG 1992), LVO (1990); s of John Frank Wright, of Wolverhampton; *b* 16 June 1944; *Educ* Wolverhampton GS, Peterhouse Cambridge; *m* 3 Feb 1968, Sally Ann Dodkin; 1 s (Nicholas b 1970), 1 da (Laura b 1973); *Career* HM Dip Serv: third sec 1966, third later second sec Tokyo 1966, second later first sec FCO 1972, Ecole Nationale d'Administration Paris 1975, first sec Paris 1976, private sec to Sec of Cabinet 1980, cnsllr (econ) Tokyo 1982, head of Personnel Servs Dept FCO 1985, dep private sec to HRH The Prince of Wales 1988–90; ambass Seoul 1990–94, dep under sec for Asia, Americas and Trade Promotion FCO 1994–96, ambass Tokyo 1996–; *Recreations* running, cooking, military history, golf; *Style—* HE Sir David J Wright, KCMG, LVO; ✉ c/o Foreign and Commonwealth Office (Tokyo), King Charles Street, London SW1A 2AH

WRIGHT, Dr David Julian Maurice; s of Herschel Wright (d 1982), and Ann, *née* Hammerman; *b* 12 May 1937; *Educ* Univ of London (MB BS, MD); *m* Rosalind, da of Alfred Kerstein; 3 da (Mandy, Pandy, Candy); *Career* reader in microbiology Charing Cross Hosp and Westminster Med Sch 1982 (conslt 1974), dir Lyme Diagnostic Serv, temp advsr WHO; author of numerous scientific papers on leprosy, syphilis, septic shock, Lyme disease and post-infection fatigue; FRCPath 1991 (MRCPath 1982); *Books* Immunology of Sexually Transmitted Diseases (1988), Molecular and Cell Biology of Sexually Transmitted Diseases (1992); *Recreations* eating, dreaming, televising and if possible all three at once; *Clubs* Willesden Discussion Group; *Style—* Dr David Wright; ✉ Microbiology, Charing Cross Hospital, Fulham Palace Road, London W6 8RF (☎ 0181 846 7262, fax 0181 846 7261)

WRIGHT, Dr David Stephen; OBE (1995); s of Edward Alfred Wright (d 1943), and Winifred May, *née* Oliver; *b* 4 Aug 1935; *Educ* Epsom Coll, Bart's (MB BS, MSc, DPH, DIH); *m* 19 Feb 1966, Caroline Auza, da of George William Black (d 1987), of Leeds; 2 s (Mark b 1967, Adam b 1969), 1 da (Alexandra b 1972); *Career* RN 1960–85 (ret with rank of Surgn Capt, final appt prof of naval occupational med and dir of health); head BP Group Occupational Health Centre 1985–91, chief med offr BP plc 1989–95; conslt occupational physician 1995–; BMA: chm Armed Forces Ctee 1985–88, memb Cncl 1985–88; dean Faculty of Occupational Med RCP 1991–94; Freeman City of London 1982, Liveryman Worshipful Soc of Apothecaries 1982; memb: Soc of Occupational Med, BMA; FFOM, FRCP, FRSM, FFOM(I); OStJ 1984; *Recreations* golf, walking, gardening; *Style—* Dr David Wright, OBE; ✉ 9 Ashburton Road, Alverstoke, Gosport, Hampshire PO12 2LH (☎ 01705 582459)

WRIGHT, Sir Denis Arthur Hepworth; GCMG (1971, KCMG 1961, CMG 1954); s of A E Wright (d 1949), and Margery Hepworth Chapman (d 1973); *b* 23 March 1911; *Educ* Brentwood Sch, St Edmund Hall Oxford; *m* 1939, Iona, da of Granville Craig (d 1941), of Bolney, Sussex; *Career* Diplomatic Serv; served (in commercial and consular capacities): Romania, Turkey, Yugoslavia, USA; asst under sec FO 1955–59, ambass Ethiopia 1959–62, asst under sec FO 1962, ambass Iran 1963–71 (formerly cnsllr 1954–55, chargé d'affaires 1953–54); non-exec dir: Shell Transport and Trading Co, Standard Chartered Bank, Mitchell Cotts Group 1971–81; govr Overseas Serv, Farnham Castle 1971–87; pres: Br Inst of Persian Studies 1978–87, The Iran Soc 1989–95; hon fellow: St Edmund Hall 1972, St Antony's Coll Oxford 1976; Sir Percy Sykes Meml Medal Royal Soc for Asian Affrs 1991; *Books* Persia (with James Morris and Roger Wood, 1968), The English Amongst the Persians (1977), The Persians Amongst the English (1985); *Clubs* Travellers'; *Style—* Sir Denis Wright, GCMG; ✉ 15 Flint Street, Haddenham, Aylesbury, Bucks HP17 8AL (☎ 01844 291086)

WRIGHT, Dermot John Fetherstonhaugh; s of J W Wright, of West Wittering, Sussex, and late Dorothy, *née* Fetherstonhaugh; *b* 5 Aug 1944; *Educ* Wellington, Trinity Coll Cambridge (MA); *m* 1, 1969 (m dis 1992), Patricia Fergie; 2 da (Emma, Louise); m 2, 1992, Bridget Bovill; 1 da (Eleanor); *Career* called to the Bar Inner Temple 1967, currently head of chambers, asst recorder SE Circuit; tstee James Peek Tst (charity); *Recreations* yachting, playing piano, golf; *Clubs* National Liberal, Chichester Yacht, Barnacle Cruising (pres); *Style—* Dermot Wright, Esq; ✉ 3 Temple Gardens, Temple, London EC4Y 9AU (☎ 0171 583 0010, fax 0171 353 3361)

WRIGHT, Edward Arnold; MBE (1991); s of John Ernest Wright (d 1976), of Hornsey, and Alice Maud, *née* Arnold (d 1968); *b* 20 Nov 1926; *Educ* Tollington GS Muswell Hill; *Career* 52 RTR 1943–45, KDG 1945–47; 1962–70: sales dir Gothic Press Ltd, md Gothic Display Ltd, md Gothic Studios Ltd; chm and md Edward Wright Ltd 1970–; former hon treas: Fauna and Flora Preservation Soc, Br Section Int Cncl for Bird Preservation; former cncl memb Br Tst for Ornithology; Freeman City of London 1980, Liveryman Worshipful Co of Gardeners 1980; *Recreations* gardening, shooting; *Clubs* MCC; *Style—* Edward Wright, Esq, MBE; ✉ Edward Wright Ltd, 5/11 Palfrey Place, London SW8 1PB (☎ 0171 735 9535, fax 0171 793 0967, mobile 0860 539806)

WRIGHT, Sir Edward Maitland; kt (1977); s of Maitland Turner Wright (d 1943), and Kate, *née* Owen (d 1954); *b* 13 Feb 1906; *Educ* Jesus Coll and ChCh Oxford, Göttingen Univ (BA, MA, DPhil); *m* 1934, Elizabeth Phyllis (d 1987), da of Harry Percy Harris, JP (d 1952); 1 s (John); *Career* Flt-Lt RAFVR, Princ Sci Offr Air Miny Intelligence 1943–45; prof mathematics Univ of Aberdeen 1936–62, princ and vice chllr 1962–76, res fell 1976–83; hon fell Jesus Coll Oxford 1963, Hon DSc Strathclyde; Hon LLD: St Andrews, Pennsylvania, Aberdeen; Order of Polonia Restituta 1978; FRSE 1937; *Books* Theory of Numbers (with G H Hardy, 1 edn 1938, 5 edn 1979); *Clubs* Caledonian (London); *Style—* Sir Edward Wright, FRSE; ✉ 16 Primrosehill Ave, Cults, Aberdeen AB1 9NL (☎ 01224 861185)

WRIGHT, Gerald; s of William Arthur Reginald Wright (d 1967), and Olive Annie Neal Wright (d 1995); *b* 9 Sept 1935; *Educ* Monmouth, Queens' Coll Cambridge (MA); *m* 1959, Elizabeth Ann, da of Dr William Edward Harris (d 1974), of Llandaff; 3 s (Jeremy, Mathew, William); *Career* Nat Serv 2 Lt Welch Regt 1954–56; dir Lintas London 1972–73, chm Lintas Scandinavia 1973–74, dep chm and md Lintas London 1974–80, md Thresher and Co Ltd 1980–81; Whitbread & Co: mktg dir (UK) 1981–82, chm Nat Sales Div 1982–83; chm and chief exec Lintas London 1983–89, regnl dir Eastern Europe, Austria and Switzerland Lintas Worldwide 1989–94, dir Posmark Ltd 1994–96; conslt Harris Wright & Associates 1994–; FIPA, FRSA; *Recreations* reading, opera, walking, cycling, rugby, cricket, bridge, travel; *Clubs* Reform, Solus; *Style—* Gerald Wright, Esq; ✉ Harris Wright & Associates, 25 Crown Lane, Chislehurst, Kent BR7 5PL (☎ and fax 0181 325 6899)

WRIGHT, Graham John; s of Reginald Steer Wright (d 1973), and Phyllis Eileen, *née* Brooks (d 1987); *b* 18 May 1939; *Educ* St Clement Dane's GS; *m* 8 July 1961, Sandra Judith, da of Wilfred Sidney Chitty; 2 s (Andrew John b 17 Feb 1968, Adam John b 27 May 1971); *Career* actuarial student Law Union and Rock Insurance Co 1956; pensions mangr: Philips Electronics 1972–80 (asst pensions mangr 1963–72), Courtaulds plc 1980–; dir Courtaulds Pensions Investment Tstees Ltd; former tutor Inst of Actuaries, former Speaker Nat Assoc Pension Funds; chm: Purley Bury Tennis Club 1981–, Argonauts Club 1991–92; memb Cncl Occupational Pensions Advsy Serv (dir OPAS Ltd); FIA 1967, FPMI 1977; *Recreations* tennis, bridge, football (supporter), chess, theatre; *Style—* Graham Wright, Esq; ✉ Courtaulds plc, 50 George Street, London W1A 2BB (☎ 0171 612 1000, fax 0171 612 1500, telex 28788)

WRIGHT, Gregory Arthur; s of Ernest Arthur Wright, and Florence, *née* Swindells; *b* 1 Nov 1946; *Educ* Bournville Tech GS; *m* 21 Nov 1970, Christine, da of late Stanley Allen Tongue, of Northfield, Birmingham; 2 s (Dale b 1974, Adam b 1977), 1 da (Emma b 1982); *Career* Josolyn Layton-Bennett CAs 1969–72; Ernst & Whinney: ptnr Birmingham 1980 (joined 1972), managing ptnr Cardiff 1985 and Edinburgh 1988–89; Ernst & Young: ptnr Edinburgh 1989–91, ptnr Leicester 1991–, managing ptnr East Midlands Area Office 1995–; FCA 1979; *Recreations* chess, cricket, gardening; *Style—* Gregory Wright, Esq; ✉ Paddock House, 31 Cedar Drive, Market Bosworth, Warwicks CV13 0LW (☎ 01455 291285); Ernst & Young, Provincial House, 37 New Walk, Leicester LE1 6TU (☎ 0116 254 9818, fax 0116 255 1357)

WRIGHT, Hugh Raymond; s of Rev Raymond Blayney Wright (d 1980), of Macclesfield, and Alys Mary, *née* Hawksworth (d 1972); *b* 24 Aug 1938; *Educ* Kingswood Sch Bath, The Queen's Coll Oxford (MA); *m* 7 April 1962, Jillian Mary, da of Peter McIldowie Meiklejohn (d 1959), of Bedford; 3 s (Andrew b 1963, William b 1967, James b 1970); *Career* asst master Brentwood Sch 1961–64; Cheltenham Coll: joined 1964, head of classics 1967–72, house master Boyne House 1971–79; headmaster: Stockport GS 1979–85, Gresham's Sch Holt 1985–91; chief master King Edward's Sch Birmingham 1991–; HMC: chm NW Dist 1983, chm Community Serv Sub Ctee 1985–90 (memb 1980–90), memb Assisted Places Working Pty 1992–, nat rep HMC Ctee 1993–94, chm HMC 1995; memb: Panel Admty Interview Bd 1982–, ABM 1987–, ISJC Europe Ctee 1991–96, Ctee Bloxham Project 1992–, Court Univ of Birmingham 1992–, Cncl Univ of Birmingham 1995–; lay reader Dio Birmingham, treas Eastern Div ISIS 1988–90; *Publications* film strips and notes on The Origins of Christianity and the Medieval Church (1980); *Recreations* walking, ornithology, music, theatre; *Clubs* East India; *Style—* Hugh Wright, Esq; ✉ King Edward's School, Birmingham B15 2UA (☎ 0121 472 1672)

WRIGHT, Ian; *b* 3 Nov 1963; *Career* professional footballer (forward); clubs: Crystal Palace 1985–91 (117 goals), Arsenal FC (joined for 2.5m) 1991–; honours with Arsenal: Golden Boot 1992, League Cup and FA Cup double 1993; England: 21 full caps and 5 goals (as at Jan 1997); *Style—* Ian Wright; ✉ c/o Jerome Anderson Management, 248 Station Road, Edgware, Middx HA8 7AU (☎ 0181 958 7799)

WRIGHT, Ian; s of Peter Wright, of Maidenhead, Berks, and Gladys, *née* Green; *b* 4 April 1958; *Educ* Desborough Sch Maidenhead, St Catharine's Coll Cambridge (exhibitioner, MA); *m* 23 Dec 1987, Judith, da of Eric Gilboy, of Dean, Cumbria; *Career* pres Cambridge Student Union 1980–81, political organiser SDP 1981–85, PR conslt Gwynne Hart (Grayling Group) 1985–87, gp account dir Chilmark Public Relations 1987–88, dir Communications Partnership 1988–89, md Golley Slater Brooker 1989–94, head of PR Boots Healthcare International 1994–; vice pres SDP 1989–91, chm Lib Dems in PR and Public Affrs 1995–; tstee Norman Hart Meml Fund 1986–; MIPR; *Books* Reviving the Centre (with Roger Fox, 1989); numerous articles in nat press and other pubns; *Recreations* cricket, football, gardening; *Style—* Ian Wright, Esq; ✉ Boots Healthcare International, D 6 Building, 1 Thane Road, Beeston, Nottingham NG3 2AA (☎ 0115 955 4400, fax 0115 968 9212)

WRIGHT, Ian James; s of James Wilson Wright (d 1987), of Wishaw, and Dorothy, *née* Ormerod (d 1961); *b* 28 May 1948; *Educ* Liverpool Coll of Art (BA), RCA (MA); *m* 1976, Glenda, da of William Laverick Tindale; 3 s (Stewart James b 1978, Steven William b 1981, James Lewis b 1987); *Career* Kinneir Calvert Tuhill Design Consultants 1973–75; currently design dir The Jenkins Group (joined 1975); *Style—* Ian James Wright, Esq; ✉ 61 Warren Road, Chingford, London E4 6QR (☎ 0181 529 8231); The Jenkins Group, 9 Tufton Street, Westminster London SW1P 3QB (☎ 0171 799 1090, fax 0171 222 6751)

WRIGHT, Ian Wheeler; s of Rev Ernest Wright (d 1961), and Nancy, *née* Wheeler (d 1991); *Educ* Kingswood Sch Bath, Ch Ch Oxford (MA); *m* 1968, (Janet) Lydia, da of Norman Giles (d 1983); 1 s (Oliver b 1973); *Career* HM Overseas Civil Serv Kenya 1956–59; ed Elliot Lake Standard Ontario Canada 1960; The Guardian: joined 1961, film critic, dep features ed 1964, special corr Sudan Aden 1967, Far East corr, war corr Vietnam 1968–70, foreign ed 1970–76, managing and dep ed 1977–95; dir Guardian Newspapers 1984–95; tstee Children's Express, chm Tech Advsy Gp RNIB; *Style—* Ian Wright, Esq; ✉ c/o The Guardian, 119 Farringdon Rd, London EC1 (☎ 0171 607 2406)

WRIGHT, James Robertson Graeme; DL (Tyne and Wear 1995); s of John Wright, and Elizabeth Calder, *née* Coghill; *b* 14 June 1939; *Educ* Inverness Royal Acad, Dundee HS, Univ of Edinburgh (Guthrie fell, C B Black scholar, MA), St John's Coll Cambridge (major scholar, Henry Arthur Thomas student, Denney student, Ferguson scholar, MA); *m* 1966, Jennifer Susan, *née* Greenberg; 2 da; *Career* Univ of Edinburgh: lectr in humanity (Latin) 1966–78 (asst lectr 1965), sr warden Pollock Halls of Residence 1973–78, memb Univ Ct 1975–78; St Catharine's Coll Cambridge: fell 1978–87, professorial fell 1987–91, hon fell 1992–, dir of studies in classics 1978–87, bursar 1979–87, chm Cambridge Bursar's Ctee 1986–87 (sec 1983–86); sec-gen of the Faculties Univ of Cambridge 1987–91; vice-chllr Univ of Newcastle upon Tyne 1992–; dir The Newcastle Initiative 1993–; assoc cmmr Hamlyn Nat Cmmn on Educn 1992–93; non-exec memb: Cambridge District Health Authy 1990–91, Northern and Yorks Regnl Health Authy 1993–96; memb: Governing Body Shrewsbury Sch 1986–, Scottish HE Funding Cncl 1992–97, Ctee of Vice-Chllrs and Principals 1992– (memb Cncl 1995–), Advsy Gp Newcastle Common Purpose 1992–, Ctee for Int Co-operation in HE Br Cncl 1992–; *Recreations* walking, travel in France, food, wine; *Clubs* Athenaeum, Northern Counties (Newcastle upon Tyne); *Style—* James Wright, Esq, DL; ✉ The Vice-Chancellor's Office, University of Newcastle upon Tyne, Newcastle upon Tyne NE1 7RU (☎ 0191 222 6064, fax 0191 222 6828)

WRIGHT, Jerry; s of Gerald Wright, of Chislehurst, Kent, and Elizabeth, *née* Harris; *b* 28 Oct 1960; *Educ* Eltham Coll, Univ of Bristol (BA History); *m* 15 July 1989, Ann Clare, *née* Faller; 1 s (Christopher James Faller b 14 April 1995); *Career* business gp dir Homecare and Personal Wash Lever Brothers Ltd 1993–; *Recreations* rugby, cricket, music (especially opera), travel, food and drink, bridge, reading, crosswords; *Style—* Jerry Wright, Esq; ✉ Lever Brothers Ltd, 3 St James Road, Kingston-upon-Thames, Surrey KT1 2BA (☎ 0181 541 8366, fax 0181 974 5021, mobile 0802 472062)

WRIGHT, Joe Booth; CMG (1979); s of Joe Booth Wright (d 1967), of Notts, and Annie Elizabeth, *née* Stockdale (d 1964); *b* 24 Aug 1920; *Educ* King Edward VI GS Retford, Univ of London (BA); *m* 1, 1945, Pat, *née* Beaumont; 1 s (Christopher), 2 da (Helen, Annie); m 2, 1967, Patricia Maxine, da of Albert Nicholls (d 1955); *Career* serv in Armed Forces 1941–46; HM Dip Serv 1947–79 in Jerusalem, Munich, Basrah, Formosa, Indonesia, Cyprus and Tunisia; HM consul-gen: Hanoi 1971–72, Geneva 1973–75; HM ambass Ivory Coast, Upper Volta & Niger 1975–78, ret 1979; writer, lectr, translator; memb Inst of Linguists and Translators Guild 1982; *Books* Francophone Black Africa Since Independence (1981), Zaire Since Independence (1983), Paris As It Was (1985), Who Was the Enemy ? (1993), Security and Cooperation in Europe: The View from the East (1993); *Recreations* cricket, Chinese painting, music, cinema; *Clubs* Royal Over-Seas League; *Style—* Joe Wright Esq, CMG; ✉ 29 Brittany Rd, St Leonards-on-Sea, E Sussex TN38 0RB (☎ 01424 439563)

WRIGHT, Brig John Anthony; CBE (1992, MBE 1973); s of Col Thomas Wright, CBE (d 1989), and Joyce Mary, *née* Walker (d 1993); *b* 10 Oct 1940; *Educ* Wellington, RMA Sandhurst; *m* 4 March 1967, Anstice Gillian, da of Wing Cdr (Charles Percy) Vernon Hervey (d 1993); 1 s (Peter b 1971), 2 da (Claudia b 1969, Alicia b 1983); *Career* RMAS 1959, 2 Lt RTR 1960, ADC and PS to High Cmmr Aden 1964, Adj RHKR(V) 1969, transferred 16/5 Lancers 1970, RN Staff Coll 1973, NDC 1980, CO 16/5 Lancers 1982, DPSO/CDS 1987, DJPS 1992, ret Brig; chm: Pony Club Polo 1989, FIP Jr Ctee 1992; mangr Tidworth Polo Club 1995–; *Recreations* polo; *Style*— Brig John Wright, CBE; ✉ Tidworth Polo Club, Tedworth Park, Tidworth, Hants SP9 7AH (☎ 01980 846705, fax 01980 842558)

WRIGHT, John Edward; s of John Nicholas Wright (d 1962), and Ellen Bullen, *née* Mulloy; *b* 23 May 1933; *Educ* Mold GS, Univ of Liverpool (MB ChB, MD); *m* 23 May 1959, Kathleen Teresa, da of John Reid (d 1938); 1 s (John b 1960), 1 da (Elizabeth b 1966); *Career* Nat Serv RAMC 1957–60; conslt ophthalmic surgn St Mary's Hosp London 1969–73; sr lectr in ophthalmology Univ of London 1969–73, conslt ophthalmic surgn Moorfields Eye Hosp London 1973– (sr registrar 1964–67), conslt ophthalmic surgn Royal ENT Hosp London 1973–; Wendel Hughes Lectr USA 1982, Doyne Lectr Oxford 1987; numerous pubns on orbital disease; past sec of the Ophthalmological Soc, pres Int Orbital Soc, past bd memb Moorfields Eye Hosp; memb: RSM, Coll of Ophthalmologists, American Acad of Ophthalmology; FRCS 1966; *Recreations* golf, fishing; *Clubs* Denham Golf and Piscatorial Soc; *Style*— John Wright, Esq; ✉ 44 Wimpole St, London W1M 7DG (☎ 0171 580 1251, fax 0171 224 3722)

WRIGHT, John Gordon Laurence; s of Rev William Henry Laurence Wright (d 1993), of Edinburgh, and Mary Campbell, *née* Macdonald (d 1995); *b* 6 June 1944; *Educ* Glenalmond, BNC Oxford (MA); *m* 16 July 1974, (Faith) Alison, da of Dr John Allan Guy (d 1986, Capt RAMC 1939–45), of Kendal; 2 s (Thomas b 1977, Richard b 1981); *Career* Hambros Bank Ltd 1967–71, pres Stewart Ivory & Co Ltd (formerly Stewart Fund Managers Ltd) 1971– (apptd dir 1972); MSI; *Recreations* photography, skiing, shooting; *Clubs* New (Edinburgh); *Style*— John Wright, Esq; ✉ 34 Greenhill Gardens, Edinburgh EH10 4BP; Stewart Ivory & Co Ltd, 45 Charlotte Sq, Edinburgh EH2 4HW

WRIGHT, John Trevor; OBE (1987); s of George Leslie Wright (d 1988), and Anne, *née* McCracken (d 1992); *b* 7 Feb 1935; *Educ* Univ of Leeds (MA); *m* 1, 1957 (m dis 1981), Grace, *née* Williams; m 2, 1982, Nuala June, da of Robert Warren Maguire; 2 s (Christopher b 13 Oct 1957, Philip b 14 July 1964), 1 da (Julia b 15 Oct 1961); *Career* asst lectr in English Univ of Leeds 1961–62 (res fell 1957–59), lectr in linguistics SOAS 1962–67; British Council: prof Regnl Inst of English Bangalore 1967–70, English language offr W India 1971, English Teaching Information Centre London 1971–73, dir English Language Centre Chalimbana Zambia 1973–76, English language offr Spain 1979–82 (Jakarta 1976–79), dir Ecuador 1982–88, head Overseas Appointments Gp London 1988–89, dir Bahrain 1989–94, advsr Civil Service Bureau Cncl of Ministers Govt of Bahrain 1994–; *Books* Speaking English (2 Vols and 7 tapes); *Recreations* computers, music, golf; *Clubs* RAF, Royal Over-Seas League; *Style*— John Wright, Esq, OBE; ✉ British Council, PO Box 452, Manama, Bahrain (e-mail jwright@batelco.com.bh)

WRIGHT, Karen Jocelyn Wile; da of Louis David Wile (d 1972), and Grace Carlin Wile; *b* 15 Nov 1950; *Educ* Princeton HS, Brandeis Univ (BA), Univ of Cambridge (MA), London Business Sch Univ of London (MSc); *m* 23 May 1981, Richard Bernard Wright, s of Bernard Gilbert Wright; 2 da (Louisa Karen b 17 April 1985, Rebecca Katherine b 21 Oct 1986); *Career* fndr and proprietor Hobson Gallery Cambridge 1975–84, Bernard Jacobson Gallery Cork St 1985, worked on Victor Willing catalogue Whitechapel Art Gallery 1986; Modern Painters magazine: fndr with Peter Fuller 1987, asst ed 1987–89, managing ed 1989–91, ed 1991–; AICA 1988; *Recreations* art, tennis, swimming, reading, playing with the children; *Clubs* Groucho; *Style*— Mrs Karen Wright; ✉ Modern Painters, Universal House, 251 Tottenham Court Road, London W1P 9AD (☎ 0171 436 0076, fax 0171 580 5615)

WRIGHT, Keith Elliot; s of Wilfred Stratten Wright (d 1961), and Dorothea, *née* Elliot (d 1961); *b* 20 Nov 1920; *Educ* Giggleswick Sch, Selwyn Coll Cambridge (BA); *m* 20 Feb 1954, Patricia Ann, da of Raymond Tustin Taylor (d 1985); 1 s (David b 1956), 2 da (Catherine b 1958, Sally b 1959); *Career* WWII offr Duke of Wellington Regt 1939–45; sr ptnr Slaughter & May 1976–84 (slr 1950, ptnr 1955); memb: Cncl King Edward VII's Hosp for Offrs 1986–95, London Advsy Bd Salvation Army, Cncl Offrs' Assoc; chm Wilts Rural Housing Assoc 1991–96; memb Law Soc 1950; *Recreations* theatre, walking, gardening; *Style*— Keith Wright, Esq; ✉ Kestrels, Oak Lane, Easterton, nr Devizes, Wilts SN10 4PD (☎ 01380 812573)

WRIGHT, Dr Kenneth Campbell; CMG (1987), OBE (1973); s of James Edwin Wright (d 1981), of Colinton, Edinburgh, and Eva Rebecca, *née* Sayers (d 1964); *b* 31 May 1932; *Educ* George Heriot's Sch, Univ of Edinburgh (MA, PhD), Univ of Paris (Licence-ès-Lettres); *m* 19 April 1958, Diana Yolande, da of Geoffrey Morse Binnie, FRS (d 1989), of Benenden, Kent; 1 s (David b 1963), 2 da (Jacqueline b 1964, Vanessa b 1968); *Career* cadet pilot RAFVR 1950, cmmnd RAFVR 1954, short serv reg cmmn RAF 1957–60 (Flt Lt 1959); lectr: Lovanium Univ and Institut Politique Congolais 1960–63, Univ of Ghana 1963–65 (sr lectr 1964–65); HM Dip Serv: FO 1965–68, first sec (econ) Bonn 1968–72, FCO 1972–75 and 1979–82, first sec later cnsllr UK Rep EEC Brussels 1975–79, cnsllr Paris 1982–85, asst under sec of state 1985–89; dir: Brit Invisible Exports Cncl 1989–91 (British Invisibles wef Oct 1990), City Communications Centre 1989; political affrs advsr Saferworld Fndn 1992–, Res Dept The Economist 1992–; *Recreations* people, places, books; *Clubs* Athenaeum; *Style*— Dr Kenneth Wright, CMG, OBE; ✉ Leven House, 2 The Meadway, Heath Lane, London SE3 0UP (☎ 0181 852 3650)

WRIGHT, Rev Canon Kenyon Edward; s of Charles James Wright (d 1975), and Mary Dunbar, *née* Adamson (d 1992); *b* 31 Aug 1932; *Educ* Paisley GS, Univ of Glasgow (MA), Univ of Cambridge (MA), Univ of Serampore India (MTh); *m* 18 Aug 1955, Betty, da of Arthur Robinson (d 1958); 3 da (Lindsey Jane b 1959, Shona May b 1961, Shelagh Ann b 1964); *Career* minister Durgapur United Church Bengal India 1955–59, dir Ecumenical Social and Industl Int India 1961–70, canon residentiary and dir of int ministry Coventry Cath 1970–81, gen sec Scottish Churches Cncl 1981–90, dir KAIROS (Scottish Churches Agency for Social and Environmental Studies) 1990–; chm exec Scottish Constitutional Convention, chm Scottish Environmental Forum, gen sec Christian Peace Conference; patron Scottish Refugee Cncl; exec memb Scottish Cncl Devpt and Indust; *Books* Structures for a Missionary Congregation (1965), Ecology and Christian Responsibility (1974), By Word and Deed (1992); *Style*— The Rev Canon Kenyon Wright; ✉ KAIROS Centre, Glencarse, Perth PH2 7LX (☎ and fax 01738 860386)

WRIGHT, Malcolm Carter; s of Edward Wright (d 1977); *b* 11 April 1938; *Educ* King's Sch Macclesfield; *m* 1, 1964 (m dis 1980), Susan Helen, *née* Winter; 2 s (Nicholas Richardson b 1967, Matthew Carter b 1969); m 2, 9 Dec 1989, Margaret Anne, *née* Phillips; *Career* R Bailey & Son plc: joined 1954, dir 1967, jt md 1977, chm and md 1993–95, non-exec dir 1995–; chm Surgical Dressings Manufacturers' Assoc 1980–83; past provincial offr Utd Grand Lodge and Supreme Grand Chapter; memb: RYA, Manchester Cruising Assoc; *Recreations* yachting (yacht 'Sunchase'); *Clubs* South Caernarvon Yacht, Pwllheli Sailing, Rudyard Lake Sailing; *Style*— Malcolm Wright, Esq; ✉ Carters Bottom, Longhurst Lane, Mellor, Stockport, Cheshire SK6 5AH (☎ and fax 0161 427 4506)

WRIGHT, Dr Martin; s of Clifford Kent Wright (d 1969), of Sheffield, and Rosalie, *née* Mackenzie (d 1967); *b* 24 April 1930; *Educ* Repton, Jesus Coll Oxford (MA), LSE (PhD); *m* 26 July 1957, Louisa Mary (Lisa), da of John Osborne Nicholls (d 1974), of Yoxall, Staffordshire; 3 s (Edward b 1960, James b 1961, William b 1963), 2 da (Sophie b 1960 d 1993, Ellie b 1968); *Career* librarian Inst of Criminology Cambridge 1964–71, dir Howard League for Penal Reform 1971–81, information/policy devpt offr Victim Support 1985–94, conslt on mediation 1994–; visiting scholar Centre for Criminological and Legal Research Univ of Sheffield 1994–, visiting research fell Centre for Legal Studies Univ of Sussex 1995–; chm Lambeth Mediation Serv 1989–92; memb: Br Society of Criminology, Mediation UK, Howard League for Penal Reform, Inst for the Study and Treatment of Delinquency; *Books* The Use of Criminology Literature (ed, 1974), Making Good: Prisons, Punishment and Beyond (1982), Mediation and Criminal Justice: Victims, Offenders and Community (jt ed with B Galaway, 1989), Justice for Victims and Offenders: A Restorative Response to Crime (1991, 2 edn 1996); *Recreations* suggesting improvements; *Style*— Dr Martin Wright; ✉ 19 Hillside Rd, London SW2 3HL (☎ 0181 671 8037)

WRIGHT, Hon Mr Justice; Hon Sir (John) Michael; kt (1990); s of Prof John George Wright (d 1971), and Elsie Lloyd, *née* Razey (d 1955); *b* 26 Oct 1932; *Educ* The King's Sch Chester, Oriel Coll Oxford (BA, MA); *m* 25 July 1959, Kathleen Esther Gladys Wright, JP, da of Frederick Arthur Meanwell, MM (d 1945); 1 s (Timothy b 1965), 2 da (Elizabeth b 1961, Katharine b 1963); *Career* Nat Serv RA 1951–53, 2 Lt 1952, Lt 1953, TA 1953–56, TARO 1956–; called to the Bar Lincoln's Inn 1957, recorder of the Crown Ct 1974–90, QC 1974, ldr SE Circuit 1981–83, bencher 1983–, chm Bar 1983–84 (vice chm 1982–83), legal assessor RCVS 1984–90, judge of the High Court of Justice (Queen's Bench Div) 1990–, presiding judge SE Circuit 1995–; *Style*— The Hon Mr Justice Wright; ✉ c/o Royal Courts of Justice, London WC2

WRIGHT, Prof Michael Thomas; s of William George Wright (d 1985), and Lily May, *née* Turner; *b* 11 April 1947; *Educ* Sheldon Heath Sch Birmingham, Aston Univ (BSc, PhD); *m* 29 Aug 1970, Patricia Eunice, da of Stanley Douglas Cox; 1 da (Rebecca Michelle b 19 Sept 1977); *Career* apprentice EPE Co Birmingham 1963–68, res engr Redman Heenan Froude Worcs 1969–76, engrg dir Linear Motors Ltd Loughborough 1976–78, tech dir NEI Peebles Ltd Edinburgh 1978–82, engrg dir GEC Large Machines Rugby 1982–85, Molins PLC 1985–90 (md Tobacco Div then gp md); Aston Univ: prof and head Dept of Mechanical and Electrical Engrg 1990–92, chm Aston Business School 1992–93, sr pro-vice chllr 1994–96, vice chllr 1996–; non-exec chm The 600 Group plc 1993–, non-exec dir ERA Technology 1994–; governing dir Scot Engrg Trg Scheme Glasgow 1978–82; IEE Student Paper Award 1970, IEEE Petrochemical Indust Author Award 1981, IEE Power Div Premium for published work 1983; FIEE 1981, sr memb IEEE (USA) 1981, FEng 1988, FIMechE 1989, FRSA 1989, CMath 1994, FIMA 1994; *Style*— Prof Michael Wright, FEng; ✉ Vice Chancellor's Office, Aston University, Aston Triangle, Birmingham B4 7ET (☎ 0121 359 3611)

WRIGHT, Miles Francis Melville; s of Montague Francis Melville Wright (d 1968), and Marjorie Isobel, *née* Brook (d 1968); *b* 3 Dec 1943; *Educ* Ampleforth, Ch Ch Oxford (MA); *Career* dir American Int Underwriters (UK) Ltd 1982–84 (asst md 1984–87), md Polwring Underwriting Agency at Lloyd's 1988–96, currently arbitrator and expert witness in insurance disputes; Freeman: Worshipful Co of Glaziers & Painters of Glass, Worshipful Co of Insurers; *Recreations* cricket, tennis, shooting, gardening; *Clubs* 1900 Club, MCC, I Zingari, Free Foresters, Emeritus & Old Amplefordian CCS; *Style*— Miles Wright, Esq; ✉ The Barracks, Cranbrook, Kent TN17 2LG (☎ 01580 712209)

WRIGHT, Prof Nicholas Alcwyn; s of Glyndwr Alcwyn Wright (d 1980), and Hilda Lilian, *née* Jones (d 1978); *b* 24 Feb 1943; *Educ* Bristol GS, Univ of Durham (MB BS), Univ of Newcastle upon Tyne (MD, PhD, DSc), MA (Oxon); *m* 1966, Vera, da of George Matthewson; 1 da (Claire Louise b 8 Aug 1968), 1 s (Graeme Alcwyn b 18 Dec 1969); *Career* Univ of Newcastle upon Tyne: demonstrator in pathology 1966–71, research fell 1971–74, lectr in pathology 1974–76, sr lectr 1976–77; Univ of Oxford: clinical reader in pathology 1977, Nuffield reader 1978, fell Green Coll 1979–80; dir of histopathology Hammersmith Hosp 1980–96; Royal Postgraduate Med Sch: dean 1996–, vice princ Imperial Coll Sch of Med 1996–; Imperial Cancer Research Fund: dir Histopathology Unit 1988–, dir of clinical research 1991–96; chm Research for Health Charities Gp 1994; memb Cncl: Royal Coll of Pathologists 1982–, Br Soc of Gastroenterology 1986–; FRCPath 1986; *Recreations* rugby football, cricket, squash, military history, cooking; *Clubs* Athenaeum; *Style*— Prof Nicholas Wright; ✉ Royal Postgraduate Medical School, Hammersmith Hospital, Du Cane Road, London W12 0NN (☎ 0181 383 3200, fax 0181 383 3203)

WRIGHT, Sir (John) Oliver; GCMG (1981, KCMG 1974, CMG 1964), GCVO (1978), DSC (1944); s of Arthur Wright (d 1963), of Seaford; *b* 6 March 1921; *Educ* Solihull Sch, Christ's Coll Cambridge (MA); *m* 1942, (Lillian) Marjory, da of Hedley Vickers Osborne, of Solihull; 3 s (Nicholas b 1946, John b 1949, Christopher b 1950); *Career* RNVR WWII; joined HM Dip Serv 1945; served: NY, Bucharest, Singapore, Berlin, Pretoria; private sec to: Foreign Sec 1960–63, PM 1964–66; ambass Denmark 1966–69, seconded to Home Office, UK rep to NI Govt 1969–70, chief clerk 1970–72, dep under sec FCO 1972–75; ambass: FRG 1975–81, ret then recalled from retirement to be ambass to Washington 1982–86; dir: Siemens Ltd 1981–82, Savoy Hotel plc 1987–94, Enviromed Plc 1993–; pres German Chamber of Indust and Commerce 1989–92 (vice pres 1986–89 and 1992–95); chm: Br Konigswinter Conf Steering Ctee 1986, Bd of Govrs Reigate GS 1989–, Anglo-Irish Encounter 1986–91; hon fell Christ's Coll Cambridge 1982– (master designate May-June 1982); memb Bd Br Cncl 1981–82 and 1986–91; tstee: Br Museum 1986–91, Shakespeare Int Globe Centre (vice chm of Int Cncl 1986–); Hon DHL Univ of Nebraska 1983; Grand Cross German Order of Merit 1978, King of Arms Order of St Michael and St George 1987–96; *Recreations* theatre, opera; *Clubs* Travellers'; *Style*— Sir Oliver Wright, GCMG, GCVO, DSC; ✉ Burstow Hall, Horley, Surrey RH6 9SR (☎ 01293 783494)

WRIGHT, (Lester) Paul; s of Christopher Percy Wright (d 1985), and Mary, *née* Sutton; *b* 2 July 1946; *Educ* Bedford Sch, Gonville and Caius Coll Cambridge (MA, PhD), Kennedy Sch of Govt Harvard Univ (Harkness fell); *m* 1969, Jill, *née* Wildman; 1 s (Barnaby b 1976); *Career* fell Inst of Historical Res Univ of London 1969–70, lectr in history Univ of Reading 1970–71; Home Office: asst private sec to Home Sec 1972–73, private sec to Perm Sec 1980–82, head of Prison Bldg Div 1983–87, head of Bdcasting Div 1987–91, head of Drugs Div 1991–92; Dept of Nat Heritage: head of Bdcasting Film and Sport Gp 1992–93, head of Bdcasting and Media Gp 1993–96, head of Arts Buildings and Millennium Gp 1996–; *Recreations* music, theatre, walking, looking at pictures; *Style*— Paul Wright, Esq; ✉ Head of Art, Building and Millennium Group, Department of National Heritage, 2–4 Cockspur Street, London SW1Y 5DH (☎ 0171 211 6122)

WRIGHT, Sir Paul Hervé Giraud; KCMG (1975, CMG 1960), OBE (1952); s of Richard Hervé Giraud Wright (sec of White's Club), and Ellen Margaret, da of Lewis Mercier; *b* 12 May 1915; *Educ* Westminster; *m* 1942, Beatrice Frederika Wright, MP Bodmin 1941–45, da of Frank Roland Clough and wid of Flt-Lt John Rankin Rathbone, MP, RAFVR (ka 1940); 1 da; *Career* served WWII, Maj KRRC, HQ 21 Army Gp (despatches); contested (Lib) Bethnal Green 1945; asst dir PR NCB 1946–48, PR dir Festival of Britain 1948–51; joined HM Foreign Serv 1951, Paris and NY 1951–54, FO 1954–56, The Hague 1956–57, head of Info Policy Dept FO 1957–60, Cairo 1960–61, cnsllr UK Delgn to NATO 1961–64, dir gen Br Info Services NY 1964–68, min (info) Washington 1965–68; ambass: Congo (Kinshasa) and Republic of Burundi 1969–71, Lebanon 1971–75, ret; special rep of Sec of State for Foreign and Cwlth Affrs 1975–78, hon sec London Celebrations Ctee for Queen's Silver Jubilee 1977; chm: Irvin GB Ltd 1979–88, chm Br American Arts Assoc 1983–88, Br Lebanese Assoc 1987–90; chm of Govrs Westminster Cathedral Choir

Sch 1993– (govr 1981–), pres The Elizabethan Club 1988–94, memb Trusthouse Forte Cncl 1987–; hon fell Westminster Sch 1992–, Hon RCM; KSG 1996, FRSA; *Books* A Brittle Glory (autobiography); *Clubs* Garrick; *Style*— Sir Paul Wright, KCMG, OBE; ✉ 62 Westminster Gardens, London SW1P 4JG

WRIGHT, Peter; s of Nigel Wright, and June, *née* Oxnam; *b* 13 Aug 1953; *Educ* Marlborough, Clare Coll Cambridge; *m* 3 Aug 1974, Dorothy; 3 s (Ben b 9 Sept 1981, William b 25 May 1987, Edward b 21 Sept 1990), 1 da (Alice b 30 March 1984); *Career* reporter Evening Post - Echo Hemel Hempstead 1975–78; Daily Mail: reporter 1979, asst news ed 1979–85, assoc news ed (foreign) 1985–86, asst features ed 1986–88, ed Femail 1988–91, asst ed (features) 1991–92, assoc ed 1992–95, dep ed 1995–; *Style*— Peter Wright, Esq; ✉ Daily Mail, Northcliffe House, 2 Derry Street, Kensington, London W8 5TT (☎ 0171 938 6000, fax 0171 937 4463)

WRIGHT, Peter Hugh; s of William Wright, of Bonnyrigg, and Elizabeth, *née* Kerr; *b* 30 Dec 1967; *Educ* Lasswade HS; *m* 24 April 1993, Audrey Anne, da of Gordon Gray; 1 da (Eilidh Elizabeth b 11 Sept 1995); *Career* Rugby Union prop; former clubs: Lasswade RFC 1984–86, Boroughmuir RFC; currently with Melrose RFC; Scotland: former memb under 18, 19 and 21 teams, first full cap v Australia 1992, 21 caps; memb: Br Lions tour to NZ 1992–93, Scottish World Cup squad 1995; John Monteith Builders 1984–89, McDonald Ross Structural Engineers 1989–; *Recreations* travel, cinema, real ale; *Style*— Peter Wright, Esq

WRIGHT, Peter Michael; s of Dudley Cyril Brazier Wright, of Finchley, London, and Pamela Deirdre, *née* Peacock; *b* 6 March 1954; *Educ* Highgate Sch London, RCM (Organ exhibitioner, ARCM, LRAM), Emmanuel Coll Cambridge (Organ scholar, MA); *Career* sub organist Guildford Cathedral 1977–89, asst music master Royal GS Guildford 1977–89, organist and dir of music Southwark Cathedral 1989–; conductor: Edington Festival 1984–90, Guildford Chamber Choir 1985–94, Surrey Festival Choir 1987–; several recordings as organist and conductor released; memb: Cncl RCO 1990–, Cathedral Organists' Conference; FRCO; *Recreations* opera, theatre, travel, reading; *Style*— Peter Wright, Esq; ✉ 52 Bankside, Southwark, London SE1 9JE (☎ 0171 261 1291); Southwark Cathedral, Montague Close, London Bridge, London SE1 9DA (☎ 0171 407 3708, fax 0171 357 7389)

WRIGHT, Sir Peter Robert; kt (1993), CBE (1985); s of Bernard Wright (d 1981), and Hilda Mary, *née* Foster (d 1973); *b* 25 Nov 1926; *Educ* Bedales, Leighton Park; *m* 1954, Sonya Hana, da of Yoshi Sueyoshi (d 1931); 1 s (Jonathan), 1 da (Poppy); *Career* dancer Ballet Jooss and Sadler's Wells Theatre Ballet 1947–55, ballet master Sadler's Wells Opera Ballet and teacher Royal Ballet Sch 1955–58, ballet master Stuttgart Ballet 1960–63, guest prodr BBC TV 1963–65, freelance choreographer and prodr 1965–69, assoc dir Royal Ballet 1970–76, dir Sadler's Wells Royal Ballet (relocated and renamed The Birmingham Royal Ballet in 1990) 1976–95 (dir laureate 1995–); special prof Sch of Performance Studies Univ of Birmingham 1990–96; memb: Cncl Friends of Covent Garden, Exec Cncl Royal Acad of Dancing; govr: Royal Ballet Sch, Sadler's Wells Fndn, Rambert Dance Co; pres: Benesh Inst of Choreology, Cncl for Dance, Education and Training 1994–, Friends of Sadler's Wells 1995–; vice-pres: Myashthenia Gravis Assoc, Royal Acad of Dancing; Hon DMus Univ of London 1990, Hon DLitt Univ of Birmingham 1994; fell Birmingham Conservatoire of Music 1991; *Prodns* noted for prodns of 19th century classical ballets incl The Sleeping Beauty, Swan Lake, Giselle, The Nutcracker, and Coppelia, for most major cos in Europe and USA, Dutch and Canadian Nat Ballets, Royal Winnipeg Ballet, The Houston Ballet, Ballet de Rio de Janeiro, Stuttgart Ballet, Bavarian State Opera Ballet, Vienna State Opera Ballet, Star Dancers Ballet Tokyo, Ballet of the Colon Theatre Buenos Aires; *Own Creations* The Mirror Walkers, The Great Peacock, A Blue Rose, Dance Macabre, Summertide, Namouna, Designs for Dancers, Quintet, Summer's Night, El Amor Brujo; *Awards* Standard Award for Most Outstanding Achievement in Ballet 1981, John Newson Award for Greatest Contribution to SWRB 1988, Queen Elizabeth II Coronation Award Royal Acad of Dancing 1990, Digital Premier Award 1991, Critics Circle Award for Distinguished Contribution to The Arts 1996; *Recreations* gardening, ceramics; *Style*— Sir Peter Wright, CBE; ✉ 10 Chiswick Wharf, London W4 2SR

WRIGHT, Samantha; *b* 1 Sept 1966; *Educ* Wreake Valley Coll Leicester, Coll of St Paul's and St Mary's Cheltenham; *ptnr* Ian P Jennings (England hockey player); *Career* hockey player; debut Leicester Ladies 1979, currently memb Slough Ladies Hockey Club (nat outdoor and Euro champions); England: jr debut 1982, sr debut 1983, 38 full caps outdoor, 30 full caps indoor, capt 1992–; GB: 25 sr outdoor caps, tour NZ and Aust 1990, memb Olympic training squad 1991–92, tour S Africa England 1993, memb World Cup team 1993–94; awards: Player of the Year 1989, top indoor 1990–91, top goalscorer indoor 1989–90; teacher Wreake Valley Coll Leicester 1986–87, currently corp sales exec; *Recreations* most sports, keeping fit; *Style*— Ms Samantha Wright; ✉ 8 Mole Close, Cove, Farnborough, Hants GU14 2NY

WRIGHT, Stanley Harris; s of John Charles Wright (d 1965); *b* 9 April 1930; *Educ* Bolton Sch, Merton Coll Oxford (MA); *m* 1; 1 s; m 2, 1973, Hon Alison Elizabeth, *qv*, da of Baron Franks, PC, OM, GCMG, KCB, CBE (Life Peer); 1 s; *Career* Bd of Trade 1952, HM Foreign Serv 1955–57, HM Treasy 1958, first sec (fin) Br Embassy Washington DC 1964–66, HM Treasy 1966–72 (under sec 1970–72), dir Lazard Bros & Co Ltd 1972–81; exec chm Inter Commercial Bank 1981–83; non-exec dir: Wilkinson Match Ltd 1974–81, Scripto Inc 1977–81, Law Land Co Ltd 1979–81, Royal Tst Bank 1984–88, Stadium Ltd 1990–96, Wolstenholme Rink plc 1991–93 (chm 1982–91); ptnr Price Waterhouse & Partners 1985–88; hon treas and memb Cncl Queen Mary & Westfield Coll London 1989–; *Recreations* various; *Clubs* Reform, MCC; *Style*— S H Wright, Esq; ✉ 6 Holly Place, London NW3 6QU (☎ 0171 435 0237)

WRIGHT, Dr Stephen Geoffrey; s of Stanley and Betty Wright, of Stoke-on-Trent; *b* 31 May 1944; *Educ* Longton HS, King's Coll Hosp Sch of Med London (MB BS); *m* Jennifer Lynn, da of Francis T Clay; 2 s (Matthew Stephen b 13 April 1979, Alexander Francis Stanley b 16 June 1982); *Career* jr med posts in UK and Nigeria, sr lectr London Sch of Hygiene and Tropical Med and hon conslt Physician Hosp for Tropical Diseases 1980–95, assoc prof of med Coll of Med King Saud Univ Riyadh Saudi Arabia 1985–88, conslt physician Hosp for Tropical Diseases Univ Coll London Hosp Tst 1995–; hon physician King Edward VII's Hosp for Offrs London; FRCP 1991; *Books* Hunter's Tropical Medicine (assoc ed, 7 edn 1991); *Recreations* sport, gardening, music; *Style*— Dr Stephen Wright; ✉ Hospital for Tropical Diseases, 4 St Pancras Way, London NW1 0PE (☎ 0171 530 3473); Private Patients Wing, University College Hospital, 25 Grafton Way, London WC1E 6DB (☎ 0171 383 7916)

WRIGHT, Susan; da of Kenneth Sidney Wright, and Janet Audrey, *née* Coffin; *b* 28 June 1970; *Educ* Charles Darwin Sr Sch Biggin Hill; *Career* squash professional; began playing aged 12, first title Wimbledon Under 14 Open 1983, winner numerous under 16 and 19 tournaments incl Under 16 Br Open; clubs: Raquets Fitness Centre Thame, Biggin Hill Squash; also plays in German and Dutch leagues and Ladies Nat League, rep Kent at jr and sr level 1985–, memb world circuit 1988–; titles won incl: Middx Open twice, Beds Open twice, Kent Closed, Dunlop Champion of Champions twice, Bamberg Cup Germany 1988, Br Nat Doubles Championship 1987 (with sister Debbie) and 1989, OSC Cup 1990, Br Nat 1992; runner-up: Br Open 1991, Dutch Open 1991, Singapore Open 1992; England caps: 5 under 16 1985–86, 29 under 19 1985–89, 15 sr 1989–; England honours: jr team Home Int champions 1985–89, sr team Home Int champions 1989–92, capt jr team winners world under 19 event Brighton 1987, capt sr team Euro Championship winners 1990; Avia Jr Player of the Year 1985–86, Squash Writers' Award Br Open 1991, Squash Rackets Assoc Player of the Year 1992; currently studying for fitness and nutrition dip; *Recreations* skiing, listening to most music, eating out, going to the cinema; *Style*— Miss Susan Wright; ✉ c/o Richard Grummitt, 14 Linden Rise, Bourne, Lincs PE10 9TD

WRIGHT, Very Rev Dr (Nicholas) Thomas (Tom); s of Nicholas Irwin Wright, of Morpeth, Northumberland, and Rosemary, *née* Forman; *b* 1 Dec 1948; *Educ* Sedbergh, Exeter Coll Oxford (MA, DPhil, Rugby Fives half blue), Wycliffe Hall Oxford; *m* 14 Aug 1971, Margaret Elizabeth Anne, da of Frank Albert Fiske; 2 s (Nicholas Julian Gregory b 9 June 1974, Oliver Thomas Irwin b 1 March 1981), 2 da (Rosamund Sarah Margaret b 17 March 1976, Harriet Elizabeth Ruth b 9 Feb 1979); *Career* ordained: deacon 1975, priest 1976; Merton Coll Oxford: jr res fell 1975–78, jr chaplain 1976–78; fell and chaplain Downing Coll Cambridge 1978–81, asst prof of New Testament lit McGill Univ Montreal 1981–86, hon prof Diocesan Coll Montreal 1981–86, fell, tutor and chaplain Worcester Coll Oxford 1986–93, univ lectr in theol Univ of Oxford 1986–93, canon theologian Coventry Cathedral 1992–, dean of Lichfield 1993–; memb Doctrine Cmmn C of E 1979–81 and 1989–95, fell Inst for Christian Studies Toronto 1992–; memb: Soc of Biblical Lit 1982, Soc of New Testament Studies 1988; *Books* Small Faith, Great God (1978), The Work of John Frith (1983), The Epistles of Paul to the Colossians and to Philemon (1987), The Glory of Christ in the New Testament (1987), The Interpretation of the New Testament 1861–1986 (1988), The Climax of the Covenant (1991), New Tasks for a Renewed Church (1992), The Crown and the Fire (1992), The New Testament and the People of God (1992), Who Was Jesus? (1992), Following Jesus (1994), The Lord and His Prayer (1996), Jesus and the Victory of God (1996), The Original Jesus (1996), For All God's Worth (1997); *Recreations* music, hill walking, poetry, cricket, golf; *Style*— The Very Rev Dr Tom Wright; ✉ The Deanery, Lichfield, Staffs WS13 7LD (☎ 01543 256120, fax 01543 411154)

WRIGHT, Thomas William John; s of John William Richard Wright (d 1977), of Canterbury, Kent, and Jane Elizabeth, *née* Nash (d 1978); *b* 5 Aug 1928; *Educ* Kent Coll, Simon Langton Sch Canterbury, Wye Coll London (BSc); *m* 4 Jan 1956, Shirley Evelyn, da of Henry Parkinson (d 1943), of Beckenham, Kent; 2 da (Geraldine Anne b 1959, d 1994, Jane b 1962); *Career* garden estate mgmnt conslt and int lectr; tea plantation mangr Kenya and govt horticultural res offr UK 1953–58, mangr Nursery and Landscape Co Devon 1956–60; lectr Pershore Coll 1962–68, sr lectr in landscape horticulture Wye Coll London 1968–90; conslt on restoration and mgmnt of historical gardens; visiting prof Univs of Beijing and Shanghai China, lectr Univ of Kent's Summer Acad on Kent's Historic Gdns; Veitch Memorial medal RHS 1989; tstee: Landscape Design Tst, Cobham Hall Heritage Tst, Fortescue Gardens Tst; memb: Gdns Ctee HHA, Gdns Panel Nat Tst, Shows Ctee RHS, Govt Royal Parks Review Gp 1991–95, Scientific Ctee Benetton Fndn Italy, Strategy and Standing Advsy Ctee Harold Hiller Arboretum, Garden Restoration Design Gp Hampton Ct Palace; judge Chelsea Show Gardens; ALI 1978, FIHort 1986; *Books* The Gardens of Kent, Sussex and Surrey (No 4 in Batsford Series, 1978), Large Gardens and Parks, Management and Design (1982), RHS Dictionary of Gardening (1992), RHS Encyclopedia of Gardening (contrib, 1990 and 1992); *Recreations* travel, natural history, gardening, music, climatology; *Style*— Thomas Wright, Esq; ✉ Nyewood Lodge, Nyewood, Rogate, Petersfield, Hampshire GU31 5JL (☎ 01730 821375, fax 01730 821922)

WRIGHT, Col Timothy Blake (Tim); s of Maj Harold Stanley Wright, TD (d 1989), and Gladys Mabel Wright; *b* 18 June 1936; *Educ* Hurstpierpoint Coll; *m* 27 April 1963, Leoné Shirley, da of Clifford Hare Harris (d 1938); *Career* Royal Sussex Regt 1954–57, 5 Battalion The Queen's Regt (Volunteers) 1967–69; trainee John Dickinson and Co Ltd 1957, chief inspr Northern Rhodesia Police 1964 (asst inspr 1957, inspr 1960), ret Zambia Police 1967, slr 1970, Capt Army Legal Servs 1970, ADALS Hong Kong 1972–82, DADALS HQ NI 1977–78, Col 1986; memb: Police History Soc, Western Front Assoc, Soc for Army Historical Res; memb Law Soc; *Recreations* model soldiers, gardening, walking; *Style*— Col T B Wright; ✉ Legal Branch Headquarters, 4th Division, Mons Barracks, Aldershot, Hants GU11 2LF

WRIGHT, Prof Verna; s of Thomas William Wright (d 1934), and Nancy Eleanor, *née* Knight (d 1978); *b* 31 Dec 1928; *Educ* Bedford Sch, Univ of Liverpool (MB ChB 1953, MD 1956); *m* 8 Aug 1952, Esther Margaret, da of John Bruce Brown (d 1962), of Kings Walden, Hertfordshire; 5 s (Stephen b 1953, Paul b 1955, Andrew b 1958, Mark b 1964, James b 1970), 4 da (Susannah b 1956, Miriam b 1959, Deborah b 1962, Philippa b 1968); *Career* res asst Univ of Leeds 1956–58; res fell Div of Applied Physiology Johns Hopkins Hosp Baltimore 1958–59; Univ of Leeds: lectr Dept of Clinical Medicine 1960–64, sr lectr 1964–70, ARC prof of rheumatology 1970–94; conslt physician in rheumatology Utd Leeds Teaching Hosp 1964–1994; former pres Heberden Soc, Br Assoc for Rheumatology and Rehabilitation; pres Creation Res Soc; vice-pres Biblical Creation Soc; former chm: Standing Advsy Ctee for Rheumatology Royal Coll of Physicians, United Beach Mission, Young Life Assoc; chm Exec and Fin Ctee Arthritis and Rheumatism Cncl; FRCP 1970 (MRCP 1958); *Books* Bone and Joint Disease in the Elderly (1983), Integrated Clinical Science: Musculoskeletal Disease (1984), Personal Peace in a Nuclear Age (1985), Arthritis and Joint Replacement (1987), Introduction to the Biomechanics of Joints and Joint Replacement (1981), Applied Drug Therapy of the Rheumatic Diseases (1982), Diagnostic Picture Tests in Rheumatology (1987), Clinical Rheumatology, Pain (1987), Mechanics of Human Joints (1993), Understanding Arthritis and Joint Replacement (1993); *Recreations* reading; *Style*— Professor Verna Wright; ✉ Inglehurst, Park Drive, Harrogate HG2 9AY (☎ 01432 502326, fax 01423 521981); Rheumatology and Rehabilitation Research Unit, Department of Medicine, University of Leeds, 36 Clarendon Road, Leeds LS2 9NZ (☎ 0113 233 4940, fax 0113 244 5533, telex 336017)

WRIGHT, Wendy (Mrs S B Beresford-Davies); da of Gp Capt Desmond Robert Morane-Griffiths, DFC, and Daphne Eve, *née* Fawke; *b* 9 Aug 1947; *Educ* Kent Coll Pembury, Mme Anita's Villa de L'Assomption Paris, Inchbald Sch of Design (Dip ISGD); *m* 1, 25 Sept 1971 (m dis 1978), Robert Sullivan Thomas; m 2, 2 June 1978 (m dis 1994), John Charles Wright, er s of Sir Rowland Sydney Wright, CBE; 1 s (William Rowland Hawksworth b 1984), 1 da (Clemency Sarah b 1980); m 3, 11 July 1994, Sydney Bjarne Beresford-Davies; *Career* garden designer, landscape conslt; lectr The English Gardening Sch, princ The Garden Sch in the North 1989–; memb advsy Cncl Inchbald Sch of Design; FSLGD 1987; *Recreations* gardening, horses, bridge; *Style*— Ms Wendy Wright; ✉ Glasdir Bach, Nevern, Pembrokeshire, Dyfed SA42 0NQ (☎ 01239 820623)

WRIGHT OF RICHMOND, Baron (UK 1994), of Richmond upon Thames, London; Sir Patrick Richard Henry Wright; GCMG (1989, KCMG 1984, CMG 1978); s of Herbert Wright (d 1977), of Chetwode, Buckingham, and Rachel, *née* Green; *b* 28 June 1931; *Educ* Marlborough, Merton Coll Oxford; *m* 1958, Virginia Anne, step da of Col Samuel John Hannaford (d 1983), of Hove; 2 s (Hon Marcus b 1959, Hon Angus b 1964), 1 da (Hon Olivia (Mrs McDonald) b 1963); *Career* Nat Serv Lt RA; entered Foreign Serv 1955; served: Beirut, Washington, Cairo, Bahrain; private sec (overseas affrs) to PM 1974–77; ambass: Luxembourg 1977–79, Syria 1979–81; dep under sec FCO Jan 1982–84, ambass Saudi Arabia 1984–86, perm under sec FCO and head Dip Serv 1986–91; dir: Barclays plc 1991–96, Unilever, The British Petroleum Company plc, De La Rue plc 1991–, BAA plc 1992–; memb Security Cmmn 1993–; memb Cncl: Royal Inst of Int Affairs (chm 1995–), Royal Coll of Music, Utd World Coll of the Atlantic; vice pres Home-Start; govr Wellington Coll, Ditchley; hon fell Merton Coll Oxford 1987; memb Cncl and dir Overseas Relations Order of St John; KStJ 1990; FRCM 1994; *Clubs* Oxford and Cambridge; *Style*— The Rt Hon Lord Wright of Richmond, GCMG; ✉ c/o House of Lords, Westminster, London SW1A 0PW

WRIGHTON, John Derek; s of Thomas Alfred Haken Wrighton, and Elslie Evelyn, *née* Field; *b* 10 March 1933; *Educ* East Barnet GS, Univ of London (MB BS); *m* 1967, Jean; 1 da (Jane b 5 Nov 1967), 1 s (David b 19 Nov 1969); *Career* Nat Serv Surgn Lt RN 1958–61; med offr British European Airways 1961–62, in gen practice Witham Essex 1962–63, surgical registrar London 1963–67, orthopaedics registrar then sr registrar Princess Elizabeth Hosp Exeter 1967–72, orthopaedic conslt W Dorset 1972–93, currently in private practice Winterbourne Hosp Dorchester and conducting lecture and operating tours abroad; memb Br Athletics Team 1955–60 (winner 400m Euro Championships Stockholm 1958, winner 440 yards Br AAA Championships 1959, capt Br Athletics Team 1959, capt Men's Team Olympics Rome 1960); High Sheriff of Dorset 1995–96; *Recreations* skiing, water-skiing, tennis, swimming; *Style*— John Wrighton, Esq; ✉ Cleaves Cliff, 39 Bowleaze Coveway, Preston, Weymouth, Dorset DT3 6PL (☎ and fax 01305 832418)

WRIGHTSON, Dr Keith Edwin; s of Robert Wrightson (d 1968), and Evelyn, *née* Atkinson (d 1987); *b* 22 March 1948; *Educ* Dame Allan's Boys' Sch Newcastle, Fitzwilliam Coll Cambridge (Reddaway Scholar, Sr Scholar, MA, PhD); *m* 19 Aug 1972, Eva Mikušová, da of Jozef Mikuš; 1 s (Nicholas Mikuš b 6 Aug 1982), 1 da (Eliška Anne b 13 April 1989); *Career* research fell in history Fitzwilliam Coll Cambridge 1972–75, lectr in modern history Univ of St Andrews 1975–84; Univ of Cambridge: univ lectr in history 1984–93, reader in English social history 1993–; Jesus Coll Cambridge: fell 1984–, dir of studies in history 1990–; visiting prof: Univ of Toronto, Univ of Alberta; memb Bd Euro Grad Sch for Training in Economic and Social Historical Research 1990–; memb Editorial Bd: Social History 1979–, Law and History 1982–89, Continuity & Change 1985–90, The Seventeenth Century 1985–, Rural History 1989–; Canadian Cwlth fell 1983–84; FRHistS 1986, FBA 1996; *Books* Poverty and Piety in an English Village. Terling 1525–1700 (with David Levine, 1979, 2 edn, 1995), English Society 1580–1680 (1982), The World We Have Gained (co-ed, 1986), The Making of an Industrial Society. Whickham 1560–1745 (with David Levine, 1992); also author of numerous essays and articles on English social history; *Recreations* modern jazz; *Style*— Dr Keith Wrightson, FBA; ✉ Jesus College, Cambridge CB5 8BL (☎ 01223 339449, fax 01223 324910)

WRIGHTSON, Sir (Charles) Mark Garmondsway; 4 Bt (UK 1900), of Neasham Hall, Co Durham; s of Sir John Wrightson, 3 Bt, TD, DL (d 1983), and Hon Lady Wrightson; 1 Bt, chm of Head Wrightson & Co Ltd (bridge builders), and MP (C) for Stockton-on-Tees and E Div of St Pancras; *b* 18 Feb 1951; *Educ* Eton, Queens' Coll Cambridge; *m* 1975, Stella, da of late George Dean; 3 s (Barnaby, James, William); *Heir* s, Barnaby Thomas Garmondsway Wrightson b 5 Aug 1979; *Career* dir Hill Samuel Bank Ltd 1984; Liveryman Worshipful Co of Haberdashers; *Style*— Sir Mark Wrightson, Bt; ✉ 39 Westbourne Park Road, London W2 5QE

WRIGLEY, Prof Christopher John (Chris); s of Arthur Wrigley, of Shipton Gorge, Dorset, and Eileen Sylvia, *née* Herniman; *b* 18 Aug 1947; *Educ* Kingston GS, UEA (BA), Birkbeck Coll London (PhD); *m* 11 Sept 1987, Margaret, da of late Anthony Walsh, of Wigton, Cumbria; *Career* lectr in econ history Queen's Univ Belfast 1971–72; reader in econ history: Loughborough Univ 1984–88 (lectr 1972–78, sr lectr 1978–84); prof of modern Br History Univ of Nottingham 1991– (reader in econ hist 1988–91); chm Loughborough Lab Pty 1977–79 and 1980–85 (treas 1973–77), exec memb Loughborough Trades Cncl 1981–86; Leics cncllr 1981–89 (ldr of Lab Gp 1986–89), Charnwood borough cncllr and dep ldr Lab Gp 1983–87; Parly candidate (Lab): Blaby 1983, Loughborough 1987; ed The Historian 1993–; Historical Assoc: memb Cncl 1980–, a vice pres 1992–95, dep pres 1995–96, pres 1996–; memb: Econ History Soc Cncl 1983–92 and 1994–, Exec Ctee Labour History Soc 1983– (vice chm 1994–); FRHistS; *Books* David Lloyd George and The British Labour Movement (1976), A J P Taylor - A Complete Bibliography (1980), A History of British Industrial Relations Vol 1 1875–1914 (ed, 1982), Vol 2 1914–1939 (ed, 1986), and Vol 3 1939–78 (ed, 1996), William Barnes - The Dorset Poet (1984), Warfare Diplomacy and Politics (ed, 1986), Arthur Henderson (1990), Lloyd George and the Challenge of Labour (1990), On the Move (jt ed, 1991), Lloyd George (1992), Challenges of Labour (ed, 1993); *Recreations* swimming, walking; *Style*— Prof Chris Wrigley; ✉ Department of History, University of Nottingham, Nottingham, Notts NG7 2RD (☎ 0115 951 5945)

WRIGLEY, Prof Sir Edward Anthony (Tony); kt (1996); s of Edward Ernest Wrigley (d 1953), and Jessie Elizabeth, *née* Holloway (d 1976); *b* 17 Aug 1931; *Educ* King's Sch Macclesfield, Univ of Cambridge (BA, MA, PhD); *m* 2 July 1960, Maria Laura, da of Everhard Dirk Spelberg (d 1968); 1 s (Nicholas b 1963), 3 da (Marieke b 1961, Tamsin b 1966, Rebecca b 1969); *Career* William Volker res fell Univ of Chicago 1953–54, lectr in geography Univ of Cambridge 1958–74; Peterhouse Cambridge: fell 1958–, tutor 1962–64, sr bursar 1964–74; Hinkley visiting prof Johns Hopkins Univ 1975, Tinbergen visiting prof Erasmus Univ Rotterdam 1979, prof of population studies LSE 1979–88, sr res fell All Souls Coll Oxford 1988–94; Univ of Cambridge: prof of economic history 1994–, master Corpus Christi Coll 1994–; co dir Cambridge Gp for the History of Population and Social Structure 1974–95; memb Inst for Advanced Study Princeton 1970–71, pres Manchester Coll Oxford 1987–96, pres British Academy 1997– (treas 1989–95); laureate Int Union for the Scientific Study of Population 1993; FBA 1980; *Books* Industrial Growth and Population Change (1961), English Historical Demography (ed, 1966), Population and History (1969), Nineteenth Century Society (ed, 1972), Towns in Societies (ed with P Abrams, 1978), Population History of England (ed with R S Schofield, 1981), Works of Thomas Robert Malthus (ed with D Souden, 1987), People, Cities and Wealth (1987), Continuity, Chance and Change (1988); *Recreations* gardening; *Style*— Prof Sir Tony Wrigley, FBA; ✉ 13 Sedley Taylor Rd, Cambridge CB2 2PW (☎ 01223 247614); Corpus Christi College, Cambridge CB2 1RH (☎ 01223 338029)

WRIGLEY, (William) Matthew; s of Rev William Vickers Wrigley, of Rillington, nr Malton, N Yorks, and Margaret, *née* Hunter; *b* 3 July 1947; *Educ* Westminster (Queen's scholar), King's Coll Cambridge (scholar, MA); *m* 17 July 1971, Susan Jane, da of Percival Thomas Pratt; *Career* admitted slr 1972; ptnr: Biddle & Co London 1975–78 (articled clerk 1968–72), Dibb Lupton Broomhead Leeds 1978–96, Wrigleys Leeds 1996–; cncllr N Yorks CC 1985–89; memb Law Soc 1972; *Style*— Matthew Wrigley, Esq; ✉ Wrigleys, 5 Butts Court, Leeds LS1 5JS (☎ 0113 244 6100, fax 0113 244 6101)

WRIGLEY, Thomas James Borgen; s of Edmund Wrigley (d 1963), of Skipton, and Karen Olga, *née* Borgen (d 1961); *b* 31 Aug 1936; *Educ* Merchant Taylors Sch; *m* 1961, Catherine Ethel, da of Sqdn Ldr Clement James Gittins (d 1969), of Herts; 2 s (Edmund b 1967, Michael b 1970), 1 da (Sarah b 1965); *Career* CA; gp chief exec First National Finance Corporation plc until 1993, md First National Bank until 1993; memb Mgmnt Ctee Fin and Leasing Association until 1990, memb Deposit Protection Bd until 1993; currently non-exec dir: First National Credit plc, Tennis Management International Ltd (chm), Pay and Play Tennis Ltd, Poco Loco Ltd; *Recreations* golf, gardening, bridge; *Style*— Thomas Wrigley; ✉ The Old Malt House, St Peter Street, Marlow, Bucks SL7 1NQ (☎ 01628 482677, fax 01628 478672)

WRIXON-BECHER, John William Michael; s and h of Sir William Wrixon-Becher, 5 Bt, MC, *qv*, by his 1 w, later Countess of Glasgow (d 1984); *b* 29 Sept 1950; *Educ* Harrow, Neuchâtel Univ Switzerland; *Career* Lloyd's underwriter G N Rouse 1971–74, Lloyd's Brokers 1974–87, dir Wise Speke Financial Services 1987–93, fin conslt HSBC Gibbs Ltd 1993–; CII Fin Planning Certs; memb: Soc of Fin Advsrs, Lloyd's; *Recreations* shooting, fishing, golf; *Clubs* White's, MCC, I Zingari, Swinley Forest, BFSS; *Style*— John Wrixon-Becher, Esq

WRIXON-BECHER, Maj Sir William Fane; 5 Bt (UK 1831), of Ballygiblin, Cork, MC (1943); s of Sir Eustace William Windham Wrixon-Becher, 4 Bt, of Mallow, Co Cork, Ireland (d 1934), and Hon Constance Gough-Calthorpe (d 1957); *b* 7 Sept 1915; *Educ* Harrow, Magdalene Coll Cambridge (BA); *m* 1, 1946 (m dis 1960), Hon Mrs (Ursula Vanda Maud) Bridgewater (later Countess of Glasgow, d 1984), 2 da of 4 Baron Vivian; 1 s, 1 da; m 2, 1960, Yvonne Margaret, former w of Hon Roger Lloyd-Mostyn (now 5 Baron Mostyn, *qv*), and da of A Stuart Johnson, of Henshall Hall, Congleton, Cheshire (d 1970); *Heir* s, John William Michael Wrixon-Becher, *qv*; *Career* Temp Maj Rifle Bde (Supp Reserve), served West Desert, Tunisian Campaign 1940–43, (wounded, POW escaped), liaison offr to Gen Strafer Gott (Cdr 13 Corps) at Battle of Sidi Rezegh 1941, Italian Campaign 1944, ADC to FM Lord Wilson, Supreme and Allied Cdr Mediterranean; Lloyd's underwriter 1950; memb: British Boxing Bd of Control 1961–82, Nat Playing Fields Assoc 1953–65; pres Wilts Branch NPFA 1950–56; played cricket Sussex 1939, capt Wiltshire 1949–53; *Recreations* cricket, golf, reading biographies and autobiographies of famous men and women; *Clubs* Royal Green Jackets, MCC, I Zingari (sec 1952–92); *Style*— Maj Sir William Wrixon-Becher, Bt, MC; ✉ 13 Montpelier Crescent, Brighton BN1 3JF

WROBEL, Brian John Robert Karen; s of Charles Karen Wrobel, of USA, and Marian, *née* Wiseman; *b* 4 Sept 1949; *Educ* Stowe, Univ of London (LLB, LLM); *Career* called to the Bar Lincoln's Inn 1973, also Gray's Inn and Bars State of California and US Supreme Ct; former memb Ctee of Mgmnt of the Inst of Advanced Legal Studies Univ of London; hon legal advsr to All Party Br Parly Human Rights Gp; participant in human rights fact-finding missions 1975–: Iran (before and after revolution), S Korea, S Africa, USA; memb Br Legal Delgns to Poland, USSR and China; election observer Zimbabwe 1985; govr Br Inst of Human Rights, chm Readers Int (Publishers), conslt on legal colloquia to GB-USSR Assoc; author of various legal papers, reports and articles; *Style*— Brian Wrobel, Esq; ✉ Mitre Court Chambers, 3rd Floor, Temple, London EC4Y 7BP (☎ 0171 353 9394, fax 0171 353 1488)

WRONG, Henry Lewellys Barker; CBE (1986); s of Henry Arkel Wrong, and Jean, *née* Barker; *b* 20 April 1930; *Educ* Trinity Coll Univ of Toronto (BA); *m* 18 Dec 1966, Penelope Hamilton, da of Mark Richard Norman, CBE, of Much Hadham, Herts; 2 s (Mark Henry b 1967, Sebastian Murray b 1971), 1 da (Christina Jocelyn b 1970); *Career* admin Met Opera NY 1952–64; dir: programming Nat Arts Centre Ottawa 1964–68, Festival Canada Centennial Prog 1967, Barbican Centre 1970–90, Euro Arts Fndn 1990–; chm Spencer House (London) 1990–93; memb Advsy Ctee: ADAPT 1988–96, LSO; memb RSA 1988 (fell Arts Ctee), tstee Royal Opera House 1989–95, tstee Royal Fine Arts Cmmn 1995; Liveryman Worshipful Co of Fishmongers 1987; Hon DLitt City Univ 1985; Order of Merit France Offr Class 1985, Hungarian Medal of Culture 1989, Centennial medal Canada 1967; *Clubs* White's, Badminton and Racket (Toronto); *Style*— Henry Wrong, Esq, CBE; ✉ Yew Tree House, Much Hadham, Herts (☎ 01279 842106)

WROTTESLEY, 6 Baron (UK 1838); Sir Clifton Hugh Lancelot de Verdon Wrottesley; 14 Bt (E 1642); s of Hon Richard Wrottesley (d 1970), and Georgina, now Mrs Jonathan Seddon-Brown; suc gf (5 Baron, sixteenth in descent from Sir Walter Wrottesley, a chamberlain of the Exchequer under Edward IV and himself third in descent from Sir Hugh de Wrottesley, KG (one of the original members of the Order), who fought with the Black Prince at Crécy) 1377; *b* 10 Aug 1968; *Educ* Eton, Univ of Edinburgh; *Heir* half unc, Hon Stephen John Wrottesley, *qv*; *Career* patron of three livings; *Clubs* Carlton, Lansdowne, Cavalry and Guards, St Moritz Tobogganing, Skinner's Guild; *Style*— The Rt Hon the Lord Wrottesley; ✉ c/o C Hoare & Co, 32 Lowndes Street, London SW1X 9HZ

WROTTESLEY, Hon Stephen John; s of 5 Baron Wrottesley (d 1977); half-uncle and h of 6 Baron Wrottesley, *qv*; *b* 21 Dec 1955; *Educ* Harrow; *m* 16 Dec 1982, Mrs Rosamund Clare Fletcher, *née* Taylor; 2 da (Alexandra Wynne Marie b 11 May 1985, Stephanie Victoria b 1988); *Style*— The Hon Stephen Wrottesley

WROUGHTON, Dr John Presbury; s of Robert Wystan Wroughton (d 1936), of Swadlincote, Derbyshire, and Kathleen, *née* Harrison; *b* 27 Oct 1934; *Educ* Ashby-de-la-Zouch GS, Hertford Coll Oxford (BA, DipEd, MA), Univ of Bristol (PhD); *Career* asst master Dame Allan's Sch Newcastle upon Tyne 1959–62, asst master Ashby-de-la-Zouch GS 1962–65; King Edward's Sch Bath: head of History Dept 1965–74, second master 1974–82, headmaster 1982–93; pt/t lectr Depts of Continuing Educn Univs of Bristol and Bath; sch master student Pembroke Coll Oxford 1987, visiting fell Fitzwilliam Coll Cambridge 1971; memb: HMC 1982–93, SHA 1982–93; FRHistS 1972; *Books* Cromwell and the Roundheads (1969), Plots, Traitors and Spies (1970), Smuggling (with John Paxton, 1971), Documents on British Political History (1971), Bath in the Age of Reform (1972), The Civil War in Bath and North Somerset (1973), Documents on World History (with Denys Cook, 1976), English Historical Facts 1603–1688 (with Chris Cook, 1980), King Edward's School at Bath 1552–1982 (1982), A Community at War 1642–1650 (1992); gen ed 30 vols of Documents and Debates; contrib to History Today, History Review, Bath History; *Recreations* writing, sport, oil painting, world travel; *Clubs* Bath & County, Bath RFU, Bath Rotary; *Style*— Dr John Wroughton; ✉ 41 The Empire, Grand Parade, Bath BA2 4DF (☎ and fax 01225 420050)

WROUGHTON, Philip Lavallin; *b* 1933; *Educ* Eton; *Career* chm C T Bowring & Co Ltd insurance brokers until 1996 (joined 1961), vice chm Marsh & McLennan Companies 1994–96 (previously chm Marsh & McLennan Inc); memb Cncl Lloyd's of London 1992–95; former High Sheriff Royal County of Berkshire, Lord Lt Royal County of Berkshire 1995–; *Recreations* racing, shooting; *Style*— Philip Wroughton, Esq; ✉ The Bowring Building, Tower Place, London EC3P 3BE (☎ 0171 357 3000, fax 0171 283 0290)

WULSTAN, Prof David; s of Rev Norman B Jones (d 1948), and (Sarah) Margaret, *née* Simpson (d 1973); *b* 18 Jan 1937; *Educ* Royal Masonic Sch, Coll of Tech Birmingham, Magdalen Coll Oxford (BSc, ARCM, MA, BLitt); *m* 9 Oct 1965, Susan Nelson, da of Frank Nelson Graham (d 1963); 1 s (Philip Richard James b 1969); *Career* fell and lectr Magdalen Coll Oxford 1964–78, visiting prof Univ of California Berkeley USA 1978, statutory lectr Univ Coll Cork 1979–80 (prof of music 1980–83), Gregynog prof of music Univ Coll of Wales 1983–92, research prof Univ of Wales Aberystwyth 1992–; dir The Clerkes of Oxenford 1964–; numerous recordings and appearances for TV and radio, appearance at festivals, recordings of incidental music for TV and cinema, composer of church music; *Books* Gibbons Church Music (Early English Church Music) Vol 3 (1964) and vol 27 (1979), Anthology of English Church Music (1968), Play of Daniel (1976), Coverdale Chant Book (1978), Sheppard, Complete Works (1979), Tudor Music (1985), Musical Language (1991), and many other editions, articles and reviews; *Recreations* tennis, badminton, food and drink, bemoaning the loss of the English language; *Style*— Prof David Wulstan; ✉ Ty Isaf, Llanilar, Aberystwyth SY23 4NP (☎ 01970 241229); Music Dept, Univ of Wales Aberystwyth, Cardiganshire SY23 2AX (☎ 01970 622095)

WURTZEL, David Ira; s of late Paul Bernard Wurtzel, of LA, Calif, and Shirley Lorraine, *née* Stein; *b* 28 Jan 1949; *Educ* Univ of California Berkeley (BA), QMC London (MA) Fitzwilliam Coll Cambridge (MA); *Career* called to the Bar 1976; arts corr The

Diplomat 1989–; novelist; author of articles in Town and Country (NY); memb Laurence Olivier Awards Panel; *Books* Thomas Lyster, A Cambridge Novel (1983); *Recreations* theatre, opera, travelling abroad, taking exercise, architecture, conservation; *Style*— David Wurtzel, Esq; ✉ 57 Round Hill Crescent, Brighton, East Sussex BN2 3FQ

WYATT, Arthur Powell; s of Dr Henry George Wyatt (ka 1938), and Edith Maud, *née* Holden (d 1972); *b* 14 Oct 1932; *Educ* Taunton Sch, Eltham Coll, Bart's Med Sch (MB BS); *m* 20 Aug 1955, Margaret Helen, da of Rev W H Cox (d 1988); 4 s (John b 1958, Robert b 1961, David b and d 1964, Andrew b 1966); *Career* lectr in surgery Bart's 1961–63, sr registrar in surgery KCH 1964–67, postgrad res surgn Univ of California San Francisco 1965–66, conslt surgn Greenwich Healthcare Tst 1967–; hon surgical advsr No 2 Hosp Liangshan Sichuan and Municipal People's Hosp Taiyuan China; pres RSM Surgery Section 1989–90, chm Greenwich and Bexley Div BMA 1995–96; memb Ct of Examiners RCS; past pres: W Kent Medico Chirurgical Soc, Eltham Combined Div St John Ambulance; memb: BMA, Vascular Surgery Soc, Br Soc of Gastroenterology, Soc of Minimally Invasive Gen Surgns; fell Assoc of Surgns of GB and I, FRCS, FICS; *Recreations* orchid growing, travel, skiing; *Clubs* Woolwich Rotary, Huntarian Society; *Style*— Arthur Wyatt, Esq; ✉ The Cottage, 72 Camden Park Rd, Chislehurst, Kent BR7 5HF (☎ and fax 0181 467 9477); The Blackheath Hospital, 40–42 Lee Terrace, Blackheath, London SE3 9UD (☎ 0181 318 7722, fax 0181 318 2542); The Queen Elizabeth Hospital, Stadium Road, Woolwich, London SE18 4QH (☎ 0181 856 5533); Greenwich District Hospital, Vanbrugh Hill, London SE10 9EH (☎ 0181 858 8141)

WYATT, David Joseph; CBE (1977); s of Frederick Wyatt (d 1967), and Selina, *née* Parr (d 1990); *b* 12 Aug 1931; *Educ* Leigh GS Lancs; *m* 1, 1957, Annemarie (d 1978), da of Jakob Angst, of Zurich; 2 s (Simon b 1960, Antony b 1961), 1 da (Caroline b 1967); m 2, 1990, Wendy Baron, OBE, da of Dr S B Dimson (d 1991); *Career* Nat Serv RAF 1950–52; HM Foreign then Dip Serv: joined 1949, Berne 1954–57, Vienna 1961–64, Canberra 1965–69, Ottawa 1971–74, Stockholm 1976–79, under sec on loan to Home Civil Serv 1979–82, ambass UK Mission to UN 1982, min and dep commandant Br Military Govt Berlin 1983–85; dir Int Div BRCS 1985–92 (acting dir gen Jan-July 1990), int relations advsr Br Red Cross Soc 1992–, chm Int Advsy Cmmn on Red Cross/Crescent Movement 1995–; *Style*— David Wyatt, Esq, CBE; ✉ c/o British Red Cross Society, 9 Grosvenor Crescent, London SW1X 7EJ (☎ 0171 201 5121, fax 0171 267 2428)

WYATT, Jeremy Gaylord; s of Maj Alan Wyatt (d 1992), of W Sussex, and Pamela, *née* Jermy; *b* 31 Oct 1943; *Educ* Goring Hall, Salisian Coll; *m* 29 Oct 1968, Jenifer Ann Perry, da of Maj John Moore (d 1958); 1 s (Rupert), 1 da (Charlotte); *Career* RA 1962–67, Capt South Arabian Army 1965–67; PR exec ICI Ltd 1969–73, head PR Fisons Ltd 1973–81, dir of communications John Brown plc 1981–83, Main Bd dir and md Corp Div Good Relations Gp Plc 1983–86, dep md Biss Lancaster Plc 1986–91, dir of communications The Prudential Corporation 1991–; *Books* Marketing for Lawyers (1985); *Recreations* garden design, mil history, sailing; *Style*— Jeremy Wyatt, Esq

WYATT, Mark Anthony; s of Anthony John Francis Wyatt, of Brecon, Powys, and Edwina Dawn, *née* Games; *b* 19 Feb 1957; *Educ* Brecon GS, UC Swansea (BSc); *m* 6 Oct 1984, Fiona Mary, da of James McDonald; 3 da (Katherine Leigh b 31 Aug 1988, Hannah Eve b 10 Aug 1990, Megan Rachel b 26 June 1996); *Career* rugby union player (full back); over 300 appearances Swansea RFC 1977–; represented: Swansea Univ 1975–82 (capt 1978–79), Welsh Univs (capt), Br Univs (capt), UAU, Barbarians, Welsh Academicals (capt), Brecon Co; Wales: rep XV v Maoris and Japan, full debut v England 1983, 10 caps; holder of points record in a season Swansea RFC; res UC Swansea; currently dir Gower Business Systems; *Recreations* golf, squash; *Style*— Mark Wyatt, Esq; ✉ Swansea RFC, Bryn Rd, Swansea (☎ 01792 464918)

WYATT, Robert Laurence (Bob); s of Charles Wyatt (d 1987), and Phyliss Muriel, *née* Wheeler; *b* 20 Jan 1943; *Educ* Portsmouth Northern GS; *m* 15 May 1965, Linda Doreen, da of Alan Patrick Mullin; 2 s (James b 1968, David b 1971); *Career* Midland Bank plc: joined Portsmouth branch 1959, seconded to Bank of Bermuda 1967, asst gen mangr 1981, gen mangr 1984, vice chm/chief exec Forward Trust Gp Ltd (lease finance subsid of Midland Bank Gp) 1987, rejoined Midland Bank as gen mangr London Div, chm Forward Trust Group 1992–; vice-chm Finance Houses Assoc 1988; AIB 1964; *Recreations* golf, gardening, ballet; *Style*— Bob Wyatt, Esq; ✉ Midland Bank plc, 27–32 Poultry, London EC2P 2BX

WYATT, (Christopher) Terrel; s of Lionel Harry Wyatt, and Audrey Vere Wyatt; *b* 17 July 1927; *Educ* Kingston GS, Battersea Poly, Imperial College (BSc, DIC); *m* 1 (m dis); 4 s; m 2, 1990, Patricia; *Career* RE 1946–48; Charles Brand & Son Ltd 1948–54; Richard Costain Ltd: joined 1955, dir 1970, gp chief exec 1975–80, dep chm 1979–80; chm Costain Group plc 1980–87, chm W S Atkins Ltd 1987– (chief exec 1987–92), non-exec dir Blue Circle Industries plc 1991–96; FEng 1980, FICE, FIStructE; *Recreations* sailing; *Style*— Terrel Wyatt, Esq, FEng; ✉ The White House, St Martin's Avenue, Epsom, Surrey KT18 5HS; W S Atkins Ltd, Woodcote Grove, Ashley Rd, Epsom, Surrey KT18 5HW (☎ 013727 26140)

WYATT, (Richard) Wesley; s of James Richard Dinham Wyatt (d 1985), of Croford, Wiveliscombe, Somerset, and Elsie, *née* Reed (d 1977); *b* 16 April 1932; *Educ* Taunton Sch; *m* 1; 1 s (Robert Hugh b 1958), 1 da ((Maria) Jayne b 1959); m 2, 22 April 1989, Olive Louisa, da of Fred Parsons (d 1957); *Career* farmer; dir Rural Devpts of Portugal; chm: Farm Advsy Ctee Liscombe Experimental Husbandry Farm 1983–89, Liscombe Research Ltd 1989–90; memb: R & D Ctee Home Grown Cereals Authy 1986–90, Advsy Sectoral Gp (Ruminants) Priorities Bd 1990–93; organist Wiveliscombe Methodist Church 1951–86, chm Taunton Constituency Young Cons 1959–62, vice pres Somerset Young Cons 1962, memb Wiveliscombe Parish Cncl 1970–87, pres Old Tauntonian Assoc 1979, chm Burnham & Berrow GC 1986–88 and 1989–90 (Centenary capt 1990–91); ARAgS; *Recreations* golf, gardening, classical music, rugby, cricket; *Clubs* Burnham & Berrow Golf; *Style*— Wesley Wyatt, Esq; ✉ Tommy Brewers Barn, Fitzhead, Taunton, Somerset TA4 3JZ (☎ 01823 400156, fax 01823 401023)

WYATT, (Alan) Will; s of Basil Wyatt, of Oxford, and Hettie Evelyn, *née* Hooper; *b* 7 Jan 1942; *Educ* Magdalen Coll Sch Oxford, Emmanuel Coll Cambridge (BA); *m* 2 April 1966, Jane Bridgit, da of Beauchamp Bagenal (d 1959), of Kitale, Kenya; 2 da (Hannah b 1967, Rosalind b 1970); *Career* reporter Sheffield Morning Telegraph 1964–65, sub ed BBC Radio News 1965–68; BBC TV: prodr 1968– (programmes include Robinsons Travels, B Traven - A Mystery Solved, Late Night Line Up, The Book Programme), head presentation programmes 1977–80, head documentary features 1981–87, head features and documentaries gp 1987–88, md Network Television 1991–97 (asst md 1988–91), chief exec BBC Broadcast 1996–; dir BBC Enterprises 1991–94; chm Ctee on Violence in TV Programmes BBC 1983 and 1987; tstee Br Video History Tst, dir Broadcasting Audience Research Bd (BARB) 1989–91, govr London Inst 1990, govr Nat Film and Television Sch 1996–; FRTS 1992; *Books* The Man Who Was B Traven (1980); *Recreations* walking, horse racing, theatre; *Style*— Will Wyatt, Esq; ✉ BBC Television Centre, London W12 7RJ (☎ 0181 743 8000)

WYATT OF WEEFORD, Baron (Life Peer UK 1987), of Weeford, Co Staffs; Sir Woodrow Lyle; kt (1983); s of Robert Harvey Lyle Wyatt (d 1932), and Ethel, *née* Morgan (d 1974); descended from Humphrey Wyatt (1540–1610), the ancestor of the Wyatt architects, painters, sculptors and inventors; *b* 4 July 1918; *Educ* Eastbourne Coll, Worcester Coll Oxford (MA); *m* 1, 1939 (m dis 1944), Susan Cox; m 2, 1948 (m dis 1956), Nora Robbins; m 3, 1957 (m dis 1966), Lady Moorea Hastings (now Black), da of 15 Earl of Huntingdon by his 1 w, Cristina; 1 s (Pericles); m 4, 1966, Verushka, *née* Racz, widow of Baron Dr Lazlo Banszky von Ambroz; 1 da (Petronella); *Career* Maj WWII (despatches); journalist; MP (Lab): Aston 1945–55, Bosworth 1959–70; Parly under sec of state and fin sec War Office 1951; chm Horserace Totalisator Bd 1976–1997; *Books* incl: The Jews at Home (1950), Turn Again Westminster (1973), What's Left of the Labour Party, The Exploits of Mr Saucy Squirrel (1976), The Further Exploits of Mr Saucy Squirrel, To the Point (1981), Confessions of an Optimist (1985), High Profiles (play, 1992), Into the Dangerous World; *Style*— The Rt Hon the Lord Wyatt of Weeford; ✉ 19 Cavendish Ave, London NW8 9JD

WYBREW, John; *b* 28 Oct 1941; *Educ* Queens' Coll Cambridge (MA); *m*; 3 da; *Career* Royal Dutch Shell Group 1964–96: various positions London and The Netherlands 1964–74, head of special projects Shell UK Exploration and Production 1974–77, southern ops mangr 1977–80, tech dir and dep md Brunei Shell Petroleum Co Ltd 1980–82, head of supply devpt Supply Oil Co-ordination Div Shell International Petroleum Co Ltd 1982–83, head of economic and sector planning for exploration and prodn Shell International Petroleum Maatschappij The Hague 1983, seconded as advsr on energy and tport policies PM's Policy Unit 1984–88, exec dir Mgmnt Charter Initiative Working Pty 1987, bd dir Shell UK 1989–96 (planning and public affrs dir 1989–95, corp affrs dir 1995–96); exec dir (i/c strategic planning, corp affrs, health safety & environment and gp info servs) British Gas plc 1996–; memb: Europe Ctee CBI, Cncl Indust and Parl Tst, Bd Corporate Responsibility Gp; offr Parly Gp for Energy Studies; *Recreations* theatre, tennis, golf; *Style*— John Wybrew, Esq; ✉ British Gas plc, The Adelphi, John Adam Street, London WC2N 6HT (☎ 0171 269 4874, fax 0171 269 4933)

WYBREW, John Leonard; s of Leonard Percival Wybrew, of Radlett, Herts, and May Edith Wybrew; *b* 27 Jan 1943; *Educ* Bushey GS, Sir John Cass Coll; *m* 1967 (m dis 1990), Linda Gillian, da of Wing Cdr John James Frederick Long, of Goddards Lane, Camberley; 1 s, 2 da; *Career* life mangr and actuary Time Assur Soc 1971-72, gen mangr and dir: Windsor Life Assur Co Ltd 1972–76 (md 1976–, chm 1988–90 and 1992–), World-Wide Assur Co Ltd 1972–76 (dir 1982–); pres and chief exec offr Br-American Life Assur Co Pte Singapore 1990–92, md Windsor Gp Ltd; chm: Windsor Investmnt Mgmnt 1986–90, Windsor Tst Mangrs 1986–90; memb ctee of mgmnt Family Assurance Soc 1987–90; Liveryman Worshipful Co of Actuaries; *Recreations* horses, sailing, reading, golf; *Clubs* Tanglin, Oriental, Annabel's; *Style*— John Wybrew Esq; ✉ Gosland Green, Bunbury, Cheshire CW6 9PY (☎ 01829 260220); Windsor Group Ltd, Windsor House, Telford Centre, Salop TF3 4NB (☎ 01952 292929, telex 849780)

WYFOLD, 3 Baron (UK 1919); Sir Hermon Robert Fleming Hermon-Hodge; 3 Bt (UK 1902); s of 2 Baron Wyfold, DSO, MVO (d 1942), and Dorothy, da of Robert Fleming and aunt of Peter Fleming, the travel writer, and Ian Fleming, the creator of James Bond; *b* 26 June 1915; *Educ* Eton, Le Rosey Switzerland; *Heir* none; *Career* Capt Grenadier Gds (reserve); dir Robert Fleming Holding & other cos; ret; *Recreations* gardening; *Clubs* Carlton, Pratt's, Metropolitan (New York); *Style*— The Rt Hon the Lord Wyfold; ✉ c/o Robert Fleming Holdings, 25 Copthall Avenue, London EC2R 7DR (☎ 0171 638 5858)

WYKE, Prof John Anthony; s of Eric John Edward Wyke (d 1979), and Daisy Anne, *née* Dormer; *b* 5 April 1942; *Educ* Dulwich Coll, St John's Coll Cambridge (scholar, MA, VetMB, coll prizes), Univ of London (PhD); *m* 1968, Anne Wynne, da of John Mitchell; 1 s (Robert Andrew b 1977); *Career* postdoctoral res Univ of Washington and Univ of Southern California 1970–72, head Tumour Virology Lab Imperial Cancer Res Fund (ICRF) Laboratories 1976–83 (scientific staff 1972–76), head ICRF Laboratories Bart's 1983–87 (asst dir 1985), dir Beatson Inst for Cancer Res 1987–; hon prof Univ of Glasgow 1991–96; fell Leukemia Soc of America 1970–72; MRCVS 1967, FRSE 1989; *Recreations* hill walking, ski touring, gardening; *Style*— Prof John Wyke, FRSE; ✉ Beatson Institute for Cancer Research, Garscube Estate, Switchback Road, Bearsden, Glasgow G61 1BD (☎ 0141 942 9361, fax 0141 943 0372)

WYKES-JOYCE, Max Stephen Holmes; s of Frederick Bicknell, MM (d 1965), of Marston Green, Warwicks, and May Elizabeth, *née* Ballard (d 1990); *b* 26 Dec 1924; *Educ* Prince Henry's GS Evesham, LSE, Anglo-French Art Centre London, Goldsmiths' Coll Sch of Art London; *m* 30 Oct 1947 (m dis 1967), Liza Margaret, da of Walter Langley-Kemp (d 1972), of Perth, W Aust; 1 da (Sianna b 1949); *Career* WWII, RAF 1943–47; London art critic Int Herald Tribune 1967–87, fine arts corr Antique Dealer and Collectors Guide 1967–, saleroom corr Arts Review 1986–92; contrib to: The Collector, Galleries magazine, The Independent and many other newspapers and periodicals; Accademico d'Italia con Medaglia d'Oro 1980; hon life memb Int Assoc of Art Critics 1996; *Books* Triad of Genius - Edith and Osbert Sitwell (1953), 7000 Years of Pottery and Porcelain (1958), Cosmetics and Adornment - Ancient and Contemporary Usage (1961), Les Instants Immobiles - The Work of Bouvier de Cachard (1973), Seven Archangels - The Art of Marian Bohusz-Szyszko (1977), My Heart has Opened unto Every Form - The Art of Basil Alkazzi (1982), A New Season... (1993), Charlotte Kell - Collages, Art Boxes and Sculptures (1995); *Recreations* fencing, gardening, walking, cat watching; *Style*— Max Wykes-Joyce, Esq; ✉ 8 Elm Road, Evesham, Worcestershire WR11 5DL (☎ 01386 40214)

WYLD, David John Charles; s of John Hugh Gilbert Wyld, TD, and Helen Selina, *née* Leslie Melville (d 1946); *b* 11 March 1943; *Educ* Harrow, ChCh Oxford (MA); *m* 1, 19 Dec 1970 (m dis), Sally, da of Ellis Morgan, CMG, of Penhenllan, Cusop, Hay on Waye, Herefordshire; 2 s (Barnaby b 1972, Jonathan b 1973); m 2, 20 June 1987, Caroline Mary, da of Walter Ronald Alexander, CBE, of Moonzie Mill, Balmullo, St Andrews, Fife; 3 da (Charlotte b 1988, Alexandra b 1989, Rachel b 1991); *Career* called to the Bar 1968, admitted slr 1974; practising slr Linklaters & Paines 1974–79, ptnr Macfarlanes 1981–; sec gen Int Law Assoc 1993–, pres London Slrs' Litigation Assoc 1992–94; memb Law Soc 1974; *Recreations* reading, walking, golf; *Clubs* Hon Co of Edinburgh Golfers, MCC, Berkshire Golf, Liphook Golf; *Style*— David Wyld, Esq; ✉ Macfarlanes, 10 Norwich St, London EC4A 1BD (☎ 0171 831 9222, fax 0171 831 9607, telex 296381 MACFAR G)

WYLDBORE-SMITH, Maj-Gen Sir (Francis) Brian; kt (1980), CB (1964), DSO (1943), OBE (1944); yr s of Rev William Reginald Wyldbore-Smith (d 1943, sometime domestic chaplain to the Marquess of Londonderry and ggs of Sir John Wyldbore Smith, 2 Bt); *b* 10 July 1913; *Educ* Wellington, RMA Woolwich; *m* 1944, Hon Molly Angela Cayzer, yr da of 1 Baron Rotherwick; 1 s, 4 da; *Career* GOC 44 Div (TA) and Home Counties dist 1965–68, Maj-Gen ME, Far E, France, Italy, Germany, Col 15/19 Hussars 1970–77, dep constable Dover Castle 1965–68, ret 1968; dir Cons Bd of Fin 1970–92, appeals dir Margaret Thatcher Fndn 1992–; *Recreations* shooting; *Clubs* Buck's, Naval and Military; *Style*— Maj-Gen Sir Brian Wyldbore-Smith, CB, DSO, OBE; ✉ Grantham House, Grantham, Lincs (☎ 01476 564705)

WYLDBORE-SMITH, William Francis; s of John Henry Wyldbore-Smith (d 1982), of Scaynes Hill, Sussex, and Tighnabruaich, Argyll, and Robina, *née* Ward (d 1993); *b* 15 Jan 1948; *Educ* Marlborough; *m* 27 Dec 1974, Prisca Faith, da of Rev Peter Nourse (d 1992), of Leominster, Herefordshire; 1 da (Philippa b 15 April 1977); *Career* admitted slr 1972; ptnr: Osborne Clarke 1977–85, Wood Awdry Wansbroughs (formerly Wood & Awdry) 1986– (managing ptnr 1990–95); chm: N Wilts Business Assoc 1985–88, N Wilts Enterprise Agency 1986–93, Wilts Rural Enterprise Agency 1989–92; non-exec dir Great Western Enterprise 1993–94, non-exec memb Wiltshire and Bath Health Authy 1994–; Under Sheriff of Wilts 1987–; Freeman City of London, Liveryman Worshipful Company of Musicians; memb Law Soc; *Recreations* gardening, shooting, reading; *Clubs* Brooks's;

Style— W F Wyldbore-Smith, Esq; ✉ Bremhill Manor, Calne, Wilts SN11 9LA (☎ 01249 814969); Wood Awdry Wansbroughs, 3 St Mary Street, Chippenham, Wilts SN15 3JE (☎ 01249 444422, fax 01249 443666)

WYLES, Andrew Tobias Michael (Toby); s of Michael Ronald Vincent Wyles, and Patricia Mary, *née* Davies; *b* 16 Nov 1960; *Educ* Solihull Sch, Jesus Coll Cambridge (capt boat club, BA, titular exhibitioner), Harvard Graduate Sch of Business Admin (MBA); *Career* asst fund mangr Hoare Govett Ltd London 1983–84, assoc conslt corp strategy consltg The LEK Partnership London and Boston Mass 1984–87, MBA Harvard 1987–89, summer assoc Leverage Capital Gp Citibank NA London 1988, M&A assoc Morgan Stanley International London 1989–90, dir venture capital (i/c N of England) Apax Partners & Co London and Leeds 1990–; conslt V&A Museum 1989; *Recreations* rowing, cooking, the arts; *Clubs* Cambridge in the City, Harvard Business Sch of London, Harvard (London); *Style—* Toby Wyles, Esq; ✉ Apax Partners & Co, 15 Portland Place, London W1N 3AA (☎ 0171 872 6300)

WYLIE, Alexander Featherstonhaugh; QC (Scot 1991); s of Ian Hamilton Wylie (d 1991), and Helen Jane, *née* Mearns (d 1993); *b* 2 June 1951; *Educ* Univ of Edinburgh (LLB Hons); *m* 12 July 1975, Gail Elizabeth Watson, da of Winifred and William Duncan; 2 da (Claire Elizabeth b 4 Aug 1981, Nicola Jane b 1 April 1985); *Career* admitted slr Scotland 1976, admitted Faculty of Advocates 1978, in practice 1978–, standing jr counsel to Accountant of Ct 1986, advocate depute 1989–92, called to the English Bar Lincoln's Inn 1990; jt chm Discipline Ctee ICAS 1994–, pt/t memb Scottish Legal Aid Bd 1994–; FCIArb 1991 (ACIArb 1977); *Style—* Alexander Wylie, Esq, QC; ✉ c/o Advocates' Library, Parliament House, Edinburgh EH1 1RF (☎ 0131 226 2881 (Clerk))

WYLIE, Prof John Cleland Watson; s of George Stewart Wylie (d 1966), of Belfast, and Phyllis Ann, *née* Watson; *b* 6 July 1943; *Educ* Methodist Coll Belfast, Queen's Univ Belfast (LLB, LLD), Harvard (LLM); *m* 22 Sept 1973, Gillian Lindsey, da of Eric Sidney Edward Gardner, of London; 1 s (Nicholas George b 1977), 1 da (Emma Louise b 1979); *Career* lectr in law Queen's Univ Belfast 1965–71, Frank Knox fell Harvard 1966–67; Univ of Wales Coll of Cardiff: sr lectr 1972–76, reader 1976–79, prof of law 1979–, dean faculty of law 1980–83, dep princ 1990–93, head Cardiff Law Sch 1991–96; ed: N Ireland Legal Quarterly 1970–76; editorial dir: Professional Books Ltd 1981–87, Butterworth (Ireland) Ltd 1987–; land law conslt: Trinidad and Tobago Govt 1978–83, N Ireland Office 1980–90; memb Legal Studies Bd CNAA 1984–87, pres SPTL 1994–95, chm Ctee of Heads of Univ Law Schs 1993–94; *Books* Irish Land Law (2 edn, 1986), Land Laws of Trinidad and Tobago (1986), Irish Landlord and Tenant Law (1990), Irish Conveyancing Statutes (1994), Irish Conveyancing Law (2nd ed 1996); *Recreations* reading, swimming, gardening; *Style—* Prof John Wylie; ✉ Cardiff Law School, University of Wales College of Cardiff, PO Box 427, Cardiff CF1 1XD (☎ 01222 874177, fax 01222 874097)

WYLIE, Rt Hon Lord; Norman Russell Wylie; VRD (1961), PC (1970), QC (1964); s of late William Wylie; *b* 26 Oct 1923; *Educ* Paisley GS, St Edmund Hall Oxford, Univ of Glasgow, Univ of Edinburgh; *m* 1963, Gillian, da of late Dr Richard Verney, of Edinburgh; 3 s (Julian b 1964, Russell b 1966, Philip b 1968); *Career* Lt Cdr RNR, served Fleet Air Arm and Russian and Atlantic Convoys; advocate 1952, standing counsel to Air Miny Scotland 1956–59, crown counsel 1959–64, slr-gen Scotland 1964 (April-Oct), MP (C) Edinburgh Pentlands 1964–74, lord advocate 1970–74, Scottish Lord of Session (senator of the Coll of Justice) 1974–90, justice of appeal Republic of Botswana 1994–; hon fell St Edmund Hall 1975–; *Recreations* sailing (yacht 'Niarana'), shooting; *Clubs* New (Edinburgh), Royal Highland Yacht, RNSA; *Style—* The Rt Hon Lord Wylie, VRD, PC; ✉ 30 Lauder Rd, Edinburgh EH9 (☎ and fax 0131 667 8377)

WYLIE, Dr Ronald James; OBE (1984); s of James Baird Wylie (d 1977), of Edinburgh, and Christina, *née* Mathieson (d 1977); *b* 31 Aug 1930; *Educ* Melville Coll, Univ of Edinburgh (CA, JDipMA); *m* 17 Sept 1955, Brenda Margaret, da of George Paterson Wright (d 1952), of Leeds; 2 s (Roderick b 1957, Stuart b 1960); *Career* Tullis Russell Co Ltd: md 1973–81, chief exec 1981–85; chief exec Young Enterprise Scotland 1986–94, ret; Hon DBA Univ of Strathclyde 1995; *Recreations* sailing, photography, music; *Clubs* Burntisland Sailing; *Style—* Dr Ronald J Wylie, OBE; ✉ Treetops, 123 Dysart Road, Kirkcaldy KY1 2BB (☎ 01592 651597)

WYLLIE, Douglas Stewart; s of (Matthew) Stewart Wyllie, of Edinburgh, and Rowena Margaret Wyllie; *b* 20 May 1963; *Educ* Dulwich, Daniel Stewart's and Melville Coll Edinburgh; *Career* rugby union fly-half/centre; formerly played soccer for England Under 13 schoolboys; clubs: Stewart's Melville FP RFC (over 600 appearances) 1981–96, Boroughmuir 1996–; Barbarians RFC (8 appearances); capt and memb Scotland under 21, Scotland B (3 caps); Scotland: 18 full caps, debut v Australia 1984, Five Nations debut v Wales 1985, tour Romania 1984, tour France and Spain 1986, tour USA and Canada 1985, tour NZ 1987 and 1990, tour Zimbabwe 1988, tour Japan 1989, capt tour USA and Canada 1991, memb World Cup squad 1991, tour Western Samoa, Tonga and Fiji 1993; winner Middx sevens 1982; bank offr Bank of Scotland 1981–88, sales exec Equity & Law Assurance Co 1988–89, sales exec Bukta Sportswear 1989–92, sales rep Nike (UK) Ltd 1992–93, sales rep Russell Athletic 1993–96, sales exec Whyte & Mackay 1996–; *Recreations* all sports; *Style—* Douglas Wyllie, Esq; ✉ Scottish Rugby Union, Murrayfield, Edinburgh EH12 5PJ

WYLLIE, Dr George Ralston; s of Andrew Wyllie (d 1965), and Harriet Mills Wyllie (d 1979); *b* 31 Dec 1921; *Educ* Allan Glen's Sch Glasgow, Bellahouston Acad Glasgow; *m* 16 Sept 1944, Daphne Winifred, da of William Herbert Watts, BEM (d 1965); 2 da (Louise b 28 July 1950, Elaine b 7 May 1954); *Career* sculptor, writer and performer; electrical engr (petty offr) RN 1942–46, served HMS Argonaut; Civil Serv: Post Office 1938–42 and 1946–47, Customs & Excise 1948–80; Exhibitions in UK, USA and Europe; exhibited and performed Glasgow Edinburgh and London 1982– (incl Edinburgh Festival 1994); sculpture events: Straw Locomotive Glasgow 1987, Paper Boat Gulbenkein award event 1989; works included and installed in: Glasgow Cathedral, Glasgow Kelvingrove Museum, World HQ GA Insurance Perth, Atrium and UFA-Fabrik Berlin, Getty Fndn Fluxus Archives, Arts Cncls of Scotland and England, Worcester Museum Mass USA, Whitworth Art Gallery Manchester; film: The Why's Man; play: A Day Down A Goldmine (1982); fell Hand Hollow Fndn E Chatham NY 1982–83; Hon DLitt Univ of Strathclyde; ARSA; *Clubs* Royal Gourock YC; *Style—* Dr George Wyllie; ✉ 9 McPherson Drive, Gourock, Renfrewshire PA19 1LJ (☎ and fax 01475 632810)

WYLLIE, Gordon Malcolm; WS (1982); s of Thomas Smith Wyllie, of Dallas House, Troon, and Margaret Hutton Gordon Malcolm; *b* 20 July 1951; *Educ* Dunoon GS, Univ of Glasgow (LLB); *Career* law apprentice McGrigor Donald Glasgow 1972–74, head Executry Dept Strathern & Blair WS Edinburgh 1974–77, ptnr Biggart Baillie & Gifford 1980– (sr law asst 1977–80); clerk: Grand Antiquity of Glasgow 1984–, Trades House of Glasgow and sister bodies 1987–, Gen Cmmrs of Income Tax Glasgow North 1990– (depute 1983) and Glasgow South 1992–; dir: Bailford Trustees Ltd, Grand Antiquity Soc of Glasgow; sec Trades Hall of Glasgow Building Preservation Tst; deacon Incorporation of Hammermen of Edinburgh, memb Incorporations of Tailors and Bonnetmakers and Dyers of Glasgow and Hammermen of Irvine; memb: Soc of Tst and Estate Practitioners, Soc of Antiquaries of Scotland, Soc for Promotion of Hellenic Studies, Int Bar Assoc, Action Research, Edinburgh West End Community Cncl, St Andrew's Soc of Glasgow; *Recreations* history, music and the arts generally, architecture and design, country dancing, country walks; *Clubs* Scottish Arts (Edinburgh), Western (Glasgow); *Style—* Gordon M Wyllie, Esq, WS; ✉ Biggart Baillie & Gifford and The Trades House of Glasgow, 310 St Vincent Street, Glasgow G2 5QR (☎ 0141 228 8000, fax 0141 228 8310)

WYMAN, Peter Lewis; s of late John Bernard Wyman, MBE, of Sharpthorne, Sussex, and Joan Dorethea, *née* Beighton; *b* 26 Feb 1950; *Educ* Epsom Coll; *m* 16 Sept 1978, Joy Alison, da of Edward George Foster, of Horsted Keynes, Sussex; 1 s (John b 1985), 1 da (Gemma b 1988); *Career* chartered accountant; articled clerk Ogden Parsons & Co and Harmood Banner 1968–73; Coopers & Lybrand (formerly Deloitte Haskins & Sells): mangr 1974–78, ptnr 1978–, head of tax 1993–; memb Ctee London Soc of CAs 1981–90 (chm 1987–88); ICAEW: memb Cncl 1991–, chm Faculty of Taxation 1991–95, chm Educn and Training Directorate 1995–, memb Exec Ctee 1996–; special advsr on deregulation and taxation to Parly Under Sec of State for Corp Affairs (Neil Hamilton, MP) 1993–94, memb Deregulation Task Force 1994–, external overseer Contribs Agency/Inland Revenue Jt Working Prog 1995–; Freeman: Worshipful Co of CAs 1988, City of London 1988; FCA 1978 (ACA 1973), FIMgt 1978, FRSA 1993; *Recreations* twentieth century history, equestrian sports, gardening; *Style—* Peter L Wyman, Esq; ✉ Reapyears Corner, Streeters Rough, Chelwood Gate, W Sussex RH17 7LL (☎ 01825 740243); Coopers & Lybrand, 1 Embankment Place, London WC2N 6NN (☎ 0171 213 4777, fax 0171 213 2415, car 0374 259723)

WYMER, Dr John James; s of Bertram Osborne Wymer (d 1959), and Leah, *née* Vidal (d 1981); *b* 5 March 1928; *Educ* Richmond and East Sheen Co Sch, Shoreditch Training Coll; *m* 1, 1948 (m dis 1972), Pauline, da of E G May; 3 da (Miranda, Tessa and Lucille), 2 s (Leigh Daniel and Charles Bertram); m 2, 1976, Eunice Mollie, da of Alfred Spurling; 1 step s (Michael); *Career* archaeologist Reading Museum 1956–65, research assoc Univ of Chicago 1965–78, research assoc Univ of East Anglia 1979–80, field offr Essex Archaeological Unit 1981–82, field offr Norfolk Archaeological Unit 1983–90, dir Southern Rivers Palaeolithic Survey for English Heritage 1992–94, dir English Rivers Palaeolithic Survey for English Heritage 1995–97; sometime lectr Workers Educational Assoc; pres Quaternary Research Assoc 1975–77; vice-pres: Suffolk Inst of Archaeology and History 1985–, Prehistoric Soc 1991–93, Norfolk and Norwich Archaeological Soc 1994– (pres 1990–93), Berkshire Archaeological Soc 1995–; chm Cncl for Br Archaeology of East Anglia 1990–95; memb Inst of Field Archaeologists 1992; Stopes Meml Medal 1972; Hon MA Univ of Durham 1969, Hon DSc Univ of Reading 1995; FSA 1963, FBA 1996; *Books* Lower Palaeolithic Archaeology in Britain (1968), Gazetteer of Mesolithic Sites (1977), The Palaeolithic Age (1982), The Middle Stone Age Site at Klasies River Mouth in South Africa (with R Singer, 1982), The Palaeolithic Sites of East Anglia (1985), The Lower Palaeolithic Site at Hoxe, England (with Singer and Gladfelter, 1993); also author of numerous papers and reports in archaeological and geological jls; *Recreations* travelling, reading, gardening, carpentry; *Style—* Dr John Wymer, FBA; ✉ The Vines, The Street, Great Cressingham, Thetford, Norfolk IP25 6NL

WYN-ROGERS, Catherine; da of Geoffrey Wyn Rogers, and Helena, *née* Webster; *b* 24 July 1954; *Educ* St Helena HS for Girls Chesterfield, RCM (fndn scholar, ARCM, Dame Clara Butt Award); *Career* mezzo-soprano; studied with Meriel St Clair, Ellis Keeler, Diane Forlano; concerts with: Bach Choir, Royal Choral Soc, Huddersfield Choral Soc, RPO, English Chamber Orch, Bournemouth Symphony Orch, Royal Liverpool Philharmonic Orch, Philharmonia, City of Birmingham Symphony Orchs, Three Choirs Festival, Aldeburgh Festival, The Sixteen, English Concert, Acad of Ancient Music; opera cos appeared with: Scottish Opera, Welsh Nat Opera, Opera North, ENO; Royal Opera House roles incl: Mrs Sedley in Peter Grimes, First Norn and Erda in Wagner's Ring Cycle, Sosostris in The Midsummer Marriage; also worked with: Bernard Haitink, Andrew Davis, Sir Charles Mackerras, Richard Hickox, Mark Elder, Roger Norrington; soloist Last Night of the Proms 1995; pres Derby Bach Choir 1995, patron Amadeus Choir of Toronto; *Recordings* Haydn's Harmoniemesse (with Winchester Cathedral Choir under David Hill), John Gay's Beggar's Opera, Teixeira's Te Deum and Bach's Christmas Oratorio (with The Sixteen and Orch for Collins Classics), Mozart's Vespers (with Trevor Pinnock), Vaughan Williams' Serenade to Music (with Roger Norrington), Elgar's The Dream of Gerontius (EMI), Graham Johnson's Complete Schubert Edition (Hyperion); *Recreations* drawing, painting; *Style—* Ms Catherine Wyn-Rogers; ✉ c/o Lies Askonas Ltd, 6 Henrietta Street, London WC2E 8LA (☎ 0171 379 7700, fax 0171 242 1831)

WYNDHAM, Henry Mark; s of Hon Mark Wyndham, OBE, MC, and Anne, *née* Winn; *b* 19 Aug 1953; *Educ* Eton, Sorbonne; *m* 21 Dec 1978, Rachel Sarah, da of Lt-Col Leslie Francis Gordon Pritchard, MBE, TD (d 1977), of Wadhurst, E Sussex; 3 s (Ned b 1983, Leo b 1985, William b 1988); *Career* Christies International 1974–87 (dir 1983–87), fndr Henry Wyndham Fine Art 1987, chm Sotheby's UK 1994–; expert BBC Antiques Road Show 1987–94, govr Thomas Coram Fndn, fell Rupert Morgan Library NY; memb Patrons of British Art Tate Gallery (memb Ctee 1993–); Freeman Worshipful Co of Goldsmiths; *Recreations* cricket, soccer, golf, tennis, travelling, shooting and fishing, looking at pictures; *Clubs* White's, MCC (memb Ctee 1994–), Pratt's; *Style—* Henry Wyndham, Esq; ✉ The Old Rectory, Southease, Lewes, E Sussex BN7 3HX; Sotheby's UK, 34 New Bond Street, London W1 (☎ 0171 493 8080)

WYNESS, James Alexander Davidson; s of Dr James Alexander Davidson Wyness (d 1984), of Dyce, Aberdeen, and Millicent Margaret, *née* Beaton (d 1996); *b* 27 Aug 1937; *Educ* Stockport GS, Emmanuel Coll Cambridge (MA, LLB); *m* 18 June 1966, Josephine Margaret, da of Lt-Col Edward Stow Willard Worsdell, MBE, TD, of Eynsford, Kent; 3 da (Rachel b 28 July 1968, Emily b 3 Feb 1971, Jeannie b 27 Aug 1974); *Career* Nat Serv 2 Lt RA; slr; articled clerk AF & RW Tweedie 1964–66; Linklaters & Paines 1966–: ptnr 1970–, managing ptnr 1987–91, jt sr ptnr 1991–93, sr ptnr 1994–96; non-exec dir Bowthorpe plc 1979–; pres Saracens FC RFU 1993–96, non-exec chm Saracens PLC 1996–; memb Worshipful Co of City of London Slrs; memb Law Soc; *Recreations* visiting France, growing vegetables, rugby football (captain Saracens FC RFU 1962–65, Middx RFU and London RFU), reading; *Style—* James Wyness, Esq; ✉ Linklaters & Paines, Barrington House, 59–67 Gresham St, London EC2V 7JA (☎ 0171 606 7080, fax 0171 606 5113)

WYNFORD, 8 Baron (UK 1829); Robert Samuel Best; MBE (Mil 1952), DL (Dorset 1970); s of 7 Baron Wynford (d 1942), and Evelyn (d 1929), da of Maj-Gen Sir Edward Sinclair May, KCB, CMG; *b* 5 Jan 1917; *Educ* Eton, Sandhurst; *m* 1941, Anne, da of Maj-Gen John Minshull-Ford, CB, DSO, MC (d 1948); 1 s, 2 da; *Heir* s, Hon John Best, *qv*; *Career* Army offr; landowner and farmer, formerly Instructor Jt Serv Staff Coll 1957–60; Croix de Guerre; *Recreations* field sports, walking; *Clubs* Army and Navy; *Style—* The Rt Hon the Lord Wynford, MBE, DL; ☎ 01300 320241

WYNN, Cdr Andrew Guy; LVO (1984); yr s of Lt Cdr Hon Charles Wynn, RN, and Hon Hermione Willoughby, da of 11 Baron Middleton; *b* 26 Nov 1950; *Educ* Eton, Gonville and Caius Coll Cambridge (MA); *m* 1, 1978 (m dis 1987), Susanjane, da of Selwyn Willis Fraser-Smith, CBE, MC, of Crowborough; 1 s (Alexander Charles Guy b 1980); m 2, 1988, Shelagh Jean MacSorley, yr da of Prof I K M Smith, of Welwyn Garden City; *Career* Lt Cdr RN, Equerry to HRH The Duke of Edinburgh 1982–84, Dep Supply Offr HMS Ark Royal 1984–86, Cdr RN, Offr Policy Section 1987–88; sch bursar Eton Coll 1988–, chm Schs and Univs Polo Assoc 1996– (sec 1991–96); *Style—* Cdr Andrew Wynn, LVO; ✉ Eton College, Windsor SL4 6DB

WYNN, Hon Robert Vaughan; s and h of 7 Baron Newborough, DSC, *qv*, of Rhug, Corwen, N Wales, by his 1 w, Rosamund, da of late Maj Robert Barbour, of Bolesworth Castle, Tattenhall, Cheshire; *b* 11 Aug 1949; *Educ* Milton Abbey; *m* 1, 1981, Mrs Sheila Christine Wilson, da of William A Massey; 1 da (Lucinda Rosamond b 1982); m 2, 16

April 1988, Mrs Susan E Hall, da of late Andrew Lloyd, of Malta; *Career* landowner and farmer; dir Peplow Training and Recruitment Services Ltd; *Recreations* skiing, sailing; *Clubs* Royal Thames Yacht; *Style*— The Hon Robert Wynn; ✉ Peplow Hall, Peplow, Market Drayton, Shropshire TF9 3JP (☎ 01952 78230, fax 01952 78403)

WYNN, Terence; MEP (Lab) Merseyside East and Wigan (majority 74,087); s of Ernest Wynn (d 1979), and Lily, *née* Hitchen (d 1976); *b* 27 June 1946; *Educ* Leigh Tech Coll, Riversdale Marine Coll, Univ of Salford (MSc); *m* 7 March 1967, Doris, da of Ernest Ogden (d 1971); 1 s (David Mark b 4 March 1968), 1 da (Terry Joanne b 20 Nov 1970); *Career* trg exec MTA 1985–89; councillor Wigan Met Borough Cncl 1979–90; MEP (Lab): Merseyside E 1989–94, Merseyside E and Wigan 1994–; *Recreations* reading, theatre, swimming, music, rugby league; *Style*— Terence Wynn, Esq, MEP; ✉ European Office, 105 Corporation St, St Helens, Merseyside WA10 1SX (☎ 01744 451609, fax 01744 29832)

WYNN, Terence Bryan; s of Bernard Wynn (d 1971), of Newcastle upon Tyne, and Elsie, *née* Manges; *b* 20 Nov 1928; *Educ* St Cuthbert's GS Newcastle upon Tyne; *Career* jr reporter Hexham Courant 1945–47; reporter: Blyth News 1947–48, Shields Evening News 1948–50, Sunderland Echo 1950–53, Daily Sketch 1953–58; head of news and current affrs Tyne Tees TV 1958–66, editorial planning BBC TV News 1966–67; sr press offr: The Land Cmmn 1967–71, HM Customs and Excise 1971–72; ed: The Universe 1972–77, Lib News Lib Pty Orgn 1977–83; press offr Central Office of Info 1983–85, ed Your Court Lord Chllr's Dept 1985–88, dir More Publicity 1989–, ed Brentwood News 1990–; author Walsingham (a modern mystery play prod at Walsingham and in Westminster Cathedral) 1975; hon vice pres Catholic Writers' Guild 1970– (chm 1967–70); MIPR 1971; *Recreations* reading, writing, talking; *Clubs* Press, Nat Lib; *Style*— Terence Wynn, Esq; ✉ Bosco Villa, 30 Queens Road, South Benfleet, Essex SS7 1JW (☎ 01268 792033)

WYNN PARRY, Dr Christopher Berkeley (Kit); MBE (1954); s of Hon Mr Justice (Sir Henry) Wynn Parry, KBE (d 1962), of Harpenden, Herts, and Hon Shelagh Berkeley, *née* Moynihan (d 1975), da of 1 Baron Moynihan; *b* 14 Oct 1924; *Educ* Eton, Univ of Oxford (DM, MA); *m* 25 July 1953, Lamorna Cathleen, da of Albert George W Sawyer (d 1970), of Clavering, Essex; 1 s (Simon b 1961), 3 da (Charlotte b 1954, Sarah b 1957, Jane b 1959); *Career* RAF 1948–75, Gp Capt Med Branch, conslt advsr in rheumatology and rehabilitation, dir of rehabilitation Jt Servs Med Rehabilitation Units RAF Chessington and RAF Headley Court; dir of rehabilitation Royal Nat Orthopaedic Hosps 1975, hon conslt in applied electrophysiology Nat Hosp for Nervous Diseases Queen Square 1975, civil conslt in rheumatology and rehabilitation RAF 1975, chm Disability Ctee RCP London 1978–88, past dir of rehabilitation King Edward VII Hosp Midhurst Sussex; winner William Hyde award for sport and med; author of articles on: rehabilitation, rheumatology, orthopaedics, pain, peripheral nerve injuries, resettlement, backpain, organisation of servs; author of chapters in 22 books; fndr and first pres Int Rehabilitation Med Assoc, sec Int Fedn of Physical Med, past pres Physical Med Section and Kovacs Prizeman RSM, Stanford Cade medallist RAF Med Branch, advsr in rehabilitation to Chief Med Offr 1979–86, member Mac Coll Working Pty into Artificial Limb and Appliance Serv 1986–88, pres Br Soc for Surgery of the Hand; Br Cncl visiting lectr and scholar to: Russia, Hungary, Czechoslovakia; hon pres French Soc for Orthoses of the Upper Limb, co ed International Journal of Rehabilitation Studies, memb Editorial Bd Pain Br Soc for Surgery of the Hand Injury, bd memb Opera Factory, memb Ct of Assts Worshipful Co of Dyers (Prime Warden 1981–82 and 1984–85); memb: Br Soc for Surgery of the Hand, Br Soc of Rheumatology, Br Soc for Relief of Pain, RSA, Bd Opera Factory; FRCP, FRCS; *Books* Rehabilitation of the Hand (4 edn, 1982); *Recreations* gardening, music, the arts, walking, wine and food; *Clubs* Savile; *Style*— Dr Kit Wynn Parry, MBE; ✉ 51 Nassau Road, Barnes, London SW13 9QJ (☎ 0181 748 6288); Devonshire Hospital, 29 Devonshire Street, London W1

WYNNE, David; OBE (1994); s of Cdr Charles Edward Wynne, RNR, and Millicent, *née* Beyts; *b* 25 May 1926; *Educ* Stowe, Trinity Coll Cambridge; *m* 1968, Gillian Mary Leslie (d 1990), da of Leslie Grant, of Argentina and Switzerland; 2 s (Edward, Roland), and 2 step children; *Career* served WWII Sub Lt RNVR; sculptor; numerous important public works worldwide over the last 36 years; *Recreations* active sports, poetry, travel; *Clubs* Garrick, Leander, Queen's, Hurlingham, Cresta Run; *Style*— David Wynne, Esq, OBE; ✉ 5 Burlington Lodge Studios, Buer Road, London SW6 (☎ 0171 731 1071)

WYNNE, Thomas Meirion; s of Rev E E Wynne (d 1981), of Flint; *b* 26 April 1934; *Educ* UCW (LLB); *m* 21 June 1958, Elizabeth Gwenda; 2 s (Michael Vaughan b 1960, Gareth Dylan b 1961); *Career* slr; former clerk to Justices of Dolgellau and Barmouth; clerk to Cmmrs of Taxes, former Mental Health cmmr; *Style*— T Meirion Wynne, Esq; ✉ Llifor, Friog, Fairbourne, Gwynedd LL38 2RX (☎ 01341 250428); J Charles Hughes & Co, Solicitors, Dolgellau, Gwynedd (☎ 01341 422464)

WYNNE-MORGAN, David Wynne; s of Col John Wynne-Morgan, and Marjorie Mary (Marcie), *née* Wynne (d 1992); *b* 22 Feb 1931; *Educ* Bryanston; *m* 1 (m dis), Romaine Chevers, *née* Ferguson; 2 s (Nicholas b 1956, Adrian b 1957); m 2 (m dis), Sandra, *née* Paul; m 3, 26 June 1973, Karin Elizabeth, da of Daniel Eugene Stines; 2 s (Jamie b 1975, Harry b 1980); *Career* journalist: Daily Mail 1951–54, Daily Express 1954–57; fndr Partnerplan PR (sold to Extel Group 1980); chm: Hill and Knowlton (UK) Ltd 1984–92, Marketing Group GB 1989–91; pres and chief exec Europe, ME and Africa Region Hill and Knowlton 1990–94 (chm Worldwide Exec Ctee, conslt 1994–); co-fndr WMC Communications 1995–; played squash for Wales 1953–56; memb Cncl Lord's Taverners' 1990–95 (chm Commercial Ctee 1992–94); dir Horsham Corporation 1995–; MIPR; *Books* autiobiography of late Pres Gamal Abdel Nasser (serialised Sunday Times), biography of Pietro Annigoni (serialised Daily Express), I Norman Levy; *Recreations* cricket, tennis, riding, squash; *Clubs* Turf, Annabel's, Bath and Rackets, Queen's; *Style*— David Wynne-Morgan, Esq; ✉ 8 Unwin Mansions, Queens Club Gardens, London W14; WMC Communications, Elsinore House, 77 Fulham Palace Road, London W6 8JA (☎ 0181 741 7444, fax 0181 741 7333)

WYNNE-PARKER, Michael; s of David Boothby Wynne-Parker (d 1955); *b* 20 Nov 1945; *Educ* Lady Manners Sch; *m* 1975 (m dis 1991); 2 da (Sarah Ruth Isabella b 1978, Fiona Alice Elizabeth b 1981); m 2, 1995, Mandana Farzaneh; *Career* chief exec Introcom Ltd; dir: Access to Justice Ltd, Interlink Jordan Ltd, Geographical Mining and Surveying Corporation Ltd, Jacqueline Stallone's Hollywood Horoscope (UK) Ltd, Joan Collins Productions Ltd, Stone Music Ltd; conslt to various public and private cos and govt ministers and charities; pres ESU of South Asia; vice pres: ESU of Sri Lanka, ESU of Nepal, ESU of India; former govr ESU; fndr patron Pensthorpe Waterfowl Tst; tstee: Wellington Pier Charitable Tst, The Japanese Br Charitable Tst, ESU Sri Lanka Educnl Tst, Mencap City Fndn (fndr tstee and govr); fell Atlantic Cncl of the UK; fndr: Knockie Stalking Club, Utd Charities Unit Tst (formerly Mencap Unit Tst); former vice chm Norfolk Beagles; life memb: Royal Soc of St George, Sri Lanka Friendship Assoc (fndr memb), Norfolk Naturalist Tst; memb: Royal Soc for Asian Affrs, CLA, Salisbury Gp, The Pilgrims; *Books* Bridge over Troubled Water (1988); *Recreations* field sports, travelling, gardens, books; *Clubs* Carlton, Mark's, Clermont, Annabel's, Puffin's (Edinburgh), Les Ambassadeurs; *Style*— Michael Wynne-Parker, Esq; ✉ 38 Marlborough Court, Pembroke Road, London W8 6DL; Introcom Ltd, 1–11 Hay Hill, Berkeley Square, London W1X 7LF (☎ 0171 493 4517, fax 0171 409 2557); Introcom House, 88 Kingsway, London WC2B 6AA

WYNNE-WILLIAMS, John Anthony; s of John Gabriel Wynne-Williams, MBE, and Mary Adele Josephine, *née* Corazza; *b* 8 Nov 1949; *Educ* Farleigh House Sch Farleigh Wallop Hants, Stonyhurst; *Career* dir D'Arcy Macmanus and Masius 1970–79; dep chm: Ryman plc 1981–87, Levelmill Ltd 1987–; dir: Holland and Holland Ltd 1989–92, Kiki McDonough Ltd 1990–; chm Moyses Stevens Group Ltd 1989–; chm Royal Marsden Hosp Appeal Coordinating Ctee, memb Devpt Bd Ballet Rambert; memb Worshipful Co of Fanmakers; *Recreations* shooting, Cresta Run, backgammon, theatre; *Clubs* White's, Marks, RAC, St Moritz Tobogganing; *Style*— John Wynne-Williams, Esq

WYVILL, (Marmaduke) Charles Asty; Lord of the Manor of Constable Burton and patron of three livings; s of Marmaduke Frederick Wyvill (d 1953, 7 in descent from D'Arcy Wyvill, yr bro of Sir Marmaduke Wyvill, 5 Bt, unc of 6 Bt and great unc of 7 Bt, since whose death in 1774 the Btcy has been dormant; D'Arcy was himself 11 in descent from Richard Wyvill, one of the 25,000 supporters of Henry VI killed at the rout of Towton 1461), and May Bennet; *b* 30 Aug 1945; *Educ* Stowe, RAC Cirencester; *m* 1972, Margaret Ann, da of Maj Sydney Hardcastle, RA; 3 s (Marmaduke b 1975, Edward b 1977, Frederick b 1983), 1 da (Katherine b 1981); *Career* land agent; patron of the livings of Spennithorne, Fingall and Denton; ARICS; landowner (3000 acres); High Sheriff of North Yorkshire 1986; *Recreations* shooting, fishing; *Clubs* Brooks's; *Style*— Charles Wyvill, Esq; ✉ Constable Burton Hall, Leyburn, N Yorks DL8 5LJ

Y

YACOUB, Prof Sir Magdi Habib; kt (1992); *b* 16 Nov 1935; *Educ* Cairo Univ (MB BCh), FRCS, FRCS(Ed), FRCS(Glas) 1961, MRCS, LRCP (London) 1966, MRCP 1986; *Career* rotating house offr Cairo Univ Hosp 1958–59, surgical registrar Postgrad Surgical Unit Cairo Univ 1959–61; resident surgical offr: London Chest Hosp 1962–63, Brompton Hosp May-Oct 1963; surgical registrar London Chest Hosp 1963–64, rotating sr surgical registrar Nat Heart and Chest Hosps 1964–68, instr and asst prof Section of Cardiovascular Surgery Univ of Chicago 1968–69; Harefield Hosp: conslt cardiac surgn 1969–, dir of med research and educn 1992–; conslt cardiac surgn Nat Heart Hosp 1973–89, Br Heart Fndn prof of cardiothoracic surgery Nat Heart and Lung Inst Royal Brompton NHS Tst 1986–; hon conslt Royal Free Hosp Med Sch London and King Edward's Coll of Med Lahore Pakistan, hon prof of surgery Univ of Sienna Italy and hon prof of cardiac surgery Charing Cross and Westminster Hosp Med Schs London; ed: Annual in Cardiac Surgery, Current Opinion in Cardiology: Coronary Artery Surgery; memb various Editorial Bds incl: Jl of Cardiac Surgery, Current Opinion in Cardiology, Transplantation, Cardiovascular Pharmacology and Therapeutics; various visiting professorships and named/guest lectures incl: The Bradshaw Lecture RCP London 1988, honoured guest lecture Assoc of American Thoracic Surgns Washington DC 1991, The Frances Rather Seybold Lectr and visiting prof Texas Children's Hosp Houston 1992, The Tudor Edwards Lecture RCP London 1992, visiting prof and O T Clagett lectr Mayo Clinic Rochester Minnesota 1993, visiting prof in cardiac surgery and Hubbard lectr Brigham and Women's Hosp Boston Mass 1994, Claude S Beck visiting lectr Univ Hosps of Cleveland Ohio 1994, Stikeman visiting prof McGill Univ Montreal 1994, visiting prof Hartford Hosp Hartford Connecticut 1994, 17th Leonard Abrahamson Meml Lecture Dublin 1995; Clement Price Thomas Award RCS (England) 1989, Ambuj Nath Bose Prize RCP 1992; Hon DSc: Brunel Univ 1985, American Univ at Cairo 1989, Loughborough Univ 1990, Univ of Keele 1995; Hon MCh Univ of Cardiff 1986, Hon PhD Univ of Lund 1988, Hon FRCP 1990; memb: Soc of Thoracic Surgns of GB and Ireland, Br Cardiac Soc, RSM, German Soc of Thoracic and Cardiac Surgery, German Cardiac Soc, Scandinavian Soc of Thoracic Surgns, Japanese Soc of Surgns, Int Soc of Thoracic and Vascular Surgery, Euro Soc of Cardiothoracic Surgns, Thai Soc of Cardiothoracic Surgns, Egyptian Soc of Cardiology, South African Soc of Cardiology, Cardiac Soc of Australia and NZ, Pakistan Cardiac Soc, Indian Soc of Cardiothoracic Surgns; fell American Coll of Cardiology; *Style—* Professor Sir Magdi Yacoub; ✉ Cardiothoracic Surgery, National Heart and Lung Institute, Imperial College of Science, Technology and Medicine, Dovehouse Street, London SW3 6LY (☎ 0171 351 8534/3, fax 0171 351 8229)

YAFFÉ, Paul; s of David Yaffe (d 1976), of Manchester, and Dinah Pash; *b* 21 April 1946; *Educ* Delamere Forest Sch, Cheetham Secdy Sch; *m* 21 June 1967, Janis Andrea, da of Eric Brown; 2 s (Mark Daniel b 22 July 1968, Adam James b 23 Oct 1972); *Career* environmental portrait photographer 1961–; worked in family photographic firm, opened own studio in Southport 1967, numerous exhibitions UK and abroad, lectr on photography and modern promotional methods in photography; chm Judging Panel BIPP (portraiture, wedding and theatrical photography) 1978 (memb 1974, dep chm 1976), chm Admissions and Qualifications Bd BIPP 1983–87 (dep chm 1980); fell Master Photographers Assoc 1981, hon PFP Norwegian Fame Assoc, 4 times memb Kodak Gold Circle; memb Professional Photographers Assoc of America; FBIPP 1972, FRPS 1979, FRSA, MIMgt 1993; *Style—* Paul Yaffé, Esq; ✉ Paul Yaffé Ltd, Wayfarers Arcade, Lord St, Southport, Merseyside PR8 1NT (☎ 01704 550000/01704 544004/0831 250217)

YAPP, Sir Stanley Graham; kt (1975); s of William Yapp; *m* 1 (m dis); 1 da; m 2 (m dis), Carol; 1 s; m 3, 1983, Christine, da of Ernest Horton, former Lord Mayor of Birmingham; *Career* ldr Birmingham City Cncl 1972–74; W Midlands CC: ldr 1973–77, vice chm 1982–83, chm 1983–84; chm Birmingham Int Airport 1988–94, chm various bodies; vice-chm Local Authorities' Mgmnt Services & Computer Ctee; *Style—* Sir Stanley Yapp; ✉ 172 York Road, Hall Green, Birmingham B28 8LW

YARBOROUGH, 8 Earl of (UK 1837); Charles John Pelham; also Baron Yarborough (GB 1794) and Baron Worsley (UK 1837); s of 7 Earl of Yarborough, JP (d 1991), and (Florence) Ann Petronel, *née* Upton; *b* 5 Nov 1963; *Educ* Eton, Bristol Univ; *m* 26 Jan 1990, Anna-Karin, da of George Zecevic, of Montreux, Switzerland; 3 s (George John Sackville, Lord Worsley b 9 Aug 1990, Hon William Charles John Walter b 28 Dec 1991, Hon James Marcus b 8 March 1994); *Heir* s, George Pelham, Lord Worsley b 9 Aug 1990; *Style—* The Rt Hon the Earl of Yarborough; ✉ Brocklesby Park, Lincolnshire DN37 8PL (☎ 01469 560242)

YARDLEY, Prof Sir David Charles Miller; kt (1994); s of Geoffrey Miller Yardley (d 1987), and Doris Woodward, *née* Jones (d 1934); *b* 4 June 1929; *Educ* Ellesmere Coll, Univ of Birmingham (LLB, LLD), Lincoln Coll Oxford (DPhil, MA); *m* 30 Aug 1954, Patricia Anne Tempest (Patsy), da of Lt-Col Basil Harry Tempest Olver, MBE (d 1980); 2 s (Adrian b 1956, Alistair b 1962), 2 da (Heather b 1958, Briony b 1960); *Career* Nat Serv Flying Offr Educn Branch RAF 1949–51; called to the Bar Gray's Inn 1952; fell St Edmund Hall Oxford 1954–74 (emeritus 1974–), Barber prof of law Univ of Birmingham 1974–78, head of Dept of Law Politics and Econs Oxford Poly 1978–80, Rank Fndn prof of law Univ of Buckingham 1980–82 (hon prof 1994–), visiting prof Oxford Brookes Univ 1995–; chm Cmmn for Local Admin in Eng 1982–94, complaints cmmr Securities and Investments Bd 1994–; chm: rent assessment ctees, rent tbnls and nat insur local tbnls 1963–82 and 1995–, Oxford Preservation Tst 1989–; FRSA 1991; *Books* Introduction to Constitutional and Administrative Law (1960, 8 edn 1995), A Source Book of English Administrative Law (1963, 2 edn 1970), The Future of the Law (1964), Principles of Administrative Law (1981, 2 edn 1986), Geldarts Introduction to English Law (ed 1995), Hanbury and Yardley's English Courts of Law (1979), The Protection of Freedom (with I Stevens, 1982); *Recreations* lawn tennis, opera, cats; *Clubs* RAF; *Style—* Prof Sir David Yardley; ✉ 9 Belbroughton Rd, Oxford OX2 6UZ (☎ 01865 554831)

YARDLEY, Gordon J; *Career* md Newey & Eyre Ltd 1974–88 (joined 1951, Newey & Eyre purchased by BTR plc 1983); BTR plc: exec dir Europe 1988–91, non-exec dir 1991–; *Style—* Gordon Yardley, Esq; ✉ BTR plc, Silvertown House, Vincent Square, London SW1P 2PL (☎ 0171 834 3848)

YARKER, Peter Francis; *b* 25 June 1943; *Educ* St Michael's Sch Ingoldisthorpe, Ealing Sch of Hotel Keeping & Catering (Musketeers cup); *m* Rosemary Margaret, *née* Allday; 3 s (James Francis b 1969, Edward Timothy b 1972, William Daniel b 1974); *Career* admin trainee Grosvenor House Park Lane 1965; asst mangr: Dudley Hotel Hove 1966, Grosvenor House Sheffield 1967; mangr Burlington Hotel Eastbourne 1969–72 (sr asst mangr 1968), gen mangr Beaufort Hotel Bath 1972–77, dir Myddleton Hotels Ltd 1977–81, regnl dir Ladbroke Hotels 1980–83, proprietor Dukes Hotel Bath 1983–91, proprietor Savoy Hotel Cheltenham 1993; currently dir: Dukes Norton Management Ltd, Leisure Partnership Ltd; winner Master Innholder award 1978; Freeman City of London, Liveryman Worshipful Co of Basketmakers; FHCIMA, memb CIM; *Style—* Peter Yarker, Esq; ✉ Dukes Norton Management Ltd, The White House, High Street, Norton St Philip, Bath BA3 6LH (☎ 01373 834716, fax 01373 834716)

YARMOUTH, Earl of; Henry Jocelyn Seymour; s and h of 8 Marquess of Hertford, *qv*; *b* 6 July 1958; *Educ* Harrow, RAC Cirencester; *m* 15 Dec 1990, Beatriz, da of Jorge Karam, of Copacabana, Rio de Janeiro, Brazil; 2 s (Baron Conway of Ragley b 2 Nov 1993, Hon Edward George Seymour b 24 Jan 1995), 1 da (Lady Gabriella Helen Seymour b 23 April 1992); *Heir* s, William Francis, Baron Conway of Ragley b 2 Nov 1993; *Career* farm manager; *Style—* Earl of Yarmouth; ✉ Ragley Hall, Alcester, Warwickshire B49 5NJ (☎ 01789 762090, fax 01789 764791); Ragley Home Farms, Alcester, Warwickshire B49 5LZ (☎ 01789 763131, car 0836 355512)

YARNOLD, Rev Edward John; s of Edward Cabré Yarnold, MM (Sgt Queen's Westminster Rifles and civil servant, d 1972), of Burley-in-Wharfedale, W Yorks, and Agnes, *née* Deakin; *b* 14 Jan 1926; *Educ* St Michael's Coll Leeds, Heythrop Coll, Campion Hall Oxford (MA, DD); *Career* entered Soc of Jesus 1943, ordained 1960; tutor in theology Campion Hall 1964– (Master 1965–72), visiting prof Univ of Notre Dame Indiana 1982–, research lectr Univ of Oxford 1991–; Murray prof of Catholic thought Univ of Toledo Ohio 1995; memb Anglican-RC Int Cmmn 1970–81 and 1982–91, pres Catholic Theological Assoc of GB 1986–88; Cross of Order of St Augustine of Canterbury 1981; *Books* The Theology of Original Sin (1971), The Awe-Inspiring Rites of Initiation (1972, new edn 1994), The Second Gift (1974), The Study of Liturgy (ed with C Jones and G Wainwright, 1978, new edn 1992), They Are in Earnest (1982), Seven Days with the Lord (1984), The Study of Spirituality (ed with C Jones and G Wainwright, 1986), In Search of Unity (1989), Time for God (1991), Anglicans and Roman Catholics: The Search for Unity (ed with C Hill, 1994), Anglican Orders: The Documents in the Case (ed with C Hill, 1996); *Recreations* opera, cricket; *Style—* The Rev Edward Yarnold, SJ; ✉ Campion Hall, Oxford OX1 1QS (☎ 01865 286111, fax 01865 286148)

YARNOLD, Patrick; s of Leonard Francis Yarnold (d 1963), of Hassocks, Sussex, and Gladys Blanche, *née* Merry; *b* 21 March 1937; *Educ* Bancroft's Sch Woodford Green Essex; *m* 14 Jan 1961, Caroline, da of Andrew James Martin (d 1988), of Maida Vale, London; 2 da (Louise b 2 Feb 1962, Frances b 12 Feb 1964); *Career* Nat Serv 1955–57; joined HM Foreign Serv (now Dip Serv) 1957: FO 1957–60, Addis Ababa 1961–64, Belgrade 1964–66, FO (later FCO) 1966–70; 1 sec and head of chancery Bucharest 1970–73, 1 sec (commercial) Bonn 1973–76, 1 sec FCO 1976–79, cnsllr (econ and commercial) Brussels 1980–83, consul gen Zagreb 1983–85, cnsllr, head of chancery and consul gen Belgrade 1985–87, cnsllr FCO 1987–90, consul gen Hamburg 1990–94, consul gen Marseilles 1994–97; *Recreations* travel, photography, walking, genealogy, chinese cooking, local history, reading, etc; *Style—* Patrick Yarnold, Esq; ✉ c/o Foreign and Commonwealth Office, King Charles Street, London SW1A 2AH

YARRANTON, Sir Peter George; kt (1992); s of Edward John Yarranton (d 1955), of London NW9, and Norah Ellen, *née* Atkins (d 1978); *b* 30 Sept 1924; *Educ* Willesden Tech Coll; *m* 10 April 1947, Mary Avena, da of Sydney Flowitt, MC (d 1957), of Scarborough; 1 s (Ross b 9 Sept 1952), 1 da (Sandy (Mrs Turnbull) b 16 Oct 1950); *Career* RAF 1942–57; WWII Pilot Offr 1944, Flying Offr 1945, served Liberators Burma and SE Asia, Flt Lt 1949; served: Canada, USA, Bahamas, Ceylon, Malaya, India, Australia, UK; Shell Mex and BP Ltd: trg 1957–58, ops offr Reading 1958–61, UK industl relations liaison offr 1961–63, i/c industl relations 1963–66, mangr industl relations 1966–69, regnl ops mangr SE Region 1969–75; mangr Plant and Engrg Distribution Div Shell UK Oil Ltd 1975–77, gen mangr Lensbury Club 1978–92; pres: Lensbury RFC 1979–, Wasps RFC 1982–85, Middx Co RFU 1986–88, RFU 1991–92; England rugby international (5 caps); former capt Barbarians, London, Middx, Wasps, Br Combined Servs and RAF Rugby Clubs; former chm of selectors for London and Middx; chm: London Regnl Cncl for Sport and Recreation 1983–89, UK Sports Cncl 1989–94, Sports Partner Ltd 1991–95; non-exec dir Drugcheck (UK) Ltd 1995–; conslt Stuart Canvas Products; former: PR advsr RFU, outside broadcast commentator BBC, presenter on the world's largest TV screen at Twickenham; former capt RAF Swimming and Water Polo Teams; pres The Great River Race 1994–; govr: Sports Aid Fndn, Queen's Coll Taunton 1993–; tstee: The Richmond Boat Project, RFU Castlecroft; memb: Jet Heritage Tst, Wooden Spoon Soc; patron Royal Canoe Club Tst - The Comet Fndn 1988–; life vice-pres Recreational Mangrs' Assoc; Freeman City of London 1977, memb Worshipful Co of Gold and Silver Wyre Drawers 1977 (memb Ct of Assts 1987); Hon DArts De Montfort Univ 1993; FIMgt, FIPD; *Recreations* all sports; *Clubs* RAF, East India, Rugby Club of London, MCC, Surrey CCC, Lensbury, Surbiton Croquet (chm 1988–), Molesey Boat (hon life memb), Lord's Taverners'; *Style—* Sir Peter Yarranton; ✉ Broom Point, Broom Water West, Teddington TW11 9QH; Sunnydale Villas, Durlston Road, Swanage, Dorset

YARROW, Sir Eric Grant; 3 Bt (UK 1916), of Homestead, Hindhead, Frensham, Co Surrey; MBE (1946), DL (Renfrewshire 1970); s of Sir Harold Yarrow, 2 Bt, GBE (d 1962), by his 1 w, Eleanor; *b* 23 April 1920; *Educ* Marlborough, Univ of Glasgow; *m* 1, Rosemary Ann (d 1957), da of late H T Young; 1 s (Richard d 1987); m 2, 1959 (m dis 1975), Annette Elizabeth Françoise, da of late A J E Steven; 3 s (Norman b 1960, Peter (twin) b 1960, David b 1966); m 3, 1982, Caroline Joan Rosa, da of late R F Masters, of Piddinghoe, Sussex, and former w of Philip Botting; *Heir* gs, Ross b 1985; *Career* served RE Burma 1939–45, Maj 1944; former chm and md Yarrow PLC, former chm Clydesdale Bank PLC, former dir Standard Life Assur Co, former dir Nat Australian Bank; hon pres Princess Louise Scottish Hosp at Erskine, pres Scot Area Burma Star Assoc, pres Scottish Convalescent Home for Children 1957–70; former memb Cncl IOD, deacon Incorpn of Hammermen of Glasgow 1961–62, Prime Warden of Worshipful Co of Shipwrights 1970, pres Smeatonian Soc of Civil Engrs 1983, pres Marlburian Club 1984, chm Blythe Sappers 1989, hon vice pres Cncl of Royal Inst of Naval Architects; hon memb Inst of Engrs and Shipbuilders in Scotland; FRSE 1974; OStJ 1970; *Style—* Sir

Eric Yarrow, Bt, MBE, DL, FRSE; ✉ Cloak, Kilmacolm, Renfrewshire PA13 4SD (☎ 01505 872067)

YARWOOD, Michael Edward (Mike); OBE (1976); s of Wilfred Yarwood (d 1993), and Bridget Yarwood (d 1983); *b* 14 June 1941; *Educ* Bredbury Secdy Sch Cheshire; *m* 1969 (m dis 1987), Sandra Jean, da of Eric Burville; 2 da (Charlotte b 1970, Clare b 1972); *Career* first TV appearance 1963; BBC: Three of a Kind 1967, Look - Mike Yarwood, Mike Yarwood in Persons (series) 1971–82; ATV: Will the Real Mike Yarwood Stand Up? (series) 1968; Thames: Mike Yarwood in Persons 1983–87, Mike Yarwood Christmas Show 1984–87, One For The Pot (nat tour) 1988; Royal Variety performances 1968, 1972, 1976, 1981, 1987 and 1993; Variety Club of GB Award for BBC TV Personality of The Year 1973, Royal Television Soc Award for outstanding creative achievement in front of camera 1978; memb Grand Order of Water Rats; *Books* And This Is Me (1974), Impressions of My Life (1986); *Recreations* golf, tennis; *Clubs* Lord's Taverners; *Style*— Mike Yarwood, Esq, OBE; ✉ c/o International Artistes Ltd, Mezzanine Floor, 235 Regent Street, London W1R 8AX (☎ 0171 439 8401, fax 0171 409 2070)

YASS, Irving; CB (1993); s of Abraham Yass (d 1961), and Fanny, *née* Caplin (d 1980); *b* 20 Dec 1935; *Educ* Harrow Co GS, Balliol Coll Oxford (BA); *m* 14 Aug 1962, Marion Ruth, da of Benjamin Leighton (d 1979); 2 s (David b 1965, Michael b 1966), 1 da (Catherine b 1963); *Career* asst princ Miny of Transport and Civil Aviation 1958, private sec to jt parly sec 1960, princ HM Treasy 1967–70, asst sec DOE 1971, sec Ctee of Inquiry into Local Govt Fin 1974–76; Dept of Transport 1976–: under-sec fin 1982–86, dir tport policy for London 1992–94; dir of planning and tport Government Office for London 1994–95, dir of tport and planning London First Ltd 1995–; *Style*— Irving Yass, Esq, CB; ✉ London First Ltd, Caxton House, 6 Tothill Street, London SW1H 9NA (☎ 0171 222 1445, fax 0171 222 1448)

YASSUKOVICH, Stanislas Michael; CBE (1991); s of Dimitri Yassukovich, and Denise Yassukovich; *b* 5 Feb 1935; *Educ* Deerfield Acad Mass, Harvard Univ; *m* Diana Veronica, da of Ralph Obre Crofton Townsend; 2 s (Michael, Nicholas), 1 da (Tatyana); *Career* served US Marine Corps 1957–61; White Weld & Co: joined in Zurich 1961, London 1962, gen ptnr NY 1969, md London until 1973; EuroBanking Co Ltd London: md 1973, dep chm 1983–85; chm Merrill Lynch Europe Ltd 1985–91, currently chm S M Yassukovich & Co Ltd; non-exec chm: Flextech plc, Hemingway Properties PLC, Gallo & Co Ltd, Park Place Capital Ltd, Henderson EuroTrust PLC, EASDAQ SA; vice chm Bristol & West Building Society, dep chm ABC International Bank PLC; non-exec dir: Henderson Administration Group PLC, South West Water PLC, Unionamerica Holdings plc; a dep chm Stock Exchange 1986–89, chm The Securities Assoc 1987–91; chm City Disputes Panel, chm City Research Project, memb City Advsy Gp CBI; *Recreations* hunting, shooting, polo; *Clubs* Buck's, Turf, The Brook (USA), Union (USA), Travellers (Paris); *Style*— Stanislas Yassukovich, Esq, CBE; ✉ SM Yassukovich & Co Ltd, 42 Berkeley Square, London W1X 5DB (☎ 0171 318 0825, fax 0171 318 0826)

YATES, Prof Bernard; s of John Gordon Yates (d 1972), of York, and Beatrice May, *née* Rawlings (d 1993); *b* 17 Feb 1929; *Educ* Archbishop Holgate's GS York, Univ of Leeds (BSc, PhD), Univ of Salford (DSc); *m* 10 Sept 1955, Muriel, da of Robert Parvin (d 1954), of Thirsk, N Yorks; *Career* Nat Serv RAF 1947–49; memb: sci staff GEC Res Laboratories Wembley 1955–58, academic staff Bradford Inst of Technol 1958–64; Univ of Salford: reader 1964–80, prof of physics 1980–92, chm Dept of Pure and Applied Physics 1982–92, pro-vice chllr 1985–89, research prof in physics 1992–; FInstP 1964, CEng 1989; *Style*— Prof Bernard Yates; ✉ Joule Laboratory, Department of Physics, University of Salford, Salford M5 4WT (☎ 0161 745 5000, fax 0161 745 5999, telex 668680 Sulib)

YATES, Brian Douglas; s of Bertram Yates (d 1994), of Birmingham, and Barbara, *née* Wenham (d 1985); *b* 1 May 1944; *Educ* Uppingham, Clare Coll Cambridge (MA), London Business Sch (MBA); *m* 1971, Patricia, da of Arthur Hutchinson, of Dublin; 1 s (Justin b 1976); *Career* various engrg appointments with Molins, RHP Bearings, Thorn EMI and Dexion; dir: Morris Mechanical Handling Ltd 1988–, Euroconsumer Publications Ltd 1992–, Trading Standards Services Ltd 1992–; Consumers' Assoc: memb Cncl 1986–, chm Business Ctee 1989, chm Cncl 1994–; memb: Northampton BC 1979–83, Hants CC 1985–89, Heathrow Airport Consultative Ctee 1992–; Eur Ing, CEng, MIM, FRSA; *Recreations* real and lawn tennis, ski touring; *Clubs* Hatfield House Tennis, Harpenden Lawn Tennis; *Style*— Brian Yates, Esq; ✉ 19 Park Avenue South, Harpenden, Herts AL5 2DZ (☎ 01582 768484, fax 01582 767989); Consumers' Association, 2 Marylebone Road, London NW1 4DF (☎ 0171 830 6000, fax 0171 830 7650)

YATES, Prof (Anthony) David; s of Cyril Yates, and Violet Ethel, *née* Man; *b* 5 May 1946; *Educ* Bromley GS, St Catherine's Coll Oxford (David Blank exhibitioner, MA Jurisprudence, Frank Alan Bullock Prize), Coll of Law Guildford (slr); *m* 1 (m dis 1989), Carolyn Paula, *née* Hamilton; 3 da (Sarah Olivia Ann, Katherine Lucy Hannah, Rachel Jane Louise); m 2, Susanna Margaret, *née* McGarry; *Career* Univ of Hull: asst lectr in law 1969–72, dep warden Morgan Hall of Residence 1969–70, warden Newholme Student Residence 1970–72; Univ of Bristol: lectr in law 1972–74, dep warden Wills Hall of Residence 1972–74, visiting lectr 1974–75; Univ of Manchester: lectr in law 1974–76, warden Chandos Hall of Residence UMIST 1975–76, sr lectr in law 1976–79, princ Dalton Hall 1976–80 (pt/t 1979–80), visiting prof 1979–80; Univ of Essex: chm Dept of Law 1979–83, dean Sch of Law 1979–84, Fndn prof of law 1979–87, pro-vice-chllr Univ of Essex 1985–87, visiting prof 1987–89; currently ptnr and dir of professional devpt Baker & McKenzie; visiting prof of law Univ of NSW 1985, Parsons visiting fell Univ of Sydney 1985; sometime external examiner univs of: London, Sheffield, Warwick, E Anglia, Loughborough, NUI, Dublin, Keele, Cambridge, Leeds, Bristol and Manchester; Law Soc of Eng and Wales: memb Cncl 1992–, memb Trg Ctee 1993–, chm Legal Practice Course Bd 1995–, chm Working Party on review of Legal Practice Course 1996; memb Ctee City of London Law Soc 1993–; memb: Advsy Ctee for Law Trg Within the Office American Bar Assoc 1988–, Advsy Bd Orientation in American Law Prog Univ of California 1990–, Advsy Ctee Centre for Advanced Legal Studies Univ of Leuven Belgium 1994–; Public Housing Law ed Encyclopaedia of Social Welfare Law 1973–80, gen ed The Professional Lawyer 1991–93; memb: Advsy Bd Urban Law and Policy 1978–, Editorial Bd Review of International Business Law 1988–, Editorial Bd Jl of Contract Law 1988–; Freeman City of London 1993; memb Law Soc 1969; *Publications* Exclusion Clauses in Contracts (1978, 2 edn 1982), Leases of Business Premises (1979), Landlord and Tenant Law (with A J Hawkins, 1981, 2 edn 1986), Standard Business Contracts (with A J Hawkins, 1986), The Carriage of Goods by Land, Sea and Air (ed-in-chief and contrib, 1993); also author of numerous articles in various jls; *Recreations* opera, food and wine, rugby football; *Clubs* United Oxford & Cambridge University, City Livery, Law Society; *Style*— Prof David Yates; ✉ Baker & McKenzie, 100 New Bridge Street, London EC4V 6JA (☎ 0171 919 1253, fax 0171 919 1263, mobile 0385 242557, e-mail david_yates@bakermck.com)

YATES, Douglas Martin; s of Albert Sidney Yates, of Pinner, Middx, and Lily Gertrude, *née* Jones; *b* 16 Jan 1943; *Educ* St Clement Danes GS, LSE (BSc); *m* 1967, Gillian, da of Edward Gallimore, of Ealing, London; 1 s (Nicholas b 1972), 2 da (Lindsay b 1969, Alexandra b 1979); *Career* chartered accountant; The Rank Group plc: finance dir 1982–87, commercial dir 1987–; dir: Camus PLC 1994, Rank Xerox Ltd 1983; *Recreations* tennis, badminton, bridge, music; *Style*— Douglas M Yates, Esq; ✉ The Rank Group plc, 6 Connaught Place, London W2 2EZ (☎ 0171 706 1111)

YATES, Ian Humphrey Nelson; CBE (1991); s of James Nelson Yates (d 1954), of Carnforth, Lancs, and Martha Wyatt, *née* Nutter (d 1965); *b* 24 Jan 1931; *Educ* Lancaster Royal GS, Canford; *m* 16 June 1956, Daphne June, da of Cyril Henry Hudson (d 1985), of Sanderstead, Surrey; 3 s (David b 1958, Nicholas b 1960, Simon b 1963); *Career* Nat Serv cmmnd Lt Royal Scots Greys Germany and ME 1951–53; mgmnt trainee Westminster Press Ltd 1953–58; Bradford and Dist Newspapers: asst gen mangr 1960, gen mangr 1964, md 1969–75; dir and chief exec Press Assoc Ltd 1989–90 (gen mangr and chief exec 1975); chm: Tellex Monitors Ltd 1987–90, Universal News Services Ltd 1989–90, CRG Communications Group 1990; pres: Young Newspapermen's Assoc 1966, Yorks Newspaper Soc 1968; memb: Cncl Newspaper Soc 1970–75, Cncl Cwlth Press Union 1977–90; pres Alliance of Euro News Agencies 1987–88, chm New Media Ctee of Alliance of Euro News Agencies 1984–90; FRSA 1989; *Recreations* walking, reading, theatre; *Style*— Ian Yates, Esq, CBE; ✉ Woodbury, 11 Holmwood Close, East Horsley, Surrey (☎ 01483 283873)

YATES, Ivan Ray; CBE (1982); *b* 22 April 1929; *Educ* Collegiate Sch Liverpool, Univ of Liverpool (BEng); *m* Jennifer Mary, *née* Halcombe; 1 s (Mark b 9 Jan 1970), 1 da (Jane b 21 Sept 1971); *Career* English Electric Co (now British Aerospace plc): joined as graduate apprentice 1950, pioneered use of computers to study aircraft dynamics and mgmnt, chief project engr TSR-2 (based Warton) 1960–65, project mangr Jaguar project 1966, dir BAC Preston 1973 (special dir 1970), dir Aircraft Projects 1974 (incl Tornado, ldr UK industl consortium developing UK Experimental (fighter) programme (EAP) culminating in launch of Euro Fighter programme (EFA) 1986), md Warton Div and Bd memb Aircraft Gp (following nationalisation) 1978, chief exec Aircraft Gp and dir British Aerospace plc 1982, Bd memb BAe Inc 1983–88, dep chief exec BAe 1986, left gp 1990; sometime former dir and chm: SEPECAT SA (Jaguar), PANAVIA Aircraft GmbH (Tornado), Eurofighter GmbH; visiting prof in principles of engrg design Univ of Cambridge (by-fell Churchill Coll), Wright Brothers lectureship AIAA; pres SBAC 1988–89 (ldr first delgn to USSR 1989); memb Cncl Design Cncl 1990–, chm RSA's Mfrg Initiative, govr Imperial Coll; former memb Cncl: Royal Academy of Engineering, Royal Utd Servs Inst, Royal Aeronautical Soc (winner Gold and Silver Medals); cmmr Royal Cmmn 1851; pres R J Mitchell Museum of Aviation Southampton; Hon DSc Loughborough Univ of Technol 1989, Hon DSc City Univ 1991; foreign memb Royal Swedish Acad of Engrg Scis 1990; FIMechE, FRAeS, FAIAA, FRSA, CIMgt, FEng 1983; *Style*— Ivan Yates, Esq, CBE, FEng; ✉ Ivan Yates & Associates (fax 01273 480695)

YATES, Rt Rev John; s of Frank Yates and Edith Ethel Yates, of Burslem; *b* 17 April 1925; *Educ* Battersea GS, Blackpool GS, Jesus Coll Cambridge, Lincoln Theological Coll; *m* 1954, Jean Kathleen Dover; 1 s, 2 da; *Career* served RAFVR 1943–47; curate Christ Church Southgate 1951–54, tutor and chaplain Lincoln Theological Coll 1954–59, vicar Bottesford-with-Ashby 1959–65, princ Lichfield Theological Coll 1966–72, suffragan bishop Whitby 1972–75, bishop of Gloucester 1975–91, bishop at Lambeth 1991–94, ret; sat in House of Lords 1981–91; Hon DLitt NCAA 1992; *Clubs* RAF; *Style*— The Rt Rev John Yates; ✉ 14 Belle Vue Road, Andover, Hants SP10 2DF

YATES, Matthew Stewart; s of Michael Yates, of Basildon, and Sylvia, *née* Hepton; *b* 4 Feb 1969; *Educ* Mayflower Sch; *Career* athlete; memb Newham & Essex Beagles; England debut 800m 1989, GB debut 1500m 1990, also represented England under 23 and S England 1989; achievements incl: runner up 800m AAA Championships 1989, Bronze medal 800m Cwlth Games 1990, runner up 1500m GB v E Germany 1990, European 800m finalist 1990, winner Madrid Mile 1991, winner New York Mile 1991, winner 1500m AAA Championships 1991, finalist 1500m World Championships 1991, fourth place overall 1500m Grand Prix 1991, Gold medal 1500m Euro Indoor Championships 1992; Sports Aid Fndn award, Basildon Cncl Sports award; *Recreations* music, art, rugby union, football; *Clubs* Nike International; *Style*— Matthew Yates, Esq; ✉ c/o British Athletic Federation, 225a Bristol Road, Edgbaston, Birmingham B5 7UB

YATES, Peter James; s of Lt-Col Robert Latimer Yates (d 1980), and Constance Leah, *née* Aitken (d 1940); *b* 24 July 1929; *Educ* Charterhouse, RADA; *m* 8 Oct 1960, Virginia Sue, da of Charles Quentin Pope (d 1961); 2 s (Toby Robert Quentin b 1962, Andrew b 1971), 2 da (Victoria Camilla b 1964 d 1965, Miranda Jane b 1965); *Career* film and theatre dir-prodr; films directed incl: Summer Holiday 1962, One Way Pendulum 1964, Robbery 1966, Bullitt 1968, John and Mary 1969, Murphy's War 1970, The Hot Rock 1971, The Friends of Eddie Coyle 1972, For Pete's Sake 1973, Mother Jugs and Speed 1975, The Deep 1976, Breaking Away 1978 (also prodr, Acad Award nominations incl best film and best direction), Eyewitness (also prodr) 1980, Krull 1982, The Dresser 1983 (also prodr, Acad Award nominations incl best film and best direction), Eleni 1985, The House on Carroll Street (also prodr) 1986, Suspect 1987, An Innocent Man 1989, Year of the Comet (also prodr) 1992, Roommates 1993, The Run of the Country (also prodr) 1994; plays directed incl: Passing Game 1975, Interpreters 1985; *Clubs* Garrick; *Style*— Peter Yates, Esq; ✉ William Morris Agency, 151 El Camino Drive, Beverly Hills, CA 90212, USA

YATES, Rodney Brooks; s of Henry Bertram Yates, OBE (d 1993), of Alvechurch, Birmingham, and Emily Barbara, *née* Wenham (d 1984); *b* 7 June 1937; *Educ* Uppingham; *m* 1 (m dis); 2 s (Mark b 1965, Duncan b 1966), 1 da (Camilla b 1970); m 2, 16 Sept 1983, Hazel, *née* Brown; 1 s (Benjamin b 1986); *Career* dir: Akroyd & Smithers plc 1976–86, Mercury Group Management 1986–87, Hemsley & Co Securities Ltd 1988–89; md Madoff Securities International Ltd 1987–88, dir Olliff & Partners plc 1987–95 (chm 1987–93), dir Bentley Capital (Europe) Ltd 1991–; memb: Cambs Family Health Serv Authy 1990–96, North West Anglia Health Authy 1996– govr Peterborough HS 1992–, memb Gen Med Cncl 1993–; Liveryman Worshipful Co of Tallow Chandlers; FCA, MSI (memb Stock Exchange 1971); *Recreations* tennis, reading; *Clubs* RAC; *Style*— Rodney Yates, Esq; ✉ The Old Rectory, Marholm, Peterborough PE6 7JA (☎ 01733 269466, fax 01733 330127)

YATES, Roger Philip; s of Eric Yates, of Warrington, and Joyce Mary, *née* Brown; *b* 4 April 1957; *Educ* Boteler GS Warrington, Worcester Coll Oxford (BA), Univ of Reading; *m* 7 Sept 1985, Kim Patricia, da of Anthony Gerald Gibbons, of Abinger, Surrey; 3 s (Max b 1987, Jeremy b 1989, Robert Alexander b 1992); *Career* joined GT Management Ltd 1981, dir GT Management (UK) Ltd 1984–88, dir GT Management plc 1986–88, investmt dir GT Unit Managers Ltd 1988; dir and chief investment offr Morgan Grenfell Investment Management 1988–, dir Morgan Grenfell Asset Management 1991–94, dir and chief investment offr LGT Asset Management plc 1994–; *Recreations* golf, skiing, tennis; *Style*— Roger Yates, Esq; ✉ 6 Nicosia Road, London SW18 3RN; LGT Asset Management plc, Alban Gate, 125 London Wall, London EC2 (☎ 0171 710 4567)

YATES, Prof William Edgar; s of Douglas Yates (d 1955), and Doris, *née* Goode (d 1990); *b* 30 April 1938; *Educ* Fettes, Emmanuel Coll Cambridge (MA, PhD); *m* 6 April 1963, Barbara Anne, da of Wolfgang Fellowes (d 1984); 2 s (Thomas b 1971, Paul b 1974); *Career* 2 Lt RASC 1957–58; lectr in German Univ of Durham 1963–72, prof of German Univ of Exeter 1972– (dep vice chllr 1986–89), Germanic ed Modern Language Review 1981–88; corresponding fell Austrian Acad of Sciences 1992; memb: Modern Humanities Res Assoc (memb Ctee 1980–), Eng Goethe Soc (memb Cncl 1984–), Int Nestroy Soc (memb Cncl 1986–), The Viennese Shakespeare Soc (vice-pres 1992–); chm of govrs Exeter Sch 1994–; *Books* Grillparzer: A Critical Introduction (1972), Nestroy: Satire and Parody in Viennese Popular Comedy (1972), Humanity in Weimar and

Vienna: The Continuity of an Ideal (1973), Tradition in the German Sonnet (1981), Nestroy (ed Stücke 12–14 1981–82, Stücke 34 1989, Stücke 18/1 1991)), Viennese Popular Theatre (ed with J R P McKenzie, 1985), Grillparzer und die europäische Tradition (ed with R Pichl and others, 1987), Schnitzler, Hofmannsthal, and the Austrian Theatre (1992), Nestroy and the Critics (1994), Vom schaffenden zum edierten Nestroy (ed, 1994), Theatre in Vienna: A Critical History, 1776–1995 (1996); *Recreations* music; *Style—* Prof W E Yates; ✉ 7 Clifton Hill, Exeter EX1 2DL; Dept of German, University of Exeter, Queen's Building, Exeter EX4 4QH (☎ 01392 264337, fax 01392 264339)

YATES, William Hugh; s of Brig Morris Yates, DSO, OBE, and Kathleen Rosanna, *née* Sherbrooke; *b* 18 Dec 1935; *Educ* Lancing, RMA Sandhurst, Coll of Estate Mgmnt; *m* 1, 1963 (m dis 1972), Celia Geraldine, *née* Pitman; 1 s; m 2, 1979, Elizabeth Susan Mansel-Pleydell, *née* Luard; 4 step s; *Career* served Army 1955–61; asst Rylands & Co 1961–64; Knight Frank & Rutley (now Knight Frank): negotiator 1964–67, md Knight Frank & Rutley SA Geneva 1968–72, ptnr i/c international investmts 1972–78, managing ptnr 1978–82, head Residential Div 1982–92, sr ptnr 1992–May 1996, ret; dir: EUPIC Services BV 1973–82, Ecclesiastical Insurance Group 1985– (dep chm 1995–), Woolwich Building Society 1990– (dep chm 1996–), Woolwich Europe Ltd 1991–95, Woolwich Surveyors Ltd; hon treas Save the Children Fund 1986–92 (chm fund raising 1980–86); FRICS 1965; *Recreations* riding, gardening, golf, music; *Clubs* Turf, Cavalry and Guards', Wentworth Golf; *Style—* William Yates, Esq; ✉ 42 Bloomfield Terrace, London SW1W 8PQ (☎ 0171 730 8701); Upper Farmhouse, Milton Lilbourne, Pewsey, Wilts SN9 5LQ (☎ 01672 563438); 3rd Floor, 9 Cavendish Place, London W1M 9DL (☎ 0171 580 1787, fax 0171 580 1790)

YEA, Philip Edward; s of John Alfred William Yea (d 1971), and Elsie Beryl, *née* Putman; *b* 11 Dec 1954; *Educ* Wallington HS for Boys, Brasenose Coll Oxford (MA); *m* 5 Dec 1981, Daryl, da of William Anthony Walker; 2 s (William b 24 May 1984, Daniel b 6 Dec 1986), 1 da (Georgina b 20 Feb 1992); *Career* Perkins Engines Ltd 1977–80, Moteurs Perkins SA France 1980–82, Foursquare Div Mars Ltd 1982–83, Guinness PLC 1984–88 (dir of business devpt United Distillers Group 1987–88), fin dir Cope Allman Packaging plc 1989–91 (joined 1988), fin dir Guinness PLC 1993– (rejoined 1991); also chm: Gleneagles Hotels PLC, Guinness Publishing; non-exec dir William Baird PLC; FCMA 1982, FRSA 1993; *Recreations* family, cinema; *Style—* Philip Yea, Esq; ✉ Guinness PLC, 39 Portman Square, London W1H 0EE (☎ 0171 486 0288, fax 0171 486 4862)

YEATES, Andrew; *b* 27 Sept 1957; *m*; 2 c; *Career* admitted slr 1981; contracts mangr Thames Television and Thames Television International 1981–87, company lawyer Phonographic Performance Ltd 1987–88; Channel Four Television: prog acquisition exec 1988–89, sr prog acquisition exec 1989–90, head of acquisitions and business affrs 1991–94, corporation sec and head of rights 1994–; vice chm The Educational Recording Agency Ltd; Liveryman Worshipful Co of Haberdashers; memb Law Soc; *Recreations* theatre, amateur operatics, music; *Clubs* Copinger Society; *Style—* Andrew Yeates; ✉ Channel Four Television Corporation, 124 Horseferry Road, London SW1P 2TX (☎ 0171 306 8505, fax 0171 306 8366)

YEATES, William Ronald; s of Richard Henry Yeates (d 1972), of Coatbridge, Strathclyde, and Caroline McAra Barclay (d 1983); *b* 24 June 1929; *Educ* Kildonan HS Coatbridge, Cranfield Business Sch; *m* 4 Sept 1955, Jean Valentine, da of Frederick Ernest Boxall (d 1960); 2 s (Douglas b 5 Feb 1957, Colin b 30 Oct 1958); 2 da (Cheryl b 23 Sept 1961, Heather b 18 Nov 1963); *Career* Nat Serv RAF 1947–49; J Sainsbury plc: branch mangr 1964–74, dist mangr 1974–76, area dir 1976–83, md Savacentre Ltd 1982–90; charitable activities: Marwell Zoological Tst, Guide Dogs for the Blind, Cancer Research; MInstD 1983; *Recreations* golf; *Clubs* Ampfield Golf, Bramshaw Golf; *Style—* Ronald Yeates, Esq; ✉ Bruma, Southdown Rd, Shawford, Winchester, Hampshire

YELDON, Peter James; s of John Gordon Yeldon (d 1980), and Joan, *née* Wilson (d 1974); *b* 7 May 1962; *Educ* St Ivo Sch Cambs, Univ of Newcastle (BA); *m* 1, 17 Aug 1985, Elizabeth Anne, *née* Fozard; 1 s (Timothy John b and d 12 February 1991), 2 da (Charlotte Alice b 14 Dec 1991, Berlinda Claire b 1 Dec 1993); m 2, 30 Sept 1995, Judith Ann, da of Barry Matthiae; 1 s (Thomas Barry b 30 Dec 1994), 1 da (Harriet Joan (twin) b 30 Sec 1994); *Career* Arthur Andersen & Co: articled clerk 1983–86, CA 1986, licensed insolvency practitioner 1989; Smith and Williamson: ptnr 1989–, head of insolvency 1989–, head of corp servs 1993–, memb Bd 1993–, chm Mktg Ctee, insolvency work incl Palace Pictures/Palace Group, Maxwell Offshore Companies and Poland and Wellington Lloyd's Action Groups, corp advice to insurance, construction and media entities; dir: Smith and Williamson Securities, Smith and Williamson Insurance Consultants, Smith and Williamson Group Management Services, Smith and Williamson Trust Corporation, Smith and Williamson Unit Trust Managers, Smith and Williamson Insurance Cash Fund Ltd, Smith and Williamson Management Consultancy Ltd, CPP Investments Ltd; memb Courses and Conferences Ctee Soc of Practitioners in Insolvency 1993–; fndr chm West End Business Club 1993, treas Assoc for Spinal Injury Research, Rehabilitation and Reintegration 1994; ACA, MInstD, MSPI; *Recreations* sea fishing, Rolls Royce enthusiast, art, fast cars, running; *Style—* Peter Yeldon, Esq; ✉ The Tythings, West Winterslow, Salisbury, Wilts SP5 1RE (☎ 01980 862892); Smith and Williamson, 1 Riding House Street, London W1A 3AS (☎ 0171 637 5377, fax 0171 323 5683)

YELLOLY, Prof Margaret Anne; da of Samuel Webster Yelloly (d 1976), and Rowena Emily, *née* Bull (d 1989); *b* 7 June 1934; *Educ* Queen Margaret's Sch, Univ of St Andrews (MA), Univ of Liverpool (MA), Univ of Leicester (PhD); *Career* lectr Univ of Leicester Sch of Social Work 1966–72, lectr LSE 1973–76, head Dept of Applied Social Studies Goldsmiths' Coll 1976–86, prof of social work and dir of social work educn Univ of Stirling 1986–91, Tavistock Clinic prof of social work Brunel Univ 1991–93 (hon prof 1994–); memb Central Cncl for Educn and Training in Social Work 1989–92, chm Social Work Educn Ctee Jt Univ Cncl 1988–91; *Books* Social Work Theory and Psychoanalysis (1985), Social Work and the Legacy of Freud (1989), Learning and Teaching in Social Work (1994); *Recreations* classical music, harpsichord; *Style—* Prof Margaret Yelloly; ✉ 10 King George Street, London SE10 8QJ (☎ 0181 692 3627)

YENTOB, Alan; *b* 11 March 1947; *Career* BBC: joined as gen trainee 1968, prodr/presenter BBC Radio and External Broadcasting 1968–69, asst dir Arts Features TV 1969–73, prodr and dir Omnibus strand BBC2 1973–75, fndr ed Arena arts strand BBC2 1978–85, head of music and arts BBC TV 1985–87, controller of BBC2 1988–93, controller of BBC1 1993–96, dir of progs BBC TV 1996–; govr Nat Film and TV Sch, memb Cncl English Stage Co Royal Ct Theatre, memb Advsy Ctee ICA; hon fell: RCA, RIBA; *Programmes* Arena documentaries incl: The Orson Welles Story, Billie Holiday - The Long Night of Lady Day, The Private Life of the Ford Cortina, My Way, The Chelsea Hotel; responsible for progs, films and series for BBC2 incl: The Late Show, Oranges Are Not The Only Fruit, The Snapper, Truly Madly Deeply, Have I Got News For You, Absolutely Fabulous, Rab C Nesbitt, Troubleshooter, Pandora's Box, Video Diaries, live relays of operas Tosca and Stiffelio, opera series The Vampyr; for BBC1 incl: introduction of Monday episode of EastEnders, re-introduction of Sunday afternoon family serial (incl Just William and The Borrowers); *Awards* incl: Best Arts Series Br Academy Awards for Arena 1982, 1983 and 1984, Best Arts Series Broadcasting Press Guild Awards for Arena 1985, Gold Award NY Film Festival and Int EMMY for Omnibus film The Treble 1985; *Style—* Alan Yentob, Esq; ✉ BBC Television Centre, Wood Lane, London W12 7RJ (☎ 0181 743 8000)

YEO, Diane Helen; da of Brian Harold Pickard, FRCS, and Joan Daisy, *née* Packham; *b* 22 July 1945; *Educ* Blackheath HS, Univ of London, Institut Francais de Presse; *m* 30 March 1970, Timothy Stephen Kenneth Yeo, MP, *qv*, s of Dr Kenneth John Yeo; 1 s (Jonathan b 1970), 1 da (Emily b 1972); *Career* BBC Radio prodn 1968–74, dir clearing house scheme Africa Educnl Tst 1974–79, head of fundraising Girl Guides' Assoc 1979–82; dir: appeals and public rels YWCA 1982–85, Inst of Charity Fundraising Mangrs 1985–88; conslt Centre for Voluntary Organisation LSE 1988–, charity cmmr 1989–95, dir Charity Appointments 1987–, chief exec The Malcolm Sargent Cancer Fund for Children 1995–, conslt Centre for Charity and Trust Research South Bank Univ 1995–; FICFM 1983, FRSA 1989; *Recreations* photography, music, tennis, swimming; *Style—* Mrs Diane Yeo; ✉ Malcolm Sargent Cancer Fund for Children, 14 Abingdon Road, London W8 6AF (☎ 0171 937 4548)

YEO, Jacinta Marina; *b* 23 Jan 1962; *Educ* Trinity Coll Dublin (BA, BDentSci, MA, Irish Dental Bd prize in periodontology, oral med, oral pathology and oral surgery), Primary FRCS (first place), accredited American Nat Dental Bd, Dip in Gemology (part one); *Career* dentist/broadcaster; house surgn Dublin Dental Hosp 1984–85, in private practice 1985–; advsr BUPA 1994–95, spokesman BDA 1995–; various TV and radio appearances on dentistry and gen topics 1993–; FRSM 1986; memb: BDA 1986, Br Endodontic Assoc 1987; FRSH 1995; *Recreations* polo, gemology, photography; *Clubs* Sloane, RAC; *Style—* Miss Jacinta Yeo; ✉ 40 Harley Street, London W1N 1AB (☎ 0171 323 2057)

YEO, Timothy Stephen Kenneth (Tim); MP (C) Suffolk South (majority 17,289); s of Dr Kenneth John Yeo (d 1979), and Norah Margaret Yeo; *b* 20 March 1945; *Educ* Charterhouse, Emmanuel Coll Cambridge; *m* 1970, Diane Helen, *qv*, da of Brian Harold Pickard; 1 s (Jonathan b 1970), 1 da (Emily b 1972); *Career* Parly candidate (C) Bedwellty 1974, MP (C) Suffolk South 1983–; jt sec: Cons Back-Bench Fin Ctee 1984–87, Social Services Select Ctee 1985–88; PPS to Rt Hon Douglas Hurd 1988–90, Parly under sec Dept of Environment 1990–92, Parly under sec Dept of Health 1992–93, min of state Dept of Environment 1993–94 (resigned); memb Select Ctee on Employment 1994–96, memb Treasy Select Ctee 1996–; chm Univent plc 1995–; dir Worcester Engrg Co Ltd 1975–86, asst treas Bankers Trust Company 1970–73, treas Int Voluntary Service 1975–78, dir The Scope (formerly Spastics Soc) 1980–83, tstee Tanzania Devpt Tst 1980–, chm Charities VAT Reform Gp 1981–88, chm Tadworth Ct Tst 1983–91; *Publications* Public Accountability and Regulation of Charities (1983); *Recreations* skiing; *Clubs* Carlton, Royal St George's Golf; *Style—* Tim Yeo, Esq, MP; ✉ House of Commons, London SW1A 0AA (☎ 0171 219 3000)

YEOMAN, Maj-Gen Alan; CB (1987); s of George Smith Patterson Yeoman (d 1978), and Wilhelmina Tromans Elwell (d 1944); *b* 17 Nov 1933; *Educ* Dame Allan's Sch Newcastle upon Tyne, RMA Sandhurst; *m* 12 March 1960, Barbara Joan, da of Norman Albert Davies (d 1975); 2 s (Timothy b 1 May 1961, Michael b 1 April 1965), 1 da (Sally b 29 Jan 1963); *Career* cmmnd RCS 1954; served 1954–70: Korea, Malaysia, Singapore, Cyprus, UK, BAOR, Canada; Staff Coll 1963, CO 2 Div Signals Regt BAOR 1970–73; HQ 1 (Br) Corps 1973–74, MOD 1974–77, Col AQ HQLF Cyprus 1978–79, Cdr Trg Gp Royal Signals and Catterick Garrison 1979–82, Brig AQ HQ 1 (Br) Corps BAOR 1982–84, Cdr Communications BAOR 1984–87, ret 1988; Hon Col 37 Signals Regt (V) 1987–96, Col Cmdt Royal Signals 1987–93; dir Army Sport Control Bd 1988–95; chm Royal Signals Assoc 1995–; *Recreations* golf, cricket, skiing; *Clubs* Army and Navy, MCC; *Style—* Maj-Gen A Yeoman, CB; ✉ c/o Lloyds Bank, Catterick Garrison, North Yorks

YEOMAN, Martin; s of Arthur John Yeoman (d 1993), and Gladys Dorothy, *née* Illsley; *b* 21 July 1953; *Educ* RA Schs (Silver medal for drawing); *Career* artist; David Murray Landscape scholar 1978, Richard Ford scholar 1979, Elizabeth Greenshield scholar 1980, Hamerson Purchase Prize 1984; occasional painting companion to HRH The Prince of Wales; RP; *Solo Exhibitions* Highgate Gall 1986, Two Tours of the Middle East (Agnews) 1987, New Grafton Gall 1990, The Queen's Grandchildren (National Portrait Gall) 1993, Selected Works (Mompesson House) 1994, Christopher Wood Contemporary Art 1995; *Group Exhibitions* Royal Acad Summer Exhbn 1976–77, 1979–90 and 1992–96, Imperial Tobacco Portrait Award (Nat Portrait Gall) 1981 and 1985, Six Young Artists (Agnews) 1985, Four Painters (New Grafton Gall) 1987, The Long Perspective (National Tst Exhbn, Agnews) 1987, A Personal Choice (Fermoy Gall) 1988, Salute to Turner (Nat Tst Exhbn, Agnews) 1989, The Order of Merit (Nat Portrait Gall) 1992; *Work in Collections* HM The Queen, HRH The Prince of Wales, Sir Brinsley Ford, Diocese of Birmingham, Baring Brothers, Grimsby Sch of Art, Nat Portrait Gall; *Style—* Martin Yeoman, Esq, RP

YEOMANS, Richard David; s of Richard James Yeomans (d 1964), of Eversley, Basingstoke, Hants, and Elsie Marian, *née* Winson; *b* 15 Feb 1943; *Educ* Hartley Wintney Co Secdy Modern Sch, Hants Coll of Agric, Shuttleworth Coll (NDA); *m* 6 April 1968, Doreen Ann, da of William Herring, of Aldershot; 1 s (Jonathon b 24 Feb 1976), 1 da (Claire b 14 Dec 1972); *Career* with Milk Mktg Bd 1965–71; Unigate plc: area mangr (tport) 1971, gen mangr (milk) 1975, latterly bd dir; md: Wincanton Transport Ltd 1978–, Wincanton Group Ltd 1982–91; ops dir Milk Marketing Bd 1994, chief exec Milk Marque 1996– (ops dir 1994–96); chm TLS Range Plc 1992, princ David Yeomans Associates 1991; tstee Nat Motor Museum Beaulieu; Liveryman Worshipful Co of Carmen; memb Wine Guild of UK; FIMgt 1982, FCIT 1989, FRSA 1990; *Recreations* shooting, opera, gardening, photography; *Clubs* RAC; *Style—* David Yeomans, Esq; ✉ Sandwood, Curlew Drive, West Chorleton, Kingsbridge, Devon TQ7 2AA (☎ 01548 53133); Milk Marque, Cleeve House, Lower Wick, Worcester WR2 4YB (☎ 01905 858500, fax 01905 858600)

YEOWART, Geoffrey Bernard Brian; s of Brian Albert Yeowart, of Chailey, Sussex, and Vera Ivy, *née* Goring; *b* 28 March 1949; *Educ* Ardingly Coll, Univ of Southampton (LLB), King's Coll London (LLM); *m* 6 Oct 1979, Patricia Eileen, da of Oswald Anthony (d 1984); 2 s (Thomas b 8 June 1983, Matthew b 30 Sept 1986), 1 da (Clare b 7 Nov 1980); *Career* admitted slr 1975 (admitted Hong Kong 1982); ptnr: Durrant Piesse 1985–88, Lovell White Durrant 1988–; memb: Law Soc, City of London Law Soc; *Recreations* sailing, skiing, reading; *Style—* Geoffrey Yeowart, Esq; ✉ Lovell White Durrant, 65 Holborn Viaduct, London EC1A 2DY (☎ 0171 236 0066, fax 0171 248 4212, telex 887122 LWD G)

YERBURGH, Capt the Hon Robert Richard Guy; o s and h of 2 Baron Alvingham, CBE, *qv*; *b* 10 Dec 1956; *Educ* Eton; *m* 1, 1981 (m dis 1993), Vanessa Kelty, yr da of Capt Duncan Kinloch Kirk; 2 s (Robert William Guy b 16 Sept 1983, Edward Alexander Henry b 6 April 1986); m 2, 1994, Karen L, elder da of Antony Baldwin, of Great Missenden, Bucks; 1 s (Charles Antony George b 19 Sept 1995); *Career* Lt 17/21 Lancers 1978, Capt 1980, attached to Army Air Corps as pilot 1979–83, resigned 1983; *Recreations* shooting, fishing, skiing (jt services instr); *Clubs* Cavalry & Guards'; *Style—* Capt the Hon Robert Yerburgh; ✉ Valley Farm House, Bix Bottom, Henley-on-Thames, Oxon (☎ 01491 576043)

YHAP, Laetitia Karoline; da of Leslie Neville Yhap (d 1987), and Elizabeth, *née* Kogler; *b* 1 May 1941; *Educ* Fulham Co GS, Camberwell Sch of Arts and Crafts (NDD), Slade School (DFA); *m* 1963 (m dis 1980), Jeffrey Camp; 1 s (Ajax b 1984); *ptnr* 1983–, Michael Rycroft; *Career* artist in oils; Leverhulme Res award (travel in Italy) 1962–63; first solo show Norwich Sch of Art 1964, Young Contemporaries FBA galleries and tour 1965, various showings with London Gp 1965–, three solo shows Piccadilly Gallery 1968, 1970 and 1973, solo summershow Serpentine Gallery 1975, Drawings of People (mixed exhibition, Serpentine Gallery London) 1975, John Moores (mixed exhibition) Liverpool, The British Art Show 1979, Art and The Sea (ICA and tour) 1981, Tolly Cobbold 1983, solo show Air Gallery London 1984, The Hard-Won Image (Tate Gallery) 1984, solo show touring The Business of the Beach (Laing Art Gallery Newcastle) 1988, Picturing People (Br Cncl Exhibition touring Far East) 1990, solo show Rye Art Gallery 1991, solo show Worthing Art Gallery and Museum 1992, Life at the Edge (The Charleston Gallery) 1993, solo show Bound by the Sea (Gymnasium Gallery Berwick-upon-Tweed) 1994, solo show Maritime Counterpoint (Boundary Gallery London) 1996; memb London Gp; *Recreations* badminton, concert going; *Style*— Ms Laetitia Yhap; ✉ 12 The Croft, Hastings, East Sussex TN34 3KH

YONACE, Dr Adrian Harris; JP (Dorset 1989); s of Dr Jack Yonace (d 1975), of Salford, and Bryna, *née* Fidler; *b* 26 Nov 1943; *Educ* Manchester GS, Univ of Manchester, Univ of Nottingham (BMedSci, BM BS); *m* 9 March 1989, Maureen Wilson, da of Thomas Wilson Ramsay, of Gullane; 2 c (Tristan Jack and Giselle Isla (twins) b 23 Aug 1995); *Career* computer systems analyst IBM 1965–67, computer conslt 1967–70; house physician and house surgn Univ Dept Manchester Royal Infirmary 1976–77, lectr in psychiatry Royal Free Hosp Univ of London 1980–83, conslt and hon sr lectr Friern Hosp and Univ of London 1983–89; conslt psychiatrist: St Ann's Hosp Poole 1989–93, Marchwood Priory Hosp Southampton 1993–; hon clinical res fell Univ of Southampton 1993–; examiner MRCPsych 1993–, sr examiner MB ChB Finals Univ of London; sec E Dorset BMA 1993–; Silver Dip Eng Bridge Union Teachers Assoc; JP Inner London Juvenile Bench 1985–89, Ct chm Poole Bench 1989–; FRCPsych 1994 (MRCPsych 1983); *Recreations* scrabble, bridge, golf; *Style*— Dr Adrian Yonace, JP; ✉ Marchwood Priory Hospital, Hythe Road, Marchwood, Southampton SO40 4WU (☎ 01703 840044)

YORATH, Terence Charles (Terry); s of David Yorath, of Cardiff, and Mary, *née* Sigallias; *b* 27 March 1950; *Educ* Cathays GS Cardiff; *m* 1971, Christine, da of Fred Kay (d 1990); 2 s (Daniel Aidan b 25 July 1976 d 25 May 1992, Jordan Lloyd b 8 Feb 1986), 2 da (Gabrielle Nicole b 24 April 1973, Louise Jayne b 18 April 1974); *Career* former professional footballer, now manager; clubs as player: Leeds Utd 1966–76 (capt, 250 appearances), Coventry City 1976–79 (capt, 100 appearances), Tottenham Hotspur 1979–81 (60 appearances), Vancouver Whitecaps 1981–83; honours with Leeds Utd: League Championship 1968, European Cup 1969, FA Cup 1972, runners-up European Cup Winners' Cup 1974; 59 Welsh caps 1969–80 (a record 42 as capt); Welsh Sports Personality of the Year 1974, Welsh Sportsman of the Year 1976; player/asst manager Bradford City 1983–86 (champions Div 3); manager: Swansea City 1986–88 and 1989–90, Bradford City 1988–89, Welsh National Team 1991–93 (pt/t 1988–91); general mangr Cardiff City 1994–95, int mangr Lebanese FA 1995–; regular TV football commentator, co-presenter football prog on HTV, involved in estab of schools of excellence for 9 to 16 year olds in Wales; fndr Terry Yorath Sports Consultancy Ltd 1994; vice pres Glamorgan CCC, memb National Sports Medicine Inst, patron Hypertrophic Cardiomyopathy Assoc (memb Ctee on Cardiac Screening for Adults); *Recreations* golf, horse racing; *Style*— Terry Yorath, Esq; ✉ Val d'Or, 28 The Ring Road, Shadwell, Leeds, W Yorks LS17 8NJ (☎ 0113 265 1146, fax 0113 265 0979, mobile 0836 737300)

YORK, Archdeacon of; *see:* Austin, Ven George Bernard

YORK, 96 Archbishop of 1995–; Most Rev and Rt Hon Dr David Michael Hope; KCVO (1995), PC (1991); patron of many livings, the Archdeaconries of York, Cleveland and the East Riding, and the Canonries in his Cathedral; the Archbishopric was founded AD 625, and the Province comprises fourteen Sees; s of Jack Hope, by his w Florence; *b* 14 April 1940; *Educ* Queen Elizabeth GS Wakefield, Univ of Nottingham (BA), Linacre Coll Oxford (DPhil, hon fell 1993), St Stephen's House Oxford; *Career* asst curate St John Tuebrook Liverpool 1965–70, chaplain Bucharest 1967–68, vicar St Andrew Warrington 1970–74, princ St Stephen's House Oxford 1974–82; vicar of All Saints' Margaret St London 1982–85, bishop of Wakefield 1985–91, bishop of London 1991–95; dean of HM's Chapels Royal 1991–95; *Recreations* theatre, walking, travel; *Style*— The Most Rev and Rt Hon the Lord Archbishop of York, KCVO; ✉ Bishopthorpe Palace, Bishopthorpe, York, N Yorks YO2 1QE (☎ 01904 707021/2, fax 01904 709204)

YORK, Col Edward Christopher; TD (1978), DL (N Yorks, 1988); s of Christopher York, and Pauline Rose Marie, *née* Fletcher; *b* 22 Feb 1939; *m* 28 April 1965, Sarah Ann, da of Maj James Kennedy Maxwell, MC (d 1980), of Buckby Folly, Northants; 1 s, 1 da; *Career* 1 Royal Dragoons (ret 1964), CO Queen's Own Yeomanry 1979–81, Dep Cdr 15 Inf Bde 1981–85, ADC (TAVR) to HM The Queen 1982–86; farmer and horticulturist; chm Thirsk Race Course Co Ltd; memb: Cncl RASE (hon dir 1992–96, pres 1996), Cncl CLA, Yorkshire Agric Soc (pres 1989); vice pres Northern Assoc of Building Socs; vice chm Yorks and Humberside TAVRA, Hon Col Y Sqdn The Queen's Own Yeo 1991–, Col Cmdt Yeomanry 1994–; chm Leeds Charitable Tst Royal Armouries International plc 1995–; High Sheriff N Yorks 1988; *Clubs* Boodle's, Pratt's; *Style*— Col E C York, TD, DL; ✉ Hutton Wandesley Hall, York YO5 8NA (☎ home 01904 738240, office 01904 738462/755, fax 01904 738468)

YORK, Michael; OBE (1996); s of Joseph Gwynne Johnson, and Florence Edith May Chown; *b* 27 March 1942; *Educ* Hurstpierpoint Coll, Bromley GS, Univ Coll Oxford (BA); *m* 1968, Patricia Frances; *Career* actor; Chevalier de L'Ordre National des Arts et Lettres (France) 1995; *Theatre* Dundee Repertory Theatre 1964, Nat Theatre Co 1965; credits incl: Outcry (NY) 1973, Bent (NY) 1980, Cyrano de Bergerac (Santa Fe) 1981, Whisper in the Mind (Phoenix) 1991, The Crucible (NY) 1992, Someone to Watch Over Me (NY) 1993; *Television* Jesus of Nazareth 1976, A Man Called Intrepid 1978, For Those I Loved 1981, The Weather in the Streets 1983, The Master of Ballantrae 1983, Space 1984, The Far Country 1985, The Four Minute Mile 1988, The Heat of the Day 1988, Till We Meet Again 1989, The Night of the Fox 1990, Fall From Grace 1994; *Films* Accident 1966, The Taming of the Shew 1967, Romeo and Juliet 1967, England Made Me 1971, Cabaret 1972, The Three Musketeers 1973, Murder on the Orient Express 1974, Conduct Unbecoming 1975, Logan's Run 1975, The Riddle of the Sands 1978, Success is the Best Revenge 1984, Dawn 1985, Vengence 1986, The Return of the Three Musketeers 1988, The Long Shadow 1992, Rochade 1992, Eline Vere 1992, Wide Sargasso Sea 1993, Discretion Assured 1993, The Shadow of a Kiss 1994, Gospa 1995; *Books* Travelling Player (autobiog, 1991), The Magic Paw Paw (1994); *Style*— Michael York, Esq, OBE; ✉ c/o London Management, 2–4 Noel Street, London W1V 3RB (☎ 0171 287 9000, fax 0171 287 3036)

YORK, Susannah Yolande; da of (William Peel) Simon Fletcher, and late Joan Nita Mary, *née* Bowring; *b* 9 Jan 1942; *Educ* Marr Coll Troon, E Haddon Hall Northants; *m* 2 May 1960 (m dis 1980), Michael Barry Wells; 1 s (Orlando Wells b June 1973), 1 da (Sasha Wells b May 1972); *Career* actress, writer, director; *Theatre* incl: Wings of a Dove, A Singular Man, Man and Superman, Private Lives, Hedda Gabler (London and New York); London and Paris performances: Peter Pan, Cinderella, The Singular Life of Albert Nobbs, Penthesilea, Fatal Attraction, The Women, The Apple Cart, Agnes of God, The Human Voice, Multiple Choice, A Private Treason, Lyric for a Tango, The Glass Menagerie, A Streetcar Named Desire, Noonbreak, September Tide (Comedy Theatre) 1994, Independent State (Grace Theatre and Aust tour) 1995; as dir: Revelations (Edinburgh Festival) 1991, The Eagle has Two Heads (Lilian Bayliss) 1994, First Years, Beginnings (Grace Theatre) 1995; *Television* incl: The Crucible, The Rebel and the Soldier, The First Gentleman, The Richest Man in the World, Fallen Angels, Second Chance, We'll Meet Again, The Other Side of Me, Star Quality, The Two Ronnies, Yellow Beard, A Christmas Carol, Bonnie Jean, Macho, Love Boat - USA, Return Journey, After the War, The Man from the Pru, The Haunting of the New, Devices and Desires, Boon, Trainer; *Films* incl: Tunes of Glory, Greengage Summer, Freud, Tom Jones, The Seventh Dawn, Act One Scene Nun, Sands of the Kalahari, Scruggs, Kaleidoscope, A Man for All Seasons, Sebastian, Duffy, Lock up your Daughters, The Killing of Sister George, Images (Best Actress Award at Cannes Film Festival), They Shoot Horses Don't They?, Country Dance, Happy Birthday Wanda June, Conduct Unbecoming, That Lucky Touch, Sky Riders, Eliza Fraser, Zee and Co, Silent Partner, The Shout, Memories, The Awakening, Gold, Jane Eyre, The Maids, Loophole, Superman I and II, Golden Gate Murders, Alice, Christmas Carol, Yellowbeard, Mio My Mio, Bluebeard, A Summer Story, Just ask for Diamond, Melancholia, Barbarblu Barbarblu, Little Women; *Books* In Search of Unicorns (2 edns, republished 1985), Larks Castle (1976, republished 1986); *Recreations* gardening, reading, writing, walking, travelling, films and theatre; *Style*— Ms Susannah York; ✉ Peters Fraser & Dunlop Ltd, 503 The Chambers, Chelsea Harbour, Lots Road, London SW10 0XF (☎ 0171 352 4446, fax 0171 352 7356)

YORK-JOHNSON, Michael; *see:* York, Michael

YORKE, David Harry Robert; CBE (1993); s of Harry Reginald Francis Yorke (d 1958), and Marie Christine, *née* Frost (d 1994); *b* 5 Dec 1931; *Educ* Dean Close Sch Cheltenham, Coll of Estate Mgmnt; *m* 23 April 1955, Patricia Gwynneth, da of Henry Arthur Fowler-Tutt (d 1975); 1 da (Sarah b 1960); *Career* Nat Serv RA 1954–56 (2 Lt 1955); chartered surveyor; Weatherall Green & Smith: ptnr London 1961–84, sr ptnr 1984–89, gp chm 1989–92, conslt 1992–; memb: Bristol Devpt Corp 1988–96, Cncl Br Property Fedn 1989–94; chm: RICS Insurance Services Ltd 1992–96, Belgravia Property Co 1993–95; dir Br Waterways Bd 1988–96; pres RICS 1988–89; Freeman City of London 1978, Liveryman Worshipful Co of Chartered Surveyors 1979; FRICS 1966 (ARICS 1956), FCIArb 1993; *Publications* Essentials of Rent Review (conslt ed, 1996); *Recreations* boating, crosswords, swimming, occasional cookery; *Clubs* Buck's; *Style*— David Yorke, Esq, CBE; ✉ Penolva, St Mawes, Cornwall TR2 5DR (☎ 01326 270235); 2 Chester Cottages, London SW1 (☎ 0171 823 4015)

YORKE, Margaret; da of John Peel Alexander Larminie (d 1958), and Alison Yorke, *née* Lyle (d 1978); *b* 30 Jan 1924; *Educ* Prior's Field Godalming Surrey; *m* 1945 (m dis 1957), Basil Nicholson; 1 da, 1 s; *Career* served WRNS 1942–45; author; asst librarian: St Hilda's Coll Oxford 1959–60, Christ Church Oxford 1963–65; sometime school secretary and bookseller; memb: Crime Writers' Assoc (chm 1979–80), Soc of Authors, PEN, Mystery Writers of America; *Books include* The Cost of Silence (1977), The Point of Murder (1978), Death on Account (1979), The Scent of Fear (1980, Best Translated Novel Swedish Acad of Detection 1982), The Hand of Death (1981), Devil's Work (1982), Find Me a Villain (1983), The Smooth Face of Evil (1984), Intimate Kill (1985), Safely to the Grave (1986), Evidence to Destroy (1987), Speak for the Dead (1988), Crime in Question (1989), Admit to Murder (1990), A Small Deceit (1991), Criminal Damage (1992), Dangerous to Know (1993), Almost The Truth (1994), Pieces of Justice (collected short stories, 1994), Serious Intent (1995), A Question of Belief (1996); series featuring the detective Patrick Grant: Dead in the Morning (1970), Silent Witness (1972), Grave Matters (1973), Mortal Remains (1974), Cast for Death (1976); *Recreations* swimming, reading, gardening, theatre, travel; *Clubs* Royal Over-Seas League; *Style*— Mrs Margaret Yorke; ✉ c/o Curtis Brown, 4th Floor, Haymarket House, 28–29 Haymarket, London SW1Y 4SP (☎ 0171 396 6600)

YORKE, Very Rev Michael Leslie; s of Leslie Henry Yorke (d 1996), of Worthing, and Brenda Emma, *née* Linnell; *b* 25 March 1939; *Educ* Midhurst GS, Brighton Coll, Magdalene Coll Cambridge (BA), Cuddesdon Coll Oxford (MA); *m* 1, 6 June 1964, Michal Sara (d 1987), da of Christopher Vigor Dadd; 1 da (Philippa Clare b 14 Nov 1965), 1 s (Christopher Tobias b 3 April 1969); m 2, 22 Oct 1988, Frances Grace Archer, da of David Parry-Williams; *Career* ordained: deacon 1964, priest 1965; curate Croydon Parish Church 1964–67, precentor Chelmsford Cathedral 1968–73, dep dir Res and Trg 1973–75, rector Ashdon with Hadstock 1974–78, canon residentiary Chelmsford Cathedral 1978–88, concurrently vice provost 1984–88, vicar St Margaret's Church Kings Lynn 1988–94, hon canon Norwich Cathedral 1993–94, provost Portsmouth Cathedral 1994–; nat chm Samaritans 1976–79; *Recreations* contemporary art, military history, long country walks; *Style*— The Very Rev Michael Yorke; ✉ Provost's House, Pembroke Road, Old Portsmouth, Hampshire PO1 2NS (☎ and fax 01705 824400); Portsmouth Cathedral Office, St Thomas' Street, Hampshire PO1 2HH (☎ 01705 823300, fax 01705 295480)

YOSHIDA, Miyako; da of Eiji Yoshida, of Tokyo, and Etsuko, *née* Fukuda; *Career* ballet dancer; with Sadler's Wells Royal Ballet (now Birmingham Royal Ballet) 1984–95, princ Royal Ballet 1995–; *Performances* incl leading roles in: Swan Lake, Sleeping Beauty, The Nutcracker, Giselle, Elite Syncopations, La Fille Mal Gardée, Hobson's Choice, The Dream, Don Quixote, Paquita, Allegri Diversi, Theme and Variations, Concerto Barrocco, Les Sylphides, Divertimento No 15, Dance Concertantes, Symphony in 3 Movements, Choreartium, Five Tangos, Pavane pas de deux, Sylvia; *Awards* Prix de Lausanne 1983, Global Award 1989, Dance and Dancer magazine Dancer of the Year 1991, E Nakagawa Award 1995, A Tachibana Award 1996; *Recreations* reading, watching films; *Style*— Miss Miyako Yoshida; ✉ The Royal Ballet, Covent Garden, London WC2E 9DD (☎ 0171 240 1200)

YOUARD, Richard Geoffrey Atkin; s of Lt-Col Geoffrey Youard, MBE (d 1987), and Hon Mrs Rosaline Joan, *née* Atkin (d 1973); *b* 27 Jan 1933; *Educ* Bradfield, Magdalen Coll Oxford (BA); *m* 31 Dec 1960, Felicity Ann, da of Kenneth Valentine Freeland Morton, CIE, of Great Wilbraham, Cambridge; 1 s (Andrew b 1964), 2 da (Penelope b 1961, Elizabeth b 1966); *Career* Nat Serv 1951–53, cmmnd RA 1952, Lt TA; admitted slr 1959, Slaughter and May 1956–89 (ptnr 1968–89); the Investment Ombudsman (formerly Investment Referee) 1989–96; chm: Islington Consumers' Gp 1965, Nat Fedn of Consumer Gps 1968; memb Home Office Ctee on London Taxicab and Car Hire Trade 1967, inspr DTI 1987, memb Governing Body Bradfield Coll 1968–95 (clerk and govr); hon res fell King's Coll London 1988; memb Cncl Pali Text Soc 1991; memb Law Soc 1968; *Books* various works on banking law and practice incl Butterworths Banking Forms and Precedents (ed 1986); *Recreations* gardening, electronics, beekeeping, map collecting, reading, Welsh language; *Clubs* Garrick; *Style*— Richard Youard, Esq; ✉ 12 Northampton Park, London N1 2PJ (☎ 0171 226 8055); Cwm Mynach Ganol, Bontddu, Dolgellau, Gwynedd LL40 2TU

YOUD, Sam (pen name John Christopher); s of Sam Youd (d 1966), and Harriet, *née* Hawkins (d 1949); *b* 16 April 1922; *Educ* Peter Symonds Sch; *m* 1, 1946 (m dis 1978), Joyce, *née* Fairbairn; 1 s (Nicholas b 20 June 1951), 4 da (Rose b 1 July 1953, Elizabeth b 14 Sept 1955, Sheila b 27 July 1957, Margret b 11 April 1959); m 2, 24 Dec 1980, Jessica, *née* Ball; *Career* writer; Atlantic award in lit 1947, Guardian award 1971, Christopher award 1971, Jugendbuchpreis 1976, George Stone children's book award 1977; Soc of Authors: memb 1948–, memb Children's Writers Gp 1977– (chm 1983–85); fiction for adults as John Christopher incl: The Death of Grass (1956), The World in Winter (1962), The Possessors (1965), A Wrinkle in the Skin (1965), The Little People (1966), Pendulum (1968); fiction for young people as John Christopher incl: The Tripods trilogy (1967–68), The Lotus Caves (1969), The Guardians (1970), The Sword trilogy (1970–72), Dom and Va (1973), Wild Jack (1974), Empty World (1977), The Fireball trilogy (1981–86), When The Tripods Came (1988), A Dusk of Demons (1993); has also written as Hilary Ford, William Godfrey, Peter Graaf, Anthony Rye and Samuel Youd; *Recreations* dogless dog walking and counting blessings; *Clubs* United (Guernsey), Royal

Channel Islands Yacht (Guernsey), Academy; *Style*— Sam Youd, Esq; ✉ One Whitefriars, Rye, E Sussex TN31 7LE (☎ 01797 224557, fax 01797 224654)

YOUENS, Sir Peter William; kt (1965), CMG (1962), OBE (1960); s of Rev Canon Fearnley Algernon Cyril Youens (d 1968), and Dorothy Mary, *née* Ross (d 1975); *b* 29 April 1916; *Educ* King Edward VII Sch Sheffield, Wadham Coll Oxford (MA); *m* 1943, Diana Stephanie (d 1990), da of Edward Hawkins; 2 da (Stephanie (Mrs Richard Worsley), Sarah (Mrs Christopher Nevile)); *Career* joined Colonial Admin Serv 1938, naval serv 1939–40; Sierra Leone: asst dist cmmr 1942, dist cmmr 1948, colony cmmr and memb Legislative Cncl 1950; dep chief sec Nyasaland 1953–63 (asst sec 1951), memb Nyasaland Legislative Cncl 1954–61; sec to PM and Cabinet: Nyasaland 1963–64, Malawi 1964–66; exec dir Lonrho plc 1966–69 and 1981–94 (non-exec dir 1980–81), ptnr John Tyzack and Partners Ltd 1969–81; *Recreations* walking, theatre; *Clubs* East India and Sports, Vincent's (Oxford); *Style*— Sir Peter Youens, CMG, OBE; ✉ Hillview, Primrose Hill Road, London NW3

YOUNG, Angus Graham Ferguson; s of Fergus Ferguson Young (d 1976), and Helen Frances Graham, *née* Murphy (d 1976); *b* 22 July 1933; *Educ* Aymestrey Sch Crown East Worcester, King's Sch Bruton Somerset, Christ's Coll Cambridge (BA, MA); *m* 6 Oct 1962, Sheila Ann, da of Frank Kemp, of Thetford, Norfolk; 2 da (Nicola Frances b 22 Sept 1963, Katharine Ann b 24 March 1965); *Career* Nat Serv 2 Lt Somerset LI 1951–53 (served with 3 Bn Gold Coast Regt RWAFF); Radcliffes & Co: articled clerk to Sir Edmund Sargant 1956, admitted slr 1960, ptnr 1962–95, sr ptnr 1990–95; dir CMG plc 1993–; tstee and chm Queen Elizabeth Hosp for Children Res Appeal Tst 1960–; memb Cncl: Royal London Aid Soc 1961–, Animal Health Tst 1991–; tstee Help the Aged 1996–; memb: Law Soc 1960, Westminster Law Soc 1962; *Recreations* reading, walking, fishing, theatre, occasional sailing and shooting; *Clubs* St Stephen's Constitutional, RAC; *Style*— Angus Young, Esq; ✉ Radcliffes Crossman Block, 5 Great College Street, Westminster, London SW1P 3SJ (☎ 0171 222 7040, fax 0171 222 6208/6754)

YOUNG, Anthony Elliott (Tony); s of Prof Leslie Young, of Esher, Surrey, and Ruth, *née* Elliott; *b* 20 Dec 1943; *Educ* Epsom Coll, St John's Coll Cambridge (MA, MB MChir), St Thomas' Hosp Med Sch; *m* 6 July 1968, Dr Gwyneth Vivien Wright, da of Prof Eldred Walls, of Edinburgh, Scot; 3 s (Adam Elliott b 1974, Oliver Elliott b 1975, Toby Elliott b 1977); *Career* dir of surgery St Thomas' Hosp 1988–93 (conslt surgn 1981–); med dir Guy's and St Thomas' NHS Tst 1993–; memb BMA 1968, FRSM 1970, FRCS 1971; *Books* Vascular Malformations (1988), Companion in Surgical Studies (1992); *Recreations* fishing, painting, reading; *Style*— Anthony Young, Esq; ✉ 63 Lee Rd, Blackheath, London SE3 9EN (☎ 0181 852 1921); St Thomas' Hospital, London SE1 7EH (☎ 0171 928 9292); 38 Devonshire Place, London W1N 1PE (☎ 0171 580 3612, fax 0181 244 5467)

YOUNG, Prof Archie; s of Archibald Young, TD, of Glasgow, and Mary Downie, *née* Fleming (d 1995); *b* 19 Sept 1946; *Educ* Glasgow HS, Univ of Glasgow (BSc, MB ChB, MD); *m* 24 Dec 1973 (m dis 1995), Sandra, da of Archibald Clark (d 1969), of Glasgow; 1 s (Archie b 1980), 1 da (Sula b 1979); *Career* clinical lectr Univ of Oxford 1978–85, prof of geriatric med Royal Free Hosp Med Sch London 1988– (conslt physician 1985–88); memb: Research Advsy Cncl Research into Ageing, Scientific Advsy Ctee Rehabilitation and Medical Research Tst; Prince Philip Medal Inst of Sports Med 1995; Scottish swimming int 1965–70 (British 1970), Scottish water polo int 1968; memb: Medical Research Soc, Euro Soc for Clinical Investigation, American Coll of Sports Medicine; memb Incorporation of Tailors Glasgow; FRCPG 1985, FRCP 1989; *Recreations* physical; *Clubs* London Scottish Football, Junior Mountaineering Club of Scotland; *Style*— Prof Archie Young; ✉ University Dept of Geriatric Medicine, Royal Free Hosp Sch of Medicine, London NW3 2PF (☎ 0171 794 0500 ext 5240, fax 0171 830 2202)

YOUNG, Barbara Scott; da of George Young (d 1981), of Perth, Scotland, and Mary, *née* Scott; *b* 8 April 1948; *Educ* Perth Acad, Univ of Edinburgh (MA), Univ of Strathclyde; *Career* sr admin Gtr Glasgow Health Bd 1973–78, dir of planning & devpt St Thomas's Health Dist 1978–79, dist gen admin NW Dist Kensington, Chelsea & Westminster AHA 1979–82, dist admin Haringey Health Authy 1982–85; dist gen mangr: Paddington & North Kensington Health Authy 1985–88, Parkside Health Authy 1988–91; chief exec RSPB 1991–; pres Inst of Health Servs Mgmnt 1987–88 (dip 1971), patron Inst of Environmental & Ecological Mgmnt 1993–, tstee Nat Cncl for Voluntary Orgns 1993–; memb: World Cncl Birdlife Int 1994–, Ctee of Sec of State for Environment's UK Round Table on Sustainability, Cmmn on Future of the Voluntary Sector, Ctee on the Public Understanding of Sci (COPUS) 1996–; Hon Doctorate Univ of Stirling 1995; AHSM 1971; *Books* What Women Want (contrib, 1990), Medical Negligence (contrib, 1990); *Recreations* cinema, gardening; *Style*— Miss Barbara Young; ✉ Chief Executive, RSPB, The Lodge, Sandy, Beds SG19 2DL (☎ 01767 680551, fax 01767 692365)

YOUNG, Bertram Alfred; OBE (1980); s of Bertram William Young, and Dora Elizabeth, *née* Knight; *b* 20 Jan 1912; *Educ* Highgate Sch; *Career* HM Forces 1939–48 (Lancashire Fusiliers, King's African Rifles); Amalgamated Press 1930–35, asst ed Punch 1948–63, drama critic and arts ed Financial Times 1964–77; *Books* Tooth and Claw (1958), Bechuanaland (1966), Cabinet Pudding (1967), The Mirror up to Nature (1982), The Rattigan Version (1986); *Recreations* surviving; *Clubs* Garrick; *Style*— B A Young, Esq, OBE; ✉ 1 Station St, Cheltenham, Gloucestershire GL50 3LX (☎ 01242 581485)

YOUNG, Sir Brian Walter Mark; kt (1976); er s of Sir Mark Young, GCMG (d 1974), sometime Govr of Barbados, Tanganyika and Hong Kong; ggs of Sir George Young, 2 Bt, of Formosa Place; *b* 23 Aug 1922; *Educ* Eton, King's Coll Cambridge; *m* 1947, Fiona Marjorie, only da of Allan Stewart, 16 of Appin; 1 s (Timothy b 1951), 2 da (Joanna b 1949, Deborah b 1953); *Career* serv WWII RNVR; asst master Eton 1947–52, headmaster Charterhouse 1952–64, memb Central Advsy Cncl on Educn 1956–59; dir Nuffield Fndn 1964–70 (managing tstee 1978–90), dir-gen IBA (previously ITA) 1970–82; memb Arts Cncl 1983–88, chm Christian Aid 1983–90; Hon DLitt Heriot-Watt Univ; Hon RNCM 1987; FSA 1994; *Style*— Sir Brian Young, FSA; ✉ Hill End, Woodhill Ave, Gerrards Cross, Bucks (☎ 01753 887793)

YOUNG, Charles Whiteford; s of John Whiteford Young (d 1975), of Glasgow, and Jean-Kay Ralston, *née* Miller; *b* 18 May 1953; *Educ* Glasgow Acad, Trinity Coll Glenalmond, Univ of Aberdeen (LLB), Univ of Glasgow (dip Accountancy); *m* 27 Aug 1981, Sharon Midgley Moiran, da of Alexander Kilpatrick Stevenson; 3 da (Victoria Louise Midgley b 22 Nov 1985, Alexandra Jane Whiteford b 25 May 1987, Katherine Elizabeth Wallace b 3 Oct 1988); *Career* trainee accountant Arthur Young McClelland Moores Glasgow 1975–78, dir and memb Court British Linen Bank Ltd 1991– (joined 1979); MICAS 1978; *Recreations* golf, skiing, tennis, swimming, cycling; *Clubs* Bruntsfield Links Golf, Elie Golf House, East India, Devonshire, Sports and Public Schools; *Style*— Charles Young, Esq; ✉ 8 Succoth Place, Edinburgh EH12 6BL (☎ 0131 539 2628); The British Linen Bank Ltd, 4 Melville Street, Edinburgh EH3 7NS (☎ 0131 243 8326)

YOUNG, His Hon Judge; Christopher Godfrey; s of Dr H G Young (d 1949); *b* 9 Sept 1932; *Educ* Bedford Sch, King's Coll London (LLB); *m* 1969, Jeanetta Margaret, *née* Vaughan (d 1984); 1 s; *Career* called to the Bar Gray's Inn 1957, Midland and Oxford Circuit 1959–75, recorder 1975–79, circuit judge (Midland and Oxford Circuit) 1980–; liaison judge with magistrates: for Peterborough, Huntingdon and Toseland 1980–87, for Leicestershire 1987–; memb Parole Bd 1990–93, hon pres Sch of Law de Montfort Univ 1996–; *Recreations* music, natural history, Byzantium, foreign travel; *Style*— His Hon Judge Young; ✉ Stockshill House, Duddington, Stamford, Lincs PE9 3QQ

YOUNG, Prof Daniel Greer; s of Gabriel Young, and Julia, *née* McNair; *b* 22 Nov 1932; *Educ* Wishaw HS, Univ of Glasgow; *m* 2 Aug 1957, Agnes Gilchrist (Nan), da of Joseph Donald; 1 s (Kenneth Donald b 1962), 1 da (Rhoda Agnes (Mrs Abel) b 1958); *Career* Nat Serv 1957, special short serv cmmn to Ghana Govt 1959; hon conslt paediatric surgn: The Hosp for Sick Children Gt Ormond St London (formerly sr registrar and resident asst surgn), Queen Elizabeth Hosp London; sr lectr in paediatric surgery Inst of Child Health Univ of London, hon conslt paediatric surgn Greater Glasgow Health Bd, prof of paediatric surgery Univ of Glasgow 1992– (formerly reader); ex chm Intercollegiate Bd in Paediatric Surgery, memb Cncl RCPS Glasgow, ex pres Royal Medico-Chirurgical Soc of Glasgow, ed for the Br Isles - Journal of Paediatric Surgery UK, chm W of Scotland Surgical Assoc, past pres Br Assoc of Paediatric Surgns, memb Exec Ctee World Fedn of Paediatric Surgical Assocs; hon memb: Hungarian Assoc of Paediatric Surgns, South African Assoc of Paediatric Surgns, American Paediatric Surgical Assoc; FRCSEd, FRCS Glasgow; *Books* Baby Surgery (with B F Weller, 1971), Baby Surgery (with E J Martin, 2 edn, 1979), Children's Medicine and Surgery (jtly, 1995); *Recreations* curling, gardening, fishing; *Style*— Prof Daniel Young; ✉ 49 Sherbrooke Avenue, Glasgow G41 4SE (☎ 0141 427 3470); Royal Hospital for Sick Children, Yorkhill, Glasgow G3 8SJ (☎ 0141 201 0000, fax 0141 201 0858)

YOUNG, David Edward Michael; QC (1980); s of George Henry Edward Young, and Audrey, *née* Seymour; *b* 30 Sept 1940; *Educ* Monkton Combe Sch Somerset, Univ of Oxford (MA); *m* 1967, Anne, da of John Henry de Bromhead, of Ireland; 2 da (Yolanda b 1970, Francesca b 1972); *Career* called to the Bar Lincoln's Inn 1966, bencher 1989, head of chambers; recorder SE Circuit 1987–, dep High Ct judge Chancery Div 1993–; chm Plant Varieties and Seeds Tbnl 1987–; *Books* Terrell on the Law of Patents (1994), Passing Off (1994); *Recreations* tennis, skiing, walking, country pursuits; *Style*— David Young, Esq, QC; ✉ Three New Square, Lincoln's Inn, London WC2A 3RS (☎ 0171 405 1111)

YOUNG, David Ernest; s of Harold Ernest Young (d 1971), of Sheffield, and Jessie, *née* Turnbull; *b* 8 March 1942; *Educ* King Edward VII Sch Sheffield, Corpus Christi Coll Oxford (BA); *m* 8 Feb 1964 (m dis), Norma, da of Alwyn Robinson (d 1979); 2 da (Wendy b 1965, Michele b 1968); *Career* asst princ Air Miny 1963; private sec: Chief of Air Staff 1968–70, Min State of Def 1973–75; asst sec Central Policy Review Staff Cabinet Office 1975–77; John Lewis Partnership: joined 1982, md Peter Jones Sloane Square 1984–86, fin dir 1987–, dep chm 1993–; chm: Halos Ltd 1994–96, Audit Ctee Open Univ 1994–, Cncl Open Univ 1996–; ind memb Steering Bd of Companies House 1988–93, memb Hansard Soc Cmmn on Regulation of Privatised Utilities 1996; *Recreations* walking, opera, theatre; *Style*— David Young, Esq; ✉ John Lewis Partnership plc, 171 Victoria St, London SW1E 5NN (☎ 0171 828 1000, fax 0171 828 6609)

YOUNG, Rt Rev David Nigel de Lorentz; *see:* Ripon, Bishop of

YOUNG, Lt-Gen Sir David Tod; KBE (1980), CB (1977), DFC (1952); s of William Young (d 1930), by his w Davina Tod, *née* Young (d 1974); *b* 17 May 1926; *Educ* George Watson's Coll Edinburgh; *m* 1, 1950, Joyce Marian Melville (d 1987); 2 s; m 2, 11 June 1988, Mrs Joanna M Oyler, *née* Torin; *Career* cmmnd Royal Scots 1945, Col GS Staff Coll 1969–70, Cdr 12 Mechanized Bde 1970–72, Dep Mil Sec MOD 1972–74, Cdr Land Forces NI 1975–77, Col The Royal Scots 1975–80, Dir Infantry 1977–80, Col Cmdt Scottish Div, GOC Scotland 1980–82; govr Edinburgh Castle 1980–82, ret; chm Cairntech Ltd 1983–92 (non-exec dir 1992–); HM cmmr Queen Victoria Sch Dunblane 1984–93, pres Army Cadet Force Assoc Scotland 1984–96, Col Cmdt Ulster Def Regiment 1986–91, chm Scottish Ctee Marie Curie Memorial Fndn 1986 (memb 1983), govr St Columba's Hospice 1986, chm St Mary's Cathedral Workshop 1986–92 (pres 1993), vice-pres Scottish Partnership Agency for Palliative and Cancer Care 1993; *Recreations* golf, shooting; *Clubs* New, Royal Scots (both Edinburgh); *Style*— Lt-Gen Sir David Young, KBE, CB, DFC; ✉ c/o Adam & Co plc, 22 Charlotte Sq, Edinburgh EH2 4DF

YOUNG, David Tyrrell; s of Tyrrell Francis Young, of London, and Patricia Morrison, *née* Spicer; *b* 6 Jan 1938; *Educ* Charterhouse; *m* 11 Sept 1965, Madeline Helen Celia, da of Anthony Burton Capel Philips (d 1983), of Tean, Stoke-on-Trent; 3 da (Melanie Rosamond b 1969, Annabel Katharine b 1971, Corinna Lucy b 1974); *Career* TA 1 Regt HAC 1955–67, ret Capt 1967; trainee CA Gerard Van De Linde & Son 1955–60, audit mangr James Edwards Dangerfield & Co 1961–65; Spicer & Oppenheim (formerly Spicer & Pegler): audit mangr 1965–68, ptnr 1968–82, managing ptnr 1982–88, sr ptnr and int chm 1988–90; dep chm Touche Ross & Co 1990–93; chm: N Herts NHS Tst 1994–, City Capital Counselling UK 1996–; dir: Lombard Insurance Group plc 1993–, Asprey plc 1993–, Wates City of London Properties plc 1994–, Nomura Bank International plc 1996–; cncl memb ICEAW 1979–82; memb HAC; Freeman City of London, Memb Ct Worshipful Co of Fishmongers, memb Ct of Assts Worshipful Co of CAs; FCA, FRSA, Hon FCGI; *Recreations* golf, tennis; *Clubs* Royal St George's Golf, Royal Worlington Golf, City of London; *Style*— David T Young, Esq; ✉ Overhall, Ashdon, Saffron Walden, Essex CB10 2JH (☎ 01799 584556); Eastgate House, 40 Dukes Place, London EC3A 7LP (☎ 0171 204 1000, fax 0171 397 4588)

YOUNG, David Wright; MP (Lab) Bolton South East (majority 12,691); *Educ* Greenock Acad, Univ of Glasgow, St Paul's Coll Cheltenham; *Career* formerly: cncllr Coventry Co Borough Cncl, alderman Nuneaton Borough Cncl, cncllr Nuneaton DC; chm Coventry E Lab Pty 1964–68; Parly candidate (Lab): S Worcs 1959, Banbury 1966, Bath 1970; MP (Lab): Bolton E Feb 1974–1983, Bolton SE 1983–; PPS to Sec of State for Def 1977–79, offr CPA and IPU Gps House of Commons; former memb: Public Accounts Cmmn Select Ctee on Employment, Pty Ctees of Foreign Affairs and Def; All Pty Ctees and Parly Gps: vice chm Burmese, Gibralta, Danish, Ecuador, Japan, Lebanon, Malawi, Mongolian, Indonesian, Mauritius, Morocco, Peru, Singapore, Swedish, Belize and Venezuela, treas Iranian, jt sec Malaysian, sec Finland; vice chm House of Commons Motor Club; *Style*— David Young, Esq, MP; ✉ House of Commons, London SW1A 0AA

YOUNG, Donal Richard William (Don); s of Rupert Meyer Young (d 1974), and Euphemia Charlotte, *née* Cuthbert; *b* 18 April 1939; *Educ* City Sch Lincoln, LSE (BSc (Econ)); *m* Charlotte; 2 s; *Career* Unilever Ltd 1961–69, sr trg advsr and devpt mangr Food, Drink and Tobacco Training Board 1969–71, gp mgmnt devpt exec Plessey Company 1971–74, gp head of personnel and orgn Ellerman Group 1974–82, dir personnel and orgn Thorn EMI plc 1982–90, dir Young Samuel Chambers Ltd (strategy, orgn and devpt consultancy) 1990–93, dir of orgn and human resources Redland PLC 1993–; chm YSC Ltd; qualified pilot, hon citizen City of New Orleans; *Publications* Improving Work Groups (revised, 1992), Top Team Development (1990); *Recreations* sailing and adventure, gardening, community life, pubs, beer, wine and conversation; *Style*— Don Young, Esq; ✉ Redland plc, Redland House, Reigate, Surrey RH2 0SJ (☎ 01737 233234, fax 01737 223527)

YOUNG, Prof Douglas Wilson; s of John Robert Young (d 1992), and Christina, *née* Martin; *b* 15 Jan 1939; *Educ* Eastwood Sch Glasgow, Univ of Glasgow (BSc, PhD, Carnegie Scholar); *m* 1971, Ruth Lilian, da of Brian Welch; 1 da (Janet Mary b 1973), 1 s (Malcolm John b 1976); *Career* research fell Harvard Univ 1963–65; Univ of Sussex: lectr in chemistry 1965–84, reader 1984–88, prof of chemistry 1988–; visiting scholar Uppsala Univ 1985, visiting prof Univ of Nantes 1989; Royal Soc of Chemistry: chm Bio-organic Gp 1991–94, Tilden lectr and medal 1993–94, vice pres Perkin Div 1995–97; FRSC, FRSE 1996; *Publications* author of over 130 books and articles; *Recreations* listening to music, DIY; *Style*— Prof Douglas Young, FRSE; ✉ School of Chemistry and Molecular Sciences, University of Sussex, Falmer, Brighton, Sussex BN1 9RH (☎ 01273 678327, fax 01273 677196, e-mail D.W.YOUNG@SUSSEX.ac.uk)

YOUNG, Elizabeth Jane; da of Philip John Grattidge, of Wareham, Dorset, and Marion Elizabeth, *née* Dixon; *b* 9 Jan 1957; *Educ* Bedford HS for Girls, Sidney Sussex Coll Cambridge (MA); *m* 11 April 1981, John Todd Young, *qv*, s of Ian Taylor Young, of Rugby, Warwickshire; *Career* slr; Clifford Chance (formerly Coward Chance): articled clerk 1980–82, admitted slr 1982, ptnr 1988–; memb: Law Soc, City of London Slrs' Co; *Recreations* mountaineering, windsurfing; *Clubs* Cannons; *Style*— Mrs Elizabeth Young; ✉ Clifford Chance, 200 Aldersgate St, London EC1A 3JJ (☎ 0171 600 1000, fax 0171 600 5555)

YOUNG, Prof the Rev Frances Margaret; da of Alfred Stanley Worrall, CBE, of Belfast, and Mary Frances, *née* Marshall; *b* 25 Nov 1939; *Educ* Bedford Coll London (BA), Girton Coll Cambridge (MA, PhD); *m* 20 June 1964, Dr Robert Charles Young, s of Lt Charles William Young (d 1978), of Sherborne, Dorset; 3 s (Arthur Thomas b 1967, Edward Stanley b 1969, William Francis b 1974); *Career* ordained Methodist minister 1984; Univ of Birmingham: temporary lectr in theol 1971–73, lectr in New Testament studies 1973–82, sr lectr 1982–86, Edward Cadbury prof of theology 1986–, dean Faculty of Arts 1995–; Hon DD Univ of Aberdeen 1994; *Books* Sacrifice and the Death of Christ (1975), Can These Dry Bones Live? (1982), From Nicaea to Chalcedon (1983), Face to Face (1985, revised edn 1990), Focus on God (with Kenneth Wilson, 1986), Meaning and Truth in 2 Corinthians (with David Ford, 1987), The Art of Performance (1990), The Making of the Creeds (1991); *Recreations* music, walking, cycling, camping, poetry; *Style*— Prof the Rev Frances Young; ✉ 142 Selly Park Rd, Birmingham B29 7LH (☎ 0121 472 4841); Office of the Dean of the Faculty of Arts, University of Birmingham, PO Box 363, Birmingham B15 2TT (☎ 0121 414 5657)

YOUNG, (Russell) Francis; s of Canon (Cecil) Edwyn Young, CVO (Queen's chaplain, d 1988), of Hove, Sussex, and Beatrice Mary, *née* Rees; *b* 27 Feb 1953; *Educ* Radley, Blackpool Coll of Hotel Mgmnt (HND Catering and Hotel Admin); *m* 9 May 1981, Anne, da of Charles Edward Williams; 1 s (Edward Francis Charles b 30 May 1982), 1 da (Alexandra Anne Mary b 1 May 1985); *Career* hotelier; asst food and beverage mangr Grosvenor Hotel Chester 1975–76 (trainee mangr 1974–75), mangr HM King Hussein of Jordan's summer palace Aqaba Jordan 1975–78 (i/c entire running of palace except security and the royal yachts), food and beverage mangr Sandy Lane Hotel St James Barbados 1978–80; Marriot Corporation 1980–84: dir of restaurant Hunt Valley Marriott Baltimore Maryland 1980–81, opened as food and beverage dir Longwharf Marriott Boston Mass 1981–82 then London Marriott 1982–84; gen mangr Oakley Court Hotel Windsor 1985–86, gp ops dir Select Country Hotels 1986–87; restored semi-derelict vicarage and opened as proprietor The Pear Tree at Purton 1987– (National Westminster Bank Award for Business Development 1992 and RAC Blue Ribbon 1993, 1994 and 1995); chm Swindon Hotelier Assoc, vice chm Thames Valley Hotels, chm Bd of Govrs Bradon Forest Sch; Freeman City of London, MI 1994, FHCIMA; *Recreations* cricket, family, walking; *Clubs* Purton Cricket; *Style*— Francis Young, Esq; ✉ The Pear Tree at Purton, Church End, Purton, Swindon, Wilts SN5 9ED (☎ 01793 772100, fax 01793 772369)

YOUNG, Gavin David; s of Lt Col Gavin David Young (d 1978), and Daphne, *née* Forestier-Walker (d 1981); *b* 24 April 1928; *Educ* Rugby, Trinity Coll Oxford (MA); *Career* Nat Serv Welsh Gds 1946–48, served in Palestine 1947–48; Ralli Brothers Iraq 1950–52, Desert Locust Control Tihama and Asir Provinces of Saudi Arabia 1954–56; foreign corr The Observer in Africa Far E and ME 1959–90 (corr in NY 1962–63 and Paris 1967); FRSL 1987, FRGS 1989; *Books* Return to the Marshes (1977), Iraq: Land of Two Rivers (1979), Slow Boats to China (1981), Slow Boats Home (1985), Worlds Apart (1987), Beyond Lion Rock (1988), In Search of Conrad (1991, jt winner Thomas Cook Travel Award), From Sea to Shining Sea: A Present-Day Journey Through America's Past (1995), A Wavering Grace: A Vietnamese Family in War and Peace (1997); *Recreations* travel in remote places, reading, walking, music, talking late; *Clubs* Cavalry and Guards', Pratt's, Brooks's, Beefsteak, Shikar, Foreign Correspondents (Hong Kong); *Style*— Gavin Young, Esq, FRSL; ✉ c/o Well, 49 Earls Court Road, London W8 6EE (☎ and fax 0171 937 3538)

YOUNG, George Horatio (Gerry); s and h of Rt Hon Sir George Samuel Knatchbull Young, 6 Bt, MP, and Aurelia, *née* Nemon; *b* 11 Oct 1966; *Educ* Windsor CFE, Christ Church Oxford; *Career* chartered accountant and investment banker; *Recreations* cricket, tennis, classical guitar; *Style*— Gerry Young, Esq; ✉ Flat 4, 27 Elsham Road, London W14 8HB

YOUNG, Rt Hon Sir George Samuel Knatchbull; 6 Bt (UK 1813), of Formosa Place, Berks; MP (C) Ealing Acton (majority 7,007); PC (1993); s of Sir George Young, 5 Bt, CMG (d 1960), by his w Elisabeth (herself er da of Sir Hugh Knatchbull-Hugessen, KCMG, who was in turn n of 1 Baron Brabourne); *b* 16 July 1941; *Educ* Eton, Christ Church Oxford; *m* 1964, Aurelia, da of Oscar Nemon, and Mrs Nemon-Stuart, of Boars Hill, Oxford; 2 s, 2 da; *Heir* s, George Horatio Young; *Career* economist NEDO 1966–67, Kobler res fell Univ of Surrey 1967–69, memb Lambeth Borough Cncl 1968–71, econ advsr Post Office Corporation 1969–74, memb GLC (Ealing) 1970–73; MP (C) Ealing Acton Feb 1974–, oppn whip 1976–79, under sec of state DHSS 1979–81, under sec of state DOE 1981–86, comptroller of HM Household (sr Govt whip) 1990, min of state for the environment 1990–92, min for housing and inner cities 1992–94, fin sec to the Treasy 1994–95, sec of state for tport 1995–; tstee Guinness Tst 1986–90; *Books* Tourism, Blessing or Blight?; *Style*— The Rt Hon Sir George Young, Bt, MP, PC; ✉ House of Commons, London SW1A 0AA

YOUNG, Gerard Francis; CBE (1967), DL (S Yorkshire 1973); s of Smelter Joseph Young (d 1954), of Richmond Park, Sheffield, and Edith, *née* Aspinall (d 1983); *b* 5 May 1910; *Educ* Ampleforth; *m* 7 Aug 1937, Diana, da of Charles Murray, MD; 2 s (Hugo b 13 Oct 1938, Charles b 29 April 1947), 3 da (Jane b 6 March 1945, Sarah b 8 Dec 1950, Caroline b 8 June 1980); *Career* The Tempered Spring Co Ltd 1930–81 (chm 1954–78); chm Sheffield area Sun Alliance and London Insurance Group 1967–79 (dir 1958), dir Nat Vulcan Engineering Insurance Group 1960–79, chm Radio Hallam Ltd 1973–79, dir Crucible Theatre Trust Ltd 1967–75; memb Fin Bd RC Dio of Hallam 1981–95; memb: Nat Bd for Prices and Incomes 1968–71, Top Salaries Review Body, Armed Forces Pay Review Body 1971–74; tstee: Sheffield Town Tst (town collector 1978–81), J G Graves Charitable Tst (chm 1974–86); Freshgate Tst Fndn (chm 1980–86), govr United Sheffield Hosps 1945–53, memb Cncl Univ of Sheffield 1943–84 (pro chllr 1951–67), gen cmmr of income tax 1947–74; JP Sheffield 1950–74, High Sheriff Hallamshire 1973–74, Lord-Lt S Yorks and Custos Rotolorum 1974–85; KStJ 1976; memb Co of Cutlers in Hallamshire (Master 1961–62); Hon LLD Univ of Sheffield 1962; FIMechE; GCSG (Vatican) 1974; *Recreations* gardening, 13 grandchildren; *Clubs* Sheffield; *Style*— Gerard Young, Esq, CBE, DL; ✉ Roundfield, 69 Carsick Hill Crescent, Sheffield S10 3LS (☎ 0114 230 2834)

YOUNG, (John Andrew) Gordon; s of Harold James Young, of Grantown on Spey, and Agnes Elizabeth, *née* Wilson; *b* 19 March 1945; *Educ* King's Coll Sch Wimbledon; *m* 1, 30 Nov 1968, Jane Pamela (d 1988), da of Ronald Victor Seyd, of W Sussex; 1 s (Angus b 17 Jan 1972), 1 da (Suzanna b 9 May 1969); m 2, 27 Oct 1989, Sylvie Claire, da of George Seassau, of Aix En Provence; 1 da (Margaux b 16 Oct 1990); *Career* Baring Bros & Co Ltd 1970–73; NM Rothschild & Sons Ltd: joined 1973, exec dir 1981–87; exec dir Smith New Court plc 1987, md Smith New Court International Equities until 1995, md Merrill Lynch International Ltd 1995–; MICAS; *Recreations* golf, travel; *Clubs* Oriental, Hurlingham, West Sussex Golf, Hong Kong; *Style*— Gordon Young, Esq; ✉ 30 Walpole Street, London SW3 4QS (☎ 0171 730 3401); Merrill Lynch International Ltd, 20 Farringdon Road, London EC1M 3NH (☎ 0171 772 1000, fax 0171 772 2929)

YOUNG, Graham Christopher McKenzie; DL (Wiltshire 1996); s of Archibald Hamilton Young (d 1966), of Caterham, and Lurline, *née* Chandler; *b* 20 Dec 1935; *Educ* Culford Sch, Trinity Coll Cambridge (MA, LLM); *m* 15 Dec 1962, Pamela Frances, da of Geoffrey Frances Anthony Bisley (d 1989), of Kempsford, Glos; 1 s (Jonathan Graham b 1965), 2 da (Alison b 1964, Caroline b 1968); *Career* admitted slr 1962; ptnr Townsends Swindon 1964–96; pt/t chm: rent assessment panels, social security, child support and disability appeal tbnls; pres: Swindon Lions Club 1970, Glos and Wilts Inc Law Soc 1986; tstee Fairford Town Charity; formerly: memb and co sec Prospect Fndn Swindon, chm Swindon Alcohol for Enjoyment Forum; Parly candidate (C) Swindon 1974; memb Law Soc; *Books* A Little Law (1991), Townsends, Solicitors, Swindon and Newbury - from the 18th Century to 1996 (1996); *Recreations* swimming, DIY, driving 1996 MG, collecting Edward VIII memorabilia; *Style*— Graham Young, Esq, DL; ✉ New Milton, Back Lane, Fairford, Glos (☎ 01285 712317); Townsends, 42 Cricklade St, Swindon, Wilts (☎ 01793 410800, fax 01793 512452)

YOUNG, Hugh Kenneth; TD (1992); s of John Young (d 1974), and Monica, *née* Auckland (d 1936); *b* 6 May 1936; *Educ* Edinburgh Acad; *m* 19 Sept 1962, Marjory Bruce, da of Charles Wilson (d 1987), of Edinburgh; 2 s (Hugh b 1967, Angus b 1970), 1 da (Susan b 1965); *Career* TA 1957–59, Nat Serv 2 Lt Royal Scots 1960, served Libya, TA 1961–69 (Capt 1966) and 1986–92 (Maj 1989); Bank of Scotland: exec dir subsid British Linen Bank Ltd 1978–84, gen mangr, sec and memb Mgmnt Bd Bank of Scotland 1984–96, chm Bank of Scotland (Jersey) Ltd 1986–96, dir Bank of Wales (Jersey) 1986–96; dir Scottish Agricultural Securities Corporation plc 1988–96, dir First Mortgage Securities Ltd 1992–; chm Tstees Royal Scots Benevolent Soc, vice chm Lowland Employers Liaison Ctee; CA, FCIBS; *Recreations* squash, tennis, hill-walking; *Clubs* Army and Navy, Edinburgh Sports; *Style*— Hugh K Young, Esq, TD; ✉ 30 Braid Hills Road, Edinburgh EH10 6HY (☎ 0131 447 3101)

YOUNG, Prof Ian Robert; OBE (1986); s of John Stirling Young (d 1971), and Ruth Muir, *née* Whipple (d 1975); *b* 11 Jan 1932; *Educ* Sedbergh, Univ of Aberdeen (BSc, PhD); *m* 1956, Sylvia Marianne Whewell, da of Frederick George Ralph; 2 s (Graham John b 1958, Neil George b 1960), 1 da (Fiona Marianne b 1966); *Career* Hilger & Watts Ltd 1955–59, Evershed & Vignoles Ltd 1959–67, Evershed Power Optics Ltd 1967–76, EMI Central Res Laboratory 1976–81, sr res fell GEC Hirst Res Centre, vice pres Res Picker International Inc Cleveland Ohio 1981–, visiting prof RPMS Hammersmith Hosp 1983–; Duddell Medal Inst of Physics 1983, Gold Medal Soc of Magnetic Resonance in Med 1988, Silver Medal Soc of Magnetic Resonance 1994; Hon DSc Univ of Aberdeen 1992; pres Soc of Magnetic Resonance in Medicine 1991–92, hon memb Soc of Magnetic Resonance Imaging 1989; FIEE 1967, FEng 1988, FRS 1989, hon FRCR 1990, FInstP 1991; *Recreations* ornithology, DIY, walking; *Style*— Prof Ian Young, OBE, FRS, FEng; ✉ Church Hill Cottage, West Overton, Marlborough, Wiltshire SN8 4ER (☎ 01672 861615); Robert Steiner MRI Unit, Hammersmith Hospital, Ducane Road, London W12 0HS (☎ 0181 383 3298/3777)

YOUNG, James Drummond (Jim); s of James Henry Young, of Glasgow, and Mary, *née* Moore (d 1988); *b* 26 Feb 1950; *Educ* Hutchesons' GS, Univ of Glasgow (LLB); *m* 26 Sept 1973, Gillian Anne, da of William Boyd, MBE; 1 da (Jennifer Anne b 9 Dec 1976), 1 s (Graham James b 7 Jan 1979); *Career* trainee McGrigor Donald & Co 1971–73, slr West Lothian DC 1975–77; ptnr: Moncrieff Warren Paterson 1979–85, McGrigor Donald 1985–; accredited specialist in employment law Law Soc of Scot (memb Employment Ctee); memb Law Soc of Scot 1975; *Recreations* golf, cricket, contemporary art; *Clubs* Clydesdale Cricket, Merchants of Edinburgh Golf, Glasgow Art; *Style*— Jim Young, Esq; ✉ 5 Braid Hills Avenue, Edinburgh (☎ 0131 447 1951); McGrigor Donald, 68/73 Queen Street, Edinburgh EH2 4NF (☎ 0131 226 7777, fax 0131 226 7700, e-mail postmaster@mcgrigor.demon.co.uk)

YOUNG, Baroness (Life Peer UK 1971), of Farnworth, Co Palatine of Lancaster; Janet Mary Young; PC (1981), DL (Oxon 1989); da of John Norman Leonard Baker, and Phyllis, *née* Hancock; *b* 23 Oct 1926; *Educ* Headington Sch Oxford, Prospect Hill Sch New Haven Conn USA, Mount Holyoke Coll USA, St Anne's Coll Oxford (MA); *m* 1950, Dr Geoffrey Tyndale Young (fellow Jesus Coll Oxford); 3 da (Hon Alexandra Janet (Hon Mrs Slater) b 1951, Hon Rosalind Ann (Hon Mrs McIntyre) b 1954, Hon Juliet Marguerite (Hon Mrs Brown) b 1962); *Career* sits as Cons peer in House of Lords; memb Oxford City Cncl 1957–72 (alderman and ldr Cons Gp 1967–72); Baroness-in-Waiting to HM The Queen (first ever Cons woman govt whip in upper chamber) 1972–73, Parly under-sec of state DOE 1973–74, vice chm Cons Pty Orgn (with special responsibility for women's orgns) 1975–83 (dep chm 1977–79); min of state DES 1979–81, chllr Duchy of Lancaster 1981–82, Cons ldr House of Lords Sept 1981–83, Lord Privy Seal 1982–83, min of state FCO 1983–87; dir: National Westminster Bank plc 1987–96, Marks and Spencer plc 1987–97; former dir UK Provident, former memb BR Western Region Advsy Bd, pres W India Ctee 1996– (vice pres 1987–96); chm: Independent Schs Jt Cncl 1989–92 and 1994–, Governing Bodies of Girls' Schs 1989–, Cncl Headington Sch 1993–, Assoc of Cons Peers 1995–; memb Cncl Ditchley Fndn 1990–; chllr Univ of Greenwich 1993–; hon fell: Inst of Civil Engrs, St Anne's Coll Oxford; tstee Lucy Cavendish Coll Cambridge 1988; Hon DLL Mt Holyoke Coll USA; *Clubs* Univ Women's; *Style*— The Rt Hon the Baroness Young, PC, DL; ✉ House of Lords, London SW1A 0PW

YOUNG, Jimmy Leslie Ronald; CBE (1993, OBE 1979); s of Frederick George Young (d 1989), and Gertrude Jane *née* Woolford (d 1972); *b* 21 Sept 1923; *Educ* East Dean GS Cinderford Gloucestershire; *m* 1, 1946 (m dis), Wendy Wilkinson; 1 da; m 2, 1950 (m dis), Sally Douglas; m 3, 1996, Alicia Plastow; *Career* WWII RAF, Sgt (physical trg instructor); broadcaster; first BBC radio bdcast Songs at Piano 1949, pianist/singer/bandleader 1950–51, first theatre appearance Empire Theatre Croydon 1952 (numerous subsequent appearances); BBC Radio series 1953–67 incl: Housewives Choice, The Night is Young, 12 O' Clock Spin, Younger Than Springtime, Saturday Special, Keep Young, Through Till Two; presenter of: Radio Luxembourg programmes 1960–68, Jimmy Young Programme BBC Radio Two 1973– (Radio One 1967–73); TV work incl: Pocket Edition (BBC) 1955, Jimmy Young Asks (BBC) 1972, Whose Baby (ITV) 1973, Jim's World (ITV) 1974, The Jimmy Young Television Programme (ITV) 1984–87, host of first Br Telethon (Thames) 1980; bdcasts live from various countries; records: Too Young 1951, Unchained Melody (number one hit) 1955, The Man from Laramie (number one hit) 1955, Chain Gang 1956, More 1956, Miss You 1963; first Br singer to have two consecutive number one hit records; Radio Personality of the Year Variety Club of GB 1968, HM The Queen's Silver Jubilee medal 1977, Radio Industries Club Award for Programme of the Year 1979, Sony Award for Broadcaster of the Year 1985, Daily Mail/BBC Nat Radio Award for Best Current Affrs Programme 1988, Sony Roll of Honour Award 1988, TV and Radio Industries Club Award for Best Radio Programme of the Year 1989, Broadcasting Press Guild Award for Radio Broadcaster of the Year 1994, Sony Gold Award for Men Matters - Service to the Community 1995; hon memb Cncl NSPCC; Freeman City of London 1969, Liveryman Worshipful Co of Carmen 1969; *Books* Jimmy Young Cookbooks (1968, 1969, 1970, 1972), JY (autobiography, 1973), Jimmy Young (autobiography, 1982); *Clubs* Wigan Rugby League

Social & Working Mens; *Style*— Jimmy Young, Esq, CBE; ✉ BBC Broadcasting House, London W1A 1AA (☎ 0171 580 4468 ext 55360)

YOUNG, John A; *Career* Hewlett-Packard Company: joined 1958, exec vice pres and memn Bd of Dirs 1974–92, pres and chief exec offr 1978–92, ret; non-exec dir: SmithKline Beecham plc 1993–, Chevron Corporation, Wells Fargo Bank, Affymetrix Inc, Shaman Pharmaceuticals Inc, Ciphergen, General Magic, Novell; numerous awards incl: US Cncl for International Business Leadership Award 1985, US Nat Science Fndn Distinguished Public Achievement Award 1990, Prime Minister's Trade Award Japan 1990, Soc of Mfrg Engrs Total Excellence in Electronics Mfrg Award 1993; *Style*— John Young, Esq; ✉ 3200 Hillview Avenue, Palo Alto, California 94304, USA (☎ 00 1 415 857 2057, fax 00 1 415 857 2677)

YOUNG, John Adrian Emile; s of John Archibald Campbell Young (d 1979), of Plaxtol, Kent, and Irene Eugenie, *née* Bouvier (d 1976); *b* 28 July 1934; *Educ* Cranbrook Sch Kent, Univ of London (LLB); *m* 20 June 1959, Yvonne Lalage Elizabeth, da of John Digby Hyde Bankes (d 1976), of Otford, Kent; 3 s (Charles b 1961, Paul b 1962, Simon b 1965), 1 da (Anna b 1963); *Career* ptnr Cameron Markby Hewitt Slrs 1965–95, legal offr Office of the Banking Ombudsman 1996–; nat chm Young Slrs Gp 1965–66, pres Association Internationale des Jeunes Avocats 1968–69, memb Cncl Int Bar Assoc 1983–94, choirmaster/organist of local church; Master City of London Slrs Co 1989–90 (Freeman 1967); pres British Middle East Law Cncl 1994–95; Law Soc: memb 1958, asst sec 1958–64, memb Cncl 1971–95, dep vice-pres 1993–94, vice pres 1994–95; FRSA 1989; *Recreations* music, gardening, foreign travel; *Style*— John Young, Esq; ✉ Stonewold House, The Street, Plaxtol, Kent (☎ and fax 01732 810289)

YOUNG, Sir John Kenyon Roe; 6 Bt (UK 1821), of Bailieborough Castle, Co Cavan; s of Sir John William Roe Young, 5 Bt (d 1981), by his 1 w, Joan Minnie Agnes, *née* Aldous (d 1958); *b* 23 April 1947; *Educ* Hurn Ct Sch Christchurch, Napier Coll; *m* 1977, Frances Elise, only da of W R Thompson; 1 s, 1 da (Tamara Elizabeth Eve b 9 Nov 1986); *Heir* s, Richard Christopher Roe Young, b 14 July 1983; *Career* former hydrographic surveyor; purchasing mangr; *Recreations* golf; *Style*— Sir John Young, Bt; ✉ Bolingey, 159 Chatham Rd, Maidstone, Kent ME14 2ND

YOUNG, John Robert Chester; CBE (1992); s of Robert Nisbet Young (d 1956), and Edith Mary, *née* Roberts (d 1981); bro of Louise Botting, *qv*, the broadcaster and financial consultant; *b* 6 Sept 1937; *Educ* Bishop Vesey's GS, St Edmund Hall Oxford (MA); *m* 1963, Pauline Joyce, da of George Yates (d 1966); 1 s (and 1 s decd), 1 da; *Career* ptnr Simon & Coates stockbrokers 1965–82; Stock Exchange: memb 1965–82, memb Cncl 1978–82, dir of policy and planning 1982–87; vice chm Exec Bd Int Stock Exchange 1987–90; chief exec: Securities Assoc 1987–91, Securities and Futures Authy 1991–93, Securities and Investments Bd 1993–95 (non-exec dir 1996–); non-exec dir: East Surrey NHS Tst 1992–96, Gartmore Venture Capital Trust 1996–, Darby Group plc 1996–; nominated memb Cncl Lloyds and memb Lloyds Regulatory Bd 1996–; Freeman City of London; *Recreations* rugby football, cooking; *Clubs* Harlequins, Vincent's, City of London; *Style*— J R C Young, Esq, CBE; ✉ Richmond House, Falkland Grove, Dorking RH4 3DL

YOUNG, John Robertson (Rob); s of Francis John Young (d 1982), and Marjorie Elizabeth, *née* Imrie; *b* 21 Feb 1945; *Educ* Norwich Sch, Univ of Leicester (BA); *m* 15 July 1967, Catherine Suzanne Françoise, da of Jean Houssait (d 1945); 1 s (Jerome Robertson b 9 Jan 1971), 2 da (Isabelle b 10 April 1969, Juliette Claire b 29 Oct 1978); *Career* joined Diplomatic Service 1967, first sec Cairo 1970, FCO 1972, Paris 1976, FCO 1981, cnsllr Damascus 1984, head of Middle E Dept FCO 1987, min Paris 1991, dep under sec of state FCO 1994–; *Recreations* sailing, theatre, music (playing piano and organ and collecting records); *Clubs* Cruising Assoc; *Style*— Rob Young, Esq; ✉ c/o Foreign and Commonwealth Office, King Charles St, London SW1

YOUNG, John Todd; s of Ian Taylor Young, of Rugby, Warwicks, and Flora Leggett, *née* Todd; *b* 14 Jan 1957; *Educ* Manchester GS, Sidney Sussex Coll Cambridge (BA, MA); *m* 11 April 1981, Elizabeth Jane Young, *qv*, da of Philip John Grattidge, of Wareham, Dorset; *Career* Lovell White Durrant (formerly Lovell, White & King): articled clerk 1979–81, slr 1981–, ptnr 1987–; memb Worshipful Co of Slrs; memb Law Soc; *Recreations* mountaineering, windsurfing; *Clubs* Cannons; *Style*— John Young, Esq; ✉ Lovell White Durrant, 65 Holborn Viaduct, London EC1A 2DY (☎ 0171 236 0066, fax 0171 248 4212, telex 887122 LWD)

YOUNG, John William Garne; s of David Richard Young, of Shaftesbury, Dorset, and Pamela Mary, *née* Garne; *b* 6 Jan 1945; *Educ* Shaftesbury GS; *m* 1 Jan 1971, (Eleanor) Louise, da of Abryn Walsh Sparks (d 1980), of Swinburne, SA; 3 s (Michael b 1972, David b 1974, Peter b 1980); *Career* dir Parmiter Ltd 1967–87 (md 1973–87), chief exec Wolseley plc 1996– (dir and div chief exec 1982–95); pres Agric Engrs Assoc 1987–88, govr BBSRC Silsoe Res Inst, pres Comité Européen de Constructeurs de Mechanisme Agricole 1995–96; CIAgrE; *Recreations* cricket, tennis; *Style*— John Young, Esq; ✉ The Gables, Hindon Lane, Tisbury, Wilts SP3 6QF (☎ 01747 870756); PO Box 18, Vines Lane, Droitwich, Worcs WR9 8ND (☎ 01905 794444, fax 01905 776704)

YOUNG, Jonathan Piers; s of Peter Alan George Young, of Chudleigh, Devon, and Mavis Irene Young; *b* 23 Sept 1959; *Educ* Blundell's, Univ of Leicester (BA); *m* 1993, Caroline Margaret, o da of John Jervis Murray Bankes, of Tempus House, Hinton Ampner, Alresford, Hants; 1 da (Henrietta b 1994), 1 s (Fergus b 1996); *Career* ed: Shooting Times and Country magazine 1986–90, The Field 1991–; Freeman City of London, Liveryman Worshipful Co of Gunmakers; *Books* A Pattern of Wings (1989); *Recreations* shooting, fishing, falling off horses, cooking vast stews; *Clubs* Buck's; *Style*— Jonathan Young, Esq; ✉ The Field, King's Reach Tower, Stamford Street, London SE1 9LS (direct ☎ 0171 261 6221, fax 0171 261 5358)

YOUNG, (David) Junor; s of David Young (d 1974), and Margaret Mellis; *b* 23 April 1934; *Educ* Robert Gordon's Coll Aberdeen; *m* 6 Nov 1954, Kathleen, da of E Brooks, of Eastbourne; 2 da (Stephanie b 1955, Philippa b 1967), 2 s (Ashley b 1958, Jonathan b 1964); *Career* joined FO 1951, consul Stuttgart 1978–81, first sec Kampala 1981–84, consul-gen Hamburg 1984–86, cnsllr (commercial) British Embassy Bonn 1986–88, British high cmmr Honiara Solomon Islands 1988–90, dep high cmmr Karachi 1991–94; tstee Victor Ratte Lay Tst; *Recreations* fishing, shooting; *Style*— D J Young, Esq; ✉ Pine Cottage, Hintlesham, Suffolk

YOUNG, Dr Kate; da of Rev W P Young (d 1969), and Ann Nielson Cumming (d 1941); *b* 13 June 1938; *Educ* Oxenford Castle Sch Ford Midlothian, LSE (PhD); *ptnr* Charles Legg; 1 s (Justin Dubon b 1965), 1 step s (Jake Legg b 1970), 1 step da (Jessica Legg 1969); *Career* worked with How (of Edinburgh) and Doubleday (in NY), worked in FAO, Inst of Devpt Studies (Univ of Sussex, promoted study of the impact of devpt on women, set up 18 week course for policy makers and activists on gender relationships and economic devpt and MA course Gender and Devpt) 1975–88, fndr and exec-dir Womankind (Worldwide) 1989; *Books* ed: Of Marriage and the Market (1981), Women and Economic Development (1988), Serving Two Masters (1989), Planning Development With Women (1993); *Recreations* gardening, talking with friends over a good meal, walking; *Style*— Dr Kate Young; ✉ Executive Director, Womankind (Worldwide), 3 Albion Place, London W6 0LT (☎ 0181 563 8607, fax 0171 563 8611)

YOUNG, Prof Kenneth George (Ken); s of Henry George Young, of Christchurch, Hants, and Olive, *née* Heybeard; *b* 3 Jan 1943; *Educ* Brockenhurst GS, LSE (BSc, MSc, PhD); *Career* res offr LSE 1966–73, res fell Univ of Kent 1974–77, sr res fell Univ of Bristol 1977–79, sr fell Policy Studies Inst 1979–87, prof and dir Inst of Local Govt Studies 1987–89, head Sch of Public Policy Univ of Birmingham 1989–90, prof of politics and head Dept of Political Studies Queen Mary and Westfield Coll London 1990–92 (vice princ 1992–); FRHistS 1983; *Books* Local Politics and the Rise of Party (1975), Metropolitan London (1982), Managing the Post-Industrial City (1983), New Directions for County Government (1989); *Recreations* reading, travel; *Style*— Prof Ken Young; ✉ 2 Devonshire Road, Chiswick, London W4 2HD (☎ 0181 747 0718); Queen Mary and Westfield College, University of London, Mile End Rd, London E1 4NS (☎ 0171 975 5555)

YOUNG, Kenneth Middleton; CBE (1977); s of Cyril William Dix Young, of Cardiff, and Gwladys, *née* Middleton (d 1991); *b* 1 Aug 1931; *Educ* Neath GS, Univ of Wales Aberystwyth (BA), Univ of Manchester (Dip Personnel Mgmnt); *m* 25 Aug 1958, Brenda May, da of John Thomas (d 1951), of Connahs Quay; 1 s (Michael b 1964), 1 da (Pamela b 1961); *Career* cmmnd Pilot Offr and navigator RAF 1952–54; collective agreements mangr Massey-Ferguson (UK) Ltd 1959–64, personnel advsr Aviation Div Smiths Industries Ltd 1964–66, GEC 1966–71 (gp personnel mangr and dir GEC (Management) Ltd); The Post Office: bd memb 1972, vice chm 1986, dep chm 1990–92, chm Subscription Services Ltd 1988–92, chm Girobank plc 1989–90, chm Post Office Counters Ltd 1990–92; memb Employment Appeal Tbnl; chm Student Loans Co Ltd 1992–, chm Further Education Development Agency 1994–, dir Courage Pensions Ltd 1993–; tstee Post Office Pension Funds 1992–; chm Roehampton Inst 1992–95; hon fell Univ of Wales Aberystwyth 1991; FIPM 1986, CIMgt 1990; *Recreations* Wales rugby, Chelsea AFC, photography, theatre; *Style*— Kenneth Young, Esq, CBE; ✉ The Student Loans Company, 100 Bothwell Street, Glasgow G2 7JD (☎ 0141 306 2000)

YOUNG, Sir Leslie Clarence; kt (1984), CBE (1980), DL (1983); s of late Clarence James Young, and Ivy Isabel Young (d 1984); *Educ* LSE (BSc (Econ)); *m* 1949, Muriel Howard Pearson; 1 s, 1 da; *Career* formerly with Courtaulds Ltd; chm: NW Regnl Cncl CBI 1976–78, NW Industl Devpt Bd 1978–81, J Bibby & Sons PLC 1979–84, Merseyside Devpt Corpn 1980–84, Br Waterways Bd 1984–87, NatWest Bank 1986–90 (dir Northern Region 1975–84), Hoskins Healthcare Ltd 1991–95; non-exec dir: Mersey Docks and Harbour Bd 1979–80, Granada TV 1979–83, Bank of England 1980–84, Swiss Pioneer Life PLC 1986–92, Lancashire Enterprises PLC 1992–; chm of Tstees Nat Museum and Galleries in Merseyside 1986–95; Hon LLD Univ of Liverpool; *Style*— Sir Leslie Young, CBE, DL; ✉ Gloverstone Court, Castle Street, Chester

YOUNG, (Peter) Miles; s of Matthew Derek Young (d 1989), and Joyce Doreen, *née* Robson (d 1976); *b* 12 June 1954; *Educ* Bedford Sch, New Coll Oxford (MA); *Career* advertising; Lintas London 1976–79, Allen Brady & Marsh 1979–83, dir client service Ogilvy & Mather Ltd 1983–90; Ogilvy & Mather Direct Ltd: md 1990–92, dep chm and chief exec 1992–93, chm 1993–95; pres Ogilvy & Mather Asia/Pacific 1995–; ldr Westminster Cncl 1993–95 (memb 1986–); chm: New Technology Ctee 1986–87, Environment Ctee 1987–90; Burdett-Coutts Fndn 1986, govr Harper Tst 1989–, vice chm Conserve 1990, chm Bedford Prep Sch Ctee 1992–; Liveryman Worshipful Co of Curriers; MIPA 1990; *Recreations* gastronomy, walking, Balkan travel; *Clubs* Carlton; *Style*— Miles Young, Esq; ✉ c/o 10 Lesley Court, Strutton Ground, London SW1P 2HZ

YOUNG, (Roderic) Neil; s of Frederick Hugh Young, OBE (d 1969), of Oxted, Surrey, and Stella Mary, *née* Robinson; *b* 29 May 1933; *Educ* Eton, Trinity Coll Cambridge (MA); *m* 16 June 1962, Gillian Margaret, da of Col William Alexander Salmon, OBE, of Balcombe, W Sussex; 2 s (Peter b 1964, Rupert b 1969), 1 da (Jennifer b 1966); *Career* 2 Lt Queen's Own Royal W Kent Regt 1952; dir: Murray Johnstone Ltd 1969–70, Kleinwort Benson Ltd 1972–86, Globe Investment Trust plc 1973–90, Brunner Investment Trust plc 1975–92, Merchants Trust plc 1975–85, Kleinwort Grieveson Investment Management Ltd 1986–88, Aberdeen Petroleum plc 1988–93, Malvern UK Index Trust plc 1990–, London & SE Bd Bradford & Bingley Building Society 1990–; dep chm Assoc of Investmt Tst Cos 1987–89; memb Advsy Ctee Greenwich Hosp, Alderman and JP City of London 1982–94, Sheriff City of London 1991–92; memb Ct of Assts Worshipful Co of Gunmakers (former Master); FCA 1969 (ACA 1959); *Recreations* shooting, gardening, DIY, golf, tennis; *Clubs* Rye Golf; *Style*— Neil Young, Esq; ✉ Pembury Hall, Pembury, Kent TN2 4AT (☎ 01892 822971)

YOUNG, Nicholas Charles; s of Leslie Charles Young (d 1986), of Dorking, Surrey, and Mary Margaret, *née* Rudman; *b* 16 April 1952; *Educ* Wimbledon Coll, Univ of Birmingham (LLB), Coll of Law; *m* 1977, Helen Mary Ferrier, da of William Renwick Hamilton; 3 s (Edward b 1980, Alexander b 1982, Thomas b 1984); *Career* supervisor residential unit HM Prison Grendon Underwood 1974–75, slr Freshfields 1977–78 (articled clerk 1975–77), travelled Europe and Asia 1978–79, ptnr Turner Martin & Symes 1981–85 (joined as slr 1979), sec for devpt Sue Ryder Foundation 1985–90, dir of UK ops British Red Cross 1990–95 (Cabinet Office Top Mgmnt Prog 1993), chief exec Cancer Relief Macmillan Fund 1995–; vice chm Nat Cncl for Hospice and Specialist Palliative Care Servs, memb Policy and Research Task Gp ACENVO; memb Law Soc 1975; *Recreations* amateur drama, running, cricket, literature, theatre and cinema; *Clubs* Stumblers' Association; *Style*— Nicholas Young, Esq; ✉ Cancer Relief Macmillan Fund, Anchor House, 15–19 Britten Street, London SW3 3TZ (☎ 0171 351 7811, fax 0171 376 8098)

YOUNG, Prof Peter Colin; s of John William Young (d 1958), and Naomi Bessie, *née* Crane (d 1987); *b* 5 Dec 1939; *Educ* Loughborough Univ (BTech, MSc), Univ of Cambridge (MA, PhD); *m* 31 Aug 1963, Wendy Anne; 2 s (Timothy John b 2 Jan 1966, Jeremy Peter b 26 May 1973), 1 da (Melanie Clare b 28 Aug 1967); *Career* control and systems engr US Navy China Lake Calif 1967–69, sr industrial res fell ICI and Dept of Engrg Univ of Cambridge 1970–71, lectr in engrg and fell Clare Hall Cambridge 1971–75, professorial fell Aust Nat Univ 1975–81, prof of environmental sci Univ of Lancaster 1981– (dir Centre for Res in Environmental Systems); MRAeS, MIEE, CEng, FIMA, FRSA; *Books* Modelling and Data Analysis in Biotechnology and Medical Engineering (ed with G C Vansteenkiste, 1983), Recursive Estimation and Time Series Analysis (1984), Identification and System Parameter Estimation vols 1 and 2 (ed with H A Barker, 1985), Concise Encyclopedia of Environmental Systems (ed and author, 1993); *Recreations* fell walking, drawing; *Style*— Prof Peter Young; ✉ Director, Centre for Research on Environmental Systems (CRES), Institute of Environmental and Biological Sciences, University of Lancaster, Lancaster LA1 4YQ (☎ 01524 65201, fax 01524 63806, telex 65111 LANCUL G)

YOUNG, Richard Aretas Lewry; s of Dr Carmichael Aretas Young (d 1987), and Marie Ethel, *née* Lewry; *b* 17 Jan 1943; *Educ* Haileybury England, Haileybury Melbourne Aust, St Catharine's Coll Cambridge (MA, MB BChir), St Mary's Hosp Med Sch London (LRCP, FRCS); *m* 8 July 1972, Lesley Rita, da of Gerald Duckett; 3 s (Simon, Andrew, Peter); *Career* Bernard Sunley res fell RCS 1974–75, surgical registrar Royal Free Hosp 1976–78, sr surgical registrar St Mary's Hosp London 1978–82, conslt gen and vascular surgn W Middx Hosp 1982–, teacher Univ of London, hon sr lectr Charing Cross and Westminster Hosps Med Sch; memb BMA, FRSM; *Recreations* golf, sailing; *Clubs* Fulwell Golf; *Style*— Mr Richard Young; ✉ 26 Strawberry Hill Rd, Twickenham, Middx TW1 4PU (☎ 0181 891 0638, fax 0181 287 2778); West Middlesex University Hospital, Twickenham Rd, Isleworth, Middx TW7 6AF (☎ 0181 565 5768)

YOUNG, Sir Richard Dilworth; kt (1970); s of Philip Young, by his w Constance Maria Lloyd; *b* 9 April 1914; *Educ* Bromsgrove, Univ of Bristol; *m* 1951, Jean Barbara Paterson, *née* Lockwood; 4 s; *Career* Boosey & Hawkes Ltd: dep chm 1978–79, chm 1979–84; dir Tube Investmts Ltd 1958 (md 1961–64), chm Alfred Herbert Ltd 1966–74 (dep chm 1965–66); dir: Rugby Portland Cement Co 1968–88, Cwlth Finance Development Corp 1968–83, Ingersoll Engineers Inc (USA) 1966–71; memb: Central Advsy Cncl on Sci and Technol 1967–70, Cncl CBI 1967–74, Cncl Univ of Warwick 1966–89, Cncl SSRC 1973–75, SRC Engrg Bd 1974–76; Hon DSc Univ of Warwick; FIMechE (memb Cncl 1969–76), CIMgt; *Clubs* Athenaeum; *Style—* Sir Richard Young

YOUNG, Richard Stuart; s of David Young (d 1991), and Hilda, *née* Ellison; *b* 17 Sept 1947; *m* 1, 13 Nov 1975, Riita Sinikka Harju (d 1983); 2 s (Danny Eemil b 27 April 1977, Sammy Richard b 27 April 1979); m 2, 28 June 1985, Susan Manije Walker; 1 da (Hannah Harley b 31 Oct 1987); *Career* photographer 1974–; *Books* By Invitation Only (1981), Paparazzo (1989); *Recreations* riding my Harley Davidson; *Clubs* Guards Polo; *Style—* Richard Young, Esq

YOUNG, Robert; s of Walter Horace Young (d 1963), of Wood Green, London, and Evelyn Joan, *née* Jennings; *b* 27 March 1944; *Educ* The Boys' GS Tottenham, Magdalen Coll Oxford (BA); *m* 18 Dec 1965, Patricia Anne, da of Robert Archibald Cowin, of Hest Bank, Lancs; 2 s (Matthew b 1969, Alec b and d 1972), 1 da (Judith b 1974); *Career* dir Rolls-Royce Motors Diesel Div 1977–81, gp commercial dir Vickers plc 1981–83; on secondment from Vickers: memb Central Policy Review Staff Cabinet Office 1983, memb 10 Downing St Policy Unit 1983–84; md Crane Ltd 1985–88, chief exec Plastics Div McKechnie plc 1988–90; dir: Beauford plc 1990–92, Casindell Ltd mgmnt conslts 1993–94; competition policy conslt Coopers & Lybrand 1993–; CBI: regnl cncllr W Mids 1980–81, chm Shropshire 1981; memb: Monopolies and Mergers Cmmn 1986–92, Fulbright Cmmn 1994–; FInstD 1985; *Recreations* music, photography, cats, horse-riding; *Clubs* IOD; *Style—* Robert Young, Esq; ✉ 54 Fordhook Ave, Ealing Common, London W5 3LR (☎ 0181 992 2228)

YOUNG, Robin Urquhart; s of Ian Urquhart Young, and Mary Hamilton, *née* West; *b* 7 Sept 1948; *Educ* Fettes, Univ Coll Oxford (Open scholar, BA); *Career* DOE: joined 1973, various positions in housing and local govt fin, private sec to Under Sec for Local Govt (Guy Barnett) 1976, to Housing Min (John Stanley) 1980 and successively to Secs of State (Patrick Jenkin, Kenneth Baker and Nicholas Ridley) 1985, worked in local govt fin 1981–85, under sec and head Housing Directorate 1988–91, headed team responsible for White Paper on the Environment 1990–91, head Local Govt Review Team 1991–92, head Local Govt Directorate 1992–94; dep sec and first dir Government Office for London 1994–; *Style—* Robin Young, Esq; ✉ Government Office for London, Room 10.01, Riverwalk House, 157–161 Millbank, London SW1P 4RR (☎ 0171 217 3098, fax 0171 217 3465)

YOUNG, Sir Roger William; kt (1983); s of Charles Bowden Young (d 1963), and Dr Ruth Young, *née* Wilson (d 1983); *b* 15 Nov 1923; *Educ* Dragon Sch, Westminster, Christ Church Oxford (MA, STh, LHD); *m* 1950, Caroline Mary, da of Lt-Cdr Charles Perowne Christie, RN (d 1929); 2 s (Patrick, Christopher), 2 da (Elizabeth, Janet); *Career* Sub Lt RNVR (Navigating Offr) 1943–45; res tutor St Catharine's Cumberland Lodge Windsor Gt Park 1949–51, asst master Manchester GS 1951–58, princ George Watson's Coll Edinburgh 1958–85, chm Cheltenham Ladies Coll 1986–93, memb Public Schs Cmmn 1968–70, pres Head Teachers Assoc of Scotland 1972–74; chm Headmasters' Conf 1976, memb GBA Ctee 1986–94 (dep chm 1987), memb Cncl Univ of Bath 1993–96; Scottish nat govr BBC 1979–84; FRSE 1965; *Books* Lines of Thought (1958), Everybody's Business (1968); *Recreations* gardening, hill-climbing, photography, knitting, opera, cinema; *Clubs* E India; *Style—* Sir Roger Young, FRSE; ✉ 11 Belgrave Terrace, Somerset BA1 5JR (☎ and fax 01225 336940)

YOUNG, Prof Stephen John; s of John Leonard Young (d 1994), and Joan Young; *b* 23 Jan 1951; *Educ* Univ of Cambridge (MA, PhD); *m* (m dls), Jayne Elizabeth Young; 2 da (Emma and Claire); *Career* UMIST Manchester: lectr Control Systems Centre 1978–79, Computation Dept 1979–84; Engrg Dept Univ of Cambridge: lectr 1984–94, reader in info engrg Oct-Dec 1994, prof of info engrg Dec 1994–; fell Emmanuel Coll Cambridge; tech dir Entropic Cambridge Research Lab; chm Inst of Acoustics Speech Gp; co-ed Computer Speech and Language; MBCS, MIEE, FIOA, CEng; *Publications* author of numerous conference papers and articles in learned jls; *Recreations* tennis, skiing, music; *Style—* Prof Stephen Young; ✉ Engineering Department, University of Cambridge, Trumpington Street, Cambridge CB2 1PZ (☎ 01223 332654, fax 01223 332662, e-mail SJY@ENG.CAM.AC.UK)

YOUNG, Sir Stephen Stewart Templeton; 3 Bt (UK 1945), of Partick, Co City of Glasgow; s of Sir Alastair Spencer Templeton Young, 2 Bt, DL (d 1963), and (Dorothy Constance) Marcelle (d 1964), widow of Lt John Hollington Grayburn, VC, and da of Lt-Col Charles Ernest Chambers; *b* 24 May 1947; *Educ* Rugby, Trinity Coll Oxford, Univ of Edinburgh; *m* 1974, Viola Margaret, da of Prof Patrick Horace Nowell-Smith (whose mother was Cecil, ggda of Most Rev Hon Edward Vernon-Harcourt, sometime Archbishop of York and yr bro of 3 Baron Vernon) by his 1 w Perilla (da of Sir Richard Southwell and who m subsequently, as his 2 w, Baron Roberthall); 2 s (Charles, Alexander David b 6 Feb 1982); *Heir* s, Charles Alastair Stephen Young b 21 July 1979; *Career* advocate; Sheriff of: Glasgow and Strathkelvin March-June 1984, North Strathclyde at Greenock 1984–; *Style—* Sir Stephen Young, Bt; ✉ Glen Rowan, Shore Rd, Cove, Dunbartonshire G84 0NU

YOUNG, Susan Caroline; da of David Robert Young, of Alcester, and Pamela Ann, *née* Gee; *b* 7 July 1961; *Educ* Lady Manner Sch Bakewell Derbys, Malvern Hall Warks, Solihull Coll of Technol, Liverpool Poly (BA), Royal Coll of Art Sch of Film and TV (Princess of Wales scholarship, MA, RCA); *Career* animation film and commercials director; with Barrie Joll Associates until 1987; freelance dir: Practical Pictures 1987–89, Felix Films 1989–91; fndr memb and film dir Mojo Working 1991–94, directing through Susan Young Ltd 1994–; represented by Claire-Garret in the USA 1996–; *Clients* incl: Arts Channel, United Nations, WEA Records, C4, BBC, Levis, Bic, Island Records, Polygram, Decca, A & M Records, Budweiser, Classic FM, General Foods, David Byrne, Jimi Hendrix Estate, Hitatchi; *Films* incl: Peyote Hunt 1981, Thin Blue Lines 1982, Trafalgar Square 1983, Tempting Fate 1984, Carnival 1985, The Doomsday Clock 1987, Beleza Tropical 1989; *Exhibitions* incl: Animation (Tate Gallery) 1983, Young Blood (Barbican) 1984, European Illustration Annual 1985, Los Angeles Animation Festival (touring) 1986, Br Design and Art Directors Annual 1990 and 1991; *Awards* numerous int film festivals and awards incl recently: Prix D'Italia (for Orchestra) 1991, Gold medal NY Advtg Awards (for Classic FM) 1994, Clio award (for Holland - Flower of Europe) 1995, BAFTA nomination (for American Football - Big Match) 1996; *Recreations* conversation, painting, poetry, literature, travel; *Style—* Ms Susan Young; ✉ Susan Young Ltd, 3–7 Harbour Yard, Chelsea Harbour, London SW10 0QL (☎ 0171 823 3006)

YOUNG, Hon (William Aldus) Thoby; s and h of 2 Baron Kennet; *b* 24 May 1957; *Educ* Marlborough, Univ of Sussex; *m* 25 April 1987, Hon Josephine Mary Keyes, 2 da of 2 Baron Keyes; 1 s (Archibald Wayland Keyes b 7 June 1992), 1 da (Maud Elizabeth Aurora b 8 March 1989); *Career* staff SDP 1980–83, md and chm Offshore Productions Ltd 1984–88, owner The Fresh Food Co 1989–; winner Soil Assoc Organic Fresh Produce Award 1995; *Recreations* playing the trumpet, writing; *Style—* The Hon Thoby Young; ✉ 41A Loftus Road, Shepherds Bush, London W12 7EH (☎ 0181 740 6433)

YOUNG, Thomas Nesbitt; s of Sir Frank Young, FRS (d 1988), former master of Darwin Coll and prof of biochemistry Cambridge, and Dr Ruth Young, DPM; *b* 24 July 1943; *Educ* The Leys Sch Cambridge, Pembroke Coll Oxford (MA); *m* 1971, Elisabeth Ann Shepherdson, da of Harry Hick, of Wakefield, W Yorks; 1 da (Harriet b 1973), 1 s (Simon b 1975); *Career* secdy sch teacher Uganda 1962; HM Dip Serv: entered 1966, Ankara 1969–72, Madrid 1973–76, Ankara 1978–80, NY 1981, Washington DC 1981–84, dep high cmmr Ghana (Accra) 1987–90, dir of trade promotion Canberra 1991–93, ambass Azerbaijan (Baku) 1993–; *Recreations* sailing, hill walking, Renaissance music; *Style—* Mr Thomas Young; ✉ c/o FCO (Baku), King Charles Street, London SW1A 2AH (☎ 00 873 144 6455 and 00 994 12 985558, fax 00 873 144 6456 and 00 994 12 922739)

YOUNG, Timothy Nicholas; QC (1996); s of William Ritchie Young, and Patricia Eileen, *née* Greig; *b* 1 Dec 1953; *Educ* Malvern, Madgalen Coll Oxford (exhibitioner, BA Jurisprudence, BCL); *m* 6 June 1981, Susan Jane, da of Wing Cdr Eamon St Brendan Kenny; 2 s (William Henry b 6 Oct 1983, Charles Frederick b 3 Jan 1986), 1 da (Frances Elizabeth b 26 July 1988); *Career* lectr in law St Edmund Hall Oxford 1976–80, called to the Bar Gray's Inn 1977, in practice at Commercial Bar 1978–; *Books* Voyage Charters (1993); *Recreations* watching and playing cricket and golf, watching rugby, drawing and watercolours, music; *Clubs* RAC, Alleyn's Old Boys' Cricket; *Style—* Timothy Young, Esq, QC; ✉ 20 Essex Street, London WC2R 3AL (☎ 0171 583 9294, fax 0171 583 1341)

YOUNG, Hon Toby Daniel Moorsom; s of Baron Young of Dartington, *qv*, by his 2 w Sasha; *b* 1963; *Educ* Brasenose Coll Oxford, Harvard, Trinity Coll Cambridge; *Career* journalist; columnist The Evening Standard, contributing ed Vanity Fair; *Recreations* food and drink; *Clubs* Groucho; *Style—* Toby Young; ✉ Vanity Fair, 350 Madison Avenue, New York, NY 10017, USA

YOUNG, William Chalmers (Bill); s of William Henry Young (d 1967), of Reigate, Surrey, and Joan Margaret, *née* McGlashan (d 1978); *b* 8 Oct 1919; *Educ* King's Sch Canterbury, Clare Coll Cambridge (MA); *m* 12 April 1944, Elizabeth Irene, da of Maj Alfred Russel Marshall, DSO, MC; 1 s (Martin), 3 da (Jane, Francesca, Rosemary); *Career* Nat Serv WWII cmmnd RA 1939, Lt Kent Yeo 143 Field Regt, Capt IORA HQ RA 49 Div, Capt OC 60 Field Security Section Intelligence Corps; chm Smith & Young Ltd family business 1980–84 (jt md 1947–84); chm: Nat Assoc Engravers and Diestampers 1957–58, Envelope Makers and Mfrg Stationers Assoc 1963–66; pres: SE Dist London Masterprinters Assoc 1960–61, London Printing Industs Assoc 1973–74; pres Inst of Printing 1976–78 (cncl memb 1969–81); memb Educn Ctee Surrey CC 1970–74, govr (later vice chm and chm) Camberwell Sch of Arts and Crafts, hon sec (later dir) Surrey Co Playing Fields Assoc 1958–85 (Nat Playing Fields Assoc Duke of Edinburgh Award), chm Surrey Play Cncl 1976–79; chm Marshall Tst (C of E charity) 1982–87 (currently tstee), pres Old Boys' Assoc King's Sch Canterbury 1970–73, memb Royal Inst of Int Affrs, general cmmr of Income Tax 1973–94; Worshipful Co of Stationers and Newspaper Makers: Liveryman 1952, Renter Warden, Chm Livery Ctee 1969–71, memb Ct of Assts 1982–94, Under Warden 1989–90, Upper Warden 1990–91, Master 1991–92, currently Ct Emeritus; FIOP, FRSA; *Recreations* beagling, tennis, jogging, music (opera, ballet); *Clubs* Hawks (Cambridge), Cwlth Tst; *Style—* Bill Young, Esq; ✉ Rushpond Cottage, School Lane, Winfrith Newburgh, Dorset DT2 8JX (☎ 01305 852951)

YOUNG, Sir William Neil; 10 Bt (GB 1769), of North Dean, Buckinghamshire; s of Capt William Elliot Young (ka 1942), and gs of Sir Charles Young, 9 Bt, KCMG, MVO (d 1944); Sir Charles's w was Clara, da of Sir Francis Elliot, GCMG, GCVO (gs of 2 Earl of Minto, also Envoy Extraordinary & Min Plenipotentiary to the King of the Hellenes 1903–17); *b* 22 Jan 1941; *Educ* Wellington, RMA Sandhurst; *m* 1965, Christine Veronica, o da of Robert Boland Morley, of Buenos Aires; 1 s (William Lawrence Elliot b 1970), 1 da (Catherine Clare (Mrs Hugh E Powell, *see* Sir Charles Powell, KCMG) b 1967); *Heir* s, William Lawrence Elliot Young, b 26 May 1970; *Career* Capt 16/5 Queen's Royal Lancers, ret 1970; stockbroker with Phillips & Drew, dir Kleinwort Benson International Investment Ltd 1982–87, head of investmt mgmnt Saudi International Bank 1987–91, int private banking (head of Middle East) Coutts & Co 1991–94, currently dir Barclays International Private Banking; *Recreations* skiing, tennis, sailing, shooting; *Clubs* Cavalry and Guards', Hong Kong; *Style—* Sir William Young, Bt; ✉ Penchrise Peel, Hawick, Roxburghshire

YOUNG OF DARTINGTON, Baron (Life Peer UK 1978), of Dartington, Co Devon; Michael Young; s of Gibson Young (musician), and Edith Young (writer); *b* 9 Aug 1915; *Educ* Dartington Hall, Univ of London (BSc, PhD); *m* 1, 1945, Joan Lawson; 2 s (Hon Christopher Ivan b 1946, Hon David Justin b 1949), 1 da (Hon Emma Dorothy b 1956); m 2, 1960, Sasha (d 1993), da of Raisley Stewart Moorsom; 1 s (Hon Toby Daniel Moorsom b 1963), 1 da (Hon Sophie Ann b 1961); m 3, 1995, Dorit Uhlemann; 1 da (Hon Gaia Inigo); *Career* sits as Labour peer in House of Lords; called to the Bar Gray's Inn 1939; sec Lab Pty Res Dept 1945–51, dir Inst for Community Studies 1953–, fell Churchill Coll Cambridge 1961–66, fndr and chm Social Sci Res Cncl 1965–68, memb NEDC 1975–78; pres: Consumers' Assoc 1965– (chm 1956–65), Nat Extension Coll 1971–, Advsy Centre for Educn 1976–, Coll of Health 1983–; chm: Mutual Aid Centre 1977–, Tawney Soc (SDP think tank) 1982–84, Open Coll of the Arts 1986–91, Open Sch 1988–; pres Birkbeck Coll London; tstee Dartington Hall 1942–92; Albert Medal RSA; hon fell LSE 1978, hon fell Churchill Coll Cambridge; hon degrees: Univ of Sheffield, Univ of Adelaide, Univ of Exeter, Queen Mary Coll, Open Univ, Univ of Keele, Univ of East London, Univ of Southampton; Hon FBA; *Books* incl: Family and Kinship in East London (with Peter Willmott, 1957), The Rise of the Meritocracy (1958), Learning Begins at Home (with Patrick McGeeney, 1968), The Symmetrical Family (with Peter Willmott, 1974), The Elmhirsts of Dartington - The Creation of an Utopian Community (1982), Social Scientist as Innovator (1984), The Metronomic Society - Natural Rhythms and Human Timetables (1988), Life After Work - The Arrival of the Ageless Society (with Tom Schuller, 1991), Your Head in Mine (poetry, with Sasha Moorsom, 1993), A Good Death (with Lesley Cullen, 1996); *Style—* The Rt Hon the Lord Young of Dartington, FBA; ✉ 18 Victoria Park Square, London E2 9PF

YOUNG OF GRAFFHAM, Baron (Life Peer UK 1984), of Graffham, Co W Sussex; David Ivor Young; PC (1984); s of late Joseph Young and his w, Rebecca; *b* 27 Feb 1932; *Educ* Christ's Coll Finchley, Univ Coll London (LLB, Capt London Univ Golf 1954); *m* 1956, Lita Marianne, da of Jonas Shaw; 2 da (Hon Karen Debra b 1957 m 1983, Hon Mr Justice Rix, *qv*, Hon Judith b 1960); *Career* admitted slr 1956; chm Eldonwall Ltd 1961–74, dir Town & City Properties Ltd 1971–74; chm: Manufacturers Hanover Property Services 1974–80, Greenwood Homes Ltd 1976–82; dir Centre for Policy Studies 1979–82 (memb Mgmnt Bd 1977–82); special advsr: Dept of Indust 1979–82, Dept of Educn and Sci 1981–82; chm Manpower Servs Cmmn 1982–84, memb/chm NEDC 1982–89; min without portfolio 1984–85, sec of state for employment 1985–87, sec of state for trade and indust and pres of the Bd of Trade 1987–89, retired from Govt 1989; dep chm Cons Pty 1989–90; dir Salomon Inc 1990–94; chm: Cable & Wireless plc 1990–95, Young Associates Ltd 1996–; currently dir: Annes Gate Property plc, Chelsea and Greenwich Land Development Corporation plc, Combined Services Estates plc, European Land & Property Corporation (KC & UDMS) plc, European Land & Property Developments plc, Richmond Retail Corporation plc, Second Opinion Investments Ltd, Southside Land Corporation plc, St John's Gardens Developments plc, The South Bank Foundation Ltd, UK Lotteries Ltd, Whitehall Corporation plc, Powerdesk plc; chm: Br Orgn for Rehabilitation by Training (ORT) 1975–80, Admin Ctee World ORT Union 1980–84, Int Cncl of Jewish Social and Welfare Servs 1981–; pres: Jewish Care 1990–, World ORT Union 1990–, IOD 1993–; chm: EU-Japan Assoc 1991–, Cncl Univ Coll London 1995–, London Philharmonic Tst 1995–; dir Prince of Wales Business Leaders Forum; Hon FRPS 1981; *Publications* The Enterprise Years

(1990); *Recreations* music, book collecting, photography and golf; *Clubs* Savile; *Style—* The Rt Hon Lord Young of Graffham, PC; ✉ Young Associates Ltd, Harcourt House, 19 Cavendish Square, London W1M 9AB (☎ 0171 447 8800, fax 0171 447 8849)

YOUNGER, Capt (John) David Bingham; JP (1994); s of Maj Oswald Bingham Younger, MC (d 1989), of Etal, Cornhill-On-Tweed, Northumberland, and Dorothea Elizabeth, *née* Hobbs (d 1996); *b* 20 May 1939; *Educ* Eton, RMA Sandhurst; *m* 1 Dec 1962, Anne Rosaleen, da of Lt-Col John Logan, TD, DL (d 1987), of Wester Craigend, Stirlingshire; 1 s (Mark Robert b 1972), 2 da (Sarah Juliet (Mrs Peter Landale) b 1964, Camilla Jane b 1966); *Career* Argyll and Sutherland Highlanders cmmnd 1959, Adj 1 Bn Borneo and Singapore 1965–67 (GSM Clasps Borneo and Malaysia), GSO 3 Directorate of Mil Ops MOD 1967–69, ret 1969; sec Queen's Body Guard for Scotland (Royal Co of Archers) 1993 (memb 1969–); Scottish & Newcastle Breweries Ltd: joined 1969, sr exec London 1971–73, sr exec Glasgow 1973–76, sr exec Edinburgh (incl 8 months secondment to GEC Marconi Space and Defence Systems) 1976–79; co-fndr and md Broughton Brewery Ltd 1979–94, dir Broughton Ales Ltd 1995–96; memb Argyll and Sutherland Highlanders Regtl Tst and Ctee 1985–92; chm Scottish Borders Tourist Bd 1989–91, vice pres Royal Highland and Agricultural Soc of Scotland 1994; chm of Govrs Belhaven Hill Sch Dunbar 1988–94; dir Queen's Hall Edinburgh 1992–; Borders Region dist of Tweeddale: DL 1987, Vice Lord-Lt 1992–94, Lord-Lt 1994–96; Lord-Lt of Tweeddale 1996–; MInstD 1984; *Recreations* country pursuits; *Style—* Capt David Younger, JP; ✉ Kirkurd House, Blyth Bridge, Peeblesshire EH46 7AH (☎ and fax 01721 752223)

YOUNGER, Gordon; *b* 4 Nov 1945; *Educ* Gateshead GS for Boys; *m* 5 Oct 1968, Pat; 2 da (Susan b 12 March 1973, Carol b 28 March 1975); *Career* Co-operative Bank: joined in Newcastle 1962, Inspection and Advances Depts Head Office Manchester 1969–74, various mgmnt appts in branches 1974–84, head of clearing London 1984–87, exec dir Transmissions Div 1992–94 (asst gen mangr 1987–90, gen mangr 1990–92); chief exec BACS Ltd 1994– (dir 1987–90 and 1994–); chm Cheque and Credit Clearing Ltd 1991–94 (dir 1986–94); alternate then full memb Cncl APACS 1987–94 (memb Strategy Gp 1992–94); FCIB 1992; *Recreations* walking, reading, gardening, swimming, travel, watching football (especially Newcastle United); *Style—* Gordon Younger, Esq; ✉ BACS Ltd, De Havilland Road, Egware, Middx HA8 5QA (☎ 0181 952 2333)

YOUNGER, James Samuel (Sam); s of Rt Hon Sir Kenneth Gilmour Younger (d 1976), of London, and Elisabeth Kirsteen, *née* Stewart; *b* 5 Oct 1951; *Educ* Westminster Sch, New Coll Oxford (BA); *m* 5 May 1984, Katherine Anne, da of Cyril Kenneth Spencer; 1 s (Edward Spencer Younger b 6 June 1986); *Career* asst ed Middle East International magazine 1972–78; BBC World Service: sr asst Central Current Affrs Talks 1979–84, sr prodr Current Affrs World Service 1984–85 (exec prodr 1985–86), asst head BBC Arabic Service 1986–87, head Current Affrs World Service in English 1987–89, head BBC Arabic Service 1989–92, controller Overseas Services 1992–94, dir of bdcasting 1994, md BBC World Service 1994–; *Recreations* choral singing, sport; *Style—* Sam Younger; ✉ 28 Rylett Crescent, London W12 9RL (☎ 0181 743 4449); BBC World Service, PO Box 76, Bush House, London WC2B 4PH (☎ 0171 240 3456, fax 0171 379 6841)

YOUNGER, (Roland) Nicholas; s of Henry Johnston Younger (d 1940), and Anna, *née* Marshall (d 1989), of Baro, Haddington; *b* 23 Dec 1934; *Educ* Winchester, Magdalene Coll Cambridge (MA); *m* 30 June 1962, Mary Younger, da of Maj-Gen R C A Edge; 3 s (Alexander William b 1963, Henry Benjamin b 1965, Simon Clovis b 1970); *Career* Nat Serv Subalt Royal Scots Greys 1953–55; research offr The Welding Institute 1958–62, tech mangr Davy Ashmore Ltd 1962–68, project mangr Imperial Smelting Corporation (subsid of Rio Tinto Zinc Corp) 1968–75, tech dir Davy International 1976–96; chm: Davy Roll Co Ltd, Formet Ltd, Turner Chilled Rolls Ltd; former non-exec dir: Clecim SA, Davy McKee (Stockton) Ltd; memb Cncl The Welding Inst; memb Cleveland Inst of Engrs; FIM (former vice pres), FEng 1995; *Recreations* music, field sports; *Style—* Nicholas Younger, Esq, FEng; ✉ Thirkleby House, Thirsk, North Yorkshire YO7 2AY (☎ 01845 501481)

YOUNGER, Hon Sheriff Robert Edward Gilmour; 3 s of 3 Viscount Younger of Leckie, OBE, TD, DL; bro of Rt Hon Lord Younger of Prestwick, TD, DL, MP, *qqv*; *b* 25 Sept 1940; *Educ* Winchester, New Coll Oxford, Univ of Edinburgh, Univ of Glasgow; *m* 1972, Helen, da of Eric Hayes (d 1959), and Margaret, sis of Sir John Muir, 3 Bt, TD; 1 s, 1 da; *Career* advocate 1968; Sheriff: Glasgow and Strathkelvin at Glasgow 1979–82, Tayside Central and Fife at Stirling and Falkirk 1982–87, Stirling and Alloa 1987–92, Stirling 1992–; *Style—* The Hon Sheriff Robert Younger; ✉ Old Leckie, Gargunnock, Stirling (☎ 01786 860213)

YOUNGER OF LECKIE, 3 Viscount (UK 1923); Sir Edward George Younger; 3 Bt (UK 1911), OBE (1940), TD, DL; s of 2 Viscount Younger of Leckie, DSO, TD, JP, DL (d 1946), and Maud (d 1957), er da of Sir John Gilmour, 1 Bt; *b* 21 Nov 1906; *Educ* Winchester, New Coll Oxford (BA); *m* 7 June 1930, Evelyn Margaret, MBE (d 1983), da of late Alexander Logan McClure, KC, sometime Sheriff of Aberdeen, Kincardine and Banff; 3 s, 1 da; *Heir* s, Rt Hon Lord Younger of Prestwick, TD, DL, *qv*; *Career* Capt A Staff, France 1940, Col Gen Staff, France 1939–40, UK 1940–45, Col Argyll and Sutherland Highlanders (TA); Lord-Lt Stirling and Falkirk 1964–79; *Clubs* New (Edinburgh); *Style—* The Rt Hon the Viscount Younger of Leckie, OBE, TD, DL; ✉ Wester Leckie, Kippen, Stirling FK8 3JL

YOUNGER OF PRESTWICK, Baron (Life Peer UK 1992), of Ayr in the District of Kyle and Carrick; Sir George Kenneth Hotson Younger; KT (1995), KCVO (1993), TD (1964), PC (1979), DL (Stirlingshire 1968); s and h of 3 Viscount Younger of Leckie, OBE, TD, *qv*; *b* 22 Sept 1931; *Educ* Winchester, New Coll Oxford (MA); *m* 7 Aug 1954, Diana Rhona, er da of Capt Gerald Seymour Tuck, DSO, RN (d 1984), of Little London, Chichester, Sussex; 3 s (Hon James Edward George b 11 Nov 1955, Hon Charles Gerald Alexander b 4 Oct 1959, Hon Andrew Seymour Robert b 19 Nov 1962), 1 da (Hon Joanna Rosalind (Hon Mrs Davidson) b 16 Jan 1958); *Career* 2 Lt Argyll and Sutherland Highlanders 1950, with 1 Bn BAOR and Korea 1951, 7 Bn (TA) 1952–65; Hon Col 154 (Lowland) Tport Regt RCT TA & VR 1977–85; pres cncl TA & VRA 1993–; contested (C) N Lanarks 1959 and stood down from Kinross and W Perths 1963 in favour of Sir Alec Douglas-Home, MP (C) Ayr 1964–92; govr Royal Scottish Acad of Music 1960–70, Scottish Cons whip 1965–67, dir Charrington Vintners Ltd 1966–68, dep chm Cons Pty in Scotland 1967–70 and chm 1974–75, parly under sec of state for Devpt Scottish Office 1970–74, min of state for Defence Jan-March 1974; sec of state for: Scotland May 1979–Jan 1986, Defence Jan 1986–July 1989; dir: Tennant Caledonian Breweries 1977–79, Murray International Trust plc 1989–, Murray Smaller Markets Trust plc 1989–, Murray Income Trust plc 1989–, Murray Ventures plc 1989–, Scottish Equitable Life Assurance Society 1990–, BCH Property Limited 1991–, Banco de Santander SA 1991–; chm: The Royal Bank of Scotland plc 1989–, The Royal Bank of Scotland Gp plc 1989–, Siemens Plessey Electronic Systems Ltd 1990–, PIK (Holdings) Ltd 1991–, SPEED Ltd 1991–, BCH Property 1992–; vice-pres Inst of Banking 1993–; chllr Napier Univ 1993–; fell Winchester Coll 1992–; delivered Sir Andrew Humphrey Meml lectr on The Future of Air Power 1988; pres Nat Union of Cons Assocs 1987–88; Brig Queen's Body Guard for Scotland (Royal Co of Archers); fell Winchester Coll; regent Royal Coll of Surgns of Edinburgh; Hon LLD Glasgow 1992, Hon DLitt Napier Univ 1992, Hon LLD Univ of Liverpool 1995; Hon DUniv: Edinburgh 1993, Paisley 1994; FRSE 1993; *Recreations* tennis, sailing; *Clubs* Caledonian (London), Highland Brigade; *Style—* The Rt Hon Lord Younger of; ✉ Leckie, Gargunnock, Stirlingshire FK8 3BN (☎ 01786 86274)

YOUNGSON, Prof Alexander John; CBE (1987); s of Dr Alexander Brown (d 1954), and Helen Youngson (d 1945); *b* 28 Sept 1918; *Educ* Aberdeen GS, Univ of Aberdeen (MA, DLitt), Univ of California; *m* 14 Sept 1948, Elizabeth Gisborne, da of Leonard Brown Naylor, CBE (d 1957); 1 s (Graeme b 1952), 1 da (Sheila b 1954); *Career* Lt RNVR S Atlantic and Europe 1939–45; lectr Univ of Cambridge 1950–58, prof Univ of Edinburgh 1958–74, dir RSSS Aust Nat Univ 1974–80, chm Royal Fine Art Cmmn for Scot 1983–90; *Books* Possibilities of Economic Progress (1959), The Making of Classical Edinburgh (1966), After the '45 (1973), The Prince and the Pretender (1985), Urban Development (1990), Edinburgh and the Border Country (1993); *Recreations* gardening; *Style—* Prof Alexander Youngson, CBE; ✉ 17 The Horseshoe, York Y02 2LY

YOUNGSON, George Gray; s of Alexander Keay Youngson, MBE, of Glenrothes, Fife, and Jean Oneil, *née* Kelly; *b* 13 May 1949; *Educ* Buckhaven HS, Univ of Aberdeen (MB ChB, PhD); *m* 17 March 1973, Sandra Jean, *née* Lister; 1 s (Calum Lister b 1981), 2 da (Kellie Jane b 1973, Louise b 1975); *Career* Univ of Aberdeen: lectr in surgery 1979–82, res fell 1974–76; res in cardiothoracic surgery Univ of W Ontario Canada 1977–79, clinical fell in paediatric surgery Hosp for Sick Children Toronto Ontario Canada 1983, conslt surgn Aberdeen Royal Hosp Tst 1985; sec Scot Surgical Paediatric Soc; memb: Br Assoc of Paediatric Surgns, Assoc of Surgns GB and Ireland; FRCSEd 1977 (examiner 1991); *Recreations* bagpipe music, sport (fishing, tennis, squash, golf); *Style—* George Youngson, Esq; ✉ 10 Kennerty Park, Peterculter, Aberdeen AB1 0LE (☎ 01224 734403); Royal Aberdeen Children's Hospital, Cornhill Road, Aberdeen (☎ 01224 681818)

YOUNIS, Dr Farouk Mustafa; s of Mustafa Younis, of Amman, Jordan, and Wasila Mahmoud Khader; *b* 1 March 1947; *Educ* Markaziyah All HS Baghdad Iraq, Baghdad Univ Med Sch (MB ChB); *m* 13 Sept 1975, Cynthia Karen, da of George Gadsby (d 1992), of Ilkeston, Derbyshire; 1 s (Sami Farouk b 15 Feb 1977); *Career* surgeon; started career in Palestinian refugee camps in Lebanon with Red Crescent Soc Med and Health Prog 1971–72; trg posts UK 1973–: casualty, gen surgery, orthopaedics, thoracic, vascular and urologic surgery; casualty post Chesterfield, gen surgery posts Harrogate, Barrow in Furness and Huddersfield, orthopaedics post Cambridge, kidney transplant and gen surgery post Royal Free Hosp London, gen and vascular surgery Chelmsford, conslt surgeon Whittington Hosp 1981–83, private surgical practice 1981–; memb: BMA, RSM, Ind Doctors' Forum; FRCS 1977; *Recreations* tennis, golf, travel, chess; *Clubs* David Lloyd Tennis (Finchley); *Style—* Dr Farouk Younis; ✉ 129 Harley Street, London W1N 1DJ (☎ 0171 487 4897, fax 0171 224 6398)

YOXALL, George Thomas; s of George Thomas Yoxall (d 1983), of Sandbach, Cheshire, and Mary, *née* Bunn (d 1990); *b* 22 Feb 1949; *Educ* Crewe Co GS, Hertford Coll Oxford (MA); *m* 10 April 1976, Barbara Elizabeth, da of Thomas Donald Gorrie, of Liverpool; 2 s (Matthew b 1980, Richard b 1982); *Career* admin sci offr Sci Res Cncl 1970–72, actuarial student Duncan C Fraser & Ptnrs 1972–73, asst to investmt mangr Nat Farmers Union Mutual Insur Soc 1973–76, UK equity mangr Airways Pension Scheme 1976–82, asst investmt mangr Central Fin Bd Methodist Church 1982–84, sr portfolio mangr Abbey Life N America 1984–86, dir investmts Abbey Life Assurance Co 1989–94; md: Abbey Life Investments Services 1989–94 (dir N America 1986–88), Exeter Fund Managers 1994; dir: Abbey Unit Trust Managers 1989–94, Regent Global Fund 1989–, First Phillipines Investment Trust 1989–94, Exeter Investment Group 1994, Exeter Asset Management 1994, Malaysia Equity Fund 1996–; business conslt 1995–; memb Investmt Ctee ABI 1989–93; Liveryman Worshipful Co of Actuaries; AIA 1978; *Recreations* hockey, sailing, skiing, civil aviation; *Style—* George Yoxall, Esq; ✉ 98 Canford Cliffs Road, Poole, Dorset BH13 7AE (☎ and fax 01202 700609)

YUASA, Takuo; *b* 27 July 1949; *Educ* Coll/Conservatory of Music Univ of Cincinnati (BMus), Vienna Hochschule für Musik (Dip); *m* 1982, Shigeko Takaoka; 1 da (Michika b 1984); *Career* conductor Gumma Symphony Orch 1984–88, princ guest conductor BBC Scottish Symphony Orch 1989–93; UK debut 1988, Proms debut 1989; conducted orchs incl: Tonkünstlerorchester Vienna, Japan Philharmonic, Tokyo Met Symphony, Warsaw Nat Philharmonic, Polish Radio Nat Symphony, London Philharmonic, Yomiuri Nippon Symphony, Oslo Philharmonic, Ulster Orchestra, Bournemouth Symphony, Royal Liverpool Philharmonic, Hong Kong Philharmonic, Syndey Symphony, Berlin Symphony; venues incl: Vienna Konzerthaus, Royal Festival Hall, opening concert Glasgow Euro City of Culture Festival 1990, Sydney Opera House, Berlin Philharmonic Hall, numerous others in UK, Japan, Scandinavia, Australia and Europe; *Recordings* Rimsky-Korsakov's Sheherazade (with London Philharmonic Orch), Benjamin Britten's Four Sea Interludes and others (with Royal Liverpool Philharmonic Orch, on EMI label); *Style—* Takuo Yuasa, Esq; ✉ Hakata 2–1–28, Izumi, Osaka, 594 Japan; c/o Patrick Garvey Management, 59 Landsdown Place, Hove, E Sussex BN3 1FL (☎ 01273 206623, fax 01273 208484)

YULE, (Duncan) Ainslie; s of Edward Campbell Yule (d 1974), and Elizabeth Morgan Ainslie; *b* 10 Feb 1941; *Educ* North Berwick HS, Edinburgh Coll of Art (DA); *m* 1, 1963 (m dis 1982), Patricia Carlos; 1 da (b 1963); m 2, 1982, Mary Johnson; *Career* sculptor; work in several public and private collections; teaching posts: lectr in design Gray's Sch of Art Aberdeen 1966–79; sessional lectr: Univ of Reading 1978–81, Middx Poly (Hornsey Sch of Art) 1979–81; visiting lectr RCA 1984–87; head of sculpture Kingston Univ 1982– (reader 1987–); *Solo Exhibitions* incl: New 57 Gallery Edinburgh 1969, Serpentine Gallery 1973, Richard Demarco Gallery Edinburgh 1972/73/82/88, Leeds Univ 1973, Park Square Gallery Leeds 1976, Editions Alecto 1977, Fruitmarket Gallery Edinburgh and travelling 1977, St Paul's Gallery Leeds 1981, Angela Flowers Gallery 1986, Kingston Poly 1990; *Mixed Exhibitions* incl: Earth Images Whitechapel Art Gallery 1973, Gubbio Biennale 1973, Leeds Univ 1975, Scottish Arts Cncl 1975/77, Silver Jubilee Exhbn of Br Sculpture Battersea Park 1977, Belgrade '77 1977, Scottish Nat Gallery of Modern Art 1978, first Sculpture Biennial Toronto 1978, Scottish Artists in Finland 1978, The British Art Show Sheffield, Bristol and Newcastle 1979–80, Scottish Contemporary Art Robinson Galleries Houston Texas 1985, Scottish Gallery London 1989/90/91, Chicago Art Fair 1990, Museum of Fine Arts Budapest 1992, Villa Foscarini-Rossi Venice 1993; *Awards* Andrew Grant scholarship 1963, Scottish Arts Cncl award 1973 and 1975, Gregory fell in Sculpture Univ of Leeds 1974–75, memb Faculty of Prix de Rome 1980–84, Rainbow Wood scholarship Japan 1996; *Clubs* Chelsea Arts; *Style—* Ainslie Yule, Esq; ✉ 218 Sheen Lane, London SW14 8LB (☎ 0181 876 5047, fax 0181 547 7133)

Z

ZACCOUR, Makram Michel; s of Michel Zaccour (former MP and Foreign & Interior Min of Lebanon, d 1937), and Rose, *née* Gorayeb; *b* 19 Aug 1935; *Educ* Berkeley Coll California Univ (BSc); *Career* gen mangr Industrias Textiles Ultratex (Colombia) 1964–66 (sales 1957–64); Merrill Lynch: fin conslt ME 1967–73, mangr Beirut office 1973, Beirut and Paris 1976, London 1977–83, regnl dir Merrill Lynch Pierce Fenner & Smith Ltd 1983–92, vice chm Int Private Banking Gp 1992–, chm Middle East 1992–, co-chm Merrill Lynch Bank (Suisse) 1993–; memb Arab Bankers' Assoc; Phi Beta Kappa; *Clubs* Annabel's, Harry's Bar, Mark's; *Style*— Makram M Zaccour, Esq; ✉ Merrill Lynch International Bank, 33 Chester Street, London SW1X 7XD (☎ 0171 867 6210, fax 0171 629 0622)

ZACHARY, Stefan Hedley; s of Jan Bronislaw Zacharkiewicz (d 1987), and Thelma Joyce, *née* Mortimer; *b* 30 June 1948; *Educ* Roundhay Sch Leeds, Leeds Coll of Art (BA); *m* 7 Aug 1971, (Margaret) Patricia, da of Stanley George Wright, of Great Kingshill, Bucks; 2 s (Alexander Adam, Christopher Jan), 1 da (Halina Patricia); *Career* Royal Yeomanry TA&VR 1972–73, 5 Bn The Queen's Regt TA&VR 1973–76, RMA Sandhurst 1975; interior designer Conran Design Group 1970–71, assoc ptnr Howard Sant Partnership 1971–77, md and dir McColl Group plc 1977–92, princ Zachary Design 1992–; pres CSD 1994–96 (vice pres 1986–89), memb RIBA Mktg Gp 1987–88, jt hon pres Design Business Assoc 1989– (founding chm 1986–89); Freeman City of London 1988, Liveryman Worshipful Co of Painter Stainers 1989 (Freeman 1988); FCSD 1981, FBID 1979, FRSA 1979, FIMgt 1984; *Books* CSD Works Agreement User's Guide (1983); *Recreations* flying, gliding, shooting, travel, driving, painting and drawing; *Style*— Mr Stefan Zachary, PPCSD; ✉ Zachary Design, Little Moseley House, Naphill, Bucks HP14 4RE (☎ 01494 562592, car 0836 202419, mobile 0836 326932)

ZAFIROPOULOS, HE Vassilis S; *b* 24 Jan 1934, Corfu; *Educ* Univ of Athens (Political Sci and Law); *m*; 1 s; *Career* Greek diplomat; entered Greek Civil Serv 1962, Miny of Fin 1962–67, on secondment i/c press matters UN Info Centre for Greece, Israel, Turkey and Cyprus (Athens) 1967–71, joined Diplomatic Serv 1971, third sec Central Serv Miny of Foreign Affrs 1971–73, second sec Consul Liege Belgium 1973–76, first sec Greek Embassy Nicosia and dir Greek Press Office Cyprus 1976–78, cnsllr Greek Embassy Nicosia 1978–80, cnsllr for political affrs Greek Embassy London 1980–84, head of Cyprus affrs Miny of Foreign Affrs 1984–86, min cnsllr Dep Perm Rep of Greece to NATO Brussels 1986–90, min plenipotentiary 1990, ambass of Greece to Aust and NZ 1991–93, perm rep of Greece to NATO 1993–96, ambass of Greece to the Ct of St James's 1996–; *Style*— HE Mr Vassilis S Zafiropoulos; ✉ Embassy of Greece, 1a Holland Park, London W11 3TP (☎ 0171 229 3850, fax 0171 229 7221)

ZAGO, Paolo Bruno; s of Augusto Zago (d 1969), and Axelina, *née* Bonali (d 1993); *b* 20 Sept 1932; *Educ* Istituto Tecnico Commerciale Treviso Italy; *m* Evelyn; *Career* served Italian Air Force 1950–52; hotelier; varied hotel experience 1952–57 (family business/hotel companies in Italy and abroad); CIGA Hotel Co: reception and front of the house mangr The Gritti Palace Hotel Venice 1957–66, asst gen mangr Excelsior Palace Hotel Lido Venice 1966–71; The Savoy Co: joined 1971, asst gen mangr The Berkeley Hotel Knightsbridge 1972–73, md and gen mangr The Connaught Hotel Mayfair 1980– (gen mangr 1973, dir 1975); Personnalité de l'Année 1988; Confrérie des Chevaliers du Tastevin 1976; fndr memb Euro Hotel Mangrs Assoc, hon fndr memb Academie Culinaire de France (GB) 1980; Cavaliere al Merito della Repubblica Italiana 1995; fell City and Guilds of London Inst 1996; *Recreations* oil painting, gardening, antiques, travel; *Style*— Paolo Zago, Esq; ✉ The Connaught Hotel, Carlos Place, Mayfair, London W1Y 6AL (☎ 0171 499 7070)

ZAIWALLA, Sarosh Ratanshaw; *b* 27 Sept 1947; *Educ* Univ of Bombay (BCom, LLB); *children* 1 da (Freya b 1981), 1 s (Varun (b 1983); *Career* admitted slr 1978; fndr ptnr Gagrat & Co London 1978–82, sr ptnr Zaiwalla & Co London 1982–; specialist in international commercial contracts and maritime disputes and immigration and nationality cases; memb: Law Soc, Maritime Arbitrators' Assoc, Baltic Exchange London, Int Ct of Arbitration of Int C of C Paris, London Ct of Int Arbitration (fndr memb), Indian Cncl of Arbitration Delhi, London Maritime Arbitrators' Assoc (supporting memb); pres Soc of Friends of the Lotus Children, memb One Nation Forum; FRSA; *Style*— Sarosh Zaiwalla, Esq; ✉ Zaiwalla & Co, Chancery Lane, London WC2A 1ZZ (☎ 0171 312 1000, fax 0171 312 1100)

ZAKHAROV, Prof Vasilii; s of Viktor Nikiforovich Zakharov (d 1976), and Varvara Semyenovna, *née* Krzak (d 1962); *Educ* Latymer Upper Sch, Univ of London (BSc, MSc, PhD, DIC, DSc); *m* 1959, Jeanne, da of Horace Hopper (d 1988), of Canterbury; 1 s (Oleg b 1959), 1 da (Anna b 1962); *Career* res in computer systems and applications Birkbeck Coll London 1953–56, res in digital systems Rank Xerox 1956–57, res fell in physics Imperial Coll (RCS) 1957–60, physicist CERN 1960–65, univ reader in experimental physics QMC 1965–66, head Computer Systems and Electronics Div SRC Daresbury Laboratory 1966–78, dir Computer Centre and prof of computer systems Univ of London 1978–80, sr assoc CERN Geneva 1980–83 (res assoc 1971–72), prof Univ of Geneva 1984–87, dir of info processing Int Orgn for Standards Geneva 1989–95, ret 1996; visiting prof of physics: QMC 1968, Westfield Coll London 1974–78; visiting scientist JINR Dubna USSR 1965, conslt AERE Harwell 1965; memb SRC Computer Sci Ctee 1974–77; numerous pubns and contribs to scientific and tech literature; *Books* Digital Systems Logic (1968); *Recreations* rough shooting, amateur radio, collecting Russian miscellania, skiing; *Style*— Prof Vasilii Zakharov; ✉ 74 route de Chêne, CH-1208 Geneva, Switzerland; The Firs, Old Castle, Malpas, Cheshire SY14 7NE; ISO, 1 rue de Varembé, CH-1211 Geneva 20, Switzerland (☎ 00 41 22 749 0228, fax 00 41 22 733 3430)

ZAMBONI, Richard Frederick Charles; s of Alfred Charles Zamboni (d 1957), and Frances, *née* Hosler (d 1983); descendant of a Swiss (Engiadina) family with lineage traceable to 1465; *b* 28 July 1930; *Educ* Monkton House Sch Cardiff; *m* 1, 2 Jan 1960, Pamela Joan (d 1993), da of Laurence Brown Marshall; 2 s (Edward b 1962, Rupert b 1967), 1 da (Charlotte b 1964); m 2, March 1996, Deirdre Olive, da of John Reginald Kingham; *Career* Br Egg Mktg Bd 1959–70; chm: Sun Life Investment Management Services Ltd 1985–89, Sun Life Trust Management Ltd 1985–89; vice chm Sun Life Assurance Society plc 1986–89 (md 1979–89); dep chm Assoc of Br Insurers 1986–88 (chm Life Insur Cncl 1986–88); chm: Avon Enterprise Fund plc 1990– (dir 1984), AIM Distribution Trust Plc 1996–; chm Cncl of Mgmnt Grange Centre for People with Disabilities 1991–; Liveryman Worshipful Co of Insurers; FCA; *Recreations* ornithology, gardening, golf; *Style*— Richard Zamboni, Esq; ✉ The Old Vicarage, Church Street, Leatherhead, Surrey KT22 8ER (☎ 01372 812398)

ZAMOYSKI, Count Adam Stefan; s of Lt-Col Count Stefan Zamoyski, OBE, VM, LLD, Order of Polonia Restituta (d 1976, fifth in descent from Andreas Zamoyski, cr Count 1778 (confirmed 1780) by Empress Maria Teresa of Austria at the time of the Partitions of Poland) by his w Princess Elizabeth Czartoryska (d 1989); the Princess's gf was Prince Wladyslaw Czartoryski (s of Tsar Alexander I's Foreign Minister Prince Adam, who was also briefly head of Independent Poland 1830), while her grandmother (Wladyslaw's w) was HRH Princess Marguerite d'Orléans (da of HRH The Duc de Nemours, 2 s of Louis Philippe, King of the French); *b* 11 Jan 1949, in New York; *Educ* Downside, Queen's Coll Oxford; *Career* historian and author, books include a biography of Chopin and a History of Poland; recent books incl The Last King of Poland (1992), The Forgotten Few (1995); tstee Czartoryski Fndn Krakow and several Polish charities in England; Knight of Honour & Devotion Sov Mil Order of Malta 1977, Kt of Justice Constantinian Order of St George (House of Bourbon Sicily) 1978, Order of Polonia Restituta 1982; *Clubs* Pratt's, Puffin's, Polish Hearth; *Style*— Count Adam Zamoyski; ✉ 33 Ennismore Gdns, London SW7 (☎ 0171 584 9053); Wilcza 19 m7, 00–544 Warszawa, Poland (☎ 00 48 2 628 5281)

ZAMOYSKI, Count Wojciech Michal; er s of Count Michal Zamoyski (2 s of Count Adam Zamoyski, sometime ADC to Tsar Nicholas II, by his marriage with Countess Maria Potocka; Adam the ADC was youngest bro of Count Stefan, who was the ggf of Count Adam Stefan Zamoyski, *qv*); *b* 12 Sept 1927, Kozlowka Palace; *Educ* Poland, Angola, S Africa; *m* 1955, Isobel Zamoyska, er da of William Forbes-Robertson Mutch; 2 s (Count Paul b 1957, Count Alexander b 1962), 1 da (Countess Anna Isabella b 1960); *Career* Formerly official at Rhodesian High Cmmn and Overseas Devpt Admin; *Recreations* Poland, the Third World, travel; *Style*— Count Wojciech Zamoyski; (☎ 0171 581 0998)

ZANDER, Prof Michael; s of Dr Walter Zander (d 1993), and Margaret, *née* Magnus (d 1968); *b* 16 Nov 1932; *Educ* RGS High Wycombe, Jesus Coll Cambridge (BA, LLB), Harvard Law Sch (LLM); *m* 27 Aug 1965, Elizabeth Treeger (Betsy), da of Clarence R Treeger, of NYC; 1 da (Nicola b 1969), 1 s (Jonathan b 1970); *Career* 2 Lt RA; admitted slr 1962, Sydney Morse & Co 1962–63; LSE: asst lectr 1963, lectr 1965, sr lectr 1970, reader 1970, prof 1977–, convenor Law Dept 1984–88; memb Royal Cmmn on Criminal Justice 1991–93; regular broadcasts on radio and TV, legal corr The Guardian 1963–87; *Books* Lawyers and the Public Interest (1968), Legal Services for the Community (1973), The Law-Making Process (1980, 4 edn 1994), The Police and Criminal Evidence Act (1984, 3 edn 1995), A Bill of Rights? (4 edn 1996), Cases and Materials on English Legal Systems (7 edn 1996), A Matter of Justice: The Legal System in Ferment (revised edn, 1989); *Recreations* learning the cello, swimming; *Style*— Prof Michael Zander; ✉ 12 Woodside Ave, London N6 4SS (☎ 0181 883 6257, fax 0181 444 3348); LSE, Houghton St, London WC2 (☎ 0171 955 7268, fax 0171 242 0392)

ZAPHIRIOU-ZARIFI, Ari Charles; s of Prof George Aristotle Zaphiriou, of Washington DC, and Frosso, *née* Zarifi; *b* 10 March 1946; *Educ* Stowe, LSE (BSc); *m* 27 Dec 1973 (m dis 1990), Yana, da of Ulysses Sistovaris (d 1985); 1 s (Stefan b 1975), 1 da (Viki b 1978); m 2, 30 April 1995, Heba, da of Jad Kabban; 1 da (Anna b 1996); *Career* Peat Marwick Mitchell 1967–70, J Henry Schroder Wagg 1970–73, chm and chief exec The Heritable and General Investment Bank Ltd 1988– (dir 1975, md 1979); chm: Alpha Gamma Group 1983–, Beeson Gregory Holdings Ltd; FCA 1970; *Recreations* tennis, swimming, sailing, theatre, gardening; *Style*— Ari Zaphiriou-Zarifi, Esq; ✉ 31 Gloucester Square, London W2 (☎ 0171 262 2112); Spence House, Dock Lane, Beaulieu, Hants

ZATOUROFF, Dr Michael Argo; s of Argo Arakel Zatouroff (d 1980), of New York, and Nina, *née* Dragounova (d 1979); *b* 23 Oct 1936; *Educ* Seaford Coll Sussex, Royal London Hosp (MB BS, DCH, FRCP); *m* 13 May 1961, Diana, da of Alan Curtis Heard; 1 s (Justin Alan b 7 Sept 1965), 2 da (Anna Eugenie b 22 July 1963, Catherine Morwenna b 20 April 1968); *Career* house offr Royal London Hosp 1961, sr house offr Royal United Hosp Bath 1962–63; med registrar: UCH Ibadan Nigeria 1963–64, Royal Northern Hosp London 1964–66; conslt physician Kuwait Govt 1966–76; present appts: hon sr lectr in Med Royal Free Hosp London, conslt physician The London Clinic London, lectr in med The London Foot Hosp London, examiner in med (United Exam Bd UK, Soc of Chiropodists, Med Artists' Assoc of GB), memb Editorial Bd Medicine International; winner Horder Prize in Med 1966; Freeman City of London, Liveryman Worshipful Co of Barber Surgeons; memb: Soc of Authors, RSM 1965, Med Soc of London 1966, Harvian Soc 1966, Osler Club 1966; hon fell Soc of Chiropodists; *Books* Physical Signs in General Medicine (1976, 2 edn 1995), Diagnostic Studies in General Medicine (1989), The Foot in Clinical Diagnosis (1993); *Recreations* cross-country cycling, med photography, carriage driving, theatre, eating, reading, dieting; *Clubs* Garrick; *Style*— Dr Michael Zatouroff; ✉ 25 Fordington Rd, Highgate, London N6 4TD (☎ 0181 883 5118); The London Clinic, 149 Harley St, London W1N 1HF (☎ 0171 935 4444, fax 0171 935 2725)

ZATZ, Paul Simon Jonah; s of Samuel Zatz (d 1981), and Stella Rachel Morgan, *née* Levy; *b* 21 April 1938; *Educ* King William's Coll, Sidney Sussex Coll Cambridge (MA, LLM); *m* 5 Sept 1965, Patricia Ann, da of Sidney Landau (d 1971); 1 s (Joshua b 1969), 1 da (Rachel b 1967); *Career* admitted slr 1964; ptnr Lawrance Messer & Co 1968–81; Clyde Petroleum plc: co sec 1980, legal and corp dir 1983, fin dir 1989–; dir English String Orchestra Ltd 1991–; *Recreations* opera, walking; *Clubs* City Univ; *Style*— Paul Zatz, Esq; ✉ Clyde Petroleum plc, Coddington Court, Coddington, Ledbury, Herefordshire HR8 1JL (☎ 01531 640811, fax 01531 640519)

ZEALLEY, Christopher Bennett; s of late Sir Alec Zealley, of Devon, and late Nellie Maude, *née* King; *b* 5 May 1931; *Educ* Sherborne, King's Coll Cambridge (choral scholarship, MA); *m* 23 April 1966, Ann Elizabeth Sandwith; 1 s (Robert Paul b 1969), 1 da (Elizabeth Victoria b 1972); *Career* cmnnd RNVR 1953; ICI 1955–66, IRC 1966–70; dir: Dartington Hall Tst 1970–88, JT Group Ltd, Grant Instruments Ltd; chm: Public Interest Res Centre 1972–, Social Audit Ltd 1972–, Consumers Assoc (Which?) 1976–82, Consumers Assoc Ltd 1991–93, Dartington and Co Group plc 1979–91, Charity Appointments Ltd 1986–92, Dartington Coll of Art 1973–91, Morwellham Recreation Co Ltd 1978–; memb Cncl Univ of Exeter 1988–; tstee various orgns incl Charities Aid

Fndn 1981–90; *Books* Creating a Charitable Trust; *Recreations* music; *Clubs* Naval; *Style*— Christopher Zealley, Esq; ✉ Sneydhurst, Broadhempston, Totnes, Devon TQ9 6AX

ZEEGEN, Dr Ronald; OBE (1994); *b* 30 Oct 1938; *Educ* Battersea GS, Bart's Med Coll (MB BS, LRCP, MRCS, DObstRCOG, FRCP); *m*; 3 c; *Career* jr registrar and res fell Bart's 1965–69 (temp sr registrar 1971), sr registrar Westminster Hosp 1971–74 (registrar 1970), conslt physician i/c Depts of Gastro-enterology Westminster and St Stephen's Hosp 1974–93, conslt physician and gastroenterologist Westminster and Chelsea Hosp 1993–; receiving conslt physician Westminster Hosp for Palace of Westminster 1985–93; hon conslt gastro-enterologist: Royal Marsden Hosp 1986–, Royal Brompton and Nat Heart Hosps 1986–; hon conslt physician: Newpaper Press Fund 1986–, Royal Hosp Chelsea 1994–; former memb Editorial Bd Medical Digest; contrib to books and published papers for several med jls incl Br Med Jl, Br Jl of Clinical Practice, Gut, Lancet and Quarterly Jl of Medicine; memb: BMA, Br Soc of Gastro-enterology, Liver Club, Med Soc of London, Harveian Soc, Hunterian Soc; FRCP 1980; *Recreations* horology, antique walking sticks, fine wines, canal restoration; *Clubs* Garrick; *Style*— Dr Ronald Zeegen, OBE; ✉ Westminster and Chelsea Hospital, 369 Fulham Road, London SW10 9NH (☎ 0181 746 8007)

ZEEMAN, Prof Sir (Erik) Christopher; kt (1991); s of Christian Zeeman (d 1929), of Aarhus and Yokohama, and Christine, *née* Bushell (d 1968); *b* 4 Feb 1925; *Educ* Christ's Hospital, Christ's Coll Cambridge (BA, MA, PhD); *m* 1, June 1950 (m dis 1959), Elizabeth, da of Evan Jones; 1 da (Nicolette b 1956); m 2, 30 Jan 1960, Rosemary, da of Harold Samuels Gledhill; 3 s (Tristan b 1960, Crispin b 1965, Samuel Christian b 1970), 2 da (Mary Lou b 1961, Francesca b 1967); *Career* Flying Officer RAF 1943–47; fell Gonville & Caius Coll Cambridge 1953–64, Cwlth fell Univ of Chicago and Princeton Univ 1954–55, lectr Univ of Cambridge 1955–64, memb Institut des Hautes Etudes Scientifiques Paris 1962–63, fndn prof and dir Mathematics Research Centre Univ of Warwick 1964–88 (hon prof 1988–), visiting prof Univ of California Berkeley 1966–67, sr fell SERC 1976–81, prof Royal Instn 1983–, visiting fell CCC Oxford 1985–86, princ Hertford Coll Oxford 1988–95, Gresham prof of geometry Gresham Coll London 1988–94; visiting prof: Inst for Advanced Study Princeton, Institut des Hautes Etudes Scientifique Paris, Instituto de Matematica Pura e Aplicada Rio de Janeiro, Int Centre for Theoretical Physics Trieste, Univ of Maryland, Florida State Univ, Univ of Pisa; chm Mathematic Ctee SERC 1982–85, pres London Mathematical Soc 1986–88, vice pres Royal Soc 1989–90, fndr chm Scientific Steering Ctee Isaac Newton Inst Cambridge 1990–; Queen's Jubilee medal 1977, Senior Whitehead prize London Mathematical Soc 1982, Faraday medal Royal Soc 1988; Hon DSc: Univ of Hull 1984, Claremont Univ Centre & Graduate Sch 1986, Univ of Leeds 1990, Univ of Durham 1990, Univ of Hartford 1992; Hon DSc & Hon Prof Univ of Warwick 1988, Hon DUniv York 1988, Docteur honoris causa Univ of Strasbourg 1974, hon fell Christ's Coll Cambridge 1989; FRS 1975, memb Brazilian Acad of Sciences 1972; *Books* Catastrophe Theory (1977), Geometry and Perspective (1987), Gyroscopes & Boomerangs (1989); many research papers; *Recreations* family, music, carpentry, walking; *Style*— Prof Sir Christopher Zeeman; ✉ 23 High Street, Woodstock, Oxon OX20 1TE (☎ 01993 813402)

ZEFFERT, Clive Lewis; s of Henry Zeffertt (sic), of Portsmouth, and Ann, *née* Levison; *b* 11 Aug 1938; *Educ* Portsmouth GS, Portsmouth Sch of Architecture (Dip Arch); *m* 21 April 1966, Sherry Lynn, da of Charles Weinstein (d 1966), of Portland, Oregon, USA; 1 s (Simeon b 1977), 1 da (Sara b 1973); *Career* architect; princ Clive Zeffert Assocs 1978; dir Thames Housing Ltd 1981; dir Easefern Ltd 1984; ARIBA; *Recreations* Tai Chi, flying, squash, sailing; *Style*— Clive Zeffert, Esq; ✉ 32 Crouch Hall Rd, London N8 8HJ (☎ 0181 341 3375, (work) 0181 340 3963)

ZEKI, Prof Semir; *b* 8 Nov 1940; *Educ* UCL (BSc, PhD); *m* 1967, Anne-Marie Claire, *née* Blestel; 1 da (Isabelle b 24 June 1973), 1 s (Sebastian b 13 Jan 1977); *Career* res assoc St Elizabeth's Hosp Washington DC 1967–68, asst prof of anatomy Univ of Wisconsin 1968–69, Henry Head res fell Royal Soc 1975–80; UCL: asst lectr in anatomy 1966–67, lectr in anatomy 1969–75, reader in neurobiology 1980–81, prof of neurobiology 1981–, co-head Wellcome Dept of Cognitive Neurology 1996–; visiting prof: Duke Univ Durham N Carolina 1977, Institut für Medizinische Psychologie Ludwig Maximilians Univ Munich 1982–87, Univ of California Berkeley 1984; visiting lectr Univ of St Andrews 1985; given numerous special lectures; memb: Bd of Advisors Beit Meml Tst 1984–89, Scientific Advsy Bd The Neurosciences Institute NY 1986–, Bd of Scientific Govrs Scripps Res Inst Calif 1992–, Bd of Govrs Int Brain Res Orgn (IBRO) 1993–; chm Vision Res Working Pty Wellcome Tst 1987– (memb 1985–87); tstee Fight for Sight 1992–, guarantor Brain 1994–; Hocart Prize Royal Anthropological Inst 1961, Minerva Fndn Prize California 1985, Prix Science Pour l'Art LVMH Paris 1991, Rank prize in opto-electronics 1992, Zotterman prize Swedish Physiological Soc 1993; assoc ed and memb Ed Bds of scientific jls; Hon DSc Aston Univ 1994; FRSM 1972, memb Physiological Soc 1978, FZS 1980, MRI 1985, assoc Neurosciences Res Program NY 1985, hon memb Italian Primatological Assoc 1988, FRS 1990, memb Academia Europea 1990, memb European Acad of Sciences and Arts Salzburg 1992; *Books* A Vision of the Brain (1993), La Quête de l'Essentiel (with Balthus, 1995); author of papers and articles in scientific jls; *Recreations* reading (especially about the darker side of man), music (especially opera), deep sleep; *Style*— Prof Semir Zeki, FRS; ✉ Department of Anatomy and Developmental Biology, University College London, Gower Street, London WC1E 6BT (☎ 0171 380 7316, fax 0171 380 7316)

ZELKHA, Morris Sion; s of Eliahou Sion Zelkha (d 1988), of London, and Dinah, *née* Sopher; *b* 22 June 1948; *Educ* St Paul's; *m* 1, (m dis 1984); m 2, 2 Sept 1993, Jacqueline Marjorie Gosling; 1 da (Sarah Diana); *Career* articled clerk rising to sr tax mangr Deloitte & Co (formerly Deloitte Plender Griffiths) 1966–77, joined Tansley Witt & Co (merged with Arthur Andersen & Co 1979) as tax mangr 1977, tax ptnr Arthur Andersen 1981–; ACA 1970, AInstT 1970; *Recreations* bridge, snooker, reading; *Style*— Morris S Zelkha, Esq; ✉ Arthur Andersen, 1 Surrey Street, London WC2R 2PS (☎ 0171 438 3420, fax 0171 438 5163)

ZELLICK, Prof Graham John; s of Reginald Zellick (d 1993), of Windsor, Berks, and Beana, *née* Levey; *b* 12 Aug 1948; *Educ* Christ's Coll Finchley, Gonville and Caius Coll Cambridge (MA, PhD), Stanford Univ Sch of Law California (Ford Fndn fell); *m* 18 Sept 1975, Prof Jennifer Zellick, da of Michael Temkin (d 1993), of London; 1 s (Adam b 1977), 1 da (Lara b 1980); *Career* Queen Mary and Westfield Coll (formerly Queen Mary Coll) Univ of London: lectr in laws 1971–78, reader in law 1978–82, prof of public law 1982–88, dean Faculty of Laws 1984–88, head Dept of Law 1984–90, Drapers' prof of law 1988–91, sr vice principal and actg principal 1990–91, prof of law 1991–, principal 1991–; Univ of London: dean Faculty of Laws 1986–88, senator 1985–94, dep chm Academic Cncl 1987–89, memb Cncl 1994–, dep vice-chllr 1994–97, vice-chllr 1997–; visiting prof of law Univ of Toronto 1975 and 1978–79, visiting scholar St John's Coll Oxford 1989; called to the Bar Middle Temple 1992; ed: Euro Human Rights Reports 1978–82, Public Law 1981–86; memb Editorial Bds: British Journal of Criminology 1980–90, Public Law 1981–91, Howard Journal of Criminal Justice 1984–87, Civil Law Library 1987–; chm: Tel Aviv Univ Tst Lawyers' Gp 1984–89, Prisoners' Advice and Law Serv 1984–89, Legal Ctee All Party Parly War Crimes Gp 1988–91, Ctee of Heads of Univ Law Schs 1988–90, E London Strategic Forum for Nat Educn and Training Targets 1993–95; dep chm Justice Ctee on Prisoners' Rights 1981–83; memb: Cncl Howard League for Penal Reform 1973–82, Jellicoe Ctee on Bds of Visitors of Prisons 1973–75, Newham Dist Ethics Ctee 1985–86, Data Protection Tbnl 1985–96, Lord Chancellor's Advsy Ctee on Legal Aid 1985–88, Lord Chancellor's Advsy Ctee on Legal Educn 1988–90, Cncl West London Synagogue 1990–93 (chm Educn Ctee 1990–93, memb Exec Ctee 1991–93), Cncl City and East London Confedn for Medicine and Dentistry 1991–95, Bart's Med Coll 1991–95, Cncl of Govrs The London Hosp Med Coll 1991–95, Bd of Dirs and Exec Ctee Inst of Citizenship Studies 1991–93, Cncl Spitalfields Heritage Centre 1992–, Cncl Ctee of Vice Chancellors and Principals 1993–, Bd of Dirs UCAS 1994–, Main Bd E London Partnership 1994–95; vice chm of Cncl Academic Study Gp for Israel and the Middle East 1995–; non-exec memb: S Thames Regnl Health Authy 1994–95, E London and City Health Authy 1995–; govr: Central London Poly 1973–77, Pimlico Sch 1973–77, Queen Mary Coll then Queen Mary and Westfield Coll 1983–, Univ Coll Sch 1983–92, N London Poly 1986–89, Univ of Greenwich 1994–; patron Redress Tst 1993–; JP Inner London 1981–85; Freeman City of London 1992, Liveryman Worshipful Co of Drapers 1995 (Freeman 1991); FIMgt 1991, FRSA 1991, FRSM 1996, FInstD 1996; *Books* Justice in Prison (with Sir Brian MacKenna, 1983), The Law Commission and Law Reform (ed 1988), Prisons in Halsbury's Laws of England (4 edn, with Sir Louis Blom-Cooper, QC); *Clubs* Reform; *Style*— Prof Graham Zellick; ✉ Queen Mary and Westfield College, London E1 4NS (☎ 0171 975 5001, fax 0181 981 2848, telex 891750); University of London, Senate House, London WC1E 7HU

ZEMAN, Prof Zbyněk Anthony Bohuslav; s of Jaroslav Zeman (d 1972), and Růzena Zemanová, *née* Pětníková (d 1980); *b* 18 Oct 1928; *Educ* Prague Univ, Univ of London (BA), Univ of Oxford (DPhil); *m* 1956, Anthea, da of Norman Collins; 2 s (Adam b 1957, Alexander b 1964), 1 da (Sophia b 1967); *Career* res fell St Antony's Coll Oxford 1958–61, memb editorial staff The Economist 1959–62, lectr in modern history Univ of St Andrews 1962–70, head of res Amnesty Int 1970–73, dir East-West SPRL (Brussels) and Euro Co-operation Res Gp 1974–76, prof of Central and SE Euro studies and dir Comenius Centre Univ of Lancaster 1976–82; Univ of Oxford: res prof in Euro history 1982–96 (prof emeritus 1996–), professorial fell St Edmund Hall 1983–96; visiting prof Univ of Prague 1990–91, Leverhulme res fell 1993–95, visiting fell Inst of the History of the Czech Army Prague 1994–95; *Books* The Break-up of the Habsburg Empire 1914–18 (1961), Nazi Propaganda (1964), The Merchant of Revolution, A Life of Alexander Helphand (with W B Scharlau, 1964), Prague Spring (1969), A Diplomatic History of the First World War (1971), International Yearbook of East-West Trade (co-ed, 1975), The Masaryks Selling the War: art and propaganda in the First World War (1978), Heckling Hitler: caricatures of the Third Reich (1984), Pursued by a Bear, The Making of Eastern Europe (1989), The Making and Breaking of Communist Europe (1991); *Recreations* tennis, skiing, cooking; *Style*— Prof Zbyněk Zeman; ✉ St Edmund Hall, Oxford; Činská 18, Prague 6, Czech Republic

ZEPHANIAH, Benjamin Obadiah Iqbal; s of Valerie Ebanks; *b* 15 April 1958; *m* 17 March 1990, Amina Iqbal Zephaniah; *Career* poet; one year as writer-in-residence Africa Arts Collective City of Liverpool, TV and radio presenter (incl Passport to Liverpool, Radio 4), chm Hackney Empire Theatre; patron: Irie Dance Co, Tom Allen Centre, Market Nursery Hackney, Newham Young People's Theatre Scheme, Umoja Housing Co-op; pres SHOP (self-help organisation for ex-prisoners); short listed: creative artist in residence Univ of Cambridge 1986, prof of poetry Univ of Oxford; subject of two C4 documentaries, toured Europe, Canada, USA and the Caribbean, regular appearances on TV and radio; *Films* Didn't You Kill My Brother (Comic Strip), Farendg; *Records* Big Boys Don't Make Girls Cry, Free South Africa (with The Wailers), Dub Ranting, Rasta, Us and Dem (Island/Mango, 1990), Back to Roots (Acid Jazz Records, 1995), Belly of de Beast (Ariwa Records, 1996); *Plays* Playing the Right Tune, Job Rocking, Hurricane Dub (BBC Young Playwrights award 1988), Streetwise, Delirium; *Books* Pen Rhythm (Page One Books), The Dread Affair (Arena), In a Liverpool (Africa Arts Collective), Rasta Time in Palestine (Shakti), City Psalms (Bloodaxe), Talking Turkeys (Penguin, 1994), Funky Chickens (Penguin, 1996), Propa Propaganda (Bloodaxe, 1996); *Style*— Benjamin Zephaniah, Esq; ✉ B Z Associates, PO Box 673, East Ham, London E6 3QD; c/o Sandra Boyce Management, 1 Kingsway House, Albion Rd, London N16 0TA (☎ 0171 923 0606, fax 0171 241 2313)

ZERNY, Richard Guy Frederick; s of Marcus Zerny (d 1984), and Eunice Irene Mary, *née* Diggle (d 1982); *b* 27 June 1944; *Educ* Charterhouse; *m* 11 Sept 1970, Jane Alicia, da of Albert George Steventon (d 1984); 2 s (Charles Marcus Stephen b 1972, Miles Patrick Richard b 1973), 1 da (Clare Louise b 1979); *Career* Zernys Ltd: dir 1969–95, md 1979–83, chm 1989–95; dir Johnson Group Cleaners Properties plc 1983, chief exec (UK) Johnson Group Cleaners plc 1989– (dir 1983), chm Johnson Cleaners UK Ltd 1995–; dir Cleaning Tokens Ltd 1986–; chm: Joseph Harris Ltd 1989–95 (md 1983–89), Bollom Ltd 1989–95, Kneels Ltd 1989–95, James Hayes & Sons Ltd 1989–95, Johnson Bros (Cleaners) Ltd 1989–95, JAS Smith & Sons (Cleaners) Ltd 1989–95, John Crockatt Ltd 1989–95, Hartonclean Ltd 1989–95, J Pullar & Sons Ltd 1989–95, Johnson Micronclean Ltd 1989–95, Apparelmaster UK Ltd 1995–; md Johnson Group Management Services Ltd 1989–; Hull and Dist Lifeboat Branch: memb Ctee 1967–83, sec 1975–83; Liveryman Worshipful Co of Launderers 1987, Freeman City of London 1986; *Recreations* sailing, golf, squash, bridge; *Clubs* Royal Yorks Yacht, Formby Golf; *Style*— Richard G F Zerny, Esq; ✉ Clayton House, Liverpool Rd South, Burscough, Lancashire, L40 7TP; Johnson Group Cleaners plc, Mildmay Rd, Bootle, Merseyside L20 5EW (☎ 0151 933 6161)

ZETLAND, 4 Marquess of (UK 1892); Sir Lawrence Mark Dundas; 7 Bt (GB 1762), DL (N Yorkshire 1994); also Earl of Ronaldshay (UK 1892), Earl of Zetland (UK 1838), and Baron Dundas (GB 1794); eldest s of 3 Marquess of Zetland, DL (d 1989), and Penelope, Marchioness of Zetland; *b* 28 Dec 1937; *Educ* Harrow, Christ's Coll Cambridge; *m* 4 April 1964, Susan Rose, 2 da of Guy Richard Chamberlin, of Great Shefford, Newbury, Berks; 2 s (Earl of Ronaldshay b 5 March 1965, Lord James Edward b 2 May 1967), 2 da (Lady Henrietta Kate (Lady Henrietta Stroyan) b 9 Feb 1970, Lady Victoria Clare b 2 Jan 1973); *Heir* s, Earl of Ronaldshay; *Career* late 2 Lt Grenadier Gds; landowner; dir: Redcar Racecourse, Catterick Racecourse, Escor Toys Ltd, Barony Fishing Co Ltd, Racing Five Ltd; steward of the Jockey Club 1992–94, dir British Horseracing Bd 1993–; *Recreations* tennis (lawn and Royal), squash, racing (racehorses Foggy Buoy, Tatiana and Chance Command); *Clubs* All England Lawn Tennis, Jockey; *Style*— The Most Hon the Marquess of Zetland, DL; ✉ Aske, Richmond, North Yorkshire DL10 5HJ (☎ 01748 823222, fax 01748 823252); 44 Bramerton Street, London SW3 (☎ 0171 351 2324)

ZETTER, Paul Isaac; CBE (1981); s of late Simon Zetter, and Esther Zetter; *b* 9 July 1923; *Educ* City of London Sch; *m* 1954, Helen Lore Morgenstern; 1 s (Adam), 1 da (Carolyn); *Career* chm Zetters Group plc and assoc cos 1972–; memb Sports Cncl 1985–87, chm S Region Sports Cncl 1985–87, chm Sports Aid Fndn 1976–85 (hon vice pres 1985–); pres: John Carpenter Club 1987–88, The Restricted Growth Assoc 1993–; vice pres Ice Skating Championships 1994, tstee Fndn for Sport and the Arts 1991–; Freeman City of London 1981, Liveryman Worshipful Co of Glovers; *Books* It Could Be Verse (1976), Bow Jest (1992); *Recreations* walking, writing, fishing; *Clubs* East India; *Style*— Paul Zetter, Esq, CBE; ✉ Zetters Group plc, 86–88 Clerkenwell Rd, London EC1 (☎ 0171 253 5376)

ZEUNER, Christopher Stephan Hugh; OBE (1990); s of Prof Frederick E Zeuner (d 1963), of London, and Ilse Henrietta, *née* Levin (d 1979); *b* 23 Sept 1945; *Educ* Seaford Coll Petworth, Bishop Otter Coll Chichester (Cert Ed); *m* 1975, Diana Elizabeth, da of Margaret and Derrick Sharp; 2 da (Francesca Elizabeth b 12 Aug 1979, Anna Henrietta b 14 Feb 1984); *Career* museum dir; mgmnt trainee Metal Box Co; teacher Hayling Island Hants, dir Weald and Downland Museum (Museum of the Yr Award 1975, Times/Shell Community Museum of the Yr Award 1989); chm Assoc of Ind Museums 1989–91, pres Euro Assoc of Open Air Museums 1990–93; tstee: Museum of Kent Life, VIVAT Tst; Freeman Worshipful Co of Plumbers; FMA 1995; *Style*— Christopher Zeuner, Esq, OBE; ✉ Weald & Downland Open Air Museum, Singleton, nr Chichester, West Sussex PO18 0EU (☎ 01243 63348)

ZHUKOV, Yuri Olegovich; *b* 12 Nov 1964; *Educ* Vaganova Ballet Academi St Petersburg; *Career* Kirov Ballet 1982–89, princ San Francisco Ballet 1992–95 (soloist 1989–92), princ Birmingham Royal Ballet 1995–; roles with Kirov Ballet incl: Prince in The Nutcracker, Poet in Les Sylphides, Albrect in Giselle, Poet in Balanchine's Scotch Symphony, Prince in Cinderella; roles with San Francisco Ballet incl: Prince in Swan Lake, Prince in Sleeping Beauty, James in La Sylphide, Cavalier in The Nutcracker, princ in Balanchine's Serenade, Agon, Symphony in C, Four Temperaments, Tudor's Dark Elegies, Robbins's In the Night; *Style*— Yuri Zhukov, Esq; ✉ The Birmingham Royal Ballet, Birmingham Hippodrome, Thorp Street, Birmingham B5 4AU (☎ 0121 622 2555)

ZIEGLER, Philip Sandeman; CVO (1991); s of Maj Colin Louis Ziegler, DSO, DL (d 1977); *b* 24 Dec 1929; *Educ* Eton, New Coll Oxford; *m* 1, 1960, Sarah (decd), da of Sir William Collins (d 1976); 1 s, 1 da; m 2, 1971, Mary Clare, *née* Charrington; 1 s; *Career* HM Dip Serv 1952–67, editorial dir William Collins and Sons (joined 1967); chm: Soc of Authors 1988–90, Public Lending Right Advsy Ctee 1994–; *Books* Duchess of Dino (1962), Addington (1965), The Black Death (1968), William IV (1971), Melbourne (1976), Crown and People (1978), Diana Cooper (1981), Mountbatten (1985), The Sixth Great Power: Barings 1762–1929 (1988), King Edward VIII (1990), Harold Wilson (1993), London at War (1995); *Clubs* Brooks's; *Style*— Philip Ziegler, Esq, CVO; ✉ 22 Cottesmore Gardens, London W8 (☎ 0171 937 1903, fax 0171 937 5458)

ZIENKIEWICZ, Prof Olgierd Cecil; CBE (1989); s of Casimir Rafael Zienkiewicz (d 1958), of Edinburgh, and Edith Violet, *née* Penny (d 1974); *b* 18 May 1921; *Educ* Imperial Coll of Sci and Technol London (BSc, ACGI), Univ of London (PhD, DSc, DIC); *m* 15 Dec 1952, Helen Jean, da of Albert Fleming; 2 s (Andrew Olgierd b 17 Sept 1953, John David b 4 May 1955), 1 da (Krystyna Helen (Mrs Beynon) b 3 March 1958); *Career* conslt engr Sir William Halcrow & Partners 1945–49, lectr Univ of Edinburgh 1949–57, prof of structural engrg Northwestern Univ Evanston Illinois USA 1957–61, prof and head of Dept of Civil Engrg Univ of Wales Swansea 1961–88, dir Inst for Numerical Methods in Engrg 1970–; written circa 500 papers on: solid and fluid mechanics, stress analysis of dams, nuclear reactors, lubrication theory, devpt of the finite element method; fndr and chief ed Int Jl for Numerical Methods in Engrg; memb numerous editorial bds of jls incl: Solids & Structures, Earthquake Engrg, Rock Mechanics; memb Cncl ICE 1972–76, chm Ctee of Analysis and Design Int Congress of Large Dams 1973–85, holder visiting res chair of naval sea systems cmd Naval Postgrad Sch Monterey California 1979–80, visiting Jubilee prof Chalmers Univ of Technol Göteborg Sweden 1990 and 1992, UNESCO chair of numerical methods Tech Univ of Catalunya Barcelona 1989, 1990, 1991, 1992, 1993, 1994 and 1995, Chair prof Univ of Texas Austin 1989, 1990, 1991, 1993, 1994 and 1995, pres Int Assoc of Computational Mechanics 1986–90; recipient: James Alfred Ewing medal ICE 1980, Nathan Newmark medal American Soc of Engrs 1980, Worcester Warner Reid medal American Soc of Mechanical Engrs 1980, Carl Friedrich Gauss medal W German Acad of Sci 1987, Royal medal Royal Soc 1990, Gold medal Inst of Structural Engrs 1992, Gold medal Inst of Mathematics and its Applications 1992; hon prof Dalian China 1988; Hon DSc: Lisbon 1972, Univ of Ireland 1975, Univ of Brussels 1982, Northwestern Univ USA 1984, Univ of Trondheim Norway 1985, Chalmers Univ of Technol Sweden 1987, Univ of Technol Warsaw 1989, Univ of Technol Krakow Poland 1989, Univ of Hong Kong 1992, Tech Univ of Budapest 1992, Univ of Padua 1992, Tech Univ of Compiegne France 1992, Univ of Thessaloniki 1993, Brunel Univ 1993, Univ of Wales 1993, Tech Univ of Vienna 1993; hon fell: Univ of Wales Swansea 1989, Imperial Coll London 1993; Hon DLitt Univ of Dundee 1987; fell City and Guilds Inst of London 1979; Chevalier dans l'Ordre des Palmes Académiques (France) 1996; foreign memb: US Nat Acad of Engrs 1981, Polish Acad of Sci 1985; FRS 1978, FEng 1979; *Books* The Finite Element Method in Structural Mechanics (1967), The Finite Element Method in Engineering Science (1971), The Finite Element Method (1977, 4 edn with R L Taylor, vol I 1989, vol II 1991), Finite Elements and Approximations (with K Morgan, 1980); *Recreations* sailing, diving; *Clubs* Athenaeum; *Style*— Prof Olgierd Zienkiewicz, CBE, FRS, FEng; ✉ 29 Somerset Road, Mumbles, Swansea SA3 4PG (☎ 01792 368776)

ZIERKE, Ulrich; s of Dr Erwin Zierke, of Frankfurt, Germany, and Elsbeth Zierke; *b* 24 June 1944; *Educ* GS Germany, J W Goethe Univ Frankfurt (Diplom Kaufmann); *m* 4 April 1975, Kornelia, da of Robert Saur; *Career* Nat Serv 1965–67, banking apprentice 1963–65; Westdeutsche Landesbank: banker 1972, seconded Libra Bank London and Mexico City 1974–78, various assignments to NY Tokyo and Madrid 1978–90, sr vice pres 1983–, dep chief exec Chartered WestLB Ltd London 1990–92, gen mangr Westdeutsche Landesbank London 1992–95; chief exec The Thomas Cook Group Limited 1995–; MInstD; *Recreations* travelling, arts, skiing; *Clubs* Arts, RAC; *Style*— Ulrich Zierke, Esq; ✉ The Thomas Cook Group Ltd, 45 Berkeley Street, London W1A 1EB (☎ 0171 499 4000, fax 0171 408 4129)

ZIFF, (Robert) Paul; JP (Bradford 1991); s of Max Ziff (d 1954), by his w Annie (d 1953); *b* 20 Dec 1935; *Educ* Giggleswick Sch; *m* 29 April 1987, Lea, da of late Irving Charles Bambage, of Yorks; *Career* chm: Finest Brands International Ltd, Champion Manufacturing (Safety Headwear) Ltd, Phoenix Sports Footwear Ltd, Harwood Antiques Ltd; Barker Variety Club of GB (chm Leeds Regnl Ctee 1975 and 1981); Freeman City of London, Liveryman Worshipful Co of Pattenmakers; *Recreations* mechanical music and automata; *Clubs* City Livery, Queen's; *Style*— Paul Ziff, Esq, JP; ✉ Gallogate House, Weeton, nr Leeds LS17 0BA; Finest Brands International Ltd, FBI House, Low Fields Way, Leeds LS12 6HQ (☎ 0113 270 7007)

ZIGMOND, Jonathan Peter; s of His Hon Judge Joseph Zigmond (d 1980), and Muriel, *née* Lermon; *Educ* Cheadle Hulme Sch, Univ of Reading (BSc); *m* 11 Sept 1976, Sarah Angela Barbara, *née* Roff; 2 s (Andrew Morris b 3 Jan 1981, Robin James b 13 Dec 1982); *Career* articled clerk Hogg Bullimore Chartered Accountants 1972–75, qualified 1975; Coopers & Lybrand: joined 1976, City practice 1976–82, Leeds 1982–, ptnr 1983–, head of tax practice Leeds 1983–95, memb Tax Bd 1993–96; memb: Inheritance Tax and Tsts Sub Ctee ICAEW 1988–, Capital Taxes Ctee Chartered Inst of Taxation 1995–; FCA (ACA 1975), ATII 1975, STEP 1992; *Books* Tax Digest: Inheritance Tax on Discretionary and Accumulation Trusts (1987, 2 edn 1988), Inheritance Tax Planning (1987, 2 edn 1988), Tax Digest: Capital Gains Tax and Offshore Trusts (1992); *Style*— Jonathan Zigmond, Esq; ✉ Coopers & Lybrand, Albion Court, 5 Albion Place, Leeds LS1 6JP (☎ 0113 243 1343, fax 0113 231 4598)

ZILKHA, Dr Kevin Jerome; s of Joseph Zilkha (d 1989), and Daisy, *née* Shohet; *b* 4 Dec 1929; *Educ* Alliance Sch, Guy's Hosp Med Sch London (MD); *m* 10 Sept 1958, Judith Diana, da of Walter Mogridge; 2 s (Timothy b 22 Nov 1960, Jonathan b 29 Oct 1965), 1 da (Caroline b 16 March 1964); *Career* neurological house physician Guy's Hosp 1953–54 (former house offr posts), RAMC Egypt and Cyprus 1954–56, med registrar Guy's and New Cross Hosps 1956–58, resident MO Nat Hosp Queen Square 1961–62 (jr resident posts 1958–61), research fell Dept of Chemical Pathology Guy's Hosp Med Sch 1962–63, sr registrar Nat Hosp and Hosp for Sick Children Gt Ormond St 1963 and 1965–94, conslt neurologist Nat Hosp for Neurology and Neurosurgery and KCH 1965–94; hon neurologist to: Maudsley Hosp 1965–94, Royal Hosp and The Army 1972–; pres Harveian Soc of London 1981; chm: Research Ctee and Research Ethics Ctee KCH 1968–, Conslts Ctee KCH 1985–87, Conslts Ctee Nat Hosp 1989–91, Ethics Ctee Nat Hosp 1993–94, Med Advsy Ctee Cromwell Hosp 1988–90, Bd of Dirs Cromwell Hosp 1990–; tstee Med Research Tst KCH 1994–; memb: BMA 1965, Assoc of Br Neurologists 1965, RSM 1965; FRCP; *Recreations* sailing; *Clubs* MCC, Garrick, Chichester Yacht; *Style*— Dr Kevin Zilkha; ✉ The Cromwell Hospital, Cromwell Road, London SW5 (☎ 0171 460 2000)

ZIMAN, Lawrence David; *b* 10 Aug 1938; *Educ* City of London Sch, Trinity Hall Cambridge (MA), Univ of Michigan Law Sch (post-grad fell); *m* Joyce; 2 s; *Career* slr; Herbert Oppenheimer Nathan & Vandyk: articled clerk 1960–63, asst slr 1963–65, ptnr 1965–66; founding ptnr Berwin & Co (now Berwin Leighton) 1966–70, seconded to Industrial Reorganisation Corporation 1969–70, fndr Ziman & Co 1970 (merged with Nabarro Nathanson 1977), ptnr Nabarro Nathanson 1977–95, gen counsel TI Group plc 1995–; dir N Brown Group plc; inspr under Companies Act to investigate affrs of Barlow Clowes/James Ferguson 1988 (report published 1995); *Books* Butterworths Company Law Service (consulting ed, 1985–95); *Clubs* Lansdowne; *Style*— Lawrence Ziman, Esq; ✉ TI Group plc, 50 Curzon Street, London W1Y 7PN (☎ 0171 499 9131, fax 0171 493 6533)

ZIMMER, Dr Robert Mark; s of Norman Zimmer, NY, USA, and Lenore *née* Wasserman; *Educ* Churchill Coll Cambridge, MIT (SB), Columbia Univ NY (MA, MPhil, PhD); *m* 23 July 1983, Joanna Elizabeth Marlow, da of Thomas Gondris, of Ipswich, Suffolk; 1 s (Edmund b 31 Jan 1992); *Career* lectr: Columbia Univ 1982–85, Brunel Univ 1985–; visiting scholar Dept of Sanskrit and Indian Studies Harvard Univ 1989, visiting prof Univ of Ottawa 1989; published poetry and articles on mathematics, computer science, electrical engrg and 18th century Eng lit; *Recreations* food, books; *Clubs* Young Johnsonians; *Style*— Dr Robert Zimmer; ✉ 4 Selwyn Court, Richmond, Surrey TW10 6LR (☎ 0181 948 3772); Department of Computer Science, Brunel University, Uxbridge, Middx, UB8 3PH (☎ 01895 274000 ext 2756, fax 01895 232806, telex 261173 G)

ZIMMERMANN, Frank Peter; *b* 1965; *Career* violinist; studied with Valery Grodov, Sashko Gawriloff, Herman Krebbers; awarded Premio dell Accademia Musicale Chigiana Siena 1990; orchs appeared with incl: Philadelphia Orch, Chicago Symphony Orch, Boston Symphony Orch, The Cleveland Orch, Los Angeles Philharmonic, Toronto Symphony Orch, Gustav Mahler Youth Orch, Berlin Philharmonic Orch, Gewandhausorchstra Leipzig, Munich Philharmonic, Bayerische Rundfunk, Vienna Philharmonic, Chamber Orch of Europe, Orchestre de Paris, Oslo Philharmonic Orch, Royal Concertgebouw Orch, Russian Nat Orch, NHK Symphony Orch, LSO, Hallé Orch, English Chamber Orch, The London Philharmonic, Philharmonia Orch; conductors worked with incl: Lorin Maazel, Barenboim, Andrew Davis, Sir Colin Davis, Wolfgang Sawallisch, Dohnanyi, Bernard Haitink, André Previn, Kurt Sanderling, Franz Welser-Möst; special concerts incl: Mozart Sinfonia Concertante for Violin and Viola (with Tabea Zimmermann and English Chamber Orch) Buckingham Palace 1991, May Day concert Royal Albert Hall (televised all over world); *Recordings* all for EMI incl: Saint-Saëns Concerto No 3, Stravinsky Concerto, Ravel Tzigane, all Mozart Sonatas, all Prokofiev Sonatas, works by Berg/Stravinsky/Ravel (Edison Award 1992, Diapason d'Or de l'Année 1992), works by Debussy/Ravel/Janacek (with Alexander Lonquich, Diapason d'Or 1992), works by Groupe des Six (Edison Award 1994), Eugène Ysaye 6 Solo Sonatas (Prix Cecilia, ECHO/Deutscher Schallplattenpreis), Brahms Violin Concerto with Mozart Violin Concerto No 3 (with Berlin Philharmonic Orch and Wolfgang Sawallisch), Tchaikovsky Concerto and Prokofiev Concerto No 1 (with Berlin Philharmonic Orch and Lorin Maazel); *Style*— Frank Peter Zimmermann, Esq; ✉ c/o Intermusica Artists' Management, 16 Duncan Terrace, London N1 8BZ (☎ 0171 278 5455, fax 0171 278 8434)

ZINKIN, Peter John Louis; *b* 23 July 1953; *Educ* Winchester, Magdalene Coll Cambridge (BA), London Business Sch (MSc(Econ)); *Career* London Business Sch 1978–81; BICC plc: various appts 1981–88, gp planning & devpt mangr 1988–91, chm BICC Developments 1991–, main bd dir 1991–; MCT; *Style*— Peter Zinkin, Esq; ✉ BICC plc, Devonshire House, Mayfair Place, London W1X 5FH (☎ 0171 629 6622, fax 0171 409 0070)

ZINNEMANN, Fred; s of Dr Oskar Zinnemann (d 1941), and Anna (d 1942); *b* 29 April 1907; *Educ* Vienna Univ Law Sch (BA), Ecole Technique de Cinematographie Paris; *m* 1936, Renée Bartlett; 1 s (Tim); *Career* film director; Hon tstee Artists Rights Fndn (USA); fell: BAFTA, BFI; Hon DLitt Univ of Durham 1994; memb: Dir's Guild of America (second vice pres 1961–64), American Film Inst (co-fndn and ex-tstee 1967–71), Acad of Motion Picture Arts; since 1985 campaigner for moral rights of film authors & fight against mutilation of existing and future heritage of films (USA/UK); *Films* The Wave 1934, The Seventh Cross 1942, The Search 1947, Act of Violence 1948, The Men 1949, Teresa 1950, High Noon 1951, A Member of The Wedding 1952, From Here To Eternity 1953, Oklahoma! 1955, A Hatful of Rain 1956, The Nun's Story 1958, The Sundowners 1960, Behold A Pale Horse 1963, A Man For All Seasons 1967, The Day Of The Jackal 1973, Julia 1977, Five Days One Summer 1982; *Exhibition* photographs taken in Manhattan in 1932 (V&A 1992); *Awards* incl: Acad Awards (Oscars) 1951, 1954 and twice winner 1967, BAFTA Awards 1967 and 1978, other awards incl NY Film Critics 1952, 1954, 1959 and 1967, Directors' Guild 1954 and 1967, Moscow Festival 1965, Golden Thistle (Edinburgh) 1965, D W Griffith (Directors' Guild US) 1970, Donatello (Italy) 1978, US Congressional Life achievement Award 1987, Order of Arts and Letters (France) 1982, Gold Medal City of Vienna (Austria) 1967, John Huston Award (Artists' Right Fndn USA) 1994; *Publications* autobiography (published 1992); *Recreations* mountaineering, chamber music; *Clubs* Sierra (San Francisco); *Style*— Fred Zinnemann, Esq; ✉ 98 Mount Street, London W1Y 5HF (☎ 0171 499 0179, fax 0171 493 1783)

ZINS, Stefan; s of Maximilian Zins (d 1966), and Zofia, *née* Kurzman; *b* 5 June 1927; *Educ* Hammersmith Coll of Art and Architecture, UCL (Cert Town Planning); *m* 17 Aug 1959, Harriet Norah, da of Henry Frank Back (d 1968); 1 da (Deborah b 1962); *Career* architect, planning conslt; fndr and dir Stefan Zins Associates Ltd; i/c numerous residential building schemes in SE England, for public and private sectors, also hotels, youth hostels, old peoples' homes and commercial projects; FRIBA; *Recreations* tennis, skiing, swimming, wine tasting; *Clubs* Confrerie des Compagnons Haut Normands du Gouste-Vin; *Style*— Stefan Zins, Esq; ✉ 31 Valiant House, London SW11 3LU; 71 Warwick Road, London SW5 9HB (☎ 0171 370 3129, fax 0171 373 5993)

ZOCHONIS, Sir John Basil; kt (1997), DL (1989); s of Constantine Zochonis (d 1951), of Altrincham, and Nitza Octavia, *née* Stavridi (d 1981); *b* 2 Oct 1929; *Educ* Rugby, Univ of Oxford (BA); *m* 14 Sept 1990, Brigid Mary Evanson, da of Dr George Smyth; *Career* chm Paterson Zochonis plc 1970–93 (joined 1953, dir 1957); chm Cncl Univ of Manchester 1987–90; memb: Cncl Royal Africa Soc 1984, Cncl Br Exec Serv Overseas 1988, Bd Commonwealth Development Corp 1992–95; pres: Greater Manchester Youth Assoc (now FIRST) 1980–93 (vice pres 1979), Manchester Univ Settlement 1989– (memb 1982–); tstee Police Fndn 1994– (memb Exec Ctee 1989–); High Sheriff for Co of Greater Manchester 1994–95; Hon LLD Univ of Manchester 1991; Freeman City of London 1978, Liveryman Worshipful Co of Tallow Chandlers 1978; *Recreations* reading and cricket; *Clubs* Travellers', MCC; *Style*— Sir John Zochonis, DL; ✉ c/o Paterson Zochonis plc,

Cussons House, Bird Hall Lane, Stockport SK3 0XN (☎ 0161 491 8000, fax 0161 491 8090)

ZOUCHE, 18 Baron (E 1308); Sir James Assheton Frankland; 12 Bt (E 1660); s of Hon Sir Thomas Frankland, 11 Bt (d 1944, s of Sir Frederick Frankland, 10 Bt, by his w Baroness Zouche (d 1965), 17 holder of the Peerage and descendant of Eudes La Zouche, yr bro of Sir Roger La Zouche of Ashby after whose family Ashby-de-la-Zouch is named); Lord Zouche is coheir to Barony of St Maur (abeyant since 1628); *b* 23 Feb 1943; *Educ* Lycée Jacard Lausanne; *m* 1978, Sally, da of Roderic M Barton, of The Red House, Bungay, Suffolk; 1 s, 1 da; *Heir* s Hon William Thomas Assheton b 23 July 1984; *Career* Capt 15/19 King's Roy Hussars (ret 1968), ADC to Govr Tasmania 1965–68, Hon ADC to Govr Victoria 1975–; pres Multiple Sclerosis Soc Victoria 1981–84; co dir; *Recreations* shooting; *Clubs* Cavalry & Guards', Melbourne (Australia); *Style*— The Rt Hon the Lord Zouche; ✉ The Abbey, Charlton Adam, Somerton, Somerset TA11 7BE

ZUCKER, His Hon Judge; Kenneth Harry; QC (1981); s of Nathaniel Zucker (d 1989), of London, and Norma Zucker, *née* Mehlberg (d 1937); *b* 4 March 1935; *Educ* Westcliff HS, Exeter Coll Oxford; *m* 1961, Ruth Erica, da of Dr Henry Brudno (d 1967); 1 s (Jonathan), 1 da (Naomi); *Career* called to the Bar Gray's Inn 1959, recorder 1982–89, circuit judge (SE Circuit) 1989–; *Recreations* reading, walking, photography, bookbinding; *Style*— His Hon Judge Zucker, QC; ✉ Wood Green Crown Court, Woodall House, Lordship Lane, London N22 5LF

ZUCKERMAN, Prof Arie Jeremy; *b* 30 March 1932; *Educ* Univ of Birmingham (BSc, MSc, DSc), Univ of London (MB BS, MD, DipBact, Univ Gold medal, Evans prize, A B Cunning prize, A B Cunning award); *Career* Flt Lt then Sqdn Ldr RAF Med Branch 1959–61; first obstetric house surgn Royal Free Hosp 1957–58, casualty surgn and admissions offr Whittington Hosp London 1958–59 (house physician in gen med Jan-July 1958), Med Branch RAF 1959–62; registrar Public Health Laboratory Serv Central, secondment as hon registrar Dept of Pathology Guy's Hosp Med Sch 1962–63, sr registrar Public Health Laboratory 1963–65; London Sch of Hygiene and Tropical Med: sr lectr Dept of Bacteriology and Immunology 1965–68, reader in virology 1968–72, prof of virology 1972–75, dir Dept of Med Microbiology 1975–88; prof of microbiology Univ of London 1975–, dean of Royal Free Hosp Sch of Med 1989–; WHO: conslt on hepatitis 1970–, memb Expert Advsy Panel on Virus Diseases 1974–, dir Collaborating Centre for Ref and Res on Viral Hepatitis 1974–89, dir Collaborating Centre for Ref and Res on Viral Diseases 1990–; hon conslt virologist: N E Thames Regnl Blood Transfusion Centre 1970–94, Charing Cross Hosp 1982–, Nat Blood Authy 1994–; hon conslt microbiologist Royal Free Hosp 1989–, non-exec dir Royal Free Hampstead NHS Tst 1990–, dir Anthony Nolan Bone Marrow Tst; memb: Cncl Royal Coll of Pathologists 1983–86, Bd Public Health Laboratory Serv 1983–89, Cncl Univ Coll London 1996–, Cncl Zoological Soc of London; ed: Journal of Medical Virology 1976–, Journal of Virological Methods 1979–; contrib to numerous other learned jls; Stewart prize of the BMA 1981, James Blundell Medal and Award Br Blood Tranfusion Soc 1992; MRCS, DObstRCOG 1958, FRCPath 1977 (MRCPath 1965), FRCP 1982 (LRCP 1957, MRCP 1977); *Books* Virus Diseases of the Liver (1970), Hepatitis-associated Antigen and Viruses (1972), Human Viral Hepatitis (2 edn, 1975), Hepatitis Viruses of Man (with C R Howard, 1979), A Decade of Viral Hepatitis (1980), Viral Hepatitis (ed, 1986), Viral Hepatitis and Liver Disease (ed, 1988), Recent Development in Prophylactic Immunization (ed, 1989), Viral Hepatitis (ed, 1990), Principles and Practice of Clinical Virology (3 edn, 1994), Viral Hepatitis: Scientific Basis and Clinical Management (with H Thomas, 1993); *Style*— Prof Arie Zuckerman; ✉ Royal Free Hospital School of Medicine, Rowland Hill Street, Hampstead, London NW3 2PF (☎ 0171 794 0500)

ZUCKERMAN, Hon Paul Sebastian; s of Baron Zuckerman, OM, KCB, FRS (Life Peer; d 1993), and Lady Joan Rufus Isaacs, da of 2 Marquess of Reading; *b* 1945; *Educ* Rugby, Trinity Coll Cambridge (MA), Univ of Reading (PhD); *m* 1972 (m dis 1986), Mrs Janette Hampel, da of R R Mather, of Stoke-by-Clare, Suffolk; *Career* formerly: dir S G Warburg & Co Ltd, chm Intermediate Technol Devpt Gp; currently md Caspian Securities Ltd; tstee William Walton Fndn; *Clubs* Brooks's; *Style*— The Hon Paul Zuckerman; ✉ The Old Rectory, Grosvenor Rd, London SW1; Caspian Securities Ltd, 199 Bishopsgate, London EC2

ZUKERMAN, Pinchas; *b* 1948; *Educ* began musical training with father, Israel Conservatory (with Ilona Feher), Acad of Music Tel Aviv, Julliard Sch USA (scholar, studied with Ivan Galamian); *Career* musician; violinist, violist, teacher and conductor; as soloist performs with major orchestras worldwide; soloist and conductor with many maj orchestras incl: New York Philharmonic, Boston Symphony, Los Angeles Philharmonic, Nat Symphony Orchestra and San Francisco, Montreal, Toronto and Ottawa Symphonies, Berlin Philharmonic, Philharmonia, Eng Chamber Orchestra, Israel Philharmonic; former music dir: South Bank Festival, St Paul Chamber Orchestra; princ guest conductor Dallas Symphony Orchestra's Int Music Festival 1990–; artist dir Baltimore Symphony Orchestra's Summer Musicfest 1996; extensive recital tours with Marc Neikrug, chamber music collaborations with Itzhak Perlman, Daniel Barenboim, Ralph Kirshbaum; discography incl over 75 recordings widely representative of violin and viola repertoires; exclusive artist for BMG Classics; *Awards* first prize Twenty-Fifth Leventritt Int Competition 1967, Achievement award Int Center in NY, King Solomon award America-Israel Cultural Fndn, Medal of Arts 1983; Hon DUniv Browns USA; *Style*— Pinchas Zukerman; ✉ c/o Shirley Kirshbaum & Assoc Inc, 711 West End Avenue, Suite SKN, New York, NY 10025, USA (☎ 00 1 212 2224843)

ZULUETA, *see:* de Zulueta

ZUNZ, Sir Gerhard Jacob (Jack); kt (1989); s of Wilhelm Zunz (d 1959), of Johannesburg, South Africa, and Helene (d 1973); *b* 25 Dec 1923; *Educ* Athlone HS Johannesburg SA, Univ of The Witwatersrand Johannesburg SA (BSc); *m* 1948, Babs Maisel; 1 s (Leslie Mark b 1956), 2 da (Marion Erica b 1952 d 1992, Laura Ann b 1955); *Career* served WWII SA Artillery Egypt and Italy 1943–46; asst engr Alpheus Williams & Dowse 1948–50; Ove Arup & Partners: structural and civil engr London 1950–54, co fndr and ptnr SA 1954–61, assoc ptnr and ptnr in all overseas partnerships 1965–77; chm Ove Arup & Partners 1977–84; Ove Arup Partnership: dir 1977–84, co chm 1984–89, conslt 1989–95, chm Ove Arup Foundation 1993–96; non-exec dir Innisfree PFI Fund 1995–; pres CIRIA 1995–; Industl Commoner Churchill Coll 1967–68; Hon DSc West Ontario 1993, Hon DEng Glasgow 1994; FEng 1983, Hon FRIBA 1990, FCGI 1991, FICE, FIStructE *Awards* Oscar Faber Silver medal (with Sir Ove Arup) 1969, Inst Structural Engrs Gold medal 1988, Oscar Faber Bronze medal (with M Manning & C Jofeh) 1990; *Recreations* theatre, music, golf; *Style*— Sir Jack Zunz, FEng; ✉ Ove Arup Partnership, 13 Fitzroy St, London W1P 6BQ (☎ 0171 636 1531, fax 0171 580 3924)

ZUTSHI, Dr Derek Wyndham Hariram; s of Lambodha Zutshi (d 1964), of Srinagar, Kashmir and London, and Eileen Dorothy Wyndham Lord (d 1944); *b* 26 April 1930; *Educ* Epsom Coll, Univ of Bristol (MB ChB); *m* 11 May 1974, Marguerite Elizabeth, da of Edgar Montague Smith (d 1944), of Lima, Peru and Bournemouth; *Career* rheumatology conslt 1973–; med registrar MRC Rheumatism Res Unit Canadian Red Cross Meml Hosp Taplow 1966–68, sr registrar in rheumatology and clinical tutor med The London Hosp 1968–73, med dir Sch of Physiotherapy Prince of Wales's Gen Hosp 1973–77, rheumatology conslt Gen Hosps Tottenham (Prince of Wales, St Ann's) 1973–77, sr med offr Medicines and Communicable Disease Divs DHSS 1977–86; examiner: Chartered Soc of Physiotherapy 1974–78, Coll of Occupational Therapists 1980–89; chm Federal Cncl of Indian Orgns 1994–95 (hon treas 1974–94); memb: Cncl and hon sec Br Assoc for Rheumatology and Rehabilitation 1974–78, Cncl Med Soc of London 1977–80, Cncl Hunterian Soc 1978–96 (hon treas 1979–92, pres 1993–94, vice pres 1995–96); Univ of Bristol: memb Ct 1958–, memb Cncl 1988–, memb Standing Ctee of Convocation 1981– (chm 1988–); memb: Bd of Tstees The Hindu Centre London 1962–95 (chm 1984–95, patron 1996–), Bd of Govrs Tottenham Coll of FE 1974–90 (dep chm 1978–87); Nat Rubella Cncl (Nat Cncl for Childhealth): memb Advsy Panel 1988–, memb Mgmnt Ctee 1989–90; memb Disability Appeal Tbnls 1992–; Freeman City of London, Liveryman Worshipful Co of Apothecaries; FRSA, FRSM, FRCP; *Recreations* travel, music, reading; *Clubs* Athenaeum; *Style*— Dr Derek Zutshi; ✉ 36 Eton Court, Eton Ave, Hampstead, London NW3 3HJ (☎ 0171 722 6316)